Master Index to Poetry

An Index to Poetry
in Anthologies & Collections

DISCARD

Poetry Index Press

Poetry Index Annual
American Poetry Index
Annual Index to Poetry in Periodicals
Master Index to Poetry

Master Index to Poetry

An Index to Poetry
in Anthologies & Collections

Volume I
First Edition

Prepared by
The Editorial Board, Roth Publishing, Inc.

Copyright © 1988 Roth Publishing, Inc.
All rights reserved
Preliminary Edition
© 1985 Granger Book Co., Inc.

International Standard Book Number 0-89609-273-9
Library of Congress Number 85-81058

Manufactured in the U.S.A.

Poetry Index Press is a
division of Roth Publishing, Inc.

Contents

Preface vii

Introduction ix

List of Works Indexed xi

Master Index to Poetry 1

Appendix I: Title Reference 2041

Appendix II: Author Reference 2059

Appendix III: Subject Classification ... 2069

Preface

The **MASTER INDEX TO POETRY** is being developed to provide author, title, and first line access to poetry which is reproduced on microfiche (CoreFiche). This tandem of index and poetry, enabling users to identify, locate, and access poems in one fully integrated resource, provides a unique and effective reference utility.

The projected universe of index/fiche is the entire range of poetry in the English language. The undertaking, vast in scope and massive in detail, requires a substantial commitment of time and effort. A Preliminary Edition of the **MASTER INDEX** to Phase I of CoreFiche was published in 1985; this First Edition is a revision and correction of its predecessor, and an enlargement in that it also includes Phase II of CoreFiche.

Additional CoreFiche phases, containing poems not previously reproduced, will be issued; supplementary editions of the **MASTER INDEX** accessing this material will be published. While it is anticipated that the optimum utilization of the **MASTER INDEX** will be in conjunction with the fiche, it has collateral stand-alone utility.

Introduction

This First Edition of the **MASTER INDEX** analyzes 1,032 poetry book titles in 1,079 volumes (containing approximately 250,000 individual poem citations) which have been republished in microfiche (CoreFiche) in two phases. Phase I contains 747 anthologies (781 volumes) listed in *Granger's Index to Poetry*; Phase II contains 295 titles (298 volumes) listed in *Granger's* and other leading poetry indexes.

Each of the 1,032 poetry titles indexed has been assigned a five digit identifying code number (e.g. 6001-3) which, together with the micropublisher's prefix (0-8486), constitutes the book's ISBN. The code number is given in each entry of the **MASTER INDEX** to identify the source book for each poem. The complete ISBN appears on the eye-legible header of each fiche. Thus, reference from an entry can be made to the "List of Works Indexed" (see page xi) to identify the book wherein the poem appears, and then to the poem itself via the fiche. (Note that if a poem appears in more than one book, each code number is given; as a general rule, however, poems that appear in both phases bear only Phase I code numbers.)

The "List of Works Indexed" contains bibliographic information in two alpha-sequences (one for each Phase) but in one continuous numeric code sequence. It follows this Introduction. In addition, to facilitate greater utility, the titles of both phases are merged in two separate appendices: (1) an alphabetical listing by title, beginning on page 2,041, and (2) an alphabetical listing by author/editor, beginning on page 2,059.

Arrangement. The filing in the index proper is generally alphabetical word by word (i.e. "my world" precedes "myself"). Articles at the beginning of titles are retained but disregarded in the alphabetizing (except articles in dialect and foreign languages). Common abbreviations like Dr. and St. are alphabetized as though spelled out ("Doctor," "Saint"), as are numbers (i.e. 1232 is filed as "one thousand thirty two"). "McAllister" is interfiled with "MacArthur" under "Mac"; the interjections "O" and "Oh" are interfiled together under "O." Punctuation is not disregarded in filing. A word with punctuation will follow an identical word without punctuation.

    1. *Author Entry*. Author, title, translator, and code number are given in this entry. There is no entry for anonymous poems; they are indexed only by title and first line (and translator if any). Where authorship is not certain, the abbreviation "atr" (attributed) is given with the putative author. The name by which a poet is indexed is generally the best known

writing name, whether a pseudonym, married, or legal name; it is not necessarily the name used in the source anthology. Cross reference from variant names is made to the main author entry.

2. *Title Entry*. This entry contains the title of the poem, its author, translator, and the five digit book code. The first word of the title is printed in boldface; the title appears in quotation marks when it is the first line. If only a portion of the poem is contained in the work, the abbreviation "sels" (selections) follows the title.

3. *First Line Entry*. Access by first line in addition to title is provided when the first line is not similar to the title. This entry applies generally only to poems contained in the 298 volumes constituting Phase II, although such entries for poems in Phase I have also been made (there are 36,000 first line entries in this edition); future editions will provide additional first line entries for those omitted in this edition. The first line entry is always printed in quotations; the first word is printed in boldface.

4. *Translator Entry*. Translated poems are also indexed by a separate translator entry in which, title, author, and book code symbol are provided.

Subject Classification. The 1,032 book titles indexed are arranged by subject classification (where practicable) in Appendix III, beginning on page 2,069.

List of Works Indexed

The following anthologies and collections are the source books used to create the **MASTER INDEX**. Each is available on CoreFiche and is identified by the five digit code on the left. The date of original publication appears at the end of the listing.

Phase I publications were selected from anthologies used in Granger's Index to Poetry. Phase II publications were selected from additional reference indexes. These are indicated after the date by the following bold face symbols.

G = Granger's Index to Poetry
* = Brewton's Index to Children's Poetry
B = Bruncken's Subject Index to Poetry
P = Roth's Poetry Index Annual
S = Sell's Subject Index to Poetry for Children and Young People

PHASE I: 6001-3 to 6747-6

6001-3 **Advanced Elocution.** Rachel W. Shoemaker. 1896.
6002-1 **All the Best Dog Poems.** Edwin Burtis, comp. 1946.
6003-X **American Ballads and Songs.** Louise Pound, ed. 1922.
6004-8 **American Familiar Verse:** vers de societe. Brander Matthews, ed. 1904.
6005-6 **American Idea;** as expounded by American statesmen. Joseph B. Gilder, comp. 1902.
6006-4 **American Lyrics.** Edith Rickert, comp. 1912.
6007-2 **American Mystical Verse.** Irene Hunter, comp. 1925.
6008-0 **American Poems (1625-1892).** Walter C. Bronson, ed. 1912.

6009-9 **American Poetry.** Alban De Mille, ed. 1923.
6010-2 **American Poetry, 1922:** a miscellany. Louis Untermeyer, ed. 1925.
6011-0 **American Poetry, 1925:** a miscellany. Louis Untermeyer, ed. 1925.
6012-9 **American Poetry, 1927:** a miscellany. Louis Untermeyer, ed. 1927.
6013-7 **American prose.** Horace Scudder, ed. 1880.
6014-5 **American Star Speaker & Model Elocutionist.** Charles W.
6015-3 **American War Ballads & Lyrics, Volume I.** George C. Eggleston, ed. 1889.

List of Works Indexed

6016-1 **American War Ballads & Lyrics, Volume II.** George C. Eggleston, ed. 1889.

6017-X **American Writing, 1943:** (magazine verse). Alan Swallow, ed. 1944.

6018-8 **Another Book of Verses for Children.** Edward V. Lucas, ed. 1907.

6019-6 **Answering Voice:** love lyrics by women. New ed. Sara Teasdale, comp. 1928

6020-X **Anthology of American Poetry** ("Lyric America"). Alfred Kreymborg, ed. 1935.

6021-8 **Anthology of Canadian Poetry (English).** Ralph Gustafson, comp. 1942.

6022-6 **Anthology of Catholic Poets.** Shane Leslie, comp. 1925.

6023-4 **Anthology of English Verse.** John Drinkwater, ed. 1924.

6024-2 **Anthology of English Poetry: Dryden to Blake.** Kathleen Campbell, comp. 1930.

6025-0 **Anthology of French Poetry:** 10th-19th centuries. Henry Carrington, tr. 1900.

6026-9 **Anthology of Light Verse.** Louis Kronenberger, ed. 1935.

6027-7 **Anthology of Mazazine Verse for 1913.** William S. Braithwaite, ed. 1913.

6028-5 **Anthology of Magazine Verse for 1914.** William S. Braithwaite, ed. 1914.

6029-3 **Anthology of Magazine Verse for 1915.** William S. Braithwaite, ed. 1915.

6030-7 **Anthology of Magazine Verse for 1916.** William S. Braithwaite, ed. 1916.

6031-5 **Anthology of Magazine Verse for 1917.** William S. Braithwaite, ed. 1917.

6032-3 **Anthology of Magazine Verse for 1918.** William S. Braithwaite, ed. 1918.

6033-1 **Anthology of Magazine Verse for 1919.** William S. Braithwaite, ed. 1919.

6034-X **Anthology of Magazine Verse for 1920.** William S. Braithwaite, ed. 1920.

6035-8 **Anthology of Magazine Verse for 1921.** William S. Braithwaite, ed. 1921.

6036-6 **Anthology of Magazine Verse for 1922.** William S. Braithwaite, ed. 1922.

6037-4 **Anthology of Magazine Verse for 1923.** William S. Braithwaite, ed. 1923.

6038-2 **Anthology of Magazine Verse for 1924.** William S. Braithwaite, ed. 1924.

6039-0 **Anthology of Magazine Verse for 1925.** William S. Braithwaite, ed. 1925.

6040-4 **Anthology of Magazine Verse for 1926.** William S. Braithwaite, ed. 1926.

6041-2 **Anthology of Magazine Verse for 1928.** William S. Braithwaite, ed. 1928.

6042-0 **Anthology of Magazine Verse for 1935.** Alan Pater, ed. 1936.

6043-9 **Anthology of New Zealand Verse.** Robert M. Chapman, comp. 1956.

6044-7 **Anthology of Recent Poetry.** Enl. ed. L. D'O. Walters, comp. 1932.

6045-5 **Anthology of Swedish Lyrics from 1750 to 1925.** Charles W. Stork, comp. 1930.

6046-3 **Anthology of Victorian Poetry.** Sir M.E. Grant Duff, ed. 1902.

6047-1 **Arbor Day** (Our American Holidays Series). Robert H. Schauffler, ed. 1909.

6048-X **Arbor Day in the Primary Room.** Susie M. Best. 1899.

List of Works Indexed

6049-8 **Arbor Day Manual.** Charles R. Skinner, ed. 1890.

6050-1 **Armenian Legends and Poems.** Zabelle C. Boyajian, comp. 1916.

6051-X **Armistice Day** (Our American Holidays Series). Anne P. Sanford, ed. 1927.

6052-8 **Art of Reading Poetry.** Earl Daniels, ed. 1941.

6053-6 **Atlantic Prose & Poetry.** Charles S. Thomas, ed. 1919.

6054-4 **Author's Birthdays:** Volume 1. Alice M. Kellogg, comp. 1896.

6055-2 **Ballad Book.** William Allingham, ed. 1864.

6056-0 **Ballad Book.** Katharine L. Bates, ed. 1890.

6057-9 **Ballads and Sea Songs from Nova Scotia.** William R. Mackenzie, comp. 1938.

6058-7 **Ballads and Songs from Ohio.** Mary O. Eddy, comp. 1939.

6059-5 **Ballads and Songs of Southern Michigan.** Emelyn E. Gardner, ed. 1939.

6060-9 **Ballads for Little Folks.** Alice & Phoebe Cary. 1874.

6061-7 **Ballads Migrant in New England.** Helen H. Flanders, comp. 1953.

6062-5 **Ballads of American Bravery.** Clinton Scollard, ed. 1900

6063-3 **Ballads of Books.** Brander Matthews, ed. 1887.

6064-1 **Barton's Comic Recitations.** Jerome Barton, ed. 1871.

6065-X **Beautiful Poems on Jesus.** Basil Miller, comp. 1948.

6066-8 **Because I Love You.** Anna E. Mack, comp. 1894.

6067-6 **Best English and Scottish Ballads.** Edward A. Bryant, comp. 1911.

6068-4 **Best of Modern European Literature** ("Heart of Europe"). Klaus Mann, ed. 1943.

6069-2 **Best Poems of 1923.** Leonard A.G. Strong, ed. 1924.

6070-6 **Best Poems of 1924.** Leonard A.G. Strong, ed. 1924.

6071-4 **Best Poems of 1925.** Leonard A.G. Strong, ed. 1925.

6072-2 **Best Poems of 1926.** Leonard A.G. Strong, ed. 1926.

6073-0 **Bird-Lovers' Anthology.** Clinton Scollard, comp. 1930.

6074-9 **Blue & The Gray:** the best poems of the Civil War. Claudius M. Capps, ed. 1943.

6075-7 **Blue Poetry Book.** Andrew Lang, ed. 1891.

6076-5 **Book of American Poetry.** Edwin Markham, comp. 1934.

6077-3 **Book of American Verse.** Alfred C. Ward, ed. 1935.

6078-1 **Book of Baby Verse.** Joseph Morris (Bachelor), ed. 1923.

6079-X **Book of Ballads.** John R. Crossland, comp. 1940.

6080-3 **Book of British Ballads.** Reginald B. Johnson, comp. 1912.

6081-1 **Book of Canadian Poetry.** Arthur J.M. Smith, ed. 1943.

6082-X **Book of Christmas.** Introd. by Hamilton W. Mabie. 1909.

6083-8 **Book of Fireside Poems.** William R. Bowlin, ed. 1937.

6084-6 **Book of Friendship.** Introd. by Samuel McChord Crothers. 1910.

6085-4 **Book of Friendship Verse.** Joseph Morris (Bachelor), ed. 1924.

6086-2 **Book of Georgian Verse.** 2 vols. William S. Braithwaite, comp. 1909.

6087-0 **Book of Heroic Verse.** Arthur Burrell, comp. 1920.

6088-9 **Book of Historical Poems.** William R. Bowlin, comp. 1939.

6089-7 **Book of Humorous Verse.** Rev. ed. Carolyn Wells, comp. 1934.

List of Works Indexed

6090-0 **Book of Irish Poetry.** Alfred P. Graves, ed. 1907.
6091-9 **Book of Joyous Children.** James W. Riley. 1902.
6092-7 **Book of Light Verse.** Robert M. Leonard, ed. 1910.
6093-5 **Book of Living Poems.** William R. Bowlin, comp. 1934.
6094-3 **Book of Love.** Introd. by Madison Cawein. Jessie Reid, comp. 1891.
6095-1 **Book of Lullabies.** Elva S. Smith, comp. 1925.
6096-X **Book of Modern Catholic Verse.** Theodore Maynard, comp. 1926.
6097-8 **Book of Mother Verse.** Joseph Morris (Bachelor), ed. 1924.
6098-6 **Book of Old English Ballads.** Hamilton W. Mabie, comp. 1896.
6099-4 **Book of Old English Love Songs.** Hamilton W. Mabie, comp. 1897.
6100-1 **Book of Personal Poems.** William R. Bowlin, comp. 1936.
6101-X **Book of Poems.** Oliphant Gibbons, ed. 1938.
6102-8 **Book of Poetry.** 2 vols. Edwin Markham, comp. 1927.
6103-6 **Book of Russian Verse.** Cecil M. Bowra, ed. 1943.
6104-4 **Book of Treasured Poems.** William R. Bowlin, comp. 1928.
6105-2 **Book of Verse for Children.** Edward V. Lucas, comp. 1897.
6106-0 **Book of Winter.** Edith Sitwell, comp. 1951.
6107-9 **Boy's Book of Verse.** Rev. ed. Helen D. Fish, comp. 1951.
6108-7 **Brief Anthology of Poetry.** Stephen F. Fogle, ed. 1951.
6109-5 **Bright Side.** Charles R. Skinner, comp. 1909.
6110-9 **British Poets of the Nineteenth Century.** Rev. ed. Curtis H. Page, ed. 1910.
6111-7 **British Popular Ballads.** John E. Housman, ed. 1952.

6112-5 **Broadway Book of English Verse**—The Sacred Fire. 4th ed. William B. Honey, ed. 1946.
6113-3 **Bugle Echoes: a collection of the poems of the Civil War.** Francis F. Browne, ed. 1916.
6114-1 **Cambridge Book of Poetry for Children.** Kenneth Grahame, ed. 1916.
6115-X **Canadian Poets.** John W. Garvin, ed. 1916.
6116-8 **Cap & Gown: 1st Series.** Joseph Le Roy Harrison, ed. 1893.
6117-6 **Cap & Gown: 2nd Series.** Frederic L. Knowles, comp. 1897.
6118-4 **Cap & Gown: 3rd Series.** R.L. Paget (Knowles), ed. 1902.
6119-2 **Cape Cod Ballads.** Joe Lincoln. 1902.
6120-6 **Cat in Verse.** Carolyn Wells, comp. 1935.
6121-4 **Century Readings in American Literature.** Rev. ed. Fred L. Pattee, comp. 1932.
6122-2 **Century Readings in English Literature.** Rev. ed. John W. Cunliffe, comp. 1910.
6123-0 **Certain Poets of Importance: Victorian verse.** Hattie H. Sloss, comp. 1929.
6124-9 **Chatto Book of Modern Poetry, 1915-1955.** New ed. Cecil Day Lewis, ed. 1959.
6125-7 **Cherry-Tree.** Geoffrey Grigson, comp. 1959.
6126-5 **Chief American Poets.** Curtis H. Page, ed. 1905.
6127-3 **Child Life.** John Greenleaf Whittier, ed. 1871.
6128-1 **Child World.** James W. Riley. 1893.
6129-X **Childhood Songs: (poems).** Lucy Larcom. 1874.
6130-3 **Children's Book.** Frances (Hodgson) Burnett, ed. 1909.

List of Works Indexed

6131-1 **Children's Book of Poetry.**
Henry T. Coates, comp. 1879.
6132-X **Children's First Book of Poetry.**
Emilie K. Baker, comp. 1915.
6133-8 **Children's Garland.** Coventry
Patmore, comp. 1862.
6134-6 **Children's Garland of Verse.**
Grace (Little) Rhys, comp.
1921.
6135-4 **Children's Poems That Never Grow Old.** Clement F. Benoit, comp. 1922.
6136-2 **Children's Second Book of Poetry.** Emilie K. Baker, comp. 1915.
6137-0 **Child's Own Speaker.** Emma Cecilia & Elizabeth Rook. 1895.
6138-9 **Chilswell Book of English Poetry.** Robert S. Bridges, comp. 1924.
6139-7 **Choice Dialect & Other Characterizations.** Charles C. Shoemaker, comp. 1893.
6140-0 **Choice Dialogues.** Rachel W. Shoemaker, ed. 1888.
6141-9 **Choice Readings.** New ed. Robert M. Cumnock, ed. 1913.
6142-7 **Choice Readings, from Standard & Popular Authors.** Robert I. Fulton, comp. 1887.
6143-5 **Choric Interludes.** Mildred J. Keefe, ed. 1942.
6144-3 **Christ in Poetry.** Thomas C. Clark, ed. 1952.
6145-1 **Christmas** (Our American Holidays Series) Robert H. Schauffler, ed. 1907.
6146-X **Christmas Anthology of Poetry & Painting.** Vivian Campbell, ed. 1947.
6147-8 **Christmas Entertainments.** Alice M. Kellogg, comp. 1918.
6148-6 **Classic Dialogues & Dramas.** Rachel W. (Hinkle) Shoemaker, comp. 1888.
6149-4 **Coal Dust on the Fiddle.** George Korson, comp. 1943.
6150-8 **Collected English Verse.** Margaret Bottrall, ed. 1946.
6151-6 **Collected Poems.** 3 vols. Alfred Noyes. 1913-20.
6152-4 **Collection of English Poems, 1660-1800.** Ronald S. Crane, ed. 1932.
6153-2 **College Book of Verse, 1250-1925** ('Riverside Book of Verse'). Robert M. Gay, comp. 1927.
6154-0 **College Readings in Poetry.** Frances K. Del Plaine, ed. 1933.
6155-9 **Comic Recitations & Readings.** Charles W. Brown, comp. 1901.
6156-7 **Commencement Parts.** Harry C. Davis, comp. 1929.
6157-5 **Common Muse.** Vivian de Sola Pinto, ed. 1957.
6158-3 **Complete George Washington Anniversary Programs.** Alma Kaird, ed. 1931.
6159-1 **Complete Poems.** Robert Service. 1921.
6160-5 **Contemporary German Poetry.** Babette Deutsch, ed. 1923.
6161-3 **Contemporary Poetry.** Marguerite Wilkinson, ed. 1923.
6162-1 **Contemporary Verse.** New ed. A. Marion Merrill, ed. 1936.
6163-X **Copeland Reader.** Charles T. Copeland, ed. 1926.
6164-8 **Cradle Book of Verse.** Louise Hovde, comp. 1927.
6165-6 **Cumnock's School Speaker.** Robert M. Cumnock, comp. 1904.
6166-4 **Delsarte Recitation Book.** 4th ed. Elsie M. Wilbor, comp. 1905.
6167-2 **Delsarte Speaker.** Henry D. Northrop, ed. 1895.
6168-0 **Dialogues and Dramas.** Lewis B. Monroe, ed. 1873.
6169-9 **Dick Turpin's Ride and Other Poems.** Alfred Noyes. 1927.

List of Works Indexed

6170-2 **Dick's Comic Dialogues.** William B. Dick, ed. 1886.
6171-0 **Dick's Festival Reciter.** William B. Dick, ed. 1892.
6172-9 **Dreams & Images:** anthology of Catholic poets. Joyce Kilmer, ed. 1917.
6173-7 **Drills and Marches.** Emma Cecilia & Elizabeth Rook. 1890.
6174-5 **Dublin Book of Irish Verse, 1728-1909.** John Cooke, ed. 1909.
6175-3 **Dutch Dialect;** recitations, readings & jokes. 1902.
6176-1 **Early American Poets.** Louis Untermeyer, ed. 1952.
6177-X **Easter** (Our American Holidays Series). Susan T. Rice, ed. 1916.
6178-8 **Ebony Rhythm.** Beatrice M. Murphy, ed. 1948.
6179-6 **Echoing Green,** Books I-III: anthology of verse. 3v in 1. Cecil Day Lewis, ed. 1937-43.
6180-X **Edinburgh Book of Scottish Verse, 1300-1900.** Macneile Dixon, ed. 1910.
6181-8 **Elizabethan Lyrics:** critical anthology. Kenneth Muir, ed. 1953.
6182-6 **Elizabethan Lyrics.** 3rd ed. Norman Ault, ed. 1949.
6183-4 **Elocution and Action.** Enl. ed. Frank T. Southwick. 1928.
6184-2 **Enchanted Years.** John C. Metcalf, ed. 1921.
6185-0 **English & Scottish Popular Ballads.** Francis J. Child, ed. 1904.
6186-9 **English Anthology of Prose & Poetry.** Henry Newbolt, comp. 1921.
6187-7 **English Galaxy of Shorter Poems.** Gerald Bullett, ed. 1933.
6188-5 **English History as Told by English Poets.** Katharine L. Bates, ed. 1902.
6189-3 **English Lyric Poetry, 1500-1700.** Frederic I. Carpenter, ed. 1906.
6190-7 **English Pastoral Poetry:** from the beginnings to Marvell. Frank Kermode, ed. 1952.
6191-5 **English Pastorals.** Edmund K. Chambers, ed. 1906.
6192-3 **English Poems.** Edward C. Baldwin, ed. 1908.
6193-1 **English Poems,** Vol. 1. Old English & middle periods, 450-1550. Walter C. Bronson, ed. 1910.
6194-X **English Poems,** Vol. 2. Elizabethan age & puritan period. Walter C. Bronson, ed. 1909.
6195-8 **English Poems,** Vol. 3. Restoration & 18th century. Walter C. Bronson, ed. 1908.
6196-6 **English Poems,** Vol. 4. 19th century. Walter C. Bronson, ed. 1907.
6197-4 **English Poems from Chaucer to Kipling.** Thomas M. Parrott, ed. 1902.
6198-2 **English Poetry, 1170-1892.** John M. Manly, comp. 1907.
6199-0 **English Poetry of the 19th Century.** G.R. Elliott, ed. 1923.
6200-8 **English Satires.** William O. Smeaton, ed. 1899.
6201-6 **English, Scottish & Welsh Landscape, 1700-c.1860.** Sir John Betjeman, comp. 1944.
6202-4 **English Sonnets.** New ed. Sir Arthur Quiller-Couch, ed. 1935.
6203-2 **Entertainments for All the Year.** Clara J. (Fort) Denton. 1910.
6204-0 **Eternal Passion in English Poetry.** Edith Wharton, ed. 1939.
6205-9 **Eureka Entertainments.** 1894.

List of Works Indexed

6206-7 **Every Soul Is a Circus.** Vachel Lindsay. 1929.

6207-5 **Excelsior Dialogues.** Phineas Garrett, ed. 1904.

6208-3 **Faber Book of English Verse.** John Hayward, ed. 1958.

6209-1 **Faber Book of Modern Verse.** New ed. Michael Roberts, ed. 1951.

6210-5 **Faber Book of 20th Century Verse:** in Britain, 1900-1950. John Heath-Stubbs, ed. 1953.

6211-3 **Facing Forward.** Joseph Morris (Bachelor), ed. 1925.

6212-1 **Famous Poems Explained.** Waitman Barbe. 1909.

6213-X **Favorite Poems:** selected from English & American authors. 1884.

6214-8 **Favorite Poems of Faith & Comfort.** Barbara M. Olds, ed. 1942.

6215-6 **Favorite Speaker.** T.G. La Moille, comp. 1885.

6216-4 **Fifty Christmas Poems for Children.** Florence B. Hyett, comp. 1923.

6217-2 **Fifty Poets.** William R. Benet, ed. 1933.

6218-0 **Fire and Sleet and Candlelight.** August Derleth, ed. 1961.

6219-9 **Fireside Encyclopedia of Poetry.** Henry T. Coates, comp. 1901.

6220-2 **Fireside Poems.** Veronica S. Hutchinson, ed. 1930.

6221-0 **Five-Minute Declamations,** Part I. Walter K. Fobes, ed. 1885.

6222-9 **Five-Minute Declamations,** Part II. Walter K. Fobes, ed. 1890.

6223-7 **Flag Day** (Our American Holidays Series). Robert Haven Schauffler, ed. 1912.

6224-5 **Flying Colours.** Sir Charles G. Roberts, ed. 1942.

6225-3 **For His Sake.** Anna E. Mack,

6226-1 **For Thee Alone.** Grace Hartshorne, comp. 1899.

6227-X **Formal Spring:** French renaissance poems. R.N. Currey, tr. 1950.

6228-8 **Four Winds,** Books I-III. 3v in 1. Jean Edwards, comp. 1939.

6229-6 **Friday Afternoon Series of Dialogues.** Thomas S. Denison, ed. 1907.

6230-X **Friendly Town.** Edward V. Lucas, comp. 1905.

6231-8 **G.I. Songs.** Edgar A. Palmer, ed. 1944.

6232-6 **Garden Book of Verse.** 2v in 1. William Griffith, ed. 1932.

6233-4 **Garland of Childhood:** little book for all lovers of children. Percy Withers, comp. 1910.

6234-2 **Georgian Poetry, 1911-1912.** Prefatory note by E.H. Marsh. 1914.

6235-0 **Georgian Poetry, 1913-1915.** Prefatory note by E.H. Marsh. 1916.

6236-9 **Girl's Book of Verse.** Rev. ed. Mary G. Davis, comp. 1952.

6237-7 **Give Out!** Eric Posselt, ed. 1943.

6238-5 **Golden Gleams of Thought.** S.P. Linn, comp. 1881.

6239-3 **Golden Numbers.** Kate D. Wiggin, ed. 1902.

6240-7 **Golden Poems by British & American Authors.** Francis F. Browne, ed. 1882.

6241-5 **Golden Songs of the Golden State.** Marguerite Wilkinson, comp. 1917.

6242-3 **Golden Staircase.** Louey Chisholm, ed. 1906.

6243-1 **Golden Treasury of American Songs & Lyrics.** Frederic L. Knowles, ed. 1897.

6244-X **Golden Treasury of Irish Verse.** Lennox Robinson, ed. 1925.

6245-8 **Golden Treasury of Longer Poems.**

xvii

List of Works Indexed

Ernest Rhys, ed. 1921.

6246-6 **Golden Treasury of the Best Songs & Lyrical Poems**...New ed. C. Day Lewis & Francis T. Palgrave, eds. 1954.

6247-4 **Good Humor for Reading & Recitation.** Henry F. Wood, comp. 1893.

6248-2 **Good Things for Washington & Lincoln Birthdays.** Marie Irish. 1907.

6249-3 **Grace Marie Stanistreet's Recitations for Children.** Grace M. Stanistreet, comp. 1930.

6250-4 **Great Poems of the English Language.** New ed. by W.R. Benet. Wallace A. Briggs, ed. 1941.

6251-2 **Greek Poetry for Everyman.** F.L. Lucas, ed. 1951.

6252-0 **Gypsy Trail,** Volume 1. Pauline Goldmark, comp. 1914.

6253-9 **Gypsy Trail,** Volume 2. Pauline Goldmark, comp. 1930.

6254-7 **Hallowe'en** (Our American Holidays Series). Robert H. Schauffler, comp. 1933.

6255-5 **Handbook of Best Readings.** Solomon H. Clark, ed. 1902.

6256-3 **Harper's Anthology for College Courses,** Volume 2, Poetry. Frederick A. Manchester, ed. 1926.

6257-1 **Harrap Book of Modern Verse.** Maurice Wollman, comp. 1958.

6258-X **Harrap Book of Sea Verse.** Ronald Hope, ed. 1960.

6259-8 **Harvest of German Verse.** Margarete A. Munsterberg, comp. 1916.

6260-1 **Heart Throbs.** Joe M. Chapple, comp. 1905.

6261-X **Heaven's Distant Lamps.** Anna E.

6262-8 **Here We Come A'Piping.** Rose Fyleman, ed. 1937.

6263-6 **Heroic Ballads.** David H. Montgomery, ed. 1890.

6264-4 **Heroic Tales in Verse.** E.J. Pratt, ed. 1941.

6265-2 **High Lights in American Literature.** Ola P. Srygley, ed. 1940.

6266-0 **High Tide.** Gertrude M. Richards, comp. 1916.

6267-9 **Historic Poems & Ballads.** Rupert S. Holland, ed. 1912.

6268-7 **Holiday Entertainments.** Charles C. Shoemaker, ed. 1888.

6269-5 **Holyrood.** W.H. Hamilton, ed. 1929.

6270-9 **Homespun:** ...Poetry by General Federation of Women's Clubs. Anita Browne, comp. 1936.

6271-7 **Household Book of Poetry.** Charles A. Dana, ed. 1882.

6272-5 **How to Celebrate Thanksgiving & Christmas.** Alice M. Kellogg, ed. 1894.

6273-3 **Humbler Poets,** 1st Series: 1870-85. Slason Thompson, ed. 1885.

6274-1 **Humbler Poets,** 2nd Series: 1885-1910. Wallace Rice, comp. 1911.

6275-X **Humorous Dialogues.** H. Elliott McBride. 1879.

6276-8 **Humorous Dialogues & Dramas.** Charles C. Shoemaker, comp. 1888.

6277-6 **Humorous Hits & How to Hold an Audience.** Grenville Kleiser. 1908.

6278-4 **Humorous Poetry of the English Language, Chaucer to Saxe.** James Parton, ed. 1884.

6279-2 **Humorous Readings.** Lewis B. Monroe, ed. 1871.

6280-6 **Humorous Speaker.** Paul M.

6281-4 **I Hear America Singing.** Ruth Barnes, comp. 1937.

6282-2 **I Sing of a Maiden:** the Mary book of verse. Sister M.

xviii

List of Works Indexed

Therese, ed. 1947.
6283-0 **Icelandic Poems & Stories.** Richard Beck, ed. 1943.
6284-9 **Ideal Drills.** Marguerite W. Morton, comp. 1900.
6285-7 **In Praise of Nuns.** James M. Hayes, ed. 1942.
6286-5 **Independence Day** (Our American Holidays Series). Robert H. Schauffler, ed. 1912.
6287-3 **Innocent Merriment.** Franklin P. Adams, comp. 1942.
6288-1 **Introduction to American Poetry.** Frederick C. Prescott, ed. 1932.
6289-X **Introduction to Poetry.** Jay B. Hubbell, ed. 1922.
6290-3 **Invitation to Verse.** A.E.M. Bayliss, ed. 1943.
6291-1 **It Can Be Done.** Joseph Morris (Bachelor), ed. 1921.
6292-X **Joyce Kilmer's Anthology of Catholic Poets.** New ed. Joyce Kilmer, ed. 1926.
6293-8 **Kavanaugh's Juvenile Speaker, for Very Little Boys & Girls.** Mrs. Russell Kavanaugh. 1877.
6294-6 **Kidd's New Elocution & Vocal Culture.** Robert Kidd. 1883.
6295-4 **Lamb's Poetry for Children.** Charles & Mary Lamb. 1903.
6296-2 **Land of Song,** Book I. Katharine H. Shute, ed. 1898.
6297-0 **Lang's Ballads of Books.** Andrew Lang. 1888.
6298-9 **Last Voyage.** Alfred Noyes. 1930.
6299-7 **Lays of the New Land.** Charlie M. Simon, ed. 1943.
6300-4 **Le Gallienne Book of American Verse.** Richard Le Gallienne, ed. 1925.
6301-2 **Le Gallienne Book of English Verse.** Richard Le Gallienne, ed. 1922.
6302-0 **Library of Poetry & Song.** 12th ed. William C. Bryant, ed. 1874.
6303-9 **Light of the World.** Joseph Morris (Bachelor), ed. 1928.
6304-7 **Lincoln Literary Collection.** John P. McCaskey, comp. 1897.
6305-5 **Lincoln's Birthday** (Our American Holidays Series). Robert H. Schauffler, ed. 1909.
6306-3 **Listening Child.** Lucy W. Thacher, comp. 1899.
6307-1 **Little Book of American Humorous Verse.** T.A. Daly, comp. 1926.
6308-X **Little Book of Limericks.** H.I. Brock, comp. 1947.
6309-8 **Little Book of American Poets.** Jessie B. Rittenhouse, comp. 1915.
6310-0 **Little Book of Modern Verse.** Jessie B. Rittenhouse, comp. 1913.
6311-X **Little-Folk Lyrics.** Frank D. Sherman. 1897.
6312-8 **Little Folks Speaker.** Charles W. Brown, comp. 1903.
6313-6 **Little People's Dialogues.** Clara J. (Fort) Denton. 1888.
6314-4 **Little People's Speaker.** Rachel W. Shoemaker. 1886.
6315-2 **London Book of English Verse.** Herbert E. Read, ed. 1949.
6316-0 **Look to This Day.** Poetry Society of Southern California. 1944.
6317-9 **Love.** Walter De La Mare, ed. 1946.
6318-7 **Love Songs of Childhood.** Eugene Field. 1894.
6319-5 **Love's Enchantment.** Helen Ferris, comp. 1944.
6320-9 **Love's High Way.** Gertrude M. Richards, comp. 1927.
6321-7 **Lover's Treasury of Verse.** John W. Chadwick, comp. 1891.
6322-5 **Lyra Heroica.** William E. Henley, ed. 1891.

List of Works Indexed

6323-3 **Lyra Historica.** M.E. Windsor, comp. 1911.
6324-1 **Lyric Moderns in Brief.** Tom Boggs, ed. 1940.
6325-X **Lyric Poetry of the Italian Renaissance.** L.R. Lind, comp. 1954.
6326-8 **Lyric South.** Clarence A. Hibbard, ed. 1928.
6327-6 **Lyric Year.** Ferdinand Earle, ed. 1912.
6328-4 **Lyrics from the Old Song Books.** Edmonstoune Duncan, ed. 1927.
6329-2 **McBride's Choice Dialogues.** H. Elliott McBride. 1893.
6330-6 **McBride's New Dialogues.** H. Elliot McBride. 1883.
6331-4 **Magic Carpet.** Gertrude M. Richards, comp. 1924.
6332-2 **Magic Casements.** George S. Carhart, comp. 1926.
6333-0 **Major American Poets to 1914.** Francis Murphy, ed. 1967.
6334-9 **Many Voices,** Books I-II. 1 vol. ed. Mona Swann, ed. 1934.
6335-7 **Master of Men.** Thomas C. Clark, comp. 1930.
6336-5 **Masterpieces of Modern Verse.** Edwin D. Shurter, comp. 1926.
6337-3 **Masterpieces of Religious Verse.** James D. Morrison, ed. 1948.
6338-1 **Melody of Earth.** Gertrude M. Richards, comp. 1918.
6339-X **Memorable Poetry.** Sir Francis Meynell, ed. 1956.
6340-3 **Memorial Day** (Our American Holidays Series). Robert H. Schauffler, ed. 1911.
6341-1 **Metaphysical Lyrics & Poems of the 17th Century.** Herbert J. Grierson, ed. 1921.
6342-X **Minnesota Skyline.** Carmen N. Richards, ed. 1944.
6343-8 **Mirror for French Poetry, 1840-1940.** Cecily Mackworth (De Chanannes La Palice), ed. 1947.

6344-6 **Miscellaneous Readings.** Lewis B. Monroe, ed. 1872.
6345-4 **Miscellany of American Poetry, 1920.** Louis Untermeyer, ed. 1920.
6346-2 **Model Dialogues.** William M. Clark, comp. 1897.
6347-0 **Modern American Lyrics.** Stanton A. Coblentz, comp. 1924.
6348-9 **Modern American Poets.** Conrad Aiken, ed. 1927.
6349-7 **Modern Australian Poetry.** 2nd ed. rev. Henry M. Green, ed. 1952.
6350-0 **Modern British Lyrics.** Stanton A. Coblentz, comp. 1952.
6351-9 **Modern French Poetry.** Joseph T. Shipley, comp. 1926.
6352-7 **Modern Greek Poetry.** Rae Dalven, ed. 1949.
6353-5 **Modern Muse:** poems of today, British & American. English Association. 1934.
6354-3 **Modern Poet.** Gwendolen Murphy, ed. 1938.
6355-1 **Modern Poetry for Children,** Book 6. James J. Reynolds, ed. 1928.
6356-X **Modern Poetry for Children,** Book 8. James J. Reynolds, ed. 1928.
6357-8 **Modern Poets' World.** James Reeves, ed. 1957.
6358-6 **Modern Reader & Speaker.** George Riddle, ed. 1900.
6359-4 **Modern Religious Verse & Prose.** Fred Merrifield, ed. 1925.
6360-8 **Modern Welsh Poetry.** Keidrych Rhys, ed. 1954.
6361-6 **Monologues and Novelties.** Benjamin L.C. Griffith, ed. 1896.
6362-4 **Moorish Poetry.** A.J. Arberry, ed. 1953.
6363-2 **Mother Goose.** William R. Benet, comp. 1943.
6364-0 **Mother Goose on the Rio Grande.** Frances Alexander, ed. 1944.

List of Works Indexed

6365-9 Mothers' Anthology. William L. Phelps, comp. 1941.
6366-7 Mother's Day (Our American Holidays Series). Susan T. Rice, comp. 1915.
6367-5 Music Makers. Stanton A. Coblentz, ed. 1945.
6368-3 My Caravan. Eulalie O. Grover, ed. 1913.
6369-1 My Favorite English Poems. John Masefield, ed. 1950.
6370-5 My Recitations. Cora U. Potter. 1886.
6371-3 Narrative and Lyric Poetry. James W. Tupper, ed. 1927.
6372-1 National Epics. Kate M. Rabb. 1896.
6373-X Nature in Verse. Mary I. Lovejoy, comp. 1895.
6374-8 Nature Lover's Knapsack. Enl. ed. Edwin O. Grover, ed. 1947.
6375-6 New Anthology of Modern Poetry. Selden Rodman, ed. 1938.
6376-4 New Arbor Day Exercises. Alice M. Kellogg, comp. 1901.
6377-2 New Book of Dialogues. Sarah A. Frost (Shields). 1872.
6378-0 New Book of English Verse. Charles Williams, ed. 1935.
6379-9 New British Poets. Kenneth Rexroth, ed. 1949.
6380-2 New Canon of English Poetry. James Reeves, ed. 1967.
6381-0 New Century Speaker. Henry A Frink. 1898.
6382-9 New Dialogues and Plays. 3 vols. in 1. Binney Gunnison.
6383-7 New Golden Treasury of Songs & Lyrics. Ernest Rhys, comp.
6384-5 New Land, New Language. Judith Wright, comp. 1957.
6385-3 New Library of Poetry & Song. 2 vols. William C. Bryant, ed. 1877.
6386-1 New Patriotism. Thomas C. Clark, comp. 1927.

6387-X New Pieces That Will Take Prizes in Speaking Contests. Harriet Blackstone, comp. 1901.
6388-8 New Poems by American Poets, #2. Rolfe Humphries, ed. 1957.
6389-6 New Poems, 1940. Oscar Williams, ed. 1941.
6390-X New Poems, 1942. Oscar Williams, ed. 1942.
6391-8 New Poems, 1943. Oscar Williams, ed. 1943.
6392-6 New Science of Elocution. Rev. ed. S.S. Hamill. 1914.
6393-4 New Voices. New ed. Marguerite Wilkinson, ed. 1928.
6394-2 New Year & Midwinter Exercises. Alice M. Kellogg, ed. 1907.
6395-0 Off the Ground, Books I-IV. 4 vols. William Kerr, ed. 1945.
6396-9 Off to Arcady. Max J. Herzberg, ed. 1933.
6397-7 Oklahoma Anthology for 1929. Joseph F. Paxton, ed. 1929.
6398-5 Old English Songs. Austin Dobson, ed. 1894.
6399-3 100 American Poems. Selden A. Rodman, ed. 1948.
6400-0 One Hundred & One Famous Poems, with a Prose Supplement. Roy J. Cook, comp. Rev. ed. 1929.
6401-9 One Hundred & Ten Favorite Children's Poems. H.G. Platt, ed. 1943.
6402-7 One Hundred Choice Selections, #1. Phineas Garrett, ed.
6403-5 One Hundred Choice Selections, #2. Phineas Garrett, ed.
6404-3 One Hundred Choice Selections, #4. Phineas Garrett, ed.
6405-1 One Hundred Choice Selections, #5. Phineas Garrett, ed.
6406-X One Hundred Choice Selections, #7. Phineas Garrett, ed.
6407-8 One Hundred Choice Selections, #8. Phineas Garrett, ed.
6408-6 One Hundred Choice Selections,

List of Works Indexed

#9. Phineas Garrett, ed.
6409-4 One Hundred Choice Selections, #10. Phineas Garrett, ed.
6410-8 One Hundred Choice Selections, #15. Phineas Garrett, ed.
6411-6 One Hundred Choice Selections, #18. Phineas Garrett, ed.
6412-4 One Hundred Choice Selections, #19. Phineas Garrett, ed.
6413-2 One Hundred Choice Selections, #20. Phineas Garrett, ed.
6414-0 One Hundred Choice Selections, #22. Phineas Garrett, ed.
6415-9 One Hundred Choice Selections, #23. Phineas Garrett, ed.
6416-7 One Hundred Choice Selections, #26. Phineas Garrett, ed.
6417-5 One Hundred Choice Selections, #31. Phineas Garrett, ed.
6418-3 One Hundred Great Religious Poems. Randolph Ray, ed. 1951.
6419-1 One Hundred Narrative Poems. George E. Teter, ed. 1918.
6420-5 One Hundred Poems of Peace. Thomas C. Clark, comp. 1934.
6421-3 Open Door to Poetry. Anne K. Stokes, ed. 1931.
6422-1 Open Gates. Susan T. Spaulding, comp. 1924.
6423-X Open Road. Edward V. Lucas, comp. 1905.
6424-8 Open Sesame!, Parts I-III. 3 vols. Blanche W. Bellamy, ed. 1889-90.
6425-6 Orator's Manual. Rev. ed. George L. Raymond. 1910.
6426-4 Original Recitations with Lesson Talks. Enl. ed. Emma D. Banks. 1908.
6427-2 Other Men's Flowers. A.P. Wavell, Lord Wavell, comp. 1944.
6428-0 Our Heritage of World Literature. Rev. ed. 2 vols. in 1. Stith Thompson, ed. 1942.
6429-9 Out of the Heart. John W. Chadwick, ed. 1891.
6430-2 Oxford Anthology of English Poetry. Howard F. Lowry, ed. 1935.
6431-0 Oxford Book of American Verse. Bliss Carman, ed. 1927.
6432-9 Oxford Book of Ballads. Sir Arthur Quiller-Couch, ed. 1910.
6433-7 Oxford Book of Canadian Verse. William W. Campbell, comp. 1914.
6434-5 Oxford Book of English Verse, 1250-1900. Sir Arthur Quiller-Couch, ed. 1900.
6435-3 Oxford Book of Greek Verse in Translation. T.F. Higham, ed. 1938.
6436-1 Oxford Book of Sixteenth Century Verse. Edmund K. Chambers, comp. 1932.
6437-X Oxford Book of Victorian Verse. Sir Arthur Quiller-Couch, ed. 1912.
6438-8 Parnassus. Ralph W. Emerson, ed. 1874.
6439-6 Parnassus En Route. Mrs. Kenneth Horan, comp. 1929.
6440-X Parody Anthology. Carolyn Wells, comp. 1904.
6441-8 Patrician Rhymes. Clinton Scollard, ed. 1932.
6442-6 Patriotic Anthology: poems of American history...Peter Pauper Press. 1940.
6443-4 Patriotic Pieces from the Great War. Edna D. Jones, comp. 1918.
6444-2 Patriotic Readings & Recitations. Josephine Stafford, ed. 1902.
6445-0 Peerless Reciter. Henry D. Northrop, ed. 1894.
6446-9 Penguin Book of Canadian Verse. Ralph Gustafson, ed. 1958.
6447-7 Penguin Book of Sonnets. Carl Withers, ed. 1943.

List of Works Indexed

6448-5 **Persian Poems.** A.J. Arberry, ed. 1954.
6449-3 **Pieces for Every Day the Schools Celebrate.** Rev. ed. Norma H. Deming, comp. 1949.
6450-7 **Pieces for Prize Speaking.** A.H. Craig, ed. 1931.
6451-5 **Pieces That Have Won Prizes.** Enl. ed. Frank McHale, comp. 1930.
6452-3 **Pinafore Palace.** Kate D. Wiggin, ed. 1907.
6453-1 **Pipe & Pouch.** Joseph Knight, comp?. 1894.
6454-X **Pocketful of Rhymes.** Katherine Love, ed. 1946.
6455-8 **Poems by Contemporary Women.** Theodora Roscoe, comp. 1944.
6456-6 **Poems by Grades,** Vol. 1. For grades 1-4 (primary). Ada Harris, comp. 1907.
6457-4 **Poems by Grades,** Vol. 2. For grades 5-8 (grammar). Ada Harris, comp. 1907.
6458-2 **Poems, Chiefly Narrative.** New rev. ed. Wilbert L. Macdonald, ed. 1938.
6459-0 **Poems Children Love.** Penrhyn W. Coussens, comp. 1908.
6460-4 **Poems for a Machine Age.** Horace J. McNeil, ed. 1941.
6461-2 **Poems for Daily Needs.** Thomas C. Clark, ed. 1936.
6462-0 **Poems for Enjoyment.** Elias Lieberman, ed. 1931.
6463-9 **Poems for Great Days.** Thomas C. Clark, comp. 1948.
6464-7 **Poems for Modern Youth.** Adolph Gillis, ed. 1938.
6465-5 **Poems for Red Letter Days.** Elizabeth H. Sechrist, comp. 1951.
6466-3 **Poems for the Children's Hour.** Josephine Bouton, comp. 1927.
6467-1 **Poems for Youth.** William R. Benet, comp. 1925.

6468-X **Poems from the Desert.** Members of the Eighth Army. 1944.
6469-8 **Poems I Remember.** John Kieran, comp. 1942.
6470-1 **Poems of American Patriotism.** Brander Matthews, ed. 1882.
6471-X **Poems of American Patriotism.** R.L. Paget (Knowles), ed. 1898.
6472-8 **Poems of Death.** Phoebe Pool, comp. 1945.
6473-6 **Poems of the English Race.** Raymond M. Alden, ed. 1921.
6474-4 **Poems of the Great War.** John W. Cunliffe, ed. 1916.
6475-2 **Poems of This War by Younger Poets.** Patricia Ledward, ed. 1942.
6476-0 **Poems of Today.** Alice C. Cooper, ed. 1924.
6477-9 **Poems of Today.** 1st & 2nd series. 2v in 1. English Association. 1924.
6478-7 **Poems of Youth.** Alice C. Cooper, ed. 1928.
6479-5 **Poems That Every Child Should Know.** Mary E. Burt, ed. 1904.
6480-9 **Poems Worth Knowing.** Rev. ed. Claude E. Lewis, comp. 1958.
6481-7 **Poems You Ought to Know.** Elia W. Peattie, ed. 1902.
6482-5 **Poet Physicians.** Mary L. McDonough, comp. 1945.
6483-3 **Poet to Poet.** Houston Peterson, ed. 1945.
6484-1 **Poetic New-World.** Lucy H. Humphrey (Smith), comp. 1910.
6485-X **Poetic Old-World.** Lucy H. Humphrey (Smith), comp. 1908.
6486-8 **Poetical Favorites-Yours & Mine.** Warren Snyder, comp. 1910.
6487-6 **Poetical Works.** One vol. ed. (excluding 8 dramas). Robert Bridges. 1953.
6488-4 **Poetry & Life:** introduction to poetry. Clyde S. Kilby, ed. 1953.

List of Works Indexed

6489-2 **Poetry & Life:** anthology of English Catholic poetry. F.J. Sheed, comp. 1942.

6490-6 **Poetry Arranged for the Speaking Choir.** Marion P. Robinson. 1936.

6491-4 **Poetry as Experience.** Norman C. Stageberg, ed. 1952.

6492-2 **Poetry Book,** Volume 1. Miriam B. Huber, ed. 1926.

6493-0 **Poetry Book,** Volume 2. Miriam B. Huber, ed. 1926.

6494-9 **Poetry Book,** Volume 3. Miriam B. Huber, ed. 1926.

6495-7 **Poetry Book,** Volume 4. Miriam B. Huber, ed. 1926.

6496-5 **Poetry Book,** Volume 5. Miriam B. Huber, ed. 1926.

6497-3 **Poetry Book,** Volume 6. Miriam B. Huber, ed. 1926.

6498-1 **Poetry Book,** Volume 7. Miriam B. Huber, ed. 1926.

6499-X **Poetry Book,** Volume 8. Miriam B. Huber, ed. 1926.

6500-7 **Poetry Book,** Volume 9. Miriam B. Huber, ed. 1926.

6501-5 **Poetry Cure.** Robert H. Schauffler, comp. 1925.

6502-3 **Poetry for Children.** Samuel Eliot, ed. 1879.

6503-1 **Poetry for Junior High Schools,** Book 1. Elias Lieberman, ed. 1926.

6504-X **Poetry for School Reading.** Marcus White, ed. 1889.

6505-8 **Poetry of American Wit & Humor.** R.L. Paget (Knowles), ed. 1899.

6506-6 **Poetry of Our Times.** Sharon O. Brown, ed. 1928.

6507-4 **Poetry of the Nineties.** C.E. Andrews, ed. 1926.

6508-2 **Poetry of the Transition, 1850-1914.** Thomas M. Parrott, ed. 1932.

6509-0 **Poetry of Today.** Rosa M. Mikels, ed. 1927.

6510-4 **Poetry's Plea for Animals.** Frances E. Clarke, comp. 1927.

6511-2 **Poet's Cat.** Mona Gooden, comp. 1946.

6512-0 **Poet's Craft.** Helen F. Daringer, comp. 1935.

6513-9 **Poet's Gold.** Davis Ross, ed. 1933.

6514-7 **Poets Laureate.** Kenneth Hopkins. 1954.

6515-5 **Poets of the Pacific,** 2nd series. Yvor Winters, ed. 1949.

6516-3 **Poets Speak, 1943.** May Sarton, ed. 1943.

6517-1 **Point Lace & Diamonds.** George A. Baker Jr. 1875.

6518-X **Popular British Ballads,** Vols I-IV. 4 vols. Reginald B. Johnson, ed. 1894.

6519-8 **Posy Ring.** Kate D. Wiggin, ed. 1903.

6520-1 **Practical Dialogues.** Amos M. Kellogg, comp. 1903.

6521-X **Practical Elocution.** Enl. ed. Jacob W. Shoemaker. 1893.

6522-8 **Practical Public Speaking.** Solomon H. Clark. 1899.

6523-6 **Practical Recitations.** Amos M. Kellogg. 1903.

6524-4 **Praise of Lincoln.** A. Dallas Williams, ed. 1911.

6525-2 **Prayer Poems.** O.V. Armstrong, comp. 1942.

6526-0 **Pre-Raphaelites in Literature & Art.** D.S.R. Welland, ed. 1953.

6527-9 **Preface to Poetry.** Charles W. Cooper. 1946.

6528-7 **Presenting Welsh Poetry.** Gwyn Williams, ed. 1959.

6529-5 **Primary Recitations.** Amos M. Kellogg, comp. 1897.

6530-9 **Primary Speaker.** Amos M. Kellogg, comp. 1903.

6531-7 **Prize Poems, 1913-1929.** Charles A. Wagner, ed. 1930.

List of Works Indexed

6532-5 **Questing Spirit.** Halford E. Luccock, ed. 1947.
6533-3 **Quiet Hour.** FitzRoy Carrington, ed. 1915.
6534-1 **Quiz Kids' Book:** stories & poems chosen by the Quiz Kids. 1947.
6535-X **Rainbow Gold.** Sara Teasdale. comp. 1922.
6536-8 **Reading Poems.** Wright Thomas, ed. 1941.
6537-6 **Readings & Monologues of Distinction.** Frances L. Hess, comp. 1925.
6538-4 **Readings from the New Poets.** William W. Ellsworth, ed. 1928.
6539-2 **Recitations for Younger Children.** Grace Gaige, comp. 1927.
6540-6 **Recitations:** old & new, for boys & girls. Grace Gaige, comp. 1924.
6541-4 **Reciter's Treasury of Scenes & Poems.** Ernest G. Pertwee, ed. 1934.
6542-2 **Red Harvest.** Vincent G. Burns, ed. 1930.
6543-0 **Red Letter Poems by English Men & Women.** Thomas Y. Crowell, comp. 1884.
6544-9 **Restoration Carnival.** Vivian de Sola Pinto, ed. 1954.
6545-7 **Romantics.** Geoffrey Grigson, ed. 1942.
6546-5 **Russian Poetry, 1917-1955.** Jack Lindsay, ed. 1957.
6547-3 **Sailor's Garland.** New ed. John Masefield, ed. 1924.
6548-1 **Sara Shriner's Selections.** Sara V. Shriner, comp. 1924.
6549-X **Saucy Sailor & Other Dramatized Ballads.** Alice M.G. White, comp. 1940.
6550-3 **School & College Speaker.** Wilmot B. Mitchell. ed. 1901.
6551-1 **School & Parlor Comedies.** Benjamin L.C. Griffith. 1894.

6552-X **School Speaker & Reader.** William D. Hyde, ed. 1900.
6553-8 **Schoolday Dialogues.** Alexander Clark, comp. 1897.
6554-6 **Science & Art of Elocution.** F.H. Fenno, ed. 1878.
6555-4 **Second Book of Danish Verse.** Charles W. Stork, tr. 1947.
6556-2 **Second Book of Modern Verse.** Jessie B. Rittenhouse, ed. 1919.
6557-0 **Second Book of Russian Verse.** Cecil M. Bowra, ed. 1948.
6558-9 **Second Daffodil Poetry Book.** Ethel L. Fowler, comp. 1931.
6559-7 **Select Speeches for Declamation.** John H. Bechtel, comp. 1898.
6560-0 **Selection from the Great English Poets.** Sherwin Cody, comp. 1905.
6561-9 **Seven Poets in Search of an Answer.** Thomas Yoseloff, ed. 1944.
6562-7 **Seventeenth-Century English Poetry.** R.C. Bald, ed. 1959.
6563-5 **Seventeenth Century Lyrics.** 2nd ed. Norman Ault, ed. 1950.
6564-3 **Seventeenth Century Songs & Lyrics.** John P. Cutts, ed. 1959.
6565-1 **Shoemaker's Best Selections, #1.** Jacob W. Shoemaker, ed.
6566-X **Shoemaker's Best Selections, #2.** Jacob W. Shoemaker, ed.
6567-8 **Shoemaker's Best Selections, #3.** Jacob W. Shoemaker, ed.
6568-6 **Shoemaker's Best Selections, #4.** Jacob W. Shoemaker, ed.
6569-4 **Shoemaker's Best Selections, #5.** Jacob W. Shoemaker, ed.
6570-8 **Shoemaker's Best Selections, #6.** Jacob W. Shoemaker, ed.
6571-6 **Shoemaker's Best Selections, #7.** Jacob W. Shoemaker, ed.
6572-4 **Shoemaker's Best Selections, #9.** Jacob W. Shoemaker, ed.

List of Works Indexed

6573-2 Shoemaker's Best Selections, #10. Jacob W. Shoemaker, ed.
6574-0 Shoemaker's Best Selections, #11. Jacob W. Shoemaker, ed.
6575-9 Shoemaker's Best Selections, #14. Jacob W. Shoemaker, ed.
6576-7 Shoemaker's Best Selections, #21. Jacob W. Shoemaker, ed.
6577-5 Shoemaker's Best Selections, #22. Jacob W. Shoemaker, ed.
6578-3 Shoemaker's Best Selections, #23. Jacob W. Shoemaker, ed.
6579-1 Shoemaker's Best Selections, #25. Jacob W. Shoemaker, ed.
6580-5 Shoemaker's Best Selections, #26. Jacob W. Shoemaker, ed.
6581-3 Shorter Modern Poems, 1900-1931. David Morton, comp. 1932.
6582-1 Silver Branch. Sean O'Faolain, comp. 1938.
6583-X Silver Linings. Joseph Morris (Bachelor), comp. 1927.
6584-8 Silver Poets of the Sixteenth Century. Gerald Bullett, ed. 1947.
6585-6 Silver Treasury. Jane Manner, ed. 1934.
6586-4 Sixteenth-Century English Poetry. Norman E. McClure, ed. 1954.
6587-2 "Smiles." Alice L. Richards. 1899.
6588-0 Smiles Yoked with Sighs. Robert J. Burdette. 1900.
6589-9 Soldiers' Collection of Poems & Ballads. William A. Brooks, ed. 1941.
6590-2 Soldiers' Verse. Patric Dickinson, comp. 1945.
6591-0 Songs & Ballads from Over the Sea. E.A. Helps, comp. 1912.
6592-9 Songs & Ballads of Greater Britain. E.A. Helps, comp. 1913.
6593-7 Songs from the Land of Dawn. Lois J. Erickson, tr. 1949.
6594-5 Songs of American Folks. Satis N. Coleman, ed. 1942.
6595-3 Songs of American Sailormen. Enl. ed. Joanna C. Colcord, ed. 1938.
6596-1 Songs of Childhood. Walter Ramal (De La Mare). 1902.
6597-X Songs of Nature. John Burroughs, comp. 1901.
6598-8 Songs of the Cattle Trail & Cow Camp. John A. Lomax, comp. 1919.
6599-6 Songs of the Sea & Sailors' Chanteys. Robert Frothingham, comp. 1924.
6600-3 Songs of Three Centuries. New rev. ed. John G. Whittier, ed. 1875.
6601-1 Special Day Exercises. Amos M. Kellogg, comp. 1903.
6602-X Speech Choir. Marjorie Gullan, ed. 1937.
6603-8 Standard Dialogues. Alexander Clark, comp. 1898.
6604-6 Standard English Poems: Spenser to Tennyson. Henry S. Pancoast,
6605-4 Standard Selections. Robert I. Fulton, comp. 1907.
6606-2 Standard Speaker. Epres Sargent, comp. 1852.
6607-0 Star-Points. Gertrude M. Richards, comp. 1921.
6608-9 Stardust & Holly. Dorothy M. Shipman, comp. 1932.
6609-7 Steamboatin' Days. Mary Wheeler, comp. 1944.
6610-0 Steps to Oratory. F. Townsend Southwick, ed. 1900.
6611-9 Sterling Dialogues. William M. Clark, comp. 1929.
6612-7 Stories & Poems for Children. Celia Thaxter. 1883.
6613-5 Story-Telling Ballads. Frances J. Olcott, comp. 1920.
6614-3 Story-Telling Poems. Frances J. Olcott, comp. 1913.

List of Works Indexed

6615-1 **Sunflowers.** Willard Wattles, comp. 1916.
6616-X **Tableaux, Charades & Pantomimes.** Emma C. Rook, comp. 1889.
6617-8 **Temperance Selections.** John H. Bechtel, ed. 1893.
6618-6 **Thanksgiving** (Our American Holidays Series). Robert H. Schauffler, ed. 1907.
6619-4 **Third Book of Modern Verse.** Jessie B. Rittenhouse, ed. 1927.
6620-8 **This Is for You.** William S. Lord, comp. 1902.
6621-6 **Three Minute Declamations for Men.** Harry C. Davis, ed. 1890.
6622-4 **Three Russian Poets.** Vladimir Nabokov, tr. 1944.
6623-2 **Three Years with the Poets.** Bertha Hazard, comp. 1904.
6624-0 **Through Italy with the Poets.** Robert H, Schauffler, comp. 1908.
6625-9 **Thudding Drums.** G.M. Miller, comp. 1942.
6626-7 **Tiny Tots Speaker.** Elizabeth J. Rook. 1895.
6627-5 **To Mother.** Elizabeth McCracken, ed. 1917.
6628-3 **Today's Literature.** Dudley C. Gordon, ed. 1935.
6629-1 **Tommy's First Speaker.** Thomas W. Handford, ed. 1885.
6630-5 **Tommy's Second Speaker.** Thomas W. Handford, ed. 1900.
6631-3 **Traveler's Book of Verse.** Frederick E. Emmons, ed. 1928.
6632-1 **Treasury of American Verse.** Walter Learned, ed. 1897.
6633-X **Treasury of British Humor.** Morris Bishop, ed. 1942.
6634-8 **Treasury of English Verse, New & Old.** A.S. Collins, ed. 1931.
6635-6 **Treasury of Irish Poetry in the English Tongue.** Stopford A. Brooke, ed. 1900.
6636-4 **Treasury of Middle English Verse.** Margot R. Adamson, comp. 1930.
6637-2 **Treasury of Satire.** Edgar Johnson, ed. 1945.
6638-0 **Treasury of Verse for Little Children.** Rev. ed. Madalen G. Edgar, ed. 1927.
6639-9 **Treasury of Verse for School & Home.** Madalen G. Edgar, ed. 1926.
6640-2 **Trial Balances.** Ann Winslow, ed. 1935.
6641-0 **Triumph of Life.** Horace Gregory, ed. 1943.
6642-9 **12 Spanish American Poets.** H.R. Hays, ed. 1943.
6643-7 **Twentieth-Century German Verse.** Herman Salinger, ed. 1952.
6644-5 **Twentieth Century Verse.** Ira Dilworth, ed. 1945.
6645-3 **Two Hundred Poems.** Ricardo Quintana, ed. 1947.
6646-1 **Types of Poetry.** Rev. ed. Howard J. Hall, ed. 1931.
6647-X **Types of Poetry.** Jacob Zeitlin, ed. 1926.
6648-8 **Unseen Wings.** Stanton A. Coblentz, comp. 1949.
6649-6 **Up from the Earth.** Sylvia Spencer, comp. 1935.
6650-X **Valiant Muse.** Frederick W. Ziv, ed. 1936.
6651-8 **Vermont Chap Book.** Helen H. Flanders, comp. 1941.
6652-6 **Vers de Societe Anthology.** Carolyn Wells, ed. 1902.
6653-4 **Verse of Our Day.** Margery Gordon, ed. 1923.
6654-2 **Verses I Like.** Major Edward Bowes, comp. 1937.
6655-0 **Victorian & Later English Poets.** James B. Stephens, ed. 1934.
6656-9 **Victorian Anthology, 1837-1895.** Edmund C. Stedman, ed. 1895.
6657-7 **Victorian Poetry.** Edward K.

List of Works Indexed

Brown, ed. 1942.
6658-5 **Victorian Songs.** Edmund H. Garrett, comp. 1895.
6659-3 **Vintage Verse.** Clifford Bax, comp. 1945.
6660-7 **Vista of English Verse.** Henry S. Pancoast, comp. 1911.
6661-5 **Voice, Speech & Gesture.** Hugh Campbell. 1895.
6662-3 **Voices from the Fields.** Russell Lord, ed. 1937.
6663-1 **Voices from the Past.** James M. Todd, ed. 1955.
6664-X **Waggon of Life, & Other Lyrics by Russian Poets...** Sir Cecil Kisch, tr. 1947.
6665-8 **War & The Poet...From Ancient Times to the Present.** Richard Eberhart, ed. 1945.
6666-6 **War Poets.** Oscar Williams, ed. 1945.
6667-4 **Washington's Birthday** (Our American Holidays Series). Robert H. Schauffler, ed. 1910.
6668-2 **Way of Poetry.** John Drinkwater, ed. 1922.
6669-0 **Werner's Readings & Recitations, #1.** Sara S. Rice, comp. 1928.
6670-4 **Werner's Readings & Recitations, #2.** 1910.
6671-2 **Werner's Readings & Recitations, #3.** George Kyle, ed. 1891.
6672-0 **Werner's Readings & Recitations, #4.** Elsie M. Wilbor, comp. 1891.
6673-9 **Werner's Readings & Recitations, #5.** Sara S. Rice, comp. 1913.
6674-7 **Werner's Readings & Recitations, #6.** Elsie M. Wilbor, comp. 1892.
6675-5 **Werner's Readings & Recitations, #7.** Elsie M. Wilbor, comp. 1892.
6676-3 **Werner's Readings & Recitations, #8.** Jean Carruthers, comp. 1892.
6677-1 **Werner's Readings & Recitations, #9.** Jean Carruthers, comp. 1892.
6678-X **Werner's Readings & Recitations, #10.** Caroline B. Le Row, comp. 1892.
6679-8 **Werner's Readings & Recitations, #11.** Sara S. Rice, comp. 1899.
6680-1 **Werner's Readings & Recitations, #12.** Elsie M. Wilbor, comp. 1893.
6681-X **Werner's Readings & Recitations, #13.** Rev. ed. Francis P. Richardson, comp. 1928.
6682-8 **Werner's Readings & Recitations, #15.** Rev. ed. Caroline E. Dickenson, comp. 1928.
6683-6 **Werner's Readings & Recitations, #16.** 1896.
6684-4 **Werner's Readings & Recitations, #17.** Rev. ed. Stanley Schell, ed. 1929.
6685-2 **Werner's Readings & Recitations, #18.** 1898.
6686-0 **Werner's Readings & Recitations, #19.** Pauline Phelps, comp. 1898.
6687-9 **Werner's Readings & Recitations, #21.** Pauline Phelps, comp. 1899.
6688-7 **Werner's Readings & Recitations, #22.** Rev. ed. Elise West, comp. 1929.
6689-5 **Werner's Readings & Recitations, #23.** Rev. ed. Howell L. Piner, comp. 1929.
6690-9 **Werner's Readings & Recitations, #24.** Rev. ed. Miriam Nelke, comp. 1926.
6691-7 **Werner's Readings & Recitations, #25.** Rev. ed. Rachel Baumann, comp. 1929.
6692-5 **Werner's Readings & Recitations, #26.** Rev. ed. 1923.
6693-3 **Werner's Readings & Recitations, #27.** 1891.

List of Works Indexed

6694-1 Werner's Readings & Recitations, #29. Enl. ed. Elise West, comp. 1908.
6695-X Werner's Readings & Recitations, #30. Anna Randall-Diehl, comp. 1903.
6696-8 Werner's Readings & Recitations, #31. Stanley Schell, ed. 1903.
6697-6 Werner's Readings & Recitations, #32. Enl. ed. Stanley Schell, ed. 1904.
6698-4 Werner's Readings & Recitations, #34. Elise West, comp. 1905.
6699-2 Werner's Readings & Recitations, #35. 1906.
6700-X Werner's Readings & Recitations, #36. Pauline Phelps, ed. 1906.
6701-8 Werner's Readings & Recitations, #37. Elise West, comp. 1906.
6702-6 Werner's Readings & Recitations, #39. Elise West, comp. 1907.
6703-4 Werner's Readings & Recitations, #40. Rev. ed. Stanley Schell, comp. 1928.
6704-2 Werner's Readings & Recitations, #41. Rev. ed. Stanley Schell, comp. 1929.
6705-0 Werner's Readings & Recitations, #42. 1908.
6706-9 Werner's Readings & Recitations, #43. 1908.
6707-7 Werner's Readings & Recitations, #44. Elise West, comp. 1908.
6708-5 Werner's Readings & Recitations, #45. Stanley Schell, ed. 1910.
6709-3 Werner's Readings & Recitations, #46. Stanley Schell, ed. 1910.
6710-7 Werner's Readings & Recitations, #47. Stanley Schell, ed. 1910.
6711-5 Werner's Readings & Recitations, #48. Stanley Schell, ed. 1911.
6712-3 Werner's Readings & Recitations, #49. Stanley Schell, ed. 1912.
6713-1 Werner's Readings & Recitations, #50. Stanley Schell, ed. 1912.
6714-X Werner's Readings & Recitations, #51. Stanley Schell, ed. 1912.
6715-8 Werner's Readings & Recitations, #52. Rev. ed. Stanley Schell, ed. 1929.
6716-6 Werner's Readings & Recitations, #53. Rev. ed. Stanley Schell, ed. 1929.
6717-4 Werner's Readings & Recitations, #54. Stanley Schell, ed. 1915.
6718-2 Werner's Readings & Recitations, #55. Rev. ed. Stanley Schell, ed. 1929.
6719-0 Werner's Readings & Recitations, #56. Stanley Schell, ed. 1915.
6720-4 Werner's Readings & Recitations, #57. Stanley Schell, ed. 1916.
6721-2 Werner's Readings & Recitations, #58. Rev. ed. Stanley Schell, ed. 1929.
6722-0 What Cheer. David McCord, ed.
6723-9 What I Like in Poetry. William L. Phelps. comp. 1934.
6724-7 Whimsey Anthology. Carolyn Wells, ed. 1906.
6725-5 White House Handbook of Oratory. Charles E. Chadman, comp. 1899.
6726-3 Winged Horse Anthology. Joseph Auslander, ed. 1929.
6727-1 With Harp & Lute. Blanche J. Thompson, comp. 1935.
6728-X With Trumpet & Drum. Eugene Field. 1892.
6729-8 World Literature. Arthur E. Christy, ed. 1947.
6730-1 World's Great Religious Poetry. Caroline M. Hill, ed. 1923.
6731-X World's Greatest Short Stories. Sherwin Cody, ed. 1902.
6732-8 World's One Thousand Best Poems. 10 vols. Berton Braley, ed. 1929.
6733-6 Worldly Muse. Arthur J.M. Smith, ed. 1951.
6734-4 Wreath of Christmas Poems. Albert M. Hayes, ed. 1942.
6735-2 Yale Book of American Verse.

List of Works Indexed

Thomas R. Lounsbury, ed. 1912.

6736-0 **Yankee Doodles.** Ted Malone (Russell), ed. 1943.

6737-9 **Year Book of Famous Lyrics.** Frederic L. Knowles, comp. 1901.

6738-7 **Young American's Speaker.** Henry D. Northrop, ed. 1895.

6739-5 **Young Folks' Book of Mirth.** Mary R. Thomas, comp. 1924.

6740-9 **Young Folks' Dialogues.** Charles C. Shoemaker, ed. 1885.

6741-7 **Young Folks' Entertainments.** Emma C. Rook. 1886.

6742-5 **Young Folks' Readings.** Lewis B. Monroe, ed. 1904.

6743-3 **Young Folks' Recitations.** Rachel W. Shoemaker, comp. 1888.

6744-1 **Young People's Speaker.** Henry D. Northrop, ed. 1895.

6745-X **Young People's Speaker.** Emma C. Rook, comp. 1892.

6746-8 **Yule Fire.** Marguerite Wilkinson, comp. 1925.

6747-6 **Yule Tide Cheer.** Edward A. Bryant, comp. 1912.

Phase II: 6748-4 to 7042-6

6748-4 **All in a Lifetime.** Edgar A. Guest. 1938. **G**

6749-2 **The Alps as Seen by the Poets.** J. Walker McSpadden, ed. 1912. **B**

6750-6 **The American Album of Poetry;** from the bookends of Ted Malone (F. Alden Russell). 1938.

6751-4 **An American Anthology:** 67 poems now in anthology form for the first time. Tom Boggs, ed. 1942.

6752-2 **The American Common-place Book of Poetry.** George Cheever, ed. 1846.

6753-0 **American Poetry.** Percy H. Boynton, ed. 1918. **G**

6754-9 **American Poetry, 1671-1928.** Conrad Aiken, ed. 1918. **G**

6755-7 **The American Village & Other Poems.** Charles W. Denison. 1845.

6756-5 **Ancient English Christmas Carols, MCCC to MDCC.** Edith Rickert, ed. 1928. **G**

6757-3 **Ancient Spanish Ballads;** historical & romantic. John G. Lockhart, tr. New rev. ed. 1856.

6758-1 **Another Republic:** 17 European & South American writers. Charles Simic & Mark Strand, eds. 1985. **P**

6759-X **Anthology of Contemporary Latin-American Poetry.** Dudley Fitts, ed. Rev. & enl. ed. 1947. **G**

6760-3 **An Anthology of Humorous Verse:** Herrick to Owen Seaman. Helen & Lewis Melville (i.e. Helen & Lewis Benjamin), eds. 1910.

6761-1 **Anthology of Magazine Verse for 1938-1942, & Yearbook of American Poetry.** Alan F. Pater, ed. 1942. **G**

6762-X **Anthology of Massachusetts Poets.** William Stanley Braithwaite, ed. 1922.

6763-8 **An Anthology of Modern Bohemian Poetry.** Paul Selver, comp. & tr. 1912.

6764-6 **An Anthology of New Hampshire**

List of Works Indexed

Poetry. Edith Haskell Tappan, ed. 1938.
6765-4 **Anthology of Serbian Poetry:** the golden age; English & Serbo-Croatian in parallel columns. Milhailo Dordevic, tr. 1984. P
6766-2 **Arabic Poetry:** a primer for students. A.J. Arberry, tr. 1965.
6767-0 **Arrivals:** Canadian poetry in the eighties. Bruce Meyer, ed. 1986. P
6768-9 **Australian Ballads & Rhymes:** poems inspired by life and scenery in Australia & New Zealand. B.W. Sladen, ed. 1888.
6769-7 **Austrian Poetry Today.** Milne Holton & Herbert Kuhner, eds. & trs. 1985. P
6770-0 **Ballades & Rondeaus, Chants Royal, Sestinas, Villanelles & Etc.** Joseph William Gleeson White, ed. 1887.
6771-9 **Ballads & Lyrics of Old France, with Other Poems.** Andrew Lang. New ed. 1907.
6772-7 **Ballads of Babyland, English & American.** Robert Ford, ed. 1905.
6773-5 **Ballads of Old New York.** Arthur Guiterman. 1920.
6774-3 **Beautiful Snow & Other Poems.** J.W. Watson. New & enl. ed. 1871.
6775-1 **Best Loved Poems of Korea:** selected for foreigners. Chang-soo Koh, tr. 1984. P
6776-X **The Best Poems of 1922.** Thomas Moult, ed. 1923. G
6777-8 **The Best Poems of 1923.** Thomas Moult, ed. 1925. G
6778-6 **The Best Poems of 1924.** Thomas Moult, ed. 1925. G
6779-4 **The Best Poems of 1926.** Thomas Moult, ed. 1927. G
6780-8 **The Best Poems of 1930.** Thomas Moult, ed. 1930. G
6781-6 **The Best Poems of 1931.** Thomas Moult, ed. 1931. G
6782-4 **The Best Poems of 1932.** Thomas Moult, ed. 1932. G
6783-2 **The Best Poems of 1941.** Thomas Moult, ed. 1942. G
6784-0 **A Book of Australasian Verse.** Walter Murdoch, ed. 2nd ed. 1924. G
6785-9 **The Book of Bodley Head Verse:** being a selection of poetry published at the Bodley Head. J.B. Priestly, ed. 1926.
6786-7 **Book of Cheerful Cats & Other Animated Animals.** J.G. Francis. 1903. *
6787-5 **Book of Humorous Poetry.** William P. Nimmo, publisher, 18?
6788-3 **The Book of South African Verse.** Guy Comp Butler. 1959. G
6789-1 **The Bookfellow Poetry Annual, 1941.** George Steele Seymour & Rachel Albright, eds. 1941.
6790-5 **Breaking Silence:** an anthology of contemporary Asian-American poets. Joseph Bruchac, ed. 1983. P
6791-3 **Burdett's Dutch Dialect Recitations & Humorous Readings.** James S. Burdett, comp. 1884. G
6792-1 **California Bicentennial Poets Anthology.** A.D. Winans, ed. 1976.
6793-X **The Call of the Homeland;** a collection of English verse. R.P. Scott & Katharine T. Wallas, eds. 1907.
6794-8 **Campion's Works.** Thomas Campion. Percival Vivian, ed. 1909.
6795-6 **Canadian Poems & Lays:** selections of native verse,

List of Works Indexed

reflecting the seasons, legends & life of the dominion. William Douw Lighthall, ed. 18-.

6796-4 **Canadian Singers & Their Songs:** a collection of portraits & autograph poems. Edward S. Caswell, comp. New ed. 1919.

6797-2 **Canadian Verse for Boys & Girls.** John W. Garvin, ed. 1930.

6798-0 **Cape Cod in Poetry.** Joshua Freeman Crowell & Florence Hathaway Crowell, eds. 1924. B

6799-9 **The Caravan of Verse.** Milton J. March, ed. 1938.

6800-6 **The Centenary Book of South African Verse, 1820 to 1925.** Francis Carey Slater, ed. 1925.

6801-4 **A Century of French Poets:** being a selection illustrating the history of French poetry during the last hundred years. Francis Yuon Eccles, ed. 1909.

6802-2 **A Century of Parody & Imitation.** Walter Jerrold & R.M. Leonard, eds. 1913. B

6803-0 **Chelsea Retrospective 1958-1983.** Sonia Rauziss, ed. 1984. P

6804-9 **Child Verses from "Punch".** Phyllis Chase, ill. 1925.

6805-7 **The Children's Third Book of Poetry.** Emilie Kip Baker. 1915. G

6806-5 **Christmas in Poetry:** 2nd series. Carnegie. 1923. G

6807-3 **Christmas Selections for Reading & Recitations.** Rosamund Livingstone McNaught, ed. 1906. G

6808-1 **The City Day;** an anthology of recent American poetry. Eda Lou Walton, comp. 1929.

6809-X **The Collected Poems of T.E. Brown.** H.F. Brown, H.G. Dakyns, & W.E. Henley, eds. 1900.

6810-3 **Collected Verse of Rudyard Kipling.** 1907. G

6811-1 **The Complete Limerick Book:** the origin, history & achievement of the limerick, with about 350 selected examples. Langford Reed. 1924.

6812-X **The Complete Poems of Francis Ledwidge.** 1919.

6813-8 **The Complete Poetical Works of Joanna Baillie.** 1832.

6814-6 **The Complete Poetical Works of William Cowper.** H.S. Milford, ed. 2nd ed. 1905.

6815-4 **Complete Poetical Works.** Benjamin Franklin Taylor. 1886.

6816-2 **The Complete Poetical Works of James Thomson.** A. Logie Robertson, ed. 1908.

6817-0 **The Coning Tower Book:** being a selection of the best verses published in the Coning Tower. Franklin P. Adams, ed. 1926.

6818-9 **Contemporary American Poets.** Horace C. Baker, ed. 1928.

6819-7 **Contemporary Scottish Verse.** Sir George Douglas, ed. 1893.

6820-0 **Days and Deeds:** a book of verse. Burton Egbert Stevenson & Elizabeth B. Stevenson, comps. 1906. G

6821-9 **The Denny Poems/1982.** David R. Pichaske, ed. 1983. P

6822-7 **The Denny Poems/1983.** David R. Pichaske, ed. 1984. P

6823-5 **Dick's Dutch, French & Yankee Dialect Recitations.** William Brisbane Dick, ed. G

6824-3 **Dick's Ethiopian Scenes, Variety Sketches & Stump Speeches.** William Brisbane Dick, ed. 1879. G

6825-1 **Dick's Irish Dialect Recitations.** William Brisbane Dick, ed. 1879. G

6826-X **East Tennessee & Western Virginia Mountain Ballads:** the last stand of American

List of Works Indexed

civilization. Celestin Pierre Cambiaire, ed. 19-.

6827-8 **Elizabethan Songs:** in honour of love & beautie. Edmund H. Garrett, comp. 1891. G

6828-6 **Eminent British Poets of the Nineteenth Century,** Vols I-II. 2 vols. Paul Robert Lieder, ed. 1938. G

6829-4 **English & Scottish Ballads.** Robert Graves, ed. 1957. G

6830-8 **English Lyrics, Chaucer to Poe, 1340-1809.** William Ernest Henley, ed. 1897.

6831-6 **English Poems from Dryden to Blake.** James W. Tupper, ed. 1933.

6832-4 **The English Poets: Vol. IV. Wordsworth to Rossetti.** Thomas Humphry Ward, ed. 2nd ed. rev. 1892. G

6833-2 **The Eternal Sea:** an anthology of sea poetry. W.M. Williamson, ed. 1946. G

6834-0 **Eugene Field Book:** verses, stories & letters. Mary E. Burt & Mary B. Cable, eds. 1898. G

6835-9 **Eugene Field Reader.** Alice L. Harris, ed. 1905.

6836-7 **Evenings with Colorado Poets:** an anthology of Colorado verse. Francis S. Kinder & F. Clarence Spender, eds. 1926.

6837-5 **Flint & Feather:** the complete poems of E. Pauline Johnson (Tekahionwake). 12th ed. 1928.

6838-3 **A Florentine Cycle & Other Poems.** Gertrude Huntington McGiffert. 1915.

6839-1 **From One Word:** selected poems from "Spirit", 1944-1949. John Gilland Brunini, ed. 1950. G

6840-5 **The Fugitives & Other Poems.** John E. Barrett. 1897.

6841-3 **Georgia Poets:** an anthology of 33 contemporaries. 1932.

6842-1 **German Ballads.** Elizabeth Craigmyle, tr. & ed. 18-.

6843-X **The Golden Treasury of Canadian Verse.** A.M. Stephen, ed. 1928.

6844-8 **The Golden Treasury of Modern Lyrics.** Laurence Binyon, comp. 1924. G

6845-6 **The Golden Treasury of Scottish Poetry.** Hugh MacDiarmid, ed. 1940. G

6846-4 **Great Poems of the World War.** William Dunseath Eaton, ed. 1922.

6847-2 **A Half-Century of Song:** an anthology of Hunter College verse. George Mason Whicher, ed. 1935.

6848-0 **A Hebrew Anthology:** a collection of poems & dramas inspired by the Old Testament and post-Biblical tradition gathered from the writing of English poets. George Alexandra Kohut, ed. 2 Vols. 1913. B

6849-9 **The High School Prize Speaker.** William Leonard Snow, ed. 1916. G

6850-2 **The Hollow Reed.** Mary J.J. Wrinn, ed. 1935. B

6851-0 **Humorous & Exhibition Dialogues.** Sarah Annie Shields Frost. 1870. G

6852-9 **A Hundred Verses from Old Japan:** being a translation of the Hyakunin-isshiu. William N. Porter, tr. 1909.

6853-7 **Hurdy-gurdy on Olympus.** Berton Braley. 1927. B

6854-5 **Icelandic Lyrics:** originals & translation. Richard Beck, ed. 1930.

6855-3 **In the Dreamlight:** twenty-one Alaskan writers. Robert Hedin & David Stark, eds. 1984. P

6856-1 **India's Love Lyrics:** including the Garden of Kama. Laurence

List of Works Indexed

Hope, ed. 1906.

6857-X **The Inkling Selection:** a poetry anthology. John Hall, ed. 1984. **P**

6858-8 **Irish Minstrelsy:** a selection of Irish songs & ballads; original & translated. Hallidy H. Sparling, ed. 3rd ed. rev.

6859-6 **Jacobite Songs & Ballads.** G.S. Macquoid, ed. 18-.

6860-X **Jumping Pond:** poems & stories from the Ozarks. Michael Burns & Mark Sanders, eds. 1983. **P**

6861-8 **The Junior Poetry Cure.** Robert Haven Schauffler, ed. 1931. **G**

6862-6 **Just Glad Things.** Edgar A. Guest. 1911.

6863-4 **Kingdom of Love & How Salvator Won.** Ella Wheeler Wilcox. 1902.

6864-2 **Kuloskap the Master & Other Algonkin Poems:** translated metrically. Charles Godfrey Leland & John Dyneley Prince, trs. & eds. 1902. **B**

6865-0 **The Last Poems of Alice & Phoebe Cary.** Mary Clemmer Ames, ed. 1873.

6866-9 **The Late Augustans:** longer poems of the later eighteenth century. Donald Davie, ed. 1958. **G**

6867-7 **The Laureates of England:** from Ben Johnson to Alfred Tennyson; with selections from their works & an introduction dealing with the origin & significance of the English laureateship. Kenyon West. 1895.

6868-5 **Leaves from Maple Lawn.** William White. 1885.

6869-3 **Life's Highway.** Edgar A. Guest. 1933.

6870-7 **The Light from Another Country:** poetry from American prisons. Joseph Bruchac, ed. 1984. **P**

6871-5 **Lincoln & The Poets.** William W.

Betts Jr., ed. 1965. **G**

6872-3 **The Little Book of Modern British Verse.** Jessie B. Rittenhouse, ed. 1924. **G**

6873-1 **Lyra Celtica:** an anthology of representative Celtic poetry; ancient Irish, Alban, Gaelic, Breton, Cymric, & Modern Scottish & Irish Celtic Poetry. E.A. Sharp & J. Matthay, eds. 2nd ed. rev. 1924.

6874-X **Lyra Elegantiarum:** a collection of some of the best specimens of vers de societe & vers d'ocassion in the English language, by deceased authors. Frederick Locker, ed. 1884.

6875-8 **Lyric Forms from France:** their history & their use; with an anthology of ballades, chants royal, rondels, rondeaus, triolets, villanelles, sestinas, in English verse. Helen Louise Cohen. 1922. **B**

6876-6 **Lyrics.** Cora Fabbri. 1892.

6877-4 **Lyrics & Narrative Poems.** Herbert Trench. n.d.

6878-2 **Lyrics of the Law:** a recital of songs & verses pertinent to the law & the legal profession, selected from several sources. J. Greenbag Croke, comp. 1884. **B**

6879-0 **Man Answers Death:** an anthology of poetry. Corliss Lamont, ed. 2nd ed. enl. 1952. **G**

6880-4 **May Days:** an anthology of verse from Masses-Liberator. Genevieve Taggard, ed. 1925. **B**

6881-2 **Medieval English Lyrics:** a critical anthology. R.T. Davies, ed. 1964. **G**

6882-0 **The Merry-Go-Round.** Carolyn Wells. 1901.

6883-9 **The Message in the Mirror:** writing by students on the brink

List of Works Indexed

of the new age. Mary Ellis Peterson, ed. 1983. P
6884-7 **A Miscellany of British Poetry, 1919.** William Kean Seymour, ed. 1919.
6885-5 **Miscellaneous Poems.** Edward R. Huxley. 1906.
6886-3 **Modern Czech Poetry:** selected texts with translation & an introduction. Paul Selver, comp. & tr. 1920.
6887-1 **Modern Literature for Oral Interpretation.** Gertrude E. Johnson. Rev. ed. 1930. B
6888-X **Moods, Songs & Doggerels.** John Galworthy. 1912.
6889-8 **More Heart Throbs.** Joe Mitchel Chapple. 1911. G B
6890-1 **More Songs from Vagabondia.** Bliss Carman & Richard Hovey. 1896.
6891-X **My Poetry Book.** Grace Thompson Huffard, Laura Mae Carlisle & Helen Ferris, comps. 1934. G S
6892-8 **Neighborly Poems & Dialect Sketches.** James Whitcomb Riley. 1897.
6893-6 **Neo-Georgian Poetry, 1936-1937.** 1937.
6894-4 **New England Poets:** an anthology of verse by the residents of Connecticut, Maine, Vermont, Massachusetts, New Hampshire, Rhode Island. 1948.
6895-2 **New Lyrical Ballads:** anthology. Maurice Carpenter, Jack Lindsay & Honor Srundel, eds. 1945.
6896-0 **New Plays for Christmas.** Anne Putnam Sanford. 1935. G
6897-9 **The New Poetry.** Harrie Monroe & Alice Corbin Henderson, eds. 1917. G S
6898-7 **New Rain, Volume III.** C.D. Grant, ed. 1984. P
6899-5 **New Rain, Volume IV.** C.D. Grant, ed. 1984. P
6900-2 **New Voices:** selected university & college prize-winning poems, 1979-1983. May Swenson, ed. 1984. P
6901-0 **19+1:** an anthology of San Francisco poetry. A.D. Winans, ed. 1978.
6902-9 **A Nonsense Anthology.** Carolyn Wells, ed. 1902. G
6903-7 **Nothing to Wear & Other Poems.** William Allen Butler. New ed. 1899.
6904-5 **Nursery Rhyme Book.** Andrew Lang, ed. 1904 *
6905-3 **O Lovely England & Other Poems.** Walter De La Mare. 1953.
6906-1 **Ohio Poets,** an Anthology of 90 Contemporaries. 1934.
6907-X **Old English Ballads.** Francis B. Gummere, ed. & comp. 1894. B
6908-8 **Olive, Cypress & Palm:** an anthology of love & death. Mina Curtiss, comp. 1930. B
6909-6 **One Hundred Choice Selections, #3.** Phineas Garrett, ed. G
6910-X **One Hundred Choice Selections, #6.** Phineas Garrett, ed. G
6911-8 **One Hundred Choice Selections, #11.** Phineas Garrett, ed. G
6912-6 **One Hundred Choice Selections, #12.** Phineas Garrett, ed, G
6913-4 **One Hundred Choice Selections, #13.** Phineas Garrett, ed. G
6914-2 **One Hundred Choice Selections, #14.** Phineas Garrett, ed. G
6915-0 **One Hundred Choice Selections, #16.** Phineas Garrett, ed. G
6916-9 **One Hundred Choice Selections, #17.** Phineas Garrett, ed. G
6917-7 **One Hundred Choice Selections, #21.** Phineas Garrett, ed. G
6918-5 **One Hundred Choice Selections, #24.** Phineas Garrett, ed. G
6919-3 **One Hundred Choice Selections, #25.** Phineas Garrett, ed. G

List of Works Indexed

6920-7 One Hundred Choice Selections, #27. Phineas Garrett, ed. G
6921-5 One Hundred Choice Selections, #28. Phineas Garrett, ed. G
6922-3 One Hundred Choice Selections, #29. Phineas Garrett, ed. G
6923-1 One Hundred Choice Selections, #30. Phineas Garrett, ed. G
6924-X One Hundred Choice Selections, #32. Phineas Garrett, ed. G
6925-8 One Hundred Choice Selections, #33. Phineas Garrett, ed. G
6926-6 One Hundred Choice Selections, #34. Phineas Garrett, ed. G
6927-4 One Hundred Choice Selections, #35. Phineas Garrett, ed. G
6928-2 One Hundred Choice Selections, #36. Phineas Garrett, ed. 1897. G
6929-0 One Hundred Choice Selections, #37. Charles C. Shoemaker, ed. 1899. G
6930-4 1000 Years of Irish Poetry. Kathleen Hoagland, ed. 1947. G
6931-2 The Oxford Book of Christian Verse. Lord David Cecil, ed. 1940. G
6932-0 The Oxford Book of Eighteenth Century Verse. David Nichol Smith, ed. 1926. G
6933-9 The Oxford Book of Seventeenth Century Verse. H.J.C. Grierson & G. Bullough, eds. 1934. G
6934-7 The Pageant of English Poetry: being 1150 poems & extracts by 300 authors. R.M. Leonard, comp. 1916.
6935-5 A Paradise of English Poetry. Henry C. Beeching, ed. 2 Vols. 1892.
6936-3 Pennsylvania's Verse. William Otto Miller, ed. 1902.
6937-1 The Pink Book of Verse for Very Little Children. Augusta Monteith, comp. 1934. G
6938-X Poems. Brian Brooke. 1918.

6939-8 Poems. Edward Farquhar. 1905.
6940-1 Poems. Jan Ingelow. 1867.
6941-X Poems. Robert Loveman. 1896.
6942-8 Poems. Francis Thompson. 1893.
6943-6 Poems About Birds: from the Middle Ages to the present day. H.J. Massingham, ed. B
6944-4 Poems & Ballads. Herman Hagedorn. 1913.
6945-2 The Poems and Dramas of Lord Byron. Crowell, ed. n.d.
6946-0 Poems of American History. Burton Egbert Stevenson, ed. 1908. G B S
6947-9 The Poems of Matthew Arnold. 1849-1867. Sir Arthur Quiller-Couch, ed. 1906.
6948-7 Poems of William Edmondstoune Aytoun. F. Page, ed. 1920.
6949-5 The Poems of Eugene Field. Eugene Field. 1910. G
6950-9 Poems of Richard Lawson Gales. Anthony C. Deane, ed. 1930.
6951-7 The Poems of Adam Lindsay Gordon. Douglas Sladen, ed. 1912.
6952-5 Poems of Home and Country. James A. Martling. 1884.
6953-3 Poems of Inspiration: poems of courage, cheer & faith. Joseph Morris & St. Clair Adams, comps. 1940. G
6954-1 Poems of Justice. Thomas Curtis Clark, comp. 1929. B
6955-X The Poems of Alice Meynell. Complete ed. 1923.
6956-8 Poems of Passion. Ella Wheeler Wilcox. 1883.
6957-6 The Poems of Adelaide A. Procter. Complete ed. 1858.
6958-4 Poems of Sleep and Dream. Carol Stewart, comp. 1947.
6959-2 Poems of the Dance: an anthology 1500 B.C.- 1920 A.D. Edward R. Dickson, ed. 1921. B
6960-6 Poems of the Scottish Minor

List of Works Indexed

Poets, from the age of Ramsay to David Gray. Sir George Douglas, ed. 1819.
- 6961-4 **Poems of Henry Van Dyke.** Henry Van Dyke. 1920. **G**
- 6962-2 **Poems on Several Occasions.** Thomas Warton the Elder. 1930.
- 6963-0 **Poems Teachers Ask For:** Book one. 1925. **G**
- 6964-0 **Poems Teachers Ask For:** Book two. 1925. **G**
- 6965-7 **The Poet & the Children:** carefully selected poems from the works of the best & most popular writing for children. Matthew Henry Lothrop, ed. 1882.
- 6966-5 **The Poet Dreaming in the Artist's House:** contemporary poems about the visual arts. Emilie Buchwald & Ruth Roston, eds. 1984. **P**
- 6967-3 **The Poetical & Dramatic Works of Samuel Taylor Coleridge.** New ed. Crowell, ed. n.d.
- 6968-1 **The Poetical Works of Armstrong, Dyer & Green.** George Gilfillan, ed. 1858.
- 6969-X **The Poetical Works of Alice & Phoebe Cary.** 1822.
- 6970-3 **The Poetical Works of John Dryden;** with memoir & introduction to poems. Crowell, ed. n.d.
- 6971-1 **The Poetical Works of William Falconer.** John Nitford, ed. 1870.
- 6972-X **The Poetical Works of John Gay.** G.C. Faber, ed. 1925.
- 6973-8 **The Poetical Works of Mrs. Hermans** (Felicia Dorothea Hermans); reprinted from the early editions. 1890.
- 6974-6 **The Poetical Works of Thomas Hood;** with memoir & notes. 18-.
- 6975-4 **The Poetical Works of Johnson, Parnell, Gray & Smolett;** with memoirs, critical dissertations, & explanatory notes. George Gilfillan, ed. 1855.
- 6976-2 **The Poetical Works of Bayard Taylor.** 1880.
- 6977-0 **The Poetical Works of Alfred Tennyson.** Complete ed. 18-.
- 6978-9 **The Poetry of Flight.** Selden Rodman, ed. 1941. **G**
- 6979-7 **The Poetry Society of America Anthology.** Amy Bonner & others, eds. 1946. **G**
- 6980-0 **The Poets & Poetry of England in the 19th Century:** with additions R.H. Stoddard. Rufus W. Griswold, ed. Rev. & enl. ed. 1874.
- 6981-9 **Poets Behind Barbed Wire:** tanka poems. Jiro Nakano & Kay Nakano eds. & trs. 1983. **P**
- 6982-7 **The Poets in the Nursery.** Charles Powell, ed. 1920.
- 6983-5 **Princeton Verse.** Raymond Blaine Fosdick, ed. 1904.
- 6984-3 **Pulitzer Prize Poems.** Marjorie Barrows, comp. 1941. **G**
- 6985-1 **Recent Poetry, 1923-1933.** Alida Monro, ed. 1933.
- 6986-X **Renascence & Other Poems.** Edna St. Vincent Millay. 1917. **G**
- 6987-8 **Rhymes A La Mode.** Andrew Lang. 5th ed. 1895.
- 6988-6 **Rhymes of Vermont Rural Life:** 1st Series. Daniel L. Cady. 1919.
- 6989-4 **Rhymes of Vermont Rural Life:** 2nd Series. Daniel L. Cady. 1922.
- 6990-8 **Riley Child-Rhymes.** James Whitcomb Riley. 1898. **G**
- 6991-6 **Riley Farm-Rhymes.** James Whitcomb Riley. 1905.
- 6992-4 **Riley Love-Lyrics.** James Whitcomb Riley. 1905.

List of Works Indexed

6993-2 **Riley Songs of Summer.** James Whitcomb Riley. 1908.

6994-0 **The Rising Tide & Other Poems.** Charles Whitby. 1920.

6995-9 **Roosevelt as the Poets Saw Him:** tributes from the singers of America & England to Theodore Roosevelt. Charles Hanson Towne, ed. 1923. **B**

6996-7 **A Satire Anthology.** Carolyn Wells, eds. 1905. **G**

6997-5 **Sea Music:** an anthology of poems & passages descriptive of the sea. Mrs, William Sharp, ed. n.d.

6998-3 **Secong Coming Anthology:** ten years in retrospect. A.D. Winans, ed. 1984. **P**

6999-1 **Secrets.** Jessie O. Jones. 1945. *

7000-0 **Selected Poems by Edith Sitwell.** 1937.

7001-9 **Selected Poems on Woodrow Wilson:** a memorial by American poets. C.B. McAllister, ed. 1926.

7002-7 **Shoemaker's Best Selections #17.** Jacob W. Shoemaker, ed. 1917. **G**

7003-5 **The Son of the Male Muse:** new gay poetry. Ian Young, ed. 1983. **P**

7004-3 **Songs After Work.** Louis J. Magee. 1907.

7005-1 **Songs from This Earth on Turtle's Back:** contemporary American Indian poetry. Joseph Bruchac, ed. 1926. **B**

7006-X **Songs from Vagabondia.** Bliss Carman & Richard Hovey. 1984.

7007-8 **Songs of Adventure.** Robert Frothingham, ed. 1926. **B**

7008-6 **Songs of Dogs:** an anthology. Robert Frothingham, ed. 1920. **B**

7009-4 **Songs of Freedom.** H.S. Salt, ed. n.d.

7010-8 **Songs of Horses:** an anthology. Robert Frothingham, ed. 1920. **B**

7011-6 **Songs of Labor & Other Poems.** Morris Rosenfeld. 1914.

7012-4 **Songs of Men:** an anthology. Robert Frothingham, ed. 1918. **B**

7013-2 **Songs of Nepal:** an anthology of Nevar folksongs & hymns. Siegfried Lienhard, ed. & tr. 1984. **P**

7014-0 **Songs of Science:** an anthology. Virginia Shortridge, ed. 1930. **B**

7015-9 **Sonnets of This Century.** William Sharp, ed. 1886.

7016-7 **South Carolina Poets,** an Anthology of Contemporary Verse by 28 Poets; foreword by Ellen M. Carrol. 1936.

7017-5 **Southern Poets.** Edd Winfield Parks, ed. 1936. **G**

7018-3 **Special New Zealand Anthology.** A.D. Winans, ed. 1974.

7019-1 **The Spirit of St. Louis:** 100 poems. Charles Vale, comp. 1927. **B**

7020-5 **The Squirrel's Granary:** a countryman's anthology. Sir William Beach Thomas, comp. 1936. **B**

7021-3 **Taken from Life:** verses. 1897. **G**

7022-1 **Three Minute Readings for College Girls.** Harry Cassell Davis, ed. 1897. **G B**

7023-X **Through High Windows.** Lilian Sauter. 1911.

7024-8 **Today's Negro Voices.** Beatrice M. Murphy, ed. 1970. **G**

7025-6 **A Treasure of Humorous Poetry.** Frederic Lawrence Knowles, ed. 1902. **G B**

7026-4 **A Treasury of War Poetry:** 1st

List of Works Indexed

series. George Herbert Clarke, ed. 1919. **G B S**

7027-2 **A Treasury of War Poetry:** 2nd series. George Herbert Clarke, ed. 1919. **G B S**

7028-0 **Types of Children's Literature.** Walter Barnes, comp. 1919. *

7029-9 **Valour & Vision:** poems of the war 1914-18. Jacqueline Trotter, ed. New ed. 1920.

7030-2 **Vermont Verse:** an anthology. Walter John Coates & Frederick Tupper, eds. 1932. **B**

7031-0 **War Verse.** Frank Foxcroft, ed. 1918. **B**

7032-9 **Warnings:** an anthology on the nuclear peril. John Witte, ed. 1984. **P**

7033-7 **When Day Is Done.** Edgar A. Guest. 1921.

7035-3 **Winter Sports Verse.** William Haynes & Joseph LeRoy Harrison, eds. 1919. **B**

7036-1 **Woman Who Has Sprouted Wings:** poems by contemporary Latin American women poets. Mary Crow, ed. 1984. **P**

7037-X **Women Poets of the Victorian Era.** Mrs. William Sharp, ed. n.d.

7038-8 **Women's Poetry To-day.** Lewis Worthington Smith, ed. 1929. **B**

7039-6 **The World's Best Poems.** Mark Van Doren & Garibaldi M. Lapola, eds. 1929. **G**

7040-X **The Yoke of Thunder.** Robert P. Tristram Coffin. 1932.

7041-8 **Younger American Poets, 1830-1890.** Douglas Gladen, ed. 1891.

7042-6 **Zoar:** a book of verse. Helen & Bernard Bosanquet.

A B C of literature. Carolyn Wells. 7021-3
A B C's garden. Leonora Speyer. 6421-3
A B C's in green. Leonora Speyer. 6374-8,6478-7,6607-0, 6510-4,6585-6
A Becket, Gilbert Abbott
    A holiday task. 6902-9
A [pseud.]
    The child and the fairies. 6368-3
A clymene. Paul Verlaine. 7039-6
A David, statuaire. Charles Augustin Sainte-Beuve. 6801-4
A deux. Eugene Aubert. 6847-2
A dieu! and au revoir. John Oxenham. 6337-3
"A for the ax you very well know". Unknown. 6059-5
"A ho hi! hirrum bo!/Early sails she". The reiving ship. Kenneth Macleod. 6873-1
A is an apple. Unknown. 6722-0
"A is for Anthony Hope". A B C of literature. Carolyn Wells. 7021-3
"A is for apple that hangs on the tree". A Christmas alphabet. Carolyn Wells. 6882-0
A la belle Helene. Andrew Lang. 6771-9
A la belle imperieuse. Victor Hugo. 6801-4
A la Claire Fontaine. Unknown (French Canadian) 6795-6
"A la claire fontaine" Frank Oliver Call. 6797-2
A la mode. Clara Marcelle Greene. 6670-4
"A pas lents et suivis du chien de la maison". Automne. Albert Samain. 6801-4
"A Potsdam les totaux absteneurs". Limerick:"A Potsdam les totaux absteneurs." Unknown. 6308-X
"A Saint-Blaise, a la Zuecca". Chanson ("A Saint-Blaise"). Alfred de Musset. 6801-4
A quelques poetes. Emile Deschamps. 6801-4
A quoi bon? Jules Wynn Smith. 6178-8
A se stesso. Giacomo Leopardi. 7039-6
A terre. Wilfred Owen. 6666-6
A toi. Alys Hungerford. 6784-0
"A travers le bois fauve et radieux". Sous bois. Theodore de Banville. 6801-4
A une tulipe. Francois Coppee. 6801-4
"A voir une maison commode, propre & belle". Le bonheur de ce monde. Plantin. 7020-5
"A was an affluent ape". A marvelous menagerie. Carolyn Wells. 6882-0
"A was an andiron". Alphabet of inanimates. Carolyn Wells. 6882-0
A was an ant. Edward Lear. 6452-3
"A was an apple-tart". Unknown. 6363-2
"A was an Archer...". Unknown. 6363-2
"A was an army to settle". Monorhymed alphabet. Unknown. 6724-7
"A was an auk". Alphabet antics. Carolyn Wells. 6882-0
A! mercy, fortune. Unknown. 6881-2
A' aboot it. William Lyle. 6166-4
A' for our rightfu' king. Robert Burns. 6934-7
"A' nicht it was freezin', a' nicht I was...". Curling song. Norman Macleod. 7035-3
"A' night I'm haunted by a shape". The bachelor's dream. John Rankine. 6878-2
"A'n't the stars purty". At the hospital window. Carl Smith. 6929-0
A, a, a, a, nunc gaudet ecclsia. Unknown. 6756-5
A, a, a, a, nunc gaudet Maria. Unknown. 6756-5
"A, B, C, tumble-down D". Unknown. 6363-2
A,B,C. Charles Stuart Calverley. 6724-7,6092-7
"A-B-C-D".. Unknown. 6364-0
"A-coming o'er the crags o' Kyle". Unknown. 6059-5
"A-E-I-O-U".. Unknown. 6364-0
"A-dipping candles used to be". Dipping candles in Vermont. Daniel L. Cady. 6988-0
A-feared of a gal. Unknown. 6277-6
A-helpin' save with Hoover. Ruth Collins Dixon. 6681-X
A-hunting we will go. Henry Fielding. 6385-3,6398-5,6153-2
A-Maying. Irwin Shupp Jr. 6936-3
A-Maying. Unknown. 6189-3
A-Maying, a-playing. Thomas Nashe. 6182-6
A-roving. Victor Daley. 6784-0
A-sitting on a gate. Charles Lutwidge ("Lewis Carroll") Dodgson. 6179-6
A-soak in 'wum barrels'. Delia A. Heywood. 6927-4
"A-sway/On red rose". Shadow. Adelaide Crapsey. 6850-2

A-tishoo. Walter De La Mare. 6596-1
A-visitin' the school. Unknown. 6927-4
"A-walking and a-talking". Sweet Willie. Unknown. 6826-X
"A-when we used to shear the sheep". Vermont wool carding. Daniel L. Cady. 6988-0
A-working on the railway. Arthur H. Clark. 6281-4
A. Apple pie. Edward Lear. 6452-3
A.,C.
    The doughboy and the gob. 6817-0
A.,F.C.
    Nestlings. 6273-3
A.,H.
    A Flemish village. 6589-9,6846-4
A.,J.W.
    Litany in war time. 7031-0
A.,K.H.
    Their turn. 7021-3
A.,L.T.
    Song of the smoke-wreaths. 6453-1
A.,M.
    "And I shall never trace this path again". 6817-0
    Beatrice dead. 6817-0
    Variation on an old theme. 6817-0
A.,W.B.
    The fall of Corydon. 7021-3
A.B.C.. Unknown. 6502-3
An A.B.C. of devotion. Unknown. 6881-2
A.D. 1608. William Miller Gamble. 6983-5
A.E. Housman and a few friends. Humbert Wolfe. 6722-0
A.E. See Russell, George William
A.E.F.. Carl Sandburg. 6289-X,6345-4,6542-2,665-8
The A.E.F. to T.R. Corinne Roosevelt Robinson. 6995-9
A.R. Ammons amid the fungi. Diane Ackerman. 6803-0
A.S.K.. A. S. K. 6474-4
Aakjaer, Jeppe
    The oats. Charles Wharton Stork (tr.). 6555-4
    The rye field. Charles Wharton Stork (tr.). 6555-4
    The stonebreaker. Charles Wharton Stork (tr.). 6555-4
Aaron. George Herbert. 6430-2,6431-1,6933-9
Aaron Burr's wooing. Edmund Clarence Stedman. 6946-0
Aaron Hatfield. Edgar Lee Masters. 6897-9
Aaron on Mount Hor. Lydia Huntley Sigourney. 6848-0
Aaron Stark. Edwin Arlington Robinson. 6850-2
Aaron's breastplate. Anna Shipton. 6848-0
Aaron, Madeleine
    God is here. 6337-3
Aaronson, Leonard [Lazarus]
    The baptism. 6210-5
    The homeward journey. 6210-5
    Pesci misti. 6210-5
Aasrestrup, Emil
    Evening sigh. Charles Wharton Stork (tr.). 6555-4
    Punishment. Charles Wharton Stork (tr.). 6555-4
    To a friend. Charles Wharton Stork (tr.). 6555-4
Ab astris. Anne C. Lynch Botta. 7030-2
An abalone shell. Grace MacGowan Cooke. 6241-5
Abandoned brothel. C.R. Holmes. 6515-5
The abandoned church. Milan Rakic. 6765-4
The abandoned farm. Louis J. Magee. 7004-3
The abandoned mine. D.E. Griffith. 6149-4
The abandoned mine. Charles Claybrooke Woollacott. 6625-9
The abandoned mine. Charles Claybrook Woollacott. 6800-6
"Abandoned to the antique auction". Picture of a Victorian lady 1839-1896 Eupha Whitworth Richie. 6857-X
A abandoned tow-path. Elias Lieberman. 6072-2
Abandoned woman's lament. Jackson Holland Patterson. 6841-3
Abandonment. John Galsworthy. 7008-6
Abasshyd. [James] Pittendrigh Macgillivray. 6269-5
Abba-labba-la. David Stefansson. 6283-0
Abbe, George
    Black lake. 6761-1
    The clean gentleman. 6218-0
    Death is a little thing. 6218-0
    The harbor longs for shouting. 6764-6
    The minister. 6764-6
    Telephone wires in winter. 6761-1
    You were at the dead river. 6218-0
The abbess. Sir Walter Scott. 6285-7
Abbey Asaoe. William Allingham. 6930-4

ABBEY!

"**Abbey!** for ever smiling pensively". Fountains abbey. Ebenezer Elliott. 7015-9
Abbey, Henry
    The draw-bridge keeper. 6909-6
    The stranger's alms. 6621-6
    "What do we plant when we plant a tree?" 6171-0
Abbie Ben Adams. Carolyn Wells. 6120-6
The **Abbot** M'Kinnon. James Hogg. 6219-9
"**Abbot** is painting me so true". On his portrait. William Cowper. 6814-6
The **abbot** of Derry. John Bennett. 6619-4
The **abbot** of Inisfalen. William Allingham. 6079-X,6614-3
"An **abbot** rich (whose taste was good)". The equivocation. John Gay. 6972-X
"The **abbot** willed it, and it was done". The Jew's gift. Thomas Bailey Aldrich. 6848-0
The **abbot's** blessing on the Bruce. Sir Walter Scott. 6424-8
Abbot, Celinda Bishoprick
    To Ethel Dummer Mintzer. 6789-1
    To Eva. 6789-1
Abbot, Frances
    April, fr. Calendar. 6764-6
    Calendar, sels. 6764-6
    January, fr. Caledndar. 6764-6
    July, fr. Calendar. 6764-6
    October, fr. Calendar. 6764-6
Abbott, Anne
    The veil. 6648-8
Abbott, Claude Colleer
    Bunch: a cat. 6511-2
Abbott, Edgar Wade
    Her majesty. 7022-1
    The poppy-land express. 6978-1,6075-1,6274-1
    Rapid transit. 6576-7
Abbott, Edwin M.
    The cosmic trail. 6799-9
Abbott, Elsie
    Ride not too fast with beauty. 6799-9
Abbott, Gwynne
    The mermaids. 6799-9
Abbott, H.H.
    The weathercock. 6639-9
Abbott, Howard S.
    With colors gay. 6818-9
Abbott, J.H.M.
    The song of the dead. 6846-4
Abbott, Lyman
    He worried about it. 6744-1
    Patriotic son. 6051-X
Abbott, Steve
    Sonnet 007 ("Really"). 7003-5
    To a Soviet artist in prison. 7003-5
Abbreviated rumination. P.L. Jacobs. 6870-7
Abdel-hassan. Unknown. 6409-4
"**Abdhur** Rahman, the Durani chief, of him...". The ballad of the king's mercy. Rudyard Kipling. 6810-3
The **abdication** of Charles V. Sir William Stirling-Maxwell. 6960-6
Abdiel. John Milton. 6302-0;6385-3
Abdiel-the-Syrian's chant of the kiss. Hermann Hagedorn. 6944-4
Abdul, the Bulbur ameer. Unknown. 6237-7
Abdy, Mrs. ?
    In the street of by-and-by. 6916-9
Abe No Nakamaro
    "While gazing up into the sky". William N. Porter (tr.). 6852-9
Abel. Demetrios Capetanakis. 6665-8
"**Abelard**, my wisdom's saint". Lute song of the lady Heloise. Herbert Edward Palmer. 6780-8
The **Abencerrage**, sels. Felicia Dorothea Hemans. 6439-6
The **Abencerrage**. Felicia Dorothea Hemans. 6973-8
Aber stations. Thomas Edward Brown. 6809-X
Abercrombie, Lascelles
    All last night. 6210-5
    Balkis, fr. Emblems of love. 6102-8,6301-2
    Ceremonial ode intended for a university. 6437-X
    Epilogue. 6250-4,6393-4,6437-X
    Epitaph. 6023-4
    Hymn to love. 6437-X
    Inscription. 6879-0
    Margaret's song. 6872-3
    Marriage song. 6102-8
    Marriage song, sels. 6301-2
    The sale of St. Thomas. 6872-3
    The seeker. 6730-1
    Small fountains. 6861-8
    Woman's beauty. 6513-9
Aberg, William
    Diving the field. 6870-7
    The harvest. 6870-7
    Poem for John my brother. 6870-7
    The sleepers. 6870-7
    The weight. 6870-7
Aberpennar, Davies
    Beware, wass. 6360-8
    For Gwenhwyfar and Blodeuwedd. 6360-8
    Poem for D. Robert Griffiths. 6360-8
    Poem for Gwyn and Kathe. 6360-8
    Poem for Keith Scott. 6360-8
    Poem for M.A.J.D. 6360-8
    Tudur aled. 6360-8
Abertawy. Walter Savage Landor. 6828-6
Abhain au bhuideil. Joseph Sheridan Le Fanu. 6174-5
Abi, viator--. Unknown. 7031-0
Abide in me, sels. Harriet Beecher Stowe. 6144-3
Abide with me. Henry Francis Lyte. 6730-1,6219-9,6656-9, 6102-8,6214-8,6238-5,6014-5,6001-3,6240-7,6418-3, 6732-8,6337-3,6479-5
Abide with me. William H. Monk. 6304-7,6889-8
'**Abide** with me.' Stephen H. Thayer. 6744-1,6925-8
Abide with us. Horatius Bonar. 6065-X,6656-9
The **abiding** three. William White. 6868-5
Abigail Becker. Amanda T. Jones. 6274-1,6416-7,6566-X
Abla. Antara. 7039-6
The **able** sailor. Unknown. 6583-X
The **able** seaman's story. Archie Binns. 7007-8
Ablution. Sappho. 6102-8
Abnegation. Christina Georgina Rossetti. 6122-2,6656-9
Abner and the widow Jones. Robert Bloomfield. 6919-3
Abner's second wife. P.C. Fossett. 6922-3
Abner's second wife. Unknown. 6744-1
Abney, Louise
    A carol for Christmas Eve. 6143-5
    Common things. 6143-5
    Dance of the leaves. 6143-5
    Easter morning. 6143-5
Aboard at a ship's helm. Walt Whitman. 6126-5
"**Aboard** o' the good ship Margaret Ann". Sentence of death on the high seas. Arthur Matthison. 6915-0
Abode divine. Al Rusafi. 6362-4
The **abode** of young maidens early dead, fr. Tree of time. Gertrude Huntington McGiffert. 6838-3
An **abondoned** abode. Rose Henderson. 6653-4
An **Aboriginal** chant. Unknown. 6247-4
An **Aboriginal** mother's lament. Charles Harper. 6627-5,6656-9,6768-9
Aboriginal sin. John Hay. 6388-8
Abou Ben Adhem. Leigh Hunt. 6101-X,6102-8,6109-5,6134-6, 6136-2,6138-,6133-8,6392-6,6600-3,6732-8,6186-9,6198-2,6236-9,6239-3,6242-3,6260-,6271-7,6291-1,6294-6, 6302-0,6332-2,6337-,6339-X,6370-5,6385-3,6401-9,6418-9,6426-,6437-X,6451-5,6457-4,6459-0,6473-6,6478-, 6479-5,6481-7,6486-8,6501-5,6502-3,6503-,6504-X,6534-1,6605-2,6614-3,6623-2,6730-,6723-9,6737-9,6424-8, 6419-1,6639-9,6301-2,6131-1,6219-9,6212-1,6104-4, 6199-0,6383-7,6250-4,6135-4,6461-2,6192-3,6155-9, 6560-0,6102-8,6304-7,6808-1,6214-8,6438-8,6421-3, 6543-0
"**Abou** Ben Halstead - may his tribe increase!". A good man's sorror. Eugene Field. 6949-5
Abou Ishak. Hafiz. 6102-8
About 'two'. Fred W. Leu. 6906-1
"**About a week before town meeting**". Pre-townmeeting talk in Vermont. Daniel L. Cady. 6988-6
"**About** ane bank, where birdis on bewis". The cherry and the slae, sels. Alexander Montgomerie. 6845-6
About children. Edgar A. Guest. 6869-3
About contributions. Unknown. 6680-1

About Eleanor Rumming. John Skelton. 6659-3
"About fifty years since, in the days of...". Paddy's metamorphosis. Thomas Moore. 6930-4
"About his brow the laurel and the bay". A man! Clinton Scollard. 6995-9
"About its lip winds ivy, ivy flecked". Theocritus. 6435-3
About May. Ella Wheeler Wilcox. 6863-4
About Savannah. Unknown. 6946-0
"About six weeks from squirrel cup". Planting potaters in Vermont. Daniel L. Cady. 6989-4
"About the blamedest bird I know". The Vermont crow. Daniel L. Cady. 6989-4
"About the break of day". Alfred Noyes. 6298-9
"About the cottage, cold and white". Breaking the roads. Phoebe Cary. 6865-0;6969-X
About the fairies. Unknown. 6165-6,6373-X,6131-1
"About the field they piped right". Tyrle, tyrlow... So merrily the shepherds began to blow. Unknown. 6756-5
"About the field they piped right". Unknown. 6334-9
"About the last of husking time". A Vermont drove of cattle. Daniel L. Cady. 6989-4
"About the ocean there is witchery". A seashell. Fred Keller Dix. 6906-1
"About the room the Christmas greens". God bless our school. Unknown. 6913-4
About the second-last rose of summer. Charles Plumb. 7020-5
About the Shelleys. William Wordsworth. 6722-0
"About the time Christ was born". Baile and Aillinn, sels. William Butler Yeats. 6844-8
"About the time of Christmas". Jane Conquest. Unknown. 6963-0
"About the time of Michael's feast". At Michelmas. Bliss Carman and Richard Hovey. 6890-1
"About with this brimmer my bullyes." Unknown. 6563-5
"About Yule, when the wind blew...". Unknown. 6518-X
"About, by George! the biggest thing". A Vermont railroad scurzion. Daniel L. Cady. 6989-4
Above St. Irenee. Duncan Campbell Scott. 6656-9
"Above all controversy/Celestial beauty glows". February 3, 1924. Katharine Lee Bates. 7001-9
"Above him the wild skies bending". The escort of the yellowstone. John Steven McGroarty. 6995-9
"Above me are the Alps". Murat. George Gordon, 6th Baron Byron. 6385-3,6438-8,6749-2
"Above sleeping yard light, you wait". Raven at Lemon Creek jail. Thomas Waltner. 6870-7
"Above the battlements of stolid stone". City rain storm. Anderson M. Scruggs. 6841-3
"Above the broken walls the apple boughs". Vision. Dorothy Paul. 6846-4
Above the dark. Jarl Hemmer. 6045-5
"Above the din of commerce, above the clamor..". The falling of thrones. Ella Wheeler Wilcox. 6863-4
Above the dock. T.E. Hulme. 6209-1
Above the fresh ruffles of the surf. Hart Crane. 6258-X
"Above the frozen floods". The skaters. Grace W. Leach. 7035-3
"Above the gabled houses, blanched and bright". Copernicus. Thomas S. Jones Jr.. 6850-2
"Above the gleaming lake, against the..sky". The forest guardian. Sylvia Clark. 6764-6
"Above the high hills of endeavour...". Yonder. Charles Whitby. 6994-0
Above the hills of time. Thomas Tiplady. 6337-3
"Above the housetops eight dives fly". Eight doves. Jane Dransfield. 6979-7
"Above the mountain, bleak and bare". The winter camp fire. Unknown (Shoshone Indian). 7035-3
"Above the palms, the peaks of pearly gray". Canopus. Bayard Taylor. 6976-2
"Above the pines the moon was slowly drifting". Dickens in camp. Francis Bret Harte. 6385-3,6240-7,6406-X,6465-5,6478-7,6632 ,6600-3,6707-7,6309-8,6300-4,6304-7, 6291 ,6250-4,6188-1,7041-8
"Above the ridges of roofs". Mattersburg/judengasse. Gunter Unger. 6769-7
"Above the russet clods athe corn is seen". The skylark. John Clare. 6943-6
"Above the seven planets' range". All saints. Alice L. Rostetter. 6847-2
"Above the town a monstrous wheel is turning". Sunset in the city. Richard Le Gallienne. 7014-0
"Above them spread a strange sky". The indian's welcome to the pilgrim fathers. Lydia Huntley Sigourney. 6820-0
"Above us hangs the jewelled night". Waking. John Le Gay Brereton. 6784-0
"Above us radiant sun, the charm of green...". From a walk. Vojislav Ilic Jr.. 6765-4
"Above white clouds I hear sweet." Kyoroku. 6027-7
"Above yon sombre swell of land". In Berkshire. Richard Hengist Horne. 6793-X
"Above you burns a molten-copper sun". The ski-runner. Unknown. 7035-3
"Above, in the castle-land". The lower Rhine. Louis J. Magee. 7004-3
Abr-ar-Rahman I
  The palm tree. J.B. Trend (tr.). 7039-6
Abraham. John Stuart Blackie. 6848-0
Abraham. Edmund Vance Cooke. 6532-5
Abraham. Earl B. Marlatt. 6143-5
Abraham and Ephraim. Sam Walter Foss. 6505-8
Abraham and his gods. Richard Monckton Milnes; 1st Baron Houghton. 6848-0
Abraham and the fire-worshipper. Leigh Hunt. 6848-0
Abraham and the idolater. Sadi [or Saadi] (Mushlih-ud-Din) 6848-0
Abraham at Machpelah. Lydia Huntley Sigourney. 6848-0
Abraham Davenport. John Greenleaf Whittier. 6496-5,6552-X, 6153-2,6126-5,6008-0,6288-1,6431-0
Abraham Lincoln. Joseph Auslander. 6736-0
Abraham Lincoln. Fred Clare Baldwin. 6524-4
Abraham Lincoln. Rosemary and Stephen Vincent Benet. 6871-5
Abraham Lincoln. Joel Benton. 6305-5,6524-4
Abraham Lincoln. Virginia Frazer Boyle. 6102-8,6076-5,6524-4
Abraham Lincoln. Henry Howard Brownell. 6113-3,6239-3,6709-3,6305-5,6524-4
Abraham Lincoln. William Cullen Bryant. 6074-9,6288-1,6126-5
Abraham Lincoln. Mary Livingston Burdick. 6524-4
Abraham Lincoln. Alice Cary. 6524-4
Abraham Lincoln. Thomas Curtis Clark. 6037-4,6449-3
Abraham Lincoln. Samuel Valentine Cole. 6449-3
Abraham Lincoln. Amasa Stetson Condon. 6524-4
Abraham Lincoln. Rose Terry Cooke. 6305-5,6524-4
Abraham Lincoln. P.C. Croll. 6524-4
Abraham Lincoln. Ralph Waldo Emerson. 6449-3
Abraham Lincoln. John W. Fentress. 6178-8
Abraham Lincoln. J.T. Goodman. 6524-4
Abraham Lincoln. Eugene J. Hall. 6524-4
Abraham Lincoln. Leon Huhner. 6887-1
Abraham Lincoln. Harry Elmore Hurd. 6761-1
Abraham Lincoln. Edward R. Huxley. 6885-5
Abraham Lincoln. James Nicoll Johnston. 6524-4
Abraham Lincoln. Mark Lemon. 6304-7
Abraham Lincoln. James Russell Lowell. 6302-0,6385-3,6552-X,6442-6,6470-1,6304-7,6396-9
Abraham Lincoln. Walter Malone. 6524-4
Abraham Lincoln. Francesca Falk Miller. 6449-3
Abraham Lincoln. Frank Moore. 6305-5,6524-4
Abraham Lincoln. Florence Evelyn Pratt. 6305-5,6524-4
Abraham Lincoln. Franklin Benjamin Sanborn. 6524-4
Abraham Lincoln. Margaret Elizabeth Sangster. 6524-4
Abraham Lincoln. Samuel Francis Smith. 6524-4
Abraham Lincoln. Monroe Sprowl. 6524-4
Abraham Lincoln. Edmund Clarence Stedman. 6524-4
Abraham Lincoln. Richard Henry Stoddard. 6305-5,6524-4, 6449-3,6113-3
Abraham Lincoln. Tom Taylor. 6088-9,6219-9,6656-9,6102-8, 6305-5,6263-6,6438-8,6332-2,6385-3,6600-3,6610-0, 6672-0,6732
Abraham Lincoln. George Alfred Townsend. 6524-4
Abraham Lincoln. Unknown. 6438-8
Abraham Lincoln. William Henry Venable. 6524-4
Abraham Lincoln ("This man"). Richard Henry Stoddard. 6239-3
Abraham Lincoln - 1863. Richard Realf. 6524-4
Abraham Lincoln - 1865. Lewis V.F. Randolph. 6524-4

ABRAHAM

Abraham Lincoln walks at midnight. Vachel Lindsay. 6088-9,
   6375-6,6431-0,616-3,6542-2,6449-3,6653-4,6289-X,6299-
   7,6332-2,6337-3,6347-0,6465 ,6474-4,6538-4,6556-2,
   6583-X,6108-7,6641
Abraham Lincoln's Christmas gift. Nora Perry. 6305-5,6524-
   4,7041-8
Abraham's bread. Sir Edwin Arnold. 6848-0
Abraham's offense. Sir Edwin Arnold. 6848-0
Abraham's sacrifice. Unknown. 6193-1
Abraham, H.V.
   Limerick:"A Jew and a Scotchman, found 'tight'". 6811-1
Abrahams, J. Fox
   Tim Titus. 6925-8
Abrahams, Robert D.
   1941. 6761-1
Abrahams, William
   In the Henry James country. 6666-6
   The museum. 6666-6
   Poem in time of war. 6666-6
Abram and Zimri. Clarence Chatham Cook. 6848-0,6385-3,6407-
   8
Abram, Sydney S.
   Street player. 6850-2
Abram, Sylvia S.
   Skyscraper. 6850-2
Abril, Xavier
   Elegy to the invented woman. Muna Lee (tr.). 6759-X
   Elegy to the lost and already blurred by time. Blanca
      Lopez Castellon (tr.). 6759-X
   Exaltation of elementary materials. H.R. Hays (tr.).
      6759-X
   Nocturne. H.R. Hays (tr.). 6759-X
Abroad. Sophus Claussen. 6555-4
Abroad and at home. Jonathan Swift. 6722-0
"Abroad was shed the thickly falling mist". Icicles.
   William White. 6868-5
Absalom. Nathaniel Parker Willis. 6402-7,6744-1,6121-4,
   6848-0
Absalom and Achitophel. John Dryden. 6562-7,6152-4,6430-2
Absalom and Achitophel, sels. John Dryden. 6637-2,6195-0,
   6250-4,6024-2,6179-6,6198-2,6208-3,6726-3,6733
Abschied. Count Joseph von Eichendorff. 6252-0
Abse, Dannie
   Letter to Alex Comfort. 6210-5
Absence. Matthew Arnold. 6094-3
Absence. John Arthur Blaikie. 6656-9
Absence. Robert Burns. 6240-7
Absence. Heloise Davison. 6847-2
Absence. Walter De La Mare. 6905-3
Absence. John Donne. 6250-4,6301-2
Absence. Cora Fabri. 6876-6
Absence. Edgar A. Guest. 6748-4
Absence. Richard Jago. 6102-8,6086-2,6383-7
Absence. Frances Anne Kemble. 6219-9,6226-1,6066-8,6045-1,
   6271-7,6302-0,6385-3,6358-6,6620
Absence. Joyce Lancaster. 6850-2
Absence. Walter Savage Landor. 6086-2
Absence. Sir Philip Sidney. 6584-8
Absence. Sara Teasdale. 6777-8
Absence. Unknown. 6436-1,6732-8,6226-1,6737-9
Absence. Nathaniel Parker Willis. 6097-8
Absence and presence. Fulke Greville; 1st Baron Brooke.
   6436-1
The absence of little Wesley. James Whitcomb Riley. 6243-1
Absence of occupation, fr. Retirement. William Cowper.
   6932-0
"Absence, absenting causeth me to complain." Sir Thomas
   Wyatt. 6584-8
Absence, fr. A pastoral ballad. William Shenstone. 6024-2
"Absence, hear thou my protestation". Ode ("Absence").
   John Donne. 6182-6,6189-3
"Absence, hear thou my protestation." John Hoskins. 6181-8,
   6182-6,6187-7,6341-1
"Absence, the noble truce" Fulke Greville; 1st Baron
   Brooke. 6380-2
Absences. Paul Eluard. 6351-9
Absent. William Shakespeare. 6385-3
The absent boy. Margaret Elizabeth Sangster. 6274-1,6486-8,
   6385-3
Absnt creation. Derek S. Savage. 6379-9

4

An absent friend. Sappho. 6435-3
Absent friends. Ibn Hazm. 6362-4
"Absent from thee I languish still". A song ("Absent").
   John Wilmot, 2d Earl of Rochester. 6562-7,6544-9,
   6195-0,6315-2,6150-8
"Absent from thee". John Wilmot, 2d Earl of Rochester.
   6208-3,6563-5,6023-4
The absent lover. Edmund Spenser. 6935-5
The absent minded birch tree. Kathleen Millay. 6449-3
"Absent or present, still to thee". Lines written on a
   blank leaf of The pleasures...memory. George Gordon,
   6th Baron Byron. 6945-2
The absent soldier's son. Sydney Dobell. 6302-0,6385-3,
   6627-5
Absent yet present. Edward Bulwer-Lytton; Baron Lytton.
   6437-X
The absentee. Edgar A. Guest. 6748-4
The absinthe drinkers. Robert Service. 6159-1
The absinthe-drinker. Arthur Symons. 6210-5
Absolute and Abitofhell. Ronald Arbuthnott Knox. 6096 X
"Absolute knowledge I have none". The source of news.
   Unknown. 6846-4
Absolutely inexcusable. Unknown. 6847-2
Absolution. Arthur Davison Ficke. 6217-2
Absolution. Edith (Bland) Nesbit. 6166-4
Absolution. Siegfried Sassoon. 6393-4
"Absolve me for a while, undo". Ideal beauty. E.S. Hall.
   6768-9
Abstemia. Gelett Burgess. 6902-9
The abstinent lover. Abul Bahr. 6362-4
Abstract of the surgeon-general's report, fr. Croaker.
   Fitz-Greene Halleck and Joseph Rodman Drake. 6753-0
"Abstracted and alone sat Saul the king". Saul. G. M.
   Bell. 6848-0
Abstrosophy. Gelett Burgess. 6902-9
Abt Vogler. Robert Browning. 6198-2,6641-0,6657-7,6730-1,
   6723-9,6656 ,6102-8,6110-9,6655-0,6560-0,6430-2,6250
   ,6196-6,6199-0,6245-8
Abt Vogler, sels. Robert Browning. 6123-0,6337-3
Abu 'L-'Atahiya
   "Alas for the (all too) short time passed". A.J.
      Arberry (tr.). 6766-2
Abu Abd Allah
   Scurvy entertainment. A.J. Arberry (tr.). 6362-4
   The water-wheel. A.J. Arberry (tr.). 6362-4
   Wine and citron. A.J. Arberry (tr.). 6362-4
Abu Aiyub
   The gift. A.J. Arberry (tr.). 6362-4
Abu Amr
   Bad company. A.J. Arberry (tr.). 6362-4
Abu Bakr (of Marrakesh)
   The sword. A.J. Arberry (tr.). 6362-4
Abu Bakr Muhammad
   Panegyric. A.J. Arberry (tr.). 6362-4
Abu Dharr
   The oranges. A.J. Arberry (tr.). 6362-4
Abu Firas
   "Ladies, have you no reward for one whose actions".
      A.J. Arberry (tr.). 6766-2
Abu Hafs
   Beauty. A.J. Arberry (tr.). 6362-4
   Hips. A.J. Arberry (tr.). 6362-4
   Sunburn. A.J. Arberry (tr.). 6362-4
Abu Ishaq
   Changefulness. A.J. Arberry (tr.). 6362-4
Abu Jaafar
   Magian wine. A.J. Arberry (tr.). 6362-4
   Wine, my love. A.J. Arberry (tr.). 6362-4
Abu Midran. Eugene Field. 6949-5
Abu Nuwas
   "The man burdened with passion is a weary man." A.J.
      Arberry (tr.). 6766-2
Abu Shamaqmaq
   Hungry master and hungry cat. A.S. Tritton (tr.). 6511-
      2
Abu Tammam
   "The sword is nearer in tidings than (any) writings".
      A.J. Arberry (tr.). 6766-2
Abu Yahya
   Bloom of age. A.J. Arberry (tr.). 6362-4

The moth. A.J. Arberry (tr.). 6362-4
Abu Zaid
    The army. A.J. Arberry (tr.). 6362-4
Abu Zakariya
    Bubbling wine. A.J. Arberry (tr.). 6362-4
    The spear. A.J. Arberry (tr.). 6362-4
Abul Arab
    The gift. A.J. Arberry (tr.). 6362-4
Abul Bahr
    The abstinent lover. A.J. Arberry (tr.). 6362-4
Abul Fadl
    Body and soul. A.J. Arberry (tr.). 6362-4
Abul Hajjaj
    The reed. A.J. Arberry (tr.). 6362-4
Abul Hasan (of Badajoz)
    In battle. A.J. Arberry (tr.). 6362-4
Abul Hasan (of Santa Maria).
    Revel. A.J. Arberry (tr.). 6362-4
Abul Hasan (of Seville)
    The dove. A.J. Arberry (tr.). 6362-4
    Golden glow. A.J. Arberry (tr.). 6362-4
Abul Mughira
    Moon and Venus. A.J. Arberry (tr.). 6362-4
Abul Qasim (of Alcira)
    Rider. A.J. Arberry (tr.). 6362-4
Abul Qasim (of Silves)
    Unexpected fortune. A.J. Arberry (tr.). 6362-4
Abul-Ala
    Quatrains. 6102-8
Abus Salt
    Bounty. A.J. Arberry (tr.). 6362-4
    The incense burner. A.J. Arberry (tr.). 6362-4
    Sun and cloud. A.J. Arberry (tr.). 6362-4
    Two seas. A.J. Arberry (tr.). 6362-4
    The white charger. A.J. Arberry (tr.). 6362-4
Abuse of authority, fr. Measure for measure. William Shakespeare. 6302-0,6543-0
Abuse of the gospel. William Cowper. 6814-6
Abusive snatches. Unknown. 6582-1
The **abyss**. Feodor Ivanovich Tyutchev. 6622-4
"The **acacia** is heavy with blossom". The death of a horse. Jodi Ann Johnson. 6900-2
The **acacia** leaves. Allen Upward. 6897-9
Academe. Henry Alford. 6980-0
Academe. Sir Edwin Arnold. 6484-1
The **academy** bell. Unknown. 6523-6
Acateon. John Erskine. 6253-9
Acbar and Nourmahal. Thomas Moore. 6302-0;6385-3
Accent on paths. Mary Ernestine Clark. 6789-1
"**Accept** 'em Tommy as they're meant". Presentation inscription to Mr. Tommy Potter. John Gay. 6972-X
"**Accept** a bit of scrapbook rhyme". To Miss R.G. Louis J. Magee. 7004-3
Accept my full heart's thanks. Ella Wheeler Wilcox. 6085-4
Accept our tribute. Isaac Watts. 6065-X
"**Accept** thou shrine of my dead saint". The exequy to his matchlesse never to be forgotten... Henry King. 6908-8
"**Accept**, dear girl, this little token". A valentine to my wife. Eugene Field. 6949-5
"**Accept**, dear maid, this little token". With a golden necklace. Johann Wolfgang von Goethe. 6948-7
"**Accept**, loved nymph, this tribute due". To Amanda ("Accept"). James Thomson. 6816-2
"**Accept**, O sacred shade, this artless verse". Ode on the death of the author, by a lady. J. W.. 6962-2
Accept, my love, as true a heart. Matthew Prior. 6226-1
"**Accept**, young prince, the moral lay". The lyon, the tyger, and the traveller. John Gay. 6972-X
Acceptance. Robert Frost. 6879-0
Acceptance. Marie Emilie Gilchrist. 6906-1
Acceptance. Langston Hughes. 6388-8
Acceptance. Willard Wattles. 6007-2,6556-2
Acceptation. John Galsworthy. 6888-X
Acceptation. Margaret Junkin Preston. 6946-0
Accepted and will appear. Parmenas Mix. 6505-8
Accepted and will pay. Parmenas Mix. 6089-7
"An **accident** happened to the sky". Patches. Betty Myers. 6841-3
Accident in art. Bliss Carman and Richard Hovey. 6890-1

Accident in art. Richard Hovey. 6527-9
"**Accidents** will happen...". The little streets. Edgar A. Guest. 6748-4
Accidia. Henry Charles Beeching. 6437-X
Accinge sicut. Bible. 6830-8
An **acclamation**. Sir John Davies. 6584-8
The **accolade**. Bayard Taylor. 6976-2
Accompanied thus. Charles H. Howe. 6799-9
Accomplices. Thomas Bailey Aldrich. 6524-4
Accomplished facts. Carl Sandburg. 6726-3,6034-X
Accomplishment. Jackson Holland Patterson. 6841-3
According to scripture. Jean Starr Untermeyer. 6012-9
According to St. Mark. Thomas S. Jones Jr. 6335-7
"**According** to the degree of the people of resolve". al-Mutanabbi. 6766-2
According to thy gracious word. James Montgomery. 6337-3
According to your dream. Joseph Auslander. 6761-1
Accordion. Robert Service. 6159-1
Accordionist. Vladimir Kazin. 6546-5
An **account** of the greatest English poets, sels. Joseph Addison. 6191-5,6195-0
An **account** of the greatest English poets. Joseph Addison. 6831-6
Accountability. Paul Laurence Dunbar. 6736-0
The **accounte** of W. Canynges feast. Thomas Chatterton. 6086-2,6195-0,6198-2
Accursed. Unknown. 6273-3
"**Accursed** by sin, where shall I flee?". Words of Jesus. William White. 6868-5
Accusation. Helen Petkanich. 6799-9
Accusation against the forgiving friend. Francis D. Clare. 6839-1
The **accusation**. Edgar Lee Masters. 6538-4
"**Accuse** me thus: that I have scanted all". Sonnet 117 ("Accuse me"). William Shakespeare. 6447-7
"**Accused** though I be without desert." Sir Thomas Wyatt. 6584-8
Aceldama. George F. Butler. 6846-4
Aceldama, sels. Hugh Chisholm. 6390-X
"**Ach**, faeder bed! mein faeder bed!". Mein faeder bed. Eugene Field. 6949-5
"**Ach**, mein dog Pete". Hans' dog, Pete. Irene Davis Grueninger. 6906-1
"**Achaemenides** once, Menippus now...". Unknown. 6251-2
"**Achaians** have got Troy, upon this very day". Aeschylus. 6665-8
Acharya, Sri Ananda
    My faith. 6730-1
    Realization. 6730-1
Acheloos. Angelos Sikelianos. 6352-7
Acherontic chill. Detlev von Liliencron. 6160-5
Achievement. Edgar A. Guest. 6869-3
Achievement. Florence Jenney. 6034-X
Achievement. Berta Hart Nance. 6337-3
Achievement. Milton Purdy. 6850-2
"**Achievin'** sech distinction with his moddel...". Prof. Vere de Blaw. Eugene Field. 6949-5
Achilles. Ernest Myers. 6483-3
"**Achilles** and Hector and Homer and all". On Hayley's portrait. William Cowper. 6814-6
Achilles and Lycaon, fr. The Iliad. Homer. 6435-3
Achilles and Patroclus, fr. The Iliad. Homer. 6435-3
Achilles and the maiden. John Erskine. 6184-2
Achilles and the Scamander, fr. The Iliad. Homer. 6435-3
Achilles and Thetis, fr. The Iliad. Homer. 6435-3
Achilles on the rampart, fr. The Iliad. Homer. 6435-3
Achilles over the trench. Alfred Lord Tennyson. 6977-0
Achilles rallies the Greeks. Homer. 6102-8
Achilles shows himself in the battle by the ships. Homer. 6933-9
"**Achilles** then within his tent...", fr. The Iliad. Homer. 6435-3
Achilles to Lycaon, fr. The Iliad. Homer. 6665-8
Achilles' prayer, fr. The Iliad. Homer. 6435-3
The **Achilles'** reply to the embassy. Homer. 6435-3
Achilles: an opera. John Gay. 6972-X
Achitophel, fr. Absalom and Achitophel. John Dryden. 6660-7,6102-8
Achleitner, Friedrich
    "Biii bibibibibi." Milne Holton and Herbert Kuhner

(tr.). 6769-7
"Bix/bum." Milne Holton and Herbert Kuhner (tr.). 6769-7
"Oooooooooooooooooooooo." Milne Holton and Herbert Kuhner (tr.). 6769-7
"A so." Milne Holton and Herbert Kuhner (tr.). 6769-7
"The acid smell of my body, the propped". 8/2. John Campbell. 7032-9
The acid test. Mark Guy Pearse. 6461-2
Acis and Galatea: an English pastoral opera. John Gay. 6972-X,6250-4
Acker, Peter
   On hearing of a man's death in a hang glider accident. 6767-0
Acker, William (tr.)
   Long I have loved to stroll. T'ao Yuan-Ming, 6125-7
Ackerley, J.R.
   On a photograph of myself as a boy. 6776-X
Ackerly, W.A.
   Prayer of an unemployed man. 6337-3
Ackerman, Diane
   A.R. Ammons amid the fungi. 6803-0
Ackerman, Edwin N.
   Infinity. 6750-6
Ackerman, Mora L.
   Mahmed. 6818-9
Ackerman, Zoe
   My canary's rhapsody. 6653-4
Ackerson, John
   Ecce homo. 6337-3
Ackland, Valentine
   Night driving. 6761-1
Acknowledgment. Sidney Lanier. 6153-2,6250-4,6753-0
An acknowledgment. Henry King. 6150-8
Acluin - his epitaph. Helen Waddell. 6641-0
Acolyte. Mary Brent Whiteside. 6326-8
Acon. Hilda ("H.D.") Doolittle. 6331-4
Acon and Rhodope; or, inconstancy, sels. Walter Savage Landor. 6198-2,6110-9
Acorn. Unknown. 6272-5
Acorn, Milton
   The dolphin-walk. 6767-0
   A good sight of Andromeda. 6767-0
   Gull passage by moonlight. 6767-0
The acorn. Grace O. Kyle. 6529-5
The acquaintaceship. Jovan Ducic. 6765-4
Acquaintance. David Morton. 6332-2
An acquaintance declined. Margaret Eytinge. 6965-7
Acquainted with the night. Robert Frost. 6339-X,6125-7
The acquiescence of pure love. Madame De la Mothe Guion. 6814-6
The acquired art. Annie Higgins. 6037-4
Acquisition. Howard McKinley Corning. 6039-0
Acquisition. Clara Hyde. 6750-6
Acquittal. Leonie Adams. 6012-9
An acre of grass. William Butler Yeats. 6246-6
Acres of power. Randall Swingler. 6895-2
"Acrobats, a coloured flock". Tumbler leaves. Mary Josephine Benson. 6797-2
Acropolis. Catherine Patrick. 6799-9
Across a gaudy room. Michael (Katherine Bradley & Edith Cooper) Field. 6507-4
Across Illinois. John Stoltze. 6476-0
"Across a pasture of yellow lillies". Blue horses: west winds. Anita Endrezze-Danielson. 7005-1
"Across a thousand miles of sea...". Arrival. Henry Van Dyke. 6961-4
"Across a wintry wind-swept plain". No room. Winnifred Elliot. 6799-9
"Across in my neighbor's window...". My neighbor's baby. Unknown. 6913-4
"Across my keyboard, dreaming, you evoke". Clan call. Powers. Rose Mills. 7038-8
"Across my senses, faintly borne, a still". I hear a call. Avis H. Grant. 6906-1
"Across th' ensanguined sea the sun". Stormy sunset, fr. The south foreland. William ("Fiona Macleod") Sharp. 6997-5
"Across the barren moor". A song of the storm. Philip Bourke Marston. 6997-5

"Across the battlements of Saint Michel". Mont Saint Michel. Emily Taylor Perkins. 6799-9
"Across the bitter leagues of sundering brine". Wentworth Place. George Meason Whicher. 6847-2
"Across the boulder'd majesty". Sunset amid..mountains, fr. Australian transcripts. William ("Fiona Macleod") Sharp. 6768-9
Across the bridge. Clem Portman. 6857-X
Across the Delaware. Will Carleton. 6946-0
"Across the dark waves of the sea". A Cape Cod home, sels. Thomas Franklin Hall. 6798-0
Across the door. Padraic Colum. 6581-3
"Across the door-step, worn and old". The buried ring. John James Piatt. 7041-8
"Across the eastern sky has glowed". The crowing of the red cock. Emma Lazarus. 7041-8
"Across the empty garden-beds". The sailing of the sword. William Morris. 6828-6
"Across the far-stretched carpet...". Sunrise on the veld. Robert Alexander Nelson. 6800-4
Across the fens. Gilbert Thomas. 6257-1
Across the fields. Walter Crane. 6656-9
"Across the fields and marshes". Creltholme. Joshua Freeman Crowell. 6798-0
Across the fields to Anne. Richard Burton. 6310-1,6476-0, 6632-1
"Across the forest unbroken". Thoughts of Mashpee. Nelson D. Simons. 6798-0
"Across the glittering snow stretches...". In hospital. Annie Rothwell. 6795-6
"Across the heath, the monolith's public arch". Sonnet ("Across the heath"). Alfred Jarry. 6343-8
"Across the heaving ocean's billowy flow". Sonnet ("Across the heaving"). Edmond Gore Alexander Holmes. 6331-4
"Across the heights the June",fr. Children of the sun. Wallace Gould. 6031-5
"Across the inlet's ebb and rise". A scandal in New Amsterdam. Arthur Guiterman. 6773-5
"Across the lonely beach we flit". The sandpiper. Celia Thaxter. 6861-8
'Across the lot'. C. S. 6273-3
"Across the mesh fo feathered pine". There might be glory in the night. Ann [or Annie E.] Hamilton. 6782-5
"Across the moorlands of the Not". Moorlands of the Not. Unknown. 6902-9
"Across the narrow [or lonely] beach we flit". The sandpiper. Celia Thaxter. 6271-7,6073-0,6239-3,6479-5,6597-X,6623 ,6006-4,6102-8,6127-3,6242-3,6385-3, 6612 ,6632-1,6510-4,6121-4,6424-8,6212-1,6104 ,6076-5,6309-8,6456-6,6300-4
"Across the pew, with complaisance". My little sweetheart. Arthur G. Wright. 6770-0
"Across the places deep and dim". The road to anywhere. Bert Leston Taylor. 6891-X
"Across the plain the wind whines through...". The snowstorm. Pearl Riggs Crouch. 6836-7
"Across the quiet bay/At end of day". The sirens. Sir Edwin Arnold. 6980-0
Across the river. Lucy Larcom. 6407-8
"Across the road a mountain rose of rock". The pass of Ampezzo. Helen Hunt Jackson. 6749-2
"Across the room, within the narow molding". The picture. Marjorie Meeker. 6808-1
"Across the sands by Mary's well". Nazareth. L.. 6846-4
Across the sea. William Allingham. 6658-5
"Across the sea, along the shore". Arthur Hugh Clough. 6980-0
"Across the silken couch of sand". Bather sleeping. James E. Warren Jr.. 6979-7
"Across the stars float fleecy clouds". Passing souls. Gertrude Huntington McGiffert. 6838-3
"Across the Stony Mountains, o'er the desert". The crisis. John Greenleaf Whittier. 6946-0,6753-0
"Across the swiffline waves they went". The cruise of the 'P.C.' Unknown. 6902-9
Across the table. Bliss Carman and Richard Hovey. 6890-1
"Across the tinsel of my dreams". The builder. Maud Morrison Huey. 6818-9
"Across the trackless seas I go". To my sister. Adam Lindsay Gordon. 6951-7

"Across the tropic land, once more across". Copper kettle. Estelle Rooks. 6850-2
Across the world I speak to thee. Edith M. Thomas. 6331-4
Across the world I speak to thee. Edith Matilda Thomas. 6770-0
Across the years. Harriet Stanton Place. 6789-1
Across the years. Alise Williams Whitelaw. 6789-1
"Across the years he could recall". The secret heart. Robert P. Tristram Coffin. 6979-7
"Across what calm of tropic seas". To -, of her dark eyes. Alice Meynell. 6955-X
Acrostic. J. H. 6453-1
An acrostic ("A boat"). Charles Lutwidge ("Lewis Carroll") Dodgson. 6724-7
Acrostic ("Are you deaf"). Charles Lutwidge ("Lewis Carroll") Dodgson. 6724-7
Acrostic ("E.L.M."). James Abraham Martling. 6952-5
Acrostic ("Earth"). Sir John Davies. 6724-7
Acrostic ("Eulalie"). James Abraham Martling. 6952-5
An acrostic ("Friendship"). Unknown. 6724-7
Acrostic ("Go, little poem"). Charles Lamb. 6724-7
Acrostic ("Making"). Louis J. Magee. 7004-3
Acrostic exercise. Unknown. 6709-3
Acrostic on William Paddy. Unknown. 6753-0
An acrostic plant. R.S. P. 7021-3
Acrostic: Abraham Lincoln. Hartie I. Phillips. 6708-5
An acrostical valentine. Frank Dempster Sherman. 6770-0
Acrostics ("Lovely"). ? Bogart. 6724-7
Act 005 (midnight). Thomas Bailey Aldrich. 6467-1
Act of creation. Peter Stevens. 6767-0
An act of faith. Paul Potts. 6895-2
Act of love. Nicholas Moore. 6379-9
Act the man. Earl Alonzo Brininstool. 6109-5
Actaeon. (?) Bewe. 6436-1
Actaeon. Rayner Heppenstall. 6210-5
Actaeon. Alfred Noyes. 6151-6
Actaeon. Sir Charles George Douglas Roberts. 7041-8
Actea. James Rennell Rodd; 1st Baron Rennell. 6656-9
Action. Robert Loveman. 6941-X
Action. Daniel Webster. 6294-6
"Action is transitory", fr. The borderers. William Wordsworth. 6867-7
Actions speak louder. Peter A. Lea. 6249-0
Active Christian benevolence...source of...happiness. Carlos Wilcox. 6752-2
Acton, Ellen M.
    Dream. 6818-9
    Prediction. 6750-6
Acton-Bond, Marion
    Sunset on an English hill. 6541-4
The actor. Constance Farmar. 6777-8
The actor. John ("Peter Pindar") Wolcott. 6089-7
The actress. Dorothy Parker. 6052-8
Actual willow. Winifred Welles. 6038-2
Actuality. Sir John Suckling. 6315-2
Ad amicos. Bayard Taylor. 6976-2
Ad aristus fuscus. Unknown. 6936-3
Ad astra. Jean M. Batchelor. 7019-1
Ad astra. Martha Martin. 6585-6
Ad Astra. Thomas Walsh. 6096 X
Ad bellonam. Frank Lillie Pollock. 6471-X
Ad castitatem. Francis Thompson. 6489-2
Ad chloen, M.A. Mortimer Collins. 6089-7,6092-7
Ad Christum. Charles Whitby. 6994-0
Ad domnulam suam. Ernest Dowson. 6513-9
Ad Dorotheam. Edward Verrall Lucas. 6772-7
Ad finem. Heinrich Heine. 7039-6
Ad finem. Ella Wheeler Wilcox. 6956-8
Ad impudentissimam. Unknown. 6116-8
Ad Inuictissimum, Serenissimumque Iacobvm. Thomas Campion. 6794-8
Ad lesbiam. Caius Catallus. 6945-2
Ad leuconoen. Horace. 7039-6
Ad majorem dei gloriam. Frederick George Scott. 6337-3, 6656-9
Ad Mariam. Sister M. Edwardine. 6543-0
Ad matrem. Julian Henry Fane. 6097-8,6627-5
Ad matrem amantissimam et carissiman filii... John Myers O'Hara. 6556-2
Ad Matrem, in Caelis. Charles L. O'Donnell. 6096-X,6727-1

Ad ministram. William Makepeace Thackeray. 6092-7,6230-X
Ad mortem. Unknown. 6724-7
Ad patriam. Clinton Scollard. 6449-3
Ad patriam, sel. William Dudley Foulke. 6954-1
Ad Pyrrha. Horace. 6732-8
Ad uxorem. James Abraham Martling. 6952-5
Ad vivos. Kate Stephens. 6615-1
Ad Xanthiam phoceum. Horace. 7039-6
Ada, Sister Mary
    Approach. 6839-1
Adagio. Bo Bergman. 6045-5
Adagio. Jaroslav Vrchlicky. 6886-3
Adagio, fr. Summer night. Bayard Taylor. 6976-2
Adagio: a duet. Alfred Kreymborg. 6010-2
Adair, Ivan
    In war. 7031-0
    Real presence. 6730-1
Adair-Macdonald, Mary
    Epiphany vision (in the ward). 7031-0
    In last year's camp. 7031-0
    'V.A.D.' 7031-0
Adam. Honor Arundel. 6895-2
Adam. Stephen Vincent Benet. 6732-8
Adam. John Freeman. 6777-8
Adam and Eve. Eleazar Dexter. 7030-2
Adam and Eve's morning hymn. John Milton. 6543-0
Adam Bell, Clim of the Clough, and William of Cloudesly. Unknown. 6185-0,6518-4
Adam canoes sthe Meramac river. Walter Bargen. 6860-X
Adam describing Eve. John Milton. 6302-0;6142-7
Adam Gorman. Unknown. 6061-7
Adam lay ybounden. Unknown. 6756-5
"Adam lay ybounden". Unknown. 6106-0,6378-0,6489-2,6317-9, 6187-7,6334 ,6125-7,6150-8,6430-2
"Adam never knew what 'twas to be a boy". What Adam missed. Unknown. 6917-7
Adam never was a boy. Thomas Chalmers Harbaugh. 6926-6
Adam never was a boy. Thomas Chalmers Harbaugh. 6701-8
Adam posed. Anne Finch, Countess of Winchilsea. 6733-9
Adam to Eve. John Milton. 6848-0
Adam to Eve. John Milton. 6302-0;6385-3
Adam's account of his creation. John Milton. 6142-7
Adam's choice. Edward Farquhar. 6939-8
Adam's complaint. Theophanes. 6848-0
Adam's hymn in paradise. Joost van den Vondel. 6730-1
Adam's morning hymn in paradise. John Milton. 6848-0
Adam's morning hymn in paradise. John Milton. 6302-0;6385-3;6730-1
Adam's warning, fr. As you like it. William Shakespeare. 6001-3
Adam's wonder. George O'Neil. 6217-2
Adam, Helen
    The fair young wife. 6218-0
    The step mother. 6218-0
Adam, James (tr.)
    The hymn of Cleanthes (or, Hymn to Zeus). Cleanthes, 6337-3
Adam, Jean
    The mariner's wife. 6219-9
    There's nae luck about the house. 6271-7
Adam, Lilith, and Eve. Robert Browning. 6110-9,6196-6
"Adam, who thought himself immortal still". The discovery. Monk Gibbon. 6930-4
"Adamastor, whom Camoens and the sea". A voyage to Africa, sels. David Wright. 6788-3
Adams and liberty. Robert Treat Paine. 6946-0
Adams, Anna Mary
    Time. 6799-9
Adams, Arthur
    The Australian. 6784-0
    Fleet Street. 6784-0
    A pair of lovers in the street. 6784-0
    The Pleiades. 6784-0
    The weakling. 6784-0
    Written in Australia. 6784-0
Adams, Bill
    The ballad of the Ivanhoe. 6107-9
    The homeward bound (landfall). 6833-2
    Light of morning. 7007-8
    Peg-leg's fiddle. 6107-9,6833-2

ADAMS

Adams (cont.)
    Shore roads of April. 6833-2
    Stowaway. 6833-2
    Tramp's lyric. 7007-8
Adams, Cedric
    Intelligence test. 6491-4
Adams, Charles Follen
    Der coming man. 6565-1,6921-5
    Der Deutscher's maxim. 6923-1
    Der drummer. 6791-3,6823-5,7041-8
    Der oak und der vine. 6505-8,7920-7
    Der spider and der fly. 6924-X
    Der vater-mill. 6920-7,7041-8
    Dot baby off mine. 6175-3,6505-8,6573-2
    Dot lambs vot Mary haf got. 6175-3
    'Dot leedle Loweeza'. 6791-3
    Dot long-handled dipper. 6247-4,6505-8
    Fritz und I. 6791-3,6823-5
    Hans and Fritz. 6791-3,6823-5,6914-2
    He gets dhere shust der same! 7041-8
    Johnny Judkins. 6917-7
    Leedle Yawcob Strauss. 6505-8,6739-5
    Mine Katrine. 6517-6,6791-3,6823-5
    Mine mother-in-law. 6247-4,6505-8
    Mine shildren. 6791-3
    Mine vamily. 6572-4,6917-7,6572-4
    Mother's doughnuts. 6920-7
    Pat's criticism. 6825-1
    Shonny Schwartz. 6175-3,6791-3
    Strauss' boedry. 6922-3
    A tale of the nose. 6505-8
    A trapper's story. 6913-4
    "Vas marriage a failure?" 6505-8,6505-8
    Yaw, dot is so! 6280-6
    Yawcob's tribulations. 6924-X
    A zoological romance. 6916-9
    Zwei lager. 6791-3,6823-5
Adams, Elmer C.
    To a country hotel towel. 6750-6
Adams, Francis
    The rape of the nest. 6510-4,6943-6
    To the Christians. 6730-1
Adams, Francis W.
    Spring morning. 6591-0,6592-9
Adams, Francis W.L.
    'Anarchism'. 7009-4
    In Trafalgar Square. 7009-4
    Outside London. 7009-4
    To England. 7009-4
Adams, Franklin Pierce
    Ballade of the annual query. 6761-1
    Ballade of Schopenhauer's philosophy. 6875-8
    The cataract of T.R. 6995-9
    Jim and Bill. 6307-1
    Metaphysics. 6307-1
    An ode to T.R. 6995-9
    "Perscios odi". 6464-7
    The piker's Rubaiyat. 6274-1
    R.I.P. 6850-2
    The rich man. 6861-8
    Simplicity. 6464-7
    The slump in Sybaris. 6464-7
    'Such stuff as dreams' 6875-8
    Those two boys. 6026-9
    To a young woman on the 'World" staff. 6026-9
    To his lyre. 6307-1
    Villanelle, with Stevenson's assistance. 6850-2,6861-8, 6875-8
Adams, Franklin Pierce (tr.)
    Ad leuconoen. Horace, 7039-6
    Ad Pyrrha. Horace, 6732-8
    Ad Xanthiam phoceum. Horace, 7039-6
    He advances his modest boast to fame. Horace, 6637-2
    To Chloris, sels. Horace, 6732-8
Adams, Henry
    Prayer to the Virgin of Chartres. 6282-2
Adams, James Barton
    At a cowboy dance. 6281-4
    Bill's in trouble. 6889-8
    Billy, he's in trouble. 6736-0
    The dance at the little gila ranch. 6959-2

Adams, John Coleman
    Cape Cod. 6798-0
Adams, John Quincy
    The lip and the heart. 6004-8,6026-9,6307-1
    Man wants little here below. 6569-4
    Send forth, O God, thy light and truth. 6337-3
    To Sally. 6092-7
    The wants of man. 6438-8,6910-X
Adams, John Quincy (tr.)
    Psalm 033. Sing to Jehovah a new song. Bible, 6848-0
    To Sally. Horace, 7039-6
    Version of the 107th psalm. Bible, 6848-0
Adams, Jon
    Lady Grace. 7018-3
    Poem for Janis Joplin. 7018-3
Adams, Joseph V.
    The last raft. 6799-9
Adams, Katharine Rebecca
    I must forget. 7016-7
    Perhaps I shan't remember. 7016-7
    Reflection. 7016-7
    Sonnet ("All this"). 7016-7
    Sonnet ("Now tenderly"). 7016-7
    To one beloved. 7016-7
Adams, Leonie
    Acquittal. 6012-9
    At tea one bitter afternoon. 6808-1
    The barouche. 6808-1
    Bell tower. 6012-9
    Bird and bosom. 6071-4
    Country of the proud. 6012-9
    Country summer. 6012-9
    Evening sky. 6012-9
    Every bird of nature. 6012-9
    Ghostly tree. 6012-9
    The gift. 6012-9
    Home-coming. 6253-9,6393-4
    The horn. 6012-9
    The lonely host. 6012-9
    The moon and the spectator. 6012-9
    The mount. 6217-2
    The mysterious thing. 6012-9
    Quiet. 6880-4
    The river in the meadows. 6012-9,6250-4,6012-9, 6250-4
    Sight. 6808-1
    Spire of Saint Patrick's and the moon. 6808-1
    Sundown. 6012-9
    To the waterfront pigeons. 6808-1
    Twilit revelation. 6019-6, 6150-8
Adams, Louise B.
    Oklahoma hail! 6397-7
Adams, Marguerite Janvrin
    Prayer in an artic season. 6979-7
    They who posssess the sea. 6833-2
Adams, Mary M.
    Lincoln at Gettysburg. 6524-4
Adams, Myrtle
    One word. 6750-6
Adams, Oscar Fay
    Beaten. 7041-8
    Where are the pipes of Pan? 6770-0
Adams, Paul
    Peg-leg's fiddle. 6107-9
Adams, Saint Clair
    Playing off base. 6211-3
    A problem to be solved. 6291-1
Adams, Sarah Flower
    Father, Thy will be done. 6219-9
    Hymn. 6656-9
    Love. 6656-9
    The mourners came at break of day. 6214-8
    "Nearer, my God, to thee". 6219-9,6271-7,6337-3,6656-9, 6730-1,6723
Adamson, Sir John Ernest
    Green and gold. 6800-6
    The heart of the hills. 6800-6
    The moon's trek. 6800-6
    The quivering gum. 6800-6
Adan, Martin
    Nativity. Muna Lee (tr.). 6759-X,6734-4

Adanac, Ian
   The silent army. 6846-4
Adaptable poem. Thomas Masson. 6698-4
Adcock, Arthur St. John
   By deputy. 6760-3
   My neighbour. 6760-3
Addaeus
   "His yoke-ox, growing feeble...". F.L. Lucas (tr.). 6251-2
   An ox past service. Walter Leaf (tr.). 6435-3
Addict. Mabel MacDonald Carver. 6218-0
Addios. Donald C. Babcock. 6388-8
Addison. Alexander Pope. 6385-3,6102-8
Addison County, Vermont, clay. Daniel L. Cady. 6988-6
Addison, Joseph
   An account of the greatest English poets, sels. 6191-5, 6195-0
   An account of the greatest English poets. 6831-6
   Blenheim. 6932-0
   The campaign, sels. 6191-5
   The campaign. 6152-4
   Cato. 6250-4
   Cato's solilioquy on immortality. 6424-8
   Cato's soliloquy, fr. Cato. 6102-8,6304-7,6337-3,6424-8, 6541-4,6543
   Cato, sels. 6879-0
   Cato, sels. 6102-8
   The Countess of Manchester. 6278-4
   How are thy servants blest. 6931-2
   Hymn. 6543-0
   Hymn ("How are thy servants blest"). 6219-9,6271-7
   Hymn ("When all thy mercies"). 6271-7
   Hymn ("When rising from the bed"). 6271-7
   Hymn to the creation. 6820-0
   Immortality. 6461-2
   "It must be so - Plato, thou reason'st well", fr. Cato. 6934-7
   Italy. 6543-0
   Italy and Britain. 6932-0
   A letter from Italy, sels. 6831-6
   A letter from Italy. 6152-4
   Lines. 6648-8
   Love is not to be reasoned down or lost. 6066-8
   Ode ("The spacious firmament"). 6102-8,6271-7,6337-3, 6301-2,6543-0
   Ode to the creation. 6639-9
   Pastoral hymn. 6932-0
   Psalm 023. 6543-0,6219-9
   Rosamond's song. 6543-0
   The spacious firmament on high. 6102-8,6304-7,6438-8, 6660-7,6424-8,6250 ,6152-4,6219-9,6723-9,6737-9,6101-X,6457-4,6604-6,6641-0,6214-8,6464
   Speech of Sempronius. 6304-7
   To a capricious friend. 6278-4
   To a rogue. 6278-4
   To an ill-favored lady. 6278-4
   To spring gardens. 6230-X
   When all thy mercies, O my God. 6219-9,6931-2
   With what a graceful tenderness he loves. 6066-8
Addison, Joseph (tr.)
   The Po. Lucan, 6624-0
   Psalm 019. Bible, 6848-0,6730-1
   Psalm 023. Bible, 6848-0
   Psalm 115. Bible, 6848-0
   Temperament. Martial, 7039-6
   Vesuvius ("Vesuvio, covered"). Martial, 6624-0
Addison, Medora
   Wasted hours. 6347-0
Addison, fr. Epistle to Dr. Arbuthnot. Alexander Pope. 6934-7
Addison, fr. Moral essays. Alexander Pope. 6934-7
Addit. ms. 17492, British museum, sels. Sir Thomas Wyatt. 6586-4
Addition of the disk by King Akhnaten... Unknown (Egyptian) 7039-6
Additional verses to Hail Columbia. Oliver Wendell Holmes. 6946-0
Addleshaw, Percy ("Percy Hemingway")
   The happy wanderer. 6437-X
   It may be. 6656-9

   Travellers. 6656-9
Address at Gettysburg. Abraham Lincoln. 6503-1
Address delivered at...new theatre at Richmond. Henry Timrod. 6753-0
Address intended to be recited at the Caledonia meeting. George Gordon, 6th Baron Byron. 6945-2
Address of Leonidas. Richard Glover. 6344-6
Address of Ruth to Naomi, fr. The bible. Unknown. 6236-9
Address of the sylph of autumn to the bard. Washington Allston. 6752-2
Address on closing a performance. Unknown. 6064-1
Address spoken at the opening..Drury-Lane Theatre,1812. George Gordon, 6th Baron Byron. 6945-2
Address to a canoe-birch. Vachel Lindsay. 6206-7
Address to a child during a boisterous winter evening. Dorothy Wordsworth. 6018-8
Address to a Haggis. Robert Burns. 6180-X
Address to a lady. Robert Burns. 6271-7,6152-4
Address to a steam-vessel. Joanna Baillie. 6813-8
Address to a wild deer. Christopher (John Wilson) North. 6980-0
Address to an Egyptian mummy. Horace Smith. 6600-3
Address to Bellona and King James V. John Bellenden. 6180-X
Address to certain gold-fishes. Hartley Coleridge. 6219-9
Address to Edinburgh. Robert Burns. 6191-5
Address to fancy. Felicia Dorothea Hemans. 6973-8
An **address** to his elbow chair, new cloath'd. William Somervile. 6152-4
Address to his native vale. Robert Bloomfield. 6980-0
Address to liberty. William Cowper. 6286-5
Address to light. John Milton. 6543-0
Address to Miranda. William Falconer. 6971-1
Address to Mr. Cross, of Exeter Change... Thomas Hood. 6974-6
Address to music. Felicia Dorothea Hemans. 6973-8
Address to my soul. Elinor Wylie. 6531-7
Address to the alabaster sarcophagus. Horace Smith. 6302-0;6385-3
Address to the Deil. Robert Burns. 6278-4,6024-2,6102-8, 6180-X,6198-2,6152-4,6430
Address to the doomed, fr. The flowering stone. George Dillon. 6979-7
Address to the indolent. James Thomson. 6294-6
An **address** to the mob on occasion of the late riot... William Cowper. 6814-6
Address to the mummy at Belzoni's exhibition. Horace Smith. 6219-9,6639-9,6092-7,6271-7,6302-0,6385-3, 6331-4,6543-0
An **address** to the mummy in Belzoni's exhibition, sels. Horace Smith. 6934-7
Address to the new year. Dinah Maria Mulock Craik. 6449-3, 6820-0
Address to the nightingale. Richard Barnfield. 6271-7,6302-0,6385-3
Address to the ocean. George Gordon, 6th Baron Byron. 6585-6
Address to the ocean. Bryan Waller ("Barry Cornwall") Procter. 6302-0;6385-3
Address to the old year. Henry Timrod. 6753-0
Address to the poets. John Keble. 6980-0
Address to the reviewers. John ("Peter Pindar") Wolcott. 6760-3
Address to the scholars of New England. John Crowe Ransom. 6389-6
Address to the soul. Augustus Montague Toplady. 6219-9
An **address** to the steam washing company. Thomas Hood. 6974-6
Address to the toothache. Robert Burns. 6089-7,6302-0,6385-3,6219-9,6278-4
Address to the toothache, sels. Robert Burns. 6102-8
Address to the unco guid, or the rigidly righteous. Robert Burns. 6250-4,6430-2,6153-2,6024-2,6154-0,6198-2, 6200-8,6315-2,6152
Address to the unco guid, sels. Robert Burns. 6337-3
Address to the wood-lark. Robert Burns. 6102-8
Address to thought. Felicia Dorothea Hemans. 6973-8
Address to tragedy. Olga Berggolts. 6546-5
Address unknown. Josephine Louise Byrne. 6839-1
Address unspeakable. Lioel Wiggam. 6042-0

ADDRESS

An **address** without a phoenix. Horace Smith. 6802-2
An **address**, fr. Croaker papers. Fitz-Greene Halleck and Joseph Rodman Drake. 6753-0
Addressed to a clergyman. Thomas Rowley. 7030-2
Addressed to Haydon. John Keats. 6828-6
Addressed to Haydon. John Keats. 6543-0
Addressed to Miss Macartney. William Cowper. 6814-6
Ade, George
    R=e=m=o=r=s=e. 6026-9
Adeane, Louis
    Four poems for April. 6379-9
    The night loves us. 6379-9
    Poem on Hampstead Heath. 6379-9
Adee, David Graham
    The lone star of Cuba. 7022-1
Adelaide Anne Procter. Sir Edwin Arnold. 6046-3
Adelaide Crapsey. Carl Sandburg. 6031-5
Adelaide Neilson. William Winter. 7041-8
Adelied. Alice Cary. 6969-X
Adeline. Alfred Lord Tennyson. 6977-0
Adelman, Sylvia
    Fog. 6850-2
    Loneliness. 6850-2
    Onward and upward. 6850-2
Aden, ?
    Where's Annette. 6574-0
Adequacy, fr. Mother-songs. Marian Williams McGaw. 6906-1
Adeste fideles. Saint (atr) Bonaventure. 6543-0
Adeste fideles. Saint (atr) Bonaventure. 6608-9
Adeste fideles. M. Portugal. 6608-9
Adeste fideles. Unknown. 6730-1
Adests fideles. Unknown (Latin) 6337-3,6418-3
Adieu. Thomas Carlyle. 6240-7
Adieu. Leon Dierx. 6351-9
Adieu. Eleanor Elizabeth Montgomery. 6656-9
Adieu. Constantia E. Riley. 6178-8
"**Adieu** awhile, forsaken flood". The grotto. Matthew Green. 6968-1
Adieu l'amour. George Granville; Baron Lansdowne. 6024-2
Adieu love, untrue love. Unknown. 6182-6
Adieu to Argyll. Charles Larcom Graves. 6760-3
"**Adieu** to Belashanny! where I was bred & born". The winding banks of Erne. William Allingham. 6858-8
Adieu to France, fr. De roberval. John Hunter-Duvar. 6795-6
Adieu to his mistress. Alexander Montgomerie. 6180-X
"**Adieu** to kindred hearts and home". Early adieux. Adam Lindsay Gordon. 6951-7
"**Adieu** to thee, fair Rhine". George Gordon, 6th Baron Byron. 6331-4
Adieu! Farewell earth's bliss! Thomas Nashe. 6182-6, 6181-8,6536-8,6194-X,6430
"**Adieu**! al vaine delightes". Melancholye. William Motherwell. 6960-6
"**Adieu**! Monseigneur rises now". Monseigneur plays. Theodosia Garrison. 7038-8
"**Adieu**, adieu! my native shore." George Gordon, 6th Baron Byron. 6302-0,6385-3,673-9,6890-0
"**Adieu**, adieu! our dream of love." Thomas Kibble Hervey. 6302-0;6385-3
"**Adieu**, farewell earth's bliss". A lament. Thomas Nashe. 6935-5
"**Adieu**, O daisy of delight!". A farewell. Alexander Montgomerie. 6830-8
"**Adieu**, Romauld! But thou canst not forget me". The farewell of Clarimonde. Ella Wheeler Wilcox. 6956-8
Adieu, fond love, fr. The lover's progress. Francis Beaumont. 6328-4
"**Adieu**, sweet Angus, Maeve, and Fand". The passing of the shee. John Millington Synge. 6930-4
"**Adi·u**, sweet haven! lovely vale, farewell!". On leaving Limpley Stoke. Charles Whitby. 6994-0
"**Adieu**, thou hill! where early joy". The adieu. George Gordon, 6th Baron Byron. 6945-2
"**Adieu**, ye joys of La Valette!". Farewell to Malta. George Gordon, 6th Baron Byron. 6092-7,6945-2
An **adieu**. Florence Earle Coates. 6027-7
The **adieu**. George Gordon, 6th Baron Byron. 6945-2
The **adieu**. William Robert Spencer. 6086-2
"**Adieu**? why so? deare Castaminda stay." Unknown. 6563-5

Adieux a Marie Stuart. Algernon Charles Swinburne. 6828-6
Adieux au college de Belley. Alphonse Marie Louis de Lamartine. 6718-2
"' **Adiew**, madam my mother dear". Unknown. 6111-7
Adios. Joaquin Miller. 6753-0
Adioux among the Sioux. Unknown. 6724-7
Adirondack evening. Chard Powers Smith. 6038-2
The **Adirondacs**, sels. Ralph Waldo Emerson. 6484-1
Adjustment. Robinson Jeffers. 6012-9
Adjustment. Gertrude W. Robinson. 6906-1
Adjustment. John Greenleaf Whittier. 6730-1
Adler, Felix
    The city of our hopes. 6337-3
    The city of the light. 6954-1
    Hail! the glorious golden city. 6730-1
Adler, Frederick Herbert
    Changed thought-birds. 6906-1
    Cocoons. 6906-1
    A final spring. 6906-1
    Give me your hand. 6906-1
    The road. 6906-1
    Scandal monger. 6906-1
    September. 6906-1
    To A -. 6906-1
Adlestrop. Edward Thomas. 6506-6,6634-8,6464-7,6650-X
Administration hall. Francis Paxton. 6397-7
An **admirable** new northern story of two constant lovers. Unknown. 6547-3
Admiral Benbow. Unknown. 6547-3
Admiral Byrd. Ogden Nash. 6736-0
Admiral death. Sir Henry Newbolt. 6087-0,6395-0,6250-4
Admiral dugout. Cicely Fox Smith. 7031-0
The **admiral** Guarinos. Unknown (Spanish) 6757-3
Admiral Hosier's ghost. Unknown. 6547-3
Admiral Rodney's triumph on the 12th of April. Unknown. 6547-3
The **admiral** walks his quarterdeck. Unknown. 6237-7
The **admiral's** ghost. Alfred Noyes. 6290-3;6151-6
Admirals all. Sir Henry Newbolt. 6211-3,6242-3,6639-9
Admire not, shepherd's boy. George Wither. 6191-5
"**Admit** thou darlinge of myne eyes." Unknown. 6563-5
Admonition. William Wordsworth. 6198-2
Admonition for spring. Louis Alexander Mackay. 6021-8,6446-9
Admonition to a traveller. William Wordsworth. 6246-6,6737-9,6543-0
An **admonition** to young lasses. Alexander Montgomerie. 6180-X
Admonition to youth. Melba Williams. 6906-1
The **admonition**: to Betsey. Helen Parry Eden. 7029-9
Adobe wall and Indian Joe. Laban Thomas Johnston. 6316-0
Adolescence. Mavis Clare Barnett. 6039-0
Adolescence. Bernard K. Kay. 6764-6
Adolescence. Alice M. Shepard. 6764-6
Adolescence. Melba Williams. 6906-1
Adolescents in the dusk. Ian Fletcher. 6209-1
Adolphus Elfinstone. Gelett Burgess. 6465-5
Adolphus, Duke of Guelders. Owen (Edward Bulwer-Lytton, Earl Lytton) Meredith. 6669-0
Adolphus, Gustavus. See Gustavus II, King
Adon olam. Unknown. 6848-0
Adonais. Will Wallace Harney. 7041-8
Adonais. Percy Bysshe Shelley. 6660-7,6560-0,6430-2,6196-6, 6199-0,6250 ,6245-8,6102-8,6192-3,6150-8,6110-9,6219 ,6660-7,6560-0,6430-2,6196-6,6199-0,6250 ,6245-8, 6102-8,6192-3,6150-8,6110-9,6219 ,6023-4,6086-2,6424-8,6122-2,6154-0,6198-2,6315-2,6332-2,6483 ,6536-8, 6604-6,6641-0,6726-3,6732-8,6543
Adonais, sels. Percy Bysshe Shelley. 6980-0
Adonais, sels. Percy Bysshe Shelley. 6369-1,6214-8,6301-2, 6648-8,6646-1,6378-0,6634-8,6730-1,6102-8,6208-3, 6339
Adonis. Hilda ("H.D.") Doolittle. 6077-3,6619-4
Adonis. John Keats. 6980-0
Adonis. Blanche Shoemaker Wagstaff. 6327-6
Adonis sleeping. John Keats. 6980-0
The **adopted** child. Felicia Dorothea Hemans. 6973-8
The **adopted** child. Felicia Dorothea Hemans. 6271-7
Adoration. Jeanne Marie Bouvier de la Motte Guyon. 6730-1
Adoration. James Pul Heady. 6894-4

Adoration. Laurence (Adele Florence Nicolson) Hope. 6856-1
Adoration. David Morton. 6337-3
The adoration. William Rose Benet. 6320-9
"Adored heart's dearest!". Morning. Annie Edgerly Thayer. 6764-6
Adoro te devote. Saint Thomas Aquinas. 6543-0
"Adown beside an old stone wall". Four pictures. Harriet E. Durfee. 6926-6
"Adown the dim-lit gallery I stept". Ladye Maude. Cora Fabri. 6876-6
Adown the years. Robert Loveman. 6941-X
Adown the years. Ada Simpson Sherwood. 6926-6
Adrian Block's song. Edward Everett Hale. 6946-0
Adrian's address to his soul when dying. George Gordon, 6th Baron Byron. 6945-2
"Adriana—Nay, said I not—". Sir Henry Taylor. 6238-5
Adriani morientis ad animam suam. Matthew Prior. 6152-4
Adriano, sels. Pietro Mestastio. 6975-4
Adrift. Elizabeth Dickinson West. 6090-0,6174-5
Adrift. James Chapman Woods. 6997-5
Adul Tima [pseud].
    Sense. 6817-0
"Adullam's sheltering cavern bent". Filial piety of David. Lydia Huntley Sigourney. 6848-0
An adult lullaby. Unknown. 6881-2
Adultery at a Las Vegas bookstore. Stephen Shu Ning Liu. 6790-5
The advance guard. Berton Braley. 6853-7
The advance of the Trojans, fr. The Iliad. Homer. 6435-3
"Advance your chorall motions now". A song ("Advance"). Thomas Campion. 6794-8
'Advance, America'. John Helston. 7027-2
Advance, Australia. Andrew Lang. 6323-3
'Advance.'. Frank H. Gassaway. 6673-9
An advanced thinker. Brander Matthews. 6996-7
The advantage of foreknowledge. Sir John Suckling. 6874-X
Advantages of nudism. Erich Fried. 6769-7
Adveniat regnum tuum. Katharine (Hinkson) Tynan. 6533-3
Advent. Howard McKinley Corning. 6039-0
Advent. John Gould Fletcher. 6337-3,6345-3
Advent. Christina Georgina Rossetti. 6655-0
Advent meditation. Alice Meynell. 6746-8
The advent of peace. Arthur Hugh Clough. 7014-0
Advent of spiritualism. Edward R. Huxley. 6885-5
Advent Sunday. John Keble. 6980-0
Advent, fr. St. Paul. Frederick W.H. Myers. 6337-3
The advent. William White. 6868-5
Adventure. Henry Holcomb Bennett. 6088-9
Adventure. Hilda Conkling. 6368-3
Adventure. Adelaide Crapsey. 6897-9
Adventure. Sally Bruce Kinsolving. 6102-8
Adventure. William Alexander Percy. 6326-8,6421-3
Adventure. John Runcie. 6591-0,6592-9
Adventure. Clark Ashton Smith. 6628-3
Adventure. Willoughby Weaving. 7014-0
Adventure on the wings of morning. Rachel Albright. 6750-6
An adventure on wheels. Unknown. 6889-8
The adventurer. Dana Burnet. 6732-8
The adventurer. Odell Shepard. 6029-3,6431-0
The adventurer. Royall Snow. 6906-1
Adventurers of science. Berton Braley. 6853-7
The adventurers. May C. ([Mary] Gillington) Byron. 6478-7
The adventurers. Bliss Carman and Richard Hovey. 7007-8
Adventures. Robert Norwood. 6797-2
Adventures in Mother Gooseland. Grace Marie Stanistreet. 6249-0
The adventures of Harriet Simper,fr.Progress of dulness. John Trumbull. 6008-0,6288-1
The adventures of John Brainless,fr.Progress of dulness. John Trumbull. 6009-9
The adventures of Miss Harriet Simper, fr. The progress. John Trumbull. 6753-0
Adventures of Robinson Crusoe. Unknown. 6131-1
Adventuring. Lalia Mitchell Thornton. 6654-2
"Adventuring in golden glory". Coals and ashes: 1916 Sylvester Baxter. 6798-0
The adventurous kangaroo. Carolyn Wells. 6882-0
Adverse desires. Edward R. Huxley. 6885-5
Adversity. William Shakespeare. 6294-6
Adversity. Ruth Smeltzer. 6270-9

"Adversity confronts the weary world". Wings of adversity. Rose Jane Ward. 6799-9
Advertisement. John Gay. 6972-X
Advertisement. Alfred Kreymborg. 6069-2
The advertisement answered. Frank M. Thorn. 6916-9,6742-5
Advertising. Ingeborg Bachmann. 6769-7
Advice. Le Baron Cooke. 6039-0
Advice. William Henry Davies. 6334-9
Advice. Austin Dobson. 6652-6
Advice. L.L. H. 7021-3
Advice. Lindley Williams Hubbell. 6039-0
Advice. Unknown. 6302-0
Advice. Ella Wheeler Wilcox. 7041-8
The advice of a judge. Everett C. Richmond. 6799-9
Advice of Polonius to his son, fr. Hamlet. William Shakespeare. 6552-X,6543-0
Advice to a boy. Robinson Kay Leather. 6301-2
Advice to a clam-digger. Wilbert Snow. 6038-2,6070-6
Advice to a clansman. Thomas Pattison. 6180-X
Advice to a girl. Thomas Campion. 6732-8,6737-9
Advice to a lady in autumn. Philip Dormer Stanhope, 4th Earl of Chesterfield. 6092-7,6152-4
Advice to a lover. S. Charles Jellicoe. 6174-5
Advice to a lover. Sir John Suckling. 6153-2
Advice to a lover, fr. Perikeiromene. Menander. 6435-3
Advice to a young lawyer. Joseph Story. 6878-2
Advice to a young lawyer. Joseph Story. 6142-7
Advice to a young man wishing to wed. Winifred Johnston. 6397-7
Advice to a young prophet. J.M. S. 6817-0
Advice to a young romanticist. Allen Tate. 6619-4,6071-4, 6039-0
Advice to Amanda. Francis Hopkinson. 6753-0
Advice to an advocate. Joseph Story. 6294-6
Advice to gardeners, fr. The gardens. Abbe de Lille. 6649-6
Advice to leesome merriness. Sir Richard Maitland. 6180-X
Advice to my young wife. Maxwell Bodenheim. 6037-4
Advice to red leaves. Muriel F. Hochdorf. 6850-2
Advice to small children. Edward Anthony. 6396-9
Advice to the ladies of London in the choice... Unknown. 6157-5
Advice to the Marquis of Rockingham. David Garrick. 6874-X
Advice to the old beaux. Sir Charles Sedley. 6152-4
Advice to the same. Sir Philip Sidney. 6584-8
Advice to the young. Unknown. 6410-8
Advice to travelers. Walker Gibson. 6388-8
Advice to worriers. George S. Kaufman. 6026-9,6501-5
Advice to young lawyers. Joseph Story. 6142-7
Advice to young women. John ("Peter Pindar") Wolcott. 6278-4
Advice to youth. Countee Cullen. 6817-0
Advice: a satire. Tobias George Smollett. 6975-4
The advice. Sir Walter Raleigh. 6380-2
The advice. Charles Sackville; 6th Earl of Dorset. 6250-4, 6092-7
"Adze and hammer and anvil stroke". The whaling town. Arthur Wentworth Hamilton Eaton. 7041-8
"Ae a fond mother, when the day is o'er". Nature. Henry Wadsworth Longfellow. 6097-8,6176-1,6303-9,6337-3, 6365-9,6243 ,6126-5,6153-2,6300-4,6214-8,6464-7,6723 ,6627-5,6726-3,6473-6,6250-4,6288-1,6431 ,6491-4, 6737-9
Ae fond kiss. Robert Burns. 6086-2,6195-0,6430-2,6152-4, 6250-4,6737 ,6301-2,6396-9,6102-8,6154-0,6186-9,6198-2,6204-0,6536-,6180-X,6240-7,6302-0,6307-9,6385-3, 6659
"Ae morning near the dawning, I saw a counsel". The circuiter's lament. David Crichton. 6878-2
Aedh wishes for the clothes of heaven. William Butler Yeats. 6437-X,6477-9
Aegean islands 1940-41. Bernard Spencer. 6379-9
Aeglamour seeks his shepherdess. Ben Jonson. 6150-8
Aeglamour's lament. Ben Jonson. 6191-5
"Aegle, beauty and poet, has two little crimes". Unknown (French) 6945-2
Aeliana's diary. Henry Chettle. 6436-1
Aeliana's duty. Henry Chettle. 6026-9
Aella, sels. Thomas Chatterton. 6086-2,6250-4
Aella, sels. Thomas Chatterton. 6726-3

AENEID,

Aeneid, sels. Vergil. 6484-1
The *Aeneid,* sels. Vergil. 6372-1
The *Aeneid,* sels. Vergil. 6198-2,6186-9,6194-X
The *Aeneid.* Vergil. 6483-3
An *aenigma.* Vincent Bourne. 6814-6
AEnone. William Edmonstoune Aytoun. 6980-0
Aeolian harp. William Allingham. 6090-0,6438-8
The *Aeolian* harp. Herman Melville. 6333-0
An *Aeolian* harp. Michael (Katherine Bradley & Edith Cooper) Field. 6656-9
"*Aeons* ago the river's fangs struck deep". Grand Canyon. Lilian White Spencer. 6836-7
Aere Perennius. Charles Hanson Towne. 6338-1
The *aeronaut* to his lady. Frank Sidgwick. 6722-0
An *aeroplane* against a daylit moon. Robert P. Tristram Coffin. 7040-X
"A *aeroplane* came whirring through the sky". Flight Commander Stork. Marian Osborne. 6797-2
Aeroplane factory. Mary Carolyn Davies. 7038-8
Aeroplanes. Walter James Turner. 7029-9
Aeschylos and Sophocles. Walter Savage Landor. 6102-8,6110-9,6102-8,6483-4
Aeschylus
   "Achaians have got Troy, upon this very day". Richard Lattimore (tr.). 6665-8
   Agamemnon, sels. 6435-3
   "Behold the tyrants that oppressed your land". G.M. Cookson (tr.). 6435-3
   "The bow of Zeus has twanged...", fr. Agamemnon. Jack Lindsay (tr.). 6435-3
   Chorus, fr. Agamemnon. Gilbert Murray (tr.). 7039-6
   Chorus, fr. Seven against Thebes. Alfred Edward Housman (tr.). 7039-6
   Chorus, fr. The seven against Thebes. 6102-8
   "Come, dance and song, in linked round". G.M. Cookson (tr.). 6435-3
   The daughters of Atlas. Cecil Maurice Bowra (tr.). 6435-3
   Death. Andrew Lang (tr.). 6987-8,6879-0
   Epitaph on himself. 6102-8
   "The god of war, money changer of dead bodies". Richard Lattimore (tr.). 6665-8
   The gods' children. Cecil Maurice Bowra (tr.). 6435-3
   A grave on Ossa. T.F. Higham (tr.). 6435-3
   Hymn to Zeus, fr. Agamemnon. 6730-1
   "I call on Zeus...", fr. Agamemnon. Jack Lindsay (tr.). 6435-3
   "If I were to tell of our labours, our hard lodging." Louis MacNeice (tr.). 6665-8
   Inexorable death. Cecil Maurice Bowra (tr.). 6435-3
   Io. Walter Headlam (tr.). 6435-3
   Justice protects the dead. Cecil Maurice Bowra (tr.). 6435-3
   Laughter of the waves. 7020-5
   The marriage of heaven and earth. Cecil Maurice Bowra (tr.). 6435-3
   "My reverend Elders, worthy...", fr. Agamemnon. Walter Headlam (tr.). 6435-3
   News of war. Edwyn R. Bevan (tr.). 6435-3
   Nysa. Andrew Lang (tr.). 6987-8
   "O father, fwther of our woe". G.M. Cookson (tr.). 6435-3
   "O woman very unhappy...", fr. Agamemnon. Louis MacNeice (tr.). 6435-3
   "One Aeschylus, Athenian born". T.F. Higham (tr.). 6435-3
   The overthrow of Zeus. G.M. Cookson (tr.). 6435-3
   "Pallas' home contenteth me". G.M. Cookson (tr.). 6435-3
   The Persians, sels. John Stuart Blackie (tr.). 6484-1
   Philoctetes calls for death. Cecil Maurice Bowra (tr.). 6435-3
   Prayer for deliverance. Gilbert Murray (tr.). 6435-3
   Prometheus bound. G.M. Cookson (tr.). 6435-3
   Prometheus in the earthquake. Jack Lindsay (tr.). 6435-3
   Prometheus the teacher of men. G.M. Cookson (tr.). 6435-3
   Prometheus vinctus, sels. George Gordon, 6th Baron Byron (tr.). 6945-2
   The Red Sea. Cecil Maurice Bowra (tr.). 6435-3
   Salamis. G.M. Cookson (tr.). 6435-3,6665-8
   "There is the sea...", fr. Agamemnon. Walter Headlam (tr.). 6435-3
   Thetis ("He praised the greatness of the child..."). Cecil Maurice Bowra (tr.). 6435-3
   The wail of Prometheus bound. Elizabeth Barrett Browning (tr.). 6730-1
   "What courier could arrive...", fr. Agamemnon. Walter Headlam (tr.). 6435-3
   The worship of cotys. 6435-3
   The wounded eagle. Cecil Maurice Bowra (tr.). 6435-3
   Xerxes defeated. G.M. Cookson (tr.). 6435-3
   "Zeus is the air, Zeus earth, and Zeus the sky". Cecil Maurice Bowra (tr.). 6435-3
Aeschylus. Aubrey Thomas De Vere. 7015-9
Aesop
   The ass in the lion's skin. William Ellery Leonard (tr.). 7039-6
   The shepherd-boy and the wolf. William Ellery Leonard (tr.). 7039-6
   The swan and the goose. William Ellery Leonard (tr.). 7039-6
Aesop. Andrew Lang. 6732-8,6656-9
Aesop at play. Phaedrus. 7039-6
Aesopus
   The way of life. A.J. Butler (tr.). 6435-3
The *aesthete* to the rose. Unknown. 6440-X
The *aesthete.* Sir William Schwenck Gilbert. 6026-9
Aesthetics. C.T. Lanham. 6039-0
Aestivation. Oliver Wendell Holmes. 6089-7,6722-0,6724-7
Aetate XIX. Herman Charles Merivale. 6656-9
Aeternae memoriae patris. Leon Paul Fargue. 6343-8
Aetius the unbeliever. William Herbert; Earl of Pembroke. 6980-0
"*Afar* in the ages of quaint renown". William the testy. Arthur Guiterman. 6773-5
Afar in the desert. Thomas Pringle. 6800-6,6788-3
"*Afar* in the desert." Thomas Pringle. 6302-0,6385-3,6219-9,6304-7,6591-0,6592
Afar in Tuna. Ethel May Ericson. 6847-2
"*Afar* in the midst of the forest". A Delaware youth and his uncle. Unknown (Algonquin Indian). 6864-2
Afar on the floodways. Unknown. 6489-2
"*Afar,* where the rugged northland". The first Christmas-tree. Myra A. Goodwin. 6927-4
"*Afar/In* heaven's space". Token. Charlotte Hazlewood. 6789-1
Afeared of a gal. Unknown. 6273-3,6632-1,6672-0,6505-8
An *afernoon* in Artillery walk. Leonard Bacon. 6527-9
"The *affairs* of the world are all hurry and trouble..." Unknown (Chinese) 6545-7
Affectation in the pulpit. William Cowper. 6045-1,6605-2
Affection. Letitia Elizabeth ("L.E.L.") Landon. 6980-0
Affection and desire. Sir Walter Raleigh. 6436-1
"*Affection's* charm no longer gilds". The personified sentimental. Francis Bret Harte. 6902-9
"*Affections* lose their object; time brings". Sonnet, to an octogenarian. William Wordsworth. 6828-6
"*Affections,* instincts, principles, and powers". Written in Butler's sermons. Matthew Arnold. 6947-9
Aferte domino. Bible. 6830-8
Affinity. Mrs. A.J. ("Ricketty Kate") Filson. 6349-7
Affinity. George William ("A.E.") Russell. 6320-9
Affinity. Leonora Speyer. 6984-3
Affinity. Ronald Stuart Thomas. 6257-1
Affinity. Unknown. 7021-3
The *affinity.* Anna Wickham. 6102-8
An *affirmation.* Minot Judson Savage. 6337-3
Affliction. Sir John Davies. 6436-1
Affliction. George Herbert. 6315-2,6378-0,6150-8,6341-1,6438-8
Affliction. W. Wesley Trimpi. 6515-5
The *affliction* of Margaret, sels. William Wordsworth. 6934-7
The *affliction* of Margaret. William Wordsworth. 6246-6,6365-9,6086-2,6110-9
The *affliction* of Richard. Robert Bridges. 6487-6,6641-0
Afflictions sanctioned by the word. William Cowper. 6814-6
"*Affrighted* down death's realms I fled". Post tenebras

lux. Gertrude Huntington McGiffert. 6838-3
The **Afghani** nomad coat (part V) Rita Dove. 7032-9
Afoot. Sir Charles George Douglas Roberts. 6374-8,6656-9
Afoot. Cicely Fox Smith. 6374-8,6423-X
Afoot and light-hearted. Walt Whitman. 6374-8
"**Afore** the game of goff come 'round". Playing checkers in Vermont. Daniel L. Cady. 6988-6
"**Afore** we went to Denver we heerd..Tabor Grand". Modjesky as cameel. Eugene Field. 6949-5
Afore yo' daddy comes. Lalia Mitchell. 6690-9
Aforetime. Thomas Sturge Moore. 6884-7
Afraid of a wetting. Unknown. 6130-3
Afraid? Of whom am I afraid? Emily Dickinson. 6177-X
Africa. Claude McKay. 6880-4
Africa. Unknown. 6335-7,6337-3
The **African** chief. William Cullen Bryant. 6732-8
The **African** mother. Unknown. 6683-6
An **African** song. Thomas Chatterton. 6315-2,6545-7
African witchcraft. Arthur Shearly Cripps. 6625-9
Afridi love. Laurence (Adele Florence Nicolson) Hope. 6856-1
Afrikaans homestead. Peter Jackson. 6788-3
After. Theodora Bates. 6118-4
After. Robert Browning. 6102-8
After. Florence Earle Coates. 6051-X,6607-0
After. Francis Ledwidge. 6812-X
After. Victor F. Murray. 6269-5
After. Lizette Woodworth Reese. 6326-8
"**After** 18". Austrians. Josef Mayer-Limberg. 6769-7
After a city winter. Haniel Long. 6039-0
After a dance. John Moran. 6680-1
After a Dolmetsch concert. Arthur Upson. 6310-1,6464-7
"**After** a day of horizontal rain". Atlas of Oregon. Madeline DeFrees. 7032-9
After a game of squash. Samuel L. Albert. 6388-8
"**After** a generation the graves gape lean and". Each year's song. Walter Benton. 6761-1
"**After** a heart disease, Aunt Li died". A pair of fireflies. Stephen Shu Ning Liu. 6790-5
After a hundred storms. Helene Mullins. 6042-0
After a journey. Thomas Hardy. 6208-3,6246-6,6150-8
After a lecture om Wordsworth. Oliver Wendell Holmes. 6126-5
After a lecture on Keats. Oliver Wendell Holmes. 6483-3, 6431-0
After a lecture on Shelley. Oliver Wendell Holmes. 6126-5
"**After** a long half year" Keiho Soga. 6981-9
"**After** a man has been married awhile". The kick under the table. Edgar A. Guest. 7033-7
After a parting. Alice Meynell. 6955-X
After a proposal. Edgar A. Guest. 6862-6
After a retreat. Robert Hugh Benson. 6172-9,6292-X
"**After** a sandstorm left them worn and spent". Ramadan in the desert. May Folwell Hoisington. 7038-8
After a summer shower. Andrews Norton. 6285-3;6600-3
"**After** a supper of mountain rice". Hometown. Luis Cabalquinto. 6790-5
After a tempest. William Cullen Bryant. 6752-2
After a year in the city. Risa Alice Lowie. 6847-2
"**After** a youth by woes o'ercast". Queen Mary's return to Scotland. James Hogg. 6980-0
After action. Robert Haven Schauffler. 7027-2
After all. Thomas S. Jones Jr. 6653-4
After all. Arthur Upson. 6441-8
After all. William Winter. 6113-3,6243-1,6471-X,6016-2, 6470-1,6304
After all and after all. Mary Carolyn Davies. 6031-5
After all splendors. Mary Brent Whiteside. 6326-8
After an interval. Walt Whitman. 6126-5
After apple-picking. Robert Frost. 6399-3,6488-4,6536-8, 6556-2,6602-X
After Aughrim. Arthur Gerald Geoghegan. 6090-0,6174-5,6088-9
After aughrim. Emily Lawless. 6244-X
After awhile. Unknown. 6294-6
After Barabbas. Gus Pelletier. 6857-X
After battle. Duncan Campbell Scott. 6021-8,6051-X
After battle. Unknown. 6337-3
After battle, fr. The Bhagavad-gita. Unknown (Sanskrit) 6337-3

After being discharged. Howard Griffin. 6839-1
After Blenheim. Robert Southey. 6132-X,6133-8,6134-6,6107-9,6542-2,6188 ,6339-X,6501-5,6504-X,6733-6,6464-7
After blok. William Sydney Thayer. 7014-0
After bombardment. John Pudney. 6666-6
After Browning. Unknown. 6440-X
After business hours. Richard Hovey. 6753-0
After Chagall. Rene Wenger. 6966-5
After Christmas. Consuelo Valencia. 6337-3
After civilization. Edward Carpenter. 6252-0
"**After** clouds have passed and dropped..wetness". Your eyes. E.O. De Camp. 6906-1
After construing. Arthur Christopher Benson. 6473-6,6656-9
After Corunna. Charles Wolfe. 6322-5
After court martial. Francis Ledwidge. 6812-X
After dark vapors have oppressed our plains. John Keats. 6110-9,6371-3,6086-2
"**After** dark vapors have oppressed our plains" John Keats. 6828-6
"**After** dear old grandma died". Little Homer's slate. Eugene Field. 6834-0;6949-5
After death. Sir Edwin Arnold. 6424-8
After death. Louise Chandler Moulton. 7041-8
After death. Frances Isabel Parnell. 6090-0,6174-5,6244-X, 6656-9
After death. Christina Georgina Rossetti. 6600-3,6508-2, 6648-8,6655-0,6656-9
After death. Sara Teasdale. 6897-9
After death in Arabia. Sir Edwin Arnold. 6337-3,6730-1, 6102-8,6177-X,6656-9,6303
"**After** death nothing is, and nothing death". Seneca. 6544-9,6879-0
After depression came soul. Tommy Witaker. 7024-8
After dilettante concetti. Henry Duff Traill. 6089-7,6724-7,6092-7
"**After** dinner a few drinks then bed". There is of course a legend. Al Purdy. 6767-0
After disaster. Lizette Woodworth Reese. 6619-4
After discussion. Agnes Ryan. 6764-6
After drought. Alta Booth Dunn. 6662-3
After Frost. Unknown. 6675-5
After Grace. Unknown. 6688-7
After great pain a formal feeling comes. Emily Dickinson. 6491-4
"**After** great storms the calm returns." Sir Thomas Wyatt. 6584-8
After grey vigils. George Santayana. 6726-3
After grieving. Aline Kilmer. 6607-0
After harvest, fr. The year of the soul. Stefan George. 6643-7
After hearing a waltz by Bartok. Amy Lowell. 6959-2
After Horace. Alfred Dennis Godley. 6089-7
After Jutland. Katharine (Hinkson) Tynan. 7027-2
"**After** life's departing sigh". Second life. Johann Wolfgang von Goethe. 6948-7
"**After** long months abroad". American birds. Thomas Caldecot Chubb. 6761-1
"**After** long peace there comes...silver chatter". Now it is summer. Margaret Elizabeth Rhodes. 6761-1
"**After** long riot". Requiem for a courtesan. G.M. Hort. 6780-8
"**After** long searching through..thousand volume". Escape. Alfred Noyes. 6781-6
"**After** long storms and tempests sad assay". Sonnet 063 ("After long "), fr. Amoretti. Edmund Spenser. 6181-8
"**After** long years sweet feeling came to me". Yearning in early spring. Karel Cervinka. 6763-8
"**After** long, after vague leagues". Sonata and destruction. Pablo (Neftali Ricardo Reyes Basualto) Neruda. 6759-X
After looking into Carlyle's reminiscences. Algernon Charles Swinburne. 6657-7
After loos. Patrick MacGill. 6542-2
After love. Arthur Symons. 6301-2
After lovers. Roberta Holloway. 6808-1
After man's massacre. Carol Del Guidice. 6883-9
After many days. Robert Fuller Murray. 6269-5
After many years. Henry Clarence Kendall. 668-9,6591-0, 6592-9

AFTER

After Mardi Gras. Sister Mary Honora. 6388-8
After Mary Howitt. Charles Lutwidge ("Lewis Carroll") Dodgson. 6739-5
After midnight. Charles Vildrac. 7039-6
After my last song. Francis Ledwidge. 6812-X
"After nightfall" Sojin Takei. 6981-9
"After October, comes November". Samuel Hoffenstein. 6817-0
"After our Aesop's fable shown to-day". Epilogue to Albion and Albanius. John Dryden. 6970-3
After partridge shooting. Detlev von Liliencron. 6160-5
After poems (1913,1916,1911,1959). Anna Akhmatova. 6803-0
After rain. Archibald Lampman. 6115-X
After rain. Alfred Noyes. 6151-6
After rain. Adele Zimmerman. 6850-2
"After rain he ventures out". The photographer. Roger Pfingston. 6966-5
After reading a chapter by Henry James. Unknown. 6274-1
After reading a life of Mozart. William Goldberg. 6585-6
After reading Ajax. William Johnson Cory. 6483-3
After reading an anthology of fugitive verse. Henry Aylett Sampson. 6032-3
After reading Antony and Cleopatra. Robert Louis Stevenson. 6659-3
After reading Psalms XXXIX, XL, etc. Thomas Hardy. 6378-0
After reading Tamburlaine the great. Sir William Watson. 6483-3,6102-8
After reading the reviews of Finnegans Wake. Melville Cane. 6722-0
After reading Trollope's History of Florence. Eugene Field. 6949-5
After seeing a masque. William Shakespeare. 6935-5
After seeing Hampden as Cyrano. Ruth Esther Salley. 6847-2
After seeing the collection of pictures at Wilton House. Thomas Warton Jr. 6086-2
"After seventy-nine years in the same house". Departure. J. Charles Green. 6870-7
After six thousand years. Victor Hugo. 6665-8
"After snow, after snow". Resignation. Carl Ludwig Franke. 6952-5
After so long. Unknown. 6689-5
After so much loss. Laura Riding. 6354-3
After sorrow. Margaret E. Bruner. 6461-2
"After sorrow's night." Richard Watson Gilder. 6370-5
After St. Augustine. Mary Elizabeth Coleridge. 6337-3,6641-0
"After split skies and tardy thunder, rain". Rococo summer. Lawrence Perry Spingarn. 6979-7
"After strange stars, inscrutable, on high". Broken promise. Sarah Morgan Bryan Piatt. 7041-8
"After such years of dissension and strife". Epigram. Thomas Hood. 7025-6
After summer. Philip Bourke Marston. 6656-9
After sunset. William Allingham. 7015-9
After sunset. Hall Caine. 7015-9
After sunset. Grace Hazard Conkling. 6232-6,6102-8,6337-3, 6653-4,6253-9,6393 ,6374-8,6076-5,6636-5,6509-0,6656-2
AAter sunset. Algernon Charles Swinburne. 6198-2,6199-0
After sunset, sels. Algernon Charles Swinburne. 6123-0
After the accident. Francis Bret Harte. 6565-1
After the Annunciation. Eileen Duggan. 6282-2
After the apple-picking. Robert Frost. 6338-1,6300-4,6491-4,6723-9
After the ball. Samuel Minturn Peck. 6693-3
After the ball. Nora Perry. 6240-7,6385-3,6410-8,6600-3, 6735-2,6219 ,7041-8
After the ball. Unknown. 6826-X
After the battle. Mary E. Braddon. 6424-8
After the battle. Robert J. Burdette. 6588-0
After the battle. Victor Hugo. 6351-9
After the battle. Thomas Moore. 6090-0,6174-5,6086-2
After the battle. V. Stuart Mosby. 6744-1,6167-2,6922-3
After the battle. William Shakespeare. 6087-0
After the battle. Richard Chenevix Trench. 6656-9
After the battle. Unknown. 6408-6,6589-9,6167-2,6403-5, 6444-2
After the battle of Aughrim. Thomas Moore. 6090-0
After the battle of Bull Run. Unknown. 6008-4
"After the blast of lightning from the east". The end. Wilfred Owen. 6879-0
"After the brown bull passed from Cooley's fie". The death of Sualtem. Francis Ledwidge. 6812-X
After the burial. James Russell Lowell. 6600-3,6126-5,6076-5,6723-9,6102-8,6304 ,6076-5,6288-1
After the burial, sels. James Russell Lowell. 6102-8
"After the busy day has ended". In my hammock. Laura Vandivier. 6799-9
After the centennial. Christopher Pearse Cranch. 6946-0
After the chariot race, fr. The Iliad. Homer. 6435-3
After the circus. Raymond Holden. 6037-4
"After the cloud and the whirlwind". The dawn of peace. Alice Cary. 6969-X
After the club-dance, fr. At Casterbridge fair. Thomas Hardy. 6828-6
After the Comanches. Unknown. 6946-0
"After the coffee and the cognac...". Valmondois: from a suite for France. Clark Mills. 6761-1
After the cows. John Vance Cheney. 6632-1
After the curfew. Oliver Wendell Holmes. 6126-5,6288-1
After the engagement. Ella Wheeler Wilcox. 6863-4
"After the eyes that looked, the lips...spake". Gettysburg ode. Bayard Taylor. 6976-2
After the fair, fr. At Casterbridge fair. Thomas Hardy. 6828-6
After the fall. Edwin Muir. 6781-6
"After the final no there comes a yes". The well dressed man with a beard. Wallace Stevens. 6751-4
After the fire. Oliver Wendell Holmes. 6946-0
After the flood. Arthur Rimbaud. 6343-8
After the flood. Arthur Rimbaud. 6106-0
After the Fourth of July. M. Phelps Dawson. 6580-5,6820-0
After the funeral. Dylan Thomas. 6209-1
After the gale. Robert Bridges. 6315-2
After the German. George A. Baker. 6517-1
After the holidays. Eliazbeth Guion Hess. 6799-9
"After the honey drops of pearly showers". To his sister, Mrs. S.: the rose. William Hammond. 6933-9
"After the hurricane the rocky chasms churned". The skeleton on the shore. Starr Nelson. 6979-7
"After the Maytime and after the Junetime". Midsummer. Ella Wheeler Wilcox. 7041-8
After the martyrdom. Scharmel Iris. 6144-3,6337-3
After the opera. Ben Wood Davis. 6927-4
After the order of Melchisedec. Robert Norwood. 6337-3
"After the pangs of a desperate lover". Song ("After"). John Dryden. 6430-2
After the pioneers, fr. Texas. Henry Van Dyke. 6961-4
After the play. Burton Egbert Stevenson. 6116-8
After the pleasure party. Herman Melville. 6333-0
"After the poetry of outwaiting the line-up". Mexico City, 150 pesos to the dollar. Jim Mitsui. 6790-5
After the pow-wow, sel. Harold Littlebird. 7005-1
After the quarrel. Adam Lindsay Gordon. 6437-X
After the quarrel, fr. The road to Avernus. Adam Lindsay Gordon. 6951-7
After the rain. Thomas Bailey Aldrich. 6008-0, 6121-4
After the rain. Arthur A. Greve. 6857-X
After the rain. Jaroslav Vrchlicky. 6763-8
"After the rain stops". Summer morning after a rain. Kwang-sup Kim. 6775-1
After the ring. Unknown. 6661-5
After the sea-ship. Walt Whitman. 6258-X,6331-4,6547-3
"After the sharp salt kiss". On a violet leaf from Keats' grave. Marjorie L.C. Pickthall. 6796-4
After the skirmish. Sir Alfred Comyn Lyall. 6046-3
"After the song the love,and after..love..play". A banquet. Ernest Benshimol. 6762-X
After the storm. Louise Imogen Guiney. 7041-8
After the storm. William Makepeace Thackeray. 6519-8
After the strike. Joseph A. Siemer. 6149-4
"After the sun has turned him". Autumn. Hesiod. 6251-2
"After the sunset in the mountains". Flat waters of the west in Kansas. Carl Sandburg. 6778-6
"After the tanks and gun machines". Cavalry charge. Folger McKinsey. 7010-8
After the theatre. Unknown. 6414-0
After the tornado. Paul Hamilton Hayne. 7041-8
After the visit. Thomas Hardy. 6208-3,6246-6
After the waltz. Ben Wood Davis. 6928-2

After the war. Richard Le Gallienne. 6946-0,7027-2
After the wedding. William L. Keese. 6693-3
After the wedding. Unknown. 6691-7
"After the whipping, he crawled into bed". Portrait of a boy. Stephen Vincent Benet. 6861-8
"After the winter rain the linnets come again". May: lady of poppies. Eugene Dimon Preston. 6836-7
"After these weeks at sea, my native land". Durban revisited. Ralph Nixon Currey. 6788-3
"After they have tired." Stephen Spender. 6209-1
"After this feud of yours and mine". Making peace. Sarah Morgan Bryan Piatt. 7041-8
"After this flood" Ingeborg Bachmann. 6769-7
"After those reverend papers, whose soul is". Letter to Sir H. Wotton at his going ambassador..Venice. John Donne. 6933-9
"After three months treatment". The crazyman. Arthur Baysting. 7018-3
After three years. Arthur Shearly Cripps. 6625-9
After twenty years. Louis Aragon. 6068-4
After twenty years. Unknown. 6744-1
After two years. Richard Aldington. 6161-3,6513-9, 6393-4
After Watteau. Austin Dobson. 6875-8
After wings. Sarah Morgan Bryan Piatt. 6309-8
After winter. Carolyn Sherwin Bailey. 6466-3
The after woman. Francis Thompson. 6828-6
The after woman. Francis Thompson. 6282-2
After work. John Oxenham. 6337-3
"After your life of steadfast faith". Mother. M.E. Peteet. 6799-9
After, fr. In hospital. William Ernest Henley. 6250-4
After-days. Eric Chilman. 7031-0
The after-dinner smoke. Edgar A. Guest. 6862-6
The after-echo. Henry Van Dyke. 6983-5
The after-echo. Henry Van Dyke. 6961-4
After-glow. Mary Elizaᵃeth Mahnkey. 6662-3
After-song. Richard Watson Gilder. 6066-8,6309-8
After-thought [to Duddon sonnets]. William Wordsworth. 6208-3,6625-9,6110-9,6371-3,6250-4,6634-8,6086-2, 6122-2,6430-2,6199-0
An after-thought. Unknown. 6936-3
After-thoughts. Louis J. Magee. 7004-3
After-word. Josephine Preston Peabody. 6861-8
The after. Paul Fericano. 6901-0
Afterbirth (sculpture #4-bronze). Beryle Williams. 6966-5
Afterglow. Charles G. Blanden. 6274-1,6620-8
Afterglow. Amelia Josephine Burr. 7038-8
Afterglow. Amy Lowell. 6984-3
Afterglow. Dona Wayland. 6270-9
The afterglow. Marianne Clarke. 6799-9
The afterglow. Margaret Clyde Robertson. 6836-7
Aftermath. Louise Bryant. 6036-6
Aftermath. Henry Wadsworth Longfellow. 6333-0
Aftermath. Sara V. Prueser. 6906-1
Aftermath. Sydney King Russell. 6648-8
Aftermath. Siegfried Sassoon. 6850-2
Aftermath. Siegfried Sassoon. 6051-X,6332-2,6337-3,6490-6, 6506-6,6666 ,6250-4,6542-2,6102-8,6464-2
Aftermath. D. Howard Tripp. 6474-4
Aftermath. Raymond W. Walker. 6118-4
Aftermath. Lolly Williams. 6750-6
The Aftermath, fr. Iphigenia in Aulis. Euripides. 6665-8
The aftermath.. James Hendry. 6273-3
The aftermath. Samuel Waddington. 7015-9
"The afternnon/Flutters and dies". Nox mortis. Paul Bewsher. 7029-9
Afternoon. Fannie Stearns Davis. 6607-0,6476-0
Afternoon. Beatrice Goldsmith. 6640-2
Afternoon at a parsonage. Jean Ingelow. 6940-1
Afternoon at a parsonage, sels. Jean Ingelow. 6934-7
"The afternoon burns up from a gravel hotbed". The flea market. Patricia M. Johnson. 6857-X
Afternoon call. Donald Davidson. 6326-8
An afternoon call. Harriet Nutty. 6130-3
Afternoon class. Isabel Alden Kidder. 6764-6
Afternoon in a church. Raymond Kresensky. 6144-3,6335-7
"An afternoon like hunger/like solitude". Under the sun. Cecilia Bustamante. 7036-1
The afternoon nap. Charles Gamage Eastman. 6127-3
The afternoon of a faun. Stephane Mallarme. 6351-9

Afternoon off. Lucia M. Pitts. 6178-8
Afternoon on a hill. Edna St. Vincent Millay. 6300-4,6421-3,6653-4,6076-5,6581-3,6723 ,6102-8,6338-1,6374-8, 6476-0,6556-2
Afternoon tea. Abbie Farwell Brown. 6713-1
Afternoon tea. Robert Service. 6159-1
"The afternoon was one that might have merged". Wild swans. Robert P. Tristram Coffin. 7040-X
"Afterthought of summer's bloom!". A November daisy. Henry Van Dyke. 6961-4
An afterthought on apples. Helen Parry Eden. 6096-X
An afterthought. George A. Baker. 6187-7
An afterthought. Samuel Minturn Peck. 7041-8
Afterthoughts. Malcolm de Chazal. 6803-0
Afterthoughts. Edwin Arlington Robinson. 6184-2
Afterthoughts. Unknown (Greek) 6435-3
Afterthoughts of Donna Elvira. Carolyn Kizer. 6388-8
Afterward. Gerhard Fritsch. 6769-7
Afterward. P.J. (Polly) Holt. 6883-9
Afterward. Cyril Morton Horne. 6650-X
Afterward. Wilbur Dick Nesbit. 6303-9
Afterward. Charles Hanson Towne. 6846-4
Afterward. Elizabeth Stuart Phelps Ward. 7041-8
Afterwards. Peter Baker. 6475-2
Afterwards. Debbie Balsaitis. 6883-9
Afterwards. Violet Fane; Baroness Currie. 6656-9,6046-3
Afterwards. Mahlon Leonard Fisher. 6556-2
Afterwards. Edgar A. Guest. 6748-4
Afterwards. Thomas Hardy. 6655-0,6208-3,6541-4,6375-6,6125-7,6653-4,6723
Afterwards. Burton Egbert Stevenson. 6116-8
Afterwards. Mary Dixon Thayer. 6937-1
Afterwards. Mark Van Doren. 6984-3
Afterwhile. James Whitcomb Riley. 6260-1
Afton water. Robert Burns. 6152-4,6513-9,6560-0,6545-7, 6430-2,6543 ,6240-7,6289-X,6302-0,6385-3,6597-X,6737
Again. Unknown. 6600-3
"Again 'twas evening," fr. The minstrel girl. John Greenleaf Whittier. 6752-2
"Again - again she comes! methinks I hear". Hope. Thomas Kibble Hervey. 6980-0
"Again a February sun". February, 1897. Louis J. Magee. 7004-3
"Again Columbia's stripes, unfurl'd". Enterprise and Boxer. Unknown. 6946-0
"Again I see my bliss at hand". The lake. Matthew Arnold. 6947-9
"Again I see you, ah my queen". Juana. Alfred de Musset. 7039-6,6732-8
"Again I walk at twilight". In an old garden. Terry B. Dinkel. 6906-1
Again among the hills. Richard Hovey. 6374-8
Again and again. Doris Muhringer. 6769-7
"Again I saw another angel". Margaret L. Woods. 6648-8
Again I sing my songs. Morris Rosenfeld. 7011-6
'Again rejoicing nature sees'. Robert Burns. 6597-X
"Again that lovely lamp from half its orb". The fire-flies. Sir Humphry Davy. 6980-0
"Again the harvests of white and gold". September. Benjamin Franklin Taylor. 6815-4
Again the late last night. Karel van Woestijne. 6068-4
"Again the royal streamers play!". Ode on the Duke of York's second departure from England. William Falconer. 6971-1
Again the story is told. Ada Jackson. 6337-3
"Again the veld revives". Namaqualand after rain. William Plomer. 6788-3
"Again there rises from memory the beat". Where there used to be badlands. Circe Maia. 7036-1
"Again there's a golden haze". Fort Tryon. Arthur Guiterman. 6773-5
"Again thou reignest in thy golden hall". To the harvest moon. William Stanley Roscoe. 7015-9
Again to thy dear name. John Ellerton. 6304-7
"Again will I buid thee". The dancer. Jeremiah. 6959-2
"Again! oH! send that anthem-peal again". The music of St. Patrick's. Felicia Dorothea Hemans. 6973-8
Again, Sappho. Mary Brent Whiteside. 6326-8
"Again, in darkness". Sheepherder's wind. Wilson O. Clough. 6761-1

AGAIN,

"Again, in the Book of Books, to-day". Prodigals. Phoebe Cary. 6969-X
"Again, the ruddy mud crusts my shoe". Clay. Paul Gianoli. 6860-X
"Again," fr. Morpheus. Hilda ("H.D.") Doolittle. 6012-9
Against a romantic interpretation. John Chamberlain. 6761-1
"Against an elm a sheep was ty'd". The wild boar and the ram. John Gay. 6972-X
Against dress, to a lady. Thomas Warton (the Elder) 6962-2
Against fruition. Sir John Suckling. 6378-0
Against hope. Abraham Cowley. 6315-2,6341-1
Against idleness and mischief. Isaac Watts. 6152-4
"Against infection and the hand of war" William Shakespeare. 7020-5
Against interested life. William Cowper. 6814-6
Against irresolution. Richard Crashaw. 6931-2
Against marriage. William Walsh. 6092-7
"Against my love shall be, as I am now". Sonnet 063 ("Against my love"). William Shakespeare. 6436-1, 6560-0
"Against my second coming..." Willard Wattles. 6032-3
Against platonick love. Unknown. 6933-9
Against publishing satires. Colin Ellis. 6339-X
Against quarelling and fighting. Isaac Watts. 6932-0
Against sloth, fr. The bible, Proverbs 6:6-11. Unknown. 6496-5
"Against that time (if ever that time come).". Sonnet 049 ("Against that time"). William Shakespeare. 6447-7
Against the barons' enemies. Unknown. 6881-2
"Against the dim hot summer blue". Wild-roses. William ("Fiona Macleod") Sharp. 6793-X
Against the fear of death. John Dryden. 6472-8
Against the fear of death. Lucretius. 7039-6
"Against the horizon I have seen their heads". Range cattle. Glenn Ward Dresbach. 6761-1
"Against the huge black door of the night". The guest. Jorge Carrera Andrade. 6759-X
Against the native hour lets down the locks. Allen Tate. 6527-9
"Against the planks of the cabin side". Sea song. Laurence (Adele Florence Nicolson) Hope. 6019-6,6102-8,6856-1
"Against the rails he leant/To take a last...". The policeman's tear. Shirley Brooks. 6760-3
"Against the shabby house I pass each day". To happier days. Mabel McElliott. 6846-4
"Against the shadowed pane". A tree in winter. Julia Ross Alden. 6906-1
"Against the sky a sea bird's breast of cloud". The mind has studied flight. Raymond Holden. 6979-7
"Against the sun there sets a moon". Take away the darkness. Witter Bynner. 6761-1
"Against the sunset's glowing wall". The wife of Manoah to her husband. John Greenleaf Whittier. 6848-0
Against the wall. Aline Kilmer. 6393-4
"Against the wall of this sky". Elegy on an empty skyscraper. John Gould Fletcher. 6782-4
Against them who lay unchastity to the sex of woman. William Habington. 6562-7
Against weeping. Henry King. 6935-5
Against women. Unknown. 6881-2
Against women either good or bad. Thomas Norton. 6182-6
Against women's fashions. John Lydgate. 6022-6
Against writers that carp at other men's books. Sir John Harrington. 6092-7
Agamede's song. Arthur Upson. 6310-1,6300-4
Agamemnon's children, fr. Iphigenia in Tauris. Euripides. 6435-3
Agamemnon, sels. Aeschylus. 6435-3
Aganis the thievis of Liddisdale. Sir Richard Maitland. 6180-X
Agassiz. James Russell Lowell. 6126-5
Agatha. Alfred Austin. 6656-9
Agatha. Will Hubbard Kernan. 6670-4
Agatha's song. Harriet Prescott Spofford. 7041-8
Agathias
    Not such your burden. William M. Hardinge (tr.). 7039-6
    Plutarch. John Dryden (tr.). 7039-6
Agathias Scholasticus
    The best memorial. George Allen (tr.). 6435-3
    Dicing. Sir William Marris (tr.). 6435-3
    The girls' lot. Sir William Marris (tr.). 6435-3
    Leave a kiss within the cup. J.M. Edmonds (tr.). 6435-3
    Rest in death. W. Shepherd (tr.). 6879-0
    The swallows ("Night long I sigh, and soon..."). Sir William Marris (tr.). 6435-3
Age. Anacreon (atr) 7039-6
Age. Berton Braley. 6853-7
Age. Jean Follain. 6803-0
Age. Richard Garnett. 7015-9
Age. Richard Garnett. 6656-9
Age. Richard Garnett. 7015-9
Age. Arthur Seymour John Tessimond. 6893-6
Age. Edward Tuck. 6465-5
Age and song. Algernon Charles Swinburne. 6219-9
Age and youth. Kathryn Cross. 6799-9
Age and youth. Letitia Elizabeth ("L.E.L.") Landon. 6980-0
"Age cannot reach me where the veils of God...". Immortality. Susan L. Mitchell. 6930-4
"Age cannot wither her...", fr. Antony and Cleopatra. William Shakespeare. 6339-X
"The age demanded an image", fr. Hugh Selwyn Mauberley. Ezra Pound. 6399-3
"Age forty, Rosetta shudders as she gives...". Paolo Dipietro. Joseph Maviglia. 6767-0
"An age in her embraces past". The mistress. A song. John Wilmot, 2d Earl of Rochester. 6933-9
Age in prospect. Robinson Jeffers. 6012-9
Age in youth. Trumbull Stickney. 6380-2
Age intercedes for youth. Rachel Annand Taylor. 6180-X
Age invading. Aline Kilmer. 6031-5
The age is great and strong. Victor Hugo. 6730-1
"Age is oppurtunity". Henry Wadsworth Longfellow. 6109-5
Age not to be rejected. Unknown. 6933-9
The age of a dream. Lionel Johnson. 6507-4
The age of bronze. George Gordon, 6th Baron Byron. 6945-2
The age of children happiest. Henry Howard, Earl of Surrey. 6133-8
The age of Herbert and Vaughan. Edmund Blunden. 6483-3
The age of ink. Edgar A. Guest. 7033-7
The age of Queen Anne. Alexander Pope. 6188-5
The age of wisdom. William Makepeace Thackeray. 6656-9, 6652-6,6737-9,6219-9,6102-8,6026-9,6092-7,6732-8, 6722-0,6271-7,6302-0,6385-3,6301
"Age shall no' daunt me, nor sorrow for youth". The strange spirit. Walter De La Mare. 6985-1
"Age sits gracefully upon old canvasses". Muesum. John Ciardi. 6761-1
"Age takes in pitiless hands". '...All gone...' Walter De La Mare. 6905-7
Age talks to youth. Edgar A. Guest. 6748-4
"Age upon age your solitary height". Stone mountain. Jessie Young Norton. 6841-3
Age, fr. Two moods from the hill. Ernest Benshimol. 6762-X
"Age, with stealing steps...," fr. Tales of the hall. George Crabbe. 6301-2,6659-3
The age-long war, fr. Towards democracy. Edward Carpenter. 7009-4
The age. Herbert Edwin Clarke. 6656-9
The aged aged man. Charles Lutwidge ("Lewis Carroll") Dodgson. 6150-8
The aged bard's wish. Unknown. 6873-1
The aged Carle. Sir Walter Scott. 6430-2
The aged Christ. Gertrude Huntington McGiffert. 6838-3
The aged Indian. Felicia Dorothea Hemans. 6973-8
The aged Indian. Unknown. 6003-X
The aged louer renounceth loue. Henry Howard, Earl of Surrey. 6586-4
The aged lover renounceth love. Unknown. 6066-8
The aged lover renounceth love. Sir Thomas Wyatt. 6543-0
An aged man who loved to doze away. Walter Savage Landor. 6110-9,6086-2
"The aged man, when he beheld winter coming...". The acacia leaves. Allen Upward. 6897-9
The aged man-at-arms. George Peele. 6219-9
"The aged man/Had placed his trust...". Picture of a beggar. William Wordsworth. 6980-0
Aged ninety years. Wilbert Snow. 6039-0,6071-4
The aged oak at Oakley. Henry Alford. 6219-9
The aged prisoner. Unknown. 6411-6,6744-1,6167-2

The **aged** stranger. Francis Bret Harte. 6889-8
The **aged** stranger. Francis Bret Harte. 6732-8,6307-1,6572-4
Agee, James
    Millions are learning how. 6375-6
    Permit me voyage. 6641-0
    Rapid transit. 6375-6
The **ageless** Christ. B.L. Byer. 6065-X
"**Ages** elapsed ere Homer's lamp appeared". Milton, fr. Table talk. William Cowper. 6934-7
"**Ages** of earth are in me. I am made". Strange splendour. Ernest Hartsock. 6780-8
The **ages** of man. Hesiod. 6435-3
The **ages.** John Sterling. 6980-0
Aghadoe. John Todhunter. 6244-X,6437-X
Agincourt. Michael Drayton. 6659-3,6371-3,6419-1,6332-2, 6179-6,6182-6,6186-9,6228-8,6323-3,6726-3,6733-6, 6473-6,6301-2,6660-7
Agincourt. William Shakespeare. 6935-5
Agincourt ("O that we now had here"). William Shakespeare. 6087-0
Agincourt, fr. Henry V ("Now all the youth..."). William Shakespeare. 6473-6
Agincourt, sels. Michael Drayton. 6339-X,6322-5
Aging poet, fr. Poetical sketches. Robert Hillyer. 6761-1
Aging poetess, fr. Poetical sketches. Robert Hillyer. 6761-1
Aglaia. Nicholas Breton. 6436-1
Agnes. Mah-do-ge Tohee. 7005-1
Agnes and the hill-man. William Morris. 6110-9
Agnes the martyr. Ellen Murray. 6416-7
Agnes, I love thee! Unknown. 6277-6,6155-9
Agnew, Georgette
    Auto-suggestion. 6804-9
Agnostic. Helen G. Ladd. 6764-6
The **agnostic's** prayer. Demps Alexander Oden. 6799-9
Agolanti and his lady, fr. The legend of Florence. Leigh Hunt. 6980-0
The **agonie.** George Herbert. 6378-0
Agony bells. Allie Wellington. 6406-X
The **agony** of God. Georgia Harkness. 6337-3
Agosin, Marjorie (tr.)
    The blue bottles. Delia Dominguez, 7036-1
    I read fortunes in dreams. Delia Dominguez, 7036-1
    The sun looks back. Delia Dominguez. 7036-1
The **agricultural** Irish girl. Unknown. 6930-4
Agrikler [pseud].
    Proverbeel feelossify. 6913-4
Agro-dolce. James Russell Lowell. 6429-9,6321-7,6226-1
Aguila, Pancho
    Birthing: 2000 6870-7
    E.P.A. 6870-7
    Folsom, August 11th: a question of races. 6792-1, 6998-3
    Nuclear racial lockdowns. 6870-7
    A prison bi-centennial address. 6792-1
    St. Valentine. 6870-7
    The turnaround for higherground. 6870-7
    Woman guard. 6870-7
Aguinaldo. Bertrand Shadwell. 6946-0
"**Ah** bonnie darling, lift your dark eyes...". An old tale of three. Una Uraqhart. 6873-1
"**Ah** brother poet! send me of your shade". William Cowper. 6814-2
"**Ah** Cloris! that I now...", fr. The mulberry garden. Sir Charles Sedley. 6544-9,6430-2
"**Ah** Cupid, I mistook thee". Francis Davison. 6187-7
"**Ah** cease thy tears and sobs, my little life". To an infant. Samuel Taylor Coleridge. 6967-3
"**Ah** changed and cold, how changed and very...". Dead before death. Christina Georgina Rossetti. 6828-6
"**Ah** fading joy". Song ("Ah fading joy"). John Dryden. 6187-3,6430-2
Ah fading joy. John Dryden. 6315-2,6125-7
Ah Gabriel. Winifred Welles. 6036-6
"**Ah** hate to see de evenin' sun go down." Unknown. 6375-6
"**Ah** lady, lady, leave the creeping mist". In Tintagel. Andrew Lang. 6987-8
"**Ah** little mill, you're rumbling still". An Oxford idyll. Thomas Edward Brown. 6809-X

"**Ah** lonely isles, fragments...". Antipater of Thessalonica. 6251-2
"**Ah** loue! where is thy Abydinge?" Unknown. 6563-5
Ah love! could you and I with him conspire,fr. Rubaiyat. Omar Khayyam. 7039-6
"**Ah** me! for aught that ever I could read". William Shakespeare. 6238-5
"**Ah** me! fully sorely is my heart forlorn". The schoolmistress, sels. William Shenstone. 6831-6
"**Ah** me! How slow the sad years pass". Song ("Ah me!"). Beatrice Rosenthal. 6274-1
"**Ah** me! the mighty love that I have borne." George Frederick Cameron. 6433-7,6115-X
"**Ah** me! those joyous days are gone!". My boyhood. John Godfrey Saxe. 6772-7
"**Ah** me! those old familiar bounds!". Ode on a distant prospect of Clapham academy. Thomas Hood. 6874-X
"**Ah** me! what causes such complaining breath". Elegy on David Laing, Esq. Thomas Hood. 6974-6
"**Ah** me! with what a witching grace". Triolets of tennis. Marion M. Miller. 6983-5
"**Ah** me!/Am I the swaine". George Wither. 6933-9
"**Ah** me!/It was God's choice ere mine...". All Saints' Day. Arthur Shearly Cripps. 6800-6
"**Ah** me, ah me, how neigborly the..Junes become". Two birds of June. Benjamin Franklin Taylor. 6815-4
"**Ah** me, but it might have been!". On a nankin plate. Austin Dobson. 6875-8
"'**Ah** me, but it might have been!'". On a nankin plate. Austin Dobson. 6770-0
"**Ah** me, do you remember still". An Italian garden. Agnes Mary F. ("Madame Duclaux") Robinson. 6872-3
Ah me, do you remember still. Agnes Mary F. ("Madame Duclaux") Robinson. 6726-3
"**Ah** me, my friend! it will not, will not last!". Elegy. He complains how soon...life is over. William Shenstone. 6932-0
"**Ah** me, once Archeades pressed...". Asclepiades. 6251-2
"**Ah** moon, how slender sliced tonite". Introspection. Ruth D. McGinnis. 6750-6
"**Ah** Nellie, you were always fair, and you were". An ode to Nellie. Edgar A. Guest. 6862-6
"**Ah** my dere, ah my dere Son". Unknown. 6106-0
"**Ah** my heart, ah, what aileth thee?" Sir Thomas Wyatt. 6584-8
"**Ah** no. To distant climes, a dreary scene" Oliver Goldsmith. 6935-5
"**Ah** robin." Sir Thomas Wyatt. 6584-8
"**Ah** stay! ah turn!". Song ("Ah stay!"). William Congreve. 6315-2
"**Ah** stern cold man". A woman and her dead husband. David Herbert Lawrence. 6897-9
Ah sunflower [weary of time]. William Blake. 6660-7,6179-6, 6536-8,6086-2,6250-4,4430-2,6301 ,6187-7,6246-6,6604-6,6615-1,6378-0,6154-7
"**Ah** take those lips away; no more". Deadly kisses. Pierre de Ronsard. 6771-9
"**Ah** thou! that, undeceived and unregretting". Jacques Tahareau, 1530. Andrew Lang. 6771-9
"**Ah** voices sweet as honey, ah maiden songs divine". Alcman. 6251-2
"**Ah** what is love? It is a pretty thing". Happy as a shepherd. Robert Greene. 6793-X
"**Ah** wherefore with infection should he live". Sonnet 067 ("Ah wherefore with infection"). William Shakespeare. 6560-0
"**Ah** with what heart of wonder...". Oppian. 6251-2
"**Ah** yes, I see the sunshine play". Waiting. Alice Cary. 6865-0;6969-X
"**Ah!** 'barefoot boy!' you have led me back". 'The barefoot boy'. Phoebe Cary. 6969-X
"**Ah!** bah! Sir Coo, is that thy way". Cibber's ironical lines on himself. Colley Cibber. 6867-7
"**Ah!** cease - those fruitless tears restrain". Pietro Metastasio. 6973-8
"**Ah!** cease this kind of persuasive strain". Ode to a friend. William Mason. 6831-6
"**Ah!** cease this kind persuasive strain". Ode to a friend. William Mason. 6932-0
"**Ah!** Chloris, 'tis true to disarm...". Song ("Ah!

AH!

Chloris"). Charles Sackville; 6th Earl of Dorset. 6544-9
"Ah! could my Agnes rove these favorite shades". To Agnes. Felicia Dorothea Hemans. 6973-8
"Ah! Country guy, the hour is nigh". Song ("Ah! Country guy"). Sir Walter Scott. 6830-8
"Ah! County guy, the hour is nigh". County guy, fr. Quentin Durward. Sir Walter Scott. 6828-6
"Ah! do not drive off grief, but place your...". To one in grief. Walter Savage Landor. 6874-X
"Ah! gentle, fleeting, wavering sprite". Adrian's address to his soul when dying. George Gordon, 6th Baron Byron. 6945-2
"Ah! give me, Lord, the single eye". Augustus Montague Toplady. 6931-2
"Ah! gone so soon? So early from us fled". The dead mariner. Charles W. Denison. 6755-7
"Ah! happy life it was to live!...". Robert Louis Stevenson. John E. Barrett. 6840-5
"Ah! how compassion comes, like spring". Ballad: the spring rain. Raymond Ellsworth Larsson. 6783-2
"Ah! I remember well (and how can I". Reminiscence. Samuel Daniel. 6935-5
"Ah! if our souls but poise and swing". Ever true. Unknown. 6889-8
"Ah! Love was never yet without". Romaic love song. Unknown. 6945-2
"Ah! languid hand, safe in some scented glove". Sarah Morgan Bryan Piatt. 6238-5
"Ah! lovely faded plant, the blight I mourn". To a dying exotic. Felicia Dorothea Hemans. 6973-8
"Ah! Marianson, my beauteous dame". Marianson. Unknown (French Canadian). 6795-6
Ah! me. Unknown. 6273-3
"Ah! no, not these!". Parentage. Alice Meynell. 6955-X
"Ah! now farewell thou sweet and gentle maid". Sonnet ""Ah! now farewell"). Felicia Dorothea Hemans. 6973-8
"Ah! on Thanksgiving Day...". The pumpkin. John Greenleaf Whittier. 6889-8
"Ah! poor Psyche". Psyche. Victor Rydberg. 6045-5
"Ah! que de joie, la flute et la musette...". Ballades. Paul Fort. 6801-4
"Ah! reign, wherever man is found". The triumph of heavenly love desired. Madame De la Mothe Guion. 6814-6
"Ah! that half bashful and half eager face!". Bird-nesting. Charles Tennyson Turner. 6980-0,6943-6
"Ah! the end of it all". The end of it all. Frank Putnam. 6889-8
"Ah! the moment flew fast". The haven, fr. A tiny trip. Joseph Ashby Sterry. 6770-0
"Ah! the tang o' the snell hill-air". Ski-song of the Braemar postman. Unknown. 7035-3
"Ah! the world has many a Horner". Jack Horner [for grown people]. Unknown. 6909-6
"Ah! then and there was hurrying to and fro". The call to battle. Felicia Dorothea Hemans. 6973-8
"Ah! they were strong, those men of". The cabala. Clifford Harrison. 6848-0
"Ah! this is life". Interpretations. Ralph Duffield Small. 6983-5
"Ah! trouble and trouble and sorrow!". Countryman's song. John Galsworthy. 6888-X
"Ah! urged too late, from beauty's bondage...". To Amanda (Ah! urged"). James Thomson. 6816-2
"Ah! were she pitiful as she is fair". Robert Greene. 6181-8,6187-7
"Ah! what a weary race my feet have run". Sonnet to the river Lodon. Thomas Warton Jr.. 6932-0
"Ah! what is life! a dream within a dream". Life. Edward Moxon. 6980-0
"Ah! what is love! It is a pretty thing". Happy as a shepherd. Robert Greene. 6874-X
"Ah! what is love? It is a pretty thing". Robert Greene. 6181-8,6187-7,6302-0,6385-3,6122-2
Ah! What woes are mine. Edmond O'Ryan. 6930-4
"Ah! what time will thou come?...". The dawning. Henry Vaughan. 6931-2
"Ah! what will become of the lily". Providence. Phoebe Cary. 6865-0;6969-X
"Ah! What woes are mine to bear". Ah! What woes are mine. Edmond O'Ryan. 6930-4
"Ah! when will all be ended? If the dead". William Morris. 6238-5
"Ah! wherefore do I haunt the shadowy tomb". By the sea. Roden Noel. 7015-9
"Ah! wherefore should my weeping maid suppress". On her endeavouring to conceal her grief at parting. William Cowper. 6814-6
"Ah! whither doost thou now thou greater muse". Canto 007, fr. Two Cantos of Mvtabilitie. Edmund Spenser. 6586-4
"Ah! who can say-however fair his view". Henry Kirke White. 6407-8
"Ah! why did thy rude hand molest". The petition of the red-breast. Felicia Dorothea Hemans. 6973-8
"Ah! why does love distract my thoughts". Toru Minamoto (Kawara No Sadaijin) 6852-9
"Ah! with what freedom could I once...pray'd". The sigh. Nathaniel Wanely. 6931-2
"Ah! with what freedome could I once...pray'd". The sigh. Nathaniel Wanley. 6933-9
"Ah! wonderful moon!". Little poem. Narihira. 6879-0
Ah! yet consider it again. Arthur Hugh Clough. 6110-9,6655-0,6656-9,6491-4
Ah! Yet consider it again! Arthur Hugh Clough. 6828-6
"Ah's easin' up mah sandals, Lawd". Marse Jesus - will it be long? Alida Dickerman Hodges. 6764-6
"Ah, ah ye falce fatall tale I read." Unknown. 6563-5
"Ah, are you digging on my grave?" Thomas Hardy. 6506-6, 6527-9
Ah, be not false. Richard Watson Gilder. 6735-2
"Ah, beyond contempt and all blame". The leafy dead. Humbert Wolfe. 6780-8
Ah, bring it not. Dollie Radford. 6656-9
"Ah, cease to plead with that sweet...voice". The widow to her son's betrothed. Caroline Elizabeth Sarah Sheridan Norton. 6980-0
"Ah, Circe, Circe! in the wood we cried". Circe's island revisited. Andrew Lang. 6771-9
"Ah, could I my poet only draw". My poet. Alice Cary. 6865-0;6969-X
"Ah, dear papa, did you but know". Jane Taylor. 6105-2
"Ah, dismal, grey-cowled April, that with...". April. James Abraham Martling. 6952-5
"Ah, drimin dubh dilis, ah pride of the flow". Drimin dubh. Unknown (Irish). 6858-8
"Ah, Eros does not always smite". Eros does not always smite. Michael (Katherine Bradley & Edith Cooper) Field. 6872-3
"Ah, Faustus/Now hast thou but one bare hour..". Faustus' dying soliloquy, fr. Faustus. Christopher Marlowe. 6934-7
"Ah, God! but we were nigh undone". General James B. Steedman at Chickamauga. Benjamin Franklin Taylor. 6815-4
"Ah, God, for a man with a heart, head, hand". Prayer ("Ah, God"). Alfred Lord Tennyson. 6337-3
Ah, friend let us be true. Matthew Arnold. 6084-6
"Ah, had I ever thought the world would care". Francesco Petrarch. 6325-X
"Ah, happiness". A song of happiness. Ernest Rhys. 6897-9
"Ah, happy-hearted bird". My lady sleeps. Robert Burns Wilson. 7041-8
Ah, he who forgets. Jos. Vacl. Sladek. 6763-8
"Ah, heart, this is our summer passing--this". Sonnet. Lillah A. Ashley. 6799-9
"Ah, heedless girl! why thus disclose". To a vain lady. George Gordon, 6th Baron Byron. 6945-2
"Ah, help me! but her face and brow". Her face and brow. James Whitcomb Riley. 6992-4
"Ah, here it is! I'm famous now". First appearance in type. Oliver Wendell Holmes. 6910-X
"Ah, hoop of gold that binds the maid". The gemless ring. Herbert Trench. 6877-4
"Ah, how she is lovely, my Louisiana!". Louisiana. K. O. Hass. 6818-9
Ah, how sweet! John Dryden. 6302-0,6385-3,6219-9,6301-2
Ah, I have striven, I have striven. Mary Elizabeth

Coleridge. 6186-9
"Ah, Juliet, if the measure...", fr Romeo and Juliet. William Shakespeare. 6392-6
"Ah, how the eye on the picture stops". My picture. Alice Cary. 6969-X
"Ah, how the human mind wearies her self". Nature unimpaired by time. John Milton. 6814-6
"Ah, I remember well (and how can I).". Hymen's triumph, sels. Samuel Daniel. 6827-8
"Ah, I see you at your window". I must write. Hattie Horner Louthan. 6836-7
"Ah, if what energy I have". Uncircumventible. Walter De La Mare. 6905-3
"Ah, it's home, dearie, home, that my heart...". The little house. Grace Noll Crowell. 7038-8
Ah, lassie fair! S.G. Tenney. 6116-8
"Ah, Leipsydrion, thou hast betrayed...". Unknown. 6435-3
"Ah, look/How sucking their last sweetness...". The divers. Peter Quennell. 6985-1
Ah, love! let us be true. Matthew Arnold. 6066-8
Ah, love, but a day. Robert Browning. 6320-9,6199-0,
"Ah, lovely weed, and yet it seems a shame". Lines to a milkweed. Galdys Higbee Polinske. 6799-9
"Ah, Mamon, say, why is it we". Rondeau. Ernest Dowson. 6875-8
Ah, make the most of what we yet may spend, fr.Rubaiyat. Omar Khayyam. 7039-6
"Ah, me mither ment me auld breeks". Unknown. 6059-5
"Ah, me! when shall I marry me?". Song ("Ah, me!"). Oliver Goldsmith. 6244-1
Ah, mighty boisterous blown breath..siren song for me. Roden Noel. 6997-5
"Ah, misty Gereneia, ill cra·g, thou shouldst...". Simonides. 6251-2
"Ah, my beloved, fill the cup that clears, fr. Rubaiyat. Omar Khayyam. 7039-6
"Ah, my brave Vitellius!". To one who eats larks. William Kean Seymour. 6884-7
"Ah, my dear angry Lord". Bitter-sweet. George Herbert. 6931-2
"Ah, my heart, the storm and sadness!". Liebesweh. Dora Wilcox. 6784-0
Ah, my sweet sweeting. Unknown. 6317-9,6328-4
"Ah, never in all my life". Alone. John Hall Wheelock. 6897-9
"Ah, none can know how soon..world forgets, fr. Hannibal. John Nichol. 6819-7
Ah, now the summer. Helen Morrow. 6761-1
Ah, Ronin! Sir Thomas Wyatt. 6328-4
"Ah, our passed life we know". The seeds we sow. Edward R. Huxley. 6885-5
"Ah, Postumus, my postumus, the years are...". Lugubrious villanelle of platitudes. Louis Untermeyer. 6875-8
"Ah, seek me, life". Seek me, life. Ralph Douberly. 6841-3
"Ah, she was not an angel to adore". Safe. Alice Cary. 6865-0;6969-X
Ah, stay! ah, turn!, fr. The fair penitent. William Congreve. 6328-4
"Ah, sweet Kitty Neil! rise up from your wheel". An Irish melody. Denis Aloysius McCarthy. 6805-7
"Ah, sweet Kitty Neil, rise up from that wheel". Kitty Neil. John Francis Waller. 6858-8
"Ah, sweet Tipperary in the springtime...". Tipperary in the spring. Denis Aloysius McCarthy. 6887-1
Ah, sweet content. Barnabe Barnes. 6194-X
"Ah, sweet Content! where is thy mild abode?" Barnabe Barnes. 6181-8,6186-6,6189-3
Ah, sweet is Tipperary. Denis Aloysius McCarthy. 6096-X, 6162-1,6266-0,6583-X,6476-0
"Ah, sweet Kitty Neil." Denis Florence MacCarthy. 6302-0;6385-3
"Ah, tell me not that memory". Despondency. Letitia Elizabeth ("L.E.L.") Landon. 6980-0
"Ah, the dull round, the littleness of things!". The teacher. Helen Gray Cone. 6847-2
"Ah, the poor shepherd's mournful fate". The despairing lover. William Hamilton. 6874-X
"Ah, there are mighty things under the sun". God is love. Alice Cary. 6969-X
"Ah, there be souls none unerstand". Joaquin Miller. 6238-5

"Ah, to be by Mooni now!". Mooni. Henry Clarence Kendall. 6784-0,6437-X
Ah, we are neither heaven nor earth. John Masefield. 6199-0
"Ah, we are neither heaven nor hell, but men". Sonnet ("Ah, we are neither"). John Masefield. 6879-0
"Ah, well-a-day! The grandames say". The Puritan maiden's May-day. Margaret Junkin Preston. 6965-7
"Ah, what a change! Thou, who didst emptily...". Robert Bridges. 6487-6
Ah, what avails the sceptered race. Walter Savage Landor. 6604-6,6196-6,6660-7,6187-7,6328-4
"Ah, what is life?-what is joy?-but Aphrodite...". Mimnermus. 6251-2
"Ah, what is love? it is a pretty thing". Love in Arcady. Robert Greene. 6830-8
"Ah, what is this you draw ashore". But still intrepid Icarus. Louise Crenshaw Ray. 7014-0
"Ah, what time wilt thou come? When shall". The second advent. Henry Vaughan. 6935-5
"Ah, when shall all men's good." Alfred Lord Tennyson. 6225-3
"Ah, when the gentle breath of spring comes...". Life. Henry Denison. 7030-2
"Ah, wherefore sing? The soft, sweet air...". June. Isabel Beulah Schein. 6847-2
"Ah, who are these on whom the vital bloom". Children of toil, fr. 'Who follow the flag' Henry Van Dyke. 6954-1
"Ah, who will tell me, in these leaden days". Spring in the north. Henry Van Dyke. 6961-4
"Ah, why may I not speak? Thou speak'st to me". To my guitar. Adelma H. Burd. 6847-2
"Ah, wife, sweet wife, what name". Hippolytus, sels. Euripides. 6879-0
Ah, with the grape my fading life provided,fr. Rubaiyat. Omar Khayyam. 7039-6
"Aha! A guest!/within my master's house, a...". Morgiana dances. William Rose Benet. 6959-2
"Aha! a traitor in the camp". To a usurper. Eugene Field. 6834-0;6949-5
Ahab Mohammed. James Matthews Legare. 6459-0
Ahab the builder. John Elliott Bowman. 6848-0
Ahern, Maureen (tr.)
    Empty house. Rosario Castellanos, 7036-1
    Home economics. Rosario Castellanos, 7036-1
    Malinche. Rosario Castellanos, 7036-1
    Silence near an ancient stone. Rosario Castellanos, 7036-1
The Ahkond of swat. Edward Lear. 6089-7,6026-9
The Ahkoond of swat. George Thomas Lanigan. 6021-8,6089-7, 6732-8,6505-8
"Ahoy there dada! and how are you". Villanelle to my dad. Ethel Greenfield. 6850-2
Ahrend, Evelyn
    Icarus. 6850-2
Aichinger, Ilse
    Belonging. Milne Holton and Herbert Kuhner (tr.). 6769-7
    Edge of the mountain. Milne Holton and Herbert Kuhner (tr.). 6769-7
    Late. Milne Holton and Herbert Kuhner (tr.). 6769-7
    Thought out. Milne Holton and Herbert Kuhner (tr.). 6769-7
Aide, Hamilton
    The Danube river. 6656-9
    The forsaken. 6656-9
    In the evening. 6226-1
    Lost and found. 6304-7,6370-5,6744-1,6569-4,6911-8
    Love, the pilgrim. 6658-5
    Oh, let me dream. 6658-5
    Remember or forget. 6737-9
    Story of George Lee. 6167-2
    When we are parted. 6656-9
Aignish on the Machair. Agnes Mure Mackenzie. 6873-1
Aiken Drum. Unknown. 6179-6
Aiken, Conrad
    And in the hanging gardens. 6011-0,6649-6
    Annihilation. 6012-9

AIKEN

The argument. 6012-9
Asphalt. 6034-X
At a concert of music. 6012-9
Atlantis. 6984-3
The bright moon. 6253-9
Chance meetings. 6076-5,6102-8
Changing mind. 6012-9
Concert pitch. 6007-2
Dancing Adairs. 6897-9
The day ended, fr. The pilgrimage of Festus. 6984-3
Dead Cleopatra. 6897-9
Discordants. 6513-9
Evening song of Senlin. 6628-3
Evensong. 6030-7,6513-9
Exile. 6778-6
Fade, then-die, depart, and come no more. 6779-4
Five sonnets. 6783-2
The four appearances. 6389-6
God's acre. 6011-0
The going forth. 6761-1
The house. 6069-2
Meeting. 6012-9
Miracles. 6030-7
Morning song of Senlin. 6153-2,6808-1,6393-4
Music I heard. 6250-4,6300-4
Nuit blanche: north end. 6391-8
An old man sees himself. 6393-4
The pilgrimage of Festus, sels. 6345-4
The pomecitron tree. 6012-9
Portrait of one dead. 6033-1
Poverty grass. 6011-0
Prelude. 6781-6
Prelude 029 ("What shall"). 6209-1
Prelude 056 ("Rimbaud"). 6375-6,6209-1,6375-6
Priaps and the pool. 6010-X
Priapus and the pool, sels. 6649-6
Psychomachia. 6011-0
The road. 6011-0
The room. 6011-0
Sea holly. 6011-0,6072-2
See, as the carver carves a rose. 6467-1
Seven twilights. 6010-2
Seven twilights, sels. 6798-0
Sonnet ("Broad"). 6012-9
Sonnet ("Green"). 6783-2
Sonnet ("How many clouds"). 6783-2
Sonnet ("How then the winged"). 6783-2
Sonnet ("Imprimis"). 6012-9
Sonnet ("My love"). 6012-9
Sonnet ("Sun-born"). 6783-2
Sonnet ("Think"). 6012-9
Sonnet ("What music's"). 6012-9
Sonnet ("Shape has no shape"). 6783-2
Tetelestai. 6010-2,6071-4
This is the shape of the leaf. 6581-3
Time in the rock, sels. 6209-1
The unknown soldier. 6666-6
The vampire. 6542-2, 6070-6
Variations, sels. 6393-4
Variations, XIV. 6513-9
The verge. 6780-8
The wars, and the Unknown Soldier. 6665-8
The wedding. 6011-0
When trout swim down Great Ormond Street. 6467-1

Aiken, Lucy
The beggar-man. 6131-1

Aikin, Anna Letitia. See Barbauld
Aileen aroon. Gerald Griffin. 6930-4
The **ailing** parent. Lora Dunetz. 6388-8
Ailleen. John Banim. 6858-8
"The **ailments** of advancing years". Princess Shikishi. 6852-9
Ailsie, my bairn. Eugene Field. 6949-5
Aim high. Ernest Neal Lyon. 6701-8
The **aim** of life. Philip James Bailey. 6240-7
The **aim** was song. Robert Frost. 6250-4
The **aim**. Irene Rutherford McLeod. 6266-0
The **aim**. Sir Charles George Douglas Roberts. 6337-3,6446-9
Ain't got no place to lay my head. Unknown. 6609-7
Ain't he cute. Unknown. 6917-7

Ain't he cute. Unknown. 6744-1
Ain't it awful, Mabel? John Edward Hazzard. 6089-7
"**Ain't** they lookin' rosy". In Santa Claus time. Frank Lebby Stanton. 6807-3
"**Ainsi**, quand l'aigle du tonnerre". L'enthousiasme. Alphonse Marie Louis de Lamartine. 6801-4
"**Ainsi**, quand Mazeppa, qui rugit et qui pleure". Mazeppa. Victor Hugo. 6801-4
"**Ainsi**, toujours pousses vers de nouveaux...". Le lac. Alphonse Marie Louis de Lamartine. 6801-4

Ainslie, Caroline
Orphans. 6799-9

Ainslie, Douglas
Good Friday's hoopoe. 6180-X
Lines prefixed to St John of Damascus. 6046-3
A stirrup-cup. 6180-X

Ainslie, Douglas (tr.)
Apprehension. Unknown (Sanskrit), 6437-X
The archer. Unknown (Sanskrit), 6437-X

Ainslie, Hew
I left ye, Jeanie. 6180-X
It's dowie in the hint o' hairst, fr. Mary. 6180-X
Sir Arthur and Lady Ann. 6518-X
Willie and Helen. 6180-X,6518-X

Ainsworth, Lillian M.
Chelsea. 7030-2

Ainsworth, Percy Clough
'And the life everlasting.' 6337-3
The kingdom within. 6337-3

Air castles. Clara H. Bradner. 6920-7
"The **air** comes forth this morning". Little song in the air. Genaro Estrada. 6759-X
"The **air** cool and soft". Chaka. Frank Templeton Prince. 6788-3
Air corps roar. Robert R. Selway Jr. 6237-7
"The **air** falls chill". September dark. James Whitcomb Riley. 6991-6
"The **air** grew black with menace, as the sun". The storm. Grace Bentley Beach. 6847-2
"The **air** is ecstasy; to breathe is joy". Do not love me now. Viola Cornett. 6750-6
"The **air** is filled with sunlight". Spring. Thorsteinn Gislason. 6854-5,6283-0
"The **air** is full of dawn and spring". Spring. John Hall Wheelock. 6897-9
"The **air** is full of diamond dust tonight". Frozen fire. Floris Clark McLaren. 6750-6
"The **air** is heavy with a mist of spice". The monk in his garden. Helen Hay Whitney. 7038-8
"The **air** is light with a twinkling nimble tune". Comparison. Maxwell Bodenheim. 6880-4
"The **air** is like a butterfly". Easter. Joyce Kilmer. 6850-2,6897-9,6891-X
"The **air** is like a jarring bell". Pedagogues, fr. Marine. Edith Sitwell. 7000-0
"The **air** is soft as the clouds above". Rhythm of the palms: Rio de Janeiro - the minuet. Winifred Huff Gill. 6789-1
"The **air** is steeped in scent of berries...". Ecologue. Jaroslav Vrchlicky. 6763-8
"The **air** is still and col. It comes not". The fall of Jerusalem. Henry Hart Milman. 6848-0
"The **air** is white with snow-flakes clinging". Villanelle. John Payne. 6770-0
"The **air** is white with snowflakes clinging". John Payne. 6850-2
"The **air** is white with snowflakes". Villanelle. John Payne. 6875-8
The **air** mail. Berton Braley. 6853-7
An **air** of coolness plays upon his face. Sarah N. Cleghorn. 6501-5
Air raid. Clifford Dyment. 6475-2
Air raid. Theodore Spencer. 6389-6,6666-6,6645-3
Air raid. John Allen Wyeth. 6482-5
Air raid, old style. Helen Bryant. 6761-1
Air raid: Barcelona. Langston Hughes. 6761-1
The **air** raid. Archibald MacLeish. 6978-9
"**Air** sleeps - from strife or stir the clouds..". Childhood. William Wordsworth. 6980-0
Air, fr. The art of preserving heath. John Armstrong.

6968-1
Air-raid casualties: Ashridge hospital. Patricia Ledward. 6475-2
Air-raid warning. Douglas Gibson. 6475-2
Air-raid, fr. In war time. Wilfred Wilson Gibson. 6884-7
The **air**.. Marguerite Wilkinson. 6607-0
"An **aircraft** is landing with a hundred...". Peace conference. Hans Magnus Enzensberger. 7032-9
Aird, Thomas
    The swallow. 6656-9
Aire and angels. John Donne. 6106-0,6341-1
Airly beacon. Charles Kingsley. 6123-0,6204-0,6658-5,6737-9
The **airman's** alphabet. Wystan Hugh Auden. 6375-6
The **airman's** battle hymn. James A. Mackreth. 7012-4
Airman's certificate, fr. Exploration by air. Fleming MacLeish. 6978-9
An **airman's** prayer. Hugh R. Brodie. 6337-3
"**Airman**, so free in the morning sun". The builders. Josephine A. Meyer. 6847-2
The **airman**.. Gregg Goddard. 6474-4
The **airman**. William Robert Rodgers. 6472-8,6666-6
Airmen from overseas. Laurence Binyon. 6224-5
The **airmen's** hymn. Harry Webb Farrington. 6337-3
The **airmen**. Cecil Roberts. 7014-0
The **airmen**. Frederick George Scott. 6021-8
"An **airport** and a beacon-light shining". Beacon lights. Nellie E. Warren. 6799-9
Airs for a flute. Marjorie Meeker. 6038-2
The **airs** of Palestine, sels ("On Arno's"). John Pierpont. 6752-2
The **airs** of Palestine, sels ("Where lies"). John Pierpont. 6752-2
The **airs** of spring. Thomas Carew. 6271-7,6219-9
"**Airs!** that wander and murmur round". The siesta. Unknown (Spanish). 7039-6
Airth, Frances
    Author to his child. 6750-6
    The dream that cracked a whip. 6750-6
"**Airy** del Castro was as bold a knight". Anti-Thelyphthora. William Cowper. 6814-6
Airy nothings, fr. The tempest. William Shakespeare. 6914-2
Airy nothings, fr. The tempest. William Shakespeare. 6302-0;6385-3
"**Airy**, fairy Lillian". Lillian's reading. Edgar A. Guest. 6862-6
Aishah Schechinah. Robert Stephen Hawker. 6096-X,6378-0, 6282-2,6323-3,6022-6
Aix-La-Chapelle. Bayard Taylor. 6331-4,6439-6
Aix-la-Chapelle. William Wordsworth. 6484-1
"**Aj!** he was carried on his back". Tlingit burial. Tom Lowenstein. 6855-3
Ajanta: five poems. Muriel Rukeyser. 6390-X
Ajax. Phoebe Cary. 6060-9
Ajax and Ulysses, sels. James Shirley. 6427-2
Ajax in flight, fr. The Iliad. Homer. 6435-3
Ajax on the decks, fr. The Iliad. Homer. 6435-3
Ajruna's debate with Sri Krishna, fr. Bhagavad-Gita. Unknown (Sanskrit) 6665-8
The **akathistos** hymn. Unknown. 6282-2
Akawense. Phyllis Wolf. 7005-1
Akazome Emon
    "Waiting and hoping for thy step". William N. Porter (tr.). 6852-9
"**Akbeit** the Venice girls get praise". Ballad of the women of Paris. Francois Villon. 7039-6
Akenside, Mark
    Benevolence. 6932-0
    Early influences. 6932-0
    England, unprepared for war. 6932-0
    For a grotto. 6831-6
    The hand of nature, fr.The pleasures of the imagination. 6934-7
    "He many a creature did anatomize", fr. The virtuoso. 6934-7
    Hymn to science. 6152-4
    Inscription. 6932-0
    Inscription for a statue of Chaucer at Woodstock. 6219-9
    [Inscription] For a grotto. 6152-4,6195-0
    Invocation to the genius of Greece. 6932-0
    The mingled pain and pleasure arising from virtuous emotions. 6543-0
    Nature's influence on man. 6932-0
    The nightingale, fr. Ode to the evening star. 6545-7
    Ode 001: Allusion to Horace. 6152-4
    Ode 017: On a sermon against glory. 6152-4
    Ode to the evening star. 6152-4
    On a sermon against glory. 6271-7
    On taste. 6543-0
    The pleasures of cultivated imagination. 6543-0
    The pleasures of imagination, sels. 6831-6
    The pleasures of imagination, sels. 6152-4,6195-0,6438-8,6122-2
    Poets. 6932-0
    The virtuoso. 6102-8
Akerman, J.Y.
    The harnet and the bittle. 6125-7
Akerman, Lucy Evelina
    Another little wave. 6131-1
    Nothing but leaves. 6219-9
Akers, Dana Kneeland
    Mongol. 6646-8
Akers, Elizabeth. See Allen, Elizabeth Akers
Akers, J. Milton
    What I saw. 6913-4
Akhmatova, Anna
    After poems (1913,1916,1911,1959). Stephen Berg (tr.). 6803-0
    All is gold. Babette Deutsch (tr.). 6546-5,6160-5
    In the pioneer camp. Jack Lindsay (tr.). 6546-5
    It's good up here. Jack Lindsay (tr.). 6546-5
The **akhoond** of swat. Eugene Field. 6949-5
Aki-suke
    "See, how the wind of autumn drives". William N. Porter (tr.). 6852-9
Akin. Herbert Everell Rittenburg. 6662-3
Akins, Zoe
    A cabaret dancer. 6959-2
    Conquered. 6897-9
    I am the wind. 6019-6,6076-5,6102-8
    Lethargy. 6327-6
    Norah. 6019-6
    One woman. 6300-4
    Rain, rain! 6019-6, 6394-X
    "She loved/Shakespeare's sonnets". 6850-2
    The snow-gardens. 6649-6
    This is my hour. 6300-4
    The tragedienne. 6897-9
    Villanelle of city and country. 6875-8
    The wanderer. 6076-5,6102-8,6300-4,6396-9
Al Aaraff, sels. Edgar Allan Poe. 6008-0,6288-1
"**Al Brannock** said he'd build a barn". A Vermont raising. Daniel L. Cady. 6989-4
Al Rusafi
    Abode divine. A.J. Arberry (tr.). 6362-4
    The stream. A.J. Arberry (tr.). 6362-4
    The weaver's apprentice. A.J. Arberry (tr.). 6362-4
    The young carpenter. A.J. Arberry (tr.). 6362-4
Al far della notte. William ("Fiona Macleod") Sharp. 6507-4
Al fresco. James Russell Lowell. 6049-8
Al the meryere. Unknown. 6106-0
"**Al the meryere** is that place." Unknown. 6378-0
Al-Asamm
    Excuses. A.J. Arberry (tr.). 6362-4
    The unripe orange. A.J. Arberry (tr.). 6362-4
Al-Assal
    Toledo captured by the Franks. A.J. Arberry (tr.). 6362-4
Al-Barraq
    The inky mouth. A.J. Arberry (tr.). 6362-4
    Lyric. A.J. Arberry (tr.). 6362-4
al-Barudi
    "Was it the unsheathing of a sword". A.J. Arberry (tr.). 6766-2
al-Buhturi
    "I have guarded my soul from that which would defile." A.J. Arberry (tr.). 6766-2

Al-Buqaira
    The bow. A.J. Arberry (tr.). 6362-4
    The camomile. A.J. Arberry (tr.). 6362-4
    The singer. A.J. Arberry (tr.). 6362-4
Al-Dabbaj
    Two suns. A.J. Arberry (tr.). 6362-4
Al-Dhahabi
    The introduction. A.J. Arberry (tr.). 6362-4
Al-Fata al-Kafif
    White for mourning. A.J. Arberry (tr.). 6362-4
Al-Ghassani
    Eclipse. A.J. Arberry (tr.). 6362-4
    Roses. A.J. Arberry (tr.). 6362-4
Al-Hadrami
    Beauty's armoury. A.J. Arberry (tr.). 6362-4
    Departure. A.J. Arberry (tr.). 6362-4
Al-Haitham
    Meteor. A.J. Arberry (tr.). 6362-4
    Rich and poor. A.J. Arberry (tr.). 6362-4
    The rising sun. A.J. Arberry (tr.). 6362-4
Al-Hajjam
    The broken water-wheel. A.J. Arberry (tr.). 6362-4
    The candle. A.J. Arberry (tr.). 6362-4
    False friend. A.J. Arberry (tr.). 6362-4
    The pen. A.J. Arberry (tr.). 6362-4
    The stork. A.J. Arberry (tr.). 6362-4
    The toothpick. A.J. Arberry (tr.). 6362-4
    Vultures. A.J. Arberry (tr.). 6362-4
Al-Husri
    The breeze. A.J. Arberry (tr.). 6362-4
    The trees. A.J. Arberry (tr.). 6362-4
Al-Isra'ili
    The sprouting board. A.J. Arberry (tr.). 6362-4
    Trees and waves. A.J. Arberry (tr.). 6362-4
Al-Jaziri
    Forgiveness. A.J. Arberry (tr.). 6362-4
Al-Jazzar
    Moon of grace. A.J. Arberry (tr.). 6362-4
Al-Kasad
    The lost angel. A.J. Arberry (tr.). 6362-4
al-Khansa
    "I was sleepless, and I passed the night keeping vigil. A.J. Arberry (tr.). 6766-2
Al-Kutandi
    Elegy for a dead king. A.J. Arberry (tr.). 6362-4
    River of Seville. A.J. Arberry (tr.). 6362-4
Al-Lama'i
    Night storm. A.J. Arberry (tr.). 6362-4
Al-Liss
    The mountain. A.J. Arberry (tr.). 6362-4
    Night. A.J. Arberry (tr.). 6362-4
    The thimble. A.J. Arberry (tr.). 6362-4
al-Ma'arri
    "Souls stretching out their necks". A.J. Arberry (tr.). 6766-2
Al-Mahdi
    The preacher. A.J. Arberry (tr.). 6362-4
Al-Mu'tamid
    The handsome knight. A.J. Arberry (tr.). 6362-4
    The king's hand. A.J. Arberry (tr.). 6362-4
    The letter. A.J. Arberry (tr.). 6362-4
    Moon of loveliness. A.J. Arberry (tr.). 6362-4
    Night by the river. A.J. Arberry (tr.). 6362-4
    The vine. A.J. Arberry (tr.). 6362-4
Al-Munfatil
    Enchantress. A.J. Arberry (tr.). 6362-4
    The mole. A.J. Arberry (tr.). 6362-4
Al-Munsafi
    Colloquy. A.J. Arberry (tr.). 6362-4
    The skiff. A.J. Arberry (tr.). 6362-4
Al-Mushafi
    Pearls. A.J. Arberry (tr.). 6362-4
Al-Mustazhir
    The banished lover. A.J. Arberry (tr.). 6362-4
al-Mutanabbi
    "According to the degree of the people of resolve". A.J. Arberry (tr.). 6766-2
Al-Mutawakkil
    Invitation. A.J. Arberry (tr.). 6362-4
al-Nabigha
    "(News) came to me - may you spurn the curse!" A.J. Arberry (tr.). 6766-2
Al-Nashshar
    The garden. A.J. Arberry (tr.). 6362-4
Al-Nasir
    Royal pride. A.J. Arberry (tr.). 6362-4
Al-Qalami
    Ramadan. A.J. Arberry (tr.). 6362-4
Al-Radi Billah
    The passers by. A.J. Arberry (tr.). 6362-4
Al-Ramadi
    The shaven beauty. A.J. Arberry (tr.). 6362-4
al-Rusafi
    "Comrade, affairs are in a ferment". A.J. Arberry (tr.). 6766-2
al-Samau'al
    "When a man's honour is not defiled by baseness". A.J. Arberry (tr.). 6766-2
al-Sharif al-Radi
    "O sickness of your heart". A.J. Arberry (tr.). 6766-2
al-Shidyaq
    "In the west hath arisen a light". A.J. Arberry (tr.). 6766-2
Al-Sumaisir
    The glutton. A.J. Arberry (tr.). 6362-4
    Mosquitoes. A.J. Arberry (tr.). 6362-4
Al-Taliq
    Saki. A.J. Arberry (tr.). 6362-4
Al-Tulaitili
    The ant. A.J. Arberry (tr.). 6362-4
Al-Tutili
    Battle. A.J. Arberry (tr.). 6362-4
    Contentment. A.J. Arberry (tr.). 6362-4
    Lion fountain. A.J. Arberry (tr.). 6362-4
    Sacrifice. A.J. Arberry (tr.). 6362-4
    Seville. A.J. Arberry (tr.). 6362-4
Alabama. Julia Tutwiler. 6074-9,6465-5
Alabama bound. Unknown. 6594-5
The **Alabama**.. Maurice Bell. 6113-3
"**Alack**! 'tis melancholy theme to think". The Irish schoolmaster. Thomas Hood. 6802-2,6974-6
"**Alack**! I am afriad they have awaked", fr. Macbeth. William Shakespeare. 6392-6
"**Alack**! why am I sent for...", fr. Richard II. William Shakespeare. 6323-3
"**Alack**, it is a dismal night". The daughter. Alice Cary. 6969-X
"**Alack**, what poverty my muse brings forth". Sonnet 103 ("Alack, what poverty"). William Shakespeare. 6447-7
Aladdin. James Russell Lowell. 6077-3,6136-2,6243-1,6331-4, 6473-6,6478 ,6496-5,6583-X,6631-3,6421-3,6396-9,6288-1,6126-5,6371-3,6004-8,6212-2,6107-9
Aladdin and the jinn. Vachel Lindsay. 6619-4,6393-4
Alamance. Seymour W. Whiting. 6946-0
Alameda. Mary Stewart. 6928-2
Alan. Raymond F. Roseliep. 6218-0
Alan Seeger. John L. Jones. 6799-9
Alan Seeger. Washington Van Dusen. 6846-4
"**Alan-wart** loon", sels. J.G. Horne. 6269-5
"**Alanus** calvus". An epitaph ("Alanus calvus"). Unknown. 6881-2
Aladdin's paradise. Robert Southey. 6980-0
The **alaphet**.. Unknown. 6466-3
Alaric in Italy. Felicia Dorothea Hemans. 6973-8
Alarm. Margaret Forst. 6906-1
The **alarmed** skipper. James Thomas Fields. 6089-7,6279-2, 6307-1,6736-0
The **alarming** progress of luxury in New England. Benjamin Tompson. 6077-3
Alarming prospect. Unknown. 6278-4
"**Alas** for grim old age! Alas for youth...". Theognis. 6251-2
"**Alas** for him that for any of the vile...". He who forsakes the clerkly life, fr. 'Life of St....' Unknown. 6930-4
"**Alas** for the (all too) short time passed". Abu 'L-'Atahiya. 6766-2
"**Alas** for the voyage, O high king of heaven". Farewell to Ireland. Colum-Cille (atr). 7039-6
Alas for youth. Firdusi] (Abul Kasin Mansur) Firdausi [or

Firdawsi. 7039-6
Alas that spring should vanish with the rose. Edward Fitzgerald. 6090-0
"Alas the grief, and deadly woeful smart." Sir Thomas Wyatt. 6584-8
Alas!. Phoebe Cary. 6735-2,6969-X,6309-8
Alas!. Muriel F. Hochdorf. 6850-2
"Alas! 'tis true I have gone here and there". Sonnet 110 ("Alas! 'tis true"). William Shakespeare. 6436-1, 6378-0
"Alas! alas! the while". A night with a holy-water clerk. Unknown. 6881-2
"Alas! alas! this wasted night". Protest: by Zahir-u-Din. Laurence (Adele Florence Nicolson) Hope. 6856-1
"Alas! by what mean may I make ye to know" John Heywood. 6182-6
"Alas! For saturn's days of gold" William Morris. 6828-6
"Alas! deceite that in truste is nowe". Trust only yourself. Unknown. 6881-2
"Alas! how bitter are the wrongs of love!" George (Mary Ann Cross) Eliot. 6238-5
"Alas! how dismal is my tale". The curse of Doneraile. Patrick O'Kelly. 6930-4
"Alas! how light a cause may move." Thomas Moore. 6198-2;6302-0;6385-3
"Alas! how many hopes of life". Realizations. William White. 6868-5
"Alas! I do not know on what sad ay". 'Quelque part une enfance tres douce doit mourir'. Olive Custance. 6785-9
"Alas! I have lost my God". Rejected. Lord Alfred Bruce Douglas. 6785-9
Alas! madam, for stealing a kiss. Sir Thomas Wyatt. 6430-2
Alas! Poor queen. Marion Angus. 6845-6
"Alas! my child, where is the pen". The hen. Oliver Herford. 6902-9
"Alas! my dear friend, what a state of affairs". Epistle of condolence. Thomas Moore. 6930-4
"Alas! my Lord is going/Oh my woe!". Comfort in extremity. Christopher Harvey. 6931-2
"Alas! now wilt thou chide, and say (I deem).". Epilogue to the poet's sitter. Francis Thompson. 6942-8
"Alas! O Hellas lorn and whist". Nostalgia. Thomas Sturge Moore. 6780-8
"Alas! our glories float between the earth...". Ambition and glory. Edward Bulwer-Lytton; Baron Lytton. 6980-0
"Alas! our pleasant moments fly". On parting. Edward Coote Pinkney. 7017-5
"Alas! so all things now do hold their peace". Henry Howard, Earl of Surrey. 61h1-8,6584-8
"Alas! so all things now do hold their peace". Night. Henry Howard, Earl of Surrey. 6436-1
"Alas! that breathing vanity should go". The two peacocks of Bedfont. Thomas Hood. 6974-6
"Alas! that Mary should unfaithful be". A moan from the San Francisco bar. Mary MacH.. 6878-2
"Alas! the blush upon my cheek". Taira No Kanemori. 6852-9
"Alas! the little child is dead". On the death of an infant. Margaret L. Woods. 6785-9
Alas! the love of women, fr. Don Juan. George Gordon, 6th Baron Byron. 6934-7
"Alas! They had been friends in youth" Samuel Taylor Coleridge. 6935-5
"Alas! the weary hours pass slow". The countersign. Unknown. 6916-9
"Alas! they had been friends in youth". They had been friends in youth, fr. Christabel. Samuel Taylor Coleridge. 6934-7
"Alas! upon some starry height". Prelude ("Alas"). Robert Service. 6159-1
"Alas! We live in days of shame". Time's justice. William Henry Davies. 7014-0
"Alas! what boots the long". Sonnet ("Alas!"). William Wordsworth. 6438-8
"Alas! what pity 'tis that regularity". Toby tosspot. George Colman the Younger. 6787-5,6787-5,6302-0,6385-3,6410-8
Alas! what shall I do for love? Henry VIII; King of England. 6328-4,6528-7

"Alas! what shul we freres do". A friar complains. Thomas Phillips (atr). 6881-2
"Alas! what stay is there in human state". John Dryden. 6867-7
"Alas! with swift and silent pace". Autumn. Samuel Johnson. 6975-4
"Alas! youth fades, the inmost longing wanes". Autumn causerie. Jan Svatopluk Machar. 6763-8
"Alas, 'tis true I have gone here and there". William Shakespeare. 6198-2,6204-0,6122-2,6600-3
Alas, alack. Walter De La Mare. 6538-4,6454-X
"Alas, alas! Where shall I go to search..my children?" Unknown (Newari) 7013-2
"Alas, alas! how many sighs". The unhonored. Phoebe Cary. 6969-X
"Alas, alas, eheu!". Song ("Alas"). Ronald Campbell Macfie. 6873-1
Alas, for man!, fr. Mont Blanc revisited. John Ruskin. 6934-7
Alas, for the fleet wings of time. Clinton Scollard. 6875-8
"Alas, for the land where 'God's acres'...vain". Monuments. Benjamin Franklin Taylor. 6815-4
"Alas, for us no second spring". Triolets after Moschus. Andrew Lang. 6987-8,6879-0,6875-8
"Alas, Fra Giacamo/Too late!". Fra Giacamo. Robert Buchanan. 6918-5
"Alas, have I not paindenough, my friend?" Sir Philip Sidney. 6645-3
"Alas, how bitter are the wrongs of love". The wrongs of love. Letitia Elizabeth ("L.E.L.") Landon. 6980-0
"Alas, how easily things go wrong!" fr. Phantastes. George Macdonald. 6383-7
Alas, how soon. Walter Savage Landor. 6110-9,6199-0
"Alas, how soon the hours are over" Walter Savage Landor. 6828-6
"Alas, my God". Thomas Shepherd. 6931-2
"'Alas, my brother!'/All the land is still". The man of God from Judah. Barbara Miller Macandrew. 6848-0
"Alas, my hart will brek in three". Fearful death. Unknown. 6881-2
Alas, so long! Dante Gabriel Rossetti. 6197-4
"Alas, that even in a heavenly marriage". Marriage unequal. Johann Wolfgang von Goethe. 6948-7
"Alas, that fancy's pencil still portrays". The memory of the past. John Leyden. 6980-0
"Alas, that spring should vanish with the rose". Omar's lament. Edward Fitzgerald. 6844-8
"Alas, the path is lost, we cannot leave". A lost path. Andrew Lang. 6771-9
"Alas, where have been, oh husband?..." Unknown (Newari) 7013-2
Alaska. Joaquin Miller. 6946-0
Alaska. Unknown. 6465-5
Alastor and the swan. Percy Bysshe Shelley. 6980-0
Alastor, sels. Percy Bysshe Shelley. 6980-0
Alastor, sels. Percy Bysshe Shelley. 6102-8,6198-2,6726-3, 6196-0,6199-0,6648
Alastor; or, the spirit of solitude. Percy Bysshe Shelley. 6138-9,6110-9,6430-2,6250-4
Albatross. Charles Burgess. 6388-8
Albatross. J.E. Scruggs. 6396-9
Albatross. Charles Warren Stoddard. 6073-0,6096-X,6597-X
"An albatross goes flapping high". The sailor. Horace Gregory. 6751-4
The albatross.. Roy Campbell. 6625-9
The albatross. Charles Baudelaire. 6351-9
The albatross. Celia Thaxter. 6612-7
Albaugh, Dorothy P.
  Communion. 6750-6
  Prayer for a boy with a kite. 6750-6
Albee, John
  Landor. 6300-4
"Albeit nurtured in democracy". Libertatis sacra fames. Oscar Wilde. 7015-9
"Albeit the Venice girls get praise". Ballad of the women of Paris. Algernon Charles Swinburne. 6875-8
'Albemarle' Cushing. Herman Melville. 6946-0
'Albemarle' Cushing. Herman Melville. 6946-0
Albert. Dennis Kelly. 7003-5

ALBERT

Albert Durer's studio. Josiah Gilbert Holland. 6331-4,6631-3
Albert Graeme's song. Sir Walter Scott. 6518-X
Albert Sidney Johnston. Kate Brownlee Sherwood. 6074-9
Albert Sidney Johnston. Francis Orrery Ticknor. 6946-0
Albert the good, fr. The idylls of the king. Alfred Lord Tennyson. 6123-0,6102-8,6424-8
Albert, Edith
   Credo. 6847-2
   Ecce homo! 6847-2
   Keats. 6847-2
   Triptolemus. 6847-2
Albert, Samuel L.
   After a game of squash. 6388-8
   All of her. 6388-8
   Near the base line. 6388-8
   One, two, three. 6388-8
   Street-walker in March. 6388-8
"Albert, in thy race we cherish". Ode on Prince Albert, sels. William Wordsworth. 6867-7
Alberta. John D.S. Campbell; 9th Duke of Argyle. 6433-7
Alberta, let yo' hair hang low. Unknown. 6609-7
Alberti, Rafael
   A spectre is haunting Europe. Ira J. Wallach and Angel Flores (tr.). 6068-4
Alberto Rojas Jimenez comes flying. Pablo (Neftali Ricardo Reyes Basualto) Neruda. 6642-9
Albertson, Charles Carroll
   The holy child. 6337-3
Albertson, Cyrus E.
   Reflections. 6337-3
Albino. Ambrose Philips. 6191-5
Albion and Albanius, sels. John Dryden. 6208-3
Albion's England, sels. William Warner. 6547-3
Albright, Rachel
   Adventure on the wings of morning. 6750-6
   Best stories. 6789-1
   Bibliophile's library. 6789-1
   On reading Books alive by Vincent Starrett. 6789-1
Albro, John
   A tale of the east (side). 6247-4
Album verses. Oliver Wendell Holmes. 6121-4
Album verses. Washington Irving. 6240-7,6004-8
The **album.** Cecil Day Lewis. 6208-3
Albums. Jules Laforgue. 6351-9
Alcaeus
   Antimenidas. Sir William Marris (tr.). 6435-3
   An armoury. Gilbert Highet (tr.). 6435-3,6665-8
   Castor and Polydeuces. Cecil Maurice Bowra (tr.). 6435-3
   "Drink! Why wait for lamps? The day". Cecil Maurice Bowra (tr.). 6435-3
   Helen and Thetis. Sir William Marris (tr.). 6435-3
   Immortalia ne speres. Cecil Maurice Bowra (tr.). 6435-3
   "Now bind the woven necklaces". Cecil Maurice Bowra (tr.). 6435-3
   Poverty. 6954-1
   "Soak your lungs with wine, for now". Cecil Maurice Bowra (tr.). 6435-3
   Storm at sea. Cecil Maurice Bowra (tr.). 6435-3
   To Athena. T.F. Higham (tr.). 6435-3
   To Sappho ("Violet-haired, holy, sweetly..."). 6435-3
   "Zeus rains; a storm comes in its might". Cecil Maurice Bowra (tr.). 6435-3
Alcaeus of Messene
   Pan's piping. John William Mackail (tr.). 6423-X
   Philip, king of Macedon. Sir William Marris (tr.). 6435-3
Alcaeus of Messene. Philip V; King of Macedon. 6435-3
Alcaeus of Mytilene
   "The flowery spring-I heard her, coming upon her way". F.L. Lucas (tr.). 6251-2
   "Homeward from earth's far ends thou art returned". F.L. Lucas (tr.). 6251-2
   "It is not streets where proud-roofed mansions stand". F.L. Lucas (tr.). 6251-2
Alcaics: to H.F.B. Robert Louis Stevenson. 6437-X
Alcatraz. Ina D. Coolbrith. 6484-1
Alcestis. Vittorio Alfieri. 6973-8
Alcestis. Anne Goodwin Winslow. 6039-0
Alcestis in Ely. Nicholas Moore. 6379-9
Alcestis, sels. Euripides. 6879-0
The **alchemist,** sels. Ben Jonson. 6317-9,6369-1,6378-0
The **alchemist.** Louise Bogan. 6036-6
The **alchemist.** Thomas Noel Wrenn. 6983-5
Alchemy. Francis Carlin. 6032-3,6292-X
Alchemy. Christine Park Hankinson. 6841-3
Alchemy. Ibn Abil Khayal. 6362-4
Alchemy. Sarah Litsey. 6750-6
Alchemy. Sara Teasdale. 6338-1
Alchin, Gordon
   A song of the air. 6846-4
Alcman
   "Ah voices sweet as honey, ah maiden songs divine". F.L. Lucas (tr.). 6251-2
   Hagesichora. Gilbert Highet (tr.). 6435-3
   The halycons. W.T. Wade-Gery (tr.). 6435-3
   "The mountain summits sleep, glens, cliffs, and caves". Thomas Campbell (tr.). 7039-6
   The mountain summits sleep. 6125-7
   Night. W.T. Wade-Gery (tr.). 6435-3
   On the mountains. Cecal Maurice Bowra (tr.). 6435-3
Alcock, Mary (tr.)
   Psalm 057. Bible, 6848-0
   Psalm 063. Bible, 6848-0
Alcoeus
   The storm. John Hermann Merivale (tr.). 7039-6
Alcohol. Louis MacNeice. 6391-8
Alcoholic goblins. Thomas Jefferson Savage. 6482-5
Alcott, Amos Bronson
   Approaching God. 6288-1
   Emerson. 6431-0
   Excellence. 6288-1
   Garrison. 6431-0,6820-0
   Hawthorne. 6820-0
   Thoreau. 6309-8, 6431-0
   Wendell Phillips. 6300-4,6820-0
Alcott, Louisa May
   My kingdom. 6337-3
   Thoreau's flute. 6309-8
   Transfiguration. 6879-0,7041-8
Alcyone. Sir Edmund Gosse. 7015-9
Alcyone. Frances Laughton Mace. 6300-4
Aldan, Daisy (tr.)
   Afterthoughts. Malcolm de Chazal, 6803-0
Aldana, Francisco de
   The image of God. Henry Wadsworth Longfellow (tr.). 6730-1
Aldaramy, Meskin
   On his friends. 6424-8
Aldaran. Annie Campbell Huestis. 6115-X
Aldborough, fr. The village. George Crabbe. 6934-7
The **alde..** John Freeman. 6477-9
Aldebaran at dusk. George Sterling. 6347-0,6607-0,6253-9, 6467-1
Alden, Ada
   As a star from the dust. 6850-2
   Psyche's lamp. 6076-5,6102-8
   The star of peace. 7001-9
   Unhearing. 6850-2
Alden, Henry Mills
   The magic mirror. 7030-2
Alden, Julia Ross
   Crows flying. 6906-1
   Hunger. 6906-1
   If I come back. 6906-1
   Prayer ("Dismayed"). 6906-1
   A tree in winter. 6906-1
Alden, Raymond Macdonald
   Carmen amoebaeum. 6936-3
   Mabel. 6936-3
   May. 6456-6
   With a gift of flowers. 6936-3
"The **alder** by the river". Spring. Celia Thaxter. 6135-4, 6049-8,6356-X,6519-8,6612-7,6165-6,6623
Alder, Alice Mabel
   The street of peacocks. 6800-6
Alder-trees. Antonin Sova. 6763-8
"The **alderman** woke from his nightmare...". A vision of siren soup. Shirley Brooks. 6760-3

Alderson, Althea Todd
    The spirit of St. Louis. 7019-1
Aldfrid's itinerary through Ireland. Flann (atr.) Fionn. 6930-4
Aldfrid's itinerary through Ireland. Flann (atr.) Fionn. 6930-4
Aldington, Mrs. Richard. See Doolittle, Hilda
Aldington, Richard
    After two years. 6161-3,6513-9, 6393-4
    At the British Museum. 6439-6
    Choricos. 6153-2
    Dawn. 6393-4
    Epitaph in ballade form. 6875-8
    A garden homily. 6069-2
    Images. 6102-8
    In the trenches. 6542-2
    Inscriptions. 6581-3,6780-8
    Lesbia. 6897-9
    The poplar. 6897-9,6509-7
    Possession. 6985-1
    Prayer ("I am a garden"). 6649-6
    Rhapsody in a third-class carriage. 6985-1
    Song 003, fr. Songs for puritans. 6985-1
    A sophistry of duration. 6776-X
    To Cynthia. 6070-6
    Vicarious atonement. 6542-2,6730-1
    The wine-cup. 6872-3
Aldington, Richard (tr.)
    The dream. Gaspara Stampa, 6325-X
    Flowers and love, fr. The decameron. Giovanni Boccaccio, 6325-X
    In absence. Gaspara Stampa, 6325-X
    Song of the girls and the tattlers (cicadas). Lorenzo de' Medici, 6325-X
    To a balcony. Matteo Maria Boiardo, 6325-X
    To Alcestis, fr. Alcestis. Euripides, 6435-3
    Triumph of Bacchus aand Ariadne. Lorenzo de' Medici, 6325-X
Aldis, Dorothy
    The ballad of a daft girl. 6039-0
    Hiding. 6891-X
    Inanimates. 6808-1
    Little. 6850-2
    Maine shore. 6396-9
    Radiator lions. 6891-X
    Setting the table. 6891-X
Aldis, Mary
    Barberries. 6897-9
    Flash-lights. 6076-5,6102-8
    The happening. 6037-4
    The other one comes to her. 6037-4
    She remembers. 6037-4
    She thinks of the faithful one. 6037-4
    The sisters. 6030-7
    They meet again. 6037-4
    The wandering one makes music. 6037-4
    When you come. 6897-9
Aldrich, Anne Reeve
    Color song. 7041-8
    Fanny. 6004-8
    A little parable. 6076-5,6102-8,6300-4,6309-8,6337-3
    Love's change. 6019-6, 6309-8
    Recollection. 6076-5,6102-8,6300-4
    A song of life. 7041-8
    Souvenirs. 6004-8
    The wish. 7041-8
Aldrich, Henry
    A catch. 6933-9
    Christ Church bells. 6563-5
    Reasons for drinking. 6092-7,6736-0
    Why I drink. 6026-9
Aldrich, James
    A death-bed. 6214-8,6219-9,6271-7,6737-9,6911-8,6309-8
Aldrich, Thomas Bailey
    Accomplices. 6524-2
    Act 005 (midnight). 6467-1
    After the rain. 6008-0, 6121-4
    Alec Yeaton's son. 6614-3
    An alpine picture. 6439-6,6749-2,
    Amontillado. 6004-8
    Apparitions. 6076-5,6102-8,6648-8
    An Arab welcome. 6424-8
    At Bay Ridge. 6484-1
    Baby Bell. 6219-9,6889-8
    The ballad of Babie Bell. 6008-0
    Before the rain. 6008-0, 6121-4
    The bells at midnight. 6946-0
    The bluebird. 6820-0
    By the Potomac. 6946-0
    Comedy. 6887-1
    The crescent and the cross. 6177-X
    Dirge. 6431-0
    Enamored architect of airy rhyme. 6309-8,6431-0
    The faded violet. 6121-4
    The flight of the goddess. 6309-8
    Forever and a day. 6307-1
    Fredericksburg. 6076-5,6102-8,6271-7,6470-1,6737-9,6442,6121-4,6467-1
    Friar Jerome's beautiful book. 6396-9,6614-3
    Guilielmus rex. 6439-6,6484-1
    Heredity. 6300-4
    Hesperides. 6121-4
    I vex me not with brooding o'er the years. Carl Friedrich (into German) Kayser (tr.). 6847-2
    I vex me not with brooding on the years. 6648-8,6431-0
    I'll not confer with sorrow. 6431-0
    Identity. 6076-5,6102-8,6464-7,6468-8,7041-8
    If all be true that I do think. 6563-5
    In an artist's studio. 6887-1
    In an atelier. 6358-6
    In the belfry of the Nieuwe Kerk. 6484-1
    In Westminster Abbey. 6484-1
    The Jew's gift. 6848-0
    Judith. 6848-0
    Kriss Kringle. 6747-6
    L'eau dormante. 6004-8
    Lady of Castlenoire. 6319-5
    The Lorelei. 6439-6
    Love's calendar. 6226-1
    The lunch. 6652-6
    The man and the hour. 6121-4
    Maple leaves. 6820-0
    Marjorie's almanac. 6135-4
    Memory. 6076-5,6102-8,6464-7,6439-6,6309-8,6431,6153-2, 6396-9,6737-9
    The metemspsychosis. 6648-8
    Miracles. 6121-4
    No songs in winter. 6431-0
    Nocturne. 6004-8,6271-7
    An ode on the unveiling of the Shaw Memorial...Boston. 6946-0
    Oh, sad are they who know not love. 6226-1
    An old castle. 6439-6
    On an intaglio head of Minerva. 6004-8,6219-9
    On Lynn terrace. 6288-1
    Outward bound. 6833-2
    Palabras carinosas. 6226-1,6309-8,6321-7,7041-8,6429-4
    Palinode ("Who is Lydia..."). 6320-9
    Pampinea. 6008-0,6009-9
    A Persian love song. 6260-1
    The piazza of St. Mark at midnight. 6484-1,6631-3,6485-X
    Piscataqua river. 6121-4,6484-1,6121-4
    Prescience. 6437-X
    Sea drift. 6997-5
    Sleep. 6121-4,6288-1
    Song from the Persian. 6309-8,6431-0
    Sunset. 6214-8
    Thalia. 6004-8, 6307-1, 6431-0
    Three flowers. 6484-1
    Tiger-lilies. 6121-4,6431-0
    The tragedy. 6573-2
    A Turkish legend. 6424-8
    Two songs from the Persian. 6121-4
    Unguarded gates. 6946-0
    Unsung. 6648-8
    An untimely thought. 6887-1
    Wedded. 6121-4
    When the sultan goes to Ispahan. 6076-5,6102-8,6121-4
    Who know not love. 6321-7

Aldridge, Richard
    The world's way. 6307-1
Aldridge, Richard
    By return mail. 6388-8
    A serendipity of love. 6388-8
    Weeping willow. 6388-8
Ale. William Henry Davies. 6501-5
Ale. John Still. 6092-7
Alec Yeaton's son. Thomas Bailey Aldrich. 6614-3
Alec. Dunham's boat. Charles Henry ("John Paul") Webb. 6632-1
Alegria, Claribel
    Flowers from the volcano. Darwin J. Flakoll (tr.). 7036-1
    I'm a mirror. Darwin J. Flakoll (tr.). 7036-1
    Little cambric tamales. Darwin J. Flakoll (tr.). 7036-1
Aleppo. Ibn Kharuf. 6362-4
"**Alert** as bird or early worm". A portrait. Harry Graham. 6995-9
Alex tells a bear story. James Whitcomb Riley. 6128-1
Alexander. Alexander Geddes. 6929-0
Alexander Aetolus
    Euripides. Cecil Maurice Bowra (tr.). 6435-3
Alexander at the gates of paradise. Richard Chenevix Trench. 6848-0
Alexander breaking Bucephalus. George Lansing Taylor. 6552-X,6673-9
Alexander Pope at Stanton Harcourt. Sidney Keyes. 6210-5
Alexander Selkirk during his solitary abode... William Cowper. 6138-9,6543-0,6659-3,6424-8
Alexander Sergeyevich. Hugh Western. 6761-1
Alexander taming Bucephalus. Park Benjamin. 6410-8,6478-7
Alexander the Great. Unknown. 6090-0,6732-8
Alexander Throckmorton. Edgar Lee Masters. 6102-8,6076-5
Alexander Ypsilanti. Unknown. 6183-4
Alexander's feast, sels. John Dryden. 6427-2
Alexander's feast; or, the power of music. John Dryden. 6102-8,6189-3,6322-5,6660-7,6560-0,6152 ,6438-8,6022-6,6023-4,6197-4,6430-2,6195 ,6424-8,6491-4,6543-0, 6154-0,6246-5,6473-6,6562-7,6198-2,6315 ,6239-3,6302-0,6385-3,6726-3,6646-1,6219
Alexander, A. Crighton
    Song for a holiday. 6461-2
Alexander, Cecil Frances
    All things bright and beautiful. 6337-3,6638-0
    The burial of Moses. 6909-6
    The burial of Moses. 6131-1,6212-2,6219-9,6304-7,6438-8, 6614 ,6565-1
    The creation. 6891-X
    Dreams. 6930-4
    Dreams. 6090-0
    Evening song. 6638-0
    He is risen. 6177-X
    The Irish mother's lament. 6090-0
    Jesus calls us o'er the tumult. 6337-3
    Once in royal David's city. 6337-3
    The place of remembrance. 6174-5
    There is a green hill far away. 6304-7,6337-3,6730-1, 6656-9
Alexander, Dai
    The miner. 6895-2
Alexander, Eleanor
    Now. 6090-0
    Song ("He climbs"). 6090-0
    Who sleeps? 7029-9
Alexander, F.D.
    On the recovery of the cannon. 6983-5
Alexander, Frances
    Old women. 6265-2
Alexander, Griffith
    My sweetheart. 6770-0
Alexander, H.W. (tr.)
    Poor fisher folk. Victor Hugo, 6102-8,6344-6,6385-3
Alexander, Hartley
    The blizzard. 6143-5
Alexander, Joseph Addison
    The doomed man. 6337-3
Alexander, Louise Alexander
    Loki bound. 6021-8
Alexander, Richard
    The altar stone. 6818-9

Alexander, S.J.
    To San Francisco. 6946-0
Alexander, Sidney
    The plane. 6978-9,6761-1
Alexander, W.H. (tr.)
    The poor fisher folk, sels. Victor Hugo, 6849-9
Alexander, William
    The birthday crown. 6437-X
    Epitaph in Fahan churchyard. 6046-3
    Epitaph in the cathedral of Derry. 6046-3
    A fine day on Lough Swilly. 6090-0
    Frost-morning. 6090-0
    Oxford and her chancellor. 6046-3
    Oxford in 1845. 6046-3
    Preface to The finding of the book and other poems. 6046-3
    A vision of Oxford, sels. 6437-X
Alexander; Earl of Stirling, Sir William
    An echo. 6134-6
    "I envy not Endymion now no more" 6182-6
    Illusion. 6180-X
    "Let others of the world's decaying tell". 6181-8,6182-6
    Madrigal ("When in her face mine eyes I fix") 6182-6
    "Oh, if thou knew'st how thyself doest harm" 6182-6
    To Aurora. 6180-X
    The tragedy of Croesus. 6908-8
Alexandra's fourteenth birthday. Albert Paris Gutersloh. 6769-7
Alexis
    The confident scientist. T.F. Higham (tr.). 6435-3
"**Alexis,** here she stay'd; among these pines". Sonnet ("Alexis"). William Drummond of Hawthornden. 6908-8
"**Alexis,** here she stayed; among these pines" William Drummond of Hawthornden. 6182-6
"**Alexis,** here shee stay'd among these pines". Sonnet 046 ("Alexis, here shee stay'd..."). William Drummond of Hawthornden. 6933-9
Alfieri, Vittorio
    Alcestis. Felicia Dorothea Hemans (tr.). 6973-8
    Battle of Maclodio [or Macalo], fr. Conte di Carmagnola. Felicia Dorothea Hemans (tr.). 6973-8
    To Dante. Lorna de' Lucchi (tr.). 7039-6
Alford, Henry
    Academe. 6980-0
    The aged oak at Oakley. 6219-9
    Baptismal hymn. 6219-9
    Be just, and fear not. 6911-8
    Beauty of nature. 6980-0
    A churchyard soliloquy. 6980-0
    Colonos. 6656-9
    Contentment. 6568-6
    A doubt. 6980-0
    Easter eve. 7015-9
    Filiolae dulcissimae. 6046-3
    A funeral. 6980-0
    Harvest home. 6214-8,6337-3,6730-1
    Hymn for All-Saints Day in the morning. 6980-0
    Lady Mary. 6046-3
    'The master is come, and calleth for thee'. 6980-0
    A memory. 6980-0
    A spiritual and well-ordered mind. 6980-0
    Thanksgiving Day. 6424-8
    Thanksgiving hymn. 6219-9
Alford, Henry (tr.)
    A lover. Plato, 6732-8
Alford, Janie
    Thanks be to God. 6337-3,6461-2
Alfred and his descendants. William Wordsworth. 6188-5
Alfred Lord Tennyson: Sing a song of sixpence. Charles Powell. 6982-7
Alfred Noyes: Ride a cock-horse. Charles Powell. 6982-7
Alfred Tennyson. Wilfrid Scawen Blunt. 6483-3,6655-0
Alfred the Great to his men. James Sheridan Knowles. 6621-6,6606-2
Alfred the harper. John Sterling. 6980-0
Alfred the harper. John Sterling. 6271-7,6385-3,6438-8
"**Alfred,** I would say that you behold me now". A scene in summer. Arthur Henry Hallam. 6980-0
Alfred, a masque, sels. James Thomson. 6198-2

Algebra of divorce. L.F. Gerlach. 6515-5
"The **algebra** of miracles, that". The streets. Yvor Winters. 6808-1
Algeciras seen over a stormy sea. Ibn Malik (of Granada) 6362-4
Alger Jr., Horatio
    John Maynard. 6565-1,6964-9
Alger, Gertrude
    The daisy. 6798-0
    The dandelion. 6798-0
    A dream. 6798-0
    Fireflies. 6798-0
    A friend. 6798-0
    The ideal. 6798-0
    In a snowstorm. 6798-0
    Indian love song. 6798-0
    November night. 6798-0
    Out of the gray. 6798-0
    Song ("On every"). 6798-0
    Summer rain. 6798-0
    The wind. 6798-0
Alger, William R.
    The masque and the reality. 6577-5
    The parting lovers. 6385-3
    Petisson and Mlle. de Sardery. 6084-6
Alger, William Rounseville
    Charity's eye. 7008-6
Alger, William Rounseville (tr.)
    The parting lovers. Unknown (Chinese), 6302-0;6385-3
    To heaven approached a Sufi saint. Unknown (Persian), 6302-0;6385-3
    True friendship. Jamee, 6085-4
Algernon Charles Swinburne: Curly locks. Charles Powell. 6982-7
Alguire, Annie B.
    Expression. 6789-1
    Growing old. 6789-1
    Your ambition. 6789-1
Alhama. George Gordon, 6th Baron Byron. 6322-5
The **Alhambra**, sels. Washington Irving. 6484-1
The **Alhambra**. George Croly. 6980-0
Ali Ben Abu Taleb
    Make friends. Ralph Waldo Emerson (tr.). 6337-3
"**Ali** Ben Ali (did you never read).". The stag-eyed lady. Thomas Hood. 6974-6
Ali and the Jew. Sir Edwin Arnold. 6848-0
Ali, Agha Shahid
    The butcher. 6900-2
Alibi. Anne V. Kelly. 6249-0
Alice. Herbert Bashford. 6078-1
Alice. Denis Florence MacCarthy. 6302-0;6385-3
Alice. Christina Georgina Rossetti. 6123-0
Alice Ayres. Emilia Aylmer Blake. 6695-X
Alice Brand, fr. The lady of the lake. Sir Walter Scott. 6086-2,6558-9,6075-7,6290-3,6457-4,6604-6,6732-8, 6610 ,6558-9,6518-X,6219-9,6639-9,6613-5,6438
Alice du Clos. Samuel Taylor Coleridge. 6677-1
Alice fell. William Wordsworth. 6133-8,6134-6,6496-5
Alice in Wonderland, sels. Charles Lutwidge ("Lewis Carroll") Dodgson. 6523-6
"**Alice** is tall and upright as a pine". Charles Cotton. 6187-7
Alice Maud. Unknown. 6675-5
Alice of Monmouth, sels. Edmund Clarence Stedman. 6066-8
"**Alice** says we're marionettes". The weight. William Aberg. 6870-7
Alice's supper. Laura E. Richards. 6891-X
Alien. Margaret J.E. Brown. 6316-0
Alien. Helen Frazee-Bower. 6777-8
Alien. Ann Louise Hayes. 6515-5
Alien. Archibald MacLeish. 6649-6
Alien sun-flowers. Rea Woodman. 6327-6
Alien to the earth. Lilith Lorraine. 6648-8
The **alien**. Charles Murray. 6800-6
Alienation. Harry Kemp. 6102-8,6076-5
Alighieri, Dante
    Nimrod and the monsters of hell. Leigh Hunt (tr.). 6102-8
    Of Beatrice de Portinari. 6102-8
    Paolo and Francesca, sels. Stephen Phillips (tr.). 6046-

3,6541-4
Aline's love song. Emma Dunning Banks. 6426-4
Alington, C.A.
    The trust. 7029-9
Alison. Unknown. 6186-9,6153-2
Alison and Willie. Unknown. 6185-0
Alison Gross. Unknown. 6055-2,6056-0,6558-9,6067-6
Alison's mother to the brook. Josephine Preston Peabody. 6627-5
Alison, R.
    There is a garden in her face. 6219-9
Alisoun. Geoffrey Chaucer. 6150-8
Alive for evermore. Amos Niven Wilder. 6337-3
Alkman
    Hypnosis. Florence Mary Bennett (tr.). 6847-2
All. Francis A. Durivage. 6481-7,6693-3
All. Antoni Slonimski. 6068-4
All. Cyril G. Taylor. 6541-4
All. Unknown. 6260-1
"**All** Afric, winged with death and fire". A double ballad of August. Algernon Charles Swinburne. 6875-8
"**All** afternoon wind and rain". Radio. Dorothy Beedy. 6750-6
"**All** ages shall speak with amaze and applause". Massachusett's song of liberty, sels. Mercy Warren. 6798-0
"**All** alone I visit a deserted well". Self-portrait. Dong-ju Yun. 6775-1
"**All** alone in the tield". John S. Crow. Kirke Monroe. 6965-7
"**All** alone on the hillside". The grey horse troop. Robert W. Chambers. 7012-4
The **all** alone tree. F. O'Neil Gallagher. 6466-3
The **all** alone tree. F. O'Neill Gallagher. 6368-3
"**All** along the Brazos river". The wild-bees, fr. Texas. Henry Van Dyke. 6961-4
All are busy. Mary N. Prescott. 6530-9
"**All** are but parts of one stupendous whole" Alexander Pope. 6935-5
"**All** are indebted much to thee". Gratitude and love to God. Madame De la Mothe Guion. 6814-6
"**All** are players of destiny, playing roles...". The stage of destiny. Beaumont Claxton. 6928-2
"**All** around me". The old spinner. Virginia Lyne Tunstall. 6776-X
"**All** around the water tank". Railroad bum. Unknown. 6826-X
"**All** bars now/are wet with scotch and". The after. Paul Fericano. 6901-0
"**All** bathed in pearl and amber light". The flight of Nicolete. Rosamund Marriott ("Graham R. Tomson") Watson. 6875-8
All beautiful the march of days. Frances Whitmarsh Wile. 6337-3
All before. Unknown. 6240-7
All bells in paradise. Unknown. 6756-5
"**All** beneath the white-rose tree". The three captains. Unknown (French). 6771-9
"**All** blessings which the Fates, Propheticke...". The second squire (2). Thomas Campion. 6794-8
"**All** bones but yours will rattle when I say". The sea-serpent. James Robinson Planche. 6902-9
"**All** buildings are but monuments of death". Epigram: fatum supremum. Unknown. 6933-9
All busy. Unknown. 6114-1
All but blind. Walter De La Mare. 6102-8
"**All** by the sides of the wide wild river". Cradle song. Alice Cary. 6865-0;6969-X,6969-X
"**All** common things, each day's events". Henry Wadsworth Longfellow. 6238-5
"**All** day I have been broken". Content. Elisabeth Kuskulis. 6836-7
All day I hear. James Joyce. 6491-4
All day I hear the noise of waters. James Joyce. 6930-4
"**All** day long he kept the sheep". The prophet. Josephine Preston Peabody. 6762-X
"**All** day long the guns at the forts". The surrender of New Orleans. Marion Manville. 6946-0
"**All** day long the river flowed". Daniel Periton's ride. Albion W. Tourgee. 6922-3
"**All** day long they come and go". Pittypat and tipptoe.

Eugene Field. 6834-0;6949-5
"All day long till the west was red". Making port. J.T. McKay. 6833-2
"All day long upon her throne". Through the wood. Victor Plarr. 6785-9
"All day long, all day long". The boy and his mother. Hermann Hagedorn. 6944-4
"All day long/The gray rain beating". Rain. Seumas (James Starkey) O'Sullivan. 6930-4
"All day pounding nails". The horn blow. Jeff Tagami. 6790-5
All day rain. Larry Gould. 6750-6
"All day the cool waters". The swimmer's song. Lydia Gibson. 6880-4
"All day the curlew wailed and screamed". The weird of Michael Scott, sels. William ("Fiona Macleod") Sharp. 6819-7
"All day the dreaming magic of a hill". Day on a hill. Oliver Jenkins. 6764-6
"All day the dreamy sunshine steeps". An Indian summer carol. Fidelis [pseud].. 6795-6
"All day the great guns barked and roared". Molly Pitcher. Laura E. Richards. 6478-7,6736-0,6946-0
"All day the lark has struck its golden chord". Sonnet ("All day"). Mabel Posegate. 6906-1
"All day the mallet thudded far below". Gold. Wilfred Wilson Gibson. 6897-9
"All day the moments gathered for the moment". Instant out of time. Amanda Benjamin Hall. 6979-7
"All day the sky had worn a lurid hue". Saved. Stockton Bates. 6921-5
"All day through woodland stillnesses". The shooting of the moose. Theodore Roberts. 7035-3
"All day, all day, round the clacking net". The weaver. Archibald Lampman. 7041-8
"All day, all night, I hear the jar". The loom of life. Unknown. 6923-1
"All day, safe in the sun, the wall grew". 'Builder, what do you build?' John Ritchey. 6761-1
"All day/The bird sits in his cage.". Isas. 6027-7
"All de chillens am growed up and gone...". Song of desolation. Just Johnson. 6750-6
"All down the years thy tale has rolled—". To Homer. John Malcolm Bulloch. 6770-0
"All earthly beauty hath one cause and proof". Robert Bridges. 6186-9,6487-6
All ending in 'O'. A.F. Caldwell. 6684-4
"All evening the smell of wet goats". Grandfather. Andrew Murray. 6821-9
All fellows, sels. Laurence Housman. 6730-1
All flesh. Francis Thompson. 6477-9
"All flesh is grass". 'The voice of one saying, cry'. Mary Hume Mills. 7016-1
"All folks hev some soft spot". Pa's soft spot. D.A. Ellsworth. 6929-0
All fools' day. Unknown. 6465-5
All for a man. Helen M. Winslow. 6688-7
All for love. George Gordon, 6th Baron Byron. 6246-5,6737-9
All for love, or the world well lost, sels. John Dryden. 6106-0
All for the best. Edgar A. Guest. 7033-7
All for the best. Unknown. 6530-9
All for the cause. William Morris. 6879-0
All for the cause! William Morris. 7009-4
All for you. Samuel Minturn Peck. 6226-1
"All glory else besides ends with our breath". Justice. Samuel Daniel. 6935-5
All goats. Elizabeth J. Coatsworth. 6070-6
All gone. Cecil Day Lewis. 6209-1
'...All gone...' Walter De La Mare. 6905-3
"All good things have not kept aloof". To - ("All good things..."). Alfred Lord Tennyson. 6977-0
"All Greece hates". Helen. Hilda ("H.D.") Doolittle. 6777-8
"All hail the dawn of a new day breaking". What we want. Ella Wheeler Wilcox. 6863-4
"All hail the sturdy vats and tanks". Heroic ballad 1976. Will Irwin. 6817-0,6732-8
All hail to a night. William Douw Lighthall. 7035-3

"All hail to Thee, child Jesus, fr. Hymns and anthems... Caroline Hazard. 6762-X
"'All hail to a night when the stars...'". All hail to a night. William Douw Lighthall. 7035-3
"All hail! Eternal day breaks on the earth". Easter day. William White. 6868-5
"All hail! the prince of peace on earth". At Bethlehem. William White. 6868-5
"All hail! thou noble land". America to Great Britain. Washington Allston. 6300-4,6752-2
"All hail! unfurl the stripes and stars". God save our president. Francis De Haes Janvier. 6913-4
"All hail! Unfurl the stripes and stars!". God save our president. Francis De Haes Janvier. 6946-0
"All hail, friends and neighbors...". An honest rum-seller's advertisement. A. McWight. 6914-2
"All hail, immortal company". Moloch, Limited. Charles Whitby. 6994-0
All hail, pioneers! John Morgan Thew. 6342-X
All hail, the pageant of the years. John Haynes Holmes. 6337-3
All Hallow Eve. Carolyn Wells. 6820-0
"All hail, thou child of love's immortal love". Love's aforetime. William White. 6868-5
"All hail, ye famous farmers!". Ars agricolaris. Henry Van Dyke. 6961-4
"All hail/Ever borne back to mind". Mrs Kimber. Osbert Sitwell. 6985-1
All hands unmoor! William Falconer. 6833-2
All have work to do. R.P. S. 6131-1
"All heaven and earth are still...". Night. George Gordon, 6th Baron Byron. 6240-7
"All heavy minds." Sir Thomas Wyatt. 6187-7,6584-8
All here. Oliver Wendell Holmes. 6753-0
All here. Oliver Wendell Holmes. 6126-5,6288-1
All here. Oliver Wendell Holmes. 6753-0
All I know. Edgar A. Guest. 6748-4
"All honor be to merchantmen". Merchantmen. Cicely Fox Smith. 7031-0
"'All honour to him who sall win the prize'". For those who fail. Joaquin Miller. 6861-8
"All human race, from China to Peru". Of the universal love of pleasure. Thomas Warton (the Elder). 6962-2
"All human things are subject to decay". On Shadwell. John Dryden. 6996-7
"All humane things are subject to decay". The primacy of dullness, fr. MacFlecknoe. John Dryden. 6933-9
"All Hybla's honey, all that sweetnesse can". Steps to the temple, sels. Richard Crashaw. 6908-8
"All I ask is a night wind". Wish. Muriel F. Hochdorf. 6850-2
All ignorance toboggans into know. Edward Estlin Cummings. 6666-6
"All in a dreary April day". Inconstancy. Phoebe Cary. 6865-0;6969-X
"All in a garden green." Unknown. 6317-9
All in a lifetime. Edgar A. Guest. 6748-4
"All in a rainy hazel wood". Two lyrics. Marjorie L.C. Pickthall. 6785-9
All in all. Alice Cary. 6969-X
All in all. Edith (Bland) Nesbit. 7009-4
"All in an April wood". A song ("All"). Lizette Woodworth Reese. 6274-1
"All in the centre of the choir Bernardo's...". The funeral of the Count of Saldana. Unknown (Spanish). 6757-3
"All in the dark we grope along". Life. Ella Wheeler Wilcox. 6291-1
All in the day's work. Edgar A. Guest. 6748-4
All in the downs. Thomas Hood. 6026-9
"All in the early time". The dance of old age. Unknown (Algonquin Indian). 6864-2
All in the family. Berton Braley. 6853-7
"All in the gay and golden weather". Maid and man. Alice Cary. 6865-0;6969-X
"All in the mirk midnight when I was beside...". The tell-tales. Unknown (Greek). 6771-9
"All in the olden time". Kuloskap and Winpe; or, the master's first victory. Unknown (Algonquin Indian). 6864-2

All in the wind. R.E. Gibbs. 6118-4
"All in this pleasnat evening...". Unknown. 6334-9
"All is best, though we oft doubt",fr.Samson Agonistes. John Milton. 6933-9
"All is best...", fr. Samson agonistes. John Milton. 6334-9;6634-8
All is gold. Anna Akhmatova. 6546-5,6160-5
"All is over! fleet career". The last leap. Adam Lindsay Gordon. 6951-7,6784-0
"All June I bound the rose in sheaves". One way of love. Robert Browning. 6828-6
All is spirit and part of me. L. D'O. Walters. 6044-7
All is truth. Walt Whitman. 6560-0
All is vanity. James O'Neill. 6848-0
All is vanity. John Webster. 6150-8
'All is vanity, saith the preacher'. George Gordon, 6th Baron Byron. 6945-2
All is vanity, sels. Anne Finch, Countess of Winchilsea. 6472-8
All is well. Arthur Hugh Clough. 6828-6
All is well. Arthur Hugh Clough. 6110-9
All is well. Alfred Lord Tennyson. 6240-7
"All knobs and knuckles, hammer knees and...". Folk tale. Linda Pastan. 6803-0
All last night. Lascelles Abercrombie. 6210-5
All life moving to one measure. Wilfred Wilson Gibson. 6464-7
"All listlessly we float". Where shall we land? James Whitcomb Riley. 6992-4
"All lookes be pale, harts cold as stone" Thomas Campion. 6794-8
"All love that has not friendship for its base". Upon the sand. Ella Wheeler Wilcox. 6956-8
All lovely things. Christopher Morley. 6875-8
All mah sins been taken away. Unknown. 6594-5
All mankind are trees. Unknown. 6672-0
"All mankind by Love...", fr. Ode to music. Robert Bridges. 6487-6
"All men are born free, and..with equal rights". Slavery. Carlos Wilcox. 6752-2
"All men are equal in God's mighty plan". Abraham Lincoln. Leon Huhner. 6887-1
All men are free! Elliott Napier. 6784-0,6289-X
"'All men created equal' - black and bold". Monticello. Ruth H. Hausman. 6850-2
"All men must live the life in them". The ballad of Guy Moquet. Maurice Carpenter. 6895-2
"All morning long". Question. Le Baron Cooke. 6038-2
All mother. Eliza Sproat Turner. 6429-9,6321-7
All mountains. Hilda ("H.D.") Doolittle. 6253-9
"All my boasting friends". Unknown. 6364-9
"All my daily tasks were ended". The single head of wheat. Unknown. 7002-7
"All my feelin's in the spring". Me and Mary. James Whitcomb Riley. 6993-2
All my heart this night rejoices. Paul Gerhardt. 6337-3
"All my life I have been blind". Blind. Jean Milne Gower. 6836-7
"All my life is joy and pleasure". Fairy song. Felicia Dorothea Hemans. 6973-8
"All my love for my sweet". Song ("All my love"). John Hall Wheelock. 6897-9
All my luve, leave me not. Unknown. 6845-6
"All my past life is mine no more". Song ("All my"). John Wilmot, 2d Earl of Rochester. 6527-9
"All my past life is mine no more". John Wilmot, 2d Earl of Rochester. 6187-7
"All my plans/we cannot run". On the hospitalization of my daughter for diabetes. Lynne Saviatt. 6998-3
"All my world is glad today". Rhapsody of peonies. Sallie Garland Pippen. 6818-9
All nature danceth. William Henry Davies. 6935-5
"All nature is but art unknown to thee". Essay on man. Alexander Pope. 7014-0
"All nature seems at weowrk. Slugs leave...". Work without hope. Samuel Taylor Coleridge. 6828-6
"All night before the brink of death". The school at war. Sir Henry Newbolt. 6793-X
"All night by the shore". Edward Carpenter. 6997-5
"All night I muse, all day I cry." Unknown. 6317-9

"All night he galloped alone, in wild...". Alone with his work. Yannis Ritsos. 6758-1
"All night I sit and ponder". Dilemma. Viola Brothers Shore. 6817-0
"All night I've heard the marsh-frog's croak". An unfinished poem. Adam Lindsay Gordon. 6951-7
"All night in a cottage far". The vision of spring, 1916. Sir Henry Howarth Bashford. 7027-2
"All night long falling from wing-struck air". Elegy for a lost continent. Margaret R. Richter. 6979-7
"All night long rocked in my bed". No one is asleep even while dreaming. Michelle Roberts. 6870-7
"All night long they heard, in the house...". Avery. William Dean Howells. 7041-8
"All night long, by a distant bell". The window. Henry Van Dyke. 6961-4
"All night the booming minute gun". The wreck. Felicia Dorothea Hemans. 6973-8
"All night the boy from Cluny has lain in...". Long narrow roadway. Kim Maltman. 6767-0
"All night the chimes". The chimes. Richard Lawson Gales. 6950-9
All night the lone cicada. Sir Charles George Douglas Roberts. 6501-5,6115-X
"All night the waves of darkness roar". A stormy night. Robert Loveman. 6941-X
"All night under the moon," fr. For G. Wilfred Wilson Gibson. 6317-9
All night! Leon Baker. 6870-7
"All night, through Daisy's sleep, it seems". Daisy's valentines. Austin Dobson. 7272-7
All of her. Samuel L. Albert. 6388-8
All of roses. David Herbert Lawrence. 6301-2
"All of the boxes and cartons of glass". Business. Charles Grenville Hamilton. 6954-1
"All of the olden time". How Kuloskap was conquered by the babe. Unknown (Algonquin Indian). 6864-2
"All of the olden time!". How Kuloskap went whale-fishing. Unknown (Algonquin Indian). 6864-2
All of them. Unknown. 6403-5
All on one side. Harry Romaine. 7021-3
All or nothing. Bayard Taylor. 6802-2
"All other joy of life he strove to warm" George Meredith. 6828-6
"All other joys," fr. Modern love. George Meredith. 6656-9
"All other storms were playthings to this...". Storm. Louis Golding. 6782-4
All our griefs to tell. John Newton. 6065-X
All over the world. Geoffrey Johnson. 6257-1
"All over the world we sing of fame". Fame. James Herbert Morse. 6996-7
All passes into dust save deathless art alone. Erinna. 6102-8
"All people hearken and give care". Psalm 049. Bible. 6848-0
"All people that on earth do dwell". Psalm 100. Bible. 6848-0
"All perfect things are saddening in effect". Perfectness. Ella Wheeler Wilcox. 6956-8
"All power is in essence poetical" Eusebius of Tyre. 7014-0
All quiet along the Potomac. Ethel Lynn Beers. 6113-3,6340-3,6732-8,6219-9,6300-4,6484-1
All quiet along the Potomac tonight. Lamar Fontaine. 6074-9
"'All quiet along the Potomac', they say". The picket-guard. Ethel Lynn Beers. 6946-0
"'All quiet along the Potomac,' they say". The picket-guard. Ethel Lynn Beers. 6753-0
"All red with leaves Tatsuta's stream". Ariwara No Narihira. 6852-9
"All right, I've done something I shouldn't". To any wife, fr. Matrimonial melodies. Berton Braley. 6853-7
All rose before the aged apparition, fr. America. William Blake. 6106-0
"All round the sea wet shining nets were spread". Philip Bourke Marston. 6997-5
All ruin is the same. Emmanuel Litvinoff. 6666-6
All saints. Wyn Griffith. 6360-8
All saints. Alice L. Rostetter. 6847-2

ALL   30

All Saints' Day. Arthur Shearly Cripps. 6800-6
All Saints' Day. John Keble. 6543-0
"All science seems placed on high" Sir Francis Bacon. 7014-0
All serene. Nellie R. Nesselroade. 6662-3
"All service ranks the same". Song ("All service"). Robert Browning. 6315-2
"All shapes of beauty on this earth are laid". The words of Keats. Jeannette Sewell. 6847-2
All shrines are one. Hinton White. 6303-9
"All sights are fair to the recovered blind". Colonization of Africa. John Gardiner Calkins Brainard. 6752-2
"All silent now the clash of war...". 'Scipio'. Walter S. Keplinger. 6922-3
"All singers have shadows". The green singer. John Shaw Neilson. 6784-0
"All so late, you too heard those". In your sleep, sels. Vittorio Sereni. 6803-0
All sorts. Unknown. 6247-4
All Soul's Day. Siegfried Sassoon. 6532-5,6072-2
"All Soul's day. Rosamund Marriott ("Graham R. Tomson") Watson. 6274-1
All Soul's eve. Florence Kilpatrick Mixter. 6036-6
All Soul's night. Dora Sigerson Shorter. 6656-9
All souls. Liboria E. Romano. 6218-0
All souls. Katharine (Hinkson) Tynan. 6102-8
All Souls night. F.L. Montgomery. 6850-2
All Souls' night. Gertrude Huntington McGiffert. 6838-3
"All still, all silent, save the sobbing rush". Adelaide Anne Procter. 6997-5
"All strangest things the multitudinous years". Sophocles. 6435-3
"All summer I've worn a shocking hat". To Phyllis returned to town. MacGregor Jenkins. 7021-3
"All summer long the people knelt". At the president's grave. Richard Watson Gilder. 6946-0,6820-0
"All summer long, your crowding planes". To the aviators of Leaside and Armour Heights. James B. Dollard. 6796-4
"All summer the green that I let go...". When a tree turns yellow early. David McCord. 6761-1
All sung. Richard Le Gallienne. 6785-9
"All sweet and startled gravity". Promenade. John Galsworthy. 6888-X
"All tam w'en de leaf turn yeller". Antoine's song. Rowland Evans Robinson. 7030-2
All that 'lieve in Christian lay, worship every... Unknown. 6756-5
All that I ask. Bert Leston Taylor. 6274-1
"All that a man might ask thou hast given...". A petition. Robert Ernest Vernede. 7026-4
"All that can be witnessed from my window...". Winter in the garden. Edgar A. Guest. 6748-4
"All that I am is thine". A toi. Alys Hungerford. 6784-0
"All that is dearest to me thou didst give". England. Walter De La Mare. 6905-3
"All that is finished, finished, finished" Alexander Blok. 6103-6
All that is left. Basho (Matsuo Basho) 6665-8
All that is left. Basho (Matsuo Basho). 6665-8
"All that is nobly beautiful or true". Saint Joan: a. Herbert Edward Palmer. 6781-6
All that jazz. Yasmeen Jamal. 6870-7
All that summer. Lora Dunetz. 6388-8
"All that was euer ask't, by vow of Ioue". The first squire (2). Thomas Campion. 6794-8
All that was mortal. Sara Teasdale. 6781-6
"All that's bright must fade". Thomas Moore. 6980-0
All that's past. Walter De La Mare. 6477-9,6250-4,6150-8, 6464-7,6726-3,6508-2
"All the bells were ringing". The broken doll. Christina Georgina Rossetti. 6891-X
"All the bright hues from Eastern garlands...". Picture of the infant Christ with flowers. Felicia Dorothea Hemans. 6973-8
"All the buds and bees". May. Leigh Hunt. 6049-8,6385-3
All the children. Unknown. 6416-7
"All the dead kings came to me". The dead kings. Francis Ledwidge. 6812-X
"All the dog-wood blossoms are underneath the tree". Edna St. Vincent Millay. 6986-X
All the dry-veined watchers of the sky. Vernon Patterson. 6037-4
"All the earth's ores, unmixed with air & fire". Here is the world. Raymond Holden. 6761-1
"All the field is white with lace". Lace. Doris V. Lecky. 6850-2
"All the flowers dance for you". For a child. Eleanor Vinton. 6764-6
All the flowers of the spring. John Webster. 6182-6,6187-7
"All the fluttering wishes". Wishes. Adelaide Anne Procter. 6957-6
"All the here and all the there". Our two worthies. John Crowe Ransom. 7017-5
'All the hills and vales along'. Charles Hamilton Sorley. 6474-4
"All the house is sad to-day". Tuffy. Edgar A. Guest. 6869-3
"All the house was asleep". Sly Santa Claus. Mrs. S.C. Stone. 6807-3
"All the lights are gleaming where the towns..". Commencement: June 1929. Muriel F. Hochdorf. 6850-2
"All the long day the vapours played". The lifting of the muse. Emily Pauline ("Tekahionwake") Johnson. 6837-5
"All the maidens were merry and wed". Iannoula. Unknown (Greek). 6771-9
All the march of the things divine, fr. The Guru Granth. Puran Singh. 6732-8
"All the meadowlands were gay". A spring trouble. William Macdonald. 6873-1
All the merrier is that place. Unknown. 6756-5
"All the mystery of the ages". Moon mountain. Katherine Hunter Coe. 6906-1
'All the night and all the day,' fr. Fiametta. Agnes Mary F. ("Madame Duclaux") Robinson. 6770-0
"All the rest were full of knowledge...". Our lady's fool. Dorothy Eileen Sangster. 6761-1
All the rights she wants. Carl Spencer. 6675-5
All the rivers. Elizabeth Stuart Phelps. 6600-3
All the rivers. Elizabeth Stuart Phelps Ward. 7041-8
"All the running waves of eager life". Alfred Austin. 6997-5
All the same. Frederic Edward Weatherley. 6928-2
All the same in the end. Isaac Ross. 6273-3,6724-7
All the squires together. Thomas Campion. 6794-8
"All the stars, gold-footed, wander". Heinrich Heine. 6876-6
"All the striving, all the failing". Depression. Morris Rosenfeld. 7011-6
"All the sunlit fields are gay". Summer wind. William Roehrick. 6850-2
"All the thin shadows". Autumn evening in Serbia. Francis Ledwidge. 6812-X,7027-2
"All the things that call a man to the...". White magic. Berton Braley. 6853-7
"All the things that have been done...". Australia. Agnes Neale. 6768-9
"All the time my soul is calling". Whither. Alice Cary. 6969-X
"All the trees are sleeping, all winds...still". Hide and seek. Henry Van Dyke. 6961-4
"All the tulips by her yard/ Were warped...". Tulip blooms. Barbara Ruth Collins. 6799-9
"All the vision of springtime". Promise. Sara Ware Basset. 6798-0
"All the wide world now I sway". Aristophanes. 6435-3
"All the women tell me". Unknown (Greek) 6251-2
"All the world is bright". A madrigal. Frank Dempster Sherman. 7041-8
All the world's a stage. Palladas. 6435-3
All the world's a stage. Sir Walter Raleigh. 6436-1
"All the world's a stage", fr. As you like it. William Shakespeare. 6610-0
All the year round. Ellen Mackay Hutchinson Cortissoz. 6066-8
"All these hours she sits and counts". Passing feet. Phoebe Cary. 6969-X
"All these nights, all these traffic lights". Crossing with the light. Dwight Okita. 6790-5
"All things are bound together by a tie". The ond. Archag

Tchobanian. 6889-8
All things are current found. Henry David Thoreau. 6176-1
"All things are doubly fair". Art. Theophile Gautier. 7039-6,6879-0
"All things are wrought of melody". Unheard. Madison Cawein. 6889-8
All things be dear..., or The sad complaint of...people. Unknown. 6157-5
All things beautiful. John Keble. 6131-1,6449-3
"All things bright and beautiful". The creation. Cecil Frances Alexander. 6891-X
All things bright and beautiful. Cecil Frances Alexander. 6337-3,6638-0
All things come right. Reynale Smith Pickering. 6109-5
All things except myself I know. François Villon. 6652-6
All things flow. Charles R. Murphy. 6038-2
"All things have something more than barren use". Alexander Smith. 6238-5
"All things lie hushed and quiet". A serenade, fr. Kafir songs. Francis Carey ("Jan van Avond") Slater. 6800-6
All things love me. Unknown. 6629-1
"All things proceed as though the stage". At Sagamore hill. Edgar Lee Masters. 6995-9
All things shall pass away. Theodore Tilton. 7022-1
"All things thou bringest, Hesper...". Sappho. 6251-2
All things to all men. Robert J. Burdette. 6588-0
All things to all men. Theognis. 6435-3
"All things upon the blessed earth". A Christmas chant. John E. Barrett. 6840-5
All things wait upon thee. Christina Georgina Rossetti. 6239-3,6510-4
"All things wax old. What voice shall chase...". Stanzas ("All things"). Aubrey Thomas De Vere. 6980-0
All things will die. Alfred Lord Tennyson. 6977-0
"All this (said he) we know". Achilles shows himself in the battle by the ships. Homer. 6933-9
"All this day/you've pulled at my womb". Lunar eclipse. Jessica Scarbrough. 6870-7
All this is ended. Rupert Brooke. 6051-X
"All this night shrill canticleer". Chanticleer. William Austin. 6931-2
"All this night shrill chanticleer". Sun of righteousness. Unknown. 6756-5
All this time this song is best. Unknown. 6756-5
"All this will change: the slowly-waking trees". Sonnet ("All this"). Katharine Rebecca Adams. 7016-7
"All those sharp fancies, by down-lapsing...". A dream of fair women, sel. Alfred Lord Tennyson. 6958-4
"All those treasures that lie...". Slow movement. William Carlos Williams. 6897-9
"All thoughts, all creeds, all dreams are true". Oi peovres. Alfred Lord Tennyson. 6977-0
"All thoughts, all passions". Love. Samuel Taylor Coleridge. 6315-2
"All thro' the breathing night there seemed...". A Venetian night. Hugo von Hofmannsthal. 7039-6
All through that year. N.K. Cruickshank. 6475-2
"All through the castle of high-bred ease". The princess's finger-nail. Ella Wheeler Wilcox. 6863-4
"All through the dark before dawn." May C. ([Mary] Gillington) Byron. 6720-4
"All through the day, in the shadows". The song of the hammock. Pax P. Hibben. 6983-5
"All through the long and dreary night". Udaisho Michitsuna No Haha. 6852-9
"All through the never-ending night". Sun-ye. 6852-9
"All through the smiling, resting land". The sword. Helen Booth. 6923-1
"All through the troubled night the service...". Service stars. Mabel Kingsley Richardson. 7014-0
All too slowly. Lucia Trent. 6144-3
"All true glory rests". The power of virtue. William Wordsworth. 6980-0
All turns into yesterday. Unknown. 6881-2
"All under the leaves, the leaves of life". The seven virgins. Unknown. 6931-2
"All up and down New England streets". The old guard. Marguerite Emilio Buxton. 6764-6
"All victory is struggle, using chance". Progress.

Unknown. 6916-9
"All vision fades, but splendor does not die." Samuel Roth. 6393-4
"All was dark, the city slumbered". Daybreak. Hazel May Oyler. 6799-9
"All we ask is to be let alone". Henry Howard Brownell. 6402-7
All we do. Unknown. 6237-7
All well. Horatius Bonar. 6271-7
All will be well. Amory Hare. 6619-4
"All wind and rain, the clouds fled fast...". The 'Orion's' figurehead at Whitehall. Unknown. 7031-0
"All women are lovely and radiantly fair". Magazine girls. Edgar A. Guest. 6862-6
"All women born are so perverse". Triolet ("All women"). Robert Bridges. 6487-6,6770-0
"All wordly shapes shall melt in gloom". The last man. Thomas Campbell. 6075-7,6086-2,6219-9,6648-8,6600-3, 6910
"All words are born of Janus". Duplicity. David Ray. 6761-1
"All worldly dreams I would resign". If some true maiden's love were mine. Samuel Minturn Peck. 6770-0
"All ye that pass along love's trodden way". La vita nuova, sels. Dante Alighieri. 7039-6
"All ye that passe by this holy place". A second epitaph. Unknown. 6881-2
"All ye who fought since England was a name". To the men who have died for England. Unknown. 7031-0
"All yee forsaken louers come & pitty my distress." Unknown. 6563-5
All yellow. Unknown. 6049-8
"All yesterday the thought of you was resting". Day dawn. Emily Pauline ("Tekahionwake") Johnson. 6837-5
All you that are good fellows. Unknown. 6756-5
"All you that are too fond of wine". Lieutenant Luff. Thomas Hood. 6974-6
"All you that e'er tasted of swatful-hall beer". The country wedding. Unknown. 6874-X
"All you that in this house be here". Old Christmas. Unknown. 6806-5
All you that in this house be here. Unknown. 6756-5
"All you whose eyes would learn to weep...". Funeral elegies, sels. Francis Quarles. 6908-8
"All you young men, I pray attend...". The Irish sailor. Unknown. 6858-8
"All you've got to do is to fuck a great...". How to be a great writer. Charles Bukowski. 6998-3
"All young men should take note of the case". Limerick:"All young men should take note of the case." M.B. Thornton. 6308-X
All your fortunes we can tell ye, fr. Masque of gipsies. Ben Jonson. 6125-7
"All's but naught", fr. Antony and Cleopatra. William Shakespeare. 6339-X
"All's dust, all's laughter...". Glycon. 6251-2
All's for the best. Martin Farquhar Tupper. 6543-0
All's for the best. Unknown. 6910-X
"All's over, then: does truth sound bitter". The lost mistress. Robert Browning. 6828-6
All's to gain. Anne Whitney. 6006-4
All's well. Francis William Bourdillon. 7031-0
All's well. William Allen Butler. 6271-7
All's well. Thomas Dibdin. 6302-0;6385-3
All's well. Harriet McEwen Kimball. 6385-3,6600-3
All's well. William A. Quayle. 6337-3,6461-2
All's well. Unknown. 6407-8,6636-4
All's well. David Atwood Wasson. 6102-8,6600-3,6076-5
All's well. John Greenleaf Whittier. 6437-X
All's well that ends well. Unknown. 6089-7
All, all a-lonely. Unknown. 6125-7
"All, all of a piece throughout." John Dryden. 6125-7
"All, all that once was mine is mine for ever" Afanasi Fet. 6103-2
"All-ador'd, all glorious...". Robert Bridges. 6487-6
An all-around intellectual man. Thomas Masson. 6417-5
The all-golden. James Whitcomb Riley. 6993-2
All-Hallowe'en. Thomas Dickson Finletter. 6936-3
All-Hallowe'en. Mary E. (Freeman) Wilkins. 6965-7
All-Hallows eve. Francis Ledwidge. 6812-X

ALL-LOVING,

The **all-loving**, fr. An epistle. Robert Browning. 6337-3
All-over love. Abraham Cowley. 6563-5
All-Saints. Edmund Yates. 6089-7
"**All-worshipp'd** gold! thou mighty mystery!". R.S.S. William Cowper. 6814-6
The **Allagash** Falls. Henrietta M. Dow. 6894-4
Allah. Siegfried A. Mhalman. 6102-8
"**Allan** Ian Og Macleod of Raasay". Macleod's lament. Neil Munro. 7029-9
Allan Percy. Caroline Elizabeth Sarah Sheridan Norton. 6271-7
Allan, Catherine
   The rabbit on the wall. 6131-1
Allan, Robert
   To a linnet. 6180-X
Allard, Leo J.
   This I know. 6799-9
"**Allas** the wo! Allas, the peynes stronge." Geoffrey Chaucer. 6317-9
Allatoona. Samuel H.M. Byers. 6946-0
"**Alle** that beth of herte trewe". The death of King Edward I. Unknown. 6881-2
Allegiance. Zoe A. Tilghman. 6397-7
Allegory. Thomas Hood. 6974-6
Allegory. Howard Mumford Jones. 6347-0
Allegory of the vine... Alfhild Wallen. 6857-X
Allegory of torment. Pablo de (Carlos Diaz Loyola) Rokha. 6759-X
An **allegory** on man. Thomas Parnell. 6975-4
An **allegory**. Percy Bysshe Shelley. 6828-6
Allegra agonistes. Grace Fallow Norton. 6897-9
Allegro. McM [pseud]. 6817-0
"**Allelluia** to God! Missouri is free!". Jan. 11, 1865, 3 o'clock p.m. James Abraham Martling. 6952-5
Alleluai, alleluai, alleluai, now sing we. Unknown. 6756-5
Allelui, allelui. Unknown. 6756-5
Alleluia. William White. 6868-5
Alleluia! aleluia! Deo patri sit gloria. Unknown. 6756-5
Alleluia, alleluia, alleluia..Deo patri sit gloria. Unknown. 6756-5
Alleluia, alleluia, de virgine Maria. Unknown. 6756-5
Allen, Alice E.
   Crocus bells. 6048-X
   Dance of the snowflakes. 6147-8
   Life's common things. 6654-2
Allen, Cecil Maurice Bowra and G. (tr.)
   The moving rocks. Apollonius Rhodius. 6435-3
Allen, Charles Fletcher
   Inter vias. 6836-7
Allen, E.C.A.
   Now they'll have enough of food. 6772-7
Allen, Elisabeth Channing
   This I remember. 6750-6
Allen, Elizabeth Akers
   "Blush, happy maiden, when you feel". 6226-1,6508-2
   Endurance. 6219-9
   Four words. 6066-8, 6226-1
   In a garret. 6300-4
   My dearling. 6309-8
   My ship. 6219-9
   Rock me to sleep. 6219-9,6431-0,6304-7
   Sea-birds. 6309-8
   True. 6889-8
   The willow. 6424-8
Allen, Ernest Bourner
   A hymn of peace. 6337-3
Allen, George
   In your life we shall live. 6761-1
   Return to war. 6761-1
Allen, George (tr.)
   Amor omnipotens. Apollonius Rhodius, 6435-3
   Andromache's wedding. Sappho, 6435-3
   The best memorial. Agathias Scholasticus, 6435-3
   A charioteer. Unknown (Greek), 6435-3
   Chorus: The kings of Troy, fr. Andromache. Euripides, 6665-8
   Croesus. Bacchylides, 6435-3
   A dedication to Athene. Archias, 6435-3
   Dirge, fr. Supplices. Euripides, 6435-3
   Electra and Orestes, fr. Electra. Euripides, 6435-3
   Eros and his mother. Apollonius Rhodius, 6435-3
   Eteocles and Polynices, fr. Phoenissae. Euripides, 6435-3
   Europa and the bull. Moschus, 6435-3
   Freedom. Palladas, 6435-3
   "From Zeus begin we, never nameless we". Aratus, 6435-3
   The furies, fr. Orestes. Euripides, 6435-3
   His anthology. Meleager, 6435-3
   His death, fr. Hippolytus. Euripides, 6435-3
   Hylas. Apollonius Rhodius, 6435-3
   Jason's sowing and reaping. Apollonius Rhodius, 6435-3
   The kings of Troy, fr. Andromache. Euripides, 6435-3
   Lament for Adonis. Bion, 6435-3
   Maidens at rest. Chaeremon, 6435-3
   Medea's dream. Apollonius Rhodius, 6435-3
   Medea's hesitation. Apollonius Rhodius, 6435-3
   Medea's parting words. Apollonius Rhodius, 6435-3
   The meeting. Apollonius Rhodius, 6435-3
   Mocaria and Iolaus, fr. Heraclidae. Euripides, 6435-3
   "My Constantine, why sleep in bronze? Awaken". Unknown, 6435-3
   "On Dido's famous image, friend, you stare". Unknown, 6435-3
   Orpheus. Phanocles, 6435-3
   A painting of Dido. Unknown (Greek), 6435-3
   Polyxena, fr. Hecuba. Euripides, 6435-3
   Primitive man. Moschion, 6435-3
   Remorse. Apollonius Rhodius, 6435-3
   A riddle, fr. Ichneutae. Sophocles, 6435-3
   The sailing of the argo. Apollonius Rhodius, 6435-3
   The trial of the dog. Aristophanes, 6435-3
   When justice dwelt on earth. Aratus, 6435-3
   A young mother. Dioscorides, 6435-3
   Youth, fr. Hercules Furens. Euripides, 6435-3
Allen, Grant
   A ballade of evolution. 6770-0,6875-8
   A prayer ("A crowned caprice"). 6301-2,6071-4
Allen, Hervey
   Beyond debate. 6326-8
   Black roses. 6037-4
   The blind man. 6542-2,6628-3
   Carolina spring song. 6076-5,6102-8
   Chicken blood. 6217-2
   Christmas epithalamium. 6746-8
   Dead men, to a metaphysician. 6036-6
   Funeral at high tide. 6326-8
   Gargantua. 6076-5,6102-8,6462-1.6464-2
   La Fayette's lands. 6421-3
   The leaping poll. 6037-4
   Middleton garden. 6649-6
   Northern earth mood. 6039-0
   Palmetto town. 6265-2,6326-8,6431-0
   The priest and the pirate. 6326-8
   Refuge. 6037-4
   Saga of Leif the lucky, sels. 6833-2
   Shadows. 6036-6
   Southward Sidonian Hanno. 6833-2
   Walls. 6037-4
   Whim alley. 6039-0,6071-4,6153-2
   The wingless victory. 6542-2
Allen, James Lane
   On the mantlepiece. 6034-X
Allen, Leslie Holdsworth
   Memnon. 6784-0
   The reaper. 6349-7,6384-5
Allen, Lucy Branch
   The bird man. 6510-4
Allen, Lyman Whitney
   The coming of his feet. 6337-3
   The people's king. 6463-9
   The stroke of justice. 6524-4
   The voice of destiny. 6524-4
Allen, Margaret Buller
   The new bonnet. 6937-1
Allen, Marie Louise
   Angels. 6906-1
   Dryads. 6906-1
   Fountain. 6906-1
   Intuition. 6906-1
   Secret ways. 6906-1

Symbol. 6906-1
To one who is silent. 6906-1
Allen, Mary Dell
The night song. 6818-9
Allen, Pattie
The old mill. 6397-7
Allen, Paula Gunn
Grandmother. 7005-1
Kopis'taya (a gahtering of spirits) 7005-1
Pocahontas to her English husband, John Rolfe. 7005-1
Powwow 79, durango. 7005-1
Recuerdo. 7005-1
Allen, Percy (tr.)
A mystic song. Unknown (French), 6730-1
Allen, Sara Van Alstyne
The children's hour. 6761-1
Sweeter than rain. 6761-1
The zoo in the city. 6979-7
Allen, T.F. Higham and G. (tr.)
Medea betrayed. Apollonius Rhodius, 6435-3
"Now hear the old rule". Aristophanes, 6435-3
Allen, William Boyd
Thalatta. 6833-2
Allen-a-Dale. Sir Walter Scott. 6075-7,6102-8,6136-2,6290-3,6498-1,6459 ,6502-3,6504-X,6602-X,6732-8,6086-2, 6110 ,6438-8,6219-9,6639-9
Allenby enters Jerusalem! Stephen Chalmers. 7014-0
Aller, Katharine L.
God of a universe within whose bounds. 6337-3
Allerton, Ellen P.
Beautiful things. 6461-2
Allestry, Jacob
What art thou, love? 6563-5
Alley cat. Frank Stevens. 6120-6
An **alley** cat. Nancy Byrd Turner. 6780-8
An **alley** cat. Nancy Byrd Turner. 6120-6,6464-7
Alley, Rewi (tr.)
Under the frontier post. Wang Chang-Ling, 6125-7
War. Li Po, 6125-7
The white horse. Tu Fu, 6125-7
Allgood, Joseph
Uncle Pete's plea. 6924-X
Allhusen, Beatrice
From Bosrah. 7031-0
In the desert. 6800-6
The **alliance** of education and government. Thomas Gray. 6152-4
Allies. George Edward Woodberry. 6032-3
"**Alligator,** hedgehog, anteater, bear". Unknown. 6059-5
The **alligator.** Beatrice Ravenel. 6326-8,6628-3
Alling, Kenneth Slade
Beauty. 6037-4
February thaw. 6036-6
First ice. 6036-6
On the passing of the last fire horse from Manhattan Island . 6510-4
Pebbles. 6038-2
Portrait of the artist in death. 6072-2
Return. 6039-0
Summer night. 6036-6
This flesh. 6039-0
To a birch tree. 6039-0
To a woman. 6037-4
To one who asked. 6037-4
The unscarred fighter remembers France. 6036-6
Wind, wind. 6653-4
Allingham, William
Abbey Asaroe. 6930-4
The abbot of Inisfalen. 6079-X,6614-3
Across the sea. 6658-5
Aeolian harp. 6090-0,6438-8
After sunset. 7015-9
Autumnal sonnet. 7015-9
The bird. 6438-8
The bubble. 6930-4
Day and night songs. 6656-9
A day dream's reflection. 6997-5
A day'dream's reflection. 7015-9
Death deposed. 6930-4
The dirty old man. 6358-6,6512-0,6927-4

A dream. 6090-0,6102-8,6383-7,6153-2,6656-9,6648
The fairies. 6301-2,6421-3,6454-X,6543-0,6638-0,6090-0, 6133-8,6271-7,6328-4,6437-X,6534 ,6131-1,6219-9,6135-4,6125-7,6383-7,6639 ,6102-8,6104-4,6114-1,6252-0, 6656-9
The fairy folk. 6368-3,6424-8,6456-6,6614-3
The faithless knight. 6518-X
Four ducks on a pond. 6052-8,6090-0,6102-8,6368-3,6396-9,6660
Half-waking. 6660-7
Homeward bound. 6660-7
The lepracaun or fairy shoemaker. 6090-0
Lovely Mary Donnelly. 6271-7,6543-0,6656-9,6658-5,6438-8,6219
The lover and birds. 6437-X
The lupracaun, or fairy shoemaker. 6930-4
The maids of Elfin-Mere. 6518-X
A memory. 6437-X
The milkmaid. 6518-X
The mill. 6125-7
Morning. 6438-8
The nobleman's wedding. 6518-X
The pilot's daughter. 6438-8
Robin redbreast. 6114-1,6131-1,6424-8,6449-3,6639-9, 6133-8,6271-7,6552-X,6219-9,6739-9,6638
The sailor. 6133-8,6438-8,6656-9
St. Margaret's Eve. 6518-X
Serenade. 6658-5
Song. 6658-5
A swing song. 6454-X,6512-0
These little songs. 6301-2
The touchstone. 6090-0,6438-8,6304-7,6613-5,6219-9
Venus of the needle. 6278-4,6787-5
A wife. 6219-9
The winding banks of Erne. 6858-8
Wishing. 6502-3,6114-1,6131-1,6424-8,6456-6,6638-0,6639
The witch-bride. 6518-X
Would I knew! 6980-0
Allinson, Brent Dow
Christmas, 1917. 6542-2
Harvard declares war. 6542-2
Hymn of Halsted Street. 6954-1
'One world.' 6337-3
Prayer in the trenches. 6051-X
Allison Gross. Unknown. 6185-0
Allison, Annye Lewis
Aunt Caroline. 6799-9
Cheer. 6818-9
Allison, David Paul
A Scot's lament. 7001-9
Allison, Drummond
The brass horse. 6210-5
Dedication. 6210-5
My sister Helen. 6210-5
Allison, Flora Cecile
The solitude of space. 6799-9
Allison, Joy
Which loved [her] best? 6131-1,6449-3
Allison, Margaret (tr.)
Remembrance. Francisco Castillo Najera, 6482-5
Suicide? Elias Nandino, 6482-5
Surgical art versus beauty. Rudolfo Figueroa, 6482-5
Allison, Richard
Cherry-ripe. 6652-6
Allison, Richard (tr.)
Psalm 003. Bible, 6848-0
Allison, William Talbot
At a toboggan meet. 6591-0,6592-2
Cartier arrives at Stadacona. 6591-0,6592-2
The rum maniac. 6403-5
Ships of the north. 7035-3
Sic transit gloria. 6796-4
Allison, Young Ewing
The dead man's song. 6300-4
Derelict. 6107-9
Alliteration, or The siege of Belgrade. Unknown. 6125-7
Allnut, Alice Duer
A bread and butter letter. 6653-4
Allonby, Margaret
A book for Christmas. 6788-3

Eurydice. 6788-3
For Sheila. 6788-3
Lustration of the winter tree, sels. 6788-3
O Theophilus. 6788-3
Reflection. 6788-3
Alloquy. Amabel King. 6224-5
Allott, Kenneth
Cheshire cat. 6379-9
Departure platform. 6379-9
"**Allotted** a four-by-four square". Sapling. Yvette Johnson. 7024-8
Allouette. Robert Service. 6159-1
Allston, Joseph Blyth
Stack arms. 7017-5
Allston, Washington
Address of the sylph of autumn to the bard. 6752-2
America to Great Britain. 6300-4,6752-2
Boyhood. 6219-9,6271-7
The paint king. 6752-2
An **allusion** to Horace the 10th satyr... John Wilmot, 2d Earl of Rochester. 6562-7
Allwood, Brian
No laws. 6666-6
Alma. Sir Franklin Lushington. 6046-3
Alma. Richard Chenevix Trench. 6793-X
Alma Tadema, L.
A little song. 6937-1
Alma mater. Thomas Edward Brown. 6809-X
Alma mater. Robert Dye. 6527-9
Alma mater. Louis J. Magee. 7004-3
Alma mater. Sir Arthur Quiller-Couch. 6437-X,6477-9
Alma mater. Unknown. 6156-7,6718-2
Alma perdida. Valery Larbaud. 6351-9
Alma redemptoris mater. Hermanus Contractus. 6282-2
Alma redemptoris mater. Unknown. 6756-5
The **almack's** adieu. William Makepeace Thackeray. 6802-2
Almae matres. Andrew Lang. 6269-5,6508-2
The **almanack** for 1733, sels. Nathaniel Ames. 6753-0
The **almanack** for 1738, sels. Nathaniel Ames. 6753-0
The **almanack** for 1743, sels. Nathaniel Ames. 6753-0
Almansor. Heinrich Heine. 6484-1
Almanzor and Almahide, sels. John Dryden. 6562-7
Almeria. Ibn Safar. 6362-4
Almeria. Pablo (Neftali Ricardo Reyes Basualto) Neruda. 6665-8
Almighty God! Thomas Moore. 6848-0
Almighty Lord, with one accord. W. Woolsey Stryker. 6337-3
"**Almighty** crowd, thou shorten'st all dispute". Vox populi, fr. The medall. John Dryden. 6933-9
"**Almighty** Father! let thy lowly child". A poet's prayer. Ebenezer Elliott. 6934-7
"**Almighty** God! when round thy shrine". Almighty God! Thomas Moore. 6848-0
"**Almighty** God, fader of hevene". A prayer to the Trinity. Unknown. 6881-2
"**Almighty** king! whose wond'rous hand". Grace and providence. William Cowper. 6814-6
"**Almighty** wisdom made the land". The sea is his. Edward Sandford Martin. 6833-2
Almon Keefer. James Whitcomb Riley. 6128-1
Almond blossoms ("'Tis not summer yet...") Unknown. 6720-4
"The **almond** tree has bought herself a dress". Spring & co. Jorge Carrera Andrade. 6759-X
The **almond** tree. Georgios Drossinis. 6352-7
Almond, wild almond. Herbert Trench. 6877-4
Almond-blossom. Sir Edwin Arnold. 6219-9
Almost. Vesle Fenstermaker. 6857-X
Almost a man. Emma Celia & Lizzie J. Rook. 6137-0
"**Almost** alone in/death". Jean-Louis. David Slater. 6998-3
"**Almost** any man can say it". On Christmas eve. Judd Mortimer Lewis. 6807-3
"**Almost** any rainbow". Rainbow-room. Lillian Everts. 6750-6
"**Almost** I feel the pulse-beat of the ages". A shelf of old books. Grace Noll Crowell. 6761-1
Almost attained. John Girdler. 6836-7
Almost beyond endurance. James Whitcomb Riley. 6277-6,6605-4
Almost everybody is dying here: only a few actually... Daniel Berrigan. 6870-7
Almost time. Unknown. 6373-X

Alms. Edna St. Vincent Millay. 6320-9
Alms. Josephine Preston Peabody. 6476-0;6607-0
The **alms** house. George Crabbe. 6378-0
Alms in autumn. Rose Fyleman. 6044-7,6374-8,6466-3,6253-0
Almswomen. Edmund Blunden. 6506-6,6250-4
Almy, Frederic
To Vice-President Roosevelt. 6995-9
Alnwick castle. Fitz-Greene Halleck. 6302-0-6385-3,6735-2, 6288-1,6219-9
The **aloe.** Laurence (Adele Florence Nicolson) Hope. 6856-1
"**Aloft** in the gray tower". The bell of old north. S.X. E.. 6983-5
"**Aloft** on footless levels of the night". Night flying. Frederick Victor Branford. 7014-0
Aloha. Lulu Bradley Cram. 6764-6
Aloha. William Griffith. 6478-7,6607-0
Alone. Kit Blomer. 6883-9
Alone. Robert J. Burdette. 6260-1
Alone. Alice Cary. 6969-X
Alone. Walter De La Mare. 6125-7
Alone. John Chipman Farrar. 6607-0
Alone. Robert Finch. 6021-8,6446-9
Alone. Mary Garbarini. 6789-1
Alone. Hermann Hesse. 6643-7
Alone. Leigh Mitchell Hodges. 7019-1
Alone. Alexander Laing. 7019-1
Alone. Dorothy Leonard. 6039-0
Alone. Gertrude Huntington McGiffert. 6838-3
Alone. Edgar Allan Poe. 6176-1,6333-0,6299-7,6250-4
Alone. Phillips Stewart. 7041-8
Alone. Louise Goodson Tennyson. 6316-0
Alone. Jamie Tobias. 6883-9
Alone. Unknown. 6902-9
Alone. John Hall Wheelock. 6897-9
Alone - with one fair star. Mathilde Blind. 6747-6
"**Alone** above the sea, alone/Above the land...". Alone. Leigh Mitchell Hodges. 7019-1
"**Alone** amid the battle-din untouched". Courage. Dyneley Hussey. 7026-4
"**Alone** and ever weary with dark care". Francesco Petrarch. 6325-X
"**Alone** by a starless sea". Dance motive. Percy MacKaye. 6959-2
Alone by the bay. Louise Chandler Moulton. 6240-7
Alone by the lake. Verner von Heidenstam. 6045-5
"**Alone** he soars, this eagle of our time". 'Lindbergh flies alone' Cornelia Fulton Crary. 7019-1
"**Alone** I drift upon a sea of sound". Song ("Alone"). Sara Ware Basset. 6798-0
"**Alone** I sit and remember". Sound. Margaret Haynes Foster. 7016-7
"**Alone** I walked the ocean strand". A name in the sand. Hannah Flagg Gould. 6912-6
Alone in Arcady. Clinton Scollard. 6875-8
"**Alone** in desert dreary". In the wilderness. Morris Rosenfeld. 7011-6
"**Alone** in Rome. Why, Rome is lonely too". Written at Rome. Ralph Waldo Emerson. 6753-0
"**Alone** in his own cabin". Alfred Noyes. 6298-9
Alone in spring. Caroline Giltinan. 6619-4,6034-X,6326-8
Alone in the big town she dreams. Frank (Michael O'Donovan) O'Connor. 6779-4,6096-X
"**Alone** in the desert sand". The kiss of Allah. Celestin Pierre Cambiaire. 6826-X
"**Alone** in the dreary, pitiless street". Nobody's child. Phila H. Case. 6565-1,6964-9,6554-6
"**Alone** in the hot sun". The song maker. Kingsley Fairbridge. 6788-3
Alone into the mountain. Katharine Lee Bates. 6144-3,6337-3
"**Alone** on a hillock brown-tufted". Edgar Allen Poe: Little Miss Muffet. Charles Powell. 6982-7
"**Alone** on Lykaion since man hath been". Mt. Lykaion. Trumbull Stickney. 6754-9
Alone on the hill. Frederick R. McCreary. 6036-6
"**alone** on the hill-top,/Sadly and silently". Song for Macleod of Macleod. Mary Macleod. 6873-1
"**Alone** on the white earth beneath her". Eternity. William Sydney Thayer. 7014-0
"**Alone** one noon on a sheet of igneous rock". Myths. Guy

Butler. 6788-3
"**Alone** sat Hagar in the wild". To Jane. Rufus Wilmot Griswold. 7030-2
"**Alone** she sate by the hearth-place biding". The bride's slippers. David Stefansson fra Fagraskogi. 6854-5
"**Alone** stands the willow on a rock above...". The sea willow. Jovan Ducic. 6765-4
"**Alone** they walked - their fingers knit...". The lost path. James Whitcomb Riley. 6992-4
"**Alone** through gloomy forest-shades". The fall of D'Assas. Felicia Dorothea Hemans. 6973-8
"**Alone** walking". Wishing my death. Unknown. 6881-2
Alone with his work. Yannis Ritsos. 6758-1
Alone with my conscience. Unknown. 6260-1
"**Alone** with natue's breathing things". The royal aspects of the earth. John B.L. Warren, 3d Baron De Tabley. 7020-5
"**Alone** within my house I sit". My dream of dreams. Alice Cary. 6865-0;6969-X
Alone! Stark alone! Harriet Hamilton Cowell. 6799-9
"**Alone**, alone on the mountains, the". Jephtha's daughter. Rose Terry Cooke. 6848-0
"**Alone**, alone, let me wander alone". Fallow. Charles Mackay. 6980-0
"**Alone**, as was her wont, she sat...". Count Alarcos and the infanta Solisa. Unknown (Spanish). 6757-3
"**Alone**, I wait, till her twilight gate". Reverie: Zahir-u-Din. Laurence (Adele Florence Nicolson) Hope. 6856-1
"**Alone**, upon a summer's eve". Swansong on the moorlands. Steingrimur Thorsteinsson. 6854-5
"**Along** a backroad to Oregon, leaving". Highway 299 Gerald Cable. 6855-3
"**Along** a mile of mud the tide". The horseshoes. Robert P. Tristram Coffin. 7040-X
"**Along** before Marchmeeting day". Looking over Vermont town resorts. Daniel L. Cady. 6988-6
"**Along** dim lanes lit only by the stars". Wild geese go over. Edwin Carlile Litsey. 6750-6
"**Along** in November, when chill was the weather". The twin ballots. Unknown. 6928-2
Along the beach, fr. James Lee's wife. Robert Browning. 6655-0
"**Along** the blushing borders, bright with dew". Spring flowers, fr. The seasons (Spring). James Thomson. 6932-0
"**Along** the country roads there grow". Samuel Hoffenstein. 6817-0
"**Along** the crowded streets I walk and think". Pulvis et umbra. Agnes Mary F. ("Madame Duclaux") Robinson. 6770-0
"**Along** the east, where late the dark impended". Morning. Bayard Taylor. 6976-2
Along the field. Alfred Edward Housman. 6508-2
"**Along** the fields we came by." Alfred Edward Housman. 6430-2
"**Along** the garden terrace, under which," fr. Modern love. George Meredith. 6659-3
"**Along** the grassy lane one day". The special darling. Alice Cary. 6969-X
Along the highway. Ethel Turner. 6042-0
"**Along** the hot and endless road". His rubies: told by Valgovind. Laurence (Adele Florence Nicolson) Hope. 6856-1
"**Along** the ice I see her fly". The skater belle. Samuel Minturn Peck. 7035-3
"**Along** the line of smoky hills". Indian summer. William Wilfred Campbell. 6021-8,6795-6
"**Along** the margin-sand large foot-marks went". Hyperion, sel. John Keats. 6958-4
Along the noisy streets. Alexander Pushkin. 6879-0
"**Along** the outposts of time's stately march". St. Albans. Sarah Ann Watson. 7030-2
"**Along** the Rand in eighty-five". Johannesburg. William Plomer. 6788-3
Along the road. Douglas Mackintosh. 7016-7
Along the Wallawhatoola. Mary Stuart Wamsley. 6799-9
"**Along** the rosy cloud light steals and...". The black panther. Charles Marie Leconte de Lisle. 6873-1
"**Along** the seaweed margined shore". Along the way. Joshua Freeman Crowell. 6798-0

"**Along** the serried coast the southerly raves". Sea-grief. Dowell O'Reilly. 6784-0
"**Along** the shaded, lone concession way". The perfume of the sods. Robert Kirkland Kernighan. 6797-2
"**Along** the shore the slimy brine-pits yawn". The witch's whelp. Richard Henry Stoddard. 6753-0,6753-0,6300-4
"**Along** the slopes of an ancient hill". The Christmas light. Frank Walcott Hutt. 6807-3
"**Along** the starlit Seine went music swelling". Pauline, fr. Records of woman. Felicia Dorothea Hemans. 6973-8
"**Along** the sunlit Nepperhan". Andre passes. G.S. B.. 6817-0
"**Along** the sunny lane". Idyl, fr. In Tuscany. Cora Fabri. 6876-6
"**Along** the turner turnpike at a rest stop...". Poem near midway truck stop. Lance Henson. 7005-1
"**Along** the valley's narrow gorge". How the fifty-first took the bridge. Jeff. H. Nones. 6923-1
Along the way. James Buckham. 6303-9
Along the way. Joshua Freeman Crowell. 6798-0
Along the way. John S. Thomson. 6433-7
"**Along** the wayside path she comes". One of many. Minnie D. Bateham. 6928-2
"**Along** the Woodford road there comes a noise". Sonnet ("Along the Woodford road"). Thomas Hood. 6974-6
Along the wind. Chard Powers Smith. 6619-4
Along this front. James Herbert Morse. 6997-5
"**Along** this secret and forgotten road". A forest path in winter. Archibald Lampman. 7035-3
Alons au bois le may cueillir. Charles, Duc d' Orleans. 6850-2,7039-6
Alonzo the brave and the fair Imogene. Matthew Gregory Lewis. 6406-X,6086-2,6219-9,6518-X
Alonzo the brave, and the fair Imogene. Unknown. 6554-6
Aloof. Christina Georgina Rossetti. 6437-X
"**Aloof**, aloof, and come no near". The sea mark. Captain Smith. 7017-5
Alp's decision. George Gordon, 6th Baron Byron. 6621-6
Alpenjager's lied. Johann C. Friedrich von Schiller. 6252-0
Alpermann, Joan
A spring message. 6368-3
Alpha and Omega, fr. two sonnets. Kathryn Bruchholz Thomson. 6270-9
Alpha the dog. Robert Sward. 6767-0
Alphabet. Susan Fromberg Schaeffer. 6803-0
Alphabet antics. Carolyn Wells. 6882-0
Alphabet of inanimates. Carolyn Wells. 6882-0
Alphabet of quotations. Unknown. 6530-9
Alphabet of summer. Mrs. J.M. Dana. 6715-8
Alphabet verse. Unknown. 6724-7
An **alphabetical** wooing. Unknown. 6724-7
Alpheus
"Lost now are the homes...". F.L. Lucas (tr.). 6251-2
"Still we behold Troy city...". F.L. Lucas (tr.). 6251-2
Alphonsa, Mother Mary
Impress of the Crucifix. 6285-7
Alpine descent, fr. The prelude. William Wordsworth. 6726-3
The **alpine** flowers. Lydia Huntley Sigourney. 6752-2
Alpine heights. Friedrich Adolf Krummacher. 6302-0;6385-3
The **Alpine** horn. Felicia Dorothea Hemans. 6973-8
The **alpine** hospital, fr. The prelude. William Wordsworth. 6958-4
Alpine hunter on an opposite crag, fr. Songs of Lucerne. Johann C. Friedrich von Schiller. 6749-2
Alpine minstrelsy. Johann C. Friedrich von Schiller. 6142-7
An **alpine** picture. Thomas Bailey Aldrich. 6439-6,6749-2,
The **Alpine** sheep. Maria White Lowell. 6600-3
The **Alpine** shepherd. Felicia Dorothea Hemans. 6973-8
An **Alpine** village. Anne Goodwin Winslow. 6326-8
The **Alps** at daybreak. Samuel Rogers. 6749-2
The **Alps** in summer. John Addington Symonds. 6749-2
The **Alps** in summer. William Wordsworth. 6749-2
The **Alps** in winter. John Addington Symonds. 6749-2
The **Alps**. Oliver Goldsmith. 6749-2
The **Alps**. James Montgomery. 6749-2

ALPS

The **Alps**. Bryan Waller ("Barry Cornwall") Procter. 6749-2
The **Alps**. William Wordsworth. 6484-1
Alqamah
   His camel. Sir Charles Lyall (tr.). 7039-6
Already. Stephen Spender. 6209-1
"**Already** I grow weary thinking how". Francesco Petrarch. 6325-X
"**Already** evening! In the duskiest nook". Evening. Owen (Edward Bulwer-Lytton, Earl Lytton) Meredith. 7015-9
"**Already** the tarpaper of the sky". Husband shoveling snow from the roof. William Meissner. 6821-9
Alsatian sketch. Gertrude Huntington McGiffert. 6838-3
Alspach, Russell K. (tr.)
   Sweet Jesus. Friar Michael of Kildare, 6930-4
Alston, Joseph Blynth
   'Stack arms'. 6946-0
Alta
   San Lorenzo: library. 6998-3
Alta quies. Alfred Edward Housman. 6536-8,6733-6
Alta quies, fr. More poems. Alfred Edward Housman. 6828-6
Altar boy. Sister Mary Immaculata. 6839-1
The **altar** boy. Leonard Feeney. 6543-0
Altar of liberty. Sophia Mavroidi Papadaky. 6352-7
"The **altar** stone we made". The altar stone. Richard Alexander. 6818-9
The **altar**. George Herbert. 6491-4
The **altar**. Jean Starr Untermeyer. 6102-8,6076-5
Altars. Bernard Freeman Trotter. 6337-3
Altenburg, Michael
   Swedish battle-song. 6424-8
Altenburg, Michael (tr.)
   The battle-song of Gustavus Adolphus. Unknown (German), 6302-0;6385-3
Alter ego. John Banister Tabb. 6007-2
Alter? when the hills do. Emily Dickinson. 6006-4,6646-1
Alteram partem. Arthur Hugh Clough. 6123-0,6110-9
The **alternative**. Aphra Behn. 6874-X
The **alternative**. John Henry Owens. 6178-8
Alternatives. DuBose Heyward. 6038-2
"**Altho** I be the basest of mankind". St. Simeon stylites. Alfred Lord Tennyson. 6977-0
"**Although** at the lim'ricks of Lear". Limerick:"Although at the lim'ricks of Lear". Edward Lear. 6811-1
"**Although** beneath this grave-mound...". Simonides. 6251-2
"**Although** I decked a chamber for my bride. George Santayana. 6347-0
"**Although** I had a check." Henry Howard, Earl of Surrey. 6584-8
Although I know the gentle night. Fujiwara No Michinobu. 6852-9
"**Although** great queen thou now in silence lye". Queen Elizabeth. Anne Bradstreet. 6753-0
"**Although** his back be at the wa'.". Here's his health in water. Unknown. 6859-6
"**Although** I ever did my best". The failure. Merle Kulow Sherrill. 6818-9
"**Although** I'm oldest I can't". Daughter. Kimiko Hahn. 6790-5
"**Although** I've writ of many a task". Vive Vermont. Daniel L. Cady. 6989-4
"**Although** it hides the mountains in its mist". On the mountain. Anna Spencer Twitchell. 6836-7
"**Although** it is not plainly visible to the eye". Fujiawara no Toshiyuki. 7039-6
"**Although** the world may think of you as old". For a certain beloved gentleman. Margaret E. Bruner. 6799-9
"**Although** Ulysses to undreamed-of seas". Ulysses - and after. Justin Huntly McCarthy. 6793-X
"**Although** we lie/heart-and skin". Our child of pain. Christine Busta. 6769-7
"**Although** with joy intense my heart is". 'Gam ze ya'avor' James O'Neill. 6848-0
"**Although** you east me to the root". The vine and the goat. Euenus. 6961-4
Alton Locke's song. Charles Kingsley. 6123-0
Alton, Ralph
   My delftware maid. 7022-1
Altrocchi, Julia Cooley
   Autumn and spring. 6039-0

Altrocchi, Rudolph
   Ode in memory of Theodore Roosevelt. 6995-9
Altruism. Robertson Trowbridge. 6566-X
Altruism. Unknown. 6486-8
Altruism ("The God of things as they are"). David Starr Jordan. 6473-6
The **altruist** order, sels. Rene Ghil. 6351-9
Alulvan. Walter De La Mare. 6596-1
Alumni greeting song. Mary A. McClelland. 6717-4
Alumnus football, sels. Grantland Rice. 6337-3
Alvar's address to the spirits of the dead. Samuel Taylor Coleridge. 6828-6
Alvarez, Lynne (tr.)
   Exile. Alejandra Pizarnik, 7036-1
   From a copy of 'Les chants de maldoror' Alejandra Pizarnik, 7036-1
   From the other side. Alejandra Pizarnik, 7036-1
Alvord, James Church
   Drum taps to heaven. 6542-2
Always a pulse. Hal Saunders White. 6808-1
"**Always** an ending. Shall I never see". Endings. Daniel Whitehead Hicky. 6841-3
"**Always** before your voice my soul". Poem ("Always before"). Edward Estlin Cummings. 6036-6
"**Always** before, the clear unbroken snow". In winter. Bernice Lesbia Kenyon. 6880-4
"'**Always** begin a poem/with the last line'". Lesson. J. Whitebird. 6901-0
"**Always** I loved a baby". Song ("Always"). Charles L. O'Donnell. 6214-8
"**Always** birds/in the sky" H. C. Artmann. 6769-7
Always last (valedictory poem). Unknown. 6718-2
"**Always** laugh when you can". George Gordon, 6th Baron Byron. 6109-5
"**Always** quiet". Unknown. 6364-0
Always right. Eugene Field. 6949-5
Always saying 'don't'. Edgar A. Guest. 7033-7
"**Always** the poor are with us". The tread of the poor. Lee Spencer. 6954-1
"**Always** thorns with roses grow". The common lot. Frederick A. Hinckley. 6798-0
"**Always** waiting at the back of the mind". Landscape with children. Sister Maris Stella. 6761-1
Always we watch them. Paul Mariah. 6870-7
"**Always** when I wake at night". In the dark. Lucy Wilson Buxton. 7016-7
Always with song. Mary B. Ward. 6750-6
"**Always** you will be young". Youth. George Elliston. 6906-1
"**Always** you've hung in the dim old hall". To a picture of a lady. Sara Kane. 6799-9
Alyea, Dorothy
   The aviator. 7019-1
   Portrait of two unhappy young people. 6979-7
Alyona. Alexsandr Yashin. 6546-5
Alysoun. Unknown. 6198-2,6193-1,6383-7
"**Am** I despis'd because, you say". Age not to be rejected. Unknown. 6933-9
"**Am** I failing? For no longer can I cast". George Meredith. 6508-2
"**Am** I failing? For no longer can I cast" George Meredith. 6828-6
Am I in Italy? Samuel Rogers. 6484-1
"**Am** I kin to sorrow". Kin to sorrow. Edna St. Vincent Millay. 6986-X
"**Am** I myself in every careless mirror?". Reflections. Lucile Enlow. 6841-3
"**Am** I not the nobler through my love?" Alfred Lord Tennyson. 6066-8
"**Am** I paler than is my wont, my love?". What I saw. John Whitaker Watson. 6774-3
"**Am** I waking? Was I sleeping?". Podas okus. Adam Lindsay Gordon. 6951-7
Am I with you, fr. Songs in absence. Arthur Hugh Clough. 6199-0
"**Am** I with you, or you with me?" Arthur Hugh Clough. 6828-6
Amala's bridal song, fr. Death's jest book. Thomas Lovell Beddoes. 6832-4
Amalfi. Henry Wadsworth Longfellow. 6624-0,6631-3
Amalfi by the sea. Ella Colter Johnston. 6906-1

Amanda. Coventry Patmore. 6383-7
"Amanda is sending messages again". Amanda, playing. C.W. Truesdale. 6966-5
"Amanda, since thy lovely frame". Advice to Amanda. Francis Hopkinson. 6753-0
Amantium irae amoris redintegratio. Richard Edwardes. 6436-1,6383-7,6301-2
Amantium irae amoris..., fr. The paradise of dainty... Richard Edwards. 6182-6,6315-2,6586-4
The amaranth. Coventry Patmore. 6315-2
"Amarillis teare thy haire." Unknown. 6563-5
Amaryllis. Thomas Campion. 6182-6,6187-7,6191-5,6301-2, 6099-4
Amaryllis. Unknown. 6926-6
"Amaryllis I did woo". George Wither. 6187-7,6092-7
"Amaryllis I did woo/And I courted Phillis too". A madrigal. George Wither. 6874-X
"Amaryllis, Chloris, Phyllis". Their turn. K.H. A.. 7021-3
Amaryllis, fr. Idylls. Theocritus. 6987-8
Amasis. Laurence Binyon. 6437-X
The amateur flute. Unknown. 6440-X
The amateur Orlando. George Thomas Lanigan. 7025-6
Amateur photography. Nathan Haskell Dole. 6670-4
An amateur, driving too fast, fr. The wasps. Aristophanes. 6308-X
Amateurs. Geroid Robinson. 6241-5
Amatores ambo. Norman T. Boggs. 6320-9
The amatory sonnets of Abel Shufflebottom. Robert Southey. 6278-4
Amaturus. William Johnson Cory. 6094-3
Amazing facts about food. Unknown. 6089-7
"Amazing, beauteous change!" Philip Doddridge. 6302-0;6385-3
The amazons. Richard A. Crouch. 7031-0
The Amazons. Yvonne Ffrench. 6782-4
Ambassador Extraordinary. R.L. Townsend. 7019-1
"Ambassador of Christ you go". Chaplain to the forces. Winifred M. Letts. 7031-0,7026-4
Amber. Holger Drachmann. 6555-4
"Amber and gold and a trail of mist". A lover speaks. Elizabeth Greene Thomas. 7016-7
The amber bead. Robert Herrick. 6125-7
"Amber clouds on a cobalt sky". A very weary actor. Eugene Field. 6949-5
Amber from Egypt. Agnes Kendrick Gray. 6478-7
"Amber the sky" Rokwaho. 7005-1
"The amber-tinted level sands". The rocky-lily, fr. Australian transcripts. William ("Fiona Macleod") Sharp. 6768-9
The ambience of love. Isidor Schneider. 6513-9
Ambient, Mark
    What May said to December. 6280-6
Ambiguous lines. Unknown. 6089-7,6724-7
Ambition. Berton Braley. 6887-1
Ambition. Edmund Palmer Clarke. 6764-6
Ambition. Samuel Johnson. 6087-0
Ambition, Charles Rann Kennedy. 6980-0
Ambition. Aline Kilmer. 6031-5,6556-2,6307-1,6727-1
Ambition. Maybel le McLaurin Kinsey. 7016-7
Ambition. Edward Lysaght. 6086-2
Ambition. Gertrude Huntington McGiffert. 6838-3
Ambition. John Neal. 6600-3
Ambition. Cotton Noe. 6499-X
Ambition. Elsie Ruth Schloss. 6847-2
Ambition. Robert Service. 6159-1
Ambition ("He who ascends"). George Gordon, 6th Baron Byron. 6294-6,6610-0
Ambition ("Nature"). Christopher Marlowe. 6294-6,6150-8
Ambition and glory. Edward Bulwer-Lytton; Baron Lytton. 6980-0
Ambition in Cuffe street. Unknown. 6506-6
"Ambition with her sire had kept her word". Success in New York, fr. Fanny. Fitz-Greene Halleck. 6753-0
The ambitious Marguerite. Agnes Carr Sage. 6675-5
The ambitious mouse. John Chipman Farrar. 6466-3,6368-3
The ambitious oyster. Joseph Morris. 6211-3
Ambitious Sophy. Elizabeth Turner. 6105-2
Ambivalence. Anita Patterson. 6857-X
Ambrose. James Russell Lowell. 6600-3
Ambrose, Saint

'How far, o rich' 6954-1
Veni creator. 6271-7
The ambrosian song of praise. Unknown. 6952-5
An ambulance driver's prayer. Thomas F. Coakley. 6846-4
"The ambulance stood near the paddock gate". The lay of the hospital race. Hugh Edmund Keough. 7010-8
The ambuscade. Florence Cecilia Roberts. 6648-8
Ambushed by angels. Gustav Davidson. 6218-0
"Amd while they sat at speech as at a fast". The coming of storm, fr. Tristram of Lyonesse. Algernon Charles Swinburne. 6997-5
Amelia. Coventry Patmore. 6508-2
Amelia mixed the mustard. Alfred Edward Housman. 6722-0, 6633-X
Amen. Arthur Christopher Benson. 6437-X
Amen. Georg Trakl. 6160-5
Amen-Hotep IV
    Hymn to the sun. James Henry Breasted (tr.). 6879-0
The amende honorable. Unknown. 6278-4
Amends to nature. Arthur Symons. 6232-6,6102-8,6153-2
"Amereic where freedom thrives". America is free. Dorothy McGraw Kenton. 6789-1
Amergin. Susan L. Mitchell. 6174-5
Amergin. Susan L. Mitchell. 6174-5
Amergin (atr.)
    The incantation. George Sigerson (tr.). 6930-4
    Invocation to Ireland. R.A.S. Macalister and Eoin MacNeill (tr.). 6930-4
    The mystery. Douglas Hyde (tr.). 6930-4
America. Stephen Vincent Benet. 6464-7
America. John Henrik Clarke. 6178-8
America. Florence Earle Coates. 6449-3
America. Arthur Cleveland Coxe. 6946-0
America. Sydney Dobell. 6198-2,6473-6,6656-9,6102-8,6250-4, 6607
America. Marjorie Frost Fraser. 6042-0
America. Charles Haseloff. 6998-3
America. Alfred Kreymborg. 6897-9
America. Henry Wadsworth Longfellow. 6337-3
America. Raul Otero Reiche. 6759-X
America. Herman Scheffauer. 6327-6
America. Samuel Francis Smith. 6456-6,6449-3,6300-4,6267-9, 6265-2,6121-4,6088-9.6131-1,6219-9,6101-X,6260-1, 6471-X,6486-2,6521-X,6623 ,6156-7,6136-2,6286-5,6401-9,6736-0,6125 ,6289-X,6459-0,6465-5,6479-5,6706-9, 6732
America. Bayard Taylor. 6223-7,6265-2
America. Henry Van Dyke. 6265-2
America. Marguerite Weed. 6847-2
America. A.D. Winans. 6901-0
America ("Oh, mother of a mighty race"). William Cullen Bryant. 6014-5,6176-1,6086-5,6302-0,6385-3,6678
America ("She is young and beautiful-my country"). Harriet Monroe. 6607-0
America ("Where the wings of a sunny Dome expand"). Herman Melville. 6333-0
America and England. George Huntington. 6711-5
America and England. George Edward Woodberry. 6473-6
America and France. Alan Seeger. 6030-7
America at St. Paul's. Margaretta Byrde. 7031-0,7027-2
America awakes. Mary Ernestine Clark. 6789-1
America comes in. Klaxon (John Graham Bower) 6224-5
America first! G. Ashton Oldham. 6386-1;6337-3
America for me. Henry Van Dyke. 6101-X,6102-8,6103-1,6503-1,6512-0,6104-5,6396-0,6076-5
'America for me'. Henry Van Dyke. 6961-4
America for me, sels. Henry Van Dyke. 6337-3
"America grew in me with my years". Spoken for many mouths. Troy Garrison. 6761-1
America independent. Philip Freneau. 6753-0
America is free. Dorothy McGraw Kenton. 6789-1
America politica historia, in spontaneity. Gregory Corso. 6803-0
America remembers, sels. Paul Engle. 6375-6
America speaks. Ella Wheeler Wilcox. 6681-X
America the beautiful. Katharine Lee Bates. 6051-X,6101-X, 6162-1,6337-3,6332-2,6465-,6466-3,6476-0,6509-0,6730-1,6736-0,6431 ,6161-3,6214-8,6265-2,6336-5,6396-9, 6449
America to England. M.J. Savage. 6889-8
America to Great Britain. Washington Allston. 6300-4,6752-

AMERICA

America triumphant. Elvira Bush Smith. 6818-9
"America! America! She maketh loud complaint". St. Rooseveltius. C. D.. 6995-9
"America! dear brother land!". Greeting from England. Unknown. 6946-0
"America! thou fractious nation". A proclamation. Unknown. 6946-0
America's answer. R.W. Lillard. 6476-0,6548-1,6449-3
America's early settlers. Martin Luther Peter. 6818-9
America's flags. Unknown. 6158-3
America's gift to France. John Jay Chapman. 6681-X
America's gospel. James Russell Lowell. 6337-3
America's peace cry. Hephzibah Elizabeth Spencer Kendrick. 6799-9
America's prosperity. Henry Van Dyke. 6961-4
America's task, fr. The second inaugural address. Abraham Lincoln. 6386-1
America's triumvirate. Isabel Fiske Conant. 6995-9
America's welcome home. Henry Van Dyke. 6961-4
America, 1750 George Berkeley. 6606-2
"America, America!/We chant thy note of praise". Ode to America. Mary P. Denny. 6799-9
"America, my own!". National song. William Henry Venable. 6946-0
America, my sweet. Jacinto Fombona Pachano. 6642-9
America, my sweet. Jacinto Fombona Pachano. 6642-9
"America, our country". America. Marguerite Weed. 6847-2
America, sels. Sydney Dobell. 6199-0
America, sels. William Blake. 6106-0
"America, thou peerless one". America triumphant. Elvira Bush Smith. 6818-9
"America/Drummed out of". America. A.D. Winans. 6901-0
American aristocracy. John Godfrey Saxe. 6302-0;6385-3
American birds. Thomas Caldecot Chubb. 6761-1
An American creed. Everard Jack Appleton. 6846-4
American culture, fr. Fanny. Fitz-Greene Halleck. 6753-0
The American eagle, sels. Charles West Thompson. 6171-0
The American eagle. Elizabeth Sampson. 7019-1
The American eagle. C.W. Thompson. 6921-5
An American exile. Isaac Hinton Brown. 6014-5,6414-0,6444-2
The American feast. Unknown. 6693-3
The American fireman. Christopher Bannister. 6274-1
The American flag, sels. Joseph Rodman Drake. 6239-3
The American flag. Charles Constantine Pise. 6096 X
The American flag. Unknown. 6314-4,6601-1
The American flag. Joseph Rodman Drake. 6077-3,6176-1,6240-7,6302-0,6385-3,6402-7,6425-6,6473-6,6486-8,6600-3, 6735-2,6401-9,6606-2,6639-9,6424-8,6396-9,6457-9, 6309-8,6219-9,6304-7,6135-4,6223-7,6228-1,6442-6, 6431-1,6212-1,6265-2,6470-1,6131-1,6212-1,6470-1, 6131-1,6121-4,6102-8,6076-5,6396-9,6457-9,6309-8, 6219-9,6304-7,6135-4,6223-7,6228-1,6442-6,6431-1, 6212-1,6265-2,6470-1,6131-1,6212-1,6470-1,6131-1, 6121-4,6102-8,6076-5,6300-4
The American flag. Lena E. Faulds. 6529-5,6684-4
The American forest girl, fr. Records of woman. Felicia Dorothea Hemans. 6973-8,6980-0,6929-0
The American freedom. Matthew Biller. 6761-1,6465-5
"An American frigate from Baltimore came". Paul Jones (2). Unknown. 6946-0
An American girl. Brander Matthews. 6875-8
An American girl. Brander Matthews. 6732-8,6652-6
The American hero. Nathaniel Niles. 6288-1
American ideals. Theodore Roosevelt. 6449-3
American independence. Francis Hopkinson. 6946-0
American independence. Alfred Billings Street. 6449-3
"The American land is a land of freedom". The American freedom. Matthew Biller. 6761-1,6465-5
American landscape. Charles Edward Eaton. 6761-1
American liberty. Philip Freneau. 6753-0
An American love-ode. Thomas Warton (the Elder) 6962-2, 6152-4
"American muse, whose strong & diverse heart". Invocation, fr. John Brown's body. Stephen Vincent Benet. 6891-X
"American muse, whose strong and diverse heart". Invocation, fr. John Brown's body. Stephen Vincent Benet. 6984-3
American names. Stephen Vincent Benet. 6299-7,6513-9,6736-

American Negra. Anita Scott Coleman. 6178-8
The American patriot's prayer. Unknown. 6946-0
The American poets. Joel Barlow. 6121-4
American prelude. Axton Clark. 6761-1
American radio. Maxwell Bodenheim. 6561-9
American Rhapsody to Lindbergh. Willis A. Boughton. 7019-1
The American rural home, sels. Thrope Greenleaf. 6171-0
American scene. Josephine Johnson. 6761-1
The American soldier's hymn. Unknown. 6946-0
The American soldier. Philip Freneau. 6753-0
"The American spirit speaks". The choice. Rudyard Kipling. 7026-4
American spring. Michael David Madonick. 7032-9
The American times, sels. Jonathan Odell. 6008-0
The American times. Jonathan Odell. 6753-0
An American to his mother. Unknown. 6741-X
The American traveler. Robert Henry ("Orpheus C. Kerr") Newell. 6915-0
The American traveller. Robert Henry ("Orpheus C. Kerr") Newell. 6722-0,6505-8,6089-7
The American village. Charles W. Denison. 6755-7
American woods. Harvey Shapiro. 6803-0
The American's creed. William Tyler Page. 6449-3
An American, one of the roughs, a kosmos. Unknown. 6440-X
An American. Rudyard Kipling. 6810-3
The American. James Bertolino. 7032-9
Americana, sels. Carl Rakosi. 6803-0
Americans. W. Cephas Cunningham. 6799-9
Americans all. Minna Irving. 6449-3
The Americans come! Elizabeth A. Wilbur. 6443-4,6478-7
"The Americans make many spectacular movies". The cinema. Bill Manhire. 7018-3
"Americans! revenge your country's wrongs". America independent. Philip Freneau. 6753-0
"Americans, we've built a nation great". Challenge to Americans. Dora Ward. 6799-9
"Americus, as he did wend". The noble tuck-man. Jean Ingelow. 6902-9
Amers, Grace H.
    My calvary. 6818-9
Ames, Eleanor Kirk
    Wash dolly up like that. 6451-5
Ames, Eva Edgerton
    Way up in old Vermont. 7030-2
Ames, Marilyn Grace
    'What's that white lady doing in your house' 6857-X
Ames, Mary Clemmer. See Clemmer, Mary
Ames, Nathaniel
    The almanack for 1733, sels. 6753-0
    The almanack for 1738, sels. 6753-0
    The almanack for 1743, sels. 6753-0
Ametas and Thestylis making hay-ropes. Andrew Marvell. 6563-5,6026-9
"Ami, notre pere est le tien". La vision. Alfred de Musset. 6801-4
Amibtion's trail. Ella Wheeler Wilcox. 6211-3
Amichai, Yehuda
    "If I forget thee, Jerusalem" 6758-1
    "My mother once told me" 6758-1
    "Out of three or four in a room" 6758-1
    A pity. We were such a good invention. 6758-1
    Rain on a battlefield. 6758-1
    Tourist. 6758-1
    We did it. Harold Schimmel (tr.). 6758-1
Amico suo. Herbert P. Horne. 6274-1,6656-9
"Amid a flurry of laces and frills". Prom night. Linda Beth Toth. 6857-X
"Amid conversation/& whiskey". I go to whiskey bars. Raymond Thompson. 6870-7
"Amid the channel's wiles and deep decoys". Love brings warning of natura maligns,fr.Coming of love. Theodore Watts-Dunton. 6997-5
"Amid the fading browns and greens and blues". Beeches. Helen Gross Hume. 6847-2
Amid the flowers. Osbert W. Warmingham. 6143-5
"Amid the loud ebriety of war". The Birkenhead. Sir Henry Yule. 6934-7
"Amid the nut grove, still and brown". The faerie's child. Thomas Caulfield Irwin. 6930-4

"Amid the scene, like some dark towering fiend". Tecumseh's death. Major Richardson. 6795-6
Amid the shadows. Anthero de Quental. 6648-8
"Amid the shining swords and lances". Fragment ("Amid the shining swords"). Sharaf al-Din. 6362-4
"Amid the silver music of the bells". George Eliot. John E. Barrett. 6840-5
"Amid the stress of high-embattled strife". Ruskin. Sir Owen Seaman. 6793-X
"Amid the throng that treads the busy city". The sister of charity. James Abraham Martling. 6952-5
"Amid the treasures strewn around". Daniel Webster's plow. Benjamin Franklin Taylor. 6815-4
"Amid this life, where age by age are pressed". Ritournelles. Bohdan Kaminsky. 6763-8
Amid, John
  The tail of the world. 6880-4
"Amidst a wood of oaks with canvas leaves". Description of a ninety-gun ship. William Falconer. 6971-1
"Amidst the massive sideboard's burnished...". A little tin plate. Garnet Walch. 6768-9,6681-X
"Amidst the peopled and regal isle". Dartmoor. Felicia Dorothea Hemans. 6973-8
"Amidst the thrilling leaves, thy voice". The voice of God. Felicia Dorothea Hemans. 6973-8
"Amidst these scenes, O pilgrim! seek'st Rome!". Rome buried in her own ruins. Francisco de Quevedo y Villegas. 6973-8
Amiel. Robert Bridges. 6487-6
Amiel's garden. Gertrude Huntington McGiffert. 6232-6,6338-1,6649-6
Amiel, H.F.
  The dew-drop. 6424-8
Amiens's songs, fr. As you like it. William Shakespeare. 6436-1,6600-3
Aminta, the golden age. Torquato Tasso. 6325-X
Amintas and Claudia, or The merry shepherdess. Unknown. 6157-5
"Amintor oh thou faithless swane." Unknown. 6563-5
Ammianus
  Omnes eodem cogimur. Sir William Marris (tr.). 6435-3
Ammons, A. R.
  Two motions. 6803-0
Ammunition column. Gilbert Frankau. 7027-2
Amnesiac. Mark Osaki. 6790-5
'Amo, amas, amat'. Murdock Pemberton. 6817-0
"Amo, amas/I love a lass." John O'Keefe. 6317-9,6125-7
Amohia's flight. Alfred Domett. 6591-0,6592-9
Amon-Re
  Hymn of victory: Thyutmose III. James Henry Breasted (tr.). 6665-8
Among all lovely things my love had been. William Wordsworth. 6369-1
Among green pleasant meadows. Unknown. 6127-3
"Among his fellows he was smitten". Portrait. Amanda Benjamin Hall. 6042-0
Among my books. Francis R.S. Erskine; Earl of Rosslyn. 6297-0
Among my books. Mark Houston. 6118-4
Among my books. Samuel Minturn Peck. 6297-0
"Among my several memories of fear". A buck's head on the wall. Robert P. Tristram Coffin. 7040-X
"Among polychromed/Songs...". Insanity. William Roehrick. 6850-2
Among school children. William Butler Yeats. 6208-3,6659-3,6645-3,6150-8
Among shadows. Leonard Clark. 6258-X
Among shadows. Arthur Davison Ficke. 6897-9
Among the animals. Mary Mapes Dodge. 6131-1
Among the animals. Emma Celia & Lizzie J. Rook. 6137-0
"Among the awful forms that stand assembled". Don Garzia. Samuel Rogers. 6980-0
Among the blind. Yannis Ritsos. 6803-0
"Among the carven images". The sparrow. I. Henry Wallis. 6785-9
Among the caves. Frederic Prokosch. 6390-X
"Among the changing months May stands confest". The month of May. James Thomson. 6816-2
"Among the crumbling arches of decay". Poem. Iris Tree. 6785-9

Among the ferns. Edward Carpenter. 6730-1,6252-0
"Among the flock of clouds that browse the fir". Anniversary. Arturo Giovannitti. 6880-4
"Among the flowers of summer-time she stood". A garden piece. Sir Edmund Gosse. 6770-0
"Among the flowers, like flowers, her slow...". The gardener. Francis Ledwidge. 6812-X
"Among the guava trees I sit". I love her still. William White. 6868-5
Among the heather. George Arnold. 6066-8, 6253-9
Among the hills. Richard Hovey. 6121-4
Among the hills. John Greenleaf Whittier. 6597-X,6126-5
"Among the hills of night my thoughts". The shepherd. Elizabeth Roberts MacDonald. 6796-4
"Among the hills of St. Jerome". At St. Jerome. Susan ("Seranus") Frances. 6797-2
"Among the legends sung or said". The wishing bridge. John Greenleaf Whittier. 6964-9
"Among the mad, none madder...". Theognis. 6251-2
"Among the maple-buds". April. Lloyd Mifflin. 6047-1
Among the millet. Archibald Lampman. 6433-7
"Among the mountains I wandered and saw...". The poor. Carl Sandburg. 6897-9,6954-1
Among the mountains, fr. The excursion. William Wordsworth. 6832-4
Among the multitude. Walt Whitman. 6560-0
"Among the mystical murmur of waves". Old captains. Joshua Freeman Crowell. 6798-0
"Among the Sinai monks the Brother John". John of Mt. Sinai. A.L. Frisbie. 6922-3
Among the names. E.L. Cassauria. 6097-8
Among the pines. Helena Coleman. 6591-0,6592-2
"Among the pitfalls in our way". Alice Cary. 6969-X,6238-5
Among the rocks, fr. James Lee's wife. Robert Browning. 6655-0,6196-6,6252-0,6560-0
Among the roses. Thornton W. Burgess. 6798-0
'Among the savages' Ralph Salisbury. 7005-1
"Among the smoke and fog...December afternoon". Portrait of a lady. Thomas Stearns Eliot. 6897-9
"Among the smoke of December". Portrait of a lady. Thomas Stearns Eliot. 6076-5,6020-X,6348-9
"Among the stars my dreams I set". Adventure. Willoughby Weaving. 7014-0
"Among the tombs". Elegy ("Among"). Robert Bridges. 6487-6
Among the trees. William Cullen Bryant. 6049-8
Among the violets, fair lilies and roses. Unknown. 6563-5
Among these turf-stacks. Louis MacNeice. 6666-6
"Among this somber tone, bend low in sadness". Pathetique. Nelson Hanback. 6799-9
"Amongst the myrtles as I walk'd". The inquiry. Thomas Carew. 6874-X
"Amongst the sights that Mrs. Bond". The drowning ducks. Thomas Hood. 6974-6
Amonson, Louis S.
  My country. 6925-8
Amontillado. Thomas Bailey Aldrich. 6004-8
Amor aeternalis. Clark Ashton Smith. 6218-0
Amor fons amoris. Edmond Gore Alexander Holmes. 6090-0
Amor mundi. Christina Georgina Rossetti. 6657-7,6508-2,6655-0
Amor mysticus. Sister Marcela de Carpio de San Felix. 7039-6
Amor omnia vincit. William Shakespeare. 6429-9,6226-1,6321-7
Amor omnipotens. Apollonius Rhodius. 6435-3
Amor profanus. Ernest Dowson. 6507-4,6648-8,6655-0
Amores, sels. Ovid. 6380-2
Amoret. William Congreve. 6244-X,6195-0
Amoret, sels. John Fletcher. 6935-5
Amoretti. Edmund Spenser. 6122-2,6436-1,6586-4
Amoretti, sels. Edmund Spenser. 6430-2,6194-X,6645-3,6154-0,6198-2,6208-3,6536-8,6250-4
Amoretti, sels. Edmund Spenser. 6908-8
Amoretti, sels. Edmund Spenser. 6908-8
Amoris finis. George Frederick Cameron. 6115-X
The amorist. Nahum Tate. 6563-5
"An amorous M.A.". Limerick:"An amorous M.A." Unknown. 6308-X
An amorous dialogue between John and his mistress. Unknown. 6157-5

AMOROUS

The **amorous** warre, sels. Jasper Mayne. 6562-7
Amos, amas. John O'Keefe. 6092-7
Amour de voyage. Rudyard Kipling. 6652-6
Amours de voyage. Arthur Hugh Clough. 6828-6
Amours de voyage. Arthur Hugh Clough. 6430-2
Amours de voyage, sel. Arthur Hugh Clough. 7014-0
Amours de voyage, sels. Arthur Hugh Clough. 6110-9,6199-0
Amours de voyage, sels. Arthur Hugh Clough. 6123-0,6246-5
Ampelopsis (virgina creeper). Ronald Campbell Macfie. 6269-5
Amphimachos the dandy. Vincent McHugh. 6388-8
Amphion. Alfred Lord Tennyson. 6691-7
Amphipolis. Antipater of Thessalonica. 6435-3
Amphis
    The solace of art. T.F. Higham (tr.). 6435-3
The **amphitheatre** at Pozzuoli. Sir Henry Taylor. 6624-0
The **amphora**. Fedor Sologub. 7039-6
"The **ample** proposition that hope makes". The uses of ill success. William Shakespeare. 6935-5
Ample, fr. Matrimonial melodies. Berton Braley. 6853-7
Amran's wooing. Bayard Taylor. 6976-2
Amsbary, Wallace Bruce
    Mon Pierre. 6280-6
    Rubaiyat of Mathieu Lettellier. 6280-6
Amsterdam. Francis Jammes. 7039-6
Amulet. Ibn Sa'id (of Alcala La Real) 6362-4
The **amulet**.. Ralph Waldo Emerson. 6429-9,6321-7
Amy Wentworth. John Greenleaf Whittier. 6126-5,6484-1,6429-9,6438-8,6288-1,6321-7,6419-1
Amy's cruelty. Elizabeth Barrett Browning. 6302-0;6385-3, 6092-7,6652-6
Amy's love-letter. Phoebe Cary. 6969-X
Amyata. Sir Gilbert Elliot. 6219-9
Amycus, fr. Idyll xxii. Theocritus. 6435-3
Amynta. Sir Gilbert Elliott. 6934-7
"**Amyntichus** the aged, when his fisher's days...". Macedonius. 6251-2
Amyntor. Thomas Godfrey. 6288-1
An den mond. Johann Wolfgang von Goethe. 6252-0
An thou were my ain thing. Allan Ramsay. 6180-X,6195-0
"**An'** noo that the Laird has exit had made". The laird o'cockpen (additional stanzas) Susan Ferrier. 6760-3
Ana, Zipporah, Huldah. James Abraham Martling. 6952-5
Anabasis. Eithne Wilkins. 6379-9
Anabasis, sels. St.-J. (Alexis Saint-Leger Leger) Perse. 6343-8
Anach. Darrell Figgis. 6090-0
Anacre oink verse. Robert Herrick. 6732-8
Anacreon
    Anacreon's dove. Samuel Johnson (tr.). 7039-6
    The cheat of Cupid. Robert Herrick (tr.). 6271-7
    Drinking. Abraham Cowley (tr.). 6271-7
    The golden mean. T.F. Higham (tr.). 6435-3
    "I wish to tune my quivering lyre". George Gordon, 6th Baron Byron (tr.). 6945-2
    Love. T.F. Higham (tr.). 6435-3
    Nunc est bibendum. T.F. Higham (tr.). 6435-3
    Old age. T.F. Higham (tr.). 6435-3
    On the grasshopper. William Cowper (tr.). 6271-7
    Spring. Thomas Moore (tr.). 6271-7
    Take her, break her. Walter Headlam (tr.). 6435-3
    "Thracian filly, why so heartless...". F.L. Lucas (tr.). 6251-2
    "Timocritus fought well. This is his grave". F.L. Lucas (tr.). 6251-2
    To Artemis ("To Artemis I kneel..."). T.F. Higham (tr.). 6435-3
    To Cleobulus. T.F. Higham (tr.). 6435-3
    To Dionysus ("Roving god, whose playfellows"). T.F. Higham (tr.). 6435-3
    "'Twas now the hour when night had driven". George Gordon, 6th Baron Byron (tr.). 6945-2
    When I drain the rosy bowl. Francis Fawkes (tr.). 6328-4
    Youth and pleasure. Thomas Moore (tr.). 6879-0
Anacreon. Anitpater of Sidon. 6879-0
Anacreon (atr)
    Age. Abraham Cowley (tr.). 7039-6
    Beauty. Thomas Stanley (tr.). 7039-6
    The grasshopper. Abraham Cowley (tr.). 7039-6,6271-7

    The picture. Thomas Stanley (tr.). 7039-6
    Spring. Thomas Stanley (tr.). 7039-6
    The wish. Thomas Stanley (tr.). 7039-6
    Youthful age. Thomas Stanley (tr.). 7039-6
Anacreon to the sophist. B. H. 6817-0
Anacreon's dove. Anacreon. 7039-6
Anacreon's ode. Henry Lawes. 6328-4
Anacreon's tomb. Unknown (Greek) 6435-3
Anacreon, ode ninth. Samuel Johnson. 6975-4
Anacreontic. Robert Herrick. 6189-3,6430-2
Anacreontic. Thomas Parnell. 6244-X
Anacreontic (1). Thomas Parnell. 6975-4
Anacreontic (2). Thomas Parnell. 6975-4
Anacreontic to a little pig's tail. Isaac Story. 6787-5
Anacreontic-drinking. Abraham Cowley. 6186-9
Anacreontics. Alfred Lord Tennyson. 6977-0
Anacreontique. Thomas Moore. 6278-4
Anacreontiques, sels. Abraham Cowley. 6562-7
Anacreontiques. Drinking. Abraham Cowley. 6152-4
Anactoria. Algernon Charles Swinburne. 6828-6
"**Anais**". Ruth Weiss. 6901-0
Analog for love. Helen Goldbaum. 6640-2
Analogies. Gerd Aage Gilhoff. 6798-0
The **analysis** of love. Herbert Read. 6209-1
'**Anarchism**'.. Francis W.L. Adams. 7009-4
Anarchy. Sir John Collings ("Solomon Eagle") Squire. 6072-2
Anarchy slain by true liberty. Percy Bysshe Shelley. 6543-0
"**Anastasia**, fair blossom...". Julianus [or Julian the Egyptian]. 6251-2
Anastasis. Albert E.S. Smythe. 6433-7,6115-X
Anathema. George S. Bryan. 6037-4
Anathema. Josephine Hancock Logan. 6789-1
Anathemata. Franklin Benjamin Sanborn. 6438-8
The **anathemata**, sels. David Jones. 6528-7
Anatolius, Saint
    Fierce was the wind billow. John Mason Neale (tr.). 6337-3
    Peace. 6214-8
Anatomical observation. Lenore Eversole Fisher. 6750-6
The **anatomy** of humor. Morris Bishop. 6722-0
Anatomy of melancholy. Ralph Gustafson. 6767-0
The **anatomy** of melancholy. Terence. 6317-9
An **anatomy** of the world. John Donne. 6378-0,6369-1
Anatomye, sels. John Halle. 6482-5
Anawrok, Edgar
    "Each time" 6855-3
    Silhouettes in flight. 6855-3
Anaxilas
    The cautious householder. T.F. Higham (tr.). 6435-3
    Human worms. T.F. Higham (tr.). 6435-3
Ancestor. Jimmy Santiago Baca. 6870-7
"The **ancestor** remote of man". Man and the Ascidian. Andrew Lang. 6987-8
Ancestors. Amory Hare. 7038-8
Ancestors' graves in Kurakawa. Joy Kogawa. 6790-5
The **ancestors**. Dorothy Livesay. 6767-0
Ancestral. Jessica Nelson North. 6850-2
Ancestral burden. Alfonsina Storni. 6759-X
Ancestral caste. Edward R. Huxley. 6885-5
The **ancestral** dwellings. Henry Van Dyke. 6265-2
Ancestral home. Aidna Van Orden. 6847-2
The **ancestral** song. Felicia Dorothea Hemans. 6973-8
"**Ancestral**, and pre-natal traits". Man's inante powers. Edward R. Huxley. 6885-5
The **ancestress**, sels. Letitia Elizabeth ("L.E.L.") Landon. 6066-8
Ancestry. Stephen Crane. 6861-8
Ancestry. Stephen Crane. 6300-4
Anchor song. Rudyard Kipling. 6507-4
Anchorage. Joy Harjo. 7005-1
Anchored to the infinite. Edwin Markham. 6162-1;6266-0;6337-3
Anchusa [pseud].
    Freud in New England. 6817-0
Ancient. George William ("A.E.") Russell. 6253-9
The **ancient** Abe. Charles G. ("Miles O'Reilly") Halpine. 6524-4
"**Ancient** and leaden-lidded he treads". Chameleon. Anthony

Delius. 6788-3
"Ancient Barbarossa, the kaiser Friedrich old".
   Barbarossa. Friedrich Ruckert. 6842-1
Ancient and modern Greece. George Gordon, 6th Baron Byron.
   6543-0
Ancient and modern Italy compared, part 001,fr. Liberty.
   James Thomson. 6816-2
The ancient and modern muses. Francis Turner Palgrave.
   6656-9
Ancient April. Elizabeth Ball. 6397-7
Ancient battle-song. Felicia Dorothea Hemans. 6973-8
Ancient beautiful things. Fannie Stearns Davis. 6556-2,
   6688-7,6019-6,6102-8,6026-5
An ancient chess king. Jean Ingelow. 7015-9
An ancient chess king. Jean Ingelow. 7015-9,7037-X
An ancient chess king. Jean Ingelow. 7015-9
An ancient chess king. Jean Ingelow. 7015-9,7037-X
An ancient Christmas carol. Unknown. 6466-3
"Ancient dame, how wide and vast". Ode on the death of a
   lady who lived one hundred years. Vincent Bourne.
   6814-6
The ancient doctrine. Robert Browning. 6437-X
"An ancient duck, complacent, fat". The duck and the
   nightingale. William Ellery Leonard. 6887-1
"An ancient enemy have I". Grief. Adelaide Anne Procter.
   6957-6
Ancient forests of the Near East. Gerald Cable. 6855-3
Ancient Greek song of exile, fr. Lays of many lands.
   Felicia Dorothea Hemans. 6973-8
"The ancient greybeard shoulders on his load". Francesco
   Petrarch. 6325-X
An ancient grievance. Unknown. 6936-3
Ancient hymn. Unknown. 6385-3
Ancient Irish rann. Unknown. 6090-0
The ancient mariner among the dead bodies of sailors.
   Samuel Taylor Coleridge. 6543-0
The ancient mariner finds a voice to bless and pray.
   Samuel Taylor Coleridge. 6543-0
The ancient mariner, sel. Samuel Taylor Coleridge. 6958-4
The ancient mariner, sels. Samuel Taylor Coleridge. 6317-9
The ancient mariner. Unknown. 6440-X
The ancient mariner. Samuel Taylor Coleridge. 6023-4,6197-
   4,6133-8,6138-9
Ancient music. Ezra Pound. 6536-8
Ancient night. Jacqueline Hoyt. 6850-2
"The ancient of cities!- the lady of nations!". Jerusalem.
   John Kebble Hervey. 6848-0
The ancient one. Charles Culhane. 6870-7
Ancient Phyllis. William Congreve. 6563-5
"Ancient pile, which sends from the past a...". Acropolis.
   Catherine Patrick. 6799-9
An ancient prayer. Thomas H.B. Webb. 6107-9
An ancient prophecy. Philip Freneau. 6015-3
The ancient race. Michael Tormey. 6174-5,6292-X
An ancient rhyme. Walter Savage Landor. 6092-7
An ancient rhyme. John O'Hagan. 6858-8
Ancient riddle. Jean Starr Untermeyer. 6012-9
The ancient sage. Alfred Lord Tennyson. 6730-1,6199-0,6655-
   0
Ancient seminary maid. Margherita Arlina Hamm. 6718-2
Ancient song of victory. Felicia Dorothea Hemans. 6973-8
An ancient stutters. Charles Monroe Walker. 6764-6
An ancient tale. John O'Hagan. 6090-0;6174-5
The ancient thought. Watson Kerr. 6730-1
An ancient to ancients. Thomas Hardy. 6776-X
An ancient to ancients. Thomas Hardy. 6641-0,6102-8,6023-4,
   6659-3
An ancient toast. Unknown. 6097-8,6260-1,6478-7
"The ancient tribes, when they and earth...". Pueblo
   legend. Lilian White Spencer. 6779-4,6836-7
"The ancient wood is white and still". Ballade of the
   pipesmoke carry. Bert Leston Taylor. 6875-8
Ancients of New England. John Farrar. 7030-2
And 'I know why the caged bird sings': a villanelle.
   Geroge Mosby Jr. 6870-7
"And a calm caught my little finger". The little girl that
   lost a finger. Gabriela (Lucila Godoy Alcayaga)
   Mistral. 6759-X
"And a great sign appeared in heaven", fr. Apocalypse.
   Unknown. 6282-2

"And a perfect feast of nectar'd sweets" John Milton. 7014-
   0
And after all. Halle W. Warlow. 6270-9
"And after all, it's there for the listening". The oracle
   of Delphi. Adele Naude. 6788-3
"And after all, what is there here to thrill". Greek
   temples. Irwin [pseud].. 6817-0
"And after Winthrop's, Hooker's...hearse". A funeral elegy
   upon the death of...John Cotton... John Norton. 6753-
   0
"And all night long, in dreams, he heard...sea". Rain in
   the night. Norah Lilian D'Altera Dowsley. 6800-6
"And all the long night through I heard...". The sound of
   rain. Barbara Young. 7038-8
"And are ye one of hermitage". The inquiry, fr. At
   Casterbridge fair. Thomas Hardy. 6828-6
"And are ye sure the news is true?" William Julius Mickle
   (atr.) 6317-9
"And art thou come, blest babe?" Unknown. 6931-2
"And art thou weary, without health". The dark house.
   Francis Carey ("Jan van Avond") Slater. 6800-6
"And as I sat, over the light blue hills". The dance of
   the merry damsels. John Keats. 6959-2
"And as a bird each fond endearment tries". Oliver
   Goldsmith. 6238-5
"And as a full field charging was the sea". Algernon
   Charles Swinburne. 6997-5
"And as the august blossom of the dawn". Algernon Charles
   Swinburne. 6997-5
"And by her side went Eros, and Passion...". Hesiod. 6251-
   2
And can the physician. Unknown. 6179-6,6334-9
"And can the physician make sick men well?". Song ("And
   can"). Unknown. 6182-6,6315-2,6334-9
"And certainly they say, for fine behaving". The monks and
   the giants, sels. John Hookham Frere. 6832-4
"And constant shells that evermore retain". Richard
   Garnett. 6997-5
"And could we choose the time and choose aright". John
   Dryden. 6867-7
And day is done. Le Garde S. Doughty. 6042-0
And death shall have no dominion. Dylan Thomas. 6339-X,
   6390-X,6472-8,6379-9
"And deep-eyed children cannot long be...". Ballad of the
   outer life. Hugo von Hofmannsthal. 7039-6
"And did those feet in ancient time". 'Till we have built
   Jerusalem' William Blake. 6954-1
"And did those feet in ancient time," fr. Milton. William
   Blake. 6023-4,6052-8,6187-7,6536-8,6668-2,6793
"And did you never lie upon the shore". Alfred Lord
   Tennyson. 6997-5
"And didst thou fear the queen of night". Poem
   written...opinions of a deaf and dumb child, sels.
   James Abraham Hillhouse. 6752-2
"And dirge to dirge than answers...". Unknown. 6251-2
"And do I then behold again the secne". Scenes of
   childhood. Edward Moxon. 6980-0
"And do they so? have they a sense". Etenim res creatae
   exerto capite observantes... Henry Vaughan. 6935-5
And do they so? have they a sense. Henry Vaughan. 6341-1
"And do they so? have they a sense". Henry Vaughan. 6933-9
"And doth not meeting like this make amends?". Thomas
   Moore. 6085-4
And dust to dust. Charles David Webb. 6388-8
"And dwells there in a female heart". Addressed to Miss
   Macartney. William Cowper. 6814-6
"And each good thought or action moves". John Greenleaf
   Whittier. 6623-2
And each man's leave. Roland Robinson. 6384-5
"And either tropic now". A night storm. John Milton. 6935-
   5
"And Elijah said unto Ahab, get thee up...". A little
   cloud. Bible. 7020-5
"And especially as the hours". Coma. Liane Heller. 6767-0
"And even as I listen, charmed and mute". Listening. Don
   Marquis. 6761-1
And far away, the azure peaks. Eliska Krasnohorska. 6763-8
And fare thee well, my own green, quiet vale. Richard
   Henry Dana. 6752-2
"And first within th porch and jaws of hell". The gates

of hell. Thomas Sackville; 1st Earl of Dorset. 6935-5
"And five of us those summer days". To Barbary land. Agnes E. Mitchell. 7002-7
"And folks are beginning to think it looks odd". A fable for critics, sels. James Russell Lowell. 6959-2
"And for the few that only lend their ear". The poet's audience. Samuel Daniel. 6935-5
"And God spake unto Noah, and to his sons...". The first rainbow. Bible. 7020-5
'And forbid them not'. Benjamin Franklin Taylor. 6815-4
...And free. Lindamichellebaron. 6899-5
"And from steep to steep/Of heaven..." Algernon Charles Swinburne. 6997-5
And God created the great whales. John Milton. 6833-2
And God shall be king over the whole earth. Arno Nadel. 6542-2
And grow. John Hay. 6666-6
"And happy they who thus in faith obey". Impulse. Robert Southey. 6867-7
"And has the earth lost its spacious round". Lines on seeing my wife and two children sleeping... Thomas Hood. 6974-6
"And have we done with war at last?". Two fusiliers. Robert Graves. 7029-9
"'And have you not seen Evans?' 'Evans? Yes!". The inner vision. Maude Freeman Osborne. 6836-7
"And he cast it down, down, on the green grass". The new ghost. Fredegond Shove. 6393-4,6931-2,6931-2
'And he said, fight on'. Emily Pauline ("Tekahionwake") Johnson. 6837-5
"And he spake many things unto them in...". A sower. Bible. 7020-5
"And her lips (that show no dulness).". A song to her beauty, fr. The mistress of Philaeete. George Wither. 6827-8
And here the hermit sat, and told his beads. William Ellery Channing. 6399-3,6176-1
"And here the precious dust is laid". The inscription on the tomb of the Lady Mary Wentworth. Thomas Carew. 6933-9,6933-9,6150-8
"And here was peace, in purple hill". Peace. Ann Lavoie Morrow. 6894-4
"And here we are, alive in time and space". Time: twentieth century. Virginia Earle. 6839-1
"And here, sweet friend, I go my way". Adios. Joaquin Miller. 6753-0
"And I could weep! - the Oneyda chief". Dirge of Outalissi. Thomas Campbell. 6980-0
"And I have come upon this place". Einstein. Archibald MacLeish. 6754-9
"And I have seen again the marvellous child". Sonnet ("And I have seen"). Paul Verlaine. 6343-8
"And I looked long and I could not descry". The soul of swans. Mary Siegrist. 7014-0
"And I mankind". My love that mourneth for me. John Gwynneth. 6756-5
"And I must have my little symbols, too". Postscript to a song. Thomas Hornsby Ferril. 6836-7
"And I must say that God is Christ". Faith. Edwin McNeill Poteat. 6144-3,6337-3
"And I remember that this room was mine". A memory. Milicent Laubenheimer. 6799-9
"And I rode the greyhound down to Brooklyn". Wild strawberry. Maurice Kenny. 7005-1
"And I'm afraid of leaves, of the highway". Clouds and men, sels. Alistair Paterson. 7018-3
"And history". Alexander Smith. 6238-5
"And I shall never trace this path again". M. A. 6817-0
And I too in Arcadia. Felicia Dorothea Hemans. 6973-8
"And I, too, sing the song of all creation". Unknown. 6109-5
"And if an eye may save or slay." Sir Thomas Wyatt. 6584-8
And if he die? Arthur Davison Ficke. 6879-0
And if I cry release... Sarah-Elizabeth Rodger. 6781-6
'And if I did what then?'. George Gascoigne. 6182-6,6208-3,6380-2
And if I say. Maxwell Bodenheim. 6037-4
"And if he ever should come back". The last words. Maurice Maeterlinck. 7039-6

"And if I cannot see the gleam". For those who follow. Bertye Young Williams. 6906-1
"And if I do not go to sleep". Going to sleep. George Elliston. 6861-8
"And if the fight I lose, what then?". The fighter. Edgar A. Guest. 6869-3
"And if the trees were gone and their...leaves". Trees needed. John Ritchey. 6761-1
"And if your own and time alike betray you". To dreamers everywhere. Amelia Josephine Burr. 6954-1
"And if/This bit of new". Late blossom. Joyce Lancaster. 6850-2
"And in haste the refluent ocean". Henry Wadsworth Longfellow. 6997-5
And in her morning. Jessica Powers. 6282-2
And in that twilight. Lucy Larcom. 6066-8
"And in the after silences". After. Francis Ledwidge. 6812-X
"And in the frosty season...", fr. The prelude. William Wordsworth. 6289-X,6395-0
And in the hanging gardens. Conrad Aiken. 6011-0,6649-6
"And in those days she made a little song". Song, fr. Lancelot and Elaine. Alfred Lord Tennyson. 6867-7
And is it night? Unknown. 6182-6
"And is it thus, ye base and blind". An address to the mob on occasion of the late riot... William Cowper. 6814-6
"And is there care in heaven? and is there love". Edmund Spenser. 6931-2
"And is there glory from the heavens departed?". The lost pleiad. Felicia Dorothea Hemans. 6980-0
"And is there sadness in thy dreams, my boy?". The dreaming child. Felicia Dorothea Hemans. 6973-8
"And is there then no earthly place". Rhymes on the road. Thomas Moore. 6760-3
"And is this all? Can reason be no more". A reflection on the ode Horace, Book II. Ode 010. William Cowper. 6814-6
And it is among rude untutored dales, sels. William Wordsworth. 6867-7
And it was windy weather. James Stephens. 6253-9
"And i[t] fayrlye befell so fayr me bethought." Unknown. 6378-0
"And Jacob went out from Beersheba..." Bible. 6958-4
And Jesus wept. Matthew Bridges. 6065-X
And Joe went. Unknown. 6741-X
"And it will bring you back—". Longing. Blanche Kendall McKey. 6818-9
"And Jacob went out from Beersheba, and...". The book of Genesis. Bible. 6958-4
"And let the canakin clin, [clink]," fr. Othello. William Shakespeare. 6308-X,6328-4
"And let this feeble body fail." Charles Wesley. 6302-0
"And light and sound ebbed from the earth". Percy Bysshe Shelley. 6997-5
And lightly, like the flowers. Pierre de Ronsard. 6102-8
And lightly, like the flowers. Pierre de Ronsard. 6732-8
'And lightly, like the flowers' William Ernest Henley. 6770-0
"And like the moan of lions hurt to death". Algernon Charles Swinburne. 6997-5
"And lo! the sea that fleets about the land". The sea danceth. Sir John Davies. 6833-2
"And lo! upon the murmuring waves". The ship. Christopher (John Wilson) North. 6980-0
"And lo, the prison door was closed at night!". Rizal the immortal. Januario Puruganan. 6906-1
"And love? What was love, then." Edward Bulwer-Lytton; Baron Lytton. 6066-8
"And Medon answer made...", fr. The Odyssey. Homer. 6435-3
"And meet lone death on the drear ocean's waste". Percy Bysshe Shelley. 6997-5
"And Nestor, the Geranian...", fr. The Odyssey. Homer. 6435-3
"And my whole soul revolves, the cup runs over". Eden remembered. Robert Browning. 7020-5
"And my young sweetheart sat at board with me". Idyl. Alfred Mombert. 7039-6
"And Naomi said to her daughters-in-law". Ruth, fr. The story of Ruth. Bible. 6805-7

"And night came down over the solemn waste". The river oxus. Matthew Arnold. 7020-5
"And Noa went up into the ship, and sat". The entrance into the ark. Jean Ingelow. 6848-0
"And now 'tis night. A myriad stars have come". Night in the Thousand Isles. Charles Sangster. 6795-6
"And now Cyllenian...", fr. The Odyssey. Homer. 6435-3
"And now before young David could". David and Goliah. Michael Drayton. 6848-0
"And now the bell - the bell". Little Nell's funeral, fr. Old curiosity shop. Charles Dickens. 6909-6
"And now the city smoke begins to rise". Summer evening at a short distance from the city. Alonzo Lewis. 6752-2
"And now the devil's voice rose up and out". News of the devil, sels. Humbert Wolfe. 6985-1
"And now the end of Ahab's house had". The death of Jezebel. Unknown. 6848-0
"And now the mists are lifting". Unknown. 6109-5
"And now the next you'll scarce hold true". Charles F. Smith. 6254-7
"And now the parting time has come". Unknown. 6601-1
"And now the sacred rite was done". The lay of Mr. Colt. William Edmonstoune Aytoun. 6948-7
"And now the storm-blast came, and he". The rime of the ancient mariner, sel. Samuel Taylor Coleridge. 6935-5
"And now there is nothing l ft to celebrate" George Barker. 6379-9
And now these jonquils. David Morton. 6850-2
"And now we climb this bare eroded hill". Dombashawa. Peter Jackson. 6788-3
"And now we only ask to serve." M.E. Townsend. 6225-3
And O the wind. Witter Bynner. 6653-4
"And now, electing the illumined air". The gargantuan flight. Lynn Riggs. 6808-1
"And now, gentlemen/A word I ive to remain...". The base of all metaphysics. Walt Whitman. 6753-0,6126-5
"And now, man-slaughtering Pallas took in hand". The end of the suitors, fr. The Odyssey. Homer. 6933-9
"And now, while the dark vast earth shakes...". The stars in their courses. John Freeman. 7027-2
"'And now,' said the Governor, gazing...". The first Thanksgiving day. Margaret Junkin Preston. 7041-8
"And nowm in accents deep and low". Address of the sylph of autumn to the bard. Washington Allston. 6752-2
"And O! ye solitudes of rocks and waters". The solitudes of Malbay, fr. Atlantic coast scenery. Sir Aubrey De Vere. 6997-5
"And oft the stars above me". The dreamer. John Harsen Rhoades. 6789-1
"And oft, while wonder thrill'd my breast...". Waterspout. Luis de Camoens [or Camoes]. 6833-2
"And oh! what odours the voluptous vale". Alaodin's paradise. Robert Southey. 6980-0
"And oh, ;to think the sun can shine". Adelaide Neilson. William Winter. 7041-8
"And on the smalle greene twistis sat". A May burden. James I; King of Scotland. 6943-6
And one is two? Winifred Virginia Jackson. 6039-0
"And one man said". The choice. Edgar A. Guest. 6869-3
"And only where the forest fires have sped". Fire-flowers. Emily Pauline ("Tekahionwake") Johnson. 6837-5
"And over the waste of barren moorland...". Sonnet: aftermath of storm and war. Herbert Edward Palmer. 6780-8
"And owe we not these visions". The power of the bards, sels. Philip Pendleton Cooke. 7017-5
"And panoplied alike for war or peace". Victoria. Alfred Austin. 7022-1
"And Rachel lies in Ephrath's land". Dirge of Rachel. William Knox. 6848-0
"And present gratitude." John Greenleaf Whittier. 6225-3
"And reared you tenderly...", fr. Hachi no ki. Seami. 6106-0
"And ride in triumph...", fr. The conquests... Christopher Marlowe. 6726-3
"And round the sleep that fell around then...". The last sleep of Tristram and Iseult. Algernon Charles Swinburne. 6997-5
And sae came of it. Johann Wolfgang von Goethe. 7042-6

"And see the biped soaring up". On hearing of a man's death in a hang glider accident. Peter Acker. 6767-0
'And seven more redskins bit the dusts' Quincy Kilby. 7007-8
And shall Trelawny die? Robert Stephen Hawker. 6427-2,6102-8,6668-2
"And shall we light the candle now?". After-word. Josephine Preston Peabody. 6861-8
"'And shall we say, forever?' I had cried". Vista, fr. Once again the Eden. Noel Hudson Stearn. 6789-1
And she cried. Minna Irving. 6277-6
"And she is sleeping now without a dream". Died young. Cora Fabri. 6876-6
'And she is spoke'. Unknown. 6846-4
And she said and I said. Alfred Kreymborg. 6070-6
And she washed his feet with her teares... Sir Edward Sherburne. 6562-7,6563-5,6023-4
"And she washed his feet with her tears." Sir Edward Sherburne. 6125-7
"And shining with gloom, the water grey". Elizabeth Barrett Browning. 6997-5
"And Simeon blessed them...", fr. Luke. Unknown. 6282-2
"And shrink ye from the way". The departed. Felicia Dorothea Hemans. 6973-8
"And shure, I was tould to come in till..". The Irishwoman's letter. Unknown. 6909-6
"And sitt'st thou there, O losteJerusalem!". Jerusalem. Sir Aubrey De Vere. 7015-9
"And sleeps thy heart when flower and tree". Summer. Johannes Carl Andersen. 6784-0
"And small are the white-crested that play". Walter Savage Landor. 6997-5
"And so an easier life our Cyclops drew". The Cyclops. Theocritus. 7039-6
And so at last. David Starr Jordan. 6337-3,6461-2
"And so he is done with roaming". The dead rover. Berton Braley. 6853-7
"And so I am rejected with a phrase". Rispetto. O.M. Dennis. 6850-2
"And so I aeard a voice say What is freedom?". What is freedom? Edward Carpenter. 7009-4
"And so he lingered on the trackless way". Anna Bromberger. 6847-2
"And so in Sparta long ago the maids". The marriage of Helen and Menelaus. Theocritus. 6959-2
"And so love comes again on flashing wings". Echoed music. Ruth Peiter. 6906-1
"And so my fairy little elf". My beautiful 'tick-a-tock'. Louise S. Upham. 6965-7
"And so old Betsey Green is dead!". The oldest pauper on the town. John Whitaker Watson. 6774-3
And so the word had breath, fr. In memoriam. Alfred Lord Tennyson. 6335-7
And so to-day. Carl Sandburg. 6010-2
And so tomorrow. Samuel E. Boyd. 6178-8
"And so we part, with shout and song". Farewell, thou lovely wood. H. Hoffman Von Fallersleben. 6952-5
"And so you wonder, do you, why the jury...". Juror number six. Unknown. 6878-2
"And so, o'er many a league of sea". On dream water. Francis Ledwidge. 6812-X
"And so--you are afraid of death!". Accusation. Helen Petkanich. 6799-9
"And somewhere yet in the hill-tops." Unknown. 6225-3
"And soon, when this life with its waiting is over". Marianne Farningham. 6407-8
And still. Leonard Feeney. 6214-8
"And still I changed; I was a boy no more". Jean Ingelow. 6238-5
And still the heart. Robert Nathan. 6761-1
"And strew faint sweetness...", fr. Paracelsus. Robert Browning. 6726-3
"And suddenly there springs", fr. Anchored. Sir Lewis Morris. 6997-5
And that inverted bowl they call the sky, fr. Rubaiyat. Omar Khayyam. 7039-6
And the band played. Maurice E. McLaughlin. 6451-5
"And the blear-eyed filmy sea did boom". Owen (Edward Bulwer-Lytton, Earl Lytton) Meredith. 6997-5
"And the breezes havewhispered to me". Whispers. James

Abraham Martling. 6952-5
And the cock crew. Amelia Josephine Burr. 6542-2
"And the crest/Of every mounting wave..." Richard Garnett. 6997-5
And the days were accomplished. Mary Ballard Duryee. 6979-7
And the dead. Sean Jennett. 6379-9
And the dreamers of dreams. John Oscar Beck. 6039-0
"And the first gray of morning filled the east". Sohrab and Rustum. Matthew Arnold. 6271-7,6110-9,6199-0, 6264-4,6371-3,6419 ,6828-6
And the gas chamber drones in the distance. Greg Forker. 6870-7
And the greatest of these. Unknown. 6750-6
"And the hatch-board where Sir Andrew lay". Unknown. 6518-X
"And the hypocrites/resurrected Cain". Those not confused are prisoners of war. Noah Mitchell. 6870-7
"'And the judge said: 'What! no money to pay". Prisoner at the bar. Edgar A. Guest. 6869-3
"And the Lord God caused a deep sleep to...". The book of Genesis. Bible. 6958-4
"And the Lord God planted a garden eastward...". The garden of Eden. Bible. 7020-5
'And the life everlasting.' Percy Clough Ainsworth. 6337-3
And the little wind. John G. Neihardt. 6347-0
"And the Lord God caused a deep sleep...". Bible. 6958-4
"And the next ship I got was the Auburn of...". The able seaman's story. Archie Binns. 7007-8
"And the night shall be filled with music". Henry Wadsworth Longfellow. 6238-5
"And the old folks said" Diane Mei Lin Mark. 6790-5
And the pear trees shiver. Jocelyn Macy Sloan. 6218-0
"And the rainbow lives in the curve of the sand". Alfred Lord Tennyson. 6997-5
"And the raven takes but a single wife..life". The raven. Marguerite Young. 6979-7
"And the realized vision is clasped to...heart". At Vallambrosa, sels. William Wordsworth. 6867-7
And the rivers run south. Frederick R. McCreary. 6072-2
"And the robins/have packed their songs". Variations on a late October day. Geroge Mosby Jr.. 6870-7
"And the seer's words take measure". Stanzas ("And the seer's"), fr. The golden city. John ("Evelyn Douglas") Barlas. 7009-4
"And the spray of myrtle chases". Stanzas ("And the spray.."), fr. The golden city. John ("Evelyn Douglas") Barlas. 7009-4
"And the sun outpouring like a crowd". Fifth Avenue at noon. Eve Merriam. 6761-1
"And the voice that was softer than silence...". The vision of Sir Launfal, sel. James Russell Lowell. 6954-1
"And Thebes, how fallen now! Her storied gates". Thebes. William Whitehead. 6911-8
"And the voice that was softer...", fr. The vision... James Russell Lowell. 6335-7
And the winner is. Greg Forker. 6870-7
"And the world was made flesh." Laurence Housman. 6337-3
And the world's face. Julian Symons. 6666-6
"And then from sullen clouds the storm...". Broken trees. Edna Davis Romig. 6836-7
"And then he danced;- all foreigners excel". Don Juan. George Gordon, 6th Baron Byron. 6198-2,6959-2
"And then I fell asleep, and had a dream". To Mr. Simon Wolf. Frank Claudy. 6848-0
"And then I sat me down, and gave the rein". Sonnet ("And then I sat"). Gustav Rosenhane. 7039-6
And then no more. James Clarence Mangan. 6244-X
"And then she saw me creeping". Fossils. James Stephens. 6930-4
"And then they moved. Sunlight covered them...". The heroes. Frederic Prokosch. 6761-1
"And then, monsieur, I am so fond". A perogative of the king. Felix E. Schelling. 6936-3
"And then?". Robert Underwood Johnson. 6585-6
"And there are hearts like richest wines". E.H. Keene. 6109-5
"And there shall come forth a rod...", fr. The bible. Unknown. 6334-9

"And there they sat, a popping corn". Popping corn. Unknown. 6912-6
"And there they sleep! - the men who stood". The tombs of Plataea. Felicia Dorothea Hemans. 6973-8
'And there was a great calm.' Thomas Hardy. 6125-7
"And there was stormy silence in that city". Petrograd. Babette Deutsch. 6880-4
"And there were in the same...", fr. The Bible. Unknown. 6466-3
"And these all night...", fr. The Iliad. Homer. 6435-3
"And these all reach from east to west". Unknown. 66601-1
"And they divied Poland - three times...". Wandering woman. Rosalie Moore. 6761-1
"And they murmured again, 'Could'.". The murmuring flock. F.J. Ottarson. 6848-0
"and they were talking, in the dark...". Hell's purgatory, sels. Edoardo Sanguineti. 6803-0
"And they who do their souls no wrong." James Russell Lowell. 6225-3
"And this is how I/memorized your body". Excerpts from 'Riffs' (a work in progress) Dennis Lee. 6767-0
"And this is life: to live, to love, to lose!" Unknown. 6238-5
"And this reft house is that which he built". Sonnet: on a ruined house in a romantic country. Samuel Taylor Coleridge. 6802-2
And this reviving herb whose tender green, fr. Rubaiyat. Omar Khayyam. 7039-6
"And this thought will be our comfort." Charlotte Murray. 6225-3
"And this was once Esoeris". Esoeris. Lydia Gibson. 6880-4
"And this was your cradle? Why surely,my Jenny". The old cradle. Frederick Locker-Lampson. 6772-7
"And this, O Spain...". Maria Jane Jewsbury. 6402-7
"And thither thou, beloved, and thither I." Christina Georgina Rossetti. 6225-3
"And tho' when wearied some dear one lies down." A.H. Parry. 6225-3
"And those two young ladies of Birmingham". Limerick:"And those two young ladies of Birmingham." Unknown. 6308-X
"And thou art dead, as young and fair." George Gordon, 6th Baron Byron. 6086-2,6219-9,6110-9,6543-0,6828-6
"And thou art now no longer near!". To the parted one. Johann Wolfgang von Goethe. 7039-6
"And thou hast walked about (how strange...).". An address to the mummy in Belzoni's exhibition, sels. Horace Smith. 6934-7
"And thou wert sad - yet I was not with thee". Lines on hearing that Lady Byron was ill. George Gordon, 6th Baron Byron. 6945-2
"And thou wert sad- yet I was not with thee". Lines. George Gordon, 6th Baron Byron. 6828-6
"And thou woult'st not!" Winifred Stoddard LeBar. 6144-3
"And thou wouldst know this wicked world?". To a would-be new woman. ? Metcalfe. 7021-3
"And thou, gray voyager to the breezeless sea". To the dying year. John Greenleaf Whittier. 6752-2
"And thou, o life, the lady of all bliss". Newborn death (2). Dante Gabriel Rossetti. 6828-6
"And thou, twin orbs of love and joy!". To a sleeping baby's eyes. Eugene Field. 6949-5
"And thus as we were talking to and for". Complaint of the common weill of Scotland. Sir David Lyndsay. 6845-6
"And thus Narcissus, cunning with a hand-glass". Prelude. Conrad Aiken. 6781-6
"And Timur again set out for the wars". Double-focus. Al Purdy. 6767-0
"And thus they fought...", fr. The Iliad. Homer. 6435-3
And to such as play only the bass viol. John Finley. 6607-0
And to the young men. Merrill Moore. 6527-9
"And truly I would rather be struck dumb" John Keats. 6935-5
"And turn," fr. Myrtle bough. Hilda ("H.D.") Doolittle. 6012-9
"And was the day of my delight", fr. In memoriam. Alfred Lord Tennyson. 6867-7
"And was this all? He died! He who did wait". Methuselah. Lydia Huntley Sigourney. 6848-0

"And was thy home, pale withered thing". On a leaf from the tomb of Virgil. Felicia Dorothea Hemans. 6973-8
"And we shall build upon the earth". From dust thou art. Frances Waddle. 6750-6
"And we vowed it then and there". Good resolutions, fr. Gedichte. Johann Wolfgang von Goethe. 7042-6
"And we, poor waifs, whose life term seems". Paul Hamilton Hayne. 6238-5
And we, that now make merry in the room, fr. Rubaiyat. Omar Khayyam. 7039-6
"And welcome now (great monarch) to your own". John Dryden. 6933-9
"And what if cheerful shouts, at noon". June, sels. William Cullen Bryant. 6934-7
"And what Mantle dreams of". Even the best. Gary Allan Kizer. 6870-7
"And what of all remained to me". Fragment ("And what of"). Jan z Wojkowicz. 6763-8
"And what of old age without memories". Reply to advice to youth. Marion Doyle. 6750-6
And what shall you say? Joseph Seamon Cotter Jr. 6532-5
"And what was Stella but a haughty dame". To - ("And what"). Edward Moxon. 6980-0
"And what, my thoughtless sons, should fire...". Britannia's empire, fr. Britannia. James Thomson. 6932-0
"And when at last, with priestly pray'r". The kissing of the bride, fr. The white house ballads. Eugene Field. 6949-5
"And when he died the flesh that was young...". Remembering Woodrow Wilson. Edward A. Richards. 6761-1
"...And when he was in bed, after his prayers". Passing understanding. C.F. MacIntyre. 6751-4
"And when it comis to the ficht". Bruce addresses his army. John Barbour. 6845-6
And when like her, Oh Saki, fr. Rubaiyat. Omar Khayyam. 7039-6
"And when night comes they will sing". Evening. Walter James Turner. 6331-4
"And when the summer heat is great". Story of Udaipore: told by Lalla-ji, the priest. Laurence (Adele Florence Nicolson) Hope. 6856-1
"And when they came to merry Carlisle". Unknown. 6518-X
"And whence thy loveliness, child of the wave?". The pearl. Wilfred M. Post. 6983-5
"And where are you going, bouchelleen-bawn". Bouchelleen-bawn. John Banim. 6858-8
"And where we love is home". Oliver Wendell Holmes. 6109-5
"And while the wind began to sweep". Alfred Lord Tennyson. 6997-5
"And who is he of regal mien". Ode for the new year, 1761. William Whitehead. 6867-7
"And who so coy? what is yor rose." Unknown. 6563-5
"And why are you so pale, my Nora?". Growing rich. Alice Cary. 6969-X
"And why not I, as hee". To himselfe and the harpe. Michael Drayton. 6933-9
"And will he not come again?," fr. Hamlet. William Shakespeare. 6187-7,6328-4,6194-X
"And will they cast the altars down". In Portugal, 1912. Alice Meynell. 6955-X
"And Willy, my eldest-born, is gone...". The grandmother. Alfred Lord Tennyson. 6977-0
And wilt thou leave me thus? Sir Thomas Wyatt. 6182-6,6187-7,6430-2,6646-1
And wilt thou weep when I am low? George Gordon, 6th Baron Byron. 6945-2
"And with it fled the tempest, so that ocean". Percy Bysshe Shelley. 6997-5
And with no language but a cry. Amos Niven Wilder. 6337-3, 6532-5
"And witness, dear companion of my walks". The task, sels. William Cowper. 6831-6
"And would you faine the reason know". A booke of Ayres (VIII). Thomas Campion. 6794-8
"And would you see my mistress' face?". Song ("And would"). Unknown. 6436-1
"And would you see my mistress' face?" Thomas Campion. 6935-5

"And would you see my mistris face?". A booke of Ayres (II). Thomas Campion. 6794-8
"And ye are strong to shelter! all meek things". Thoughts connected with trees (2). Felicia Dorothea Hemans. 6973-8
And ye shall walk in silk attire. Susanna Blamire. 6086-2
And yet. Maimie A. Richardson. 6269-5
"And yet God's world is speaking". A new mother. Adelaide Anne Procter. 6957-6
"And yet I am one who looks behind". Seeking forgetfulness. William Bell Scott. 7015-9
And yet fools say. George Sanford Holmes. 6464-7
And yet, because thou overcomest so. Elizabeth Barrett Browning. 6430-2
"And yet, for chastisement of these regrets". Morning after the ball, fr. The prelude. William Wordsworth. 6832-4
"And you as well must die, beloved dust". Sonnet ("And you as well"). Edna St. Vincent Millay. 6102-8,6076-5
"--And you begin to grow, but no one notices". 'Grow in hope and grace'. Barbara Anne Baker. 7024-8
"And you that glisten through the lovely blue". St. Francis to the birds, sel. William Alexander Percy. 7014-0
"And you will never find me". Fugitive. Blanche Waltrip Rose. 6906-1
And your young men shall see visions. Margaret Mead. 6808-1
"And Zion be the glory yet' Unknown. 6848-0
And, as the cock crew, those who stood..., fr.Rubaiyat. Omar Khayyam. 7039-6
"And, father cardinal, I have heard..", fr. King John. William Shakespeare. 6879-0
"And, lo, leading a blessed host comes one". Lincoln. Harriet Monroe. 6871-5
"And, O beloved voices, upon which". Futurity. Elizabeth Barrett Browning. 7037-X
"And, therefore, when I look into my heart". The perplexity. Frederick William Faber. 6980-0
And/or. Clarence Day. 6722-0
An Andalusian folk song. Richard Lawson Gales. 6950-9
Andante for autumn. Herman Salinger. 6799-9
Andante, fr. Summer night. Bayard Taylor. 6976-2
Andean crossing. Alejandro Peralta. 6759-X
Andersdatter, Karla Margaret
  "Shoshone father" 6998-3
Andersen, Hans Christian
  Little Gretchen. 6131-1
  New Year's eve. 6424-8
  The pearl. Charles Wharton Stork (tr.). 6555-4
  The rosebud. Charles Wharton Stork (tr.). 6555-4
Andersen, Johannes Carl
  Summer. 6784-0
Anderson, Alexander ("Surfaceman")
  The Apollo Belvidere, fr. In Rome. 6819-7
  Big fittie Jock. 6819-7
  Bowl aboot. 6819-7
  Cuddle doon. 6889-8
  Cuddle doon. 6271-7
  How little Tom was saved. 6167-2,6652-6
  Jenny wi' the airn teeth. 6819-7
  "Langsyne, when life was bonnie". 6819-7
  Nottman. 6819-7
  O, mither, sing a sang to the bairns. 6929-0
  Toshie Norrie. 6180-X
Anderson, Alice D.
  The poet. 6178-8
  The poet. 6178-8
Anderson, Bernice Gibbs
  Isn't it true! 6799-9
Anderson, Dorothy
  Dust. 6034-X
Anderson, Edna L.
  It seems to me. 6178-8
Anderson, Ethel
  Flood. 6384-5
  Love in age. 6349-7
  Yesterday. 6384-5
Anderson, Isabel
  In a Sudan village. 6894-4

Anderson, J. Redwood
    Mary O'Brian. 6872-3
    A prayer in war-time. 6783-2
Anderson, Jack
    Astounding tales. 7003-5
    The invention of New Jersey. 6803-0
    A lecture on avant-garde art. 7003-5
    A not uncommon case: a melodrama. 7003-5
Anderson, Jack L.
    Antother letter to Joseph Bruchac. 6870-7
    Face in a mirror. 6870-7
    Faces. 6870-7
    Reading sign. 6870-7
    Visit to the hermitage. 6870-7
Anderson, Jessie Annie
    Prayer to the sacred heart. 6295-5
Anderson, Jo
    The piddlin' pup. 6231-8
Anderson, John
    Clipper ships. 6833-2
    Shadows of sails. 6833-2
Anderson, Joseph M.
    He's just a dog. 7008-6
Anderson, Katherine Finnigan
    My little Cape Cod maiden. 6818-9
Anderson, Margaret Steele
    Madison Cawein. 6029-3
    Somebody's garden. 6820-0
Anderson, Mary Louisa
    Now, Lord, upon thy sea of air. 6337-3
Anderson, Maxwell
    Epilogue. 6039-0
    Full-circle. 6034-X
    Prayer after youth. 6039-0
    Telemachus muses. 6396-9
    "The time when I was plowing." 6036-6
    Toll the bell for Damon. 6817-0
    Youth's songs. 6241-5
Anderson, May M.
    The child martyr. 6574-0
Anderson, Mrs. (tr.)
    Flower dances. Unknown (German), 6373-X
Anderson, Oma Carlyle
    If you have a little boy. 6750-6
    Let me forget. 6750-6
Anderson, Patrick
    Cold colloquy. 6446-9
    Drinker. 6446-9
    My bird-wrung youth. 6446-9
Anderson, Robert
    Buck o' Kingwatter. 6328-4
Anderson, Robert Gordon
    Leader of men. 6995-9
Anderson, W.H.
    In welcome to the president. 7001-9
Andrade, Carlos Drummond de
    The dead in frock coats. 6758-1
    The dirty hand. 6758-1
    Don't kill yourself. 6758-1
    The elephant. 6758-1
    Quadrille. 6758-1
    Souvenir of the ancient world. 6758-1
    Your shoulders hold up the world. 6758-1
Andrade, E.N. da C.
    Song ("Nothing I have"). 6072-2
Andrade, Jorge Carrera
    Biography. H.R. Hays (tr.). 6642-9
    Bulletin of bad weather. H.R. Hays (tr.). 6642-9
    Dining-room mirror. H.R. Hays (tr.). 6642-9
    Dust, corpse of time. H.R. Hays (tr.). 6642-9
    Election handbill of green. H.R. Hays (tr.). 6642-9
    Hydrographic poem. H.R. Hays (tr.). 6642-9
    Indian rbellion. H.R. Hays (tr.). 6642-9
    Nameless islands. H.R. Hays (tr.). 6642-9
    Nothing belongs to us. H.R. Hays (tr.). 6642-9
Andre. Charlotte Fiske Bates. 6946-0
Andre passes. G.S. B. 6817-0
Andre's last request. Nathaniel Parker Willis. 6424-8
Andre's request to Washington. Nathaniel Parker Willis. 6946-0
Andre, John
    The cow-chace. 6946-0
Andrea del Sarto. Robert Browning. 6154-0,6484-1,6488-4, 6527-9,6536-8,6604-,6655-0,6657-7,6726-3,6660-7,6631-3,6723 ,6102-8,6110-9,6199-0,6192-3,6430-2
Andrea del Sarto, sels. Robert Browning. 6337-3
Andreas, sels. Unknown. 6489-2
Andrew Batan. Unknown. 6061-7
Andrew Hofer. Julius Mosen. 6424-8
Andrew Jackson, fr. The tall men. Donald Davidson. 7017-5
Andrew Lammie. Unknown. 6057-9,6185-0,6185-0
Andrew M'Crie. Robert Fuller Murray. 6802-2
Andrew Magrath's reply to John O'Tuomy. Andrew Magrath. 6930-4
Andrew Marteen. Unknown. 6061-7
Andrew Rykman's prayer. John Greenleaf Whittier. 6126-5
Andrew Rykman's prayer, sels. John Greenleaf Whittier. 6337-3
Andrew of Crete
    Christian, dost thou see them? John Mason Neale (tr.). 6337-3
Andrew, Father
    Love's argument. 6337-3
Andrew-caretaker. Arthur Wallace Peach. 6038-2
Andrews, Albert Charlton
    The maker's image. 6889-8
Andrews, Charlton
    Our modest doughboys. 6946-0
Andrews, Francis
    Phyllis inamorata. 6563-5
Andrews, George Lawrence
    At Ellis Island. 6039-0
    The charwoman. 6039-0
    Dawn. 6037-4
    Wild geese. 6039-0
Andrews, Joan
    Autumn in a New Hampshire village. 6764-6
    I watched spring. 6764-6
Andrews, John Williams
    New wonder. 6979-7
Andrews, Margaret Lovell
    At a Breton sea-blessing. 6875-8
Andrews, Mark
    John Peel. 7008-6
Andrews, Mary Raymond Shipman
    A call to arms. 6946-0
Andrews, Maude
    The fad obsolete. 7021-3
Andro and his cutty gun. Unknown. 6180-X
"Androcles from his injur'd lord, in dread". Reciprocal kindness the primary law of nature. Vincent Bourne. 6814-6
Andromache's lament. Unknown (Latin) 6948-7
Andromache's wedding. Sappho. 6435-3
Andromache, fr. The Iliad. Homer. 6435-3
Andromeda. Euripides. 6435-3
Andromeda. Gerard Manley Hopkins. 6209-1
Andromeda. James Jeffrey Roche. 6022-6,6096-X,6172-9
Andromeda. James Jeffrey Roche. 7041-8
Andromeda and the sea-nymphs. Charles Kingsley. 6656-9
Andros, R.S.S.
    Perseverance. 6302-9,6304-7
Andy Youngblood. Mary Elizabeth Mahnkey. 6662-3
Ane by ane. George Macdonald. 6180-X
"Ane doolie sessoun to ane cairfull dyte". The testament of Cresseid. Robert Henryson. 6845-6
Ane sang of the birth of Christ. Martin Luther. 6125-7
Ane satire of the three estaitis, sels. Sir David Lyndsay. 6845-6
Ane supplication in contemplation of syde taillis. Sir David Lyndsay. 6845-6
" .Anear the centre of that northern crest, fr. The city..." James ("B.V.") Thomson. 6508-2
Anecdote for fathers. William Wordsworth. 6867-7,6828-6
Anecdote of the jar, fr. Pecksniffiana. Wallace Stevens. 6531-7
Anemones. Robert P. Tristram Coffin. 7040-X
Anemones ("Under the soil."). Unknown. 6720-4
Anemones for Miss Austen. Bernard Bergonzi. 6257-1
Anetta ones- her book. Frank Lebby Stanton. 6576-7

Aneurin
  Odes of the months. 6873-1
Angel. Alexander Pushkin. 6103-6
The angel and the child, fr. Jean Reboul. Henry Wadsworth Longfellow. 6772-7
The angel and the rose. Carlos Oquendo de Amat. 6759-X
The angel at the ford. William James Dawson. 6656-9
"An angel came, of her rank the fairest". Painting. Edward Farquhar. 6939-8
Angel court. Grace Coolidge. 6629-1
An angel describes truth. Ben Jonson. 6933-9
Angel faces. Dinah Maria Mulock Craik. 6304-7
The angel ferry. Henry S. Cornwell. 6404-3
Angel guidance. Edward R. Huxley. 6885-5
"The angel host that sped last night". Christmas morning. Eugene Field. 6949-5
Angel hosts. Edward R. Huxley. 6885-5
"An angel in black" Christine Busta. 6769-7
The angel in the house, sels. Coventry Patmore. 6123-0, 6198-2,6066-8,6508-2,6560-0,6250-4,6656-9
An angel in the house. Leigh Hunt. 6737-9,6219-9,6321-7, 6543-0,6271-7,6429-9,6600-3
The angel in the house. Coventry Patmore. 6908-8
The angel mother. Edward R. Huxley. 6885-5
Angel neighbors. James Abraham Martling. 6952-5
"The angel of death through the dry earth slid". Music of the spheres. William Bell Scott. 6819-7
The angel of death, sels. Johan Olof Wallin. 6045-5
The angel of death. Adelaide Anne Procter. 6957-6
The angel of life. Richard Rowe. 6784-0
The angel of patience. John Greenleaf Whittier. 6302-0, 6385-3,6418-3,6730-1
Angel of peace. Unknown. 6274-1
An angel of Peruginio. Arthur Symons. 6655-0
Angel of the agony, fr. The dream of Gerontius. John Henry, Cardinal Newman. 6931-2
"The angel of the morning, garbed in gold". Sonnet ("The angel"). Edwin Justus Mayer. 6880-4
The angel of the sombre cowl. Alma Frances McCollum. 6115-X
The angel of the sun. Felicia Dorothea Hemans. 6973-8
The angel of the world. George Croly. 6980-0
Angel or woman. Thomas Parnell. 6153-2
"Angel spirits of sleep". Robert Bridges. 6487-6
The angel that missed Christmas. William E. Brooks. 6039-0
Angel thoughts. John Keats. 7020-5
An angel touched your forehead. Ernst von der Recke. 6555-4
An angel unawares. Unknown. 6337-3
Angel visits. Felicia Dorothea Hemans. 6973-8
Angel voices. Mary B. Stevenson. 6144-3
"The angel voices of the sky". Christmas hymn. Alice Polk Hill. 6836-7
Angel wings. Harriet Holman. 7016-7
"An angel with a radiant face". The angel and the child, fr. Jean Reboul. Henry Wadsworth Longfellow. 6772-7
The angel's bidding. Adelaide Anne Procter. 6957-6
"Angel's blessings all around". Sarah's prayer for dark nights. Sarah Morse. 6883-9
The angel's kiss. Alma Frances McCollum. 6115-X
Angel's serenade. Unknown. 6706-9
The angel's song. John Henry, Cardinal Newman. 6328-4
The angel's song. Edmund Hamilton Sears. 6006-4,6065-X, 6449-3
The angel's story. Adelaide Anne Procter. 6694-1,6742-5, 6747-6
An angel's visit. Eliza Sproat Turner. 6385-3,6600-3
"Angel's voice rose recently cut". The angel and the rose. Carlos Oquendo de Amat. 6759-X
The angel's whisper. Samuel Lover. 6219-9,6424-8,6658-5, 6543-0,6078-1,6174-5,6302-0,6385-3,6502-3,6519
The angel's whisper. Unknown. 6616-X
The angel, fr. Four songs, after Verlaine. Alfred Noyes. 6151-6
Angel, fr. The dream of Gerontius. John Henry, Cardinal Newman. 6931-2
Angel-nocturne. Xavier Villaurrutia. 6759-X
"The angel/against a backdrop of gold". Annunciation. John Minczeski. 6966-5
The angel. William Blake. 6086-2

The angel. Mildred Focht. 6847-2
The angel. Jeannette Bliss Gillespy. 6118-4
The angel. Carl Horn. 6249-0
The angel. Mikhail Lermontov. 6103-6
The angel. Unknown. 6920-7
Angela. Philip James Bailey. 6980-0
The angelic chorus. D.J. Donahoe. 6172-9,6292-X
Angelic ministry. Edmund Spenser. 6600-3
Angelic service. Winifred M. Letts. 6162-1
The angelic song. Ivy English. 6745-X
Angelic songs are swelling. Frederick William Faber. 6304-7
The angelic workshop. John Milton. 6543-0
Angelica and the ork. Sir John Harington. 6436-1
Angelina ("When de fiddle gits to singing..."). Paul Laurence Dunbar. 6274-1,6653-4
"Angelina, you who know how to sew...". The dead grenadier. Pedro Juan Vignale. 6759-X
Angeline. Harry Lee. 6607-0
Angeline, Sister Mary
  Laughter in heaven. 6285-7
Angelita, Sister Mary
  Signum cui contradicetur. 6292-X
Angellier, Auguste
  Dreams. Henry Van Dyke (tr.). 6961-4
  An evocation. Henry Van Dyke (tr.). 6961-4
  Eyes and lips. Henry Van Dyke (tr.). 6961-4
  The garland of sleep. Henry Van Dyke (tr.). 6961-4
  The ivory cradle. Henry Van Dyke (tr.). 6961-4
  L'habitude. 6801-4
  La grele. 6801-4
  The old bridge. Henry Van Dyke (tr.). 6961-4
  Resignation. Henry Van Dyke (tr.). 6961-4
  Tranquil habit. Henry Van Dyke (tr.). 6961-4
Angelo. Stuart Sterne. 6673-9
Angelo orders his dinner. Bayard Taylor. 6089-7,6440-X
Angels. Marie Louise Allen. 6906-1
Angels. Edmund Spenser. 6935-5
Angels and ministers of grace, fr. Hamlet. William Shakespeare. 6328-4,6392-6
"Angels at the foot,/And angels at the head". Sing-song. Christina Georgina Rossetti. 6828-6
The angels for the nativity of our Lord. William Drummond of Hawthornden. 6931-2
"Angels have talked with him and showed him...". The mystic. Alfred Lord Tennyson. 6977-0
"Angels holy,/High and lowly". Psalm 148. Bible. 6848-0
"Angels in heaven, you've held him so long!". Little blue shoes. Maybelle McLaurin Kinsey. 7016-7
"The angels in high places". Azrael. Robert Gilbert Walsh. 6337-3,6102-8,6310-1,6076-5
Angels of Bethlehem. Edmund Hamilton Sears. 6304-7
The angels of Buena Vista. John Greenleaf Whittier. 6126-5, 6219-9,6419-1,6568-6,6142-7,6358-6,6486-8,6457-4, 6552-X6610
"Angels of light, spread your bright wings...". Ministering angels. Adelaide Anne Procter. 6957-6
Angels of snow. Lorna Crozier. 6767-0
Angels of the spring. Robert Stephen Hawker. 6374-8
The angels' call. Felicia Dorothea Hemans. 6973-8
"Angels, roll the rock away!". Thomas Scott. 6065-X
"Angels, where you soar". A prayer ("Angels"). Alfred Noyes. 6169-9
The angels.. William Drummond of Hawthornden. 6145-1,6239-3,6438-8,6746-8
Angelus. Carmen Alicia Cadilla. 6759-X
Angelus Silesius. See Scheffler, Johannes
"Angelus inquit pastoribus". Now the mosy high is born. James Ryman. 6881-2
Angelus song. Austin Dobson. 6240-7
The Angelus. Florence Earle Coates. 6631-3
The angelus. Francis Bret Harte. 6241-5
The angelus. Robert Loveman. 6941-X
Anger. Cesar Vallejo. 6642-9
Anglais mort a Florence. Wallace Stevens. 6751-4
"The angle of the sun, declining, lifts". Envoi. John Barton. 6767-0
Angler. Isabel Fiske Conant. 6501-5
The angler's ballad. Charles Cotton. 6152-4
The angler's farewell. Thomas Hood. 6974-6

ANGLER'S

Angler's fireside song. Henry Van Dyke. 6961-4
The angler's invitation. Thomas Tod Stoddart. 6239-3
The angler's reveille. Henry Van Dyke. 6457-4,6497-3
The angler's song. William Basse. 6398-5
The angler's song. John Chalkhill. 6328-4
The angler's song. John Dennys. 6182-6
The angler's song. Isaac McLellan Jr. 6752-2
The angler's song. Unknown. 6563-5
The angler's trysting tree. Thomas Tod Stoddart. 6271-7, 6302-0,6385-3,6219-2
The angler's vindication. Thomas Tod Stoddart. 6180-X
An angler's wish. Henry Van Dyke. 6478-7,6300-4,6431-0, 6336-5
The angler's wish. Izaak Walton. 6271-7,6302-0,6385-3,6563-5,6219-9,6737
The angler. John Chalkhill. 6302-0,6385-3,6271-7,6219-9
The angler. Felicia Dorothea Hemans. 6973-8
The angler. Thomas Buchanan Read. 6302-0;6385-3
The anglers' grave. Thomas Tod Stoddart. 6960-6
Anglesburg, Eva R.
    Pioneer woman. 6270-9
"Anglice, et vnanimis Scotice pater, anne...". Ad Inuictissimum, Serenissimumque Iacobvm. Thomas Campion. 6794-8
Anglicised Utopia. Sir William Schwenck Gilbert. 6996-7
Angling. Thomas Doubleday. 7015-9
Angling. Ada E. Hall. 6818-9
Angling. Caroline Anne Bowles Southey. 6980-0
Angling, fr. Spring. James Thomson. 6302-0;6385-3
Anglo-Norman carol. Unknown. 6747-6
Anglo-Norman carol. Unknown. 6756-5
The Anglo-Saxon brood. Arthur Stringer. 6224-5
The Anglo-Saxon language. Vachel Lindsay. 6345-4
"An Angora cat sat quietly in his home". A concatenation. Carolyn Wells. 6882-0
The angora cat. Frederick Locker-Lampson. 6760-3
Angosto Theo. Thomas Hardy. 6730-1
Angry admonition. Dorothy Jane Deuell. 6750-6
An angry anarchist. Unknown. 6486-8
"Angry domed silo mouths/with long". The death penalty. Ross Laurse. 6792-1
The angry ones. Berton Braley. 6853-7
"The angry sunset fades from out the west". On the shore. Augusta Webster. 6997-5
Angry words. Unknown. 6919-3
"A angry young husband called Bicket". Limerick:"An angry young husband called Bicket". John Galsworthy. 6811-1
"An angry, muttering private shivered and...". Confederate wall. Greg Giles. 6883-9
Anguish. Adelaide Crapsey. 6850-2
Anguish. Henry Vaughan. 6250-4
Anguish. Paul Verlaine. 6102-8
Anguita, Eduardo
    Passage to the end. Lloyd Mallan (tr.). 6759-X
    Service. Lloyd Mallan (tr.). 6759-X
Angus Armstrong, fr. Casualties. Wilfred Wilson Gibson. 6653-4
Angus remembers. William Jeffrey. 6269-5
Angus, Marion
    Alas! Poor queen. 6845-6
"Anicent mounds upon Ohio's hills". To the Indian mounds of Ohio. Gertrude W. Robinson. 6906-1
"Anigowanotenu!/Oft these lovely days...". Passamaquoddy love song. Unknown (Algonquin Indian). 6864-2
Anima Christi. Saint Ignatius of Loyola. 6543-0
An animal alphabet ("A-the absolutely abstemious..."). Edward Lear. 6724-7
An animal alphabet ("Alligator, beetle,..."). Unknown. 6724-7
Animal crackers. Christopher Morley. 6368-3
Animal disputans. S. Milton Rose. 6039-0
Animal fair. Philip Booth. 6388-8
Animal havens, sels. John Varney. 6808-1
An animal song. Kathleen Conyngham Greene. 6510-4
Animal tranquility and decay. William Wordsworth. 6196-6
Animality of man. Edward R. Huxley. 6885-5
The animals in the ark, fr. The Chester play of the deluge. Unknown. 6125-7
The animals' fair. Carolyn Wells. 6882-0

"The animals, as once in Eden, lived". The millennium. Robert Pollock. 6980-0
Animals, fr. Song of myself. Walt Whitman. 6332-2,6396-9
The animals. Edwin Muir. 6357-9
Animated film, a sequence of emblem poems, sels. James Reaney. 6767-0
Animula. David Wevill. 6767-0
Animus. Mary Baron. 6855-3
Anita, fr. In Tuscany. Cora Fabri. 6876-6
Anitpater of Sidon
    Anacreon. Thomas Moore (tr.). 6879-0
    Erinna. A.J. Butler (tr.). 6879-0
Annderson, W.H.
    Our brother's keeper. 6542-2
Ann. William Roehrick. 6850-2
Ann Curtis. Babette Kurtz. 6850-2
Ann Peters. Florence Crocker Comfort. 6782-4
Ann Rutledge. Edwin Markham. 6619-4
Ann's way. Estelle E. Wilson. 6750-6
Anna. Babette Deutsch. 6959-2
"Anna Elsie, she jumped with surprise". Unknown. 6363-2
Anna Pavlowa (1885-1931). Charles Edward Butler. 6640-2
"'Anna'! Insipid and weak as gruel". Austin Dobson. Louis Untermeyer. 6875-8
"Anna-Marie, love, up is the sun" Sir Walter Scott. 6828-6
Annabel Lee. Stanley Huntley. 6089-7,6280-6,6440-X
Annabel Lee. Edgar Allan Poe. 6723-9,6126-5,6107-9,6560-0, 6288-1,6431-0,6513 ,6006-4,6045-1,6077-3,6102-8,6134-6,6176 ,6186-9,6240-7,6243-1,6255-5,6328-4,6332 , 6333-0,6339-X,6344-6,6370-5,6427-2,6481 ,6385-3,6639-9,6300-4,6104-4,6219-9,6226 ,6473-6,6498-1,6632-1, 6732-8,6735-2,6302 ,6076-5,6008-0,6250-4,6319-5,6396-9,6585
Annan water. Thomas Heywood. 6134-6
Annan water. Unknown. 6055-2,6075-7,6098-6,6228-8,6067-6, 6153-
Anne. Lizette Woodworth Reese. 6441-8,6632-1,6484-1
Anne Boleyn. Barbara Bingley. 6541-4
Anne Boleyn O'Shaugennessy. Ruth Crary Clough. 6750-6
Anne Greville, Countess Temple. Horace Walpole; 4th Earl of Orford. 6086-2
Anne Hathaway. Edmund ("Edmund Falconer") O'Rourke. 6922-3
Anne Hathaway. William Shakespeare. 6302-0,6429-9,6321-7, 6578-3
Anne Hathaway. Unknown. 6166-4,6385-3
Anne Hathaway alone at Avon. Anna Catherine Markham. 6327-6
"Anne Hutchinson did not believe". Glory. Estelle Rooks. 6850-2
Anne Hutchinson's exile. Edward Everett Hale. 6946-0
Anne Rutledge. Edgar Lee Masters. 6076-5,6161-3,6121-4, 6653-4,6393-4,6102-8,6332-2,6538-4,6583-X,6732-8, 6646
Anne's curls. Stan Rice. 6901-0
Annie. Edwin Ford Piper. 6031-5
"Annie Winne and me". The confession of Annaple Gowdie, witch. Walter Chalmers Smith. 6819-7
Annie and Willie's prayer. Sophia P. Snow. 6045-1,6142-7, 6165-6,6554-6,6131-1,6565
Annie Bolanny. Unknown. 6125-7
Annie in the grave-yard. Caroline Gilman. 6271-7
Annie Laurie. Lady John Scott and William Douglas. 6289-X, 6737-9
Annie Laurie. William Douglas. 6104-4,6486-8,6289-X,6396-9, 6250-4,6066-8,6239-3,6240-7,6136-2,6332-2,6479-5
Annie Laurie. Lady John Scott. 6732-8,6304-7
Annie Laurie. Unknown. 6014-5,6180-X,6204-0,6302-0,6129-9, 6094
Annie of Lochroyan. Unknown. 6056-0
Annie Pickens. Eugene J. Hall. 6921-5
Annie Protheroe. Sir William Schwenck Gilbert. 6410-8
Annie Shore and Johnnie Doon. Patrick Orr. 6897-9
Annie Smith. John Davidson. 6383-7
Annie's garden. Eliza Lee Follen. 6452-3,6135-4
Annie's ticket. Unknown. 6914-2
Annie's ticket. Unknown. 6139-7
Annie, Harriet
    Death of Gaudentis. 6910-X
Annie, dear. Thomas Osborne Davis. 6858-8
Annihilation. Conrad Aiken. 6012-9

Annihilation. George Chinn. 6672-0
Annis Vane - A.D. 1558. Margaret Junkin Preston. 6965-7
Anniversaries. Aldous Huxley. 6872-3
Anniversary. Robert Bridges. 6487-6
Anniversary. Arturo Giovannitti. 6880-4
Anniversary. Hermann Hagedorn. 6347-0
Anniversary. Heloise M.B. Hawkins. 6836-7
Anniversary. Arthur Winfield Knight. 6998-3
Anniversary. Kevin Sullivan. 6839-1
An **anniversary** ("Bright, my beloved..."). Robert Bridges. 6487-6
Anniversary ("See Love, a year is pass'd..."). Unknown. 6487-6
The **anniversary** deaths. Charles W. Denison. 6755-7
Anniversary for armistice. Muriel F. Hochdorf. 6850-2
Anniversary hymn. George Houghton. 7041-8
Anniversary ode. Charles Dickens. 6168-0
Anniversary of the birth of Abraham Lincoln. Levi Lewis Hager. 6524-4
Anniversary sonnet. Sue Marra. 6857-X
An **anniversary.** Richard Lovelace. 6315-2
The **anniversary.** Gamaliel Bradford. 6036-6
The **anniversary.** John Donne. 6150-8,6341-1,6023-4,6430-2, 6186-9,6562-7,6536-8,6634-8,6317-9
The **anniversary.** Wilfred Wilson Gibson. 6071-4
The **anniversary.** Sir Ronald Ross. 6482-5
The **anniverse.** Henry King. 6378-0
Anniversry toast. Luna Craven Osburn. 6799-9
Anno 1829. Heinrich Heine. 7039-1
Anno domini. John Bellenden. 6022-6
Anno santo. Stephen Spender. 6209-1
Annot Lyle's song: 'Birds of omen,' fr. The legend... Sir Walter Scott. 6828-6
Annotation. Eleanor [pseud]. 6817-0
Announcement. Harry Brown. 6761-1
The **annoyer.** Nathaniel Parker Willis. 6271-7
Annual legend. Winfield Townley Scott. 6390-X,6666-6
The **Annuciation** ("Not yesterday, nor yet a day"). Margaret Devereaux Conway. 6282-2
The **annuitant's** answer. George Outram. 6878-2
The **annuity.** George Outram. 6878-2,6912-6
The **annuity.** George Outram. 6089-7,6554-6,6180-X,6385-3, 6568-6
"**Annunciata** stands". Pavane. Edith Sitwell. 7000-0
Annunciation. Ken Etheridge. 6360-8
Annunciation. John Minczeski. 6966-5
Annunciation. John Minczeski. 6966-5
The **Annunciation** ("'Fiat'-The flaming word"). John Banister Tabb. 6282-2
The **Annunciation** ("Mary, Mother of our Maker"). Saint Nerses. 6282-2
The **Annunciation** ("Our lady went forth pondering") Unknown. 6282-2
Annunciation ("Salvation to all that will is nigh") . John Donne. 6282-2
Annunciation night. Katherine Eleanor Conway. 6144-3
Annunciation night, fr. Mary of Nazareth. Abby Maria Hemenway. 6282-2
Annunciation to all women. Agnes C. Foote. 6144-3
The **annunciation,** fr. Davideis. Abraham Cowley. 6931-2
The **annunciation.** Felicia Dorothea Hemans. 6973-8
The **annunciation.** Margot Kriel. 6966-5
The **Annunciation.** Unknown. 6881-2
The **annunication.** Adelaide Anne Procter. 6674-4,6172-9
Annus memorabilis, 1789. William Cowper. 6814-6
Annus Mirabilis. John Dryden. 6208-3
Annus Mirabilis (1902). Laurence Housman. 6477-9
Annus Mirabilis, sels. John Dryden. 6198-2,6562-7,6195-0
Anodyne. Harriet Gray Blackwell. 6750-6
An **anodyne** ("As in the night I restless lie"). Thomas Ken. 6533-3
An **anodyne.** Thomas Ken. 6931-2
The **anodyne.** Sarah N. Cleghorn. 6501-5
"**Anon** the murky cloud is riven". Unknown. 6902-9
Anonymous. John Banister Tabb. 6102-8,6076-5,6431-0,6300-4
Anonymous speech. Jorge Carrera Andrade. 6642-9
Anonymous speech. Ramon Lopez Velarde. 6642-9
The **anonymous** valentine. Wilbur Dick Nesbit. 6401-9
Another. Ann Buddy. 6249-0
Another. William Cowper. 6250-4

Another. Robert Herrick. 6879-0
"**Another** April dared to come and flaunt". From a sonnet sequence. Bernard K. Kay. 6764-6
'**Another** Athens shall arise'. A.M. Stephen. 6224-5
Another beetle. Jean Diefenbach. 6262-8
"**Another** call to higher spheres". Parent's solace. Edward R. Huxley. 6885-5
Another chance. Henry Van Dyke. 6961-4
Another cross. John Masefield. 6337-3
Another day. Douglas Malloch. 6583-X
Another day. Betsy Winter. 6799-9
"**Another** day awakes. And who". West wind in winter. Alice Meynell. 6955-X
Another dialogue, to be sung at the same time. Thomas Campion. 6794-8
"**Another** flagon, old friend! O course". Told at The Falcon. Edwin Coller. 6925-8
Another generation. Sir John Collings ("Solomon Eagle") Squire. 6069-2
Another grace for a child. Robert Herrick. 6562-7,6645-3, 6194-X
Another kind of autumn. Patricia M. Johnson. 6857-X
"**Another** land has crashed into the deep". Roumania. George Edward Woodberry. 7027-2
"**Another** Leonora once inspir'd". To Leonora singing at Rome. John Milton. 6814-6
Another life. Philip Levine. 6792-1,6998-3
Another little wave. Lucy Evelina Akerman. 6131-1
Another man's poison. Constance Milton. 6750-6
Another match. Unknown. 6453-1
"**Another** new gown, as I declare!". Grandmother. May Probyn. 6770-0
"**Another** nickel in the slot". A hero in the land of dough. Robert Clairmont. 6751-4
Another ode to the north-east wind. Unknown. 6802-2
Another of the same..., fr. The Phoenix Nest. Sir Edward Dyer. 6586-4
Another old song. Barney Bush. 7005-1
Another on her. Robert Herrick. 6194-X
"**Another** one of God's pictures". January sunrise. Hattie B. Terril. 6799-9
"**Another** part (a prospect differing...", fr. The Iliad. Homer. 6435-3
Another plum cake. Ann and Jane Taylor. 6105-2
Another plum cake. Jane Taylor. 6131-1
Another poem. Edward Farquhar. 6939-8
"**Another** reason why you have not died". To Knute Rockne. Estelle Rooks. 6850-2
"**Another** side, unbrageous grots and caves". Paradise, fr. Paradise lost. John Milton. 6933-9
Another song. William Ross. 6845-6
Another sonnet to black it self. Edward Herbert, 1st Baron Herbert of Cherbury. 6562-7
Another spirit advances. Jules Romains. 6351-9
Another spirit advances. Jules Romains. 7039-6,6343-8
"**Another** stiff, another midriff". America. Charles Haseloff. 6998-3
Another sunset. John Minczeski. 6966-5
Another tribute to Wyatt. Henry Howard, Earl of Surrey. 6584-8
Another visit of St. Nicholas. Carolyn Wells. 6882-0
Another visit of St. Nicholas. Carolyn Wells. 6882-0
Another Washington. Joel Benton. 6708-5
"**Another** warning sound! the funeral bell". Stanzas to the memory of George the Third. Felicia Dorothea Hemans. 6973-8
Another way. Ambrose Bierce. 6076-5,6006-4,6102-8,6732-8, 6076-5,6307-1,6300
Another way. Andrew Lang. 6180-X
Another way of love. Robert Browning. 6828-6
Another way of love. Robert Browning. 6110-9,6655-0
Another year. Katharine Lee Bates. 6747-6
Another year. Thomas O'Hagan. 6449-3
Another year. A.M. Walton. 6662-3
"**Another** year - and I am twenty-five". Anniversary. Kevin Sullivan. 6839-1
"**Another** year! Time marks them fast". To J.A.S. on his -- tieth birthday. Louis J. Magee. 7004-3
"**Another** year!-another deadly blow!". William Wordsworth. 6323-3

"Another year/Of sighs and song". Triolet. J.O. L.. 6817-0
"Another! 'tis a sad word to the heart". On the death of Mr. Woodward, at Edinburgh. John Gardiner Calkins Brainard. 6752-2
"'Another', says the child we love". Another poem. Edward Farquhar. 6939-8
"Anout the time of Christmas". Jane Conquest. Unknown. 6915-0
Anschusa [pseud].
    The goldenrod. 6846-4
Anspacher, Louis K.
    The future speaks. 6799-9
Anster, John
    The fairy child. 6271-7
    If I might choose. 6930-4
Anstey, Christopher
    Letter containing a panegyric on Bath. 6932-0
    The new Bath guide, sels. 6152-4
    The public breakfast. 6996-7
Anstey, F. See Gutherie, Thomas A.
Answer. Isabel Fiske Conant. 6619-4
Answer. Harriet Hoock. 6543-0
Answer. Sir Walter Scott. 6861-8
Answer. Leonora Speyer. 6513-9
Answer for hope. Richard Crashaw. 6341-1
Answer from Assisi. Isabel Harriss Barr. 6979-7
Answer of the mummy at Belzoni's exhibition. Unknown. 6910-X
Answer of the mummy at Belzoni's exhibition. Unknown. 6302-0;6385-3
"The answer that ye made to me, my dear." Sir Thomas Wyatt. 6584-8
Answer to 'I am dying'. William Laurie. 6910-X
Answer to a beautiful poem entitled The common lot. George Gordon, 6th Baron Byron. 6945-2
Answer to a charge of inconstancy. John Herman Merivale. 6980-0
Answer to a child's question. Samuel Taylor Coleridge. 6302-0,6385-3,6519-8,6133-8,6138-9,6066-8,6135-4, 6638-0,6449-3,6424-8,6131-1
Answer to a timid lover. Bernice Lesbia Kenyon. 6036-6
Answer to Chloe jealous. Matthew Prior. 6563-5,6026-9,6152-4,6092-7
Answer to Cui Bono. Jane Welsh Carlyle. 6424-8
Answer to Lines written in Rousseau's Letters of...nun. George Gordon, 6th Baron Byron. 6945-2
Answer to Marlowe. Sir Walter Raleigh. 6436-1
Answer to Master Wither's song, 'Shall I, wasting...' Ben Jonson. 6089-7,6440-X
Answer to one. Louise McNeill. 6761-1
Answer to pauper. Thomas Hood. 6974-6
An answer to Rock me to sleep. Unknown. 6963-0
Answer to some elegant verses sent by a friend... George Gordon, 6th Baron Byron. 6945-2
Answer to stanzas addressed to Lady Hesketh. William Cowper. 6814-6
Answer to the "Hour of death". Mrs. C.B. Wilson. 6403-5
Answer to the following question of Mrs. Howe. Alexander Pope. 6874-X
The answer to the objection. Sir John Davies. 6584-8
Answer to the passionate shepherd. Sir Walter Raleigh. 6543-0
Answer to 'Five o'clock in the morning'. Unknown. 6406-X
Answer to 'Leona'. Unknown. 6406-X
"The answer which our faith receives". Such as I have give I unto thee. William White. 6868-5
Answer world!. Angela Morgan. 6542-2
"Answer, ye chiming waves". The voice of the waves. Felicia Dorothea Hemans. 6973-8
The answer.. Grantland Rice. 6291-1
An answer. Robert Browning. 7015-9
An answer. George Frederick Cameron. 6115-X
An answer. Perceval Gibbon. 6793-X
An answer. S. St. G. Lawrence. 6510-4
An answer. Sir Toby Matthews. 6563-5
An answer. Bayard Taylor. 6976-2
An answer. Ella Wheeler Wilcox. 6956-8
The answer. Sara Hamilton Birchall. 6374-8
The answer. Katherine (Amelia Beers Warnock Garvin) Hale. 6115-X

The answer. Rudyard Kipling. 6810-3
The answer. Isabella Bryans Longfellow. 6750-6
The answer. James Abraham Martling. 6952-5
The answer. Geoffrey Matthews. 6895-2
The answer. Josephine A. Meyer. 6847-2
The answer. John Henry Owens. 6178-8
The answer. Sara Teasdale. 6029-3
The answer. Sara Teasdale. 6897-9
The answer. Alfred Lord Tennyson. 6977-0
Answered. Phoebe Cary. 6969-X,6461-2
Answered. Ella Wheeler Wilcox. 6956-8,6863-4
Answered. Ella Wheeler Wilcox. 7041-8
The answered prayer. Unknown. 6260-1
Answered prayers. Ella Wheeler Wilcox. 6415-9
Answering to roll-call. Frank Lebby Stanton. 6471-X
Answering wind. Ida E. Sprague. 6857-X
The answers, fr. Eight doorknobs to a door. Robert Clairmont. 6324-1,6722-0
The ant an engineer. Unknown. 6373-X
The ant and the cricket. Unknown. 6639-9,6165-6,6401-9, 6519-8,6614-3,6135-4,6424
The ant and the grasshopper. Joseph Crosby Lincoln. 6119-2
"Ant grist for the mill?". The water-mill. Ann ("Aunt Effie") Hawkshawe. 6937-1,6018-8
The ant in office. John Gay. 6972-X
The ant. Al-Tulaitili. 6362-4
The ant. Isaac Watts. 6502-3
Antaeus. Daphne Muir. 6800-6
The antagonist. David Ferry. 6388-8
Antara
    Abla. Edward Powys Mathers (tr.). 7039-6
    "Make war on me, O vicissitudes of the nights". A.J. Arberry (tr.). 6766-2
Antarctic from New England. Winfield Townley Scott. 6640-2
Ante mortem. Robinson Jeffers. 6012-9
Antelope with cattle. Robert McBlair. 6850-2
"The antennae of a dream/Reaching for honey". Desire. Emma Hicks McDonald. 6799-9
Anteros. William Johnson Cory. 6437-X
Anthem. Joseph Hall. 6830-8
Anthem for doomed youth. Harold Monro. 6581-3
Anthem for doomed youth. Wilfred Owen. 6666-6,6153-2,6464-7,6209-1,6125-7,6650 ,6246-6,6337-3,6357-8,6726-3, 6542-2,6653
Anthem of the angelic quires after the last temptation. John Milton. 6334-9
Anthems for the inauguration of Jerusalem. Bible. 6488-4
Anthias, Tefcros
    The clown. Rae Dalven (tr.). 6352-7
    Epilogue. Rae Dalven (tr.). 6352-7
    Hands thrust in pockets. Rae Dalven (tr.). 6352-7
Anthologistics. Arthur Guiterman. 6722-0
Anthology of Oom. Isidor Schneider. 6039-0
Anthony Ashley Cooper, Earl of Shaftesbury, fr. Absalom. John Dryden. 6934-7
Anthony Crundle. John Drinkwater. 6506-6
Anthony, Edward
    Advice to small children. 6396-9
    Ballade of dottiness. 6875-8
    Epitaph for a deserving lady. 6875-8
    'He collected his thoughts' 6875-8
    The old watchdog to his sons. 6396-9
Anthony, Joseph
    A four-line philosophy. 6396-9
Anti-desperation. Matthew Arnold. 6947-9
Anti-Thelyphthora. William Cowper. 6814-6
Anticipation. Emily Bronte. 6123-0
Anticipation. John B.L. Warren, 3d Baron De Tabley. 6246-5
Anticipation. Amy Lowell. 6300-4
Anticipation. Lucilius. 6850-2
Anticipation. Jonathan Slocum. 6817-0
Anticipation. Jennifer Watters. 6883-9
Anticipations. Edward Verrall Lucas. 6793-X
Anticipations and recollections, sels. Samuel Bartlett Parris. 6482-5
Anticipatory dirge on Professor Buckland, the geologist. Archbishop Whately. 6787-5
Antietam. James Abraham Martling. 6952-5
WAntigone. John Reade. 7041-8
Antigone, sels. Sophocles. 6527-9

Antigonish. Hughes Mearns. 6722-0
Antimenidas. Alcaeus. 6435-3
Antin, David
    Constructions and discoveries. 6803-0
Antinous. Narcisse Wood. 6037-4
"**Antiochus.** O Antioch, my Antioch". Judas Maccabaeus. Henry Wadsworth Longfellow. 6848-0
Antipater
    "Damis the Nysaean of a little bark...". F.L. Lucas (tr.). 6251-2
    "The hunting-hound of Midas...". F.L. Lucas (tr.). 6251-2
    "No more shall stones nor oakwoods...". F.L. Lucas (tr.). 6251-2
    "Terse-tongued and sparely worded...". F.L. Lucas (tr.). 6251-2
    "Where are the towers that crowned...". F.L. Lucas (tr.). 6251-2
Antipater of Sidon
    Erinna, sels. A.J. Butler (tr.). 6435-3
    Greater love. T.F. Higham (tr.). 6435-3
    On Anacreon. Thomas Moore (tr.). 6271-7
    Orpheus ("No more with rocks..."). A.J. Butler (tr.). 6435-3
    The ruins of Corinth. Walter Leaf (tr.). 6435-3
    "This rudely sculptured porter-pot". 6637-2
Antipater of Sidon. Hilda ("H.D.") Doolittle. 7014-0
Antipater of Thessalonica
    "Ah lonely isles, fragments...". F.L. Lucas (tr.). 6251-2
    Amphipolis. Sir William Marris (tr.). 6435-3
    "Cythere the Bithynian...". F.L. Lucas (tr.). 6251-2
    Drowned in harbour. Sir William Marris (tr.). 6435-3
    "Here it was once Leander crossed...". F.L. Lucas (tr.). 6251-2
    A water mill. Sir William Marris (tr.). 6435-3
Antiphanes
    Not dead, but gone before. T.F. Higham (tr.). 6435-3
    The profession of flattery. T.F. Higham (tr.). 6435-3
Antiphilus
    "Give me a mattress...". F.L. Lucas (tr.). 6251-2
    "Long, O Protesilaus, long shall thy fame...". F.L. Lucas (tr.). 6251-2
Antiphilus of Byzantium
    A freshet. Sir William Marris (tr.). 6435-3
    Noontide rest. Sir William Marris (tr.). 6435-3
    The old ferryman. Sir William Marris (tr.). 6435-3
    Once in a way. J.E. B. (tr.). 6435-3
Antiphon. Joseph ("Seosamh MacCathmhaoil") Campbell. 6143-5
Antiphon. George Herbert. 6138-9,6527-9,6334-9
An **antiphonal** (Psalm XXIV) Bible. 6153-2
Antiphony. William Morris. 6123-0,6656-9
Antiphony for Thursday. Philip Horton. 6640-2
Antipodal. Joseph Auslander. 6039-0
Antiquated volumes. William M. Gamble. 6983-5
Antique. Elizabeth Thomas. 6880-4
The **antique** at Paris. Johann C. Friedrich von Schiller. 6424-8
Antique Greek lament. Felicia Dorothea Hemans. 6973-8
Antique harvesters. John Crowe Ransom. 6208-3
The **antique** sepulchre. Felicia Dorothea Hemans. 6973-8
Antique shop. Marguerite Steedman. 6841-3
Antiquities. Louis J. Magee. 7004-3
Antiquity. E. Merrill Root. 6880-4
The **antiquity** of art. Sir George Douglas. 6819-7
The **antiquity** of fashions. Mary J.J. Wrinn. 6850-2
Antiquity of freedom. William Cullen Bryant. 6126-5,6049-8, 6286-5,6385-3,6457-4,6288-1,6304
Antiquity of freedom, sels. William Cullen Bryant. 6176-1
Antiseptics- lenses. Isabel Fiske Conant. 7014-0
Antler
    What every boy knows. 7003-5
Antoine et Cleopatre. Jose Maria de Heredia. 6801-4
Antoine's song. Rowland Evans Robinson. 7030-2
Antolius, Saint
    Peace. 6214-8
Antoninus, Marcus Aurelius
    Even in a palace. 6424-8
Antonio. James Abraham Martling. 6952-5

Antonio. Laura E. Richards. 6554-X
Antonio Oriboni. Margaret Junkin Preston. 6411-6
Antonio ploughs. Charles Erskine Scott Wood. 6880-4
Antonio's revenge, sels. John Marston. 6315-2;6378-0
Antonio's wooing. Miguel de Saavedra Cervantes. 6732-8
Antony and Cleopatra. William Haines Lytle. 6370-5,6408-6, 6273-3,6481-7,6385-3,6486 ,6735-2,6732-8,6431-0,6219-9
Antony and Cleopatra. Eugene Mason. 6884-7
Antony and Cleopatra, sels. William Shakespeare. 6301-2, 6088-9,6472-8
Antony and Cleopatra, sels. William Shakespeare. 6186-9, 6083-8,6378-0,6186-9,6102-8,6186 ,6204-0,6339-X,6408-6,6527-9,6634-8,6192
Antony and the soothsayer. William Shakespeare. 6438-8
Antony in arms. Robert Buchanan. 6889-8
Antony on Julius Caesar. William Shakespeare. 6534-1
Antony on the death of Caesar, fr. Julius Caesar. William Shakespeare. 6552-X,6743-3
Antony over the dead body of Caesar. William Shakespeare. 6438-8
"**Antony'a** dead!", fr. Antony and Cleopatra. William Shakespeare. 6339-X
Antony's eulogy on Caesar, fr. Julius Caesar. William Shakespeare. 6457-4
Antony's oration, fr. Julius Caesar. William Shakespeare. 6294-6,6302-0
Antony's speech to Roman citizens, fr. Julius Caesar. William Shakespeare. 6552-X
Anotother letter to Joseph Bruchac. Jack L. Anderson. 6870-7
Antrin Thochts. Gilbert Rae. 6331-4
Ants. Alfred Kreymborg. 6348-9
"**Ants** are the busiest people I know". Jessie Orton Jones. 6999-1
"**Ants** climbing up my foot" Sojin Takei. 6981-9
The **ants.** John Clare. 6510-4
Antwerp. Ford Madox (Hueffer) Ford. 6897-9
Antwerp and Bruges. Dante Gabriel Rossetti. 6484-1
The **anvil.** Laurence Binyon. 7026-4
The **anvil.** Alfred Noyes. 6169-9
Anxiety. George Macdonald. 6373-X
The **anxious** anthemist. Guy Forrester Lee. 6846-4
The **anxious** dead. John McCrae. 7031-0
The anxious dead. John McCrae. 6482-5,6650-X,6104-4
The **anxious** farmer. Burges Johnson. 6338-1
"Anxious, they waited in the anteroom". The transfusion. George Sterling. 7014-0
Any boy to his first love. Edward Davison. 6779-4
"**Any** color, so long as it's red". Red. Eugene Field. 6949-5
"**Any** emotion, even joy, is wearing". Choice. Grace Blanchard. 6764-6
Any lover to his lass. Berton Braley. 6853-7
"**Any** one can hang a curtain". Burton's curtains. Robert C.V. Meyers. 6925-8
Any one will do. Unknown. 6089-7,6273-3,6505-8
Any saint. Francis Thompson. 6828-6
Any soldier son to his mother. N.G. H. 7031-0
Any time, O Lord. Josephine Van Dolzen Pease. 6037-4
Any town. Charles Norman. 6076-5
"**Any** way the old world goes". The song on the way. Unknown. 6891-X
Any wife. Albertine H. Miller. 6750-6
Any wife to any husband. Robert Browning. 6828-6
Any wife to any husband. Robert Browning. 6204-0,6208-3, 6427-2,6110-9,6094-3
Anybody's. Alice Stettiner. 6818-9
"**Anyone** can write revolution - revolution...". Revolution. William Rose Benet. 6880-4
Anyte
    "Beside the grey sea-shingle...". F.L. Lucas (tr.). 6251-2
    Death the leveller. Sir William Marris (tr.). 6435-3
    The goat. W.H.D. Rouse (tr.). 6435-3
    "in life, Manes the slave...". F.L. Lucas (tr.). 6251-2
    "Never again rejoicing in the surges...". F.L. Lucas (tr.). 6251-2
    On a cave. Thomas Warton (the Elder) (tr.). 6962-2
    A statue of Cypris. Sir William Marris (tr.). 6435-3

Under a laurel. R.A. Furness (tr.). 6435-3
Anywhere, nowhere. J. William Lloyd. 6799-9
Apache. William Haskell Simpson. 6628-3
"**Apache** dance!". Impressions of Paris. Norma Paul Ruedi. 6750-6
The **Apache** in ambush. Bailey Millard. 6102-8,6076-5
Apache-wife-Arizona. Lilian White Spencer. 6038-2
Apart. Margaret J.E. Brown. 6316-0
Apart. John James Piatt. 6243-1,7041-8
"**Apart** from the woes that are dead and gone". Alice Cary. 6969-X
"**Apart**, thank heaven, from all to do". The owl. Walter De La Mare. 6905-3
Apartment partners. Francis M. Botelho. 6750-6
The **ape** and the lady. Sir William Schwenck Gilbert. 6280-6
THe **ape** and the thinker. Owen Wister. 6579-1
The **ape's** shop. John Greenleaf Whittier. 6530-9
"The **ape**, the monkey and baboon did meet" Unknown. 6380-2
The **ape**.. Roland Young. 6722-0
Apelles' song. John Lyly. 6052-8,6189-3,6660-7,6192-3,6186-9,6198 ,6604-6
Apelles' song ("Cupid and my Campaspe played"). John Lyly. 6092-7
"**Apelles**, hearing that his boy". The tears of a painter. Vincent Bourne. 6814-6
Apes in Avernus. William Rose Benet. 6012-9
Apex. Baron Ireland [pseud]. 6722-0
Aphrodite. George William ("A.E.") Russell. 6872-3
Aphrodite. John Sterling. 6980-0
Aphrodite and the knife-grinder. Count Carl Snoilsky. 6045-5
Aphrodite metropolis (1). Kenneth Fearing. 6751-4
Aphrodite on Ida. Unknown (Greek) 6435-3
"**Aphrodite**, daughter of Zeus, undying". Sappho. 6251-2
Apocalypse. Theodore Maynard. 6172-9,6292-X
Apocalypse. Richard Realf. 6113-3,6240-7,6470-1
Apocalypse. Ronald Ross. 7027-2
Apocalypse, sels. Unknown. 6282-2
An **apocalypse**. Edward Shillito. 7031-0
Apocrypha. Babette Deutsch. 6777-8
Apocrypha. Evelyn Scott. 6761-1
Apocrypha, sels. Unknown. 6625-9
Apocryphal soliloquies. Louis Untermeyer. 6012-9,6072-2
Apolinaire, Guillaume
 Pont Mirabeau. W.J. Strachan (tr.). 6343-8
Apollinaire, Guillaume
 Hunting horns. W.J. Strachan (tr.). 6343-8
 Shadow. Jessie Degen and R. Eberhart (tr.). 6665-8
 War. Jessie Degen and R. Eberhart (tr.). 6665-8
 Zone. W.J. Strachan (tr.). 6343-8
Apollo. Matthew Arnold. 6322-5
Apollo. Thomas Holley Chivers. 7017-5
Apollo. Thomas Holley Chivers. 6176-1
Apollo and the seaman. Herbert Trench. 6877-4
The **Apollo** Belvidere, fr. In Rome. Alexander ("Surfaceman") Anderson. 6819-7
Apollo destroys his horses, fr. The Iliad. Homer. 6435-3
"**Apollo** hearing this, passed quickly on". Homer. 6435-3
"**Apollo** left the golden muse". Villanelle. Andrew Lang. 6875-8
Apollo the betrayer, fr. Ion. Euripides. 6435-3
"**Apollo** through the woods came down". Apollo and the seaman. Herbert Trench. 6877-4
Apollo troubadour. Witter Bynner. 6336-5
Apollo's song. Ben Jonson. 6315-2
Apollo's song ("My Daphne's hair is twisted gold"). John Lyly. 6092-7,6250-4
Apollonides
 The poor farmer's offering. Sir William Marris (tr.). 6435-3
Apollonius
 "But far astern of Argo her whitening wake...". F.L. Lucas (tr.). 6251-2
 "Now night drew darkness...". F.L. Lucas (tr.). 6251-2
 "So he spoke in her honour...". F.L. Lucas (tr.). 6251-2
 "So without voice, without murmur...". F.L. Lucas (tr.). 6251-2
Apollonius Rhodius
 Amor omnipotens. George Allen (tr.). 6435-3

Eros and his mother. George Allen (tr.). 6435-3
 Hylas. George Allen (tr.). 6435-3
 Jason's sowing and reaping. George Allen (tr.). 6435-3
 Medea betrayed. T.F. Higham and G. Allen (tr.). 6435-3
 Medea's dream. George Allen (tr.). 6435-3
 Medea's hesitation. George Allen (tr.). 6435-3
 Medea's parting words. George Allen (tr.). 6435-3
 The meeting. George Allen (tr.). 6435-3
 The moving rocks. Cecil Maurice Bowra and G. Allen (tr.). 6435-3
 Remorse. George Allen (tr.). 6435-3
 The sailing of the argo. George Allen (tr.). 6435-3
Apologia. Samuel Hoffenstein. 6217-2
Apologia for a druid. W.M. Bronk. 6764-6
Apologia pro poemate meo. Wilfred Owen. 6250-4
Apology. Stephen Vincent Benet. 6761-1
Apology. Phoebe Cary. 6969-X
Apology. Arthur Guiterman. 6875-8
Apology. Ibn al-Haddad. 6362-4
Apology. Amy Lowell. 6556-2,6019-6,6431-0,6653-9
Apology. John McClure. 6619-4,6326-8
Apology for bad dreams. Robinson Jeffers. 6399-3,6012-9
Apology for gazing at a young lady in church. Unknown. 6770-0
An **apology** for having loved before. Edmund Waller. 6430-2, 6438-8
Apology for kings. John ("Peter Pindar") Walcott. 6278-4
An **apology** for not showing her what I had wrote. William Cowper. 6814-6
Apology for vagrants, fr. The country justice. John Langhorne. 6932-0
Apology to my heirs. Carolyn Wilson Link. 6979-7
An **apology** to the harp. Thomas D'Arcy McGee. 6244-X
An **apology**, fr. The earthly paradise. William Morris. 6289-X,6604-6,6655-0,6660-7,6110-9,6199-0,6430-2,6196-6, 6508-2
The **apology**, sels. Charles Churchill. 6198-2
The **apology**, sels. Charles Churchill. 6191-5
The **apology**. Ralph Waldo Emerson. 6077-3,6176-1,6600-3, 6126-5,6288-1,6008 ,6121-4,6431-0
"**Apon** the midsummer evin, mirriest of nichtis". The tretis of the tua mariit wemen and the edo. William Dunbar. 6845-6
Apostacy. Berton Braley. 6853-7
The **apostate**. Alfred Edgar Coppard. 6070-6
"**Apostle** of the 'open door' in lands". To Mr. and Mrs. R.P. Louis J. Magee. 7004-3
Apostle of the helpless. Helen Irene Garvey. 6342-X
Apostrophe to a fighter plane. Virginia Taylor McCormick. 6979-7
Apostrophe to death. Caelius Sedulius. 6930-4
Apostrophe to light, fr. Paradise lost. John Milton. 6372-1
Apostrophe to the deity. William Wordsworth. 6980-0
Apostrophe to the island of Cuba. James Gates Percival. 6946-0
Apostrophe to the Mississippi. Mrs. A.M. Wilcox. 6417-5
Apostrophe to the ocean. George Gordon, 6th Baron Byron. 6392-6,6504-X,6610-0,6574-0,6304-7
An **apostrophe** to the oyster. J.W. Gesnard. 6919-3
Apostrophe to the sun. James Gates Percival. 6752-2
Apostrophe to the watermelon. Unknown. 6693-3
The **apothecary** man. Unknown. 6413-2
Apotheosis. Russell J. Wilbur. 6995-9
The **apotheosis** of Hercules. John Gay. 6972-X
The **apothesis** of vice. Alexander Pope. 6733-6
Apparent failure, sels. Robert Browning. 6123-0,6501-5, 6337-3
Apparently with no surprise. Emily Dickinson. 6754-9
Apparition. John Erskine. 6034-X
Apparition. William Ernest Henley. 6186-9,6659-3,6250-4, 6508-2
Apparition. Henri de Regnier. 6801-4
Apparition. Raymond de la Tailhede. 6351-9
The **apparition** of his mistress calling him to Elysium. Robert Herrick. 6369-1,6733-6
Apparition on the lake, fr. The prelude. William Wordsworth. 6832-4
The **apparition**, fr. America. William Blake. 6106-0
The **apparition**.. Herman Melville. 6333-0

The apparition. George Gordon, 6th Baron Byron. 6438-8
The apparition. John Donne. 6315-2,6562-7
The apparition. Stephen Phillips. 6844-8
Apparitions. Thomas Bailey Aldrich. 6076-5,6102-8,6648-8
Apparitions. Robert Browning. 6198-2
Apparitions. Thomas Curtis Clark. 6490-6,6337-3,6542-2
Apparitions. Alice Corbin. 6897-9
Apparuit. Ezra Pound. 6754-9
Appassionato, fr. Summer night. Bayard Taylor. 6976-2
A appeal for are to the sextant of the old brick...
    Unknown. 6724-7
A appeal for are to the sextant of..brick meetinghouse.
    Arabella M. ("A. Gasper") Willson. 6089-7
Appeal for illumination, fr. Morgante Maggiore. Luigi
    Pulci. 6282-2
The appeal of the phoenix, fr. The Iliad. Homer. 6435-3
The appeal to Harold. Henry Cuyler Bunner. 7041-8
An appeal to Lyce. Horace. 6949-5
An appeal to the "sextant" for air. J.S. Buckminster. 6404-3
An appeal to the goddess A. Thomas Russell Ybarra. 6118-4
An appeal to the sexton for air. Arabella M. ("A. Gasper")
    Willson. 6568-6
An appeal.. Emily Lawless. 6090-0
An appeal.. Sir Thomas Wyatt. 6436-1
An appeal. Emily Lawless. 6090-0
An appeal. Adelaide Anne Procter. 6957-6
An appeal. Jessie Scott. 6965-7
An appeal. Algernon Charles Swinburne. 6110-9
The appeal. Emily Bronte. 6315-2
The appeal. Walter Savage Landor. 6086-2
Appearance. Norman H. Russell. 7005-1
Appearance and reality. Alfred Noyes. 6169-9
The appearance of Cromwell's ghost..battle of Culloden.
    Unknown. 6859-6
Appearances. Robert Browning. 6110-9
Appearnance of the spectre horse and the burning ship..
    Richard Henry Dana. 6752-2
Appeasement. Martha Keller. 6761-1
Appeasement. Feodor Ivanovich Tyutchev. 6622-4
"Applauding youths laughed with young...". The Harlem
    dancer. Eli Edwards. 6959-2
Apple and rose. Karle Wilson Baker. 6506-6
Apple blossom. Estelle Rooks. 6850-2
Apple blossom time. Jessie H. Wixom. 6818-9
Apple blossoms. Ludvig Holstein. 6555-4
Apple blossoms. Amanda T. Jones. 6554-8
Apple blossoms. William Wesley Martin. 6255-5,6707-7,6478-7,6143-5,6585-6
Apple blossoms. Arthur L. Phelps. 6796-4
Apple blossoms. Elizabeth Stuart Phelps. 6240-7
Apple blossoms. Unknown. 6373-X,6706-9
"Apple blossoms softly falling". Apple blossom time.
    Jessie H. Wixom. 6818-9
"Apple man upon the corner worries me a lot". The apple
    vendor. Edgar A. Guest. 6869-3
The apple of life. Owen (Edward Bulwer-Lytton, Earl
    Lytton) Meredith. 6848-0
An apple orchard in the spring. William Wesley Martin.
    6239-3
Apple pickers. Carl Carmer. 6761-1
The apple seed. C.A.M. Webb. 6745-X
Apple tree. Edgar A. Guest. 6869-3
Apple tree. John Maher Murphy. 6761-1
The apple tree. Oliver St. John Gogarty. 6532-5
The apple tree. Jane Taylor. 6131-1
"Apple trees reveal their souls". Triolet. Gilbert
    O'Connon. 6850-2
The apple vendor. Edgar A. Guest. 6869-3
Apple wine. Elizabeth Grey Stewart. 6761-1
"Apple, beech, and cedar fair". Song ("Apple"). Unknown.
    6047-1
The apple-barrel. Edwin L. Sabin. 6820-0
The apple-dumplings and George the Third. John ("Peter
    Pindar") Wolcott. 6621-6
Apple-paring night in Vermont. Daniel L. Cady. 6988-6
Apple-pie and cheese. Eugene Field. 6004-8,6307-1
Apple-seed John. Lydia Maria Child. 6614-3
The apple-tree. Nancy Campbell. 6478-7
The apple. Grace O. Kyle. 6529-5

The apple. Lady Margaret Sackville. 6437-X
Appledore in a storm. James Russell Lowell. 6344-6
Applegate, Joseph H.
    Woodrow Wilson (a fragment). 7001-9
Appleget, Thomas B.
    Lost and found. 6567-8
Apples. Lisel Mueller. 6388-8
Apples. Lizette Woodworth Reese. 6039-0
"The apples I ate in Bedfordshire". Calendar song. Arnold
    Rattenbury. 6895-2
Apples falling. Louise Townsend Nicholl. 6037-4
Apples for sale. Lewis M. Knapp. 6039-0
"Apples on the table an' the grate-fire blazin". Autumn
    evenings. Edgar A. Guest. 7033-7
Apples, fr. Verses made for Women who cry apples, &c.
    Jonathan Swift. 6380-2
The apples. (Frederick) Ridgely Torrence. 6034-X
Appleton, Everard Jack
    An American creed. 6846-4
    The fighting failure. 6736-0
    The one. 6337-3
    Soldiers of the soil. 6846-4
Appleton, Thomas Gold
    Lauterbrunnen. 6749-2
Applied astronomy. Esther B. Tiffany. 6280-6,6441-8,6505-8,
    6652-8
Appomattox. Benjamin Davenport House. 6074-9
The appraisal. Sara Teasdale. 6850-2
Appreciation. William Judson Kibby. 6085-4,6291-1
Appreciation. George Meredith. 6828-2
The appreciation of Lincoln. Robertus Love. 6524-4
Apprehension. James Anderson Fraser. 6337-3
Apprehension. Unknown (Sanskrit) 6437-X
Apprehension (I). Agnes Mary F. ("Madame Duclaux")
    Robinson. 7015-9
Apprehension (II). Agnes Mary F. ("Madame Duclaux")
    Robinson. 7015-9
Apprehension: fantasy: memory. Sir John Davies. 6584-8
Apprenticed. Jean Ingelow. 6437-X
"Apprenticed angels everywhere". The morning, fr. Life on
    the farm. Benjamin Franklin Taylor. 6815-4
Apprisals. Richard Eugene Burton. 7041-8
Approach. Sister Mary Ada. 6839-1
Approach. Grace Fallow Norton. 6761-1
The approach of age. George Crabbe. 6302-0;6385-3
The approach of cold weather. Sir Egerton Brydges. 6980-0
The approach of evening. Unknown. 6724-7
Approach of morning, fr. Philip Van Artevelde. Henry
    Taylor. 6980-0
Approach of night. Clarence Urmy. 6274-1
The approach of Pharaoh, fr. Genesis. Caedmon. 6665-8
The approach of pharaoh. Caedmon. 6022-6
The approach of the fairies. William Shakespeare. 6133-8
The approach of the storm. Unknown. 6118-4
The approach of winter, fr. The seasons (Winter). James
    Thomson. 6932-0
The approach of winter. Thomas Sackville; 1st Earl of
    Dorset. 6150-8
Approach to Florence. George Gordon, 6th Baron Byron. 6631-3
Approach to Genoa. Samuel Rogers. 6624-0
The approach. Thomas Traherne. 6931-2
Approaches. George Macdonald. 6337-3
Approaching God. Amos Bronson Alcott. 6288-1
An appropriate keepsake. H.M. Stone. 6116-8
Appropriation. Harrison Robertson. 6004-8
Apres. Arthur J. Munby. 6385-3,6656-9
Apres moi le deluge. Unknown (Greek) 6435-3
The apricot tree. Ibn A'isha. 6362-4
April. Mabel W. Arnold. 6799-9
April. Rubye Arnold. 7016-7
April. Janet Norris Bangs. 6799-9
April. Remy Belleau. 6771-9
April. Alice Cary. 6865-0;6969-X
April. John Vance Cheney. 6374-8
April. Edmund Palmer Clarke. 6764-6
April. Elizabeth L. Cushing. 6433-7
April. Emily Dickinson. 6374-8
April. Theodosia Garrison. 6374-8,6478-7,6503-1,6653-4
April. Louis Ginsberg. 6034-X

APRIL

April. William Z. Gladwin. 6529-5
April. Avis H. Grant. 6906-1
April. Florence Hamilton. 6076-5
April. Mary Howitt. 6456-6
April. Thomas S. Jones Jr. 6653-4
April. John Keble. 6271-7
April. Sally Bruce Kinsolving. 6039-0
April. Mary Sinton Leitch. 6326-8
April. Henry Wadsworth Longfellow. 6047-1
April. Samuel Longfellow. 6597-X
April. Robert Loveman. 6941-X
April. James Abraham Martling. 6952-5
April. Jessie McDermott. 6049-8
April. Isobel McFadden. 6337-3
April. Lloyd Mifflin. 6047-1
April. William Morris. 6186-9
April. Mok-wol Park. 6775-1
April. Naomi Rogin. 6850-2
April. Estelle Rooks. 6850-2
April. George Montagu, Earl of Sandwich. 6331-4
April. Lou Saulmon. 6799-9
April. William Shakespeare. 6049-8
April. Frank Dempster Sherman. 6311-X
April. Edmund Spenser. 6191-5
April. Benjamin Franklin Taylor. 6815-4
April. Sara Teasdale. 6466-3
April. Alfred Lord Tennyson. 6737-9
April. Celia Thaxter. 6456-6
April. Karel Toman. 6886-3
April. Jaime Torres Bodet. 6759-X
April. Sir William Watson. 6044-7,6374-8,6423-X
April. John Greenleaf Whittier. 6049-8,6126-5
April. Joseph Clinton Williams. 6316-0
April. Anne Wolf. 6750-6
April ("My name is April"). Unknown. 6623-2
April - North Carolina. Harriet Monroe. 6556-2
April 2nd. Theodosia Garrison. 6031-5
April afternoon, Point Loma (1769). Winifred Davidson. 6039-0
"April again - bringing pain". April. Rubye Arnold. 7016-7
April air. Alfred Noyes. 6169-9
April and May. Celia Thaxter. 6049-8,6612-2
April and May. fr. 'May-Day'. Ralph Waldo Emerson. 6239-3
"April came: her eyes, opaquely gray". April. Naomi Rogin. 6850-2
"April comes tearfully". April. Estelle Rooks. 6850-2
An April day. Henry Wadsworth Longfellow. 6049-8
An April day. Anna Maria Pratt. 6529-5
An April day. Caroline Anne Bowles Southey. 6639-9
April days, fr. In memoriam. Alfred Lord Tennyson. 6047-1, 6597-X
April dusk. Lucy Atkinson McIlwaine. 6799-9
April fantasie. Ellen Mackay Hutchinson Cortissoz. 6820-0
April flower-song. Harold Kellock. 6118-4
April fool's day. Unknown. 6466-3
"An April fool, I swear is one". An April fool. Henry Cuyler Bunner. 6875-8
"April fool, go to school". Unknown. 7028-0
An April fool. Henry Cuyler Bunner. 6875-8
The April fool. Eugene Field. 6949-5
April fools. Kate Masterson. 6682-8
April fools. Emily Huntington Miller. 6373-X,6456-6
April fools. Winthrop Mackworth Praed. 6424-8
April ghost. Lizette Woodworth Reese. 6019-6
"April has dipped/To earth again". April. Lou Saulmon. 6799-9
April in England. Robert Browning. 6239-3,6424-8
April in England. Norah M. Holland. 6474-4
April in Ireland. Nora Hopper. 6873-1
April in New England. Nancy Byrd Turner. 6764-6
April in the city. Elisabeth Scollard. 6510-4
April in the hills. Archibald Lampman. 6115-X,6253-9
April in the woods. Mary McKinley Cobb. 6841-3
April in Vermont. Daniel L. Cady. 6988-6
"April is a gypsy girl". April. Avis H. Grant. 6906-1
"April is in my mistress' face". Song ("April"). Unknown. 6436-1
"April is in my mistress' face". Unknown. 6187-7
April ladies. Grace Brown Putnam. 6818-9
April longing. Mary Wilkerson Cleaves. 6178-8

April love. Ernest Dowson. 6513-9
April midnight. Arthur Symons. 6959-2
The April morn. Felicia Dorothea Hemans. 6973-8
April morning. George Elliston. 6374-8
April morning at t'Eagle. Dorothy Una Ratcliffe. 6785-9
April morning, sels. William Wordsworth. 6545-7
An April morning. Bliss Carman. 6236-9,6503-1,6393-4,6236-9,6338-1,6053-6,6162-1,6653-4
April music. Clinton Scollard. 6374-8
April night. Archibald Lampman. 6115-X
April night. Richard Le Gallienne. 6252-0
April night. Maye DeWeese Porter. 6906-1
April on the battlefields. Leonora Speyer. 6032-3,6051-X, 6556-2,6431-0
April on the half moon mountain. C.L. Edson. 6615-1
April on Tweed. Andrew Lang. 6180-X
April rain. Robert Loveman. 6102-8,6368-3,6396-6,6076-5, 6300-4,6108 ,6232-6,6374-8,6337-3,6356-X,6476-0,6583
April rain. Marian Williams McGaw. 6906-1
April rain song. Langston Hughes. 6554-X
"April rain/Brings tender buds and grass". To M.L.A. Ethel Emily Fels. 6906-1
"April rains are shod with silver". April ladies. Grace Brown Putnam. 6818-9
April rise. Laurie Lee. 6246-6
An April romance. Arthur Guiterman. 6773-5
April shower. Unknown. 6373-X
An April shower. Nellie Burget Miller. 6836-7
April showers. Mary E. (Freeman) Wilkins. 6137-0
"April showers/Bring May flowers". A mean trick. Dorothy Quick. 6750-6
"The April sky sags low and drear", fr. Hawthorn. William Ernest Henley. 6123-0
April song. Don Marquis. 6732-8
An April song. George C. Michael. 6846-4
An April song. Charles Hanson Towne. 6654-2
April speaks. Lloyd Mifflin. 6476-0
"April still is far away". Treasure. Beryl V. Thompson. 6750-6
"April sun breaks through what's left". For Cleo Wright. Corrine Hales. 6900-2
April theology. John G. Neihardt. 6300-4
April to March. Mildred I. McNeal. 6702-6
An April violet. Unknown. 6385-3
"April walks behind me still...". Hurdy-gurdy days. Martha Haskell Clark. 6891-X
April ways. Lucile S. Kappeler. 6906-1
April weather. Bliss Carman. 6374-8,6252-0
April weather. Jessie McDermott. 6466-3
April weather. Lizette Woodworth Reese. 6338-1,6374-8,6326-8,6653-4,6503-1
An April welcome. Phoebe Cary. 6865-0;6969-X
April! April! are you here? Dora Read Goodale. 6964-9
April's amazing meaning. George Dillon. 6619-4,6581-3,6071-4
April's charms. William Henry Davies. 6253-9
April's coming. Lancaster Pollard. 6374-8
April's daughter. Virginia Lyne Tunstall. 6979-7
April's fools. Mrs. A. Giddings Park. 7022-1
April's lambs. William Henry Davies. 6884-7
April's return. Grace Richardson. 6053-6
April's trick. Robert Palfrey Utter. 6131-4
April, 1885. Robert Bridges. 6487-6
April, 1942. Mark Van Doren. 6666-6
"April, and wind, and frozen rutted roads". Four Aprils. Ann Draper Forrestt. 6671-1
"April, April!". Song ("April"). Sir William Watson. 6232-6, 6266-0,6437-X,6465-5,6490-5,6423 ,6239-3,6102-8,6301-2,6250-4
April, fr. Calendar. Frances Abbot. 6764-6
April, fr. Sonnets of the months. Folgore da San Gemignano. 6325-X
April, fr. The fields of dawn. Lloyd Mifflin. 6597-X
"April, pride of woodland ways". April. Remy Belleau. 6771-9
April, sels. Irene Rutherford McLeod. 6338-1,6161-3,6368-3, 6653-4
"April. You hearken, my fellow". Earth's lyric. Bliss Carman and Richard Hovey. 6890-1
"Aprils have lived in my heart". Maturity. Ellen M.

Carroll. 7016-7
Aprocrypha. Babette Deutsch. 6037-4
The **Aprodite** of Praxiteles. Unknown (Greek) 6435-3
Aprons of silence. Carl Sandburg. 6345-4
Apuleius
    The coming of Isis, fr. Metamorphoses. Andrew Lang (tr.). 6987-8
    Invocation of Isis, fr. Metamorphoses. Andrew Lang (tr.). 6987-8
Apuleius, Lucius
    Eros and Psyche. Robert Bridges (tr.). 6487-6
Aquarium. Eugenio Florit. 6642-9
Aquarium. Jose Gorostiza. 6759-X
"**Aqui/you** can't loosen up". Real deal revelation. Raymond Ringo Fernandez. 6870-7
An **Arab** and his donkey. Unknown. 6724-7
Arab love song. Francis Thompson. 6339-X,6427-2,6301-2, 6655-0,6108-2,6507
Arab song. Hermann Hagedorn. 6944-4
Arab song. Richard Henry Stoddard. 6431-0
An **Arab** to his mistress. Walter Savage Landor. 6980-0
The **Arab** to the palm. Bayard Taylor. 6302-0,6385-3,6271-1
An **Arab** welcome. Thomas Bailey Aldrich. 6424-8
The **Arab's** farewell to his horse. Caroline Elizabeth Sarah Sheridan Norton. 6980-0
The **Arab's** farewell to his steed. Caroline Elizabeth Sarah Sheridan Norton. 6242-3,6510-4,6131-1,6219-9,7010-8
"**Arab**, Egyptian, English - by the sword". Gordon (II). Sir William Watson. 7015-9
The **Arab.** Charles Stuart Calverley. 6385-3
Arabella and Sally Ann. Paul Carson. 6919-3
Arabella Stuart, fr. Records of woman. Felicia Dorothea Hemans. 6973-8
"**Arabella** as a school-girl". Arabella and Sally Ann. Paul Carson. 6919-3
Arabesque. Robert Hillyer. 6649-6
Arabia. James Abraham Martling. 6952-5
Arabia infelix. Aldous Huxley. 6779-4
Arabia, fr. The listeners. Walter De La Mare. 6234-2,6726-, 6250-4,6668-2
"**Arabian** fiction never fill'd the world". A lover. William Wordsworth. 6980-0
An **Arabian** tale. Unknown. 6744-1
Arabs. Alfred Kreymborg. 6348-9
Araby's daughter. Thomas Moore. 6744-1,6438-8
Arac's song. Sir William Schwenck Gilbert. 6722-0
Arachne. William Empson. 6985-1
Arachnida, female. Aletha Humphreys. 6218-0
Aragon, Louis
    After twenty years. Rolfe Humphries (tr.). 6068-4
    Dirge for the barrel-organ of the new barbarism. Selden Rodman (tr.). 6665-8
    Elsa's eyes. W.J. Strachan (tr.). 6343-8
    Pastoral ("The great voice".). Joseph T. Shipley (tr.). 6351-9
    The phoenix reborn from its ashes. Joseph T. Shipley (tr.). 6351-9
    Tcheliabtraktrostroi waltz, sels. Nancy Cunard (tr.). 6343-8
    Zone libre. Louis MacNeice (tr.). 6343-8
Arakoon. Henry Clarence Kendall. 6997-5
Araminta. John Gay. 6972-X
Aran. Sean O'Faolain. 6582-1
Aratus
    "From Zeus begin we, never nameless we". George Allen (tr.). 6435-3
    "Often the birds of mere or main...". F.L. Lucas (tr.). 6251-2
    When justice dwelt on earth. George Allen (tr.). 6435-3
Araxes came devouringly. Hovhannes Hovhannessian. 6050-1
Arbasto's song, fr. Arbasto. Robert Greene. 6934-7
Arbasto, sels. Robert Greene. 6586-4
Arberry, A.J. (tr.)
    Abode divine. Al Rusafi, 6362-4
    Absent friends. Ibn Hazm, 6362-4
    The abstinent lover. Abul Bahr. 6362-4
    "According to the degree of the people of resolve". al-Mutanabbi, 6766-2
    "Alas for the (all too) short time passed". Abu 'L-'Atahiya, 6766-2

    Alchemy. Ibn Abil Khayal, 6362-4
    Aleppo. Ibn Kharuf, 6362-4
    Algeciras seen over a stormy sea. Ibn Malik (of Granada), 6362-4
    Almeria. Ibn Safar, 6362-4
    Amulet. Ibn Sa'id (of Alcala La Real), 6362-4
    The ant. Al-Tulaitili, 6362-4
    Apology. Ibn al-Haddad, 6362-4
    The apricot tree. Ibn A'isha, 6362-4
    Archery. Ibn Sa'id (of Alcala La Real), 6362-4
    The army. Abu Zaid, 6362-4
    The artichoke. Ibn al-Talla, 6362-4
    "As salt resolved in the ocean". Jalal [or Jelal] ed-din Rumi, 6448-5
    "Ask the backs of horses on the day of battle". Ibn 'Unain, 6766-2
    Aspiration. Ibn Hani, 6362-4
    Aubade. Ibn Hani, 6362-4
    Aubergines. Ibn Sara, 6362-4
    Bacchanal. Ibn Baqi, 6362-4
    Bad company. Abu Amr, 6362-4
    The banished lover. Al-Mustazhir, 6362-4
    Battle. Al-Tutili, 6362-4
    Battle song. Ibn Farsan, 6362-4
    The beard. Ibn al-Hajj, 6362-4
    Beardless youth. Ibn Iyad, 6362-4
    Beauty. Abu Hafs, 6362-4
    Beauty in rags. Ibn al-Arabi, 6362-4
    Beauty's armoury. Al-Hadrami, 6362-4
    The benefactor. Ibn Sara, 6362-4
    Benevolence. Siraj, 6362-4
    Beside a stream. Hamda, 6362-4
    Betrayal. Ibn Sa'id (of Alcala La Real), 6362-4
    A black horse with a white breast. Ibn Sa'id (of Alcala La Real), 6362-4
    The blind man. Nazhun, 6362-4
    The bloody sword. Ibn al-Zaqqaq, 6362-4
    Bloom of age. Abu Yahya, 6362-4
    Blue and gold. Ibn Burd, 6362-4
    Body and soul. Abul Fadl, 6362-4
    Bounty. Abus Salt, 6362-4
    The bow. Al-Buqaira, 6362-4
    "The breeze of the morn". Jalal [or Jelal] ed-din Rumi, 6448-5
    The breeze. Al-Husri, 6362-4
    The broken water-wheel. Al-Hajjam, 6362-4
    Bubbling wine. Abu Zakariya, 6362-4
    The camomile. Al-Buqaira, 6362-4
    The candle. Al-Hajjam, 6362-4
    Carousal. Ibn Khafaja, 6362-4
    Carousal. Ibn Safar, 6362-4
    The champion. Ibn Baqi, 6362-4
    Changefulness. Abu Ishaq, 6362-4
    Changes. Ibn Sa'id (of Alcala La Real), 6362-4
    Chess. Ibn Sharaf, 6362-4
    Clemency. Ibn al-Hajj, 6362-4
    Coat of mail. Ibn Abdul Ghafur, 6362-4
    Coat of mail. Asa the Blind, 6362-4
    Colloquy. Al-Munsafi, 6362-4
    The comely warrior. Ibn Sa'id (of Alcala La Real), 6362-4
    Community. Iqbal, 6448-5
    Compliment. Ibn al-Haddad, 6362-4
    "Comrade, affairs are in a ferment". al-Rusafi, 6766-2
    Concert. Ibn Sharaf, 6362-4
    Contentment. Al-Tutili, 6362-4
    Continence. Ibn Faraj, 6362-4
    <u>Continuing love. Ibn Rashiq, 6362-4</u>
    Corn in the wind. Iyad, 6362-4
    Courtship. Ibn Sa'id (of Alcala La Real), 6362-4
    The crow. Ibn Sa'id (of Alcala La Real), 6362-4
    Cruel masters. Ibn Zaidun, 6362-4
    The curtain fell. Gulchin, 6448-5
    The dancer. Ibn Kharuf, 6362-4
    Dawn. Ibn Billita, 6362-4
    Dawn. Ibn Muqana, 6362-4
    Dawn song. Ibn Sa'id (of Alcala La Real), 6362-4
    Daybreak. Ibn Burd, 6362-4
    Debauch. Ibn Rashiq, 6362-4
    Departure. IbnMujbar, 6362-4

Departure. Al-Hadrami, 6362-4
Descent. Jalal [or Jelal] ed-din Rumi, 6448-5
The devil's complaint. Sana'i, 6448-5
Dialogue. Ibn Munakhkhal, 6362-4
"Do you know, daughter of the Persians". Mihyar al-Dailami, 6766-2
The dove. Abul Hasan (of Seville), 6362-4
The down. Ibn Rashiq, 6362-4
Drinking song ("A house well supplied."). Avenzoar, 6362-4
Drinking song ("Hasten hither, saki mine.") Ubada, 6362-4
Drunken beauty. Ibn Billita, 6362-4
The eagle. Khanlari, 6448-5
Early pleasure. Ibn Hamdis, 6362-4
"The earth had put on a green robe". Ibn Sahl, 6766-2
Ebony and ivory. Ibn Hamdin, 6362-4
Eclipse. Al-Ghassani, 6362-4
Elegy for a dead king. Al-Kutandi, 6362-4
Enchantress. Al-Munfatil, 6362-4
Epitaph. Iraj, 6448-5
"Every thing from you is accepted". Baha' al-Din Zuhair, 6766-2
Exchange. Hafsa, 6362-4
Excuses. Al-Asamm, 6362-4
Exposure. Ibn al-Zaqqaq, 6362-4
Eye and heart. Ibn al-Batti, 6362-4
Eyelashes. Ibn al-Hammara, 6362-4
False friend. Al-Hajjam, 6362-4
Family tree. Ibn al-Qaffun, 6362-4
Fate. Ibn Abdun, 6362-4
Fate's malignity. Ibn Wahbun, 6362-4
Favourites. Ibn Abd Rabbihi, 6362-4
Fidelity. Ibn Zaidun, 6362-4
Fire. Ibn Sara, 6362-4
Flirtation. Ibn Zaidun, 6362-4
Flow and ebb. Ibn Safar, 6362-4
"Flowers every night". Jalal [or Jelal] ed-din Rumi, 6448-5
Flowing stream. Ibn Hamdis, 6362-4
Forgiveness. Al-Jaziri, 6362-4
The fountain. Ibn al-Ra'i'a, 6362-4
Fragment ("Amid the shining swords"). Sharaf al-Din, 6362-4
Fragment ("Praise not"). Ibn al-Missisi, 6362-4
Frankincense. Ibn al-Zaqqaq, 6362-4
Fruit tree. Ibn Qadi Mila, 6362-4
The galley. Ibn Hariq, 6362-4
Gamble. Iraqi, 6448-5
Garden at sunset. Marj Kuhl, 6362-4
The garden. Al-Nashshar, 6362-4
Gazelle. Ibn al-Qabila, 6362-4
The gift. Abu Aiyub, 6362-4
The gift. Abul Arab, 6362-4
Gilliflower. Ibn al-Abbar, 6362-4
The glance. Ibn Iyad, 6362-4
The glutton. Al-Sumaisir, 6362-4
Golden glow. Abul Hasan (of Seville), 6362-4
The guardians. Ibn Sa'id (of Alcala La Real), 6362-4
The handsome knight. Al-Mu'tamid, 6362-4
"Happy was I". Jalal [or Jelal] ed-din Rumi, 6448-5
The hawk. Ibn al-Qabturnu, 6362-4
"He raised up and raised high, and built". Matran, 6766-2
"He set the world aflame". Jalal [or Jelal] ed-din Rumi, 6448-5
"He that is my soul's repose". Jalal [or Jelal] ed-din Rumi, 6448-5
"The heavenly rider passed". Jalal [or Jelal] ed-din Rumi, 6448-5
Held fast. Sadi [or Saadi] (Mushlih-ud-Din), 6448-5
Hips. Abu Hafs, 6362-4
Hopes. Ibn al-Imam, 6362-4
The house of the heart. Siraj, 6362-4
The house. Ibn al-Hammara, 6362-4
The hypocrites. Ibn al-Batti, 6362-4
"I have guarded my soul from that which would defile." al-Buhturi, 6766-2
"I sought a soul in the sea". Jalal [or Jelal] ed-din Rumi, 6448-5

"I was sleepless, and I passed the night keeping vigil. al-Khansa, 6766-2
"If life be gone, fresh life to you". Jalal [or Jelal] ed-din Rumi, 6448-5
Immunity. Ibn Maimun, 6362-4
In absence. Avenzoar, 6362-4
In battle. Abul Hasan (of Badajoz), 6362-4
In praise of the king. Ibn Ammar, 6362-4
In the mosque. Ibn Malik (of Murcia), 6362-4
"In the west hath arisen a light". al-Shidyaq, 6766-2
The incense burner. Abus Salt, 6362-4
"Indeed I remembered you yearningly". Ibn Zaidun, 6766-2
The inkstand. Ibn Lubbal, 6362-4
The inky mouth. Al-Barraq, 6362-4
The introduction. Al-Dhahabi, 6362-4
Inverted eyelids. Ibn Haiyun, 6362-4
Invitation. Ibn Sa'id (of Seville), 6362-4
Invitation. Al-Mutawakkil, 6362-4
Jessamine. Ibn al-Abbar, 6362-4
Joy and sorrow. Sadi [or Saadi] (Mushlih-ud-Din), 6448-5
The king who died young. Ibn al-Khabbaza, 6362-4
The king's hand. Al-Mu'tamid, 6362-4
The knights. Ibn Sa'id (of Alcala La Real), 6362-4
"Ladies, have you no reward for one whose actions". Abu Firas, 6766-2
The letter. Al-Mu'tamid, 6362-4
Lilies. Ibn Darraj, 6362-4
Lilies and roses. Ibn al-Qutiya, 6362-4
Lion fountain. Al-Tutili, 6362-4
"Long has grown my night through the love of one". Bashshar ibn Burd, 6766-2
The lost angel. Al-Kasad, 6362-4
Love the foe. Sadi [or Saadi] (Mushlih-ud-Din), 6448-5
Love's code. Mutarrif, 6362-4
Love's evidence. Ibn Baqi, 6362-4
Love's storm. Ibn Sa'id (of Alcala La Real), 6362-4
Lovely maid. Ibn Khafaja, 6362-4
Lovely river. Ibn Khafaja, 6362-4
The lute. Ibn Qadi Mila, 6362-4
Lyric. Al-Barraq, 6362-4
Magian wine. Abu Jaafar, 6362-4
"Make war on me, O vicissitudes of the nights". Antara, 6766-2
Man and wife. Parvin, 6448-5
"The man burdened with passion is a weary man." Abu Nuwas, 6766-2
"March has arrived; stand up with us, companion". Shauqi, 6766-2
Marguerite. Ibn Billita, 6362-4
Mary. Tavallali, 6448-5
Meteor. Al-Haitham, 6362-4
The miracle of spring. Bahar, 6448-5
The mirror. Ibn al-Sabuni, 6362-4
Mist. Ibn Bassam, 6362-4
Modest blush. Ibn Abd Rabbihi, 6362-4
The mole. Al-Munfatil, 6362-4
Moles. Ibn Haiyun, 6362-4
Moon and Venus. Abul Mughira, 6362-4
Moon in eclipse. Ibn Hamdis, 6362-4
Moon in mist. Ibn Burd, 6362-4
Moon of beauty. Ibn al-Faras, 6362-4
Moon of grace. Al-Jazzar, 6362-4
Moon of loveliness. Al-Mu'tamid, 6362-4
Mosquitoes. Al-Sumaisir, 6362-4
The moth. Abu Yahya, 6362-4
Mother. Iraj, 6448-5
The mountain. Al-Liss, 6362-4
Mutability. Ibn Hazm, 6362-4
"My heart doth fly." Unknown (Arabic), 6362-4
My miser. Ibn Sa'id (of Alcala La Real), 6362-4
"(News) came to me – may you spurn the curse!" al-Nabigha, 6766-2
Night. Al-Liss, 6362-4
Night and day. Ibn Darraj, 6362-4
Night by the river. Al-Mu'tamid, 6362-4
Night of bliss. Ibn al-Zaqqaq, 6362-4
Night of joy. Ibn Abi Ruh, 6362-4
Night storm. Al-Lama'i, 6362-4

Night the plunderer. Khanlari, 6448-5
The night traveller. Ibn Atiya, 6362-4
Night visitor. Ibn Hamdis, 6362-4
Nightfall. Siraj, 6362-4
Noblesse oblige. Ibn Sa'id (of Alcala La Real), 6362-4
Nocturne ("When I am alone, to dream"). Shahriyar, 6448-5
The nuptials. Ibn Sa'id (of Alcala La Real), 6362-4
"O sickness of your heart". al-Sharif al-Radi, 6766-2
Odi et amo. Ibn al-Hajj, 6362-4
"Oft-times a guest of a phantom of one". Ibn Khafaja, 6766-2
The old toper. Ibn Sa'id (of Alcala La Real), 6362-4
On hearing al-Mutanabbi praised. Ibn Wahbun, 6362-4
On taking up a humble place at court. Ibn Adha, 6362-4
On the death of his wife. Ibn al-Hammara, 6362-4
Oranges. Ibn Sara, 6362-4
The oranges. Abu Dharr, 6362-4
The Palanquins. Ibn Sa'id (of Alcala La Real), 6362-4
Panegyric. Abu Bakr Muhummad, 6362-4
The party. Ibn al-Qabturnu, 6362-4
"Pass round the cups of the wine of the lips' deep red. Ibn Zakur, 6766-2
The passers by. Al-Radi Billah, 6362-4
Patronage. Ibn al-Labbana, 6362-4
Pearls. Al-Mushafi, 6362-4
The pen. Al-Hajjam, 6362-4
Perfect love. Sana'i, 6448-5
Poet's pride. Ibn Ammar, 6362-4
Poor lodgings. Ibn Abdun, 6362-4
The portent. Ibn al-Zaqqaq, 6362-4
The preacher. Al-Mahdi, 6362-4
Pretences. Ibn Rashiq, 6362-4
The protector. Ibn Sharaf, 6362-4
The quince. Ibn Sara, 6362-4
The radish. Ibn Quzman, 6362-4
Rain and lightning. Ibn Shuhaid, 6362-4
Rain at festival. Ibn Rashig, 6362-4
Rain at festival. Ibn Rashiq, 6362-4
Ramadan. Al-Qalami, 6362-4
Random thoughts. Bahar, 6448-5
Ransom. Ibn Ammar, 6362-4
The raven. Kuthiyir, 6362-4
The red gown. Ibn al-Sabuni, 6362-4
Red wine in a black glass. Ibn Mujbar, 6362-4
Red wine in a black glass. Inb Mujbar, 6362-4
The reed. Abul Hajjaj, 6362-4
"Remembering thy li." Jalal [or Jelal] ed-din Rumi, 6448-5
"Resign the affair to destiny". Ibn Zuhr, 6766-2
Revel. Abul Hasan (of Santa Maria)., 6362-4
Revenge. Hamda, 6362-4
Revenge. Avenzoar, 6362-4
Rich and poor. Al-Haitham, 6362-4
Rider. Abul Qasim (of Alcira), 6362-4
Riposte. Nazhun, 6362-4
The rising sun. Al-Haitham, 6362-4
Ritual. Ibn Abd Rabbihi, 6362-4
River of Seville. Al-Kutandi, 6362-4
The river. Ibn Sa'id (of Alcala La Real), 6362-4
The roan. Ibn Khafaja, 6362-4
Rose-petals. Ibn al-Zaqqaq, 6362-4
Roses. Al-Ghassani, 6362-4
Royal bounty. Ibn Hani, 6362-4
Royal bounty. Ibn Sa'id (of Alcala La Real), 6362-4
Royal pride. Ibn al-Nasir, 6362-4
Sacrifice. Al-Tutili, 6362-4
Sad love. Tavallali, 6448-5
Sails. Ibn Billita, 6362-4
Saki. Al-Taliq, 6362-4
A saki refusing to drink wine. Ibn al-Tarawa, 6362-4
Sand. Ibn al-Arabi, 6362-4
Schooners. Ibn Lubbal, 6362-4
Scurvy entertainment. Abu Abd Allah, 6362-4
Sea of night. Ibn Sa'id (of Alcala La Real), 6362-4
Sequence. Jami, 6448-5
Serpent curls. Ibn Jakha, 6362-4
The setting sun. Ibn Sa'id (of Alcala La Real), 6362-4
Seville. Al-Tutili, 6362-4
The shaven beauty. Al-Ramadi, 6362-4

The shield. Hafsa, 6362-4
Ship in storm. Ibn Darraj, 6362-4
The ship. Ibn Safar, 6362-4
The singer. Al-Buqaira, 6362-4
Sister sun. Ibn Malik (of Granada), 6362-4
The skiff. Al-Munsafi, 6362-4
Slander. Ibn Hazm, 6362-4
Sleep. Unknown (Arabic), 6362-4
Socrates' house. Yasimi, 6448-5
"Souls stretching out their necks". al-Ma'arri, 6766-2
Spare. Ibn Ammar, 6362-4
The spear. Abu Zakariya, 6362-4
The sprouting board. Al-Isra'ili, 6362-4
Star flowers. Ibn al-Zaqqaq, 6362-4
The stolen penknife. Ibn Sa'id (of Alcala La Real), 6362-4
Stolen pleasure. Ibn Shuhaid, 6362-4
The stork. Al-Hajjam, 6362-4
Storm. Ibn al-Bain, 6362-4
Strategy. Ibn Sa'id (of Alcala La Real), 6362-4
The stream. Al Rusafi, 6362-4
The striking of the tent. Ibn al-Khabbaza, 6362-4
Sun and cloud. Abus Salt, 6362-4
Sunburn. Abu Hafs, 6362-4
Sunlight on the sea. Ibn Sa'id (of Alcala La Real), 6362-4
Sunshine. Ibn Abi Bishr, 6362-4
"Sweet sleep has been barred from my eyes". Ibn al-Rumi, 6766-2
The swimmer. Ibn Khafaja, 6362-4
Sword and lance. Ibn Shuhaid, 6362-4
"The sword is nearer in tidings than (any) writings". Abu Tammam, 6766-2
The sword. Abu Bakr (of Marrakesh), 6362-4
The tailor's apprentice. Ibn Kharuf, 6362-4
The tale of battle. Ibn Sa'id (of Alcala La Real), 6362-4
The thimble. Al-Liss, 6362-4
"This pretty, twanging boy poured out for me". Ibn al-Khaiyat, 6766-2
"Thou who lovest, like a crow". Jalal [or Jelal] ed-din Rumi, 6448-5
"Though every way I try". Jalal [or Jelal] ed-din Rumi, 6448-5
"Time bringeth swift to end". Jalal [or Jelal] ed-din Rumi, 6448-5
Toledo captured by the Franks. Al-Assal, 6362-4
The toothpick. Al-Hajjam, 6362-4
Treachery. Ibn Khafaja, 6362-4
Trees and waves. Al-Isra'ili, 6362-4
The trees. Al-Husri, 6362-4
Two seas. Abus Salt, 6362-4
Two suns. Al-Dabbaj, 6362-4
Ugliness. Ibn Shakil, 6362-4
Unexpected fortune. Abul Qasim (of Silves), 6362-4
The unripe orange. Al-Asamm, 6362-4
Victory. Ibn Hani, 6362-4
The vine. Al-Mu'tamid, 6362-4
Violet. Ibn A'isha, 6362-4
Virgin earth. Ibn al-Bain, 6362-4
The virgin. Ibn Sa'id (of Alcala La Real), 6362-4
Vultures. Al-Hajjam, 6362-4
Wages. Ibn Kharuf, 6362-4
The walnut. Ibn al-Qutiya, 6362-4
"Was it the unsheathing of a sword". al-Barudi, 6766-2
Water. Ibn Saad al-Khair, 6362-4
The water-cooler. Sharaf al-Din, 6362-4
Water-lilies. Ibn Hamdis, 6362-4
The water-wheel. Abu Abd Allah, 6362-4
Wave wing. Ibn Sa'id (of Alcala La Real), 6362-4
"We dra k upon the remembrance of therbeloved". Ibn al-Farid, 6766-2
The weaver's apprentice. Al Rusafi, 6362-4
The wheel. Ibn al-Abbar, 6362-4
"When a man's honour is not defiled by baseness". al-Samau'al, 6766-2
"When the horizon burst forth with light". Ibn al-Mu'tazz, 6766-2
White and black. Ibn al-Attar, 6362-4
The white charger. Abus Salt, 6362-4

White for mourning. Al-Fata al-Kafif, 6362-4
White hair. Ibn Ghaiyath, 6362-4
A white horse with a crimson flash. Ibn Abdus, 6362-4
"Who lifteth up the spirit". Jalal [or Jelal] ed-din Rumi, 6448-5
"Who was he that said". Jalal [or Jelal] ed-din Rumi, 6448-5
Wild deer. Hafiz, 6448-5
The wind. Ibn Sa'id (of Alcala La Real), 6362-4
Wine and citron. Abu Abd Allah, 6362-4
Wine at dawn. Ibn Sa'id (of Alcala La Real), 6362-4
Wine at morning. Ibn Safar, 6362-4
Wine, my love. Abu Jaafar, 6362-4
The wine-bearer. Habib, 6362-4
Wings of wine. Ibn al-Yamani, 6362-4
"Would that hind had fulfilled to us her promise". Umar ibn Abi Rabi'a, 6766-2
A yellow horse with a blaze and a black mane. Ibn Sa'id (of Alcala La Real), 6362-4
A yellow horse with a blaze. Ibn Sa'id (of Alcala La Real), 6362-4
The young carpenter. Al Rusafi, 6362-4
The young pilgrim. Ibn Faddal, 6362-4
The youth. Ibn Sara, 6362-4
The **arbiter**. Edward Farquhar. 6939-8
Arbor amoris. Francois Villon. 6102-8
Arbor amorsis. Francois Villon. 6771-9
Arbor day ("Again we come this day to greet..."). Seymour S. Short. 6049-8
Arbor day ("Now a strong, fair shoot..."). Unknown. 6049-8
Arbor day ("Plant in the springtime..."). Unknown. 6049-8
Arbor Day alphabet. Ada Simpson Sherwood. 6047-1
Arbor Day exercises. Lucia M. Mooney. 6684-4
Arbor day invocation ("Like the glad birds..."). Emma S. Thomas. 6049-8
Arbor day march. Ellen Beauchamp. 6049-8,6171-0
Arbor day ode. Parr Harlow. 6049-8
Arbor day poem ("Come thou, my oftimes...") Anna R. Pride. 6049-8
Arbor day poem ("Listen! the grand old forests..."). Lillian E. Knapp. 6049-8
Arbor Day song. Mary A. Heermans. 6047-1
Arbor Day song. Alice S. Webber. 6376-4
An Arbor Day tree. Unknown. 6047-1
Arbor day tribute. Jared Barhite. 6049-8
Arbor vitae. Coventry Patmore. 6315-2
Arbor vitae, sels. Coventry Patmore. 6123-0
Arboricide. Louise Imogen Guiney. 6096 X
Arbuthnot, George
   The vicar's tribute. 7008-6
Arbuthnot, John
   Preface to John Bull and his law-suit. 6200-8
Arbutus. Adelaide Crapsey. 6338-1
Arbutus. Elaine Goodale. 6049-8
Arbutus. Anne Hall. 6049-8
Arbutus. Helen Hunt Jackson. 6049-8
Arbutus. Unknown. 6049-8
Arbutus. Isaac Watts. 6049-8
Arbutus and spring. Helen M. Parsons. 6799-9
"Arbutus, thou dost faintly swing". Arbutus. Unknown. 6049-8
The **arbutus**. Unknown. 6373-X
The **arc-lamps**. Theodor Daubler. 6160-5
Arcades. John Milton. 6250-4
Arcades ambo. Robert Browning. 6123-0
Arcades, sels. John Milton. 6301-2
Arcadia. John Gay. 6092-7
"Arcadia was of old (said he) a state". Rhotus on Arcadia. John Chalkhill. 6933-9
Arcadia, sels. Sir Philip Sidney. 6378-0,6586-4,6301-2
"Arcadian bliss was long since past". 'Tis ever so. William T. MacIntyre. 6983-5
Arcadian dialogue. Sir Philip Sidney. 6584-8
Arcadian dialogue (2). Sir Philip Sidney. 6584-8
An **Arcadian** flirtation. Unknown. 7021-3
"Arcadian scenes adieu! in Cyrrha's vale". A farewell to poetry. Thomas Warton (the Elder). 6962-2
Arcadians confer in exile. James Branch Cabell. 6875-8
Arcadius' song to Sepha. William Bosworth. 6194-X
Arcady. Mary Leslie Newton. 6118-4

Arcady in England. Victoria Mary Sackville-West. 6785-9
Arcana sylvarum. Charles De Kay. 7041-8
The **arch** armadillo. Carolyn Wells. 6466-3
An **archaeological** congress. Robert J. Burdette. 6588-0
The **archaeologist** of the future. Leonard Bacon. 6722-0
Archaeology. Babette Deutsch. 7014-0
The **archangel**, fr. Vision of judgment. George Gordon, 6th Baron Byron. 6315-2
The archbishop and Gil Blas. Oliver Wendell Holmes. 6413-2
Archbishop Tait. Unknown. 6125-7
"Archduke Francis Ferdinand, Austrian heir...". The retinue. Katharine Lee Bates. 6846-4
Archeanassa. Asclepiades. 6435-3
Archedike. Simonides. 6435-3
Archer song. Johann C. Friedrich von Schiller. 6952-5
Archer, William (tr.)
   Hannele, sels. Gerhart Hauptmann, 6681-X
The **archer**. Frank Dempster Sherman. 6311-X
The **archer**. Arthur James Marshall Smith. 6446-9
The **archer**. Unknown (Sanskrit) 6437-X
The **archer**. Crawford Williams. 6750-6
The **archers**. Emily Pauline ("Tekahionwake") Johnson. 6837-5
Archery. Ibn Sa'id (of Alcala La Real) 6362-4
The archery meeting. Thomas Haynes Bayly. 6092-7
"The arches of the red bridge". The red bridge. Skipwith Cannell. 6897-9
"Archfiends of history: Herod, Judas". Master mind. Katheryn Ullmen. 6761-1
Archias
   A dedication to Athene. George Allen (tr.). 6435-3
   Echo. Sir William Marris (tr.). 6435-3
   Imitatrix ales. Sir William Marris (tr.). 6435-3
   A tomb by the sea. Sir William Marris (tr.). 6435-3
Archibald Higbie. Edgar Lee Masters. 6897-9
Archibald, Mrs. G.
   A law agin it. 6920-7
Archie. Phoebe Cary. 6969-X
Archie Dean. Gail Hamilton. 6914-2
Archie Dean. Gail Hamilton. 6554-6,6569-4
Archie o Cawfield. Unknown. 6185-0
Archie's mother. Rose Hartwick Thorpe. 6672-0
Archilochus
   Be still, my soul. Cecil Maurice Bowra (tr.). 6435-3
   "A branch of myrtle in her happiness". F.L. Lucas (tr.). 6251-2
   "For me my spear is kneaded bread...". F.L. Lucas (tr.). 6251-2
   A girl. John Addington Symonds (tr.). 6435-3
   God punishes. Cecil Maurice Bowra (tr.). 6435-3
   "Heart, my heart, with cares past curing thou...". F.L. Lucas (tr.). 6251-2
   "A henchman sworn of Ares, Lord God of wat, I live". F.L. Lucas (tr.). 6251-2
   The ideal general. A. Watson Bain (tr.). 6435-3
   Knowledge. 6435-3
   "Many a trick the wise fox knows". F.L. Lucas (tr.). 6251-2
   Rough sea. Cecil Maurice Bowra (tr.). 6435-3
   Simple tastes. Cecil Maurice Bowra (tr.). 6435-3
   "Some Thracian now goes strutting with the shield...". F.L. Lucas (tr.). 6251-2
   Thasos. Cecil Maurice Bowra (tr.). 6435-3
   There is nothing strange. 6435-3
Archimago's hermitage, fr. the Fairie Queene. Edmund Spenser. 6102-8
"Archin' here and arrachin' there". Water music. Christopher M. ("Hugh MacDiarmid") Grieve. 6845-6
Archipelagoes. Bartolo Cattafi. 6803-0
The **architect**. Molly Anderson Haley. 6144-3,6335-7
Architects. Edith Claire Cam. 6799-9
Architects of dream. Lucia Trent. 6420-5,6461-2
Architectural atoms. Horace Smith. 6802-2
Architecture. Wallace Stevens. 6808-1
Archy a low brow. Don Marquis. 6722-0
Archy experiences a seizure. Don Marquis. 6722-0
archygrams. Don Marquis. 6722-0
Arcita's dying address. Geoffrey Chaucer. 6543-0
The **Arctic** herd. John Morgan. 6855-3
The **arctic** Indian's faith. Thomas D'Arcy McGee. 6433-7

An **Arctic** vision. Francis Bret Harte. 6946-0
Arcturus in autumn. Sara Teasdale. 6619-4,6217-2,6393-4
Arcturus, fr. Pictures of autumn. Sara Teasdale. 6011-0
Arcum conteret. Sister Mary Therese. 6285-7
Ardan mor. Francis Ledwidge. 6244-X
Arden of Feversham, sels. Unknown. 6317-9
Ardor. Gamaliel Bradford. 6032-3
"**Are** God and Nature then at strife". Alfred Lord Tennyson. 6289-X
"**Are** lovers full of fire". Francis Davison. 6187-7
Are the children at home? Margaret Elizabeth Sangster. 6365-9
Are the children at home? Unknown. 6910-X
"**Are** there holier ones/Than these?". Anna. Babette Deutsch. 6959-2
"**Are** there not lofty moments when the soul". Josiah Gilbert Holland. 6238-5
"**Are** there not, then, two musics unto men?", fr Music. Arthur Hugh Clough. 6123-0
Are these God's children? Sarah M. Chatfield. 6575-9
"**Are** these the ancient, holy hills". The Jewish pilgrim. Frances Browne. 6848-0
"**Are** these the flow'ry banks". Sonnet ("Are these"). William Drummond of Hawthornden. 6908-8
"**Are** these the honors they reserve for me". Columbus in chains. Philip Freneau. 6946-0
Are they not all ministering spirits. Robert Stephen Hawker. 6199-4
"**Are** they shadows that we see?". Song ("Are they"). Samuel Daniel. 6189-3
Are they shadows that we see? Samuel Daniel. 6182-6,6733-6, 6315-2
"**Are** we not nobles? we who trace". Our titles. Adelaide Anne Procter. 6957-6
Are women fair? Francis Davison. 6089-7
"**Are** ye for ever to your skies departed?". Angel visits. Felicia Dorothea Hemans. 6973-8
"**Are** ye no gaun to wauken the day, ye rogue?". The sleepy laddie. William Miller. 6960-6
Are you a mason? Rev. Magill. 6407-8
"**Are** you anxious to bewitch?". The radenovitch: a song of the new dance. Unknown. 6787-5
"**Are** you deaf, Father William?". Acrostic ("Are you deaf"). Charles Lutwidge ("Lewis Carroll") Dodgson. 6724-7
Are you from Bevan? James (Shaky) Robertson. 6149-4
"**Are** you looking for someone...". Thoughts of Thomas Hardy. Edmund Blunden. 6783-2
"**Are** you not weary in your distant places". To exiles. Neil Munro. 6793-X
"**Are** you ready for your steeple-chase". Ballad ("Are you ready"). Charles Kingsley. 6661-5
Are you ready? Louis Eisenbeis. 6927-4
Are you so lovely? Walter De La Mare. 6905-3
"**Are** you there? Can you hear?". Better than love. Ruth Pitter. 6783-2
'**Are** you there?' Strickland Gillilan. 6303-9
"**Are** you, what your faire lookes expresse?" Thomas Campion. 6794-8
Aren't we all. Norman Hills Stateman. 6178-8
"The **arena** of self/is great within you". Querencia. Megan E. Boyd. 6900-2
Arensberg, Walter Conrad
    At daybreak. 6897-9
    Dialogue. 6897-9
    Out of doors. 6076-5,6464-7
    Song of the souls set free. 6897-9
    To Hasekawa. 6897-9
    Voyage a l'infini. 6029-3
Ares. Albert Ehrenstein. 6160-5
"**Ares**, in might surpassing...". Unknown. 6251-2
Arethusa. Percy Bysshe Shelley. 6134-6,6136-2,6179-6,6228-8,6239-3,6271 ,6484-1,6219-9,6639-9,6086-2,6110-9, 6199 ,6134-6,6136-2,6179-6,6228-8,6239-3,6271 ,6484-1,6219-9,6639-9,6086-2,6110-9,6199
The **Arethusa**. Prince Hoare. 6328-4,6547-3,6322-5,6639-9, 6086-2
Aretina's song. Sir Henry Taylor. 6656-9
Arevalo Martinez, Rafael
    Clean clothes. Muna Lee (tr.). 6759-X

Arey, Harriet Ellen (Grannis)
    Myself. 7030-2
    Thanksgiving. 6820-0
Areytos. Jean Brierre. 6178-8
Argemone. Adam Lindsay Gordon. 6951-7
Argenteuil, 1128. George Moore. 6779-4
Arglwydd Arwain. William Williams. 6024-2,6528-7
Argow, W.W.W.
    Outward bound. 6143-5
    A Thanksgiving litany. 6143-5
Argument. Edgar A. Guest. 6748-4
Argument. Stanley Johnson. 6039-0
Argument. Unknown. 6294-6
Argument. Mildred Weston. 6722-0
An **argument** addressed to Christ. Gervase Toelle. 6839-1
The **argument** of his book. Robert Herrick. 6562-7,6726-3
The **argument** of the Hesperides. Robert Herrick. 6189-3, 6543-0
Argument of the second sestiad, fr. Hero and Leander. Christopher Marlowe. 6430-2
Argument to Hesperides. Robert Herrick. 6604-6
The **argument**. Conrad Aiken. 6012-9
Argumentative theology. Samuel Butler. 6543-0
Argus. Eleanor Farjeon. 6236-9
Argus. Alexander Pope. 6478-7
Argyle, Duke of. See Campbell, John D.S.
Argyll tour. Eugenio Montale. 6803-0
Aria. Comte Robert de Montesquiou. 6351-9
Ariadne. Geoffrey Chaucer. 6438-8
Ariadne's farewell. Helen Hunt Jackson. 6438-8
Ariadne, sels. Leigh Hunt. 6980-0
Ariail, Warren
    At dawn. 7016-7
    Essie smiles. 7016-7
    Necessity. 7016-7
    Poverty. 7016-7
    Sympathy. 7016-7
    That is enough. 7016-7
Ariara No Yuki-hira
    "If breezes on Inaba's peak". William N. Porter (tr.). 6852-9
"An **arid** plain of stillness". On the desert. Josephine S. Brooks. 6894-4
Aridity. Michael (Katherine Bradley & Edith Cooper) Field. 6931-2
Ariel. Paul Hamilton Hayne. 7041-8
Ariel and the suicide. Thomas Hood. 6980-0
Ariel in the cloven pine. Bayard Taylor. 6976-2
Ariel sings. William Shakespeare. 6138-9
Ariel's song. William Shakespeare. 6150-8,6396-9,6438-8, 6138-9,6271-7,6315-2,6660-7,6456-6,6424
Ariel's song ("Come unto these yellow sands.") William Shakespeare. 6228-8
Ariel's song ("Full fathom five thy father lies.") William Shakespeare. 6228-8
Ariel's song ("Where the bee sucks, there suck I.") William Shakespeare. 6436-1
Ariel's song, fr. Songs. William Shakespeare. 6600-3
Ariel's song, fr. The tempest. William Shakespeare. 6208-3, 6466-3,6315-2,6512-0,6239-3,6332 ,6623-2
Ariel's songs. William Shakespeare. 6131-1,6197-4,6219-9, 6099-4,6436-1,6634-8,6421-3,6560-0
"**Ariel**, O, -my angel, my own". Robert Bridges. 6487-6
Arion
    Hymn to Poseidon. Herbert Kynaston (tr.). 6435-3
Arion. George (Mary Ann Cross) Eliot. 7037-X
Arion. Zbigniew Herbert. 6758-1
Arion Anadyomenos. Ronald Bottrall. 6150-8,6354-3
"**Arion**, whose melodic soul". Arion. George (Mary Ann Cross) Eliot. 7037-X
Ariosto, Ludovico
    Orlando furioso, sels. W.S. Rose (tr.). 6372-1
Ariphron of Sicyon
    The song of health. Robert Bland (tr.). 6879-0
"**Arise** up, England, from the smoky cloud". England. John Hanmer, Baron Hanmer. 7015-9,6793-X,6793-X
Arise ye Nova Scotia slaves. P.J. Lynch. 6149-4
Arise!. Roden Noel. 7009-4
"**Arise!** and see the glorious sun". A morning hymn. Francis Hopkinson. 6753-0

ARISE!

"**Arise!** O, my soul, on this Christmas so blest". The Christmas glory. William White. 6868-5
"**Arise!** old Norway sends the word". Old Norway. Felicia Dorothea Hemans. 6973-8
"**Arise!** this day shall shine". The first sorrow. Adelaide Anne Procter. 6957-6
"**Arise!** Why kneel to one who envies thee?". A dialogue. Gertrude Huntington McGiffert. 6838-3
Arise, my thoughts. Unknown. 6830-8
"**Arise**, oh, my country! Arise in thy glory". My country. Louis S. Amonson. 6925-8
"**Arise**, shine; for thy light is come". Surge, illuminare. Bible. 6830-8
Arise, ye men of strength and might. Charles James. 6274-1
"**Arise**, ye prisoners of starvation!". The internationale. Eugene Pottier. 6954-1
"**Arise**-'tis the day of our Washington's glory". Crown our Washington. Hezekiah Butterworth. 6465-5,6449-3,6820-0
Arisen at last. John Greenleaf Whittier. 6753-0
Arisen at last. John Greenleaf Whittier. 6126-5,6288-1
Arisen at last. John Greenleaf Whittier. 6753-0
"**Arist**, whose hand with horror wing'd...". To George Cruikshank, esq. Matthew Arnold. 6947-9
"**Aristion**, so swift once...". Thyillus. 6251-2
The **aristocracy** of France, sels. Viscount Strangford; George Sydney Smythe. 6046-3
The **aristocrat**. Elizabeth Stanton Hardy. 6979-7
Aristodicus
  A dead locust. Humbert Wolfe (tr.) 6435-3
"**Ariston** had a sling, wherewith he got". Unknown. 6435-3
Aristophanes
  "All the wide world now I sway". 6435-3
  An amateur, driving too fast, fr. The wasps. F.A. Wright (tr.). 6308-X
  "Bear me no grudge, spectators...". B.B. Rogers (tr.). 6435-3
  Chorus of birds. Algernon Charles Swinburne (tr.). 7039-6
  A chorus of women, fr. Thesmophoriazusae. 6996-7
  The cloud chorus. Andrew Lang (tr.). 6987-8
  "Clouds, ever drifting in air". T.F. Higham (tr.). 6435-3
  "Come on then, ye dwellers by nature in darkness". Algernon Charles Swinburne (tr.). 6435-3
  Dancing in the meadow. 6959-2
  "Dear comrade, arise, from slumber awake". T.F. Higham (tr.). 6435-3
  "Dere now bemoany to de ouder air". B.B. Rogers (tr.). 6435-3
  "Easy, Ned, easy, go soft...". T.F. Higham (tr.). 6435-3
  "Fiercely, methinks, will he rage in his heart...". Marshall MacGregor (tr.). 6435-3
  The frogs' song. T.F. Higham (tr.). 6435-3
  The frogs, sels. 6337-3
  "Gloom of the night, gloom of the night". T.F. Higham (tr.). 6435-3
  The happy dancer. 6959-2
  "Here in thy home we await thy tread". 6435-3
  "How Hellas' youth". T.F. Higham (tr.). 6435-3
  How the women will stop war, fr. Lysistrata. B.B. Rogers (tr.). 6658-8,6665-8
  "If one of the comedy-makers of old had attempted...". Gilbert Murray (tr.). 6435-3
  Life of men, fr. The birds. John Hookham Frere (tr.). 6545-7
  "Nay, I'll not chip and scratch them line by line". Marshall MacGregor (tr.). 6435-3
  "Now for the Chorus, the Graces, the". B.B. Rogers (tr.). 6435-3
  "Now hear the old rule". T.F. Higham and G. Allen (tr.). 6435-3
  "Now peace, and be still! A seal on your lips...". Gilbert Murray (tr.). 6435-3
  "Since first to exhibit his Plays he began". B.B. Rogers (tr.). 6435-3
  The trial of the dog. George Allen (tr.). 6435-3
  "Well, I must go. Why keep on loitering here". T. Mitchell (tr.). 6435-3
  "Wh-wh--wh-wh...where's". T.F. Higham (tr.). 6435-3
  "When Olympus Hera was given". T.F. Higham (tr.). 6435-3
  "With reverence to your worships...". T. Mitchell (tr.). 6435-3
  Women's chorus. 6585-6
  "You, I presume, could adroitly and gingerly". B.B. Rogers (tr.). 6435-3
  "You, too, retire and sit you down again". B.B. Rogers (tr.). 6435-3
'An **Aristotelian** elegy'. Donald E. Bogle. 7024-8
Aristotle
  An inscription for all council-chambers, fr. Eth. Nic. Bernard Bosanquet (tr.). 7042-6
  To virtue. T.F. Higham (tr.). 6435-3
Arithmetic. Walter De La Mare. 6905-3
Arithmetic in life. M. Truesdell Cooper. 6926-6
Ariwara No Nari-hira
  "All red with leaves Tatsuta's stream". William N. Porter (tr.). 6852-9
Arizona. Margaret Rowe Clifford. 6465-5
Arizona. John Gould Fletcher. 6509-0
Arizona. Sharlot M. Hall. 6946-0
Arizona. Thomas W. Stevens. 6484-1
Arizona Jim. Charles F. Lummis. 6670-4
Arizona nights. Berta Hart Nance. 6265-2
Arizona poems: Mexican quarter. John Gould Fletcher. 6506-6
Arizona summer. Eleanor Baldwin. 6750-6
The **Ark** and the Dove. Daniel Sargent. 6833-2
The **ark** and the dove. Lydia Huntley Sigourney. 6848-0
The **ark**. John Milton. 6833-2
The **ark**. Jones Very. 6288-1
Arkansas post. James Abraham Martling. 6952-5
The **Arkansas** traveler. Sanford C. Faulkner. 6465-5
Arkwright, John S.
  The supreme sacrifice. 6730-1
Arkwright, Pegleg. See Proudfit, David Law
Arlington Heights. Benjamin Franklin Taylor. 6815-4
Arlo Will. Edgar Lee Masters. 6897-9
"An **arm** of aid to the weak." Richard Monckton Milnes; 1st Baron Houghton. 6225-3
Arm of the lake. Robert Wallace. 6860-X
"**Arm'd** in the cause on Chalgrove's...plain". Naucratia, or naval dominion, sels. Henry James Pye. 6867-7
Arma virumque. Harold Kellock. 6118-4
The **armada**, sels. Thomas Babington Macaulay, 1st Baron Macaulay. 6427-2,6239-3
The **armada**. Thomas Babington Macaulay, 1st Baron Macaulay. 6087-0,6232-3,6290-3,6186-9,6669-0,6188,6459-0,6732-8,6322-5,6639-9,6046-3,6263-6,6808-1,6079-X
The **armada**. Algernon Charles Swinburne. 6122-2
Armageddon. Sir Edwin Arnold. 6212-1
Armand Dussault. Wilson MacDonald. 6722-0
Armbuster, Anna A.
  The storm. 6818-9
Armed. William Shakespeare. 6087-0
The **armed** liner. H. Smalley Sarson. 7031-0,6846-4
"**Armed** soul that ridest through a land". 'Songs of a semite' Helen Gray Cone. 6848-0
Armenia's love to Shakespeare. Zabelle C. Boyajian. 6050-1
The **Armenian** mother. Eugene Field. 6949-5
The **Armenian** poet's prayer. Alexander Dzadourian. 6050-1
Armenian song. Anne Stoddard. 6478-7
Armer, Laura Adams
  Prayer of the Navajos. 6490-6
Armida's garden, fr. Jerusalem delivered. Torquato Tasso. 6649-6
The **arming** of Pigwiggen, fr. 'Nymphidia'. Michael Drayton. 6239-3
Armistice. Charles Buxton Going. 6051-X,6309-8
Armistice. Eunice Mitchell Lehmer. 6420-5,6461-2,6542-2
Armistice. Thomas Lodge. 6436-1
Armistice. Frederick George Scott. 6797-2
Armistice. Louis Untermeyer. 6542-2
Armistice (November, 1928). Margaret Elizabeth Sangster. 6449-3
Armistice Day. Edmund Vance Cooke. 6542-2
Armistice Day. Mary Carolyn Davies. 6051-X
Armistice Day. Roselle Mercier Montgomery. 6465-5,6542-2

Armistice Day. John J. Willoughby. 6542-2
The Armistice Day parade. Nancy Boyd. 6817-0
Armistice Day, 1918-1928. Nancy Byrd Turner. 6051-X
Armistice Day, 1920. Curtis Wheeler. 6542-2
Armistice Day, 1926. Lucia Trent. 6051-X
Armistice Day, 1926. Curtis Wheeler. 6732-8
Armistice Day, 1928 Ernest Hartsock. 6542-2
Armistice Day, 1938. G.M. Miller. 6625-9
Armistice, 1928 Kenneth Groesbeck. 6542-2
The armony of byrdes. Unknown. 6943-6
Armor. Georgia Douglas Johnson. 6038-2
The armoraider's song. Winston Johnson. 6237-7
Armored. Lucile Hargrove Reynolds. 6750-6
"Armored in fashionable layers". Grace be with them all that love. Shelley Jones. 7003-5
The armorer cruiser squadron. Unknown. 6237-7
The armorer's errand. Julia C.R. Dorr. 7030-2
The armorer's errand. Julia C.R. Dorr. 6673-9
The armour of innocence. Thomas Campion. 6604-6,6660-7
Armour, Richard
    Do not disturb. 6761-1
An armoury. Alcaeus. 6435-3,6665-8
Arms and the boy. Wilfred Owen. 6375-6,6666-6
"Arms and the leader I sang whose piety". Torquato Tasso. 6325-X
Arms and the muse. John Milton. 6322-5
"Arms for the slaves! Let all be set". Of arming the slaves! James Abraham Martling. 6952-5
The arms of 'eighty-two'. Michael Jozeph Barry. 6858-8
Arms, M.W. (tr.)
    In the piazza of San Petronio. Giosue Carducci, 6624-0
The Armstrong at Fayal. Wallace Rice. 6946-0
Armstrong's good-night. Unknown. 6219-9
Armstrong, D. Hercules
    Do they mean me? 6761-1
Armstrong, E.J.
    The ladye's rock. 6518-X
Armstrong, Hamilton Fish
    Lines for the hour. 6034-X,6076-5,6102-8,6337-3
Armstrong, Jennifer M.
    Florida. 6900-2
Armstrong, John
    Air, fr. The art of preserving health. 6968-1
    The art of preserving health, sels. 6831-6
    The art of preserving health. 6968-1
    Blest winter nights, fr.The art of preserving health. 6932-0
    A day: an epistle to John Wilkes, of Aylesbury, Esq. 6968-1
    Diet, fr. The art of preserving health. 6968-1
    Exercise, fr. The art of preserving health. 6968-1
    The home of the Naiads, fr.The art of preserving health. 6932-0
    An imitation of Spencer. 6968-1
    Imitations of Shakespeare. 6968-1
    Of benevolence: an epistle to Eumenes. 6968-1
    The passions, fr. The art of preserving health. 6968-1
    Taste. 6968-1
Armstrong, Martin
    The buzzards. 6943-6
    The cage. 6779-4
    Cathedral at night. 6071-4
    The explorers. 7014-0
    Going up the line. 7029-9
    The Naiad. 6072-2
    Poetry and the subconscious. 6776-X
Armstrong, Mary J.
    Peace guaranteed. 6270-9
Armstrong, Thomas M.
    The story of Rebekak. 6921-5
Army. Ken LaMere. 6883-9
Army. Kenneth Neal. 6475-2
Army air force ground crew song. Richard Black. 6237-7
The army bean. Unknown. 6205-9
An army corps on the march. Walt Whitman. 6288-1
Army correspondent's last ride. George Alfred Townsend. 6340-3
The Army flying corps. Unknown. 6237-7
The army horse. McLandburgh Wilson. 6510-4
The army mule, the navy goat & the kick of the kangaroo.

Alfred Eiseman et al. 6237-7
The army of despair. John Chalmers DaCosta. 6482-5
The army of spring. Mary Barker Dodge. 6965-7
The army of the dead. Barry Pain. 7029-9,7027-2
The army of the Lord. Adelaide Anne Procter. 6957-6
Army of the Potomac. Joaquin Miller. 7002-7
The army of the Red Cross. Katrina Trask. 6449-3
The army of Xerxes. Delphic Oracle. 6435-3
The army surgeon, fr. Sonnets. Sydney Dobell. 6380-2
The army. Abu Zaid. 6362-4
Armytage, Faulkner
    Friday afternoon at the Boston Symphony Hall. 6996-7
Arnason, Magnus A. (tr.)
    Sorrow. Johann Sigurjonsson. 6854-5,6283-0
Arndt, Ernst Moritz
    The field marshal. James Abraham Martling (tr.). 6952-5
    The German fatherland. J. Macray (tr.). 6484-1
Arndt, G. M.
    To the Bible. James Abraham Martling (tr.). 6952-5
Arne, Thomas Augustine
    Water parted. 6328-4
Arnett, Joseph W.
    Launch out into the deep. 6799-9
Arnold at Stillwater. Thomas Dunn English. 6062-5,6674-4, 6419-1
Arnold Bennett: Robert Bridges. Humbert Wolfe. 6781-6
Arnold the vile traitor. Unknown. 6946-0
Arnold von Winkleried. James Montgomery. 6409-3,6479-5, 6498-1,6552-X,6554-6,6419-1,6424-8,6566-X
"Arnold! the name, as heretofore". Arnold the vile traitor. Unknown. 6946-0
Arnold's departure. Philip Freneau. 6753-0
Arnold's departure. Philip Freneau. 6121-4
Arnold's departure. Philip Freneau. 6753-0
Arnold, Alexander S.
    The dying soldier of Joshua. 6848-0
    Samson: champion and judge of Israel. 6848-0
Arnold, Alice
    December. 6807-3
Arnold, Emily Gail
    In April. 6449-3
Arnold, George
    Among the heather. 6066-8, 6253-9
    Beer. 6004-8,6300-4
    Farewell to summer. 6820-0
    A farewell. 6066-8
    "Here,/ With my beer" 7041-8
    The jolly old pedagogue. 6004-8,6219-9,6304-7,6910-X
    Jubilate. 6833-2
    The merry Christmas time. 6272-5
    October. 6272-5
    September. 6820-0,6219-9,6964-9
    September days. 6456-6
    A sunset fantasie. 7041-8
    Sweet September. 6820-0
    Youth and age. 6004-8
Arnold, John (tr.)
    Psalm 004. Bible, 6848-0
Arnold, Josias Lyndon
    Ode to the Connecticut River. 7030-2
Arnold, Mabel W.
    April. 6799-9
    The bus. 6799-9
    Companionship. 6799-9
    The Messiah. 6799-9
    Morning mist. 6799-9
    The weaver. 6894-4
Arnold, Matthew
    Absence. 6094-3
    Ah, friend let us be true. 6084-6
    Ah, love! let us be true. 6066-8
    Anti-desperation. 6947-9
    Apollo. 6322-5
    "As the stars come out, and the night-wind". 6793-X
    Atossa. 6511-2
    Austerity of poetry. 6102-8,6110-9,6199-0,6250-4,6430-2, 6437 ,6655-0,6828-6
    Bacchanalia; or, The new age. 6110-9,6271-7,6655-0
    Balder dead. 6947-9
    Balder dead, sels. 6656-9

The better part. 6110-9,6199-0,6337-3,6196-6,6250-4,
     6371 ,6737-9,6543-0
'The bloom is gone' 6943-6
The buried life. 6199-0,6250-4,6430-2,6655-0,6828-6
The burning of Balder's ship. 6102-8
But the majestic river. 6252-0
Cadmus and Harmonia. 6046-3,6437-X
Calais sands. 6430-2,6560-0,6253-9
Callicles' song, fr. Empedocles on Etna. 6102-8,6110-9,
     6125-7,6828-6
Calm soul of all things. 6730-1
The canticle of the sun. 6250-4
A caution to poets. 6947-9
The church of Brou. 6947-9,6828-6
Consolation. 6947-9
Contagion of courage, fr. Rugby chapel. 6337-3
Continued. 6655-0
Courage. 6541-4
The cuckoo's parting cry, fr. Thyrsis. 6153-2
The death of Nelson. 6502-3
The death of Sohrab. 6322-5
Desire. 6730-1
Destiny. 6250-4
The divinity. 6199-0
Dover beach. 6052-8,6208-3,6337-3,6178-0,6437-X,6604 ,
     6371-3,6192-3,6250-4,6301-2,6439-6,6650 ,6023-4,6046-
     3,6102-8,6150-8,6110-9,6199 ,6153-2,6196-6,6430-2,
     6560-0,6659-3,6646 ,6513-9,6645-3,6723-9,6660-7,6491-
     4,6656 ,6585-6
Dover beach, sels. 6589-9
A dream. 6947-9
Early death and fame. 6641-0
East and west. 6110-9
East London. 6337-3,6730-1,6660-7,6655-0,6430-2,62 0 ,
     6102-8,6110-9,6199-0
Empedocles on Etna. 6250-4,6947-9
Empedocles on Etna, sels. 6934-7
Empedocles on Etna, sels. 6102-8,6199-0,6301-2,6378-
     0.6430-2,6656
Empedocles on Etna, sels. 6879-0
Empedocles' song, fr. Empedocles on Etnaa. 6828-6
Epilogue to Lessing's 'Laocoon'. 6250-4
Euphrosyne. 6219-9,6250-4,6560-0
Excuse. 6271-7,6321-7
"Far on its rocky knoll descried", fr. Stanzas..Carnac.
     6997-5
A farewell. 6947-9
Flee fro' the press. 6322-5
The forsaken merman. 6046-3,6102-8,6153-2,6196-6,6199-0,
     6558 ,6114-1,6110-9,6197-4,6252-0,6430-2,6558 ,6319-
     5,6424-8,6371-3,6383-7,6656-9,6723 ,6646-1,6639-9,
     6828-6,6133-8,6271-7,6437-X,6512-0,6655-0
Fragment of a chorus of 'Dejaneira'. 6250-4
Fragment of a chorus of a Dejaneira. 6947-9
Fragment of an 'Antigone'. 6947-9
The future. 6177-X,6196-6,6430-2,6828-6
Geist's grave. 6230-X,6604-6,6656-9,6660-7
"Go, for they call you, shepherd, from the hill!" 7020-
     5
"Goethe in Weimar sleeps", fr. Memorial verses. 6793-X
The good shepherd with the kid. 6102-8
Growing old. 6110-9,6828-6
Haworth churchyard. 6655-0
The Hayswater boat. 6947-9
"Headlands stood out into the moon-lit deep". 6997-5
Heine. 6439-6
Heine's grave. 6848-0,6828-6,6250-4
Heine's grave, sels. 6110-9
Horatian echo. 6947-9
Human life. 6199-0,6828-6
Hymn of Empedocles. 6437-X
Immortality. 6337-3,6110-9,6250-4,6199-0,6354-3,6373 ,
     6655-0
In harmony with nature. 6337-3,6430-2,6199-0,6655-0
In utrumque paratus. 6378-0;6655-0,6430-2
Indifference. 6271-7
Inward peace, fr. Lines written in Kensington gardens.
     6337-3
Isolation. 6437-X,6110-9,6250-4,6383-7,6655-0
Kaiser dead. 6196-6

The lake. 6947-9
Last song of Callicles. 6655-0
The last word. 6052-8,6208-3,6271-7,6337-3,6378-0,6437-,
     6102-8,6110-9,6250-4,6513-9,6543-0,6737 ,6371-3,6655-
     0
Lines written by a death-bed. 6947-9
Lines written by a death-bed, sels. 6934-7
Lines written in Kensington Gardens. 6046-3,6199-0,6110-
     9,6649-6,6604-6;6655 ,6110-9,6196-6,6660-7
Lines written in Kensington Gardens, sels. 6301-2
Longing. 6226-1,6430-2
Lovers. 6066-8
Lyric stanzas of Empedocles. 6110-9
Memorial verses. 6046-3,6102-8,6199-0,6250-4,6430-2,
     6641 ,6655-0,6656-9,6645-3,6828-6
Men of genius. 6947-9
Merope. 6947-9
Midsummer, fr. Thyrsis. 6558-9
A modern Sappho. 6655-0,6947-9
Morality. 6110-9,6199-0,6250-4,6828-6
Mycerinus. 6655-0,6828-6
A nameless epitaph (1). 6947-9
A nameless epitaph (2). 6947-9
The neckan. 6457-4,6219-9,6639-0
The new sirens: a palinode. 6947-9
Obermann once more. 6110-9,6199-0,6749-2
On the Rhine. 6934-7,6947-9
Pagan and Christian. 6424-8
The pagan world. 6250-4
Palladium. 6208-3,6621-6,6252-0,6430,6110-9,6252-0,6655-
     0,6110-9,6196-6,6199-0
Parting. 6282-0,6383-7
Philomela. 6198-2,6246-6,6332-2,6423-X,6052-8,6271-7,
     6102-8,6153-2,6219-9,6110 ,6430-2,6250-4,6252-0,6655-
     0,6656-9,6558
A picture at Newstead. 6947-9
Pis-aller. 6102-8,6110-9,6199-0,6828-6
Pis-aller. 6110-9,6150-4,6199-0
Progress. 6199-0,6337-3,6199-0
The progress of poesy. 6250-4
The progress of poetry. 6233-4
Progress, sels. 6144-3
A question. 6655-0
Quiet work. 6138-9,6457-4,6110-9,6430-2,6541-4,6250 ,
     6199-0,6301-2,6655-0,6639-9
Rachel. 6848-0
Rachel, I. 6947-9
Rachel, II. 6947-9
Rachel, III. 6947-9
Religious isolation. 6199-0,6828-9
Requiescat. 6199-0,6383-7,6250-4,6430-2,6437-X,6655 ,
     6046-3,6301-2,6102-8,6153-6,6371-3,6197 ,6110-9,6513-
     9,6560-0
Resignation. 6430-2,6828-6
Revolutions. 6199-0,6828-6
The river oxus. 7020-5
The river. 6947-9
Rugby chapel. 6110-9,6052-8,6655-0,6730-1,6199-0,6110-9,
     6430
Rugby chapel, sels. 6337-3
Saint Brandan. 6747-6
St. Brandan. 6558-9
The scholar gipsy. 6208-3,6437-X,6655-0,6023-4,6046-3,
     6301 ,6196-6,6420-3,6245-8,6250-4,6199-0,6125 ,6110-
     9,6150-8,6668-2,6828-6
The scholar-gipsy, sels. 6543-0
"The sea is calm to-night", fr. Dover beach. 6997-5
Second best. 6110-9,6199-0,6828-6
Self-deception. 6110-9,6828-6
Self-dependence. 6192-3,6585-6,6250-4,6396-9,6579-1,
     6660 ,6604-6;6655-0;6730-1,6110-9,6196-6,6430 ,7022-
     1,6828-6
Separation. 6250-4
Shakespeare. 6437-X,6604-6,6655-0,6023-4,6102-8,6607 ,
     6558-9,6110-9,6646-1,6301-2,6464-7,6196 ,6430-2,6560-
     0,6192-3,6541-4,6250-4,6199 ,6371-3,6723-9,6828-6
The sick king in Bokhara. 6655-0,6828-6
Sohrab and Rustum, sels. 6378-0,6656-9
Sohrab and Rustum. 6271-7,6110-9,6199-0,6264-4,63713,
     6419 ,6828-6

The song of Callicles. 6437-X,6252-0
Sonnet ("One lesson"). 6947-9
Sonnet to the Hungarian nation. 6947-9
Sonnet: Monica's last prayer. 6947-9
Sonnet: quiet work. 6828-6
A southern night. 6947-9
Stagirius. 6947-9
Stanzas composed at Carnac. 6947-9
Stanzas from the Grande Chartreuse. 6046-3,6102-8,6110-9,6196-6,6430-2,6199 ,6052-8,6604-6,6655-0
Stanzas in memory of Edward Quillinan. 6947-9
Stanzas in memory of the author of Obermann. 6046-3, 6199-0,6250-4,6947-9
The strayed reveller, sels. 6369-1,6655-0
The strayed reveller. 6110-9
A summer night. 6199-0,6430-2,6560-0,6828-6
Switzerland. 6430-2,6560-0
Switzerland, sels. 6110-9
The terrace at Berne. 6749-2,6947-9
"Though the muse be gone away". 6947-9
Thyrsis. 6437-X,6655-0,6438-3,6110-9,6250-4,6430 ,6252-0,6301-2,6084-6
Thyrsis, sels. 6378-0,6558-9,6102-8,6649-6,6543-0
To a friend. 6196-6,6199-0,6430-2,6828-6
To a gipsy child by the sea-shore. 6947-9
To a republican friend, 1848. 6828-6,6199-0,6655-0
To a republican friend, 1848, continued. 6828-6,6199-0
To an independent preacher. 6947-9,6828-6
To Fausta. 6947-9,6828-6
To George Cruikshank, esq. 6947-9
To Marguerite, fr. Switzerland. 6655-0,6737-9,6110-9, 6208-3,6102-8,6110-9,6250-4,6199-0,6150
To my friends who ridiculed a tender leave-taking. 6947-9
To the Duke of Wellington on hearing him mispraised. 6947-9
The tomb - at the church of Brou. 6046-3,6641-0
Too late. 6947-9
Tristram and Iseult. 6046-3,6655-0
Tristram and Iseult, sels. 6541-4,6560-0
Urania. 6219-9, 6250-4, 6560-0
The voice. 6250-4
"We cannot kindle when we will", fr. Morality. 6793-X
West and east. 6114-1
West London. 6196-6,6199-0,6430-2,6828-6
A wish. 6271-7,6199-0,6110-9,6655-0
Wordsworth and Goethe, fr. Stanzas...author of Obermann. 6934-7
The world and the quietest. 6656-9
The world's triumphs. 6250-4,6947-9
Worldly place. 6828-6,6102-8,6110-9,6199-0,6655-0,6660-7
Written in Butler's sermons. 6947-9
Written in Emerson's essays. 6828-6
Yes, in the sea of life enisled. 6196-6
Youth and calm. 6271-7,6199-0,6655-0
The youth of man. 6947-9
The youth of nature. 6828-6,6110-9
Youth's agitations. 6543-0
Arnold, Matthew (tr.)
Canticle of the creatures (or, Canticle of the sun). Saint Francis of Assisi, 6337-3
Thekla's answer. Johann C. Friedrich von Schiller, 6947-9
Arnold, Mrs. J.O.
To 'him that's awa'. 7031-0
Arnold, Richard K.
Eight o'clock. 6515-5
Five o'clock. 6515-5
Arnold, Rubye
April. 7016-7
The awakening. 7016-7
Disillusion. 7016-7
Eyes. 7016-7
Forget. 7016-7
Spring. 7016-7
Waiting. 7016-7
Why? 7016-7
Arnold, Samuel J.
The battle of Trafalgar. 6552-X

Arnold, Sarah Louise
The mother. 6449-3
Arnold, Sir Edwin
Abraham's bread. 6848-0
Abraham's offense. 6848-0
Academe. 6484-1
Adelaide Anne Procter. 6046-3
After death. 6424-8
After death in Arabia. 6337-3,6730-1,6102-8,6177-X,6656-9,6303
Ali and the Jew. 6848-0
Almond-blossom. 6219-9
Armageddon. 6212-1
Azar and Abraham. 6848-0
Azrael and the indian prince. 6848-0
Berlin - the sixteenth of March. 6046-3
The book of love, sels. 6066-8
The caliph's draught. 6656-9
Darien. 6946-0
Destiny. 6337-3,6226-1
The Egyptian princess. 6980-0
Flowers. 6980-0
Give a man a horse he can ride. 6301-2
"God doth suffice! O thou, the patient one." 6225-3
'He and she.' 6370-5,6102-8,6066-8
He who died at Azan. 6271-7
Iblis and Abraham. 6848-0
The law of death. 6573-2
The light of Asia, sels. 6046-3
A love song of Henri Quatre. 6658-5
The lover with his loved one sailed the sea. 6066-8
A ma future. 6226-1
Mahmud and Ayaz, fr. Sa'id in the garden. 6656-9
Making of man. 6848-0
Moses and the angel. 6848-0
Mount Pilate. 6484-1,6749-2
The musmee. 6656-9
Naught is the same "as if love had not been" 6066-8
Nimrud and the gnat. 6848-0
Not death is strong enough to part asunder. 6066-8
Obscure martyrs. 6793-X
Oh, if thou be'st true lover. 6066-8
On a cyclamen. 6066-8
The order of valour. 6793-X
Ozair the Jew. 6848-0
Pearl seventy-eight. 6510-4
Pontius Pilate. 6679-8
Raglan. 6656-9
A Rajput nurse. 6921-5
Serenade. 6658-5
"She and he". 6648-8
The sirens. 6980-0
Solomon and the ant. 6848-0
Solomon's signet. 6848-0
The song of the devas. 6271-7
Song without a sound, fr. Sa'di in the garden. 6656-9
The sorrow of Buddha. 6929-0
The swallows. 6368-3,6820-0
To a pair of Egyptian slippers. 6437-X
Too full of love my soul is to find the place. 6066-8
We are the voices of the whispering wind. 6301-2
With Sa'di in the garden, sels. 6656-9
Woman's voice. 6271-7
Wreck of the Northern Belle. 6578-3
Arnold, Sir Edwin (tr.)
After battle, fr. The Bhagavad-gita. Unknown (Sanskrit), 6337-3
Bustan, sels. Sadi [or Saadi] (Mushlih-ud-Din), 7039-6
Courage, fr. the Gulistan. Sadi [or Saadi] (Mushlih-ud-Din), 7039-6
The dancer, fr. the Bustan. Sadi [or Saadi] (Mushlih-ud-Din), 7039-6
The Darweesh. Sadi [or Saadi] (Mushlih-ud-Din), 6448-5
Death, fr. The Bhagavad-gita. Unknown (Sanskrit), 6337-3
Forgiveness. Sadi [or Saadi] (Mushlih-ud-Din), 6448-5
Friendship, fr. the Gulistan. Sadi [or Saadi] (Mushlih-ud-Din), 7039-6
The great journey, fr. Maha-Bharata. Unknown (Sanskrit), 6372-1

Gulistan, sels. Sadi [or Saadi] (Mushlih-ud-Din), 7039-6
Help, fr. the Gulistan. Sadi [or Saadi] (Mushlih-ud-Din), 7039-6
Maha-Bharata, sels. Unknown (Sanskrit), 6372-1
Mesnevi, fr. the Gulistan. Sadi [or Saadi] (Mushlih-ud-Din), 7039-6
Prudence. Sadi [or Saadi] (Mushlih-ud-Din), 6448-5
Resurrection of Abdullah. Unknown (Arabic), 6304-7
Savitri; or love and death, fr. Maha-Bharta. Unknown (Sanskrit), 6372-1
Song celestial, fr. The Bhagavad-gita. Unknown (Sanskrit), 6337-3

Arnold, Walter G.
Entreaty. 6178-8
Interrogation. 6178-8

Arnold, master of the Scud. Bliss Carman. 6833-2
"Arose a mammouth arch as in a dream". The court of lights. Lucy H. King Smith. 6906-1
"Around are the orchards and the...hills". Baie des Chaleur. Henry Duncan Chisholm. 6764-6
"Around me cluster quaint cloud-berry flowers". The cloud-berry flower, fr. On the scrape. John Veitch. 6819-7
"Around me rise/The 'hills' of God...". Mansfield. Ada J. (Ellen Eliza Philips) Moore. 7030-2
"Around me rose the phantoms of the dark". Gerald Massey. 6648-8
"Around Mount Miyoshino's crest". Masatsune. 6852-9
Around Thanksgiving time. Unknown. 6703-4
"Around me stand the everlasting hills". Mount Agassiz. William White. 6868-5
"Around no fire the soldiers sleep to-night". The battlefield. Sydney Oswald. 7026-4
"Around our center meetinghouse". Our old center-town Vermont meetinghouse. Daniel L. Cady. 6988-6
"Around stones called precious". Black meat. Jean Follain. 6758-1
"Around the cage, around the cage". The fox. Francis Maguire. 6761-1
"Around the Chattanooga gate". Lookout Mountain. Benjamin Franklin Taylor. 6815-4
Around the child. Walter Savage Landor. 6934-7,6102-8
Around the corner. Charles Hanson Towne. 6654-2
"Around the dusky brow of night". Vespers. Arthur Wallace Peach. 7030-2
"Around the good world's wide expanse". Names of romance. Berton Braley. 6853-7
"Around the last bend". Adam canoes sthe Meramac river. Walter Bargen. 6860-X
"Around the manger at his birth". The Ascension. William White. 6868-5
"Around the moon glide ghosts on nights". Grotesque. Gerd Aage Gilhoff. 6798-0
"Around the rocky headlands, far and near". The sea's voice. William Prescott Foster. 6833-2,7041-8
Around the sun. Katharine Lee Bates. 6327-6,6393-4
"Around the time" Frank LaPena Tauhindauli. 7005-1
"Around the time-scarred battlefield where now". Brook sound at evening. August Derleth. 6783-2
"Around the walls of Jericho". Jericho. Frank Foxcroft. 6848-0
Around the world. Kate Greenaway. 6452-3
Around the world. Thomas Tapper. 6368-3
"Around thee, barefoot girl, there float". To a dancer of Tanagra. Thomas Walsh. 6959-2
"Around were all the roses red". Spleen. Paul Verlaine. 7039-6
"Arouse, arouse, each kilted clan!". Welcome, Charlie, o'er the main. Unknown. 6859-6

Arrabal, Fernando
The stone of madness, sels. Laurence Lewis (tr.). 6803-0

Arracombe Wood. Charlotte Mew. 6331-4;6506-6
"Arraign'd poore captiue at the barre I stand," Bartholomew Griffin. 6586-4
Arraignment. Lizette Woodworth Reese. 6031-5,6653-4
The arraignment of a louer. George Gascoigne. 6586-4
The arraignment of Paris, sels. George Peele. 6122-2
Arraignment, sels. William Rose Benet. 6337-3
Arran. Unknown (Irish) 6125-7

An arrangement for an inquiring oboe of philosphic bent. Raymond Ellsworth Larsson. 6038-2
Arrangement in black and gold, New Orleans, 1821. Walter McClellan. 6036-6
"Arrayed in snow-white pants and vest". Ain't he cute. Unknown. 6917-7
Arrest. Sojin Takei. 6981-9

Arrieta, Rafael Alberto
"January night, quiet and luminous". Muna Lee (tr.). 6759-X

Arrival. Henry Van Dyke. 6961-4
Arrival and departure. Charles Eglinton. 6788-3
arrival and welcome, fr. Tahiti. John Liddell Kelly. 6768-9
Arrival of the conqueror. Norman Rosten. 6561-9
The arrival of the crusaders. Saint Nerses Shnorhali. 6050-1
The arrival of the greenhorn. Unknown. 6281-4
The arrival of the post, fr. The task. William Cowper. 6195-0
The arrival, fr. The day dream. Alfred Lord Tennyson. 6676-3
The arrival.. William Rose Benet. 6532-5
The arrow and the song. Henry Wadsworth Longfellow. 6431-0, 6560-0,6135-4,6250-4,6300-4,6006-4,6102-8,6288-1, 6076-5,6304-7,6461 ,6060-1,6623-2,6337-3,6401-9,6501-5,6632 ,6085-4,6605-4,6479-5,6176-1,6291-1,6486 , 6107-9,6457-4,6104-4,6126-5,6457-4,6639
The arrow of acestes. Thomas Hornsby Ferril. 7019-1
The arrow's death. Allan D. Dowling. 6979-7
The arrow. Theodore Maynard. 6042-0
The arrow. Richard Henry Stoddard. 6337-3
The arrow. William Butler Yeats. 6187-7
Arrowhead aisles. Lillian Reiquam Sandberg. 6342-X
Arrows for love. John Lyly. 6827-8
Ars agricolaris. Henry Van Dyke. 6961-4
Ars amatoria, sels. Ovid. 6637-2
Ars dura. Christopher Morley. 6030-7
Ars longa. Adam Lindsay Gordon. 6951-7
Ars poetica. Archibald MacLeish. 6052-8,6527-9,6619-4,6645-3,6491-4
Ars victrix. Austin Dobson. 6527-9,6102-8,6508-2,6655-0, 6656-9
The arsenal at Springfield. Henry Wadsworth Longfellow. 6176-1,6481-7,6332-2,6473-6,6735-2,6240 ,6420-5,6610-0,6560-0,6484-1,6585-6
The arsenal at Springfield. Henry Wadsworth Longfellow. 6665-8,6250-4,6288-1,6126-5,6219-9
Arsinoe's cats. Rosamund Marriott ("Graham R. Tomson") Watson. 6120-6,6511-2
Art. Richard Burton. 6184-2
Art. Ralph Waldo Emerson. 6753-0
Art. Theophile Gautier. 6732-8
Art. Theophile Gautier. 7039-6,6879-0
Art. Herman Melville. 6333-0
Art. James ("B.V.") Thomson. 6198-2,6437-X
Art ("When, from the sacred garden driven") Charles Sprague. 6605-2
Art above nature. Robert Herrick. 6827-8
Art and heart. Ella Wheeler Wilcox. 6956-8
Art and life. Henry Dawson Lowry. 6793-X
Art and nature. William Shakespeare. 6438-8
An art critic. Sam Walter Foss. 6690-9
Art in the service of love. Michelangelo Buonarroti. 6102-8
An art master. John Boyle O'Reilly. 6004-8
The art of Alma-Tadema. Emily Pauline ("Tekahionwake") Johnson. 6837-5
The art of book-keeping. Laman Blanchard. 6089-7,6297-0
The art of book-keeping. Thomas Hood. 6606-2,6424-8,6219-9
The art of bringing up children, sels. Scevola de Sainte-Marthe. 6482-5
"The art of good driving's a paradox quite". Unknown. 6904-5
The art of holding on. Dwight Okita. 6790-5
The art of love. Sir John Suckling. 6317-9
The art of our necessities is strange. Forrest Izard. 6722-0
The art of poetry. Vicente Huidobro. 6759-X
The art of preserving health, sels. John Armstrong. 6831-6

The art of preserving health. John Armstrong. 6968-1
The art of succeeding. Johan Henrik Kellgren. 6045-5
The art of the arts. Robert Underwood Johnson. 6585-6
The art of writing, fr. Essay on criticism. Alexander Pope. 6934-7
The art of writing. Alexander Pope. 6732-8
"Art such as this has power to withstand". Sargent's portrait of Theodore Roosevelt. Margaret Ridgely Partridge. 6995-9
"Art thou a statist in the van". A poet's epitaph. William Wordsworth. 6110-9,6828-6,6250-4
"Art thou a thing of mortal birth". To a sleeping child. Christopher (John Wilson) North. 6980-0
"Art thou already weary of the way". Sonnet ("Art thou already"). Frances Anne Kemble. 7037-X
"Art thou come from the far-off land at last?". The palmer. Felicia Dorothea Hemans. 6973-8
"Art thou gon in haste Ile not forsake thee." Unknown. 6563-5
"Art thou gone in haste," fr. The Thracian wonder. John Webster and William Rowley. 6317-9
Art thou gone in haste? Unknown. 6182-6
"Art thou Heywood with the mad mery wit" John Heywood. 6380-2
"Art thou in loeu? it cannot be." Henry Hughes (atr) 6563-5
Art thou living yet? James G. Clarke. 6913-4
Art thou living yet? Unknown. 6304-7
"Art thou not glad to close". Address to the old year. Henry Timrod. 6753-0
"Art thou not hungry for thy children, Zion". To Zion. Jehuda [or Judah] Halevi. 7039-6
"Art thou poor, yet hast thou golden slumbers". Thomas Dekker. 6187-7,6198-2,6430-2
"Art thou solicitor for all thy tribe". To a sparrow. Unknown. 6878-2
"Art thou some individual of a kind". On a miser (3). Unknown (Greek). 6814-6
Art thou that she. Unknown. 6563-5
"Art thou that shee." Unknown. 6563-5
"Art thou the voice of God, thou tremulous sea". Sea voices. Charles A. Fox. 6997-5
Art thou weary, art thou troubled. Saint Stephen the Sabaite. 6337-3,6304-7
Art thou weary? Frances Anne Kemble. 6046-3
Art thou weary? John Mason Neale. 6490-6,6219-9
Art's martyr. Andrew Lang. 6987-8
Art, fr. A lover's diary. Gilbert Parker. 6656-9
Art, sels. James ("B.V.") Thomson. 6150-4,6070-6
Artaud, Antontin
   Black poet. Paul Zweig (tr.). 6803-0
Artegall and Radigund, fr. The faerie queene. Edmund Spenser. 6436-1
Artemis on Latmos. Amelia Josephine Burr. 6031-5
Artemis prologuizes. Robert Browning. 6980-0
Artemis visits the Cyclopes. Callimachus. 6435-3
Artevelde's character of his wife, fr. Philip Van... Henry Taylor. 6980-0
Artevelde's love for Adriana, fr. Philip Van Artevelde. Henry Taylor. 6980-0
Artevelde's vision of his wife, fr.Philip Van Artevelde. Henry Taylor. 6980-0
Artevelde, sels. Henry Taylor. 6066-8
'Artful dodger.' Mary Swain Paxton. 6397-7
Arthur passes in the dawn. Alfred Lord Tennyson. 7020-5
Arthur's farewell to Guinevere. Alfred Lord Tennyson. 6543-0
Arthur's wife. Phoebe Cary. 6969-X
Arthur, sels. William Winter. 6300-4
The **artichoke**. Ibn al-Talla. 6362-4
Articles of war. Dunstan Thompson. 6666-6
Articulate thrush. Lew Sarett. 6073-0
Artie's "amen". Paul Hamilton Hayne. 6745-X,6155-9,6917-7
Artifice disowned by love. James Sheridan Knowles. 6980-0
An **artifice** of dust. Lionel Wiggam. 6640-2
Artificial beauty. Lucianus. 7039-6
Artillery shoot. James Forsyth. 6666-6
Artist. Alexander Blok. 6103-6
Artist. Unknown. 6713-1
Artist and mode, sels. Robert Buchanan. 6934-7

An **artist** draws a peach. Patricia Hampl. 6966-5
"The **artist** has slipped her spiral shell". 'That first gulp of air we all took when first born' Nancy Paddock. 6966-5
The **artist** speaks. Don Erman. 6789-1
The **artist's** morning song. Johann Wolfgang von Goethe. 6948-7
The **artist**, fr. The picture of St. John. Bayard Taylor. 6976-2
The **artist-eye**. Josephine Hoshaw. 6906-1
The **artist**.. Owen (Edward Bulwer-Lytton, Earl Lytton) Meredith. 6600-3
The **artist**.. Sir Walter Raleigh. 6722-0
The **artist**. Henry Bellamann. 6326-8
The **artist**. Stewart Brisby. 6870-7
The **artist**. Oscar Levertin. 6045-5
The **artist**. Peter Meinke. 6966-5
The **artist**. Gene Moore. 6750-6
Artistry. M. Florence Hay. 6316-0
Artists. Alice Stettiner. 6818-9
Artists east and west. Diane Chang. 6790-5
The **artists**.. Jalal [or Jelal] ed-din Rumi. 6448-5
Artmann, H. C.
   "Always birds/in the sky" Milne Holton and Herbert Kuhner (tr.). 6769-7
   "The drum/whips up steam" Milne Holton and Herbert Kuhner (tr.). 6769-7
   "A rose/five roses/thirteen roses" Milne Holton and Herbert Kuhner (tr.). 6769-7
   "The sun is a new house" Milne Holton and Herbert Kuhner (tr.). 6769-7
   "A water-blue tree/rises high" Milne Holton and Herbert Kuhner (tr.). 6769-7
The **arts** come to America. Joel Barlow. 6121-4
The **arts** of death. William Blake. 6150-8
Arturo [pseud.]
   Gratitude. 6817-0
Artz, Ethel Mae
   Flowers. 6799-9
   My hero. 6799-9
Arundel, Earl of. See **Howard, Philip**
Arundel, Honor
   Adam. 6895-2
   His mother. 6895-2
   Morning shift. 6895-2
   The musician. 6895-2
   Refugees. 6895-2
"as". Psalm 046. Bible. 6271-7
"As 'mid the tuneful choir to keep". Sir Walter Scott. 6997-5
As 'Old Giles' saw it. D.S. Cohen. 6406-X
As a beam o'er the face of the waters may glow. Thomas Moore. 6102-8,6543-0
"As a beauty I am not a star". Limerick:"As a beauty I am not a star". Woodrow Wilson. 6811-1
"As a beauty I'm not a great star". Limeratomy. Anthony Euwer. 6861-8
"As a bird may pause, partway in its...flight". Reunion. Charlotte Hazlewood. 6789-1
"As a boy with a richness of needs I wandered" Clifford Dyment. 6257-1
"As a boy, just before sleeping". The young man's song. Wayne McNeill. 7003-5
"As a critic, the poet, Buchanan". Limerick:"As a critic, the oetp Buchanan". Dante Gabriel Rossetti. 6811-1
"As a decrepit father takes delight". Sonnet 037 ("As a decrepit father"). William Shakespeare. 6447-7
"As a drenched dorwned bee". A baby asleep after pain. David Herbert Lawrence. 6872-3
"As a drenched, drowned bee". A baby asleep after pain. David Herbert Lawrence. 6958-4
"As a fair maid was walking down by the banks...". Unknown. 6059-5
'As a flower'. Mary McKinley Cobb. 6841-3
"As a golfer I'm not one who cops the money". Golf luck. Edgar A. Guest. 7033-7
"As a handful of sand". A handful of sand. Lydia Gibson. 6880-4
As a little child. Florence Wilkinson. 6006-4
As a man soweth. Johann Wolfgang von Goethe. 6337-3

AS

As a star from the dust. Ada Alden. 6850-2
As a strong bird on pinions free. Walt Whitman. 6954-1
"As a sunset fades". Inscription for a book. W.A. Barton Jr.. 7016-7
'As a watch in the night'. R.C. Hollock. 6983-5
As Adam early in the morning. Walt Whitman. 6333-0
"As a white candle/In a holy place". The old woman. Joseph ("Seosamh MacCathmhaoil") Campbell. 6332-2,6096-X, 6607-0,6244-X,6365-9,6930
"As a young stag the thicket past". The tame stag. John Gay. 6972-X
"As a youth". Yesterday's child. Robert Reedburg. 7024-8
"As Abraham, the friend of God, once". Abraham and the idolater. Sadi [or Saadi] (Mushlih-ud-Din). 6848-0
"As Aesop was with boys at play". Aesop at play. Phaedrus. 7039-6
As all things pass. Diana Bickston. 6870-7
"As Amoret with Phyllis sat. Sir Carr Scrope. 6563-5
"As an unperfect actor on the stage". Sonnet 023 ("As an unperfect"). William Shakespeare. 6430-2,6560-0
"As Annie was carrying the baby one day". A question. Unknown. 6167-2,6913-4
"As an unperfect actor on the stage". William Shakespeare. 6204-0
"As anybody seen Bill 'Awkins?". Bill 'Awkins. Rudyard Kipling. 6810-3
"As are our hearts, our way is one". Joanna Baillie. 6973-8
"As at noon Dulcina rested" Unknown. 6874-X
"As at their work two weavers sat". The two weavers. Hannah More. 6918-5
As at thy portals also death. Walt Whitman. 6097-8
"As balmy as the breath of her you love". Fragment ("As balmy"). Dante Gabriel Rossetti. 6545-7
"As beats the sea against the rocks!...". Stornelli and Strambotti, sels. Agnes Mary F. ("Madame Duclaux") Robinson. 6997-5
"As beats the sun from mountain crest". The partridge. Eugene Field. 6949-5
"As beautiful Kitty one morning was tripping". The broken pitcher. Unknown. 6914-2
"As billows upon billows roll". The surrender at Appomattox. Herman Melville. 6946-0
"As birds their infant brood protect". Jehovah-Shammah. William Cowper. 6814-6
"As brave man faces the foe". At sea. Richard Hovey. 7006-X
"As by Salamanca's city". The student. Johann Ludwig Uhland. 6948-7
As by fire. Ella Wheeler Wilcox. 6956-8
"As by some tyrant's stern command". The lawyer's farewell to his muse. Sir William Blackstone. 6889-8,6219-9
"As by the shore, at break of day." Thomas Moore. 6302-0, 6385-3,6219-9
"As by the streames of Babilon" Thomas Campion. 6794-8
"As careful emrchants do expecting stand". The heart's venture. William Browne. 6935-5
"As center-rush he was our pride". Our hero. Harry Romaine. 7021-3
"As children keep". Epilogue. Edwina Stanton Babcock. 6331-4
"As children, told to go to bed". In a churchyard. Walter De La Mare. 6905-3
"As Cupid in Cyther's grove". Cupid, hymen and plutus. John Gay. 6972-X
"As Darwin catalogued each bird and beast". Voyage of discovery. Alice Mackenzie Swaim. 6857-X
As consequent, etc. Walt Whitman. 6333-0
As day begins to wane. Helena Coleman. 6021-8,6115-X
As dead leaves fall. Kathleen Nicholson. 6799-9
"As death was journeying through the land". Death's choice. George Halse. 6916-9
"As Dick and I/Were a-sailing by". Lines left at Mr. Theodore Hook's house in June, 1834 Richard Harris ("Thomas Ingoldsby") Barham. 6874-X
As dew in April. Unknown. 6756-5
As dew in April. Unknown. 6734-4
As dies the year. Alfred Austin. 6580-5
"As down in the meadows I chanced to pass". Susan's complaint and remedy. Unknown. 6874-X

As down in the sunless retreats. Thomas Moore. 6102-8
"As down the distant halls of time..". Adown the years. Ada Simpson Sherwood. 6926-6
"As down the street she wambled slow". Bessie Bobtail. James Stephens. 6897-9
"As dozing I sat in my chair by the fire". A visit to Hades. Stockton Bates. 6921-5
"As dreams the fasting nun of paradise". Apprehension (II). Agnes Mary F. ("Madame Duclaux") Robinson. 7015-9
"As due by many titles I resigne". John Donne. 6562-7
"As dying Roland to God solemnly". Sonnet 026 ("As dying Roland"). Arlo Bates. 7041-8
"As every prospect opens on my view". Changes of home. John Leyden. 6980-0
As falling frost. Lionel Wiggam. 6640-2
"As falls the fragment of a mighty star". Quentin Roosevelt. Leon Huhner. 6887-1
"As fast as thou shalt wane, so fast thou grow". Sonnet 011 ("As fast as thou"). William Shakespeare. 6447-7
"As fickle as the mountain gusts". Daini No Sammi. 6852-9
"As fire tempers the iron, so." Alice Cary. 6225-3
As for me, I have a friend. Ernest McGaffey. 6620-8
"As frank as a mirror was Anne". Ann. William Roehrick. 6850-2
"As fresh as a pink, on the other side". Law at our boarding-house. A.C. Gordon. 6878-2
"As frightened as a child I came to you". Returning. Janet Newmane Preston. 6841-3
As from a flower's chalice. Unnur ("Hulda") Benediktdottir. 6854-5
"As from his work, the veill that long...". Unveiling the statue. James Abraham Martling. 6952-5
"As from the Orient the sun". The prayer of Daniel. Robert Morris. 6848-0
"As gallant ships as ever ocean stemm'd". On the British commercial depredations. Philip Freneau. 6753-0
"As gaudy flies across a pewter plate". In war-time, fr. In war time. Wilfred Wilson Gibson. 6884-7
As ghosts may walk. Richard Lawson Gales. 6950-9
"As gilly-flowers do but stay". Upon a lady that died in child-bed, and left a... Robert Herrick. 6874-X
"As gloaming comes, the music knells". Cowbells at midnight. Florence Randal Livesay. 6797-2
"As God leads, I am content". Being conent. Unknown. 6889-8
"As good be out of the world as out of fashion". Love's last shift, sels. Colley Cibber. 6867-7
"As hang two mighty thunderclouds". The guns in the grass. Thomas Frost. 6946-0
As happy dwellers by the seaside hear. Celia Thaxter. 6833-2
"As has been said a thousand times". Until the cows come home. Arthur R. Macdougal Jr.. 6761-1
"As he that loves oft looks on the dear form". On the 'vita nuova' of Dante. Dante Gabriel Rossetti. 6828-6
As he walked with us. Harry Webb Farrington. 6144-3
"As he who sails aloof". Aetius the unbeliever. William Herbert; Earl of Pembroke. 6980-0
"As I am not/Pythagorean". Posterity. Cyril Dabydeen. 6790-5
"As I am sitting in the sun upon the porch...". The fire-hangbird's nest. Eugene Field. 6949-5
"As I approach the last of all my days". Sonnet ("As I approach"). Francesco Petrarch. 6879-0
"As I came by a green forest-side". A carol of hunting. Unknown. 6756-5
"As I came by Lochmaben gate". Lochmaben gate. Unknown. 6859-6
"As I came by the way". Man, move thy mind, and joy this feast. Unknown. 6756-5
"As I came down from Trouble town". Trouble town. Robert Loveman. 6941-X
"As I came down the Highgate hill". Highgate hill. Sir Henry Howarth Bashford. 7007-8
"As I came in by Achindown". The haughs of Cromdale. Unknown. 6859-6
"As I came through the valley of despair". Through the valley. Ella Wheeler Wilco. 6956-8

"As I came to the edge of the woods". Come in. Robert Frost. 6783-2
"As I enter the living room". The news. Jennifer Watters. 6883-9
"As I feel very queer, my will I now make". The will of James Bigsby. James Bigsby. 6878-2
"As I gaed down the water-side". 'The bells o' Banff'. Neil Munro. 7031-0
"As I go home at end of day, the old road". The old country. Katharine (Hinkson) Tynan. 6779-4
"As I go up and down these days". The passing of the old Vermont meetinghouse. Daniel L. Cady. 6988-6
"As I hear the breath of the mother". Past and present. Francis Turner Palgrave. 6980-0
"As I lay asleep, as I lay asleep". The dead mother. Robert Buchanan. 6819-7
"As I lay at your feet that afternoon", Regardant. Colonel John Hay. 7041-8
"As I lay in my bed slepe full unmete". Sleep and poetry. John Keats. 6828-6
"As I lay in the early sun". Song ("As I lay"). Edward Shanks. 6102-8
"As I lay in the trenches". In the trenches. Maurice Hewlett. 7026-4
"As I lay quietly in the grass". Four children. Robert Graves. 6779-4
"As I lay upon a night". Alma redemptoris mater. Unknown. 6756-5
"As I lie at rest on a patch of clover". Black swans. Andrew Barton Paterson. 6793-X
"As I loitered through the village". Blowing bubbles. Eugene H. Munday. 6919-3
"As I passed by a river-side". The carnal and the crane. Unknown. 6756-5
"As I rode one day on a Loita track...". 'On the Loita plains'. Brian ("Korongo") Brooke. 6938-X
"As I rode over the dusty waste". The ballad of Hadji and the boar. Ian Hamilton. 7010-8
"As I roved out on a summer's morning down...". Castlehyde. Unknown. 6930-4
"As I roved out one summer's morning...". Colleen Rue. Unknown. 6930-4
"As I sail home to Galveston". A sailor's song. Hazel Harper Harris. 6833-2
"As I sat musing in my study one day". Where is heaven. Edward R. Huxley. 6885-5
"As I sat sorrowing,/Love came and bade me...". Spring sadness. John Payne. 6770-0
"As I sate down to breakfast in state". The country clergyman's trip to Cambridge. Thomas Babington Macaulay, 1st Baron Macaulay. 6874-X
"As I sit here reflecting on my life". The nuclear family. Melvin Douglass Brown. 6870-7
"As I sit hunting for the word". The robin. John Galsworthy. 6888-X
"As I stand here beside you". The ancestors. Dorothy Livesay. 6767-0
"As I strolled on the beach with...Isabella". Flirtation. Unknown. 6919-3
"As I sunbathe in the prison yard". Reaching. William Carson Fagg. 6870-7
"As I sunk the lobster-pots". Fisherman's luck. Wilfred Wilson Gibson. 6833-2
"As I travell'd o'er the plain". Date oblym bellesario. Francis Hopkinson. 6753-0
"As I up rose in a morning". Mother, white as lily flower. Unknown. 6756-5
"As I walk through the streets". Prayer ("As I walk"). Francis Stewart Flint. 6161-3,6393-4
"As I walk'd thinking through a little grove". Catch: On a wet day. Franco Sacchetti. 7039-6
"As I walked by myself". A song on King William III. Unknown. 6902-9
"As I walked me this endurs day". Here I sit alone. Unknown. 6931-2
"As I walked my pardner to the gate today". The gate. Yasmeen Jamal. 6870-7
"As I walked out one morning for pleasure". Whoopee ti yi yo, git along, little dogies. John A. Lomax. 6891-X
"As I walked over the hill one day". Nursery song. Ann A.G. Carter. 6373-X,6452-3,6131-1,6373-X,6502-3
"As I walked past the". Spring breeze. Unknown (Japanese). 6850-2
"As I was a-walking upon my wedding-day". The drowned lover. Lady Margaret Sackville. 6777-8
"As I was climbing Ardan Mor". The herons. Francis Ledwidge. 6930-4,6812-X
"As I was going to market-town". A timely hint. Unknown. 6922-3
"As I was out a-swinging". Swinging. M.K. Westcott. 6937-1
"As I was spittin' into the ditch...". 'Soldier an' sailor too'. Rudyard Kipling. 6810-3
"As I was walkin' the jungle round". A ballad ("As I was walkin'"). Guy Wetmore Carryl. 6440-X
"As I was walking down the road". The happy toad. Edgar A. Guest. 6869-3
"As I was walking down the street". Flirtation. Edgar A. Guest. 6748-2
"As I was walking in the gardens where". The heart's journey (1). Siegfried Sassoon. 6985-1
"As I went down by Hastings Mill I lingered...". Hastings Mill. Cicely Fox Smith. 7012-4
"As I went down the village green". Ducks. Norman Ault. 6937-1
"As I went down to Derby town". Folk song. Unknown. 6179-6
"As I went down to Dymchurch wall". In Romney marsh. John Davidson. 6873-1
"As I went out for to take a little walk". Wild Bill Jones. Unknown. 6826-X
"As I went out walking for pleasure one day". The pretty Mauhee. Unknown. 6826-X
"As I went walking down the way I met a...miss". The temptress. Edgar A. Guest. 6869-3
"As I went walking up and down". The ghosts of Oxford. W. Snow. 7027-2
"As I write poetry in the middle of night". Chuang-Tze's butterfly. Chang-soo Koh. 6775-1
"As I'm sitting all alone in the gloaming". Bantry bay. James Lyman Molloy. 6930-4
"As heaven and earth are fairer," fr. Hyperion. John Keats. 6438-8
As Helen once. Muna Lee. 6619-4
As Hermes once took to his feathers light. John Keats. 6086-2
"As high as the trumpet's blast". Pindar. 6230-X
"As his who on some midnight hears". Philip Bourke Marston. 6997-5
"As I cam in by Dunidier". Unknown. 6111-7
As I came down from Lebanon. Clinton Scollard. 6300-4,6250-4,6310-1,6509-0,6102-8,6476-0,6076-5
"As I came down from Lebanon" Clinton Scollard. 7041-8
As I came down Mount Tamalpais. Clarence Urmy. 6241-5,6484-1
"As I doze at dawn" Keiho Soga. 6981-9
As I ebb'd with the ocean of life. Walt Whitman. 6315-2,6333-0,6399-3
"As I gird on for fighting," fr. Last poems. Alfred Edward Housman. 6828-6
As I grew older. Langston Hughes. 6628-3
As I grow old. Douglas Malloch. 6303-9
As I grow old. Herbert Everell Rittenburg. 6662-3
As I grow old. Unknown. 6337-3
"As I in hoary winter's night stood shivering in". Robert Southwell. 6181-8,6187-7
As I lay a-thynkynge. Richard Harris ("Thomas Ingoldsby") Barham. 6046-3
As I lay dreaming abed. John McClure. 6326-8
As I lay musing. Unknown. 6157-5
"As I lay sleeping." Unknown. 6187-7,6317-9
As I lay with my head in your lap camerado. Walt Whitman. 6126-5,6288-1
"As I me walk'd in one morning." Unknown. 6645-3
As I on go my way. Strickland Gillilan. 6337-3
As I pondered in silence. Walt Whitman. 6726-3,6288-1,6300-4
"As I rode out one evening, all in the month of May". Unknown. 6059-5
"As I rode to Grecian, to Grecian's fair home". Unknown. 6059-5
"As I roved down through Irish town one evening...".

Unknown. 6059-5
As I sat alone by blue Ontario's shore, sels. Walt Whitman. 6753-0
' As I sat at my spinning-wheel'. Unknown. 6157-5
"As I sat on the sunny bank". Unknown. 6059-5,6125-7
As I sat under a sycamore tree. Unknown. 6756-5
"As I sit by the fireside a-thinking". Unknown. 6059-5
As I stood by yon roofless tower. Robert Burns. 6180-X
"As I took a walk one May morning...". Unknown. 6059-5
"As I walked by myself". Unknown. 6363-2,6125-7
As I walked forth. Robert Underwood Johnson. 6328-4
As I walked out one evening. Wystan Hugh Auden. 6472-8
"As I walked out one evening fair...". Unknown. 6059-5
"As I walked out one evening just as the sun...". Unknown. 6059-5
"As I walked out one evening, I roamed...". Unknown. 6059-5
"As I walked out one morning in June". Unknown. 6059-5
"As I walked out one night, it being dark all over." Unknown. 6317-9
"As I was going along, long, long". Unknown. 6363-2
"As I was going o'er Westminster bridge." Unknown. 6452-3
"As I was going to sell my eggs". Unknown. 6363-2
"As I was going to St. Ives." Mother Goose. 6452-3
"As I was going up Pippen Hill". Unknown. 6363-2
"As I was going up the hill". Unknown. 6363-2
As I was laying on the green. Unknown. 6722-0,6733-6
"As I was standing on a corner". Unknown. 6059-5
"As I was walking all alone". Unknown. 6317-9,6518-X
As I was walking in the gardens. Siegfried Sassoon. 6649-6
"As I went by". Rose O'Neill. 6102-8,6076-5
"As I went down to Darby". Unknown. 6059-5
"As I went out walking one evening of late". Unknown. 6059-5
"As I went out walking one morning in May". Unknown. 6059-5
"As I went through a garden green. Unknown. 6756-5
"As I went through the garden gap". Unknown. 7028-0
"As I went through the garden gap." Mother Goose. 6452-3
"As I went through the garden gap." Unknown. 6452-3
"As I went to Bonner". Unknown. 6363-2
"As I went to the wake that is held on the green" Unknown. 6874-X
As if carbon is nothing. Bernice Lever. 6767-0
"As if fell upon a day". An ode ("As if"). Richard Barnfield. 6182-6,6436-1,6315-2,6250-4
"As if he had crawled from the sea". Warrior with shield. Michael Dennis Browne. 6966-5
"As if one were the Count of Monte Cristo". Conspiracy at midnight. John Maher Murphy. 6839-1
"As if spring's fresh groves should change...". Nature's fountain of youth, fr. The coming of love. Theodore Watts-Dunton. 6997-5
As if the sea should part. Emily Dickinson. 6154-0
"As if to relish" Muin Ozaki. 6981-9
"As if, in grief of chains and modest shame". Power's greek slave. James Abraham Martling. 6952-5
"As if/these northern lights confirm". Russian Easter, 1981 Richard Dauenhauer. 6855-3
"As in a duskie and tempestuous night". Sonnet 012 ("As in a duskie and tempestuous night"). William Drummond of Hawthornden. 6933-9
"As in a duskie and tempestuous night". William Drummond of Hawthornden. 6208-3
"As in a glass at evening, dusky-grey". Evening, fr. Parted love. William Bell Scott. 6819-7
As in a picture-book. Fannie Stearns Davis. 6619-4
As in a rose-jar. Thomas S. Jones Jr. 6006-4,6338-1,6347-0, 6476-0,6653-4
"As in a theatre the amused sense". At the play. Thomas Edward Brown. 6809-X
"As in a vision/I beheld the long, long trail". Vision. Anne Cleveland Cheney. 6954-1
"As in battailes, so in all other actions...". The description of a maske presented before the... Thomas Campion. 6794-8
"As in her ancient mistress' lap". Familiarity dangerous. Vincent Bourne. 6814-6,6511-2
"As in my chambers, all alone". The brief. Unknown. 6878-2
"As in the boughs of a tall poplar-tree". Sophocles. 6435-3
"As in the gardens, all through May, the rose". His lady's tomb. Pierre de Ronsard. 6771-9,7039-6
"As in the house I sate". Poverty. Thomas Traherne. 6931-2
As in the midst of battle. George Santayana. 6102-8,6347-0, 6310-1,6536-8,6076-5,6300
"As in the night I restless lie". An anodyne. Thomas Ken. 6931-2
As in the woodland I walk. Richard Le Gallienne. 6162-1
"As is the mainland to the sea". What science says to truth. Sir William Watson. 7014-0
"As it befell in midsummer time". Unknown. 6518-X
As it began to dawn. George Edward Hoffman. 6144-3
"As it fell one holy-day". Unknown. 6111-7,6518-X
"As it fell out on a holy day". The bitter withy. Unknown. 6756-5
"As it fell out on a long summer's day". Unknown. 6518-X
"As it fell out one May morning". The holy well. Unknown. 6931-2,6756-5
"As it fell out upon a day". Ballad ("As it fell"). Unknown. 6179-6
"As it fell out upon a day". Unknown. 6111-7
"As it fell upon a day". The plaint of the nightingale. Richard Barnfield. 6934-7
As it fell upon a day. Richard Barnfield. 6122-2,6181-8, 6187-7,6198-2,6301-2
As it fell upon a day. Thomas Hood. 6974-6
'As it is in heaven'. I. Edgar Jones. 6923-1
As it looked then. Edwin Arlington Robinson. 6038-2
As it was in the beginning. Daisy Arnold Maude. 6841-3
As Jacob served for Rachel. Unknown. 6922-3,6848-0
As Jimmie sees it. Charles C. Jones. 6697-6
"As Johnny came home from seashore". Unknown. 6059-5
As Johnny walked out. Unknown. 6518-X
As Joseph was a-walking. Unknown. 6466-3,6623-2
"As it was promised them so I beheld". All Souls' night. Gertrude Huntington McGiffert. 6838-3
"As it were upon the sea.Under the wind's hand". The desert travellers. Laurence David Lerner. 6788-3
"As it's give' me to perceive". On any ordenary man in a high state of laughture... James Whitcomb Riley. 6892-8
"As Jove the Olympian (who both I & you know).". The political balance. Philip Freneau. 6753-0
"As Jupiter I made my court in vain". Epilogue intended to have been spoken..Lady Wentworth. John Dryden. 6970-3
"As Jupiter's all-seeing eye". The eagle, and the assembly of animals. John Gay. 6972-X
"As kingfishers catch fire, dragonflies draw flame." Gerard Manley Hopkins. 6209-1,6491-4
"As laborers set in a vineyard". Figs of thistles. Phoebe Cary. 6969-X
"As lamps burn silent with unconscious light" Aaron Hill. 6874-X
As lamps into the pen. Dorothy Wellesley. 6210-9
"As late each flower that sweetest blows". The rose. Samuel Taylor Coleridge. 6967-3
"As late I rov'd by Lodon's whispering stream". To the right honourable George Dodington, Esq. Thomas Warton (the Elder). 6962-2
"As leaden as the aftermath of wine". Elegy. Alexander Pushkin. 6103-6
As life what is so sweet. Unknown. 6563-5
"As little Jenny Wren". Unknown. 6363-2
"As little sunflowers you see us now!" Unknown. 6205-9
As Lucy went a-walking. Walter De La Mare. 6596-1
"As long ago with psalm and rite". The aged Christ. Gertrude Huntington McGiffert. 6838-3
"As long as faith and freedom last". The living line. Harold Begbie. 7031-0
"As long as I can watch the blue". Satisfied. Fay Goode Haring. 6799-9
"As long as I have memory I shall live". Nocturne for Chopin, fr. Processional. Rachel Mack Wilson. 6906-1
"As love is cause of joy". Love. Anthony Munday. 6436-1
"As lovers, banished from their lady's face". Before her portrait in youth. Francis Thompson. 6942-8
"As manager of horses, Mr. Merryman is". Punch's apotheosis. Horace Smith. 6802-2

As many questions as answers. Laura Riding. 6354-3
"As many thousands come and go". A beautiful life. Delphia L. Hopper. 6906-1
"As men talk in a dream, so Corinth all". Lamia, sel. John Keats. 6958-4
"As men who fought for home and child and wife". The battle of Oriskany. Charles D. Helmer. 6946-0
"As misfortune made the throne her seat". The fair penitent, sels. Nicholas Rowe. 6867-7
"As Mister B. and Mistress B". A report from below. Thomas Hood. 6974-6
"As music builds a bright impermanent tower". A prologue for poems. John A. Holmes. 6780-8
"As Nancy at her toilet sat". Her right name. Matthew Prior. 6874-X
"As near beauteous Boston lying". The Boston tea party. Unknown. 6753-0
"As needy gallants in the scriveners' hands". Prologue to Amboyna. John Dryden. 6970-3
"As Nora on the pavement". Nora on the pavement. Arthur Symons. 6959-2
"As o'er old '89 the veil was dropped". The trotting wonders of 1889 Em. Pierce. 7010-8
"As o'er the glacier's frozen sheet", sels. Oliver Wendell Holmes. 6601-1
"As o'er the highland hills I hied". On the restoration of the forfeited estates, 1784. Unknown. 6859-6
"As o'er the hill we roam'd at will". Wanderers. Charles Stuart Calverley. 6802-2,7025-6
"As o'er the vessel's side she leant". The first lover. Laurence (Adele Florence Nicolson) Hope. 6856-1
"As ocean murmurs when the storm is past". Robert Buchanan. 6997-5
"As oft as I behold and see." Henry Howard, Earl of Surrey. 6584-8
"As oft I doe record." Unknown. 6563-5
"As old I am as that white, throbbing star". With star and grass. Anna Spencer Twitchell. 6836-7
"As on a branch, in May". Sonnet ("As on a branch"). Pierre de Ronsard. 6227-X
"As on a dark guitar". Ballad of love and blood. Angel Miguel Queremel. 6759-X
"As on a daye Clorinda fayre was bathinge." Unknown. 6563-5
"As on a dull day in an ocean cave". Alfred Lord Tennyson. 6997-5
As on a hidden voyage. William Elijah Hunter. 6800-6
"As on a hill-top rude, when closing day". Sonnet ("As on a hill-top"). John Milton. 6814-6
"As on a time my warlike sister strayd". The story of Fiordispina. John Gay. 6972-X
"As on along through life I go". Our old Vermont apple pole. Daniel L. Cady. 6988-6
"As on Antonio's waist the miner halteth". Midway. James Abraham Martling. 6952-5
"As on Euphrates shady banks we lay". Psalm 137 ("As on Euphrates shady banks we lay"). George Sandys. 6933-9
"As on my roving way I go". A song of the Christmas wind. Eugene Field. 6949-5
"As on the fiery lightning followeth the thunder". Solon. 6251-2
"As on the Sea of Galilee." John Greenleaf Whittier. 6225-3
"As on the front/Of some cathedral pile...". A spiritual and well-ordered mind. Henry Alford. 6980-0
"As on the night before this happy morn". Christmas day. George Wither. 6756-5
"As on the sea-boat shore Britannia sat". Britannia. James Thomson. 6816-2
"As on through life's journey we go,day by day". Dwarf and giant. William Allen Butler. 6903-7
"As once I rambled in the woods". Mysterious doings. Eugene Field. 6887-1,6949-5
"As one by one, in dread Medea's train." Unknown. 6559-7
As one finding peace. Sister Mary Madeleva. 6292-X
As one finding peace. Sister Mary of the Visitation. 6292-X
"As one in sorrow looks upon". The old year and the new. James Whitcomb Riley. 6992-4

"As one invulnerable. Jessica Nelson North. 6039-0
"As one lamp lights another, nor grows less". Jottings for sportsmen. James Russell Lowell. 6861-8
"As one may sip a stranger's bowl". Song of Khan Zada. Laurence (Adele Florence Nicolson) Hope. 6856-1
"As one that leadeth a blind man". The saddest sight. Alice Cary. 6969-X
"As one who cleaves the cirumambient air". Timon of Archimedes. Charles Battell Loomis. 6902-9
"As one who long in populous city pent". A summer's morning. John Milton. 6935-5
As one who stands. Unknown. 6097-8
"As one who wanders into old workings." Cecil Day Lewis. 6209-1
"As one who, journeying, checks the rein...". Honors II: The answer. Jean Ingelow. 6940-1
"As one who, long in thickets and in brakes". The garden, fr. The task. William Cowper. 6814-6
"As one, at midnight, wakened by the call". Prelude ("As one"). Wilfred Wilson Gibson. 6289-X
"As other men have creed, so have I mine". Theodore Tilton. 6238-5
"As other Men, so I my selfe doe Muse," Michael Drayton. 6586-4
As others see us, fr. To a louse. Robert Burns. 6337-3
"As our mother the frigate, bepainted and fine". Cruisers. Rudyard Kipling. 6810-3
"As over Gladsmuir's blood-stained field". Gladsmuir. Unknown. 6859-6
"As over the fresh grass her golden feet". Francesco Petrarch. 6325-X
"As pants the hart for cooling streams". Psalm 042. Nahum Tate. 6867-7
"As passed the rector of All-Saints one day". Little turncoats. Georgia A. Peck. 6920-7
As pebbles in the sea. Unknown. 6273-3
"As pines, that to the mountain summits...". Aspiration. James Abraham Martling. 6952-5
"As power and wit will me assist." Sir Thomas Wyatt. 6584-8
As precious stone... Jaroslav Vrchlicky. 6886-3
"As puritans they prominently wax". A certain people. George Meredith. 6828-6
"As quivering aspen leaves reflect". Aspens. Olive Watkins. 6818-9
"As Richard and I sat together one day". The hole in the patch. Unknown. 6916-9
As red men die. Emily Pauline ("Tekahionwake") Johnson. 6115-X
"As rising from the vegetable world". The bird nation. James Thomson. 6943-6
"As rising on its purple wing". The fate of beauty. George Gordon, 6th Baron Byron. 6980-0
As rivers of water in a dry place. Anna Bunston De Bary. 6776-X,6253-9
"As rock to sun or storm". Poem. Niall Sheridan. 6930-4
"As rolls a wave of perfume o'er the sea". From Enamorado. John Hunter Duvar. 7041-8
"As round as an apple, as deep as a cup." Mother Goose. 6452-3
"As sailors loitering in a luscious isle". Outward bound. Arthur Christopher Benson. 7014-0
"As salt resolved in the ocean". Jalal [or Jelal] ed-din Rumi. 6448-5
"As seamen, shipwreck'd on some happy shore". To the Lady Castlemain -afterwards Duchess of Cleveland. John Dryden. 6970-3
As seen in later years. Delia A. Heywood. 6927-4
"As shadows slipping along the wall, women". Largo. Farona Konopak. 6979-7
"As Shakespeare couldn't write his plays". By deputy. Arthur St. John Adcock. 6760-3
"As Sir Launfal made morn through the...gate". The vision of Sir Launfal, sels. James Russell Lowell. 6753-0
As she says. Joseph Bert Smiley. 6926-6
"As ships becalmed." Arthur Hugh Clough. 6302-0;6385-3
"As slaughter red the long creek crawls". The heron. Madison Cawein. 7041-8
"As slow I climb the cliff's ascending side". Retrospection. William Lisle Bowles. 6980-0

As slow our ship. Thomas Moore. 6174-5,6328-4,6459-0,6302-0,6604-6,6385 ,6086-2,6250-4,6660-7
"As slowly, as carefully as a wading bird". The water lily. David Wagoner. 6966-5
"As so we two came". The question. Frank Templeton Prince. 6124-9
"As soft as silk, as white as milk." Mother Goose. 6452-3
"As some cathedral, wehre a holy relic". Love's miracle. James Abraham Martling. 6952-5
"As some flame-crooked venomed Malay blade". Sonnet 025 ("As some"). Arlo Bates. 7041-8
"As some lone miser isiting his store". The patriot's boast. Oliver Goldsmith. 6793-X
"As sometimes in a dead man's face", fr. Memoriam. Alfred Lord Tennyson. 6536-8
"As soon as I". Sonnet ("As soon"). Louise Labe. 6227-X
"As soon as woman begins to be ashamed". Livy. 6083-8
"As soon as you have let the job". Fixing over the barns in Vermont. Daniel L. Cady. 6989-4
"As spring tripped blithely through the air". Debut of spring. Jeannette Carter Brautigan. 6789-1
"As still the waters as the woods are still". Dawn on Chateaugay. Constance Deming Lewis. 6841-3
"As strangers, you and I are here". Recollections. Adelaide Anne Procter. 6980-0,6957-6
"As streams the sun in golden gleams". Realization. Edla Park Peck. 6836-7
"As sure as midnight by the clock". The night watchman. Robert P. Tristram Coffin. 7040-X
"As swift as a bird in flight". Skating song. Arthur Griscom. 7035-3
"As swift as time put round the glass". Song ("As swift"). Unknown. 6024-2
"As t'other day o'er the green meadow I pass'd" Unknown. 6874-X
"As tender lambs with wolves agree". Horace, epod. 004, imitated. John Gay. 6972-X
"As the ambitious sculptor, tireless, lifts". A sculptor. Ella Wheeler Wilcox. 6956-8
"As the child rocks on his playhorse". Playhorse. Loren Stream. 6883-9
"As the cold wind rushes through her hair". Broken birds. Tracy Martin. 6883-9
"As the day sets silently into a stone". Interfusion. Han-mo Chung. 6775-1
"As the days grow longer." Mother Goose. 6452-3
"As the days lengthen". Unknown. 6904-5
As the Greek's signal flame. Walt Whitman. 6126-5
"As the devil lay dying". The patient. Michael Guttenbrunner. 6769-7
"As the fog lifts over". Snacks, fr. Ogesa Ondo. Ronald P. Tanaka. 6790-5
"As the full moon shining there". The moon to the sun. Alice Meynell. 6955-X
"As the hart panteth after the water brooks". Quemadmodum. Bible. 6830-8
"As the hart panthet after the water brooks". Psalm 042, fr. The book of psalms. Bible. 7039-6
"As the hot day swooned into afternoon". Storm in the tropics, fr. The human inheritance. William ("Fiona Macleod") Sharp. 6997-5
"As the hush of early evening". Woodland fantasy. C.P. Kendall. 6764-6
"As the hyacinth high on the mountains...". Sappho. 6251-2
"As the inhastening tide doth roll". Song ("As the inhastening"). Alice Meynell. 6997-5
As the larks rise. Theodosia Garrison. 7007-8
"As the liberty lads o'er the sea". Song for the Luddites. George Gordon, 6th Baron Byron. 6945-2
"As the meek doe, climbing the mountain steeps". Paraphrase of a portion of the forty-second psalm. Bible. 6848-0
"As the moon's reflection trembleth". Heinrich Heine. 6876-6
As the moon's soft splendour. Percy Bysshe Shelley. 6328-4
"As the mute nightingale in closest groves". To the blessed Virgin Mary. Gerald Griffin. 6930-4
"As the parson sat at his books one day". A minister's quarter pay-day. C.B. Lewis. 6910-X
As the pigeon flies. C.B. Lewis. 6415-9,6167-2

"As the professor speaks". Several short poems. George Swede. 6767-0
"As the proud horse with costly trappings gay". Shortening sail. William Falconer. 6833-2
"As the proud horse...", fr. The shipwreck. William Falconer. 6547-3
As the seasons roll. Unknown. 6847-2
"As the slanting sun drowsed lazily". Cape coloured batman. Guy Butler. 6788-3
"As the stars come out, and the night-wind". Matthew Arnold. 6793-X
"As the still hours towards midnight wore". How peace came. Alice Cary. 6865-0;6969-X
"As the sunbeams stream...", fr. Woodnotes. Ralph Waldo Emerson. 6047-1
"As the sweet apple reddens, high up against the sky". Sappho. 6251-2
As the tide comes in. Cale Young Rice. 6374-8,6653-4
"As the tired voyager on stormy seas". Invocation, fr. Female characters of scripture. Felicia Dorothea Hemans. 6973-8
"As the tree does not end". Appearance. Norman H. Russell. 7005-1
As the trucks go rollin' by. L.W. Suckert. 6846-4
"As the uncertain twittering of the birds". Sonnet: grief. Thomas Holley Chivers. 7017-5
As the wind. Laurence E. Estes. 6342-X
"As the wind at play with a spark". Louisa May Alcott. Louise Chandler Moulton. 6820-0
"As their listless eyes bore into your heart". Spectator. Karin McGowan. 6883-9
"As there is music uninform'd by art". To my honoured friend Sir Robert Howard. John Dryden. 6970-3
As they fell. Edward Augustus Blount Jr. 6482-5
As they leave us. Florence Earle Coates. 6443-4
"As they listened eagerly to all the master...". The last hymn. Blanche Lee. 6818-9
"As they sat in English-wood". Unknown. 6518-X
As things are. Unknown. 6589-9
"As things come tumbling down around". Courage. Jeannette Carter Brautigan. 6789-1
"As this Jew, this Simon Peter...". Petrus. ? Kinkel. 6842-1
"As this life must soon end, and frame...decay". The last will and testament of William Ruffell, Esq. Unknown. 6878-2
"As those who eat a luscious fruit". No rival like the past. Laurence (Adele Florence Nicolson) Hope. 6856-1
"As thou light a candle". An internee mourns for his son who died in Italy. Sojin Takei. 6981-9
"As though a potter made his clay". Portrait of a lady. Mary Brent Whiteside. 6037-4
"As though all the stars should fall down...". My poem to the children killed in the war in Spain. Jose Ramon Heredia. 6793-X
As though from love. Leonore G. Marshall. 6979-7
"As though with new eyes I have seen the dawn". Outlook. Ivan Swift. 6799-9
"As threads spilling dew-drops". The dolphins. Hamish Maclaren. 6833-2
"As thro' the land at eve we went". Song ("As thro'"). Alfred Lord Tennyson. 6437-X;6655-0
"As through life's changeful course you move". You are not alone. Edward R. Huxley. 6885-5
"As through the dawn-mist gray...formlessness". Home, fr. Once again the Eden. Noel Hudson Stearn. 6789-1
As through the land at eve we went, fr. The princess. Alfred Lord Tennyson. 6337-3,6260-1,6154-0,6123-0, 6543-0,6110-9,6656-9,6560-0,6250-4,6737-9
"As thro gh the wild green hills of Wyre." Alfred Edward Housman. 6138-9
"As thus I stand beside the murmuring stream". Sonnet 005 ("As thus I stand..."). Robert Southey. 6867-7
'As thy day, so shall thy strength be.' Lydia Huntley Sigourney. 6752-2
"As thy ship sails o'er life's ocean". A birthday wish. Mary Lydia Carpenter. 6799-9
' As thyself'. Unknown. 6274-1
As time goes on. Emilio Adolfo von Westphalen. 6759-X

As time one day by me did pass. Henry Vaughan. 6341-1
"As to kidnap the congress has...been my aim". General Howe's letter. Unknown. 6946-0
As to moonlight. Witter Bynner. 6037-4
As to the weather. Unknown. 6083-8,6089-7
"As to-night you came your way". To the passing saint. Eugene Field. 6949-5
As toilsome I wander'd. Walt Whitman. 6006-4,6186-9,6317-9, 6085-4,6512-0,6542 ,6288-1,6659-3,6084-6,6126-5,6396-9,6639-9
As toilsome I wander'd Virginia's woods. Algernon Charles Swinburne. 6289-X
"As Tommy Snooks and Bessie Brooks." Mother Goose. 6739-5
"As Tommy Snooks and Bessy Brooks". Mother Goose. 6363-2, 6452-3
"As towering through the height". Bacchylides. 6251-2
"As trees accept the winter, take your grief". In this gray season. Ralph Friedrich. 6761-1
"As trees stand/it was not a very grand tree". Tree perjury. Wayne Miller. 6901-0
As true as thy faith, this riddle thus saith. Thomas Tusser. 6586-4
"As turned harp-strings sad noates take." Unknown. 6563-5
As Vesta was from Latmos Hill descending. Unknown. 6430-2
"As two proud ships upon the pathless main". Fate. Unknown. 6273-3
"As underneath the trees I pass". Miss Nettybun and the satyr's child, fr. Metropolitan. Edith Sitwell. 7000-0
"As vanquished years behind me glide". Faith's surrender. Rossiter Johnson. 7041-8
"As violets, modest, tender-eyed". My lady. Phoebe Cary. 6969-X
"As waves that up a quiet cove". Eleanore, sels. Alfred Lord Tennyson. 6997-5
"As we come marching, marching, in the...". Bread and roses. James Oppenheim. 6954-1
As we forgive. Alfred Noyes. 6151-6
As we go on. Struthers Burt. 6607-0
"As we hammer out iron we shall hammer out...". Tomorrow. Regino Pedroso. 6759-X
"As we look at these gay flowers". Rondel ("As we look"). Charles, Duc d' Orleans. 6227-X
"As Wednesbury there was a cocking". Wednesbury cocking. Unknown. 6829-4
As we pray. John Keble. 6303-9,6337-3,6214-8
As we rush in the train. James Thomson. 6934-7
As we rush in the train. James ("B.V.") Thomson. 6180-X, 6508-2
As we were a sailing. Unknown. 6547-3
As we were a-sailing. Unknown. 6057-9,6547-3
'As weary pilgrim'. Anne Bradstreet. 6176-1,6288-1
As well as any other. Laura Riding. 6072-2
"As when a scout/Through dark & desart wayes..". New worlds, fr. Paradise lost. John Milton. 6933-9
"As when a traveller, whose journey lies". The picture, fr. The picture of St. John. Bayard Taylor. 6976-2
"As when a tree's cut down, the secret root". Prolgue to The tempest. John Dryden. 6970-3
"As when a wretch (who conscious of his crime)". Priam and Achilles, fr. The Iliad. Homer. 6932-0
"As when desire, long darkling, dawns, and". Bridal bath, fr. The house of life. Dante Gabriel Rossetti. 6828-6
"As when far off the warbled strains are heard". La Fayette. Samuel Taylor Coleridge. 6828-6
"As when from his mountain-outlook...", fr. The Iliad. Homer. 6251-2
As when Saint Francis walked the ways of. James L. McLane Jr. 6607-0
"As when some bowlder, black and massy...". The falling bowlder. James Abraham Martling. 6952-5
"As when some great and gracious monarch dies". Eleanora; a panegyrical poem. John Dryden. 6970-3
"As when some skilful cook, to please each ...". To Bernard Lintott. John Gay. 6972-X
"As when the billow gathers...", fr. The Iliad. Homer. 6435-3
"As when the deep lies heaving...", fr. The Iliad. Homer. 6251-2
"As when the haze of some wan moonlight makes". Metempsychosis of the pine. Bayard Taylor. 6976-2
"As when the shadow of the sun's eclipse". Sonnet ("As when the shadow..."). George Edward Woodberry. 7026-4
"As when with downcast eyes we muse and brood". Sonnet ("As when with downcast eyes..."). Alfred Lord Tennyson. 6977-0
"As when with downcast eyes". Alfred Lord Tennyson. 6085-4
"As when, from some proud capital that crowns". Close of the vision of judgment. James Abraham Hillhouse. 6752-2
"As when, high up...", fr. The Iliad. Homer. 6251-2
"As when, upon a tranced summer night". Dreaming oaks. John Keats. 6793-X
As winds that blow against a star. Joyce Kilmer. 6096 X
"As withereth the primrose by the river". Edmund Bolton. 6181-8
"As wrinkled as the wind-swept firth". The Russian immigrant grandmother. Fanny Bixby Spencer. 6954-1
"As ye came from the holy land". The holy land of Walsinghame. Unknown. 6829-4
As ye came from the holy land. Unknown. 6186-9,6187-7,6659-3,6513-9
As ye do it unto these. Unknown. 6144-3,6335-7
"As ye go through these palm-trees". A song of the Virgin Mother, fr. Los pastores de Belen. Lope de Vega Carpio. 7039-6
"As ye see, a mountaine lion fare". Sarpedon's speech, fr. The Iliad. Homer. 6933-9
As ye would. Edith Virginia Bradt. 6928-2
"As yet a stranger to the gentle fires". Elegy 007 ("As yet a stranger..."). John Milton. 6814-0
"As yonder lamp in my vacated room". Charles Whitehead. 7015-9
"As you came from the holy land". How should I your true love know. Sir Walter Raleigh. 6934-7
"As you came from the holy land". Sir Walter Raleigh. 6181-8,6125-7,6153-2
As you go through life. Ella Wheeler Wilcox. 6654-2
"As you go through the countryside". A Vermont barn. Daniel L. Cady. 6989-4
As you like it, sels. William Shakespeare. 6250-4,6430-2, 6560-0,6107-9,6192-3,6104 ,6047-1,6102-8,6122-2,6182-6,6198-2,6332 ,6049-8,6083-8,6154-0,6179-6,6242-3, 6317 ,6339-X,6392-6,6395-0,6473-6,6610-0,6623 ,6634-8,6732-8,6239-3,6466-3,6585-6,6301
"As you sow, so shall you reap". The advice of a judge. Everett C. Richmond. 6799-9
As you used to do. Unknown. 6097-8
"As you would speak of flowers...". Legend. David Morton. 6850-2
"As you're growing old". Growing old. Annie B. Alguire. 6789-1
"As you, dear Lamon, soundly slept". To Ward H. Lamon, asleep on his library floor. Eugene Field. 6949-5
"As, even today, the airman, feeling the...". Icarus. Valentin Iremonger. 6930-4
"As, I have learned - how strange though!...". The flame. Robert Paul Turbeville. 7016-7
"As, long ago, the Trojan slaves were awed". To one who waits. Charles Monroe Walker. 6764-6
"As, seeking broader lands to gain". Palm Beach. Mary Leighton. 6818-9
"As, when in days of old, God said, 'Arise'.". The return to Bethel. Schuyler E. Sears. 6906-1
"As, when the seaward ebbing tide doth pour". Regrets. Alice Meynell. 6955-X
"As, with enforced yet unreluctant pace". The social future. John Kells Ingram. 6930-4
Asa the Blind
Coat of mail. A.J. Arberry (tr.). 6362-4
Asa trot. Unknown. 6303-9
Asa-tada
"To fall in love with womankind". William N. Porter (tr.). 6852-9
Ascending footsteps. Josephine Byington. 6799-9
"**Ascending** through the twilit wood". The lonely unicorn. Frederic Prokosch. 6782-4
The **Ascension** and the Assumption. Raon Lopez Velarde.

ASCENSION

6642-9
Ascension day. Richard Lawson Gales. 6950-9
Ascension day. Henry Vaughan. 6931-2
Ascension hymn. The Venerable Bede. 6337-3
The **ascension** of Christ. William Drummond of Hawthornden. 6302-0
The **ascension** of Elijah. James Stephenson. 6848-0
Ascension-hymn. Henry Vaughan. 6341-1
The **Ascension..** Edwin Markham. 6335-7
The **ascension.** Joseph Beaumont. 6931-2
The **Ascension.** William White. 6868-5
Ascent. Melba Williams. 6906-1
The **ascent** of Elijah. Winthrop Mackworth Praed. 6848-0
The **ascent** of F 6, sels. Wystan Hugh Auden. 6375-6
The **ascent** of Snowdon. William Wordsworth. 6395-0
Ascent of the Alps. Adam Gottlob Oehlenschlager. 6749-2
The **ascent.** Helen Parry Eden. 6785-9
The **ascent.** James Abraham Martling. 6952-5
The **ascent.** David O'Neil. 6032-3
Ascention. John Donne. 6933-9
"The **asceticism** of this rock". Realization. George Kuznets. 6850-2
Asclepiades
    "Ah me, once Archeades pressed...". F.L. Lucas (tr.). 6251-2
    Archeanassa. R.A. Furness (tr.). 6435-3
    Dewy garlands. Andrew Lang (tr.). 6819-7
    "Drink, drink, Asclepiades...". F.L. Lucas (tr.). 6251-2
    Eumares. Richard Garnett (tr.). 7039-6
    His son. George B. Grundy (tr.). 7039-6
    "O sweet is snow to June...". F.L. Lucas (tr.). 6251-2
    Preface to Erinna's poems. R.A. Furness (tr.). 6435-3
    Seasons. Henry Van Dyke (tr.). 6961-4
    There is no loving after death. R.A. Furness (tr.). 6435-3
    Timon's epitaph. William Shakespeare (tr.). 7039-6
    A tomb by the sea. Walter Leaf (tr.). 6435-3
    Why plague me, loves?. John Swinnerton Phillimore (tr.). 6435-3
    "With Hermione the witching as I played...". F.L. Lucas (tr.). 6251-2
    "Your maidenhead-you grudge it...". F.L. Lucas (tr.). 6251-2
    Zeus too is a victim. Walter Leaf (tr.). 6435-3
Asclepius. Pindar. 6435-3
Ascription. Arthur Shearly Cripps. 6625-9
The **Ascutney** charades. Julia A. Sabine. 6616-X
"**Ase** I me rod this ender day". The five joys of Mary. Unknown. 6881-2
Ase's death. Gertrude Huntington McGiffert. 6838-3
Ase's death, fr. Peer Gynt. Henrik Ibsen. 6585-6
"**Asenath** Osgood, fair and straight". To a daguerreotype. Jean Decker. 6850-2
Aseyev, Nikolai
    Black hussars. Jack Lindsay (tr.). 6546-5
The **ash** and the leaping spark. Boris Todrin. 6764-6
The **ash** pool. Unknown. 6273-3
Ash Wednesday. Thomas Bernhard. 6769-7
Ash Wednesday. John Erskine. 6393-4
Ash Wednesday. Rosa Zagnoni Marinoni. 6465-5,6727-1
Ash Wednesday day. Louis Untermeyer. 6011-0
Ash Wednesday I. Thomas Stearns Eliot. 6645-3
Ash Wednesday, sels. Thomas Stearns Eliot. 6317-9,6315-2
"The **ash** suddenly flames". Dunkerqure-Paris line. Naomi Mitchison. 6782-4
Ash-Wednesday VI. Thomas Stearns Eliot. 6208-3
Ashamed of Jesus. Joseph Grigg. 6065-X
Ashbee, Charles and Janet (tr.)
    "Ich stand auf hohen Berge". Unknown, 6547-3
Ashbury, William
    Father in heaven. 6566-X
Ashby. John Reuben Thompson. 6113-3,6074-9
Ashby-Sterry, Joseph
    Kindness to animals. 6902-9
    The little rebel. 6656-9
    A Marlow madrigal. 6656-9
    Pet's punishment. 6652-6,6089-7,6889-8
    A portrait. 6656-9
    Saint May: a city lyric. 6652-6

    A street sketch. 6652-6
Ashcake. Thomas Nelson Page. 6431-0
Ashcroft, Edward
    Song for Telemachus. 6782-4
Ashe, Marjorie Dugdale
    Friend. 6799-9
Ashe, Thomas
    At Altenahr. 6658-5
    The city clerk. 6437-X
    Fay. 6772-7
    The guest. 6094-3
    A machine hand. 6437-X
    Marian. 6656-9
    Marit. 6658-5
    Meet we no angels, Pansie? 6437-X
    No and yes. 6658-5
    Phantoms. 6656-9
    Poeta nascitur. 6656-9
    A vision of children. 6656-9
Ashes. Mary Kate Hunter. 6799-9
Ashes. De Witt Sterry. 6453-1,6576-7
The **ashes** in the sea. George Sterling. 6310-1
Ashes of glory. Augustus Julian Requier. 6074-9,6113-3
Ashes of life. Edna St. Vincent Millay. 6986-X
Ashes of life. Edna St. Vincent Millay. 6019-6
Ashes of roses. Elaine Goodale Eastman. 6431-0
Ashes of roses. Elaine Goodale. 6240-7
Ashes on the slide. Eugene Field. 6949-5
Ashes to ashes, fr. Matrimonial melodies. Berton Braley. 6853-7
Ashleigh, Charles
    Vespers. 6880-4
    When I go out. 6880-4
Ashley, Kenneth H.
    Close of play. 6785-9
    Points of view. 6350-0
    Rudkin. 6069-2
    The two-seater. 6785-9
    'Who's there?' 6785-9
Ashley, Lillah A.
    Sonnet. 6799-9
Ashley, Margaret Lee
    In April. 6027-7,6431-0
Ashley, Paul David
    Beauty. 6870-7
    Prison. 6870-7
    The ritual. 6870-7
    Song from the unfinished man. 6870-7
    Sounds. 6870-7
Ashore. Laurence (Adele Florence Nicolson) Hope. 6102-8, 6301-2
Ashour, Gladys Brierly
    Expectation. 6750-6
Ashtabula. Berton Braley. 6853-7
Ashtaroth: a dramatic lyric. Adam Lindsay Gordon. 6951-7
Ashton, E.B. (tr.)
    My death. Carl Zuckmayer, 6068-4
    To a young leader of the first world war. Stefan George, 6068-4,6665-8
Ashworth, Margaret
    Heigh ho! 6937-1
Asia. Jean Follain. 6758-1
Asia. Jean Follain. 6803-0
Asia's reply. Percy Bysshe Shelley. 6186-9
"**Asia's** rock-hollow'd fanes,first-born of time". Moral ruins. Horace Smith. 6980-0
Asia's song. Percy Bysshe Shelley. 6252-0
Asia, fr. Prometheus unbound. George Gordon, 6th Baron Byron. 6659-3
Asian birds. Robert Bridges. 6487-6,6656-9
Asian birds. Robert ("Droch") Bridges. 6656-9
Asis. Percy Bysshe Shelley. 6102-8
Ask and it shall be given unto you. Gertrude Huntington McGiffert. 6838-3
Ask and ye shall receive. Alice B. Haven. 6260-1
"**Ask** any question in this town". 'Round Cape Horn'. Unknown. 6833-2
"**Ask** for no mild millennium". The millennium. James Oppenheim. 6954-1
"**Ask** him who knows the secret of the seed". What is a

poem? Carmen Judson. 6750-6
Ask mamma. A. Melville Bell. 6411-6
Ask me no more. Thomas Carew. 6023-4,6383-7,6197-4,6563-5
Ask me no more. Alfred Lord Tennyson. 6250-4,6560-0,6543-0,
    6737-9,6199-0,6737 ,6655-0,6656-9,6219-9,6321-7,6110-
    9,6154-0,6240-7,6271-7,6122-2,6429-9
"Ask me no more where Jove bestows". Song ("Ask me no
    more"). Thomas Carew. 6154-0,6052-8,6102-8,6271-7,
    6301-2,6560 ,6317-9,6250-4,6513-9,6341-1,6189-3,6562
    ,6198-2,6150-8,6186-9,6315-2,6634-8,6186
"Ask me no more where Jove bestows". Thomas Carew. 6726-3,
    6271-7,6219-9,6187-7,6208-3,6023-4,6383-7,6197-4,
    6250-4,6543-0,6099-4,6430-2,6092-7,6219-9,6271-3
"Ask me no more whither do stray" Thomas Carew. 6935-5
"Ask me no more, why there appears". Pyms anarchy. Thomas
    Jordan. 6933-9
"Ask me nothing now, my dear/The stars are...". Warning.
    Amelia Josephine Burr. 7038-8
"Ask me to remember and all that I could tell". Alchemy.
    Sarah Litsey. 6750-6
"Ask not if love no passion knows". A villanelle of love.
    R. L. Mergoz. 6875-8
"Ask not my name, O friend!". A nameless epitaph (2).
    Matthew Arnold. 6947-9
Ask not of me, love, what is love. Philip James Bailey.
    6094-3
Ask not one least word of praise, fr. Ferishtah's fancies.
    Robert Browning. 6655-0
"Ask not the cause, why sullen spring". To a fair young
    lady, going out of the town in spring. John Dryden.
    6970-3
"Ask of voices in the twilight". 'Barnaval,' sel. Charles
    De Kay. 7041-8
"Ask the backs of horses on the day of battle". Ibn
    'Unain. 6766-2
"Ask what is human life - the sage replies". Hope. William
    Cowper. 6814-6
"Ask you what provocation I have had?". Satire. Alexander
    Pope. 6932-0
Ask your mother. Edgar A. Guest. 6748-4
"Ask'st thou my home? my pathway wouldst..know". Thekla's
    song; or, the voice of the spirit. Johann C.
    Friedrich von Schiller. 6973-8
Ask, is love divine. George Meredith. 6198-2,6560-0
Askew, we ask you. Melville Cane. 6979-7
Asking. Unknown. 6273-3
Asking forgiveness. Arthur Symons. 6102-8
Asleep. Will Chamberlain. 7001-9
Asleep. Ethelreda Lewis. 6800-6
Asleep. Wilfred Owen. 6958-4
Asleep. J. Ernest Whitney. 6836-7
Asleep. William Winter. 6431-4
"Asleep at last! For fourscore years". Oliver Wendell
    Holmes. William Hamilton Hayne. 6820-0
Asleep at the switch. George Hoey. 6915-0
Asleep at the switch. George Hoey. 6451-5
Asleep by the Irish Sea. Elizabeth Glendenning Ring. 6443-
    4
Asleep in Jesus. Margaret Mackay. 6065-X
"Asleep or waking is it? for her neck". Laus veneris.
    Algernon Charles Swinburne. 6828-6
"Asleep! O sleep a little while, white pearl!". O sleep a
    little while. John Keats. 6958-4
Asmenius
    Thoughts in a garden. E.E. Sikes (tr.). 6649-6
Asolando, sels. Robert Browning. 6430-2
Asolo. Robert Browning. 6331-4
Asparagus, fr. Verses made for women who cry apples...
    Jonathan Swift. 6380-2
Aspatia's song. Francis Beaumont and John Fletcher. 6301-2,
    6383-7
Aspatia's song. Francis Beaumont. 6933-9
Aspatia's song. John Fletcher. 6102-8,6186-9
Aspatia's song, fr. The maid's tragedy. John Fletcher.
    6102-8,6186-9,6328-4,6153-2,6396-9
Aspecta Medusa. Dante Gabriel Rossetti. 6610-0,6110-9
Aspects of the pines. Paul Hamilton Hayne. 7017-5,6753-0,
    6265-2,6288-1
Aspen tree. Paul Celan. 6758-1
Aspens. Olive Watkns. 6818-9

"The aspens yesterday/intolerant and drawn". Did you not
    see. Alex Kuo. 6790-5
Asphalt. Conrad Aiken. 6034-X
Asphodel. Willa Sibert Cather. 6274-1
Asphodel. Rosamund Marriott ("Graham R. Tomson") Watson.
    6875-8
Aspinall, George
    The leap of Curtius. 6912-6
Aspinwall, Alicia
    Patrick goes to school. 6891-X
Aspiration. Eva Gore-Booth. 6174-5
Aspiration. William Elijah Hunter. 6800-6
Aspiration. Ibn Hani. 6362-4
Aspiration. James Abraham Martling. 6952-5
Aspiration. Peter McArthur. 6433-7
Aspiration. C.E.D. Phelps. 6274-1
Aspiration. Clinton Scollard. 6607-0
Aspiration. John Banister Tabb. 6317-9
Aspiration. Edward William Thomson. 6437-X
Aspiration. George Wither. 6337-3
The aspiration. John Norris. 6931-2
The aspiration. John Norris. 6315-2,6737-9
Aspirations. Unknown. 6911-8
Aspirations. Osbert W. Warmingham. 6143-5
Aspirations of the soul after God. Madame De la Mothe
    Guion. 6814-6
Aspirations of youth. James Montgomery. 6459-0,6543-0
Asquith, Herbert
    The fallen subaltern. 7026-4
    A Flemish village. 7027-2
    Nightfall. 6354-3
    On a troopship, 1915. 7027-2
    Volunteer. 7031-0
    The volunteer. 7029-9,6872-3,7026-4
    Youth in the skies. 6783-2
The Asra. Heinrich Heine. 6842-1
The ass and his master. Tomaso de Yriarte. 6278-4
The ass in the lion's skin. Aesop. 7039-6
The ass of heaven. Katharine (Hinkson) Tynan. 6069-2
"An ass put on a lion's skin and went". The ass in the
    lion's skin. Aesop. 7039-6
The ass speaks. Katharine (Hinkson) Tynan. 6337-3
The ass's legacy. Ruteboeuf. 6996-7
The assault heroic. Robert Graves. 6393-4
The assault on the fortress. Timothy Dwight. 6946-0
The assault.. J.B.B. Nichols. 6477-9
The assault.. Robert Nichols. 6332-2,6108-2,6542-2
The assayer's story. Unknown. 6274-1
"Assemble, all ye maidens, at the door". Elegy
    ("Assemble"). Robert Bridges. 6487-6
The assertion. Cecil Day Lewis. 6391-8
Asses. Padraic Colum. 6779-4
Asshole poem. Jim Holmes. 7003-5
The assignation. Herbert Edwin Clarke. 7015-9
"Assist me, ye muses (whose harps are in tune)". The
    progress of balloons. Philip Freneau. 6753-0
Assonance. Barry Callaghan. 6767-0
Assumpta est Maria. Liam Brophy. 6282-2
Assumpta Maria. Francis Thompson. 6096-X,6282-2
The Assumption ("Behold! the mother bird"). John Banister
    Tabb. 6282-2
Th Assumption ("O heart submissive in this martyrdom").
    John Gilland Brunini. 6282-2
The assumption of Troilus. Geoffrey Chaucer. 6150-8
The Assumption. Sir John Beaumont. 6022-6
Assunpink and Princeton. Thomas Dunn English. 6946-0
Assurance. Grace Noll Crowell. 6465-5
Assurance. George Herbert. 6931-2
An assurance. Nicholas Breton. 6436-1
Assurances. Walt Whitman. 6126-5,6288-1
"Assured that you are doomed to die, do as your". Unknown.
    6435-3
Assyrian night-song. Bayard Taylor. 6976-2
Aster. Plato. 6435-3
Asteria. W. Wesley Trimpi. 6515-5
"Astonished children" Ronald R.W. Lightbourne. 6898-7
The astonished tippler. Thomas Chalmers. 6404-3
Astounding tales. Jack Anderson. 7003-5
Astra [pseud].
    Cloudland scenes. 7014-0

ASTRA

The gift of flight. 7014-0
Astraea. John Greenleaf Whittier. 6126-5,6288-1
Astraea redux. John Dryden. 6152-4
Astraea redux. Percy Bysshe Shelley. 6830-8
Astraea redux, sels. John Dryden. 6933-9
Astraea redux, sels. John Dryden. 6106-0,6198-2,6195-0
An astral romance. Gustave V. Drake. 7021-3
Astrantia. Lilian Sauter. 7023-X
Astray. Walter De La Mare. 6905-3
Astray. Xaver Dovrak. 6763-8
Astrid. Alfred Noyes. 6151-6
Astrid, sels. Alfred Noyes. 6289-X
"Th'astrologers did all alike presage". On the astrologers. Unknown (Greek). 6814-6
The astrological tower. Johann C. Friedrich von Schiller. 6142-7
Astrology. George Croly. 6980-0
Astrology. Leslie Nelson Jennings. 6072-2
Astrology. Sennett Stephens. 6441-8
The astronaut. Cecilia Bustamante. 7036-1
An astronomer muses. Nellie Burget Miller. 6836-7
Astronomical. Unknown. 6273-3
"The astronomy class was told of a star". Another visit of St. Nicholas. Carolyn Wells. 6882-0
Astrophel. Edmund Spenser. 6732-8,6543-0
Astrophel and Stella. Sir Philip Sidney. 6186-9,6198-2, 6584-3
Astrophel and Stella, sels. Sir Philip Sidney. 6102-8,6208-3,6108-7,6378-0,6536-8,6586,6604-6,6645-3,6646-1, 6194-X,6430-2,6491
Astrophil to his son, aged seven months. Thomas Warton (the Elder) 6962-2
Asturias, Miguel Angel
The Indians come down from Mixco. Donald Devenish Walsh (tr.). 6759-X
"Asunder shall the clouds be rolled". The day of judgment. Unknown (Gaelic). 6845-6
Asutralia's men. Dorothea MacKellar. 6846-4
Asyev, Nikolai
To a shining falcon. Jack Lindsay (tr.). 6546-5
Asylum. John Theobald. 6761-1
The asylum.. William Rose Benet. 6031-5
"At 12:30 sharp/as though to underscore". Almost everybody is dying here: only a few actually... Daniel Berrigan. 6870-2
"At 8 a.m./in waking light". 8 a.m. Tom Mitchelson. 6899-5
At a Breton sea-blessing. Margaret Lovell Andrews. 6875-8
At a burial. Sir William Watson. 6337-3
At a Chinaman's grave. Wing Tek Lum. 6790-5
"At a city hotel an enormous giraffe". The gorgeous giraffe. Carolyn Wells. 6882-0
At a concert of music. Conrad Aiken. 6012-9
At a cowboy dance. James Barton Adams. 6281-4
At a funeral. Unknown. 6952-5
At a house in Hampstead. Thomas Hardy. 6828-6
At a meeting of friends. Oliver Wendell Holmes. 6753-0
At a meeting of friends. Oliver Wendell Holmes. 6126-5
At a meeting of friends. Oliver Wendell Holmes. 6753-0
At a parade. Frank Templeton Prince. 6379-9,6666-6
At a poet's grave. Francis Ledwidge. 6812-X
"At a roundup on the Gily". The legend of boastful Bill. Charles Badger Clark Jr.. 7010-8
At a sheep-shearing. George Wither. 6935-5
At a solemn music. John Milton. 6102-8,6246-6,6315-2,6634-8,6187-7,6328 ,6562-7,6563-5,6430-2,6737-9,6194-X, 6230
"At a springe wel under a thorn". The spring under a thorn. Unknown. 6881-2
"At Aachen in his kingly might". The Count of Hapsburg. Johann C. Friedrich von Schiller. 6842-1
At a toboggan meet. William Talbot Allison. 6591-0,6592-2
At a vacation exercise. John Milton. 6933-9
At a wedding. Sir John Suckling. 6959-2
At a window. Carl Sandburg. 6512-0,6531-7,6300-4
At a window sill. Christopher Morley. 6431-0
At a women's club. Lawrence K. Russell. 6929-0
At Altenahr. Thomas Ashe. 6658-5
At Amalfi. Richard Monckton Milnes; 1st Baron Houghton. 6624-0
At Amalfi ("Here might I rest forever;here"). John Addington Symonds. 6624-0,6631-3
At an outpost. H. Woolley. 6793-X
At Assisi. William Vaughn Moody. 6624-0,6300-4
At Auchindown. Unknown. 6859-6
"At an upper window-pane". Silhouette. Denys Lefebvre. 6800-6
At aunty's house. James Whitcomb Riley. 6990-8
At Baia. Hilda ("H.D.") Doolittle. 6348-9
At Bay Ridge. Thomas Bailey Aldrich. 6484-1
"At bed-sides, in dusk of forebodings...". Gaze of death. Otakar Brezina. 6886-3
At bedtime. Unknown. 6684-4
At Beechwood. Louis J. Magee. 7004-3
At benediction. Eleanor Rogers Cox. 6172-9
At best. John Boyle O'Reilly. 6240-7,6309-8
At best, poets. Robert Graves. 6339-X
At Bethlehem. Richard Crashaw. 6737-9
At Bethlehem. N.W. Rand. 6926-6
At Bethlehem. John Banister Tabb. 6627-5
At Bethlehem. William White. 6868-5
At Billings' bridge graveyard. Robert Billings. 6767-0
At boarding-school. Mary Chahoon. 6684-4
At Burgos. Arthur Symons. 6655-0
At Burntside lake. Selma Saari Evans. 6342-X
At Camden. Katharine Lee Bates. 6036-6
"At call of roll he answered not". The old minister. William White. 6868-5
"At Cato's head in Russell street". Ona the fly-leaf of a book of old plays. Walter Learned. 7041-8
"At Christmas time it seems to me". Friends. Esther Bergman Narey. 6799-9
"At Christmas-time Dan Cupid plays". Christmas. Nora Chesson. 6807-3
"At Christmas-time, poor papa tries...". Poor papa. Elsie Duncan Yale. 6807-3
At candle time. Ben H. Smith. 6662-3
At candle-lightin' time. Paul Laurence Dunbar. 6254-7,6696-8,6281-4
At Carcassonne. Winfred Ernest Garrison. 6542-2
At Carcassonne. George Craig Stewart. 6439-6
At Castellamare. John Addington Symonds. 6624-0,6631-3
At Casterbridge fair, sels. Thomas Hardy. 6828-6
At Casterbridge fair: former beauties. Thomas Hardy. 6208-3
At Castle Boterel. Thomas Hardy. 6208-3,6246-6,6150-8
At castle wood. Emily Bronte. 6655-0
At chadwicks bar and grill. Lance Henson. 7005-1
At chambers. Sir Lewis Morris. 6772-7
At Cheyenne. Eugene Field. 6949-5
At Christmas. Arthur Shearly Cripps. 6747-6
At Christmas-tide. Susie M. Best. 6807-3
At Christmas-time. W.G. Park. 6807-3
At church. S.T. Livingston. 6116-8
At close of day. Stephan G. Stephansson. 6283-0,6854-5
At colon. C.E. Hudeburg. 6640-2
At Coruna. Robert Southey. 6188-5
At court. Edmund Spenser. 6424-8
At Crow's Nest Pass. Emily Pauline ("Tekahionwake") Johnson. 6837-5
At Currabwee. Francis Ledwidge. 6812-X
At dancing school. Unknown. 6710-7
At dawn. Warren Ariail. 7016-7
At dawn. William Shakespeare. 6396-9
At dawn. Arthur Symons. 6655-0
At dawn. Charles Williams. 6210-9
"At dawn in silence moves the mighty stream". The glacier, fr. Three Alpine sonnets. Henry Van Dyke. 6961-4
"At dawn they came to the stream Hiddekel". The death of Eve. William Vaughn Moody. 6753-0
"At dawn/grinding machines". Dawn. Ilse Brem. 6769-7
At daybreak. Walter Conrad Arensberg. 6897-9
"At daybreak Maeve rose up from where..prayed". Before the war of Cooley. Francis Ledwidge. 6812-X
"At daybreak, when the falcon claps his wings". Ballad written for a bridegroom. Algernon Charles Swinburne. 6875-8
"At Derby Haven in sweet Manx land". 'God is love'. Thomas Edward Brown. 6809-X
At de cake-walk. Martha Young. 6711-5
At dead o' the night, Alanna. James B. Dollard. 6115-X

At Delos. Duncan Campbell Scott. 6021-8,6446-9
At Dieppe. William Wetmore Story. 6219-9
At Dingle Bank. Edward Lear. 6722-0
"At dinner, she is hostess, I am host". George Meredith. 6508-2
"At dinner, she is hostess, I am host," fr. Modern love. George Meredith. 6659-3
At dusk. Mary Dixon Thayer. 6039-0
At Easter. Amy J. Dolloff. 6764-6
At Easter time. Laura E. Richards. 6177-X
At Eden gates. Alfred Noyes. 6151-6
"At dusk in the small midwestern towns". The passage. William Meissner. 7032-9
"At dusk the narrow street is a landscape...". The narrow street. Menotti Del Picchia. 6759-X
"At dusk/from the island in the river". If the owl calls again. John Haines. 6855-3
"At early dawn I once had been". The dawning of the day. Unknown. 6930-4
"At early dawn through London you must go". Good counsel. John Davidson. 6793-X
"At early morn I watched, scarce consciously". A symbol. William Bell Scott. 6819-7
At eighty-three, sels. Thomas Durley Landels. 6045-1;6337-3
At Eleusis. Hilda ("H.D.") Doolittle. 6070-6
At Eleusis. Ella Wheeler Wilcox. 6956-8
At Ellis Island. George Lawrence Andrews. 6039-0
At end. Louise Chandler Moulton. 7041-8
At end. Louise Chandler Moulton. 6066-4
"At end of love, at end of life". At end. Louise Chandler Moulton. 7041-8
At even. Thomas S. Jones Jr. 6320-9
At even. Frederick Manning. 6897-9
"At even o'Hallowmas no sleep I sought". The spell. John Gay. 6820-0
At even, when the sun was set. Henry Twells. 6337-3
At evening. J.T. Newcomb. 6693-3
At evening. Dora Wilcox. 6784-0
At evening time it shall be light. William White. 6868-5
At eventide. Joseph Crosby Lincoln. 6119-2
At eventide. Unknown (German) 6337-3
At eventide. John Greenleaf Whittier. 6126-5
"At every heart-beat". Time. George William ("A.E.") Russell. 6879-0
"At fierce Sidero's word the thralls drew near". The taming of Tyro. Sophocles. 6987-8
At first. Nigel Heseltine. 6360-8
At Florence. William Wordsworth. 6631-3
At Fontainbleau. Arthur Symons. 6656-9
"At first the hum through sagging leaves". Mosquitoes. David Baker. 7032-9
"At first the infant". A soliloquy. Unknown. 6995-9
"At five he wants to be a fireman". Youth's ambition. Anna Grace Boyles. 6750-6
"At five o'clock the fear began". Forerunner to rain. Virginia Moore. 6780-8
"At Florence, in a listless street". Prince Charlie's weather-vane. Eugene Lee-Hamilton. 6793-X
At four-score. Richard Watson Gilder. 6429-9,6321-7
At fourscore. Eben Eugene Rexford. 6097-8
At Fredericksburg. John Boyle O'Reilly. 6074-9
At Fredericksburg - Dec. 13, 1862. John Boyle O'Reilly. 6917-7
At Gettysburg. George Wharton Pepper. 6936-3
At Gettysburg. Unknown. 6113-3,6016-2
At Gibraltar. George Edward Woodberry. 6431-0,6300-4,6076-5,6102-8,6239-3,6243-1,6310-4,6076-5
At Glastonbury. Henry Kingsley. 6339-X
"At fourteen her breasts were flabby". Merlene. Kell Robertson. 6998-3, 6901-0
"At Glendalough lived a young saint". St. Kevin. Samuel Lover. 6825-1,6930-4
"At good cheer house on friendship street". Joseph Morris. 6085-4
At graduating time. Unknown. 6465-5,6449-3
At Grafton. John Drinkwater. 6477-9
At grandfather's. John French Wilson. 6037-4
At grandmother's. Arthur Wentworth Hamilton Eaton. 7041-8
At grass. Philip Larkin. 6257-1

At half-mast. Emily Pauline ("Tekahionwake") Johnson. 6837-5
At harvest. Joseph ("Seosamh MacCathmhaoil") Campbell. 6897-9
"At her easel, brush in hand". A contrast. Eleanor C. Donnelly. 6918-5,6579-9
At her fair hands. Walter Davison. 6182-5,6436-1,6726-3, 6317-9
"At her fair hands how have I grace entreated". A dialogue between him and his heart. W. Davison. 6935-5
At her grave. Arthur O'Shaughnessy. 6656-9
At her wedding. Edgar A. Guest. 6869-3
At her window. Frederick Locker-Lampson. 6301-2
At his feet. Lois R. Carpenter. 6065-X
At his grave (Hughenden, May, 1881). Alfred Austin. 6656-9
At home. Bernard Barton. 6273-3
At home. Thomas Augustin Daly. 6875-8
At home. Christina Georgina Rossetti. 6186-9,6648-8,6655-0, 6656-9
At home. Bayard Taylor. 6260-1
At home in heaven. James Montgomery. 6656-9
"At home it seems to be the rule". Ma's tools. Unknown. 6889-8
"At home to-night, alone with Dot". At home. Thomas Augustin Daly. 6875-8
"At Kangaroo Gully in 'fifty-two'.". Catching the coach. Alfred T. Chandler. 6768-9
"At Kotri, by the river, when evening's sun...". Kotri, by the river. Laurence (Adele Florence Nicolson) Hope. 6856-1
At home, fr. Studies for pictures. Bayard Taylor. 6976-2
At husking time. Emily Pauline ("Tekahionwake") Johnson. 6476-0,6656-9
At Isola Bella. Jessie B. Rittenhouse. 6338-1
At Ithaca. Hilda ("H.D.") Doolittle. 6069-2
At Katherine Walton's bluff on the Ashley. Kadra Maysi. 6039-0
At Kew. Alfred Noyes. 6639-9
At Lac Labelle. Susan ("Seranus") Frances. 6797-2
At lake Sullivan. Josepha Contoski. 6342-X
At Lanuvium. James Rennell Rodd; 1st Baron Rennell. 6624-0
At last. George E. Bowen. 6274-1
At last. Stopford Augustus Brooke. 6321-7,6429-9
At last. Clarkson Clothier. 6406-X
At last. Paul Hamilton Hayne. 6177-X
At last. Helen Hunt Jackson. 7041-8
At last. Philip Bourke Marston. 6656-9
At last. Thomas Masson. 7021-3
At last. Gertrude Huntington McGiffert. 6838-3
At last. Sir Lewis Morris. 6656-9
At last. Richard Henry Stoddard. 6243-1
At last. Unknown. 6273-3
At last. John Greenleaf Whittier. 6303-9,6730-1,6214-8
"'At last 'tis finished!' cried the...painter". Picture of the last supper. Louise E.V. Boyd. 6927-4
"At last I have a Sabine farm". My Sabine farm. Eugene Field. 6949-5
"At last I'm with thee, long-reknowned Cape...". Cape Cod. James T. Gallagher. 6798-0
"At last a soft and solemn-breathing sound" John Milton. 6935-5
At last post. Walter Lightowler Wilkinson. 6650-X
"At last the bird that sang so long". Good Friday night. William Vaughn Moody. 6753-0
"At last the dream that clad the field". In my vineyard. Bayard Taylor. 6976-2
"At last the golden oriental gate", fr. Romeo...Juliet. William Shakespeare. 6240-7
"At last there'll dawn the last of the...year". Optimism. Alfred Victor Ratcliffe. 7026-4,6650-X
"At last we parley: we so strangely dumb" George Meredith. 6828-6
"At last withdraw your cruelty." Sir Thomas Wyatt. 6584-8
"At last, a stroke has fall'n; Toulon is ours". Napoleon in regeneration. Edward Farquhar. 6939-8
"At last, beloved nature! I have met". Sonnet ("At last"). Henry Timrod. 6753-0
"At last, we parley: we so strangely dumb". George Meredith. 6508-2
'At least for now' Tanya Tyler. 6899-5

At Leeds. Unknown. 6722-0
At Lemnos. Thomas Russell. 7015-9
"At length 'tis done, the glorious conflict's". Louisbourg. Francis Hopkinson. 6753-0
"At length a reverend sire among them came". The ark. John Milton. 6833-2
"At length appears the wish'd-for night". Another runic ode. Thomas Warton (the Elder). 6962-2
"At length must Suffolk beauties shine in vain". To Lady Firebrace. Samuel Johnson. 6975-4
"At length the gusts of anguish cease". A death-bed. Francis Turner Palgrave. 6980-0
"At length the winter's h;owling blasts are...". The swallows. Richard Jago. 6943-6
"At length the wintry horrors disappear". A journey from Patapsco in Maryland to Annapolis. R. Lewis. 6753-0
"At length their long kiss severed...". Nuptial sleep. Dante Gabriel Rossetti. 6980-0
"At length they all to merry London came". Sonnet ("At length"). Edmund Spenser. 6301-2
"At length thy golden hours have winged...". Anacreon. Anitpater of Sidon. 6879-0
"At length upon the lone Chorasmian shore". Alastor and the swan. Percy Bysshe Shelley. 6980-0
"At length, by demonstration me to teach". The ruines of time, sel. Edmund Spenser. 6958-4
"At length, my friend, the far-sent letters...". Elegy 001: To Charles Deodati. John Milton. 6814-6
"At Madge, ye hoyden, gossips scofft". Madge: ye hoyden. Eugene Field. 6949-5
"At Mantua long had lain in chains". The death of Hofer. Julius Mosen. 6914-2
"At length/His senses yiellding", fr. The prelude. William Wordsworth. 6958-4
At les eboulements. Duncan Campbell Scott. 6547-3,6656-9
At Lexington. Benjamin Sledd. 6074-9
At life's best. Alfred Lord Tennyson. 6429-9,6321-7
At Lincoln's tomb. Robertus Love. 6524-4
At Lord's. Francis Thompson. 6659-3
At Lord's cricket ground. Francis Thompson. 6179-6,6339-X
At Lulworth cove a century back. Thomas Hardy. 6659-3
At magnolia cemetery. Henry Timrod. 6289-X,6431-0,6309-8, 6464-7
At Manilla. Unknown. 6589-9
At Manly. Leonard Mann. 6349-7
At Mass. Unknown. 6244-X
At Melville's tomb. Hart Crane. 6399-3,6641--0
At Mexican Springs. Laura Tohe. 7005-1
At Michelmas. Bliss Carman and Richard Hovey. 6890-1
At midnight. Kurt Heynicke. 6160-5
At midnight. Sir Lewis Morris. 6383-7
"At midnight by the stream I roved". Lewti. Samuel Taylor Coleridge. 6828-6
At midnight of All Souls. Mary Cowden Clarke. 6997-5
At midnight of All Souls. Mary Cowden-Clark. 7037-X
"At midnight, death's and truth's unlocking...". The crystal. Sidney Lanier. 7041-8
"At moost mischief". My lute and I. Sir Thomas Wyatt. 6881-2
"At morn - at noon - at twilight dim". Hymn ("At morn - at noon - at twilight dim"). Edgar Allan Poe. 6753-0
"At morn we placed on his funeral bier". Callimachus. 6814-6
"At morn when first the rosy gleam". Bob White. Francis Charles McDonald. 6983-5
At morning. Arthur Snover. 6249-0
At morning an iris. Patrick Evans. 6379-9
At Mosgiel, sels. William Wordsworth. 6867-7
"At morning many a doting dad". Walking the boy. Edgar A. Guest. 6748-4
"At morning, silence reigns supreme". On the glacier. Henry Van Dyke. 6983-5
"At most mischief." Sir Thomas Wyatt. 6584-8
At musing hour. Thomas Wells. 6752-2
At Neponsit. Ruth Lewisohn. 6847-2
At Niagara. Richard Watson Gilder. 6484-1
"At my father's wake/The old people". Desmet, Idaho, March 1969 Janet Campbell Hale. 7005-1
At night. Mary Baldwin. 6274-1
At night. Winifred Adams Burr. 6648-8

At night. Frances Cornford. 6497-3
At night. Richard Watson Gilder. 6243-1
At night. Alice Meynell. 6477-9,6393-4,6508-2
At night. Sergei Smirnov. 6546-5
At night. Theodore Spencer. 6389-6
"At night I like to snuggle in my pillow". Jessie Orton Jones. 6999-1
"At night before my final sleep, I know". Unrelated thoughts. Nancy Walsh. 6799-9
"At night he hears the robbers". The owner. Peter Wild. 6998-3
"At night I dreamt I was back in Ch'ang-an". Dreaming that I went with Li and Yu to visit Yuan Chen. Po Chu-I. 6958-4
"At night the sky is full of stars". The stars. Alice Barkley. 6789-1
"At night when rain falls on the roof". Rain. Virginia Wilson Lachicotte. 7016-7
"At night you scratched". Sarah. Harold Marcus. 6900-2
"At night, in my dream, I stoutly climbed...". A dream of mountaineering. Po Chu-I. 6958-4
"At night, the coffeepot stands upended in...". Parachute. Dwight Okita. 6790-5
"At night, when mummy's tucked me in". The children in the chair. Ethel Talbot. 6804-9
"At night, when passion's ebbing tide". Yasmini. Laurence (Adele Florence Nicolson) Hope. 6856-1
At night: the sleeper. Jessica Nelson North. 6069-2
At nightfall. Lucy Larcom. 6129-X
At nightfall. Charles Hanson Towne. 6654-2
At nineteen. William Sawyer. 6841-3
At ninety in the shade. James Whitcomb Riley. 6993-2
At Noey's house. James Whitcomb Riley. 6128-1
At noon. Katherine (Amelia Beers Warnock Garvin) Hale. 6115-X
At noon and midnight. James Whitcomb Riley. 6066-8
"At noon-time I stood in the door-way to see". The summer storm. Alice Cary. 6969-X
At odds with life. David Law ("Pegleg Arkwright") Proudfit. 7041-8
"At once with him they rose". Hell, fr. Paradise lost. John Milton. 6933-9
"At once, she wen, and found the Cyclopes." Callimachus. 6435-3
"At one time/he had called himself/a poet". 'An Aristotelian elegy'. Donald E. Bogle. 7024-8
"At one time/we aQe our rice". A sometimes love poem. George Leong. 6790-5
"At our gate he groaneth, groaneth". At our golden gate. Joaquin Miller. 6753-0
At parting. E. Pearl Dancey. 6750-6
At parting. Marie Shields Halvey. 6654-X
At parting. Haniel Long. 6033-1
At parting. Algernon Charles Swinburne. 6508-2
At parting. Katharine (Hinkson) Tynan. 7027-2
At parting. Unknown. 6563-5
At peep of dawn. Clinton Scollard. 6770-0,6875-8
At Penshurst. Edmund Waller. 6430-2
"At peep of dawn the daffodil". At peep of dawn. Clinton Scollard. 6770-0,6875-8
"At Pievenick in the marketplace". The marketplace in Pievenick. Hermann Hagedorn. 6944-4
At play. Eugene Field. 6949-5
At play. Unknown. 6621-6
At Port Royal. John Greenleaf Whittier. 6113-3,6438-8,6470-1,6442-6
At Putney. Rudolph Chambers Lehmann. 6785-9
At Pylos, fr. The Odyssey. Homer. 6435-3
At Queen Maude's banquet. Lucy Larcom. 6129-X
At Rainbow lake. Arthur Weir. 7041-8
"At precisely three o'clock Don Pedro...". Marvels of the will. Octavio Paz. 6758-1
At rehearsal. Alice Cary. 6865-0;6969-X
At rest in the National Cathedral. C.N. Lund. 7001-9
At Richmond. William Allen Butler. 6903-7
At Rome. William Wordsworth. 6631-3
At Roncevaux. Alfred Noyes. 6169-9
At Sagamore hill. Edgar Lee Masters. 6033-1
At Sagamore hill. Edgar Lee Masters. 6995-9
At Saint Patrick's purgatory. Donnchadh (atr.) Mor O'Dala.

6930-4
At Saint Patrick's purgatory. Sean O'Faolain. 6582-1
At Sainte-Marguerite. Trumbull Stickney. 6380-2
"At rivermouth/wharves wait". Southern coast. Erick Brenstrum. 7018-3
"At Sagamore the chief lies low". Sagamore. Corinne Roosevelt Robinson. 6995-9
"At Sansuena,in the tower,fair Melisendra lies". Melisendra. Unknown (Spanish). 6757-3
"At school, during class". Graffiti in a university rest;room: 'killing people...' Jim Mitsui. 6790-5
At school-close. John Greenleaf Whittier. 6465-5
At sea. Francis William Bourdillon. 6273-3
At sea. Alice Cary. 6865-0;6969-X
At sea. Allan Cunningham. 6242-3,6504-X
At sea. Vera Elizabeth Guerard. 7024-8
At sea. Richard Hovey. 7006-X
At sea. William Bell Scott. 6997-5
At sea. Phillips Stewart. 7041-8
At sea. Algernon Charles Swinburne. 6875-8
At sea. John Townsend Trowbridge. 6240-7,6600-3,6742-5, 6271-7,6438-8,6219 ,6302-0,6385-3
At sea. Jean Starr Untermeyer. 6012-9
"At sea are tossing ships". Apart. John James Piatt. 6243-1,7041-8
At sea on the sabbath. Charles W. Denison. 6755-7
"At Sestos Hero dwelt...", fr. Hero and Leander. Christopher Marlowe. 6726-3
"At sea their mischeifes grewe, but ours at...". The third squire. Thomas Campion. 6794-8
"At Selinonto where the city stood". Selinonto. Leonard Shoobridge. 6785-9
At set of sun. Christina Georgina Rossetti. 6461-2
At set of sun. Unknown. 6914-2
At setting and rising morn. Allan Ramsay. 6219-9
"At setting day and rising moon". Song ("At setting"). John Gay. 6240-7
"At seven you just nick it". A public dinner. Thomas Hood. 6974-6
"At Sidon lived a husband with his wife". The wife's treasure. Sabine Baring-Gould. 6848-0
"At Silver Lake three fishermen got up...". The gullible fishermen. Edgar A. Guest. 6748-4
At seventy-two, sels. Thomas Dunn English. 6482-5
At singing time. Anne P.L. Field. 6097-8
At Sparta, fr. The Odyssey. Homer. 6435-3
At St. Jerome. Susan ("Seranus") Frances. 6797-2
At St. Paul's. Hardwicke Drummond Rawnsley. 7026-4
At Stratford. Louis J. Magee. 7004-3
At Stratford-on-Avon. Mackenzie Bell. 6656-9
"At sixty years, when April's face". To Austin Dobson. Sir Owen Seaman. 6875-8
"At slumber time the nodding heads". A slumber story. Robert J. Irish. 6818-9
"At Strasburg on the moat". The switzer. Unknown. 6952-5
At sundown. Mary H. Cabaniss. 6841-3
At sundown. Friedrika Heyl. 6253-9
At sunrise. John E. Barrett. 6840-5
At sunrise. E.J. Barton. 6468-X
At sunrise. John Gould Fletcher. 6345-4
At sunset. Mattie A.W. Clark. 6373-X
At sunset. Emily Pauline ("Tekahionwake") Johnson. 6837-5
At sunset. James Benjamin Kenyon. 6347-0
At sunset. Steingrimur Thorsteinsson. 6283-0
At sunset. William White. 6868-5
"At sunset sad, at dawning wild". Tangola's refusal, fr. The story of Balladeadro. George Gordon McCrae. 6768-9
"At sunset, when the rosy light was dying". Wings of a dove. Henry Van Dyke. 6961-4
"At sunset-I have a vision of 10,000 carabos". The new Manong. Luis Syquia. 6790-5
"At Tara to-day in this fateful hour". The rune of St. Patrick. Unknown. 6873-1
"At Thames faire port". Praise of poets, fr. Britannias pastorals. William Browne. 6933-9
At tea. Thomas Hardy. 6491-4
At tea one bitter afternoon. Leonie Adams. 6808-1
At the 'ye that do truly'. Charles Williams. 6931-2
At the altar. Mary Kyle Dallas. 6671-2

At the Ambassadeurs. Arthur Symons. 6659-3
At the aquarium. Max Eastman. 6102-8,6506-6,6730-1,6076-5, 6300-4
At the ball game. Horace. 6949-5
"At the bar of Judge Conscience, stood Reason". A flight of fancy. Frances Sargent Osgood. 6878-2
At the barricade. Victor Hugo. 7022-1
"At the battle of the Nile". Unknown. 6363-2
"At the beginning of the meat". Po, po, po, po, [I] love brawn and so do mo. Unknown. 6756-5
At the bottom of the well. Louis Untermeyer. 6012-9
At the British Museum. Richard Aldington. 6439-6
At the burial of a scholar. Staub. 6952-5
At the Cafe de la Paix. Georgianna Livinston. 6906-1
At the camp-fire. Sarah F. Meader. 6928-2
At the cedars. Duncan Campbell Scott. 6681-X,6458-2,6115-X, 6591-0,6592-9,6656-9
At the cenotaph. Christopher M. ("Hugh MacDiarmid") Grieve. 6375-6
At the ceramic exhibition. Harriet Stanton Place. 6789-1
At the church gate. William Makepeace Thackeray. 6660-7, 6046-3,6321-7,6226-1,6092-7,6199 ,6250-4,6122-2,6429-9,6271-7,6302-0,6385-3,6481 ,6600-3,6656-9,6658-5, 6219-9,6737-9,6102
"At the close of a winter day". The rhyme of the three captains. Rudyard Kipling. 6810-3
"At the close of the day". The coquet mother and coquet daughter. John Gay. 6972-X
At the comedy. Arthur Stringer. 6115-X
At the coming of the wild swans. William ("Fiona Macleod") Sharp. 6134-4
At the concert. James Lindsay Gordon. 6682-8
At the concert. Ray Clarke Rose. 6274-1
At the convent gate. Austin Dobson. 6655-09
At the convent near Saint Gall. James Cochrane. 6749-2
At the corner. Hazel Hall. 6628-3
"At the corner of Wood street, when daylight appears" William Wordsworth. 6935-5
"At the corner of Wood street, when daylight..". The reverie of poor Susan. William Wordsworth. 6832-4, 6075-7,6228-8,6332-2,6395-0,6623-2,6737 ,6246-6,6138-9,6419-1,6250-4,6086-2,6110
"At the corner of Wood Street, when daylight..". The vision of home. William Wordsworth. 6793-X
"At the corners of my house". Four trees. Mildred Focht. 6847-2
At the cottage. Edgar A. Guest. 6862-6
At the council. John B.L. Warren, 3d Baron De Tabley. 6046-3
At the court-house door. Unknown. 6273-3
"At the crematorium for my first visit". As if carbon is nothing. Bernice Lever. 6767-0
At the crossroads. Richard Hovey. 6161-3
"At the cry of the first bird". The crucifixion. Unknown. 6930-4
At the dance. Arthur Crew Inman. 6959-2
At the dark hour. Paul Dehn. 6666-6
At the dawn. Alice Macdonald Kipling. 6337-3
"At the dead of night by the side of the sea". The seaside cave. Alice Cary. 6969-X
At the dog show. Christopher Morley. 6510-4
At the Dogana. Arthur Symons. 6624-0
At the door. Eugene Field. 6772-7
At the door. Eugene Field. 6834-0;6949-5
At the door. Wendy Wood. 6269-5
At the door. Bertha Gerneaux Woods. 6042-0
"At the door of his hut sat Massasoit". The peace message. Burton Egbert Stevenson. 6946-0
At the draper's. Thomas Hardy. 6637-2
At the ebony circle. Helen G. Quigless. 7024-8
At the edge. Harriet Monroe. 6628-3
"At the edge of her sofa". Rapist. Jose Y. Teran Jr.. 6870-7
At the edge of the bay. Thomas Caldecot Chubb. 6396-9,6288-1
At the edge of the garden. Joyce Lancaster. 6850-2
At the embassy. Louis J. Magee. 7004-3
At the end of a book. Langdon Elwyn ("John Philip Varley") Mitchell. 6431-0
At the end of play. Bertel Gripenberg. 6045-5

AT the end of the day. Bliss Carman and Richard Hovey. 6890-1
At the end of the day. Richard Hovey. 6224-5,6310-1,6473-6, 6501-5,6735-2
At the end of the king's highway. Unknown. 6461-2
At the end of the way. Verner von Heidenstam. 6045-5
At the end of things. Arthur Edward Waite. 6730-1
"At the entrance, there where all roads begin". Song of Thomas, departed. Winett de Rokha. 6759-X
"At the feet of Don Henrique now King Pedro...". The proclamation of King Henry. Unknown (Spanish). 6757-3
3t the ferry. Emily Pauline ("Tekahionwake") Johnson. 6795-6
At the florists. Louis J. Magee. 7004-3
At the florists' feast in Norwich. Matthew Stevenson. 6563-5
"At the foot of the hill the milk-house stands". Milking time, fr. Life on the farm. Benjamin Franklin Taylor. 6815-4
At the fountain. Marcabrun. 7039-6
"At the fountain of youth, I drank, one day". Give me youth and the world is mine. Celestin Pierre Cambiaire. 6826-X
At the funeral. Lorraine Mozee Taylor. 6662-3
At the funeral of --. Kristjan N. ("K.N.") Julius. 6854-5
At the furrier's. William Heer Wright. 6396-9
"At the game which is my life". The game. Conrado Nale Roxlo. 6759-X
At the games. Robert Graves. 6070-6
At the garden gate. Unknown. 6411-6
At the gate. Sir Henry Howarth Bashford. 7007-8
At the gate. Mae Clover Winters. 6270-9
"At the gate of old Granada...". The lamentation for Celin. Unknown (Spanish). 6757-3,7039-6
At the gates. Isabel Harriss Barr. 6839-1
At the gates. Alfred Noyes. 6169-9
At the gates of spring. Sir Charles George Douglas Roberts. 6115-X
At the gates of the tombs. Carl Sandburg. 6880-4
At the grave of a land-shark. Ernest G. Moll. 6722-0
At the grave of Burns. William Wordsworth. 6198-2,6483-3, 6110-9,6828-6
At the grave of Cecil Rhodes. Peter Jackson. 6788-3
At the grave of Charles Lamb in Edmonton. Sir William Watson. 6793-X
At the grave of Dante Gabriel Rossetti. Mackenzie Bell. 6656-9
At the grave of Henry Vaughan. Siegfried Sassoon. 6483-3, 6641-0,6071-4
At the grave of my grandfather. Pearce Young. 6515-5
At the grave of Poe. Clinton Scollard. 6184-2
At the grave of Walker. Joaquin Miller. 6431-0
At the Great Wall of China. Edmund Blunden. 6257-1
At the grindstone; or, a home view of the battle field. Robert Buchanan. 6344-6
At the hacienda. Francis Bret Harte. 6431-0
"At the harbor/in Frederiksted". 'A palette' Rochelle DuBois. 6898-7
"At the head of Wear Water...". Unknown. 6258-X
At the heart. M.A. DeWolfe Howe. 6051-X
At the hearthside. John Vance Cheney. 6632-1
At the hospital window. Carl Smith. 6929-0
At the Jewish museum. Olga Cabral. 6966-5
At the King of Prussia. Thomas Dickson Finletter. 6936-3
"At the jungle's edge, torn open". Lan Nguyen: the uniform of death 1971 David Mura. 6790-5
"At the kennel where they bred you were...". You're a dog. C. L. Gilman. 7008-6
At the last. James Berry Bensee. 6304-7
At the last. Richard Doddridge Blackmore. 6641-0
At the last. Will H. Hendrickson. 7007-8
At the last. Philip Bourke Marston. 6656-9
At the last. Arthur O'Shaughnessy. 6174-5
At the last. William ("Fiona Macleod") Sharp. 6655-0
At the last. Mrs. J.M. Winton. 6413-2
At the lattice. Alfred Austin. 6652-6
At the leap of the waters. Edward F. Garesche. 6172-9
At the loom. Unknown. 6273-3
At the lowest ebb of night. Robert P. Tristram Coffin. 7040-X
At the Luxembourg. Guy-Charles Cros. 6351-9
"At the magic hour of twilight/Day merges...". Commutation to heaven. Ann Strickland. 6799-9
At the making of man. Bliss Carman. 6115-X
At the manger. Wystan Hugh Auden. 6391-8
At the manger. John Banister Tabb. 6053-6
At the manor house. Christian Winther. 6555-4
At the medding march. Gerard Manley Hopkins. 6292-X,6489-2
At the mercy of the wind. Violeta Parra. 7036-1
At the Mermaid cafeteria. Christopher Morley. 6102-8,6076-5,6464-7,6467-1
At the Mermaid, fr. Letter to Ben Jonson. Francis Beaumont. 6934-7
At the mid hour of night. Thomas Moore. 6174-5,6186-9,6244-X,6328-4,6246-6,6208 ,6301-2,6648-8,6383-7,6543-0, 6153-2,6086-2,6430-2
At the mid hour of night. Unknown (Greek) 6435-3
"At the midnight in the silence". Epilogue ("At the midnight"). Robert Browning. 6473-6,6196-6
At the mill. Unknown (Greek) 6435-3
At the movies. Florence Ripley Mastin. 7027-2
"At the north end of our village stands". The washerwoman. Alice Cary. 6969-X
"At the old Genevan wharf she lay". Lake Leman and Chillon. Henry Morford. 6749-2
At the old ladies' home. Ruth Guthrie Harding. 6030-7
"At the one shot". The caged eagle's death dream, fr. Cawdor. Robinson Jeffers. 6978-9
At the opera. George H. Jessop. 6414-0
At the opera. Owen (Edward Bulwer-Lytton, Earl Lytton) Meredith. 6661-5
At the opera. E. De Lancey Pierson. 7021-3
At the opera. Unknown. 7021-3
At the oratorio. Unknown. 6415-9
At the pantomime. Oliver Wendell Holmes. 6848-0
"At the peeping of the morning". the rabbi's son-in-law. Sabine Baring-Gould. 6848-0
At the piano. Unknown. 6273-3
At the picture-show. Karle Wilson Baker. 6030-7
At the play. Thomas Edward Brown. 6809-X
At the police station. Raymond Souster. 6767-0
At the portal of heaven, fr. Suite Belgique. Gertrude Huntington McGiffert. 6838-3
At the president's grave. Richard Watson Gilder. 6946-0, 6820-0
At the pyramid of Cestius near the graves of Shelley... Thomas Hardy. 6331-4
At the rendezvous. A.W. Schack von Stahheldt. 6555-4
At the rendezvous. A.W. Schack von Stahheldt. 6555-4
At the roadhouse: in memory of Robert Louis Stevenson. Bliss Carman. 6890-1
At the rock. William Smith Pettit. 6118-4
"At the round earth's imagined corners, blow". John Donne. 6369-1,6536-8,6562-7,6315-2,6179-6
"At the round earth's imagined corners, blow." John Donne. 6645-3
At the Sand island camp. Keiho Soga. 6981-9
At the Saturday Club. Oliver Wendell Holmes. 6126-5,6288-1
"At the round earths imagin'd corners". Sonnet ("At the round"). John Donne. 6341-1,6472-8,6430-2
"At the safari's end a porter". The luck in the square stone, sels. Herman Charles Bosman. 6788-3
"At the Salvation Army/a clerk". From Sand Creek, sel. Simon J. Ortiz. 7005-1
At the school exercises. Edgar A. Guest. 6869-3
At the sea. Henry Hunter Welsh. 6936-3
At the seaside. George Ewart Evans. 6360-8
At the seaside. Robert Louis Stevenson. 6368-3
At the set of sun. Mary Ashley Townsend. 6484-1
At the set of the sun. Unknown. 6303-9
At the shore. Edwin Morgan. 6979-7
At the shrine. Richard Kendall Munkittrick. 6431-0
At the sign of the cleft heart. Theodosia Garrison. 6166-4
At the sign of the cock. Sir Owen Seaman. 6089-7,6440-X
At the sign of the golden key, fr. Suite Belgique. Gertrude Huntington McGiffert. 6838-3
At the sign of the jolly jack. Geoffrey Smith. 6230-X, 6747-6
At the signof the spade. John Vance Cheney. 6006-4

"At the sound of the wild geese". Wild geese. Ella Moore Marshall. 6799-9
"At the spraygun stands large heroic Ted". Portrait of a gentleman. Ruth Pitter. 6985-1
"At the spring". Song ("At the spring.") Jasper Fisher. 6334-9
At the stage door. James Clarence Harvey. 6923-1
At the stage-door. Arthur Symons. 6301-2
At the Stevenson fountain. Wallace Irwin. 6476-0,6241-5
At the summer cottage. Edgar A. Guest. 6862-6
At the sunrise in 1848. Dante Gabriel Rossetti. 6110-9
At the symphony. Robert Nathan. 6465-5,6036-6
At the tavern. Alice Cary. 6060-9
At the theater. Rachel (Lyman) Field. 6891-X
At the three anchors, fr. Suite Belgique. Gertrude Huntington McGiffert. 6838-3
"At the time of Matines, Lord, thu were itake". The hours of passion. Unknown. 6881-2
At the tomb of Washington. Clinton Scollard. 6449-3
At the tombs of the House of Savoy. William Jay Smith. 6388-8
At the top of the road. Charles Buxton Going. 6274-1
At the tunnel's mouth. Frederic Lyster. 6166-4
At the turn of the year. Clifford Bax. 6069-2
At the turn of the year. Ben H. Smith. 6662-3
At the Villa Conti. William Wetmore Story. 6624-0
"At the unseen portal waiting". Go to sleep. Ella Warner Fisher. 7030-2
"At the village emporium in Woodstock". Frederick Winsor. 6722-0
At the volcano internment camp. Muin Ozaki. 6981-9
At the wars. J.B.B. Nichols. 6477-9
At the water. Elizabeth Madox Roberts. 6326-8
"At the western window I paused from...". Being on duty all night in the palace and dreaming... Po Chu-I. 6958-4
At the window. Praxilla. 6435-3
At the window. Alfred Lord Tennyson. 6977-0
"At the window Chloe stands". The serenade. Thompson Seiser Wescott. 6936-3
At the window, sels. Alfred Lord Tennyson. 6045-1
At the workers' benches. Raymond Kresensky. 6954-1
At the worst. Israel Zangwill. 6730-1
At the yellow of the leaf. Bliss Carman. 6252-0
At the zoo. Anne May Smith. 6466-3
At the zoo. Israel Zangwill. 6510-4
"At thee the mocker sneers in cold derision". The maid of Orleans. Johann C. Friedrich von Schiller. 7039-6
At their place. Paul Mariah. 6870-7
At Thermopylae. Simonides. 6435-3,6665-8
At thirty-five. Robert Service. 6159-1
At this farewell. William Wordsworth. 6465-5
At Tiber mouth. James Rennell Rodd; 1st Baron Rennell. 6271-7,6624-0
"At three-score winter's end I died". An epitaph ("At three-score..."). Unknown (Greek). 6814-6
At tide water. Sir Charles George Douglas Roberts. 6021-8, 6446-9
At Timon's villa. Alexander Pope. 6733-6
At Tintagil. Sara Teasdale. 6320-9,6039-0
"At times the air is sad". Sad air. Carmen Alicia Cadilla. 6759-X
"At times when under cover I 'ave said". The instructor. Rudyard Kipling. 6810-3
"At times/You are so still". To one who is silent. Marie Louise Allen. 6906-1
"At Trin. Col. Cam. - which means...". The collegian and the porter. James Robinson Planche. 6909-6,6787-5
"At Trin. Col. Cam.--which means, in proper...". The collegian and the porter. Horace Smith. 6760-3
At twilight. Marian Buxton Clark. 6906-1
At Tynemouth priory. William Lisle Bowles. 6196-6
At Uncle Dock's. Elsie Malone McCollum. 6692-5
At Vallambrosa, sels. William Wordsworth. 6867-7
At Venice. Arthur Hugh Clough. 6624-0,6657-7
At Verona. Oscar Wilde. 6624-0
"At twilight, when I am alone". Evening. Stephan G. Stephansson. 6283-0
"At twilight, when I am alone with my thoughts". Evening. Stephan G. Stephansson. 6854-5

"At two years old the world he sees". For a birthday. Christopher Morley. 6875-8
"At Wapping I landed, and called to hail Mog". Jack at the opera. Charles Dibdin. 7025-6
At waking. Ethelwyn Wetherald. 6115-X
At war. Charles Madge. 6209-1
At warm springs. William Rose Benet. 6465-5
At Welbedacht. A.M. Buckton. 6788-3
At whose sheltering shall the day sea. William Sydney Graham. 6209-1
At winter's end. Sister Mary Madeleva. 6292-X
At wonder donut. Laureen Mar. 6790-5
At world's end. Robert Desnos. 6803-0
At worst. Edward Farquhar. 6939-8
"At worthingan exile from Geraldine G--". My life is a-- Frederick Locker-Lampson. 6760-3
"At yestere'en the world was dull and bare". The coming of the snow. Marion L. Bertrand. 6799-9
"At York, Pennsylvania, recently died". Variation of the rule in Shelley's case. Unknown. 6878-2
Atalanta. James Maurice Thompson. 6431-0
Atalanta conquered. William Morris. 6302-0;6385-3
Atalanta in Calydon. Algernon Charles Swinburne. 6657-7
Atalanta in Calydon, sels. Algernon Charles Swinburne. 6154-0,6122-2,6208-3,6527-9,6634-8,6726 ,6437-X,6655-0,6732-8,6543-0,6656-9,6197 ,6110-9,6192-3,6250-4, 6199-0,6655-0
Atalanta in Camden-town. Charles Lutwidge ("Lewis Carroll") Dodgson. 6440-X
Atalanta victorious. William Morris. 6302-0;6385-3
Atalanta's defeat, fr. The earthly paradise. William Morris. 6656-9
Atalanta's race, fr. The earthly paradise. William Morris. 6122-2,6657-7,6110-9,6102-8
Atalanta's victory, fr. The earthly paradise. William Morris. 6656-9
Ataraxia. Caroline Elizabeth Sarah Sheridan Norton. 6980-0
Atavism. Cale Young Rice. 6102-8,6347-0,6076-5,6648-8
Atavism. Elinor Wylie. 6218-0
The atavist. Robert Service. 6159-1
The atavistic maid. Berton Braley. 6853-7
Atchley, T.J.
    Maybe so, maybe. 6789-1
    Quatrain. 6789-1
Athabaska dick. Robert Service. 6159-1
Athaliah. Jean Baptiste Racine. 6848-0
Athanase Diakos. Aristote Valaoritis. 6352-7
Athanasius, Sister Mary
    Truth and beauty. 6761-1
Athanasy. Rose Scorgie. 6799-9
Athassel abbey. Louise Imogen Guiney. 6431-0
Athearn, Sarah A.
    Fast or slow time. 6764-6
    Postlude, fr. Program notes. 6764-6
    Prelude, fr. Program notes. 6764-6
    Program notes, sels. 6764-6
Atheism. Arthur Hugh Clough. 7025-6
Atheism. Arthur Hugh Clough. 6438-8
The atheist's wail. Dorothy Ducas. 6532-5
The atheist. William Knox. 6505-1
"Athelstan King/Lord among earls". Battle of Brunanburgh. Alfred Lord Tennyson. 6977-0
The Athenian dead. Simonides. 6435-3
An Athenian garden. Trumbull Stickney. 6380-2
The Athenian monument, fr. Platea. Simonides. 6435-3
The Athenian's confirmation vow. Unknown (Greek) 7042-6
Athens. George Gordon, 6th Baron Byron. 6543-0
Athens. Kostas Kariotakis. 6352-7
Athens. Rita Boumy Pappas. 6352-7
Athens. Nicephorus Vrettakos. 6352-7
Athens, fr. Paradise regained. John Milton. 6933-9
Atherstone, Edwin
    The last days of Herculaneum, sels. 6570-8
    The plague of hailstones. 6848-0
    Sunrise at sea. 6833-2
"Athirst in spirit, through the gloom". The prophet. Alexander Pushkin. 7039-6
"Athirst, anhungered, comfortless, alone". The mantle of the years. Gertrude Huntington McGiffert. 6838-3
"An Wathletic young lady of Clewer". Limerick:"An athletic

ATHLETIC

young lady of Clewer". Unknown. 6811-1
Athol cummers. James Hogg. 6180-X
Athulf and Ethilda. Sir Henry Taylor. 6385-3,6438-8
Athulf's death song, fr. Death's jest-book. Thomas Lovell Beddoes. 6656-9
"**Athwart** that land of bloss'ming vine". The battle-line. James B. Dollard. 6846-4
"**Athwart** the path of years deep shadows rest". Flag of liberty and light. George Sanford Holmes. 6836-7
"**Athwart** the unclear ages whirled". Discouragement. Phillip A. M. Villiers de l'isle-Adam. 6873-1
Atkins, David
   The trail. 6241-5
Atkins, Henry
   To Virginia. 6241-5
Atkins, John
   War aims: planning. 6895-2
Atkinson, Elmina
   Gray gauntlet. 7031-0
Atkinson, J.A.
   Father Christmas' message. 6147-8
Atkinson, James (tr.)
   The death of Kais. Nizami, 6448-5
   The death of Liali. Nizami, 6448-5
   Envoi ("O ye"). Nizami, 6448-5
   Kais declares his love. Nizami, 6448-5
   Kais in the desert. Nizami, 6448-5
   Laili disconsolate. Nizami, 6448-5
   Modena. Alessandro Tassoni, 6624-0
   Rustem slays Sohrab. Firdusi] (Abul Kasin Mansur) Firdausi [or Firdawsi, 6448-5
   Sohrab is born. Firdusi] (Abul Kasin Mansur) Firdausi [or Firdawsi, 6448-5
Atlantic. Eugenio Florit. 6642-9
Atlantic. Benjamin Franklin Taylor. 6815-4
Atlantic Charter: 1942. Francis Brett Young. 6107-9
Atlantic City. Henry Cuyler Bunner. 6735-2
Atlantic City waiter. Countee Cullen. 6976-5
Atlantic City water. Countee Cullen. 6102-8,6076-5
Atlantic combers. William ("Fiona Macleod") Sharp. 6997-5
Atlantic grain. Charles Plumb. 7020-5
"The **Atlantic** rolls around a fort of Spain". San Sebatian. John Nichol. 7015-9
Atlantis. Conrad Aiken. 6984-3
Atlantis. Wystan Hugh Auden. 6210-5
Atlantis. Gordon Bottomley. 6023-4
Atlantis. Stanton A. Coblentz. 6218-0
Atlas of Oregon. Madeline DeFrees. 7032-9
"**Atlas** perceiv'd the load of heav'n's new...". The transformation of Galanthis. John Gay. 6972-X
"**Atlas**! who for a moment held a world". Woodrow Wilson. Laura Simmons. 7001-9
"**Atlive**, alive/Ah, Pablo, Your name so...". Style 7. William Wantling. 6998-3
Atoll. Robert Service. 6159-1
The **atoll** in the mind. Alex Comfort. 6209-1,6391-8
An **atom** of celestial beauty. Lorna Greene. 7030-2
The **atom**.. Thomas Thornely. 6532-5
Atonement. Margaret E. Bruner. 6337-3
Atonement. Aline Kilmer. 6250-4
Atonement. Marie LeNart. 6144-3
Atonement. Bayard Taylor. 6976-2
"**Atonement** Day - evening pray'r - sadness...". Atonement evening prayer. Morris Rosenfeld. 7011-6
The **atonement**, fr. Paradise lost. John Milton. 6933-9
"**Atop** its mound frosted white". 'Among the savages' Ralph Salisbury. 7005-1
The **atophier**. Eric Silvernale. 6883-9
Atossa. Matthew Arnold. 6511-2
"**atqui** sciebat quae sibi barbarus". Regulus returns to Carthage. Horace. 7020-5
Atropos. John Myers O'Hara. 6076-5,6556-2
The **attack**.. Siegfried Sassoon. 6332-2,6542-2
The **attack**. Thomas Buchanan Read. 6946-0
Attainment. Madison Cawein. 6730-1
Attainment. Ella Wheeler Wilcox. 6730-1
An **attempt** at a city sunset. Francis Ledwidge. 6812-X
An **attempt** at the manner of Waller. William Cowper. 6814-5
"**Attempt** the end and never stand to doubt". Robert Herrick. 6623-2

'**Attempted** suicide'. Thomas Frost. 6926-6
"**Attend** my fable if your ears be clean". The wayzgoose, sels. Roy Campbell. 6788-3
Attendants. David Morton. 6746-8
"**Attending** for instructions, when". A whimsical attorney's bill. Unknown. 6878-2
Atterbury, Francis
   Written on the leaves of a white fan. 6563-5
"**Atthis**, our own loved Anactoria". Sappho. 6251-2
Attic. Arthur Davison Ficke. 6880-4
"**Attic** maid! with honey fed". To the swallow. Unknown (Greek). 6814-6
The **attic**, fr. The homestead. Gertrude Huntington McGiffert. 6838-3
The **attic**.. Rose Fyleman. 6466-3
Attica is. Stewart Brisby. 6870-7
Atticus, fr. Epistle to Dr. Arbuthnot. Alexander Pope. 6932-0
Attidudinist. Paul (J.G. Clemenceau Le Clerq) Tanaquil. 6039-0
Attila. G.R. Glasgow. 7031-0
Attila's sword. ? Lingg. 6842-1
"**Attired** in black, spangled with flames of...". Spirit of night. Thomas Rogers. 6908-8
Attitude. Robert E. Brittain. 6397-7
"An **attorney** was taking a turn". The briefless barrister. John Godfrey Saxe. 6878-2,6787-5
Attraction. Ella Wheeler Wilcox. 6956-8
Attraction of the east. Felicia Dorothea Hemans. 6980-0
Attractions of the east. Felicia Dorothea Hemans. 6973-8
Attune. Joshua Freeman Crowell. 6798-0
Atwater, Amy
   Baby picture. 6750-6
Atwood, Margaret
   Cave series, sel. 6767-0
Au bal mnasque. Unknown. 6983-5
Au Clair de la lune. Viola Gerard Garvin. 6781-6
"**Au** declin de l'automne, il est souvent des...". Pensee d'automne. Charles Augustin Sainte-Beuve. 6801-4
Au nord. Emile Verhaeren. 6801-4
Aubade. Madison Cawein. 6266-0
Aubade. Sir William Davenant. 6186-9
Aubade. William Empson. 6210-5,6391-8
Aubade. Ibn Hani. 6362-4
Aubade. Alexander Montgomerie. 6830-8
Aubade. William Shakespeare. 6102-8,6732-8
Aubade. Edith Sitwell. 6052-8,6491-4
Aubade: Dick, the donkey boy. Osbert Sitwell. 6257-1
Auber, Harriet
   The holy spirit. 6337-3
Aubergines. Ibn Sara. 6362-4
Aubert, Brenda
   Gracie's fancies. 6965-7
Aubert, Eugene
   A deux. 6847-2
   Le passage de la barre. 6847-2
   Ou je voudrais aller. 6847-2
The **auburn** lock. Unknown. 6874-X
Auburn, fr. The deserted village. Oliver Goldsmith. 6932-0
Aucassin and Nicolete. Unknown. 6850-2
Aucassin et Nicolete. Grace Duffield Goodwin. 6274-1
"**Auckland**, you great arshole". Ode to Auckland. James Baxter. 7018-3
Auction. Leone Rice Grelle. 6750-6
The **auction** sale. Robert Service. 6159-1
Auction: Anderson Galleries. Louis Untermeyer. 6034-X
The **auctioneer** and the lawyer. ? Smith. 6064-1
The **auctioneer's** gift. Sam Walter Foss. 6923-1
"The **auctioneer**, then, in his labor began". Bernard Barton. 6402-7
Auctioning off the baby. Unknown. 6166-4
The **audacious** kitten. Oliver Herford. 6699-2
Audelay, John
   Be true to your condition in life. 6881-2
   In his utter wretchedness. 6881-2
Auden, Wystan Hugh
   The airman's alphabet. 6375-6
   As I walked out one evening. 6472-8
   The ascent of F 6, sels. 6375-6
   At the manger. 6391-8

Atlantis. 6210-5
August for the people. 6666-6
Ballad ("Oh what is that sound"). 6666-6
A bride in the '30's. 6209-1
Carry her over the water. 6210-5
Chorus, fr. Paid on both sides. 6150-8
The cultural presupposition. 6645-3
The dog beneath the skin, sels. 6375-6
"Far from the heart of culture". 6665-8
First things first. 6388-8
Get there if you can and see the land... 6375-6
Happy ending. 6645-3
He is the way. 6337-3
Hearing of harvests rotting in the valleys. 6641-0
If, on account of the political situation. 6666-6
In memory of Sigmund Freud. 6209-1
In memory of W.B. Yeats. 6125-7,6389-6,6645-3,6491-4
In memory of W.B. Yeats, sels. 6210-5
In war time. 6645-3
The island cemetery. 6388-8
"The Jew wrecked in the German cell" 6666-6
Journal of an airman, sels. 6978-9
Law like love. 6210-5
"Lay your sleeping head, my love". 6208-3
The lesson. 6209-1
Letter to Lord Byron: part V. 6354-3
Look, stranger, at this island now. 6354-3
The maze. 6391-8
Miranda's song. 6209-1
Mundus et infans. 6391-8
Munitions expert, fr. On this island. 6337-3
Musee des Beaux Arts. 6391-8,6645-3
New Year letter, sels. 6208-3
The night mail. 6125-7
"O love, the interest itself in thoughtless heaven".
   6150-8
O what is that sound. 6257-1
"O, where are you going" 6150-8
Objects. 6388-8
1st September 1939. 6208-3
Petition. 6645-3
Portrait. 6072-2
Prologue. 6209-1,6375-6
Prologue. 6390-X
Pur. 6645-3
The sea and the mirror, sels. 6210-5
September 1, 1939. 6666-6,6389-6,6645-3
"Sing, Ariel, sing," fr.T he sea and the mirror. 6645-3
Sir, no man's enemy, forgiving all. 6209-1,6375-6,6150-
   8
Song ("So large a morning"). 6388-8
Song ("Warm are the still"). 6209-1
Song for St. Cecilia's day. 6210-5
Spain. 6666-6
"Taller to-day, we remember." 6209-1
There will be no peace. 6388-8
Truth. 6337-3
"Watch any day." 6209-1
Who's who. 6491-4
The witnesses. 6354-3
Audi et Alteram Partem. M.C. Conway Poole. 6591-0,6592-9
Audience to poet. Hazel Hall. 6038-2
Audiences. Howard Mumford Jones. 6347-0
Audit, September 1939. James Walker. 6783-2
Audley court. Alfred Lord Tennyson. 6977-0
Auersperg, Graf von
   Monch and Jungfrau. 6749-2
   St. Martin's wall. 6749-2
Auf ein altes bild. Eduard Friedrich Morike. 6838-3
Auf wiedersehen! James Russell Lowell. 6302-0,6385-3,6735-
   2,6441-8,6077-3,6004-8,6092-7,6126-5,6219-9,6288-1,
   6226-1,6560-0
Auf wiedersehen, sels. James Russell Lowell. 6732-8
Auguries. Robert Bridges. 6232-6
Auguries of innocence. William Blake. 6024-2,6208-3,6315-2,
   6337-3,6427-2,6641-,6086-2,6195-0,6430-2,6730-1
Auguries of innocence, sels. William Blake. 7009-4
Auguries of innocence, sels. William Blake. 6179-6,6317-9,
   6634-8,6648-8
Augury. Edmund Blunden. 6943-6

Augury. Josephine Jacobsen. 6839-1
August. William Davis Gallagher. 6597-X
August. Hamlin Garland. 6396-9
August. Ivan Kershner. 6857-X
August. Francis Ledwidge. 6812-X
August. Muna Lee. 6038-2
August. Louis MacNeice. 6208-3
August. Betty Myers. 6841-3
August. James Whitcomb Riley. 6993-2
August. Schuyler E. Sears. 6906-1
August. Frank Dempster Sherman. 6311-X
August. Edmund Spenser. 6239-3
August. Bayard Taylor. 6976-2
August. Celia Thaxter. 6597-X
August. Willoughby Weaving. 6506-6
August. Elinor Wylie. 6077-3,6464-7
August. A.J. Young. 6779-4
August. A.J. Young. 6269-5
August (1). Andreas Okopenko. 6769-7
August (2). Andreas Okopenko. 6769-7
August 1918. Maurice Baring. 7029-9
August 6 Bruce Spang. 7032-9
"**August** 6, 1945. City of Hiroshima". The day after
   Trinity. Richard Oyama. 6790-5
"**August** Strindberg. Brutal wars with women". Dionysians in
   a bad time. Irving Layton. 6767-0
August afternoon. Hilda Conkling. 6421-3
An **August** afternoon. J.P. Irvine. 6597-X
August for the people. Wystan Hugh Auden. 6666-6
August in the new all-glass General Motors plant... Mary
   Rinehart. 6761-1
August lilies. Benjamin Franklin Taylor. 6815-4
An **August** midnight. Thomas Hardy. 6828-6
An **August** mood. Duncan Campbell Scott. 6501-5
August moon. Gerhard Fritsch. 6769-7
August moonrise. Sara Teasdale. 6033-1
August night. Ronald Walker Barr. 6906-1
August night. Sara Teasdale. 6619-4,6393-4
August night in the city. Charles Hanson Towne. 6347-0
August of life. Albert Paris Gutersloh. 6769-7
August on the Roman Campagna. Frederic Crowninshield. 6624-
   0
The **August** second syndrome. J.A. Hines. 6870-7
The **August** sky. Edith Wyatt. 6252-0
August song. William Griffith. 6347-0
"The **August** sun is setting". The reaper's song. Thomas
   D'Arcy McGee. 7009-4
An **august** wood road. Sir Charles George Douglas Roberts.
   6591-0,6592-9
August, 1914, sels. Don Marquis. 6538-4
August, 1914. Robert Bridges. 6224-5
August, fr. Love's calendar. Max Dauthendey. 6160-5
August, fr. The earthly paradise. William Morris. 6110-9
"**August./Say** it slow". August. Ivan Kershner. 6857-X
August?: hottest day of the year. Brander Matthews. 6875-8
Augustine. Earl B. Marlatt. 6143-5
Augustine, Saint
   "Great art thou, O Lord." 6337-3
   Te deum laudamus. 6543-0
"**Augustus** stills survives in Maro's strain". Epigram on
   George nI and Colley Cibber, Esq. Samuel Johnson.
   6975-4
The **auld** ash tree. Thomas Davidson. 6960-6
Auld daddy darkness. James Ferguson. 6132-X,6466-3,6519-8,
   6627-5,6690-9,6368
Auld fermer's address to the 'prodigal' sun. James Logie
   ("Hugh Haliburton") Robertson. 6819-7
The **auld** house. Carolina Oliphant, Baroness Nairne. 6365-9,
   6086-2
The **auld** Kirk of Scotland. George Murray. 6180-X
Auld lanɪ syne. Robert Burns. 6086-2,6084-6,6219-9,6197-4,
   6153-2,6301 ,6192-3,6152-4,6560-0,6430-2,6150-4,6371
   ,6195-0,6723-9,6014-5,6024-2,6085-4,6102-8,6138-9,
   6180-,6186-9,6198-2,6240-7,6260-1,6271-7,6289-,6302-
   0,6328-4,6332-2,6385-3,6486-8,6501-,6527-9,6732-8,
   6646-1,6438-8,6543-0,6304
Auld lang syne. John White Chadwick. 6337-3,6730-1
The **auld** man's mear's dead. Patrick Birnie. 6845-6
Auld matrons. Unknown. 6185-0
Auld Rb Morris. Robert Burns. 6302-0,6737-9,6571-6

AULD

"Auld neebor/I'm three times...your debtor". To Davie: a brother poet, sels. Robert Burns. 6831-6
Auld robin gray. Lady Anne Lindsay. 6024-2,6240-7,6271-7, 6302-0,6385-3,6600 ,6086-2,6153-2,6438-8,6491-4,6560-0,6019-6,6102-8,6138-9,6180-X,6219-9,6410 ,6134-6, 6138-9,6198-2,6228-8,6246-6,6732 ,6102-8,6543-0
The auld smiddy end. James (1827-1888) Thomson. 6960-6
"The auld Stuarts back again". Unknown. 6859-6
"The auld wife sat at her ivied door". Ballad ("The auld wife"). Charles Stuart Calverley. 6440-X,6722-0,6512-0,6089-6,6501-5,6802-2
The auld wife. Charles Stuart Calverley. 6490-6
Ault, Norman
    Ducks. 6937-1
    The pig's tail. 6937-1
    A pinch of salt. 6937-1
    Without and within. 6337-3
'Aunt 'Mandy.' Joseph Crosby Lincoln. 6119-2
Aunt Beulah's wisdom. Earl Gene Box. 6870-7
Aunt Caroline. Annye Lewis Allison. 6799-9
Aunt Clara [pseud].
    Pussy's hiding place. 6131-1
Aunt Eliza. Harry ("Col. D. Streamer") Graham. 6722-0,6026-9,6125-7,6026-9,6125-7
Aunt Hannah. Harmon C. Wade. 6071-4
Aunt Jane. Alden A. Nowlan. 6218-0
Aunt Lizzie in who's who. E. Brightwen. 7020-5
Aunt Mary. Robert Stephen Hawker. 6292-X,6172-9
"Aunt Nellie had fashioned a dainty thing". Baby in church. Unknown. 6918-5
Aunt Phoebe's remonstrance. R.F. Williams Jr. 6116-8
Aunt Rhody's dream. Emma Dunning Banks. 6426-4
Aunt Selina. Carol Haynes. 6036-6
Aunt Shaw's pet jug. Holman F. Day. 7025-6
Aunt Sophy's notable experiment. Edward R. Huxley. 6885-5
Aunt Tabitha. Oliver Wendell Holmes. 6142-7,6249-0,6409-4, 6661-5,6739-5
Aunt Tabitha. Unknown. 6963-0
Aunt Tabitha. Unknown. 7022-1
Aunt Zillah speaks. Herbert Edward Palmer. 6210-5
Auqarius. Robert J. Burdette. 6588-0
Auras of delight, fr. The unknown eros. Coventry Patmore. 6315-2,6022-6
Auras on the interstates. Gerald Vizenor. 7005-1
Aurednicek, Otakar
    My deity. Paul Selver (tr.). 6763-8
Aurelia's valentine. Mary Kyle Dallas. 6671-2
Aurelius, Marcus. See Antoninus, Marcus
Aureng-Zebe, sels. John Dryden. 6562-7,6152-4,6195-0
Aurin, Emil Carl
    The conqueror. 6889-8
Auringer, O.C.
    God's country. 6920-7
Aurora. Peter Stevens. 6767-0
An aurora borealis. George Croly. 6980-0
Aurora Leigh, sels. Elizabeth Barrett Browning. 6123-0, 6239-3,6484-1,6730-1,6655-0,6656
Aurora's home. Elizabeth Barrett Browning. 6543-0
Aurousseau, Marcel
    The navigator. 6782-4
Aurum potabile. Bayard Taylor. 6976-2,6848-0
Auslander, Joseph
    Abraham Lincoln. 6736-0
    According to your dream. 6761-1
    Antipodal. 6039-0
    A blackbird suddenly. 6337-3,6076-5,6253-9,6653-4
    Cesar Franck. 6037-4
    Channel port. 6783-2
    Chart. 6039-0
    Crying, 'Thalassus!' 6036-6
    Dragnet. 6393-4
    Enigma. 6778-6
    An eye. 6779-4
    Foam stray. 6039-0
    Fog. 6071-4
    Gifts without season. 6337-3
    He is risen, sels. 6337-3
    Hill hunger. 6653-4
    Home-bound. 6762-X
    I come singing. 6034-X,6336-5
    In envy of cows. 6037-4,6777-8
    In memoriam. 6879-0
    Interval. 6070-6
    Interview with Lazarus. 6879-0
    Is this the lark! 6464-7,6581-3,6776-X
    Marked. 6070-6
    Not even Dante. 6879-0
    Now in the night. 6761-1
    Pendulum. 6076-5,6102-8
    The poets, sels. 6464-7
    The return. 6347-0
    The riveter. 6464-7
    Saint of France. 6439-6
    A sandal string. 6850-2
    Severus to Tiberius greatly. 6039-0
    Somewhere a lonely bird. 6036-6
    Somewhere I know. 6007-2
    Spilled flame. 6102-8,6076-5
    Steel. 6072-2,6217-2,6250-4,6808-1
    Sunrise trumpets. 6036-6
    Tangent. 6071-4
    Ten years after. 6542-2
    These evenings. 6761-1
    Three things. 6777-8,6102-8,6076-5,6037-4
    To my despoiler. 6777-8
    Touch. 6850-2
    Ulysses in autumn. 6464-7
    Water. 6850-2
    Where your feet go. 6039-0
    Wings at dawn. 6102-8,6069-2,6076-5,6076-5,6253-9
    Words. 6653-4
Auslander, Joseph (tr.)
    "Ah, had I ever thought the world would care". Francesco Petrarch, 6325-X
    "Already I grow weary thinking how". Francesco Petrarch, 6325-X
    "As over the fresh grass her golden feet". Francesco Petrarch, 6325-X
    "I find no peace and bear no arms for war". Francesco Petrarch, 6325-X
    "Rain fire from heaven down upon thy head." Francesco Petrarch, 6325-X
Ausonius, Decimus Magnus
    Idyll of the rose. John Addington Symonds (tr.). 6649-6
    To his wife. Terrot Reaveley Glover (tr.). 7039-6
Auspex. James Russell Lowell. 6243-1,6288-1,6126-5,6153-2, 6309-8
Auspice of jewels. Laura Riding. 6209-1
"Auspicious poet, wert thou not my friend". To Mr. Granville, afterwards Lord Lansdowne. John Dryden. 6970-3
Austen, Sarah (tr.)
    The passage. Johann Ludwig Uhland, 6606-2
Austerity of poetry. Matthew Arnold. 6102-8,6110-9,6199-0, 6250-4,6430-2,6437 ,6655-0,6828-6
Austin Dobson. Christopher Morley. 6483-3
Austin Dobson. Louis Untermeyer. 6875-8
Austin Dobson recites a ballade by way of retort. Louis Untermeyer. 6850-2
Austin Dobson: Mary, Mary. Charles Powell. 6982-7
"Austin! accept a grateful verse from me!". To Dr. Austin, of Cecil Street, London. William Cowper. 6814-6
Austin, Adam
    For lack of gold. 6180-X,6086-2
Austin, Alfred
    Agatha. 6656-9
    "All the running waves of eager life". 6997-5
    As dies the year. 6580-5
    At his grave (Hughenden, May, 1881). 6656-9
    At the lattice. 6652-6
    Ave Maria. 6570-8
    Britannia to Columbia. 6946-0
    "But when a sunny sevennight had passed". 6997-5
    Chorus of islanders. 7022-1
    Elegy. 6102-8
    England to America. 6084-6
    "Far off, the silent sea gloomed cold and gray". 6997-5
    "Feeble, shadowy, shallow?" 6997-5
    Grave-digger's song, fr. Prince Lucifer. 6656-9
    The haymaker's song. 6656-9

The human tragedy, sels. 6997-5
Is life worth living, sels. 6337-3
Is life worth living? 6793-X,6322-5
The last redoubt. 6744-1
"The long lithe wave/Now white fringed..." 6997-5
Love's blindness. 7015-9
Love's supremacy. 6094-3
Love's trinity. 6437-X
Love's wisdom. 7015-9
The lover's song. 6437-X
Mother-song, fr. Prince Lucifer. 6656-9
A night in June. 6658-5
Primroses. 6102-8,6437-X
Primroses. 6198-2,6102-8,6437-X
Prince Lucifer, sels. 6656-9
Savonarola and Lorenzo. 6382-9
A sleepless night. 7015-9
"Soon as they were afresh upon the sea". 6997-5
"The tide comes rolling in in ridgy sheets". 6997-5
Unseasonable snows. 7015-9
Victoria. 7022-1
A voice from the west. 6889-8,6639-9
A wild rose. 6226-1

Austin, Clarke
    Celibacy. 6022-6
Austin, Henry W.
    Legend of Crystal Spring. 6920-7
    The prince's hunting. 6921-5
Austin, J.O.
    A nun. 6285-7
Austin, John
    Blest be thy love, dear Lord. 6219-9
    Fain would my thoughts. 6931-2
    Hark, my soul. 6931-2
Austin, Mary
    The brown bear. 6891-X
    The eagle's song. 6979-7
    The rocky mountain sheep. 6891-X
    The shepherds in Judea. 6820-0,6608-9
    Women's war thoughts. 6036-6
    You go by in that street. 7038-8
Austin, Mary (tr.)
    Come not near my songs. Unknown (Shoshone Indian), 7039-6,6513-9
    The grass on the mountain. Unknown (Paiute Indian), 7039-6,6602-X
    Lament of a man for his son. Unknown (Paiute Indian), 7039-6,6602-X
    Love song. Unknown (Papago Indian), 7039-6
    Neither spirit nor bird. Unknown (Shoshone Indian), 6513-9,6241-5,7039-6
Austin, Sarah (tr.)
    The passage. Johann Ludwig Uhland, 6271-7,6385-3
Austin, William
    Carol ("All this night shrill chanticler"). 6563-5
    Chanticleer. 6931-2
    lullaby ("Sweet baby, sleep! what ails my dear"). 6931-2
    To a musician. 6931-2
Austral. See Wilson, Mrs. J.G.
Australasia. William Charles Wentworth. 6768-9
Australasia, sels. William Charles Wentworth. 6784-0
Australia. A.D. Hope. 6349-2
Australia. Agnes Neale. 6768-9
Australia. Bernard O'Dowd. 6384-5
Australia. Dowell O'Reilly. 6784-0
Australia. J. Laurence Rentoul. 6784-0
Australia infelix. William Gay. 6784-0
Australia to England. Archibald T. Strong. 6224-5,6474-4
Australia, 1894. William Gay. 6784-0
Australia, 1905. Archibald T. Strong. 6784-0
Australia, 1914. Archibald T. Strong. 6784-0
Australia, our land. C. Venn Pilcher. 6224-5
Australian federation. William Gay. 6784-0
An Australian girl. Ethel Castilla. 6656-9
An Australian girl. Sir John Suckling. 6768-9
Australian spring. Hugh McCrae. 6784-0
An Australian symphony. George Essex Evans. 6784-0
Australian transcripts, sels. William ("Fiona Macleod") Sharp. 6768-9

The Australian. Arthur Adams. 6784-0
Australians to the front! John Sandes. 6474-4
Australie. See Heron, Mrs. Hubert
Austrians. Josef Mayer-Limberg. 6769-7
Aut Caesar aut Nullus. Lilian White Spencer. 6096-X,6619-4
Autermont, Harriet du
    Some faith at any cost. 6337-3
The author and the statesman. Henry Fielding. 6278-4
The author loving these homely meats... John Davies of Hereford. 6182-6
"Author of light" Thomas Campion. 6794-8
The author of the "Pobble". Edward Lear. 6105-2
The author to her book. Anne Bradstreet. 6333-0,6288-1
The author to his booke. Thomas Heywood. 6933-9
Author to his child. Frances Airth. 6750-6
"An author who laid down the law". Limerick:"An author who laid down the law". Helen Taylor. 6811-1
The author's abstract of melancholy. Robert Burton. 6563-5
The author's account of himself. Robert Pollock. 6980-0
Author's entreaty for his lay, fr. Lilya. Eysteinn of Asgrimsson. 6282-2
The author's epitaph, made by himselfe. Sir Walter Raleigh. 6208-3,6430-2,6586-4
The author's miseries. Alexander Pope. 6302-0;6385-3
The author's purpose, fr. Don Juan. George Gordon, 6th Baron Byron. 6199-0
The author's resolution in a sonnet. George Wither. 6604-6, 6189-3,6660-7
The author's resolution. George Wither. 6102-8
"An author, by name Gilbert St. John". Limerick:"An author, by name Gilber St. John". P.T. Mannock. 6811-1
"An authoress, living at Trim". Limerick:"An authoress, living at Trim". Unknown. 6811-1
The authorised version of the bible, sel. gospel of St. Matthew. 6958-4
Authority. Samuel Butler. 6294-6
Authors and critics. Edward Young. 6250-4
"Authors are judg'd by strange capricious...". Three hours after marriage. John Gay. 6972-X
The authour's dreame. Francis Quarles. 6933-9
Auto wreck. Karl Shapiro. 6390-X,6491-4
Auto-da-fe. George A. Baker. 6187-7
Auto-suggestion. Georgette Agnew. 6804-9
Autobiographical. Douglas Barbour. 6767-0
Autobiographical. William Cowper. 6543-0
Autobiography. Louis MacNeice. 6210-5
Autobiography. Dorothy Parker. 6722-0
Autobiography. Mary Willis Shuey. 6761-1
Autobiography in fourteen chapters. R. L. 6662-3
Autobiography, chapter XVII: floating the big piney. Jim Barnes. 7005-1
An autobiography. Ernest Rhys. 6437-X,6656-9
Autochthon. Sir Charles George Douglas Roberts. 6597-X,6656-9
The autocrat of the breakfast table, sels. Oliver Wendell Holmes. 6332-2,6399-3
The autograph book of blue. H.W. Jakeway. 6688-7
An autograph. John Greenleaf Whittier. 6126-5
Autolicus's song, fr. The winter's tale. William Shakespeare. 6208-3,6315-2,6436-1,6722-0,6153-2
Autolycus' song (in basic English). Richard L. Greene. 6722-0
Automedon
    "O man, on thyself have mercy...". F.L. Lucas (tr.). 6251-9
Automne. Albert Samain. 6801-4
Automobile. Delmore Schwartz. 6850-2
The automobile. Percy MacKaye. 6102-8,6310-1,6509-0,6732-8, 6076-5,6464 ,6396-9
Autonomous. Mark Van Doren. 6391-8
Autres betes, autres moeurs. Ogden Nash. 6375-6
Autum' time. Jewell Bell McMurtrey. 6799-9
Autumn. William Aspenwall Bradley. 6031-5
Autumn. Myrtle W. Campbell. 6799-9
Autumn. Roy Campbell. 6044-7,6491-4
Autumn. Bliss Carman. 6053-6,6506-6,6653-4
Autumn. Alice Cary. 6865-0;6969-X
Autumn. John Clare. 6246-5
Autumn. John Clare. 6466-3
Autumn. John Clare. 6668-2

AUTUMN

Autumn. Walter De La Mare. 6246-5
Autumn. Emily Dickinson. 6307-1,6421-3,6723-9,6374-8,6466-3,6250-4,6253-9,6307-1
Autumn. Jean J. Eastly. 6799-9
Autumn. William Davis Gallagher. 6385-3
Autumn. John Galsworthy. 6888-X
Autumn. Jose Gorostiza. 6642-9
Autumn. Edgar A. Guest. 6869-3
Autumn. Edgar A. Guest. 6862-6
Autumn. Mrs. Hawtrey. 6131-1
Autumn. Hesiod. 6251-2
Autumn. Thomas Hood. 6018-8,6271-7,6272-5,6302-0,6385-3, 6334-9,6512
Autumn. Josef Hora. 6068-4
Autumn. Josephine Hoshaw. 6906-1
Autumn. T.E. Hulme. 6315-2,6209-1,6491-4
Autumn. Samuel Johnson. 6975-4
Autumn. John Keats. 6634-8
Autumn. Albert Laighton. 6373-X;6529-5
Autumn. Walter Savage Landor. 6086-2
Autumn. Francis Ledwidge. 6812-X
Autumn. Detlev von Liliencron. 7039-6
Autumn. Henry Wadsworth Longfellow. 6077-3,6558-9,6456 6
Autumn. James McAuley. 6349-7
Autumn. Harriet Monroe. 6959-2
Autumn. John Richard Moreland. 6326-8
Autumn. Rosa Mulholland; Lady Gilbert. 6174-5
Autumn. Nagata. 6027-7
Autumn. Thomas Nashe. 6315-2;6436-1;6182-6;6181-8
Autumn. John Frederick Nims. 6761-1
Autumn. William Oliver Bourne Peabody. 6752-2
Autumn. Hans Hartvig Seedorff Pederson. 6555-4
Autumn. Forrest Reid. 6244-X
Autumn. Rainer Maria Rilke. 6160-5
Autumn. Elizabeth Madox Roberts. 6037-4,6736-0
Autumn. William Robert Rodgers. 6379-9
Autumn. William Roehrick. 6850-2
Autumn. Christina Georgina Rossetti. 6828-6
Autumn. Christina Georgina Rossetti. 6828-6
Autumn. Arthur L. Salmon. 6782-6
Autumn. Will H. Skaling. 6799-9
Autumn. Ben H. Smith. 6662-3
Autumn. Edmund Spenser. 6820-0,6254-7,6239-3
Autumn. Carol Stein. 6850-2
Autumn. Rabindranath Tagore. 6730-1,6214-8
Autumn. James Thomson. 6315-2,6604-6,6660-7
Autumn. Feodor Ivanovich Tyutchev. 6622-4
Autumn. Unknown. 6273-3
Autumn. Unknown. 6752-2
Autumn. Jean Starr Untermeyer. 6332-2,6509-0,6556-2,6336-5, 6467-1
Autumn. Sir William Watson. 6437-X,6301-2
Autumn. Clement Wood. 6607-0
Autumn ("Sweet sabbath of the year"). Unknown. 6752-2
Autumn ("The dying year..."). William Oliver Bourne Peabody. 6752-2
"The autumn afternoon is dying o'er". The flight of crows. Emily Pauline ("Tekahionwake") Johnson. 6837-5
Autumn again. Stirling Bowen. 6880-4
Autumn alchemy. Luna Craven Osburn. 6799-9
Autumn and death. Amy Lowell. 6619-4
Autumn and spring. Julia Cooley Altrocchi. 6039-0
Autumn and winter, fr. Elegy to the memory of Mr. T. Philips. Thomas Chatterton. 6545-7
Autumn at Anoka. Florence Kreeger Hunting. 6342-X
Autumn ballet. Charles Wharton Stork. 6959-2
"Autumn blew out last night with the...stars". For my son on his twelfth birthday. Frances Frost. 6761-1
"The autumn breeze/Strips the last vestiges...". Plea. Sylvia Lapidus. 6850-2
"Autumn breezes through the branches". Picture songs. Edla Park Peck. 6836-7
Autumn by the sea. John Galsworthy. 6888-X
Autumn causerie. Jan Svatopluk Machar. 6763-8
Autumn chant. Edna St. Vincent Millay. 6102-8,6232-6,6250-4,6161-3,6076-5,6581
"The autumn comes, a maiden fair". Autumnn, fr. The seasons. Kalidasa. 7039-6
Autumn communion. Gladys Cromwell. 6032-3
Autumn crickets. Glenn Ward Dresbach. 6850-2

The autumn cry. Unknown. 6118-4
Autumn dawn. Helen B. L. Bayley. 6798-0
An autumn day. George Crabbe. 6659-3
An autumn day. John Addington Symonds. 6252-0
Autumn daybreak. Edna St. Vincent Millay. 6299-7
Autumn days. Maybelle Mayne Porter. 6841-3
"Autumn deepens" Sojin Takei. 6981-9
Autumn dialogue. Louis Untermeyer. 6012-9
Autumn dusk. Sara Teasdale. 6070-6
Autumn dusk, fr. Berkshire notes. Sara Teasdale. 6778-6
"Autumn eats its leaf out of my hand: we...". Corona. Paul Celan. 6758-1
Autumn evening. Francis Scarfe. 6895-2
Autumn evening in Serbia. Francis Ledwidge. 6812-X,7027-2
The autumn evening. William Oliver Bourne Peabody. 6752-2
Autumn evenings. Edgar A. Guest. 7033-7
Autumn evensong. George Meredith. 6383-7
Autumn fancies. Unknown. 6496-5
Autumn fashions. Edith Matilda Thomas. 6820-0
"The autumn fills the sky". Counting the stars. Dong-ju Yun. 6775-1
The autumn fire. Geoffrey Johnson. 6761-1
Autumn fires. Robert-Louis Stevenson. 6232-6,6623-2,6252-0
Autumn flight. Alexander Karanikas. 6764-6
An autumn flitting. George Cotterell. 6656-9
Autumn flowers. Caroline Anne Bowles Southey. 6271-7
Autumn flowers. Jones Very. 6333-0
Autumn fruits, fr. Aella. Thomas Chatterton. 6545-7
An autumn garden. Bliss Carman. 6374-8
Autumn glory. Edith Edwards Waldron. 6894-4
Autumn glow. Joshua Freeman Crowell. 6798-0
An autumn god. Margaret W. Paradise. 7014-0
"Autumn hath all the summer's fruitful treasure". Autumn. Thomas Nashe. 6315-2;6436-1;6182-6;6181-8
Autumn haze. Richard Kendall Munkittrick. 6465-5
Autumn healing. Jean Ward. 6299-7
Autumn hickory trees. George A. Scarborough. 6761-1
"Autumn hides behind the summer sun". Barely autumn. Jean Levicki. 6857-X
The autumn house. George M. Brady. 6930-4
Autumn hunter. Mary Howard. 6857-X
Autumn idleness, fr. The house of life. Dante Gabriel Rossetti. 6123-0,6526-0,6655-0
Autumn in a New Hampshire village. Joan Andrews. 6764-6
Autumn in Carmel. George Sterling. 6619-4
Autumn in Connecticut. Henrietta Cholmeley-Jones. 6894-4
Autumn in England. Colin Mitchell. 6650-X
Autumn in my garden. Marion MacKenzie. 6818-9
Autumn in spring. John Summers. 7018-3
Autumn in the garden. Henry Van Dyke. 6961-4
Autumn in the highlands. John Campbell Shairp. 6253-9
Autumn in the park. Thomas Hardy. 7020-5
"Autumn is weary, halt, and old". The October redbreast. Alice Meynell. 6955-X
Autumn journal VII. Louis MacNeice. 6666-6
Autumn leaf. John Richard Moreland. 6042-0
An autumn leaf. Harry Emerson Fosdick. 6118-4
Autumn leaves. Celestin Pierre Cambiaire. 6826-X
Autumn leaves. William Wilfred Campbell. 6843-X
Autumn leaves. Emily Collins. 6764-6
Autumn leaves. Janie Screven Heyward. 6036-6
Autumn leaves. Thomas Wentworth Higginson. 6049-8
Autumn leaves. George Kett. 6800-6
Autumn leaves. Elizabeth Dimon Preston. 6836-7
Autumn leaves. Margaret P. Sutphen. 6466-3
Autumn leaves. Unknown. 6373-X
Autumn leaves. William White. 6868-5
Autumn leaves. Angelina Wray. 6964-9
"Autumn leaves in flaming flight". To D.M. Gilbert O'Connon. 6850-2
"The autumn leaves went whispering by". A ballad. Riccardo Stephens. 6873-1
The autumn leaves. Unknown. 6049-8
Autumn love. Alexander Blok. 6103-6
Autumn love. John Crowe Ransom. 7017-5
Autumn love. William Fred Sachs. 6906-1
Autumn memories. George F. Savage-Armstrong. 6656-9
Autumn moon. Marcia G. Kester. 6857-X
Autumn morning at Cambridge. Frances Cornford. 6331-4,6437-X,6506-6

Autumn movement. Carl Sandburg. 6033-1,6556-2
Autumn musing. Marie T. Copp. 6799-9
Autumn night in Fresno. Eda Lou Walton. 6777-8
Autumn pageant. Mary Hume Mills. 7016-7
Autumn ploughing. Hesiod. 6251-2
An autumn riddle. Unknown. 6623-2
The autumn river glowing with lamentation. Jae-sam Park. 6775-1
An autumn rose-tree. Michael Earls. 6096-X,6172-9,6292-X
Autumn scene. Edgar A. Guest. 6869-3
Autumn sea. George Edward Woodberry. 6253-9
An autumn serenade. John B.L. Warren, 3d Baron De Tabley. 7020-5
Autumn silence. Arthur S. Bourinot. 6115-X
Autumn song. Padraic Colum. 6582-1
Autumn song. Edward Dowden. 6930-4
Autumn song. Lydia Gibson. 6880-4
Autumn song. William Griffith. 6102-8,6076-5
Autumn song. Conrad Orton Milliken. 6936-3
Autumn song. Dante Gabriel Rossetti. 6110-9
Autumn song. Duncan Campbell Scott. 6433-7
Autumn song. Edmund Clarence Stedman. 6373-X
Autumn song. Unknown. 6272-5
An autumn song. Bliss Carman. 6653-4
The autumn stroll. Virgie Rucker Howerton. 6906-1
"The autumn sun is shining, round and gay". Laughter. Mary Craig Sinclair. 6954-1
Autumn tourists. Unknown. 6358-6
Autumn tree. Witter Bynner. 6783-2
An autumn trinket. Thomas Edward Brown. 6809-X
Autumn tumbleweeds. Orpha Gullickson. 6342-X
"The autumn upon us was rushing". Ravings. Thomas Hood Jr. 6802-2
Autumn voices. F.W. B. 6049-8
An autumn walk with Deborah. Aline Kilmer. 6033-1
An autumn wedding song. Algernon Tassin. 6116-8
Autumn wind. Alfred D. Butts. 6799-9
Autumn wind. George Dillon. 6253-9
"The autumn wind-oh, hear it howl!". Hallowe'en. Arthur Cleveland Coxe. 6820-0
Autumn woods. William Cullen Bryant. 6126-5
Autumn Woods. Blanche Shoemaker Wagstaff. 7038-8
Autumn's altar. Etta M. Graves. 6764-6
Autumn's gypsies. Laurel Jane Spitler. 6799-9
Autumn's mirth. Samuel Minturn Peck. 6239-3
Autumn's orchestra. Emily Pauline ("Tekahionwake") Johnson. 6837-5
Autumn's processional. Dinah Maria Mulock Craik. 6239-3, 6239-3
Autumn's sighing. Thomas Buchanan Read. 6271-7
Autumn's work. Unknown. 6529-5
"Autumn, be kind to her, slow your arrival". Prayer for a girl no longer young. Ina Draper DeFoe. 6750-6
Autumn, forsake these hills. Frank Ernest Hill. 6808-1
Autumn, fr. Four songs, after Verlaine. Alfred Noyes. 6151-6
Autumn, fr. In memoriam. Alfred Lord Tennyson. 6597-X
Autumn, fr. The fields of dawn. Lloyd Mifflin. 6597-X
Autumn, fr. Thistledown. Cora Fabri. 6876-6
"Autumn, here, is always a tug at the gut". Journal entries written by light through a Princeton... Geraldine Little. 7032-9
Autumn, sels. James Thomson. 6122-2,6198-2
Autumn: a dirge. Percy Bysshe Shelley. 6133-8,6302-0,6385-3,6023-4,6219-9,6668-2,6179-6,6271-7,6328-4,6228-8, 6334-9
Autumn: allegro con fuoco, fr. Time is a dream. Lillian V. Inke. 6640-2
Autumn: or Hylas and Aegon. Alexander Pope. 6191-5
Autumn; each in his own tongue. William Herbert Carruth. 6891-X
The autumn. Elizabeth Barrett Browning. 6123-0
The autumn. Unknown. 6529-5
Autumnal. Marie Emilie Gilchrist. 6619-4
Autumnal. Ann Louise Hayes. 6515-5
Autumnal. Richard Middleton. 6338-1
Autumnal. Lewis Spence. 6269-5
Autumnal beauty. John Donne. 6935-5
Autumnal clouds. John Gould Fletcher. 6348-9
Autumnal dreams. Bayard Taylor. 6976-2

Autumnal ecstasy. Charles Wharton Stork. 6038-2
An autumnal evening. William ("Fiona Macleod") Sharp. 6236-9
Autumnal ode, sels. Thomas Hood. 6395-0
The autumnal rain song. Stevan Lukovic. 6765-4
Autumnal rhythm. Laban Thomas Johnston. 6316-0
Autumnal sonnet. William Allingham. 7015-9
Autumnal strolls 1 Milutin Bojic. 6765-4
Autumnal vespers. Bayard Taylor. 6976-2
The autumnall. John Donne. 6378-0,6562-7
Autumn, fr. The seasons. Kalidasa. 7039-6
Autumnus. Joshua Sylvester. 6182-6,6317-9,6562-7
Autumnus. Joshua Sylvester. 6933-9
Auvache, Elizabeth V.
    December. 6799-9
Auvergnat. Hilaire Belloc. 6339-X,6423-X
Aux carmelites. Katharine (Hinkson) Tynan. 6930-4
Aux Italiens. Owen (Edward Bulwer-Lytton, Earl Lytton) Meredith. 6046-3,6155-9,6304-7,6585-6,6277-6,6413-2, 6605-4,6378-5,6732-8,6656 ,6302-0,6385-3,6219-9,6102-8,6451-5
The auxiliary cruiser. N.M.F. Corbett. 7027-2
The avalanche. Unknown. 6410-8
Avalanches. Helen Hunt Jackson. 7041-8
Avalanches. Helen Hunt Jackson. 6749-2
Avalon. Thomas Holley Chivers. 6754-9
Avalon. Donald Davidson. 6326-8
Avar inroad. Jan Svatopluk Machar. 6886-3
Avarice. Howard Kohner. 6850-2
Avarice. William Langland. 6489-2
Avaro. Samuel Taylor Coleridge. 6278-4
Avaro, a tale. Thomas Warton (the Elder) 6962-2
"Avast, honest Jack! now, before you...mellow". The battleof Erie. Unknown. 6946-0
Avatar and the manger. Harry William Nelson. 6799-9
The avatar. W.E. Davenport. 7001-9
Avatars. Babette Deutsch. 6037-4
Ave. Walter Adolphe Roberts. 6034-X
Ave. Dante Gabriel Rossetti. 6282-2,6657-7,6508-2,6655-0
Ave. Dante Gabriel Rossetti. 6931-2
"Ave Maria! bright and pure". Ora pro me. Adelaide Anne Procter. 6957-6
Ave atque vale. Aubrey Beardsley. 6096-X
Ave atque vale. Algernon Charles Swinburne. 6483-3,6102-8, 6250-4,6430-2,6508-2,6301-2,6655-0
Ave atque vale. John Banister Tabb. 6006-4
Ave atque vale. Rosamund Marriott ("Graham R. Tomson") Watson. 6656-9
Ave atque vale (I). Thomas S. Jones Jr. 6653-4
Ave atque vale, fr. Sigismonda and Guiscardo. John Dryden. 6933-9
Ave Caesar! Rudolph Chambers Lehmann. 7008-6
Ave crux, spes unica! Edward Shillito. 6144-3,6337-3
Ave imperatrix. Oscar Wilde. 6271-7,6656-9
Ave imperatrix, sels. Oscar Wilde. 6427-2
Ave Maria. Alfred Austin. 6570-8
Ave Maria. Florence Mary Bennett. 6847-2
Ave Maria. Henriette Charasson. 6282-2
Ave Maria. John Jerome Rooney. 6022-6,6172-9
Ave Maria bells. Charles Warren Stoddard. 6292-X,6282-2, 6172-9
Ave Maria gratia plena. Oscar Wilde. 6022-6,6144-3,6335-7, 6096-X,6282-6,6292
Ave Maria, fr. Don Juan. George Gordon, 6th Baron Byron. 6282-2,6332-2
Ave Maria, fr. The lady of the lake. Sir Walter Scott. 6282-2
Ave maris stella. Unknown. 6282-2,6214-8
Ave regina coelorum. Unknown. 6282-2
"Ave rosa sine spinis." Unknown. 6563-5
"'Ave you 'eard o' the window at Windsor". The window at Windsor. Rudyard Kipling. 6810-3
"Ave! now let prayer and music". Spanish evening hymn. Felicia Dorothea Hemans. 6973-8
Ave, Caesar!, fr. In hospital. William Ernest Henley. 6508-2
Ave, fr. Ane Ballat of our Lady. William Dunbar. 6324-1
Ave, mater--atque vale. William Noel Hodgson. 6477-9
Ave, vita nostra. Clifford J. Laube. 6282-2
Ave: Sidney anier. John Banister Tabb. 6121-4

Avenel Gray. Edwin Arlington Robinson. 6531-7,6069-2,6037-4
"Avenge O Lord thy slaughter'd Saints, whose bones". John Milton. 6562-7;6087-0
"Avenge, O Lord! thy slaughtered saints". Sonnet ("Avenge, O Lord"). John Milton. 6563-5,6023-4
Avenged!. Alfred Berlyn. 6681-X
The avenger. Berton Braley. 6853-7
The avenging childe. John Gibson Lockhart. 6344-6
The avenging childe. Unknown (Spanish) 6757-3
The avenging childe. Unknown (Spanish) 6676-3
"The Avenue of the Allies". Alfred Noyes. 6151-6
The avenue, fr. Facade. Edith Sitwell. 7000-0
Avenzoar
    Drinking song ("A house well supplied.") A.J. Arberry (tr.). 6362-4
    In absence. A.J. Arberry (tr.). 6362-4
    Revenge. A.J. Arberry (tr.). 6362-4
The average boy. Pauline Phelps. 6687-9
The average man. William Langland. 6489-2
The average man. Margaret Elizabeth Sangster. 6583-X
The average man. Edgar A. Guest. 6862-6
Averill, Anna Boynton
    A little milkmaid. 6965-7
Avery. William Dean Howells. 7041-8
Avery Anameer. Joseph Payne Brennan. 6218-0
Avery, Claribel Weeks
    Death and a rose. 6764-6
    The door is now shut. 6789-1
    Rose of remembrance. 6764-6
Avery, Selina B.
    Mirage. 6764-6
Avgeris, Markos
    Granny Tassia. Rae Dalven (tr.). 6352-7
    Plebian song. Rae Dalven (tr.). 6352-7
The aviator. Dorothy Alyea. 7019-X
The aviator. Alexander Blok. 6978-9
The aviator. Lilian Sauter. 7023-X
"Avid of life and love, insatiate vagabond". Verlaine. Bliss Carman and Richard Hovey. 6890-1
Avila, Anne Harley
    Grime. 6750-6
Avis. Oliver Wendell Holmes. 6127-3
Avison, Margaret
    Goal far and near. 6767-0
    Knowledge of age. 6446-9
    Meeting together of poles and latitudes: in prospect. 6446-9
    Perspective. 6446-9
    Setting for the portrait. 6767-0
    Tennis. 6446-9
"Avoid them, as a serpent's hiss". Gossipers. Edward R. Huxley. 6885-5
Avoirdupois. Unknown. 6724-7
The Avon and the Thames. Arthur Upson. 6331-4,6631-3
Avon memories. Leyland Huckfield. 6033-1
The Avon valley. William Cobbett. 7020-5
"Avon, thy rural views, thy pastures wild". Monody written near Stratford-upon-Avon. Thomas Warton Jr.. 6867-7
Avond, Jan van. See Slater, Francis Carey
Avowal. Minnie Markham Kerr. 6750-6
Avowal. A.M. Sullivan. 6292-X
Avrett, Robert
    The wake. 6648-8
Avril. Remi Belleau. 7020-5
Aw gee whiz! Edgar A. Guest. 7033-7
"Aw, Billy, good sowl! don't cuss! don't cuss!". Mater dolorosa. Thomas Edward Brown. 6809-X
"Aw, I daresay you'll hardly cwedit the stowy". A gallant wescue. W. Sapte Jr.. 6920-7
Awa, Whigs, awa. Unknown. 6859-6
Awaiting the barbarians. Constantine P. Cavafy. 6352-7
Awake. Cecilia Bustamante. 7036-1
"Awake - again the gospel-trump is blown". Advent Sunday. John Keble. 6980-0
"Awake and mourn; let all the nations shed". Eulogy. Leonard G. Foster. 6820-0
"Awake faire muse, for I intend". An ode ("Awake"). William Browne. 6562-7
Awake in arkness. John James Piatt. 7041-8

"Awake thee, my Bessy, the morning is fair". Song ("Awake thee"). Jeremiah [or James] Joseph Callanan. 6930-4
Awake under the stars. Raymond Holden. 6979-7
"Awake without knowing it". In the middle of the night. Duncan Mitchel. 7003-5
Awake!. William Robert Rodgers. 6390-X,6666-6
Awake!. Sir Walther von der Vogelweide. 7039-6
"Awake! arise, ye men of might!". To arms. Paul Benjamin. 6946-0
"Awake! arise, ye patriot brave". A war-song. Eugene Field. 6949-5
Awake! awake! Elmer Ruan Coates. 6403-5
Awake! awake! Unknown. 6720-4
"Awake! awake! my gallant friends". The battle of Tippecanoe. Unknown. 6946-0
"Awake! The day is coming now". Awake! Sir Walther von der Vogelweide. 7039-6
"Awake! awake! the stars are pale..." John Ruskin. 6478-7
"Awake! ye forms of verse divine". The national painting, fr. Croaker papers. Fitz-Greene Halleck and Joseph Rodman Drake. 6753-0
"'Awake, arise, or be for ever fall'n'". Satan awakens all his legions, fr. Paradise lost. John Milton. 6958-4
"Awake, arise, pull out your eyes". Unknown. 6363-2
Awake, arise, thy light is come. Thomas Moore. 6848-0
"Awake, arise, you dead men all-dead women...". Hallowe'en. Nora Hopper. 6820-0
Awake, awake my lyre! Abraham Cowley. 6563-5
"Awake, awake! Thou heavy sprite. Thomas Campion. 6214-8, 6794-8
'Awake, awake!' Frank Dempster Sherman. 6875-8
"Awake, awake, O gracious heart". Frank Dempster Sherman. 6850-2
"Awake, awake, nay, slumber not, nor sleep!". The new epiphany. Samuel Waddington. 6875-8
"Awake, awake, nay, slumber not, not sleep!". The new epiphany. Samuel Waddington. 6770-0
"Awake, awake, o gracious heart". 'Awake, awake!' Frank Dempster Sherman. 6875-8
"Awake, awake/Put on thy strength, O Zion". Consurge, consurge. Bible. 6830-8
Awake, mine eyes! Unknown. 6182-9
"Awake, my glory, ere the rosy morn". Psalm 057. Bible. 6848-0
Awake, my heart. Robert Bridges. 6186-9,6204-0,6266-0,6437-X,6477-9,6487,6655-0,6656-9,6737-9
Awake, my love. Allan Cunningham. 6980-0
Awake, my soul. James O. Walker. 6894-4
Awake, my soul! Philip Doddridge. 6214-8
"Awake, my soul". Thomas Ken. 6931-2
"Awake, my soul, and with the sun". A morning hymne. Thomas Ken. 6933-9
"Awake, my soul, stretch every nerve." Philip Doodridge. 6001-3
'Awake, psaltery and harp; I myself will awake early'. Unknown. 6752-2
"Awake, sad heart, whom sorrow ever drowns" George Herbert. 6935-5
"Awake, thou spring of speaking grace, mute rest..." Thomas Campion. 6794-8
"Awake, ye nations, slumbering supine". Sonnet ("Awake, ye nations"). George Edward Woodberry. 7026-4
"Awaken! For the servitors of spring". The conqueror passes. James Branch Cabell. 6875-8,6850-2
The awakened war god. Margaret Widdemer. 6730-1
Awakening. Rose Terry Cooke. 6177-X
Awakening. Julia C.R. Dorr. 6327-6
Awakening. Edward Dowden. 7015-9
Awakening. Dorothy Hobson. 6979-7
Awakening. Mabel Endresen Miller. 6342-X
Awakening. Mildred Solwan. 6850-2
Awakening. H. Stuart. 6072-2
Awakening of Endymion. Letitia Elizabeth ("L.E.L.") Landon. 6219-9
The awakening of Italy, fr. The dead year. James ("B.V.") Thomson. 7009-4
The awakening of man, fr. Paracelsus. Robert Browning. 6730-1
The awakening of spring. Alfred Lord Tennyson. 6457-4,6669-0

The awakening of Uncle Sam. Sam Walter Foss. 6741-X
The awakening year. Thomas Buchanan Read. 6049-8
The awakening, fr. Lily and lute. Jean Ingelow. 6689-5
The awakening.. Angela Morgan. 6338-1
The awakening.. Cyrus L. Sulzberger II. 6640-2
An awakening. Alice Furlong. 6090-0
The awakening. Rubye Arnold. 7016-7
The awakening. Patrick Reginald Chalmers. 6249-0
The awakening. Jeanne Robert Foster. 6320-9
The awakening. Harry Lee. 6761-1
The awakening. Bernard Welland. 6799-9
Awaking, Belinda prepares for the day..., fr. Rape. Alexander Pope. 6637-2
Aware of spring. Lionel Wiggam. 6640-2
Awareness. Miriam Teichner. 6291-1,6337-3,6490-6
Away. James Whitcomb Riley. 6260-1,6303-9,6337-3,6730-4
"Away beyond the Jarboe house". Strange tree. Elizabeth Madox Roberts. 6891-X
"Away by the lands of the Japanee". Rhyme of the three sealers. Rudyard Kipling. 6810-3
"Away down east where I was reared". Mary Smith. Eugene Field. 6949-5
"Away from city chafe and care". Triolets ("Away from"). Cotsford Dick. 6770-0
"Away from home I am nothing...". Sophocles. 6435-3
"Away from the din of the city". Call of the open. Laura E. Bradshaw. 6799-9
Away from the wine-cup, away!. Unknown. 6408-6
"Away goes Sussex William and his pack". William Cowper. 6814-6
Away in a manger. Martin Luther. 6337-3
"Away in the dim and distant past". Sunset. Phoebe Cary. 6969-X
"Away my verse; and never fear." Walter Savage Landor. 6086-2,6110-9
"Away on the glist'ning plain we go". The skaters song. Unknown. 7035-3
Away out on the mountain. Kelly Harrell. 6179-6
Away to Twiver, away, away! Unknown. 6182-6
"Away to the Alps". The chamois hunters. Charles Swain. 6980-0
"Away to the sea! the sea!/Cheerily!". Song of the brook-ripples. James Abraham Martling. 6952-5
"Away with all life's memories". Trust (2). Alice Cary. 6969-X
Away with bloodshed. Alfred Edward Housman. 6722-0
"Away with ferrets, traps and cats". Warning the rats in Vermont. Daniel L. Cady. 6989-4
"Away with the blast of the wind that blows". The mermaids. Gwynne Abbott. 6799-9
"Away with this cash." Unknown. 6563-5
"Away with your fictions of flimsy romance". The first kiss of love. George Gordon, 6th Baron Byron. 6945-2
"Away yee barb'rous woods", fr. Polyolbion. Michael Drayton. 6933-9
Away!. Bertha Ochsner. 6887-1
"Away! The moor is dark beneath the moon." Percy Bysshe Shelley. 6138-9
"Away! ancestral caste, away!". Ancestral caste. Edward R. Huxley. 6885-5
"Away! away! our fires stream bright". The skater's song. Ephraim Peabody. 7035-3
"'Away! away! to the ocean's blue!'". A fable. James Abraham Martling. 6952-5
"Away! the moor is dark". Stanzas ("Away"). Percy Bysshe Shelley. 6315-2
"Away! though still thy sword is red". Song, founded on an Arabian anecdote. Felicia Dorothea Hemans. 6973-8
"Away, 'way off' cross the seas and such". The little toy land of the Dutch. Unknown. 6891-X
"Away, away in the northland". A legend of the northland. Phoebe Cary. 6135-4,6964-9,6060-9
"Away, away o'er the glittering snow". A snow-shoe tramp. Beatrice Harlowe. 7035-3
Away, away! Percy Bysshe Shelley. 6634-8
Away, away, vex me no more. Unknown. 6563-5
"Away, away, ye notes of wo". Stanzas ("Away, away"). George Gordon, 6th Baron Byron. 6980-0
Away, away, ye notes of woe! George Gordon, 6th Baron Byron. 6945-2

"Away, away, youf flattering arts". Lines written in Rousseau's Letters of an Italian nun.. George Gordon, 6th Baron Byron. 6945-2
"Away, delights! go seek some other dwelling." John Fletcher. 6317-9,6182-6
"Away, far off in China, many, may years ago". Cho-che-Bang and Chi-chil-Bloo. Unknown. 6911-8
"Away, fond dupes! who, smit with sacred love". Architectural atoms. Horace Smith. 6802-2
"Away, let nought to love displeasing". Winifreda. Unknown. 6874-X
"Away, sad th ughts, and teasing". The children dancing. Laurence Binyon. 6884-7
"Away, those cloudy looks, that lab'ring sigh". Lines addressed to a friend, in answer to..melancholy letter. Samuel Taylor Coleridge. 6967-3
"Away, useless trifles!...". Of the sad lot of the humanists in Paris. George Buchanan. 6845-6
"Away, ye gay landscapes, ye gardens of roses". Lachin y Gair. George Gordon, 6th Baron Byron. 6110-9,6196-6, 6438-3,6859-6,6945-2
"Away; let nought to love displeasing". Unknown. 6932-0
Awdlay (atr), John
  The flower of Jesse. 6756-5
"Aweary, wounded unto death". All in all. Alice Cary. 6969-X
"Awed by thy firmament above/Confused by...". The agnostic's prayer. Demps Alexander Oden. 6799-9
Awee. Nia Francisco. 7005-1
An awful fate. Carolyn Wells. 6882-0
Awful hazardous. Charles Irvin Junkin. 6274-1
"The awful line between north and south". Poem written before Mother's day for Mrs. Lopez from... R. Wayne Hardy. 6870-7
An awful responsibility. Keith Preston. 6722-0
"An awful storm has wrecked our bark". Wrecked. William White. 6868-5
'Awful!'. Peter Remsen Strong. 6004-8
"Awhile forget the scene of woe". Ode on the birthday of Princes Charles Edward Stuart. Unknown. 6859-6
Awkward. J. Cheever Goodwin. 6416-7
The awkward squad. Unknown. 6859-6
The axolotl.. David McCord. 6722-0
Axon, W.E.A.
  New Year's day. 6747-6
Ay. Alfred Lord Tennyson. 6977-0
"Ay me! for aught that ever...", fr. A midsummer... William Shakespeare. 6726-3
"Ay me, alas! the beautiful bright hair". Canzone: His lament for Selvaggia. Cino da Pistoia. 7039-6
"Ay me, ay me! I sigh to see the scythe afield". Thomas Proctor. 6181-8
"Ay me, ay me, I sigh to see...". Unknown. 6334-9
"Ay me, ay me, the mallow in the mead". Unknown. 6435-3
Ay waukin, O. Robert Burns. 6180-X
"Ay! drop the treacherous mask! throw by". Butler's proclamation. Paul Hamilton Hayne. 6946-0
"Ay, build her long and narrow and deep". Atlantic. Benjamin Franklin Taylor. 6815-4
Ay, but to die, fr. Measure for measure. William Shakespeare. 6634-8,6102-8
"Ay, give all honor to the man". A vision of hands. Benjamin Franklin Taylor. 6815-4
"Ay, gloriously thou standest there". The skies. William Cullen Bryant. 6752-2
"Ay, guitarrist of the roots". Romanza of the guitarrist. Raul Otero Reiche. 6759-X
"Ay, if a madman could have leave." John Keats. 6482-5
"Ay, it is fitting on this holiday". Ode in memory of the American volunteers fallen..France. Alan Seeger. 6946-0
"Ay, let it rest! And give us peace". The gospel of peace. James Jeffrey Roche. 6946-0
"Ay, many flowering islands lie". The rooks. Percy Bysshe Shelley. 6943-6
"Ay, me, poor soul, whom bound in sinful...". A dialogue. A. W.. 6935-5
"Ay, pale and silent maiden". A requiem. James Russell Lowell. 6486-8
"Ay, ring thy shout to the merry hours". Lines occasioned

AY, 88

by hearing a little boy mock...clock.. Lydia Maria
  Child. 6752-2
"Ay, shout and rave, thou cruel sea". Herndon. Silas Weir
  Mitchell. 6946-0
"Ay, take them to the college! let them be". The dying
  missionary. Charles W. Denison. 6755-7
"Ay, there they are/Nobles, and sons of nobles". The royal
  masque, fr. Charles the first. Percy Bysshe Shelley.
  7009-4
"Ay, this was wont to be a festal time". The vespers of
  Palermo. Felicia Dorothea Hemans. 6973-8
"Ay, thou art for the grave; thy glances shine". Sonnet to
  ---. William Cullen Bryant. 6752-2
"Ay, thou art welcome - heaven's...breath!". Sonnet ("Ay,
  thou art welcome"). William Cullen Bryant. 6752-2
"Ay, thou art welcome, heaven's". October ("Ay, thou art
  welcome"). Unknown. 6523-6
"Ay, warrior, arm! and wear thy plume". Death and the
  warrior. Felicia Dorothea Hemans. 6973-8
"Aya ahaniquo/I am here only". Ayohu Kanogisdi death song.
  Carroll Arnett Gogisgi. 7005-1
"Aye me can love and bewtie soe conspire." Unknown. 6563-5
"Aye me! that loue should natures workes...". A booke of
  Ayres (XIII). Thomas Campion. 6794-8
Aye waukin' O! Unknown. 6845-6
"Aye! exactly - that's the name". The Indiaman. Thomas
  Edward Brown. 6809-X
Aye, but to die, fr. Measure for measure. William
  Shakespeare. 6934-7
"Aye, ladsm aye, we fought 'em". 'Off Manilly'. Edmund
  Vance Cooke. 6946-0
"Aye, not a doubt 'twas dark without". The storm. Arthur
  Patchett Martin. 6768-9
"Aye, Silver Street is where I lodge". Write I will.
  Nanita MacDonell Balcom. 6761-1
"Aye, snows are rife in December". Doubtful dreams. Adam
  Lindsay Gordon. 6951-7
"Aye, that's our woman's way. We lean on faith". Woman's
  way. Cora Fabri. 6876-6
Aye-Williams, Ernest
  Mid the breakers. 6927-4
Ayer, Ethan
  An exceeding great army. 6218-0
Aylmer's field. Alfred Lord Tennyson. 6669-0
Aylmer's field, sels. Alfred Lord Tennyson. 6239-3
Ayme, ayme, I sigh to see the scythe field. Unknown. 6472-8
Ayne, Blythe
  "This trip" 6998-3
Ayohu Kanogisdi death song. Carroll Arnett Gogisgi. 7005-1
Ayres, Alfred (tr.)
  Lenora. August Burger, 6675-5
Ayres, Philip
  Complains, being hindered the sight of his nymph. 6563-5
  Endymion and Diana. 6023-4
  On a fair beggar. 6563-5
  On old Rome. 6023-4
  A sonnet. On the death of Sylvia. 6908-8
  To love. 6152-4
  To the nightingale. 6152-4
  To the winds. 6152-4
Ayres, Philip (tr.)
  Dream of his lady ("Fair eyes, ye mortal..."). Giovanni
    Battista Guarini, 6325-X
Ayroun, William
  Puffa poetical. 6278-4
Ayscough and Amy Lowell, Florence (tr.)
  The battle to the south of the city. Li Po, 6102-8
  The blue-green stream. Wang Wei, 6253-9
  On hearing a bamboo flute. Li Po, 6649-6
  Once more fields and gardens. T'ao Yuan-Ming, 6649-6
  Written in early autumn at the pool of sprinkling
    water. Chao-ti of Han, 6253-9
Ayton, Sir Robert
  I do confess thou'rt smooth and fair. 6092-7
  "I lov'd thee once, I'll love no more". 6933-9
  I'll love no more. 6934-7
  Inconstancy reproved. 6180-X
  To an inconstant mistress. 6180-X

To his forsaken mistress. 6102-8,6219-9
Upon a diamond cut in forme of a heart set with a
  crown. 6933-9
"When thou did thinke I did not love". 6933-9
Woman's inconstancy. 6092-7
"Wrong not sweete empress of my heart". 6933-9
Aytoun, William Edmonstoune
  AEnone. 6980-0
  The ballad of Lycaon. 6948-7
  The battle of the boulevard. 6278-4
  The biter bite. 6278-4
  Blind old Milton. 6948-7
  Bothwell. 6948-7
  The broken pitcher. 6948-7
  Burial march of Dundee. 6219-9
  The buried flower. 6948-7
  Charles Edward at Versailles. 6948-7
  Comfort in affliction. 6278-4
  The crusaders' march. 6948-7
  Dame Fredegonde. 6278-4
  Danube and the Euxine. 6948-7
  Dead Dundee, fr. The burial march of Dundee. 6934-7
  The dirge of the drinker. 6278-4
  Edinburgh after Flodden. 6219-9,6370-5,6263-6
  The elder's warning. 6948-7
  The empty bottle. 6278-4
  The execution of Montrose. 6370-5,6552-X,6167-2,6291-9,
    6263-6,6424,6656-9
  The execution of Montrose. 6948-7
  The fight with the snapping turtle. 6948-7
  Firmilian. 6948-7
  Francesca da Rimini. 6278-4
  The golden age. 6948-7
  The heart of the Bruce. 6370-5,6613-5,6263-6
  Hermotimus. 6437-X
  Homer. 6948-7
  The husband's petition. 6278-4
  Idees Napoleoniennes. 6278-4
  The island of the Scots. 6948-7,7022-1
  James IV at Flodden. 6046-3
  La mort d'Arthur. 6948-7
  A lament for Percy Bysshe Shelley. 6948-7
  Latimer and Ridley, burned at the stake in Oxford,1851.
    6948-7
  The laureate. 6996-7
  The lay of Mr. Colt. 6948-7
  The lay of the Levite. 6092-7
  The lay of the lover's friend. 6278-4
  The lay of the legion. 6948-7
  The lay of the Levite. 6948-7
  Lays of the Scottish cavaliers. 6948-7
  Little John and the red friar. 6948-7
  Louis Napoleon's address to his army. 6278-4
  Magus Muir. 6948-7
  Massacre of the Macpherson. 6271-7,6125-7,6219-9
  The mausoleum. 6948-7
  A midnight meditation. 6278-4
  Nuptial ode on the marriage of...the Prince of Wales.
    6948-7
  Ode to the past. 6948-7
  Oenone. 6948-7
  The old camp. 6948-7
  The old Scottish cavalier. 6552-X,6079-X,6656-9
  On Miss Helen Faucit's Juliet. 6948-7
  Paris and Helen. 6278-4
  Poland. 6948-7
  Puffs poetical. 6278-4
  The queen in France. 6948-7
  The refusal of Charon. 6180-X
  The rhyme of Sir Launcelot Bogle. 6948-7
  Shadows of recollection. 6948-7
  Sonnet to Britain. 6948-7
  Tarquin and the augur. 6278-4
  Tarquin and the augur. 6948-7
  The wandering Jew. 6948-7
  The widow of Glencoe, sels. 6934-7
  The widow of Glencoe. 6948-7
Aytoun, William Edmonstoune (tr.)
  Andromache's lament. Unknown (Latin), 6948-7
  The artist's morning song. Johann Wolfgang von Goethe,

6948-7
The brothers. Johann Wolfgang von Goethe, 6948-7
The castle by the sea. Johann Ludwig Uhland, 6948-7
The cavalier's choice. Johann Wolfgang von Goethe, 6948-7
The Count of Greiers. Johann Ludwig Uhland, 6948-7
Cupid as a landscape painter. Johann Wolfgang von Goethe, 6948-7
De amore et spinis. Unknown (Latin), 6948-7
The doleful lay of the wife of Asan Aga. Johann Wolfgang von Goethe, 6948-7
The dream. Johann Ludwig Uhland, 6948-7
Durand. Johann Ludwig Uhland, 6948-7
Early spring. Johann Wolfgang von Goethe, 6948-7
The elf-stroke. Unknown (Danish), 6948-7
Epitaph of Constantine Kanaris. Wilhelm Muller, 6948-7
Exculpation. Johann Wolfgang von Goethe, 6948-7
The happy pair. Johann Wolfgang von Goethe, 6948-7
Holy family. Johann Wolfgang von Goethe, 6948-7
The hymn of King Olaf the Saint. Unknown (Icelandic), 6948-7
Ilia's dream. Unknown (Latin), 6948-7
Iotis dying. Unknown (Greek), 6948-7
The king in Thule. Johann Wolfgang von Goethe, 6948-7
Lament of Richard during his imprisonment. Richard I; King of England, 6188-5
Lili's park. Johann Wolfgang von Goethe, 6948-7
Longing. Johann Wolfgang von Goethe, 6948-7
Love's hour-glass. Johann Wolfgang von Goethe, 6948-7
Love's witness. Unknown (Greek), 6948-7
Marriage unequal. Johann Wolfgang von Goethe, 6948-7
Midnight music. Johann Ludwig Uhland, 6948-7
The minstrel's curse. Johann Ludwig Uhland, 6948-7
The Musagetes. Johann Wolfgang von Goethe, 6948-7
On the lake. Johann Wolfgang von Goethe, 6948-7
The pariah. Johann Wolfgang von Goethe, 6948-7
Poesy. Johann Wolfgang von Goethe, 6948-7
Prologue of Laberius. Unknown (Latin), 6948-7
Psyche. Johann Wolfgang von Goethe, 6948-7
The refusal of Charon. Unknown (Greek), 6948-7
Sacred ground. Johann Wolfgang von Goethe, 6948-7
The scheik of Sinai in 1830. Ferdinand Freiligrath, 6948-7
Second life. Johann Wolfgang von Goethe, 6948-7
Separation. Johann Wolfgang von Goethe, 6948-7
The seven sleepers of Ephesus. Johann Wolfgang von Goethe, 6948-7
The shepherd's lament. Johann Wolfgang von Goethe, 6948-7
Sorrow without consolation. Johann Wolfgang von Goethe, 6948-7
Spring-time, fr. Tristia. Ovid, 6948-7
The story of Orpheus. Unknown (Latin), 6948-7
The student. Johann Ludwig Uhland, 6948-7
Tarquin's dream. Unknown (Latin), 6948-7
To a golden heart. Johann Wolfgang von Goethe, 6948-7
To Lina. Johann Wolfgang von Goethe, 6948-7
To Luna. Johann Wolfgang von Goethe, 6948-7
To the moon. Johann Wolfgang von Goethe, 6948-7
The treacherous maid of the mill. Johann Wolfgang von Goethe, 6948-7
The treasure-seeker. Johann Wolfgang von Goethe, 6948-7
The voice from the tomb. Unknown (Greek), 6948-7
Warning. Johann Wolfgang von Goethe, 6948-7
The wedding feast. Johann Wolfgang von Goethe, 6948-7
Who'll buy a cupid? Johann Wolfgang von Goethe, 6948-7
With a golden necklace. Johann Wolfgang von Goethe, 6948-7
The wreaths. Johann Wolfgang von Goethe, 6948-7
The youth and the mill-stream. Johann Wolfgang von Goethe, 6948-7
Azalea flowers. Yun-hyn Cho. 6775-1
Azalea flowers. So-wol Kim. 6775-1
"Azalea, jessamine, have vanished". Mallows of the marshes. Mary Sinton Leitch. 7038-8
The **Azalea**.. Coventry Patmore. 6096-X,6508-2,6655-0
Azaleas. Muda. 6027-7
"Azaleas are eaten in my native land". Azalea flowers. Yun-hyn Cho. 6775-1
Azar and Abraham. Sir Edwin Arnold. 6848-0

The **Aziola**. Percy Bysshe Shelley. 6383-7
The **azra**. Heinrich Heine. 7039-6
Azrael. Henry Wadsworth Longfellow. 6848-0
Azrael. Henry Wadsworth Longfellow. 6396-9
Azrael. Gertrude Huntington McGiffert. 6102-8,6076-5
Azrael. Robert Gilbert Walsh. 6337-3,6102-8,6310-1,6076-5
Azrael. Robert Gilbert Welsh. 6076-5
Azrael. William Winter. 6600-3
Azrael and the indian prince. Sir Edwin Arnold. 6848-0
The **azure** grotto. Charles Dent Bell. 6624-0
"The **azure** lake is argent now". Midnight at Geneva. Francis Turner Palgrave. 6749-2
"**Azure**, I come! from the caves of death...". Helen, the sad queen. Paul Valery. 7039-6
"The **azured** vault, the crystal circles bright" James I; King of Scotland. 6182-6

B
  A tale of a walled town, sels. 6538-4
  What may happen to a thimble. 6519-8
B# sharp portrait of a blues singer. Catherine Sanders. 6898-7
B'y Sara burned down. Unknown. 6609-7
B-B-B. Unknown. 6396-9
B., E. B.
  On Judah. 6848-0
B., M. E.
  Gamaliel of Jerusalem. 6848-0
  Hadasseh of Tiberias. 6848-0
B.,A.J.
  Kitchener's march. 7031-0
B.,C.
  The child and the star. 6131-1
B.,C.E.
  The robin's Christmas. 6131-1
B.,C.G.
  To be continued. 6817-0
  To be continued. 6817-0
  To be continued. 6817-0
  To be continued. 6817-0
B.,C.T.
  Cousin John. 6889-8
B.,E.
  Life or death. 6273-3
  The shepherd's carol. 6387-7
  A trenodia, sels. 6008-0
B.,E.G.
  To Betty. 6466-3
B.,E.L.
  "Come this way", sels. 6601-1
  "I shake the snow on the ground below", sels. 6601-1
  "When the autumn comes its round", sels. 6601-1
B.,F.W.
  Autumn voices. 6049-8
B.,G.S.
  Andre passes. 6817-0
  The motorist's guide. 6817-0
  A rime of an ancient gentleman. 6817-0
  The sons of Mary. 6817-0
B.,H.R.
  Wait and see. 6589-9
B.,J.C.
  There is a time. 6116-8
B.,J.E. (tr.)
  Once in a way. Antiphilus of Byzantium, 6435-3
B.,K.N.
  Dr. Buttonhook. 6130-3
B.,L.
  The biologic face. 6118-4
B.,L.F.
  Sunset. 6118-4
B.,M.E.
  A bird story. 6965-7
  A catastrophe. 6965-7
  A dandy lion. 6965-7
  Do you know him? 6965-7
  If I were a little baby! 6965-7

B.

    If wishes were horses! 6965-7
    A little sister's story. 6965-7
    A receipt for a ticket. 6680-1
    A riddle. 6965-7
    Teddy the teazer. 6965-7
    Two faces under a hood. 6965-7
    A youthful martyr. 6965-7
B.,M.K.
    The four sunbeams. 6638-0
B.,P.
    Helping. 7031-0
    A message. 6741-X
B.,R.F.
    The golf fiend. 7021-3
B.,R.K.
    Limerick:"Should a plan we suggest, just that minute." 6308-X
    Limerick:"You remember that pastoral frolic." 6308-X
B.,S.L.
    My room-mate. 6118-4
B.,W.
    Mary ("Beside the empty sepulcher she lingered"). 6144-3
B.,W.C.
    To a rose. 6118-4
B.,W.H.
    On receipt of a rare pipe. 6453-1
"Ba-ba, baby sheep". A hushaby. Eugene Field. 6949-5
Baa, baa black sheep. Mother Goose. 6362-2,6452-3,6466-3
Baa, baa, black sheep. Mother Goose. 6135-4
Baal-Moloch. Florence Tanenbaum. 6880-4
Baar, Amelia
    A Christmas camp on the San Gabr'el. 6274-1
Baath, Albert Ulrik
    "If I were a poet." Charles Wharton Stork (tr.). 6045-5
Bab-lock-hythe. Laurence Binyon. 6477-9
Babanek, Karel
    I go, nor know wither. Paul Selver (tr.). 6763-8
Babb, J. Franklin
    Keep a little moment. 6764-6
Babb, Stanley E.
    High noon: Galveston beach. 6265-2
    A masque of dead queens. 6039-0
    Midwinter monochrome. 6265-2
    Wild geese in midwinter. 6265-2
The babbitt and the bromide. Ira Gershwin. 6026-9
"Babble in bower". Marjory's song from Becket, fr. Locksley hall. Alfred Lord Tennyson. 6867-7
Babcock, Charlotte Farrington
    Edge. 6253-9
Babcock, Donald C.
    Addios. 6388-8
    Meditation by Mascoma Lake. 6388-8
Babcock, Edwina Stanton
    Epilogue. 6331-4
    The little shade. 6076-5,6102-8
    May-day in Kalamata. 6331-4
    Sunset on the Acropolis. 6331-4
Babcock, Emma D.
    Wind of the Matawan prairie. 6342-X
Babcock, Maltbie Davenport
    Be strong. 6109-5,6337-3,6260-1,6461-2
    Companionship. 6007-2
    Death. 6303-9,6337-3,6730-1
    'Give us this day our daily bread.' 6337-3
    No distant lord. 6337-3
    Not to be ministered to. 6525-2
    Prayer ("God the dew.") 6461-2
    School days. 6337-3,6486-3
    This is my father's world. 6337-3
Babcock, Mary Lowrey
    These remain. 6847-2
Babcock, W.H.
    Bennington. 6946-0
"A babe is born, to bliss us bring". Now sing we with angelis. Unknown. 6756-5
"A babe is bornb all of a may". Nowell, ell, ell, ell, now is well that ever was woe. Unknown. 6756-5
"Babe Jesu lying/On my little pallet lonely". Saint Ita's fostering. Saint (atr.) Ita. 6930-4

The babe of Bethlehem. Henry Beer. 6065-X
The babe of Bethlehem. Conde Benoist Pallen. 6172-9,6292-X
The babe. Sir William Jones. 6240-7,6102-8,6219-9
Babel. Louis MacNeice. 6391-8
Babel. Caroline Elizabeth Sarah Sheridan Norton. 7037-X
Babel and Bethel. Frank Buchanan. 6532-5
Babel: the gate of God, fr. Chambers of Imagery. Gordon Bottomley. 6234-2
The babes in the wood. Unknown. 6078-1,6105-2,6242-3,6003-X,6135-4,6131
The babes in the woods. Francis Bret Harte. 6077-3
Babette. Unknown. 6274-1
The babiaantje. Frank Templeton Prince. 6788-3
The babie ("Nae shoon to hide her tiny taes"). Jeremiah Eames Rankin. 6078-1,6479-5,6219-9
The babie.. Hugh Miller. 6623-2,6086-2,6134-6,6656-9
The babies are all grown. Ethel M. Colson. 6577-5
"The babies born in tiny towns". The heavenly runaway. John Daniel Logan. 6797-2
"Babies short and babies tall". Unknown. 6205-9
Baboon. Charles Hanson Towne. 6102-8,6076-5,6300-4,6510-4
The baboon and the poultry. John Gay. 6972-X
Babushkaa. Edith M. Thomas. 6614-3,6746-8,6608-9
Baby. Elaine Goodale. 6429-9,6321-7
Baby. George Macdonald. 6424-8,6456-6,6639-9,6656-9,6638-0, 6078-1,6165-6,6127-3,6385-3,6242-3
Baby. Fern L. Molloy. 6750-6
Baby. William Brighty Rands. 6772-7
Baby. Unknown. 6629-1
The baby across the street. Unknown. 6078-1
Baby and I. Anna E. Pickens. 6078-1
Baby and Mary. Unknown. 6902-9
A baby asleep after pain. David Herbert Lawrence. 6958-4
A baby asleep after pain. David Herbert Lawrence. 6872-3
Baby Bell. Thomas Bailey Aldrich. 6219-9,6889-8
"Baby blew a bubble". The bubble. F. Hoatson. 6937-1
Baby bobolink's cradle. L.G. Warner. 6965-7
"The baby brought us luck". Lucky. Cathy Song. 6790-5
Baby bunting. Mother Goose. 6135-4
Baby bunting. Unknown. 6078-1
Baby bye. Theodore Tilton. 6183-4,6302-0,6424-8,6456-6
Baby Charley. Sidney Lanier. 6078-1
Baby corn. Unknown. 6519-8
Baby corn. Lydia Avery Coonley Ward. 6135-4
Baby faith. Unknown. 6742-5
The baby girl. Eugenio Florit. 6759-X
Baby hair. Constance Nichols. 6178-8
Baby in a manger. Alice Barkley. 6789-1
Baby in church. Winnie M. Gow. 6450-7
Baby in church. Unknown. 6918-5
Baby in church. Unknown. 6078-1,6273-3,6744-1
A baby in the house. Ella Wheeler Wilcox. 6078-1
Baby is a sailor. Unknown. 6629-1
"A baby is borne us blis to bring". Jesus comforts his mother. Unknown. 6881-2
Baby is creeping. Unknown. 6078-1
Baby is king. Unknown. 6078-1
"A baby is the best to love". A baby's love. Edgar A. Guest. 6862-6
A baby kangaroo. K.B. Ford. 6530-9
Baby land. Unknown. 6312-8
Baby logic. Elizabeth W. Bellamy. 6137-0,6680-1,6585-6
Baby logic. Helen M. Winslow. 6677-1
Baby Louise. Margaret Eytinge. 6385-3,6219-9
Baby May. William Cox Bennett. 6078-1,6271-7,6302-0,6385-3, 6131-1,6219 ,6656-9
Baby mine. Robert J. Burdette. 6588-0
Baby mine. Frederick Locker-Lampson. 6078-1,6429-9,6321-7
Baby Nell. Unknown. 6312-8
Baby O'Grundy. Marion Couthouy Smith. 6130-3
The baby of Saint Brigid. Francis Carlin. 6285-7
"A baby on a woman's breast". The four kisses. George M. Vickers. 6927-4
The baby over the way. Washington Gladden. 6078-1,6273-3
Baby Paul. Mrs. Bishop Thompson. 6078-1,6131-1
Baby picture. Amy Atwater. 6750-6
Baby reigns supreme. Henry Wadsworth Longfellow. 6078-1
"Baby sat on the window-seat". Baby and Mary. Unknown. 6902-9
Baby seed song. Edith (Blad) Nesbit. 6105-2,6466-3,6519-8,

90

6135-4,6639-9,6638
Baby seeds. Unknown. 6466-3
"A baby shines as bright". Babyhood. Algernon Charles Swinburne. 6875-8
A baby show. H. H. 6965-7
Baby sister. Lucy S. Ruggles. 6629-1
"The baby sits in her cradle." Unknown. 6385-3
Baby sleeps. Unknown. 6413-2
The baby sleeps. Unknown. 6629-1
"A baby smiled in its mother's face". Infection. Louis de Louk. 6889-8
"Baby smiled today". Baby. Fern L. Molloy. 6750-6
A baby song. Elizabeth Stoddard. 6078-1
A baby song. Alfred Lord Tennyson. 6772-7
Baby thankful. Caroline Metcalf. 6965-7
Baby toes. Carl Sandburg. 6299-7
The baby tramp. B.E. Todd. 6804-9
"The baby trilliums heard the rain". Bairnies, cuddle doon. Robert Kirkland Kernighan. 6797-2
"Baby wants a lullaby". Lullaby ("Baby wants") William Brighty Rands. 6452-3
The baby who was three-fourths good. Ethelwyn Wetherald. 6797-2
Baby Zulma's Christmas carol. Augustus Julian Requier. 6385-3
"The baby won't go to anyone but me". Grizzly. Ann Chandonnet. 6855-3
Baby!. Unknown. 6629-1
The baby's birthday. Eliza Lee Follen. 6452-3
"A baby's boot, and a skein of wool". Unfinished still. Unknown. 6912-6
Baby's breakfast. Anne Emilie Poullson. 6452-3
Baby's complaint. L.J. H. 6131-1
Baby's correspondence. Alice P. Carter. 6672-0
Baby's cradle is green. Unknown. 6629-1
Baby's day. Lucy Larcom. 6129-X
A baby's death. Algernon Charles Swinburne. 6655-0
The baby's debut. James Smith. 6089-7,6092-7,6219-9,6278-4
Baby's drawer. Emma Celia & Lizzie J. Rook. 6741-7
Baby's dreams. Edgar Fawcett. 6632-1
Baby's face-song. Unknown. 6078-1
A baby's feet and hands. Unknown. 6629-1
"A baby's feet, like sea-shells pink". Etude realiste. Algernon Charles Swinburne. 6875-8
A baby's feet. Algernon Charles Swinburne. 6289-X,6424-8
The baby's footprint. Mary E. (Freeman) Wilkins. 6965-7
"Baby's gone awandering". Babyhood. Berton Braley. 6853-7
Baby's got a tooth. Edgar A. Guest. 6078-1
"The baby's hair is just a timid fuzz". Prediction. Ellen M. Acton. 6750-6
Baby's hands. Gomei. 6891-X
A baby's hands. Algernon Charles Swinburne. 6424-8
The baby's kiss. G.R. Emerson. 6412-4,6572-4
The baby's kiss. Unknown. 6260-1
Baby's letter. Louise E.V. Boyd. 6965-7
Baby's letter. Kate Upson Clark. 6312-8
Baby's letter. Unknown. 6273-3
Baby's logic. Elizabeth W. Ballamy. 6744-1
A baby's love. Edgar A. Guest. 6862-6
The baby's name. Unknown. 6690-9
The baby's Omar. Carolyn Wells. 6440-X
The baby's prayer. Elizabeth Stuart Phelps. 6965-7
The baby's protest. Joseph Morris. 6078-1
A baby's rattle. Unknown. 6273-3
A baby's reflections. Unknown. 6167-2
Baby's reply. Unknown. 6273-3
Baby's ring. Phoebe Cary. 6060-9
The baby's secret. Frances Hodgson Burnett. 6130-3
Baby's shoes. William Cox Bennett. 6271-7,6302-0,6385-3, 6424-8,6543-0
Baby's skies. M.C. Bartlett. 6078-1,6627-5,6321-7,6429-9
Baby's skies. Unknown. 6312-8,6629-1
Baby's soliloquy. Unknown. 6744-1
The baby's stocking. Unknown. 6601-1
The baby's thoughts. Lucy Larcom. 6129-X
The baby's thoughts. Unknown. 6675-5
Baby's valentine. Laura E. Richards. 6338-1
"Baby, baby, hush-a-bye". A lullaby ("Baby, baby". Laurence Alma Tadema. 6242-3
"Baby, O baby, fain you are for bed". Cradle song. Louis Esson. 6784-0
The baby, fr. Dovecote mill. Phoebe Cary. 6865-0;6969-X
Baby, open your eyes. William Cox Bennet. 6078-1
"Baby-child/Mystery of mysteries". Multum in parvo. Darrell Figgis. 6785-9
Baby-land. George Cooper. 6273-3,6452-3,6131-1,6627-5,6078-1
The baby. Kalidasa. 6385-3,6438-8
The baby. Ann and Jane Taylor. 6078-1,6627-5
The baby. Jane Taylor. 6078-1,6131-1,6627-5
The baby. Elizabeth W. Townsend. 6684-4,6131-4
Babyhood. Berton Braley. 6853-7
Babyhood. Josiah Gilbert Holland. 6481-7
Babyhood. James Whitcomb Riley. 6078-1
Babyhood. Algernon Charles Swinburne. 6875-8
Babyland. Ella Wheeler Wilcox. 6178-1,6661-5
Babylon. Laura Benet. 6218-0
Babylon. Viola Gerard Garvin. 7007-8
Babylon. Edwin Markham. 6076-5
Babylon. Virgil Markham. 6102-8,6076-5
Babylon. Arthur Patchett Martin. 6591-0,6592-9
Babylon. James Jeffrey Roche. 7041-8
Babylon. George William ("A.E.") Russell. 6634-8,6659-3
Babylon. Robert Southey. 6848-0
Babylon. A.G. Stephens. 6784-0
Babylon. Alfred Lord Tennyson. 6848-0
Babylon. Unknown. 6848-0
"Babylon - where I go dreaming". Ralph Hodgson. 6897-9
"Babylon has fallen! Aye, but Babylon endures". Babylon. A.G. Stephens. 6784-0
Babylon, Babylon, Bayblon the great. Vachel Lindsay. 6871-5
Babylon; or, The bonnie banks o Fordie. Unknown. 6185-0, 6193-1,6067-6
The Babylonian captivity. Joel Barlow. 6735-2
Baca, Jimmy Santiago
    Ancestor. 6870-7
    The county jail. 6870-7
    I am sure of it. 6870-7
    It started. 6870-7
    The new warden. 6870-7
Bacarole. Knud Ludvig Rahbek. 6555-4
Baccalaureate. David McCord. 6722-0
Baccalaureate hymn. Winifred H. Phillips. 6847-2
A Baccanal. Aurelian Townsend. 6328-4
Bacchae, sel. Euripides. 7014-0
The bacchae, sels. Euripides. 6334-9
Bacchanal. Babette Deutsch. 6959-2
Bacchanal. Ibn Baqi. 6362-4
Bacchanal, fr. Baccae. Euripides. 6435-3
Bacchanal, fr. In war time. Wilfred Wilson Gibson. 6884-7
Bacchanalia; or, The new age. Matthew Arnold. 6110-9,6271-7,6655-0
A Bacchanalian song. Bryan Waller ("Barry Cornwall") Procter. 6658-5
A Bacchanalian toast. Robert Herrick. 6724-7
Bacchante. Alice Louise Jones. 6959-2
The Bacchante to her babe. Eunice Tietjens. 6029-3
A Bacchic ode. Bayard Taylor. 6976-2
Bacchus. Ralph Waldo Emerson. 6077-3,6176-1,6250-4,6300-4, 6309-8
Bacchus. William Empson. 6390-X
Bacchus. John Keats. 6423-X,6543-0
Bacchus. Frank Dempster Sherman. 7041-8
Bacchus. Frank Dempster Sherman. 6102-8,6310-1,6632-1,6732-8,6076-5
Bacchus and Ariadne, fr. Scaramouch in Naxos. John Davidson. 6819-7
Bacchus and the pirates. Alfred Noyes. 6151-6
"Bacchus by the lonely ocean". The vengeance of Bacchus, fr. Rhododaphne. Thomas Love Peacock. 6832-4
Bacchus in Tuscany, sels. Francesco Redi. 6482-5
Bacchylides
    "As towering through the height". F.L. Lucas (tr.). 6251-2
    Croesus. George Allen (tr.). 6435-3
    The eagle of song. T.F. Higham (tr.). 6435-3
    Fecundi calices. Cecil Maurice Bowra (tr.). 6435-3
    Heracles and Meleager. Cecil Maurice Bowra (tr.). 6435-3

"Lord of Athene's holy hill". F.L. Lucas (tr.). 6251-2
"Lord of Athens' holy ground", fr. Theseus. Cecil Maurice Bowra (tr.). 6435-3
"Once the sacker of towns...". F.L. Lucas (tr.). 6251-2
Peace on earth. John Addington Symonds (tr.). 7039-6
"So said the valiant master...", fr. Theseus. John Swinnerton Phillimore (tr.). 6435-3
Theseus, sels. Cecil Maurice Bowra (tr.). 6435-3
Theseus, sels. John Swinnerton Phillimore (tr.). 6435-3
Theseus, sels. 6435-3
"Thronged now the shrines with revel...". F.L. Lucas (tr.). 6251-2
Bach. Leonard Lanson Cline. 6880-4
Bach's organ works. Thomas Edward Brown. 6230-X
Bach, in the fugues and preludes. Sir William Watson. 7014-0
Bache, Anna
  The ill-natured briar. 6131-1
  The quilting. 6910-X
Bachelder, Phoebe Smith
  Communion ("Not to the twelve alone"). 6144-3
  Holy week ("And having taken bread, he broke it"). 6144-3
Bacheller, Irving
  Ballad of the Sabre Cross and 7. 6274-1
  The mocking bird ("Lord of the odored alleys green!"). 6073-0
  Whisperin' Bill. 6923-1,6670-4
"The **bachelor** 'e fights for one". The married man. Rudyard Kipling. 6810-3
The **bachelor** and the bride. Unknown. 6064-1
"A **bachelor** born (a common fate).". My widow. David Crichton. 6878-2
The **bachelor** coat. Unknown. 6929-0
The **bachelor** girl. Oliver Herford. 6652-6
Bachelor hall. Eugene Field. 6949-5
The **bachelor** sale. Unknown. 6916-9
The **bachelor** sale. Unknown. 6402-7
The **bachelor**'s cane-bottom chair. William Makepeace Thackeray. 6278-4
The **bachelor**'s dream. Thomas Hood. 6089-7,6680-1,6219-9, 6278-4
The **bachelor**'s dream. John Rankine. 6878-2
A **bachelor**'s growl. Unknown. 6415-9
Bachelor's hall. John Finley. 6302-0,6385-3,6219-9
Bachelor's hall. Unknown. 6404-3,6742-5,6742-5
The **bachelor**'s hope. Malcolm M. Luzader. 6924-X
A **bachelor**'s invocation. Unknown. 6453-1
A **bachelor**'s love-song. J.H. Ryan. 6675-5
A **bachelor**'s mono-rhyme. Charles Mackay. 6089-7
The **bachelor**'s reasons for taking a wife. Unknown. 6064-1
The **bachelor**'s regret. Edward R. Huxley. 6885-5
A **bachelor**'s reverie. Unknown. 6417-5
The **bachelor**'s soliloquy. George R. Russell. 6402-7
The **bachelor**'s soliloquy. Unknown. 6280-6,6425-6,6440-X, 6453-1,6155-9
The **bachelor**'s song. Thomas Flatman. 6152-4
A **bachelor**'s views. Tom Hall. 6453-1
Bachelors' landlady. Hyde Clayton. 6750-6
The **bachelors**. Unknown. 6408-6
Bachmann, Ingeborg
  Advertising. Milne Holton and Herbert Kuhner (tr.). 6769-7
  "After this flood" Milne Holton and Herbert Kuhner (tr.). 6769-7
  Enigma. Milne Holton and Herbert Kuhner (tr.). 6769-7
  Exile. Milne Holton and Herbert Kuhner (tr.). 6769-7
  Hotel de la paix. Milne Holton and Herbert Kuhner (tr.). 6769-7
Back. Wilfred Wilson Gibson. 6337-3,6464-7,6542-2
"Back above the world". Imperial airways. Louis Untermeyer. 7014-0
Back and forth in a rocker. Richard Kendall Munkittrick. 6097-8
Back and side go bare, go bare. William Stevenson. 6430-2
"Back and side go bare, go bare". Unknown. 6187-7,6723-8
Back from London. David Meltzer. 6792-1, 6998-3
"Back from battle, torn and rent". In the morning. Klaxon (John Graham Bower). 7031-0
Back home. May Williams Ward. 6750-6

Back home again. Grantland Rice. 6088-9
"Back home/in the p.i.". Manong Federico Delo Reyes and his golden banjo. Al Robles. 6790-5
"Back in her box by the curtains shaded". The old stage queen. Ella Wheeler Wilcox. 6863-4
Back in the mountains. Mary Elizabeth Mahnkey. 6662-3
'Back in the return.' Huw Menai. 6360-8
The back of God. J.R. Perkins. 6337-3
"Back of the mountaintops at dawn". Morning star. Ida May Borncamp. 6799-9
The back stairs, fr. The homestead. Gertrude Huntington McGiffert. 6838-3
"Back then, once more to the breast the waves". Recovery. Felicia Dorothea Hemans. 6973-8
"Back through misty scenes of yore". Evolution of man. Edward R. Huxley. 6885-5
Back to London: a poem of leave. Joseph Johnston Lee. 7027-2,7031-0
Back to mother's arms. Frances Dana Barker ("Aunt Fanny") Gage. 6097-8
Back to rest. William Noel Hodgson. 6477-9
Back to school. Edgar A. Guest. 6862-6
'Back to the army again'. Rudyard Kipling. 6810-3
Back to the border. Laurence (Adele Florence Nicolson) Hope. 6856-1
"Back to the flower-town, side by side". In memory of Walter Savage Landor. Algernon Charles Swinburne. 6828-6
"Back to the grand Apollo! Tell me not". The Apollo Belvidere, fr. In Rome. Alexander ("Surfaceman") Anderson. 6819-7
"Back up old age and wrinkled face". Christmas eve. Edgar A. Guest. 6862-6
Back yard. Carl Sandburg. 6121-4
"Back, then, once more to breast the waves...". Recovery, fr. Thoughts during sickness. Felicia Dorothea Hemans. 6980-0
"Back, ye phantoms of the past". Phantoms. Adelaide Anne Procter. 6957-6
Back-log moods. James B. Hunt. 6983-5
The back-log; or, uncle Ned's little game. Innes Randolph. 6411-6
The back-work club. H.S. Chamberlain Jr. 6118-4
"Backbone of the nation is the happy..throng". Real people. Edgar A. Guest. 6869-3
Background. Un-kyo Kang. 6775-1
Background with revolutionaries. Archibald MacLeish. 6645-3
Backing the favourite. Thomas Hood. 6974-6
The backlog. Edward Farquhar. 6939-8
Backsliding brother. Frank Lebby Stanton. 6696-8
The backslider.. Jeanne Robert Foster. 6607-0
Backstair ballad. David McCord. 6089-7
Backstrom, Edvard
  A song of Sten Sture. Charles Wharton Stork (tr.). 6045-5
"Backtracking/Fifty miles past Bakersfield". Visiting father. Genny Lim. 6790-5
Backus, Bertha Adams
  Then laugh. 6736-0
The backward look. William Cowper. 6233-4
Backwards. Nancy Lee Couto. 6900-2
The backwoodsman, sels. James Kirke Paulding. 6077-3
Backyard swing. Janet Campbell Hale. 7005-1
Bacon and eggs. Sir Alan Patrick Herbert. 6722-0
Bacon's epitaph. John Cotton (of Queens Creek) 6008-0,6288-1
Bacon's epitaph, made by his man. John Cotton (atr) 6946-0
Bacon's epitaph, made by his man. Unknown. 7017-5
Bacon's epitaph, made by his man. Unknown. 6176-1
Bacon, George Vaux
  'Jew!' 6848-0
Bacon, Helen C.
  A song of spring. 6373-X,6456-6
Bacon, Josephine Daskam
  An Omar for ladies. 6440-X
  The sleepy song. 6452-3,6466-3
Bacon, Leonard
  An afernoon in Artillery walk. 6527-9
  The archaeologist of the future. 6722-0

The ballad of Angel May. 6506-6
Color line. 6984-3
A concert. 6506-6
"Dante was naif although he had an inkling". 6619-4
Epitaph in anticipation. 6722-0
Fame. 6464-7
Forefather's hymn. 6473-6
High summer. 6761-1
I saw that shadowed thing. 6619-4
"Idiots will prate and prate of suicide". 6619-4
"Io ritornai dalla santissima onda" 6217-2,6250-4
Lyric XXVII, fr. Animula vagula. 6393-4
The mirrors of Grub Street. 6070-6
Night laughter. 6076-5,6102-8
The Pilgrim fathers. 6337-3
The reason. 6736-0
Sunderland capture. 6984-3
"Thirty-eight years. Yes, neither less nor more". 6619-4
Tower of ivory. 6722-0
Bacon, Mrs. L.B.
    Naming the chickens. 6720-1,6742-5
Bacon, Peggy
    Hearth. 6891-X
Bacon, Sir Francis
    "All science seems placed on high" 7014-0
    "Knowledge and poer are reciprocal," fr. Novum organum. 7014-0
    Life. 6219-9,6246-6,6560-0
    The life of man. 6182-6,6726-3,6436-1
    Novum Organum, sel. 7014-0
    Of gardens. 7020-5
    Paraphrase of Psalm 090. 6186-9
    "The world's a bubble, and the life of man" 6935-5
    The world's a bubble. 6934-7
    The world. 6189-3
    Worth of knowledge. 6304-7
The bad adder. Carolyn Wells. 6882-0
The bad axe fair. Edgar A. Guest. 6723-9
Bad boy. Unknown. 6715-8
The bad boy. Norman Gale. 6242-3
A bad cold. H. Elliott McBride. 6416-7
Bad company. Abu Amr. 6362-4
Bad dream. Unknown. 6713-1
Bad dreams, sels. Robert Browning. 6430-2
The bad girl's lament. Unknown. 6057-9
The bad kittens. Elizabeth J. Coatsworth. 6465-5,6071-4, 6464-7
The bad lands. Roy B. Herrick. 6799-9
Bad luck to this marching. Charles Lever. 6930-4
Bad Peter, bad Joe. Unknown. 6692-2
"Bad news will come". I read fortunes in dreams. Delia Dominguez. 7036-1
Bad poets. Samuel Taylor Coleridge. 6278-4
The bad season makes the poet sad. Robert Herrick. 6430-2
Bad squire, sel. Charles Kingsley. 6954-1
The bad squire. Charles Kingsley. 6934-7
Bad times. Joseph Beaumont. 6337-3
"Bad was the wife of Barney O'Linn". Barney O'Linn and the leeches. Unknown. 6920-7
The bad workman. Anatole France. 6351-9
Bad writers. Samuel Butler. 6278-4
"A bad-tempered bully of Thurso". Limerick:"A bad-tempered bully of Thurso". Langford Reed. 6811-1
Badcombe Fair: night. Laurence Housman. 6069-2
Badger. John Clare. 6380-2
Badlam, Anna E.
    Human body lesson in rhyme. 6314-4
Badley, Mary Esther
    The parade. 6449-3
Baer, Charles E.
    Postponed. 6249-0
Baer, Libbie C.
    A little girl's wish. 6684-4
    Long ago. 6674-4
    An unrepentant rebel. 6694-1
Baerlein, Henry
    The fool. 6541-4
Baetman, F. (tr.)
    Salutation. Zerea Jacob, 6282-2

The baffled knight. Unknown. 6058-7,6185-0,6278-4
Bafflement. Neeta Marquis. 6316-0
A bag o' wind. Unknown. 6983-5
The bag of the bee. Robert Herrick. 6194-X,6430-2
A bag of tools. R.L. Sharpe. 6337-3,6583-X,6736-0
The bag pudding. Unknown. 6466-3
Bag-pipes at sea. Clinton Scollard. 6310-1,6734-8,6250-4
A bagatelle. James G. Burnett. 6652-6
Bagby, J.R.
    The empty sleeve. 6074-9
Bagg, Robert
    Ballad in blond hair foretold. 6388-9
    For her on the first day out. 6388-8
    Oracle at Delphi. 6388-8
    Speak this kindly to her. 6388-8
The baggage coach ahead. Unknown. 6003-X
The baggage fiend. Unknown. 6407-8
Bagged the wrong bird. John P. Lyons. 7021-3
Bagger, Carl Christian
    The departure. Charles Wharton Stork (tr.). 6555-4
Baggesen, Jens
    Childhood. Henry Wadsworth Longfellow (tr.). 7039-6
Baggot, Mary
    No death. 6799-9
Bagley wood. Lionel Johnson. 6655-0
The bagman's dog. Richard Harris ("Thomas Ingoldsby") Barham. 6278-4
Bagpipe music. Louis MacNeice. 6930-4
Bagpipe music. Louis MacNeice. 6390-X,6733-6,6536-8
Bagpipe player. Leonora Speyer. 6331-4,6631-3
Bagpipe song. Unknown. 6228-8
Bagpipes. Shaemas O'Sheel. 6979-7
Baha' al-Din Zuhair
    "Every thing from you is accepted". A.J. Arberry (tr.). 6766-2
Bahar
    The miracle of spring. A.J. Arberry (tr.). 6448-5
    Random thoughts. A.J. Arberry (tr.). 6448-5
The Bahristan of Jami, sel. Unknown. 6120-6
Baiae ("But Baiae, soft retreat in days of yore"). Nicholas Michell. 6624-0
Baiae ("There Baiae sees no more the joyous throng"). James Thomson. 6624-0
Baie des Chaleur. Henry Duncan Chisholm. 6764-6
Baile and Aillinn, sels. William Butler Yeats. 6844-8
Bailey ballads, sels. Thomas Hood. 6974-6
The bailey beareth the bell away. Unknown. 6383-7
Bailey, Alfred G.
    Shrouds and away. 6446-9
    Whistle and wheels. 6446-9
Bailey, Alice Ward
    The iceboat. 7035-3
Bailey, Carolyn Sherwin
    After winter. 6466-3
    A Christmas party. 6466-3
    If. 6466-3
Bailey, H. Sewall
    Sailor man. 6833-2
Bailey, Ira J.
    The island of home. 6416-7
Bailey, J.H.
    No smoking allowed. 6414-0
Bailey, John (tr.)
    Primo vere. Giosue Carducci, 7039-6
Bailey, L.H.
    Miracle. 6338-1
Bailey, Lansing C.
    Eight volunteers. 6741-X
Bailey, Margaret Emerson
    Close to the earth. 6780-8
    Prayer. 6654-2
    White Christmas. 6581-3
Bailey, Philip James
    The aim of life. 6240-7
    Angela. 6980-0
    Ask not of me, love, what is love. 6094-3
    "The beautiful are never desolate". 6238-5
    Calmness of the sublime. 6980-0
    "The day hath gone to God". 6238-5
    "Death is another life; we bow our heads". 6238-5

BAILEY

The end of life. 6543-0
Faith. 6980-0
Festus describes his friend, fr. Festus. 6980-0
Festus, sels. 6198-2,6225-3,6238-5,6337-3,6317-9,6693, 6656-9
Forecast. 6438-8
The great black crow. 6089-7
Great thoughts. 6980-0,6543-0
"Humility is the base of every virtue". 6238-5
I remember the only wise thing I ever did. 6066-8
If aught can make me seek. 6066-8
It has been such a day as that, thou knowest. 6066-8
"Let each man think himself an act of God". 6402-7
A letter. 6980-0
Life. 6461-2
Like an island in a river. 6543-0
Love of God and man. 6543-0
Lucifer's song. 6102-8
My lady. 6437-X
The poet. 6980-0
Truth and sorrow. 6980-0
"We live in deeds, not years;in thoughts,not breaths." 6102-8,6225-3,6238-5,6109-5,6693-3
What is heaven? 6014-5

Bailey, Robert S.
Now. 7016-7
Worthwhile. 7016-7

Bailie, Mary
De tired pickaninny's star-song. 6692-5

The **bailiff's** daughter of Islington. Unknown. 6055-2,6239-3,6290-3,6518-X,6634-8,6098-,6185-2,6271-7,6549-X, 6319-5,6430-2,6659 ,6067-6

Baillie, Joanna
Address to a steam-vessel. 6813-8
"As are our hearts, our way is one". 6973-8
A Basil: a tragedy. 6813-8
The beacon. 6813-8
Birthday lines to Agnes Baillie. 6980-0
The black cock. 6219-9,6271-7
The brave man. 6294-6
The bride: a drama. 6813-8
The chough and crow. 6832-4,6383-7
Christopher Columbus. 6980-0,6813-8,6813-8
Constancy. 6980-0
Constantine Paleologus: a tragedy. 6813-8
The country inn: a comedy. 6813-8
De Monfort: a tragedy. 6813-8
Deceit. 6294-6
The dream: a tragedy. 6813-8
The elden tree. 6813-8
The election: a comedy. 6813-8
Ethwald: a tragedy. 6813-8
Family legend. 6813-8
Fisherman's song. 6180-X
The ghost of Fadon. 6813-8
The gowan glitters on the sward. 6600-3
The heath-cock. 6302-0;6385-3
The highland shepherd. 6543-0
The kitten. 6120-6,6219-9,6511-2
Lady Griseld Baillie. 6813-8
Lord John of the east. 6813-8
The maid of Llanwellyn. 6086-2
Malcolm's heirs. 6813-8
The martyr: a drama. 6813-8
Morning song. 6219-9
"No fish stir in our heaving net", fr. The beacon. 6997-5
A November night's traveller. 6813-8
Orra: a tragedy. 6813-8
The outlaw's song. 6086-2
Patriotism and freedom. 6304-7
Poverty parts gude companie. 6086-2
Rayner: a tragedy. 6813-8
Saw ye Johnnie comin'? 6086-2,6180-X
The second marriage: a comedy. 6813-8
The shepherd's song. 6180-X
The siege: a comedy. 6813-8
Sir Maurice. 6813-8
A soldier. 6294-6
Song. 6543-0
Song ("Oh welcome"). 6219-9
Song ("The bride..."). 6832-4
Song ("The morning air plays on my face"). 6980-0
Song ("They who may"). 6086-2
To a child. 6233-4
To a kitten. 6086-2,6092-7
To Mrs. Siddons. 6813-8
Traveller by night, sels. 6980-0
The tryal: a comedy. 6813-8
"Up! quit thy bower." 6302-0;6385-3
A volunteer song. 6813-8
William Wallace. 6813-8
Woo'd and married and a' 6086-2,6198-2

Baillie, Lady Grisell [or Grizel]
The ewe-buchtin's bonnie. 6086-2
Were na my heart light I wad die. 6086-2,6180-X
Werena my heart licht I wad dee. 6960-6

Bain, A. Watson (tr.)
The ideal general. Archilochus, 6435-3

Bain, C.
In the night. 6216-4

Bain, Read
The secret. 6037-4

Bain, Robert
King James the First of Scotland, sels. 6269-5

Bainbridge, Katharine
Wherever my boat is sailing. 6316-0

Baine, W.
Nola Kosmo. 6414-0,6744-1

Baines Carew, gentleman. Sir William Schwenck Gilbert. 6878-2

Baird, George M.P.
A ballad of wise men. 6608-9

"The **bairnies** cuddle doon at nicht". Cuddle doon. Alexander ("Surfaceman") Anderson. 6889-8
Bairnies, cuddle doon. Robert Kirkland Kernighan. 6797-2
Bait. Norah Lilian D'Altera Dowsley. 6800-6
Bait of the average fisherman. H.C. Dodge. 6724-7,6505-8
The **bait.** John Donne. 6536-8,6722-0,6092-7,6430-2,6191-5, 6191-5
Baith gude and fair and womanly. Unknown. 6845-6
Baitsy and I are oudt. George M. Warren. 6918-5
The **baker's** tale. Charles Lutwidge ("Lewis Carroll") Dodgson. 6371-3,6861-8

Baker, ?
"There are some deeds so grand". 6238-5

Baker, Barbara Anne
'Grow in hope and grace'. 7024-8

Baker, Bess Kine
An evening prayer ("If I have done an unkind act..."). 6303-9

Baker, David
First auction. 6860-X
How old I have become. 6860-X
Looking in both directions from inside the covered... 6860-X
Mosquitoes. 7032-9

Baker, Emilie K. (tr.)
The Lorelei. Heinrich Heine, 6805-7

Baker, F.M.
Mother's hired man. 6684-4

Baker, Gene
A brother gone. 6995-9

Baker, George A.
After the German. 6517-1
An afterthought. 6187-7
Auto-da-fe. 6187-7
Chinese lanterns. 6517-1
Chivalrie. 6517-1
Christmas greens. 6187-7
De lunatico. 6004-8
Easter morning. 6187-7
Fishing. 6187-7
Frost-bitten. 6187-7
An idyl of the period. 6517-1,6392-6
Jack and me. 6517-1
Lake Mahopac-Saturday night. 6187-7
"Le dernier jour d'un Condamne". 6004-8,6187-7,6632-1, 6652-6
A legend of St. Valentine. 6187-7

Les enfants perdus. 6517-1
Love your neighbor as yourself. 6568-6
Love's young dream. 6517-1
Making new year's calls. 6517-1
Matinal musings. 6187-7
Nocturne. 6187-7
Old photographs. 6187-7
A piece of advice. 6517-1
Pyrotechnic polygot. 6187-7
Reverie in church. 6409-4,6567-8,6744-1
A romance of the saw-dust. 6187-7
Sleeping beauty. 6187-7
A song ("I shouldn't like"). 6517-1
A song ("Spring time"). 6187-7
"The stay-at home's paean." 6517-1
Ten hours a day. 6187-7
Thoughts on the commandments. 6517-1
Up the aisle-Nell Latine's wedding. 6517-1
Zwei konige auf orkadal. 6517-1
Baker, George H.
   The ballad of New Orleans. 6403-5
Baker, George Linville
   Rondeau. 6936-3
   To the friar's senior society. 6936-3
Baker, George M.
   The cruise of the Monitor. 6678-X
   The red jacket. 6167-2,6566-X,6744-1,6964-9
   The red jacket. 6911-8
   Thoughts during Easter service. 6720-4
Baker, Glen
   Simon the Cyrenian speaks. 6144-3
Baker, Gulielma A. Wheeler
   Consecration of the temple. 6848-0
Baker, Harry T.
   To a patriot. 6995-9
Baker, Henry W.
   Christ the consoler. 6065-X
   The King of love. 6065-X,6337-3
Baker, Julia A.
   Mizpah. 6889-8
   Mizpah. 6303-9
Baker, Karkle Wilson
   Old lace. 6777-8
Baker, Karle Wilson
   Apple and rose. 6506-6
   At the picture-show. 6030-7
   A child's game. 6512-0
   City lights. 6512-0
   A clear night. 6031-5
   Courage ("Courage is armor"). 6337-3,6501-5,6464-7
   Creeds. 6250-4,6730-1
   Days. 6250-4,6556-2
   Eagle youth. 6051-X
   Good company. 6374-8,6476-0,6556-2,6730-1,6393-4,6421 ,
      6030-7,6265-2,6253-9,6509-0,6510-4,6653
   Grey. 6326-8
   Growing old. 6585-6
   Half way stone. 6585-6
   The hill steps. 6506-6
   The housewife: winter afternoon. 6326-8
   I love the friendly faces of old sorrows. 6501-5
   I shall be loved as quiet things. 6250-4,6332-2,6506-6,
      6619-4
   Leaf-burning. 6607-0
   Morning song. 6076-5,6102-8,6512-0,6534-1,6607-0
   The old inn. 6653-4
   The ploughman. 6032-3,6607-0,6730-1
   Pronouns. 6326-8
   Rondel for Christmas. 6653-4
   Rondel for September. 6875-8
   Some towns of Texas. 6265-2
   Song of the forerunners. 6265-2
   Thrushes. 6073-0
   Vanity. 6032-3
   W.V.M. 6031-5
   The world at the bottom of the lake. 6326-8
Baker, Leon
   All night! 6870-7
   Cap'n & me. 6870-7
   Getting back to work (in solitary confinement) 6870-7
   Jackson state prison (with a touch of Shakespeare) 6870-7
   On youth, the warden & solitary! 6870-7
Baker, M.E.
   Yankee revenants. 6761-1
Baker, N.R.
   Indian Summer. 6799-9
Baker, Peter
   Afterwards. 6475-2
   Come! let us dance. 6475-2
   In Memoriam-- P. W. 6475-2
   Line after line. 6475-2
   Wartime love-song. 6475-2
Baker, S.H.
   New dresses. 6131-1
Baker, Stacy E.
   Willie's dream. 6807-3
The **baker**. Lida Wilson Turner. 6841-3
Bakewell, John
   Hail, thou once despised Jesus. 6065-X,6219-9,6065-X
Baking for the party. Grace Livingston Hill. 6713-1
The **baking** of a man. D.E. Wheeler. 6033-1
Bakke, Th. M.
   Farewell to the Pilgrims. 6818-9
Bal masque: 1915. M.C. Sinclair. 6542-2
Balaam. John Keble. 6848-0
Balaam. John Keble. 6437-X
Balaban, John
   Mau than, sel. 6803-0
The **balad** of dead ladies. Francois Villon. 7039-6
Balade ("Hyd, Absolon, thy gilte tresses clere"). Geoffrey
   Chaucer. 6315-2,6125-7,6250-4
Balade de Bon Conseyl. Geoffrey Chaucer. 6198-2
Balaklava. Alexander Smith. 6573-2
Balance. Edward Farquhar. 6939-8
Balance. Melanie Hyman. 6515-5
Balance. Eden Phillpotts. 7014-0
Balance. Charles Hanson Towne. 6761-1
Balance a straw, fr. Reprisal. Tobias George Smollett.
   6328-4
"The **balance** sheet" Walther Nowotny. 6769-7
The **balance** wheel. Elmer Ruan Coates. 6045-1
The **balance**. William Sterling. 6501-5
Balaustion's adventure, sels. Robert Browning. 6483-3
Balboa. Nora Perry. 6946-0
Balcom, Nanita MacDonell
   Write I will. 6761-1
Balcony scene, fr. Romeo and Juliet. William Shakespeare.
   6148-6,6585-6
The **balcony**. Charles Baudelaire. 6732-8
The **bald** eagle and the barber. J.G. Francis. 6786-7
"A **bald-headed** judge called Beauclerk". Limerick:"A bald-
   headed judge called Beauclerk". Unknown. 6811-1
Balder. Unknown. 6271-7
Balder dead. Matthew Arnold. 6947-9
Balder dead, sels. Matthew Arnold. 6656-9
Balder's wife. Alice Cary. 6969-X
Balder, sels. Sydney Dobell. 6102-8
The **baldness** of chewed-ear. Robert Service. 6159-1
Baldwin, Astley H.
   Little brown bushy-tail. 6629-1
   On the threshold. 6394-2,6449-3
Baldwin, E.N.
   The watermelon season. 6687-9
Baldwin, Eleanor
   Arizona summer. 6750-6
   The calf. 6510-4
   Polo ponies. 6510-4
Baldwin, Faith
   Vigil. 6337-3,6076-5
Baldwin, Fred Clare
   Abraham Lincoln. 6524-4
Baldwin, Mary
   At night. 6274-1
   Winter. 6274-1
Baldwin, Mary Newton
   Chapel in the woods. 6646-8
Baldwin, Rose Linda
   I pray. 6799-9
Baldwin, William

BALDWIN

The beloved to the spouse. 6436-1
"Beware, take heede, take heede, beware, beware" 6380-2
Christ to his spouse. 6182-6
Christ, my beloved. 6182-6
The spouse to the beloved. 6436-1
Bale, John
Wassail. 6756-5
Wassail, wassail. 6125-7,6334-9
Balfe, Michael W.
I dreamt that I dwelt in marble halls. 6706-9
Balin and Balan, sels. Alfred Lord Tennyson. 6199-0
Balinski, Stanislaw
Chopin's motherland. Marion Moore Coleman (tr.) 6068-4
Balkis, fr. Emblems of love. Lascelles Abercrombie. 6102-8, 6301-2
Balkwill, Michael (tr.)
Chalcomede wards off her lover. Nonnus, 6435-3
Hymn to Zeus ("Most glorious of immortals..."). Cleanthes, 6435-3
Leander's death. Musaeus, 6435-3
The snow of stones, fr. The Iliad. Homer, 6435-3
"A story of passion's conflict that the laughter...". Nonnus, 6435-3
"Thus shouting onward...", fr. The Iliad. Homer, 6435-3
"The time was night, when the most violent...". Musaeus, 6435-3
Ball. Kate Greenaway. 6466-3
Ball's bluff. Herman Melville. 6077-3
Ball, Alice M.
The doctor's choice. 6611-9
Ball, Caroline A.
The jacket of gray. 6074-9
Ball, Elizabeth
Ancient April. 6397-7
Flame and gray. 6397-7
Outlook. 6397-7
People. 6397-7
Poems of rebellion. 6397-7
Ball, William
Praise to Jesus. 6065-X
Praise to Jesus! 6065-X
A ball-room madrigal. W.C. Nichols. 6116-8
Ballad. Charles Stuart Calverley. 6656-9,6534-1
Ballad. Leonard Cohen. 6446-9
Ballad. Thomas Hood. 6656-9
Ballad ("...But little wist Marie Hamilton.") Unknown. 6179-6
Ballad ("Are you ready"). Charles Kingsley. 6661-5
A ballad ("As I was walkin'"). Guy Wetmore Carryl. 6440-X
Ballad ("As it fell"). Unknown. 6179-6
Ballad ("Butter and eggs"). Charles Stuart Calverley. 6092-7
Ballad ("Dark forests"). Raffi. 6050-1
A ballad ("Dear Betty"). Sir Charles Hanbury Williams. 6230-X
Ballad ("Hie upon hielands.") Unknown. 6179-6
Ballad ("In the summer"). Harriet Prescott Spofford. 6243-1,6309-8
Ballad ("It was Earl Haldan's"). Charles Kingsley. 6239-3
Ballad ("It was not in the winter"). Thomas Hood. 6271-7, 6423-X
Ballad ("O stoodent"). Unknown. 6902-9
Ballad ("O! shairly"). William Soutar. 6379-9
Ballad ("Of all the girls"). John Gay. 6157-5
Ballad ("Oh what is that sound"). Wystan Hugh Auden. 6666-6
Ballad ("Oh, come my joy"). Henry Treece. 6666-6
A ballad ("Rise, rise"). Unknown. 6753-0
Ballad ("She's up"). Thomas Hood. 6974-6
Ballad ("Sigh on"). Thomas Hood. 6271-7
Ballad ("Soft white lamb"). Christina Georgina Rossetti. 6772-7
Ballad ("Spring"). Thomas Hood. 6974-6
Ballad ("The auld wife"). Charles Stuart Calverley. 6440-X, 6722-0,6512-0,6089-7,6501-5,6802-2
A ballad ("The biggest man") Williams [pseud]. 6880-4
A ballad ("The Druid Urien"). Sir Walter Scott. 6087-0
Ballad ("What do we"). John Payne. 6770-0
A ballad ("You gallants"). Sir Charles Sedley. 6157-5,6544-9

Ballad against the enemies of France. Algernon Charles Swinburne. 6875-8
A ballad at parting. Algernon Charles Swinburne. 6875-8
A ballad for a boy. Unknown. 6479-5
A ballad for a boy. William Johnson Cory. 6014-8,6079-X
A ballad for brave women. Charles Mair. 6795-6,6797-2
Ballad for Cape Henry Day. Virginia Lyne Tunstall. 6038-2
Ballad for gloom. Ezra Pound. 6897-9
A ballad for Katharine of Aragon. Charles Causley. 6210-5
A ballad for May Day, sels. Paul Potts. 6895-2
"A ballad from the sevep dials press...". Unknown. 6157-5
Ballad in blond hair foretold. Robert Bagg. 6388-9
A ballad in the manner of R-dy-rd K-pl-ng. Guy Wetmore Carryl. 6089-7
A ballad maker. Padraic Colum. 6628-3
The ballad of 'La tribune' Archibald MacMechan. 6797-2
The ballad of 'Teddy's terrors' Stephen French Whitman. 6995-9
A ballad of 1941. Francis Gelder. 6475-2
The ballad of a barber. Aubrey Beardsley. 6507-4
Ballad of a bridal. Edith (Bland) Nesbit. 6656-9
The ballad of a butcher and the dear little children. Unknown. 6916-9
Ballad of a careless man. Edgar A. Guest. 6748-4
Ballad of a child. John G. Neihardt. 6556-2
Ballad of a cruel fate. Dana Burnet. 6732-8
The ballad of a daft girl. Dorothy Aldis. 6039-0
Ballad of a gray cloak. Elizabeth Buell. 6799-9
The ballad of a little fun. James Maurice Thompson. 6062-5
The ballad of a lost house. Leonora Speyer. 6531-7,6619-4, 6039-0
A ballad of a nun. John Davidson. 6102-8,6250-4,6301-2
The ballad of Adam's first. Leland Davis. 6037-4
Ballad of Admiral Hosier's ghost. Richard Glover. 6086-2
Ballad of Agincourt. Michael Drayton. 6303-2,6331-4,6385-3, 6504-X,6536-8,6536-8,6634-8,6634-8,6331-4,6023-4, 6197-4,6102-8,6219-9,6302-0;6385-3
The ballad of Agincourt. Michael Drayton. 6263-6
A ballad of all the trades. Unknown. 6157-5
Ballad of Amaryllis in the shade. Richard Le Gallienne. 6029-3
Ballad of amateur hour. Phyllis McGinley. 6654-2
The ballad of Ameighlia Maireigh. Unknown. 6724-7
A ballad of an anti-Puritan. Gilbert Keith Chesterton. 6089-7
A ballad of an artist's wife. John Davidson. 6274-1
A ballad of ancient oaths. Eugene Field. 6949-5
The ballad of Andrew Symington. Richard Lawson Gales. 6950-9
The ballad of Andrew. Kostas Varnalis. 6352-7
The ballad of Angel May. Leonard Bacon. 6506-6
Ballad of another Orphelia. David Herbert Lawrence. 6125-7
A ballad of antiquaries. Austin Dobson. 6508-2
A ballad of appeal.l Algernon Charles Swinburne. 6875-8
The ballad of Babie Bell. Thomas Bailey Aldrich. 6008-0
The ballad of baby bunting. Henry Sambrooke Leigh. 6078-1
A ballad of badlam. Unknown. 6089-7
A ballad of bath. Algernon Charles Swinburne. 6770-0,6875-8
The ballad of Beau Brocade. Austin Dobson. 6046-3
Ballad of bedlam. Unknown. 6902-9
A ballad of bedlam. Unknown. 6278-4
Ballad of Benny roads number 65943 Jack Micheline. 6901-0
The ballad of blasphemous Bill. Robert Service. 6159-1
The ballad of Boh Da Thone. Rudyard Kipling. 6810-3
The ballad of bouillabaisse. John James Ingalla. 6026-9, 6439-6,6652-6,6656-9,6092-7
The ballad of bouillabaisse. William Makepeace Thackeray. 6331-4,6732-8,6271-7,6437-X,6484-1,6089
The ballad of bouillabiasse. William Makepeace Thackeray. 6230-X
The ballad of Bunker Hill. Edward Everett Hale. 6946-0
A ballad of burdens. Algernon Charles Swinburne. 6828-6
A ballad of burdens. Algernon Charles Swinburne. 6110-9
The ballad of Calnan's Christmas. Helen Gray Cone. 6062-5
Ballad of Camden Town. James Elroy Flecker. 6371-3
A ballad of Cape St. Vincent. John Masefield. 6395-0
A ballad of Capri. Unknown. 6414-0
The ballad of Captain Kidd. Unknown. 6732-8
The balad of Casey's billy-goat. Robert Service. 6159-1

The ballad of Cassandra Brown. Helen Gray Cone. 6089-7,
    6652-6
The ballad of Cassandra Brown. Coroebus Green. 6918-5
A ballad of charity. Charles Godfrey Leland. 6089-7,6508-8
The ballad of Chickamauga. James Maurice Thompson. 6074-9
>The ballad of Christmas. Walter De La Mare. 6746-8
A ballad of Claremont hill. Henry Van Dyke. 6961-4
A ballad of college days. Unknown. 6118-4
The ballad of crossing the brook. Sir Charles George
    Douglas Roberts. 6797-2
A ballad of Dansekar the Dutchman. Unknown. 6547-3
A ballad of dead camp-fires. Robert Cameron Rogers. 6006-4
Ballad of dead girls. Dana Burnet. 6431-0
The ballad of dead ladies, fr. Francois Villon. Dante
    Gabriel Rossetti. 6198-2,6289-X,6527-9,6026-9,6301-2,
    6646-1,6656-9,6508-2,6655-0
The ballad of dead ladies. Dante Gabriel Rossetti. 6875-8
The ballad of dead ladies. Francois Villon. 6879-0
The ballad of dead men's bay. Algernon Charles Swinburne.
    6518-X
Ballad of death and the lady. Unknown. 6328-4
A ballad of death. Algernon Charles Swinburne. 6526-0,6655-
    0
A ballad of departure. Unknown (Greek) 6771-9
A ballad of despair. Wade Wellman. 6218-0
The ballad of Dick Turpin. Alfred Noyes. 6079-X
A ballad of Dick Whittington. Richard Lawson Gales. 6950-9
Ballad of Douglas Bridge. Francis Carlin. 6244-X
The ballad of Dowsabell. Michael Drayton. 6315-2
A ballad of dreamland. Algernon Charles Swinburne. 6770-0
A ballad of dreamland. Algernon Charles Swinburne. 6732-8,
    6199-0,6473-6,6655-0,6110-9
Ballad of Earl Haldan's daughter. Charles Kingsley. 6136-2,
    6518-X
A ballad of earth and sky. Bertha Lee Gardner. 7019-1
A ballad of east and west. Rudyard Kipling. 6419-1,6656-9,
    6322-5,6107-9,6161-3,6660 ,6675-5,6473-6,6337-3,6101-
    X,6395-0,6476
A ballad of Easter eve. Richard Lawson Gales. 6950-9
Ballad of Edgehill. Hubert Nicholson. 6895-2
The ballad of Eliza Davis. William Makepeace Thackeray.
    6278-4
A ballad of Emma Samson. John Trotwood Moore. 6074-9
The ballad of Father Gilligan. William Butler Yeats. 6639-
    9,6508-2,6727-1,6458-2,6371-3,6396 ,6060-0,6266-0,
    6290-3,6473-6,6518-X,6162
The ballad of Fisher's boarding-house. Rudyard Kipling.
    6518-X
Ballad of Florentin. Georges Duhamel. 6351-9
A ballad of forgotten tunes. Agnes Mary F. ("Madame
    Duclaux") Robinson. 6770-0
ballad of Francois V. Algernon Charles Swinburne. 6071-4
A ballad of Francois Villon. Algernon Charles Swinburne.
    6828-6
A ballad of Francois Villon. Algernon Charles Swinburne.
    6483-3,6732-8,6110-9,6655-0,6102-8
Ballad of Frederico Garcia Lopez. Luis Cardoza y Aragon.
    6759-X
Ballad of good counsel. Geoffrey Chaucer. 6022-6
The ballad of Grizzly Gulch. Wallace Irwin. 6995-9
The ballad of gum-boot Ben. Robert Service. 6159-1
The ballad of Guy Moquet. Maurice Carpenter. 6895-2
The ballad of Hadji and the boar. Ian Hamilton. 7010-8
The ballad of Hampstead Heath. James Elroy Flecker. 6079-X
The ballad of Hank the Finn. Robert Service. 6159-1
Ballad of Hans Breitmann. Charles Godfrey Leland. 6089-7
The ballad of hard-luck Henry. Robert Service. 6159-1,6519-
    0
A ballad of heaven. John Davidson. 6655-0,6507-4,6656-9,
    6371-3,6648-8,6102-8
A ballad of hell. John Davidson. 6518-X,6726-3,6153-2,6655-
    0
A ballad of heroes. Austin Dobson. 6289-X,6340-3,6465-5,
    6476-0
A ballad of heroes. Agnes Mary F. ("Madame Duclaux")
    Robinson. 6770-0
A ballad of heroes. Agnes Mary F. ("Madame Duclaux")
    Robinson. 6875-2
A ballad of higher endeavor. Unknown. 6089-7
The ballad of Hiram Hover. Bayard Taylor. 6802-2

Ballad of hope and fear. Charles Madge. 6209-1
The ballad of how Macpherson held the floor. Robert
    Service. 6159-1
Ballad of human life. Thomas Lovell Beddoes. 6656-9
The ballad of imitation. Austin Dobson. 6770-0
The ballad of imitation. Austin Dobson. 6655-0
The ballad of Ishmael day. Fitz-Greene Halleck. 6402-7
The ballad of Ismael Day. Unknown. 6946-0
Ballad of Jack Jouett. Julia Johnson Davis. 6042-0
Ballad of Jasper road. Katherine (Amelia Beers Warnock
    Garvin) Hale. 6797-2
A ballad of jealousy. Leland Davis. 6880-4
The ballad of Jenny the mare. Unknown. 6105-2,6423-X
The ballad of Jesse James. William Rose Benet. 6399-3
Ballad of John Camplejohn. Bliss Carman. 6301-2
Ballad of John Nameless. Maurice Carpenter. 6895-2
A ballad of John Nicholson. Sir Henry Newbolt. 6371-3
The ballad of John Paul Jones. Arthur Guiterman. 6773-5
A ballad of John Silver. John Masefield. 6162-1,6079-X
The ballad of Judas Iscariot. Robert Buchanan. 6473-,6518-
    X,6732-8,6656-9,6646-1,6102
The ballad of Keith of Ravelston. Sydney Dobell. 6046-3,
    6301-2
The ballad of Kind Kittok. William Dunbar. 6636-4
The ballad of Lager Bier. Edmund Clarence Stedman. 6735-2
A ballad of Lauderdale. Phoebe Cary. 6865-0;6969-X
The ballad of Lenin's tomb. Robert Service. 6159-1
A ballad of life. Algernon Charles Swinburne. 6655-0
The ballad of London river. May C. ([Mary] Gillington)
    Byron. 6793-X
A ballad of London. Richard Le Gallienne. 6507-4,6102-8,
    6439-6
A ballad of lost lovers. Agnes Mary F. ("Madame Duclaux")
    Robinson. 6770-0
Ballad of love and blood. Angel Miguel Queremel. 6759-X
A ballad of love in London. Charles Hanson Towne. 6331-4
Ballad of lovely Bridget. Marjorie Allen Seiffert. 6628-3
The ballad of Lycaon. William Edmonstoune Aytoun. 6948-7
A ballad of Manila Bay. Sir Charles George Douglas
    Roberts. 6062-5
A ballad of Marjorie. Dora Sigerson Shorter. 6174-5
The ballad of McCarthy's trombone. Joseph Crosby Lincoln.
    6119-2
The ballad of Mean Marks. Amanda Benjamin Hall. 6039-0
The ballad of meikle-mousels. Unknown. 6191-5
The ballad of Melicertes. Algernon Charles Swinburne. 6875-
    8
The ballad of Moll Magee. William Butler Yeats. 6473-6,
    6646-1
The ballad of nails. Nikolai Tikhonov. 6546-5
The ballad of Nathan Hale. Unknown. 6015-3
The ballad of New Orleans. George H. Baker. 6403-5
The ballad of New Orleans. George Henry Boker. 6946-0
The ballad of O'Bruadir. Frederick Robert Higgins. 6833-2
Ballad of old Doc Higgins. Leonora Speyer. 6850-2
A ballad of old metres. Unknown. 6770-0
The ballad of one-eyed Mike. Robert Service. 6159-1
Ballad of Oriana. Alfred Lord Tennyson. 6328-4
A ballad of Orleans. Agnes Mary F. ("Madame Duclaux")
    Robinson. 6323-3,6656-9
Ballad of our dear lady of the railway carriage. Rene
    Schickele. 6160-5
Ballad of our lady. William Dunbar. 6282-2,6022-6
Ballad of Paco Town. Clinton Scollard. 6062-5
Ballad of past delight. John Payne. 6770-0
A ballad of past meridian. George Meredith. 6828-6
A ballad of past meridian. George Meredith. 6508-2
Ballad of Pentyre town. Rosamond Marriott ("Graham R.
    Tomson") Watson. 6997-5
Ballad of Pentyre town. Rosamund Marriott ("Graham R.
    Tomson") Watson. 6793-X
Ballad of piny ridge. Ben Lucien Burman. 6778-6
The ballad of pious Pete. Robert Service. 6159-1
A ballad of Port Royal. Jamesuis Hannay. 7041-8
A ballad of prose and rhym. Austin Dobson. 6508-2
The ballad of prose and rhym. Austin Dobson. 6301-2
A ballad of Queen Elizabeth. Margaret Widdemer. 6037-4
The ballad of reading gaol, sel. Oscar Wilde. 6958-1
The ballad of Reading gaol, sels. Oscar Wilde. 6096-X,6244-
    X,6337-3,6507-4,6726-3,6732

BALLAD

The ballad of reading gaol. Oscar Wilde. 6930-4
The ballad of Reading gaol. Oscar Wilde. 6427-2,6250-4, 6304-2,6022-6,6655-0
A ballad of Redhead's Day. Richard Butler Glaenzer. 6946-0
A ballad of Robin Hood. Unknown. 6625-9
A ballad of Roncesvalles. Felicia Dorothea Hemans. 6832-4
The ballad of Sagamore hill. Wallace Irwin. 6995-9
A ballad of Saint Christopher. Richard Lawson Gales. 6950-9
The ballad of salvation Bill. Robert Service. 6159-1
A ballad of Santa Claus. Henry Van Dyke. 6961-4
A ballad of Sark. Algernon Charles Swinburne. 6770-0,6875-8
A ballad of sea fardingers, describing evil fortune. Unknown. 6547-3
The ballad of Semmerwater. Sir William Watson. 6290-3,6490-6
Ballad of Simple Simon. J. Corson Miller. 6039-0
A ballad of Sir John Franklin. George Henry Boker. 6473-6, 6396-9
The ballad of soulful Sam. Robert Service. 6159-1
Ballad of Sparrow. Maurice Carpenter. 6895-2
The ballad ofs plendid silence. Edith (Bland) Nesbit. 6661-5;6670-4
The ballad of St. Barbara. Gilbert Keith Chesterton. 6884-7
The ballad of St. Barbara. Gilbert Keith Chesterton. 7027-2
A ballad of St. Christopher. Richard Lawson Gales. 6079-X
A ballad of St. Swinthin's day. Emily Henrietta Hickey. 6424-8
A ballad of strawberry Sunday. Katherine Drayton Simons. 7016-2
A ballad of suicide. Gilbert Keith Chesterton. 6732-8,6089-7,6026-9,6633-X
The ballad of sweet P. Virginia Woodward Cloud. 6946-0
The ballad of Sweet P. Virginia Woodward Cloud. 6688-7
The ballad of the "Laughing Sally" Sir Charles George Douglas Roberts. 6610-0
The ballad of the 'Eastern crown'. Cicely Fox Smith. 7031-0
Ballad of the afternoon tea. H.P. Huntress. 6118-4
The ballad of the army. Tu Fu. 6542-2
Ballad of the banshee. James B. Dollard. 6115-X
Ballad of the bells, sels. Paul Fort. 6351-9
The ballad of the Billycock. Anthony C. Deane. 6026-9,6102-8
The ballad of the black fox skin. Robert Service. 6159-1
Ballad of the black kitten. Marjorie Allen Seiffert. 6628-3
The ballad of the boat. Richard GarneAt. 6138-8,6457-4, 6481-7,6046-3,6656-9
The ballad of The Bolivar. Rudyard Kipling. 6810-3
The ballad of the bore. Austin Dobson. 6655-0
A ballad of the Boston tea party. Oliver Wendell Holmes. 6323-3
The ballad of the brand. Robert Service. 6159-1
Ballad of the brave. Grantland Rice. 6583-X
Ballad of the brides of Quair. Isa Craig Knox. 6518-X,6600-3
Ballad of the canal. Phoebe Cary. 6089-7,6724-7
A ballad of the captains. E.J. Brady. 6044-7
Ballad of the careless lover. Marjorie Allen Seiffert. 6628-3
Ballad of the cats of bygone days. Michael Scot. 6511-2
A ballad of the champions. Unknown. 6274-1
The ballad of the children of the czar. Delmore Schwartz. 6389-6
The ballad of the circus. Charles Hanson Towne. 6162-1
The ballad of the Clampherdown. Rudyard Kipling. 6479-5
The ballad of the colors. Thomas Dunn English. 6451-5,6576-7
Ballad of the common man. Alfred Kreymborg. 6561-9
A ballad of the Conemaugh flood. Hardwicke Drummond Rawnsley. 6946-0
A ballad of the courtier and the country clown. Unknown. 6157-5
The ballad of the cross. Theodosia Garrison. 6509-0,6393-4
The ballad of the dark ladie. Samuel Taylor Coleridge. 6527-9,6110-9,6086-2

Ballad of the dead king. Dana Burnet. 6347-0
Ballad of the dolphin's daughter. Marjorie Allen Seiffert. 6628-3
Ballad of the doorstone. Louise Ayres Garnett. 6619-4
The ballad of the easier way. Alfred Noyes. 6151-6
The ballad of the Emeu. Francis Bret Harte. 6089-7
Ballad of the equinox. Vernon Watkins. 6528-7
Ballad of the Erie Canal. Unknown. 6281-4
The ballad of the fiddler. Seumas (James Starkey) O'Sullivan. 6497-3,6628-3
A ballad of the fleet. Alfred Lord Tennyson. 6290-3,6625-9, 6322-5
Ballad of the followers. Franz Werfel. 6160-5
The ballad of the fox. Unknown. 6134-6
The ballad of the foxhunter. William Butler Yeats. 6478-7
A ballad of the French fleet. Henry Wadsworth Longfellow. 6473-6,6552-X,6126-5,6484-1
A ballad of the French fleet. Henry Wadsworth Longfellow. 6946-0
Ballad of the Gaspereau. Arthur Wentworth Hamilton Eaton. 6797-2
Ballad of the gibbet. Andrew Lang. 6875-8
Ballad of the gibbet. Francois Villon. 6771-9,7039-6
Ballad of the gold country. Helen Hunt Jackson. 6241-5
Ballad of the golden vanity. Unknown. 6328-4
A ballad of the good Lord Nelson. Lawrence Durrell. 6733-6
Ballad of the goodly fere. Richard Hovey. 6076-5
Ballad of the goodly fere. Ezra Pound. 6052-8,6102-8,6527-9,6536-8,6300-4,6076
A ballad of the great war. Flaccus [pseud]. 6817-0
Ballad of the Guije. Nicolas Guillen. 6642-9
Ballad of t^{e}e harper. Johann Wolfgang von Goethe. 6328-4
The ballad of the ice-worm cocktail. Robert Service. 6159-1
Ballad of the imperial goldfish. Dennis Kelly. 7003-5
The ballad of the Ivanhoe. Bill Adams. 6107-9
Ballad of the jelly-cake. Eugene Field. 6949-5
The ballad of the king's jest. Rudyard Kipling. 6236-9
The ballad of the king's jest. Rudyard Kipling. 6810-3
The ballad of the king's mercy. Rudyard Kipling. 6810-3
Ballad of the lady in hell. Annette Patton Cornell. 6750-6
The ballad of the Lady Lorraine. Padraic Gregory. 6541-4
A ballad of the lakes. Laura E. McCully. 6115-X
The ballad of the leather medal. Robert Service. 6159-1
Ballad of the Lincoln penny. Alfred Kreymborg. 6736-0
Ballad of the little black hound. Dora Sigerson Shorter. 6930-4
Ballad of the long-legged bait. Dylan Thomas. 6390-X
Ballad of the lords of old time. Algernon Charles Swinburne. 6875-8
Ballad of the lords of old time. Francois Villon. 7039-6
The ballad of the lost bride. Unknown. 6693-3
Ballad of the mermaid. Charles Godfrey Leland. 7025-6,6760-3
The ballad of the merry ferry. Emma Rounds. 6891-X
The ballad of the midnight sun. H.E. Hamilton-King. 6518-X
The ballad of the northern lights. Robert Service. 6159-1
Ballad of the outer life. Hugo von Hofmannsthal. 7039-6
The ballad of the overconfident pollywog. F.R. DuBois. 6118-4
The ballad of the oysterman. Oliver Wendell Holmes. 6126-5, 6396-9,6419-1,6464-7,6136-2,6478-7,6497-3,6512-0, 6610-0,6613,6165-6,6176-1,6290-3,6332-2,6735-2,6089
Ballad of the Philippines. Frank Lebby Stanton. 6589-9
The ballad of the pipe. Hermann Rave. 6453-1
Ballad of the primrose way. Rose Edith Mills. 6274-1
Ballad of the rag-bag heart. Marjorie Allen Seiffert. 6019-6
The ballad of the Rawalpindi. Nathaniel A. Benson. 6224-5
The ballad of the rising. Unknown. 6022-6
A ballad of the road. Constance D'Arcy Mackay. 6336-5
Ballad of the rough riders. Marion Couthouy Smith. 6995-9
The ballad of the rubberplant and palm. Alice Wellington Rollins. 6529-5
Ballad of the Sabre Cross and 7. Irving Bacheller. 6274-1
The ballad of the shamrock. Fitz-James O'Brien. 6414-0
Ballad of the Spanish armada. Austin Dobson. 6610-0,6322-5
A ballad of the strange and wonderful storm of hail. Unknown. 6157-5
Ballad of the summoning. Federico Garcia Lorca. 6068-4

The **ballad** of the Taylor pup. Eugene Field. 6949-5
Ballad of the tempest. James Thomas Fields. 6271-7,6412-4, 6219-9
Ballad of the Thanksgiving pilgrim. Clinton Scollard. 6618-6
The **ballad** of the three sons. Amanda Benjamin Hall. 6531-7, 6039-0
Ballad of the two grandfathers. Nicolas Guillen. 6642-9
Ballad of the unsuccessful. Richard Burton. 6274-1
The **ballad** of the Vermont calf. Daniel L. Cady. 6989-4
A **ballad** of the war. George Herbert Sass. 6074-9
A **ballad** of the war. Frank H. Staffer. 6529-5
A **ballad** of the were-wolf. Rosamund Marriott ("Graham R. Tomson") Watson. 6670-4
The **ballad** of the white horse, sels. Gilbert Keith Chesterton. 6234-2
The **ballad** of the white horse. Gilbert Keith Chesterton. 6102-8,6541-4,6301-2
Ballad of the wicked nephew. James Thomas Fields. 6575-9
A **ballad** of the wise men. Margaret Widdemer. 6331-4
Ballad of the women of Paris. Algernon Charles Swinburne. 6875-8
Ballad of the women of Paris. Francois Villon. 7039-6
The **ballad** of the young queen. Eleanor Widdis. 6249-0
Ballad of thread for a needle. Marjorie Allen Seiffert. 6619-4
The **ballad** of ths solemn ass. Henry Van Dyke. 6961-4
The **ballad** of Titus Labienus. Laura E. Richards. 7022-1
The **ballad** of touch-the-button Nell. Robert Service. 6159-1
A **ballad** of trees and the master. Sidney Lanier. 6121-4, 6467-1,6730-1,6723-9,6250-4,6288-1,6431-0,6104 ,6047-1,6077-3,6144-3,6337-3,6465-5,6478 ,6299-7,6333-0, 6335-7,6423-X,6473-6,6006 ,6501-5,6509-0,6632-1,6309-8,6464-7,6727
A **ballad** of trees. Robert Norwood. 6797-2
The **ballad** of True Thomas. Unknown. 6138-9
Ballad of two kings. Grant H. Code. 6218-0
Ballad of Ulysses. Marjorie Allen Seiffert. 7038-8
Ballad of Uncle Joe. Alice Cary. 6865-0;6969-X
A **ballad** of war. Menella Bute Smedley. 6919-3
A **ballad** of Weenen. Olive R. Bridgman. 6625-9
The **ballad** of William Sycamore. Stephen Vincent Benet. 6891-X
The **ballad** of William Sycamore. Stephen Vincent Benet. 6506-6,6527-9,6619-4,6037-4,6581-3,6250 ,6467-1,6628-3
A **ballad** of wise men. George M.P. Baird. 6608-9
Ballad of women I love. Eugene Field. 6949-5
A **ballad** of wonder. Eleanor Slater. 6337-3
The **ballad** of Yaada. Emily Pauline ("Tekahionwake") Johnson. 6797-2
The **ballad** of Yaada. Emily Pauline ("Tekahionwake") Johnson. 6837-5,6843-X
A **ballad** on ale. John Gay. 6972-X
A **ballad** on quadrille. John Gay. 6972-X
A **ballad** on quadrille. John Gay. 6092-7
The **ballad** singer. Thomas Hardy. 6186-9,6317-9
A **ballad** to Queen Elizabeth. Austin Dobson. 6123-0,6258-X, 6026-9,6639-9
A **ballad** upon a wedding, sels. Sir John Suckling. 6317-9, 6194-X
A **ballad** upon a wedding. Sir John Suckling. 6301-2,6230-X, 6197-4,6099-4,6315-2,6378-0,6481-7,6563-5,6634 ,6157-5,6562-7,6733-3,6092-7,6659-3,6250
A **ballad** upon the popish plot. John Gadbury. 6157-5
A **ballad** warning men to beware of deceitful women, sels. John Lydgate. 6317-9
A **ballad** when at sea. Charles Sackville; 6th Earl of Dorset. 6092-7
Ballad written for a bridegroom. Algernon Charles Swinburne. 6875-8
Ballad, fr. The rivals. Sir William Davenant. 6867-7
A **ballad-maker**.. Padraic Colum. 6477-9
Ballad: Alice Brand, fr. Lady of the lake. Sir Walter Scott. 6604-6,6660-7
Ballad: before my bookshelves. Nelson Rich Tyerman. 6875-8
Ballad: Le pere severe. Unknown (French) 7039-6
Ballad: Lembek's will. Charles Whitby. 6994-0
Ballad: Lost for a rose's sake. Unknown (French) 7039-6

Ballad: The elected knight. Unknown (Danish) 7039-6
Ballad: The mer-man, and Marstig's daughter. Unknown (Danish) 7039-6
Ballad: the spring rain. Raymond Ellsworth Larsson. 6783-2
A **ballad**. Thomas Campion. 6794-8
A **ballad**. John Gay. 6191-5,6152-4,6219-9
A **ballad**. Riccardo Stephens. 6873-1
Ballade. James Elroy Flecker. 7014-0
Ballade. Paul Fort. 7039-6
Ballade. John Cameron Grant. 6770-0
Ballade. E. Adelaide Hahn. 6847-2
Ballade. William Ernest Henley. 6724-7
Ballade. W. H. Jewitt. 6770-0
Ballade. Don Marquis. 6722-0
Ballade. Unknown. 6770-0
Ballade. Francois Villon. 6227-X
Ballade ("Far in the depths"). Unknown. 6118-4
Ballade ("One day"). Charles, Duc d' Orleans. 6227-X
Ballade a double refrain. Edwin Meade Robinson. 6850-2, 6875-8
Ballade a la lune. Alfred de Musset. 6801-4
Ballade against the enemies of France. Richard Le Gallienne. 6875-8
Ballade against the enemies of France. Francois Villon. 6102-8
Ballade by the fire. Edwin Arlington Robinson. 6476-0
A **ballade** catalogue of lovely things. Richard Le Gallienne. 6490-6
Ballade d'aujourd'hui. Coates Chapman. 6274-1
Ballade de bon conseil. Gertrude Marie Purcell. 6847-2
Ballade de Marguerite. Unknown (French) 7039-6
Ballade de Victor Hugo. Theodore de Banville. 6801-4
Ballade dedicatory to Mrs. Elton of White Staunton. Andrew Lang. 6987-8
Ballade des enfants sans souci. Oliver Elton. 6875-8
Ballade des pendus (gringoire) Andrew Lang. 6875-8
Ballade for missionaries. Squidge [pseud]. 6817-0
Ballade for peace ("O pray"). Charles, Duc d' Orleans. 6227-X
Ballade for the laureate. Andrew Lang. 6770-0,6875-8
Ballade made in the hot weather. William Ernest Henley. 6770-0
Ballade made in the hot weather. William Ernest Henley. 6508-2
Ballade of a backslider. Edwin Meade Robinson. 6875-8
A **ballade** of a book-revviewer. Gilbert Keith Chesterton. 6875-8
Ballade of a conspicuous omission. Carolyn Wells. 6089-7
Ballade of a dream addict. Virginia Scott. 6750-6
Ballade of a friar. Clement Marot. 6987-8
Ballade of a garden. Arthur Reed Ropes. 6770-0,6875-8
Ballade of a summer hotel. Junia. 6722-0
Ballade of a Toyokuni colour print. William Ernest Henley. 6875-8
Ballade of Acheron. Rosamund Marriott ("Graham R. Tomson") Watson. 6770-0
The **ballade** of adaptation. Brander Matthews. 6501-5
Ballade of antique dances. William Ernest Henley. 6770-0, 6875-8
A **ballade** of any father to any son. Sir John Collings ("Solomon Eagle") Squire. 6722-0
Ballade of Asphodel. Rosamund Marriott ("Graham R. Tomson") Watson. 6770-0
Ballade of aspiration. William Ernest Henley. 6770-0,6875-8
Ballade of Aucassin. Andrew Lang. 6850-2
Ballade of August. Patrick Reginald Chalmers. 6875-8
A **ballade** of ballade-mongers. Augustus M. Moore. 6770-0, 6875-8
A **ballade** of ballade-mongers. Augustus M. Moore. 6089-7;6440-X
Ballade of barren roses. Gertrude Bartlett. 6115-X
Ballade of belief. Cotsford Dick. 6770-0
Ballade of biblioclats. Rosamund Marriott ("Graham R. Tomson") Watson. 6770-0
Ballade of big plans. Dorothy Parker. 6817-0
Ballade of blue china. Andrew Lang. 6732-8,6102-8,6424-8, 6656-9
Ballade of books unbought. Christopher Morley. 6875-8
A **ballade** of bothers. Unknown. 6770-0

BALLADE

A ballade of boyhood. Alfred Noyes. 6781-6
A ballade of brides. Thomas Augustine Daly. 6875-8
Ballade of broken flutes. Edwin Arlington Robinson. 6875-8
A ballade of broken things. Blanche Weitbrec. 7027-2
Ballade of burial. Cotsford Dick. 6770-0
A ballade of busy doctors. James Newton Matthews. 6482-5
A ballade of Calypso. Sir Charles George Douglas Roberts. 6770-0
A ballade of calypso. Sir Charles George Douglas Roberts. 6875-8
Ballade of caution. Arthur Guiterman. 6875-8
The ballade of charitie. Thomas Chatterton. 6604-6,6102-8, 6660-7,6659-3
Ballade of Charon and the river girl. J.B. Morton. 6722-0
Ballade of Christmas ghosts. Andrew Lang. 6145-1,6608-9
Ballade of colleens. Hamish Maclaren. 6779-4
Ballade of cricket. Andrew Lang. 6802-2,6987-8,6770-0
A ballade of crying for the moon. Patrick Reginald Chalmers. 6875-8
Ballade of dead actors. William Ernest Henley. 6875-8
Ballade of dead actors. William Ernest Henley. 6026-9
Ballade of dead cities. Sir Edmund Gosse. 6473-6,6732-8, 6102-8
Ballade of dead cities. Andrew Lang. 6875-8
Ballade of dead ladies. Andrew Lang. 6875-8
Ballade of dead ladies. Francois Villon. 6102-8
The ballade of dead ladies. Francois Villon. 6652-6
Ballade of dead poets. Clinton Scollard. 6770-0
Ballade of dead poets. Clinton Scollard. 6875-8
Ballade of dead thinkers. Unknown. 6770-0
A ballade of death and time. Bert Leston Taylor. 6875-8
A ballade of death. Hunter MacCulloch. 6770-0
Ballade of dime novels. Arthur Guiterman. 6875-8
A ballade of diminishing control. Sir John Collings ("Solomon Eagle") Squire. 6722-0
Ballade of dottiness. Edward Anthony. 6875-8
Ballade of dreams. Rose E. Macaulay. 6875-8
Ballade of dreams transposed. Gelett Burgess. 6652-6
Ballade of Easter dawn. Edwin Meade Robinson. 6875-8
Ballade of envy. Ted Robinson. 6817-0
A ballade of evolution. Grant Allen. 6770-0,6875-8
Ballade of Exmoor. F.S. P. 6770-0
Ballade of expansion. Hilda Johnson. 6996-7
Ballade of expansion. Hilda Johnson. 6946-0
The ballade of fact and fiction. Brander Matthews. 6875-8
Ballade of fairy gold. Rosamund Marriott ("Graham R. Tomson") Watson. 6770-0
Ballade of farewell. Brian Hooker. 6875-8
Ballade of fog in the Canon. Gelett Burgess. 6875-8
Ballade of forgotten loves. Arthur Grissom. 7021-3
Ballade of forgotten loves. Arthur Grissom. 6089-7
Ballade of his lady. J.B.B. Nichols. 6770-0
Ballade of his own country. Andrew Lang. 6331-4
A ballade of inaction. Mary Muriel Rochester. 6847-2
Ballade of incipient lunacy. Sir Alan Patrick Herbert. 6875-8
A ballade of indignation. Carolyn Wells. 6875-8
A ballade of irresolution. Bert Leston Taylor. 6875-8
Ballade of June. William Ernest Henley. 6320-9,6473-6,6652-6
A ballade of kings. Arthur Symons. 6875-8
A ballade of kings. Arthur Watson Symons. 6770-0
A ballade of labor and love. Unknown. 6274-1
Ballade of ladies' names. William Ernest Henley. 6652-6
Ballade of literary fame. Andrew Lang. 6987-8,6996-7
The ballade of lovelace. George Moore. 6770-0,6875-8
A ballade of memorie. Janet Hamilton. 7037-X
Ballade of middle age. Andrew Lang. 6770-0,6850-2
Ballade of middle age. Andrew Lang. 6301-2
Ballade of middle age. Andrew Lang. 6850-2,6987-8
Ballade of midsummer days and nights. William Ernest Henley. 6123-0
A ballade of midsummer. Brander Matthews. 6770-0,6875-8
A ballade of midsummer. Clinton Scollard. 6875-8
Ballade of might-be. Rosamund Marriott ("Graham R. Tomson") Watson. 6770-0
Ballade of misery and iron. George Carter. 6954-1
Ballade of Muhammad Din Tilai. Edward Powys Mathers. 6513-9
Ballade of my lady's beauty. Joyce Kilme. 6310-1,6320-9, 6441-8,6300-4
Ballade of neglected merit. Andrew Lang. 6987-8
Ballade of Nicolete. Rosamund Marriott ("Graham R. Tomson") Watson. 6481-7
Ballade of Nicolete. Rosamund Marriott ("Graham R. Tomson") Watson. 6850-2
Ballade of old instruments. Mortimer Wheeler. 6770-0
Ballade of old laughter. Richard Le Gallienne. 6875-8
A ballade of old loves. Carolyn Wells. 6145-1
A ballade of old loves. Carolyn Wells. 6807-3
Ballade of old plays. Andrew Lang. 6875-8
A ballade of old sweethearts. Richard Le Gallienne. 6770-0, 6875-8
A ballade of Philomela. Sir Charles George Douglas Roberts. 6770-0
A ballade of playing cards. Gleeson White. 6656-9
Ballade of primitive man. Andrew Lang. 6770-0,6875-8
Ballade of professional pride. Cecil Chesterton. 6096 X
Ballade of queen's lace. Richard Le Gallienne. 6162-1
Ballade of railway novels. Andrew Lang. 6987-8
Ballade of rhyme. Frank Dempster Sherman. 6770-0
Ballade of riches. Edward Wilbur Mason. 6889-8
Ballade of riches. Edward Wilbur Mason. 6583-X
A ballade of roses. Justin Huntly McCarthy. 6875-8,6770-0
Ballade of Schopenhauer's philosophy. Franklin Pierce Adams. 6875-8
Ballade of sea-music. Mortimer Wheeler. 6997-5
Ballade of sea-music. Mortimer Wheeler. 6770-0
Ballade of sleep. Andrew Lang. 6770-0
Ballade of solitude. William Black. 6770-0,6875-8
A ballade of souls. Edmund Clerihew Bentley. 6659-3
Ballade of spring. William Ernest Henley. 6770-0,6875-8
A ballade of spring's unrest. Bert Leston Taylor. 6875-8
Ballade of summer. Andrew Lang. 6987-8,6770-0
Ballade of the ancient wheeze. Newman Levy and Nate Salsbury. 6875-8
Ballade of the annual query. Franklin Pierce Adams. 6761-1
Ballade of the bard. Clinton Scollard. 6770-0
Ballade of the book-hunter. Andrew Lang. 6186-9,6297-0, 6656-9,6186-9
The Ballade of the book-man's paradise. Andrew Lang. 6987-8
Ballade of the bookworm. Andrew Lang. 6226-1
Ballade of the bourne. Rosamund Marriott ("Graham R. Tomson") Watson. 6770-0
Ballade of the Caxton Head. Lionel Johnson. 6875-8
Ballade of the Cognescenti. Gelett Burgess. 6875-8
The ballade of the coming rain. James Whitcomb Riley. 6993-2
Ballade of the devil-may-care. Gelett Burgess. 6652-6
The ballade of the dream-ship. Joseph Crosby Lincoln. 6119-2
Ballade of the dreamland rose. Brian Hooker. 6338-1,6347-0, 6250-4
Ballade of the engaged young man. Richard Kendall Munkittrick. 6441-8
Ballade of the fan. William F. Kirk. 6274-1
A ballade of the first rain. Gilbert Keith Chesterton. 6875-8
Ballade of the forest in summer. Patrick Reginald Chalmers. 6875-8
Ballade of the forlorn lady. Creighton Brown Burnham. 6397-7
A ballade of the game. Unknown. 6274-1
Ballade of the gamefish. Grantland Rice. 6211-3
Ballade of the Gibbet. Francois Villon. 6102-8
Ballade of the Girton girl. Andrew Lang. 6987-8
Ballade of the Girton girl. Andrew Lang. 6875-8
Ballade of the golfer in love. Clinton Scollard. 6089-7
Ballade of the Goth. Sir Walter Raleigh. 6722-0
Ballade of the hanging gardens of Babylon. Richard Le Gallienne. 6875-8
Ballade of the hanging gardens of Babylon. Richard Le Gallienne. 6732-8
Ballade of the ideal waiter. Berton Braley. 6853-7
The ballade of the incompetent ballade-monger. James Kenneth Stephen. 6875-8
Ballade of the journey's end. Lady Margaret Sackville. 6875-8
Ballade of the junk-man. Richard Le Gallienne. 6732-8

Ballade of the little things that count. Burges Johnson. 6875-8
Ballade of the lords of old time. Francois Villon. 6102-8
Ballade of the lost refrain. Christopher Morley. 6875-8
A ballade of the night. Margaret L. Woods. 6875-8
Ballade of the nightingale. Archibald T. Strong. 6875-8
A ballade of the nurserie. John Twig. 6902-9
Ballade of the optimist. Rosamund Marriott ("Graham R. Tomson") Watson. 6770-0
Ballade of the oubliette. Bert Leston Taylor. 6875-8
Ballade of the pipesmoke carry. Bert Leston Taylor. 6875-8
Ballade of the poetic life. Sir John Collings ("Solomon Eagle") Squire. 6722-0
Ballade of the primitive jest. Andrew Lang. 6089-7
Ballade of the real and ideal. Andrew Lang. 6875-8
Ballade of the road unknown. Richard Le Gallienne. 6162-1
Ballade of the Scottyshe kinge. John Skelton. 6157-5
Ballade of the sea-folk. William ("Fiona Macleod") Sharp. 6770-0,6875-8
Ballade of the second-best bed. Karl Shapiro. 6391-8
Ballade of the ship. Louis J. Magee. 7004-3
Ballade of the song of the sea-wind. William ("Fiona Macleod") Sharp. 6770-0,6875-8
Ballade of the southern crosse. Andrew Lang. 6289-X
The ballade of the summer-boarder. Henry Cuyler Bunner. 6770-0,6875-8
The ballade of the summer-boarder. Henry Cuyler Bunner. 6652-6
Ballade of the table d'hote. G.S. K. 6817-0
Ballade of the tempting book. Thomas Augustine Daly. 6875-8
Ballade of the things that remain. Richard Le Gallienne. 6875-8
Ballade of the thrush. Austin Dobson. 6073-0,6424-8
A ballade of the thuner-see. Emily Pfeiffer. 6770-0
Ballade of the unattainable. Andrew Lang. 6875-8
Ballade of the unchanging beauty. Richard Le Gallienne. 6488-4
Ballade of things known and unknown. Francois Villon. 6102-8
The ballade of tobacco. Brander Matthews. 6453-1
Ballade of Tristram's last harping. Gertrude Bartlett. 6115-X
Ballade of true wisdom. Andrew Lang. 6297-0
Ballade of truisms. William Ernest Henley. 6770-0
Ballade of truisms. William Ernest Henley. 6123-0
Ballade of unfortunate mammals. Dorothy Parker. 6089-7, 6026-9
Ballade of vain hopes. William ("Fiona Macleod") Sharp. 6770-0,6875-8
A ballade of wattle blossom. Robert Richardson. 6793-X
Ballade of windy nights. William Henry Ogilvie. 6875-8
Ballade of wisdom and folly. Carolyn Wells. 6875-8
Ballade of women. Archibald T. Strong. 6875-8
Ballade of women I love. Eugene Field. 6875-8
Ballade of youth and age. William Ernest Henley. 6123-0
Ballade of Yule. Andrew Lang. 6770-0
Ballade to his lady. Geoffrey Chaucer. 6830-8
Ballade to our lady of Czestochowa. Hilaire Belloc. 6282-2, 6532-5
Ballade to our lady, fr. The ship of fools. Alexander Barclay. 6282-2
Ballade to patience and you. Georgia H. Cooper. 6850-2
Ballade to Rosamund. Geoffrey Chaucer. 6881-2
Ballade to the women. Thomas Augustine Daly. 6875-8
Ballade to Theocritus, in winter. Andrew Lang. 6289-X,6501-5,6656-9,6543-0
Ballade to Villon. Clinton Scollard. 6770-0
Ballade un peu banale. Arthur James Marshall Smith. 6733-6
A ballade-catalogue of lovely things. Richard Le Gallienne. 6476-0,6607-0,6509-0,6153-2,6161-3
Ballade-Lilith. John Cameron Grant. 6770-0
Balladeadro in captivity, fr. The story of Baladeadro. George Gordon McCrae. 6768-9
Ballades. Paul Fort. 6801-4
Ballades des pendus. Andrew Lang. 6770-0
Ballamy, Elizabeth W.
    Baby's logic. 6744-1
Ballantyne, James
    Castles in the air. 6127-3,6131-1,6219-9

Creep afore ye gang. 6233-4,6131-1
Muckle-mou'd Meg. 6656-9
Naebody's bairn. 6960-6
Ballantyne, John F.
    Thine eyes. 6273-3
Ballard, C.R.
    The Pacific railway. 6946-0
Ballard, Charles
    Summer arabesque. 6232-6
Ballard, Charles Rollin
    How does the rain come? 7030-2
Ballard, Dorothy Scott
    The father. 6144-3
Ballard, Harlan House
    In the catacombs. 6089-7,6415-9,6736-0
    'Man that ought to be.' 6717-4
    A Welsh classic. 6415-9,6521-X,6630-5
Ballard, Julia P.
    Two little roses. 6049-8
    The verdict. 6685-2
Ballard, Lowell C.
    Wooden wheels. 6799-9
Ballard, Sallie M.
    To my soldier brother. 6074-9
Ballata: He will gaze upon Beatrice. Dante Alighieri. 7039-6
Ballata: In exile at Sarzana. Guido Cavalcanti. 7039-6
Ballenberg, Kay
    Reminder. 6750-6
Ballerina. Bernice Lesbia Kenyon. 7038-8
The ballet girl. Unknown. 6693-3
Ballet russe. John W. Draper. 6959-2
The ballet school. Russell Hughes. 6959-2
"Balling".. Charlene Jones. 7018-3
The Balliol rooks. Frederick S. Boas. 6073-0,6477-9
The balloon man. Howard Mumford Jones. 6039-0
Balloon over the Rhondda. Roland Mathias. 6360-8
The ballot. John Pierpont. 6289-X,6465-5,6396-9,6300-4
The Ballotville female convention. Unknown. 6914-2
Ballou, A.L.
    Dead in his bed. 6273-3
Ballou, Adin
    Westminster Abbey. 6224-5
Ballou, William Hosea
    My John. 6370-5
Ballyvourney. Thomas Boyd. 6244-X
Balmont, Konstantin
    "I came into this world to see the sunlight" Washington Matthews (tr.). 6103-6
    The reed. Cecil Maurice Bowra (tr.). 6103-6
Balmy June. William Fred Sachs. 6906-1
"The balmy south a genle sigh releases". A greeting. Jonas Hallgrimsson. 6854-5
"Balmy zephyrs, lightly flitting". Drury's dirge. Horace Smith. 6802-2
"Baloo, loo, lammy, now baloo, my dear". Lullaby ("Baloo, loo"). Carolina Oliphant, Baroness Nairne. 6078-1, 6424-8
Balow. Unknown. 6317-9,6395-9,6533-3
"Balow, my babe! lie still and sleep". Lady Anne Bothwell's lament, sels. Unknown. 6934-7
Balow, my bonnie. Eugene Field. 6949-5
Balsaitis, Debbie
    Afterwards. 6883-9
    Haze. 6883-9
Balske, Glennys
    A fringe of snow. 6342-X
Balthasar's song, fr. Much ado about nothing. William Shakespeare. 6436-1,6026-9
Balthazar and the quack. John Tobin. 6606-2
Baltimore. B. Rush Plumly. 6008-0
The Baltimore grays. Unknown. 6074-9
Balulalow. John and James Webberburn. 6931-2
Balulalow. John and James Webberburn. 6315-2
Bamberg, sels. Frederick William Faber. 6046-3
Bamberger, Augustus Wright
    Out of the vast. 6337-3
"Bambi-eyed rich girls". Poem for Edie Sedgwick who slep in a swimming pool. Stewart Brisby. 6870-7
Bambino (Corsican lullaby). Eugene Field. 6949-5

BAMBOO

The bamboo briars. Unknown. 6003-X
Bamboozling grandma. Unknown. 6684-4
Bamborough castle. William Lisle Bowles. 6543-0
Bampfylde, John
    Sonnet: to the redbreast. 6219-9
Banal sojourn, fr. Pecksniffiana. Wallace Stevens. 6531-7
Banana. Charles G. Bell. 6388-8
"A banana boat drifting with the tide". Dreams of lost Atlantis. Alejandro Murguia. 6792-1
Bancroft, Elizabeth Jane
    Loyalty to God. 6894-4
"The band blares". Circus. Eleanor Farjeon. 6891-X
The band in the pines. John Esten Cooke. 6113-3
"The band is on the quarter-deck...". The man behind. Douglas Malloch. 6846-4
"A band of beggars out to view." Kohei. 6027-7
"A band of sweet blue violets". White violets. John Russell Hayes. 6936-3
"A band, a bob-wig and a feather". Fable, related by a beau to Aesop. Sir John Vanbrugh. 6874-X
The banded. Edwin Ford Piper. 6032-3
Bandeira, Manuel
    Dead of night. Dudley Poore (tr.). 6759-X
    The highway. Dudley Poore (tr.). 6759-X
    In soapsuds street. Dudley Poore (tr.). 6759-X
    Mozart in heaven. Dudley Poore (tr.). 6759-X
    Salute to Recife. Dudley Poore (tr.). 6759-X
    The woods. Dudley Poore (tr.). 6759-X
    The woods. Dudley Poore (tr.). 6759-X
"Bandinello slouches on a chair". Geo-politics. Alvaro Cardona-Hine. 6966-5
The bandit's fate. Unknown. 6787-5
The bands and the beautiful children. Patricia K. Page. 6446-9
The bane of poverty. Theognis. 6435-3
Baneful paths. Edward R. Huxley. 6885-5
Banfield, Edith Colby
    Glamour. 6836-7
    Indian names. 6836-7
    Infancy. 6836-7
    Mother earth. 6836-7
    To a portrait of Abraham Lincoln. 6524-4
Bangay, Evelyn D.
    Thoughts out riding. 6782-4
Bangham, Mary Dickerson
    Come, holy babe! 6144-3
Bangkolidye. Barry Pain. 6089-7
Bangs, Edward
    Yankee Doodle. 6307-1,6465-5
    The Yankee's return from camp. 6946-0
Bangs, Ella M.
    Was Lincoln king? 6708-5
Bangs, Ella Matthews
    Revisited. 6798-0
Bangs, Janet Norris
    April. 6799-9
    Care. 6037-4
    Time and the woman. 6789-1
Bangs, John Kendrick
    Before the toy shop window. 6691-7
    Blind. 6303-9,6337-3
    Boy baby's protest. 6715-8
    Boy so different from daddy! 6715-8
    The catch. 6510-4
    Christmas day. 6069-2,6747-6
    Deliverance. 6654-2
    Faith. 6214-8
    Gardening. 6654-2
    The gifts divine. 6303-9
    The hazard. 6441-8
    I never knew a night so black. 6337-3
    If ("If I were fire I'd seek the frozen north"). 6291-1
    The kingdom of man. 6291-1
    The little elf man. 6466-3
    The little elf. 6135-4,6401-9,6519-8
    Little orphant Teddy. 6995-9
    Little toy-dog. 6714-X
    'Mona Lisa.' 6089-7
    My dog. 6510-4
    My share. 6109-5
    Nature's hired man. 6006-4
    The note within. 6711-5
    On being good. 6441-8
    A philosopher. 6006-4,6291-1
    The richer mines. 6291-1
    The seeing eye. 6510-4
    Small but noisy. 6715-8
    A smiling paradox. 6291-1
    Success ("Success?). 6109-5
    A thanksgiving. 6303-9,6337-3
    To a withered rose. 6047-1
    To melancholy. 6291-1
    Today. 6461-2
    What really is the trouble. 6280-6
    The word. 6053-6,6291-1
Banim, John
    Ailleen. 6858-8
    Bouchelleen-bawn. 6858-8
    Damon and Pythias, sels. 6148-6
    Damon to the Syracusans. 6406-X,6606-2
    He said that he was not our brother. 6930-4
    The Irish maiden's song. 6858-8
    Soggarth Aroon. 6090-0,6656-9
Banish sorrow. George Ogle. 6086-2
The banish'd beauty. John Gay. 6972-X
The banished Bejant. Robert Fuller Murray. 7025-6
Banished duke living in the forest, fr. As you like it. William Shakespeare. 6138-9
The banished Duke of Grantham. Unknown. 6829-4
The banished kings. Richard Chenevix Trench. 6980-0
The banished kings. Richard Chenevix Trench. 6848-0
The banished lover. Al-Mustazhir. 6362-4
The banished wife's lament. Unknown. 6193-1
The banishment, fr. Paradise lost. John Milton. 6933-9
Banjo mine. Unknown. 6116-8
Banjo Sam. A.M. McCullough. 6397-7
A banjo song. Paul Laurence Dunbar. 6274-1
The bank clerk. Edgar A. Guest. 6862-6
The bank roll. Edgar A. Guest. 6862-6
The bank-swallows. Unknown. 6373-X
"Banked in a serried drift beside the sea". Ballade of fog in the Canon. Gelett Burgess. 6875-8
Banker Jr., William
    The battle of Queenstown. 6946-0
Banker's dream, fr. Hippdromania. Adam Lindsay Gordon. 6951-7
Bankers are just like anybody else, except richer. Ogden Nash. 6733-6
Banking up Vermont houses. Daniel L. Cady. 6988-6
The bankis of Helicon. Alexander Montgomerie. 6180-X
Banko, ?
    Cattle. 6891-X
The bankrupt's visitor. Thomas Dunn English. 6411-6
Banks Jr., Theodore Howard
    In memoriam. 6347-0
    The return. 6846-4
The banks o' Doon. Robert Burns. 6219-9,6438-8,6152-4,6250-4,6219-9,6153 ,6075-7,6180-X,6186-9,6240-7,6332-2, 6427-,6302-0,6315-2,6385-3,6668-2,6660-7,6646 ,6481-7,6479-5,6484-1,6604-6,6726-3,6560
The banks o' Yarrow. Unknown. 6055-2,6098-6,6056-0
The banks of Brandywine. Unknown. 6057-9
The banks of Brandywine. Unknown. 6059-5
The banks of Claudie. Unknown. 6057-9,6058-7
The banks of low Lee. Unknown. 6061-7
The banks of Newfoundland. Unknown. 6057-9
The banks of sweet Dundee. Unknown. 6057-9,6058-7
The banks of the Lee. Thomas Osborne Davis. 6302-0;6385-3
The banks of the Sacramento. Unknown. 6547-3
Banks, Emma Dunning
    Aline's love song. 6426-4
    Aunt Rhody's dream. 6426-4
    Battle cry. 6426-4
    Bridget's mission jug. 6426-4
    Diamond cut diamond. 6426-4
    Dot's Christmas; or, the sober hat. 6426-4
    Flossie Lane's marriage. 6426-4
    Flying Jim's last leap. 6412-4,6426-4,6964-9
    The gipsy bride. 6686-0
    Grandma Robbin's temperance mission. 6426-4

How congress fought for Sheridan. 6426-4
Laureame: the marble dream. 6426-4
A legend of rose Sunday. 6426-4
A lesson of obedience. 6426-4
A man's story. 6426-4
Medley. 6426-4
Mein Katrine's brudder Hans. 6426-4
Memorial Day at the farm. 6426-4
The mother's Easter scarf. 6426-4
Off for slumber-land. 6426-4
The old, old story. 6426-4
One Thanksgiving day out west. 6426-4
Pat and the Yankee. 6426-4
Prince Eric's Christ maid. 6426-4
Prince Eric's Christ-maid. 6426-4
Princess Imra and the goatherd. 6426-4
Princess Irma and the goatherd. 6426-4
A quart of milk. 6426-4
A Roman valentine. 6426-4
A Russian Christmas. 6426-4
Ruthie's faith in prayer. 6426-4
St. Valentine's and St. Patrick's day. 6426-4
Society flirtation. 6426-4
The soldier's joy. 6426-4
A squeeze in the dark. 6426-4
Two Thanksgiving dances. 6426-4
Van Bibber's rock. 6426-4

Banks, George Linnaeus
I live for those who love me. 6456-6
Mrs. Brown and Mrs. Green. 6408-6
My aim. 6273-3
What I live for. 6337-3,6415-9,6260-1,6109-5
What to live for. 6523-6,6654-2

Banks, Madge S.
Beyond Cathay. 6269-5

Banks, Martha Burr
Flag Day. 6684-4
A small seamstress. 6130-3

Bannard, Edward W.
Betty to herself. 6274-1

The banner Betsey made. Thomas Chalmers Harbaugh. 6444-2
Banner of America. Denis Aloysius McCarthy. 6162-1,6143-5
The banner of England. Susanna Strickland Moodie. 6796-4
"The banner of freedom high floated unfurled". The United States and Macedonian (2). Unknown. 6946-0
The banner of freedom, fr. Song of the union. Jeremiah W. Cummings. 6171-0
The banner of love. Edward R. Huxley. 6885-5
The banner of the covenanters. Caroline Elizabeth Sarah Sheridan Norton. 6344-6
The banner of the cross. George Washington Doane. 6065-X
The banner of the Jew. Emma Lazarus. 7041-8
The banner of the Jew. Emma Lazarus. 6431-0
The banner of the stars. Rossiter W. Raymond. 6471-X
The banner that welcomes the world. Hezekiah Butterworth. 6451-5,6926-6

Banner, Brandon
Coming from the picnic. 6247-4
The banner. Alfred Noyes. 6151-6
Bannerman of the Dandenong. Alice Werner. 6639-9
"Banners hung drooping from on high". The two monuments. Felicia Dorothea Hemans. 6973-8
Banners of flame. Virginia Scott. 6799-9

Banning, Kendall
The great adventure. 6846-4
Heart's haven. 6337-3
In Arcady by moonlight. 6347-0
Once on a time. 6076-5,6102-8,6347-0,6441-8,6732-8
The phantom caravan. 6347-0
Quatrain. 6118-2
The wander lure. 6374-8

Bannister, Christopher
The American fireman. 6274-1
Compensations. 6274-1
A mother's heart. 6097-8
A thread of hair. 6097-8
Three things. 6097-8
To a maid of thirteen. 6274-1

Bannockburn. Robert Burns. 6075-7,6102-8,6239-3,6240-7, 6271-7,6302-,6385-3,6457-4,6479-5,6552-X,6438-8,6543 ,6086-2,6219-9,6212-1,6263-6,6267-9,6424 ,6560-0, 6569-4,6737-9,6188-5,6323-3
"Bannocks o' bear meal, bannocks o' barley". Bannocks of barley. Unknown. 6859-6
The banquet of sense, fr. The poetaster. Ben Jonson. 6827-8
Banquet song. Edwin Osgood Grover. 6441-8
A banquet. Ernest Benshimol. 6762-X
The banquet. Ernest Myers. 7015-9
The banshee.. John Todhunter. 6174-5,6656-9
Bantry bay. James Lyman Molloy. 6930-4
The Bantry girls' lament for Johnny. Unknown. 6858-8
Banty Tim. John Hay. 6385-3,6550-3

Banville, Theodore de
Ballade de Victor Hugo. 6801-4
La montagne. 6801-4
The laurels are felled. 6351-9
Mourir, dormir. 6801-4
"Nous n'irons plus au bois, les lauriers sont coupes" 6801-4
Praise of water. Henry Carrington (tr.). 6025-0
Sous bois. 6801-4
To Adolphe Gaiffe. 6351-9

Baptism on Armistice Day. Chad Walsh. 6839-1
The baptism. Leonard [Lazarus] Aaronson. 6210-5
Baptismal hymn. Henry Alford. 6219-9
The Baptist parsonage. James W. Stanistreet. 6249-0
"A bar of steel—it is only". Smoke and steel, sels. Carl Sandburg. 6954-1
The bar-tender's story. David Law ("Pegleg Arkwright") Proudfit. 6273-3
Barabas in his counting-house. Christopher Marlowe. 6150-8
Barabbas speaks. Edwin McNeill Poteat. 6337-3

Baratynsky, Evgeni
Death. Cecil Maurice Bowra (tr.). 6103-6

Barb-wire Bill. Robert Service. 6159-1,6211-3
Barbara. Eugene Field. 6949-5
Barbara. Alexander Smith. 6344-6,6437-X,6102-8,6094-3
Barbara Allen. Unknown. 6826-X
Barbara Allen. Unknown. 6180-X,6659-3,6491-4,6003-X
Barbara Allen's cruelty. Unknown. 6055-2,6098-6,6102-8.6613-5,6153-2,6067 ,6219-9,6301-2
Barbara at the window. Alice Cary. 6865-0;6969-X
Barbara Blue. Alice Cary. 6683-6,6683-6
Barbara Ellen. Unknown. 6281-4
Barbara Frietchie. John Greenleaf Whittier. 6300-4,6219-9, 6460-1,6126-5,6107-9,6736 ,6442-6,6228-1,6434-1,6016-2,6008-0,6808 ,6267-9,6322-5,6484-1,6639-9,6444-2, 6014-5,6062-5,6077-3,6113-3,6134-6,6176 ,6211-3,6239-3,6242-3,6260-1,6271-7,6302 ,6370-5,6385-3,6401-9, 6402-7,6479-5,6457 ,6558-9,6661-5,6706-9,6732-8,6735-2,6263
Barbara Frietchie [in Dutch]. John Greenleaf Whittier. 6175-3
Barbara in the meadow. Alice Cary. 6865-0;6969-X
Barbara's cannery ritual. David McElroy. 6855-3
Barbara's land revisited-August 1978 Geary Hobson. 7005-1
Barbarossa. Friedrich Ruckert. 6842-1
Barbarossa. Friedrich Ruckert. 6614-3
The barbarous bird-gods: a savage parabasis. Andrew Lang. 6987-8

Barbauld, Anna Letitia
The cheerful way. 6889-8
Christ risen. 6219-9
Come unto me. 6271-7
Come, says Jesus' voice. 6065-X
Death of the virtuous. 6219-9,6271-7,6600-3
Life. 6102-8,6198-2,6600-3,6240-7,6271-7,6260 ,6086-2, 6104-4,6438-8,6301-2,6219-9,6737 ,6238-5,6402-7,6530-9,6732-8,6250-4,6543 ,6302-0,6337-3,6385-3,6481-7, 6486-8,6502
Life and death. 6291-1
"Life! I know not what thou art". 6230-X,6396-9,6246-6, 6479-5
"Life! we've been long together". 6238-5,6402-7
Life's good-morning. 6424-8
Life, I know not what thou art. 6964-9
The mouse's petition. 6133-8
Ode to spring. 6543-0
Praise to God. 6214-8,6219-9,6271-7

BARBAULD

Priase to God. 6214-8,6219-9,6271-7,6438-8
The sabbath of the soul. 6303-0,6303-9,6385-3,6600-3
Spring, fr. Ode to spring. 6934-7
A summer evening's meditation, sels. 6102-8
A summer evening's meditation. 6302-0;6385-3
The vowels. 6018-8
Words. 6304-2
"The **barber** shaved the mason". Unknown. 6363-2
"A **barber** who lived in Batavia". Limerick:"A barber who lived in Batavia". Unknown. 6811-1
The **barber's** nuptials. Unknown. 6787-1
The **barber's**. Walter De La Mare. 6466-3
Barber, Joseph
   A modern version of The Merchant of Venice. 6166-4
   Shad punctual at Easter time. 6720-4
Barber, Margaret
   The knitting. 6750-6
Barber, Mary Finette
   Sky writing. 6818-9
"**Barber**, barber, shave a pig". Mother Goose. 6363-2
The **barber**. Edward Verrall Lucas. 6018-8
"'A **barbered** woman's man", - yes, so". Contemporaries. Richard Hovey. 7006-X
Barberini, Francesco da
   Of caution. Dante Gabriel Rossetti (tr.). 6325-X
   A virgin declares her beauties. Dante Gabriel Rossetti (tr.). 6325-X
Barberino, Francesco da
   Of caution. Dante Gabriel Rossetti (tr.). 7039-6
Barberries. Mary Aldis. 6897-9
The **barberry** bush. Grace Hazard Conkling. 6029-3
The **barberry-bush**. Jones Very. 6438-8
Barbie, Mary Helen
   Death. 7016-7
   Life gives to me. 7016-7
   Little things. 7016-7
   Magnolia. 7016-7
   Pastel. 7016-7
   Swift be the passing. 7016-7
Barbier, Auguste
   La curee. 6801-4
   Prologue. 6801-4
   Titien. 6801-4
Barbour, Douglas
   Autobiographical. 6767-0
   The image repetition. 6767-0
Barbour, John
   The battle of Bannockburn. 6180-X
   Bruce addresses his army. 6845-6
   Bruce consults his men. 6845-6
   The Bruce, sels. 6180-X
   The eve of Bannockburn. 6180-X
   Freedom. 6180-X,6250-4,6383-7
   Loyalty. 6180-X
   Sorrow of the knights at Bruce's death. 6180-X
Barbusse, Henri
   The letter. 6351-9
   The seamstress. 6351-9
Barcarole. Arthur Guiterman. 6331-4,6439-6
Barcarolle. Ben Wood Davis. 6927-4
Barcarolle. Theophile Gautier. 6801-4
Barcelona. Vincent Sheehan. 6761-1
Barcelona celebrates three years of Franco. Aaron Kramer. 6561-9
Barclay of Ury. John Greenleaf Whittier. 6263-6,6126-5, 6288-1,6613-5,6271-7,6302-0,6385-3,6610-0,6735-2
Barclay, Alexander
   Ballade to our lady, fr. The ship of fools. 6282-2
   Geographers. 6022-6
   Preachment for preachers. 6022-6
   The ship of fools, sels. 6282-2
   Star of the sea. 6022-6
   The Tudor rose. 6022-6
Barclay, Sheppard
   In woman's praise. 6878-2
"The **bard** addresses whisky-/Why liquor of...". Why, liquor of life? Turlough Carolan. 6930-4
The **bard** and the cricket. Robert Browning. 6676-3
"The **bard** must have a kind, courageous heart". The poet. Philip James Bailey. 6980-0

The **bard** of auld lang syne. James Main Dixon. 6476-0
"The **bard** received me with open-heartedness...". A visit to the poet. Rodolfo Pucelli. 6799-9
The **bard** speaks, fr. Epistle to my brother George. John Keats. 6832-4
"The **bard** who first adorn'd our native tongue". To the Duchess of Ormond, fr. Tales from Chaucer. John Dryden. 6970-3
Bard's chant. James Shirley. 6022-6
A **bard's** epitaph. Robert Burns. 6198-2,6289-X,6302-0,6385-3,6600-3,6543 ,6737-9
A **bard's** lament over his children. Padraic Gregory. 6090-0
The **bard's** last song. James Abraham Martling. 6952-5
The **bard's** summons to war. Owen (Edward Bulwer-Lytton, Earl Lytton) Meredith. 6606-2
Bard, Milford
   Burning of the Lexington. 6914-2,6744-1
Bard, Robert M.
   The mendicant. 6294-6
Bard, W.E.
   Mesa trail, sels. 6265-2
Bard, Wilkie
   Limerick:"..young lady of Jarrow". 6811-1
"The **bard**, if e'er he feel at all". To Mrs, King on her kind present to the author. William Cowper. 6814-6
The **bard**, sels. Thomas Gray. 6258-X
The **bard**. William Blake. 6730-1
The **bard**. Thomas Gray. 6543-0,6322-5,6660-7,6438-8,6086-2, 6087-0,6075-7,6246-6,6271-7,6323-3,6122 ,6198-2,6604-6,6192-3,6195-0,6430-2,6219
Bardel, John
   Carol to our lady. 6490-6
Bardin, James C.
   Tropic beach song. 6184-2
"A **bardling** came where by a river grew". Invita Minerva. James Russell Lowell. 6753-0
"**Bards** of passion and of mirth". Ode ("Bards"). John Keats. 6122-2,6198-2,6527-9,6271-7,6110-9,6430-2, 6199-0,6219-9,6371-3
Bards of passion and of mirth. John Keats. 6483-3,6732-8, 6086-2,6102-8
The **bards** we quote. Bert Leston Taylor. 6722-0
The **bards**. Robert Graves. 6209-1
The **bards**. Felicia Dorothea Hemans. 6973-8
Bardy, E.J.
   Trade. 6639-9
Bare almond trees. David Herbert Lawrence. 6354-3
"A **bare** strand/Of hillcocks...", fr. Julian and Maddalo. Percy Bysshe Shelley. 6793-X
"The **bare** trees look like spectres...". Winter, fr. Thistledown. Cora Fabri. 6876-6
"A **bare** uncovered bulb". Reality. Yvette Johnson. 7024-8
Bare, Matthias
   Only a baby small. 6743-3
"**Bare**, as a wild wave in the wild North Sea". Alfred Lord Tennyson. 6997-5
"**Bare**, brown, and barren, clas in driest dust". The veld, sels. Mary Rosalie Boyd. 6800-6
Bare-bosom'd night. Walt Whitman. 6597-X
The **barefoot** boy that drives the cattle home. Unknown. 6530-9
'The **barefoot** boy'. Phoebe Cary. 6969-X
The **barefoot** boy. John Greenleaf Whittier. 6456-6,6309-8, 6396-9,6216-5,6121-4,6076 ,6008-0,6135-4,6560-0,6288-1,6431-0,6300 ,6004-8,6464-7,6585-6,6127-3,6176-1, 6239-3,6299-7,6423-X,6473 ,6233-4,6302-0,6385-3,6437-X,6632-1,6732 ,6486-8,6583-X,6597-X,6006-4,6101-X, 6102
The **barefooted** boys. Unknown. 6113-5
The **barefooted** friar, fr. Ivanhoe. Sir Walter Scott. 6828-6
Barely autumn. Jean Levicki. 6857-X
Barely possible. Inez George Gridley. 6750-6
"**Barendt** Cuyler, Indian trader". A deal in real estate. Arthur Guiterman. 6773-5
Barfield, Owen
   Day. 6777-8
Bargain. Mabel Natalie Ericksen. 6750-6
Bargain. Florence Dickinson Stearns. 6979-7
Brgain basement. F.T. Macartney. 6349-7

The **bargain** of Faust. Hazel Nicholson. 6818-9
A **bargain** sale. Samuel Ellsworth Kiser. 6583-X
A **bargain's** a bargain. Unknown. 6134-6
A **bargain**. Abbie Farwell Brown. 6162-1
The **bargain**. Claire Stewart Boyer. 6818-9
The **bargain**. Sir Philip Sidney. 6138-9,6427-2,6513-9
The **bargain**. Henry Van Dyke. 6961-4
Bargains in hearts. Maud Hosford. 7021-3
"The **barge** she sat in...", fr. Antony and Cleopatra. William Shakespeare. 6339-X,6408-6,6527-9
Barge song on the Schuylkill River. Charles H.A. Esling. 6936-3
A **barge** wife. John Chipman Farrar. 6619-4
Bargen, Walter
    Adam canoes sthe Meramac river. 6860-X
    Trickle down on Jimerson creek. 6860-X
Barham, Richard Harris ("Thomas Ingoldsby")
    As I lay a-thynkynge. 6046-3
    The bagman's dog. 6278-4
    City bells. 6302-0;6385-3
    The confession. 6089-7
    The demolished farce; or, who is the author? 6802-2
    Eheu fugaces. 6092-7,6278-4
    The execution. 6219-9,6579-1
    Family poetry. 6278-4
    The forlorn one. 6089-7
    The ghost. 6278-4
    The inebriate. 6302-0
    The jackdaw of Rheims. 6064-1,6089-7,6290-3,6302-0,6385-3,6473 ,6464-7,6656-9,6808-1,6800-3,6732-8
    The knight and the lady. 6302-0,6089-7,6045-7
    Last lines. 6437-X
    The lay of St. Cuthbert. 6427-2
    A lay of St. Gengulphus. 6278-4
    The legend of a shirt. 6302-0
    Lines left at Mr. Theodore Hook's house in June, 1834 6874-X
    Lines on the birthday of Sir Thomas White. 6018-8
    The little vulgar boy. 6279-2
    The London University. 6278-4
    Look at the clock. 6278-4,6219-9
    "Look at the clock." 6302-0
    Lurline; or, the knight's visit to the mermaids. 6669-0
    Margate. 6802-2
    Misadventures at Margate. 6089-7,6232-4,6302-0,6385-3, 6278-4
    Misadventures at Margate. 7025-6
    More walks. 6089-7
    Mr. Barney Maguire's <u>account of the cornonation. 6656-9,</u> 6219-9
    Mr. Barney Maguire's account of the coronation. 6787-5
    My letters. 6092-7,6278-4
    My lord Tomnoddy. 6402-7
    Nell Cook. 6633-X
    Netley abbey. 6278-4
    New-made honour. 6092-7,6278-4
    Not a sou had he got. 6278-4,6440-X
    Nursery reminiscences. 6064-1,6233-4
    On the death of a daughter. 6385-3
    On the windows of King's College. 6278-4
    The poplar. 6092-7,6278-4
    Raising the devil. 6278-4
    Sir Rupert the fearless. 6278-4
    The witches' frolic. 6669-0
Barhite, Jared
    Arbor day tribute. 6049-8
Baril, Melanie
    "A cold eerie silence..." 6883-9
"**Baring** its breast to the sun as of yore". The legend of Glooscap. Arthur Wentworth Hamilton Eaton. 7041-8, 6797-2
Baring, Maurice
    August 1918. 7029-9
    Circe. 6785-9
    The dying reservist. 6785-9
    In memoriam, A.H. 6096 X
    Julian Grenfell. 7029-9
    Leirioessa kalyx. 6437-X
    Moan in the form of a ballade. 6722-0
    Song ("The sky is stormy and red"). 6785-9
    Vale. 6785-9
Baring, Maurice (tr.)
    The beauty. Alexander Pushkin, 6103-6
    <u>"Do you remember, Mary." Alexey Tolstoy, 6103-6</u>
    Elegy. Alexander Pushkin, 6103-6
    "Good-bye! Forget the days of wane" Nikolay Nekrasov, 6103-6
    "I've lived to bury my desires." Alexander Pushkin, 6103-6
    "Outside it is blowing and raining." Alexey Tolstoy, 6103-6
    A prayer. Alexander Pushkin, 6103-6
    The prophet. Alexander Pushkin, 6103-6
    The rosy wreath. Rufinus, 6435-3
    The testament. Mikhail Lermontov, 6103-6
    "Through the slush and the ruts of the highway" Alexey Tolstoy, 6103-6
    To -. Alexander Pushkin, 6103-6
    Troparian. Alexey Tolstoy, 6103-6
Baring-Gould, Sabine
    Child's evening hymn. 6132-X,6418-3,6214-8,6656-9,6737-9
    The gift of the king. 6848-0
    The loan. 6848-0
    Now the day is over. 6373-X,6466-3,6104-4,6723-9
    The olive tree. 6239-3,6242-3
    Onward, Christian soldiers. 6337-3,6466-3,6418-3,6730-1, 6214-8
    The Rabbi Joachim. 6848-0
    the rabbi's son-in-law. 6848-0
    Turn again! 6848-0
    The two rabbins. 6848-0
    The wife's treasure. 6848-0
Baring-Gould, Sabine (tr.)
    The pilgrim's song. Bernard S. Ingeman, 6214-8,6730-1
Baris, Amanda
    "Mother moon". 6130-3
The **bark** 'True Love'. Benjamin Franklin Taylor. 6815-4
The **bark** of Clanranald. Alexander (Alasdair MacMhaighstir A.) Macdonald. 6180-X
"**Bark** that bare me through foan and squall". Boatman's hymn. Andrew Magrath. 6930-4
"**Bark** that bears my name through foam & squall". Song of the boatman (duan an bhadora). Unknown (Irish). 6858-8
"The **bark** that held a prince went down". He never smiled again, fr. Lays of many lands. Felicia Dorothea Hemans. 6973-8
Bark, Matthias
    The dying street Arab. 6407-8
Bark-bound, fr. Pictures of women. Agnes Lee. 6033-1
A **barker** incites an old man..., fr. Old and new New York. Alfred Kreymborg. 6012-9
Barker, Edna L.S.
    Words above a lamp. 6761-1
Barker, Edward D.
    Go sleep, ma honey. 6006-4
Barker, Eliza H.
    Shun the bowl. 6410-8
Barker, Elsa
    Breshkovskaya, sels. 6076-5,6102-8
    The Easter children. 6954-1
    The frozen grail. 6300-4,6310-1,6732-8,6396-9
    I know. 6019-6
    A prayer for love. 6461-2
    Song of the North Pole flag. 6714-X
    Sonnet ("The sweet caresses"). 6338-1
    The two selves. 6320-9,6648-8
    The vigil of Joseph. 6393-4,6746-8
    "When I am dead and sister to the dust". 6076-5,6102-8, 6310-1
    The word of summer. 7030-2
Barker, Eric Wilson
    The dark inanimate. 6648-8
Barker, George
    "And now there is nothing left to celebrate" 6379-9
    Delilah poem. 6390-X
    Eight secular elegies. 6391-8
    Elegy. 6390-X
    Elegy on the eve. 6665-8

Elegy V. 6210-5
"Everywhere is our wilderness everywhere" 6379-9
First American ode. 6389-6
Five sacred elegies. 6391-8
Galway Bay. 6209-1
Love poem ("Less the dog begged to die...") 6379-9
Love poem ("My joy, my jockey, my Gabriel") 6379-9
Love poem ("O tender under her right breast") 6379-9
Love poem ("They like the ship at rest in the bay.") 6209-1
Munich elegy No. 1 6666-6
News of the World I. 6209-1
News of the world II. 6210-5
News of the world III. 6210-5
O dog my God how can I cease to praise. 6390-X
"O golden fleece she is where she lies tonight". 6379-9
"O who will speak from a womb or a cloud?" 6389-6
Ode ("O to us speak"). 6985-1
Requiem anthem for the Austrian constitution. 6390-X
Resolution of dependence. 6210-5
Second American ode. 6389-6
Seven Pacific sonnets. 6389-6
"So in one man Europe I sit here". 6379-9
Sonnet of fishes. 6209-1
Sonnet to my mother. 6339-X,6390-X,6666-6
Summer idyll. 6209-1
Summer song. 6246-6,6210-5
"This is that month, Elizabeth" 6379-9
Three elegies. 6389-6
Three memorial sonnets (for two young seamen lost overboard). 6666-6,6389-6
To any member of my generation. 6666-6
To my mother. 6246-6,6209-1,6491-4
Triumphal ode MCMXXX. 6389-6,6666-6
The true confession of George Barker, sels. 6210-5
Two epistles. 6389-6
Barker, J.W.
    By-and-by. 6523-6
    Waiting by the shore. 6523-6
Barker, Johnson
    The house full of wine. 6617-8
Barker, Mary Lucretia
    The music at the gate. 6789-1
    To my mother. 6789-1
Barker, S. Omar
    Batchin'. 6281-4
    The law west of the Pecos. 6281-4
    Memorial Day, 1925. 7001-9
    The sheep beezness. 6281-4
    To a jack rabbit. 6281-4
    Where Billy the Kid still rides. 6265-2
    Woodland magic. 6265-2
Barker, Shirley
    Child that I never had. 6761-1
    Sandwich fair. 6764-6
Barkers, i.e. the critics, fr. Gedichte. Johann Wolfgang von Goethe. 7042-6
Barkley, Alice
    Baby in a manger. 6789-1
    Buttercups. 6789-1
    Colorland. 6789-1
    I'd like to be a white girl. 6789-1
    A little birdie in a cage. 6789-1
    A mountain. 6789-1
    My boats. 6789-1
    The river. 6789-1
    Seaweed. 6789-1
    The stars. 6789-1
Barlas, John ("Evelyn Douglas")
    Covering hair. 6659-3
    The golden city, sels. 7009-4
    Le jeune Barbaroux. 7009-4
    Noblesse oblige. 6659-3
    Stanzas ("And the seer's"), fr. The golden city. 7009-4
    Stanzas ("And the spray.."), fr. The golden city. 7009-4
    Stanzas ("Of the dim-eyed"), fr. The golden city. 7009-4
    Stanzas ("There gorgeous Plato"), fr. The golden city. 7009-4
    Stanzas ("They be happy"), fr. The golden city. 7009-4
Barley water, fr. The poetical cookbook. Unknown. 6278-4
The barley-mow and the dunghill. John Gay. 6972-X
The barley-mowers' song. Mary Howitt. 6334-9
Barlow, Fanny
    Taken on trial. 6247-4
Barlow, George
    The compact. 6280-6
    The dead child. 6274-1,6437-X,6656-9
    If only thou art true. 6656-9
    Life's gifts. 6066-8
    Love on deck. 6066-8
    Love's final powers. 6066-8
    The old maid. 6656-9
    The soul. 6437-X
    Spiritual passion. 6437-X
    Together. 6066-8
Barlow, Jane
    Christmas rede. 6437-X
    A curlew's call. 6656-9
    An errand. 6090-0
    Inish Fay. 6793-X
    Out of hearing. 6090-0
    A song of sun setting. 6090-0
Barlow, Joel
    The American poets. 6121-4
    The arts come to America. 6121-4
    The Babylonian captivity. 6735-2
    A choice in spoons, fr. The hasty pudding. 6399-3
    The columbiad, sels. 6008-0,6288-1
    The first American Congress. 6946-0
    Freedom. 6176-1
    The hasty pudding, sels. 6008-0,6121-4,6399-3
    The hasty pudding: canto III. 6077-3
    The hasty pudding. 6753-0
    The hasty pudding. 6288-1
    The hasty pudding. 6753-0
    Hymn to peace. 6176-1
    On the discoveries of Captain Lewis. 6946-0
    The pudding eaten. 6176-1
    The pudding praised. 6176-1
    The pudding prepared. 6176-1
    Vision of Columbus, sels. 6753-0
    The vision of Columbus, sels. 6008-0
Barlow, Nellie
    Those who fail. 6744-1
Barlow, Robert H.
    Edgar Allan Poe. 6218-0
    Mythological episode. 6218-0
    Warning to snake-killers. 6218-0
Barmaid, fr. London types. William Ernest Henley. 6507-4
The Barmecides. Richard Chenevix Trench. 6980-0
The barn owl. Samuel Butler. 6943-6
The barn owl. Jean Follain. 6758-1
The barn owl. Eugene Edmund Murphey. 6723-9
Barn sounds. Daniel Smythe. 6761-1
"The barn that's built from plans that's sound". A Vermont lean-to. Daniel L. Cady. 6989-4
The barn window. Lucy Larcom. 6129-X
The barn. Edmund Blunden. 6844-8
The barn. Stephen Spender. 6257-1
Barnaby, Goodman
    Give me the hand. 6911-8
Barnack, Joachim August Christian
    Spring evening. James Abraham Martling (tr.). 6952-5
Barnacles. Sidney Lanier. 6479-5,6288-1
The barnacles. Robert P. Tristram Coffin. 7040-X
Barnard, Ana
    Telling tales. 6687-9
Barnard, Anne. See Lindsay, Lady Anne
Barnard, E.Y.
    "There was the richness of our former living". 6468-X
Barnard, Edward W.
    Modern romance. 6694-1
Barnard, Seymour
    Ku Klux Klanthem. 6880-4
Barnard, Thomas
    Improvement in the forties. 6092-7
Barnard; Bishop of Limerick, Dr.
    On mending his thoughts. 6874-X

'Barnaval,' sel. Charles De Kay. 7041-8
'Barnaval,' sel. Charles De Kay. 7041-8
Barnefield, Richard. See Barnfield, Richard
Barnes, Barnabe
   Ah, sweet content. 6194-X
   "Ah, sweet Content! where is thy mild abode?" 6181-8, 6186-6,6189-3
   "A blast of wind, a momentary breath". 6181-8,6586-4
   Content. 6436-1
   God's virtue. 6436-1
   "Gracious, Diune, and most omnipotent." 6586-4
   The life of man. 6436-1
   Ode ("Behold"). 6189-3
   Ode ("Why doth heaven"). 6182-6,6436-1
   The world's bright comforter. 6931-2
   "The worldes bright comforter (whose beamsome light)." 6182-6,6586-4
Barnes, Charles Lee
   The kingfisher. 6795-6
Barnes, Djuna
   Lines to a lady. 6032-3
   To the dead favourite of Liu Ch'e. 6034-X
Barnes, Earl B.
   A trubute. 6880-4
Barnes, Elizabeth I.
   Peace pictures. 6270-9
Barnes, G.H.
   The bricklayers. 6915-0,6167-2
Barnes, James
   Bill Sweeny of the Black Gang. 6274-1
   Inscriptions. 6983-5
   The song of then and now. 6471-X
   The torpedo=boat. 6471-X
Barnes, James Allison
   A nobler way. 6109-5
Barnes, Jim
   Autobiography, chapter XVII: floating the big piney. 7005-1
   Comcomly's skull. 7005-1
   Four Choctaw songs. 7005-1
   Four things Choctaw. 7005-1
   Wolf hunting near Nashoba. 7005-1
Barnes, Joseph Hood
   Evening near ragged mountain. 6764-6
   Memory. 6764-6
Barnes, M.C.
   The little woman. 6576-7
Barnes, Natalie (tr.)
   Daylight. Unknown (Pawnee Indian), 6891-X
   Ke-ni-ga song. Unknown (American Indian), 6891-X
Barnes, Nellie
   Prayer to Dsilyi Neyene. 6490-6
   Ritual song. 6490-6
Barnes, Nellie (tr.)
   Mountain song. Unknown (American Indian), 6396-9
Barnes, Ronald Gorell. See Gorell, Lord
Barnes, Verne
   Way down south in Mississippi. 6465-5
Barnes, William
   Bees a-zwarmen. 6018-8
   The blackbird. 6423-X
   Blackmwore maidens. 6199-0
   Bleake's house in Blackmwore. 6092-7
   Carn a-turnen yoller. 6423-X
   The castle ruins. 6656-9
   Christmas invitation. 6018-8
   The clote. 6246-6
   The d'rection post. 6018-8
   Evenen in the village. 6423-X,6660-7
   Evening, and maidens. 6437-X
   False friends-like. 6133-8,6134-6
   The farmer's invitation. 6747-6
   The fireside chairs. 6980-0
   Good night. 6546-7
   Guy Faux's night. 6018-8
   Harvest hwome: second part. 6659-3
   Harvest hwome: the vu'st part. 6659-3
   The head-stone. 6437-X
   The heare. 6656-9
   Heedless o' my love. 6545-7
   Home's a nest. 6980-0
   In the spring. 6545-7
   "In the stillness o' the night." 6302-0,6383-7
   Jeane. 6317-9
   The leaves. 6125-7
   Lullaby ("The rooks' nests"). 6242-3,6533-3
   The maid var my bride. 6423-X
   Mary-Ann's child. 6133-8
   Mater dolorosa. 6102-8,6214-8,6337-3,6395-9,6533-3
   May. 6125-7,6246-6,6545-7
   The may tree. 6315-2
   The mother's dream. 6134-6,6339-X,6545-7,6737-9
   Mother, never mourn. 6097-8
   The motherless child. 6934-7
   The motherless child. 6102-8
   The motherless child. 6934-7
   My fore-elders. 6980-0
   My love's guardian angel. 6545-7
   The new house a-getten wold. 6545-7
   Night a-zetten in. 6545-7
   The oak-tree. 6437-X
   The old house. 6437-X
   The peasant's return. 6438-8
   Readen ov on. 6134-6,6808-1
   The settle. 6383-7
   The shepherd o' the farm. 6423-X
   The sky a-clearen. 6545-7
   The spring. 6423-X
   The turnstile. 6437-X
   Uncle an' Aunt. 6423-X
   Vo'k a-comen into church. 6931-2
   Walking home at night. 6980-0
   White an' blue. 6545-7
   The white road up Athirt the Hill. 6423-X
   The wife a-lost. 6246-6,6437-X
   The wind at the door. 6317-9,6545-7
   A winter night. 6125-7
   A witch. 6133-8
   Withstanders. 6931-2
   Woak hill. 6844-8
   The woodlands. 6246-6,6437-X,6423-X,6383-7,6301-2
   Woodley. 6331-4
   Woone smile mwore. 6656-9
Barnes, William (tr.)
   Cynddylan's hall. Unknown (Welsh), 6528-7
   The hearth of Urien. Unknown (Welsh), 6125-7
   In wintry midnight. Unknown (Welsh), 6125-7
   In wintry midnight. Francesco Petrarch, 6125-7
Barnet, Mavis Clare
   Romance. 6076-5,6102-8
Barnett, Margaret H.
   Thy sorrows. 6461-2
Barnett, Mavis Clare
   Adolescence. 6039-0
   Silence. 6037-4
   Spring song. 6039-0
Barney and Katey. Unknown. 6061-7
Barney and Katie. Unknown. 6058-7
Barney McGee. Richard Hovey. 6089-7,6732-8,6102-8,6076-2
Barney O'Hea. Samuel Lover. 6930-4
Barney O'Lean. Unknown. 6058-7
Barney O'Linn and the leeches. Unknown. 6920-7
Barney's invitation. Philip Freneau. 6946-0
Barney's invitation. Philip Freneau. 6288-1
Barney, Anna Louise
   The cloak. 6750-6
Barney, William D.
   The gourd-heads. 6218-0
   In the beginning. 6218-0
   The panther possible. 6218-0,6218-4
Barnfield, Richard
   Address to the nightingale. 6271-7,6302-0,6385-3
   As it fell upon a day. 6122-2,6181-8,6187-7,6198-2,6301-2
   A comparison of the life of man. 6023-4,6436-1
   Daphnis to Ganymede. 6182-6
   "England his heart; his corpse the waters have". 6258-X
   The nightingale ("As it fell upon a day"). 6073-0,6075-7,6133-8,6246-6,6219-9,6639 ,6737-9
   The nightingale. 6438-8

BARNFIELD

An ode ("As if"). 6182-6,6436-1,6315-2,6250-4
Philomel. 6102-8,6186-9,6191-5,6301-2,6328-4,6732
The plaint of the nightingale. 6934-7
A shepherd's complaint. 6436-1
To his friend Master R.L., in praise of music... 6182-6
The unknown shepherd's complaint. 6182-6
Whilst as fickle fortune smiled. 6219-9
Barnfloor and winepress. Gerard Manley Hopkins. 6022-6
Barnouw, A.J. (tr.)
   Columbus. J. Slauerhoff, 6068-4
   From time to eternity. Henriette Roland Holst, 6068-4
Barns in November. James Hearst. 6491-4
Barnstone, Willis
   Wandering loos in Shaoshan. 6803-0
Barnstorming. John Morgan. 6855-3
Barnyard melodies. Fred Emerson Brooks. 6921-5,6695-X
Barnyard symphony. Marie Emilie Gilchrist. 6906-1
The **barnyard**.. Maud Burnham. 6452-3,6466-3
The **barnyard**. Maud Burnham. 6135-4
Baro, Gene
   Lament for better or worse. 6218-0
Baron Giovanni Nicotera. Harriet Eleanor Hamilton
   (Baille) King. 7037-X
Baron Grimalkin's death. Will Carleton. 6692-2
The **baron** o Leys. Unknown. 6185-0
The **baron** of Brackley. Unknown. 6185-0,6180-X,6055-2,6518-X
The **baron** prays for victory..., fr. Rape. Alexander Pope. 6637-2
Baron Renfrew's ball. Charles G. ("Miles O'Reilly") Halpine. 6946-0
The **baron's** last banquet. Albert Gorton Greene. 6425-6, 6486-8,6552-X,6606-2,6392-6,6909 ,6567-8,6219-9,6744-1
The **baron's** wars, sels. Michael Drayton. 6194-X
Baron, Jacques
   The finest day of one's life. 6351-9
   Long live life. 6351-9
   Romance of brunettes and blondes. 6351-9
Baron, Linda Michelle. See Lindamichellebaron
Baron, Mary
   Animus. 6855-3
   Card for my mother's birthday. 6855-3
   Christening. 6855-3
   Penelope at the loom. 6855-3
   Sea otter woman/instructions. 6855-3
Baron, Robert
   To Eliza, upon May day morning, 1649 6563-5
The **barons** bold. William Johnson Fox. 6188-5,6656-9
Baronti, Gerve
   Sahara. 6031-5
   Seasons ("How lovely these trees are"). 6031-5
The **barouche**. Leonie Adams. 6808-1
Barr, Alice
   The steamer Capitol. 6342-X
Barr, Amelia E.
   A Christmas camp on the San Gabr'el. 6273-3
   The new year ledger. 6486-8
   The new-year ledger. 6921-5
   Thanksgiving. 6703-4,6449-3
Barr, Elizabeth N.
   Nirvana. 6039-0
Barr, Isabel Harriss
   Answer from Assisi. 6979-7
   At the gates. 6839-1
   Clock in the capitol - Williamsburg. 6761-1
Barr, Lillie E.
   Household thrush. 6711-5
   A king in disguise. 6523-6
   A mother's answer. 6917-7
   A mother's answer. 6097-8
   Nay, I'll stay with the lad. 6573-2
   Ten robber toes. 6166-4
Barr, Mary A.
   The bottom drawer. 6273-3
   "I wouldna gie a copper plack". 6102-8
   I wouldne gie a copper plack. 6102-8
   The lost colors. 6621-6
   "Now, soul, be very still and go apart". 6238-5
   Petit Jean. 6917-7

   When I'm a man. 6530-9
Barr, Matthias
   Hetty and the fairies. 6131-1
   Jesus, see a little child. 6131-1
   Mary's pet. 6131-1
   Moon so round and yellow. 6135-4,6368-3
   Only a baby small. 6078-1,6240-7,6502-3,6131-1,6639-9
   The organist. 6680-1
   The sailor boy and his mother. 6131-1
   The shepherd's dog. 6131-1
Barr, Ronald W.
   The organ grinder. 6039-0
Barr, Ronald Walker
   August night. 6906-1
   The devil prompts a sonnet. 6906-1
   Poe's poem. 6906-1
   Requiem for Rupert Brooke. 6906-1
   Vincit omnia veritas. 6906-1,6779-4
Barra. Robert Lawrence. 6767-0
The **barrack** yard. Nettie Palmer. 6384-5
Barracks apt. 14. Theodore Weiss. 6388-8
Barraud, C.W.
   Saint Winefride. 6285-7
Barred. Naomi Evans Vaughn. 6178-8
Barrel house: industrial city. Langston Hughes. 6561-9
The **barrel** organ. Alfred Noyes. 6332-2,6732-8,6723-9,6653-4,6371-3,6464
The **barrel-organ**, sels. Alfred Noyes. 6102-8,6649-6
The **barren** Easter. Clinton Scollard. 6177-X
The **barren** shore. Coventry Patmore. 6123-0
Barren spring, fr. The House of life. Dante Gabriel Rossetti. 6208-3,6378-0,6110-9,6655-0
"The **barren** wasteland". Death at the camp. Keiho Soga. 6981-9
Barret, Pringle
   A hint to the wise. 6466-3
   The old woman who lives in the town. 6466-3
   Perhaps. 6466-3
Barrett, Alfred
   Chant of departure. 6282-2
   Mary's Assumption. 6282-2
Barrett, Eaton Stannard
   Woman. 6240-7,6250-4,6214-8
Barrett, John E.
   At sunrise. 6840-5
   A blast of autumn. 6840-5
   A Christmas chant. 6840-5
   Christmas pearls. 6840-5
   The city of Scranton. 6840-5
   The classes and masses. 6840-5
   A cry in the night. 6840-5
   The day of peace. 6840-5
   The dead minstrel. 6840-5
   The death of Hamlet. 6840-5
   Do you remember? 6840-5
   The double crown. 6840-5
   The edelweiss. 6840-5
   The enchanted vest. 6840-5
   The engineer. 6840-5
   The flag at Gettysburg. 6840-5
   A friend of mine. 6840-5
   The fugitives; a tale of slavery. 6840-5
   George Eliot. 6840-5
   A girl from Ireland. 6840-5
   The growing of the Christmas tree. 6840-5
   A hero of the mine. 6840-5
   Hymn to Saint Patrick. 6840-5
   Life's journey. 6840-5
   Lincoln. 6840-5
   Lincoln. 6524-4
   The Magdalene. 6840-5
   May Day. 6840-5
   The midnight storm. 6840-5
   Milicent May's valentine. 6840-5
   The miner. 6840-5
   The misanthrope. 6840-5
   A mother's treasure. 6840-5
   Nancy Flannigan. 6840-5
   The oak. 6840-5
   Richand poor. 6840-5

Robert Louis Stevenson. 6840-5
The slate pickers. 6840-5
Song of the steel mill. 6840-5
Tessie. 6840-5
Thanksgiving chimes. 6840-5
To a little girl of ten. 6840-5
Tragedy of a fishing village. 6840-5
A tree. 6840-5
The unknown soldiers' monument. 6840-5
The water lily. 6840-5
When pussy went a-fishing. 6840-5
Barrett, Louise
  Ifs. 6249-0
Barrett, Ruth J.
  Perennials. 6764-6
Barrett, Wilson Agnew
  A New England church. 6730-1
  "That night I danced" 6959-2
The barricades. Walter Adolphe Roberts. 6880-4
Barrick, J.R.
  No land like ours. 6074-9
Barrier. Dorothy Quick. 6648-8
"The barrier stone has rolled away". Easter. Edwin L. Sabin. 6820-0
The barrier. Louis Lavater. 6349-7
The barrier. Clyde McKay. 6880-4
Barriers. Joyce Lancaster. 6850-2
Barriers. Ellinor Norcross. 6039-0
The barring o' the door. Unknown. 6600-3
Barringer, Ethel Skipton
  Three guests. 6799-9
Barrington, Margaret
  Ships. 6070-6
Barrington, Patrick
  Here a nit-wit lies. 6722-0
  I was a bustle-maker once, girls. 6722-0
  Take me in your arms, Miss Moneypenny-Wilson. 6633-X, 6722-0
Barrington, Pauline B.
  In a garden. 6241-5
  A white iris. 6232-6,6338-1,6509-0,6393-X
Barris, Amanda
  Mother moon. 6130-3
  "Too early, robin". 6130-3
  "The world is gay". 6130-3
Barron, W.F.
  In olden style. 6118-4
Barrow, Elfrida De Renne
  Penetralia. 6040-4
Barrow, Kate T.
  Contrasted valentines. 6719-0
Barrows, O.R.
  Swinging neath the old apple tree. 6304-7
Barry's attack upon Sir Joshua Reynolds. John ("Peter Pindar") Walcott. 6278-4
Barry, Beatrice
  The medical corps. 6449-3
  Twa lassies. 6681-X
Barry, Iris
  Lost. 6071-4
  Virgin moon. 6069-2
Barry, K.E.
  Caught. 6671-2
Barry, L.E.F.
  Mad girl's song. 6541-4
Barry, Mary
  Elswitha. 6273-3
Barry, Michael Joseph
  The arms of 'eighty-two'. 6858-8
  Dear Carrigaline. 6858-8
  The place to die. 6219-9
  The place where man should die. 6240-7,6271-1,6219-9, 6263-6,6240-7,6271-7,6263-6
  The sword. 6090-0
  The Wexford massacre. 6858-8
  "Whether on the scaffold, high ". 6238-5
The bars of fate. Ellen M.H. Gates. 6291-1
"The bars on my cell have rusted". Rust. Michael Hogan. 6870-7
"The bars were nothing brave or strange...". Farmer's borderland. Edward Farquhar. 6939-8
Barstow, Henry H.
  If Easter be not true. 6337-3
The bartender's story. David Law ("Pegleg Arkwright") Proudfit. 6913-4
Barter. John Richard Moreland. 6461-2
Barter. Genevieve Parris. 6799-9
Barter. Sara Teasdale. 6052-8,6332-2,6338-1,6478-7,6503-1, 6583 ,6431-0,6143-5,6371-3,6253-9,6431-0,6653-4,6723
Barter. Margaret Widdemer. 6007-2,6730-1
Barter our northern darkness. Nigel Heseltine. 6360-8
Barter, Charles
  Stray memories of Natal and Zululand, sels. 6788-3
Barthel, Max
  The plow. 6643-7
Barthelemy, Eleanor
  Portrait of an old woman. 6640-2
  Sonnet in anger. 6640-2
  This is the worth. 6640-2
  This: to be calm. 6640-2
The Bartholdi statue. John Greenleaf Whittier. 6126-5
Bartholomew. Norman Gale. 6078-1,6242-3
"Bartholomew Benjamin Bunting". The singular sangfroid of baby Bunting. Guy Wetmore Carryl. 6902-9
Bartholomew Gosnold's dream. Benjamin Drew. 6798-0
Barthram's dirge. Robert Surtees. 6075-7
Bartimeus. Laura Simmons. 6144-3,6335-7
Bartimeus to the bird. John Banister Tabb. 6943-6
Bartleson, F.A.
  New Year's eve. 6113-3,6470-1
Bartlett, Elizabeth
  Behold this dreamer. 6388-8
  The cage. 6388-8
  Dark angel. 6388-8
  Private hurricaine. 6792-1
  The question is proof. 6388-8
Bartlett, George B.
  Mignonette. 6438-8
Bartlett, Gertrude
  Ballade of barren roses. 6115-X
  Ballade of Tristram's last harping. 6115-X
  The gunners. 6115-X
  Put by the flute. 6115-X
Bartlett, M.C.
  Baby's skies. 6078-1,6627-5,6321-7,6429-9
Bartlett, Ruth Fitch
  Portrait in the horizontal. 6040-4
  Possessed. 6039-0
  Put by the flute. 6115-X
  She looks beyond tomorrow. 6039-0
The Bartley explosion. Orville J. Jenks. 6149-4
Bartley mine disaster. Unknown. 6149-4
Barton Jr., W.A.
  Common people. 7016-7
  Immortality. 7016-7
  Infatuation. 7016-7
  Inscription for a book. 7016-7
  Rest. 7016-7
  To a critic. 7016-7
  To a dead moth. 7016-7
  Your hands. 7016-7
Barton, A. Russell
  The symphony. 6342-X
Barton, Bernard
  At home. 6273-3
  "The auctioneer, then, in his labor began". 6402-7
  The battle of Gibeon. 6848-0
  British oak. 6304-7
  Bruce and the spider. 6267-9
  Children of light. 6980-0
  An evening prayer. 6127-3
  Farewell. 6980-0
  "Hush! 'tis a holy hour...". 6402-7
  The land which no mortal may know. 6014-5
  Not ours the vows. 6271-7,6337-3,6600-3,6620-8,6226-1, 6219
  "Now in thy youth, beseech of Him". 6973-8
  Robert Bruce and the spider. 6918-5
  Seaside thoughts. 6014-5
  Spiritual worship. 6980-0

BARTON

Spring. 6131-1
The squirrel. 6529-5,6135-4,6131-1
"There be those." 6271-7,6219-9
To a profile. 6980-0
To Mary. 6980-0
To the skylark. 6980-0
The translation of Enoch. 6848-0
The word of God. 6525-2

Barton, Clara
Marmara. 7022-1

Barton, E.J.
At sunrise. 6468-X

Barton, Joan
One sharp delight. 6780-8

Barton, John
Envoi. 6767-0
Metropolitan life. 6767-0

Barton, Marie
Home of my thoughts. 6525-2
New Year. 6525-2
Peace on earth. 6525-2
Thanksgiving Day. 6525-2
What is prayer? 6525-2

Bartscher, Lyle
Hunger. 6799-9
Reminiscence. 6799-9

Baruch, Dorothy W.
Riding in a motor boat. 6891-X

Barzillai the Gileadite. Lydia Huntley Sigourney. 6848-0

Bas-Quercy, ?
Carol of the birds. 6608-9

Bas-bleu. Unknown. 6278-4
Base details. Siegfried Sassoon. 6339-X
The base of all metaphysics. Walt Whitman. 6753-0,6126-5
"Base oppressors, leave your slumbers". Song ("Base oppressors"). J.A. Leatherland. 7009-4
Baseball by the old. Unknown. 6274-1
Baseball game. John Maher Murphy. 6761-1

Bashaw, Thomas P.
Columbia's prayer. 6846-4

Bashford, Herbert
Alice. 6078-1
By the Pacific. 6102-8,6076-5
Cuba, 1897. 6471-X
Morning in camp. 6076-5,6102-8,6476-0,6241-5
Mount Rainier. 6484-1
Night in camp. 6241-5

Bashford, Sir Henry Howarth
At the gate. 7007-8
The gypsies. 6490-6
Highgate hill. 7007-8
L'envoi. 7007-8
Parliament Hill. 6653-4
The philosopher. 6070-6
The philospher. 6070-6
Romances. 6439-6
A song of settlement. 6793-X
The stranger. 6778-6
The vision of spring, 1916. 7027-2
Where do the gipsies come from? 6026-9,6334-9
Woodford fair. 6071-4

"A bashful junior, who stood". Slow. G.W. Gilmore. 6983-5
The bashful lover. James Thomson. 6816-2
The bashful Marguerite. Alice Wellington Rollins. 6529-5
"A bashful swain loved a pretty maid". A sermon in stone. Unknown. 6983-5
Bashfulness. Robert Herrick. 6194-X

Basho (Matsuo Basho)
All that is left. Curtis Hidden Page (tr.). 6665-8
"A bright red pepper-pod - but lo!" Curtis Hidden Page (tr.). 6850-2
"Butterfly, awake, awake!" Curtis Hidden Page (tr.). 6850-2
"Even the rocks of Futami." Lois J. Erickson (tr.). 6027-7
Green leaves. 6510-4
Hail on the pine trees. 6891-X
"An island etched on a silver sky." Lois J. Erickson (tr.). 6027-7
"A lonely pond in age-old stillness sleeps". Curtis Hidden Page (tr.). 7039-6
"O cricket, from your cheery cry". Curtis Hidden Page (tr.). 7039-6
"Old battlefield, fresh with spring flowers again". Curtis Hidden Page (tr.). 6850-2
"Old men, white-haired, beside the ancestral graves". Curtis Hidden Page (tr.). 7039-6
"The old pond, aye! and". 6850-2
Perfume of plum upon the air. Lois J. Erickson (tr.). 6027-7
Quick-falling dew." Curtis Hidden Page (tr.). 7039-6
Reminder. Curtis Hidden Page (tr.). 6102-8
"Still chirp the crickets." Lois J. Erickson (tr.). 6027-7
"This, then, the end of a dream of power." Lois J. Erickson (tr.). 6027-7
"The waving ripe fields glow with gold." Lois J. Erickson (tr.). 6027-7
"White of the first light snow." Lois J. Erickson (tr.). 6027-7

Basho (Matsuo Basho).
All that is left. Curtis Hidden Page (tr.). 6665-8
Reminder. Curtis Hidden Page (tr.). 6102-8

Bashshar ibn Burd
"Long has grown my night through the love of one". A.J. Arberry (tr.). 6766-2

Basic communication. Thomas Hornsby Ferril. 6388-8
"The basic language of the soul". What is poetry? Nellie Burget Miller. 6836-7
Basic writing 702 John Paul Minarik. 6870-7
A Basil: a tragedy. Joanna Baillie. 6813-8
Basis of friendship. Allan Ramsay. 6085-4
A basket of flowers. Adam Lindsay Gordon. 6951-7
A basket-maker's song. Thomas Dekker. 6436-1
The basket-maker. Virginia Taylor McCormick. 6036-6
Basketball. James Lewisohn. 6870-7

Baskett, N.M.
Orpheus and Eurydice. 6918-5
The substitute. 6415-9

Basking. Sydney Dobell. 6240-7
"Basking in peace in the warm spring sun". Romance of a carpet. Unknown. 6914-2

Basse, William
The angler's song. 6398-5
Clorus' song. 6191-5
Elegy on Mr. William Shakespeare. 6483-3,6250-4
Elegy on Shakespeare. 6933-9
An epitaph. 6102-8
The hunter's song. 6563-5
A memento for mortality. 6182-6,6150-8
On Mr. Wm. Shakespeare. 6182-6,6562-7
Renowned Spenser, lie a thought more nigh. 6301-2

Basselin and Jean Le Houx, Olivier
To his nose. Ralph Nixon Currey (tr.). 6227-X
War and wine. Ralph Nixon Currey (tr.). 6227-X

Basset, Sara Ware
Promise. 6798-0
Song ("Alone"). 6798-0

Bast. William Rose Benet. 6511-2
Bastard. Robert Service. 6159-1
The bastard king of England. Unknown. 6237-7
The bastard's lot. Richard Savage. 6932-0

Bastard, Thomas
De naevo in facie faustinae. 6317-9
Methinks 'tis pretty sport. 6182-6

The bastard. Kingsley Fairbridge. 6591-0,6592-9

Bastian, Walter M.
Rime of retrospection. 6761-1

The Bastile, fr. The task. William Cowper. 6195-0,6545-7
Bastinado. Lynn Riggs. 6397-7
A basting thread. Unknown. 6426-4
The basvigliana. Vincenzo Monti. 6973-8
Bat chimney. Glenn Ward Dresbach. 6789-1
The bat potato. Carolyn Wells. 6882-0
"Bat, bat, come under my hat". Unknown. 6904-5
The bat. Charles Lutwidge ("Lewis Carroll") Dodgson. 6440-X
The bat. Theodore Roethke. 6761-1

Bataille, Henry
The fountain of pity. 6351-9

The last lullaby. 6351-9
Memories. 6351-9
Batchelder, Anna
Warum? 7030-2
Batchelor, Jean M.
Ad astra. 7019-1
Batchin'.. S. Omar Barker. 6281-4
Bate, John
Cologne. 6379-9
Bate, R. Alexander
The sister at a maternity hospital. 6818-9
Bateham, Minnie D.
The legend of Innisfallen. 6415-9
One of many. 6928-2
Bateman, Edgar
Limerick:"Said I to my friend, Mrs. Lee". 6811-1
Bateman, Henry
The ship on fire. 6344-6,6630-5
Bates and Brainard Bates, Esther
Ipswich bar. 6053-6
Bates, Arlo
In thy clear eyes. 6770-0,6875-8
Might love be bought. 6770-0,6875-8
On the road to Chorrera. 7041-8
One. 6620-8
The pool of sleep. 6309-8,6501-5,6441-8,6652-6
Quite a history. 6015-2
A rose. 6770-0
A rose. 6441-8,6652-6
A shadow boat. 6632-1
A shadow boat. 7041-8
Sonnet 024 ("When two souls"). 7041-8
Sonnet 025 ("As some"). 7041-8
Sonnet 026 ("As dying Roland"). 7041-8
Sonnet 027 ("We must be"). 7041-8
Sonnets in shadow, sels. 7041-8
To my infant son. 7041-8
Triolet ("Wee rose"). 6770-0
A woodland tragedy. 6632-1
Bates, Charlotte Fiske
Andre. 6946-0
Last days of Byron. 7041-8
Springs. 7041-8
Bates, Charlotte Fiske (tr.)
The escurial. Theophile Gautier, 6424-8
The last sigh of the moor. Theophile Gautier, 6484-1
Bates, Clara Doty
The bed-time story. 6131-1
Blue and gold. 6965-7
Catkins. 6965-7
A fashionable lady. 6965-7
Golden rod. 6529-5
The last of the pippins. 6965-7
The lilac. 6049-8,6373-X,6529-5
Our grandmothers. 6965-7
Roasting corn. 6965-7
A sad case. 6314-4,6699-2
Snow stories. 6965-7
The spinner. 6621-6
Spring questions. 6452-3
The story of nobody's cat. 6965-7
Ted's rubber boots. 6965-7
Who likes the rain? 6132-X,6373-X,6466-3,6452-3
Bates, David
Speak gently. 6260-1,6632-1,6922-3
Bates, Eleanor
College daughter - lonely parents. 6718-2
Bates, Herbert
On the prairie. 6274-1
Pioneers. 6274-1
The pioneers. 6274-1
There is a music in the march of stars. 6274-1
Bates, Katharine Lee
Alone into the mountain. 6144-3,6337-3
America the beautiful. 6051-X,6101-X,6162-1,6337-3,6332-2,6465-,6466-3,6476-0,6509-0,6730-1,6736-0,6431 ,
6161-3,6214-8,6265-2,6336-5,6396-9,6449
Another year. 6747-6
Around the sun. 6327-6,6393-4
At Camden. 6036-6

"But thou go forth and do thy deed." 6225-3
By the sea of Galilee. 6144-3
Christmas after war. 6746-8,6608-9
Come unto me. 6144-3
The creed of the wood. 6501-5
Dawn at Lexington. 6039-0
"Does he hunt with the great Orion" 6995-9
The dogs of Bethlehem. 6162-1
Don't you see? 6274-1
Ecco il santo. 6532-5
The Falmouth bell. 6798-0
February 3, 1924. 7001-9
The fellowship. 6006-4
The first bluebirds. 6510-4
The first voyage of John Cabot. 6162-1
Gardens. 6232-6
Graves at Christiania. 6331-4
Grotto of the nativity. 6331-4
Gypsy-heart. 6266-0,6476-0,6374-8
Hills and sea. 6798-0
Home, sels. 6798-0
The home-coming. 6039-0
The horses. 6510-4
The ideal. 6798-0
Idealists. 7001-9
Indian bearers. 6798-0
The kings of the east. 6144-3,6337-3,6730-1,6608-9
Laddie. 6476-0,6510-4
The lame shepherd. 6746-8,6608-9
Let life be royal. 7038-8
Love planted a rose. 6338-1,6653-9
Mine own countree. 6928-2
The new crusade. 6162-1
Only mules. 6510-4
Out of sight of land, sels. 6798-0
The pilgrim ship. 6039-0
Poetry. 6798-0
Rebecca and Abigail. 6162-1
The retinue. 6846-4
Roosevelt's guest. 6995-9
Sarah Threeneedles. 6102-8
The schoolroom I love the best. 6684-4
Sea birds. 6798-0
Shut out. 6036-6
Soldiers of freedom. 6443-4
Somebody's boy. 6449-3
A song of waking. 6820-0
The song that shall atone. 6542-2
Splendid isolation. 6039-0,6307-1
The star of Bethlehem. 6607-0
Success. 6347-0
Tempted. 6144-3
Thanksgiving. 6006-4
This tattered catechism. 6031-5
To peace ("The cup, the ruby cup"). 6051-X
To Sigurd. 6162-1,6030-7,6510-4
To the old year. 6747-6
Vigi. 6512-0
Wild weather. 6542-2
Woodrow Wilson. 6184-2
Yellow clover. 6031-5
Yellow warblers. 6338-1,6374-8,6509-8,6556-2
Bates, L.J.
Why little birds hop, and other birds walk. 6965-7
Bates, Lewis J.
Some sweet day. 6273-3,6303-9,6491-4
Bates, Lilybell
The spell of provincetown. 6798-0
Bates, Mrs. E.C.
Naming the baby. 6131-1
Bates, Stockton
Fathoming brains. 6923-1
Friend death, fr. Thoughts on birth, life and death. 6928-2
Out of the east. 6927-4
Saved. 6921-5
South fork. 6923-1
The starry flag. 6922-3
The starry flag. 6444-2
A visit to Hades. 6921-5

Bates, Theodora
    After. 6118-4
    The hall of sleep. 6118-4
    Rondeau. 6118-4
The bath tub. Ezra Pound. 6536-8
Bath, Earl of. See Pulteney, Sir William
The bath. Rudolph Chambers Lehmann. 7008-6
The bath. Bayard Taylor. 6976-2
"Bathed in unfallen sunlight". Horatius Bonar. 6238-5
Bathed in war's perfume. Walt Whitman. 6126-5
Bather sleeping. James E. Warren Jr. 6979-7
The bather's dirge. Tennyson Minor. 6440-X
A bather.. Amy Lowell. 6031-5
The bather. Bliss Carman and Richard Hovey. 6890-1
Bathers. Terence Tiller. 6209-1,6379-9
The bathers. H.L. Doak. 6506-6
Bathgate, Alexander
    Our heritage. 6768-9
    To the moko-moko, or bell-bird. 6768-9
    The woman in the moon. 6591-0,6592-9
Bathing. John Keble. 6459-0
A bathing girl. Johannes V. Jensen. 6555-4
A bathing snatch. James ("B.V.") Thomson. 6997-5
Bathing: from the Bothie of Tober na Vuolich. Arthur Hugh Clough. 6438-8
Baths. Mary Campbell Monroe. 6710-7
Bathtub gin. Philip H. Rhinelander. 6722-0
Bathurst, John Killick
    Love's pilgrim. 6433-7
Bathurst, William Hiley
    A faith that will not shrink. 6461-2
    The triumphs of thy conquering power. 6065-X
Bats. Robert P. Tristram Coffin. 7040-X
Bats. Comte Robert de Montesquiou. 6351-9
Batson, Robert
    Guinevere to Lancelot. 6385-3
Battarias. Miltiades Malakassis. 6352-7
Batte's song. Michael Drayton. 6315-2
"Batter in the home place". Sounds from the baseball field. Ella Wheeler Wilcox. 6863-4
"Batter my heart, three peron'd God; for, you". John Donne. 6562-7,6634-8,6150-8
"Batter my heart, three person'd God". Sonnet ("Batter my heart"). John Donne. 6341-1,6430-2
"Batter the doors of heaven". Douleur. Lulu Brunt Dawson. 6750-6
Battersby, C. Maude
    An evening prayer. 6525-2,6461-2
Battery. Jean Cocteau. 6351-9
"The battery grides and jingles". The day's march. Robert Nichols. 6872-3,7026-4
Battery moving up to a new position from rest camp:dawn. Robert Nichols. 6532-5
Battery Park. Leonard Cline. 6441-8
Battery Park. L. 6817-0
Battery Park. David McCord. 6506-6
The battery. C.G. Thompson. 7016-7
Battin, Wendy
    The lives we invite to flower among us flower beyond us. 6900-2
Battle. Al-Tutili. 6362-4
Battle. Wilfred Wilson Gibson. 7031-0
Battle. Wilfred Wilson Gibson. 6897-9
Battle. Christine Park Hankinson. 6841-3
The battle above the clouds. Theron Brown. 6630-5,6678-8
The battle autumn of 1862. John Greenleaf Whittier. 6074-9, 6113-3,6271-7
A battle ballad. Francis Orrery Ticknor. 6074-9
Battle bunny-- Malverne hill. Francis Bret Harte. 6743-3, 6808-1
The battle by moonlight, fr. The story of Baladeadro. George Gordon McCrae. 6768-9
Battle cry. Emma Dunning Banks. 6426-4
Battle cry. John G. Neihardt. 6291-1,6102-8,6076-2
Battle cry. William Henry Venable. 6946-0
The battle cry of freedom. George F. Root. 6589-9,6121-4, 6736-0
A battle cry. Lee Shippey. 6274-1,6337-3,6583-X
The battle eve of the brigade. Thomas Osborne Davis. 6930-4

The battle field, sels. William Cullen Bryant. 6337-3
The battle field. William Cullen Bryant. 6219-9,6271-7, 6302-0,6340-3,6385-3,6600-3,6605-,6153-2,6444-2,6288-1,6126-5,6263-6,6735
The battle field. William Herbert; Earl of Pembroke. 6980-0
The battle flag at Shenandoah. Joaquin Miller. 6419-1
The battle flag of Earl Sigurd. Unknown. 6889-8
Battle hymn. Gustavus II (G. Adolphus); King of Sweden. 6730-1
Battle hymn. Donald Goold Johnson. 6650-X
Battle hymn. Karl [or Charles] Theodore Korner. 6606-2
Battle hymn of the republic. Julia Ward Howe. 6014-5,6102-8,6134-6,6165-6,6243-4,6302-,6077-3,6113-3,6239-3, 6240-7,6337-3,6459-,6260-1,6427-2,6471-X,6552-X,6600-3,6605-,6289-X,6340-3,6385-3,6399-3,6418-3,6437-, 6473-6,6486-8,6496-5,6552-X,6589-9,6623-,6610-0,6632-1,6693-3,6730-1,6732-8,6735-,6470-1,6088-9,6431-0, 6560-0,6250-4,6008-0,6016-2,6288-1,6442-6,6214-8, 6219-9,6736-0,6300-4,6114-1,6121-4,6737-9,6214-8, 6219-9,6263-6,6267-9,6309-8,6639-9,6304-7,5668-6, 6424-8,6438-8,6076-5,6309-8,6639-9,6304-7,5668-6, 6424-8,6438-8,6076-5
Battle hymn of the Russian republic. Louis Untermeyer. 6031-5
Battle hymn of the Spanish rebellion. Louis Alexander Mackay. 6733-6
A battle hymn. George Henry Boker. 6753-0
The battle in the clouds. William Dean Howells. 6113-3
The battle in the west, fr. The passing of Arthur. Alfred Lord Tennyson. 6378-0
A battle in Yellowstone Park. Eugene Field. 6949-5
Battle interlude. I. Celner. 6468-X
Battle of Actium, fr. Aeneid. Vergil. 6933-9
Battle of Agincourt. Michael Drayton. 6188-5,6239-3,6808-1, 6424-8,6543-0
The battle of Ai. Timothy Dwight. 6077-3
The battle of Ardnocher. Arthur Gerald Geoghegan. 6518-X
The battle of Argoed Llwyfain. Taliesin. 6528-7
The battle of Baltimore. Unknown. 6946-0
The battle of Bannockburn, fr. Bruce. John Davidson. 6819-7
The battle of Bannockburn. Robert Burns. 6188-5
The battle of Bannockburn. John Barbour. 6180-X
The battle of Bannockburn. Sir Walter Scott. 6192-3,6543-0
Battle of Beal and Duine. Sir Walter Scott. 6567-8
Battle of Beal and Duine, fr. The lady of the lake. Sir Walter Scott. 6832-4
The battle of Beal-an-atha-buidhe. William Drennan. 6858-8
The battle of Belleau Wood. Edgar A. Guest. 6846-4
The battle of Bennington. Julia Douglas Fay. 7030-2
The battle of Bennington. Thomas P. Rodman. 6946-0
The battle of Blenheim. Robert Southey. 6089-7,6101-X,6102-8,6122-2,6127-3,6242 ,6271-7,6302-0,6385-3,6457-4, 6459-0,6502 ,6503-1,6552-X,6604-6,6614-3,6732-8,6660 ,6646-1,6543-0,6639-9,6424-8,6419-1,6267 ,6304-7, 6219-9,6131-1,6104-4,6199-0,6458-2,6212-1,6086-2
The battle of Bridgewater. Unknown. 6946-0
Battle of Brunanburgh. Alfred Lord Tennyson. 6977-0
The battle of Brunanburh. Unknown. 6665-8
Battle of Bunker Hill. Frederick Swartwout Cozzens. 6409-4, 6744-1,6568-6
The battle of Bunker Hill. Unknown. 6946-0
The battle of Bunkers-Hill, sels. Hugh H Brackenridge. 6008-0
The battle of Charleston harbor. Paul Hamilton Hayne. 6113-3,6062-5,6340-3,6016-2
The battle of Charlestown. Henry Howard Brownell. 6946-0
The battle of Eutaw. William Gilmore Simms. 6946-0
Battle of Fontenoy. Thomas Osborne Davis. 6404-3,6630-5
The battle of Fontenoy. Bartholomew Dowling. 6219-9
The battle of Fredericksburg. Unknown. 6057-9
The battle of Gettysburg. Howard (Laura C. Redden Searing) Glyndon. 6402-7
The battle of Gibeon. Bernard Barton. 6848-0
The battle of Grand Pre. M.J. Katzmann Lawson. 6795-6
Battle of Harlaw. Sir Walter Scott. 6438-8
The battle of Harlaw. Unknown. 6180-X,6185-0
The battle of Hohenlinden. Thomas Campbell. 6606-2,6424-8
The battle of Inkerman. George W. Bungay. 6919-3

Battle of Ivry. Thomas Babington Macaulay, 1st Baron
　　Macaulay. 6554-6,6240-7,6604-6,6045-1,6240-7,6328,
　　6606-2,6610-0,6425-6,6570-8,6660-7,6424
The battle of Jarama. Pablo (Neftali Ricardo Reyes
　　Basualto) Neruda. 6665-8
The battle of King's Mountain. Unknown. 6946-0
The battle of King's mountain. Unknown. 7017-5
The battle of Kossovo. Unknown (Servian) 6424-8
The battle of La Prairie. William Douw Lighthall. 6433-7,
　　6656-9
The battle of Lake Champlain. Philip Freneau. 6946-0
The battle of Lake Regillus. Thomas Babington Macaulay,
　　1st Baron Macaulay. 6250-4
The battle of Lepanto. Unknown. 6674-4
The battle of Lexington, sels. Ralph Waldo Emerson. 6601-1
The battle of Lexington. George W. Bungay. 6911-8
The battle of Lexington. Sidney Lanier. 6240-7,6267-9,6470-1
The battle of Liege. Dana Burnet. 7026-4
The battle of Limerick. William Makepeace Thackeray. 6271-7,6092-7
The battle of Lockout Mountain. George Henry Boker. 6403-5,
　　6678-X
The battle of Lovell's pond. Henry Wadsworth Longfellow.
　　6946-0
Battle of Maclodio [or Macalo], fr. Conte di Carmagnola.
　　Vittorio Alfieri. 6973-8
The battle of Maldon, sels. Unknown. 6489-2
The battle of Maldon. Unknown. 6102-8
Battle of Manila. Sarah Beaumont Kennedy. 6580-5
The battle of Manilla, sels. Richard Hovey. 6946-0
The battle of Manilla. Amelia Josephine Burr. 6690-9
The battle of Monmouth. Thomas Dunn English. 6946-0
The battle of Monmouth. R. H. 6946-0
The battle of Morgarten. Felicia Dorothea Hemans. 6744-1,
　　6575-9,6267-9,6749-2
The battle of Morris' Island. Unknown. 6946-0
The battle of Murfreesboro. Kinahan Cornwallis. 6946-0
The battle of Muskingum; or, the defeat of the Burrites.
　　William Harrison Safford. 6946-0
The battle of Naseby, sels. Thomas Babington Macaulay, 1st
　　Baron Macaulay. 6395-0
The battle of Naseby. Thomas Babington Macaulay, 1st Baron
　　Macaulay. 6192-3,6197-4,6419-1,6560-0,6639-9,6554-6,
　　6188-5,6323-3,6504-X,6228-8,6656
The battle of Navarino. Unknown. 6157-5
The battle of New Orleans. Thomas Dunn English. 6267-9,
　　6470-1
The battle of New Orleans. Thomas Dunn English. 6946-0
The battle of Niagara, sels. John Neal. 6008-0
The battle of Oriskany. Charles D. Helmer. 6946-0
The battle of Oriskany. Benjamin Franklin Taylor. 6815-4
The battle of Otterbourne, sels. Unknown. 6427-2,6067-6
The battle of Otterbourne. Unknown. 6075-7,6180-X,6198-2,
　　6098-6,6185-0,6395-0,6518-4
The battle of Otterburn. Unknown. 6188-5,6056-0,6197-4,
　　6419-1
"The battle of our life is brief". Henry Wadsworth
　　Longfellow. 6238-5
The battle of peace. Wilson MacDonald. 6337-3
The battle of Philiphaugh. Unknown. 6185-0
The battle of Plattsburg Bay. Clinton Scollard. 6946-0
The battle of Plattsburg. Unknown. 6946-0
The battle of Point Pleasant. Unknown. 6003-X
The battle of Queenstown. William Banker Jr. 6946-0
The battle of Sempach. George Walter Thornbury. 6749-2
The battle of Sheriff-muir. Unknown. 6859-6
Battle of Somerset. Cornelius C. Cullen. 6946-0
Battle of St. Crispian's day. William Shakespeare. 6438-8
The battle of Stonington on the seaboard of Connecticut.
　　Philip Freneau. 6946-0
Battle of the Baltic. Thomas Campbell. 6239-3,6263-6,6267-9,6639-9,6424-8,6322 ,6240-7,6197-4,6438-8,6219-9,
　　6660-7,6659 ,6086-2,6196-6,6246-5,6302-0,6504-X,6732
　　,6188-5,6473-6,6242-6,6258-X,6323-3,6604 ,6075-7,
　　6180-X,6271-7,6552-X,6457-4
The battle of the bight. Sir William Watson. 7027-2
The battle of the books, fr. Aetia. Callimachus. 6435-3
The battle of the boulevard. William Edmonstoune Aytoun.
　　6278-4

The battle of the Boyne. Unknown. 6090-0,6518-X
The battle of the Cowpens. Thomas Dunn English. 6678-X,
　　6470-1
Battle of the frogs and mice. Pigres (atr.) 6679-8
The battle of the kegs. Francis Hopkinson. 6015-3,6176-1,
　　6399-3,6008-0,6288-1,6121-4,6265-2
The battle of the king's mill. Thomas Dunn English. 6946-0
The battle of the Lake Regillus, sels. Thomas Babington
　　Macaulay, 1st Baron Macaulay. 6427-2,6648-8
The battle of the Marne. Wilhelm Klemm. 6160-5
The battle of the Nile. Unknown. 6057-9
The battle of the Shannon and the Chesapeake. Unknown.
　　6057-9
The battle of the summer islands, sels. Edmund Waller.
　　6152-4,6194-X
The battle of Tippecanoe. Unknown. 6946-0
The battle of Tippecanoe. Unknown. 6678-X
The battle of Trafalgar. Samuel J. Arnold. 6552-X
The battle of Trafalgar. Unknown. 6547-3
The battle of Trenton. Unknown. 6946-0
The battle of Trenton. Unknown. 6015-3,6286-5,6552-X,6712-3,6470-1
Battle of Val. Unknown. 6859-6
The battle of Valparaiso. Unknown. 6946-0
Battle of Waterloo. George Gordon, 6th Baron Byron. 6504-X,
　　6304-7,6542-2
A battle poem. Benjamin Franklin Taylor. 6678-X
Battle prayer. Karl [or Charles] Theodore Korner. 6949-5
The battle rainbow. John Reuben Thompson. 6074-9
Battle sleep. Edith Wharton. 6029-3
Battle song. Ebenezer Elliott. 6102-8,6323-8,6383-7,6322-5
Battle song. Ibn Farsan. 6362-4
Battle song. Robert Burns Wilson. 6946-0
Battle song ("Arm, arm..."). John Fletcher. 6334-9
A battle song for freedom. Gail Hamilton. 6165-6
Battle song, fr. The mad lover. John Fletcher. 6334-9
The battle to the south of the city. Li Po. 6102-8
Battle until victory. Unknown. 6717-4
The battle within. Christina Georgina Rossetti. 6337-3
The battle-cry of freedom. Unknown. 6389-6
The battle-eve of the brigade. Thomas Osborne Davis. 6046-3
The battle-field. Felicia Dorothea Hemans. 6973-8
The battle-fields. Max Eastman. 6037-4
The battle-flag of Sigurd. Dora Greenwell. 6437-X
The battle-flag of Sigurd. William Motherwell. 6960-6
The battle-line. James B. Dollard. 6846-4
Battle-ship and torpedo-boat. J.W. M. 6471-X
"The battle-smoke still fouled the day". The Red Cross
　　nurse. Edith M. Thomas. 7027-2
The battle-song of Gustavus Adolphus. Unknown (German)
　　6302-0;6385-3
Battle-song of the Oregon. Wallace Rice. 6946-0
The battle-word. Robert Nicoll. 7009-4
The battle.. Thomas Babington Macaulay, 1st Baron
　　Macaulay. 6087-0
Battle: hit. Wilfred Wilson Gibson. 6332-2
The battle=cry of freedom. Unknown. 6471-X
The battle. Chu Yuan. 6665-8
The battle. Johann C. Friedrich von Schiller. 6294-6,6621-6
The battle. Johann C. Friedrich von Schiller. 6344-6,6404-3,6606-2
Battledore and shuttlecock. Amy Lowell. 6030-7
Battledores. Fitz-James O'Brien. 6441-8
The battlefield: Gettysburg. Lloyd Mifflin. 6946-0
The battlefield. Sydney Oswald. 7026-4
The battlefield. Walt Whitman. 6542-2
The battlefields of the future. Sir William Watson. 7014-0
The battleof Erie. Unknown. 6946-0
"The battles for the pickle dish once more are". The card
　　club's first meeting. Edgar A. Guest. 6862-6
Battles, William Snowden
　　The doctor's dream, sels. 6482-5
Battleships. Arthur William Beer. 6789-1
Battleships. Lori Petri. 6542-2
"TheBarke battleships move slowly down the bay".
　　Battleships. Arthur William Beer. 6789-1
Baubie, William Edward
　　The race at Petit Cote. 7035-3

Baucis. Erinna. 6435-3
Baucis and Philemon. Jonathan Swift. 6133-8,6239-3,6679-8, 6152-4,6219-9,6424 ,6278-4
Baucis and Philemon, fr. Metamorphoses. Ovid. 7039-6
Baudelaire. Eugene Lee-Hamilton. 6301-2
Baudelaire. Humbert Wolfe. 6483-3
Baudelaire, Charles
    The albatross. 6351-9
    The balcony. 6732-8
    Beauty. Alan Conder (tr.). 6317-9
    Cats. D.S. MacColl (tr.). 6511-2
    The cats. Sir John Collings ("Solomon Eagle") Squire (tr.). 6343-8
    The clock. Alan Conder (tr.). 6317-9
    Comes the charming evening. David Paul (tr.). 6343-8
    Correspondences, sels. 6351-9
    Don Juan in hell. James Elroy Flecker (tr.). 6343-8
    The fair Dorothy. Arthur Symons (tr.). 6343-8
    Giantess. Karl Shapiro (tr.). 6343-8
    Harmonie du soir. Lord Alfred Bruce Douglas (tr.). 7039-6
    "J'aime le souvenir de ces epoque nues" 6801-4
    L'irreparable. 6801-4
    La beatrice. 6801-4
    La beaute. Lord Alfred Bruce Douglas (tr.). 7039-6
    Le beau navire. 6801-4
    Le vin de l'assassin. 6801-4
    Les hiboux. Arthur Symons (tr.). 7039-6
    Les sept viellards. 6106-0
    The little old women. F.P. Sturm (tr.). 6102-8
    My cat. 6120-6,6692-2
    Parfum exotique. 6801-4
    A poet's pipe. Richard Herne Shepherd (tr.). 6453-1
    Preface. 6801-4
    The ransom. Alan Conder (tr.). 6317-9
    Robed in a silken robe. 6732-8
    Sad madrigal, sels. 6351-9
    The seven old men. 6102-8
    Sois sage o ma douleur. Lord Alfred Bruce Douglas (tr.). 7039-6
    Spleen. David Paul (tr.). 6343-8
    The sun. David Paul (tr.). 6343-8
    Une charogne. 6801-4
Baughan, Blanche Edith
    Five prayers. 6784-0
    God's acre. 6784-0
    The greatest gift. 6784-0
    The Mary Ross. 6784-0
    The old place. 6784-0
    On the just and the unjust. 6784-0
Baugher, Ruby Dell
    A Christmas prayer. 6525-2
Bauldy Fraser. James Hogg. 6859-6
Baum, Esther J.
    Home. 6847-2
    "Were there no fair dawn". 6847-2
Baum, L. Frank
    Captain Bing. 6274-1
    Father Goose. 6274-1
Bavarian gentians. David Herbert Lawrence. 6641-0,6209-1
Bavarian roadside. Leonora Speyer. 6039-0,6393-4
Bavieca. John Gibson Lockhart. 7010-8
Bavieca. Unknown (Spanish) 6757-3
"Bawcocks and bullyes alle, who ys for ye...". The elixir. Unknown. 7007-8
"The bawl of a steer". The cowboy's life. John A. Lomax. 6891-X
Bax, Clifford
    At the turn of the year. 6069-2
    In the train. 6090-6,6250-4
    Turn back, O man. 6337-3
Baxter, Carolyn
    Houston street, N.Y. 6870-7
    Lower court. 6870-7
    Masochistic tendencies (/a caustic bastard) 6870-7
    Toilet bowl congregation (holding cell in criminal...) 6870-7
    Warden's day, Capt. America (Who is that masked man...) 6870-7
Baxter, James
    The boobhead & the girl. 7018-3
    Ode to Auckland. 7018-3
    The parting, fr. Cressida. 6043-9
    Poem in the Matukiyuki valley. 6043-9
    A rope for Harry Fat. 7018-3
    A small ode on mixed flatting. 7018-3
Baxter, Richard
    Entering by his door. 6065-X
    Lord, it belongs not to my care. 6931-2,6337-3,6931-2
    A preacher's urgency. 6337-3
    Resignation. 6219-9,6600-3
    The valediction. 6302-0,6219-9
Baxter, Sylvester
    Coals and ashes: 1916 6798-0
    Forever? 6798-0
    Good-will and God's peace. 6798-0
    The oak by the sea. 6798-0
    October days. 6798-0
    The returning. 6762-X
    The returning. 6798-0
    The storm in the valley. 6798-0
    Wherefore? 6798-0
    Young springtime. 6798-0
Bay Billy. Frank H. Gassaway. 6370-5,6413-2,6521-X,6510-4, 6639-9
The bay fight. Henry Howard Brownell. 6113-3,6678-X,6438-8, 6462-1
The bay fight. Henry Howard Brownell. 6016-2,6470-1
"The bay lies steely gray/And cold the sky". Mirror. Katherine Gleeson McAleer. 6799-9
The Bay of Biscay. Andrew Cherry. 6302-0,6385-3,6502-3, 6258-X
Bay of Guanabara. Menotti Del Picchia. 6759-X
"The bay was bronze with sunset and so light". Wings. William Rose Benet. 7014-0
The bayadere. Francis Saltus Saltus. 6431-0
Bayard. Mary Louise Ritter. 6385-3
Bayard Taylor. John Greenleaf Whittier. 6240-7
Bayberry candle. Muriel F. Hochdord. 6850-2
The bayberry candle. Samuel W. Hallett. 6798-0
Bayberry dips. Ellen Vane. 6817-0
Bayer, Konrad
    "First I want to be happy" Milne Holton and Herbert Kuhner (tr.). 6769-7
    "I and my body" Milne Holton and Herbert Kuhner (tr.). 6769-7
    "I'm a true child" Milne Holton and Herbert Kuhner (tr.). 6769-7
    "Nobody helps me" Milne Holton and Herbert Kuhner (tr.). 6769-7
Bayles, James C.
    In the gloaming. 6902-9
Bayley, Helen L.
    Autumn dawn. 6798-0
    The beach plum. 6798-0
    Cape Cod color. 6798-0
    The glory of God. 6798-0
    The greater moment. 6798-0
    The village library. 6798-0
Bayley, L.M. Laning
    The grave by the sorrowful sea. 6923-1
The Bayliffe's daughter of Isington. Unknown. 6499-X,6668-2
Baylis, Samuel M.
    The birth of the snowshoe. 7035-3
    The fur king. 7035-3
    Gather round, all ye good men. 7035-3
    Tally-ho. 7035-3
Baylis, Samuel Mathewson
    Montreal. 6591-0,6592-2
    The music of the reel. 6591-0,6592-2
Bayliss, A.E.M.
    Sir Septimus. 6290-3
Bayliss, John
    October. 6379-9
Bayly, Thomas Haynes
    The archery meeting. 6092-7
    A fashionable novel. 6874-X
    The first gray hair. 6980-0,6543-0
    Hark! the convent bells are ringing. 6543-0

The hunting season. 7025-6
I must come out next spring. 6652-6
"I never was a favourite". 6980-0
"I turn to thee in time of need". 6980-0
I' saddest when I sing. 6980-0
I'd be a butterfly. 6874-X
I'd be a butterfly. 6652-6
Isle of beauty. 6543-0,6744-1
The man with a tuft. 6760-3
The mistletoe bough. 6302-0,6385-3,6424-8
Nightingale's song. 6438-8
A novel of high life. 6092-7
"Oh no! we never mention her". 6980-0
Oh! where do the fairies hide their heads? 6132-X,6271-7,6656-9
Oh, no! we never mention him. 6543-0
The old kirk yard. 6980-0
Out. 6409-4
The pilot. 6605-2
Reading a tragedy. 6064-1
"The rose that all are praising". 6980-0
"She never blamed him, never". 6980-0
She wore a wreath of roses. 6271-7,6656-9
"She would not know men were she now to view me". 6980-0
The soldier's tear. 6980-0
To my wife. 6219-9
What is London's new lion? 6652-6
Where do the fairies hide their heads? 6368-3
"Why don't the men propose?" 6089-7,6280-6,6652-6
Wither away. 6980-0
Won't you? 6066-8,6226-1,6620-8

Baynes, Ernest Harold
Death and Roosevelt. 6995-9
The last race. 6039-0

Baynes, O'Hara
The scene lends its aid. 7035-3

Bayonet and chisel. Shirley Brooks. 6760-3
The **bayonet** charge. Nathan D. Urner. 6294-6,6404-3
The **bayonet**. Shawn O'Leary. 6349-7

Baysting, Arthur
The crazyman. 7018-3

Bazell, Lenard M.
Smoke. 6818-9

Be a 'try' boy. Unknown. 6684-4
Be a woman. Edward Brooks. 6575-9
Be careful what you say. Unknown. 6928-2
Be cheerful. Unknown. 6109-5,6654-2
Be comforted, fr. The death of the Duke of Clarence... Alfred Lord Tennyson. 6337-3
Be content. Unknown. 6139-7,6165-6
Be contented. Unknown. 6274-1
Be different to trees. Mary Carolyn Davies. 6232-6,6184-2
Be each a gentleman. William Makepeace Thackeray. 6747-6
"Be faithful, O my soul! 'tis grand to live". Fides probata coronat. William White. 6868-5
"Be for a little while eternal". O mors aeterna. Horace Gregory. 6780-8
"Be frank with me, and I accept my lot". Sonnet ("Be frank"). Caroline Elizabeth Sarah Sheridan Norton. 6980-0
Be glad. Edith Virginia Bradt. 6720-4
Be glad and full of joy to-day. Unknown. 6720-4
"Be glad, lordings, be ye more and less". Puer nobis natus est, de virgine Maria. Unknown. 6756-5
"Be good, my dear, let who will be clever". Charles Kingsley. 6238-5
"Be good, sweet maid, and let who will be...". Charm. Bertha Strong Cooley. 6894-4
Be hopeful. Francis Strickland. 6583-X
Be humble. ? Jones. 6752-2
"Be hushed, all voices and untimely laughter". A dead march. May C. ([Mary] Gillington) Byron. 7037-X
"Be hushed, my soul, to rest". God knoweth best. William White. 6868-5
"Be in me as the eternal moods". Doria. Ezra Pound. 6897-9
"Be in me as the eternal moods". Ezra Pound. 6619-4
Be in time. Unknown. 6530-9,6167-2
"Be it a weakness, it deserves some praise". William Cowper. 6238-5

"Be it mine to peruse/Old prints and editions". Triolet of the bibliophile. Charles Sayle. 6875-8
"' Be it right or wrong...". Unknown. 6518-X
"Be judged, mysterious blood...". Your weight and your fortune - 1c. Henry Rago. 6761-1
Be just, and fear not. Henry Alford. 6911-8
Be kind. Dora Donn. 6529-5
Be kind te me dowter. Unknown. 6149-4
"Be kind to me as lang's I'm yours". He's coming here. Unknown. 6859-6
Be kind to the birds. Unknown. 6530-9
"Be kind to the panther!". The panther. Unknown. 6902-9
Be kind-- a quartette for four little children. Unknown. 6629-1
"Be life what it has been, and let us hold". To his wife. Decimus Magnus Ausonius. 7039-6
"Be like a bird, that, halting in her flight." Victor Hugo. 6238-5
Be like George Washington. S. Jennie Smith. 6712-3
"Be like the twisted polyp that coiling round...". Theognis. 6251-2
Be merciful to horses. Robert Kirkland Kernighan. 6591-0, 6592-2
Be merry. Unknown. 6756-5
Be merry. Unknown. 6746-8
"Be merry, all birds, to-day". Ay. Alfred Lord Tennyson. 6977-0
"Be merry, be merry, I pray you". Be merry. Unknown. 6756-5
"'Be mine', said the ardent young Sawmilegoff". A Russian courtship. Unknown. 6926-9
Be mine, and I will give thy name. William Cox Bennett. 6656-9
Be my sweetheart. Eugene Field. 6949-5
Be near me. Cy Warman. 6836-7
"Be near me when my light is low", fr. Memoriam. Alfred Lord Tennyson. 6536-8
"Be near me, dearest, till my task is done". Be near me. Cy Warman. 6836-7
"Be noble, and the nobleness that lies." James Russell Lowell. 6225-3,6238-5
"Be not afeard...", fr. The tempest. William Shakespeare. 6395-0
Be not afraid. Herbert Trench. 6877-4
Be not afraid of beauty. Edward Sapir. 6039-0
"Be not afraid to pray - to pray is right". Prayer ("Be not afraid to pray"). Hartley Coleridge. 6337-3,6202-4,6337-3
Be not afraid, fr. The song of the open road. Walt Whitman. 6337-3
"Be not afraid, God." Rainer Maria Rilke. 6160-5
'Be not afraid...'. Robert Nathan. 6236-9
"Be not displeased, but pardon me". Sagami. 6852-9
"Be not much troubled about many things". Light. Alice Cary. 6865-0;6969-X
"Be not proud pritty one." Unknown. 6563-5
"Be not proud, nor coye nor cruell." Unknown. 6563-5
"Be not simply good, be good for something". Henry David Thoreau. 6623-2
"Be not simply good, but good for something." James Russell Lowell. 6225-3
"Be not thou silent now at length". Psalm 083. Bible. 6848-0
"Be not too proud, imperious dame". The defiance. Thomas Flatman. 6933-9
"Be not too quick to carve our rhyme". A song ("Be not"). Herbert P. Horne. 6301-2
"Be off, Krnsa! Do not behave like this!..." Unknown (Newari) 7013-2
"Be off, wind, vagabond - scare". Fool's songs in a windmill. Hamish Maclaren. 6780-8
Be patient. Georgiana Klingle ("George Klingle") Holmes. 6461-2
Be patient. Unknown. 6271-7,6629-1,6742-5
"Be patient, gentle queen...", fr. Henry VI. William Shakespeare. 6323-3
"Be patient, life, when love is at the gate". Dialogue. Walter Conrad Arensberg. 6897-9
"Be patient, O be patient! Put your ear..earth". Patience. William James Linton. 7009-4

Be perfect. Iris Tree. 6320-9
Be polite. Emma Celia & Lizzie J. Rook. 6741-7
Be polite. Unknown. 6626-7
Be quiet, wind. Sir Charles George Douglas Roberts. 6021-8
'Be quiet: fear not.' Frances Ridley Havergal. 6461-2
"Be rootfast. Never yield". Last rally. Clifford J. Laube. 6761-1
"Be sad, be cool, be kind". The long shadow of Lincoln. Carl Sandburg. 6871-5
Be she fair as lillies be. Unknown. 6563-5
"Be silent here amid this desolation". Poe's poem. Ronald Walker Barr. 6906-1
Be still. Alice Cary. 6865-0;6969-X
Be still. William Closson Emory. 6464-7
Be still. Katharina von Schlegel. 6337-3
Be still to-day. Joseph Freeman. 6778-6
"Be still, mad world, cease from thy..strife". Introspection. John M. Dean. 7001-9
Be still, my soul. Archilochus. 6435-3
"Be still, my soul, be still." Alfred Edward Housman. 6102-8,6430-2,6508-2
"Be still, my soul, be still; the arms you...". Injustice. Alfred Edward Housman. 6954-1
"Be still, my sweet sweeting...". Lullaby ("Be still"). John Phillip. 6182-6
"Be still. The hanging gardens were a dream" Trumbull Stickney. 6310-1,6380-2
"Be still: be still: nor dare". A holy hill. George William ("A.E.") Russell. 7039-6
Be strong. Maltbie Davenport Babcock. 6109-5,6337-3,6260-1, 6461-2
Be strong. Adelaide Anne Procter. 6337-3;6583-X
Be strong! Duncan Campbell Scott. 6501-5
"Be strong, nor let thy heart nor faint...fall". Faith's victory. William White. 6868-5
"Be strong, O warring soul! For very sooth". To the heroic soul. Duncan Campbell Scott. 6843-X
Be sure. Frank W. Gunsaulus. 6889-8
Be the best of whatever you are. Douglas Malloch. 6291-1, 6736-0,6654-2
"Be the day weary." Unknown. 6225-3
"Be then your counsels, as your subject, great". To the federal convention. Timothy Dwight. 6946-0
"Be this our trust, that ages...". Thought. Sir Humphry Davy. 6980-0
"Be thou my vision, o Lord of my heart". A prayer. Unknown. 6930-4
Be thou then my beauty. Thomas Campion. 6328-4
"Be thou, in all my falling". Wall crucifix. John Duffy. 6839-1
"Be thou, O God! by night, by day". A sacred melody. Unknown. 6752-2
"Be tranquil, Dellius, I pray". To Quintus Dellius. Horace. 6949-5
Be true. Horatius Bonar. 6239-3,6242-3,6337-3
Be true. Robert Collyer. 7022-1
Be true. Unknown. 6165-6,6416-7
Be true to your condition in life. John Audelay. 6881-2
Be true, fr. Hamlet. William Shakespeare. 6512-0
"Be useful where thou livest, that they may". George Herbert. 6239-3,6242-3,6623-2
Be vigilant. Edward R. Huxley. 6885-5
"Be warned! Thou canst not break nor 'scape...". The death of sin and the life of holiness. Richard Henry Dana. 6752-2
"Be wise as thou art cruel, do not press". Sonnet 140 ("Be wise"). William Shakespeare. 6447-7
"Be wise to day, 'tis madness to defer". Procrastination. Edward Young. 6932-0
"Be wise to-day! Tis madness to defer" Edward Young. 6935-5
"Be wise to-day: 'tis madness to defer". Procrastination, fr. Night thoughts. Edward Young. 6934-7
"Be with me, O Lord,when my life hath increase". A canticle. Phoebe Cary. 6865-0;6969-X
Be ye also ready, fr. Thanatopsis. William Cullen Bryant. 6337-3
Be ye in love with April-tide. Clinton Scollard. 6441-8, 6652-6
"Be ye kind", fr. The bible, Ephesians IV. Unknown. 6623-2

Be ye ready. J.B. Walter. 6417-5
Be yourself. Julia A. Booth. 6883-9
Beach. Glyn Jones. 6360-8
Beach burial. Kenneth Slessor. 6349-7
"Beach fires and lanterns". A fisher-folk legend of Picardie. Gertrude Huntington McGiffert. 6838-3
Beach plum. Joshua Freeman Crowell. 6798-0
Beach plum blossom time. Florence Hathaway Crowell. 6798-0
The beach plum. Helen L. Bayley. 6798-0
The beach road by the wood. Geoffrey Howard. 7026-4
Beach trails. Martha Haskell Clark. 6798-0
Beach, Byron
    The questions. 6486-8
Beach, Ella M.
    One heart - one way. 6717-4
Beach, Grace Bentley
    November. 6847-2
    Outside my window. 6847-2
    The storm. 6847-2
    To a wren. 6847-2
Beach, H. Prescott
    Hither, meadow gossip, tell me! 6373-X
Beach, Joseph Warren
    Cave talk. 6029-3
    The dance in the steerage. 6959-2
    Power. 6342-X
    Rue Bonaparte. 6897-9
    The view at Gunderson's. 6897-9
Beach, Mrs. H.H.A.
    Ecstasy. 6764-6
    Within thy heart. 6764-6
Beach, V. Louise
    A tribute. 6799-9
Beach-comber. Edith Ballinger Price. 6861-8
The beach. Robinson Jeffers. 6012-9
The beach. David O'Neil. 6032-3
Beachcomber. Robert Service. 6159-1
Beachcroft, T.O.
    Emblem to be cut on a lonely rock at sea. 6781-6
Beachler, Rosetta Thorson
    A tribute to Will Rogers and Wiley Post. 6799-9
Beachy head, sels. Charlotte Smith. 6649-6
Beacon light. Leslie Savage Clark. 6144-3
Beacon lights. Nellie E. Warren. 6799-9
Beacon of trust. Marjorie Herrmann Cox. 6342-X
The beacon-light. Murray Ketcham Kirk. 6995-9
The beacon. Joanna Baillie. 6813-8
The beacon. Paul Moon James. 6385-3
Beads. Chapman J. Milling. 7016-7
The beads. Jaime Jacinto. 6790-5
The beagle's cry. Unknown. 6930-4
Beagles. William Robert Rodgers. 6210-5,6930-4
Beagles at twilight. Edward A. Briggs. 6761-1
Beal' an Dhuine. Sir Walter Scott. 6385-3
Beale, Mary
    Peeping thru the snow. 6048-X
Beale, William
    Go, rose, go. 6328-4
Beall, Dorothy Landers
    The young god wish. 6327-6
Beals, Jessie Tarbox
    Destiny. 6232-6
"The beam on the streamlet was playing". Mo cailin deas cruidhte na m-bo. Unknown (Irish). 6858-8
Beam, Jeffery
    Knight, death and devil. 7003-5
    The silent speak for you. 7003-5
Beamish, Richard J.
    Caesar Rodney's ride. 6249-0
"The beams of April, ere it goes". The silk worm. Vincent Bourne. 6814-6
"The bean!/Say, buddy, the more I have seen". The bean. Berton Braley. 6853-7
Bean, Helen Mar
    Pet and bijou. 6166-4
Bean-blossoms. Unknown. 6273-3
The bean-stalk. Edna St. Vincent Millay. 6538-4;6531-7
The bean. Berton Braley. 6853-7
"Beaneath fair Magdalen's storied towers". Oxford revisited in war-time. Tertius Van Dyke. 7026-4

The **beanfield**. John Clare. 6668-2
Beans for breakfast. Unknown. 6237-7
Bear a horn and blow it naught. Unknown. 6334-9
Bear Butte Mountain. David Wilson. 6917-7
Bear dance. Ronald Rogers. 7005-1
Bear dance. Lilian White Spencer. 6490-6
A **bear** family. James Whitcomb Riley. 6091-9
"**Bear** him, comrades, to his grave". Burial of Barber. John Greenleaf Whittier. 6946-0
The **bear** hunt. Margaret Widdemer. 6891-X
The **bear** in a boat. John Gay. 6972-X
"**Bear** in mind". Drum. Langston Hughes. 6879-0
"**Bear** me no grudge, s ectators...". Aristophanes. 6435-3
The **bear** pit. Frederick Locker-Lampson. 6760-3
The **bear** river murder. Unknown. 6057-9
The **bear** story. James Whitcomb Riley. 6990-8
"**Bear** them not from grassy dells". The dying girl and flowers. Felicia Dorothea Hemans. 6973-8
Bear up a while. James ("B.V.") Thomson. 6211-3,6337-3
"**Bear** with him, he is old". The negationist. Mary H. Cabaniss. 6841-3
Bear's heart. Walter Stanley ("Stanley Vestal") Campbell. 6628-3
The **bear's** song. Edward Abbott Parry. 6242-3
The **bear's** song. Unknown (Haida Indian) 7039-6
Bear, Ray A. Young
    A drive to lone ranger. 7032-9
    Grandmother. 7005-1
    "In the first place of my life" 7005-1
    The last dream. 7005-1
    "one chip of human bone" 7005-1
    Poem for Viet nam. 7005-1
The **bear**. Edith Sitwell. 7000-0
Beard and baby. Eugene Field. 6078-1,6318-7
Beard, George P.
    The farmer's life. 6571-6
Beard, Theresa Virginia
    The death of Roosevelt. 6995-9
    Heritage. 6029-3
The **beard**. Ibn al-Hajj. 6362-4
Bearded oaks. Robert Penn Warren. 6389-6
"The **bearded** one sees the joy". Wayward child. David Llorens. 7024-8
"**Bearded** with dewy grass the mountains thrust". On a hilltop. George Russell. 6958-4
Beardless youth. Ibn Iyad. 6362-4
Beardsley, Aubrey
    Ave atque vale. 6096-X
    The ballad of a barber. 6507-4
    Catallus, carmen CI. 6785-9
    The three musicians. 6022-6,6292-X,6507-4
Beardsley, Aubrey (tr.)
    On the burial of his brother. Caius Catallus, 7039-6
"**Bearing** His cross, while Christ passed...", sels. Unknown. 6601-1
Bearing sorrow. James Thomson. 6211-3
"**Bears** lie wasting". Bears' bones. Dennis List. 7018-3
Beast and man in India. John Lockwood Kipling. 6510-4
The **beast** that rode the unicorn. Conny Hannes Meyer. 6769-7
The **beast's** confession. Jonathan Swift. 6152-4,6278-4
The **beasts** in the tower. Charles and Mary Lamb. 6295-4
The **beasts**. Sara Henderson Hay. 6979-7
The **beasts**. Walt Whitman. 6437-X,6501-5
Beat against me no longer. Lew Sarett. 6033-1
"**Beat** on proud billowes, boreas blow". Loyalty confin'd. Sir Roger L'Estrange. 6933-9
"**Beat** on, proud billows; Boreas, blow". Loyalty confined. Arthur Lord Capel. 6874-X
Beat! beat! drum! Walt Whitman. 6322-5,6288-1,6126-5,6121-4,6252-0
Beat! beat! drums! Walt Whitman. 6113-3,6340-3,6224-5,6299-7,6334-9
Beata Beatrix. Samuel Waddington. 6331-4,6046-3,6439-6
Beata solitudo. Ernest Dowson. 6508-2
Beaten. Oscar Fay Adams. 7041-8
The **beaten** path. Anne Goodwin Winslow. 6778-6
The **beaten** path. Anne Goodwin Winslow. 6619-4
Beathen paths. Ethel Turner. 6070-6
Beati mortui. Louise Imogen Guiney. 6309-8

The **beatific** sea. Thomas Campbell. 6833-2
Beatitudes. Bible. 6143-5,6491-4,6503-1,6304-7
The **beatitudes** of Jesus, fr. Matthew. Bible. 6337-3
Beatrice. Dante Alighieri. 6679-8
Beatrice. Oscar Levertin. 6045-5
Beatrice. William Shakespeare. 6543-0
Beatrice Cenci. Percy Bysshe Shelley. 6302-0;6385-3
Beatrice Cenci in her cell. Percy Bysshe Shelley. 6541-4
Beatrice dead. M. A. 6817-0
Beatrice, sels. Joseph Sheridan Le Fanu. 6174-5
Beattie, James
    Benevolence. 6409-4
    But who the melodies of morn can tell? 6180-X
    Different tastes. 6402-7
    Epitaph, intended for himself. 6086-2,6180-X,6641-0
    An epitaph. 6339-X
    The hermit. 6219-9,6271-7,6302-0,6385-3,6600-3
    His own epitaph. 6960-6
    Law. 6302-0,6385-3,6410-8
    Life beyond the tomb. 6606-2
    The minstrel, sels. 6831-6
    The minstrel, sels. 6191-5
    The minstrel, sels. 6831-6
    The minstrel. 6198-2,6302-0,6152-4
    Morning. 6302-0,6385-3,6543-0
    Morning sounds. 6793-X
    Nature. 6438-8
    Nature and the poets, fr. The minstrel. 6932-0
    Nature's charms, fr. The minstrel. 6932-0
    Night. 6438-8
    Reasons for humility. 6402-7
    Retrement: an ode. 6960-6
    Solitude. 6932-0
    A summer morn. 6240-7
Beattie, Robert Brewster
    A way to a happy new year. 6654-2
Beattie, William
    Evening hymn of the Alpine shepherds. 6219-9
Beatty, Pakenham
    Charles Lamb. 6656-9
    The death of Hampden. 6656-9
    To thine own self be true. 6273-3,6481-7
    When will love come? 6273-3,6652-6
Beatty, William A.
    Three songs of love. 6818-9
Beatus vir. Richard Le Gallienne. 6253-9
Beau Tibbs, his character and family. Oliver Goldsmith. 6200-8
The **beau's** receipt for a lady's dress. Unknown. 6157-5
Beau's reply. William Cowper. 6519-8,6086-2
Beauchamp, Ellen
    Arbor day march. 6049-8,6171-0
    A hymn in praise of the natural world. 6049-8
    Song oi dedication ("The tree we are planting..."). 6049-8
Beaudin, Nicolas
    Music hall. 6351-9
The **Beaufort** exile's lament. Unknown. 6074-9
Beaufort, Aileen
    My nursery walls. 6249-0
Beaumont (atr), Francis
    "Eies look off theires no beeholdinge." 6563-5
Beaumont and Fletcher. Algernon Charles Swinburne. 6250-4
Beaumont and John Fletcher, Francis
    Aspatia's song. 6301-2,6383-7
    Beauty clear and fair. 6099-4,6271-7
    The bloody brother, sels. 6208-3
    Bonduca. 6438-8
    Bridal song, fr. The little French lawyer. 6827-8
    A bridal song. 6737-9
    A burlesque of 1612. 6186-9
    The captain, sels. 6208-3,6562-7
    Care charming sleep...", fr. The valentinian. 6562-7
    The chances, sels. 6369-1
    Come sleep. 6383-7
    Come, sleep. 6383-7
    Cupid's revenge, sels. 6208-3
    A dirge. 6383-7
    The disguised maiden. 6385-3
    Drink and drown sorrow, fr. The bloody brother. 6934-7

BEAUMONT

The elder brother, sels. 6369-1
The faithful shepherdess. 6369-1
The farewell to love. 6641-0
Folding the flocks. 6271-7,6302-0,6385-3,6219-9,6424-8, 6737
"Hence, all ye vain delights." 6271-7,6302-0,6385-3
The honest man's fortune, sels. 6369-1
Hymn to Pan. 6099-4
I did hear you talk far above singing. 6066-8
Invocation to sleep. 6099-4,6302-0,6385-3
Lay a garland on my hearse. 6430-2
Lines on the tombs in Westminster. 6197-4
Look out, bright eyes. 6219-9
Love at first sight. 6438-8
Love song, fr. The bloody brother. 6208-3
Love song, fr. Valentinian. 6208-3
Lovers rejoyce, fr. Cupid's revenge. 6208-3
Lullaby, fr. The woman-hater. 6208-3
The mad love, sels. 6369-1
The maid's tragedy, sels. 6543-0
Mirth. 6383-7
Misfortune. 6294-6
The night-walker: or, the little thief, sels. 6369-1
Pan. 6271-7
Philaster, sels. 6302-0,6369-1
Poet's mood. 6438-8
The power of love. 6219-9
The queen of Corinth, sels. 6369-1
The river god's song. 6134-6,6466-3,6421-3
Roses, their sharp spines being gone. 6197-4
Rule a wife and have a wife, sels. 6369-1
The sad song, fr. The captain. 6208-3
The scornful lady, sels. 6369-1
Song. 6737-9
Song ("Lay a garland"). 6219-9
Song ("Shake off"). 6438-8
Song for the sick emperor, fr. Valentinian. 6208-3
Song in the wood, fr. The little French lawyer. 6827-8
The Spanish curate, sels. 6369-1
Speak, love. 6271-7
Spring. 6271-7,6737-9
"Take, O take those lips away". 6240-7,6219-9
"Tell me dearest what is Love", fr. The captaine. 6562-7
Thierry and Theodoret. 6958-4
Thierry and Theodoret, sel. 6958-4
To Pan. 6271-7,6219-9
To the blest evanthe, fr. A wifp for a moneth. 6562-7
To Venus. 6438-8
Valentinian, sels. 6208-3,6562-7
Wake, gently wake, fr. Wit at several weapons. 6827-8
Wedding song, fr. The maid's tragedy. 6827-8
A wife for a moneth, sels. 6369-1,6562-7
The woman-hater, sels. 6208-3

Beaumont, Francis
Adieu, fond love, fr. The lover's progress. 6328-4
Aspatia's song. 6933-9
At the Mermaid, fr. Letter to Ben Jonson. 6934-7
Bridal song. 6182-6
"Come, sleep, and with thy sweet deceiving". 6181-8, 6182-6
Fit only for Apollo. 6125-7
In Westminster Abbey. 6322-5
The indifferent. 6182-6
Jillian of Berry. 6182-6
Letter to Ben Jonson. 6933-9
A letter to Ben Jonson. 6315-2,6250-4,6301-2
'Like to the falling of a star" 6935-5
Lines on the tombs in Westminster. 6198-2,6337-3,6189-3, 6543-0
Lovers, rejoice! 6182-6
The masque of the gentlemen of Gray's Inn..., sels. 6933-9
Master Francis Beaumont's letter to Ben Jonson. 6198-2, 6483-3,6562-7
Mirth ("'Tis mirth that fills the veins with blood") 6182-6
The month of May. 6125-7
On the life of man. 6198-2,6604-6,6726-3,6153-2,6189-3, 6660

On the tombs in Westminster Abbey. 6022-6,6102-8,6289-X, 6246-6,6484-1,6604 ,6194-X,6219-9,6250-4,6660-7,6631-3,6737
Song ("More pleasing were these sweet delights"). 6933-9
Song ("On blessed youths, for Jove doth pause"). 6933-9
Song ("Peace and silence be the guide"). 6933-9
Song ("Shake off your heavy trance"). 6933-9
Song ("You should stay longer if we durst"). 6933-9
Song for a dance ("Shake off your heavy trance!") 6182-6
Songs, fr. The masque of the gentlemen of Gray's Inn... 6933-9
"'Tis mirth that fills the veins with blood". 6181-8
True beauty. 6182-6

Beaumont, Irwin
The ride from Ghent to Aix. 7021-3

Beaumont, Joseph
The ascension. 6931-2
Bad times. 6337-3
Biothanatos. 6933-9
The garden. 6931-2,6933-9,6931-2,6933-9
The garden. 6562-7,6563-5
The gentle check. 6563-5
The gnat. 6315-2
Home. 6245-8
House and home. 6933-9
Love. 6933-9
Morning hymn. 6931-2
Purification of the blessed virgin. 6282-2
Whit Sunday. 6931-2
Whiteness, or chastity. 6315-2

Beaumont, Sir John
The Assumption. 6022-6
Of my dear son, Gervase Beaumont. 6562-7,6563-5,6291-9, 6737-9
Of the epiphany. 6747-6
Of true liberty. 6933-9
On my dear son. 6934-7
On the Annuniciation and Resurrection. 6022-6
Time. 6294-6
To his last maiesty, concerning the trve forme... 6562-7
To his late majesty, concerning...English poetry. 6933-9

Beaumont, Thomas
His despair. 6563-5
To his mistress, sending her the Arcadia. 6563-5

Beaumont-Hamel. Alan Mackintosh. 6542-2
Beauregard. Catherine Anne Warfield. 6946-0
Beauregard's appeal. Paul Hamilton Hayne. 7041-8

Beausoleil, Beau
Half and half again. 6901-0
Passage #3 6901-0
Poem for a Cuban brigade of women cane cutters. 6901-0
Remain. 6901-0
"Your thick hair" 6901-0

"Beaute des femmes, leur faiblesse, et ces mains..." Paul Verlaine. 6801-4
"Beaute, secret d'en haut, rayon, divin embleme" Alphonse Marie Louis de Lamartine. 6801-4
"Beauteous and bright is he among the". Joab's description of David. George Peele. 6848-0
Beauteous death. Henry Vaughan. 6383-7
"Beauteous machine! let love thy movements...". Written in a lady's watch-case. Thomas Warton (the Elder). 6962-2
The beauties around us. Jesse Sill. 6799-9
Beauties eclipsed. Francis Lenton. 6328-4
The beauties of English orthography. Unknown. 6724-7
The beauties of nature. Anthony C. Deane. 6996-7
The beauties of Santa Crux, sels. Philip Freneau. 6008-0, 6288-1
The beauties of Santa Cruz. Philip Freneau. 6333-0
Beauties of the morning. Unknown. 6935-5
"Beauties, have ye seen this toy". Song ("Beauties"). Ben Jonson. 6430-2
"Beautiful arch of the protal where thought...". To my mistress's eyebrow. James Abraham Martling. 6952-5
"The beautiful are never desolate". Philip James Bailey.

6238-5
"Beautiful are thy works and ways, O god...". God of the young. William Rose Benet. 6761-1
"Beautiful as a wave before it breaks". A dancer. Cale Young Rice. 6959-2
"Beautiful as the flying legend...some leopard". Judith of Bethulia. John Crowe Ransom. 7017-5
"Beautiful Bermuda, sunny, sleepy isle". Impressions of Bermuda. Madeline B. Foster. 6799-9
'The beautiful blue Danube'. Ella Wheeler Wilcox. 6956-8, 6863-4
Beautiful child. William Andrew H. Sigourney. 6772-7
"Beautiful child! by thy mother's knee". My beautiful child. William Andrew H. Sigourney. 6909-6
Beautiful city, fr. The promise of May. Alfred Lord Tennyson. 6867-7
The beautiful damsel; or, the undaunted female. Unknown. 6018-8
Beautiful death. John Lancaster Spalding. 6274-1
"Beautiful deeds are like beautiful flowers". The flowery path of life. Clara Degman Hook. 6906-1
Beautiful dreams. Unknown. 6407-8
"Beautiful face and heart". The good angel of the household. Gertrude Huntington McGiffert. 6838-3
"Beautiful from the coiled and angry seed". A woman to her world. Ruth Forbes Sherry. 6761-1
The beautiful gate. Unknown. 6486-8
The beautiful gift. Grace Noll Crowell. 6449-3
"Beautiful golden-rod!/Up from the...". Golden-rod. Isabell Sherrick Wardell. 6836-7
Beautiful grandmama. Unknown. 6742-5
Beautiful grandmamma. Mary A. Denison. 6131-1
Beautiful grandmamma. Unknown. 6273-3
"A beautiful guitar/in a pawnshop window...". Poem for Elizabeth. Wayne Miller. 6998-3, 6901-0
Beautiful hands. Ellen M.H. Gates. 6097-8,6260-1
Beautiful hands. Unknown. 6014-5,6530-9
The beautiful horses. Donald Hall. 6388-8
The beautiful incendiary. Horace Smith. 6802-2
"Beautiful is she, this woman". Love song. Unknown (American Indian). 6021-8
The beautiful island of Ceylon. Phillips Brooks. 6373-X
"A beautiful lady named Psyche". Unknown. 6722-0
"A beautiful lady named Psyche". Limerick:"A beautiful lady named Psyche." Unknown. 6308-X
A beautiful lady. Elizabeth Madox Roberts. 6037-4
The beautiful land of Nod. Ella Wheeler Wilcox. 6014-5, 6632-1,6530-9
The beautiful land. Eric Chilman. 6639-9
A beautiful legend. K.N. E. 6294-6
A beautiful legend. Unknown. 6848-0
Beautiful lie the dead. Stephen Phillips. 6785-9,6872-3
A beautiful life. Delphia L. Hopper. 6906-1
Beautiful lily. Alice Mortenson. 6065-X
Beautiful May. Benjamin Franklin Taylor. 6815-4
"A beautiful maid of Madrid". Limerick:"A beautiful maid of Madrid". Unknown. 6811-1
"A beautiful maiden was little Min-Ne". Ho-ho of the golden belt. John Godfrey Saxe. 6787-5
Beautiful meals. Thomas Sturge Moore. 6668-2
"A beautiful night, and I returning home". From inward shining. Robert Wayne. 6839-1
A beautiful night. Thomas Lovell Beddoes. 6315-2
Beautiful on the bough. Alfred Noyes. 6151-6
"A beautiful place is the town of Lo-yang". Lo-yang. Ch'ien Wen-ti. 7039-6
'Beautiful proud sea'. Sara Teasdale. 6779-4
The beautiful river. Benjamin Franklin Taylor. 6385-3
Beautiful saviour. Charlotte M. Kruger. 6065-X
"The beautiful scenes around us". The beauties around us. Jesse Sill. 6799-9
Beautiful snow. Major Sigourney. 6273-3
Beautiful snow. Unknown. 6440-X
Beautiful snow. John W. Watson. 6889-8
Beautiful snow. John Whitaker Watson. 6142-7,6273-3,6344-5, 6302-0,6385-3,6706 ,6732-8,6219-9,6304-7
The beautiful snow. Caroline Griswold. 6909-6
Beautiful soup. Charles Lutwidge ("Lewis Carroll") Dodgson. 6802-2
"Beautiful sprite!/Sporting in golden light". To the oriole. James Abraham Martling. 6952-5
"Beautiful star, that dawned in the Orient". Star of the east. Mary B. Sleight. 6807-3
"Beautiful stories, by tongue and pen". A monkish legend. Phoebe Cary. 6969-X
"Beautiful symbol of a freer life". On seeing a wild bird. Alice Cary. 6969-X
Beautiful things. Ellen P. Allerton. 6461-2
Beautiful things. Jane Taylor. 6456-6
Beautiful things. Unknown. 6049-8,6629-1
Beautiful trees. A.L. R. 6049-8
A beautiful unknown. Celestin Pierre Cambiaire. 6826-X
"Beautiful was Wetu as a blue shadow". Lament for a dead crow. Francis Carey ("Jan van Avond") Slater. 6788-3
"The beautiful wild wind". The exorcism. Norman Moser. 6998-3
Beautiful women. Walt Whitman. 6300-4
Beautiful Yosemite. Viva I. Stark. 6270-9
"Beautiful world of new, buperber birth...". As a strong bird on pinions free. Walt Whitman. 6954-1
"Beautiful, beautiful the mother lay". Robert Buchanan. 6997-5
"Beautiful, brief, flame up and die". Advice to red leaves. Muriel F. Hochdorf. 6850-2
"A beautiful, delicate, fragile vase". The mended vase. William R. Sims. 6924-X
"Beautiful, distracting Hetty,/This was how...". Villanelle. Cosmo Monkhouse. 6770-0
A beautifull mistress. Thomas Carew. 6933-9
Beauty. Abu Hafs. 6362-4
Beauty. Kenneth Slade Alling. 6037-4
Beauty. Anacreon (atr) 7039-6
Beauty. Paul David Ashley. 6870-7
Beauty. Charles Baudelaire. 6317-9
Beauty. Henry Charles Beeching. 6785-9
Beauty. Abraham Cowley. 6150-8
Beauty. John Cross. 6037-4
Beauty. Alice Booth Day. 6750-6
Beauty. William Foster Elliott. 6071-4
Beauty. Edgar A. Guest. 6748-4
Beauty. Edgar A. Guest. 6869-3
Beauty. L. L. Hershberger. 6818-9
Beauty. Nora Hopper. 6507-4
Beauty. Edward Hovell-Thurlow; 2d Baron Thurlow. 6302-0, 6385-3,6737-9
Beauty. Armel O'Connor. 6034-X
Beauty. Yannis Ritsos. 6758-1
Beauty. Naomi Rogin. 6850-2
Beauty. Alexander Smith. 6656-9
Beauty. Edmund Spenser. 6436-1,6438-8
Beauty. Joel Elias Spingarn. 6250-4
Beauty. Thomas Stanley. 6513-9
Beauty. Unknown. 6436-1
Beauty. Gretchen O. Warren. 6762-X
Beauty ("A thing of beauty is a joy forever"). John Keats. 6183-4,6232-6,6610-0,6102-8,6543-0
Beauty ("Beauty is but a vain and doubtful good"). Unknown. 6436-1
Beauty ("Beauty, that burns enshrined.."). Charles Maurras. 6351-9
Beauty ("I have seen dawn and sunset on moors ..."). John Masefield. 6423-X,6477-9,6634-8,6723-9
Beauty ("You bid me stay; I go"). Clinton Scollard. 6607-0
Beauty accurst. Richard Le Gallienne. 6507-4
"A beauty all stainless, a pearl of a maiden". The Geraldine's daughter. Egan O'Rahilly. 6930-4
Beauty and beauty. Rupert Brooke. 6234-2
"Beauty and song and Christ". Essentials. Sister Mary St. Virginia. 6761-1
Beauty and sorrow. Robert Liddell Lowe. 6640-2
Beauty and terror. Lesbia Harford. 6349-7
Beauty and the beast. Charles and Mary Lamb. 6295-4
Beauty and the beast. Sylvia Lynd. 6781-6
Beauty and the bird. Dante Gabriel Rossetti. 7020-5
Beauty and time. J. C. 6189-3
"Beauty and truth and all that these contain." James Russell Lowell. 6225-3
Beauty and youth. John Dryden. 6867-7
Beauty at the plough, fr. Dorothy. Arthur J. Munby. 6656-9
Beauty awake. Maybelle McLaurin Kinsey. 7016-7

BEAUTY

Beauty bathing. Anthony Munday. 6934-7
Beauty beyond praise. William Shakespeare. 6634-8
"Beauty blue and beauty white". Shopping day. Orrick Johns. 6817-0
Beauty builds. Evelyn Elster. 6342-X
"Beauty came out of the early world". Isadora. Witter Bynner. 6959-2
"Beauty clear and fair". Song ("Beauty clear and fair"). John Fletcher. 6933-9
Beauty clear and fair. Francis Beaumont and John Fletcher. 6099-4,6271-7
Beauty clear anB fair. John Fletcher and Philip Massinger. 6430-2
Beauty clear and fair. John Fletcher. 6198-2,6563-5,6317-9, 6562-7,6189-3
Beauty crowds me. Emily Dickinson. 6300-4
"Beauty deserves the homage of the muse". On beauty. James Thomson. 6816-2
Beauty everywhere. W.L. Smith. 6629-1
Beauty extoll'd. Unknown. 6933-9
Beauty extolled. Henry Noel. 6125-7
Beauty fades. William Drummond of Hawthornden. 6219-9
"Beauty fled from her, into far places". Beauty returned. Elizabeth Greene Thomas. 7016-7
Beauty in darkness. Alfred Noyes. 6151-6
Beauty in excellence. Henry Noel. 6328-4
Beauty in exile, sels. Arthur Davison Ficke. 6320-9
The beauty in my heart. Maude Zobel. 6799-9
Beauty in rags. Ibn al-Arabi. 6362-4
Beauty in the grave. Robert Blair. 6543-0
Beauty in worship, fr. A poem...Christ-Church. Unknown. 6933-9
"Beauty in your silent towers". Beauty and the beast. Sylvia Lynd. 6781-6
"Beauty is a fragile/And a tender thing". Song against beauty. Bertye Young Williams. 6906-1
"Beauty is but a painted hell" Thomas Campion. 6794-8
Beauty is elsewhere. Boyce House. 6265-2
"Beauty is my creed,/From sordidness may...". My creed. Elsie Conley. 6818-9
Beauty is vain. Christina Georgina Rossetti. 6980-0
"Beauty like hers is genius. Not the call". Genius in beauty, fr. The house of life. Dante Gabriel Rossetti. 6828-6
"Beauty lives, awake, my soul, to song!". Awake, my soul. James O. Walker. 6894-4
"Beauty never visits mining places". Out of the coalfields, sels. Frederick C. Boden. 6954-1
The beauty of death. Benjamin Franklin Taylor. 6815-4
The beauty of England. Elizabeth Barrett Browning. 6543-0
Beauty of Greece and the Grecian isles. George Gordon, 6th Baron Byron. 6543-0
"The beauty of Israel is slain...", fr. The bible. Unknown. 6334-9
"The beauty of her hair bewilders me". Her hair. James Whitcomb Riley. 6992-4
"The beauty of Israel is slain...". Inclyti Israel. Bible. 6830-8
"Beauty of ladies of compassionate heart". Guido Cavalcanti. 6325-X
Beauty of nature. Henry Alford. 6980-0
'A beauty of St. Giles.' William Aspenwall Bradley. 6118-4
The beauty of terror. William Blake. 6322-5
The beauty of the Unakas. Edward Farquhar. 6939-8
Beauty of the world. Frank ("Furnley Maurice") Wilmot. 6349-7
The beauty of the world. William Brighty Rands. 6648-8, 6383-9
Beauty paramount. Sir William Killigrew. 6563-5
"Beauty remembered may be more than sorrow". Mine is the choice. Margery Howell. 6761-1
Beauty returned. Elizabeth Greene Thomas. 7016-7
Beauty Rohtraut. Eduard Friedrich Morike. 7039-6
"Beauty sat bathing by a spring". Beauty bathing. Anthony Munday. 6934-7
"Beauty sat bathing by a spring". Anthony Munday. 6181-8;6182-6;6238-2
Beauty shop. Mary Brent Whiteside. 6841-3
Beauty should not last forever. Harriet Holman. 7016-7
"Beauty smiles from the rugged hills". Beauty. L. L. Hershberger. 6818-9
"Beauty stooped and chose us early". Asylum. John Theobald. 6761-1
Beauty the pilgrim. Gerald Gould. 6625-9
Beauty triumphant. John Keats. 6423-X
"Beauty wch all men admire." Unknown. 6563-5
Beauty's a flower. Moira (Nesta Higginson Skrine) O'Neill. 6320-9,6102-8
Beauty's armoury. Al-Hadrami. 6362-4
Beauty's burden. Charles Wharton Stork. 6034-X
Beauty's nomads. Vyacheslav Ivanov. 6103-6
Beauty's pageant, fr. The house of life. Dante Gabriel Rossetti. 6110-9
"Beauty, a silver dew that falls in May". Epigram. Unknown. 6436-1
"Beauty, alas! where wast thou born". Do me right, and do me reason. Thomas Lodge. 6827-8
Beauty, alas, where wast thou born. Robert Greene. 6182-6
Beauty, alas, where wast thou born. Thomas Lodge. 6182-6
Beauty, arise! Thomas Dekker. 6182-6
Beauty, fr. Once again the Eden. Noel Hudson Stearn. 6789-1
"Beauty, since you so much desire" Thomas Campion. 6794-8
"Beauty, sweet love, is like the morning dew" Samuel Daniel. 6182-6,6436-1
"Beauty, thou secret lamp, awake!". An ode to beauty. Herbert Trench. 6877-4
Beauty, time, and love, sels. Samuel Daniel. 6317-9,6102-8
"Beauty, truth and rarity". Mutations of the phoenix (1). Herbert Read. 6985-1
The beauty. Alexander Pushkin. 6103-6
"The beautye of the lande ys slayne". Kynge David, hys lamente over the bodyes of Kynge... Sir Philip Sidney. 6848-0
Beaver brook. James Russell Lowell. 6008-0,6288-1
Beaver Brook, West Windsor, Vermont. Daniel L. Cady. 6989-4
Beaver pond meadow. Henry Augustin Beers. 7041-8
Beaver, Dorothy
Timeless things. 6461-2
The beaver. Mary Howitt. 6510-4
Beazley, Samuel
"When I'm dead, on my tomb-stone I hope they will say" 6874-X
Bebb, F.G. Montfort
On one George Bennett, a butler. 6072-2
Becalmed. Samuel K. Cowan. 6919-3
Becalmed at sea. Samuel K. Cowan. 6674-7
Because. Helen Eikamp. 6857-X
Because. Edward Fitzgerald. 6652-6
Because. Adelaide Anne Procter. 6066-8
Because. Unknown. 6451-5,6576-7
"Because at fifty miles he drives". The railroad engineer. Edgar A. Guest. 6748-4
"Because each act of creation is a miracle". Boschka Layton 1921-1984 Irving Layton. 6767-0
"Because for once the sword broke in her hand". France. Cecil Chesterton. 7026-4
Because he (John Careless) maketh mention... Unknown. 6586-4
"Because he heard a sweet voice call". The seaside grave. Harold Fehrsen Sampson. 6800-6
"Because he is more my own". Gossamer. Virginia Moore. 6761-1
Because he is young. Okura. 7039-6
Because he lived. Edgar A. Guest. 6869-3
"Because he seemed to walk", fr. The city of dreadful-James ("B.V.") Thomson. 6819-7
"Because I could not stop for death." Emily Dickinson. 6348-9,6491-4
"Because I love her." Gerald Bullett. 6317-9
"Because he sulked and held his head". The quitter. Edgar A. Guest. 6748-4
"Because her eyes were far too deep". 'Dream'. James Whitcomb Riley. 6992-4
"Because I am idolatrous and have besought". Epigram. Ernest Dowson. 6022-6
"Because I am/So short and fat". Query. Helen Young. 6750-6
"Because I could not stop for death" Time and eternity:

XXVII. Emily Dickinson. 6879-0
"Because I have made light of death". Death. Alan Mackintosh. 6872-3
"Because I have not done he things I know". One of many (1). Alice Cary. 6865-0;6969-X
"Because I hold it sinful to despond". Courage. Celia Thaxter. 6764-6
"Because I love, I weep". Song ("Because I love"). Mary Carolyn Davies. 6619-4
"Because I oft in dark abstracted guise". Sonnet ("Because I oft"). Sir Philip Sidney. 6219-9
"Because I sat upon a hill". A lonely, swimming bird. Robert P. Tristram Coffin. 7040-X
"Because I think not ever to return". Ballata: In exile at Sarzana. Guido Cavalcanti. 7039-6
"Because I used to shun". The spark. Joseph Mary Plunkett. 7039-6
"Because I was too carefully correct...". Causes. Marion Thomas. 6750-6
"Because in the night Ar of Moab is laid waste". Quia nocte. Bible. 6830-8
"Because man's soul is man's God still", fr. Sunrise. Algernon Charles Swinburne. 6123-0
"Because men saw a vision, dreamed a dream". Stone walls of New England. Catherine Cate Coblentz. 7030-2
"Because mine eyes can never have their fill". Ballata: He will gaze upon Beatrice. Dante Alighieri. 7039-6
"Because my face is black". Blackamoor's lament. Edward Harry William Meyerstein. 6893-6
"Because my faltering feet may fail to dare". Hilaire Belloc. 6931-2
"Because my fathers gave not grace". To Madonna in Quaker. Waldeen H. White. 6761-1
"Because no other dream my childhood knew". Proem: to the artist, fr. The picture of St. John. Bayard Taylor. 6976-2
"Because of death hold not thy life too cheap". Death and life. Herbert Edward Clarke. 6793-X
Because of her who flowered..., fr. Song for a listener. Leonard Feeney. 6282-3
"Because of love, oh friend, he and I are one". Unknown (Newari) 7013-2
Because of some good act. Unknown. 6889-8
"Because of someone's death". The night they kept vigil in the south. Jorge Luis Borges. 6759-X
"Because of the fullness of what I had". Penalty. Ella Wheeler Wilcox. 6956-8
"Because of the memory of one we held dear". In a province. Frank Templeton Prince. 6788-3
Because of you. W. Cestrian. 6589-9
"Because of you we will be glad and gay". Julian Grenfell. Maurice Baring. 7029-9
Because our past lives every day. Ed Lipman. 6870-7
"Because river-fog". Kiyowara Fukuyabu. 7039-6
Because San Quentin killed two more today. Ed Lipman. 6870-7
Because she's a woman, not her learning. Unknown. 6718-2
"Because some men in khaki coats". A lullaby ("Because some men"). G.R. Glasgow. 7031-0
"Because the blood of Christ". Christian's poem. Jorge de Lima. 6759-X
"Because the chalice of your mouth your...". Intercession. Cordelia Cox. 6799-9
"Because the Chiricahuas formed a haven". Warriors. Michael Hogan. 6870-7
"Because the city gave him of her gold". Evarra and his gods. Rudyard Kipling. 6810-3
"Because the thing was finished in a tomb". Juliet protests. Wendy Marsh. 6799-9
"Because the world is falling". War. Jock Curle. 6475-2
"Because they thought his doctrines...not just". Shelley. Paul Hamilton Hayne. 7017-5
"Because they were so brave and young". Fingal's weeping. Neil Munro. 6873-1
"Because thou hast believ'd, the wheels of life". To the Duke of Wellington on hearing him mispraised. Matthew Arnold. 6947-9
"Because thou hast the power and own'st the grace." Elizabeth Barrett Browning. 6560-0
"Because thy prayer hath never fed". They said. Edith M. Thomas. 6996-7
"Because Vermonters like a knife". Whittling in Vermont. Daniel L. Cady. 6989-4
"Because wet knew not a single". Why we didn't rent the cabin. Donald Finkel. 6860-X
"Because we live in the browning season". Kopis'taya (a gahtering of spirits) Paula Gunn Allen. 7005-1
"Because we loved the land we lost". Warsaw - Poland. Martha Keller. 6761-1
"Because you are fair as souls of the lost...". To a gitana dancing. Arthur Symons. 6959-2
"Because you could not choose to cramp". To a revolutionary poet. Sydney Olivier. 6793-X,7009-4
Because you love me. Unknown. 6889-8
"Because you were, Marie, Marie". Austin Dobson: Mary, Mary. Charles Powell. 6982-7
"Because your voice was at my side",fr. Chamber Music. James Joyce. 6536-8
Bech, Bodil
　In the train. Charles Wharton Stork (tr.), 6555-4
Becher, Johannes R.
　The children's crusade. Babette Deutsch (tr.). 6160-5
Becher, Ulrich
　Vow of the European. 6643-7
The Bechuana boy. Thomas Pringle. 6980-0
Beck, Agnes Stewart
　Who knows where beauty lies? 6799-9
Beck, Doris R.
　Seeking waters. 6799-9
Beck, Elizabeth
　To our unknown dead. 6691-7
Beck, Fernand
　To a weary Ford. 6850-2
Beck, Gary
　Grandmother. 6900-2
Beck, John Oscar
　And the dreamers of dreams. 6039-0
　Roland Holst. 6068-4
Beck, L. Adams
　A Chinese scroll picture, sels. 6649-6
Beck, Laura S.
　Winter wizardry. 6799-9
Beck, Richard
　The pioneer's field. 6799-9
Beck, Thomas
　Bless, dear saviour, this child. 6065-X
Becker, Bessie
　"I would make a fiddle cry". 6847-2
Becker, Charlotte
　The feast of the dead. 6274-1
　Life. 6109-5
　Pierrot goes. 6846-4
　Progress. 6338-1
　Thackeray's creed. 6109-5
Becker, Edna
　Reconnaissance. 6750-6
　Reflections. 6337-3
Becker, Edna M.
　A moth found at the door. 6750-6
Becker, N. R. A.
　Conviction. 6818-9
Becker, R.N.A.
　Soliloquy. 6542-2
Becket. Alfred Lord Tennyson. 6188-5
Becket saves Rosamund, fr. Becket. Alfred Lord Tennyson. 6382-9
Becket's diadem. Unknown. 6022-6
Becket, sels. Alfred Lord Tennyson. 6382-9,6541-4
Beckett, Samuel (tr.)
　Universe-solitude. Paul Eluard, 6343-8
Beckwith tragedy. Unknown. 6651-8
Becky Miller. Unknown. 6175-3,6277-6
Becoming a man. Strickland Gillilan. 6211-3
Becquer, Gustavo Adolfo
　They closed her eyes. John Masefield (tr.). 7039-6
Bed. Charles Simic. 6803-0
The bed by the window. Robinson Jeffers. 6628-3
Bed in summer. Robert Louis Stevenson. 6122-2,6623-2,6456-6,6723-9,6132-X,6242-3,6401-9,6466-3,6529-5,6533
The bed of fleur-de-lys. Charlotte Perkins Steson Gilman.

BED

    6241-5
Bed time. Grace May North. 6130-3
Bed-charm. Unknown. 6466-3,6018-8
The bed-post doll. Kate Lawrence. 6965-7
Bed-rock. John Oxenham. 6461-2
Bed-time. Katharine Newbold Birdsall. 6130-3
Bed-time. Hilda Conkling. 6421-3
Bed-time. Francis R.S. Erskine; Earl of Rosslyn. 6519-8, 6656-9,6092-7,6627-5,6078-1
Bed-time. Ralph Mortimer Jones. 6250-4
Bed-time philosopher. Unknown. 6715-8
The bed-time story. Clara Doty Bates. 6131-1

Beda
    A hymn of glory let us sing. 6065-X

Beddoes, Thomas Lovell
    Amala's bridal song, fr. Death's jest book. 6832-4
    Athulf's death song, fr. Death's jest-book. 6656-9
    Ballad of human life. 6656-9
    A beautiful night. 6315-2
    Bridal song and dirge. 6271-7
    Bridal song to Amala. 6437-X
    The brides tragedy, sels. 6378-0,6656-9
    Broadside and street ditties, sels. 6334-9
    A crocodile. 6378-0
    "A cypress-bough, and a rose-wreath sweet". 6980-0
    The daisy and the flood. 6545-7
    "Dear, I could weep, but that my brain is dry." 6317-9
    Death's jest book. 6545-7
    Death's jest book, sel. 6958-4
    Death's jest book, sel. 6958-4
    Death's jest book, sels. 6472-8,6198-2,6317-9,6378-0, 6482-5,6199-0,6656
    Dirge. 6217-7,6302-0,6656-9
    Dirge. 6908-8
    Dirge. 6317-7,6328-4
    Dirge. 6641-0
    Dirge. 6315-2,6437-X,6383-7
    Dirge for Wolfram, fr. Death's jest book. 6832-4
    A dirge. 6879-0
    A dirge. 6908-8
    Dream of dying. 6958-4
    Dream of dying, sels. 6545-7
    Dream-pedlary. 6186-9,6198-2,6315-2,6427-2,6437-X,6482-, 6199-0,6301-2,6102-8,6512-0,6533-3,6732 ,6656-9,6658-5,6668-2,6737-9
    Dreams to sell. 6114-1
    "Durst thou again say life and soul has lifted." 6317-9
    Epitaph. 6908-8
    Fragment ("Or I will burst"). 6545-7
    The ghosts' moonshine. 6317-9,6378-0
    "Has no one seen my heart of you?" 6187-7
    Hesperus sings, fr. The bride's tragedy. 6656-9
    "Hist, oh hist". 6187-7
    How many times do I love thee. 6240-7,6328-4,6429-9, 6620-8,6246-6,6383 ,6226-1,6219-1,6321-7
    If there were dreams to sell. 6187-7,6328-4
    "If thou wilt ease thine heart". 6187-7,6385-3
    L'envoi. 6317-9
    A lament. 6908-8
    The lily of the valley. 6187-7
    Love goes a-hawking, fr. The bride's tragedy. 6656-9
    Love's last messages. 6980-0
    Mandrake's song. 6378-0
    Mariners' song. 6328-4,6437-X,6383-7
    "The mighty thought of an old world". 6150-8,6187-7, 6378-0
    The milking-pail, fr. Broadside and street ditties. 6334-9
    "My will lies there, my hope, and all my life." 6317-9
    Och, Johnny, I hardly knew ye. 6334-9
    The phantom-lover. 6317-9
    The phantom-wooer, sels. 6472-8
    The phantom-wooer. 6378-0
    Sailor's song. 6423-X
    The sea. 6133-8,6253-9
    Sibylla's dirge. 6179-6,6246-6,6378-0,6641-0
    Song. 6737-9
    Song ("Hither haste"). 6187-7
    Song ("How many times"). 6512-0
    Song ("Old Adam"). 6473-6
    Song by two voices. 6658-5,6737-9
    Song from the ship, fr. Death's jest-book. 6246-6,6334-9,6658-5
    Song of the Stygian naiades. 6378-0
    Song on the water. 6187-7
    Songs at Amala's wedding. 6315-2
    A subterranean city. 6980-0
    The swallow leaves her nest, fr. Death's jest-book. 6199-0
    Sweet to die. 6980-0
    "Then all the minutes of my life to come." 6317-9
    Threnody. 6641-0
    To night ("So thou art come again..."). 6315-2
    To sea, to sea! 6385-3,6457-3,6484-3,6478-7,6512-0,6656
    Torrisnind, sels. 6656-9
    "The wanton water leaps in sport". 6997-5
    'We have bathed, where none have seen us'. 6208-3
    Wolfram's dirge. 6543-0
    Wolfram's song. 6102-8,6179-6,6383-7,6437-X,6246-6

Beddoes, Thomas Lovell (tr.)
    Under the lime tree. Sir Walther von der Vogelweide, 6545-7

Beddome, Benjamin
    The glorious gift of God. 6065-X
    Jesus wept. 6219-9

Bede, Cuthbert (Edward Bradley)
    In immemoriam. 6440-X
    In memoriam. 6089-7
    On a toasted muffin. 6802-2

Bede, The Venerable
    Ascension hymn. Elizabeth Charles (tr.). 6337-3
    Hymn ("A hymn of glory"). Elizabeth Charles (tr.). 6730-1
    Sparrows and men. 6943-6

"Bedecked with trinkets and with pretty frock". Dance of a Nautch girl. Unknown. 6959-2

Bedingfield, William
    Contentment. 6874-X
    A lover's choice. 6874-X

Bedlam song. Unknown. 6324-1
Bedlam town. Ella Wheeler Wilcox. 6629-1
The Bedouin child. Theodore Watts-Dunton. 6233-4
Bedouin love song. Bayard Taylor. 6302-0,6385-3,6331-4, 6481-7,6076-5
Bedouin song. Bayard Taylor. 6102-8,6236-9,6243-1,6332-2, 6632-7,6732 ,6008-0,6288-1,6560-0,6467-1,6396-9,6226 ,6094-3,6431-0,6107-9,6560-0,6121-4,6219-9,6300-4, 6309-8

Bedregal de Conitzer, Yolanda
    Facing my portrait. Donald Devenish Walsh (tr.). 6759-X

A bedroom on the East River. Edith Ballinger Price. 6861-8
The bedspread. Katharine Duncan ("Jerry Doane") Morse. 6396-9
Bedtime. Carol Florence Derby. 6249-0
Bedtime. Edgar A. Guest. 7033-7
Bedtime comes too soon. Burges Johnson. 6715-8
Bedtime in Galilee. Berenice Rice. 6750-6
Bedtime tales. Joseph Joel Keith. 6218-0
"Bedtime's come fu' little boys". Lullaby ("Bedtime's come"). Paul Laurence Dunbar. 6891-X
"A bee allur'd by the perfume". The bee and the pine-apple. William Cowper. 6814-6
Bee and the butterfly. Unknown. 6312-8,6629-1
The bee and the flower. Alfred Lord Tennyson. 6496-5
The bee and the lily. Thomas Westwood. 6638-0
The bee and the pine-apple. William Cowper. 6814-6
The bee and the rose. Unknown. 6629-1
Bee balm. Frederick Lewis Pattee. 6764-6
The bee in church. Alfred Noyes. 6151-6,6510-4
A bee in late autumn. William Force Stead. 6779-4
"The bee is not afraid of me". Emily Dickinson. 6299-7, 6239-3
"The bee of night hums/among abundant leaves". Awake. Cecilia Bustamante. 7036-1
"Bee quick my boyes drinke off yr wine." Unknown. 6563-5
A bee sets sail. Katharine Duncan ("Jerry Doane") Morse. 6510-4,6368-3
Bee song. Unknown. 6952-5
"Bee to the blossom, moth to the flame". Vanity f vanities. Helen Hunt Jackson. 7041-8

The bee to the blossom. James Abraham Martling. 6952-5
"The bee to the heather". Song ("The bee to the heather").
    Sir Henry Taylor. 6437-X,6732-8
The bee's mission. Marion Short. 6700-X
The bee's sermon. Unknown. 6674-7
The bee-boy's song. Rudyard Kipling. 6655-0
The bee-hive. Unknown. 6859-6
A bee-keeper. Unknown (Greek) 6435-3
Bee-master. Victoria Mary Sackville-West. 6257-1
The bee-orchis. Andrew Young. 6125-7
Bee-song. Unknown. 6334-9
"Bee-ull! Bee-ull! O Bee-ull! my gracious". Wakin' the
    young uns. John Boss. 6924-X
The bee. Charles Fitz-Geffrey. 6182-6
The bee. Henry Hawkins. 6022-6
The bee. Felicia Dorothea Hemans. 6973-8
The bee. Sidney Lanier. 6753-0
The bee. Ruth Manning-Sanders. 6071-4
The bee. Unknown. 6466-3,6563-5
Beebe, Lucius
    Pietro Aretino. 6038-2
Beebe, Lucius M.
    Volatus triumphans. 6039-0
Beebe, Minnie Mason
    For the master's sake. 6818-9
The beech and the sapling oak, fr. Maid Marian. Thomas
    Love Peacock. 6934-7
"The beech is bare, and bare the ash". December. Bayard
    Taylor. 6976-2
The beech tree's petition. Thomas Campbell. 6597-X,6047-1,
    6049-8,6086-2
Beech trees. Sister Mary Madeleva. 6107-9
The beech-nut gatherer. Pamela Vining Yule. 6591-0,6592-9
The beech-tree. Rose Fyleman. 6262-8
Beecham, Audrey
    Ditty ("If this town should tumble down.") 6472-8
    Exile. 6379-9
    Sonnet. 6958-4
Beecher, Henry Ward
    In change unchanging. 6177-X
    Our flag. 6684-4
Beeches. Helen Gross Hume. 6847-2
Beeching, Henry Charles
    Accidia. 6437-X
    Beauty. 6785-9
    Bicycling song. 6239-3
    The blackbird. 6437-X
    A boy's prayer. 6239-3,6243-3,6465-5
    Fatherhood. 6477-9
    Going down hill on a bicycle. 6423-X,6437-X,6107-9,6161-3
    Knowledge after death. 6447-X,6656-9
    Loca senta situ. 6785-9
    Prayers ("God who created me"). 6303-9,6337-3,6161-3,
        6322-5,6639-9,6656-9,6477-9,6437 ,6322-5
    A summer day. 6656-9
    To my totem. 6656-9
Beeching, Henry Charles (tr.)
    A bride. Meleager, 6435-3
Beeching, Jack
    1944 - the invasion coast. 6666-6
Beede, A.M. (tr.)
    The land of the evening mirage. Unknown (Sioux Indians),
        6730-1
Beede, Charles Gould
    The maniac. 6686-0
Beede, Clara M.
    Evening. 6799-9
    My garden. 6799-9
    A tribute to dad. 6799-9
Beede, Eva J.
    The golden rod. 6049-8
    Why cats wash after eating. 6699-2
Beedome, Thomas
    The broken heart. 6933-9
    The choice. 6563-5
    Epitaph on Drake. 6339-X
    To the noble Sir Francis Drake. 6562-7
Beedy, Dorothy
    Radio. 6750-6

Beefsteak when I'm hungry. Unknown. 6609-7
Beelzebub and Job. Samuel Taylor Coleridge. 6278-4
Been all aroun' the whole roun' worl' Unknown. 6609-7
"Been out in the lifeboat often?". The liefboat. George
    Robert Sims. 6918-5
"Been workin' on de levess". Mississippi levee. Langston
    Hughes. 6751-4
Beeny cliff. Thomas Hardy. 6645-3
Beer. George Arnold. 6004-8,6300-4
Beer. Charles Stuart Calverley. 6092-7
Beer. Flavius Claudius Julianus Imperator. 6435-3
Beer, Arthur William
    Battleships. 6789-1
    Heart's-ease. 6789-1
Beer, Henry
    The babe of Bethlehem. 6065-X
Beer, Morris Abel
    A boy of old Manhattan - Theodore Roosevelt. 6503-1
    "A boy of old Manhattan" 6995-9
    Broken dreams. 6347-0
    The church in the heart. 6337-3
    The conqueror. 6607-0
    The conqueror. 6861-8
    I found a beggar starving. 6347-0
    Manhattan. 6102-8,6076-5,6088-9
    Old garrets. 6300-4
    Piety. 6040-4
    Poets ("If a poet sings because he must"). 6040-4
    The puddle. 6300-4
Beers, Ethel Lynn
    All quiet along the Potomac. 6113-3,6340-3,6732-8,6219-9,6300-4,6484-1
    The boys. 6408-6
    Disproving a legend. 6155-9
    Kept in. 6424-8
    Not one to spare. 6240-7
    Old-fashioned flowers. 6049-8
    On the shores of Tennessee. 6392-6,6402-7
    Our folks. 6045-1,6142-7,6344-6,6392-6,6554-6,6565
    The picket guard. 6016-2,6288-1,6309-8,6370-5,6470-1,
        6589
    The picket-guard. 6753-0
    The picket-guard. 6121-4,6288-1,6309-8,6422-1,6471-X,
        6502
    The picket-guard. 6946-0
    Weighing the baby. 6078-1,6131-1
    Which shall it be. 6260-1,6219-9,6304-7,6424-8,6497-3
    Which? 6097-8
Beers, Henry Augustin
    Beaver pond meadow. 7041-8
    Biftek aux champignons. 6652-6
    Carcamon. 6219-9
    Ecce in deserto. 6431-0
    A fish story. 6089-7,6723-9
    Hugh Latimer. 7041-8
    Nunc dimittis. 6723-9
    The rising of the curtain. 7041-8
    A shades. 6004-8
    The singer of one song. 6347-0,6723-9
    The upland. 7007-8
    Ye laye of ye woodpeckore. 6902-9
Beers, Lorna
    Soft sell. 6218-0
    Top hat and tales. 6218-0
Bees. Frank Dempster Sherman. 6311-X,6452-3
Bees. Unknown. 6018-8
Bees a-zwarmen. William Barnes. 6018-8
"The bees about the linden-tree". November's cadence, fr.
    Jonas Fisher. James Carnegie; Earl of Southesk. 6180-X,6656-9,6819-7,6819-7
"Bees are resting sugary thighs". Cradle song. Norman
    Gale. 6772-7
"Bees are robbers, fleet and daring". Avarice. Howard
    Kohner. 6850-2
"Bees build around red liver". A poor Christian looks at
    the ghetto. Czeslaw Milosz. 6758-1
"Bees hummed and rooks called hoarsely outside". Gervais.
    Margaret Adelaide Wilson. 7027-2
Bees in peach blossom. Louis Golding. 6069-2
"The bees in the clover are making honey...". The mower in

Ohio. John James Piatt. 7041-8
The bees of Myddleton Manor. May Probyn. 6172-9,6656-9
"Bees over the gooseberry bushes". The bees. Lola Ridge. 6891-X
"The bees were holding levees in the flowers". Inamorata. Francis Ledwidge. 6812-X
The bees' song. Walter De La Mare. 6722-0
The bees. Monk Gibbon. 6930-4
The bees. Lola Ridge. 6891-X
Beet farmer. Mark Mirich. 6750-6
Beethoven. Edward Carpenter. 7014-0
Beethoven. Roden Noel. 6102-8
Beethoven. Lucy H. King Smith. 6799-9
Beethoven and Angelo. John Banister Tabb. 6250-4
A Beethoven andante. Grace Hazard Conkling. 6467-1
Beethoven in Central Park. Alfred Noyes. 6151-6
Beethoven's third symphony. Richard Hovey. 7041-8
The beetle. Edith King. 6262-8
The beetle. James Whitcomb Riley. 6512-0
"BeeyBessy Mell and Mary Gray." Unknown. 6452-3
Befooled. Mary Elizabeth Mahnkey. 6324-1
Before. Mary Sinton Leitch. 6954-1
"Before Granada's fated walls, encamped...". The Moor's revenge. Adam Mickiewicz. 6928-2
Before a midnight breaks in storm. Rudyard Kipling. 6810-3
Before a monument. Alexander Young. 6178-8
Before a saint's picture. Walter Savage Landor. 6233-4
Before a trophy case. Elinor Lennen. 6316-0
Before action. Wilfred Wilson Gibson. 6653-4
Before action. William Noel Hodgson. 7026-4
Before action. William Noel Hodgson. 6337-3,6477-9,6501-5, 6730-1,6650-X,6542
Before Agincourt, fr. Henry V. William Shakespeare. 6125-7
Before and after. Oliver Madox Brown. 6656-9
Before and after. Charles T. Grilley. 6277-6
Before and behind. Abbott Lawrence. 6685-2
Before battle. Habberton Lulham. 7031-0
Before dawn. Walter De La Mare. 6216-4
Before dawn. Algernon Charles Swinburne. 6655-0
Before dawn in the wood. Marguerite Wilkinson. 6501-5,6300-4
Before dawn, sels. Harold Monro. 6234-2
Before day. Siegfried Sassoon. 6730-1
Before death, fr. Ajax. Sophocles. 6435-3
Before disaster. Yvor Winters. 6751-4
Before exile. Louise Mack. 6784-0
Before Ginchy. E. Armine Wodehouse. 7027-2
"Before Grenada's fated walls..." Mickiewicz. 6606-2
"Before her flew affliction girt in storms". A procession of peace. George Chapman. 6935-5
"Before her knee the boy did stand...". The escape of Gayferos. Unknown (Spanish). 6757-3
Before her portrait in youth. Francis Thompson. 6942-8
Before her portrait in youth. Francis Thompson. 6507-4, 6199-0
Before I knocked and flesh let me enter. Dylan Thomas. 6210-5
"Before him rolls the dark, relentless ocean". 1620-1920. Le Baron Russell Briggs. 6762-X
"Before I brand a brother". Before. Mary Sinton Leitch. 6954-1
"Before I came across the sea". The native Irishman. Unknown. 6930-4
"Before I eat my pudding". The spoon. Elizabeth Fleming. 6937-1
"Before I go/I'm supposed to get a last wish". I take back everything I've said. Nicanor Parra. 6758-1
"Before I joined the army". Death and the fairies. Patrick MacGill. 6872-3
"Before I leave you, child, I must insist...". Achilles: an opera. John Gay. 6972-X
"Before I pass from youth". Transition. Jesse Lynch Williams. 6983-5
"Before I saw the fall". The secret sun. Virginia Moore. 6761-1
"Before I trust my fate to thee". A woman's question. Adelaide Anne Procter. 6910-X
"Before I was born my mother drowned". Arm of the lake. Robert Wallace. 6860-X
Before it is too late. George Bancroft Griffith. 6097-8, 6274-1
"Before Jehovah's awful throne." Isaac Watts. 6302-0
"Before man parted for this earthly strand". Revolutions. Matthew Arnold. 6199-0,6828-6
Before marching, and after. Thomas Hardy. 6051-X
Before Mary of Magdala came. Edwin Markham. 6338-1
Before my face the picture hangs. Robert Southwell. 6489-2
Before night. Hedwig Katscher. 6769-7
Before Orleans. Katherine Kelley Taylor. 6906-1
"Before our eyes a pageant rolled". After the centennial. Christopher Pearse Cranch. 6946-0
"Before Saint Stephen of Gormaz". The knight of Saint George. Johann Ludwig Uhland. 6903-7
Before parting. Robert Burns. 6322-5
Before pilate. Leslie Savage Clark. 6144-3
Before playing Tinkertown. Edmund Vance Cooke. 6280-6
Before quiet, fr. Songs of farewell. Hazel Hall. 6778-6
Before sailing. Unknown. 6273-3
Before Sedan. Austin Dobson. 6915-0
Before Sedan. Austin Dobson. 6240-7,6046-3,6424-8,6660-7
Before Sedan. Unknown. 6385-3
Before sentence is passed. Richard P. Blackmur. 6389-6
"Before she has her floor swept". Portrait by a neighbor. Edna St. Vincent Millay. 6891-X
Before sleep. Sir Thomas Browne. 6438-8
Before sleep. Anne Ridler. 6379-9
Before sleeping. Unknown. 6732-8
Before sunrise, in the vale of Chamouni. Samuel Taylor Coleridge. 6749-2
"Before sunrise/think of brushing out an...". Song for my name. Linda Hogan. 7005-1
"Before that ship, there was no motion". At the shore. Edwin Morgan. 6979-7
Before the Apollo of the Belvedere. Rene Francois Armand Sully-Prudhomme. 6351-9
Before the Aragava at night. Nikolai Tikhonov. 6546-5
"Before the altar the candles are laid". Candlemas. Mary Saint-Amand. 7016-7
Before the assault. Robert Ernest Vernede. 7029-9
"Before the barn-door crowing", fr. The beggar's opera. John Gay. 6733-6
"Before the beginning of years". The life of man. Algernon Charles Swinburne. 6828-6
Before the beginning of years. Algernon Charles Swinburne. 6199-0,6508-2,6655-0,6122-2,6123-0,6486-8,6726-3, 6430-2
"Before the big shop window stood". Peggy's doubt. Rosa Graham. 6965-7
Before the birth of one of her children. Anne Bradstreet. 6333-0
"Before the bleak era by providence set". Years of discretion. Frederic F. Vandewater. 7007-8
Before the blossom. Robert Underwood Johnson. 6652-6
Before the burial. Bayard Taylor. 6976-2
Before the Cenotaph. Dorothy Margaret Stuart. 6044-7
Before the charge. Patrick MacGill. 7027-2
Before the coming of the planes that burn the cities. Otto D'Sola. 6759-X
Before the crib. Kevin Jarlath Sullivan. 6761-1
Before the crucifix. Amelia Josephine Burr. 6184-2
Before the curfew. Oliver Wendell Holmes. 6632-1
"Before the dawn begins to glow". 'Before the dawn' Samuel Minturn Peck. 6875-8,6770-0
"Before the dawn begins to glow". Samuel Minturn Peck. 6646-1
'Beforr the dawn' Samuel Minturn Peck. 6875-8,6770-0
"Before the day the gleaming dawn doth flee". Academe. Henry Alford. 6980-0
Before the fair. Anna Hempstead Branch. 6441-8
"Before the fiery sun". The bowl of liberty. Felicia Dorothea Hemans. 6973-8
Before the gate. William Dean Howells. 6429-9,6600-3,6670-4,6321-7
"Before the glare o' dawn I rise". The shearer's wife. Louis Esson. 6784-0
Before the glass. Gail French. 6659-3
"Before the great round sun came up". Buttercups. Alice Barkley. 6789-1
"Before the hot dog had grown stylish...". The old hot-dog wagon. Edgar A. Guest. 6748-4

Before the ikon of the mother of God. Constantine of Rhodes. 6282-2
Before the iron gate. E.L. Mayo. 6751-4
Before the life-mask of Keats. Alfred Noyes. 6169-9
Before the mirror. Algernon Charles Swinburne. 6437-X
"Before the night/Before its confusion". Half and half again. Beau Beausoleil. 6901-0
Before the old castle of Verona. Giosue Carducci. 6624-0
Before the paling of the stars. Christina Georgina Rossetti. 6144-3,6337-3,6746-8,6639-9,6608-9
Before the party. A.C. Gordon. 6686-0
Before the phantom of false morning died, fr. Rubaiyat. Omar Khayyam. 7039-6
"Before the pharaohs in their crimson halls". To an orchard. Victor Sampson. 6800-6
Before the rain. Thomas Bailey Aldrich. 6008-0, 6121-4
Before the robin dates. Rose Morgan. 6615-1
Before the sacrament. Reginald Heber. 6086-2
"Before the scarlet of this autumn dies". Sonnet 006, fr. Sonnet sequence. Isabel Alden Kidder. 6764-6
Before the shower. Margaret Johnson. 6965-7
"Before the shrine they lit the flame". Forever? Sylvester Baxter. 6798-0
"Before the silos come to stay". 'Haying the oats' in Vermont. Daniel L. Cady. 6988-6
Before the squall. Arthur Symons. 6507-4,6655-0
Before the starry threshold of Jove's court. John Milton. 6543-0
Before the storm. Richard Dehmel. 7039-6
Before the storm. Robert Loveman. 6941-X
Before the storm. William Plomer. 6985-1
Before the tears. Francis Ledwidge. 6812-X
"Before the tears of autumn shed". An autumn serenade. John B.L. Warren, 3d Baron De Tabley. 7020-5
"Before the temple walls the shadows meet". Surya, the sun god. John Proctor Mills. 6799-9
"Before the town had lost its wits". Ballade of antique dances. William Ernest Henley. 6770-0,6875-8
Before the toy shop window. John Kendrick Bangs. 6691-7
Before the war of Cooley. Francis Ledwidge. 6812-X
Before Vicksburg. George Henry Boker. 6946-0
"Before the wind that greets the sun". The old 'constitution' Arthur Guiterman. 6773-5
"Before thy door too long of late". Extremum tanain. Horace. 7039-6
"Before thy leaves thou comest once more". The dying boy to the sloe blossom. Ebenezer Elliott. 6980-0
"Before time they were sound". Grandfathers. Dennis Shady. 6870-7
"Before VEspasian's regal throne". Death of Gaudentis. Harriet Annie. 6910-X
"Before we shall again behold". Song ("Before"). Sir William Davenant. 6562-7,6341-1
Before winter. Frederick R. McCreary. 6038-2
Before you came. Marjorie Meeker. 6019-6
Before you came. Mary Siegrist. 7001-9
"Before yu leave my hands' abuses". To an old quill of Lord Dunsany's. Francis Ledwidge. 6812-X
"Before, before he was aware". Comrades: an episode. Robert Nichols. 7027-2
Before, fr. In hospital. William Ernest Henley. 6102-8, 6250-4,6659-3
Before, sels. Robert Browning. 6144-3
Beg parding. Unknown. 6125-7
Beg-innish. John Millington Synge. 6174-5,6244-X
Begbie, Agnes H.
  Unto us a child is born. 6095-1
Begbie, Harold
  Britons beyond the seas. 6793-X
  England ("Who would not live for her"). 6224-5
  Grounds of the terrible. 6481-7
  The living line. 7031-0
  The swords of India. 6224-5
Begbie, Joan
  The sailing ship. 7020-5
Beggar. Dorothy Grey Smith. 6799-9
Beggar. A.R. Ubsdell. 6782-4
The beggar and burglar..., fr. Old and new New York. Alfred Kreymborg. 6012-9
The beggar at the door. Henry Constable. 6383-7

Beggar Bill. Walter Hendricks. 6542-2
The beggar family. Morris Rosenfeld. 7011-6
A beggar for God. John Stigall. 6285-7
A beggar in paradise. Verne Bright. 6954-1
The beggar laddie. Unknown. 6185-0
Beggar maid. Lillie Hall. 7016-7
The beggar maid. Alfred Lord Tennyson. 6133-8,6136-2,6613-5,6668-2,6737-9
"The beggar through the world so wide". The beggar. Johann Ludwig Uhland. 6903-7
"A beggar to the graveyard hied". Poverty, fr. The Panchatantra. Unknown (Indian). 6879-0
The beggar woman. Gestur Palsson. 6854-5
The beggar's child. Padraic Colum. 6244-X
The beggar's daughter of Bednall-Greene. Unknown. 6669-0
The beggar's gift. S. Decatur Smith Jr. 6580-5
The beggar's holiday. John Gould Fletcher. 6194-X
The beggar's opera, sels. John Gay. 6733-6,6637-2,6152-4, 6491-4
The beggar's opera. John Gay. 6972-X
The beggar's petition. Thomas Moss. 6219-9,6912-6
Beggar's rhyme. Unknown. 6466-3,6608-9
Beggar's serenade. John Heath-Stubbs. 6379-9
The beggar's soliloquy. George Meredith. 6828-6
"Beggar, you say- in the entrt? A tramp?". The tramp. James Abraham Martling. 6952-5
The beggar-girl. Unknown. 6131-1
The beggar-maid and King Cophetua. Alfred Lord Tennyson. 6616-X
"beggar-man crept to my side". Human nature. Eugene Field. 6949-5
The beggar-man. Lucy Aiken. 6131-1
A beggar. Adelaide Anne Procter. 6957-6
The beggar. Michael Drayton. 6383-7
The beggar. Edgar A. Guest. 6748-4
The beggar. James Russell Lowell. 6502-3
The beggar. Johann Ludwig Uhland. 6903-7
Beggarly. Josephine A. Meyer. 6847-2
Beggars. Ella Higginson. 6309-8
Beggars' song. Richard Brome. 6334-9
The beggars. Sylvia Plath. 6803-0
The beggars. Arthur Symons. 6507-4
The beggars. Margaret Widdemer. 6897-9
Begging another, on colour of mending the former. Ben Jonson. 6317-9
Begging epistle to the chancellor of the exchequer. Ben Jonson. 6867-7
Begin again. Sarah ("Susan Coolidge") Woolsey. 6583-X,6260-1
"Begin by parting your hair". Parting: a game. Lynne Sukenick. 6792-1
Begin the beguine. Cole Porter. 6527-9
Begin the day with God. Unknown. 6337-3
"Begin the song! to God the timbrels strike". The song of Judith, paraphas'd from the Apocrypha. Thomas Warton (the Elder). 6962-2
"Begin we from the muses, o my song!". The dance of the muses. Hesiod. 6959-2
Begin your reform today. Unknown. 6715-8
"Begin, my lord, in early youth". The pack-horse and the carrier. John Gay. 6972-X
"Begin, my soul, the exalted lay". Psalm 148 (hymn). Bible. 6848-0
Beginners. Walt Whitman. 6288-1
Beginning again. Unknown. 6409-4
Beginning haying in Vermont. Daniel L. Cady. 6989-4
The beginning of creation, fr. The paraphrase. Caedmon. 6102-8
The beginning of day, fr. Phaethon. Euripides. 6435-3
The beginning of the wrath, fr. The Iliad. Homer. 6435-3
"A beginning storm sets my blood racing". Lives. Cyril Dabydeen. 6790-5
Beginnings. Mary Allen Edge. 6037-4
The beginnings of faith. Sir Lewis Morris. 6730-1
Begone dull care! Unknown. 6600-3
"Begone, pernicious baneful tea". Virginia banishing tea. Unknown. 6753-0
"Begone, you, sir! Here, shepherd, call..dog". The shepherd dog of the Pyrenees. Ellen Murray. 6919-3
Behave yoursel' before folk. Alexander Rodger. 6180-X

BEHAVE
126

Behave yoursel' before folk. Unknown. 6721-2
The **behavior** of mirrors on Easter island. Julio Cortazar. 6758-1
Behemb, Martin
   I shall be satisfied. 6065-X
"**Behind** a flake of cloudy fire". To whom they sing. Eden Phillpotts. 6780-8
"**Behind** a thick and cloudy door". The same story. Fannie Williams. 6850-2
"**Behind** are the guns drilled by their daughter". Embarkation song. Geoffrey Matthews. 6895-2
Behind dark places. Melville Cane. 6979-7
"**Behind** dept. stores, in/3rd st. bars". You see them in the alleys. Al Masarik. 6792-1, 6998-3
Behind her fan. Frank Dempster Sherman. 6770-0
Behind Mount Spokane, the beehive mountain. Vachel Lindsay. 6206-7
"**Behind** her fan of downy fluff". Behind her fan. Frank Dempster Sherman. 6770-0
"**Behind** me lie the clumping streets". Battery Park. L.. 6817-0
"**Behind** me lies the mistress of the east". The pilgrim. Eleanor Downing. 6172-9
"**Behind** some palms I saw her stand". Au bal mnasque. Unknown. 6983-5
"**Behind** steel bars a drift of snow". Snow-leopard. Berenice Van Slyke. 6808-1
"**Behind** that dark mysterious curtain drear". Silent guests. Edla Park Peck. 6836-7
Behind the Arras - A.D. 1486. Margaret Junkin Preston. 6965-7
Behind the arras, sels. Bliss Carman. 6102-8,6076-5
"**Behind** the back of our time" Christine Lavant. 6769-7
"**Behind** the barn was mystery". The pines. Robert P. Tristram Coffin. 6984-3
"**Behind** the board fence at the banker's house". The last antelope. Edwin Ford Piper. 6861-8
Behind the closed eye. Francis Ledwidge. 6266-0,6332-2, 6653-4
"**Behind** the cottage the mill-creek flowed". The playmates, fr. Dovecote mill. Phoebe Cary. 6865-0;6969-X
Behind the door. Bert Leston Taylor. 6307-1
"**Behind** the higher hill". Slate. David Gascoyne. 6985-1
Behind the house is the millet plot. Muna Lee. 6556-2
"**Behind** the house of a friend". Smoke. John Morgan. 6855-3
Behind the lines. Sir John Collings ("Solomon Eagle") Squire. 6659-3
"**Behind** the manor lies the mere". En roulant ma boule. Unknown (French Canadian). 6795-6
"**Behind** the New Jersey shore". Obon by the Hudson. Richard Oyama. 6790-5
"**Behind** the moving train" Keiho Soga. 6981-9
Behind the muzzle. W. Livingston Larned. 7008-6
"**Behind** the prison bars of mind". Hunger. Lyle Bartscher. 6799-2
Behind the waterfall. William Schroll. 6857-X
"**Behind** the wolden,/And sky all golden". The cow-boy's vision. James Abraham Martling. 6952-5
"**Behind** this latticed door of ivied green". Inscription for a garage door. Doris V. Lecky. 6850-2
Behn (atr), Aphra
   Of love. 6563-5
Behn, Aphra
   The alternative. 6874-X
   Love armed. 6563-5
   Love enthroned. 6830-8
   Love in fantastic triumph (sat) 6092-7,6430-2
   "O love, that stronger art than wine." 6317-9
   Serenade. 6563-5
   Song ("Love in fantastic"). 6191-5
   Song. Love arm'd. 6933-9
   Song: Love arm'd. 6150-8
Behn, Harry
   Hallowe'en. 6236-9
"a**ehold** a star appearing in the south". The lone star, fr. Texas. Henry Van Dyke. 6961-4
"**Behold** a type: lo how, in her own land". In memoriam: Lydia F. Wadleigh. Helen Gray Cone. 6847-2
"**Behold** a wonder here". Song ("Behold a wonder"). Unknown. 6436-1

"**Behold** Champlain sail to and fro". Champlain and Lake Champlain. Daniel L. Cady. 7030-2
Behold a wonder here. John Dowland. 6026-9
"**Behold** from sluggish winter's arm". Primo vere. Giosue Carducci. 7039-6
"**Behold** great Neptunes risen from ye deep." Henry Hughes (atr) 6563-5
"**Behold** her seven hills loom white". Resurge San Francisco. Joaquin Miller. 6946-0
"**Behold** her talons drag to view". Scandal, fr. Thumb nail sketches. Mary H. Cabaniss. 6841-3
"**Behold** her, single in the field". The solitary reaper. William Wordsworth. 6396-9,6464-7,6301-2,6371-3,6197- 4,6153 ,6150-8,6199-0,6250-4,6196-6,6430-2,6560 , 6086-2,6023-4,6110-9,6828-6,6075-7,6102-8,6122-2, 6138-9,6154-0,6271 ,6186-9,6198-2,6208-3,6236-9,6332- 2,6423 ,6289-X,6315-2,6395-0,6488-4,6512-0,6604 , 6473-6,6499-X,6536-8,6625-9,6634-8,6052 ,6726-3,6645- 3,6723-9,6646-1,6660-7,6585
"**Behold** I stand in the street without". Hear ye his voice. Robert Kirkland Kerrighan. 6796-4
"**Behold** her, single in the field". William Wordsworth. 6187-7
"**Behold** in us three parties known as 'supers'.". 'Supers'. H. Chance Newton. 6920-7
"**Behold** me! with swift foot across the land". The questioner of the sphinx. Virginia Donaghe McClurg. 6836-7
"**Behold** me, bound between the shafts". 'Number 7' Edith Musgrave. 7010-8
"**Behold** me, in my chiffron, gauze and tinsel". Dancing Adairs. Conrad Aiken. 6897-9
Behold my hands. Lula G. Winston. 6799-9
"**Behold** now, praise the Lord, all ye servants". Psalm 134. Bible. 6848-0
"**Behold** the arena cleared". The glove. Johann C. Friedrich von Schiller. 6842-1
Behold the deeds! Henry Cuyler Bunner. 6770-0
Behold the deeds! Henry Cuyler Bunner. 6089-7,6440-X,6732- 8,6026-9,6300-4
"**Behold** the gentle waters lap against...side". The legend of thunder. H.R.A. Pocock. 6795-6
"**Behold** the glorious morn! and where art thou". To the memory of a brother. Unknown. 6752-2
"**Behold** the mansion reared by daedal Jack". The modern house that Jack built. Sallie Ada Vance. 6909-6
"**Behold** the mystery!/Like to a meteor". Salve. Patience Worth. 7019-1
Behold the sun that seemed but now. George Wither. 6934-7
"**Behold** the tyrants that oppressed your land". Aeschylus. 6435-3
"**Behold** the vast concourse drifting along". The ship of Zion. Edward R. Huxley. 6885-5
"**Behold** the western evening light!". The autumn evening. William Oliver Bourne Peabody. 6752-2
"**Behold** the wonders of the mighty deep". The sea. Unknown. 6902-9
"**Behold** the young, the rosy spring". Spring. Anacreon. 6271-7
"**Behold** these maidens in a row". The dancers. Richard Watson Gilder. 6959-2
"**Behold** this Easter guest who goes". Mouse in a florist's window. Virginia Scott Miner. 6979-7
Behold this dreamer. Elizabeth Bartlett. 6388-8
"**Behold** this needle; when the artick stone". On the needle of a sun-dial. Francis Quarles. 6933-9
"**Behold** this ruin! 'Twas a skull". Lines to a skeleton. Unknown. 6889-8
"**Behold** this sorry garden rake". The heedless rake. Carolyn Wells. 6882-0
'**Behold** thy mother and they brother.' William Heribert. 6636-4
"**Behold** what homage to his idol paid". With Petrarch's sonnets. Walter Savage Landor. 6874-X
"**Behold** what homage to his idol paid". Walter Savage Landor. 6289-X
"**Behold** where night clutches the cup of heaven". Sunset. Percy MacKaye. 6764-6
"**Behold** yon new-born infant, griev'd". The ignorance of man. James Merrick. 6931-2

Behold your king! Frances Ridley Havergal. 6065-X
"Behold your mountain's hoary height". To Thaliarchus. Horace. 7039-6
"Behold! here comes a man of peace". The man of peace. Grace Guille Purse. 7001-9
Behold! the dreamer cometh!. Lady Margaret Sackville. 6269-5
"Behold, a silly tender babe". Robert Southwell. 6187-7, 6216-4
"Behold, above the mountains there is light". The praise of Dionysus (1). Sir Edmund Gosse. 6770-0,6875-8
"Behold, behold! the granite gates unclose". The praise of Dionysus (2). Sir Edmund Gosse. 6959-2
"Behold, dear mistress, how each pleasant green". Thomas Watson. 6181-8
Behold, I stand at the door and knock. William Walsham How. 6219-9
"Behold, how good and now pleasant it is...". Psalm 123, fr. The book of psalms. Bible. 7039-6
"Behold, I teach you beyond-man!". Thus spake Zarathustra, sels. Friedrich Nietzsche. 6879-0
Behold, my cross was gone! Alice Mortenson. 6065-X
Behold, O Aspasia! I send you verses. Walter Savage Landor. 6315-2
Behold, O man. Edmund Spenser. 6182-6
"Behold, our walking in these valleys". Ode ("Behold"). Barnabe Barnes. 6189-3
"Behold, the Lord God will come," fr. Isaiah. Bible. 6136-2
"Behold, this dreamer cometh!" Gustaf Froding. 6045-5
"Behold, thou art all fair, my love". The chief among ten thousand. Horatius Bonar. 6848-0
"Behold, thou art fair, my love". Quam pulchra. Bible. 6830-8
"Behold, thou hast instructed many". Ecce domisti. Bible. 6830-8
"Behold, within the leafy shade". A sister. William Wordsworth. 6668-2,6935-5
"Behold/The time is now!". The fold. Alice Meynell. 6955-X
Beignet de pomme, fr. Poetry cook book. Unknown. 6278-4
"Bein' uncle to the kids". An uncle. Edgar A. Guest. 6862-6
Being a man. Unknown. 6529-5
Being a mother. Elizabeth Barrett Browning. 6097-8
"Being a ship-blessing, together...". Birlinn Chlannraghnaill. Alexander (Alasdair MacMhaighstir A.) Macdonald. 6845-6
Being but men. Monk Gibbon. 6780-8
Being conent. Unknown. 6889-8
Being Danish. Kaj Munk. 6555-4
Being forsaken of his friend he complaineth. E. S. 6182-6
Being her friend. John Masefield. 6102-8
Being his mother. James Whitcomb Riley. 6097-8
"Being in thought of love I came upon". Guido Cavalcanti. 6325-X
"Being my selfe captyved here in care". Sonnet 073 ("Being my selfe"), fr. Amoretti. Edmund Spenser. 6315-2
Being on duty all night in the palace and dreaming... Po Chu-I. 6958-4
"Being one day at my window all alone". Visions. Francesco Petrarch. 7039-6
Being walkers with the dawn. Langston Hughes. 6954-1
Being young. John Holmes. 6265-2
"Being your slave, what should I do but tend". William Shakespeare. 6187-7,6204-0,6246-6
"Being your slave, what should I do but tend". Sonnet 057 ("Being your slave"). William Shakespeare. 6250-4, 6447-7
The beings of the mind. Felicia Dorothea Hemans. 6973-8
Beining, Guy R.
   Ogden as Texas traveller. 6998-3
Bek, Herschell
   To a man sleeping in a subway train. 6072-2
   Tropic dawn. 6070-6
Bel
   The Taj at Agra. 6591-0,6592-9
Bel m'es quan lo vens m'alena. Arnaut Daniel. 7039-6
Belagcholly days. Unknown. 6089-7,6277-6,6724-7
Belated. John Greenleaf Whittier. 6049-8
The belated Christ. Gertrude Huntington McGiffert. 6838-3

Belden, Charlotte
   Wild moccasins for me. 6342-X
The beleaguered city. Henry Wadsworth Longfellow. 6641-0, 6121-4,6648-8,6288-1,6126-5,6133
Beleagured cities. F.L. Lucas. 6257-1
The belfries. Alys Fane Trotter. 7029-9
The belfry of Bruges. Henry Wadsworth Longfellow. 6331-4, 6126-5,6648-8,6288-1,6121-4,6126-5,6439-6,6631-3
The belfry of Ghent. Robert Maguire. 6554-6,6912-6
The belfry of Mons. Wilfrid Thorley. 6542-2
The belfry pigeon. Nathaniel Parker Willis. 6271-7,6302-0, 6385-3,6510-4
The belfy of Bruges, sels. Henry Wadsworth Longfellow. 6288-1
A Belgian Christmas Eve. Alfred Noyes. 6151-6
The Belgian flag. E. Cammaerts. 6443-4
Belgium. Hardwicke Drummond Rawnsley. 7031-0
Belgium. Edith Wharton. 6474-4
Belgium the bar-lass. Agnes Mary F. ("Madame Duclaux") Robinson. 6474-4,6331-4,6474-4
"Belgium, 1944, is another place I've never...". Foot soldier. Rhea Tregebov. 6767-0
Belial's address, opposing war. John Milton. 6606-2
The belief in astrology. Johann C. Friedrich von Schiller. 6606-2
Believe and take heart. John Lancaster Spalding. 6292-X, 6172-9
"Believe it or not, as you choose". Catharina, the second part. William Cowper. 6814-6
"Believe me not, friend, when in grief's unreason" Alexey Tolstoy. 6103-6
Believe me, if all those endearing young charms. Thomas Moore. 6332-2,6481-7,6289-X,6527-9,6302-0,6385 ,6102-8,6732-8,6086-2,6250-4,6226-1,6094-3,6219-9,6543-0
"Believe me/I wouldn't laugh". Space age. Ken Wainio. 6901-0
Believe not him. Unknown. 6563-5
"Believe thou, O my soul", fr. Religious musings. Samuel Taylor Coleridge. 6545-7
Believe, o friend. Edwin Markham. 6303-9
"Believing you were pure and virginal". Immunity of beauty. Clarence L. Haynie. 6481-3
Belinda. Virginia Taylor McCormick. 6039-0
Belinda. Alexander Pope. 6302-0;6365-3
Belinda Bumble. Carolyn Wells. 6882-0
Belinda's fan. Samuel Minturn Peck. 6441-8
Belinda's window. Margaret Widdemer. 6449-3
Belisarius. Henry Wadsworth Longfellow. 6077-3,6631-3
Belitt, Ben
   Brief for a future defense. 6640-2
   Contentious heart. 6640-2
   Field left fallow. 6640-2
   Hermes genetic. 6640-2
   Song of the King's huntsmen. 6640-2
   This our grief. 6640-2
Belivest thou this? William C. Paris. 6764-6
"Beliza shade your shining eyes." Unknown. 6563-5
Belknap, Jessie Downs
   If I am sitting close to you. 6799-9
Bell & Charles Maurron, Julian (tr.)
   The drunken boat. Arthur Rimbaud, 6343-8
The bell at sea. Felicia Dorothea Hemans. 6973-8
Bell birds. Henry Clarence Kendall. 6768-9,6784-0
The bell buoy. Rudyard Kipling. 6508-2
Bell carol. Louise Morey Bowman. 6779-4
A bell in the Orthodox steeple. Thomas Waltner. 6870-7
"The bell in the convent tower swung". The book of hours of Sister Clotilde. Amy Lowell. 6754-9
The bell of Atri. Henry Wadsworth Longfellow. 6478-7,6498-1,6623-2,6419-1,6510-4,6614
The bell of Christmas. Clinton Scollard. 6608-9
Bell of dawn. Paul Fort. 6607-0
The bell of Innisfare. Unknown. 6166-4
The bell of old north. S.X. E. 6983-5
The bell of the angels. Unknown. 6922-3
The bell of the Atlantic. Lydia Huntley Sigourney. 6403-5
"Bell rings, the key clicks, the door swings". Gray's inn. Wilfred Wilson Gibson. 6779-4
"A bell sings, 'Children! Children!'". A bell in the Orthodox steeple. Thomas Waltner. 6870-7

BELL

Bell tower. Leonie Adams. 6012-9
Bell, A. Melville
    Ask mamma. 6411-6
    A helpmate. 6279-2
    A helpmate. 6912-6
    War's end. 6344-6
Bell, Alexander
    An orator's first speech in parliament. 6279-2
Bell, Alfred Henry Haynes
    Love at first sigh. 6800-6
    The thrush. 6800-6
    To a sea conch. 6800-6
    To Viola. 6800-6
Bell, Anne
    Pride. 6249-0
    Pride ("The maple tree one autumn day"). 6249-0
Bell, Arthur W.
    Case history. 6722-0
Bell, Beulah Allyne
    For Noel. 6799-9
    Scherzo. 6906-1
    To a deserted lake. 6906-1
    To a fellow traveler. 6585-6
    To a fellow traveler. 6906-1
Bell, Charles A.
    Tim Twinkleton's twins. 6406-X
Bell, Charles Dent
    The azure grotto. 6624-0
    Solemn rondeau. 6437-X
    The sweet, sad years. 6770-0
    A wish. 6770-0
Bell, Charles G.
    Banana. 6388-8
    Girl walking. 6388-8
    Island dogs. 6388-8
    Love in age. 6388-8
    Termites. 6388-8
    Windowed habitations. 6388-8
Bell, G. L. (tr.)
    The diwan of Hafiz, sels. Hafiz, 6732-8
Bell, G. M.
    Saul. 6848-0
Bell, Gertrude (tr.)
    Comfort. Hafiz, 6448-5
    Desire. Hafiz, 6448-5
    Rose bloom. Hafiz, 6448-5
    Tidings of union. Hafiz, 6448-5
Bell, Gertrude Lowthian
    To Hafiz of Shiraz. 6483-3
Bell, Gertrude Lowthian (tr.)
    Ode 006. Hafiz, 7039-6
Bell, Harriet Dayton
    Spring. 6750-6
Bell, Hattie F.
    'Obbie Dobbie'. 6965-7
    Trundle-bed treasures. 6918-5
Bell, Henry Glassford
    The end. 6960-6
    The fate of Sergeant Thin. 6787-5
    Mary, Queen of Scots. 6451-5,6744-1,6167-2
    Milan cathedral. 6624-0
    My alpenstock. 6749-2
    The road to Appenzell. 6749-2
    To a lady. 6787-5
    The uncle. 6408-6,6451-5
Bell, Jerome B.
    Mystery. 6337-3
Bell, John Joy
    "Blackie". 6639-9
    The choice. 6242-3
    The lights. 6242-3
    On the quay. 6242-3
    The ships. 6242-3,6639-9
Bell, Julian
    Pluviage. 6124-9
    The redshanks. 6317-9
Bell, Lida
    The dark man. 6906-1
    Reunion 6906-1
    Solitudes. 6906-1
    Venice. 6906-1
    Watts' paintings. 6906-1
Bell, Mackenzie
    At Stratford-on-Avon. 6656-9
    At the grave of Dante Gabriel Rossetti. 6656-9
    Spring's immortality. 6656-9
Bell, MacKenzie
    Wild roses and snow. 6274-1
Bell, Maud Anna
    From a trench. 7027-2
Bell, Maurice
    The Alabama. 6113-3
    The men. 6016-2,6074-9
Bell, Neil
    The cry of the children. 6804-9
Bell, Olive
    The outcast's dream. 6273-3
Bell, Robert
    Master and man. 7020-5
Bell, Robert Mowry
    For Cuba. 6471-X
    The second volume. 6431-0
Bell, Sir Idris (tr.)
    Epilogue to Alun Mabon. Ceirog, 6528-7
    Ode to Rhys ap Maredudd of Tywyn. Dafydd Nanmor, 6528-7
Bell, Walker Meriwether
    Jefferson Davis. 6946-0,6088-9
Bell, William
    Elegy 008. 6210-5
    Elegy 012. 6210-5
    Sonnet ("You whispered"). 6210-5
    A young man's song. 6210-5
"Bell, thou soundest gaily". The village church bell. Aloys Wilhelm Schreiber. 6952-5
The bell-bird, fr. Australian transcripts. William ("Fiona Macleod") Sharp. 6768-9
The bell-birds. William ("Fiona Macleod") Sharp. 6768-9
The bell-flower tree. Eugene Field. 6949-5
Bell-horses. Unknown. 6937-1
The bell-man. Robert Herrick. 6228-8,6254-7,6512-0,6194-X
The bell-ringers. James Rorty. 6979-7
A bell. Clinton Scollard. 6266-0,6653-4,6608-9
The bell. William Henry Davies. 6491-4
The bell. Stella Gibbons. 6893-8
The bell. Alfred Noyes. 6151-6
The bell. James Rorty. 6501-5
Bella Gorry. Thomas Edward Brown. 6809-X
Bellaman, Henry
    The gypsy. 6778-6
Bellamann, Henry
    The artist. 6326-8
    A Charleston garden. 6326-8,6649-6
    Cups of illusion. 6037-4
    The deeper seas. 6833-2
    Gardens of the Santee. 6649-6
    God. 6036-6
    The gulf stream. 6833-2
    Home-sickness. 6776-X
    Homesickness. 6037-4
    Magnolia gardens. 6649-6
    Pause. 6326-8
    Pause ("The wind blows tonight"). 6326-8
    Portrait sonnets. 6036-6
    The pursuit ("I know you now"). 6037-4
    The pursuit. 6037-4
    A sound of going in the tops of the mulberry trees... 6619-4
    The upward pass. 6326-8
Bellamy & Maud Wilder Goodwin, Blanche
    The nine muses. 6424-8
    The seven wonders of the world. 6424-8
Bellamy, Elizabeth W.
    Baby logic. 6137-0,6680-1,6585-6
Bellamy, W.H.
    Kirtle red. 6652-6
Bellaw, A.W.
    Christmas-tide. 6148-6
    Conjugal conjugations. 6089-7,6724-7,6505-8
    The fiddler. 6675-5
    Husking song. 6682-8

Jim. 6925-8
Knittin' at the 'stockin'. 6505-8
The mitten. 6682-8
The old line fence. 6089-7,6724-7
The Sunday fisherman. 6724-7
Bellay, Joachim du. See Du Bellay, Joachim
A belle of praeneste. Margaret Junkin Preston. 7041-8
The belle of the Balkans. Newman Levy. 6026-9
The belle of the ball-room. Winthrop Mackworth Praed. 6122-2,6198-2,6600-3,6732-8,6089-7,6302 ,6385-3,6473-6, 6652-6,6026-9,6278-4,6092
Belleau, Remi
Avril. 7020-5
Belleau, Remy
April. Andrew Lang (tr.). 6771-9
The sweet month of April. Henry F. Cary (tr.). 6545-7
Bellenden, John
Address to Bellona and King James V. 6180-X
Anno domini. 6022-6
A starscape. 6022-6
The traduction of Titus Livius, sels. 6180-X
Bellerophon. George Meredith. 6198-2
Bellerophon. Pindar. 6435-3
The belles ryngeth to evensonge. Stephen Hawes. 6733-6
Bellinger, Alfred R.
We launhed and parted, never more to meet. 6347-0
Bellis, Daisy Maud
Think-abouts. 6799-9
The bellman's good-morrow. Unknown. 6489-2
The bellman's song. Unknown. 6182-6,6189-3,6194-X,6383-7
Bellman, Karl Mikael
Concerning Mollberg's parade to Coporal Boman's grave. Charles Wharton Stork (tr.). 6045-5
Fredman's epistles, sels. Charles Wharton Stork (tr.). 6045-5
A nota bene. Charles Wharton Stork (tr.). 6045-5
Of Haga. Charles Wharton Stork (tr.). 6045-5
Of Madame Bergstrom's portrait at the inn of Lilya... Charles Wharton Stork (tr.). 6045-5
On fishing. Charles Wharton Stork (tr.). 6045-5
To old Movitz, with consumption. Charles Wharton Stork (tr.). 6045-5
To Ulla at a window in Fishertown, noon of a summer day. Charles Wharton Stork (tr.). 6045-5
Belloc, Elizabeth
Pelion. 6782-4
Belloc, Hilaire
Auvergnat. 6339-X,6423-X
Ballade to our lady of Czestochowa. 6282-2,6532-5
"Because my faltering feet may fail to dare". 6931-2
The big baboon. 6018-8
The birds. 6172-9,6216-4,6292-X,6421-3
The bison. 6179-6
Charles Augustus Fortescue. 6633-X
Courtesy. 6746-8,6102-8,6172-9,6608-9,6292-X,6427-2, 6477
The death and last confession of Wandering Peter. 6339-X,6427-2
Dedicatory ode, sels. 6477-9
The dodo. 6125-7
The dromedary. 6722-0
Duncton Hill. 6250-4
The early morning. 6044-7,6292-X,6246-6,6423-X,6301-2, 6172 ,6102-8
East and west. 6723-9
The elm. 6844-8
Epigrams ("When I am dead...") 6427-2
Fatigued. 6633-X
The frog. 6089-7,6232-6,6102-8,6664-7,6421-3
G. 6018-8
The gnu. 6102-8
Godolphin Horne. 6228-2
'He does not die' 7012-4
Henry King. 6861-8
The hills of the south country. 6084-6
The hippopotamus. 6179-6,6722-0
How did the party go? 6339-X
In a boat. 6282-2
Jim. 6861-8
Jim. 6096-X,6179-6,6125-7

Lines to a don. 6427-2,6633-X
The llama. 6089-7
Matilda. 6290-3
The microbe. 6089-7
The modern traveller, sels. 6427-2
The night. 6096-X,6437-X,6501-5
Noel. 6172-9,6216-4,6292-X
On a great election. 6722-0,6633-X
On a politician. 6722-0
On his books. 6722-0
On Lady Poltagrue, a public peril. 6722-0
On mundane acquaintances. 6633-X
Our lord and lady. 6292-X,6282-2,6172-9,6727-1
The politician of the Irish earldom. 7014-0
The prophet lost in the hills at evening. 6931-2
The prophet lost in the hills at evening. 6292-X,6172-9
The python. 6861-8
The python. 6018-8
The rebel. 6102-8
The rhinoceros. 6125-7
Sedan. 7031-0,7027-2
Song ("You wear"). 6250-4
Song of the Pelagian heresy. 6096-X
Song: inviting the influence of a young lady... 6437-X
Sonnet 021: Sonnets and verse. 6532-5
The south country. 6172-9,6506-6,6292-X,6250-4,6439-6, 6044-7,6096-X,6331-7,6423-X,6477-9,6437
Tarantella. 6096-X,6228-8,6427-2,6732-8
The telephone. 7014-0
They say, and I am glad they say. 6026-9
To dives. 6096-X
To the Balliol men still in Africa. 6292-X,6172-9,6250-4
The viper. 6089-7
The vulture. 6018-8
W. 6018-8
The yak. 6089-7,6466-3,6026-9,6368-3,6454-X,6808
Belloc, Joseph Hilaire. See Belloc, Hilaire
Bellona. Adam Lindsay Gordon. 6951-7
Bellows, Isabel Frances
Some of the children. 6629-1
Three naughty kittens. 6692-2
Bellows, Silence Buck
Last cargo. 6833-2
The bells ("Hear the sledges with the bells"). Edgar Allan Poe. 6008-0,6250-4,6121-4,6219-9,6396-9,6265 ,6288-1, 6560-0,6107-9,6431-0,6457-7,6504-X,6706-9,6732-8, 6302-0,6365 ,6735-2,6142-7,6344-6,6392-6,6402-7,6451 ,6294-6,6459-0,6486-8,6496-5,6554-6,6600 ,6661-5, 6239-3,6466-3,6724-7,6475-4,6464 ,6466-3,6421-3,6131-1,6639-9,6143-5,6126
Bells across the snows. Frances Ridley Havergal. 6145-1, 6147-8
"The bells are ringing merrily". Independence Day. William Lloyd Garrison. 7009-4
The bells at midnight. Thomas Bailey Aldrich. 6946-0
Bells for John Whitesides' daughter. John Crowe Ransom. 6038-2,6052-8,6246-6,6488-4,6326-8
Bells from out of the past. Joellen Ingram. 6799-9
Bells in the country. Robert Nathan. 6466-3
Bells in the rain. Elinor Wylie. 6501-5
'The bells o' Banff'. Neil Munro. 7031-0
The bells of Aberdovey. Unknown. 6331-4
The bells of Allah. John Runcie. 6800-6
The bells of Califon. Harry Lee. 6083-8
Bells of Flanders. Dominique Bonnaud. 6443-4
The bells of Fossombrone. Clinton Scollard. 6624-0
"The bells of Mount Vernon are ringing to-day". Washington's birthday. Hezekiah Butterworth. 6964-9
"The bells of Sunday rang us down". Song ("The bells of Sunday"). John Ciardi. 6666-6
The bells of heaven. Ralph Hodgson. 6102-8,6044-7,6427-2, 6477-9,6532-5,6634-8,6339 ,6501-5,6510-4,6668-2,6581-3,6723-9,6393
The bells of London. Unknown. 6466-3
The bells of Lynn. Frederic Edward Weatherley. 6165-6
The bells of Lynn. Henry Wadsworth Longfellow. 6006-4,6484-1
The bells of Malines. Henry Van Dyke. 6961-4
The bells of Notre Dame. Eugene Field. 6949-5

BELLS

The bells of Notre Dame. Unknown. 6927-4
The bells of Ostend. William Lisle Bowles. 6964-9
The bells of peace. John Galsworthy. 6509-0
The bells of Roncevaux. Thomas Walsh. 6331-4
The bells of San Blas. Henry Wadsworth Longfellow. 6288-1
The bells of San Gabriel. Charles Warren Stoddard. 6292-X, 6172-9,6241-5
The bells of San Juan Capistrano. Charles Augustus Keeler. 6241-5
The bells of Shandon. Francis Sylvester ("Father Prout") Mahony. 6022-6,6046-3,6102-8,6125-7,6439-6,6658-5, 6219-9,6424-8,6543-0,6174-5,6183-4,6090-0,6096-X, 6240-7,6302 ,6385-3,6331-4,6481-7,6484-1,6344-6,6554 ,6600-3,6706-9,6732-8,6304-7,6566-X
Bells of Varenna. Eden Phillpotts. 6331-4
"The bells of the dawn ring". Senses of life. Kwang-sup Kim. 6775-1
The bells of youth. William ("Fiona Macleod") Sharp. 6541-4
The bells of Yule. Alfred Lord Tennyson. 6747-6
Bells toll. Vojislav Ilic Jr. 6765-4
"Bells upon the city are ringing in the night". The north countrie. Robert Louis Stevenson. 6793-X
The bells, fr. In memoriam. Alfred Lord Tennyson. 6216-4, 6459-0
Bells, fr. The dark cup. Sara Teasdale. 6531-7
The bells, Ostend. William Lisle Bowles. 6196-6
The bells.. Judy [pseud]. 6440-X
The bells. Gertrude Huntington McGiffert. 6838-3
The bells. Unknown. 6089-7,6732-8
Belly and mind. Unknown (Greek) 6435-3
The belly of the land. Luci Tapahonso. 7005-1
Belonging. Ilse Aichinger. 6769-7
Beloved. Elizabeth Barrett Browning. 6337-3,6019-6
"A beloved land is yon land in the east". Deirdre's farewell to Scotland. Unknown. 6930-4
"Beloved one, for thy sweet sake". Unknown. 6050-1
The beloved stranger, sels. Witter Bynner. 6033-1
Beloved Syracuse. Unknown. 6118-4
The beloved to the spouse. William Baldwin. 6436-1
The beloved vagabond. W.G. Tinckom-Fernandez. 6083-8,6374-8
"Beloved vagrant of the ample ear". Burro. O. R.. 7010-8
"Beloved! your hair was golden". Song by Sitara, of Kashmir. Laurence (Adele Florence Nicolson) Hope. 6856-1
"Beloved, can you hear me? Take this lantern". The flight. Richard Church. 6778-6
"Beloved, do you pity not my doleful case". Lament of the mangaire sugach. Andrew Magrath. 6930-4
"Beloved, if you love me, leave me free". Not wholly chained. Florence B. Jacobs. 6750-6
"Beloved, in the noisy city here". James Russell Lowell. 6126-5
Beloved, it is morn. Emily Henrietta Hickey. 6096-X,6292-X, 6172-9,6656-9
"Beloved, it is morn!". Song ("Beloved"). Emily Henrietta Hickey. 6437-X
"Beloved, little beloved, where shall I find..". The voice of Rachel weeping. Beatrice Cregan. 7031-0
"Beloved, may your sleep be sound". Lullaby ("Beloved"). William Butler Yeats. 6210-5
"Beloved, my beloved, when I think." Elizabeth Barrett Browning. 6430-2,6560-0
Beloved, my glory. Michael (Katherine Bradley & Edith Cooper) Field. 6250-4
"Beloved, this, the heart I offer thee". Love's prayer. Lucy Maud Montgomery. 6796-4
Beloved, thou hast brought me many flowers. Elizabeth Barrett Browning. 6430-2
"Beloved, thou hast brought me many flowers". Sonnet ("Beloved"). Elizabeth Barrett Browning. 6232-6
The beloved.. Hafiz. 6448-5
The beloved. Bertha Newberry. 6327-6
The beloved. Sara Teasdale. 6777-8
Below San Gimignano. John V.A. MacMurray. 6624-0
"Below lies one whose name was traced in sand". His epitaph. David Gray. 6960-6
"Below me in the garden there". Two kisses. Richard Stillman Powell. 7021-3

"Below me, always below me is water...". Water. Francis Ponge. 6758-1
"Below the cliff an overhanging rock". Myrtle in the mist. Rosemary Trebon. 6799-9
"Below the flying hosts of routed night". The threshing. Pearl Riggs Crouch. 6836-7
Below the heights. Walter Herries Pollock. 6656-9
Below the old house. William Bell Scott. 6180-X,6046-3
"Below they watch us winging mile on mile". Formation. Frank Ernest Hill. 7014-0
"Below this marble monument is laid". On the monument of Miss Mary Frampton. John Dryden. 6970-3
"Below, the Doctor's garden lay", fr. The drama. Austin Dobson. 6123-0
"Belphage wrote well...". Belphage: a biography. E.L. Mayo. 6751-4
Belshazzar. George Croly. 6404-3,6585-6
Belshazzar. Heinrich Heine. 6732-8
Belshazzar. Edward Maturin. 6848-0
Belshazzar. Henry Hart Milman. 6848-0
Belshazzar. Hannah More. 6848-0
Belshazzar. Bryan Waller ("Barry Cornwall") Procter. 6848-0
Belshazzar and Daniel. W. H. Roberts. 6848-0
"Belshazzar is king! Belshazzar is". Belshazzar. Bryan Waller ("Barry Cornwall") Procter. 6848-0
"Belshazzar! from the banquet turn". To Belshazzar. George Gordon, 6th Baron Byron. 6945-2
Belshazzar's downfall. Heinrich Heine. 6415-9
Belshazzar's feast. Felicia Dorothea Hemans. 6973-8
Belshazzar's feast. T.S. Hughes. 6606-2
Belshazzar's feast. Thomas Smart Hughes. 6848-0
"The belt goes by for days". Barbara's cannery ritual. David McElroy. 6855-3
Belted will. Frederick Sheldon. 6613-5
"Belted with stars and with a crown of stars". Origen's dream. William Elijah Hunter. 6800-6
Belts. Rudyard Kipling. 6810-3
"Belts of woodland, wigwam haystacks". A ramble in Normandie. Gertrude Huntington McGiffert. 6838-3
The Belvedere torso. Gertrude Huntington McGiffert. 6838-3
Bembo, Pietro
    "Thou, the stern monarch of dismay". Felicia Dorothea Hemans (tr.). 6973-8
Bemis, Katherine Prescott
    The parting ways. 6836-7
    The road to Spain. 6836-7
    To my mother. 6836-7
    Waking. 6836-7
    We pay. 6836-7
    The yoke. 6836-7
Bemiss, J.M.
    A minister's prayer. 6525-2
Ben Apfelgarten. Eugene Field. 6949-5
Ben Bluff. Thomas Hood. 6089-7
Ben Bolt. Thomas Dunn English. 6085-4,6451-5,6632-1,6732-8, 6744-1,6723 ,6300-4,6431-0,6121-4
"Ben Butler, on a summer's day". The political Maud. Eugene Field. 6949-5
Ben Dorain. Duncan Ban MacIntyre. 6873-1
Ben Fisher. Frances Dana Barker ("Aunt Fanny") Gage. 6407-8
"Ben Fisher had finished his hard day's work". Unknown. 6059-5
"Ben Fisher had finished his hard day's work". A home picture. Frances Dana Barker ("Aunt Fanny") Gage. 6910-X
Ben Franklin, Esq. Charles Irvin Junkin. 6936-3
Ben Hafed. William Whitehead. 6917-7
Ben Hafiz, the muezzin. Richard Henry Savage. 6580-5
Ben Hassan's dream. Waldo Messaros. 6928-2
Ben Hazard's guests. Anna P. Marshall. 6915-0
Ben invites a friend. Ben Jonson. 6230-X
Ben Isaac's vision. Annie M. Lawrence. 6411-6
Ben Jonson. Algernon Charles Swinburne. 6198-2,6483-3,6196-6,6250-4,6655-0
Ben Jonson entertains a man from Stratford. Edwin Arlington Robinson. 6348-9,6288-1,6646-1
Ben Jonson's commonplace book. Lucius Cary; Lord Falkland. 6385-3

Ben Karshook's wisdom. Robert Browning. 6848-0
Ben Karshook's wisdom. Robert Browning. 6110-9,6430-2
Ben Milam. William H. Wharton. 6946-0
Ben-ammi and the fairies. John Godfrey Saxe. 6848-0
Benardo's revenge. Unknown. 6294-6
Benares. Jorge Luis Borges. 6642-9
The bench-legged fyce. Eugene Field. 6949-5
"Bend low your ear, my music passes". The earth speaks. Lilian Sauter. 7023-X
The bended bow, fr. Lays of many lands. Felicia Dorothea Hemans. 6973-8
Bendig, Edna
    Craftsman. 6750-6
The bending of the bow, fr. The Odyssey. Homer. 6372-1
"The bending sails shall whiten on the sea". The ships. Theodore Maynard. 6833-2
"Bending, I bow my head". Combing. Gladys Cardiff. 7005-1
"Beneath a democratic flag". Les miserables de luxe. Ernest Hyett. 6818-9
"Beneath a fruitful apple tree". Prince Pompom. Oliver Herford. 6861-8
"Beneath a lime, remoter from the scene". Death of Lara. George Gordon, 6th Baron Byron. 6980-0
"Beneath a placid brow". William Motherwell. 6980-0
"Beneath a shady elm tree". Selling the baby. Ada Carleton. 6922-3
Beneath a shady tree. Elizabeth Voss. 6906-1
"Beneath an ancient bridge,...straitened flood". A Suffolk fen. George Crabbe. 6793-X
"Beneath brown earth I gently press". Planting bulbs. Clair [pseud].. 6817-0
"Beneath each lovers' parting". Prescience. Simon Glass. 6818-9
"Beneath fair Magdalen's storied towers". Oxford revisited in war time. Tertius Van Dyke. 7031-0
"Beneath her skates the curved steel bars". The skater. Orth Harper Stein. 7035-3
"Beneath its vaulted cover richly blue". Child of Arabia. Maude Freeman Osborne. 6836-7
"Beneath my dog-furred leaves you see". The strawberry. Edith Sitwell. 7000-0
"Beneath my dreaa a field of flowers". From a copy of 'Les chants de maldoror' Alejandra Pizarnik. 7036-1
"Beneath my shady tree I rest". Beneath a shady tree. Elizabeth Voss. 6906-1
"Beneath my window lies the busy street". Two Viaducts. Alice C. Weitz. 7038-8
"Beneath our consecrated elm". The new-come chief, fr. Under the old elm. James Russell Lowell. 6946-0
"Beneath our feet and o'er our head". The holy field. Henry Hart Milman. 6931-2
Beneath such rains. James E. Warren Jr. 6144-3
"Beneath th' triumphal blue, th' riotous day". Antony and Cleopatra. Eugene Mason. 6884-7
Beneath the apple tree. Delphia L. Hopper. 6906-1
"Beneath the arches of the leaves I lie". Villanelle of city and country. Zoe Akins. 6875-8
Beneath the beam. W.E. Manning. 6681-X
Beneath the Belgium watertank. Unknown. 6237-7
Beneath the Cross. Elizabeth Cecilia Clephane. 6337-3
"Beneath the beech's shade I read". Holiday. Hermann Hagedorn. 6944-4
"Beneath the blistering tropical sun". Wheeler's brigade at Santiago. Wallace Rice. 6946-0
"Beneath the branch of the green may". Song ("Beneath the branch"). Unknown (French). 7039-6
"Beneath the brown, lustrous haze". Reflection. Margaret Allonby. 6788-3
"Beneath the deep and solemn midnight sky". Father an child. Richard Watson Gilder. 7041-8
Beneath the flag. Unknown. 6471-X,6223-7
"Beneath the flat and paper sky". Clowns' houses, fr. Facade. Edith Sitwell. 7000-0
"Beneath the flow of words". Foundation. Frances Minturn Howard. 6979-7
Beneath the forms of outward rite. James A. Blaisdell. 6337-3
"Beneath the fourteen pointed arches". Cataclysm. Noel Harry Brettell. 6788-3
"Beneath the full-eyes Syrian moon". Abraham and his ods.

Richard Monckton Milnes; 1st Baron Houghton. 6848-0
"Beneath the gilt capricorn". Said the noctambulo, fr. Facade. Edith Sitwell. 7000-0
"Beneath the hedge, or near the stream". The glow-worm. Vincent Bourne. 6814-6
"Beneath the hill, athwart the stream". So is he made. Sarah Litsey. 6750-6
"Beneath the hot midsummer sun". His mother's song. Unknown. 6097-8,6964-9
"Beneath the hot, midsummer sun". His mother's song. Unknown. 7022-1
"Beneath the loveliest dream there coils..fear". A dream. Theodore Watts-Dunton. 7015-9
"Beneath the low-hung night cloud". The Three Bells. John Greenleaf Whittier. 6833-2
Beneath the mound. R. T. Smith. 7005-1
Beneath the mountains. Ruzena Jesenka. 6763-8
"Beneath the ocean's sapphire lid". The gardens of the sea. George Sterling. 6833-2
"Beneath the palace of the king". The shepherd. Johann Ludwig Uhland. 6903-7
"Beneath the pale skies, dreaming". Memoria in eterna. Cora Fabri. 6876-6
"Beneath the rocky peak that hides". The garden of the gods. William Allen Butler. 6903-7
Beneath the sanctuary lamp. Elenita Thompson Kirkpatrick. 6285-7
"Beneath the shadow of a beaver hat". The espousal. John Gay. 6972-X
"Beneath the shadow of the cross". Samuel Longfellow. 6065-X
"Beneath the silent chambers of the earth". Hell, fr. Davideis. Abraham Cowley. 6931-2
"Beneath the stars one August night". August night. Ronald Walker Barr. 6906-1
"Beneath the Tao tree at Waikiki". Dead volcano. Helen Louise Stapleford. 6799-9
Beneath the surface. W.F. Fox. 6408-6
"Beneath the vast stretched skies each thing..". Understanding. Halley W. Groesbeck. 6906-1
Beneath the wattle boughs. Frances Tyrrell Gill. 6274-1, 6656-9
Beneath the wattle boughs. Frances Tyrrell Gill. 6768-9
"Beneath these fruit-tree boughs that shed". William Wordsworth. 6084-6
"Beneath this green and". R.I.P. Franklin Pierce Adams. 6850-2
"Beneath this narrow jostling street". Fleet Street. Arthur Adams. 6784-0
"Beneath this quiet, turfy". An epitaph. Richard Kendall Munkittrick. 6274-1
"Beneath this sodden ground lies one". Rose Ann Murray. 6850-2
"Beneath this starry arch". Onward. Harriet Martineau. 7037-X
"Beneath this starry arch". Harriet Martineau. 6238-5
"Beneath this stone brave Braddock lies". Braddock's fate and an encitement to revenge, sels. Stephen Tilden. 6753-0
"Beneath this stone in hopes of Zion". Unknown. 6083-8
"Beneath this stone our baby lies,". Unknown. 6722-0
"Beneath this vast serene of sky". Time. John Galsworthy. 6888-X
"Beneath thy all-directing rod". The Lord the creator. Sir John Bowring. 7020-5
"Beneath thy spell, O radiant sea". The sea' spell. Susan Marr Spalding. 6833-2
"Beneath unfathomable seas". Elfin dancer. Bernard Gilbert. 6959-2
"Beneath yon ruin'd abbey's moss-grown piles". The solemn noon of night,fr.The pleasures of melancholy. Thomas Warton Jr. 6932-0
"Beneath you eastern ridge, the craggy bound". Inscription for a seat in the groves of Coleorton. William Wordsworth. 6980-0
Benedic, anima mea. Bible. 6830-8
Benedicite. Richard Wilton. 6770-0
Benedict Brosse. Susan Frances ("Seranus") Harrison. 6115-X
"A Benedict youth known as Rutters". Limerick:"A Benedict

Benedict, E.L.
    youth known as Rutters". Edward Minshall. 6811-1
Benedict, E.L.
    Dandelions. 6529-5
    The four points. 6530-9
    A January thaw. 6394-2
    March. 6529-5
    A November evening. 6530-9
Benedict, Georgia
    Queen Anne's lace. 6118-4
Benedict, Hester A.
    Good-night. 6085-4,6273-3
    If only you were here. 6226-1
    A little story. 6131-1
    Only a woman. 6167-2,6273-3,6911-8
    Satisfied. 6273-3
Benedicte, fr. Snow bound. John Greenleaf Whittier. 6066-8, 6288-1,6126-5,6226-1,6302-0,6385-3,6620-8,6226-1, 6066-8
"**Benedicte**, what dreamed I this night?" Unknown. 6317-9, 6380-2
Benedictio domini. Ernest Dowson. 6507-4,6292-X,6508-2, 6172-9
Benediction. Valery Bryusov. 6103-6
Benediction. Arthur Shearly Cripps. 6800-6
The **benediction** ("In the year eighteen and nine..."). Clifford Harrison. 6661-5
Benediction ("Let no blasphemer till the sacred earth") Mark Turbyfill. 6619-4
Benediction ("The sun be warm and kind") Eleanor Powers. 6490-6
The **benediction** line. Mildred Maralyn Mercer. 6906-1
Benediction, fr. Herod. Stephen Phillips. 6337-3
Benediction, fr. The Canterbury tales. Geoffrey Chaucer. 6337-3
A **benediction**.. Alice Milligan. 6090-0;6174-5
The **benediction**. Francois Coppee. 6411-6,6451-5,6576-7, 6610-0,6550-3,6692
Benedictus, fr. Luke. Bible. 6337-3
Benedikt, Michael
    Definitive things. 6803-0
Benedikt, Michael (tr.)
    The tornado. Aime Cesaire, 6803-0
Benediktdottir, Unnur ("Hulda")
    As from a flower's chalice. Skuli Johnson (tr.). 6854-5
    If the moonbeam. Skuli Johnson (tr.). 6854-5,6283-0
    Lilies of white. Watson Kirkconnell (tr.). 6283-0
Benediktsson, Einar
    Northern lights. Jakobina Johnson (tr.). 6283-0
    Northern lights. Jakobina Johnson (tr.). 6854-5
    Rain. Watson Kirkconnell (tr.). 6283-0
    Surf. Jakobina Johnson (tr.). 6854-5
The **benefactor**. Ibn Sara. 6362-4
Beneficence. Sadi [or Saadi] (Mushlih-ud-Din) 6448-5
The **benefit** of trouble. Edgar A. Guest. 6862-6
Benet, Laura
    Babylon. 6218-0
    The bird of paradise. 6073-0
    Crowning. 6979-7
    Gardens of Babylon. 6880-4
    The hedgehog. 6464-7
    The rowers. 6218-0
    'She wandered after strange gods.' 6347-0
    The thrush. 6073-0
    The working children to the story teller. 6954-1
Benet, Rosemary and Stephen Vincent
    Abraham Lincoln. 6871-5
    Christopher Columbus. 6554-X
    Johnny Appleseed. 6891-X
    Nancy Hanks (1784-1818). 6076-5,6299-7,6236-9
    Peregrine white and Virginia Dare. 6554-X
Benet, Stephen Vincent
    Adam. 6732-8
    America. 6464-7
    American names. 6299-7,6513-9,6736-0
    Apology. 6761-1
    The ballad of William Sycamore. 6891-X
    The ballad of William Sycamore. 6506-6,6527-9,6619-4, 6037-4,6581-3,6250 ,6467-1,6628-3
    A book of Americans, sels. 6375-6
    Carol, new style. 6070-6,6746-8
    A Confederate prison. 6542-2
    The death of Stonewall Jackson. 6879-0
    Death-chant of the centaurs, sels. 6300-4
    Flood tide. 6467-1
    Going back to school. 6299-7
    The guns. 6542-2
    The hemp. 6030-7
    The hidden place. 6253-9
    The hiders' song, fr. John Brown's body. 6217-2
    If this should change. 6761-1
    Invocation, fr. John Brown's body. 6891-X
    Invocation, fr. John Brown's body. 6984-3
    "John Brown's body lies a-mouldering in the grave". 6984-3
    John Brown's body, sels. 6217-2,6527-9,6726-3
    Jubili, jubilo!, fr. John Brown's body. 6984-3
    King David. 6037-4,6069-2,6531-7
    Lincoln and Davis. 6542-2
    Litany for dictatorships. 6375-6
    Lonely burial. 6076-5,6102-8,6556-2
    Mad Blake. 6076-5
    Moonrider. 6037-4
    Mortuary parlors. 6393-4
    The mountain whippoorwill. 6265-2
    The mountain whippoorwill. 6039-0,6071-4,6281-4,6464-7, 6399-3,6619 ,6464-7,6736-0
    Now that I am clean again. 6339-X
    Ode to Walt Whitman. 6483-3
    1935. 6042-0
    "Out of John Brown's...", fr. John Brown's body. 6726-3
    Pickett's charge. 6464-7
    Portrait of a boy. 6332-2,6501-5,6327-6
    Portrait of a boy. 6861-8
    Rain after a vaudeville show. 6031-5
    A sad song. 6393-4
    To Rosemary. 6299-7
    Unfamiliar quartet. 6722-0
    War. 6542-2
    Winged man. 6347-0,6653-4
    The years ride out, fr. John Brown's body. 6984-3
Benet, William Rose
    The adoration. 6320-9
    Apes in Avernus. 6012-9
    Arraignment, sels. 6337-3
    The arrival. 6532-5
    The asylum. 6031-5
    At warm springs. 6465-5
    The ballad of Jesse James. 6399-3
    Bast. 6511-2
    Brazen tongue. 6012-9
    Dead letter office. 6217-2
    The death of Robin Hood. 6781-6
    Debutantrum. 6307-1
    Dedication to a first book. 6320-9
    Deer in Mooreland. 6782-4
    Eternal masculine. 6012-9
    The falconer of God. 6007-2,6102-8,6162-1,6347-0,6476-0, 6501 ,6076-5,6161-3,6012-9,6250-4,6513-9,6300 ,6007-2,6730-1,6732-8,6337-3,6393-4,6236-9,6506-6,6509-0, 6532-5,6556-2,6607
    The fawn in the snow. 6011-0
    Fire and glass. 6011-0
    Front line. 6032-3,6051-X
    God of the young. 6761-1
    Her way. 6034-X,6607-0
    His ally. 6291-1,6501-5
    Home defense. 6817-0
    The horse thief. 6861-8
    The horse thief. 6030-2,6107-9,6253-9
    The house at evening. 6034-X,6619-4
    How to catch unicorns. 6162-1
    Inscription for a mirror in a deserted dwelling. 6641-0
    Jesse James: American myth. 6011-0,6107-9,6375-6,6464-7, 6488-4,6527
    Judgment. 6076-5
    'Junkets,' immortal. 6331-4
    The last ally. 6464-7
    Late summer. 6979-7
    Lindbergh. 7019-1
    Lullaby of the catfish and the crab. 6722-0

Mad Blake. 6102-8,6556-2,6250-4,6030-7,6076-5
The marvelous Munchausen. 6027-7
Merchants from Cathay. 6162-1,6393-4,6396-9
Mimi and the foreboding frost. 6012-9
Mistress Fate. 6291-1
Moon rider. 6011-0
Morgiana dances. 6959-2
Mustang. 6253-9,6037-4
Ode for an epoch. 6764-6
The old Adam. 6736-0
On Edward Webbe, English gunner. 6032-3
The pale dancer. 6959-2
Paternity. 6327-6
Pearl diver. 6020-X
Poor girl. 6880-4
Primum mobile. 6012-9
Prium mobile. 6012-9
The red country. 6051-X,6542-2
Revolution. 6880-4
Ritual. 6887-1
Rogues' apocalypse. 6011-0
S.V.B. 6483-3,6516-3
The sea dream. 6347-0
The skater of ghost lake. 6619-4
Sky writers. 6978-9
Stage directions. 6011-0
Street of cats. 6511-2
There lived a lady in Milan. 6506-6
Third row, centre. 6722-0
Trammeled swimmer. 6979-7
Tricksters. 6032-3
Two north shore poems. 6979-7
The unjust word. 6012-9
Whale. 6011-0,6039-0,6619-4
Wings. 7014-0
The wood-cutter's wife. 6039-0,6012-9
Woolworth Tower. 6509-0

Benevenuta, Sister Mary
Mater incognita. 6282-2

Benevolence. Mark Akenside. 6932-0
Benevolence. James Beattie. 6409-4
Benevolence. Siraj. 6362-4

Bengough, John Wilson
Sympathy. 6796-4

Benham, Ida W.
The little brown seed in the furrow. 6049-8

"Benign accoucheur moving there". Earth speaks. Ethel Case Cook. 6799-9
Benign neglect. Lindamichellebaron. 6899-5
Benina to Belshazzar. Henry Hart Milman. 6980-0
Benjamin Harrison. Charles E. Russell. 6820-0
Benjamin Pantier. Edgar Lee Masters. 6646-1

Benjamin and George D. Sutton, Charles L.
The flag that has never known defeat. 6471-X

The Benjamin's lamentations. Unknown. 6547-3

Benjamin, Isaac
For a crippled girl. 6249-0
Prayer ("Not for a long"). 6249-0

Benjamin, Park
Alexander taming Bucephalus. 6410-8,6478-7
The chosen ones of Israel. 6848-0
The old sexton. 6240-7
Press on. 6045-1,6291-1,6213-8,6291-1,6405-1
The sexton. 6407-8

Benjamin, Paul
To arms. 6946-0

Benlowes, Edward
Theophila, sels. 6208-3
To his muse. 6563-5

Benn, Gottfried
Man and woman go through the cancer ward. Babette Deutsch (tr.). 6160-5
Morgue. Babette Deutsch (tr.). 6160-5
Songs. Babette Deutsch (tr.). 6160-5

Benners Jr., William J.
Gloria belli. 6923-1
Old letters. 6923-1

Bennet, N.M.
Honeycomb. 6799-9

Bennet, William Cox
Baby, open your eyes. 6078-1

Bennett Jr., J.
To the essential poet. 6998-3

Bennett, Anna Elizabeth
Laughing woman. 6640-2
Renuncio. 6640-2
The skeptic. 6640-2
Wind. 6640-2

Bennett, Arnold
Limerick:"..young man of Montrose". 6811-1
Limerick:"..young plumber of Leigh". 6811-1

Bennett, E.M.
Cold front. 7018-3
Electronic art. 7018-3

Bennett, Florence Mary
Ave Maria. 6847-2
The New Englander speaks. 6847-2

Bennett, Florence Mary (tr.)
Hypnosis. Alkman, 6847-2

Bennett, Gertrude Ryder
These times. 6337-3
Tropical fish. 6979-7
Wayside shrine. 6144-3

Bennett, Henry Holcomb
Adventure. 6088-9
The flag goes by. 6239-3,6479-5,6457-4,6356-X,6465-5, 6478 ,6223-7,6107-9,6736-0,6300-4,6449-3,6654 ,6503-1,6512-0,6579-1,6639-9
St. Patrick was a gentleman. 6219-9,6271-7,6465-5

Bennett, Jack
Missing Bobby Shaftoe. 6702-6

Bennett, John
The abbot of Derry. 6619-4
The dead pussy-cat. 6120-6
God bless you, dear, to-day. 6274-1
I want an epitaph. 6764-6
The last visitor. 6764-6
Over the rose-leaves, under the rose. 6274-1
The skylark's song. 6820-0
The song of the Spanish Main. 6274-1
To Marie. 6902-9
To Marie. 6089-7
What troubled Poe's raven. 6440-X

Bennett, Julia M.
A cup of water. 6685-2

Bennett, Rowena Bastin
Join the caroling. 6608-9

Bennett, William Cox
Baby May. 6078-1,6271-7,6302-0,6385-3,6131-1,6219 ,6656-9
Baby's shoes. 6271-7,6302-0,6385-3,6424-8,6543-0
Be mine, and I will give thy name. 6656-9
A Christmas song ("Blow, wind, blow,"). 6145-1,6656-9
Come home, my sailor. 6747-6
Cradle song. 6658-5
From India. 6408-3
Invocation to rain in summer. 6239-3,6302-0,6385-3,6771-7
Lullaby, O lullaby. 6078-1
My roses blossom the whole year round. 6658-5
Rain in summer. 6373-X
The right above the wrong. 7009-4
The slaver's wreck. 7009-4
To a cricket. 6239-3,6271-7
The wife's appeal. 6911-8
A winter song ("Crackle and blaze"). 6466-3,6747-6
The worn wedding-ring. 6302-0,6385-3,6620-8

Bennington. W.H. Babcock. 6946-0
Bennington lake. Gene Fendt. 6857-X
Benny. Mrs. Burroughs. 6131-1
Benny. Annie Chambers Ketchum. 6385-3
Benny. Unknown. 6127-3

Benoit, Pierre
Diaduminius. 6351-9
For Berenice. 6351-9
The return. 6351-9

Bensee, James Berry
At the last. 6304-7

Bensel, James Berry
February. 6456-6

BENSEL

Lones to a friend. 6358-6
My sailor. 7041-8
Benshimol, Ernest
Age, fr. Two moods from the hill. 6762-X
A banquet. 6762-X
Sonnet of life. 6037-4
Two moods from the hill, sels. 6762-X
Youth, fr. Two moods from the hill. 6762-X
Benson, Arthur Christopher
After construing. 6473-6,6656-9
Amen. 6437-X
Chalvey. 6793-X
An English sheel. 6656-9
The hawk ("The hawk slipped out of the pine..."). 6073-0,6395-0
In the garden. 6649-6
Knapweed. 6656-9
Lord Vyet. 6437-X
My old friend. 6085-4
My will. 6793-X
Ode on Rt. Hon. W.E. Gladstone. 6323-3
Ode to music. 7014-0
Outward bound. 7014-0
The phoenix. 6437-X
Prelude ("Hush'd"). 6301-2
The prelude. 6437-X,6301-2
Prid. Kal. Oct. 6785-9
The pursuit. 6785-9
Realism. 6656-9
The stage of heaven. 6785-9
The toad. 6510-4
A trio. 6793-X
The water-ousel. 6785-9
Wounds. 6510-4
Benson, Arthur Christopher (tr.)
Love's precinct. Mnasalcas, 6102-8
On deck. Theognis, 6102-8
Benson, Edward Frederick
Prayer ("The dawn"), fr. The image in the sand. 6501-5
Benson, Edward W.
Character. 6529-5
Benson, Irene Chapman
In memoriam ("Canadian soldiers-valorous and true"). 6224-5
Benson, L.L.
'Come unto to'. 6927-4
Benson, Louis FitzGerald
Dedication. 6337-3,6525-2
The light of God is falling. 6337-3
O thou whose feet have climbed life's hill. 6337-3
Songs of Jesus. 6337-3
Benson, Louis Fitzgerald (tr.)
Near the Cross. Unknown (Latin), 6337-3
Benson, Margaret
Once upon a time. 6510-4
Pets. 6230-X
Benson, Mary A.
The fairies' Christmas. 6684-4
Benson, Mary Josephine
The blackbird troubadour. 6797-2
The book-binder. 6797-2
Noon-day on Lake Ontario. 6796-4
Tumbler leaves. 6797-2
Benson, Nathaniel A.
The ballad of the Rawalpindi. 6224-5
Elegy in spring. 6021-8
Benson, Robert Hugh
After a retreat. 6172-9,6292-X
The priest's lament. 6022-6
The Teresian contemplative. 6096-X,6022-6,6285-7,6172-9,6292-X
Benson, Stella
Thanks to my world for the loan of a fair day. 6019-6
The **bent** sae brown. Unknown. 6185-0
Bentivoglio, Il Marchese Cornelio
"The sainted spirit which, from bliss on high". Felicia Dorothea Hemans (tr.). 6973-8
Bentley, Edmund Clerihew
A ballade of souls. 6659-3
Envoi ("Prince"). 6659-3

J.S. Mill. 6089-7,6722-0
Lord Clive. 6089-7,6722-0
Sir Christopher Wren. 6089-7,6722-0
Bentley, Richard
A reply to an imitation of the second ode... of Horace. 6932-0
Benton, Joel
Abraham Lincoln. 6305-5,6524-4
Another Washington. 6708-5
Dakota. 6484-1
December. 6006-4,6597-X
Grover Cleveland. 6946-0
Hallowe'en ("Pixie, kobold, elf, and sprite"). 6254-7, 6465-5
A kiss - by mistake. 6652-6
The poet. 6730-1
The pretty maid of Kissimmee. 6417-5
The scarlet tanager. 6073-0
Benton, Myron B.
Midsummer invitation. 6597-X
The mowers. 6385-3
"There is one spot for which my soul will yearn". 6597-X
Benton, Rita
Our daily bread. 6954-1
Benton, Walter
Each year's song. 6761-1
Summary of the distance between the bomber and the objective. 6666-6
With the most susceptible element, the mind...toxic action. 6666-6
Benvenuta, Sister Mary
The contemplative. 6285-7
A song of the white and red. 6292-X
Benvenuto Cellini. Count Carl Snoilsky. 6045-5
Benyon, James
Limerick:"A motorist, out on a spree". 6811-1
Beowulf
Sole survivor. Charles W. Kennedy (tr.). 6879-0
Beowulf, sels. Unknown. 6179-6
Beowulf, sels. Unknown. 6102-8
Beowulf, sels. Unknown. 6646-1
Beowulf: Book XII. Unknown. 6732-8
Beowulf: Book XIII. Unknown. 6732-8
Beppo. Ella Wheeler Wilcox. 6956-8
Beppo: a Venetian story. George Gordon, 6th Baron Byron. 6945-2
Bequests, fr. The will. John Donne. 6324-1
Bera, Michael
The mad March wind. 6130-3
Beralde tries to convince his brother..., fr. Invalid. Moliere (Jean Baptiste Poquelin) 6637-2
Beranger, Pierre Jean de
Broken fiddle. Eugene Field (tr.). 6949-5
Cricket on the hearth. 6424-8
The dead alive. Robert B. Brough (tr.). 6787-5
The king of Yvetot. 6102-8,6732-8
The king of Yvetot. Robert B. Brough (tr.). 6787-5
The king of Yvetot. William Toynbee (tr.). 7039-6
Le petit homme rouge. 6801-4
Le vieux caporal. 6801-4
Les bohemiens. 6801-4
Les souvenirs du peuple. 6732-8
Ma vocation. Eugene Field (tr.). 6949-5
Ma vocation. 6801-4
My last song perhaps. Eugene Field (tr.). 6949-5
Rosette. 6652-6
She is so pretty. 6652-6
The song of the cossack to his horse. Francis Sylvester ("Father Prout") Mahony (tr.). 6344-6
Tiresome spring. 6652-6
To my old coat. Eugene Field (tr.). 6949-5
Berceuse, fr. Bread out of iron. Marjorie Allen Seiffert. 6531-7
Berchan, ?
The fort of Rathangan. 6125-7
Berchenko, Frank
Inscription for a clock. 6396-9
"Bereave me not of these delightful dreams". Dreams of outh. William Lisle Bowles. 6980-0

Bereaved. James Whitcomb Riley. 6076-5,6121-4,6300-4,6309-8,6102-8,6243-1,6260-1,6337-3,6431-0
"Bereaved of all, I went abroad". Emily Dickinson. 6348-9
The bereaved swan. Stevie Smith. 6210-5
Bereavement. William Lisle Bowles. 6086-2
Bereavement. John Godfrey Saxe. 6735-2
Bereavement. Chauncey Devereux Stillman. 6879-0
Bereavement. Viola Bailey Wilson. 6750-6
Bereavement, fr. Alcestis. Euripides. 6435-3
"Bereft of all, alone he dies". Watching at the Easter tomb. William White. 6868-5
"Bereft the house without its ancient glass". The mirrors, fr. The homestead. Gertrude Huntington McGiffert. 6838-3
Berenberg, David P.
Men. 6042-0
Two sonnets. 6036-6
Berg, Sharon
The birth poem. 6767-0
Breastfeeding at the art gallery of Ontario... 6767-0
Berg, Stephen (tr.)
After poems (1913,1916,1911,1959). Anna Akhmatova, 6803-0
The berg.. Herman Melville. 6333-0
Bergen, Grace Updegraff
Minneapolis. 6342-X
Bergen, Helen Corinne
Even in death. 6686-0
Berger, Gottfried A.
Earl Walter. Elizabeth Craigmyle (tr.). 6842-1
Lenore. Elizabeth Craigmyle (tr.). 6842-1
The wild huntsman. 6842-1
Berggolts, Olga
Address to tragedy. Jack Lindsay (tr.). 6546-5
Endpiece. Jack Lindsay (tr.). 6546-5
Parting. Jack Lindsay (tr.). 6546-5
Songs of the Spanish children. Jack Lindsay (tr.). 6546-5
Bergin, Osborn
A court poet in trouble. 6582-1
In praise of a harp. 6582-1
On the breaking up of a school. 6582-1
Bergin, T.G. (tr.)
"Alone and ever weary with dark care". Francesco Petrarch, 6325-X
"Determined with one sally to erase". Francesco Petrarch, 6325-X
Good Friday 1327. Francesco Petrarch, 6325-X
"In what divine ideal, what lofty sphere". Francesco Petrarch, 6325-X
Lament for the sailing of the crusade. Rinaldo D'Aquino, 6325-X
"Now perish, Baia, root and stock and name". Giovanni Boccaccio, 6325-X
"Now while the wind and earth and heavens rest". Francesco Petrarch, 6325-X
"O unforgiving thoughts, I pray you: peace!". Francesco Petrarch, 6325-X
"Through savage woods I walk without demur". Francesco Petrarch, 6325-X
"Through twenty-one long years...". Francesco Petrarch, 6325-X
"To that fair kingdom, o my gentle lord". Giovanni Boccaccio, 6325-X
To the Emperor Charles V and to King Francis I... Veronica Gambara, 6325-X
Bergman, Bo
Adagio. Charles Wharton Stork (tr.). 6045-5
Bergman, Harold
Change of mood. 7030-2
Bergonzi, Bernard
Anemones for Miss Austen. 6257-1
Bering, Betsy
Still life. 6966-5
Berke, Judith
The red room. 6966-5
Berkeley, George
America, 1750 6606-2
On the prospect of planting arts and learning... 6271-7, 6219-9,6737-9,6271-7

The prospect in America, sels. 6102-8
Verses on the prospects of planting arts...in America. 6152-4
Westward ho! 6385-3
Westward the course of empire. 6240-7
Berkley, Sir William
Where did you borrow that last sigh? 6563-5
Berkshire hills. Will H. Skaling. 6799-9
Berkshire notes. Sara Teasdale. 6778-6
Berkshires in April. Clement Wood. 6556-2,6653-4
Berlein, E.
Cape Town from Platte Klip. 6800-6
Capetown from Platte Klip. 6625-9
Rachel. 6800-6
Berlin - the sixteenth of March. Sir Edwin Arnold. 6046-3
Berlin air raid. Aaron Kramer. 6561-9
Berlin masque. John Hejduk. 6803-0
Berlyn, Alfred
Avenged! 6681-X
Berlyn, Louis P.
Limerick:"In the famed Scottish castle of Glamis". 6811-1
Berman, Fred
The cemetery beside the road. 6841-3
Love's call. 6841-3
When the shadows deepen. 6841-3
The wildflower. 6841-3
Berman, Rita
Pilot! 7019-1
Berman, Ruth
Snow Queen's portrait. 6966-5
Bermudas. Andrew Marvell. 6179-6,6208-3,6239-3,6258-X,6315-2,6562 ,6563-5,6600-3,6634-8,6641-0,6152-4,6430 , 6250-4,6150-8,6214-8,6125-7,6645-3
Bermudas, sels. Andrew Marvell. 6369-1
Bernal Diaz' preface to his book. Archibald MacLeish. 6375-6
Bernard of Clairvaux (atr), Saint
Jesus the very thought of thee. Edward Caswall (tr.). 6337-3
Bernard of Clairvaux, Saint
Hail, thou head! 6065-X
"Jesus, the very thought of thee". 6065-X
Jesus, thou joy of living hearts. 6730-1
Of our lord's passion, sels. 6144-3
Thou light of life. 6065-X
Bernard of Cluny
The celestial country. John Mason Neale (tr.). 6219-9
Jerusalem, the golden. 6730-1,6304-7,6214-8
Jerusalem, the golden. John Mason Neale (tr.). 6337-3
Jesus, thou joy of living hearts. 6730-1
Bernard, Henry
Marie. 6423-X
Bernardine du born. Lydia Huntley Sigourney. 66601-1
Bernardo and Alphonso. John Gibson Lockhart. 6242-3,6403-5
Bernardo and Alphonso. Unknown (Spanish) 6757-3
Bernardo del Carpio. Felicia Dorothea Hemans. 6973-8
Bernardo del Carpio. Felicia Dorothea Hemans. 6134-6,6302-0,6706-9,6744-1,6014-5,6142 ,6242-3,6392-6,6606-2, 6661-5,6403-5,6419 ,6294-6,6419-1
Bernardo's revenge. Unknown. 6913-4
Bernardo's revenge. Unknown. 6242-3
Berneval. Jack Lindsay. 6895-2
Bernhard, Robert E.
Happy days. 6894-4
Bernhard, Thomas
Ash Wednesday. Milne Holton and Herbert Kuhner (tr.). 6769-7
Imprisoned. Milne Holton and Herbert Kuhner (tr.). 6769-7
No tree. Milne Holton and Herbert Kuhner (tr.). 6769-7
Tired. Milne Holton and Herbert Kuhner (tr.). 6769-7
Bernheisel, Jesse L.
A dream realized. 6654-2
Bernhoff, John
The witch-song. 6716-6
Berni, Francesco
Portrait. L.R. Lind (tr.). 6325-X
Berning, Helen Darby
To a young mother. 6750-6

Berries and nettles. William Force Stead. 6778-6
Berrigan, Daniel
    Almost everybody is dying here: only a few actually... 6870-7
    Living I shall live. 6839-1
    Man is more. 6803-0
    Patience, hard virtue. 6870-7
    Piper. 6839-1
    Rehabilitative report: we can still laugh. 6870-7
    A typical 6:00 p.m. in the fun house. 6870-7
    We were permitted to meet together in prison to... 6870-7
Berry, H.W.
    To an Egyptian boy. 6722-0
Berry, R.G.
    Tramp philosophy. 6719-0
Berry, Wendell
    A music. 6803-0
Berry, William
    Thunder on, you silver stallions! 6096 X
Berrying song. Lucy Larcom. 6129-X
Berryman, John
    Boston Common. 6391-8
    Conversation. 6389-6,6666-6
    Desires of men and women. 6389-6
    The disciple. 6391-8
    The moon and the night and the men. 6389-6,6666-6
    The spinning heart. 6389-6
    The statue. 6391-8
Bersohn, Robert
    The dignity of labor. 6722-0
Berssenbrugge, Mei-mei
    Farolita. 6790-5
Berstecher, Thekla N.
    The closed door. 6906-1
    Comradeship. 6906-1
    Home. 6906-1
    Joan. 6906-1
    Sultry days. 6906-1
    Winter. 6906-1
Bert Kessler. Edgar Lee Masters. 6723-9
Berte, Hal
    The spring poet. 6695-X
Bertha. Anne Whitney. 6600-3
Bertha in the lane. Elizabeth Barrett Browning. 6271-7, 6302-0,6385-3,6600-3,6572-4
Berthoff, Helen Tappan
    To life. 6799-9
Bertie's philosophy. Eva March Tappan. 6273-3
Bertolino, James
    The American. 7032-9
Bertram, Anthony
    The demi-gods. 6781-6
Bertrand [or Bertrans]
    Song of battle. Ezra Pound (tr.). 6665-8
Bertrand, Marion L.
    The coming of the snow. 6799-9
    Compensation. 6799-9
    My demand. 6799-9
    Of such as these. 6799-9
Bertrand, Sister Mary
    Our lady of mercy. 6282-2
Beruria. Unknown. 6690-9
A besetting sin. Edmund Vance Cooke. 6697-6
Beshigtashlian, Muggurdich
    Spring. 6050-1
"Beshrew that heart that makes my heart to groan". Sonnet 133 ("Beshrew that heart"). William Shakespeare. 6447-7
Beside a brook at Mokanshan. Witter Bynner. 6778-6
Beside a fountain. Thomas Morley. 6328-4
"Beside a river that I know, shrined in..grove". The pilgrims of liberty. Thomas D'Arcy McGee. 7009-4
Beside a stream. Hamda. 6362-4
"Beside a tomb I saw a crimson tree". The crimson tree. Elsie J. Cosler Campbell. 6799-9
Beside chrysanthemums. Jung-ju Suh. 6775-1
Beside flowers. Marie Sercombe. 6270-9
Beside her carriage. Vachel Lindsay. 6206-7
"Beside her father's house is the black loss". Like a shadow. David Coy. 6860-X
"Beside his head there sat a fair young man". Angels. Edmund Spenser. 6935-5
"Beside love, what jewel has mystery". Love. Stella Gibbons. 6893-6
"Beside our gathered sheaves to rest". Nooning. William White. 6868-5
"Beside that tent and under guard". Geronimo. Ernest McGaffey. 6946-0
"Beside the dark Utawa's stream...". How Canada was saved (May 1660). George Murray. 6795-6
"Beside the engine-driver grim". A night ride on the engine. Emma Shaw. 6922-3
"Beside the garve's new-rounded sod". Sympathy. John Wilson Bengough. 6796-4
"Beside the grey sea-shingle...". Anyte. 6251-2
Beside the idle summer sea, fr. Bric-a-brac. William Ernest Henley. 6123-0
"Beside the lonely river". Little Big Horn. Ernest McGaffey. 6946-0
"Beside the pale water". The pool. Fritz S. Burnell. 6784-0
Beside the sea. Thornton W. Burgess. 6798-0
Beside the sea. Robert Louis Stevenson. 6937-1
"Beside the sea, metallic bright". Minstrels, fr. Marine. Edith Sitwell. 7000-0
Beside the seaside, sels. Sir John Betjeman. 6258-X
"Beside the smooth black lacquer sea". Rain, fr. Two promenades sentimentales. Edith Sitwell. 7000-0
"Beside the stream and in the alder-shade". Lovers' quarrel. Sir Edmund Gosse. 6770-0
"Beside the streams of Babylon, in tears". From psalm 137 (1). Bible. 6848-0
Beside the way. Jeannette Marks. 6320-9
"Beside the weather-boarded shanty". Neglected. Monica Shipp Cline. 6799-9
The besom-man. Joseph ("Seosamh MacCathmhaoil") Campbell. 6930-4
Bess. Alfred T. Chandler. 6681-X
Bess. Alfred T. Chandler. 6768-9
Bess. Orrick Johns. 6032-3
Bess the gawkie. James Muirhead. 6180-X
"Bess went to church one sultry day". Please, preacher man, can I go home? Unknown. 6923-1
Besse Bunting. Unknown. 6881-2
Bessie. W. Wetherbee. 6116-8
Bessie Bell and Mary Gray. Mother Goose. 6055-2,6180-X, 6395-0,6466-3,6185-0,6067 ,6153-2
Bessie Bo Peep of Engle Steepe. T.W. Handford. 6629-1
Bessie Bobtail. James Stephens. 6897-9
Bessie Brown, M.D. Samuel Minturn Peck. 6089-7,6441-8,6441-8,6505-8
Bessie of Ballington Brae. Unknown. 6057-9
Bessie's boil. Robert Service. 6159-1
Bessie's Christmas dream. Unknown. 6927-4
Bessie's dilemma. Mary Kyle Dallas. 6671-2
Bessie's first party. Belle Marshall Locke. 6927-4
Bessie's letter. Emma Celia & Lizzie J. Rook. 6137-0
Bessy Bell and Mary Gray. Unknown. 6904-5
Best. Helen Hunt Jackson. 6632-1
"Best and brightest, come away!". To Jane: the invitation. Percy Bysshe Shelley. 6828-6
"Best I like your title won". An epistle in June. Helen Gray Cone. 6847-2
The best beauty. Emma Celia & Lizzie J. Rook. 6137-0
The best cow in peril. Unknown. 6409-4
The best day. Unknown. 6109-5
Best days. Unknown (Greek) 6435-3
The best dog. Unknown. 7008-6
The best faith. Edward Payson Powell. 6109-5
The best firm. Walter G. Doty. 6861-8
The best firm. Walter G. Doty. 6135-4
The best friend. William Henry Davies. 6607-9
The best friend. Norman Gale. 6510-4
The best is yet to come. Annie E. Smiley. 6583-X
The best judgment. Alice Cary. 6969-X
The best memorial. Agathias Scholasticus. 6435-3
"The best men, doing their best", sels. Elizabeth Barrett Browning. 6601-1
Best o' fellers. Frank Lebby Stanton. 6211-3

Best of all meals. Edgar A. Guest. 6748-4
"Best of artists! mark for me". My alpenstock. Henry Glassford Bell. 6749-2
The best of husbands. John Godfrey Saxe. 6787-5
"The best of men". Deckar. 6238-5
The best of the ball. William Sawyer. 6652-6
"The best of what we do and are". Thoughts on the banks of the Nile, sels. William Wordsworth. 6867-7
The best of wives. Unknown. 6787-5
The best prayer. Samuel Taylor Coleridge. 6543-0
The best road of all. Charles Hanson Towne. 6374-8,6476-0, 6607-0
The 'best room'. Oliver Wendell Holmes. 7022-1
The best sewing machine. Unknown. 6744-1
The best sewing-machine. Unknown. 6917-7
The best spare room. Joseph Crosby Lincoln. 6119-2
Best stories. Rachel Albright. 6789-1
Best that I can. Unknown. 6312-8
The best thing in the world. Elizabeth Barrett Browning. 6410-8
The best thing in the world. Unknown. 6014-5,6629-1,6652-6
"The best things are nearest". Unknown. 6109-5
The best times. James Whitcomb Riley. 6091-9
The best treasure. John J. Moment. 6337-3
The best tree. Unknown. 6274-1
The best way. Walter Chalmers Smith. 6180-X
Best, Charles
    Looke how the pale queene. 6833-2
    The moon. 6182-6,6436-1
Best, Eva
    The dog and the tramp. 6923-1
    Don't tell. 6137-0
Best, Susie M.
    At Christmas-tide. 6807-3
    A catastrophe. 6147-8
    Decoration Day. 7022-1
    Herein is love. 6066-8
    A hymn for America. 6926-6
    Is it success? 6109-5
    "A king may knight a knave, but God." 6225-3
    Kriss Kringle. 6147-8
    The loud silence. 6750-6
    The miracle dreams. 6532-5
    Musical martyrdom. 6711-5
    Our nation's dead. 6529-5
    Put it off. 6529-5
    Rum and ruin. 6685-2
    Santa Claus' visit. 6147-8
    Statesman, ruler, hero, martyr. 6708-5
    The story of Peterkin Paul. 6529-5
    Summer-time. 6529-5
    A surprise for Santa Claus. 6272-5
    Thanksgiving. 6532-5
    Thanksgiving acrostic. 6703-4
    The Thanksgiving feast. 6529-5
    Tiny trees. 6048-X
    We are the trees. 6048-X
    Winter. 6529-5
    A zealous patriot. 6529-5
Best, Theodore
    Lindbergh. 7019-1
Best, to the best. Alice Cary. 6969-X
"The best-off folks, I've heard folks say". Working by the day in Vermont. Daniel L. Cady. 6989-4
The best. Elizabeth Barrett Browning. 6437-X
The best. Carl Sandburg. 6337-3
The best. Jesse Lynch Williams. 6983-5
Bester, Laura Heebner
    The orphan moon. 6249-0
    To Tommy. 6249-0
A bestiary, sels. Unknown. 6193-1
"Bestow, dear Lord, upon our youth". Prayer for a blessing. William Cowper. 6814-6
Bestowal. Margaret Fuller. 6006-4
Bete humaine. Francis Brett Young. 6861-8
Bete humaine. Francis Brett Young. 6510-4
Beth Gelert. W.R. Spencer. 6912-6
Beth Gelert. William Robert Spencer. 6132-X,6134-6,6271-7, 6302-0,6370-5,6385 ,6497-3,6614-3,6661-5,6219-9,6304-7,6510-4,6131-1

Beth Marie. William Alexander Percy. 6036-6
Beth-El. Louis Albert Lamb. 6274-1
Betham-Edwards, Matilda Barbara
    A child's prayer. 6519-8,6456-6
    A child's hymn. 6638-0,6639-9
    Evening hymn. 6636-9
    Gethsemane. 6065-X
Bethel. Augustine Joseph Hickey Duganne. 6015-3,6113-3, 6062-5,6678-X
Bethel, Mary Ursul
    Pause. 6043-9
Bethesda. Edward Farquhar. 6939-8
Bethesda (a sequel). Arthur Hugh Clough. 6110-9
Bethesda, a sequel. Arthur Hugh Clough. 6198-2
Bethlehem. Phillips Brooks. 6006-4
Bethlehem. Bliss Carman. 6608-9
Bethlehem. Clinton Scollard. 6337-3
Bethlehem. Katharine (Hinkson) Tynan. 6216-4,6746-8,6747-6, 6608-9
The Bethlehem road. Ida Norton Munson. 6144-3
The Bethlehem star shines on! Alice Mortenson. 6065-X
Bethlehem town. Eugene Field. 6949-5
Bethlehem-town. Eugene Field. 6007-2
Bethrothed anew. Edmund Clarence Stedman. 6385-3,6429-9, 6321-7
Bethsabe bathing. George Peele. 6182-6;6315-2
Bethsabe's song. George Peele. 6436-1,6150-8
Bethune, George Washington
    Cling to thy mother. 6097-8,6627-5
    Fourth of July. 6414-0,6678-X
    He died for me. 6065-X
    Hymn to night. 6385-3
    My mother. 6097-8,6395-9
    "O Jesus! when I think of thee". 6065-X
Bethune, John
    Hymn of the church yard. 6271-7
Bethune, Norman
    A compressionist's creed. 6482-5
    Red moon. 6482-5
    The T.B.'s progress. 6482-5
Betjeman, Sir John
    Beside the seaside, sels. 6258-X
    Distant view of a provincial town. 6633-X
    East Anglian bathe. 6246-6
    The fete champetre. 6733-6
    Hunter trials. 6339-X
    A Lincolnshire tale. 6218-0
    'New king arrives in his capital by air...'. 6722-0
    Parliament Hill fields. 6210-5,6257-1
    Potpourri from a Surrey garden. 6733-6
    Upper Lambourne. 6246-6,6210-5
    Youth and age on Beaulieu River, Hants. 6210-5
Betrand Hume. Edgar Lee Masters. 6300-4
Betrayal. Hester H. Cholmondeley. 6337-3
Betrayal. Emily Dickinson. 6179-6
Betrayal. Ibn Sa'id (of Alcala La Real) 6362-4
Betrayal. John Banister Tabb. 6022-6
Betrayal. Sir Thomas Wyatt. 6436-1
The betrayal. Robert P. Tristram Coffin. 7040-X
The betrayal. Alice Furlong. 6090-0
Betrayed. Lizette Woodworth Reese. 6619-4
Betrayed. William White. 6868-5
Betrothal. Martha Ostenso. 6320-9
Betrothal. Estelle Rooks. 6850-2
The betrothal of Sigurd. William Morris. 6094-3
A betrothal. Frank Dempster Sherman. 7041-8
The betrothal. Edna St. Vincent Millay. 6513-9
The betrothed.. Rudyard Kipling. 6453-1,6732-8,6688-7,6576-7
Betsey. Unknown. 6058-7,6061-7
Betsey. W. Dayton Wegefarth. 6537-6
Betsey and I are out. Will Carleton. 6404-3,6344-6,6565-1
Betsey Baker. Unknown. 6057-9
Betsey destroys the paper. Will Carleton. 6404-3
Betsey Trotwood's cat. Louella C. Poole. 6120-6
Betsey und I hafe bust ub. James S. Burdett. 6791-3,6823-5
Betsy Bobbity's bun. Unknown. 6692-5
Betsy Lee. Thomas Edward Brown. 6809-X
Betsy's battle flag. Minna Irving. 6274-1,6356-X,6465-5, 6449-3

BETTER

Better a day of faith. Henry Burke Robins. 6337-3
"Better a rocky shore where waters run". Paradox. Margaret I. Simpson. 6764-6
A better answer (to Chloe jealous). Matthew Prior. 6152-4, 6633-X,6024-2,6208-3,6733-6,6604-6,6660-7
"Better be with the dead", fr. Macbeth. William Shakespeare. 6879-0
The better country. Oliver Goldsmith. 6240-7
Better far to pass away. Richard Molesworth Dennys. 6650-X
Better in the morning. Leander S. Coan. 6014-5
"Better it were to abide by the sea". Pace implora. Joaquin Miller. 7041-8
"Better it were to sit still by the sea". Pace implora. Unknown. 6889-8
The better job. Edgar A. Guest. 7033-7
The better land. Felicia Dorothea Hemans. 6502-3,6219-9, 6131-1
Better late than never. A.W. Curtis. 6523-6
'Better love ––'. Brian ("Korongo") Brooke. 6938-X
Better off than Lincoln. Unknown. 6248-2
The better part. Matthew Arnold. 6110-9,6199-0,6337-3,6196-6,6250-4,6371 ,6737-9,6543-0
"A better prize/There is for man...". Washington. William Herbert; Earl of Pembroke. 6980-0
A better resurrection. Christina Georgina Rossetti. 6657-7, 6737-9,6214-8,6655-0,6508-2
"Better stop dis kickin'." Unknown. 6109-5
Better than gold. Abram Joseph Ryan. 6337-3
Better than gold. Alexander Smart. 6304-7
Better than gold. Unknown. 6911-8
Better than gold. Mrs. J.M. Winton. 6167-2
"Better than grandeur, better than gold". Better than gold. Unknown. 6911-8
"Better than granite, Spoon River". Aaron Hatfield. Edgar Lee Masters. 6897-9
Better than love. Ruth Pitter. 6783-2
"Better the morsel, dry and stale". The first eight verses of chapter seventeen of the... William Dearness. 6848-0
Better things. Leigh Hunt. 6620-8,6066-8
Better things. George Macdonald. 6165-6
Better things. George McDonald. 6914-2
Better to climb and fall. Unknown. 6273-3,6583-X
"Better to mourn a blossom snatched away". Ella Wheeler Wilcox. 6238-5
"Better to smell the violet cool...". Better things. George McDonald. 6914-2
"Better to walk the realm unseen." George Macdonald. 6225-3
"Better trust all and be deceived". Frances Anne Kemble. 6238-5
Better walk than ride. Unknown. 6787-5
The better way. Lurana W. Sheldon. 6583-X
The better way. Jean Ingelow. 6240-7
Betterton or John Dryden, Thomas
What shall I do? 6563-5
Betterton, Thomas
The magnificent lover. 6830-8
Betts, Craven Langstroth
Emerson. 6820-0
Longfellow. 6820-0
Betts, Frank
The pawns. 6532-5
Betts, Gregory
Hearing Heaney read. 6767-0
Stormwatch: Fogo island. 6767-0
Betts, Idella Campbell
I can and I will. 6461-2
Betts, Maud L.
Santa Claus is coming. 6147-8
Betts, Ostie Vernona
The Evangeline trail. 6265-2
Betty and the bear. Unknown. 6909-6
Betty and the bear. Unknown. 6260-1
Betty Botter's batter. Unknown. 6697-6
Betty Lee. Elisha Norman Gunnison. 6167-2,6569-4
Betty Pringle. Mother Goose. 6135-4
"Betty Pringle had a little pig." Unknown. 6452-3
Betty to herself. Edward W. Bannard. 6274-1
Betty Zane. Thomas Dunn English. 6946-0

Betty's song to her doll. Charles Lutwidge ("Lewis Carroll") Dodgson. 6249-0
"Between Awaji and the shore". Minamoto No Kanemasa. 6852-9
Between Brielle and Manasquan. Oliver St. John Gogarty. 6930-4
"Between Cordova and Seville", fr. Images. Valery Larbaud. 6351-9
"Between a garbage pile and a peddler's tray". Yule fire in a slum. Robert Haven Schauffler. 6764-6
"Between broaf fields of wheat and corn". The stranger on the still. Thomas Buchanan Read. 6219-9,6964-9
"Between cleft foot and seraph wings". Equilibrium. Gemma D'Auria. 6839-1
"Between foam and tide/his back rises up". To a boy. Nancy Morejon. 7036-1
"Between life and life's image, battling". Allegory of torment. Pablo de (Carlos Diaz Loyola) Rokha. 6759-X
Between midnight and morning. Sir Owen Seaman. 6337-3
Between Namur and Liege. William Wordsworth. 6332-2,6199-0
"Between nose and eyes a strange contest arose". Report of an adjudged case. William Cowper. 6787-5
Between our folding lips. Thomas Edward Brown. 6809-X
Between reaches of stone. Roberta Holloway. 6808-1
"Between the amber portals of the sea". The peach tree. Edith Sitwell. 7000-0
Between the battles. Francis Sherman. 6433-7
"Between the bookends/Of my heart". Bookends. R. Scott Bowen. 6750-6
"Between the circling ocean sea". The limit of lands. Andrew Lang. 6771-9
"Between the dreamy waltzes". De trop. L. W.. 7021-3
"Between the dusk of a summer night", fr. Hawthorn. William Ernest Henley. 6123-0
"Between the fragrant rows of corn he strides". Illinois farmer. Beulah Jackson Charmley. 6750-6
"Between the grasses in the marsh". The marsh-spider. Robert P. Tristram Coffin. 7040-X
"Between the hands, between the brows". Love-lily. Dante Gabriel Rossetti. 6828-6
"Between the heart and the lips we stay..words". To all our dead. Lucy Masterman. 7031-0
"Between the hedges of the centuries." Gilbert Waterhouse. 6589-9
Between the lights. Unknown. 6889-8
Between the lines. Wilfred Wilson Gibson. 6332-2,6474-4, 6542-2
Between the lines. Ernest Radford. 6875-8
Between the lines. Ernest Radford. 6770-0
"Between the lion and the lamb". Song for March. Robert P. Tristram Coffin. 7040-X
"Between the midnight and the morn". Ballade of Acheron. Rosamund Marriott ("Graham R. Tomson") Watson. 6770-0
"Between the moondawn and the sundwon here". On the cliffs. Algernon Charles Swinburne. 6828-6
Between the rapids. Archibald Lampman. 7041-8
"Between the roadside and the wood". A windflower. Bliss Carman. 6656-9,7041-8
"Between the salt sea-send before". A green wave. William ("Fiona Macleod") Sharp. 6997-5,6793-X
Between the showers. Amy Levy. 6875-8
"Between the songs and silences of the flicker". The flicker on the fence. S.M. McManus. 6929-0
Between the sunken sun and the new moon. Paul Hamilton Hayne. 6300-4,6121-4
Between the sunset and the sea. Algernon Charles Swinburne. 6052-8
Between the two poles of politeness. Paul Eluard. 6803-0
Between two loves. Thomas Augustine Daly. 6089-7,6320-9, 6653-4,6464-7
"Between two unknown trees I stood". Fantasy in a forest. Leah Bodine Drake. 6783-2
"Between us, stone on stone, we built a tall". Misunderstanding. May Richstone. 6750-6
"Betwen the moaning of the mountain stream". In shadowland. Sir Joseph Noel Paton. 6873-1
"Betwixt mine eye and heart a league is took". Sonnet 047 ("Betwixt mine eye"). William Shakespeare. 6447-7
"Betwixt he actual and unseen, alone". Beethoven. Edward

Carpenter. 7014-0
"Betwixt the quarters, flows a golden sea". Battle of Actium, fr. Aeneid. Vergil. 6933-9
"Betwixt two fires, the suna and the earth...". Thus sang the waters. Otakar Brezina. 6763-8
Betz, Annette
   Memory. 6799-9
Bevan, Edwyn R. (tr.)
   News of war. Aeschylus, 6435-3
   An only son. Leonidas of Tarentum, 6435-3
   Shepherd. Leonidas of Tarentum, 6435-3
   Time. Leonidas of Tarentum, 6435-3
   A wayside grave. Leonidas of Tarentum, 6435-3
Bevare of the vidders. Unknown. 6139-7
The beverley maid and the tinker. Unknown. 6157-5
Beverly, Katharine
   Dreams are so pale. 6178-8
   Night song. 6178-8
Beville, Anna McIntosh
   Twilight time. 6818-9
Bevington, L. S.
   Roses. 6770-0
Bevington, Laura S.
   Love's depth. 7015-9
Bevington, Louisa S.
   The valley of remorse. 7037-X
Bevvenuto's valentine. Elinor Wylie. 6019-6,6037-4
"Bewail not much, my parents! me, the prey". On an infant. Unknown (Greek). 6814-6
"Bewailing in my chamber thus allone". The coming of love, fr. The kingis quhair. James I; King of Scotland. 6845-6
"Bewar, squier, yeman, and page". A warning to those who serve lords. Unknown. 6881-2
Beware. Henry Wadsworth Longfellow. 6083-8,6441-8,6004-2, 6560-0,6652-6
Beware. Sir Walter Scott. 6438-8
Beware. Dora Sigerson Shorter. 6844-8
"Beware fair maide of muskie courtiers oathes". Unknown. 6933-9
"Beware of building! I intended". Epigram on his garden shed (1). William Cowper. 6814-6
"Beware of her fair hair, for she excels". Percy Bysshe Shelley. 6238-5
Beware of the silver grizzly. Vachel Lindsay. 6206-7
Beware of the wolf. A.L.O. E. 6131-1
Beware the hawk. Frances B. Huston. 6799-9
"Beware the lurking scorpion, friend". Unknown. 6435-3
"Beware this man who carries in". Martyr. Frances Minturn Howard. 6979-7
Beware!. Unknown (German) 6004-8,6288-1,6560-0
"'Beware!' 'Tis a voice from the". Pharaoh to Alexander. Unknown. 6848-0
'Beware'.. John C. Mathis. 6983-5
"Beware, my friend! of crystal brook". On an ugly fellow. Unknown (Greek). 6814-6
"Beware, take heede, take heede, beware, beware" William Baldwin. 6380-2
Beware, wass. Davies Aberpennar. 6360-8
Bewe, (?)
   Actaeon. 6436-1
"Bewhiskered sprite/Of unrestrained delight". I had a dog. O. R.. 7008-6
Bewick and Graham. Unknown. 6185-0
The bewildered guest. William Dean Howells. 6102-8,6076-5
Bewildering emotions. James Whitcomb Riley. 6128-1
"Bewitching drowned what time it is". Vicente Huidobro. 6759-X
Bewsher, Paul
   The dawn patrol. 7026-4
   Nox mortis. 7029-9
   Searchlights. 7027-2
The bewteis of the flute-ball. Unknown. 6845-6
Bey (William Manns, II), Yillie
   Making of a militant. 7024-8
Beyond. Phoebe Cary. 6969-X
Beyond. Rose Terry Cooke. 6749-2,6919-3
Beyond. Alma Robison Higbee. 6761-1
Beyond. Lionel Johnson. 6250-4
Beyond. Thomas S. Jones Jr. 6338-1,6619-4
Beyond. John Gibson Lockhart. 6337-3
Beyond. James Abraham Martling. 6952-5
Beyond. John Richard Moreland. 6648-8
Beyond. Allan Munier. 6274-1
Beyond. Adelaide Anne Procter. 6957-6
Beyond. Unknown. 6926-6
Beyond. Unknown. 6014-5
Beyond ("What is there beyond?"). William Cullen Bryant. 6303-9
Beyond a mountain. Witter Bynner. 6347-0
Beyond Cathay. Madge S. Banks. 6269-5
Beyond Connecticut, beyond the sea. John Peale Bishop. 7017-5
"Beyond a ridge of pine with russet tips". Thistle-down. Emily Pauline ("Tekahionwake") Johnson. 6837-5
Beyond death. Alfred Noyes. 6151-6
Beyond debate. Hervey Allen. 6326-8
Beyond grief. Richard Leon Spain. 6750-6
Beyond Kerguelen. Henry Clarence Kendall. 6784-0
Beyond knowing. Nina Willis Walter. 6316-0
Beyond knowledge. Alice Meynell. 6955-X
Beyond lies America. Carlos Bulosan. 6761-1
"Beyond Ortygia there lies an isle", fr. The Odyssey. Homer. 6251-2
Beyond Rathkelly. Francis Carlin. 6441-8
Beyond Rhodope, once. Leslie Nelson Jennings. 6038-2
"Beyond resilient flow and black-sand beach". The flow of eternal light and power. Mary Mullis Hinricks. 6857-X
"Beyond that mist-blue, light-shy blur...". 'Yea, a sword shall pierce through thy own soul...' Mary Belden James. 6847-2
"Beyond the angles of the cube it lies". Fourth dimension. Jessie Young Norton. 6841-3
Beyond the bars. George E. Bowen. 6274-1
"Beyond the bay of silver grey". Eventide at Muizenberg. Francis Watermeyer. 6800-6
"Beyond the black hole of the open door". A mystery. Godfrey Green. 6857-X
Beyond the blue. Emily Pauline ("Tekahionwake") Johnson. 6837-5
"Beyond the branches of the pine" Richard Watson Gilder. 7041-8
Beyond the breakers, sels. George Sterling. 6954-1
"Beyond the cheat of time, here where you...". The light of the house. Louise Imogen Guiney. 7041-8
Beyond the dunes. Muriel F. Hochdorf. 6850-2
"Beyond the end of paradise". A ballad of lost lovers. Agnes Mary F. ("Madame Duclaux") Robinson. 6770-0
"Beyond the farthest glimmering star". George Denison Prentice. 6238-5
Beyond the final breath. Lilith Lorraine. 6648-8
"Beyond the forbidding fence" Keiho Soga. 6981-9
"Beyond the gate I see a hand". At the gate. Sir Henry Howarth Bashford. 7007-8
"Beyond the harbour bar the sun goes down". Adrift. James Chapman Woods. 6997-5
Beyond the haze. Unknown. 6273-3
"Beyond the hill's gray". Unknown. 6364-0
Beyond the horizon. Robert Freeman. 6337-3
"Beyond the howl and hiccough of the tune". Jazz on the island. Leonora Speyer. 7038-7
"Beyond the lake it is gleaming...". Shattered dreams. Clara Keck Heflebower. 6906-1
"Beyond the midland rocky range". The California year. Benjamin Franklin Taylor. 6815-4
Beyond the night. Samuel Minturn Peck. 6461-2
Beyond the path of the outmost sun. Rudyard Kipling. 7012-4
Beyond the Potomac. Paul Hamilton Hayne. 6074-9,6113-3
"Beyond the path of the outmost sun...". Dedication, fr. Barrack room ballads. Rudyard Kipling. 6810-3
"Beyond the sea there's much contented". 'Bwana Tumbo'-the great hunter. Walter Beverly Crane. 6995-9
"Beyond the smiling and the weeping." Horatius Bonar. 6240-7,6302-0,6385-3
Beyond the stars. Charles Hanson Towne. 6347-0,6336-5,6648-8
"Beyond the stars that shine in golden glory". Unknown. 6238-5

BEYOND

Beyond the storm. Janice Blanchard. 6750-6
Beyond the veil. Henry Vaughan. 6189-3,6250-4
Beyond the violet rays. Helena Coleman. 6115-X
Beyond the wall. J.J. Maloney. 6870-7
Beyond the war. Olive Tilford Dargan. 6029-3
"Beyond the window is a windy hill". Faculty meeting. David Morton. 6880-4
Beyond tomorrow. Minnie Hite Moody. 6841-3
Beyond understanding. Marion Walley. 6750-6
Beyond wars. David Morton. 6946-0
"Beyond, beyond the mountain line". Dreams. Cecil Frances Alexander. 6930-4
The beyond. Ella Wheeler Wilcox. 6303-9,6337-3
Beyond?. George Arthur Greene. 6174-5,6507-4
Bezruc, Petr
    I, sels. Paul Selver (tr.). 6763-8,6886-3
    Kijov. Paul Selver (tr.). 6886-3
    Kyjov. Paul Selver (tr.). 6763-8
    Moravian village. Paul Selver (tr.). 6763-8
    Ostrava. Paul Selver (tr.). 6763-8
    Peterswald. Paul Selver (tr.). 6763-8
    The pitman. Paul Selver (tr.). 6886-3
    Thou and I. Paul Selver (tr.). 6763-8
    Who will take my place? Paul Selver (tr.). 6763-8
The Bhagavad Gita, sels. Unknown (Sanskrit) 6337-3
Bhartrihari
    Peace. Paul Elmer More (tr.). 6253-9
    Peace. Paul Elmer More (tr.). 6253-9
    Time. Paul Elmer More (tr.). 7039-6,6879-0
Bhavani. Unknown (Newari) 7013-2
Bhimasena. Unknown (Newari) 7013-2
Bhimasena (2). Unknown (Newari) 7013-2
"Bi a forrest as I gan fare" Unknown. 6380-2
Bi-focal trouble. Edgar A. Guest. 6869-3
Bialik, Chaim Nachman
    The death of the wilderness, sels. Maurice Samuel (tr.). 7039-6
    Songs of the people, sels. Maurice Samuel (tr.). 7039-6
Bianca among the nightingales. Elizabeth Barrett Browning. 6657-7
"Bianca! fair Bianca! who could dwell". Bianca's dream. Thomas Hood. 6974-6
Bianchi, Martha Gilbert Dickinson
    The night-watch. 6006-4
    One day. 6320-9
    Twilight at Florence. 6331-4
    The watcher. 6006-4
    "What heart but fears a fragrance?". 6338-1
    The worlds. 6762-X
Bianor
    "This man that is mean...". F.L. Lucas (tr.). 6251-2
    Unseen riches. Walter Leaf (tr.). 6435-3
"Bibamus hilares." Unknown. 6563-5
Bibesco, Elizabeth
    Sonnet ("There is no comfort"). 6780-8
Bible
    Accinge sicut. 6830-8
    Afferte domino. 6830-8
    "And Jacob went out from Beersheba..." 6958-4
    "And the Lord God caused a deep sleep..." 6958-4
    Anthems for the inauguration of Jerusalem. 6488-4
    An antiphonal (Psalm XXIV) 6153-2
    Beatitudes. 6143-5,6491-4,6503-1,6304-7
    The beatitudes of Jesus, fr. Matthew. 6337-3
    "Behold, the Lord God will come," fr. Isaiah. 6136-2
    Benedic, anima mea. 6830-8
    Benedictus, fr. Luke. 6337-3
    "Blessed are the poor in spirit," fr. St. Matthew. 6183-4
    "Blessed of the Lord of his land," fr. Deuteronomy. 6466-3
    The book of Ecclesiastes, sels. 6879-0
    The book of Ezekiel. 6958-4
    The book of Genesis. 6958-4
    The book of Genesis. 6958-4
    Canite tuba. 6830-8
    Cantemus domino. 6830-8
    Cast thy bread upon the waters, fr. Ecclesiastes. 7039-6
    The Christmas story, fr. Luke. 6337-3
    The closing doxology, fr. Psalm 150. 6337-3
    Come unto me, fr. Matthew. 6337-3
    Consurge, consurge. 6830-8
    Creation, fr. Ecclesiasticus. 6179-6
    The creation, fr. Genesis. 6143-5
    Cujus adjutor es. 6830-8
    David's lament for Jonathan. 6084-6
    David's lament, fr. Book of Samuel. 6125-7,6143-5
    De profundis, fr. Psalm 130. 6337-3
    Death of the King of Babylon, fr. Isaiah XIV. 6472-8
    Death's conqueror, fr. Corinthians. 6337-3
    The deliverance of Jehovah, fr. Psalm 27. 6730-1
    Deus, quis similis. 6830-8
    Deutero, fr. Isaiah. 6143-5
    Domine probasti. 6830-8
    Domine, audivi. 6830-8
    Domini est terra. 6830-8
    "Doth the hawk fly by thy widom, and stretch" 7020-5
    The eagle. 7020-5
    Ecce domisti. 6830-8
    Ecclesiastes, sels. 6282-2,6490-6,6143-5
    Ecclesiasticus, sels. 6252-0
    Ego flos campi. 6830-8
    Ephesians, sels. 6143-5
    The eternal quest, fr. Job. 6337-3
    The everlasting arms, fr. Psalm 91. 6730-1
    Evil unbounded and infinite good. 6488-4
    Exodus 15. 6732-8
    Famous men, fr. Ecclesiasticus. 6179-6
    Fear not: for behold, I bring..good tidings, fr. St. Luke. 6747-1
    Fili mi, custodi. 6830-8
    Finis venit. 6830-8
    The first Christmas, fr. St. Luke. 6465-5
    First Corinthians, sels. 6107-9
    First Corinthinans, sels. 6143-5,6527-9
    The first flight. 7020-5
    The first rainbow. 7020-5
    The first six verses of the ninetieth psalm. Robert Burns (tr.). 6848-0
    From psalm 137 (1). and Felicia Hemans, Luis de Camoens (tr.). 6848-0
    From psalm 137 (2). and Felicia Hemans, Luis de Camoens (tr.). 6848-0
    The garden of Eden. 7020-5
    Genesis VI. 6732-8
    Genesis, sels. 6282-2,6193-1
    Glory of God revealed in Jesus, fr. Second Corinthians. 6337-3
    The glory of God, fr. Psalms. 6136-2
    The, fr. The Book of Job glory of the horse. 7010-8
    'Go to now, ye rich' 6954-1
    God our refuge, fr. Psalm 91. 6337-3
    God, our dwelling place, fr. Psalm 90. 6337-3
    'Good tidings unto the meek' 6954-1
    Good tidings, fr. Luke. 6337-3
    The goodness of God. 6396-9
    Gospel according to St. Luke, sels. 6243-5
    Gospel according to St. Matthew, sels. 6143-5
    The gospel of Saint Matthew. 6958-4
    The greatness of love, fr. First Corinthians. James Moffatt (tr.). 6337-3
    A hallelujah chorus, fr. Psalm 248. 6337-3
    "The hand of the Lord was upon me..." 6958-4
    "Hast thou entered into the treasures of the snow?" 7020-5
    Hast thou given the horse strength?, fr. Book of Job. 6125-7
    The heavens above and the law within, fr. Psalm 19. 6730-1
    The heavens declare the glory of God, fr. Psalm 19 6337-3
    The heavens, fr. Psalm 19 6125-7
    Ho, everyone that thirsteth, fr. Isaiah. 6337-3
    Homo natus de muliere. 6830-8
    Hosea. 6143-5
    How is the gold become dim, fr. Lamentations of Jeremiah. 6125-7
    How the mighty have fallen, fr. Samuel. 6665-8
    The hymn of the world within, fr. Psalm 103. 6730-1

BIBLE

Hymn of the world without, fr. Psalm 104. 6730-1
I am the rose of Sharon, fr. Song of Solomon. 6125-7
I will lift up mine eyes, fr. Proverbs. 6132-X
"I will put enmities", fr. Genesis. 6282-2
Immortality, fr. Job. 6730-1
Imputantur. 7020-5
In convertendo. 6830-8
In dimido dierum. 6830-8
Inclyti Israel. 6830-8
Intemperance, fr. Isaiah. 6337-3
Isaiah LII, sels. John Wycliffe (tr.). 6334-9
Isaiah XL. 6490-6
Isaiah, sels. 6334-9,6134-5
Isiah XIV, sels. 6472-8
Jeremiah's lamentation. 6143-5
Jevohah's immovable throne, fr. Psalm 93. 6730-1
Job 14. 6732-8
Job longeth for death, fr. Job. 6472-8
Job's comforters, fr. Job. 6730-1
Job's curse, fr. The book of Job. 7039-6
Job's entreaty, fr. The book of Job. 7039-6
Job, sels. 6472-8
Joel. 6143-5
Judith 16. 6732-8
"Keep thy tongue from evil", fr. Psalms. 6623-2
The king of glory. 6373-X
Knowledge and wisdom. 6574-0
A lament in exile (Psalm 137) 6153-2
The lament of David over Saul and Jonathan. 6228-8,6396-9
The lament of David, fr. Samuel. 6334-9
Lament over Saul, fr. Samuel. 6087-0
Laudate dominum. 6125-7
Laudate dominum. 6830-8
The law within, fr. Psalm 19. 6337-3
The leader. 6512-0
Leave it all quietly So God, fr. Psalm 62. James Moffatt (tr.). 6337-3
Legislators. 6954-1
"Let the day perish wherein I was born", fr. Job. 6879-0
Let us now praise famous men, fr. Ecclesiasticus. 6087-0,6334-9,6625-9,6125-7
Levate signum. 6830-8
Lift up your heads, O ye gates! 6512-0
A little cloud. 7020-5
The Lord is a man of war, fr. Exodus. 6665-8
The Lord is my light, fr. Psalms. 6805-7
The Lord is my shepherd, fr. Psalm 23 6183-4,6132-X, 6337-3,6527-9
"The Lord possessed me," fr. Proverbs. 6282-2
The Lord's prayer, fr. St. Matthew. 6337-3,6418-3
Lord, thou hast been our refuge. Psalm 90. 6472-8
A love idyl, fr. The song of songs. 6153-2
Love, fr. Corinthians. 6179-6
Love, fr. The song of Solomon. 6153-2,6337-3
Luke, sels. 6282-2
The magnificat, fr. Luke. 6337-3
Man that is born of a woman, fr. Job. 6472-8
"Man that is born of woman", fr. Job. 6879-0
Matthew 6. 6732-8
Matthew 7. 6732-8
A message to the young. 6396-9
Micah. 6143-5
Momento creatoris tui. 6830-8
Mulierem fortem. 6830-8
My light and my salvation, fr. Psalm 27 6337-3
"My son, keep my words," fr. Proverbs. 6317-9
The mystery of death, fr. First Corinthians. 6107-9
Nunc dimittis, fr. St. Luke. 6543-0
"Oh that I knew where I might find him," fr. Job. 6337-3
The ocean, fr. Psalm 107. 6730-1
Omnes gentes plaudite. 6830-8
Omnia haec. 6830-8
On death - a sonnet, fr. Ecclesiasticus. 6337-3
The one hundred and forty-eighth psalm paraphrased. George Wither (tr.). 6848-0
Osculetur me. 6830-8
Our refuge, fr. Psalm 46. 6337-3

Out of the whirlwind, fr. The book of Job. 7039-6
Palaces. 6954-1
Paraphrase of a portion of the forty-second psalm. Ibbie McColm Wilson (tr.). 6848-0
Paraphrase of psalm 137. Henry Carrington (tr.). 6848-0
Paraphrase of psalm 148. Felicia Dorothea Hemans (tr.). 6848-0
A paraphrase on psalm 114 John Milton (tr.). 6848-0
Pereat dies. 6830-8
The pilgrim's song, fr. Psalm 121. 6730-1
Praeparate scutum. 6830-8
Praise of famous men, fr. Ecclesiastes. 6337-3
Praise of famous men, fr. Ecclesiastics. 6337-3
The praise of God. 6396-9,6288-1
Prophecy. 7020-5
A prophecy. 6179-6
Prosperity. 6954-1
The protection of Jehovah, fr. Psalm 13. 6730-1
Proverbs. 6958-4
Proverbs 005. 6732-8
Proverbs 030. 6732-8
Proverbs 031. 6732-8
Proverbs, sel. 6958-4
Proverbs, sels. 6143-5,6282-2,6282-2,6143-5,6317-9
Psalm ("I will lift"). 6466-3
Psalm 001. John Milton (tr.). 6848-0
Psalm 001, fr. The book of psalms. 7039-6
Psalm 001. 6418-3
Psalm 001. Richard Mather et al. (tr.). 6121-4
Psalm 002. Peter McNeill (tr.). 6848-0
Psalm 003. Richard Allison (tr.). 6848-0
Psalm 004. John Arnold (tr.). 6848-0
Psalm 005 Charles Wesley (tr.). 6848-0
Psalm 006. John Playford (tr.). 6848-0
Psalm 007. Thomas Sternhold (tr.). 6848-0
Psalm 008 Emily F. Carleton (tr.). 6848-0
Psalm 008. 6143-5,6153-2,6418-3,6143-5,6163-X
Psalm 009. Isaac P. Noyes (tr.). 6848-0
Psalm 010. George Wither (tr.). 6848-0
Psalm 011. Abraham Coles (tr.). 6848-0
Psalm 012 6848-0
Psalm 013. Francis Davidson (tr.). 6848-0
Psalm 013. Francis Davison (tr.). 6271-7
Psalm 014 Giovanni Battista Cotta (tr.). 6848-0
Psalm 015. 6421-3
Psalm 017. 6848-0
Psalm 019. Joseph Addison (tr.). 6848-0,6730-1
Psalm 019, fr. The book of psalms. 7039-6
Psalm 019. 6253-9,6418-3,6421-3,6490-6,6498-1,6501
Psalm 019. Richard Mather et al. (tr.). 6121-4
Psalm 019. Isaac Watts (tr.). 6271-7
Psalm 015. Nahum Tate and Nicholas Beady (tr.). 6848-0
Psalm 020. George Wither (tr.). 6848-0
Psalm 021. Peter McNeill (tr.). 6848-0
Psalm 022. Cotton Mather (tr.). 6848-0
Psalm 022. 6732-8
Psalm 023. Joseph Addison (tr.). 6848-0
Psalm 023 (He leadeth me). 6848-0
Psalm 023. 7039-6,6143-5,6373-X,6418-3,6464-7,6534-1, 6565 ,6501-5,6503-1,6654-2,6623-2,6732-8,6491 ,6585-6
Psalm 024. Horatius Bonar (tr.). 6848-0
Psalm 024, fr. The book of psalms. 7039-6
Psalm 024. 6052-8,6143-5,6153-2,6421-3,6418-3,6565 , 6490-6,6585-6,6143-5
Psalm 024. Richard Mather et al. (tr.). 6008-0
Psalm 025 Edward Clare (tr.). 6848-0
Psalm 026 6848-0
Psalm 027 Archibald Ross (tr.). 6848-0
Psalm 028. Thomas Sternhold (tr.). 6848-0
Psalm 029. James I; King of Scotland (tr.). 6848-0
Psalm 030. George Wither (tr.). 6848-0
Psalm 031:15. My times are in thy hand. Anna Letitia Waring (tr.). 6848-0
Psalm 032:8. The still small voice. Anna Shipton (tr.). 6848-0
Psalm 033. 6143-5
Psalm 033. Sing to Jehovah a new song. John Quincy Adams (tr.). 684-0
Psalm 034 6848-0

BIBLE

Psalm 035. Abner Jones (tr.). 6848-0
Psalm 036 6848-0
Psalm 037. Isaac Watts (tr.). 6848-0
Psalm 038. George Wither (tr.). 6848-0
Psalm 039. George Wither (tr.). 6848-0
Psalm 040 6848-0
Psalm 041. George Wither (tr.). 6848-0
Psalm 042, fr. The book of psalms. 7039-6
Psalm 042. 6143-5,6418-3,6490-6,6143-5
Psalm 043. George Wither (tr.). 6848-0
Psalm 043. 6143-5
Psalm 044. Abraham Coles (tr.). 6848-0
Psalm 044. 6282-2
Psalm 045. Peter McNeill (tr.). 6848-0
Psalm 046 and Martin Luther, Thomas Carlyle (tr.). 6848-0
Psalm 046 and Thomas Carlyle, Martin Luther (tr.). 6848-0
Psalm 046. 6051-X,6334-9,6490-6,6501-5,6143-5,6418
Psalm 046. Thom Carlyle (fr. tr. of Martin Luther) (tr.). 6271-7
Psalm 046. George Sandys (tr.). 6198-2
Psalm 046. Isaac Watts (tr.). 6271-7
Psalm 047. Abner Jones (tr.). 6848-0
Psalm 048 6848-0
Psalm 049. Thomas Sternhold (tr.). 6848-0
Psalm 050. Thomas Ravenscroft (tr.). 6848-0
Psalm 051. Michelangelo Buonarroti (tr.). 6848-0
Psalm 051, stanzas suggested by. Archdeacon Moore (tr.). 6848-0
Psalm 052. Abraham Coles (tr.). 6848-0
Psalm 053 Charles Haddon Spurgeon (tr.). 6848-0
Psalm 054. John Hopkins (tr.). 6848-0
Psalm 055. 6848-0
Psalm 056. 6861-8
Psalm 056. George Wither (tr.). 6848-0
Psalm 057. Mary Alcock (tr.). 6848-0
Psalm 058. John Hopkins (tr.). 6848-0
Psalm 059. Nahum Tate and Nicholas Brady (tr.). 6848-0
Psalm 060. Peter McNeill (tr.). 6848-0
Psalm 061. Isaac Watts (tr.). 6848-0
Psalm 062. Isaac Watts (tr.). 6848-0
Psalm 063. Mary Alcock (tr.). 6848-0
Psalm 064. Abraham Coles (tr.). 6848-0
Psalm 065. Henry Vaughan (tr.). 6848-0
Psalm 066. Abner Jones (tr.). 6848-0
Psalm 067. 6848-0
Psalm 068 George Sandys (tr.). 6848-0
Psalm 069. Isaac Watts (tr.). 6848-0
Psalm 070. John Hopkins (tr.). 6848-0
Psalm 071. Robert Grant (tr.). 6848-0
Psalm 072. James Montgomery (tr.). 6219-9
Psalm 073 Henry Howard, Earl of Surrey (tr.). 6848-0
Psalm 074. Thou art, o God. Thomas Moore (tr.). 6848-0
Psalm 075. Peter McNeill (tr.). 6848-0
Psalm 076. Abraham Coles (tr.). 6848-0
Psalm 077. Isaac Watts (tr.). 6848-0
Psalm 078. Abraham Coles (tr.). 6848-0
Psalm 079. John Hopkins (tr.). 6848-0
Psalm 080. John Milton (tr.). 6848-0
Psalm 081. John Milton (tr.). 6848-0
Psalm 082. John Milton (tr.). 6848-0
Psalm 083. John Milton (tr.). 6848-0
Psalm 084. Henry Francis Lyte (tr.). 6219-9
Psalm 085. John Milton (tr.). 6848-0
Psalm 086. John Milton (tr.). 6848-0
Psalm 087. John Newton (tr.). 6848-0
Psalm 087. John Newton (tr.). 6219-9
Psalm 088. John Milton (tr.). 6848-0
Psalm 088. 6641-0
Psalm 089 6848-0
Psalm 084. John Milton (tr.). 6848-0
Psalm 090. 6143-5,6472-8,6490-6
Psalm 090. Isaac Watts (tr.). 6219-9
Psalm 091 6861-8
Psalm 091 James Montgomery (tr.). 6848-0
Psalm 091. 6143-5,6490-6,6501-5
Psalm 092. Abraham Coles (tr.). 6848-0
Psalm 093. 6848-0
Psalm 093. Richard Mather et al. (tr.). 6008-0,6121-4

Psalm 093. Sir Philip Sidney (tr.). 6438-8
Psalm 094. Abner Jones (tr.). 6848-0
Psalm 095 6861-8
Psalm 095 6848-0
Psalm 095, fr. The book of psalms. 7039-6
Psalm 095. 6501-5,6575-9
Psalm 096. Philip Sidney (tr.). 6848-0
Psalm 096. 6143-5
Psalm 096. Thomas Steinhold (tr.). 6438-8
Psalm 097. John Hopkins (tr.). 6848-0
Psalm 097. 6421-3
Psalm 098. Abraham Coles (tr.). 6848-0
Psalm 098. 6418-3,6641-0
Psalm 098. Isaac Watts (tr.). 6219-9
Psalm 099. Abraham Coles (tr.). 6848-0
Psalm 100. William Kethe (tr.). 6848-0
Psalm 100. 6490-6,6219-9,6271-7
Psalm 100. Richard Mather et al. (tr.). 6121-4
Psalm 100. Isaac Watts and Charles Wesley (tr.). 6219-9
Psalm 101. Isaac Watts (tr.). 6848-0
Psalm 102, verses 6 and 7. Robert Southwell (tr.). 6848-0
Psalm 103 6861-8
Psalm 103, fr. The book of psalms. 7039-6
Psalm 103. 6143-5,6421-3,6501-5,6143-5
Psalm 103. The divine love unchangeable. James Montgomery (tr.). 6848-0
Psalm 104. 6253-9
Psalm 104. Paraphrased. James Thomson (tr.). 6848-0
Psalm 105. 6848-0
Psalm 106. Abraham Coles (tr.). 6848-0
Psalm 107 6125-7
Psalm 107, sels. 6107-9,6228-8
Psalm 108. Thomas Norton (tr.). 6848-0
Psalm 109. Abraham Coles (tr.). 6848-0
Psalm 110. Abraham Coles (tr.). 6848-0
Psalm 111. Isaac Watts (tr.). 6848-0
Psalm 112. Isaac Watts (tr.). 6848-0
Psalm 113. Isaac Watts (tr.). 6848-0
Psalm 114. C.H. Terrot (tr.). 6848-0
Psalm 115. George Wither (tr.). 6848-0
Psalm 115. Joseph Addison (tr.). 6848-0
Psalm 116 6848-0
Psalm 117. Isaac Watts (tr.). 6848-0
Psalm 117. Isaac Watts (tr.). 6219-9,6271-7
Psalm 118 Edward Clare (tr.). 6848-0
Psalm 119. Abraham Coles (tr.). 6848-0
Psalm 120. 6848-0
Psalm 121 6861-8
Psalm 121, fr. The book of psalms. 7039-6
Psalm 121. 6107-9,6179-6,6252-0,6228-8,6143-5,6501 , 6418-3,6421-3,,6143-5,6107-9,6179-6,6228-8
Psalm 121. Richard Mather et al. (tr.). 6121-4
Psalm 121. Isaac Watts (tr.). 6219-9
Psalm 121. Divine protection. Isaac Watts (tr.). 6848-0
Psalm 122. Abraham Coles (tr.). 6848-0
Psalm 123. Cotton Mather (tr.). 6848-0
Psalm 123, fr. The book of psalms. 7039-6
Psalm 124 6848-0
Psalm 125 6848-0
Psalm 126 6848-0
Psalm 126. 6334-9
Psalm 127, sel. 6958-4
Psalm 127. The sleep. Elizabeth Barrett Browning (tr.). 6848-0
Psalm 128. Isaac Watts (tr.). 6848-0
Psalm 129. Isaac Watts (tr.). 6848-0
Psalm 137, sels. Felicia Dorothea Hemans and Luis de Camoens (tr.). 6848-0
Psalm 130. James Montgomery (tr.). 6848-0
Psalm 130. Paraphrase. Sir Thomas Wyatt (tr.). 6848-0
Psalm 131. Cotton Mather (tr.). 6848-0
Psalm 132. Isaac Watts (tr.). 6848-0
Psalm 133. Sir John Bowring and Gerbrand Brederode (tr.). 6848-0
Psalm 133 Gerbrand Brederode and John Bowring (tr.). 6848-0
Psalm 133. 6008-0
Psalm 134. Isaac P. Noyes (version of Edward VI) (tr.). 6848-0

Psalm 135. Abner Jones (tr.). 6848-0
Psalm 136. John Milton (tr.). 6848-0
Psalm 137. Fitz-Greene Halleck (tr.). 6848-0
Psalm 137. J.F. Simmons (tr.). 6848-0
Psalm 137. William Dearness (tr.). 6848-0
Psalm 137, fr. The book of psalms. 7039-6
Psalm 137, sels. 6490-6,6732-8
Psalm 137. 6143-5
Psalm 137. Timothy Dwight (tr.). 6121-4
Psalm 137. Richard Mather et al. (tr.). 6121-4
Psalm 137. By the rivers of Babylon we sat down and...
  George Gordon, 6th Baron Byron (tr.). 6848-0
Psalm 137. By the waters of Babylon. Christina Georgina
  Rossetti (tr.). 6848-0
Psalm 137. The Jewish captive. Elizabeth Oakes (Prince)
  Smith (tr.). 6848-0
Psalm 138. Thomas Norton (tr.). 6848-0
Psalm 139. Sir Philip Sidney (tr.). 6438-8
Psalm 139. 'Whither shall I flee from thy presence?'
  Lydia Huntley Sigourney (tr.). 6848-0
Psalm 140. George Wither (tr.). 6848-0
Psalm 141. Abraham Coles (tr.). 6848-0
Psalm 142. Cotton Mather (tr.). 6848-0
Psalm 143. Nahum Tate and Nicholas Brady (tr.). 6848-0
Psalm 144. 6848-0
Psalm 145 6848-0
Psalm 146. Abraham Coles (tr.). 6848-0
Psalm 147. Isaac Watts (tr.). 6848-0
Psalm 147. 6490-6,6163-X
Psalm 148. John Stuart Blackie (tr.). 6848-0
Psalm 148. Richard Mant (tr.). 6848-0
Psalm 148 (hymn). John Ogilvie (tr.). 6848-0
Psalm 148. 6143-5,6252-0,6418-3,6490-6,6545-7,6641
Psalm 148. George Wither (tr.). 6219-9
Psalm 149. Cotton Mather (tr.). 6848-0
Psalm 149. 6163-X
Psalm 150 6125-7
Psalm 150. Peter McNeill (tr.). 6848-0
Psalm 150. 6334-9,6143-5,6163-X
Psalm 156. 6334-9
Psalm o23. 6143-5
Psalm o23. James Merrick (tr.). 6271-7
Psalm of David ("The earth is the Lord's..."). 6466-3
A psalm of David. Richard Mather et al. (tr.). 6008-0,
  6121-4
A psalm of praise. 6153-2
Psalms, sels. 6304-7
Quaerite me. 6830-8
Quam pulchra. 6830-8
Quam pulchri. 6830-8
Quare mater. 6830-8
"The queen stood on thy right hand," fr. Psalms. 6282-2
Quemadmodum. 6830-8
Qui est iste. 6830-8
Quia nocte. 6830-8
Quomodo sedet. 6830-8
Quotations for peace day. 6051-X
A rebuke to the proud, fr. The Book of Job. 6625-9
The refuge, fr. Psalm 46 6730-1
Remember now thy creator, fr. Ecclesiastes. 6153-2,6304-
  7,6337-3,6464-7,7039-6
Requirite in libro. 6830-8
Romans, sels. 6143-5
Ruth and Naomi. 6143-5
Ruth to Naomi, fr. Ruth. 6337-3
Ruth, fr. The story of Ruth. 6805-7
Ruth, sels, fr. Ruth. 6732-8
Satan's speech, fr. Genesis. 6193-1
The search, fr. Psalm 42. 6730-1
The searcher of hearts (Psalm CXXXIX) 6153-2
The searcher of hearts is thy maker, fr. Psalm 139.
  6730-1
The seasons. 7020-5
Selections. 6052-8,6214-8,6087-0,6623-2,6289-X,6334-9,
  6416-7,6466-3,6490-6,6496-,6501-5,6527-9,6601-1,6625-
  9,6732-8,6602-
The sermon on the mount, fr. Matthew. 6732-8,6418-3
The shepherd's psalm. 6512-0
The silver cord. 7020-5
The sluggard - a sonnet, fr. Proverbs. 6337-3,6488-4

Solomon, sels. 6730-1
Song of Moses, fr. Exodus. 6567-8
Song of Solomon. 6732-8,6649-6,6143-5
Song of Solomon. 6958-4
Song of Solomon II:8-17. 6490-6
The song of songs, fr. Solomon. 6236-9,6232-6,6153-2,
  6513-9
Song of the thunderstorm. 6488-4
A song of trust. 6512-0
Sorrow, fr. Daniel. 6294-6
A sower of discord, fr. Proverbs. 6337-3
A sower. 7020-5
Spring. 6512-0
Super flumina. 6830-8
Suretyship. 6488-4
Surge, illuminare. 6830-8
The tears of the oppressed. 6954-1
The ten commandments. 6131-1
That they go down to the sea. 6125-7
Then the Lord answered, fr. Job. 6179-6
Then the Lord answered, fr. The book of Job. 7039-6
Things stately in their going. 6488-4
To truth, fr. Solomon. 6730-1
Translation of psalm 137. William Cowper (tr.). 6848-0
The tree and the chaff, fr. Psalm I. 6730-1
The twenty-third psalme. George Herbert (tr.). 6848-0
The two paths. 6488-4
Ululate naves. 6830-8
Vanitas vanitatum. 6830-8
Veni in hortum. 6830-8
Vere scio. 6830-8
Verses, fr. The song of Solomon. 6623-2
Version of the 107th psalm. John Quincy Adams (tr.).
  6848-0
The virtuous wife, fr. Proverbs. 6337-3
Vision of the day of judgment, fr. Isaiah. 6730-1
Voice of God out of the whirlwind, fr. Job. 6337-3,6153-
  2
What doth the Lord require?, fr. Micah. 6337-3
What is man?, fr. Psalm 8. 6337-3
"Whatsoever things are true", fr. Philippians. 6109-5
"Whatsoever thy hand findeth to do..." 6623-2
"Where shall wisdom be found?" G.R. Noyes (tr.). 6606-2
"While the earth remaineth, seedtime and harvest" 7020-
  5
"Who hath sent out the wild ass free? Or who hath" 7020-
  5
Wine and woe, fr. Proverbs. 6337-3
The wine glass, fr. Proverbs. 6724-7
Wings. 6512-0
Wisdom can be obtained only from God, fr. Job. 6418-3
The wisdom of Solomon, sels. 6334-9
The wisdom of Solomon. 6179-6
Wisdom, fr. Job. 6087-0
The word, fr. John. 6337-3
'You hands are full of blood' 6954-1
The **Bible** in harmony with temperance. Felicia Dorothea
  Hemans. 6404-3
The **Bible** my mother gave me. Unknown. 6260-1
Bible stories. Lizette Woodworth Reese. 6421-3
Bible, George P.
  Little Dorothy's sayings. 6579-1
A **bible-story** for mothers. Nathaniel Parker Willis. 6848-0
The **Bible**. Thomas Traherne. 6315-2
The **Bible**. John Greenleaf Whittier. 6337-3
Bibliolatres. James Russell Lowell. 6288-1
The **bibliomania**. John Ferriar. 6297-0
Yhe **bibliomaniac's** bride. Eugene Field. 6949-5
The **bibliomaniac's** prayer. Eugene Field. 6735-2
Bibliophile's library. Rachel Albright. 6789-1
Bibo and Charon. Matthew Prior. 6278-4
Bickel, Nancy
  When you have seen the brown November wood. 6761-1
Bickers, D.G.
  To keep the peace. 6542-2
  The verdict. 7001-9
  Woodrow Wilson. 7001-9
Bickerstaffe, Isaac
  An expostulation. 6092-7
  I cre nobody, not I, fr. Love in a village. 6934-7

BICKERSTAFFE

Song ("How happy"). 6932-0
Song, fr. Love in a village. 6930-4
There was a jolly miller. 6502-3
What are outward forms? 6930-4
Bickersteth, Edward Henry
Give us men! 6337-3
Peace, perfect peace. 6065-X
The prince of peace. 6065-X
Bickley, Beulah Vick
Daybreak. 6789-1
The flowering rod. 6789-1
Bickley, Francis
The players. 7026-4
Bickston, Diana
As all things pass. 6870-7
Collect calls. 6870-7
For Chicle & Justina. 6870-7
For Zorro. 6870-7
Pipe dreams. 6870-7
The **bicycle** and the pup. Unknown. 6744-1
The **bicycle** ride. James Clarence Harvey. 6923-1
Bicycling in the sky. Arthur Lewis Tubbs. 6579-1
Bicycling song. Henry Charles Beeching. 6239-3
The **bicycle** ride. J.G, Francis. 6786-7
Bid adieu to girlish days. James Joyce. 6174-5
Bid adieu, adieu, adieu. James Joyce. 6244-X
"Bid adieu, my sad heart, bid adieu to thy peace". William Cowper. 6814-6
"Bid him to dine that loves thee, leave him...". Hesiod. 6251-2
Bid me discourse, fr. Venus and Adonis. William Shakespeare. 6328-4
"Bid me not go where neither suns nor showers". William Cartwright. 6187-7,6830-8
"Bid me not go where neither suns nor show'rs". A valediction. William Cartwright. 6933-9
Bid me sin no more. Charles Wesley. 6065-X
"Bid not farewell for fate can ne're divorce." Unknown. 6563-5
"Bid thee to my mystic feast". The feast of life. Letitia Elizabeth ("L.E.L.") Landon. 6980-0
Bidden word. Clifford J. Laube. 6042-0
Bidder, George
Two and forty-two. 6233-4
Bidding, Rudolf G.
Erdgewalt. 6253-9
Biddle, E.K.
To a student. 6954-1
Biddle, Francis
Sunday morning. 6880-4
Biddle, Livingston L.
In a garden. 6338-1
Biddle, Virginia
Silence. 6032-3
Biddles, Adelaide
The flight of the Gods. 6411-6
Bide a wee, and dinna fret. Unknown. 6583-X,6687-9
'Bide a wee, and dinna fret.' S.E. G. 6273-3
Bidwell, Margaret J.
How the revival came. 6680-1
Licensed to sell; or, thy little blossom. 6567-8
Bienseance. John ("Peter Pindar") Walcott. 6278-4
Bierbaum, Otto Julius
Blacksmith pain. Jethro Bithell (tr.). 7039-6
Kindly vision. Jethro Bithell (tr.). 7039-6
Oft in the silent night. Ludwig Lewisohn (tr.). 7039-6
Bierce, Ambrose
Another way. 6076-5,6006-4,6102-8,6732-8,6076-5,6307-1, 6300
The bride. 6307-1
Creation. 6307-1
The death of Grant. 6076-5,6102-8,6340-3
The hero. 6465-5
An invocation. 6076-5,6102-8
Montefiore. 6076-5,6102-8,6467-1
My country, 'tis of thee. 6736-0
The politician. 6076-5,6102-8,6732-8,6076-5,6102-8
Rebuke. 6076-5,6102-8
Religion. 6076-5,6102-8
T.A.H. 6102-8,6732-8,6076-5,6736-0,6300-4

To a critic of Tennyson. 6076-5,6102-8
"Bierstadt! In my stupidity". Bierstadt's 'storm in the rocky mountains' James Abraham Martling. 6952-5
Biftek aux champignons. Henry Augustin Beers. 6652-6
Big Eagle, Duane
Birthplace. 7005-1
Elegy. 7005-1
My grandfather was a quantum physicist. 7005-1
Recollection. 7005-1
Wind and impulse. 7005-1
Big and little things. Alfred H. Miles. 6459-0,6135-4
"**Big** at the bottom and little at the top". Unknown. 7028-0
The **big** baboon. Hilaire Belloc. 6018-8
Big bedtime. Edith Ballinger Price. 6861-8
Big Ben Bolton. Eugene J. Hall. 6414-0
The **big** black trawler. Alfred Noyes. 6151-6
"**Big** blue overcoat and breeches red as red". Paris again. Unknown. 7031-0
"**Big** Fanny & stromin vinne deal". Suicide. Bob Kaufman. 6792-1
Big boat's up the rivuh. Unknown. 6609-7
Big brother. Elizabeth Madox Roberts. 6891-X
Big Chief Wotapotami. David McCord. 6722-0
Big dog. Edgar A. Guest. 6748-4
Big fine woman from Ruleville. Jayne Cortez. 6898-7
Big fittie Jock. Alexander ("Surfaceman") Anderson. 6819-7
Big fun. Diane Burns. 7005-1
The **big** game. Alex. C. D. Noe. 6818-9
The **big** mystical circus. Jorge de Lima. 6759-X
The **big** one. Luis Cabalquinto. 6790-5
The **big** rocky candy mountains. Unknown. 6125-7
The **big** shoe. Unknown. 6745-X
The **big** shoe. Adeline Dutton (Train) Whitney. 6414-0
Big sister's lullaby. Unknown. 6466-3
Big Smith. Juliana Horatia Ewing. 6242-3,6808-1,6639-9, 6638-0
Big spring 1972 Dick Turner. 6860-X
Big Stone Lake. Nina Pride Hoag. 6342-X
Big Thursday. Eugene Field. 6949-5
"The **big** teetotum twirls". Double ballade of the nothingness of things. William Ernest Henley. 6770-0, 6875-8
The **big** trimmer, fr. Ogesa Ondo. Ronald P. Tanaka. 6790-5
"The **big-eyed** baby, just across the way". Humanity. Eugene Field. 6949-5
Big-lipped Negro. Nicolas Guillen. 6642-9
Bigelow mountain. Norman W. Sturtevant. 6799-9
Bigelow, Walter Storrs
The poet's morn. 6247-4
Bigg, Louisa
The child is father to the man. 6575-9
Bigg, Stanyan
Night and the soul. 6102-8
Biggers, Earl Derr
The German band. 6274-1
"The **biggest** basket 'round our place". Apple-paring night in Vermont. Daniel L. Cady. 6988-6
"The **biggest** man in creation?". A ballad ("The biggest man") Williams [pseud]. 6880-4
The **bigler's** crew. Unknown. 6578-1
The **Biglow** papers, sels. James Russell Lowell. 6176-1,6600-3,6008-0,6288-1,6542-2
The **Biglow** papers. James Russell Lowell. 6597-X
The **Biglow** papers. James Russell Lowell. 6126-5,6739-5
Bigot. Eleanor Slater. 6337-3
The **bigot's** garb. Edward R. Huxley. 6885-5
Bigsby, James
The will of James Bigsby. 6878-2
"**Biii bibibibibi**." Friedrich Achleitner. 6769-7
Bijah. Charles M. Lewis. 6683-6
Bijah's story. Unknown. 6415-9
Bile dem cabbage down. Unknown. 6594-5
Bilin' sap. Charles Hawkes. 6497-3
Bilin' sap. Clarence Hawkes. 7035-3
Bill 'Awkins. Rudyard Kipling. 6810-3
Bill and Belle. Arden S. Fitch. 6682-8
Bill and I. George Henry Miles. 6409-4
Bill and Joe. Oliver Wendell Holmes. 6045-1,6085-4,6385-3, 6512-0,6004-8,6288 ,6575-9,6126-5
Bill and the supe. Berton Braley. 6853-7

Bill Dubbins. Unknown. 6149-4
"Bill could take a puppy and teach him...". Dog trainer. Edgar A. Guest. 6748-4
A bill from Cupid. Arthur Guiterman. 6320-9
Bill George, fr. Blue Juanita. Malcolm Cowley. 6531-7
Bill Hopkin's colt. Unknown. 6651-8
Bill Manning. Joseph I.C. Clarke. 6292-X
Bill Mason's bride. Francis Bret Harte. 6910-X
Bill Mason's bride. Unknown. 6294-6,6370-5
The bill of landing, fr. A tiny trip. Joseph Ashby Sterry. 6770-0
Bill Peters, the stage driver. Unknown. 6281-4
Bill Sweeny of the Black Gang. James Barnes. 6274-1
Bill the bomber. Robert Service. 6159-1
Bill the weaver. Unknown. 6057-9
Bill's grave. Robert Service. 6159-1
Bill's in the legislature. Unknown. 6964-9
Bill's in trouble. James Barton Adams. 6889-8
Bill's tenor and my bass. Eugene Field. 6085-4
Biller, Matthew
    The American freedom. 6761-1,6465-5
    A man and his house. 6761-1
A billet-doux. Unknown. 6416-7,6724-7
Billings, Georgiana
    Was pa ever a boy? 6715-8
Billings, Lydia Rader
    Night comes to the ninnescah. 6316-0
    Our children's children. 6316-0
    Return. 6316-0
Billings, Robert
    At Billings' bridge graveyard. 6767-0
"The billows swell, the winds are high". Temptation. William Cowper. 6814-6
"The billows up the broad bay crawl and creep". The waves' confessional. William Lindsey. 6798-0
"The billowy headlands swiftly fly". Battle-song of the Oregon. Wallace Rice. 6946-0
Bills, Grace R.
    The wall within the wood. 6764-6
Billson, C.J. (tr.)
    Asclepius. Pindar, 6435-3
    Bellerophon. Pindar, 6435-3
    Castor and Polydeuces. Pindar, 6435-3
    The childhood of Achilles. Pindar, 6435-3
    Evadne and her son. Pindar, 6435-3
    The hyperboreans. Pindar, 6435-3
    The infant Heracles. Pindar, 6435-3
    The island of Blest. Pindar, 6435-3
    The marriage of Thetis. Pindar, 6435-3
    The quest of the Golden Fleece. Pindar, 6435-3
    The sons of Aeacus. Pindar, 6435-3
    Strepsiades of Thebes. Pindar, 6435-3
Billy and his drum. James Whitcomb Riley. 6091-9
Billy Boy. Unknown. 6826-X
Billy boy. Unknown. 6058-7,6228-8,6281-4
Billy Grimes, the drover. Unknown. 6915-0
Billy in the Darbies. Herman Melville. 6315-2;6333-0;6380-2
Billy K. Simes. Elmer Ruan Coates. 6920-7
Billy McGinnis agrees. James Logie ("Hugh Haliburton") Robertson. 6149-4
Billy O'Rourke. Unknown. 6058-7
"Billy put the puppy-dog". Naughty Billy. Laura E. Richards. 6937-1
Billy the kid. Shuntaro Tanikawa. 6803-0
Billy the kid. Unknown. 6594-5
Billy's rose. George Robert Sims. 6417-5
Billy's rose. Unknown. 6273-3
Billy, he's in trouble. James Barton Adams. 6736-0
Bilsford, Guy
    A century of peace. 6088-9
Bilton, Ernest
    Dives and Lazarus. 7009-4
Binckli, Stephanie L.
    Misappellation. 6750-6
    My new clam. 6750-6
"Bind fast thyself with silvery ties". Right building. William J. Duncan. 6927-4
Bind-weed. Sarah ("Susan Coolidge") Woolsey. 6239-3
"The binder of books is paring his leather". The book-binder. Mary Josephine Benson. 6797-2
Binding sheaves. Jean Ingelow. 6543-0
Binding, Rudolph G.
    Love song ("The deer stand still now ..."). 6643-7
Bindlestiff. Edwin Ford Piper. 6034-X
Bingen on the Rhine. Caroline Elizabeth Sarah Sheridan Norton. 6014-5,6370-5,6481-1,6402-7,6552-X,6486, 6600-3,6706-9,6439-6,6424-8,6304-7,6484-1,6219-9
Bingham, Charles D.
    The building of the barn. 6691-7
    Too old for father's kisses. 6691-7
Bingham, Clifton
    When. 6132-X
Bingham, Norman W.
    Song of owl's head. 7030-2
Bingham, Ralph
    Op'ra-house piano in the one-night stand. 6719-0
    Why uncle Ben back-slid. 6926-6
Bingley, Barbara
    Anne Boleyn. 6541-4
Bingo. Unknown. 6732-8
"A bingo bird once nestled her nest". The dismal dole of the doodledoo. Eugene Field. 6949-5
"Bingo pup and I went walking". Tiny quail. Blanche Elliott. 6906-1
Binley and '46'. Unknown. 6408-6
Binney, Thomas
    Eternal light! 6337-3,6730-1
Binnorie. Unknown. 6180-X,6186-9,6228-8,6625-9,6634-8,6726-,6490-6,6153-2,6067-6,6307-2
Binns, Archie
    The able seaman's story. 7007-8
Binns, Henry Bryan
    Injunction. 6506-6
    Ultimate act. 6291-1
Binny and bunny. Unknown. 6720-4
Binsey poplars (felled 1879). Gerard Manley Hopkins. 6187-7,6491-4
Binyon, Laurence
    Airmen from overseas. 6224-5
    Amasis. 6437-X
    The anvil. 7026-4
    Bab-lock-hythe. 6477-9
    The bowl of water. 6266-0
    The burning of the leaves, sels. 6246-6
    The children dancing. 6884-7
    Commercial. 6884-7
    A day this is boundless. 6233-4
    Day's end. 6437-X
    The dead to the living. 6476-0
    The dray. 6507-4
    Edith Cavell. 7026-4
    England. 6477-9
    Ferry Hinksey. 6138-9
    Fog. 6507-4
    "For mercy, courage, kindness, mirth." 6138-9,6501-5
    For the fallen. 6224-5,6289-X,6337-3,6477-9,6639-9
    The forest pine. 6253-9
    The fourth of August. 7029-9
    Harebell and pansy. 7020-5
    The healers. 6542-2
    Hearken to the hammers! 6777-8
    Hunger. 6625-9
    In misty blue. 6477-9
    Initiation. 6253-9
    Invocation to youth. 6437-X
    John Winter. 6258-X,6290-3,6547-3
    Kennack sands. 6793-X
    The lamp of Greece. 6783-2
    The little dancers. 6395-0,6437-X,6477-9,6507-4
    The little dancers. 6959-2
    Little hands. 6233-4,6320-9,6337-3
    Louvain. 7031-0
    Magnets. 6069-2
    Men of Verdun. 7026-4
    Nature. 6138-9,6102-8
    The new world. 7027-2
    Nothing is enough. 6250-4
    Numbers. 6884-7
    O summer sun. 6477-9

BINYON

O world, be nobler! 6102-8,6301-2,6646-1
One year old. 6266-0
Oxford in war-time. 7027-2
The porch of stars. 6320-9
A prayer to time. 7020-5
A prayer. 6532-5
Red night. 6507-4
The road menders. 6477-9
Seven years. 6266-0
The sirens, sels. 6334-9
Song ("For mercy"). 6102-8,6161-3,6250-4
song ("For mercy, courage..."). 6884-7
A song. 6668-2
Sorrow. 6879-0
The statues. 6437-X
The things that grow. 6607-0
The things that grow. 6649-6
Thinking of shores. 6250-4
To the Belgians. 7026-4
To women. 6161-3,6250-4
Trafalgar Square. 6046-3
Umbria. 6331-4,6631-3
Virgil's farewell to Dante. 6210-5
We have planted a tree. 6872-3
Woe to him. 6337-3
Youth. 6253-9
Binyon, Laurence (tr.)
    Little poem. Narihira, 6879-0
Bio-poetic statement: instruction to warriors on...
    Carroll Arnett Gogisgi. 7005-1
Biographies. Dorothy Parker. 6506-6
Biography. Jorge Carrera Andrade. 6642-9
Biography. Charles Bruce. 6446-9
Biography. Jorge Carrera Andrade. 6642-9
Biography. Anna Lovelace Gorsuch. 6750-6
Biography. Ralph Gustafson. 6021-8
Biography. Abraham M. Klein. 6042-0
Biography. John Masefield. 6234-2;6488-4
Biography. Aleksey Nedogonov. 6546-5
Biography. Idella Purnell. 6038-2
Biography for the use of the birds. Jorge Carrera Andrade.
    6759-X
The biologic face. L. B. 6118-4
Bion
    "Hesper, thou golden light...". F.L. Lucas (tr.). 6251-
    2
    Idyl (1). Eugene Field (tr.). 6949-5
    Idyl (2). Eugene Field (tr.). 6949-5
    "A lad that was a fowler...". F.L. Lucas (tr.). 6251-2
    Lament for Adonis. George Allen (tr.). 6435-3
    Lament of Adonis, sels. John Addington Symonds (tr.).
    7039-6
    Song of Eros. Eugene Field (tr.). 6949-5
    A spring poem. Eugene Field (tr.). 6949-5
Biothanatos. Joseph Beaumont. 6933-9
"Birch and green holly, boys". Unknown. 6904-5
Birch and paddle. Sir Charles George Douglas Roberts. 6795-
    6
The birch canoe, fr. The song of Hiawatha. Henry Wadsworth
    Longfellow. 6252-0
Birch tree. Yung-gul Lee. 6775-1
The birch tree at Loschwitz. Amy Levy. 6019-6
"A birch tree stands in graceful beauty". A day dream.
    Nelly Miller Seely. 6799-9
"The birch tree swang her fragrant hair" Alfred Lord
    Tennyson. 6049-8
The birch tree. Edgar A. Guest. 6869-3
The birch tree. Detlev von Liliencron. 6160-5
The birch tree. Addie V. McMullen. 6049-8
Birch trees. John Richard Moreland. 6036-6
Birch, Frank
    "War is dread when battle shock and fierce affray".
    6238-5
Birch, Minerva
    Farewell to school days. 6717-4
"The birch, the myrtle, and the bay", sels. John Dryden.
    6601-1
Birch-Bartlett, Helen
    The lake. 6037-4
    Lola wears lace. 6037-4

Birch-Reynardson, Henry
    Evening in the desert. 7029-9
The birch-tree. James Russell Lowell. 6077-3,6049-8
Birchall, Sara Hamilton
    The answer. 6374-8
    A conversation. 6374-8
    Gipsy song. 6374-8
    The gipsy wedding. 6374-8
    September. 6374-8
    Song of the open. 6374-8
    Vagabonds. 6374-8
Birches. Robert Frost. 6029-3,6257-1,6288-1,6336-5,6396-9,
    6300-4,6646-1,6723-9,6265-2,6217-2,6161-3,6121-4,
    6162-1,6332-2,6348-9,6509-0,6527-9,6556-,6332-2,6467-
    1,6300-4,6646-1,6491-4
The birches. William White. 6868-5
The bird among the blooms. Marion Short. 6166-4
Bird and bosom. Leonie Adams. 6071-4
Bird and brook. William Henry Davies. 6884-7
The bird and the baby. Alfred Lord Tennyson. 6743-3
The bird and the maid. Unknown. 6131-1
The bird and the tree. (Frederick) Ridgely Torrence. 6102-
    8,6619-4,6393-4,6029-3,6076-5,6153
The bird at dawn. Harold Monro. 6073-0;6607-0
The bird at sea. Felicia Dorothea Hemans. 6973-8
The bird bath. Edith Harriet Jones. 6799-9
"A bird came down the walk". Emily Dickinson. 6348-9,6454-
    X,6513-9
Bird carol. Louise Morey Bowman. 6797-2
A bird committee. Alexander Montgomerie. 6943-6
Bird companies. Edmund Spenser. 7020-5
Bird cry. Lynn Riggs. 6397-7
A bird from the west. Dora Sigerson Shorter. 6437-X
The bird in a cage. William Lisle Bowles. 6638-0
A bird in hand. Norman Gale. 6510-4
"The bird in my heart's a-calling through a...". 'The
    crier by night,' sels. Gordon Bottomley. 6873-1
'A bird in the hand is worth two in the bush' Unknown.
    6127-3
A bird in the hand. Frederic Edward Weatherley. 6089-7,
    6605-4,6656-9
Bird in the sun. Elizabeth Grey Stewart. 6761-1
Bird language. Emeline Sherman Smith. 6385-3
The bird let loose in eastern skies. Thomas Moore. 6240-
    7;6302-0
The bird man. Lucy Branch Allen. 6510-4
Bird music. James Rorty. 6073-0
The bird nation. James Thomson. 6943-6
Bird neighbors. Arlyle Mansfield. 6799-9
The bird nest is transparent by Qudrat. Jeff Jentz. 6900-2
Bird o'er the battlefield. Isabel Fiske Conant. 6542-2
"The bird of felicity flew". The bird of felicity.
    Willoughby Weaving. 7014-0
The bird of hope. Charles Swain. 6980-0
The bird of Jesus. Padraic Colum. 6096-X
The bird of paradise. William Henry Davies. 6234-2
The bird of paradise. Laura Benet. 6073-0
Bird of passage. Edgar Fawcett. 6240-7
Bird of passion. Rollo Britten. 6897-9
The bird of sadness. Christian Morgenstern. 6160-5
"Bird of the bitter bright gray golden morn". A ballad of
    Francois Vill n. Algernon Charles Swinburne. 6828-6
"Bird of the broad and sweeping wing". To the eagle. James
    Gates Percival. 6752-2
"Bird of the broud and sweeping wing!". The eagle. James
    Gates Percival. 6820-0
"Bird of the free and fearless wing!". To the skylark.
    Bernard Barton. 6980-0
"Bird of the greenwood!". The bird at sea. Felicia
    Dorothea Hemans. 6973-8
"Bird of the heavens! whose matchless eye". The American
    eagle. C.W. Thompson. 6921-5
"Bird of the morn,/When roseate clouds begin". To the
    lark. John Clare. 6943-6
Bird of the sea, fr. Iphigenia in Taurus. Euripides. 6435-
    3
Bird on a rock. John Logan. 6966-5
Bird on the rifle range. Daniel Smythe. 6761-1
The bird on the telegraph wire. Unknown. 6273-3
The bird on Ygdrasil. James A. Mackeret. 6070-6

Bird raptures. Christina Georgina Rossetti. 6657-7,6655-0
A bird sings at night. Hildegarde Flanner. 6808-1
A bird sings at night. Hildegarde Flanner. 6073-0
Bird song. Edwina Cushing Gifford. 6894-4
Bird song. John Hay. 6388-8
Bird song. Alfred Noyes. 6073-0
Bird songs. Kathie Moore. 6049-8
A bird speaks. Mary Frances Butts. 6965-7
A bird story. M.E. B. 6965-7
Bird talk. Carl Sandburg. 6012-9
Bird that art singing on Ebro's side. Felicia Dorothea Hemans. 6973-8
The bird that bears the bell. Unknown. 6943-6
The bird that sings. Emma Celia & Lizzie J. Rook. 6137-0
"The bird that soars on highest wing". Humility. Unknown. 6914-2
"The bird that sometime built within my breast". The lover to his love having forsaken him and... Unknown. 6943-6
Bird trades. Unknown. 6049-8,6312-8,6373-X,6529-5
"A bird whirrs against the window". Intangible. Max Holzer. 6769-7
Bird with bosom red. Unknown. 6373-X
The bird with the coppery, keen claws. Wallace Stevens. 6036-6
A bird wooing. Herbert Price. 6800-6
The bird's funeral. Unknown. 6740-9
A bird's house. Anna F. Burnham. 6965-7
A bird's life. May Swenson. 6803-0
A bird's ministry. Margaret Junkin Preston. 6600-3
Bird's music. Frank Dempster Sherman. 6311-X
A bird's nest. James Hurdis. 6385-3
A bird's nest. Florence Percy. 6373-X,6449-3
The bird's nest. Alexander Smart. 6131-1
The bird's nest. Elizabeth Turner. 6242-3,6135-4
Bird's nests. Unknown. 6049-8,6629-1,6304-7
The bird's release, fr. Lays of many lands. Felicia Dorothea Hemans. 6973-8
Bird's song at morning. William James Dawson. 6656-9
Bird's song in spring. Edith (Bland) Nesbit. 6519-8
The bird's song, the sun, and the wind. Sir Charles George Douglas Roberts. 6656-9
A bird's-eye view. Unknown. 6127-3,6742-5
Bird, M.
 The herdman's happy life, fr. M. Bird's set songs. 6198-2
 M. Bird's set songs, sels. 6198-2
Bird, Robert
 The crofter's farewell. 7009-4
 The fairy folk. 6132-X,6519-8,6135-4,6639-9,6638-0
 The freedom of the hills. 7009-4
Bird, Stephen Moylan
 What if the lapse of ages were a dream? 6347-0
"A bird, a man, a loaded gun,". Unknown. 6722-0
The bird-boy. Robert Bloomfield. 6980-0
A bird-eye's view. Unknown. 6131-1
A bird-loving Don. R. H. Coon. 7020-5
Bird-nesting. Charles Tennyson Turner. 6980-0,6943-6
The bird-scarer's song. Unknown. 6114-1
The bird-shop. Alfred Noyes. 6169-9
Bird-song and wire, fr. Desert adrift. Alice Corbin. 6628-3
Bird-songs. John Lyly. 6558-9
The bird-watcher. Frederic Prokosch. 6390-X
"A bird/a bone/a glass". Ballad of Benny roads number 65943 Jack Micheline. 6901-0
"A bird/while you watch through the window". Discontinuity. Ulalume Gonzalez de Leon. 7036-1
The bird. William Allingham. 6438-8
The bird. Robert Greacen. 6475-2
The bird. Jorge de Lima. 6759-X
The bird. Max Michelson. 6897-9
The bird. Henry Vaughan. 6943-6
The bird. Henry Vaughan. 6563-5
Birdcatcher's song, fr. The paradise of birds. William James Courthope. 6656-9
Birdie's secret. Unknown. 6312-8
Birdies with broken wings. Mary Mapes Dodge. 6519-8,6135-4
Birds. James Montgomery. 6302-0;6385-3
Birds. Katharine Duncan ("Jerry Doane") Morse. 6510-4

Birds. Richard Henry Stoddard. 6243-1,6459-0,6309-8
The birds ("I thought to shoulder time"). Herbert S. Gorman. 6073-0,6619-4
Birds ("Sure maybe ye've heard the storm-thrush"). Moira (Nesta Higginson Skrine) O'Neill. 6073-0,6090-0,6266-0,6175-5
Birds ("The fierce musical cries..."). Robinson Jeffers. 6073-0
The birds ("Within mankind's duration..."). Sir John Collings ("Solomon Eagle") Squire. 6073-0,6102-8
The birds and the children. E.T. Sullivan. 6049-8
The birds and the pheasant. Unknown. 6440-X
"The birds are in full song". April morning at t'Eagle. Dorothy Una Ratcliffe. 6785-9
"The birds are quiet on the boughs". Lyric ("The birds are quiet..."). Arthur K. Sabin. 6884-7
Birds are seen approaching in the air carrying nests... William John Courthope. 6943-6
Birds are singing round my window. Richard Henry Stoddard. 6424-8
"Birds are singing, blossoms blooming". Traveling song. H. Von Fallersleben. 6952-5
Birds at my window. Edward Spencer. 6385-3
The birds flit unafraid. Herbert Trench. 7031-0
"The birds fly low at Oyster bay". Sagamore. Coletta Ryan. 6995-9
"Birds fly south, and dancing snowflakes fall". Winter. Thekla N. Berstecher. 6906-1
The birds go by. John Shaw Neilson. 6349-7
"Birds hung poised on the granite.The big wind". Going into exile. Frederic Prokosch. 6761-1
Birds in autumn. Louise Townsend Nicholl. 6761-1
"The birds in kind have each obeyed". Birds are seen approaching in the air carrying nests... William John Courthope. 6943-6
The birds in spring Thomas Nashe. 6519-8
Birds in spring, fr. The seasons (Spring). James Thomson. 6932-9
Birds in summer. Felicia Dorothea Hemans. 6049-8
Birds in summer. Mary Howitt. 6496-5,6519-8,6304-7,6135-4, 6131-1,6156-6
Birds in summer, sels. Mary Howitt. 6334-9,6156-6
Birds in the fens, fr. Polyolbion. Michael Drayton. 6125-7
Birds in the flax. Stanley Snaith. 6257-1
"Birds in the high hall-garden", fr. Maud. Alfred Lord Tennyson. 6122-2,6110-9,6153-2
Birds of a feather flock together. Unknown. 6363-2
The birds of Endermay [or Invermay]. David Mallet [or Malloch]. 6932-0
The birds of god, fr. Hippolytus. Euripides. 6435-3
The birds of Killingworth. Henry Wadsworth Longfellow. 6510-4,6288-1,6458-2,6212-1
Birds of no feather. Maggie B. Peeke. 6965-7
"Birds of omen dark and foul". Annot Lyle's song: 'Birds of omen,' fr. The legend... Sir Walter Scott. 6828-6
Birds of paradise. Christina Georgina Rossetti. 6123-0
Birds of passage. Henry Wadsworth Longfellow. 6753-0
Birds of passage. Esaias Tegner. 6045-5
The birds of passage. Felicia Dorothea Hemans. 6973-8
Birds of prey march. Rudyard Kipling. 6542-2
The birds of Rhiannon. Euros Bowen. 6528-7
The birds of Scotland. Hugh Macdonald. 6597-X
The birds of steel. William Henry Davies. 7029-9
"The birds of the air, they sing it". Song ("The birds of the air"). John Vance Cheney. 6374-8
The birds of the air. Felicia Dorothea Hemans. 6973-8
The birds of tin. Charles Madge. 6379-9
The birds of Whitby. Thomas S. Jones Jr. 6073-0
Birds on a telegraph wire. Count Carl Snoilsky. 6045-5
Birds over New York. William Thomas Walsh. 6761-1
"The birds put off their ev'ry hue". On Mrs. Montague's feather-hangings. William Cowper. 6814-6
"Birds sit and sing among the flowers." Shou. 6027-7
"The birds stitch/Back and forth". Criss-cross pattern. Ethel Brodt Wilson. 6789-1,6039-0
"The birds that sing on autumn eves". Robert Bridges. 6487-6
"The birds they sing". Unknown. 6334-9
"Birds to her music were whirring outside". A spring song. Margaret Sidney. 6965-7

BIRDS

"The birds turned/stopping". Wrapped hair bundles. Frank LaPena Tauhindauli. 7005-1
"The birds were beating north again with...". Wanderlust. Odell Shepard. 7012-4
The birds' convention. Miller Hageman. 6682-8
The birds' departure. Unknown. 6672-0
Birds' food. Sara Coleridge. 6334-9
Birds' food, sels. Sara Coleridge. 6334-9
The birds' lawn party. Unknown. 6373-X
The birds' lullaby. Emily Pauline ("Tekahionwake") Johnson. 6602-X
Birds' nests. M.S. C. 6131-1
The birds' nests. Unknown. 6891-X
The birds' orchestra. Celia Thaxter. 6612-7
Birds'-nesting time. Joseph Crosby Lincoln. 6119-2
Birds, beasts, and fishes. Ann and Jane Taylor. 6105-2
"Birds, joyous birds of the wandering wing!". The birds of passage. Felicia Dorothea Hemans. 6973-8
The birds, the beasts, and the bat. Francis Hopkinson. 6753-0
Birds, why are ye silent? John Clare. 6943-6
The birds. Hilaire Belloc. 6172-9,6216-4,6292-X,6421-3
The birds. William Blake. 6943-6
The birds. Felicia Dorothea Hemans. 6973-8
The birds. Sir John Collings ("Solomon Eagle") Squire. 6943-6
The birds. Sir John Collings ("Solomon Eagle") Squire. 6510-4

Birdsall, Katharine Newbold
    Bed-time. 6130-3
    The squabble bird. 6130-3
Birdseye. Charles Madge. 6985-1
Birdseye, George
    A fair exchange. 6505-8
    The Hindoo's death. 6273-3
    How Tom saved the train. 6672-0
    June 21st. 6505-8
    The miser's will. 6917-7
    The miser's will. 6744-1
    Paradise. 6089-7,6505-8
    The policeman's story. 6917-7
    Too much of it. 6505-8
Birdwatcher. Henry Treece. 6666-6
Birge, Paul Relland
    Mirage. 6327-6
The Birkenhead, sels. Sir Henry Yule. 6427-2,6322-8
'The Birkenhead.'. Hattie Tyng Griswold. 6686-0
The Birkenhead. Sir Henry Yule. 6934-7
Birkhead, Matthew
    The entered apprentices' song. 6328-4
The birks of Aberfeldie. Robert Burns. 6180-X,6250-4,6383-7
The birks of Invermay [or Endermay]. David Mallet [or Malloch]. 6180-X
Birlinn Chlann-raghnaill. Alexander (Alasdair MacMhaighstir A.) Macdonald. 6845-6
Birney, Earle
    Bushed. 6446-9
    For Steve. 6666-6
    Man is a snow. 6446-9
    Mappemounde. 6446-9
    On going to the wars. 6666-6
    Pacific door. 6446-9
    Rot below Adam's peak (Sri Lanka*) 6767-0
    Slug in woods. 6021-8,6446-9
    Still life near Bangalore. 6767-0
    This page my pigeon. 6446-9
Birnie, Patrick
    The auld man's mear's dead. 6845-6
Biron's canzonet, fr. Love's labour's lost. William Shakespeare. 6827-8
Birrel, G.B.
    A thought on peace conferences. 6880-4
Birt, Josephine Sievers
    Changeling. 6906-1
    Crying Cupid. 6906-1
    In a garden. 6906-1
    Please. 6906-1
    The sandy soul. 6906-1
    Sorrow. 6906-1

Birth. Stanton A. Coblentz. 6750-6
Birth. Sulamith Ish-Kishor. 6847-2
Birth. George Burt Lake. 6482-5
Birth. Henri Michaux. 6758-1
Birth. E. Merrill Root. 6619-4
Birth. Annie R. ("Grace Raymond") Stillman. 6097-8,6627-5
Birth and death. Algernon Charles Swinburne. 6123-0
Birth and death. Thomas Wade. 6656-9
The birth and death of pain, sels. Silas Weir Mitchell. 6482-5
The birth at Bethlehem. Thomas Campbell. 6747-6
The birth o' Robin Hood. Unknown. 6613-5
The birth of Australia. Percy Russell. 6768-9,6656-9
The birth of Christ. Alfred Lord Tennyson. 6145-1,6424-8
Birth of Henri Quatre. Elizabeth J. Coatsworth. 6039-0
The birth of Ireland. Unknown. 6165-6
Birth of June. Olive Waldron Warner. 6799-9
birth of Kuloskap, the lord of beasts and men...The. Unknown (Algonquian Indian) 6864-2
The birth of Pierrot. Thomas Walsh. 6266-0
The birth of portraiture. Thomas Moore. 6302-0;6385-3
The birth of Robin Hood. Unknown. 6055-2,6518-X,6613-5
The birth of Rustem. Firdusi] (Abul Kasin Mansur) Firdausi [or Firdawsi. 6448-5
The birth of Saint Patrick. Samuel Lover. 6089-7,6165-6, 6412-4,6465-5,6219-9
The birth of speech. Hartley Coleridge. 6656-9
The birth of St. Patrick. Samuel Lover. 6825-1
The birth of the flowers. Mary McNeil Fenollosa. 6338-1
The birth of the harp, fr. The Kalevala. Unknown (Finnish) 6372-1
The birth of the opal. Ella Wheeler Wilcox. 6863-4
The birth of the Prophet. Bayard Taylor. 6976-2
The birth of the snowshoe. Samuel M. Baylis. 7035-3
The birth of the squire. John Gay. 6972-X
'The birth of Venus'. John Galsworthy. 6888-X
The birth of Venus, sels. Thomas Gordon Hoke. 6997-5
The birth of Venus. Walter De La Mare. 6905-3
The birth of Venus. Unknown. 6833-2
The birth of woman. Helen Higgins. 6396-9
The birth poem. Sharon Berg. 6767-0
The birth song of Christ. Edmund Hamilton Sears. 6065-X
The birth tokens. Anne Goodwin Winslow. 6038-2
The birth-bed prayer. [James] Pittendrigh Macgillivray. 6269-5
The birth-bond, fr. The house of life. Dante Gabriel Rossetti. 6186-9,6430-2,6110-9,6508-2
The birth-bond. Dante Gabriel Rossetti. 6828-6
A birth-day. Benjamin Franklin Taylor. 6815-4
The birth.. Don Marquis. 6607-0,6746-8
The birth. Don Marquis. 6393-4
Birthday. Jean Starr Untermeyer. 6011-0
The birthday crown. William Alexander. 6437-X
A birthday gift. Christina Georgina Rossetti. 6519-8
Birthday gifts. Adelaide Anne Procter. 6957-6
A birthday greeting. M.E. F. 6273-3
A birthday greeting. Julia Hazel Frank. 6847-2
The birthday lesson. Mary Livingston Burdick. 6712-3
Birthday lines to Agnes Baillie. Joanna Baillie. 6980-0
Birthday messages. Caroline Bowers Tombo. 6654-2
Birthday ode for the year 1800. Henry James Pye. 6867-7
The birthday of Abraham Lincoln. Mary Clement Leavitt. 6524-4
Birthday of Daniel Webster. Oliver Wendell Holmes. 6126-5
Birthday of Daniel Webster, sels. Oliver Wendell Holmes. 6820-0
The birthday of Washington ever honored. William Howitt. 6171-0,6712-3
The birthday of Washington. Silas Weir Mitchell. 6936-3
Birthday on deathrow. Harold LaMont Otey. 6870-7
Birthday poem, Nov. 4th. John Thompson Jr. 6666-6
A birthday song. Richard Watson Gilder. 6465-5
A birthday song. Jonathan Odell. 6288-1,6753-0
Birthday sonnet. Elinor Wylie. 6641-0
A birthday sonnet. Floyd Dell. 6880-4
A birthday thought. Charles and Mary Lamb. 6295-4
Birthday thoughts. Mabel Celia Saunders. 6799-9
A birthday treat. Carolyn Wells. 6882-0
A birthday verse. M.A. DeWolfe Howe. 6006-4
Birthday verses. Thomas Hood. 6974-6

The **birthday** week. Unknown. 6424-8
A **birthday** wish. Mary Lydia Carpenter. 6799-9
A **birthday**. Margaret McCarthy. 6887-1
A **birthday**. Christina Georgina Rossetti. 6861-8
A **birthday**. Christina Georgina Rossetti. 6123-0,6153-2,
     6301-2,6092-7,6655-0,6102 ,6198-2,6204-0,6657-7,6526-
     0,6052-8,6315 ,6508-2,6585-6,6659-3,6560-0,6430-2,
     6383-7,6019-6,6508-2,6585-6,6659-3,6560-0,6430-2,
     6383-7,6019-6
Birthdays. Unknown. 6132-X
Birthing. Jean Hollander. 6821-9
Birthing: 2000 Pancho Aguila. 6870-7
A **birthnight** candle. John Finley. 6476-0,6607-0
Birthplace. Duane Big Eagle. 7005-1
The **birthplace**. Robert Frost. 6012-9
The **birthplace**. Elisabeth Kuskulis. 6836-7
Birthright. John Drinkwater. 6726-3
Birthright. Geraldine Kudaka. 6790-5
Birthsong. Jessica Scarbrough. 6870-7
Bisby, Grace Griswold
    Eternity. 6818-9
Bishop Blougram's apology. Robert Browning. 6657-7
Bishop Blougram's apology, sel. Robert Browning. 6958-4
Bishop Blougram's apology, sels. Robert Browning. 6337-3,
     6427-2
Bishop Bruno. Robert Southey. 6086-2,6196-6
Bishop Butler of Kilcash. Unknown. 6930-4
Bishop Doane on his dog. George Washington Doane. 6107-9
Bishop Doane's tribute to his dog Cluny. George Washington
     Doane. 6510-4
Bishop Hatto. Robert Southey. 6105-2,6133-8,6134-6,6290-3,
     6473-6,6639-9,6079-X,6125-7,6131-1
"A **bishop** and a preacher too...". A ballad of Santa Claus.
     Henry Van Dyke. 6961-4
The **bishop** of Ross. Richard Robert Madden. 6858-8
The **bishop** orders his tomb at Saint Praxed's Church.
     Robert Browning. 6046-3,6102-8,6110-9,6656-9,6646-1,
     6659 ,6199-0,6052-8,6154-0,6198-2,6427-2,6484-1,6657
     ,6150-8,6196-6,6430-2,6472-8,6655-0,6682
Bishop Patteson. Menella Bute Smedley. 6046-3
Bishop Ravenscroft. George Washington Doane. 6752-2
Bishop Spaniel's sermons. Colin Ellis. 6339-X
The **bishop's** harp. Richard Manning of Brunne. 6022-6
The **Bishop's** see. Unknown. 6157-5
Bishop, Daisy Marita
    Water tower at Waldo. 6818-9
Bishop, Elizabeth
    The fish. 6399-3
    The map. 6640-2
    The reprimand. 6640-2
    Roosters. 6389-6
    Squatter's children. 6388-8
    Three valentines. 6640-2
    The wit. 6388-8
Bishop, John Peale
    Beyond Connecticut, beyond the sea. 7017-5
    The death of a dandy. 6036-6
    Encounter. 6979-7
    The hours. 6390-X
    The mothers. 7017-5
    The return. 6390-X,6666-6
    Speaking of poetry. 6751-4
Bishop, John Peale (tr.)
    The peasant declares his love. Emile Roumer, 6759-X
    Then twist the neck this delusive swan. Enrique
        Gonzalez Martinez, 6759-X
Bishop, Julia Truitt
    Robert. 6686-0
Bishop, Margery
    Ruth to Naomi. 6316-0
    Winter window. 6316-0
Bishop, Morris
    The anatomy of humor. 6722-0
    "A clergyman out in Dumont". 6722-0
    Drinking song for present-day gatherings. 6026-9
    Ecclesiastes. 6036-6
    Eschatology. 6722-0
    The immoral arctic. 6722-0
    Limerick:"A clergyman out in Dumont." 6308-X
    Limerick:"Said a girl from beyond Pompton Lakes." 6308-X
    Limerick:"There's a vaporish maiden in Harrison." 6308-X
    Lines written in a moment of vibrant ill-health. 6722-0
    Merry old souls. 6722-0
    Mournful numbers. 6722-0
    A New Hampshire boy. 6036-6
    No more of the moon. 6628-3
    Public aid for Niagara Falls. 6287-3
    "Said old Peeping Tom of Fort Lee:". 6722-0
    A salute to the modern language association... 6722-0
    Sing a song of the cities. 6722-0
    The tales that barbers tell. 6026-9
    "There's a vaporish maiden in Harrison". 6722-0
    A tonversation with baby. 6722-0
    We have been here before. 6722-0
Bishop, Morris (tr.)
    "The ancient greybeard shoulders on his load".
        Francesco Petrarch, 6325-X
    "Diana, naked in the shadowy pool". Francesco Petrarch,
        6325-X
    "From thought to thought, from mountain-peak...".
        Francesco Petrarch, 6325-X
    "It is the evening hour; the rapid sky". Francesco
        Petrarch, 6325-X
    "Life hurries on, a frantic refugee". Francesco
        Petrarch, 6325-X
    "Now I go grieving for the days on earth". Francesco
        Petrarch, 6325-X
    "O little room, my harbor from the sea". Francesco
        Petrarch, 6325-X
    "O lovely little bird, I watch you fly". Francesco
        Petrarch, 6325-X
    "She used to let her golden hair fly free". Francesco
        Petrarch, 6325-X
    "That window where the sun at midday shows". Francesco
        Petrarch, 6325-X
    "You who give ear to sorrow, as you scan". Francesco
        Petrarch, 6325-X
    "Zephyr returns, and scatters everywhere". Francesco
        Petrarch, 6325-X
Bishop, Samuel
    Fati valet hora benigni. 6086-2
    The second marriage. 6086-2
    To his wife, with a knife. 6874-X
    To his wife on the fourteenth anniversary... 6092-7,
        6317-9
    To his wife on the sixteenth anniversary of their
        wedding. 6092-7
    To his wife...with a ring. 6153-2
    To Mary. 6219-9
    The touch stone. 6086-2
Bisinger, Gerald
    Epilogue in Berlin. Milne Holton and Herbert Kuhner
        (tr.). 6769-7
    Intermezzo: noon in the bazaar cafe. Milne Holton and
        Herbert Kuhner (tr.). 6769-7
    "Poate/Nu vom mai fi nici!" Milne Holton and Herbert
        Kuhner (tr.). 6769-7
Bismarck. K.G. Ossian-Nilsson. 6045-5
Bismillah. David Law ("Pegleg Arkwright") Proudfit. 6614-3,
     6424-8
The **bison** track. Bayard Taylor. 6976-2
A **bison-king**. Joaquin Miller. 6510-4
The **bison**. Hilaire Belloc. 6179-6
Bispham Jr., George Tucker
    The realm of love. 6118-4
Bispham, Caroline Russell
    The eagle. 6995-9
Bispham, George Tucker
    The moon. 6983-5
Bissell, Emma Magin
    Life's curtain. 6799-9
Bissett, Bill
    Dew yu know. 6767-0
    Its past th green margarine now. 7003-5
    Looking for the innr life in 100 mile. 6767-0
    Sailor. 7003-5
    Th lovr sighs if it all revolvs around yu. 6767-0
    Wer they angels I didint know. 7003-5

Bit by bitter. Ralph Cheyney. 6750-6
A bit of lace. Arthur Hobson Quinn. 6936-3
A bit of pottery. Unknown. 6629-1
A bit of shopping for the country. Unknown. 6922-3
A bit of shopping for the country. Unknown. 6744-1
A bit of stone. Gertrude Huntington McGiffert. 6838-3
"A bit of sun in my window-nook". Gold. Helen M. Shuster. 6799-9
Bite bigger. Unknown. 6240-7
The bite. Emma Celia & Lizzie J. Rook. 6137-0
The biter bite. William Edmonstoune Aytoun. 6278-4
Bithell, Jethro (tr.)
    After midnight. Charles Vildrac, 7039-6
    Amsterdam. Francis Jammes, 7039-6
    Awake! Sir Walther von der Vogelweide, 7039-6
    Ballad of the outer life. Hugo von Hofmannsthal, 7039-6
    Blacksmith pain. Otto Julius Bierbaum, 7039-6
    A childish game. Sir Reinmar von Hagenau, 7039-6
    From summer hours. Emile Verhaeren, 7039-6
    He that loves a rosy cheek. Sir Heinrich von Rugge, 7039-6
    His own true wife. Sir Wolfram von Eschenbach, 7039-6
    Hours grey. Francis Viele-Griffin, 6343-8
    Kindly vision. Otto Julius Bierbaum, 7039-6
    The laborer. Richard Dehmel, 7039-6
    A leave-taking. Arno Holz, 7039-6
    Lonely. Andre Spire, 7039-6
    Love, whose month was ever May. Sir Ulrich von Liechtenstein, 7039-6
    Many indeed must perish in the keel. Hugo von Hofmannsthal, 7039-6
    Most quietly at times. Casar Flaischlen, 7039-6
    On the mountain. Sir Neidhart von Reuental, 7039-6
    Prayer to go to paradise with the asses. Francis Jammes, 7039-6
    Sensation. Arthur Rimbaud, 7039-6
    Sleeping they bear me. Alfred Mombert, 7039-6
    Song ("Three little maidens..."). Maurice Maeterlinck, 7039-6
    With a rod no man alive. Sir Walther von der Vogelweide, 7039-6
"Biting down my overgrown nails" Muin Ozaki. 6981-9
Biting through. Traise Yamamoto. 6790-5
Bits and pieces. Gregory J. Ford. 7024-8
"Bits of song..what else?" Yone Noguchi. 6850-2
"Bits of white on bands of blue". Scallop boats. Joshua Freeman Crowell. 6798-0
The bitten grass. Edward Shanks. 6778-6
Bitter bread and weak wine. Jean Starr Untermeyer. 6619-4, 6011-0
"The bitter burden of little things!". The yoke. Katherine Prescott Bemis. 6836-7
Bitter chill. John Keats. 6083-8
The bitter cry of the children. Elizabeth Barrett Browning. 6954-1
Bitter disappointment. George Croly. 6294-6
Bitter experience. Letitia Elizabeth ("L.E.L.") Landon. 6980-0
Bitter fruit. Margaret E. Bruner. 6789-1
Bitter fruit. Maye DeWeese Porter. 6906-1
"Bitter hate and harsh reproaches no more...". Woodrow Wilson arisen. Janet Bolton. 7001-9
The bitter herb. Jeanne Robert Foster. 6556-2
The bitter purple willows. Allen Upward. 6897-2
The bitter river. Langston Hughes. 6561-9
Bitter sanctuary. Harold Monro. 6209-1
Bitter serenade. Herbert Trench. 6877-4
Bitter serenade. Herbert Trench. 6090-0
Bitter stream. Leo Kennedy. 6021-8
Bitter summer thoughts: no. 3. Carl Sandburg. 6011-0
Bitter sweet, fr. The four winds. Ralph Cheever Dunning. 6531-7
The bitter withy. Unknown. 6756-5
The bitter withy. Unknown. 6071-4
"Bitter, the bread produced by those enslaved". Self conviction. Edward R. Huxley. 6885-5
Bitter-sweet. George Herbert. 6931-2
Bitter-sweet. Elisabeth Scollard. 6619-4
Bitter-sweet. Henry Van Dyke. 6961-4
Bitter-sweet. J. Roy Zeiss. 6039-0

The bittern. Julia Boynton Green. 6039-0
Bitterness. Eldon George McLean. 6178-8
Bitters. Rose Porter. 6750-6
Bittersweet. Kenneth C. Kaufman. 6397-7
Bivalves. Christopher Morley. 6538-4
Bivouac by the Rappahannock. Grace Duffie Roe. 6675-5
The bivouac in the snow. Margaret Junkin Preston. 6113-3
The bivouac of the dead. Theodore O'Hara. 6015-3,6465-5, 6074-9,6486-8,6735-2,6271 ,6340-3,6385-3,6459-0,6471-X,6424-8,6309 ,6304-7,6470-1,6088-9,6121-4,6442-6, 6431
Bivouac on a mountain side. Walt Whitman. 6113-3,6126-5, 6288-1,6125-7
"Bix/bum.". Friedrich Achleitner. 6769-7
Bixley, Barbara Brooks
    My hiding place and me. 6799-9
Biyng a pyg. John Heywood. 6586-4
Bjarnason, Bogi (tr.)
    At the funeral of --. Kristjan N. ("K.N.") Julius, 6854-5
Bjarnason, Paul (tr.)
    My land of dreams. Gudmundur Magnusson, 6854-5
Bjornson, Bjornstjerne
    The boy and the flute. Sir Edmund Gosse (tr.). 7039-6
    The boy and the flute. 6732-8
    The princess. 6585-6
    The ski-journey. 7035-3
    The tree ("The tree's early leaf-buds..."). 6047-1,6049-8,6127-3,6373-X,6466-3,6502-,6131-1,6519-8,6546-6
Black. Wilfred Wilson Gibson. 6102-8
Black. Sarah Foss Wolverton. 6316-0
Black Aiken's lot. Winifred Virginia Jackson. 6038-2
Black and blue eyes. Thomas Moore. 6302-0;6385-3
Black and gold. Nancy Byrd Turner. 6143-5
Black and tan. J. Farley Ragland. 6178-8
Black and white shuffle. Harry Elmore Hurd. 6722-0
Black are the stars. Raymond F. Roseliep. 6218-0
"Black as a nun." Christian Morgenstern. 6160-5
"Black ash/photographs of". Pine point, you are: Gordon Henry. 7005-1
Black ashes. Martha Haskell Clark. 6374-8
"Black beauty, which above that common light". Edward Herbert, 1st Baron Herbert of Cherbury. 6106-0
Black Bill's honey-moon. Alfred Noyes. 6458-2
"Black beneath as the night". The red-winged blackbird. Ethelwyn Wetherald. 6797-2
The black birds. Henry Van Dyke. 6961-4
"The black boy rose from his bed". Samuel. Alan Paton. 6788-3
"'Black boy', I said to him...". Dusky answer. Jack Conroy. 6906-1
Black bunny. William Brighty Rands. 6114-1
Black cameo on pink quartz. John W. Burton. 6178-8
Black cat. Lora Dunetz. 6388-8
Black cat in prunus-tree. Joseph Braddock. 6511-2
The black Christ. Arthur Shearly Cripps. 6788-3
Black Christmas. DuBose Heyward. 6038-2,6326-8
"Black clouds that hide the blue of sky". When the shadows deepen. Fred Berman. 6841-3
The black cock. Joanna Baillie. 6219-9,6271-7
"The black con getting out with me stood there". Getting out. J.J. Maloney. 6870-7
The black cottage, sels. Robert Frost. 6052-8
The black cottage. Robert Frost. 6162-1,6399-3,6121-4
"Black crows out on the grey and white". Crows on the river. Theodore Goodridge Roberts. 6797-2
"Black damp earth of the badlands". Let's go again. Circe Maia. 7036-1
The black death of Bergen. Frederick Temple Blackwood, Baron Dufferin. 6580-5
The black dice. Henry Christeen Warnack. 6327-6
The black dudeen. Robert Service. 6159-1
"The black earth's always drinking". Unknown (Greek) 6251-2
"The black earth, the red earth". Thompson's last stand. Maurice Carpenter. 6895-2
Black elk steps upon Alcatraz. Eugene Ruggles. 6901-0
Black eyes. William Wetmore Story. 6735-2
"Black eyes if you seem dark". To her eyes. Edward Herbert, 1st Baron Herbert of Cherbury. 6933-9

Black faces. Anita Scott Coleman. 6178-8
"Black faces lifted to the heavens - searching".
    Evolution. Thelma Parker Cox. 7024-8
Black fear. Elizabeth Woody. 7005-1
Black feathered mules. Jayne Cortez. 6898-7
Black Friday. Louella C. Poole. 6120-6
Black frost. May Folwell Hoisington. 7038-8
Black funnel spouting black. Michael Roberts. 6985-1
Black gauntlet. William Cousins. 6178-8
"A black guard motions me into an airway full". City jail.
    J.J. Maloney. 6870-7
Black hat. Paul Evison. 7018-3
Black Hills survival gathering, 1980 Linda Hogan. 7005-1
The Black Hills. Nellie H. Evans. 6799-9
Black hole in space. Clem Portman. 6857-X
A black horse with a white breast. Ibn Sa'id (of Alcala La
    Real) 6362-4
The black hound bays. George Sterling. 6880-4
Black hussars. Nikolai Aseyev. 6546-5
Black is beautiful. Townsend T. Brewster. 7024-8
"Black is the beauty...", fr. The bloody... Christopher
    Marlowe. 6106-0;6726-3
Black judgement. Nikki Giovanni. 7024-8
The black knight. John Todhunter. 6437-X
Black lake. George Abbe. 6761-1
The black leopard. Frances Crawford. 6515-5
Black lightning. Arthur Sze. 6790-5
Black Magdalens. Countee Cullen. 6532-5
Black magic. Robert Hillyer. 6039-0
Black mammies. John Wesley Holloway. 6365-9
Black Mammy. Edith Tatum. 6083-8
Black man. William Yandell Elliott. 6071-4,6039-0
"Black man in a white dress shirt". Man's world
    dissolving. Derek Butler. 6870-7
The black man speaks. Langston Hughes. 6561-9
"Black man, white man, brown man, yellow man". West India
    dock road. Thomas Burke. 7012-4
Black meat. Jean Follain. 6758-1
Black men. Lucia Trent. 6954-1
Black Mesa. Ronald Rogers. 7005-1
The Black Messengers. Cesar Vallejo. 6642-9
Black Mrs. Behemoth, fr. Facade. Edith Sitwell. 7000-0
"Black men are the tall trees that remain...".
    Portraiture. Anita Scott Coleman. 6818-9
"Black milk of daybreak we drink it at...". Fugue of
    death. Paul Celan. 6758-1
Black music. Frances Smith Johnson. 6316-0
The black nun. Winifred Welles. 6037-4
The black panther. Charles Marie Leconte de Lisle. 6873-1
The black panther. James Mooney. 6850-2
The black panther. John Hall Wheelock. 6102-8,6347-0,6506-
    6,6076-5,6467-1
"Black people, arise". There are seeds to sow. Bernette
    Golden. 7024-8
"Black people/have got to be Black". Number 28. Doughtry
    ("Doc") Long Jr.. 7024-8
"Black pitchy night, companion of my woe". Sonnet ("Black
    pitchy"). Michael Drayton. 6315-2,6436-1
Black poet. Antontin Artaud. 6803-0
Black poppies. Wayne Miller. 6792-1
The black prince. Sir Walter Scott. 6114-1
The black prince. William Shakespeare. 6438-8
Black Ranald. Phoebe Cary. 6566-X
Black recruit. Georgia Douglas Johnson. 6178-8
The black regiment. George Henry Boker. 6946-0
The black regiment. George Henry Boker. 6062-5,6113-3,6271-
    7,6239-3,6402-7,6471-,6302-0,6385-3,6016-2
The black riders. Stephen Crane. 6121-4,6736-0
Black rock. William Roehrick. 6850-2
The black rock of Kiltearn. Andrew Young. 6210-5
The black rock. John Gould Fletcher. 7017-5
The black rock. John Gould Fletcher. 6034-X
Black rocks. Laureen Mar. 6790-5
The black rose. Clement Wood. 6619-4
Black roses. Hervey Allen. 6037-4
Black sailor's chanty. Charles Augustus Keeler. 6833-2
"Black shadows fall/From the lindens tall". Birds of
    passage. Henry Wadsworth Longfellow. 6753-0
Black sheep. Richard Burton. 6260-1,6310-1,6431-0
Black sheep. Margaret Ballard McCann. 6764-6

The black sheep. Edgar A. Guest. 6869-3
The black sheep. Robert Service. 6159-1
"Black smoke of sound". Air raid: Barcelona. Langston
    Hughes. 6761-1
Black soldier. Elizabeth J. Buchtenkirk. 6979-7
Black soldier. Mary Wilkerson Cleaves. 6178-8
Black spirit. Tom Poots. 6218-0
"Black swallows swooping or gliding". The skaters. John
    Gould Fletcher. 6850-2
Black swans. Andrew Barton Paterson. 6793-X
Black swans. Count Carl Snoilsky. 6045-5
Black swans..Murray lagoons, fr. Australian transcripts.
    William ("Fiona Macleod") Sharp. 6768-9
Black tambourine. Hart Crane. 6375-6
"Black time, soulless and hungered, like a...". Hymn to
    man. Royall Snow. 7019-1
The black trout. Eugenio Montale. 6803-0
The black virgin. Gilbert Keith Chesterton. 6282-2
The black vulture. George Sterling. 6083-8,6073-0,6102-8,
    6509-0,6310-1,6732 ,6396-9,6393-4,6431-0,6250-4,6467-
    1,6510 ,6076-5,6121-4,6241-5,6300-4
The black wall-flower. Frances Anne Kemble. 6656-9
"The black walnut logs in the chimney". The picture-book.
    Alice Cary. 6969-X
"Black was the oozy lift". Storm, fr. Meg Blane. Robert
    Buchanan. 6997-5
Black water side. Unknown. 6061-7
"Black we are but much admired". Unknown. 6904-5
"Black with the blackness of hell and despair". Let there
    be light! Ruth Wright Kauffman. 6846-4
"Black within and red without." Mother Goose. 6452-3
Black your shoes, your Honour? Banbury Chapbook. 6466-3
'The black' country. D.J. Enright. 6257-1
"Black'on frowns east on Maidon". After the club-dance,
    fr. At Casterbridge fair. Thomas Hardy. 6828-6
Black, John
    Song comes like a frustrated flower. 6979-7
Black, Leon
    Long time ago. 6237-7
Black, MacKnight
    Fulfilling. 6954-1
    Give not with your hands. 6039-0
    Lenin. 6880-4
    Morning. 6808-1
    Poems of the machine age. 6464-7
    Structural iron workers. 6808-1
    Turbines. 6808-1
Black, Richard
    Army air force ground crew song. 6237-7
Black, William
    Ballade of solitude. 6770-0,6875-8
    Infant joy. 6424-8
"The black, carved writing desk, the two...". The poet's
    place. Yannis Ritsos. 6758-1
"The black-bird whistles from the thorny brake". Birds in
    spring, fr. The seasons (Spring). James Thomson.
    6932-0
Black-eyed Susan. John Gay. 6250-4,6560-0,6092-7,6543-0,
    6198-2,6328-4,6246-6,6302-0,6385-3,6502
"Black-eyed pickaninny". Pickaninny. Ellen Earl. 6750-6
Black-out. Robinson Jeffers. 6666-6
"Black/wings sun glanced". Leaving smoke's. Gordon Henry.
    7005-1
Blackall, C.W.
    The padre. 6846-4
Blackall, Captain
    Seven days' leave. 6443-4
Blackamoor's lament. Edward Harry William Meyerstein. 6893-
    6
Blackberry briars. Albert Frederick Wilson. 6036-6
The blackberry farm. John James Piatt. 7041-8
"Blackberry, elderberry". Berries and nettles. William
    Force Stead. 6778-6
Blackbird. Ronald Bottrall. 6985-1
Blackbird. John Drinkwater. 6073-0,6477-9,6639-9,6668-2
Blackbird. Frederick Tennyson. 6385-3,6600-3,6656-9
The blackbird ("In the far corner..."). Humbert Wolfe.
    6073-0,6374-8,6466-3,6368-3
The blackbird ("The nightingale has a lyre of gold").
    William Ernest Henley. 6073-0,6464-7,6104-4,6102-8

BLACKBIRD

The blackbird ("When smoke stood up from Ludlow"). Alfred Edward Housman. 6073-0
"The blackbird always makes me laugh". Sobersides. Gertrude Ewing. 6799-9
The blackbird in the town. Oliver St. John Gogarty. 6482-5
"The blackbird is singing on Michigan's shore". Geehale, an Indian lament. Unknown. 6752-2
The blackbird of Daricarn. George Sigerson. 6174-5,6582-1
The blackbird of Derrycairn. Sean O'Faolain. 6582-1
"A blackbird singing". To one dead. Francis Ledwidge. 6812-X
The blackbird song. Marjory Christmas. 6541-4
A blackbird suddenly. Joseph Auslander. 6337-3,6076-5,6253-9,6653-4
The blackbird troubadour. Mary Josephine Benson. 6797-2
The blackbird's song, fr. The boy in grey. Henry Kingsley. 6518-X
The blackbird, or, Logan's lament. Unknown. 6058-7
The blackbird.. William Barnes. 6423-X
A blackbird. Marcus Argentarius. 6435-3
The blackbird. Henry Charles Beeching. 6437-X
The blackbird. Francis William Bourdillon. 6943-6
The blackbird. Alice Cary. 6073-0,6006-4,6309-8
The blackbird. Charles and Mary Lamb. 6242-3
The blackbird. Alfred Lord Tennyson. 6597-X,6123-0,6092-7
The blackbird. Unknown. 6182-6
The blackbird. Unknown. 6859-6
The blackbird. Unknown (Irish) 6858-8
"Blackbirds feeding in a field of grass". White whale specked black. Randolph Outlaw. 6870-7
The blackbirds: an elegy. Richard Jago. 6943-6
The blackbirds. Francis Ledwidge. 6812-X
Blackburn, Alexander
    What makes a nation great? 6461-2
Blackburn, Grace
    The chant of the woman. 6115-X
    The cypress-tree. 6115-X
    Epic of the Yser. 6115-X
    The evening star. 6115-X
    If winter come. 6115-X
    Sing ho for the herring. 6115-X
    Twilight. 6691-7
Blackburn, Paul
    Newsclips 2. (Dec/6-7) 6803-0
Blackburn, Thomas
    An easter hymn. 6271-7,6429-9
"Blacke pytchy Night, companyon of my woe." Michael Drayton. 6586-4
"Blacken thy heavens, Jove". Prometheus. Johann Wolfgang von Goethe. 7039-6,6879-0
"Blackened and bleeding, helpless, painting...". Chicago. Francis Bret Harte. 6820-0
"Blacker than black of the plum-tree bough". One black crow. Ann Bradshaw. 6979-7
"Blacker than e'er the inky waters roll". Wool is down. Garnet Walch. 6768-9,6591-0,6592-9
Blacker, William
    Oliver's advice. 6858-8
    Protestant boys.
"The blackest day in the history of". Walking. Trevor Reeves. 7018-3
Blackford, Byron Haverly
    The end. 6818-9
Blackham, H.H.
    Forsaken homes and graves. 6768-9
"Blackie".. John Joy Bell. 6639-9
Blackie, John Stuart
    Abraham. 6848-0
    Chinese Gordon. 6819-7
    David. 6848-0
    The death of Columba. 6819-7
    Moses. 6848-0
    Musical frogs. 6711-5
    The musical frogs. 6916-9
    My faithful fond one. 6180-X
    My loves. 6180-X,6437-X
    The old soldier in the Gareloch head. 6873-1
    A song of geology, fr. Musa Burschicosa. 6819-7
    A song of good counsel. 6134-4
    The song of Mrs. Jenny Geddes. 6819-7
    A song of Scottish heroes. 7009-4
    The song of the highland river. 6819-7
    The well of Bethlehem. 6848-0
    The working man's song. 6819-7
    The working man't song. 6820-0
Blackie, John Stuart (tr.)
    The Persians, sels. Aeschylus, 6484-1
    Psalm 148. Bible, 6848-0
Blackman, Louise
    Miracle. 6178-8
    Rain wish. 6178-8
Blackmore, Richard Doddridge
    At the last. 6641-0
    Creation, sels. 6482-5
    Dominus illuminatio mea. 6337-3,6437-X,6303-9,6723-9
    Reunited love. 6273-3
    Yes (They stood above the world.") 6273-3,6226-1
Blackmur, Richard P.
    Before sentence is passed. 6389-6
    The dead ride fast. 6390-X
    Missa Vocis. 6390-X
    Twelve scarabs for the living. 6391-8
Blackmore maidens. William Barnes. 6199-0
The blacksmith of Bottledell. James Maurice Thompson. 6742-5
The blacksmith of Limerick. Robert Dwyer Joyce. 6858-8
The blacksmith of Ragenbach. frank Murray. 6912-6
Blacksmith pain. Otto Julius Bierbaum. 7039-6
Blacksmith's song (no. 1). I.E. Diekenga. 6711-5
Blacksmith's song (no. 2). G. Lemoine. 6711-5
The blacksmith's story. Frank Clive. 6742-5
The blacksmith's story. Frank Olive. 6045-1,6142-7,6392-6,6451-5,6566-X
The blacksmith. G. Lemoine. 6701-8
The blacksmith. Edward Verrall Lucas. 6018-8
Blackstone, Sir William
    The lawyer's farewell to his muse. 6889-8,6219-9
Blackwell, Alice Stone (tr.)
    The bond. Archag Tchobanian, 6889-8
    The Chragan palace. Thomas Terzyan, 6050-1
    Cradle song ("Nightingale, oh, leave..."). Raphael Patkanian, 6050-1
    "The lips of the Christ-child are like to twin leaves". Saint Gregory of Narek, 6050-1
    The little lake. Bedros Tourian, 6050-1
    The tears of Araxes. Raphael Patkanian, 6050-1
    The wandering Armenian to the swallow. C.A. Dodochian, 6050-1
Blackwell, Dorothy F
    Crescendo. 6178-8
    Nocturne. 6178-8
Blackwell, Dorothy F.
    Echo. 6178-8
Blackwell, Harriet Gray
    Anodyne. 6750-6
Blackwell, W.A.
    'Let go!'. 6274-1
"The blade I bear". Unknown. 6435-3
Blade of grass. S. Prochazka. 6763-8
A blade of grass. Frederick Victor Branford. 6269-5
A blade of grass. John F.G. Holmes. 6764-6
The blades of grass. Stephen Crane. 6232-6,6102-8,6076-5,6337-3,6464-7
The blades of Harden, fr. Whaup o' the rede. William Henry Ogilvie. 6845-6
The Blaeberry courtship. Unknown. 6057-9
Blagden, Isa
    Endurance. 7037-X
    Sorrow. 7037-X
Blaikie, John Arthur
    Absence. 6656-9
    Love's secret name. 6274-1,6656-9
    Song. 6656-9
Blaine of Maine. Eugene Fitch Ware. 6820-0
Blair, Avanelle Wilmeth
    Knife of nostalgia. 6750-6
Blair, George
    The dying Kafir. 6800-6
Blair, Margaret
    Night-club. 6490-6

Blair, Robert
   Beauty in the grave. 6543-0
   Church and church-yard at night, fr. The grave. 6932-0
   The end of life, fr. The grave. 6934-7
   The grave, sels. 6198-2,6294-6,6195-0,6152-4
   The grave, sels. 6831-6
   The grave. 6086-2
   Oft in the lone church-yard. 6543-0
   Pride ("When self-esteem, or other's adulation"). 6294-6
   Strength in the grave. 6543-0
Blair, the regular. Ida Reed Smith. 6889-8
Blaisdell, Hosea Q.
   Sometime. 6411-6
Blaisdell, James A.
   Beneath the forms of outward rite. 6337-3
Blaising, Charlotte
   Futility. 6750-6
Blake. John Gould Fletcher. 6289-X,6345-4
Blake's testament. William Blake. 6659-3
Blake, Clifton E.
   Par. 7030-2
Blake, Emilia Aylmer
   Alice Ayres. 6695-X
   The glacier-bed. 6167-2,6744-1
   The glacier-bed. 6925-8
   A juryman's story. 6924-X
Blake, James Vila
   In him. 6730-1
   Wedded. 6066-8,6620-8
Blake, Katherine D.
   The road to Laughertown. 6109-5
Blake, Katherine Devereux
   Laughertown. 6847-2
   "Of old when shepherds watched". 6847-2
   When would I die? 6847-2
Blake, Mary Elizabeth
   The dawning o' the year. 6309-8
   A dead summer. 7041-8
   Going and coming. 7041-8
   Heartsick! 7041-8
   In exile. 6309-8
Blake, Rodney
   Hoch! der Kaiser. 6089-7,6274-1
Blake, Willa
   Mourning. 6750-6
Blake, William
   Ah sunflower [weary of time]. 6660-7,6179-6,6536-8,6086-2,6250-4,6430-2,6301 ,6187-7,6246-6,6604-6,6615-1, 6378-0,6154-
   All rose before the aged apparition, fr. America. 6106-0
   America, sels. 6106-0
   "And did those feet in ancient time," fr. Milton. 6023-4,6052-8,6187-7,6536-8,6668-2,6793
   The angel. 6086-2
   The apparition, fr. America. 6106-0
   The arts of death. 6150-8
   Auguries of innocence. 6024-2,6208-3,6315-2,6337-3,6427-2,6641-,6086-2,6195-0,6430-2,6730-1
   Auguries of innocence, sels. 7009-4
   Auguries of innocence, sels. 6179-6,6317-9,6634-8,6648-8
   The bard. 6730-1
   The beauty of terror. 6322-5
   The birds. 6943-6
   Blake's testament. 6659-3
   Blind-man's bluff. 6018-8,6086-2
   The blossom. 6943-6
   The book of Thel, sels. 6208-3,6317-9
   The book of Thel. 6152-4,6195-0
   Brotherhood. 6150-8
   The building of Jerusalem. 6639-9
   The caverns of the grave I've seen. 6380-2
   The child and the piper. 6133-8
   Childhood. 6233-4
   chimney sweeper, fr. The songs of innocence. 6105-2, 6086-2,6152-4
   The chimney sweeper. 6102-8,6106-0,6134-6,6233-4,6075-7, 6634-,6086-2,6153-2,6723-9
   The clod and the pebble. 6024-2,6198-2,6208-3,6315-2, 6427-2,6430 ,6150-8,6250-4,6371-3
   Cradle so^{n}g ("Sleep, sleep, beauty bright"). 6134-6, 6216-4,6395-9,6627-5,6737-9,6491 ,6078-1,6533-3,6214-8,6491-4,6328-4,6086
   Cromek. 6545-7
   The crystal cabinet. 6086-2,6380-2
   Cupid. 6089-7,6732-8
   Dedication of the designs to Blair's 'Grave'. 6086-2
   The defiled sanctuary. 6191-5
   "The desire of man being infinite" 7014-0
   A divine image. 6024-2,6086-2,6152-4,6250-4,6430-2,6150 ,6125-7,6208-3,6337-3,6339-X,6526-8,6730
   Doctor Johnson, fr. An island in the moon. 6545-7
   The door of death. 6125-7,6461-2
   A dream. 6134-6,6378-0,6479-5,6454-X,6638-0,6639 ,6086-2,6195-0,6378-0
   The echoing green. 6086-2,6454-X,6371-3,6491-4,6195-0, 6152 ,6018-8,6138-9,6179-6,6228-8,6236-9,6466
   "England! awake! awake! awake!" 6138-9
   Enitharmon's song, fr. Vala. 6125-7
   Epigram ("He who bends"). 6179-6
   Epigram ("I give"). 6179-6
   Epigram ("The sword"). 6179-6
   Epilogue to the accuser who is the God of this world. 6378-0
   Eternity ("He who bends to himself a Joy"). 6315-2,6339-X
   Ethinthus, queen of waters, fr. Europe. 6125-7,6545-7
   Evening. 6487-6
   The everlasting gospel, sels. 6931-2
   The everlasting gospel, sels. 6191-5
   The everlasting gospel, sels. 6931-2
   Fair Eleanor. 6518-X
   The fields from Islington to Marybone. 6125-7
   The four zoas, sels. 6106-0
   Fragment ("Spirit"). 6545-7
   From Islington to Marybone. 6641-0
   The garden of love. 6232-6,6271-7,6302-0,6315-2,6317-9, 6385-,6086-2,6195-0,6301-2,6430-2
   The gates of paradise. 6208-3
   Good English hospitality. 6157-5
   "Great things are done when men and mountains meet." 6501-5
   The grey monk, sels. 6301-2
   The grey monk. 6250-4
   The happy piper. 6114-1
   "He who binds to himself a joy." 6187-7,6317-9
   "He who sees the infinite" 7014-0
   Hear the voice. 6086-2
   "Hear the voice of the Bard!". 6186-9,6246-6
   Heaven and hell, fr. The marriage of heaven and hell. 6545-7
   Holy Thursday. 7009-4
   Holy Thursday. 6233-4,6339-X,6478-7,6536-8,6634-8,6737 , 6086-2,6152-4,6214-8,6421-3,6430-2
   "How sweet I roam'd from field to field". 6187-7,6208-3, 6733-6
   How sweet is the shepherd's sweet lot. 6228-8
   The human abstract. 6831-6
   Humility and doubt, sels. 6545-7
   I asked a thief. 6733-6
   I cry: Love, love!, fr. The vision of the three daughters. 6545-7
   I heard an angel. 6502-3,6659-3
   I loved the jocund dance. 6187-7,6328-4
   I saw a chapel all of gold. 6154-0,6488-4
   I saw a monk of Charlemaine. 6378-0
   I told my love. 6934-7
   "I wander thro' each chartered street." 6317-9
   "I was angry with my friend". 6187-7
   Ideas of good and evil, auguries of innocence. 6198-2, 6254-0
   "If it were not for the poetic" 7014-0
   Immortal tent. 6978-9
   The immortal. 6315-2
   In a wife I would desire. 6733-6
   Infant joy. 6078-1,6102-8,6134-6,6186-9,6233-4,6242-, 6086-2,6301-2,6737-9,6315-2,6339-X,6502-3,6519-8, 6533-3

BLAKE   154

Infant sorrow. 6078-1,6086-2,6208-3,6233-4,6533-3
Introduction, fr. Songs of innocence. 6219-9,6371-3,
  6543-0,660-7,6024-2,6198-2,6315-2,6488-4,6604-6,6634-
Introduction: "Piping down the valleys." 6271-7
Jerusalem. 6228-8,6334-9,6339-X,6395-0,6427-2,6658 ,
  6107-9,6150-8,6665-8
Jerusalem, sels. 6334-9,6378-0
Joy is my name. 6328-4
Jubilance. 6943-6
The lamb. 6024-2,6075-7,6078-1,6102-8,6134-6,6154 ,6086-
  2,6104-4,6152-4,6195-0,6114-1,6131 ,6183-4,6216-4,
  6242-3,6315-2,6337-3,6339 ,6371-3,6430-2,6424-8,6456-
  6,6510-X,6454 ,6418-3,6481-7,6519-8,6604-6,6726-3,
  6730 ,6630-7,6639-9,6543-0,6638-0,6645-3,6723 ,6634-
  8,6964-9
The lament of Thel. 6634-8
The land of dreams. 6134-6,6186-9,6233-4,6533-3,6086-2,
  6114
The lapwing. 6545-7
A laughing song. 6334-9,6466-3,6585-6,6454-X,6153-2,
  6668 ,6086-2
Lessons on cruelty. 6134-6
Life. 6138-9
Life, sels. 6018-8
The little black boy. 6102-8,6228-8,6233-4,6249-0,6271-
  7,6369-,6086-2,6152-4,6430-2,6219-9,6150-8,6214 ,
  6395-9,6627-5,6737-9
The little boy found. 6086-2
A little boy lost, fr. Songs of Innocence. 6430-2,6086-
  2,6152-4
The little boy lost, fr. Songs of innocence. 6086-2
Little lamb. 6502-3
The little vagabond. 6089-7,6271-7,6328-4,6733-6,6152-4
London. 6086-2,6152-4,6208-3,6378-0,6150-8,6125 ,6491-4,
  6645-3,6250-4
London, fr. The human image. 6125-7
Long John Brown and little Mary Bell. 6633-X
"Love seeketh not itself to please." 6317-9,6066-8
Love's prisoner. 6250-4
Love's secret. 6102-8,6198-2,6427-2,6250-4,6513-9,6153 ,
  6464-7,6737-9
Mad song. 6102-8,6328-4,6378-0,6152-4
"Man's perceptions are not bounded by organs" 7014-0
The manuscript book, sels. 6179-6
The marriage of heaven and hell, sels. 6315-2,6152-4
"Memory, hither come". 6187-7,6328-4,6258-4
The men of Thames. 6125-7
The mental traveller. 6086-2,6195-0
Milton. 6102-8,6315-2,6195-0,6301-2,6723-9
Milton, sels. 6186-9,6208-3,6334-9,6152-4,6195-0,6430 ,
  6107-9,6334-9,6337-3,6378-0,6730-1,6527-9,6427-
Mock on, mock on, Voltaire, Rousseau. 6086-2,6430-2
"Mock on, mock on, Voltaire, Rousseau". 6931-2
The monk. 6315-2
The Moon, like a flower. 6395-0
Morning. 6187-7,6315-2
The morning comes, fr. America. 6545-7
Mr Cromek. 6125-7
My pretty rose tree. 6086-2
"My silks and fine array." 6138-9,6187-7,6208-3,6328-4,
  6301-2,6383 ,6125-7
My spectre around me night and day. 6380-2,6086-2
Never seek to tell thy love, fr. Love's secret. 6187-7,
  6430-2,6092-7,6317-9,6246-6,6634
The new dispensation, fr. The everlasting gospel. 6934-
  7
New Jerusalem. 6634-8,6138-9
Night. 6252-0
Night. 6024-4,6138-9,6246-6,6369-1,6423-X,6604-,6152-4,
  6153-2,6252-0,6543-0,6646-1,6660 ,6075-7,6086-2,6102-
  8,6668-2,6737-9,6808
Nightingale and flowers. 6315-2
Nurse's song. 6421-3,6075-7,6138-9,6228-8,6242-3,6533-5,
  6737 ,6086-2,6668-2
Nurse's song, fr. Songs of experience. 6152-4
Nurse's song, fr. Songs of innocence. 6152-4
O lapwing! 6125-7
"O Rose, thou art sick". 6187-7
"O thou with dewy locks, who lookest down". 6187-7
On another's sorrow. 6271-7,6337-3,6502-3,6604-6,6660-7,
  6219 ,6152-4,6808-1,6271-7,6337-3,6502-3,6604-6,6660-
  7,6219 ,6152-4,6808-1
Our lesser kindred, fr. Auguries of innocence. 6102-8
Pipe a song. 6732-8
The piper. 6127-3,6131-1
Piping down the valleys wild. 6236-9,6328-4,6395-0,6519-
  8,6726-3,6639 ,6104-4,6454-X,6723-9,6127-3,6131-3,
  6469
The poet's voice. 6125-7
Poetical sketches, sels. 6208-3,6152-4
A poison free, r. Songs of experience. 6154-0,6301-2,
  6427-2
A poison tree. 6154-0,6198-2,6430-2,6427-2,6527-9,6301
"Prayer is the study of art" 7014-0
Preface, fr. Milton. 6152-4
The price of experience, fr. Zala. 6545-7
Prophetic books, sels. 6198-2
Prophetic books, universal humanity. 6198-2
Proverbs. 6198-2
The proverbs of hell, fr. The marriage of heaven and
  hell. 6545-7
Proverbs, sels. 6198-2
The question answer'd. 6733-6
"Reason, or the ration of all we have" 7014-0
Reeds of innocence. 6102-8,6086-2,6301-2
A robin redbreast. 6421-3
The schoolboy. 6086-2,6179-6,6246-6,6634-8
The shepherd. 6315-2,6328-4,6086-2,6639-9,6454-X,6638
The sick rose. 6106-0,6179-6,6198-2,6208-3,6228-8,6246-,
  6315-2,6430-2,6125-7,6086-2,6645-3
Sleep, sleep, beauty bright. 6958-4
Soft snow. 6106-0
Song. 6543-0
Song ("Fresh from the dewy hill"). 6086-2
Song ("How sweet"). 6086-2,6430-2,6560-0,6659-3,6383-7,
  6371 ,6086-2,6383-7,6371-3,6659-3,6560-0,6430 ,6102-
  8,6232-6,6423-X,6726-3,6125-7,6195
Song ("I love the jocund dance.") 6086-2
Song ("Love and harmony"). 6943-6
Song ("Little boy"). 6233-4
Song ("Memory, hither come"). 6102-8,6086-2
Song ("My silks"). 6086-2,6153-2,6371-3,6430-2,6152-4,
  6472 ,6254-4,6560-0,6246-6,6315-2
Song ("Never seek"). 6315-2
A song of liberty. 6334-9
A song of singing. 6134-6,6383-7
Songs of experience The. 6430-2
Songs of experience, sels. 6198-2,6208-3
Songs of experience: introduction. 6315-2
Songs of innocence. 6186-9,6430-2,6421-3,6560-0
Songs of innocence, sels. 6152-4,6192-3,6668-2,6105-2,
  6208-3,6289-X,6726-3,6104-4,6195
The spirit's warfare. 6138-9
Spring. 6334-9,6018-8
Spring. 6138-9
"Still the faint harps...", fr. The four zoas. 6106-0
The sunflower. 6385-3,6438-8,6125-7
The sword and the sickle. 6125-7
A tear is an intellectual thing. 6102-8
Thel's motto. 6125-7
Three things to remember. 6073-0,6512-0,614-1,6510-4
Thy Maker is near. 6303-9
The tiger, sels. 6289-X
The tiger. 6125-7,6131-1,6114-1,6438-8,6086-2,6424 ,
  6023-4,6660-7,6152-4,6195-0,6430-2,6513 ,6250-4,6150-
  8,6107-9,6383-7,6219-9,6252 ,6153-2,6301-2,6371-3,
  6396-9,6421-3,6510 ,6464-7,6491-4,6543-0,6646-1,6639-
  9,6723 ,6668-2,6737-9,6645-3,6024-2,6138-9,6186-9,
  6198-2,6239-3,6337-,6052-8,6102-8,6133-8,6134-6,6136-
  2,6154-,6242-3,6271-7,6332-2,6369-1,6385-3,6395-,
  6328-4,6625-9,6634-8,6726-3,6730-1,6427-2,6473-6,
  6481-7,6488-4,6501-5,6504-,6527-9,6534-1,6536-8,6597-
  X,6600-3,6604-,6383-7,6430-2,6195-0,6152-4
'Till we have built Jerusalem' 6954-1
To autumn ("O Autumn, laden with fruit..."). 6334-9,
  6018-8
"To find the western path." 6250-4
To memory. 6830-8
To mercy pity peace and love. 6317-9
To morning. 6334-9,6018-8,6252-0

"To see a world in a grain of sand." 6187-7,6250-4
"To see the world in a grain." 6250-4
To spring. 6328-4,6334-9,6250-4,6018-8,6152-4,6086-2
To summer ("O thou who passest..."). 6334-9,6018-8,6152-4
To the Christians. 6730-1
To the divine image. 6604-6,6660-7
To the evening star. 6024-2,6102-8,6154-0,6236-9,6315-2, 6423-,6332-2,6334-9,6488-9,6604-6,6645-3,6152 ,6192-3,6252-0,6430-2,6125-7,6543-0,6545
To the muses. 6102-8,6186-9,6315-2,6395-0,6600-3,6604-, 6726-3,6660-7,6545-7,6152-4,6092-7,6250
To the muses. 6935-5
To the muses. 6430-2,6125-7,6086-2,6543-0
To the queen. 6191-5
To Tirzah. 6317-9
To winter ("'O Winter! bar thine..."). 6018-8,6334-9
True and false love. 6935-5
"'Twas on a Holy Thursday, their innocent faces". 6187-7
Two epigrams. 6633-X
Two kinds of riches. 6198-2
The two songs. 6198-2,6153-2
The tyger. 6179-6,6187-7,6208-3,6246-6,6315-2,6339-, 6732-8
The voice of the ancient bard. 6934-7
The voice of the bard. 6301-2
A war song to Englishmen. 6395-0,6665-8,6545-7
A war song. 6328-4
When a man has married a wife. 6733-6
When early morn walks forth. 6328-4
When the green woods laugh, fr. Songs of innocence. 6328-4
Why was Cupid a boy. 6092-7
The wild-flower's song. 6250-4
William Bond. 6369-1,6380-2
William Bond, sels. 6317-9
Written 1811. 6337-3
Blakely, Roger
  Winslow Homer, prisoners from the front. 6966-5
Blakeney, Bruce
  Carmen. 6397-7
  Chanson tendre. 6397-7
Blakeney, Lena Whittaker
  The covered wagon. 6397-7
  Goldfish. 6397-7
  Leaving England. 6397-7
  Night on the Irish Sea. 6397-7
  The prairie ("Today at dusk I crossed the...prairie"). 6397-7
  The prairie. 6397-7
  Quest. 6397-7
  Quest ("So long as beauty calls me"). 6397-7
  Sketches from the Dolomites. 6397-7
  Strangers. 6397-7
"Blame not my cheeks, though pale with love". Thomas Campion. 6187-7
"Blame not my cheeks, though pale with loue...". A booke of Ayres (XIV). Thomas Campion. 6794-8
"Blame not my lute, for he must sound." Sir Thomas Wyatt. 6182-6,6584-8,6250-4,6072-9,6219-9
"Blame not thyself too much", fr. The princess. Alfred Lord Tennyson. 6867-7
"Blameless as daylight I stood looking". The eye-mote. Sylvia Plath. 6803-0
Blamire, Susanna
  And ye shall walk in silk attire. 6086-2
  In silk attire. 6086-2,6383-7
  The nabob. 6086-2,6219-9
  The siller crown. 6019-6,6219-9
  What ails this heart o' mine? 6600-3,6219-9
Blanch, F.D.
  Bulwarks. 6857-X
"Blanch-amiced, roseal nursling, resupine". Francis Thompson: Hush-a-bye, baby. Charles Powell. 6982-7
Blanchard, Amy Ella
  Rest. 6927-4
Blanchard, Edith Richmond
  Cats. 6120-6
Blanchard, Grace
  Choice. 6764-6
Blanchard, Janice
  Beyond the stom. 6750-6
  Old barn. 6750-6
Blanchard, Laman
  The art of book-keeping. 6089-7,6297-0
  Dolce far niente. 6874-X
  False love and true logic. 6089-7
  Hidden joys. 6656-9
  The mother's hope. 6097-8,6271-7,6302-0,6385-3,6219-9
  Nell Gwynn's looking-glass. 6656-9
  Ode to a human heart. 6089-7
  Whatever is, is right. 6089-7,6724-7
  Wishes of youth. 7015-9
Blanchard, Mary E.
  A glance backward. 6414-0,6686-0
Blanchard, S.L.
  Hidden joys. 6793-X
Blanche. A. Bernard Miall. 6274-1
Blancheflour and Jellyflorice. Unknown. 6185-0,6518-X,6613-5
Bland, Edith. See Nesbit, Edith
Bland, Henry Meade
  Divine rhythm. 6303-9
  The pioneer. 6102-8
Bland, Imogene
  Emotions. 6857-X
Bland, James
  Carry me back to old Virginny. 6465-5
Bland, Robert (tr.)
  All the world's a stage. Palladas, 6435-3
  Home. Unknown (Greek), 6385-3
  The song of health. Ariphron of Sicyon, 6879-0
Blanden, Charles G.
  Afterglow. 6274-1,6620-8
  The first bud o' the year. 6274-1
  Little windows. 6036-6
  Over the hills. 6461-2
  Overtones. 6036-6
  The passion flower. 6144-3,6006-4,6144-3
  Quatrain ("Christ bears a thousand crosses now.") 6144-3
  Quatrain ("Delve not so deep..."). 6038-2
  A rose ("All day with bright, appealing face"). 6274-1
  Song ("What trees"). 6144-3
  A song the grass sings. 6232-6,6374-8
  Time may steal the dewy bloom. 6620-8
  Until the morning break. 6461-2
  Valentine. 6820-0
  The weaver. 6036-6
  Yesterday. 6036-6
Blanding, Don
  Foreboding. 6143-5
  Hollywood. 6736-0
  A journey ends. 6337-3
  Soldier, what did you see? 6337-3,6107-9
Blane, William
  Cecil John Rhodes. 6800-6
  Pioneer's epitaph. 6625-9
  Pioneer's epitaph. 6800-6
Blank misgivings of a creature moving about in two worlds.... Arthur Hugh Clough. 6655-0
'Blank misgivings of a creature moving about in...' Arthur Hugh Clough. 6828-8
Blank misgivings, sels. Arthur Hugh Clough. 6110-9,6199-0
"Blank seems my life, and all unblest its toil". Song birth. Herbert Tucker. 6800-6
Blank verse. Muriel F. Hochdorf. 6850-2
Blank verse in rhyme. Thomas Hood. 6255-5
"A blanket of snow about my feet". December child. Virginia Wuerfel Slayton. 6906-1
Blarney Castle. Samuel Lover. 6331-4,6484-1,6439-6
The blas bleu, sels. Hannah More. 6932-0
Blasphemy, fr. The heretic. Louis Untermeyer. 6083-8
"The blast from freedom's northern hills". Massachusetts to Virginia. John Greenleaf Whittier. 6753-0
A blast of autumn. John E. Barrett. 6840-5
"The blast of common censure could I fear". To Mr. Lee, on his tragedy of Alexander the Great. John Dryden. 6970-3

BLAST

"A blast of wind, a momentary breath". Barnabe Barnes. 6181-8,6586-4
The blast-1875.. Robert Louis Stevenson. 6508-2
The blasted herb. Mesech Weare. 6946-0
"Blasted with sighs, and surrounded with tears". Twicknham garden. John Donne. 6933-9
Blasting. Kathryn White Ryan. 6039-0
Blasting rocks in Vermont. Daniel L. Cady. 6988-6
"The blasts of autumn drive the winged seeds". Spring. Percy Bysshe Shelley. 6980-0
Blatchford, P.L.
    The vision of Handel. 6674-4
Blauss, John Lincoln
    Master of hearts of men. 6995-9
Blazek, Douglas
    Handgrenades in my grapefuit. 6998-3
    The human firewood piano. 6792-1
    Revelation of the bare ass. 6792-1
    Testimony concerning a sickness. 6792-1
Bleaching a web of cotton in Vermont. Daniel L. Cady. 6989-4
Bleak weather. Ella Wheeler Wilcox. 6956-8
"Bleak were the hills and the cold wind...". The pauper's child. Augusta Moore. 6924-X
"The bleak wind is howling". The prairie. Josephine Hoshaw. 6906-1
"Bleak-faced winter, with his braggart winds". Australian spring. Hugh McCrae. 6784-0
Bleake's house in Blackmwore. William Barnes. 6092-7
A bleeding heart aflame. James M. Hayes. 6285-7
Bleheris. Archibald MacLeish. 6012-9
A blemished offering. Margaret Junkin Preston. 7041-8
Blencowe, J. W.
    The Jew's appeal to the Christian. 6848-0
Blend. Ed Lee. 6178-8
"A blend of mirth and sadness, smiles and tears". Walter Malone. 6289-X
"Blended by fading moonlight with the grass". Yellow eyes. Kingsley Fairbridge. 6800-6
Blenheim. Joseph Addison. 6932-0
Blennerhasset's island, fr. The new pastoral. Thomas Buchanan Read. 6946-0
"Bless God, my soul! thou, Lord, alone". Psalm 104, sels. Nahum Tate. 6867-7
"Bless God, ye happy lands". The jubilee of 1850. Adelaide Anne Procter. 6957-6
Bless the blessed morn. Horatius Bonar. 6065-X
Bless the dear old verdant land. Denis Florence MacCarthy. 6656-9
"Bless the lord, o my soul". Psalm 103 Bible. 6861-8
"Bless the Lord, O my soul". Psalm 103, fr. The book of psalms. Bible. 7039-6
"Bless the Lord, O my soul!". Benedic, anima mea. Bible. 6830-8
"Bless us, and save us! What's here". The ground squirrel. Paul Hamilton Hayne. 6965-7
"Bless you, bless you, burnie bee". Unknown. 6363-2
"Bless'd be that king, which evermore". A prayer of Tobias. Michael Drayton. 6848-0
Bless, dear saviour, this child. Thomas Beck. 6065-X
The blessed agitator. Lucia Trent. 6144-3
"Blessed angel! Blessed angel!". Peace. James Abraham Martling. 6952-5
"Blessed are the poor in spirit," fr. St. Matthew. Bible. 6183-4
"Blessed are they that mourn." William Cullen Bryant. 6240-7,6302-0,6385-3
"Blessed are they who die for God." Adelaide Anne Procter. 6225-3
"Blessed be God for flowers!" Mrs. Charles Tinsley. 6049-8
"Blessed be that lady bright". A cause for wonder. Unknown. 6881-2
Blessed be that lady bright. Unknown. 6756-5
"Blessed be that maid Mary". Eia Jesus hodie natus de virgine. Unknown. 6756-5
"The blessed Christ on Calvary". Ressurection. Hazel Hanna. 6799-9
Blessed be the holy will of God. Unknown. 6930-4
A blessed bird, as I you say, that died and rose... Unknown. 6756-5

"A blessed cooling fount thou art". The tear. Kristjan Jonsson. 6854-5
The blessed damozel. Dante Gabriel Rossetti. 6186-9,6198-2, 6236-9,6634-8,6604-6,6655 ,6657-7,6052-8,6122-2,6240-7,6302-0,6385 ,6536-8,6656-9,6660-7,6196-6,6430-2, 6560 ,6315-2,6437-X,6501-5,6526-0,6661-5,6726 ,6732-8,6250-4,6646-1,6199-0,6110-9,6219 ,6023-4,6046-3, 6508-2,6150-8,6153-2,6245
The blessed face. Ray Palmer. 6065-X
"Blessed is the man that walketh not...". Psalm 001, fr. The book of psalms. Bible. 7039-6
"Blessed is the man who hath not walked astray". Psalm 001. Bible. 6848-0
"Blessed Mary, moder virginal". A short prayer for Mary. Unknown. 6881-2
Blessed may thou be, sweet Jesus. Unknown. 6756-5
"Blessed of the Lord of his land," fr. Deuteronomy. Bible. 6466-3
The blessed rain. Frank Lebby Stanton. 6274-1
The blessed rain. Jennie Schmitz. 6270-9
The blessed road. Charles Buxton Going. 6144-3,6335-7
The blessed task. Harriet McEwen Kimball. 6065-X
The blessed trail. Thomas B. Livingston. 6799-9
The blessed Virgin compared to the air we breathe. Gerard Manley Hopkins. 6282-2,6489-2
The blessed virgin Mary compared to a window. Thomas Merton. 6282-2
The blessed virgin's expostulation. Nahum Tate. 6282-2
"Blessed, yet sinful one, and broken hearted!". Mary Magdalen. Bartolome Leonardo de Argensola. 6752-2
"Blessed/are the injured animals". Blessing. Linda Hogan. 7005-1
A blessing for the blessed. Laurence Alma Tadema. 6242-3, 6519-8
Blessing myself. David Ignatow. 6803-0
The blessing of a smoke. Ray D. Smith. 6274-1
"The blessing of my later years" William Wordsworth. 6867-7
The blessing of song. Unknown. 6925-8
The blessing of the beds. Elizabeth J. Coatsworth. 6217-2
The blessing of the Bruce. Sir Walter Scott. 6669-0
Blessing of toil. Samuel Ellsworth Kiser. 6449-3
Blessing on little boys. Arthur Guiterman. 6619-4
A blessing on the dance. Unknown. 6915-0
"Blessing she is; God make her so." James Russell Lowell. 6225-3
"Blessing, my God: one shaft can sink...". Prospect from Gilboa. Edward Farquhar. 6939-8
The blessing. Mary Colborne-Veel. 6784-0
Blessinger, Jerry
    Words. 6857-X
Blessings. Winifred M. Letts. 6090-0
Blessings along the way. Joel Swartz. 6583-X
Blessings of peace. Henry Wadsworth Longfellow. 6719-0
Blessings on Doneraile. Patrick O'Kelly. 6930-4
"The blessings which the weak & poor...scatter". Kindness. Sir Thomas Noon Talfourd. 6980-0
"Blessings, alas! unmerited". Too late. Phoebe Cary. 6969-X
Blessington, Countess of
    A friend. 6787-5
"Blesssings, O Father! shower". A prayer of affection. Felicia Dorothea Hemans. 6973-8
"Blest are the immortal gods." Sappho. 6271-7,6385-3
"Blest are the perfect in the way". Psalm 119. Bible. 6848-0
"Blest be the boat". Unknown. 6334-9
Blest be the ties that bind. John Fawcett. 6304-7
Blest be thy love, dear Lord. John Austin. 6219-2
"Blest is the turf, serenely blest". Dirge. Leigh Hunt. 6934-7
"Blest leaf! whose aromatic gales dispense". In imitation of Pope, fr. A pipe of tobacco. Isaac Hawkins Browne. 6932-0
"Blest leaf! whose aromatic gales...", fr. A pipe... Isaac Hawkins Browne. 6092-7
"Blest of God, the God of nations". Columbia's jubilee. Granville B. Putnam. 6925-8
"Blest pair of sirens, pledges of heav'ns joy". John Milton. 6931-2

Blest statesman he. William Wordsworth. 6199-0
Blest winter nights, fr.The art of preserving health. John Armstrong. 6932-0
"Blest! who far from all mankind". Repose in God. Madame De la Mothe Guion. 6814-6
Blest, blest and happy he. Unknown. 6845-6
Blethen, Joseph
    The mushers. 7008-6
    The passing of barbary Tim. 7007-8
Blew, William John
    O Lord, thy wing outspread. 6656-9
Blewett, Jean
    The boy of the house. 7022-1
    Chore time. 6115-X
    For he was Scotch, and so was she. 6115-X
    A good woman. 6591-0,6592-2
    Her lesson. 6797-2
    Love's lesson. 6796-4
    Margaret. 6433-7
    The native born. 6793-X
    The native born. 6797-2
    The passage. 6115-X
    Quebec. 6115-X
    She just keeps house for me. 6433-7
    Song of the golden sea. 6591-0,6592-2
    Spring. 6433-7
    The usurer. 6115-X
    What time the morning stars arise. 6115-X
Blicher, Steen Steensen
    The heather. Charles Wharton Stork (tr.). 6555-4
    The Jutlander. Charles Wharton Stork (tr.). 6555-4
    Prelude, fr. Birds of passage. Charles Wharton Stork (tr.). 6555-4
    To sorrow. Charles Wharton Stork (tr.). 6555-4
Blight. Ralph Waldo Emerson. 6077-3,6288-1
Blight. Edna St. Vincent Millay. 6986-X
"The blight of time is on that giant tor". Pike's Peak. Milton S. Rose. 6836-7
Blight, John
    The cat-o-nine-tails. 6384-5
    Stonefish and starfish. 6384-5
Blighted love. Luis de Camoens [or Camoes]. 6385-3
'Blighters.'. Siegfried Sassoon. 6210-5
Blighty. Theodosia Garrison. 6331-4
Blighty. Siegfried Sassoon. 6846-4
Blind. John Kendrick Bangs. 6303-9,6337-3
Blind. Fanny Crosby. 6337-3
Blind. Jean Milne Gower. 6836-7
Blind. Harry Kemp. 6076-5,6250-4,6467-1,6102-8,6338-1,6374-8,6476-0,6556-2
Blind. June Lucas. 6954-1
Blind. Norman V. Pearce. 6337-3
Blind. Adeline Rubin. 6397-7
Blind. Isabel Beulah Schein. 6847-2
"Blind Cyclops, hurling stones of destiny". To nature (III). Emily Ffeiffer. 7015-9
Blind alley. F.B. Caperil. 6039-0
Blind alley. Tae-jin Park. 6775-1
The blind and the dead. Robert Service. 6159-1
The blind archer. Sir Arthur Conan Doyle. 6702-6
Blind Bartimeus. Henry Wadsworth Longfellow. 6144-3;6335-7
The blind beggar of Alexandria, sels. George Chapman. 6378-0
The blind beggar's daughter of Bednall Green. Unknown. 6058-7,6518-4,6067-6,6319-5
The blind beggar's daughter. Unknown. 6061-7
The blind beggar. Mary [or Mollie] Evelyn Moore Davis. 7021-3
Blind Boone. Dorothy Belle Flanagan. 6396-9
The blind boy's pranks. William Thom. 6180-X
The blind boy. Colley Cibber. 6246-5,6133-8,6328-4,6219-9, 6424-8,6302-0,6385-3,6152-4,6131-1,6639-9,6519
The blind boy. Hannah Flagg Gould. 6131-1
The blind boy. F. Lister Hawks. 6131-1
The blind boy. Unknown (Algonquin Indian) 6864-2
Blind but happy. Fanny Crosby. 6337-3
The blind child's Christmas. Edith Ballinger Price. 6861-8
The blind child. Unknown. 6303-9,6337-3
Blind clay. Mary Fleming Labaree. 6036-6
The blind fiddler. William Wordsworth. 6142-7,6304-5

The blind flower girl of Pompeii. Ella Lindsey Matchett. 6417-5
"A blind girl/stares at me". Black lightning. Arthur Sze. 6790-5
The blind girl. Nathalia Crane. 6506-6,6332-2
"Blind guardians of the glory of our land". On the senate's repudiation of an honorable compact. Hermann Hagedorn. 6944-4
Blind guides. Thomas Curtis Clark. 6037-4
The blind highland boy. William Wordsworth. 6142-7,6459-0
The blind king. Johann Ludwig Uhland. 6842-1
The blind lady. Max Jacob. 6351-9
The blind lamb. Celia Thaxter. 6612-7,6573-2
Blind love. Rosamund Marriott ("Graham R. Tomson") Watson. 6875-8
The blind man at the fair. Joseph ("Seosamh MacCathmhaoil") Campbell. 7039-6
The blind man speaks. Howard Kenneth Preston. 6042-0
The blind man to his bride. Caroline Elizabeth Sarah Sheridan Norton. 6980-0
"A blind man walked down the street, his...". The blind man. Godfrey Green. 6857-X
Blind man's bluff. Unknown (Greek) 6435-3
The blind man's lament. James Wallis Eastburn. 6752-2
The blind man's morning. Viola Meynell. 6042-0;6339-X
The blind man. Hervey Allen. 6542-2,6628-3
The blind man. Godfrey Green. 6857-X
The blind man. James Lewisohn. 6870-7
The blind man. Nazhun. 6362-4
The blind man. Margaret Elizabeth Sangster. 6654-2
The blind men and the elephant. Sana'i. 6448-5
The blind men and the elephant. John Godfrey Saxe. 6165-6, 6176-1,6228-8,6290-3,6279-2,6404 ,6337-3,6512-0,6527-9,6639-9,6107-9,6464
The blind men. Ethelwyn Wetherald. 6433-7
Blind moone of London. Alfred Noyes. 6151-6
The blind nun. Thomas S. Jones Jr. 6285-7
The blind old man. Unknown (Greek) 6435-3
Blind old Milton. William Edmonstoune Aytoun. 6948-7
The blind pedlar. Osbert Sitwell. 6102-8
The blind poet's wife. Edwin Coller. 6744-1
The blind poet. Unknown. 6090-0
The blind poet. Anthony Raftery. 6090-0
The blind preacher. Yakov Polonsky. 6103-6
The blind rower. Wilfred Wilson Gibson. 6508-2
The blind sailor. Theodore Goodridge Roberts. 6115-X
Blind spots. Lois Ethleen Schmidt. 6270-9
The blind steed. Unknown (German) 6131-1
The blind stranger. Wilfred Wilson Gibson. 6780-8
The blind traveler. Alice Cary. 6969-X
The blind youth. Clive Sansom. 6339-X
Blind, Mathilde
    Alone - with one fair star. 6747-6
    The blind. 6437-X
    Chants of life. 7037-X
    Cleave thou the waves. 7015-9,6997-5,7015-9,6997-5
    Dare quam accipere. 6437-X,6730-1
    The dead. 6199-0,6383-7
    Humn to Horus. 6437-X
    L'envoy. 7037-X
    Love in exile, sels. 6656-9
    Love's completeness. 7037-X
    A love-triology, sels. 6656-9
    The mirror of Diana. 6624-0
    The reapers. 7037-X
    Return of the fishing fleet, fr. The heather on fire. 6997-5
    St. Oran, sels. 6997-5
    The storm, fr. The heather on fire. 6997-5
    The street children's dance. 6772-7
Blind-man's bluff. William Blake. 6018-8,6086-2
Blind-man's-bluff. Gertrude Hall. 6672-0
The blind.. Thomas Walsh. 6096-X,6102-8,6076-5
The blind. Mathilde Blind. 6437-X
"Blinded and deafened by the seas". Meditation. Blanaid Salkeld. 6930-4
The blinded bird. Thomas Hardy. 6102-8
The blinded soldier to his love. Alfred Noyes. 6169-9
"Blindfolded and alone I stand". Not as I will. Helen Hunt Jackson. 6836-7

BLINDING

The **blinding** of Tiresias. Callimachus. 6435-3
Blindman's bluff. Horace Smith. 6742-5
Blindness. Mary A. Hipple. 6249-0
Blindness. John Milton. 6240-7
Blindness, fr. Oedipus tyrannus. Sophocles. 6435-3
Blinn, Lucy Marion
    The land of nod. 6682-8
    Little Mary's wish. 6406-X
    Nutting. 6411-6
    Poor house Nan. 6451-5,7022-1
    Poorhouse Nan. 6963-0
    Rispah. 6573-2
    Sue's Thanksgiving. 6702-6
    Two of them. 6965-7
Blins, Lucy
    Rizpah. 6848-0
Bliss, Diane
    Fire. 6900-2
Bliss, Jane Wells
    Me. 6818-9
Bliss, Sylvia Hortense
    The cloister of the falling snow. 7030-2
    Evening. 7030-2
The **blissful** day. Robert Burns. 6271-7
A **blith** and bonny country lass. Thomas Lodge. 6026-9
Blithe are we set wi' ither. Ebenezer Picken. 6086-2
The **blithe** mask. Dallett Fuguet. 6337-3
"**Blithe** was the youth that summer day". Barbara. Eugene Field. 6949-5
"**Blithest** spirit of the earth". To the cicala. Frederick Tennyson. 6980-0
Blizzard, April 6, 1982 Sheila C. Forsyth. 6857-X
The **blizzard**. Hartley Alexander. 6143-5
Bloch, Robert
    Nightmare number four. 6218-0
Block city. Robert Louis Stevenson. 6401-9,6466-3,6135-4, 6368-3
Block, Louis James
    The final struggle, fr. The new world. 6946-0
    Suffrage marching song. 6274-1
    Woman suffrage marching-song. 6711-5
The **block-house** in the park. Arthur Guiterman. 6773-5
The **blockader**. DuBose Heyward. 6326-8
Blocking the pass. Charles Madge. 6354-3
Blodgett, Arthur S.
    Lonesome. 6764-6
Blodgett, Harriet F.
    December. 6145-1
Blodgett, Mary H.
    Wings of youth. 7019-1
Bloede, Gertrude. See "Sterne, Stuart"
Blok, Aleksandr
    The Scythians. Babette Deutsch and Avrahm Yarmolinsky (tr.). 6546-5
    The Scythians. Jack Lindsay (tr.). 6665-8
Blok, Alexander
    "All that is finished, finished, finished" Cecil Maurice Bowra (tr.). 6103-6
    Artist. Cecil Maurice Bowra (tr.). 6103-6
    Autumn love. Cecil Maurice Bowra (tr.). 6103-6
    The aviator. Payson Loomis (tr.). 6978-9
    "Dead roses and dying" Cecil Maurice Bowra (tr.). 6103-6
    Demon. Cecil Maurice Bowra (tr.). 6103-6
    "I have forebodings of Thee. Time is going" Cecil Maurice Bowra (tr.). 6103-6
    A little black man. 7014-0
    "A maiden's song in the choir was telling" 6103-6
    Russia. Babette Deutsch and Avrahm Yarmolinsky (tr.). 7039-6
    "Russia, my life! are we tied to one fate for us?" Cecil Maurice Bowra (tr.). 6103-6
    Shadows on the wall. Cecil Maurice Bowra (tr.). 6103-6
    The steps of the commander. Cecil Maurice Bowra (tr.). 6103-6
    "Those who were born in years of quiet" Cecil Maurice Bowra (tr.). 6103-6
    Voice from the chorus. Cecil Maurice Bowra (tr.). 6103-6
    Vulture. Cecil Maurice Bowra (tr.). 6103-6
    "Wild wind batters" Cecil Maurice Bowra (tr.). 6103-6
    "Yes, I have loved. And the mad glowing" Cecil Maurice Bowra (tr.). 6103-6
    "You say I am frozen. and dry, and apart" Cecil Maurice Bowra (tr.). 6103-6
    "You say that I'm asleep, and you" Cecil Maurice Bowra (tr.). 6103-6
Blomberg, Erik
    Dead gods. Charles Wharton Stork (tr.). 6045-5
    Duet. Charles Wharton Stork (tr.). 6045-5
    Night. Charles Wharton Stork (tr.). 6045-5
    Truth. Charles Wharton Stork (tr.). 6045-5
Blomer, Kim
    "Smokey blue eyes" 6883-9
Blomer, Kit
    Alone. 6883-9
    "Golden leaves" 6883-9
    Song for the mountains. 6883-9
Blomfield, Bishop
    Limerick:"..young lady of Cirencester". 6811-1
Blomfield, D. F.
    Roundel ('Love, though I die, and dying lave') 6770-0
    Roundel ('My lips refuse to take farewell of bliss') 6770-0
    Roundel ('Other lips than you intreat') 6770-0
"A **blond** girl is bent over a poem...". Episode in a library. Zbigniew Herbert. 6758-1
Blondel. Clarence Urmy. 6467-1
Blondel's song, fr. Richard Coeur-de-Lion. Michel J. Sedaine. 6424-8
Blondie goes to heaven. Unknown. 6339-X,6427-2
Blood. Barney Bush. 7005-1
Blood and the moon. William Butler Yeats. 6645-3
The **blood** horse. Bryan Waller ("Barry Cornwall") Procter. 6102-8,6302-0,6385-3,6239-3,6656-9,6084-6,6219-9, 6510-4
Blood is thicker than water. Wallace Rice. 6946-0
blood is thicker than water. Wallace Rice. 6062-5,6224-5
Blood of our fathers. Brian ("Korongo") Brooke. 6938-X
Blood on a stone. Francisco Mendez. 6759-X
Blood on the saddle. Everett Cheetham. 6594-5
"**Blood** thirtsy care goe packe." Unknown. 6563-5
Blood, Grace Holbrook
    Defenceless. 6764-6
    Night call. 6764-6
    Vision. 6764-6
Blood, Henry Ames
    The fighting parson. 6286-5
    Pro mortuis. 7041-8
    The rock in the sea. 6997-5
    Shakespeare. 7041-8
    The two enchantments. 7041-8
"**Blood**, wind, and glee". The dance of the sword. Unknown. 6873-1
The **blood-guilty**. Empedocles. 6435-3
The **blood-red** Fourragere. Robert Service. 6159-1
"**Blood-red** ball in the milky sky". Before night. Hedwig Katscher. 6769-7
A **blood-red** ring hung round the moon. John E. ("Barry Dane") Logan. 6274-1,6656-9
Blood-root. E.S. F. 6597-X
The **blood-stained** cross. Mary Carolyn Davies. 6032-3
The **bloodhound**. Bryan Waller ("Barry Cornwall") Procter. 7008-6
The **bloodless** sportsman. Sam Walter Foss. 6510-4
Bloodworth, Fannie
    The minuet. 6710-7
The **bloody** brother, sels. Francis Beaumont and John Fletcher. 6208-3
The **bloody** conquests of mighty Tamburlaine. Christopher Marlowe. 6726-3,6125-7
Bloody sire. Robinson Jeffers. 6389-6
The **bloody** son. Unknown. 6732-8
The **bloody** sword. Ibn al-Zaqqaq. 6362-4
"The **bloody** trunk of him who did possess". The fall. Sir Richard Fanshawe. 6933-9
Bloom. Alfred Kreymborg. 6776-X
The **bloom** hoists its banner. Jose Gorostiza. 6642-9
'The **bloom** is gone' Matthew Arnold. 6943-6
Bloom of age. Abu Yahya. 6362-4

"The bloom of the mimosa". Mimosa. Perceval Gibbon. 6800-6
"Bloom the dogwoods down in Texas". Homing. Mary S. Fitzgerald. 6789-1
"Bloom you flowers while you can". Pro-nuke blues. Alan Dugan. 7032-9
Bloom, beauteous blossoms. Sir Patrick Fells. 6724-7
The bloom. Herbert Trench. 6877-4
Bloomfield, Robert
    Abner and the widow Jones. 6919-3
    Address to his native vale. 6980-0
    The bird-boy. 6980-0
    The Fakenham ghost. 6105-2,6079-X
    The farmer's boy, sels. 6302-0,6385-3
    Harvest-home. 6980-0
    Lambs at play. 6302-0;6385-3
    Lines addressed to my children. 6543-0
    Moonlight in summer. 6302-0;6385-3
    The soldier's return. 6302-0,6385-3,6600-3
    Why he thinks she loves him. 6874-X
    The widow to her hour-glass. 6980-0
Bloomgarden, Solomon. See Yehoash
The blooming of the rose. Anna Hempstead Branch. 6232-6, 6338-1
Blooms of May. James Whitcomb Riley. 6992-4
"Blooms the Duomo, lustrous, exquisite". The city of flowers, fr. A Florentine cycle. Gertrude Huntington McGiffert. 6838-3
Bloomsbury. Wilfred Whitten. 6230-X
Blossom. Chun-soo Kim. 6775-1
Blossom and bird. Arthur E.J. Legge. 6793-X
"A blossom drops from the tree". Blossom. Chun-soo Kim. 6775-1
Blossom time. Ethelwyn Wetherald. 6797-2
"The blossom's tint is washed away". Ono No Komachi. 6852-9
"Blossom, that to the night alone". To the night blooming cereus. James Abraham Martling. 6952-5
Blossom-time. Hazel Hall. 7038-8
The blossom. William Blake. 6943-6
The blossome. John Donne. 6562-7,6189-3,6341-1
Blossoms. Frank Dempster Sherman. 6311-X
Blossoms. Jewell Bothwell Tull. 7038-8
"Blossoms as old as May I scatter here". The place. Francis Ledwidge. 6812-X,7027-2
"Blossoms of babies". Handfuls. Carl Sandburg. 6897-9
The blossomy barrow. Thomas Augustine Daly. 6338-1,6307-1
A blot in the 'scutcheon, sels. Robert Browning. 6123-0
Blount Jr., Edward Augustus
    As they fell. 6482-5
    A crew poem. 6501-5
    The hunchback. 6482-5
    The stranger's evidence. 6417-5
Blount, Annie R.
    Revenge. 6677-1
    Under the lamplight. 6909-6
Blouzelinda's funeral. John Gay. 6932-0
Blouzelinda's funeral, fr. Shepherd's week. John Gay. 6932-0
"Blow gently passion in my faire ones breast." Unknown. 6563-5
Blow high, blow low. Charles Dibdin. 6086-2,6383-7
Blow my eyes! Wallace Irwin. 6083-8,6089-7
Blow softly, thrush. Joseph Russell Taylor. 6073-0
Blow the man down. Unknown. 6057-9,6490-6,6547-3,6281-4
"Blow there, sweet Zephyrus!". Song ("Blow there!"). Unknown. 6563-5
Blow thy horn, hunter. William Cornish. 6328-4
A blow up. Thomas Hood. 6974-6
"Blow winds, and crack your cheeks...", fr. King Lear. William Shakespeare. 6726-3
"Blow ye the trumpet in Zion.. ". Canite tuba. Bible. 6830-8
"Blow ye trumpet, gather from afar". Sonnet on hearing of the...Polish insurrection. Alfred Lord Tennyson. 6977-0
Blow your trumpets, angels. John Donne. 6125-7
Blow! Bugle, Blow! Alfred Lord Tennyson. 6260-1,6125-7, 6102-8,6114-1
Blow, J.H.
    The maiden husking corn. 6578-3

"Blow, blow your trumpets till they crack". Fame's penny trumpet. Charles Lutwidge ("Lewis Carroll") Dodgson. 6996-7
"Blow, blow, thou winter wind". Song ("Blow, blow"), fr. As you like it. William Shakespeare. 6820-0
"Blow, blow, thou winter wind", fr. As you like it. William Shakespeare. 6192-3,6189-3,6197-4,6639-9, 6219-9,6371-3,6646-1,6737-9,6122-2,6271-7,6536-8, 6726-8,6085-4,6102 ,6187-7,6246-6,6182-6,6134-6,6502-3,6317 ,6395-0,6534-1,6099-4,6154-0,6101-X,6328 , 6473-6,6490-6,6302-0,6385-3,6052-8,6634 ,6732-8,6438-8,6143-5,6102-8,6194-X,6104
"Blow, blow, winds below, braggart winds...". Wind-song. Nora Chesson. 6793-X
Blow, boys, blow. Unknown. 6057-9,6281-4
Blow, boys, blow! Unknown. 6281-4
Blow, bullies, blow. Unknown. 6547-3
Blow, northern wind. Unknown. 6434-5
"Blow, northerne wind". Love for a beautiful lady. Unknown. 6881-2
Blow, wind, blow. Mother Goose. 6452-3,6466-3,6114-1,6135-4
"Blow, winds of God/The bugle's call". The winds of God. Marguerite A. Whitcomb. 6799-9
Blow, ye winds. Unknown. 6278-4
"Blowe there sweet Zephyrus where thou shalt finde." Thomas Carew (atr.) 6563-5
"Bloweth like snow/From the grey thistles". Thistledown. William ("Fiona Macleod") Sharp. 6793-X
Blowing bubbles. Beatrice Paula Byrnes. 6750-6
Blowing bubbles. Burges Johnson. 6368-3
Blowing bubbles. Eugene H. Munday. 6919-3
Blowing bubbles. O.F. Starkey. 6743-3
"Blowing was made for grete game". Unknown. 6334-9
Blows the wind to-day. Robert Louis Stevenson. 6228-8,6315-2
"Blows the wind to-day, and the sun...". Exiled. Robert Louis Stevenson. 6793-X
Bloy, Leon
    A prayer for those who weep for the world. 6016-0
The bludy serk. Robert Henryson. 6180-X
The bludy serk. Robert Henryson. 6931-2
Blue Cloud, Peter
    Coyote, coyote, please tell me. 7005-1
    Dogwood blossoms. 7005-1
    Elderberry flute song. 7005-1
    Sweat song. 7005-1
    To-ta Ti-om. 7005-1
"Blue against the bluer heavens". Listening angels. Adelaide Anne Procter. 6957-6
Blue and gold. Clara Doty Bates. 6965-7
Blue and gold. Ibn Burd. 6362-4
"The blue and gold-the blue and gold expand". The Canadian west. Robert Kirkland Kernighan. 6797-2
Blue and gray. Unknown. 6486-8
The blue and the gray in France. George M. Mayo. 6846-4
The blue and the gray. Francis Miles Finch. 6263-6,6300-4, 6121-4,6102-8,6076-5,6309 ,6304-7,6642-2,6104-1,6449-3,6470-1,6396-3,6442-6,6565 ,6045-1,6344-6,6014-5, 6600-3,6215-6,6610 ,6136-2,6240-7,6271-7,6340-3,6385-3,6478 ,6273-3,6113-3,6486-8,6006-4,6053-6,6101 , 6512-0,6589-9,6732-8,6016-2,6431-0,6288 ,6706-9,6074-9,6102-8,6451-5,6457-4,6471
The Blue and the Gray. Ellen H. Flagg. 6304-7
The blue and the gray. Unknown. 6273-3,6340-3,6003-0
Blue and white. Mary Elizabeth Coleridge. 6437-X
Blue Annajo n. Bliss Carman and Richard Hokey. 6890-1
"Blue as the Danube leaps the flame". Premiere danseuse. Fanny Hodges Newman. 6959-2
The blue bells of Scotland. Unknown. 6732-8
!"Blue bells, on blue hills, where..sky is blue". Harebells. Emily Henrietta Hickey. 7037-X,6046-3
Blue bird's song. Emily Huntington Miller. 6304-7
The blue bird. Mary Elizabeth Coleridge. 6134-6
Blue birds. Ha-woon Han. 6775-1
Blue bonnets over the border. Robert Gilfillan. 6802-2
Blue bonnets over the border. Sir Walter Scott. 6328-4
The blue bottles. Delia Dominguez. 7036-1
Blue bowl. Emmet Pendleton. 6750-6
"A blue circus/a spotlght, and a red girl". A Chagall

BLUE

(#1) Dan Propper. 6998-3, 6901-0
The **blue** closet. William Morris. 6657-7,6110-9,6655-0,6656-9
Blue days. Jung-ju Suh. 6775-1
"**Blue** diamonds/stacked in a claws laughter". Captured bird. George Rachow. 6870-7
"The **Blue** Horizon was a mine...". Our lady of the mine. Eugene Field. 6949-5
Blue dreamlight Shaman song. Tom Lowenstein. 6855-3
Blue evening. Emanuel Leseticky z Lesehradu. 6763-8
Blue ey'd Mary. Unknown. 6157-5
"**Blue** eye beauty". Unknown. 6363-2
Blue eyes. Unknown. 6826-X
The **blue** forget-me-not. Isabella Valancy Crawford. 6797-2
The **blue** gentians. Edward Ryan Woodle. 6274-1
Blue girls. John Crowe Ransom. 6357-8,6619-4,6125-7
Blue grass portrait. Mabel Posegate. 6906-1
Blue harvest. Frances Frost. 6396-9
The **blue** hen's chickens. Arthur Guiterman. 6817-0
Blue heron. Yetza Gillespie. 6979-7
Blue heron. Mary Brent Whiteside. 6039-0
Blue heron near the old mill bridge. Raymond Souster. 6767-0
The **blue** heron. Theodore Goodridge Roberts. 6021-8,6446-9
The **blue** heron. James Maurice Thompson. 6073-0
Blue hills beneath the haze. Charles Goodrich Whiting. 6431-0
The **blue** hills. Philip Francis Little. 6244-X
Blue homespun. Frank Oliver Call. 6021-8
"**Blue** horizons with speckled clouds". Clouds. John Edwards. 6799-9
Blue horses: west winds. Anita Endrezze-Danielson. 7005-1
Blue hyacinths. Adelaide Crapsey. 6850-2
Blue hydrangeas. Rainer Maria Rilke. 6160-5
"**Blue** is the sea below you". Farewell to the Pilgrims. Th. M. Bakke. 6818-9
Blue island intersection. Carl Sandburg. 6345-4
Blue jay. Hilda Conkling. 6421-3
Blue jay. Leonora Speyer. 6073-0
The **blue** jay. Louise Driscoll. 6073-0,6232-6,6653-4
The **blue** jay. Susan Hartley Sweet. 6457-4
The **blue** jay. Susan Hartley Swett. 6519-8
Blue Juanita, sels. Malcolm Cowley. 6531-7
The **blue** lake - Mount Gambier. Agnes Neale. 6768-9
"**Blue** light and rancid slate is this...soil". Under a garden stone. Clara Hyde. 6750-6
Blue melody. William I. Powell. 6178-8
The **blue** men of the Minch. Donald A. Mackenzie. 6180-X
"**Blue** mists lie curled along the sullen stream". A crucifix in the Etsch Thal. John Addington Symonds. 7015-9
"**Blue** mists of morning filled it to the brim". The Colorado canyon. Georgiana Hodgkins. 6799-9
Blue moonshine. Francis G. Stokes. 6902-9
Blue mounds near Luvnrne. Carmen Suurmeyer. 6342-X
"The **blue** night, like an angel, came into...". Nocturne: In Provence. Bliss Carman and Richard Hovey. 6890-1
Blue norther. Isaac W. Wade. 6039-0
Blue October at Indian reservation. Stella Jeanne Skinaway. 6342-X
Blue Persian. Isabel Fiske Conant. 6120-6
Blue Peter. Stanislaus Lynch. 6930-4
"The **blue** of the heavenly deeps above". Cape Cod. John Coleman Adams. 6798-0
"**Blue** open seas/Sleep". An evening at Skolje. Aleksa Santic. 6765-4
Blue ribbon cats. Lalia Mitchell Thornton. 6120-6
Blue roses. Eloise Robinson. 6032-3
"The **blue** sea bares". Spring day. Ji-hoon Cho. 6775-1
Blue shoes. Kate Greenaway. 6891-X
"**Blue** skies mighty temptin', an' the ...". Fishin'-hunger. Edgar A. Guest. 6862-6
"**Blue** sky, grey stones, and the far sea". Acceptation. John Galsworthy. 6888-X
The **blue** spruce. Edgar A. Guest. 6869-3
Blue squills. Sara Teasdale. 6032-3,6232-6,6556-2,6653-4, 6439-6
"**Blue** stars of evening". Christmas eve: New York. Hal Saunders White. 6808-1
Blue symphony. John Gould Fletcher. 6348-9

160

Blue tropic. Luis Cabalquinto. 6790-5
"**Blue** turquoise waves,/Opal green sprays". Sea gems. Evon DesSins. 6818-9
A **blue** valentine. Joyce Kilmer. 6031-5,6096-X,6292-X,6282-2,6307-1
"The **blue** was gone from the lake...". Laneer. Hermann Hagedorn. 6944-4
"**Blue** was the loch, the clouds were gone". Loch-long. Samuel Rogers. 6980-0
Blue water. John Gould Fletcher. 6776-X
Blue water. John Gould Fletcher. 6010-2
"The **blue** waves are sleeping". Serenade ("The blue"). Jeremiah [or James] Joseph Callanan. 6930-4
Blue willow. Mildred D. Shacklett. 6750-6
The **blue** wind of the Yangtse valley. Hamish Maclaren. 6893-6
The **blue**, blue smoke. Unknown. 6090-0
"The **blue**, deep, glorious heavens!". A poet's dying hymn. Felicia Dorothea Hemans. 6973-8
"'**Blue**, purple and scarlet and...'". Color. Jane Blakeslee Richards. 6818-9
Blue-beard. Theodore Pease Cooke. 6004-8
"A **blue-bell** springs upon the ledge". Spring song. Paul Laurence Dunbar. 6820-0
"A **blue-bird** sings his heart out...". Unseeing eyes. Gertrude S. Stinson. 6750-6
The **blue-bird**.. Marion Thornton Egbert. 6274-1
The **blue-bird**. Alexander Wilson. 6219-9
"The **blue-black** mountains are etched". The chance. Arthur Sze. 6790-5
"A **blue-black** Nubian plucking oranges". Color. Wilfred Wilson Gibson. 6897-9
Blue-butterfly day. Robert Frost. 6076-5
"A **blue-eyed** lad was seated". The study hour. Flaccus [pseud].. 6817-0
"A **blue-eyed** phantom far before". Christina Georgina Rossetti. 6187-7
The **blue-green** stream. Wang Wei. 6253-9
"The **blue-leaved** fig-trees swell with laughter". The five musicians. Edith Sitwell. 7000-0
The **blue-tit**. Norman Gale. 6510-4
"**Blue/on/blue**". Pinay. Virginia Cerenio. 6790-5
Bluebeard. Josiah Gilbert Holland. 6413-2
Bluebeard. Edna St. Vincent Millay. 6077-3
Bluebeard. Unknown. 6616-X
Bluebeard's castle. Rose Terry Cooke. 6431-0
The **bluebell** of Scotland. Unknown. 6479-5
The **bluebell**.. Emily Bronte. 6123-0
The **bluebell**. Margaret Deland. 6652-6
The **bluebell**. Unknown. 6049-8
Bluebells. Walter De La Mare. 6596-1
"**Bluebells** are nodding/So quaintly nearby". My garden. Hazel Hanna. 6799-9
Blueberries. Frank Prentice Rand. 6762-X
The **bluebird** ("'Tis early spring...") C.F. Gerry. 6049-8
The **bluebird** ("Before you thought of spring"). Emily Dickinson. 6073-0
The **bluebird** ("I know the song...") Emily Huntington Miller. 6529-5,6623-2,6127-3,6519-8,6556-6,6135-4, 6131-1,6368-3
The **bluebird** ("When ice is thawed..."). James Maurice Thompson. 6073-0
The **Bluebird** cafe. Jo McDougall. 6860-X
The **bluebird's** song. Unknown. 6049-8
The **bluebird**. Thomas Bailey Aldrich. 6820-0
The **bluebird**. Eben Eugene Rexford. 6449-3
Bluebirds. Helen Merrill Egerton. 6796-4
Bluebirds. Helen M. Merrill. 6115-X
Bluebirds in autumn. Celia Thaxter. 6612-7
A **bluebrid** in March, sels. Bliss Carman. 6021-8
The **bluefinch**. L. 6084-6
Blues. Mary du Passage. 6899-5
"**Blues** & rum & big fat". The history of weather. George Mattingly. 6792-1
"The **blues**, spreading their robes...". Natural being. Octavio Paz. 6758-1
The **blues**; a literary eclogue. George Gordon, 6th Baron Byron. 6945-2
The **bluff**. Kimberly A. Brown. 6857-X
Blumenthal, Walter Hart (tr.)

Moses on the Nile. Victor Hugo, 6848-0
Blunden, Edmund
  The age of Herbert and Vaughan. 6483-3
  Almswomen. 6506-6,6250-4
  At the Great Wall of China. 6257-1
  Augury. 6943-6
  The barn. 6844-8
  Cloudy June. 6044-7
  Country sale. 6776-X
  Country sale. 6393-4
  The daimyo's pond. 6071-4
  The fine nature. 6783-2
  A 'first impression': Tokyo. 6778-6
  Ghost of the beautiful past. 6655-0
  The giant puffball. 6210-5
  The haunted house. 6648-8
  If we had met. 6655-0
  In a country churchyard. 6072-2
  Juliet. 6659-3
  Lark descending. 6354-3
  The meadow stream. 6781-6
  The memory of Kent. 6331-4,6472-8
  Midnight skaters. 6179-6,6246-6,6210-5,6150-8
  Omen. 6071-4
  The poor man's pig. 6044-7,6150-8,6044-7
  A psalm. 6532-5
  Report on experience. 6208-3,6317-9
  Reunion in war. 7029-9
  Sheet lightning. 6257-1
  Solutions. 6210-5
  The spell. 6777-8
  The sunlit vale. 6246-6
  The survival. 6780-8
  Thoughts of Thomas Hardy. 6783-2
  The Wartons. 6483-3
  Water moment. 6069-2
  What is winter? 6246-6
  A yeoman. 6070-6,6393-4
Blunden, Edmund (tr.)
  Cicada. Unknown (Greek), 6435-3
  A Maltese dog. Tymnes, 6435-3
The **blunder**. Jan (Joyce A. Maxtone Graham) Struther. 6778-6
Blunt, Hugh Francis
  The dreamer. 6954-1
  God's handmaid. 6285-7
Blunt, John Franklin
  An Irish fantasy. 6799-9
Blunt, Wilfrid Scawen
  Alfred Tennyson. 6483-3,6655-0
  The camel rider. 6210-5
  Chanclebury ring. 6477-9
  A day in Sussex. 6331-4,6477-9
  The desolate city. 6437-X,6172-9,6292-X
  Esther, sels. 6301-2
  An exhortation. 7015-9
  The falcon. 6022-6
  Gibraltar. 6096-X,6437-X,6484-1,6656-9,6439-6,6022
  "How shall I build". 6292-X, 6172-9
  Laughter and death. 6102-8
  The morte d'Arthur. 6655-0
  The oasis of Sidi Kahled. 6271-7
  The old squire. 6096-X,6437-X,6656-9
  On a lost opportunity. 6204-0
  A plea for Egypt, fr. The wind and the whirlwind. 7009-4
  The pride of unbelief. 7015-9
  Recollections of childhood. 6233-4
  Red, red gold. 6233-4
  Roumeli hissar. 6659-3
  St. Valentine's Day. 6096-X,6204-0,6437-X,6477-9
  The sinner-saint. 6022-6
  Song ("O fly not"). 6292-X,6437-X,6172-9
  Sonnet ("Long have I"). 7009-4
  The sublime. 6102-8
  They shall not know. 6655-0
  Think no more of me. 6655-0
  To Manon, comparing her to a falcon. 6437-X,6656-9
  To Manon, on her lightheartedness. 6656-9
  To Manon, on his fortune in loving her. 6301-2
  To one excusing his poverty. 6271-7
  To one who would make a confession. 6271-7,6301-2
  The two highwaymen. 6879-0
  Vanitas vanitatis. 7015-9
  The Venus of Milo. 6331-4,6439-6,6631-3
  With Esther. 6437-X
  Written at Florence. 6437-X,6439-6
  You have let the beauty of the day go over. 6655-0
Blunt, Wilfrid Scawen (tr.)
  The days of our youth. Unknown (Arabic), 7039-6
Bluntness. William Shakespeare. 6294-6
"**Blurred** figures in the twilight hurry by". Twilit street. Margaret Forst. 6906-1
"**Blurred** formations". Penetralia. Elfrida De Renne Barrow. 6040-4
Blurred memories of mama are skeltons I long to see... Catherine Sanders. 6898-7
"**Blurred** tombstone, hidden in the woods". Elegy to the lost and already blurred by time. Xavier Abril. 6759-X
Blurt, master constable, sels. Thomas Middleton. 6317-9
"The **blush** is on the flower & the bloom...tree". Mo cailin donn. George Sigerson. 6858-8
"The **blush** is on the flower, and the bloom...". Ma cailin donn. George Sigerson. 6873-1
Blush not redder than the morning. Nathaniel Lee. 6563-5
"The **Blush** not redder thaought of me." Nathaniel Lee. 6092-7
"**Blush,** happy maiden, when you feel". Elizabeth Akers Allen. 6226-1,6508-2
The **blushing** maple tree. Unknown. 6049-8
The **blushing** rose and purple flower. Philip Massinger. 6934-7
"**Blusin** bebopin". Fading notes. Garey D. Frierson. 6898-7
Bly blue and his gun. Nellie M. Garabrant. 6699-2
Bly, Robert
  "Dark eyebrows swim like turtles" 6803-0
  "How beautiful the shiny turtle" 6803-0
  Merchants have multiplied. 6803-0
  Poems for Max Ernst, sels. 6803-0
Bly, Robert (tr.)
  Monologue with its wife. Gunnar Ekelof, 6803-0
"**Blythe**, blythe, and merry are we!". The social cup. Charles Gray. 6960-6
"**Blyther** than the burnie." Marion Hubbard. 6116-8
The **blythsome** bridal. Unknown. 6180-X
Bo. Robert C.V. Meyers. 6926-6
Bo's'n Jack of the "Albatross". E. Stanway Jackson. 6417-5
Bo-peep. Anthony C. Deane. 6440-X
"**Bo-talee** rode easily among his enemies...". The fear of Bo-talee. N. Scott Momaday. 7005-1
The **boa** and the blanket. Unknown. 6278-4
Boadicea. William Cowper. 6188-5,6424-8,6543-0,6302-0,6385-3,6322 ,6323-3,6473-6,6679-8,6732-8,6438-8,6250 , 6075-7,6102-8,6133-8,6217-7,6304-7,6263 ,6301-2,6197-4,6086-2
Boadicea. Alfred Lord Tennyson. 6977-0
Boake, Barcroft
  Where the dead men lie. 6384-5
The **boar** and the shibboleth. Edward Doro. 6250-4
The **boar** is dead. Unknown. 6756-5
The **boar's** head carol. Unknown. 6145-1,6328-4,6383-7
The **boar's** head carol. Unknown. 6881-2
"The **boar's** head in hand I bring". Hey, hey, hey, hey, the boar's head is armed gay. Unknown. 6756-5
The **boar's** head in hand bear I. Unknown. 6756-5
"The **boar's** head that we bring here". In die nativitatis. Unknown. 6756-5
Boar, Arthur
  The breeding lark. 6438-8
A **board** school pastoral. May Kendall. 6274-1,6656-9
Boarding the birds. Edgar A. Guest. 6748-4
Boas, Frederick S.
  The Balliol rooks. 6073-0,6477-9
"**Boast** not these titles of your ancestors". A fragment ("Boast not these titles..."). Ben Jonson. 6867-7
"The **boast** of heraldry, the pomp of power". Thomas Gray. 6238-5
The **boasting** of Sir Peter Parker. Clinton Scollard. 6946-0
"A **boat** a boat aste to the ferry." Unknown. 6563-5

BOAT

"Boat after boat". Tunny-fish. George Rostrevor Hamilton. 6782-4
"The boat is chafing at our delay". Song ("The boat is chafing"). John Davidson. 6102-8,6252-0
"The boat is hauled upon the hardening sand". Rest. John Charles Earle. 7015-9
Boat o' dreams. Loren Palmer. 6118-4
The boat of grass. Kemble Butler. 6344-6
The boat of grass. Sarah Kemble Wister. 6502-3
The boat of my lover. Dinah Maria Mulock Craik. 6066-8
A boat on the sea. Ethel Turner. 6784-0
The boat on the Serchio. Percy Bysshe Shelley. 6369-1
Boat race, 1915. Unknown. 7031-0
The boat race, fr. Queen Hynde. James Hogg. 6001-3
The boat sails away. Kate Greenaway. 6262-8
Boat song. Adelaide Cilley Waldron. 6764-6
A boat song, fr. Hypatia. Charles Kingsley. 6832-4
Boat song, fr. The lady of the lake. Sir Walter Scott. 6371-3,6219-9,6543-0,6180-X,6049-8,6087-0,6331-4, 6732-8,6328
A boat song. Unknown. 6873-1
"A boat, beneath a sunny sky". An acrostic ("A boat"). Charles Lutwidge ("Lewis Carroll") Dodgson. 6724-7
Boat-building in Spain. Ray Ledyard. 6116-8
The boat-horn.. Unknown. 6273-3
The boat. George Macdonald. 6337-3
The boatie rows. John Ewen. 6180-X,6086-2,6219-9
The boatie rows. Unknown. 6600-3,6438-8
Boatman of Kinsale. Thomas Osborne Davis. 6656-9
Boatman's hymn. Andrew Magrath. 6930-4
"Boatman, boatman! my brain is wild". Comfort. Alice Cary. 6969-X
The boatman.. Christina Georgina Rossetti. 6466-3
The boatman. Thomas Pattison. 6180-X
Boats. Dorothy Viertel. 6850-2
"The boats are out, and the storm is high". Fishers of men. Adelaide Anne Procter. 6957-6
Boats at night. Edward Shanks. 6332-2
"The boats go out and the boats come in". The fisher's widow. Arthur Symons. 6793-X
Boats sail on the rivers. Christina Georgina Rossetti. 6466-3,6656-6,6368-3,6262-8,6434-X
"Boats that carry sugar". Freight boats. James S. Tippett. 6891-X
Boatswain's' monument. Charles Gordon Byron. 7008-6
"Bob Brown's gone globe-gliding". The gastronaut. Jonathan Williams. 6803-0
Bob and the Bible. Unknown. 6314-4
Bob Anderson, my beau. Unknown. 6946-0
Bob Sawyer. Unknown. 6547-3
"Bob went lookin' for a job". Plain Bob and a job. James William Foley. 6963-0
Bob white. Dora Read Goodale. 6073-0,6272-5
Bob white. Edgar A. Guest. 6510-4
Bob White. Francis Charles McDonald. 6983-5
Bob white. Francis Charles McDonald. 6688-7
"Bob white". Unknown. 6529-5
'Bob white'. Eleanor Kirk. 6314-4
Bob-o'-Lincoln. William Cullen Bryant. 6772-7
"Bobbie Burns and Bobbie Browning". The two Bobbies. Bliss Carman. 7006-X
Bobby Shafto's gone to sea. Mother Goose. 6134-6,6132-X, 6401-9,6452-3,6363-2,6135
Bobby Shafto, fr. Under a fool's cap. Daniel Henry Jr. 6605-4
Bobby's Thanksgiving. Unknown. 6130-3
The bobolink's song. Stanley Waterloo. 6675-5
The bobolink. Thomas Hill. 6271-7,6597-X,6529-5,6302-0;6385-3
The bobolink. James Russell Lowell. 6073-0
The bobolink. Unknown. 6049-8,6165-6,6392-6,6574-0
Bobolinks. Eugene Edmund Murphey. 6723-9
The bobolinks.. Christopher Pearse Cranch. 6239-3
Bobrowski, Johannes
    Cathedral 1941 6758-1
    Childhood. 6758-1
    Kaunas 1941 6758-1
    Latvian songs. 6758-1
    North Russian town. 6758-1
    On the Jewish dealer A.S. 6758-1

    The spoor in the sand. 6758-1
Bobwhite. George Cooper. 6891-X
Boccaccio. Thomas Edward Brown. 6809-X
Boccaccio. Thomas Edward Browne. 6230-X
Boccaccio. Eugene Field. 6949-5
Boccaccio, Giovanni
    Cymon and Iphigenia. John Dryden (tr.). 6970-3
    Dante. Francis C. Gray (tr.). 6624-0
    The decameron, sels. 6325-X
    Flowers and love, fr. The decameron. Richard Aldington (tr.). 6325-X
    "Now perish, Baia, root and stock and name". T.G. Bergin (tr.). 6325-X
    Of three girls and their talk. 6429-9,6321-7
    The queen of angels. Thomas Walsh (tr.). 6282-2
    Sigismonda and Guiscardo. John Dryden (tr.). 6970-3
    Sonnet 108. Francis C. Gray (tr.). 6484-1
    Sonnet: Inscription for a portrait of Dante. Dante Gabriel Rossetti (tr.). 7039-6
    Sonnet: Of his last sight of Fiammetta. Dante Gabriel Rossetti (tr.). 7039-6
    Theodore and Honoria. John Dryden (tr.). 6970-3
    "To that fair kingdom, o my gentle lord". T.G. Bergin (tr.). 6325-X
"Boccaccio, for you laughed all laughs...". Boccaccio. Thomas Edward Brown. 6809-X
Boccace, sels. John Dryden. 6562-7
Bocock, John Paul
    Rough riding at El Caney. 6995-9
    The table d'hote. 6274-1
    Thanksgiving in old Virginia. 6703-4
    The twins in the turret. 6471-X
    Washington. 7022-1
Boden, Frederick C.
    How shall I sing? 6542-2
    Out of the coalfields, sels. 6954-1
    The son of man. 6072-2
Bodenheim, Maxwell
    Advice to my young wife. 6037-4
    American radio. 6561-9
    And if I say. 6037-4
    The camp-follower. 6542-2
    City girl. 6069-2
    Comparison. 6880-4
    Dear Minna. 6036-6
    Death. 6102-8,6348-9,6076-5,6467-1
    Discovery ("On this March day the ferns in milk-green") 6561-9
    Ending. 6034-X
    Finalities. 6776-X
    Forgetfulness. 6348-9
    The game. 6561-9
    Hill-side tree. 6348-9
    Instructions for a ballet. 6036-6
    Interlude. 6348-9
    The interne. 6897-9
    The king of Spain. 6779-4
    Manhattan, 1943. 6561-9
    The measuring ones. 6561-9
    The miner. 6897-9
    Minna. 6348-9
    New York City. 6037-4
    The old Jew. 6102-8,6076-5,6300-4
    An old poet to his love. 6102-8,6076-5
    Poem to gentiles. 6561-9
    Poem to religion. 6561-9
    Poet's story. 6561-9
    The rear-porches of an apartment-building. 6897-9
    Rhymed conversation with money. 6070-6
    Sentimentality. 6072-2
    A sister writes. 6561-9
    Soldiers. 6348-9
    Sonnet ("Like wine"). 6034-X
    Sonnet to a Negro girl. 6561-9
    Still free. 6561-9
    Technique. 6561-9
    To a baby. 6070-6
    To a discarded steel rail. 6467-1
    To a friend. 6300-4
    To an enemey. 6897-9

Two sonnets to my wife. 6036-6
Voices. 6033-1
Bodensee. John Addington Symonds. 6749-2
"**Bodies** on fire/the monks in orange cloth". Black Hills survival gathering, 1980 Linda Hogan. 7005-1
Bodtcher, Ludvig
Footprints. Charles Wharton Stork (tr.). 6555-4
Body. Mabel Simpson. 6039-0,6396-7
Body and soul. Abul Fadl. 6362-4
The **body** fair. Mark Andre Raffalovitch. 7015-9
"The **body** is never silent. Aristotle said...". Talk. William Matthews. 6803-0
"The **body** is no prison where we lie". Shakespeare himself. Bliss Carman. 6890-1
Body of Jesus. Arthur Cleveland Coxe. 6065-X
The **body** of man. Sir Charles Scott Sherrington. 6482-5
Body remembered. Constantine P. Cavafy. 6352-7
Body's beauty. Dante Gabriel Rossetti. 6828-6
Body's beauty, fr. The house of life. Dante Gabriel Rossetti. 6508-2,6110-9
The **body's** eye. Anne Welsh. 6788-3
The **body.** Otakar Brezina. 6763-8
The **body.** Ruth Herschberger. 6390-X
The **body.** Rachel Annand Taylor. 6844-8
The **body.** Unknown. 6373-X
The **Boer** War. William Plomer. 6788-3
Boethius. Samuel Johnson. 6641-0
Boethius - si vis celsi iura tonantis. Helen Waddell. 6641-0
The **Bofors** A.A. gun. Gavin Ewart. 6666-6
The **bog** lands. William A. Bryne. 6292-X
Bogan, Jim
The discriminations: virtuous amusements and wicked... 6966-5
Bogan, Louise
The alchemist. 6036-6
Cassandra. 7038-8
The changed woman. 6037-4
Chanson un peu naive. 6070-6,6250-4
'Come, sleep...' 6399-3
The crows. 6619-4,6036-6
July dawn. 6388-8
March twilight. 6388-8
The mark. 6217-2
Medusa. 6250-4
The meeting. 6388-8
Memory. 6036-6
Men loved wholly beyond wisdom. 6619-4,60196
My voice not being proud. 6880-4
Portrait. 6880-4
Pyrotechnics. 6880-4
Roman fountain. 6052-8
The romantic. 6037-4
Several voices out of a cloud. 6733-6
Solitary observation brought back from a short sojourn. 6052-8
Song ("Love me"). 6019-6
To a dead lover. 6037-4
Women. 6726-3,6036-6
Words for departure. 6808-1
Bogart, ?
Acrostics ("Lovely"). 6724-7
Bogart, Elizabeth
He came too late. 6219-9
Bogart, Ernest Ludlow
An unknown hero. 7022-1
Bogen, Laurel Ann
27 years of madness. 6998-3
Bogert, Harry Howe
The cross triumphant. 6799-9
Bogg's dogs. Unknown. 6064-1
Boggs, Minnie McKinnon
Memories. 6799-9
Boggs, Norman T.
Amatores ambo. 6320-9
Boggs, Tom
Conclusion. 6761-1
Every man is inner dark. 6761-1
Rogue's gallery. 6324-1
Wolves. 6761-1

Bogie side; or, Huntly's raid. Unknown. 6859-6
Bogle, Donald E.
'An Aristotelian elegy'. 7024-8
Now. 7024-8
Bohemia. Robert Loveman. 6941-X
Bohemia. Dorothy Parker. 6375-6
Bohemia. Unknown. 7012-4
"**Bohemia** is the land for me". Bohemia. Robert Loveman. 6941-X
"**Bohemia!** Bohemia! The land of art and song". Bohemia. Unknown. 7012-4
The **bohemian** dreams. Robert Service. 6159-1
A **Bohemian** drinking song. Thomas Truxtun Hare. 6936-3
The **Bohemian** hymn. Ralph Waldo Emerson. 6730-1,6126-5,6214-8,6250-4,6288-1,6467
The **bohemian.** Robert Service. 6159-1
The **bohemians** of Boston. Gelett Burgess. 7025-6
Bohernabreena. Leslie Daiken. 6930-4
Bohm, Elizabeth
Tracks. 6979-7
Bohun-Greene, Marius
Not one thing alone. 6482-5
Boiardo, Matteo Maria
"Give me, full-handed, lilies, give me the rose". L.R. Lind (tr.). 6325-X
"Once in good hour there came in company". L.R. Lind (tr.). 6325-X
"Poor drooping flowers and pallid violets". Peter Russell (tr.). 6325-X
"Sing with me, you little amorous birds". L.R. Lind (tr.). 6325-X
"Song of birds which leaps from leaf to leaf". Peter Russell (tr.). 6325-X
To a balcony. Richard Aldington (tr.). 6325-X
Boice, Dorothy Wardell
Home from town. 6662-3
In memoriam. 6662-3
Boie, Mildred
Five o'clock hour. 6761-1
Boies, Lura Anna
The rain. 6131-1
Boiled dish in Vermont. Daniel L. Cady. 6989-4
Boiling sap at night in Vermont. Daniel L. Cady. 6988-6
Bois de Boulogne, fr. Pictures of autumn. Sara Teasdale. 6011-0
Bois, Gertrude du
Meditation in St. Mary's. 6144-3
Bois-etoile. Ethel M. Hewitt. 7027-2
Boise, F. Irene
My trip to the moon. 6702-6
Bojic, Milutin
Autumnal strolls 1 6765-4
The crows. 6765-4
The kiss. 6765-4
The legend of woman. 6765-4
Bok, Edward W.
The glory of all England. 6039-0
"The **boke** of Phyllyp sparowe", sels. John Skelton. 6733-6
Boke of two ladies, sels. David Morton. 6282-2
Boker, George Henry
The ballad of New Orleans. 6946-0
A ballad of Sir John Franklin. 6473-6,6396-9
A battle hymn. 6753-0
The battle of Lockout Mountain. 6403-5,6678-X
Before Vicksburg. 6946-0
The black regiment. 6946-0
The black regiment. 6062-5,6113-3,6271-7,6239-3,6402-7,6471-,6302-0,6385-3,6016-2
Count Candespina's standard. 6294-6,6392-6,6409-4,6742-5
Countess Laura. 6302-0,6385-3,6673-9
The crossing at Fredericksburg. 6946-0
The cruise of the Monitor. 6946-0
Dirge for a soldier. 6946-0,6309-8,6470-1,6121-4,6288-1,6291-9,6300-4,6396-9,6113-3,6240-7,6271-7,6302-0,6385-3,6437-,6471-X,6473-6,6481-7,6486-8,6490-6,6552-,6600-3,6732-8,6737-7,6665-8,6431-0,6304
The ferry. 6431-0
The fever in my blood has died. 6288-1
The flag. 6223-7

Hooker's across. 6946-0
Lincoln. 6305-5,6524-4
On board the 'Cumberland' 6016-2,6288-1
On board the Cumberland, March 7, 1862. 6402-7,6678-X
Our heroic themes, sels. 6524-4
Prince Adeb. 6302-0,6385-3
Sir John Franklin. 6402-7
The sword-bearer. 6016-2
To America. 6121-4
To England. 6121-4
Upon the hill before Centreville. 6015-3
The 'Varuna.' 6016-2
Zagonyi. 6946-0
Bokujin
"Lightly, lightly/Summer breezes playing." Lois J. Erickson (tr.). 6027-7
Bold. Unknown. 6983-5
"**Bold** and brave, and strong and stalwart". The story of Abel Tasman. Frances Sesca Lewin. 6768-9
"**Bold** bad pirates on a bold bad craft". Buccaneers. Berton Braley. 6853-7
"**Bold** captain of the body-guard". Zagonyi. George Henry Boker. 6946-0
Bold dighton. Unknown. 6057-9
The **bold** dragoon. Sir Walter Scott. 6087-0
The **bold** dragoon. Unknown. 6919-3
The **bold** fisherman. Unknown. 6061-7
Bold Hathorne. Unknown. 6281-4
Bold Hawthorne. Unknown. 6753-0
Bold Kidd, the pirate. Unknown. 6061-7
"**Bold** is the attempt,in these licentious times". The demagogue. William Falconer. 6971-1
"**Bold** lady, with your lazy, haughty grace". To ignorance. Theressa M. DeFosset. 6906-1
"**Bold** Robin Hood is a forester good". Friar Tuck. Sidford F. Hamp. 6926-9
The **bold** peddler and Robin Hood. Unknown. 6136-2,6185-0
Bold Phelim Brady, the Bard of Armagh. Unknown. 6930-4
The **bold** privateer. Unknown. 6058-7,6547-3
Bold Robert Emmet. Tom Maguire. 6930-4
Bold Robin Hood. Thomas Love Peacock. 6334-9
Bold Robin Hood and the pedlar. Unknown. 6061-7
Bold Robin Hood rescuing the three squires. Unknown. 6061-7
"The **bold** young autumn came riding along". The foolish elm. Ella Wheeler Wilcox. 6863-4
Bold, Henry
"Chloris, forbear a while, do not o'erjoy me." 6317-9, 6563-5
Fire, fire! 6328-4
"**Boldly** enter into your own house of silence". Spirit quickened. Grace H. Thompson. 6799-9
"**Boldly** we go to the battle, the Knights...". Klan song. Morrie [pseud].. 6817-0
Boldness in love. Thomas Carew. 6562-7,6563-5
Boldyreff, John W.
Defiance. 6818-9
Bolehill trees. James Montgomery. 6049-8
Bolelyn, Anne
Defiled is my name. 6328-4
O death, rock me to sleep. 6328-4,6125-7
Boles, Pearl
Morning. 6764-6
Boles, Vivian Pike
The single error. 6750-6
Bolingbroke's entrance into London. William Shakespeare. 6438-8
Bolingbroke,..having heard..banishment..,fr. Richard II. William Shakespeare. 6138-9
The **boll** weevil song. Unknown. 7017-5
The **boll** weevil. Unknown. 6594-5
Bolles, D.H.
Washington. 6712-3
Bolles, Frank
The oven-bird. 6597-X
Bolles, Jason
Let me praise once your body. 6042-0
My brother. 6042-0
Bolling, Bertha
Pan's garden. 6649-6

Bolton, Edmund
"As withereth the primrose by the river". 6181-8
A carol ("Sweet music, sweeter far"). 6931-2
A palinode ("As withereth the primrose by the river") 6182-6,6334-9
The shepherd's song. 6145-1
The shepherd's song. 6756-5
To Favonius. 6436-1
Bolton, Janet
Woodrow Wilson arisen. 7001-9
Bolton, John Johnson
Doctor and clergyman. 6694-1
Bolton, Lois Arnold
The farmer's wife. 6761-1
Bolton, Ruby E.
Finesse. 6750-6
Bolton, Sarah Knowles
Faith. 6303-9,6525-2
The inevitable. 6260-1,6337-3,6512-0,6730-1,6924-X
Live in the present. 6461-2
Live today. 6337-3
"O glorious Easter morning!" 6225-3
One face. 6066-8,6226-1
Paddle your own canoe. 6294-6,6211-3
Bolton, Sarah Tittle
Left on the battle-field. 6016-2
The **Boltons**, 22. Eugene Field. 6949-5
Bolts. Unknown. 7010-8
Bombardment and aftermath. John Henrik Clarke. 6178-8
The bombardment of Bristol. Unknown. 6946-0
The bombardment of Vicksburg. Paul Hamilton Hayne. 6552-X
The bombardment. Amy Lowell. 6029-3
Bombed last night. Unknown. 6237-7
Bombers. Cecil Day Lewis. 6491-4
Bombing casualties in Spain. Herbert Read. 6210-5
A bome, god wot. Unknown. 6756-5
Bomke, Mary Cockburn
A roving alley-cat. 6120-6
"**Bon** chevalier masque qui chevaucheen silence" Paul Verlaine. 6801-4
Bon jour, bon soir. Unknown. 6669-0
Bon voyage. Helen Hunt Jackson. 7041-8
Bon voyage. William White. 6868-5
Bonaparte. Alfred Lord Tennyson. 6977-0
Bonar, A. R.
The palm tree. 6848-0
Bonar, Horatius
Abide with us. 6065-X,6656-9
All well. 6271-7
"Bathed in unfallen sunlight". 6238-5
Be true. 6239-3,6242-3,6337-3
"Beyond the smiling and the weeping." 6240-7,6302-0, 6385-3
Bless the blessed morn. 6065-X
The chief among ten thousand. 6848-0
Christ is all. 6065-X
Cross and throne. 6065-X
The everlasting memorial. 6417-5,6304-7
The fairest he. 6065-X
The first and the last. 6065-X
Gain of loss. 6304-7
God's way. 6337-3,6525-2
He liveth long who liveth well. 6238-5,6294-6
He took my place. 6065-X
His glory tell. 6065-X
How long? 6385-3
How to live. 6240-7
How we learn. 6240-7,6214-8
I heard the voice of Jesus say. 6065-X,6337-3
I lay my sins on Jesus. 6065-X
"I was a wandering sheep". 6065-X
The inner calm. 6418-3,6600-3,6219-9
Is he not fair? 6848-0
Is this all. 6302-0
It is finished. 6065-X
Jerusalem's dayspring. 6848-0
Life from death. 6910-X
A little while. 6271-7,6219-9,6656-9
Lost but found. 6656-9
Love is of God. 6337-3

The master's touch. 6065-X,6240-7,6303-9,6337-3,6600-3, 6571 ,6214-8,6656-9
"More in the garden grows than what is sown." 6225-3
Mount Hor. 6848-0
Mount Sinai. 6848-0
The new song. 6214-8
Not very far. 6406-X
Only one life. 6014-5
Patience. 6014-5
Perseverance. 6261-X
Reappearing. 6177-X
The same forever. 6065-X
Thy way not mine. 6732-8,6656-9
The voice from Galilee. 6656-9
We shall meet and rest. 6304-7
Who liveth well. 6337-3
The work that saves. 6065-X
Zion's morning. 6848-0
Zion, awake! 6848-0
Bonar, Horatius (tr.)
Psalm 024. Bible, 6848-0
Bonar, John Henry
Poe's cottage at Fordham. 6250-4,6309-8
Bonaventure, Saint
Psalter of the blessed virgin Mary. Sister M. Emmanuel (tr.). 6282-2
Bonaventure, Saint (atr)
Adeste fideles. 6543-0
Adeste fideles. Frederick Oakeley (tr.). 6608-9
Bond and free. Robert Frost. 6320-9
The **bond** of blood. Will Henry Thompson. 6062-5
The **bond** of love. Paul Fort. 6351-9
Bond, Carrie Jacobs
The perfect day. 6732-8
Bond, Freda C.
Over the hills by Fortingall. 6782-4
Snow scene. 6780-8
The **bond**. Archag Tchobanian. 6889-8
The **bondage** of drink. Unknown. 6912-6
Bonds. Laurence Housman. 6337-3
Bonds of affection. Letitia Elizabeth ("L.E.L.") Landon. 6014-5
Bonduca. Francis Beaumont and John Fletcher. 6438-8
Bone county. Jane M. Fink. 6900-2
Bone, Florence
Prayer for a little home. 6337-3,6396-6,6466-3,6509-0, 6525-5
A prayer for a little home. 6396-9
Bone, Gertrude
The mystic. 6532-5
The **bone-duster**. John Morgan. 6855-3
Bonehead hill. Robert Service. 6159-1
Boner, H.
For our lady of sorrow. 6779-4
Reflection. 6396-9
Boner, John Henry
The light'odd fire. 7041-8
The light'ood fire. 6006-4
Poe's cottage at Fordham. 6250-4,6309-8,6431-0,6483-3, 6484-1
We walked among the whispering pines. 7041-8
Bones of a house, fr. Blue Juanita. Malcolm Cowley. 6531-7
The **bones** of Chuang Tzu. Arthur Waley. 6069-2
Boneset tea. Jennie Talladay. 6707-7
The **bonfire**. Robert Frost. 6031-5,6542-2
Bonfires. Edith Haskell Tappan. 6270-9
Bongwi. Kingsley Fairbridge. 6800-6
Bongwi. Kingsley Fairbridge. 6625-9
Bonham, Thomas
In praise of ale. 6563-5,6026-9
The **Bonhomme** Richard and Serapis. Philip Freneau. 6946-0
Bonnaud, Dominique
Bells of Flanders. 6443-4
Bonne entente. Francis Reginald Scott. 6446-9
Bonnell, Margaret Boyce
Election day. 6995-9
Man of straight word. 6995-9
Bonnelycke, Emil
My soul. Charles Wharton Stork (tr.). 6555-4
Bonner, Amy

House long known. 6979-7
Bonner, John H.
Remembrance. 6097-8,6274-1
Bonnet sonnet. Jacqueline Embry. 6039-0
Bonnets indispensable to Easter. William B. Chishold. 6720-4
Bonnets of Bonnie Dundee. Sir Walter Scott. 6271-7,6610-0, 6219-9,6263-6,6267-9
Bonney, Callie L.
Keeping an ancient custom. 6720-4
Bonnie Annie. Unknown. 6185-0,6732-8,6067-6
"**Bonnie** Charlie's noo awa'.". The king over the water. Unknown. 6793-X
The **bonnie** bairns. Allan Cunningham. 6960-6
The **bonnie** banks o' Fordie. Unknown. 6136-2
The **bonnie** banks o' Loch Lomond. Unknown. 6180-X
Bonnie belle. Samuel Minturn Peck. 6770-0
Bonnie Bessie Lee. Robert Nicoll. 6656-9
The **bonnie** blue flag. Harry McCarthy. 6074-9
The **bonnie** blue flag. Annie Chambers Ketchum. 6015-3,6113-3,6223-7
The **bonnie** broukit bairn. Christopher M. ("Hugh MacDiarmid") Grieve. 6845-6
The **bonnie** brukit lassie. James Tytler. 6180-X
Bonnie Doon. Robert Burns. 6024-2,6198-2,6102-8,6597-X, 6543-0,6737 ,6150-8,6301-2,6304-7,6371-3
Bonnie Dundee, sels. Sir Walter Scott. 6424-8
The **bonnie** Earl of Murray. Unknown. 6180-X,6395-0
Bonnie George Campbell. William Motherwell. 6134-6,6383-7
Bonnie George Campbell. Unknown. 6055-2,6132-X,6180-X,6271-7,6395-0,6600-,6604-6,6193-1,6153-2,6219-9,6660-7
The **bonnie** house o' Airlie. Unknown. 6180-X,6185-0,6067-6
Bonnie James Campbell. Unknown. 6185-0
Bonnie Kilmeny gaed up the glen. James Hogg. 6845-6
Bonnie Lady Ann. Allan Cunningham. 6543-0
Bonnie Lady Ann. Allan Cunningham. 6830-8
Bonnie lasses. Unknown. 6629-1
Bonnie Lesley. Robert Burns. 6086-2,6198-2,6271-7,6246-6, 6634-8,6219-9,6092
Bonnie Mary. Robert Burns. 6240-7
The **bonnie** milk-cow. Alexander Smart. 6131-1
Bonnie Prince Charlie. James Hogg. 6180-X,6395-0,6219-9, 6267-9
Bonnie ran the burnie doun. Carolina Oliphant, Baroness Nairne. 6086-2
Bonnie sweet Jessie. Unknown. 6139-7
Bonnie twinkling starnies. James McKowen. 6090-0;6174-5
Bonnie wee Eric. Frances Ridley Havergal. 7002-7
Bonnie wee thing. Robert Burns. 6302-0,6385-3,6737-9
Bonnie Wood o' Craigie-lea. Robert Tannahill. 6180-X
The **bonniest** bairn in a' the warl'. Robert Ford. 6239-3
Bonny Annie. Unknown. 6518-X
Bonny baby Livingston. Unknown. 6185-0,6613-5
Bonny Barbara Allan. Unknown. 6056-0,6057-9,6058-7,6108-7, 6154-0,6518 ,6319-5,6491-4
Bonny Bee Hom. Unknown. 6185-0
The **bonny** birdy. Unknown. 6185-0
The **bonny** bunch of roses. Unknown. 6057-9
Bonny Charlie. Unknown. 6859-6
Bonny Dundee, fr. The doom of Devorgoil. Sir Walter Scott. 6180-X,6136-2,6323-3,6634-8,6087-0,6473 ,6481-7,6196-6,6110-9,6438-8,6086-2,6322
The **bonny** Earl of Moray. Unknown. 6179-6,6067-6
The **bonny** Earl of Murray. Unknown. 6185-0,6228-8,6518-4, 6668-2
Bonny Eloise. J.R. Thomas. 6074-9
Bonny George Campbell. Unknown. 6512-0,6067-6
The **bonny** highland laddie. Unknown. 6859-6
The **bonny** hind. Unknown. 6185-0,6518-X
The **bonny** house of Airly. Unknown. 6518-X
Bonny James Campbell. Unknown. 6518-X
Bonny John Seton. Unknown. 6185-0
The **bonny** lass of Anglesey. Unknown. 6185-0,6518-4
The **bonny** light horseman. Patrick Joseph McCall. 6174-5
Bonny Lizie Baillie. Unknown. 6185-0
The **bonny** moorhen. Unknown. 6859-6
The **bonny** Tweed for me. William A. Foster. 6180-X
"**Bonny** sweet-marjoram was in flower". The tithing-man. Mary E. (Freeman) Wilkins. 6965-7
The **bonny** wee hoose. William Lyle. 6695-X

BONNYBELL:

Bonnybell: the gray sphex. Edgar Lee Masters. 6033-1
Bonta, Edwin W.
    The heights. 7019-1
Bonte, George Willard
    The seven words. 6818-9
Bonum est mihi quod humiliasti me. Henry Howard, Earl of Surrey. 6584-8
The boobhead & the girl. James Baxter. 7018-3
The booby-trap. Robert Service. 6159-1
Boodson, Alison
    Carol. 6379-9
    Night alert. 6379-9
    Poem ("He lying"). 6379-9
    Poem ("I do not want"). 6379-9
Boodson, Sergeant N.
    Cyprus. 6468-X
The boogah man. Paul Laurence Dunbar. 6653-4
'Booh!'. Eugene Field. 6078-1,6318-7
Book & bookplate. John Masefield. 6722-0
"A book and a jug and a dame". Limerick:"A book and a jug and a dame." Unknown. 6308-X
The book and the cup. Jessica Powers. 6839-1
"Book falls from the table crying 'Leave me!'". The sound track jumps. John Ciardi. 6751-4
"The book I read by no design or plan". Chance. Ruth H. Hausman. 6850-2
A book for Christmas. Margaret Allonby. 6788-3
Book I, fr. Paradise lost. John Milton. 6122-2
Book I, fr. The prelude. William Wordsworth. 6122-2
Book I, satire III (With some pot-fury,...). Joseph Hall. 6198-2
Book I, sels. John Gay. 6198-2
Book II, fr. Paradise lost. John Milton. 6122-2
"Book larnin'". M.H. Turk. 6139-7
"The book lay unread in my lap". Going home. Maurice Kenny. 7005-1
The book line. Arthur Guiterman. 6773-5
A book of Americans, sels. Stephen Vincent Benet. 6375-6
The book of books. Sir Walter Scott. 6337-3
The book of books. John Greenleaf Whittier. 6097-8
The book of Ecclesiastes, sels. Bible. 6879-0
A book of economics. Haniel Long. 6102-8,6076-5
The book of Ezekiel. Bible. 6958-4
The book of Genesis. Bible. 6958-4
The book of Genesis. Bible. 6958-4
A book of gold. John James Piatt. 6620-8
The book of hours of Sister Clotilde. Amy Lowell. 6754-9
The book of hours, sels. Rainer Maria Rilke. 6648-8
The book of joyous children. James Whitcomb Riley. 6091-9
Book of Leinster, sels. Whitley Stokes. 6174-5
The book of life. Richard Thomson. 6297-0
The book of love, sels. Sir Edwin Arnold. 6066-8
The book of memory. Edgar A. Guest. 7033-7
The book of nature. Phoebe Cary. 6969-X
The book of nature. William Drummond of Hawthornden. 6934-7
A book of remembrance. Mazie V. Caruthers. 6750-6
Book of songs, sonnets, Dresden poetry, sels. Heinrich Heine. 6439-6
The book of the duchess, sels. Geoffrey Chaucer. 6726-3
The book of the duchess,, sels. Geoffrey Chaucer. 6193-1
The book of Thel, sels. William Blake. 6208-3,6317-9
The book of Thel. William Blake. 6152-4,6195-0
"A book of verses beneath the bough," fr. Rubaiyat. Omar Khayyam. 6232-6
"A book of Verses underneath the Bough". Edward Fitzgerald. 6187-7
A book of verses underneath the bough, fr. Rubaiyat. Omar Khayyam. 7039-6
Book review. Louis Untermeyer. 6011-0
A book was writ of late. John Milton. 6733-6
"The book, by George! I'd rather own". Thompson's Vermont. Daniel L. Cady. 6988-6
The book-binder. Mary Josephine Benson. 6797-2
The book-hunter. Frank Dempster Sherman. 6297-0
The book-keeper's dream. Unknown. 6155-9
The book-path, fr. The five seals in the sky. Vachel Lindsay. 6206-7
The book-plate's petition. Austin Dobson. 6297-0
The book-stalls on the Seine. Charles Lewis Sattery. 6331-4,6439-6,6631-3
The book-worm.. C.W. Pearson. 6274-1
The book-worms. Robert Burns. 6125-7,6297-0,6545-7
The book.. William Drummond of Hawthornden. 6332-2
A book. Emily Dickinson. 6478-7
A book. Hannah More. 6465-5
The book. William Carson Fagg. 6870-7
The bookdealer's daughter. Jan Chisholm. 6900-2
A booke of Ayres (I). Thomas Campion. 6794-8
A booke of Ayres (II). Thomas Campion. 6794-8
A booke of Ayres (III). Thomas Campion. 6794-8
A booke of Ayres (IV). Thomas Campion. 6794-8
A booke of Ayres (IX). Thomas Campion. 6794-8
A booke of Ayres (IX). Thomas Campion. 6794-8
A booke of Ayres (V). Thomas Campion. 6794-8
A booke of Ayres (V). Thomas Campion. 6794-8
A booke of Ayres (VI). Thomas Campion. 6794-8
A booke of Ayres (VII). Thomas Campion. 6794-8
A booke of Ayres (VII). Thomas Campion. 6794-8
A booke of Ayres (VIII). Thomas Campion. 6794-8
A booke of Ayres (X). Thomas Campion. 6794-8
A booke of Ayres (XI). Thomas Campion. 6794-8
A booke of Ayres (XI). Thomas Campion. 6794-8
A booke of Ayres (XII). Thomas Campion. 6794-8
A booke of Ayres (XIII). Thomas Campion. 6794-8
A booke of Ayres (XIV). Thomas Campion. 6794-8
A booke of Ayres (XIV). Thomas Campion. 6794-8
A booke of Ayres (XIX). Thomas Campion. 6794-8
A booke of Ayres (XV). Thomas Campion. 6794-8
A booke of Ayres (XVI). Thomas Campion. 6794-8
A booke of Ayres (XVII). Thomas Campion. 6794-8
A booke of Ayres (XX). Thomas Campion. 6794-8
Bookends. R. Scott Bowen. 6750-6
Booker T. Washington. John W. Fentress. 6178-8
Booker, Stephen Todd
    Flash. 6870-7
    Look away/look away. 6870-7
    Lynched. 6870-7
    No fig. 6870-7
    Paperweight escape. 6870-7
Bookes of Ayres, sels. Thomas Campion. 6208-3
A bookkeeper's son. Edgar A. Guest. 6748-4
Bookra. Charles Dudley Warner. 6083-8,6309-8
Books. E.J.H. Goodfellow. 6137-0
Books. Sara Josepha Hale. 6294-6
Books. Hermann Hesse. 6643-7
Books. John Higgins. 6385-3
Books. Unknown. 6385-3
Books and flowers. Felicia Dorothea Hemans. 6973-8
Books and love. Carl David af Wirsen. 6045-5
Books and reading. John Jay Chapman. 6036-6
The books I ought to read. Abbie Farwell Brown. 7021-3
"Books are a part of man's perogative". Man's perogative, fr. The wife. Sir Thomas Overbury. 6934-7
"Books are not seldom talismans and spells". Books, fr. The task. William Cowper. 6934-7
"The books I cannot hope to buy". Ballade of the unattainable. Andrew Lang. 6875-8
"Books I would read, but most will go unread". Unrest. Bernice Lesbia Kenyon. 6880-4
Books of the Bible. John Nelson Davidson. 6274-1,6714-X
"Books rule thy mind, so let it be!". Triolet to her husband. Andrew Lang. 6875-8
Books, fr. Personal talk. William Wordsworth. 6934-7
Books, fr. The library. George Crabbe. 6932-0
Books, fr. The library. George Crabbe. 6934-7
Books, fr. The library. George Crabbe. 6932-0
Books, fr. The library. George Crabbe. 6934-7
Books, fr. The task. William Cowper. 6934-7
Bookshelf. Robert Service. 6159-1
"The bookshelf hoards the wealth worth...". Bibliophile's library. Rachel Albright. 6789-1
The bookworm. Thomas Parnell. 6297-0
The bookworm. Royall Tyler. 6004-8
The bookworm. Carolyn Wells. 6739-5
The boola-boola maid, fr. Five frivolous songs. Robert Service. 6159-1
"Boom and crash of the breech-block guns". To Charles Lindbergh. W.L. Werner. 7019-1
Boomer, Paul C.

Life. 6482-5
Mind. 6482-5
Boomerang. Emily Porter St. John. 6316-0
"Booming and quaking". Skarphedinn among the flames. Hannes Hafstein. 6854-5
The boon companion. Oliver St. John Gogarty. 6427-2
The boon companion. Johann Ludwig Uhland. 6952-5
The boon of memory. Felicia Dorothea Hemans. 6973-8
Boone, Stanley
    The county jail. 6880-4
Boot and saddle. Robert Browning. 6198-2,6328-4,6395-0, 6732-8,6723-9,6656
"Boot and saddle, see, the slanting". Finis exoptatus, fr. Ye wearie wayfarer. Adam Lindsay Gordon. 6951-7
Boot hill. Sharlot M. Hall. 7012-4,7038-8
Boot saddle. Robert Browning. 6197-4,6153-2,6655-0,6383-7, 6430-2,6110
The boot's song. Unknown. 6237-7
The bootblack. Unknown. 6409-4
The booted hens. Francis Carlin. 6032-3
Booth, Barbara M.
    Love's melody. 6799-9
Booth, Barton
    Sweet are the charms. 6219-9
Booth, Carrie Belle
    Mumble and grumble. 6799-9
Booth, Eva Gore
    Crucifixion. 6730-1
    Harvest. 6730-1
    The little waves of Breffny. 6423-X,6477-9
Booth, Helen
    The hostage. 6920-7
    The little sister of Mercy. 6922-3
    The old organ. 6922-3
    Renyi. 6920-7
    The rose of Avondale. 6921-5
    The sword. 6923-1
Booth, Helena
    Passing hours. 6799-9
Booth, Julia A.
    Be yourself. 6883-9
    War. 6883-9
    What's the difference? 6883-9
Booth, Philip
    Animal fair. 6388-8
    Catwise. 6388-8
    Nebraska, U.S.A. 6803-0
    The turning. 6388-8
Boots. Rudyard Kipling. 6726-3
Boots and saddles. Nicholas Saboly. 6608-9
Boots, W. E.
    Wild geese over Winona. 6342-X
Booz endormi. Victor Hugo. 6801-4
Bora ring. Judith Wright. 6384-5
Borawski, Walta
    God, the unplucked notes. 7003-5
    Invisible history. 7003-5
    Things are still sudden & wonderful. 7003-5
Border. Isabel Fiske Conant. 6076-5,6102-8
Border affair. Charles B. Clarke. 6714-X
A border affair. Charles Badger Clark Jr. 6274-1
Border ballad. Betty Bridgman. 6342-X
Border ballad, fr. The monastery. Sir Walter Scott. 6239-3, 6087-0,6239-3,6242-3,6271-7,6481-7,6512
A border ballad. Harry ("Col. D. Streamer") Graham. 6724-7
A border ballad. Thomas Love Peacock. 6802-2
The border land. Marie L. Moffatt. 6919-3
Border march, fr. The monastery. Sir Walter Scott. 6604-6, 6458-2
A border memory. Florence L. Snow. 6615-1
Border song. Sir Walter Scott. 6240-7,6192-3,6304-7
Border-land. Phoebe Cary. 6969-X
Border-songs. Witter Bynner. 6628-3
The borderers, sels. William Wordsworth. 6867-7,6958-4
Borderland. Ellen M. Carroll. 7016-7
Borderland. Laura Simmons. 6320-9
Borderline. Paul Fericano. 6901-0
Borderline. R.H. Grenville. 6218-0
Bordewich, Hattie S
    Minnesota battle flags from Gettysburg. 6342-X

Bordy, Alter
    Ma. 6033-1
The bore.. John Godfrey Saxe. 6294-6
Borecky, Jaromir
    To a new morning. Paul Selver (tr.). 6763-8
The bores. Unknown. 6921-5
Borger Joris's hammer. Arthur Guiterman. 6773-5
Borges, Jorge Luis
    Benares. H.R. Hays (tr.). 6642-9
    Butcher shop. H.R. Hays (tr.). 6642-9
    Cyclical night. Robert Lima (tr.). 6803-0
    A day's run. H.R. Hays (tr.). 6642-9
    General Quiroga rides to death in a crriage. H.R. Hays (tr.). 6642-9
    General Quiroga rides to death in a carriage. H.R. Hays (tr.). 6642-9
    Houses like angels. Robert Stuart Fitzgerald (tr.). 6759-X
    July avenue. H.R. Hays (tr.). 6642-9
    Love's priority. Robert Stuart Fitzgerald (tr.). 6759-X
    Natural flow of memory. H.R. Hays (tr.). 6642-9
    The night they kept vigil in the south. Robert Stuart Fitzgerald (tr.). 6759-X
    Patio. Robert Stuart Fitzgerald (tr.). 6759-X
    A patio. H.R. Hays (tr.). 6642-9
    The Recoleta. H.R. Hays (tr.). 6642-9
    Sepulchral inscription. Robert Stuart Fitzgerald (tr.). 6759-X
    To Rafael Cansinos Assens. Robert Stuart Fitzgerald (tr.). 6759-X
"Born by the hills of hard grey weather...". Leichhardt. Henry Clarence Kendall. 6768-9
A born fisherman. Joe Cone. 6694-1
"Born in the garret, in the kitchen bred". A sketch. George Gordon, 6th Baron Byron. 6378-0,6945-2
"Born in the purple! born in the purple!". Porphyrogenitus. Bayard Taylor. 6976-2
Born is the babe. Unknown. 6756-5
Born of tears. William Henry Davies. 6246-5
"Born of the earth, my mother". Daughter of Pan. Nancy Telfair. 6841-3
"Born of the prairie and the wave...". Fort Dearborn, Chicago. Benjamin Franklin Taylor. 6344-6
"Born on an island and raised near the sea". Answering wind. Ida E. Sprague. 6857-X
"Born on the breast of the prairie...". Brandon. Emily Pauline ("Tekahionwake") Johnson. 6837-5
"Born rangers both of us and we were young". The lost trail. Henry Herbert Knibbs. 7008-6
Born to the purple. James Whitcomb Riley. 6091-9
"Born with all the arms sought..separate peace". The deserter. John Streeter Manifold. 6895-2
"Born with the vices of my kind". Thomas D'Urfey. 6933-9
Born yesterday. Philip Larkin. 6257-1
"Born, nurtered, wedded,prized,within the pale". La Fayette. Dolly Madison. 6946-0
Bornberger, August W.
    Out of the vast. 6303-9
Borncamp, Ida May
    Morning star. 6799-9
Borne. Daniel Walter Owens. 7024-8
"Borne by the tempest, on we sail". Hymn ("Borne by the tempest, on we sail"). John Pierpont. 6752-2
"Borne on the wings of time another year". On the prospect of a revolution in France. Philip Freneau. 6753-0
The borough, sels. George Crabbe. 6831-6
The borough, sels. George Crabbe. 6482-5,6317-9,6195-0
The borough. George Crabbe. 6208-3
Borrioboola gha. Orrin Goodrich. 6344-6,6406-X
Borrow, George
    Lavengro, sels. 6107-9
    Svend Vonved. 6438-8
Borrow, George (tr.)
    Adon olam. Unknown, 6848-0
    The invitation. Goronwy Owen, 6528-7
    The mist. Unknown (Welsh), 6528-7
    The mother. Unknown, 6097-8
    The snow on Evia. Unknown, 6331-4
The borrowed book. Charles Nodier. 6297-0
The borrowedchild. Howard Weeden. 6691-7

BORROWED

Borrowed feathers. Joseph Morris. 6291-1
Borrowed plumes. Adam Lindsay Gordon. 6951-7
Borrowed thoughts, sels. Adelaide Anne Procter. 6957-6
Borrowin' the baby. Wilbur Dick Nesbit. 6889-8
Borrowing. Ralph Waldo Emerson. 6302-0,6385-3,6722-0,6735-2
Borson, Roo
    City. 6767-0
Borst, Richard Warner
    The challenge of the tillers. 6954-1
    For the new age. 6954-1
    Traffic warning. 6542-2
Borthwick, James Drummond
    'Speak, Lord, for thy servant heareth' 6848-0
Borthwick, Jane L. (tr.)
    Be still. Katharina von Schlegel, 6337-3
Bosanquet, Bernard (tr.)
    And sae came of it. Johann Wolfgang von Goethe, 7042-6
    The Athenian's confirmation vow. Unknown (Greek), 7042-6
    Barkers, i.e. the critics, fr. Gedichte. Johann Wolfgang von Goethe, 7042-6
    Constancy, fr. Gedichte. Johann Wolfgang von Goethe, 7042-6
    The dance of death. Unknown (Greek), 7042-6
    Good resolutions, fr. Gedichte. Johann Wolfgang von Goethe, 7042-6
    The good will, fr. Pharsalia. Lucan, 7042-6
    "Great nature's inmost heart". Haller, 7042-6
    Heredity. Johann Wolfgang von Goethe, 7042-6
    The higher shrewdness. Johann Wolfgang von Goethe, 7042-6
    An inscription for all council-chambers, fr. Eth. Nic. Aristotle, 7042-6
    The master. Johann Wolfgang von Goethe, 7042-6
    Mephistopheles to the student, fr. Faust. Johann Wolfgang von Goethe, 7042-6
    Our ignorance in asking. Johann Wolfgang von Goethe, 7042-6
    Philistine mysticism. Johann Wolfgang von Goethe, 7042-6
    The researcher, fr. Gedichte. Johann Wolfgang von Goethe, 7042-6
    Salvation, fr. Faust. Johann Wolfgang von Goethe, 7042-6
    To joy, or freedom, fr. Gedichte. Johann C. Friedrich von Schiller, 7042-6
    To the originals, fr. Gedichte. Johann Wolfgang von Goethe, 7042-6
    The true life-passion. Johann Wolfgang von Goethe, 7042-6
    A voice from old Germany. Johann Wolfgang von Goethe, 7042-6
Bosanquet, Helen
    Boys and men. 7042-6
    A brithday greeting. 7042-6
    Dreamland. 7042-6
    Gleaners. 7042-6
    Low life. 7042-6
    Non tali auxilio. 7042-6
    Old age: 1916. 7042-6
    The old woman's war work. 7042-6
    Oxshott common in war-time. 7042-6
    The puzzled conscience. 7042-6
    The rock. 7042-6
    They shall renew their youth. 7042-6
    The wanderers. 7042-6
Boschka Layton 1921-1984 Irving Layton. 6767-0
Bosco, Louis J.
    The radiant stone. 7032-9
Bosher, Kate Langley
    Lee. 6184-2
Bosley, Jose
    City of healing. 6342-X
Bosman, Herman Charles
    The luck in the square stone, sels. 6788-3
    The poet. 6788-3
    Recovery from mental illness. 6788-3
    Seed. 6788-3
Boss, John
    Wakin' the young uns. 6924-X
Bosschere, Jean de
    This is the end. 6351-9
    Ulysses builds his bed. 6351-9
Bossidy, John Collins
    A Boston toast. 6736-0
    On the aristocracy of Harvard. 6722-0
Bossy and the daisy. Margaret Deland. 6937-1
Bostelmann, Carl John
    The call to arms. 6542-2
    Christ in the Andes. 6144-3
    Conquerors. 6542-2
    Harper's Ferry. 6979-7
    The poet. 6041-2
Boston. Berton Braley. 6853-7
Boston. Ralph Waldo Emerson. 6267-9,6470-1
Boston. Sam Walter Foss. 6088-9
Boston. John Boyle O'Reilly. 6946-0
The Boston burglar. Unknown. 6058-7,6003-X
The Boston cats. Arthur Macy. 6120-6
Boston Common. John Berryman. 6391-8
Boston Common. Oliver Wendell Holmes. 6484-1
The Boston Evening Transcript. Thomas Stearns Eliot. 6399-3
"A Boston gentleman declares". A plea for the classics. Eugene Field. 6949-5
Boston hymn. Ralph Waldo Emerson. 6014-5,6113-3,6299-7,6302-0,6385-3,6473 ,6600-3,6730-1,6288-1,6126-5
Boston hymn, sel. Ralph Waldo Emerson. 6954-1
Boston hymn, sels. Ralph Waldo Emerson. 6102-8,6076-5
A Boston lullaby. James Jeffrey Roche. 6505-8
A Boston lullaby. Unknown. 7021-3
Boston nursery rhymes. Joseph Cook. 6089-7
The Boston symphony orchestra. James Fenimore Cooper. 6476-0
Boston tea. David Wadsworth Cannon Jr. 6178-8
Boston tea party. Maurice Kenny. 7003-5
The Boston tea party. Unknown. 6753-0
A Boston toast. John Collins Bossidy. 6736-0
Boston, Everett
    Psalms at sea: the convert. 6039-0
    Pslams of the sea: the convert. 6039-0
Bostwick, Grace G.
    The reward. 6303-9,6337-3,6461-2
Bostwick, Helen B.
    The king's picture. 6889-8,6912-6
Bostwick, Helen Louise Barron
    Drafted. 6045-1
    How the gates came ajar. 6404-3,6682-8,8889-8
    The king's picture. 6273-3
    Litle dandelion. 6132-X,6127-3,6502-3,6519-8,6135-4,6131
    Urvasi. 6066-8,6600-3
"Bosun's whistle piping...". Watchin' out for subs. U.A.L.. 6846-4
Boswell, Arthur
    Roughchin, the pirate. 6833-2
Boswell, James
    A justiciary opera. 6787-5
    To Mrs. Thrale on her thirty-fifth birthday. 6724-7
Boswell, Robert Bruce (tr.)
    Athaliah. Jean Baptiste Racine, 6848-0
Boswell, Sir Alexander
    Good night, and joy be wi' you a' 6383-7
    Jenny dang the weaver. 6180-X
    Jenny's bawbee. 6180-X
    March of the men of Harlech. 6328-4
Bosworth, William
    Arcadius' song to Sepha. 6194-X
    See'st not, my love. 6563-5
The botanic garden, sels. Erasmus Darwin. 6482-5
Botanical. Marie Emilie Gilchrist. 6906-1
Botanist on Alp (No. 2). Wallace Stevens. 6751-4
Botany. Walter Savage Landor. 6092-7
Botany bay. Unknown. 6826-X
Botelho, Francis M.
    Apartment partners. 6750-6
"Both Cherokee and Samek saw you, and tell". Bear dance. Ronald Rogers. 7005-1
Both less and more. Richard Watson Dixon. 6315-2

"Both sexes now deprave...", fr. The happy pair. Sir
    Charles Sedley. 6544-9
Both sides. Mary Abigail ("Gail Hamilton") Dodge. 6120-6
Both sides. Gail Hamilton. 6742-5
Both sides of the Tweed. Unknown. 6859-6
Both worshipped the same great name. Unknown. 6443-4
The bothie of tober-vrolich, sels. Arthur Hugh Clough.
    6656-9
Bothwell. William Edmonstoune Aytoun. 6948-7
Bothwell. Ebenezer Elliott. 6980-0
Bothwell bank. John Pinkerton. 6086-2
Bothwell bridge. Unknown. 6185-0
Bothwell, sels. Algernon Charles Swinburne. 6656-9
Botkin, Benjamin Albert
    Chalk. 6397-7
    Faculty recital. 6397-7
    Field wireless. 6397-7
    The fish. 6397-7
    Going to the store. 6397-7
    Meteor. 6850-2
    Moon-miracle. 6397-7
    People riding. 6397-7
    Sanctuary. 6397-7
    Spiders. 6397-7
Botkin, Coe
    For sustenance. 6799-9
    Night wind. 6799-9
Botsford, Allan
    Such a friend. 6085-4
Botta, Anne C. Lynch
    Ab astris. 7030-2
    In the library. 7030-2
    Love. 6600-3
    Thoughts in a library. 6219-9
    Until death. 7030-2
A Botticelli face. Humbert Wolfe. 6634-8
The bottle and the bird. Eugene Field. 6949-5
The bottle genie. Rhys Pasley. 7018-3
"The bottle of perfume that Willie sent". Unknown. 6722-0
"The bottle of perfume that Willie sent". Limerick:"The
    bottle of perfume that Willie sent". Unknown. 6811-1
The bottle tree. Eugene Field. 6318-7
The bottom drawer. Mary A. Barr. 6273-3
The bottom of the car. Tom James. 6149-4
Bottomley, Gordon
    Atlantis. 6023-4
    Babel: the gate of God, fr. Chambers of Imagery. 6234-2
    A carol for Christmas Day before dawn. 6532-5
    Chambers of imagery, sels. 6234-2
    'The crier by night,' sels. 6873-1
    Dawn. 6897-9
    Eager spring. 6161-3,6430-2
    Elegiac mood. 6897-9
    Elegiac mood. 6872-3
    The end of the world, fr. Chambers of imagery. 6234-2,
      6393-4
    In memoriam A.M.W. 6250-4,6301-2
    King Lear's wife. 6234-2
    A louse crept out of my lady' shift. 6125-7
    My moon. 6897-9
    Netted strawberries. 6668-2
    New Year's Eve, 1913. 6477-9,6102-8
    Night and morning songs. 6897-9
    A song of apple gathering. 6541-4
    To iron-founders and others. 6437-X,6477-9
Bottoms up! Berton Braley. 6853-7
'Bottoms up' ad finem. Percy Adams Hutchinson. 6118-4
Bottrall, Ronald
    Arion Anadyomenos. 6150-8,6354-3
    Blackbird. 6985-1
    The future is not for us. 6354-3
    Genesis. 6150-8
    On a grave of the drowned. 6985-1
    Ploughing. 6985-1
    Preamble to a great adventure. 6354-3
Bottrall, Ronald (tr.)
    Dream of his lady ("O eyes, you mortal stars").
      Giovanni Battista Guarini, 6325-X
Botwood, Edward
    Hot stuff. 6946-0

The Bouchaleen bawn. Patrick Joseph McCall. 6174-5
Bouchalleen bawn. John Keegan. 6174-5
Bouchelleen-bawn. John Banim. 6858-8
Boucicault, Dion
    Green upon the cape. 6858-8
    I'm very happy where I am. 6858-8
    A peasant woman's song. 6090-0,6244-X,6090-0,6174-5,
      6244-X
    The shan van vocht. 6858-8
    Wearing of the green. 6694-1
    The wearing of the green. 6858-8
The bough of time. Ella Young. 6090-0
"The boughs that bend over". By the light of the moon.
    Robert Kelley Weeks. 7041-8
"The boughs they blow across the pane". A wintery waste.
    Alice Cary. 6865-0;6969-X
Bought. Francis Davison. 6379-9
A bought embrace. George S. Fraser. 6666-6
"Bought him of the Navajos- shadow of a pony". Largo.
    Henry Herbert Knibbs. 7010-8
Bought locks. Martial. 7039-9
Boughton, Willis A.
    American Rhapsody to Lindbergh. 7019-1
Bouilhet, Louis
    La colombe. 6801-4
Boulder. Morris Zwart. 6850-2
Boulders. Charles Wharton Stork. 6338-1
Boule's hop. Unknown. 6281-4
Boulmier, Joseph
    Old books, fresh flowers. Rosamund Marriott ("Graham R.
      Tomson") Watson (tr.). 6297-0
    Vng livra viel. 6297-0
"Bounce buckram, velvet's dear". Unknown. 6363-2
Bouncing-bet. Rose Morgan. 6615-1
Bound for harvest-home, Idyll vii. Theocritus. 6435-3
Bound for Sourabaya! Charles Henry Souter. 6784-0
Bound to the mast. Francis Ledwidge. 6812-X
Bound upon th' accursed tree. Henry Hart Milman. 6219-9
The boundary rider. Thomas Heney. 6784-0
"A bounding satyr, golden in the beard". The tomb of
    Sophocles. Sir Edmund Gosse. 7015-9
Bounds. Eleanor Price. 6396-9
Boundy, Rex
    A virile Christ. 6144-3,6337-3,6730-1
Bounty. Abus Salt. 6362-4
The bounty of our age. Henry Farley. 6563-5
Bouquet for Judas. Charles Henry Tenney. 6723-9
Bouquet of belle scavoir. Wallace Stevens. 6761-1
A bouquet of flowers. Unknown. 6171-0
Bouquet, John Alexander
    The epitaph. 6337-3
    Sorrow turned into joy. 6337-3
Bourbon, Nita
    Fourwheeling to the gravel pit. 6857-X
Bourdeux, Nellie G.
    Sunday afternoon. 6761-1
Bourdillon, Francis William
    All's well. 7031-0
    At sea. 6273-3
    The blackbird. 6943-6
    Caeli. 6652-6
    The call. 7031-0
    The call. 7027-2
    The debt unpayable. 6542-2
    Eurydice. 6250-4
    The heart-cry. 6476-0
    Light. 6219-9,6654-2,6371-3,6737-9,6226-1,6273-3,6477-9,
      6486-8,6620-8
    Light and love. 6337-3
    A lost God, sels. 6730-1
    A lost legend. 6610-0
    A lost voice. 6658-5
    Love's meinie. 6658-5
    Night. 6204-0
    "The night has a thousand eyes." 6138-9,6260-1,6332-2,
      6497-3,6437-X,6481-,6656-9,6658-5,6250-4,6646-1,6560-
      0,6660 ,6046-3,6102-8,6104-4,6732-8
    "O! winter twilight, while the moon". 6238-5
    Old and young. 6656-9
    Outwards or hmewards. 6273-3,6104-4

BOURDILLON

Song ("The night has a thousand eyes"). 6320-9
To a lark. 6943-6
Two robbers. 6273-3
Upon the valley's lap. 6260-1
A violinist. 6437-X, 6656-9
Where runs the river? 6730-1, 6046-3

Bourinot, Arthur S.
Autumn silence. 6115-X
A flower in the city street. 6115-X
The harvest wind. 6115-X
Immortality. 6796-4
Returning. 6115-X
Sleeping now in Coventry. 6224-5
Snow shadows. 6021-8
To the memory of Rupert Brooke. 6115-X
What far kingdom. 6021-8

Bourke, W.P.
When my cousin comes to town. 7021-3

Bourne, David
Parachute descent. 6666-6

Bourne, Vincent
An aenigma. William Cowper (tr.). 6814-6
"Busy, curious, thirsty fly." 6302-0; 6385-3
The cantab. William Cowper (tr.). 6814-6
The cause won. William Cowper (tr.). 6814-6
The cricket. William Cowper (tr.). 6814-6, 6271-7
Denner's old woman. William Cowper (tr.). 6814-6
Familiarity dangerous. William Cowper (tr.). 6814-6, 6511-2
The glow-worm. William Cowper (tr.). 6814-6
The innocent thief. William Cowper (tr.). 6814-6
Invitation to the redbreast. William Cowper (tr.). 6814-6
The jackdaw. William Cowper (tr.). 6814-6
A manual more ancient that the art of printing... William Cowper (tr.). 6814-6
The maze. William Cowper (tr.). 6814-6
No sorrow peculiar to the sufferer. William Cowper (tr.). 6814-6
Ode on the death of a lady who lived one hundred years. William Cowper (tr.). 6814-6
On the picture of a sleeping child. William Cowper (tr.). 6814-6
The parrot. William Cowper (tr.). 6814-6
Reciprocal kindness the primary law of nature. William Cowper (tr.). 6814-6
The silk worm. William Cowper (tr.). 6814-6
The snail. 6133-8
The snail. William Cowper (tr.). 6814-6, 6454-X
Sparrows self-domesticated in Trinty College, Cambridge. William Cowper (tr.). 6814-6
Strada's nightingale. William Cowper (tr.). 6814-6
The tears of a painter. William Cowper (tr.). 6814-6
The Thracian. William Cowper (tr.). 6814-6
Verses to the memory of Dr. Lloyd (1). William Cowper (tr.). 6814-6
Verses to the memory of Dr. Lloyd (2). William Cowper (tr.). 6814-6

The **Bourne**. Walter De La Mare. 6905-3
The **bourne**. Christina Georgina Rossetti. 6208-3, 6315-2, 6508-2, 6655-0

Bourniot, Arthur S.
An indian arrow head. 6797-2
Padded footsteps. 6797-2
The pine tree swing. 6797-2
"To-day there came a pedlar" 6797-2

Bousquet, Louis
Madelon. 6732-8

Boutelle, Mary Keeley
Grandmother Gray. 6742-5
Grandmother Gray. 6915-0

Bouton d'or. Jessie B. Rittenhouse. 6441-8

Bouton, Elizabeth
The woodland lesson. 6411-6

Boutwell, Martha M.
Camp fire. 6764-6

Boutwell, Mary S.
In an old cemetery. 6764-6

Bouve, Thomas Tracy
'The Shannon' and the 'Chesapeake'. 6062-5

"The **bow** of Zeus has twanged...", fr. Agamemnon. Aeschylus. 6435-3
A **Bow** Street ballad. William Makepeace Thackeray. 6760-3
"**Bow** the head! For through the door". The cross triumphant. Harry Howe Bogert. 6799-9
"**Bow**, daughter of Babylon, bow thee". Babylon. Alfred Lord Tennyson. 6848-0
The **bow-leg** boy. Eugene Field. 6949-5
A **bow-meeting** song. Reginald Heber. 6102-8
"**Bow-wow** says the dog". Unknown. 6363-2
"**Bow-wow-wow!/Whose** dog are thou?" Mother Goose. 6452-3, 6363-2
The **bow**. Al-Buqaira. 6362-4

Bowdish, Luman R.
December. 6799-9
When love grows cold. 6799-9

Bowdler Jr., John
"Children of God, who, faint and slow." 6302-0

"**Bowed** low on his ancient loom". The weaver. Caroline Sparks. 6799-9
"**Bowed** with grief and sorrow". The soldier's grave. John C. Long. 6799-9

Bowen, Anna C.
A love idyll. 6799-9

Bowen, Charles Synge Bowen, Baron
Good-night, good-morning. 6046-3
Just & unjust. 6722-0

Bowen, E.E.
Doer and dreamer. 6793-X
Willow the king. 6290-3

Bowen, Edward
Forty years on. 6046-3
Shemuel. 6046-3

Bowen, Euros
The birds of Rhiannon. Gwyn Williams (tr.). 6528-7

Bowen, George E.
At last. 6274-1
Beyond the bars. 6274-1
Despoiled. 6274-1
Porto Rico. 6274-1

Bowen, H. Courthope
To a doleful poet. 6770-0

Bowen, John Eliot
The man who rode to Conemaugh. 7041-8, 6062-5
To Wilding, my polo-pony. 7041-8

Bowen, Mary M.
Cradle song. 6131-1

Bowen, Nettie Stephenson
May I walk with you? 6799-9
My garden of friends. 6799-9

Bowen, R. Scott
Bookends. 6750-6

Bowen, Stirling
Autumn again. 6880-4
There being no new oceans to explore. 6880-4
There is a farmer. 6880-4
A thrush high as a star. 6880-4

The **bower** of bliss, fr. The fairie queene. Edmund Spenser. 6150-8, 6102-8, 6302-0, 6385-3, 6315-2, 6436-1, 6600
The **bower** of peace. Robert Southey. 6946-0

Bower, A.V.
Whims. 6918-5

Bower, Amy
Wedding feast. 6750-6

Bower, John Graham. See "Klaxon"

The **bower**, fr. The old Scotch house. William Bell Scott. 6819-7

"The **bowers** whereat, in dreams, I see". To - ("The bowers"). Edgar Allan Poe. 6126-5, 6288-1, 6545-7

Bowers, Edgar
'Dear mother, I've come home to die'. 6074-9
Epigram on the passing of Christmas. 6515-5
For W.A. Mozart. 6515-5
From J. Haydn to Constanze Mozart (1791). 6515-5
The mountain cemetery. 6515-5
The stoic: for Laura von Courten. 6515-5
Two poems on the Catholic Bavarians. 6515-5
Venus. 6515-5
The virgin Mary. 6515-5
The wise men. 6515-5

The **Bowery**. Charles Sumner Hoyt. 6736-0
Bowes, Margaret Illington
   The trail. 6654-2
Bowes-Lyon, Lilian
   The passive hands. 6052-8
   A shepherd's coat. 6246-6
Bowie, Walter Russell
   The continuing Christ. 6144-3,6337-3
   A declaration of belief. 6532-5
   The empty soul. 6337-3
   God of the nations. 6337-3
   The holy city. 6337-3
   O love that triumphs over loss. 6337-3
Bowing her head. Unknown. 6074-9
Bowker, R.R.
   Toll, then, no more. 6183-4,6302-0
Bowl aboot. Alexander ("Surfaceman") Anderson. 6819-7
"The **bowl** has very graceful lines". Blue bowl. Emmet Pendleton. 6750-6
"A **bowl** of daffodils". The casualty clearing station. Gilbert Waterhouse. 7026-4,6650-X
The **bowl** of liberty. Felicia Dorothea Hemans. 6973-8
The **bowl** of water. Laurence Binyon. 6266-0
The **bowl**. Walter Clarke Rodman. 6936-3
Bowled. Unknown. 6724-7
Bowles, Caroline Anne
   The pauper's deathbed. 6889-8
Bowles, Fred G.
   A song of the road. 6337-3,6374-8
Bowles, O.J.
   Clouds. 6036-6
   Walls. 6037-4
Bowles, William Lisle
   At Tynemouth priory. 6196-6
   Bamborough castle. 6543-0
   The bells of Ostend. 6964-9
   The bells, Ostend. 6196-6
   Bereavement. 6086-2
   The bird in a cage. 6638-0
   The butterfly and the bee. 6479-5
   The cliff. 6543-0
   Come to these scenes of peace. 6271-7,6302-0,6385-3
   Discovery of Madeira. 6980-0
   Dover cliffs. 6543-0
   Dreams of youth. 6980-0
   Evening. 6543-0
   The greenwood. 6085-4,6271-7,6302-0,6385-3,6428-8
   Influence of time on grief. 6086-2
   Lucerne. 6749-2
   Matilda. 6980-0
   November, 1793. 6086-2
   "O time! who know'st a lenient hand to lay." 6317-9
   On a distant view of England. 6219-9
   On the funeral of Charles I. 6271-7,6219-9
   On the Rhine. 6302-0;6385-3,6543-0
   Ostend. 7015-9
   Remembrance. 6980-0
   Retrospection. 6980-0
   The Rhine. 6219-9
   Sonnet ("Evening, as slow"). 6152-4
   Sonnet ("Languid, and sad"). 6152-4
   Sonnet ("O time"). 6152-4
   Sonnet (July 18th 1787). 6208-3
   Sonnet at Ostend, June 22, 1787. 6932-0
   Sonnet: at Dover cliffs, July 20, 1787. 6152-4
   Sonnet: Netley abbey. 6152-4
   Sonnet: on a distant view of England. 6219-9,6152-4
   Swallow and redbreast. 6131-1
   Thermopylae. 6396-9
   Time and grief. 6102-8,6541-1,6250-4
   "'Tis the first primrose...", sels. 6601-1
   To him is reared no marble tomb. 6086-2
   To time. 6543-0
   Written at Ostend. 6086-2
Bowles, William Lisle (tr.)
   Thermoplyae. Simonides, 7039-6
The **bowline**.. Sir Alan Patrick Herbert. 6722-0
Bowling green. Arthur Guiterman. 6773-5
Bowman, Archibald Allan
   Rastatt, fr. Sonnets from a prison camp. 6785-9
   Sonnets from a prison camp, sels. 6785-9
   Thoughts of home, fr. Sonnets from a prison camp. 6785-9
Bowman, C.E.
   The sphere of woman. 6260-1
Bowman, John Elliott
   Ahab the builder. 6848-0
Bowman, Louise Morey
   Bell carol. 6797-2
   Bird carol. 6797-2
   The clover field. 6797-2
   The lost shepherd. 6843-X
   Mermaid. 6021-8
"**Bowmen**, shout for Gamelbar!". The war-song of Gamelbar. Bliss Carman. 7006-X,6873-1
Bowra, Cecil Maurice (tr.)
   An absent friend. Sappho, 6435-3
   Achilles and Lycaon, fr. The Iliad. Homer, 6435-3
   "Ah, Leipsydrion, thou hast betrayed...". Unknown, 6435-3
   "All that is finished, finished, finished" Alexander Blok, 6103-6
   Angel. Alexander Pushkin, 6103-6
   Apollo the betrayer, fr. Ion. Euripides, 6435-3
   Artist. Alexander Blok, 6103-6
   Autumn love. Alexander Blok, 6103-6
   "Away from home I am nothing...". Sophocles, 6435-3
   Be still, my soul. Archilochus, 6435-3
   Beauty's nomads. Vyacheslav Ivanov, 6103-6
   "Believe me not, friend, when in grief's unreason" Alexey Tolstoy, 6103-6
   Benediction. Valery Bryusov, 6103-6
   Bereavement, fr. Alcestis. Euripides, 6435-3
   The bricklayer. Vasili Kazin, 6103-6
   The captains. Nikolai Gumilev, 6103-6
   Castor and Polydeuces. Alcaeus, 6435-3
   Chalcomede prays to be saved from love. Nonnus, 6435-3
   Chance. Unknown (Greek), 6435-3
   "Chance, in whom men start and end". Unknown, 6435-3
   Chivalry, fr. Supplices. Euripides, 6435-3
   The climb to virtue. Simonides, 6435-3
   The cloud. Alexander Pushkin, 6103-6
   The coming huns. Valery Bryusov, 6103-6
   The common lot. Menander, 6435-3
   Complaint. Vyacheslav Ivanov, 6103-6
   Conscience doth make cowards of us all. Menander, 6435-3
   The convicts. Alexey Tolstoy, 6103-6
   Cossack cradle=song. Mikhail Lermontov, 6103-6
   A Cretan merchant. Simonides, 6435-3
   The cup of life. Mikhail Lermontov, 6103-6
   The daughters of Asopus. Corinna [pseud]., 6435-3
   The daughters of Atlas. Aeschylus, 6435-3
   Dawn, fr. Ion. Euripides, 6435-3
   "Day's rain is done. The rainy mist of night" Alexander Pushkin, 6103-6
   "Dead roses and dying" Alexander Blok, 6103-6
   "Dear son of Aegeus, to the gods alone". Sophocles, 6435-3
   Death. Unknown (Greek), 6435-3
   Death. Evgeni Baratynsky, 6103-6
   Delos. Pindar, 6435-3
   Demon. Alexander Blok, 6103-6
   Devils. Alexander Pushkin, 6103-6
   A distaff. Erinna, 6435-3
   "Do not rustle, rye" Alexey Koltsov, 6103-6
   "Do you remember how together" Mikhail Lermontov, 6103-6
   The doom of Hippolytus. Euripides, 6435-3
   "Drink! Why wait for lamps? The day". Alcaeus, 6435-3
   Earth and sky, fr. Chrysippus. Euripides, 6435-3
   An eclipse. Pindar, 6435-3
   An epilogue to Polycrates. Ibycus, 6435-3
   Euripides. Alexander Aetolus, 6435-3
   Everything decays, fr. Oedipus coloneus. Sophocles, 6435-3
   The family dinner-party. Menander, 6435-3
   Fecundi calices. Bacchylides, 6435-3
   Flowers for the graces. Sappho, 6435-3
   Flowery garments. Cypria, 6435-3

"For the last time I risk caresses" Alexander Pushkin, 6103-6
Foreboding. Alexander Pushkin, 6103-6
The garland, fr. Hippolytus. Euripides, 6435-3
"Gladly they saw me sleeping on the shore". Sophocles, 6435-3
The god of war. Sophocles, 6435-3
God punishes. Archilochus, 6435-3
"God, who created me from sodden clay" Fedor Sologub, 6103-6
The gods' children. Aeschylus, 6435-3
Gratitude. Mikhail Lermontov, 6103-6
"Hail to thee, boy, mighty one". Unknown, 6435-3
Hecate, fr. Rhizotomi. Sophocles, 6435-3
Helicon and Cithaeron. Corinna [pseud]., 6435-3
Heracles and Meleager. Bacchylides, 6435-3
The herd of horses. Sergei Esenin, 6103-6
Hope. Mikhail Lermontov, 6103-6
"How he departed hence, you who stood by". Sophocles, 6435-3
Hymn of the Curetes. Unknown (Greek), 6435-3
"I have a child; so fair". Sappho, 6435-3
"I have forebodings of Thee. Time is going" Alexander Blok, 6103-6
"I loved you once, in in my soul maybe" Alexander Pushkin, 6103-6
"I loved you, Atthis, once, long, long ago...". Sappho, 6435-3
Immortalia ne speres. Alcaeus, 6435-3
"In the breeze, on a bough that is asking" Boris Pasternak, 6103-6
In the leaves the raindrops gently. Alexey Tolstoy, 6103-6
Inexorable death. Aeschylus, 6435-3
"It chanced when the dance was pealing" Alexey Tolstoy, 6103-6
"It is not true, this tale". Unknown, 6435-3
"It was an early day of spring" Alexey Tolstoy, 6103-6
"It was not Zeus, I think, made this decree". Sophocles, 6435-3
The jar. Fedor Sologub, 6103-6
Justice protects the dead. Aeschylus, 6435-3
"Land of mine, where I was bred" Alexey Tolstoy, 6103-6
Leipsydrion. Unknown (Greek), 6435-3
Loneliness. Nikolai Gumilev, 6103-6
"Lord of Athens' holy ground", fr. Theseus. Bacchylides, 6435-3
Love. Sappho, 6435-3
Love. Ibycus, 6435-3
Love is idle, fr. Danae. Euripides, 6435-3
"Maidenhood, O Maidenhood". Sappho, 6435-3
Marching song. Tyrtaeus, 6435-3
Marriage - two views. Menander, 6435-3
The marriage of heaven and earth. Aeschylus, 6435-3
May 26, 1828. Alexander Pushkin, 6103-6
Message to Siberia. Alexander Pushkin, 6103-6
Monument. Alexander Pushkin, 6103-6
My own, my native land. Menander, 6435-3
A national anthem. Lamprocles, 6435-3
Never. Afanasi Fet, 6103-6
"No, not for you, for you, does my love flame". Mikhail Lermontov, 6103-6
"Now bind the woven necklaces". Alcaeus, 6435-3
"O flame and horror, masterpiece of evil". Sophocles, 6435-3
"Oh gloomy and dreary! and no one to stretch out..." Mikhail Lermontov, 6103-6
Old age, fr. Erechtheus. Euripides, 6435-3
Old man's song. Alexey Koltsov, 6103-6
The old men, fr. Aeolus. Euripides, 6435-3
On. Alexander Pushkin, 6103-6
"On the horizon rises holy night". Feodor Ivanovich Tyutchev, 6103-6
On the mountains. Alcman, 6435-3
Orpheus and Eurydice. Valery Bryusov, 6103-6
Our march. Vladimir Mayakovsky, 6103-6
Palinode on Helen. Stesichorus, 6435-3
Parting. Sappho, 6435-3
The passing of Oedipus, fr. Oedipus coloneus. Sophocles, 6435-3

Pelops. Pindar, 6435-3
Philoctetes calls for death. Aeschylus, 6435-3
Philoctetes deserted. Sophocles, 6435-3
Pindarum quisquis... Corinna [pseud]., 6435-3
The poet. Alexander Pushkin, 6103-6
The poet. Alexander Pushkin, 6103-6
The power of custom. Pindar, 6435-3
Prayer ("When life's"). Mikhail Lermontov, 6103-6
The prisoner. Afanasi Fet, 6103-6
Pure love, fr. Theseus. Euripides, 6435-3
The Red Sea. Aeschylus, 6435-3
The reed. Konstantin Balmont, 6103-6
The road to Emmanus. Vyacheslav Ivanov, 6103-6
The road to Emmanus. Ida Norton Munson, 6144-3
Rough sea. Archilochus, 6435-3
"Russia, my life! are we tied to one fate for us?" Alexander Blok, 6103-6
A sail. Mikhail Lermontov, 6103-6
Shadows on the wall. Alexander Blok, 6103-6
Simple tastes. Archilochus, 6435-3
Six letters, fr. Theseus. Euripides, 6435-3
A small city on a rock. Phocylides, 6435-3
So did the son of Priam...", fr. The Iliad. Homer, 6435-3
"So vainly through the night prayed Morreus...". Nonnus, 6435-3
"Soak your lungs with wine, for now". Alcaeus, 6435-3
Song ("Sing not"). Alexey Koltsov, 6103-6
Sparta. Terpander, 6435-3
Stanzas. Alexander Pushkin, 6103-6
The steps of the commander. Alexander Blok, 6103-6
Stillness and sound. Simonides, 6435-3
The stolen bow, fr. Philoctetes. Sophocles, 6435-3
The stonecutter. Valery Bryusov, 6103-6
Storm at sea. Alcaeus, 6435-3
"Take not away my wits, O God" Alexander Pushkin, 6103-6
Temptation. Vladislav Khodasevich, 6103-6
Thasos. Archilochus, 6435-3
Themostocles. Timocreon, 6435-3
"Then shall he lie in the earth". Unknown, 6435-3
Theoxenus. Pindar, 6435-3
Theseus, sels. Bacchylides, 6435-3
Thetis ("He praised the greatness of the child..."). Aeschylus, 6435-3
"Those who were born in years of quiet" Alexander Blok, 6103-6
Thou shall not die, fr. Hercules furens. Euripides, 6435-3
Threats. Menander, 6435-3
Timocreon. Simonides, 6435-3
"'Tis time, my friend, 'tis time! For rest the heart." Alexander Pushkin, 6103-6
To A.P. Kern. Alexander Pushkin, 6103-6
To Apollo and the muses. Terpander, 6435-3
To Atthis. Sappho, 6435-3
To Zeus. Terpander, 6435-3
Tristia. Osip Mandelstam, 6103-6
Two voices. Valery Bryusov, 6103-6
The undying law, fr. Antigone. Sophocles, 6435-3
Voice from the chorus. Alexander Blok, 6103-6
Vulture. Alexander Blok, 6103-6
Wedding song. Sappho, 6435-3
"A well, and the cherry-trees blowing." Alexey Tolstoy, 6103-6
"What an evening! Streamlets run" Afanasi Fet, 6103-6
What is life?, fr. Polyidus. Euripides, 6435-3
What is man? Palladas, 6435-3
"Where, my childhood's home, art thou". Sergei Esenin, 6103-6
"Wild wind batters" Alexander Blok, 6103-6
Winter evening. Alexander Pushkin, 6103-6
Winter morning. Alexander Pushkin, 6103-6
Womankind, fr. Tereus. Sophocles, 6435-3
The wounded eagle. Aeschylus, 6435-3
"Yes, I have loved. And the mad glowing" Alexander Blok, 6103-6
"You say I am frozen. and dry, and apart" Alexander Blok, 6103-6
"You say that I'm aslep, and you" Alexander Blok, 6103-

6
"Zeus is the air, Zeus earth, and Zeus the sky".
    Aeschylus, 6435-3
"Zeus rains; a storm comes in its might". Alcaeus, 6435-3

Bowring and Gerbrand Brederode, Sir John (tr.)
Psalm 133. Bible, 6848-0

Bowring, Edgar Alfred (tr.)
An old song. Heinrich Heine, 6879-0
Song ("In the Rhine"). Heinrich Heine, 6484-1
Submission. Heinrich Heine, 6097-8

Bowring, Sir John
"From the recesses of a lowly spirit." 6302-0,6385-3, 6600-3,6656-9
God. 6240-7
God is love. 6014-5,6219-9.6337-3
Hymn ("Father, thy paternal care"). 6600-3
In the cross of Christ I glory. 6251-X,6337-3,6730-1, 6214-8
"Look above thee-never eye". 6238-5
The Lord the creator. 7020-5
Not ripe for political power. 6385-3
Our duty here. 6049-8
The soul eternal. 6337-3
Towering o'er the wrecks of time. 6065-X
The watchman's report. 6271-7
Watchman, tell of the night. 6219-9
What of the night? 6732-8,6656-9

Bowring, Sir John (tr.)
Adam's hymn in paradise. Joost van den Vondel, 6730-1
God. Gabriel Romanovitch Derzhavin, 6385-3,6964-9,6392-6,6404-3
The mother nightingale. Estevan Manuel de Villegas, 6302-06385-3
The nightingale. Maria Tesselchade Visscher, 6302-0, 6385-3
Ode to the deity. Gabriel Romanovitch Derzhavin, 6568-6
The rich and the poor man. Kremnitzer, 6996-7
The rich man and the poor. Khemnitzer, 6606-2

The box upon her head. Unknown. 6057-9

Box, Earl Gene
Aunt Beulah's wisdom. 6870-7
Butch is back. 6870-7
Midwife. 6870-7
Old man con. 6870-7
Trash. 6870-7

The box. Dawad Philip. 6899-5
A boxer called Panther. Reuel Denney. 6527-9
Boxer shorts named champion. Melvin Douglass Brown. 6870-7
The boxer turned bartender. Gary Allan Kizer. 6870-7
A boxer. Simonides. 6435-3
Boxiana. Unknown. 6787-5
Boxing, fr. Verses on games. Rudyard Kipling. 6427-2
Boy. Dong-ju Yun. 6775-1
"A boy I loved sweet Sally Pine". Cupid peeped in through the blinds. Richard Casper Dillmore. 6927-4
Boy and girl. Mary Emily Bradley. 6682-8
Boy and girl of Plymouth. Helen L. Smith. 6964-9
A boy and his dad. Edgar A. Guest. 7033-7
A boy and his dog. Edgar A. Guest. 6510-4
The boy and his mother. Hermann Hagedorn. 6944-4
The boy and his playthings. Anna Maria Lenngren. 6045-5
A boy and his pup. Arthur Guiterman. 6510-4
A boy and his stomach. Edgar A. Guest. 6401-9,6135-4
A boy and his stomach. Unknown. 6963-0
Boy and lark. Lydia Huntley Sigourney. 6131-1
The boy and the angel. Robert Browning. 6828-6
The boy and the angel. Robert Browning. 6198-2,6473-6,6610-0,6655-0,6419-1,6424
The boy and the blue-bird. Celestin Pierre Cambiaire. 6826-X
The boy and the boot. Unknown. 6629-1
The boy and the flag. Edgar A. Guest. 6135-4
The boy and the flute. Bjornstjerne Bjornson. 7039-6
The boy and the flute. Bjornstjerne Bjornson. 6732-8
The boy and the frog. Unknown. 6743-3
The boy and the mantle. Unknown. 6185-0
The boy and the ring. Unknown. 6165-6
The boy and the robin. F.C. Woodworth. 6131-1
The boy and the sheep. Ann Taylor. 6519-8

The boy and the skylark. Charles and Mary Lamb. 6459-0
The boy and the wolf. John Hookham Frere. 6401-9,6135-4
The boy at the nore. Thomas Hood. 6760-3,6974-6
The boy awakens. Albert Paris Gutersloh. 6769-7
Boy baby's protest. John Kendrick Bangs. 6715-8
Boy Brittan. Forceythe Willson. 6113-3,6554-6,6678-X,6016-2
The boy decides. Rickman Mark. 6105-2
Boy dressing. Mark Van Doren. 6984-3
The boy engineer. George Lansing Taylor. 6701-8
The boy fishing. E.J. Scovell. 6210-5,6257-1
The boy from Ballytearim. Moira (Nesta Higginson Skrine) O'Neill. 6393-4,6161-3
A boy hero. Unknown. 6918-5
A boy hero. Unknown. 6744-1
A boy I know. Unknown. 6889-8
The boy I love. Unknown. 6629-1
Boy in a coal car. Glenn Ward Dresbach. 6761-1
The boy in armor. Hermann Hagedorn. 6490-6,6542-2
A boy in church. Robert Graves. 6634-8
"Boy in khaki, boy in blue". Columbia's prayer. Thomas P. Bashaw. 6846-4
The boy in the house. Robert P. Tristram Coffin. 7040-X
Boy in the wind. George Dillon. 6619-4,6779-4
Boy killed by a falling tree in Hartford. Unknown. 6061-7
The boy lives on our farm. James Whitcomb Riley. 6018-8
the boy mind. Edgar A. Guest. 6862-6
The boy next door. Samuel Ellsworth Kiser. 6846-4
Boy o' mine. Edgar A. Guest. 7033-7
The boy of Egremond. William Wordsworth. 6438-8
A boy of old Manhattan - Theodore Roosevelt. Morris Abel Beer. 6503-1
"A boy of old Manhattan" Morris Abel Beer. 6995-9
The boy of the Alps. Thomas Moore. 6749-2
A boy of the ghetto. Margaret Widdemer. 6162-1
The boy of the house. Jean Blewett. 7022-1
A boy of twenty. Horace Gregory. 6393-4
"The boy on the bicycle blends with the night". Mystic on wheels. Margery Swett Mansfield. 6808-1
The boy on the prairie. Edwin Ford Piper. 6031-5
"A boy out hunting". Pelion. Elizabeth Belloc. 6782-4
The boy patriot. James Whitcomb Riley. 6091-9
The boy poet. William Wordsworth. 6438-8
"The boy poses as a heron-all knees". Manalmedu. Maurya Simon. 6900-2
Boy reading. John Holmes. 6761-1
Boy remembers in the field. Raymond Knister. 6021-8
Boy riding forward backward. Robert Francis. 6388-8
The boy she used to know. (Alfred) Damon Runyon. 6836-7
"A boy should have an open fireplace". A boy's need. Herbert Clark Johnson. 6761-1
Boy sleeping. Robert Francis. 6761-1
Boy so different from daddy! John Kendrick Bangs. 6715-8
"The boy still small enough to be kissed". Raccoon hunt. Robert P. Tristram Coffin. 6761-1
"The boy that built our schoolhouse fires". Building the schoolhouse fires in Vermont. Daniel L. Cady. 6989-4
The boy to the school-master. Edward J. Wheeler. 6530-9, 6552-X,6632-1
The boy to the schoolmaster. Unknown. 6415-9
"A boy upon a Shetland pony". Adventure on the wings of morning. Rachel Albright. 6750-6
Boy waking. Roberta Holloway. 6808-1
A boy was born at Bethlehem. Edward Hilton Young. 6337-3
"A boy went looking for Puck one day". The boy who found Puck. Orford Young. 6804-9
The boy who couldn't say 'no!'. Unknown. 6630-5
The boy who didn't pass. Unknown. 6964-9
The boy who found Puck. Orford Young. 6804-9
The boy who never told a lie. Unknown. 6479-5,6135-4
The boy who went from home. Emma M. Johnston. 6406-X
Boy with a silver plow. Dennis Murphy. 6076-5
Boy with his hair cut short. Muriel Rukeyser. 6375-6
Boy with pony. Samuel Ellsworth Kiser. 6715-8
The boy with the hoe. T.B. Weaver. 6964-9
The boy with the little bare toes. William Harvey. 6368-3
"Boy! I detest all Persian fopperies". Ode ("Boy! I detest..."). Horace. 6814-6
A boy's aspirations. Menella Bute Smedley. 6242-3
Boy's bear story. James Whitcomb Riley. 6166-4

BOY'S

Boy's complaint about butter. Caroline Gilman. 6131-1
A boy's complaint. Unknown. 6248-2
A boy's complaint. Annie H. Streeter. 6530-9
The boy's complaint. Unknown. 6743-3
A boy's conclusion. Unknown. 6166-4
Boy's day. Ruth Evelyn Henderson. 6861-8
Boy's great schemes. Tudor Jenks. 6715-8
A boy's hands. Albert Edmund Trombly. 6036-6
"A boy's heart is a light heart". Hero wanted. Berton Braley. 6853-7
Boy's idea of Christmas. Lulu M. Rorke. 6702-6
A boy's king. Samuel Ellsworth Kiser. 6690-9
The boy's last request. Unknown. 6911-8
Boy's letter to Santa Claus. Unknown. 6715-8
A boy's likes and dislikes. Elsie Day Cruthirds. 6799-9
A boy's mercy. Bessie G. Hart. 6670-4
Boy's mission. Ella Wheeler Wilcox. 6715-8
A boy's mother. James Whitcomb Riley. 6097-8,6452-3,6605-4,6632-1
A boy's need. Herbert Clark Johnson. 6761-1
A boy's opinion. Emma Celia & Lizzie J. Rook. 6137-0
A boy's opinion. Unknown. 6744-1,6167-2
Boy's play and girl's play. Mrs. Hawtrey. 6127-3,6502-3
A boy's plea. Unknown. 6530-9
A boy's pocket. Unknown. 6314-4
A boy's prayer. A.B. Ponsonby. 6337-3
A boy's prayer. Henry Charles Beeching. 6239-3,6243-3,6465-5
Boy's resolution("This school year I mean to do better") Unknown. 6715-8
Boy's rights. Carrie May. 6273-3
A boy's song, sels. James Hogg. 6934-7
A boy's song. James Hogg. 6250-4,6114-1,6131-1,6301-2,6639-9,6454,6086-2,6638-0,6668-2,6543-0,6105-2,6373-X,6519-8,6466-3,6479-5,6496,6242-3,6249-0,6401-9,6459-0,6552-X,6135,6623-2,6634-8,6075-7,6132-X,6134-6,6180
A boy's tent. Malville Haller. 6038-2
A boy's Thanksgiving. Lydia Maria Child. 6701-8
Boy's wanted. Unknown. 6743-3
Boy's Washington composition. Emma C. Dowd. 6712-3
A boy's whistle. Judd Mortimer Lewis. 6274-1
"Boy, I detest the Persian pomp". The preference declared. Horace. 6949-5
"Boy, I hate their empty shows". Ode ("Boy, I hate..."). Horace. 6814-6
A boy, a lake, a sun. Robert P. Tristram Coffin. 6984-3
Boy, bare your head. Nancy Byrd Turner. 6466-3,6512-0
A boy, fr. The prelude. William Wordsworth. 7020-5
A boy. Nathaniel Parker Willis. 6911-8
The boy. Eugene Field. 6949-5,6902-9
The boy. Hertha Kraftner. 6769-7
The boy. Nathaniel Parker Willis. 6304-7
Boyajian, Zabelle C.
Armenia's love to Shakespeare. 6050-1
Boyang the wandering recluse. Al Robles. 6790-5
Boyce, Florence J.
The party at Crogan's. 6887-1
Boyce, S. Minerva
Out of the silence. 7030-2
Boyd, David
The prospect for peace. 6789-1
Boyd, Le Roy J.N.
On the threshold. 6818-9
Boyd, Louise E.V.
Baby's letter. 6965-7
Picture of the last supper. 6927-4
Wopsenonic. 6927-4
Boyd, Marion M.
White dusk. 6253-9
Boyd, Mark Alexander
Cupid and Venus. 6845-6
Sonnet ("Fra bank"). 6180-X,6317-9,6380-2
Boyd, Mary Rosalie
The veld, sels. 6800-6
Boyd, Mary S.
Miss Kitty Manx to Sir Thomas Angora. 6692-2
Boyd, Megan E.
Querencia. 6900-2
Boyd, Nancy
The Armistice Day parade. 6817-0
I like Americans. 6736-0
Boyd, Samuel E.
And so tomorrow. 6178-8
Dance finale. 6178-8
Rebel. 6178-8
Tomorrow's winds. 6178-8
Boyd, Thomas
Ballyvourney. 6244-X
The heath. 6930-4
The king's son. 6090-0,6244-X
Love on the mountain. 6244-X
To the Leanan Sidhe. 6090-0,6244-X
Boyden, Polly Chase
Mud. 6891-X
Boyer and Mary Crow, Patsy (tr.)
Let's go again. Circe Maia, 7036-1
Possibilities. Circe Maia, 7036-1
Wet grapes... Circe Maia, 7036-1
Where there used to be badlands. Circe Maia, 7036-1
"A wind will come from the south" Circe Maia, 7036-1
Boyer, Claire Stewart
The bargain. 6818-9
Boyer, Isabel R.
Shadows. 6818-9
Boyesen, Hjalmar Hjorth
Brier-rose. 6413-2,6550-3,6572-4
Brier-rose, sels. 6614-3
Calpurnia. 6673-9
Earl Sigurd's Christmas Eve. 6578-3
Evolution. 7041-8
Hilda's little hood. 6577-5
Inge, the boy king, sels. 7002-7
Jarl Sigurd's Christmas Eve. 6676-3
Little Sigrid. 6676-3
The lost hellas. 7041-8
Thora. 6574-0
Boyhood. Washington Allston. 6219-9,6271-7
Boyhood ambitions. Edgar A. Guest. 6748-4
Boyhood and girlhood. Hartley Coleridge. 6233-4
Boyhood friends. Edgar Lee Masters. 6031-5
Boyhood of Columbus. James Russell Lowell. 6624-0
Boyhood, fr. The prelude. William Wordsworth. 6726-3
Boylan, Grace Duffie
By and by. 6579-1
The old house. 6274-1
Who goes there? 6995-9
Boylan, M. Nora
The brownie men. 6147-8
Christmas morn. 6147-8
Christmas time. 6147-8
The mousie. 6147-8
Old Santa Claus. 6272-5,6147-8
Saint Nick. 6147-8
Santa's helpers. 6147-8
Time for Santa Claus. 6147-8
Boyle, Kay
Hunt. 6781-6
Monody to the sound of zithers. 6037-4
Boyle, Magdelen Eden
Paradox. 6750-6
Ultimation. 6799-9
Boyle, Mary E.
Invocation ("Oh! glen of mine"). 6269-5
Mairi dancing. 6269-5
Boyle, Roger. See Orrery, Earl of
Boyle, Sarah Roberts
The voice of the grass. 6006-4,6356-X,6466-3,6519-8,6597-X
Boyle, Virginia Frazer
Abraham Lincoln. 6102-8,6076-5,6524-4
Her wedding eve. 6686-0
I kilt er cat. 6120-6
I know that my redeemer liveth. 6065-X
Tennessee. 6946-0
Boyles, Anna Grace
Youth's ambition. 6750-6
The Boyne Water. Unknown. 6174-5,6732-8
Boynton, H.W.
The golfer's Rubaiyat. 6440-X

Boynton, M.P.
    Preparedness. 6542-2
Boys and banties. J.K. Nutting. 6965-7
Boys and girls. Emma Celia & Lizzie J. Rook. 6137-0
Boys and girls. Florence Wilkinson. 6274-1
Boys and men. Helen Bosanquet. 7042-6
Boys and tadpoles. Louis Untermeyer. 6345-4
The boys and the apple tree. Ann and Jane Taylor. 6105-2
The boys I used to know, sels. Mary B. Plummer. 6149-4
Boys in the grass. Florence Hynes Willette. 6761-1
Boys make men. Unknown. 6530-9
"Boys need the sabbath for solemn meditation". Sunday afternoon. Nellie G. Bourdeux. 6761-1
The boys of Kilkenny. Unknown. 6858-8
"Boys of mine, I send you forth". Highest education. Grace D. Ford. 6764-6
The boys of the island. Unknown. 6281-4
The boys of Wexford. Robert Dwyer Joyce. 6858-8
The boys that run the furrow. Frank Lebby Stanton. 6486-8
"Boys twain/Banties twain". Boys and banties. J.K. Nutting. 6965-7
Boys wanted. Unknown. 6629-1,6744-1,6167-2
The boys we need. Unknown. 6529-5
The boys we want. A. Sargent. 6617-8
The boys who never grew up. Charles Law Watkins. 7012-4
The boys' candidate. James Whitcomb Riley. 6990-8
Boys' play and girls' play. Mrs. Hawtrey. 6131-1
Boys' rights. Unknown. 6215-6,6312-8
"Boys, take another! To-night we'll be gay". 'Swore off'. John N. Fort. 6923-1
"Boys, to the hunting field! Though't is...". 'Nota bene' Unknown. 7010-8
The boys. Ethel Lynn Beers. 6408-6
The boys. Oliver Wendell Holmes. 6404-3,6610-0,6621-6,6565-1,6396-9,6304 ,6486-8,6521-X,6006-4,6102-8,6142-7, 6260 ,6008-0,6288-1,6076-5,6126-5,6121-4,6219 ,6265-2
The boys. Unknown. 6742-5
Brabbham, Mouzon W.
    A father's prayer. 6525-2
"Brace thee, my friend, when times are hard". To Dellius. Horace. 6879-0
Brace up. Unknown. 6744-1
Brace, Arty
    Nancy. 6451-5
Brace, Letitia A.
    A point of view. 6799-9
The bracelet: to Julia. Robert Herrick. 6488-4,6194-X,6092-7,6652-6
Brachlow, Marjorie W.
    In memory. 6342-X
Bracken, John
    Discovery. 6761-1
Bracken, Thomas
    Not understood. 6927-4,6085-4
    Pax vobiscum. 6784-0
Brackenridge, Hugh H
    The battle of Bunkers-Hill, sels. 6008-0
Bracker, Jon
    Last night. 7003-5
Bracker, Milton
    P is for paleontology. 6722-0
Bradbury, Bianca
    Farmer's wife. 6979-7
    Nor'easter. 6833-2
Bradbury, Mrs. L.A.
    A Christmas pastime; or, the crying family. 6268-7
    Long ago. 6268-7
Bradbury, William B.
    Marching along. 6074-9,6471-X,6016-2
Bradby, Godfrey Fox
    'Could ye not watch one hour?' 6337-3
    The flowing tide. 6639-9
    In hoc signo. 6337-3
    Lyonesse. 6541-4
    Marsh marigolds. 6541-4
    Versailles. 6631-3
Braddan vicarage. Thomas Edward Brown. 6809-X
Braddan village. Thomas Edward Brown. 6084-6
Braddock's fate and an encitement to revenge, sels.
    Stephen Tilden. 6753-0
Braddock's fate, with an incitement to revenge. Stephen Tilden. 6946-0
Braddock, Emily A.
    The burghers of Calais. 6621-6
    How the laurel went to church. 6965-7
    Pussy willow and the south wind. 6965-7
    Regulus. 6677-1
Braddock, Joseph
    Black cat in prunus-tree. 6511-2
Braddon, Mary E.
    After the battle. 6424-8
Braden, Charles S.
    The cross. 6144-3
Braden, Mrs. Findley
    Thae auld laird's secret. 6687-9
    What the Lord had done for him. 6675-5
Bradford, Ellen Knight
    How the refugees were saved. 6928-2
Bradford, Gamaliel
    The anniversary. 6036-6
    Ardor. 6032-3
    Can't you. 6441-8
    Cherry-buds. 6036-6
    A common case. 6036-6
    The congregation. 6033-1
    Deeds undone. 6072-2
    The divagator. 6032-3
    Dreams. 6039-0
    Exit God. 6032-3,6337-3,6532-5
    The fabric. 6036-6
    Flight of kisses. 6070-6
    God. 6291-1,6303-9,6337-3,6532-5,6730-1
    Heinelet. 6032-3,6291-1
    Hope ("When I was a little boy"). 6607-0
    Hunger. 6762-X
    Illimitable. 6036-6,6619-4
    The joy of living. 6291-1
    The lot. 6039-0
    Love's detective. 6441-8
    Mare amoris. 6037-4
    Napoleon. 7027-2
    Ode to Thomas Jefferson. 6184-2
    Porcelain vase. 6040-4
    The pursuit. 6032-3
    Rain. 6039-0
    The riot. 6762-X
    Robert E. Lee. 6032-3
    Roses. 6037-4
    Rousseau. 6762-X
    Song of the sea rover. 6037-4
    The surprise. 6036-6
    The thing to do. 6036-6
    Things of clay. 6032-3
    Thomas Jefferson. 6184-2
    Three portraits. 6037-4
    The thyroid gland. 6039-0
    The topmost bough. 6033-1
    The villa of Hadrian. 6624-0
Bradford, May N.
    U.S. spells "US". 6690-9
Bradford, Sarah H.
    Resurrection. 6177-X
Bradford, William
    New England's growth, fr. New England. 6946-0
    The Plymouth harvest. 6466-3
Bradley, A.F. Kent
    hands drop off. 6925-8
Bradley, Berton
    Gentlemen adventures. 7007-8
Bradley, Dwight
    The disciple. 6144-3
Bradley, Edward. See "Bede, Cuthbert"
Bradley, Jonathan Dorr
    To my dog, Jowler. 7030-2
Bradley, Kate A.
    Cupid's exchange. 6719-0
    How the organ was paid for. 6672-0
    The king's joy-bells. 6674-4
Bradley, Katherine. See Field, Michael

Bradley, Mary Emily
   Boy and girl. 6682-8
   A chrysalis. 6479-5,6597-X
   Little Christel. 6744-1
   "Of all the bonny buds that blow", sels. 6601-1
   The reason why. 6682-8
Bradley, Mary Linda
   The last heifer. 6894-4
Bradley, Sam
   Declaring the male. 6803-0
Bradley, Samuel M.
   Roc's brood. 6218-0
   This here is hell. 6218-0
Bradley, William Aspenwall
   Autumn. 6031-5
   'A beauty of St. Giles.' 6118-4
   Fult Faithorne. 6102-8,6076-5
   Island tea. 6441-8
   Love and the stars. 6320-9
   Men of Harlan. 6476-0,6556-2
   Sancta Ursula. 6031-5
   Summer. 6031-5
   Will Warner. 6102-8,6076-5
Bradley, William B.
   Chide mildly the erring. 6304-7
Bradley, William Czar
   Verses in a watch. 7030-2
Bradnack, Fowler
   The mysterious guest. 6294-6
Bradner, Clara H.
   Air castles. 6920-7
Bradshaw, Ann
   One black crow. 6979-7
Bradshaw, Catherine
   Night. 6799-9
Bradshaw, Laura E.
   Call of the open. 6799-9
Bradstreet, Anne
   'As weary pilgrim'. 6176-1,6288-1
   The author to her book. 6333-0,6288-1
   Before the birth of one of her children. 6333-0
   Contemplations. 6176-1,6330-0,6121-4,6008-0,6288-1
   Contemplations, sels. 6077-3,6337-3
   The flesh and the spirit. 6333-0,6288-1
   The four ages of man. 6673-9
   The four monarchyes, sels. 6008-0
   The four seasons of the year, sels. 6008-0
   In memory of my dear grandchild Ann Bradstreet... 6077-3
   A letter to her husband, absent upon public employment. 6333-0,6088-0,6288-1
   Letters to her husband. 6753-0
   Longing for heaven. 6008-0
   Of the four ages of man, sels. 6008-0
   The prologue. 6077-3,6288-1,6008-0
   The prologue. 6753-0
   Queen Elizabeth. 6753-0
   Spring, fr. The four seasons of the year. 6008-0
   To her most honoured father, Thomas Dudley Esq. 6753-0
   To my dear and loving husband. 6077-3,6333-0,6121-4
   Verses upon the burning of our house. 6333-0
Bradt, Edith Virginia
   As ye would. 6928-2
   Be glad. 6720-4
Brady, E.J.
   A ballad of the captains. 6044-7
   The great grey water. 6784-0
   Lost and given over. 6784-0
   Southerly. 6384-5
Brady, George M.
   The autumn house. 6930-4
   The generation. 6930-4
The braes o Yarrow. Unknown. 6185-0,6458-2
The braes o' Balquhither. Robert Tannahill. 6180-X,6600-3, 6086-2,6219-9,6543-0
The braes of Gleniffer. Robert Tannahill. 6086-2
The braes of Yarrow. William (of Bangour) Hamilton. 6180-X, 6152-4,6240-7,6271-7,6600-3,6086-2,6219-9,6438
The braes of Yarrow. John Logan. 6180-X,6086-2,6219-9,6438-8,6246-6

Braganca, Nadejda de
   Prayer ("O God"). 6337-3
Braggart!. Denis Wrafter. 6930-4
Brahma. Ralph Waldo Emerson. 6006-4,6077-3,6102-8,6176-1, 6186-9,6246 ,6302-0,6385-3,6399-X,6726-3,6730-1,6732 ,6735-2,6088-0,6250-4,6560-0,6126-5,6396 ,6288-1, 6431-0,6153-2,6467-1,6300-4,6309-8,6252-0,6121-4, 6076
Brahma. Andrew Lang. 6802-2
Brahma's answer. Richard Henry Stoddard. 6385-3
The Brahmin's son. Richard Henry Stoddard. 6673-9
The Brahmns. Herbert Morris. 6388-8
Braid claith. Robert Fergusson. 6180-X,6086-2,6195-0,6152-4,6383-7
Brainard, John Gardiner Calkins
   The captain, sels. 6752-2
   The captain. 6632-1
   Colonization of Africa. 6752-2
   The dead leaves strew the forest-walk. 6752-2
   The deep. 6385-3
   Departure of the pioneer. 6752-2
   Epithalamium. 6271-7,6600-3,6291-9
   The fall of Niagara. 6385-3,6600-3,6632-1
   "I saw two clouds at morning." 6240-7,6302-0,6385-3
   If I could love. 6441-8
   The Indian summer. 6752-2
   Isaiah 035 6848-0
   Isaiah XXXV. 6752-2
   Jerusalem. 6752-2
   Niagara. 6219-9
   On the death of Commodore Oliver H. Perry. 6946-0
   On the death of Mr. Woodward, at Edinburgh. 6752-2
   On the loss of a pious friend. 6752-2
   On the loss of Professor Fisher. 6752-2
   Salmon River. 6752-2
   Sonnet to the sea serpent. 6833-2
   Stanzas ("The dead leaves"). 6077-3
   The sweet brier. 6752-2
   To a friend. 6570-8
   To the dead. 6752-2
Brainard, Mary Gardner
   Faith and sight. 6337-3
   God knoweth. 6600-3
   Not knowing. 6303-9,6632-1,6889-8
Brainerd, Ethel M.
   Fairy antics. 6906-1
   Fate. 6906-1
   Love song. 6906-1
   My ship. 6906-1
   The pessimist and the optimist. 6906-1
   To a bit of a girl. 6906-1
Brainerd, Mary Beale
   Her laddie's picture. 6575-9
Braithwaite, W.C.
   Christ our contemporary. 6337-3
Braithwaite, William Stanley
   Sandy star. 6102-8,6076-5
   A sea-prayer. 6525-2,6431-0
   "Sic vita." 6310-1,6374-8,6161-3
   Twenty stars. 7007-8
   The vision. 6266-0
The brakeman's sweetheart. Robert J. Burdette. 6588-0
Brakle, John Van
   Easter ("Today unnumbered church bells ring") 6144-3
   Easter message. 6144-3
Braley, Benjamin
   The recipe. 6654-2
Braley, Berton
   The advance guard. 6853-7
   Adventurers of science. 6853-7
   Age. 6853-7
   The air mail. 6853-7
   All in the family. 6853-7
   Ambition. 6887-1
   Ample, fr. Matrimonial melodies. 6853-7
   The angry ones. 6853-7
   Any lover to his lass. 6853-7
   Apostacy. 6853-7
   Ashes to ashes, fr. Matrimonial melodies. 6853-7
   Ashtabula. 6853-7

The atavistic maid. 6853-7
The avenger. 6853-7
Babyhood. 6853-7
Ballade of the ideal waiter. 6853-7
The bean. 6853-7
Bill and the supe. 6853-7
Boston. 6853-7
Bottoms up! 6853-7
The bread line. 6954-1
Buccaneers. 6853-7
Business is business. 6853-7
By degrees. 6853-7
By request. 6853-7
A canto of Khans. 6853-7
Carcassone. 6853-7
A career. 6853-7
The champion. 6853-7
Chef Pernollet. 6853-7
Chicago. 6853-7
Childhood. 6853-7
The choice. 6853-7
Cliff Dweller lyrics. 6853-7
The comb band. 6443-4
Company. 6853-7
Consequences. 6853-7
The dead broncho-buster. 6853-7
The dead rover. 6853-7
The desert disillusion. 6853-7
Deserted roads. 7012-4
Dimensions. 6853-7
The direful tale of horror. 6853-7
Do it now. 6853-7
Don't be down-hearted. 6853-7
The drums. 6853-7
The drums. 6732-8
A dull life. 6853-7
The electrician. 7014-0
Empty. 6732-8
The endless battle. 6853-7
Enough. 6995-9
Essential. 6853-7
The exile. 6853-7
A fable for poets. 6853-7
The failures. 6853-7
The farmer's wife. 6853-7
A few left. 6853-7
The fighting word. 6853-7
Five little wandersongs. 6853-7
For service. 6853-7
Frankness between friends. 6085-4
Futility. 6853-7
A gift. 6853-7
Gifts and givers. 6853-7
The glow within. 6761-1
A gothamite in Camelot. 6853-7
The great adventure. 6853-7
Guess who? 6995-9
Hero wanted. 6853-7
Heroes. 6478-7
The hills. 6336-5,6332-2,6336-5,6476-0
Ho for noa noa. 6853-7
Hoboes. 6853-7
The honker. 6853-7
The hopeless passion. 6853-7
Immutable. 6853-7
In the king's english. 6853-7
In the subjunctive. 6853-7
The indian sign. 6853-7
Invocation. 7007-8
It's hard to say. 6853-7
It's only fair. 6853-7
J. K. 6853-7
The jay walker. 6853-7
The jazz baby. 6853-7
Joseph's reform. 6853-7
The jungle wallah. 6853-7
Kisses. 6853-7
A large evening at the club. 6853-7
The life of Riley. 6853-7
Lightfoot Larry. 6853-7

The living epitaph. 6085-4,6303-9
The main drag. 6853-7
Man. 6853-7
Manhood. 6853-7
Matrimonial melodies, sels. 6853-7
Mercenaries. 6853-7
Merchant adventurers. 6853-7
The method of the mad mullah. 6853-7
The milkman. 6853-7
The millennnium. 6853-7
'Mind the paint' 6853-7
The miracle. 6853-7
Moderation. 6853-7
The modern version. 6853-7
Monochrome. 6853-7
Monogamy. 6853-7
Mother-1927 model. 6853-7
The mother. 6097-8
Names of romance. 6853-7
Names of romance. 6732-8
Necessary. 6853-7
Negation. 6853-7
New Orleans. 6853-7
The new route. 7012-4
New York. 6853-7
No rule to be afraid of. 6853-7
Nobody home. 6853-7
A non-wander song. 6853-7
Nuthin' 6853-7
The old cowpuncher speaks. 6853-7
Old lady necessity. 6853-7
Old stuff. 6853-7
The old top sergeant. 6846-4
Once on a time. 6853-7
Opportunity. 6291-1
An oriental ballad. 6853-7
Pan in pandemonium. 6853-7
Pan in pandemonium. 6307-1
Paradise lost. 6853-7
Pardners. 7010-8
The permanent brand. 6853-7
Philadelphia. 6853-7
The philanderer. 6853-7
The pioneers. 6211-3
Pittsburgh. 6853-7
Playing the game ("Yes, he went an' stole our steers").
   6291-1
The poetess. 6853-7
A prayer ("Lord, let me"). 6211-3
Prayer of a sportsman. 6853-7
A prayer. 6853-7
Preference. 6853-7
The price. 6853-7
Red meat. 6853-7
A regular girl. 6853-7
The regular story. 6853-7
Restoration, fr. Matrimonial melodies. 6853-7
Riches. 6853-7
Road law. 6853-7
The sailing list. 6853-7
Salt fish. 6853-7
San Francisco. 6853-7
The shadow of the years. 6853-7
Sonnets of seven cities, sels. 6853-7
Space. 6853-7
Speaking of driving, fr. Matrimonial melodies. 6853-7
Start where you stand. 6291-1
Submarine badinage. 6853-7
Success. 6291-1
Such stuff as dreams are made on. 6853-7
A suggestion. 6853-7
Sure he will. 6853-7
The swamp angel. 6817-0
System, fr. Matrimonial melodies. 6853-7
Take it from father. 6853-7
Terminals. 6853-7
That's her privilege. 6853-7
There he goes. 6853-7
The thinker. 6476-0,6104-4,6449-3
Three minus one. 6853-7

To 'the wife' 6853-7
To a flapper. 6853-7
To a photographer. 6476-0,6104-4,6449-3
To a photographer. 6853-7
To a voyager. 7007-8
To an antique stiletto. 6853-7
To any wife, fr. Matrimonial melodies. 6853-7
Ulysses. 6853-7
Undomesticated animals. 6853-7
Valhalla inn. 6853-7
Volapuk. 6853-7
The warmth of memory. 6853-7
The watchers. 6853-7
What's in a name. 6853-7
White magic. 6853-7
The widest hearthstone. 6853-7
Windows. 6853-7
The worm turns. 6853-7
Youth. 6853-7

Braley, Bertonne
Pardners. 6598-8

The bramble brier. Unknown. 6058-7
The bramble flower. Ebenezer Elliott. 6127-3

Bramhall, Mary Bradley
Lake scene. 6764-6
Loss. 6764-6

Bramley, H.R.
A cradle-song of the Virgin. 6095-1

Bramston, James
Time's changes. 6932-0

Bran. Unknown. 6873-1
"A branch of myrtle in her happiness". Archilochus. 6251-2
"The branch of plum". Imperious design. Maureen Cobb Mabbott. 6979-7
"The branch of that oak jutting into the air". Fey. Walter De La Mare. 6905-3

Branch, Anna Hempstead
Before the fair. 6441-8
The blooming of the rose. 6232-6,6338-1
Connecticut road song. 6431-0
Dream. 6007-2,6556-2
Ere the golden bowl is broken. 6348-9,6217-2
First sight. 6266-0
Gladness. 6266-0,6501-5
Grieve not, ladies. 6102-8,6310-1,6441-8,6732-8,6076-5, 6300
The heart of the road. 7012-4
Her hands. 6101-X
Her words. 6509-0,6393-4,6723-9
I think of him as one who fights. 6184-2
In the beginning was the word. 6619-4,6393-4
Inheritance. 6619-4
The monk in the kitchen, sels. 6337-3
The monk in the kitchen. 6007-2,6102-8,6348-9,6532-5, 6556-2,6300 ,6076-5,6161-3
My mother's clothes. 6006-4,6395-9
My mother's words. 6162-1
The name. 6032-3
Nimrod, sels. 6102-8,6076-5
A nut shell. 6861-8
Service. 6019-6
The silence of the poets. 6723-9
So I may feel the hands of God. 6501-5
Song of the wandering dust. 6006-4
Songs for my mother. 6310-1,6476-0,6627-5,6431-0,6336-5
Songs for my mother: her hands. 6266-0,6465-5
Songs for my mother: her stories. 6395-9
The storm. 6607-0
To a New York shop-girl dressed for Sunday. 6162-1,6310-1
Two inscriptions for the Christmas candle. 6337-3
An unbeliever. 6337-3,6730-1,6467-1
'Under the trees', sels. 6338-1
The warrior maid. 6319-5

Branch, Frederick W.
The keeper of the wall. 6764-6
The Yankees. 6764-6

Branch, Mary Lydia Bolles
I am seven and can sew. 6713-1
The petrified fern. 6304-7,6523-6,6600-3,6621-6,6964-9, 6006-4,6049-8,6183-4,6385-3,6162-1,6478
The petrified fern. 6006-4,6162-1
A poor little mother. 6314-4,6312-8
The wild poppy. 6529-5

The branch. Jones Very. 6641-0
Branches. Carl Sandburg. 6602-X
Branches of Adam, sels. John Gould Fletcher. 6012-9
Branches of trees. Jennie D. Moore. 6048-X
Brand fire new whaling song...from the Pacific Ocean. Unknown. 6833-2
Brand loyalty. Dennis Schmitz. 7032-9
Brand speaks. Henrik Ibsen. 6730-1

Brand, Millen
The honeymoon, fr. Local lives. 6803-0
Local lives, sel. 6803-0

Brandenburgh harvest-song. Felicia Dorothea Hemans. 6973-8

Brandies, Irma
For Betalo. 6847-2
Memory. 6847-2
"She will be here when I am gone". 6847-2

The branding.. Farrukhi. 6448-5

Brandis, Annette von
The May bug. 6680-1

Brandon. Emily Pauline ("Tekahionwake") Johnson. 6837-5

Brandt, C. Margaret
Sometimes. 6818-9

Brandy and soda. Hugh Howard. 6273-3
Brandy pond. Winifred Virginia Jackson. 6039-0

Branford, Frederick Victor
A blade of grass. 6269-5
The cockney's dream. 6269-5
Dying airman to nature. 7014-0
Farewell to mathematics. 6884-7
Flanders. 6269-5
The gleeman. 6071-4
The idiot. 6778-6
The idiot. 6070-6
Night flying. 7014-0
Novissima verba. 6069-2
Ode to sorrow. 6777-8
Ode to sorrow. 6269-5
Over the dead. 6884-7
Return. 6884-7
The siren rocks. 6779-4
Sonnet ("We thought"). 6269-5

Branford, William
Trooper Temple Pulvermacher. 6788-3

Branigan, Johanna Rachel
Meditation on Jesus Christ. 6532-5

Branksome Hall, fr. The lay of the last minstrel. Sir Walter Scott. 6424-8

Brannock, Fowler
The mysterious guest. 6923-1

Brant, Beth
For all my grandmothers. 7005-1
Native origin. 7005-1
Ride the turtle's back. 7005-1

Branwen, sels. Wyn Griffith. 6360-8

Brasch, Charles
Poland, October, fr. Nineteen thirty-nine. 6043-9

Brasch, Thomas
Prewar. Reinhold Grimm (tr.). 7032-9

Brasfield, Philip
Censorship. 6870-7
Inebriates. 6870-7
An interview. 6870-7
Rune. 6870-7
Trouble. 6870-7

The brass horse. Drummond Allison. 6210-5
Brathay church. William Wordsworth. 6484-1

Brathwaite, Richard
My mistress. 6563-5
The nightingale ("Jug, jug! Fair fall the nightingal") 6182-6
Of maids' inconstancy. 6182-6

"Brauely deckt, come forth, bright day" Thomas Campion. 6794-8

Brautigan, Jeannette Carter
Courage. 6789-1
Debut of spring. 6789-1

Bravado. Marie M. Mott. 6799-9
Brave and true. Henry Downton. 6743-3,6167-2
The **brave** at home. Thomas Buchanan Read. 6097-8,6302-0, 6260-1,6385-3,6471-X,6632 ,6113-3,6403-5,6737-9,6470-1,6569-4,6403 ,6309-8,6304-7,6121-4,6219-9,6309-8
"**Brave** bastion of a faith outworn". In a two million dollar chapel. Richard M. Steiner. 6954-1
"**Brave** Chickatawbut was the chief". Indian names. Phebe T. Chamberlain. 6798-0
A **brave** boy. Unknown. 6248-2,6744-1
A **brave** epitaph. John Milton. 6087-0
"**Brave** flowers, that I could gallant it like you". Henry King. 6187-7
Brave Kate Shelley. Mrs. M.L. Rayne. 6744-1,6167-2
"**Brave** flowers, that I could gallant it...". A contemplation upon flowers. Henry King. 6933-9
"**Brave** hearts were they". Our lost aviators. Isola M. Ohaver. 6818-9
"**Brave** lads in olden musical centuries". Robert Louis Stevenson. 6187-7
Brave life. Grantland Rice. 6291-1
A **brave** little girl. Unknown. 6451-5
A **brave** little Quakeress. Unknown. 6249-0
Brave Lord Willoughby. Unknown. 6322-5
Brave love. Unknown. 6260-1,6672-0
The **brave** man. Joanna Baillie. 6294-6
"**Brave** men go out to sea/Inships of wood...". Peace, be still. James C. Haupt. 6799-9
"The **brave** Shoshones much revere". A Shoshone legend. Eugene Field. 6949-5
"**Brave** Sir Count Ricci, in feudal days of yore". The trfiumph o the rich. Edith Wordsworth. 6925-8
Brave news. Unknown. 6937-1
Brave news from admiral Vernon. Unknown. 6547-3
"**Brave** news is come to town." Unknown. 6452-3
The **brave** old oak. Henry Fothergill Chorley. 6302-0;6385-3, 6543-0
Brave Paulding and the spy. Unknown. 6946-0
Brave retreats. William O. Perkins Jr. 6799-9
"**Brave** spirit! mourned with fond regret". To the memory of General Sir Edward Pakenham. Felicia Dorothea Hemans. 6973-8
The **brave** tars of old England. Unknown. 6547-3
Brave Wolfe. Unknown. 6946-0
Brave wolfe. Unknown. 6057-9,6061-7
A **brave** woman. John F. Nocholls. 6923-1
The **brave** women of Tann. William James Linton. 6087-0
A **brave-hearted** maid. Unknown. 6489-2
A **brave-hearted** maid. Unknown. 6282-2
The **brave**.. Nicholas Rowe. 6211-3
Bravery. William Shakespeare. 6087-0
Braves of the hunt. Henry Herbert Knibbs. 6510-4
"The **bravest** battle that ever was fought!". Mothers of men. Joaquin Miller. 6964-9,6963-0
The **bravest** battle that ever was fought. Joaquin Miller. 7002-7
The **bravest** battle. Joaquin Miller. 6097-8;6260-1
"The **bravest** names for fire and flames". General John. Sir William Schwenck Gilbert. 6902-9
Bravest of the brave. Robert J. Burdette. 6139-7,6588-0
The **bravo**. Jean Moreas. 6351-9
Braw lads o' Galla water. Robert Burns. 6180-X
Brawn of England's lay. John Hunter-Duvar. 6656-9
Bray, Mary Matthews
    O, quaint little town. 6798-0
    Old Yarmouth. 6798-0
    Wayside blossoms. 6798-0
Brayton, Teresa
    A Christmas song. 6172-9,6292-X
"The **brazen** form of the great god Pan". Ballade for missionaries. Squidge [pseud].. 6817-0
Brazen tongue. William Rose Benet. 6012-9
Braziel, Arthur
    Virgin field. 6178-8
"The **braziers**, it seems, are preparing to pass". Epigram on the braziers' company having resolved... George Gordon, 6th Baron Byron. 6945-2
Brazil. Ronaldo de Carvalho. 6759-X
The **brdie-ale**. Alfred Noyes. 6151-6
Bre'r Jason's sermon. Unknown. 6312-8

Bread. Leslie Savage Clark. 6144-3
Bread. Abraham Moses Klein. 6446-9
Bread. Unknown. 6337-3
Bread. Unknown (French) 6166-4
A **bread** and butter letter. Alice Duer Allnut. 6653-4
Bread and cherries. Walter De La Mare. 6937-1
"Bread and milk for breakfast". Winter. Christina Georgina Rossetti. 6466-3
Bread and roses. James Oppenheim. 6954-1
Bread and wine. Margaret J.E. Brown. 6316-0
"'Bread for my mother!' said the voice". Rizpah with her sons. Nathaniel Parker Willis. 6848-0
The **bread** is all baked. Unknown. 6328-4
Bread line. Florence Converse. 6490-6
The **bread** line. Berton Braley. 6954-1
The **bread** line. Dana Burnet. 6431-0
The **bread** line. Edgar A. Guest. 6869-3
Bread of the world. Reginald Heber. 6337-3
Bread on the water. Nell Chapman. 6178-8
"Bread on which angels feed". This is that bread, fr. Hymns and anthems... Caroline Hazard. 6762-X
Bread out of iron, sels. Marjorie Allen Seiffert. 6531-7
Bread winners. David Greenhood. 6042-0
"Bread, breadbaker". Unknown. 6364-0
The **bread-knife** ballad, fr. Five frivolous songs. Robert Service. 6159-1
"Break cloudless bright, thy silver day". Silver wedding day. Benjamin Franklin Taylor. 6815-2
"Break forth in song, long-silent earth". Zion, awake! Horatius Bonar. 6848-0
"Break forth in song, ye trees". Hymn for the second centennial anniversary of...Boston. John Pierpont. 6752-2
"Break me a wand from the willow bough". A song of spring. Mary A. Brooks. 6764-6
Break my heart of stone. Charles Wesley. 6065-X
Break of day. John Donne. 6182-6,6634-8,6491-4
Break of day in the trenches. Isaac Rosenberg. 6209-1,6354-3,6666-6
The **break** of day. John Shaw Neilson. 6784-0
"Break off! Dance no more!". War-music, fr. Music. Henry Van Dyke. 6961-4
Break thou the bread of life. Mary Artemisia Lathbury. 6337-3
"Break, O wind!/Break against the trees". Autumn wind. Alfred D. Butts. 6799-9
Break, break, break. Alfred Lord Tennyson. 6723-9,6660-7, 6543-0,6565-1,6658-5,6656 ,6424-8,6646-1,6371-3,6639-9,6304-7,6301 ,6219-9,6104-4,6659-3,6212-1,6199-0, 6250 ,6193-3,6430-2,6102-8,6560-0,6110-9,6197 ,6196-6,6396-6,6464-7,6138-9,6478-7,6208-3,6240-7,6358-X, 6610 ,6228-8,6260-1,6289-X,6271-7,6332-2,6597 ,6328-4,6657-7,6198-2,6726-3,6600-3,6123 ,6337-3,6655-0, 6634-8,6536-8,6481-7,6488 ,6392-6,6122-2,6142-7,6187-7,6459-X,6277 ,6,73-6,6604-6,6385-3,6052-8,6645-3, 6737
Break, fancy, from thy cave. Ben Jonson. 6328-4
"Breake hart in twayne, fayre Ronile may se." Unknown. 6563-5
"Breake now, my heart, and dye! Oh no, she may relent" Thomas Campion. 6794-8
Breaker and maker. Grantland Rice. 6211-3
Breakers of bronchos. Lew Sarett. 6037-4,6265-2
"The **breakers** pound the rocks and the". Roosevelt. Hermann Hagedorn. 6995-9
"The **breakers** pound upon the yellow strand". The surf at Chatham. William Chase Greene. 6798-0
The **breakers**. E.H. Brodie. 6997-5
Breakfast. Wilfred Wilson Gibson. 6393-4
The **breakfast** and dinner trees. Vachel Lindsay. 6206-7
The **breakfast** food family. Bert Leston Taylor. 6274-1
The **breakfast** table, August 5, 1945 Geraldine Little. 7032-9
Breaking a colt in Vermont. Daniel L. Cady. 6989-4
"Breaking a scarlet pomegranate with his teeth". The pomegranate. Berenice Van Slyke. 6808-1
Breaking billows. William ("Fiona Macleod") Sharp. 6997-5
Breaking billows..Sorrento, fr. Australian transcripts. William ("Fiona Macleod") Sharp. 6768-9
WBreaking in a tenderfoot. Unknown. 6003-X,6281-4

The breaking plow. Nixon Waterman. 6889-8
Breaking silence. Janice Mirikitani. 6790-5
Breaking the day in two. Ella Wheeler Wilcox. 6863-4
Breaking the molds. Hortense Flexner. 6954-1
Breaking the moulds. Hortense Flexner. 7038-8
Breaking the roads. Phoebe Cary. 6865-0;6969-X
"Breaking through the brambles...". The wind is my neighbor. Margery Swett Mansfield. 6850-2
Breaking tradition. Janice Mirikitani. 6790-5
"The breaking waves dashed high." Felicia Dorothea Hemans. 6001-3
Breast forward. Robert Browning. 6260-1
"Breast to breast of a sun-kissed rock". The cave woman. Gulielma Day Orr. 6906-1
Breasted, James Henry (tr.)
 Hymn of victory: Thyutmose III. Amon-Re, 6665-8
 Hymn to the sun. Amen-Hotep IV, 6879-0
 The song of the Egyptian minstrel. Unknown (Egyptian), 6879-0
Breastfeeding at the art gallery of Ontario... Sharon Berg. 6767-0
Breasting the storm. Allen Eastman Cross. 6764-6
The breastplate of Saint Patrick. Unknown. 6107-9
The breastplate of St. Patrick. Unknown. 6090-0,6107-9
Breath. Arthur Smith. 6792-1
"A breath from the tropics broke winter' spell". The silver frost. Barry Straton. 6795-6
The breath of Avon. Theodore Watts-Dunton. 6656-9
"The breath of air, that stirs the harp's...". On the loss of Professor Fisher. John Gardiner Calkins Brainard. 6752-2
"A breath of air/A delicate ball". Blowing bubbles. Beatrice Paula Byrnes. 6750-6
The breath of light. A. E. 6873-1
A breath of mint. Grace Hazard Conkling. 6338-1
Breath of pines. Mildred Kleinschmidt. 6397-7
"Breath of sweetgrass, blown through...evening". Departure. Muriel F. Hochdorf. 6850-2
Breath of the briar. George Meredith. 6508-2
"The breath of the morn is sharp and chill". Fishing song. Conrad Orton Milliken. 6936-3
The breath of the spirit. Unknown. 6156-7
Breath on the oat. Joseph Russell Taylor. 6946-0
"A breath, like the wind's breath, may carry". The measure of time. Alice Cary. 6969-X
A breath. William Lindsey. 6798-0
"Breathe againe, while we with musicke". The maskers second dance. Thomas Campion. 6794-8
"Breathe not the tomorrow in her ears". The cabaret dancer. Hermann Hagedorn. 6959-2
Breathe on me, breath of God. Edwin Hatch. 6337-3
Breathes there a man. Samuel Hoffenstein. 6722-0
Breathes there a man. Sir Walter Scott. 6134-6,6138-9,6211-3,6481-7,6087-0,6457,6238-5,6395-0,6302-0,6385-3, 6486-8,6337,6461-2,6107-9,6197-4,6457-4,6737-9
"Breathes there the man, with soul so dead". A bridal. Sir Walter Scott. 6980-0
"Breathes there the man," fr.The lay of...last minstrel. Sir Walter Scott. 6793-X
"Breathing do I draw that air to me". Song of breath. Peire Vidal. 7039-6
"Breathing/heart to heart". City boy. Stephanie Herbst. 6883-9
Breathings of spring. Felicia Dorothea Hemans. 6049-8
Breathless awe. Edwin Markham. 6337-3
"Breathless we watch the fight in the saloon". Cinema. Gwendolen Haste. 6808-1
Breathnach, Michael
 Man-child. 6292-X
"The breaths of kissing night and day". Dream-tryst. Francis Thompson. 6828-6,6942-8
Brebeuf and his breathen, sels. Edwin John Pratt. 6446-9
Brebeuf and Lalemant. Alan Sullivan. 6115-X
Brecha's harp-song. Ernest Rhys. 6656-9
Brecht, Bert
 Yes, I live in a dark age. R. Landshoff and J.T. Latouchie (tr.). 6068-4
Brecht, Vincent B.
 Happy ghosts. 6936-3
Breck, Mrs. Frank A.
 A Christmas thought. 6065-X
The Brecknock beacons. Martin Farquhar Tupper. 7015-9
"Brederen, listen ter de words I say". De gospel train. Julia Johnson Davies. 6778-6
Brederode and John Bowring, Gerbrand (tr.)
 Psalm 133 Bible, 6848-0
Bredon hill. Alfred Edward Housman. 6506-6,6538-4,6726-3, 6508-2,6491-4
Breed, Eleanor
 Scapegoats. 6337-3
Breed, fr. The testament of beauty. Robert Bridges. 6487-6
Breed, women, breed. Lucia Trent. 6542-2
The breeding lark. Arthur Boar. 6438-8
The breedyen. Douglas Hyde. 6873-1
Breen, Genevieve R.
 Henry Hastings Sibley. 6342-X
The breeze after the calm. Samuel Taylor Coleridge. 6543-0
Breeze and billow. Albert Durrant Watson. 6115-X
The breeze from shore. Felicia Dorothea Hemans. 6973-8
"The breeze has swelled the whitening sail". Song of the Pilgrims (1). Thomas Cogswell Upham. 6752-2,6946-0
"The breeze of the morn". Jalal [or Jelal] ed-din Rumi. 6448-5
A breeze through the forest. Richard Dalton Williams. 6174-5
The breeze.. Unknown. 6466-3
The breeze. Al-Husri. 6362-4
The breeze. Ruth Wellman. 6798-0
"The breezes freshen; orient rays". A day in Palestine. Robert Needham Cust. 6848-0
"Breezes went steadily thro' the tall pines". Nathan Hale. Unknown. 6946-0
Bregenz. Adelaide Anne Procter. 6749-2
Bregy, Katherine
 Gethsemane's gift. 6337-3
 Japanese cherries. 6292-X
 Song of a smiling lady. 6249-0
Breining, June
 Inexperience. 6396-9
Breitmann, Hans. See Leland, Charles Godfrey
Breitt, Luke
 Night atlas. 6792-1
 Poem for Valerie. 6792-1
"Brekekekew! coax! coax! O happy, happy frogs!". The musical frogs. John Stuart Blackie. 6916-9
Brell, William J. (tr.)
 Fourth station ("They say this is his mother-"). Ruth Shaumanm, 6282-2
Brem, Ilse
 Dawn. Milne Holton and Herbert Kuhner (tr.). 6769-7
 Late days. Milne Holton and Herbert Kuhner (tr.). 6769-7
 Roses. Milne Holton and Herbert Kuhner (tr.). 6769-7
 Sometimes. Milne Holton and Herbert Kuhner (tr.). 6769-7
Bremer, Frederika
 The heavenly dove. Mary Howitt (tr.). 6424-8
 A little brawl. Mary Howitt (tr.). 6424-8
 Swedish mother's lullaby. 6627-5
Brenan, Joseph
 "Come to me, dearest!" 6385-3,6226-1
Brenda at thirty. Gertrude Joan Buckman. 6850-2
"Brendan, holy Brendan of the blessed beard". Saint Brendan's prophecy. Unknown. 6930-4
Brennan on the moor. Unknown. 6057-9
Brennan, Christopher J.
 The burden of Tyre, sels. 6384-5
 Fire in the heavens. 6384-5,6349-7
 The grand cortege. 6349-7
 I said, this misery must end. 6384-5
 My heart was wandering in the sands. 6784-0
 O white wind. 6349-7
 The pangs that guard the gates of joy. 6784-0
 The point of noon. 6349-7
 The wanderer, sels. 6349-7
 What do I know? 6384-5
Brennan, Eileen
 Thoughts at the museum. 6930-4
Brennan, Gerald
 Shanahan's ould queen. 7007-8

Brennan, Joseph
    Come to me, dearest. 6600-3,6620-8
    The exile to his wife. 6219-9,6407-8
Brennan, Joseph Payne
    Avery Anameer. 6218-0
    The chestnut roasters. 6218-0
    Ghost-town saloon: winter. 6218-0
    Grandfather's ghost. 6218-0
    The humming stair. 6218-0
    The last pagan mourns for dark Rosaleen. 6218-0
    The man I met. 6218-0
    Nightmare. 6218-0
    One day of rain. 6218-0
    Ossian. 6218-0
    Recognition of death. 6218-0
    The scythe of dreams. 6218-0
    The serpent waits. 6218-0
    The wind of time. 6218-0
Brenner, Irving
    Echoes from camp Upton. 7007-8
Brenstrum, Erick
    Late testament. 7018-3
    Southern coast. 7018-3
Brent, Hally Carrington
    I think I know no finer things than dogs. 6107-9
Brereton, Ethel C.
    Pussy cat. 6262-8
Brereton, Jane
    On Beau Nash's picture at Bath, which once stood... 6874-X
    "This picture placed these busts...". 6289-X
Brereton, John Le Gay
    Buffalo creek. 6784-0
    The dead. 6784-0
    The robe of grass. 6784-0
    Waking. 6784-0
Brereton, M.G.
    The old brocade. 6338-1
Bresca. Lucy Barbour Ewing. 6926-6
Breshkovskaya, sels. Elsa Barker. 6076-5,6102-8
Bresler, Elya
    Lullaby ("In your little armored bed"). 6761-1
Brest left behind. John Chipman Farrar. 6051-X,6452-2
The **brestplate** of St. Patrick. Saint Patrick (atr) 6090-0
"The **brethering** in Lucre Hollow were disturbed". The church in Lucre Hollow. Louis Eisenbeis. 6925-8
Bretherton, Cyril
    To Towser. 7008-6
Breton, Andre
    Broken line. 6351-9
Breton, Nicholas
    Aglaia. 6436-1
    An assurance. 6436-1
    The Christmas now is past. 6756-5
    "Come, little babe, come silly soul". 6181-8
    Coridon's supplication to Phillis. 6586-4
    The country lad. 6383-7
    A cradle song. 6233-4,6395-9,6301-2
    A displeasure against loue, fr. Melancholic humors. 6586-4
    Farewell to town, sels. 6934-7
    A farewell to town. 6092-7
    "Good muse, rock me asleep" 6935-5
    His wisdom. 6436-1,6026-9,6436-1
    Hymn ("When the angels..."). 6271-7
    "I have neither plums nor cherries". 6187-7
    "I would I were an excellent devine." 6302-0
    I would thou wert not fair. 6182-6,6189-3
    "In the merry month of May". 6181-8,6187-7
    Ipsa quae. 6436-1
    Lovely kind and kindly loving. 6189-3
    Melancholic humors, sels. 6586-4
    Melancholic humors, sels. 6586-4
    The merry country lad. 6182-6,6315-2
    Now Christmas draweth near. 6756-5
    An odd conceit. 6182-6,6436-1,6586-4
    Olden love-making. 6436-1,6191-5
    "On a hill there grows a flower." 6317-9
    A passage in the life of St. Augustine. 6385-3
    Pastoral. 6830-8
    A pastoral ("On a hill"). 6182-6,6219-9
    A pastoral ("Sweet birds"). 6182-6,6586-4,6153-2
    A pastoral of Phillis and Coridon. 6383-7,5686-4
    A pastoral. 6219-9
    Phillida and Corydon. 6827-8
    Phillida and Corydon. 6014-5,6182-6,6198-2,6102-8,6271-7,6328 ,6092-7,6194-X,6191-5,6219-9,6430-2,6258 , 6385-3,6652-6,6732-8,6737-9,6733-6,6014-5,6092-7, 6102-8,6122-2,6182-6,6194-X,6198-2,6219-9,6250-4, 6271-7,6328
    Phillis. 6436-1
    Phillis the fair. 6302-0,6385-3,6302-9
    The ploughman's song. 6026-9,6208-3
    The ploughman's [or plowman's] song. 6026-9,6208-3,6436-1
    A prayer for gentlewomen and others to use. 6586-4
    Pretty twinkling sparkling eyes. 6182-6
    Pretty twinkling starry eyes. 6182-6
    The priest. 6219-9,6271-7
    A report song. 6436-1
    Say that I should say I love ye. 6182-6
    The second pastor's song. 6191-5
    Shall we go dance the hay? 6328-4
    Shepherd and shepherdess. 6436-1
    A solemne concept, fr. Melancholic humors. 6586-4
    A sonet to the tune of a hone a hone. 6586-4
    Song ("Lovely kind"). 6317-9
    A supplication. 6436-1
    "Sweet birds that sit and sing amid the shady". 6187-7
    A sweet lullaby ("Come, little babe...") 6182-6,6436-1, 6533-3,6586-4,6194-X,6189
    A sweet pastoral. 6271-7,6317-9,6586-4,6250-4,6383-7, 6191
    The third pastor's song. 6191-5
    To his muse. 6436-1
    Who can live in heart so glad. 6423-X
    Worldly paradise. 6194-X
Brettell, Noel Harry
    Cataclysm. 6788-3
    Elephant. 6788-3
    Giraffes. 6788-3
    Outside Kimberley. 6788-3
    Wind and an eagle owl, sels. 6788-3
Breviary, Roman
    "The morning purples all the sky". 6065-X
Brevities. Siegfried Sassoon. 6357-8
"A **brewer** in a country town". Patent brown stout. Unknown. 6787-5
The **brewer's** man. Leonard Alfred George Strong. 6506-6, 6538-4,6722-0,6633-X
Brewer, Daniel Chauncey
    Softly the evening shadows. 6066-8,6226-1
Brewer, Ebenezer Cobham
    Little things. 6479-5
Brewer, Layton
    A terrible example. 7021-3
    Traced. 7021-3
Brewer, Wilmon
    Peaceful Thames. 6894-4
"A **brewer,** in a country town". Brown stout. Unknown. 6926-6
A **brewer..** Unknown. 6722-0
Brewster, Elizabeth
    Is the pathetic fallacy true? 6767-0
Brewster, Margaret
    Moods. 6396-9
Brewster, Marguerite A.
    The dark-jut stone. 6857-X
Brewster, Townsend T.
    Black is beautiful. 7024-8
Brezee, Wellington
    Sonnet. 6799-9
Brezina, Otakar
    The body. Paul Selver (tr.). 6763-8
    The brotherhood of the believers. Paul Selver (tr.). 6886-3
    Dithyramb of the worlds. Paul Selver (tr.). 6763-8
    Earth? Paul Selver (tr.). 6886-3
    Gaze of death. Paul Selver (tr.). 6886-3
    Legend of secret guilt. Paul Selver (tr.). 6886-3

BREZINA

A mood. Paul Selver (tr.). 6886-3
My mother. Paul Selver (tr.). 6763-8
Nature. Paul Selver (tr.). 6763-8
Pure morning. Paul Selver (tr.). 6763-8
Responses. Paul Selver (tr.). 6763-8
Spring night. Paul Selver (tr.). 6763-8,6886-3
Thus sang the burning stars. Paul Selver (tr.). 6763-8
Thus sang the waters. Paul Selver (tr.). 6763-8
Woe of man. Paul Selver (tr.). 6763-8
Women. Paul Selver (tr.). 6763-8
"Brian O'Lin, and his wife, and wife's mother". Unknown. 6904-5
Brian O'Linn. Unknown. 6930-4
Brian O'Linn. Unknown. 6613-5
"Brian O'Linn was a gentleman born". Brian O'Linn. Unknown. 6930-4
Bric-a-brac, sels. William Ernest Henley. 6123-0
Brice, Beatrix
    To the vanguard. 7029-9
"Brick walls built by labor". Labor. Edith Thomas. 6880-4
Brick, Norman
    Of snow. 6666-6
brick-dust. Louise Brooke. 6034-X
Brickhead, William Hunter
    He was a friend indeed. 6066-8
The bricklayer. Vasili Kazin. 6103-6
The bricklayers. G.H. Barnes. 6915-0,6167-2
Brickman, Irving
    Dirt song. 6237-7
    Maneuver song. 6237-7
Bridal ballad. Edgar Allan Poe. 6m41-0,6288-1
Bridal bath, fr. The house of life. Dante Gabriel Rossetti. 6828-6
Bridal birth, fr. The house of life. Dante Gabriel Rossetti. 6110-9,6430-2,6508-2
The bridal day. Felicia Dorothea Hemans. 6973-8
The bridal day. Edmund Spenser. 6543-0
The bridal feast. F.C. Long. 6404-3;6554-6
The bridal hour. Alice Cary. 6969-X
The bridal in Eden. F.J. Ottorson. 6918-5,6848-0
Bridal night. Don Marquis. 6619-4
The bridal o 't. Christina Georgina Rossetti. 6180-X
Bridal of Andalla. Unknown (Spanish) 6438-8,6219-9
The bridal of Andalla. Unknown. 6271-7
The bridal of Andalla. Unknown (Spanish) 6757-3
The bridal of Malahide. Gerald Griffin. 6174-5,6518-X,6576-7
The bridal of Pennacook, sels. John Greenleaf Whittier. 6484-1
Bridal song. Francis Beaumont. 6182-6
Bridal song. John Fletcher. 6733-6,6153-2
Bridal song. Henry Hart Milman. 6219-9
Bridal song ("Now, Sleep, bind fast the flood of air") George Chapman. 6182-6,6102-8
A bridal song ("Roses, their sharp spines being gone"). William Shakespeare. 6436-1
Bridal song and dirge. Thomas Lovell Beddoes. 6271-7
Bridal song to Amala. Thomas Lovell Beddoes. 6437-X
A bridal song unsung. Alfred Noyes. 6169-9
Bridal song, fr. The little French lawyer. Francis Beaumont and John Fletcher. 6827-8
A bridal song, fr. Two noble kinsmen. William Shakespeare. 6436-1
A bridal song. Francis Beaumont and John Fletcher. 6737-9
A bridal song. Thomas Dekker. 6436-1
A bridal song. Hugh McCrae. 6784-0
A bridal song. Percy Bysshe Shelley. 6328-4
Bridal veil. Joseph Clinton Williams. 6316-0
The bridal veil. Alice Cary. 6969-X
A bridal. Sir Walter Scott. 6980-0
The bridal. Heinrich Heine. 6842-1
The briddes in May. Geoffrey Chaucer. 6943-6
The bride and the matron. Helen Hoyt. 6038-2
A bride in the '30's. Wystan Hugh Auden. 6209-1
The bride of Abydos, sels. George Gordon, 6th Baron Byron. 6289-X,6332-2,6439-6
The bride of Abydos. George Gordon, 6th Baron Byron. 6110-9,6430-2
The bride of Corinth. Johann Wolfgang von Goethe. 6842-1
The bride of Lammermoor, sels. Sir Walter Scott. 6427-2

The bride of the Greek isle. Felicia Dorothea Hemans. 6554-6,6569-4
Bride or handmaiden?. Lewis Spence. 6269-5
The bride reluctant. Harriet Eleanor Hamiliton (Baille) King. 6096 X
"The bride she is winsome and bonny". Song ("The bride..."). Joanna Baillie. 6832-4
"Bride! upon thy marriage-day". The bridal day. Felicia Dorothea Hemans. 6973-8
The bride's dream. Adelaide Anne Procter. 6957-6
The bride's farewell. Felicia Dorothea Hemans. 6980-0
Bride's mother. Christie Lund. 6750-6
The bride's prelude. Dante Gabriel Rossetti. 6997-5
The bride's reply. George Henry Miles. 6096 X
The bride's slippers. David Stefansson fra Fagraskogi. 6854-5
The bride's tragedy. Algernon Charles Swinburne. 6518-X
The bride-song, fr. The prince's progress. Christina Georgina Rossetti. 6198-2,6204-0,6437-X
The bride: a drama. Joanna Baillie. 6813-8
A bride. Meleager. 6435-3
The bride. Ambrose Bierce. 6307-1
The bride. Ralph Hodgson. 6023-4
The bride. Edmund Spenser. 6302-0,6438-8
The bride. Sir John Suckling. 6302-0,6385-3,6438-8
The bride. Unknown. 6752-2
The bride. Thomas Wade. 6980-0
"Bridegroom dear, to what shall I compare thee". Sappho. 6435-3
Bridegroom Dick, sels. Herman Melville. 6399-3
The bridegroom of Cana. Marjorie L.C. Pickthall. 6433-7, 6115-X
The, sels bridegroom. Charles Julian Downey. 6836-7
The brides of Enderby. Jean Ingelow. 6479-5,6403-5
The brides tragedy, sels. Thomas Lovell Beddoes. 6378-0, 6656-9
Bridge builders. Evelyn Simms. 6478-7
The bridge keeper's story. W.A. Eaton. 6922-3
The bridge o'er the river of death. Edward R. Huxley. 6885-5
The bridge of death. Unknown (French) 6771-9
The bridge of Glen Aray. Charles Mackay. 6924-X
The bridge of Glen Aray. Charles Mackay. 6167-2
The bridge of life. Unknown. 6273-3
The bridge of sighs. Thomas Hood. 6301-2,6122-2,6344-6, 6014-5,6198-2,6486-8,6246 ,6271-7,6289-X,6302-0,6385-3,6370-5,6402 ,6425-6,6437-X,6501-5,6604-6,6610-0, 6661 ,6726-3,6732-8,6660-7,6570-8,6646-1,6543 ,6102-8,6560-0,6513-9,6153-2,6192-9,6656
The bridge of truth. Unknown. 6407-8
The bridge you'll never cross. Grenville Kleiser. 6337-3, 6583-X
Bridge, Elizabeth Brown Du. See Du Bridge
The bridge, sels. Hart Crane. 6399-3,6052-8,6375-6
Bridge-guard in the Karroo. Rudyard Kipling. 6810-3,6788-3
The bridge. Arthur Wentworth Hamilton Eaton. 6115-X
The bridge. John Gawsworth. 6893-6
The bridge. Henry Wadsworth Longfellow. 6006-4,6732-8,6554-6,6597-X,6142-7,6215 ,6457-4,6457-4,6858-6,6126-5, 6304-7,6706-9,6288-1,6560-0
The bridge. Frederick Peterson. 6431-0
The bridge. James ("B.V.") Thomson. 6437-X
The bridge. Nikolai Tikhonov. 6546-5
Bridgeman, Amy Sherman
    John Masefield. 6762-X
Bridges, Elizabeth
    "Use me, England". 7029-9
Bridges, Joseph
    Close up this house. 6042-0
Bridges, Mabel Rutherford
    My son's son to his son's son--perhaps. 6799-9
Bridges, Madeline. See De Vere, Mary Ainge
Bridges, Matthew
    And Jesus wept. 6065-X
    Crown him with many crowns. 6337-3
    Rise, glorious conqueror! rise. 6065-X
Bridges, Robert
    The affliction of Richard. 6487-6,6641-0
    After the gale. 6315-2
    "Ah, what a change! Thou, ho didst emptily...". 6487-6

"All earthly beauty hath one cause and proof". 6186-9,
   6487-6
"All mankind by Love...", fr. Ode to music. 6487-6
"All-ador'd, all glorious...". 6487-6
Amiel. 6487-6
"Angel spirits of sleep". 6487-6
Anniversary. 6487-6
An anniversary ("Bright, my beloved..."). 6487-6
April, 1885. 6487-6
"Ariel, O, -my angel, my own". 6487-6
Asian birds. 6487-6,6656-9
Auguries. 6232-6
August, 1914. 6224-5
Awake, my heart. 6186-9,6204-0,6266-0,6437-X,6477-9,
   6487 ,6655-0,6656-9,6737-9
"The birds that sing on autumn eves". 6487-6
Breed, fr. The testament of beauty. 6487-6
Britannia victrix. 6487-6
Buch der lieder. 6487-6
"But when the winds...", fr. Ode to music. 6487-6
Cheddar pinks. 6487-6
The chivalry of the sea. 6487-6
Chorus of Oceanides, fr. Demeter. 6334-9
Chorus of Scyrian maidens, fr. Achilles in Scyros. 6334-9
Christmas eve, 1917. 6487-6
'Clear and gentle stream'. 6476-0,6487-6
The cliff-top. 6487-6
"The clouds have left the sky". 6187-7,6487-6
The college garden. 6487-6
Come se quando. 6487-6
"Crown winter with green". 6487-6
The curfew tower. 6487-6
"Dear lady, when thou frownest". 6487-6
Dejection. 6487-6
Demeter. 6487-6
Democritus. 6487-6
The downs. 6395-0,6423-X,6487-6,6477-9,6541-4
A dream. 6487-6
Dunstone hill. 6487-6
The duteous heart. 6487-6
Elegy ("Among"). 6487-6
Elegy ("Assemble"). 6487-6
Elegy ("Clear"). 6487-6,6250-4,6430-2
Elegy ("How well"). 6487-6
Elegy ("The wood"). 6154-0,6487-6,6507-4,6250-4,6430-2
Elegy - the summer house on the mound. 6186-9,6245-8,
   6487-6
Elegy on a lady, whom grief...killed. 6437-X,6477-9,
   6508-2,6301-2
Emily Bronte. 6487-6
England to India. 6487-6
"England will keep her dearest...". 6487-6
Eros. 6317-9
Ethick, fr. The testament of beauty. 6487-6
"The evening darkens over". 6487-6,6508-2
The excellent way. 6487-6
The fair brass. 6186-9,6487-6
"Fight well, my comrades...". 6487-6
"Fire of heaven, whose starry arrow". 6487-6
First spring morning. 6242-3,6334-9,6487-6
The flowering tree. 6487-6
Flycatchers. 6487-6
For 'Pages inedites'. 6487-6
Fortunatus nimium. 6482-5,6487-6
Founder's day. 6437-X,6487-6
The fourth dimension. 6487-6
Fourth of June at Eton. 6487-6
Friendship, fr. The testament of beauty. 6337-3
"The full moon from her cloudless skies". 6487-6,6655-0
The garden in September. 6232-6,6487-6,6649-6
"Gay Robin is seen no more". 6242-3,6487-6
Gheluvelt. 6487-6
Ghosts. 6487-6,6201-5
Giovanni Dupre. 6487-6
"Gird on thy sword...", fr. A hymn of nature. 6487-6
"Gloom and the night...", fr. A hymn of nature. 6487-6
The great elm. 6487-6
The growth of love, sels. 6154-0
The growth of love. 6487-6

Hark to the merry birds. 6266-0,6478-7,6487-6
"Hark! What spirit...", fr. A hymn of nature. 6487-6
"Haste on, my joys! your treasure lies". 6487-6
Hell and hate. 6487-6
The hill pines were sighing. 6187-7,6477-9,6487-6,6430-
   2,6508-2
'His poisoned shafts' 6770-0
Hodge. 6487-6
A hymn of nature, sels. 6487-6
"I climb the mossy bank of the glade". 6487-6
"I died in very flow'r...". 6487-6
"I found to-day out walking". 6487-6
I have loved flowers that fade. 6187-7,6232-6,6246-6,
   6317-9,6487-6,6507 ,6102-8,6250-4,6396-9,6508-2,6655-
   0
I heard a linnet courting. 6339-X,6487-6
"I love all beauteous things" 6339-X,6477-9,6487-6,6507-
   4,6625-9,6655 ,6250-4,6301-2,6508-2,6581-3
"I made another song". 6487-6
I never shall love the snow again. 6477-9,6487-6,6430-2,
   6508-2,6655-0
"I praise the tender flower". 6187-7,6487-6
"I travel to thee with the sun's first rays". 6186-9,
   6487-6
I will not let thee go. 6320-9,6477-9,6487-6,6508-2,
   6656-9
The idle flowers. 6487-6,6125-7
The idle life I lead. 6187-7,6339-X,6487-6
In der fremde. 6487-6
"In still midsummer night". 6487-6
"In ways of beauty...", fr. A hymn of nature. 6487-6
Indolence. 6487-6
Introduction, fr. The testament of beauty. 6487-6
Invitation to the country, fr. Spring. 6487-6
An invitation to the Oxford pageant, July 1907. 6487-6
The isle of Achilles. 6487-6
January. 6487-6
Jesus, fr. The testament of beauty. 6337-3
Johannes Milton, senex. 6487-6,6375-6
"Joy, sweetest lifeborn joy, where dost thou dwell".
   6487-6
Kate's mother. 6487-6
La gloire de Voltaire. 6487-6
"Lament, fair hearted...", fr. Ode to music. 6487-6
Larks. 6487-6
Last week of February, 1890. 6487-6,6508-2
Late spring evening. 6487-6
Laus Deo. 6487-6,6641-0
London snow. 6154-0,6186-9,6315-2,6395-0,6473-6,6477 ,
   6125-7,6135-2,6487-6,6507-4,6464-7,6655
"Long are the hours the sun is above." 6187-7,6317-9,
   6487-6,6508-2
Lord Kitchener. 7029-9,7026-4
A love lyric. 6487-6
"Love on my heart from heaven fell". 6487-6
"Love to Love calleth", fr. Ode to music. 6487-6
Low barometer. 6487-6
"Man born of desire", fr. Ode to music. 6487-6
"Man, born to toil...", fr. A hymn of nature. 6487-6
Matres dolorosae. 6097-8,6627-5
Melancholy. 6487-6,6199-0
Millicent. 6487-6
The months. 6487-6
Morning hymn. 6487-6
"My bed and pillow are cold". 6487-6
My delight and thy delight. 6186-9,6488-4,6487-6,6430-2,
   6250-4,6508
"My eyes for beauty pine". 6487-6,6655-0
"My spirit kisseth thine". 6487-6
"My spirit sang all day". 6487-6
"Myriad-voiced Queen...", fr. Ode to music. 6487-6
Narcissus. 6487-6
Nightingales. 6052-8,6073-0,6186-9,6208-3,6437-X,6487 ,
   6536-8,6250-4,6253-9,6301-2,6464-7,6653 ,6655-0
Noel: Christmas Eve, 1913. 6487-6
"The north wind came up yesternight". 6487-6
North wind in October. 6487-6,6253-9
November. 6487-6
"O love, I complain". 6487-6
"O love, my muse, how was't for me". 6487-6

"O my vague desires". 6487-6
"O thou unfaithful, still as ever dearest". 6487-6
"O youth whose hope is high". 6473-6,6487-6,6656-9
October. 6487-6
Ode on the tercentenary commemoration... 6487-6
Ode to music, sels. 6487-6
On a dead child. 6186-9,6477-9,6487-6,6482-5,6430-2
On the hill. 6995-9
"One grief of thine". 6487-6
Open for me the gates of delight. 6186-9,6487-6
Our lady. 6282-2,6487-6,6532-5
"The palm willow". 6487-6
A passer-by. 6052-8,6258-X,6331-4,6437-X,6487-6,6547 , 6250-4,6430-2,6301-2,6508-2,6631-3,6656 ,6506-6,6507-4,6150-8,6655-0
Pater filio. 6437-X,6487-6,6508-2,6655-0
The philosopher to his mistress. 6430-2,6487-6,6508-2, 6655-0
The pinks along my garden walks. 6487-6
Poor child. 6487-6
Poor poll. 6487-6
"Poor withered rose and dry." 6487-6,6656-9
A poppy grows upon the shore. 6487-6,6507-4
The portrait of a grandfather. 6487-6
"Power eternal...," fr. A hymn of nature. 6487-6
Prometheus the firegiver. 6487-6
The psalm. 6487-6,6210-5
Pythagoras. 6487-6
Recollections of solitude. 6487-6
Regina cara. 6487-6
"Rejoice, ye dead...", fr. Ode to music. 6487-6
Reply, fr. Spring. 6487-6
"Riding down the country lanes." 6487-6
A robin. 6487-6
Rondeau. 6875-8
Rondeau ("His poisoned shafts, that fresh he dips") 6875-8
Rondeau ("His poisoned shafts..."). 6487-6
Roosevelt in Wyoming. 6995-9
"Say who is this with silvered hair". 6487-6
School-days. 6473-6
Screaming tarn. 6487-6,6655-0
"The sea keeps not the Sabbath day". 6487-6
"The sea with melancholy...", fr. Ode to music. 6487-6
Selfhood, fr. The testament of beauty. 6487-6
Septuagesima. 6487-6
Simpkin. 6487-6
"Since thou, O fondest and truest". 6487-6
"Since to be loved endures". 6487-6
"Since we loved,-(the earth that shook". 6487-6
The sleeping mansion. 6487-6
"The snow lies sprinkled on the beach". 6258-X,6487-6
"So sweet love seemed that April morn". 6187-7,6204-0, 6487-6,6199-0,6655-0,6656
"Sometimes when my lady sits by me". 6487-6
Song ("I love my lady's"). 6487-6
"A song of my heart, as the sun peered o'er the sea". 6487-6
"Sorrow and joy...". 6487-6
The south wind. 6487-6
Spirits. 6437-X
Spring goeth all in white. 6477-9,6478-7,6487-6,6253-9, 6581-3,6125
Spring, sels. 6487-6
"The storm is over, the land hushes to rest". 6487-6
The summer trees are tempest-born. 6487-6
"Sweet compassionate tears", fr. A hymn of nature. 6487-6
The tapestry. 6487-6
The testament of beauty, sels. 6317-9,6337-3,6483-3, 6487-6
Thanksgiving day. 6337-3
"Thee fair Poetry...", fr. Ode to music. 6487-6
"There is a hill beside the silver Thames". 6331-4,6477-9,6487-6,6430-2,6508-2,6655
"This world is unto God a work of art". 6186-9,6487-6
"Thou didst delight my eyes". 6179-6,6246-6,6487-6,6656-9,6655-0
To a socialist in London. 6487-6
To Catullus. 6487-6
To Francis Jammes. 6487-6
To Harry Ellis Wooldridge. 6487-6
To his excellency. 6487-6
To Joseph Joachim. 6487-6,6641-0
"To me, to me...", fr. Ode to music. 6487-6
"To my love I whisper, and say". 6487-6
To Percy Buck. 6487-6
To Robert Burns. 6487-6
To Sir Thos. Barlow, P.R.C.P. 6487-6
To the president of Magdalen college, Oxford. 6487-6
To the United States of America. 6946-0,7026-4
To Thos. Floyd. 6487-6
"To us, O Queen...", fr. Ode to music. 6487-6
Trafalgar Square. 6186-9,6487-6
The tramps. 6487-6
Triolet. 6094-3,6488-4,6507-4
Triolet ("All women"). 6487-6,6770-0
Triolet ("When first"). 6487-6,6770-0
"Turn, O return...", fr. Ode to music. 6487-6
The unillumined verge. 6085-4,6303-9
"The upper skies are palest blue". 6487-6
Verses written for Mrs. Daniel. 6487-6
A vignette ("Among the meadows"). 6487-6
A villager. 6487-6
Vision. 6487-6
Vivamus. 6487-6
The voice of nature. 6487-6
A water-party. 6487-6
"Weep not to-day: why should this sadness be". 6437-X, 6487-6
The west front. 6487-6
When death to either shall come. 6204-0,6482-5,6487-6
"When I see childhood on the threshold seize". 6844-8
"When June is come, then all the day". 6477-9,6487-6
"When my love was away." 6317-9,6487-6
"When thou didst give thy love to me". 6187-7
"When thou, my beloved, diedst, I saw heaven open". 6487-6
"Where San Miniato's convent from the sun". 6186-9
"Where thou art better I too were, dearest...". 6487-6
"Who builds a ship must first lay down...". 6289-X
"Who goes there? God knows. I'm nobody...". 6487-6
"Who has not walked upon the shore". 6487-6
"Why hast thou nothing in thy face". 6487-6
The widow. 6487-6
"Will Love again wake". 6487-6
The windmill. 6487-6,6668-2
The winnowers. 6487-6,6430-2,6508-2,6639-9
Winter. 7035-3
Winter nightfall. 6179-6,6246-6,6487-6,6506-6
"A winter's night with the snow about". 6487-6
Wintry delights. 6487-6
Wishes. 6487-6
Wooing. 6487-6
"Ye thrilled me once, ye mournful strains". 6487-6
"Yet shall his storm...", fr. Ode to music. 6487-6

Bridges, Robert (tr.)
At eventide. Unknown (German), 6337-3
Communion of saints. Andre Chenier, 6487-6
Communion of saints. Andre Chernier, 6487-6
Country music. Plato, 6435-3
Eros and Psyche. Lucius Apuleius, 6487-6
The Iliad, sels. Homer, 6487-6
"Mortal though I be, yea ephemeral...". Unknown, 6487-6
Povre ame amoureuse. Louise Labe, 6958-4,6487-6
Priam and Achilles, fr. The Iliad. Homer, 6435-3
Revenants. Unknown, 6487-6
Starry heavens without. Ptolemaeus, 6435-3
"These grey stones have rung with mirth...". Unknown, 6487-6
"Thousand threads of rain...". Unknown, 6487-6
"Thus sed-he, & Hermes hearing...", fr. The Iliad. Homer, 6487-6
"With these words Hermes sped...", fr. The Iliad. Homer, 6435-3

Bridges, Robert ("Droch")
Asian birds. 6656-9
A Christday day prayer. 6747-6
Elegy. 6508-2
Erwpiov axoos apoupns [Etosian achthos aroures]. 6210-5

Father to mother. 6006-4
The garden in september. 6649-6
Hector in Hades. 6143-2
The hothouse violet speaks. 6983-5
James McCosh. 6983-5
To a friend dying. 6006-4
To L.B.C.L.M. 6430-2
A toast to our native land. 6265-2
The towers of Princeton. 6983-5
Upon the shore. 6656-9
When first we met. 6396-9,6646-6
Bridge[s], Madeline. See De Vere, Mary Ainge
Bridget's mission jug. Emma Dunning Banks. 6426-4
Bridgett, Fr. (tr.)
Inscription on an ancient bell. Unknown, 6282-2
Bridgman, Amy Sherman
The christening. 6031-5
Bridgman, Betty
Border ballad. 6342-X
Bridgman, L.J.
On knowing when to stop. 6089-7
Bridgman, M.A.
God knoweth. 6304-7
Bridgman, Olive R.
A ballad of Weenen. 6625-9
Three ships. 6625-9
Bridgman, Theo.
His name was Keko. 6799-9
"The **bridle-reins** hang loose in the hold...". The boundary rider. Thomas Heney. 6784-0
Bridled. Cynthia Ozick. 6803-0
"**Brief** are the days and few". Notwithstanding. James Buckham. 7030-2
Brief biography. Marguerite George. 6218-0
A **brief** description. Harry Romaine. 7021-3
Brief enterprise. Alice Monks Mears. 6979-7
Brief for a future defense. Ben Belitt. 6640-2
Brief life. Ernest Dowson. 6274-1
Brief moment. Faith E. Packard. 6799-9
Brief pledge. Clarissa Hall. 6789-1
The **brief** present. Unknown (Greek) 6879-0
A **brief** puff of smoke. Selim. 6453-1
Brief worship. Virginia Scott Miner. 6750-6
The **brief.** Unknown. 6878-2
The **briefless** barrister. John Godfrey Saxe. 6724-7,6278-4, 6219-9
The **briefless** barrister. John Godfrey Saxe. 6878-2,6787-5
Brier. Emily Pauline ("Tekahionwake") Johnson. 6337-3
Brier-rose. Hjalmar Hjorth Boyesen. 6413-2,6550-3,6572-4
Brier-rose, sels. Hjalmar Hjorth Boyesen. 6614-3
The **brier.** Walter Savage Landor. 6980-0
Brierre, Jean
Areytos. 6178-8
Harlem. 6178-8
To Paul Robeson. 6178-8
Brierwood pipe. Charles Dawson Shanly. 6385-3
'The **brigade** must not know, sir!'. John James Piatt. 6113-3
'The **brigade** must not know, sir!' Unknown. 6946-0
'The **brigade** must not know, sir'. Unknown. 7017-5
The **brigand** leader and his wife. Felicia Dorothea Hemans. 6973-8
The **brigand's** grave. Unknown (Greek) 6771-9
Briggs Jr., Thomas H.
Inopportune. 6274-1
With you. 6274-1
Briggs, Edward A.
Beagles at twilight. 6761-1
Briggs, Ernest
The lonely child. 6384-5
While immortality endures. 6384-5
Briggs, George Wallace
Knowledge through suffering. 6337-3
Briggs, Greta
London under bombardment. 6427-2
Briggs, Le Baron Russell
1620-1920. 6762-X
Briggs, Margaret Perkins
Harvesters. 7038-8
In autumn ones. 6039-0

Old house. 7038-8
Pastures. 6040-4
"**Brighidin** Bhan of the lint-white locks". A northern love song. Seosamh Maccathmhaoil. 6873-1
Brighidin ban mo stor. Edward Walsh. 6174-5
"**Bright** and blooming as the spring". John Sheffield; Duke of Buckingham. 6544-9
"**Bright** as among the stars...", fr. The Iliad. Homer. 6606-2
Bright be the place of thy soul. George Gordon, 6th Baron Byron. 6543-0,6828-0
"**Bright** be the skies that cover thee". To Laura, two years of age. Nathaniel Parker Willis. 6752-2
"The **bright** blue water of the sea". The sandy soul. Josephine Sievers Birt. 6906-1
"**Bright** Dorothy, with eyes of blue". My grandchildren at church. Richard Wilton. 6770-0
"**Bright** cap and streamers", fr. Chamber Music. James Joyce. 6536-8
Bright day-grey day. William Shakespeare. 6634-8
"**Bright** flower! whose home is everywhere". To the daisy ("Bright flower"). William Wordsworth. 6199-0,6250-4
"**Bright** flowers, of varied tender-tinted hues". Cosmos. Francis Ernley Walrond. 6800-6
"**Bright** gloried children of the year's late...". Autumn leaves. William Wilfred Campbell. 6843-X
Bright hours. Margaret Husted. 6922-5
"The **bright** hours return...". The lament of Llywarch Hen [Llywarch the Aged]. Felicia Dorothea Hemans. 6973-8
Bright intervals. Jessie Haefner. 6799-9
The **bright** little dandelion. Unknown. 6530-9,6629-1
The **bright** moon. Conrad Aiken. 6253-9
"**Bright** Phoebus had risen and shone o'er the sea". Unknown. 6059-5
"A **bright** new church for god they made". Religion. Ruth Fenisong. 6818-9
"A **bright** or dark eternity in view". Live for eternity. Carlos Wilcox. 6752-2
"**Bright** portalles of the skie". An hymne of the ascension. William Drummond of Hawthornden. 6933-9
"A **bright** red pepper-pod - but lo!" Basho (Matsuo Basho) 6850-2
"**Bright** shine the golden summits in the light". A calm sea. Robert Southey. 6833-2
"**Bright** shines the sun; play, beggars, play!" A. W. 6181-8
Bright side. Unknown. 6304-7
The **bright** side. Edgar A. Guest. 6862-6
The **bright** side. Mary A. Kidder. 6260-1,6583-X,6404-3
"**Bright** skies, bright sea". In memoriam: A.F. Thomas Edward Brown. 6809-X
"**Bright** soule, instruct poore mortalls how to mourne." Unknown. 6563-5
Bright spirit. Josephine Royle. 6076-5
"**Bright** spirit now one hundred years at rest". Remembering Keats. Edward Sandford Burgess. 6847-2
Bright star! would I were steadfast as thou art. John Keats. 6154-0,6527-9,6726-3,6198-2,6154-0,6122 ,6246-6,6536-8,6208-3,6737-9,6110-9,6371 ,6122-2,6317-9, 6527-9,6726-3,6198-2,6154 ,6199-0,6196-6,6430-2,6560-0,6464-7,6646 ,6086-2,6491-4,6723-9
"**Bright** star, would I were steadfast as thou". Sonnet ("Bright star"). John Keats. 6052-8,6204-0,6659-3
"**Bright** Stella! form'd for universal reign". To Miss Hickman. Samuel Johnson. 6975-4
"**Bright** starre of Beauty, on whose eye-lids sit" Michael Drayton. 6586-4
"**Bright** sun! before whose glorious ray". Irish war-song. Edward Walsh. 6858-8
"**Bright** though the garden was and Eden-sweet". The autumn fire. Geoffrey Johnson. 6761-1
"**Bright** universe unseen, yet seen awhile". Renewal of fountains. Marya Alexandrovna Zaturenska. 6984-3
"**Bright** was the moon as from thy gates I went". Rouen. Edward Moxon. 6980-0
"**Bright** was the morning, and cool the air". Thomas D'Urfey. 6933-9
Bright, Henry Hepburn
Painted ladies. 6800-6
Bright, John
When I am dead. 6768-9

Bright, Verne
   A beggar in paradise. 6954-1
   Comrade Christ. 6144-3
Bright, W.
   Crowned and discrowned. 6046-3
The **brighter** day. Unknown. 6014-5
"**Brighter** than the sunshine on a...April day". Sunshine in the house. Clara Louise Burnham. 6965-7
Brightest and best of the sons of the morning. Reginald Heber. 6337-3,6730-1,6304-7,6214-8,6608-9
Brightest and best of the sons of the morning. Reginald Herber. 6239-3
"**Brightest** and best of the sons of the morning". Christmas hymn. Reginald Heber. 6980-0
"**Brightly** beams the moon to-night". Sleighing. Orrin Chalfont Painter. 7035-3
"**Brightly** for him the future smiled". Mother and son. Phoebe Cary. 6969-X
"**Brightly** the morning sunshine glowed". The wife, fr. Dovecote mill. Phoebe Cary. 6865-0;6969-X
Brightly thou hast fled. Felicia Dorothea Hemans. 6973-8
Brightness falls from the air. Thomas Nashe. 6733-6
"The **brightness** of blown water was her brow". Character. David Morton. 6779-4
Brighton pier. Clement Scott. 6652-6
Brightwen, E.
   Aunt Lizzie in who's who. 7020-5
Brigid, St. (atr.)
   The feast of Saint Brigid of Kildare. Eugene O'Curry (tr.). 6930-4
Brignal banks, fr. Rokeby. Sir Walter Scott. 6180-X,6102-8, 6186-9,6395-0,6458-2,6086 ,6428-8,6110-9
The **brigs** of Ayr, sels. Robert Burns. 6332-2,6484-1
The **brillancies** of winter. Thomas Love Peacock. 6334-9
Brimiga's woe. Benjamin Lee. 6936-3
Brinckerhoff, Julia
   A dream. 6686-0
Brind, John
   Merry little toddlekins. 6713-1
Brine, Mary D.
   Total annihilation. 6917-7
Brine, Mary Dow
   How little it costs. 6654-2
   March, and the boys. 6965-7
   The prettiest girl. 6167-2
   The road to slumber-land. 6078-1,6627-5
   Somebody's mother. 6451-5
   Total annihilation. 6426-4
   The valentine. 6404-3,6451-5
Bring back my flowers. Lucy Larcom. 6129-X
"**Bring** cypress, rosemary and rue". Grover Cleveland. Joel Benton. 6946-0
Bring flowers. Felicia Dorothea Hemans. 6973-8,6049-8
"**Bring** flowers, ye grateful millions of...land". Decoration ode. Ben Wood Davis. 6927-4
"**Bring** fluted asphodel," fr. Songs from Cyprus. Hilda ("H.D.") Doolittle. 6011-0
"**Bring** from the craggy haunts of birch & pine". Song ("Bring from"). John Todhunter. 6090-0,6437-X,6253-9
"**Bring** from the craggy haunts of birch...". O mighty, melancholy wind. John Todhunter. 6930-4
"**Bring** games". Vicente Huidobro. 6759-X
"**Bring** hemlock, black as Cretan cheese". Epigram. Robert Hillyer. 6722-0
Bring home the poet. Patrick MacDonough. 6930-4
Bring laurel. S.B. Dunn. 6709-3
"**Bring** me a tiny mouse's skin". Her fairy feet. Eugene Field. 6949-5
"**Bring** me my helmet and spear...". Via rosinante. Dorothy E. Reid. 6906-1
"**Bring** me some oranges on blue china". Siesta. William Kean Seymour. 6884-7
Bring me the sunset in a cup. Emily Dickinson. 6374-8
"**Bring** me the vinegar jug of water...". A young man to his wife. Clarence Lawson. 6761-1
"**Bring** music! stir the brooding air". Music at a deathbed. Felicia Dorothea Hemans. 6973-8
"**Bring** myrrh and myrtle bud," fr. Songs from Cyprus. Hilda ("H.D.") Doolittle. 6011-0
"**Bring** one rosette of alien mistletoe". For Noel. Beulah Allyne Bell. 6799-9
'**Bring** out your dead.' Margaret H. Lawless. 6690-9
"**Bring** the bowl which you boast". Here's a health to King Charles, fr. Woodstock. Sir Walter Scott. 6828-6
Bring us in good ale. Unknown. 6756-5,6881-2,6187-7,6732-8, 6733-6,6334-9,6732-8
"**Bring** us in no brown bread...". Unknown. 6334-9
"**Bring** with you, for me to have,a spray..olive". October letter. Helen Hoyt. 6777-8
"**Bring** your roses to the valley". Memorial day. Edgar A. Guest. 6862-6
"**Bring**, novelist, your note-book!". Women of Mumbles Head. Clement Scott. 6277-6,6661-5,6706-9,6964-9
Bringers of the hemlock. Stanton A. Coblentz. 6144-3
Brininstool, Earl Alonzo
   Act the man. 6109-5
   A cattle range at night. 6628-3
   Happiness. 6274-1
   His dad. 6889-8
   A prairie mother's lullaby. 6095-1
   Rock-a-by land. 6078-1
   The short-grass country. 6628-3
   The west for me. 6628-3
   When papa was a boy. 6964-9
   Where the sagebrush billows roll. 6628-3
Brink, Carol Ryrie
   The creche. 6608-9
Brinkley, May
   Pebbles ("Your little words"). 6041-2
Brinnin, John
   Prague. 6391-8
Brinnin, John Malcolm
   Every earthly creature. 6391-8
   For my pupils in the war years. 6391-8
   Observatory hill. 6391-8
   Prague. 6391-8
   Views of the favorite colleges. 6391-8
Brinninstool, E. A.
   The ol' cow hawse. 7010-8
Brinton, D.G. (tr.)
   A dance chant. Unknown (Osage Indians), 6730-1
Brisby, Stewart
   The artist. 6870-7
   Attica is. 6870-7
   The cyclone. 6870-7
   Poem for Edie Sedgwick who slep in a swimming pool. 6870-7
   Public school 168 6870-7
Briscoe, W.A.
   'What think ye?' 6846-4
Briseis. Charles Williams. 6884-7
"**Brisk** as a plague of frogs, the pale-skinned". Furnace wharf. Geoffrey Johnson. 6761-1
"**Briskly** and lightly". Fall leaves. Josephine Franco. 6850-2
"**Brissit** brawnis and broken banis". The bewteis of the flute-ball. Unknown. 6845-6
Brister, Iola M.
   Epigram. 6178-8
   A Negro speaks of night. 6178-8
The **Bristol** channel, fr. Clevedon verses. Thomas Edward Brown. 6809-X
A **Bristol** figure. Cosmo Monkhouse. 6677-1
Bristol, George Digby, 2d Earl of
   Song ("See, O see!"). 6563-5,6389-3,6385-3
Bristol, John Digby, 1st Earl of
   Grieve not, dear love. 6563-5
Bristol, Mrs. Royal A.
   Little Martha Washington. 6712-3
Bristowe tragedie: or, the death of Syr Charles Bawdin. Thomas Chatterton. 6086-2,6152-4,6438-8
Bristowe tragedie: or, the death of Syr Charles Bawdin, sels. Thomas Chatterton. 6191-5
Bristowe tragedie; or, the dethe of Syr Charles... Thomas Chatterton. 6198-2
Brita's wedding. W.W. Marsh. 6166-4
Britain ("There is a beauty time cannot destroy"). A.M. Stephen. 6224-5
"**Britain!** you with a heart of flame". To Great Britain. Hardwicke Drummond Rawnsley. 7031-0

Britain, France, America. Henry Van Dyke. 6961-4
Britain, part 004, fr. Liberty. James Thomson. 6816-2
Britain-to the empire (1924). Alfred Noyes. 6169-9
Britannia. James Thomson. 6816-2
Britannia ("Men deemed her changed, and lo!"). H. de Vere Stacpoole. 6224-5
Britannia rediviva;..the birth of James Prince of Wales. John Dryden. 6970-3
Britannia rules of orthography. Firth. 6722-0
Britannia to Columbia. Alfred Austin. 6946-0
Britannia victrix. Robert Bridges. 6487-6
Britannia's empire, fr. Britannia. James Thomson. 6932-0
"Britannia's gallant streamers". Yankee thunders. Unknown. 6946-0
Britannia's pastorals, sels. William Browne. 6198-2,6547-3, 6649-6,6034-X
"Britannia, mother, hear our joyous hymn". A hymn of love. Richard Hope. 7031-0
A brithday greeting. Helen Bosanquet. 7042-6
The British army of 1914. Alfred W. Pollard. 6846-4
"The British bard who looked on Eton's walls". Spirit of the everlasting boy. Henry Van Dyke. 6961-4
The British bow. Reginald Heber. 6980-0
British Canada to Mr. Louis H. Frechette. John Reade. 7041-8
British climate and freedom. Oliver Goldsmith. 6935-5
British commerce. John Dyer. 6932-0
British commerce, fr. Liberty. James Thomson. 6932-0
British freedom. William Wordsworth. 6634-8
The British grenadier. Unknown. 6946-0
The British grenadiers. Unknown. 6105-2
The British heritage. William Wordsworth. 6793-X
The British light infantry. Unknown. 6589-9,6008-0
The British lyon roused. Stephen Tilden. 6946-0
British merchant service. Cicely Fox Smith. 7026-4
British merchant service, 1915. Cicely Fox Smith. 7031-0
The British Museum reading room. Louis MacNeice. 6666-6
British oak. Bernard Barton. 6304-7
The British prison ship, sels. Philip Freneau. 6753-0
The British prison ship, sels. Philip Freneau. 6008-0,6288-1
The British prison ship, sels. Philip Freneau. 6753-0
"A British ship at anchor lay". The nine suitors. Unknown. 6927-4
"British soldiers, once again". To the British Expeditionary Force. Ronald Gorell Barnes, Lord Gorell. 7029-9
The British tar. Sir William Schwenck Gilbert. 6026-9
British tribute to Lincoln. Tom Taylor. 6260-1
British war song. F.G. Scott. 7041-8
Briton, Eloise
 To my vagrant love. 6327-6
"A Briton, even in love, should be/A subject". Ere with cold beads of midnight dew, sels. William Wordsworth. 6867-7
Britons beyond the seas. Harold Begbie. 6793-X
"Britons grown bid with pride". A poem containing some remarks on the present war. Unknown. 6946-0
"Britons who dare to claim". Unknown. 6859-6
"Britons, guard your own. Alfred Lord Tennyson. 6977-0
"Britons, now retrieve your glory". Unknown. 6859-6
Britons, strike home!, fr. Bonduca. John Fletcher. 6328-4
Brittain, Robert E.
 Attitude. 6397-7
 Casual suggestion. 6397-7
 Light and shadow. 6397-7
 Mood. 6397-7
 A silver bowl. 6397-7
Brittany, fr. Geography. Edward Verrall Lucas. 6018-8
Britten, Rollo
 Bird of passion. 6897-9
"Brittle beauty, that nature made so frail." Henry Howard, Earl of Surrey. 6584-8
Brittle, Gath
 'It war crackit afore.' 6687-9
Britton, Donald
 History. 7003-5
 Sonnet. 7003-5
Brizeux, Auguste
 Invocation. 6801-4

Marie. 6801-4
"Broad expanse of shiny shirt-front". Romance of a 'cuss-word'. Eugene Field. 6949-5
"A broad green sea the vineyard lay". Anita, fr. In Tuscany. Cora Fabri. 6876-6
"The broad of silvery noon!". Going to the spelling school. Benjamin Franklin Taylor. 6815-4
"Broad on the sunburnt hill". Sonnet ("Broad"). Conrad Aiken. 6012-9
"Broad smiles that flash at sight of cash". Dimensions. Berton Braley. 6853-7
"Broad were the bases of all being laid". Evolution. Hjalmar Hjorth Boyesen. 7041-8
Broadcast to the scholars in the eyrie. David Ross. 6979-7
The broadcast. John W. Simons. 6839-1
Broadhead, Grace Lowe
 I know. 6906-1
 Make way for spring! 6906-1
 Nocturne. 6906-1
 Only a day! 6906-1
 The typhoon. 6906-1
Broadside and street ditties, sels. Thomas Lovell Beddoes. 6334-9
The broadswords of Scotland. John Gibson Lockhart. 6302-0, 6219-9
Broadway. William Allen Butler. 6484-1
Broadway. Elizabeth J. Coatsworth. 6808-1
Broadway. Hermann Hagedorn. 6250-4
Broadway. Edith M. Thomas. 6484-1
Broadway. Nathaniel Parker Willis. 6934-7
A Broadway pageant. Walt Whitman. 6126-5
"Broadway reaches northward from fair bowling". Dutchman's quirk. Arthur Guiterman. 6773-5
Broadway's canyon. John Gould Fletcher. 6289-X
Brock. Charles Sangster. 6433-7,6115-X
Brock, David
 For the dead on the mountains. 6761-1
Brock, S.A.
 Out of the window. 6927-4
Brock: valiant leader. John Daniel Logan. 6115-X
Brockes, Barthold Heinrich
 Kirschblute bie nacht. 6253-9
Brod, Max
 Goldfish on the writing desk. Babette Deutsch (tr.). 6160-5
Brodie, E.H.
 The breakers. 6997-5
 Childhood, fr. By the sea. 6997-5
 "A glorious headland bare to sun and sky". 6997-5
 "Therefore sound on, whether with crash and din". 6997-5
 Tidal music. 6997-5
 "To the evening's golden gate". 6997-5
Brodie, Hugh R.
 An airman's prayer. 6337-3
Brodribb, C.W.
 Expeditional. 7027-2
Brody, Alter
 Portrait of the artist as a ghost. 6040-4
 Psalm 151. 6532-5
Brody, Ella
 The window. 6750-6
Brogan's lane. Louis Esson. 6784-0
The broke brigade. Frank Lillie Pollock. 7012-4
Broken. Virginia Stait. 6038-2
A broken appointment. Thomas Hardy. 6506-6,6657-7,6150-8
The broken appointment. John Kenyon. 6980-0
The broken banjo. Warren Fenno Gregory. 6116-8
"Broken battle vessels sinking with the". 'Kishinex' Strickland Gillilan. 6848-0
Broken birds. Tracy Martin. 6883-9
Broken bodies. Louis Golding. 6337-3,6490-6
The broken chain. Felicia Dorothea Hemans. 6973-8
The broken charm. Joshua Sylvester. 6383-7
A broken child from heaven. Connie Mann. 6898-7
The broken dish, fr. Domestic didactics. Thomas Hood. 6974-6
The broken dish. Thomas Hood. 6092-7
The broken doll. Christina Georgina Rossetti. 6891-X
Broken drake. Lew Sarett 6076-5

BROKEN

Broken dreams. Morris Abel Beer. 6347-0
Broken dreams. Celestin Pierre Cambiaire. 6826-X
Broken dreams. Mary Kyle Dallas. 6671-2
Broken fiddle. Pierre Jean de Beranger. 6949-5
The broken field. Sara Teasdale. 6030-7
The broken flower. Felicia Dorothea Hemans. 6973-8
The broken heart, sels. John Ford. 6198-2,6562-7,6472-8, 6186-9
A broken heart. John Ford. 6830-8
The broken heart. Thomas Beedome. 6933-9
The broken heart. John Ford. 6934-7
The broken heart. James Hogg. 6980-0
"A broken kite/Caught in a tree". A kite. Irene Davis Grueninger. 6906-1
Broken line. Andre Breton. 6351-9
Broken lines. Benjamin Rosenbaum. 6038-2
The broken lute. Felicia Dorothea Hemans. 6973-8
The broken men. Rudyard Kipling. 6810-3
"The broken moon lay in the autumn sun". To - ("The broken moon"). Alexander Smith. 6960-6
The broken mug. John Esten Cooke. 6074-9
Broken music, fr. The house of life. Dante Gabriel Rossetti. 6655-0
The broken pianola. Ralph Gustafson. 6767-0
The broken pinion. Hezekiah Butterworth. 6260-1,6337-3
The broken pitcher. William Edmonstoune Aytoun. 6948-7
The broken pitcher. Unknown. 6914-2
Broken promise. Sarah Morgan Bryan Piatt. 7041-8
The broken ring. Eugene Field. 6949-5
The broken soldier. Katharine (Hinkson) Tynan. 7031-0
A broken song. Moira (Nesta Higginson Skrine) O'Neill. 6437-X,6490-6,6732-8,6182-8,6513-9
The broken spell, fr. The story of Baladeadro. George Gordon McCrae. 6768-9
The broken sword. W.R. Titterton. 6884-7
The broken tie, fr. Pictures of women. Agnes Lee. 6033-1
The broken token. Unknown. 6518-X
The broken tower. Hart Crane. 6399-3,6641-0
Broken trees. Edna Davis Romig. 6836-7
The broken tryst. Francis Ledwidge. 6812-X
Broken voices. Lynette Roberts. 6360-8
The broken wall. L. Ashton Thorp. 6764-6
The broken water-wheel. Al-Hajjam. 6362-4
The broken wing. Unknown. 6304-7
"Broken wings in flaming sky". Requiem of the air. Robert Allison Evans. 6761-1
A broken-down actor. John Ferguson. 6269-5
Broken-face gargoyles. Carl Sandburg. 6217-2
The broken-hearted gardener. Unknown. 6125-7
Broken-hearted, weep no more. Unknown. 6752-2
Broker cupid. Frank Dempster Sherman. 6441-8
Brokken, David
  First snowfall. 6857-X
Broman, Jessie Goddard
  Open-pit mine. 6342-X
Bromberger, Anna
  "And so he lingered on the trackless way". 6847-2
  "I am to you all things majestical". 6847-2
Brome, Alexander
  I have been in love and in debt. 6328-4,6026-9
  Love's without reason. 6562-7
  Love, drink, and debt. 6427-2
  The mad lover. 6562-7,6633-X
  A mock song. 6563-5
  Now I'm resolved. 6328-4,6026-9
  The pastoral on the king's death...1648. 6933-9
  Plain dealing. 6933-9
  The resolve. 6317-9
  The riddle. 6933-9,6793-X,6933-9,6793-X
  Song of the beggars. 6563-5
  "Tell me not of a face that's fair". 6187-7
  To a coy lady. 6874-X
  Why I love her. 6317-9
Brome, Richard
  Beggars' song. 6334-9
  The forsaken maid. 6328-4
  Love unaccountable. 6092-7
  The merry beggars. 6189-3,6252-0
  Song ("Peace, wayward barne"). 6563-5
Bromeliad. Cathy Matyas. 6767-0

Bromley, Beatrice Marian
  Camp fire. 6800-6
  Camp fire. 6625-9
  Chant of the blue-gums. 6800-6
  Lament of the veld. 6800-6
  Nachtmaal eve. 6800-6
  Trekkers. 6800-6,6625-9
The broncho that would not be broken of dancing. Vachel Lindsay. 6031-5,6299-7,6162-1,6619-4,6732-8,6393 , 6102-8,6076-5,6107-9,6161-3,6510-4,6467
Bronk, W.M.
  Apologia for a druid. 6764-6
  The fungi. 6764-6
  A winter's tail. 6764-6
Bronson, Carrie E.
  Turning. 6927-4
Bronson, Carrie W.
  Housecleaning. 6707-7,6711-5
  Jack Frost's little sister. 6713-1
  Lady golden-rod. 6049-8,6629-1
  What Bessie saw. 6745-X
Bronte, Anne
  The captain's dream. 6648-8
  The doubter's prayer. 6337-3,6730-1,6214-8
  He doeth all things well. 6303-9,6337-3
  A hope. 6337-3
  A prayer. 6656-9
Bronte, Charlotte
  Christ in introspect. 6337-3
  Good cheer. 6424-8
  He saw my heart's woe. 6641-0
Bronte, Emily
  Anticipation. 6123-0
  The appeal. 6315-2
  At castle wood. 6655-0
  The bluebell. 6123-0
  "The captive raised her face...", fr. The prisoner. 6123-0
  "Child of delight, with sun-bright hair". 6123-0
  A day dream. 6648-8
  Death. 6023-4
  Death. 6123-0
  A death scene. 7037-X,6832-4
  A death-scene. 6828-6
  The elder's rebuke. 6123-0
  Encouragement. 6123-0
  Enough of thought, philosopher. 6380-2
  The evening primrose. 6253-9
  Faith and despondency. 6828-6
  Fall, leaves, fall. 6246-6,6315-2
  Harp of wind and dream-like strain. 6655-0
  Heaven's glory shone. 6828-6
  Her last lines. 6656-9
  How clear she shines. 6655-0
  How clear she shines, sels. 6123-0
  How long will you remain? 6655-0
  I am the only being whose doom. 6317-9,6380-2,6655-0
  I gazed upon the cloudless moon. 6125-7
  I know not how it falls on me. 6655-0
  "I'll think, there's not one world above",fr How clear. 6123-0
  I've been wandering. 6253-9
  If grief can touch thee. 6908-8
  The lady to her guitar. 6123-0
  Last hymn. 6424-8
  Last lines. 6090-0,6123-0,6186-9,6337-3,6339-X,6418 , 6102-8,6250-4,6383-7,6150-8,6543-0,6301 ,6437-X,6501-5,6726-3,6730-1,6723-9,6214
  Lines. 6648-8
  Lines ("Shall earth"). 6315-2
  Lines by Claudia. 6648-8
  "A little while, a little while". 6123-0,6244-X,6430-2
  "Loud without the wind was roaring". 6123-0
  Love and friendship. 6246-6
  The morning star. 6125-7
  My lady's grave. 6437-X
  The night is darkening. 6828-6
  The night-wind. 6380-2,6430-2,6125-7
  "No coward soul is mine". 6844-8
  "No coward soul is mine." 6138-9,6244-X,6208-3,6430-2,

6199-0,6655
Oh for the time when I shall sleep, fr. The philosopher. 6472-8
"O, stars, and dreams, and gentle night", fr. Stars. 6123-0
"Oh, fairly spread thy early sail", fr. The wanderer. 6123-0
The old stoic. 6123-5,6437-X,6501-5,6543-0,6430-2,6250 , 6383-7,6396-9,6646-1,6656-9,6123-5,6437-X,6501-5, 6543-0,6430-2,6250 ,6383-7,6396-9,6646-1,6656-9
The outcast mother. 6123-0
The philosopher, sels. 6879-0
The philosopher, sels. 6472-8
The philosopher. 6828-6
The philosopher. 6655-0
Plead for me? 6828-6
The prisoner. 6186-9,6246-6,6437-X,6250-4,6648-8,6301 , 6383-7,6430-2,6186-9,6246-6,6250-4,6301-2
Redbreast, early in the morning. 6380-2
Remembrance. 6046-3,6109-6,6150-8,6430-2,6090-0,6204-0, 6208-3,6246-6,6271-7,6244 ,6317-9,6481-7,6655-0,6102-8,6472-8,6723
Self-interrogation. 6828-6
"Shall earth no more inspire thee". 6246-6
Silent is the house. 6179-6,6732-8
Sleep not, dream not. 6315-2
Song. 6656-9
Song ("The linnet in the rocky dells"). 6123-0,6430-2
Speak, God of visions. 6844-8
Stanzas. 6437-X,6150-8,6656-9,6543-0
Stanzas ("Often rebuked"). 6828-6
Stanzas ("I'll not weep"). 6123-0,6315-2
Stanzas ("Often rebuked"). 6208-3,6315-2,6430-2
Stanzas to --- ("Well, some may hate..."). 6315-2
Stanzas to---. 6123-0
Stars, sels. 6123-0
"Still let my tyrants, I am not doom'd to". 6187-7
Sympathy. 6430-2
Tell me, tell me. 6315-2,6430-2
That dreary lake. 6655-0
That wind, I used to hear. 6828-6
There was a time. 6828-6
To a bluebell. 6655-0
To imagination. 6655-0
The visionary. 6246-6,6315-2,6317-9,6378-0,6641-0,6430 , 6648-8
The wanderer from the fold, sels. 6123-0
The wanderer from the fold. 6828-6
Warning and reply. 6244-X,6437-X,6641-0,6655-0,6656-9
The weary task. 6828-6
Bronte, Patrick
The cottager's hymn. 6337-3
The **bronze** Christ. Clinton Scollard. 6335-7
Bronze law. Je-chun Park. 6775-1
Bronze queen. Gertrude Parthenia McBrown. 6178-8
"**Bronzed** by the western sun, and wind...". The Madonna of the plains. Honora Carroll Hurd. 6750-6
"**Brood**, brood on this". The fountain. Lynn Riggs. 6808-1
Brooding. Jan Svatopluk Machar. 6886-3
Brooding grief. David Herbert Lawrence. 6315-2
"The **brook** and road/Were fellow-travellers". Defile of Gondo, fr. The prelude. William Wordsworth. 6832-4
The **brook** behind the Waumbek house. Martha P. Lowe. 6965-7
Brook farm. Nathaniel Hawthorne. 6484-1
A **brook** in the city. Robert Frost. 6010-2,6510-4
The **brook** in winter, fr. The vision of Sir Launfal. James Russell Lowell. 6239-3
Brook nostalgia. Herbert Edward Palmer. 6893-6
The **brook** Rhine. Augusta Webster. 6749-2,7015-9,6749-2, 7015-9
A **brook** song. Eugene Field. 6273-3
The **brook** song. James Whitcomb Riley. 6143-5
Brook sound at evening. August Derleth. 6783-2
The **brook** that ran into the sea. Lucy Larcom. 6129-X
The **brook** that runs to France. John Clair Minot. 6032-3;6478-7
Brook's song. Unknown. 6312-8
The **brook**, sels. Alfred Lord Tennyson. 6339-X
The **brook-song**. James Whitcomb Riley. 6991-6
The **brook**.. John Banister Tabb. 6473-6

The **brook**. Eugene Field. 6949-5
The **brook**. Gertrude Huntington McGiffert. 6838-3
The **brook**. Alfred Lord Tennyson. 6543-0,6668-2,6456-6,6569-4,6639-9,6424 ,6114-1,6421-3,6135-4,6192-3,6199-0, 6250 ,6560-0,6808-1,6110-9,6196-6,6133-8,6332-2,6479-5,6498-1,6239-3,6597 ,6228-8,6127-3,6136-2,6334-9, 6401-9,6459 ,6334-9,6478-7,6501-5,6504-X,6423-X,6623
The **brook**. William Wordsworth. 6543-0
Brooke, Arthur Spayd
Lines ("Though the night"). 6936-3
May-day. 6936-3
The red and blue. 6936-3
Brooke, Baron. See Greville, Fulke
Brooke, Brian ("Korongo")
'Better love --'. 6938-X
Blood of our fathers. 6938-X
'The bush crank'. 6938-X
'Bush versus London'. 6938-X
'call of the wild'. 6938-X
Coward. 6938-X
The dying pioneer. 6938-X
The fall of the mighty. 6938-X
A father's advice. 6650-X
'A father's advice'. 6938-X
'For the sake of a joke'. 6938-X
The great adventure. 6938-X
A hunter's requiem. 6938-X
The hunter. 6938-X
In adversity. 6938-X
'Magadi'. 6938-X
The missing something. 6938-X
'Nature'. 6938-X
The new year. 6938-X
'On the Loita plains'. 6938-X
Only a volunteer. 6650-X
'Only a volunteer'. 6938-X
The outlaw: or, a night on the German border. 6938-X
A rolling stone. 6938-X
Smoke of the camp fire. 6788-3
'Smoke of the camp fire'. 6938-X
The song of the bamboos. 6938-X
'That ride'. 6938-X
"The thing that I knew". 6938-X
'Through other eyes'. 6938-X
'Under the mists of the Kenia snow'. 6938-X
Waiting for news on the frontier. 6938-X
When two pals part. 6938-X
'When you're down'. 6938-X
The whine of the boozer. 6938-X
Brooke, Caris
Cradle song. 6373-X
Brooke, Charlotte
Pulse of my heart. 6090-0
Brooke, Charlotte (tr.)
Ah! What woes are mine. Edmond O'Ryan, 6930-4
Brooke, Louise
brick-dust. 6034-X
Brooke, Rupert
All this is ended. 6051-X
Beauty and beauty. 6234-2
The busy heart. 6339-X
A channel passage. 6258-X,6210-5
The Chilterns. 6508-2
Clouds. 6234-2
The dead ("Blow out, you bugles"), fr. 1914. 6250-4
The dead ("These hearts were woven"), fr. 1914. 6250-4
The dead, I. 6224-5,6332-2,6653-4
The dead, II. 6224-5,6332-2,6161-3,6653-4
The dead. 6214-8,6491-4,6301-2,6542-2,6371-3,6464 ,6044-7,6051-X,6465-5,6477-9,6427-2,6393
Dear, they have poached the eyes you loved so well. 6722-0
Death. 6730-1
Dining-room tea. 6234-2
Dust. 6234-2,6437-X,6026-9
Finding. 6320-9
The fish. 6234-2,6510-4
The funeral of youth: threnody. 6210-5
Gifts of the dead. 6650-X
The great lover, sels. 6491-4

BROOKE
190

The great lover. 6044-7,6234-2,6332-2,6477-9,6732-8,
    6538 ,6154-0,6320-9,6476-0,6506-6,6464-7,6666 ,6508-
    2,6653-4
The great lover. 6102-8
Heaven. 6199-0
Heaven ("Fish fly-replete, in depth of June"). 6234-2,
    6426-6,6339-X,6730-1,6733-6,6199
The hill. 6153-2,6301-2,6659-3
If I should die. 6538-4
The little dog's day. 6228-8
Mary and Gabriel. 6282-2
Mummia. 6581-3
Mutability. 6508-2
Nineteen-fourteen. 6153-2
Not with vain tears. 7031-0
"Now, God be thank'd who has match'd us with his hour"
    6138-9
The old vicarage, Grantchester. 6234-2,6331-4,6477-9,
    6508-2,6723-9
The one before the last. 6437-X
1914, sels. 6250-4
Peace. 6051-X,6199-0,6337-3,6730-1,6051-X,6199-0,6301-2,
    6337-3,6508-2,6650
Pine trees and the sky: evening. 6266-0,6332-2,6332-2
Retrospect. 6897-9
Safety. 6653-4
Second best. 6437-X
The soldier ("If I should die, think only this of me").
    6250-4,6371-3,6581-3,6161-3,6396-9,6371 ,6650-X,6668-
    2,6542-2,6646-1,6639-9,6666 ,6023-4,6102-8,6104-4,
    6250-4,6199-0,6301 ,6044-7,6051-X,6224-5,6234-2,6303-
    9,6509 ,6332-2,6477-9,6052-8,6154-0,6208-3,6289 ,
    6337-3,6470-0,6506-6,6527-9,6726-3,6732
Song ("Oh! Love"). 6266-0
The song of the pilgrims. 6334-9,6532-5
Sonnet ("I said"). 6508-2
Sonnet ("Not with vain tears"). 6234-2
Sonnet ("Oh! death"). 6250-4
Tiare Tahiti. 6234-2,6508-2
Town and country. 6234-2
The treasure. 6250-4
Wagner. 6375-6
Brooke, Stopford Augustus
    At last. 6321-7,6429-9
    Courage. 6303-9,6730-1
    The earth and man. 6090-0,6250-4,6478-7
    The jungfrau's cry. 6656-9
    May and love. 6066-8
    Nature and love. 6090-0
    The noble lay of Aillinn. 6090-0
    Prince Riquet's song, fr. Riquet of the tuft. 6656-9
    Queen's song, fr. Riquet of the tuft. 6656-9
    Riquet of the tuft, sels. 6656-9
    Song, fr. Six days. 6873-1
    Versailles (1784). 6656-9
Brooke, Stopford Augustus (tr.)
    The storm on sea. Unknown, 6334-9
    "Whiles, my way I take...". Unknown, 6334-9
Brooker, Louisa J.
    A party. 6249-0
Brookfield. William E. Marshall. 6115-X
The brooklet. Sir Robert Grant. 6302-0;6385-3
The Brooklyn at Santiaga. Wallace Rice. 6946-0
Brooklyn Bridge. Sir Charles George Douglas Roberts. 6484-
    1
The Brooklyn Bridge. Edna Dean Proctor. 6946-0
The Brooklyn bridge. Edna Dean Proctor. 7041-8
The Brooklyn Bridge. Henry Firth Wood. 6247-4
Brooklynese champion. Margaret Fishback. 6722-0
Brooks, Alice
    Herod. 6576-7
Brooks, Andrew
    For Barbara. 6767-0
Brooks, Charles Shirley
    Home they brought her lap-dog dead. 7025-6
    The philosopher and his daughter. 6385-3
Brooks, Charles Timothy
    The fisherman's hut. 7022-1
    God save the state. 6171-0
    The old thirteen. 6916-9

Our native land. 6449-3
A plea for Flood Ireson. 6946-0
Brooks, Charles Timothy (tr.)
    Alpine heights. Friedrich Adolf Krummacher, 6302-0;6385-
    3
    The blind steed. Unknown (German), 6131-1
    The fisher. Johann Wolfgang von Goethe, 6302-0;6385-3
    Good night. Karl [or Charles] Theodore Korner, 6302-
    0;6385-3
    The greeting of Kynast. Friedrich Ruckert, 6613-5
    Hermann and Thusnelda. Friedrich Gottlieb Klopstock,
    6302-0;6385-3
    The monk of Heisterbach. Karl Wilhelm Muller, 6614-3
    Night song. Matthias Claudius, 6271-7
    The nobleman and the pensioner. Gottlieb K. Pfeffel,
    6302-0,6385-3
    Nurse's watch. Unknown (German), 6302-0;6385-3
    Seeing and not seeing. Unknown, 6402-7
    The sword song. Karl [or Charles] Theodore Korner, 6302-
    0,6385-3
    Time not to be recalled. Unknown, 6402-7
    The widow. Christian Furchtegott Gellert, 6279-2
    Wilhelm Tell, sels. Johann C. Friedrich von Schiller,
    6484-1
    Winter song. Unknown (German), 6302-0;6385-3
Brooks, Charles William Shirley
    Dixit, et in mensam-. 6092-7
    For a'that and a'that. 6802-2
    To my five new kittens. 6802-2
Brooks, Edward
    Be a woman. 6575-9
Brooks, Elbridge Streeter
    Caesar Rodney's ride. 6621-6
    The Liberty bell. 6552-X
    Rodney's ride. 6922-3
    Rodney's ride. 6614-3,6744-1
Brooks, Florence
    The steel age. 6327-6
Brooks, Francis
    Down the Little Big Horn. 6062-5
    Jesus wept. 6274-1
    Livingstone. 6274-1
    Love and hope. 6274-1
    Mount Rainier. 6484-1
Brooks, Fred Emerson
    Barnyard melodies. 6921-5,6695-X
    The California flea. 6923-1
    The dog sale. 6701-8
    Don't you think so, Bill? 6579-1
    Drummer boy of the Rappahannock. 6707-7
    Foreign views of the statue. 6451-5,6687-9,6920-7
    Foreigners at the fair. 6691-7
    The funeral of the mountains. 6674-7
    The ghost of an old continental. 6920-7
    The jealous wife. 6921-5
    Jennie. 6670-4
    The kindergarten tot. 6702-6
    A man's debt. 6097-8
    The miller's maid. 6921-5,6682-8
    The miracle of Cana. 6922-3,6682-8
    'Oh, yeh-yus!' 6694-1
    Old ace. 6672-0
    Old ace. 6924-X
    The orthod-ox team. 6451-5,6687-9
    Paddy Moore. 6683-6
    Palestine. 6672-0
    The remainder of the year. 6694-1
    Shall Bess come hame? 6921-5
    The sheriff of Cerro-Gordo. 6687-9
    Silly Billy. 6691-7
    The stuttering lover. 6697-6
    Tramp and cur. 6710-7
    Uncle Eph's heaven. 6683-6
    Watchin' the sparkin'. 6280-6
    The whistling boy. 6701-8
Brooks, Jerry
    Minutes. 6799-9
Brooks, Josephine S.
    On the desert. 6894-4
Brooks, Louise Upham

Crowns. 6144-3
Brooks, Maria Gowen
   "Day, in melting purple dying." 6302-0;6385-3
   Disappointment. 6385-3
   Song ("Day, in melting"). 6271-7,6219-9
   Song of Egla. 6077-3,6300-4
   Zophiel, sels. 6077-3,6102-8,6076-5
Brooks, Mary A.
   A song of spring. 6764-6
Brooks, Mrs. James Gorden
   Hebrew melody. 6848-0,6752-2
Brooks, Mrs. Pope
   I planted flowers today. 7016-7
   Westward. 7016-7
   Youth and age. 7016-7
Brooks, Phillips
   The beautiful island of Ceylon. 6373-X
   Bethlehem. 6006-4
   The child of Bethlehem. 6007-2
   Christmas carol ("The earth has grown old..."). 6608-9, 6145-1,6337-3,6466-3,6692-5,6449-3,6654
   Christmas everywhere. 6337-3
   Christmas once is Christmas still. 6746-6
   Easter angels. 6225-3
   Easter morning. 6337-3
   Everywhere, everywhere Christmas tonight. 6465-5,6747-6
   "How silently, how silently." 6225-3
   O little town of Bethlehem. 6746-8,6278-4,6145-1,6183-4, 6239-3,6466-3,6486-8,6730 ,6143-5,6608-9,6456-6,6337-3
   Our burden bearer. 6337-3,6525-2
   Present and future faiths. 6424-8
   The voice of the Christ-child. 6747-6
Brooks, S.
   Havelock. 6323-3
Brooks, Shirley
   Bayonet and chisel. 6760-3
   A dreary song. 6440-X
   The policeman's tear. 6760-3
   Saint Pancras bell. 6424-8
   A vision of siren soup. 6760-3
   Waggawocky. 6440-X
Brooks, William E.
   The angel that missed Christmas. 6039-0
   Memorial Day. 6037-4,6337-3,6465-5,6449-3,6542-2
   Pilate remembers. 6779-4
   The rich young ruler questions. 6039-0
   The shrine of the lion. 6995-9
   Spoil. 6532-5
   Three wise kings. 6144-3
Brooks, William Grant
   Tramp musician. 6702-6
"Brooks, for they call'd you so that knew you". To the Rev. W.H. Brookfield. Alfred Lord Tennyson. 6977-0
The **brookside**. Richard Monckton Milnes; 1st Baron Houghton. 6658-5,6543-0,6321-7,6396-9,6656-9,6385-3, 6429-9,6260-1,6240-7,6600-3,6620 ,6219-9,6226-1,6737-9
The **broom** flower. Mary Howitt. 6271-7,6302-0,6385-3,6424-8
"The **broom** looks tattered and tired to-day". The cat and the broom. A.A. Kenny. 6804-9
The **broom** of Cowdenknowes. Unknown. 6180-X,6185-0
The **broom** of the Cowdenknowes. Robert Crawford. 6960-6
Broome, J.
   M. E. Medley. 6468-X
Broome, William
   Habakkuk's prayer. 6848-0
   The rose-bud. 6932-0,6315-2,6152-4
The **broomfield** hill. Unknown. 6185-0,6518-4
Broomstick train; or return of the witches. Oliver Wendell Holmes. 6254-7,6698-8,6332-2,6126-5
Broomwell, Myron
   Precaution. 6751-4
Brophy, Liam
   Assumpta est Maria. 6282-2
Brophy, Liam (tr.)
   Notre dame des petits. Louis Mercier, 6282-2
Brosius, Letitia W.
   Spare the youth. 6685-2
Brother (pseud.)

   Evidence. 6662-3
   Familiar things. 6662-3
   If we could hear with God. 6662-3
   Little towns at dusk. 6662-3
   Mountain women. 6662-3
   Of all good medicines I label best. 6662-3
   Our grief will pass. 6662-3
   To losers of Earth and God. 6662-3
   Who die, loving the good earth. 6662-3
   Winter twilight. 6662-3
Brother and sister. Charles Lutwidge ("Lewis Carroll") Dodgson. 6125-7
Brother and sister. George (Mary Ann Cross) Eliot. 6772-7
Brother and sister. George (Mary Ann Cross) Eliot. 6233-4, 6239-3,6424-8,6321-7,6429-9,6429-9
Brother and sister, sels. George (Mary Ann Cross) Eliot. 6543-0
"**Brother** bards of every region". Aurum potabile. Bayard Taylor. 6976-2,6848-0
Brother beasts. Cale Young Rice. 6510-4
Brother Ben. Robert C.V. Meyers. 6919-3
Brother bunnies. B.R. M. 6937-1
Brother death. Edward Dowden. 7015-9
Brother fire. Louis MacNeice. 6357-8,6209-1,6665-8
Brother Gian. Cale Young Rice. 6326-8
A **brother** gone. Gene Baker. 6995-9
Brother Hubert. Unknown. 6614-3
Brother Jonathan's lament for sister Caroline. Oliver Wendell Holmes. 6015-3,6113-3,6340-3,6471-X,6288-1, 6126
Brother juniper. Blanche Mary Kelly. 6292-X,6172-9
Brother man. Eden Phillpotts. 7014-0
"**Brother** man, awake!". New Year's hymn. Oscar Edward Maurer. 6894-4
The **brother** of a weed. Arthur Symons. 6510-4
Brother Rugino. Ann [or Annie E.] Hamilton. 6037-4
Brother Toper. Richard R. Kirk. 6118-4
"**Brother**! awake from thy long lethargy". Purpose. Unknown. 6920-7
The **brother's** dirge. Felicia Dorothea Hemans. 6973-8
A **brother's** tribute. Unknown. 6744-1
"' call the gulls **Brother**, brother,'". Lindbergh. Hilda Ziegler. 7019-1
"**Brother**, lost brother!". The wood-god. Bliss Carman and Richard Hovey. 6890-1
"**Brother**, my brother! whoever you are". A song of the all. Robert Norwood. 7014-0
Brother, tell me of the battle. George F. Root. 6074-9
"**Brother**, thou hast gone before us". Funeral anthem. Henry Hart Milman. 6980-0
'**Brother.**'. Virginia Lyne Tunstall. 6326-8
Brotherhood. William Blake. 6150-8
Brotherhood. Josiah Gilbert Holland. 6911-8
Brotherhood. Robert de Lamennais. 6420-5
Brotherhood. Edwin Markham. 6337-3,6386-1,6665-5,6476-0, 6107-9
Brotherhood. James Oppenheim. 6607-0
Brotherhood ("God, what a world, if men in street..."). Ella Wheeler Wilcox. 6335-7
Brotherhood ("O brother man! fold to thy heart..."). John Greenleaf Whittier. 6386-1,6420-5
Brotherhood ("There shall rise from this..."). Sir Lewis Morris. 6420-5
Brotherhood of man. Edward R. Huxley. 6885-5
The **brotherhood** of man. Archibald Ross. 6848-0
The **brotherhood** of the believers. Otakar Brezina. 6886-3
Brotherhood, sels. Sir Lewis Morris. 6335-7
Brotherly love. Unknown. 6848-0
Brothers. Gerard Manley Hopkins. 6430-2
Brothers. James Weldon Johnson. 6527-9
Brothers. Heinrich Lersch. 6643-7
Brothers all. Edgar A. Guest. 7033-7
"**Brothers** among men who after us shall live". Epitaph in ballade form. Richard Aldington. 6875-8
"**Brothers** and men that shall after us be". Ballad of the gibbet. Andrew Lang. 6875-8
Brothers in arms. Alfred Perceval Graves. 6474-4
"**Brothers** in blood! They who this wrong began". To the United States of America. Robert Bridges. 6946-0, 7026-4

BROTHERS

Brothers of the faith. John Oxenham. 6144-3
Brothers of the sea. J.H. Macnair. 7029-9
Brothers once more. W.J.C. Train. 6171-0
Brothers, and a sermon. Jean Ingelow. 6940-1
"Brothers, in a ring recline we". The song of the free. Unknown. 6952-5
The brothers, sels. William Wordsworth. 6867-7
The brothers: Henry and John Shears. Lady Jane F. ("Speranza") Wilde. 6518-X
The brothers. Wilfred Wilson Gibson. 6628-3
The brothers. Johann Wolfgang von Goethe. 6948-7
The brothers. Amy Grosebeck. 6218-0
The brothers. Arthur Vine Hall. 6800-6
The brothers. Marietta Holley. 6695-X
The brothers. Dante Gabriel Rossetti. 6802-2
The brothers. Algernon Charles Swinburne. 6518-X
Brotherson, Frances B.M.
  Which could I spare? 6404-3
Brotherton, Alice Williams
  The first Thanksgiving day. 6618-6
  Plighted, A.D. 6695-X
  The ragged regiment. 6374-8
  The sailing of King Olaf. 6053-6,6521-X,6572-4
  Unawares. 6053-6
  Woman and artist. 6097-8
Brotherton, Mary
  Human love. 6785-9
Brough bells. Robert Southey. 6134-6,6600-3
Brough, Robert B. (tr.)
  The dead alive. Pierre Jean de Beranger, 6787-5
  The king of Yvetot. Pierre Jean de Beranger, 6787-5
Brough, Robert Barnabas
  An early Christian. 6437-X
  'A gentleman'. 7009-4
  I'm a shrimp! 6802-2
  My lord Tomnoddy. 6633-X,6656-9
  My Lord Tomnoddy. 6996-7,7025-6
  Neighbor Nelly. 6385-3
  The strawberry leaf. 7009-4
  'Vulgar declamation'. 7009-4
Brougham, Henry Peter Brougham, Lord
  The orator's epitaph. 6278-4
Brougham, John
  Persevere. 6406-X
  Summer friends. 6569-4
Brought to trial for blowin'. Unknown. 6744-1
"Brought to trial, she has agreed". The injunction. Christopher Bursk. 7032-9
Broughty wa's. Unknown. 6185-0
"Brow bender/Eye peeper." Unknown. 6452-3
"A brow that rises lofty and serene". On Lincoln's portrait. Unknown. 6936-3
Brower, Laura Helena
  Et nunc et semper. 7001-9
  Heritage. 6542-2
Brower, Pauline Florence
  Dedication. 6327-6
Brown Adam. Unknown. 6055-2,6185-0,6518-X,6067-6
"Brown and furry". The caterpillar. Christina Georgina Rossetti. 6891-X
Brown as any thrush is. Pierson Underwood. 6320-9
The brown bear. Mary Austin. 6891-X
Brown bee. William Brighty Rands. 6496-5
The brown bird. Walt Whitman. 6437-X
The brown dwarf of Rugen. John Greenleaf Whittier. 6614-3
"Brown fiddle, you are a gypsy!". The gypsy. Henry Bellaman. 6778-6
"A brown field jabbed a finger into a grove...". Firefly. George Uba. 6790-5
A brown girl dead. Countee Cullen. 6538-4
The brown girl or fair Ellender. Unknown. 7017-5
The brown girl. Unknown. 6826-X
Brown is my love. Unknown. 6182-6,6187-7,6189-3
"Brown is my love, but graceful". Song ("Brown is my love"). Unknown. 6436-1
The brown jug. Francis Fawkes. 6385-3
Brown of Ossawatomie. John Greenleaf Whittier. 6946-0
Brown of Ossawatomie. John Greenleaf Whittier. 6087-0,6484-1,6126-5,6219-9,6300-4
"The brown of her eyes in the oaken leaf". A lilt in fall. Arthur Guiterman. 6773-5
Brown on England's lay. John Hunter Duvar. 7041-8
The brown owl. Unknown. 6937-1
Brown Robin's confession. Unknown. 6022-6
The brown robin. Unknown. 6518-X,6185-0
Brown Robyn's confession. Unknown. 6055-2,6185-0,6547-3, 6067-6
Brown stout. Unknown. 6926-6
The brown thrush. Lucy Larcom. 6449-3,6510-4,6638-0,6049-8, 6623-2,6127-3,6452-3,6135-2,6129
The brown thrush. Unknown. 6820-0
Brown's descent, or, The willy-nilly slide. Robert Frost. 6162-1,6722-0,6393-4
Brown, Abbie Farwell
  Afternoon tea. 6713-1
  A bargain. 6162-1
  The books I ought to read. 7021-3
  Clothes. 6452-3
  The cross-current. 6032-3
  East wind. 6331-4
  The fairy fort. 6029-3
  The fisherman. 6833-2
  The flowerphone. 6338-1
  Grandser. 6102-8,6076-5,6037-4
  Green crosses. 6162-1,6607-0
  The heritage. 6266-0,6473-6
  In the king's garden. 7022-1
  Kindred. 6006-4
  Learning to play. 6452-3
  The lost playmate. 6242-3,6607-0
  A music box. 6452-3
  Names ("From Somerset and Devon,"). 6331-4,6476-0
  Papa's calendar. 6713-1
  Peace with a sword. 6443-4
  Pirate treasure. 6619-4
  A September birthday in Brittany. 6331-4
  Spring patchwork. 6338-1
  To the dogs of the great St. Bernard. 6510-4
  The vigil. 6162-1,6478-7
  The wall. 6338-1
  A wasted morning. 6510-4
  Windows. 6266-0,6476-0
  Work. 6337-3
Brown, Alan
  Vernal frequency. 6021-8
Brown, Alice
  Candlemas ("O hearken, all ye little weeds"). 6006-4, 6310-1,6465-5,6478-7
  Cloistered. 6102-8,6337-3,6076-5,6300-4,6076-5
  Forewarned. 6441-8
  Hora Christi. 6007-2,6310-1,6337-3,6418-3,6532-5,6730 , 6608-9,6746-8
  Pagan prayer. 6730-1
  Revelation. 6730-1
  Sunrise on Mansfield Mountain. 6762-X
  To an enchantress. 6120-6
  A west-country lover. 6310-1,6441-8,6300-4
Brown, Alison
  They shall not pass. 6846-4
Brown, Alison [or Allison]
  If ever time shall come. 6449-3
  Since you went away. 6443-4
Brown, Audrey Alexandra
  In time of invasion. 6224-5
  Laodamia, sels. 6021-8
Brown, B. Curtis
  Jonathan Bing. 6512-0,6534-1
Brown, C. Hilton
  '--a scotch terrier Hamish' 7008-6
Brown, C.F.
  A hundred years to come. 6912-6
Brown, Campbell Rae
  Kissing cup's race. 6451-5
Brown, Charlotte
  The encounter. 6396-9
Brown, Clara T.
  Flowers. 6906-1
  The garden. 6906-1
  His legacy. 6906-1
  Idols. 6906-1

192

The little town. 6906-1
Our busy street. 6906-1
Brown, Delores A.
Upon looking at love. 6178-8
Brown, Earl Bigelow
Daily cross. 6144-3
New crucifixion ("Now, around the world, the mills"). 6144-3
Streets of gold. 6954-1
Brown, Emma Alice
Measuring the baby. 6912-6
Measuring the baby. 6260-1
Brown, Emma E.
The first St. Martin's summer. 6965-7
'Where the brook and river meet'. 6965-7
Brown, Emma K.
Ned's wonderings. 6965-7
Brown, Flora Warren
Pity. 6270-9
Brown, Ford Madox
For the picture, the last of England. 6656-9
O.M.B. 6656-9
Brown, Frances
The greatest loss. 6337-3
If that were true! 6271-7
"Is it come?" 6271-7,6219-9
Losses. 6001-3,6271-7
"O the pleasant days of old." 6271-7,6302-0,6385-3,6219-9,6424-8
The pleasant days of old. 6155-9
The rabbi's vision. 6413-2
Songs of our land. 6858-8
The streams. 6858-8
Brown, Frank E.
Christmas eve. 6807-3,6147-8
Brown, Frank S.
Fall in. 6650-X
Brown, Grace Evelyn
Faith. 6818-9
Brown, H.H.
The old man's ship comes home. 6690-9
Brown, Harry
Announcement. 6761-1
The drill. 6665-8
Questions to be put to a biographer. 6761-1
The words of the excited boy. 6761-1
Brown, Harry Duane
Life. 6396-9
Brown, Helen E.
The rainbow. 6677-1
The shower. 6677-1
The sunbeam. 6677-1
Brown, Henry E.
The pipe you make yourself. 6453-1
Brown, Hilton
Dead-sea fruit. 6269-5
'Glen,' a sheep-dog. 6269-5
I.M. 'Hamish,' a Scotch terrier. 6269-5
The little ships. 6269-5
'Nicky', a hospital dog. 6269-5
Brown, Ina Ladd
Fog. 6799-9
My star. 6799-9
Brown, Irene Fowler
The rear guard. 6074-9
Brown, Isaac Hinton
An American exile. 6014-5,6414-0,6444-2
Hans Bleimer's mool. 6014-5
The honest deacon. 6014-5
Lay of the madman. 6014-5
Nathan Hale, the martyr spy. 6014-5,6417-5
Only a pin. 6014-5,6155-9
Which one? 6014-5,6579-1
Brown, J.A.
Robinson Crusoe. 6566-X
Sadness mingles with joy. 6717-4
Brown, J.T.
A Dutchman's dog story. 6505-8
Brown, Jane
The girl in the laboratory thinks of her grandmother. 7014-0
Brown, Jessie H.
The finding of the cross. 6575-9
Brown, Joe C.
Rustic love. 6178-8
Signs of sleep. 6178-8
Brown, John Henry
Night. 6433-7
Brown, Joseph Brownlee
Thalassa. 6481-7
Thalatta! Thalatta! 6007-2,6102-8,6076-5,6309-8,6737-9, 6104
Brown, Julian
Mr. Ripley parodies Mr. Nash - or vice versa. 6218-0
Brown, Kate Louise
Cherry ripe. 6049-8
The Christ candle. 6653-4
The Christmas candle. 6465-5
Dandelion. 6373-X,6639-9,6638-0
Gentian. 6373-X
Good-bye, little flowers. 6529-5
The leaflets. 6373-X
The little plant. 6143-5,6177-X
Pussy willow. 6452-3,6466-3,6135-4
The tree buds. 6638-0
Brown, Kimberly A.
The bluff. 6857-X
Brown, L.G.
Trundle-bed theology. 6682-8
Brown, Mabel
Who plants a dogwood tree. 6374-8
Brown, Margaret J.E.
Alien. 6316-0
Apart. 6316-0
Bread and wine. 6316-0
Unknown tongue. 6316-0
Brown, Margaret Marchand
Pottery maker. 6270-9
Brown, Marian L.
Flood legend. 6857-X
Brown, Marion Francis
Ghosts. 6039-0
Brown, Martha Taylor
We know. 6750-6
Brown, Melvin Douglass
Boxer shorts named champion. 6870-7
The dirt doctor. 6870-7
A message from Reverend Fat Back made possible by... 6870-7
The nuclear family. 6870-7
The steelworker. 6870-7
Brown, Mrs. Cecil D.
They pity us. 6662-3
Brown, Nellie M.
Merry Christmas. 6272-5
Plant song. 6373-X
Brown, Olive Boda
Riches. 6818-9
Wild flowers. 6818-9
Brown, Olive Stevens
My kittens. 6692-2
Brown, Oliver Madox
Before and after. 6656-9
Laura's song. 6437-X,6656-9
The past world. 7015-9
Requiescant. 7015-9
"With desperate longing, more than foam which lies". 6997-5
Brown, Phoebe Hinsdale
I love to still awhile away. 6525-2
Private devotion. 6632-1,6735-2
Brown, R. Grant
In the forest. 6591-0,6592-9
Love ditty. 6591-0,6592-9
A lover's lament. 6591-0,6592-9
Brown, Rosellen
The crossroads of the south. 6803-0
Brown, Ruth
May 20-21 1927 7019-1
Brown, Slater

BROWN

The ersatz bread. 6761-1
Brown, T. Clarke
   Rhode Island. 6465-5
Brown, T. E.
   Evensong. 7020-5
   Scarlett Rocks. 7020-5
Brown, Theron
   The battle above the clouds. 6630-5,6678-8
   The critical moment. 6926-6
   Master sweet-tooth. 6965-7
   The old wife. 6577-5
Brown, Thomas (Tom)
   A catch. 6328-4
   Doctor Fell. 6152-7,6464-7
   I do not love thee, Doctor Fell. 6722-0,6396-9
   I'm glad he knows. 6680-1
   The warning. 6482-5
Brown, Thomas (Tom) (tr.)
   Non amo te. Martial, 7039-6
   Written while a student at Christ church, Oxford. Martial, 6527-9
Brown, Thomas Edward
   Aber stations. 6809-X
   Alma mater. 6809-X
   At the play. 6809-X
   An autumn trinket. 6809-X
   Bach's organ works. 6230-X
   Bella Gorry. 6809-X
   Betsy Lee. 6809-X
   Between our folding lips. 6809-X
   Boccaccio. 6809-X
   Braddan vicarage. 6809-X
   Braddan village. 6084-6
   The Bristol channel, fr. Clevedon verses. 6809-X
   Canticle. 6655-0
   Canticle. 6809-X
   Captain Tom and Captain Hugh. 6809-X
   Carol ("Three kings from out of the Orient"). 6655-0
   Carol ("Three kings..."). 6809-X
   Catherine Kinrade. 6437-X
   Chalse a killey. 6508-2
   Chalse a killey. 6809-X
   The childhood of Kitty of the Sherragh Vane. 6873-1
   The christening. 6809-X
   Christmas rose. 6809-X
   Clevedon verses, sels. 6508-2,6809-X
   Clifton. 6477-9,6508-2
   Climbing. 6655-0
   Climbing. 6809-X
   Cui bono?, fr. Clevedon verses. 6809-X
   Dante and Ariosto. 6809-X
   Dartmoor: sunset at Chagford: Homo loqvitvr. 6809-X
   Dartmoor: sunset at Chagford: Respondent dhmioyptoe. 6809-X
   Dedication, fr. Fo'c's'le yarns: 1st series. 6809-X
   Dedication, fr. Fo'c's'le yarns: 2d series. 6809-X
   The Dhoon. 6508-2
   The dhoon. 6809-X
   A dialogue between Hom-Veg and Ballure's river. 6809-X
   Disguises. 6730-1
   The doctor. 6809-X
   Dora. 6395-9,6536-8,6250-4,6508-2
   Dora, fr. Clevedon verses. 6809-X
   Dreams. 6655-0
   Dreams. 6809-X
   Dunoon. 6809-X
   Ecclesiastes. 6809-X
   The empty cup. 6809-X
   Envoy to Fo'c's'le yarns: Go back! 6809-X
   Epistola ad Dakyns. 6809-X
   Euroclydon. 6809-X
   Evensong. 6809-X
   Ex ore infantis. 6809-X
   Exile. 6809-X
   A fable, for Henricus D., Esq., Jr. 6809-X
   Failand. 6809-X
   Fives'-court. 6809-X
   A fragment ("Yon bird..."). 6809-X
   Gob-ny-ushtey (Water's mouth). 6809-X
   'God is love'. 6809-X
   Hallam's church, fr. Clevedon verses. 6809-X
   Hotwells. 6809-X
   I bended unto me. 6809-X
   Ibant obscurae. 6809-X
   IIoihmation. 6809-X
   In a fair garden. 6809-X
   In Gremio. 6809-X
   In memoriam. 6655-0
   In memoriam. 6809-X
   In memoriam: A.F. 6809-X
   In memoriam: J. Macmeikin. 6809-X
   In memoriam: Paul Bridson. 6809-X
   In the coach. 6809-X
   In the coach, sels. 6508-2
   The Indiaman. 6809-X
   Indwelling. 6655-0
   Indwelling. 6809-X
   The intercepted salute. 6508-2
   The intercepted salute. 6809-X
   Is it amavi or is it amo? 6809-X
   Israel and Hellas. 6809-X
   Jessie. 6204-0
   Job the white. 6809-X
   Juventa perennis. 6809-X
   Kitty of the Sherragh Vane. 6809-X
   Land, ho! 6809-X
   The laugh. 6809-X
   Life. 6809-X
   The lily-pool and the cow. 6339-X
   Lime street. 6809-X
   Lynton verses. 6423-X
   M.T.W. 6809-X
   The Manx witch. 6809-X
   Mary Quayle. 6809-X
   Mater dolorosa. 6809-X
   Metaboah. 6809-X
   A morning walk. 6809-X
   My garden. 6052-8,6236-9,6477-9,6501-5,6503-1,6730 , 6102-8,6143-5,6301-2,6250-4,6396-3,6508 ,6101-X,6232-6,6337-3,6423-X,6437-X,6732 ,6653-4,6655-0,6737-9
   Nature and art. 6809-X
   'Ne sit ancillae'. 6809-X
   Norton wood, fr. Clevedon verses. 6809-X
   'Not willing to stay'. 6809-X
   O God to thee I yield. 6508-2,6809-X
   Obviam. 6809-X
   Octaves. 6809-X
   Old John. 6809-X
   On the sinking of the Victoria. 6809-X
   Opifex. 6437-X
   The organist in heaven. 6315-2,6437-X,6508-2
   An Oxford idyll. 6655-0
   An Oxford idyll. 6809-X
   Pain. 6809-X
   The Pazons, fr. In the coach. 6508-2
   The Peel life-boat. 6809-X
   Peggy's wedding. 6655-0
   Peggy's wedding. 6809-X
   Per omnia deus, fr. Clevedon verses. 6809-X
   The pessimist, or the rave and the jackdaw. 6809-X
   The pitcher. 6809-X
   Planting. 6809-X
   Poets and poets. 6809-X
   Portbury. 6809-X
   Praesto. 6144-3
   The prayers. 6809-X
   Prelude, fr. Fo'c's'le yarns: 3d series. 6809-X
   Preparation. 6437-X,6650-0
   Prologue: Spes altera, fr' Fo'c's'le yarns: 1st series. 6809-X
   Reconciliation. 6809-X
   Risus Dei. 6809-X
   Roman women. 6809-X
   Sad! sad! 6655-0
   Sad! sad! 6809-X
   St. Bee's head. 6655-0
   St. Bee's head. 6809-X
   Salve! 6437-X
   Scarlett rocks. 6809-X
   The schoolmasters. 6809-X

The schooner. 6477-9
Secuturus, fr. Clevedon verses. 6809-X
A sermon at Clevedon. 6809-X
'Social science'. 6809-X
Song ("Look at me..."). 6809-X
Song ("Weary wind..."). 6809-X
Specula. 6809-X
Star-steering, fr. Clevedon verses. 6809-X
To E.M.O. 6809-X
To E.M.O. 6722-0
To G. Trustrum. 6809-X
To K.H. 6655-0
To K.H. 6809-X
To W.E. Henley. 6809-X
Tommy big-eyes. 6809-X
Tommy big-eyes, sels. 6233-4
Trito Esuriens. 6809-X
Veris et favoni. 6809-X
Vespers. 6339-X
The voices of nature, fr. Clevedon verses. 6809-X
Wastwater to Scawfell. 6809-X
The well. 6809-X
When love meets love. 6437-X
White foxglove. 6809-X
Whitehaven harbour. 6809-X
A wish. 6230-X
A wish. 6809-X
Xpiema. 6809-X
Brown, Thomas Wilson
"Is life worth living?" 6109-5
Brown, Vandyke. See Cook, Marc Eugene
Brown, William C.
An ode to rum. 6408-6
Brown, William Goldsmith
The hills were made for freedom. 6240-7
A hundred years to come. 6240-7,6219-9
Mother, home, heaven. 6240-7
Ne'er shall I forget. 6097-8,6395-9
"Brown-faced sailor, tell me true". At sea. Alice Cary. 6865-0;6969-X
Brown-headed nuthatch. Eugene Edmund Murphey. 6723-9
Browne of Tavistock, William
The concert. 6943-6
Browne, Charles Farrar ("Artemus Ward")
Uncle Simon and Uncle Jim. 6089-7
Browne, E.G. (tr.)
The blind men and the elephant. Sana'i, 6448-5
The branding. Farrukhi, 6448-5
Good night. Sana'i, 6448-5
Message ("Bear from me to Khurasan, Zephyr..."). Nasir-i Khusrau, 6448-5
Mystic cups. Iraqi, 6448-5
Shiraz. Sadi [or Saadi] (Mushlih-ud-Din), 6448-5
Thy love. Sana'i, 6448-5
Browne, Elizabeth
England beseiged. 6789-1
Browne, Emma E.
The ferns and the flakes. 6965-7
Browne, F.F.
Santa Barbara. 6484-1
Browne, Felicia Dorothea. See Hemans, F.D.
Browne, Frances
The hope of the resurrection. 6177-X
The Jewish pilgrim. 6848-0
Losses. 6914-2
Losses. 6600-3,6543-0
Browne, Francis
Origin of the printer's devil. 6787-5
Browne, Francis Fisher
Vanquished. 6113-3,6273-3,6340-3
Browne, George B.
The train ride. 6178-8
Browne, H.J.D.
The voice of the Oregon. 6471-X
Browne, Irving
Man's pillow. 6300-4
My new world. 6300-4
Psalm of law. 6878-2
Venice ("Out of the land and in the sea"). 6624-0
Browne, Isaac Hawkins

"Blest leaf! whose aromatic gales...", fr. A pipe... 6092-7
The fire side: a pastoral soliloquy. 6932-0
In imitation of Pope, fr. A pipe of tobacco. 6932-0
In imitation of Young, fr. A pipe of tobacco. 6932-0
"Little tube of mighty power", fr. A pipe of tobacco. 6092-7
A pipe of tobacco, sels. 6092-7
A pipe of tobacco. 6024-2,6092-7
Browne, M. Hedderwick
My love of long ago. 6689-5
Browne, Mary Ann
Last prayers. 6752-2
Browne, Mathew
The world. 6466-3
Browne, Maurice
To her who passes. 6034-X
Browne, Michael Dennis
To my wife in time of war. 7032-9
Warrior with shield. 6966-5
Browne, R.A.
Measuring the baby. 6772-7
Browne, Sir Thomas
Before sleep. 6438-8
A colloquy with God. 6563-5
Even tavern-musicke. 6230-X
Evening hymn. 6600-3,6291-9,6737-9,6337-3
The night is come. 6958-4
Spirit. 7020-5
Browne, Sir William
Oxford & Cambridge. 6722-0
Whigs and Tories. 6733-6
Browne, Thomas Edward
Boccaccio. 6230-X
Browne, Virgil
Created clay. 6799-9
Browne, William
Britannia's pastorals, sels. 6198-2,6547-3,6649-6,6034-X
Carpe diem. 6189-3
Celadyne's song. 6933-9
Celia is gone. 6563-5
The charm. 6533-3
A country danger. 6191-5
Dawn of day. 6182-6
The death of Philarete. 6191-5
A description of a musical consort of birds. 6191-5
A dirge. 6191-5
Down in a valley. 6527-9
An elegy. 6230-X
An elegy. 6908-8
Epitaph. 6189-3
Epitaph. 6198-2,6512-0
Epitaph on the countess dowager of Pembroke. 6315-2, 6189-3,6250-4,6150-8,6301-2
Epitaph on the Countess of Pembroke. 6250-4
An epitaph on Mrs. El: Y. 6908-8
Epitaph: in obitum M.S. X Maij, 1614. 6933-9
A fairy banquet, fr. Britannia's pastorals. 6194-X
A fragrant grove. 6935-5
The frolic mariners of Devon. 6125-7
Gentle nymphs, be not refusing. 6182-6
Glide soft, ye silver floods. 6182-6,6023-4
"Hail thou, my native soil! Thou blessed plot" 6935-5
He that looks still on your eyes. 6934-7
The heart's venture. 6935-5
In obitum M.S. X May 1614. 6182-6,6562-7,6250-4,6153-2
An invitation. 6191-5
A landscape. 6191-5
"Like to a silkworm of one year". 6334-9
Love who will. 6563-5
Love's reasons. 6189-3
A lover's greeting. 6830-8
Memory. 6935-5
Memory. 6153-2
My choice. 6102-8,6302-0
Now that the spring hath filled our veins. 6328-4
An ode ("Awake"). 6562-7
On his wife, an epitaph. 6908-8
Onthe countess dowager of Pembroke. 6186-9,6187-7,6198-

2,6562-7,6641-0,6646 ,6194-X
On the death of Marie, countess of Pembroke. 6726-3
On the right honourable Charles, Lord Herbert... 6908-8
Praise of poets, fr. Britannias pastorals. 6933-9
The praise of Spencer. 6543-0
Riot's climbing of a hill. 6191-5
A rose, as fair as ever saw the north. 6194-X
The rose. 6135-4
"Shall I tell you whom I love." 6182-6,6271-7,6385-3, 6226-1,6219-9
The shepherdesses' garlands. 6191-5
Sic vita. 6334-9
The siren's song, fr. A masque of the inner temple. 6827-8
The siren's song. 6102-8,6258-X,6385-3,6600-3,6189-3, 6737
"So shuts the marigold her leaves". 6187-7,6125-7
Song ("For her gait"). 6102-8,6186-9
Song ("Hearken then"). 6250-4
Song ("Love, that looks"). 6187-7
Song ("Shall I tell"). 6600-3
Song ("Welcome..."). 6827-8
The song in the wood. 6189-3
The song of Celadyne. 6099-4
Song of the sirens. 6182-6,6334-9,6150-8,6125-7
Song of the syrens. 6933-9
Sorrow. 6383-7
Spring morning. 6668-2
squirrel hunt, fr. Britannia's pastorals. 6194-X
The squirrel. 6179-6
"Steer hither, steer your winged pines". 6187-7
The subject of all verse. 6934-7
Sweeter scents than in Arabia found,fr Britannia's pastorals. 6194-X
Thirsis' praise of his mistress. 6191-5
"Underneath this sable hearse". 6289-X
Venus and Adonis. 6182-6
"Venus by Adonis' side". 6092-7,6562-7
Vision 5. 6562-7
Vision of the rose. 6189-3
A vision. 6563-5
Walking in a garden, fr. Britannia's pastorals. 6649-6
Walla, the fairest nymph, fr. Britannia's pastorals. 6194-X
"Welcome, welcome, I do sing." 6271-7,6302-0,6385-3, 6189-3,6737-9
A welcome. 6219-9,6250-4
What wight he loved. 6092-7
Willy, or glide soft ye silver floods. 6543-0

Brownell (atr.), Henry Howard
Original version of the John Brown song. 6753-0

Brownell, Adelia
Flights. 7019-1

Brownell, Edith
Motherhood ("Gray gloomed the hillside..."). 6097-8
October. 6820-0

Brownell, Florence Keer
Strawberry mark. 6979-7

Brownell, Henry Howard
Abraham Lincoln. 6113-3,6239-3,6709-3,6305-5,6524-4
"All we ask is to be let alone". 6402-7
The battle of Charlestown. 6946-0
The bay fight. 6113-3,6678-X,6438-8,6462-1
The bay fight. 6016-2,6470-1
The burial of the Dane. 6385-3,6600-3,6300-9,6309-8, 6407-8
The burial of the dead. 6431-0
Bury them. 6946-0
The eagle of Corinth. 6062-5
Honest Abe. 6524-4
John Brown. 6589-9,6121-4
The lawyer's invocation to spring. 6089-7,6240-7,6302-0, 6385-3,6441-8,6505 ,6219-9,6652-6
A lawyer's poem to spring. 6629-1
"Let us alone." 6302-0,6385-3,6505-8
Night quarters. 6239-3
The old cove. 6438-8
The river fight. 6062-5,6113-3,6470-1,6016-2
Sumter. 6946-0

The **brownie** men. M. Nora Boylan. 6147-8

The **brownie** of Blednoch. William Nicholson. 6960-6
"The **brownie** who lhves in the forest". The brownie's Christmas. Mary E. (Freeman) Wilkins. 6965-7
The **brownie's** Christmas. Mary E. (Freeman) Wilkins. 6965-7
The **brownies**. M.M. Grant. 6715-8

Browning (atr.), Elizabeth Barrett
Out in the fields with God. 6337-3
The sweetest lives. 6337-3

Browning at Asolo. Robert Underwood Johnson. 6102-8'6331-4, 6624-0,6076-5,6309-8,6631

Browning, Elizabeth Barrett
Amy's cruelty. 6302-0;6385-3,6092-7,6652-6
"And shining with gloom, the water grey". 6997-5
And yet, because thou overcomest so. 6430-2
Aurora Leigh, sels. 6123-0,6239-3,6484-1,6730-1,6655-0, 6656
Aurora's home. 6543-0
The autumn. 6123-0
The beauty of England. 6543-0
"Because thou hast the power and own'st the grace." 6560-0
Being a mother. 6097-8
Beloved. 6337-3,6019-6
"Beloved, my beloved, when I think." 6430-2,6560-0
Beloved, thou hast brought me many flowers. 6430-2
Bertha in the lane. 6271-7,6302-0,6385-3,6600-3,6572-4
"The best men, doing their best", sels. 6601-1
The best thing in the world. 6410-8
The best. 6437-X
Bianca among the nightingales. 6657-7
The bitter cry of the children. 6954-1
"But when the thrushes sang", fr. Aurora Leigh. 6123-0
"Can it be right to give what I can give?" 6560-0
Casa Guidi windows, sels. 6832-4
Casa Guidi windows, sels. 6123-0,6479-5,6484-1,6656-9, 6543-0
Cheerfulness taught by reason. 6123-0,6604-6,6177-X, 6660-7,6177-X
The child and the watcher. 6271-7,6219-9
A child asleep. 6233-4
A child's thought of God. 6123-0,6198-2,6303-9,6466-3, 6127-3,6249 ,6356-X,6519-8,6575-9,6131-4,6219-9,6368 ,6424-8,6456-6
Choruses of Eden spirits, fr. A drama of exile. 6334-9
The chrism and crown of love. 6014-5
Comfort. 6934-7
Confessions. 6437-X,6655-0
Consolation. 6655-0
Content. 6337-3
Content in service. 6177-X
A court lady. 6302-0,63385-3,6486-3,6219-9,6656-9
Cowper's grave. 6219-9,6543-0,6655-0,6271-7,6437-X,6483- 3,6600-3,6657-7,6304
Cowper's grave, sels. 6198-2
Critics. 6996-7
Crowned and wedded. 6188-5
The cry of the children. 6383-7,6560-0,6655-0,6102-8, 6219-9,6134-6,6233-4,6337-3,6481 ,6188-5,6198-2,6473-6,6657-7,6732-8,6656
The cry of the human, sels. 6337-3
A curse for a nation. 6198-2,6358-6
The cygney finds the water, fr. Aurora Leigh. 6934-7
De profundis. 6240-7,6302-0,6385-3
A dead rose. 6123-0,6383-7,6543-0
Death and love. 6383-7
A denial. 6301-2
The deserted garden. 6232-6,6302-0,6655-0,6649-6
Do you think of me? 6085-4
Duchess May. 6669-0
England ("Whoever lives true life will love true love") 6123-0
Exaggeration. 6965-7
The face of all the world is changed, I think. 6199-0, 6430-2
A false step. 6732-8,6655-0
Far, and yet near. 6429-9,6321-7
Farewells from paradise. 6437-X
"Fasten your souls so high, that constantly". 6238-5
First news from Villafranca. 6123-0

"First time he kiss'd me, he but only kiss'd." 6560-0
First, second, third. 6429-9,6321-7
Flush or faunus. 6934-7
The forced recruit. 6219-9,6196-6
Fullness of love. 6429-9,6226-1,6321-7
Futurity. 6123-0
Futurity. 7037-X
"Get leave to work". 6238-5
The gift. 6383-7
Glory in the commonplace, fr. Aurora Leigh. 6337-3
Go from me. 6339-X,6019-6,6199-0,6250-4
"Go, travel 'mid the hills!...",fr.Seaside meditation. 6123-0
"God did anoint thee with his odorous oil", sels. 6601-1
"God, set our feet low and our forehead high", sels. 6601-1
'Good from a book'. 6465-5
Grief. 6246-6,6315-2,6437-X,6657-7,6737-9,6383 ,6214-8, 6543-0
He giveth his beloved sleep. 6304-7,6424-8,6569-4
Hiram Powers' Greek slave. 6102-8
Hiram Powers's Greek slave. 6934-7
His mother's face. 6097-8
The house of clouds. 6682-8
"How do I love thee? Let me count the ways." 6240-7, 6289-X,6337-3,6465-5,6488-4,6527 ,6199-0,6192-3,6513-9,6430-2,6560-0,6107 ,6019-6,6094-3,6250-4,6536-8, 6620-8,6726 ,6464-7
"Howe'er the uneasy world is vexed...",fr. Casa Guidi. 6123-0
"I am prescient by the very hope". 6238-5
"I call you hard", fr. Aurora Leigh. 6123-0
"I fain would ask thee to forget". 6238-5
I lived with visions for my company. 6430-2
"I never gave a lock of hair." 6250-4
I think of thee. 6199-0
"I thought once how Theocritus had sung". 6204-0,6246-6, 6430-2,6560-0,6396-9,6199 ,6088-9
"If I leave all for thee, wilt thou exchange". 6238-5
If thou must love me. 6337-3,6339-X,6646-1,6513-9,6585-6,6250 ,6019-6,6153-2,6199-0
Inclusions. 6437-X
Insufficiency. 6123-0,6019-6
"Is it indeed so? If I lay here dead." 6560-0
Italy ("The darling of the earth"). 6302-0,6624-0
Joy. 6134-6
Lady Geraldine's courtship. 6271-7,6677-1,6438-8,6219-9
The lady's yes. 6123-0,6302-0,6385-3,6438-8,6219-9
The lay of the rose. 6980-0
A lay of the early rose. 7037-X
"The least flower, with a brimming cup...", sels. 6601-1
Lessons from the gorse. 6123-0
"Let star-wheels and angel-wings, with their holy...". 6238-5
Like a sick child. 6097-8
Little Mattie. 6014-5,6134-6
"Live and love". 6402-7
The look. 6337-3
"The Lord turned, and looked upon Peter" 6144-3
Lord Walter's wife. 6302-0,6385-3,6671-1
The lost bower. 6114-1
Love. 6123-0
Love for love's sake. 6094-3,6321-7
Love letters. 6737-9
Loved once. 6980-0
Man and nature. 6123-0
A man's requirements. 6123-0,6198-2,6092-7
Man, fr. Aurora Leigh. 6102-8
Marian's child. 6543-0
The mask. 6437-X
May's love. 6092-7
The meaning of the look. 6144-3,6337-3
The measure. 6848-0
Mother and poet. 6097-8,6271-7,6302-0,6344-6,6385-3, 6395 ,6543-0.6656-9,6197-4,6219-9,6655-0,6550-3,6624-0,6627-5
The mother's prayer. 6097-8,6365-9
Motherless, fr. Aurora Leigh. 6097-8,6123-0,6627-5

Mountaineer and poet. 6749-2
The mourning mother. 6097-8
A musical instrument. 6828-6
A musical instrument. 6123-0,6198-2,6236-9,6290-3,6332-2,6479 ,6197-4,6196-6,6301-2,6396-9,6304-7,6421 , 6228-8,6339-X,6385-3,6437-X,6600-3,6657-,6046-3,6102-8,6219-9,6253-9,6383-7,6543 ,6465-5,6478-7,6604-, 6655-0,6732-8,6541,6192-3,6430-2,6560-0,6656-9,6639-9,6660
"My child, we were two children", fr. Translations. 6123-0
My doves. 6980-0
My heart and I. 6240-7,6656-9
My Kate. 6123-0,6066-8,6092-7
My letters. 6066-9
"My poet, thou canst touch all the notes." 6483-3,6726-3
Mystery. 6437-X
"The nail that holds the wood...", sels. 6601-1
Napoleon's final return. 6424-8
Nevermore alone. 6337-3
"The night has a thousand eyes." 6238-5
The north and the south. 6437-X
Nothing small. 6102-8
"Of all the thoughts of God that are", sels. 6601-1
Oh, fear to call it loving. 6226-1
On a portrait of Wordsworth by B.R. Haydon. 6385-3,6483-3
Only a curl. 6014-5,6408-6,6744-7
Out in the fields with God. 6589-9,6214-8,6461-2,6368-3
Parting lovers. 6302-0;6385-3
Patience taught by nature. 6931-2
Perplexed music. 6198-2
Perplexed music. 7037-X
The pet name. 6302-0,6385-3,6302-9,6384-5
The poet. 6214-8
The poet. 6102-8,6214-8,6585-6,6730-1
The poets, fr. Lady Geraldine's courtship. 6934-7
A portrait ("Face"). 6934-7
The portrait of a friend. 6084-6
A portrait. 6239-3,6250-4,6302-0,6385-3
A portrait ("I will paint"). 6239-3,6302-9
Praise of earth. 6437-X
The prospect. 6123-0,6461-2,6604-6,6660-7,6123-7
Reading, fr. Aurora Leigh. 6239-3
A reed. 6980-0
A rhapsody of life's progress. 7037-X
Rime of the Duchess May. 6473-6,6438-8
The romance of the swan's nest. 6127-3,6239-3,6302-0, 6370-5,6385-3,6457 ,6133-8,6249-0,6575-9,6219-9,6518-X
Romaunt of Margret. 6980-0
The romaunt of the page. 6166-4,6518-X
Round our restlessness. 6337-3
Santa Maria Novella. 6624-0
"Say never, ye loved once". 6238-5
The sea-mew. 6123-0,6510-4
A sea-side meditation, sels. 6123-0
Seraph and the poet. 6980-0
"The shadow of her face upon the wall", fr. Sketches. 6123-0
A simile, fr. Aurora Leigh. 6832-4
The sleep. 6046-3,6585-6,6078-1,6271-7,6337-3,6219-9, 6543-0,6656 ,6123-0,6198-2,6302-0,6385-3,6600-3,6730-
Sleeping and watching. 6965-7,6772-7
Song of the rose. 6049-3
Sonnet ("Beloved"). 6232-6
Sonnet ("Go from me"). 6236-9,6604-6,6226-1
Sonnet ("How do I love thee?"). 6154-0,6317-9,6604-6
Sonnet ("I thought once"). 6154-0,6604-6,6197-4
Sonnet ("If I leave"). 6604-6
Sonnet ("If thou must"). 6154-0
Sonnet ("The face of all"). 6934-7
Sonnet ("Yet, love"). 6934-7
Sonnets from the Portuguese, sels. 6196-6,6430-2,6560-0, 6192-3,6250-4,6199 ,6107-9,6088-9,6543-0,6219-9,6371-3,6660 ,6102-8,6301-2,6723-9,6737-9
Sonnets from the portuguese. 6828-6
Sonnets from the Portuguese. 6110-9,6655-0
Sonnets from the Portuguese, sel. 6123-0,6186-9,6198-2,

BROWNING

6271-7,6302-0,6385-,6154-0,6317-9,6337-3,6437-X,6483-3,6604-,6204-0,6240-7,6657-7,6726-3,6732-8,6656
Sonnets to George Sand. 6385-3
The soul's expression. 6198-2
The soul's expression. 7037-X
"Speak low to me, my Saviour, low and sweet", sels. 6601-1
Substitution. 6214-8,6337-3,6730-1
The sweetness of England. 6423-X
Tears ("Thank God, bless God, all ye who suffer not"). 6501-5
"Thou hast thy calling to some palace-floor." 6483-3
A thought for a lonely death-bed. 6337-3
Three kisses. 6240-7,6066-8,6226-1
To Flush, my dog. 6075-7
To George Sand. 6123-0
To George Sand, a recognition. 6198-2
To L.E.L. on the death of Felecia Hemans. 6046-3
Traveling south toward Italy. 6102-8
A tribute to woman, fr. Drama of exile. 6001-3
True peace, fr. 'Casa guidi windows' 6954-1
The two sayings. 6337-3
Two sketches. 6123-0
"Unlike are we, unlike." 6250-4
Vallombrosa. 6439-6
Vallombrosa ("And Vallombrosa, we went to see"). 6331-4, 6624-0
A view across the Roman compagna. 6302-0;6385-3
The virgin Mary to the child Jesus. 6282-2
A vision of poets, sels. 6483-3,6046-3
A vision of poets. 6669-0
The ways of love. 6429-9,6226-1,6321-7
"What can I give thee back." 6250-4
When our two souls stand up erect and strong. 6199-0, 6250-4,6430-2,6204-0,6536-8,6726-3,6153-2,6192-3, 6560
'Where there is no vision--,' fr. Aurora Leigh. 6337-3
Wine of Cyprus, sels. 6483-3
Wisdom unapplied. 6123-0,6601-1
A woman's answer. 6486-8
A woman's question. 6889-8
A woman's question. 6370-5
A woman's shortcomings. 6198-2,6066-8
Work. 6198-2,6501-5,6604-6,6660-7
"Yet, love, mere love, is beautiful indeed". 6844-8
"You who keep account". 6238-5

Browning, Elizabeth Barrett (tr.)
Ad finem. Heinrich Heine, 7039-6
The Cyclops. Theocritus, 7039-6
Mein kind, wir waren kinder. Heinrich Heine, 7039-6
Our lady of the passion. John Mauropus, 6282-2
Psalm 127. The sleep. Bible, 6848-0
Selections. Heinrich Heine, 6123-0
The wail of Prometheus bound. Aeschylus, 6730-1

Browning, Ophelia G.
Sometime, somewhere. 6303-9,6525-2
Sometime, somewhere. 6889-8

Browning, Robert
Abt Vogler. 6198-2,6641-0,6657-7,6730-1,6723-9,6656 , 6102-8,6110-9,6655-0,6560-0,6430-2,6250 ,6196-6,6199-0,6245-8
Abt Vogler, sels. 6123-0,6337-3
Adam, Lilith, and Eve. 6110-9,6196-6
After. 6102-8
Ah, love, but a day. 6320-9,6199-0,
The all-loving, fr. An epistle. 6337-3
Along the beach, fr. James Lee's wife. 6655-0
Among the rocks, fr. James Lee's wife. 6655-0,6196-6, 6252-0,6560-0
The ancient doctrine. 6437-X
"And strew faint sweetness...", fr. Paracelsus. 6726-3
Andrea del Sarto. 6154-0,6484-1,6488-4,6527-9,6536-8, 6604-,6655-0,6657-7,6726-3,6660-7,6631-3,6723 ,6102-8,6110-9,6199-0,6192-3,6430-2
Andrea del Sarto, sels. 6337-3
Another way of love. 6828-6
Another way of love. 6110-9,6655-0
An answer. 7015-9
Any wife to any husband. 6828-6
Any wife to any husband. 6204-0,6208-3,6427-2,6110-9, 6094-3
Apparent failure, sels. 6123-0,6501-5,6337-3
Apparitions. 6198-2
Appearances. 6110-9
April in England. 6239-3,6424-8
Arcades ambo. 6123-0
Artemis prologuizes. 6980-0
Ask not one least word of praise, fr. Ferishtah's fancies. 6655-0
Asolando, sels. 6430-2
Asolo. 6331-4
The awakening of man, fr. Paracelsus. 6730-1
Bad dreams, sels. 6430-2
Balaustion's adventure, sels. 6483-3
The bard and the cricket. 6676-3
Before, sels. 6144-3
Ben Karshook's wisdom. 6848-0
Ben Karshook's wisdom. 6110-9,6430-2
Bishop Blougram's apology. 6657-7
Bishop Blougram's apology, sel. 6958-4
Bishop Blougram's apology, sels. 6337-3,6427-2
The bishop orders his tomb at Saint Praxed's Church. 6046-3,6102-8,6110-9,6656-9,6646-1,6659 ,6199-0,6052-8,6154-0,6198-2,6427-2,6484-1,6657 ,6150-8,6196-6, 6430-2,6472-8,6655-0,6682
A blot in the 'scutcheon, sels. 6123-0
Boot and saddle. 6198-2,6328-4,6395-0,6732-8,6723-9, 6656
Boot saddle. 6197-4,6153-2,6655-0,6383-7,6430-2,6110
The boy and the angel. 6828-6
The boy and the angel. 6198-2,6473-6,6610-0,6655-0,6419-1,6424
Breast forward. 6260-1
By the fireside. 6186-9,6597-X,6655-0,6230-X,6102-8
Caliban upon Setebos. 6828-6
Caliban upon Setebos. 6657-7,6730-1,6430-2,6199-0,6110-9,6655
Cavalier tunes. 6828-6
Cavalier tunes. 6188-5,6332-2,6334-9,6358-6,6490-6,6527- ,6657-7,6196-6,6430-2,6656-9,6110-9
Cavalier tunes, sels. 6334-9,6732-8,6199-0,6301-2,6655-0
Childe Roland to the dark tower came. 6198-2,6427-2, 6657-7,6656-9,6655-0,6430
Childe Roland to the darl tower. 6102-8,6110-9,6192-3, 6196-6,6723-9,6472
Christmas eve, sels. 6144-3
A Christmas sermon. 6747-6
Cleon. 6657-7,6430-2,6655-0
Cleon, sels. 6427-2
"Cliffs, an earthquake suffered jut", fr. Sordello. 6997-5
Clive. 6576-7
The confessional. 6427-2
Confessions. 6246-6,6657-7,6110-9,6199-0,6655-0
Count Gismond. 6166-4,6102-8,6518-X,6578-3
Cristina. 6200-8,6657-7,6110-9,6199-0,6430-2,6655
Cristina, sels. 6123-0
"Dance, yellows and whites and reds",fr. Parleyings. 6123-0
A daughter of the leech. 6094-3
David's journey after comforting Saul. 7020-5
David's song before Saul. 6179-6
Day. 6625-9
De gustibus. 6043-6,6199-0,6110-9,6541-4,6430-2,6655 , 6123-0,6154-0,6473-6,6624-0,6657-7,6656
De gustibus, sels. 6464-7
Deaf and dumb. 6337-3
The death in the desert, sels. 6144-3
A death in the desert. 6931-2
A death in the desert. 6245-8
A death in the desert. 6931-2
Development. 6110-9
The development of man, fr. Paracelsus. 6199-0
Doctor- 6848-0
Donald and the stag. 6669-0
Dubiety. 6123-0,6657-7
Duty. 6964-9
"Earth's crammed with beauty." 6225-3
Earth's immortalities. 6110-9,6383-7

Earth's immortalities, sels. 6655-0
Echetlos. 6657-7,6110-9
Eden remembered. 7020-5
The Englishman in Italy. 6484-1,6655-0,6657-7
Epilogue. 6437-X,6657-7,6656-9,6655-0,6464-7,6214 ,6102-8,6214-8,6250-4,6199-0
Epilogue ("At the midnight"). 6473-6,6196-6
Epilogue to Asolando. 6123-0,6154-0,6198-2,6208-3,6337-3,6501 ,6023-4,6110-9,6301-2,6660-7,6723-9,6737 , 6604-6,6657-7
Epilogue to the Pacchiarotto volume. 6110-9
Epilogue, fr. Dramatis personae. 6144-3,6110-9
Epilogue, fr. Pacchiarotto volume. 6110-9
Epilogue, sels. 6144-3
An epistle containing the strange medical experience... 6655-0
An epistle of Kaeshish. 6199-0
An epistle. 6657-7
An epistle. 6828-6
Epitaph (Levi Lincoln Thaxter). 6656-9
Eurydice to Orpheus. 6641-0,6199-0
Evelyn Hope. 6014-5,6123-0,6198-2,6240-7,6271-7,6302-,6301-2,6291-9,6110-9,6046-3,6560-0,6655 ,6303-9,6370-5,6385-3,6473-6,6486-8,6600-,6023-4,6102-8,6383-7,6543-0,6655-0,6656 ,6657-7
Eyes calm. 6723-9
A face. 6123-0,6110-9,6655-0,6543-0,6656-9
Faith. 6214-8
Fame, fr. Earth's immortalities. 6655-0
Fears and scruples. 6110-9
Ferishtah's fancies, sels. 6110-9
Fifine at the fair, sels. 6997-5
Fifine at the fair, sels. 6110-9
Fifine at the fair, sels. 6997-5
Filippo Baldinucci on the privilege of burial. 6848-0
Fire is in the flint, fr. Ferishtah's fancies. 6655-0
The flight of the duchess, sels. 6123-0
The flight of the duchess. 6271-7,6655-0
The flower's name, fr. Garden fancies. 6321-7
The flower's name. 6123-0,6232-6,6246-6,6302-0,6385-3,6677-,6199-0,6250-4,6429-9,6655-0,6585-6
For life, with all its yields of joy or woe. 6066-8
"For music (which is earnest of a heaven", fr.Pauline. 6123-0
A forgiveness, sels. 6541-4
Fra Lippo Lippi. 6154-0,6198-2,6427-2,6488-4,6536-8,6657-,6196-6,6430-2,6110-9,6199-0,6655-0,6723
Fra Lippo Lippi. 6828-6
Garden fancies, sels. 6649-6
Garden-fancies. 6429-9,6092-7,6321-7,6652-6,6655-0
Gibraltar. 6331-4
Give a rouse. 6198-2,6271-7,6328-4,6334-9,6501-5,6732-,6110-9,6199-0,6430-2,6655-0,6656-9,6723 ,6271-7
Give her but a least excuse, fr. Pippa passes. 6199-0
The glove. 6271-7,6527-9,6458-2,6419-1,6655-0
God's in hiks heaven. 6654-2
Good morning. 6401-9,6519-8,6135-4,6424-8
A grammarian's funeral, sels. 6123-0
A grammarian's funeral. 6198-2,6315-2,6337-3,6358-6,6657-7,6730-,6102-8,6196-6,6430-2,6046-3,6110-9,6199 ,6250-4,6301-2,6655-0
A grammarian's funeral. 6828-6
Greece, fr. Cleon. 6427-2
"The grey sea and the long black land". 6997-5
Grow old along with me. 6654-2
The guardian angel. 6484-1,6604-6,6624-0,6110-9,6660-7
Gypsies. 6466-3
He who aspires. 6303-9
"Heap cassia...", fr. Paracelsus. 6726-3,6110-9,6196-6
Helen's tower. 7015-9
Her perfect praise. 6429-9,6321-7
'Here's to Nelson's memory'. 6657-7
The heretic's tragedy. 6378-0
Herve Riel. 6183-4,6228-8,6239-3,6271-7,6294-6,6331-,6110-9,6424-8,6419-1,6371-3,6322-5,6267 ,6332-2,6344-6,6370-5,6385-3,6395-0,6406-,6155-9,6192-3,6250-4,6421-3,6573-2,6219 ,6427-2,6473-6,6478-7,6479-5,6504-X,6550-,6552-X,6621-6
Holy Cross day, sels. 6046-3
Holy-cross day. 6427-2
Holy-cross day. 6848-0
Home thoughts from abroad. 6047-1,6101-X,6123-0,6133-8,6134-4,6138-,6107-9,6110-9,6102-8,6046-3,6104-4,6196 ,6154-0,6186-9,6187-7,6198-2,6208-3,6232-,6430-2,6560-0,6250-4,6383-7,6199-0,6114 ,6331-4,6332-2,6339-X,6423-X,6427-2,6437-,6153-2,6301-2,6668-2,6396-9,6439-6,6646 ,6466-3,6473-6,6597-X,6604-6,6655-0,6657-,6464-7,6656-9,6586-6,6631-3,6660-7,6737 ,6723-9,6726-3,6828-6
Home thoughts, from the sea. 6123-0,6154-0,6198-2,6258-X,6395-0,6437 ,6196-6,6430-2,6114-1,6110-9,6322-5,6439 ,6473-6,6484-1,6655-0,6657-7
House. 6527-9,6657-7,6110-9,6430-2,6655-0
The householder. 6378-0
How it strikes a contemporary. 6657-7
How they brought the good news from Ghent to Aix. 6014-5,6101-X,6133-8,6136-2,6228-8,6239-,6046-3,6102-8,6110-9,6131-1,6197-4,6419 ,6134-6,6198-2,6332-2,6478-7,6610-0,6657-,6219-9,6263-6,6267-9,6396-9,6510-4,6585 ,6242-3,6271-7,6302-0,6385-3,6339-X,6401-,6438-8,6424-8,6518-X,6543-0,6560-0,6655 ,6425-6,6457-4,6473-6,6479-5,6501-5,6504-,6196-6,6383-7,6371-3,6639-9,6656-9,6512-0,6521-X,6534-1,6552-X,6606-2,6732-
I go to prove my soul, fr. Paracelsus. 6337-3
The illimitable God, fr. A death in the desert. 6337-3
In a gondola. 6186-9,6204-0,6437-X,6657-7,6199-0,6439 , 6110-9,6655-0,6656-9
In a year. 6271-7,6302-0,6385-3,6543-0,6655-0,6219 , 6102-8,6199-0
In doubt of doubt, fr. Bishop Blougram's apology. 6337-3
In the doorway. 6380-2
In three days. 6204-0,6429-9,6110-9,6199-0,6321-7
An incident at Ratisbon. 6424-8
Incident of the French camp. 6861-8
Incident of the French camp. 6123-0,6183-4,6198-2,6239-3,6242-3,6271-,6046-3,6102-8,6263-6,6110-9,6267-9,6560 ,6302-0,6332-2,6385-3,6395-0,6410-8,6473-,6107-9,6199-0,6419-1,6421-3,6371-3,6560 ,6550-3,6552-X,6614-3,6625-9,6732-8,6479-,6131-1,6197-4,6219-9,6464-7,6656-9
Instans tyrannus. 6473-6,6655-0
"It's wiser being good than bad", fr.Apparent failure. 6123-0,6102-8
The Italian in England. 6473-6,6657-7,6655-0,6110-9,6430-2,6458 ,6419-1
The Italian in England. 6828-6
Italy, fr. De Gustibus. 6934-7
Ivan Ivanovitch. 6669-0
James Lee's wife. 6204-0
James Lee's wife, sels. 6199-0,6560-0
Jochanan Hakkadosh. 6848-0
Johannes Agricola in meditation. 6437-X,6657-7
Karshish, sels. 6144-3
Karshish, the Arab physician. 6730-1
The king is cold. 6385-3
A king. 6438-8
La Saisiaz. 6828-6
La saisiaz, sels. 6110-9
The laboratory. 6052-8,6154-0,6437-X,6657-7,6677-1,6655 ,6153-2,6196-6,6541-4
The last ride together. 6196-6,6301-2,6655-0,6154-0,6198-2,6315-2,6437-X,6726-3,6723 ,6102-8,6110-9,6153-2,6250-4,6430-2,6560
Life in a love. 6429-9,6437-X,6655-0,6321-7,6430-2,6102
A light woman. 6023-4
A likeness. 6378-0,6110-9
The lost leader. 6828-6
The lost leader. 6154-0,6246-6,6271-7,6289-X,6328-4,6483-,6046-3,6084-6,6438-8,6424-8,6560-0,6219 ,6198-2,6332-2,6427-2,6600-3,6657-7,6683-,6102-8,6110-9,6197-4,6304-7,6219-4,6250 ,6196-6,6655-0,6656-9.6543-0,6723-9,6199 ,6092-7,6552-X
The lost mistress. 6828-6
The lost mistress. 6023-4,6208-3,6437-X,6371-5,6543-0,6737 ,6655-0
Love among the ruins. 6828-6
Love among the ruins. 6154-0,6204-0,6320-9,6332-2,6437-X,6473-,6196-6,6199-0,6430-2,6655-0,6560-0,6541 ,6110-9,6371-3,6066-8,6543-0,6723-9,6657

Love among the ruins, sels. 6123-0
Love in a life. 6429-9,6437-X,6430-2,6199-0,6655-0,6321
 ,6102-8,6110-9
Love is the only good in the world. 6066-8
Love, fr. Earth's immortalities. 6655-0
A lover's quarrel. 6204-0
Lyric love, fr. The ring and the book. 6437-X
Magical nature. 6110-9,6655-0
Man I am and man would be, fr. Ferishtah's fancies.
 6655-0
Man's destiny, fr. Paracelsus. 6337-3
Man, bird and God. 6291-1
Marching along. 6198-2,6328-4,6334-9,6473-6,6732-8,6656
 ,6102-8,6110-9,6199-0,6219-9,6430-2,6723 ,6655-0
Marching along, sels. 6395-0
Martin Relph. 6686-0
Mary Wollstonecraft and Fuseli. 6094-3
May and death. 6085-4
"The mayor was dumb...", fr. Pied piper. 6123-0
Meeting. 6302-0,6385-3,6737-9
Meeting at night. 6828-6
Meeting at night. 6123-0,6198-2,6204-0,6208-3,6236-9,
 6246-,6199-0,6110-9,6102-8,6656-9,6646-1,6464 ,6258-
 X,6320,9,6332-2,6358-6,6512-0,6657-,6046-3,6250-4,
 6196-6,6491-4,6723-9,6655 ,6430-2,6464-7,6659-3,6682-
 8
Memorabilia. 6123-0,6154-0,6208-3,6315-2,6483-3,6657-,
 6656-9,6655-0,6430-2,6301-2,6464-7,6250 ,6726-3,6732-
 8,6108-2,6646-1,6110-9,6657 ,6737-9
Men and women, sels. 6369-1,6439-6
Mertoun's song, fr. A blot in the 'scutcheon. 6123-0,
 6383-7
"'Mid the sharp, short emerald wheat", sels. 6601-1
Misconceptions. 6110-9,6204-0,6271-7,6437-X,6481-7,6732-
 8,6250 ,6199-0,6655-0,6656-9
"The morn when first it thunders in March",fr.Pictures.
 6123-0
Morning. 6109-5
"The moth's kiss, first!" 6302-0,6385-3,6429-9,6321-7
Muckle-mouth Meg. 6427-2,6689-5,6655-0,6656-9,6110-9
Muleykeh. 7010-8
Music, fr. Abt Vogler. 6123-0
My last duchess. 6828-6
My last duchess. 6123-0,6154-0,6198-2,6208-3,6289-X,
 6332-,6579-1,6585-6,6645-3,6723-9,6660-7,6577 ,6427-
 2,6473-6,6488-4,6536-8,6604-6,6655-,6102-8,6150-8,
 6153-2,6371-3,6646-1,6430 ,6046-3,6197-4,6199-0,6196-
 6,6192-3,6110 ,6656-9,6657-7,6682-8,6726-3
My lode-star, fr. Pauline. 6337-3
My star. 6198-2,6320-9,6429-9,6501-5,6657-7,6543 ,6102-
 8,6110-9,6250-4,6430-2,6321-7,6491 ,6585-6,6655-0,
 6199-0
My sun sets to rise again, fr. At the Mermaid. 6337-3
The names. 6848-0
The names. 6483-3
Nationality in drinks. 6092-7
Natural magic. 6110-9,6655-0
Nay but you. 6250-4
Ned Bratts. 6655-0
Never the time and the place. 6198-2,6204-0,6657-7,6655-
 0,6723-9,6737 ,6102-8,6199-0,6110-9,6250-4
The new boy and the angel. 6102-8,6177-X
New Year's hymn, fr. Pippa passes. 6102-8
Night and morning. 6527-9
The north country. 6466-3
"Not alone when life flows still, do truth". 6238-5
Now. 6655-0
"O lyric Love, half angel and half bird", fr. The ring.
 6123-0,6204-0,6199-0
Oft have I stood by thee, fr. Pauline. 6337-3
Oh, good gigantic smile, fr. Jame Lee's wife. 6199-0
"Oh, to be in England now that April's there" 7020-5
"Oh, we're sunk enough here, God knows!", fr Cristina.
 6123-0
Old pictures in Florence. 6624-0,6110-9,6655-0
Old pictures in Florence, sels. 6123-0
One more word, sels. 6934-7
One reason for industry. 6861-8
One way of love. 6271-7,6427-2,6676-3,6732-8,6737-9,
 6655 ,6094-3,6110-9,6543-0,6656-9

One way of love. 6828-6
One word more. 6154-0,6198-2,6204-0,6427-2,6655-0,6656 ,
 6102-8,6110-9,6250-4
One word more, sels. 6123-0
Ottima and Sebald, two lovers, fr. Pippa passes. 6102-8
"Ours is a great wild country", fr. The flight... 6123-
 0
"Over the sea our galleys went", fr. Paracelsus. 6547-3,
 6250-0,6110-9
Pambo. 6655-0
Paracelsus. 6828-6
Paracelsus, sel. 7014-0
Paracelsus, sels. 6123-0,6369-1,6547-3,6726-3,6484-1,
 6199 ,6110-9
Parleyings with certain people of importance, sels.
 6123-0,6483-3
Parting and meeting. 6732-8
Parting at morning. 6123-0,6198-2,6204-0,6208-3,6236-9,
 6332-,6046-3,6102-8,6199-0,6110-9,6196-6,6430 ,6339-
 X,6358-6,6437-X,6512-0,6657-7,6656 ,6301-2,6646-1,
 6655-0,6723-9,6122-2
Parting at morning. 6828-6
The patriot. 6114-1,6246-6,6339-X,6395-0,6457-4,6473 ,
 6110-9,6196-6,6199-0,6458-2,6655-0,6624 ,6552-X,6163-
 X,6199-0,6246-6,6110-9
Pauline, sels. 6123-0,6144-3,6369-1,6483-6,6730-1,6144-
 3,6337-3,6359-4,6123-0
A pearl, a girl. 6321-7,6429-9
A pearl-a girl. 6110-9,6321-7,6429-9,6655-0
Phases of the moon. 6125-7
The phases of the moon, fr. One word more. 6125-7
Pheidippides. 6154-0,6473-6,6550-3,6669-0,6424-8,6122-2,
 6163-8,6424-8
Pictor Ignotus. 6110-9,6655-0,6657-7
Pictor ignotus. 6110-9
The pied piper of Hamelin, sels. 6123-0
The pied piper of Hamelin. 6089-7,6179-6,6302-0,6358-3,
 6484-1,6614 ,6105-2,6127-3,6133-8,6239-3,6290-3,6427
 ,6136-2,6242-3,6271-7,6401-9,6504-X,6732 ,6304-7,
 6131-1,6135-4,6107-9,6102-8,6110 ,6219-9,6421-3,6371-
 3,6668-2,6419-1,6639 ,6304-7,6131-1,6135-4,6107-9,
 6102-8,6110 ,6219-9,6421-3,6371-3,6668-2,6419-1,6639
 ,6861-8,6828-6
Pippa passes. 6110-9,6250-4,6466-3,5697-X
Pippa passes, sels. 6047-1,6123-0,6332-2,6560-0,6655-0,
 6250 ,6192-3,6197-4,6199-0,6094-3,6232-6,6732 ,6337-
 3,6418-3,6479-5,6484-1,6732-8,6047-1,6123-0,6332-2,
 6560-0,6655-0,6250 ,6192-3,6197-4,6199-0,6094-3,6232-
 6,6732 ,6337-3,6418-3,6479-5,6484-1,6732-8
Pippa's morning sing, fr. Pippa passes. 6134-6
Pippa's song. 6861-8
Pippa's song, fr. Pippa passes. 6047-1,6104-4,6242-3,
 6328-4,6466-3,6421 ,6252-0,6291-1,6374-8,6437-X,6501-
 5,6604 ,6534-1,6047-1,6104-4,6242-3,6328-4,6466-3,
 6421 ,6252-0,6291-1,6374-8,6437-X,6501-5,6604 ,6534-
 1
"The poet's age is sad: for why?", fr. Asolando. 6123-0
Poetics. 6110-9
Poetics ("So say the foolish..."). 6110-9
"The poets pour us wine," fr. the Pacchiarotto volume.
 6110-9
Pompilia speaks. 6233-4
Pompilia speaks, sels. 6233-4
Pompilia, fr. The ring and the book. 6123-0,6657-7
The pope and the net. 6089-7,6092-7
The pope, fr. The ring and the book. 6657-7
Popularity. 6110-9,6483-3,6110-9
Porphyria's lover. 6110-9,6301-2,6430-2,6655-0,6657-7,
 6723 ,6645-3,6110-9,6301-2,6430-2,6655-0,6657-7,6723
 ,6645-3,6301-2,6110-9
Porphyria's lover. 6828-6
The professor's Christmas sermon, fr. Christmas eve.
 6082-X
Prologue, fr. Asolando. 6123-0,6657-7
Prologue, fr. La Saisiaz. 6123-0,6110-9
Prologue, fr. The two poets of Croisic. 6110-9
Prologue, fr. The two poets of Crossic. 6723-9
Prospice. 6001-5,6123-0,6154-0,6208-3,6289-X,6291 ,6328-
 4,6332-2,6337-3,6437-X,6473-6,6479 ,6501-5,6604-6,
 6655-0,6657-7,6730-1,6732 ,6102-8,6110-9,6196-6,6199-

0,6301-2,6737 ,6023-4,6214-8,6371-3,6560-0,6656-9, 6660 ,6107-9,6212-1,6250-4,6430-2,6723-9,6820 ,6001-3,6123-0,6154-0,6208-3,6289-X,6291 ,6328-4,6332-2, 6337-3,6437-X,6473-6,6479 ,6501-5,6604-6,6655-0,6657-7,6730-1,6732 ,6102-8,6110-9,6196-6,6199-0,6301-2, 6737 ,6023-4,6214-8,6371-3,6560-0,6656-9,6660 ,6107-9,6212-1,6250-4,6430-2,6723-9

Rabbi Ben Ezra. 6198-2,6291-1,6337-3,6437-X,6479-5,6527 ,6600-3,6604-6,6655-0,6657-7,6730-1,6723 ,6102-8, 6110-9,6560-0,6250-4,6199-0,6660 ,6107-9,6214-8
Rabbi Ben Ezra, sels. 6332-2
Ratisbon. 6370-5,6621-6
Religion, fr. Mr. Sludge, the medium. 6337-3
Rephan. 6655-0
Respectability. 6828-6
Respectability. 6110-9,6199-0
Rest remaineth. 6465-5
The ride from Ghent to Aix. 6370-5,6403-5
The ring and the book, sels. 6123-0,6144-3,6154-0,6204-0,6378-0,6484 ,6655-0,6657-7,6403-5,6430-2,6199-0, 6110
Rosny. 6110-9
"Round the cape of a sudden came the sea". 6997-5
"Round us the wild creatures," fr. Ferishtah's fancies. 6110-9,6655-0
Rudel to the lady of Tripoli. 6315-2,6378-0,6427-2,6110-9
Saint and sinner. 6094-3
Saul. 6110-9,6430-2,6199-0,6107-9,6646-1,6196 ,6655-0, 6110-9,6430-2,6199-0,6107-9,6646-1,6196 ,6655-0,6337-3,6527-9,6657-7,6726-3,6730-1,6723
Saul, sels. 6123-0,6144-3,6198-2,6315-2,6427-2,6716-
Scene in a garden. 6466-3
A serenade at the villa. 6378-0;6655-0
Shelley. 6560-0
Shop. 6023-4,6655-0,6657-7
Sirandus Schafnaburgensis. 6733-6,6655-0
The soldier relieved. 6114-1
Soliloquy of the Spanish cloister. 6192-3,6199-0,6655-0, 6153-2,6430-2,6102 ,6154-0,6427-2,6527-9,6657-7,6732-8,6733-
Solomon and Balkis. 6848-0
Something to remember. 6114-1
Song ("All service"). 6315-2
Song ("Nay but you"). 6198-2,6110-9,6199-0,6655-0
Song ("Overhead the tree-tops"). 6233-4
Song ("The moth's kiss, first"). 6620-8
Song ("The year's at the spring"), fr. Pippa passes. 6236-9,6332-2,6337-3,6423-X,6478-7,6604-,6730-1,6192-3,6301-2,6368-3
Song ("There's a woman"). 6094-3,6560-0
Song from 'pippa passes' 6820-0
Song, fr. In a gondola. 6301-2
Song, fr. Paracleus. 6543-0
Song, fr. Pippa passes. 6543-0
Song: "Nay but you, who do not love her" 6828-6
Songs from Paracelsus. 6828-6
Sordello, sels. 6123-0,6369-1
Speculative. 6199-0
The statue and the bust. 6102-8,6110-9,6484-1,6624-0, 6655-0,6676-3,6430-2,6199
The statue and the bust. 6828-6
Strafford. 6188-5,6323-3
"Such a starved bank of moss",fr two poets of Croisic. 6123-0,6199-0,6430-2,6585-6,6655-0,6737
Summum bonum. 6110-9,6301-2,6321-7,6491-4,6655-0,6123-0, 6320-9,6429-9,6199-0,6196-6,6737
Sunrise. 6374-8,6252-0
"Take the cloak from his face, and at first". 6187-7
"That autumn eve was stilled", fr. Sordello. 6123-0
"That low man seeks a little thing to do", fr funeral. 6123-0
That one face, fr. Dramatis personae. 6337-3
"Then all is still...", fr. Paracelsus. 6123-0
"Then I tuned my harp-took off the lilies...",fr Saul. 6123-0
"There's a fancy some lean to...", fr Old Pictures. 6123-0
There's a woman like a dewdrop. 6620-8,6110-9
This is a spray... 6943-6

Through the Metidja to Abd-el-Kadr. 6328-4,6110-9
Thus the mayne glideth. 6252-0
Time's revenges. 6110-9,6655-0
To E.B.B. 6321-7,6429-9
A toccata of Galuppi's. 6046-3,6110-9,6250-4,6301-2, 6186-9,6331-4,6427-2,6536-8,6624-0,6657-,6315-2,6380-2,6726-3,6655-0,6560-0,6300
Too late. 6828-6
Touch him n'eer so lightly. 6110-9
Transcendentalism: a poem in twelve books. 6655-0
Tray. 6110-9
Truth is within, fr. Paracelsus. 6337-3
Truth, fr. A death in the desert. 6337-3
The twins. 6621-6
Two in the campagna. 6204-0,6208-3,6246-6,6331-4,6624-0, 6657-,6102-8,6110-9,6150-8,6430-2,6560-0,6726 ,6655-0
The two poets of Croisic, sels. 6123-0,6102-8
The two poets of Croisic, sels. 6110-9,6723-9
The two poets of Croisic. 6250-4
Up at a villa--down in the city. 6289-X,6395-0,6473-6, 6657-7,6733-6,6723 ,6110-9,6199-0,6655-0
Verse-making -- love-making, fr. Ferishtah's fancies. 6328-4,6110-9
The wanderers. 6437-X
"Wanting is- what?" 6828-6
Wanting is--what? 6198-2,6110-9,6196-6,6199-0,6655-0, 6737
Waring. 6934-7
Waring: part 2. 6258-X
"The water's in stripes like a snake, olive-pale". 6997-5
"What were seen? None knows", fr. One word more. 6123-0
When a man's busy. 6722-0
"Where the quiet-colored end of evening...", fr. Ruins. 6123-0
White witchcraft. 6123-0
"Why come temptations but for man to meet." 6225-3
"Why from the world," fr. Ferishtah's fancies. 6110-9
Why I am a liberal. 6123-0,6110-9,6199-0,6250-4
The wild joys of living. 6501-5
The wise thrush. 6073-0
A woman's last word. 6123-0,6186-9,6246-6,6317-9,6657-7, 6655
A woman's last word. 6102-8,6110-9,6199-0,6250-4,6650-0
Women and roses. 6828-6
Women and roses. 6199-0
Women and roses, sels. 6232-6
"Words break no bones". 6889-8
"The year's at the spring", fr. Pippa passes. 6197-4, 6196-6,6199-0,6371-3,6396-9,6473 ,6023-4,6123-0,6136-2,6289-X,6465-5,6481 ,6214-8,6456-6,6737-9
You'll love me yet, fr. Pippa passes. 6102-8,6199-0
Youth and art. 6092-7,6094-3,6110-9,6655-0,6656-9,6089-7,6123-0,6657-7,6683-6,6732-8,6585

Browning, Robert (tr.)
Death the enemy, fr. Alcestis. Euripides, 6435-3
The greatest tribute. Philemon, 6435-3
Hospitality, fr. Alcestis. Euripides, 6435-3
"**Browning**, old fellow". In a copy of Browning. Bliss Carman and Richard Hovey. 6890-1
Brownjohn, John
The Indian attack. 6580-5
Miltiades gets the best of Santa Claus. 6167-2,6415-9
Miltiades Peterkin Paul. 6410-8,6744-1
Brownlee, Robert Earl
The moth. 6347-0
Brownlow, Edward B.
The song of Orpheus. 6433-7
Brownrigg, Shirley
The dark song. 6850-2
The **Browns**. Thomas Dunn English. 6912-6
Brownson, William Green
The consultation, fr. The country doctor. 6482-5
The country docotr, sels. 6482-5
Getting gray. 6482-5
"**Browsing** among old books long laid away". Guests. David Morton. 6850-2
Bruce addresses his army. John Barbour. 6845-6
Bruce and the abbot. Sir Walter Scott. 6438-8

BRUCE

Bruce and the spider. Bernard Barton. 6267-9
Bruce consults his men. John Barbour. 6845-6
Bruce to his men at Bannockburn. Robert Burns. 6301-2
Bruce's address to his army at Bannockburn. Robert Burns. 6289-X,6604-6,6250-4,6660-7
The **Bruce's** locket. ? Strachwitz. 6842-1
Bruce, **Aubert Edgar**
    Contrast ("What wrote he on the parched and dusty...") 6144-3
    Provincialism. 6954-1
Bruce, **Charles**
    Biography. 6446-9
    Eastern shore. 6446-9
    Words are never enough. 6021-8
Bruce, **George**
    Kinnaird head. 6379-9
Bruce, **Michael**
    The complaint of nature. 6086-2
    The elegy to spring, sels. 6960-6
    Elegy written in spring. 6086-2
    The fly. 6131-1
    Ode to the cuckoo. 6180-X,6086-2
    Spring pointing to God. 6049-8
Bruce, **R.L.**
    Prohibition's might. 6685-2
Bruce, **Robert Michael**
    Nomente. 6800-6
Bruce, **Wallace**
    'Inasmuch'. 6139-7
    Memorial Day. 6340-3
    No life is so strong and complete. 6066-8
    The old homestead. 6575-9
    Ole Bull's Christmas. 6688-7
    One word. 6676-3
    Our nation forever. 6449-3
    Parson Allen's ride. 6946-0
The **Bruce**, sels. John Barbour. 6180-X
Bruchac, **Joseph**
    The buffalo skull. 6998-3
Brudder Jones's heterodxy. Unknown. 6687-9
Bruff, **Nancy**
    The one ambassador. 6979-7
Bruges. William Wordsworth. 6484-1
Bruise. Nancy McCleery. 6855-3
"Bruised by a heel he strove to die". The death of a snake. William Plomer. 6985-1
Bruised knuckles: S & M valentines. Wayne McNeill. 7003-5
Brumana. James Elroy Flecker. 6044-7,6477-9,6659-3,6508-2
Brun, **Yung-ro**
    Spring rain. 6775-1
Brundisium. Lucan. 6624-0
Bruner, **Margaret E.**
    After sorrow. 6461-2
    Atonement. 6337-3
    Bitter fruit. 6789-1
    Christmas eve meditation. 6337-3
    The comforting. 6750-6
    Cruelty. 6120-6
    Elegy. 6120-6
    Epitaph for a cat. 6120-6
    For a certain beloved gentleman. 6799-9
    The grocery store cat. 6120-6
    An old cat meditates. 6120-6
    Selfishness. 6337-3
    Sonnet ("There have been"). 6120-6
    Souvenirs. 6120-6
    Unbidden mood. 6789-1
    The way of a cat. 6120-6
Brunini, **John Gilland**
    Th Assumption ("O heart submissive in this martyrdom"). 6282-2
    Mary, Martha, Mary. 6839-1
    The resurrection. 6337-3
    Silent sufferer. 6292-X
    To Mary at Christmas. 6282-2
Brunn, **Friederike**
    Chamouny at sunrise. 6749-2
Brunnen. James Montgomery. 6749-2
Bruno, **Giordano**
    The philosophic flight. John Addington Symonds (tr.). 6325-X
    The philosophic flight. John Addington Symonds (tr.). 7039-6
Bruns, **John Dickson**
    The foe at the gates. 6113-3
    Our Christmas hymn. 6113-3
    Sir Pronto's party. 6131-1
Bruns, **K. von K.**
    Freedom. 6799-9
Brush, **Christine Chaplin**
    The cornstalk's lesson. 6965-7
    The mother apple-blossom. 6965-7
Brushed by the master's hand. Paul Floyd Cornish. 6818-9
The **brut**, sels. Unknown. 6198-2,6193-1
The **brute**. William Vaughn Moody. 6250-4
Bruton town. Unknown. 6829-4
Brutus. William Shakespeare. 6102-8
Brutus and Cassius, fr. Julius Caesar. William Shakespeare. 6138-9
Brutus and Titus. Nathaniel Lee. 6606-2
Brutus on the death of Caesar. William Shakespeare. 6304-7
Brutus's oration over the body of Lucretia. John Howard Payne. 6302-0,6385-3
"Bryan O'Lynn and his wife and wife's mother". Unknown. 6363-2
Bryan, **G.S.**
    Old roads. 6764-6
    Preference. 6764-6
Bryan, **George S.**
    Anathema. 6037-4
    A modern Lochinvar. 6441-8
Bryant dead. Paul Hamilton Hayne. 6820-0
Bryant on his birthday. John Greenleaf Whittier. 6126-5
Bryant's seventieth birthday. Oliver Wendell Holmes. 6753-0
Bryant's seventieth birthday. Oliver Wendell Holmes. 6126-5
Bryant's seventieth birthday. Oliver Wendell Holmes. 6753-0
Bryant, **Ann**
    Gladioli. 6750-6
Bryant, **Blanche Browne**
    Queen mountain. 6270-9
Bryant, **Florence Estelle**
    The Empire State Building. 6799-9
Bryant, **Helen**
    Air raid, old style. 6761-1
    But sing your love. 6761-1
Bryant, **John Howard**
    Close to ninety. 7022-1
    The Indian summer. 6618-6
    The little cloud. 6302-0;6385-3
    The valley brook. 6302-0;6385-3
    Winter. 6385-3
Bryant, **Lesbia**
    A Thanksgiving dinner. 6703-4
Bryant, **Louise**
    Aftermath. 6036-6
Bryant, **M. Alice**
    Washington's life. 6171-0,6712-3
Bryant, **May**
    The plucky prince. 6614-3
Bryant, **T.H.**
    Limerick:"..young Birton B.A." 6811-1
Bryant, **William Cullen**
    Abraham Lincoln. 6074-9,6288-1,6126-5
    The African chief. 6732-8
    After a tempest. 6752-2
    America ("Oh, mother of a mighty race"). 6014-5,6176-1, 6086-5,6302-0,6385-3,6678
    Among the trees. 6049-8
    Antiquity of freedom. 6126-5,6049-8,6286-5,6385-3,6457-4,6288-1,6304
    Antiquity of freedom, sels. 6176-1
    Autumn woods. 6126-5
    The battle field, sels. 6337-3
    The battle field. 6219-9,6271-7,6302-0,6340-3,6385-3, 6600-3,6605-,6153-2,6444-2,6288-1,6126-5,6263-6,6735
    Be ye also ready, fr. Thanatopsis. 6337-3
    Beyond ("What is there beyond?"). 6303-9

"Blessed are they that mourn." 6240-7,6302-0,6385-3
Bob-o'-Lincoln. 6772-7
The burial of love. 6271-7,6600-3
The burial place, sels. 6049-8
Catterskill Falls. 6484-1
Centennial hymn. 6946-0
Christmas. 6144-3,6337-3
Christmas in 1875. 6753-0
The conjunction of Jupiter and Venus. 6288-1
The conqueror's grave. 6735-2
The crowded street. 6271-7,6302-0,6457-4,6735-2,6219-9, 6304
The damsel of Peru. 6412-4
Dante. 6483-3
The death of flowers. 6239-3,6271-7,6303-9,6486-8,6600-3,6632-
The death of Lincoln. 6008-0,6288-1,6077-3,6176-1,6289-X,6265-2,6524-4,6126
The death of slavery. 6340-3,6403-5
The death of the flowers. 6121-4,6309-8,6396-9,6438-8, 6219-9,6304 ,6560-0,6639-9,6232-6,6240-7,6302-0,6385-3,6288-1,6431
Dedication ("We dedicate a church today"). 6525-2
The dream of Schiller. 6648-8
The embargo, sels. 6008-0
An evening revery. 6431-0
The evening wind. 6753-0
The evening wind. 6077-3,6102-8,6240-7,6271-7,6299-7, 6291 ,6076-5,6126-5,6304-7,6008-1,6288-1,6302-0,6385-3
Fatima and Raduan. 6302-0;6385-3
"Few, few were they whose swords of old", sels. 66601-1
The flood of years. 6385-3,6304-7,6569-4,6288-1,6126-5, 6265
A forest hymn, sels. 6102-8,6076-5,6126-5
A forest hymn. 6014-5,6047-1,6049-8,6407-8,6473-6,6735-, 6008-0,6288-1,6431-0,6076-5,6121-4,6214 ,6302-0,6385-3,6457-4,6673-9,6304-7
The forest maid. 6437-X
The fountain, sels. 6049-8
The fountain. 6673-9
The fringed gentian. 6621-6
The future life. 6240-7,6385-3,6735-2
The gladness of nature. 6047-1,6049-8,6127-3,6457-4, 6597-X,6135
God's first temples. 6392-6,6521-X,6376-4
The Greek boy. 6965-7
The Greek partisan. 7009-4
The Green Mountain Boys. 6267-9
Green River. 6523-6,6288-1,6126-5,6121-4,6484-1,6376
"The groves were God's first temples", sels. 6047-1
The groves. 6629-1
The holy star. 6065-X
A home mission prayer. 6525-2
"How shall I know thee in the sphere which keeps". 6238-5
The hunter of the prairies. 6271-7,6484-1,6219-9
The hunter's vision. 6271-7,6648-8
The hurricane. 6302-0,6457-4
Hymn of the city. 6077-3,6288-1,6126-5,6121-4
A hymn of the sea. 6258-X,6302-0
Hymn to death. 6126-5,6288-1,6753-0
Hymn to the north star. 6457-X
I broke the spell that held me long. 6732-8,6288-1,6431-0
I cannot forget with what fervid devotion. 6121-4,6288-1
"I cannot forget with what fervid devotion". 6753-0
Inscription for an entrance to a wood. 6047-1,6049-8, 6077-3,6332-2,6333-0,6288 ,6008-0,6121-4,6126-5
An invitation to the country. 6047-1,6049-8,6597-X
Jack Frost. 6242-3
June. 6240-7,6735-2,6288-1,6126-5
June, sels. 6934-7
The lapse of time. 6077-3
A lifetime. 6126-5,6288-1,6753-0
Lines on revisiting the country. 6484-1
The little people of the snow. 6126-5
The living lost. 6219-9
The love of God. 64612

March. 6820-0,6239-3,6502-3,6304-7,6456-6
The May-sun sheds an amber light. 6077-3
A meditation on Rhode Island coal. 6484-1,6753-0
The mocking bird and the donkey. 6512-0
"Modest and shy as a nun is she", sels. 6601-1
Monument mountain. 6008-0,6126-5,6288-1,6753-0
The mosquito. 6278-4
A mother's charge. 6143-5
The mother's hymn. 6097-8,6302-0,6337-3,6365-9
The murdered traveller. 6752-2
The murdered traveller. 6438-8
The murdered traveller. 6752-2
Mutation. 6077-3
My autumn walk. 6113-3,6302-3,6385-3,6288-1,6126-5
"My heart is awed within me, when I think". 6238-5
'No man knoweth his sepulchre' 6848-0
A noon scene. 6752-2
Not yet. 6113-3
November. 6121-4
O fairest of the rural maids. 6299-7,6102-8,6076-5,6008-8,6250-4,6288 ,6076-5,6431-0,6126-5,6219-9
"Oh fairest of the rural maids". 6965-7
O mother of a mighty race. 6486-8,6126-5,6271-7,6735-2, 6288-1
"O mother of a mighty race". 6753-0
October. 6126-5,6288-1
Ode for the burial of Abraham Lincoln. 6709-3
"Oh, mother of a mighty race". 6946-0
The old man's counsel. 6049-8
The old man's funeral. 6438-8
On Jefferson. 6088-9
Our country's call. 6015-3,6113-3,6403-5,6126-5
"Our hopes like towering falcons aim". 6238-5
The painted cup. 6484-1
The part. 6219-9,6288-1
The past, sels. 6102-8,6076-5
The past. 6077-3,6735-2,6288-1,6431-0,6126-5,6219 ,6304-7
The path, sels. 6333-0
The path. 6597-X
The planting of the apple tree. 6006-4,6047-1,6049-8, 6239-3,6356-X,6300 ,6299-7,6302-0,6385-3,6479-5,6486-8,6497 ,6597-X,6672-0,6735-2,6126-5,6304-7,6457 , 6006-4,6047-1,6049-8,6239-3,6356-X,6300 ,6299-7,6302-0,6385-3,6479-5,6486-8,6497 ,6597-X,6672-0,6735-2, 6126-5,6304-7,6457 ,6239-3,6820-0
The poet. 6288-1
The poet. 6288-1,6289-X,6333-0,6126-5
The prairies. 6008-0,6126-5,6121-4,6288-1,6333-0,6484 , 6020-X,6121-4,6008-0,6288-1
The return of the birds. 6049-8,6529-5
"The rivulet", sels. 6600-3
The rivulet. 6438-8
Rizpah. 6848-0
Robert of Lincoln. 6006-4,6073-0,6127-3,6302-0,6373-X, 6385 ,6392-6,6466-3,6473-6,6479-5,6519-8,6742 ,6088-0,6570-8,6288-1,6135-4,6004-8,6126 ,6131-1,6456-6, 6088-0,6570-8,6288-1,6135-4,6004-8,6126 ,6131-1,6456-6
Sella's fairy slippers. 6302-0
Seventy-six. 6753-0,6946-0,6820-0
Seventy-six - the American War of Independence. 7009-4
The siesta. 6302-0;6385-3
The skies. 6752-2
The snow-shower. 6302-0,6373-X,6385-3,6735-2,6300-4
"So live, that when thy summons comes to join". 6238-5, 6461-2
Song. 6652-6
A song for New Year's Eve. 6465-5,6267-9
Song of Marion's men. 6015-2,6062-5,6136-2,6176-1,6271-7,6410-,6286-5,6302-0,6385-3,6732-8,6735-2,6442 , 6457-4,6471-X,6504-X,6552-X,6589-9,6706-
Song of the Greek Amazon. 6732-8
The song of the sower, sels. 6334-9
The song of the sower. 6753-0
Song of the stars. 6438-8
Song of the stars, sels. 6334-9
Sonnet ("A power"). 6752-2
Sonnet ("Ay, thou art welcome"). 6752-2
Sonnet to ---. 6752-2

"Soon, over half the earth". 6272-5
Spring in town. 6752-2
The star of Bethlehem. 6385-3
The story of seventy-six. 6444-2
A summer ramble. 6008-0
Summer wind. 6077-3,6008-0
Thanatopsis. 6008-0,6250-4,6560-0,6288-1,6431-0,6214 ,6309-8,6467-1,6300-4,6304-7,6438-8,6219 ,6008-0,6250-4,6560-0,6288-1,6431-0,6214 ,6309-8,6467-1,6300-4, 6304-7,6438-8,6219 ,6006-4,6014-5,6077-3,6102-8,6176-1,6183-,6271-7,6299-7,6302-0,6385-3,6303-9,6332-, 6333-0,6402-7,6418-3,6425-6,6437-X,6457-,6473-6,6481-7,6486-8,6600-3,6610-0,6632-,6726-3,6730-1,6732-8, 6735-2,6723-9,6570 ,6076-5,6126-5,6121-4,6371-3,6424-8,6585 ,6424-8
Thanatopsis, sels. 6049-8,6260-1,6289-X
"There is a power whose care." 6225-3
"There is a sacred dread of death". 6238-5
"These are the gardens of the Desert, these". 6289-X
Those glorious stars. 6304-7
"Thou hast put all things under his feet." 6302-0
Thou, whose unmeasured temple stands. 6337-3
"'Tis sweet, in the green spring..." 6049-8
To a mosquito. 6385-3
To a waterfowl. 6008-0,6250-4,6288-1,6431-8,6121-1,6104 ,6214-8,6121-4,6219-9,6300-4,6309-8,6304 ,6265-2, 6371-3,6126-5,6076-5,6421-3,6438 ,6396-9,6008-0,6250-4,6288-1,6431-8,6121-1,6104 ,6214-8,6121-1,6219-9, 6300-4,6309-8,6304 ,6265-2,6371-3,6126-5,6076-5,6421-3,6438 ,6396-9,6006-4,6007-2,6073-0,6075-7,6077-3, 6101-,6102-8,6133-8,6176-1,6208-3,6239-3,6246-,6238-5,6597-X,6600-3,6632-1,6730-1,6732-,6271-7,6289-X, 6302-0,6332-2,6333-0,6385-,6337-3,6457-4,6473-6,6481-7,6503-1,6589-,6646-1,6639-9,6464-7,6737-9,6735-2, 6510
To Cole, the painter, departing for Europe. 6333-0
"To him who in the love of nature holds", sels. 6047-1
To the Apennines. 6624-0
To the evening wind. 6332-2
To the fringed gentian. 6219-9,6121-4,6153-2,6126-5, 6431-0,6288 ,6008-0,6304-7,6396-9,6424-8,6560-0,6219-9,6121-4,6153-2,6126-5,6431-0,6288 ,6008-0,6304-7, 6396-9,6424-8,6560-0,6006-4,6101-X,6176-1,6239-3, 6271-7,6302-,6303-9,6385-3,6457-4,6488-4,6497-3,6523-,6600-3,6641-0,6654-2,6737-9,6438-8,6250
To the memory of Abraham Lincoln. 6088-9,6305-5
To the river Arve. 6749-2
Tree burial. 6049-8
"Truth crushed to earth shall rise again". 6102-8,6238-5,6260-1,6523-6,6076-5
The twenty-second of December. 6239-3
The twenty-second of February. 6465-5,6712-3,6575-9
Upon the mountain's distant head. 6456-6
Waiting by the gate. 6271-7,6409-4
A walk at sunset. 6077-3,6121-4
Washington. 6964-9,6820-0
Washington's birthday. 6486-8
The water fowl. 6260-1
The western world. 6752-2
"What cordial welcomes greet the guest". 6238-5
"Where fall the tears of love..." 6049-8
The white-footed deer. 6457-4,6614-3
William Tell. 6749-2
William Tell. 6331-4,6439-6
The wind and stream. 6008-0
A winter piece. 6008-0,6121-4,6126-5
The yellow violet. 6077-3,6176-1,6333-0,6457-4,6536-8, 6431 ,6008-0,6288-1,6126-5,6121-4
"Yet nerve thy spirit to the proof". 6238-5
The yew, fr. The burial place. 6049-8
Bryant, William Cullen (tr.)
The bending of the bow, fr. The Odyssey. Homer, 6372-1
The donkey and the mocking-bird. Jose Rosas, 6614-3
The elm and the vine. Jose Rosas, 6614-3
Helen at the Scaean gates, fr. The Iliad. Homer, 6372-1
The Iliad, sels. Homer, 6372-1,6610-0
The life of the blessed. Luis Ponce de Leon, 6752-2
The love of God, fr. The provencal. Bernard Rascas, 6385-3
The love of God. Unknown (French), 6385-3
Mary Magdalen. Bartolome Leonardo de Argensola, 6752-2
The Odyssey, sels. Homer, 6372-1,6484-1
Palace of Alcinous, fr. The Odyssey. Homer, 6372-1
The parting of Hector and Andromache, fr. The Iliad. Homer, 6372-1,6102-8
The siesta. Unknown (Spanish), 7039-6
Sonnet ("It is a fearful night"). Semedo, 6732-8
Ulysses and Achilles, fr. The Odyssey. Homer, 6879-0
The victory of Hector, fr. The Iliad. Homer, 6610-0
The woodman and the sandal tree. Jose Rosas, 6614-3
Brydges, Matthew. See Bridges, Matthew
Brydges, Sir Egerton
The approach of cold weather. 6980-0
"But in this rural life," fr. Hastings' sonnets. 6980-0
"But is congenial quiet," fr. Hastings sonnets. 6980-0
"A century did not thy vigour pale"fr.Hastings' sonnets. 6980-0
Hastings' sonnets. 6980-0
"A hundred years to live," fr. Hastings' sonnets. 6980-0
"Old Harry Hastings!", fr. Hastings' sonnets. 6980-0
On Moor Park. 6980-0
On Moor Park - written at Lee priory, 8/10/1826 6980-0
On Moor Park - written at Paris, May 10, 1825. 6980-0
On Moor Park - written at Paris, May 11, 1826. 6980-0
On Moor Park - written August 20, 1807. 6980-0
"Then comes the rude," fr. Hastings' sonnets. 6980-0
"There is exhalaration in the chase," fr. Hastings' 6980-0
To a lady in illness. 6980-0
To autumn, near her departure. 6980-0
To evening. 6980-0
To Mary. 6980-0
"To-morrow will the music," fr. Hastings' sonnets. 6980-0
The winds. 6980-0
Brydges, Sir Samuel Egerton
Echo and silence. 6240-7,6086-2,6291-9
Bryne, William A.
The bog lands. 6292-X
Bryngynge in the bore's head. Unknown. 6747-6
Bryom, John
Self-rightousness. 6337-3
Bryon's farewell. George Gordon, 6th Baron Byron. 6301-2, 6383-7
Bryson, Lyman
The prophet. 6028-5
Bryusov, Valery
Benediction. Cecil Maurice Bowra (tr.). 6103-6
The coming huns. Cecil Maurice Bowra (tr.). 6103-6
Mowers in the line of fire. Jack Lindsay (tr.). 6456-5
Orpheus and Eurydice. Cecil Maurice Bowra (tr.). 6103-6
Radiant ranks of seraphim. Babette Deutsch and Avrahm Yarmolinsky (tr.). 7039-6
Remote in a closed space. Jack Lindsay (tr.). 6456-5
The stonecutter. Cecil Maurice Bowra (tr.). 6103-6
To comrade intellectuals. Jack Lindsay (tr.). 6456-5
Two voices. Cecil Maurice Bowra (tr.). 6103-6
Bubble-blowing. William Canton. 6639-9
The **bubble.** William Allingham. 6930-4
The **bubble.** William Drummond of Hawthornden. 6737-9
The **bubble.** F. Hoatson. 6937-1
Bubbles. Alfred Kreymborg. 6010-2
Bubbles. George H. Shorey. 6466-3
"Bubbles that burst in seething flood". Champagne. Thomas Blaine Donaldson. 6936-3
Bubbling wine. Abu Zakariya. 6362-4
Buccaneer. Charles Kingsley. 6732-8
A **buccaneer chorus.** Clark B. Firestone. 7007-8
The **buccaneer,** fr. Rokeby. Sir Walter Scott. 6832-4
The **buccaneer.** Sir Walter Scott. 6543-0
Buccaneers. Berton Braley. 6853-7
The **buccaneers.** Richard Hovey. 7006-X
Buch der lieder. Robert Bridges. 6487-6
Buchan, John
Fisher Jamie. 6269-5,6331-4
Fratri Dilectissimo. 6427-2
Home-thoughts from abroad. 6269-5
In praise of the Royal Scots Fusiliers. 6476-0
The shorter catechism. 6269-5

Buchanan, Charles L.
    Wood magic. 6269-5
    Sonnet ("For all"). 6327-6
Buchanan, David K.
    A spellin' school. 6928-2
Buchanan, Dugald (tr.)
    The day of judgment. Unknown (Gaelic), 6845-6
    Omnia vanitas. Unknown (Gaelic), 6845-6
Buchanan, Frank
    Babel and Bethel. 6532-5
    I must to prayer. 6532-5
Buchanan, George
    Epithalamium for Mary Stuart and the Dauphin of France. 6845-6
    Of the sad lot of the humanists in Paris. 6845-6
Buchanan, J.A.
    Oregon state song. 6465-5
Buchanan, Robert
    Antony in arms. 6889-8
    Artist and model, sels. 6934-7
    "As ocean murmurs when the storm is past". 6997-5
    At the grindstone; or, a home view of the battle field. 6344-6
    The ballad of Judas Iscariot. 6473-,6518-X,6732-8,6656-9,6646-1,6102
    "Beautiful, beautiful the mother lay". 6997-5
    The churhyard. 6656-9
    The dead mother. 6819-7
    The death of Roland the knight. 6134-6
    The death of Roland. 6669-0
    "The dim star of the ocean lieth cool". 6997-5
    The dream of the world without death, fr. The book of Orum. 6656-9
    The faery foster-mother. 6656-9
    The faery reaper. 6437-X
    "Far beneath/Sleepeth the glassy ocean like a sheet". 6997-5
    Fides amantis. 6819-7
    The fiery birth of the hills. 6819-7
    Flower of the world. 6873-1
    Fra Giacamo. 6918-5
    Fra Giacomo. 6385-3
    Freedom's ahead. 6001-3
    The green gnome. 6136-2,62424-3,6271-7,6302-0,6600-3
    Hans Vogel. 6672-0
    Hermione. 6219-9
    The hills on their thrones. 6819-7
    Hugh Sutherland's pansies. 6669-0
    Hugo the bastard. 7007-8
    "I saw below me", fr. The lifting of the veil. 6997-5
    The image in the forum. 6144-3
    In London on Saturday night. 6092-7
    In the garden, sels. 6066-8
    January wind. 6424-8
    Judas Iscariot. 6437-X,6301-2
    King Blaabhein. 6819-7
    L'envoi. 6639-9
    Langley lane. 6925-8
    Langley lane. 6183-4,6242-3,6344-6,6219-9
    The light of freedom. 7009-4
    The little fay. 6424-8
    The little milliner. 6302-0;6385-3
    Little Ned. 6302-0
    Liz. 6934-7
    Nell. 6410-8,6744-1
    The new Rome. 6954-1
    O mither, dinna dee. 6240-7
    "O what is this moaning so faint and low?" 6648-8
    "O what is this morning so faint and low". 6997-5
    The old politician. 6271-7
    On a young poetess's grave. 6656-9
    "One night if storm". 6997-5
    Penelope. 6980-0
    The perfect state, fr. The drama of kings. 7009-4
    Phil Blood's leap. 6410-8,6518-X,6410-8
    The pilgrim and the herdboy. 6437-X
    Pygmalion the sculptor. 6980-0
    Quiet waters. 6383-7
    The runes. 6383-7
    Sea-wash. 997-5
    Serenade. 6658-5
    Song. 6658-5
    Spring song in the city. 6183-4,6597-X,6656-9
    The starling. 6344-6
    Storm and calm. 6997-5
    Storm, fr. Meg Blane. 6997-5
    The strange country. 6873-1
    Summer moon. 6424-8
    The summer pool. 6656-9
    Tiger bay. 6926-6
    To Harriett. 6066-8
    Tom Dunstan. 6219-9
    Two sons. 6233-4,6639-9,6656-9
    The vision of the man accurst, fr. The book of Orm. 6819-7
    The wake of Tim O'Hara. 6825-1
    The wake of Tim O'Hara. 6139-7,6385-3,6732-8,6656-9
    We are children. 6656-9
    The wedding of Shon Maclean. 6180-X,6574-0
    "When the great seas roar". 6997-5
    When we are all asleep. 6656-9
    White rose and red, sels. 6543-0
    The widow Mysie. 6579-1
Buchebner, Walter
    Extinguish the hyacinth. Milne Holton and Herbert Kuhner (tr.). 6769-7
    "I'm capable of loving" Milne Holton and Herbert Kuhner (tr.). 6769-7
    My poem. Milne Holton and Herbert Kuhner (tr.). 6769-7
    "Ne pas se pencher en dehors" Milne Holton and Herbert Kuhner (tr.). 6769-7
Bucher, Helen Hall
    Pennsylvania. 6465-5
Buchtenkirk, Elizabeth J.
    Black soldier. 6979-7
Buchwald, Emilie
    Still lives. 6966-5
The **buck** in the snow. Edna St. Vincent Millay. 6979-7
Buck o' Kingwatter. Robert Anderson. 6328-4
A **buck's** head on the wall. Robert P. Tristram Coffin. 7040-X
Buck, Charles Gurdon
    An idyl. 7025-6,6675-5
Buck, Howard
    Plush. 6039-0
Buck, Mary K.
    The children. 6097-8
Buck, Nellie Manley
    Itasca in October. 6342-X
Buck, Richard Henry
    Kentucky babe. 6006-4,6078-1,6132-X,6732-8
The **bucket**.. Samuel Woodworth. 6077-3,6176-1,6243-1,6271-7,6600-3,6431
Buckham, David
    David Shaw, hero. 7022-1
Buckham, James
    Along the way. 6303-9
    The heart's proof. 6461-2
    The kitten of the regiment. 6621-6
    The music of the hounds. 7008-6
    My best Kentucky reel. 6798-0
    Notwithstanding. 7030-2
    Passed off the stage. 6675-5
    Rover in church. 6695-X
    The smallest of the drums. 6062-5,6340-3,6471-X
    The song in the night. 6373-X
    The song of the market-place. 6451-5,6676-3
    The song of the storm. 6373-X
    Star-fancies. 7030-2
    The tattered flag. 6223-7
    Tomorrow. 7030-2
Buckham, John
    A wasted day. 6889-8
Buckhorn cactus. Emma Ghent Curtis. 6836-7
"The **buckhounds** went on under the rain". Hunt. Kay Boyle. 6781-6
Buckhurst, Lord. See Sackville, Thomas
Buckingham & Normanby, Duke of. See Sheffield, John
Buckingham's address, fr. King Henry VIII. William Shakespeare. 6001-3

BUCKINGHAM

Buckingham, George Villiers, 2d Duke of
    Consolation. 6778-6
    An epitaphn upon Thomas, Lord Fairfax. 6934-7
    Harvest home. 6071-4
    To his mistress. 6563-5
Buckle in. Edgar A. Guest. 6862-6
The **buckle**. Walter De La Mare. 6421-3,6596-1
Buckley, Christopher
    On being whole. 6803-0
Buckman, Gertrude Joan
    Brenda at thirty. 6850-2
    Confession. 6850-2
    Merle. 6850-2
    Rejuvenation. 6850-2
    Vagabondia. 6850-2
Buckminster, J.S.
    An appeal to the "sextant" for air. 6404-3
Buckram, James
    Kitten of the regiment. 6699-2
    The race at devil's elbow. 6690-9
Buckton, A.M.
    At Welbedacht. 6788-3
Buckton, Alice M.
    Old Yule night. 6793-X
Bud and lamb. Marie de L. Welch. 6781-6
A **bud** in the frost. Moira (Nesta Higginson Skrine) O'Neill. 6244-X
"**Bud** into blossom, flower into fruit". Song ("Bud into blossom"). Robert Germain Cole. 6118-4
"A **bud** of red geranium". The naughty little geranium. Carolyn Wells. 6882-0
"The **bud** that looked out with a wistful smile". Spring, fr. Thistledown. Cora Fabri. 6876-6
Bud's fairy tale. James Whitcomb Riley. 6128-1
"**Bud**, come here to your uncle a spell". A home-made fairy-tale. James Whitcomb Riley. 6990-8
The **bud**. Edmund Waller. 6328-4
Buddha. Unknown (Newari) 7013-2
Buddha Guatama
    Psalms of Buddha, sels. 6732-8
The **Buddha** at Kamakura. Rudyard Kipling. 6315-2
Buddha descends to Lumbini. Unknown (Newari) 7013-2
Buddha Sakyamuni. Unknown (Newari) 7013-2
Buddha the world idea, fr. Rig-Veda. Unknown. 6730-1
Buddhist dance. Ji-hoon Cho. 6775-1
Buddhist hymn. Henry Clinton Webster. 7030-2
Buddhist song. Leolyn Louise Everett. 6785-9
Budding author's behest. Jan Dougher. 6857-X
"The **budding** floweret blushes at the light". The want. Thomas Chatterton. 6935-5
'Budding life' John D. Costlow. 6818-9
The **buddy** system (...a release for my cynicism...) Terri Jewell. 6899-5
Buddy, Ann
    Another. 6249-0
    Eddy and Davy have teeth and teeth. 6249-0
    Some man. 6249-0
Budge, Sir E.A. Wallis (tr.)
    Kebra Nagast, sel. Unknown, 7014-0
    The one God. Unknown (Egyptian), 6337-3
    Weddase Maryam. Unknown, 6282-2
Budget. Elspeth Macduffie O'Halloran. 6441-8
Budget, Boston
    Saint Nick. 6745-X
Budmouth dears. Thomas Hardy. 6733-6
Buds and babies. Christina Georgina Rossetti. 6772-7
"The **buds** that bloom on Easter day". Easter buds. Wood Levette Wilson. 7021-3
Buell, C.J.
    A factory girl. 6097-8
    Only a factory girl. 6274-1,6714-X
Buell, Elizabeth
    Ballad of a gray cloak. 6799-9
Buen matina. Sir John Salusbury. 6182-6
Buena Vista. Albert Pike. 6015-3;6471-X
Buers, Edwin (tr.)
    Mary on her way to the temple. Ruth Shaumanm, 6282-2
Buffalo. Florence Earle Coates. 6946-0
Buffalo Bill. Carl Sandburg. 6491-4
Buffalo creek. John Le Gay Brereton. 6784-0

A **buffalo** dance at Santo Domingo. Witter Bynner. 6039-0
Buffalo dusk. Carl Sandburg. 6602-X
The **buffalo** hunters. Unknown. 6278-4
Buffalo marrow on black. Lance Henson. 7005-1
The **buffalo** skinners. Unknown. 6003-X
The **buffalo** skull. Joseph Bruchac. 6998-3
The **buffalo** waiting room. David Ray. 6803-0
The **buffalo**. Herbert Price. 6800-6
Bufo, fr. Epistle to Dr. Arbuthnot. Alexander Pope. 6932-0
Buford, Naomi E.
    Heritage. 6178-8
"A **bug** is looking at me". Reflection. Francis H. Deter. 6906-1
Bug spots. Carl Sandburg. 6011-0
The **bugaboo**. Eugene Field. 6949-5
Bugbee, Emily J.
    Growth. 6049-8
    In memoriam-A. Lincoln. 6392-6
The **bugle** call. Thomas O'Hagan. 6115-X
Bugle song of peace. Thomas Curtis Clark. 6449-3,6542-2, 6730-1
Bugle song, fr. The princess. Alfred Lord Tennyson. 6212-1, 6192-3,6104-4,6392-6,6504-X,6600-3,6604-6,6610-0, 6479 ,6457-4,6706-9,6142-7,6183-4,6240-7,6271 ,6481-7,6552-X,6302-0,6385-3,6543-0,6565 ,6503-1,6498-1, 6332-2,6136-2,6425-6,6512 ,6554-6,6123-0,6623-2,6239-3,6486-8,6134 ,6424-8,6421-3,6660-7,6656-9,6658-5, 6403 ,6304-7,6371-3,6153-2,6219-9,6438-8,6560
The **bugle**. Minna Irving. 6471-X
The **bugle**. Alfred Lord Tennyson. 6737-9
"The **bugleman** heard the bugle sound". Beth Gelert. W.R. Spencer. 6912-6
"The **bugler** sent a call of high romance". The last post. Robert Graves. 7027-2
The **bugler's** first communion. Gerard Manley Hopkins. 6508-2
The **bugler**. Lin Davies. 6542-2
The **bugler**. Frederick W. Harvey. 6477-9,6102-8
The **bugler**. Ernest Rhys. 6783-2
Bugles in the dawning. Frances Hanson. 6224-5
"The **bugles** of departure blow the call". Woodrow Wilson. Edythe C. Toner. 7001-9
"**Bugles** of England were blowing o'er the sea". For England. J.D. Burns. 6784-0
The **bugles** of dreamland. William ("Fiona Macleod") Sharp. 6499-X,6252-0
"**Bugles!**/And the great nation thrills...". The call of the bugles. Richard Hovey. 6753-0
Buick. Karl Shapiro. 6390-X
Build a fence of trust. Mary Frances Butts. 6461-2
Build a little fence. Mary Frances Butts. 6109-5
Build a little fence. Unknown. 6211-3,6260-1
"**Build** me straight, O worthy master". Henry Wadsworth Longfellow. 66601-1
"**Build** thee more stately mansions, O my soul." Oliver Wendell Holmes. 6225-3,6238-5
Build thy dream. Winifred Webb. 6461-2
'Builder, what do you build?' John Ritchey. 6761-1
The **builder**. Caroline Giltinan. 6619-4,6036-6,6328-8
The **builder**. Maud Morrison Huey. 6818-9
The **builder**. Duncan Campbell Scott. 6115-X
The **builder**. Unknown. 6337-3
The **builder**. Willard Wattles. 6102-8,6619-4,6746-8,6467-1, 6076-5,6464
The **builder**. George Meason Whicher. 6847-2
Builders of ruins. Alice Meynell. 7037-X
Builders of ruins. Alice Meynell. 6955-X
Builders of the state. Richard Watson Gilder. 6465-5
The **builders**. Ebenezer Elliot. 6656-9
The **builders**. Henry Wadsworth Longfellow. 6498-1,6523-6, 6337-3,6457-4,6571-6,6126-5,6104-4,6560-0,6288-1
The **builders**. Josephine A. Meyer. 6847-2
The **builders**. Henry Van Dyke. 6961-4
The **builders**. Robert Whitaker. 6954-1
Building. Sarah ("Susan Coolidge") Woolsey. 6925-8
Building a skyscraper. James S. Tippett. 6891-X
The **building** of Jerusalem. William Blake. 6639-9
"**building** of a home! Ah! joy supreme!The". Home. Esther J. Baum. 6847-2
Building of sand. Grant H. Code. 6218-0

The building of Solomon's temple. Unknown. 6057-9
The building of Springfield. Vachel Lindsay. 6473-6
The building of the barn. Charles D. Bingham. 6691-7
The building of the canoe. Henry Wadsworth Longfellow. 6136-2
The building of the house. Charles Mackay. 6669-0
Building of the Hudson River Bridge. John Gould Fletcher. 6781-6
The building of the Long Serpent. Henry Wadsworth Longfellow. 6833-2
Building of the palace of Poseidon, fr. Orion. Richard Hengist Horne. 6980-0
The building of the ship, sels. Henry Wadsworth Longfellow. 6753-0
The building of the ship, sels. Henry Wadsworth Longfellow. 6258-X,6265-2
The building of the ship. Henry Wadsworth Longfellow. 6049-8,6176-1,6499-X,6457-4,6126-5,6322-5,6250-4,6288-1, 6736-0,6121-4
Building the bridge. Benjamin Franklin Taylor. 6815-4
Building the bridge for him. William Allen Dromgoole. 6303-9
Building the schoolhouse fires in Vermont. Daniel L. Cady. 6989-4
"A building there is, well known, I conjecture". The sexton and the thermometer. William Allen Butler. 6903-7
"The buildings are vomiting pink blood". Notes for a basterd angel. Neeli Cherkovski. 6998-3, 6901-0
"Buildings are waterfalls of stone". Waterfalls of stone. Louis Ginsberg. 6880-4,6808-1
"'Built by the convicts,' we are told". Sky-line drive. Jean Milne Gower. 6836-7
Buirgy, Mary
    Two heritages. 6750-6
Buk of Eneados, sels. Gavin [or Gawain] Douglas. 6193-1
Bukowski, Charles
    The crunch. 6998-3
    Don't come around but if you do... 6998-3
    For Jane. 6792-1
    He beats his women. 6998-3
    How to be a great writer. 6998-3
    The priest and the matador. 6792-1
    Something for the touts, the nuns, the grocery... 6792-1
    The tragedy of the leaves. 6792-1
Bulbs. Louise Driscoll. 6232-6
The Bulbul. Maud Wynn Cole. 6800-6
Bulcke, Karl
    There is an old city. Ludwig Lewisohn (tr.). 7039-6
Bulfinch, Maria H.
    An Easter-tide deliverance. 6177-X
"'Bulger said, 'After pineapple...'". A duck for dinner, fr. Owl's clover. Wallace Stevens. 6751-4
Bulkley (atr.), Edward
    Threnodia on Samuel Stone. 6753-0
Bulkley, Vivien
    Cat of cats. 6511-2
The bull and the mastiff. John Gay. 6972-X
The bull fight of Gazul. Unknown. 6271-7
Bull Run. Alice B. Haven. 6678-X
"Bull terrier? Sure she's a white 'un...". My bull terrier. Wex Jones. 7008-6
Bull, A.J. (tr.)
    Landscape of evil. Tristan Corbiere, 6343-8
Bull, Philip J.
    The new preacher. 6916-9
"The bull, the fleece are c amm'd & not a room". Audley court. Alfred Lord Tennyson. 6977-0
The bull-fight of Gazul. Unknown (Spanish) 6757-3
The bull-fight.. George Gordon, 6th Baron Byron. 6407-8
Bull-terrier—frost. Unknown. 6719-0
The bull.. Ralph Hodgson. 6234-2,6726-3
"A bull/a fence". Kandinsky: 'improvisation no. 27' Edward Tick. 6966-5
The bull. Margaret Johnson. 6690-9
Bullard, Harold
    The tree ("O fair and forest tree"). 6031-5
The bulldozer. Donald A. Stauffer. 6666-6
Bullen, Arthur Henry
    By Avon stream. 6477-9
    Mid-May, 1918. 6477-9
Bulletin of bad weather. Jorge Carrera Andrade. 6642-9
Bulletin of bad weather. Jorge Carrera Andrade. 6642-9
Bullett, Gerald
    "Because I love her." 6317-9
The bullfight. Federico Garcia Lorca. 6068-4
The bullfinch. Edward Verrall Lucas. 6018-8
The bullfrog serenade. Joseph Crosby Lincoln. 6119-2
Bullington. Cicely Fox Smith. 6846-4
Bulloch, John Malcolm
    To Homer. 6770-0
Bullock-Willis, Virginia
    The two mothers. 6818-9
The bullocks. Alex Comfort. 6210-5
Bullocky. Judith Wright. 6384-5,6349-7
Bullwinkle, Christine Wood
    Night. 6466-3
Bulosan, Carlos
    Beyond lies America. 6761-1
    History of a moment. 6761-1
"A bulrush stood on a river's rim". The vainglorious oak and the modest bulrush. Guy Wetmore Carryl. 6861-8
Bulteel, John
    I grant your eyes are much more bright. 6563-5
The bulwark of liberty. Abraham Lincoln. 6337-3;6420-5
Bulwarks. F.D. Blanch. 6857-X
Bulwer-Lytton, Edward R. See Meredith, Owen
Bulwer-Lytton; Baron Lytton, Edward
    Absent yet present. 6437-X
    Ambition and glory. 6980-0
    "And love? What was love, then." 6066-8
    The cardinal's soliloquy, fr. Richilieu. 6656-9
    Claude Melnotte's apology and defence. 6385-3
    Consequences of the Reformation. 6046-3
    Cromwell's reflections on Killing no murder. 6980-0
    Cromwell's soliloquy over the dead body of Charles. 6980-0
    Euripides. 6980-0
    Fox. 6046-3
    The hollow oak. 6543-0
    In the Etrurian valley. 6385-3
    The language of the eyes. 6980-0
    The language of the eyes. 6543-0
    The language of the eyes. 6980-0
    Ther last crusader. 6980-0
    Last days of Queen Elizabeth. 6980-0
    Little Ella. 6772-7
    Lord John Russell. 6046-3
    Lord Melbourne. 6046-3,6389-6
    Lord Ronald's ride. 6677-1
    Love and fame. 6980-0
    Nydia's song. 6437-X
    O'Connell. 6046-3
    "O, near ones, dear ones." 6066-8
    The orator. 6046-3
    Patience and hope. 6980-0
    The pen. 6424-8
    Pitt. 6046-3
    Richlieu and France. 6294-6,6606-2
    Richlieu, sels. 6416-7
    The sabbath. 6980-0
    St. James's Street on a summer morning, fr. New Timon. 6046-3
    The secret way. 6543-0
    Sir Robert Walpole. 6046-3
    A spendthrift. 6980-0
    "Standing by the river, gazing on the river". 6238-5
    The successful politican. 6046-3
    Tears. 6585-6
    When stars are in the quiet skies. 6656-9
Bulwer-Lytton; Baron Lytton, Edward (tr.)
    The battle. Johann C. Friedrich von Schiller, 6344-6, 6404-3,6606-2
    The chariot race, fr. Electra. Sophocles, 6621-6
    Damon and Pythias. Johann C. Friedrich von Schiller, 6606-2
    Electra, sels. Sophocles, 6621-6
    The glove. Johann C. Friedrich von Schiller, 6732-8
    The invincible armada. Johann C. Friedrich von Schiller,

BULWER-LYTTON;

6424-8
    The world. Johann C. Friedrich von Schiller, 6424-8
Bumbers, Squire Jones. Arthur Dawson. 6858-8
The **bumble** bee. Unknown. 6629-1
Bumble-bee. James Whitcomb Riley. 6710-7
Bumble-bee and clover. Unknown. 6132-X
Bumblebee. Edna D. Wood. 6466-3
The **bumboat** woman's story. Sir William Schwenck Gilbert. 6572-4,6219-9
A '**bump** supper'. Heathcote William Garrod. 6785-9
Bumpety bump. Unknown. 6937-1
The **bumps**.. Unknown. 6149-4
Bumstead, Eudora S.
    In the swing. 6373-X
    Indian summer. 6618-6
    Margie's Thanksgiving. 6618-6
    A summer lullaby. 6373-X
Bumstead, Eudora S. (tr.)
    The canary's story. E.V. S., 6373-X
    Good-night. Sydney Dayre, 6373-X
    The little pine tree. Unknown (German), 6373-X,6049-8
Bunbury, Henry Shirley
    The joys of Jamaica. 6591-0,6592-9
    The West Indies. 6591-0,6592-9
A **bunch** of flowers. Unknown. 6740-9
A **bunch** of flowers. Emma Celia & Lizzie J. Rook. 6137-0
A **bunch** of forget-me-nots. Thomas Hood. 6974-0
"A **bunch** of golden keys is mine". Golden keys. Unknown. 6963-0
A **bunch** of primroses. George Robert Sims. 6928-2
A **bunch** of roses. John Banister Tabb. 6519-8
A **bunch** of sweets. George Gordon, 6th Baron Byron. 6543-0
A **bunch** of trout-flies. Henry Van Dyke. 6961-4
Bunch: a cat. Claude Colleer Abbott. 6511-2
Bunches of grapes. Walter De La Mare. 6089-7,6459-0,6114-1, 6596-1,6454-X,6018-8
Bunches of grapes. Walter Rand. 6136-2
Bundle of letters. Blanche Baird Winfield. 6711-5
A **bundle** of letters. Frank Dempster Sherman. 6441-8
A **bundle** of loves. Mary L. Gaddess. 6672-0
Bundles. John Chipman Farrar. 6466-3
Bundy, Alison
    Deads. 6900-2
    This is a poem, that is a snake. 6900-2
Bung yer eye. Stewart Edward White. 6281-4
Bungay, George W.
    The battle of Inkerman. 6919-3
    The battle of Lexington. 6911-8
    Creeds of the bells. 6014-5,6392-6,6404-3,6565-1
    Heads, hearts, and hands. 6273-3
    Labor. 6920-7
    Old Tennant Church. 6922-3
    Our ships at sea. 6913-4
    The sad sweet bells. 6155-9
    The Statue of Liberty unveiled. 6920-7
    Ten pound ten. 6416-7
    This old world of ours. 6919-3
    The town pump. 6416-7
    A vegetable convention. 6912-6
    Wide-awake. 6709-3
Bunge, Mabel E.
    Plea for a miracle. 6857-X
Bungiana, sels. Unknown. 6722-0
Bunhill's fields. Anne Ridler. 6379-9
Bunin, Ivan
    Flax. Babette Deutsch and Avrahm Yarmolinsky (tr.). 7039-6
Bunk Johnson's grave at New Iberia. Jonathan Williams. 6803-0
Bunker Hill. George H. Calvert. 6678-X
Bunker Hill. Grenville Mellen. 6438-8
Bunker Hill. Benjamin Franklin Taylor. 6815-4
Bunker's Hill. John Neal. 6678-X
Bunker, John
    The look. 6096 X
    Saint's gold. 6032-3
    Soliloquy at St. Helena. 6761-1
Bunky. Billie Marie Crabb. 6750-6
Bunn, William M.
    My ships. 6926-6

Bunner, Henry Cuyler
    The appeal to Harold. 7041-8
    An April fool. 6875-8
    Atlantic City. 6735-2
    The ballade of the summer-boarder. 6770-0,6875-8
    <u>The ballade of the summer-boarder. 6652-6</u>
    Behold the deeds! 6770-0
    Behold the deeds! 6089-7,6440-X,6732-8,6026-9,6300-4
    Candor. 6004-8,6166-4,6441-8,6632-1,6732-8,6735-2,6505
    Chakey Einstein. 6735-2
    The chaperon. 6735-2
    The chaperon. 6004-8,6092-7,6336-5
    Da capo. 6441-8,6735-2
    Envoy. 6307-1
    Feminine. 6441-8,6735-2
    Forfeits. 6004-8
    Grandfather Watts's private fourth. 6105-2,6166-4
    Haro. 6721-2
    The heart of the tree. 6047-1,6143-5
    Hide and go seek. 6260-1
    Holiday home. 6632-1
    Home sweet home with variations. 6440-X
    Imitation ("My love she leans from the window"). 6440-X
    Interesting. 6652-6
    Just a love-letter. 6735-2
    Kitty's summering. 6652-6
    Les morts vont vite. 6770-0
    Les morts vont vite. 6875-8
    A lost child. 6441-8
    The maid of Murray Hill. 6652-6
    My Shakespere. 6297-0
    O honey of Hymettus Hill. 6770-0
    O honey of Hymettus hill. 6121-4
    "O honey of Hymettus hill" 6875-8
    The old flag. 6632-1
    On Newport beach. 6770-0,6875-8
    <u>On Newport beach. 6121-4</u>
    One, two, three. 6183-2,6242-3,6289-X,6466-3,6519-8, 6534 ,6135-4,6004-8,6368-3,6456-6,6639-9,6638 ,6632-1,6701-8,6732-8,6964-9
    'One, two, three'. 7022-1
    A pitcher of mignonette. 6723-9,6047-1,6464-7,6467-1, 6121-4,6300-4,6646 ,6121-4,6300-4,6467-1,6501-5,6770-0
    Poetry and the poet. 6724-7
    Ready for the ride - 1795 6770-0
    Ready for the ride - 1795 6121-4
    Ready for the ride-1795 6875-8
    Saint Valentine. 6875-8
    Salute the flag. 6471-X
    September. 6770-0
    Shake, Mulleary and go-ethe. 6089-7,6724-7,6026-9
    She was a beauty. 6735-2,6121-4
    Sonnet to order. 6724-7
    Strong as death. 6006-4,6431-0,6309-8
    That New Year's call. 6875-8
    To a dead woman. 6431-0
    Triumph. 6431-0
    Triumph, sels. 6102-8,6076-5
    The wail of the 'personally conducted'. 6724-7
    The way to Arcady. 6004-8,6431-0,6467-1,6652-6,6089-7, 6166-4,6320-9,6473-6,6732-8,6735-
    The way to Arcady. 7041-8
    Wed. 6735-2
    Written on Valentine's Day. 6121-4
    Yes? ("Is it true, then, my girl?"). 6273-3
Bunny did it. Emma Celia & Lizzie J. Rook. 6137-0
"A **bunny** once made up his mind". The valiant rabbit. Carolyn Wells. 6882-0
A **bunny** romance. Oliver Herford. 6018-8
Bunston, Anna
    Under a Wiltshire apple tree. 6214-8
Bunting, Basil
    'Villon', sels. 6733-6
Bunton, Frederica Katheryne
    You taught me love. 6178-8
The **bunty** shoe. James E. Richardson. 6031-5
Bunya No Asayasu
    "This lovely morn the dewdrops flash". William N. Porter (tr.). 6852-9

Bunya No Yasudide
"The mountain wind in autumn time". William N. Porter (tr.). 6852-9
Bunyan, John
Enough! 6461-2
The frog. 6179-6
"He that is down, needs fear no fall". 6562-7
The hog. 6179-6
"My little bird, how canst thou sit". 6933-9
Of the boy and the butterfly. 6018-8
Of the child with the bird at the bush. 6562-7,6563-5, 6675-5
Of the fatted swine. 6018-8
The pilgrim song, fr. Pilgrim's progress. 6933-9
Pilgrim song, fr. The pilgrim's progress. 6157-5,6334-9
Pilgrim's progress, sels. 6334-9,6339-X
The pilgrim. 6466-3,6613-5,6075-7,6239-9,6242-3,6271-7, 6337-3,6427
The shepherd boy sings in the valley of humiliation. 6187-7,6236-9,6239-3,6418-3,6730-1,6214
The shepherd boy's song, The pilgrim's progress. 6242-3, 6337-3,6466-3,6560-0,6301-2,6639
The shepherd's song. 6931-2
Song ("He that is down"). 6481-7
Song in the valley of humiliation. 6102-8
Sunset. 6732-8
To be a pilgrim, fr. The pilgrim's progress. 6934-7
To his reader. 6186-9
True valour. 6613-5
Upon the snail. 6125-7
The valley of humiliation. 6732-8
The bunyip and the whistling kettle. John Streeter Manifold. 6384-5
The bunyip and the whistling kettle. John Streeter Manifold. 6666-6
The bunyip. Douglas Stewart. 6349-7
Buon, Maida
La tour d'Auvergne. 6417-5
Buonaparte. Alfred Lord Tennyson. 6323-3,6655-0
Buonaparte. William Wordsworth. 6543-0
The buoy-bell. Charles Tennyson Turner. 6833-2,6656-9
Burbidge, Thomas
Eventide. 6600-3,6656-9
If I desire with pleasant songs. 6271-7,6302-0,6620-8, 6627-5,6656-9
Mother's love. 6097-8,6271-7,6656-9
To Imperia. 6656-9
Burch, Adelle E.
Lesson that Easter teaches. 6720-4
Burch, Loren W.
Communion ("I would be one with Thee") 6144-3
"Into thy hands." 6144-3
Burd Ellen. Unknown. 6055-2
Burd Ellen and young Tamlane. Unknown. 6185-0
Burd Helen. Unknown. 6302-0,6219-9
Burd Isabel and Earl Patrick. Unknown. 6185-0
Burd, Adelma H.
Our privilege. 6847-2
To my guitar. 6847-2
"The burden of an ancient rhyme." Walter Savage Landor. 6513-9
The burden of eternity. Jiri Karascek ze Lvovic. 6763-8
The burden of Itys, sels. Oscar Wilde. 6655-0
"The burden of fair women. Vain delight". A ballad of burdens. Algernon Charles Swinburne. 6828-6
"The burden of hard hitting: slog away!". Ballade of cricket. Andrew Lang. 6802-2,6987-8,6770-0
The burden of lost souls. Herve-Noel Le Breton. 6873-1
The burden of night. Samuel R. Elliot. 6632-1
The burden of Nineveh. Dante Gabriel Rossetti. 6828-6
The burden of Nineveh. Dante Gabriel Rossetti. 6110-9,6430-2
The burden of strength. George Meredith. 6199-0
The burden of the day. Bayard Taylor. 6976-2
The burden of time. Charles Lotin Hildreth. 7041-8
The burden of time. Frederick George Scott. 6115-X
The burden of Tyre, sels. Christopher J. Brennan. 6384-5
Burden-bearers. John Oxenham. 6461-2
The burden. Toyohiko Kagawa. 6337-3
The burden. Marta of Sillen. 6045-5
The burden. Lucy Rider Meyer. 6260-1
The burden. Jessica Nelson North. 6781-6
Burdens. Edward Dowden. 6383-7
Burdens of unrest. Thomas Holley Chivers. 7017-5
Burder, Henry Foster
Christ the conqueror. 6065-X
Burdett, James S.
Betsey und I hafe bust ub. 6791-3,6823-5
Der mule shtood on der steamboad deck. 6791-3,6823-5
Burdette, R.N.
The little hatchet story. 6570-8
Burdette, Robert J.
After the battle. 6588-0
All things to all men. 6588-0
Alone. 6260-1
An archaeological congress. 6588-0
Auqarius. 6588-0
Baby mine. 6588-0
The brakeman's sweetheart. 6588-0
Bravest of the brave. 6139-7,6588-0
A cataracket. 6588-0
Christ. 6065-X
The comet. 6588-0
Consequences. 6588-0
The countermarch. 6588-0
The cricket. 6588-0
The day we do not celebrate. 6588-0
Dogmatic philosophy. 6588-0
Don't fret. 6588-0
Engineers making love. 6415-9
Evening. 6588-0
Festina lente. 6588-0
Finis. 6588-0
The funny old clown. 6588-0
Getting even. 6588-0
Glory in the northwest. 6588-0
The good old times. 6712-3
The gray day. 6610-2
The hod-fellow. 6588-0
In medio tutissimus ibis. 6588-0
In time of peace. 6588-0
The inside track. 6588-0
James Whitcomb Riley. 6588-0
"Keep sweet and keep movin'". 6260-1
Lines to a mule. 6588-0
The main hatch. 6588-0
The man and the picnic. 6889-8
March. 6588-0
Margins. 6588-0
The master sleeps. 6588-0
May day. 6588-0
The mendicant. 6588-0
Morning. 6588-0
My first cigar. 6588-0
My guide. 6337-3
The odd I see. 6588-0
Old wine in new bottles. 6588-0
On the coast of man. 6588-0
Orphan born. 6089-7,6588-6
The Pierian spring. 6588-0
The plaint of Jonah. 6588-0
The postmaster. 6588-0
The private's glory. 6588-0
Pulmonic passion. 6588-0
Putting his armor on. 6588-0
The putty man. 6588-0
Realization. 6588-0
Rime of the ancient miller. 6588-0
The romance of the carpet. 6089-7,6732-8,6505-8
Running the weekly. 6588-0
Russian soldier, rest! 6693-3
School "takes up". 6588-0
The school ma'am. 6588-0
The seedsman. 6588-0
Sic transit. 6588-0
Since she went home. 6921-5,6689-5
Sisyphus. 6588-0
Soldier, rest! 6089-7,6588-0,6724-7
'Songs without words'. 6089-7,6440-X,6588-0
A spell of rhyme. 6588-0

Sunday talk in the horse sheds. 6680-1
'Teamster Jim'. 6139-7
Then and now. 6523-6
The tramp. 6588-0
Trolley la la! 6588-0
Two rag men. 6588-0
Under the purple and motley. 6926-6
Utopia. 6588-0
What lack we yet? 6588-0
What will we do? 6089-7,6505-8
When my ship comes in. 6273-3,6964-9
When Washington was president. 6674-7
Wilhelmj. 6724-7
Burdick, Arthur J.
Keep up with the times. 6928-2
Washington's birthday. 6712-3
Burdick, Mary Livingston
Abraham Lincoln. 6524-4
The birthday lesson. 6712-3
Burdick, Rose M.
A last desire. 6818-9
Burfitt, Mary F.
Talking to a chicken. 6713-1
"Burgeis, thou haste so blowen atte the cole". Too much sex. Unknown. 6881-2
Burger, August
Lenora. Alfred Ayres (tr.). 6675-5
Burgess, Charles
Albatross. 6388-8
Five serpents. 6388-8
Lady and crocodile. 6388-8
Two garden scenes. 6388-8
Burgess, Dorothy
The unknown wind. 6039-0
Water I'll have. 6039-0
Burgess, Edward Sandford
Octette (001). 6847-2
Octette (002). 6847-2
Octette (003). 6847-2
Octette (004). 6847-2
Octette (005). 6847-2
Octettes. 6847-2
Remembering Keats. 6847-2
The sea-goddess restores the rapt Shelley. 6847-2
To one waering arbutus. 6847-2
Burgess, Gelett
Abstemia. 6902-9
Abstrosophy. 6902-9
Adolphus Elfinstone. 6465-5
Ballade of dreams transposed. 6652-6
Ballade of fog in the Canon. 6875-8
Ballade of the Cognescenti. 6875-8
Ballade of the devil-may-care. 6652-6
The bohemians of Boston. 7025-6
The butterfly's madrigal. 6652-6
The chant royal of pure romance. 6850-2
Chant-royal of California. 6875-8
Chant-royal of the true romance. 6875-8
The cradle. 6817-0
Darkness before dawn. 6880-4
A daughter of the north. 6875-8
Dighton is engaged. 6089-7,6441-8,6732-8
Ebb tide at noon. 6241-5
Extracts from the Rubaiyat of Omar Cayenne. 6089-7
The floorless room. 6534-1
Fourth dimension. 6817-0
Goop rhymes. 6861-8
Helen's face a book. 6652-6
"I wish that my room had a floor". 6026-9,6722-0
I'd rather have fingers than toes. 6534-1,6724-7
The invisible bridge. 6089-7
Kitty wants to write. 6089-7,6732-8
The lazy roof. 6089-7
Limerick:"I wish that my room had a floor." 6308-X
The magic month. 6608-9
My feet. 6466-3
Psycholophon. 6902-9
The purple cow. 6736-0,6739-5,6089-7,6289-X,6300-4,6464-7,6534-1,6732 ,6089-7
Rondeau: Oh, in my dreams I flew! 6875-8

Rondel of perfect friendship. 6875-8
The roof. 6723-9
Sestina of youth and age. 6875-8
A song of the New Year. 6241-5
Ubasti. 6120-6
Villanelle of things amusing. 6089-7,6724-7
Willy and the lady. 7007-8
Burgess, George
The heavenly breeze. 6065-X
Burgess, Helen M.
Mother's petition, in wartime. 6144-3
Burgess, Robert Louis
Girls. 6037-4
Prayer for strength to hate fools. 6880-4
Burgess, Stella Fisher
One there was. 6144-3
Burgess, Thornton W.
Among the roses. 6798-0
Beside the sea. 6798-0
A deep revenge. 6798-0
Easter. 6798-0
The first frost. 6798-0
The marshes by the sea. 6798-0
'My dad an' me' 6798-0
My old maid aunt. 6798-0
A peach. 6798-0
Resurrection. 6798-0
The swimming hole. 6798-0
Thanksgiving at Grandpa's. 6798-0
This little pig went to market. 6798-0
The **burgesses** of Calais. Laurence Minot. 6022-6
The **burghers** of Calais. Emily A. Braddock. 6621-6
The **burghers'** battle. William Morris. 6334-9,6110-9,6656-9
Burghley, William Cecil, 1st Baron
To Mistress Anne Cecil, upon making her a ...gift. 6182-6,6436-1
Burglar Bill. Thomas Anstey ("F. Anstey") Gutherie. 6633-X
Burglar Bill. Unknown. 6139-7
Burgman, Lucy
The empire state. 6799-9
Memories of pioneer days. 6799-9
The **burgomaster** gull. Celia Thaxter. 6612-7
Burgon, John William
Petra. 6046-3
Burgoyne's elm. Lucia M. Mooney. 6684-4
Burgoyne, John
The dashing white sergeant. 6328-4
Burham-beeches. Henry Luttrell. 6086-2,6092-7
Burial. Struthers Burt. 6646-8
Burial. Gertrude Callaghan. 6096 X
Burial. Kingsley Fairbridge. 6800-6
The **burial** ("When that great Kings return to clay"). Rudyard Kipling. 6625-9
Burial ("Yowe, yowe, mwanango duku!"). Kingsley Fairbridge. 6625-9
Burial hymn. Henry Hart Milman. 6219-9
The **burial** in the desert. Felicia Dorothea Hemans. 6973-8
Burial in the east. Pablo (Neftali Ricardo Reyes Basualto) Neruda. 6759-X
Burial march of Dundee. William Edmonstoune Aytoun. 6219-9
Burial of an emigrant's child in the forest. Felicia Dorothea Hemans. 6973-8
The burial of an infant. Henry Vaughan. 6430-2
The **burial** of Arnold. Nathaniel Parker Willis. 6392-6
Burial of Barber. John Greenleaf Whittier. 6946-0
The **burial** of Diarmuid. Alice Milligan. 6628-3
The **burial** of Grant. Richard Watson Gilder. 6340-3
The **burial** of Gustaf Froding. Verner von Heidenstam. 6045-5
The **burial** of King Cormac. Sir Samuel Ferguson. 6244-X, 6639-9
The burial of Knowles. Charles W. Denison. 6755-7
The **burial** of Latane. John Reuben Thompson. 6113-3,6016-2
Burial of Lincoln. Richard Henry Stoddard. 6302-0,6385-3
The **burial** of love. William Cullen Bryant. 6271-7,6600-3
The **burial** of Moses. Unknown. 6554-6
The **burial** of Moses. Cecil Frances Alexander. 6909-6
The **burial** of Moses. Cecil Frances Alexander. 6131-1,6212-2,6219-9,6304-7,6438-8,6614 ,6565-1
The **brial** of poor Cock Robin. Unknown. 6459-0

The **burial** of Robert Browning. Michael (Katherine Bradley
  & Edith Cooper) Field. 6656-9
The **burial** of Sir John Moore at [or after] Corunna.
  Charles Wolfe. 6646-1,6543-0,6639-9,6304-7,6301-2,
  6131 ,6219-9,6125-7,6114-1,6212-1,6104-4,6199 ,6107-
  9,6250-4,6560-0,6438-8,6263-6,6665 ,6014-5,6134-6,
  6479-5,6228-8,6606-2,6732 ,6087-0,6090-0,6174-5,6188-
  5,6239-3,6290 ,6122-2,6198-2,6052-8,6075-7,6289-X,
  6504 ,6242-3,6244-X,6246-6,6271-7,6459-0,6484 ,6323-
  3,6302-0,6385-3,6370-5,6407-8,6457 ,6473-6,6600-3,
  6090-0,6136-2,6138-9,6240 ,6486-8,6621-6,6186-9,6332-
  2,6102-8,6339 ,6502-1,6512-0,6726-3,6457-4,6424-8,
  6737
The **burial** of Sophocles. Geoffrey Bache Smith. 6650-X
The **burial** of St. Brendan. Padraic Colum. 6071-4
The **burial** of the bachelor. Unknown. 6440-X
The **burial** of the cat. R.K. Hutchinson. 6314-4
The **burial** of the Dane. Henry Howard Brownell. 6385-3,6600-
  3,6300-9,6309-8,6407-8
The **burial** of the dead, fr. The waste land. Thomas Stearns
  Eliot. 6531-7
The **burial** of the dead. Henry Howard Brownell. 6431-0
The **burial** of the linnet. Juliana Horatia Ewing. 6519-8
Burial of the Minnisink. Henry Wadsworth Longfellow. 6299-
  7,6502-3,6126-5,6008-0
The **burial** place, sels. William Cullen Bryant. 6049-8
A **burial-urn**, fr. Electra. Sophocles. 6435-3
The **burial**. Unknown. 6752-2
The **burial**. John Webster. 6315-2
Buried alive, fr. Antigone. Sophocles. 6435-3
The **buried** boy to his mother. Charles W. Denison. 6755-7
The **buried** child. Dorothy Wellesley. 6246-6
Buried cities. William Allen Butler. 6903-7
"**Buried** deep beneath an oak-tree". Attila's sword. ?
  Lingg. 6842-1
The **buried** flower. William Edmonstoune Aytoun. 6948-7
Buried gold. Alice Cary. 6060-9
The **buried** life. Matthew Arnold. 6199-0,6250-4,6430-2,6655-
  0,6828-6
The **buried** love. Rufus Dawes. 6752-2
The **buried** ring. John James Piatt. 7041-8
"**Buried** today." Dinah Maria Mulock Craik. 6302-0;6385-3
Buried treasure. Eva Dean. 6486-8
Burk, Edmund J.
  The origin of shoes. 6936-3
Burke
  "Teach me, O lark! with thee to greatly rise", sels.
    6601-1
Burke and Wills, sels. Colin Thiele. 6384-5
Burke, Christian
  A Christmas carol. 6807-3,6145-1
  'Until the daybreak'. 6260-1
Burke, Francis
  The mediatrix of grace. 6282-2
Burke, Henrietta
  Prophecy for a friend. 6839-1
Burke, Kenneth
  For a modernist sermon. 6532-5
Burke, M.L.S.
  Turned out for rent. 6273-3
Burke, Richard
  We will not die, these lovers say. Robin Flower (tr.).
    6244-X
Burke, Roydon
  Reverie. 6042-0
Burke, Thomas
  Shops. 6331-4
  West India dock road. 7012-4
Burket, Gail Brook
  Northward flight at dawn. 6750-6
Burkett, Winifred
  Waiting. 6750-6
Burkholder, Brad
  Copperheads. 6900-2
Burklund, Carl Edwin
  Gamaliel Bradford. 6761-1
  Preludes at evening. 6042-0
Burl veneer. Lillian Stickney. 6764-6
Burleigh, George S.
  Mother Margery. 6271-7

A prayer for life. 6385-3
The puzzled bird-beast. 6530-9
What to drink. 6617-8
Burleigh, William Cecil, Lord. See Burghley
Burleigh, William H.
  Freedom's gathering. 6709-3
  Satan and the grog-seller. 6411-6,6507-8
  The weaver. 6406-X
Burler, Jennie McBride
  Wind of the south. 6241-5
Burlesque. Samuel Johnson. 6228-8
Burlesque ode. Tobias George Smollett. 6975-4
A **burlesque** of 1612. Francis Beaumont and John Fletcher.
  6186-9
Burlesque on the modern versification of ancient..tales.
  Samuel Johnson. 6975-4
A **burlesque** rondo. Louis Untermeyer. 6875-8
Burlin, Helen
  Caterpillar. 6979-7
The **burly**, burly banks of Barbry-o. Unknown. 6061-7
Burma hills. Bernard Gutteridge. 6666-6
Burman, Ben Lucien
  Ballad of piny ridge. 6778-6
  O, they're seekin' Jamie Tolliver. 6779-4
"**Burn** me, tongue of fire!". Paraclete. Jorge de Lima. 6759-
  X
Burn, Minstrel
  Leader Haughs. 6075-7
Burnaby, Charles or William
  Upon a sickly lady. 6563-5
Burnard, Sir Francis Cowley
  The fisherman's chant. 6089-7,6724-7
  Oh, my Geraldine. 6089-7
  True to Poll. 6089-7
"**Burned** from the ore's rejected dross". The anvil.
  Laurence Binyon. 7026-4
Burnell, Fritz S.
  The isle of apple-trees. 6784-0
  The pool. 6784-0
Burnell, Mary A.
  High ideals not lost. 6718-2
Burnet, Dana
  The adventurer. 6732-8
  Ballad of a cruel fate. 6732-8
  Ballad of dead girls. 6431-0
  Ballad of the dead king. 6347-0
  The battle of Liege. 7026-4
  The bread line. 6431-0
  Gayheart, a story of defeat. 6029-3
  The gift. 6761-1
  Harvest. 6029-3
  The homeland. 6478-7,6556-2
  Hunger. 6320-9
  Lord of the city. 7014-0
  Marching song. 6051-X
  Napoleon's tomb. 7027-2
  Paper roses. 6393-4
  Peace at morning. 6051-X
  Portrait of an old sea captain. 7012-4
  The ragged piper. 6431-0
  The riddle. 6431-0
  The road to Vagabondia. 7008-6
  The road to vagabondia. 6374-8,6476-0,6510-4
  Roses in the subway. 6102-8,6338-1,6476-0,6393-4,6070-5
  The sack of old Panama, sels. 6467-1
  The sack of old Panama. 6464-7
  Song ("Love's on the highroad") 6266-0,6320-9,6441-8,
    6476-0,6653-4
  Song for youth. 6891-X
  Three swords. 6607-0
  To a logician. 6031-5
  Wayfarers. 6833-2
  Who dreams shall live. 6431-0
Burnett, Frances Hodgson
  The baby's secret. 6130-3
Burnett, James G.
  A bagatelle. 6652-6
Burnett, Mary E.
  Did not pass. 6629-1
Burney, Chrles

Burnham, Anna F.
  Valentine's day. 6328-4
Burnham, Anna F.
  A bird's house. 6965-7
  Her name. 6426-4
  Homesick. 6965-7
  In mourning. 6965-7
  An incursion of the Danes. 6965-7
  Mehitabel Sapphira Jones. 6451-5
  Nobody. 6965-7
  Pretty Polly Pansy. 6965-7
  True to life. 6673-9
Burnham, Clara Louise
  Contrary town. 6965-7
  Sunshine in the house. 6965-7
Burnham, Creighton Brown
  Ballade of the forlorn lady. 6397-7
  Prairie night. 6397-7
  Rainbow. 6397-7
Burnham, Maud
  The barnyard. 6452-3,6466-3
  The barnyard. 6135-4
  The five little fairies. 6452-3,6466-3
  The pigeons. 6135-4,6452-3,6466-3,6135-4
Burnham, Raymond
  Her answer to his verses. 6118-4
Burnham, Richard
  Friend of sinners. 6065-X
"Burnie bee, burnie bee". Unknown. 6904-5
The burning babe. Robert Southwell. 6122-2,6182-6,6233-4, 5 631 -2,6337-3,6436 ,6198-2,6208-3,6436-1,6489-2,6634-8,6106 ,6586-4,6737-6,6150-8,6214-8,6747-6,6537 , 6023-4,6746-8,6022-6,6438-8,6189-3,6608
"Burning between the beanfields and the corn". Strange fields. Randall Swingler. 6895-2
Burning brush in Vermont. Daniel L. Cady. 6988-6
Burning bush. S. Foster Damon. 6506-6
Burning bush, sels. John Drinkwater. 6320-9
The burning bush. Herbert S. Gorman. 6032-3
The burning bush. Norman Nicholson. 6379-9
The burning bush. Marian Storm. 6039-0
Burning candle. Edgar A. Guest. 6748-4
The burning city. Norman Rosten. 6561-9
"A burning glass of burnished brass". De te. Adam Lindsay Gordon. 6951-7
"The burning golden rose of the day". By the sea. James ("B.V.") Thomson. 6997-5
Burning haystack. Marie Emilie Gilchrist. 6906-1
The burning of Balder's ship. Matthew Arnold. 6102-8
The burning of Jamestown. Thomas Dunn English. 6946-0
"The burning of a man's abode". Law-love. Unknown. 6878-2
The burning of the leaves, sels. Laurence Binyon. 6246-6
Burning of the Lexington. Milford Bard. 6914-2,6744-1
The burning of the love letter. Thomas Hood. 6874-X
The burning of the love-letter. Thomas Hood. 6974-6
The burning of the temple. Isaac Rosenberg. 6209-1
The burning prairie. Alice Cary. 6744-1,6568-6,6909-6
"The burning sands!". Love in the desert. Gertrude Huntington McGiffert. 6838-3
The burning ship. J.H. McNaughton. 6695-X
The burning ship. Unknown. 6554-6,6744-1
"The burning skies are steel". Drought. David John Darlow. 6800-6
Burning the bee-tree. Ruth Pitter. 6893-6
"Burning, burning, burning for ever...". The glacier-bed. Emilia Aylmer Blake. 6925-8
The burning-glass. George William ("A.E.") Russell. 6301-2
The burning-glass. Laurence Whistler. 6475-2
Burns. Ebenezer Elliott. 6302-0,6385-3
Burns. Fitz-Greene Halleck. 6302-0,6385-3,6600-3,6735-2, 6219-9
Burns. Horatio Nelson Powers. 6385-3
Burns. Jeremiah Eames Rankin. 6385-3
Burns. William Roscoe. 6302-0
Burns. John Greenleaf Whittier. 6271-7,6302-0,6385-3,6483-3,6288-1,6126
Burns monument. John Singer. 6895-2
Burns' century song. Benjamin Franklin Taylor. 6815-4
Burns, Diane
  Big fun. 7005-1
  DOA in Dulse. 7005-1
  Gadoshkibos. 7005-1
  Our people. 7005-1
  Sure you can ask me a personal question. 7005-1
Burns, Edward F.
  Hobson and his men. 6741-X
Burns, Elizabeth
  Joan of Arc. 6900-2
Burns, J.D.
  For England. 6784-0
Burns, John Dickson
  O, tempora! O, mores! 6074-9
  Our Christmas hymn. 6074-9
Burns, Michael
  A drunken satyr from Newton County tells how he met... 6860-X
  When all else failed. 6860-X
Burns, Ralph
  Only one-after a painting by Georgian O'Keeffe. 6966-5
Burns, Robert
  A' for our rightfu' king. 6934-7
  Absence. 6240-7
  Address to a Haggis. 6180-X
  Address to a lady. 6271-7,6152-4
  Address to Edinburgh. 6191-5
  Address to the Deil. 6278-4,6024-2,6102-8,6180-X,6198-2, 6152-4,6430
  Address to the toothache. 6089-7,6302-0,6385-3,6219-9, 6278-4
  Address to the toothache, sels. 6102-8
  Address to the unco guid, or the rigidly righteous. 6250-4,6430-2,6153-2,6024-2,6154-0,6198-2,6200-8, 6315-2,6152
  Address to the unco guid, sels. 6337-3
  Address to the wood-lark. 6102-8
  Ae fond kiss. 6086-2,6195-0,6430-2,6152-4,6250-4,6737 , 6301-2,6396-9,6102-8,6154-0,6186-9,6198-2,6204-0, 6536-,6180-X,6240-7,6302-0,6307-9,6385-3,6659
  Afton water. 6152-4,6513-9,6560-0,6545-7,6430-2,6543 , 6240-7,6289-X,6302-0,6385-3,6597-X,6737
  'Again rejoicing nature sees'. 6597-X
  As I stood by yon roofless tower. 6180-X
  As others see us, fr. To a louse. 6337-3
  Auld lang syne. 6086-2,6084-6,6219-9,6197-4,6153-2,6301 ,6192-3,6152-4,6560-0,6430-2,6150-4,6371 ,6195-0, 6723-9,6014-5,6024-2,6085-4,6102-8,6138-9,6180-,6186-9,6198-2,6240-7,6260-1,6271-7,6289-,6302-0,6328-4, 6332-2,6385-3,6486-8,6501-,6527-9,6732-8,6646-1,6438-8,6543-0,6304
  Auld Rob Morris. 6302-0,6737-9,6571-6
  Ay waukin, O. 6180-X
  The banks o' Doon. 6219-9,6438-8,6152-4,6250-4,6219-9, 6153 ,6075-7,6180-X,6186-9,6240-7,6332-2,6427-,6302-0,6315-2,6385-3,6668-2,6660-7,6646 ,6481-7,6479-5, 6484-1,6604-6,6726-3,6560
  Bannockburn. 6075-7,6102-8,6239-3,6240-7,6271-7,6302-, 6385-3,6457-4,6479-5,6552-X,6438-8,6543 ,6086-2,6219-9,6212-1,6263-6,6267-9,6424 ,6560-0,6569-4,6737-9, 6188-5,6323-3
  A bard's epitaph. 6198-2,6289-X,6302-0,6385-3,6600-3, 6543 ,6737-9
  The battle of Bannockburn. 6188-5
  Before parting. 6322-5
  The birks of Aberfeldie. 6180-X,6250-4,6383-7
  The blissful day. 6271-7
  Bonnie Doon. 6024-2,6198-2,6102-8,6597-X,6543-0,6737 , 6150-8,6301-2,6304-7,6371-3
  Bonnie Lesley. 6086-2,6198-2,6271-7,6246-6,6634-8,6219-9,6092
  Bonnie Mary. 6240-7
  Bonnie wee thing. 6302-0,6385-3,6737-9
  The book-worms. 6125-7,6297-0,6545-7
  Braw lads o' Galla water. 6180-X
  The brigs of Ayr, sels. 6332-2,6484-1
  Bruce to his men at Bannockburn. 6301-2
  Bruce's address to his army at Bannockburn. 6289-X,6604-6,6250-4,6660-7
  Ca' the yowes to the knowes. 6737-9,6180-X,6271-7,6302-0,6385-3,6086-2,6250
  The carles of Dysart. 6383-7
  Castle Gordon. 6328-4

Charlie he's my darling. 6737-9
The chevalier's lament. 6859-6
A child's grace. 6132-X,6519-8,6466-3
Chloe. 6239-3
Chorus, fr. The jolly beggars. 7009-4
Cock up your beaver. 6138-9,6334-9
Coming through the rye. 6180-X,6385-3,6383-7,6301-2, 6543-0
Contented wi' little. 6831-6
Corn rigs. 6180-X
The cotter's Saturday night, sels. 7009-4
The cotter's Saturday night, sels. 6260-1,6395-0
The cotter's Saturday night, sels. 7009-4
The cotter's Saturday night. 6014-5,6101-X,6198-2,6271-7,6302-0,6332-,6370-5,6385-3,6604-6,6730-1,6732-8, 6660
A curler's elegy. 7035-3
"The day returns, my bosom burns." 6302-0,6385-3,6250-4, 6737-9
Death and Doctor Hornbook. 6180-X
The death and dying words of poor Mailie,... 6198-2
Defiance. 6322-5
The deil's awa' wi' the exciseman. 6328-4,6430-2
Devotion. 6322-5
"Does haughty Gaul invasion threat?" 6830-8
Duncan Gray. 6154-0,6180-X,6198-2,6246-6,6332-2,6634-, 6302-0,6328-4,6385-3,6560-0,6737-9,6737
Elegy on Captain Matthew Henderson. 6271-7,6385-3,6423-X,6600-3,6291-9
Epistle to a young friend. 6260-1,6332-2,6370-5,6543-0
Epistle to Davie, a brother poet. 6180-X
Epistle to Dr. Blacklock. 6932-0
Epistle to John Lapraik, an old Scottish bard. 6430-2, 6152-4,6150-8
Epistle to John Lapraik, sels. 6332-2,6195-0
Epistle to the Rev. John M'Math. 6831-6
Epitaph for James Smith. 6026-9
Epitaph on a friend. 6337-3
Epitaph on Holy Willie. 6200-8,6278-4
Epitaph on my father. 6337-3
Epitaph on W—. 6278-4
Epitaph to James Smith. 6932-0
The exciseman. 6845-6
"Fair maid, we need not take the hint". 6104-4
Farewell to Nancy. 6024-2,6271-7,6219-9,6560-0,6094-3, 6543
The farewell, sels. 6472-8
A farewell. 6075-7,6228-8,6246-6,6737-9
Flow gently, sweet Afton. 6183-4,6198-2,6706-9,6219-9, 6304-7
For a' that and a' that. 6024-2,6102-8,6157-5,6186-9, 6457-4,6479-,6102-8,6153-2,6394-2,6453-0,6737-9,6464 ,6302-0,6332-2,6385-3,6395-0,6732-8,6560 ,6104-4, 6152-4,6197-4,6430-2
For an altar to independence. 6793-X
The gloomy night is gathering fast. 6180-X,6332-2
Go fetch me a pint o' wine. 6198-2,6328-4
The goal of life. 6322-5
The golden locks of Anna. 6830-8
The good heart. 6438-8
Grace before eating. 6303-9,6214-8
Green grow the rashes. 6180-X,6302-0,6385-3,6726-6,6732-8,6646 ,6026-9,6152-4,6086-2,6301-2,6195-0,6659 , 6491-4,6737-9
Gude'en to you, Kimmer. 6633-X
Had I a cave. 6302-0
Hallowe'en ("Upon that night, when fairies light"). 6254-7
Happiness. 6654-2
The happy trio. 6830-8
"He's gane, he's gane!". 6085-4,6438-8
The heather was blooming. 6943-6
"Here lies Johnny Pidgeon". 6289-X
Here's a health to Ane. 6271-7
Here's a health to them that's awa. 6271-7
Hey, the dusty miller. 6805-7
Highland Harry. 6859-6
Highland Mary. 6102-8,6154-0,6180-X,6198-2,6240-7,6246 , 6219-9,6723-9,6152-4,6430-2,6560-0,6195 ,6271-7,6289-X,6302-0,6385-3,631-4,6473-,6023-4,6104-4,6250-4,

6301-2,6371-3,6439 ,6086-2,6226-1,6481-7,6486-8,6600-3,6732 ,6102-8,6197-4,6394-2,6631-3,6543-0,6737
The highland widow's lament. 6383-7
The holy fair. 6198-2,6430-2,6195-0,6152-4
Holy Willie's prayer. 6089-7,6180-X,6200-8,6733-6,6438-8,6152 ,6278-4,6633-X,6637-2
Honest poverty. 6271-7,6438-8,6131-1
"I am my mammie's ae bairn." 6317-9
I love my Jean. 6075-7,6239-3,6152-4
I murder hate by field or flood. 6380-2
"I once was a maid...", fr. The jolly beggars. 6733-6
I'm owre young to marry yet. 6180-X
"If happiness has not her seat". 6238-5
Inspiration. 6438-8
Is there for honest poverty. 6180-X,6604-6,6195-0,6250-4,6660-7
It was a' for our rightfu' king. 6024-2,6180-X,6086-2
Jean. 6246-6,6332-2,6560-0,6301-2,6226-1,6737 ,6104-4, 6219-9,6250-4
Jessy. 6219-9
John Anderson, my jo. 6246-6,6271-7,6289-X,6339-X,6395-0,6475 ,6086-2,6195-0,6153-2,6192-3,6301-2,6491 , 6101-X,6180-X,6198-2,6328-4,6332-2,6337 ,6152-4,6373-9,6668-2,6543-0,6438-8,6560 ,6138-9,6240-7,6302-0, 6385-3,6427-2,6481 ,6250-4,6371-3,6219-9,6639-9,6646-1,6430 ,6488-4,6536-8,6610-0,6625-9,6726-3,6634
John Barleycorn. 6024-2,6089-7,6179-6,6385-3,6479-5, 6502 ,6105-8,6023-4,6518-X,6732-8,6733-6
The jolly beggars, sels. 6733-6
The jolly beggars. 6732-8,6026-9,6152-4,6430-2
The joyful widower. 6760-3
Kenmure's on and awa'. 6271-7
King Coal to Uncle Sam. 6741-X
Lady Mary Ann. 6518-X
Lament for Culloden. 6188-5,6246-6,6088-9
Lament for Glencairn. 6304-7
Lament for James, Earl of Glencairn. 6438-8
Lament of Mary,Queen of Scots,on the approach of spring. 6188-5,6438-8,6088-9,6543-0
The lass o' Ballochmyle. 6180-X,6271-7
Lassie wi' the lint-white locks. 6191-5,6545-7
Last May a braw wooer. 6024-2,6545-7,6518-X,6195-0
Lauth. 6510-4
The lea-rig. 6180-X
"Let not a woman e'er complain." 6302-0;6385-3
Life. 6302-0
Lines to John Lapraik, sels. 6198-2
Lines, written on the window of the Globe tavern, Dumfries. 6723-9
The linnet. 6943-6
Logan braes. 6365-9,6545-7
Long is the night. 6328-4
Love song. 6625-9
The lovely lass of Inverness. 6180-X,6323-3,6086-2
Luath, fr. 'The twa dogs' 7008-6
Macpherson's [or M'Pherson's] farewell. 6180-X,6271-7, 6332-2,6334-9,6395-0,6427-,6383-7
Mally's meek, Mally's sweet. 6250-4
Man was made to mourn. 6302-0,6486-8,6152-4
A man's a man for a' that. 6138-9,6154-0,6198-2,6291-1, 6328-4,6337-,6086-2,6143-5,6424-8,6219-9,6568-6,6478-7,6490-6,6521-X,6315-2,6706-9
Man's inhumanity to man, fr. Man was made to mourn. 6260-1,6337-3
Mary Morison. 6154-0,6180-X,6240-7,6246-6,6302-0,6332-, 6543-0,6737-9,6219-9,6086-2,6152-4,6430 ,6385-3,6395-0,6600-3,6726-3,6560-0,6195
Melancholy. 6294-6
A mountain daisy. 6659-3
The muse of Burns, fr. The vision. 6545-7
My ain kind dearie, O! 6543-0
My bonie Mary. 6250-4
My bonnie Mary. 6634-8,6086-2,6301-2
My heart's in the highlands. 6134-6,6136-2,6180-X,6239-3,6242-3,6271-,6737-9,6631-3,6152-4,6129-9,6424-8, 6723 ,6138-9,6302-0,6328-4,6457-4,6669-0,6732-,6639-9
My Jean. 6634-8,6066-8,6226-1
My love is like a red, red rose. 6024-2,6150-8,6491-4, 6723-9

BURNS

My love, she's but a lassie yet. 6180-X
My Nanie's awa. 6180-X
My Nanie, O. 6180-X,6195-0,6371-3
"My wife's a winsome wee thing." 6271-7,6302-0,6385-3, 6620-8,6737-9,6491
A night ride, fr. Tam o'Shanter. 7020-5
O Mally's meek, Mally's sweet. 6239-3
"O Mary, at thy window be". 6187-7
O May, thy morn. 6830-8
"O my love's [or luv's] like a red, red rose." 6513-9, 6464-7,6138-9,6246-6,6302-0,6726-3,6438-8,6396-9, 6543 ,6192-3,6195-0,6550-0,6152-4,6250-4,6430
O were my love yon lilac fair. 6125-7,6086-2
O wert thou in the cauld blast. 6024-2,6075-7,6102-8, 6134-6,6180-X,6604 ,6723-9,6660-7,6737-9,6383-7,6371-3,6646 ,6236-9,6536-8
O'er the water to Charlie. 6180-X
O, ay my wife she dang me. 6491-4
"O, leeze me on spinnin wheel". 6830-8
"O, saw ye bonnie Lesley?" 6240-7,6302-0,6385-3
O, were my love. 6250-4
O, wert thou in the cauld blast. 6153-2,6195-0,6430-2
O, whistle an' I'll come to ye, my lad. 6180-X,6560-0
Of a' the airts the wind can blaw. 6154-0,6180-X,6302-0, 6385-3,6600-3,6543 ,6086-2,6371-3,6438-8,6197-4,6195-0,6430 ,6154-0,6180-X,6302-0,6385-3,6600-3,6543 , 6086-2,6371-3,6438-8,6197-4,6195-0,6430
Oh, Willie brewed a peck o' maut. 6154-0
Old Scotia's grandeur, fr. The cotter's Saturday night. 6934-7
On a celebrated ruling elder. 6278-4
On a Scotch coxcomb. 6278-4
On a suicide. 6278-4
On a wag in Mauchline. 6278-4
On Andrew Turner. 6278-4
On Grizzel Grim. 6278-4
On John Dove. 6278-4
On Maria dancing. 6959-2
On scaring some waterfowl in Loch-Turit. 6510-4
On seeing a wounded hare. 6597-X
On the birth of a posthumous child. 6543-0
Open the door to me, oh! 6395-0,6491-4
"Pleasures are like poppies spread." 6238-5
The poet's choice. 6278-4
A poet's welcome to his love begotten daughter. 6164-8
Poetical inscription for an altar of independence. 7009-4
Poor Mailie's elegy. 6180-X,6195-0
Posie. 6302-0,6385-3,6195-0
Prayer for Mary. 6560-0
Prayer for my native land, fr. Cotter's Saturday night. 6337-3
A prayer in the prospect of death. 6337-3,6418-3,6730-1, 6108-2,6195-0,6214
The rantin dog the daddie o't. 6830-8
A red, red rose. 6102-8,6154-0,6180-X,6204-0,6271-7, 6332 ,6339-X,6427-2,6465-5,6512-0,6527-9,6604 ,6634-8,6732-8,6668-2,6737-9,6153-2,6301 ,6086-2,6219-9, 6371-3,6066-8,6646-1,6023 ,6114-1,6125-7,6226-1,6639-9,6545-7,6660
The rigs o'barley. 6315-2
The river's supplication. 6049-8
Robert Bruce's address to his army before Bannockburn. 6024-2,6323-4
The Ronalds of the Bennals. 6760-3
A rose-bud by my earlt walk. 6543-0
Saw ye bonnie Lesley. 6180-X,6195-0,6250-4
Scotland. 6438-8
Scots wae hae [wi' Wallace bled]. 6646-1,6481-7,6726-3, 6192-3,6430-2,6195-0,6152 ,6052-8,6154-0,6180-X,6198-2,6328-4,6473-
Scots! wha hae wi' Wallace bled. 6639-9
Scroggam. 6545-7
"See the smoking bowl before us", fr. Jolly beggars. 6845-6
"See the smoking bowl...", fr. 'The jolly beggars'. 6733-6
Sic a wife as Willie had. 6845-6
The silver tassie. 6180-X
"Some hae meat that canna eat". 66601-1

Song ("My luve is like"). 6315-2,6423-X,6501-5
Song of the old soldier. 6733-6
Song: Green grow the rashes. 6198-2
Song: Mary Morison. 6198-2
Song: My Nanie, O. 6198-2
Sonnet. 6943-6
Strathallan's lament. 6859-6
Summer's a pleasant time. 6383-7
Tam Glen. 6180-X,6198-2,6152-4,6195-0,6430-2,6026
Tam o' shanter. 6153-2,6646-1,6419-1,6086-2,6291-9,6023 ,6438-8,6245-8,6430-2,6394-2,6560-0,6660 ,6152-4, 6195-0,6371-3,6543-0,6371-3,6024-2,6089-7,6102-8, 6154-0,6180-X,6254-,6198-2,6685-2,6726-3,6732-8,6733-6,6491 ,6271-7,6302-0,6385-3,6473-6,6484-1,6604-
"Then gently scan your brother man". 6238-5
There was a lad. 6180-X
There'll never be peace. 6138-9
There'll never be peace till Jamie comes home. 6075-7, 6086-2
"There's nae luck about the house." 6385-3
Thou lingering star. 6180-X
To a field-mouse. 6634-8,6510-4
To a louse. 6195-0,6430-2,6302-0,6385-3,6473-6,6733-6, 6371-3,6152
To a mountain daisy. 6646-1,6438-8,6219-9,6086-2,6152-4, 6430 ,6560-0
To a mountain daisy. 6891-X
To a mountain daisy. 6047-1,6049-8,6102-8,6180-X,6239-3, 6271-,6198-2,6660-7,6192-3,6195-0,6250-4,6543 ,6302-0,6385-3,6479-5,6597-X,6604-6,6634-
To a mouse. 6192-3,6152-4,6195-0,6560-0,6660-7,6250 , 6104-0,6430-2,6438-8,6396-9,6086-2,6219 ,6371-3,6464-7,6491-4,6543-0,6024-2,6597-X,6604-6,6726-3, 6732-,6102-8,6138-9,6180-X,6246-6,6302-0,6315-,6332-2,6385-3,6473-6,6479-5,6527-9,6534-
To Davie Sillar. 6385-3
To Davie: a brother poet, sels. 6831-6
To J.S. 6186-9
To John Taylor. 6722-0
To Mary in heaven. 6102-8,6154-0,6186-9,6271-7,6302-0, 6385-,6198-2,6600-3,6086-2,6301-2,6219-9,6723 ,6430-2,6560-0
To the devil. 6438-8
To the toothache. 6787-5
To the unco guid. 6302-0,6385-3,6438-8
To the woodlark. 6943-6
To William Simpson of Ochiltree. 6180-X,6332-2
The toad-eater. 6545-7
The true pathos. 6250-4
True until death. 6322-5
The twa dogs. 6191-5,6545-7,6394-2
Up in the morning early. 6466-3,6383-7,6143-5
The vision. 6271-7,6600-3,6438-8
Wandering Willie. 6180-X
War song. 6328-4
Wee Willie Gray. 6138-9
Wha is that at my bower door? 6545-7
Whan I sleep I dream. 6024-2
When she cam ben, she bobbed. 6180-X
"Whistle and I will come to you, my lad." 6302-0;6385-3
Whistle o'er the lave o 't. 6180-Y
The whistle. 6518-X
"Why am I loth to leave this earthly scene?" 6238-5
Willie brew'd a peck o' maut. 6180-X,6430-2,6086-2,6152-4,6192-3
The winsome wee thing. 6219-9
Winter. 6438-8
A winter night, sels. 6332-2
A winter night. 6024-2,6438-8
The wounded hare. 6510-4
Writing verses. 6438-8
Ye banks and braes. 6631-3
Ye flowery banks o' bonnie Doon. 6187-7,6328-4,6395-0, 6634-8,6152-4,6195 ,6246-6,6395-0,6536-8,6430-2

Burns, Robert (tr.)
The first six verses of the ninetieth psalm. Bible, 6848-0

Burns, Robetr
The poet's choice. 6178-4
Poor Mailie's elegy. 6195-8

The posie. 6302-9
Burns, Vincent Godfrey
　　Eloquent rags. 6042-0
　　An ex-serviceman makes a vow. 6542-2
　　The farmers outlaw weeds. 6542-2
　　Hell a la mode. 6542-2
　　A Hun. 6542-2
　　If Jesus came back today, sels. 6144-3
　　Making cannon in Bethlehem. 6542-2
　　The march of the ghosts. 6542-2
　　The passing of Woodrow Wilson, prophet of peace. 6542-2
　　Picking skulls at Verdun. 6542-2
　　Sonnet for Christmas. 6337-3
　　To a certain very ugly building. 6542-2
　　To the preachers on Armistice Day. 6542-2
　　Transformation. 6542-2
Burns: an ode. Algernon Charles Swinburne. 6655-0
Burnshaw, Stanley
　　I, Jim Rogers. 6042-0
Burnt are the petals of life. Elsie Pumpelly Cabot. 6762-X
Burnt lands. Sir Charles George Douglas Roberts. 6656-9
Burnt Norton. Thomas Stearns Eliot. 6645-3
The burnt offering. James Abraham Martling. 6952-5
A burnt ship. John Donne. 6665-8
Burnt ships. Helen Hunt Jackson. 6066-8
Burr, Amelia Josephine
　　Afterglow. 7038-8
　　And the cock crew. 6542-2
　　Artemis on Latmos. 6031-5
　　The battle of Manilla. 6690-9
　　Before the crucifix. 6184-2
　　The child in black. 7038-8
　　The cricket in the path. 6338-1
　　End and beginning. 6030-7
　　Exempt. 6847-2
　　Fall in! 6031-5
　　Father O'Shea. 6032-3
　　For remembrance. 6320-9
　　The furnace man. 6750-6
　　Gipsy-heart. 7012-4
　　Gone? 6847-2
　　Gorgio lad. 6102-8,6076-5,6253-9
　　Herb of grace. 6338-1
　　In bozen of a Sunday. 6847-2
　　In deep places. 6019-6,6464-7,6847-2
　　In memory of a dumb friend. 6510-4
　　Kitchener's march. 6224-5
　　Lie-awake songs. 6266-0
　　The loon. 6510-4
　　A Lynmouth widow. 6102-8,6556-2,6019-6,6076-5,6393-4
　　The meeting. 6032-3
　　Mother moon. 6638-0
　　The mother of Judas. 6543-0
　　Mr. Valiant passes over. 6995-9
　　My mother. 6847-2
　　Night at sea. 6331-4,6631-3
　　Night magic. 6607-0
　　Nocturne. 6030-7
　　On the way of the cross. 6032-3
　　The Patteran. 6847-2
　　Pershing at the tomb of Lafayette. 6846-4,6946-0
　　Perugia. 6027-7
　　The poppies. 6030-7
　　The prayer ("You say"). 6443-4
　　The prayer. 6419-1,6443-4
　　Rain in the night. 6338-1
　　Reality. 6144-3
　　Romany gold. 6607-0
　　Sentry-go. 6861-8
　　A song of living. 6476-0,6431-0
　　A spring symphony. 6029-3
　　To dreamers everywhere. 6954-1
　　To lovers. 6441-8,6619-4
　　Two viewpoints. 6846-4
　　A type. 7038-8
　　Ulysses in Ithaca. 6029-3
　　The vagabond grown old. 7012-4
　　The voice of the unborn. 6266-0
　　Warning. 7038-8
　　'We'. 7019-1

　　Where love is. 6556-2,6847-2
Burr, Jennie M.
　　A letter and a crown. 6965-7
Burr, Winifred Adams
　　At night. 6648-8
　　Ghosts. 6218-0
　　Opening door. 6218-0
Burrell, David J.
　　The shepherd's story. 6923-1
Burrell, Mary A.
　　Seniors' farewell song. 6717-4
Burris, Sidney
　　Still life, but one. 6900-2
Burro. Henry Herbert Knibbs. 6506-6
Burro. O. R. 7010-8
Burroughs, Alethea S.
　　Savannah. 6113-3
Burroughs, Ellen. See Jewett, Sarah
Burroughs, Jack
　　A friend in need. 6510-4
Burroughs, John
　　The crow. 6073-0
　　The downy woodpecker. 6073-0
　　Golden Crown sparrow of Alaska. 6597-X
　　My own shall come to me. 6183-4,6479-5
　　The return. 6337-3
　　The swallow. 6073-0
　　To the Lapland Longspur. 6073-0,6597-X
　　Waiting. 6006-4,6007-2,6085-4,6102-8,6240-7,6266-,6273-3,6600-3,6076-5,6250-4,6104-4,6309 ,6303-9,6337-3, 6501-5,6730-1,6732-8,6300 ,6252-0
Burroughs, Mrs.
　　Benny. 6131-1
Burroughs, W.F.
　　The young bootblack. 6417-5
Burroway, Jan
　　Owed to Dickens, 1956 6388-8
　　Song ("With whomsoever"). 6388-8
Burrs and brambles. Robert Graves. 6778-6
Bursaw, Mike
　　"The key set me" 6883-9
Bursk, Christopher
　　The injunction. 7032-9
　　Outside the gates of Norristown prison. 7032-9
"Burst is the iron gate!". Titian's Assumption. William Allen Butler. 6903-7
"A burst of sudden wings at dawn". Home. Francis Ledwidge. 6812-X
"Bursts from a rending east in flaws". Hard weather. George Meredith. 6828-6
Burt Sr. & George F. Brigel, R.J.
　　Song of the army engineers. 6237-7
Burt Sr., R.J.
　　The infantry - kings of the highway. 6237-7
Burt, Jean Brooks
　　The things divine. 6964-9
Burt, Katharine Brown
　　Chant for the salt marsh. 6789-1
　　Elysian trail. 6799-9
　　First maternity. 6750-6
　　Prayer before work. 6789-1
Burt, Katharine Newlin
　　Old America speaks. 6761-1
Burt, Mary E.
　　The flying squirrel. 6479-5
Burt, Maxwell Struthers. See Burt, Struthers
Burt, Nathaniel
　　Eden. 6761-1
　　Rain in spring. 6761-1
Burt, Struthers
　　As we go on. 6607-0
　　Burial. 6646-8
　　Dawn. 6253-9
　　Fifty years spent. 6556-2
　　The hill-born. 6337-3,6501-5,6607-0
　　Horizons. 6619-4
　　The land. 6031-5,6051-X
　　Love in marriage. 6320-9
　　May. 6102-8,6076-5
　　No one knows the countryside. 6619-4

BURT

Pack trip suite. 6253-9
Pierrot at war. 7027-2
Princeton to Virginia. 6184-2
To a friend wanting war. 6542-2
We are wonderful, we are wise. 6979-7
The young dead. 6032-3,6051-X
The **burthen** of the ass. John Banister Tabb. 6510-4
Burton's curtains. Robert C.V. Meyers. 6925-8
Burton, Ernest De Witt
    The way O Christ thou art. 6337-3
Burton, Henry
    The ivy. 6049-8
    A light upon the mountains. 6337-3
    Pass it on. 6109-5,6337-3,6654-2
    Patience. 6014-5
    "Were there no night we could not read the stars". 6238-5
Burton, John
    New York. 6490-6
    Prayer ("I often say"). 6337-3
Burton, John W.
    Black cameo on pink quartz. 6178-8
    Pride. 6178-8
    Vignette. 6178-8
Burton, Katherine
    November eleventh. 6465-5,6761-1
    The way. 6214-8
Burton, R.F. (tr.)
    On the death of Catarina de Attayda. Luis de Camoens [or Camoes], 7039-6
Burton, Richard
    Across the fields to Anne. 6310-1,6476-0,6632-1
    Art. 6184-2
    Ballad of the unsuccessful. 6274-1
    Black sheep. 6260-1,6310-1,6431-0
    The Camberwell garden. 6327-6
    The city of the dead. 6300-4
    The city. 6632-1,6309-8
    The claim of kindred. 6006-4
    The cloister garden at Certosa. 6338-1,6649-6
    The comfort of the stars. 6266-0,6374-8
    Factory children. 6337-3
    A faithful dog. 6476-0,6510-4
    Faithful follower, gentle friend. 7008-6
    Fate. 6029-3
    The forefather. 6431-0
    God's garden. 6338-1,6632-1,6730-1
    Here lies Pierrot. 6027-7
    Human. 6027-7
    The human touch. 6266-0,6309-8
    If we had the time. 6887-1
    In a sweatshop. 6954-1
    In the Place de la Bastille. 6102-8,6076-5
    Mary Magdalene. 6144-3
    Masks. 6632-1
    May-lure. 6374-8
    The miner. 6509-0
    Mortis dignitas. 6102-8,6632-1,6076-5
    The national air. 6461-2
    The old Sante Fe Trail. 6265-2,6484-1
    On Syrian hills. 6144-3
    The plan. 6476-0
    Shakespeare reads the King James version. 6464-7
    Song of the sea. 6374-8
    The song of the unsuccessful. 6006-4,6730-1,6310-1
    Strength in weakness. 6337-3
    Summer. 6374-8
    The symbol. 6887-1
    "Tomorrow has a rare alluring sound". 6109-5
    Two mothers. 6097-8
    The vanished voice. 6232-6
Burton, Richard Eugene
    Apprisals. 7041-8
    The city. 7041-8
    Song of the sea. 7041-8
Burton, Robert
    The author's abstract of melancholy. 6563-5
Burton, Robert (tr.)
    The anatomy of melancholy. Terence. 6317-9
Bury her at even. Michael (Katherine Bradley & Edith Cooper) Field. 6844-8
Bury me in the morning. Stephen A. Douglas. 6889-8
"**Bury** the dragon's teeth!". Bury them. Henry Howard Brownell. 6946-0
Burying ground by the ties. Archibald MacLeish. 6375-6
"The **bus** winds down through the busy street". The bus. Mabel W. Arnold. 6799-9
The **bush** aboon traquair. Robert Crawford. 6250-4,6383-7
The **bush** aboon Traquair. John Campbell Shairp. 6180-X,6437-X,6046-3
'The **bush** crank'. Brian ("Korongo") Brooke. 6938-X
Bush goblins. H.M. Green. 6784-0
A **bush** idyl. Alfred T. Chandler. 6768-9
A **bush** study, a la watteau. Arthur Patchett Martin. 6677-1
A **bush** study, a la Watteau. Arthur Patchett Martin. 6768-9
The **bush** that burned. Lois Moyes. 6799-9
'**Bush** versus London'. Brian ("Korongo") Brooke. 6938-X
Bush, Barney
    Another old song. 7005-1
    Blood. 7005-1
    It is finished. 7005-1
    Voice in the blood. 7005-1
    Whose voice. 7005-1
Bush, Elizabeth
    Fantasia in E minor. 6799-9
Bush, Jocelyn
    The little red sled. 6466-3
The **bush**, sels. Bernard O'Dowd. 6784-0
The **bush**. James Lister Cuthbertson. 6784-0
Bushby, D. Maitland
    China town, San Francisco. 6954-1
    Ten years have passed. 6542-2
Bushed. Earle Birney. 6446-9
The **bushed** burned with fire. Judah M. Turkat. 6839-1
The **bushman's** cave, sels. William Charles Scully. 6800-6
The **bushman's** cave. William Charles Scully. 6591-0,6592-9
A **bushman's** song. Andrew Barton Paterson. 6784-0
The **bushman**. A.C. Smith. 6768-9
The **bushmen**.. Francis Carey ("Jan van Avond") Slater. 6625-9
Bushnell, Louisa
    Once upon a time. 6569-4
Bushnell, Samuel G.
    On the aristocracy of Harvard. 6089-7
Bushnell, William H.
    A touch of nature. 6926-6
"**Busie** old fool, unruly Sun". John Donne. 6187-7
Busied youth. Earle Henry MacLeod. 6818-9
The **busines** of an uncle. Edgar A. Guest. 6869-3
Business. Edgar A. Guest. 6862-6
Business. Charles Grenville Hamilton. 6954-1
Business is business. Berton Braley. 6853-7
"'**Business** is business,' he said to me". Business. Edgar A. Guest. 6862-6
"'**Business** is business,' the little man said". Business is business. Berton Braley. 6853-7
"The **business** that one big deal". Washington Square bar, lunchtime. George Tsongas. 6901-0
Buson
    "The fireflies massed upon the palm fronds." Lois J. Erickson (tr.). 6027-7
    "Look! On the great great bronze bell." Lois J. Erickson (tr.). 6027-7
    Mists of daybreak. 6891-X
    "A summer night/With breezes sweet." Lois J. Erickson (tr.). 6027-7
"**Buson**, Goshun, Kinkoku". Artists east and west. Diane Chang. 6790-5
Busse, Carl
    The quiet kingdom. Ludwig Lewisohn (tr.). 7039-6
Bussy D'Ambois, sel. George Chapman. 6958-4
Bussy D'Ambois, sels. George Chapman. 6317-9,6378-0,6369-1
A **bust**. Unknown. 6983-5
Busta, Christine
    "An angel in black" Milne Holton and Herbert Kuhner (tr.). 6769-7
    Drought. Milne Holton and Herbert Kuhner (tr.). 6769-7
    Hoarfrost. Milne Holton and Herbert Kuhner (tr.). 6769-7
    Miserere. Milne Holton and Herbert Kuhner (tr.). 6769-7

Our child of pain. Milne Holton and Herbert Kuhner (tr.). 6769-7
"They've cut down/the sunflower" Milne Holton and Herbert Kuhner (tr.). 6769-7
Bustamante y Ballivian, Enrique
   Telegraph pole. Muna Lee (tr.). 6759-X
Bustamante, Cecilia
   The astronaut. Mary Crow (tr.). 7036-1
   Awake. Mary Crow (tr.). 7036-1
   Resonances. David Tipton (tr.). 7036-1
   Under the sun. Mary Crow (tr.). 7036-1
Bustan, sels. Sadi [or Saadi] (Mushlih-ud-Din) 7039-6
A **busted** dolly. Josephine Merwin Cook. 6711-5
The **buster**. Sam Walter Foss. 6926-6
The **bustle** in a house. Emily Dickinson. 6288-1
The **busts** of Goethe and Schiller in Walhalla. William Allen Butler. 6903-7
"Busy and happy young housekeepers we". Unknown. 6205-9
Busy bee. John W. Garvin. 6797-2
The **busy** bee. Unknown. 6629-1
The **busy** bee. Isaac Watts. 6183-4,6373-X,6466-3,6502-3, 6456-6
A **busy** day. Unknown. 6466-3
A **busy** day. Marguerite Wilkinson. 6880-4
"A **busy** dream, forgotten ere it fades". Life ("A busy dream"). Unknown. 6273-3
The **busy** heart. Rupert Brooke. 6339-X
"Busy little boy,/With so much to do". Busied youth. Earle Henry MacLeod. 6818-9
The **busy** mule. Unknown. 6629-1
A **busy** person. Alfarata Hilton. 6466-3
"The **busy** waters multitudinous". The tide coming in. J. Pierce. 6997-5
"Busy with thoughts;/I'm busy all day". On thoughts. Margaret E. Hendrickson. 6818-9
"The **busy** world has time and space". Beauty. Edgar A. Guest. 6869-3
Busy, curious, thirsty fly! William Oldys. 6328-4,6219-9, 6092-7
"Busy, curious, thirsty fly." Vincent Bourne. 6302-0;6385-3
But. A.D. Winans. 6901-0
"But 'nameless somethings'...". The veld ecologue: the pioneers, sels. Roy Campbell. 6788-3
"But 'three brief years'! beloved, is it so?". I learned to know. Mary Cromwell Low. 6847-2
But -. Belle Hunt. 6675-5
But a moment. Florence Maxine Movshovitch. 6847-2
But a short time to live. Leslie Coulson. 6589-9,6650-X, 7026-4,6846-4
"But about his house peered...", fr. The Odyssey. Homer. 6435-3
"But Achilles, by the breakers...", fr. The Iliad. Homer. 6251-2
"But Alcimus and Automedon...", fr. The Iliad. Homer. 6251-2
"But ah, though peace indeed is here". Lines written by a death-bed, sels. Matthew Arnold. 6934-7
"But all through life I see a cross". Olrig Grange. 6238-5
"But anxious cares the pensive nymph oppressed". Canto 004, fr. The rape of the lock. Alexander Pope. 6122-2
"But art thou co e, dear Saviour?" Unknown. 6931-2
"But as bees or supple-waisted...", fr. The Iliad. Homer. 6251-2
"But as for thee". Ulysses and Achilles, fr. The Odyssey. Homer. 6879-0
"But as in a garden a poppy...", fr. The Iliad. Homer. 6251-2
"But as o'er some parched mountain...", fr. The Iliad. Homer. 6251-2
"But as on a day in winter...", fr. The Iliad. Homer. 6251-2
"But as some star of bale...", fr. The Iliad. Homer. 6251-2
"But as they talked, laid near...", fr. The Odyssey. Homer. 6251-2
"But be contented: when that fell arrest". Sonnet 074 ("But be contented"). William Shakespeare. 6369-1, 6369-1,6436-1
"But be contented: when that fell arrest". William Shakespeare. 6473-6
"But beware the month of Lenaion". Winter. Hesiod. 6251-2
"But chief by numbers of industrious hands". A nation's wealth. John Dyer. 6932-0
"But deeper shadows gather o'er". Unknown. 6902-9
"But Delos is pleasant, O Phoebus...". Homer. 6435-3
"But do not go - I like to have you near me". A modern Psyche. Eliza Calvert Hall. 7021-3
"But do thy worst to steal thyself away". Sonnet 092 ("But do thy worst"). William Shakespeare. 6560-0
"But France got drunk with blood...vomit crime". Stanzas ("But France"). George Gordon, 6th Baron Byron. 7009-4
But don't be humble, fr. Working gang poems. Byron Herbert Reece. 6761-1
"But far astern of Argo her whitening wake...". Apollonius. 6251-2
But for lust. Ruth Pitter. 6210-5
"But grant, in public, men sometimes are shown". Woman's ruling passions, fr. Of the characters of women. Alexander Pope. 6932-0
"But grant, the virtues of a temp'rate prime". Life's last scene, fr. The vanity of human wishes. Samuel Johnson. 6932-0
"But he his wonted pride". Satan and his host, fr. Paradise lost. John Milton. 6933-9
"But he is oft the wisest man". The oak and the broom, sels. William Wordsworth. 6867-7
"But heaven hath a hand in these events." William Shakespeare. 6225-3
"But Hector, when he saw...", fr. The Iliad. Homer. 6435-3
But helpless pieces of the game he plays, fr. Rubaiyat. Omar Khayyam. 7039-6
"But her knees are at his words...", fr. The Odyssey. Homer. 6251-2
"But here's the sunset of a tedious day.". Robert Herrick. 6083-8
But I don't know. Delova Durnford. 6750-6
"But I have sinuous shells of pearly blue". Walter Savage Landor. 6997-5
"But how can I live without you? - she cried". Testament (2). Anne Morrow Lindbergh. 6879-0
"But hushed be every thought that springs". To Sir George Beaumont, sels. William Wordsworth. 6867-7
"But I didn't expect such a crowd". Malay shopping carol. Mary J.J. Wrinn. 6850-2
"But I hae dream'd a dreary dream". The Douglas' dream. Unknown. 6958-4
"But I must leave thee, Italy! To-day". The distant Alps. Florence Smith. 6749-2
"But I suppose you could not know that...". Flight. Margaret Widdemer. 7038-8
"But if as not by that the soul desired." Arthur Hugh Clough. 6110-9
"But if I should say" Edward Estlin Cummings. 6531-7
"But in this rural life," fr. Hastings' sonnets. Sir Egerton Brydges. 6980-0
"But is congenial quiet," fr. Hastings sonnets. Sir Egerton Brydges. 6980-0
"But it starts with the picture of my...". The cloud unfolding. Ernesto Trejo. 6792-1,6998-3
"But labour is now free, and there is hope!". The enfranchised labourer. Wathen Mark Wilks Call. 7009-4
"But list! a low and moaning sound". The shipwreck, fr. The isle of Palms. Christopher (John Wilson) North. 6997-5
"...But little wist Marie Hamilton". Ballad ("...But little wist Marie Hamilton.") Unknown. 6179-6
"But lo! the Alps ascending white in air". Chartreuse. William Wordsworth. 6749-2
"But love whilst that thou may'st be loved again" Samuel Daniel. 6182-6,6436-1
"But minuets are no more!". The death of the minuet. Catherine Maria Fanshaw. 6959-2
"But Miss Ambition as, as I was saying". American culture, fr. Fanny. Fitz-Greene Halleck. 6753-0
"But most by numbers judge a poet's song". The art of writing, fr. Essay on criticism. Alexander Pope. 6934-7

BUT

But my dolls. Unknown. 6314-4
But never life-- Lillian R. Wagner. 6799-9
"But no one seemed to guess, nor guessing". What never happened, sels. Alistair Paterson. 7018-3
...But not forgotten. Gunner P. J. Flaherty. 6468-X
"But now a herald...", fr. The Odyssey. Homer. 6251-2
"But now the Sun, great Hyperion's child". Unknown. 6435-3
"But now Zeus throned in...", fr. The Iliad. Homer. 6251-2
"But now the hero of immortal birth". The apotheosis of Hercules. John Gay. 6972-X
"But now, the o'erhanging Alps,...near". Hannibal's [assage of the Alps. Silius Italicus. 6749-2
"But now-as ravening wolves...", fr. The Iliad. Homer. 6251-2
"But now/From the brow". Envoy to Fo'c's'le yarns: Go back! Thomas Edward Brown. 6809-X
"But O, my muse, what numbers wilt thou find". Blenheim. Joseph Addison. 6932-0
"But of these ladies he despairs to-day". On Dryden's heroic tragedies, fr. The virtuoso. Thomas Shadwell. 6867-7
"But Olaf's heart, albeit on English soil". The Viking battle, fr. The deeds of King Olaf. Charles Whitby. 6994-0
"But oh! 'twas hard to have him go, -- to know." Celia E. Gardiner. 6066-8,6226-1
But one. Ella Wheeler Wilcox. 6956-8
"But one month more I shall be". Rendezvous. Lenora Speyer. 7038-8
"But pleasures are like poppies spread". A night ride, fr. Tam o'Shanter. Robert Burns. 7020-5
"But science also is man's destiny". The telegraph. Richard Hengist Horne. 7014-0
"But see the fading many-colored woods", fr. Autumn. James Thomson. 6122-2
"But see, the fading many coloured woods". Autumn. James Thomson. 6315-2,6604-6,6660-7
But sing your love. Helen Bryant. 6761-1
But still intrepid Icarus. Louise Crenshaw Ray. 7014-0
"But that entrance, mother". The foster-mother's tale. Samuel Taylor Coleridge. 6967-3
"But that night/When on my bed", fr. The prelude. William Wordsworth. 6958-4
"But that which most makes sweet thy...". A country life, sel. Robert Herrick. 6958-4
"But the chief/Are poets...". Poets. Mark Akenside. 6932-0
"But the eternal father...", fr. The Iliad. Homer. 6435-3
"But the flesh" Peter Henisch. 6769-7
But the majestic river. Matthew Arnold. 6252-0
"But the whippoorwill wails on the moor", sels. James G. Clarke. 6601-1
But then. Ben King. 6211-3,6707-7
"But these are scenes where nature's...hand". The village, sels. George Crabbe. 7009-4
But this is also everlasting life. Sarah N. Cleghorn. 6532-5
"But this may not be. Age is shrouding you...". Homer. 6435-3
"But this my need". My creed. Gertrude Huntington McGiffert. 6838-3
"But thou are terrible, with the unrevealed". Ernest Dowden. 6997-5
"But thou go forth and do thy deed." Katharine Lee Bates. 6225-3
"But thou, O Hope! with eyes so fair". Unknown. 6392-6
"But through the night with torch in hand". Nysa. Aeschylus. 6987-8
But to his mother Mary. John Milton. 6282-2
"But to tell the white-armed...", fr. The Iliad. Homer. 6251-2
"But to you, o Lord, what can we offer?". Lukanin beach I. Richard Dauenhauer. 6855-3
"But twelve short years you lived, my son". His son. Asclepiades. 7039-6
But two I love. James M. Hayes. 6285-7
"But up soon swims our mullet...". Oppian. 6251-2
"But vain the tears for darken'd years". Song ("But vain the tears"), fr. The ancient sage. Alfred Lord Tennyson. 6867-7
'But we did walk in Eden.' Josephine Preston Peabody. 6338-1
"But were I loved, as I desire to be". Love defiant. Alfred Lord Tennyson. 7015-9
But what of song? Sophie Himmell. 6761-1
"But when a sunny sevennight had passed". Alfred Austin. 6997-5
"But when came early morning...", fr. The Odyssey. Homer. 6251-2
"But when her heart...", fr. The Odyssey. Homer. 6435-3
But when I saw Grand Canyon. Byrdie L. Martin. 6799-9
"But when the bands were mustered...", fr. The Iliad. Homer. 6251-2
"But when the mother...", fr. The Odyssey. Homer. 6435-3
"But when the queen immersed in such a trance". The farewell of Arthur, fr. Guinevere, fr. The idylls.. Alfred Lord Tennyson. 6867-7
"But when the sunset smiled". Sunset from the train. Richard Watson Gilder. 7041-8
"But when the thrushes sang", fr. Aurora Leigh. Elizabeth Barrett Browning. 6123-0
"But when the winds...", fr. Ode to music. Robert Bridges. 6487-6
"But when through Troy's wide...", fr. The Iliad. Homer. 6251-2
"But when up stalks from the ground". Summer. Hesiod. 6251-2
"But when we in our viciousness grow hard". William Shakespeare. 6238-5
"But when we were come...", fr. The Odyssey. Homer. 6251-2
"But wherefore do not you a mightier way". Sonnet 016 ("But wherefore"). William Shakespeare. 6208-3
"But who art thou, with curious beauty graced". Opportunity. Niccolo Machiavelli. 7039-6
"But who comes/Brushing the floor with what...". Italy, sels. Samuel Rogers. 6832-4
"But who is he with modest looks", fr. Poet's epitaph. William Wordsworth. 6867-7
"But who is he, with modest looks", fr. A poet's epitaph. William Wordsworth. 6934-7
"But who is this, what thing on sea or land," fr. Samson. John Milton. 6088-9
"But who shall see the glorious day". But who shall see? Thomas Moore. 6848-0
"But who the melodies of morn can tell?". Morning sounds. James Beattie. 6793-X
But who the melodies of morn can tell? James Beattie. 6180-X
"But why did I kill him? Why? Why?". After hearing a waltz by Bartok. Amy Lowell. 6959-2
"But why/Waste that on the sky?". To a skylark. A.R. Ubsdell. 6781-6
"But winter has yet brighter scenes; he boasts". A winter scene. Unknown. 6752-2
"But Wordsworth's eyes avert their ken". Wordsworth and Goethe, fr. Stanzas...author of Obermann. Matthew Arnold. 6934-7
"But wise Telemachus...", fr. The Odyssey. Homer. 6435-3
But yesterday. William White. 6868-5
"But yesterday the world was steeped". In welcome to the president. W.H. Anderson. 7001-9
"But yesterday thine eyes were bright". The cathara. Walter Colton. 7030-2
"But yesterday!/O blooms of May". Blooms of May. James Whitcomb Riley. 6992-4
'But, Walt, it may not hold' Joel Cox. 6860-X
"But, the dancing- ah! parlez-moi, Dolly...". The fudge family in Paris. Thomas Moore. 6959-2
Butch is back. Earl Gene Box. 6870-7
Butchart, Isabel
  Dawn. 6653-4
Butcher & Andrew Lang, S.H. (tr.)
  Menelaus and Proteus, fr. The Odyssey. Homer. 6435-3
The butcher boy. Unknown. 6057-9,6058-7
The butcher boy. Unknown. 6059-5
Butcher shop. Jorge Luis Borges. 6642-9
The butcher's boy. Unknown. 6003-X
Butcher, Theodora Starr
  The two towns. 6130-3
The butcher-bird. Celia Thaxter. 6612-7
A butcher. Thomas Hood. 6974-6

The butcher. Agha Shahid Ali. 6900-2
Butchering day. C.L. Edson. 6615-1
'Butchering in the fall' in Vermont. Daniel L. Cady. 6988-6
Butchers. Redmond Phillips. 6384-5
Butler Jr., Benjamin F.
    Fauntleroy. 6417-5
Butler's proclamation. Paul Hamilton Hayne. 6946-0
Butler, A.J. (tr.)
    Apres moi le deluge. Unknown (Greek), 6435-3
    "Come pure in heart before this hallowed fane". Unknown, 6435-3
    Erinna. Anitpater of Sidon, 6879-0
    Erinna, sels. Antipater of Sidon, 6435-3
    God's concern. Palladas, 6435-3
    A joyful mother of children. Unknown (Greek), 6435-3
    Love and music. Meleager, 6102-8
    Love or death. Paulus Silentiarius, 6435-3
    Naked I came. Palladas, 6435-3
    "Now I am dead, be earth devoured of hell". Unknown, 6435-3
    "Of children nine and twenty that I bore". Unknown, 6435-3
    An old fishing net. Julianus [or Julian the Egyptian], 6435-3
    Orpheus ("No more with rocks..."). Antipater of Sidon, 6435-3
    Plato, a musician. Leontius, 6435-3
    A Pythian oracle. Unknown (Greek), 6435-3
    A Spartan's death. Unknown (Greek), 6732-8
    Thermopylae. Simonides, 6732-8,6102-8
    The vain farewell. Paulus Silentiarius, 6435-3
    The way of life. Aesopus, 6435-3
Butler, Alpheus
    Maid and violinist. 6178-8
    Portrait of a poet. 6178-8
    Primrose and thistle. 6178-8
Butler, Arthur Gray
    Edith and Harold. 6437-X
    Oh! to see him once again. 6226-1
    Two long vacations: Grasmere. 6437-X
Butler, Charles Edward
    Anna Pavlowa (1885-1931). 6640-2
    Eulogy. 6640-2
    Holy Thursday. 6640-2
    Of falcons. 6640-2
    Song for a stranger's sake. 6640-2
Butler, Derek
    Man's world dissolving. 6870-7
    Parole board. 6870-7
    Pigeons in prison. 6870-7
    School days/rule days. 6870-7
    Tryst. 6870-7
Butler, Edward H.
    A faun song. 6983-5
    From an old boat. 6983-5
Butler, Ellis Parker
    Nature's wisdom. 6628-3
    The secret combination. 6089-7
    The secret combination. 7021-3
Butler, Florence Hascall
    Grandma'a radio. 6249-0
Butler, Frances Kemble. See Kemble, Frances
Butler, George F.
    Aceldama. 6846-4
Butler, Guy
    Cape coloured batman. 6788-3
    David. 6788-3
    Home thoughts. 6788-3
    Myths. 6788-3
    Pieta. 6788-3
    Stranger to Europe. 6788-3
Butler, Henry Montague
    Lift up your hearts! 6337-3
Butler, Hood C.
    Ebony rhythm. 6178-8
Butler, Kemble
    The boat of grass. 6344-6
Butler, Samuel
    Argumentative theology. 6543-0
    Authority. 6294-6
    Bad writers. 6278-4
    The barn owl. 6943-6
    The character of a small poet. 6200-8
    The character of Hudibras. 6200-8
    Confession. 6278-4
    Courtiers. 6278-4
    Critics. 6278-4
    Distichs and saws. 6543-0
    Fear. 6278-4
    A fragment of science, fr. Hudibras. 6787-5
    Godly casuistry, fr. Hudibras. 6933-9
    The godly. 6278-4
    Good writing. 6278-4
    Holland. 6278-4
    Honor. 6543-0
    Hudibras and the Presbyterians, fr. Hudibras. 6637-2
    Hudibras' sword and dagger. 6302-0;6385-3
    Hudibras' weapon and charger, fr. Hudibras. 6637-2
    Hudibras, sels. 6637-2,6102-8,6188-5,6198-2,6208-3,6315-2,6562-,6192-3,6195-0,6152-4,6637-2,6378-0,6732
    Hypocrisy. 6089-7,6092-7,6278-4
    Inventions. 6278-4
    Laborious writers. 6278-4
    Language of the learned. 6278-4
    The law. 6278-4
    The life after death. 6879-0
    The logic of Hudibras. 6302-0;6385-3
    Logicians. 6278-4
    Love. 6563-5,6737-9
    Marriage. 6278-4
    The metaphysical sectarian. 6341-1
    Modern prowess in war, fr. Hudibras. 6934-7
    The morn, fr. Hudibras. 6934-7
    Morning. 6543-0
    Not on sad Stygian shore. 6250-4
    On a club of Scots. 6278-4
    On loyalty in the cavaliers. 6328-4
    Opinion. 6278-4
    The opinionative. 6278-4
    Philosophy of Hudibras. 6302-9
    The philosophy of the Hudibras. 6302-2,6385-3
    Piety. 6278-4
    Poets. 6278-4
    Polish. 6278-4
    Politicians. 6278-4
    Presbyterian church government, fr. Hudibras. 6933-9
    Presbyterian knight and independent squire,fr. Hudibras. 6933-9
    The Presbyterian knight. 6150-8,6150-6
    The Presbyterians, fr. Hudibras. 6188-5,6543-0
    A psalm of Montreal. 6633-X
    Puffing. 6278-4
    The Puritan knight errant, sels. 6186-9
    The puritan knight errant. 6186-9
    Puritans. 6438-8
    The rabble, or who pays? 6278-4
    The religion of Hudibras. 6089-7,6302-0,6385-3,6092-7
    Saintship versus conscience. 6102-8
    The sectarian knight. 6733-6
    Smatters. 6089-7,6278-4
    Spiritual trimmers. 6543-0
    To a bad poet. 6760-3
    To his mistress. 6563-5
    Upon the weakness and misery of man. 6543-0
    Women. 6278-4
Butler, Samuel (tr.)
    Andromache, fr. The Iliad. Homer, 6435-3
    At Sparta, fr. The Odyssey. Homer, 6435-3
    Eumaeus the swineherd. Homer, 6435-3
    Sailing weather, fr. The farmer's year. Hesiod, 6435-3
    When the snail climbs, fr. The farmer's year. Hesiod, 6435-3
Butler, Thomas
    Song of little. 6214-8
Butler, Thomas Meek
    Columbia comes. 6443-4
Butler, William Allen
    All's well. 6271-7
    At Richmond. 6903-7

Broadway. 6484-1
Buried cities. 6903-7
The busts of Goethe and Schiller in Walhalla. 6903-7
The carnival of 1848. 6903-7
Cast-off garments, fr. Nothing to wear. 6064-1
Columbus. 6903-7
Cornelia's reply. 6903-7
Dobbs his ferry. 6903-7
Dwarf and giant. 6903-7
The equestrian statue of Washington. 6903-7
F.B.C.; Chancellorsville, May 3, 1863. 6903-7
The garden of the gods. 6903-7
A golden wedding. 6903-7
The graveyard at West Point. 6903-7
"I can't" and "I can" 6629-1
In memoriam: T.S.K. 6903-7
The incognita of Raphael. 6735-2
The Inversnaid inn. 6903-7
A midnight sun episode. 6903-7
Miss Flora M'Flimsey. 6505-8
Miss nobody's Christmas dinner. 6903-7
The new argonauts. 6903-7
Nobody to blame. 6787-5
Nothing to wear. 6219-9,6903-7
Nothing to wear, sels. 6064-1,6404-3,6008-0
Notre Dame de Rouen. 6903-7
Oberammergau, 1890. 6903-7
Old and new. 6903-7
Old Pone. 6903-7
The old woman of Troyes. 6903-7
Our fifty-fifth. 6903-7
Psyche. 6903-7
The salle Montesqieu. 6903-7
The sexton and the thermometer. 6903-7
A silver wedding. 6903-7
'Somebody'. 6903-7
Sunbeam and shadow. 6903-7
Titian's Assumption. 6903-7
Tom Twist. 6903-7
The torture-chamber at Ratisbon. 6903-7
Two cities. 6903-7
Uhland. 6903-7
Uhland. 6271-7
Vaucluse. 6484-1
The wanderer. 6903-7
Work and worship. 6903-7
Butler, William Allen (tr.)
The beggar. Johann Ludwig Uhland, 6903-7
The knight of Saint George. Johann Ludwig Uhland, 6903-7
The landlady's daughter. Johann Ludwig Uhland, 6903-7
The minstrel's curse. Johann Ludwig Uhland, 6903-7
The mournful tournament. Johann Ludwig Uhland, 6903-7
The nun. Johann Ludwig Uhland, 6903-7
The shepherd's sabbath song. Johann Ludwig Uhland, 6903-7
The shepherd. Johann Ludwig Uhland, 6903-7
The three songs. Johann Ludwig Uhland, 6903-7
The wreath. Johann Ludwig Uhland, 6903-7
Buttadeus. William Samuel Johnson. 6030-7
Buttcane, Maude
Tragedy. 6799-9
"**Butter** and eggs and a pound of cheese". Ballad ("Butter and eggs"). Charles Stuart Calverley. 6092-7
Butter and eggs, and a pound of cheese. Charles Stuart Calverley. 6732-8
Butter and something. Charles Lutwidge ("Lewis Carroll") Dodgson. 6249-0
Butterbaugh, D.S.T.
Nothing and something. 6670-4
The **butterbean** tent. Elizabeth Madox Roberts. 6326-8
Buttercup. Unknown. 6529-5
Buttercup cow. Elizabeth Rendall. 6262-8
Buttercup, poppy, forget-me-not. Eugene Field. 6684-4
A **buttercup.** K. C. 6049-8
Buttercups. Alice Barkley. 6789-1
Buttercups. Wilfrid Thorley. 6437-X,6501-5,6374-8
Buttercups and daisies. Mary Howitt. 6127-3,6479-5,6529-5, 6638-0,6135-4,6114-1,6131-1
"The **buttercups,** bright-eyed and bold", sels. Julia C.R. Dorr. 6601-1
The **buttercups.** Francis H. Deter. 6906-1
Buttered pippin-pies. John Davies. 6125-7
Butterfield, Frances Westgate
Le printemps empoissone. 6979-7
Butterflies. Francois Coppee. 6585-6
Butterflies. John Davidson. 6301-2
Butterflies. Saint-Paul Roux. 6351-9
Butterflies. Unknown. 6529-5
"The **butterflies** can scarcely find." Kyoshi. 6027-7
"**Butterflies** with filmy, fantastic...". Butterfly parade. Edwin C. Graber. 6799-9
"**Butterflies,** butterflies". Corn-grinding song. Unknown (Laguna Indian). 7039-6
"**Butterflies/Alighting** on larkspur". Flights. Adelia Brownell. 7019-1
Butterfly. D. English. 6804-9
The **butterfly** and the bee. William Lisle Bowles. 6479-5
The **butterfly** and the snail. John Gay. 6133-8
Butterfly blue and grasshopper yellow. Olive A. Wadsworth. 6131-1
Butterfly dance-song. Tawakwaptiwa. 6959-2
Butterfly in the Boston Athenaeum. Clarissa Hall. 6789-1
Butterfly laughter. Katherine Mansfield. 6777-8
A **butterfly** of fashion. Oliver Herford. 6996-7
A **butterfly** on baby's grave. Unknown. 6629-1
Butterfly parade. Edwin C. Graber. 6799-9
Butterfly picture-writing. Vachel Lindsay. 6206-7
"**Butterfly** silver and butterfly gold". Butterfly. D. English. 6804-9
Butterfly weed - Indian fire. Florence Randal Livesay. 6115-X
"A **butterfly** will find the milkweed plant". Jessie Orton Jones. 6999-1
"A **butterfly** with velvet wings that go". Wings. Minnie S. Hunter. 6799-9
The **butterfly's** ball. Mrs. Henry Roscoe (atr.) 6683-6,6105-2,6131-1
The **butterfly's** ball. Thomas Roscoe (atr.) 6105-2,6142-7, 6459-0,6131-1,6683-6
The **butterfly's** ball. William Roscoe. 6114-1,6639-9
The **butterfly's** first flight. Unknown. 6135-4
The **butterfly's** journey. Han-mo Chung. 6775-1
The **butterfly's** lesson. Unknown. 6373-X
The **butterfly's** madrigal. Gelett Burgess. 6652-6
The **butterfly's** toilet. Nixon Waterman. 6529-5
"**Butterfly, awake, awake!**" Basho (Matsuo Basho) 6850-2
"**Butterfly,** butterfly, brilliant and bright". To a butterfly. Lady Flora Hastings. 6772-7
The **butterfly..** Edwin Markham. 6338-1
The **butterfly..** Alice Freeman Palmer. 6303-9;6266-0;6337-3;6476-0
The **butterfly..** John Banister Tabb. 6473-6
The **butterfly.** Samuel Taylor Coleridge. 6086-2
The **butterfly.** Francis Ponge. 6803-0
The **butterfly.** Joseph Skipsey. 6656-9
The **butterfly.** Edmund Spenser. 6935-5
The **butterfly.** Unknown. 6373-X
Buttermilk channel. Arthur Guiterman. 6773-5
Butterworth, Hezekiah
The banner that welcomes the world. 6451-5,6926-6
The broken pinion. 6260-1,6337-3
By Chickamauga river. 6113-3
The church of the revolution. 6946-0
The clocks of Kenilworth. 7041-8
Crown our Washington. 6465-5,6449-3,6820-0
The death of Jefferson. 6946-0
Decoration Day. 7022-1
The first Thanksgiving. 7002-7
Five kernels of corn. 6703-4
The Florida ibis. 7041-8
For Christmas day. 6673-9
The fountain of youth, sels. 6614-3,6484-1
The fountain of youth: a dream of Ponce de Leon. 6552-X
Garfield's ride at Chickamauga. 6074-9
Immortal morn. 6465-5,6143-5,6449-3
In Bay Chaleur. 6273-3,6670-4
The legend of Waukulla. 6946-0
Lincoln's heart. 6260-1
Lincoln's last dream. 6524-4

The nation's defenders. 6578-3
Nix's mate. 6565-1
The old flower beds. 6578-3
Ortiz. 6946-0
Roger Williams. 6946-0
Salve! 6580-5
The snow-bird. 6135-4,6466-3,6519-8
The stately minuet. 6166-4
The taper. 6260-1
The thanksgiving for America. 6946-0
The Thanksgiving in Boston harbor. 6618-6,6484-1
That gray, cold christmas day. 6621-6
Verazzano at Rhodes and Rhode Island. 6946-0
Washington. 6712-3,6143-5
Washington's birthday. 6964-9
Whitman's ride for Oregon. 6946-0
"A buttery, sugary, syrupy waffle". The groaning board. Pink [pseud].. 6817-0
Buttonholes. Hazel Hall. 6880-4
Buttons. Frederick R. McCreary. 6038-2
Buttons. Carl Sandburg. 6542-2
Butts, Alfred D.
    Autumn wind. 6799-9
Butts, Mary Frances
    A bird speaks. 6965-7
    Build a fence of trust. 6461-2
    Build a little fence. 6109-5
    Changelings. 6373-X
    The child and the gentian. 6965-7
    A child's thought. 6965-7
    The Christmas trees. 6519-8,6135-4
    Corporal Clover. 6965-7
    "Every evening baby goes." 6452-3
    The happy hour. 6097-8
    In Galilee. 6848-0
    Keeping store. 6452-3,6466-3,6135-4
    A little shopper. 6965-7
    May miracles. 6965-7
    A mother's song. 6097-8
    Mother's work. 6097-8
    Nature's thoughfulness. 6373-X
    Night. 6519-8
    Shadow and echo. 6965-7
    The silver boat. 6965-7
    The sun will shine. 6109-5
    The sweetest place. 6137-0,6452-3
    To-day. 6337-3
    Tree planting. 6049-8
    Trot, trot! 6078-1
    The voice of the chestnut tree. 6965-7
    Water jewels. 6638-0
    The water-lily. 6273-3,6260-1
    Wild winds. 6519-8,6135-4
    Winter night. 6519-8,6135-4
Buxom Joan. William Congreve. 6089-7
Buxton, Esther W.
    Putting the world to bed. 6529-5,6638-0,6639-9
Buxton, Ida M.
    Faded flowers. 6919-3
Buxton, John
    From a prisoner of war. 6761-1
Buxton, Lucy Wilson
    Dedication. 7016-7
    The foot prints and the wave. 7016-7
    In the dark. 7016-7
    Winter's garden. 7016-7
    The wood-thrush sings. 7016-7
Buxton, Marguerite Emilio
    Fog at the isles of shoals. 6764-6
    The old guard. 6764-6
"Buy a fresh chicken". Sweet 'n sour. Genny Lim. 6790-5
Buzz and hum. Ben Jonson. 6383-7
Buzz! quoth the blue-fly. Ben Jonson. 6189-3
"Buzz, buzz, buzz". Unknown. 6334-9
"Buzz, quoth the blue fly". Unknown. 6363-2
Buzzard. William Roehrick. 6850-2
Buzzard's point. George M. Vickers. 6921-5
Buzzard, C.N.
    The lady of snows. 7035-3
The buzzards. Martin Armstrong. 6943-6

'Bwana Tumbo'-the great hunter. Walter Beverly Crane. 6995-9
By a bank as I lay. Unknown. 6328-4
By a bier-side. John Masefield. 6477-9
By a chapel as I came. Unknown. 6125-7
"By a gay and sunny sprite". The playful sun-beam. Lucile S. Kappeler. 6906-1
"By a grey stone pile". The old. Geroge Mosby Jr.. 6870-7
By a lover. Thomas Hood. 6980-0
By a mountain-stream at rest. Felicia Dorothea Hemans. 6973-8
"By a route obscure and lonely". Dream-land. Edgar Allan Poe. 6753-0
"By a window overlooking tv antennas and...". Reflections on the death of a parrot. Jaime Jacinto. 6790-5
"By all means, use sometime to be alone". George Herbert. 6238-5
"By all the glories of the day". Before action. William Noel Hodgson. 7026-4
"By Babylon's still waters we sat down". Paraphrase of psalm 137. Bible. 6848-0
"By Babylonian flowing streams". Psalm 137. Bible. 6848-0
"By all thy gloryes willingly I goe." Thomas Jordan (atr) 6563-5
By an ancient sea. Thomas Curtis Clark. 6144-3,6532-5
By an ant-heap. Terence Heywood. 6788-3
By an evolutionist. Alfred Lord Tennyson. 6198-2,6199-0, 6473-6,6655-0
By an evolutionist, sels. Alfred Lord Tennyson. 6337-3
By an Indian grave. Mildred Plew Merryman. 6039-0
By an iris-shadowed pool. Mary Carolyn Davies. 6619-4
By an open window in church. Corinne Roosevelt Robinson. 6266-0,6476-0
By and by. Grace Duffie Boylan. 6579-1
By and by. Unknown. 6273-3,6583-X
By Avon stream. Arthur Henry Bullen. 6477-9
"By banks where burned awhile the rose". Renascence. Muredach J. Dooher. 6930-4
"By blazing homes, through forests torn". War. William Lightfoot Visscher. 6846-4
"By Cavite on the bay". The battle of Manilla, sels. Richard Hovey. 6946-0
By blue Ontario's shore, sels. Walt Whitman. 6288-1,6300-4
By Celia's arbour. Thomas Moore. 6328-4
By Chickamauga river. Hezekiah Butterworth. 6113-3
By Clodagh's stream. Francis Carlin. 6032-3
By Coelia's arbor. Richard Brinsley Sheridan. 6930-4
"By chance they met in the doctor's room". X-ray pictures of two men. Edgar A. Guest. 6748-4
"By Coelia's arbor, all the night". By Coelia's arbor. Richard Brinsley Sheridan. 6930-4
By cool Siloam's shady rill. Reginald Heber. 6337-3,6519-8, 6086-2,6304-7
"By day she wooes me, soft, exceeding fair". The world. Christina Georgina Rossetti. 7037-X
"By day she wooes me, softly, exceeding fair". The world. Christina Georgina Rossetti. 7015-9
"By day the bat is cousin to the mouse". The bat. Theodore Roethke. 6761-1
"By day, by night, along the lines...". The challenge of the guns. A.N. Field. 7026-4
By degrees. Berton Braley. 6853-7
By deputy. Arthur St. John Adcock. 6760-3
"By dim light, there not being much". Obligatory love poem. P.L. Jacobs. 6870-7
By doing good we live. Josephine Troup. 6418-3
By earth restored. Inez George Gridley. 6662-3
By Edina mill pond. Edith Schussler and Otto Schussler. 6342-X
By Faughan. Francis Ledwidge. 6812-X
"By easy slope to west, as if it had". Cheyenne mountain. Helen Hunt Jackson. 7041-8
"By ev'ry sweet tradition of true hearts". Sonnet ("By ev'ry sweet"). Thomas Hood. 6974-6
"By every stream, by every way". Song ("By every stream"). Karel Toman. 6763-8
"By every sweet tradition of true hearts". By a lover. Thomas Hood. 6980-0
By flood and field, fr. Ye wearie wayfarer. Adam Lindsay Gordon. 6951-7

"By gad I'm awake, a quiver and a shake". The dying pioneer. Brian ("Korongo") Brooke. 6938-X
"By giddy stairway led". Tapestries. George Houghton. 7041-8
"By her exulting outside look of youth",fr.The prelude. William Wordsworth. 6867-7
"By her lisping tongue". Mother's love. John S. Reid. 6097-8
"By Killarney's lakes and fells". Killarney. Edmund ("Edmund Falconer") O'Rourke. 6858-8
"By Logan's streams that rin sae deep". Logan braes, sels. John Mayne. 6934-7
"By him lay heavy sleep...", fr. The induction. Thomas Sackville; 1st Earl of Dorset. 6726-3,6198-2
By his bedside. Fern Mary Munsell. 6799-9
By jes' laughin' Unknown. 6583-X
By Kandy lake. J.H. S. 6591-0,6592-9
By Lough-na-Gar: green light. Arthur Symons. 6793-X
"By long observation I have understood". Wood an insect. Jonathan Swift. 6831-6
By lovely within. Celia Thaxter. 6612-7
"By man imprisoned, ocean wondrous vast". A drop of brine. Kristinn Stefansson. 6854-5
By memory inspired. Unknown. 6174-5,6244-X
By Menec'hi shore. Louis Tiercelin. 6873-1
"By miracles exceeding power of man". Crucifying. John Donne. 6933-9
By momba tracks. Roderick Quinn. 6384-5
By my own sweat. Alex R. Schmidt. 6750-6
By Ned! Unknown. 6689-5
"By myself walking". Hypochondriacus. Charles Lamb. 6802-2
"By Nebo's lonely mountain". The burial of Moses. Cecil Frances Alexander. 6909-6
By night. Philip Jerome Cleveland. 6337-3
"By night there came a clearing in th sky". And now these jonquils. David Morton. 6850-2
"By night we lingered on the lawn", fr. Memoriam. Alfred Lord Tennyson. 6536-8
"By night, came a dream to Ros-crana!". Fingal and Ros-crana. Unknown. 6873-1
"By O'Neill close beleaguered...". The battle of Beal-an-atha-buidhe. William Drennan. 6858-8
By now. Ralph Salisbury. 7005-1
"By one great heart, the universe is stirred". Life. Margaret Deland. 7041-8
"By our pastor perlext". Addressed to a clerygman. Thomas Rowley. 7030-2
By parcels post. George Robert Sims. 6089-7
By poverty depressed, fr. London. Samuel Johnson. 6934-7
"By reason of thy law". Francis Thompson. 6655-0
By request. Berton Braley. 6853-7
By return mail. Richard Aldridge. 6388-8
By riversides. Antonin Sova. 6886-3
"By Saint Mary, my lady". John Skelton. 6187-7
"By robe or plume or equipage of king". The death of Ahad. Richard Wilton. 6848-0
"By Rufus' hall, where Thames polluted flows". On the report of a wooden bridge. James Thomson. 6816-2
"By rules of fitness and of tense". Remarks to my grown-up pup. Burges Johnson. 7008-6
"By Saint Mary, my lady". In praise of Isabel Pennell. John Skelton. 6830-8
By some strange way. Katharine Tonkin. 6032-3
By stubborn stars, sels. Kenneth Leslie. 6021-P
By summer woods. Unknown. 6049-8
"By that lake, whose gloomy shore". Thomas Moore. 6518-X, 6086-2
"By that name you will not know her". Theodora. Phoebe Cary. 6969-X
'By that way pass the gods', fr. A Florentine cycle. Gertrude Huntington McGiffert. 6838-3
By the Alma. James Dawson. 6577-5
By the Alma river. Dinah Maria Mulock Craik. 6302-0,6385-3, 6409-4
By the Arno. Oscar Wilde. 6331-4,6624-0,6439-6,6331-3
By the autumn sea. Paul Hamilton Hayne. 6219-9
By the beautiful sea. Thomas Cole. 6388-8
By the bivouac's fitful flame. Walt Whitman. 6126-5,6252-0, 6288-1
By the Conemaugh. Florence Earle Coates. 6946-0

"By the blue waters -the restless ocean-waters". Antique Greek lament. Felicia Dorothea Hemans. 6973-8
"By the blue wooden sea". Switchback, fr. Marine. Edith Sitwell. 7000-0
By the cross of Monterey. Richard Edward White. 6922-3
"By the dark mountains guarded well". Sabbation. Richard Chenevix Trench. 6848-0
"By the dark stillness brooding in the sky". On a picture of Christ bearing the cross. Felicia Dorothea Hemans. 6973-8
By the deep nine. W. Pearce. 6125-7
"By the door in the wall of Saint Symeon's...". Moyen age. Wilfred Rowland Childe. 6893-6
"By the dread and viewless powers". Druid chorus on the landing of the Romans. Felicia Dorothea Hemans. 6973-8
By the earth's corpse. Thomas Hardy. 6657-7
"By the edme of the chasm is a slippery track". Saint Gotthard pass. Johann C. Friedrich von Schiller. 6749-2
By the evening fire. Edward Sandford Martin. 6097-8
By the fire. Aldous Huxley. 6320-9,
By the fireside. Robert Browning. 6186-9,6597-X,6655-0, 6230-X,6102-8
By the fireside. Lucy Larcom. 6385-3;6600-3
By the fireside. Thomas J. Mohn. 6799-9
"By the fireside there are old men seated". Unknown. 6240-7
"By the five subtle senses is the mind". The senses. Theodore Maynard. 6839-1
By the fountain. George Frederick Cameron. 7041-8
By the gray sea. John Hall Wheelock. 6619-4
By the grey-gulf water. Andrew Barton Paterson. 6639-9
By the lake. Edith Sitwell. 6019-6
"By the lamplit stall I loitered, feasting...". Sight. Wilfred Wilson Gibson. 6861-8
By the light of the moon. Robert Kelley Weeks. 7041-8
By the lightning we lost our sight. Unknown. 6057-9
"By the little river". The willows. Walter Prichard Eaton. 6891-X
"By the lone sea shore". Charles Mackay. 6997-5
"By the lordly Hudson River". Foresight saga. William Roehrick. 6850-2
"By the margin of the fountain, in the...". By the fountain. George Frederick Cameron. 7041-8
By the margin of the great deep. George William ("A.E.") Russell. 6437-X,6253-9,6723-9
"By the memory of olden deeds heroic which...". An invitation. James Abraham Martling. 6952-5
"By the mighty minister's bell". Last rites. Felicia Dorothea Hemans. 6973-8
"By the moon we sport and play". The urchins' dance. John M. Lyly. 6959-2
"By the moon we sport and play". Unknown. 6181-8
By the North Sea. Algernon Charles Swinburne. 6828-6
By the North Sea. Algernon Charles Swinburne. 6250-4
By the North Sea, sels. Algernon Charles Swinburne. 6997-5
By the ocean. Ruzena Jesenka. 6763-8
By the Pacific. Herbert Bashford. 6102-8,6076-5
By the Pacific Ocean. Joaquin Miller. 6753-0
By the Pacific Ocean. Joaquin Miller. 6484-1
By the Pacific Ocean. Joaquin Miller. 6753-0
"By the pale marge of Acheron". Villanelle of Acheron. Ernest Dowson. 6875-8
"By the path of winter-mutilated clouds...". Last song to a girl of the waterfront. Otto D'Sola. 6759-X
"By the pleasant fire they sat one night". True worth. Unknown. 6926-6
By the pool at the Third Roses. Arthur Symons. 6508-2
By the Potomac. Thomas Bailey Aldrich. 6946-0
"By the promise of noon's splendor in the...". The ideal. Katharine Lee Bates. 6798-0
"By the pure spring, whose haunted waters flow". A promise. Frances Anne Kemble. 6980-0
"By the ripple, ripple of the shallow sea". Song of the water-nixies. Sarah Williams. 6997-5,7037-X
"By the river of lead/The night-factory". River of lead. Iwan [or Yvan] Goll. 6803-0
"By the rivers of Babylon". Super flumina. Bible. 6830-8
By the rivers of Babylon we sat down and wept. George

Gordon, 6th Baron Byron. 6945-2
"By the rivers of Babylon, there we sat down". Psalm 137, fr. The book of psalms. Bible. 7039-6
By the road to the Sunnyvale air-base. Yvor Winters. 6628-3
"By the road to the contagious hospital". Poem ("By the road"). William Carlos Williams. 6069-2
"By the roadside, 'neath the shade". Rest. William White. 6868-5
"By the roadside, rain or shine". Ragged robin and bouncing bet. Alice Reid. 6820-0
"By the rosy cliffs of Devon, on a green hill's". Where love is. Amelia Josephine Burr. 6556-2,6847-2
By the sea. Elsie Cooper. 6997-5
By the sea. William Dean Howells. 6997-5
By the sea. Roden Noel. 7015-9
By the sea. Christina Georgina Rossetti. 6258-X
By the sea. Bayard Taylor. 6440-X
By the sea. James ("B.V.") Thomson. 6997-5
By the sea. Steingrimur Thorsteinsson. 6854-5
By the sea. Unknown. 6926-6
By the sea. Unknown. 6273-3
By the sea. Philip H. Welsh. 6415-9
By the sea. William White. 6868-5
By the sea. William Wordsworth. 6246-6,6668-2,6737-9
By the sea of Galilee. Katharine Lee Bates. 6144-3
By the sea-wall. Vincent O'Sullivan. 6174-5
By the seaside. William Wordsworth. 6997-5
"By the shore of Gitche Gumee". Hiawatha's departure, fr. The song of Hiawatha. Henry Wadsworth Longfellow. 6753-0
By the shore of the river. Christopher Pearse Cranch. 6406-X
"By the side of a country kirk wall". Unknown. 6859-6
"By the side of a green stagnate pool". A pastoral ("By the side"). George Alexander Stevens. 6157-5
"By the side of the Hoongtide bridge..." Unknown (Chinese) 6545-7
By the side of the Rydal Mere, sels. William Wordsworth. 6867-7
"By the soft green light in the woody glade". The spells of home. Felicia Dorothea Hemans. 6973-8
By the statue of King Charles at Charing Cross. Lionel Johnson. 6301-2,6383-7,6250-4,6102-8,6655-0,6508, 6044-7,6096-X,6244-X,6437-X,6477-9,6022
"By the storm invaded". Zelneth's lament, fr. Phantasmion. Sara Coleridge. 7037-X
By the sun-down seas. Joaquin Miller. 6121-4
By the swinging seas. William Ernest Henley. 6429-9,6321-7
By the turret stair. Clinton Scollard. 7041-4
"By the vats of Dionysus...". Unknown. 6251-2
"By the warm hearthstone and the Yule-tree's..". Two homelands. Lance Fallaw. 6800-4
By the waters of Babylon. Edgar Lee Masters. 6619-4
"By the waters of life we sat together". An old man's idyl. Richard Realf. 6921-5
By the well. Sir Edmund Gosse. 6770-0
By the Wissahickon. Charles R. Murphy. 6036-6
By the wood. Robert Nichols. 6542-2
"By this he knew she wept with waking eyes". George Meredith. 6508-2
"By this he knew she wept with waking eyes" George Meredith. 6828-6
"By this the Northern waggoner had set" Edmund Spenser. 6935-5
"By this the northerne wagoner had set". Canto 002, fr. The faerie queene. Edmund Spenser. 6122-2
"By this white hand, thus shook...". A lover's oath. George Croly. 6980-0
"By this, the dreadfull beast...", fr. The...queen. Edmund Spenser. 6726-3
"By this, the sun his westering car drove low". The last evening before eternity. James Abraham Hillhouse. 6752-2
"By thy birth, thou blessed Lord". Blessed may thou be, sweet Jesus. Unknown. 6756-5
"By Tweed, by Teviot's winding tide". Elegy on Thomas Tod Stoddart, the angler-poet. Sir George Douglas. 6819-7
By thy life I live. Jeanne Marie Bouvier de la Motte Guyon. 6337-3
By valiant still. Unknown. 6859-6
By wave and war. Albert E.S. Smythe. 6115-X
"By ways remote and distant waters sped". Catallus, Carmen CI. Aubrey Beardsley. 6785-9
"By what appalling dim upheaval". Simon Gerty. Elinor Wylie. 6880-4
"By what law fell King Charles? By all the laws" Owen (Edward Bulwer-Lytton, Earl Lytton) Meredith. 6606-2
"By what word's power, the key of paths untrod". Heart's hope, fr. The house of life. Dante Gabriel Rossetti. 6110-9,6199-0,6250-4,6828-6
"By white wool houses thick with sleep". Poor Martha. Edith Sitwell. 7000-0
"By whom was David taught". Jehovah-Nissi. William Cowper. 6814-6
"By windowless and gutted shops where rain". Refugees. E.L. Mayo. 6751-4
By wood and wold. Adam Lindsay Gordon. 6784-0
By wood and wole, fr. Ye wearie wayfarer. Adam Lindsay Gordon. 6951-7
By world laid low. Unknown (Irish) 6125-7
By yon burn side. Robert Tannahill. 6086-2
"By Zeus I charge thee, whose clear lightnings...". Sophocles. 6435-3
"By yon castle wa', at the close of the day". There'll never be peace till Jamie comes hame. Unknown. 6859-6
"By your fingertips". Wonder. Lucy A. Jochen. 6857-X
By-and-by. J.W. Barker. 6523-6
By-by, lullaby. Unknown. 6756-5
By-the-way. Patrick MacGill. 6102-8
Byard, Dorothy Randolph
  Together at dawn. 6761-1
"Bye, baby bunting." Mother Goose. 6452-3
Bye, baby, bye. Unknown. 6078-1
Byedny, Demyan
  My voice. Jack Lindsay (tr.). 6546-5
  None knew. Jack Lindsay (tr.). 6546-5
Byely, Andrei
  Native land. Jack Lindsay (tr.). 6546-5
Byer, B.L.
  The ageless Christ. 6065-X
Byers, Samuel H.M.
  Allatoona. 6946-0
  The marriage of the flowers. 6049-8,6166-4
  News at the White House. 6708-5
  Sherman's march to the sea. 6113-3,6016-2,6442-6,6470-1
  The song of Iowa. 6465-5
  The watcher at the gate. 6542-2
  With corse at Allatoona. 6946-0
The bygone year. Arthur Ketchum. 6747-9
Bygones. Bert Leston Taylor. 6089-7
Byington, Josephine
  Ascending footsteps. 6799-9
Byles, Mather
  elegy address'd to his Excellency Governour Belcher, sels. 6008-0
Bynner and Kiang Kangohu, Witter (tr.)
  The moon at the fortified pass. Li Po, 6665-8
Bynner, Witter
  And O the wind. 6653-4
  Apollo troubadour. 6336-5
  As to moonlight. 6037-4
  Autumn tree. 6783-2
  The beloved stranger, sels. 6033-1
  Beside a brook at Mokanshan. 6778-6
  Beyond a mountain. 6347-0
  Border-songs. 6628-3
  A buffalo dance at Santo Domingo. 6039-0
  Changes. 6779-4
  The chaplet. 6467-1
  Chinese procession. 6037-4
  Consummation, fr. To Celia. 6897-9
  The coquette. 6441-8
  A country cottage. 6232-6
  A dance for rain. 6619-4,6581-3,6265-2
  The day. 6542-2
  Defeat. 6979-7
  Donald Evans. 6036-6

During a chorale by Cesar Franck, fr. To Celia. 6897-9
Eagle dance. 6628-3
The early gods. 6338-1
Ecce homo. 6730-1
El Gallo. 6072-2
Endyion. 6780-8
Epithalamium and elegy. 6619-4
The eternal Helen. 6070-6
A farmer remember Lincoln. 6102-8,6076-5
The fields. 6509-0,6556-2
Ghosts of Indians. 6506-6,6431-0,6421-3,6653-4,6464-7
Gipsying. 6628-3
God's acre. 6556-2
The golden heart. 6031-5
A goodbye from the ship. 6776-X
Grenstone. 6031-5
A Grenstone elm. 6653-4
Grenstone Falls. 6628-3
Grenstone river. 6467-1
Grieve not for beauty. 6336-5,6393-4
The heart of gold. 6320-9
Hills of home. 6102-8,6556-2,6732-2,6076-2,6431-0,6439
The hills of San Jose. 6628-3
The home-land. 6607-0
Hurt child. 6761-1
Isadora. 6959-2
Joe and Jack and Jennie. 6017-X
Journey's end. 6320-9
Kids. 6891-X,6887-1
Lest I learn. 6027-7
The light-bringer. 6542-2
Lindbergh. 7019-1
The little farm. 6030-7
'The loves of every day' 6875-8
A mocking-bird. 6338-1,6253-9,6653-4
The mystic ("By seven vineyards on one hill"). 6310-1, 6300-4
Neighbors. 6607-0
The new God. 6730-1,6542-2
The new life. 6310-1,6653-4
The new world, sels. 6393-4
The new world. 6250-4
Nocturne. 6347-0
Not in Russia. 6042-0
Not only swords. 6619-4
An ode to a dancer. 6959-2
The old men and the young men. 6071-4
Outlaws. 6880-4
Passages from a poem: the new world. 6029-3
The poet. 6100-1,6730-1
Point Bonita. 6628-3
Premonition. 6037-4
Prepare. 6542-2,6420-5,6463-9
Property. 6331-4
Republic to republic. 6946-0
The sandpiper ("Along the sea-edge..."). 6073-0,6421-3
Sentence. 6310-1
Shame on you, Lenin! 6880-4
She slept like a lady. 6808-1
The skeptic. 6441-8
"Somebody called Walt Whitman". 6289-X
A song of Liang-Chou. 6628-3
A song of the palace. 6628-3
Songs ascending, fr. To Celia. 6897-9
Sonoma. 6628-3
Take away the darkness. 6761-1
A tent song. 6217-2
Thoughts of old time on the Ch'u river. 6628-3
Three men. 6039-0
Three poplars. 6347-0
Through a gateway in Japan. 6506-6
A thrush in the monlight. 6073-0,6506-6,6556-2,6030-7, 6628-3
To a phoebe bird. 6073-0,6102-8,6266-0,6509-0,6076-5, 6161 ,6464-7,6653-4
To any one. 6556-2,6542-2
To Ceclia. 6897-9
To Edna St. Vincent Millay. 6817-0
To no one in particular. 6441-8,6030-7
To Robert Browning. 6327-6

Train-mates. 6027-7,6467-1
The unknown soldier. 6542-2
Vagrant. 6628-3
Voices. 6466-3,6464-7
War. 6542-2
Winter sonnets. 6782-4
Wistaria. 6069-2,6777-8
Woman of China. 6761-1
A word to the wise. 6070-6
Words on public affairs. 6037-4
A young girl. 6071-4
Bynner, Witter (tr.)
My retreat at Mount Chung=Nan. Wang Wei, 6482-5
Spring heart-break. Liu Fang-p'ing, 6232-6
Byrd (atr), William
Love's immortality. 6153-2
Byrd, William
Long has the furious priest. 7017-5
My mind to me a kingdom is. 6271-7,6302-0,6600-3,6571-6, 6438-8,6219 ,6304-7
My sweet little baby, what meanest thou to cry? 6328-4
Song ("In crystal towns"). 6022-6
Song ("Let not"). 6022-6
Song ("What pleasure"). 6271-7
This sweet and merry month. 6328-4
Byrde, Margaretta
America at St. Paul's. 7031-0,7027-2
Byrne, Donn
The piper. 6327-6
To the world's edge. 6396-9
Byrne, Florence M.
Sestina. 6770-0
Byrne, J. Patrick
Disinherited. 6761-1
Byrne, Josephine Louise
Address unknown. 6839-1
Byrne, Patrick
Cold, cold, cold. 6475-2
Byrnes, Beatrice Paula
Blowing bubbles. 6750-6
Byrnes, Clara
The city speaks. 6847-2
To E.F.K.V.E. 6847-2
Byrnes, Evelyn
Pioneer mothers. 6342-X
Byrnes, Jane Luelling
The omen. 6799-9
Byrom, John
Careless content. 6600-3,6152-4,6219-9
Careless content, sels. 6317-9
Christians, awake! 6747-6
Christmas carol ("Christmas, awake, salute the happy morn") . 6219-9
Contentment: or, The happy workman's song. 6152-4
The countrymen and the ass. 6064-1
The desponding soul's wish. 6932-0
Epigram on Handel and Bononcini. 6932-0
Epigram on the feuds between Handel and Bononcini. 6152-4
Extempore verses ("God bless"). 6932-0
Extempore verses ("Long was"). 6831-6
Extempore verses upon a trial of skill...Figg & Sutton. 6932-0
Hymn for Christmas day. 6337-3
An hymn to the omnipresence. 6152-4
Jacobite toast. 6427-2,6733-6,6092-7,6219-9
My spirit longeth for thee. 6271-7
On the origin of evil. 6831-6
A pastoral ("My time"). 6024-2,6219-9
The pond. 6621-6
The salutation of the blessed virgin. 6282-2
The soul's tendency towards its true centre. 6152-4
Three black crows. 6089-7
Tom the porter. 6152-4
Which is which. 6089-7,6278-4
Byron. Joaquin Miller. 6501-5,6309-8
Byron. Robert Pollok. 6302-0;6385-3
Byron. Herbert Trench. 6877-4
Byron. Albert Edmund Trombly. 6037-4
Byron. Sir William Watson. 6737-9

Byron and Childe Harold, fr. Childe Harold's pilgrimage. George Gordon, 6th Baron Byron. 6196-6
Byron and the rest. Walter Savage Landor. 6186-9
"**Byron** lay, lazily lay". Doer and dreamer. E.E. Bowen. 6793-X
Byron the voluptuary. Sir William Watson. 6656-9
"**Byron**! 'tis thine alone on eagles' pinions". To Lord Byron. Richard Henry Wilde. 7017-5
Byron's conspiracy, sels. George Chapman. 6378-0
Byron's farewell to his native land. Unknown. 6630-5
Byron's grave. Roden Noel. 6046-3
Byron, Charles Gordon
    Boatswain's' monument. 7008-6
Byron, George Gordon, 6th Baron
    Address intended to be recited at the Caledonia meeting. 6945-2
    Address spoken at the opening..Drury-Lane Theatre,1812. 6945-2
    Address to the ocean. 6585-6
    "Adieu to thee, fair Rhine". 6331-4
    "Adieu, adieu! my native shore." 6302-0,6385-3,673-9, 6980-0
    The adieu. 6945-2
    Adrian's address to his soul when dying. 6945-2
    The age of bronze. 6945-2
    Alas! the love of women, fr. Don Juan. 6934-7
    Alhama. 6322-5
    All for love. 6246-5,6737-9
    'All is vanity, saith the preacher'. 6945-2
    Alp's decision. 6621-6
    "Always laugh when you can". 6109-5
    Ambition ("He who ascends"). 6294-6,6610-0
    Ancient and modern Greece. 6543-0
    "And thou art dead, as young and fair." 6086-2,6219-9, 6110-9,6543-0,6828-6
    And wilt thou weep when I am low? 6945-2
    Answer to a beautiful poem entitled The common lot. 6945-2
    Answer to Lines written in Rousseau's Letters of...nun. 6945-2
    Answer to some elegan verses sent by a friend... 6945-2
    Apostrophe to the ocean. 6392-6,6504-X,6610-0,6574-0, 6304-7
    The apparition. 6438-8
    Approach to Florence. 6631-3
    The archangel, fr. Vision of judgment. 6315-2
    Asia, fr. Prometheus unbound. 6659-3
    Athens. 6543-0
    The author's purpose, fr. Don Juan. 6199-0
    Ave Maria, fr. Don Juan. 6282-2,6332-2
    Away, away, ye notes of woe! 6945-2
    Battle of Waterloo. 6102-8,6304-7,6542-2
    Beauty of Greece and the Grecian isles. 6543-0
    Beppo: a Venetian story. 6945-2
    The blues; a literary eclogue. 6945-2
    The bride of Abydos, sels. 6289-X,6332-2,6439-6
    The bride of Abydos. 6110-9,6430-2
    Bright be the place of thy soul. 6543-0,6828-6
    Bryon's farewell. 6301-2,6383-7
    The bull-fight. 6407-8
    A bunch of sweets. 6543-0
    By the rivers of Babylon we sat down and wept. 6945-2
    Byron and Childe Harold, fr. Childe Harold's pilgrimage. 6196-6
    Cain: a mystery. 6848-0,6945-2
    The carnival. 6624-0
    The castled crag of Drachenfels. 6383-7
    Cecilia Metella. 6980-0
    The charity ball. 6945-2
    Childe Harold's address to the ocean. 6889-8
    Childe Harold's farewell to England. 6552-X
    Childe Harold's pilgrimage. 6198-2,6088-9,6828-6
    Childe Harold's pilgrimage, sels. 6660-7,6107-9,6250-4, 6545-7,6110-9,6199 ,6102-8,6188-5,6208-3,6239-3,6483-3,6527-,6258-X,6289-X,6395-0,6427-2,6547-3,6604-, 6332-2,6726-X,6732-8,6196-6,6430-2,6560
    Childish recollections. 6945-2
    Childish recollections (2). 6945-2
    Chillon. 6102-8,6424-8

    Churchill's grave. 6945-2,6828-6
    The Cincinnatus of the west. 6465-5
    Clarens. 6749-2
    "Clarens! sweet Clarens." 6484-1
    "Clime of the unforgotten brave". 7009-4
    Coliseum by moonlight. 6302-0,6358-6,6385-3
    The Coliseum, sels, fr. Childe Harold's pilgrimage. 6196-6
    The Coliseum. 6424-8,6302-0,6332-2,6385-3,6484-1,6624-0, 6199
    Communion with nature. 6143-5
    Condolatory address to Sarah, Countess of Jersey... 6945-2
    The conquest. 6945-2
    Conrad and the dead body of Medora. 6543-0
    Conrad's love for Medora. 6543-0
    Conscience. 6337-3
    The cornelian. 6945-2
    The corsair. 6438-8
    Corsairs' song. 6252-0
    Could love for ever. 6086-2
    A country house party. 6996-7
    "Cruel Cerinthus! does the fell disease". 6945-2
    The curse of Minerva. 6945-2
    Damaetas. 6945-2
    Daniel Boone, fr. Don Juan. 6302-0;6385-3
    Darkness. 6102-8,6392-6,6110-9,6430-2,6199-0
    The days are done. 6945-2
    The death of Calmar and Orla. 6945-2
    Death of Lara. 6980-0
    Death, fr. The giaour. 6302-0;6385-3
    The dedication in Don Juan. 6200-8,6110-9
    Deep and dark blue ocean, fr. Childe Harold. 6125-7
    Deep in my soul. 6328-4
    Defiance, fr. Childe Harold's pilgrimage. 6545-7
    The deformed transformed: a drama. 6945-2
    The degeneracy of Greece. 6606-2
    Desire and disillusion, fr. Childe Harold's pilgrimage. 6199-0
    The destruction of Sennacherib, sels. 6395-0,6419-1
    The destruction of Sennacherib. 6075-7,6101-X,6183-4, 6289-X,6478-7,6504-,6102-8,6239-3,6323-2,6271-7,6339-X,6479-,6473-6,6481-7,6490-6,6512-0,6527-9,6600-, 6606-2,6732-8,6438-8,6114-1,6219-9,6267 ,6263-3,6192-3,6430-2,6560-0,6104-4,6212 ,6131-1,6214-8,6304-7, 6018-8,6424-8,6723 ,6543-0,6737-9,6421-3,6086-2,6110-9,6547 ,6639-9
    "Devil returned to hell by two", fr. The Devil's drive. 6996-7
    The devil's drive. 6945-2
    Don Juan. 6198-2,6959-2
    Don Juan adolescent. 6633-X
    Don Juan's arrival in England. 6633-X
    Don Juan, sels. 6102-8,6154-0,6282-2,6302-0,6315-2,6332-,6385-3,6395-0,6483-3,6527-9,6604-6,6726-,6732-8, 6733-6,6322-2,6196-6,6430-2,6250 ,6560-0,6472-8,6199-0,6659-3,6660-7,6110
    Donna Julia's letter, fr. Don Juan. 6832-4
    Drachenfels. 6331-4,6439-6,6631-3
    The dream. 6102-8,6271-7,6302-0,6385-3,6291-9
    Ducal palace. 6624-0
    The dying boys on the raft. 6543-0
    The dying gladiator. 6138-9,6402-7,6602-2,6424-8,6304-7
    Dying speech of Marino Faliero. 6606-2
    Elegiac stanzas on the death of Sir Peter Paerker, Bart. 6945-2
    Elegy. 6246-5
    Elegy on Newstead abbey. 6945-2
    Elegy on Thryza. 6246-5
    Endorsement to the deed of separation, in...1816. 6945-2
    English bards and Scotch reviewers. 6196-6
    English bards and Scotch reviewers, sels. 6934-7,6102-8, 6483-3,6198-2
    Epigram on my wedding day. 6945-2
    Epigram on the braziers' company having resolved... 6945-2
    Epigram, fr. Tom Paine. 6945-2
    Epigrams on Castlereagh. 6733-6,6945-2
    The episode of Nisus and Euryalus. 6945-2

BYRON

Epistle from Mr. Murray to Dr. Polidori. 6945-2
Epistle to a friend, in answer to some lines...cheerful. 6945-2
Epistle to Augusta. 6110-9,6828-6,6945-2,6945-2
Epistle to Mr. Murray. 6945-2
Epistle to Thomas Moore, sels. 6945-2
Epitaph for Joseph Blackett, late poet and shoemaker. 6945-2
Epitaph for William Pitt. 6945-2
Epitaph on a friend. 6945-2
Epitaph on Castlereagh. 6945-2
Epitaph on John Adams, of Southwell. 6945-2
Eternal spirit of the chainless mind. 6240-7
Euthanasia. 6543-0
The eve of Quatre Bras. 6793-X
The eve of Waterloo, fr. Childe Harold. 6188-5,6242-3, 6375-5,6427-2,6479-5,6552-,6114-1,6107-9,6621-6,6263-6,6267-9,6964
Evening, fr. Don Juan. 6302-0;6385-3
The execution of Hugo. 6980-0
The execution. 6438-8
Exhortation to the Greeks. 6610-0
Fair Greece! sad relic of departed worth. 6240-7
The fall of Greece. 6240-7
The falls of Terni. 6624-0
"Fare thee well! and if forever." 6219-9,6302-0,6486-8, 6543-0,6438-8,6086-2,6110
A farewell to land. 6136-2
Farewell to Malta. 6092-7,6945-2
Farewell to the muse. 6945-2
"Farewell! if ever fondest prayer." 6302-0,6543-0,6737-9,6828-6
The fate of beauty. 6980-0
The field of Waterloo. 6294-6,6402-7
Filial love. 6302-0;6385-3
Fill the goblet again. 6092-7
The first kiss of love. 6945-2
First love. 6240-7,6385-3,6092-7
For music. 6086-2
The fountain of Egeria. 6543-0
A fragment ("Could I remount"). 6945-2
fragment ("When, to their airy"). 6945-2
Fragment written shortly after the marriage...Chaworth. 6945-2
Freedom's hero, fr. The prisoner of Chillon. 6337-3
Freedom's true heroes. 6543-0
Friendship. 6322-5
The giaour. 6250-4
The girl of Cadiz. 6271-7,6331-4,6439-6,6219-9
The gladiator. 6438-8
The glory that was Greece. 6198-2,6114-1,6322-5
Good night. 6732-8
Greece. 6424-8
Greece, fr. Childe Harold. 6302-0,6385-3,6196-6,6304-7
Greece, fr. The giaour. 6302-0;6385-3
Haidee and Juan, fr. Don Juan. 6832-4
Haidee, fr. Canto II. 6110-9
Hail and farewell. 6322-5
Harold the wanderer, fr. Chile Harold's Pilgrimage. 6832-4
The harp the monarch minstrel swept. 6848-0,6543-0
"He that hath sail'd...", fr. Childe Harold's... 6547-3
Heaven and earth: a mystery. 6945-2,6848-0
Hebrew melodies, sels. 6945-2
The Hellespont. 6543-0
Herod's lament for Mariamne. 6945-2,6848-0
Heroes of Greece. 6406-X
Hesperus. 6153-2
"High and inscrutable...", fr. Don Juan. 6726-3
Hints from Horace. 6945-2
"His classic studies...", fr. Don Juan. 6726-3
Hours of idleness, sels. 6945-2
"However, I still think, will all due deference". 7025-6
Hurts of time. 6438-8
"Hush'd is the din of tongues...", fr. Childe... 6395-0
"I do believe". 6238-5
"I saw thee weep - the big bright tear". 6945-2
I stood in Venice, on the bridge of sighs. 6484-1
I would I were a careless child. 6945-2

Idleness. 6294-6
If sometimes in the haunts of man. 6543-0
If that high world. 6014-5,6543-0
Imaginative sympathy with nature. 6240-7
The immortal mind. 6600-3,6730-1
Impromptu, in reply to a friend. 6945-2
Impromtu. 6110-9
"In digging up your bones, Tom Paine". 6088-9
In praise of the Turk. 6633-X
In Seville. 6484-1
"In the first year of freedom's second dawn". 6289-X
Incantation, fr. Manfred. 6438-8
Inscription on the monument of a Newfoundland dog. 6945-2,6510-4,6945-2
Invocation to the spirit of Achilles. 6086-2
Invocation, fr. Don Juan. 6315-2,6543-0
The Irish avatar. 6945-2
Island (the sea cave) 6438-8
The island. 6945-2,6438-8,6945-2
The isles of Greece. 6186-9,6208-3,6331-4,6339-X,6481-7, 6484-,6301-2,6125-7,6383-7,6192-3,6199-0,6110 ,6726-3,6023-4,6086-2,6104-4,6252-0,6212 ,6439-6,6639-9, 6668-2,6543-0,6723-9
The isolation of genius. 6543-0
Jephtha's daughter. 6438-8,6543-0,6828-6
John Keats. 6102-8
Juan and Haidee, fr. Don Juan. 6094-3,6196-6,6199-0
The Jura mountains. 6749-2
"The kiss, dear maid." 6302-0;6385-3
Know ye the land?, fr. The bride of Abydos. 6198-2,6332-2,6543-0
L'amitie est l'amour sans ailes. 6945-2
Labuntur, fr. Canto I. 6110-9
Lachin y Gair. 6110-9,6196-6,6438-3,6859-6,6945-2
Lake Leman. 6331-4,6385-3,6196-6
The lake of Geneva. 6600-3,6543-0,6631-3
Lambro's return. 6302-0
The lament of Tasso. 6980-0,6945-2,6828-6
Lara. 6945-2
Latest verses. 6302-0;6385-3
Leucadia. 6484-1
Liberty and America. 6323-3
"A light broke in upon my soul". 66601-1
Lines. 6828-6
Lines addressed to a young lady. 6945-2
Lines addressed to the Rev. J.T. Becher. 6945-2
Lines in the traveller's book at Orchomenus. 6945-2
Lines inscribed upon a cup formed from a skull. 6545-7, 6945-2
Lines on hearing that Lady Byron was ill. 6945-2
Lines to Mr. Hodgson. 6092-7
Lines written beneath a picture. 6945-2
Lines written beneath an elm in the churchyard...Harrow. 6945-2
Lines written in an album at Malta, sels. 6289-X
Lines written in Rousseau's Letters of an Italian nun.. 6945-2
Lines written on a blank leaf of The pleasures...memory. 6945-2
The Lisbon packet. 6278-4
London literature and society, fr. Canto XI. 6110-9
London, fr. Don Juan. 6439-6
Longing. 6086-2
Love. 6066-8
Love of England. 6438-8
Love unseen, fr. Child Harold's pilgrimage. 6545-7
Love's last adieu. 6945-2
Maid of Athens [ere we part]. 6154-0,6271-7,6302-0,6328-4,6332-2,6385-,6543-0,6723-9,6219-9,6430-2,6560-0, 6226 ,6481-7,6484-1,6086-2,6110-9
Man - woman. 6302-0;6385-3
"A man must serve his time", fr. English bards. 6996-7
Man's love. 6102-8
Manfred. 6110-9,6196-6,6438-3,6828-6
Manfred on the Jungfrau. 6749-2
Manfred to the sorceress. 6980-0
Manfred's midnight thoughts. 6543-0
Manfred's soliloquy on the jungfrau. 6543-0
Manfred, sels. 6102-8,6332-2,6541-4,6648-8
Maino faliero to the Venetian conspirators. 6606-2

Marino Faliero, doge of Venice. 6945-2
Martial, lib. I, epig. I. 6945-2
Matrons and maids. 7025-6
Mazeppa. 6828-6
Mazeppa's ride. 6302-0,6358-6,6385-3
Mazeppa, sels. 6392-6
Midnight in the east. 6543-0
A mighty mass of brick. 6484-1
Money, fr. Don Juan. 6787-5
Monody on the death of the Right Hon. R.B. Sheridan. 6945-2,6980-0
Mont Blanc. 6749-2,6600-3,6749-2
A moonlight night at Venice. 6543-0
Murat. 6385-3,6438-8,6749-2
My boat is on the shore. 6481-7,6102-8,6199-0,6301-2, 6383-7
My epitaph. 6945-2
My native land - good night. 6543-0
"My soul is dark - Oh! quickly string". 6945-2
Napoleon's farewell. 6716-6
Napoleon, fr. Childe Harold. 6302-0;6385-3
Nature's daughter. 6370-5
Nevermore. 6240-7
New duet. 6945-2
Night. 6597-X
Night. 6240-7
Night and storm in the Alps, fr. Childs Harold's... 6332-2
Night and tempest, fr. Childe Harold's pilgrimage. 6832-4
The night before Waterloo. 6484-1,6737-9,6543-0,6088-9, 6212-2
Night, fr. Childe Harold's pilgrimage. 6315-2
No more. 6438-8
"Oh Rome! my country...", fr. Childe...pilgrimage. 6289-X
"O snatch'd away in beauty's bloom." 6543-0,6102-8,6138-9,6198-2,6289-X,6302-0,6385-,6271-7,6315-2,6560-0, 6250-4,6110-9,6219
O, talk not to me. 6830-8
An occasional prologue. 6945-2
The ocean, fr. Childe Harold's pilgrimage. 6138-9,6332-2,6337-3,6240-7,6374-8,6706-,6543-0,6150-8,6252-0, 6424-8,6199-0
Ode ("Oh Venice"). 6198-2
Ode from the French. 6250-4
Ode on Venice. 6631-3,6828-6
Ode to Napoleon. 6102-8,6385-3,6086-2
Ode to Napoleon Bonaparte. 6110-9
An ode to the framers of the frame bill. 6157-5
Oh! snatch'd away in beauty's bloom. 6086-2,6828-6
Oh! weep for those. 6945-2,6848-0
"Oh, talk not to me of a name great in story." 6138-9, 6289-X,6092-7
On a carrier... 6278-4
On a change of masters at a great public school. 6945-2
On a Cornelian heart which was broken. 6945-2
On a distant view o fthe village and school of Harrow. 6945-2
On being asked what the 'origin of love'. 6945-2
On Chillon. 6192-3,6199-0,6430-2,6102-8
On finding a fan. 6945-2
On himself and his epic. 6186-9
On leaving Newstead abbey. 6945-2
On Lord Thurlow's poems. 6945-2
On Moore's last operatic farce, or farcical opera. 6945-2
On my thirty-third birthday. 6945-2
On my wedding day. 6945-2
On Napoleon's escape from Elba. 6945-2
On parting. 6945-2
On revisiting Harrow. 6945-2
On Samuel Rogers. 6278-4
On the birth of John William Rizzo Hoppner. 6945-2
On the bust of Helen by Canova. 6945-2,6828-6
On the castle of Chillon. 6625-9,6737-9,6143-5,6371-5, 6246-5
On the day of the destruction of Jerusalem by Titus. 6945-2,6848-0
On the death of a young lady. 6945-2

On the death of Mr. Fox. 6945-2
On this day I complete my thirty-sixth year. 6332-2, 6110-9,6430-2,6560-0,6086-2,6196 ,6250-4,6219-9,6197-4,6199-0,6371-3
One struggle more and I am free. 6945-2,6543-0,6945-2
The Orient. 6302-0;6385-3
Oscar of Alva. 6945-2
Outward bound. 6385-3,6438-8
Paranthetical address, by Dr. Plagiary. 6945-2,6808-2
Parisina. 6945-2
Parnassus. 6484-1,6543-0
The parting of Conrad and Medora. 6543-0
Petrarch's tomb, fr. Childe Harold's pilgrimage. 6331-4, 6439-6,6624-0
Poems to Thyrza. 6472-8
Poems to Thyrza, sels. 6472-8
Poetical commandments, fr. Canto I. 6110-9
Poetical commandments, fr. Don Juan. 6110-9
The power of money, fr. Don Juan. 6150-8
The prayer of nature. 6213-8,6945-2
The Princess Charlotte. 6302-0,6385-3
The prison of Tasso. 6624-0,6631-3
The prisoner of Chillon. 6192-3,6196-6,6560-0,6264-4, 6458-2,6197 ,6110-9,6438-8,6086-2,6219-9,6371-3,6631
The prisoner of Chillon. 6646-1,6569-4,6543-0,6419-1, 6192-3,6196-6,6560-0,6264-4,6458-2,6197 ,6110-9,6438-8,6086-2,6219-9,6371-3,6631 ,6646-1,6569-4,6543-0, 6419-1,6828-6
Procreative virtue of great examples. 6606-2
Prometheus. 6086-2,6199-0,6110-9,6828-6
Prometheus unbound, sels. 6659-3
The prophecy of Dante. 6945-2
The prophecy of Dante. 6828-6
A publisher to his client. 6138-9
The pursuit of beauty. 6543-0
The race with death. 6322-5
The rainbow. 6438-8
Ravenna. 6624-0
Ravenna, sels. 6484-1
Real and unreal solitude. 6543-0
Realm of the sea. 6385-3
Remember him, who passion's power. 6945-2
Remember thee! remember thee! 6945-2
Remembrance. 6945-2
Remind me not, remind me not. 6945-2
Remorse, fr. On this day I complete my 36th year. 6337-3,6543-0
Reply to some verses of J.M.B. Pigot. 6945-2
The return of Beppo. 6302-0
The Rhine. 6302-0, 6385-3,6484-1,6543-0
"Roll on, thou deep nd dark blue ocean..." 6402-7
Rome. 6624-0,6610-0,6624-0,6543-0,6424-8,6631
Rome and freedom, fr. Childe Harold's pilgrimage. 6196-6,6199-0
The ruins of Rome. 6153-2
St. Peter's. 6624-0
Santa Croce. 6624-0,6631-3
Sardanapalus: a tragedy. 6945-2
Saul. 6945-2
The sceptic and his poem, fr. Don Juan. 6196-6
Sea grot. 6385-3
The sea. 6302-0,6385-3,6732-8,6438-8
Sennacherib. 6322-5
Serenity. 6291-1
She walks in beauty. 6154-0,6198-2,6208-3,6236-9,6246-5, 6271-,6187-7,6302-0,6317-9,6385-3,6732-8,6196 ,6228-8,6289-X,6315-2,6332-2,6423-X,6473-,6328-4,6430-2, 6560-0,6250-4,6199-0,6513 ,6328-4,6481-7,6536-8,6600-3,6604-6,6726-,6301-2,6104-4,6197-4,6110-9,6438-8, 6086 ,6153-2,6219-9,6371-3,6737-9,6723-9,6396 ,6646-1,6543-0,6660-7,6302-0,6385-3,6317 ,6023-4,6828-6
The shipwreck, fr. Don Juan. 6110-9,6196-6,6560-0,6332-2
Siege and conquest of Alhambra. 6438-8
The siege of Corinth. 6679-8,6438-8,6245-8
A sketch. 6378-0,6945-2
The skull. 6294-6,6385-3,6438-8
"The sky is changed...", fr. Childe Harold... 6726-3
So, we'll go no more a-roving. 6075-7,6106-0,6198-2, 6208-3,6317-9,6369-,6187-7,6302-0,6315-2,6385-3,6527-

BYRON

9,6536-,6726-3,6199-0,6430-2,6659-3,6383-7,6301
Solitude. 6597-X,6438-8,6543-0
Song for the Luddites. 6945-2
Song of Saul before his last battle. 6438-8,6110-9,6086-2,6848-0
Song of the corsairs. 6833-2
Song of the Greek poet. 6302-0,6385-3,6271-7,6153-2, 6219-9,6424
Song of the rover. 6302-0;6385-3
Sonnet on Chillon, fr. The prisoner of Chillon. 6439-6, 6660-7,6197-4,6110-9,6086-2,6543 ,6301-2,6154-0,6289-X,6315-2,6331-4,6488-4,6604-
Sonnet to George the Fourth. 6945-2
Sonnet to Lake Leman. 6484-1,6110-9,6749-2
Sonnet, to Genevra. 6945-2
Sonnet, to Genevra (2). 6945-2
Southey. 6302-0
Spain, fr. Childe Harold's pilgrimage. 6196-6
The spell is broken, the charm is flown! 6945-2
A spirit passed before me. 6848-0
A spirit passed before. 6945-2
Stanza to Augusta, sels. 6934-7
Stanzas. 6075-7
Stanzas ("Away, away"). 6980-0
Stanzas ("But France"). 7009-4
Stanzas ("Can tyrants"). 7009-4
Stanzas ("Could love"). 6945-2,6832-4
Stanzas ("Oh, talk not"). 6271-7,6732-8,6219-9
Stanzas ("Though the day of") 6438-8
Stanzas ("Yet, freedom"). 7009-4
Stanzas composed during a thunderstorm. 6945-2
Stanzas for music. 6086-2,6110-9,6543-0,6250-4,6219-9, 6430 ,6198-2,6271-7,6332-2,6604-0,6660-7,6737
Stanzas for music ("I speak not"). 6945-2
Stanzas for music ("There be none"). 6199-0,6828-6
Stanzas for music ("There's not"). 6110-9,6199-0,6828-6
Stanzas for music ("They say"). 6110-9,6828-6
Stanzas to a Hindoo air. 6945-2
Stanzas to a lady. 6945-2
Stanzas to a lady, on leaving England. 6945-2
Stanzas to Augusta. 6102-8,6271-7,6328-4,6092-7,6110-9, 6383-7,6543-0,6560-0
Stanzas to Augusta. 6828-6
Stanzas to Augusta ("Through the day..."). 6945-2
Stanzas to Augusta ("When all around grew..."). 6945-2
Stanzas to the Po. 6624-0,6631-3
Stanzas written in passing the Ambracian Gulf. 6945-2
Stanzas written on the road between Florence and Pisa. 6075-X,6332-2,6110-9
Stars. 6240-7,6543-0
The statue of Apollo. 6543-0
"Stop! for thy tread is on...", fr. Childe Harold's... 6395-0
Storm at night on Lake Leman. 6385-3
The storm. 6438-8
The storming of Corinth. 6322-5
Sublime tobacco. 6092-7
Substitute for an epitaph. 6945-2
"Sun of the sleepless! melancholy star!" 6945-2
Sunset. 6385-3,6438-8
Sunset in the Morea. 6543-0
Swimming. 6239-3,6385-3,6438-8
The tear. 6486-8
There be none of beauty's daughters. 6138-9,6246-5,6328-4,6536-8,6315-2,6110
"There is a pleasure in the pathless woods". 6238-5, 6395-0,6547-3,6726-3
"There was a sound...", fr. Childe Harold... 6726-3
There was a time, I need not name. 6945-2
"There's doubtless something in domestic doings". 7025-6
There's not a joy the world can give. 6219-9
They accuse me. 6733-6
"They never fail who die". 6238-5
They say that hope is happiness. 6086-2
Thou art not false, but thou art fickle. 6945-2,6828-6
Thoughts suggested by a college examination. 6945-2
A thunder-storm in the Alps. 6240-7
"'Tis being and doing and having that make". 6109-5
'Tis sweet to hear, fr. Don Juan. 6332-2

To a beautiful Quaker. 6945-2
To a lady (Mrs. Musters). 6945-2
To a lady who presented the author...velvet band. 6945-2
To a lady who presented to the author a lock of hair... 6945-2
To a lady,on being asked my reason for quitting England. 6945-2
To a vain lady. 6945-2
To a youthful friend. 6945-2
To an oak at Newstead. 6945-2
To Anne. 6945-2
To Anne (2). 6945-2
To Augusta. 6302-0,6385-3,6086-2
To Belshazzar. 6945-2
To Caroline. 6945-2
To Caroline (2). 6945-2
To Caroline (3). 6945-2
To D--. 6945-2
To Dives. 6945-2
To E--. 6945-2
To Edward Noel Long, Esq. 6945-2
To Eliza. 6945-2
To Ellen. 6945-2
To Emma. 6945-2
To England, fr. Childe Harold's pilgrimage. 6726-3
To Florence. 6945-2
To Ginevra. 7015-9
To Greece. 6395-0
To Ianthe, fr. Childe Harold. 6208-3
To Inez. 6732-8
To Lesbia. 6945-2
To Lord Thurlow. 6945-2
To M--. 6945-2
To M.S.G. 6945-2
To M.S.G. (2). 6945-2
To Marion. 6945-2
To Mary. 6980-0
To Mary, on receiving her picture. 6945-2
To Mr. Hodgson. 6874-X
To Mr. Murray ("To hook"). 6945-2
To Mr. Murray ("Strahan"). 6945-2,6802-2
To Mr. Murray ("For Orford"). 6945-2
To my son. 6945-2
To romance. 6945-2
To the author of a sonnet beginning 'Sad is my verse'. 6945-2
To the author of a sonnet... 6278-4
To the Countess of Blessington. 6945-2
To the Duke of Dorset. 6945-2
To the Earl of Clare. 6945-2
To the memory of Kirke White, fr. English bards... 6934-7
To the ocean, fr. Childe Harold's pilgrimage. 6239-3, 6214-8,6301-2,6631-3,6331-4,6730
To the Rhine. 6631-3
To the sighing strephon. 6945-2
To Thomas Moore ("Oh you"). 6945-2
To Thomas Moore ("My boat"). 6945-2
To Thomas Moore. 6196-6,6430-2,6110-9,6560-0,6396-9, 6154-0,6240-7,6271-7,6289-X,6302-0,6332-,6385-3,6483-3,6092-7,6086-2,6659-3,6737
To Thyrza ("Without a stone"). 6980-0,6945-2
To Thyrza. 6543-0
To Thyrza ("One struggle more, and I am free"). 6980-0
To time. 6945-2
To woman. 6945-2,6996-7
Tom Paine, sels. 6945-2
Transient beauty, fr. The giaour. 6302-0;6385-3
Triumph of the defeated. 6337-3
Turkish beauty. 6302-0
"'Twas twilight, and the sunless day...", fr. Don Juan. 6395-0,6726-3
Twilight. 6543-0
The two Foscari, sels. 6239-3,6258-X
The two Foscari. 6945-2
The unreturning brave. 6240-7
The Vatican. 6624-0
Venice. 6624-0,6439-6,6543-0,6242-8
Venice and Rome, fr. Childe Harold's pilgrimage. 6332-2

Venice and sunset, fr. Childe Harold's pilgrimage. 6199-0
Venice, fr. Childe Harold. 6331-4,6732-8,6196-6,6439-6
Venice: a fragment. 6631-3
The Venus de Medici. 6624-0
Verses found in a summer house at Hales-Owen. 6945-2
Versicles. 6945-2
A very mournful ballad on...siege & conquest of Alhama, 6219-9,6945-2
Vision of Belshazzar. 6848-0,6134-6,6395-0,6552-X,6614-3,6438-8,6192
The vision of judgment. 6200-8,6315-2,6378-0,6536-8, 6637-2,6110
The vision of judgment, sels. 6150-8,6196-6
The vision of judgment. 6828-6
"Voices, sweeping through all time, peal". 6238-5
Voltaire and Gibbon. 6150-8
The waltz. 6200-8
Washington. 6484-1,6820-0
Waterloo. 6240-7,6302-0,6323-3,6331-4,6332-2,6385-,6395-0,6457-4,6610-0,6438-8,6196-6,6560 ,6424-8,6457-4, 6631-3,6665-8,6639-9
We'll go no more a-roving. 6339-X,6427-2,6086-2
Wellington, fr. Don Juan. 6324-1
"Were my bosom as false as thou deem'st it to be". 6945-2
Werner, or, the inheritance. 6945-2
When a man hath no freedom. 6199-0
When coldness wraps this suffering clay. 6014-5,6219-9, 6648-8,6543-0
When I roved a young highlander. 6945-2
When we two parted. 6102-8,6134-6,6186-9,6246-5,6271-7, 6302-,6328-4,6726-3,6732-8,6219-9,6371-3,6430 ,6393-9,6543-0,6737-9,6196-6,6560-0,6199-0,6110-9,6513-9, 6086-2,6094
"Where may the wearied eye repose." 6712-3
Where none intrudes. 6501-5
"Where rose the mountains...", fr. Childe Harold... 6395-0
The wild gazelle. 6945-2
The wild gazelle. 6848-0
Windsor poetics. 6278-4
'With a swimmer's stroke'. 6423-X
"Words are things, and a small drop of ink". 6238-5
"The world is a bundle of hay". 6052-8
Written after swimming from Sestos to Abydos. 6089-7, 6026-9,6464-7,6278-4,6945-2
Written on road between Florence and Pisa. 6086-2
"Yet still there whispers the small voice within". 6238-5
Youth and age. 6246-5,6737-9
Zuleika. 6543-0

Byron, George Gordon, 6th Baron (tr.)
Ad lesbiam. Caius Catallus, 6945-2
"Aegle, beauty and poet, has two little crimes". Unknown (French), 6945-2
Appeal for illumination, fr. Morgante Maggiore. Luigi Pulci, 6282-2
The chain I gave. Unknown (Turkish), 6945-2
Epigram. Rulhieres, 6945-2
Epitaph on Virgil and Tibullus. Domitius Marsus, 6945-2
Francesca of Rimini, fr. The divine comedy. Dante Alighieri, 6945-2
Greek war-song. Unknown (Greek), 6945-2
Hesperus the bringer. Sappho, 7039-6
"I wish to tune my quivering lyre". Anacreon, 6945-2
"The man of firm and noble soul". Horace, 6945-2
Medea, sels. Euripides, 6945-2
The morganna maggiore, sels. Luigi Pulci, 6945-2
Morgante Maggiore, sels. Luigi Pulci, 6282-2
Ode ("We do not curse thee, Waterloo!). Unknown (French), 6945-2
On a nun. Jacopo Vittorelli, 7039-6,6945-2
Post-obits and the poets. Martial, 7039-6
Prometheus vinctus, sels. Aeschylus, 6945-2
Psalm 137. By the rivers of Babylon we sat down and... Bible, 6848-0
Romaic love song. Unknown, 6945-2
Romaic song. Unknown, 6945-2
Tu me chamas. Unknown (Portuguese), 6945-2
Tu me chamas (2). Unknown (Portuguese), 6945-2
"'Twas now the hour when night had driven". Anacreon, 6945-2
Whom the gods love. Menander, 6435-3
"Ye cupids, droop each little head". Caius Catallus, 6945-2

Byron, Mary C. See Byron, May C.
Byron, May C. ([Mary] Gillington)
The adventurers. 6478-7
"All through the dark before dawn." 6720-4
The ballad of London river. 6793-X
The cactus. 6800-6
The call of the veld. 6591-0,6592-9
The conqueror. 7014-0
A dead march. 7037-X
Drought. 6800-6
The fairy thrall. 6274-1
Good-bye. 6800-6
The herd-boy in the rain. 6800-6
The home coming. 7037-X
If death were good. 6800-6
Intra muros. 6481-7
The little son. 6800-6
My ten dollies. 6713-1
"O far away, green waves, your voices call". 6997-5
"O wild black sea that flashes fitful light". 6997-5
The pageant of seamen. 6079-X
Pastoral. 6800-6
"The sea-weed rises, sunset-red". 6997-5
"The sunrise flashes and floats and flickers..." 6997-5
The tryst of the night. 6873-1
Vigil. 6997-5
A wave. 6997-5
Byron, sels. Joaquin Miller. 6107-9
"Byron, what clash in thee of sea and wind". Byron. Herbert Trench. 6877-4
Byson, Eva
Now bar the door. 6532-5
Byu-lo, baby-bunting! Unknown. 6424-8
Byun, Yung-ro
Nongae, who died for her country. 6775-1
Byway in biography. Maurice Hare. 6339-X
Byzantium. William Butler Yeats. 6354-3,6150-8,6208-3,6315-2,6536-8,6209-1,6645-3

"C is for Christmas, best day of the year!". Christmas acrostic. Rosamund Livingstone McNaught. 6807-3
"C'est un bazar, au bout des faubourgs rouges". Le bazar. Emile Verhaeren. 6801-4
"C'etait dans la nuit brune". Ballade a la lune. Alfred de Musset. 6801-4
The c'rrect card. George Robert Sims. 6451-5
C-C-C cootie. Unknown. 6589-9
C.,A.
The venturesome buds. 6373-X
C.,A.E.
Snow. 6373-X
C.,A.L.
To him all life was beauty. 6144-3
C.,C.L.
A little April fool. 6965-7
C.,E.
Emaricdulfe. 6182-6
C.,E.F.L.
The centipede's dilemma. 6965-7
C.,E.P.
Fuzzy wuzzy leaves us. 6440-X
C.,G.A.J.
Ireland. 6474-4
C.,H.D.
Sonnet to the South Street Bridge. 6936-3
C.,J.
Beauty and time. 6189-3
The frailty of beauty. 6182-6
C.,J.F.
The caliph and satan. 6302--0
C.,K.

C.
    A buttercup. 6049-8
C.,M.E.
    Wondrous wine class. 6717-4
C.,M.H.
    Spring on the heights. 6118-4
C.,M.S.
    Birds' nests. 6131-1
C.,N.
    Life. 6563-5
C.,R.
    The mandolin. 6118-4
C.,W.C.
    Fly, little letter. 6116-8
C.L.M.. John Masefield. 6365-9,6102-8,6508-2
C.R.R.
    Mycenae. 6799-9
C.S.A.. Abram Joseph Ryan. 7041-8
The C.S.A. commissioners. Unknown. 6946-0
Ca' the yowes. Isobel Pagan. 6198-2,6086-2
Ca' the yowes to the knowes. Robert Burns. 6737-9,6180-X, 6271-7,6302-0,6385-3,6086-2,6250
Ca' the yowes to the knowes. Unknown. 6180-X
Caaryl, Guy Wetmore
    Red Riding Hood. 6736-0
Cab-driver's lament. Norman Moser. 6998-3
The cabala. Clifford Harrison. 6848-0
Cabalquinto, Luis
    The big one. 6790-5
    Blue tropic. 6790-5
    Eating lechon, with my brothers and sisters. 6790-5
    The flower vendor. 6790-5
    Hometown. 6790-5
Cabaniss, Mary H.
    At sundown. 6841-3
    The jest, fr. Thumb nail sketches. 6841-3
    The mourner. 6841-3
    The negationist. 6841-3
    The saint. 6841-3
    Scandal, fr. Thumb nail sketches. 6841-3
    Shangaied. 6841-3
    The spendthrift. 6841-3
    Thumb nail sketches, sels. 6841-3
    Truth, fr. Thumb nail sketches. 6841-3
A cabaret dancer. Zoe Akins. 6959-2
The cabaret dancer. Hermann Hagedorn. 6959-2
Cabbages. William Makepeace Thackeray. 6802-2
Cabell, James Branch
    Arcadians confer in exile. 6875-8
    The conqueror passes. 6875-8,6850-2
    Easter eve. 6337-3
    Fancies in Filigree. 6875-8
    Foot-note for idyls. 6875-8
    Garden song. 6250-4
    Grave gallantry. 6875-8
    The Hoidens. 6875-8
    One end of love. 7017-5
    Story of the flowery kingdom. 6512-0
    Villon quits France. 6875-8
The cabin at the end of the road. Helen Haynes. 6799-9
Cabin love-song. John Alfred Macon. 6139-7
Cabin of my dreams. Lillian Stickney. 6764-6
Cabin philosophy. Unknown. 6687-9
The cabin where Lincoln was born. Robert Morris. 6524-4
The cable hymn. John Greenleaf Whittier. 6126-5
Cable, Catherine
    The shining road. 6461-2
Cable, George Washington
    An editor's first-born. 6004-8
    The last arrival. 6273-3
    A new arrival. 6078-1,6280-6,6479-5,6440-X
Cable, Gerald
    Ancient forests of the Near East. 6855-3
    Highway 299 6855-3
    The illumination of George Jr. 6855-3
    Mr. Pete Totten. 6855-3
"Cables entangling her". She is far from the land. Thomas Hood. 6974-6
Cableton, Will
    The prayer ("Twas a night"). 6139-7
Caboose thoughts. Carl Sandburg. 6808-1

Caboose thoughts. Carl Sandburg. 6399-3,6288-1,6628-3
Cabot, Elsie Pumpelly
    Burnt are the petals of life. 6762-X
Cabral, Olga
    At the Jewish museum. 6966-5
    Hokusai's wave. 6966-5
    Mother and sister of the artist. 6966-5
    Picasso's women. 6966-5
The Cachalot, sels. Edwin John Pratt. 6021-8
Cacoethes scribendi. Oliver Wendell Holmes. 6089-7
Cacophony for clarinet. Edith Sitwell. 7000-0
Cactus. Terence Heywood. 6788-3
"The cactus has its spike". I am desert-born. Vaida Stewart Montgomery. 6979-7
"A cactus shields me from the sun". The cactus. May C. ([Mary] Gillington) Byron. 6800-6
The cactus, fr. Desert drift. Alice Corbin. 6628-3
The cactus. May C. ([Mary] Gillington) Byron. 6800-6
The cactus. Laurence (Adele Florence Nicolson) Hope. 6338-1
The cad.. Sean O'Faolain. 6582-1
Cadenabbia. Henry Wadsworth Longfellow. 6331-4,6624-0,,6631-3
Cadences. Samuel T. Clover. 6476-0
Cadences. John Payne. 6656-9
Cadgwith. Lionel Johnson. 6096-X,6282-2,6437-X,6292-X,6172-9,6301
Cadilla, Carmen Alicia
    Angelus. Dudley Fitts (tr.). 6759-X
    Responsories. Dudley Fitts (tr.). 6759-X
    Sad air. Dudley Fitts (tr.). 6759-X
Cadmus and Harmonia. Matthew Arnold. 6046-3,6437-X
Cadmus, Will H.
    A wife's lament. 6166-4
Cadwalder Fry and his theory. Robert C.V. Meyers. 6924-X
Cady, Daniel L.
    Addison County, Vermont, clay. 6988-6
    Apple-paring night in Vermont. 6988-6
    April in Vermont. 6988-6
    The ballad of the Vermont calf. 6989-4
    Banking up Vermont houses. 6988-6
    Beaver Brook, West Windsor, Vermont. 6989-4
    Beginning haying in Vermont. 6989-4
    Blasting rocks in Vermont. 6988-6
    Bleaching a web of cotton in Vermont. 6989-4
    Boiled dish in Vermont. 6989-4
    Boiling sap at night in Vermont. 6988-6
    Breaking a colt in Vermont. 6989-4
    Building the schoolhouse fires in Vermont. 6989-4
    Burning brush in Vermont. 6988-6
    'Butchering in the fall' in Vermont. 6988-6
    Canaan avd. Vermont. 6989-4
    Candidating in Vermont. 6988-6
    Champlain and Lake Champlain. 7030-2
    'Changing works' in Vermont. 6988-6
    Choir troubles in Vermont. 6989-4
    Cleaning out the suller in Vermont. 6988-6
    Closing a trade in Vermont. 6989-4
    Cording up the ned in Vermont. 6989-4
    Courting in Vermont. 6989-4
    Croquet in Vermont. 6989-4
    Cutting corn in Vermont. 6988-6
    Digging potaters in Vermont. 6988-6
    Dipping candles in Vermont. 6988-6
    Doing chores in Vermont. 6989-4
    Driving oxen in Vermont. 6989-4
    Early candle writing in Vermont. 6989-4
    Early days in Vermont. 6988-6
    Early spring in Vermont. 6988-6
    Farmers' teas in Vermont. 6989-4
    'Farming it' in Vermont. 6988-6
    Fashion in Vermont. 6989-4
    Feeling big in Vermont. 6989-4
    <u>Fireworks in Vermont. 6989-4</u>
    The first snow in Vermont. 6988-6
    Fixing over the barns in Vermont. 6989-4
    Fourth of July in Vermont. 6988-6
    General Ira Allen: founder of the state... 6989-4
    Getting ready to go to meeting in Vermont. 6989-4
    Getting up the winte wood in Vermont. 6988-6

Going crosslots in Vermont. 6988-6
Greasing boots in Vermont. 6988-6
'Hailing the doctor' in Vermont. 6988-6
'Half a crop' in Vermont. 6988-6
A happy Vermonter. 6989-4
Harvest time in Vermont. 6988-6
'Having the thrashers' in Vermont. 6988-6
'Haying the oats' in Vermont. 6988-6
Haying time in Vermont. 6988-6
Haying, Vermont and ginger drink coordinated. 6988-6
Helps in Vermont haying. 6989-4
The hills of old Vermont. 6988-6
Hoeing corn in Vermont. 6989-4
Holding town office in Vermont. 6989-4
'Hopping mad' in Vermont. 6988-6
Housecleaning day in Vermont. 6988-6
How Barre, Vermont, was named. 6988-6
Husking corn in Vermont. 6989-4
Jericho, Vermont. 6988-6
The last of May in Vermont. 6988-6
'Leaving it out' in Vermont. 6989-4
Looking over Vermont town resorts. 6988-6
Making soap in Vermont. 6988-6
Making Vermont piccalilli. 6989-4
Managing Vermont boys. 6989-4
May in Vermont. 6989-4
Mending brush fence in Vermont. 6988-6
Mid-April in Vermont. 6988-6
The Middlebury, Vermount, Fair. 6988-6
Nature fakirs in Vermont. 6988-6
Neighboring in Vermont. 6989-4
New goods at a Vermont store. 6989-4
New Vermont names. 6988-6
An old Vermont cellar hole. 7030-2,6989-4
The old Vermont farm. 6988-6
An old Vermont red cow. 6989-4
Old Vermont roads. 6988-6
Old-fashioned Vermont flowers. 6988-6
Our old center-town Vermont meetinghouse. 6988-6
Our old Vermont apple pole. 6988-6
Our old Vermont lumber wagon. 6988-6
Our old Vermont parlor-room. 6988-6
Our Vermont brick oven. 6989-4
Our Vermont pie-safe button. 6989-4
Our Vermont woodhouse chamber. 6989-4
An 'over the mountain' Vermont frock. 6989-4
Padua. 7030-2
Passing a subscription paper in Vermont. 6989-4
The passing of the old Vermont meetinghouse. 6988-6
Picking apples in Vermont. 6988-6
'Picking stone' in Vermont. 6988-6
Pitching hay in Vermont. 6988-6
Pitching the last tumble in Vermont. 6989-4
Planting corn in Vermont. 6988-6
Planting potaters in Vermont. 6989-4
Playing checkers in Vermont. 6988-6
Pre-townmeeting talk in Vermont. 6988-6
The Proctorsville and Windsor, Vermont, stage. 6988-6
Putting the cream in the well of Vermont. 6988-6
Raising Hubbard squash in Vermont. 6988-6
Raking after the cart in Vermont. 6989-4
Riding horse to cultivate in Vermont. 6988-6
'Round the railroad in Vermont. 6989-4
Rutland County, Vermont. 6989-4
Saint Albans, Vermont. 6989-4
Seeing the girls home in Vermont. 6989-4
Selling a cow in Vermont. 6988-6
Selling a farm in Vermont. 6989-4
Setting the table in Vermont. 6989-4
'Settled going' in Vermont. 6989-4
Shall Vermonters raise sheep? 6988-6
'Shopping' in Vermont. 6988-6
Simple remedies in Vermont. 6989-4
Singns of spring in Vermont. 6989-4
Smoking meat in Vermont. 6989-4
The south side of the barn in Vermont. 6989-4
Sparking a girl in Vermont. 6989-4
Special message to the Vermont legislature. 6988-6
Spring on the Vermont farm. 6988-6
Spring's work in Vermont. 6989-4

Sprouting potaters in Vermont. 6989-4
Stock and Vermont punkins. 6988-6
'The straight and narrow' in Vermont. 6989-4
Sunday buggy riding in Vermont. 6989-4
That's Vermont. 6988-6
Thompson's Vermont. 6988-6
Too much Lake Champlain in Vermont. 6988-6
Trout fishing in Vermont. 6989-4
The 'true Vermonter'. 6988-6
Two Vermont roads. 6989-4
The University of Vermont service flag - 1517 stars. 6988-6
Vacation hints for young Vermonters. 6988-6
Vermont 'clips' and 'cases'. 6989-4
A Vermont 'donation'. 6988-6
The Vermont 'hired man'. 6988-6
Vermont 'tavern stands'. 6988-6
A Vermont appreciation. 6989-4
A Vermont auctioneer. 6988-6
A Vermont barn. 6989-4
A Vermont basket. 6989-4
A Vermont bootmaker. 6988-6
A Vermont breakfast. 6988-6
Vermont brownbread. 6989-4
Vermont buckwheat batter. 6988-6
A Vermont buttery. 7030-2,6989-4
A Vermont castor. 6989-4
Vermont cheesemaking. 6988-6
A Vermont chicken buyer. 6988-6
Vermont corn meal. 6988-6
A Vermont cosset. 6989-4
Vermont country life. 6989-4
A Vermont country store. 6988-6
The Vermont crow. 6989-4
Vermont deestrict school. 6989-4
Vermont district school recollections. 6989-4
Vermont dried beef. 6988-6
A Vermont drove of cattle. 6989-4
Vermont fall feed. 6988-6
Vermont farm lore. 6989-4
Vermont farming tools. 6988-6
Vermont foliage. 6989-4
Vermont freestones. 6989-4
A Vermont general-utility man. 6988-6
A Vermont grinstone. 6988-6
Vermont haying tools. 6989-4
A Vermont horseshed talk. 6989-4
Vermont housekeeping. 6988-6
Vermont in late September. 6988-6
A Vermont justice court. 6989-4
A Vermont kitchen. 6988-6
A Vermont lean-to. 6989-4
Vermont Morgans. 6988-6
Vermont oyster suppers. 6988-6
A Vermont pasture. 7030-2,6989-4
Vermont preachers. 6989-4
A Vermont putterer. 6989-4
A Vermont railroad scurzion. 6989-4
A Vermont raising. 6989-4
A Vermont rascal. 6988-6
A Vermont reading circle. 6989-4
A Vermont rock maple. 6989-4
A Vermont sawmill. 6989-4
A Vermont sheriff. 6989-4
A Vermont sleigh. 6989-4
A Vermont spring smudge. 6989-4
Vermont stone wall. 6989-4
A Vermont stoneboat. 6989-4
A Vermont Sunday dinner. 6988-6
The Vermont thrashers are coming. 6988-6
A Vermont train of cars. 6989-4
A Vermont village fool. 6989-4
Vermont wild flowers in August. 6988-6
Vermont will do her part. 6988-6
Vermont wool carding. 6988-6
Vive Vermont. 6989-4
Voting the paupers in Vermont. 6988-6
Walton's Vermont register. 6989-4
Warm clothes in Vermont. 6989-4
Warning the rats i Vermont. 6989-4

Washing sheep in Vermont. 6988-6
Washing the buggy in Vermont. 6989-4
Whittling in Vermont. 6989-4
Why district school used to keep in Vermont. 6988-6
Windsor, Vermont. 6988-6
Winter churning in Vermont. 6988-6
Working by the day in Vermont. 6989-4
'Working on the road' in Vermont. 6988-6
'Working up the woodpile' in Vermont. 6988-6
Cadyow castle. Sir Walter Scott. 6110-9
Caedmon
    The approach of Pharaoh, fr. Genesis. Charles W.
        Kennedy (tr.). 6665-8
    The approach of pharaoh. 6022-6
    The beginning of creation, fr. The paraphrase. 6102-8
    The creation. 6489-2
    Fall of angels and of man, fr. Genesis. 6489-2
    The fall of man. 6848-0
    Far and wide she went. 6833-2
    Genesis, sels. 6489-2
    The paraphrase, sels. 6102-8
    The paraphrase. 6102-8
    Satan's presumption and fall. 6269-5
Caedmon. George Garrett. 6388-8
Caedmon. Norman Nicholson. 6210-5
Caedmon's hymn. Unknown. 6193-1
Caeli. Francis William Bourdillon. 6652-6
The Caelian hill. Bessie Rayner Parkes. 6624-0
Caelica. Fulke Greville; 1st Baron Brooke. 6186-9,6380-2,
    6436-1
Caelica and Philocell. Fulke Greville; 1st Baron Brooke.
    6436-1,6195-5
Caelica, sels. Fulke Greville; 1st Baron Brooke. 6931-2,
    6378-0,6317-9,6586-4,6931-2
Caelum non animum. William Habington. 6793-X
Caesar. Paul Valery. 6665-8
Caesar and Christ. Thomas Curtis Clark. 6542-2
Caesar in Egypt, sels. Colley Cibber. 6867-7
Caesar remembers. William Kean Seymour. 6464-7
Caesar Rodney's ride. Richard J. Beamish. 6249-0
Caesar Rodney's ride. Elbridge Streeter Brooks. 6621-6
"A Caesar tinting red the sands of Gaul". Strange love.
    Edward Wurtzebach. 6761-1
"Caesar, afloat with his fortunes!". The turtle. Unknown.
    6946-0
Caesura. Glory E. Scott. 6799-9
Caesura. Berenice Van Slyke. 6808-1
The Cafe Molineau. Eugene Field. 6949-5
Cafe scene. Saunders Lewis. 6528-7
The cafe singer. Margaret Widdemer. 7038-8
Cafes. Robert B. Smith. 6870-7
Cafeteria afternoon. Oscar Williams. 6761-1
Cage, John
    Three mesostics. 6803-0
The cage. Martin Armstrong. 6779-4
The cage. Elizabeth Bartlett. 6388-8
The cage. Geoffrey Chaucer. 6943-6
The cage. Jean Garrigue. 6390-X
The cage. James Stephens. 6510-4
Caged. Grace Denio Litchfield. 6510-4
A caged bird. Sarah Orne Jewett. 6597-X,6073-0
The caged bird. Maimie A. Richardson. 6269-5
The caged eagle's death dream, fr. Cawdor. Robinson
    Jeffers. 6978-9
The caged squirrel. Janet Gargan. 6510-4
Cagobens village. Unknown (American Indian) 6396-9
The cailin deas. George Sigerson. 6858-8
Cailleach bein-y-vreich. John Campbell Shairp. 6656-9
Cain. Victor Hugo. 6102-8
Cain. Louis Untermeyer. 6011-0
Cain: a mystery. George Gordon, 6th Baron Byron. 6848-0,
    6945-2
Caine, Hall
    After sunset. 7015-9
    How long, o Lord! 6954-1
    Where lies the land? 7015-9
Cainsmorning. Dom Moraes. 6339-X
The caique, fr. The ghazul. William Makepeace Thackeray.
    6802-2
Cairn builders. John Hackett ("An Pilibin") Pollock. 6244-X

Cairncross, Thomas S.
    Grey Galloway. 6269-5
The caissons go rolling along. Edmund L. Gruber. 6237-7
Caius Gracchus. Vincenzo Monti. 6973-8
Cake on Sunday, fr. Old and new New York. Alfred
    Kreymborg. 6012-9
The cake walk. Unknown. 6247-4
Cake, Lu B.
    Ghosts in the barn. 6696-8
    Mister, yer gittin' old. 6927-4
Cakes and ale. Unknown. 6733-6
Cakes and pies. Emeroy Hayward. 6684-4
Cakes o' croudy. Unknown. 6859-6
The cakewalk. Wilfred Wilson Gibson. 6959-2
The Calais disaster. Unknown. 6651-8
Calais sands. Matthew Arnold. 6430-2,6560-0,6253-9
Calais, 1802, sels. William Wordsworth. 6867-7
Calais, August 1802. William Wordsworth. 6659-3
"Calamus budded in the bottomland". Wild apples. August
    Derleth. 6979-7
Calantha's dirge. John Ford. 6189-3
Calderon de la Barca, Pedro
    The dream called life. Edward Fitzgerald (tr.). 7039-6
    Thou art of all created things. 6433-7
Calderon, Pedro de la Barca
    Justina's temptation. Denis Florence MacCarthy (tr.).
    6102-8
Caldwell of Springfield. Francis Bret Harte. 6742-5,6444-2
Caldwell of Springfield. Unknown. 6294-6
Caldwell, A.F.
    All ending in 'O'. 6684-4
Caldwell, George W.
    The doctor, sels. 6482-5
    The surgeon. 6482-5
    The trail of life. 6482-5
Caldwell, James E.
    Ottawa. 6433-7
Caldwell, Richard
    Conspiracy. 6397-7
    Leaves. 6397-7
    Old folks. 6397-7
    Once. 6397-7
    Romance. 6397-7
Caldwell, W.W.
    Washington. 6684-4
Caldwell, William W.
    In summer time. 6385-3
    Robin's come. 6135-4,6273-3,6597-X
Caldwell, William W. (tr.)
    A Rhine legend. Emanuel Geibel. 6484-1
    The rose-bush. Unknown (German), 6385-3
The Caledonian market. William Plomer. 6257-1
Calenberg, Connie
    I love thee, Lord. 6065-X
    "Take my hand, O blessed master". 6065-X
Calendar song. Arnold Rattenbury. 6895-2
Calendar, sels. Frances Abbot. 6764-6
The calendar. Unknown. 6466-3,6424-8
"Calenus owed a single pound, which yet". Minimum de
    malis. Unknown. 6878-2
Calf in the goldenrod. Julia Van der Veer. 6850-2
The calf-path. Sam Walter Foss. 6162-1,6486-8
The calf. Eleanor Baldwin. 6510-4
Calgary of the plains. Emily Pauline ("Tekahionwake")
    Johnson. 6837-5
Calhoun, Robert D.
    Definition. 6017-X
Caliban in the coal mines. Louis Untermeyer. 6102-8,6337-3,
    6490-6,6509-0,6602-X,6336
Caliban on the island. William Shakespeare. 6150-8
Caliban upon Setebos. Robert Browning. 6828-6
Caliban upon Setebos. Robert Browning. 6657-7,6730-1,6430-
    2,6199-0,6110-9,6655
The calico cat. Vachel Lindsay. 6206-7
Calico pie. Edward Lear. 6891-X,6722-0
Calico, cantle, scythe and snath, fr. Inner song... Thomas
    Hornsby Ferril. 6751-4
Calidasa. See Kalidasa
Calidore. John Keats. 6828-6

California. Ina D. Coolbrith. 6241-5
California. Mary Carolyn Davies. 6241-5
California. Rolfe Humphries. 6038-2
California. Joaquin Miller. 6484-1
California. Lydia Huntley Sigourney. 6946-0
California. Unknown. 6058-7
A California Christmas. Joaquin Miller. 6431-0
A California city landscape. Carl Sandburg. 6010-2
A California Easter mass. Charles K. Field. 6241-5
The California flea. Fred Emerson Brooks. 6923-1
A California garden, fr. Emilia. Robinson Jeffers. 6649-6
California landscape. Leona Bishop Mealey. 6316-0
California of the south. Grace Ellery Channing-Stetson. 6241-5
California orchard. Elsa Gidlow. 6628-3
California poppies. Mary Carolyn Davies. 6241-5
A California song. Clarence Urmy. 6241-5
A California vignette, fr. Tamar. Robinson Jeffers. 6501-5
California winter. Edward Rowland Sill. 6484-1
The California year. Benjamin Franklin Taylor. 6815-4
Californina- the invitation. James Abraham Martling. 6952-5
The caliph and satan. J.F. C. 6302--0
The caliph's draught. Sir Edwin Arnold. 6656-9
The caliph's encampment. Thomas Moore. 6438-8
Calisthenics. Lolly Williams. 6750-6
Calkins, S.S.
    The world is waiting for you. 6649-3
"The call 'To arms!' resounded...". The veteran. J.A. Fraser. 6795-6
Call and T.F. Higham, W.M.W. (tr.)
    Demeter at Elusis. Unknown (Greek), 6435-3
    "Of great Demeter here begins my lay". Homer, 6435-3
    The rape of Persephone. Unknown (Greek), 6435-3
    "She, with heavy heart". Homer, 6435-3
"Call back your odours, lovely flowers!". The wanderer and the night-flowers. Felicia Dorothea Hemans. 6973-8
The call for five hundred thousand more. James Abraham Martling. 6952-5
"Call for the robin redbreast and the wren". Daniel Webster. 6395-0
"Call for the robin-red-brest and the wren". Cornelia's song. John Webster. 6933-9,6150-8
"Call for the robin-redbreast and the wren". John Webster. 6181-8,6536-8,6125-7,6430-2,6189-3
"Call for the robin-redbreast and the wren". A dirge. John Webster. 6182-6,6276-3,6533-3
Call him high Shelley now. Alfred Kreymborg. 6619-4
"Call him the child of God" William H. Draper. 6995-9
"Call it not loneliness to dwell". The caravan in the desert. Felicia Dorothea Hemans. 6973-8
"Call it survival/But who is the fittest". Canteen pimpin' Yasmeen Jamal. 6870-7
"Call Jehovah thy salvation". Psalm 091 Bible. 6848-0
Call loudly, Chantecler! Pauline Starkweather. 6761-1
"Call me friend or foe". The comrade. Lee Wilson Dodd. 6897-9
Call me not dead. Richard Watson Gilder. 6730-1
"Call me not dead when I, indeed, have gone". Unknown. 6238-5
"Call me not dead when I, indeed, have gone". 'Call me not dead' Richard Watson Gilder. 7041-8
The call of brotherhood. Corinne Roosevelt Robinson. 6420-5
The call of Colorado. Eugene Dimon Preston. 6836-7
The call of David. John Henry, Cardinal Newman. 6848-0
The call of England. Sir Owen Seaman. 7031-0
The call of Kansas. Esther M. Clark. 6615-1
"The call of homing rooks, the shrill". Desiderium: in memoriam, S.F.A. Andrew Lang. 6987-8
The call of the adventurers. Orrin K. Charles. 7007-8
The call of the bugles. Richard Hovey. 6753-0
The call of the Carillon. Annie Charlotte Dalton. 6224-5
The call of the city. Amy Levy. 6793-X
The call of the countryside. J. M. Meador. 6818-9
The call of the drum. J. Willey Owen. 6130-3
The call of the heart. Madison Cawein. 6094-3
The call of the hour. Marion Couthouy Smith. 6995-9
The call of the morning. George Darley. 6930-4
Call of the open. Laura E. Bradshaw. 6799-9

The call of the Scot. Ruth Guthrie Harding. 6088-9
The call of the spring. Alfred Noyes. 6151-0,6266-0,6478-7, 6653-4,6660-7
The call of the stream. Charles H. Crandall. 6274-1
The call of the unbeaten. Grantland Rice. 6291-1
The call of the veld. May C. ([Mary) Gillington) Byron. 6591-0,6592-9
Call of the west. Eugene Carroll Nowland. 6719-0
'call of the wild'. Brian ("Korongo") Brooke. 6938-X
The call of the wild. Robert Service. 6159-1,6433-7,6374-8, 6433-7,6115-X
The call of the wild. Daisy Sherman. 6270-9
The call of the woods. Edgar A. Guest. 7033-7
The call of the woods. William Shakespeare. 6114-1
A call on a ball. Carolyn Wells. 6882-0
"Call out the roll call of the dead, that we". Requiem mass. Jack Lindsay. 6895-2
"Call them all together at a white round table". The end of the quest. Dorothy Stott Shaw. 6836-7
"Call them gladiolas! That's how mother knew..". Gladiolas. Edgar A. Guest. 6869-3
A call to action. Callinus. 6435-3,6665-8
Call to arms. Helene Mullins. 6420-5
The call to arms in our street. Winifred M. Letts. 7031-0
The call to arms in our street. Winifred M. Letts. 7027-2
A call to arms. Mary Raymond Shipman Andrews. 6946-0
The call to arms. Carl John Bostelmann. 6542-2
The call to battle. Felicia Dorothea Hemans. 6973-8
A call to the builders. Helen Gray Cone. 6848-0
Call to the colors. Arthur Guiterman. 6274-1
The call to the colors. Unknown. 6741-X
A call to the cow ponies. William Henry Ogilvie. 7010-8
A call t the wild. Edward John Plunkett, 18th Baron Dunsany. 6930-4
A call to youth. Elise Jean Jacobs. 6847-2
"Call ye these appearances", fr. The prelude. William Wordsworth. 6867-7
Call, Frank Oliver
    "A la claire fontaine" 6797-2
    Blue homespun. 6021-8
    Calvary. 6796-4
    Hidden treasure. 6797-2
    La terre. 6021-8
    An old habitant. 6021-8
    The raconteur. 6021-8
    "Unto a fountain clear" 6797-2
Call, Wathen Mark Wilks
    The enfranchised labourer. 7009-4
    The haunted shore. 7015-9
    Hymn ("When by the marbled lake I lie and listen"). 6437-X
    Kossuth and the Hungarians. 7009-4
    Mazzini. 7009-4
    The people's petition. 6437-X,6656-9,6186-6
    Protection. 7009-4
    Renunciation. 6437-X,6730-1
    The Virgin Mary's bank. 6518-X
Call, Wathen Marks Wilks
    Summer days. 6656-9
The call.. Jones Very. 6333-0
A call. George William ("A.E.") Russell. 6393-4
The call. Francis William Bourdillon. 7031-0
The call. Francis William Bourdillon. 7027-2
The call. Daniel Corkery. 6930-4
The call. George Darley. 6219-9
The call. Cora D. Fenton. 6374-8
The call. Edgar A. Guest. 6374-8
The call. John Hall. 6317-9,6208-3,6563-5,6341-1,6023-4
The call. John Hall. 6933-9
The call. George Herbert. 6271-7
The call. Harry Kemp. 7007-8
The call. Charlotte Mew. 6354-3
The call. Thomas Osbert Mordaunt. 6339-X
The call. Robert Service. 6159-1
The call. Alan Sullivan. 6727-6
The call. Katharine (Hinkson) Tynan. 6102-8
'Calla all'. Unknown. 6946-0
Callaghan, Barry
    Assonance. 6767-0
    Mother and son. 6767-0

CALLAGHAN

Snowfall. 6767-0
So it was done. 6767-0
Callaghan, Gertrude
Burial. 6096 X
Caution. 6039-0
Hurricane. 6096 X
I shall break a heavy bough. 6619-4
To Rodin's statue of an old courtesan. 6039-0
Callanan, Jeremiah [or James] Joseph
Gougaune Barra. 6302-0,6385-3,6409-4,6858-6
Lines to the blessed sacrament. 6930-4
Moonlight. 6090-0
O say, my brown Drimin. 6858-8
Serenade ("The blue"). 6930-4
Song ("Awake thee"). 6930-4
Callanan, Jeremiah [or James] Joseph (tr.)
The convict of Clonmell. Unknown (Irish), 6244-X,6858-8
Dirge of O'Sullivan Bear. Unknown (Irish), 6858-8
The girl I love. Unknown (Irish), 6858-8,6930-4
Lament of O'Sullivan Bear. Unknown (Irish), 6244-X
O say, my briwb drimin. Unknown (Irish), 6930-4
The outlaw of Lough Lene. Unknown (Irish), 6244-X,6930-4,6930-4,6090-0,6545-7
Callao. Crosbie Garstin. 6464-7
Called back. Emily Dickinson. 6102-8
Called back. Orellius [pseud]. 7031-0
A **caller** for Samuel Taylor Coleridge. Elinor Lennen. 6316-0
Caller Herrin'. Carolina Oliphant, Baroness Nairne. 6258-X, 6332-2,6086-2
Caller herrin'. Unknown. 6687-9
Caller water, sels. Robert Fergusson. 6198-2,6086-2
Callicles' song, fr. Empedocles on Etna. Matthew Arnold. 6102-8,6110-9,6125-7,6828-6
Callimachus
Artemis visits the Cyclopes. T.F. Higham (tr.). 6435-3
"At morn we placed on his funeral bier". William Cowper (tr.). 6814-6
"At once, she wen, and found the Cyclopes." T.F. Higham (tr.). 6435-3
The battle of the books, fr. Aetia. T.F. Higham (tr.). 6435-3
The blinding of Tiresias. R.A. Furness (tr.). 6435-3
D$_h$ybreak in the city, fr. Hecale. T.F. Higham (tr.). 6435-3
Delos. R.A. Furness (tr.). 6435-3
Dialogue with the dead, fr. Epigrams. G.M. Young (tr.). 6435-3
The epiphany of Apollo. R.A. Furness (tr.). 6435-3
Epitaph on Charidas of Cyrene. George B. Grundy (tr.). 6879-0
Epitaph on Heraclitus. 6102-8
Erysichthon. T.F. Higham (tr.). 6435-3
"For Crethis the teller of stories..." F.L. Lucas (tr.). 6251-2
The good live for ever, fr. Epigrams. H. Macnaghten (tr.). 6435-3,6046-3,6253-9
Heraclitus, fr. Epigrams. William Johnson Cory (tr.). 6435-3,6046-3,6253-9,6879-0,6230-x,6396 ,6052-8,6437-X,6668-2,6250-4,6301-2,6246-5,6512-0,6186-9,6246-5, 6639-9,6656
"Here lies the son of Battus..." R.A. Furness (tr.). 6435-3
His son. George B. Grundy (tr.). 6879-0
"The huntsman, Epicydes, across the mountains..." F.L. Lucas (tr.). 6251-2
"I loathe bards' commonplaces." F.L. Lucas (tr.). 6251-2
Love's capriciousness, fr. Epigrams. R.A. Furness (tr.). 6435-3
"Maidens, in Thebes Athene loved once.." F.L. Lucas (tr.). 6251-2
The nether world. 6102-8
Nicoteles, fr. Epigrams. R.C.K. Ensor (tr.). 6435-3
"Now you are buried, Timon..." F.L. Lucas (tr.). 6251-2
Odi profannum vulgus, fr. Epigrams. R.A. Furness (tr.). 6435-3
On Pallas bathing, fr. A hymn. William Cowper (tr.). 6814-6
"Once in the ear of Apollo said envy..." F.L. Lucas (tr.). 6251-2
"One single nymph all other nymphs above." R.A. Furness (tr.). 6435-3
"One told me, Heraclitus." F.L. Lucas (tr.). 6251-2
The poet's father. R.A. Furness (tr.). 6435-3
Saon of Acanthus. John Addington Symonds (tr.). 6850-2
"Sleeps Charidas beneath you..." F.L. Lucas (tr.). 6251-2
They told me, Heraclitus, you were dead. 6102-8
To Aratus, fr. Epigrams. R.A. Furness (tr.). 6435-3
Calling me. Ruby Alora Peaplon. 6799-9
Calling the doctor. John Wesley Halloway. 6281-4
Calling the roll. ? Sheppard. 6889-8
Calling the violet. Lucy Larcom. 6891-X
Calling the violet. Lucy Larcom. 6129-X
Calling them up. George Cooper. 6049-8
"**Calling** to mind since first my love". Sonnet ("Calling to mind"). Michael Drayton. 6436-1
"**Calling** to minde since first my Loue begun," Michael Drayton. 6586-4
Calling-one's own. Unknown (American Indian) 6393-4
The **calling**. George Sigerson. 6292-X
Callinus
A call to action. T.F. Higham (tr.). 6435-3,6665-8
Callirhoe, sels. Michael (Katherine Bradley & Edith Cooper) Field. 6477-9
Callistratus
Harmodius and Aristogeiton. Sir John Denman (tr.). 6271-1
Callum-a-glen. James Hogg. 6859-6
Calm. Stanton A. Coblentz. 6833-2
Calm. Thomas Moore. 6294-6
Calm. William Wordsworth. 7020-5
"**Calm** and clear! the bright day is declining". 'Twixt the cup and the lip, fr. Hippodromania. Adam Lindsay Gordon. 6951-7
Calm and full the ocean. Robinson Jeffers. 6666-6
The **calm** and silent night. Alfred Domett. 6747-6
"**Calm** and unruffled is the bay". Charles Mackay. 6997-5
Calm as the cloudless heaven. Christopher (John Wilson) North. 6833-2
"**Calm** heights of God on which I stand". From Pisgah. William White. 6868-5
"**Calm** is all nature as a resting wheel". Written in very early youth. William Wordsworth. 6828-6
"**Calm** is mine and peace forever". Freedom. Mabel Crehore Greene. 6841-3
Calm is the fragrant air. William Wordsworth. 6196-6
"**Calm** is the morn without a sound". A Lincolnshire landscape. Alfred Lord Tennyson. 6793-X
"**Calm** is the morn without a sound", fr. Memoriam. Alfred Lord Tennyson. 6536-8,6125-7
"**Calm** martyr of a noble cause". Jefferson Davis. Walker Meriwether Bell. 6946-0,6088-9
Calm morning at sea. Sara Teasdale. 6833-2
"**Calm** nature, old and withered, seeks the rest". Years end. Evelyn Swanson. 6750-6
"**Calm** on the bosom of thy God". A dirge. Felicia Dorothea Hemans. 6973-8,6934-7
"The **calm** Rappahannock flowed on to the sea". On the Rappahannock. Charles H. Tiffany. 6924-X,6451-5
"**Calm** on the bosom of thy God." Felicia Dorothea Hemans. 6302-0
Calm on the listening ear of night. Edmund Hamilton Sears. 6304-7,6278-4,6747-6
"**Calm** scenes of patriarch life!...". Images of patriarchal life. Felicia Dorothea Hemans. 6973-8
A **calm** sea. Robert Southey. 6833-2
Calm soul of all things. Matthew Arnold. 6730-1
"**Calm** the city lay in midnight silence". The homeless poor. Adelaide Anne Procter. 6957-6
"**Calm** was the day, and through the...air". Prothalamion, sels. Edmund Spenser. 6934-7
"**Calm** was the even, and clear was the sky". Song ("Calm was the even"). John Dryden. 6152-4,6430-2
The **calm.** John Donne. 6315-2,6547-3,6562-7
Calmerton, Gail
Old man shadow. 6799-9
"**Calmly** and alone/He lives his life". To the leader of a great nation. Ernestine Renee Sllier. 6799-9

"Calmly the earth survives the storm". Solidity. Paul F. Keen. 6799-9
Calmness and retrospection, fr. Edward the fair. Henry Taylor. 6980-0
"The calmness of an August afternoon". August. Schuyler E. Sears. 6906-1
Calmness of the sublime. Philip James Bailey. 6980-0
Calomel. Unknown. 6003-X
Calouri, Mary
    Night is so long. 6750-6
Calpurnia. Hjalmar Hjorth Boyesen. 6673-9
Calpurnia. Mary Muriel Rochester. 6847-2
Calthrop, Samuel Robert
    Where Baby Joy comes from. 6321-7,6429-9
Calumny. Frances Sargent Osgood. 6273-3
Calvary. Frank Oliver Call. 6796-4
Calvary. William Dean Howells. 6144-3
Calvary. Jessie B. Rittenhouse. 6850-2
Calvary. Edwin Arlington Robinson. 6337-3,6532-5,6730-1, 6144-3
Calvary. John Rothschild. 6542-2
Calvary ("A dying figure against the sky") Mary Hallet. 6144-3
Calvary ("Five thousand followed him...") Hugh Robert Orr. 6144-3
Calvary song. Elbridge Jefferson Cutler. 6008-0
Calvary's cry. John William Cunningham. 6065-X
Calverley's. Edwin Arlington Robinson. 6310-1
Calverley, Charles Stuart
    A,B,C. 6724-7,6092-7
    The Arab. 6385-3
    The auld wife. 6490-6
    Ballad. 6656-9,6534-1
    Ballad ("Butter and eggs"). 6092-7
    Ballad ("The auld wife"). 6440-X,6722-0,6512-0,6089-7, 6501-5,6802-2
    Beer. 6092-7
    Butter and eggs, and a pound of cheese. 6732-8
    The cat. 6125-7
    Changed. 6026-9
    The cock and the bull. 6385-3,6089-7,6440-X
    Companions. 6089-7,6732-8,6656-9
    Contentment. 6026-9
    Disaster. 6440-X,6089-7
    First love. 6633-X,6518-X,6089-7,6732-8
    Flight. 6652-6
    'Forever'. 6722-0,6026-9
    Gemini and virgo. 6722-0,6233-4
    "Hic vir, hic est". 6200-8,6092-7
    In the gloaming. 6440-X
    Lines suggested by the fourteenth of February. 6026-9
    Love. 6026-9
    Lovers, and a reflection. 6092-7,6633-X,6722-0,6089-7, 6440-X
    Motherhood. 6690-9
    Ode to tobacco. 6026-9,6092-7,6722-0,6089-7,6732-8
    Ode--'On a distant prospect' of making a fortune. 6760-3
    Of friendship. 6440-X
    Of propriety. 6996-7
    Of reading. 6440-X
    On the beach. 6026-9
    On the brink. 6656-9,6676-3
    Peace. 6633-X
    Peace: a study. 6996-7
    Play. 6512-0
    Precious stones. 6287-3
    Proverbial philosophy. 6092-7
    Sad memories. 6518-X,6120-6
    The schoolmaster abroad with his son, sels. 6339-X,6089-7
    The schoolmaster abroad with his son. 6996-7,7025-6
    Shelter. 6046-3,6512-0
    Striking. 6440-X,6228-8,6760-3
    To Leuconoe. 6315-2
    Tommy's first love. 6918-5
    Under the trees. 6724-7
    Wanderers. 6802-2,7025-6
Calverley, Charles Stuart (tr.)
    "All strangest things the multitudinous years".

Sophocles, 6435-3
    Amycus, fr. Idyll xxii. Theocritus, 6435-3
    Anno 1829. Heinrich Heine, 7039-6
    The death of Daphnis. Theocritus, 7039-6
    The dogs at the homestead, fr. Idyll xxv. Theocritus, 6435-3
    Hylas, fr. Idyll xiii. Theocritus, 6435-3
    Incantation from the sorceress. Theocritus, 6102-8
    The incantation. Theocritus, 7039-6
    Sirmio. Caius Catullus, 7039-6
    Universal change, fr. Ajax. Sophocles, 6435-3
Calvert, George H.
    Bunker Hill. 6678-X
Calvin, John
    Salutation to Jesus Christ. 6418-3
Calvino, Italo
    Cities & desire 005. 6758-1
    Cities & signs 001. 6758-1
    Cities & signs 002. 6758-1
    Cities & signs 005. 6758-1
    Cities & the dead 003. 6758-1
    Cities & the sky 005. 6758-1
    Continuous cities 004. 6758-1
    Hidden cities 001. 6758-1
    Trading cities 001. 6758-1
Calvos, Andreas
    The lover of his country. Rae Dalven (tr.). 6352-7
    The ocean. Rae Dalven (tr.). 6352-7
    To the sacred battalion. Rae Dalven (tr.). 6352-7
Calypso. William Carlos Williams. 6388-8
Calypso to Ulysses. William Alexander Percy. 6038-2
Calypso watching the ocean. Letitia Elizabeth ("L.E.L.") Landon. 6980-0
Calypso's island, fr. The Odyssey. Homer. 6435-3
Cam, Edith Claire
    Architects. 6799-9
Camadeva. Bayard Taylor. 6976-2
The Camberwell garden. Richard Burton. 6327-6
Cambiaire, Celestin Pierre
    Autumn leaves. 6826-X
    A beautiful unknown. 6826-X
    The boy and the blue-bird. 6826-X
    Broken dreams. 6826-X
    Christmas legend. 6826-X
    Christmas night in France. 6826-X
    Fairies and flowers. 6826-X
    Give me youth and the world is mine. 6826-X
    God forgives, but men do not. 6826-X
    An hour with you. 6826-X
    I love you. 6826-X
    Inspiration. 6826-X
    The kiss of Allah. 6826-X
    Lief's trail. 6826-X
    The morrow. 6826-X
    My rosary of dreams, sels. 6826-X
    Opportunity. 6826-X
    School memories. 6826-X
    September dream. 6826-X
    Sleep, baby, sleep. 6826-X
    Symphony. 6826-X
    Those we left behind. 6826-X
    Years gone by. 6826-X
    You. 6826-X
Cambrai and Marne. Sir Charles George Douglas Roberts. 6115-X
The Cambrian in America. Felicia Dorothea Hemans. 6973-8
The Cambridge ladies. Edward Estlin Cummings. 6491-4
Cambridge, Ada
    Honour. 6784-0
Cambridgeshire. Frances Cornford. 6071-4
Cambyses and the Macrobian bow. Paul Hamilton Hayne. 6411-6
Camden, Harriet Parker
    Oklahoma. 6465-5
Camden, William
    On a puritanicall lock-smith. 6722-0
Came the great popinjay, fr. Facade. Edith Sitwell. 7000-0
Came those who saw. Alan Sullivan. 6433-7,6115-X
"Came ye o'er frae France?" Unknown. 6859-6
The camel rider. Wilfrid Scawen Blunt. 6210-5

CAMEL'S

Camel's hump. Perrin Bachellor Fisk. 7030-2
The camel's hump. Rudyard Kipling. 6242-3
The camel's nose. Lydia Huntley Sigourney. 6519-8,6424-8
The camel. Mary Howitt. 6131-1
Cameos. Andrew Lang. 6987-8
Camerados. Bayard Taylor. 6089-7,6440-X,6440-X
Cameron, Everett
    Harvest. 6761-1
Cameron, George Frederick
    "Ah me! the mighty love that I have borne." 6433-7,6115-X
    Amoris finis. 6115-X
    An answer. 6115-X
    By the fountain. 7041-8
    Death. 7041-8
    The future. 6433-7
    The golden text. 6656-9,6861-8
    I am young. 6115-X
    In after days. 6021-8,6115-X
    My political faith. 6446-9
    On leaving the coast of Nova Scotia. 6795-6
    On life's sea. 7041-8
    Our poets. 7041-8
    Relics. 6446-9,7041-8
    Shelley. 7041-8
    Standing on tiptoe. 6433-7,6115-X
    To the west wind. 6115-X
    True greatness. 6433-7
    True love and tried. 7041-8
    The way of the world. 6115-X,6843-X,7041-8
    What matters it? 6433-7,7041-8,6115-X,6656-9
    Wisdom. 6115-X
Cameron, Nellie R.
    Guess who. 6713-1
Cameron, Norman
    El Aghir. 6210-5
    Fight with a water-spirit. 6257-1
    The firm of happiness, limited. 6210-5
    Lucifer. 6339-X
    Moonlight, waterlight and opal. 6354-3
    Three love poems. 6210-5
    The wanton's death. 6210-5
Cameron, Norman (tr.)
    Evil. Arthur Rimbaud, 6665-8
    Sonnet ("Dead men"). Arthur Rimbaud, 6665-8
    The stolen heart. Arthur Rimbaud, 6343-8
    Voyels. Arthur Rimbaud, 6343-8
Cameron, W.J.
    Outward. 6486-8
The Cameronian cat. Unknown. 6089-7,6120-6
The Cameronian's dream. James Hyslop. 6271-7,6383-7
Caminsky, Eva
    Equality. 6818-9
Cammack, Kay
    The young mother. 6097-8
Cammaerts, E.
    The Belgian flag. 6443-4
Cammaerts, Emile
    The flight into Egypt. George Nathaniel, Marquis Curzon Curzon (tr.). 6785-9
    Fuite en Angleterre. 6785-9
    A war-lullaby. 6542-2
Camo, Pierre
    The tomb of Gaugin. 6351-9
    Volupte. 6351-9
Camoens. Herman Melville. 6483-3
Camoens [or Camoes], Luis de
    Blighted love. Viscount Strangford; George Sydney Smythe (tr.). 6385-3
    Ecologue 015, sels. Felicia Dorothea Hemans (tr.). 6973-8
    Inez de Castro, fr. The lusiad. William Julius Mickle (tr.). 6372-1
    The lusiad, sels. William Julius Mickle (tr.). 6372-1
    "No searching eye can pierce the veil". Felicia Dorothea Hemans (tr.). 6973-8
    On the death of Catarina de Attayda. R.F. Burton (tr.). 7039-6
    Sonnet ("How strange a fate"). Felicia Dorothea Hemans (tr.). 6973-8
    Sonnet ("Leave me"). Richard Garnett (tr.). 7039-6
    Sonnet 019. ("Spirit beloved"). Felicia Dorothea Hemans (tr.). 6973-8
    Sonnet 023: to a lady who died at sea. Felicia Dorothea Hemans (tr.). 6973-8
    Sonnet 058 ("Should love"). Felicia Dorothea Hemans (tr.). 6973-8
    <u>Sonnet 070 ("High in the glowing"). Felicia Dorothea</u> Hemans (tr.). 6973-8
    Sonnet 080 ("Saved from the perils"). Felicia Dorothea Hemans (tr.). 6973-8
    Sonnet 108 ("Fair Tajo"). Felicia Dorothea Hemans (tr.). 6973-8
    Sonnet 128 ("There blooms"). Felicia Dorothea Hemans (tr.). 6973-8
    Sonnet 133 ("Waves of Mondego"). Felicia Dorothea Hemans (tr.). 6973-8
    Sonnet 178 ("Oft have I sung"). Felicia Dorothea Hemans (tr.). 6973-8
    Sonnet 181. ("Where shall I find"). Felicia Dorothea Hemans (tr.). 6973-8
    Sonnet 186 ("Those eyes"). Felicia Dorothea Hemans (tr.). 6973-8
    Sonnet 205 ("He who proclaims"). Felicia Dorothea Hemans (tr.). 6973-8
    Sonnet 239 ("Beside the stream"), fr. Psalm 137. Felicia Dorothea Hemans (tr.). 6973-8
    Sonnet 271 ("This mountain"). Felicia Dorothea Hemans (tr.). 6973-8
    Sonnet 278 ("Exempt from every grief"). Felicia Dorothea Hemans (tr.). 6973-8
    Sonnet 282 (Wrapt in sad"), fr. Psalm 137. Felicia Dorothea Hemans (tr.). 6973-8
    The spirit of the cape, fr. The lusiad. William Julius Mickle (tr.). 6372-1
    Waterspout. 6833-2
Camoens, and Felicia Hemans, Luis de (tr.)
    From psalm 137 (1). Bible, 6848-0
    From psalm 137 (2). Bible, 6848-0
The camomile. Al-Buqaira. 6362-4
Camouflage. M. G. 6589-9
Camouflage. John Streeter Manifold. 6666-6
Camouflage of the willow ptarmigan. Mary Owings Miller. 6979-7
The camp at night. George Chapman. 6186-9
Camp ballad. Francis Hopkinson. 6936-3
Camp chums. Rose Waldo. 6891-X
Camp fire. Martha M. Boutwell. 6764-6
Camp fire. Beatrice Marian Bromley. 6800-6
Camp fire. Beatrice Marian Bromley. 6625-9
Camp fire in Alaska. John Muir. 6253-9
Camp fire musings. Guy Eden. 6591-0,6592-9
Camp follower's song, Gomal River. Laurence (Adele Florence Nicolson) Hope. 6856-1
Camp of the fallen. Imogen Clark. 6461-2
The camp within the waste. Roderick Quinn. 6784-0
Camp, Pauline Frances
    His name. 6995-9
    Little helper. 6713-1
The camp, fr. Marmion. Sir Walter Scott. 6832-4
The camp-fire. Charles Claybrook Woollacott. 6800-6
The camp-follower. Maxwell Bodenheim. 6542-2
A camp-meeting hymn. Unknown. 6693-3
A camp. Robert Louis Stevenson. 6395-0,6252-0,6655-0
Campaign song. Ben H. Smith. 6662-2
The campaign, sels. Joseph Addison. 6191-5
The campaign. Joseph Addison. 6152-4
Campanella, Tomasso
    The people. John Addington Symonds (tr.). 7039-6,6102-8
Campanile di Pisa. Thomas William Parsons. 6600-3;6624-0
Campaspe. John Lyly. 6935-5
Campbell. Winthrop Mackworth Praed. 6385-3
Campbell, Alice
    Constancy. 6764-6
    Footprints in the snow. 6764-6
Campbell, Anne
    The keyboard. 6799-9
    A ten year old's vacation. 6249-0
    To mother. 6461-2
Campbell, Archibald Young

The dromedary. 6510-4,6044-7
Sonnet ("Think not of Christ"). 6779-4
There are still kingfishers. 6073-0,6253-9
Campbell, Bartley T.
That baby in Tuscaloo. 6911-8
That baby in Tuscaloo. 6155-9
Campbell, David
The possum and the moon. 6349-7,6349-7,6384-5
The stockman. 6349-7
Campbell, Edward R.
The old beech tree. 7030-2
Campbell, Elizabeth K.
Ski patrol. 6783-2
Campbell, Elsie J. Cosler
The crimson tree. 6799-9
Campbell, Ethel
Sunrise: the valley of a thousand hills. 6800-6
Campbell, Eva M.
The spirits of St. Louis. 7019-1
Campbell, Fay Strawn
Chantey. 6316-0
Romany dance. 6316-0
Campbell, Frank E.
November 11th. 6542-2
Campbell, Isabel Jones
Love songs. 6397-7
Campbell, Ivar
The marriage of earth and spring. 6650-X
Campbell, James
The gilly of Christ. 6244-X
Campbell, James E.
Disciplinin' sistah Brown. 6710-7
Campbell, Jane
The gray kitten. 6510-4
Campbell, Jane M. (tr.)
We plow the fields. Matthias Claudius, 6337-3
Campbell, Joan
The pools of peace. 6253-9,6421-3
A sealess world. 7020-5
A song for Anne. 6253-9
Campbell, John
8/1. 7032-9
8/19. 7032-9
8/2. 7032-9
8/24 (The farmhouse finally speaks). 7032-9
7/28. 7032-9
Campbell, Joseph ("Seosamh MacCathmhaoil")
Antiphon. 6143-5
At harvest. 6897-9
The besom-man. 6930-4
The blind man at the fair. 7039-6
Cloud and sun. 6134-6
The dancer. 6959-2,6244-X
A fighting-man. 6930-4
Fires. 6069-2
Ghosts. 6090-0
Go, ploughman, plough. 6891-X
The herb-leech. 6930-4
I am the gilly of Christ. 6872-3,6930-4
I am the mountainy singer. 6332-2,6102-8,6292-X,6506-6
"I will go with my father a-ploughing" 6478-7,6292-X
The ninepenny fidil. 6506-6
O glorious childbearer. 6930-4
The old woman. 6332-2,6096-X,6607-0,6244-X,6365-9,6930
On waking. 6897-9
The poet loosed a winged song. 6930-4
Saturn. 6096-X
Three colts exercising in a six-acre. 6930-4
The tinkers. 6930-4
The unfrocked priest. 6930-4
When rooks fly homeward. 6096-X
Campbell, Laura
Pilgrimage. 6028-5
Campbell, Margaretta P.
October. 6799-9
Campbell, Marion Susan
Riding through Jerusalem. 6144-3
Campbell, Myrtle W.
Autumn. 6799-9
The prophet. 6799-9

Campbell, Nancy
The apple-tree. 6478-7
The child. 6781-6
Like one I know. 6090-0,6172-9
The monkey. 6510-4,6476-0
Campbell, Robert
Praise to the lamb. 6177-X
Campbell, Robert (tr.)
Praise to the lamp. Unknown, 6177-X
Campbell, Roy
The albatross. 6625-9
Autumn. 6044-7,6491-4
Choosing a mast. 6246-5,6258-X,6210-5
The dark champion. 6800-6
The death of Polybius Jubb. 6722-0
Death of the bull. 6210-5
Dreaming spires. 6788-3
The fall of Satan, fr. The flaming terrapin. 6788-3
Hialmar and the Aasvogel. 6800-6
Home thoughts in Bloomsbury. 6633-X
Horses on the Camargue. 6625-9,6780-8,6985-1
Invocation to the African muse, fr.The flaming
   terrapin. 6788-3
Luis de Camoes. 6210-5
Noah, fr. The flaming terrapin. 6788-3
On Professor Drennan's verse. 6722-0
On some South African novelists. 6633-X,6722-0
Out of the ark. 6625-9
Rounding thr cape. 6625-9
The serf. 6375-6,6625-9
The sisters. 6210-5
The sling. 6788-3
The theology of Bangwi. 6800-6
To a pet cobra. 6625-9
To the springboks in England, 1932. 6625-9
To the sun. 6210-5
Toledo, July 1936. 6210-5
Tristan di Cunha. 6150-8
The veld ecologue: the pioneers, sels. 6788-3
The wayzgoose, sels. 6788-3
The zebras. 6246-5,6250-4
The Zulu girl. 6625-9
Campbell, Roy (tr.)
The louse-catchers. Arthur Rimbaud, 6343-8
Campbell, Thomas
The battle of Hohenlinden. 6606-2,6424-8
Battle of the Baltic. 6239-3,6263-6,6267-9,6639-9,6424-
   8,6322 ,6240-7,6197-4,6438-8,6219-9,6660-7,6659 ,
   6086-2,6196-6,6246-5,6302-0,6504-X,6732 ,6188-5,6473-
   6,6242-3,6258-X,6323-3,6604 ,6075-7,6180-X,6271-7,
   6552-X,6457-4
The beatific sea. 6833-2
The beech tree's petition. 6597-X,6047-1,6049-8,6086-2
The birth at Bethlehem. 6747-6
Caroline. 6980-0
Description of Wyoming. 6980-0
Dirge of Outalissi. 6980-0
Downfall of Poland. 6240-7
A dream, sels. 6648-8
Drinking song of Munich. 6934-7
The dying Gertrude to Waldegrave. 6302-0;6385-3
Earl March look'd on his dying child. 6737-9
Elijah's interview. 6848-0
Epistle from Algiers. 6092-7
The evening star. 6302-0;6385-3
Exile of Erin. 6198-2,6302-0,6385-3,6543-0,6291-9,6457-
   4,6744-1
The fall of Poland. 6980-0
Fall of Warsaw, 1794 6606-2,6425-6
Field flowers. 6543-0
The final triumph of hope. 6543-0
The first kiss. 6226-1,6302-0;6385-3
Florine. 6934-7
Fragment of an oratorio. 6848-0
Freedom and love. 6543-0,6246-5
The friars of Dijon. 6787-5
Gertrude of Wyoming, sels. 6980-0
Glenara. 6600-3,6606-2,6438-8,6613-5
Hallowed ground. 6302-0,6385-3,6271-7,6337-3,6219-9,
   6404 ,6250-4

CAMPBELL

The harper. 6380-2
Hohenlinden. 6014-5,6212-1,6104-4,6125-7,6131-1,6737 , 6075-7,6102-8,6180-X,6271-7,6457-4,6484 ,6186-9,6192-3,6560-0,6196-6,6250-4,6543 ,6153-2,6639-9,6660-7, 6665-8,6219-9,6438 ,6198-2,6263-6,6267-9,6304-7,6726-3,6732 ,6086-2,6239-3,6240-7,6246-5,6302-0,6385 , 6479-5,6504-X,6610-0
Hope. 6438-8
The Irish harper and his dog. 6891-X
The lament of the Outalissi. 6543-0
The last man. 6075-7,6086-2,6219-9,6648-8,6600-3,6910
Lochiel's warning. 6302-0,6385-3,6438-8,6219-9,6606-2, 6086-2,6148-6,6271-7,6409-4,6606-2,6601
Lord Ullin's daughter. 6134-6,6370-5,6502-3,6552-X,6614-3,6646 ,6136-2,6196-6,6131-1,6560-0,6668-2,6419 , 6079-X,6219-9,6319-5,6396-9,6543-0,6518 ,6239-3,6242-3,6246-5,6478-7,6479-5,6486 ,6086-2,6600-3,6639-9, 6675-5
The maid of Neidpath. 6246-5
The maid's remonstrance. 6302-0;6385-3
Margaret and Dora. 6092-7
Men of England. 6219-9
Mighty sea! cameleon-like thou changest. 6833-2
"Mighty sea!/Cameleon-like thou changest..." 6997-5
The mother. 6543-0
The mountain summits sleep. 6125-7
Napoleon and the British sailor. 6302-0,6385-3,6131-4, 6808-1,6614-3
O'Connor's child. 6219-9
Ode to the Germans. 7009-4
Ode to winter. 6246-5,6086-2,6180-X
"Oh, leave this barren spot to me", sels. 6601-1
"Old ocean was/Infinity of ages ere we breated". 6997-5
"On Linden, when the sun was low". 6601-1
The Oneyda's death-song, fr. Gertrude of Wyoming. 6832-4
The parrot. 6290-3,6133-8,6552-X,6614-3,6396-9,6046-3, 6131-1
"Pleasant sea!/Earth has not a plain". 6997-5
Poland. 6302-9,6385-3
Poor dog Tray. 6084-6,6018-8,6083-8,6133-8,6306-3
The power of Russia. 7009-4
The rainbow. 6479-5,6134-6
The river of life. 6086-2,6246-5,6302-0,6385-3
Soldier and sailor. 6322-5
The soldier's dream. 6131-1,6332-2,6219-9,6424-8,6438-8, 6104-4,6543 ,6134-4,6304-7,6419-1,6560-0,6737-9,6246 ,6018-8,6086-2,6302-0,6385-3,6504-X,6606
Song. 6737-9
Song ("Withdraw not"). 6226-1
Song of Hybrias the Cretan. 6934-7
Song of the Greeks, 1822. 6606-2
Song to the evening star. 6086-2,6660-7,6533-3,6604-6, 6737-9,6291-9,6291-9
The spectre boat. 6648-8
Stanzas on the battle of Navarino, 1827. 7009-4
The statue of Arnold von Winkelried, Stanz. 6749-2
Switzerland. 6749-2
Taste. 6102-8
To a beautiful Jewish girl of Altona. 6848-0
To the evening star. 6086-2,6180-X,6271-7
To the evening star ("Gem of the crimson-colour'd..."). 6246-5
To the evening star ("Star that bringest home..."). 6246-5
To the rainbow. 6597-X,6606-2,6438-8
"Warsaw's last champion...", fr. The pleasures of hope. 66601-1
What's hallowed ground? 6294-6,6605-2,6621-6
"When Jordan hushed his waters still." 6302-0
"Wide o'er Bannock's heathy wold". 6601-1
Ye mariners of England. 6105-2,6197-4,6196-6,6199-0, 6102-8,6114 ,6186-9,6438-8,6086-2,6301-2,6219-9,6267 ,6188-5,6639-9,6660-7,6424-8,6263-6,6322 ,6239-3, 6240-7,6242-3,6331-4,6473-6,6543 ,6504-X,6625-9,6732-8,6302-0,6385-3,6198 ,6075-7,6133-8,6138-9,6180-X, 6271-7,6328 ,6246-5,6552-X,6604-6,6102-8
Young love's a gallant boy. 6874-X

Campbell, Thomas (tr.)
Martial elegy. Tyrtaeus, 6385-3
"The mountain summits sleep, glens, cliffs, and caves". Alcman, 7039-6
A soldier's riches. Hybrias, 6435-3
Youthful valor. Tyrtaeus, 6621-6

Campbell, Walter Stanley ("Stanley Vestal")
Bear's heart. 6628-3
Cynthia Ann. 6397-7
Deadwood. 6628-3
Fandango. 6281-4
King David. 6397-7
Oliver Wiggins. 6281-4
Prairie battle. 6628-3
Riding song. 6397-7
Saddle song. 6397-7
Sand creek. 6628-3

Campbell, William Wilfred
Autumn leaves. 6843-X
Canadian folk song. 6466-3,6053-6
A Canadian folk-song. 6656-9
A Canadian Galahad. 6433-7
The children of the foam. 6115-X
The dreamers. 6115-X
England. 6224-5,6433-7,6115-X
The heart of the lakes. 6795-6
The Hebrew father's prayer. 6848-0
How one winter came in the lake region. 6446-9
Indian summer. 6021-8,6795-6
Keziah. 7041-8
Lake Huron. 6591-0,6592-2
A lake memory, fr. The century. 6656-9,7041-8
Langemarck at Ypres. 6443-4
The last prayer. 6115-X
The last scene from Mordred. 6433-7
Lines on a rereading of parts of the Old Testament. 6433-7
Lines on a skeleton. 6433-7
The lyre of life. 6433-7
Manitou. 6795-6,7041-8
Margery maketh the tea. 6274-1,6478-7
A mid-winter night's dream. 6795-6
The month of ripeness. 6433-7
The mother. 6115-X,6433-7
Not unto endless dark. 6796-4
October morning. 6433-7
Pan the fallen. 6053-6
Stella Flammarum. 6433-7,6115-X
Sunset, Lake Huron. 6843-X
Three things. 7041-8
To the lakes. 6656-9
The tragedy of man. 6433-7
Vapour and blue. 6591-0,6592-2
The were-wolves. 6274-1
The were-wolves. 6656-9
Where Kitchener sleeps. 7027-2
Wind. 6433-7
With Cortez in Mexico. 6946-0

Campbell; 9th Duke of Argyle, John D.S.
Alberta. 6433-7
Canada. 6433-7
Qu' appelle valley. 6433-7
Quebec. 6021-8
Unto the hills (adp. fr. Psalm 121). 6337-3

Camper's night song. Robert Louis Stevenson. 6107-9,6421-3
The camper. Emily Pauline ("Tekahionwake") Johnson. 6837-5
The camper. Jeanne Showers Knoop. 6342-X
The campfire. Margaret Adelaide Wilson. 6241-5
Camping. Margaret Southgate Rucker. 6789-1
Camping out. William Empson. 6209-1
Camping song. Bliss Carman. 6374-8

Campion (atr.), Thomas
Doe not, O doe not prize thy beauty at too high a rate. 6378-0

Campion, ?
Ninety-eight. 6918-5

Campion, John T.
The felons. 6858-8

Campion, Thomas
Ad Inuictissimum, Serenissimumque Iacobvm. 6794-8
Advice to a girl. 6732-8,6737-9
"All lookes be pale, harts cold as stone" 6794-8

All the squires together. 6794-8
Amaryllis. 6182-6,6187-7,6191-5,6301-2,6099-4
"And would you see my mistress' face?" 6935-5
Another dialogue, to be sung at the same time. 6794-8
"Are you, what your faire lookes expresse?" 6794-8
The armour of innocence. 6604-6,6660-7
"As by the streames of Babilon" 6794-8
"Author of light" 6794-8
Awake, awake! Thou heavy sprite. 6214-8,6794-8
"Awake, thou spring of speaking grace, mute rest..." 6794-8
A ballad. 6794-8
Be thou then my beauty. 6328-4
"Beauty is but a painted hell" 6794-8
"Beauty, since you so much desire" 6794-8
"Blame not my cheeks, though pale with love". 6187-7
A booke of Ayres (XII). 6794-8
A booke of Ayres (I). 6794-8
A booke of Ayres (II). 6794-8
A booke of Ayres (III). 6794-8
A booke of Ayres (IV). 6794-8
A booke of Ayres (IX). 6794-8
A booke of Ayres (IX). 6794-8
A booke of Ayres (V). 6794-8
A booke of Ayres (V). 6794-8
A booke of Ayres (VI). 6794-8
A booke of Ayres (VII). 6794-8
A booke of Ayres (VII). 6794-8
A booke of Ayres (VIII). 6794-8
A booke of Ayres (X). 6794-8
A booke of Ayres (XI). 6794-8
A booke of Ayres (XI). 6794-8
A booke of Ayres (XIII). 6794-8
A booke of Ayres (XIV). 6794-8
A booke of Ayres (XIV). 6794-8
A booke of Ayres (XIX). 6794-8
A booke of Ayres (XV). 6794-8
A booke of Ayres (XVI). 6794-8
A booke of Ayres (XVII). 6794-8
A booke of Ayres (XX). 6794-8
Bookes of Ayres, sels. 6208-3
"Brauely deckt, come forth, bright day" 6794-8
"Breake now, my heart, and dye! Oh no, she may relent" 6794-8
Canto quarto. 6794-8
Canto quinto. 6794-8
Canto secundo. 6794-8
Canto tertio. 6794-8
Chance and change. 6198-2
The charm. 6189-3,6250-4
Cherry ripe. 6233-4,6099-4,6092-7,6250-4,6153-2,6646 , 6481-7,6301-2,6737-9,6634-8,6198-2,6246-5,6339-X
Chorus ("Vanish"). 6794-8
Chorus ("Since knights"). 6794-8
Chorus ("That pleasure"). 6794-8
Chorus ("Vertue"). 6794-8
Come away, armed with love's delights. 6328-4,6189-3, 6794-8
"Come follow me, my wandring mates" 6794-8
"Come, cheerful day, part of my life to me". 6187-7, 6182-6,6383-7,6794-8
Come, let us sound with melody. 6328-4
"Come, O come, my life's delight." 6317-9,6187-7,6328-4, 6182-6,6935-5
"Come, you pretty false-eyed wanton". 6733-6,6181-8, 6794-8
Conjuration. 6153-2
Content. 6436-1
Corinna. 6383-7
"Could my heart more tongues imploy" 6794-8
The cypress curtain of the night. 6315-2,6328-4,6533-3
The dance. 6794-8,6182-6
Day and night. 6189-3
De instituto authoris. 6794-8
"Deare if I with guile would guild a true intent" 6794-8,6380-2
The description of a maske on S. Stephens night. 6794-8
The description of a maske presented before the... 6794-8
Description, speeches, and songs of the Lords Maske.

6794-8
Devotion. 6186-9,6102-8,6737-9
A dialogue sung the first night, the king... 6794-8
Dismissal. 6436-1
Doctor in physicke. 6794-8
A dying fall. 6935-5
Elegiarvm liber (in Latin) 6794-8
An epigram. 6794-8
Epigramma. 6794-8
Epigrammatvm (in Latin) 6794-8
"Eu'ry dame affects good fame, what ere her doings be" 6794-8
Fain would I wed. 6733-6
"Faine would I my loue disclose" 6794-8
"Faine would I wed a faire yong man that day and..." 6794-8
Fair, if you expect admiring. 6328-4
The fairy queen Proserpina. 6733-6
The farewell song. 6794-8
"Fire that must flame is with apt fuell fed" 6794-8
Fire, fire! 6328-4
The first inuocation in a full song ("Powerfull...") 6794-8
The first squire (1). 6794-8
The first squire (2). 6794-8
"Follow thy fair sun, unhappy shadow." 6317-9,6328-4, 6430-2,6250-4,6383-7,6315 ,6194-X,6182-6
"Follow your saint, follow with accents sweet". 6182-6, 6181-8,6204-0,6328-4,6301-2,6383 ,6023-4,6250-4,6189-3,6187-7,6317-9,6536
Fortunati nimium. 6604-6,6192-3,6660-7
The fourth squire. 6794-8
A full song. 6794-8
Give beauty all her right. 6328-4,6383-7,6794-8
"Good men, shew, if you can tell" 6794-8
Good wife. 6194-X
A happy marriage. 6659-3
"Harden now thy tyred hart, with more then flinty..." 6380-2,6794-8
"Hark, all you ladies that do sleep." 6182-6,6181-8, 6430-2
"Her fayre inflaming eyes" 6794-8
"Her rosie cheekes, her euer smiling eyes" 6794-8
Her rosy cheeks. 6328-4
Hope and fear. 6482-5
The hours of sleepy night. 6182-6,6181-8
"How eas'ly wert thou chained" 6794-8
How shall I come, sweet love, to thee? 6315-2
A hymn in praise of Neptune. 6189-3,6421-3,6639-9,6794-8,6334-9
I care not for these ladies. 6733-6,6181-1,6430-2
"I must complain, yet doe enjoy my loue" 6794-8
"Iacke and Ione they thinke no ill" 6794-8
"If any hath the heart to kill" 6794-8
If I hope, I pine. 6328-4
"If loue courts truth, then women doe not loue" 6794-8
If she forsake me. 6328-4
"If thou long'st so much to learne (sweet boy)..." 6794-8
Illvstrissimo, poetentissimoqve principi, Fredrico... 6794-8
In love. 6935-5
Integer vitae. 6732-8,6102-8,6513-9
Jack and Joan [they think no ill]. 6344-9,6339-X,6187-7, 6194-X,6250-4,6383-7,6668-2,6228-8
Jvstvm et tenacem. 6935-5
"Kind are her answers". 6187-7,6181-8,6328-4,6250-4
The kings good-night. 6794-8
Kisses. 6182-6,6436-1
Lament for Prince Henry. 6641-0
A lamentation. 6179-6
Laura. 6186-9,6436-1,6182-6,6934-7
"Leaue prolonging thy distresse" 6794-8
"Lift vp to heau'n, sad wretch, thy heauy spright" 6794-8
"Lighten, heauy hart, thy spright" 6794-8
A little breath I'll borrow. 6482-5
"Loe, when backe mine eye" 6794-8
The Lords welcome, sung before the kings goodnight. 6794-8

CAMPION

"Love me or not, love her I must or die." 6182-6,6328-4, 6794-8
Love's pilgrims. 6436-1
Love's request. 6827-8
Love, and never fear. 6634-8
The man of life upright. 6194-X,6250-4,6430-2,6794-8, 6182-6,6099-4,6181-8,6337-3,6189-3,6230-X,6396-9, 6421-3,6668-2
"Markes that did limit lands in former times" 6794-8
The maskers first daunce. 6794-8
The maskers second dance. 6794-8
The maskers second daunce. 6794-8
"Maydes are simple, some men say" 6794-8
The measure of beauty. 6189-3,6250-4
Mistress, since you so much desire. 6328-4
"Most sweet and pleasing are thy wayes, o God" 6794-8
The mountebank's mask, sel. 6958-4
"My sweetest Lesbia let vs live and love." 6378-0,6315-2,6634-8,6182-6,6491-4,6099-4,6181-1,6194-X,6092-7, 6472-8
Neptune. 6436-1
Never love unless you can. 6092-7,6794-8,6182-6,6315-2, 6187-7,6733-6
"Never weather-beaten sail more willing bent". 6794-8, 6187-7,6182-6,6181-8,6194-X,6125-7,6641
"Night as well as brightest day hath her delight." 6099-4
"Now hath Flora robbed her bowers" 6935-5
Now let her change. 6328-4
Now winter nights enlarge. 6052-8,6162-6,6334-9,6315-2, 6250-4,6181-8,6328-4,6194-X
O come quickly! 6186-9,6337-3,6214-8,6737-9
"O deare that I with thee might liue" 6794-8
"O griefe, o spight, to see poore vertue scorn'd" 6794-8
"O loue, where are thy shafts, thy quiuer, and thy..." 6794-8
"O neuer to be moued" 6794-8
"O sweet delight, O more than human bliss". 6187-7,6328-4
O what unhoped for sweet. 6328-4
"O what vnhop't for sweet supply!" 6794-8
Obseruations in the art of english poesy. 6794-8
Of counterpoint. 6794-8
Of the taking of all concords, perfect and imperfect. 6794-8
Of the tones of musicke. 6794-8
Out of my soul's depth. 6931-2
"Out of my soules deapth" 6794-8
The peaceful western wind. 6099-4,6328-4,6315-2,6328-4
"The peacefull westerne winde" 6794-8
'A pilgrimage towards loues holy land', fr.Bookes..Ayres. 6208-3
"Pin'd I am and like to die" 6794-8
The preface. 6794-8
Relation of royal entertainment giuen by Lord Knowles. 6794-8
A renunciation. 6732-8
"Respect my faith, regard my seruice past" 6794-8
Rose-cheeked Laura. 6315-2,6536-8,6634-8,6181-8,6189-3, 6194-X,6430-2
Roses. 6436-1
Rustic joys. 6737-9
The second inuocation to the tune of the first. 6794-8
The second squire (1). 6794-8
The second squire (2). 6794-8
A secret love or two I must confess. 6733-6,6794-8
See where she flies. 6328-4
Seek the Lord. 6931-2,6794-8
The shadow. 6189-3
Shall I come, sweet love, to thee. 6182-6,6328-4,6430-2, 6383-7,6187-7
Shall I, then, hope when faith is fled. 6194-X,6794-8
Sic transit. 6879-0
"Silly boy, 'tis full moon yet, thy night as day..." 6317-9,6794-8,6935-5
Since she, even she, for whom I lived. 6328-4
"Sing a song of joy" 6794-8
Sleep, angry beauty. 6737-9
"Sleep, angry beauty, sleep, and fear not me." 6317-9,

6182-6,6380-2,6187-7,6794-8
"So many loues haue I neglected" 6794-8
"So quicke, so hot, so mad is thy fond sute" 6380-2, 6794-8
So sweet is thy discourse to me. 6328-4,6491-4,6794-8
"So tir'd are all my thoughts". 6315-2,6794-8
Song. 6639-9
A song ("Advance"). 6794-8
A song ("Cease"). 6794-8
A song ("Come away"). 6794-8
A song ("Come triumphing"). 6794-8
Song ("Come, O!"). 6436-1
Song ("Come, you pretty"). 6436-1
Song ("Follow thy fair sun"). 6436-1
Song ("Follow your saint"). 6436-1
Song ("Give beauty"). 6436-1
Song ("I care not"). 6436-1
Song ("I must complain"). 6026-9
Song ("Jack and Joan"). 6436-1
Song ("Kind are her answers.") 6436-1
Song ("My sweetest Lesbia"). 6436-1
Song ("Never weather-beaten"). 6436-1
The song ("No longer wrong the night") 6794-8
Song ("Now winter nights"). 6436-1
Song ("O sweet delight"). 6423-X
Song ("Shall I come"). 6436-1
Song ("Sweet, exclude me not"). 6026-9
Song ("Tenants"). 6026-9
Song ("The man of life upright.") 6436-1
Song ("There is a garden"). 6423-X
Song ("There is none"). 6436-1
Song ("Thou art not fair"). 6436-1
Song ("Though you are young"). 6436-1
Song ("Thrice toss"). 6436-1
Song ("Turn all"). 6026-9
Song ("When thou must home"). 6436-1
Song ("When to her lute"). 6436-1
Song ("Where are all thy beauties"). 6436-1
The song ("Wooe her, and win her, he that can") 6794-8
A song and dance triumphant of the maskers. 6794-8
A song from a booke of ayres. 6106-0
Song from a masque. 6383-7
Song from the lute books. 6150-8
Song of pleasure and pain. 6659-3
A song of three voices continuing while the presents... 6794-8
A song of three voyces with diuers instruments. 6794-8
A song. 6794-8
Songs from lute books. 6436-1
Songs of mourning. 6794-8
The stars dance. 6436-1
"Sweet, exclude mee not, nor be divided" 6794-8
There is a garden in her face. 6182-6,6328-4,6430-2, 6194-X,6723-9,6726 ,6488-4,6527-9,6536-8,6794-8
There is none, oh, none but you. 6182-6,6328-4,6189-3, 6794-8
"Think'st thou to seduce me then with words..." 6182-6, 6181-8,6733-6,6092-7,6794-8
The third squire. 6794-8
"Thou art not fair, for all thy red and white". 6187-7, 6182-6,6181-8,6328-4,6383-7,6092
"Thou joy'st, fond boy, to be by many loved". 6794-8, 643-=2
"Though you are young, and I am old." 6099-4,6328-4
"Though your strangenesse frets my hart" 6794-8
Thrice toss these oaken ashes in the air. 6182-6,6194-X, 6315-2
"Thus I resolue, and time hath taught me so" 6794-8
"To his sweet lute apollo sung the motions of the..." 6794-8
To Laura. 6935-5
To Lesbia. 6604-6,6189-3,6660-7,6827-8
To music bent is my retired mind. 6931-2,6641-0,6931-2
"To musicke bent is my retyred minde" 6794-8
To my honovrable friend, Sr Thomas Movnson... 6794-8
To my worthy friend, Mr. Iohn Mounson... 6794-8
To shades of underground. 6125-7
To the flowre of princes, Charles, Prince of Great... 6794-8
To the masqers representing stars. 6315-2

To the most disconsolate. 6794-8
To the most high and mighty. 6794-8
To the most illvstriovs and mighty. 6794-8
To the most princely and vertuovs the Lady Elizabeth. 6794-8
To the most puisand and gratious Iames king of great. 6794-8
To the most scared (1). 6794-8
To the most scared (2). 6794-8
To the right honovrable, both in birth and vertve... 6794-8
To the right noble and verutous Theophilus Howard... 6794-8
To the right noble and worthily honourd, the Lord... 6794-8
To the right noble, and vertvovs Henry Lord Clifford... 6794-8
To the right vertuous, and honorable, the Lord... 6794-8
To the world. 6794-8
To the worthy avthor. 6794-8
The torch-bearers daunce. 6794-8
Triumph now. 6188-5
"Truth, sprung from heauen, shall shine" 6794-8
"Tune thy musicke to thy hart" 6794-8
Turn all thy thoughts to eyes. 6181-8,6328-4
Turn back, you wanton flier. 6181-8,6328-4
"Unless there were consent 'twixt hell and heauen." 6317-9
"Vaile, loue, mine eyes; o hide from me" 6794-8
"Vain men, whose follies make a god of love." 6317-9, 6794-8
View me, Lord, a work of thine. 6931-2,6794-8,6337-3
Vivamus mea Lesbia atque amemus. 6187-7,6733-6
Vmbra (in latin) 6794-8
Vobiscum est iope. 6186-9,6102-8,6301-2
Were my heart as some men's are. 6934-7,6794-8
"What harvest half so sweet is". 6187-7,6328-4,6733-6, 6794-8
What if a day or a month or a year. 6182-6
What is a day? 6328-4
"What is it all that men possesse, among..." 6794-8
"What meanes this folly, not to braue it so" 6794-8
When thou must home to shades of underground. 6182-6, 6189-3,6250-4,6315-2,6317-9
"When to her lute Corinna sings". 6187-7,6328-4,6250-4, 6092-7
"Where are all thy beauties now?" 6794-8,6472-8
"Where shall I refuge seeke, if you refuse mee?" 6794-8
Where she her sacred bower adorns. 6315-2,6099-4,6794-8
Whether men do laugh or weep. 6328-4
"Why presumes thy pride on that that must so..." 6794-8
Winter nights. 6189-3,6230-X,6383-7
"Wise men patience neuer want" 6794-8
Women only are men's good. 6733-6
The writer to his book. 6430-2,6794-8
Yet still I live. 6482-5
Young and old. 6482-5
Young and simple thoughts I am. 6733-6,6794-8
"Your faire lookes vrge my desire" 6794-8
Campion, Thomas (tr.)
My sweetest Lesbia. Caius Catallus, 7039-6
When thou must home. Sextus Propertius, 7039-6
Campione, Michael J.
Musings. 6799-9
Campkin, H.
Palindromes. 6724-7
Camptown. John Ciardi. 6666-6
Campus. Ted Olson. 6761-1
Campus song. Louis J. Magee. 7004-3
The camstairie. Lewis Spence. 6269-5
"Can a poem say my heart/While I stand apart?". Poem to be danced. Helen Hoyt. 6959-2
"Can any pleasure in 6ife compare". Old ace. Fred Emerson Brooks. 6924-X
"Can I forget that beauteous day". The grotto of Egeria. William Sotheby. 6980-0
"Can I not sin, but thou wilt be". To his conscience. Robert Herrick. 6931-2
"Can I not syng but hoy". The shepherd on the hill. Unknown. 6931-2
"Can I, who have for others oft compiled". On my dear son. Sir John Beaumont. 6934-7
Can do. Everett C. Richmond. 6799-9
"Can he yt loves be man." Unknown. 6563-5
Can I forget?. Sidney Goodsir Smith. 6379-9
"Can I not syng but hoy." Unknown. 6378-0
"Can it be right to give what I can give?" Elizabeth Barrett Browning. 6560-0
"Can it be smoke and steam that rise". The old sap-house. Henry Duncan Chisholm. 6764-6
"Can it be that it is morning". May. William G. Park. 6049-8
"Can life be a blessing". Song ("Can life be a blessing"). John Dryden. 6733-6,6152-4
"Can life be a blessing". John Dryden. 6562-7
"Can love be controll'd by advice?". Song ("Can love"). John Gay. 6315-2
"Can man, O God! the tale of man repeat". Hymn 004, fr. Hymns of a hermit. John Sterling. 6980-0
"Can the choice mislead". Choice of the home at Grasmere, fr. The recluse. William Wordsworth. 6867-7
"Can the depths of the ocean afford you...". The Munster war-song. Richard Dalton Williams. 6858-8
"Can there be a moon in heaven to-night". Isabelle. James Hogg. 6802-2
"Can this be your face, this whose calm". To Fraser's death-mask of Roosevelt. L. Upton Wilkinson. 6995-9
"Can tyrants but by tyrants conquer'd be". Stanzas ("Can tyrants"). George Gordon, 6th Baron Byron. 7009-4
"Can we believe - by an effort". Cities. Hilda ("H.D.") Doolittle. 6808-1
"Can we not consecrate". Love and sacrifice. Bernard O'Dowd. 6784-0
Can you count the stars? Unknown. 6373-X
"Can you divide seed". Answer from Assisi. Isabel Harriss Barr. 6979-7
"Can you forget me? I who have so cherished". Letitia Elizabeth ("L.E.L.") Landon. 6980-0
Can you give gladness to me? S. Charles Jellicoe. 6174-5
"Can you go to another who wins in the fight". Other's success. Edgar A. Guest. 6862-6
Can you hear me? Katherine Hunter Coe. 6906-1
"Can you imahine anyone selling his kittens?". Sign by the road: kittens for sale. Bettie Sale. 6750-6
"Can you listen a heart-thrilling story". Lotty's message. Alexander G. Murdoch. 6692-5,6923-1
"Can you not let me sleep? Why for your sake". Sonnet† ("Can you not"). Floyd Dell. 6880-4
"Can you open that ebony casket?". A contrast. Adelaide Anne Procter. 6957-6
Can you paint a thought. John Ford. 6430-2
"Can you paint a thought? or number." John Ford (atr) 6317-9
"Can you picture a/roach playing". After man's massacre. Carol Del Guidice. 6883-9
Can you read these? Unknown. 6861-8
"Can you remember John's great boast". A ballad of jealousy. Leland Davis. 6880-4
Can you sing a song? Joseph Morris. 6291-1
"Can you, the author of our ioy". A song of three voices continuing while the presents... Thomas Campion. 6794-8
Can't. Edgar A. Guest. 6291-1
Can't. Harriet Prescott Spofford. 6946-0,6820-0
Can't be president. Unknown. 6248-2
"Can't read nuthin'". Nuthin' Berton Braley. 6853-7
Can't you. Gamaliel Bradford. 6441-8
Cana. James Freeman Clarke. 6600-3
Canaan avd. Vermont. Daniel L. Cady. 6989-4
Canada. John D.S. Campbell; 9th Duke of Argyle. 6433-7
Canada. Guttormur J. Guttormsson. 6854-5
Canada. Emily Pauline ("Tekahionwake") Johnson. 6837-5
Canada. Sir Charles George Douglas Roberts. 7041-8
Canada ("O child of nations, giant-limbed"). Sir Charles George Douglas Roberts. 6433-7,6656-9,6446-9
Canada ("Topping the hill, the long white road"). J. Edgar Middleton. 6433-7
Canada not last. William Douw Lighthall. 6795-6
Canada not last. William Douw Lighthal. 7041-8

This **Canada** of ours. Sir James Edgar. 6224-5
Canada speaks of Britain. Sir Charles George Douglas
  Roberts. 6021-8,6224-5
Canada to Australia. Frederick George Scott. 6224-5
Canada to England. Marjorie L.C. Pickthall. 6224-5;6474-4
Canada to England. Arthur Stringer. 6224-5
Canada to England. Unknown. 6795-6
The **Canada** wind. Helen M. Merrill. 6433-7
"**Canada**, Canada!". Salutation. Charles Whitby. 6994-0
Canaday, Elizabeth Barbara
  Earth's breast. 6039-0
Canadian. A.M. Stephen. 6843-X
The **Canadian** authors meet. Francis Reginald Scott. 6722-0
Canadian boat song. Unknown. 6180-X,6378-0,6395-0
Canadian boat song, sels. Unknown. 6427-2
A **Canadian** boat song. Thomas Moore. 6438-8,6219-9,6252-0,
  6424-8,6543-0,6014-5,6459-0,6133-8,6302-0,6385-3,
  6328
The **Canadian** boat song. J. Wilson. 6934-7
Canadian born. Emily Pauline ("Tekahionwake") Johnson.
  6837-5
Canadian camping song. Sir James Edgar. 6591-0,6592-2
Canadian folk song. William Wilfred Campbell. 6466-3,6053-6
A **Canadian** folk-song. William Wilfred Campbell. 6656-9
A **Canadian** Galahad. William Wilfred Campbell. 6433-7
The **Canadian** herd-boy. Susanna Strickland Moodie. 6433-7,
  6591-0
Canadian hunter's song. Susanna Strickland Moodie. 6656-9
The **Canadian** rossignol. Edward William Thomson. 6115-X
The **Canadian** song-sparrow. Sir James Edgar. 6795-6
A **Canadian** summer evening. Mrs. Leprohon. 6795-6
Canadian twilight. Lucy Maud Montgomery. 6797-2
The **Canadian** west. Robert Kirkland Kernighan. 6797-2
The **Canadian** whitethroat. Sir James Edgar. 6591-0,6592-2
Canadian winter song. William Wye Smith. 7035-3
The **Canadian**.. J. Edgar Middleton. 6224-5
Canadians. William Henry Ogilvie. 6474-4
The **Canadians** on the Nile. W. Wye Smith. 6591-0,6592-9
The **Canadians** on the Nile. William Wye Smith. 6795-6
A **canary** at the farm. James Whitcomb Riley. 6670-4
The **canary**'s story. E.V. S. 6373-X
The **canary**. Morris Rosenfeld. 7011-6
The **canary**. Frank Dempster Sherman. 6311-X
The **canary**. Elizabeth Turner. 6135-4
Cancel my subscription. J.A. Hines. 6870-7
Cancel the past. Thomas M. Kettle. 6244-X
Cancion ("O love..."). Juan II; King of Castile. 7039-6
Candida. B.A. Gould Jr. 6116-8
The **candidate**'s creed. James Russell Lowell. 6089-7,6736-0,
  6278-4
The **candidate**, sels. Charles Churchill. 6024-2
The **candidate**. Unknown. 6928-2
Candidating in Vermont. Daniel L. Cady. 6988-6
Candle and cross. Elisabeth Scollard. 6320-9
Candle and cup. Helen T.D. Robinson. 6799-9
The **candle** and the flame. George Sylvester Viereck. 6102-8,
  6076-5,6300-6
The **candle** indoors. Gerard Manley Hopkins. 6828-6,6931-2
The **candle** indoors. Gerard Manley Hopkins. 6209-1
The **candle** indoors. Gerard Manley Hopkins. 6931-2
"The **candle** is out-/It has crashed to...". The lady.
  Elizabeth J. Coatsworth. 6861-8
Candle light. John Cowper Powys. 6300-4
Candle lights. Edna Allen Wright. 6270-9
The **candle** seller. Morris Rosenfeld. 7011-6
Candle-light. Thomas S. Jones Jr. 6653-4
Candle-light. Helen Myra Ross. 6906-1
Candle-light. Jules Supervielle. 6343-8
The **candle-light**'s lament. Unknown. 6118-4
Candle-lighted faces. Gertr de W. Robinson. 6906-1
Candle-lighting song. Arthur Ketchum. 6478-7,6607-0
The **candle**.. Leroy F. Jackson. 6466-3
The **candle**. Al-Hajjam. 6362-4
The **candle**. Walter De La Mare. 6905-3
The **candle**. Ethel Emily Fels. 6906-1
The **candle**. Unknown. 6937-1
Candlemas. Arthur Ketchum. 6053-6
Candlemas. Mary Saint-Amand. 7016-7
Candlemas ("If Candlemas day be dry and fair"). Unknown.
  6465-5
Candlemas ("O hearken, all ye little weeds"). Alice Brown.
  6006-4,6310-1,6465-5,6478-7
Candler, George H.
  Now. 6654-2
Candles. Babette Deutsch. 6653-4
Candles. Harriet Holman. 7016-7
"The **candles** are white". Sexton. Richard Ronan. 7003-5
Candor. Henry Cuyler Bunner. 6004-8,6166-4,6441-8,6632-1,
  6732-8,6735-2,6505
Candor. Thomas Otway. 6294-6
Candor. Unknown. 6927-4
"**Candor** compels me, Becher! to commend". Answer to some
  elegant verses sent by a friend... George Gordon,
  6th Baron Byron. 6945-2
A **candy-pull**. Unknown. 6529-5
Cane, Luis
  Prayer for each awakening. Dudley Fitts (tr.). 6759-X
Cane, Melville
  After reading the reviews of Finnegans Wake. 6722-0
  Askew, we ask you. 6979-7
  Behind dark places. 6979-7
  Hail to the major. 6654-2
  Hymn to night. 6979-7
  A winter night. 6118-4
The **cane-bottom'd** chair. William Makepeace Thackeray. 6085-4,6738-8,6092-7,6230-X,6570-8
Canfield, Arthur G.
  My faith. 6303-9
Canfield, Flavia Camp
  Shall I? 7030-2
  The triangle. 7030-2
Canfield, Hattie G.
  Changing color. 6672-0
Canite tuba. Bible. 6830-8
Cannady, Criss E.
  In the sitting room of the opera. 6966-5
  Sunlight in a cafeteria. 6966-5
Cannan, Edward
  An unexpected fact. 6089-7
Cannan, May Wedderburn
  Lamplight. 7029-9
Cannell, Skipwith
  The king. 6897-9
  The lean gray rats. 6954-1
  The red bridge. 6897-9
"A **canner** remarkably canny". Limerick:"A canner remarkably
  canny." Unknown. 6308-X
"A **canner**, exceedingly canny,". Carolyn Wells. 6724-7
The **cannibal** and the skeleton. Hector Fezandie. 6361-6
"A **cannibal** bold of Penzance". Limerick:"A cannibal bold
  of Penzance.". Unknown. 6308-X
The **cannibal** flea. Thomas Hood Jr. 6440-X
The **cannibal** Zeus. Unknown (Greek) 6987-8
"A **cannibal** maid and her Hottentot blade". How three were
  made one. Unknown. 6936-3
Canning (et al.), George
  New morality. 6152-4
Canning and John Hookham Frere, George
  The friend of humanity and the knife grinder. 6152-4,
  6733-6
  Imitation of Southey. 6092-7
  Inscription. 6802-2
  The progress of man, sels. 6152-4
  Sapphics (Needy knife-grinder). 6092-7
  The soldier's wife. 6802-2
  The soldiers' friend. 6802-2
Canning, George
  The cat and the bird. 6125-7
  The elderly gentleman. 6089-7,6440-X
  Epistle from Lord Borington to Lord Granville. 6200-8,
  6086-2
  Epitaph on the tombstone erected over the
  Marquis...leg. 6219-9
  Epitaph, for the tombstone erected...Marquis of
  Angelsea... . 6086-2
  Fragment of an oration. 6874-X
  Friend of humanity and the knife-grinder. 6385-3,6271-7,
  6438-8,6086-2,6219-9
  Inscription for Brownrigg's cll. 6302-0

Ipecacuanha. 6125-7
The knife-grinder. 6089-7,6102-8,6279-2,6732-8
The pilot that weathered the storm. 6793-X,6934-7
A political dispatch. 6092-7,6874-X
Sapphics. 6150-8
The soldier's friend. 6932-0
Song ("The University of Gottingen"). 6732-8
Song ("Whene'er with haggard"). 6026-9,6278-4
Song by Rogero, fr. The rovers. 6092-7,6152-4
Song of one eleven years in prison. 6089-7
Song, sung by Rogero. 6219-9
To Mrs. Leigh upon her wedding day. 6026-9
The University of Gottingen. 6787-5,6302-0,6279-2,6424-8

Canning, Right Hon. George
A political despatch. 6874-X

Cannon Jr., David Wadsworth
Boston tea. 6178-8
Dark love. 6178-8
Insight. 6178-8
Mountains. 6178-8
To Nita. 6178-8
World weariness. 6178-8

Cannon song. H.P. Peck. 6453-1
"The cannon's voice is dumb". Peace. Harold Trowbridge Pulsifer. 6051-X,6449-3

Cannon, Edward
An unsuspected fact. 6902-9

"The cannons roar and trumpets sound". Lowland lassie. Unknown. 6859-6
Cannot forget. So-wol Kim. 6775-1
"A canny old codger at Yalta". Limerick:"A canny old codger at Yalta." Unknown. 6308-X
"A canny Scotch lad of Pitlochry". Limerick:"A canny Scotch lad of Pitlochry". Langford Reed. 6811-1
Cano Carmen sixpence. Unknown. 6302-0
Canoe. Keith Douglas. 6379-9
Canoe song. Isabella Valancy Crawford. 6795-6
Canoe song at twilight. Laura E. McCully. 6115-X
The canoe. Isabella Valancy Crawford. 6795-6,6930-4,7041-8
Canon. Jackson Holland Patterson. 6841-3

Canon, Lima Boyd
Unborn day. 6799-9

Canonicus and Roger Williams. Unknown. 6946-0
The canonization. John Donne. 6182-6,6198-2,6315-2,6562-7,6494-1
Canons of descent. Unknown. 6878-2
Canopus. Bayard Taylor. 6976-2
Canopus. Bert Leston Taylor. 6102-8,6722-0,6076-5,6026-9
"Canst thou not minister to a mind diseased". William Shakespeare. 6238-5
"Canst thou, O cruel, say I love thee not". Sonnet 149 ("Canst thou, O cruel"). William Shakespeare. 6447-7
The cantab. Vincent Bourne. 6814-6
Cantaliso in a bar. Nicolas Guillen. 6759-X
The cantaloupe. Julia Boynton Green. 6039-0
Cantata, sels. John Howell. 6768-9
Canteen pimpin' Yasmeen Jamal. 6870-7
The canteen. Charles G. ("Miles O'Reilly") Halpine. 6412-4
The cantelope. Bayard Taylor. 6089-7,6440-X
Cantemus domino. Bible. 6830-8
The Canterbury pilgrims. Geoffrey Chaucer. 6302-0;6385-3
The Canterbury tales, sels. Geoffrey Chaucer. 6200-8,6732-8,6198-2,6369-1,6726-3,6228 ,6378-0,6102-8,6484-1, 6337-3,6193-1,6430 ,6250-4,6197-4,6301-2
Cantica: our lord Christ: of order. Jacopone da Todi. 6325-X
Canticle. Thomas Edward Brown. 6655-0
Canticle. Thomas Edward Brown. 6809-X
Canticle. William Griffith. 6161-3,6073-0,6347-0,6509-0, 6253-9,6393-4
Canticle. Francis Quarles. 6208-3
Canticle de profundis. Lucy Larcom. 6340-3
Canticle for the doomed. Ruth Forbes Sherry. 6316-0
Canticle for three voices, sels. Paul Claudel. 6343-8
The canticle of brother sun. Saint Francis of Assisi. 6334-9
Canticle of Canticles, sels. Unknown. 6282-2
Canticle of the creatures (or, Canticle of the sun). Saint Francis of Assisi. 6337-3

Canticle of the sun. Saint Francis of Assisi. 6730-1
The canticle of the sun. Matthew Arnold. 6250-4
The canticle of the sun. Saint Francis of Assisi. 6143-5, 6252-0
The canticle of the sun. Unknown. 6541-4
Canticle, sels. John Norris. 6562-7
A canticle. Phoebe Cary. 6865-0;6969-X
A canticle. William Alexander Percy. 6037-4
Cantiga de Maria das Estrelas. Nancy Lee Couto. 6900-2
Canto 001, fr. The faerie queene. Edmund Spenser. 6122-2
Canto 001, fr. The locvsts, or apollyonists. Phineas Fletcher. 6562-7
Canto 001, fr. The rape of the lock. Alexander Pope. 6122-2;6733-6
Canto 002 John Gay. 6972-X
Canto 002, fr. The faerie queene. Edmund Spenser. 6122-2
Canto 002, fr. The rape of the lock. Alexander Pope. 6122-2
Canto 003, fr. The rape of the lock. Alexander Pope. 6122-2
Canto 004, fr. The rape of the lock. Alexander Pope. 6122-2
Canto 005, fr. The rape of the lock. Alexander Pope. 6122-2
Canto 006, fr. Two Cantos of Mvtabilitie. Edmund Spenser. 6586-4
Canto 007, fr. Two Cantos of Mvtabilitie. Edmund Spenser. 6586-4
Canto 013 ("Kung walked"). Ezra Pound. 6209-1
Canto 017 ("So that the vines"). Ezra Pound. 6375-6
Canto 045 ("With Usura"). Ezra Pound. 6399-3
A canto of Khans. Berton Braley. 6853-7
Canto quarto. Thomas Campion. 6794-8
Canto quinto. Thomas Campion. 6794-8
Canto secundo. Thomas Campion. 6794-8
Canto tertio. Thomas Campion. 6794-8

Canton, Wilberto L.
Island. Dudley Fitts (tr.). 6759-X
On Lake Llanquihue. Donald Devenish Walsh (tr.). 6759-X

Canton, William
Bubble-blowing. 6639-9
Carol. 6608-9
Carol ("When the herds"). 6216-4
Children's new prayer. 6713-1
The comrades. 6250-4
The crow. 6102-8
The death of Anaxagoras. 6250-4
Envoy. 6233-4
The god and the schoolboy. 6250-4
Heights and depths. 6477-9
In the shadow. 6250-4
Karma. 6656-9
Laus infantium. 6250-4,6656-9,6274-1
Moonlight. 6250-4
A new poet. 6102-8,6250-4,6274-1,6478-7,6732-8
A philosopher ("Yes, you may let them creep...the rug") 6250-4
A philsopher. 6250-4
Rhymes about a little woman. 6452-3
She was a treasure. 6638-0
Suspirium. 6250-4
This grace vouchsafe me. 6250-4
This is the way the ladies ride. 6937-1
Through the ages. 6250-4
Trafalgar. 6639-9
The wanderer. 6274-1
When the herds were watching. 6747-6

Canute. William Wordsworth. 6484-1
Canute the Dane. Michael (Katherine Bradley & Edith Cooper) Field. 6188-5
Canute the Great, sels. Michael (Katherine Bradley & Edith Cooper) Field. 6656-9

Canute, King
Merrily sang the monks in Ely. 6301-2

"The canvas speaks; again we see". Charlotte Corday. Robert Loveman. 6941-X
Canyon people. Josephine Miles. 6640-2
Canyon walls. Iris Sparks. 6799-9
Canzone. John Milton. 6814-6
Canzone: He perceives his rashness in love... Guido

CANZONE:

        Guinicelli. 7039-6
Canzone: His lament for Selvaggia. Cino da Pistoia. 7039-6
Canzone: of distance. Ruggeri D'Amici. 6325-X
Canzone: Of his dead lady. Giacomino Pugliesi. 7039-6
Canzone: of the gentle heart. Guido Guinicelli. 6325-X
Canzone: to love and to his lady. Guido Delle Colonne. 6325-X
Canzonet. Unknown. 6182-6
Canzonet. Henry Kirke White. 6980-0
Canzonetta. Sir James Marriott. 6024-2
Canzonetta. Betty Myers. 6841-3
Canzonetta: A bitter song to his lady. Pier Moronelli di Fiorenza. 7039-6
Caoch O'Lynn. Arthur Stringer. 6797-2
Caoch the piper. John Keegan. 6174-5,6451-5,6404-3,6518-X
The cap and bells. William Butler Yeats. 6437-X,6102-8, 6125-7,6301-2
Cap'n & me. Leon Baker. 6870-7
Cap'n Paul. Unknown. 6061-7
Cap'n storm-along. Alfred Noyes. 6151-6
'Cap'n'.. Arthur Wallace Peach. 6833-2
Cape Cod. John Coleman Adams. 6798-0
Cape Cod. Sarah A. Dixon. 6798-0
Cape Cod. James T. Gallagher. 6798-0
Cape Cod color. Helen L. Bayley. 6798-0
A Cape Cod home, sels. Thomas Franklin Hall. 6798-0
Cape Cod memory. A. Pearle Carter. 6039-0
A Cape Cod native. Henry David Thoreau. 6484-1
Cape Cod pines. Sarah A. Dixon. 6798-0
"Cape Cod's our mother; we her sons". The sons of old Cape Cod, sels. Thomas N. Stone. 6798-0
Cape Cod, sels. Joshua Freeman Crowell. 6798-0
Cape coloured batman. Guy Butler. 6788-3
A Cape homestead. Lance Fallaw. 6800-6
The cape in June. Sarah A. Dixon. 6798-0
Cape of Good Hope. William Rodger Thomson. 6800-6
Cape St. Vincent. G.D. Martineau. 6072-2
Cape Town from Platte Klip. E. Berlein. 6800-6
Cape, Fred
    The tin gee gee. 6964-9
Cape-cottage at sunset. William Belcher Glazier. 6271-7, 6302-0,6385-3
The Cape. M.H. Crowell. 6798-0
Capel, Arthur Lord
    Loyalty confined. 6874-X
Capell, William
    I saw death slain. 6144-3
Caperil, F.B.
    Blind alley. 6039-0
Capern, Edward
    Tim Tuff. 6909-6
Capernaum at eventide. William White. 6868-5
Capers et caper. Eugene Fitch Ware. 7025-6
Capes, F.M. (tr.)
    A little song. Robert Grosseteste, 6282-2
Capes, Molly
    Hallowe'en ("Bolt and bar the front door"). 6254-7
Capetanakis, Demetrios
    Abel. 6665-8
Capetanakis, Demetrios (tr.)
    Two poems. Pantelis Prevelakis, 6068-4
Capetown from Platte Klip. E. Berlein. 6625-9
Capilano. A.M. Stephen. 6843-X
Capital punishment. Myra Townsend. 6402-7
Capital punishment. Unknown. 6260-1
Cappleman, Josie Frazee
    The resurrected hearts. 6675-5
Capri. Sara Teasdale. 6331-4
Capriccioso, fr. Summer night. Bayard Taylor. 6976-2
Caprice. William Dean Howells. 6429-9,6026-9,6321-7,6652-5
Caprice. Rose Marie. 6750-6
Caprice. Clara Shanafelt. 6897-9
Caprice. Unknown. 6312-8
Caprice at home. Unknown. 6701-8
"'Capt'n Bill, I've come to see your...'". Attune. Joshua Freeman Crowell. 6798-0
Capt. Sally Tompkins, C.S.A. Beverly Randolph Tucker. 6482-5
Captain Bing. L. Frank Baum. 6274-1
Captain Bover. Unknown. 6547-3
Captain Brazenhead. John D. Swain. 7007-8
Captain Car, or Edom O Gordon. Unknown. 6907-X
Captain Car, or, Edom o Gordon. Unknown. 6185-0,6198-2, 6430-2,6518-4
Captain Carpenter. John Crowe Ransom. 6038-2,6733-6,6209-1, 6070-6
Captain Charles Lindbergh. Robert Normile Rose. 7019-1
Captain Craig, sels. Edwin Arlington Robinson. 6501-5
"Captain Weeks, your right hand...". To Captain Seaman Weeks, fr. Croaker papers. Fitz-Greene Halleck and Joseph Rodman Drake. 6753-0
"Captain Wolf, he says, sailed three times...". Captain Wolf. Lilian B. Miner. 6799-9
Captain death. Unknown. 6157-5,6328-4
Captain Glen. Unknown. 6057-9,6547-3,6547-3
Captain Gold and French Janet. Agnes Mary F. ("Madame Duclaux") Robinson. 6518-X
Captain Guynemer. Florence Earle Coates. 7027-2
Captain Guynemer. Florence Earle Coates. 6051-X
Captain Hill. Jock Vanderbilt. 6396-9
Captain Jim Rees an' the Katie. Unknown. 6609-7
Captain Jinks. Unknown. 6826-X
Captain Joe. William L. Keese. 6451-5
Captain Kempthorn, fr. John Endicott. Henry Wadsworth Longfellow. 6382-9
Captain Kidd. Unknown. 6057-9,6003-X,6281-4
Captain Latane. John Reuben Thompson. 6074-9
Captain Lean. Walter De La Mare. 6596-1
Captain Loredan. Edward King. 6467-1
The captain of St. Kitts. Beulah May. 6833-2
Captain of the nine. J. Warren Merrill. 6715-8
A captain of the press-gang. Bliss Carman. 7006-X
"Captain or Colonel, or Knight in Arms". John Milton. 6562-7
Captain Paton. John Gibson Lockhart. 6787-5
Captain Paton's lament. John Gibson Lockhart. 6960-6
Captain Paton's lament. John Gibson Lockhart. 6180-X
Captain Reece of the mantlepiece. Sir William Schwenck Gilbert. 6412-4,6732-8,6239-3,6219-9
The captain stood on the carronade. Frederick Marryat. 6105-2;6258-X;6547-3
Captain sword. Leigh Hunt. 6239-3,6046-3
Captain Tom and Captain Hugh. Thomas Edward Brown. 6809-X
Captain Ward and the rainbow. Unknown. 6061-7,6185-0,6518-X,6518-X
Captain Wedderburn's courtship. Unknown. 6057-9,6058-7, 6185-0,6185-0
Captain Wolf. Lilian B. Miner. 6799-9
The captain's daughter. James Thomas Fields. 6356-X,6052-8, 6479-5,6127-3,6614-3,6131 ,6214-8
The captain's dream. Anne Bronte. 6648-8
The captain's drum. Benjamin Franklin Taylor. 6815-4
The captain's feather. Samuel Minturn Peck. 6309-8
The captain's last hail. William Edward Penney. 6018-8
The captain's song. Ethel Clifford. 6785-9
Captain's walk. Oliver Jenkins. 6764-6
The captain's wife. Theodore Tilton. 6113-3
"Captain, for what brave hire". Ballade of dreams. Rose E. Macaulay. 6875-8
"Captain, I have seen". A warning for Abraham Lincoln. Jacinto Fombona Pachano. 6759-X
The captain, sels. Francis Beaumont and John Fletcher. 6208-3,6562-7
The captain, sels. John Gardiner Calkins Brainard. 6752-2
The captain. John Gardiner Calkins Brainard. 6632-1
The captain. Alfred Lord Tennyson. 6610-0
The captain. Unknown. 6589-9
Captains adventurous. Norah M. Holland. 7027-2
The captains of the years. Arthur R. MacDougall Jr. 6335-7, 6542-2,6144-3,6337-3
The captains. Nikolai Gumilev. 6103-6
Capte Hatteras, fr. The bridge. Hart Crane. 6399-3
Caption for one's own photograph. N.K. Cruickshank. 6475-2
Captive. Fay Slobod Greenfield. 6799-9
The captive bee. Robert Herrick. 6219-9
The captive bird. Percy Bysshe Shelley. 6943-6
The captive butterfly. Helen Granville-Barker. 6510-4
The captive humming bird. Joel T. Hart. 6273-3
The captive knight and the blackbird. Unknown (Spanish) 6757-3

The captive lion. June Daly. 6625-9
The captive lover. Henry Lawes. 6328-4
The captive polar bear. Stephen Lucius Gwynn. 6510-4
"The captive raised her face...", fr. The prisoner. Emily Bronte. 6123-0
The captive ships at Manila. Dorothy Paul. 6946-0
The captive's hymn. Edna Dean Proctor. 6946-0
The captive. William ("Wild Bill") Franklin. 6870-7
The captive. Rudyard Kipling. 6655-0
The captive. Enrique Gonzalez Martinez. 6482-5
Captives. Leo Konopka. 6249-0
Captives going home. Unknown. 6074-9
The captives. A tragedy. John Gay. 6972-X
Captivity. Geoffrey Chaucer. 6023-4,6250-4
Captivity. Oliver Goldsmith. 6250-4
Captivity. Samuel Rogers. 6208-3
Captivity narrative: September 1981 Adrian C. Louis. 7005-1
The captivity, sels. Oliver Goldsmith. 6174-5
The capture of Athens. Oracle of Serapis. 6435-3
Capture of Little York. Unknown. 6946-0
Captured. Archibald MacLeish. 6778-6
Captured. Archibald MacLeish. 6038-2
Captured bird. George Rachow. 6870-7
The captured bumble-bee. Nellie Wood. 6684-4
The captured eagle. Janet Gargan. 6510-4
The captured flag. Arthur Weir. 6795-6
Capua
 In a theater. A. Werner (tr.). 6610-0
Capua. John Nichol. 6624-0
Caput Mortuum. Edwin Arlington Robinson. 6052-8
"Caput apri refero". The boar's head carol. Unknown. 6881-2
Car six. Americo Casiano. 6898-7
Caractacus. Augustine Joseph Hickey Duganne. 6924-X
Caradoc, the bard, to the Cymrians. Owen (Edward Bulwer-Lytton, Earl Lytton) Meredith. 6606-2
Caravaggio and his models. Rene Ricard. 7003-5
A caravan from China comes. Richard Le Gallienne. 6310-1;6499-X;6509-0
The caravan in the desert. Felicia Dorothea Hemans. 6973-8
Caravan of longing. Iwan [or Yvan] Goll. 6160-5
The caravan. Madeleine Nightingale. 6368-3
Caravans. Emily Patterson. 6144-3
Caravans. P.A.A. Thomas. 6468-X
The caravels of Columbus. Elias Lieberman. 6336-5
Carbaugh, Frank
 The fields of the Marne. 6589-9,6650-X
Carbery, Ethna (Anna Johnson MacManus)
 In Tir-na'n-og. 6292-X,6172-9
 The love-taler. 6090-0,6102-8,6930-4
 Mea culpa. 6292-X,6172-9
 Niamh. 6252-0
 The other. 6019-6
 The passing of the gael. 6793-X
 The shadow house of Lugh. 6096-X
Carcamon. Henry Augustin Beers. 6219-9
Carcassone. Berton Braley. 6853-7
Carcassonne. Robert Loveman. 6941-X
Carcassonne. Gustave Nadaud. 6255-5,6484-1,6451-5,6424-8,6631-3,6102
Carcassonne. Gustave Nadaud. 6370-5,6605-4,6439-6,6331-4
Carcassonne. Gustave Nadaud. 6631-3
Carcassonne. M.E.W. Sherwood. 6277-6,6358-6
Carcassonne. Unknown. 7002-7
Carco, Francis
 Carnival. 6351-9
 Is he dead? 6351-9
Carcosa. Lin Carter. 6218-0
The card club's first meeting. Edgar A. Guest. 6862-6
Card for my mother's birthday. Mary Baron. 6855-3
A card game: kinjiro sawada. Patricia Y. Ikeda. 6790-5
Card houses. Unknown. 6273-3
A card of invitation to Mr. Gibbon...1781. William Hayley. 6932-0
The card-dealer.. Dante Gabriel Rossetti. 6657-7,6110-9
A card. William Cowper. 6814-6
Cardiff, Gladys
 Combing. 7005-1
 Long person. 7005-1
 Owl and rooster. 7005-1
 Tlanusi' Yi, the leech place. 7005-1
 To frighten a storm. 7005-1
Cardinal. Avis H. Grant. 6906-1
"A cardinal awakened me". Four tunes. Helen Gross Hume. 6847-2
The cardinal bird. William Davis Gallagher. 6006-6,6073-0, 6597-X,6265-2
Cardinal Fisher. John Heywood. 6022-6
Cardinal Manning. Aubrey Thomas De Vere. 6172-9,6292-X, 6656-9
Cardinal Wolsey. Samuel Johnson. 6543-0
Cardinal Wolsey. William Shakespeare. 6621-6
Cardinal Wolsey on being cast off by Henry VIII. William Shakespeare. 6424-8
Cardinal Wolsey's farewell, fr. King Henry VIII. William Shakespeare. 6014-5,6337-3
The cardinal's soliloquy, fr. Richilieu. Edward Bulwer-Lytton; Baron Lytton. 6656-9
The cardinal-bird.. Arthur Guiterman. 6338-1
Cardona-Hine, Alvaro
 Geo-politics. 6966-5
Cardoza y Aragon, Luis
 Ballad of Frederico Garcia Lopez. Donald Devenish Walsh (tr.). 6759-X
Cardozo, Elizabeth C.
 We met them on the common way. 6337-3
Cardozo, Nancy
 In the depot...refugees. 6761-1
Cards and kisses. John Lyly. 6102-8,6328-4,6732-8
"Cards, and swords, and a lady's love". When George was king. Emily Pauline ("Tekahionwake") Johnson. 6837-5
Carducci, Giosue
 Before the old castle of Verona. 6624-0
 In the piazza of San Petronio. M.W. Arms (tr.). 6624-0
 Monte Cavo. Robert Haven Schauffler (tr.). 6624-0
 The ox. 6510-4
 The ox. Frank Sewall (tr.). 6102-8
 Primo vere. John Bailey (tr.). 7039-6
 Rome. 6624-0
 Snowfall. Romilda Rendel (tr.). 7039-6
Care. Janet Norris Bangs. 6037-4
Care. Alice Cary. 6969-X
Care. Virginia Woodward Cloud. 6309-8
"Care away away away." Unknown. 6378-0
"Care away goe thow from me." Unknown. 6563-5
Care charming sleep...", fr. The valentinian. Francis Beaumont and John Fletcher. 6562-7
Care I for roses so? Arthur Forbes. 6761-1
"Care flieth,/Hope and fear together". Autumn. Christina Georgina Rossetti. 6828-6
"Care is like a husbandman". Care. Alice Cary. 6969-X
"Care keeps his watch in every old man's eyes." William Shakespeare. 6686-0
"The care of sheep, the labours of the loom". The fleece. John Dyer. 6968-1
Care's confessor. Unknown. 6383-7
"Care, charming sleep". Song ("Care, charming sleep.") John Gould Fletcher. 6102-8
Care-charmer sleep. Samuel Daniel. 6737-9,6315-2,6182-6, 6187-7,6246-5,6436-1,6536-8,6634-8,6533-3,6102-8, 6153-2
"Care-charmer sleep, son of the sable night". Sonnet ("Care-charmer sleep"). Samuel Daniel. 6189-3,6150-8
"Care-charmer sleepe, sweet ease in restles miserie," Bartholomew Griffin. 6586-4
Care-charming sleep. John Fletcher. 6194-X,6052-8,6501-5, 6737-9,6430-2,6383-7
Career. W.W. Christman. 6662-3
The career of the cooky-cat. Carolyn Wells. 6882-0
A career. Berton Braley. 6853-7
Careers. Robert Graves. 6506-6
"Carefree sweet child! Straighten your curls!". Gypsy. Vojislav Ilic. 6765-4
The careful husband. Unknown. 6930-4
"Careful observers may foretell the hour". A description of a city shower. Jonathan Swift. 6930-4
The careful penman. Unknown. 6089-7
Carefully. Ethel Jacobson. 6750-6
"Careles of love and free from feares." Thomas Carew

(atr.) 6563-5
Careless. Edgar A. Guest. 6869-3
Careless. Charles Mackay. 6980-0
Careless. George Sterling. 6121-4
"Careless as a butterfly". At last. Gertrude Huntington McGiffert. 6838-3
The **careless** bottle. Carolyn Wells. 6882-0
Careless content. John Byrom. 6600-3,6152-4,6219-9
Careless content, sels. John Byrom. 6317-9
"Careless forever, beautiful proud sea". 'Beautiful proud sea'. Sara Teasdale. 6779-4
The **careless** gallant, or A farewell to sorrow. Peter Anthony Motteux. 6157-5
The **careless** gallant. Thomas Jordan. 6563-5,6092-7
The **careless** good fellow. John Oldham. 6152-4
Careless love. Stanley J. Kunitz. 6666-6
Careless love. Unknown. 6609-7
The **careless** lover. Sir John Suckling. 6874-X
The **careless** maid. Unknown. 6134-6,6383-7
"Careless she lies along the southern main". Australia, 1905. Archibald T. Strong. 6784-0
The **careless** word. Caroline Elizabeth Sarah Sheridan Norton. 6980-0
"Careless/but not fearless". Urn I: silent for twenty-five. Walter Lew. 6790-5
The **carelesse** nurse mayd. Thomas Hood. 6724-7
Carelton, Will
  The prize of the Margaretta. 6946-0
"The cares of the day". Travail. Gertrude Fitzpatrick. 6789-1
"Caress'd or chidden by the dainty hand". Sonnet to a coquette (1). Alfred Lord Tennyson. 6977-0
"Carest Thou not? O Thou that givest life". Unknown. 6238-5
Carew (atr.), Thomas
  "Blowe there sweet Zephirus where thou shalt finde." 6563-5
  "Careles of love and free from feares." 6563-5
  "Had I a trumpet, and that trumpet fames." 6563-5
  "Poor Pensiue I o're chargde with woe." 6563-5
  "Still Amathea thou art fayre." 6563-5
Carew or James Shirley or Samuel Pick, Thomas
  To his mistress confined. 6563-5
Carew [or Carey], Lady Elizabeth
  Revenge of injuries. 6385-3,6600-3
  True greatness. 6737-9
Carew, Thomas
  The airs of spring. 6271-7,6219-9
  Ask me no more. 6023-4,6383-7,6197-4,6563-5
  "Ask me no more where Jove bestows". 6726-3,6271-7,6219-9,6187-7,6208-3,6023-4,6383-7,6197-4,6250-4,6543-0, 6099-4,6430-2,6092-7,6219-9,6271-3
  "Ask me no more whither do stray" 6935-5
  A beautifull mistress. 6933-9
  Boldness in love. 6562-7,6563-5
  Celia singing. 6733-6,6563-5,6430-2
  Chloris in the snow. 6099-4
  The compliment. 6250-4
  A deposition from love. 6341-1,6378-0,6430-2,6194-X, 6150-8,6933
  Disdain returned. 6562-7,6099-4,6271-7,6563-5,6604-6, 6250 ,6189-3,6194-X,6092-7,6438-8,6291-9,6660
  An.elegie upon the death of the dean of Pauls, Dr.John Donne. 6341-1,6562-7
  An elegy upon the death of Doctor Donne, dean of Paul's. 6483-3
  Epitaph. 6301-2
  Epitaph on Lady Mary Villiers (I) 6908-8
  Epitaph on Lady Mary Villiers (II) 6908-8
  Epitaph on the Lady Mary Villers. 6562-7,6563-5,6430-2, 6194-X,6189-3
  An epitaph. 6198-2
  Eternity of love protested. 6341-1,6933-9
  "Give me more love or more disdain." 6302-0,6385-3,6328-4,6226-1,6737-9
  Good counsell to a young maid. 6933-9
  He that loves a rosy cheek. 6600-3,6328-4,6668-2,6543-0, 6302-0,6385-3,6187-7
  "How ill doth he deserve a lover's name". 6187-7,6935-5
  "I do not love thee for that fair." 6302-0;6385-3,6737-9
  "If when the sun at noon displays". 6187-7
  In praise of his mistress. 6827-8
  Ingrateful beauty threatened. 6198-2,6317-9,6562-7,6150-8,6153-2,6341-1
  The inquiry. 6874-X
  The inscription on the tomb of the Lady Mary Wentworth. 6933-9,6933-9,6150-8
  "Know, Celia, since thou art so proud". 6187-7
  Lady Mary Villiers. 6659-3
  Love's errand. 6830-8
  Maria Wentworth. 6562-7,6641-0,6341-1
  "Mark how the bashful morn, in vain". 6187-7,6328-4
  Mediocrity in love rejected. 6562-7,6102-8,6563-5,6092-7,6543-0,6026-9,6341-1
  Murdering beauty. 6430-2
  Night and day to his mistress. 6328-4
  "Now that the winter's gone, the earth hath lost". 6187-7
  Now that winter's gone. 6668-2
  On Celia's singing. 6543-0
  A pastoral dialogue. 6191-5,6190-7
  Persuasions to enjoy. 6563-5,6737-9
  Persuasions to joy: a song. 6198-2,6122-2
  A prayer to the wind. 6543-0
  The primrose. 6189-3,6383-7
  The protestation. 6543-0,6122-2
  Red and white roses. 6543-0
  Secrecy protested. 6430-2
  Song. 6645-3
  Song ("Ask me no more"). 6154-0,6052-8,6102-8,6271-7, 6301-2,6560 ,6317-9,6250-4,6513-9,6341-1,6189-3,6562 ,6198-2,6150-8,6186-9,6315-2,6634-8,6186
  Song ("How ill"). 6562-7
  Song ("If when the sun"). 6562-7
  Song ("The purest soule"). 6562-7
  Song ("This little vault"). 6562-7
  Song ("When thou, poore excommunicate"). 6562-7
  Song ("Would you know"). 6198-2
  Song ("You that thinke"). 6562-7
  A song. 6723-9
  Spring. 6239-3
  The spring. 6208-3
  "Sweetly breathing, vernal air." 6302-0;6385-3
  To a lady that desired I would love her. 6315-2,6563-5, 6341-1,6150-8,6562-7
  To A.L. 6935-5
  To Celia singing. 6099-4
  To my inconstant mistress. 6315-2,6563-5,6341-1,6317-9
  To my worthy friend Mr. George Sandys. 6341-1,6562-7
  To Saxham. 6933-9
  To the Countess of Anglesey. 6908-8
  The true beauty. 6246-5,6332-2,6732-8,6737-9,6226-1
  The unfading beauty. 6102-8,6560-0,6153-2
  Ungrateful beauty. 6102-8,6092-7,6543-0,6827-8
  Upon Master W. Mountague his returne from travell. 6562-7
  When on the altar of my hand. 6328-4
  "When thou, poor excommunicate". 6187-7,6830-8
  "Would you know what's soft? I dare". 6187-7
  "You that think love can convey". 6187-7,6317-9
Carew, Will
  The six road ends. 6090-0
Carey, Bernice H.
  Waiting. 6397-7
Carey, Henry
  Cato's advice. 6874-X
  "Expect great things from God." 6225-3
  God save the king. 6219-9,6126-5,6240-7,6732-8
  Harry Carey's reply. 6230-X
  A loyal song. 6934-7
  The maiden's choice. 6219-9
  A maiden's ideal of a husband. 6620-8
  Mrs. Stuart's retirement. 6423-X
  "Of all the girls that are so smart." 6317-9
  Roger and Dolly. 6157-5
  Sally in our alley. 6024-2,6089-7,6157-5,6246-5,6339-X, 6481-7,6486-8,6732-8,6302-0,6385-3,6092-7,6104-4, 6560-0,6030-7
  Saly sweetbread. 6157-5

"With an honest old friend and a merry old song" 6874-X
Carey, Lady Elizabeth. See Carew, Lady Elizabeth
Carey, Patrick
    Chains. 6563-5
    Christ in his passion, fr. Hymn: crucifixus pro nobis. 6931-2
    Christ in the cradle, fr. Hymn: crucifixus pro nobis. 6931-2
    Christ in the garden, fr. Hymn: crucifixus pro nobis. 6931-2
    Crucifixion pro nobis. 6563-5
    Hymn ("Whilest I beheld the neck o' the dove"). 6563-5
    Hymn: crucifixus pro nobis. 6931-2
    Nulla fides. 6562-7
    Triolets. 6023-4
Carey, of Carson. Charles Godfrey Leland. 7025-6
Cargoes. Edgar Daniel Kramer. 7007-8
Cargoes. John Masefield. 6102-8,6458-2,6143-5,6153-2,6161-3,6723 ,6138-9,6154-0,6246-6,6274-1,6331-4,6332 , 6427-2,6466-3,6477-9,6538-4,6732-8,6464 ,6639-9,6653-4,6301-2,6393-4,6396-9,6491
Carillon. Henry Wadsworth Longfellow. 6302-0;6385-3
Caring. Francis Reginald Scott. 6446-9
Caring for one's mother. Alexander Pope. 6097-8
"A **carion** crow sat on an oak". Unknown. 6363-2
Caritas. Hollis Russell. 6397-7
Carl [pseud]
    The valley of rest. 6983-5
"**Carle**, an' the king come". Unknown. 6859-6
Carle, now the king's come. Sir Walter Scott. 6180-X
The **carles** of Dysart. Robert Burns. 6383-7
Carleton, Ada
    Selling the baby. 6922-3
Carleton, Emily F. (tr.)
    Psalm 008 Bible, 6848-0
Carleton, Emma
    Faith. 6337-3
Carleton, Guy
    The old clock. 6414-0
Carleton, Sara King
    Cathedral. 6979-7
    Grand finale. 6218-0
Carleton, Will
    Across the Delaware. 6946-0
    Baron Grimalkin's death. 6692-2
    Betsey and I are out. 6404-3,6344-6,6565-1
    Betsey destroys the paper. 6404-3
    The Christmas baby. 6414-0
    Coasting down the hill. 7035-3
    Cuba to Columbia. 6946-0
    The dead stowaway. 6155-9
    The dead student. 6412-4
    The death-bridge of the Tay. 6550-3,6919-3
    Dialogue of the horses. 6510-4
    Difficult love-making. 6671-2
    Elder Lamb's donation. 6505-8,6672-0
    Farm ballads, sels. 6155-9
    Farmer and wheel; or, the new Lochinvar. 6919-3
    Farmer Stebbins at football. 6926-6
    Farmer Stebbins at Ocean Grove. 6917-7,6155-9
    Farmer Stebbins on rollers. 6416-7
    The first settler's story. 6281-4,7041-8,6413-2,6550-3, 6706-9
    Flash: The fireman's story. 6465-5,6451-5,6497-3,6107-9, 6574-0
    The funeral. 6139-7
    Goin' home today. 6155-9,6409-4
    Gone with a handsomer man. 6911-8
    How Betsey and I made up. 6045-1
    How Jamie came home. 6406-X
    How we fought the fire. 7002-7
    How we kept the day. 6155-9
    The lightning-rod dispenser. 6630-5
    The little black-eyed rebel. 6267-9,6470-1
    Little golden hair. 6413-2
    Makin' an editor outen o' him. 6014-5,6913-4
    The mother and her child. 6404-3
    The new church organ. 6089-7,6370-5,6566-X,6155-9,6505-8,6910 ,6240-7,6385-3
    The old reading class. 6415-9,6630-5
    Our traveled parson. 6571-6,6411-6
    Out of the old house, Nancy. 6281-4,6300-4,6407-8
    Over the hill from the poor-house. 6964-9
    Over the hill to the poor-house. 6404-3,6732-8,6412-4, 6566-X
    The ride of Jennie McNeal. 6062-5,6392-6,6478-7,6552-X, 6570-8,6916
    The sandal-maker of Babylon. 6739-5
    The schoolmaster's guests. 6281-4,6914-2
    The second settler's story. 6281-4
    A sigh for Knockmany. 6090-0
    Sir Turlough; or, the churchyard bride. 6518-X
    To a skeleton. 6404-3
    Took Johnnie to the show. 6929-0
    Uncle Sammy. 6505-8
    Under the wheels. 6924-X
    Up in the loft. 6929-0
    The victory-wreck. 6946-0
    "The way at times may dark and weary seem." 6225-3
    The wedding of the towns. 6630-5
Carlin, Francis
    Alchemy. 6032-3,6292-X
    The baby of Saint Brigid. 6285-7
    Ballad of Douglas Bridge. 6244-X
    Beyond Rathkelly. 6441-8
    The booted hens. 6032-3
    By Clodagh's stream. 6032-3
    Child dear. 6096 X
    Counsel. 6039-0
    The cuckoo. 6393-4
    The deaf-mute sermon. 6032-3
    Filial deity. 6839-1
    The golden nickel. 6037-4
    The grey plume. 6619-4
    Her reverie. 6250-4
    Hope's song. 6607-0
    The Irish. 6292-X
    Joy to you. 6607-0,6467-1
    Maureen Oge. 6032-3
    My neighbor. 6096 X
    The only-born. 6096-X
    The parish bard. 6250-4
    Pax. 6036-6
    Perfection. 6250-4
    The philomath speaks. 6070-6
    Plea for hope. 6096-1
    The rivals. 6096-X
    The solar road. 6292-X
    The two nests. 6073-0,6619-4,6467-1
    Under an Irish lark. 6250-4
    The Virgin's slumber song. 6282-2,6746-8,6393-4
    Wine. 6292-X
Carlin, George W.
    In Palestine. 6144-3
Carlino, Don Santiago
    The soldier tramp. 6920-7
Carlisle ha'. Unknown. 6859-6
Carlisle yetts. Unknown. 6859-6
Carlos Lopez, Luis
    The mayor. H.R. Hays (tr.). 6642-9
    Old maids. H.R. Hays (tr.). 6642-9
    Rubbish VII. H.R. Hays (tr.). 6642-9
    Rubbish, IV. H.R. Hays (tr.). 6642-9
    To a dog. H.R. Hays (tr.). 6642-9
    To my native city. H.R. Hays (tr.). 6642-9
    To Satan. H.R. Hays (tr.). 6642-9
"**Carlos**, calm down, love". Don't kill yourself. Carlos Drummond de Andrade. 6758-1
Carlotta mia. Thomas Augustine Daly. 6707-7
Carlsbad. Eugene Field. 6949-5
Carlyle (fr. tr. of Martin Luther), Thom (tr.)
    Psalm 046. Bible, 6271-7
Carlyle, Jane Welsh
    Answer to Cui Bono. 6424-8
    To a swallow building under our eaves. 6656-9
    To a swallow building under the eaves at Craigenputtock. 6424-8
Carlyle, Thomas
    Adieu. 6240-7
    Cui bono? 328-4,6730-1,6424-8,6996-7

CARLYLE

From the mountains to the Champaign. 6934-7
Heard are the voices. 6240-7
The sower's song. 6732-8,6437-X,6383-7,6656-9
Speech of the Erdgeist in Faust. 6046-3
This mysterious mankind. 6102-8
To-day. 6239-3,6136-2,6180-X,6337-3,6457-4,6730-1,6639
To-day. 6242-3,6424-8,6102-8,6461-2,6368-3,6046-3,6239-3,6530-9,6481-7
Two men I honor. 6954-1
Work. 6449-3

Carlyle, and Martin Luther, Thomas (tr.)
Psalm 046 Bible, 6848-0

Carlyle, J.D. (tr.)
To a cat. Ibn Alalaf Alnaharwany, 6511-2

Carlyle, Thomas (tr.)
Ballad of the harper. Johann Wolfgang von Goethe, 6328-4
Knowest thou the land. Johann Wolfgang von Goethe, 6328-4
Longing. Johann Wolfgang von Goethe, 6328-4

Carman and Richard Hovey, Bliss
Accident in art. 6890-1
Across the table. 6890-1
The adventurers. 7007-8
At Michelmas. 6890-1
At the end of the day. 6890-1
The bather. 6890-1
Blue Annajohn. 6890-1
Comrades. 6006-4
Concerning Kavin. 6890-1
Distillation. 6890-1
Earth's lyric. 6890-1
A faun's song. 6890-1
The first julep. 6890-1
A friend's wish. 6890-1
A good-bye. 6890-1
The hearse-horse. 6890-1
In a copy of Browning. 6890-1
In a garden. 6890-1
In silence. 6890-1
In the wayland willows. 6890-1
Jongleurs. 6890-1
June night in Washington. 6890-1
Karlene (1). 6890-1
Karlene (2). 6890-1
The Kavanagh. 6006-4
Kavin again. 6890-1
Lal of Kilrudden. 6890-1
Mary of Marka. 6890-1
The mother of poets. 6890-1
Nancibel. 6890-1
The night-washers. 6890-1
Nocturne: In Anjou. 6890-1
Nocturne: In Provence. 6890-1
Premonition. 6890-1
Quince to lilac. 6890-1
Secrets. 6890-1
September woodlands. 6890-1
A song for Marna. 6890-1
Speech and silence. 6890-1
Spring song. 6006-4
The unsainting of Kavin. 6890-1
Verlaine. 6890-1
When I was twenty. 6890-1
Wood-folk lore. 6890-1
The wood-god. 6890-1

A carman's account of a law suit. Sir David Lindesay. 6089-7
A carman's account of a lawsuit. Sir David Lyndsay. 6240-7

Carman, Bliss
An April morning. 6236-9,6503-1,6393-4,6236-9,6338-1,6053-6,6162-1,6653-4
April weather. 6374-8,6252-0
Arnold, master of the Scud. 6833-2
At the making of man. 6115-X
At the roadhouse: in memory of Robert Louis Stevenson. 6890-1
At the yellow of the leaf. 6252-0
Autumn. 6053-6,6506-6,6653-4
An autumn garden. 6374-8
An autumn song. 6653-4
Ballad of John Camplejohn. 6301-2
Behind the arras, sels. 6102-8,6076-5
Bethlehem. 6608-9
A bluebrid in March, sels. 6021-8
Camping song. 6374-8
A captain of the press-gang. 7006-X
The choristers. 6797-2
A Christmas eve choral. 6282-2,6746-8
Christmas song. 6446-9
Coronation ode. 6224-5
The cry of the hillborn. 6374-8
Daisies. 6374-8,6467-1,6102-8,6337-3,6497-3,6076-5,6396-6,6423-X
The dance of the sunbeams. 6959-2
Daphne. 6423-X,6250-4
The deserted pasture. 6053-6,6374-8
Earth voices. 6115-X,6843-X
The eavesdropper. 6102-8,6076-5
The enchanted traveller. 6631-3,6331-4
Envoy. 6301-2,6501-5,6732-8
The Foys of the road. 6597-X
From an old ritual. 6252-0
The garden of dreams. 6338-1,6320-9
Golden Rowan. 6656-9
The gravedigger. 6161-3,6309-8,6433-7,6509-0
Hack and hew. 6656-9,6433-7,6732-8
Heaven. 6232-6,6649-6
Hem and haw. 6337-3,6458-2,6890-1,6996-7
The heretic. 6730-1
The house of Idiedaily. 7006-X
"I loved thee, Atthis, in the long ago." 6433-7
"I think the sun when he turns at night." 6433-7
"I was a reed in the stilly stream." 6433-7
In lyric season. 6795-6
In Philistia. 6026-9
In the heart of the hills. 6433-7
In the house of Idiedaily. 6437-X,6467-1
The joys of the road. 6374-8,6437-X,6079-X,6458-2,6252-0,6423-X,6006-4
The juggler, sels. 6076-5,6102-8
The juggler. 6162-1,6309-8
"Let the red dawn surmise." 6433-7
Lord of my heart's elation. 6250-4,6252-0,6393-4,6310-1,6509-0
"Love, by that loosed hair." 6433-7
Low tide on Grand-Pre. 6115-X,6446-9,6021-8,6433-7
The man of the marne. 6051-X
The marching morrows. 6473-6
Marigolds. 6374-8
Marion Drury. 6732-8,6656-9
The mendicants. 6374-8,6656-9
A more ancient mariner. 6473-6,6597-X,6006-4,6374-8,6656-9
The mote. 7006-X
A mountain gateway. 6027-7,6253-9,6115-X
Mr. moon: a song of the little people. 6890-1,6368-3
The mysteriarchs. 6327-6
A northern vigil. 6021-8,6437-X,6446-9
Now the lengthening twilights hold. 6253-9
On the tomb of Bliss Carman, fr. Songs from vagabondia. 6337-3
Over the shoulders and slopes of the dune. 6501-5
Over the wintry threshold. 6027-7
Overlord. 6433-7
The path to Sankoty. 6484-1
Phi Beta Kappa poem. 6028-5
The rainbird. 6073-0
Resignation. 7006-X
Roadside flowers. 6250-4,6162-1,6232-6,6266-0
The rough rider. 6995-9
A rover's song. 7006-X
St. Bartholomew's on the hill. 6374-8
Sappho lyrics, sels. 6433-7
Sappho, sels. 6446-9
The sceptics. 6006-4,6996-7
A sea child. 6656-9
A seamark. 6446-9
Shakespeare himself. 6890-1
The ships of Saint John. 68332

The ships of Yule. 6797-2
A son of the sea. 6374-8,6433-7
Song. 6656-9
Song ("Love, by that loosened hair"). 6076-5,6102-8
Songs of the sea children, sels. 6433-7
Spring song. 6374-8,6433-7,6478-7,6732-8,6252-0,6301-2
Spring song, sels. 6076-5,6102-8
Spring's saraband. 6115-X
A staccato to O Le Lupe. 6440-X
Stir. 7041-8
The tent of noon. 6115-X
Threnody for a poet. 6115-X
Trees. 6232-6,6374-8,6465-5,6478-7,6797-2,6861
Trees (In the Garden of Eden, planted by God,). 6338-1
Triumphalis. 6607-0,6513-9
The twelfth night star. 6266-0,6747-4
The two Bobbies. 7006-X
The unreturning. 6250-4,6310-1
A vagabond song. 6236-9,6332-2,6336-5,6104-4,6143-5, 6252 ,6239-3,6464-7,6646-1,6310-1,6332-2,6374 ,6476-0,6490-6,6506-6,6602-X
Vestigia. 6303-9,6337-3,6730-1,6723-9,6418-3,6532
A waif. 7006-X
The war cry of the eagles. 7027-2
The war-song of Gamelbar. 7006-X,6873-1
The weather-vane. 6336-5
"When I have departed." 6433-7
Where is heaven?, fr. Here and now. 6143-5,6337-3
Why. 6310-1
A windflower. 6656-9,7041-8
The winged victory. 6439-6,6331-4
Winter. 6723-9
The winter scene. 6336-5,6031-5
Winter streams. 6478-7
The world at St. Kavin's. 6501-5
The wraith of the red swan. 6795-6
Youth in the air. 7019-1

Carmelita. Julia Mills Dunn. 6682-8
Carmell, Pamela (tr.)
Jellyfish. Raquel Jodorowsky, 7036-1
Poem in every language. Raquel Jodorowsky, 7036-1
The power of man. Raquel Jodorowsky, 7036-1
Song for vocal chords and instruments of electronic... Raquel Jodorowsky, 7036-1
Carmen. Bruce Blakeney. 6397-7
Carmen. Madison Cawein. 7041-8
Carmen. Newman Levy. 6026-9
Carmen amoebaeum. Raymond Macdonald Alden. 6936-3
Carmen Bellicosum. Guy Humphreys McMaster. 6239-3;6015-3;6240-7;6735-2
Carmen genesis. Francis Thompson. 6489-2
Carmen in celeberrimi gloveri leonidam. Thomas Warton (the Elder) 6962-2
Carmen Paschale, sels. Caelius Sedulius. 6282-2
Carmen triumphale, sels. Robert Southey. 6867-7
Carmen, Felix
The spinning wheel. 7021-3
Valentine to a flirt. 7021-3
Carmer, Carl
Apple pickers. 6761-1
Night rider. 6887-1
Carmia. Alice Cary. 6865-0;6969-X
Carmichael, Alexander (tr.)
"Blest be the boat". Unknown, 6334-9
Hebridean sea-prayer. Unknown (Gaelic), 6334-9
Carmichael, Amy
In acceptance lieth peace. 6337-3
The last defile. 6337-3
Think it not strange. 6337-3
Toward Jerusalem. 6337-3
Carmichael, Hoagy
I'm a cranky old Yank in a clanky old tank. 6237-7
Carmichael, Jennings
Tomboy Madge. 6768-9
Carmichael, Sarah E.
The origin of gold. 6302-0
Carmichiel, Ada Clarke
The ghost of St. Anthony falls. 6342-X
Carmina festiva. Henry Van Dyke. 6961-4
Carn a-turnen yoller. William Barnes. 6423-X

The **carnal** and the crane. Unknown. 6756-5
The **carnal** and the crane. Unknown. 6185-0
Carnations. Ken Etheridge. 6360-8
Carnations. Margaret Widdemer. 6019-6
Carnegie, Agnes Lindsay
Death. 6180-X
Carnegie; Earl of Southesk, James
February in the Pyrenees, fr. Jonas Fisher. 6819-7
The flitch of Dunmow. 6656-9
The German tower-keeper, fr. Jonas Fisher. 6819-7
Good old souls. 6661-5
Influence of...time on national looks, fr. Jonas Fisher. 6819-7
Jonas Fisher: a poem in brown and white, sels. 6819-7
The mountain fir, fr. Jonas Fisher. 6819-7
November's cadence, fr. Jonas Fisher. 6180-X,6656-9, 6819-7,6819-7
Pigworm and Dixie, fr. Jonas Fisher. 6819-7
The rocky mountains, fr. Jonas Fisher. 6819-7
Carney, Julia A. Fletcher
Little things. 6356-X,6401-9
Carney, Julia Fletch
Duty and kindness. 6135-4
Little things. 6135-4
Carnival. Francis Carco. 6351-9
The **carnival** of 1848. William Allen Butler. 6903-7
The **carnival**.. George Gordon, 6th Baron Byron. 6624-0
The **carnival**. Muna Lee. 6397-7
The **carnival**. Clinton Scollard. 6542-2
Caro, Francis
The poet's hour. Joseph T. Shipley (tr.). 6351-9
Carol. Alison Boodson. 6379-9
Carol. William Canton. 6608-9
Carol. Kenneth Grahame. 6478-7
Carol. Louise Imogen Guiney. 6437-X
Carol. Hamish Maclaren. 6269-5
Carol. Langdon Elwyn ("John Philip Varley") Mitchell. 6608-9
Carol. Norman Nicholson. 6379-9
Carol. William Robert Rodgers. 6210-5
Carol. John Short. 6210-5
Carol ("Adam lay ybounden.") Unknown. 6179-6
Carol ("All this night shrill chanticler"). William Austin. 6563-5
A carol ("As I in a hoarie, winter's night"). Robert Southwell. 6145-X
A carol ("He came all so still"). Unknown. 6214-8
A carol ("He came all so still.") Unknown. 6627-5
Carol ("I sing of a maiden.") Unknown. 6179-6,6395-9,6489-2,6746-8
Carol ("In the bleak mid-winter.") Christina Georgina Rossetti. 6179-6
A carol ("Sweet music, sweeter far"). Edmund Bolton. 6931-2
Carol ("The ox he openeth wide the doore.") Louise Imogen Guiney. 6746-8
Carol ("There comes a ship a-sailing.") Unknown. 6179-6
Carol ("Three kings from out of the Orient"). Thomas Edward Brown. 6655-0
Carol ("Three kings..."). Thomas Edward Brown. 6809-X
A carol ("Vines branching stilly.") Louise Imogen Guiney. 6746-8
Carol ("We bring in the holly, the ivy, and the pine"). Unknown. 6268-7
Carol ("When the herds"). William Canton. 6216-4
"A carol at the end of the war", fr. A song of victory. Edwin Markham. 6051-X;6386-1;6420-5
A carol bringing in the boar's head. Unknown. 6756-5
A carol closing sixty-nine. Walt Whitman. 6753-0,6126-5, 6753-0
Carol for Candelmas day. Unknown. 6563-5
A carol for Christmas Day before dawn. Gordon Bottomley. 6532-5
A carol for Christmas Eve. Louise Abney. 6143-5
A carol for Christmas Eve. Eleanor Farjeon. 6143-5
Carol for his darling on Christmas day. Derek Stanford. 6379-9
A carol for the twelfth day. Unknown. 6806-5
A carol from Flanders. Frederick Niven. 6420-5;6443-4
Carol naive. John McClure. 6746-8

A carol of Agincourt. Unknown. 6881-2
A carol of hunting. Unknown. 6756-5
A carol of Mother Mary. Unknown. 6102-8
A carol of St. George. Unknown. 6881-2
Carol of the birds. ? Bas-Quercy. 6608-9
A carol of the birth of Christ. Unknown. 6756-5
The carol of the fir tree. Alfred Noyes. 6746-8
The carol of the poor children. Richard Middleton. 6216-4;6532-5;6602-X
Carol of the three kings. Lady Anne Lindsay. 6747-6
Carol on Corfu. Lawrence Durrell. 6339-X
The carol singer. Eleanor Farjeon. 6339-X
Carol to our lady. John Bardel. 6490-6
Carol with variations. Phyllis McGinley. 6532-5
Carol, 15th century. Unknown. 6850-2
Carol, brothers, carol. William Augustus Muhlenberg. 6608-9
Carol, carol, tenderly. Lady Anne Lindsay. 6747-6
Carol, new style. Stephen Vincent Benet. 6070-6,6746-8
Carol: A shepherd and a shepherdess. Clement Marot. 6227-X
Carol: The five joys. Unknown. 6022-6
Carol: The five joys of the virgin. Unknown. 6282-2
Carolan and Bridget Cruise. Samuel Lover. 6518-X
Carolan and Bridget Cruise. Samuel Lover. 6858-8
Carolan's prophecy. Felicia Dorothea Hemans. 6973-8
Carolan, Turlough
    The cup of O'Hara. Sir Samuel Ferguson (tr.). 6930-4
    Why, liquor of life? John D'Alton (tr.). 6930-4
Carolina. R.W. Page. 6118-4
Carolina. Henry Timrod. 6113-3,6243-1,6459-0,6465-5,6074-9
Carolina. John A. Wagner. 6074-9
Carolina spring song. Hervey Allen. 6076-5,6102-8
Caroline. Thomas Campbell. 6980-0
Caroline (pseud.)
    Farewell to brother Jonathan. 6753-0
Caroline of Edinboro town. Unknown. 6057-9,6058-7
"Caron oh caron come away." Unknown. 6563-5
Caron, Anne Aydt
    My home town. 6342-X
Carossa, Hans
    Star-song. 6643-7
Carousal. Ibn Khafaja. 6362-4
Carousal. Ibn Safar. 6362-4
Carouse. Charles Hanson Towne. 6374-8,6653-4
The carousel. Rainer Maria Rilke. 6160-5
Carpe diem. William Browne. 6189-3
Carpe diem. Sir George Etherege. 6092-7
Carpe diem. Theophile Marzials. 6656-9
Carpe diem. Richard Monckton Milnes; 1st Baron Houghton. 6383-7
Carpe diem. Hugh Orange. 6071-4
Carpe diem. William Shakespeare. 6246-6,6732-8
Carpe Diem, fr. In the early, pearly morning. Laurence (Adele Florence Nicolson) Hope. 6427-2
Carpe diem, fr. Robert, second duke of Normandy. Thomas Lodge. 6436-1
Carpenter. Leslie Savage Clark. 6144-3
The carpenter ("I wonder what he charged..."). G.A. Studdert-Kennedy. 6144-3,6335-7
The carpenter ("Silent at Joseph's side he stood"). Phyllis Hartnoll. 6144-3,6335-7,6532-5
Carpenter of eternity. E. Merrill Root. 6144-3
The carpenter of Galilee. Hilda W. Smith. 6144-3,6337-3
The carpenter of Nazareth. Walter Smith. 6144-3
The carpenter's shop. Ann ("Aunt Effie") Hawkshawe. 6018-8
Carpenter's son. Annie Johnson Flint. 6065-X
The carpenter's son. Alfred Edward Housman. 6536-8
The carpenter's son. Kathryn Blackburn Peck. 6065-X
The carpenter's young wife. Geoffrey Chaucer. 6733-6
Carpenter, Amelia Walstein
    Old Flemish lace. 6004-8
Carpenter, Audrey F.
    Thoughts of a long-legged French doll. 6249-0
Carpenter, Edward
    After civilization. 6252-0
    The age-long war, fr. Towards democracy. 7009-4
    "All night by the shore". 6997-5
    Among the ferns. 6730-1,6252-0
    Beethoven. 7014-0
    The dead comrade. 6542-2
    England, arise! 6954-1,7009-4
    Have faith. 6730-1
    I and my joy. 6320-9
    I heard the voice of the woods. 6252-0
    In the deep caves of the heart, fr. 'Towards democracy' 6954-1
    Little heart within thy cage. 6879-0
    Love's vision. 6730-1
    Over the great city. 6730-1
    Philolaus to Diocles. 6252-0
    A smith and the king. 6688-7
    The smith and the king. 7009-4
    The songs of the birds. 6730-1
    The stupid old body. 6730-1
    The wandering lunatic mind. 6730-1
    What is freedom? 7009-4
Carpenter, Henry Bernard
    The creed of love. 7041-8
    He sang out of his soul what he found there. 6066-8
    Love's infinite made finite. 7041-8
    The sense of loss. 7041-8
Carpenter, Howard
    Solar flight. 6178-8
Carpenter, J.E.
    The Gottinger barber. 6918-5
Carpenter, Lois R.
    At his feet. 6065-X
Carpenter, Mary Lydia
    A birthday wish. 6799-9
    Making faces. 6799-9
Carpenter, Maurice
    The ballad of Guy Moquet. 6895-2
    Ballad of John Nameless. 6895-2
    Ballad of Sparrow. 6895-2
    Lament for a lover. 6895-2
    Machine shop: nightshift. 6895-2
    Moonstruck. 6895-2
    1941 - bombers in May. 6895-2
    The quick of the green. 6895-2
    The roots of songs. 6895-2
    Thompson's last stand. 6895-2
    To S.T.C. on his 179th birthday, October 12th, 1951. 6210-5
    Venus on a sea horse. 6210-5
Carpenter, Myrtle B.
    Dog that never had a chance. 6715-8
    Loves his daddy best. 6715-8
Carpenter, Rhys
    The dream of the ropemaker's son. 6037-4
    Earth: the passing of a dancer. 6959-2
    The master sings. 6730-1
    Thoughts in a cathedral. 6327-6
    Who bids us sing? 6730-1
Carpenter, W. Boyd
    Three days. 6337-3
The carpenter. William H. Hamilton. 6269-5
The carpenter. Gumpei Yamamuro. 6027-7
"The carpenters of old Saint John". Unknown. 6364-0
Carpentry. Leslie Nelson Jennings. 6979-7
Carphyllides
    A happy man. Edwin Arlington Robinson (tr.). 7039-6
Carr, Agnes
    Lost pins. 6965-7
Carr, D.
    Premature. 6397-7
Carr, Elias F.
    Ode to New Jersey. 6465-5
Carr, Jessica
    Four fountains after Respighi. 6762-X
Carr, Josephine Norfolk
    Evensong. 6799-9
Carr, Laura Garland
    Something more. 6764-6
Carr, Luella Bender
    Missabe ore docks at night. 6342-X
Carr, Mary Jane
    Undaunted evergreens. 6799-9
Carr, Robert V.
    Sleepin' out. 7012-4
    To a buffalo skull. 6510-4

To a rattlesnake. 6510-4
Trail's end. 7012-4
Carr, Winifred
Prometheus. 7019-1
Carranza, Eduardo
Sunday. Donald Devenish Walsh (tr.). 6759-X
Carranza, Maria Mercedes
From Boyaca in the country. Ellen Watson (tr.). 7036-1
Heels over head with life. Mary Crow (tr.). 7036-1
Once upon a time a woman tied to a virture. Mary Crow (tr.). 7036-1
Carrera Andrade, Jorge
Anonymous speech. H.R. Hays (tr.). 6642-9
Biography. H.R. Hays (tr.). 6642-9
Biography for the use of the birds. Donald Devenish Walsh (tr.). 6759-X
Bulletin of bad weather. H.R. Hays (tr.). 6642-9
Dining-room mirror. H.R. Hays (tr.). 6642-9
Dust, corpse of time. H.R. Hays (tr.). 6642-y
Election handbill of green. H.R. Hays (tr.). 6642-9
The guest. Muna Lee (tr.). 6759-X
Hydrographic poem. H.R. Hays (tr.). 6642-9
Ill humour. Donald Devenish Walsh (tr.). 6759-X
Indian rebellion. H.R. Hays (tr.). 6642-9
It rained in the night. Muna Lee (tr.). 6759-X
Klare von Reuter. Muna Lee (tr.). 6759-X
Nameless islands. H.R. Hays (tr.). 6642-9
Nothing belongs to us. H.R. Hays (tr.). 6642-9
The perfect life. Dudley Fitts (tr.). 6759-X
Reaping the barley. Muna Lee (tr.). 6759-X
Second life of my mother. Muna Lee (tr.). 6759-X
Sierra. Muna Lee (tr.). 6759-X
Spring & co. Richard O'Connell (tr.). 6759-X
The stranger. H.R. Hays (tr.). 6642-9
Stroke of one. Muna Lee (tr.). 6759-X
Sunday. Muna Lee (tr.). 6759-X
Vocation of the mirror. Muna Lee (tr.). 6759-X
Windy weather. H.R. Hays (tr.). 6642-9
The **carriage** and couple. Unknown. 6742-5
"The **carriage** brushes through the bright". Solo for ear-trumpet. Edith Sitwell. 6884-7
Carrick. Susan L. Mitchell. 6090-0
Carrick, Alice Van Leer
Discipline. 6130-3
A question. 6130-3
A question. 6130-3
Carrickfergus. Louis MacNeice. 6930-4
Carrie Nation. Willard Wattles. 6615-1
Carrier, Constance
Colonel B. 6388-8
Party. 6388-8
Carrier, Warren
What I saw in October. 6966-5
The **carrier-dove**. James Thomson. 6943-6
The **carrier-pigeon** returned. Letitia Elizabeth ("L.E.L.") Landon. 6980-0
A **carrier-song**. Francis Thompson. 6942-8
The **carrier**. Thomas Hardy. 6102-8
Carrington, Henry (tr.)
Paraphrase of psalm 137. Bible, 6848-0
Pastoral ("Morning poured"). Colin Muset, 6025-0
Poem ("Tircis"). Jean Francois Sarrazin, 6025-0
A poet's grave. Unknown (French), 6025-0
Praise of water. Theodore de Banville, 6025-0
Pro and contra. M.A.M. Desaugiers, 6025-0
Carrington, James B.
I planted little trees to-day. 6449-3
To a lady in her furs. 6510-4
Carrion comfort. Gerard Manley Hopkins. 6378-0,6489-2,6657-

)'arrion7¢6â56r3)6638a2d6B08ley Hopkins. 6828-6
Carrion, Alejandro
A good year. Dudley Fitts (tr.). 6759-X
Carrol, Patrick J.
Lady day in Ireand. 6292-X
St. Patrick's treasure. 6292-X
Carroll, Armond
From a city street. 6327-6
Carroll, Ellen M.
Borderland. 7016-7
Deep dusk. 7016-7
Dusk-memories. 6039-0
Fertile dawn. 7016-7
June has brought loveliness to birth. 6818-9
Maturity. 7016-7
The pampered woman. 6041-2
Carroll, Jennie
How the babies grow. 6629-1
Carroll, Lewis. See Dodgson, Charles L.
Carroll, Patrick Joseph
Johneen. 6543-0
Lady day in Ireland. 6172-9
St. Patrick's treasure. 6172-9
Carroll, Ruth
Soft feathers spurned. 6750-6
Carrothers, James D.
"De black cat crossed his luck." 6120-6,6692-2
A **carrouse** to the emperor, the royal pole... Unknown. 6157-5
Carrowmore. George William ("A.E.") Russell. 6250-4,6581-3
Carruth, Hayden
Something for Richard Eberhart. 6803-0
Carruth, Lucy
My prayer. 6525-2
Carruth, William Herbert
Autumn; each in his own tongue. 6891-X
Dreamers pf dreams. 6104-4,6337-3
Each in his own tongue. 6889-8,6006-4,6076-5,6541-1, 6250-4,6107-9,6241 ,6266-0,6104-4,6309-8,6646-1,6104-4,6464 ,6303-9,6161-3,6473-6,6476-0,6509-0,6615
John Brown. 6615-1
Tescott. 6615-1
When she was born upon that Kansas hill. 6615-1
When the cannon booms no more. 6449-3,6542-2
Carry her over the water. Wystan Hugh Auden. 6210-5
Carry me back. John Holmes. 6388-8
Carry me back to old Virginny. James Bland. 6465-5
Carry on!. Robert Service. 6159-1,6337-3
'**Carry** on'. Edgar A. Guest. 7033-7
"**Carry** your sorrows to the market-place". To a sentimental poet. Helen Mullins. 6817-0
Carryin' sacks. Unknown. 6609-7
The **carrying** of a ghost. Nelson Antrim Crawford. 6034-X
Carrying their Coracles, fr. Upon Appleton house. Andrew Marvell. 6125-7
Carryl, Charles Edward
A ferry tale. 6724-7
The ferry to nowhere. 6732-8
Memorumdrums. 6724-7
My recollectest thoughts. 6902-9,6861-8
A nautical ballad. 6132-X,6497-3
The plaint of the camel. 6464-7,6458-2
The post captain. 6512-0,6089-7
Robinson Crusoe. 6307-1,6632-1
Robinson Crusoe's island. 6732-8
Robinson Crusoe's story. 6089-7,6332-2,6503-1,6512-0, 6458-2,6300-4,6505-8,6454-X
The walloping window-blind. 6722-0
Carryl, Guy Wetmore
A ballad ("As I was walkin'"). 6440-X
A ballad in the manner of R-dy-rd K-pl-ng. 6089-7
The debutante. 6266-0,6476-0,6732-8
The embarrassing episode of Little Miss Muffet. 6732-8
The garden of years, sels. 6320-9
A girl was too reckless of grammar. 6089-7
The harmonious heedlessness of Little Boy Blue. 6891-X
How a cat was annoyed and a poet was booted. 6120-6
How Jack found that beans may go back on a chap. 6026-9
The inhuman wolf and the lamb sans gene. 6026-9

Thétmècboxcbþµe.t6086-8nd the machiavelian fisherman. 6722-0
Pallas. 6117-6
A passing song. 6117-6
The singular sangfroid of baby Bunting. 6902-9
The sycophantic fox and the gullible raven. 6464-7,6300-4,6307-1
The vainglorious oak and the modest bulrush. 6861-8
When the great gray ships come in. 6473-6,6309-8
"**Cars** drawn by rainbow-winged steeds". The hours, fr.

CARS

Prometheus. Percy Bysshe Shelley. 6980-0
Carskaden, Harriet E.
   Oh would that I could fly to you. 6818-9
Carsley, Sara
   The little boats of Britain. 6224-5
Carson, Eva Lovett
   Distinquished baby. 6312-8
   The night before Thanksgiving. 6703-4
   What might happen. 6417-5
Carson, Norma Bright
   Elizabeth Barrett Browning. 6486-8
   The eyes of the Christ. 6486-8
   The man who can fight and smile. 6443-4
Carson, Paul
   Arabella and Sally Ann. 6919-3
Carson, W.E.
   Playing the bear. 6094-3
Carstairs, Carroll
   Field burial. 6818-9
Carswell, Edward
   Caw! Caw! Caw! 6314-4,6706-9
   The temperance echo. 6414-0
   What whiskey did to me. 6916-9
Cartan, Shemus
   A lament for Ireland ("I do not know of anything...")
   Augusta Gregory, Lady Gregory (tr.). 6244-X
The **carter** and his team. Unknown. 6134-6
Carter, A. Pearle
   Cape Cod memory. 6039-0
   Trees write their thoughts. 6039-0
Carter, Agnes L.
   Whenever a little child is born. 6078-1
Carter, Alice P.
   Baby's correspondence. 6672-0
Carter, Aline Badger
   Earth bows to the new bomb. 6144-3
   Give our conscience light. 6144-3
   Immortal words. 6144-3
Carter, Ann A.G.
   Nursery song. 6373-X,6452-3,6131-1,6373-X,6502-3
   The robin to his mate. 6135-4,6452-3
Carter, Bernice E.
   Prayer ("Do you do pray..."). 6894-4
Carter, Donald Copeland
   Veteran. 6839-1
Carter, Elizabeth
   Ode to wisdom. 6932-0
Carter, George
   Ballade of misery and iron. 6954-1
Carter, Herman J.D.
   Mountain in a storm. 6178-8
   Negro audience. 6178-8
   A poetess (to E.D.D.). 6178-8
   The voice of the hill. 6178-8
Carter, Laura M.
   In memoriam. 6764-6
Carter, Lin
   Carcosa. 6218-0
   Dark Yuggoth. 6218-0
   The dream-daemon. 6218-0
   Lunae custodiens. 6218-0
   The sabbat. 6218-0
Carter, Mary Ann
   Job. 6848-0
Carthusians. Ernest Dowson. 6096-X,6507-4,6292-X,6172-9
Cartier arrives at Stadacona. William Talbot Allison. 6591-0,6592-2
Cartier: dauntless discoverer. John Daniel Logan. 6115-X
Carton, Ronald Lewis
   Hereafter. 7027-2
   Reveille. 7027-2
Cartwright, Iva Temple
   Our father's care. 6818-9
Cartwright, William
   "Bid me not go where neither suns nor showers". 6187-7, 6830-8
   Celia upon her sparrow. 6943-6
   "Come, my sweet, whiles every strain". 6187-7
   The dead sparrow. 6861-8
   Drinking song. 6563-5

A good eating song. 6563-5
A house blessing. 6125-7
Lesbia on her sparrow. 6874-X
"Seal up her eyes, O sleep, but flow". 6187-7,6563-5
A song of dalliance. 6026-9,6378-0
"Tell me not of joy; there's none." 6317-9
To a lady weeping. 6328-4
To Chloe who for his sake wished herself younger. 6317-9
To Chloe who wished her self young enough for me. 6562-7,6102-8,6563-5,6153-2
To Mr. W.B. at the birth of his first child. 6378-0
Upon the dramatick poems of Mr. John Fletcher. 6933-9
A valediction ("Bid me not go where neither Suns..."). 6562-7,6563-5
A valediction. 6933-9
Carus, Helena
   There are so many ways to love him. 6039-0
Carus, Titus Lucretius
   Concerning the nature of things, sels. John Mason Good (tr.). 6482-5
Caruthers, Mazie V.
   A book of remembrance. 6750-6
   Fish-day. 6120-6
   His name was Bob. 6510-4
   Matilda's manners. 6120-6
   Matilda, matriarch. 6120-6
   Mothering. 6120-6
   Threnody for a pet cat. 6120-6
   Two Christmas saints. 6747-6
Carvalho, Ronald de
   Brazil. Dudley Poore (tr.). 6759-X
   Interior. Dudley Poore (tr.). 6759-X
   Trinidad market. Dudley Poore (tr.). 6759-X
Carved by Obadiah verity. Don Welch. 6966-5
Carved sandal-wood. Mattie Hallam Lacy. 6750-6
"Carven with curious symbol and mystic sign". An Egyptian love charm. Gertrude Huntington McGiffert. 6838-3
Carver and the caliph. Austin Dobson. 6694-1
The **carver** in stone. John Drinkwater. 6234-2
The **carver's** lesson. Adelaide Anne Procter. 6957-6
Carver, Mabel MacDonald
   Addict. 6218-0
   Semi-private. 6218-0
The **carver.** Edgar A. Guest. 6869-3
Cary Jr., Richard L.
   The fight of Lookout. 6678-X
   The new Magdalen. 6273-3
The **Cary** tree. Lucia M. Mooney. 6684-4
Cary, Alice
   Abraham Lincoln. 6524-4
   Adelied. 6969-X
   All in all. 6969-X
   Alone. 6969-X
   "Among the pitfalls in our way". 6969-X,6238-5
   "Apart from the woes that are dead and gone". 6969-X
   April. 6865-0;6969-X
   "As fire tempers the iron, so." 6225-3
   At rehearsal. 6865-0;6969-X
   At sea. 6865-0;6969-X
   At the tavern. 6060-9
   Autumn. 6865-0;6969-X
   Balder's wife. 6969-X
   Ballad of Uncle Joe. 6865-0;6969-X
   Barbara at the window. 6865-0;6969-X
   Barbara Blue. 6683-6,6683-6
   Barbara in the meadow. 6865-0;6969-X
   Be still. 6865-0;6969-X
   The best judgment. 6969-X
   Best, to the best. 6969-X
   The blackbird. 6073-0,6006-4,6309-8
   The blind traveler. 6969-X
   The bridal hour. 6969-X
   The bridal veil. 6969-X
   Buried gold. 6060-9
   The burning prairie. 6744-1,6568-6,6909-6
   Care. 6969-X
   Carmia. 6865-0;6969-X
   A child's wisdom. 6060-9
   The chopper's child. 6865-0;6969-X

A Christmas story. 6060-9
Comfort. 6969-X
A confession. 6865-0;6969-X
Consolation. 6969-X
Contradiction. 6865-0;6969-X
Contradictory. 6969-X
Cottage and hall. 6865-0;6969-X
Counsel ("Seek not"). 6969-X
Counsel ("Though sin"). 6969-X
Cradle song. 6865-0;6969-X,6969-X
Crags. 6969-X
Crazy Christopher. 6969-X
Damaris. 6865-0;6969-X
Dan and Dimple and how they quarreled. 6060-9
The daughter. 6969-X
The dawn of peace. 6969-X
Dead and alive. 6969-X
The dead-house. 6865-0;6969-X
"Do not look for wrong and evil". 6969-X
The double skein. 6865-0;6969-X
A dream of home. 6969-X
A dream. 6969-X
Dreams. 6865-0;6969-X
A dying hymn. 6240-7,6385-3,6407-8,6007-2,6969-X
Easter bridal song. 6720-4
The edge of doom. 6865-0;6969-X
An emblem. 6865-0;6969-X
Enchantments. 6385-3
Epithalamium. 6865-0;6969-X
Evening pastimes. 6969-X
Extremities. 6969-X
A fable of cloud-land. 6865-0;6969-X
Faded leaves. 6969-X
Fairy folk. 6546-6,6060-9
The fairy of them dell. 6673-9
Faith and works. 6407-8,6969-X
Faithless. 6969-X
Fame. 6865-0;6969-X
The farmer's daughter. 6969-X
The felled tree. 6969-X
The ferry of Gallaway. 6969-X
The field sweet-brier. 6969-X
Fifteen and fifty. 6969-X
The fire by the sea. 6385-3
The fisherman's wife. 6572-4
The flax-beater. 6865-0;6969-X
The flower spider. 6060-9
For self-help. 6969-X
Forgiveness. 6865-0;6969-X
A fragment ("It was a sandy..."). 6865-0;6969-X
Genius. 6865-0;6969-X
"The glance that doth my neighbor doubt". 6969-X
God is love. 6969-X
Going to court. 6865-0;6969-X
The golden mean. 6969-X
Good and evil. 6969-X
A good rule. 6060-9
"The grace wife of Keith'. 6969-X
The grateful swan. 6060-9
The gray swan. 6127-3,6406-X,6239-3,6497-3,6964-9
The great question. 6969-X
Growing rich. 6969-X
Hagen Walder. 6969-X
"He spoils his house and throws his pains away". 6969-X
The heaven that's here. 6969-X
Her last poem. 6600-3
Her last verses. 6219-9
Her mother, fr. An order for a picture. 6097-8
Here and there. 6969-X
Hide and seek. 6060-9
Hints. 6969-X
"Hope in our hearts doth only stay". 6969-X
How and where. 6969-X
"How dreary would the garden be" 6049-8
How peace came. 6865-0;6969-X
Hugh Thorndyke. 6969-X
I hear a dear, familiar tone. 6066-8
Idle. 6969-X
Idle fears. 6969-X
If and if. 6969-X

In bonds. 6865-0;6969-X
In despair. 6969-X
In the dark (1). 6969-X
In the dark (2). 6969-X
In vain. 6969-X
An inavlid's plea. 6969-X
Intimations. 6865-0;6969-X
Invocation. 6969-X
January. 6969-X
Jennie. 6865-0;6969-X
Jenny Dunleath. 6411-6
Johnny Right. 6969-X
Jottings for sportsmen. 6861-8
Katrina on the porch. 6865-0;6969-X
Krumley. 6600-3
The lady to the lover. 6865-0;6969-X
Last and best. 6969-X
Latent life. 6969-X
The law of liberty. 6969-X
The leak in the dyke. 6267-9
A lesson (1). 6865-0;6969-X
A lesson (2). 6969-X
A lesson of mercy. 6060-9,6456-6
Life. 6865-0;6969-X
Life of life. 6969-X
Life's mysteries. 6969-X
Life's mysteries, sels. 6066-8
Life's mystery. 6969-X
Life's roses. 6865-0;6969-X
Light. 6865-0;6969-X
Light and darkness. 6969-X
The light of days gone by. 6969-X
The little blacksmith. 6969-X
The little brother. 6127-3
Little children. 6060-9
Little Cyrus. 6969-X
The little house on the hill. 6969-X
The living present. 6969-X
Look for the best. 6523-6
Lost lilies. 6969-X
Love is life. 6969-X
Love! blessed love! if we could hang our walls. 6066-8
Love's light is strange to you? Ah me! 6066-8
Love's secret springs. 6865-0;6969-X
The lover's interdict. 6969-X
Lyric. 6969-X
Maid and man. 6865-0;6969-X
Make believe. 6385-3,6441-8,6527-9,6060-9
Man:In what a kingly fashion man doth dwell. 6969-X
The measure of time. 6969-X
Mercies. 6969-X
The might of love. 6912-6,6167-2
The might of truth. 6969-X
The mines of Avondale. 6865-0;6969-X
Miriam. 6865-0;6969-X
More life. 6969-X
Morning. 6969-X
Morning in the mountains. 6969-X
Most beloved. 6969-X
The mother fairie. 6060-9
A mother's picture. 6365-9
Mourn not. 6969-X
My creed. 6014-5,6406-X,6418-3,6632-1,6730-1
My darlings (1). 6772-7,6969-X
My darlings (2). 6969-X
My dream of dreams. 6865-0;6969-X
My faded shawl. 6969-X
My good angel. 6969-X
My picture. 6969-X
My poet. 6865-0;6969-X
Mysteries. 6969-X
No ring. 6865-0;6969-X
Nobility. 6304-7,6260-1
The noble life. 6337-3,6461-2
Not now. 6969-X
November. 6060-9,6132-X,6373-X
Now and then. 6865-0;6969-X
A nut hard to crack. 6060-9
O winds! ye are too rough, too rough. 6066-8
Occasional. 6969-X

Old Adam. 6969-X
Old chums. 6739-5,6344-6,6406-X
The old homestead. 6865-0;6969-X
The old house. 6969-X
Old maxims. 6060-9
The old story. 6969-X
On seeing a drowning moth. 6969-X
On seeing a wild bird. 6969-X
On the sea. 6865-0;6969-X
One dust. 6969-X
One moment. 6865-0;6969-X
One of many (1). 6865-0;6969-X
One of many (2). 6969-X
Open secrets. 6969-X
An order for a picture, sels. 6097-8
An order for a picture. 6407-8,6486-8,6344-6,6392-6, 6385-3,6053-6,6304-7,6431-0,6451-5,6457-7,6497
The other side. 6865-0;6969-X
"Our God is love, and that which we miscall". 6969-X
Our school-master. 6969-X
"Our unwise purposes are wisely crossed". 6969-X
Parting song. 6969-X
A penitent's plea. 6969-X
Peter Grey. 6969-X,6060-9
The picture-book. 6969-X
Pictures of memory. 6014-5,6093-5,6141-9,6142-7,6240-7, 6302-9,6392-6,6486-8
The pig and the hen. 6456-6
Pitiless faith. 6865-0;6969-X
Pitiless fate. 6969-X
Plea for charity. 6865-0;6969-X
Pleasure and pain. 6969-X
Pledges. 6865-0;6969-X
Poppies. 6865-0;6969-X
A prayer ("I have been little"). 6303-9,6969-X
Prayer for light. 6969-X
Prodigal's plea. 6865-0;6969-X
Proverbs in rhyme. 6865-0;6969-X
Providence. 6969-X
The pure in heart. 6969-X
Putting off, the armor. 6969-X
Queen of roses. 6865-0;6969-X
Receipt for an appetite. 6060-9
Remember. 6969-X
Revolutionary story. 6969-X
Rich, though poor. 6969-X
The rustic painter. 6969-X
Ruth and I. 6969-X
The saddest sight. 6969-X
Safe. 6865-0;6969-X
Sandt Macleod. 6969-X
Saved. 6865-0;6969-X
A sea song (1). 6865-0;6969-X
A sea song (2). 6969-X
The sea-side cave. 6969-X
The seal-fisher's wife. 6865-0;6969-X
Second sight. 6865-0;6969-X
Secret writing. 6865-0;6969-X
Selfish sorrow. 6865-0;6969-X
A sermon for young folks. 6060-9
Sermons in stones. 6969-X
The settler's Christmas eve. 6969-X
The shadow (1). 6865-0;6969-X
The shadow (2). 6969-X
Shadows. 6865-0;6969-X
The shoemaker. 6969-X
A short sermon. 6060-9
Signs of grace. 6969-X
Sixteen. 6969-X
Snowed under. 6865-0;6969-X
"Some days must needs be full of gloom". 6109-5
Sometimes. 6969-X,6008-0
The special darling. 6969-X
Spent and misspent. 6969-X
Spider and fly. 6060-9
A spinster's stint. 6302-0,6385-3,6006-4
"Still from the unsatisfying quest". 6969-X
Story of a blackbird. 6060-9
The stream of life. 6969-X
Stroller's song. 6969-X

Substance. 6969-X
The summer storm. 6969-X
Sunday morning. 6969-X
Supplication. 6865-0;6969-X
Suppose. 6060-9,6373-X
Sure anchor. 6969-X
The sure witness. 6600-3
The sweetest picture. 6575-9
Take care. 6060-9,6629-1
Telling fortunes. 6060-9
Text and moral. 6865-0;6969-X
"Thank God there is always a light whence to borrow." 6225-3
Thanksgiving. 6969-X
This is all. 6969-X
The thistle flower. 6969-X
Thorns. 6969-X
Three bugs. 6060-9
Three little bugs. 6135-4
Time. 6969-X
The time to be. 6049-8
To a honey-bee. 6060-9
To a stagnant river. 6969-X
To mother fairie. 6132-X,6466-3
To my friend. 6865-0;6969-X
To solitude. 6969-X
To the desponding. 6575-9
To the muse. 6865-0;6969-X
To the wind. 6969-X
"Too much of joy is sorrowful". 6969-X
Tricksey's ring. 6683-6
"True worth is in being, not seeming". 6109-5,6238-5
Trust (1). 6865-0;6969-X
Trust (2). 6969-X
Two travelers. 6969-X
Uncle Jo. 6385-3
The uncut leaf. 6969-X
Under the shadow. 6969-X
Unsatisfied. 6969-X
The unwise choice. 6066-8
Vanished. 6865-0;6969-X
The victory of Perry. 6412-4
Wait. 6969-X
Waiting. 6865-0;6969-X
Waiting for something to turn up. 6060-9
A walk through the snow. 6969-X
The washerwoman. 6969-X
The water-bearer. 6969-X
"We are the mariners, and God the sea". 6969-X
The weaver's dream. 6969-X
The west country. 6865-0;6969-X
What a bird taught. 6060-9
"What comfort, when with clouds of woe". 6969-X
What to look for. 6529-5
Whither. 6969-X
"Why should our spirits be opprest". 6969-X
The window just over the street. 6865-0;6969-X
Winter and summer. 6865-0;6969-X
A wintery waste. 6865-0;6969-X
The wise fairy. 6060-9
A wonder. 6969-X
Work. 6456-6
Written on the Fourth of July, 1864. 6865-0;6969-X
The young soldier. 6969-X

Cary, Alice Louise
The master's touch. 6799-9
Rejuvenation. 6799-9

Cary, Henry F. (tr.)
"The fairest thing in mortal eyes." Charles, Duc d' Orleans, 6302-0;6385-3;6271-7
Paradise, sels. Dante Alighieri, 6428-0
Purgatory, sels. Dante Alighieri, 6428-0
Sonnet ("Two flowers"). Pierre de Ronsard, 6545-7
The sweet month of April. Remy Belleau, 6545-7

Cary, Patrick
Hymn. 6943-6

Cary, Phoebe
Ajax. 6060-9
Alas! 6735-2,6969-X,6309-8
Amy's love-letter. 6969-X

Answered. 6969-X,6461-2
Apology. 6969-X
An April welcome. 6865-0;6969-X
Archie. 6969-X
Arthur's wife. 6969-X
Baby's ring. 6060-9
The baby, fr. Dovecote mill. 6865-0;6969-X
A ballad of Lauderdale. 6865-0;6969-X
Ballad of the canal. 6089-7,6724-7
'The barefoot boy'. 6969-X
Beyond. 6969-X
Black Ranald. 6566-X
The book of nature. 6969-X
Border-land. 6969-X
Breaking the roads. 6865-0;6969-X
A canticle. 6865-0;6969-X
The chicken's mistake. 6314-4,6060-9,6373-X,6456-6
The chords of love must be strong as death. 6066-8
Christmas. 6969-X
Christmas (2). 6969-X
The Christmas sheaf. 6969-X
Coming home. 6969-X
Coming round. 6969-X,6412-4
Compensation. 6969-X
Complaint. 6969-X
The country grave-yard, fr. Dovecote mill. 6865-0;6969-X
Cowper's consolation. 6969-X
The crow's children. 6060-9,6714-X,6127-3,6131-1
The cry of the heart and flesh. 6865-0;6969-X
A cry of the heart. 6865-0;6969-X
Dappledun. 6060-9
A day dream. 6969-X
"The day is done". 6802-2,6440-X,6089-7
Dead love. 6969-X
Dickens. 6865-0,6969-X
Disenchanted. 6969-X
Do you blame her? 6969-X
Don't give up. 6060-9,6183-4,6456-6
Dorothy's dower. 6865-0;6969-X
Dovecott mill. 6865-0;6969-X
Doves' eyes. 6969-X
Drawing water. 6969-X
Dreams and realities. 6865-0;6969-X,6385-3
Dreams and realities, sels. 6337-3
Earth to earth. 6969-X,6639-9
The earthly house. 6865-0;6969-X
Easy lessons. 6060-9
Ebb-tide. 6969-X
Edgar's wife. 6865-0;6969-X
Effie's reasons. 6060-9
Enchantment. 6969-X
The envious wren. 6060-9
Equality. 6969-X
Fair Eleanor. 6865-0;6969-X
Faith. 6865-0;6969-X
Faithful. 6865-0;6969-X
Favored. 6969-X
Feathers. 6060-9
The fickle day. 6865-0;6969-X
'Field preaching'. 6969-X,6600-3
Figs of thistles. 6969-X
The fire by the sea. 6001-3
The fortune in the daisy. 6865-0;6969-X
The gardener's home, fr. Dovecote mill. 6865-0;6969-X
Garibaldi in Piedmont. 6969-X
Gathering blackberries. 6969-X
A good day. 6969-X
The good little sister. 6060-9
Gracie. 6969-X
Griselda goose. 6060-9
The happy little wife. 6060-9
Happy women. 6969-X,6006-4
The harmless luxury. 6969-X
He didn't think. 6529-5
The heir. 6865-0;6969-X
Helpless. 6865-0;6969-X
The hero of Fort Wagner. 6969-X
Hidden sorrow. 6969-X
Hives and homes. 6060-9

Homesick. 6969-X
The homestead, fr. Dovecote mill. 6865-0;6969-X
Human and divine. 6969-X
The hunchback. 6060-9
The hunter's wife. 6969-X
Hymn ("Come down, O Lord..."). 6865-0;6969-X
Hymn ("How dare I..."). 6969-X
Hymn ("When the world..."). 6865-0;6969-X
I cannot tell. 6969-X
"I know not which I love the most" 6049-8
I remember, I remember. 6440-X,6652-6
Impatience. 6969-X
In absence. 6969-X
In extremity. 6969-X
In his arms. 6865-0;6969-X
Inconstancy. 6865-0;6969-X
"It rests my weary aching eyes." 6225-3
Jacob. 6089-7,6440-X
Jealousy. 6969-X
Jennie. 6969-X
John Brown. 6969-X
John Greenleaf Whittier. 6969-X,6820-0
John Thompson's daughter. 6089-7,6440-X,6964-9
Kate Ketchem. 6406-X
Keep a stiff upper lip. 6060-9
The king's jewels. 6865-0;6969-X
The Lady Jacqueline. 6969-X
Lady Marjory. 6969-X
The lamp on the prairie. 6969-X
The landlord of "The blue hen". 6410-8
The last act. 6969-X
The last bed. 6969-X
The leak in the dike. 6451-5,6614-3,6569-4,6865-0,6969-X
A legend of the northland. 6135-4,6964-9,6060-9
Life may to you bring every good. 6066-8
Light. 6969-X
Little Gottlieb. 6638-0
Little Gottlieb's Christmas. 6574-0
Living by faith. 6969-X
Loss and gain. 6969-X
Love cannot die. 6865-0;6969-X
Love's recompense. 6969-X
Lovers and sweethearts. 6969-X
The lovers. 6240-7,6385-3
Many mansions. 6969-X
March crocuses. 6969-X
The marriage of Sir John Smith. 6440-X
"May you never, never have to say." 6225-3
Memorial. 6969-X
The mill, fr. Dovecote mill. 6865-0;6969-X
A monkish legend. 6969-X
Morning and afternoon. 6969-X
Mother and son. 6097-8,6627-5
Mother and son. 6969-X
My friend. 6969-X
My helper. 6865-0;6969-X
My lady. 6969-X
My neighbor's house. 6865-0;6969-X
My riches. 6969-X
Nearer home. 6006-4,6121-4,6219-9,6309-8,6575-9,6730 ,
    6240-7,6303-9,6385-3,6404-3,6481-7,6486 ,6600-3,6632-
    1,6392-6,6732-8,6735-2,6964 ,6969-X
Nobody's child. 6969-X
Nora's charm. 6060-9
Now. 6060-9
Obedience. 6456-6,6060-9,6183-4,6466-3
Of one flesh. 6865-0;6969-X
The old man's darling. 6969-X
Old pictures. 6969-X
On the river. 6865-0;6969-X
One sweetly solemn thought. 6706-9
The only ornament. 6969-X
Otway. 6969-X
Our good president. 6969-X
Our good president. 6524-4
Our heroes. 6580-5
Our homestead. 6127-3,6964-9,6969-X
Our pattern. 6865-0;6969-X
Our sun hath gone down. 6305-5

Over-payment. 6969-X
Passing feet. 6969-X
Peace. 6969-X,6946-0
Peccavi. 6969-X
A picture. 6865-0;6969-X
The playmates, fr. Dovecote mill. 6865-0;6969-X
The playmates. 6969-X
Plighted, fr. Dovecote mill. 6865-0;6969-X
Poor Margaret. 6969-X
Prairie on fire. 6060-9
The prairie on fire. 6969-X
A prayer ("I ask not wealth..."). 6969-X
The prize. 6969-X
Prodigals. 6969-X
Providence. 6865-0;6969-X
A psalm of life. 6440-X
Psalm of marriage. 6155-9,6403-5,6155-9
Rain and sunshine. 6060-9
Ready. 6442-6,6470-2,6062-5,6113-3,6552-X,6016-2
Ready. 6969-X
Realities. 6865-0;6969-X
Reconciled. 6969-X
Retrospect. 6969-X
Reuben. 6089-7
The robin's nest. 6060-9
The rose. 6969-X
St. Bernard of Clairvaux. 6969-X
Saint Macarius of the desert. 6865-0;6969-X
Samuel Brown. 6440-X
The schoo, fr. Dovecote mill. 6865-0;6969-X
The shadow. 6969-X
The sinner at the cross. 6865-0;6969-X
Somebody's lovers. 6969-X
Song ("I see him..."). 6969-X
Song ("Laugh out..."). 6969-X
The spiritual body. 6969-X
Spring after the war. 6969-X
Spring flowers. 6969-X
Sugar-makers, fr. Dovecote mill. 6865-0;6969-X
Sugar-making. 6969-X
Sunset. 6969-X
Suppose. 6706-9,6743-3,6060-9,6131-1
Teach us to wait! 6865-0;6969-X
A tent scene. 6969-X
Thaddeus Stevens. 6865-0,6969-X,6946-0
Thanksgiving. 6618-6
That calf. 6743-3
That calf! 6131-1,6167-2
"That very time I saw (but thou couldst not)". 6802-2
Theodora. 6969-X
There's a bower of bean-vines. 6089-7,6440-X
They didn't think. 6060-9,6530-9,6373-X,6131-1
This happy day. 6747-6
Thou and I. 6969-X
Thou knowest. 6969-X
Three bugs. 6183-4,6456-6
The three wrens. 6865-0;6969-X
To an elf on a buttercup. 6865-0;6969-X
To the children. 6060-9
Too late. 6969-X
Tried and true. 6969-X
True love. 6969-X
True love. 6620-8,6066-8
Twice smitten. 6969-X
Unbelief. 6865-0;6969-X
The unhonored. 6969-X
Up and down. 6969-X
Vain repentance. 6969-X
Via crucis, via lucis. 6865-0;6969-X
The vision of the mount. 6865-0;6969-X
Waiting the change. 6060-9
A weary heart. 6969-X
Wedded, fr. Dovecote mill. 6865-0;6969-X
What the frogs sing. 6060-9
When lovely woman. 6089-7,6280-6,6440-X,6441-8,6289-X
"Why are we so impatient of delay". 6238-5
The widow's thanksgiving. 6865-0;6969-X
The wife's Christmas. 6969-X
The wife, fr. Dovecote mill. 6865-0;6969-X
The wife. 6089-7

Winter flowers. 6969-X
A woman's answer. 6969-X
A woman's conclusions. 6969-X
Women. 6969-X
Wooed and won. 6969-X
Wooing, fr. Dovecote mill. 6865-0;6969-X
Wounded. 6865-0;6969-X
Ye did it unto me. 6865-0;6969-X
Youth and maiden, fr. Dovecote mill. 6865-0;6969-X
Cary, Robert
Vetal Guerin, voyageur. 6342-X
Cary, Thomas
On his mistress crossing the sea. 6563-5
On his mistresse going to sea. 6933-9
Cary; Lord Falkland, Lucius
Ben Jonson's commonplace book. 6385-3
'Casa Guidi windows'. Bayard Taylor. 6976-2
Casa Guidi windows, sels. Elizabeth Barrett Browning. 6832-4
Casa Guidi windows, sels. Elizabeth Barrett Browning. 6123-0,6479-5,6484-1,6656-9,6543-0
Casa Wappy. David Macbeth Moir. 6302-0,6385-3,6219-9
Casa's dirge. David Macbeth Moir. 6086-2
Casa, Della
Venice. Felicia Dorothea Hemans (tr.). 6973-8
Casabianca. Felicia Dorothea Hemans. 6133-8,6211-3,6271-7, 6459-0,6496-5,6502 ,6302-0,6404-3,6267-9,6263-6,6219-9,6322 ,6459-0,6102-8,6424-8,6639-9,6479-5,6134-6, 6602-2,6732-8,6527-9,6623
Casabona, Virginia Richards
Dearth. 6799-9
Casal, Julian de
The friar. 6543-0
Casapit, David
Dance for me. 6899-5
The cascade. Edgell Rickword. 6210-5
The case altered. Unknown. 6878-2,6787-5
Case history. Arthur W. Bell. 6722-0
The case is altered, sels. Ben Jonson. 6317-9
"The case it was this: there was tried...". Regina v. Gallars. Unknown. 6878-2
A case of highway robbery. J.G. Francis. 6786-7
A case of libel. Thomas Moore. 6878-2
A case of pedigree. Unknown. 6921-5
Case, Elizabeth York
The empty nest. 6565-1
Fairy land. 6569-4
Faith and reason. 6568-6
Southland. 6569-4
There is no unbelief. 6730-1
Unbelief. 6303-9,6337-3
Case, Josephine Young
London bells. 6761-1
Case, Laura U.
The fatal glass. 6912-6
Case, Lizzie York
Faith and reason. 6913-4
Case, Mrs. L.J.B.
Joan of Arc in prison. 6672-0
Case, Phila H.
Nobody's child. 6565-1,6964-9,6554-6
Casement, Sir Roger
Hamilcar Barca. 6096 X
Lost youth. 6292-X
Casements. Isabel Fiske Conant. 6076-5,6102-8
Casey at the bat. Ernest Lawrence Thayer. 6107-9,6723-9, 6736-0,6083-8,6527-9,6247-3,6277-6,6089-7,6274 ,6451-5,6534-1,6583-X,6732-8,6281-4,6307
Casey Jones. Unknown. 6732-8,6003-X,6281-4
Casey's little boy. Nixon Waterman. 6687-9
Casey's revenge. James Wilson. 6963-0
Casey's tabble dote. Eugene Field. 6694-1
Casey, D.A.
The spouse of Christ. 6172-9,6292-X,6285-7
Casey, John Keegan
Donal Kenny. 6090-0
Gracie Og Machree. 6873-1
Maire my girl. 6292-X
Maire, my girl. 6930-4
The rising of the moon A.D. 1798 6930-4

'Cash.'. Unknown. 6247-4
Cashel of Munster. William English. 6930-4
Cashel of Munster. Sir Samuel Ferguson. 6437-X
Cashel of munster. Unknown. 6244-X
Cashel of Munster. Edward Walsh. 6090-0
Casiano, Americo
    Car six. 6898-7
    "Deseo" 6898-7
    March nine. 6898-7
    Para Sonia. 6898-7
Casimir the Great; King of Poland
    "It kindles my soul." 6385-3
Th casket of Pandora. Marya Alexandrovna Zaturenska. 6389-6
The casket of Pandora. Marya Alexandrovna Zaturenska. 6761-1
The casket scene, fr. The merchant of Venice. William Shakespeare. 6677-1
A casket song, fr. Merchant of Venice. William Shakespeare. 6436-1
The casket songs, sels. Edmund Beale Sargant. 6234-2
The casket. Walter Savage Landor. 6874-X
The casket. Nathaniel Wanley. 6563-5
Caskey, Jessie Jane
    To the land of sleep. 6799-9
Caskey, Margaret
    I like words. 6488-4
Caskin, Lida P.
    Playing school. 6166-4
Casler, Meda G.
    Fog horns on Lake Superior. 6342-X
The casquettes, sels. Algernon Charles Swinburne. 6046-3
Cass Jr., M.M.
    Mamma's flower. 6629-1
Cass, Beryl
    Moon lady. 6764-6
    Poetry. 6764-6
    To a firelog. 6764-6
Cass, Josephine A.
    In Arcadie. 6084-6
Cassamen and Dowsabell. Michael Drayton. 6436-1,6191-5
Cassandra. Louise Bogan. 7038-8
Cassandra. Hilda ("H.D.") Doolittle. 6037-4
Cassandra. Robinson Jeffers. 6666-6
Cassandra. Edwin Arlington Robinson. 6474-4,6029-3
Cassandra Southwick. John Greenleaf Whittier. 6946-0
Cassandra Southwick. John Greenleaf Whittier. 6126-5,6288-1
Cassandre. Victor Hugo. 6801-4
Cassauria, E.L.
    Among the names. 6097-8
Cassels, Walter R.
    Love took me softly by the hand. 6066-8
Cassie, Bettie Margot
    From Mount Mansfield. 6750-6
    New England. 7030-2
Cassius. William Shakespeare. 6438-8
Cassius against Caesar. William Shakespeare. 6294-6,6407-8, 6521-X,6566-X
Cassius to Brutus. William Shakespeare. 6424-8
Casson, Herbert N.
    Zionism. 6848-0
"Cast aside dull books and thought". Invitation to the dance. Unknown. 6959-2
"Cast away those silkne clouds." Unknown. 6563-5
Cast down, but not destroyed. Unknown. 6946-0
"Cast in a rugged shape, an iron mould". Oom Paul. Denys Lefebvre. 6800-6
"Cast not the eye of scorn on humble things". The toolhouse, fr. The homestead. Gertrude Huntington McGiffert. 6838-3
Cast off all doubtful care. Unknown. 6756-5
"Cast off your dreams of gain and enterprise". Admonition to youth. Melba Williams. 6906-1
"Cast the window wider, sonny". The veld. Perceval Gibbon. 6800-6
Cast thy bread upon the waters, fr. Ecclesiastes. Bible. 7039-6
Cast your caps and cares away. John Fletcher. 6328-4
Cast your cares on God, fr. Enoch Arden. Alfred Lord Tennyson. 6337-3
Cast-off garments, fr. Nothing to wear. William Allen Butler. 6064-1
Castano, Wilfredo Q.
    Old times. 6998-3
    To people who pick food. 6998-3
Castara. William Habington. 6271-7,6302-0,6385-5,6219-9
The castaway. William Cowper. 6198-2,6645-3,6378-0,6604-6, 6641-0,6195 ,6208-3,6150-8,6430-2,6152-4,6086-2,6660 ,6371-3,6543-0
The Castellano captains. John Maher Murphy. 6839-1
Castellanos, Rosario
    Empty house. Maureen Ahern (tr.). 7036-1
    Home economics. Maureen Ahern (tr.). 7036-1
    Malinche. Maureen Ahern (tr.). 7036-1
    Silence near an ancient stone. Maureen Ahern (tr.). 7036-1
Castello. Agnes Mary F. ("Madame Duclaux") Robinson. 6872-3
Castellon, Blanca Lopez (tr.)
    April. Jaime Torres Bodet, 6759-X
    Deep sleep. Gabriela (Lucila Godoy Alcayaga) Mistral, 6759-X
    Elegy to the lost and already blurred by time. Xavier Abril, 6759-X
    God wills it. Gabriela (Lucila Godoy Alcayaga) Mistral, 6759-X
    Indian girl. Emilio Vasquez, 6759-X
Castilian. Elinor Wylie. 6331-4,6619-4,6036-6,6375-6,6631-3
Castilla, Ethel
    An Australian girl. 6656-9
    "She has a beauty of her own". 6768-9
Castillejo, Cristobal de
    Some day, some day. Henry Wadsworth Longfellow (tr.). 7039-6,6879-0
Casting all your care upon God, for he careth for you. Thomas Washbourne. 6931-2
Castle and cottage. Anna Maria Lenngren. 6045-5
The castle by the sea. Johann Ludwig Uhland. 6648-8
The castle by the sea. Johann Ludwig Uhland. 6271-7
The castle by the sea. Johann Ludwig Uhland. 6948-7
The castle by the sea. Unknown. 6061-7
Castle Gordon. Robert Burns. 6328-4
A castle in the air. C. Frisbie. 6752-2
A castle in the air. Adelaide Anne Procter. 6957-6
The castle in the air. Thomas Paine. 6385-3
The castle in the air. Richard Henry Stoddard. 6066-8,6430-2
The castle of Chillon. Letitia Elizabeth ("L.E.L.") Landon. 6749-2
The castle of friendship. Joseph Morris. 6085-4
The castle of indolence, sel. James Thomson. 6958-4
Castle of indolence, sels. James Thomson. 6289-X,6122-2, 6600-3,6102-8,6198-2,6301
The castle of indolence. James Thomson. 6024-2,6543-0,6152-4,6195-0
The castle of King Macbeth. Owen (Edward Bulwer-Lytton, Earl Lytton) Meredith. 6980-0
The castle of Norham. Sir Walter Scott. 6543-0
The castle ruins. William Barnes. 6656-9
"A castle stands in Yorkshire". The sword of Arthur. John Clair Minot. 6762-X
Castle, Horace
    My lyre. 6836-7
Castle, Mabel Wing
    Flame from ice. 6316-0
    Night sketch. 6316-0
    Silhouettes of sound. 6316-0
The castle-builder.. Jean de La Fontaine. 6105-2
The castle. Michael Roberts. 6354-3
Castlebar. Leslie Norton Jennings. 6880-4
The castled crag of Drachenfels. George Gordon, 6th Baron Byron. 6383-7
Castlehyde. Unknown. 6930-4
Castles in Spain. Henry Wadsworth Longfellow. 6331-4,6439-6,6631-3
Castles in the air. James Ballantyne. 6127-3,6131-1,6219-9
Castles in the air. William J. Lampton. 6274-1
Castles in the air. Unknown. 6530-9

CASTLES

"Castles with lofty". Soldier's song, fr. Faust. Johann Wolfgang von Goethe. 6976-2
Castor and Polydeuces. Alcaeus. 6435-3
Castor and Polydeuces. Pindar. 6435-3
Castor and Polydeukes. Pindar. 6084-6
Castor oil. Edgar A. Guest. 6548-1
Castro Z., Oscar
    Responsory for Garcia Lorca. Dudley Fitts (tr.). 6759-X
A casual song. Roden Noel. 6873-1
Casual suggestion. Robert E. Brittain. 6397-7
Casually this cup. Grace Strickler Dawson. 6042-0
Casualties. Wilfred Wilson Gibson. 6653-4
Casualty. Robert Nichols. 7029-9
Casualty. Edwin McNeill Poteat. 6337-3
The casualty clearing station. Gilbert Waterhouse. 7026-4, 6650-X
Casualty list. Henry Lamont Simpson. 6650-X
A casualty list. Mary Carolyn Davies. 6032-3
The casualty list. W. L. 7031-0
A casualty. Robert Service. 6159-1
Caswall, Edward
    Come, wandering sheep. 6065-X
    Sleep, holy babe. 6747-6
    "Sleep, holy babe". 6065-X
Caswall, Edward (tr.)
    Jesus the very thought of thee. Saint Bernard of Clairvaux (atr). 6337-3
    "Light of the soul". Unknown, 6065-X
    Morning hymn. Saint Gregory the Great, 6730-1
    "My God, I love thee." Saint Francis Xavier, 6302-0, 6385-3,6271-7,6337-3
    When the morning gilds the skies. Unknown (German), 6337-3
Caswallon's triumph. Felicia Dorothea Hemans. 6973-8
Caswell, Carri
    Friends. 6883-9
Cat and lady. Paul Verlaine. 6511-2
Cat and mouse. Unknown. 6692-2
The cat and northern lights. Elizabeth J. Coatsworth. 6120-6
"A cat and raven quarreled once". The cat, the raven, and the public. William Ellery Leonard. 6887-1
The cat and the bird and I. Henry Johnson. 6552-X
The cat and the bird. George Canning. 6125-7
The cat and the bird. Marvin Solomon. 6388-8
The cat and the bird. Unknown. 6529-5
The cat and the broom. A.A. Kenny. 6804-9
The cat and the cream. J.G. Francis. 6786-7
The cat and the fox. Jean de La Fontaine. 6511-2
The cat and the man. Oliver Edwards. 6511-2
The cat and the moon. William Butler Yeats. 6354-3,6511-2
The cat and the partridge. Damocharis the Grammarian. 6511-2
Cat calls, sels. Comte Robert de Montesquiou. 6351-9
"A cat came fiddling out of a barn". Mother Goose. 6363-2, 6452-3,6699-2
A cataracket.
The cat changed into a woman. Jean de La Fontaine. 6120-6
Cat convention. Edna A. Foster. 6692-2
The cat eater. Unknown. 6410-8
A cat law-suit. Unknown. 6692-2
Cat of cats. Vivien Bulkley. 6511-2
The cat of cats, fr. The White Princess. William Brighty Rands. 6120-6
The cat of Hindustan. Unknown. 6699-2
Cat or stomp. Laura Tohe. 7005-1
"A cat sat quaintly by the fire". Hearth. Peggy Bacon. 6891-X
Cat tails. Annie Weston Whitney. 6565-1
The cat that came to school. Unknown. 6699-2
A cat to her kittens. Eliza Grove. 6459-0
The cat's bath. Unknown. 6744-1,6167-2
A cat's birthday celebration. Gertrude Manly Jones. 6699-2
The cat's cleanliness, fr. The nature of the cat. Edward Verrall Lucas. 6018-8
The cat's conscience, fr. The nature of the cat. Edward Verrall Lucas. 6018-8,6120-6
A cat's conscience. Unknown. 6120-6
The cat's cruelty, fr. The nature of the cat. Edward Verrall Lucas. 6018-8
The cat's friends, fr. The nature of the cat. Edward Verrall Lucas. 6018-8
The cat's greediness, fr. The nature of the cat. Edward Verrall Lucas. 6018-8
Cat's meat. Harold Monro. 6228-8,6354-7,6511-2
The cat's sleeplessness, fr. The nature of the cat. Edward Verrall Lucas. 6018-8
The cat's tea party. Frederic Edward Weatherley. 6105-2, 6242-3
Cat's Thanksgiving Day. Unknown. 6699-2,6131-1
Cat's world. Bernice Lesbia Kenyon. 6120-6
Cat's-meat man; or, cupboard love. Unknown. 6699-2
The cat, fr. Jubilate Agno. Christopher Smart. 6545-7
The cat, fr. Rejoice in the lamb. Christopher Smart. 6106-0,6511-2
The cat, the raven, and the public. William Ellery Leonard. 6887-1
Cat-egorical courtship. Unknown. 6692-2
Cat-life. Lucy Larcom. 6699-2
The cat-o'-nine-tails. J.G. Francis. 6786-7
The cat-o-nine-tails.. John Blight. 6384-5
Cat-questions. Lucy Larcom. 6129-X
Cat-tails. Unknown. 6684-4
A cat. Jules Lemaitre. 6120-6
A cat. Edward Thomas. 6511-2
The cat. Charles Stuart Calverley. 6125-7
The cat. Walter Adolphe Roberts. 6120-6,6072-2
The cat. Lytton Strachey. 6511-2
Cataclysm. Noel Harry Brettell. 6788-3
The catacombs. Unknown. 6215-6
A catalectic monody. Unknown. 6089-7,6120-6,6724-7,6089-7
Cataline's defiance. George Croly. 6569-4
Catullus, Caius
    Ad lesbiam. George Gordon, 6th Baron Byron (tr.). 6945-2
    Lesbia railing. Jonathan Swift (tr.). 7039-6
    Love and death. Heathcote William Garrod (tr.). 7039-6
    My sweetest Lesbia. Thomas Campion (tr.). 7039-6
    On the burial of his brother. Aubrey Beardsley (tr.). 7039-6
    Sappho. William Ellery Leonard (tr.). 7039-6
    Sirmio. Charles Stuart Calverley (tr.). 7039-6
    Sirmio: Lago di Garda. 6631-3
    To Celia. Ben Jonson (tr.). 7039-6
    To his book. Andrew Lang (tr.). 6297-0
    To Lesbia. Samuel Taylor Coleridge (tr.). 6879-0
    True or false. Walter Savage Landor (tr.). 7039-6
    The yacht. John Hookham Frere (tr.). 7039-6
    "Ye cupids, droop each little head". George Gordon, 6th Baron Byron (tr.). 6945-2
Catullus, Carmen CI. Aubrey Beardsley. 6785-9
The catalogue. Charles Morris. 6760-3
The catalogue. Thomas Morris. 6385-3
Catalysis. Ann Menebroker. 6792-1
"The 'Catamount Tavern' is lively tonight". Parson Allen's ride. Wallace Bruce. 6946-0
A cataracket. Robert J. Burdette. 6588-0
The Cataract Isle. Christopher Pearse Cranch. 6484-1
The cataract of Lodore. Robert Southey. 6014-5,6239-3,6294-6,6358-6,6521-X,6554 ,6089-7,6302-0,6385-3,6358-6, 6451-6,6724 ,6610-0,6732-8,6808-1,6739-5,6131-1,6219-9,6464-7
The cataract of Luh Shan. Li Po. 6253-9
The cataract of T.R. Franklin Pierce Adams. 6995-9
The cataract. Kristjan Jonsson. 6854-5
Catastrophe. Robert Service. 6159-1
A catastrophe. M.E. B. 6965-7
A catastrophe. Susie M. Best. 6147-8
Catastrophic. Clarence LaFayette Stocks. 6799-9
Catawba wine. Henry Wadsworth Longfellow. 6004-8,6307-1
Catbird. Stephen Crombie. 6073-0
Catch. Sir George Etherege. 6544-9
A catch by the hearth. Unknown. 6806-5
A catch for singing. Wilfred Wilson Gibson. 6266-0
A catch for spring. Robert Nichols. 6236-9
Catch the sunshine. Emma Celia & Lizzie J. Rook. 6741-7
A catch-22 test. John L. Seller. 6870-7
Catch-on a wet day, fr. Franco Sacchetti. Dante Gabriel Rossetti. 6123-0
Catch: On a wet day. Franco Sacchetti. 7039-6
A catch. Henry Aldrich. 6933-9

A catch. Thomas (Tom) Brown. 6328-4
A catch. Thomas Dekker. 6153-2
A catch. Ben Jonson. 6182-6
A catch. Richard Henry Stoddard. 6753-0,6379-9,6300-4
A catch. Unknown. 6328-4,6562-7,6563-5
A catch. William Wager. 6861-8
The catch. John Kendrick Bangs. 6510-4
The catch. Paul Evison. 7018-3
Catching the cat. Margaret (Janvier) Vandegrift. 6131-1
Catching the coach. Alfred T. Chandler. 6768-9
Catching the colt. Marian (Annie D.G. Robinson) Douglas. 6249-0,6574-0
Cate of Ceann-Mare. Denis Florence McCarthy. 6858-8
Categorical courtship. Unknown. 6089-7,6120-6
Catena, Pauline
    Exultant. 6396-9,6288-1
Caterpillar. Helen Burlin. 6979-7
"A caterpillar squirmed". Discovery. Dorothy Sigmund. 6750-6
A caterpillar's apology for eating a favorite gladiolus. Charles Dalmon. 6510-4
A caterpillar's apology for eating a favorite... Charles Dalmon. 6861-8
The caterpillar. Unknown. 6623-2
A caterpillar. Cecil E.C. Hodgson. 6316-0
The caterpillar. E. Merrill Root. 6039-0
The caterpillar. Christina Georgina Rossetti. 6891-X
Caterpillars. John Freeman. 6250-4
Cates, Roscoe
    Temptation. 6397-7
The catfish. Oliver Herford. 6089-7
The cathara. Walter Colton. 7030-2
Catharina. William Cowper. 6092-7
Catharina, the second part. William Cowper. 6814-6
Catharine Plouffe. Susan Frances ("Seranus") Harrison. 6115-X
Catharsis. Jean Starr Untermeyer. 6011-0
Cathedral. Sara King Carleton. 6979-7
Cathedral 1941 Johannes Bobrowski. 6758-1
Cathedral at night. Martin Armstrong. 6071-4
Cathedral chimes at midnight. Florence Noar. 6490-6
Cathedral hymn. Felicia Dorothea Hemans. 6973-8
The cathedral in Trondheim. Jakob Thorarensen. 6283-0
The cathedral of Milan. Aubrey Thomas De Vere. 6631-3
The cathedral of St. Paul. Helen Lethert Meier. 6342-X
A cathedral scene. Walter Savage Landor. 6980-0
Cathedral windows. William White. 6868-5
Cathedral Woods. Augusta Wray. 6270-9
The cathedral, sels. James Russell Lowell. 6144-3,6335-7
The cathedral.. James Russell Lowell. 6333-0
The cathedral. William Congreve. 6438-8
The cathedral. George Crabbe. 6659-3
The cathedral. Thomas S. Jones Jr. 6337-3
The cathedral. William G. Shakespeare. 7027-2
Cathemerinon, sels. Aurelius Clemens Prudentius. 6282-2
Cather, Willa Sibert
    Asphodel. 6274-1
    "Grandmither, think not I forget." 6310-1,6019-6,6393-4
    The hawthorn tree. 6019-6
    L'envoi. 6274-1,6347-0,6274-1,6320-9
    A likeness. 6027-7
    The Palatine. 6509-0,6076-5,6102-8,6250-4,6300-4
    Spanish Johnny. 6732-8,6076-5,6467-1
Catherine. Charles Plumb. 7020-5
Catherine Kinrade. Thomas Edward Brown. 6437-X
Catherine, Sister Mary
    New Testament: revised edition. 6282-2
The Catholic Church, fr. The hind & the panther. John Dryden. 6933-9
The Catholic psalm. Elizabeth Ingram Hubbard. 6411-6
A cathouse in Cincinnati. Al Masarik. 6901-0
Catiline on hearing of his sentence of banishment. George Croly. 6424-8
Catiline to his army, near Faesulae. Ben Jonson. 6606-2
Catiline to his friends, after failing... George Croly. 6606-2
Catiline to the Gallic conspirators. George Croly. 6606-2
Catiline's defiance. George Croly. 6909-6
Catiline's defiance. George Croly. 6392-6,6294-6,6606-2, 6521-X,6610-0,6706

Catiline's last harangue to his army. George Croly. 6045-1, 6606-2,6294-6
Catiline, sels. George Croly. 6980-0
Catkin. Unknown. 6699-2
Catkins. Clara Doty Bates. 6965-7
Catlin, Charles T.
    Dinnis Kilboo's sanatarium. 6451-5
Catlin, Esther Trowbridge
    The voice. 6799-9
Catlin, George L.
    Cripple Ben. 6413-2
    The fire-bell's story. 6916-9
    Little Mag's victory. 6411-6,6744-1
    Lookout Mountain, 1863 - Beutelsbach, 1880. 6791-3
    Lookout Mountain. 6572-4
    My bread on the waters. 6916-9
    'One of the little ones'. 6630-5
    The Postilion of Nagold. 6927-4
    The street musicians. 6915-0
Cato. Joseph Addison. 6250-4
Cato's address to his troops in Lybia, fr. Pharsalia. Lucan. 6932-0
Cato's advice. Henry Carey. 6874-X
Cato's solilioquy on immortality. Joseph Addison. 6424-8
Cato's soliloquy, fr. Cato. Joseph Addison. 6102-8,6304-7, 6337-3,6424-8,6541-4,6543
Cato, sels. Joseph Addison. 6879-0
Cato, sels. Joseph Addison. 6102-8
Cats. Charles Baudelaire. 6511-2
Cats. Edith Richmond Blanchard. 6120-6
Cats. Francis Scarfe. 6379-9
Cats. John Banister Tabb. 6120-6
Cats. Arthur Seymour John Tessimond. 6257-1
Cats. William Wallace Whitelock. 6120-6
Cats and crocuses. Eva Martin. 6511-2
Cats and humans - all the same. Anthony Euwer. 6120-6
Cats and kings. Alfred Noyes. 6339-X
The cats have come to tea. Kate Greenaway. 6466-3
The cats of Baddeck. Phoebe Hoffman. 6120-6
The cats of Santa Anna. Torquato Tasso. 6325-X
Cats' tea party. Unknown. 6699-2,6706-9
cats' tea-party<The. Frederic Edward Weatherley. 6937-1
The cats. Charles Baudelaire. 6343-8
The cats. Unknown. 6699-2
Catskill Mountains. Washington Irving. 6484-1
Cattafi, Bartolo
    Archipelagoes. Robert White (tr.). 6803-0
    Measurements. Robert White (tr.). 6803-0
Catterskill Falls. William Cullen Bryant. 6484-1
Cattle. ? Banko. 6891-X
Cattle. Berta Hart Nance. 6265-2
Cattle before the storm. Glenn Ward Dresbach. 6510-4
Cattle bells. Lew Sarett. 6979-7
The cattle camp-dawn. Charles Erskine Scott Wood. 6628-3
The cattle camp-night. Charles Erskine Scott Wood. 6628-3
The cattle country. Emily Pauline ("Tekahionwake") Johnson. 6433-7
The cattle of his hand. Wilbur Underwood. 6730-1
A cattle range at night. Earl Alonzo Brininstool. 6628-3
Cattle show. Christopher M. ("Hugh MacDiarmid") Grieve. 6845-6
The cattle thief. Emily Pauline ("Tekahionwake") Johnson. 6837-2
The cattle train. Charlotte Perkins Stetson Gilman. 6510-4
The cattle-thief. Unknown (Greek) 6435-3
"The catts as other creatures doe." Unknown. 6563-5
Catullian hendecasyllales. Samuel Taylor Coleridge. 6204-0
Catullus
    Catullus to Lesbia. Eugene Field (tr.). 6949-5
    The rites at his brother's grave. 6102-8
    Sirmio. Thomas Moore (tr.). 6624-0
    Sparrow. 6732-8
    To Lesbia. 6732-8
    To Lesbia's sorrow. 6102-8
Catullus to Lesbia. Catullus. 6949-5
Catwalk. Daniel L. Klauck. 6870-7
Catwise. Philip Booth. 6388-8
A'Caudal'lecture. William Sawyer. 6089-7
Caughey, Elford
    First flight. 6761-1

CAUGHNAWAGA

The **Caughnawaga** beadwork-seller. William Douw Lighthall. 6795-6
Caughnawaga song. Unknown (Caughnawaga Indian) 6795-6
Caught. K.E. Barry. 6671-7
Caught by chance. T.W. Ramsey. 6257-1
Caught in the ebbing tide. Theodore Watts-Dunton. 6997-5
"**Caught** in the growing sweep of that design". Weaver. Rosa Coates Richards. 6979-7
Caught in the nets. Philip Bourke Marston. 6997-5
Cauld kail in Aberdeen. Alexander Gordon, 4th Duke of Gordon. 6180-X
The **cauld** lad's song. Unknown. 6125-7
The **cauldron** of Ceridwin, fr. The misfortunes of Elphin. Thomas Love Peacock. 6518-X
"The **cauldron.**". Francis Walker. 6241-5
The **cauliflower** worm. Vachel Lindsay. 6206-7
Cause for complaint. Unknown. 6680-1
A **cause** for wonder. Unknown. 6881-2
'**Cause** he'd nothing else to do. Herbert Grey. 6692-5
"The **cause** is in my will: I will not come". Julius Caesar, sel. William Shakespeare. 6958-4
Cause of our joy. Sister Maris Stella. 6282-2
The **cause** of this I know not. Haniel Long. 6032-3
The **cause** won. Vincent Bourne. 6814-6
The **cause.** Unknown. 6278-4
Causes. Marion Thomas. 6750-6
The **causeymire.** Alister Mackenzie. 6269-5
Causley, Charles
   A ballad for Katharine of Aragon. 6210-5
   H.M.S. Glory at Sydney. 6258-X
   Keats at Teignmouth: 1818. 6339-X
   Serenade to a cornish fox. 6258-X
Caution. Gertrude Callaghan. 6039-0
Caution. William Shakespeare. 6294-6
A **caution** to fair ladies. Henry Lawes. 6328-4
A **caution** to poets. Matthew Arnold. 6947-1
Caution's a virtue that o'ercharged is vice,fr.Hannibal. John Nichol. 6819-7
A **caution..** Unknown. 6724-7
Cautionary verses. Theodore Hook. 6089-7
Cautions. Hugh Rhodes. 6724-7
"The **cautious** collapsible cow". Limerick:"The cautious collapsible cow." Unknown. 6308-X
The **cautious** householder. Anaxilas. 6435-3
Cavafy, Constantine P.
   Awaiting the barbarians. Rae Dalven (tr.). 6352-7
   Body remembered. Rae Dalven (tr.). 6352-7
   The city. Rae Dalven (tr.). 6352-7
   Expecting the barbarians. M. Yourcenar & Wystan Hugh Auden (tr.). 6068-4
   For Ammonis who died at 29 at 610 Rae Dalven (tr.). 6352-7
   God forsakes Anthony. Rae Dalven (tr.). 6352-7
   Ionian song. Rae Dalven (tr.). 6352-7
   Ithacha. Rae Dalven (tr.). 6352-7
   Manuel Komninos. Rae Dalven (tr.). 6352-7
   Morning sea. Rae Dalven (tr.). 6352-7
   Of the ship. Rae Dalven (tr.). 6352-7
   One of the Jews (50 A.D.) Rae Dalven (tr.). 6352-7
   Return. Rae Dalven (tr.). 6352-7
   Satrapy. Rae Dalven (tr.). 6352-7
   Since nine o'clock. Rae Dalven (tr.). 6352-7
   Trojans. Rae Dalven (tr.). 6352-7
   Very seldom. Rae Dalven (tr.). 6352-7
   Walls. Rae Dalven (tr.). 6352-7
Cavalcade. Lady Margaret Sackville. 6269-5
Cavalcanti, Guido
   Ballata: In exile at Sarzana. Dante Gabriel Rossetti (tr.). 7039-6
   "Beauty of ladies of compassionate heart". George S. Fraser (tr.). 6325-X
   "Being in thought of love I came upon". Ezra Pound (tr.). 6325-X
   The effigy. Hubert Creekmore (tr.). 6325-X
   "I saw the eyes, where Amor took his place". Ezra Pound (tr.). 6325-X
   "If I should pray this lady pitiless". Ezra Pound (tr.). 6325-X
   "A lady asks for me". Ezra Pound (tr.). 6325-X
   Last song: from exile. George S. Fraser (tr.). 6325-X
   "Light do I see within my Lady's eyes". Ezra Pound (tr.). 6325-X
   Love's assize. Hubert Creekmore (tr.). 6325-X
   "My Lady's face it is they worship there". Ezra Pound (tr.). 6325-X
   Of love's power. Hubert Creekmore (tr.). 6325-X
   Sonnet: To an ill-favored lady. Dante Gabriel Rossetti (tr.). 7039-6
   Sonnet: To his lady Joan, of Florence. Dante Gabriel Rossetti (tr.). 7039-6
   "There in a woodland, to my thought more bright". George S. Fraser (tr.). 6325-X
   To Dante. Percy Bysshe Shelley (tr.). 7039-6
   "Who's this that comes, as each man looks at her". George S. Fraser (tr.). 6325-X
   "You have in you the flowers and the green grass". George S. Fraser (tr.). 6325-X
   "You, who do breach mine eyes and touch the heart". Ezra Pound (tr.). 6325-X
Cavalier song. Sir Walter Scott. 6110-9,6086-2
Cavalier tunes. Robert Browning. 6828-6
Cavalier tunes. Robert Browning. 6188-5,6332-2,6334-9,6358-6,6490-6,6527-,6657-7,6196-6,6430-2,6656-9,6110-9
Cavalier tunes, sels. Robert Browning. 6334-9,6732-8,6199-0,6301-2,6655-0
The **cavalier's** choice. Johann Wolfgang von Goethe. 6676-3
The **cavalier's** choice. Johann Wolfgang von Goethe. 6948-7
The **cavalier's** escape. George Walter Thornbury. 6239-3, 6136-2,6478-7,6424-8,6267-9
The **cavalier's** escape. George Walter Thornbury. 6263-6
A **cavalier's** lullaby for his mistress. Thomas Jordan. 6563-5
The **cavalier's** march to London. Thomas Babington Macaulay, 1st Baron Macaulay. 6980-0
Cavalier's song. Robert (Cunningham) Graham. 6086-2
The **cavalier's** song. William Motherwell. 6180-X,6239-3, 6219-9,6424-8,6737-6
The **cavalier.** Sir Walter Scott. 6075-7,6197-4,6639-9
Cavalry charge. Folger McKinsey. 7010-8
The **cavalry** charge ("With bray of trumpet"). Francis A. Durivage. 6113-3,6016-2,6566-X
The **cavalry** charge. George Parsons Lathrop. 6552-X,6673-9
The **cavalry** charge. Edmund Clarence Stedman. 6457-4,6424-8
The **cavalry** charge. Benjamin Franklin Taylor. 6113-3,6471-X,6016-2,6304-7,6580-5
Cavalry crossing a ford. Walt Whitman. 6008-0,6125-7,6288-1
The **cavalry** scout. Edmundus Scotus. 6678-X
Cavalry song. William Hamilton Hayne. 6580-5
Cavalry song. Rossiter W. Raymond. 6016-2
Cavalry song. Edmund Clarence Stedman. 6113-3,6243-1,6302-0,6385-3,6358-6,6471 ,6016-2,6219-9
Cavanagh, Michael (tr.)
   A day in Ireland. Unknown, 6244-X
Cavazza, Elizabeth
   Goose a la mode. 6440-X
   Jack and Jill ("What moan is made of the mountain..."). 6440-X
   Lullaby ("Through sleepy-land"). 6373-X
The **cave** of despair. Edmund Spenser. 6935-5
The **cave** of despair. Edmund Spenser. 6315-2
The **cave** of mammon, fr. the Fairie Queene. Edmund Spenser. 6102-8
The **cave** of Morpheus, fr. The book of the duchesse. Geoffrey Chaucer. 6958-4
The **cave** of sleep, fr. Confession amantis. John Gower. 6958-4
The **cave** of sleep. Edmund Spenser. 6302-0;6385-3
Cave of Staffa. William Wordsworth. 6438-8
Cave sedem. Theodore F. MacManus. 6083-8
Cave series, sel. Margaret Atwood. 6767-0
Cave talk. Joseph Warren Beach. 6029-3
The **cave** woman. Gulielma Day Orr. 6906-1
Cavendish; Duchess of Newcastle, Margaret
   The soul's garment. 6931-2
Cavendish; Duke of Newcastle, William
   The heaven's mould. 6317-9
   Love's vision. 6317-9
The **cavern** of the three Tells, fr. Lays of many lands. Felicia Dorothea Hemans. 6973-8

The **cavern** of the three Tells, Grutli. Felicia Dorothea Hemans. 6749-2
"The **caverns** of my mind are wrinkled". Trapped. Vernon E. Hite. 7024-8
The **caverns** of the grave I've seen. William Blake. 6380-2
The **caves** of Auvergne. Walter James Turner. 6477-9
"The **cavity** in the right side of the chest". Why most of us are limping away from life. Eugene Ruggles. 6792-1,6998-3
Caw! Caw! Caw! Edward Carswell. 6314-4,6706-9
'**Caw-caw**'.. Georgia White. 7030-2
Cawein, Madison
    Attainment. 6730-1
    Aubade. 6266-0
    The call of the heart. 6094-3
    Carmen. 7041-8
    Comradery. 6431-0
    The dancer. 6959-2
    The daughter of the snow. 7035-3
    Deserted. 6332-2,6336-5
    Dirge. 6431-0
    A fragment. 6102-8,6076-5
    Hallowe'en. 6696-8
    Here is the place where loveliness keeps house. 6300-4, 6467-1,6310-1
    The heron. 7041-8
    The house of life. 6336-5
    "I hear the woodlands calling..." 6478-7
    In an old garden. 6649-6,6232-6,6338-1
    Ku Klux. 6309-8,7017-5
    Late November morning. 6396-9
    Little bird. 6510-4
    Love and a day. 6441-8
    Lydia. 6441-8
    The magic purse. 6266-0
    The man hunt. 6464-7
    The man hunt. 7017-5
    March. 6421-3
    May. 6396-9
    Meeting in summer. 6396-9
    Mene, mene, tekel, upharsin. 6741-X
    Morning glories. 6421-3,6266-0
    Morning serenade. 6266-0
    Mosby at Hamilton. 6946-0
    The mountain still. 7017-5
    The old bayou. 6467-1
    The old home. 6476-0
    Old homes. 6338-1,6423-X
    Old man rain. 6421-3
    On the farm. 6006-4
    The path to the woods. 6887-1
    The path to the woods. 6310-1
    Penetralia. 6007-2,6161-3,6393-4,6007-2,6161-3,6359-4
    The presence of spring. 6396-9
    Prototypes. 7017-5
    The rain-crow. 6073-0,6102-8,6076-5,6300-4,6309-8
    The redbird. 6473-6
    Reed call. 6441-8
    A road song. 6266-0
    Snow. 6467-1
    Snow. 7017-5
    The speckled trout. 6027-7
    To a wind flower. 6047-1
    To a wind-flower. 6431-0
    Under arcturus. 6310-1
    Under the stars and stripes. 6471-X,6223-7
    Unheard. 6889-8
    The voice of April. 6327-6
    "When the hornet hangs in the hollyhock." 6076-5
    The whippoorwill. 6006-4
    The white evening. 7035-3
    The willow bottom. 6653-4
    The wind in the pines. 6047-1
    The winds. 7017-5
    The winds. 6161-3,6393-4
Cawna, fr. Heccar and Gaira. Thomas Chatterton. 6545-7
Cawnpore. C.W. Waddington. 6591-0,6592-9
Cawsand bay. Unknown. 6258-X
Cayley, C.B. (tr.)
    Signs of love. Francesco Petrarch, 7039-6

Cayley, George John
    An epitaph. 6092-7
    An epitaph. 6089-7
Cayzer, Charles William
    David and Bathshua. 6848-0
"**Ce** matin, nul rayon n'a penetre la brume". Journee d'hiver. Leon Dierx. 6801-4
Ce meme vieux coon. Unknown. 6724-7
Cead Mile Failte, Elim!, fr. 'The invasion'. Gerald Griffin. 6174-5
Cean dubb deelish. Sir Samuel Ferguson. 6437-X,6383-7
Cean duv deelish. Dora Sigerson Shorter. 6090-0,6244-X, 6628-3
Cean-Salla. James Clarence Mangan. 6930-4
Ceann duv dilis. George Sigerson. 6096 X
"Sea **Cease** not thou heavenly voiced glorious creature." Unknown. 6563-5
Cease not to be a mystery. Roberta Teale Swartz. 6619-4, 6071-4
Cease not to learn. Joshua Sylvester. 6934-7
"**Cease** thy wishes gentle boy." Unknown. 6563-5
"**Cease** to preen, O shining pigeons!". To the waterfront pigeons. Leonie Adams. 6808-1
"**Cease** work – have done". Vespers. Dallett Fuguet. 6936-3
"**Cease**, cease you reuels, rest a space". A song ("Cease"). Thomas Campion. 6794-8
"**Cease**, Christian, cease the word of scorn". The Jew's appeal to the Christian. J. W. Blencowe. 6848-0
"**Cease**, sorrow cease, & doe noe more torment." Unknown. 6563-5
"**Cease**, stranger, cease those piercing notes". The isles of the sirens. John Henry, Cardinal Newman. 6980-0
"**Cease**, warring thoughts, and let his brain". A lullaby, fr. The triumph of beauty. James Shirley. 6827-8
"**Ceased** now were Priam's banquets". The feast of victory. Johann C. Friedrich von Schiller. 6842-7
"**Ceased** the bold strain, then deep the Saxon..". Rowena. Henry Hart Milman. 6980-0
Cecco Angiolieri da Siena
    Sonnet: He rails against Dante. Dante Gabriel Rossetti (tr.). 7039-6
    Sonnet: In absence from Becchina. Dante Gabriel Rossetti (tr.). 7039-6
    Sonnet: Of all he would do. Dante Gabriel Rossetti (tr.). 7039-6
    Sonnet: Of Becchina in a rage. Dante Gabriel Rossetti (tr.). 7039-6
Cech, Svatopluk
    Our native tongue. Paul Selver (tr.). 6763-8
Cecidit, cecidit, Babylon magna. Theodore Maynard. 6172-9, 6292-X
Cecil. Walter De La Mare. 6596-1
Cecil John Rhodes. William Blane. 6800-6
Cecil, David
    Enchantments of the middle age. 6070-6
Cecil; Lord Burghley, William
    To Mistress Anne Cecil upon making her..new year's gift. 6528-7
Cecilia Metella. George Gordon, 6th Baron Byron. 6980-0
The **cedar** chest. Edith Osborne. 6249-0
The **Cedar** Grove. Unknown. 6057-9
Cedar Mountain. Annie Fields. 6946-0
Cedars. Grace Hazard Conkling. 6253-9
The **cedars** of Lebanon. Alphonse Marie Louis de Lamartine. 7039-6
The **cedars**. Josephine Preston Peabody. 6331-4,6509-0,6393-4
Ceirog
    Epilogue to Alun Mabon. Sir Idris Bell (tr.). 6528-7
Celadyne's song. William Browne. 6933-9
Celan, Paul
    Aspen tree. 6758-1
    Chanson of a lady in the shade. 6758-1
    Corona. 6758-1
    During the day. Milne Holton and Herbert Kuhner (tr.). 6769-7
    Erratic. Milne Holton and Herbert Kuhner (tr.). 6769-7
    Fugue of death. Christopher Middleton (tr.). 6758-1
    "It is no longer/that heaviness" Milne Holton and Herbert Kuhner (tr.). 6769-7

CELAN 262

"Narrow-wood day under a/retinerved sky-leaf..."
  Joachim Neugroschel (tr.). 6803-0
Psalm. 6758-1
Shibboleth. 6758-1
"Something dark/resembling a hand" Milne Holton and
  Herbert Kuhner (tr.). 6769-7
"You black, black/earth, mother" Milne Holton and
  Herbert Kuhner (tr.). 6769-7
Your hand full of hours. 6758-1
The **celandine**.. William Wordsworth. 6558-9
Celano, Thomas de
  Dies irae. John A. Dix (tr.). 6385-3
Celanta at the well of life. George Peele. 6315-2
The **celebes**. John Boyle O'Reilly. 7041-8
Celebration 1982 Terri Meyette Wilkins. 6870-7
A **celebration** of Charis, sels. Ben Jonson. 6179-6,6562-7,
  6228-8,6317-9,6208-3,6645
A **celebration** of Charis. Ben Jonson. 6240-7,6430-2
Celebration of love. James McAuley. 6349-7
A **celebration**. May Sarton. 6388-8
Celeste and Galileo, fr. The torch bearers. Alfred Noyes.
  6879-0
Celeste dancing. Frances Sargent Osgood. 6102-8,6076-5
The **celestial** army. Thomas Buchanan Read. 6294-6,6735-2
The **celestial** city. Giles (the Younger) Fletcher. 6933-9
The **celestial** country. Bernard of Cluny. 6219-9
The **celestial** country. Bernard de Morlaix. 6385-3
Celestial food. Cecelia Slawik Lamb. 6249-0
Celestial love. Michelangelo Buonarroti. 7039-6
Celestial music. William Shakespeare. 6543-0
The **celestial** passion. Richard Watson Gilder. 7041-8
The **celestial** passion. Richard Watson Gilder. 6300-4,6431-0
"**Celestial** poesy! whose genial sway". Australasia, sels.
  William Charles Wentworth. 6784-0
Celestial queen, fr. De partu virginis. Sincerus
  Sannazarius. 6282-2
Celestial Rhymes. Fannie Stearns Davis. 7038-8
Celestial scandal. Elva R. Ray. 6750-6
Celestial signs. Brookes More. 6032-3
The **celestial** surgeon. Robert Louis Stevenson. 6102-8,6107-9,6199-0,6250-4,6508-2,6180-X,6123-0,6491-1,6477-9,
  6501-5,6337 ,6339-X,6418-3,6730-1,6732-8,6214-8,6660
Celestial wisdom, fr. The tenth Satire. Juvenal. 7039-6
Celia. Ben Jonson. 6226-1
Celia and Belinda. Colley Cibber. 6563-5
Celia has a thousand charms. Robert Gould. 6328-4
Celia is gone. William Browne. 6563-5
Celia singing. Thomas Carew. 6733-6,6563-5,6430-2
"**Celia** turnes away her eyes." Unknown. 6563-5
Celia upon her sparrow. William Cartwright. 6943-6
Celia's home-coming. Agnes Mary F. ("Madame Duclaux")
  Robinson. 6437-X,6656-9
"**Celia**, my fairest Celia, fell." Charles Cotton. 6317-9
"**Celia**, thy sweet angels face." Anne Finch, Countess of
  Winchilsea (atr) 6563-5
Celibacy. Clarke Austin. 6022-6
Celibacy. Austin Clarke. 6292-X
Celinda. Edward Herbert, 1st Baron Herbert of Cherbury.
  6438-8,6600-3
Cell. Dennis Shady. 6870-7
Cell-rap #27 Raymond Ringo Fernandez. 6870-7
The **cell**.. George Rostrevor. 6607-0
The **cell**. George Rostrevor Hamilton. 6253-9
Cellach's poem to the dawn. Sean O'Faolain. 6582-1
Cellar. Alex Comfort. 6475-2
The **cellar**.. Hilda Conkling. 6466-3
The **cello**. Ernst Josephson. 6045-5
Cells. Rudyard Kipling. 6810-3
Celner, I.
  Battle interlude. 6468-X
The **Celtic** Cross. Thomas D'Arcy McGee. 6656-9,6930-5
Celtic speech. Lionel Johnson. 6090-0
The **Celtic** tongue. Michael Mullen. 6858-8
Celts and Saxons. Thomas Osborne Davis. 6714-X
The **Celts**. Thomas D'Arcy McGee. 6244-X,6174-5
"**Celui** qui me lira, dans les siecles, un soir" Emile
  Verhaeren. 6801-4
"A **celuy** que pluys eyme en mounde". To the one I love
  most. Unknown. 6881-2

"**Cement** house in ruins". Long haiku no. 7 Louis Cuneo.
  6792-1
Cemetery. Doris V. Lecky. 6850-2
The **cemetery** beside the road. Fred Berman. 6841-3
The **cemetery** is. Audrey McGaffin. 6388-8
The **cemetery** nightingale. Morris Rosenfeld. 7011-6
A **cemetery**. Emily Dickinson. 6153-2
Cendrars, Blaise
  The club, fr. Far west. 6351-9
  Dorypha, fr. Far west. 6351-9
  Far west, sels. 6351-9
  The mocking bird, fr. Far west. 6351-9
  Mushroom city, fr. Far west. 6351-9
Cennick, John
  Children of the heavenly king. 6219-9,6730-1
Cenotaph. Glaucus. 6435-3
The **cenotaph** of Lincoln. James Thompson McKay. 6524-4
A **cenotaph**, fr. Tegea. Simonides. 6435-3
A **cenotaph**. P. Dana. 7021-3
"The **censer** of the eglantine was moved". A song of April.
  Francis Ledwidge. 6812-X
Censorship. Philip Brasfield. 6870-7
Censorship. William Robert Rodgers. 6389-6
Censorship. Arthur Waley. 6666-6
"**Censorship** would have this pen". Censorship. Philip
  Brasfield. 6870-7
Centaur. Robert P. Tristram Coffin. 7040-X
Centaur song. Hilda ("H.D.") Doolittle. 6069-2
The **centaur**. Theodore Roethke. 6388-8
The **centaur**. Poul Sorensen. 6555-4
The **centaur**. May Swenson. 6388-8
The **centenarian's** story. Walt Whitman. 6753-0
Centennial bells. Benjamin Franklin Taylor. 6815-4
Centennial hymn. William Cullen Bryant. 6946-0
Centennial Hymn. Jay Glover Eldridge. 6799-9
Centennial hymn ("Our fathers' God"). John Greenleaf
  Whittier. 6265-2,6569-4,6286-5,6385-3,6605-4,6126-5,
  6223-7
Centennial meditation of Columbia. Sidney Lanier. 6385-3
Centennial ode. Bayard Taylor. 6385-3
The **centennial** ode, sels. Sidney Lanier. 6239-3;6386-1
Center square. Martha Keller. 6761-1
Centertown. Judith Neeld. 6821-9
A **centipede** was happy quite. Unknown. 6026-9
"A **centipede** wept as he sat on a stone". The centipede's
  dilemma. E.F.L. C.. 6965-7
A **centipede**.. Unknown. 6466-3
Centoaph songs. Brian Fitzpatrick. 6349-7
Central. John Curtis Underwood. 6509-0
The **central** I. John Masefield. 6266-0
"**Centre** of light and energy, thy way". Apostrophe to the
  sun. James Gates Percival. 6752-2
"The **centuries** have builded here". In the Yosemite. Robert
  Loveman. 6941-X
"**Centuries** old is the gullah's cry". The gullah cry.
  Eleanor Fox Ponder. 6750-6
"**Centuries** thunder/Over my head". Judas. Jessie Holt. 6789-1
The **centurion**.. Helen Purcell Roads. 6144-3,6335-7
"A **century** did not thy vigour pale"fr.Hastings' sonnets.
  Sir Egerton Brydges. 6980-0
A **century** of peace. Guy Bilsford. 6088-9
"A **century** of so ago". 'Puritan' - 'Genesta'. Eugene
  Field. 6949-5
Ceol sidhe. Francis Ledwidge. 6812-X
"**Ceptin** Jim." Lewis R. Clement. 6687-9
'**Cepting** Ike. William Devere. 6690-9
"**Cerca** un jardin". Para Sonia. Americo Casiano. 6898-7
Cercidas
  The voyage of love. Gilbert Highet (tr.). 6435-3
The **cerebralists** describe a woman. Simonetta [pseud]. 6817-0
Cerelle. Margaret Bell Houston. 6396-9
Ceremonial ode intended for a university. Lascelles
  Abercrombie. 6437-X
Ceremonies for Candlemasse eve. Robert Herrick. 6334-9,
  6562-7,6430-2
Ceremonies for Christmas. Robert Herrick. 6145-1,6239-3,
  6734-4,6230-X
Ceremonies to the maids. Robert Herrick. 6747-6

Ceremony after a fire raid. Dylan Thomas. 6666-6
A ceremony for Candlemas day. Robert Herrick. 6465-5
"The ceremony must be found". Speaking of poetry. John
    Peale Bishop. 6751-4
Cerenio, Virginia
    Manong Benny. 6790-5
    Pick-up at Chef Rizal restaurant. 6790-5
    Pinay. 6790-5
    "We who carry the endless seasons" 6790-5
    You lovely people. 6790-5
Ceres. James Maurice Thompson. 7041-8
"Ceres, most bounteous lady, thy rich leas". A masque.
    William Shakespeare. 6935-5
Cerne abbas. Hal Summers. 6257-1
A certain age. Phyllis McGinley. 6388-2
Certain American poets. Odell Shepard. 6289-X,6393-4
A certain cure. Anthony C. Deane. 6996-7
"A certain gentleman, whose yellow cheek". A good
    direction. Thomas Hood. 6974-6
Certain maxims of Hafiz, sels. Rudyard Kipling. 6427-2
"Certain pairs who had banns called...". Limerick:"Certain
    pairs who had banns...". Unknown. 6811-1
A certain people. George Meredith. 6828-6
Certain phenomena of sound. Wallace Stevens. 6017-X
A certain Saturday. Edith Lovejoy Pierce. 6144-3
"A certain sprite, who dwells below". A case of libel.
    Thomas Moore. 6878-2
The certain victory. Samuel Ellsworth Kiser. 6211-3
"The certain years moved on, intent and brief". The
    flight. Tessa Sweazy Webb. 6906-1
"A certain young fellow, named Bobbie". Limerick:"A
    certain young fellow, named Bobbie." Unknown. 6308-X
"A certain young gourmet of Crediton". Charles Inge. 6722-0
"A certain young gourmet of Crediton". Limerick:"A certain
    young gourmet of Crediton". Charles Inge. 6811-1,
    6811-1,6308-X
A certain young lady. Washington Irving. 6280-6,6441-8,
    6004-8,6652-6,6585-6
Certaine sonets neuer before printed, sels. Sir Philip
    Sidney. 6586-4
Certainties. Kenneth W. Porter. 6144-3,6335-7
"Certes, il n'aimait pas a la facon des hommes". Les
    plaintes du cyclope. Charles Marie Leconte de Lisle.
    6801-4
Cervantes, Miguel de Saavedra
    Antonio's wooing. 6732-8
Cervera. Bertrand Shadwell. 6946-0
Cervinka, Karel
    Yearning in early spring. Paul Selver (tr.). 6763-8
Cesaire, Aime
    The tornado. Michael Benedikt (tr.). 6803-0
Cesar Franck. Joseph Auslander. 6037-4
Cestrian, W.
    Because of you. 6589-9
"Cette colline est belle, inclinee et pensive". La
    colline. Henri de Regnier. 6801-4
Cezanne. Alfred Kreymborg. 6102-8,6076-5
Ch'ien Wen-ti
    Lo-yang. Arthur Waley (tr.). 7039-6
Cha till Maccruimein. Ewart Alan Mackintosh. 6477-9,6650-X
The chace, sels. William Somervile. 6831-6
Chadwick, George A.
    Weary. 6244-X
Chadwick, John A.
    The two waitings. 6385-3
Chadwick, John White
    Auld lang syne. 6337-3,6730-1
    Fate. 6321-7
    Fate ("All unconscious I beheld her"). 6429-9
    Full cycle. 6946-0
    In an unknown tongue. 6321-7
    It singeth low in every heart. 6303-9,6889-8
    King Edwin's feast. 6614-3,6424-8
    The king's diary. 6424-8
    The kiss of god. 6848-0
    The making of man. 6309-8
    Mugford's victory. 6946-0
    New house: old home. 6321-7
    The oldest story. 6321-7
    A song of trust. 6600-3
    Starlight. 6429-9,6321-7
    Tete-a-tete. 6321-7
    "To look upon the face". 6085-4
    A wedding song. 6321-7
    The yellow-hammer's nest. 6273-3
Chaeremon
    Maidens at rest. George Allen (tr.). 6435-3
Chaffee, Eleanor Alletta
    Farm boy at school. 6042-0
A Chagall (#1) Dan Propper. 6998-3, 6901-0
Chagrin. Isaac Rosenberg. 6641-0
Chahoon, Mary
    At boarding-school. 6684-4
The chain I gave. Unknown (Turkish) 6945-2
A chain of dates. Ada Simpson Sherwood. 6158-3
The chain of Princes Street. Elizabeth Fleming. 6331-4,
    6466-3,6631-3
A chain. Adelaide Anne Procter. 6226-1
The chain. John Pierpont. 7009-4
Chained. Ruth Brownlee Johnson. 6178-8
The chained bear. Gertrude W. Marshall. 6764-6
"Chained by stern duty to the rock of state". Lincoln.
    Silas Weir Mitchell. 6946-0
Chained tigers: I. Elizabeth Craigmyle. 7037-X
Chained tigers: II. Elizabeth Craigmyle. 7037-X
Chains. Patrick Carey. 6563-5
"Chains may subdue the feeble spirit, but thee". William
    Tell. William Cullen Bryant. 6749-2
"Chains on the cities! gloom in the air!". Moorish
    gathering song. Felicia Dorothea Hemans. 6973-8
"Chains, my good lord: in your good brows...". Columbus.
    Alfred Lord Tennyson. 6977-0
The chains. Kostes Palamas. 6102-8
Chairs after the Margaret Agnes Wharton show. Henry
    Petroski. 6966-5
Chaitivel, sels. Arthur O'Shaughnessy. 6655-0
Chaka. Frank Templeton Prince. 6788-3
Chakey Einstein. Henry Cuyler Bunner. 6735-2
Chalcedony. Emma Pomeroy Greenough. 6273-3
Chalcomede prays to be saved from love. Nonnus. 6435-3
Chalcomede wards off her lover. Nonnus. 6435-3
The chalice. Sybil Wynne-Jones. 6782-4
Chalk. Benjamin Albert Botkin. 6397-7
Chalk and flint. Unknown. 7031-0
Chalkhill, John
    The angler's song. 6328-4
    The angler. 6302-0,6385-3,6271-7,6219-9
    Coridon's song. 6092-7,6398-5
    Oh, the brave fisher's life. 6092-7
    "Oh, the brave fisher's life". 6334-9
    The praise of a countryman's life. 6018-8,6219-9,6108-8,
        6219-9
    Rhotus on Arcadia. 6933-9
    Song ("Oh, the sweet"). 6334-9
Challen, James
    A New Year's story. 6675-5
Challenge. Thomas Curtis Clark. 6337-3
Challenge. Jean Nette. 6291-1
Challenge. Louis Untermeyer. 6211-3
A challenge for beauty, sels. Thomas Heywood. 6317-9
The challenge of life, fr. Ulysses. Alfred Lord Tennyson.
    6337-3
The challenge of the guns. A.N. Field. 7026-4
The challenge of the tillers. Richard Warner Borst. 6954-1
The challenge of Thor. Henry Wadsworth Longfellow. 6623-2
The challenge of Thor. Henry Wadsworth Longfellow. 6850-2
Challenge to Americans. Dora Ward. 6799-9
Challenge to youth, fr. The castle builder. Henry
    Wadsworth Longfellow. 6337-3
A challenge to youth. Willard Wattles. 6615-1
Challenge, fr. Marmion. Sir Walter Scott. 6427-2
A challenge.. Willard Snowden. 6116-8
A challenge. James Clarence Harvey. 6578-3
A challenge. James Clarence Harvey. 6923-1
The challenge. Walter De La Mare. 6905-3
The challenge. Samuel A. Haynes. 6178-8
The challenge. Henry Lumpkin. 6396-9
The challenge. Calvin Murry. 6870-7
The challenge. Roger Atkinson Pryor. 6674-7

CHALLENGER

The **challenger**. Donald Wandrei. 6218-0
Challiss, James Courtney
   Mamma's pecious dirl. 6694-1
Challoner, L.
   In the desert to-day. 6468-X
   Libya. 6468-X
Chalmers, Patrick Reginald
   The awakening. 6249-0
   Ballade of August. 6875-8
   Ballade of crying for the moon. 6875-8
   Ballade of the forest in summer. 6875-8
   A dream. 6506-6
   The gardener's cat. 6120-6,6503-1,6510-4,6653-4
   Guns of Verdun. 6224-5
   "Hold." 6510-4
   If I had a broomstick. 6044-7,6638-0,6639-9
   In an old nursery. 6653-4
   Infantry. 7027-2
   The little young lambs. 6804-9
   Pan pipes. 6653-4
   Pud [or Puk]-Wudgies. 6253-9
   Roundabouts and swings. 6458-2,6044-7,6477-9,6228-8
   The steeple. 7027-2
   'Treasure island.' 6541-4
Chalmers, Stephen
   Allenby enters Jerusalem! 7014-0
   The new physician. 7014-0
   Rebellion. 7007-8
   Rebellion. 6374-8
   The song of brother Hilario. 7012-4
   Transition. 7014-0
   The voice of the city. 7014-0
Chalmers, Thomas
   The astonished tippler. 6404-3
   The drummer boy. 6404-3
Chalse a killey. Thomas Edward Brown. 6508-2
Chalse a killey. Thomas Edward Brown. 6809-X
Chalvey. Arthur Christopher Benson. 6793-X
Chamalian, George
   An epitaph. 6850-2
Chamber Music, sels. James Joyce. 6536-8
The **chamber** over the gate. Henry Wadsworth Longfellow. 6632-1,6333-0,6431-0
A **chamber** scene. Bryan Waller ("Barry Cornwall") Procter. 6980-0
"A **chamber**, myrtle-wall'd, embower'd high". Adonis sleeping. John Keats. 6980-0
The **chambered** nautilus. Oliver Wendell Holmes. 6176-1,6239-3,6243-1,6291-1,6358-6,6473 ,6258-X,6260-1,6271-7, 6337-3,6358-6,6385 ,6289-X,6601-1,6006-4,6077-3,6102-8,6183 ,6437-X,6457-4,6459-0,6478-7,6481-7,6482 , 6479-5,6499-X,6600-3,6605-4,6735-2,6332 ,6512-0,6552-X,6632-1,6730-1,6732-8,6560 ,6008-0,6250-4,6177-X, 6076-5,6126-5,6121 ,6288-1,6431-0,6104-4,6304-7,6212-1,6214 ,6219-9,6371-3,6300-4,6309-8,6421-3,6396-6, 6639-9,6219-9,6371-3,6300-4,6309-8,6421-3,6396-6, 6639-9
Chamberlain Jr., H.S.
   The back-work club. 6118-4
Chamberlain, Arthur
   Home a different place. 6715-8
Chamberlain, Brenda
   Dead ponies. 6379-9
   Fisherman husband. 6528-7
   Lament ("My man is a bone ringed with weed") 6379-9
   Poem ("You who"). 6379-9
   Song ("Heron is harsh"). 6379-9
   Song - Talysarn. 6360-8,6379-9
   To dafydd coed mourning his mountain-broken dog. 6360-8
   "You who in April laughed." 6360-8
Chamberlain, C.H.
   Illinois. 6465-5
Chamberlain, John
   Against a romantic interpretation. 6761-1
   Megalopolis. 6761-1
   Men reading: New York Public Library. 6761-1
Chamberlain, Phebe T.
   Indian names. 6798-0
   The Quaker meeting house at Spring Hill, sels. 6798-0
Chamberlain, Will
   Asleep. 7001-9
   Could they but know. 6542-2
   I am the mule. 6510-4
Chamberlayne, Lewis Parke
   Leaves from the anthology. 6030-7
Chamberlayne, William
   Chastity. 6385-3
   Pharonnida, sels. 6194-X
   The pharonnida, sels. 6194-X,6378-0
Chamberlin, Edwin
   The dervish. 6906-1
   The deserted city. 6906-1
   A sonnet to a sonnet. 6906-1
   The vegetable man. 6906-1
Chamberlin, H.H. (tr.)
   The fishermen's hut. Theocritus, 6435-3
Chambers of imagery. Archibald MacLeish. 6347-0
Chambers of imagery, sels. Gordon Bottomley. 6234-2
Chambers, ?
   To mistress Sarah Hickford. 6563-5
Chambers, Dana
   The leap. 7019-1
Chambers, E.K.
   I like to think of Shakespeare. 6477-9
   Lelant. 6477-9
Chambers, Lynne
   City after sunset. 6857-X
   Ryan. 6857-X
Chambers, Robert W.
   Dream lake. 6654-2
   The grey horse troop. 7012-4
   The 'grey horse' troop. 6946-0
   Officer Brady. 6089-7
   The recruit. 6300-4,6467-1,6089-7,6692-5,6724-7,6732-8
   The troop-ship sails. 6340-3,6471-X
   When I'se fightin' fod de Lawd. 6723-9
   Young Randal. 6180-X
Chambers, W. Francis
   Once in a while. 6274-1
Chambers, Whittaker
   Quag-hole. 6039-0
   Quag-tide. 6039-0
Chambers-Ketchum, Anne
   "I cannot tell the spell that binds thine image" 6226-1
Chameleon. Anthony Delius. 6788-3
Chameleon. Gordon LeClaire. 6833-2
Chameleon. Louise Louis. 6750-6
The **chameleon**. Sir Alan Patrick Herbert. 6512-0
The **chameleon**. James Merrick. 6600-3,6131-1,6219-9,6912-6
The **chameleon**. Matthew Prior. 6278-4
Chamisso, Adelbert von
   The toy of the giant's child. 6127-3,6614-3
   A tragic story. 6787-5
   A tragic story. William Makepeace Thackeray (tr.). 6613-5
   The widow' son. Elizabeth Craigmyle (tr.). 6842-1
The **chamois** hunter's love. Felicia Dorothea Hemans. 6973-8
The **chamois** hunters. Charles Swain. 6980-0
Chamouni. Sydney Dobell. 6832-4
Chamouny. Samuel Taylor Coleridge. 6425-6,6606-2
Chamouny. William Wordsworth. 6749-2
Chamouny at sunrise. Friederike Brunn. 6749-2
Champagne. Thomas Blaine Donaldson. 6936-3
Champagne. Franz Mikael Franzen. 6045-5
Champagne rose. John Kenyon. 6271-7,6437-X,6656-9
Champagne, 1914-1915. Alan Seeger. 6030-7
"**Champion** of human honour, let us lave". To Belgium. Eden Phillpotts. 7026-4
"**Champion** of those who groan beneath". To William Lloyd Garrison. John Greenleaf Whittier. 6753-0
The **champion** snorer. Burlington Hawkeye. 6294-6
Champion, J. (tr.)
   The birth of Rustem. Firdusi] (Abul Kasin Mansur) Firdausi [or Firdawsi, 6448-5
   Kiumers. Firdusi] (Abul Kasin Mansur) Firdausi [or Firdawsi, 6448-5
   Satire on Mahmud. Firdusi] (Abul Kasin Mansur) Firdausi [or Firdawsi, 6448-5
Champion, Martha
   Fragmenta. 6640-2

The **champion**. Berton Braley. 6853-7
The **champion**. Ibn Baqi. 6362-4
The **champion**. Lida Wilson Turner. 6750-6
Champions of the truth. John Keble. 6980-0
Champlain and Lake Champlain. Daniel L. Cady. 7030-2
Champlain: first Canadian. John Daniel Logan. 6115-X
Champney, Lizzie W.
    Daddy worthless. 6913-4
Chan Fang-sheng
    Sailing homeward. Arthur Waley (tr.). 7039-6,6253-9
Chan, Stephan
    One Christmas day. 7018-3
    The political lobbyist waits to leave the capitol. 7018-3
Chance. Ruth H. Hausman. 6850-2
Chance. Henry Herbert Knibbs. 7008-6
Chance. Unknown (Greek) 6435-3
Chance and change. Thomas Campion. 6198-2
Chance and change. Sir Lewis Morris. 6233-4
Chance meeting. Hilda ("H.D.") Doolittle. 6354-3
Chance meetings. Conrad Aiken. 6076-5,6102-8
"**Chance**, in whom men start and end". Unknown. 6435-3
Chance-fallen seed. Marie Emilie Gilchrist. 6102-8,6232-6, 6076-5
"The **chance-flung** favorite of no lucky". The man in the white house. Frederic Lawrence ("R.L. Paget") Knowles. 6995-9
A **chance**. Unknown. 6373-X
The **chance**. John Holmes. 6388-8
The **chance**. Arthur Sze. 6790-5
"The **chancellor** once was a tree full of fruit". On Thurlow. William Cowper. 6814-6
The **chancellor's** gardens. William John Courthope. 6046-3
The **chances**, sels. Francis Beaumont and John Fletcher. 6369-1
The **chances**. Wilfred Owen. 6506-6
Chanclebury ring. Wilfrid Scawen Blunt. 6477-9
Chandler Nicholas. Edgar Lee Masters. 6375-6
Chandler, A.H.
    The death-song of Chi-wee-moo. 7041-8
Chandler, Alfred
    Lights along the mile. 6784-0
Chandler, Alfred T.
    Bess. 6681-X
    Bess. 6768-9
    A bush idyl. 6768-9
    Catching the coach. 6768-9
Chandler, Amos Henry
    When Dora died. 6433-7
Chandler, Anita Gray
    The offering. 6799-9
Chandler, Anna P.
    Vacation time at grandpa's. 6715-8
Chandler, Bessie
    Mahmud and the idol. 6920-7
    The Miz. 6965-7
    My mending basket. 6097-8
    Ned's discovery. 6965-7
    Reminding the hen. 6682-8
Chandler, Elizabeth M.
    The enfranchised slaves and their benefactress. 7009-4
    Slave-produce. 7009-4
Chandler, J. (tr.)
    What star is this? Unknown (Latin), 6337-3
Chandler, Lucile
    Niagara cave. 6342-X
Chandonnet, Ann
    Grizzly. 6855-3
    In the cranberry gardens. 6855-3
Chang, Diane
    Artists east and west. 6790-5
    Codes. 6790-5
    The horizon is definitely speaking. 6790-5
    Second nature. 6790-5
    Trying to stay. 6966-5
Chang, Man-yung
    The moon, grapes, leaves. 6775-1
    Rain. 6775-1
Change. Robert Devereux, 2d Earl of Essex. 6436-1
Change. Fulke Greville; 1st Baron Brooke. 6436-1,6150-8

Change. William Dean Howells. 6431-0
Change. Raymond Knister. 6646-9
Change. Stella Reinhardt. 6397-7
Change. Percy Bysshe Shelley. 6385-3
Change. Sara Teasdale. 6538-4
Change. Lalia Mitchell Thornton. 6120-6
Change. Ella Wheeler Wilcox. 6956-8
Change. Helmut Zenker. 6769-7
Change assured. Unknown. 6274-1
"A **change** comes o'er the verdant woods". A blast of autumn. John E. Barrett. 6840-5
A **change** of face. Harrison Smith Morris. 6441-8
The **change** of flags. Arthur Guiterman. 6773-5
Change of mind. Edgar A. Guest. 6869-3
Change of mood. Harold Bergman. 7030-2
Change of voice. Unknown. 6698-4
Change should breed change. William Drummond of Hawthornden. 6931-2
Change thy mind since she doth change. Robert Devereux, 2d Earl of Essex. 6182-6
"**Change** was his mistress, chance his counselor". A vagrant's epitaph. Theodore Goodridge Roberts. 7012-4
The **change**. Abraham Cowley. 6933-9
The **change**. Abraham Cowley. 6317-9,6208-3,6341-1
The **change**. Abraham Cowley. 6933-9
The **change**. Beatrice Payne Morgan. 6841-3
The **change**. Alexander Smith. 6960-6,6980-0
The **change**. Unknown. 6859-6
Changed. Charles Stuart Calverley. 6026-9
The **changed** cross. Mrs. Charles Hobart. 6219-9
The **changed** cross. Unknown. 6909-6
Changed her mind. Unknown. 6682-8
Changed thought-birds. Frederick Herbert Adler. 6906-1
Changed voices. Sir William Watson. 6997-5
The **changed** woman. Louise Bogan. 6037-4
"**Changed**? Yes, I confess it - I have changed". Change. Ella Wheeler Wilcox. 6956-8
"**Changeful** the fair low-country, full of wiles". The lowlands. Edith L. Fraser. 7016-7
Changefulness. Abu Ishaq. 6362-4
Changeless. Martha Haskell Clark. 6374-8
Changeless. Alice Meynell. 6656-9
Changeless. John Richard Moreland. 6038-2
The **changeless** world. Sarah S. Jacobs. 6049-8
The **changeless**. Arthur Hugh Clough. 6737-9
Changeling. Josephine Sievers Birt. 6906-1
Changeling. Power Dalton. 6036-6
The **changeling**.. Charlotte Mew. 6477-9;6634-8
A **changeling**. Adelaide Anne Procter. 6957-6
The **changeling**. Agnes Lee. 6347-0
The **changeling**. James Russell Lowell. 6078-1,6127-3,6126-5
Changelings. Mary Frances Butts. 6373-X
Changes. Witter Bynner. 6779-4
Changes. Ibn Sa'id (of Alcala La Real) 6362-4
Changes. Owen (Edward Bulwer-Lytton, Earl Lytton) Meredith. 6385-3
Changes. Adelaide Anne Procter. 6957-6
Changes of home. John Leyden. 6980-0
"**Changes** of light are living things". Changes. Witter Bynner. 6779-4
Changing color. Hattie G. Canfield. 6672-0
Changing her mind. Alfred Perceval Graves. 6692-5
Changing mind. Conrad Aiken. 6012-9
'**Changing** works' in Vermont. Daniel L. Cady. 6988-6
The **changing** year. Lloyd Roberts. 6820-9
Channel firing. Thomas Hardy. 6665-8
A **channel** passage. Rupert Brooke. 6258-X,6210-5
A **channel** passage. Algernon Charles Swinburne. 6655-0
Channel port. Joseph Auslander. 6783-2
A **channel** rhyme. Cicely Fox Smith. 6258-X
Channel sunset. John Gould Fletcher. 7027-2
The **channel-stane**. John Usher. 7035-3,6960-6
Channing, Walter
    To Napoleon in exile. 6482-5
Channing, William Ellery
    And here the hermit sat, and told his beads. 6399-3, 6176-1
    The earth-spirit. 6176-1
    The earth-spirit. 6438-8

The flight of the wild geese. 6438-8,6467-1
The hillside cot. 6438-8
Hymn of the earth. 6176-1,6288-1
Memory. 6438-8
The mountain, sels. 6467-1
The mountain. 6438-8
My symphony. 6337-3
Our boat to the waves. 6385-3
A poet's hope, sels. 6300-4
A poet's hope. 6288-1,6438-8
Sea song. 6438-8
Sleepy Hollow. 6600-3
Tears in spring. 6309-8
To my companions. 6271-7
Walden Lake. 6484-1

Channing-Stetson, Grace Ellery
California of the south. 6241-5
The flag of stars. 6223-7
Flower-beds in the Tuileries. 7027-2
Qui vive? 7026-4
War. 6542-2

Chanson ("A Saint-Blaise"). Alfred de Musset. 6801-4
Chanson ("J'ai dit"). Alfred de Musset. 6801-4
Chanson ("Quand on perd"). Alfred de Musset. 6801-4
Chanson d'automne. Paul Verlaine. 6102-8
Chanson d'autrefois. Victor Hugo. 6801-4
Chanson d'or. Ann [or Annie E.] Hamilton. 6037-4
Chanson noir. Ann [or Annie E.] Hamilton. 6037-4
Chanson of a lady in the shade. Paul Celan. 6758-1
Chanson of the bells of Oseney. Cale Young Rice. 6556-2, 6326-8,6421-3
Chanson tendre. Bruce Blakeney. 6397-7
Chanson un peu naive. Louise Bogan. 6070-6,6250-4
Chansons innocentes I. Edward Estlin Cummings. 6808-1
Chansons innocentes, sels. Edward Estlin Cummings. 6527-9
Chant birds in every bush. Unknown. 6328-4
Chant du soir. Paul Fort. 6253-9
Chant for reapers. Wilfrid Thorley. 6437-X
Chant for the Bryant festival, November 5, 1864. Bayard Taylor. 6976-2
Chant for the moon-of-flowers. Lew Sarett. 6393-4
Chant for the salt marsh. Katharine Brown Burt. 6789-1
A chant of army cooks. Unknown. 6846-4
Chant of departure. Alfred Barrett. 6282-2
A chant of empire. James Rhoades. 7031-0
A chant of love for England. Helen Gray Cone. 6224-5
A chant of love for England. Helen Gray Cone. 6309-8
A chant of the ages. Alfred Noyes. 6151-6
Chant of the bards before their massacre by Edward I. Felicia Dorothea Hemans. 6973-8
Chant of the blue-gums. Beatrice Marian Bromley. 6800-6
Chant of the changing hours. Don Marquis. 6875-2
The chant of the children of the mist. Emily Pfeiffer. 6770-0,6875-8
The chant of the Colorado. Cale Young Rice. 6556-2,6336-5
The chant of the cross-bearing child. James Whitcomb Riley. 6695-X
A chant of the fought field. Edith M. Thomas. 6250-4
Chant of the old men in the woods. Charles Norman. 6076-5
The chant of the vultures. Edwin Markham. 6542-2
The chant of the woman. Grace Blackburn. 6115-X
A chant on the terrible highway. Hermann Hagedorn. 6944-4
A chant out of doors. Marguerite Wilkinson. 6476-0,6509-0, 6607-0,6143-5,6161-3
Chant royal from a copydesk for Bob Garst. Rufus Terral. 6850-2
Chant royal of August. Ethel Talbot. 6875-8
The chant royal of pure romance. Gelett Burgess. 6850-2
Chant royal of the dejected dipsomaniac. Don Marquis. 6875-8
Chant royal of the god of love. John Payne. 6875-2
Chant royal on the fixed forms. Jane Gray Ward. 6850-2
Chant sung in darkness. Herbert Trench. 6877-4
Chant-pagan. Rudyard Kipling. 6810-3
Chant-royal of California. Gelett Burgess. 6875-8
Chant-royal of the true romance. Gelett Burgess. 6875-8
A chant. Adelaide Anne Procter. 6957-6
A chanted calendar. Sydney Dobell. 6236-9
Chantey. Fay Strawn Campbell. 6316-0
A chantey for celestial vikings. Earl B. Marlatt. 7019-1

Chanticleer. William Austin. 6931-2
Chanticleer. John Chipman Farrar. 6466-3
Chanticleer. Celia Thaxter. 6519-8,6612-7,6639-9,6638-0
Chanticleer. Katharine (Hinkson) Tynan. 6242-3,6478-7,6135-4,6510-4,6639-9
Chants of life. Mathilde Blind. 7037-X
Chanty. Ronald McCuaig. 6349-7
Chanukah thoughts. Morris Rosenfeld. 7011-6
Chao-ti of Han
    Written in early autumn at the pool of sprinkling water. Florence Ayscough and Amy Lowell (tr.). 6253-9
Chaos. Alexander Pope. 6315-2
"Chaos, of old, was God's dominion". Night. Lloyd Mifflin. 6243-1
Chapbook, Banbury
    Black your shoes, your Honour? 6466-3
Chapel. Johann Ludwig Uhland. 6949-5
Chapel Hill road, N. C. James Abraham Martling. 6952-5
"The chapel bell, with hollow mournful sound". Elegy written in a college library. George Ellis. 6802-2
The Chapel in Lyoness. William Morris. 6657-7,6655-0,6543-0
The chapel in Lyoness. William Morris. 6110-9
Chapel in the woods. Mary Newton Baldwin. 6646-8
The chapel road. Mary C. Haughey. 6750-6
chapel, fr. Pictures by the way. John Nichol. 6819-7
The chapel. Bayard Taylor. 6976-2
The chaperon.. Henry Cuyler Bunner. 6735-2
The chaperon. Henry Cuyler Bunner. 6004-8,6092-7,6336-5
Chapin, Katherine Garrison
    For a British flyer. 6761-1
    From a tropical shore. 6042-0
    High wind at Spanish point. 6042-0
    Love beleaguered. 6979-7
    Memory clear. 6042-0
    Morning after. 6042-0
    Plain chant for America. 6761-1
Chaplain to the forces. Winifred M. Letts. 7031-0,7026-4
The chaplain. Unknown. 6589-9
The chaplet of Cypress. Thomas Holley Chivers. 7017-5
A chaplet of flowers. Adelaide Anne Procter. 6957-6
The chaplet. Witter Bynner. 6467-1
Chaplin, Alethea
    Hickory, dickory, dock. 6937-1
    The man in the moon. 6937-1
    The moon. 6937-1
Chaplin, Ralph
    Freedom. 6880-4
    The living dead. 6880-4
    Mourn not the dead. 6538-4,6102-8,6337-3,6542-2,6076-5
    Night in the cell house. 6538-4
    To my little son. 6036-6
    Wesley Everest. 6880-4
The chaplinade, sels. Claire Goll. 6351-9
Chaplinesque. Hart Crane. 6808-1
Chapman, Arthur
    The cliff dwelling. 6836-7
    The horseback farmer. 7012-4
    In mesa land. 6836-7
    The meeting. 6510-4
    Mother West. 6274-1
    The musings of Arroyo Al. 6486-8
    Navajo. 6836-7
    The old sheep wagon. 7008-6
    The old-timer. 7010-8
    Out where the west begins. 6836-7
    Out where the west begins. 6732-8,6102-8,6336-5,6076-5
    The pony express. 7010-8
    The ranger's life. 6478-7
    Unknown. 6542-2
    The war-horse buyers. 6510-4
    Where the west begins. 6963-0
Chapman, Coates
    Ballade d'aujourd'hui. 6274-1
Chapman, E.J.
    Lake scene in western Canada. 6591-0,6592-2
    A question. 6433-7
Chapman, E.W.
    Flowers for the brave. 6304-7

Chapman, Edward
  Columbia. 7022-1
Chapman, Ethelyn Bryant
  Snow moths. 6799-9
Chapman, George
  The blind beggar of Alexandria, sels. 6378-0
  Bridal song ("Now, Sleep, bind fast the flood of air") 6182-6,6102-8
  Bussy D'Ambois, sel. 6958-4
  Bussy D'Ambois, sels. 6317-9,6378-0,6369-1
  Byron's conspiracy, sels. 6378-0
  The camp at night. 6186-9
  The conspiracy of Charles, Duke of Byron, sels. 6369-1
  Corinna bathes. 6436-1
  De Guiana, Carmen epicum. 6436-1
  Descend, fair sun! 6182-6
  Epithalamion teratos. 6182-6,6315-2
  Eugenia. 6208-3
  Her coming. 6189-3,6250-4
  Hero and Leander, sels. 6378-0
  Homeric hymn to Neptune. 6833-2
  An invective written ...against Mr. Ben Johnson. 6200-8
  Knell. 6337-3
  Last words of Byron. 6150-8
  Love and philosophy. 6436-1
  The master spirit. 6438-8
  "Muses, that sing love's sensual emperie." 6182-6,6181-8
  Night. 6436-1
  "Now all ye peaceful regents of the night." 6317-9
  "Now sleep, bind fast the flood of air." 6317-9
  "O come, soft rest of cares! Come, night". 6187-7
  Of circumspection. 6189-3
  Ovid's banquet of Sence. 6208-3
  Paul I: Paul III. 6761-1
  The pilot. 6833-2
  The praise of Homer. 6438-8
  'Pressage of storme', fr. Eugenia. 6208-3
  A procession of peace. 6935-5
  Repentance. 6436-1
  Revenge of Bussy D'Ambois, sels. 6378-0
  The shadow of night, sel. 6958-4
  The shadow of night, sel. 6958-4
  The shadow of the night. 6380-2
  "Shine out, fair sun, with all your heat." 6125-7,6181-8
  The sixth book of Homer's Iliads, sels. 6198-2
  Sonnet ("Muses that sing"). 6315-2
  The spirit of Homer. 6186-9
  The tears of peace. 6315-2
  To Mars. 6315-2
  The tragedy of Caesar and Pompey, sels. 6378-0
  The tragedy of Charles, Duke of Byron, sels. 6369-1
  The twelfth book of Homer's Odysseys, sels. 6198-2
  Ulysses hears the prophecies of Tiresias. 6315-2
  Virtue the safest guide. 6150-8
  The wedding of Alcmane and Mya. 6436-1
Chapman, George (tr.)
  Achilles shows himself in the battle by the ships. Homer, 6933-9
  Calypso's island, fr. The Odyssey. Homer, 6435-3
  The death of Hector, fr. The Iliad. Homer, 6933-9
  The end of the suitors, fr. The Odyssey. Homer, 6933-9
  "He stoopt Pierea...", fr. The Odyssey. Homer, 6435-3
  The Iliad, sels. Homer, 6562-7,6194-X
  "In meantime flew our ships...", fr. The Odyssey. Homer, 6547-3
  Lament for Bion. Moschus, 7039-6
  Nausicaa, fr. The Odyssey. Homer, 6933-9
  The Odyssey, sels. Homer, 6527-9,6547-3
  Poetry and learning, fr. The Iliad. Homer, 6933-9
  Praise of Homer, fr. The Odyssey. Homer, 6933-9
  Priam and Achilles, fr. The Iliad. Homer, 6933-9
  The sacrifice, fr. The Odyssey. Homer, 6933-9
  Sarpedon's speech, fr. The Iliad. Homer, 6933-9
  Scylla and Charybdis, fr. The Odyssey. Homer, 6933-9
  "This said, he went to see", fr. The Iliad. Homer, 6562-7
  The Trojans outside the walls, fr. The Iliad. Homer, 6933-9
  Ulysses in the waves, fr. The Odyssey. Homer, 6933-9
Chapman, John Jay
  America's gift to France. 6681-X
  Books and reading. 6036-6
  Clouds. 6833-2
  The grandfather. 6036-6
  His vanished master. 7008-6
  No pilots we. 6071-4,6250-4
  Roosevelt. 6995-9
  Summer's adieu. 6036-6
  To a dog. 7027-2
  Toil away. 6076-5,6102-8
Chapman, Mary Berri
  Village coward. 6692-5
Chapman, Nell
  Bread on the water. 6178-8
  Requiem. 6178-8
Chapman, Violet D.
  Song of the zeppelin. 7031-0
Chappell, George S.
  Innocence. 6736-0
Chapter heading. Ernest Hemingway. 6069-2
Char, Rene
  The library is on fire. Charles Guenther (tr.). 6803-0
Char-co-o-al. Unknown. 6045-1,6566-X
Character. Edward W. Benson. 6529-5
Character. Samuel Taylor Coleridge. 6438-8
Character. Ralph Waldo Emerson. 6753-0
Character. Ralph Waldo Emerson. 6252-0,6288-1
Character. Ralph Waldo Emerson. 6753-0
Character. Johann Wolfgang von Goethe. 6109-5
Character. David Morton. 6779-4
A **character** - and a question. James Ashcroft Noble. 7015-9
A **character** and a question. Unknown. 6273-3
Character and circumstances. William Wordsworth. 6935-5
Character and love of Birtha, fr. Gondibert. Sir William Davenant. 6867-7
Character of a good parson. John Dryden. 6600-3,6543-0
The **character** of a good parson. Geoffrey Chaucer. 6970-3
Character of a happy life. Sir Henry Wotton. 6424-8,6639-9, 6543-0,6660-7,6668-2,6301 ,6194-X,6250-4,6189-3,6219-9,6371-3,6737 ,6186-9,6246-6,6291-1,6332-2,6337-3, 6473 ,6198-2,6138-9,6182-6,6562-7,6604-6,6512
The **character** of a small poet. Samuel Butler. 6200-8
Character of Artevelde, fr. Philip Van Artevelde. Henry Taylor. 6980-0
Character of Buckingham. John Dryden. 6634-8
The **character** of Holland, sels. Andrew Marvell. 6194-X
The **character** of Holland. Andrew Marvell. 6125-7
The **character** of Hudibras. Samuel Butler. 6200-8
Character of Lucile. Owen (Edward Bulwer-Lytton, Earl Lytton) Meredith. 6577-5
The **character** of the bore. John Donne. 6200-8
Character of the Earl of Shaftesbury. John Dryden. 6543-0
Character of the French. Oliver Goldsmith. 6543-0
Character of the happy warrior. William Wordsworth. 6122-2, 6138-9,6154-0,6315-2,6337-3,6501 ,6086-2,6110-9,6250-4,6199-0,6214-8
Character of the Italians. Oliver Goldsmith. 6543-0
Character of the Swiss. Oliver Goldsmith. 6543-0
Character of Villiers, Duke of Buckingham. John Dryden. 6543-0
A **character** sketch. Unknown. 6688-7
A **character..** Alfred Lord Tennyson. 6123-0
A **character.** Aubrey Thomas De Vere. 6980-0
A **character.** Menella Bute Smedley. 7037-X
Characteristics of a child. William Wordsworth. 6233-4
A **characterization-lines** on the Hon. Edward Villiers. Sir Henry Taylor. 6656-9
Characters from the satires: Atticus. Alexander Pope. 7039-6
Characters from the satires: Wharton. Alexander Pope. 7039-6
Characters of women. Edward Young. 6932-0
The **characters** of women, sels. Alexander Pope. 6637-2
Characters of women: Flavia, Atossa, and Cloe. Alexander Pope. 6932-0
Charade. Winthrop Mackworth Praed. 6239-3,6502-3,6602-2, 6302-0,6724-7,6291
Carade. Unknown. 6312-8

Charade on the name of the poet Campbell. Winthrop
    Mackworth Praed. 6874-X
Charasson, Henriette
    Ave Maria. Frederic Thompson (tr.). 6282-2
The **charcoal** man. John Townsend Trowbridge. 6142-7,6392-7,
    6279-2,6451-5,6554-6,6565
The **charcoal-burner's** son. Erik Gustaf Geijer. 6045-5
The **charcoal-burner**. Sr Edmund Gosse. 6437-X,6046-3
The **charge** at Santiago. William Hamilton Hayne. 6062-5
The **charge** at Waterloo. Sir Walter Scott. 6302-0,6385-3,
    6552-X
The **charge** by the ford. Thomas Dunn English. 6916-9
The **charge** by the ford. Thomas Dunn English. 6015-3,6113-3,
    6062-5
"The **charge** is loosed; the iron shrieks...". Eternal
    youth. A. Judson Hanna. 7007-8
The **charge** of de 'Dutch brigade'. Charles M. Connolly.
    6155-9,6791-3
The **charge** of Pickett's brigade. Unknown. 6964-9
The **charge** of the heavy brigade. Alfred Lord Tennyson.
    6473-6,6552-X
Charge of the light brigade. Alfred Lord Tennyson. 6133-8,
    6504-X,6486-8,6512-0,6621-6,6014 ,6183-4,6385-3,6425-
    6,6610-0,6271-7,6211 ,6242-3,6087-0,6473-6,6554-6,
    6239-3,6558 ,6260-1,6323-3,6392-6,6459-0,6478-7,6501
    ,6370-5,6457-4,6552-X,6732-8,6565-1,6304 ,6401-9,
    6498-1,6332-2,6479-5,6136-2,6142 ,6301-2,6403-5,6110-
    9,6192-3,6560-0,6199 ,6107-9,6212-2,6131-1,6219-9,
    6263-6,6267 ,6421-3,6424-8,6639-9,6655-0
Charge of the rough writers. Harold MacGrath. 6274-1
The **charge** on "Old Hundred". Unknown. 6417-5
A **charge** to the poets, sels. William Whitehead. 6867-7
A **charge**. Herbert Trench. 6437-X,6301-2,6396-9,6639-9
The **chargers**. Mohammed. 6732-8
"**Charging** headlong into the dawn". Lindbergh--alone! Byron
    Cooney. 7019-1
"The **chariest** maid is prodigal enought", fr. Hamlet.
    William Shakespeare. 6934-7
The **chariot** race, fr. Electra. Sophocles. 6621-6
A **chariot-race**, fr. Electra. Sophocles. 6435-3
A **charioteer**. Unknown (Greek) 6435-3
Charis. Ben Jonson. 6830-8
Charis' triumph. Ben Jonson. 6189-3
Charisius rebukes himself, fr. Epitrepontes. Menander.
    6435-3
Charitas nimia or the dear bargain. Richard Crashaw. 6489-
    2,6546-7
Charity. William Cowper. 6250-4
Charity. Charles and Mary Lamb. 6295-4
Charity. R.W. Lanigan. 6674-7
Charity. George Parsons Lathrop. 6292-X
Charity. James Abraham Martling. 6952-5
Charity. Gertrude Huntington McGiffert. 6838-3
Charity. Joaquin Miller. 7041-8
Charity. Joaquin Miller. 6303-9,6396-9,6464-7
Charity. Sir Thomas Noon Talfourd. 6408-6,6605-2
Charity. Elizabeth Turner. 6018-8
Charity. Unknown. 6260-1,6498-1,6583-X
Charity. Elizabeth H. Whittier. 6600-3
Charity ("'Mongst al your virtues"). Thomas Middleton.
    6294-6
The **charity** ball. George Gordon, 6th Baron Byron. 6945-2
Charity in thought. Samuel Taylor Coleridge. 6722-0
A **charity** sermon. Thomas Hood. 6974-6
Charity's eye. William Rounseville Alger. 7008-6
Charity's meal. Unknown. 6744-1
Charity, fr. An essay on man. Alexander Pope. 6932-0
Charity, sels. William Cowper. 6934-7
Charivari. J. Corson Miller. 6839-1
Charlemagne. Mary Sinton Leitch. 6331-4,6631-3
Charlemagne. Henry Wadsworth Longfellow. 6624-0
Charlemagne (atr.)
    Veni creator spiritus. John Dryden (tr.). 6214-8,6730-1
"**Charlemagne** carried it far". The cross. Ruby Weyburn
    Tobias. 6144-3
"**Charlemagne** had sinned a heavy sin". The confession of
    Charlemagne. Karl Simrock. 6842-1
Charlemagne's voyage. Johann Ludwig Uhland. 6842-1
"**Charlemagne**, the mighty monarch". Work and worship.
    William Allen Butler. 6903-7

"**Charles** - and I say it wond'ring...". Sonnet to Charles
    Diodati. John Milton. 6814-6
Charles Augustus Anderson. Unknown. 6057-9
Charles Augustus Fortescue. Hilaire Belloc. 6633-X
Charles D'Orleans, sels. Henry Wadsworth Longfellow. 6047-
    1
Charles Dickens. Louella C. Poole. 6476-0
Charles Dickens. Arthur Hobson Quinn. 6936-5
Charles Dickens. Sir William Watson. 6714-X
Charles Edward at Versailles. William Edmonstoune Aytoun.
    6948-7
Charles Guiteau, or, the murder of James A. Garfield.
    Unknown. 6058-7
Charles I; King of England
    Majesty in misery. 6385-3,6188-5,6014-5
    On a quiet conscience. 6228-8,6512-0,6533-3
Charles II. Nahum Tate. 6867-7
Charles II, fr. Last instructions to a painter. Andrew
    Marvell. 6933-9
Charles II, sels. Douglas Brooke Wheelton Sladen. 6656-9
Charles II; King of England
    I pass all my hours in a shady old grove. 6328-4
    Song ("I pass all"). 6563-5
"**Charles** Ives, I have heard". Ives. Richard Eberhart. 6803-
    0
Charles Kingsley. Arthur E.J. Legge. 6793-X
Charles Lamb. Pakenham Beatty. 6656-9
Charles Lamb, fr. Literary reminiscences. Thomas De
    Quincey. 6958-4
Charles Lindbergh. Huldah M. Johnson. 7019-1
"**Charles** sleeps, and feels no more the...cares".
    Cromwell's soliloquy over the dead body of Charles.
    Edward Bulwer-Lytton; Baron Lytton. 6980-0
Charles the First. Percy Bysshe Shelley. 6208-3
Charles the First, sels. Percy Bysshe Shelley. 6199-0
Charles the Second. William Wordsworth. 6188-5
Charles Webster. Edgar Lee Masters. 6628-3
Charles XII. Samuel Johnson. 6543-0,6102-8,6240-7,6302-0,
    6385-3,6250-4,6150
"**Charles**! my slow heart was only sad, when first". Sonnet
    to a friend, who asked how I felt..my infant to me.
    Samuel Taylor Coleridge. 6967-3
Charles's wain. Sir Alfred Comyn Lyall. 6793-X
Charles, Elizabeth (tr.)
    Ascension hymn. The Venerable Bede, 6337-3
    Hymn ("A hymn of glory"). The Venerable Bede, 6730-1
Charles, Mabel Munns
    The living tithe. 6144-3
Charles, Mrs.
    "Is thy cruse of comfort failing?" 6238-5
Charles, Mrs. E.R.
    Child in the judgment seat. 6304-7
Charles, Orrin K.
    The call of the adventurers. 7007-8
Charles, William Byron
    A little wrinkled soul of loveliness. 6750-6
Charleston. Richard Watson Gilder. 6946-0
Charleston. Paul Hamilton Hayne. 6074-9
Charleston. Henry Timrod. 6006-4,6113-3,6333-0,6735-2,6008-
    0,6288-1,6431-0,6396-9
A **Charleston** garden. Henry Bellamann. 6326-8,6649-6
Charleston plantations. May Sarton. 6761-1
Charlesworth, Hector
    Sonnets on the death of Stevenson. 6433-7
Charleville. John Gray. 6507-4
Charley and his father. Eliza Lee Follen. 6131-1
"**Charley** loves good cakes and ale". Unknown. 6363-2
Charley the story-teller. Unknown (German) 6614-3
"**Charley**! Here I am at last". Fragments: To Charley Walker
    (3). Adam Lindsay Gordon. 6951-7
Charley's butterfly. Unknown. 6312-8
Charley, the story-teller. Unknown. 6127-3
"**Charlie** died today". Eulogy for a tough guy. Daniel L.
    Klauck. 6870-7
Charlie he's my darling. Robert Burns. 6737-9
Charlie is my darling. James Hogg. 6136-2,6219-9
Charlie is my darling. Carolina Oliphant, Baroness Nairne.
    6323-3,6086-2
Charlie is my darling. Unknown. 6271-7,6026-9
Charlie is my darling: 2d set. Carolina Oliphant, Baroness

Nairne. 6859-6
Charlie Lucas. William Stapleton Long. 6761-1
Charlie Machree. William J. Hoppin. 6911-8
Charlie Machree. William J. Hoppin. 6142-7,6165-6,6344-6, 6385-3,6392-6,6451-5,6554-6,6567-8
Charlie MacPherson. Unknown. 6185-0
Charlie Stuart. Allan Cunningham. 6859-6
Charlie's landing. Carolina Oliphant, Baroness Nairne. 6859-6
"Charlie, he's a young man". Unknown. 6299-7
Charlie, he's my darling. Unknown. 6490-6
Charlotte Corday. Robert Loveman. 6941-X
"Charlotte lived by a mountain side". Charlotte, the frozen girl. Unknown. 6826-X
"Charlotte lived on a mountain top...". The frozen girl. Unknown. 6826-X
Charlotte, Elizabeth
    The maiden city. 6518-X
Charlotte, the frozen girl. Unknown. 6826-X
Charlton, R.M.
    The state v. Henry Day. 6878-2
Charm. Bertha Strong Cooley. 6894-4
Charm ("She wields charm"). Mark Turbyfill. 6038-2
The charm ("Thrice the brindled cat hath mewed"). William Shakespeare. 6533-3
A charm against a magpie. Unknown. 6125-7
Charm against enemies. Unknown. 6292-X
"Charm me asleep, and melt me so". Music. Robert Herrick. 7014-0
"The charm of music's soul-elating voice". Tightened strings. Elizabeth B. Robb. 6818-9
A charm to call sleep. Henry Johnstone. 6519-8,6135-4
A charm.. Rudyard Kipling. 6427-2
Charm: to be said in the sun. Josephine Preston Peabody. 6338-1
A charm. John Dryden. 6125-7
A charm. Robert Herrick. 6228-8,6125-7
A charm. Thomas Randolph. 6563-5
The charm. William Browne. 6533-3
The charm. Thomas Campion. 6189-3,6250-4
The charm. Alice Edith Egbert. 6118-4
The charm. John Fletcher. 6198-2,6189-3
Charmaid. Maude Smith Delavan. 6750-6
The charmed picture. Felicia Dorothea Hemans. 6973-8
Charmed voices. Joshua Freeman Crowell. 6798-0
The charmer. Harriet Beecher Stowe. 6304-7
Charmian. Bayard Taylor. 6976-2
Charming beauty bright. Unknown. 6058-7
The charming of the east wind. Charles Tennyson Turner. 6980-0
"A charming old lady of Settle". Limerick:"A charming old lady of Settle". Unknown. 6811-1
A charming woman. John Godfrey Saxe. 6911-8
The charming woman. Helen Selina Sheridan; Lady Dufferin. 6026-9
"A charming young lady named Nelly". Limerick:"A charming young lady named Nelly". Charles Coburn. 6811-1
Charmley, Beulah Jackson
    Illinois farmer. 6750-6
Charms. Edgar A. Guest. 6862-6
Charms. Unknown. 6193-1
The charms of nature. Joseph Warton. 6932-0
"Charms, that call down the moon from out...". To musick, to becalme a sweet-sick-youth. Robert Herrick. 6958-4
Charol and Philomel. Robert Herrick. 6943-6
"Charon! receive a family on board". On Niobe. Unknown (Greek). 6814-6
"The charred/And blackened grass". Fire. Marjorie DeGraff. 6850-2
Chart. Joseph Auslander. 6039-0
Charter oak. Lucia M. Mooney. 6684-4
The charter oak. George Denison Prentice. 6678-X
The charter of salvation. George Arthur Clarke. 6337-3
Charter-country. Arthur Shearly Cripps. 6625-9
Chartier, Allain
    Un cordier. 6724-7
Chartier, Vileta Nelson
    New England Mayflower. 6764-6
    The wind and the rain. 6764-6

Chartist chaunt. Thomas Cooper. 7009-4
Chartist song. Thomas Cooper. 6188-5,6656-9
Chartless. Emily Dickinson. 6239-3,6303-9,6331-4,6418-3, 6102-8,6096-5,6309-8,6107-9,6396-9,6250-4,6439-6, 6214-8,6300-4
Chartreuse. William Wordsworth. 6749-2
Charwoman. Dorothy Brown Thompson. 6042-0
The charwoman. George Lawrence Andrews. 6039-0
"Chas. Meech sits by the pool". My party. Florri McMillan. 6822-7
Chase after love, fr. The shepeardes calendar. Edmund Spenser. 6197-4
The chase and the race, fr. Ye wearie wayfarer. Adam Lindsay Gordon. 6427-2
"The chase is over. No noise on Ardven but...". Comala. Unknown. 6873-1
The chase of the laurel wreath. Jessie M. Wood. 7021-3
Chase, Annie
    A flock of birds. 6049-8
    Motion song--daisy fair. 6049-8
Chase, Annie E.
    Flag song for Washington's birthday. 6712-3
Chase, Clifford
    The stile. 6694-1
Chase, Edith Foster
    An old, old tree. 6342-X
Chase, Eleanor
    To A.B.C. 6817-0
Chase, Marion Monks
    One. 6177-X
Chase, Mrs. M.W.
    Growing old. 6929-0
Chase, Polly
    Hands on a card-table. 6039-0
    Little things. 6039-0
Chase, Stanley Perkins (tr.)
    The pearl, sels. Unknown, 6282-2
    The queen of courtesy, fr. The pearl. Unknown, 6282-2
The chase.. Coventry Patmore. 6600-3
The chase. James Vincent Cunningham. 6640-2
The chase. Sir Walter Scott. 6252-0,6322-5,6543-0
Chasing a rainbow of dreams. Mabel Ethleen Palmer. 6799-9
Chasing the fox. Geoffrey Chaucer. 6150-8
Chasm. Mary Lanigan Healy. 6750-6
The chasm. Hermann Hagedorn. 6347-0
The chasm. Willa Calvert Smith. 6799-9
The chaste Arabian bird. John Wilmot, 2d Earl of Rochester. 6733-6
"Chaste as the air whither she's fled". On the death of Mrs. Elizabeth Filmer. Richard Lovelace. 6934-7
Chastelard to Mary Stuart. Algernon Charles Swinburne. 6094-3
Chastelard, sels. Algernon Charles Swinburne. 6110-9,6655-0
Chastity. William Chamberlayne. 6385-3
Chastity. John Milton. 7020-5
Chastity. John Milton. 6543-0
Chastity. Susan Shogren. 6883-9
Chastity, fr. Comus. John Milton. 6933-9
Chateau de Monthiers. Katherine Mann Mann. 6180-X
Chateau Papineau. Susan Frances ("Seranus") Harrison. 6656-9
Chateaubriand, Francois de
    Comparison of Washington and Napoleon. 6424-8
Chateaux d'Espagne. Henry Sambrooke Leigh. 6802-2
Chatfield, Sarah M.
    Are these God's children? 6575-9
    Cross Betsy. 6314-4
Chatham, in seventy-eight. Edward Farquhar. 6939-8
The chatterbox. Ann Taylor. 6233-4
The chatterbox. Jane Taylor. 6424-8
Chatterton. William Wordsworth. 6980-0
Chatterton, Minnie
    A smart boy. 6312-8
Chatterton, Thomas
    The accounte of W. Canynges feast. 6086-2,6195-0,6198-2
    Aella, sels. 6086-2,6250-4
    Aella, sels. 6726-3
    An African song. 6315-2,6545-7
    Autumn and winter, fr. Elegy to the memory of Mr. T.

CHATTERTON

Philips. 6545-7
Autumn fruits, fr. Aella. 6545-7
The ballade of charitie. 6604-6,6102-8,6660-7,6659-3
Bristowe tragedie: or, the death of Syr Charles Bawdin. 6086-2,6152-4,6438-8
Bristowe tragedie: or, the death of Syr Charles Bawdin, sels. 6191-5
Bristowe tragedie; or, the dethe of Syr Charles... 6198-2
Cawna, fr. Heccar and Gaira. 6545-7
Chorus from Goddwyn. 6086-2
Eclogue: a man, a woman, Sir Roger. 6086-2
Eclogue: Elinoure and Juga. 6086-2
Eclogue: Robert and Raufe. 6086-2
Elegy, sels. 6545-7
An excellent ballad of charity. 6732-8,6102-8,6086-2, 6195-0,6152-4,6245
Faith. 6481-7
Flowers and spice, fr. Narva and Mored. 6545-7
A hymn for Christmas day. 6337-3
Last verses. 6086-2,6102-8
The minstrel's roundelay, fr. Aelia. 6108-8,6604-6,6660-7
The minstrel's song in Ella. 6600-3,6133-8,6301-2,6383-7
The minstrel's song. 6302-0,6385-3,6315-2,6271-7,6195-0, 6152-4,6219-9
My love is dead. 6240-7
Mynstrelles songe. 6024-2
"O sing unto my roundelay", fr. Aella. 6726-3,6328-4, 6560-0,6195-0
On resignation. 6543-0
Resignation. 6219-9,6271-7
Roundelay. 6153-2
Song ("O sing"), fr. Aella. 6250-4,6317-9
Song from Aella. 6086-2
Song to Aella. 6086-2
Song, fr. Aella. 6186-9
Spring song. 6328-4
Tygers, fr. The death of Nicou. 6545-7
The want. 6935-5

Chattopadhyay, Sarojini
Eastern dancers. 6507-4

Chaucer. Henry Wadsworth Longfellow. 6121-4,6126-5,6153-2, 6300-4,6230-X,6176-1,6333-0,6483-3,6288-1,6431-0
"Chaucer! when in my breast, as autumn wanes". To Chaucer. David M. Main. 7015-9
Chaucer's flower. Geoffrey Chaucer. 7020-5

Chaucer, Geoffrey
Alisoun. 6150-8
"Allas the wo! Allas, the peynes stronge." 6317-9
Arcita's dying address. 6543-0
Ariadne. 6438-8
The assumption of Troilus. 6150-8
Balade ("Hyd, Absolon, thy gilte tresses clere"). 6315-2,6125-7,6250-4
Balade de Bon Conseyl. 6198-2
Ballad of good counsel. 6022-6
Ballade to his lady. 6830-8
Ballade to Rosamund. 6881-2
Benediction, fr. The Canterbury tales. 6337-3
The book of the duchess, sels. 6726-3
The book of the duchess,, sels. 6193-1
The briddes in May. 6943-6
The cage. 6943-6
The Canterbury pilgrims. 6302-0;6385-3
The Canterbury tales, sels. 6200-8,6732-8,6198-2,6369-1, 6726-3,6228 ,6378-0,6102-8,6484-1,6337-3,6193-1,6430 ,6250-4,6197-4,6301-2
Captivity. 6023-4,6250-4
The carpenter's young wife. 6733-6
The cave of Morpheus, fr. The book of the duchesse. 6958-4
The character of a good parson. John Dryden (tr.). 6970-3
Chasing the fox. 6150-8
Chaucer's flower. 7020-5
Chauntecleer and Pertelote. 6733-6
The clerk of Oxenford [or Oxford]. 6150-8,6153-2
The cock and the fox; or, the tale of he nun's priest.

John Dryden (tr.). 6970-3
The complaint of Chaucer to his empty purse. 6726-3, 6198-2,6732-8
The complaint of Troilus. 6830-8
The complaint to his empty purse. 6301-2,6383-7
The complaynt of Chaucer to his purse. 6193-1
Counsel upon marriage. 6489-2
The cuckoo and the nightingale. 6271-7,6438-8
Daisies. 6659-3
The daisy. 6240-7
Dawn. 6153-2
Death and the ruffians, fr. The Canterbury tales. 6102-8
Description of the lists built by Theseus for the... 6935-5
The despair of Troilus. 6315-2
Destiny. 6438-8
The doctor of music, fr. The Canterbury tales. 6934-7
A dream garden. 6649-6,6153-2
A dream in May morning. 6935-5
The dream of the romaunt of the rose. 6315-2
The dream, fr. The book of the duchess. 6958-4
The dream, sels. 6301-2
Duchesse Blanche. 6438-8
An emperor's daughter stands alone. 6481-7
Exhortation to youth. 6489-2
The firste moevere of...fr. The Knightes tale. 6908-8
Flee from the press. 6328-4
The flower and the leaf; or, the lady in the arbour. John Dryden (tr.). 6970-3
Forecast. 6438-8
Fox and cock. 6438-8
The franklin's prologue, fr. the Canterbury tales. 6430-2
The franklin's tale, fr. The Canterbury tales. 6430-2
The franklin's tale, sels. 6649-6
The franklin's tale, sels. Dulcie L. Smith (tr.). 6232-6
The friar's tale, fr. The Canterbury tales. 6102-8
Gentility. 6438-8
Good counseil of Chaucer. 6102-8,6219-9,6543-0
The good parson, fr. The Canterbury tales. H.C. Leonard (tr.). 6337-3,6730-1
Griselda. 6438-8
The hous of fame, sels. 6483-3,6378-0
The house of fame, sels. 6193-1
Invocatio ad Mariam, fr. prologue to the 2nd nun's tale. Frank Ernest Hill (tr.). 6282-2
Invocation, fr. the prologue of The prioress's tale. Frank Ernest Hill (tr.). 6282-2
The knight, fr. the Canterbury tales. 6197-4,6424-8
The knightes tale. 6245-8
La prierede nostre dame. Anselm M. Townsend (tr.). 6282-2
Lack of steadfastness. 6489-2
A lady without paragon. 6881-2
Lak of steadfastnesse. 6150-8
Lat take a cat, fr. The mauciples tale. 6125-7
The legend of good women, sels. 6193-1,6378-0,6193-1
The manciple's tale, sels. 6510-4
May garden, fr. The franklin's tale. 6649-6
Merciles beaute: a triple roundel. 6732-8
Merciless beauty. 6022-6,6301-2
The milky way. 6438-8
The miller's tale, sels. 6179-6
The monk and the friar, fr. Canterbury tales. 6200-8
The monk's tale, fr. The Canterbury tales. 6369-1
Moral balade of Chaucer. 6198-2
Murder will out, fr. The Canterbury tales. 6369-1
"My thought was thus...", fr. The book of the duchess. 6726-3
Nabuchodonosor. 6848-0
'Naught may the woful spirit...fr. The knightes tale. 6908-8
The nonne preestes tale, sels. 6179-6
Now welcom somer, fr. The parlement of foules. 6560-0, 6192-3
Now welcome summer. 6489-2
The nun priest's tale, fr. The Canterbury tales. 6193-1, 6430-2

The Nun's priest's tale. Frank Ernest Hill (tr.). 6637-2
"O mooder Mayde...", fr. The prioress's tale. 6106-0
"O yonge fresshe folkes, he or she." 6317-9
"O younge freshe folkes, he or she" 6935-5
Occasional lines. 6369-1
Of his lady. 6187-7
Palamon and Arcite. John Dryden (tr.). 6679-8
Palamon and Arcite; or, the knight's tale. John Dryden (tr.). 6970-3
pardoner's tale, fr. The Canterbury tales. 6646-1,6430-2
The pardoner's tale, fr. The Canterbury tales. 6369-1
The pardoner's tale, fr. The Canterbury tales. Frank Ernest Hill (tr.). 6473-6
The pardoner's tale, sels. fr. The Canterbury tales. 6150-6,6369-1
The parish priest. 6489-2
The parlement of fools, sels. 6198-2,6378-0
The parlement of fools, sels. Dulcie L. Smith (tr.). 6232-6
The parlement of fools. 6369-1
The parlement of foules, sels. 6560-0
The parson, fr. the Canterbury tales. 6197-4
A parson. 6153-2
The perfect knight, fr. The Canterbuty tales. 6934-7
The poet. 6438-8
The poor parson, fr. The Canterbury tales. 6022-6
A poor parson. 6022-6
A praise and dream of the daisy. 6935-5
Praise of women. 6543-0
Prayer to Apollo. 6438-8
The prioress Eglantine, fr. The Canterbury tales. 6934-7
The prioress' tale, fr. The Canterbury tales. 6022-6, 6285-7,6315-2
The prioress's tale, fr. The Canterbury tales. 6022-6, 6430-2
The prioress. 6285-7,6659-3,6153-2
Prologue, fr. The Canterbury tales. 6102-8,6192-3,6193-1,6430-2,6484-1,6153-2,6186-9,6192-3,6197-4,6228-8
Prologue, fr. The prioress's tale. 6931-2
Quest for death. 6150-8,6150-6
Qui bien aime a tard oublie. 6023-4
The romaunt of the rose, sels. 6187-7
Rondel. 6383-7
A rondel. 6153-2,6659-3
Roundel ("Now welcom somer..."). 6334-9
Roundel ("Your eyen two will slay me suddenly") 6383-7
The roundel of the smale foules. 6943-6
Roundel, fr. The parlement of foules. 6198-2,6334-9
A St. Valentine rondel. 6102-8
Second nun's tale, sels. 6734-4
Seynt Valentynes Day. 6943-6
"She is the clernesse and the verray light." 6317-9
The shipman, fr. the Canterbury tales. 6022-6,6197-4
The shipman. 6258-X
A slender wench. 6659-3
Song of Troilus, fr. Troilus and Criseyde. 6317-9
A song to his purse for the king. 6881-2
The Squieres tale, fr. The Canterbury tales. 6198-2
The squire, fr. the Canterbury tales. 6197-4
The tale of the wyf of Bathe, fr. Canterbury tales. 6732-8
Tales from Chaucer, sels. John Dryden (tr.). 6970-3
"Than longen folk to goon on pilgrimages". 6153-2
"Therewith when he was ware, and gan behold." 6317-9
"These rioters, of whom I make...", fr. The...tales. 6726-3
Three rondels of love unreturned. 6881-2
To my empty purse. 6787-5
To my empty purse. 6089-7,6278-4
To Rosamounde: A balade. 6289-X,6489-2,6732-8
To Rosemounde. 6092-7
Trees, flowers, and birds. 6240-7
Troilus and Criseyde, Bk I. 6198-2
Troilus and Criseyde, Bk II. 6198-2
Troilus and Criseyde, Bk V. 6198-2
Troilus and Criseyde, sels. 6317-9,6378-0,6472-8
Troilus and Criseyde, sels. 6369-1

Troilus soliloquizes. 6187-7
Truth. 6369-1
Truth. 6489-2
Truth. 6193-1
"The truth shall make you free". 6153-2
Two invocations of the Virgin. 6022-6
Virginia. 6438-8
The wedding night of January and May. 6733-6
Welcome summer. 6383-7
The well of pity. 6489-2
"Whan that Aprille with his shoures soote". 6289-X
"Whan that Aprille with his shoures sore." 6125-7
When that April with his showers sweet. 6934-7
Wife of bath and the parson, fr. The Canterbury tales. 6378-0
The wife of Bath's fifth husband. William Van Wyck (tr.). 6633-X
A wife of Bath. 6153-2
The wife of Bath. John Dryden (tr.). 6970-3
"With-inne the temple he went him forth pleyinge." 6317-9
Written on his deathbed. 6301-2
The young squire. 6543-0
Young woman. 6106-0
Chaulieu
"Thou grot, whence flows this limpid spring". Felicia Dorothea Hemans (tr.). 6973-8
The chaunt of the brazen head. Winthrop Mackworth Praed. 6874-X
The chaunt of the brazen head. Winthrop Mackworth Praed. 6092-7,6383-7
Chauntecleer and Pertelote. Geoffrey Chaucer. 6733-6
Chauvinism. Francois Coppee. 6351-9
Chavez. Mildred McNeal Sweeney. 6310-1
Chavez, Fray Angelico
   Grey. 6761-1
   In extremis. 6839-1
   Lady of Lidice. 6282-2
   Lady of peace. 6282-2
   Mary ("Miriam, Mary, Maria, Marie,"). 6282-2
   Mulier amicta sole. 6282-2
   Sea-birds. 6282-2
   Vineyard song. 6783-2
Chayah. Thomas Moult. 6393-4
Chazal, Malcolm de
   Afterthoughts. Daisy Aldan (tr.). 6803-0
Che Sara Sara! Victor Plarr. 6872-3
the **cheap** apartment building. Yannis Ritsos. 6803-0
"**Chearonean** Plutarch, to thy deathless praise". Plutarch. Agathias. 7039-6
The **cheat** of Cupid: or the ungentle guest. Robert Herrick. 6733-6,6513-9,6383-7
The **cheat** of Cupid. Anacreon. 6271-7
Check. James Stephens. 6044-7,6102-8,6454-X
"**Check** every outflash, every ruder sally". Sonnet ("Check every outflash"). Alfred Lord Tennyson. 6977-0
Checkmate. Frederick Ebright. 6017-X
Cheddar pinks. Robert Bridges. 6487-6
Cheek, Thomas
   To Chloe. 6563-5
Cheer. Annye Lewis Allison. 6818-9
Cheer. Robert Service. 6159-1,6583-X
Cheer de union travelers. B.H. Jenkins. 6149-4
The **cheer** of the Trenton. Walter Mitchell. 6833-2
The **cheer** of those who speak English. Wallace Rice. 6459-0
Cheer up. Laura Neary. 6764-6
Cheer up. Unknown. 6406-X,6583-X
"'**Cheer** up, cheer up!' it seems to say". The chiff-chaff's message, heard in March. Richard Wilton. 6770-0
"**Cheer** up, my lads, for auld John Frost". The gude gaun game o' curlin' James A. Sidey. 7035-3
Cheer up, my mates. Abraham Cowley. 6328-4
"**Cheer** up, my young men all". Brave Wolfe. Unknown. 6946-0
Cheer, boys, cheer. Charles Mackay. 6087-0
The **cheerful** giver. John McMaster. 6817-0
Cheerful givers. Unknown. 6272-5
The **cheerful** heart. Unknown. 6273-3
A **cheerful** man's sermon. Eben Eugene Rexford. 6583-X
"A **cheerful** song from God goes up". The bells. Gertrude Huntington McGiffert. 6838-3

CHEERFUL

A cheerful song. Unknown. 6118-4
"A cheerful spirit gets on quick". William Channing
    Gannett. 6623-2
The cheerful voice. Unknown. 6530-9
The cheerful way. Anna Letitia Barbauld. 6889-8
A cheerful welcome. Unknown. 6881-2
Cheerfulness. R. McLain Fields. 6109-5
Cheerfulness taught by reason. Elizabeth Barrett Browning.
    6123-0,6604-6,6177-X,6660-7,6177-X
"Cheeriest room, that morn, the kitchen". Flying Jim's
    last leap. Emma Dunning Banks. 6412-4,6426-4,6964-9
Cheers for the living-tears for the dead. Robert G.
    Ingersoll. 6449-3
"A cheery old lady of Reading". Limerick:"A cheery old
    lady of Reading". Celia C. Stevens. 6811-1
The cheese-mites asked. Unknown. 6722-0
Cheetah. Charles Eglinton. 6788-3
Cheetham, Everett
    Blood on the saddle. 6594-5
Chef Pernollet. Berton Braley. 6853-7
Cheke, Henry
    Of perfect friendship. 6182-6
Chellis, Mary D.
    Something to be done. 6617-8
Chelsea. Lillian M. Ainsworth. 7030-2
Chelsea crypt. Robert Herring. 6360-8
Chemin des dames. Crosbie Garstin. 7029-9
The chemist to his love. Unknown. 6724-7
A chemist to his love. Unknown. 6089-7,6385-3,6488-4,6693-3,6278-4
The chemist. Edward Verrall Lucas. 6018-8
Chenery, Ruth Baldwin
    In the trolley car. 6762-X
Cheney, Anne Cleveland
    Vision. 6954-1
Cheney, Annie Elizabeth
    A coyote prowled. 6510-4
Cheney, Ednah D.
    The larger prayer. 6303-9
Cheney, Elizabeth
    Overheard in an orchard. 6337-3,6654-2
    There is a man on the cross. 6144-3,6337-3
Cheney, Ethel B.
    Healing beauty. 6662-3
Cheney, H.A.
    Mad River. 6764-6
Cheney, John Vance
    After the cows. 6632-1
    April. 6374-8
    At the hearthside. 6632-1
    At the sign of the spade. 6006-4
    Coyote. 6241-5
    Days that come and go. 6006-4,6309-8
    The dying nun. 6327-6
    Great is to-day. 6006-4
    Great is to-day. 7041-8
    The happiest heart. 6310-1,6476-0,6102-8,6337-3,6730-1,
        6076-5,6250-4,6431-0,6300-X
    Hope and tears. 6461-2
    'Is there any word from the Lord?' 6848-0
    The kitchen clock. 6724-7,6089-7,6732-8,6166-4,6451-5,
        6567
    Lincoln. 6305-5,6524-4,6449-3
    Loves of leaves and grasses. 7041-8
    The man with the hoe; a reply. 6274-1,6102-8,6076-5,
        6250-4
    The ninth symphony. 6184-2
    Old Braddock. 6062-5
    On a picture of Lincoln. 6524-4
    One. 6250-4,6309-8
    Our mother. 7041-8
    Presidio hill. 6241-5
    San Francisco. 6274-1
    The seasons. 6820-0
    Snowflakes. 7041-8
    Somewhere. 6310-1
    Song ("The birds of the air"). 6374-8
    Song of spring. 6965-7
    Song of the gloaming. 7041-8
    Spring song. 7041-8
    The strong. 6431-0
    This my life. 7012-4
    Waiting. 7041-8
    The way of it. 6632-1
    Weeds and flowers. 6820-0
    The wood-thrush. 6073-0
Cheney, Warren
    January. 6241-5
Cheney-Nichols, Beth
    Realization. 6954-1
Cheng Yu Sun (tr.)
    The long war. Li Po. 6665-8
Chenier, Andre
    Communion of saints. Robert Bridges (tr.). 6487-6
    Elegy ("A white nymph"). Arthur Symons (tr.). 7039-6
    Elegy ("Every man"). Arthur Symons (tr.). 7039-6
"Chequer'd with woven shadows as I lay". A day dream's
    reflection. William Allingham. 6997-5
Cherbury, Edward. See Herbert of Cherbury
Cherish you then the hope I shall forget. Edna St. Vincent
    Millay. 6019-6
Cherished letters. Mrs. Alexander McVeigh Miller. 6923-1
Cherkovski, Neeli
    Fresno notebook. 6792-1
    Love poem without anyone in it. 6792-1
    Notes for a basterd angel. 6998-3, 6901-0
    Thomas Merton. 6901-0
Cherner, Anne
    To Helen Frankenthaler of Circe, 1974 6966-5
    To Mark Rothko of untitled (blue, green), 1969. 6966-5
    To Morris Louis of the vlue veil 1958-9 6966-5
Chernick, Hank
    Situation normal. 6722-0
Chernier, Andre
    Communion of saints. Robert Bridges (tr.). 6487-6
The Cherokee dean. Norman H. Russell. 7005-1
Cherries. Frank Dempster Sherman. 6311-X
Cherries. Frederic Edward Weatherley. 6105-2
"Cherries, ripe cherries!". Bread and cherries. Walter De
    La Mare. 6937-1
Cherrington, Edith
    Woodrow Wilson. 7001-9
The cherry and the slae, sels. Alexander Montgomerie. 6845-6
"Cherry blossom spring festival". Sushi-Okashi and green
    tea with Mitsu Yashima. Al Robles. 6790-5
"Cherry blossom,/Know you not that I". Three songs of
    love. William A. Beatty. 6818-9
"Cherry Valley's finest raiment". When my cousin comes to
    town. W.P. Bourke. 7021-3
A cherry fair, fr. Farewell, this world! Unknown. 6125-7
The cherry fire. Mrs. George Pemble. 6149-4
"Cherry flowers." Issa. 6027-7
Cherry pie. Edgar A. Guest. 6748-4
Cherry pie, fr. The poetical cookbook. Unknown. 6278-4
Cherry pies. Mary Elizabeth Mahnkey. 6662-3
Cherry ripe. Kate Louise Brown. 6049-8
Cherry ripe. Thomas Campion. 6233-4,6099-4,6092-7,6250-4,
    6153-2,6646 ,6481-7,6301-2,6737-9,6634-8,6198-2,6246-5,6339-X
Cherry ripe. Robert Herrick. 6228-8,6732-8,6198-2,6536-8,
    6383-7,6189-3,6197-4,6219-9,6491-4,6723-9
Cherry ripe. Unknown. 6075-7
Cherry time. Sydney Dayre. 6137-0
Cherry tree. Hermann Claudius. 6643-7
Cherry trees. Alfred Edward Housman. 6625-9
Cherry trees a-bloom. Wallace Rice. 6274-1
"The cherry trees are blossoming". Masafusa. 6852-9
The cherry trees. E. Thomas. 6044-7
Cherry way. Ruth Comfort Mitchell. 6393-4
Cherry, Andrew
    The Bay of Biscay. 6302-0,6385-3,6502-3,6258-X
    The green little shamrock of Ireland. 6858-8
    The green little shamrock of Ireland. 6465-5
    Tom Moody. 6090-0
Cherry, Edith E.
    Kept for Jesus. 6065-X
Cherry, J.W.
    Shells of ocean. 6304-7
Cherry-buds Gamaliel Bradford. 6036-6

Cherry-pit. Robert Herrick. 6430-2
Cherry-ripe. Richard Allison. 6652-6
Cherry-ripe. Robert Herrick. 6250-4
"Cherry-ripe, ripe, ripe, I cry". Robert Herrick. 6187-7
Cherry-tree carol, sels. Unknown. 6459-0,6746-8,6472-8
The cherry-tree carol. Unknown. 6756-5
The cherry-tree carol. Unknown. 6052-8,6315-2,6185-0,6216-4,6003-X,6746 ,6125-7,6430-2,6608-9
The cherry-tree.. Unknown. 6248-2
The cherub-folk.. Enid Dinnis. 6096 X
The cherub. James Hogg. 6802-2
The cherubic pilgrim. Johannes ("Angelus Silesius") Scheffler. 6418-3,6730-1
The cherubim, sels. Thomas Heywood. 6730-1
Chesapeake and Shannon. Unknown. 6946-0
The Chesapeake and the Shannon. Unknown. 6057-9
A Chesapeake marsh. Lizette Woodworth Reese. 6326-8
"The Chesapeake so bold". Chesapeake and Shannon. Unknown. 6946-0
Cheshire cat. Kenneth Allott. 6379-9
The Cheshire cheese. Unknown. 6328-4
Chess. Ibn Sharaf. 6362-4
Chess. John Robert Moses. 6936-3
Chess. Unknown. 6983-5
Chess knight. Michalis Stasinopoulos. 6352-7
The chess-board. Owen (Edward Bulwer-Lytton, Earl Lytton) Meredith. 6620-8,6092-7,6543-0,6737-9,6656-9,6302-0, 6385-3,6437-X,6219-9
Chesser, Lewis
    Claude Lackey. 6860-X
    Crazy Mike. 6860-X
Chesson, Nora
    Christmas. 6807-3
    A Connaught lament. 6019-6
    Scarlett's song. 6793-X
    The sea. 6252-0
    Wind-song. 6793-X
"Chest-high in a sunshaft". The ex-priest. Kevin Clark. 6900-2
Chester, Anson G.
    The tapestry weavers. 6303-9
    Wanted. 6913-4
Chester, Harry S.
    When the light goes out. 6578-3,6964-9,6926-6
Chester, Sir Robert
    Ditty ("O holy Love, religious saint!") 6182-6
    Her hair. 6182-6
Chesterfield, Philip Dormer Stanhope, 4th Earl of
    Advice to a lady in autumn. 6092-7,6152-4
    "Immortal Newton never spoke". 6289-X
    On a full-length portrait of Beau Nash... 6278-4
    On a full length portrait of Beau Marsh. 6089-7
    On Lord Islay's garden. 6874-X
    On the above lines. 6874-X
    Verses written in a lady's Sherlock 'Upon death'. 6152-4
    Verses written in a lady's "Sherlock upon death". 6024-2
Chesterman, Hugh
    Noah and the rabbit. 6339-X
Chesteron, Frances
    How far is it to Bethlehem? 6746-8
Chesterton, Cecil
    Ballade of professional pride. 6096 X
    Envoi. 6096 X
    France. 7026-4
    Serbia to the Hohenzollerns. 7031-0
Chesterton, Frances
    How far is it to Bethlehem? 6331-4,6776-X
Chesterton, Gilbert Keith
    A ballad of an anti-Puritan. 6089-7
    The ballad of St. Barbara. 6884-7
    The ballad of St. Barbara. 7027-2
    A ballad of suicide. 6732-8,6089-7,6026-9,6633-X
    The ballad of the white horse, sels. 6234-2
    The ballad of the white horse. 6102-8,6541-4,6301-2
    A ballade of a book-revviewer. 6875-8
    A ballade of the first rain. 6875-8
    The black virgin. 6282-2
    The Christ child. 6543-0,6747-6

A Christmas carol. 6216-4,6337-3,6653-4,6465-5,6421-3, 6723-9
A cider song. 6477-9
Commercial candour. 6722-0
Commerical candour. 6026-9
The convert. 6292-X
The donkey. 6044-7,6337-3,6730-1,6102-8,6153-2,6250 , 6477-9,6510-4,6668-2,6532-5,6228-8,6246 ,6465-5,6476-0,6509-0
The earth's vigil. 7014-0
Elegy in a country churchyard. 6722-0
Elegy in a country churchyard. 6884-7
The English graves. 7029-9
The Englishman. 6722-0
Feast on wine or fast on water. 6026-9
Glencoe. 6301-2
The great minimun. 6732-8
The holy of holies. 6730-1
Home at last. 6730-1
The house of Christmas. 6532-5,6473-6,6509-0,6337-3, 6746-8
Hymn for the church militant. 6931-2
A hymn, sels. 6427-2
A hymn-O God of earth and altar. 6532-5
A hymn. 6250-4
King Alfred answers the Danes. 6931-2
The last hero. 6427-2
Lepanto. 6732-8,6052-8,6102-8,6161-3,6393-4,6331 ,6427-2,6501-5,6109-X,6476-0,6506-6,6509-0,6726-3,6491-4
Litany, fr. A hymn. 6427-2
Love's Trappist. 6320-9
Me heart. 6427-2
The merry town of Roundabout. 6096 X
Music. 6250-4
'The myth of Arthur'. 6776-X
O God of earth and altar. 6337-3
The old song. 6069-2,6210-5
The pessimist. 7014-0
The praise of dust. 6250-4
The praise of the dust. 6250-4
Prayer ("O God of earth and altar"). 6730-1
Prayer ("O God of earth"). 6730-1
A prayer in darkness. 6102-8
Regina angelorum. 6282-2
The return of Eve. 6489-2;6282-2
The rolling English road. 6631-1,6096-X,6331-4,6427-2, 6733-6
The secret people. 6427-2,6096-X
The skeleton. 6210-5
The song against grocers. 6633-X
The song against songs. 6026-9
A song of defeat. 6732-8
The song of Elf, fr. The ballad of the white horse. 6234-2
The song of right and wrong. 6427-2
Songs of education, hygiene. 7014-0
Sonnets in summer heat. 6780-8
The sword of surprise. 6250-4
To F.C. in memoriam Palestine. 6250-4
Translation from du Bellay. 6096 X
Who goes home?, sels. 6427-2
The wife of Flanders. 7029-9
The wife of Flanders. 7031-0,7026-4
The wild knight, sels. 6337-3
The wild knight. 6730-1
The chestnut burr. Unknown. 6373-X,6456-6
"The chestnut casts his flambeaux, and the flowers." Alfred Edward Housman. 6187-7,6536-8,6508-2
Chestnut Ridge, fr. Blue Juanita. Malcolm Cowley. 6531-7
The chestnut roasters. Joseph Payne Brennan. 6218-0
Chestnut Street, Boston. Harold Vinal. 6037-4
Chestnut time. Malana A. Harris. 6529-5
Chettle, Henry
    Aeliana's diary. 6436-1
    Aeliana's duty. 6026-9
    Damelus' song to his Diaphenia. 6436-1
    Diaphenia. 6187-7,6181-8
    Of Cupid. 6182-6
    "Trust not his wanton tears." 6181-8
    Wily Cupid. 61877

The chevalier's birthday. Unknown. 6859-6
The chevalier's lament. Robert Burns. 6859-6
The chevalier's muster-roll. Unknown. 6859-6
Chevalier, Albert
   A fallen star. 6701-8
   My old Dutch. 6700-X
Cheverton, E.C.
   Uncover to the flag. 6741-X,6223-7
Chevy Chace. Unknown. 6087-0,6267-9,6067-6,6239-3,6370-5
Chevy Chase. Unknown. 6301-2,632-5,6263-6,6660-7,6098-6,
   6179-6,6271-7,6604-6,6726-3,6228-
Chevy-chase. Richard Sheale. 6302-0;6385-3
Chew, Beverly
   Old books are best. 6770-0
   Old books are best. 6297-0
Chewink. Amanda T. Jones. 6615-1
Cheyenne boys. Unknown. 6003-X
Cheyenne mountain. Helen Hunt Jackson. 7041-8
Cheyne, Irene
   Old Mr Tatterlock. 6349-7
Cheyney and Lucia Trent, Ralph
   Ten years after. 6542-2
Cheyney, Edward Ralph. See Cheyney, Ralph
Cheyney, Ralph
   Bit by bitter. 6750-6
   Comrade Jesus. 6954-1
   Comrade Jesus. 6144-3
   Cynics. 6542-2
   Dark encounter. 6039-0
   Had I not loved before. 6441-8
   Joan and Jesus. 6880-4
   Love, give me the feel of to-morrow. 6051-X
   Love, give me the feel of tomorrow. 6542-2
   A lover for death. 6619-4
   Mountain night. 6619-4
   No armistice in love's war. 6954-1
   Pity Don Juan. 6040-4
   Red flag. 6542-2
   Two. 6441-8
   Unemployed. 6144-3
   Wage-slaves to war-makers. 6542-2
   You cannot kill the troubadours. 6954-1
Chez le cordonnier. Louis J. Magee. 7004-3
Chi Lien Chang. Herman Livezey. 6249-0
Chiabrera, Gabriello
   Epitaph ("Destined"). William Wordsworth (tr.). 7039-6
   Epitaph ("Not without"). Wilil am Wordsworth (tr.). 7039-6
   Epitaph ("O thou"). William Wordsworth (tr.). 7039-6
   Epitaph ("There never"). William Wordsworth (tr.). 7039-6
   Epitaph ("Weep not"). William Wordsworth (tr.). 7039-6
   Quando ride il mare. 6253-9
Chiang, Fay
   A letter to Peter. 6790-5
   Snow. 6790-5
   Voices that have filled my day. 6790-5
Chibouque. Francis Saltus Saltus. 6453-1
Chicadees. Edith M. Thomas. 6073-0
Chicago. Berton Braley. 6853-7
Chicago. Francis Bret Harte. 6820-0
Chicago. Mildred Plew Meigs. 6088-9
Chicago. John Boyle O'Reilly. 6946-0
Chicago. Wallace Rice. 6484-1
Chicago. Carl Sandburg. 6102-8,6154-0,6289-X,6498-1,6506-6,
   6527 ,6531-7,6732-7,6076-5,6300-4,6464-7,6076-5,6288-1,6736-0,6121-4,6228-3
Chicago. Benjamin Franklin Taylor. 6815-4
Chicago. Mark Turbyfill. 6396-9
Chicago. John Greenleaf Whittier. 6077-3,6465-5
Chicago. Dwight Williams. 6045-1
Chicago idyll. E. Merrill Root. 6527-9
Chicago in December. Jeanette Seletz. 6799-9
Chicago in flames. Dwight Williams. 6167-2
Chicago poems, sels. Carl Sandburg. 6531-7
Chicago weather. Eugene Field. 6949-5
Chicago: October 10, 1871 Francis Bret Harte. 6212-1,6438-8
Chick, M.P.
   Pitcher or jug. 6744-1,6314-4

Chick-a-rooster. Henry Crocker. 7030-2
Chickadee. Isaac Bassett Choate. 6394-2
Chickadee. Martha Haskell Clarke. 6073-0
Chickadee. Hilda Conkling. 6510-4
Chickadee. Ralph Waldo Emerson. 6466-3
Chickadee. Myra A. Shattuck. 6715-8
"The chickadee came in the morning". Wolverine winter.
   Paul F. Sifton. 7035-3
The Chickadee. Sydney Dayre. 6578-3
The chickadee. Sara V. Prueser. 6906-1
The chickadee. Celia Thaxter. 6612-7
"Chickadees singing in flute-notes". In a maple grove.
   Amos F. Stalcup Jr.. 6799-9
The chickadees. John Hay. 6388-8
Chickamauga. G.T. Ferris. 6340-3,6741-X
Chickamauga. Benjamin Franklin Taylor. 6815-4
Chickamauga - 1898. Unknown. 6274-1,6340-3,6741-X
Chicken blood. Hervey Allen. 6217-2
Chicken itza. Katherine Kelley Taylor. 6906-1
The chicken's mistake. Phoebe Cary. 6314-4,6060-9,6373-X,
   6456-6
"A chicken's skin hides". Anatomical observation. Lenore
   Eversole Fisher. 6750-6
The chicken; or, my first introduction to the... S.F.
   Outwood. 6274-1
Chickens come home to roost. Unknown. 6920-7
"Chickens crowing on Sourwood Mountain". Sourwood
   Mountain. Unknown. 6826-X
Chickens in trouble. Anne Emilie Poullson. 6135-4
Chickens in trouble. Unknown (Norwegian) 6452-3
The chickens. Unknown. 6529-5,6744-1,6629-1,6131-1,6167-2
Chide mildly the erring. William B. Bradley. 6304-7
The chief among ten thousand. Horatius Bonar. 6848-0
Chief Leschi of the Nisqually. Duane Niatum. 7005-1
"The chief defect of Henry King". Henry King. Hilaire
   Belloc. 6861-8
The chief mourner. Francis S. Smith. 6926-6
The chief's prayer after the salmon catch. Constance
   Lindsay Skinner. 6897-9
'The chief,' fr. In hospital. William Ernest Henley. 6250-4
"The chiefe use then in man of that he knowes". Of human
   learning. Fulke Greville; 1st Baron Brooke. 6933-9
"The chiefs were seated in a ring...". Legend of Crystal
   Spring. Henry W. Austin. 6920-7
The chieftain's son. Felicia Dorothea Hemans. 6973-8
"Chieftains, lead on! our hearts beat high". The
   Crusader's war-song. Felicia Dorothea Hemans. 6973-8
The chiff-chaff's message, heard in March. Richard Wilton.
   6770-0
Child. Carl Sandburg. 6509-0,6393-4
"A child 'midst ancient mountains I have stood". Mountain
   sanctuaries. Felicia Dorothea Hemans. 6973-8
A child ("A child's a plaything for an hour"). Mary Lamb.
   6533-3,6086-2
"Child - in all the flying sky". Poem ("Child"). Josephine
   Strongin. 6020-X
The child alone. M.A. Woods. 6134-6
"A child and a woman". Eleanor. Unknown. 6983-5
The child and dove. Felicia Dorothea Hemans. 6973-8
Child and her statue. Louis Untermeyer. 6037-4
Child and maiden. Sir Charles Sedley. 6246-6,6302-0,6385-3,
   6634-8,6092-7,6250
Child and mother. Eugene Field. 6834-0;6949-5,6891-X
Child and mother. Eugene Field. 6097-8,6365-9,6627-5,6682-8,6368-3,6576
Child and mother. Thomas Hood. 6127-3,6424-8
Child and poet. Algernon Charles Swinburne. 6828-6
Child and poet. Algernon Charles Swinburne. 6110-9,6199-0
The child and the angels. Charles Swain. 6459-0,6502-5
The child and the fairies. A [pseud.]. 6368-3
The child and the fairies. Unknown. 6132-X,6466-3
The child and the gentian. Mary Frances Butts. 6965-7
The child and the mariner. William Henry Davies. 6234-2,
   6478-7,6458-2,6508-2
The child and the mourners. Charles Mackay. 6219-9
The child and the piper. William Blake. 6133-8
The child and the star. C. B. 6131-1
The child and the star. Benjamin Franklin Taylor. 6815-4
The child and the watcher. Elizabeth Barrett Browning.

.6271-7,6219-9
The child and the world. Unknown. 6373-X
The child and the world. Kate Douglas Wiggin. 6452-3
The child and the wren. Edwin John Pratt. 6797-2
Child and the year. Unknown. 6312-8
The child and the year. Celia Thaxter. 6820-0
Child and tree. E.A. Holbrook. 6049-8
Child and wind. Lola Ridge. 6102-8,6076-5
The child angel. L.C. Whiton. 6965-7
Child asleep. Harriet Sampson. 6761-1
A child asleep. Elizabeth Barrett Browning. 6233-4
The child asleep. Clotilde de Surville. 6271-7
Child at play. Victor Hugo. 6949-5
The child at prayer. Katharine (Hinkson) Tynan. 6233-4
Child at the library. Kalfus Kurtz. 6761-1
"A child beside a hamlet's fount at play". The cottage girl. Felicia Dorothea Hemans. 6973-8
"A child building castles". Memories. Avis H. Grant. 6906-1
A child cried out at night. Ernst Wiechert. 6643-7
A child dancing at twilight. Anna Blanche McGill. 6959-2
Child dear. Francis Carlin. 6096 X
The child dying. Edwin Muir. 6246-6,6210-5
Child Dyring. Sir Walter Scott. 6438-8
A child evening prayer. Mary Lundie Duncan. 6137-0
A child for sale. Meleager. 6435-3
The child heart. Charles Augustus Keeler. 6241-5
"A child in a treetop dreamed of flying". The treetop child. Anne Lloyd. 7019-1
The child in black. Amelia Josephine Burr. 7038-8
The child in me. May Riley Smith. 6102-8,6556-2,6076-5, 6076-5,6102-8
The child in the garden. Henry Van Dyke. 6337-3
The child in the great wood. Muriel Rukeyser. 6391-8
Child in the judgment seat. Mrs. E.R. Charles. 6304-7
The child in the story awakes. Walter De La Mare. 6596-1
The child in the story goes to bed. Walter De La Mare. 6459-0,6596-1
The child in the wood. Alfred Noyes. 6169-9
"The child is father of the man". My heart leaps up, sels. William Wordsworth. 6867-7
The child is father to the man. Louisa Bigg. 6575-9
The child Jesus to Mary the rose. John Lydgate. 6282-2
"Child is thy father dead?". Song ("Child is thy father dead?"). Ebenezer Elliott. 6102-8
Child labor. Charlotte Perkins Stetson Gilman. 6102-8,6076-5
Child labor. Unknown. 6274-1
The child leans in its parent's breast. Isaac Williams. 6219-9
Child lost! Unknown. 6411-6
The child martyr. May M. Anderson. 6574-0
Child Maurice. Unknown. 6907-X
Child molester. Jay Meek. 6803-0
A child my choice. Robert Southwell. 6181-8,6489-2
A child my choice. Robert Southwell. 6931-2
The child next door. Rose Fyleman. 6891-X
"The child not yet i· lulled to rest". Cradle-song at twilight. Alice Meynell. 6955-X
"Child of a cause, whose brief archives". Winnie Davis. Mary McKinley Cobb. 6841-3
Child of a day. Walter Savage Landor. 6086-2,6656-9,6737-9, 6097-8,6233-4,6250-4,6656-9,6110-9
Child of Arabia. Maude Freeman Osborne. 6836-7
The child of Bethlehem. Phillips Brooks. 6007-2
"Child of a day, thou knowest not". To a dead child. Walter Savage Landor. 6980-0
Child of blue. Michael Hogan. 6870-7
Child of dawn, fr. Before dawn. Harold Monro. 6234-2
"Child of delight, with sun-bright hair". Emily Bronte. 6123-0
The child of earth. Caroline Elizabeth Sarah Sheridan Norton. 6980-0,6911-8
The child of Elle. Unknown. 6302-0,6219-9
A child of God longing to see him beloved. Madame De la Mothe Guion. 6814-6
The child of god. Louise Driscoll. 6031-5
A child of hers. T. Walking Eagle Marietta. 6870-7
A child of joy. Rachel Annand Taylor. 6628-3
Child of loneliness. Norman Gale. 6730-1

The child of misery, fr. The country justice. John Langhorne. 6934-7
Child of my heart. Edwin Markham. 6102-8,6076-5
"Child of my mind, my soul-child". My soul-child. Dorothy Whittington. 6906-1
"Child of my parents!sister of my soul" fr.The prelude. William Wordsworth. 6867-7
The child of nature. William Wordsworth. 6383-7
The child of peace. Selma Lagerlof. 6045-5
A child of prayer. Unknown (Japanese) 6027-7
The child of the forests. Felicia Dorothea Hemans. 6973-8
"Child of the later days! thy words..broken". Answer of the mummy at Belzoni's exhibition. Unknown. 6910-X
"Child of the lightning, alien to our dust". To Edna St. Vincent Millay. Floyd Dell. 6880-4
Child of the long grass. Roy Macnab. 6788-3
Child of the Romans. Carl Sandburg. 6299-7
"Child of the muses and the moon". Villanelle ("Child of the muses"). Unknown. 6770-0
"Child of the shifting desert sands". The traveller. Clinton Dangerfield. 7012-4
Child of the wind with harmonica. Nicephorus Vrettakos. 6352-7
A child of twelve, fr. The revolt of Islam. Percy Bysshe Shelley. 6239-3
Child on the beach. Sara Henderson Hay. 6979-7
Child owlet. Unknown. 6185-0
Child poems. Josephine Redmond Fishburn. 6033-1
A child praying. Robert Aris Wilmott. 6271-7
The child reading the Bible. Felicia Dorothea Hemans. 6973-8
The child reads an almanac. Francis Jammes. 7039-6
The child reads the almanac. Francis Jammes. 6351-9
A child said, 'What is the grass?' Walt Whitman. 6396-9
"The child sᶦt on one side of the table in...". Alphabet. Susan Fromberg Schaeffer. 6803-0
Child secret. Sylvia Lapidus. 6850-2
Child sketch in crayon. David Wevill. 6767-0
"A child sleeps under a rose-bush fair". The rose-bush. Unknown. 6929-0
A child tastes the loveliness of life... Grace Stone Coates. 6039-0
A child that has a cold. Thomas Dibdin. 6125-7
Child that I never had. Shirley Barker. 6761-1
"A child through sunny meadows toiled". The wreath. Johann Ludwig Uhland. 6903-7
Child to a rose. Charles Lutwidge ("Lewis Carroll") Dodgson. 6249-0
Child to a rose. Unknown. 6049-8,6373-X,6424-8
Child to whom all words. Frank Kendon. 6777-8
Child Vyet. Unknown. 6518-X
"The child was asleep as he lay in her arms". The child was asleep. Carol A. Frey. 6857-X
Child Waters. Unknown. 6185-0,6430-2,6518-4
"Child Waters in his stable stood". Unknown. 6518-X
"The child was living to laugh and to play". Epitaph. Victor Hugo. 6876-6
"A child was singing at his play". Child at play. Victor Hugo. 6949-5
"The child who threw away leaf after leaf". The onion. Allen Upward. 6897-9
Child wife. Joseph Joel Keith. 6218-0
A child with a shell. William Wordsworth. 6980-0
Child with malaria. Clark Mills. 6751-4,6761-1
"Child with the butterfly". Youth. Bayard Taylor. 6976-2
"A child's a plaything for an hour". A child. Charles Lamb. 6934-7
The child's appeal. Mamie Gene Cole. 6337-3
Child's carol. Eleanor Farjeon. 6421-5
A child's Christmas rhyme. Richard Lawson Gales. 6950-9
A child's Christmas song. Thomas Augustine Daly. 6431-0
A child's day. Katharine (Hinkson) Tynan. 6233-4
The child's desire. Jemima Thompson Luke. 6502-3,6459-0, 6131-1
The child's dream. Isabel Fiske Conant. 6249-0
Child's evening hymn. Sabine Baring-Gould. 6132-X,6418-3, 6214-8,6656-9,6737-9
A child's evening prayer. Samuel Taylor Coleridge. 6131-1
A child's evensong. Richard Le Gallienne. 6242-3
Child's fancies. Jennie L. Lyall. 6713-1

CHILD'S

A child's fancies. Robert Louis Stevenson. 6629-1
The child's first grief. Felicia Dorothea Hemans. 6772-7, 6973-8
A child's first impression of a star. Nathaniel Parker Willis. 6752-2
A child's future. Algernon Charles Swinburne. 6123-0,6233-4,6110-9
A child's game. Karle Wilson Baker. 6512-0
A child's garden of verses, sels. Robert Louis Stevenson. 6122-2
A child's good-bye to the old year. Unknown. 6684-4
A child's grace. Robert Herrick. 6533-3
A child's grace. Robert Burns. 6132-X,6519-8,6466-3
A child's hair. Sir William Watson. 6233-4
The child's heritage. John G. Neihardt. 6393-4
A child's hymn of praise. Jane Taylor. 6018-8
A child's hymn. Matilda Barbara Betham-Edwards. 6638-0, 6639-9
The child's hymn. Mary Howitt. 6502-3
A child's kiss. Francis Thompson. 6844-8
The child's last sleep. Felicia Dorothea Hemans. 6772-7
The child's last sleep. Felicia Dorothea Hemans. 6973-8
A child's laughter. Algernon Charles Swinburne. 6233-4, 6519-8,6682-8,6199-0,6655-0,6491,6110-9
A child's love. Unknown. 6382-9
A child's make-believe. George Macdonald. 6965-7
The child's mirror. Unknown. 6924-X
A child's mood. Juliet C. Marsh. 6965-7
The child's mother. Louise Townsend Nicholl. 6032-3
Child's natural history. Oliver Herford. 6861-8
A child's offering. Unknown. 6337-3
A child's pet. William Henry Davies. 6476-0,6510-4
A child's prayer. Matilda Barbara Betham-Edwards. 6519-8, 6456-6
A child's prayer. John Banister Tabb. 6431-0,6654-2,6736-0
A child's prayer. Francis Thompson. 6465-5,6608-9
The child's prayer. Comte Robert de Montesquiou. 6351-9
The child's prayer. Hodges Reed. 6927-4
A child's present. Robert Herrick. 6114-1
A child's protrait. William James Dawson. 6656-9
The child's quest. Frances Shaw. 6897-9
The child's return from the woodlands. Felicia Dorothea Hemans. 6973-8
A child's smile. Dinah Maria Mulock Craik. 6772-7
Child's song. Thomas Moore. 6179-6;6244-X
Child's song. Algernon Charles Swinburne. 6437-X,6110-9, 6424-8
Child's song ("The King and the Queen were riding"). Kate Greenaway. 6466-3
Child's song in spring. Edith (Bland) Nesbit. 6105-2;6423-X
A child's song overheard. Grace Hazard Conkling. 6501-5
"A child's song will find him on the hills...". The world greets him. Sophia Rogers. 7019-1
The child's soul ward. Samuel Dunievitz. 6799-9
The child's star. John Banister Tabb. 6452-3
"A child's stomach growls". Afterward. P.J. (Polly) Holt. 6883-9
Child's talk in April. Christina Georgina Rossetti. 6239-3
A child's Thanksgiving. Kate Whiting Patch. 6703-4
A child's thought of God. Elizabeth Barrett Browning. 6123-0,6198-2,6303-9,6466-3,6127-3,6249,6356-X,6519-8, 6575-9,6131-4,6219-9,6368,6424-8,6456-6
A child's thought. Mary Frances Butts. 6965-7
A child's thought. M. Marie Thyng. 6764-6
A child's wisdom. Alice Cary. 6060-9
A child's wisdom. Unknown. 6743-3
The child's wish granted. George Parsons Lathrop. 6292-X
The child's wish in June. Caroline Gilman. 6385-3,6127-3
A child's wish. Abram Joseph Ryan. 6006-4,6292-X,6172-9
The child's wonder. Margaret Johnson. 6314-4
The child's world. Unknown. 6173-7,6556-6
A child's year. T. Teignmouth Shore. 6926-6
Child, F.J.
    Overtures from Richmond. 6016-2
Child, Lydia Maria
    Apple-seed John. 6614-3
    A boy's Thanksgiving. 6701-8
    If ever I see. 6373-X,6452-3,6456-6,6510-4
    Lines occasioned by hearing a little boy mock...clock.. 6752-2
    Lines to a lady of great musical talent. 6752-2
    The little maiden and the little bird. 6242-3,6131-1
    Thanksgiving Day. 6127-3,6135-4,6449-3,6456-6,6424-8, 6132-X,6373-X,6466-3,6519-8,6618-6
    Who stole the bird's nest? 6132-X,6373-X,6519-8,6242-3, 6127-3,6131-1,6135-4,6304-7,6964-9
    The world I am passing through. 6214-8
Child, Oscar C.A.
    Tanks. 6846-4
    To a hero. 7026-4
Child, Philo H.
    Nobody's child. 6403-5
"Child, amidst the flowers at play". The hour of prayer. Felicia Dorothea Hemans. 6973-8
"Child, do not fear". Home at last. Adelaide Anne Procter. 6957-6
"A child, I chased the rainbow once, and wept". A rainbow at Victoria Falls. Frederick Charles Kolbe. 6800-6
"Child, I had spent the winters alone". Country travelled. William Sawyer. 6841-3
"A child, I saw the sky a canopy". Night skies. Edna Davis Romig. 6836-7
The child, fr. The picture of St. John. Bayard Taylor. 6976-2
"Child, why do you linger beside her portal?". Her going. Agnes Lee. 6897-9
"A child, with mystic eyes and flowing hair". Sonnet ("A child"). Philip Bourke Marston. 7015-9
"A child," fr. Echoes. William Ernest Henley. 6508-2
The child-dancers. Percy MacKaye. 6959-2
The child-judge. Unknown. 6127-3
The child-musician.. Austin Dobson. 6239-3,6424-8,6543-0
Child-songs. John Greenleaf Whittier. 6233-4,6250-4
Child-songs, sels. John Greenleaf Whittier. 6934-7
A child-thought.. Wilfrid Thorley. 6466-3
The child-world. James Whitcomb Riley. 6128-1
A child. Charles Lamb. 6934-7
A child. Unknown (Greek) 6435-3
The child. Nancy Campbell. 6781-6
The child. Ethel Clifford. 6793-X
The child. Sara Coleridge. 6233-4,6365-9
The child. John Banister Tabb. 6519-8
The child. George Edward Woodberry. 6266-0,6478-7
"Childe Dakyns, I'd have had thee born". Xpiema. Thomas Edward Brown. 6809-X
Childe Harold's address to the ocean. George Gordon, 6th Baron Byron. 6889-8
Childe Harold's farewell to England. George Gordon, 6th Baron Byron. 6552-X
Childe Harold's pilgrimage. George Gordon, 6th Baron Byron. 6198-2,6088-9,6828-6
Childe Harold's pilgrimage, sels. George Gordon, 6th Baron Byron. 6660-7,6107-9,6250-4,6545-7,6110-9,6199,6102-8,6188-5,6208-3,6239-3,6483-3,6527-,6258-X,6289-X, 6395-0,6427-2,6547-3,6604-,6332-2,6726-3,6732-8,6196-6,6430-2,6560
Childe Maurice. Unknown. 6055-2
Childe Roland to the dark tower came. Robert Browning. 6198-2,6427-2,6657-7,6656-9,6655-0,6430
Childe Roland to the darl tower. Robert Browning. 6102-8, 6110-9,6192-3,6196-6,6723-9,6472
"Childe Rowland found a damsel on the plain". The damsel of the plain. Theodore Watts-Dunton. 7015-9
Childe Vyet; or, The brothers. Unknown. 6055-2
The childe's destiny. Felicia Dorothea Hemans. 6600-3
Childe, Wilfred Rowland
    Civilization. 6893-6
    The former glory. 6096 X
    The Gothic rose. 6096 X
    The grasshopper. 6510-4
    Hardwick arras. 6780-8
    The last abbot of Gloucester. 6096 X
    Moyen age. 6893-6
    Our lady with two angels. 6282-2
    Pre-Raphaelite spring. 6893-6
    Sea garden. 6893-6
    Twelfth night. 6893-6
    Twelfth night. 6625-9
Childe-hood. Henry Vaughan. 6378-0

A childermas rhyme. Richard Lawson Gales. 6216-4
The childher.. Denis Aloysius McCarthy. 6162-1;6607-0
Childhood. Jens Baggesen. 7039-6
Childhood. William Blake. 6233-4
Childhood. Johannes Bobrowski. 6758-1
Childhood. Berton Braley. 6853-7
Childhood. Hartley Coleridge. 6772-7
Childhood. Hartley Coleridge. 6233-4
Childhood. Carlos Drummond de Andrade. 6759-X
Childhood. Frederick William Faber. 6980-0
Childhood. Edgar A. Guest. 6748-4
Childhood. Charles Lamb. 6772-7
Childhood. Jean Nuchtern. 6857-X
Childhood. Boris Pasternak. 6546-5
Childhood. Alejandra Pizarnik. 7036-1
Childhood. George William ("A.E.") Russell. 6723-9
Childhood. Alice Stettiner. 6818-9
Childhood. John Banister Tabb. 6243-1
Childhood. Henry Vaughan. 6931-2
Childhood. E.H. Visiak. 6893-6
Childhood. Henry Kirke White. 6543-0
Childhood. William Wordsworth. 6980-0
Childhood ("Long time he lay..."). Edwin Muir. 6038-2;6269-5
Childhood and age. William Wordsworth. 6935-5
Childhood and his visitors. Winthrop Mackworth Praed. 6874-X
Childhood and his visitors. Winthrop Mackworth Praed. 6772-7
Childhood and school-time, fr. The prelude. William Wordsworth. 6208-3
Childhood fancies. Unknown. 6373-X
"A childhood land of mountain ways". A lost land. Kathleen Knox. 7027-2
Childhood of a scientist. A.F. Moritz. 6767-0
The childhood of Achilles. Pindar. 6435-3
Childhood of Joan of Arc. Robert Southey. 6980-0
The childhood of Kitty of the Sherragh Vane. Thomas Edward Brown. 6873-1
The childhood of Zeus. Moero. 6435-3
"Childhood takes its hurts so lightly". Childhood. Edgar A. Guest. 6748-4
Childhood, fr. By the sea. E.H. Brodie. 6997-3
A childhood. Stephen Spender. 6379-9
A childish fancy. Unknown. 6674-7
Childish friendship. William Shakespeare. 6935-5
A childish game. Sir Reinmar von Hagenau. 7039-6
Childish recollections. George Gordon, 6th Baron Byron. 6945-2
Childish recollections (2). George Gordon, 6th Baron Byron. 6945-2
Childless. Ben Wood Davis. 6918-5
The childless father. William Wordsworth. 6737-9
The childless mother. Francis Turner Palgrave. 6365-9
Children. Mary Ainge ("Madeline Bridges") De Vere. 6274-1
Children. Walter Savage Landor. 6097-8,6627-5,6219-9
Children. Henry Wadsworth Longfellow. 6456-6,6585-6,6008-0, 6288-1,6126-5,6049-8,6233-4,6008-0,6288-1,6126-5
Children. Bernard Raymund. 6880-4
Children. Algernon Charles Swinburne. 6102-8,6193-1
"Children (as such forgive them) have I known". Religious isolation. Matthew Arnold. 6199-0,6828-9
The children and the snake. Mary Lamb. 6134-6
"Children are judges of the heart". Compensation, fr. Mother-songs. Marian Williams McGaw. 6906-1
"Children are we". The waves. Bayard Taylor. 6976-2
"Children are what the mothers are". Children. Walter Savage Landor. 6097-8,6627-5,6219-9
The children band. Sir Aubrey De Vere. 6233-4,6086-2
"The children come in with a breeze and a rush". An incursion of the Danes. Anna F. Burnham. 6965-7
The children dancing. Laurence Binyon. 6884-7
"Children far, and children near." Unknown. 6203-2
"The children finally in bed, each bare". Farm woman. Bernice Carey Fitch. 6750-6
The children in the chair. Ethel Talbot. 6804-9
The children in the moon. Unknown. 6127-3,6502-3
The children in the wood. Unknown. 6055-2,6133-6,6271-7, 6302-0,6502-3,6518 ,6067-6,6438-8,6131-1
The children in the wood. Thomas Percy. 6049-8

The children in the wood. Unknown. 6133-8
The children in the wood. Unknown. 6829-4
"The children kept coming one by one". The children we keep. Mrs. E.V. Wilson. 6964-9
"The children like the week-old zebra". Almost. Vesle Fenstermaker. 6857-X
Children look down upon the morning-gray. Cecil Day Lewis. 6491-4
The children march. Elizabeth Riddell. 6349-7
Children must be paid for. Unknown. 6278-4
Children of Britain. Sir William Watson. 6224-5
Children of darkness. Robert Graves. 6069-2
"Children of God, who, faint and slow." John Bowdler Jr. 6302-0
The children of Greenock. William Sydney Graham. 6210-5
Children of light. Bernard Barton. 6980-0
The children of Lir. Rosa Mulholland; Lady Gilbert. 7037-X
The children of Lir. Katharine (Hinkson) Tynan. 6079-X, 6244-X,6079-X
Children of love. Harold Monro. 6234-2;6320-9
"Children of night! unfolding meekly, slowly". Night-blowing flowers. Felicia Dorothea Hemans. 6973-8
The children of sorrow. Johann Gottfried von Herder. 6842-1
The children of the foam. William Wilfred Campbell. 6115-X
Children of the heavenly king. John Cennick. 6219-9,6730-1
Children of the loom. Jean Milne Gower. 6836-7
The children of the Lord's supper. Henry Wadsworth Longfellow. 6680-1,6066-8
The children of the night. Edwin Arlington Robinson. 6532-5
The children of the nights, sels. Edwin Arlington Robinson. 6274-1
The children of the poor. Victor Hugo. 6954-1
The children of the state. James Lewisohn. 6870-7
Children of the sun, sels. Wallace Gould. 6031-5
"Children of the world". Spain, take from me this cup. Cesar Vallejo. 6759-X
The children of the year. Unknown. 66601-1
Children of toil, fr. 'Who follow the flag' Henry Van Dyke. 6954-1
Children of tomorrow. Zona Gale. 6461-2
Children on a hill. Marion Ethel Hamilton. 6979-7
Children on the shore. Unknown. 6424-8
Children playing in a church-yard. Walter Savage Landor. 6772-7
Children playing in a churchyard. Walter Savage Landor. 6832-4,6874-X
"Children under the cedar tree; mushrooms...". Argyll tour. Eugenio Montale. 6803-0
The children we keep. Unknown. 6414-0
The children we keep. Mrs. E.V. Wilson. 6964-9
"The children were shouting together". Frolic. George William ("A.E.") Russell. 6478-7,6421-3
The children whom Jesus blessed. Felicia Dorothea Hemans. 6973-8
The children's appeal. Mary Howitt. 6502-3
Children's arbor day march. E.A. Holbrook. 6049-8
The children's auction. Charles Mackay. 6102-8
The children's bedtime. Unknown. 6273-3,6466-3
Children's Christmas Eve. John Keble. 6747-6
The children's crusade. Johannes R. Becher. 6160-5
The children's gardens. Sarah Doudney. 6772-7
The children's ghosts. Winifred M. Letts. 6102-8
The children's hour. Sara Van Alstyne Allen. 6761-1
The children's hour. Henry Wadsworth Longfellow. 6219-9, 6321-7,6126-5,6438-8,6288-1,6008-0,6131-1,6135-4, 6136-2,6127-3,6014-5,6176-1,6299-7,6429 ,6385-3,6401-9,6478-7,6534-1,6570-8,6230 ,6486-8,6498-1,6356-X, 6623-2,6240-7,6302
Children's joys. Sarah Doudney. 6772-7
Children's kisses. Josephine Preston Peabody. 6627-5
The children's music. F.M. Owen. 6273-3
Children's new prayer. William Canton. 6713-1
Children's praise song. W.B. Downer. 6049-8
Children's room. Ruth E. McCoy. 6750-6
Children's song. Unknown. 6003-X
The children's song. Rudyard Kipling. 6478-7,6639-9
Children's temperance song. Charles W. Denison. 6755-7
The children's theatre. Arthur Stringer. 6797-2

CHILDREN'S

"The children's world is full of sweet surprises". Sarah Doudney. 6238-5
"The children's world is full...sweet suprises". Children's joys. Sarah Doudney. 6772-7
Children, children, don't forget. Dora Owen. 6891-X
Children, fr. Danae. Euripides. 6435-3
"Children, keep up that harmless play". Children playing in a church-yard. Walter Savage Landor. 6772-7
Children, thank God. Unknown. 6502-3
"Children, to-day made fatherless". The toll-payers. Alison Lindsay. 7031-0
The children. Mary K. Buck. 6097-8
The children. Charles Dickens. 6260-1
The children. Charles M. Dickinson. 6385-3,6404-3,6742-5, 6219-9,7041-8
The children. Emily Dickinson. 6076-5,6102-8
The children. Harriet Eleanor Hamiliton (Baille) King. 6772-7
The children. Richard Realf. 6772-7
The children. William Soutar. 6783-2
The children. William Carlos Williams. 6388-8
Childress, W. Lomax
  Let us be kind. 6303-9,6964-9
Childs memory. Terri Meyette Wilkins. 6870-7
Childs, Harold
  William James. 6327-6
Childs, Mary Fairfax
  Marse Linkum's mistek. 6708-5
"Chill and mirk is the nightly blast". Stanzas composed during a thunderstorm. George Gordon, 6th Baron Byron. 6945-2
"The chill New England sunshine". The death of Goody Nurse. Rose Terry Cooke. 6946-0
A chill in summer. George Augustus Simcox. 7015-9
Chill of the eve. James Stephens. 6491-4
Chill of the eve. James Stephens. 6930-4
A chill. Christina Georgina Rossetti. 6334-9,6632-0,6519-8, 6424-8
Chillingham. Mary Elizabeth Coleridge. 6477-9
Chillon. George Gordon, 6th Baron Byron. 6102-8,6424-8
Chilman, Eric
  After-days. 7031-0
  The beautiful land. 6639-9
  Mr. Bond. 6070-6
The Chilterns. Rupert Brooke. 6508-2
The Chilterns. John Davidson. 6655-0
Chimaera in taffeta. Herbert S. Gorman. 6217-2
Chimaera sleeping. Elinor Wylie. 6628-3
Chimes. Walter Edwards Houghton Jr. 6038-2
Chimes. Henry Wadsworth Longfellow. 6431-0
Chimes. Alice Meynell. 6228-8,6477-9,6634-8,6726-3,6508-2
Chimes. Dante Gabriel Rossetti. 6198-2,6334-9,6110-9
The chimes of England. Arthur Cleveland Coxe. 6219-9
The chimes of old England. Bishop Coxe. 6273-3
The chimes of Termode. Grace Hazard Conkling. 6053-6,6331-4
The chimes. Richard Lawson Gales. 6950-9
The chimney drummer-boy. William J. Long. 6807-3
The chimney nest. Mary Barker Dodge. 6273-3,6373-X
Chimney swallow. Bertye Young Williams. 6750-6
Chimney swallows. Horatio Nelson Powers. 6240-7
The chimney sweep. E. S. H. 6438-8
chimney sweeper, fr. The songs of innocence. William Blake. 6105-2,6086-2,6152-4
The chimney sweeper. William Blake. 6102-8,6106-0,6134-0, 6233-4,6075-7,6634-,6086-2,6153-2,6723-9
"The chimney throat is old and wide". Chimney swallow. Bertye Young Williams. 6750-6
The chimney's melody. Francis Bret Harte. 6573-2
The chimney-sweep. Ellen Sturgis Hooper. 6502-3
The chimney-sweeps of Cheltenham. Alfred Noyes. 6151-6, 6653-4
Chimney-tops. Marian (Annie D.G. Robinson) Douglas. 6131-1
Chimney-tops. Unknown. 6312-8
"Chimneys with widebrimmed hats". Ill humour. Jorge Carrera Andrade. 6759-X
The chimpanzee. Oliver Herford. 6501-5
Chin Wee. L. Warner. 6118-4
"Chin tucked into collar". The flowering cacti. Gene Fowler. 6792-1

Chin, Marilyn
  A Chinaman's chance. 6790-5
  Grandmother poems. 6790-5
  The landlord's wife. 6790-5
  We are a young nation, uncle. 6790-5
  Write, do write. 6790-5
"Chin, chin, chin". Unknown. 6364-0
"A china tea set--just to own". The china tea set. Bertye Young Williams. 7038-8
The China tea set. Bertye Young Williams. 6750-6
The China tea set. Bertye Young Williams. 7038-8
The China tea set. Bertye Young Williams. 6750-6
China town, San Francisco. D. Maitland Bushby. 6954-1
The china-mender. Thomas Hood. 6974-6
Chinaman's 'Song of sixpence'. Unknown. 6710-7
A Chinaman's chance. Marilyn Chin. 6790-5
Chinatown games. Wing Tek Lum. 6790-5
Chinatown talking story. Kitty Tsui. 6790-5
The Chinese dinner. Unknown. 6912-6
The Chinese excelsior. Unknown. 6413-2
Chinese Gordon. John Stuart Blackie. 6819-7
Chinese lanterns. George A. Baker. 6517-1
Chinese laundryman. Jessie Young Norton. 6841-3
The Chinese nightingale. Vachel Lindsay. 6348-9,6531-7, 6556-2,6029-3,6288-1,6646
Chinese nursery rhyme. Isaac Taylor Headland. 6937-1,6638-0
Chinese poet among barbarians. John Gould Fletcher. 6010-2
The Chinese pot. Walter De La Mare. 6905-3
Chinese procession. Witter Bynner. 6037-4
Chinese proverb. Unknown. 7020-5
A Chinese scroll picture, sels. L. Adams Beck. 6649-6
Chinese slippers. Ben Field. 6316-0
A Chinese story. Christopher Pearse Cranch. 6911-8
Chinese sunset. Frances Hall. 6782-4
A Chinese version of Maud Muller. Joseph Bert Smiley. 6923-1
The Ching-Ting mountain. Li Po. 6102-8
"Chink, chink, chime!". Unknown. 6364-0
Chinn, George
  Annihilation. 6672-0
"Chinnie the deddy, and rethy the monkey". Cakes o' croudy. Unknown. 6859-6
Chinoiseries, sels. Amy Lowell. 6897-9
The chintz-birds. V. Fame. 6804-9
The chip on your shoulder. Edgar A. Guest. 7033-7
Chipman, Edgar M.
  Jo, the tramp. 6413-2
Chipmunk. Marie de L. Welch. 6464-7
Chipmunks. Alfred Kreymborg. 6184-2
Chipp, Eleanor
  Wild geese ("I heard the wild geese flying"). 6073-0
Chippety chin. Unknown. 6937-1
A Chippewa legend. James Russell Lowell. 6077-3
The Chippewa stream. Unknown. 6057-9
Chiquita. Francis Bret Harte. 6281-4,6467-1,6438-8,6255-5, 6165-6,6271-7,6498-1,6302-0,6735
Chiquita: a legend of the western seas. Barrett Eastman. 6274-1
"Chirp little rooster". Unknown. 6364-0
The chirping cricket. Jang-hi Lee. 6775-1
The chirrupy-cricket.. Martha Banning Thomas. 6466-3
The Christmas guests. Lindsay Duncan. 6924-X
Chishold, William B.
  Bonnets indispensable to Easter. 6720-4
Chisholm, Henry Duncan
  Baie des Chaleur. 6764-6
  Close of day. 6764-6
  Close of day. 6761-1
  The fatted calf. 6761-1
  The old sap-house. 6764-6
  The valley of beehive wells. 6761-1
Chisholm, Hugh
  Aceldama, sels. 6390-X
  Notes on progress, fr. Aceldama. 6390-X
  Ode ("The green seas"). 6389-6
  Vision, fr. Aceldama. 6390-X
  You, horse, fr. Aceldama. 6390-X
Chisholm, Ja
  The bookdealer's daughter. 6900-2

Chisholm, William B.
　'Flag the train'. 6923-1
"**Chi**to, chito when it could". Unknown. 6364-0
Chittenden, Gerald
　Gossip at Bow Mills. 6039-0
Chittenden, William Lawrence
　Dying scout. 6702-6
　My mother. 6097-8
　Neptune's steeds. 6336-5
Chitwood, William Hankins
　Life's past and future. 6799-9
Chivalrie. George A. Baker. 6517-1
Chivalry. Ben Jonson. 6438-8
Chivalry at a discount. Edward Fitzgerald. 6874-X
The **chivalry** of the sea. Robert Bridges. 6487-6
Chivalry, fr. Supplices. Euripides. 6435-3
Chivers, Thomas Holley
　Apollo. 7017-5
　Apollo. 6176-1
　Avalon. 6754-9
　Burdens of unrest. 7017-5
　The chaplet of Cypress. 7017-5
　The crucifixion. 7017-5
　The dying beauty, sels. 6482-5
　Faith. 7017-5
　Georgia waters. 7017-5
　Isadore. 7017-5
　Lily Adair. 7017-5
　The raising of Tabitha, sels. 6482-5
　Song of adoration to God. 7017-5
　Song to Isa. 7017-5
　Song to Isa singing. 6176-1
　Sonnet: grief. 7017-5
　To Allegra Florence in heaven. 7017-5
　To Idealon. 7017-5
　The voice of thought. 7017-5
Chiyo
　"Cuckoo!/Again cuckoo!" 6850-2
　"The hunter of dragon flies". Yone Noguchi (tr.). 6850-2
　"The persimmon, lo!" 6850-2
　"The well-bucket taken away". Yone Noguchi (tr.). 6850-2
Chiyo Ni
　"Small tendrils of a morning glory..." Lois J. Erickson (tr.). 6027-7
　"Smiles on my lips, while quick tears blind my eyes." Lois J. Erickson (tr.). 6027-7
Chloe. Robert Burns. 6239-3
Chloe. Charles Mordaunt; Earl of Peterborough. 6152-4,6932-0
Chloe. Matthew Prior. 6301-2,6383-7
Chloe and Euphelia. Matthew Prior. 6814-6
Chloe divine. Thomas D'Urfey. 6317-9
Chloe hunting. Matthew Prior. 6383-7
Chloe, M.A. Mortimer Collins. 6089-7
Chloe, the impeccable heartless, fr. Characters. Alexander Pope. 6637-2
"**Chloe,** you shun me like a bird". To Chloe (2). Horace. 6949-5
Chloris and Corydon. Sennett Stephens. 6441-8
Chloris and Hylas. Edmund Waller. 6563-5
"**Chloris** farewell". Song ("Chloris farewell"). Edmund Waller. 6152-4
"**Chloris** farewell, I now must go". Unknown. 6933-9
Chloris in the snow. Thomas Carew. 6099-4
Chloris in the snow. Unknown. 6250-4
Chloris properly rebuked. Horace. 6949-5
"**Chloris,** 'tis not in your power". Sir George Etherege. 6933-9
Chloris, a constant comfort. Henry Hughes. 6563-5
Chloris, forbear a while. Abraham Cowley. 6563-5
"**Chloris,** forbear a while, do not o'erjoy me." Henry Bold. 6317-9,6563-5
"**Chloris,** I cannot say your eyes." Sir Charles Sedley. 6317-9
"**Chloris,** my friend, I pray you...". Chloris properly rebuked. Horace. 6949-5
"**Chloris,** when I to thee present". A song ("Chloris, when I to thee present"). Unknown. 6933-9

Chloris, yourself you so excel. Edmund Waller. 6328-4
Cho, Byung-hwa
　Memory. 6775-1
　Seashell. 6775-1
Cho, Ji-hoon
　Buddhist dance. 6775-1
　Falling petals. 6775-1
　Flower petals on the sleeves. 6775-1
　Spring day. 6775-1
Cho, Yun-hyn
　Azalea flowers. 6775-1
Cho-che-Bang and Chi-chil-Bloo. Unknown. 6911-8
Cho-che-bang and chiea. Unknown. 6649-6
Choate, Helen
　Resurrection. 6780-8
　Wagnerian love. 6817-0
Choate, Isaac Bassett
　Chickadee. 6394-2
　The choral dance. 6959-2
　Fairies' work. 6394-2
　Tomorrow is another day. 6118-4
　Waking. 6529-5
Choc de cavaliers. Theophile Gautier. 6801-4
Chocano, Jose Santos
　The magnolia. John Pierrepont Rice (tr.). 6338-1
　The mocking-bird. Muna Lee (tr.). 6102-8
Chock, Eric
　For the field. 6790-5
　The mango tree. 6790-5
　Papio. 6790-5
　Pulling weeds. 6790-5
　Termites. 6790-5
The **chocolate** bus. Eleanor Farjeon. 6804-9
Chocolate cream, fr. Counsel to those that eat. Edward Verrall Lucas. 6018-8,6089-7
Chocorua to its neighbor. Wallace Stevens. 6391-8
"**Choctaw** death song i". Four Choctaw songs. Jim Barnes. 7005-1
Choe, Nam-sun
　The sea to the boy. 6775-1
Choice. Grace Blanchard. 6764-6
Choice. Emily Dickinson. 6019-6,6250-4,6309-8
Choice. Muna Lee. 6619-4,6393-4
Choice. Angela Morgan. 6556-2
Choice. Anna Wickham. 6532-5
A **choice** in spoons, fr. The hasty pudding. Joel Barlow. 6399-3
"The **choice** of ailment, the choice of air". The passions, fr. The art of preserving health. John Armstrong. 6968-1
The **choice** of arms. Marquis de Leuville. 6681-X
Choice of occupations. Caroline Gilman. 6131-1
The **choice** of the Cross, fr. The devil to pay. Dorothy L. Sayers. 6337-3
Choice of the home at Grasmere, fr. The recluse. William Wordsworth. 6867-7
Choice of trades. Unknown. 6314-4
"**Choice** soul, in whom, as in a glass, we see". The doom of beauty. Michelangelo Buonarroti. 7039-6
The **choice,** fr. The house of life. Dante Gabriel Rossetti. 6123-0,6198-2,6437-X,6527-9,6726-3,6110-9,6122-2, 6508-2,6250-4,6655-0
choice, sels, fr. The. Dante Gabriel Rossetti. 6369-1,6122-2,6808-2,6482-5
The **choice,** sels. John Pomfret. 6317-9;6527-9
A **choice.** Edward de Vere, 17th Earl of Oxford. 6436-1
A **choice.** Margaret Sherwood. 6184-2
The **choice.** Thomas Beedome. 6563-5
The **choice.** John Joy Bell. 6242-3
The **choice.** Berton Braley. 6853-7
The **choice.** Mary Stella Edwards. 6070-6
The **choice.** Edgar A. Guest. 6869-3
The **choice.** Rudyard Kipling. 7026-4
The **choice.** John Masefield. 7027-2
The **choice.** John Pomfret. 6152-4
The **choice.** Ezra Pound. 6897-9
The **choice.** Nahum Tate. 6339-X
The **choice.** Katharine (Hinkson) Tynan. 6338-1,6477-9,6649-6,6161-3
Choices. Carl Sandburg. 6880-4

CHOIR

The **choir** at Pixley. Edgar A. Guest. 6862-6
The **choir** invisible. George (Mary Ann Cross) Eliot. 6260-1, 6303-9,6479-5,6304-7,6424-8
"**Choir** of bright beauties in spring did appear". The May queen. John Dryden. 6970-3
"A **choir** of bright beauties in spring did...". Phillis unwilling. John Dryden. 6874-X
Choir trou'les in Vermont. Daniel L. Cady. 6989-4
"The **choir** we had in Pixley wasn't much for...". The choir at Pixley. Edgar A. Guest. 6862-6
The **choirs** of heaven. Unknown (Greek) 6435-3
Cholera camp. Rudyard Kipling. 6810-3
Cholmeley-Jones, Henrietta
    Autumn in Connecticut. 6894-4
Cholmondeley, Hester H.
    Betrayal. 6337-3
Cholmondeley-Pennell, Henry
    How the daughters came at Dunoon. 6089-7
    Lay of the deserted influenzaed. 6724-7,6089-7
    The night mail north. 6927-4
    Our traveller. 6089-7
    Waterloo place. 6724-7
    What the Prince of I dreamt. 6902-9
Choose. Carl Sandburg. 6897-9
"**Choose** me your valentine". To his mistress. Robert Herrick. 6830-8
"**Choose** your partners! Take your places!". Danse macabre. Edwin Meade Robinson. 6959-2
Choosing a kitten. Unknown. 6132-X
Choosing a mast. Roy Campbell. 6246-5,6258-X,6210-5
Choosing a name. Charles Lamb. 6242-3
Choosing a name. Mary Lamb. 6078-1,6127-3,6240-7,6302-0, 6101-1,6424-8,6808-1
Choosing a profession. Mary Lamb. 6105-2
Choosing a wife by a pipe of tobacco. Unknown. 6453-1
Choosing friends. Theognis. 6435-3
Choosing occupations. Unknown. 6684-4
"**Choosing** sides/Little girls". Chinatown games. Wing Tek Lum. 6790-5
The **choosing.** Ruth Comfort Mitchell. 7007-8
Chop-cherry. Robert Herrick. 6369-1,6562-7,6026-9,6659-3
The **chop-house** in the alley. Henry M. Hyde. 6274-1
Chopcherry. George Peele. 6383-7
Chopin prelude. Eleanour Norton. 6607-0
Chopin's motherland. Stanislaw Balinski. 6068-4
The **chopper's** child. Alice Cary. 6865-0;6969-X
Choral. Anne Goodwin Winslow. 6808-1
The **choral** dance. Isaac Bassett Choate. 6959-2
A **choral** ode to liberty, sels. Eric Mackay. 7009-4
Choral song of Illrian peasants. Samuel Taylor Coleridge. 6133-8
"The **chord,** the harp's full chord is hushed". Music of yesterday. Felicia Dorothea Hemans. 6973-8
The **chords** of love must be strong as death. Phoebe Cary. 6066-8
Chore time. Jean Blewett. 6115-X
Choric song of the lotos eaters. Alfred Lord Tennyson. 6847-2
Choric song, fr. The lotos-eaters. Alfred Lord Tennyson. 6334-9,6490-6,6143-5,6252-0,6110-9,6123-0,6634-8
Choric song, sels. Alfred Lord Tennyson. 6258-X
Choricos. Richard Aldington. 6153-2
The **chorister,** fr. In black and white: winter etchings. John Addington Symonds. 7015-9
The **choristers.** Bliss Carman. 6797-2
Chorley and John Ellerton, Henry Fothergill
    God, the omnipotent. 6337-3
Chorley, Henry Fothergill
    The brave old oak. 6302-0;6385-3,6543-0
"**Chorlis,** it is not thy disdaine". Song ("Cloris"). Sidney Godolphin. 6341-1
Chorus. Sidney Godolphin. 6317-9
Chorus. Alfred Edward Housman. 6102-8
Chorus. Algernon Charles Swinburne. 6660-7
Chorus ("Before the beginning of years"). Algernon Charles Swinburne. 6186-9,6246-6,6315-2,6219-9
Chorus ("King"). Henry Hart Milman. 6980-0
Chorus ("Life of life"). Percy Bysshe Shelley. 6315-2
Chorus ("Since knights"). Thomas Campion. 6794-8
Chorus ("Surely"). William Alexander Percy. 7017-5

Chorus ("That pleasure"). Thomas Campion. 6794-8
Chorus ("The world's great"). Percy Bysshe Shelley. 6186-9, 6315-2
Chorus ("Vain man, born to no happiness"). Sidney Godolphin. 6315-2
Chorus ("Vanish"). Thomas Campion. 6794-8
Chorus ("Vertue"). Thomas Campion. 6794-8
Chorus ("Yea, the coneys are scared"). Thomas Hardy. 6315-2
Chorus (Behold what furies still"). Samuel Daniel. 6315-2
Chorus at the Green Bear Inn. Herbert Trench. 6877-4
Chorus for Easter. David Morton. 6337-3
Chorus from Goddwyn. Thomas Chatterton. 6086-2
Chorus I, fr. The rock. Thomas Stearns Eliot. 6532-5
Chorus in a masque. Ben Jonson. 6563-5
Chorus in an unpublished drama, written very early. Alfred Lord Tennyson. 6977-0
Chorus of Anglomaniacs. Edgar Fawcett. 6505-8
Chorus of birds. Aristophanes. 7039-6
Chorus of captive Greek women, fr. Iphigenia in Tauris. Euripides. 6334-9
Chorus of English songsters. William John Courthope. 6385-3
Chorus of flowers. Leigh Hunt. 6271-7,6219-9
Chorus of islanders. Alfred Austin. 7022-1
Chorus of Oceanides, fr. Demeter. Robert Bridges. 6334-9
Chorus of Oreades, fr. The masque of Pandora. Henry Wadsworth Longfellow. 6334-9
Chorus of priests. Fulke Greville; 1st Baron Brooke. 6935-5
Chorus of satyrs, driving their goats, fr. The cyclops. Euripides. 7039-6
Chorus of Scyrian maidens, fr. Achilles in Scyros. Robert Bridges. 6334-9
Chorus of spirits. George Darley. 6930-4
Chorus of spirits of the mind, fr. Prometheus unbound. Percy Bysshe Shelley. 6935-5
Chorus of spirits, fr. Sylvia. George Darley. 6656-9
Chorus of the elements. John Henry, Cardinal Newman. 6437-X
Chorus of the flowers. Lucy Wheelock. 6049-8,6373-X,6373-X
A **chorus** of women, fr. Thesmophoriazusae. Aristophanes. 6996-7
Chorus on the death of Faustus. Christopher Marlowe. 6301-2
Chorus primus - Of time: eternitie. Fulke Greville; 1st Baron Brooke. 6933-9
Chorus Quintus- Tartarorum. Fulke Greville; 1st Baron Brooke. 6933-9
Chorus sacerdotum. Fulke Greville; 1st Baron Brooke. 6208-3,6194-X,6150-8
Chorus VI, fr. The rock. Thomas Stearns Eliot. 6532-5
Chorus X, fr. The rock. Thomas Stearns Eliot. 6532-5
Chorus, fr. Agamemnon. Aeschylus. 7039-6
Chorus, fr. Ajax. Sophocles. 7039-6
Chorus, fr. Alcestis. Euripides. 7039-6
The **chorus,** fr. Atalanta in Calydon. Algernon Charles Swinburne. 6123-0,6198-2,6023-4,6301-2,6508-2,6153-2, 6150-8
Chorus, fr. Athalie. Jean Baptiste Racine. 6730-1
The **chorus, fr. Erechtheus.** Algernon Charles Swinburne. 6334-9
Chorus, fr. Hellas. Percy Bysshe Shelley. 6154-0,6208-3, 6252-0,6150-8
Chorus, fr. Hippolytus. Euripides. 6252-0
Chorus, fr. Hippolytus. Euripides. 7039-6
Chorus, fr. Hippolytus. Gilbert Murray. 6477-9
Chorus, fr. Morpheus. Hilda ("H.D.") Doolittle. 6209-1
Chorus, fr. Oedipus rex. Sophocles. 6730-1
Chorus, fr. Paid on both sides. Wystan Hugh Auden. 6150-8
Chorus, fr. Seven against Thebes. Aeschylus. 7039-6
Chorus, fr. The Bacchae. Euripides. 6252-0
Chorus, fr. The Bacchae. Euripides. 6334-9,6102-8
Chorus, fr. The jolly beggars. Robert Burns. 7009-4
Chorus, fr. The ode for the year 1705. Nahum Tate. 6867-7
Chorus, fr. The seven against Thebes. Aeschylus. 6102-8
Chorus, fr. The Trojan women. Euripides. 6334-9
Chorus, fr. Walpurgis night. Johann Wolfgang von Goethe. 6102-8
Chorus-girl. Mary Atwater Taylor. 6039-0

Chorus: The kings of Troy, fr. Andromache. Euripides. 6665-8
Choruses from Atalanta in Cal·don. Algernon Charles Swinburne. 6828-6
Choruses from Hellas. Percy Bysshe Shelley. 6828-6
Choruses of Eden spirits, fr. A drama of exile. Elizabeth Barrett Browning. 6334-9
Choruses on the eve of Waterloo. Thomas Hardy. 6334-9
Choruses, fr. Samson Agonistes. John Milton. 6334-9
"The **chosen** ones of Israel are scatter'd". The chosen ones of Israel. Park Benjamin. 6848-0
The **chosen** path. Henry Vaughan. 6189-3
The **chosen** people. W.N. Ewer. 6026-9
Choses du soir. Victor Hugo. 6801-4
Chough. Rex E. Warner. 6179-6
The **chough** and crow. Joanna Baillie. 6832-4,6383-7
The **chough**. James Reaney. 6446-9
Chovronja-the pig. Florence Randal Livesay. 6797-2
Choyce, A. Newberry
  Let me love bright things. 6776-X
  Memory. 6542-2
  Until you pass. 6088-9
The **Chragan** palace. Thomas Terzyan. 6050-1
Chrasta, James
  We, the inheritors. 6662-3
Chrees'mas time. Thomas Augustine Daly. 6807-3
Chris. Dean. James Abraham Martling. 6952-5
The **chrism** and crown of love. Elizabeth Barrett Browning. 6014-5
The **chrism** of kings. Thomas O'Hagan. 6115-X
Chrismus on the plantation. Paul Laurence Dunbar. 6281-4
Christ. Robert J. Burdette. 6065-X
Christ. Greg Forker. 6870-7
Christ - and we. Annie Johnson Flint. 6337-3
Christ all-sufficient, fr. Saint Paul. Frederick W.H. Myers. 6337-3
Christ and the common day. Marguerite Wilkinson. 6065-X
Christ and the little ones. Julia Gill. 6127-3
Christ and the little ones. Unknown. 6918-5
Christ and the mourners. Katherine Eleanor Conway. 6144-3
Christ and the pagan. John Banister Tabb. 6292-X,6172-9, 6335-7
Christ and we. Robert Herrick. 6144-3
Christ at eight. Ernest Hartsock. 6542-2
Christ at the door. Unknown. 6065-X
Christ brought home. Unknown. 6489-2
Christ calls man home. Unknown. 6881-2
Christ calming the tempest. Horace B. Durant. 6923-1
Christ can give thee heart. Christina Georgina Rossetti. 6144-3
The **Christ** candle. Kate Louise Brown. 6653-4
Christ child. Henry Treece. 6337-3
The **Christ** child at Christmas. John Drinkwater. 6532-5
A **Christ** child book. Vachel Lindsay. 6206-7
The **Christ** child's Christmas. Laura Spencer Portor. 6449-3
The **Christ** child. Gilbert Keith Chesterton. 6543-0,6747-6
Christ Church bells. Henry Aldrich. 6563-5
Christ complains to sinners. Unknown. 6881-2
Christ crucified. Richard Crashaw. 6465-5
Christ crucified. Henry Hart Milman. 6214-8
"**Christ** for sickness...". Unknown. 6065-X
Christ has risen. Sarah ("Susan Coolidge") Woolsey. 6144-3
Christ in Crete. Eleanor Knox Farrell. 6761-1
Christ in Flanders. Unknown. 6303-9
Christ in Flanders. L. W. 7031-0
Christ in Flanders. L. W. 6930-0
Christ in Flanders. L. W. 6846-4,7027-2
Christ in Flanders. Lucy Whitmell. 6477-9,6532-5,6542-2
Christ in his passion, fr. Hymn: crucifixus pro nobis. Patrick Carey. 6931-2
Christ in introspect. Charlotte Bronte. 6337-3
Christ in the Andes. Carl John Bostelmann. 6144-3
Christ in the city. Frank Mason North. 6337-3
Christ in the cradle, fr. Hymn: crucifixus pro nobis. Patrick Carey. 6931-2
Christ in the garden. Unknown. 6061-7
Christ in the garden, fr. Hymn: crucifixus pro nobis. Patrick Carey. 6931-2
Christ in the street. Jay G. Sigmund. 6144-3
Christ in the universe. Alice Meynell. 6052-8,6096-X,6335-7,6022-6,6292-X,6172
Christ in the universe, sels. Alice Meynell. 6339-X
Christ in Woolworth's. Teresa Hooley. 6144-3,6335-7,6532-5
Christ is all. Horatius Bonar. 6065-X
Christ is arisen. Arthur Cleveland Coxe. 6177-X
Christ is coming. Heyman Wreford. 6065-X
Christ is crucified anew. John Richard Moreland. 6144-3;6335-7;6337-3
Christ is here. Robert Lowell. 6065-X
"**Christ** is risen". Christoph Christian Sturm. 6065-X
"**Christ** keep us all, as he well can". Now sing we, sing we: Gloria tibi, domine. Unknown. 6756-5
Christ liveth in me. Toyohiko Kagawa. 6027-7
"**Christ** maketh to man a fair present". Love unlike love. Unknown. 6881-2
The **Christ** militant. Thomas Curtis Clark. 6144-3
The **Christ** of common folks. George T. Liddell. 6335-7
Christ of everywhere. Henry Van Dyke. 6337-3
The **Christ** of God. Russell E. Kauffman. 6065-X
Christ of Kazan. Wilhelm Szabo. 6769-7
The **Christ** of the Andes. Edwin Markham. 6051-X,6465-5,6449-3
The **Christ** of the world's highway. Dorothy Clarke Wilson. 6337-3
Christ on Madison street. Raymond Kresensky. 6954-1
Christ our contemporary. W.C. Braithwaite. 6337-3
Christ our example. Charles Wesley. 6214-8
Christ quiets the tempest. Caelius Sedulius. 6930-4
Christ risen. Anna Letitia Barbauld. 6219-9
"**Christ** save me from half-hearted men". The glorious fool. Henry Herbert Knibbs. 7012-4
Christ speaks. Wade Oliver. 6337-3
Christ stilling the tempest. Felicia Dorothea Hemans. 6973-8
Christ tells of his passion. Cynewulf. 6489-2
"'**Christ** the Lord is risen!'". The Easter children. Elsa Barker. 6954-1
Christ the answer. George Macdonald. 6337-3
Christ the carpenter. Leslie L. Haskin. 6065-X
Christ the comrade. Padraic Colum. 6172-9,6172-9,6292-X
Christ the conqueror. Henry Foster Burder. 6065-X
Christ the consoler. Henry W. Baker. 6065-X
Christ the Lord is risen today. Charles Wesley. 6065-X
Christ the mendicant. John Banister Tabb. 6627-5
Christ to his spouse. William Baldwin. 6182-6
Christ to the sufferer, fr. Andreas. Unknown. 6489-2
Christ true love's example. Edmund Spenser. 6634-8
Christ unconquered, sels. Arthur J. Little. 6282-2
"**Christ** was born on Christmas day". Christmas carol. Thomas Helmore. 6806-5
"**Christ** was your lord & captain all your life". To his father. Robinson Jeffers. 6808-1
"The **Christ** who came of old to his own." Harriet McEwen Kimball. 6225-3
Christ's agony in the garden. Felicia Dorothea Hemans. 6973-8
Christ's bondservant. George Matheson. 6337-3
Christ's coming in triumph. Jeremy Taylor. 6065-X
Christ's gift to man. Unknown. 6022-6
Christ's giving. Ann [or Annie E.] Hamilton. 6144-3,6225-3
Christ's Nativity. Henry Vaughan. 6746-8,6747-6
Christ's pity. Elsa Gidlow. 6628-3
Christ's poverty. Warren W. Sutton. 6799-9
Christ's reign of peace. Stephen Phillips. 6144-3,6335-7
Christ's reply. Edward Taylor. 6333-0
Christ's soldier, fr. King Richard II. William Shakespeare. 6934-7
Christ's sympathy. Owen (Edward Bulwer-Lytton, Earl Lytton) Meredith. 6065-X
Christ's tear breaks my heart. Unknown. 6881-2
Christ's triumph after death. Giles (the Younger) Fletcher. 6186-9
Christ's triumph over death, sels. Giles (the Younger) Fletcher. 6315-2,6144-X
Christ's triumphant nativity. John Milton. 6634-8
Christ's victorie and triumph in heaven..., sels. Giles (the Younger) Fletcher. 6144-3,6337-3
Christ's victory. Richard Crashaw. 6337-3
"**Christ**, here's a thorn". The Lenten offering. Sylvia Townsend Warner. 6985-1

CHRIST,

Christ, my beloved. William Baldwin. 6182-6
Christ, sels. Cynewulf. 6489-2
The Christ, sels. Cynewulf. 6282-2
Christ, the good physician. Charles Wesley. 6065-X
Christ, the way. George Washington Doane. 6065-X
"Christ, whose glory fills the skies". Charles Wesley. 6931-2
"Christ,/according to/an ancient Kazan script". Christ of Kazan. Wilhelm Szabo. 6769-7
A Christ-child day in Australia. Ethel Turner. 6784-0
"The Christ-child lay in the ox's stall". Ox and donkey's carol. Sister Maris Stella. 6761-1
A Christ-cross rhyme. Robert Stephen Hawker. 6022-6
The Christ-sword. George William ("A.E.") Russell. 6785-9
The Christ. Edgar William Whan. 6144-3
Christabel. Samuel Taylor Coleridge. 6198-2,6196-6,6430-2, 6250-4,6199-0,6245 ,6646-1,6518-X,6723-9,6219-9,6110-9,6086 ,6473-6,6600-3,6634-8
Christabel, sels. Samuel Taylor Coleridge. 6332-2,6726-3, 6138-9,6369-1,6543-0,6301
"Christamas comes again with all the". A Christmas reverie. William Harper Huff. 6799-9
A Christday day prayer. Robert ("Droch") Bridges. 6747-6
'Christendom', sels. Thomas Traherne. 6208-3
Christening. Mary Baron. 6855-3
Christening Dolly. Emma Celia & Lizzie J. Rook. 6268-7
The Christening of my boy. Mrs. E.T. Corbett. 6451-5
A Christening remembered. Vernon Watkins. 6209-1
The christening.. Amy Sherman Bridgman. 6031-5
The christening. Thomas Edward Brown. 6809-X
The Christening. Walter De La Mare. 6596-1
Christensen, Holger
    Episodes of haying time. 6799-9
Christensen, Ron
    "Silence is here, silence is there" 6883-9
Christesen, Clem
    Regent-bird and girl. 6349-7
Christgau, Ferdinand G.
    Some saintly cities. 6724-7
Christian and Jew. Christina Georgina Rossetti. 6848-0
The Christian calling. Unknown. 6385-3
Christian ethics. Thomas Traherne. 6931-2
Christian forgiveness. Unknown. 6382-7
A Christian is a man who feels. Thomas Russell Ybarra. 6722-0
The Christian life. Philip Doddridge. 6411-6
The Christian life. Philip Doodridge. 6606-2
The Christian life. Samuel Longfellow. 6418-3,6730-1
Christian love. William Peter. 6980-0
The Christian maiden and the lion. Francis A. Durivage. 6412-4
The Christian paradox. Walter Chalmers Smith. 6337-3
The Christian pilgrim's hymn. William Williams. 6418-3, 6730-1
Christian Science. Edward R. Huxley. 6885-5
"Christian reads of God, the Christian sees". The presence of God. Charles W. Denison. 6755-7
The Christian slave. William Ernest Henley. 6732-8
The Christian slave. John Greenleaf Whittier. 6527-9,6126-5
The Christian soldier. G.A. Studdert-Kennedy. 6337-3
The Christian stoic. A. W. 6935-5
The Christian's confidence. Charles H. McLean. 6799-9
Christian's poem. Jorge de Lima. 6759-X
Christian, Christine
    ERA. 6857-X
Christian, Marcus B. 6178-8
    Dark heritage. 6178-8
    'Go down, Moses!' 6178-8
    Selassie at Geneva. 6178-8
Christian, dost thou see them? Andrew of Crete. 6337-3
The Christian. William Cowper. 6814-6
Christianity. Edward Farquhar. 6939-8
Christianity and war. Ernest Howard Crosby. 6542-2
Christianity in the apostles. Edward Farquhar. 6939-8
"The Christians have beleaguered...Xeres". The pounder. Unknown (Spanish). 6757-3
Christians reply to the phylosopher. Sir William Davenant. 6341-1
Christians, awake! John Byrom. 6747-6

Christie's portrait. Gerald Massey. 6656-9
Christie, Annie Rothwell
    The woman's part. 6591-0,6592-2
Christie, John
    The ruined homestead. 6591-0,6592-2
Christie, R. (tr.)
    "No sickness of the flesh is ours to-day." Feodor Ivanovich Tyutchev, 6103-6
Christie, Robert A.
    The lone woman. 7031-0
Christina Georgina Rossetti (tr.)
    Psalm 137. By the waters of Babylon. Bible, 6848-0
Christina, Sister Mary
    The day of my profession. 6285-7
"Christina, maiden of heroic mien!". To Christina, queen of Sweden with Cromwell's picture. John Milton. 6814-6
Christis Kirk of the green. Unknown. 6180-X
Christman, Elizabeth Ann
    A poet to his wife. 6761-1
Christman, Lansing
    If I sit silent. 6761-1
    Summer harvest. 6761-1
Christman, W.W.
    Career. 6662-3
    Deborah. 6662-3
    The empty cup. 6662-3
    The fox sparrow. 6073-0
    The gift of rest. 6662-3
    I give. 6662-3
    Ira and Kate. 6662-3
    The mourning dove. 6073-0
    The old mill. 6761-1
    The schoolmate. 6662-3
    The snow lies light. 6073-0
    Under the four corners' elm. 6761-1
    The untillable hills. 6662-3
Christmas. William Cullen Bryant. 6144-3,6337-3
Christmas. Phoebe Cary. 6969-X
Christmas. Nora Chesson. 6807-3
Christmas. Rose Terry Cooke. 6131-1
Christmas. Rose Terry Cooke. 6145-1
Christmas. Eugene Field. 6949-5
Christmas. Mrs. Hawtrey. 6131-1
Christmas. Felicia Dorothea Hemans. 6973-8
Christmas. George Herbert. 6138-9,6641-0,6746-3
Christmas. Arthur F. Jones. 6799-9
Christmas. Esther Bergman Narey. 6799-9
Christmas. Florence Orndorff. 6906-1
Christmas. Catherine Parmenter. 6143-5
Christmas. Harriet W. Pierson. 6799-9
Christmas. William Sawyer. 6927-4
Christmas. Betty Scott Stam. 6065-X
Christmas. Frank H. Sweet. 6807-3
Christmas. Nahum Tate. 6889-8
Christmas. Nahum Tate. 6145-1,6219-9,6449-3
Christmas. Henry Timrod. 6333-7
Christmas. Thomas Tusser. 6756-5
Christmas. Unknown. 6171-0
Christmas. Unknown. 6952-5
Christmas. Charles Williams. 6884-7
Christmas. George Wither. 6271-7
Christmas. Edward Hilton Young. 6608-9
Christmas ("Dainty little stockings"). Unknown. 6745-X
Christmas ("Once in royal David's city"). Unknown. 6145-1
Christmas ("Over the hills"). Unknown. 6807-3
Christmas (2). Phoebe Cary. 6969-X
Christmas 1930. Anderson M. Scruggs. 6781-6
Christmas 1944. Denise Levertov. 6379-9
Christmas a hundred years to come. Louis Eisenbeis. 6923-1
Christmas acrostic. Rosamund Livingstone McNaught. 6807-3
Christmas acrostic. Unknown. 6715-8,6745-X
Christmas after war. Katharine Lee Bates. 6746-8,6608-9
Christmas again. Unknown. 6171-0
A Christmas alphabet. Carolyn Wells. 6882-0
Christmas and common birth. Anne Ridler. 6210-5
Christmas and Ireland. Lionel Johnson. 6292-X,6172-9
Christmas and the old year. Rosamund Livingstone McNaught. 6807-3
The Christmas angel's message. Clare Beatrice Coffey. 692-

282

CHRISTMAS

Christmas antiphon. Algernon Charles Swinburne. 6138-9, 6144-3,6641-0,6747-6
Christmas at Babbitt's. Henry Hallam Tweedy. 6337-3
Christmas at sea. Robert Louis Stevenson. 6258-X,6332-2, 6437-X,6478-7,6486-8,6547,6634-8,6107-9,6747-6,6458-2,6723-9
Christmas at the cape. John Runcie. 6747-6
Christmas at the officers' mess. John Streeter Manifold. 6895-2
The Christmas babe. Katharine (Hinkson) Tynan. 6274-1
The Christmas baby. Will Carleton. 6414-0
The Christmas baby. Isabella Valancy Crawford. 6797-2
The Christmas ball. Mary E. (Freeman) Wilkins. 6965-7
A Christmas ballad. Mary A. Dennison. 6572-4
Christmas bells. John Keble. 6424-8
Christmas bells. Henry Wadsworth Longfellow. 6144-3,6145-7, 6272-5,6314-4,6337-3,6465,6457-4,6746-8,6457-4,6608-9
Christmas bells. Alice Mortenson. 6065-X
Christmas bells. Emma Celia & Lizzie J. Rook. 6741-7
Christmas bells. Unknown. 6145-1,6272-5,6273-3,6274-1,6131-1,6449
Christmas bells, fr. In memoriam. Alfred Lord Tennyson. 6337-3,6438-8
A Christmas bit. Edgar A. Guest. 6869-3
Christmas blessing. Franklin D. Elmer Jr. 6144-3
A Christmas blessing. Unknown. 6919-3
The Christmas box. Unknown. 6747-6
Christmas boy. Frank Lebby Stanton. 6721-2
Christmas burial. Margaret Hazelwood. 6799-9
A Christmas camp on the San Gabr'el. Amelia Baar. 6274-1
A Christmas camp on the San Gabr'el. Amelia E. Barr. 6273-3
The Christmas candle. Kate Louise Brown. 6465-5
A Christmas card, after the assassination. Mona Van Duyn. 6803-0
A Christmas Carmen. John Gr_eenleaf Whittier. 6145-1,6746-8, 6608-9
Christmas carol. Arthur Cleveland Coxe. 6219-9
Christmas carol. Kenneth Grahame. 6891-X
Christmas carol. Thomas Helmore. 6806-5
Christmas carol. Felicia Dorothea Hemans. 6424-8
Christmas carol. Felicia Dorothea Hemans. 6973-8
Christmas carol. Felicia Dorothea Hemans. 6973-8
Christmas carol. Juliet C. Marsh. 6965-7
Christmas carol. James S. Park. 6820-0
Christmas carol. James S. Park. 6145-1
Christmas carol. Unknown. 6952-5
Christmas carol. William Wordsworth. 6438-8
Christmas carol ("As Joseph was a-waukin'"). Unknown. 6145-1,6627-5,6424-8
Christmas carol ("Christmas, awake, salute the happy morn") . John Byrom. 6219-9
A Christmas carol ("God rest ye, merry gentlemen..."). Dinah Maria Mulock Craik. 6623-2,6219-9,6424-8
Christmas carol ("God rest you merry gentlemen"). Unknown. 6145-1
A Christmas carol ("Lacking samite and sable"). May Probyn. 6096-X,6282-2,6046-3,6022-6
Christmas carol ("Listen, lordings, unto me,..."). Unknown. 6145-1,6424-8
A Christmas carol ("So, now is come..."). George Wither. 6334-9,6562-7,6734-4,6668-2
Christmas carol ("The earth has grown old..."). Phillips Brooks. 6608-9,6145-1,6337-3,6466-3,6692-5,6449-3, 6654
The Christmas carol ("The minstrels played..."). William Wordsworth. 6145-1,6747-6,6424-8
A Christmas carol ("There's a song in the air"). Josiah Gilbert Holland. 6145-1,6239-3,6006-4,6627-5,6304-7, 6421
A Christmas carol ("They leave the land of gems..."). Sir Aubrey De Vere. 6145-1
Christmas carol ("What sweeter music can we bring"). Robert Herrick. 6334-2,6623-2
Christmas carol (old English). Unknown. 6239-3
A Christmas carol for children. Martin Luther. 6145-1,6747-6,6608-9
Christmas carol II. Lionel Johnson. 6490-6

The Christmas carol of the bees. Nora Archibald Smith. 6607-0
A Christmas carol, fr. Pickwick papers. Charles Dickens. 6145-1
A Christmas carol. Christian Burke. 6807-3,6145-1
A Christmas carol. Gilbert Keith Chesterton. 6216-4,6337-3, 6653-4,6465-5,6421-3,6723-9
A Christmas carol. Samuel Taylor Coleridge. 6931-2
A Christmas carol. Samuel Taylor Coleridge. 6282-2
A Christmas carol. Samuel Taylor Coleridge. 6931-2
A Christmas carol. Edgar A. Guest. 7033-7
A Christmas carol. Robert Herrick. 6216-4,6334-9,6441-0, 6473-6,6143-5,6747-6,6746-8,6114-1
A Christmas carol. Josiah Gilbert Holland. 6820-0
A Christmas carol. Laurence Housman. 6776-X
A Christmas carol. James Russell Lowell. 6144-3,6145-1, 6623-2,6478-7,6457-4,6147-8,6608-9,6746-8
A Christmas carol. James Abraham Martling. 6952-5
A Christmas carol. Mary A. O'Reilly. 6292-X,6172-9
A Christmas carol. Adelaide Anne Procter. 6957-6
A Christmas carol. Francis Quarles. 6756-5
A Christmas carol. Christina Georgina Rossetti. 6558-9, 6747-6,6734-7,6746-8,6125-7,6424,6608-9,6723-9,6214-8
A Christmas carol. Henry Charles Suter. 6799-9
A Christmas carol. Sara Teasdale. 6608-9
A Christmas carol. Unknown. 6504-X
Christmas carols. Edmund Hamilton Sears. 6214-8
Christmas carols everywhere. Charles Kingsley. 6747-6
"The Christmas carols have been sung". Toeing the line. E.J. E.. 6936-3
A Christmas carroll. George Wither. 6933-9
The Christmas cat. Frank Dempster Sherman. 6311-X
A Christmas chant. John E. Barrett. 6840-5
A Christmas chant. Alfred Dommet. 6915-0
Christmas cheer. Sir Walter Scott. 6228-8
The Christmas child. Unknown. 6466-3
The Christmas child. George Macdonald. 6216-4
A Christmas chime. Kathleen Kavanagh. 6747-6
Christmas chimes in Boston, Philadelphia, New York... Unknown. 6929-0
The Christmas chimes. Unknown. 6089-7,6413-2
Christmas comes but once a year. Thomas Miller. 6747-6
Christmas communion. Katharine (Hinkson) Tynan. 6746-8
Christmas Creek. Henry Clarence Kendall. 6591-0,6592-9
A Christmas dawn at sea. Evan Morgan. 6833-2
Christmas day. John Kendrick Bangs. 6069-2,6747-6
Christmas day. Art Cuelho. 6998-3
Christmas day. Reginald Heber. 6747-6
Christmas day. John Keble. 6046-3
Christmas day. Ruth Raymond. 6807-3
Christmas day. Margaret Elizabeth Sangster. 6449-3
Christmas Day. Christopher Smart. 6125-7
Christmas day. Caroline Eleanor Wilkinson. 6799-9
Christmas day. George Wither. 6756-5
Christmas day. George Wither. 6746-8
Christmas Day ("Hark! the herald angels sing"). Charles Wesley. 6145-1,6424-8
Christmas day and every day. George Macdonald. 6216-4
Christmas Day at sunset. Jane Broad Cole. 6764-6
Christmas day in the workhouse. George Robert Sims. 6964-9
"The Christmas day was coming". The little Christmas tree. Sarah ("Susan Coolidge") Woolsey. 6147-8,6820-0
Christmas day, 1868. Charles Kingsley. 6747-6
"The Christmas days of long ago". Christmas, today and yesterday. Gustav A. Kleinschmidt. 6799-9
Christmas dolls. Lizzie J. Rook. 6147-8
Christmas dusk. Wilbur Dick Nesbit. 6449-3
Christmas echoes. Robert Herrick. 6272-5
Christmas epithalamium. Hervey Allen. 6746-8
Christmas eve. Frank E. Brown. 6807-3,6147-8
Christmas eve. Liam P. Clancy. 6282-2
Christmas eve. Charlotte Druitt Cole. 6216-4
Christmas eve. John Davidson. 6608-9
Christmas eve. Mary Mapes Dodge. 6746-8
Christmas eve. Eugene Field. 6242-3,6147-8
Christmas eve. H.A. Foster. 6408-6
Christmas eve. Edgar A. Guest. 6862-9
Christmas eve. Hamilton Wright Mabie. 6145-1
Christmas eve. Catherine Parmenter. 6449-3

CHRISTMAS

Christmas eve. Katharine (Hinkson) Tynan. 6746-8
Christmas eve. Unknown. 6744-1
Christmas eve adventure. Unknown. 6743-3
A Christmas eve adventure. M. M. 6743-3
A Christmas eve choral. Bliss Carman. 6282-2,6746-8
Christmas eve in France. Jessie Redmond Fauset. 6032-3
Christmas eve in the Karoo. Ethelreda Lewis. 6800-6
Christmas eve meditation. Margaret E. Bruner. 6337-3
A Christmas eve monlogue. Frederick Moxon. 6739-5
Christmas eve, 1917. Robert Bridges. 6487-6
Christmas eve, sels. Robert Browning. 6144-3
Christmas eve: New York. Hal Saunders White. 6808-1
Christmas everywhere. Phillips Brooks. 6337-3
Christmas fairies. Rosamund Livingstone McNaught. 6807-3
Christmas fantasy. Loretto Troy. 6906-1
The Christmas fir. Edith Borden Greer. 6799-9
The Christmas fires. Anne P.L. Field. 6145-1
Christmas flowers. Adelaide Anne Procter. 6674-4
Christmas folk and the children. Lizzie M. Hadley. 6268-7
A Christmas folk-song. Lizette Woodworth Reese. 6454-X, 6608-9,6465-5,6509-0,6746-8,6393-4,6653-4
A Christmas ghost-story. Thomas Hardy. 6828-6
The Christmas gift for mother. Edgar A. Guest. 7033-7
A Christmas gift. Mabel L. Pray. 6147-8
A Christmas gift. David Law ("Pegleg Arkwright") Proudfit. 6695-X
The Christmas glory. William White. 6868-5
Christmas green. Lucy Larcom. 6129-X
Christmas greens. George A. Baker. 6187-7
Christmas greeting. Unknown. 6807-3
A Christmas greeting. Unknown. 6747-6
Christmas guests. Lindsay Duncan. 6676-3
Christmas guests. Lindsay (Cloud) Duncan. 6768-9
Christmas hearth rhyme. Unknown. 6466-3
Christmas holiday. Alun Lewis. 6528-7
The Christmas holly. Eliza Cook. 6519-8,6145-1,6424-8
The Christmas hunter. Clinton Scollard. 7035-3
Christmas husbandlie fare. Thomas Tusser. 6586-4
Christmas hymn. Eugene Field. 6147-8
Christmas hymn. Reginald Heber. 6980-0
Christmas hymn. Alice Polk Hill. 6836-7
Christmas hymn. Douglas Hyde. 6090-0
Christmas hymn. John Milton. 6385-3,6438-8
Christmas hymn. Edmund Hamilton Sears. 6600-3,6567-8
Christmas hymn. Unknown. 6090-0
Christmas hymn. Charles Wesley. 6746-8
A Christmas hymn ("In the fields where, long ago,"). Unknown. 6145-1
A Christmas hymn for children. Josephine Dodge Daskam. 6608-9
Christmas hymn, sels. Saint Ephrem. 6282-2
Christmas hymn, sels. John Milton. 6102-8
A Christmas hymn. Alfred Domett. 6820-0
A Christmas hymn. Alfred Domett. 6145-1,6239-3,6543-0,6639-9,6219-9,6424-8,6656-9,6102-8
A Christmas hymn. Richard Watson Gilder. 6337-3,6746-8
A Christmas hymn. Mary K. Hutchens. 6799-9
A Christmas hymn. Unknown. 6916-9
Christmas in 1875. William Cullen Bryant. 6753-0
Christmas in Carmel. Sister Mary Therese. 6285-7
Christmas in England, fr. Marmion. Sir Walter Scott. 6239-3
Christmas in freelands. James Stephens. 6628-3
Christmas in India. Rudyard Kipling. 6747-6
Christmas in olden time. Sir Walter Scott. 6142-7,6302-0, 6385-3,6465-5,6466-3,6198 ,6424-8
Christmas in Provence. Sister Mary Madeleva. 6543-0
Christmas in the forest. Aloysius Coll. 7035-3
Christmas in the heart. Unknown. 6090-0
Christmas in the north. Margaret Elizabeth Sangster. 6449-3
Christmas in Tobruk. Signalman H. G. Knight. 6468-X
A Christmas insurrection. Anne P.L. Field. 6145-1
Christmas invitation. William Barnes. 6018-8
Christmas is coming. Unknown. 6937-1,6134-6,6530-9
"Christmas knows a merry, merry place". Wassail chorus at the Mermaid. Theodore Watts-Dunton. 6793-X
Christmas legend. Celestin Pierre Cambiaire. 6826-X
A Christmas legend. Frank Sidgwick. 6668-2
A Christmas legend. Unknown. 6926-6

A Christmas letter from Australia. Douglas Brooke Wheelton Sladen. 6145-1,6656-9
A Christmas letter from Australia. Douglas Brooke Wheelton Sladen. 6768-9
The Christmas light. Frank Walcott Hutt. 6807-3
Christmas long ago. Anne H. Woodruff. 6274-1
A Christmas long ago. Unknown. 6964-9
A Christmas lullaby. John Addington Symonds. 6145-1,6519-8, 6533-3
A Christmas memory. James Whitcomb Riley. 7021-3
A Christmas memory. James Whitcomb Riley. 6091-9
Christmas merrymaking. Sir Walter Scott. 6230-X
A Christmas minuet. Minna Irving. 6807-3
Christmas morn. M. Nora Boylan. 6147-8
Christmas morning. Eugene Field. 6949-5
Christmas morning. Joaquin Miller. 6337-3
Christmas morning. Elizabeth Madox Roberts. 6891-X
Christmas morning. Elizabeth Madox Roberts. 6337-3,6466-3, 6454-X,6326-8,6727-1
Christmas morning. Unknown. 6314-4
Christmas new. Joseph Twyman. 6274-1
Christmas night. Marion Lochhead. 6337-3
Christmas night. Alice Meynell. 6508-2
Christmas night (Bless the dance) Irwin Russell. 6959-2
Christmas night in France. Celestin Pierre Cambiaire. 6826-X
Christmas night in Saint Peter's. Helen Hunt Jackson. 7041-8
Christmas night in the quarters. Irwin Russell. 6142-7, 6554-6
Christmas night in the quarters, sels. Irwin Russell. 6505-8
Christmas night of '62. W. Gordon MacCabe. 6113-3
Christmas night of '62. William Gordon McCabe. 6747-6
The Christmas now is past. Nicholas Breton. 6756-5
A Christmas of long ago. Morton Bryan Wharton. 6074-9
Christmas on the Riviera. Louis J. Magee. 7004-3
Christmas on three continents. John Peter. 6788-3
Christmas once is Christmas still. Phillips Brooks. 6746-6
Christmas out of town. James Smith. 6996-7
Christmas out of town. James Smith. 6874-X
Christmas outcasts. Unknown. 6273-3,6274-1
Christmas paradox. Unknown. 6337-3
A Christmas party. Carolyn Sherwin Bailey. 6466-3
A Christmas party. Carolyn Wells. 6882-0
A Christmas pastime; or, the crying family. Mrs. L.A. Bradbury. 6268-7
Christmas pastoral. Robert Hillyer. 6337-3
Christmas pearls. John E. Barrett. 6840-5
The Christmas pie. Robert Herrick. 6747-6
Christmas prayer. Ralph Spaulding Cushman. 6337-3
A Christmas prayer. Ruby Dell Baugher. 6525-2
A Christmas prayer. Herbert H. Hines. 6144-3,6337-3
A Christmas prayer. George Macdonald. 6216-4
A Christmas prayer. Cyril Winterbotham. 6650-X
Christmas pudding, fr. The poetical cookbook. Unknown. 6278-4
Christmas questions. Wolstan Dixey. 6147-8
The Christmas radio. Mary P. Denny. 6799-9
Christmas rede. Jane Barlow. 6437-X
A Christmas reverie. William Harper Huff. 6799-9
Christmas rose. Thomas Edward Brown. 6809-X
Christmas rose. Margaret Evelyn Singleton. 6144-3
A Christmas sermon. Robert Browning. 6747-6
Christmas service. Unknown. 6747-6
Christmas shadows. Unknown. 6273-3,6274-1
The Christmas sheaf. Phoebe Cary. 6969-X
The Christmas sheaf. Mrs. A.M. Tomlinson. 6674-4
The Christmas silence. Margaret Deland. 6145-1,6608-9,6373-X,6519-8
Christmas song. Bliss Carman. 6446-9
Christmas song. Felix E. Schelling. 6936-3
Christmas song. Edmund Hamilton Sears. 6145-1,6424-8,6608-9
Christmas song. Unknown. 6130-3
A Christmas song ("Blow, wind, blow,"). William Cox Bennett. 6145-1,6656-9
A Christmas song ("When mother-love makes..."). Tudor Jenks. 6145-1
Christmas song ("Why do bells for Christmas ring?"). Lydia

Avery Coonley Ward. 6145-1
A Christmas song. Hattie S. Russell. 6273-3
A Christmas song. Teresa Brayton. 6172-9,6292-X
A Christmas song. Florence Evelyn Dratt. 6608-9
A Christmas song. Laurence Housman. 6746-8
Christmas sonnet to E.C.S. Bayard Taylor. 6976-2
Christmas sonnet to G.H.B. Bayard Taylor. 6976-2
Christmas sonnet to J.L.G. Bayard Taylor. 6976-2
Christmas sonnet to R.H.S. Bayard Taylor. 6976-2
A Christmas sonnet. Edwin Arlington Robinson. 6337-3
Christmas sonnets, sels. Bayard Taylor. 6976-2
The Christmas spirit. Edgar A. Guest. 6862-6
Christmas star. Lettie E. Sterling. 6272-5
The Christmas star. Wolstan Dixey. 6523-6
The Christmas star. Nancy Byrd Turner. 6337-3
Christmas still lives. Clarence Hawkes. 6065-X
The Christmas stocking. Charles H. Pearson. 6147-8
Christmas stockings. Unknown. 6272-5
Christmas stories. Lettie E. Sterling. 6147-8
The Christmas story, fr. Luke. Bible. 6337-3
A Christmas story. Alice Cary. 6060-9
A Christmas story. Jane Kavanagh. 6417-5
Christmas symbols. Florence Phelps. 6799-9
A Christmas symphony. Helen Hunt Jackson. 7041-8
Christmas tears. Henry Van Dyke. 6961-4
A Christmas thought. Mrs. Frank A. Breck. 6065-X
A Christmas thought. Lucy Larcom. 6147-8
Christmas time. M. Nora Boylan. 6147-8
Christmas time. John Clare. 6747-6
Christmas time. Mrs. F. Spangenberg. 6314-4
Christmas today. Anderson M. Scruggs. 6337-3
Christmas treasures. Eugene Field. 6273-3,6670-4,6608-9, 6747-6
Christmas tree. Gertrude Fitzpatrick. 6789-1
The Christmas tree at 'The Pines.' Theodore Watts-Dunton. 6233-4
The Christmas tree in the nursery. Richard Watson Gilder 6806-5
The Christmas tree in the nursery. Richard Watson Gilder. 6807-3
The Christmas tree of the angels. Angela Morgan. 6274-1
"The Christmas tree with tapers burneth". Christmas. Unknown. 6952-5
The Christmas tree. Cecil Day Lewis. 6246-5
The Christmas tree. Margaret Elizabeth Sangster. 6915-0
The Christmas tree. Edward Shillito. 6144-3,6335-7,6608-9
The Christmas tree. Unknown. 6807-3
The Christmas tree. Unknown. 6171-0,6272-5,6529-5,6131-1
The Christmas tree. Mary E. (Freeman) Wilkins. 6449-3
The Christmas tree. Oscar Williams. 6390-X
Christmas trees. Robert Frost. 6746-8
Christmas trees. Violet Alleyn Storey. 6608-9
The Christmas trees. Mary Frances Butts. 6519-8,6135-4
Christmas vacation. Tony Esolen. 6900-2
A Christmas visitor. Unknown. 6242-3
A Christmas wail. Unknown. 6440-X
The Christmas we like. Ella M. Powers. 6147-8
The Christmas welcome. Unknown. 66601-1
A Christmas wish. Eugene Field. 6368-3
A Christmas wish. Celia Thaxter. 6608-9
Christmas, 1898 Edward Sandford Martin. 6820-0
Christmas, 1915. Percy MacKaye. 6474-4
Christmas, 1917. Brent Dow Allinson. 6542-2
Christmas, 1919. Alfred Noyes. 6151-6
Christmas, 1940. Dorothy Dumbrille. 6224-5
Christmas, 1940. Ogden Nash. 6761-1
Christmas, 1941. Flora Dingle Jesseph. 6789-1
Christmas, Edwin
  Ode to the west wind. 6541-4
Christmas, Marjory
  The blackbird song. 6541-4
Christmas, fr. Hamlet. William Shakespeare. 6125-7
Christmas, fr. In memoriam. Alfred Lord Tennyson. 6087-0, 6271-7,6552-X,6438-8
Christmas, fr. Marmion. Sir Walter Scott. 6466-3
Christmas, prithee. Unknown. 6807-3
Christmas, today and yesterday. Gustav A. Kleinschmidt. 6799-9
Christmas-day. Samuel Richards. 6142-7
Christmas-land. Unknown. 6807-3

Christmas-night in the quarters. Irwin Russell. 6915-0
Christmas-tide. A.W. Bellaw. 6148-6
Christmas-tide. Unknown. 6675-5,6153-2
A Christmas-tide shadow. Norman Howard. 6925-8
Christmas-time. Sir Walter Scott. 6600-3
Christmas: a song for the young & the wise, sels. Leigh Hunt. 6334-9
Christmastide. Emily Pauline ("Tekahionwake") Johnson. 6837-5
Christmus comin' Unknown. 6629-1
Christo paremus canticam, excelis gloria. Unknown. 6756-5
Christofor Columbo. Unknown. 6237-7
Christopher C-. Unknown. 6417-5,6678-X
Christopher Columbus. Joanna Baillie. 6980-0,6813-8,6813-8
Christopher Columbus. Rosemary and Stephen Vincent Benet. 6554-X
Christopher Columbus. Antonio Gazzoletti. 6697-6
Christopher Columbus. Edward R. Huxley. 6885-5
Christopher Marlowe. Algernon Charles Swinburne. 6122-2, 6123-0,6483-3,6250-4,6655-0
Christopher Marlowe, fr. To Henry Reynolds. Michael Drayton. 6125-7
Christopher Middleton (tr.)
  Fugue of death. Paul Celan, 6758-1
A Christopher of the Shenandoah. Edith M. Thomas. 6946-0
Christopher White. Unknown. 6185-0
Christopher, James (Nakisaki)
  Lullaby to a dream. 6178-8
Christopher, Maurette
  To Mary. 6799-9
Christs victorie on earth, sels. Giles (the Younger) Fletcher. 6562-7
Christus consolator. Rossiter W. Raymond. 6335-7,6337-3
Christus Mathaeum et discipulos alloquitur. Sir Edward Sherburne. 6022-6
Christus, sels. Henry Wadsworth Longfellow. 6144-3;6335-7
Chromatics. Emily Selinger. 6266-0
Chromis. Phineas Fletcher. 6315-2
The chronicle of the drum, sels. William Makepeace Thackeray. 6427-2,6046-3
The chronicle of the drum. William Makepeace Thackeray. 6504-X,6219-9
A chronicle. Unknown. 6902-9
The chronicle. Abraham Cowley. 6302-0,6385-3,6634-8,6302-0, 6385-3,6089 ,6271-7,6092-7,6152-4,6245-8,6230-X
The chronometer, fr. Industrial poems. A.M. Sullivan. 6839-1
The chronometer. A.M. Sullivan. 6979-7
Chrous, fr. Cleopatra. Samuel Daniel. 6436-1
A chrous, fr. Hecuba. Euripides. 6962-2
Chrous, fr. Oedipus coloneus. Sophocles. 7039-6
Chrous, fr. Philotas. Samuel Daniel. 6436-1
Chryasor. Henry Wadsworth Longfellow. 6006-4
Chrysalids. Unknown. 6274-1
Chrysalis. Lucile Enlow. 6841-3
Chrysalis, fr. two sonnets. Kathryn Bruchholz Thomson. 6270-9
A chrysalis.. Mary Emily Bradley. 6479-5,6597-X
The chrysalis. Margaret S. Hosmer. 6316-0
The chrysalis. Benjamin Franklin Taylor. 6815-4
The chrysanthemum. Frank S. Pixley. 6579-1
The chrysanthemum. Unknown. 6983-5
Chrysanthemums. Benedetta Civiletti. 6850-2
Chrysanthemums. Roberta Kerr Elliot. 6576-7
Chrysanthemums. Unknown (Japanese) 6027-7
"The chrysolites and rubies Bacchus brings". The chrysolites and rubies. Walter Savage Landor. 6828-6
The chrysolites and rubies. Walter Savage Landor. 6110-9, 6199-0
Chrystmasse of olde. Eugene Field. 6949-5
Chu Yuan
  The battle. Arthur Waley (tr.). 6665-8
Chu, Yo-han
  Sound of rain. 6775-1
Chuang-Tze's butterfly. Chang-soo Koh. 6775-1
Chuang-Tze's poem no. 7. Je-chun Park. 6775-1
Chubb, Thomas Caldecot
  American birds. 6761-1
  At the edge of the bay. 6396-9,6288-1
  How spring comes in Georgia. 6042-0

The launching of a ship. 6781-6
Two in sight of Florence. 6780-8
Wild duck song. 6979-7
Chudleigh, Mary Lee, Lady
The resolve. 6932-0
Chums. James William Foley. 6964-9
Chums. Edgar A. Guest. 6862-6
Chums. Arthur Guiterman. 6891-X
Chun, Bong-gun
Lyricism. 6775-1
Chung, Han-mo
The butterfly's journey. 6775-1
In the autumn. 6775-1
Interfusion. 6775-1
Church. Bruce Early. 6750-6
Church. Gilberto Gonzalez y Contreras. 6759-X
Church and church-yard at night, fr. The grave. Robert Blair. 6932-0
Church and state. Thomas Moore. 6278-4
Church and state. Thomas Moore. 6787-5
The **church** bell at night. Unknown. 6930-4
"The **church** bells toll a melancholy round". Written in disgust of vulgar superstition. John Keats. 6879-0
Church decking at Christmas. William Wordsworth. 6145-1
"The **church** do ze m a touchen zight". Vo'k a-comen into church. William Barnes. 6931-2
The **church** fair. Louis Eisenbeis. 6920-7
Church going. Philip Larkin. 6257-1
The **church** in 1849. Adelaide Anne Procter. 6957-6
The **church** in Lucre Hollow. Louis Eisenbeis. 6925-8
The **church** in the heart. Morris Abel Beer. 6337-3
The **church** kitten. Louis Eisenbeis. 6924-X
The **church** of a dream. Lionel Johnson. 6096-X,6244-X,6507-4
The **church** of Brou. Matthew Arnold. 6947-9,6828-6
The **Church** of England, fr. The hind & the panther. John Dryden. 6933-9
The **church** of San Salvador. William Wordsworth. 6749-2
"**Church** of the living God! in vain thy foes". William Lloyd Garrison. 6238-5
The **church** of the revolution. Hezekiah Butterworth. 6946-0
The **church** porch, sels. George Herbert. 6639-9
The **church** porch. George Herbert. 6385-3,6194-X
Church reveries of a school-girl. Mrs. Enoch Taylor. 6413-2
A **church** romance. Thomas Hardy. 6210-5
The **church** spider. Unknown. 6165-6
The **church** spider. Unknown. 6913-4
"**Church** stands there beyond the orchard blooms". A recusant. James ("B.V.") Thomson. 7015-9
The **church** steps. George T. Foster. 6273-3
The **church** the garden of Christ. Isaac Watts. 6024-2
The **church** today. Sir William Watson. 6337-3,6532-5,6730-1
Church triumphant. S. Ralph Harlow. 6337-3
The **church** universal. Samuel Longfellow. 6337-3,6730-1
Church windows. Judith Neeld. 6822-7
The **church** windows. George Herbert. 6933-9
The **church's** one foundation. Samuel J. Stone. 6337-3,6730-1,6214-8
The **church's** testimony. John Dryden. 6022-6
Church, Edward A.
The cornerstone. 6337-3
'Without are the dogs' 7008-6
Church, F.P.
Is there a Santa Claus? 6145-1
Church, Francis Pharcellus
Is there a Santa Claus? 6449-3
Church, Hubert
Rosalind. 6784-0
Spring in New Zealand. 6784-0
Church, Peggy Pond
A dower for my daughter. 6585-6
Church, Richard
Edward Millington. 6257-1
The flight. 6778-6
Hay's wharf. 6257-1
A house in war time. 6783-2
In a woman's face. 6317-9
The intruder. 6072-2
Italy. 6069-2

The Londoner in the country. 6257-1
The messenger. 6071-4
Mirage. 6779-4
Morning of the twentieth day, fr. Twentieth century psalter. 6659-3
Mud. 6354-3
Museum piece. 6780-8
Nightfall. 6072-2
Psyche goes forth to life. 6884-7
The purification. 6070-6
The question. 6070-6
A road in the weald. 6257-1
Secret service. 6354-3
Thinking of a master. 6257-1
Twentieth century love-song. 6257-1
Twentieth century psalter, sels. 6659-3
The woodpecker. 6257-1
"The **church-bells** toll to a melancholy round". Written in disgust of vulgar superstition. John Keats. 7009-4
The **church-floore**. George Herbert. 6933-9
The **church-floore**. George Herbert. 6341-1
The **church-floore**. George Herbert. 6933-9
Church-monuments. George Herbert. 6641-0
Church-music. George Herbert. 6634-8
The **church-windows**, fr. A poem...Christ-Church. Unknown. 6933-9
"A **church-yard** - aye, but spring has shaken...". Mors et vita. Cora Fabri. 6876-6
The **church**. Charles Rann Kennedy. 6490-6
The **church**. Edwin Ford Piper. 6730-1
The **church**. Jules Romains. 6730-1
Churches. Unknown. 6337-3
"**Churches** come and go, but there has ever...". The new church, fr. 'Man the social creator' Henry Demarest Lloyd. 6954-1
The **churches** of Rome and of England. John Dryden. 6022-6
"**Churchill** had strength of thought...". On one of his lampooners. William Whitehead. 6867-7
Churchill's grave. George Gordon, 6th Baron Byron. 6945-2, 6828-6
Churchill, Charles
The apology, sels. 6198-2
The apology, sels. 6191-5
The candidate, sels. 6024-2
Conscience. 6932-0
A critical fribble. 6932-0
The farewell. 6152-4
The ghost, sels. 6024-2
The ghost, sels. 6831-6
The ghost, sels. 6191-5
The ghost, sels. 6831-6
Gotham, sels. 6024-2
The journey. 6200-8
Night. 6380-2
On himself. 6932-0
The rosciad, sels. 6831-6
The rosciad, sels. 6191-5
The rosciad, sels. 6831-6
The rosciad. 6208-3
Smollett. 6302-0;6385-3
Churchill, Eva Hammond
Waiting on the quay. 6818-9
The **churchyard** on the sands, sels. John B.L. Warren, 3d Baron De Tabley. 6246-5
The **churchyard** on the sands. John B.L. Warren, 3d Baron De Tabley. 6315-2,6153-2
Churchyard roses. Bayard Taylor. 6976-2
A **churchyard** soliloquy. Henry Alford. 6980-0
Churchyard, Thomas
A farewell to a fondling. 6182-6
Old-time service. 6436-1
The **churhyard**. Robert Buchanan. 6656-9
"The **churl** that wants another's fare". The dog in the river. Phaedrus. 7039-6
Churning charm. Unknown. 6334-9
The **churning** song. Silas Dinsmore. 6273-3
The **churning**, fr. Life on the farm. Benjamin Franklin Taylor. 6815-4
Churton, J.W.
Limerick:"..young man at the war office". 6811-1

To chuse a friend, but never marry. John Wilmot, 2d Earl
    of Rochester. 6157-5
Ciardi, John
    Camptown. 6666-6
    Elegy for the face at your elbow. 6751-4
    For my 25th birthday in 1941 6666-6
    Goodmorning with light. 6666-6
    Muesum. 6761-1
    Night freight, Michigan. 6324-1
    P-151. 6527-9
    Program. 6751-4
    Song ("The bells of Sunday"). 6666-6
    The sound track jumps. 6751-4
    Twenty-three skidoo. 6761-1
Cibber's ironical lines on himself. Colley Cibber. 6867-7
Cibber, Colley
    The blind boy. 6246-5,6133-8,6328-4,6219-9,6424-8,6302-
        0,6385-3,6152-4,6131-1,6639-9,6519
    Caesar in Egypt, sels. 6867-7
    Celia and Belinda. 6563-5
    Cibber's ironical lines on himself. 6867-7
    King John, sels. 6867-7
    Love's last shift, sels. 6867-7
    An ode to his majesty for the new year, 1730-31 6867-7
    Possession is eleven points in the law, fr. Woman's
        wit. 6867-7
    Richard III, sels. 6867-7
    The rival fools, sels. 6867-7
    She wou'd and she wou'd not, sels. 6867-7
Cicada. Unknown (Greek) 6435-3
A cicada ("Chirruping grasshopper, drunken..."). Meleager.
    6435-3
Cicada days, fr. The farmer's year. Hesiod. 6435-3
The cicada. Unknown (Greek) 6435-3
The cicada. Ethelwyn Wetherald. 6797-2
Cicely and the bears. Unknown. 6742-5
Cicely croak. Emma C. Dowd. 6249-0
Cicero. Martial. 6297-0
Cicero. Minnie Obermeier. 6847-2
The cid and bavieca. Unknown. 6406-X
The Cid and the five Moorish kings. Unknown (Spanish) 6757-
    3
The Cid and the leper. Unknown (Spanish) 6757-3
Cid of the west. Edna Dean Proctor. 6995-9
The Cid's courtship. Unknown (Spanish) 6757-3
The Cid's deathbed. Felicia Dorothea Hemans. 6973-8
The Cid's departure into exile. Felicia Dorothea Hemans.
    6973-8
The Cid's funeral procession. Felicia Dorothea Hemans.
    6973-8
The Cid's rising. Felicia Dorothea Hemans. 6973-8
The Cid's wedding. Unknown (Spanish) 6757-3
The Cid, sels. Unknown (Spanish) 6372-1
The cider mill. Benjamin Franklin Taylor. 6815-4
A cider song. Gilbert Keith Chesterton. 6477-9
"Cigar lights! Yer honour? Cigar lights?". Between the
    lines. Ernest Radford. 6875-8
"Cigar lights! yer honour? Cigar lights?". Between the
    lines. Ernest Radford. 6770-0
The cigar.. Thomas Hood. 6453-1
A cigarette and pipe. Unknown. 6118-4
Cigarette for the bambino. Gavin Ewart. 6666-6
Cimabuella. Bayard Taylor. 6440-X,6092-7
The Cincinnatus of the west. George Gordon, 6th Baron
    Byron. 6465-5
The cinder king. Unknown. 6613-5
The cinder path. Charles H. Crandall. 6274-1
Cinder-fruit. Paul Jean Toulet. 6351-9
Cinderella. Miroslav Holub. 6758-1
Cinderella up to date. Carolyn Wells. 6882-0
Cinderella's song. Elizabeth Madox Roberts. 6554-X
Cindy. Unknown. 6594-5
Cinema. Gwendolen Haste. 6808-1
The cinema. Bill Manhire. 7018-3
Cinerarias. Dorothy Lowry Dolan. 6789-1
Cino da Pistoia, sels. Dante Gabriel Rossetti. 6123-0
Cinquains. Adelaide Crapsey. 6509-0,6556-2,6030-7
Cinquains, sels. Adelaide Crapsey. 6897-9
Cinquains: triad; trapped; the warning. Adelaide Crapsey.
    6332-2

A Cinque port. John Davidson. 6228-8,6477-9,6541-4,6639-9
Circassian song. Mikhail Lermontov. 6103-6
Circe. Maurice Baring. 6785-9
Circe. John B.L. Warren, 3d Baron De Tabley. 6656-9
Circe. Alfred Kreymborg. 6348-9
Circe. Louis MacNeice. 6317-9
Circe. Augusta Webster. 7037-X
Circe's island revisited. Andrew Lang. 6771-9
Circe, fr. Rose-leaves. Austin Dobson. 6770-0
A circle begins. Harold Littlebird. 7005-1
Circle day. Joseph Crosby Lincoln. 6119-2
"The circle formed, we sit in silent state". A faithful
    picture of an ordinary society. William Cowper. 6996-
    7
The circle of C. Lynette Roberts. 6360-8
Circled by a housefly. Helen G. Quigless. 7024-8
Circles. Miriam Waddington. 6446-9
Circles and squares. John Haines. 6855-3
The circlets. Frederick White. 6130-3
Circling. Ann Leventhal. 6822-7
"The circling century has brought". The battle of
    Lexington. George W. Bungay. 6911-8
The circling hearths. Roderick Quinn. 6784-0
The circling year. Ramona Graham. 6964-9
The circuiter's lament. David Crichton. 6878-2
Circumstance. Frederick Locker-Lampson. 6089-7
Circumstance. Maggie Woody Stratton. 6270-9
Circumstance. Alfred Lord Tennyson. 6046-3
Circumstance without pomp. J.K. ("Dum-Dum") Kendall. 6722-
    0
Circus. Eleanor Farjeon. 6891-X
Circus. Vine McCasland. 6034-X
The circus animals' desertion. William Butler Yeats. 6210-
    5
The circus boy. A.A. Vivyan Thomson. 6744-1
The circus boy. A.A. Vyvyan Thomson. 6925-8
The circus called 'The universe', fr. My lady... Vachel
    Lindsay. 6206-7
The circus clown. John Ferguson. 6269-5
The circus clown. Nathan D. Urner. 6410-8
Circus day. Annie H. Streater. 6530-9
Circus memories. Edgar A. Guest. 6869-3
The circus parade. James Whitcomb Riley. 6993-2
A circus wish. Rebecca Deming Moore. 6130-3
The circus-day parade. James Whitcomb Riley. 6478-7
The circus-postered barn. Elizabeth J. Coatsworth. 6464-7
The circus.. Fannie Stearns Davis. 6466-3
The circus. Elizabeth Madox Roberts. 6891-X
The circus. Robert Haven Schauffler. 6646-1
The cistern. Georgios Seferis. 6352-7
"Cisterns and stones: the fig-tree in the wall". Tuscany.
    Victoria Mary Sackville-West. 6778-6,6070-6
The cistus. Walter Savage Landor. 6092-7
Citadel. Edward Farquhar. 6939-8
Citation for Horace Gregory. Muriel Rukeyser. 6375-6
Cities. Hilda ("H.D.") Doolittle. 6808-1
Cities. Boyce House. 6265-2
Cities. Claude McKay. 6042-0
Cities. Blanche Shoemaker Wagstaff. 6331-4
Cities. Mary Brent Whiteside. 6038-2
Cities & desire 005. Italo Calvino. 6758-1
Cities & signs 001. Italo Calvino. 6758-1
Cities & signs 002. Italo Calvino. 6758-1
Cities & signs 005. Italo Calvino. 6758-1
Cities & the dead 003. Italo Calvino. 6758-1
Cities & the sky 005. Italo Calvino. 6758-1
"Cities and thrones and powers". Rudyard Kipling. 6208-3,
    6339-X,6246-6,6150-8,6250-4,6508
"The cities are full of pride". To the city of Bombay.
    Rudyard Kipling. 6810-3
"Cities are lonely, prison-like places to...". I shall go
    back. Julia Daingerfield Glass. 6799-9
"Cities are walled. It is a cruel land". Memory. Babette
    Deutsch. 6761-1
Cities behind glass. Linda Hogan. 7005-1
The cities of the plain. John Greenleaf Whittier. 6848-0
The cities of the plain. John Greenleaf Whittier. 6959-2
The cities. Jesse Stuart. 6042-0
The cities. Mildred McNeal Sweeney. 6327-6
The citizen and the red lion of Brentford. Christopher

CITIZEN

Smart. 6380-2
The **citizen** and the thieves. Unknown. 6064-1
Citizen of the world. Joyce Kilmer. 6335-7
The **citizens** defend Angiers. William Shakespeare. 6087-0
Cito pede preterit aetas, fr. Ye wearie wayfarer. Adam Lindsay Gordon. 6951-7
"The **citron-groves** their fruit and flowers...". Moorish bridal song, fr. Lays of many lands. Felicia Dorothea Hemans. 6973-8
City. Roo Borson. 6767-0
City. Jaime Torres Bodet. 6759-X
City after sunset. Lynne Chambers. 6857-X
A **city** afternoon. Edith Wyatt. 6897-9
"The **city** alights". Open and shut case. Trevor Reeves. 7018-3
City and country. Oliver Wendell Holmes. 6385-3
The **city** and the sea. Emily Pauline ("Tekahionwake") Johnson. 6837-5
City at rest. Ruth Slonim. 6342-X
City autumn. Ruth H. Hausman. 6850-2
City bells. Richard Harris ("Thomas Ingoldsby") Barham. 6302-0;6385-3
City birds. Willard Johnson. 6808-1
City blood and country jay. Unknown. 6274-1
City boy. Stephanie Herbst. 6883-9
A **city** butterfly. Victor Starbuck. 6326-8
City chap, fr. Seven movements. Alfred Kreymborg. 6011-0
The **city** child. Alfred Lord Tennyson. 6519-8,6623-2,6136-2
The **city** choir. Cy Warman. 6698-4
The **city** church. E.H. K. 6730-1
"A **city** clerk, but gently born and bred". Sea dreams. Alfred Lord Tennyson. 6977-0
The **city** clerk. Thomas Ashe. 6437-X
City comradeship. Anna Louise Strong. 6954-1
City contrasts. Unknown. 6273-3
City dawn. Naomi Rogin. 6850-2
City dawn. Margaret Elizabeth Sangster. 6042-0
The **city** dead-house. Walt Whitman. 6288-1
The **city** dweller. Bernice Lesbia Kenyon. 6509-0
The **city** elms. Elizabeth L. Cushing. 6433-7
The **city** elms. Elizabeth L. Cushing. 6433-7
City evening. Roberta Holloway. 6808-1
City fear. James Rorty. 6070-6
City ferry. Edward H. Pfeiffer. 6347-0
"The **city** from here is beautiful by night". Night city. Josephine Jacobsen. 6761-1
A **city** garden. Arthur Guiterman. 6773-5
City girl. Maxwell Bodenheim. 6069-2
City girl. Marie Medora. 6750-6
"The **city** groans and writhes upon her bed". Creation. Georgia H. Cooper. 6850-2
City growth. Naomi Rogin. 6850-2
City Hall park. Arthur Guiterman. 6773-5
"The **city** has insomnia". The city. Wilfred M. Johnson. 6857-X
The **city** horses. Helen Myers Meldrum. 6269-5
The **city** in the sea. Edgar Allan Poe. 6008-0,6250-4,6288-1, 6126-5,6300-4,6430 ,6121-4,6102-8,6076-5,6153-2,6491-4,6545 ,6176-1,6330-0,6006-4,6246-6,6258-X,6399 , 6333-0
"A **city** is a giant sound". Reminder. Kay Ballenberg. 6750-6
"The **city** is a pinball machine". The pinball machine. Wilfred M. Johnson. 6857-X
"The **city** is cutting a way". New York. Arthur Guiterman. 6773-5
"The **city** is of night", fr. The city of dreadful night. James ("B.V.") Thomson. 6508-2
"The **city** is of night, but not of sleep". The city of dreadful night, sel, James Thomson. 6958-4
City jail. J.J. Maloney. 6870-7
The **city** lieutenant. Gustaf Froding. 6045-5
City lights. Karle Wilson Baker. 6512-0
"The **city** man took off his coat and his hat". Volapuk. Berton Braley. 6853-7
City men in the country. Oliver Wendell Holmes. 6606-2
City moon. James Rorty. 6778-6
City moon. James Rorty. 6039-0
The **city** mouse and the country mouse. Christina Georgina Rossetti. 6466-3,6623-2,613-X,6452-3,6135-4

The **city** mouse and the garden mouse. Christina Georgina Rossetti. 6861-8,6891-X,6861-8,6891-X
"A **city** now we have obtain'd". The third song of Esai. George Wither. 6848-0
"The **city** nudges my vantage point". Eleventh floor view. Patricia M. Johnson. 6857-X
"The **city** of God is late become a seaport town". After Jutland. Katharine (Hinkson) Tynan. 7027-2
City of angels. Robert Nichols. 6071-4
The **city** of beggars. Alfred Hayes. 6666-6
The **city** of dreadful night, sel, James Thomson. 6958-4
The **city** of dreadful night, sels. James ("B.V.") Thomson. 6819-7,6122-2,6208-3,6198-2,6732-8,6378-0,6508 ,6315-2,6102-8,6199-0,6301-2,6655-0,6656 ,6819-7
The **city** of dreadful night. James Thomson. 6828-6
The **city** of falling leaves. Amy Lowell. 6348-9,6030-7
The **city** of flowers, fr. A Florentine cycle. Gertrude Huntington McGiffert. 6838-3
City of God. Samuel Johnson. 6337-3,6730-1
City of God. R.H. Long. 6784-0
The **city** of God. Francis Turner Palgrave. 6337-3;6418-3;6730-1
The **city** of God. Henry B. Robins. 6337-3
The **city** of God. Anna Louise Strong. 6337-3
City of granite. Eleanor Vinton. 6764-6
City of healing. Jose Bosley. 6342-X
"**City** of many, two in deep heaven are shown". Spire of Saint Patrick's and the moon. Leonie Adams. 6808-1
City of monuments. Muriel Rukeyser. 6375-6
The **city** of my love. Julia Ward Howe. 6331-4,6439-6
The **city** of our hopes. Felix Adler. 6337-3
The **city** of Scranton. John E. Barrett. 6840-5
"**City** of silence, though morning is come...". Early bells. Marjorie Meeker. 6808-1
The **city** of sleep. Laurence Housman. 6507-4
"**City** of stark desolation". Ypres. Ronald Gorell Barnes, Lord Gorell. 7027-2
City of the dead. Edward Farquhar. 6939-8
The **city** of the dead. Richard Burton. 6300-4
The **city** of the dreadful night. James ("B.V.") Thomson. 6430-2
The **city** of the light. Felix Adler. 6954-1
The **city** of the living. Unknown. 6294-6,6304-7
The **city** of the soul. Lord Alfred Bruce Douglas. 6102-8
"A **city** on destruction's border stands". Cicero. Minnie Obermeier. 6847-2
City or country. Unknown. 6314-4
The **city** park. Melrose Pitman. 6906-1
City pigeons. Edgar A. Guest. 6748-4
City quiet. Willard Johnson. 6808-1
City rain storm. Anderson M. Scruggs. 6841-3
City roofs. Charles Hanson Towne. 6162-1,6556-2
"The **city** slumbers, O'er its mighty walls". The fireman. Robert T. Conrad. 6909-4
City songs 004. Mark Van Doren. 6808-1
The **city** speaks. Clara Byrnes. 6847-2
The **city** sportsman. William H. Hills. 6745-X
City square. Leonora Speyer. 6781-6
City street. Grace Mansfield. 6750-6
A **city** tale. Alfred H. Miles. 6927-4
The **city** towers. George O'Neil. 6817-0
The **city** tree. Isabella Valancy Crawford. 6433-7
City trees. Edna St. Vincent Millay. 6299-7
A **city** voice. Theodosia Garrison. 6374-8,6653-4
"The **city** walks into the grass leaves". A spring day. Un-kyo Kang. 6775-1
"The **city** walls of Avignon are built of stone.". Spina Christi. William Kirby. 6795-6
"The **city** which thou seest no other deem". Rome, fr. Paradise regained. John Milton. 6933-9
The **city's** crown. William Dudley Foulke. 6954-1
The **city's** crown. William Dudley Foulke. 6337-3,6730-1
"The **city's** streets are hot today". Georgetown. G.A. Taylor. 6906-1
"**City**, I never told you yet". To Sydney. Louise Mack. 6784-0
The **city**, sels. Arthur Upson. 6310-1
City-weary. Edgar A. Guest. 6374-8
The **city**. Richard Burton. 6632-1,6309-8
The **city**. Richard Eugene Burton. 7041-8

The city. Constantine P. Cavafy. 6352-7
The city. John Drinkwater. 7014-0
The city. Brian Hooker. 6030-7
The city. Wilfred M. Johnson. 6857-X
The city. Ben Maddow. 6666-6
The city. James Abraham Martling. 6952-5
The city. George William ("A.E.") Russell. 7014-0
The city. George William ("A.E.") Russell. 6730-1
The city. Charles Hanson Towne. 6162-1,6556-2
The city. David Wolff. 6389-6
Civic creed. Mary McDowell. 6623-2
The civil engineers. Phoebe Hoffman. 6034-X
Civil service. Constance Nichols. 6178-8
Civil War. Charles Dawson Shanly. 6015-3,6240-7,6344-6, 6404-3,6074-9
Civil war. Unknown. 6302-0
Civil war. Unknown (French) 6166-4
Civil war - an episode of the commune. Victor Hugo. 6924-X
The civil wars, sels. Samuel Daniel. 6194-X
Civiletti, Benedetta
    Chrysanthemums. 6850-2
Civilization. Wilfred Rowland Childe. 6893-6
"Civilizations are set up and knocked down". At the gates of the tombs. Carl Sandburg. 6880-4
Civitas Dei. Edith Lovejoy Pierce. 6337-3
Cl'ar de kitchen. Unknown. 6594-5
"Clad in all their brightest green". On my mother's birthday. Felicia Dorothea Hemans. 6973-8
The claim of kindred. Richard Burton. 6006-4
Claiming the promise. Charles Wesley. 6065-X
Claine, Hall
    Graih my chree. 6873-1
Clair [pseud].
    The cynic. 6817-0
    Planting bulbs. 6817-0
    Random advice to my son. 6817-0
Clair de lune. Ford Madox (Hueffer) Ford. 6102-8
Clair de Lune. Luis Pales Matos. 6759-X
Clair de lune. Paul Verlaine. 6102-8
Clair, Olive
    Impatience. 6850-2
    Words. 6850-2
Clairmonde. Theophile Gautier. 7039-6
Clairmont, Robert
    The answers, fr. Eight doorknobs to a door. 6324-1,6722-0
    Glug-glug in salt sea. 6751-4
    Hall of primates. 6751-4
    A hero in the land of dough. 6722-0
    A hero in the land of dough. 6751-4
    Human race. 6751-4
The clam digger. Sarah A. Dixon. 6798-0
"The clam that once, on Jersey's banks". The Little-neck clam. Henry Van Dyke. 6961-4
Clam-soup. William Augustus Croffut. 6271-7
The clams. Carolyn Wells. 6882-0
Clan Alpine. Sir Walter Scott. 6438-8
Clan call. Powers. Rose Mills. 7038-8
The clan of MacCaura. Denis Florence MacCarthy. 6174-5
Clan-Ronald's men. Unknown. 6859-6
Clancy of the mounted police. Robert Service. 6159-1
Clancy of the overflow. Andrew Barton Paterson. 6784-0
Clancy's song. J.B. Connolly. 6423-X
Clancy, Liam P.
    Christmas eve. 6282-2
    A Gaelic Christmas. 6282-2
    Summer in Erin. 6761-1
Clandestine love. Rosa Zagnoni Marinoni. 6750-6
"Clang! There's a call for engine 'K'!". Fire! Sydney Flowers. 6929-0
"Clang, clang! the massive anvils ring". The song of the forge. Unknown. 6918-5
Clann Cartie. Egan O'Rahilly. 6244-X
The clans are all away. Unknown. 6859-6
The clans are coming. Unknown. 6859-6
Clapp, Frederick Mortimer
    Helen in Argos. 6118-4
    My own city. 6808-1
    Sky-signs. 6464-7
    Steam. 6653-4
    Trade. 6506-6
Clapp, Mary Brennan
    Parasols, fifty-nine cents. 6040-4
Clapsaddle, Reita M.
    Love. 6799-9
"Clara strolled in the garden with the...". Souvenir of the ancient world. Carlos Drummond de Andrade. 6758-1
Clara, Aunt
    Pussy's hiding place. 6131-1
Clarastella distrusting. Robert Heath. 6563-5
Clare coast. Emily Lawless. 6244-X
Clare market. Eugene Field. 6949-5
Clare's dragoons. Thomas Osborne Davis. 6930-4
Clare, Edward (tr.)
    Psalm 025 Bible, 6848-0
    Psalm 118 Bible, 6848-0
Clare, Francis D.
    Accusation against the forgiving friend. 6839-1
Clare, John
    The ants. 6510-4
    Autumn. 6246-5
    Autumn. 6466-3
    Autumn. 6668-2
    Badger. 6380-2
    The beanfield. 6668-2
    Birds, why are ye silent? 6943-6
    Christmas time. 6747-6
    Clock-a-clay. 6315-2,6052-8,6726-3
    A cottage garden. 6649-6
    Country letter. 6380-2
    Cowper. 6483-3,6641-0
    Death, sels. 6472-8,6545-7
    The dying child. 6934-7
    The dying child. 6380-2
    The dying child. 6934-7
    Emmonsail's heath in winter. 6208-3
    Emmonsail's heath in winter. 6943-6
    Evening primrose. 6545-7
    The evening star. 6125-7
    An evening walk. 6659-3
    The exile. 6545-7
    The fate of Amy, sels. 6934-7
    "The fir trees taper into twigs...", fr. Summer images. 6187-7
    The firetail's nest. 6943-6
    First love. 6125-7
    First sight of spring. 7015-9
    The flitting, sels. 6545-7
    The flitting. 7020-5
    The flower, fr. Pastoral poesy. 6545-7
    Fragment ("The hedgerow"). 6545-7
    The gipsy camp (in Epping Forest) 6125-7
    Graves of infants. 6383-7,6437-X
    The happy bird. 7015-9
    His last verses. 6219-9
    I am. 6208-3,6641-0,6513-9,6726-3
    I do not seek, I find, fr. Sighing for retirement. 6545-7
    I dwell on trifles, fr. The flitting. 6545-7
    I hid my love. 6380-2
    I lost the love of heaven. 6246-5,6545-7,6315-2,6441-0
    "I love at early morn...", fr. Summer images. 6187-7
    "I love the fitful gust...", fr. Summer images. 6187-7
    "I saw her crop a rose", fr. Summer images. 6187-7,6317-9
    Invitation to eternity. 6380-2,6641-0,6648-8
    July. 6219-9,6271-7
    June. 6649-6
    The laborer. 6385-3,6219-9,6438-8
    Life, death, and eternity. 6214-8
    Little trotty wagtail. 6179-6,6466-3,6668-2
    Love. 6125-7
    Love lives beyond the tomb. 6545-7
    "Love lives beyond the tomb." 6208-3,6246-5
    The love of nature. 6545-7
    Love scorned by pride. 6545-7
    Love's constancy. 6943-6
    Mary. 6208-3
    Mary Lee. 6302-0;6385-3

CLARE

Meet me in the green glen. 6246-5
The moonlit night, fr. The lover's invitation. 6545-7
Morning. 6545-7
Mouse's nest. 6125-7,6315-2
My early home. 6934-7
"The nodding oxeye bends...", fr. Summer images. 6187-7
The old year. 6513-9
"One gloomy eve I roam'd about", fr. Summer images. 6187-7
The pale sun. 6378-0
The peasant poet. 6730-1
The primrose. 6102-8
Proposals for building a cottage. 6649-6
Quail's nest. 6943-6
The ragworth. 6125-7
Remembrances. 6380-2
The rivals. 6191-5
The shepherd's calendar, sels. 6246-5,6179-6
The shepherd's calendar: February: a thaw. 6380-2
The shepherd's tree. 6186-9
The skylark. 6943-6
Song ("Love lies"). 6437-X
Song's eternity. 6334-9,6380-2,6513-9
'Song's eternity,' sels. 6943-6
Sonnet to the glow-worm. 6219-9
Spear thistle, sels. 6943-6
"The spring is coming...", fr. Summer images. 6187-7
A spring morning. 6545-7
Stone-pit. 6545-7
The stranger. 6931-2
Summer evening. 6793-X
Summer evening. 6844-8
Summer images. 6125-7
Summer images, sels. 6187-7
Summer moods. 6302-0;6385-3
Swordy well. 6726-3
Thou flower of spring. 6317-9
The thrush's nest. 6339-X,6133-8,6102-8,6668-2,6219-9, 6383-7,6565-5
To Mary: it is the evening hour. 6125-7
To the lark. 6943-6
To the snipe. 6380-2
A vision. 6380-2,6125-7
Well, honest John. 6380-2
What is love? 6380-2
"When first we hear...", fr. Summer images. 6187-7
"When once the sun sinks...", fr. Summer images. 6187-7
The wood-cutter's night song. 6186-9
A world for love. 6513-9
Written in a thunderstorm, 15 July 1841. 6545-7
Written in Northampton county asylum. 6186-9,6138-9, 6437-X
The yellowhammer. 6943-6

Clare, Shirley
Slumber song ("A song for the baby, sweet ..."). 6078-1

Clarel. Herman Melville. 6333-0
"Clarence McFaden he wanted to waltz". Unknown. 6059-5
Clarence's dream. William Shakespeare. 6438-8
"Clarendon had law and sense". On the young statesman. John Dryden. 6970-3
Clarens. George Gordon, 6th Baron Byron. 6749-2
"Clarens! sweet Clarens." George Gordon, 6th Baron Byron. 6484-1
Clari, the maid of Milan, sels. John Howard Payne. 6486-8
Claribel. Alfred Lord Tennyson. 6328-4,6334-9,6657-7,6655-0,6110-9,6196
Claribel's prayer. Lynde Palmer. 6889-8
Claribel's prayer. M.L. Parmelee. 6113-3;6165-4
Claribel's prayer. Unknown. 6240-7
Clarimonde. Theophile Gautier. 6732-8,6102-8,6468-8
Clarion. Sir Walter Scott. 6086-2,6110-9
"The clarion wind, that blew so loud at morn". Autumnal vespers. Bayard Taylor. 6976-2
Clarion, fr. old mortality. Sir Walter Scott. 6828-6
Clarissa's scissors do the fatal deed, fr. Rape. Alexander Pope. 6637-2
"Clark Colven and his gay ladie". Unknown. 6111-7

Clark Jr., B. Preston
My April. 6607-0

Clak Jr., Charles Badger
A border affair. 6274-1
Cottonwood leaves. 6490-6
A cowboy's prayer. 6303-9
The drafted man. 6032-3
The glory trail. 6281-4,6161-3,6464-7,6594-5
High-chin Bob. 7012-4
I must come back. 6042-0
The legend of boastful Bill. 7010-8
My father and I. 6542-2
A night trail. 6032-3
Pioneers. 6336-5
The plainsmen. 7012-4
Ridin'. 6281-4
The shepherder. 6281-4
The smoke-blue plains. 6736-0
The song of the leather. 7010-8
The westerner. 7012-4

Clark, A.F. Bruce
A water song. 6433-7

Clark, Alexander
My early home. 6565-1

Clark, Anne Pauline
Pansy faces. 6818-9

Clark, Arthur H.
A-working on the railway. 6281-4

Clark, Axton
American prelude. 6761-1

Clark, Charles Heber
Mrs. Jones's pirate. 7025-6

Clark, Edwin Coulson
To the memory of a poet. 6799-9

Clark, Esther M.
The call of Kansas. 6615-1
The stars above Mt. Oread. 6615-1

Clark, Eunice
Fallow land. 6375-6
The people has no obituary. 6375-6

Clark, Fanny Foster
Derby day. 6695-X

Clark, G. Orr
Spankuty man. 6715-8

Clark, G.W.
The old man's oath. 6630-5

Clark, George H.
The rail. 6302-0

Clark, H. Savile
Francesca. 6681-X
The siege of Lucknow. 6681-X

Clark, Helen Whitney
Grandpa's courtship. 6139-7
St. Valentine's day. 6680-1

Clark, Imogen
Camp of the fallen. 6461-2

Clark, J.F. and L.R. (tr.)
Self-satisfaction. Sadi [or Saadi] (Mushlih-ud-Din), 6848-0

Clark, James G.
Lincoln. 6524-4,6708-5
The voice of the people. 6695-X

Clark, John
Hector to Astyanax. 6800-6
The light of other days. 6800-6
The mercy of the Lord. 6800-6

Clark, Kate Upson
Baby's letter. 6312-8
The sea-puss. 6692-2

Clark, Kevin
The ex-priest. 6900-2

Clark, Laura Veach
Fire for the alien. 6799-9

Clark, Lavinia R.
A mountain-girded garden at Asheville. 6750-6

Clark, Leonard
Among shadows. 6258-X

Clark, Leslie Savage
Beacon light. 6144-3
Before pilate. 6144-3
Bread. 6144-3
Carpenter. 6144-3
Conquest. 6144-3

The hands of Christ. 6144-3,6337-3
Hilltops. 6144-3
Holier night. 6144-3
In Nazareth. 6144-3
Incense. 6144-3
Magi. 6144-3
Of things not seen. 6144-3
Offering. 6144-3
Remembrance. 6144-3
Son of man. 6144-3
Sovereignty. 6144-3
The Syrian's tale. 6144-3
Temple offering. 6144-3
This little earth. 6144-3
Values. 6144-3
White splendor. 6144-3
Who can forget? 6144-3
Young Jesus. 6144-3

Clark, Lewis Gaylord
The flamingo. 6902-9

Clark, Luella
The fir tree. 6049-8
Little by little. 6131-1

Clark, Lumilla Claire
Do not wait. 6109-5

Clark, Marian Buxton
At twilight. 6906-1
Hills of tomorrow. 6906-1
I put my heart in a fortress. 6906-1
My gypsy heart. 6906-1
This day. 6906-1

Clark, Martha Haskell
Beach trails. 6798-0
Black ashes. 6374-8
Changeless. 6374-8
The dreamers. 6653-4
Hurdy-gurdy days. 6891-X
In Irish rain. 6762-X
Red geraniums. 6653-4
The sea road. 6374-8
The sea road. 6798-0
Sea song. 6798-0
Sea-song. 6374-8
The stay at home. 6653-4
To a kitten. 6120-6
The villages. 6764-6

Clark, Mary Bayard
Cleopatra's soliloquy. 6273-3

Clark, Mary Ernestine
Accent on paths. 6789-1
America awakes. 6789-1

Clark, Mary Latham
Song of the moonbeam. 6764-6

Clark, Mattie A.W.
At sunset. 6373-X

Clark, Myra
Eve speaks. 6761-1

Clark, Nan M.
Frontenac Inn. 6342-X

Clark, Naomi
Late spring, sur coast. 6792-1, 6998-3
Sunup (variation on a theme by Baudelaire) 6792-1

Clark, Peter Wellington
Deserted village. 6178-8
Historic episodes. 6178-8
Paradox. 6178-8
Paradox ("How strange the fairest pearls"). 6178-8
Reality. 6178-8

Clark, Preston
Faith. 6337-3

Clark, Sylvia
The forest guardian. 6764-6
The pageant. 6764-6
West-running brook. 6764-6

Clark, Thomas Curtis
Abraham Lincoln. 6037-4,6449-3
Apparitions. 6490-6,6337-3,6542-2
Blind guides. 6037-4
Bugle song of peace. 6449-3,6542-2,6730-1
By an ancient sea. 6144-3,6532-5

Caesar and Christ. 6542-2
Challenge. 6337-3
The Christ militant. 6144-3
"Come, follow me!" 6144-3
The crusader. 7001-9
The day breaks. 6144-3
The day is brief. 6461-2
Desert wanderings. 6144-3
Disillusioned. 6144-3
Evidence. 6337-3
The faith of Christ's freemen. 6144-3
Friends. 6461-2
God give me joy. 6461-2
God's dreams. 6532-5
God's dreams. 6954-1
The happy warrior. 6995-9
"His is the way" 6144-3
In age of science. 6039-0,6337-3
It shall not be again. 6465-5,6449-3
The journey. 6337-3,6461-2
The kingdom. 6144-3,6337-3
The leader. 7001-9
Let us go back. 6461-2
Life is a feast, they say. 6954-1
Lincoln. 6036-6,6076-5,6102-8
The lost Christ ("Your skill has fashioned...") 6144-3
Mary ("With love that counted not the cost") 6144-3
My America. 6461-2,6449-3
Nazareth. 6144-3
New crucifixion ("He arose from the dead"). 6144-3
New vistas. 6954-1
O sun of life. 6144-3
One who dared to die. 6144-3
The poet's call. 6730-1
Poets ("Heralds of joy, they walk the path of sorrow"). 6037-4
A prayer for the year. 6461-2
Prayer of the poor. 6954-1
The prophet. 6449-3
Prospect. 6542-2
Redemption. 6954-1
Repentance. 6144-3
Requiem. 6449-3
Revelation. 6214-8
The road to happiness. 6461-2
The search. 6303-9,6337-3,6730-1
Take time to live. 6461-2
There lived a man. 6144-3
There shall be peace. 6461-2
There was a man. 6144-3
Thy kingdom come! 6144-3
To poets all. 6337-3
To the flag of stars. 6449-3
To the master poet. 6144-3
Today. 6144-3
The touch of human hands. 6461-2
The tragedy. 6144-3
Upon reading a volume of ancient Chinese poetry. 6036-6
The victor. 6461-2
Vision. 6954-1
Voice in a cathedral. 6144-3
Wanderers. 6144-3
We thank thee. 6449-3
Who goes there? 6461-2
Who made war? 6542-2
Woodrow Wilson. 7001-9

Clark, William M.
Song of the winter winds. 6565-1

Clark, Willis Gaylord
Last prayer of Mary, Queen of Scots. 6572-4

Clarke, ?
May. 6049-8

Clarke, Arthur H,
Poor Reuben Ranzo. 6281-4

Clarke, Augustus
The quack vendor. 6482-5

Clarke, Austin
Celibacy. 6292-X
The fair at windgap. 6930-4
Flower-quiet in the rush-strewn Sheiling. 6096 X

CLARKE 292

Flower-quiet in the rush-strewn sheiling. 6244-X
The house in the west. 6072-2
A lost heifer. 6071-4,6581-3
The lost heifer. 6071-4
O love, there is no beauty. 6244-X
Silver and gold. 6070-6
Clarke, Barney T.
To a bud. To a leaf. To a tree. 6894-4
Clarke, C.R.
Song of the mariner's needle. 6833-2
Clarke, Charles B.
Border affair. 6714-X
Clarke, Edmund Palmer
Ambition. 6764-6
April. 6764-6
Clarke, Edna Proctor. See Hays, Ednah Proctor
Clarke, Elisabeth
Gesture. 6818-9
Clarke, Frances
Who calls? 6478-7,6497-3,6368-3
Clarke, George Arthur
The charter of salvation. 6337-3
Clarke, George Herbert
A foretaste of spring. 6274-1
God's eyes. 6797-2
The last mobilization. 6224-5,6184-2
Lines written in Surrey, 1917. 7026-4
"Motionless". 6184-2
Over Saleve. 6797-2
Ruins. 7027-2
Santa Maria del Fiore. 6331-4
Sante Maria del Fiore. 6631-3
Skater and wolves. 7035-3
The Virgin of Albert. 7026-4
Clarke, H. Savile
The romance of a glove. 6652-6
A romance of the rood-loft. 6575-9
Clarke, H.E.
Lady mine. 6089-7
"No night for slumnber is this",fr. A night's rhapsody. 6997-5
A rebel riding song. 7009-4
Clarke, Hamilton
Mein schweet mossik. 6711-5
Clarke, Helen F.
Shadows. 6178-8
You are black. 6178-8
Clarke, Helen T.
Hearts of gold. 6965-7
Clarke, Herbert Edward
Death and life. 6793-X
Clarke, Herbert Edwin
The age. 6656-9
The assignation. 7015-9
A cry. 6656-9
In the wood. 6656-9
King of kings. 7015-9
Lady mine. 6652-6
Clarke, Idac M.C.
Little boy's wish. 6715-8
Clarke, J.G.
The mountains of life. 6911-8
Clarke, James Freeman
Cana. 6600-3
The difficulty. 6429-9
The difficulty. 6321-7
Love doth to her eyes repair. 6321-7
'Love doth to her eyes repair!' 6429-9
Real life. 6109-5
A reminiscence. 6321-7
Riviera di ponente. 6624-0
"When shall we meet again?" 6226-1
White-capped waves. 6833-2
Clarke, James Freeman (tr.)
Rabia. Unknown (Arabic), 6438-8
Clarke, James G.
Art thou living yet? 6913-4
"But the whippoorwill wails on the moor", sels. 6601-1
Leona. 6406-X
Clarke, John

The thrush's nest. 6134-6
Clarke, John Henrik
America. 6178-8
Bombardment and aftermath. 6178-8
Inquiry. 6178-8
Meditations of a European farmer. 6178-8
No tears. 6178-8
'Sing me a new song.' 6178-8
Clarke, Joseph I.C.
Bill Manning. 6292-X
The fighting race. 6274-1,6732-8,6102-8,6307-1,6467-1, 6732-8,6736-0
The fret of Father Carty. 6076-5
Clarke, Lewis Gaylord
The flamingo. 6089-7
Clarke, Lilian
Wer wenig sucht, der findet viel. 6429-9
Clarke, Lilian (tr.)
Wer wenig sucht, der findet viel. Friedrich Ruckert, 6321-7
Clarke, Macdonald
In the graveyard. 6481-7
Love under the ledger. 6632-1
Clarke, Marcus
In a lady's album. 6784-0
'In a lady's album'. 6768-9
Clarke, Marianne
The afterglow. 6799-9
Inspiring music. 6789-1
The road to rest. 6818-9
Clarke, Martha Haskell
Chickadee. 6073-0
Clarke, Mary Cowden
At midnight of All Souls. 6997-5
Clarke, Medora
Defiled. 6920-7
Clarke, Sara J.
"There is a grandeur in the soul that dares". 6238-5
Clarke, Sarah D.
Lastra a signa. 6624-0
A York music box. 6965-7
Clarke, Sydney Middleton
The treasure. 6258-X
Watch ashore-seletar. 6258-X
Clarke, Sylvia Storla
Devotion. 6789-1
Reflections. 6789-1
Clarke, W.G.
Last prayer of Mary Queen of Scots. 6408-6
Clarkson, M.J.
The secret of the cross. 6065-X
"Clash, roll, break!". The sea to the boy. Nam-sun Choe. 6775-1
"Clasp me a little longer, on the brink". Gertrude of Wyoming. 6973-8
"Clasp me again! my soul is very sad!". Guido and Marina. Thomas Hood. 6974-6
"Clasp mine closer, little, dear, white hand". Little hand. Cora Fabri. 6876-6
"Clasp your hands with adoration". Psalm 047. Bible. 6848-0
Class mottoes. Unknown. 6717-4,6449-3
Class song. Eleanor Guiterman. 6847-2
The class tree. Emma S. Thomas. 6049-8
A class-day Hamlet. H.P. Huntress. 6118-4
The classes and masses. John E. Barrett. 6840-5
Classic night. Benjamin Rosenbaum. 6037-4
A classic ode. Charles Battell Loomis. 6902-9
A classic waits for me. Elwyn Brooks White. 6722-0
Classified ad. Tomi Caroly Tinsley. 6178-8
Claud Halcro's song, fr. The pirate. Sir Walter Scott. 6180-X,6087-0,6134-6,6250-4,6383-7
Claude Lackey. Lewis Chesser. 6860-X
Claude Melnotte to Pauline. Owen (Edward Bulwer-Lytton, Earl Lytton) Meredith. 6661-5
Claude Melnotte's apology and defence. Edward Bulwer-Lytton; Baron Lytton. 6385-3
Claude to Eustace. Arthur Hugh Clough. 6046-3
Claudel, Paul
Canticle for three voices, sels. J. O'Connor (tr.).

6343-8
    Five great odes, sels. 6351-9
    Fourth station ("Mothers who have seen him die...") 6282-2
    The maiden Violaine, sels. 6351-9
    Our lady, help of Christians. 6282-2
    Shadows. 6351-9
Claudian
    The lonely isle. Howard Mumford Jones (tr.). 7039-6
    The old man of Verona. Abraham Cowley (tr.). 7039-6
Claudio on death, fr. Measure for measure. William Shakespeare. 6052-8
Claudio's laments, fr. Much ado about nothing. William Shakespeare. 6436-1
Claudius, Hermann
    Cherry tree. 6643-7
    Rosebush. 6643-7
    Water. 6643-7
Claudius, Matthias
    The hen. 6089-7,6996-7
    Night song. Charles Timothy Brooks (tr.). 6271-7
Claudy, Frank
    To Mr. Simon Wolf. 6848-0
Clausen, Clara A.
    Minnesota moon. 6342-X
Claussen, Sophus
    Abroad. Charles Wharton Stork (tr.). 6555-4
"Clavers and his highlandmen". Killicrankie. Unknown. 6859-6
Clawson, Barbara
    Song ("O Lord"). 6799-9
Claxton, Beaumont
    On the sunset line. 6928-2
    The stage of destiny. 6928-2
Clay. Paul Gianoli. 6860-X
Clay cattle. Francis Carey ("Jan van Avond") Slater. 6625-9
Clay hills. Jean Starr Untermeyer. 6506-6,6512-0,6161-3, 6393-4
Clay, Katharine B. (tr.)
    The Christmas child. Unknown, 6466-3
Claymore!.. Lewis Spence. 6269-5
Clayton, ?
    The rainbow. 6131-1
Clayton, Hyde
    Bachelors' landlady. 6750-6
Claytor, Gertrude
    Indian wife. 6979-7
    Sorceress. 6218-0
    The stair. 6218-0
Clean Clara. William Brighty Rands. 6290-3,6131-1,6808-1, 6131-1
Clean clothes. Rafael Arevalo Martinez. 6759-X
Clean curtains. Carl Sandburg. 6345-4
The clean gentleman. George Abbe. 6218-0
Clean hands. Austin Dobson. 6051-X
Clean pease-strae. Robert Tannahill. 6960-6
The clean platter. Ogden Nash. 6089-7,6628-3
"Clean shadows ride across the crescent moon". Gull passage by moonlight. Milton Acorn. 6767-0
Clean windows. Effie B. Collins. 6764-6
Cleaning day. Eve Gilbert Swift. 6585-6
Cleaning out the suller in Vermont. Daniel L. Cady. 6988-6
Cleaning ship. Charles Augustus Keeler. 6833-2
Cleaning the candela. Siegfried Sassoon. 6257-1
Cleaning the furnace. Edgar A. Guest. 7033-7
Cleanliness. Charles and Mary Lamb. 6519-3
Cleanliness. Unknown. 6629-1
Cleansing fires. Adelaide Anne Procter. 6730-1
Cleansing of Heorot, fr. Beowulf. Unknown. 6193-1
Cleanthes
    God leads the way. Cyril Charlie Martindale (tr.). 6435-3
    The hymn of Cleanthes (or, Hymn to Zeus). James Adam (tr.). 6337-3
    Hymn to Zeus. Edward Hayes Plumptre (tr.). 6730-1
    Hymn to Zeus ("Most glorious of immortals..."). Michael Balkwill (tr.). 6435-3
    Lead ye me on, O God. F.L. Lucas (tr.). 6435-3,6251-2
Cleanthus Trilling. Edgar Lee Masters. 6300-4

Clear and cool. Charles Kingsley. 6239-3,6501-5,6604-6, 6660-7
"Clear and gentle stream". Elegy ("Clear"). Robert Bridges. 6487-6,6250-4,6430-2
'Clear and gentle stream'. Robert Bridges. 6476-0,6487-6
"Clear as the silver call". Unknown. 6238-5
The clear blue. Jean Cocteau. 6351-9
"Clear had the day been". Lines ("Clear had the day"). Michael Drayton. 6315-2
"Clear had the day been from the dawn". A summer's eve. Michael Drayton. 6935-5
The clear may. Alfred Noyes. 6169-9
A clear midnight. Walt Whitman. 6214-8
A clear night. Karle Wilson Baker. 6031-5
"Clear o'er the turbulence that night and day". The keepers of the nation. Hermann Hagedorn. 6944-4
"Clear or cloudy, sweet as April showering". Unknown. 6181-8,6182-6
"Clear or cloudy, sweet as April showering". Song ("Clear or cloudy"). Unknown. 6436-1
Clear pools. Jeannette Marks. 6320-9,6036-6
"Clear shone the morn, the gale was fair". The Spanish armada. Robert Southey. 6867-7
Clear the way. Charles Mackay. 6915-0
Clear the way. Charles Mackay. 6014-5;6291-1
Clear the way. Unknown. 6109-5
"Clear was the orb in his holy rise". Eclipse. Edward Farquhar. 6939-8
"Clear, fresh, and dulcet streams". Francesco Petrarch. 6325-X
"Clear, placid Leman! thy contrasted lake". The Jura mountains. George Gordon, 6th Baron Byron. 6749-2
"The clear, revealing footprints in the snow". Footprints in the snow. Alice Campbell. 6764-6
"Clear-headed friend, whose joyful scorn". To - ("Clear-headed"). Alfred Lord Tennyson. 6977-0
"The clear-toned swan, to the beating of his wings". Homer. 6435-3
'Cleared'.. Rudyard Kipling. 6810-3
Clearing at dawn. Li T'ai-po. 7039-6
Clearing for the plough. Ernest G. Moll. 6349-7
The clearing. Sir Charles George Douglas Roberts. 6433-7
"Clearly the blue river chimes in its flowing". All things will die. Alfred Lord Tennyson. 6977-0
Cleator moor. Norman Nicholson. 6475-2,6210-5,6379-9
Cleator, Alice Jean
    Little dog of amusement zoo. 6510-4
    My dog and I. 7008-6
Cleave thou the waves. Mathilde Blind. 7015-9,6997-5,7015-9,6997-5
Cleaveland, C.L.
    November. 6597-X
Cleaveland, Elizabeth H. Jocelyn
    No sect [or sects] in heaven. 6273-3,6392-6
Cleaveland, Elizabeth H.J.
    The hidden path; or, the Atlantic cable. 6578-3
Cleaves, Charles Poole
    A lightkeeper. 6764-6
Cleaves, Mary Wilkerson
    April longing. 6178-8
    Black soldier. 6178-8
    Why do I love this country. 6178-8
"Cleaving their way with bomb-shell and blade". Antietam. James Abraham Martling. 6952-5
Cleburne. Unknown. 6074-9
Cleena. Ella Young. 6174-5
"Cleere had the day bin from the dawne". The sixt nimphall, sels. Michael Drayton. 6933-9
Cleghorn, Sarah N.
    An air of coolness plays upon his face. 6501-5
    The anodyne. 6501-5
    But this is also everlasting life. 6532-5
    Come, captain age. 6619-4,6653-4
    Comrade Jesus. 6076-5,6375-6,6393-4,6730-1
    Dorothea. 7030-2
    Emilia. 6467-1
    For a quick eye for beauty. 6861-8
    For sleep when overtired or worried. 6501-5
    "The gold links lie so near the mill." 6076-5,6102-8, 6464-7

Haunted village. 6030-7
If I forget thee. 7038-8
The incentive. 6954-1
Judge me, O Lord. 6337-3
Judge me, O Lord! 6144-3,6337-3
The mother at the telescope. 6039-0
The mother follows. 6880-4
Mountains. 6036-6
O altitudo! 6501-5
The Oldenburys of Sunderland. 6484-1
On reading many histories of the United States. 6184-2
Peace. 6761-1
The poltroon. 6817-0
Portrait. 6161-3
Portrait of a lady. 6034-X,6336-5
Portrait of a lady. 6034-X,6161-3
A Puritan lady's garden. 6649-6,6338-1
Quatrain. 6337-3,6375-6
Quatrain ("The golf links lie so near the mill"). 6375-6
The river. 6031-5
St. Clare hears St. Francis. 6019-6,6393-4
Saint R.L.S. 6053-6
A saint's hours. 6556-2,6476-0
A saint's hours. 6723-9
The survival of the fittest. 6076-5,6102-8
There was a moon, there was a star. 6607-0
Three great ladies. 6036-6
To safeguard the heart from hardness. 6501-5
Vermont. 6464-7,6653-4
The Vermonter departing. 6036-6
Cleirigh, Cu Chonnacht O
The ghost. James Stephens (tr.). 6244-X
Cleland et al., William
Hallow my fancie, sels. 6179-6
Clematis. Dora Read Goodale. 6049-8
Clemency. Ibn al-Hajj. 6362-4
Clemens, Samuel Langhorne. See "Twain, Mark"
Clement of Alexandria
Earliest Christian hymn. 6730-1
Shepherd of eager youth, sels. Henry M. Dexter (tr.). 6337-3
Clement, Lewis R.
"Ceptin Jim." 6687-9
Clementina and Lucilla. Walter Savage Landor. 6874-X
Clementine. Unknown. 6732-8
Clements, Albert Edward
Ghosts of the conquest. 6542-2
Song and cry of a soldier in the lines. 6542-2
Clemmer, Mary
For they alone have need of sorrow. 6066-8
Good-by, sweetheart. 6066-8
Mary in the morning-glories. 6965-7
Mother-love. 6097-8
Peace. 6240-7
Something beyond. 6461-2
"What shall I do, my friend?" 6085-4
Words for parting. 6066-8,6226-1
Cleobulus of Lindus
"Here, a maiden of bronze, I stand on Midas' grave." F.L. Lucas (tr.). 6251-2
Cleon. Robert Browning. 6657-7,6430-2,6655-0
Cleon and I. Charles Mackay. 6165-6;6291-4;6337-3;6385-3;6605-2
Cleon, sels. Robert Browning. 6427-2
Cleone to Aspasia. Walter Savage Landor. 6086-2,6110-9
Cleonicos. Theocritus. 7039-6
Cleopatra. Edgar Fawcett. 6131-1
Cleopatra. Robert Loveman. 6941-X
Cleopatra. Albert Samain. 6351-9
Cleopatra. Albert Samain. 6343-8
Cleopatra. William Shakespeare. 6438-8
Cleopatra. William Wetmore Story. 6077-3,6370-5,6385-3, 6735-2,6431-0
Cleopatra. Edith C. Tyler. 6716-6
Cleopatra and Antony ("Love-torch of all the East,"). Gretchen O. Warren. 6331-4
Cleopatra and the messenger. William Shakespeare. 6382-9
Cleopatra at Actium. Thomas Kibble Hervey. 6424-8
Cleopatra embarking on the Cydnus. Thomas Kibble Hervey. 6102-8
Cleopatra in her barge, fr. Antony and Cleopatra. William Shakespeare. 6634-8
Cleopatra on the Cydnus. William Shakespeare. 6543-0
Cleopatra to Antony. Sarah Doudney. 6273-3
Cleopatra's dream. J.J. Owens. 6273-3
Cleopatra's protest. Edward Livingston Keyes. 6671-2
Cleopatra's resolution. William Shakespeare. 6438-8
Cleopatra's soliloquy. Mary Bayard Clark. 6273-3
Cleopatra, fr. Antony and Cleopatra. William Shakespeare. 6302-0,6385-3,6150-8,6094-3
Cleopatra, sels. William Wetmore Story. 6102-8,6732-8,6076-5
"**Cleopatra,** who thought they maligned her".
Limerick:"Cleopatra, who thought they maligned her." Unknown. 6308-X
Cleora becomes a Dakotan. Harriet Seymour Popowski. 6750-6
Clephane, Elizabeth Cecilia
Beneath the Cross. 6337-3
The lost sheep. 6214-8
Ninety and nine. 6219-9,6304-7
There were ninety and nine. 6730-1
"A **clergyman** out in Dumont". Morris Bishop. 6722-0
"A **clergyman** out in Dumont". Limerick:"A clergyman out in Dumont." Morris Bishop. 6308-X
"A **clergyman,** in want". Ronald Arbuthnott Knox. 6722-0
A **cleric** courts his lady. Unknown. 6881-2
Clerical oppressions. John Greenleaf Whittier. 7009-4
Clerical oppressors. John Greenleaf Whittier. 6946-0
Clerical wit. Richard Lalor Shiel. 6404-3
Clerimont's song. Ben Jonson. 6315-2,6527-9,6491-4
Clerk Colvill. Unknown. 6185-0
"**Clerk** Colvill and his lusty dame". Unknown. 6518-X
The **clerk** of Oxenford [or Oxford]. Geoffrey Chaucer. 6150-8,6153-2
The **clerk** of the weather. P.E. Herrick. 6290-3
Clerk Sanders. Unknown. 6180-X
Clerk Saunders. Unknown. 6055-2,6102-8,6185-0,6186-9,6317-9,6518 ,6111-7,6732-8,6430-2,6067-2,6150-8,6301
Clerk Saunders and May Margaret, sels. Unknown. 6102-8, 6472-8
A **clerk** ther was of Cauntebrigge also. Walter William Skeat. 6802-2
The **clerk's** twa sons o Owsenford. Unknown. 6185-0
Clerk, Nellie S.
To my first garden flower, sels. 6768-9
Clerk, Sir John
The miller. 6125-7,6180-X
O merry may the maid be. 6086-2
The **clerk.** B.H.M. Hetherington. 6846-4
The **clerk.** B.H.M. Hetherington. 6589-9
The **clerk.** Scudder Middleton. 6030-7
Clerke, E.M.
The flying Dutchman, sels. 6997-5
Clerke, E.M. (tr.)
Quia amore langueo. Unknown, 6282-2
Clerke, William
Song ("Lo, lilies"). 6563-5
The **clerks,** fr. Children of the night. Edwin Arlington Robinson. 6274-1,6333-0,6491-4
The '**clermont'.** Arthur Guiterman. 6773-5
Cleugh, H.J.
The outcast. 6778-6
Clevedon church. Andrew Lang. 6845-6
Clevedon verses, sels. Thomas Edward Brown. 6508-2,6809-X
The **Cleveland** lyke wake dirge. Unknown. 6829-4
Cleveland's song: 'Love wake and weeps,' fr. The pirate. Sir Walter Scott. 6828-6
Cleveland, E.H.J.
Shibboleth. 6909-6
Cleveland, Elizabeth H. Jocelyn
No sects in heaven. 6403-5,6964-9
Cleveland, John
An elegy on Ben Jonson. 6933-9
An elegy on Ben Jonson. 6341-1
An elegy on Ben Jonson. 6933-9
Epitaph on the Earl of Strafford. 6933-9
Epitaph on the Earl of Strafford. 6472-8
Epitaph on the Earl of Strafford. 6933-9
From the state of love, sels. 6324-1

Gravestones ("Here lies wise...") 6427-2
Had Cain been Scot. 6092-7
Mark Anthony. 6536-8,6563-5,6026-9,6562-7
On Scotland. 6278-4,6089-7
On the memory of Mr. Edward King, drown'd... 6933-9
On the memory of Mr. Edward King, drown'd... 6562-7
The rebell Scot, sels. 6933-9
Satire on the Scots. 6996-7
The Scots apostasie, fr. Poems and satires. 6200-8
"The sluggish morn as yet undrest". 6187-7
Song ("I saw a vision"). 6324-1
To the memory of Ben Jonson. 6302-0;6385-3
Upon Phillis walking in a morning before sun-rising. 6341-1
"Whenas the nightingale chaunted her". 6187-7
Cleveland, Philip Jerome
By night. 6337-3
Cleveland, Reginald McIntosh
Destroyers off Jutland. 7026-4
The **clever** idiot. Unknown. 6064-1
Clever Tom Clinch going to be hanged. Jonathan Swift. 6175-5,6733-6,6152-4
Cleyton, James
"Who first reform'd our Stage with justest Lawes". 6562-7
Click o' the latch. Nancy Byrd Turner. 6607-0
"**Click**, click! how the needles go". Knitting socks. Unknown. 6846-4
"**Click**, click, click". Song of the type. Unknown. 6915-0
Clickstone. Rokwaho. 7005-1
The **cliff** and the cataract. Edward Farquhar. 6939-8
The **cliff** church. John Galsworthy. 6888-X
Cliff Dweller lyrics. Berton Braley. 6853-7
The **cliff** dwelling. Arthur Chapman. 6836-7
Cliff Klingenhagen. Edwin Arlington Robinson. 6491-4
"A **cliff**-locked port and a bluff sea wall". Reid at Fayal. John Williamson Palmer. 6946-0
The **cliff-top**. Robert Bridges. 6487-6
The **cliff**. William Lisle Bowles. 6543-0
Clifford, Ethel
The captain's song. 6785-9
The child. 6793-X
The harp of sorrow. 6730-1
The last hour. 6374-8
A song out of Oxfordshire. 6793-X
Clifford, George. See Cumberland, Earl of
Clifford, John
God's world. 6337-3
Clifford, Margaret Rowe
Arizona. 6465-5
Cliffs. Rin Ishigaki. 6803-0
Cliffs along the Mississippi. Emman Kinney Whaley. 6342-X
The **cliffs** of Dover. Felicia Dorothea Hemans. 6973-8
"**Cliffs** that rise a thousand feet". Sailing homeward. Chan Fang-sheng. 7039-6,6253-9
"**Cliffs**, an earthquake suffered jut", fr. Sordello. Robert Browning. 6997-5
The **cliffs**, fr. Atlantic coast scenery. Sir Aubrey De Vere. 6997-5
The **cliffside** path. Algernon Charles Swinburne. 6828-6
The **cliffside** path. Algernon Charles Swinburne. 6110-9
Cliffton, William
Mary will smile. 6077-3
Clifton. Thomas Edward Brown. 6477-9,6508-2
Clifton. Walter Savage Landor. 6980-0
Clifton chapel. Sir Henry Newbolt. 6437-X
Clifton grove. Henry Kirke White. 6543-0
"**Clifton**, in vain thy varied scenes invite". Clifton. Walter Savage Landor. 6980-0
A **climatic** madrigal. Wilbur Dick Nesbit. 6274-1
Climatic sorcery. James Whitcomb Riley. 6091-9
Climax. Alice Harrod Muir. 6799-9
Climax. Gladys Oaks. 6880-4
Climb. Winifred Welles. 6102-8,6374-8,6076-5,6393-4,6653-4,6464
The **climb** from Valle. James Logie ("Hugh Haliburton") Robertson. 6819-7
Climb to glory. Unknown. 6594-5
The **climb** to virtue. Simonides. 6435-3
Climb up to God. Jessie Corrigan Pegis. 6761-1

"**climbed** the blue staircase up to sky". Song of an initiate. Jerome Rothenberg. 6803-0
Climbing. Thomas Edward Brown. 6655-0
Climbing. Thomas Edward Brown. 6809-X
Climbing. Annie Fields. 6600-3
Climbing a mountain. James Reeves. 6354-3
Climbing a mountain. Tao Yun. 6253-9
The **climbing** road. Clinton Scollard. 6478-7
"**Clime** of the unforgotten brave". George Gordon, 6th Baron Byron. 7009-4
Cline, Leonard
Battery Park. 6441-8
"Sun go parch or cloud go pour". 6817-0
Vows. 6441-8
Cline, Leonard Lanson
Bach. 6880-4
Cline, Monica Shipp
Neglected. 6799-9
Cline, William Hamilton
The glory of the game. 6274-1
"**Cling** now to this last high rim". Prelude ("Cling now"). Leetha Journey Hofeller. 6316-0
Cling to thy mother. George Washington Bethune. 6097-8, 6627-5
Clingan, C.J.
Only a drunkard. 6415-9
Clinging to thee. Unknown (Japanese) 6027-7
The **clink** of the ice. Eugene Field. 6949-5
The **clinker**. Unknown. 6497-3,6449-3
Clinkers. Rosa Zagnoni Marinoni. 6750-6
"The **clinkum-clank** o' sabbath bells". A lowden sabbath morn. Robert Louis Stevenson. 6819-7
Clinton, Doulgas
Heritage. 6178-8
Clipped is fancy's wing. Robert Herne. 6488-4
Clipped wings. Lew Sarett. 6850-2
The **clipper** loitered south, fr. Dauber. John Masefield. 6833-2
The **clipper** seed. Edwin L. Sabin. 7035-3
Clipper ships. John Anderson. 6833-2
Clipper ships. John Gould Fletcher. 6161-3
The **clipper**. Thomas Fleming Day. 6833-2
Clive. Robert Browning. 6576-7
Clive, Caroline
Conflict. 6437-X
The queen's ball, sels. 6046-3
Clive, Frank
The blacksmith's story. 6742-5
"The **cloak** life made for her was gray in hue". The cloak. Anna Louise Barney. 6750-6
Clock. Harold Monro. 6354-3
The **clock** and dial. Allan Ramsay. 6153-2
Clock in the capitol – Williamsburg. Isabel Harriss Barr. 6761-1
Clock stop. Evelyn Hudson Rowley. 6799-9
"The **clock** stopped-not the mantel's". Emily Dickinson. 6348-9,6380-2
"The **clock** strikes one". Three strikes – out. Charles Howard Hagert. 6936-3
Clock striking. Charles and Mary Lamb. 6295-4
The **clock's** song. Rose Hawthorne Lathrop. 6172-9,6292-X
Clock-a-clay. John Clare. 6315-2,6052-8,6726-3
The **clock-tinker**. Lucy Larcom. 6129-X
The **clock**.. Unknown. 6466-3
The **clock**. Charles Baudelaire. 6317-9
The **clock**. Jovan Ducic. 6765-4
The **clock**. Francis Scarfe. 6379-9
The **clocking** hen. Unknown. 6127-3,6131-1
Clocks. Theressa M. DeFosset. 6906-1
Clocks. Tessa Sweazy Webb. 6750-6
"The **clocks** are chiming in my heart". Past. John Galsworthy. 6888-X
The **clocks** of Kenilworth. Hezekiah Butterworth. 7041-8
The **clocks** that I like best. Vachel Lindsay. 6206-7
The **clocks**, fr. The homestead. Gertrude Huntington McGiffert. 6838-3
Clockwork. Paul F. Fericano. 6792-1
The **clod** and the pebble. William Blake. 6024-2,6198-2,6208-3,6315-2,6427-2,6430,6150-8,6250-4,6371-3
The **clod**. Edwin Curran. 6076-5,6102-8

CLODIA

Clodia
"If Jove would give the leafy bowers..." 6049-8
Cloe. George Granville; Baron Lansdowne. 6562-7
Cloete, Stuart
...Of England. 6761-1
The **cloister** garden at Certosa. Richard Burton. 6338-1, 6649-6
The **cloister** garden. Ant. Klastersky. 6763-8
Cloister hymn. Emily Hanson Obear. 6799-9
The **cloister** of the falling snow. Sylvia Hortense Bliss. 7030-2
The **cloister.** Katharine R. Hegeman. 6799-9
The **cloister.** Richard Le Gallienne. 6872-3
Cloistered. Alice Brown. 6102-8,6337-3,6076-5,6300-4,6076-5
Cloistered. Mary Carolyn Davies. 6300-4
Clonard. Thomas S. Jones Jr. 6331-4,6653-4
Clonmacnoise. Thomas S. Jones Jr. 6979-7
Clonmacnoise. Angus O'Gillan. 6244-X
Clorinda and Damon. Andrew Marvell. 6935-5
Clorinda and Damon. Andrew Marvell. 6191-5
Cloris and Fanny. Thomas Moore. 6092-7
Cloris and Mertilla. Michael Drayton. 6315-2
Cloris I faine would try to love againe. Unknown. 6563-5
"**Cloris** I wish that envye were." Unknown. 6563-5
"**Cloris** when I to thee present." Unknown. 6563-5
"**Cloris,** it is not thy disdain". Sidney Godolphin. 6187-7
"**Cloris,** since my death doth com from you." Unknown. 6563-5
Clorus' song. William Basse. 6191-5
Close. Tim Dlugos. 7003-5
"**Close** at the window-pane Barbara stands". Barbara at the window. Alice Cary. 6865-0;6969-X
"**Close** beside the river Hudson stood a fortres". Mad Anthony's charge. Alexander N. Easton. 6922-3
Close by. Emily Pauline ("Tekahionwake") Johnson. 6837-5
"**Close** by a fringed banke I found." Unknown. 6563-5
"**Close** by the coal shaft the breaker stands". The slate pickers. John E. Barrett. 6840-5
"**Close** by the Mamertine". Roman women. Thomas Edward Brown. 6809-X
"**Close** by the threshold of a door nail'd fast". The colubriad. William Cowper. 6874-X
"**Close** by those meads, for ever crown'd...". Ombre at Hampton Court, fr. The rape of the lock. Alexander Pope. 6932-0
"**Close** by those meads, forever crowned with flowers". Canto 003, fr. The rape of the lock. Alexander Pope. 6122-2
"**Close** his eyes; his work is done!". Dirge for a soldier. George Henry Boker. 6946-0,6309-8,6470-1,6121-4,6288-1,6291-9,6300-4,6396-9,6113-3,6240-7,6271-7,6302-0,6385-3,6437-,6471-X,6473-6,6481-7,6486-8,6490-6,6552-,6600-3,6732-8,6737-3,6665-8,6431-0,6304
"**Close** in this deep retreat". An ode written on a grotto near Farnham in Surry... Thomas Warton (the Elder). 6962-2
"**Close** is he always to his faithful ones". Abraham's bread. Sir Edwin Arnold. 6848-0
"**Close** now thine eyes, and rest secure". A good-night. Francis Quarles. 6933-9
Close of day. Henry Duncan Chisholm. 6764-6
Close of day. Henry Duncan Chisholm. 6761-1
Close of play. Kenneth H. Ashley. 6785-9
Close of the vision of judgment. James Abraham Hillhouse. 6752-2
"**Close** ranks and ride on!". The riderless horse. Harold Trowbridge Pulsifer. 6995-9
"**Close** the door./But leave the window open". Variations on death. Kurt Klinger. 6769-7
"**Close** the windows tightly. Draw the curtains". The end of the performance. Yannis Ritsos. 6803-9
"**Close** to a nation's beating pulse he stands" Liska Stillman. 6995-9
Close to ninety. John Howard Bryant. 7022-1
Close to the earth. Margaret Emerson Bailey. 6780-8
"**Close** to the gates a spacious garden lies" Alexander Pope. 7020-5
"**Close** to the heart that is throbbing in love". A lullaby ("Close to the heart"). Willis Walton Franz. 6097-8

Close up the ranks! Edward Sims Van Zile. 6995-9,6449-3
Close up this house. Joseph Bridges. 6042-0
"**Close** your eyes and lose yourself in darkness". Oblivion. Octavio Paz. 6759-X
"**Close** your gates, O priests of Janus!". Caractacus. Augustine Joseph Hickey Duganne. 6924-X
Close your ranks. Isaac Gregory Smith. 6474-4
Close, Kathleen
Fold your pale hands. 6253-9
"**Closed** are the tear-gates of paradise". Rebecca, the Jewess. Clark B. Cochrane. 6848-0
The **closed** door. Thekla N. Berstecher. 6906-1
"**Closed** eyes can't see the white roses". Give them the flowers now. Leigh Mitchell Hodges. 6260-1,6303-9,6964-9
The **closed** gentian. Helen Philbrook Patten. 6764-6
The **closed** room. Benjamin De Casseres. 7007-8
The **closed** room. Mary Peaslee Root. 6750-6
Closet scene, fr. Hamlet. William Shakespeare. 6911-8
"The **closetful** of bottles". To a beloved alcoholic. Jean-Marie J. Crocker. 6857-X
Closing a trade in Vermont. Daniel L. Cady. 6989-4
Closing address. M. Ella Cornell. 6268-7
The **closing** doors. William ("Fiona Macleod") Sharp. 6873-1
The **closing** doxology, fr. Psalm 150. Bible. 6337-3
The **closing** scene. Thomas Buchanan Read. 6014-5,6121-4,6219-9,6309-8
The **closing** scene. Unknown. 6617-8
Closing song ("Lovely flowers, lovely flowers"). Unknown. 6601-1
Closing the doors. Irene Pettit McKeehan. 6337-3
The **closing** year. George Denison Prentice. 6142-7,6260-1,6402-7,6385-3,6554-6,6291-9,6304-7,6567-8
The **closing** year. Unknown. 6392-6
Closser, Clark
Prairie Creek landing. 6860-X
The **clote.** William Barnes. 6246-6
Cloth-of-gold. Winifred Welles. 6037-4
"**Clother** of the lily, feeder of the sparrow". A prayer ("Clother of the lily"). Christina Georgina Rossetti. 6437-X
Clothes. Abbie Farwell Brown. 6452-3
Clothes. Jean Starr Untermeyer. 6030-7
Clothes do but cheat and cozen us. Robert Herrick. 6026-9
The **clothes-pin** dollies. Camilla J. Knight. 6130-3
Clothespin Robins. Gary Jones. 6857-X
Clothier, Clarkson
At last. 6406-X
The **cloud** across the moon. E.O. De Camp. 6906-1
Cloud and flower. Agnes Lee. 6338-1
Cloud and sun. Joseph ("Seosamh MacCathmhaoil") Campbell. 6134-6
The **cloud** chamber. Arthur Sze. 6790-5
The **cloud** child. Elizabeth Jaimson. 6130-3
The **cloud** chorus. Aristophanes. 6987-8
The **cloud** confines. Dante Gabriel Rossetti. 6122-2,6198-2,6110-9,6655-0
"The **cloud** doth gather, the green wood roar". Thekla's song, fr. The piccolomini. Johann C. Friedrich von Schiller. 7039-6
Cloud fantasies: I. Christian Morgenstern. 6160-5
"A **cloud** has drifted down to rest". Night mood. Joyce Lancaster. 6850-2
The **cloud** house. Adrian Mott. 6262-8,6937-1
"A **cloud** lay cradled near the setting sun". An emblem of peace. Unknown. 6917-7
The **cloud** of carmel. Jessica Powers. 6282-2
TThe **cloud** of unknowing. Philip Murray. 6388-8
The **cloud** unfolding. Ernesto Trejo. 6792-1,6998-3
Cloud, Frederick
"Hands". 6299-7
Cloud, Marietta F.
A legend of the true. 6675-5
Woman's power. 6575-9
Cloud, Virginia Wood
Penelope's Christmas dance. 6249-0
Cloud, Virginia Woodward
The ballad of sweet P. 6946-0
The ballad of Sweet P. 6688-7
Care. 6309-8

The witch. 6688-7
The cloud, sels. Percy Bysshe Shelley. 6232-6,6369-1
The cloud, sels. Percy Bysshe Shelley. 6934-7
The cloud-berry flower, fr. On the scrape. John Veitch.
    6819-7
The cloud-capp'd towers. William Shakespeare. 7020-5
Cloud-pansy. Hilda Conkling. 6776-X
"Cloud-wreath, mist-sheath". Storm signals. Arthur
    Guiterman. 6773-5
The cloud.. Josephine Preston Peabody. 6310-1,6431-0
The cloud.. Unknown. 6273-3
The cloud. Charles Harper. 6768-9
The cloud. Oliver Herford. 6089-7
The cloud. Alexander Pushkin. 6103-6
The cloud. Percy Bysshe Shelley. 6122-2,6154-0,6183-4,6271-
    7,6289-X,6302 ,6198-2,6239-3,6332-2,6423-X,6466-3,
    6610 ,6385-3,6457-4,6552-X,6604-6,6621-6,6661 ,6473-
    6,6499-X,6536-8,6597-X,6623-2,6102 ,6677-1,6639-9,
    6660-7,6543-0,6396-9,6304 ,6421-3,6371-3,6252-0,6219-
    9,6250-4,6199-0,6153 ,6086-2,6438-8,6196-6,6430-2,
    6110-9,6560
The cloud. Sara Teasdale. 6476-0,6029-3
Cloudland scenes. Astra [pseud]. 7014-0
"A cloudless sky". This I remember. Elisabeth Channing
    Allen. 6750-6
Clouds. O.J. Bowles. 6036-6
Clouds. Rupert Brooke. 6234-2
Clouds. John Jay Chapman. 6833-2
Clouds. John Edwards. 6799-9
Clouds. Archibald Lampman. 6795-6
Clouds. Mikhail Lermontov. 6103-6
Clouds. Eden Phillpotts. 6879-0
Clouds. Sara V. Prueser. 6906-1
Clouds. Christina Georgina Rossetti. 6466-3
Clouds. Frank Dempster Sherman. 6311-X,6404-9,6519-8,6135-
    4,6639-9
Clouds. Dora Sigerson Shorter. 6174-5
Clouds. Unknown. 6373-X,6453-1
Clouds. Beulah Will. 6270-9
"Clouds above, as white as wool". In swimming-time. James
    Whitcomb Riley. 6993-2
Clouds after a storm. William Wordsworth. 6980-0
"The clouds all round the sky are black". Stroller's song.
    Alice Cary. 6969-X
Clouds and dawn. Edward Farquhar. 6939-8
Clouds and men, sels. Alistair Paterson. 7018-3
Clouds and moon. Edward Farquhar. 6939-8
"Clouds and rain and gloom are ever". April. Mabel W.
    Arnold. 6799-9
Clouds and sky. Lancaster Pollard. 6374-8
"The clouds are bunched roses". Song ("The clouds..."),
    fr. Country cousins. Edith Sitwell. 7000-0
"The clouds are fleeting by, father". The two
    interpreters. Adelaide Anne Procter. 6957-6
"The clouds are gathered and the wind blows...".
    Mesopotamia. J. Griffyth Fairfax. 7029-9
"Clouds are like pretty lambs". Clouds. Sara V. Prueser.
    6906-1
"The clouds are scudding across the moon". Storm song.
    Bayard Taylor. 6976-2
"Th cloudseare thick and darkly lower". Rain and shine.
    Brander Matthews. 6770-0,6875-8
Clouds at sunset. Harriet Rossiter Lewis. 6764-6
Clouds by night. Kuo Ch'en. 6072-2
"Clouds do not always veil the skies". Ode 009, sels.
    Horace. 6975-4
"The clouds gather fast, the oak forests moan". Theckla.
    William Peter. 6980-0
"Clouds gather, lightning flashes". Summer symphony.
    Laurel Jane Spitler. 6799-9
The clouds have already told me. Jacinto Fombona Pachano.
    6642-9
The clouds have already told me. Jacinto Fombona Pachano.
    6642-9
"The clouds have left the sky". Robert Bridges. 6187-7,
    6487-6
Clouds in the west. Augustus Julian Requier. 6074-9,6113-3
"Clouds move like sheep across the stretch...". Wind-wolf.
    Estelle Rooks. 6850-2
Clouds of evening. Robinson Jeffers. 6012-9,6628-3

Clouds of gray. Ben H. Smith. 6662-3
"Clouds raced across the sky like so many...". Sweet
    soledad. Alejandro Murguia. 6792-1, 6998-3
"The clouds roll over the pine trees". Lapooka. Charles
    Sangster. 6796-4
"Clouds spout upon her/Their waters amain". Rain on a
    grave. Thomas Hardy. 6828-6
"Clouds stream and disappear". Wistaria. Witter Bynner.
    6069-2,6777-8
The clouds that are so light. Edward Thomas. 6210-5
"The clouds that stoop from yonder sky". Implora pace.
    Bayard Taylor. 6976-2
"The clouds that watched inthe west have fled". When day
    was done. Louise Chandler Moulton. 7041-8
"Clouds walking across the sun". Spring. Ruth L. Drowns.
    6799-9
"Clouds will sail and winds will blow" Sir Walter Raleigh.
    7020-5
"Clouds, ever drifting in air". Aristophanes. 6435-3
"Clouds, forests, hills, and waters!...". Crossing the
    ford. O.W. H.. 6752-2
"Clouds, torsos, shells, peppers, trees...". Edward Weston
    in Mexico City. Philip Dacey. 6966-5
"Clouds, with a little light bewteen". Mysteries. Alice
    Cary. 6969-X
The clouds. James Stephens. 6253-9
Cloudy drop. Alfred Kreymborg. 6071-4
Cloudy June. Edmund Blunden. 6044-7
Clough, Arthur H.
    En route. 6484-1
Clough, Arthur Hugh
    "Across the sea, along the shore". 6980-0
    The advent of peace. 7014-0
    Ah! yet consider it again. 6110-9,6655-0,6656-9,6491-4
    Ah! Yet consider it again! 6828-6
    All is well. 6828-6
    All is well. 6110-9
    Alteram partem. 6123-0,6110-9
    Am I with you, fr. Songs in absence. 6199-0
    "Am I with you, or you with me?" 6828-6
    Amours de voyage. 6828-6
    Amours de voyage. 6430-2
    Amours de voyage, sel. 7014-0
    Amours de voyage, sels. 6110-9,6199-0
    Amours de voyage, sels. 6123-0,6246-5
    "Are there not, then, two musics unto men?", fr Music.
        6123-0
    "As ships becalmed." 6302-0;6385-3
    At Venice. 6624-0,6657-7
    Atheism. 7025-6
    Atheism. 6438-8
    Bathing: from the Bothie of Tober na Vuolich. 6438-8
    Bethesda (a sequel). 6110-9
    Bethesda, a sequel. 6198-2
    Blank misgivings of a creature moving about in two
        worlds.... 6655-0
    'Blank misgivings of a creature moving about in...'
        6828-6
    Blank misgivings, sels. 6110-9,6199-0
    The bothie of tober-vrolich, sels. 6656-9
    "But if as not by that the soul desired." 6110-9
    The changeless. 6737-9
    Claude to Eustace. 6046-3
    Columbus. 6424-8,6552-X
    Columbus. 6820-0
    "Come back again, my olden heart" 6380-2
    "Come back, come back, behold with straining mast" 6828-
        6
    Come back, come back, fr. Songs in absence. 6110-9,6250-
        4,6655-0
    "Come home, come home! And where is home for me" 6828-6
    Come home, come home!, fr. Songs in absence. 6655-0
    "Come near to me, my sons: your father goes",fr Jacob.
        6123-0
    Come, poet, come! 6046-3,6110-9
    Courage. 6424-8
    Currente calamo. 6315-2,6110-9
    Despondency rebuked. 6271-7
    Dipsychus. 6828-6
    Dipsychus, sels. 6331-4,6102-8,6199-0,6430-2

CLOUGH

Duty. 6828-6
Early poems. 6123-0
Early poems, sels. 6123-0
Easter day. 6198-2
Easter day, II. 6110-9,6199-0,6430-2,6655-0
Easter day: Naples, 1849. 6046-3,6102-8,6430-2,6655-0
Elspie and Philip, fr. The bothie of Tober-na-vuolich. 6832-4
En route, fr. Amours de voyage. 6110-9
England. 6383-7
"An English clergyman came spick and span", fr. Mari. 6123-0
Envoi, fr. Amours de voyage. 6110-9
An evening walk in spring. 6655-0
"Farewell, farewell! Her vans the vessel tries" 6828-6
Genesis 024 6848-0
Georgina Trevellyn to Louisa, fr. Amours de voyage. 6123-0
Green fields of England. 6934-7
"Green fields of England!" 6828-6
Green fields of England!, fr. Songs in abscence. 6110-9, 6430-2,6655-0
"Green fields of England!...", fr. Songs in absence. 6123-0,6240-7
Help, sure help, fr. Dipsychus. 6655-0
The hidden love. 6110-9,6560-0
The higher courage. 6655-0
The highland stream, fr. The bothie of Tober-na-vuolich. 6832-4
Home, rose, and home, Provence and La Palie. 6934-7
Homeward! the evening comes. 6889-8
Hope evermore and believe. 6198-2,6337-3,6730-1,6110-9, 6196-6,6199-0,6560-0,6214-8
"How often sit I, poring o'er." 6246-5
How often sit I, fr. Blank misgivings. 6199-0
I have seen higher, holier things than these. 6430-2
"If it is thou whose casual hand withdraws." 6110-9
In a lecture-room. 6657-7,6110-9,6199-0
In a London square. 6123-0,6110-9,6199-0
In stratis viarum. 6655-0
In the depths. 6828-6
In the depths. 6110-9
In the great metropolis. 6828-6
In the great metropolis. 6655-0
In Venice, Dipsychus speaks, fr. Dipsychus. 6832-4
The incoming tide. 7020-5
Isolation. 6437-X
It fortifies my soul to know. 6430-2
It is an illusion, fr. Amours de voyage. 6199-0
Ite domun saturae, venit Hesperus. 6378-0,6110-9,6655-0, 6656-9
Jacob. 6848-0
Jacob's wives. 6848-0
Keeping on. 6114-1
The latest decalogue. 6123-0,6437-X,6730-1,6092-7,6110-9,6125 ,6150-8,6655-0,6430-2,6199-0,6427-7,6657 , 6315-2,6527-9,6732-8,6733-6
The latest decalogue. 6199-0
Les vaches. 6430-2
A letter from Rome. 6315-2
Life is struggle. 6828-6
Life is struggle. 6123-0
A London idyll. 6123-0
Love and reason. 6655-0
Love, not duty. 6655-0
Mari Magno, sels. 6123-0
"The mighty ocean rolls and raves" 6828-6
The mighty ocean rolls, fr. Songs in absence. 6199-0
Minor poems, sel. 7014-0
Monte Cavallo. 6624-0
The music of the world and of the soul, sels.. 6123-0
The music of the world and of the soul. 6655-0
My wind is turned to bitter north. 6430-2
The new Sinai. 6600-3,6657-7
The new Sinai. 6110-9,6655-0
"O ship, ship, ship" 6828-6
O ship, ship, ship, fr. Songs in absence. 6655-0
"O stream descending to the sea". 6980-0
"O thou of little faith", fr. Religious poems. 6123-0
O thou whose image. 6196-6,6199-0
"O thou whose image in the shine" 6655-0
On Montorio's height, fr. Amours de voyage. 6110-9
On the Lido. 6624-0
'Our gaieties, our luxuries, fr. Dipsychus. 6110-9,6199-0
Out of sight, out of mind. 6874-X
Over the great windy waters, fr. Amours de voyage. 6199-0
Pantheon. 6110-9
The Pantheon, fr. Amours de voyage. 6110-9
'Perche pensa? Pensado s'invecchia' 6828-6
Perche pwnsa? Pensando s'invecchia. 6110-9,6196-6,6198-2
Peschiera. 6110-9,6110-9,6123-0
Philip to Adam, fr. The bothie of Tober-na-vuolich. 6832-4
Pleasure and guilt, fr. Dipsychus. 6655-0
A protest. 6656-9
Qua cursum ventus. 6198-2,6258-X,6600-3,6657-7,6271-7, 6437 ,6604-6,6543-0,6438-8,6046-3,6084-6,6737 ,6655-0,6430-2,6560-0,6250-4,6110-9,6199 ,6219-9,6371-3, 6383-7,6656-0,6660-7
The questioning spirit. 6828-6
The questioning spirit. 6110-9,6198-2,6110-9
Qui laborat, orat. 6110-9,6196-6,6199-0,6657-7,6110-9, 6199-0
The real question, fr. Amours de voyage. 6110-9
Religious poems, sels. 6123-0
Revival. 6655-0
The river Tiber. 6624-0
Rome disappoints me still, fr. Amours de voyage. 6199-0
Rome, fr. Amours de voyage. 6110-9
Say not the struggle naught availeth. 6186-9,6196-6, 6199-0,6192-3,6250-4,6430 ,6639-9,6737-9,6723-9,6660-7,6560-0,6467 ,6655-0,6665-8,6337-3,6437-X,6604-6, 6208 ,6023-4,6102-8,6371-3,6046-3,6110-9,6214 ,6150-8,6153-2,6383-7,6301-2,6501-5,6240 ,6291-1,6473-6, 6527-9,6732-8,6315-2,6610 ,6246-5,6123-0,6657-7
"Say not, the struggle nought availeth" 6828-6
Sceptic moods, fr. Amours de voyage. 6110-9
Sehnsucht. 6199-0
The shadow. 6832-4
The shady lane. 6123-0
The ship. 6383-7
Sic itur. 6380-2
A sleeping child. 6127-3,6519-8,6131-1,6135-4
"Some future day when what is now is not" 6828-6
Some future day, fr. Songs in absence. 6046-3,6110-9, 6199-0
Song ("Come home"). 6110-9
Song ("O ship"). 6110-9
Song ("Were you with me.") 6110-9
A song of autumn. 6123-0
A song of autumn. 6655-0
The song of Lamech. 6980-0,6848-0
Songs in absence. 6123-0,6655-0,6138-9,6484-1,6110-9, 6214 ,6828-6
Songs in absence, sels. 6199-0
Sonnets on the thought of death. 6110-9
Spectator ab extra. 6200-8,6733-6,6092-7
Spectator ab extra, sels. 6026-9
The spirit's song. 6315-2
The stream of life. 6123-0,6660-7,6600-3,6604-6,6110-9, 6250-4,6219-9
The stream of life. 6832-4
"That out of sight is out of mind",fr Songs in absence. 6123-0
"That out os sight is out of mind" 6828-6
'There is no God,' the wicked saith, fr. Dipsychus. 6110-9,6199-0,6655-0
"This world is very odd we see," fr. Dipsychus. 6110-9
Through a glass darkly. 6110-9
To a sleeping child. 6233-4,6242-3
To Kalon. 6110-9
Umnos aumnos. 6828-6
Umnos aumnos. 6110-9
The unchanging. 6461-2
Venice. 6250-4
"Wen Gott betrugt, ist wohl betrogen". 6655-0
"Were I with you, or you wit me" 6828-6

"Were you with me or I with you" 6828-6
Were you with me, fr. Songs in absence. 6655-0
"Were you with me, or I with you" 6828-6
What they think. 6134-6
Whate'er you dream with doubt possest. 6430-2
When the dews are earliest falling. 6430-2
"When the enemy is near thee," fr. Dipsychus. 6110-9
'Where are the great, fr. Dipsychus. 6110-9,6199-0
Where lies the land. 6123-0,6212-1,6560-0,6192-3,6655-0, 6723 ,6186-9,6250-4,6543-0,6199-0,6639-9,6730 ,6240-7,6102-8,6125-7,6219-9,6110-9,6737 ,6657-7,6656-9, 6258-X,6246-5,6332-2,6374 ,6052-8,6271-7,6437-X,6484-1,6552-X,6239 ,6828-6,6046-3
Where upon Apennine slope, fr. Amours de voyage. 6934-7
"Where, upon Apennine slope...",fr. Armours de voyage. 6123-0
With whom is no variableness, neither shadow of turning. 6828-6
With whom is no variableness, neither shadow of turning. 6198-2,6501-5,6657-7,6385-3,6337-3,6730 , 6604-6,6102-8,6110-9,6660-7,6655-0,6543 ,6199-0,6250-4
Written on a bridge. 6123-0
"Ye flags of Piccadilly" 6828-6
Ye flags of Piccadilly, fr. Songs in absence. 6655-0
Clough, Arthur Hugh (tr.)
    Slumber and sleep. Johann Wolfgang von Goethe, 6958-4
Clough, Mary L.
    The death of Jacob. 6848-0
Clough, Ruth Crary
    Anne Boleyn O'Shaugennesy. 6750-6
    A gardener walks at evening. 6789-1
Clough, Wilson O.
    Sheepherder's wind. 6761-1
Clouse, Effie
    Nature gifts. 6799-9
Clouts, Sidney
    The hawk. 6788-3
    Of Thomas Traherne and the pebble outside. 6788-3
    Roy Kloof. 6788-3
    Roy Kloof went riding. 6788-3
    The sea and the eagle. 6788-3
    The situation. 6788-3
    The sleeper. 6788-3
    Within. 6788-3
Clover. Sidney Lanier. 6753-0
Clover. Helge Rode. 6555-4
Clover. Richard Ronan. 7003-5
Clover. John Banister Tabb. 6006-4,6338-1,6374-8,6431-0
The **clover** blossoms. Oscar Laighton. 6066-8
The **clover** field. Louise Morey Bowman. 6797-2
"The **clover** in the grass is white". White clover, fr. In Tuscany. Cora Fabri. 6876-6
Clover, Madge
    In Carmel Bay. 6241-5
Clover, Samuel T.
    Cadences. 6476-0
Clover, Samuel Travers
    When zephrys blow. 6241-5
The **clover**.. James Whitcomb Riley. 6273-3
The **clover.** Margaret Deland. 6441-8
The **clown's** baby. Unknown. 6521-X,6155-9,6574-0
The **clown's** courtship. Unknown. 6089-7
The **clown's** lament. Clement Scott. 6681-X
The **clown's** reply. Oliver Goldsmith. 6228-8
A **clown's** smirk in the skull of a baboon. Edward Estlin Cummings. 6751-4
Clown's song, fr. Twelfth night. William Shakespeare. 6208-3
The **clown's** story. Marc Eugene ("Vandyke Brown") Cook. 6407-8
The **clown.** Tefcros Anthias. 6352-7
The **clown.** J.M. S. 6817-0
A **clownish** song. Thomas Nashe. 6436-1
Clowns' houses, fr. Facade. Edith Sitwell. 7000-0
Club presidents. Edgar A. Guest. 6748-4
Club woman. Phyllis McGinley. 6532-5
The **club,** fr. Far west. Blaise Cendrars. 6351-9
Clubs. Theodore Hook. 6652-6
The **clucking** hen. Ann ("Aunt Effie") Hawkshawe. 6937-1

The **clucking** hen. Unknown. 6452-3,6135-4
Clues. Mary Sinton Leitch. 6039-0,6326-8
Clump of grass. Winifred Welles. 6038-2
'**Cluny**'. William Croswell Doane. 7008-6
The **cluricaun.** Marc Connelly. 6817-0
"**Clustered** lilies in the shadows", sels. Dora Read Goodale. 6601-1
Clycine's song. Samuel Taylor Coleridge. 6086-2
Clyde, Kate
    Little things. 6530-9
Clyne, Norval
    The light of Christmas. 6747-6
Cnut, King. See Canute, King
'**Co'** boss'. E. Merrill Root. 6038-2
Co' bossy. Jennie Joy. 6670-4
Co-operation. J. Mason Knox. 6291-1,6736-0
Co-operation. Ruth Comfort Mitchell. 6718-2
Coach. Eleanor Farjeon. 6554-X
The **coach,** fr. The homestead. Gertrude Huntington McGiffert. 6838-3
Coady, Mark
    A flame. 6883-9
    Survivor. 6883-9
Coakley, Thomas F.
    An ambulance driver's prayer. 6846-4
Coal buckin' misery. Richard Lawson. 6149-4
The **Coal** Creek rebellion. Unknown. 6149-4
The **coal** digger. Jessie F. O'Donnell. 6695-X
Coal diggin' blues. Unknown. 6149-4
Coal loadin' blues. Edward Lang and Neil Orck. 6149-4
The **coal** loading machine. Unknown. 6149-4
The **coal** miner. W.B. Wilson. 6149-4
The **coal-owner** and the pitman's wife. Unknown. 6157-5
Coals and ashes: 1916 Sylvester Baxter. 6798-0
Coals of fire. Sir Alan Patrick Herbert. 6637-2,6026-9
"**Coame,** Malkyn, hurle thine oyz at Hodge Trillindle" Unknown. 6380-2
Coan, Leander S.
    Better in the morning. 6014-5
A **coarse** morning. Augusta Webster. 6997-5
Coast artillery marching song. Unknown. 6237-7
Coast artillery song. Unknown. 6237-7
Coast erosion. E.M. Wilkie. 6228-8
The **Coast** Guard of Cape Cod. Emma M. Doane. 6798-0
The **coast** of Peru. Unknown. 6833-2
The **coast** road. Robinson Jeffers. 6527-9
The **coasters.** Thomas Fleming Day. 6006-4
Coasting. Wallace E. Mather. 6965-7
Coasting cats. J.G. Francis. 6786-7
Coasting down the hill. Will Carleton. 7035-3
Coasts. Clark B. Firestone. 7007-8
Coasts. Beatrice Ravenel. 7016-7
Coasts, fr. Tidewater. Beatrice Ravenel. 6036-6,6326-8
The **coastwise** lights. Rudyard Kipling. 6331-4
The **coat** of faded gray. G.W. Harris. 6074-9
The **coat** of fire. Edith Sitwell. 6210-5
Coat of mail. Asa the Blind. 6362-4
Coat of mail. Ibn Abdul Ghafur. 6362-4
Coates, Archie Austin
    Lavender. 6032-3
Coates, Elmer Ruan
    Awake! awake! 6403-5
    The balance wheel. 6045-1
    Billy K. Simes. 6920-7
    Falling in and falling out. 6921-5
    Genius. 6920-7
    Giles and Abraham. 6910-X
    Nothing for use. 6920-7
    That autograph sale. 6922-3
    Twenty-one to-day. 6921-5
Coates, Florence Earle
    An adieu. 6027-7
    After. 6051-X,6607-0
    America. 6449-3
    The Angelus. 6631-3
    As they leave us. 6443-4
    Buffalo. 6946-0
    By the Conemaugh. 6946-0
    Captain Guynemer. 7027-2
    Captain Guynemer. 6051-X

Dream the greatest dream. 6653-4
Eros. 6320-9
For France. 6443-4
For joy. 6461-2,6232-6
A hero. 6291-1
The house of pain. 6214-8
Immortal. 6337-3
In war-time. 7026-4
Jewel-weed. 6338-1
Live thy life. 6607-0
The morning-glory. 6102-8,6076-5,6431-0
A narrow window. 6266-0
The new Mars. 6542-2
New York. 6327-6
"Not far from Paris in fair Fontainebleau". 6331-4
Per aspera. 6093-5,6291-1,6653-4
Place de la Concorde. 7026-4
The poetry of earth. 6076-5,6102-8,6266-0,6076-5,6509-0
Rhapsody. 6019-6
Serbia. 7027-2
The smile of Reims. 6031-5
The smile of Reims. 6653-4
Song. 6653-4
Song ("For me the jasmine"). 6310-1,6393-4
Song ("If love"). 6310-1
Song of life. 6476-0,6102-8,6076-5
Thanksgiving. 6303-9
Thanksgiving. 6449-3
Their victory won. 6649-3
Through the window. 6266-0
Time. 6029-3
The unconquered air. 6310-1,6473-6,6509-0,6336-5
The unconquered air. 6336-5,6509-0
War. 7031-0
The world is mine. 6431-0
Coates, Grace Stone
A child tastes the loveliness of life... 6039-0
Postscripts. 6041-2
Silenced. 6808-1
Coates, Reynell
The gambler's wife. 6916-9
The gambler's wife. 6568-6
Coates, Walter John
Looking on beauty. 7030-2
Relief. 6750-6
Coatsworth, Elizabeth J.
All goats. 6070-6
The bad kittens. 6465-5,6071-4,6464-7
Birth of Henri Quatre. 6039-0
The blessing of the beds. 6217-2
Broadway. 6808-1
The cat and northern lights. 6120-6
The circus-postered barn. 6464-7
Comments from a country garden. 6232-6
The curse. 6034-X
Daniel Webster's horses. 6218-0
Down the rain falls. 6554-X
Empty house. 6218-0
Evening. 6069-2
The fields are spread. 6554-X
The fireside kitten. 6120-6
Five inconsequential charms. 6036-6
The gate. 6034-X
Green woods. 6218-0
The lady. 6861-8
The mouse. 6512-0
Murder house. 6218-0
The Nile. 6331-4
The old mare. 6070-6
On a night of snow. 6120-6
The painted desert. 6464-7
The painted desert, sels. 6041-2
Pirates. 6072-2,6040-4,6072-2
Preparation. 6072-2
The proud dead ladies. 6037-4
Rain. 6120-6
Reflection. 6036-6
Saint John. 6070-6
Subjunctive. 6506-6
The swan. 6073-0

Syracuse. 6619-4
The three Misses Barker. 6071-4
To barns. 6396-9
To think. 6861-8,6509-0,6037-4,6891-X
The wind shrieked loud. 6218-0
The **cob** houses. Kate Putnam Osgood. 6273-3;6684-4
Cobb, Ann
Kivers. 6034-X
Up Carr Creek. 6034-X
War-time in the mountains. 6032-3
The widow-man. 6034-X
Cobb, Henry N.
"Father, take my hand". 6409-4
The gracious answer. 6409-4
Cobb, Mary McKinley
April in the woods. 6841-3
'As a flower'. 6841-3
Greetings. 6841-3
May. 6841-3
Winnie Davis. 6841-3
Cobbes, John
To Chloris. 6563-5
Cobbett, Richard
Farewell to the fairies. 6385-3
Cobbett, William
The Avon valley. 7020-5
An English village. 7020-5
Cobbler and stork. Eugene Field. 6834-0;6949-5
The **cobbler** in Willow Street. George O'Neil. 6607-0,6653-4
The **cobbler** of Glamorgan. Hermann Hagedorn. 6944-4
Cobbler! stick to your last. B.A. T. 6018-8
The **cobbler's** song. Charles Tilney. 6436-1
The **cobbler.** Unknown. 6743-3
Cobblin, Orlando Thomas
My manx minx. 6724-7
Cobhara-Lokesvara. Unknown (Newari) 7013-2
The **coble** o Cargill. Unknown. 6185-0
Coblentz, Catherine Cate
The earth worshiped! 6144-3
Hakluyt and the English voyages. 6979-7
The housewife. 6144-3
Stone walls of New England. 7030-2
The way to the arbutus. 7030-2
Coblentz, Stanton A.
Atlantis. 6218-0
Birth. 6750-6
Bringers of the hemlock. 6144-3
Calm. 6833-2
Eagles and snails. 6071-4
Fire. 6039-0
In a troubled dream. 6648-8
In a troubled world. 6144-3
In the storm. 6144-3
Land's end (Point Lobos, California). 6833-2
Last judgment. 6337-3
The lost valley. 6628-3
Memorial. 6750-6
Nephree-ti-ta. 6648-8
O prophets and redeemers. 6144-3
Omnipresence. 6337-3
Patient is time, fr. The pageant of man. 6337-3
Processional. 6648-8
The second coming. 6144-3
The unknown sculptor. 6337-3
The watcher. 6218-0
What would he say? 6144-3
Wind in the hills. 6789-1
The wolf, the hornet, and the nightingale. 6102-8,6076-5,6039-0
The woods shall not be lonely. 6979-7
The **cobra.** Miller Hageman. 6166-4
Coburn, Charles
Limerick:"A charming young lady named Nelly". 6811-1
Coburn, Louise Helen
The oriole. 6510-4
Coburn, Wallace David
The wolf hunt. 7035-3
A **cobweb** made to order. Ann ("Aunt Effie") Hawkshawe. 6131-1
Cobwebs. Ronald W. Fillmore. 6894-4

Cobwebs. Louise Imogen Guiney. 6338-1
Cobwebs. Clifford J. Laube. 6839-1
The coca tree. Jacinto Fombona Pachano. 6642-9
The coca tree. Jacinto Fombona Pachano. 6642-9
Cocaine Lil. Unknown. 6399-3
The cochero and the horse. Norbert Lyons. 7010-8
Cochineal mask. Karen Herseth Wee. 6857-X
Cochrane's bonny grizzly. Unknown. 6613-5
Cochrane, Alfred
    The eight-day clock. 6230-X
    Lazarus. 7012-4
    Life's favorite. 7031-0
    My terrier. 6230-X
Cochrane, Clark B.
    Rebecca, the Jewess. 6848-0
Cochrane, James
    At the convent near Saint Gall. 6749-2
    The lake at Zurich. 6749-2
    The monastery of Maria Einsiedeln. 6749-2
Cock a doodle doo!!! Edwin Seaver. 6880-4
"Cock a doodle doo!". Unknown. 6363-2
A cock and hen story. Robert Southey. 6278-4
The cock and the bull. Charles Stuart Calverley. 6385-3, 6089-7,6440-X
The cock and the fox; or, the tale of the nun's priest. Geoffrey Chaucer. 6970-3
The cock and the fox. Jean de La Fontaine. 6732-8
A cock crowing in a poulterer's shop. John Ferguson. 6269-5
"Cock crows in the morning." Mother Goose. 6452-3,
"The Cock doth crow". Mother Goose. 6363-2
"The cock is crowing". Written in March. William Wordsworth. 6108-7,6133-8,6134-6,6334-9,6401-9,6465 , 6466-3,6478-7,6110-9,6131-1,6086-2,6018-8
The cock of the charcoal burner. Andre Salmon. 6351-9
Cock Robin and Jenny Wren. Unknown. 6452-3,6459-0
"Cock robin got up early". Unknown. 6904-5
Cock robin's death. Unknown. 6183-4,6456-6
The cock that is the trumpet to the morn. William Shakespeare. 6558-9
Cock up your beaver. Robert Burns. 6138-9,6334-9
Cock-a-doodle-doo. Mother Goose. 6502-3
Cock-a-doodle-doo!. Richard R. Kirk. 6326-8
Cock-crow. Abbie Huston Evans. 6076-5
Cock-crow. Edward Thomas. 6464-7
Cock-crowing. Henry Vaughan. 6378-0
The cock-fighter's garland. William Cowper. 6814-6
The cock-maid, the turnspit,and the ox. John Gay. 6972-X
Cock-throwing. Martin Lluellyn. 6563-5
The cock.. Unknown. 6466-3
The cock. Unknown. 6134-6
Cockadoodledoo. Richard Lawson Gales. 6216-4
The cockatoos. Celia Thaxter. 6612-7
Cockayne country. Agnes Mary F. ("Madame Duclaux") Robinson. 6437-X,6656-9
Cockburn, Alison Rutherford
    The flowers of the forest. 6383-7
Cockburn, Mrs.
    The flowers of the forest. 6134-6
Cocke, Zitella
    'The dog I loved you so' 7008-6
    His code of honor. 7008-6
    How we celebrated. 6715-8
    Miss Nancy's gown. 6652-6
    Sir Walter's friend. 7008-6
    So very queer. 6713-1
    Thankful boy. 6715-8
    What the wind says. 6702-3
Cockerel sun. Rosemary Dobson. 6349-7
Cockin, Hereward K.
    Epitaph on an early settler. 7041-8
Cockle v. Cackle. Thomas Hood. 6200-8
Cockles and mussels. Unknown. 6930-4
Cockley Moor, Dockray, Penrith. Norman Nicholson. 6379-9
Cockney enigma on the letter H. Horace Mayhew. 6440-X
A cockney wail. Unknown. 6273-3
A cockney wail. Unknown. 6911-8
The cockney's dream. Frederick Victor Branford. 6269-5
The cockney. John Godfrey Saxe. 6302-0
The cocks have crowed. Rosemary Farrar. 6761-1,6979-7

Cocoa morning. Bob Kaufman. 6901-0
"Cocoa-nut naught". On the high price of fish. William Cowper. 6814-6
The cocoa-tree. Charles Warren Stoddard. 6431-0
The cocooning, fr. the Mireio. Frederic Mistral. 7039-6
Cocoons. Frederick Herbert Adler. 6906-1
Cocoons. Gertrude Scott Jewell. 7019-1
"Cocoons hold beauty captive for a spell". Cocoons. Frederick Herbert Adler. 6906-1
Cocotte. Robert Service. 6159-1
Cocteau, Jean
    Battery. 6351-9
    The clear blue. 6351-9
    Illusion. 6351-9
    Poem of circumstance. Joseph T. Shipley (tr.). 6351-9
The cod-fisher. Joseph Crosby Lincoln. 6119-2
Coda. Eugene Jolas. 6351-9
Coda. Dorothy Parker. 6089-7
Codd, Gertrude Jane
    The nun's diamond jubilee. 6285-7
    Song against servants. 6292-X
Code. Cosette Middleton. 6017-X
The code - heroics. Robert Frost. 6897-9
Code, Grant H.
    Ballad of two kings. 6218-0
    Building of sand. 6218-0
    Epitaph for a wooden soldier. 6218-0
    Foreboding. 6218-0
    The high place at Marib. 6218-0
    Highway to nowhere. 6218-0
    News of my friends. 6218-0
    The night refuses a dreamer. 6218-0
    Nos moraturi te salutamus. 6218-0
    Nursery rhymes for surrealists. 6218-0
    The playground of the pixie. 6218-0
    Prayer in blackout, fr. Nursery rhymes for surrealists. 6218-0
    Sea quatrains. 6036-6
    Toulouse. 6331-4
Code, H.B.
    The sprig of Shillelah. 6858-8
Code, Leslie L.
    Lake Saganaga. 6342-X
The code, fr. Translations from the Chinese. Christopher Morley. 6307-1
Codes. Diane Chang. 6790-5
Codicil. George Fox Horne. 6042-0
Codicil to a will. Nancy McCleery. 6855-3
Cody, Alexander
    The sister of charity. 6285-7
Cody, Alexander J.
    Omniscience. 6799-9
Cody, H.A.
    Glasier's men. 6797-2
    The king's and mine. 6224-5
    The old figurehead carver. 6833-2
    Old ship riggers. 6833-2
    The port of St. John. 6797-2
Coe Jr., Richard
    Life. 6632-1
Coe, E.R.
    Lindbergh. 7019-1
Coe, Katherine Hunter
    Can you hear me? 6906-1
    Impressions of the Rockies. 6906-1
    The last party. 6906-1
    Moon mountain. 6906-1
    Symbols. 6906-1
    Warning. 6906-1
Coe, Richard
    The dying soldier. 6403-5
    Emblems. 6910-X
Coelia, sels. William Alexander Percy. 6182-6
Coelo et in terra. Thomas Walsh. 6292-X,6172-9
Coelum non animum. Sir Lewis Morris. 6543-0
Coelus to Hyperion. John Keats. 6543-0
"Coesper erat: tune lubriciles ultravia". Mors iabrochii. Unknown. 6902-9
Coeur de Lion at the bier of his father. Felicia Dorothea Hemans. 6302-0

COFFEE

The coffee my mother used to make. James Whitcomb Riley. 6139-7
The coffee slips. Charles and Mary Lamb. 6295-4
A coffeepot face. Aileen Fisher. 6891-X
Coffey, Clare Beatrice
   The Christmas angel's message. 6929-0
"A coffin gray and spotted with gold". The chrysalis. Benjamin Franklin Taylor. 6815-4
Coffin, Charles
   Glad tidings from the King of kings. 6065-X
Coffin, Emma F.
   Yuletide. 6799-9
Coffin, Robert Barry
   Ships at sea. 6271-7,6358-6,6219-9,6304-7,6438-8,6735-2, 6271-7,6358-6,6219-9,6304-7,6438
Coffin, Robert P. Tristram
   An aeroplane against a daylit moon. 7040-X
   Anemones. 7040-X
   At the lowest ebb of night. 7040-X
   The barnacles. 7040-X
   Bats. 7040-X
   The betrayal. 7040-X
   The boy in the house. 7040-X
   A boy, a lake, a sun. 6984-3
   A buck's head on the wall. 7040-X
   Centaur. 7040-X
   Country church. 6984-3
   Country church. 6532-5,6337-3,6337-3
   Crystal moment. 6782-4
   Crystal moment. 6217-2,6250-4,6464-7
   The desert of Maine. 6628-3
   Eyes are lit up. 6984-3
   Fireflies. 7040-X
   Fireflies in a graveyard. 6984-3
   A flicker went free. 6761-1
   The fog. 6527-9
   The footfalls. 7040-X
   A girl shelling peas. 6761-1
   Go to the barn with a lantern. 7040-X
   Golden falcon. 6073-0,6619-4
   Good Friday song. 6532-5
   The grindstone. 7040-X
   He was of the forest. 7040-X
   The hill place. 7040-X
   The horseshoes. 7040-X
   House of eyes. 7040-X
   Humming bird ("It would take an angel's eye..."). 6073-0
   Humming-bird. 7040-X
   Hylas. 7040-X
   The jelly-fish. 7040-X
   Jethro's pet. 6628-3
   A lighted open door. 7040-X
   A lonely, swimming bird. 7040-X
   The man indoors. 7040-X
   Man of thunder. 7040-X
   The marsh-spider. 7040-X
   Midsummer evening. 7040-X
   More I cannot ask. 7040-X
   Mr. Burns starts for town. 6761-1
   Night is here. 7040-X
   The night watchman. 7040-X
   Night-hawk. 6073-0
   Night-hawk. 7040-X
   Nothing changes with the birds. 7040-X
   An old man raking leaves. 7040-X
   The older love. 7040-X
   On a day as clear as glass. 7040-X
   One in a darkness. 7040-X
   The open eye. 7040-X
   The painted gods. 7040-X
   People in high houses. 7040-X
   Pines are perilous. 7040-X
   The pines. 6984-3
   The poem. 6761-1
   Raccoon hunt. 6761-1
   Rura cano. 7040-X
   Saint Brandan of the west. 6039-0
   The sea-urchin. 7040-X
   The secret heart. 6979-7
   The secret heart. 6465-5
   The ship o' bed. 6069-2
   The ship o'bed. 6861-8
   Song for March. 7040-X
   The spider. 6464-7
   The starfish. 7040-X,6780-8
   Strange holiness. 6984-3
   Sunflowers. 7040-X,6781-6
   Sunrise. 7040-X
   Sunrise: Maine coast. 7040-X
   The swallows. 7040-X
   The swop. 6761-1
   Taking the turn. 6042-0
   Thank little boys. 6761-1
   There is no help in bees. 7040-X
   There yet sruvived a god. 7040-X
   The three songs. 7040-X
   Too late to light the lamps. 7040-X
   Towers of silence. 7040-X
   Tree-toads. 7040-X
   Two old men. 7040-X
   Unholy light. 7040-X
   The warning. 7040-X
   The way to know a father. 6465-5
   Ways to look at stars. 7040-X
   The weather vane. 7040-X
   When man swung a scythe. 7040-X
   Where I took hold of life. 7040-X
   A whippoorwill awakes. 7040-X
   Wild geese at night. 7040-X
   Wild swans. 7040-X
   Winter-piece. 7040-X
   Young farmers. 6761-1
Coffin, Robert Peter Tristram
   Lindbergh. 7019-1
Coffin, Robert Stevenson
   Ships at sea. 6385-3
The coffin. Heinrich Heine. 7039-6
Coffman, Emily Ann
   Resignation. 6750-6
Coggswell, F.H.
   The lawyer's lullaby. 6001-3
Coghill, Rhoda
   Dead. 6930-4
   The plough-hose. 6930-4
A cogie o' yill. Andrew Shirrefs. 6180-X,6086-2
Cogie, Orgill
   The ice-cream man. 6269-5
   Immanuel. 6269-5
   The rose. 6269-5
   To Sheena, beloved, thought dying. 6269-5
"Cogimur; inuitis (Clarissime) parce querelis". Illvstrissimo, poetentissimoqve principi, Fredrico... Thomas Campion. 6794-8
Cognitabo pro peccato meo. William Habington. 6189-3
Cohan, Charles C.
   Montana. 6465-5
Cohan, George M.
   Myself and me. 6889-8
   Over there. 6732-8
Cohen, D.S.
   As 'Old Giles' saw it. 6406-X
Cohen, Leonard
   Ballad. 6446-9
   Creator. 6850-2
   "When this American woman". 6446-9
Cohen, Marvin
   Past either and through both. 6803-0
"Cohorts of darkness entrenched in their lair". Fort Donelson. Thomas Hunter. 6847-2
"Coifi, the priest of King Edwin...". Out west in Queensland. Douglas Brooke Wheelton Sladen. 6768-9
The coin of pity, fr. Modern love. George Meredith. 6656-9
The coin.. Sara Teasdale. 6607-0,6161-3,6421-3
A coineachan—a highland lullaby. Unknown. 6873-1
The coins of love, fr. What of the the night? John Richard Moreland. 6337-3
Coire dubh linn. Darrell Figgis. 6090-0
Coit, Emily S.
   Hymn for Mother's Day. 6461-2

Coit, Stanton
    A nobler order. 6954-1
    A psalm of confidence, fr. 'The spirit of man' 6954-1
    Sound over all waters. 6954-1
Cokayne, Sir Aston
    Funeral elegy on the death of...Mr. Michael Drayton. 6933-9
    Of a mistress. 6563-5
The Col de Balm. Frances Ridley Havergal. 6749-2
Colborne, Mary
    Singing-lesson. 6698-4
Colborne-Veel, Mary
    The blessing. 6784-0
    Empty houses. 6784-0
    Song of the trees. 6784-0
    We go no more to the forest. 6784-0
Colburn, John Edward
    The soul's awakening. 7030-2
Colby, Joan
    Equestrienne. 6966-5
    The magician. 6966-5
Colby, Merle
    Order of service. 6780-8
Colby, Vine
    The rainbow. 6019-6
Colcord, Lincoln
    The fishing fleet. 6653-4
    Vision of war. 6542-2
Colcord, Millie
    Lift's weaving. 6926-6
Cold. Robert Francis. 6388-8
"Cold - cold! The wind howls fierce without". Bothwell. William Edmonstoune Aytoun. 6948-7
"Cold and clear-cut face...", fr. Maud. Alfred Lord Tennyson. 6122-2
"Cold and raw the north wind doth blow". Unknown. 6904-5
"Cold blew the wind along the street". What a Christmas carol did. T.A. Harcourt. 6917-7
Cold blows the wind. Unknown. 6061-7
Cold colloquy. Patrick Anderson. 6446-9
Cold consolation. Eugene Field. 6949-5
"The cold earth slept below". Lines ("The cold earth"). Percy Bysshe Shelley. 6315-2
"A cold eerie silence..." Melanie Baril. 6883-9
"Cold falls the dew,/Bright stars now gleam". Sleep boys in blue. James Abraham Martling. 6952-5
Cold front. E.M. Bennett. 7018-3
Cold harvest. Frances Taylor Patterson. 6761-1
The cold heaven. William Butler Yeats. 6375-6
"Cold Heritique Y." Unknown. 6563-5
Cold iron. Rudyard Kipling. 6532-5,6655-0
"Cold man, in whom no animating ray". To a logician. Abraham Cowley. 7014-0
"Cold mist, o'er a gray sea swelling". Impressions. Jean Mutter. 6799-9
A cold night. Kuno Meyer. 6582-1
A cold night. Bernard Spencer. 6666-6
"Cold on Canadian hills or Minden's plain". The child of misery, fr. The country justice. John Langhorne. 6934-7
"The cold strikes through me...morning comes". Winter sonnets. Witter Bynner. 6782-4
"The cold that put an end to crops". Crops. Charles Malam. 6761-1
Cold water. Lydia Huntley Sigourney. 6617-8
Cold water. Unknown. 6787-5
Cold water boys. Emma Celia & Lizzie J. Rook. 6137-0
The cold wind. Nora Hopper. 6174-5
"The cold winds swept the mountain's height". The snow-storm. Unknown. 6752-2
"Cold winter ice is fled". Summer. Unknown. 6102-8
Cold winter night. Unknown. 6826-X
"Cold's the wind,...", fr. The shoemaker's holiday. Thomas Dekker. 6198-2,6383-7
"Cold, cold is the north wind and rude..blast". The battle of Lovell's pond. Henry Wadsworth Longfellow. 6946-0
"Cold, cold!/Cold tonight is broad Moylurg". A song of winter. Unknown. 6930-4
Cold, cold, cold. Patrick Byrne. 6475-2
Cold, sharp lamentation. Douglas Hyde. 6244-X

"Cold, stiff, and dead, thou liest to-day". In memoriam - Jockie. John Veitch. 6819-7
"The cold-blooded deed upon the helpless". Kishineff and Port Arthur. Edward Sydney Tybee. 6848-0
The cold-water man. John Godfrey Saxe. 6165-6
"The cold.../With steely clutch". Winter. Adelaide Crapsey. 6891-X
Cole, A.B.
    Mr. Jonathan Bangs. 6919-3
Cole, Charlotte Druitt
    Christmas eve. 6216-4
o Cole, Eddie-Lou
    Wisteria scent. 6857-X
Cole, Elsie
    Song of the foot-track. 6784-0
Cole, Helen Wieand
    Gifts. 6144-3
    An old prima donna speaks. 6799-9
    Peace on earth. 6144-3
Cole, Jane Broad
    Christmas Day at sunset. 6764-6
Cole, Kathryne
    Patterns in our hearts. 6750-6
Cole, Mamie Gene
    The child's appeal. 6337-3
Cole, Margaret
    Treachery. 6339-X
Cole, Maud Wynn
    The Bulbul. 6800-6
    The preference. 6800-6
Cole, Robert Germain
    Song ("Bud into blossom"). 6118-4
    Spiritus intactus. 6118-4
Cole, Samuel Valentine
    Abraham Lincoln. 6449-3
    Half-mast the flag. 6995-9
    Hammer and anvil. 6266-0,6303-9
    His last victory. 6523-6
    Roosevelt. 6449-3
    The trees ("There's something in a noble tree--"). 6338-1,6374-8
Cole, Thomas
    By the beautiful sea. 6388-8
    Old woman's song. 6388-8
    Praise to light. 6388-8
Coleman, Anita Scott
    American Negra. 6178-8
    Black faces. 6178-8
    The colorist. 6178-8
    Hands. 6178-8
    Humility. 6178-8
    Portraiture. 6818-9
Coleman, Charles W.
    Love's going. 6770-0
Coleman, Helena
    Among the pines. 6591-0,6592-2
    As day begins to wane. 6021-8,6115-X
    Beyond the violet rays. 6115-X
    Dawn. 6591-0,6592-2
    Day and night. 6115-X
    Enlargement. 6115-X
    Forest tragedy. 6591-0,6592-2
    Indian summer. 6115-X
    The living dead. 6796-4
    More lovely grows the earth. 6115-X
    Night among the Thousand Isles. 6591-0,6592-2
    On the trail. 6591-0,6592-2,6433-7
    The pelican. 6591-0,6592-2
    Prairie hills. 6115-X
    The prospector. 6591-0,6592-2
    To a bluebell. 6115-X
Coleman, Jamye H.
    Impossibility. 6178-8
    The swing of life. 6178-8
Coleman, Lucille
    Echoes of Jesus. 6144-3
Coleman, Marion Moore (tr.)
    All. Antoni Slonimski, 6068-4
    Chopin's motherland. Stanislaw Balinski, 6068-4
Coleridge. Teodore Watts-Dunton. 6437-X,6483-3,6656-9

COLERIDGE

Coleridge and his child, fr. Frost at midnight. Samuel Taylor Coleridge. 6545-7
Coleridge's sky. Samuel Taylor Coleridge. 7020-5
Coleridge, E.P. (tr.)
    Oedipus at Colonus, sels. Sophocles, 6484-1
Coleridge, Ernest Hartley
    Experto crede. 6084-6,6085-4
    Song ("I lost my love long years ago"). 6785-9
Coleridge, Hartley
    Address to certain gold-fishes. 6219-9
    The birth of speech. 6656-9
    Boyhood and girlhood. 6233-4
    Childhood. 6772-7
    Childhood. 6233-4
    Early death. 6337-3
    Fear. 6980-0
    The first birthday. 6233-4
    "Full well I know..." 6380-2
    Hagar. 6848-0
    "Hast thou not seen an aged rifted tower". 6980-0
    "He lived amidst th' untrodden ways". 6802-2
    "How shall a man fore-doomed to lone estate" 6380-2
    Ideality. 6656-9
    "If I have sinn'd in act, I may repent" 6380-2
    Isaiah 046: 9 6848-0
    Jesus praying. 6337-3
    "Long time a child, and still a child, when years". 6980-0,6380-2
    May, 1840. 6437-X,6383-7,6543-0
    "Multum dilexit" 6214-8,6656-9
    Night. 6219-9
    Night. 6380-2
    Not in vain. 7015-9
    November. 6315-2,6465-5,6271-7,6271-7
    Of such is the kingdom of God. 6233-4
    'Of such is the kingdom of God'. 6772-7
    On infancy. 6233-4
    Prayer. 6737-9
    Prayer ("Be not afraid to pray"). 6337-3,6202-4,6337-3
    Prayer ("There is an awful quiet in the air"). 7015-9
    Prayer ("There is an awful"). 7015-9
    Questionings. 6233-4
    Religious unity. 6337-3
    The sabbath day's child. 6772-7
    The Sabbath day's child. 6233-4
    Sense, if you can find it. 6648-8
    "She is not fair to outward view" 6092-7,6219-9,6560-0
    "She is not fair to outward view." 6302-0,6385-3,6187-7, 6246-5
    Sin. 7015-9
    Song. 6543-0
    Song ("'Tis sweet"). 6219-9
    Song ("She is not fair"). 6107-9,6271-7,6437-X,6604-6, 6301-2,6423-X,6332-2,6271-7,6437-X,6604-6,6107
    Song ("The lark"). 6271-7
    Sonnet. 6543-0
    Sonnet ("Hast thou not"). 6545-7
    Sonnet ("How shall a man"). 6545-7
    Sonnet ("Long time"). 6832-4
    Sonnet ("The dark green"). 6545-7
    Stanzas. 6543-0
    Summer rain. 6543-0
    "'Tis strange to me, who long have seen no face" 6380-2
    To a deaf and dumb little girl. 6543-0
    To a friend. 6980-0
    To a lofty beauty, from her poor kinsman. 6437-X,6543-0
    To a proud kinswoman. 6092-7
    To Shakespeare. 6980-0
    To Shakespeare. 6483-3,6656-9
    To the nautilus. 6656-9
    "What is young Passion but a gusty breeze" 6380-2
    "What was't awaken'd first the untried ear". 6980-0
    Whither is gone the wisdom. 6199-9
    Whither is gone the wisdom and the power. 6934-7
    Whither? 6656-9
Coleridge, Hartley (tr.)
    The might of one face fair. Michelangelo Buonarroti, 6226-1
Coleridge, Mary Elizabeth
    After St. Augustine. 6337-3,6641-0
    Ah, I have striven, I have striven. 6186-9
    Blue and white. 6437-X
    The blue bird. 6134-6
    Chillingham. 6477-9
    The deserted house. 6512-0
    "Egypt's might is tumbled down". 6395-0,6186-9,6339-X
    Gibberish. 6477-9
    Gone. 6437-X
    "He knoweth not that the dead are thine." 6507-4
    A Huguenot. 6477-9,6437-X,6250-4,6639-9
    "I saw a stable, low and very bare". 6931-2
    In London town. 6861-8
    Jealousy. 6507-4
    The king. 6437-X
    L'oiseau bleu. 6253-9
    "Lord of the winds, I cry to thee". 6931-2
    A moment. 6102-8
    Mortal combat. 6437-X
    A mother to a baby. 6844-8
    Night is fallen within, without. 6186-9
    O the high valley, the little low hill. 6186-9
    On such a day. 6317-9,6246-5
    Our lady. 6844-8,6437-X,6746-8
    Prosperity. 6134-6
    Punctilio. 6437-X
    Self-question. 6507-4
    Song ("Thy hand"). 6320-9
    Street lanterns. 6044-7,6477-9
    'There was no place found'. 6931-2
    To memory. 6186-9
    Unity. 6186-9
    Unwelcome. 6246-5,6437-X,6507-4
    We were not made for refuges of lies. 6186-9
    The weapon. 6339-X
    Where a Roman villa stood, above Freiburg. 6477-9,6088-9
    "Whether I live, or whether I die". 6844-8
    The witch. 6246-5,6380-2
Coleridge, Robert Southey and Samuel Taylor
    The devil's walk. 6200-8
Coleridge, Samuel Taylor
    "Alas! They had been friends in youth" 6935-5
    Alice du Clos. 6677-1
    Alvar's address to the spirits of the dead. 6828-6
    <u>The ancient mariner among the dead bodies of sailors.</u> 6543-0
    The ancient mariner finds a voice to bless and pray. 6543-0
    The ancient mariner, sel. 6958-4
    The ancient mariner, sels. 6317-9
    The ancient mariner. 6023-4,6197-4,6133-8,6138-9
    Answer to a child's question. 6302-0,6385-3,6519-8,6133-8,6138-9,6066-8,6135-4,6638-0,6449-3,6424-8,6131-1
    Avaro. 6278-4
    Bad poets. 6278-4
    The ballad of the dark ladie. 6527-9,6110-9,6086-2
    Beelzebub and Job. 6278-4
    Before sunrise, in the vale of Chamouni. 6749-2
    "Believe thou, O my soul", fr. Religious musings. 6545-7
    The best prayer. 6543-0
    The breeze after the calm. 6543-0
    The butterfly. 6086-2
    Catullian hendecasyllales. 6204-0
    Chamouny. 6425-6,6606-2
    Character. 6438-8
    Charity in thought. 6722-0
    A child's evening prayer. 6131-1
    Choral song of Illrian peasants. 6133-8
    Christabel. 6198-2,6196-6,6430-2,6250-4,6199-0,6245 , 6646-1,6518-X,6723-9,6219-9,6110-9,6086 ,6473-6,6600-3,6634-8
    Christabel, sels. 6332-2,6726-3,6138-9,6369-1,6543-0, 6301
    A Christmas carol. 6931-2
    A Christmas carol. 6282-2
    A Christmas carol. 6931-2
    Clycine's song. 6086-2
    Coleridge and his child, fr. Frost at midnight. 6545-7
    Coleridge's sky. 7020-5

Cologne. 6089-7,6302-0,6385-3,6722-0,6732-8,6271-7,6092-7,6088-9,6219-9,6439-6
Complaint. 6722-0
The composition of a kiss. 6967-3
Concealment. 6980-0
A day-dream. 6543-0
Dead calm at sea. 6304-7
Dead calm in the tropics. 6543-0
Dejection: an ode. 6828-6
Dejection: an ode. 6315-2,6430-2,6199-0,6271-7,6378-0, 6086-2,6110-9,6208-3,6536-8
The dell. 6935-5
The desired swan-song. 6722-0
A desultory poem, written on the Christmas eve of 1794 6828-6
The devil's thoughts. 6271-7,6092-7,6219-9
"Do you ask what the birds say?" 6793-X
Domestic peace. 6543-0
A dream of spring. 6654-2
The dungeon, fr. Osorio, Act V. 6332-2
The eolian harp. 6828-6
The Eolian harp. 6545-7
Epigram. 6219-9
Epigrams. 6385-3
Epitaph on an infant. 6967-3
Epitaph. 6828-6
Epitaph. 6199-0
Epitaph on an infant. 6365-9
Epitaph on an infant. 6772-7
Epitaph on himself. 6102-8,6301-2,6337-3,6931-2
An eternal poem. 6278-4,6089-7
The exchange. 6722-0
The exchange. 6828-6
The exchange. 6092-7,6430-2
Expectoration the second. 6278-4
An expectoration. 6278-4
Fancy in Nubibus. 7015-9
Fancy in Nubibus. 6219-9,6250-4
Fancy in Nubibus. 7015-9
Fancy in Nubibus. 6302-0;6385-3
Fears in solitude. 6828-6
Fears in solitude, sels. 6527-9.6052-8,6369-1
Florence. 6624-0
The foster-mother's tale. 6967-3
Fragment ("Encinctur'd"). 6545-7
France, sels. 6198-2
France: an ode. 6828-6
France: an ode. 6192-3,6196-6,6430-2,6071-4
Friendship, fr. Christabel. 6332-2
Frost at midnight. 6208-3,6199-0,6430-2,6052-8,6378-0, 6233-4,6315-2,6634-8
Frost at midnight, sels. 6395-0
The garden of Boccaccio. 6828-6
The garden of Boccaccio. 6086-2,6110-9,6199-0
Genevieve. 6302-0,6385-3,6543-0,6102-8,6438-8,6219-9, 6600-3
Giles' hope. 6996-7
Giles's hope. 6089-7
Glycine's song. 6383-7,6395-0
Glycine's song, fr. Zapolya. 6828-6
The good great man. 6302-0,6385-3,6271-7,6604-6,6214-8, 6660 ,6110-9,6199-0,6219-9,6304-7,6737-9,6605
The good, great man. 6828-6
A green and silent spot. 6793-X
A grove. 6793-X
The happy husband. 6543-0
"He prayeth best who loveth best". 6466-3,6479-5,6238-5, 6337-3,6502-3,6456
Hexameters, sels. 6395-0
The hour when we shall meet again. 6967-3
The house that Jack built. 6440-X,6089-7
Hunting song. 6132-X,6519-8
Hymn ("Hast thou a charm to stay the morning-star"). 6331-4
Hymn ("Hast thou a charm to stay.") 6214-8
Hymn before sunrise in the vale of Chamouni. 6302-0, 6385-3,6240-7,6198-2,6600-3,6332 ,6271-7,6484-1,6730-1,6102-8,6337-3,6424 ,6086-2,6110-9,6219-9,6252-0, 6543-0
Hymn before sunrise, in the vale of Chamouni. 6192-3, 6430-2,6560-0
If I had but two little wings. 6479-5
"If I had but two little wings" 6935-5
In the manner of Spencer. 6967-3
Inscription for a fountain on a heath. 6196-6,6421-3, 6430-2,6332-2
An invocation, fr. Remorse. 6828-6
An invocation. 6430-2
"It sounds like stories from the land of spirits". 6238-5
Job. 6874-X
Job. 6089-7
Job's luck. 6848-0
Julia. 6278-4
The kiss. 6967-3
The knight's tomb. 6828-6
The knight's tomb. 6239-3,6102-8,6219-9,6301-2,6639-9, 6199 ,6023-4,6383-7,6302-0,6385-3,6134-4,6395-0,6732-8
Kubla Khan. 6154-0,6424-8,6639-9,6543-0,6464-7,6646 , 6491-4,6645-3,6634-8,6536-8,6430-2,6726 ,6179-6,6198-2,6358-6,6369-1,6501-5,6527 ,6052-8,6075-7,6102-8, 6138-9,6238-4,6271 ,6186-9,6187-7,6208-3,6228-8,6236-9,6239 ,6086-2,6560-0,6192-3,6199-0,6125-7,6252 , 6110-9,6150-8,6153-2,6219-9,6114-1,6438 ,6301-2,6396-6,6196-6,6289-X,6302-0,6315 ,6332-2,6339-X,6395-0, 6423-X,6427-2,6473 ,6481-7,6488-4
La Fayette. 6828-6
La Fayette. 6110-9
Lessons for a boy. 6512-0
A letter to Sara Hutchinson [Dejection]. 6380-2
Lewti. 6828-6
Lewti, or the Circassian love chant. 6110-9
Life. 6110-9
The life of nature, fr. Dejection: an ode. 6545-7
Limbo. 6378-0
Lines. 6828-6
Lines addressed to a friend, in answer to..melancholy letter. 6967-3
Lines composed at Clevedon. 6967-3
Lines on observing a blossom. 6967-3
Lines on an autumnal evening. 6110-9
Lines to a beautiful spring in a village. 6967-3
Lines to a friend who died of a frenzy fever. 6967-3
Lines to Joseph Cottle. 6967-3
Lines written at the King's Arms, Ross. 6967-3
Lines written at Elbingerode. 6484-1,6086-2
A little child, a limber elf. 6315-2
A little child, fr. Christable. 6934-7
Love. 6246-5,6676-3,6732-8,6271-7,6086-2,6110 ,6219-9, 6543-0,6301-2,6430-2,6560-0,6110-9,6199-0,6250-4
Love. 6315-2
Love, hope, and patience in education. 6086-2
Love, sels. 6317-9
Lovely in decay, fr. Remorse. 6545-7
Metrical feet. 6302-0;6385-3
Monody on the death of Chatterton. 6967-3
Monody on the death of Chatterton. 6483-3
Mont Blanc before sunrise. 6183-4,6571-6
Mother and child. 6097-8
"The moving moon went up the sky". 6395-0
Mythology. 6304-7
Names. 6092-7
Ne plus ultra. 6378-0
The new moon. 7020-5
Nightingale, sels. 6125-7
The nightingale. 6086-2,6271-7,6378-0
The nightingale. 6828-6
Ode on the departing year. 6967-3
Ode to Sara. 6967-3
Ode to the departing year. 6828-6
Ode to tranquility. 6110-9,6086-2
Ode to tranquillity. 6828-6
Of a bad singer. 7025-6
On a bad singer. 6089-7
On Donne's poetry. 6430-2,6483-3
On his baptismal birthday. 6337-3
On the christening of a friend's child. 6967-3
Opium jottings, fr. The Gutch memorandum book. 6545-7
Osorio, sels. 6332-2

COLERIDGE

The pains of sleep. 6086-2,6199-0,6430-2,6380-2,6086-2, 6110-9,6199-0
Part the fifth. 6943-6
Part the fourth. 6943-6
Part the second. 6943-6
Part the seventh. 6943-6
Part the sixth. 6943-6
Part the third. 6943-6
Peace on earth. 6147-8
Pensive at eve. 6491-4
Phantom. 6378-0,6641-0,6648-8
Phantom or fact. 6828-6
Phantom or fact. 6110-9
Phantom, sels. 6369-1
Praying and loving. 6424-8,6124-8
Protest against the ballet. 6199-0
The quarrel of friends, fr. Christabel. 6302-0,6385-3
The raven and the oak. 6133-8,6131-1
Rebellion, fr. France: an ode. 6545-7
Reflections on having left a place of retirement. 6828-6
Reflections on having left a place of retirement. 6110-9,6250-4
Religious musings. 6730-1
Religious musings, sels. 6828-6
A rhymester. 6089-7
The rime of the ancient mariner, sel. 6935-5
The rime of the ancient mariner, sels. 6228-8,6258-X, 6501-5,6369-1
The rime of the ancient mariner. 6136-2,6186-9,6198-2, 6302-0,6332-2,6385 ,6154-0 6179-6,6427-2,6473-6,6536-8,6732 ,6488-4,6547-3,6726-3,6723-9,6646-1,6660 , 6153-2,6301-2,6518-X,6086-2,6110-9,6196-6,6430-2, 6560-0,6371 ,6199-0,6458-2,6604-6,6150-8,6219-9,6250 ,6052-8,6271-7,6075-7,6101-X,6102-8,6552
Romance. 6322-5
The rose. 6967-3
The sacred river, fr. Kubla Khan. 7020-5
"The sea-breeze moans". 6997-5
Sentimental. 6278 4
Severed friendship. 6543-0
The sigh. 6967-3
The silent sea. 7020-5
The snow-drop. 6641-0
Something childish but very natural. 6874-X
Song ("A sunny shaft"). 6317-9
Song ("Hear, sweet spirit"). 6086-2,6271-7,6545-7
Song ("Though veiled"). 6545-7
Song from Osorio. 6110-9
Song of the pixies. 6250-4
Song, by Glycine, fr. Zapolya. 6645-3
Song, fr. Osorio. 6332-2
Song, fr. Zapolya. 6110-9
Songs of the pixies. 6932-0
Sonnet. 6543-0
Sonnet ("My heart"). 6967-3
Sonnet ("Thou gentle look"). 6967-3
Sonnet ("Sweet mercy"). 6967-3
Sonnet ("Pale roamer"). 6967-3
Sonnet ("The piteous sobs"). 6967-3
Sonnet ("As when"). 6832-4
Sonnet composed while climbing...Brockley Coomb. 6967-3
Sonnet composed on a journey homeward. 6967-3,6832-4
Sonnet on a discovery made too late. 6967-3
Sonnet to the river Otter. 6967-3
Sonnet to the author of The Robbers. 6967-3
Sonnet to a friend, who asked how I felt..my infant to me. 6967-3
Sonnet to a friend who asked how I felt... 6365-9
Sonnet: on a ruined house in a romantic country. 6802-2
Sonnet: to simplicity. 6802-2
Sonnets attempted in the manner of contemporary writers. 6802-2
Sonnets, attempted in the manner of Bowles, sels. 6967-3
"The stilly murmur of the distant sea". 6997-5
"The storms and overwhelming waves". 6997-5
Swans sing. 6339-X
Tell me, on what holy ground. 6328-4
They had been firends. 6085-4

They had been friends in youth, fr. Christabel. 6934-7
This lime-tree bower my prison. 6315-2
This lime-tree bower my prison. 6828-6
This lime-tree bower my prison. 6086-2,6110-9
Thither where he lies buried. 6066-8
Time, real and imaginary. 6533-3,6086-2,6383-7,6250-4
Time, real and immaginary. 6832-4
To a friend, together with an unfinished poem. 6967-3
To a lady. 6278-4
To a young ass. 6967-3
To a young lady, with a poem on the French Revolution. 6967-3
To a young ass. 6932-0, 6828-6
To an infant. 6967-3
To an infant. 6233-4
To an unfortunate woman. 6967-3
To C. Llyod, on his proposing to domesticate with the author. 6967-3
To nature. 6337-3
To the author of The robbers. 6483-3
To the author of The robbers (Schiller). 7015-9
To the Reverend W. L. Bowles. 6828-6
To William Wordsworth. 6483-3,6110-9
Town and country. 7020-5
The two friends. 6084-6
"Verse, a breeze 'mid blossoms straying" 6935-5
The Virgin's cradle-hymn. 6095-1
What is an epigram. 6527-9
"What is an epigram? A dwarfish whole". 6850-2
What the birds say. 6529-5,6018-8,6524-4
Whom the untaught shepherds. 6328-4
Work without hope. 6660-7,6737-9
Work without hope. 6828-6
Work without hope. 6315-2,6196-6,6250-4,6199-0,6513-9, 6545 ,6383-7,6604-6,6086-2,6110-9,6301-2
"The world so hushed!" 6997-5
"Ye clouds! That far above me float and pause" 6935-5
"You crescent moon as fixed as if it grew". 6395-0
Youth and age. 6828-6
Youth and age. 6246-5,6604-6,6250-4,6639-9,6543-0,6660 , 6086-2,6110-9,6199-0,6219-9,6371-3

Coleridge, Samuel Taylor (tr.)
The astrological tower. Johann C. Friedrich von Schiller, 6142-7
The belief in astrology. Johann C. Friedrich von Schiller, 6606-2
Dirge. Johann C. Friedrich von Schiller, 6438-8
"He is gone,--is dust!" Johann C. Friedrich von Schiller, 6606-2
Heroism. Johann C. Friedrich von Schiller, 6438-8
"Is it possible" Johann C. Friedrich von Schiller, 6606-2
Israel's lament. Hyman Hurwitz, 6848-0
Mythology. Johann C. Friedrich von Schiller, 6438-8
The tears of a grateful people. Hyman Hurwitz, 6848-0
Thekla's song. Johann C. Friedrich von Schiller, 6328-4
Thekla's song, fr. The piccolomini. Johann C. Friedrich von Schiller, 7039-6
To Lesbia. Caius Catallus, 6879-0
Westphalian song. Unknown (German), 7039-6

Coleridge, Sara
Birds' food. 6334-9
Birds' food, sels. 6334-9
The child. 6233-4,6365-9
A dedication. 6233-4
Edith alseep. 6233-4
The garden year. 6466-3
The garden year. 6649-6
Lines on the common saying that love is blind. 7037-X
The months. 6114-1,6529-5
The mother. 6437-X
O sleep, my babe! 6233-4,6365-9,6533-3
Phantasmion. 6656-9
Phantasmion's quest of Iarine. 7015-9,7037-X,7015-9, 7037-X
Phantasmion, sels. 7037-X
Song ("He came"). 6437-X
Song ("How high yon lark..."), fr. Phantasmion. 7037-X
Trees. 6262-8
Trees ("The oak is called the king of tree,"). 6466-3

Zelneth's lament, fr. Phantasmion. 7037-X
Coleridge, Stephen
   Loss. 6785-9
Coles, Abraham
   Dies irae. 6302-0
   The Microcosm, sels. 6482-5
Coles, Abraham (tr.)
   Psalm 011. Bible, 6848-0
   Psalm 044. Bible, 6848-0
   Psalm 052. Bible, 6848-0
   Psalm 064. Bible, 6848-0
   Psalm 076. Bible, 6848-0
   Psalm 078. Bible, 6848-0
   Psalm 092. Bible, 6848-0
   Psalm 098. Bible, 6848-0
   Psalm 099. Bible, 6848-0
   Psalm 106. Bible, 6848-0
   Psalm 109. Bible, 6848-0
   Psalm 110. Bible, 6848-0
   Psalm 119. Bible, 6848-0
   Psalm 122. Bible, 6848-0
   Psalm 141. Bible, 6848-0
   Psalm 146. Bible, 6848-0
   Stabat mater dolorosa. Jacopone da Todi (Jacobus de Benedictus), 6302-0
Coles, Andrew
   "The good, the brave/Whose mighty dust in glory sleeps" 6712-3
Coles, Don
   Photo. 6767-0
Coles, John F.
   What the temperance cause has done for John and me. 6914-2
Colestock, William L.
   The woes of a rookie. 6846-4
Colesworthy, Daniel Clement
   Don't kill the birds. 6356-X,6373-X,6456-6
   "A little word in kindness spoken". 6238-5
   A little word. 6654-2
Colesworthy, J.
   Trifles. 6373-X
Coley, Louis B.
   A good name more desirable than riches. 6690-9
Colin. Anthony Munday. 6122-2,6198-2,6732-8,6246-6
Colin and Lucy. Thomas Tickell. 6133-8,6152-4,6219-9
Colin Clout at court, fr. Colin Clout's come home again. Edmund Spenser. 6436-1
Colin Clout's come home again, sels. Edmund Spenser. 6258-X,6436-1
Colin Clout's songs, sels. Edmund Spenser. 6935-5
Colin Clout, sels. John Skelton. 6198-2,6586-4
Colin's cattle. Malcolm MacFarlane. 6180-X
Colin's complaint. Nicholas Rowe. 6932-0,6867-7
Colin's passion of love. George Peele. 6436-1
Colinette. Andrew Lang. 6771-9
Coliseum by moonlight. George Gordon, 6th Baron Byron. 6302-0,6358-6,6385-3
The Coliseum, sels, fr. Childe Harold's pilgrimage. George Gordon, 6th Baron Byron. 6196-6
The coliseum.. Edgar Allan Poe. 6126-5,6121-4,6331-4,6624-0,6439-6,6631-3,6288-1
The Coliseum. George Gordon, 6th Baron Byron. 6424-8,6302-0,6332-2,6385-3,6484-1,6624-0,6199
Coll, Aloysius
   Christmas in the forest. 7035-3
   Washington. 6034-X
Collage of us in May windows. Paul Fericano. 6901-0
"A collar and a tie should deck". The careless bottle. Carolyn Wells. 6882-0
the collar, sels. George Herbert. 6501-5
The collar. George Herbert. 6341-1,6214-8,6660-7,6189-3, 6723-9,6198-2,6208-3,6052-8,6122-2,6315-2,6337 ,6339-X,6378-0,6527-9,6562-7,6563-5,6604 ,6726-3,6194-4, 6430-2,6250-4,6150-8,6645
Collat, Ruth
   Questions. 6368-3
   Questions ("I visited the animals"). 6368-3,6539-2
Collect calls. Diana Bickston. 6870-7
collect for Dominion day. Sir Charles George Douglas Roberts. 7041-8

Collect for Dominion Day. Sir Charles George Douglas Roberts. 6795-6
The collection. Ernest Howard Crosby. 6954-1
The collector's discontent. Eugene Field. 6949-5
Colleen Oge Asthore. Unknown. 6930-4
Colleen Rue. Unknown. 6930-4
College 'oil cans'. Will Victor McGuire. 6920-7
"A college chap in our town". Eccentric. Unknown. 6936-3
College daughter - lonely parents. Eleanor Bates. 6718-2
College days. Carleton Hunneman. 6116-8
The college garden. Robert Bridges. 6487-6
College oil cans. Will Victor McGuire. 6963-0
A college rowing song. W.J. H. 6116-8
A college training. Joseph Crosby Lincoln. 6119-2
A college widow. Unknown. 6116-8
The collegian and the porter. James Robinson Planche. 6909-6,6787-5
The collegian and the porter. Horace Smith. 6760-3
The collegian to his bride. Unknown. 6385-3
"Collen say why sittst thou soe." Unknown. 6563-5
Coller, Edwin
   The blind poet's wife. 6744-1
   Mrs. Jones's lodger. 6918-5
   Mrs. Jones's lodger. 6918-5
   Not in the programme. 6416-7
   Sal Parker's ghost. 6744-1
   Sal Parker's ghost. 6918-5
   Told at The Falcon. 6925-8
Collester, Clinton H.
   Ephraim's storm lullaby. 6118-4
   Indian summer. 6118-4
   The morning sprite. 6118-4
   Robbie Rockaway. 6118-4
   Song of the trip-hammer. 6118-4
The collier's wife. David Herbert Lawrence. 6257-1
Collier, Johnra
   Isadora Duncan. 6959-2
Collier, Thomas S.
   The forgotten books. 6297-0
   Life's triumph. 6273-3
   Nelly tells how baby came. 6713-1,6273-3
   Not lost. 6632-1
   One land, one flag, one brotherhood. 6223-7
   The spectre ship. 6833-2
The collier. Vernon Watkins. 6210-5,6360-8
Collige rosas. William Ernest Henley. 6437-X,6513-9
Collin, David
   Pylons. 6783-2
Collingwood, W.G.
   A saint in disguise. 6747-6
Collins, Anne
   "The winter being over." 6302-0,6385-3,6271-7
Collins, Barbara Ruth
   Tulip blooms. 6799-9
Collins, Dean
   'Whose spirit is sped' 6995-9
Collins, Effie B.
   Clean windows. 6764-6
Collins, Emily
   Autumn leaves. 6764-6
Collins, Hazel Reese
   Consolation. 6799-9
Collins, John
   The golden farmer. 6874-X
   Good old things. 6874-X
   In the down-hill of life. 6219-9
   To-morrow. 6246-5,6086-2,6092-7
Collins, Michael
   On a painting by patient b. 6900-2
Collins, Mortimer
   Ad chloen, M.A. 6089-7,6092-7
   Chloe, M.A. 6089-7
   Comfort. 6385-3,6652-6
   A conceit. 6273-3
   A conceit. 6652-6
   Darwin. 6385-3
   The first of April. 6047-1,6274-1
   A game of chess. 6658-5
   A Greek idyl. 6656-9
   If. 6089-7,6440-X

COLLINS

If. 6802-2
The ivory gate. 6656-9
Kate Temple's song. 6656-9
Martial in London. 6089-7,6026-9
Merlin. 6383-7
Monorhymed alphabet ("A is my Amy, so slender..."). 6724-7
Multum in Parvo. 6658-5
My aunt's spectre. 6089-7,6652-6
My thrush. 6510-4,6073-0
The positivists. 6089-7
The positivists. 6996-7,7025-6
Queen and slave. 6437-X
Salad. 6089-7
Salad: beard. 6802-2
Salad: brow. 6802-2
Salad: hair. 6802-2
Shirley Chase. 6046-3
Sky-making. 6089-7
Snow and sun. 6620-4
A summer song. 6652-6
To a very young lady. 6772-7
To F.C. 6658-5
Two worlds. 6240-7
Violets at home. 6658-5

Collins, William
Curst be the gold and silver, fr. Persian eclogues. 6934-7
Dirge. 6639-9
Dirge for Fidele. 6092-7
Dirge in Cymbeline. 6291-9,6543-0,6250-4,6600-3,6271-7, 6604-6,6153-2,6086-2,6438
An epistle addressed to Sir Thomas Hanmer, sels. 6195-0
Fidele's dirge. 6102-8,6383-7,6301-2
How sleep the brave. 6186-9,6424-8,6102-8,6328-4,6502-3, 6114 ,6304-7,6421-3,6131-1,6219-9,6301-2,6601 ,6240-7,6395-0,6323-3,6340-3,6427-2,6479-5,6504-X,6302-0, 6385-3,6239-3,6889-8
"If aught of oaten stop, or pastoral song". 6187-7
The lookout. 6833-7
Molly Maguire at Monmouth. 6286-5,6267-9,6470-1
Ode. 6641-0,6150-8,6371-3,6668-2
Ode ("How sleep the brave"). 6228-8,6271-7,6250-4,6430-2,6438-4,6242 ,6024-2,6473-6,6315-2
Ode on the death of Mr. Thomson. 6219-9,6438-8,6483-3, 6024-2
Ode on the passions. 6567-8,6294-6,6606-2
Ode on the poetical character. 6152-4,6195-0,6430-2
Ode on the popular superstitions of the highlands. 6208-3,6102-8,6152-4,6086-2,6195-0,6430 ,6198-2
Ode to evening. 6152-4,6192-3,6430-2,6191-5,6024-2,6491-4,6543-0,6645-3,6052-8,6102 ,6023-1,6086-2,6152-4, 6150-8,6153-2,6291 ,6154-0,6371-3,6646-1,6660-7,6301-2,6430 ,6195-0,6192-3,6250-4,6192-3,6438-2, 6186-9,6198-2,6208-3,6289-X,6315-2, 6334 ,6473-6,6488-4,6527-9,6536-8,6600-3,6634 ,6726-3,6385-3,6334-9, 6024-2,6491-4,6543-0,6645-3,6052-8,6102 ,6023-1,6086-2,6152-4,6150-8,6153-2,6291 ,6154-0,6371-3,6646-1, 6660-7,6301-2,6430 ,6195-0,6192-3,6250-4,6192-3,6438-8,6732 ,6186-9,6198-2,6208-3,6289-X,6315-2,6334 , 6473-6,6488-4,6527-9,6536-8,6600-3,6634 ,6726-3,6385-3,6334-9
Ode to fear. 6152-4,6195-0,6430-2
Ode to mercy. 6543-0
Ode to music. 6143-5
Ode to pity. 6152-4,6383-7
Ode to simplicity. 6086-2,6152-4,6195-0,6024-2
Ode to the passions. 6315-2,6621-6
Ode written in 1746. 6195-0,6135-4,6527-9,6075-7,6527-9, 6246-5,6634-8,6726-3,6732-8,6527-9,6075-7,6527-9, 6246-5,6634-8,6726-3,6732-8
Ode written in the beginning of the year 1746. 6198-2, 6604-6,6086-2,6639-9,6660-7,6737-6,6153-2,6154-0, 6198-2,6604-6,6086-2,6639-9,6660-7,6737-6,6153-2, 6154-0
Ode: written in the beginning of the year 1746. 6154-0
On the death of Thomson. 6543-0
Oriental eclogues, sels. 6195-0
The passions. 6415-9,6152-4,6195-0,6250-4,6245-8,6543 , 6660-7,6102-8,6271-7,6604-6,6219-9,6438 ,6198-2,6086-2,6246-5,6302-0,6385-3,6154-0,6693-3
Persian eclogues, sels. 6152-4
Persian eclogues, sels. 6152-4
A song from Shakespeare's Cymbelyne. 6198-2,6641-0,6195-0,6152-4,6192-3,6430
To evening. 6246-5,6075-7
To music, fr. The passions. 6934-7
"Who shall awake the Spartan fife" 6935-5

"**Collision**: two seconds before, I saw the dark". Night Mare. Anita Endrezze-Danielson. 7005-1

Collop, John
The leper cleansed. 6102-8
Man a microcosm. 6482-5
To the soul. 6102-8,6023-6

Colloque metaphysique. Babette Deutsch. 6037-4
Colloque sentimentale. Paul Verlaine. 6343-8
Colloquy. Al-Munsafi. 6362-4
Colloquy. Emily Dickinson. 6076-5,6102-8
Colloquy for the states. Archibald MacLeish. 6761-1
'**Colloquy** of the ancients,' sels. Unknown. 6930-4
Colloquy on a cab-stand. Unknown. 6278-4
Colloquy on a hill top. Frances Angevine Gray. 6789-1
Colloquy with a Polish aunt, fr. Pecksniffiana. Wallace Stevens. 6531-7
A **colloquy** with God. Sir Thomas Browne. 6563-5
Collor in the wheat. Hamlin Garland. 6964-9
A **collusion** between a alegaiter and a water-snaik. J. Morris. 6438-8

Collyer, Robert
Be true. 7022-1
Saxon grit. 6263-6,6267-9,6240-7,6413-2
Under the snow. 6928-2

Colman the Younger, George
Gluggity-glug. 6385-3,6240-7
How it happened. 6302-0
Lodgings for single gentlemen. 6787-5,6760-3,6064-1
"My muse and I, ere youth and spirits fled" 6874-X
New Year's Eve. 6402-7
The Newcastle apothecary. 6787-5,6302-0,6760-3
Sir Marmaduke. 6302-0,6385-3,6271-7,6219-9
Toby tosspot. 6787-5,6787-5,6302-0,6385-3,6410-8

Colman, Sister Mary
Prayer for a silver jubilee. 6285-7

Colmon, St. (atr.)
Hymn against pestilence. Whitley Stokes and John Strachan (tr.). 6930-4

Cologne. John Bate. 6379-9
Cologne. Samuel Taylor Coleridge. 6089-7,6302-0,6385-3, 6722-0,6732-8,Y271-7,6092-7,6088-9,6219-9,6439-6
Cologne cathedral. Frances Shaw. 6509-0
"**Cologne-like** innocence that lasts too long". Straight man. Felice Picano. 7003-5
Colombine. Hugh McCrae. 6384-5
Colombine. Paul Verlaine. 6343-8
Colomen. Mary Webb. 6319-5
Colonel B. Constance Carrier. 6388-8
Colonel Burnaby. Andrew Lang. 7015-9
Colonel Ellsworth. Richard Henry Stoddard. 6946-0
Colonel Fantock. Edith Sitwell. 6250-4
Colonel Halpine's poem... George R. Russell. 6402-7
"The **colonel** has a job to do". Passing the buck. Norman E. Nygaard. 6846-4
"The **colonel** loved sweet Cicely - alas!". The colonel's orders. Robert C.V. Meyers. 6922-3
'**Colonel** on the staff.' Unknown. 6589-9
Colonel Roosevelt in Dominica. Richard Butler Glaenzer. 6995-9
The colonel's orders. Robert C.V. Meyers. 6922-3
The **colonel's** story. Robert Cameron Rogers. 7022-1
A **colonial** garden. James Benjamin Kenyon. 6338-1,6649-6
The colonial level. Unknown. 7007-8
The **colonial**. J. Edgar Middleton. 6115-X
A **colonist** in his garden. William Pember Reeves. 6591-0, 6292-9
The **colonists**. Katharine (Hinkson) Tynan. 7029-9
Colonization of Africa. John Gardiner Calkins Brainard. 6752-2
Colonized mind. Barbara Marshall. 7024-8
Colonna to the king. Richard Lalor Shiel. 6606-2

Colonna, Vittoria

"I write to soothe that inward grief alone". L.R. Lind (tr.). 6325-X
"Like some small hungry bird that sees and hears". L.R. Lind (tr.). 6325-X
Colonne, Guido Delle
Canzone: to love and to his lady. Dante Gabriel Rossetti (tr.). 6325-X
Colonos. Henry Alford. 6656-9
Colonus, fr. Oedipus. Sophocles. 6987-8
Colony, Sylvia T.
'The peace of God, which passeth any understanding'. 6270-9
Colophon. Alfred Kreymborg. 6010-2
Color. Wilfred Wilson Gibson. 6897-9
Color. Jane Blakeslee Richards. 6818-9
Color. Jeannette Sewell. 6847-2
The **color** guard. Charles W. Harwood. 6223-7
Color in November. Larah F. Wheaton. 6270-9
Color line. Leonard Bacon. 6984-3
Color notes. Charles Wharton Stork. 6338-1
Color of air. George Elliston. 6861-8
Color of dust. Ted Olson. 6039-0
Color of water. Marjorie Meeker. 6036-6
Color song. Anne Reeve Aldrich. 7041-8
Colorado. John D. Dillenbach. 6836-7
Colorado. Virginia Donaghe McClurg. 6836-7
Colorado. J. Ernest Whitney. 6836-7
Colorado anemones. Virginia Donaghe McClurg. 6836-7
The **Colorado** canyon. Georgiana Hodgkins. 6799-9
The **colored** band. Paul Laurence Dunbar. 6891-X
The **colored** dancing match. Frank Lebby Stanton. 6696-2
The **colored** marble. Benjamin Franklin Taylor. 6815-4
"A **colored** woman, bent and old and wrinkled". Aunt Caroline. Annye Lewis Allison. 6799-9
The **colorist.** Anita Scott Coleman. 6178-8
Colorland. Alice Barkley. 6789-1
"The **colorless** thin voices of the dark". Premonition. Bernice Lesbia Kenyon. 6036-6
"The **colors** come from a wonderful land". Colorland. Alice Barkley. 6789-1
The **colors** of night. N. Scott Momaday. 7005-1
"The **colors** of the rainbow". Fading away. Jessica Sybrant. 6883-9
Colour. Arthur Shearly Cripps. 6800-6
Colour. Dorothea MacKellar. 6591-0,6592-9
"The **coloured** long-shore fishermen unfurl". The gamblers. Anthony Delius. 6788-3
Colquhoun, Ithell (tr.)
Languor. Stephane Mallarme, 6343-8
The old-clothes woman. Stephane Mallarme, 6343-8
Wreathed in storm-clouds. Stephane Mallarme, 6343-8
Colson, Ethel M.
The babies are all grown. 6577-5
"**Colt** she was when I spied her, stray on...". That roan cayuse. Henry Herbert Knibbs. 7010-8
Colton, ?
Little Hal. 6889-8
Colton, Arthur
Concerning Tabitha's dancing of the minuet. 6441-8
Harps hung up in Babylon. 6310-1,6102-8,6730-1,6076-5, 6467-1
Harps in Babylon. 6467-1
Let me no more a mendicant. 6310-1
Sometime it may be. 6250-4
To Faustine. 6431-0
Troilus and Criseyde. 6723-9
Verses from the canticle of the road. 6252-0
Victory. 6820-0
Colton, Caleb C.
Irregular ode, on the death of Lord Byron. 6980-0
Life. 6980-0,6214-8
Colton, Delia Louise
The rain-drops. 6918-5
Colton, Walter
The cathara. 7030-2
A leap for lie. 6552-X
The main truck, or a leap for life. 6402-7
The **colubriad.** William Cowper. 6874-X
The **Colubriad.** William Cowper. 6089-7,6120-6,6133-8,6552-X, 6808-1,6511

Colum, Padraic
Across the door. 6581-3
Asses. 6779-4
Autumn song. 6582-1
A ballad maker. 6628-3
A ballad-maker. 6477-9
The beggar's child. 6244-X
The bird of Jesus. 6096-X
The burial of St. Brendan. 6071-4
Christ the comrade. 6172-9,6172-9,6292-X
A Connachtman. 6872-3
A cradle song. 6096-X,6477-9,6233-4,6244-X,6282-2,6581-3
The deer of Ireland. 6069-2
A drover. 6872-3
East River. 6764-6
The fair hills of Eire. 6331-4
The fair hills of Eire. 6161-3
Fourth station (Jesus his Mother meets"). 6282-2
The furrow and the hearth. 6250-4,6393-4
The furrow. 6338-1
Fuschia hedges in Connacht. 6096 X
Garadh. 6930-4
Humming bird. 6253-9
The humming bird. 6096 X
An idyll. 6320-9
Monkeys. 6464-7
No child. 6244-X
Odysseus. 6070-6
Old men complaining. 6897-9
An old woman of the roads. 6096-X,6102-8,6250-4,6292-X, 6090-0,6439 ,6513-9,6639-9,6172-9,6723-9,6161-3,6393 ,6236-9,6653-4,6331-4,6506-6,6509-0,6726 ,6096-X, 6102-8,6250-4,6292-X,6090-0,6439 ,6513-9,6639-9,6172-9,6723-9,6161-3,6393 ,6236-9,6653-4,6331-4,6506-6, 6509-0,6726
The plougher [or plower]. 6844-8,6872-3,6174-5,6244-X
The plougher. 6930-4
Polonius and the ballad singers. 6897-9
The poor girl's meditation. 6776-X
The poor scholar of the forties. 6244-X
River-mates. 6300-4
Sandalwood. 6779-4
The sea bird to the wave. 6102-8.6253-9,6300-4
She moved through the fair. 6628-3,6246-5,6320-9
The stag. 6244-X
The sunflower. 6516-3
Colum, Padraic (tr.)
The poor girl's meditation. Unknown, 6244-X
Colum-Cille (atr)
Farewell to Ireland. Douglas Hyde (tr.). 7039-6
Columba, Mother M.
From my window. 6543-0
Columba, Saint. See Columcille, Saint
Columbia. Edward Chapman. 7022-1
Columbia. Timothy Dwight. 6015-3,6077-3,6302-0,6385-3,6471-X,6286 ,6121-4,6568-6,6288-1,6444-2
Columbia. Patrick S. Gilmore. 6411-6,6444-2
Columbia. Frederic Lawrence ("R.L. Paget") Knowles. 6286-5, 6471-X
Columbia. Emma Celia & Lizzie J. Rook. 6173-7
Columbia and liberty. Robert Treat Paine. 6678-X
Columbia comes. Thomas Meek Butler. 6443-4
Columbia's banner. Edna Dean Proctor. 7022-1
Columbia's emblem. Edna Dean Proctor. 6239-3;6260-1;6678-X
Columbia's jubilee. Granville B. Putnam. 6925-8
Columbia's prayer. Thomas P. Bashaw. 6846-4
"**Columbia's** shores are wild and wide". Columbia. Edward Chapman. 7022-1
"**Columbia,** appear! - To thy mountains ascend". Perry's victory - a song. Unknown. 6946-0
"**Columbia,** large-hearted and tender". A plea. Ella Wheeler Wilcox. 6863-4
Columbia, the gem of the ocean. David T. Shaw. 6156-7,6706-9,6304-7
Columbia, the gem of the ocean. Unknown. 6471-X,6223-7
The **columbiad,** sels. Joel Barlow. 6008-0,6288-1
A **Columbian** legend. Walt Mason. 6680-1
Columbian ode. Paul Laurence Dunbar. 6465-5
Columbine. Alice Wellington Rollins. 6529-5

Columbine and Harlequin. Don Marquis. 6538-4
Columbines. Arthur Guiterman. 6232-6,6338-1
"Columbkille! Saint Columbkille!". Saint Columbkille. E.J.V. Huiginn. 6762-X
Columbkille's farewell. Douglas Hyde. 6090-0
Columbus. William Allen Butler. 6903-7
Columbus. Arthur Hugh Clough. 6424-8,6552-X
Columbus. Arthur Hugh Clough. 6820-0
Columbus. Ben Wood Davis. 6925-8
Columbus. Aubrey Thomas De Vere. 6678-X
Columbus. Charles Buxton Going. 6653-4
Columbus. Edgar A. Guest. 6748-4
Columbus. Edward Everett Hale. 6946-0
Columbus. Percy Hutchison. 6833-2
Columbus. James Russell Lowell. 6678-X,6087-0,6126-5
Columbus. Joaquin Miller. 6396-9,6300-4,6464-7,6467-1,6121-4,6212 ,6076-5,6288-1,6107-9,6431-0,6309-8,6419 , 6114-1,6104-4,6736-0,6102-8,6239-3,6260-1,6291-1, 6332-2,6465 ,6478-7,6479-5,6552-X,6678-X,6732-8,6449
Columbus. James Montgomery. 6552-X,6449-3
Columbus. Lydia Huntley Sigourney. 6678-X
Columbus. J. Slauerhoff. 6068-4
Columbus. Helen L. Smith. 6964-9
Columbus. Alfred Lord Tennyson. 6977-0
Columbus. Annette Wynne. 6356-X
Columbus and the Mayflower. Richard Monckton Milnes; 1st Baron Houghton. 6946-0
Columbus at night. Maggie Helwig. 6767-0
Columbus at the convent. John Townsend Trowbridge. 6088-9
Columbus at the court of Spain. Alexander Vinent. 6449-3
Columbus Day. Alfred Lord Tennyson. 6449-3
"Columbus braved the cruel, fickle sea". Explorer. Clarence L. Haynie. 6841-3
Columbus dying. Edna Dean Proctor. 6946-0
Columbus goes west. William Hart-Smith. 6384-5
Columbus in chains. Philip Freneau. 6946-0
"Columbus looked; and still around them spread". The first American Congress. Joel Barlow. 6946-0
"Columbus stands in the night alone...". Sonnet ("Columbus"). Sidney Lanier. 6753-0
"Columbus stood upon the deck". How Columbus found America. H.C. Dodge. 6922-3
"Columbus Verranzzo Nansen Livingstone...". An important discovery. Carolyn Wells. 6882-0
Columbus to Ferdinand. Philip Freneau. 6946-0
Columbus to Ferdinand. Jonathan Mason. 6678-X
Columbus, sels. Joaquin Miller. 6501-5
"Columbus-like, I sailed into the night". The voyager. John Banister Tabb. 6850-2
Columcille (atr.)
    Columcille the scribe. Kuno Meyer (tr.). 6930-4
    Columcille's greeting to Ireland. William Reeves and Kuno Meyer (tr.). 6930-4
Columcille (or, Columba), Saint
    The scribe. 6090-0
    There is a grey eye. 6090-0
Columcille cecenit. Unknown. 6873-1
Columcille fecit. Unknown. 6873-1
Columcille the scribe. Columcille (atr.) 6930-4
Columcille's greeting to Ireland. Columcille (atr.) 6930-4
"The column of the day now gilds". Eastern morn. William White. 6868-5
The columnist. Archibald MacLeish. 6039-0
Columns. Rudyard Kipling. 6810-3
Colvill, Helen Hester
    Unmentioned in dispatches. 7031-0
Colvin, Ian
    Flanders poppies. 6051-X
    A museum idyll. 6800-6
    To his readers. 6800-6
Colwell, Elizabeth
    I wonder. 6880-4
    Retrospection. 6880-4
Colwell, Ernest Cadman
    Jesus of Nazareth. 6144-3,6532-5,6337-3
Colwell, Lewis
    Two papers a day. 6042-0
"Com home againe!". Christ calls man home. Unknown. 6881-2
"Com, com sad turtle mateles moaninge." Unknown. 6563-5
Coma. Liane Heller. 6767-0

Comala. Unknown. 6873-1
The comb band. Berton Braley. 6443-4
"Comb between whose ivory teeth she strains". Elegy: The poet expatiates on the beauty..Delia's hair. Robert Southey. 6802-2
Combat between Fitz James and Roderick Dhu. J. Hughes. 6148-6
Combat between Paris and Menelaus, fr. The Iliad. Homer. 6679-8
The combat of Ferdiad and Cuchulain. Unknown. 6930-4
Combat of Heracles and Cycnus. Hesiod. 6435-3
A combat.. William Shakespeare. 6087-0
The combat. Edwin Muir. 6246-6
The combe. Edward Thomas. 6528-7
Combes, Helen
    The crown. 6846-4
    My goal. 6109-5
A combine. Unknown. 6670-4
Combing. Gladys Cardiff. 7005-1
Combs, Alonzo W.
    De ol' man. 6281-4
Comcomly's skull. Jim Barnes. 7005-1
Come. Sara Teasdale. 6581-3
"Come again to the city". Spring. William Roehrick. 6850-2
"Come all my good friends, I'll sing you a song". Unknown. 6059-5
"Come all ye bold heroes that plow the rough main". Unknown. 6059-5
"Come all ye bold sailors". The coast of Peru. Unknown. 6833-2
"Come all ye gents vot cleans the plate". Jeames of Buckley Square. William Makepeace Thackeray. 6760-3
"Come all ye good Centurions and wise men...". The ballad of ths solemn ass. Henry Van Dyke. 6961-4
"Come all ye jolly sailors bold". Unknown. 6059-5
"Come all ye lads and lassies and listen...". The maid f the sweet brown knowe. Unknown. 6930-4
"Come all ye lads who know no fear". Barney's invitation. Philip Freneau. 6946-0
"Come all ye landsmen, far and near". Unknown. 6059-5
"Come all ye sons of Brittany". Braddock's fate, with an incitement to revenge. Stephen Tilden. 6946-0
"Come all ye Yankee sailors, with swords". The Constellation and the Insurgente. Unknown. 6946-0
"Come all ye splendid city dells, metropolis...". Unknown. 6059-5
"Come all ye ustling shanty boys, a lesson take...". Unknown. 6059-5
"Come all you brave Americans". Brave Paulding and the spy. Unknown. 6946-0
"Come all you brave soldiers, both valiant and free". Song ("Come all you brave"). Unknown. 6589-9
"Come all you brave soldiers, both valiant...". Independence. Unknown. 6753-0
"Come all you brave soldiers..valiant and free". On independence. Jonathan Mitchell Sewall. 6946-0
"Come all you hustling gamblers". Husting glamblers. Unknown. 6826-X
"Come all you jolly river boys, I'll have you all...". Unknown. 6059-5
"Come all you laboring hands". An invitation to the poor tenants. Thomas Rowley. 7030-2
"Come all you noble bold commanders...". Unknown. 6059-5
"Come all you seamen bold". Folk song. Unknown. 6179-6
"Come all you tender Christians". Unknown. 6059-5
"Come all you Texas Rangers, wherever you may be". Unknown. 6059-5
"Come all you young ladies...". Unknown. 6059-5
"Come along, my brave clans". Gathering of the Macdonalds. Unknown. 6859-6
"Come along, true believer!". Joel Chandler Harris. 6303-9
"Come alte from the cocoon, marvelous". For an 'Homage to Rimbaud' Eugenio Montale. 6803-2
Come and go. ? Sharpe. 6064-1
Come and gone. Ebenezer Elliott. 6980-0
Come and welcome. Thomas Haweis. 6065-X
Come away. Felicia Dorothea Hemans. 6973-8
"Come away! bring on the bride". Bridal song, fr. The little French lawyer. Francis Beaumont and John Fletcher. 6827-8

"Come away! the sunny hours". The summer's call. Felicia
    Dorothea Hemans. 6973-8
Come away, armed with love's delights. Thomas Campion.
    6328-4,6189-3,6794-8
"Come away, come away from the straightness..". Song of
    the foot-track. Elsie Cole. 6784-0
"Come away, come away, death", fr. Twelfth night. William
    Shakespeare. 6182-6,6179-6,6271-7,6726-3,6246-6,6099
    ,6187-7,6328-4,6395-0,6726-3,6194-X,6645 ,6219-9,
    6250-4,6438-8,6189-3,6396-9
"Come away, come sweet love!". Song ("Come away").
    Unknown. 6436-1
"Come away, come, sweet Love! The golden morning..."
    Unknown. 6181-8,6189-3,6430-2
Come away, death. Edwin John Pratt. 6446-9
"Come away, elves! while the dew is sweet". Water-lilies.
    Felicia Dorothea Hemans. 6973-8
Come away, sweet love. John Dowland. 6315-2
"Come away, with willing feet". Evening song of maidens.
    Henry Hart Milman. 6980-0
"Come away; bring thy golden theft". A song ("Come away").
    Thomas Campion. 6794-8
Come back. Thomas Dunn English. 6410-8
Come back again, Jeanne d'Arc. Henry Van Dyke. 6961-4
"Come back again, my olden heart" Arthur Hugh Clough. 6380-
    2
"Come back to me, who wait and watch for you". Monna
    innominata. Christina Georgina Rossetti. 6828-6
"Come back to me." Christina Georgina Rossetti. 6019-6
Come back! ye friends. Henry Wadsworth Longfellow. 6085-4
"Come back, come back, behold with straining mast" Arthur
    Hugh Clough. 6828-6
Come back, come back, fr. Songs in absence. Arthur Hugh
    Clough. 6110-9,6250-4,6655-0
"Come back, ye wandering muses, come back". On the
    hellenics. Walter Savage Landor. 6828-6
"Come board my speeding chariot...". The Londoner's
    chariot. Wilfrid Thorley. 6777-8
"Come boat me o'er, come row me o'er". O'er the water to
    Charlie. Unknown. 6859-6
Come bravely on, my masters. Unknown. 6756-5
Come buy. William Shakespeare. 6634-8
Come buy my nice muffins. Unknown. 6466-3
Come by chance. Harriet Plimpton. 6799-9
Come carol, make carol. C.C. Gould. 6339-X
"Come come sweet love why dost yu stay." Unknown. 6563-5
Come down. Idris Davies. 6895-2
"Come down to the derby, come down to the race". The race
    of the year. W. Phillpotts Williams. 7010-8
"Come down to us, help and heal us". Invocation. Alice
    Cary. 6969-X
"Come down! Come down, balloon!". In soapsuds street.
    Manuel Bandeira. 6759-X
Come down, O maid. Alfred Lord Tennyson. 6187-7,6232-6,
    6726-3,6437-X,6655-0
"Come down, and dance ye in the toyle". A song to the
    maskers. Robert Herrick. 6959-2
"Come down, O Lord, and with us live!". Hymn ("Come down,
    O Lord..."). Phoebe Cary. 6865-0;6969-X
"Come drawer some wine or wele pull downe your signe."
    Unknown. 6563-5
"Come dwell with me, thou love divine". Love divine.
    William White. 6868-5
"Come every good alumnus". Outre mer. Louis J. Magee. 7004-
    3
"Come fill your pipes and puff away". A song. Edgar A.
    Guest. 6862-6
Come follow. Unknown. 6179-6
"Come follow me, my wandring mates" Thomas Campion. 6794-8
Come follow me, you country lasses. John Fletcher or
    William Rowley. 6563-5
Come follow, follow me. Unknown. 6756-5
Come for Arbutus. Sarah Louise Oberholtzer. 6597-X
"Come forth into the light of things". The tables turned,
    sels. William Wordsworth. 6867-7
Come forth! For pring ${\text{s}}$s singing in the boughs. Arthur
    Davison Ficke. 6619-4
"Come forth, and let us through our hearts...". Foliage.
    Felicia Dorothea Hemans. 6973-8
"Come forth, come forth, my maidens...". Song for the
    morning of St. John the Baptist. Unknown (Spanish).
    6757-3
"Come forth, come forth, to the festal board".
    Thanksgiving. Harriet Ellen (Grannis) Arey. 6820-0
"Come forth, my love, and greet the jocund day". A love
    idyll. Anna C. Bowen. 6799-9
"Come forth." Arthur Davison Ficke. 6581-3
"Come forward now, ye blind and sick and maimed". Francis
    X. Connolly. 6839-1
"Come from my first, ay, come". Charade on the name of the
    poet Campbell. Winthrop Mackworth Praed. 6874-X
"Come from the workshop and the farm". Californina- the
    invitation. James Abraham Martling. 6952-5
"Come from thy home in the south!". Come! James Abraham
    Martling. 6952-5
"Come gentlemen and ladies all". Unknown. 6059-5
"Come heauy hart, whose sighs thy sorrowes shew." Unknown.
    6563-5
"Come here to me, little lassie of three". The worry-
    chaser. Edgar A. Guest. 6862-6
Come here, little robin. Unknown. 6373-X,6131-1
"Come here, my sleeping darling, and climb...". On the
    road to dreamtown. Eben Eugene Rexford. 6925-8
Come hither. William Shakespeare. 6634-8
"Come hither, all sweet maidens soberly". Sonnet: On a
    picture of Leander. John Keats. 6832-4
"Come hither, child! and rest". Villanelle of sunset.
    Ernest Dowson. 6958-4,6875-8
"Come hither, child! thou silent, shy". Serapion. Bayard
    Taylor. 6976-2
"Come hither, Evan Cameron!". The execution of Montrose.
    William Edmonstoune Aytoun. 6948-7
"Come hither, Harriet, pretty miss". The adventures of
    Miss Harriet Simper, fr. The progress. John
    Trumbull. 6753-0
"Come hither, little puppy-dog." Unknown. 6452-3
"Come hither, lyttel childe, and lie...". Mediaeval
    eventide song. Eugene Field. 6949-5
"Come hither, sweet robin." Unknown. 6452-3,6510-4
"Come hither, you that love, and hear me sing". John
    Fletcher. 6187-7,6733-6
Come home. Felicia Dorothea Hemans. 6543-0
Come home again. Unknown. 6328-4
"Come home, come home". Song ("Come home"). Arthur Hugh
    Clough. 6110-9
"Come home, come home! And where is home for me" Arthur
    Hugh Clough. 6828-6
Come home, come home!, fr. Songs in absence. Arthur Hugh
    Clough. 6655-0
Come home, father. Henry Clay Work. 6736-0
"Come home, my love, come home!". Rappel d'amour. Henry
    Van Dyke. 6961-4
Come home, my sailor. William Cox Bennett. 6747-6
"Come home, sweet birds, come home". Birds in autumn.
    Louise Townsend Nicholl. 6761-1
Come in. Robert Frost. 6783-2
Come in. Robert Frost. 6339-X
"'Come in, Ankara', and a voice responds". Christ in
    Crete. Eleanor Knox Farrell. 6761-1
"'Come in, come in, loving Henry', she said". Loving
    Henry. Unknown. 6826-X
"Come in, wet wind of the west". West wind. Katharine
    (Hinkson) Tynan. 7037-X
"Come in. Everything's yours". Romance. Paul Geraldy. 6351-
    9
"Come into the garden, Maud". Song ("Come into the
    garden"). Alfred Lord Tennyson. 6437-X
"Come into the garden, Maud". Alfred Lord Tennyson. 6014-5,
    6122-6,6271-7,6302-0,6332-2,6385 ,6473-6,6110-9,6250-
    4,6560-0,6199-0,6301 ,6656-9,6543-0,6197-4,6219-9
"Come join hand in hand, brave Americans all". John
    Dickinson. 6753-0
"Come keen iambicks with your badgers feet". The rebell
    Scot, sels. John Cleveland. 6933-9
"Come kind folks, friends, and parents". Unknown. 6059-5
"Come learn with me", fr. Woodnotes, II. Ralph Waldo
    Emerson. 6250-4
"Come let us drink away the time". A song of sack.
    Unknown. 6933-9
"Come let us rejoice". About Savannah. Unknown. 6946-0

"Come let us talk together". Snowed under. Alice Cary. 6865-0;6969-X
"Come list to me a minute". Law, a comic song. Unknown. 6878-2
"Come listen a while and give ear to my song". Unknown. 6059-5
"Come listen and I'll tell you". The Yankee privateer. Arthur Hale. 6946-0
"Come listen to me, you gallants so free". Unknown. 6395-0
"Come listen to my story, Molly Bawn". Molly Bawn and Brian Oge. Unknown. 6930-4
"Come listen to my tragedy, good people...". Unknown. 6059-5
"Come listen to the story of brave Lathrop...". The lamentable ballad of the bloody brook. Edward Everett Hale. 6946-0
"Come listen, all you children who delight...". The chocolate bus. Eleanor Farjeon. 6804-9
"Come listen, good neighbors of every degree". The liberty pole. Unknown. 6946-0
"Come listen, good people, while a story..tell". Ezra House. James Whitcomb Riley. 6892-8
"Come listen, little girls and boys". Tommy and his gun. Clayton Fotterall McMichael. 6936-3
"Come listen, ye students of every degree". Song ("Come listen..."). Tobias George Smollett. 6975-4
Come little leaves. George Cooper. 6466-3,6452-3,6135-4
"Come live with me and be my love". Christopher Marlowe. 6181-8;6187-7
Come lovely and soothing death. Walt Whitman. 6472-8
"Come lust ladyes come come wth pensiue..." Unknown. 6563-5
Come morir. S.G. W. 6438-8
Come muse migrate..., fr. Song of the exposition. Walt Whitman. 6399-3
"Come muster, my lads, your mechanical tools". The new roof; a song for federal mechanics. Francis Hopkinson. 6946-0
"Come my Oenone lett us doe." Unknown. 6563-5
"Come near to me, my sons: your father goes",fr Jacob. Arthur Hugh Clough. 6123-0
"Come near! ere yet the dust". The farewell to the dead, fr. Lays of many lands. Felicia Dorothea Hemans. 6973-8
"Come near, o sun- o south wind, blow". Where are the springs of long ago? Edith Matilda Thomas. 6770-0
"Come neighbor, let us go and mend the wall". The broken wall. L. Ashton Thorp. 6764-6
Come not near. Mary Elizabeth Osborn. 6388-8
Come not near my songs. Unknown (Shoshone Indian) 7039-6, 6513-9
"Come not so near my heart!". Chrysalis. Lucile Enlow. 6841-3
"Come not when I am dead," fr. The princess. Alfred Lord Tennyson. 6385-3,6657-7,6655-0,6110-9,6737-9
Come not, oh Lord. Thomas Moore. 6848-0
Come o'er the bourn. Unknown. 6328-4
"Come o'er the green hills to the sunny sea!". Ataraxia. Caroline Elizabeth Sarah Sheridan Norton. 6980-0
Come o'er the sea. Thomas Moore. 6543-0
"Come o'er the stream, Charlie, dear Charlie..". Maclean's welcome. James Hogg. 6859-6
Come of age. Sarah Litsey. 6761-1
"Come on a little. Sit down over here. The...". Deads. Alison Bundy. 6900-2
Come on and join the air corps. Unknown. 6237-7
"Come on then, ye dwellers by nature in darkness". Aristophanes. 6435-3
"Come on then, ye dwellers by nature...". Chorus of birds. Aristophanes. 7039-6
"Come on, all you rounders, if you want to hear". Unknown. 6059-5
Come on, my pink, an' tell me what you think. Unknown. 6609-7
"Come on, you critics, find one fault who dare". Charles Sackville; 6th Earl of Dorset. 6544-9
"Come out from heaven, O Lord, and be my guide". Unsatisfied. Alice Cary. 6969-X
Come out to play. Unknown. 6132-X
Come out, love. Nathaniel Parker Willis. 6278-4

"Come over, come over the river to me". Charlie Machree. William J. Hoppin. 6911-8
"Come people, young and old, come listen to my". Unknown. 6059-5
"Come pure in heart before this hallowed fane". Unknown. 6435-3
Come quietly, Britain. Lloyd Roberts. 6224-5,6115-X
"' Come riddle your rights...". Unknown. 6059-5
Come roll him over. Unknown. 6547-3
Come se quando. Robert Bridges. 6487-6
"Come see the moon". Unknown. 6364-0
"Come shake hands, my little peach blossom". A wayside in France. Adolphe E. Smylie. 6846-4
"Come sheathe your swords! my gallant boys". Sergeant Champe. Unknown. 6946-0
Come sleep. Francis Beaumont and John Fletcher. 6383-7
"Come sleep! O sleep, the certain knot of peace". Sonnet ("Come sleep"). Sir Philip Sidney. 6271-7,6600-3, 6102-8,6150-8,6301-7
"Come sleep! O sleep, the certain...", fr. Astrophel. Sir Philip Sidney. 6181-8,6182-6,6369-1,6289-X,6533-3, 6536 ,6369-1,6645-3,6646-1
Come sleep, O sleep. Sir Philip Sidney. 6304-7
"Come sleep. Her heart's a wood-anemone". Lullaby ("Come sleep"). Florence Kilpatrick Mixter. 6036-6
"Come sorrow wrap me in thy sable cloak." Unknown. 6563-5
"Come spurre away/I have no patience...". An ode to Mr. Anthony Stafford to hasten him... Thomas Randolph. 6933-9
"Come swallow your bumpers, ye Tories, & roar". Massachusetts song of liberty. Mercy Warren (atr). 6946-0
"Come take a carouse." Unknown. 6563-5
"Come tell us the story again, papa". A Purim retrospect. W. S. Howard. 6848-0
"Come then brother loafer poet". Cock a doodle doo!!! Edwin Seaver. 6880-4
"Come then! and while the slow icile hangs". Henry Vaughan. 6230-X
"Come then, my friend! my genius come along". Henry St. John, Viscount Bolinbrooke, fr. An essay..man. Alexander Pope. 6932-0
"Come then: still the spring is new". Invitation. Heathcote William Garrod. 6785-9
"Come there now a mighty rally". Chalk and flint. Unknown. 7031-0
"Come they not down to us, those greeting kind". Greetings. Mary McKinley Cobb. 6841-3
"Come this way", sels. E.L. B. 6601-1
"Come thou at morn before I fight". A litany. Gertrude M. Hort. 7012-4
Come thou my light. Hugh Thomson Kerr. 6337-3
"Come thou, my heavy soul, and lay". Signs of grace. Alice Cary. 6969-X
"Come to Bethlehem and ye shall see". A carol of the birth of Christ. Unknown. 6756-5
Come to Britain. Sir Alan Patrick Herbert. 6722-0
Come to calvary's holy mountain. James Montgomery. 6065-X
Come to him. Orville Lawrence Kuhn. 6799-9
"Come to me with your triumphs and your woes". The beings of the mind. Felicia Dorothea Hemans. 6973-8
"Come to me, beloved". Digby Mackworth Dolben. 6931-2
Come to me, dearest. Joseph Brennan. 6600-3,6620-8
"Come to me, dearest!" Joseph Brenan. 6385-3,6226-1
Come to me, dreams of heaven! Felicia Dorothea Hemans. 6973-8
Come to me, gentle sleep. Felicia Dorothea Hemans. 6973-8
"Come to me, when my soul". The wish. Felicia Dorothea Hemans. 6973-8
Come to our land. James Abraham Martling. 6952-5
"Come to the August hills, look down the cliff". Tourist's guide. Edward Farquhar. 6939-8
"Come to the bank where the boat is moored". In the garden, fr. The road to Avernus. Adam Lindsay Gordon. 6951-7
Come to the forest. Unknown. 6049-8
Come to the Maypole! Unknown. 6787-5
"Come to the fountain and drinl with me". A faun song. Edward H. Butler. 6983-5
"Come to the house-top, Rachl! the". Hadasseh of

Tiberias. M. E. B.. 6848-0
"Come to the land of peace!". The angels' call. Felicia Dorothea Hemans. 6973-8
"Come to the moonlit lake". Skating. John Lowry Stuart. 6795-6,7035-3
"Come to the old pine grove". Pine Grove Songs. James Abraham Martling. 6952-5
"Come to the park." Stefan George. 6160-5
"Come to the south, coy elfin queen of song". South Africa's serenade to poesy. Frederick Charles Kolbe. 6800-6
"Come to the sunset tree!". Evening song of the Tyrolese peasants. Felicia Dorothea Hemans. 6749-2,6973-8
"Come to the woods, my boy!". The day of flowers. Felicia Dorothea Hemans. 6973-8
"Come to these lonely woods to die alone?". The dying raven. Richard Henry Dana. 6752-2
Come to these scenes of peace. William Lisle Bowles. 6271-7,6302-0,6385-3
"Come to your heaven, you heavenly choirs". Robert Southwell. 6187-7,6489-2
"Come triumphing, come with state". A song ("Come triumphing"). Thomas Campion. 6794-8
Come turn to mee, thou pretty little one. Unknown. 6157-5
Come under my plaidie. Hector MacNeill. 6180-X,6086-2,6960-6
"'Come unto God!' I heard a preacher call". In Gremio. Thomas Edward Brown. 6809-X
Come unto me. Anna Letitia Barbauld. 6271-7
Come unto me. Katharine Lee Bates. 6144-3
Come unto me, fr. Matthew. Bible. 6337-3
"Come unto me, ye heroes". Saratoga song. Unknown. 6946-0
"Come unto these yellow sands", fr. The tempest. William Shakespeare. 6182-6,6395-0,6328-4,6302-0,6187-7,6134,6228-8,6634-8,6099-4,6661-5,6194-X,6023 ,6723-9,6252-0,6645-3,6250-4
'Come unto to'. L.L. Benson. 6927-4
Come up from the fields father. Walt Whitman. 6101-X,6113-3,6332-2,6340-3,6344-6,6008-0,6121-4,6288-1,6265-2,6126-5
"Come Vyolle come lett me thy necke embrace." Unknown. 6563-5
"Come up the broad river, the Thames, my Dane". A wedding song. Jean Ingelow. 6940-1
"Come up, April, through the valley". An April welcome. Phoebe Cary. 6865-0;6969-X
"Come view with me this beauty rare". Consider the lily. William White. 6868-5
"Come we shepheards whose blest sight". Hymn of the nativity. Richard Crashaw. 6933-9
"Come when the ray of early morn is glowing". 'Come unto to'. L.L. Benson. 6927-4
"Come when you're called". Mother Goose. 6363-2
"Come when you're called". Unknown. 6904-5
"Come with birds' voices when the light...dim". Whitsun-eve. Evelyn Underhill. 6776-X
"Come with Carrie, Joe and me". Camping. Margaret Southgate Rucker. 6789-1
"Come with flute and violin". Rondel. Muriel F. Hochdorf. 6850-2
'come with me from Lebanan' Unknown. 7007-8
"Come with me, follow me, swift as a moth". The pool. Marjorie L.C. Pickthall. 6797-2
"Come with me-/All that live!". Autumn. Harriet Monroe. 6959-2
Come with the ring. Thomas Hood. 6917-7
"Come ye so early". Early spring. Johann Wolfgang von Goethe. 6948-7
"Come you colliers of my Gwalia". Summer holiday. Idris Davies. 6895-2
Come!. James Abraham Martling. 6952-5
"Come! for the day, thy wasted day, is closing". Cardinal Mazarin. 6238-5
"Come! let me make a sunny realm around thee". Books and flowers. Felicia Dorothea Hemans. 6973-8
"Come! Let us lay a crazy lance in rest". Errantry. John Galsworthy. 6888-X
Come! let us dance. Peter Baker. 6475-2

"Come!/Says the drum". The drum. Joseph Johnston Lee. 6846-4
"Come, all fast friends, let's jointly pray". Over the sea and far awa. Unknown. 6859-6
"Come, all ye bold Americans, to you the truth". The surrender of Cornwallis. Unknown. 6946-0
Come, all ye feathery people. Bryan Waller ("Barry Cornwall") Procter. 6934-7
Come, all ye roving rangers. Unknown. 6058-7
"Come, all ye who love her well". The call of England. Sir Owen Seaman. 7031-9
Come, all ye youths. Thomas Otway. 6430-2
"Come, all you fair and tender ladies". O waly, waly. Unknown. 6826-X
"Come, all you sons of liberty, that to..seas". The General Armstrong. Unknown. 6946-0
"Come, all you young gallants that follow...". Young Molly Bawn. Unknown. 6930-4
"Come, all young men and maidens, attend...". Unknown. 6059-5
"Come, all young men of a rambling nature". Unknown. 6059-5
"Come, be happy!- sit near me". Invocation to misery. Percy Bysshe Shelley. 6828-6
"'Come, before the summer passes'.". Travel song. Anne Glenny Wilson. 6784-0
Come, beloved. Will Smallwood. 6178-8
"Come, beneath yon verdant branches". My youth. Morris Rosenfeld. 7011-6
Come, blessed bird. Unknown. 6943-6
"Come, blessed Bird, and with thy sugred relish" Unknown. 6380-2
"Come, blessed bird, and with thy sugared...". Come, blessed bird. Unknown. 6943-6
Come, blessed sleep. Christina Georgina Rossetti. 6501-5
"Come, bring me wild pinks from the valleys". Be still. Alice Cary. 6865-0;6969-X
Come, bring with a noise. Robert Herrick. 6747-6,6608-9
"Come, brother, turn with me...". The life of god in the soul of man. Richard Henry Dana. 6752-2
"Come, brothers, share the fellowship". A drinking song. Eugene Field. 6949-5
"Come, butter, come". Mother Goose. 6334-9,6363-2
"Come, butter, come". Unknown. 6904-5,7028-0
Come, captain age. Sarah N. Cleghorn. 6619-4,6653-4
"Come, cheer up, my lads, like a..British band". Song ("Come, cheer up, my lads..."). Unknown. 6946-0
"Come, cheerful day, part of my life to me". Thomas Campion. 6187-7,6182-6,6383-7,6794-8
Come, Chloe, and give me sweet kisses. Sir Charles Hanbury Williams. 6328-4,6072-9
Come, Chloris, hie we to the bower. Henry Reynolds. 6328-4
"Come, cheerful day, part of my life, to me". Sic transit. Thomas Campion. 6879-0
"Come, Chloe, and give me sweet kisses". An epigram of Martial, imitated. Sir Charles Hanbury Williams. 6932-0
"Come, Chloe, beauteous maiden, come". A Virgilian picnic. Eugene Field. 6949-5
"Come, come away, to the tavern I say". Unknown. 6933-9
Come, come, my good shepherds. David Garrick. 6086-2
Come, come, my love. William Henry Davies. 6320-9
Come, come, thou glorious object. Sir William Killigrew. 6328-4
"Come, come, you must have another cup...". Mrs. Jones's lodger. Edwin Coller. 6918-5
"Come, come, you must have another cup///". Mrs. Jones's lodger. Edwin Coller. 6918-5
'Come, come,' said Tom's father. Thomas Moore. 6722-0
"Come, comrades! Since the road is long". A song of the road. Julie Mathilde Lippmann. 7041-8
"Come, comrades, come, your glasses clink". Down among the dead men. William Morris. 6828-6
"Come, Corporal Joe!/Tell us a tale of..Shiloh". At the camp-fire. Sarah F. Meader. 6928-2
"Come, courage, come." Clinton Scollard. 6007-2
"Come, dance a jig". Unknown. 6363-2
"Come, dance and song, in linked round". Aeschylus. 6435-3

COME, 314

"Come, dear Amanda, quit the town". To Amanda ("Come, dear"). James Thomson. 6816-2
"Come, dear children, let us away". The forsaken merman. Matthew Arnold. 6046-3,6102-8,6153-2,6196-6,6199-0, 6558 ,6114-1,6110-9,6197-4,6252-0,6430-2,6558 ,6319-5,6424-8,6371-3,6383-7,6656-9,6723 ,6646-1,6639-9, 6828-6,6133-8,6271-7,6437-X,6512-0,6655-0
"Come, dear old friend, and with us twain". To M.L. Gray. Horace. 6949-5
"Come, dear old world, and reason together". Urania. Edward Farquhar. 6939-8
"Come, dear, for it is May. Leave work & book". May. Cora Fabri. 6876-6
"Come, dearest, where the skaters gay". Skater's song. James Abraham Martling. 6952-5
Come, death — my lady is dead. Charles, Duc d' Orleans. 6881-2
"Come, death, I'd have a word with thee". The fool rings his bells. Walter De La Mare. 7026-4
"Come, each death-doing dog who dares venture". Hot stuff. Edward Botwood. 6946-0
"Come, ev'ning, once again, season of peace". Evening, fr. The task. William Cowper. 6932-0
"Come, evening, once again, season of peace". Evening, fr. The task. William Cowper. 6934-7
"Come, fill the beaker, while we chaunt...". Fort Duquesne. Florus B. Plimpton. 6946-0
Come, fill the cup, and in the fire..spring,fr.Rubaiyat. Omar Khayyam. 7039-6
"Come, fill up your glasses". The British grenadier. Unknown. 6946-0
"Come, follow me by the smell". Onions. Jonathan Swift. 6930-4
"Come, follow me!" Thomas Curtis Clark. 6144-3
"Come, freeman of the land"! Put it through. Edward Everett Hale. 6946-0
"Come, friend, I'll turn thee up again". The widow to her hour-glass. Robert Bloomfield. 6980-0
Come, gentle death! Thomas Watson. 6182-6
Come, gentle god. James Thomson. 6816-2
"Come, gentle sleep!attend thy votary's prayer". Sleep. Thomas Warton Jr. 6867-7
"Come, gentle sleep." Michelangelo Buonarroti. 6501-5
"Come, gentle venus! and assuage". A nuptial song. James Thomson. 6816-2
"Come, gentle winds, and waft". Recall. Marie H. Fleming. 6799-9
"Come, gentlemen Tories, firm, loyal, and true". Sir Henry Clinton's invitation to the refugees. Philip Freneau. 6946-0
"Come, give me back my life again...". Another chance. Henry Van Dyke. 6961-4
"Come, give us more livings and rectors". The numbering of the clergy. Thomas Moore. 6802-2
"Come, guests! and sign upon this page". To Mrs. C.W. Louis J. Magee. 7004-3
"Come, Harvey, let us sit awhile and talk". Our whippings. Eugene Field. 6949-5
"Come, healing god! Apollo, come and aid". To Amanda ("Come, healing"). James Thomson. 6816-2
"Come, hear how the brave old Columbus". The ideal India. Fred Shelley Ryman. 6919-3
"Come, heavy souls, oppressed that are". Casting all your care upon God, for he careth for you. Thomas Washbourne. 6931-2
"Come, here's to the knights of the true..oak". Come, let us be jovial. Unknown. 6859-6
"Come, Herod, my hound, from the stranger's". The bloodhound. Bryan Waller ("Barry Cornwall") Procter. 7008-6
Come, holy babe! Mary Dickerson Bangham. 6144-3
"Come, holy dove". Hymn to the holy spirit. Richard Wilton. 6931-2
"Come, I will make the continent indissoluble". A song ("Come, I will make") Walt Whitman. 6371-3,6753-0
"Come, holy spirit". Isaac Watts. 6052-8,6219-9,6304-7
Come, if you dare, our trumpets sound, fr. King Arthur. John Dryden. 6970-3
"Come, lasses and lads, get leave of your dads". Come to the Maypole! Unknown. 6787-5

"Come, leave the loathed stage,", fr. Ode to himself. Ben Jonson. 6198-2
"Come, let me write. And to what end? To ease". Sonnet 034 ("Come, let me"), fr. Astrophel and Stella. Sir Philip Sidney. 6660-7
Come, let us agree. Beatrice S. Meddins. 6799-9
Come, let us be jovial. Unknown. 6859-6
Come, let us choose. Ruth-Ellen Dodge. 6764-6
"Come, let us drink a health, boys". Unknown. 6859-6
"Come, let us kisse and parte." Michael Drayton. 6302-0;6385-3
Come, let us make love deathless. Herbert Trench. 6877-4, 6187-7,6204-0,6244-X,6320-9,6250-4,6437
"Come, let us plant the appple tree". The planting of the apple tree. William Cullen Bryant. 6006-4,6047-1, 6049-8,6239-3,6356-X,6300 ,6299-7,6302-0,6385-3,6479-5,6486-8,6497 ,6597-X,6672-0,6735-2,6126-5,6304-7, 6457 ,6006-4,6047-1,6049-8,6239-3,6356-X,6300 ,6299-7,6302-0,6385-3,6479-5,6486-8,6497 ,6597-X,6672-0, 6735-2,6126-5,6304-7,6457 ,6239-3,6820-0
"Come, let us sell the past and future, giving". Awakening. Dorothy Hobson. 6979-7
"Come, let us set our careful breasts". Ode to melancholy. Thomas Hood. 6974-6
Come, let us sound with melody. Thomas Campion. 6328-4
"Come, let us spend an idle hour in wishing". The wish. Anne Reeve Aldrich. 7041-8
Come, let us walk. Ben H. Smith. 6662-3
"Come, let's go to bed". Unknown. 6904-5
"Come, listen all unto my song". How Cyrus laid the cable. John Godfrey Saxe. 6946-0,6963-0
"Come, listen all, while I relate". The farmer's well. Unknown. 6929-0
"Come, listen to my mournful tale". Jemmy Dawson. Unknown. 6859-6
"Come, listen, good neighbors of every degree". The liberty pole satirized. Unknown. 6753-0
"Come, little babe, come silly soul". Nicholas Breton. 6181-8
"Come, little children, hand in hand". Wonderland, sels. Lloyd Roberts. 6797-2
"Come, little drummer boy, lay down...knapsack". The soldiers' friend. George Canning and John Hookham Frere. 6802-2
"Come, little drummer boy, lay down..knapsack". The soldier's friend. George Canning. 6932-0
"COme, loveliest season of the year". Spring after the war. Phoebe Cary. 6969-X
Come, lord Jesus. Charles Wesley. 6065-X
Come, love, across the sunlit land. Clinton Scollard. 6770-0
Come, love, come, the boat lies low. Unknown. 6609-7
Come, love, let's walk. Unknown. 6182-6
"Come, lovely and soothing...", fr. When lilacs... Walt Whitman. 6726-3
"Come, lovely lock of Julia's hair". The auburn lock. Unknown. 6874-X
Come, lovers, bring your cares. John Jones. 6563-5
Come, mad boys. Unknown. 6756-5
"Come, make for me a little song". A sea song (2). Alice Cary. 6969-X
"Come, May, and hang a white flag on...thorn". Thoughts at the trysting stile. Francis Ledwidge. 6812-X
"Come, my Celia, let us prove". Venetian song, fr. Volpone, or the fox. Ben Jonson. 6827-8
Come, my Celia, let us prove. Ben Jonson. 6645-3,6182-6, 6208-3,6181-8,6187-7,6536-8,6726
"Come, my crony,let's think upon far-away days". A Parthian glance. Thomas Hood. 6974-6
"Come, my lad, and sit beside me". The story of a stowaway. Clement Scott. 6927-4
"Come, my Lesbia, no repining". Catullus to Lesbia. Catullus. 6949-5
"Come, my little one, with me!". The shut-eye train. Eugene Field. 6835-9,6834-0;6949-5
"Come, my muse, a Venus draw". The picture. John Hughes. 6831-6
"Come, my sweet, whiles every strain". William Cartwright. 6187-7
"Come, my wife, put down the Bible". The lost babies.

Unknown. 6914-2
"Come, mysterious night". A hymn to night. Max Michelson. 6897-9
"Come, night...", fr. Romeo and Juliet. William Shakespeare. 6339-X
"Come, O come, my life's delight." Thomas Campion. 6317-9, 6187-7,6328-4,6182-6,6935-5
"Come, O thou traveller unknown". Charles Wesley. 6931-2
"Come, now, who is this Pasadene". The mystery of Pasadene. Eugene Field. 6949-5
"Come, o come, with sacred lays". The one hundred and forty-eighth psalm paraphrased. Bible. 6848-0
"Come, O! come, my life's delight". Song ("Come, O!"). Thomas Campion. 6436-1
"Come, oh come! In this sweetest of all nights". The triumph of Venus 'In the name of the eternal...' Svetislav Stefanovic. 6765-4
"Come, oh friend, let us secretly move around & look". Unknown (Newari) 7013-2
"Come, open your door, there's a friend...". The New Year's caller. Edgar A. Guest. 6862-6
Come, pan, and pipe. Frank Dempster Sherman. 6770-0
"Come, paraclete divine". Paraclete divine. William White. 6868-5
"Come, patient rust". An old cannon. Walter De La Mare. 6905-3
"Come, peace of mind, delightful guest!". Ode to peace. William Cowper. 6814-6
"Come, Pearl, let's take a ramble". Pearl Bryant. Unknown. 6826-X
"Come, Pepita, Phyllis, Griselda". May day. Robert J. Burdette. 6588-0
"Come, Phyllis, I've a cask of wine". To Phyllis (1). Horace. 6949-5
Come, poet, come! Arthur Hugh Clough. 6046-3,6110-9
"Come, ponder well, for 'tis no jest". The yearly distress; or, tithing time at Stock in Essex. William Cowper. 6814-6
"Come, read to me some poem". The day is done. Henry Wadsworth Longfellow. 6934-7
Come, republic. Edgar Lee Masters. 6289-X
"Come, rest in this bosom, my own stricken deer". Song ("Come, rest in this bosom"). Thomas Moore. 6513-9
"Come, rest in this bosom". Thomas Moore. 6219-9,6543-0, 6302-0,6385-3,6328-4,6486-8,6737-9
"Come, rouse up, ye bold-hearted Whigs". Old Tippecanoe. Unknown. 6946-0
Come, said my soul. Walt Whitman. 6126-5,6288-1
Come, says Jesus' voice. Anna Letitia Barbauld. 6065-X
"Come, says nurse death". Nurse death and my father. Margaret McGovern. 6761-1
"Come, see the Dolphin's anchor forged". The forging of the anchor. Sir Samuel Ferguson. 6917-2
"Come, see thy friend, retir'd without regret". Nil admirari. William Congreve. 6932-0
"Come, shake your dull noodles, ye pumpkins...". A Tory parody of 'Come join hand in hand...'. Unknown. 6753-0
"Come, shepherd swains, that wont to hear me sing". Unknown. 6830-8
Come, shepherds, come. Unknown. 6328-4
Come, shepherds, come! John Fletcher. 6182-6,6187-7
"Come, shepherds, on this grave your flourets". An elegy on an infant. Thomas Warton (the Elder). 6962-2
"Come, shut up your Blackstone,& sparkle again". To XXXX, esquire, fr. Croaker papers. Fitz-Greene Halleck and Joseph Rodman Drake. 6753-0
Come, sign the pledge. M.W. Frazer. 6417-5
Come, silence!. Patience Pollard. 6316-0
"Come, sing your songs again to me". To a mockingbird. Maybelle Mayne Porter. 6841-3
Come, sirrah Jack, ho!! Unknown. 6430-2
Come, Sirrah Jacke, hoe! Unknown. 6380-2
"Come, sit beneath". Unknown. 6435-3
Come, sleep. Francis Beaumont and John Fletcher. 6383-7
"Come, sleep, and with thy sweet deceiving". Francis Beaumont. 6181-8,6182-6
"Come, sleep, and with thy sweet deceiving." John Fletcher. 6187-7,6533-3
'Come, sleep...' Louise Bogan. 6399-3

"Come, soft and soothing". Voice of song. Steingrimur Thorsteinsson. 6854-5
"Come, soft south wind, come from the...". My treasure. James Abraham Martling. 6952-5
"Come, soldiers, arouse ye!". The dead comrade. Richard Watson Gilder. 6820-0
"Come, son of Israel, scorned in every land". The valley of Jehoshaphat. Lydia Huntley Sigourney. 6848-0
Come, sorrow, come. Unknown. 6908-8
"Come, sorrow, come! bring all thy cries". On the death of Beaumont. Unknown. 6908-8
"Come, sorrow, come, sit down and mourn...". Come, sorrow, come. Unknown. 6908-8
"Come, spur away!". An ode ("Come, spur away!") Thomas Randolph. 6194-X
"Come, spur away". Thomas Randolph. 6187-7,6374-8
"Come, swallow your bumpers, ye Tories...". The parody parodized. Unknown. 6753-0
Come, sweet lass. Unknown. 6328-4,6563-5
"Come, take the tenner, doctor...". Drought and doctrine. J. Brunton Stephens. 6768-9
"Come, take up your hats, and away let us haste". Unknown. 6904-5
"Come, tattered little pirate doll...". Pirate doll. Merry Wiggs. 6750-6
Come, thou almighty king. Charles Wesley. 6730-1,6214-8
Come, thou fount of every blessing. Robert Robinson. 6219-9
Come, thou monarch ohis last battle. William Shakespeare. 6194-X
"Come, thou old seaman, in my father's ships". Nausicaa. Richard Garnett. 6785-9
"Come, traveller, this hollow rock beneath". On a cave. Anyte. 6962-2
"Come, wander with me by the brook". West-running brook. Sylvia Clark. 6764-6
Come, wandering sheep. Edward Caswall. 6065-X
"Come, where on the moorland steep". Song, fr. Six days. Stopford Augustus Brooke. 6873-1
"Come, while in freshness and dew it lies". The world in the open air. Felicia Dorothea Hemans. 6973-8
"Come, while the blossoms of thy years...". 'They that seek me early shall find me.' Unknown. 6752-2
Come, whisper in my ear. Unknown. 6720-4
Come, ye disconsolate. Thomas Moore. 6303-9,6337-3,6418-3, 6730-1,6214-8,6304
"Come, ye heavy states of night". Song ("Come, ye heavy states"). Unknown. 6436-1
Come, ye lads, who wish to shine. Unknown. 6946-0
Come, ye little noisy crew. William Wordsworth. 6383-7
Come, ye lofty. Arthur Gurney. 6219-9
"Come, ye that despair of the land". The book line. Arthur Guiterman. 6773-5
"Come, you pretty false-eyed wanton". Song ("Come, you pretty"). Thomas Campion. 6436-1
"Come, you pretty false-eyed wanton". Thomas Campion. 6733-6,6181-8,6794-8
"Come, you seamen, deepwater mariners". Unknown. 6435-3
"Come, you whose loves are dead". A dirge. Francis Beaumont and John Fletcher. 6383-7
Come, you whose loves are dead. John Fletcher. 6182-6
"'Come— come, get up, we must be off'". The seven words. George Willard Bonte. 6818-9
Comedy. Thomas Bailey Aldrich. 6887-1
Comedy. Mark Van Doren. 6388-8
Comedy of errors, sels. William Shakespeare. 6679-8
"Comely and capable one of our race". On the portrait of a woman about to be hanged. Thomas Hardy. 6777-8
The comely warrior. Ibn Sa'id (of Alcala La Real) 6362-4
"Comes a tone, that sounds alone". The voice of the city. Stephen Chalmers. 7014-0
"Comes in flying from the street". 'Where's mamma?'. Edgar A. Guest. 7033-7
"Comes summer to the world its work to do". The work of summer. Edgar A. Guest. 6869-3
Comes the charming evening. Charles Baudelaire. 6343-8
"Comes the deer to my singing". Hunting-song. Unknown (Navaho Indian). 7039-6
"Comes the same cry from where gray Himalay". The universal prayer. Mary Sylvester Paden. 6836-7

COMET

Comet. Mary Fullerton. 6384-5
"The comet! he is on his way", sels. Oliver Wendell Holmes. 66601-1
The comet. Robert J. Burdette. 6588-0
The comet. Oliver Wendell Holmes. 6302-0,6732-8,6008-0
The comet. Albert Durrant Watson. 6115-X
Cometas
    Country gods. T.F. Higham (tr.). 6435-3
"Cometh a voice: - 'My children, hear'.". The earth-mother. John Sandes. 6784-0
"Cometh the wind from the garden". The wind. Eugene Field. 6949-5
Comfort. Elizabeth Barrett Browning. 6934-7
Comfort. Alice Cary. 6969-X
Comfort. Mortimer Collins. 6385-3,6652-6
Comfort. Hafiz. 6448-5
Comfort. Robert Herrick. 6250-4
Comfort. Archibald Lampman. 7041-8
Comfort. Miyauchi. 6027-7
Comfort. Margaret French Patton. 6501-5
Comfort. Adelaide Anne Procter. 6957-6
Comfort. Robert Service. 6159-1
Comfort. Ramona Dunning Springall. 6750-6
Comfort. Unknown. 6412-4,6226-1
Comfort in affliction. William Edmonstoune Aytoun. 6278-4
Comfort in extremity. Christopher Harvey. 6931-2
"Comfort me with apples!". Homesick. Phoebe Cary. 6969-X
"Comfort me, comfort me, great earth mother". Antaeus. Daphne Muir. 6800-6
The comfort of the stars. Richard Burton. 6266-0,6374-8
The comfort of the trees. Richard Watson Gilder. 6946-0, 6820-0
"Comfort the sorrowful with watchful eyes". Comfort. Archibald Lampman. 7041-8
Comfort through a window. Sarah Morgan Bryan Piatt. 7041-8
"Comfort thyself, my woeful heart." Sir Thomas Wyatt. 6584-8
Comfort to a youth that had lost his love. Robert Herrick. 6935-5
Comfort to a youth that had lost his love. Robert Herrick. 6908-8
Comfort, Alex
    The atoll in the mind. 6209-1,6391-8
    The bullocks. 6210-5
    Cellar. 6475-2
    Fear of the earth. 6379-9,6475-2
    Fifth elegy. 6209-1
    For sleeping now. 6475-2
    Hoc est corpus. 6391-8
    Letter from safety. 6391-8
    The level mind. 6475-2
    The lovers. 6379-9
    Notes for my son. 6379-9
    The postures of love, sels. 6209-1
    The postures of love. 6379-9
    Set on the autumn head. 6475-2
    Song for the heroes. 6379-9
Comfort, Florence Crocker
    Ann Peters. 6782-4
    He remembered. 6789-1
"Comfortably seated at twilight". By the fireside. Thomas J. Mohn. 6799-9
"The comforter of sorrow and of care". Work. Edwin L. Sabin. 6820-0
A comforter. Robert Loveman. 6941-X
A comforter. Adelaide Anne Procter. 6957-6
A comforter. Adelaide Anne Procter. 6127-3,6131-1
The comforter. Richard R. Kirk. 6118-4
The comforter. Robert Service. 6159-1
The comforters.. Dora Sigerson Shorter. 6096-X,6244-X
The comforters. Laurence Housman. 6274-1
The comforters. Dora Sigerson Shorter. 6102-8
The comforting. Margaret E. Bruner. 6750-6
Comic miseries. John Godfrey Saxe. 6089-7,6278-4
The comic valentine. Edward R. Huxley. 6885-5
"A comical camel, named Bert". Limerick:"A comical camel, named Bert". Langford Reed. 6811-1
A comical dun. John McKeever. 6045-1
The comical girl. M. Pelham. 6089-7,6808-1
Comin' Christmas morn. Ben King. 6807-3

The comin' o' the spring. Lady John Scott. 6180-X
Comin' through the rye. Unknown. 6136-2,6167-2,6219-9
The coming American, sels. Sam Walter Foss. 6337-3
The coming American. Sam Walter Foss. 6107-9
Coming and going. Grace Hyde Trine. 6102-8,6076-5
The coming child. Richard Crashaw. 6337-3
A coming cry. Ebenezer Jones. 7009-4
The coming day. William James Linton. 7009-4
The coming day. John Oxenham. 6337-3
"Coming down on the train from Kandy". Rot below Adam's peak (Sri Lanka*) Earle Birney. 6767-0
"Coming down the mountain road". The mountain road. Enid Derham. 6784-0
Coming from the picnic. Brandon Banner. 6247-4
Coming home. Phoebe Cary. 6969-X
Coming home. Dinah Maria Mulock Craik. 6600-3
Coming home from camp. Lonny Kaneko. 6790-5
Coming home in March. Harold Littlebird. 7005-1
Coming homeward out of Spain. Barnaby Googe. 6182-6
The coming huns. Valery Bryusov. 6103-6
"Coming in and out of cities". Touring. Audre Lorde. 6898-7
"The coming in of the 'Mermaiden'". Jean Ingelow. 6543-0
The coming man. Unknown. 6078-1,6273-3
The coming man. Unknown. 6772-7
The coming man. Ella Wheeler Wilcox. 6863-4
The coming of Arthur, fr. The idylls of the king. Alfred Lord Tennyson. 6655-0
The coming of Christ. Jeremy Taylor. 6014-5
The coming of Christ. Unknown. 6022-6
The coming of dawn. Grace Atherton Dennen. 6374-8,6607-0
The coming of Dian, fr. Endymion. John Keats. 6110-9
The coming of evening. Adolf Wenig. 6763-8
The coming of his feet. Lyman Whitney Allen. 6337-3
The coming of Isis, fr. Metamorphoses. Apuleius. 6987-8
The coming of Lincoln. Edwin Markham. 6524-4
The coming of love, fr. The kingis quhair. James I; King of Scotland. 6845-6
The coming of love, sels. Theodore Watts-Dunton. 6997-5, 6301-2,6997-5
The coming of love. Theodore Watts-Dunton. 6102-8
The coming of Mary Louise. Gertrude Boughton Urquhart. 6466-3
The coming of Mont Blanc. Henry Morford. 6749-2
The coming of Rebekah. Helen Myers Meldrum. 6269-5
Coming of snow. Henry Rago. 6761-1
The coming of spring. Mary Howitt. 6242-3,6530-9
The coming of spring. Agnes Maule Machar. 6433-7
The coming of spring. Nora Perry. 6136-2,6519-8,6457-4, 6135-0
The coming of spring. Unknown. 6373-X,6449-3
The coming of storm, fr. Tristram of Lyonesse. Algernon Charles Swinburne. 6997-5
The coming of the Lord. Jones Very. 6333-0
The coming of the rain, fr. Spring. James Thomson. 6198-2, 6543-0
The coming of the snow. Marion L. Bertrand. 6799-9
The coming of the sons of god. Herman Fetzer. 7007-8
The coming of the trees. Arthur Guiterman. 6449-3
The coming of war: Actaeon. Ezra Pound. 6897-9
Coming of winter. Boris Pasternak. 6546-5
The coming poet. Francis Ledwidge. 6812-X
The coming race. James Arthur Edgerton. 6836-7
Coming round. Phoebe Cary. 6969-X,6412-4
The coming rulers. Unknown. 6530-9
Coming the rye. Robert Burns. 6180-X,6385-3,6383-7, 6301-2,6543-0
Coming through the rye. Unknown. 6271-7,6737-9
"Coming to kisse her lyps (such grace I found).". Sonnet 064 (Coming to kisse), fr. Amoretti. Edmund Spenser. 6315-2
Coming to port. Max Eastman. 6509-0,6393-4
Coming to port. Max Press. 6042-0
The coming woman. Unknown. 6742-5
The coming. Anthony Delius. 6788-3
The coming. Edward Farquhar. 6939-8
Commanders of the faithful. William Makepeace Thackeray. 6026-9
Commemoration. Sir Henry Newbolt. 6437-X,6210-5
Commemoration ode. James Rusell Lowell. 6600-3,6438-8,

6424-8,6263-6,6250-4,6309
Commemoration ode, sels. James Russell Lowell. 6113-3
Commencement. Margaret Elizabeth Sangster. 6449-3
Commencement. Unknown. 6008-0
Commencement at Billville. Frank Lebby Stanton. 6698-4
Commencement essays. Unknown. 6718-2
Commencement: June 1929. Muriel F. Hochdorf. 6850-2
Commencing monk. Edward Farquhar. 6939-8
The **commendation** of music. William Strode. 6563-5
The **commendations** of Mistress Jane Scrope. John Skelton. 6436-1
Commendatory verses upon Mr. Thomas Coryat's crudities. John Donne. 6198-2
Comment. Dorothy Parker. 6817-0,6026-9
Comments from a country garden. Elizabeth J. Coatsworth. 6232-6
Commercial. Laurence Binyon. 6884-7
Commercial candour. Gilbert Keith Chesterton. 6722-0
Commerford, Charles
    A meadow lark sang. 6073-0
    A visit with a woodpecker. 6073-0
Commerical candour. Gilbert Keith Chesterton. 6026-9
Commination. Walter Savage Landor. 6026-9
Commissary report. Stoddard King. 6026-9
Committal. Helen Hartness Flanders. 7030-2
Committee meetings. Edgar A. Guest. 7033-7
Common Bill. Unknown. 6058-7
A **common** case. Gamaliel Bradford. 6036-6
The **common** cormorant or shag. Unknown. 6125-7
The common grave, fr. Sonnets. Sydney Dobell. 6380-2
Common ground. Duncan Mitchel. 7003-5
A **common** inference. Charlotte Perkins Stetson Gilman. 6730-1,6303-9,6431-0
The **common** little things. Hilda Shutts Farquhar. 6799-9
The **common** lot. John Godfrey Saxe. 6523-6
The **common** lot. Frederick A. Hinckley. 6798-0
The **common** lot. Menander. 6435-3
The **common** lot. James Montgomery. 6102-8,6180-X,6385-3, 6505-2,6600-3,6605-2,6086-2,6219-9,6543-0
The **common** lot. Ella Wheeler Wilcox. 6956-8
The **common** man, fr. The deserted village. Oliver Goldsmith. 6337-3
The **common** offering. Frances Ridley Havergal. 6225-3
Common people. W.A. Barton Jr. 7016-7
The **common** question. John Greenleaf Whittier. 6424-8
Common sense. Harry ("Col. D. Streamer") Graham. 6427-2
Common sense. William Shakespeare. 6438-8
The **common** sick. Louise Townsend Nicholl. 6033-1
Common sort of fellow. Unknown. 6710-7
The **common** street. Helen Gray Cone. 6395-0,6102-8,6509-0, 6076-5,6393-4,6396 ,6476-0
Common things. Louise Abney. 6143-5
Commonplace. Sarah ("Susan Coolidge") Woolsey. 6654-2
A **commonplace** life. Unknown. 6889-8
The **commonplace** woman. Unknown. 6167-2
The **commonplace.** Walt Whitman. 6126-5
Commonplaces. Rudyard Kipling. 6089-7,6440-X
The **commonwealth** of the bees, fr. King Henry V. William Shakespeare. 6239-3
Commonwealth vs. McAfee. C.P. Greenough. 6878-2
Communings. Robert Southey. 6214-8
Communings with thought. Felicia Dorothea Hemans. 6973-8
Communion. Dorothy P. Albaugh. 6750-6
Communion. Edward Dowden. 6214-8
Communion. Caroline Giltinan. 6292-X,6172-9
Communion. Sophie ("Ellen Burroughs") Jewett. 6501-5
Communion. Mildred Jones Keefe. 6143-5
Communion. David McCord. 6761-1
Communion. Jessie B. Rittenhouse. 6441-8
Communion. John Banister Tabb. 6303-9,6337-3,6418-3,6730-1, 6007-2
Communion. T. Turner. 6317-9
Communion. William Wordsworth. 6337-3
Communion ("I would be one with Thee") Loren W. Burch. 6144-3
Communion ("Not to the twelve alone"). Phoebe Smith Bachelder. 6144-3
Communion hymn. William Gay. 6144-3
Communion hymn. Alice Freeman Palmer. 6337-3
Communion of saints. Andre Chernier. 6487-6

Communion of saints. Andre Chernier. 6487-6
Communion song. Seymour Gordden Link. 6042-0
Communion with nature. George Gordon, 6th Baron Byron. 6143-5
Communion with nature, fr. Expostulation and reply. William Wordsworth. 6337-3
Community. Iqbal. 6448-5
Commutation to heaven. Ann Strickland. 6799-9
Commuter. Elwyn Brooks White. 6089-7,6722-0
Commuters. Adele M. Ryerson. 6799-9
Como. Joaquin Miller. 6277-6;6451-5
Como in April. Robert Underwood Johnson. 6338-1
"**Como!** thou, a treasure whom the earth". Lake Como. William Wordsworth. 6749-2
Como, sels. Samuel Rogers. 6484-1
A **comfortable** song on the poor sailors. Unknown. 6547-3
The **compact.** George Barlow. 6280-6
The **companion..** Gerald Gould. 6335-7
Companions. Charles Stuart Calverley. 6089-7,6732-8,6656-9
Companions. George William ("A.E.") Russell. 7014-0
Companions. Richard Henry Stoddard. 6297-0
Companions. Margaret Widdemer. 6218-0
Companions. Sarah ("Susan Coolidge") Woolsey. 6461-2
The **companions.** Alfred Noyes. 6151-6
Companionship. Mabel W. Arnold. 6799-9
Companionship. Maltbie Davenport Babcock. 6007-2
Companionship. Ella Wheeler Wilcox. 6523-6
Companionship of the muse. George Wither. 6600-3
Company. Berton Braley. 6853-7
Company. Le Roy Morand. 6764-6
'**Company** manners.' James Whitcomb Riley. 6091-9
The **company** of lovers. Judith Wright. 6349-7
The **company** store. Isaac Hanna. 6149-4
"**Compare** me to the child that plaies with fire," Bartholomew Griffin. 6586-4
"**Compared** with Christ". Augustus Montague Toplady. 6065-X
Comparison. Maxwell Bodenheim. 6880-4
Comparison. Mary Thomasine Downer. 6818-9
Comparison. Helen Hoyt. 6880-4
Comparison. Margaret A. Sinclair. 6591-0,6592-9
A **comparison** addressed to a young lady. William Cowper. 6814-6
A **comparison** in a seaside field. Alice Meynell. 6955-X
Comparison of love to a streame falling... Sir Thomas Wyatt. 6208-3
A **comparison** of the life of man. Richard Barnfield. 6023-4, 6436-1
Comparison of Washington and Napoleon. Francois de Chateaubriand. 6424-8
A **comparison,** addressed to a young lady. William Cowper. 6086-2,6250-4,6301-2
A **comparison.** William Cowper. 6814-6
A **comparison.** John Chipman Farrar. 6421-3,6368-3
Comparisons. Algernon Charles Swinburne. 6233-4
Compass berg. William Charles Scully. 6800-6
"A **compass** needle seldom marks the north". Ideals. Louis J. Magee. 7004-3
The **compass,** with variations. Thomas Hood. 6974-6
Compassion. Thomas Hardy. 6510-4
Compassion. Sadi [or Saadi] (Mushlih-ud-Din) 6448-5
Compassion. Ralph E. Webber. 6799-9
Compassion so divine. Anne Steele. 6065-X
"**Compassionate** eyes had our brave John Brown". John Brown: a paradox. Louise Imogen Guiney. 6946-0
"**Compatience** perses, reuth and marcy stoundes". The passion of Jesus. Unknown. 6881-2
Compel them to come in. George A. Mackenzie. 6115-X
Compensation. Marion L. Bertrand. 6799-9
Compensation. Phoebe Cary. 6969-X
Compensation. Paul Laurence Dunbar. 6309-8
Compensation. Ralph Waldo Emerson. 6753-0
Compensation. Ralph Waldo Emerson. 6288-1
Compensation. Ralph Waldo Emerson. 6753-0
Compensation. Theodosia Garrison. 6211-3,6501-5
Compensation. Gerald Gould. 6776-X
Compensation. Harry ("Col. D. Streamer") Graham. 6633-X
Compensation. Ruth H. Hausman. 6850-2
Compensation. Robinson Jeffers. 6012-9
Compensation. William Ellery Leonard. 6556-2
Compensation. Gertrude Huntington MGiffert. 6838-3

COMPENSATION

Compensation. Ruth Comfort Mitchell. 6449-3
Compensation. Franklin N. Rogers. 6764-6
Compensation. John Banister Tabb. 7017-5
Compensation. Eliza Sproat Turner. 6429-9,6321-7
Compensation. Anna Spencer Twitchell. 6836-7
Compensation. Unknown. 6045-1,6273-3,6410-8,6177-X
Compensation. Emma Boge Whisenand. 6270-9
Compensation, fr. Mother-songs. Marian Williams McGaw. 6906-1
The compensation. Ruth E.J. Sarver. 6178-8
Compensations. Christopher Bannister. 6274-1
Compensations. Alfred Noyes. 6151-6
A competent artist. Carolyn Wells. 6882-0
A complacent rondeau redouble. Louis Untermeyer. 6875-8
"Complacent they tell us, hard hearts...". Woman's future. May Kendall. 7037-X
Complaining. George Herbert. 6219-9
Complains, being hindered the sight of his nymph. Philip Ayres. 6563-5
Complaint. Phoebe Cary. 6969-X
Complaint. Samuel Taylor Coleridge. 6722-0
Complaint. Vyacheslav Ivanov. 6103-6
Complaint. William Carlos Williams. 6482-5
A complaint by night of the lover not beloved. Henry Howard, Earl of Surrey. 6182-6,6586-4,6208-3,6586-4, 6198-2,6315
The complaint of a forsaken Indian woman. William Wordsworth. 6358-6,6378-0
The complaint of a lover forsaken of his love. Unknown. 6157-5
Complaint of a lover rebuked. Henry Howard, Earl of Surrey. 6430-2
The complaint of Chaucer to his empty purse. Geoffrey Chaucer. 6726-3,6198-2,6732-8
Complaint of forgetting the dead. Jules Laforgue. 6351-9
The complaint of Lisa. Algernon Charles Swinburne. 6875-8
Complaint of love. Sir Philip Sidney. 6584-8
The complaint of nature. Michael Bruce. 6086-2
The complaint of New Amsterdam. Jacob Steendam. 6946-0
The complaint of Rosamond, sels. Samuel Daniel. 6198-2
The complaint of Rosamond. Samuel Daniel. 6430-2
Complaint of the absence of her lover being upon...sea. Henry Howard, Earl of Surrey. 6182-6,6317-9,6586-4
Complaint of the absence of his love. Sir Thomas Wyatt. 6543-0
Complaint of the common weill of Scotland. Sir David Lyndsay. 6845-6
The complaint of the Count of Saldana. Unknown (Spanish) 6757-3
Complaint of the lad with heart-disease. Jules Laforgue. 6351-9
The complaint of Troilus. Geoffrey Chaucer. 6830-8
A complaint on the miseries of life. James Thomson. 6816-2
The complaint to his empty purse. Geoffrey Chaucer. 6301-2, 6383-7
Complaint to the moon. Henry Longan Stuart. 6244-X
The complaint, sels. Edward Young. 6198-2
A complaint. Tudor Jenks. 6690-9
The complaint. Jacinto Fombona Pachano. 6642-9
The complaint. Jacinto Fombona Pachano. 6642-9
The complaint. Edward Young. 6152-4
Complainte. Jules Laforgue. 6801-4
Complaints. Bedros Tourian. 6050-1
"The complaints of the beasts in the ark". Limerick:"The complaints of the beasts in the ark". Unknown. 6811-1
The complaints of the poor. Robert Southey. 6459-0,6131-1, 6219-9
The complaynt of Chaucer to his purse. Geoffrey Chaucer. 6193-1
"The compleat angler and 'The natural history of...'" Unknown. 7020-5
Complete destruction. William Carlos Williams. 6808-1
"Complete the altar stands; my task is done". The artist, fr. The picture of St. John. Bayard Taylor. 6976-2
"Completely of our day and of our mood". A cabaret dancer. Zoe Akins. 6959-0
Completion. Victor Hugo. 6351-9
Completion. Eunice Tietjens. 6607-0,6300-4
Complexity. Judith Tractman. 6880-4

A complication. Unknown. 6118-4
Compliment. Ibn al-Haddad. 6362-4
Compliment to mariners. George Dillon. 6619-4
Compliment to Queen Elizabeth, fr. Midsummer Night's.. William Shakespeare. 6385-3,6438-8
The compliment. Thomas Carew. 6250-4
The compliment. William Habington. 6022-6
Complimentary pieces to Milton. John Milton. 6814-6
Compliments of the season. Rossiter W. Raymond. 6385-3
Composed at Cora Linn. William Wordsworth. 6142-7
Composed at Neidpath castle, 1803. William Wordsworth. 6246-6,6543-0
Composed by the sea-side near Calais August 1802. William Wordsworth. 6122-2,6488-4,6110-9,6430-2
Composed in the valley near Dover, on the day of... William Wordsworth. 6828-6
Composed on a May morning. William Wordsworth. 6198-2
Composed upon an evening of extraordinary splendor. William Wordsworth. 6110-9,6199-0,6828-6
Composed upon the beach at Calais, 1802. William Wordsworth. 6604-6,6086-2,6219-9,6230-X
Composed upon Westminster Bridge, Sept. 3, 1802. William Wordsworth. 6154-0,6473-6,6536-8,6604-6,6660-7,6197 , 6198-2,6331-4,6488-4,6527-9,6625-9,6122 ,6560-0,1696- 6,6250-4,6645-3,6110-9,6125 ,6723-9,6086-2,6023-4, 6430-2,6199-0,6659 ,6301-2,6153-2,6646-1,6371-3,6491- 4,6464 ,6560-0,1696-6,6250-4,6645-3,6110-9,6125 , 6723-9,6086-2,6023-4,6430-2,6199-0,6659 ,6301-2,6153- 2,6646-1,6371-3,6491-4,6464
The composer. Lucille Evans. 6316-0
"Composing scales besides the rails". The harmonious heedlessness of Little Boy Blue. Guy Wetmore Carryl. 6891-X
A composite cat. Maria Johns Hammond. 6699-2
Composition. George O'Neil. 6619-4,6039-0
Composition in cottons. Marie de L. Welch. 6628-3
The composition of a kiss. Samuel Taylor Coleridge. 6967-3
A compressionist's creed. Norman Bethune. 6482-5
Compton, Miriam Augusta
    Pasque flower. 6342-X
Compton-Rickett, Arthur
    O winds that wail. 6875-8
    A roundel. 6875-8
Compulsory assent. Yannis Ritsos. 6803-0
"Compunction.". Maurice Kelley. 6397-7
The computation. John Donne. 6198-2,6430-2
Comrade Christ. Verne Bright. 6144-3
Comrade Jesus. Ralph Cheyney. 6954-1
Comrade Jesus. Ralph Cheyney. 6144-3
Comrade Jesus. Sarah N. Cleghorn. 6076-5,6375-6,6393-4, 6730-1
"Comrade heart, if ever you should be tempted". The possible. Randall Swingler. 6895-2
Comrade laughter. Paul Potts. 6895-2
"Comrade thou of melancholy". The sentimental carousers. Karel Toman. 6886-3
Comrade to comrade. Marguerite Wilkinson. 6619-4
"Comrade, affairs are in a ferment". al-Rusafi. 6766-2
Comrade, remember. Raymond Kresensky. 6420-5
"Comrade, you have fought well". In memoriam: John Cookson. Harold Douglas. 6761-1
The comrade. Lee Wilson Dodd. 6897-9
Comradery. Madison Cawein. 6431-0
Comrades. Bliss Carman and Richard Hovey. 6006-4
Comrades. Jock Curle. 6475-2
Comrades. Fannie Stearns Davis. 6019-6,6327-6
Comrades. Henry R. Dorr. 6946-0
Comrades. Richard Hovey. 6310-1,6473-6,6476-0,6501-5,6464-7
Comrades ("Where are the friends that I knew..."). George Edward Woo'berry. 6310-1,6473-6,6509-0,6467-1
Comrades in death. Yiannis Griparis. 6352-7
Comrades known in marches many. Charles G. ("Miles O'Reilly") Halpine. 6113-3,6340-3
Comrades of the trail. Mary Carolyn Davies. 6374-8
Comrades! join the flag of glory. Unknown. 6015-3
"Comrades, our ranks are getting thin". Our ranks are getting thin. Louis Eisenbeis. 6927-4
Comrades, sels. Richard Hovey. 6484-1
Comrades, the morning breaks. Hafiz. 6253-9

"Comrades, you may pass the rosy...". The lay of the
    lovelorn. Sir Theodore Martin. 6802-2
Comrades: an episode. Robert Nichols. 7027-2
The comrades. William Canton. 6250-4
Comradeship. Thekla N. Berstecher. 6906-1
Comradeship. Edgar A. Guest. 6862-6
Comstock, C.H.
    "There was an old man of Dumfries". 6130-3
Comstock, Juline W.
    Hero-worship. 7019-1
Comus tempts the lady. John Milton. 6150-8
Comus, sels. John Milton. 6289-X,6369-1,6726-3,6179-6,6239-
    3,6302-0,6385-3,6138-9,6317-9,6669-0,6102 ,6219-9,
    6438-8,6649-6,6250-4,6301-2
Comus, sels. John Milton. 6934-7
"A con man in the thirties". The last ancestor. Gene
    Fowler. 6792-1
Conall's head. George Sigerson. 6582-1
Conan of Fortingall. J. Corson Miller. 6619-4
Conant, Helen Stevens
    Stavoren. 6621-6
Conant, Isabel Fiske
    America's triumvirate. 6995-9
    Angler. 6501-5
    Answer. 6619-4
    Antiseptics- lenses. 7014-0
    Bird o'er the battlefield. 6542-2
    Blue Persian. 6120-6
    Border. 6076-5,6102-8
    Casements. 6076-5,6102-8
    The child's dream. 6249-0
    Dead friend. 6850-2
    Dreamers. 6461-2
    Flower show. 6232-6
    Frail flame. 6071-4
    The great physician the doctor- Pasteur. 7014-0
    Homeless. 6850-2
    Indian graveyard--Montauk. 7038-8
    Kind sleep. 6501-5
    Kwannon, the compassionate. 6850-2
    Less than kin. 6072-2,6178-8
    The lion that Roosevelt shot. 6995-9
    Men against the sky. 6042-0
    Old Ellen. 7038-8
    Poet and merchant. 6040-4
    A queen's lament. 6037-4
    Sakura. 6850-2
    Woman. 6619-4
Conant, Wallace B.
    Spezia. 6936-3
A concatenation. Carolyn Wells. 6882-0
"Conceal not time's misdeeds, but on my brow". To a
    painter. Walter Savage Landor. 6828-6
Concealment. Samuel Taylor Coleridge. 6980-0
Conceit begotten by the eyes. Sir Walter Raleigh. 6584-8
A conceit.. Mortimer Collins. 6273-3
A conceit. Mortimer Collins. 6652-6
The conceited grasshopper. Elizabeth Turner. 6356-X
"Conceivable, after all/if not plausible". Doomsday. Hans
    Magnus Enzensberger. 7032-9
"Concentred here th' united wisdom shines". The federal
    convention. Unknown. 6946-0
Concept. Gertrude May Lutz. 6979-7
Conception. Grace Phillips. 6750-6
The conception of Christ. John Wedderburn (atr) 6756-5
Concepts. William White. 6868-5
Concerning a western mountain shaped like a whale. Vachel
    Lindsay. 6206-7
Concerning boundaries. Ethel Romig Fuller. 6461-2
Concerning Brownie. Nancy Byrd Turner. 6501-5
"Concerning brave captains". Great-heart. Rudyard Kipling.
    6995-9
Concerning death. Hovhannes Tulkourantzi. 6050-1
Concerning Geffray Teste Noire. William Morris. 6657-7,
    6655-0
Concerning Kavin. Bliss Carman and Richard Hovey. 6890-1
Concerning kisses. Unknown. 6670-4
Concerning love. Josephine Preston Peabody. 6120-6;6722-0
Concerning Mollberg's parade to Coporal Boman's grave.
    Karl Mikael Bellman. 6045-5

Concerning sisters-in-law. Unknown. 6278-4
Concerning sisters-in-law. Unknown. 6787-5
Concerning Tabitha's dancing of the minuet. Arthur Colton.
    6441-8
Concerning the nature of things, sels. Titus Lucretius
    Carus. 6482-5
Concerning usury. Koran. 6954-1
Concert. Ibn Sharaf. 6362-9
Concert at sea. Hubert Creekmore. 6666-6
A concert given by Mr. Spring. Unknown. 6629-1
The concert in the wood. Unknown. 6672-0
Concert pitch. Conrad Aiken. 6007-2
Concert: Lewisohn Stadium. Frances M. Miller. 6042-0
A concert. Leonard Bacon. 6506-6
The concert. William Browne of Tavistock. 6943-6
The concert. Unknown. 6260-1
Concession. May Frank. 6397-7
Concha. Francis Bret Harte. 6600-3
Conclusion. Tom Boggs. 6761-1
Conclusion. John Dillon Husband. 6761-1
Conclusion, fr. A dialogue between...soul and the body.
    Andrew Marvell. 6324-1
Conclusion, fr. Death's men. Walter James Turner. 6324-1
Conclusion, fr. May Queen. Alfred Lord Tennyson. 6616-X
Conclusion, fr. Sonnets of the months. Folgore da San
    Gemignano. 6325-X
The conclusion. Sir Walter Raleigh. 6088-9,6153-2,6214-8,
    6301-2,6723-9,6186-9,6198-2,6427-2,6634-8,6102-8,
    6122 ,6512-0,6730-1,6732-8,6194-X,6250-6,6461
"Concomly's skull is coming home". Comcomly's skull. Jim
    Barnes. 7005-1
The Concord fight. Ralph Waldo Emerson. 6601-1,6552-X,6263-
    6
Concord hymn. Ralph Waldo Emerson. 6449-3,6639-9,6665-8,
    6739-9,6267-9,6265 ,6223-7,6250-4,6560-0,6135-4,6288-
    1,6107 ,6104-4,0470-1,6736-0,6126-5,6153-2,6121 ,
    6300-4,6396-9,6421-3,6006-4,6208-3,6239-3,6240-7,
    6289-X,6332 ,6457-4,6641-0,6473-6,6732-8,6735-2,6723
A concord love-song. James Jeffrey Roche. 6724-7
Concord momument hymn. Ralph Waldo Emerson. 6385-3
"Condemn'd to hope's delusive mine". On the death of Mr.
    Robert Levett. Samuel Johnson. 6975-4
"Condemn'd to hope's delusive mine,". Samuel Johnson. 6208-
    3
Conder, Alan (tr.)
    Beauty. Charles Baudelaire, 6317-9
    The clock. Charles Baudelaire, 6317-9
    El desdichado. Gerard de Nerval, 6317-9
    "The gardener standing by." Unknown, 6317-9
    My little lover. Cecile Sauvage, 6317-9
    My two daughters. Victor Hugo, 6317-9
    Orinda to Lucasia. Katherine Philips, 6317-9
    The ransom. Charles Baudelaire, 6317-9
    "Seeing those mountains, distant and obscure." Mellin
        de Saint-Gelais, 6317-9
    "Sweet Adon', dar'st not glance thine eye?" Robert
        Greene, 6317-9
    When you elect to call me, God, O call. Francis Jammes,
        6317-9
Conder, Josiah
    "Through life's vapours dimly seeing." 6302-0
    Trust in Jesus. 6065-X
Conditor alme siderum externa luc credencium. Unknown.
    6756-5
Condolatory address to Sarah, Countess of Jersey... George
    Gordon, 6th Baron Byron. 6945-2
Condon, Amasa Stetson
    Abraham Lincoln. 6524-4
The condor. Michael Hogan. 6870-7
Conductor Bradley. John Greenleaf Whittier. 6911-8,6126-5
The conductor's story. Maurice E. McLoughlin. 6675-5
The conductor. Alfred Noyes. 6169-9
"A cone of dust is dancing at the lane end". Dust. Eden
    Phillpotts. 7014-0
Cone, Helen Gray
    The ballad of Calnan's Christmas. 6062-5
    The ballad of Cassandra Brown. 6089-7,6652-6
    A call to the builders. 6848-0
    A chant of love for England. 6224-5
    A chant of love for England. 6309-8

The common street. 6395-0,6102-8,6509-0,6076-5,6393-4,
    6396 ,6476-0
The dandelions. 7041-8
The dandelions. 6047-1,6519-8,6597-X,6374-8,6632-1,6421-3
An epistle in June. 6847-2
The gaoler. 6473-6
The good ship alma mater. 6847-2
Greencastle Jenny. 6419-1,6062-5
Heartbreak road. 6076-5,6102-8
In memoriam: Lydia F. Wadleigh. 6847-2
An invocation in a library. 6847-2
The ivy leaf. 6847-2
King Raedwald. 6847-2
The last cup of canary. 6467-1
The merchant of Venice. 6848-0
Of him who loved not rest. 6995-9
The ride to the lady. 6310-1
The secret of the staff. 6847-2
A song of failure. 7041-8
'Songs of a semite' 6848-0
Sonnet in memory of John Keats (1). 6847-2
Sonnet in memory of John Keats (2). 6847-2
Sonnets dedicated to the University of Virginia. 6184-2
The spark. 6501-5
The spring beauties. 6006-4,6338-1
The teacher. 6847-2
The tender heart. 6575-9,6441-8
Thisbe. 6441-8
To Belgium. 7027-2
To-day. 6310-1
To-day. 7041-8
'Under no skies but ours' 6848-0
The victor. 7019-1
Winged seeds. 6373-X
A yellow pansy. 6232-6,6266--0,6374-8,6653-4
Cone, Helen Puck
    A rhyme of Robin Puck. 6682-8
Cone, Joe
    A born fisherman. 6694-1
    Little girl of long ago. 6274-1
    The men of Monomoy. 6274-1
    Not too busy to fish. 6707-7
    When father shaves his face. 6715-8
    A young soubrette. 6700-X
Cone, N.G.
    The twelve little brothers. 6215-6
Conemaugh. Elizabeth Stuart Phelps Ward. 6946-0
Coney fourth. Marshall Schacht. 6761-1
Coney Island down der pay. Henry Firth Wood. 6413-2
The confederacy.. Jane T.H. Cross. 6074-9
The Confederate flag. Unknown. 6630-5
Confederate memorial day. Unknown. 6074-9
The confederate note. S.A. Jonas. 6074-9
A Confederate prison. Stephen Vincent Benet. 6542-2
Confederate wall. Greg Giles. 6883-9
The confederate. Whitelaw Saunders. 6039-0
"Confederates in this white field". Meeting. Charles
    Eglinton. 6788-3
"Confederates, listen...", fr. William Tell. Johann C.
    Friedrich von Schiller. 6606-2
"Confess'd from yonder slow-extinquish'd cloud". Summer
    evening and night, fr. The seasons (Summer). James
    Thomson. 6932-0
Confessio amantis. Delphine Harris Coy. 6836-7
Confession. Gertrude Joan Buckman. 6850-2
Confession. Samuel Butler. 6278-4
Confession. Evelyne Love Cooper. 6850-2
Confession. Fritz [pseud]. 6817-0
Confession. Charles, Duc d' Orleans. 6125-7
Confession. Jackson Holland Patterson. 6841-3
Confession. Jessie B. Rittenhouse. 6320-9
Confession. Frank Dempster Sherman. 6266-0
Confession. Unknown. 6690-9,6167-2,6278-4
Confession. Phillip A. M. Villiers de l'isle-Adam. 6873-1
Confession. John Hall Wheelock. 6327-6
Confession Amantis (Medea and Eson). John Gower. 6198-2,
    6193-1
A confession for forgiveness. Unknown. 6090-0
Confession of a cigar smoker. Unknown. 6453-1

Confession of a hooligan. Sergei Esenin. 6546-5
<u>Confession of a stolen kiss. Charles, Duc d' Orleans. 6881-2</u>
The confession of Annaple Gowdie, witch. Walter Chalmers
    Smith. 6819-7
The confession of Charlemagne. Karl Simrock. 6842-1
Confession of faith. Elinor Wylie. 6011-0
A confession of faith, fr. My religion. Leo Tolstoy. 6337-3,6420-5
A confession of faith. James Sprent. 7027-2
The confession of gluttony. William Langland. 6733-6
Confession overheard in the subway. Kenneth Fearing. 6666-6
Confession to J. Edgar Hoover. James Wright. 6803-0
Confession, fr. 'The book of self' James Oppenheim. 6954-1
A confession. Alice Cary. 6865-0;6969-X
A confession. Paul Verlaine. 6730-1
The confession. Richard Harris ("Thomas Ingoldsby")
    Barham. 6089-7
The confession. Kate Putnam Osgood. 6402-7
The confession. When Yi-tuo. 6125-7
Confessional. Katharine McCluskey. 6034-X
The confessional.. Robert Browning. 6427-2
The confessional.. Unknown. 6605-4
The confessional. Helen Parry Eden. 6172-9,6292-X
Confessions. Elizabeth Barrett Browning. 6437-X,6655-0
Confessions. Robert Browning. 6246-6,6657-7,6110-9,6199-0,
    6655-0
The confidant. Edward Farquhar. 6939-8
The confidant. Claude Flight. 6804-9
The confidant. Charles and Mary Lamb. 6295-4
The confidant. Leonora Speyer. 6034-X
Confidants. William Alexander Percy. 6619-4
Confided. John Banister Tabb. 6096-X,6737-9
The confident scientist. Alexis. 6435-3
Confido et conquiesco. Adelaide Anne Procter. 6957-6
The confirmation. Karl Shapiro. 6751-4
Confiteor. Adam Lindsay Gordon. 6951-7
Conflagration. John James Piatt. 7041-8
Conflict. Caroline Clive. 6437-X
Conflict. Scudder Middleton. 6038-2
Conflict. Francis Reginald Scott. 6446-9
The conflict of convictions. Herman Melville. 6333-0
The conflict. Cecil Day Lewis. 6209-1
Confluents. Christina Georgina Rossetti. 6123-0
Confucius
    Death and life. 6732-8
    The morning glory. Helen Waddell (tr.). 6232-6
    Pride in poetry. 6954-1
    The soldier. 6732-8
    Superiority. 6732-8
    Trysting time. 6732-8
    Wisdom. 6732-8
Confucius and Tsze-Lu. Edgar Lee Masters. 6042-0
"Confuse me not with impious things". A caterpillar's
    apology for eating a favorite... Charles Dalmon.
    6861-8
The confused dawn. William Douw Lighthall. 6433-7,6656-9
The conger eel. Patrick MacGill. 6930-4
The Congo, sels. Vachel Lindsay. 6527-9,6732-8,6300-4
The Congo. Vachel Lindsay. 6332-2,6726-3,6102-8,6076-5,
    6464-7,6467
The congratulation. Jonathan Odell. 6753-0
The congregation. Gamaliel Bradford. 6033-1
Congress hall, N.Y. Philip Freneau. 6753-0
The congress. Unknown. 6753-0
The Congress. Unknown. 6589-9
The congress. Unknown. 6753-0
Congressman Jones. Unknown. 6486-8
Congreve, William
    Ah, stay! ah, turn!, fr. The fair penitent. 6328-4
    Amoret. 6244-X,6195-0
    Ancient Phyllis. 6563-5
    Buxom Joan. 6089-7
    The cathedral. 6438-8
    Fair Amoret. 6733-6
    "Fair Amoret is gone astray" 6874-X
    False though she be to me and love. 6226-1
    "False though she be to me and love". 6024-2,6208-3
    A hue and cry after fair Amoret. 6932-0

A hue and cry after fair amoret. 6732-8
Lesbia. 6102-8
Letter to Viscount Cobham. 6315-2
Love for love, sels. 6562-7
"Love's but the frailty...", fr. The way of the world. 6562-7
The mourning bride, sels. 6102-8,6301-2
Music. 6302-0;6385-3
Music has charms, fr. The mourning bride. 6934-7
Nil admirari. 6932-0
"A nymph and a swain...", fr. Love for love. 6562-7
Pious Celinda. 6092-7,6026-9,6328-4
Pious Celinda [or Selinda]. 6026-9,6092-7
"Pious Selinda goes to prayers" 6874-X
Procrastination. 6302-9
Sabina wakes. 6092-7
Silly fair. 6385-3
"A soldier and a sailor." 6157-5
A soldier and a sailor. 6430-2
Song ("Ah stay!"). 6315-2
Song ("False though she be to me and love"). 6932-0
Song ("Tell me no more"). 6026-9
Tell me no more I am deceived. 6328-4
To Cynthia. 6378-0
To Cynthia weeping and not speaking. 6317-9
The way of the world, sels. 6562-7
The white rose. 6271-7
Conine, Robert
Jade and bronze. 6397-7
Conington, J. (tr.)
The Aeneid, sels. Vergil, 6372-1
Nisus and Euryalus, fr. The Aeneid. Vergil, 6372-1
Conjecture. Florence Hamilton. 6076-5
Conjugal conjugations. A.W. Bellaw. 6089-7,6724-7,6505-8
A conjugal conundrum. Unknown. 6089-7
Conjugal lament. Samuel N. Pond. 7021-3
Conjugal love. R.S. Sharpe. 6279-2
The conjunction of Jupiter and Venus. William Cullen Bryant. 6288-1
Conjuration. Thomas Campion. 6153-2
A conjuration, to Electra. Robert Herrick. 6194-X
The conjure woman. Unknown. 6691-7
The conjurer cozened. Samuel Rowlands. 6787-5
The conjurer's song, fr. The Indian queen. Sir Robert Howard. 6328-4
The conjurer. Edward Verrall Lucas. 6018-8
Conkling, Grace Hazard
After sunset. 6232-6,6102-8,6337-3,6653-4,6253-9,6393 , 6374-8,6076-5,6636-5,6509-0,6656-2
The barberry bush. 6029-3
A Beethoven andante. 6467-1
A breath of mint. 6338-1
Cedars. 6253-9
A child's song overheard. 6501-5
The chimes of Termode. 6053-6,6331-4
Cretonne tropics. 6762-X
Cretonne tropics. 6033-1
Elegy for the Irish poet Francis Ledwidge. 6653-4
Francis Ledwidge. 6556-2
Golden-throated pastoral horn. 6327-6
I have cared for you, moon. 6607-0
"I will not give thee all my heart" 6019-6
Letter to an aviator in France. 7027-2
The little rose is dust, my dear. 6431-0
Maine woods in winter. 6161-3,6184-2,6161-3
Modern sonnet. 6076-5
Morning Sonnet. 7038-8
Night song. 6253-9
Nightingales. 6338-1
The nightingales of Flanders. 6510-4,6443-4,6051-X,6510-4
On arranging a bowl of violets. 6266-0
Python. 6217-2,6250-4
The python. 6217-2
Recuerdo. 6619-4
Refugees. 6509-0
The return of Joan D'Arc. 6331-4
Rheims cathedral. 6051-X
The road to the pool. 6653-4,6338-1
The rose. 6338-1
The scissors-man. 6338-1
Song ("I will repay"). 6320-9
Steamer Letter. 7038-8
Tampico. 6556-2,6393-4
This is not loneliness. 6619-4
To a new-born baby girl. 6078-1,6266-0
To Hilda of her roses. 6762-X
To the schooner Casco, dear to R.L.S. 6030-7,6464-7
The tree of starlings. 6073-0
Victory bells. 6051-X
The whole duty of Beskshire Brooks. 6374-8,6607-0,6253-9,6431-0
You make me think of loops of water lying. 6019-6
Conkling, Hilda
Adventure. 6368-3
August afternoon. 6421-3
Bed-time. 6421-3
Blue jay. 6421-3
The cellar. 6466-3
Chickadee. 6510-4
Cloud-pansy. 6776-X
Daisies. 6393-4
Dandelion. 6538-4
Elsa. 6776-X
Evening. 6538-4
Fairies. 6368-3,6538-4
Fro you, mother. 6538-4
Hills. 6253-9,6396-9,6421-3,6236-9
Humming-bird. 6368-3
I keep wondering. 6467-1
Joy ("Joy is not a thing you can see.") 6501-5
Lilacs ("After lilacs come out"). 6619-4
A little girl's songs. 6338-1
Little green Bermuda poem. 6776-X
Little snail. 6638-0
Little snail. 6891-X
The lonesome wave. 6607-0
Moonbeam. 6861-8,6421-3
Music. 6891-X
The old bridge. 6891-X
Poems. 6396-9
Red rooster. 6762-X
Snow morning. 6776-X
Song for morning. 6421-3
Song nets. 6776-X
Spring song. 6891-X
Time. 6393-4
Tree-toad. 6478-7,6368-3
Velvets. 6762-X
Conley, Elsie
My creed. 6818-9
Conley, Robert J.
The hills of Tsa la gi. 7005-1
Ned Christie. 7005-1
The rattlesnake band. 7005-1
Tom Starr. 7005-1
Untitled. 7005-1
Wili Woyi shaman, also known as Billy Pigeon. 7005-1
A Connachtman. Padraic Colum. 6872-3
A Connaught lament. Nora Chesson. 6019-6
A Connaught lament. Nora Hopper. 6872-3
The Connaught rangers. Winifred M. Letts. 7027-2
Connecticut. Fitz-Greene Halleck. 6735-2
Connecticut road song. Anna Hempstead Branch. 6431-0
Connell, Helen
The Ysleta mission. 6396-9
Connell, Jim
New words to the tune of 'O'Donnel Abu' 6930-4
Connelly, Beverly
Testimony. 6218-0
2000 A.D.Two t. 6218-0
Connelly, Marc
The cluricaun. 6817-0
The italics are George Macdonald's. 6817-0
Connla's well. George William ("A.E.") Russell. 6090-0
Connoisseurs. D.S. MacColl. 6511-2
Connolly. Liam MacGowan. 6930-4
Connolly, Charles M.
The charge of de 'Dutch brigade'. 6155-9,6791-3
Connolly, Daniel

Knocked about. 6045-1,6344-6
Connolly, Francis X.
"Come forward now, ye blind and sick and maimed". 6839-1
No more destructive flame. 6282-2
Connolly, J.B.
Clancy's song. 6423-X
Connolly, Myles
Easter. 6096-X
The shepherd's song. 6143-5,6490-6
Connolly, Myles E.
Quo vadis? 6007-2,6292-X,6337-3
Connor, Florence Griswold
Yo' maw lubs yo' all. 6274-1
Connubial life, fr. Spring. James Thomson. 6302-0;6385-3
Connubii flores, sels. Robert Herrick. 6334-9
Conover, Marion Grace
Quest ("From a high hill"). 6041-2
"**Conquer** the proud spirit...", fr. The Iliad. Homer. 6435-3
Conquered. Zoe Akins. 6897-9
Conquered at last. Maria Louisa Eve. 6273-3
The **conquered** banner. Abram Joseph Ryan. 6300-4,6121-4, 6449-3,6431-0,6172-9,6292-X,6113-3,6243-1,6074-9, 6016-2
The **conquerer.** Ruth M. Williams. 6065-X
The **conquering** love of Jesus. Charles Wesley. 6065-X
The **conqueror** passes. James Branch Cabell. 6875-8,6850-2
The **conqueror** worm. Edgar Allan Poe. 6288-1,6126-5,6333-0, 6077-3,6735-2,6008-0,6250-4
The **conqueror's** grave. William Cullen Bryant. 6735-2
The **conqueror's** sleep. Felicia Dorothea Hemans. 6973-8
The **conqueror..** Morris Abel Beer. 6607-0
The **conqueror..** Grantland Rice. 6211-3
The **conqueror.** Emil Carl Aurin. 6889-8
The **conqueror.** Morris Abel Beer. 6861-8
The **conqueror.** May C. (Mary) Gillington) Byron. 7014-0
Conquerors. Carl John Bostelmann. 6542-2
Conquerors of death. Unknown. 6461-2
The **conquerors.** Jose Maria de Heredia. 6351-9
The **conquerors.** Harry Kemp. 6300-4,6542-2,6102-8,6335-7, 6144-3,6337-3,6732-8
Conquest. Leslie Savage Clark. 6144-3
Conquest. Unknown. 6118-4
Conquest. Ella Wheeler Wilcox. 6461-2
The **conquest** of Canaan, sels. Timothy Dwight. 6077-3,6008-0
The **conquest** of Granada, sels. John Dryden. 6152-4
The **conquest** of Louisburg, sels. John Maylem. 6008-0
Conquest of prejudice. Charles and Mary Lamb. 6295-4
The **conquest** of the air. Harold Trowbridge Pulsifer. 6473-6
Conquest, F.
A stern story. 6804-9
A **conquest.** Walter Herries Pollock. 6656-9
The **conquest.** George Gordon, 6th Baron Byron. 6945-2
The **conquests** of Tamburlaine, the Scythian..., sels. Christopher Marlowe. 6726-3
Conquistador. A.D. Hope. 6349-7
Conrad and the dead body of Medora. George Gordon, 6th Baron Byron. 6543-0
Conrad at twilight. John Crowe Ransom. 6037-4
Conrad's love for Medora. George Gordon, 6th Baron Byron. 6543-0
Conrad, Joseph
Lord Jim, sel. 6958-4
Conrad, Robert T.
The fireman. 6671-2,6744-1
The fireman. 6909-6
On the death of General Taylor. 6606-2
Conroy's gap. Andrew Barton Paterson. 7010-8
Conroy, Jack
Cornwall. 6906-1
Dusky answer. 6906-1
Journey's end. 6906-1
The quick and the dead. 6906-1
Conscience. George Gordon, 6th Baron Byron. 6337-3
Conscience. Charles Churchill. 6932-0
Conscience. Sir William Davenant. 6867-7
Conscience. George Herbert. 6378-0

Conscience. Evana Llynn. 6906-1
Conscience. James Abraham Martling. 6952-5
Conscience. Sir Edward Sherburne. 6022-6
Conscience. Henry David Thoreau. 6176-1,6399-3
Conscience ("Head bowed beneath the burden..."). Pierre Reverdy. 6351-9
Conscience ("It is a dang'rous"). William Shakespeare. 6294-6
Conscience and future judgement. Unknown. 6294-6,6964-9
Conscience and future judgment. Charles William Stubbs. 6337-3
Conscience and future judgment. Unknown. 6910-X
Conscience doth make cowards of us all. Menander. 6435-3
Conscience's song. Robert Wilson. 6436-1
Conscience, fr. Macbeth. William Shakespeare. 6337-3
The **conscientious** deacon. Vachel Lindsay. 6339-X
The **conscript.** Wilfred Wilson Gibson. 6337-3,6250-4,6464-7, 6508-2
Conscripts. Anna M. Fielding. 7010-8
Conscripts ("Related to the picnic..."). Francis King. 6475-2
Conscripts of the dream. Edwin Markham. 6954-1
The **conscripts.** Emmanuel Litvinoff. 6475-2
Consecration. Edward Farquhar. 6939-8
Consecration. Caroline Giltinan. 6037-4
Consecration. Marianne Farningham Hearn. 6337-3
Consecration. Anna Hoppe. 6065-X
Consecration. Muiredach O'Daly. 6292-X
Consecration. Muiredach O'Daly. 6090-0
The **consecration** of the common way. Edwin Markham. 6608-9
Consecration of the house. W.S. Fairbridge. 6384-5
Consecration of the temple. Gulielma A. Wheeler Baker. 6848-0
A **consecration,** sels. John Masefield. 6538-4
A **consecration..** John Masefield. 6289-X;6332-2;6427-2;6476-0;6726-3
A **consecration.** John Masefield. 6393-4,6653-4,6161-3,6458-4,6250-4,6102-8,6491,6508-2,6542-2
Consequence. Comte Robert de Montesquiou. 6351-9
Consequence of the Battle of Eddington, fr. Alfred. Henry James Pye. 6867-7
Consequences. Berton Braley. 6853-7
Consequences. Robert J. Burdette. 6588-0
Consequences. Unknown. 6260-1
The **consequences** of being a poet. Naomi Rogin. 6850-2
Consequences of the Reformation. Edward Bulwer-Lytton; Baron Lytton. 6046-3
The **conservative** man. Edward R. Huxley. 6885-5
"A **Conservative,** out on his motor". Limerick:"A Conservative, out on his motor". A.W. Webster. 6811-1
A **conservative.** Charlotte Perkins Stetson Gilman. 6431-0
A **conservative.** Charlotte Perkins Stetson Gilman. 6996-7
Consider. Christina Georgina Rossetti. 6239-3,6424-8
"**Consider** man in ev'ry sphere". The cock-maid, the turnspit,and the ox. John Gay. 6972-X
"**Consider** now the nudist's lot". Barely possible. Inez George Gridley. 6750-6
"**Consider** that the thing has died before we...". The death of the Loch Ness monster. Gwendolyn Macewen. 6767-0
'**Consider** the birds'. J.L. Foxworthy. 6269-5
"**Consider** the brave young egotism". Egotism. Anna Wickham. 6893-6
"**Consider** the heart of a perfect rose!". So blows the rose. Bertha Merena Mauermann. 6789-1
Consider the lilies. Marianne Farningham. 6918-5
Consider the lilies. William Channing Gannett. 6337-3,6730-1,6143-5
Consider the lilies. Charlotte Murray. 6225-3
Consider the lily. William White. 6868-5
"**Consider** the story of Khandahar Khan". A canto of Khans. Berton Braley. 6853-7
Consider these, for we have condemned them. Cecil Day Lewis. 6375-6
Consider well. Sir Thomas More. 6022-6
Consider, Lord, our clerk. Daniel Henderson. 6979-7
A **considerable** speck. Robert Frost. 6722-0
"**Considerate** nature, when she forms a man". The remarkable adaptedness of the African to his... James Abraham Martling. 6952-5

Consideration. Basil C. Hammond. 6799-9
Consideratus considerandus. John Wilmot, 2d Earl of
    Rochester. 6544-9
Consistency. Horace. 6949-5
Consolation. Matthew Arnold. 6947-9
Consolation. Elizabeth Barrett Browning. 6655-0
Consolation. George Villiers, 2d Duke of Buckingham. 6778-6
Consolation. Alice Cary. 6969-X
Consolation. Hazel Reese Collins. 6799-9
Consolation. Edgar A. Guest. 6862-6
Consolation. William Larminie. 6174-5
Consolation. Walter Learned. 6632-4
Consolation. John Frederick Nims. 6648-89
Consolation. Clark Ashton Smith. 6628-3
Consolation. Henry Howard, Earl of Surrey. 6436-1
Consolation. Robert Paul Turbeville. 7016-7
Consolation. Unknown. 6443-4
Consolation. Mary E. (Freeman) Wilkins. 6441-8
Consolation. William Wordsworth. 6552-X
Consolation ("Come, come, no time for lamentation now")
    John Milton. 6186-9
Consolation for early September. Roberta Holloway. 6808-1
Consolation in July. Rayner Heppenstall. 6379-9
The consolation. Anne Finch, Countess of Winchilsea. 6641-0
Consolations amidst earthly change. William Wordsworth.
    6543-0
The consolations of poetry. George Wither. 6793-X
Consolations of religion to the poor. James Gates
    Percival. 6752-2
Consolator. Mai Elmendorf Lilie. 6335-7
A consolatory poem, sels. Nicholas Noyes. 6008-0
A consolatory stanza. John ("Peter Pindar") Walcott. 6278-4
The consoler. Marion Couthouy Smith. 6995-9
The consolers. S.G. W. 6438-8
Consoling Billy. Eva Steel. 6274-1
Conspiracy. Richard Caldwell. 6397-7
Conspiracy. George Sterling. 6648-8
Conspiracy at midnight. John Maher Murphy. 6839-1
The conspiracy of Charles, Duke of Byron, sels. George
    Chapman. 6369-1
The conspiracy of Rienzi. Thomas Moore. 6631-3
Conspiracy of the clothes. Amos R. Wells. 6707-7
Conspiracy of weather-cocks. R.S. P. 6965-7
The conspirators. Frederic Prokosch. 6390-X,6666-6,6375-6
Constable, Henry
    The beggar at the door. 6383-7
    Damelus' song to his Diaphenia. 6198-2,6208-3,6191-5
    "Dear to my soul! then leave me not forsaken!" 6182-6,
        6586-4
    Diaphenia. 6182-6,6328-4,6228-8,6246-5,6634-8,6317
    "Fair sun, if you would have me praise your light."
        6586-4,6181-1
    "Hope, like the hyenna comming to be old." 6586-4
    "If ever sorrow spoke from soul that loves." 6182-6,
        6586-4
    "In that, O queen of queens, thy birth was free." 6181-8
    Love's Franciscan. 6022-6
    "Mine eye with all the deadly sinnes is fraught." 6586-4
    "Miracle of the world! I never will deny." 6181-8
    My lady's presence makes the roses red. 6301-2
    "My lady's presence makes the roses red." 6182-6,6586-4
    "Needes must I leaue, and yet needes must I loue." 6586-4
    O gracious shepherd. 6931-2
    Ode on the death of Sir Philip Sidney. 6483-3
    Of the nativity of the lady's rich daughter. 6436-1
    On Sir Philip Sidney. 6436-1
    Pain of love. 6240-7
    "Ready to seek out death, in my disgrace." 6586-4
    Sonnet ("Dear to my soul"). 6436-1
    Sonnet ("Fair sun"). 6436-1
    Sonnet ("Grace full of grace"). 6436-1
    Sonnet ("Hope"). 6436-1
    Sonnet ("Miracle of the world"). 6436-1
    Sonnet ("My lady's"). 6436-1
    Sonnet ("My tears"). 6436-1
    Sonnet ("Needs"). 6436-1
    Sonnet ("Not that thy hand"). 6436-1
    Sonnet ("Ready to seek"). 6436-1
    Sonnet ("The sun"). 6436-1
    Sonnet ("To live"). 6219-9,6436-1
    Sonnet ("Whilst Echo cries?"). 6436-1
    Sonnet ("You secret vales"). 6436-1
    Sonnets to Diana. 6436-1
    Three knights from Spain. 6228-8
    To God the father. 6489-2
    To God the son. 6436-1
    "To liue in hell, and heaven to behold," 6586-4
    To our blessed lady. 6282-2,6436-1
    To Our Blessed Lady. 6022-6
    To Saint Margaret. 6022-6
    To Sir Philip Sidney's soul. 6182-6
    To Sir Philip Sidney's soul. 6908-8
    To the blessed sacrament. 6022-6
    "When your perfections to my thoughts appeare," 6586-4
    "Whilst Eccho cyes, what shall become of mee," 6586-4
Constable, Thomas
    Old October. 6230-X,6085-4
Constance de Beverley. Sir Walter Scott. 6669-0
Constance's denunciation of King Philip, fr. King John.
    William Shakespeare. 6001-3
Constancy. Joanna Baillie. 6980-0
Constancy. Alice Campbell. 6764-6
Constancy. Samuel Daniel. 6436-1
Constancy. Charles Dibdin. 6322-5
Constancy. George Herbert. 6138-9,6438-8
Constancy. John Boyle O'Reilly. 6089-7,6505-8
Constancy. John Wilmot, 2d Earl of Rochester. 6328-4,6563-5,6250-4
Constancy. Sir Charles Sedley. 6737-9
Constancy. Sir John Suckling. 6189-3,6371-3,6737-9,6099-4,
    6315-2,6194-X,6383-7,6153-2
Constancy. Joshua Sylvester. 6250-4,6513-9,6423-X
Constancy. Edith M. Thomas. 6632-1
Constancy. Sir Thomas Wyatt. 6436-1
The constancy of nature contrasted with...human life.
    Richard Henry Dana. 6752-2
Constancy, fr. Gedichte. Johann Wolfgang von Goethe. 7042-6
Constancy. A song. John Wilmot, 2d Earl of Rochester. 6933-9
Constant. Emily Dickinson. 6620-8,6300-4
Constant. Frederic Thompson. 6292-X
Constant affection. Unknown. 6563-5
The constant cannibal maiden. Wallace Irwin. 6083-8,6089-7
The constant dove. Celia Thaxter. 6612-7
The constant farmer's son. Unknown. 6057-9,6003-X
The constant friend. Eugene Fitch Ware. 6273-3
The constant lover. Sir John Suckling. 6023-4,6250-4,6198-2,6332-2,6122-2,6527-9,6513-9
The constant north. J.F. Hendry. 6379-9
A constant reader. Parmenas Mix. 6912-6
The constant swain and virtuous maid. Unknown. 6874-X
Constantine Paleologus: a tragedy. Joanna Baillie. 6813-8
Constantine of Rhodes
    Before the ikon of the mother of God. G.R. Woodward
        (tr.). 6282-2
The Constellation and the Insurgente. Unknown. 6946-0
The Constellation and the Insurgente. Unknown. 6015-3
The constellation, fr. Texas. Henry Van Dyke. 6961-4
The constellation, sels. Henry Vaughan. 6378-0
Consternation. Unknown. 6674-4
Constitution and Guerriere. Unknown. 6015-3
The Constitution and the Guerriere. Unknown. 6946-0
The Constitution's last fight. James Jeffrey Roche. 6471-X
"The construction of lines". Physics. John Robinson. 7003-5
Constructions and discoveries. David Antin. 6803-0
Consuelo at the country club. Selden Rodman. 6375-6
Consul Romanus. Bertrand Shadwell. 7010-8
"The consul's brow was sad..." Thomas Babington Macaulay,
    1st Baron Macaulay. 6606-2
The consultation, fr. The country doctor. William Green
    Brownson. 6482-5
Consummation. James Terry Whit. 6461-2

CONSUMMATION

The **consummation** of dulness. Alexander Pope. 6634-8
Consummation, fr. To Celia. Witter Bynner. 6897-9
The **consumptive**. Unknown. 6752-2
Consurge, consurge. Bible. 6830-8
Contact. Susan Miles. 6071-4
Contact. Katie F. Nichols. 6764-6
The **contadina**. Felicia Dorothea Hemans. 6973-8
Contagion of courage, fr. Rugby chapel. Matthew Arnold. 6337-3
Contemplate all this work. Alfred Lord Tennyson. 6271-7, 6737-9,6271-7
"**Contemplate**, when the sun declines". Sunset and sunrise. John Owen. 6814-6
Contemplation. Francis Thompson. 6315-2,6507-4
A **contemplation** of night. John Gay. 6152-4
The **contemplation** of the word. Raymond Ellsworth Larsson. 6779-4
A **contemplation** upon flowers. Henry King. 6933-9
A **contemplation** upon flowers. Henry King. 6513-9,6341-1, 6737-9,6315-2,6562-7,6563-5,6194-X,6250-4
Contemplation, sels. Francis Thompson. 6208-3
Contemplations. Anne Bradstreet. 6176-1,6330-0,6121-4,6008-0,6288-1
Contemplations, sels. Anne Bradstreet. 6077-3,6337-3
The **contemplative** quarry. Anna Wickham. 6102-8
The **contemplative** sentry. Sir William Schwenck Gilbert. 6026-9
Contemplative thought. Caroline Parker Smith. 6042-0
The **contemplative**. Sister Mary Benvenuta. 6285-7
Contemporaries. Richard Hovey. 7006-X
Contemporary. Sara Bard Field. 6144-3,6532-5
Contemporary song. Theodore Spencer. 6389-6
The **contemporary** suitor. Edward Sandford Martin. 6441-8
Contempt. Sir Walter Scott. 6294-6
A **contempt** for Dylan Thomas. Wilfred Watson. 6446-9
The **contempt** of poetry. Edmund Spenser. 6436-1
Contempt of the world. Unknown. 6881-2
The **contemptible** neutral. Charlotte Perkins Stetson Gilman. 6274-1
Content. Barnabe Barnes. 6436-1
Content. Elizabeth Barrett Browning. 6337-3
Content. Thomas Campion. 6436-1
Content. Stephen Crane. 6300-4
Content. Thomas Dekker. 6423-X,6189-3,6396-9
Content. Robert Devereux, 2d Earl of Essex. 6436-1
Content. Norman Gale. 6656-9
Content. Dora Greenwell. 6461-2
Content. David Ignatow. 6803-0
Content. Elisabeth Kuskulis. 6836-7
Content. Lona C. Smith. 6799-9
Content. Richard Chenevix Trench. 6134-6
Content. Unknown. 6935-5
Content. Unknown. 6273-3,6654-2
Content. Geffrey Whitney. 6182-6
Content ("My crown is in my heart, not on my head;"). William Shakespeare. 6211-3
Content ("The bliss of man..."). Alexander Pope. 6294-6
Content and discontent. Richard Chenevix Trench. 6424-8
Content and rich. Robert Southwell. 6436-1,6586-4,6600-3
Content in service. Elizabeth Barrett Browning. 6177-X
Content thyself with thy estate. Unknown. 6182-6
"**Content** within his wigwam warm". Canonicus and Roger Williams. Unknown. 6946-0
Content, fr. Farewell to folly. Robert Greene. 6660-7,6385-3,6604-6,6383-7,6191-5,6219-5
Content, fr. King Henry VI. William Shakespeare. 6337-3
Contentation. Charles Cotton. 6934-7
Contented John. Jane Taylor. 6502-3
The **contented** lover. Unknown. 6563-5
The **contented** man. Edgar A. Guest. 6862-6
The **contented** man. Alexander Pope. 6874-X
The **contented** man. Robert Service. 6159-1
A **contented** mind. Joshua Sylvester. 6271-7,6219-9,6541-4
Contented wi' little. Robert Burns. 6831-6
"**Contentedly** with strictest strands confined". Bach, in the fugues and preludes. Sir William Watson. 7014-0
Contention between four maids... Sir John Davies. 6584-8
A **contention** betwixt a wife, a widow, and a maid. Sir John Davies. 6436-1,6584-8
The **contention** of Ajax & Ulysses, sels. James Shirley. 6108-3,6208-3,6562-7
Contentious heart. Ben Belitt. 6640-2
Contentment. Al-Tutili. 6362-4
Contentment. Henry Alford. 6568-6
Contentment. William Bedingfield. 6874-X
Contentment. Charles Stuart Calverley. 6026-9
Contentment. Charles Cotton. 6302-0;6385-3
Contentment. William Cowper. 6152-4
Contentment. Sir Edward Dyer. 6134-6,6242-3,6479-5
Contentment. Eugene Field. 6114-1
Contentment. Richard Lawson Gales. 6950-9
Contentment. Richard Greene. 6737-9
Contentment. Will S. Hayes. 6273-3
Contentment. Oliver Wendell Holmes. 6089-7,6302-0,6385-3, 6441-8,6498-1,6732 ,6745-X,6438-8,6288-1,6265-2,6230-X,6739 ,6004-8,6092-7
Contentment. Eva Wilder McGlasson. 6576-X
Contentment. M. Miller. 6952-5
Contentment. Thomas Nashe. 6600-3
Contentment. Melvin Mortimer Newberg. 6303-9
Contentment. Mark Osaki. 6790-5
Contentment. Sir Philip Sidney. 6584-8
Contentment. Willa Calvert Smith. 6799-9
Contentment. Joshua Sylvester. 6302-0,6385-3,6737-9
Contentment. Unknown. 6130-3
Contentment ("He that holds fast the golden mean"). Unknown. 6273-3
Contentment in the dark. William Bell Scott. 6180-X
Contentment is a sleepy thing, fr. Christian ethics. Thomas Traherne. 6931-2
"**Contentment**, parent of delight". A cure for the spleen, fr. The spleen. Matthew Green. 6932-0
Contentment: or, The happy workman's song. John Byrom. 6152-4
Contents of a boy's pockets. Henrietta R. Eliot. 6715-8
The **contents** of the scedule... Thomas Lodge. 6586-4
The **contessa** to her judges. Cale Young Rice. 7017-5
A **contest** between court and country. Unknown. 6563-5
A **contest**. Michael Drayton. 6191-5
Conti, Francesco Maria de
  The shore of Africa. Felicia Dorothea Hemans (tr.). 6973-8
Continence. Ibn Faraj. 6362-4
The **continental** boat basin. Rose Macaulay. 6633-X
The **continents**. Bayard Taylor. 6976-2
Contingency. W. Wesley Trimpi. 6515-5
Continuance. Dorothy Quick. 6750-6
"**Continuance/Of** remembraunce". A lover left alone. Unknown. 6881-2
Continued. Matthew Arnold. 6655-0
Continued (King's College), fr. Ecclesiastical sonnets. William Wordsworth. 6122-7
The **continuing** Christ. Walter Russell Bowie. 6144-3,6337-3
The **continuing** city. Laurence Housman. 6730-1
Continuing love. Ibn Rashiq. 6362-4
Continuities. Walt Whitman. 6177-X
Continuous cities 004. Italo Calvino. 6758-1
Continuous performanc. Kenneth Fearing. 6751-4
Contoski, Josepha
  At lake Sullivan. 6342-X
Contours. Zona Gale. 6007-2,6461-2
Contractus, Hermanus
  Alma redemptoris mater. Winfred Douglas (tr.). 6282-2
  Salve regina. Winfred Douglas (tr.). 6282-2
Contradictin' Joe. Edgar A. Guest. 7033-7
Contradiction. Alice Cary. 6865-0;6969-X
Contradiction. William Cowper. 6302-0;6385-3
Contradiction. C.G. Thompson. 7016-7
A **contradiction**. Clement Scott. 6652-6
Contradictions. Frances Archer Walls. 6906-1
Contradictory. Alice Cary. 6969-X
Contraria. Roy Meldrum. 6776-X
Contrarimes, sels. Paul Jean Toulet. 6343-8
Contrarious. R. P. 6817-0
The **contrary** experience. Herbert Read. 66209-1,6391-8
Contrary Mary. Nancy Byrd Turner. 6496-5
Contrary town. Clara Louise Burnham. 6965-7
Contrast. O.E. Enfield. 6799-9
Contrast ("And it was in the winter") Charles Granville Hamilton. 6144-3,6335-7

Contrast ("What wrote he on the parched and dusty...")
    Aubert Edgar Bruce. 6144-3
A contrast. Eleanor C. Donnelly. 6918-5,6579-9
A contrast. James Russell Lowell. 6288-1
A contrast. Adelaide Anne Procter. 6957-6
The contrast. Charles Morris. 6874-X
The contrast. Charles Morris. 6089-7,6092-7,6652-6
The contrast. Horace Smith. 6219-9
Contrasted valentines. Kate T. Barrow. 6719-0
Contrasts. Brennan McKay-Wade. 6857-X
Contrasts. John Nichol. 6819-7
Contributed by Mr. Andrew Lang. Anthony C. Deane. 6875-8
The contrite heart, sels. William Cowper. 6369-1
The contrite heart. William Cowper. 6378-0
Contrition across the waves. Caroline Giltinan. 6543-0
The conundrum of the workshops. Rudyard Kipling. 6507-4, 6102-8,6656-9
A conundrum. Unknown. 6312-8
Convalescence. Amy Lowell. 7027-2
Convalescence. David McCord. 6722-0
Convalescence. Edgar Allan Poe. 6240-7
Convalescent. William Henry Ogilvie. 6269-5
The convalescent gripster. Eugene Field. 6949-5
The convalescent. Robert Service. 6159-1
"A convalescin' woman does the stranges sort". What a sick woman does. Edgar A. Guest. 6862-6
Convent. Marcia Nichols Holden. 6979-7
The convent bell. George Roberts. 6090-0,6174-5
"The convent bells are ringing". The execution of Hugo. George Gordon, 6th Baron Byron. 6980-0
Convent echoes. Helen L. Moriarty. 6172-9,6292-X
The convent garden. Marie Kirkwood. 6285-7
The Convent Garden. Katharine (Hinkson) Tynan. 6285-7
The convent of La Verna. Bryan Waller ("Barry Cornwall") Procter. 6624-0
Convent scene, fr. Marmion. Sir Walter Scott. 6370-5
The convent. Seumas (James Starkey) O'Sullivan. 6893-6
Convention. Alfred Kreymborg. 6348-9
Convention. Agnes Lee. 6102-8,6556-2,6076-5,6396-9
Convention. Cosette Faust Newton. 6789-1
Convention song. Unknown. 6946-0
Conventionality. Eloise Wade Hackett. 6337-3
The convergence of the twain. Thomas Hardy. 6210-5
Conversation. John Berryman. 6389-6,6666-6
Conversation. William Cowper. 6230-X
Conversation. Bernice Lesbia Kenyon. 6042-0
Conversation. Louis MacNeice. 6209-1
Conversation. Benjamin Rosenbaum. 6038-2
The conversation book. Unknown. 6443-4
Conversation piece. Smith Dawless. 6527-9
Conversation piece. Jim Holmes. 7003-5
Conversation, fr. The blas bleu. Hannah More. 6932-0
Conversation, sels. William Cowper. 6102-8
Conversation, sels. William Cowper. 6198-2,6102-8
A conversation.. G.M. Miller. 6625-9
A conversation. Sara Hamilton Birchall. 6374-8
Conversational. Unknown. 6166-4,6273-3,6026-9,6088-9,6652-6
A conversational neighbor. Richard R. Kirk. 6326-8,6396-9
The conversational reformer. Harry ("Col. D. Streamer") Graham. 6736-0
The conversazzhyony. Eugene Field. 6949-5
Converse of angels. Hermann Hagedorn. 6944-4
Converse, C.C.
    Forever and forever. 6304-7
Converse, Florence
    Bread line. 6490-6
    Libertie, egalite, fraternite. 6761-1
    A rune of riches. 6368-3,6374-8
    They have blown the trumpet. 6532-5
Conversing with paradise. Howard Nemerov. 6966-5
"Conversing with your sprightly boys". owl, the swan, the cock, the spider, the ass, and... John Gay. 6972-X
Conversion. John Dryden. 6489-2,6022-6
Conversion. T.E. Hulme. 6315-2,6209-1
Conversion. Ella Wheeler Wilcox. 6956-8
Conversion, fr. Nicodemus. Andrew Young. 6337-3
Conversions/winter solstice. Aaron Shurin. 7003-5
The convert's meeting. James Abraham Martling. 6952-5
The convert. Gilbert Keith Chesterton. 6292-X

The converted cannibals. G.E. Farrow. 6089-7
Conveyancing. Thomas Hood. 6974-6
The convict clerk. James Abraham Martling. 6952-5
Convict Joe. Alexander G. Murdoch. 6921-5
The convict of Clonmell. Unknown (Irish) 6244-X,6858-8
The convict ship. Thomas Kibble Hervey. 6980-0
The convict's dream. George Crabbe. 6543-0
Conviction. N. R. A. Becker. 6818-9
The convicts. Alexey Tolstoy. 6103-6
Convoy. William Jay Smith. 6666-6
Conway, Katherine Eleanor
    Annunciation night. 6144-3
    Christ and the mourners. 6144-3
    The heaviest cross of all. 6172-9
    Saturninus. 6172-9
    Vanquished. 6285-7
Conway, Margaret Devereaux
    The Annuciation ("Not yesterday, nor yet a day"). 6282-2
Conway, Minnie
    Sunset thoughts. 6486-8
Conzonetta: of his lady in absence. Giacomino Pugliesi. 6325-X
"Coo-oo, coo-oo,/It's as much as a pigeon...". Pigeon and wren. Unknown. 6943-6
Coogee. Henry Clarence Kendall. 6656-9
Coogee, sels. Henry Clarence Kendall. 6997-5
Coogler, Gordon
    The man without the hoe. 6274-1
Cook county. Archibald MacLeish. 6374-8,6602-X
A cook of the period. Unknown. 6409-4
Cook, ?
    "So nigh is grandeur to man". 6736-0
Cook, Alice Carter
    Laughing bones. 6799-9
Cook, Clarence Chatham
    Abram and Zimri. 6848-0,6385-3,6407-8
    On one who died in May. 6300-4
Cook, Ebenezer
    The sot-weed factor, sels. 6008-0
Cook, Eliza
    The Christmas holly. 6519-8,6145-1,6424-8
    The death of master Tommy Rook. 6242-3,6502-3,6808-1
    The Englishman. 6302-0
    The fern and the moss. 6927-4
    The fisher-boat. 7037-X
    The forest trees. 6049-8
    The free. 6980-0
    Germs of greatness. 6923-1
    God bless thee, boy. 6097-8
    Good-bye. 6085-4
    Hang up his harp; he'll wake no more. 6102-8
    "Hang up his harp; he'll wake no more." 6302-0;6385-3
    "He led her to the altar". 6980-0
    "He saved his land, but did not lay his soldier..." 6712-3
    The heart's charity. 6918-5
    The holly. 6747-6
    Home for the holidays. 6242-3
    I miss thee, my mother. 6097-8
    I thank Thee, God! for weal and woe. 6303-9
    King Bruce and the spider. 6018-8
    A love song. 6980-0
    The mourners. 6980-0
    The mouse and the cake. 6242-3
    My grave. 6980-0
    "No!" 6629-1
    Norah M'Shane. 7037-X
    "Oh! Let us be happy". 6085-4
    The old arm chair. 6014-5,6502-3,6629-1,6543-0,6219-9, 6632 ,6486-8,6097-8,6260-1,6302-0,6385-3,6365 ,6627-5,6014-5,6502-3,6629-1,6543-0,6219-9,6632 ,6486-8, 6097-8,6260-1,6302-0,6385-3,6365 ,6627-5
    The old arm-chair. 6919-3
    Old Dobbin. 6127-3
    Old story-books. 6131-1
    The old water-mill. 6543-0
    Panegyric on Washington. 6171-0
    The quiet eye. 6656-9
    The rook sits high. 6073-0

COOK

    The sailor boy's gossip. 6131-1
    The scarilegious gamesters. 6919-3
    Sea murmurs. 6385-3
    The sea-child. 6656-9
    The song of the carrion crow. 6943-6
    Song of the haymakers. 7037-X
    Song of the mariners. 6328-4
    A star in the west. 6820-0
    The star in the west. 6449-3
    Summer. 6131-1
    There's a silver lining to every cloud. 6408-6
    Thy Kingdom come. 6303-9
    Tribute to Washington. 6568-6
    Trouble your head with your own affairs. 6409-4
    Try again. 6242-3
    Washington. 6260-1,6742-5
    Washington's life. 6712-3
    Water. 6927-4
    Where there's a will there's a way. 6294-6
    The willow tree. 6049-8
    The wreaths. 6980-0
Cook, Ethel Case
    Earth speaks. 6799-9
Cook, Francis S.
    Knowledge. 6750-6
Cook, Gene Seville
    Eclipse. 6799-9
Cook, Geoffrey
    Mount Tamalpais. 6792-1
Cook, Harold Lewis
    The ghost, fr. Space of breath. 6780-8
    Ode ("What is that man knows"). 6782-4
    Soliloquy in an insane asylum. 6778-6
    Time is a flower on the sea. 6232-6
Cook, John B.
    She walks in beauty. 6750-6
Cook, John Esten
    The song of the rebel, sels. 6008-0
Cook, Jonas
    Solomon Grub. 6925-8
Cook, Joseph
    Boston nursery rhymes. 6089-7
    Life. 6889-8
    Rhyme for a chemical baby. 6440-X
Cook, Josephine Merwin
    A busted dolly. 6711-5
    Signs. 6696-8
    Spooks. 6696-8
Cook, Leonard Neill
    Plymouth Sound. 6650-X
Cook, M.
    A curious want. 6505-8
Cook, Marc Eugene ("Vandyke Brown")
    The clown's story. 6407-8
    Growing old. 6441-8,6004-8
    Her opinion of the play. 6735-2,6004-8
    An honest confession. 6004-8
    Little Rocket's Christmas. 6410-8,6744-1,6410-8,6744-1, 6573-2
    Nothing new under the sun. 6271-7
    The queen of hearts. 6441-8
    A seaside incident. 6670-4,6273-3,6632-1
    To a pretty schoolma'am. 6004-8
    The weather in verse. 6416-7,6416-7
Cook, Theodore P.
    Ode for Decoration Day. 6340-3,6113-3
Cooke, Amy Buford
    Inconstant. 6750-6
Cooke, E.O.
    A slumber song ("Hush baby, hush!"). 6078-1
Cooke, Edmund Vance
    Abraham. 6532-5
    Armistice Day. 6542-2
    Before playing Tinkertown. 6280-6
    A besetting sin. 6697-6
    The coquette speaks. 6698-4
    David. 6619-4,6039-0
    Fame and fate. 6280-6
    Frenchman on the English language. 6702-6
    The hero. 7019-1
    How did you die? 6732-8,6337-3,6964-9,6291-1,6337-3, 6260-1,6274-1
    The hunter, tiring of the chase. 6995-9
    Impertinent poems, sels. 6291-1,6337-3,6260-1,6274-1
    Katie an' me. 6688-7
    Laugh a little bit. 6291-1
    The moo cow moo. 6963-0,6732-8
    'Off Manilly'. 6946-0
    On the judgmunt day. 6694-1
    The other one was Booth. 6925-8
    Ruth. 6039-0
    The third person. 6274-1
    The three crosses. 6449-3
    Uncivilized. 6076-5,6102-8
    War display. 6542-2
    Wilson. 7001-9
    The young man waited. 6929-0,6930-0
Cooke, Grace MacGowan
    An abalone shell. 6241-5
Cooke, Helen M.
    The flag at half-mast. 6695-X
Cooke, John Esten
    The band in the pines. 6113-3
    The broken mug. 6074-9
Cooke, Le Baron
    Advice. 6039-0
    The cry of the gulls. 6039-0
    Finis. 6039-0
    Question. 6038-2
Cooke, Marvin
    My treasure. 6249-0
Cooke, Philip Pendleton
    Florence Vane. 6008-0,6302-0,6385-3,6271-7,6008-0,6219-9,6735
    Life in the autumn woods. 6006-4
    The power of the bards, sels. 7017-5
Cooke, Rose Terry
    Abraham Lincoln. 6305-5,6524-4
    Awakening. 6177-X
    Beyond. 6749-2,6919-3
    Bluebeard's castle. 6431-0
    Christmas. 6131-1
    Christmas. 6145-1
    The death of Goody Nurse. 6946-0
    Fishing song. 6240-7,6271-7
    Give me a wish. 6502-3
    A great shame. 6965-7
    Hark! 6155-9
    The iconoclast. 6600-3
    In vain. 6300-4
    It is more blessed. 6303-9
    "It is more blessed." 6304-7
    Jephtha's daughter. 6848-0
    Lost on the prairie. 6127-3
    Our dead heroes. 6523-6
    Pour out thy love like the rush of a river. 6066-8
    "Pour out thy love like the rush of a river". 6066-8
    The rabbi's lesson. 6848-0
    Reve du midi. 6385-3,6271-7,6219-9
    Saint symphorien. 6424-8
    Saint Symphorien. 6632-1
    Segovia and Madrid. 6431-0
    Simon's burden. 6335-7
    The snow-filled nest. 6597-X
    The Thanksgiving magician. 6703-4
    Then. 6271-7
    The trailing arbutus. 6049-8,6271-7,6424-8
    The two villages. 6735-2,6406-X,6630-5
    A wish. 6131-1,6127-3
Cooke, Theodore Pease
    Blue-beard. 6004-8
The **cookie** jar. Edgar A. Guest. 7033-7
Cookin' things. Burges Johnson. 6700-X
Cooking and courting. Unknown. 6385-3
Cooksley, Bert
    Lullaby ("Hush my little sleepyhead..."). 6750-6
    The time of wheat. 6761-1
Cookson, G.M. (tr.)
    "Behold the tyrants that oppressed your land". Aeschylus, 6435-3

"Come, dance and song, in linked round". Aeschylus, 6435-3
"O father, father of our woe". Aeschylus, 6435-3
The overthrow of Zeus. Aeschylus, 6435-3
"Pallas' home contenteth me". Aeschylus, 6435-3
Prometheus bound. Aeschylus, 6435-3
Prometheus the teacher of men. Aeschylus, 6435-3
Salamis. Aeschylus, 6435-3,6665-8
Xerxes defeated. Aeschylus, 6435-3
"Cool beneath melon-colored cloth, your belly". For Arl in her sixth month. Al Young. 6792-1
Cool fingers. Elydia Shipman. 6799-9
The cool of the evening. Lizette Woodworth Reese. 6326-8
Cool tombs. Carl Sandburg. 6031-5,6102-8,6619-4,6726-3, 6076-5,6288 ,6393-4,6121-4
The cool web. Robert Graves. 6246-6
"Cool! cool! cool!". A faun's song. Bliss Carman and Richard Hovey. 6890-1
"The cool, blue flight of a silver flute". The flute. Dorothy O'Gara. 6764-6
Coolbrith, Ina D.
 Alcatraz. 6484-1
 California. 6241-5
 Fruitionless. 6309-8
 In blossom time. 6336-5,6478-7
 Loneliness. 6347-0
 The mariposa lily. 6484-1
 Meadow-larks. 6006-4
 A memory. 6076-5,6076-5,6102-8
 The poet. 7041-8
 The unknown great. 6214-8,6347-0
 When the grass shall cover me. 6161-3,6241-5
 "When the grass shall cover me". 6632-1
 With the caravan. 6076-5,6102-8
Coole, Ralph Garnier
 Riding at night. 7012-4
The cooleen. Douglas Hyde. 6437-X
Cooley, Bertha Strong
 Charm. 6894-4
Cooley, Hattie A.
 Grandmother's bible. 6415-9
Cooley, Julia
 The progressive. 6995-9
 Vide astra. 6300-4
Coolidge, Grace
 Angel court. 6629-1
 The open door. 6337-3
Coolidge, Richard Bradford
 The loss of the coffee pump. 6118-4
Coolidge, Susan. See Woolsey, Sarah
The Coolun. Sir Samuel Ferguson. 6090-0
The Coolun.. Martin MacDermott. 6174-5
the coolun. Maurice O'Dugan. 6930-4
The coolun. James Stephens. 6506-6
The coon's lullaby. Unknown. 6277-6
Coon, R. H.
 A bird-loving Don. 7020-5
'Coon-dog Wess'. James Whitcomb Riley. 6892-8
Cooney, Byron
 Lindbergh--alone! 7019-1
Coonjiner. Francis Paxton. 6397-7
Coop, Charles
 A point in season. 6042-0
Cooper. Unknown. 6706-9
"Cooper foreclosed a mortgage made...Bloodgood". Cooper vs. Bloodgood. William Paterson. 6878-2
The cooper o' dundee. Unknown. 6157-5
Cooper vs. Bloodgood. William Paterson. 6878-2
Cooper's hill. Sir John Denham. 6208-3,6152-4,6562-7
Cooper's hill, sels. Sir John Denham. 6198-2,6194-X
Cooper, Dennis
 David Cassidy then. 7003-5
 First sex. 7003-5
 High school basketball. 7003-5
 Kip. 7003-5
 Mark Clark. 7003-5
 My past. 7003-5
 Two friends. 7003-5
Cooper, Edith. See "Field, Michael"
Cooper, Elsie
 By the sea. 6997-5
Cooper, Evelyne Love
 Confession. 6850-2
 Cure for ennui. 6850-2
 George be quiet! 6850-2
 Guest. 6850-2
 Modern. 6850-2
 To B.C. 6850-2
Cooper, George
 Baby-land. 6273-3,6452-3,6131-1,6627-5,6078-1
 Bobwhite. 6891-X
 Calling them up. 6049-8
 Come little leaves. 6466-3,6452-3,6135-4
 Doll-baby show. 6131-1
 The doll-baby show. 6137-0
 Frogs at school. 6131-1
 In the cradle-boat. 6965-7
 Laughing boy. 6706-9
 The leaves and the wind. 6632-1,6131-1,6394-2,6143-5
 The little leaves. 6373-X
 A merry Christmas and a glad New Year. 6491-4
 Mother. 6466-3,6937-1
 The new year. 6449-3
 October's party. 6135-4,6682-8
 Only one. 6097-8,6627-5
 The rain and the flowers. 6965-7
 Roses underneath the snow. 6486-8
 Round the year. 6691-7
 The sand-man. 6922-3
 A summer day. 6456-6
 Summer games. 6137-0
 Tommy's dinner. 6703-4
 Twenty froggies. 6466-3,6452-3,6135-4
 Upside down. 6629-1
 What grandma says. 6682-8
 What robin told. 6049-8
 The wonderful weaver. 6745-X
Cooper, Georgia H.
 Ballade to patience and you. 6850-2
 Creation. 6850-2
 Dirge. 6850-2
 A garden of posies. 6850-2
 Inspiration. 6850-2
 Night muse. 6850-2
 Opportunity. 6850-2
 Poet's prospect. 6850-2
 Portrait. 6850-2
 Preference. 6850-2
 To - ("I have"). 6850-2
 To a poet. 6850-2
 Two muses. 6850-2
Cooper, Gladys H.
 Market day. 6850-2
Cooper, Gordon
 Where god walked in the calm of day. 6818-9
Cooper, James Fenimore
 The Boston symphony orchestra. 6476-0
 My brigantine. 6300-4,6302-0;6385-3
Cooper, L.S.
 St. Louie. 7019-1
Cooper, M. Truesdell
 Arithmetic in life. 6926-6
Cooper, Mary Ryan
 There are no joys. 6799-9
Cooper, Ruth
 The drunkard's wife. 6919-3
Cooper, Thomas
 Chartist chaunt. 7009-4
 Chartist song. 6188-5,6656-9
 Hail, holiest liberty. 7009-4
Cooranbean, sels. Henry Clarence Kendall. 6768-9
Coose, Nancy
 Foshay tower. 6342-X
Cootie song. Unknown. 6237-7
The cootiful dream. Unknown. 6589-9
Copa d'oro. E. Dorcas Palmer. 7030-2
"Cope sent a challenge frae Dunbar". Johnnie Cope: 2d set. Unknown. 6859-6
Cope, Mary Lovell
 Lullaby ("Sleep like a lily bud"). 6841-3

COPE

Lullaby ("The wind's in the pine tree"). 6841-3
Song ("The moon is over the poplar tree"). 6841-3
Sonnet ("I did not know"). 6841-3
Swamp mist. 6841-3
Swim song. 6841-3
Vanity. 6841-3

Copeland, Benjamin
Matters not where work is done. 6717-4
Our God is marching on. 6720-4

Copeland, Julia
Tut tut! 6799-9

Copeland, Mary Neal
Grass of the field. 6894-4

Copernicus. Thomas S. Jones Jr. 6850-2
Coplas de manrique, sels. Henry Wadsworth Longfellow. 6144-3;6335-7

Copp, Marie T.
Autumn musing. 6799-9

Coppard, Alfred E.
Stay, O stay. 6778-6

Coppard, Alfred Edgar
The apostate. 6070-6
Epitaph. 6072-2
Forester's song. 6891-X
The glorious survivors. 6210-5
The invisible rain. 6071-4
Night piece. 6069-2
The oracle. 6210-5
Pelagea. 6070-6
The shadow. 6779-4
The shadow. 6072-2
The trespasser. 6723-9
The unfortunate miller. 6210-5
The white cat. 6070-6
Winter field. 6779-4

Coppard, Alfred Edward
Forester's song. 6780-8
A lover. 6780-8
The young man under the walnut-tree. 6776-X

Coppee, Francois
A une tulipe. 6801-4
The benediction. 6411-6,6451-5,6576-7,6610-0,6550-3, 6692
Butterflies. 6585-6
Chauvinism. 6351-9
In the street. 6351-9
Innocence. 6351-9
The night-watch. 6575-9
The night-watch. 6921-5
Purgatory. Joseph T. Shipley (tr.). 6351-9
Shipwrecked. 6412-4
Une aumone. 6801-4
The wounded soldier in the convent. 6443-4

"A **copper** conclave of a sky". A Christ-child day in Australia. Ethel Turner. 6784-0
"The **copper** hills of sunset". The artist. Gene Moore. 6750-6
Copper kettle. Estelle Rooks. 6850-2
Copperheads. Brad Burkholder. 6900-3

Coppinger, Matthew
To Clelia. 6563-5

Coptiac poems. Lawrence Durrell. 6209-1
A **copy** of verses sent by Cleone to Aspasia. Walter Savage Landor. 6315-2
A **copyreader's** dream of fair women. Long John Silver [pseud.]. 6817-0
Copyright. Erich Fried. 6769-7
The **coquet** mother and coquet daughter. John Gay. 6972-X
Coquetry. Eugene Field. 6949-5
Coquette. Keith Stuart. 6374-8
The **coquette** - a portrait. John Godfrey Saxe. 6652-6
A **coquette** punished. Unknown. 6407-8
The **coquette** speaks. Edmund Vance Cooke. 6698-4
"**Coquette!** and is it flattery you ask?". Monna Vita. Hermann Hagedorn. 6944-4
The **coquette.** Witter Bynner. 6441-8
The **coquette.** John Godfrey Saxe. 6441-8
The **coquette.** Muriel Early Sheppard. 6281-4
The **coquette.** Samuel Waddington. 6770-0
The **coquetts.** Eugenia Bragg Smith. 6818-9

Cor cordium. Algernon Charles Swinburne. 6122-2,6154-0, 6657-7,6655-0,6110-9,6102-9,6199-0
Cor cordium. Wilbur Underwood. 6285-7
The **coracle**, fr. Pharsalia. Lucan. 6125-7
The **coral** fisher. Allen Upward. 6897-9
The **coral** grove. James Gates Percival. 6239-3,6302-0,6239-3,6639-9,6219-9,6385-3,6438-8,6304-7
The **coral** insect. James Montgomery. 6302-0;6385-3
The **coral** insect. Lydia Huntley Sigourney. 6302-0;6385-3
Coral lizard. Fanny de Groot Hastings. 6979-7
The **coral** vine. Lillie Mae Lumpkin. 6799-9
"The **coral-cold** snow seemed the Parthenon". Metamorphosis, fr. Three variations on a theme. Edith Sitwell. 7000-0
The **Coranna.** Thomas Pringle. 6591-0,6592-9

Corbell, E.T.
The frogs' singing-school. 6368-3
Three wise old women. 6368-3

Corbet, Richard
Country dreams. 6935-5
The fairies' farewell, sels. 6427-2
The fairies' farewell. 6052-8,6563-5,6194-X,6271-7
Farewell to the fairies. 6114-1,6301-2,6383-7,6134-6, 6600-3
Farewell, rewards and fairies. 6092-7,6315-2
A father's blessing. 6737-9
The hundredth psalm. 6427-2
Like to the thundering tone. 6089-7
On Mr. Francis Beaumont (then newly dead). 6933-9
A proper new ballad, intituled The fairies faredwell.. 6933-9
To his son, Vincent Corbet. 6562-7,6230-X,6092-7,6219-9, 6563-5
To his son, Vincent Corbet, on his birth-day...1630. 6933-9

Corbett, Mrs. E.J.
The mischievous cat. 6699-2

Corbett, Mrs. E.T.
The Christening of my boy. 6451-5
The foreclosure of the mortgage. 6916-9
The inventor's wife. 6139-7,6416-7,6964-9
The lecture. 6928-2
Miss Minerva's disappointment. 6412-4
The newsboy's cat; or the fam'ly man. 6699-2
The newsboy. 6913-4.6964-9
The old deacon's lament. 6913-4,6273-3
What Biddy said in the police court. 6411-6

Corbett, N.M.F.
The auxiliary cruiser. 7027-2
R.N.V.R. 7012-4

Corbiere, Tristan
Epitaph. 6351-9
Landscape of evil. A.J. Bull (tr.). 6343-8
Paris by day. 6351-9
Paris by night. 6351-9
Rhapsody of the deaf mute. 6351-9

Corbin, Alice
Apparitions. 6897-9
Bird-song and wire, fr. Desert adrift. 6628-3
The cactus, fr. Desert drift. 6628-3
Corn-grinding song. 6628-3
Dance. 6628-3
Desert drift, sels. 6628-3
Fiesta, fr. Desert drift. 6628-3
The foot-hills, fr. Desert drift. 6628-3
The green corn dance. 6076-5,6102-8,6628-3
Humoresque. 6897-9
In the desert. 6506-6
Juan Quintana. 6076-5,6102-8
Love me at last. 6320-9,6102-8,6109-6,6076-5
Music. 6030-7,6538-4
Muy vieja Mexicana. 6431-0
Muy vieja mexicana. 6556-2
Nodes. 6730-1
O world. 6897-9
On the Acequia Madre. 6506-6
One city only. 6897-9
The pool. 6897-9
Pueblo, fr. Desert drift. 6628-3
Red earth. 6506-6

A song from old Spain. 6320-9
Stone-pine and stream, fr. Desert d ift. 6628-3
Three men entered the desert alone. 6628-3
Two voices. 6393-4
Una anciana Mexicana. 6628-3
What dim Arcadian pastures. 6509-0,6253-9,6393-4
The wrestler, fr. Desert drift. 6628-3
Corbin, Alice (tr.)
Listening. Unknown (American Indian), 6396-9
Corbin, Inez Culver
Pine woods in winter. 6270-9
Corbin, James
The neglected grave of Lincoln's mother. 6524-4
Corby, Herbert
Missing. 6895-2
Sonnet ("He was the mutual mother"). 6895-2
Sonnet ("Jerome again"). 6895-2
Corcyra. John Henry, Cardinal Newman. 6980-0
Cordelie. Brother Paul. 6674-4
Corder, W.
The murder of Maria Marten. 6157-5
Cordial soul. Sara Henderson Hay. 6076-5
Cording up the ned in Vermont. Daniel L. Cady. 6989-4
Cords. Ruth Brownlee Johnson. 6178-8
Core. Jaime Torres Bodet. 6759-X
Coridon and Phillis. Robert Greene. 6436-1
Coridon's song. John Chalkhill. 6092-7,6398-5
Coridon's supplication to Phillis. Nicholas Breton. 6586-4
Corinna. Thomas Campion. 6383-7
Corinna. John Wilmot, 2d Earl of Rochester. 6544-9
Corinna [pseud].
The daughters of Asopus. Cecil Maurice Bowra (tr.). 6435-3
Helicon and Cithaeron. Cecil Maurice Bowra (tr.). 6435-3
Pindarum quisquis... Cecil Maurice Bowra (tr.). 6435-3
Sehnsucht; or what you will. 6817-0
Corinna bathes. George Chapman. 6436-1
Corinna goes a-singing. Frank Sidgwick. 6722-0
Corinna is divinely fair. Unknown. 6563-5
Corinna to Tanagra, from Athens. Walter Savage Landor. 6086-2,6110-9
Corinna's going a-maying. Robert Herrick. 6052-8,6527-9, 6562-7,6732-8,6102-8,6122-,6154-0,6186-9,6198-2,6385-3,6473-6,6536-,6604-6,6726-3,6733-6,6099-4,6465-5, 6723-9,6291-9,6660-7,6191-5,6197-4,6153-2,6472-8, 6250-4,6560-0,6430-2,6301-2,6194-X,6438-8,6371-3, 6646-1,6723-9,6291-9,6660-7,6191-5,6197-4,6153-2, 6472-8,6250-4,6560-0,6430-2,6301-2,6194-X,6438-8, 6371-3,6646-1
Corinna, from Athens, to Tanagra, fr. Pericles... Walter Savage Landor. 6832-4
Corinne at the capitol. Felicia Dorothea Hemans. 6973-8
Corinthian Hall. Eugene Field. 6949-5
Coriolanus. Will Victor McGuire. 6926-6
Coriolanus. William Shakespeare. 6438-8
Corkery, Daniel
The call. 6930-4
The gypsies. 6096 X
Corkine, William
Song ("Sweet Cupid"). 6315-2
"Sweet, let me go, sweet, let me go!" 6317-9
Corlett, Helen
Quiet. 6799-9
Corlis, C.T.
The two temples. 6913-4,6848-0
Cormac
The heavenly pilot. George Sigerson (tr.). 6930-4
Corman, Cid (tr.)
The pebble. Francis Ponge, 6758-1
Cormier-Shekerjian, Regina de
Skin of silence, smell of snow. 6821-9
Corn. Sidney Lanier. 6299-7,6333-0,6673-9,6121-4
Corn. James Abraham Martling. 6952-5
Corn. Emma Celia & Lizzie J. Rook. 6137-0
Corn. Unknown. 6373-X
Corn. Maud E. Uschold. 6396-9
"Corn does not hurry, and the black grape...". Second wisdom. Henry Morton Robinson. 6979-7
"Corn hangs from the rafters". Sierra. Jorge Carrera Andrade. 6759-X
The corn husker. Emily Pauline ("Tekahionwake") Johnson. 6837-5
Corn in the wind. Iyad. 6362-4
The corn lands. Unknown. 6224-5
Corn rigs. Robert Burns. 6180-X
Corn song. Benjamin Wallace Douglass. 6662-3
The corn song. John Greenleaf Whittier. 6239-3,6496-5,6135-4,6126-5,6121-4
The corn song. Unknown. 6254-7
"The corn was warm in the ground..". The holly-tree. Bayard Taylor. 6976-2
"Corn!-/Of the summery sunshine born!". Corn. James Abraham Martling. 6952-5
"The corn, in golden light". Brandenburgh harvest-song. Felicia Dorothea Hemans. 6973-8
The corn-crake. David Gray. 6180-X
Corn-fields. Mary Howitt. 6127-3,6271-7,6519-8,6597-X,6656-9
Corn-grinding song. Alice Corbin. 6628-3
Corn-grinding song. Unknown (Laguna Indian) 7039-6
Corn-grinding song. Unknown (Zuni Indian) 6538-4
Corn-law hymn. Ebenezer Elliott. 6102-8,6600-3
Corn-planter. Maurice Kenny. 7005-1
Corn-planting. Peter McArthur. 6115-X
A corn-song. Paul Laurence Dunbar. 6431-0
Corn-stalk fiddle. Paul Laurence Dunbar. 6711-5
The corn. Grace O. Kyle. 6529-5
The corncrake. James H. Cousins. 6930-4
Cornelia's reply. William Allen Butler. 6903-7
Cornelia's song. John Webster. 6933-9,6150-8
"Cornelia, a matron of ancient Rome". Cornelia's reply. William Allen Butler. 6903-7
The cornelian. George Gordon, 6th Baron Byron. 6945-2
Cornelius, Samuel
Trust. 6461-2
Cornell, Annette Patton
Ballad of the lady in hell. 6750-6
Foot note to Eden. 6750-6
Invitation to a husband. 6750-6
May road. 6750-6
Song for three sons. 6750-6
Cornell, M. Ella
Closing address. 6268-7
Opening address. 6268-7
Cornell, Marianne J.
Floating cloud. 6249-0
Corner boys. Bryan MacMahon. 6930-4
A corner fo my heart. Paul Jans. 6799-9
The corner newsboy. Victorio Acosta Velasco. 6799-9
The corner-knot. Robert Graves. 6072-2
"The cornerstone in truth is laid". For the friends at Hurstmont. Henry Van Dyke. 6961-4
The cornerstone. Edward A. Church. 6337-3
The cornet.. Henry Howard, Earl of Surrey. 6436-1
Cornett, Viola
Do not love me now. 6750-6
Cornfield myth. Mary Goose. 7005-1
Cornford, Frances
At night. 6497-3
Autumn morning at Cambridge. 6331-4,6437-X,6506-6
Cambridgeshire. 6071-4
The country bedroom. 6339-X
Dawn. 6019-6
Feri dead. 7014-0
A fragment of Empedocles. 6581-3
Grand ballet. 6354-3
In France. 6044-7,6506-6
In the backs. 6659-3
Lincolnshire remembered. 6257-1
The old nurse. 6339-X
On August thirteenth, at the mount, Marsden, Bucks. 6354-3
On Maou dying at the age of six months. 6511-2
Provence. 6778-6
The ragwort. 6044-7
To a fat lady seen from the train. 6228-8
To a lady seen from the train. 6477-9,6464-7
The woman with the baby to the philosopher. 7014-0
Youth. 6659-3

Cornford, Frances (tr.)
    Transmigration. Empedocles, 6435-3
Corning, Howard McKinley
    Acquisition. 6039-0
    Advent. 6039-0
    Farther sight. 6042-0
    Judas. 6144-3
    Oregon prologue. 6761-1
    Plowmen. 6954-1
    Question. 6144-3
    This is the death. 6782-4
Cornish (atr), William
    Pleasure it is. 6881-2
A **Cornish** carol. Robert Stephen Hawker. 6747-6
The **Cornish** emigrant's song. Robert Stephen Hawker. 6018-8
The **Cornish** miner. Walter F. Gries. 6281-4
Cornish villages. Mark Van Doren. 6039-0
Cornish wind. Arthur Symons. 6331-4,6253-9,6439-6
Cornish, Byron H.
    School of our Lord. 6713-1
Cornish, George
    To the redbreast. 6046-3
Cornish, Paul Floyd
    Brushed by the master's hand. 6818-9
Cornish, William
    Blow thy horn, hunter. 6328-4
    Desire. 6436-1
    God's blessings. 6153-2
    Gratitude. 6436-1
    "The knight knock'd at the castle gate". 6187-7
The **cornstalk's** lesson. Christine Chaplin Brush. 6965-7
"The **cornucopia** of Ceres". The Sylph's song. Edith Sitwell. 7000-0
The **cornucopia** of red and green comfits. Amy Lowell. 6032-3,6393-4
Cornwall. Jack Conroy. 6906-1
Cornwall, Barry. See Procter, Bryan Waller
Cornwall, Philip
    Twilight at the house of Morgan. 6042-0
Cornwallis Burgoyned. Unknown. 6753-0
"**Cornwallis** led a country dance". The dance. Unknown. 6946-0,6753-0
Cornwallis's surrender. Unknown. 6946-0
Cornwallis, Kinahan
    The battle of Murfreesboro. 6946-0
Cornwell, Henry S.
    The angel ferry. 6404-3
    December. 6632-1
    February. 6632-1
    January. 6632-1
    Jefferson D. 6946-0
    May. 6632-1
    My owl. 6632-1
    The stormy petrel. 6997-5
    Unrest. 6632-1
The **Coromandel** fishers. Sarojini Naidu. 6332-2,6478-7,6653-4,6107-9
Corona. Paul Celan. 6758-1
Corona borealis. Inez Barclay Kirby. 6799-9
Corona death-trap hotel, fr. On the fault line. Russell Haley. 7018-3
Corona inutilis. James Lister Cuthbertson. 6784-0
Coronach, fr. The lady of the lake. Sir Walter Scott. 6180-X,6087-0,6134-6,6228-8,6246-6,6271 ,6289-X,6512-0, 6600-3,6634-8,6732-8,6385 ,6726-3,6424-8,6304-7,6371-3,6219-3,6110 ,6438-8,6086-2,6196-6,6458-2
Coronal: a legend of the Annunication. Ruth Forbes Sherry. 6979-7
Coronation. Helen Hunt Jackson. 6431-0,6309-8,6467-1,6385-3,6600-3,6632-1,6239-3,6243-1,6438-8,6219-9
Coronation. Edward Perronet. 6337-3,6730-1,6214-8,6219-9
Coronation ode. Bliss Carman. 6224-5
The **coronation** of Inez de Castro. Felicia Dorothea Hemans. 6302-0
Coronemus nos rosis antequam marcescant. Thomas Jordan. 6733-6
The **coronet.** Andrew Marvell. 6315-2,6380-2,6302-0,6385-3, 6341-1,6150
Corp'ral's chevrons. Unknown. 6846-4
Corporal Clover. Mary Frances Butts. 6965-7

Corporal Dick's promotion. Sir Arthur Conan Doyle. 6580-5
"'**Corporal** Green!' the orderly cried". Roll-call. Nathaniel Graham Shepherd. 6016-2,6273-3,6964-9,6271-7,6273-3,6471-X,6340-3,6552-X,6165 ,6113-3,6294-6, 6404-3.6263-6,6304-7
Corporal's chevrons. Unknown. 6589-9
The **corporal.** Unknown. 6237-7,6589-9
"'**Corporale** Greene!' the orderly cried". Calling the roll. ? Sheppard. 6889-8
Corporate entity. Archibald MacLeish. 6038-2
"A **corpulent** spinster of Crewe". Limerick:"A corpulent spinster of Crewe". Unknown. 6811-1
Corpus Christi carol. Unknown. 6125-7
The **Corpus** Christi carol. Unknown. 6881-2
Corpus Christi, I, II, III. Margery Swett Mansfield. 6393-4
The **corral.** Earle Thompson. 7005-1
A **correct** compassion. James Kirkup. 6210-5
A **correction..** Robert Frost. 6722-0
Corregio. Kruna (pseud.) 6680-1
Correlated greatness. Francis Thompson. 6250-4
Correlations. Erwin F. Smith. 7014-0
Correspondence. Susan Rea. 6822-7
Correspondences. Christopher Pearse Cranch. 6385-3,6288-1
Correspondences, sels. Charles Baudelaire. 6351-9
Corrida de toros. Walter Adolphe Roberts. 6102-8
Corridan, Frances O'Connell
    First born. 6292-X
    Strong arms. 6292-X
"The **corridor** was empty". March 23, 1982 Tuesday night. Thomas Waltner. 6870-7
Corrie, C.J.
    The traitor sea. 6920-7
The **corrosive** season. Lynn Riggs. 6397-7
Corrothers, James D.
    Ghoses. 6696-8
    Paul Laurence Dunbar. 6483-3
Corruption. Henry Vaughan. 6931-2,6933-9,6931-2,6933-9
Corrymeela. Moira (Nesta Higginson Skrine) O'Neill. 6872-3
Corrymeela. Moira (Nesta Higginson Skrine) O'Neill. 6090-0, 6423-X,6477-9,6507-4,6102-8
A **corsage** bouquet. Charles Henry Luders. 6441-8,6652-6
The **corsair.** George Gordon, 6th Baron Byron. 6438-8
Corsairs' song. George Gordon, 6th Baron Byron. 6252-0
Corsellis, Timothy
    Crocus bud on a lover's grave. 6475-2
    Engine failure. 6666-6
    Repression. 6666-6
    They have taken it from me. 6666-6
    The thrush. 6666-6
    To Stephen Spender. 6666-6
    What I never saw. 6475-2
The **Corsican** vendetta; or, love's triumph. Unknown. 6675-5
Corso, Gregory
    America politica historia, in spontaneity. 6803-0
T¯e **corso:** the Roman carnival. Christopher Pearse Cranch. 6624-0
Cortazar, Julio
    The behavior of mirrors on Easter island. 6758-1
    Instructions on how to wind a watch. 6758-1
    Instructions on or rather examples of how to be afraid. 6758-1
    The lines of the hand. 6758-1
    Marvelous pursuits. 6758-1
    Progress and retrogression. 6758-1
    Theme for a tapestry. 6758-1
Cortege. Alexander Mackenzie Davidson. 6269-5
Cortege. Leopoldo Marechal. 6759-X
Cortege for Rosenbloom. Wallace Stevens. 6808-1
Cortes, Elias Hruska
    Mazeworks. 6792-1
Cortez, Jayne
    Big fine woman from Ruleville. 6898-7
    Black feathered mules. 6898-7
    I remember. 6898-7
Cortissoz, Ellen Mackay Hutchinson
    All the year round. 6066-8
    April fantasie. 6820-0
    A cry from the shore. 6271-7
    Harvest. 6271-7

Her picture. 6309-8
June. 6873-1
Moth-song. 6873-1
Priscilla. 6429-9,6226-1,6321-7
The quest. 6873-1
Corvino offers his wife..., fr. Volpone. Ben Jonson. 6637-2
Corwin, Norman
On a note of triumph. 6532-5
Cory, James M.
"Crossing the street in the rain" 7003-5
Poetry. 7003-5
Cory, William Johnson
After reading Ajax. 6483-3
Amaturus. 6094-3
Anteros. 6437-X
A ballad for a boy. 6014-8,6079-X
The hallowing of the fleet. 6793-X
Home, pup! 6018-8
An invocation. 6423-X,6437-X,6383-7
Mimnermus in church. 6317-9,6186-9
Mimnermus in church. 6199-0,6230-X,6250-4,6656-9
Oh, earlier shall the rosebuds blow. 6250-4
A poor French sailor's Scottish sweetheart. 6656-9
Remember. 6301-2,6437-X
School fencibles. 6322-5
The two captains. 6322-5
Cory, William Johnson (tr.)
Heraclitus, fr. Epigrams. Callimachus, 6435-3,6046-3, 6253-9,6879-0,6230-x,6396 ,6052-8,6437-X,6668-2,6250-4,6301-2,6246-5,6512-0,6186-9,6246-5,6639-9,6656
Corydon to his Phyllis. Sir Edward Dyer. 6182-6
"**Corydon**, arise, my Corydon!". Unknown. 6181-8
Coryell, Grace Mary Seeley
Reflection. 6799-9
A **corymbus** for autumn, sels. Francis Thompson. 6655-0
A **corymbus** for autumn. Francis Thompson. 6942-8
Cosmas, Saint
Menaion, sels. 6282-2
The purification. 6282-2
The **cosmic** egg. Unknown. 6089-7,6724-7,6438-8
Cosmic microbe. Bernard Seeman. 6799-9
The **cosmic** trail. Edwin M. Abbott. 6799-9
The **cosmis** urge. P. W. 6817-0
Cosmogony. Edgell Rickword. 6210-5
A **cosmopolitan** woman. Sam Walter Foss. 6682-4
A **cosmopolitan** woman. Unknown. 6089-7
The **cosmopolitan**. Alan Porter. 6776-X
The **cosmopolite**. Edward R. Huxley. 6885-5
Cosmos. Lillian Crellin. 6799-9
Cosmos. Lionel Day. 6850-2
Cosmos. Irwin Russell. 6004-8
Cosmos. Francis Ernley Walrond. 6800-6
Cospatrick. Unknown. 6180-X,6518-4
"**Cospatrick** has sent o'er the faem". Unknown. 6518-X
Cossack cradle=song. Mikhail Lermontov. 6103-6
Cossens, Frederick S.
To my big sweetheart. 6505-8
To my poland rooster. 6505-8
Cossimbazar. Henry Sambrooke Leigh. 6089-7
The **cost** of love. Alfred Edward Housman. 6396-9
The **cost** of praise. Edgar A. Guest. 6862-6
The **cost**. Pansy E. Howell. 6799-9
Costaniantz, Hovhannes
"No bird can reach the mountain's crest". 6050-1
Costanza, fr. Records of woman. Felicia Dorothea Hemans. 6973-8
Costanzo, Angelo di
The death of Virgil. David Wright (tr.). 6325-X
Costanzo, Rebekah Crouse
Traveler. 6461-2
Costello of Tuam, Mrs. (tr.)
The little white cat. Unknown, 6930-4
Costello, ?
Dark Rosaleen. James Clarence Mangan (tr.). 6244-X
Costello, ? (tr.)
Song ("Heaven!"). Charles, Duc d' Orleans, 6226-1
Song ("Wilt thou be mine"). Charles, Duc d' Orleans, 6226-1
"They may blame thy tenderness". Claire D'Anduze, 6226-1

Coster, Joan
Greeting. 6262-8
A song ("I am on"). 6262-8
Costlow, John D.
'Budding life' 6818-9
Cothi, Lewys Glyn
The Saxons of Flint. Mrs. M.C. Llewelyn (tr.). 6528-7
Cotswold love. John Drinkwater. 6331-4,6476-0
Cotta, Giovanni Battista (tr.)
Psalm 014 Bible, 6848-0
Cottage and hall. Alice Cary. 6865-0;6969-X
A **cottage** garden. John Clare. 6649-6
Cottage gardens, fr. Beachy head. Charlotte Smith. 6649-6
The **cottage** girl. Felicia Dorothea Hemans. 6973-8
"The **cottage** home against the wood". The past. William White. 6868-5
"A **cottage** home with sloping lawn...". The ruined merchant. Cora M. Eager. 6909-6
A **cottage** in Chine. Jean Ingelow. 6940-1
"The **cottage** was a thatch'd one". Little Jim. Edward Farmer. 6772-7
The **cottager** and his landlord. John Milton. 6814-6
The **cottager** to her infant. Dorothy Wordsworth. 6078-1, 6233-4,6519-8
The **cottager** to her infant. Dorothy Wordsworth. 6242-3
The **cottager's** hymn. Patrick Bronte. 6337-3
The **cottager's** lullaby. Dorothy Wordsworth. 6627-5
Cotter Jr., Joseph Seamon
And what shall you say? 6532-5
Rain music. 6466-3
The **cotter's** Saturday night, sels. Robert Burns. 7009-4
The **cotter's** Saturday night, sels. Robert Burns. 6260-1, 6395-0
The **cotter's** Saturday night, sels. Robert Burns. 7009-4
The **cotter's** Saturday night. Robert Burns. 6014-5,6101-X, 6198-2,6271-7,6302-0,6332-,6370-5,6385-3,6604-6,6730-1,6732-8,6660
The **Cotter's** Saturday night. Unknown. 6616-X
Cotter's song. Johan Skjoldborg. 6555-4
Cotterell, George
An autumn flitting. 6656-9
In the twilight. 6656-9
Cotterell, L.E.S.
The enduring people. 6468-X
Cotterill, H.B. (tr.)
Nausicaa, fr. The Odyssey. Homer, 6435-3
"Now when at last...", fr. The Odyssey. Homer, 6435-3
Cotton. Harry Martinson. 6420-5
Cotton (atr), John
Bacon's epitaph, made by his man. 6946-0
Cotton (of Queens Creek), John
Bacon's epitaph. 6008-0,6288-1
The **cotton** boll. Henry Timrod. 6333-0,6288-1,6121-4
The **cotton** boll. Henry Timrod. 6265-2
Cotton chorus. Virginia Moore. 6490-6
Cotton fever. Fred Ross. 6783-2
The **cotton** plant. Unknown. 6373-X
Cotton, Charles
"Alice is tall and upright as a pine". 6187-7
The angler's ballad. 6152-4
"Celia, my fairest Celia, fell." 6317-9
Contentation. 6934-7
Contentment. 6302-0;6385-3
"The day's grown old; the fainting sun". 6187-7
Evening quatrains. 6315-2,6378-0,6125-7,6023-4
"Fly, fly! The foe advances fast". 6187-7
Four sisters. 6733-6
Good night, my love. 6328-4
Invitation to Isaac Walton. 6219-9
Invitation to Izaak Walton. 6240-7
The joys of marriage. 6089-7,6724-7
Laura sleeping. 6208-3,6563-5,6189-3,6315-2
"Margaret of humbler stature by the head". 6187-7
Montross. 6563-5
The new year: to Mr. W.T. 6933-9
The new year. 6152-4,6245-8
Noon quatrains. 6315-2
Retirement. 6302-0,6385-3,6597-X,6271-7,6152-4,6219
Retirement, sels. 6378-0

COTTON

    The retirement, sels. 6934-7
    The retreat. 6563-5
    Rondeau. 6563-5
    See how the twilight slumber falls. 6328-4
    Song ("See how the twilight"). 6563-5
    Song. Set by Mr. Coleman. 6933-9
    "Thou cruel fair, I go." 6317-9
    To Calista. 6317-9
    To Chloris. 6934-7
    To Mr. Isaac Walton. 6208-3
    To my old, and most worthy friend, Mr. Izaak Walton... 6562-7
    Tomorrow. 6102-8
    Virelay. 6563-5
    The winter glass. 6230-X
    Winter's troops, fr. Winter. 6125-7
Cotton, Nathaniel
    The fireside. 6219-9,6385-3,6271-7,6620-8
    Health, sels. 6482-5
    On Lord Cobham's gardens. 6649-6
    A paradise below, fr. The fireside. 6934-7
    To a child of five years old. 6772-7
    To a child of five years old. 6233-4
    To-morrow. 6605-2
"The **cotton-still** spire". Poem ("The cotton-still"). David Evans. 6360-8
Cotton-wool. Alfred Noyes. 6151-6
Cottonwood leaves. Charles Badger Clark Jr. 6490-6
Couch, Louis Bradford
    The Lincoln boulder. 6524-4
Cough and coiffure. Camilla J. Knight. 6698-4
Coughlin, Anna B.
    Flowers. 6249-0
Could I find a bonnie glen. Anne (Mrs. Grant of Laggan) Grant. 6086-2
Could I have borne it?. May E. Dustin. 6617-8
"**Could** every blossom find a voice". The blue forget-me-not. Isabella Valancy Crawford. 6797-2
"**Could** every time-worn heart but see thee...". To the child Jesus. Henry Van Dyke. 6961-4
"**Could** he forget his death? that every hour". Upon a gardener. Unknown. 6908-8
"**Could** Homer come himself, distress'd and poor". Epigram on the refusal of Oxford to subscribe... William Cowper. 6814-6
"**Could** I bring back lost youth again". Florine. Thomas Campbell. 6934-7
"**Could** I choose the age and fortunate season". In the lists. Bayard Taylor. 6976-2
"**Could** I outwear my present state of woe". Sonnet ("Could I outwear"). Alfred Lord Tennyson. 6977-0
"**Could** I penetrate the universe". Problematic. Edward R. Huxley. 6885-5
"**Could** I pour out the nectar the gods only can". The travelling man. James Whitcomb Riley. 6889-8
"**Could** I remount the river of my years". A fragment ("Could I remount"). George Gordon, 6th Baron Byron. 6945-2
"**Could** I take me to some cavern for...hiding". Chorus, fr. Hippolytus. Euripides. 7039-6
"**Could** I win fame for the discovery". Ambition. Elsie Ruth Schloss. 6847-2
"**Could** I, from heav'n inspir'd,as sure presage". Stanzas printed on bills of mortality: 1788. William Cowper. 6814-6
"**Could** I, like God, abide in realm so small". Limitation. Douglas Mackintosh. 7016-7
Could it be? Harry Romaine. 7021-3
Could love for ever. George Gordon, 6th Baron Byron. 6086-2
"**Could** love forever/Run like a river". Stanzas ("Could love"). George Gordon, 6th Baron Byron. 6945-2,6832-4
"**Could** man be drunk for ever." Alfred Edward Housman. 6187-7,6427-2
"**Could** my heart more tongues imploy" Thomas Campion. 6794-8
Could she have guessed. Elaine Goodale. 6770-0
"**Could** then the babes from yon unshelter'd cot". Sonnet ("Could then the babes"). Thomas Russell. 6932-0

Could they but know. Will Chamberlain. 6542-2
"**Could** we but draw back the curtains". If we understood. Unknown. 6964-9
"**Could** we but govern this world as we would". Wealth's desire. Edward R. Huxley. 6885-5
Could we but know. Edmund Clarence Stedman. 6014-5
"**Could** we but see men as they are". Unknown. 6435-3
"**Could** we but see the future ere it comes". On the inscription, Keats' tombstone. William Bell Scott. 6819-7
"**Could** we forget the widow'd hour", fr. In memoriam. Alfred Lord Tennyson. 6867-7
"**Could** we look through the shadows that...". Otterbein. James Abraham Martling. 6952-5
'**Could** ye not watch one hour?' Godfrey Fox Bradby. 6337-3
"**Could** you but see her". The white swan. James Stephens. 6782-4
"**Could** you have seen the violets". Daisy. Emily Warren. 7022-1
Could you not watch with me one little hour?. Sara Bard Field. 6628-3
Couldn't keep a secret. Unknown. 6273-3
Couldn't live without you. Edgar A. Guest. 7033-7
Coulson, Leslie
    But a short time to live. 6589-9,6650-X,7026-4,6846-4
    From the Somme. 7029-9
    The god who waits. 6650-X
    Judgment. 6650-X
The **council** held by the rats. Jean de La Fontaine. 6120-6, 6679-8
The **council** of horses. John Gay. 6133-8,6239-3,6552-X
The **councillor**. Cullen Gouldsbury. 6788-3
The **counry** life. Richard Henry Stoddard. 6753-0
Counsel. Francis Carlin. 6039-0
Counsel. Mary [or Mollie] Evelyn Moore Davis. 6632-1
Counsel ("Seek not"). Alice Cary. 6969-X
Counsel ("Though sin"). Alice Cary. 6969-X
Counsel for youth. A.M. Sullivan. 6979-7
"A **counsel** in the common pleas". The farmer and the counsellor. Unknown. 6878-2,6787-5
The **counsel** of Polonius. William Shakespeare. 6639-9
Counsel to a young man. Scofield Thayer. 6039-0
Counsel to girls. Robert Herrick. 6246-6,6737-9
Counsel to those that eat. Unknown. 6089-7
Counsel to those that eat, sels. Edward Verrall Lucas. 6018-8
Counsel to virgins. Robert Herrick. 6481-7
Counsel upon marriage. Geoffrey Chaucer. 6489-2
The **counsel's** tear. Unknown. 6878-2
Counselman, Mary Elizabeth
    Room in darkness. 6218-0
Count Alarcos and the infanta Solisa. Unknown (Spanish) 6757-3
Count Albert and fair Rosalie. Sir Walter Scott. 6669-0
Count Arnaldos. Unknown (Spanish) 6757-3
Count Candespina's standard. George Henry Boker. 6294-6, 6392-6,6409-4,6742-5
Count Eberhard's hawthorn. Johann Ludwig Uhland. 6842-1
Count Filippo, sels. Charles Heavysege. 6646-9
Count Gaultier's ride. Edward Renaud. 6412-4
Count Gismond. Robert Browning. 6166-4,6102-8,6518-X,6578-3
Count Julian, sels. Walter Savage Landor. 6980-0
Count Ludwig to the wood-spirit. Dinah Maria Mulock Craik. 6676-3
"The **count** bell rings". State prison 5:00 p.m. Thomas G. Nickens. 6870-7
"**Count** Don Sancho Dias, the Signior of Saldane". The complaint of the Count of Saldana. Unknown (Spanish). 6757-3
"**Count** each affliction, whether light or grave". Sorrow. Aubrey Thomas De Vere. 7015-9,6090-0,6303-9,6214-8, 6292-X,6199-0,6250-4,6172-9,6371-3,6656-9
"**Count** not the cost of honour to the dead!". National monuments. Henry Van Dyke. 6961-4
"**Count** Richard, ruler of Normandie". Richard the fearless. Johann Ludwig Uhland. 6842-1
The **Count** of Gleichen. Bayard Taylor. 6976-2
The **Count** of Greiers. Johann Ludwig Uhland. 6948-7
The **Count** of Hapsburg. Johann C. Friedrich von Schiller.

6842-1
Count Raymond and my Cid, fr. The Cid. Unknown (Spanish) 6372-1
"Count that day lost, when it is through". The lost day. E.O. De Camp. 6906-1
"Count the sighs, and count the teares". The broken heart. Thomas Beedome. 6933-9
Countdown. Hans Magnus Enzensberger. 7032-9
Counter-attack. Siegfried Sassoon. 6527-9,6666-6
A counterblast against garlic. Horace. 6949-5
The counterblast. Robert Louis Stevenson. 6660-7
Counterfeit. James Gorham. 6850-2
Counterfeit. Clarence L. Haynie. 6841-3
The countermarch. Robert J. Burdette. 6588-0
Countersign. Arthur Ketchum. 6607-0
The countersign was Mary. Margaret Eytinge. 6273-3,6451-5
The countersign.. Unknown. 6074-9,6113-3,6340-3
The countersign. J. Hooker Hamersley. 6451-5
The countersign. Unknown. 6916-9
The countersign. Unknown. 6340-3
Countess Laura. George Henry Boker. 6302-0,6385-3,6673-9
The Countess of Manchester. Joseph Addison. 6278-4
Countess Temple, appointed Poet Laureate to the king... Horace Walpole; 4th Earl of Orford. 6024-2,6152-4
Countin the ol one hundred. Shirley Wiliams. 6792-1
Counting. Unknown. 6078-1
Counting baby's toes. Unknown. 6078-1,6131-1
Counting out. Unknown. 6452-3
Counting the family. Annie F. Redland. 6694-1
Counting the seeds. Unknown. 6927-4
Counting the stars. John Galsworthy. 6888-X
Counting the stars. Dong-ju Yun. 6775-1
Country and town. Arthur Hobson Quinn. 6936-3
The country ball, fr. The angel in the house. Coventry Patmore. 6123-0
The country bedroom. Frances Cornford. 6339-X
A country carol. Margaret Widdemer. 6746-8
The country child. Marian (Annie D.G. Robinson) Douglas. 6127-3
Country children. Unknown. 6629-1
Country church. Robert P. Tristram Coffin. 6984-3
Country church. Robert P. Tristram Coffin. 6532-5,6337-3, 6337-3
A country church. Pearce Young. 6515-5
The country clergyman's trip to Cambridge. Thomas Babington Macaulay, 1st Baron Macaulay. 6874-X
A country cottage. Witter Bynner. 6232-6
Country courtship. William D. Kelly. 6682-8
A country courtship. Francis O'Connor. 6916-9
Country cousin. Edith Sitwell. 7000-0
"A country curate visiting his flock". The lucky call. Unknown. 6911-8
Country dance. Judith Wright. 6349-7
The country dance. Arthur Guiterman. 6959-2
The country dance. Joe Jot [or Tot] Jr. 6913-4
Country dancing. Joe Jot [or Tot] Jr. 6426-2
A country danger. William Browne. 6191-5
The country docotr, sels. William Green Brownson. 6482-5
The country doctor. L. Ashton Thorp. 6764-6
Country dreams. Richard Corbet. 6935-5
Country evening. Agnes Choate Wonson. 6894-4
"The country ever has a lagging spring". Spring in town. William Cullen Bryant. 6752-2
A country fairway. James Whitcomb Riley. 6993-2
The country faith. Norman Gale. 6656-9,6374-8,6437-X,6730-1,6114-1,6808-1
Country girl. Samuel H. Stuart. 6750-6
The country girl's policy, or The cockney outwitted. Unknown. 6157-5
"Country girl, don't stay away from the market". Luis Carlos Lopez. 6759-X
Country glee. Thomas Dekker. 6436-1,6150-8,6191-5
Country gods. Cometas. 6435-3
Country gods. Plato. 6435-3
The country grave-yard, fr. Dovecote mill. Phoebe Cary. 6865-0;6969-X
A country house party. George Gordon, 6th Baron Byron. 6996-2
The country inn: a comedy. Joanna Baillie. 6813-8
"The country is like a tobacco lung". E.P.A. Pancho Aguila. 6870-7
The country justice. John Langhorne. 6866-9
Country kisses, fr. Dorothy. Arthur J. Munby. 6656-9
The country lad. Nicholas Breton. 6383-7
Country lane. Margaret Stanion Darling. 6218-0
A country lane in heaven. Alfred Noyes. 6151-6
"The country lane was full of rain". The gypsy. Wilfrid Thorley. 6778-6
The country lasses. John ("Peter Pindar") Wolcott. 6278-4
Country letter. John Clare. 6380-2
Country life. George Crabbe. 6954-1
"A country life is sweet!". The useful plough. Unknown. 6820-0
A country life, sel. Robert Herrick. 6958-4
A country life. Katherine Philips. 6934-7
The country life. Robert Herrick. 6369-1,6385-3,6194-X, 6438-8
Country music. Plato. 6435-3
Country of the proud. Leonie Adams. 6012-9
The country parson. Elizabeth Graeme Ferguson. 6004-8
The country parson. Oliver Goldsmith. 6459-0
A country pathway. James Whitcomb Riley. 6991-6
Country quiet. S.A. (Sarah Annie Shield) Frost. 6851-0
Country road. Marie Louise Hersey. 6798-0
Country road. Marie Louise Hersey. 6762-X
Country roads. Howard Ramsden. 6761-1
Country sale. Edmund Blunden. 6776-X
Country sale. Edmund Blunden. 6393-4
Country school-room, Adirondack Mountains. Louis Untermeyer. 6037-4,6736-0
Country sleighing. Edmund Clarence Stedman. 6915-0
Country sleighing. Edmund Clarence Stedman. 7035-3
Country song. Elinor Wylie. 6077-3
A country song. Sir Philip Sidney. 6436-1,6584-8,6191-5
The country squire. Tomaso de Yriarte. 6297-0
The country squire. Tomaso de Yriarte. 6787-5
Country summer. Leonie Adams. 6012-9
A country summer pastoral. Unknown. 6089-7,6724-7
A country Thanksgiving. Unknown. 6703-4,6745-X
Country towns. Kenneth Slessor. 6384-5,6349-7
Country travelled. William Sawyer. 6841-3
Country tune. Elizabeth Riddell. 6384-5
Country vegetables. Eleanor Farjeon. 6466-3
The country walk. John Dyer. 6528-7
The country wedding. Unknown. 6874-X
The country's recreations. Unknown. 6935-5
Country-bred. Cora Wilcox Dreyer. 6490-6
the countryman and jupiter. John Gay. 6972-X
Countryman's God. Roger Winship Stuart. 6337-3
Countryman's song. John Galsworthy. 6888-X
The countrymen and the ass. John Byrom. 6064-1
Countryside in New England. Mabel A. Metcalf. 6894-4
A countrywoman of mine. Elaine Goodale Eastman. 6431-0
The county clergyman's trip to Cambridge. Thomas Babington Macaulay, 1st Baron Macaulay. 6200-8,6092-7
County guy. Sir Walter Scott. 6075-7,6180-X,6102-8,6198-2, 6204-0,6604 ,6660-7,6430-2,6086-2,6110-9,6196-6,6438
County guy, fr. Quentin Durward. Sir Walter Scott. 6828-6
The county jail. Jimmy Santiago Baca. 6870-7
The county jail. Stanley Boone. 6880-4
The county mayo. Anthony Raftery. 6244-X
The county of camisards, fr. Travels with a donkey. Robert Louis Stevenson. 6123-0,6395-0
The county of Mayo. Thomas Lavelle. 6858-8,6858-8,6244-X
The county of Mayo. Unknown. See Lavelle, Thomas
County Sligo. Louis MacNeice. 6930-4
Coup d'etat. Marjorie DeGraff. 6850-2
Coup d'Etat. Ruth Herschberger. 6390-X
Coup d'etat. Dorothy Howells Walker. 6750-6
The coup de grace. Edward Rowland Sill. 6735-2
Couplet ("God loves a lovely rainbow.") Ralph Hodgson. 6102-8
Couplets in criticism. John Macy. 6037-4
Cour, Poul la
That day. Charles Wharton Stork (tr.). 6555-4
Courage. Matthew Arnold. 6541-4
Courage. Jeannette Carter Brautigan. 6789-1
Courage. Stopford Augustus Brooke. 6303-9,6730-1
Courage. Arthur Hugh Clough. 6424-8
Courage. Helen Frazee-Bower. 6347-0

COURAGE

Courage. John Galsworthy. 6888-X
Courage. John Galsworthy. 6266-0
Courage. Paul Gerhardt. 6730-1
Courage. Edgar A. Guest. 6869-3
Courage. George Herbert. 6512-0
Courage. Dyneley Hussey. 7026-4
Courage. Bernetta L. Isbell. 6799-9
Courage. O.B. Merrick. 6799-9
Courage. Margaret Ridgely Partridge. 6861-8
Courage. Robert Service. 6159-1
Courage. William Shakespeare. 6438-8
Courage. Celia Thaxter. 6764-6
Courage. Unknown. 6215-6,6654-2
Courage. Ella Wheeler Wilcox. 6956-8
Courage ("A thousand hearts are great within my bosom") William Shakespeare. 6294-6
Courage ("A valiant man"). Ben Jonson. 6211-3
Courage ("Because I coveted courage"). Virginia Moore. 6501-5
Courage ("Courage is armor"). Karle Wilson Baker. 6337-3, 6501-5,6464-7
Courage ("Courage!--Nothing can withstand"). Bryan Waller ("Barry Cornwall") Procter. 6211-3,6294-6,6606-2
Courage ("If in the past should brooding sorrow ..."). Louis Lavater. 6211-3
Courage ("Two kinds of courage..."). Louis Lavater. 6784-0
"Courage came to you with your boyhood's grace". To a soldier in hospital. Winifred M. Letts. 7026-4
Courage has a crimson coat. Nancy Byrd Turner. 6512-0
"Courage is but a word, and yet, of words". Courage. John Galsworthy. 6888-X
"Courage of heart and hand, faith first of all". Hope deferred, fr. Outside the temple. William Bell Scott. 6819-7
The courage of the lost. Edith M. Thomas. 6102-8,6076-5, 6250-4
"Courage yet, my brother or my sister!". To a foil'd European revolutionaire. Walt Whitman. 7009-4
Courage! Francis Ernley Walrond. 6800-6
"Courage! A thing inherent in the strong". Courage. O.B. Merrick. 6799-9
Courage, all! Edwin Markham. 6607-0
Courage, fr. the Gulistan. Sadi [or Saadi] (Mushlih-ud-Din) 7039-6
Courage, mon ami! Willard Wattles. 6501-5
"Courage, my son! now to the silent wood". Peace. Bhartrihari. 6253-9
"Courage, my soul, now learn to wield". Dialogue between the resolved soul & created pleasure. Andrew Marvell. 6933-9
"Courage, poor heart of stone", fr. Maud. Alfred Lord Tennyson. 6122-2
Courageous boy. Unknown. 6312-8,6629-1
The couragious Turke, sels. Thomas Goffe. 6562-7
The courier. Margaret de Kay. 6995-9
Cournos, John
    Epstein's "Christ" 6069-2
A coursage bouquet. Charles Henry Luders. 6770-0
"The course of empire, like an epic song". Tidal waves. Herbert Hough Redegar. 6789-1
The course of love. William Shakespeare. 6429-9,6321-7
"The course of the Puente hills". Puente hills. James Abraham Martling. 6952-5
The course of time. John Hookham Frere. 6802-2
The course of true love, fr. Midsummer night's dream. William Shakespeare. 6302-0;6385-3
The course of truth. John Henry, Cardinal Newman. 6980-0
The courser and the Jennet. William Shakespeare. 6315-2
The courser, fr. Venus and Adonis. William Shakespeare. 6436-1
The coursers. Percy Bysshe Shelley. 6383-7
The court historian. George Walter Thornbury. 6437-X
"The court is crowded - on the bench is seen". Punch in chancery. Unknown. 6878-2
A court lady. Elizabeth Barrett Browning. 6302-0,63385-3, 6486-3,6219-9,6656-9
The court of aldermen at Fishmonger's Hall. Unknown. 6018-8
The court of Aldermen at Fishmongers' Hall. Unknown. 6724-7
The court of Berlin. Unknown. 6273-3
The court of Berlin. Unknown. 6921-5
The court of Charles II, fr. Epistle to Augustus. Alexander Pope. 6932-0
The court of death. John Gay. 6972-X
The court of fairy, fr. Nymphidia. Michael Drayton. 6198-2, 6378-0
the court of fancy, sels. Thomas Godfrey. 6008-0
The court of lights. Lucy H. King Smith. 6906-1
The court of Neptune. John Hughes. 6833-2
A court poet in trouble. Osborn Bergin. 6582-1
Court-martial. Alfred Noyes. 6151-6
"Courteous spectators, see with your own eyes". The rehearsal at Goatham. John Gay. 6972-X
Courtesy. Hilaire Belloc. 6746-8,6102-8,6172-9,6608-9,6292-X,6427-2,6477
Courtesy. James Thomas Fields. 6654-2
Courtesy. Daniel Sargent. 6253-9
Courtesy. L.C. Whiton. 6965-7
Courtesy on departure. Edgar A. Guest. 6748-4
A courtesy. Elinor Wylie. 6012-9,6072-2
Courthope, William James
    Birdcatcher's song, fr. The paradise of birds. 6656-9
    In praise of Gilbert White, fr. The paradise of birds. 6656-9
    Ode - to the roc, fr. The paradise of birds. 6656-9
    The paradise of birds, sels. 6656-9
Courthope, William John
    Birds are seen approaching in the air carrying nests... 6943-6
    The chancellor's gardens. 6046-3
    Chorus of English songsters. 6385-3
    Dodoism, fr. The paradise of birds. 6427-2
    The paradise of birds, sels. 6427-2
    The rise of species. 6385-3
    Semi-chorus of thrushes, linnets, and blackcaps. 6943-6
    The song of man. 6943-6
The courtier and proteus. John Gay. 6972-X
The courtier's good-morrow to his mistress. Unknown. 6182-6
The courtier's health, or Merry boys of the times. Unknown. 6157-5
The courtier, fr. Mother Hubberd's tales. Edmund Spenser. 6604-6,6660-7
The courtier. Lawrence Eusden. 6867-7
Courtiers. Samuel Butler. 6278-4
A courtin' call. Unknown. 6690-9
Courtin' in the country. H. Elliott McBride. 6402-7
The courtin'.. James Russell Lowell. 6008-0,6083-8,6092-7, 6219-9,6265-2,6307 ,6121-4,6396-9,6281-4,6126-5,6288-1,6964 ,6823-5,6302-0,6385-3,6279-2,6089-7,6332-2, 6473 ,6600-3,6696-8,6732-8,6735-2,6176-1,6404 ,6610-0,6505-8,6438-8,6419-1,6431-0,6278
Courting and proverbs. W.E.P. French. 6707-7
Courting in Kentucky. Florence Evelyn Pratt. 6089-7,6505-8
Courting in Kentucky. Unknown. 6964-9
Courting in the kitchen. Unknown. 6057-9
Courting in Vermont. Daniel L. Cady. 6989-4
Courtney, W.L.
    To our dead. 7027-2
The courts. Alice Meynell. 6339-X
Courtship. Ibn Sa'id (of Alcala La Real) 6362-4
Courtship. Unknown. 6412-4
Courtship and matrimony. William Makepeace Thackeray. 6278-4
The courtship of Billy Grimes. Unknown. 6003-X
The courtship of Eve. Robert Crawford. 6269-5
The courtship of Miles Standish. Henry Wadsworth Longfellow. 6498-1,6503-1,6732-8,6126-5,6503-1
Courtship under difficulties. Unknown. 6744-1,6167-2
Courtship's end. Edgar A. Guest. 6748-4
The courtyard pigeons. Caroline Giltinan. 6073-0,6029-3
Cousin Bell's visit. Unknown. 6740-9
Cousin Florrie. Muriel F. Hochdorf. 6850-2
Cousin Floy. David Law ("Pegleg Arkwright") Proudfit. 6632-1
Cousin Jack. Unknown. 6694-1
"Cousin Jeannette hands". Midwife. Earl Gene Box. 6870-7
Cousin John. C.T. B. 6889-8
Cousin Lucrece. Edmund Clarence Stedman. 6004-8,6431-0

Cousin Nancy. Thomas Stearns Eliot. 6491-4
Cousin Rufus' story. James Whitcomb Riley. 6128-1
Cousin Zetta. Muriel F. Hochdorf. 6850-2
Cousins, James H.
    The corncrake. 6930-4
    High and low. 6930-4
    Omens. 6930-4
    The quest. 6873-1
    The wings of love. 6090-0
Cousins, William
    Black gauntlet. 6178-8
    The house of time. 6178-8
    Ultimatum. 6178-8
Couto, Nancy Lee
    Backwards. 6900-2
    Cantiga de Maria das Estrelas. 6900-2
Coutts, Francis
    Epigram. 6785-9
    The inquest. 6785-9
    Mors, morituri salutamus! 6785-9
    Oasis. 6785-9
    To England. 7031-0
Covarrubias, Juan Diaz
    A selection, sels. Edna Worthley Underwood (tr.). 6482-5
The covenant of his grace. Charles Wesley. 6065-X
The covenant. William Cowper. 6814-6,6848-0
Covenanter's battle-chant. Robert Motherwell. 6219-9
The covenanter's lament. Winthrop Mackworth Praed. 6323-3
The Coventry carol. Unknown. 6881-2
The Coventry carol. Unknown. 6179-6
Coventry, R.G.T.
    Home coming. 7029-9
"Cover the drum/with human skin". The drum. Otto Laaber. 6769-7
Cover them over with beautiful flowers. Unknown. 6340-3
Coverdale, Miles
    Of the birth of Christ. 6756-5
Covered bridges. Jennie Pendleton Hall. 6750-6
Covered bridges. Dorothy M. Ross. 6857-X
The covered wagon. Lena Whittaker Blakeney. 6397-7
Covering. Gussie Ross Jobe. 6906-1
Covering hair. John ("Evelyn Douglas") Barlas. 6659-3
"Covert and quill lie thick and white as floes". Camouflage of the willow ptarmigan. Mary Owings Miller. 6979-7
The coves of Crail. William ("Fiona Macleod") Sharp. 6656-9
The covetous knight, sels. Alexander Pushkin. 6622-4
Covington, H.F.
    The reason. 6983-5
"A cow and a calf". Unknown. 6363-2
The cow and the ass. Jane Taylor. 6242-3
The cow and the bishop. Alfred Townsend. 6744-1,6575-9
A cow at Sullington. Charles Dalmon. 6510-4
"The cow could not stand up. The deadly river". Who would be free, themselves must strike the blow. June Jordan. 7032-9
The cow herd. Diotimus. 6435-3
Th cow in apple time. Robert Frost. 6162-1,6393-4
"The cow is too well known, I fear". The cow. Oliver Herford. 6902-9
The cow slips away. Ben King. 6732-8
"The cow swings her head...". In envy of cows. Joseph Auslander. 6037-4,6777-8
"A cow, delighted, blew her horn". Ballade of dottiness. Edward Anthony. 6875-4
The cow-a bovinity. Unknown. 6724-7
The cow-boy's song. Anna Maria Wells. 6127-3,6519-8,6131-1,6135-4
The cow-boy's vision. James Abraham Martling. 6952-5
The cow-chace. John Andre. 6946-0
The cow-juice cure. Robert Service. 6159-1
Cow-puncher's song. John A. Lomax. 6711-5
A cow. Julia Van der Veer. 6850-2
The cow. Louise Ayres Garnett. 6130-3
The cow. Oliver Herford. 6902-9
The cow. Mrs. Motherly. 6937-1
The cow. Mrs. Motherly. 6452-3
The cow. Bernard O'Dowd. 6784-0

The cow. Robert Louis Stevenson. 6132-X,6242-3,6452-3,6510-4,6655-0
The cow. Ann Taylor. 6891-X
The cow. Ann and Jane Taylor. 6242-3,6114-1
Cowan, Samuel K.
    Becalmed. 6919-3
    Becalmed at sea. 6674-7
    Life. 6416-7
    Life. 6167-2
    Poor Jack. 6470-4
Coward. Brian ("Korongo") Brooke. 6938-X
Coward. Delphia L. Hopper. 6906-1
"A coward still: I've longed to fling". A coward still. John Cameron Grant. 6770-0
Coward, Noel
    Mad dogs and Englishmen. 6722-0
The coward.. Caroline Giltinan. 6031-5
A coward. Unknown. 6118-4
The coward. James Newton Matthews. 6672-0
The coward. Robert C.V. Meyers. 6927-4
The coward. Robert Service. 6159-1
Cowardliness is a dull black. Kim Fitzgerald. 6883-9
Cowards are cruel, but the brave. John Gay. 6623-2
"Cowards die many times before their deaths:". William Shakespeare. 6291-1
"Cowards die many times...", fr. Julius Caesar. William Shakespeare. 6879-0
Cowards, fr. Julius Caesar. William Shakespeare. 6337-3
Cowbells at midnight. Florence Randal Livesay. 6797-2
Cowboy song. Joseph Mills Hanson. 6889-8,7007-8
Cowboy song ("One night as I lay on the prairie."). Unknown. 6003-X
The cowboy's Christmas ball. Unknown. 6594-5
The cowboy's dream. Charles J. Finger. 6281-4
The cowboy's lament. Unknown. 6125-7
The cowboy's life. John A. Lomax. 6891-X
A cowboy's prayer. Charles Badger Clark Jr. 6303-9
The cowboy's tale. W. Kit. 6505-8
"The cowboys come charging out of the...". Salt river project. Peter Wild. 6998-3
The cowboys pass. Perry Holmes Lowrey. 7007-8
Cowden-Clark, Mary
    At midnight of All Souls. 7037-X
Cowdenknowes. Robert Crawford. 6180-X
Cowell, Harriet Hamilton
    Alone! Stark alone! 6799-9
Cowie, Alexander Gordon
    Life, death, and love. 6650-X
The cowled ape, or pretty Polly's pride. E.H. Visiak. 6777-8
Cowley's wish. Abraham Cowley. 6423-X
Cowley, Abraham
    Against hope. 6315-2,6341-1
    All-over love. 6563-5
    Anacreontic-drinking. 6186-9
    Anacreontiques, sels. 6562-7
    Anacreontiques. Drinking. 6152-4
    The annunciation, fr. Davideis. 6931-2
    Awake, awake my lyre! 6563-5
    Beauty. 6150-8
    The change. 6933-9
    The change. 6317-9,6208-3,6341-1
    The change. 6933-9
    Cheer up, my mates. 6328-4
    Chloris, forbear a while. 6563-5
    The chronicle. 6302-0,6385-3,6634-8,6302-0,6385-3,6089,6271-7,6092-7,6152-4,6245-8,6230-X
    Cowley's wish. 6423-X
    The creation, fr. Davideis. 6933-9
    Cruel beauty. 6935-5
    The cure. 6482-5
    Davideis, sels. 6562-7
    Destinie. 6341-1
    The destroying angel. 6848-0
    Drinking. 6186-9,6315-2,6427-2,6722-0,6092-7,6250-4,6513-9
    Elegie upon Anacreon. 6483-3
    The epicure. 6513-9,6482-5,6733-6
    Epigram on Drake. Ben Jonson (tr.). 6438-8
    Epigram on Francis Drake. Ben Jonson (tr.). 6867-7

COWLEY

Epitaph on a living author. 6219-9
Fill the bowl with rosy wine. 6934-7
First born of chaos...", fr. Verses written... 6562-7
The garden, sels. 6232-6
The garden. 6271-7
The grasshopper. 6133-8,6604-6,6396-9,6660-7
Great Diocletian. 6125-7
Hail, old patrician...", fr. Several discourses... 6562-7
Hell, fr. Davideis. 6931-2
An holy sister. 6760-3,6787-5
The hymn of light, sels. 6385-3
Hymn to light. 6341-1,6250-4
Hymn: to light. 6933-9
"I sing the man who Judahs scepter...", fr. Davideis. 6562-7
"If learned in other things you be," fr. Resolved... 6317-9
In defense of the Royal Society. 6250-4
In vain love, sels. 6317-9
The invocation. 6385-3
Large was his soul, fr. On the death of Willam Harvey. 6934-7
Liberty. 6600-3,6543-0
Life. 6250-4
Love. 6513-9
Love. 6339-X
Love and life. 6562-7
Love in her sunny eyes. 6543-0
A lover's chronicle. 6787-5
Mark Anthony. 6563-5
Miscellanies, sels. 6562-7
The mistress, sels. 6562-7
Mr. William Hervey. 6230-X
My diet. 6317-9,6562-7
Ode: of wit. 6152-4,6341-1,6430-2
Of drinking. 6026-9
Of myself. 6430-2,6385-3,6563-5,6430-2,6291-9,6600-3
Of solitude. 6194-X,6423-X,6563-5,6194-X,6271-7,6189-3
Of wit. 6933-9,6760-3,6933-9
On drinking. 6482-5
On the death of Mr. Crashaw. 6483-3,6250-4,6341-1,6378-0,6543-0,6562-7,6023-4
On the death of Mr. William Hervey. 6150-8,6250-4,6198-2,6562-7
On the death of Mrs. Crashaw. 6250-4,6341-1
Poet and saint, fr. On the death of Mr. Crashaw. 6934-7
The power of numbers, fr. Davideis. 6933-9
The praise of Pindar. 6152-4,6152-4,6483-3
Resolved to love, sels. 6317-9
The resurrection. 6194-X
Several discourses by way of essays, in verse..., sels. 6562-7
Sleep. 6125-7
'Solomon in all his glory was not arrayed like...' 6848-0
The soul. 6543-0
Sport. 6563-5,6250-4
Spring in a garden. 6232-6,6649-6
The spring. 6933-9
The spring. 6317-9,6194-X,6341-1
A supplication. 6219-9,6438-8,6246-5
The swallow. 6198-2,6102-8
"Tell me, O tell...", fr. Miscellanies. 6562-7
The thief. 6726-3,6563-5,6430-2
"The thirsty earth soaks up the rain". 6187-7,6562-7
"This only grant me...", fr. A vote. 6562-7
"Though you be absent...", fr. The mistress. 6562-7
To a logician. 7014-0
To his mistress. 6563-5,6092-7
To Mr. Hobbes. 6315-2
To Sir William Davenant upon...first two books of Gondibert . 6152-4
To the Royal Society. 6152-4
"Tyrian dye why do you wear". 6187-7
"Tyrian dye why do you wear" 6935-5
"Underneath this myrtle shade". 6187-7
Verses written on several occasions, sels. 6562-7
A vote, sels. 6562-7,6194-X
A vote. 6604-6,6660-7,6232-6,6604-6,6660-7

Welcome, great Stagirite. 6934-7
"Well then! I now do plainly see". 6187-7
What shall I do? 6543-0
The wish. 6562-7,6563-5,6668-2,6649-6,6659-3,6350 ,6092-7,6153-2,6301-2,6430-2,6543-0,6541 ,6198-2,6186-9, 6232-6,6726-3
Without and within. 6092-7

Cowley, Abraham (tr.)

Age. Anacreon (atr), 7039-6
Drinking. Anacreon, 6271-7
The grasshopper. Anacreon (atr), 7039-6,6271-7
The old man of Verona. Claudian, 7039-6
Procrastination. Martial, 7039-6,6428-0
To Fuscus Aristus. Horace, 7039-6

Cowley, Malcolm

Bill George, fr. Blue Juanita. 6531-7
Blue Juanita, sels. 6531-7
Bones of a house, fr. Blue Juanita. 6531-7
Chestnut Ridge, fr. Blue Juanita. 6531-7
Empty barn, dead farm, fr. Blue Juanita. 6531-7
For St. Bartholomew's eve. 6375-6
The hill above the mine. 6375-6
History. 6037-4
Laurel Mountain, fr. Blue Juanita. 6531-7
The long voyage. 6324-1,6236-9
The streets of air, fr. Blue Juanita. 6531-7
Those of Lucifer. 6808-1
Tomorrow morning. 6761-1
Tumbling mustard. 6490-6
The urn, fr. Blue Juanita. 6808-1,6531-7

Cowley, William

Epigram on Drake. Ben Jonson (tr.). 6438-8
The cowman's prayer. Unknown. 6594-5
Cowper. John Clare. 6483-3,6641-0
"Cowper had sinn'd with some excuse". On a mistake in his translation of Homer. William Cowper. 6814-6
Cowper in Bedfordshire. Sylvia Lynd. 6779-4
Cowper's consolation. Phoebe Cary. 6969-X
Cowper's grave. Elizabeth Barrett Browning. 6219-9,6543-0, 6655-0,6271-7,6437-X,6483-3,6600-3,6657-7,6304
Cowper's grave, sels. Elizabeth Barrett Browning. 6198-2

Cowper, William

Absence of occupation, fr. Retirement. 6932-0
Abuse of the gospel. 6814-6
Address to liberty. 6286-5
An address to the mob on occasion of the late riot... 6814-6
Addressed to Miss Macartney. 6814-6
Affectation in the pulpit. 6045-1,6605-2
Afflictions sanctioned by the word. 6814-6
Against interested life. 6814-6
"Ah brother poet! send me of your shade". 6814-6
Alexander Selkirk during his solitary abode... 6138-9, 6543-0,6659-3,6424-8
Annus memorabilis, 1789. 6814-6
Another. 6250-4
Answer to stanzas addressed to Lady Hesketh. 6814-6
Anti-Thelyphthora. 6814-6
An apology for not showing her what I had wrote. 6814-6
The arrival of the post, fr. The task. 6195-0
An attempt at the manner of Waller. 6814-6
Autobiographical. 6543-0
"Away goes Sussex William and his pack". 6814-6
The backward look. 6233-4
The Bastile, fr. The task. 6195-0,6545-7
"Be it a weakness, it deserves some praise". 6238-5
Beau's reply. 6519-8,6086-2
The bee and the pine-apple. 6814-6
"Bid adieu, my sad heart, bid adieu to thy peace". 6814-6
Boadicea. 6188-5,6424-8,6543-0,6302-0,6385-3,6322 ,6323-3,6473-6,6679-8,6732-8,6438-8,6250 ,6075-7,6102-8, 6133-8,6217-7,6304-7,6263 ,6301-2,6197-4,6086-2
Books, fr. The task. 6934-7
A card. 6814-6
The castaway. 6198-2,6645-3,6378-0,6604-6,6641-0,6195 , 6208-3,6150-8,6430-2,6152-4,6086-2,6660 ,6371-3,6543-0
Catharina. 6092-7
Catharina, the second part. 6814-6

Charity. 6250-4
Charity, sels. 6934-7
The Christian. 6814-6
The cock-fighter's garland. 6814-6
The colubriad. 6874-X
The Colubriad. 6089-7,6120-6,6133-8,6552-X,6808-1,6511
A comparison addressed to a young lady. 6814-6
A comparison, addressed to a young lady. 6086-2,6250-4,
   6301-2
A comparison. 6814-6
Contentment. 6152-4
Contradiction. 6302-0;6385-3
The contrite heart, sels. 6369-1
The contrite heart. 6378-0
Conversation. 6230-X
Conversation, sels. 6102-8
Conversation, sels. 6198-2,6102-8
The covenant. 6814-6,6848-0
Cowper, the religious recluse, fr. The task. 6195-0
Crazy Kate. The gipsies, fr. The task. 6543-0
The cricket. 6302-0,6385-3,6597-X,6373-X,6018-8
"Delia, th' unkindest girl on earth". 6814-6
Dependence. 6438-8
The dinner party. 6186-9
The distressed travellers; or, labour in vain. 6814-6
The diverting history of John Gilpin. 6014-5,6271-7,
   6484-1,6371-3,6131-1,6291 ,6024-2,6396-9,6152-4,6518-
   X,6086-2,6739 ,6105-2,6239-3,6486-8,6089-7,6154-0,
   6242
The dog and the water-lily. 6175-7,6133-8,6430-2
The dog and the water-lily. 6814-6
The doves. 6543-0
Dueling. 6302-0;6385-3
Early love of the country and of poetry. 6543-0
England. 6150-8
England, with all thy faults, I love thee still. 6188-5
Ephraim repenting. 6814-6
Ephraim repenting. 6848-0
Epigram. 6814-6
"An epigram is but a feeble thing". 6814-6
Epigram on his garden shed (1). 6814-6
Epigram on his garden shed (2). 6814-6
Epigram on the refusal of Oxford to subscribe... 6814-6
An epistle to a Protestant lady in France. 6814-6
An epistle to Joseph Hill, Esq. 6814-6
An epistle to Joseph Hill, esq. 6874-X
An epistle to Joseph Hill. 6153-2,6370-5
An epistle to Robert Lloyd, Esq. 6814-6
An epitaph (on a pointer) 6092-7
Epitaph on a free but tame redbreast. 6814-6
Epitaph on a hare. 6134-6,6175-7,6133-8,6092-7,6086-2,
   6131 ,6084-6,6543-0,6668-2,6228-8,6290-3,6634
Epitaph on Dr. Johnson. 6483-3
Epitaph on Dr. Johnson. 6814-6
Epitaph on Fop, a dog belonging to Lady Throckmorton.
   6814-6
Epitaph on Mr. Chester, of Chicheley. 6814-6
Epitaph on Mrs. M. Higgins, of Weston. 6814-6
An epitaph. 6814-6
Epitaphium alterum. 6814-6
Evening, fr. The task. 6932-0
Evening, fr. The task. 6934-7
Evening, fr. The task. 6932-0
Evening, fr. The task. 6934-7
Excessive modesty. 6294-6
Exhortation to prayer. 6814-6
Expostulation. 6814-6
A fable. 6814-6
The facetious story of John Gilpin. 6279-2
The faithful bird. 6133-8,6808-1
The faithful friend. 6085-4
The faithful friend. 6814-6
A faithful picture of an ordinary society. 6996-7
The flatting mill. 6814-6
Flowering shrubs, fr. The task. 6545-7
For the poor. 6814-6
Forebearance. 6337-3
The four ages. 6814-6
Fragment. 6730-1
Fragment ("He came to me..."). 6814-6

Freedom. 7009-4,6793-X
The freeman. 6302-0;6385-3
Friendship ("What virtue or what mental grace"). 6085-4
Frienship. 6814-6
The future peace and glory of the church. 6271-7,6641-0
The garden, fr. The task. 6814-6
God moves in a mysterious way. 6304-7,6737-9
Grace and providence. 6814-6
Gratitude. 6092-7
A greenhouse, fr. The task. 6649-6
The happy change. 6152-4
The happy man. 6302-0;6385-3
"Happy the man who sees a god employed." 6225-3
"Hark, my soul it is the Lord". 6065-X
Hatred of sin. 6814-6
The heart healed and changed by mercy. 6814-6
Heedless cruelty. 6102-8
Heroism. 6814-6
Heroism. 6385-3
Heu! quam remotus. 6814-6
The hidden life. 6814-6
Hope. 6814-6
"Hope, like the short-liv'd ray that gleams awhile".
   6814-6
Horace, Book II. Ode 010. 6814-6
The house of prayer. 6814-6
"How blest the youth". 6814-6
Human frailty. 6271-7
Human oppression, fr. The task. 6195-0
Humanity. 6302-0,6385-3,6410-8
Hymn ("God moves in a mysterious way") 6150-8
Hymn ("God moves in a mysterious way.") 6179-6
Hymn for the use of the Sunday school at Olney. 6814-6
I will praise the lord at all times. 6152-4
I would not enter on my list of friends, fr. The task.
   6934-7
The ice palace. 6438-8
Idem Latine redditum. 6814-6
Idem Latine redditum. 6814-6
An idler. 6861-8
Impromptu on reading the chapter on polygamy... 6814-6
Impromptu on writing a letter without...anything to
   say. 6814-6
In a mysterious way. 6461-2
In Him confiding. 6337-3
In imitation of Shakespeare. 6814-6
In memory of the late John Thornton, Esq. 6814-6
In seditionem horrendam. 6814-6
In submersionem navigii cui Georgius regale nomen...
   6814-6
Inscription for a bust of Homer. 6814-6
Inscription for a moss-house in the shrubbery at
   Weston. 6814-6
Inscription for a stone (1). 6814-6
Inscription for a stone (2). 6814-6
Inscription for an hermitage in the author's garden.
   6814-6
Inscription for the tomb of Mr. Hamilton. 6814-6
Isaiah 060: 15-20 6848-0
"It is a maxim of much weight". 6814-6
The jackdaw. 6874-X
The jackdaw. 6473-6,6328-4,6808-1,6092-7,6383-7,6153
Jehovah our righteousness. 6814-6
Jehovah-Jesus. 6814-6
Jehovah-Jireh. 6814-6
Jehovah-Nissi. 6814-6
Jehovah-nissi, the Lord my banner. 6848-0
Jehovah-Rophi. 6814-6
Jehovah-Shalom. 6814-6
Jehovah-Shammah. 6814-6
Jesus hasting to suffer. 6814-6
John Gilpin. 6127-3,6075-7,6133-8,6502-3,6614-3,6419 ,
   6136-2,6228-8,6406-X,6478-7,6504-X
Joy and peace in believing. 6219-9,6271-7
The judgment of the poets. 6814-6,6874-X
"The late Dr. Jartin/Had the good fortune". 6814-6
A law case. 6424-8
The legs without the man. 6634-8
Letter in verse. 6814-6
The light and the glory of the word. 6814-6

COWPER

Light shining out of darkness. 6154-0,6271-7,6337-3, 6730-1,6023-4,6219 ,6214-8,6723-9,6418-3
The lily and the rose. 6086-2
Lines addressed to Dr. Darwin. 6814-6
Lines after the manner of Homer,...opening of a hamper. 6814-6
Lines composed for a memorial of Ashley Cowper, Esq. 6814-6
Lines on a bill of mortality, 1790. 6931-2
Lines on receiving his mother's picture, sels. 6339-X
Lines sent with two coxcombs to Miss Green. 6814-6
Lines to my mother's picture. 6600-3,6627-5
Lines written during a period of insanity. 6378-0
Lines written on a page of the Monthly Review... 6814-6
Lines written on a window-shutter at Weston. 6814-6
Lines written...collection of handwritings & signatures. 6814-6
Lines, fr. a letter to C.P. Esq., ill with rheumatism. 6814-6
Lively hope, and gracious fear. 6814-6
A living and a dead faith. 6814-6
Longing to be with Christ. 6814-6
Looking upward in a storm. 6814-6
"The Lord will happiness divine". 6931-2
Loss of the Royal George. 6246-5,6504-X,6133-8,6138-9, 6328-4,6552 ,6131-1,6438-8,6639-9,6600-3,6726-3,6732
Love abused. 6814-6
Love constraining to obedience. 6814-6
Love of England. 6315-2
Love of liberty. 6240-7
The love of the world reproved, or hypocrisy detected. 6278-4
The love of the world reproved; or, hypocrisy detected. 6814-6
Lovest thou me? 6024-2,6378-0,6641-0,6219-9
Meditation in winter. 6543-0
Milton, fr. Table talk. 6934-7
The model preacher, fr. The task. 6195-0
The modern patriot. 6814-6
The moralizer corrected. 6814-6
The morning dream. 7009-4
The morning dream. 6814-6
"Mortals! around your destin'd heads". 6814-6
A mother's portrait. 6575-9
Motto on the king's clock. 6814-6
Mourning and longing. 6814-6
Mutual forebearance necessary to...the married state. 6814-6
My country. 6302-0;6385-3
"My former hopes are fled". 6931-2
My Mary. 6250-4,6085-4
My mother's picture. 6304-7,6014-5,6302-0,6385-3,6097-8
"My pens are all split, and ink-glass is dry". 6814-6
My soul thirsteth for God. 6814-6
Mysteries of providence. 6600-3
The narrow way. 6814-6
The needless alarm. 6814-6
The Negro's complaint. 6814-6
The new convert. 6814-6
The nightingale and the glow-worm. 6479-5,6302-0,6385-3, 6519-8,6133-8,6621-6,6131-1,6424-8
"The nose and the eyes." 6385-3,6502-3
Not of works. 6814-6
O Lord, I will praise thee. 6814-6
"O Lord, my best desire fulfil". 6931-2
Oaths. 6302-0;6385-3
Ode on reading Richardson's History..Charles Grandison. 6814-6
Ode supposed to be written on the marriage of a friend. 6814-6
Ode to Apollo. 6814-6
Ode to peace. 6814-6
An ode: secundem artem. 6814-6
Of himself. 6814-6
"Oh! for a closer walk with God". 6931-2
Old-Testament gospel. 6814-6
Olney hymns. 6814-6
On a goldfinch starved to death in his cage. 6086-2
On a letter of Miss Fanshawe. 6814-6
On a mischievous bull. 6814-6
On a mistake in his translation of Homer. 6814-6
On a plant of virgin's-bower. 6814-6
On a review condemning Thelyphthora. 6814-6
On a spaniel, called 'Beau,' killing a young bird. 6086-2
On a spaniel, called Beau, killing a young bird. 6519-8, 6075-7
On Flaxman's Penelope. 6814-6
On Hayley's portrait. 6814-6
On her endeavouring to conceal her grief at parting. 6814-6
On his approaching visit to Hayley. 6814-6
On his portrait. 6814-6
On loyalty. 6814-6
On Madan's answer to Newton's comments on Thelyphtora. 6814-6
On Mrs. Montague's feather-hangings. 6814-6
On observing some names of little note. 6659-3
On observing some names of little note. 6814-6
On observing some names on little note recorded... 6874-X
On opening a place for social prayer. 6814-6
On receipt of his mother's picture. 6726-3
On receiving Hayley's picture. 6814-6
On receiving Heyne's Virgil from Hayley. 6814-6
On that those lips had language, fr. On the receipt... 6934-7
On the author of Letters on literature. 6814-6
On the benefit received by mis majesty from sea-bathing. 6814-6
On the burning of Lord Mansfield's library (1). 6814-6
On the burning of Lord Mansfield's library (2). 6814-6
On the death of a minister. 6814-6
On the death of Mrs. Throckmorton's bullfinch. 6018-8, 6092-2,6195-0,6543-0
On the death of Sir W. Russell. 6814-6
On the high price of fish. 6814-6
On the ice islands seen floating in the German ocean. 6814-6
On the loss of the Royal George. 6024-2,6271-7,6369-1, 6604-6,6660-7,6430 ,6086-2,6197-4,6301-2,6543-0,6152-3,6560 ,6239-3,6153-2,6322-5,6258-X,6302-0,6385-3, 6547-3
On the picture of a sleeping child. 6958-4
On the promotion of Edward Thurlow, Esq. 6814-6
On the queen's visit to London. 6814-6
On the receipt of my mother's picture. 6152-4,6192-3, 6195-0
On the receipt of my mother's picture out of Norfolk. 6198-2,6271-7,6457-4,6604-6,6438-8,6660 ,6195-0,6365-9,6023-4,6543-0,6152-4,6192 ,6219-9,6430-2
On the receipt of my mother's picture out..Norfolk, sels. 6934-7
On the receipt of my mother's picture, sels. 6102-8, 6086-2
On the trial of Admiral Keppel. 6814-6
On Thurlow. 6814-6
Pairing time anticipated. 6814-6
Pairing-time anticipated. 6089-7,6133-8
Parting-time anticipated. 6089-7,6133-8
The path of sorrow. 6261-X
Peace after a storm. 6814-6
Pernicious weed. 6287-3,6453-1
The pine-apple and the bee. 6814-6
Pity for poor Africans. 6814-6
Playthings. 6665-8
Pleading for and with youth. 6814-6
The pledge of cheerfulness. 6100-1
The poet in the woods. 6543-0
The poet's New Year's gift to Mrs. Throckmorton. 6814-6
The poet, the oyster, and sensitive plant. 6814-6
A poetical epistle to Lady Austen. 6814-6
The poplar field. 6075-7,6086-2,6125-7,6491-4,6543-0, 6086-2,6125-7,6163-X,6201-6,6228-8,6246
The post. The fireside in winter, fr. The task. 6543-0
The postman. 6150-8,6150-6
Praise for faith. 6814-6
Praise for the fountain opened. 6152-4
Prayer for a blessing. 6814-6
Prayer for children. 6814-6

Prayer for patience. 6814-6
Preachers: the true vs. the insincere, fr. The task. 6337-3
Principle put to the test. 6131-1
The progress of error. 6814-6
Providence. 6438-8,6100-1,6261-X,6438-8
Psalm 137. 6814-6
R.S.S. 6814-6
R.S.S. Written in a fit of illness. 6814-6
Reasons for not writing a good letter. 6134-6
A reflection on the ode Horace, Book II. Ode 010. 6814-6
Relish of fair prospect. 6543-0
Report of an adjudged case. 6089-7
Report of an adjudged case. 6787-5
Report of an adjudged case not to be found in any...books. 6018-8,6278-4
Report of an adjudged case not to be found...any..books. 6814-6
The retired cat. 6278-4,6511-2,6089-7,6120-6,6699-2
The retirement. 6219-9
Riddle. 6814-6
The robin in winter, fr. The task. 6545-7
The rose. 6086-2,6198-2,6385-3
Rural sights and sounds, fr. The task. 6545-7
A Russian ice-palace. 6385-3
Sanctuary. 6230-X
Sardis. 6814-6
The schoolboy. 6233-4
Science and prayer, fr. The task. 6545-7
"See where the Thames". 6814-6
Seeing the beloved. 6814-6
Self-acquaintance. 6814-6
Set not thy foot on worms, fr. The task. 6195-0
The shining light. 6814-6
The shrubbery. 6380-2,6208-3,6152-4,6645-3,6086-2
Simple faith. 6932-0
Slave's complaint. 6719-0
Slavery. 6302-0;6385-3
Slavery. 6954-1
Slaves cannot breathe in England, fr. The task. 6932-0
Snow. 6543-0
The sofa, fr. The task. 6814-6
The solitude of Alexander Selkirk. 6246-5,6332-2,6479-5, 6504-X,6732-8,6560-0,6075-7,6102-8,6552-X
"Sometimes a light surprises." 6001-3
Song ("No more shall..."). 6814-6
A song ("On the green margin..."). 6814-6
The song ("The sparkling eye..."). 6814-6
A song of mercy and judgment. 6814-6
Song of peace written at the request of Lady Austen. 6814-6
Song written at the request of Lady Austen. 6814-6
Sonnet addressed to Henry Cowper, Esq. 6814-6
Sonnet to Mrs. Unwin. 6024-2,6430-2
Sonnet to William Wilberforce, Esq. 6152-4,6430-2
The sower. 6814-6
The spider and the fly. 6135-4
Stanzas on..indecent liberties taken..remains of Milton. 6814-6
Stanzas printed on bills of mortality: 1787. 6814-6
Stanzas printed on bills of mortality: 1788. 6814-6
Stanzas printed on bills of mortality: 1789. 6814-6
Stanzas printed on bills of mortality: 1790. 6814-6
Stanzas printed on bills of mortality: 1792. 6814-6
Stanzas printed on bills of mortality: 1793. 6814-6
The stateman in retirement, fr. Retirement. 6932-0
Stella's birthday. 6134-6
Strada's nightingale. 6383-7
The stream. 6317-9
The stricken deer, fr. The task. 6315-2,6337-3,6545-7
Submission. 6134-6
The succedaneum. 6423-X
Sweet meat has sour sauce; or, the slave-trader...dumps. 6814-6
"Sweet stream, that winds." 6302-0;6385-3
A sympathy with sounds, fr. The task. 6934-7
The symptoms of love. 6814-6
Table talk. 6814-6
Table talk, sels. 6831-6

Table talk, sels. 6483-3,6195-0
A tale, founded on a fact which happened in Jan. 1779 6814-6
A tale. 6018-8
The task, fr. The sofa. 6958-4
The task, fr. The sofa. 6958-4
The task, sels. 6831-6
The task, sels. 6195-0,6250-4,6545-7,6378-0,6604-6,6491 ,6024-2,6102-8,6152-4,6649-6,6301-2,6430
The task. 6198-2,6208-3
Temptation. 6814-6
Thanks for a gift of pheasants. 6814-6
This evening, Delia, you and I. 6195-0
A thunder storm. 6814-6
The time-piece, fr. The task. 6814-6
Tirocinium: or, a review of schools. 6814-6
To a lady who wore a lock of his hair set with diamonds. 6814-6
To a young friend on his arriving at Cambridge wet. 6814-6
To a young lady. 6246-5,6086-2
To a young lady who stole a pen from..Prince of Wales's. 6814-6
To Delia. 6814-6
To Dr. Austin, of Cecil Street, London. 6814-6
To George Romney, Esq. 6814-6
To Gravina, on his translating the author's song... 6814-6
To John Johnson. 6814-6
To Lady Austen, written in rainy weather. 6814-6
To Mary. 6198-2,6317-9,6086-2,6430,2,6560-0
To Mary Unwin. 6488-4,6634-8,6086-2,6153-2,6250-4
To Mary Unwin ("Mary! I want a lyre..."). 6246-5
To Mary Unwin ("The twentieth year..."). 6246-5
To Miss Creuze on her birthday. 6814-6
To Mrs, King on her kind present to the author. 6814-6
To Mrs. Newton. 6814-6
To Mrs. Throckmorton, on her transcript of Horace. 6092-7
To Mrs. Unwin. 6219-9
To my cousin Anne Bodham. 6814-6
To my cousin Anne Bodham, on receiving from her a... 6874-X
To my cousin, Anne Bodham. 6092-7
To Sir John Fenn. 6814-6
To Sir Joshua Reynolds. 6814-6
To the immortal memory of a halibut. 6092-7
To the immortal memory of the halibut on which I dined. 6814-6
To the immortal memory of the halibut... 6258-X,6378-0
To the nightingale which the author heard...1792. 6814-6
To the Rev. Mr. Newton. 6315-2
To the Rev. Mr. Newton, rector of St. Mary, Woolnoth. 6814-6
To the Rev. Mr. Newton: an invitation to the country. 6814-6
To the Rev. William Bull. 6092-7
To the Rev. William Bull. 6814-6
To the Rev. William Cawthorne Unwin. 6814-6
To the Reverend Mr. Newton on his return from Ramsgate. 6814-6
To the same (1793). 6634-8
To Warren Hastings, Esq. 6814-6
To William Hayley, Esq. 6814-6
To William Hayley, Esq. in reply to his solicitation. 6814-6
Tom Raban. 6814-6
True and false comforts. 6814-6
True pleasures. 6814-6
The true preacher, fr. The task. 6337-3
Truth. 6814-6
Truth, sels. 6831-6
The uncertain man. 6996-7
Upon a venerable rival. 6814-6
The valediction. 6814-6
The valley of the shadow of death. 6641-0
Vanity of the world. 6814-6
Verses ("I am monarch"). 6486-8
Verses supposed to be written by Alexande Selkirk.

COWPER

6131-1,6219-9,6302-0,6385-3,6271-7,6086-2,6152-4
Verses written at Bath on finding the heel of a shoe. 6814-6
Votum. 6814-6
The waiting soul. 6378-0
Walking with God. 6154-0,6271-7,6337-3,6219-9,6152-4, 6430 ,6527-9,6491-4,6723-9
Welcome cross. 6814-6
Welcome to the table. 6814-6
Which only poets know. 6634-8
Whitefield. 6302-0
Winter. 6228-8,6240-7,6302-0,6385-3,6230-X
A winter evening at home. 6240-7
The winter evening, fr. The task. 6934-7
The winter evening, fr. The task. 6814-6
The winter morning walk, fr. The task. 6814-6
The winter nosegay. 6814-6
Winter scene, fr. The task. 6932-0
Winter scenes in the country, fr. The task. 6195-0
Winter walk at noon. 6302-0;6385-3
The winter walk at noon. 6814-6
Wisdom. 6814-6
Wisdom, fr. The task. 6337-3
The woodland in spring. 6049-8
The woodman's dog. 6466-3,6512-0
Written after leaving her at New Burns. 6814-6
Written in a quarrel. 6814-6
Written under the influence of delirium. 6086-2
Yardley oak. 6814-6
Yardley Oak. 6198-2,6380-2
Yardley-oak. 6866-9
The yearly distress; or, tithing time at Stock in Essex. 6814-6

Cowper, William (tr.)
The acquiescence of pure love. Madame De la Mothe Guion, 6814-6
The advance of the Trojans, fr. The Iliad. Homer, 6435-3
An aenigma. Vincent Bourne, 6814-6
Ajax in flight, fr. The Iliad. Homer, 6435-3
"And now Cyllenian...", fr. The Odyssey. Homer, 6435-3
Anticipation. Lucilius, 6850-2
Artificial beauty. Lucianus, 7039-6
Aspirations of the soul after God. Madame De la Mothe Guion, 6814-6
"At morn we placed on his funeral bier". Callimachus, 6814-6
"Bright as among the stars...", fr. The Iliad. Homer, 6606-2
"But the eternal father...", fr. The Iliad. Homer, 6435-3
The cantab. Vincent Bourne, 6814-6
Canzone. John Milton, 6814-6
The cause won. Vincent Bourne, 6814-6
A child of God longing to see him beloved. Madame De la Mothe Guion, 6814-6
Chloe and Euphelia. Matthew Prior, 6814-6
Complimentary pieces to Milton. John Milton, 6814-6
The cottager and his landlord. John Milton, 6814-6
The cricket. Vincent Bourne, 6814-6,6271-7
Denner's old woman. Vincent Bourne, 6814-6
The description of an impertinent. Horace, 6814-6
Divine justice amiable. Madame De la Mothe Guion, 6814-6
Divine love endures no rival. Madame De la Mothe Guion, 6814-6
Elegy. Ovid, 6814-6
Elegy 001: To Charles Deodati. John Milton, 6814-6
Elegy 002: On the death of the university beadle... John Milton, 6814-6
Elegy 003: On the death of the bishop of Winchester. John Milton, 6814-6
Elegy 004: To his tutor, Thomas Young, chaplain... John Milton, 6814-6
Elegy 005: On the approach of spring. John Milton, 6814-6
Elegy 006: To Charles Deodati. John Milton, 6814-6
Elegy 007 ("As yet a stranger..."). John Milton, 6814-6
The entire surrender. Madame De la Mothe Guion, 6814-6
Epigrams, sels. John Milton, 6814-6
An epitaph ("At three-score..."). Unknown (Greek), 6814-6
An epitaph ("My name"). Unknown (Greek), 6814-6
An epitaph ("Painter"). Unknown (Greek), 6814-6
An epitaph ("Take to thy bosom"). Unknown (Greek), 6814-6
The epitaph - and the reader. Paulus Silentiarius, 6879-0
Epitaph to William Northcot. Charles Unwin, 6814-6
Expectation of death. Unknown (Greek), 6435-3
Fables. John Gay, 6814-6
Familiarity dangerous. Vincent Bourne, 6814-6,6511-2
"Far happier are the dead, methinks, than they". Unknown, 6435-3
A figurative description of...procedure of divine love. Madame De la Mothe Guion, 6814-6
"Fond youth! who dream'st that hoarded gold". Menander, 6814-6
The furnance. Homer, 6814-6
The ghost of Patroclus, fr. The Iliad. Homer, 6435-3
Glory to God alone. Madame De la Mothe Guion, 6814-6
The glow-worm. Vincent Bourne, 6814-6
God hides his people. Madame De la Mothe Guion, 6814-6
God neither known nor loved by the world. Madame De la Mothe Guion, 6814-6
Gratitude and love to God. Madame De la Mothe Guion, 6814-6
Happy solitude - unhappy men. Madame De la Mothe Guion, 6814-6
"He said, and urged him...", fr. The Odyssey. Homer, 6435-3
"He spake, to whom I...", fr. The Odyssey. Homer, 6435-3
Helen, fr. The Iliad. Homer, 6435-3
A humorous description of the author's journey... Horace, 6814-6
"I slept, when Venus entr'd: to my bed". Moschus, 6814-6
"In Cnidus born, the consort I became". Heraclides, 6814-6
The innocent thief. Vincent Bourne, 6814-6
Invitation to the redbreast. Vincent Bourne, 6814-6
The jackdaw. Vincent Bourne, 6814-6
Joy in martyrdom. Madame De la Mothe Guion, 6814-6
The joy of the cross. Madame De la Mothe Guion, 6814-6
The last journey of the wooers, fr. The Odyssey. Homer, 6435-3
Living water. Madame De la Mothe Guion, 6814-6
Love faithful in the absence of the beloved. Madame De la Mothe Guion, 6814-6
Love increased by suffering. Madame De la Mothe Guion, 6814-6
The love of God the end of life. Madame De la Mothe Guion, 6814-6
Love pure and fervent. Madame De la Mothe Guion, 6814-6
A manual more ancient that the art of printing... Vincent Bourne, 6814-6
The maze. Vincent Bourne, 6814-6
Menelaus and Odysseus, fr. The Iliad. Homer, 6435-3
The Nativity. Madame De la Mothe Guion, 6814-6
Nature unimpaired by time. John Milton, 6814-6
The necessity of self-abasement. Madame De la Mothe Guion, 6814-6
No matter. Paulus Silentiarius, 7039-6
No sorrow peculiar to the sufferer. Vincent Bourne, 6814-6
"Now marshall'd all beneath...", fr. The Iliad. Homer, 6435-3
Ode ("Boy! I detest..."). Horace, 6814-6
Ode ("Boy, I hate..."). Horace, 6814-6
Ode ("Ease is the weary..."). Horace, 6814-6
Ode ("See'st thou..."). Horace, 6814-6
An ode addressed to Mr. John Rouse, librarian... John Milton, 6814-6
Ode on the death of a lady who lived one hundred years. Vincent Bourne, 6814-6
Of the shield of Achilles, fr. The Odyssey. Homer, 6435-3
"Oft we enhance our ills by discontent". Philemon, 6814-6

On a bath. Plato, 6814-6
On a battered beauty. Unknown (Greek), 6814-6
On a fowler. Isidorus, 6850-2,6814-6
On a good man. Unknown (Greek), 6814-6
On a miser (1). Unknown (Greek), 6814-6
On a miser (2). Unknown (Greek), 6814-6
On a miser (3). Unknown (Greek), 6814-6
On a similiar character. Unknown (Greek), 6814-6
On a thief. Unknown (Greek), 6814-6
On a true friend. Unknown (Greek), 6814-6
On an infant. Unknown (Greek), 6814-6
On an old woman. Unknown (Greek), 6814-6
On an old woman. Lucilius, 6850-2
On an ugly fellow. Unknown (Greek), 6814-6
On envy. Unknown (Greek), 6814-6
On female inconstancy. Unknown (Greek), 6814-6
On flatterers. Unknown (Greek), 6814-6
On Hermocratia. Unknown (Greek), 6814-6
On invalids. Unknown (Greek), 6814-6
On late-acquired wealth. Unknown (Greek), 6814-6
On Miltiades. Unknown (Greek), 6814-6
On Niobe. Unknown (Greek), 6814-6
On one ignorant and arrogant. Owen, 6501-5
On one ignorant and arrogant. John Owen, 6814-6
On Pallas bathing, fr. A hymn. Callimachus, 6814-6
On pedigree. Epicharmus, 6814-6
On the astrologers. Unknown (Greek), 6814-6
On the death of Damon. John Milton, 6814-6
On the death of the bishop of Ely. John Milton, 6814-6
On the death of the vice-chancellor, a physician. John Milton, 6814-6
On the grasshopper. Unknown (Greek), 6814-6
On the grasshopper. Anacreon, 6271-7
On the invention of guns. John Milton, 6814-6
On the picture of a sleeping child. Vincent Bourne, 6814-6
On the Platonic idea, as it was understood by Aristotle. John Milton, 6814-6
On the reed. Unknown (Greek), 6814-6
On the shortnes of human life. Dr. Jortin, 6814-6
The parrot. Vincent Bourne, 6814-6
The perfect sacrifice. Madame De la Mothe Guion, 6814-6
Persian fopperies. Horace, 7039-6
Poem on Milton. John Dryden, 6814-6
Prudent simplicity. John Owen, 6814-6
The pursuit around the walls, fr. The Iliad. Homer, 6435-3
"Receive, dear friend, the truths I teach". Horace, 6230-X
Reciprocal kindness the primary law of nature. Vincent Bourne, 6814-6
Repose in God. Madame De la Mothe Guion, 6814-6
Retaliation. John Owen, 6814-6
The salad. Vergil (fr. the Greek of Parthenius), 6814-6
The scales of Zeus, fr. The Iliad. Homer, 6435-3
Scenes favourable to meditation. Madame De la Mothe Guion, 6814-6
The secrets of divine love are to be kept. Madame De la Mothe Guion, 6814-6
Self-diffidence. Madame De la Mothe Guion, 6814-6
Self-love and truth incompatible. Madame De la Mothe Guion, 6814-6
The silk worm. Vincent Bourne, 6814-6
Simile, fr. Paradise lost. John Milton, 6814-6
Simple trust. Madame De la Mothe Guion, 6814-6
Since God is there. Jeanne Marie Bouvier de la Motte Guyon, 6337-3
The snail. Vincent Bourne, 6814-6,6454-X
"So saying, the goddess...", fr. The Iliad. Homer, 6435-3
"So was Menoetius' valiant son...", fr. The Iliad. Homer, 6435-3
Sonnet ("As on a hill-top"). John Milton, 6814-6
Sonnet ("Enamour'd"). John Milton, 6814-6
Sonnet ("Fair lady"). John Milton, 6814-6
Sonnet ("Lady! it cannot"). John Milton, 6814-6
Sonnet to Charles Diodati. John Milton, 6814-6
"The soul came to him...", fr. The Iliad. Homer, 6435-3
The soul that loves God finds him every where. Madame De la Mothe Guion, 6814-6

Sparrows self-domesticated in Trinty College, Cambridge. Vincent Bourne, 6814-6
"A Spartan, 'scaping from the fight". Palladas, 6814-6
"A Spartan, his companion slain". Julianus [or Julian the Egyptian], 6814-6
Strada's nightingale. Vincent Bourne, 6814-6
Sunset and sunrise. John Owen, 6814-6
A swallow. Euenus, 6435-3
The swallow. Madame De la Mothe Guion, 6814-6
The tears of a painter. Vincent Bourne, 6814-6
Tellemachus finds his father, fr. The Odyssey. Homer, 6435-3
The testimony of divine adoption. Madame De la Mothe Guion, 6814-6
"Then answer thus Antenor...", fr. The Iliad. Homer, 6435-3
The Thracian. Vincent Bourne, 6814-6
"Thus Italy was moved - nor did the chief", fr. Aeneid. Vergil, 6814-6
"Thus pondering he stood...", fr. The Iliad. Homer, 6435-3
"Till sacred morn had brighten'd...", fr. The Iliad. Homer, 6435-3
To a friend in distress. John Owen, 6814-6
To Christina, queen of Sweden with Cromwell's picture. John Milton, 6814-6
To Demosthenis. Unknown (Greek), 6814-6
To Giovanni Battista Manso. John Milton, 6814-6
To health. Unknown (Greek), 6814-6
To his father. John Milton, 6814-6
To Leonora. John Milton, 6814-6
To Leonora singing at Rome. John Milton, 6814-6
To Licinius. Horace, 7039-6
To Salsillus, a Roman poet, much indisposed. John Milton, 6814-6
To the swallow. Unknown (Greek), 6814-6
Translation of psalm 137. Bible, 6848-0
The triumph of heavenly love desired. Madame De la Mothe Guion, 6814-6
Truth and devine love rejecyed by the world. Madame De la Mothe Guion, 6814-6
Vanities. Paulus Silentiarius, 6435-3
Verses to the memory of Dr. Lloyd (1). Vincent Bourne, 6814-6
Verses to the memory of Dr. Lloyd (2). Vincent Bourne, 6814-6
The vicissitudes experienced in the Christian life. Madame De la Mothe Guion, 6814-6
The wall, fr. The Iliad. Homer, 6435-3
Watching unto God in the night season. Madame De la Mothe Guion, 6814-6
Watching unto God in the night season (2). Madame De la Mothe Guion, 6814-6
Watching unto God in the night season (3). Madame De la Mothe Guion, 6814-6
Cowper, the religious recluse, fr. The task. William Cowper. 6195-0
"Cowper, whose silver, task'd sometimes hard". Sonnet addressed to Henry Cowper, Esq. William Cowper. 6814-6
"The cows are in the barnyard". A free woman. James Rorty. 6780-8
"Cows aren't clumsy". A cow. Julia Van der Veer. 6850-2
"Cows in the meadow". God's work. Gabriel (Thomas Nicoll Hepburn) Setoun. 6937-1
"The cows stood in a thunder-cloud of flies". August. A.J. Young. 6779-4
Cowslip. Unknown. 6529-5
Cowslips. Stephen Lucius Gwynn. 6174-5
"The cowslips tall her pensioners be", sels. William Shakespeare. 6601-1
Cox, C.C.
 "I love thee, gracious Lord". 6065-X
Cox, Cordelia
 Intercession. 6799-9
Cox, Donald
 Meditation. 6337-3
Cox, Eleanor Rogers
 At benediction. 6172-9
 Death of Cuchalain. 6712-9,6292-X

Cox

    The dream of Aengus Og. 6556-2
    Dreaming of cities dead. 6096-X,6292-X,6172-9
    Gods and heores at the Gael. 6172-9
    On Broadway. 6102-8,6076-5
    The return. 6946-0
    Three white birds of Aengus. 6184-2
    Three white birds of Angus. 6253-9
    To a dead poet. 6096-X,6184-2,6184-2
    To a portrait of Whistler in the Brooklyn Art Museum. 6556-2,6300-4
    To Barbary I have not sailed. 6619-4

Cox, Emma Finty
    Your cross and my cross. 6449-3

Cox, Joel
    'But, Walt, it may not hold' 6860-X
    The journeyman: blue wooden day. 6860-X

Cox, Kenyon
    Work ("Work thou for pleasure"). 6465-5,6260-1
    Work thou for pleasure. 6964-9

Cox, Lilian
    Never night again. 6144-3,6337-3

Cox, Marjorie Herrmann
    Beacon of trust. 6342-X

Cox, Palmer
    The mouse's lullaby. 6466-3

Cox, S. Donald
    The wind in the trees. 7031-0

Cox, S.K.
    A knightly welcome. 6920-7

Cox, Thelma Parker
    Evolution. 7024-8
    Frustration, a heritage. 7024-8

Coxe, Arthur Cleveland
    America. 6946-0
    Body of Jesus. 6065-X
    The chimes of England. 6219-9
    Christ is arisen. 6177-X
    Christmas carol. 6219-9
    Hallowe'en. 6820-0
    The heart's song. 6219-9
    Lake George. 6484-1
    O where are the kings and empires now. 6337-3
    The present age. 6337-3
    Song. 6608-9
    Ye shall live also. 6065-X

Coxe, Arthur Cleveland (tr.)
    Easter chorus, fr. Faust. Johann Wolfgang von Goethe, 6337-3

Coxe, Bishop
    The chimes of old England. 6273-3

Coxe, Louis O.
    Dead marine. 6666-6
    Pin-up girl. 6666-6
    Red right returning. 6666-6

The coxswain's line. H.E. Cressman. 6497-3

Coxwell, C. Fillingham (tr.)
    The peasant and the sheep. Ivan Andreevich Kriloff, 7039-6

Coy Polyphemus, fr. Idyll vi. Theocritus. 6435-3
The coy shepherdess, or Phillis and Amintas. Unknown. 6157-5

Coy, David
    Like a shadow. 6860-X
    McDougall, Jo. 6860-X
    The trout in Beartooth lake. 6860-X

Coy, Delphine Harris
    Confessio amantis. 6836-7
    Lost cabin. 6836-7
    My mother's eyes. 6836-7
    A solar myth. 6836-7
    A woman's cycle of prayer. 6836-7

Coyle, Henry
    The old apple tree. 6701-8
    Pussy's plea. 6510-4
    "She made home happy". 6097-8,6274-1

Coyote. John Vance Cheney. 6241-5
Coyote. Francis Bret Harte. 6006-4,6134-6
Coyote. Ruth Weiss. 6998-3, 6901-0
The coyote and the locust. Unknown (Zuni Indian) 7039-6
Coyote blood. Lew Sarett. 6850-2

"Coyote gives/Coyote takes". Coyote. Ruth Weiss. 6998-3, 6901-0
"Coyote kicks back". Agnes. Mah-do-ge Tohee. 7005-1
A coyote prowled. Annie Elizabeth Cheney. 6510-4
Coyote, coyote, please tell me. Peter Blue Cloud. 7005-1
"Coyote/running/running/coyote". Sweat song. Peter Blue Cloud. 7005-1

Cozens, F.H.
    Limerick:"..young curate, named Stone". 6811-1

Cozzens, Frederick Swartwout
    Battle of Bunker Hill. 6409-4,6744-1,6568-6
    An experience and a moral. 6385-3,6486-8

Cozzo grillo. H.B. Mallalieu. 6666-6
The crab and the snake. Unknown (Greek) 6435-3
"Crab man loves you" Walt Curtis. 7003-5
"The crab, the bullace and the sloe". Elegy. Alfred Austin. 6102-8
Crab-apple. Ethel Talbot. 6466-3
The crab-catchers. Celia Thaxter. 6965-7

Crabb, Billie Marie
    Bunky. 6750-6
    Honey boy. 6750-6
    Lines to a late lamented rabbit. 6750-6

Crabbe, George
    "Age, with stealing steps...," fr. Tales of the hall. 6301-2,6659-3
    Aldborough, fr. The village. 6934-7
    The alms house. 6378-0
    The approach of age. 6302-0;6385-3
    An autumn day. 6659-3
    Books, fr. The library. 6932-0
    Books, fr. The library. 6934-7
    Books, fr. The library. 6932-0
    Books, fr. The library. 6934-7
    The borough, sels. 6831-6
    The borough, sels. 6482-5,6317-9,6195-0
    The borough. 6208-3
    The cathedral. 6659-3
    The convict's dream. 6543-0
    Country life. 6954-1
    Crusty critics, fr. The library. 6932-0
    David and Saul. 6848-0
    The dean's lady. 6315-2
    The death of Ruth. 6980-0
    The demons of opium, fr. Sir Eustace Gray. 6545-7
    The dream of the condemned. 6980-0
    East Anglian seas and shores, sels. 6258-X
    The foreshore. 6150-8
    The founder of the almshouse. 6543-0
    A group of gipsies. 6980-0
    His mother's wedding-ring. 6934-7
    Inebriety. 6802-2
    Isaac Ashford. 6600-3
    Jacob and Rachel. 6848-0
    Jospeh's dream. 6848-0
    Late wisdom. 6250-4
    "Let me not have this gloomy view". 6980-0
    The library. 6186-9
    The library. 6297-0
    Life. 6932-0
    A marriage ring. 6317-9
    Meeting, sels. 6317-9
    The mourner. 6302-0;6385-3
    My Damon was the first to wake. 6086-2
    Newspapers. 6980-0
    "Oh, friendhsip, cordial of the human breast" 6935-5
    Opium dream, fr. The world of dreams. 6545-7
    The parish poor-house, fr. The village. 6932-0
    The parish register, sels. 6472-8
    The parish workhouse, fr. The village. 6301-2,6102-8, 6102-8
    Patient. 6369-1
    The pauper's funeral, fr. The village. 6150-6,6208-3
    The pauper's funeral. 6150-8
    The peasant. 6302-9,6385-3
    Peter Grimes. 6195-8,6208-3
    Peter Grimes, fr. The borough. 6195-0
    Phoebe Dawson. 6245-8
    The poor fisherman. 6793-X
    The poor, fr. The borough. 6023-4

The poor-house. 6980-0
Portrait of a vicar, sels. 6545-7
Posthumous tales. 6201-6
Practical charity. 6213-X
The preceptor husband, fr. Tales of the hall. 6195-0
Reconciliation. 6980-0
Reflections. 6641-0
Reporters. 6996-7
Resurrection. 6931-2
A retrospect. 6086-2
"A ring to me Cecilia sends" 6874-X
A sea fog. 6980-0
Sea marsh. 6545-7
The sea, fr. The borough. 6195-0
Sir Eustace Grey. 6369-1,6086-2
Sir Eustace Grey, sels. 6378-0
Sly lawyers. 6996-7
Sping to winter, fr. The ancient mansion. 6125-7
A storm on the east coast. 6943-6
A storm on the east coast. 6543-0
Strolling players. 6543-0
The sudden death and funeral. 6980-0
A Suffolk fen. 6793-X
The Suffolk shore. 6545-7
Tale X--the lover's journey, fr. Tales. 6198-2
Tales. 6208-3
Tales of the hall. 6208-3
Tales, sels. 6198-2
Truth in poetry, fr. The village. 6932-0
The village as it is. 6543-0
The village, sels. 7009-4
The village, sels. 6831-6
The village, sels. 7009-4
The village, sels. 6831-6
The village, sels. 6024-2,6102-8,6378-0,6195-0,6198-2, 6527
The village. 6186-9,6208-3,6152-4
Warwick. 6484-1
We trod the maze of error round. 6086-2
The whistling boy that holds the plough. 6086-2
The winter storm at sea. 6833-2
Woman. 6980-0
The wretched mind. 6980-0
Crabbed age and youth. Theophilus. 6435-3
"Crabbed age and youth can not live together". William Shakespeare. 6181-8,6182-6,6208-3,6271-7,6153-2
"Crabbed age and youth cannot live together". William Shakespeare. 6219-9,6250-4,6560-0
"Crabbed age and youth". Unknown. 6102-8,6194-X
A crabbed song of spring. Leonora Speyer. 6032-3
The crabfish. Unknown. 6610-0
Crabtree, Serepta A.
    What the world needs. 6717-4
The crack. J.C. Hall. 6257-1
"The crackling embers on the hearth are dead". Night. Hartley Coleridge. 6380-2
Craddle, W.
    Egoism. 6722-0
    Male and female. 6722-0
    On a certain scholar. 6722-0
"The cradle I have made for thee". The ivory cradle. Auguste Angellier. 6961-4
Cradle carol. Eleanor Slater. 6337-3
Cradle hymn ("Away in a manger, no crib for a bed"). Martin Luther. 6216-4,6466-3,6519-8,6270-7,6456-6
A cradle hymn ("Hush! my dear, lie still and slumber"). Isaac Watts. 6145-1,6519-8,6533-3
A cradle hymn. Isaac Watts. 6078-1,6198-2,6216-4,6242-3, 6315-2,6365 ,6627-5,6424-8,6131-1,6214-8,6219-9,6152-4
Cradle of peace. Marion S. O'Neil. 6662-3
The cradle of the deep. Emma Hart Willard. 6337-3
Cradle song. William Cox Bennett. 6658-5
Cradle song. Mary M. Bowen. 6131-1
Cradle song. Caris Brooke. 6373-X
Cradle song. Alice Cary. 6865-0;6969-X,6969-X
Cradle song. James Leo Duff. 6282-2
Cradle song. Louis Esson. 6784-0
Cradle song. Eugene Field. 6949-5
Cradle song. Norman Gale. 6772-7

Cradle song. Richard Gall. 6180-X,6086-2
Cradle song. Josiah Gilbert Holland. 6302-0,6385-3,6240-7, 6512-0,6627-5,6078
Cradle song. Norah M. Holland. 6115-X
Cradle song. Elizabeth Payson Prentiss. 6466-3,6219-9
Cradle song. Sir Walter Scott. 6114-1
Cradle song. Rowan Stephens. 6632-1
Cradle song. Alfred Lord Tennyson. 6638-0
Cradle song. Celia Thaxter. 6612-7
Cradle song. Unknown. 6242-3,6385-3,6413-2,6114-1
Cradle song. Unknown (German) 6131-1,6424-8,6296-2
Cradle song. Isaac Watts. 6747-6
Cradle song ("In the embers shining bright"). Richard Watson Gilder. 6623-2,6424-8
Cradle song ("Lord Gabriel, wilt thou not rejoice"). Josephine Preston Peabody. 6556-2,6506-6,6029-3
Cradle song ("Nightingale, oh, leave..."). Raphael Patkanian. 6050-1
Cradle song ("Sleep, baby, sleep!"). Unknown. 6078-1,6623-2
Cradle song ("Sleep, little baby of mine"). Unknown. 6627-5
Cradle song ("Sleep, sleep, beauty bright"). William Blake. 6134-6,6216-4,6395-9,6627-5,6737-9,6491 ,6078-1,6533-3,6214-8,6491-4,6328-4,6086
Cradle song ("Sweet slumber now creeps..."). Raphael Patkanian. 6050-1
Cradle song ("The winds are whispering over the sea"). Merle St. Croix Wright. 6365-9,6429-9,6321-7
A cradle song ("What does the little birdie say"). Alfred Lord Tennyson. 6138-9,6452-3,6304-7,6639-9
Cradle song of the poor. Adelaide Anne Procter. 6772-7
Cradle song of the virgin. Unknown. 6282-2
Cradle song to put a Negro baby to sleep. Ildefonso Pereda Valdes. 6759-X
Cradle song, sels. Isaac Watts. 6931-2
A cradle song. Nicholas Breton. 6233-4,6395-9,6301-2
A cradle song. Padraic Colum. 6096-X,6477-9,6233-4,6244-X, 6282-2,6581-3
A cradle song. John B.L. Warren, 3d Baron De Tabley. 6233-4
A cradle song. Thomas Dekker. 6436-1
A cradle song. Isaac Watts. 6233-4,6271-7,6459-0
Cradle songs ("Baby, baby bright"). Algernon Charles Swinburne. 6078-1
Cradle-song. Sarojini Naidu. 6044-7,6653-4
Cradle-song ("Madonna, Madonna"). Adelaide Crapsey. 6607-0, 6282-2
Cradle-song at twilight. Alice Meynell. 6955-X
The cradle-song of the poor. Adelaide Anne Procter. 6957-6
A cradle-song of the Virgin. H.R. Bramley. 6095-1
The cradle.. Austin Dobson. 6123-0,6240-7,6656-9
The cradle. Gelett Burgess. 6817-0
The cradle. Celia Thaxter. 6612-7
Cradled 'mid the oxen. Henry Cogswell Knight. 6747-6
"Cradled in sapphire mist, morn's sunlit deep". The morning sea. Charles A. Fox. 6997-5
"Cradled within the loving circle of your arms". To my mother. Katherine Prescott Bemis. 6836-7
Cradling wheat. Charles Erskine Scott Wood. 6039-0
Crady, Kate McAlpin
    'Memberin'. 6017-X
"The craft threads through islands without...". The Queen Charloote islands meditations. J. Michael Yates. 6767-0
Craft vs. Boite. R.H. Thornton. 6878-2
Crafton, Allen
    In time of war I sing. 6032-3
    St. Maixent. 6476-0
Craftsman. Edna Bendig. 6750-6
The craftsmen of the little box. Vasko Popa. 6758-1
The crafty farmer. Unknown. 6185-0
The crafty miss of London, or The fryar well fitted. John Wilmot, 2d Earl of Rochester. 6157-5
The crag. Mikhail Lermontov. 6103-6
Crags. Alice Cary. 6969-X
The crags. Alfred Noyes. 6151-6
Craig, Alexander
    "Go you, O winds that blow from north to south" 6182-6
    The misery of man. 6563-5

Craig, Alice B.
   Evasion. 6799-9
Craig, Flossie Deane
   Here I shall wait. 6662-3
   I have a little son. 6662-3
Craig, George D.
   Land of plenty. 6342-X
Craig, Jessie T.
   A vision. 6925-8
Craig, Marian B.
   Teach me to understand. 6461-2
Craig, Marjorie
   Poetry. 6799-9
Craig, Mary
   Plighted. 6014-5
Craig, Maurice
   Winter. 6930-4
Craig, Maurice James
   High on a ridge of tiles. 6511-2
   Three cat poems. 6511-2
Craigbilly Fair. Unknown. 6125-7
Craigie, William A. (tr.)
   Iceland. Steingrimur Thorsteinsson, 6854-5
Craigmyle, Elizabeth
   Chained tigers: I. 7037-X
   Chained tigers: II. 7037-X
   In the day of the east wind. 6997-5
   Solway sands. 6656-9
   Song or sobbing? 6997-5
   Under deep apple boughs. 7037-X
Craigmyle, Elizabeth (tr.)
   The Asra. Heinrich Heine, 6842-1
   Attila's sword. ? Lingg, 6842-1
   Barbarossa. Friedrich Ruckert, 6842-1
   The blind king. Johann Ludwig Uhland, 6842-1
   The bridal. Heinrich Heine, 6842-1
   The bride of Corinth. Johann Wolfgang von Goethe, 6842-1
   The Bruce's locket. ? Strachwitz, 6842-1
   Charlemagne's voyage. Johann Ludwig Uhland, 6842-1
   The children of sorrow. Johann Gottfried von Herder, 6842-1
   The confession of Charlemagne. Karl Simrock, 6842-1
   Count Eberhard's hawthorn. Johann Ludwig Uhland, 6842-1
   The Count of Hapsburg. Johann C. Friedrich von Schiller, 6842-1
   The cranes of Ibykus. Johann C. Friedrich von Schiller, 6842-1
   The death of Carus. Count Platen, 6842-1
   Don Ramiro. Heinrich Heine, 6842-1
   The drink from a jack-boot. Pfarrius, 6842-1
   Earl Walter. Gottfried A. Berger, 6842-1
   The erl-king. Johann Wolfgang von Goethe, 6842-1
   Est, est. Wilhelm Muller, 6842-1
   Fair Rohtraut. Eduard Friedrich Morike, 6842-1
   The feast of victory. Johann C. Friedrich von Schiller, 6842-1
   The ferry. Johann Ludwig Uhland, 6842-1
   The fight with the dragon. Johann C. Friedrich von Schiller, 6842-1
   The god and the Bayadere. Johann Wolfgang von Goethe, 6842-1
   The grave in the Busentius. Count Platen, 6842-1
   Harmosan. Count Platen, 6842-1
   Hector's farewell. Johann C. Friedrich von Schiller, 6842-1
   The horse of Vevros. Schmidt-Phiseldeck, 6842-1
   The horses of Gravelotte. ? Gerok, 6842-1
   How Christ came to a lonely child. Friedrich Ruckert, 6842-1
   Hurra, Germania! Ferdinand Freiligrath, 6842-1
   In a dream. Heinrich Heine, 6842-1
   Kassandra. Johann C. Friedrich von Schiller, 6842-1
   Lenore. Gottfried A. Berger, 6842-1
   Love's burial. Heinrich Heine, 6842-1
   The maiden from a far country. Johann C. Friedrich von Schiller, 6842-1
   The minstrel's curse. Johann Ludwig Uhland, 6842-1
   A night of spring. ? Storm, 6842-1
   A night of spring. Unknown (German), 6842-1
   The parting of the earth. Johann C. Friedrich von Schiller, 6842-1
   Petrus. ? Kinkel, 6842-1
   The pilgrim of St. Just. Count Platen, 6842-1
   The pilgrimage to Kevlaar. Heinrich Heine, 6842-1
   Retribution. Johann Ludwig Uhland, 6842-1
   Richard the fearless. Johann Ludwig Uhland, 6842-1
   The ring of polykrates. Johann C. Friedrich von Schiller, 6842-1
   The robber-brothers. Count Joseph von Eichendorff, 6842-1
   Roland, the shield-bearer. Johann Ludwig Uhland, 6842-1
   Schwerting the Saxon. ? Ebert, 6842-1
   Sir Olaf. Johann Gottfried von Herder, 6842-1,7039-6
   The smithying of Sigfrid's sword. Johann Ludwig Uhland, 6842-1
   The spectre review. ? Zedlitz, 6842-1
   The story of a night. Heinrich Heine, 6842-1
   The submerged town. Klaus Groth, 6842-1
   Sword-song. Karl [or Charles] Theodore Korner, 6842-1
   The three songs. Johann Ludwig Uhland, 6842-1
   Told by a Brahmin. Friedrich Ruckert, 6842-1
   The walk to the forges. Johann C. Friedrich von Schiller, 6842-1
   "Were I before the gates of Mecca!" Ferdinand Freiligrath, 6842-1
   The widow' son. Adelbert von Chamisso, 6842-1
Craik, Dinah Maria Mulock
   Address to the new year. 6449-3,6820-0
   Angel faces. 6304-7
   Autumn's processional. 6239-3,6239-3
   The boat of my lover. 6066-8
   "Buried today." 6302-0;6385-3
   By the Alma river. 6302-0,6385-3,6409-4
   A child's smile. 6772-7
   A Christmas carol ("God rest ye, merry gentlemen..."). 6623-2,6219-9,6424-8
   Coming home. 6600-3
   Count Ludwig to the wood-spirit. 6676-3
   A dead baby. 6980-0
   The dead Czar Nicholas. 6302-0;6385-3
   Douglas. 6732-8,6437-X
   Douglas, Douglas, tender and true. 6481-7,6109-6,6102-8,6543-0,6304-7
   A dream-child. 6772-7
   An evening guest. 6980-0
   Four years. 6046-3
   The glad new year. 6937-1
   God rest ye, merry gentlemen. 6145-1,6608-9
   The good of it. 6001-3
   Grandpa. 6684-4,6502-3
   Green things growing. 6047-1,6239-3,6597-X,6239-3,6135-4
   Guns of peace. 7015-9
   Her likeness. 6302-0;6385-3
   Highland cattle. 6239-3
   "I love you. Words are small." 6066-8
   "I said to the brown, brown thrush", sels. 6601-1
   In our boat. 6240-7
   In Swanage bay. 6669-0
   A Lancashire doxology. 6219-9
   A Lancaster doxology. 6302-0;6385-3
   Lettice. 6321-7
   The little Jew. 6848-0
   Love that asketh love again. 6226-1
   A mercenary marriage. 6302-0;6385-3
   The mill. 6183-4,6456-6
   Mine. 6321-7,6429-9
   Monsieur et mademoiselle. 6134-6
   My love Annie. 6131-1
   The new year. 6466-3,6132-X,6964-9
   North wind. 6271-7
   Now and afterwards. 6240-7,6730-1,6219-9,6302-0,6385-3
   October. 6456-6
   Only a woman. 6302-0;6385-3
   Outward bound. 6600-3
   Over the hills and far away. 6569-4
   Over the hills and far away. 6980-0
   Passing by. 6911-8
   "Peace, wild-wrung hands! hush, sobbing breath". 6066-8

Philip, my king. 6271-7,6131-1,6219-9,6656-9,6543-0,
    6078-1,6127-3,6131-3,6164-8,6219-9,6271
Plighted. 6980-0
Respect the burden. 6914-2
Rothesay bay. 7037-X
Semper fidelis. 7037-X
A silly song. 6658-5
"Sing away, ay, sing away", sels. 6601-1
Sunrise among the hills. 6416-7
Three meetings. 6066-8
To the memory of Fletcher Harper. 6385-3
Too late. 6656-9,6658-5,6737-9,6385-3,6600-3,6271-7,
    6226-1,6219-9
A true hero. 6523-6
Veronica. 6669-0
Violets. 6519-8
Winning and losing. 6424-8
Young dandelion. 6519-8,6374-8,6049-8

Crain, Emily Dawson
    Second wife. 6750-6
Cram, Lulu Bradley
    Aloha. 6764-6
Cramer, Nelly R.
    When I am a man. 6684-4
Cramming. Walter Clarke Rodman. 6936-3
Crampton, Estelle W.
    My mamma. 6713-1
Cranach. Herbert Read. 6209-1
Cranahan, Ada
    Of books. 6014-5
The cranberry bog. Sarah A. Dixon. 6798-0
Cranch, Christopher Pearse
    After the centennial. 6946-0
    The bobolinks. 6239-3
    By the shore of the river. 6406-X
    The Cataract Isle. 6484-1
    A Chinese story. 6911-8
    Correspondences. 6385-3,6288-1
    The corso: the Roman carnival. 6624-0
    Evening, fr. Sea-pictures. 6997-5
    Gnosis. 6288-1,6309-8
    I in thee, and thou in me. 6288-1
    In the forrest of Fontainebleau. 6331-4
    Knowing. 6304-7
    Magnolia-grandiflora. 6049-8
    The martyr. 6524-4
    "The mighty name of Washington." 6712-3
    Morning, fr. Sea-pictures. 6997-5
    Paestum ("There, down Salerno's bay"). 6624-0
    The pines and the sea. 6300-4
    Sea-pictures, sels. 6997-5
    Shelling peas. 6742-5
    Shelling peas. 6912-6
    So far, so near. 6337-3
    Stanzas ("Thought is deeper"). 6632-1,6600-3,6271-7,
        6219-9
    The test of sight. 6742-5
    Thought. 6240-7,6076-5,6648-8,6302-0,6385-3
    "Thought is deeper than all speech." 6718-2,6402-7
    Vesuvius ("Dread"). 6624-0
    A young poet's advice. 6770-0
Cranch, Christopher Pearse (tr.)
    Aeneid, sels. Vergil, 6484-1
    The Lorelei. Heinrich Heine, 6271-7
    To the parted one. Johann Wolfgang von Goethe, 7039-6
    The Trojan horse. Vergil, 6102-8
Crandall, Charles H.
    The call of the stream. 6274-1
    The cinder path. 6274-1
    The fair copyholder. 6620-8
    Nemesis. 6741-X
    Wayside music. 6608-9
Crane Jr., L. Burton
    The spell of the pool. 6374-8
The crane in Bloomsbury. Frank Kendon. 6072-2
The crane's message. Theognis. 6435-3
Crane, Carl
    The reader writes. 6722-0
Crane, Constance
    Washer-woman. 6750-6

Crane, Frank
    My country. 6449-3
Crane, Hart
    Above the fresh ruffles of the surf. 6258-X
    At Melville's tomb. 6399-3,6641--0
    Black tambourine. 6375-6
    The bridge, sels. 6399-3,6052-8,6375-6
    The broken tower. 6399-3,6641-0
    Capte Hatteras, fr. The bridge. 6399-3
    Chaplinesque. 6808-1
    Emblems of conduct. 6375-6
    For the marriage of Faustus and Helen, sels. 6209-1
    March. 6491-4
    North Labrador. 6209-1
    Powhatan's daughter. 6250-4,6041-2
    Praise for an urn. 6036-6
    Purgatorio. 6375-6
    Recitative. 6209-1
    The river, fr. The bridge. 6375-6
    Sunday morning apples. 6375-6
    To Emily Dickinson. 6483-3
    To Shakespeare. 6483-3
    Voyages. 6619-4
    Voyages: I. 6536-8
    Voyages: II. 6536-8,6208-3,6076-5
Crane, Lauren E.
    Th song, fr. Juanita. 6241-5
Crane, Melville
    Emily Dickinson. 6464-7
Crane, Nathalia
    The blind girl. 6506-6,6332-2
    The dust. 56012-9
    Freud. 6012-9
    The history of honey. 6393-9
    The miracle. 6012-9
    Plea for the Bonhomme Richard. 6012-9
    The proposals. 6012-9
    The royal printer. 6012-9
    Suffering. 6861-8
    The wings of lead. 7019-1
Crane, Oliver
    Waiting on the lord. 6414-0
Crane, Stephen
    Ancestry. 6861-8
    Ancestry. 6300-4
    The black riders. 6121-4,6736-0
    The blades of grass. 6232-6,6102-8,6076-5,6337-3,6464-7
    Content. 6300-4
    Eating. 6102-8,6076-5
    "Have you ever made a just man?" 6996-7
    Hymn ("A slant of sun on dull brown walls"). 6102-8,
        6076-5
    I saw a man. 6102-8,6076-5,6464-7
    I wonder. 6121-4
    If war be kind. 6732-8,6102-8,6076-5,6542-2
    In the night. 6121-4
    The little blades of grass. 6396-9
    "A little ink more or less!" 6996-7
    "A man said to the universe". 6996-7
    A man said to the universe. 6380-2
    "A man saw a ball of gold in the sky". 6996-7
    The man. 6089-7
    A newspaper is a collection of half-injustices. 6380-2
    A newspaper. 6121-4
    The pathway to truth. 6396-9
    The peaks. 6007-2,6730-1,6007-2
    "'Think as I think', said a man. 6996-7
    "Three little birds in a row". 6996-7
    "Upon the road of my life". 6996-7
    The violets. 6723-9
    War is kind. 6399-3,6121-4,6736-0,6665-8
    Wayfarer. 6102-8,6076-5,6491-4,6723-9
    "The wayfarer/Perceiving the pathway to truth". 6996-7
    Why? 6300-4
    "A youth, in apparel that glittered". 6996-7
Crane, Walter
    Across the fields. 6656-9
    The crocus. 6466-3
    Freedom in America. 7009-4
    'In love's disport' 6770-0,6875-8

CRANE

Rondel ("This book"). 6770-0,6875-8
Rondel ("When time"). 6770-0,6875-8
A seat for three: written on a settle. 6437-X,6656-9
Triolet. 6875-8
Triolet ("In the light"). 6770-0
'What makes the world?' 6770-0,6875-8

Crane, Walter Beverly
'Bwana Tumbo'-the great hunter. 6995-9

The **crane**. Hovhannes Toumanian. 6050-1
The **cranes** of Ibykus. Johann C. Friedrich von Schiller. 6842-1
Craniology. Thomas Hood. 6974-6
Cranmer's prophecy of Queen Elizabeth, fr. Henry VIII. William Shakespeare. 6730-1

Cranmer-Byng, Lancelot (tr.)
A feast of lanterns. Yuan Mei, 6649-6
On the banks of Jo-Eh. Li Po, 6732-8

Crannell, C.W.
Philosophy. 6117-6

Cranston, Claudia
If I were the lord God. 6653-4

Crape on the door. Unknown. 6045-1

Crapsey, Adelaide
Adventure. 6897-9
Anguish. 6850-2
Arbutus. 6338-1
Blue hyacinths. 6850-2
Cinquains. 6509-0,6556-2,6030-7
Cinquains, sels. 6897-9
Cinquains: triad; trapped; the warning. 6332-2
Cradle-song ("Madonna, Madonna"). 6607-0,6282-2
Dirge. 6019-6,6102-8,6431-0,6581-3,6076-5,6300-4,6653-4,
    6030-7,6019-6,6102-8,6431-0,6581-3,6076-5,6300-4,
    6653-4
Expenses. 6897-9
Fate defied. 6393-4
The fiddling lad. 6374-8
The Grand Canyon. 6464-7
The guarded wound. 6393-4
The immortal residue. 6337-3
John Keats. 6879-0
Laurel in the Berkshires. 6850-2
The lonely death. 6556-2
Niagara. 6077-3
Night winds. 6393-4
November night. 6338-1,6102-8,6076-5,6523-9,6393-4,6467
On seeing weather-beaten trees. 6153-2,6332-2,6289-X
The pledge. 6320-9
The pledge. 6897-9
Release. 6850-2
Roma aeterna. 6850-2
Shadow. 6850-2
Snow. 6850-2
Song ("I make my shroud"). 6030-7,6556-2
Song ("I make my shroud, but no one knows") 6875-8
Susanna and the elders. 6897-9
Three cinquains. 6581-3
To man who goes seeking immortality... 6879-0
To the dead in the graveyard underneath my window. 6336-5
Trapped. 6850-2
Triad. 6052-8,6102-8,6076-5,6467-1,6289-X,6732
Vendor's song. 6602-X,6431-0
The warning. 6077-3,6102-8,6076-5,6393-4,6289-X
Why. 6337-3
Winter. 6891-X

Crapsey, Edward
"Entombed within a nation's reverent love". 6238-5

Crapshooters. Carl Sandburg. 6345-4

Crary, Cornelia Fulton
'Lindbergh flies alone' 7019-1

Crash on artillery. Unknown. 6237-7
"Crash! crash! crash!". The typhoon. Grace Lowe Broadhead. 6906-1

Crashaw, Richard
Against irresolution. 6931-2
Answer for hope. 6341-1
At Bethlehem. 6737-9
Charitas nimia or the dear bargain. 6489-2,6562-7
Christ crucified. 6465-5
Christ's victory. 6337-3
The coming child. 6337-3
Description of a convent. 6285-7
Dives asking a drop. 6023-4
Divine love. 6337-3
Easter day. 6489-2
An epitaph upon a young married couple dead. 6726-3,
    6563-5,6430-2,6562-7,6179-6
An epitaph upon husand and wife who died & were buried.
    6317-9,6052-8,6337-3,6291-9,6214-8
An epitaph upon Mr. Ashton a comfortable citizen. 6933-9
Euthanasia; or, the happy death. 6250-4,6543-0
The flaming heart, sels. 6933-9
The flaming heart, sels. 6562-7
The flaming heart. 6315-2,6726-3,6285-7,6563-5,6189-3,
    6194
The good woman made welcome in heaven. 6114-1
"Her supple breasts thrills out" 6935-5
The holy nativity of our Lord God. 6473-6,6730-1
The holy Nativity, sels. 6194-X
Hymn in adoration of the blessed sacrament. 6341-1
A hymn in honor of Saint Teresa. 6208-3,6489-2,6562-7,
    6285-7,6730-1,6022 ,6341-1,6641-0,6563-5,6430-2,6150-8
Hymn of Saint Thomas in adoration of..blessed sacrament. 6489-2
The hymn of Saint Thomas in adoration... 6933-9
Hymn of the nativity. 6933-9
Hymn of the Nativity. 6191-5,6341-1
Hymn of the nativity. 6933-9
A hymn of the nativity, sels. 6144-3
Hymn to St. Theresa. 6931-2
Hymn to the name of Jesus. 6301-2
I am the door. 6430-2
In the glorious assumption of our blessed lady. 6315-2
In the holy nativity [of our Lord God]. 6198-2,6334-9,
    6562-7
In the temple. 6250-4
"Let it no longer be a forlorne hope". 6562-7
Love's nightingale. 6315-2
Loves horoscope. 6933-9
Loves horoscope. 6341-1
Loves horoscope. 6933-9
M. Crashaws answer for hope. 6933-9
M. Crashaws answer for hope, sels. 6208-3
Music's duel. 6302-0,6385-3,6562-7,6245-8
The name above every name. 6830-8
The nativity. 6489-2
New Year's Day. 6562-7
The nightingale. 6634-8
O! thou undaunted. 6543-0
On a foul morning. 6194-X
On a prayer book. 6219-9,6271-7
On a prayer-book sent to Mrs. M.R. 6102-8
On a young married couple. 6208-3
On dives. 6022-6
On Mr. G. Herbert's book...The temple of sacred poems.
    6483-3
On the assumption. 6023-4
On the blessed Virgin's bashfulness. 6430-2
On the blessed virgin's bashfulness. 6282-2
On the glorious assumption of our blessed lady. 6489-2,
    6282-2
On the glorious assumption of the blessed Virgin. 6383-7
On the miracle of Loaves. 6022-6
On the water of our lords baptisme. 6562-7
On the wounds of our crucified lord. 6562-7
Philomela. 6934-7
Psalm 023. 6219-9
Quaerit Jessum suum Maria. 6022-6
Quaerit Jesum suum Maria. 6022-6
Qui perdid animam suam. 6022-6
Qui perdiderit animan suam. 6022-6
The recommendation. 6489-2
Saint Mary Magdalene, or the weeper. 6341-1
Saint Peter's shadow. 6022-6
Saint Teresa. 6250-4
Sainte Mary Magdalene or the weeper. 6562-7

Satan. 6438-8
The shepherd's hymn, sels. 6216-4
The shepherd's hymn. 6022-6
A shepherd's song, fr. A hymn of the Nativity. 6934-7
Shepherds hymn their saviour. 6187-7
A song ("Lord, when"). 6641-0,6214-8
Song ("To thy lover"). 6271-7,6219-9
Song, fr. The flaming heart. 6645-3
Sorrow. 6935-5
Steps to the temple, sels. 6908-8
The tear. 6430-2
Temperance, or the cheap physician. 6271-7
To a young gentle-woman. 6933-9
To our blessed Lord upon the choice of his sepulchre. 6022-6
To Pontius washing his hands. 6562-7
To Saint Theresa. 6634-8
To the Countess of Denbigh. 6341-1
To the name above every name, the name of Jesus. 6214-8, 6378-0
"Two went up to the temple to pray." 6302-0,6385-3,6723-9,6337-3,6438-8,6189
Upon Bishop Andrewes his picture before his sermons. 6933-9
Upon Ford's two tragedies. 6933-9
Upon Lazarus his tears. 6491-4
Upon the body of our blessed Lord, naked and bloody. 6933-9
Upon the body of our blessed Lord, naked and bloody. 6430-2,6022-6
Upon the body of our blessed Lord, naked and bloody. 6933-9
Upon the book & picture of the seraphical Saint Teresa. 6483-3,6187-7,6102-8
Upon the death of a gentleman. 6908-8
Upon the death of the most desired Mr. Herry's. 6383-7
Verses from the shepherd's hymn. 6186-9
"Whoe'er she be." 6562-7,6099-4
The widow's mites. 6931-2
Wishes. 6600-3,6023-4,6430-2,6726-3
Wishes to his supposed mistress. 6933-9
Wishes to his supposed mistress. 6246-5,6102-8,6341-1, 6092-7,6250-4,6560 ,6302-0,6385-3,6219-9,6189-3,6732-8,6634-8,6339-X,6301-2
"The crater is deep, the lake is round". Cantiga de Maria das Estrelas. Nancy Lee Couto. 6900-2
Cratinus
Pericles. T.F. Higham (tr.). 6435-3
The poet's inspiration. Thomas Moore (tr.). 6435-3
The cravat. Unknown. 6937-1
Craven. Sir Henry Newbolt. 6063-5,6473-6,6464-7
Craven, Henry Thornton
Ennui. 6936-3
A negative ideal. 6936-3
Rudolphus at the goal. 6936-3
The crawdad song. Unknown. 6594-5
Crawford, ?
We parted in silence. 6889-8
Crawford, Charlotte Holmes
Vive la France! 6030-7,6088-9,6419-1,6846-4,6476-0,6509
Crawford, Frances
The black leopard. 6515-5
"He who would be reborn must seek." 6515-5
"I do not know if you will know." 6515-5
"Intensity abstracted in air, ready to break." 6515-5
"It is a secret sorrow." 6515-5
"The melody, from treble tones." 6515-5
"Mould sprouts in old shoes and empty heads." 6515-5
"The poplars in the fields of France". 6331-4
"A sanctuary in a maze." 6515-5
"The subtle evil that the mind engenders." 6515-5
"The supple body bends to will." 6515-5
"To face the arrows of the chance-drawn bow." 6515-5
"Uncaptured is essential death." 6515-5
"Who comforts flesh unreconciled." 6515-5
"Who sees the panic unconfessed." 6515-5
"Within the spring's bright shell of dawn." 6515-5
Crawford, Francis Marion
National hymn. 6678-X
A new national hymn. 6286-5

Petty irritations. 6094-3
Crawford, Isabella Valancy
The blue forget-me-not. 6797-2
Canoe song. 6795-6
The canoe. 6795-6,6930-4,7041-8
The Christmas baby. 6797-2
The city tree. 6433-7
The deacon and his daughter. 6591-0,6592-2
Fairy toil. 6021-8
Faith, hope and charity. 6796-4
The farmer's daughter Cherry. 6591-0,6592-2
The Helot, sel. 6021-8
The helot, sels. 6115-X
La Blanchisseuse. 6591-0,6592-2
Laughter. 6433-7
The lily bed. 6446-9
'Love me, love my dog' 6797-2
Love's land. 6433-7
Malcolm's Katie, sels. 6795-6
Malcolm's Katie, sels. 6115-X
March. 6433-7
The moon of falling leaves, fr. Malcolm's Katie. 6843-X
The mother's soul. 6115-X
The rose. 6843-X
The rose. 6102-8,6115-X
Song for the soldiers. 6115-X
Song of the axe. 6795-6
Song of the axe. 6591-0,6592-2
Crawford, J.
That was Jim. 6576-7
Crawford, Jack
If Roosevelt had been bad. 6995-9
Mother's prayer. 6685-2
The weeds of the army. 6701-8
Crawford, John
Song of the Arkansas. 6777-8
Crawford, John M. (tr.)
The birth of the harp, fr. The Kalevala. Unknown (Finnish), 6372-1
Ilmarinen's wedding feast, fr. The Kalevala. Unknown (Finnish), 6372-1
The Kalevala, sels. Unknown (Finnish), 6372-1
Wooing of the maid of beauty, fr. Kalevala. Unknown (Finnish), 6679-8
Crawford, John Wallace
Rattlin' Joe's prayer. 6274-1
Crawford, Julia
We parted in silence. 6240-7,6302-0,6385-3,6271-7,6219-9
Crawford, Louisa Macartney
Kathleen Mavourneen. 6732-8,6250-4
Crawford, Nelson Antrim
The carrying of a ghost. 6034-X
Glories. 6032-3
In the key of blue. 6033-1
The mathematician. 6032-3
Trees. 6033-1
Crawford, Robert
The broom of the Cowdenknowes. 6960-6
The bush aboon traquair. 6250-4,6383-7
The courtship of Eve. 6269-5
Cowdenknowes. 6180-X
Down the burn, Davie. 6086-2,6180-X
Hawthorn-time. 6269-5
I took my love. 6269-5
Song ("Love, love me..."). 6784-0
Tweedside. 6086-2
The U. S. air force. 6465-5
Winged words. 6784-0
Crawford, Vesta P.
The timbers of design. 6857-X
Crawford, William
On Mrs. A. H. at a concert. 6874-X
"Crawford, the ferrywoman, lampman the...". Triads II. James Reaney. 6767-0
Crawley, A.E. (tr.)
Choosing friends. Theognis, 6435-3
An oath. Theognis, 6435-3
Craytor, Hazel Fern
Dead. 6799-9

CRAZY

Crazy Christopher. Alice Cary. 6969-X
The crazy Dixie. Unknown. 6594-5
Crazy Jane talks with the bishop. William Butler Yeats. 6150-8
Crazy Kate. The gipsies, fr. The task. William Cowper. 6543-0
Crazy medicine. Lew Sarett. 6490-6
Crazy Mike. Lewis Chesser. 6860-X
Crazy song to the air of Dixie. Unknown. 6732-8
The crazy world. William Gay. 6784-0
The crazyman. Arthur Baysting. 7018-3
Creamer, Edward S.
    When Paderewski plays. 6698-4
Create great peace, fr. 1914 - and after. James Oppenheim. 6337-3
Created clay. Virgil Browne. 6799-9
The created. Jones Very. 6333-0
Creation. Ambrose Bierce. 6307-1
Creation. Georgia H. Cooper. 6850-2
Creation. Edward R. Huxley. 6885-5
Creation. John Milton. 6385-3
Creation. Alfred Noyes. 6151-6;6437-X
Creation. Carter Webster. 6178-8
Creation. Ella Wheeler Wilcox. 6956-8
Creation and fall, fr. Branches of Adam. John Gould Fletcher. 6012-9
The creation of birds. John Milton. 6943-6
The creation of man and the animals. Unknown (Algonquian Indian) 6864-2
The creation of man. John Hewitt. 6920-7
The creation of man. Morris Rosenfeld. 7011-6
Creation's Lord, we give thee thanks. William De Witt Hyde. 6337-3
"Creation's and creator's crowning good". To the body. Coventry Patmore. 6931-2
Creation's psalm. Swithin Saint Swithaine. 6848-0
The creation, fr. Davideis. Abraham Cowley. 6933-9
Creation, fr. Ecclesiasticus. Bible. 6179-6
The creation, fr. Genesis. Bible. 6143-5
Creation, sels. Richard Doddridge Blackmore. 6482-5
The creation.. Caedmon. 6489-2
The creation. Cecil Frances Alexander. 6891-X
The creation. James Weldon Johnson. 6337-3,6532-5,6527-9, 6736-0,6393-4
Creative. Etta M. Graves. 6764-6
"Creative thought drives the universe with...". Thought. Edmund Doerf. 6799-9
Creator. Leonard Cohen. 6850-2
The creator and creatures. Isaac Watts. 6271-7
The creator in creation. Unknown. 6260-1
"Creator spirit, by whose aid". Veni creator spiritus. Unknown (Latin). 7039-6
The creator.. Unknown. 6466-3
Creatrix. Anna Wickham. 6102-8
"Creature of air and light". For a design of a butterfly resting on a skull. Felicia Dorothea Hemans. 6973-8
The creche. Carol Ryrie Brink. 6608-9
Crecy. Francis Turner Palgrave. 6323-3
Credat Judaeus Apella, fr. Hippodromania. Adam Lindsay Gordon. 6951-7
Credhe's lament. Unknown. 6873-1
Credhe's lament for Cail. Unknown. 6090-0
Credidimus Jovem Regnare. James Russell Lowell. 6735-2
The creditor.. Louis MacNeice. 6532-5
The creditor. Louis MacNeice. 6354-3
Credo. Edith Albert. 6847-2
Credo. Alfred Kreymborg. 6076-5
Credo. Elias Lieberman. 6503-1
Credo. Thomas Lynn. 6857-X
Credo. Seumas (James Starkey) O'Sullivan. 6930-4
Credo. John Oxenham. 6144-3;6337-3
Credo. Edwin Arlington Robinson. 6337-3,6532-5,6730-1,6288-1,6723-9
Credo. Arthur Symons. 6437-X
Credo. Vera Wheatley. 6374-8
Credo ("God is too high to measure out each thing"). Lizette Woodworth Reese. 6532-5
Credo ("Not what, but whom, I do believe!") John Oxenham. 6335-7
Credo ("The heaven for which I wait ..."). Siegfried Sassoon. 6532-5
A credo. William Makepeace Thackeray. 6230-X
A creed ("Here is the truth in a little creed"). Edwin Markham. 6335-7,6654-2,6465-5,6291-1,6335-6,6144-3, 6266-0,6337-3
Creed and deed. Robert Loveman. 6335-7,6337-3
A creed in a garden. Norman Flower. 6337-3
The creed of desire. Bruce Porter. 6241-5
The creed of love. Henry Bernard Carpenter. 7041-8
The creed of my heart. Edmond Gore Alexander Holmes. 6648-8
Creed of the farmer. Frank I. Mann. 6715-8
The creed of the wood. Katharine Lee Bates. 6501-5
Creed worth believing. Unknown. 6109-5
A creed. Norman Gale. 6102-8,6301-2
A creed. Edgar A. Guest. 6449-3
A creed. Norman MacLeod. 6730-1
A creed. John Masefield. 6730-1
The creed. Ella Wheeler Wilcox. 6956-8
Creeds. Karle Wilson Baker. 6250-4,6730-1
Creeds. Willard Wattles. 6337-3,6501-5
Creeds of the bells. George W. Bungay. 6014-5,6392-6,6404-3,6565-1
The creek of the four graves. Charles Harper. 6768-9
The creek. Bert Leach. 6906-1
Creekmore, Hubert
    Concert at sea. 6666-6
    Dividends. 6666-6
    Music in the REC hut. 6666-6
    Pocket guide for service men. 6666-6
Creekmore, Hubert (tr.)
    Dialogue of the body with the soul, leading it... Jacopone da Todi, 6325-X
    The effigy. Guido Cavalcanti, 6325-X
    Love's assize. Guido Cavalcanti, 6325-X
    Of love's power. Guido Cavalcanti, 6325-X
    Orfeo, sacrifice of the Bacchantes in honor of Bacchus. Angelo Poliziano, 6325-X
Creel, Luke
    The wedding. 6761-1
Creelman, Josephine Rice
    Easter day. 6177-X
    My mother. 6097-8
Creep afore ye gang. James Ballantyne. 6233-4,6131-1
Creeper. Percy MacKaye. 6799-9
"The creeping incense misted all the air". The vision of Rabbi Nathan. Frederick Langbridge. 6848-0
Creeping up the stairs. W.S. McFetridge. 6273-3
The creeping vine. Aristote Valaoritis. 6352-7
Cregan, Beatrice
    The voice of Rachel weeping. 7031-0
Creighton, Alan
    Evening rift. 6021-8
    Spring workman. 6021-8
Crellin, Charles C.
    Ode to the flag. 6449-3
Crellin, Lillian
    Cosmos. 6799-9
Creltholme. Joshua Freeman Crowell. 6798-0
Cremation. William Sawyer. 6089-7
The cremation of Sam McGee. Robert Service. 6159-1,6115-X
The Creole girl. Unknown. 6003-X
Cresap, James C.
    Cruises far and wide. 6717-4
Crescendo. Dorothy F Blackwell. 6178-8
The crescent and the cross. Thomas Bailey Aldrich. 6177-X
"The crescent moon was the boomerang". Retribution. Miriam S. Lewis. 6799-9
Crescentius. Letitia Elizabeth ("L.E.L.") Landon. 6219-9
Crescentius. Letitia Elizabeth ("L.E.L.") Landon. 6980-0
Cresseid's complaint against fortune. Robert Henryson. 6881-2
Cresseid's lament. Robert Henryson. 6150-8
Cressid. Nora Perry. 7041-8
Cressman, H.E.
    The coxswain's line. 6497-3
Cresson, Abigail
    The little gods. 6396-9
Crest in the kitchen. Albert Eisele. 6799-9
Cretan idyl. William Alexander Percy. 6039-0

A **Cretan** merchant. Simonides. 6435-3
The **cretan**. Dionysios Solomos. 6352-7
"The **cretonne** in your willow chair". Cretonne tropics. Grace Hazard Conkling. 6762-X
Cretonne tropics. Grace Hazard Conkling. 6033-1
"**Creusa**, in those idyll lands delaying". Idylls. Henry Tyrrell. 7041-8
The **crew** of the Long Serpent, fr. King Olaf. Henry Wadsworth Longfellow. 6105-2
A **crew** poem. Edward Augustus Blount Jr. 6501-5
The **crew** song. Clayton Fotterall McMichael. 6936-3
Crew, Helen Coale
  A grace before reading. 6030-7
  Hearthstone and highway. 6327-6
  Irish song. 6776-X
  Irish song. 6331-4
  Sing, ye trenches! 6029-3,6542-2
Crewbawn. Francis Ledwidge. 6812-X
Crewe, Robert O.A. Crewe-Milnes, Marquess of
  A grave in Flanders. 7031-0
  Harrow and Flanders. 6477-9
  A Harrow grave in Flanders. 6250-4
  Millet and Zola. 6046-3
  Seven years. 6437-X
Crews, Judson
  In fact. 6998-3
Crichton, David
  The circuiter's lament. 6878-2
  My widow. 6878-2
Cricket. Clinton Scollard. 6102-8,6076-5,6653-4
Cricket. Vincent Starrett. 6036-6
The **cricket** ball sings. Edward Verrall Lucas. 6423-X
The **cricket** bat sings. Unknown. 6105-2
The **cricket** in the path. Amelia Josephine Burr. 6338-1
Cricket on the hearth. Pierre Jean de Beranger. 6424-8
'The **cricket** on the hearth', sels. Charles Dickens. 6724-7
"The **cricket** pipes his song again", sels. Dora Read Goodale. 6601-1
"The **cricket** sang". Emily Dickinson. 6348-9
A **cricket** singing in the market-place. Louella C. Poole. 6476-0
"The **cricket** that chirps here every night". The chirping cricket. Jang-hi Lee. 6775-1
"**Cricket**, cricket/What can you know of...". Summer night. Dorothy E. Stroh. 6799-9
The **cricket**.. Frederick Goddard Tuckerman. 6333-0
The **cricket**. Vincent Bourne. 6814-6,6271-7
The **cricket**. Robert J. Burdette. 6588-0
The **cricket**. William Cowper. 6302-0,6385-3,6597-X,6373-X, 6018-8
The **cricket**. James Benjamin Kenyon. 6006-4,6309-8
The **cricket**. Sir Charles George Douglas Roberts. 6301-2
The **cricket**. Henry B. Watterson. 6691-7
The **cricketers** of Flanders. James Norman Hall. 7026-4
Crickets at dawn. Leonora Speyer. 6034-X
"The **crickets** sing, and man's o'er-labour'd...". Cymbeline, sel. William Shakespeare. 6958-4
The **crickets**, fr. Bread out of iron. Marjorie Allen Seiffert. 6531-7
The **crickets**.. Harriet McEwen Kimball. 6597-X,6600-3,6006-4,6632-1
The **crickets**. Helen Goldbaum. 6640-2
"**Cried** a cat to his wife, 'See, my dear'.". A dutiful parent. J.G. Francis. 6786-7
"**Cried** the navy-blue ghost". Four in the morning, fr. Facade. Edith Sitwell. 7000-0
'The **crier** by night,' sels. Gordon Bottomley. 6873-1
The **crier** in the night. Hermann Hagedorn. 6944-4
The **crier**. Michael Drayton. 6182-6,6473-6,6722-0,6562-7, 6092-7,6153 ,6430-2
The **cries** of Rome, fr. The rape of Lucrece. Thomas Heywood. 6334-9
Crime. William Shakespeare. 6438-8
Crime. Robert Penn Warren. 6389-6
"**Crime** may be clear'd & sorrow's eyes be dried". The grievings of a proud spirit. George Croly. 6980-0
The **crime** took place in Granada. Antonio Machado. 6068-4
The **criminality** of war. Edward Young. 6542-2
The **crimson** and the blue. Frederick Wadsworth Loring. 6370-5

Crimson changes people. Carl Sandburg. 6345-5
The **crimson** cherry tree. Henry Treece. 6641-0,6666-6,6360-8
"**Crimson** clover I discover", sels. Dora Read Goodale. 6601-1
The **crimson** cross. Elizabeth Brown Du Bridge. 6846-4
"The **crimson** light of sunset falls". Liz. Robert Buchanan. 6934-7
"The **crimson** moon, uprising from the sea". The harvest home. Edward Hovell-Thurlow; 2d Baron Thurlow. 7015-9
"The **crimson** moon". Sonnet ("The crimson moon"). Edward Hovell-Thurlow; 2d Baron Thurlow. 6271-7
"The **crimson** roses burn and glow". Vigil. Richard Dehmel. 7039-6
Crimson sails. Alfred Noyes. 6151-6
Crimson sunset. Byrdie L. Martin. 6799-9
"The **crimson** tide was ebbing..". Very dark. Unknown. 6909-6
The **crimson** tree. Elsie J. Cosler Campbell. 6799-9
Crinagoras
  "O caves of the nymphs fresh..." F.L. Lucas (tr.). 6251-2
"**Crinog**, melodious is your song". To Crinog. Unknown. 6930-4
Cripple Ben. George L. Catlin. 6413-2
Cripple Tim. Frank Hastings. 6689-5
Crippled for life. John F. Nicholls. 6920-7
Crippled Joe. Rose Hartwick Thorpe. 6683-6
Cripps, Arthur Shearly
  African witchcraft. 6625-9
  After three years. 6625-9
  All Saints' Day. 6800-6
  Ascription. 6625-9
  At Christmas. 6747-6
  Benediction. 6800-6
  The black Christ. 6788-3
  Charter-country. 6625-9
  Colour. 6800-6
  A dead chameleon. 6800-6
  Envoi. 6800-6
  Essex. 6477-9
  Exile in August. 6625-9
  A Franciscan prayer. 6625-9,6800-6
  God's own country. 6625-9
  Holy poverty. 6844-8
  Home with dawn. 6625-9
  In deserto. 6800-6
  Lazarus. 6788-3
  'Les belles roses sans mercie.' 6437-X
  Love pagan. 6800-6
  A lyke-wake carol. 6477-9
  A Mashona husbandman. 6800-6
  My neighbor's landmark. 6625-9
  A pagan's baptism. 6788-3
  A refrain. 6477-9,6639-9
  A refrain. 6800-6
  Resurgat. 6788-3
  A rhyme for Chaminuka. 6625-9
  The signaller. 6625-9
  Spring. 6625-9
  Summer rain-song. 6625-9
  Summer rain-songs. 6800-6
  To the veld. 6800-6
  To the veld. 6625-9
  The way in Africa. 6625-9
  The way in Africa. 6800-6
  Way-song. 6800-6
  Winter veld-fires. 6800-6
Cripps, Gladys M.
  To C.A.L. 7019-1
Cripps, H.
  Limerick:"When Tommy first saw Colonel Beak". 6811-1
Crises. Gene Frumkin. 6803-0
Crises. Joseph Morris. 6211-3
Crisis. George S. Fraser. 6379-9
The **crisis**. Muriel Rice. 6327-6
The **crisis**. John Greenleaf Whittier. 6946-0,6753-0
Criseian's day, fr. King Henry V. William Shakespeare. 6621-6

CRISPUS

Crispus Attucks. John Boyle O'Reilly. 6946-0
"Crispy/Fragrant petals". To Emily Dickinson. Joyce Lancaster. 6850-2
Criss, Allen Toland
    My papa is a preacher. 6715-8
Criss-cross. Unknown. 6701-8
Criss-cross pattern. Ethel Brodt Wilson. 6789-1,6039-0
Cristina. Robert Browning. 6200-8,6657-7,6110-9,6199-0, 6430-2,6655
Cristina, sels. Robert Browning. 6123-0
Cristo morto. Francis Brett Young. 6506-6
Crites, Lucile
    The mumpy mumps. 6692-5
The critic's rules. Robert Lloyd. 6932-0
The critic.. Unknown. 6064-1
A critic. William Foster Elliot. 6506-6
A critic. William Foster Elliot. 6817-0
A critic. Walter Savage Landor. 6125-7
A critic. Harry Romaine. 7021-3
The critic. Epes Sargent. 6787-5
A critical fable, sels. Amy Lowell. 6483-3
A critical fribble. Charles Churchill. 6932-0
The critical moment. Theron Brown. 6926-6
Criticism. Sir William Watson. 6102-8
Criticism of life, fr. Hippolytus. Euripides. 6987-8
Critics. Elizabeth Barrett Browning. 6996-7
Critics. Samuel Butler. 6278-4
Critics. Jonathan Swift. 6150-8
Critics and connoisseurs. Marianne Moore. 6354-3
"Critics avaunt! Tobacco is my theme". In imitation of Young, fr. A pipe of tobacco. Isaac Hawkins Browne. 6932-0
"Critics have damned our calling, since...". The sestina of the minor poet. Norman Davey. 6875-8
The critics. Arthur Guiterman. 6773-5
"Croak -- croak -- croak!". The pessimist, or the rave of the jackdaw. Thomas Edward Brown. 6809-X
"'Croak!' said the toad, 'I'm hungry I think'". Unknown. 6904-5
' Croak,' said the toad. Unknown. 6466-3
Croaker papers, sels. Fitz-Greene Hallock and Joseph Rodman Drake. 6753-0
The croaker. Joseph Crosby Lincoln. 6119-2
Croasdale, William T.
    "I never knowed". 6274-1
Crobaugh, Emma
    He counts winter stars. 6857-X
Crocker, Harriet Francene
    My old rag doll. 6691-7
    The white ribbon. 6685-2
Crocker, Henry
    Chick-a-rooster. 7030-2
    The old, old songs. 7030-2
Crocker, Jean-Marie J.
    To a beloved alcoholic. 6857-X
Crocknaharna. Francis Ledwidge. 6331-4
The crocodile.. Charles Lutwidge ("Lewis Carroll") Dodgson. 6440-X
A crocodile. Thomas Lovell Beddoes. 6378-0
Crocus. Sarah J. Day. 6891-X
Crocus. Celia Thaxter. 6612-7
Crocus bells. Alice E. Allen. 6048-X
Crocus bud on a lover's grave. Timothy Corsellis. 6475-2
The crocus flame. Clinton Scollard. 6338-1
"Crocus had slept in his little round house". Crocus. Sarah J. Day. 6891-X
"The crocus rose from her snowy bed". Sugar-making. Phoebe Cary. 6969-X
The crocus's soliloquy. Hannah Flagg Gould. 6373-X
The crocus.. Walter Crane. 6466-3
The crocus.. Harriet Eleanor Hamiliton (Baille) King. 6597-X,6656-9
The crocus. Mary Elliott. 6135-4
The crocus. Herbert Trench. 6877-4
Crocuses. Unknown (Japanese) 6891-X
Crocuses at Nottingham. Unknown. 7031-0
"Crocuses in bloom!". Mid-March. Josie Eppert. 6906-1
Croesus. Bacchylides. 6435-3
Croffut, W.F.
    Give thanks for what? 6618-6,6171-0,6744-1
    Give thanks for what? 6917-7
Croffut, William Augustus
    Clam-soup. 6271-7
    A dirge concerning the late lamented king of..cannibal. 6089-7
Croft-Cooke, Rupert
    Kitchen garden. 6649-6
The crofter's farewell. Robert Bird. 7009-4
Crofts, George W.
    Easter lilies. 6225-3
    I love you, dear. 6620-8,6066-8
Croker, T. Crofton (tr.)
    Saint Brendan's prophecy. Unknown, 6930-4
Croll, P.C.
    Abraham Lincoln. 6524-4
Croly, George
    The Alhambra. 6980-0
    The angel of the world. 6980-0
    Astrology. 6980-0
    An aurora borealis. 6980-0
    Belshazzar. 6404-3,6585-6
    Bitter disappointment. 6294-6
    Cataline's defiance. 6569-4
    Catiline on hearing of his sentence of banishment. 6424-8
    Catiline to his friends, after failing... 6606-2
    Catiline to the Gallic conspirators. 6606-2
    Catiline's defiance. 6909-6
    Catiline's defiance. 6392-6,6294-6,6606-2,6521-X,6610-0, 6706
    Catiline's last harangue to his army. 6045-1,6606-2, 6294-6
    Catiline, sels. 6980-0
    The crucifixion. 6606-2
    Cupid grown careful. 6600-3
    Cupid's carrying provisions. 6219-9
    Death and resurrection. 6730-1
    The death of Leonidas. 6302-0,6385-3,6344-6,6606-2
    Dirge. 6271-7,6214-8
    A dirge. 6980-0,6407-8
    Domestic love. 6543-0
    Effect of oratory upon a multitude. 6980-0
    The emperor and the rabbi. 6848-0
    Evening. 6304-7
    The genius of death. 6302-0;6385-3
    The Greek and Turkman. 6606-2
    The grievings of a proud spirit. 6980-0
    Jacob. 6848-0
    Jacob's dream. 6980-0
    Jewels. 6980-0
    The last day of Jerusalem. 6848-0
    Leonidas. 6980-0
    Leonidas. 6271-7,6263-6
    Love an evil. 6980-0
    A lover's oath. 6980-0
    A meeting of magicians. 6980-0
    Mountaineers. 6980-0
    "My lack of noble blood! Then that's the bar" 6606-2
    On an antique gem bearing the heads of Pericles and Aspasia . 6086-2
    A Parisian Fauxbourg. 6980-0
    Pericles. 6046-3
    Pericles and Aspasia. 6271-7,6219-9,6219-9,6271-7,6302-9
    Rebellion. 6980-0
    The seventh plague of Egypt. 6404-3,6606-2
    Spirit of God, descend upon my heart. 6337-3
    The stars. 6980-0
Crombie, Eugene
    The dream path. 6650-X
    The gate. 6650-X
Crombie, Stephen
    Catbird. 6073-0
    A damascus nightingale. 6073-0
    Indigo bird. 6073-0
Cromek. William Blake. 6545-7
Cromer, Earl of (tr.)
    Anacreon's tomb. Unknown (Greek), 6435-3
    "Pour a libation, stranger, as you pass". Unknown, 6435-3

Crompton, Robert
    Signals of distress!. 6617-8
Cromwell. Albert Durrant Watson. 6115-X
Cromwell and Henrietta Maria, fr. Charles the First.
    William Gorman Wills. 6656-9
Cromwell and King Charles. Andrew Marvell. 6438-8
Cromwell at the corpse of Charles I. Jan Svatopluk Machar.
    6886-3
Cromwell dead, fr. A poem upon the death of O.C. Andrew
    Marvell. 6125-7
Cromwell in death. Andrew Marvell. 6250-4
Cromwell our chief of men. John Milton. 6543-0
Cromwell's reflections on Killing no murder. Edward Bulwer-
    Lytton; Baron Lytton. 6980-0
Cromwell's soliloquy over the dead body of Charles. Edward
    Bulwer-Lytton; Baron Lytton. 6980-0
Cromwell, Gladys
    Autumn communion. 6032-3
    The crowning gift. 6102-8,6076-5
    The crowning gift. 6979-7
    The deep, sels. 6501-5
    Folded power. 6032-3
    The mould. 6032-3,6556-2,6076-5,6393-4
    Star song. 6032-3,6607-0
    Winter poetry. 6033-1
    Words. 6033-1
Cromwell, Henry
    No, no! I ne'er shall love thee less. 6563-5
"**Cromwell,** I did not think to shed a tear". Thomas Wolsey,
    Cardinal Wolsey. 6289-X
"The **cronach** stills the dowie heart". The queen lilt.
    Robert Jamieson. 6960-6
Cronise, Mabel
    The legend of the fleur-de-lis. 6925-8
Cronwright-Schreiner, Samuel Cron
    A song of the wagon-whip. 6800-6
Cronyn, ? (tr.)
    Prayer to the mountain spirit. Unknown (Navajo Indians).
    6730-1
Cronyn, George
    Palinrus. 6076-5,6102-8
    Palinurus. 6076-5,6102-8
    The tree's way. 6510-4
Croodlin' doo. Eugene Field. 6949-5
The **crook** and plaid. Isobel Pagan. 6086-2
Crook, Kile
    Siege. 6750-6
Crooke, Sheila Jane
    The Statue of Liberty. 6736-0
"**Crooked** and dwarfed the tree must stay". Compensation.
    Phoebe Cary. 6969-X
Crooked corner. Percy Hasleden. 6804-9
The **crooked** footpath. Oliver Wendell Holmes. 6260-1
"**Crooked,** crawling tide with long wet fingers". Tide of
    storms. John Gould Fletcher. 6984-3
A **croon.** Unknown. 6134-6
The **croppy** boy. William B. McBurney. 6174-5
The **croppy** boy. Carroll Malone. 6858-8
The **croppy** boy. Unknown. 6179-6,6244-X
Crops. Charles Malam. 6761-1
Croquet. Unknown. 6675-5
Croquet in Vermont. Daniel L. Cady. 6989-4
Cros, Charles
    The smoked herring. A.L. Lloyd (tr.). 6343-8
Cros, Guy-Charles
    At the Luxembourg. 6351-9
    Now I have learned. 6351-9
Crosby, Elizabeth Mae
    New England. 6894-4
Crosby, Ernest
    'Rebels'. 6946-0
Crosby, Ernest Howard
    Christianity and war. 6542-2
    The collection. 6954-1
    God's gift. 6006-4
    In childhood's kingdom. 6274-1
    Life and death. 6291-1,6337-3
    Love comes. 6542-2
    The search. 6007-2,6102-8,6076-5,6461-2
    Town pictures, sels. 6501-5

    War and hell. 6542-2
Crosby, Fanny
    Blind. 6337-3
    Blind but happy. 6337-3
    The name of mother. 6097-8
    The state we honor. 6465-5
    Suppose. 6638-0
    Thy will be done in me. 6337-3
Crosby, Frank
    The professor. 6207-5
Crosby, Fred
    The lily and the linden. 6273-3
Crosby, Nora E.
    Farmer Nick's scarecrow. 6314-4
Crosland, Margaret
    Empty shells. 6475-2
Crosland, Thomas William Hodgson
    Sons. 7029-9
    Sunset. 6542-2
    Sunset. 7029-9
Cross. Langston Hughes. 6619-4,6491-4
Cross and flag. Frederick L. Hosmer. 6223-7
The **cross** and the crown. Thomas Kelly. 6337-3
The **cross** and the flag. William Henry, Cardinal O'Connell.
    6846-4
The **cross** and the tree. William L. Stidger. 6144-3
Cross and throne. Horatius Bonar. 6065-X
The **cross** at the crossways. John Oxenham. 6337-3
Cross Betsy. Sarah M. Chatfield. 6314-4
"A **cross** between blackbird and crow". Purple grackles.
    Francis Frost. 6073-0
The **cross** by the way. Unknown. 6873-1
A **cross** in Flanders. George Rostrevor Hamilton. 7031-0,
    7026-4
The **cross** in the breakers. James Abraham Martling. 6952-5
The **cross** in the wilderness. Felicia Dorothea Hemans. 6973-
    8
Cross makers. Clyde McGee. 6337-3
Cross of gold. David Gray. 7041-8
The **cross** of snow. Henry Wadsworth Longfellow. 6333-0,6337-
    3,6300-4,6288-1,6126-5,6641
The **cross** of the south. Felicia Dorothea Hemans. 6973-8
The **cross** of wood. Cyril Winterbotham. 6650-X
A **cross** on a hill. Carl S. Weist. 6065-X
Cross patch. Horace Holley. 6030-7
Cross purposes. S.A. (Sarah Annie Shield) Frost. 6851-0
Cross rhythms. Renee Roper. 6899-5
<u>The **cross** speaks. Unknown. 6489-2</u>
The **cross** triumphant. Harry Howe Bogert. 6799-9
The **cross** was his own. Unknown. 6065-X,6335-7,6337-3
Cross, Allen Eastman
    Breasting the storm. 6764-6
    The dead singer. 6848-0
    The hidden years. 6144-3
    More light shall break from out thy word. 6337-3
    Our New Hampshire. 6764-6
    A psalm of New Hampshire. 6894-4
    What doth the Lord require of thee. 6337-3
Cross, Jane T.H.
    The confederacy. 6074-9
    Over the river. 6074-9
Cross, John
    Beauty. 6037-4
Cross, Joseph C.
    A year in paradise. 6919-3
Cross, Kathryn
    Age and youth. 6799-9
    To the master. 6799-9
Cross, Zora
    When I was six. 6784-0
    Woman. 6784-0
The **cross-current.** Abbie Farwell Brown. 6032-3
Cross-currents. Winifred Virginia Jackson. 6762-X
The **cross-eyed** lovers. John H. Johnston. 6413-2
Cross-patch. Unknown. 6125-7
"**Cross-patch/Draw** the latch." Unknown. 6363-2,6452-3
The **cross.** Charles S. Braden. 6144-3
The **cross.** Donald Earl Edwards. 6144-3
The **cross.** Edward Farquhar. 6939-8
The **cross.** Leon Gllert. 6784-0

CROSS

The cross. Eva Gore-Booth. 6144-3,6337-3
The cross. Sidney Lanier. 6065-X
The cross. Charles Nelson Pace. 6065-X;6335-7
The cross. Allen Tate. 7017-5
The cross. Ruby Weyburn Tobias. 6144-3
The cross. Shirley Dillon Waite. 6144-3
The cross. Isaac Watts. 6641-0
"A cross? That?". The cross. Charles S. Braden. 6144-3
"Crosse of Jesu Christ be ever oure spede". An A.B.C. of devotion. Unknown. 6881-2
Crossed heart. Hazel Hall. 6038-2
Crosses. Mabel Hicks. 6449-3
Crosses. Edward Williams. 6335-7
"The crosses on the convent roofs". Botanist on Alp (No. 2). Wallace Stevens. 6751-4
Crossing. John Pudney. 6985-1
Crossing alone the nighted ferry. Alfred Edward Housman. 6472-8
The crossing at Fredericksburg. George Henry Boker. 6946-0
Crossing Boston Common. Louise Dyer Harris. 6722-0
Crossing Brooklyn ferry. Walt Whitman. 6333-0,6646-1,6121-4,6288-1,6126-5
Crossing Portsmouth bridge. Alan Chong Lau. 6790-5
Crossing the bar. Alfred Lord Tennyson. 6052-8,6122-2,6258-X,6260-1,6289-X,6303 ,6101-X,6332-2,6479-5,6499-X, 6657-7,6726 ,6123-0,6473-6,6456-8,6536-8,6481-7,6198 ,6154-0,6208-3,6605-4,6337-3,6418-3,6437 ,6604-6, 6650-0,6730-1,6707-7,6732-8,6737 ,6464-7,6585-6,6660-7,6723-9,6646-1,6656 ,6576-7,6645-3,6371-3,6396-9, 6252-0,6301 ,6424-8,6197-4,6167-2,6304-7,6104-4,6214 ,6177-X,6212-1,6199-0,6250-4,6461-2,6560 ,6192-3, 6196-6,6102-8,6110-9,6430-2,6820
Crossing the blackwater. Robert Dwyer Joyce. 6656-9
Crossing the border into Canada. Joy Harjo. 7005-1
Crossing the carry. W.H.H. Murray. 6744-1
Crossing the desert. Myles A.J. Rhynes. 6799-9
Crossing the ford. O.W. H. 6752-2
Crossing the plains. Joaquin Miller. 6102-8,6239-3,6510-4, 6300-4,6153-2,6076
Crossing the Rubicon. Unknown. 6878-2
"Crossing the street in the rain" James M. Cory. 7003-5
Crossing with the light. Dwight Okita. 6790-5
Crossman, Samuel
  "I said sometimes with tears". 6931-2
Crossroads of the ages. Estella Moul Miller. 6799-9
The crossroads of the south. Rosellen Brown. 6803-0
Crot, Robert J.
  The dead. 6337-3
Crotalus. Francis Bret Harte. 6467-1
The crotalus. Bailey Millard. 6102-8,6076-5
Crotchet castle, sels. Thomas Love Peacock. 6026-9,6518-X
Crouch, Pearl Riggs
  The snowstorm. 6836-7
  A story in the snow. 6891-X
  Thirst. 6836-7
  The threshing. 6836-7
Crouch, Richard A.
  The amazons. 7031-0
"Crouched on the crowded deck,we watch the sun". Leave, fr. In war time. Wilfred Wilson Gibson. 6884-7
"Crouched on the pavement, close by Belgrave". West London. Matthew Arnold. 6196-6,6199-0,6430-2,6828-6
"Crouching low, but not with fear". The thief on the cross. George M. Vickers. 6918-5
Crouse, M. Elizabeth
  Light. 6274-1
  The strength of weakness. 6274-1
  Widowhood. 6274-1
Crouse, Miriam LeFevre
  Dawn. 6144-3
  Lent. 6144-3
  Upon a hill. 6144-3
Crow. Mark Van Doren. 6778-6
Crow and pie. Unknown. 6185-0
The crow's children. Phoebe Cary. 6060-9,6714-X,6127-3, 6131-1
Crow's-foot. H.M. Leys. 6804-9
Crow, Florence
  Let me remember. 6042-0
Crow, Martha Foote
  Peace. 6164-8
  The wooden Christ. 6144-3,6542-2
Crow, Mary (tr.)
  The astronaut. Cecilia Bustamante, 7036-1
  Awake. Cecilia Bustamante, 7036-1
  Heels over head with life. Maria Mercedes Carranza, 7036-1
  Once upon a time a woman tied to a virtue. Maria Mercedes Carranza, 7036-1
  Under the sun. Cecilia Bustamante, 7036-1
The crow. John Burroughs. 6073-0
The crow. William Canton. 6102-8
The crow. Ibn Sa'id (of Alcala La Real) 6362-4
"The crowd is here, night after night". knife-thrower/The. Violet McDougal. 7038-8
The crowd. Irene McKeighan. 6144-3;6335-7;6337-3
"The crowded street, ablaze with winking eyes". Farm boy. Mary Sloane. 6761-1
The crowded street. William Cullen Bryant. 6271-7,6302-0, 6457-4,6735-2,6219-9,6304
A crowded trolley car. Elinor Wylie. 6808-1
"Crowded/People pressed together". Fallout. P.J. (Polly) Holt. 6883-9
Crowdieknowe. Christopher M. ("Hugh MacDiarmid") Grieve. 6269-5
"The crowds must be an awful strain". With sympathy. Alice Levy. 6850-2
Crowell, Florence Hathaway
  Beach plum blossom time. 6798-0
Crowell, Grace Noll
  Assurance. 6465-5
  The beautiful gift. 6449-3
  Definition. 6365-9
  The fire tenders. 6449-3
  I do not like a roof tonight. 6608-9
  I grieve for beauty wasted. 6326-8
  Let us keep Christmas. 6337-3
  The little house. 7038-8
  Love. 6750-6
  The mothers of the earth. 6449-3
  The mountain. 6039-0
  Music-mad. 6326-8
  New houses. 6449-3
  Out of a lifetime. 6461-2
  Recompense. 6512-0
  Red earth. 6265-2
  A shelf of old books. 6761-1
  Silver poplars. 6778-6
  Silver poplars. 6326-8
  So long as there are homes. 6337-3
  Some gay, adventurous thing. 6143-5
  Songs. 6326-8
  Traveler. 6042-0
  Wild geese ("I hold to my heart..."). 6073-0
  Willow whistles. 6326-8
  Young nun. 6285-7
Crowell, Joshua Freeman
  Along the way. 6798-0
  Attune. 6798-0
  Autumn glow. 6798-0
  Beach plum. 6798-0
  Cape Cod, sels. 6798-0
  Charmed voices. 6798-0
  Creltholme. 6798-0
  The dreamy dog. 6130-3
  For June. 6798-0
  Freedom's voice. 6798-0
  "From ridge to ridge". 6130-3
  I know a wood. 6798-0
  An illumination. 6130-3
  "A lady bug". 6130-3
  Mattakese. 6798-0
  Music. 6798-0
  Old captains. 6798-0
  Rebirth. 6798-0
  Scallop boats. 6798-0
  Scallop shells. 6798-0
  Scherzo. 6798-0
  The spider web. 6130-3
  The stars by night, the clouds by day. 6798-0

"The sun was up". 6130-3
To my friend the bluebird. 6130-3
Twilight song. 6798-0
Crowell, M.H.
　The Cape. 6798-0
Crowell, Norman H.
　My candidate. 6736-0
　Woodrow Wilson dead. 7001-9
Crowell, Winthrop M.
　'If' 6798-0
The crowing of the red cock. Emma Lazarus. 7041-8
The crowing of the red cock. Emma Lazarus. 6006-4,6431-0
"Crowmell, our cheif of men,who through acloud". To the Lord General Cromwell, May 1652. John Milton. 6933-9
"Crown and sceptre, how they glint". Hall of primates. Robert Clairmont. 6751-4
Crown him with many crowns. Matthew Bridges. 6337-3
Crown his bloodstained pillow. Julia Ward Howe. 6305-5, 6524-4
"The crown o' the earth...", fr. Antony and Cleopatra. William Shakespeare. 6339-X
"Crown of her, young Vancouver; crest of her..". Canada. Emily Pauline ("Tekahionwake") Johnson. 6837-5
A crown of sorrow. Adelaide Anne Procter. 6957-6
"A crown of victory! a triumphal song!". Tasso's coronation. Felicia Dorothea Hemans. 6973-8
The crown of womanhood. Frances Viola Holden. 6097-8
Crown our Washington. Hezekiah Butterworth. 6465-5,6449-3, 6820-0
"Crown us who make within". Crowning. Laura Benet. 6979-7
"Crown winter with green". Robert Bridges. 6487-6
Crown with evergreens fair. Unknown. 6708-5
The crown. Helen Combes. 6846-4
The crown. Amory Hare. 6979-7
Crowne, John
　Song ("Kind lovers"). 6-26-9,6563-5
　To many deaths decreed. 6563-5
Crowned. Mary Frances Hill. 6799-9
Crowned. Amy Lowell. 6250-4
Crowned. John Nichol. 7015-9
Crowned and discrowned. W. Bright. 6046-3
Crowned and wedded. Elizabeth Barrett Browning. 6188-5
"A crowned caprice is god of this world". A prayer ("A crowned caprice"). Grant Allen. 6301-2,6071-4
"Crowned with garlands immortal". Sunset. James Abraham Martling. 6952-5
"Crowned with silver braids—her evening...". Two generations. Zenobia Crutcher Feineman. 6799-9
"Crowned with the culture of centuries". The maker's image. Albert Charlton Andrews. 6889-8
Crowning. Laura Benet. 6979-7
"Crowning a flowery slope, it stood alone". Old church in an English park. Felicia Dorothea Hemans. 6973-8
The crowning gift. Gladys Cromwell. 6102-8,6076-5
The crowning gift. Gladys Cromwell. 6979-7
"Crowning life so over-wise". Holy poverty. Arthur Shearly Cripps. 6844-8
The crowning of Arthur. Alfred Lord Tennyson. 6438-8,6424-8
The crowning of Arthur. Charles Williams. 6209-1
The crowning of dreaming Jim. John Drinkwater. 6228-8
The crowning of the king. Robert Southey. 6927-4
Crowning of Washington. Stanley Schell. 6712-3
Crowninshield, Frederic
　August on the Roman Campagna. 6624-0
Crowns. Louise Upham Brooks. 6144-3
Crowns. William Henry Davies. 6072-2
Crowns for children. Unknown. 6424-8
Crows. Unknown. 6943-6
"Crows crowd croaking overhead". Summer evening. John Clare. 6793-X
Crows flying. Julia Ross Alden. 6906-1
Crows on the river. Theodore Goodridge Roberts. 6797-2
The crows. Louise Bogan. 6619-4,6036-6
The crows. Milutin Bojic. 6765-4
Crozier, Lorna
　Angels of snow. 6767-0
　Gorky's childhood. 6767-0
Cruciferi. Euphemia Macleod. 6818-9
Crucified to the world. Unknown. 6881-2

"Crucified, crucified every morn". Easter hymn. Ernest Jones. 7009-4
Crucifix. Edith Lovejoy Pierce. 6144-3
A crucifix in the Etsch Thal. John Addington Symonds. 7015-9
Crucifixion. Eva Gore Booth. 6730-1
Crucifixion. Eva Gore-Booth. 6337-3
Crucifixion. Unknown (Negro spiritual) 6337-3
Crucifixion. Carter Webster. 6178-8
Crucifixion ("'Lord, must I bear the whole of it...'") Frederick George Scott. 6144-3,6337-3,6335-7
Crucifixion ("Golgotha's journey is an ancient way") Hugh O. Isbell. 6144-3,6420-5
Crucifixion ("Had I been there that cruel day") Carl S. Weist. 6144-3
Crucifixion ("He sang, too") Earl B. Marlatt. 6144-3
The crucifixion ("Oh, man's capacity"). Alice Meynell. 6335-7;6489-2
Crucifixion pro nobis. Patrick Carey. 6563-5
Crucifixion to the world by the cross of Christ. Isaac Watts. 6932-0
The crucifixion. Thomas Holley Chivers. 7017-5
The crucifixion. George Croly. 6606-2
The crucifixion. Henry Hart Milman. 6065-X
The crucifixion. Unknown. 6881-2
The crucifixion. Unknown. 6930-4
Cruciform. Winifred Welles. 6317-9
Crucifying. John Donne. 6933-9
Cruel beauty. Abraham Cowley. 6935-5
The cruel boy. Elizabeth Turner. 6105-2
The cruel brother. Unknown. 6518-4,6055-2,6185-0,6193-1, 6003-X,6067-6,6319
"Cruel Cerinthus! does the fell disease". George Gordon, 6th Baron Byron. 6945-2
Cruel clever cat. Geoffrey Taylor. 6125-7
Cruel masters. Ibn Zaidun. 6362-4
The cruel mistress. William Hammond. 6563-5
"The cruel mother of the loves". To Glycera. Horace. 6949-5
The cruel mother. Unknown. 6057-9,6058-7,6061-7,6185-0, 6067-6
The cruel ship carpenter. Unknown. 6826-X
The cruel sister. Unknown. 6271-7,6613-5,6219-9
"Cruel with all its ancient cruelty". False spring. Louise Owen. 6764-6
Cruel you be. George Puttenham. 6182-6
"Cruell Clarinda tell me why." Unknown. 6563-5
Cruelty. Margaret E. Bruner. 6120-6
Cruelty and love. David Herbert Lawrence. 6234-2
Cruickshank, Helen B.
　The gipsy lass. 6269-5
　Lizzie. 6269-5
　Shy Geordie. 6269-5
Cruickshank, N.K.
　All through that year. 6475-2
　Caption for one's own photograph. 6475-2
A cruiscin lan. Unknown. 6858-8
The cruise of the 'P.C.' Unknown. 6902-9
The cruise of the Fair American. Arthur Hale. 6946-0
The cruise of the Monitor. George M. Baker. 6678-X
The cruise of the Monitor. George Henry Boker. 6946-0
Cruisers. Rudyard Kipling. 6810-3
Cruises far and wide. James C. Cresap. 6717-4
Cruising. Scott Tucker. 7003-5
Cruising the bar. Shelley Jones. 7003-5
The cruiskeen lawn. Unknown. 6174-5
The cruiskeen lawn. Unknown. 6930-4
"Crumbling a dark leaf between darker fingers". Midewiwan. Phyllis Wolf. 7005-1
Crumbs to the birds. Charles and Mary Lamb. 6018-8
Crumpets and tea. Eugene Field. 6949-5
The crumps of crumbletown. Carolyn Wells. 6882-0
"Crunch the dead leaves under thy feet". Unknown. 6238-5
The crunch. Charles Bukowski. 6998-3
The crusade, sels. Thomas Warton Jr. 6198-2
The crusade. Leitner. 7004-3
Crusader chorus, sels. Charles Kingsley. 6334-9
Crusader's hymn. Unknown (German) 6337-3
The Crusader's return. Felicia Dorothea Hemans. 6973-8
The crusader's tomb. Laurence Housman. 7029-9

CRUSADER'S

The **Crusader's** war-song. Felicia Dorothea Hemans. 6973-8
The **crusader**. Thomas Curtis Clark. 7001-9
Crusaders. Elizabeth Waddell. 6954-1,6144-3
Crusaders of the air. Kathryn Munro. 6224-5
The **crusaders'** march. William Edmonstoune Aytoun. 6948-7
"**Crush'd** by misfortune's yoke". Fragment of an oratorio. Thomas Campbell. 6848-0
"**Crushed** and thronged are all the places". A legend of Madrid. Unknown (Spanish). 6951-7
Crushed fender. Rosa Zagnoni Marinoni. 6337-3
A **crushed** hero. Joseph Crosby Lincoln. 6119-2
A **crushed** tragedian. Edward L. McDowell. 6247-4;6697-6
The **crust** of bread. Unknown. 6135-4
Crustaceans. Roy Fuller. 6379-9
"The **crusted** tree of stars soars quite". Midnight Eden. Josephine Jacobsen. 6979-7
Crusts. Walter Shea. 6144-3
Crusty critics, fr. The library. George Crabbe. 6932-0
The **crutches'** tune. Elizabeth R. Stoner. 6846-4
Cruthirds, Elsie Day
  A boy's likes and dislikes. 6799-9
The **cruxifixion**. Unknown. 6244-X
"**Cry** bravely, O town-crier". The young witch - 1698. George Sterling. 6777-8
Cry for brotherhood. Lucia Trent. 6461-2
A **cry** for conquest. Angela Morgan. 6274-1
A **cry** from an Indian wife. Emily Pauline ("Tekahionwake") Johnson. 6837-5
Cry from the battlefield. Robert Menth. 6282-2
A **cry** from the ghetto. Morris Rosenfeld. 7011-6,6102-8
A **cry** from the shore. Ellen Mackay Hutchinson Cortissoz. 6271-7
A **cry** in the night. John E. Barrett. 6840-5
The **cry** in the night. Alfred Noyes. 6151-6
Cry of a lonely heart. E. Pearl Dancey. 6750-6
The **cry** of Rachel. Lizette Woodworth Reese. 6848-0
The **cry** of the age. Hamlin Garland. 6730-1
The **cry** of the children. Elizabeth Barrett Browning. 6383-7,6560-0,6655-0,6102-8,6219-9,6134-6,6233-4,6337-3, 6481 ,6188-5,6198-2,6473-6,6657-7,6732-8,6656
The **cry** of the children. Neil Bell. 6804-9
Cry of the dead. Louis Ginsberg. 6420-5
The **cry** of the dreamer. John Boyle O'Reilly. 6260-1,6374-8, 6583-X,6576-7
The **cry** of the dreamer. John Boyle O'Reilly. 7012-4
The **cry** of the gulls. Le Baron Cooke. 6039-0
The **cry** of the heart and flesh. Phoebe Cary. 6865-0;6969-X
A **cry** of the heart. Phoebe Cary. 6865-0;6969-X
The **cry** of the hillborn. Bliss Carman. 6374-8
The **cry** of the human, sels. Elizabeth Barrett Browning. 6337-3
Cry of the people. John G. Neihardt. 6464-7
The **cry** of the uncreated. Arthur Henry Goodenough. 7030-2
A **cry** on the wind. William ("Fiona Macleod") Sharp. 6872-3
Cry out of Babylon. Clifford J. Laube. 6761-1
"**Cry** out with joy and walk among the brave". Uplifted spirit. Patricia A. Lawrence. 6857-X
"The **cry** rung from your spirit's pain." Adelaide Anne Procter. 6225-3
A **cry** to arms. Henry Timrod. 6946-0
A **cry** to arms. Henry Timrod. 6015-3,6113-3,6121-4
A **cry** to battle. Jonathan Mitchell Sewall. 6753-0
A **cry** to Mary. Saint Godric. 6881-2
A **cry** unto the Lord to stay His hand, sels. Edward Johnson. 6077-3
"**Cry**, baby, cry/Stick your finger in your eye". Unknown. 7028-0
A **cry**. Herbert Edwin Clarke. 6656-9
A **cry**. Louise Chandler Moulton. 7041-8
Crying Cupid. Josephine Sievers Birt. 6906-1
"**Crying** for her own sex". Strangers, fr. Songs for the virgin. Anne Donovan. 7018-3
Crying in the night. Annabella Milne. 6269-5
Crying, 'Thalassus!' Joseph Auslander. 6036-6
Cryptic girl. Emily Porter St. John. 6316-X
The **crystal** cabinet. William Blake. 6086-2,6380-2
The **crystal** Christ, fr. The crystal. Sidney Lanier. 6337-3
"A **crystal** clear is love, on which the light". The crystal. H.S. Gulliver. 6841-3
The **crystal** gazer. Sara Teasdale. 6036-6,60102

The **crystal** hunters. Thomas Moore. 6749-2
Crystal moment. Robert P. Tristram Coffin. 6782-4
Crystal moment. Robert P. Tristram Coffin. 6217-2,6250-4, 6464-7
The **crystal** palace. William Makepeace Thackeray. 6089-7, 6278-4
A **crystal** principle. Marguerite Young. 6391-8
The **crystal** skull. Kathleen Raine. 6209-1,6379-9
"The **crystal** spears of slantwise-drive rain". An April romance. Arthur Guiterman. 6773-5
Crystal water. Edith Wyatt. 6252-0
The **crystal**, sels. Sidney Lanier. 6144-3;6335-7;6065-X
The **crystal**. H.S. Gulliver. 6841-3
The **crystal**. Sidney Lanier. 7041-8
The **crystal**. Sidney Lanier. 6483-3
"**Crystallite** jewels harbor the moon". Sphinx. Michelle Schutts. 6883-9
Crystals and flame. Mary Cummings Eudy. 6850-2
"**Ctherine** looked, and the night rode by". Catherine. Charles Plumb. 7020-5
Cuba. James Gardner. 6471-X
Cuba. James Barron Hope. 6471-X
Cuba. Harvey Rice. 6946-0
Cuba. Edmund Clarence Stedman. 6946-0
Cuba libra. Unknown. 6118-4,6741-X
Cuba libre. Joaquin Miller. 6579-1
Cuba to Columbia. Will Carleton. 6946-0
Cuba's appeal. Carrie Shaw Rice. 6741-X
Cuba's maiden martyr. Eugenie B. Harding. 6686-0
Cuba, 1897. Herbert Bashford. 6471-X
The **Cuban** refugee. Unknown. 6689-5
A **cubic** triolet. Unknown. 6724-7
Cubism. Alfred Noyes. 6151-6
Cuchillin in his chariot. Unknown. 6873-1
Cuchulainn's lament for Ferdiad. George Sigerson. 6582-1
Cuckoo. So-wol Kim. 6775-1
Cuckoo. Katharine (Hinkson) Tynan. 6073-0,6639-9
Cuckoo. Andrew Young. 6125-7
The **cuckoo** and the nightingale. Geoffrey Chaucer. 6271-7, 6438-8
The **cuckoo** at Laverna, sels. William Wordsworth. 6867-7
"The **cuckoo** bird has long been dumb". Counting the stars. John Galsworthy. 6888-X
The **cuckoo** clock, sels. William Wordsworth. 6867-7
The **cuckoo** clock. Joseph Crosby Lincoln. 6119-2
The **cuckoo** clock. Caroline Anne Bowles Southey. 6385-3
Cuckoo lore. Unknown. 6943-6
Cuckoo poem. Ann ("Aunt Effie") Hawkshawe. 6018-8
Cuckoo song. John of Forsete. 6527-9
Cuckoo song. John of Fornsete. 6150-8
Cuckoo song. Katharine (Hinkson) Tynan. 6930-4
Cuckoo song. Unknown. 6943-6
Cuckoo song. Unknown. 6850-2
Cuckoo song. Unknown. 6052-8,6102-8,6186-9,6488-4,6732-8, 6153 ,6125-7,6193-1,6250-4
Cuckoo song. Unknown. 6850-2
Cuckoo song ("Summer is i-comen in"). Unknown. 6073-0
Cuckoo song: Dartmoor. John Galsworthy. 6888-X
The **cuckoo** wood, fr. The casket songs. Edmund Beale Sargant. 6234-2
"**Cuckoo!/Again** cuckoo!" Chiyo. 6850-2
"The **cuckoo's** a fine bird". Unknown. 6904-5
The **cuckoo's** character. Unknown. 6105-2
"The **cuckoo's** echo dies away". Fujiwara Sanseada (Go Tokudai-ji Sadajin) 6852-9
The **cuckoo's** habits. Unknown. 6105-2
The **cuckoo's** parting cry, fr. Thyrsis. Matthew Arnold. 6153-2
The **cuckoo's** song. Josui. 6891-X
The **cuckoo's** voice. John Heywood. 6105-2
The **cuckoo's** wit. Robert Stephen Hawker. 6105-2
"**Cuckoo**, cherry-tree". Unknown. 6904-5
"**Cuckoo**, cuckoo!/In April skies were blue". Cuckoo song. Katharine (Hinkson) Tynan. 6930-4
"**Cuckoo**, cuckoo". Unknown. 6904-5
"**Cuckoo**, cuckoo,/My sister who used to live". Cuckoo. So-wol Kim. 6775-1
"**Cuckoo**, this year". To be in England. Sylvia Townsend Warner. 6761-1
"The **cuckoo**, wandering in solitude...". The cuckoo at

Laverna, sels. William Wordsworth. 6867-7
The cuckoo.. Unknown. 6134-6,6724-7,6125-7,6424-8,6114-1
The cuckoo. Francis Carlin. 6393-4
The cuckoo. Rose Fyleman. 6356-X
The cuckoo. Richard Le Gallienne. 6073-0
The cuckoo. John Logan. 6127-3,6808-1
The cuckoo. George Walter Thornbury. 6658-5
The cuckoo. William Wordsworth. 6179-6,6228-8
Cuckoos. Andrew Young. 6357-8,6125-7
Cuckoos, larks, and sparrows. Camilla Doyle. 6506-6
Cuddle doon. Alexander ("Surfaceman") Anderson. 6889-8
Cuddle doon. Alexander ("Surfaceman") Anderson. 6271-7
Cuddle down, dolly. Kate Douglas Wiggin. 6452-3
The cudgeled husband. Jonathan Swift. 6278-4
Cuelho, Art
    Christmas day. 6998-3
Cui bono. Adam Lindsay Gordon. 6951-7
Cui bono. James and Horace Smith. 6802-2
Cui bono? Thomas Carlyle. 6328-4,6730-1,6424-8,6996-7
Cui bono?, fr. Clevedon verses. Thomas Edward Brown. 6809-X
Cuilinn, Sliabh
    Dear land. 6858-8
    Eire a ruin. 6858-8
    Ourselves alone. 6858-8
    Paddies evermore. 6858-8
Cuisle mo chroidhe. John Philpot Curran. 6858-8
Cujus adjutor es. Bible. 6830-8
The cul-de-sac. Jan (Joyce A. Maxtone Graham) Struther. 6317-9
Culbertson, Anne Virginia
    De wood hants. 6696-8
    Gyda of Varsland. 6680-1
    He understood. 6579-1
    My chillun's pictyah. 6675-5
    To my friend on her eighty-first irthday. 6889-8
    Triolet. 6579-1
Culennain, Cormac
    The sea-going bark. 6090-0
Culhane, Charles
    The ancient one. 6870-7
    Death row. 6870-7
    Green haven halls. 6870-7
    The straw men. 6870-7
    There isn't enough bread. 6870-7
Cullen, Cornelius C.
    Battle of Somerset. 6946-0
Cullen, Countee
    Advice to youth. 6817-0
    Atlantic City waiter. 6976-5
    Atlantic City water. 6102-8,6076-5
    Black Magdalens. 6532-5
    A brown girl dead. 6538-4
    Epitaph: for a mouthy woman. 6071-4
    For a pessimist. 6850-2
    For a pessimist. 6464-7
    For a pessimist. 6850-2
    Fruit of the flower. 6250-4
    Heritage. 6506-6,6619-4,6039-0
    I have a rendezvous with life. 6337-3,6589-9
    Incident. 6538-4
    A lady I know. 6337-3
    The litany of the dark people. 6532-5,6337-3,6393-4, 6608-9,6746-8
    The loss of love. 6072-2
    The one who said me nay. 6441-8
    The proud heart. 6041-2
    She of the dancing feet sings. 6538-4
    The shroud of color. 6250-4
    Simon the Cyrenian speaks. 6532-5,6337-3,6250-4,6107-9
    A song of praise. 6250-4
    Threnody for a brown girl. 6039-0
    To a brown girl. 6619-4
    The unknown color. 6421-3
    Wisdom cometh with the years. 6619-4
    Yet do I marvel. 6250-4
Culloden. Andrew Lang. 6793-X
Culloden day. Unknown. 6859-6
Culloden moor. Amice Macdonell. 6873-1
"Culloden, on thy swarthy brow". Lochiel's farewell.
    Unknown. 6859-6
Culmination. Marion Hendrick Ray. 6764-6
Culmination. Charles Whitby. 6994-0
The culprit and the judge. Horace Smith. 6606-2
The culprit fay, sels. Joseph Rodman Drake. 6008-0,6135-4
The culprit fay. Joseph Rodman Drake. 6121-4,6219-9,6467-1, 6102-8,6076-5,6484-1,6077-3,6239-3,6302-0,6385-3, 6673-9
A culprit. Margaret (Janvier) Vandegrift. 6575-9
The cult of the Celtic. Anthony C. Deane. 6440-X
Cultural exchange. Al Masarik. 6792-1
Cultural notes. Kenneth Fearing. 6751-4
The cultural presupposition. Wystan Hugh Auden. 6645-3
Culture in the slums. William Ernest Henley. 6770-0
Culture in the slums. William Ernest Henley. 6089-7,6440-X
"A cultured mind! Before I speak". A rondeau a la Boston,
    fr. Roundeaux of cities. Sir Robert Grant. 6850-2
A cultured mind! Before I speak. Sir Robert Grant. 6770-0
Culver, Jane
    To Katherine Mansfield. 6781-6
Culver, Mykki Verlyn
    The last renegade. 6899-5
    "Loved ones" 6899-5
    Memoir/solitaire confinement. 6899-5
    "They'll push a buzzer and" 6899-5
"Cum tu, Lydia...you know the rest". A burlesque rondo.
    Louis Untermeyer. 6875-4
The cumberbunce. Paul West. 6089-7
'Cumbered about much serving'. Bertye Young Williams. 6906-1
Cumberland, George Clifford, Earl of
    My thoughts are winged with hopes. 6182-6
    To Cynthia. 6436-1
The Cumberland. Henry Wadsworth Longfellow. 6088-9,6263-6, 6126-5,6267-9,6062-5,6113-3,6735-2,6471-X,6552-X, 6382 ,6403-5,6484-1,6016-2,6438-8,6470-1,6288
The Cumberland. Herman Melville. 6946-0
The Cumberland. Unknown. 6219-9
Cumha Ghriogair Mhic Griogair. Unknown. 6873-1
Cummaquid. Sarah A. Dixon. 6798-0
Cumming, John Palmer
    "Me, ' war goin' on." 6589-9
Cummings, Edward Estlin
    All ignorance toboggans into know. 6666-6
    "But if I should say" 6531-7
    The Cambridge ladies. 6491-4
    Chansons innocentes I. 6808-1
    Chansons innocentes, sels. 6527-9
    A clown's smirk in the skull of a baboon. 6751-4
    Dirge: 1-2-3 was the number... 6637-2
    Eight poems. 6391-8
    Four III. 6354-3
    Gee I like to think of dead. 6751-4
    Here's a little mouse. 6506-6
    "How this uncouth enchanted" 6531-7
    I am a little church (no great cathedral). 6388-8
    I go to this window. 6375-6
    "I go to this window" 6531-7
    I sing of Olaf. 6666-6
    I was sitting in McSorley's. 6491-4
    "If being morticed with a dream" 6531-7
    If I have made, my lady, intricate. 6375-6
    Impossibly, motivated by midnight. 6375-6
    Impressions 004. 6808-1
    In just-spring when the world. 6324-1
    Is 5, sels. 6736-0
    It was a goodly co. 6666-6
    Ladies and gentlemen this little girl. 6751-4
    Libration. 6880-4
    Life is more true. 6666-6
    Listen. 6665-8
    Maggie and Milly and Molly and May. 6388-8
    Maison. 6880-4
    Memorabilia. 6488-4
    My father moved through dooms of love. 6209-1,6641-0
    My sweet old etcetera. 6665-8,6666-6,6324-1
    Next to of course God America I. 6736-0,6665-8
    Noone and a star stand, am to am. 6388-8
    One x. 6052-8
    One X 'death is more than'. 6209-1

Orientale. 6513-9,6619-4
Paris; this April sunset completely utters. 6375-6
Perhaps it is to feel strike. 6324-1
"Pity this busy monster, mununkind." 6391-8
Plato told. 6666-6
Poem ("Always before"). 6036-6
Poem ("Nobody loses"). 6069-2
Poem, or beauty hurts Mr. Vinal. 6399-3
Portrait. 6020-X,6324-1
A pretty a day. 6751-4
So standing, our eyes filled with wind. 6751-4
Somewhere, I have never travelled, gladly beyond. 6399-3,6208-3
Songs ("Always before your voice my soul") 6619-4
Sonnet ("If I have made"). 6506-6
Sonnet 001 ("When learned darkness..."). 6808-1
Sonnet 015 (A fragrant sag"). 6808-1
Sonnets - unrealities 004. 6808-1
Sweet spring is your. 6399-3
What if a much of a which of a wind. 6339-X,6666-6
"Your smile eye knees and of your etcetera". 6637-2

Cummings, Jeremiah W.
The banner of freedom, fr. Song of the union. 6171-0

Cummings, Marion
Shuttle song. 6039-0

Cummings, Monette
Then- and now. 6857-X
Writing woman. 6857-X

Cummings, Philip
Whip-poor-will. 6073-0

Cummings, Philip H.
Nativity. 7030-2

Cummins, Ella Sterling
Mariquita, the bandit's daughter. 6673-9
Voices of the wildwood. 6166-4

Cummins, P.D.
Hearing, I saw. 6339-X

Cumnor Hall. William Julius Mickle. 6370-5,6459-0,6370-5, 6152-4,6219-9,6086

Cun-ne-wa-bum. Katherine (Amelia Beers Warnock Garvin) Hale. 6843-X

Cunard, L.M.
Lost. 7002-7

Cunard, Nancy
Sonnet ("The sand"). 6069-2
The white cat. 6070-6

Cunard, Nancy (tr.)
Tcheliabtraktrostroi waltz, sels. Louis Aragon. 6343-8

Cuneo, Louis
Haiku. 6792-1
Long haiku no. 7 6792-1

The **cunnin'** little thing. Eugene Field. 6949-5
"A **cunning** and curious splendour". Genius. Alice Cary. 6865-0;6969-X
Cunning bee. Unknown. 6623-2
The **cunning** cobbler done over. Unknown. 6157-5
"The **cunning** fireflies." Ryoto. 6027-7
"**Cunning** little fairy." To an elf on a buttercup. Phoebe Cary. 6865-0;6969-X
The **cunning** old crow. Unknown. 6049-8

Cunningham, A.B.
The dying soldier boy. 6074-9

Cunningham, Allan
At sea. 6242-3,6504-X
Awake, my love. 6980-0
The bonnie bairns. 6960-6
Bonnie Lady Ann. 6543-0
Bonnie Lady Ann. 6830-8
Charlie Stuart. 6859-6
A fragment. 6960-6
Gane were but the winter cauld. 6271-7,6219-9,6737-9
Gentle Hugh Herries. 6980-0
Hame, hame, hame. 6732-8,6180-X,6271-7,6383-7,6737-9, 6317
The highland laddie. 6859-6
It's hame and it's hame. 6240-7
It's hame, and it's hame. 6219-9
John Grumlie. 6089-7
The lily of Nithsdale. 6438-8
The lord's Marie. 6960-6

The lovely lass of Preston Mill. 6960-6
The lovely lass of Inverness. 6859-6
Loyalty. 6322-5,6239-3
My ain countree. 6271-7,6383-7
My Nanie, O. 6180-X,6543-0
The poet's bridal day song. 6271-7,6219-9
Poet's bridal-day song. 6219-9,6271-7,6300-9
Rob Rool and Rattlin Willie. 6180-X
A sea song. 6107-9,6322-5,6304-7,6481-7,6239-3,6134-6
She's gane to dwall in heaven. 6600-3
She's gone to bed. 6543-0
She's gone to dwell in heaven. 6219-9
The shepherd seeks his glowing hearth. 6980-0
The skylark. 6108-8
Song of the elfin miller. 6131-1,6424-8,6639-9,6127-3
The spring of the year. 6102-8
The sun rises bright in France. 6180-X,6219-9,6543-0
Thou hast sworn by thy God. 6600-3,6302-0,6385-3
Thou hast sworn by thy God, my Jeanie. 6438-8,6219-9, 6543-0
"Thou hast vowed by thy faith, my Jeanie." 6271-7
The town and country girl. 6233-4
The town child and the country child. 6808-1,6552-X
The wee, wee German lairdie. 6180-X
A wet sheet and a flowing sea. 6105-2,6466-3,6290-3, 6180-X,6271-7,6328 ,6332-2,6502-3,6102-8,6438-8,6560-0,6639 ,6600-3,6250-4,6646-1,6668-2,6543-0,6371 , 6136-2,6252-0,6737-9,6396-9,6219-9,6424 ,6258-X,6104-4,6302-0,6385-3,6374-8,6732 ,6187-7,6246-5,6478-7, 6421-3

Cunningham, James Vincent
The chase. 6640-2
The dog-days. 6640-2
Epigrams. 6017-X
The fox and the cat. 6133-8
The metaphysical moment. 6017-X
Our lady of the night. 6640-2
Retreating friendship. 6640-2

Cunningham, John
Day: a pastoral. 6932-0
Kate of Aberdeen. 6086-2
A landscape, sels. 6545-7
A landscape. 6152-4
The miller. 6152-4
Moonrise, fr. Contemplation. 6545-7
Morning. 6385-3

Cunningham, John William
Calvary's cry. 6065-X

Cunningham, Kathleen Wallace
Lullaby ("Sleepy stars..."). 6764-6

Cunningham, Martha E.
The dandelion. 6750-6

Cunningham, W. Cephas
Americans. 6799-9

Cunningham, William
Egotism. 6397-7
Old time fiddler. 6397-7
Surprise. 6397-7
This paper world. 6397-7
Understanding. 6397-7

Cunningham-Graham, Robert. See Graham, Robert
The **cup** beside the spring. Douglas Malloch. 6478-7
The **cup** of blessing. Charles Wesley. 6065-X
The **cup** of death. Louise Chandler Moulton. 7041-8
The **cup** of happiness. Gilbert Thomas. 6337-3
The **cup** of life. Mikhail Lermontov. 6103-6
The **cup** of O'Hara. Turlough Carolan. 6930-4
A **cup** of water. Julia M. Bennett. 6685-2
The **cup** of youth, sels. Silas Weir Mitchell. 6066-8
Cup us till the world goes round, fr. Antony and Cleopatra. William Shakespeare. 6192-3
"The **cup** whose shape is sound". Theme song. Theodore Spencer. 6751-4
The **cup**, fr. Idyll i. Theocritus. 6435-3
The **cup-bearer**. Meleager. 6435-3
The **cup-bearer**. Unknown. 6617-8
The **cup**.. John Townsend Trowbridge. 6597-X
The **cup**. John Galsworthy. 6888-X
The **cup**. John Oldham. 6092-7
The **cup**. Fredrick T. Roberts. 6144-3,6335-7

The cup. Sara Teasdale. 6032-3
The cup. Unknown. 6952-5
The cupboard.. Walter De La Mare. 6466-3,6262-8,6454-X
Cupid. William Blake. 6089-7,6732-8
Cupid. Ben Jonson. 6089-7,6652-6
Cupid. Sir Philip Sidney. 6584-8
Cupid & Death, sels. James Shirley. 6208-3
Cupid ("Love's god is a boy") Unknown. 6182-6
"Cupid abroad was 'lated in the night". Cupid's ingratitude. Robert Greene. 6827-8
"Cupid abroad was 'lated in the night." Robert Greene. 6099-4
Cupid acquitted, a tale. Thomas Warton (the Elder) 6962-2
Cupid and Campaspe. John Lyly. 6301-2,6104-4,6543-0,6102-8, 6182-6,6240-7,6246-6,6302-0,6385-3,6726
"Cupid and my Campaspe played". Campaspe. John Lyly. 6935-5
Cupid and my Campaspe played. John Lyly. 6479-5,6634-8, 6181-8,6536-8,6219-9,6652 ,6099-4,6430-2,6250-4,6371-3,6737-9
Cupid and the nymph. Unknown. 6110- ,6250-4
Cupid and the shepherd. Clinton Scollard. 6770-0,6875-8
Cupid and Venus. Mark Alexander Boyd. 6845-6
Cupid arraigned, fr. Galatea. John Lyly. 6827-8
Cupid as a landscape painter. Johann Wolfgang von Goethe. 6948-2
Cupid at court. Samuel Minturn Peck. 6441-8
"Cupid blushes to behold." Unknown. 6563-5
Cupid drowned. Leigh Hunt. 6479-5
Cupid grown careful. George Croly. 6600-3
"Cupid if thou tell-tale prove." Unknown. 6563-5
Cupid in a bed of roses. Unknown. 6182-6
"Cupid laid by his brand and fell asleep". Sonnet 153 ("Cupid laid by"). William Shakespeare. 6447-7
Cupid mistaken. Matthew Prior. 6026-9,6092-7
"Cupid my mris hart assaild." Unknown. 6563-5
Cupid peeped in through the blinds. Richard Casper Dillmore. 6927-4
Cupid stung. Thomas Moore. 6479-5
Cupid swallowed. Leigh Hunt. 6102-8,6280-6,6302-0,6385-3, 6737-9,6219-9,6576-7,6585-6
"'Cupid!' Venus went a-crying". Lost Cupid. Moschus. 6949-5
Cupid's alley. Austin Dobson. 6688-7
Cupid's carrying provisions. George Croly. 6219-9
Cupid's casuistry. William J. Lampton. 6277-6
Cupid's Christmas song. Elizabeth Dimon Preston. 6836-7
Cupid's curse. George Peele. 6194-X
Cupid's darts. Unknown. 6089-7
Cupid's Easter composition. Unknown. 7021-3
Cupid's exchange. Kate A. Bradley. 6719-0
Cupid's failure. Carolyn Wells. 6441-8
Cupid's garden. Unknown. 6518-X
Cupid's holiday. Floyd Dell. 6039-0
Cupid's indictment. John Lyly. 6182-6
Cupid's ingratitude. Robert Greene. 6827-8
Cupid's kiss. Walter Learned. 6004-8
Cupid's metamorphrosis. M.S W. 6118-4
Cupid's revenge, sels. Francis Beaumont and John Fletcher. 6208-3
Cupid, hymen and plutus. John Gay. 6972-X
"Cupid, I hate thee, which I'd have thee know." Michael Drayton. 6317-9
"Cupid, I scorn to beg...", fr. Love in the dark. Sir Francis Fane. 6562-7,6563-5
"Cupid, if storying legends tell aright". The composition of a kiss. Samuel Taylor Coleridge. 6967-3
"Cupid, thou naughtie Boy, when thou wert loathed" Fulke Greville; 1st Baron Brooke. 6380-2
Cupid-his mark. Theodosia Garrison. 6274-1
Cupido. Bayard Taylor. 6976-2
"Cupids wearie of the court." Unknown. 6563-5
Cups of illusion. Henry Bellamann. 6037-4
The cur and the mastiff. John Gay. 6972-X
The cur, the horse, and the shepherd's dog. John Gay. 6972-X
"The curate and churchwarden". Tom Raban. William Cowper. 6814-6
The curate thinks you have no soul. St. John Lucas. 7008-6
The curate's Christmas Eve. Harold Monro. 6210-5

Curchod, Mary M.
  I would go back. 6144-3
Curcin, Milan
  Let me do it my way! 6765-4
  The mob is an awful bunch of cattle. 6765-4
Cure for ennui. Evelyne Love Cooper. 6850-2
Cure for homesickness. Holman F. Day. 7025-6
A cure for the spleen, fr. The spleen. Matthew Green. 6932-0
Cure for the sulks. Edgar A. Guest. 6869-3
The cure for weariness. Edgar A. Guest. 7033-7
The cure of Calumette. William Henry Drummond. 6591-0,6592-2
The care of malaria. Sir Ronald Ross. 6482-5
The cure's progress. Austin Dobson. 6230-X
Cure-all. Edith M. Thomas. 6619-4
The cure. Abraham Cowley. 6482-5
Curfew. Henry Wadsworth Longfellow. 6323-3,6332-2,6692-5, 6560-0,6126-5
Curfew must not ring to-night. Rose A. Hartwick. 6392-6
Curfew must not ring to-night. Rose Hartwick Thorpe. 6219-9,6263-6,6014-5,6370-5,6211-3,6142-7,6706-9
Curfew must not ring to-night. Unknown. 6554-6,6742-5,6568-6
"The curfew tolls the knell of parting day". Mosaics. Jotham Winrow. 6913-4
"The curfew tolls the nell of parting day". Elegy. Thomas Gray. 6486-8
The curfew tower. Robert Bridges. 6487-6
Curial, Date Thomson
  Forest primeval park. 6342-X
Curing (2), fr. Songs from an invalid chair. Josephine A. Meyer. 6847-2
Curing, fr. Songs from an invalid chair. Josephine A. Meyer. 6847-2
Curiosity. Carrie Ward Lyon. 6861-8
The curiosity.. Unknown. 6740-9
A curious boy. Edgar Lee Masters. 6542-4
A curious life poem. Mrs. H.A. Deming. 6410-8
Curious observations about the weather. Unknown. 6423-X
"Curious reader, didst thou ne'er". Rondeau. Thomas Hood. 6974-6
A curious want. M. Cook. 6505-8
Curle, Jock
  Comrades. 6475-2
  Song for a failure. 6475-2
  War. 6475-2
  When love has said farewell. 6475-2
A curler's elegy. Robert Burns. 7035-3
A curlew's call. Jane Barlow. 6656-9
Curley (pseud).
  In mamma's day. 7021-3
Curley, June
  Laura Ann Phillips. 6850-2
"Curling smoke from a chimney low". The joys of home. Edgar A. Guest. 7033-7
Curling song. Henry Duncan. 7035-3
Curling song. Norman Macleod. 7035-3
The curling tongs. Unknown. 6274-1
Curly locks. Mother Goose. 6363-2,6401-9,6452-3,6466-3, 6114-1,6135-4
Curly Locks. James Whitcomb Riley. 6990-8
"Curly-haired Carl! Were a blithsome mate". For love. Unknown. 6912-6
"Curly-locks, curly-locks, brighten and beam". The passionate aethete to his love. Louis Untermeyer. 6875-8
"Curr dhoo, curr dhoo". Unknown. 6904-5
Curran, Dorothy
  An hour. 6750-6
Curran, Edwin
  The clod. 6076-5,6102-8
  The March thaw. 6032-3
  The Ohio men. 6443-4
  The painted hills of Arizona. 6102-8,6076-5,6467-1,6076-5,6102-8
  To France! 6443-4
Curran, John Philpot
  Cuisle mo chroidhe. 6858-8
  Cushla ma chree. 6439-6

CURRAN

Cushla-ma-chree. 6820-0
The deserter's meditaton. 6086-2,6545-7
The deserter. 6322-5
The monks of the screw. 6858-8
The poor man's labor. 6302-9
"The currants, moonlit as mother Bunch". The owl, fr. Facade. Edith Sitwell. 7000-0
The current coin of heaven. Charles W. Denison. 6755-7
Current of life. Unknown. 6417-5
Current of life and fire. Berenice Van Slyke. 6808-1
The current. Alice C. Weitz. 6270-9
Currente calamo. Arthur Hugh Clough. 6315-2,6110-9
Currey, Ralph Nixon
    Durban revisited. 6788-3
    Exile, a sequence, sels. 6783-2
    In memoriam: Roy Campbell. 6788-3
    Landscape. 6788-3
    Man's roots, sels. 6788-3
    Marshal Lyautey. 6788-3
    Morocco. 6788-3
    Song ("There is not joy"). 6339-X
    Song ("There is no joy..."). 6788-3
    Ultimate exile, sels. 6788-3
Currey, Ralph Nixon (tr.)
    Ballade. Francois Villon, 6227-X
    Ballade ("One day"). Charles, Duc d' Orleans, 6227-X
    Ballade for peace ("O pray"). Charles, Duc d' Orleans, 6227-X
    Carol: A shepherd and a shepherdess. Clement Marot, 6227-X
    Elegy, sels. Louise Labe, 6227-X
    Epitaph. Francois Villon, 6227-X
    Epitaph on a pet cat. Joachim Du Bellay, 6227-X,6511-2
    Epitaph on a pet dog. Joachim Du Bellay, 6227-X
    Epitaph on Rabelais. Pierre de Ronsard, 6227-X
    Farewell to France. Marie Stuart, 6227-X
    Lament of the old woman remembering her youth. Francois Villon, 6227-X
    Lines on death, and ballade of the women of the past. Francois Villon, 6227-X
    On a detractor. Mellin de Saint-Gelais, 6227-X
    Rondeau ("White as a lily.") Guillaume de Machault, 6227-X
    Rondel. Christine de Pisan, 6227-X
    Rondel ("As we look"). Charles, Duc d' Orleans, 6227-X
    Rondel ("Greet all"). Charles, Duc d' Orleans, 6227-X
    Rondel ("Stephen Le Gout"). Charles, Duc d' Orleans, 6227-X
    Rondel ("Summer has sent"). Charles, Duc d' Orleans, 6227-X
    Rondel ("The first day"). Charles, Duc d' Orleans, 6227-X
    Rondel ("The year"). Charles, Duc d' Orleans, 6227-X
    Rondel ("Winter"). Charles, Duc d' Orleans, 6227-X
    Roses: scatter by this jar of wine. Pierre de Ronsard, 6227-X
    Song ("Lovers, avoid"). Charles, Duc d' Orleans, 6227-X
    Song of the vineyard knife. Clement Marot, 6227-X
    Sonnet ("As on a branch"). Pierre de Ronsard, 6227-X
    Sonnet ("As soon"). Louise Labe, 6227-X
    Sonnet ("Happy as Ulysses"). Joachim Du Bellay, 6227-X
    Sonnet ("He who would like"). Joachim Du Bellay, 6227-X
    Sonnet ("I hate"). Joachim Du Bellay, 6227-X
    Sonnet ("Newcomer"). Joachim Du Bellay, 6227-X
    Sonnet ("O, I could wish"). Pierre de Ronsard, 6227-X
    To a fountain. Pierre de Ronsard, 6227-X
    To Cassandra. Pierre de Ronsard, 6227-X
    To his nose. Olivier Basselin and Jean Le Houx, 6227-X
    To Rimi Belleau. Pierre de Ronsard, 6227-X
    Villon's epitaph in ballade form. Francois Villon, 6227-X
    Virelay ("Am I beautiful?"). Eustache Deschamps, 6227-X
    War and wine. Olivier Basselin and Jean Le Houx, 6227-X
    A winnower of wheat to the winds. Joachim Du Bellay, 6227-X
Currie, Baroness. See "Fane, Violet"
Currie, Ernest
    Laudabunt Alii. 6793-X
Currie, John Allister
    There are no colors. 6097-8

Curry, fr. The poetical cookbook. Unknown. 6278-4
The curse and the blessing. Unknown. 6848-0
A curse for a nation. Elizabeth Barrett Browning. 6198-2, 6358-6
"The curse of Adam, the old curse of all". Sonnet ("The curse of Adam"). Thomas Hood. 6974-6
The curse of Cain. William Knox. 6606-2
The curse of Doneraile. Patrick O'Kelly. 6930-4
The curse of faint praise. Irwin [pseud]. 6817-0
The curse of Hungary. John Hay. 6610-0
The curse of Kehama, sels. Robert Southey. 6102-8,6198-2, 6395-2
The curse of Kehama. Robert Southey. 6302-0,6315-2,6092-7, 6102-8,6250-4
The curse of Kishineff. Bertrand Shadwell. 6848-0
The curse of Minerva. George Gordon, 6th Baron Byron. 6945-2
The curse of mother flood. Henry Clarence Kendall. 6768-9
The curse of the laureate. James Hogg. 6802-2
The curse of Umbawa. James Abraham Martling. 6952-5
A curse on the traitor. Sir Thomas More. 6240-7
"Curse thee, life, I will live...no more". The suicide. Edna St. Vincent Millay. 6986-X
The curse upon Edward. Thomas Gray. 6102-8
The curse. Elizabeth J. Coatsworth. 6034-X
The curse. John Donne. 6430-2
The curse. John Millington Synge. 6125-7
Cursed jealousy. Sir William Davenant. 6867-7
The curses of royalty. William Shakespeare. 6543-0
The curses. Unknown. 6859-6
Cursor Mundi (The flight into Egypt). Unknown. 6198-2,6193-1
Curst be the gold and silver, fr. Persian eclogues. William Collins. 6934-7
"The curtain falls in burst of color rare". Postlude, fr. Program notes. Sarah A. Athearn. 6764-6
The curtain falls. Mary Brent Whiteside. 6779-4
The curtain fell. Gulchin. 6448-5
"The curtain had fallen, the lights were dim". At the stage door. James Clarence Harvey. 6923-1
The curtain in the house of the metaphysician. Wallace Stevens. 6531-7
"The curtain rises on a hundred years". The old thirteen. Charles Timothy Brooks. 6916-9
"The curtain rises on the play". Blizzard, April 6, 1982 Sheila C. Forsyth. 6857-X
The curtain. Tristan Klingsor. 6351-9
Curtains for a spinster. Walter H. Kerr. 6388-8
Curtice, Louise Capron
    The model wife. 6630-5
Curtis, A.W.
    Better late than never. 6523-6
    Days that are gone. 6523-6
    The ideal girl. 6523-6
Curtis, Christine Turner
    Penitent. 6038-2
    Winter leave-taking. 6017-X
Curtis, D.W.
    Song of an old dollar bill. 6919-3
Curtis, Emma Ghent
    Buckhorn cactus. 6836-7
    Mestezo's saddle song. 6836-7
    A warning. 6836-7
Curtis, George William
    Ebb and flow. 6300-4,6309-8,6431-0
    Egyptian serenade. 6240-7,6735-2
    O listen to the sounding sea. 6735-2
    Spring song. 6735-2
Curtis, Helen B.
    May. 6373-X
Curtis, Mrs. Howard J.
    The new girl's logic. 6691-7
Curtis, Natalie (tr.)
    Corn-grinding song. Unknown (Laguna Indian), 7039-6
    Gone to war. Unknown (American Indian), 6396-9
    Hunting song. Unknown (American Indian), 6396-9
    Hunting-song. Unknown (Navaho Indian), 7039-6
    Korosta Katzina song. Unknown (American Indian), 6396-9
    Korosta katzina song. Unknown (Hopi Indian), 7039-6
    Song of the horse. Unnown (Navaho Indian), 7039-6

Song of the mocking birds. Unknown (American In, 6396-9
Song of the rain chant. Unknown (Navaho Indian), 7039-6
Wind song. Unknown (American Indian), 6396-9
Curtis, Walt
    "Crab man loves you" 7003-5
    Lost glasses. 7003-5
    Raul. 7003-5
    Salisbury by the beach, put your finger in my sea... 7003-5
    Sun-drenched branch. 7003-5
    29 reasons I luv him. 7003-5
Curtiss, F.H.
    Engaged. 6682-8
The **curtsy**. Robert C.V. Meyers. 6417-5
Curve ahead. Rosa Zagnoni Marinoni. 6750-6
"**Curved** is the line of beauty". Thomas Moody. 6238-5
Curves. Louis Ginsberg. 6037-4
Curzon, George Nathaniel, Marquis Curzon (tr.)
    The flight into Egypt. Emile Cammaerts, 6785-9
Curzon, Sarah Anne
    The loyalists. 6795-6,6433-7
"The **cushat** crouds, the corbie cries". A bird committee. Alexander Montgomerie. 6943-6
The **cushat**.. Alexander Montgomerie. 6724-7
Cusheen loo. Unknown (Irish) 6858-8
Cushing vs. Blake. William B. Gourley. 6878-2
Cushing, Anita Laurie
    New mother. 6365-9
Cushing, Elizabeth L.
    April. 6433-7
    The city elms. 6433-7
    The city elms. 6433-7
Cushing, Frank (tr.)
    The coyote and the locust. Unknown (Zuni Indian), 7039-6
Cushing, Jeannette Eugenie
    My alter ego. 6818-9
Cushions but no seats. Unknown. 6701-8
Cushla ma chree. John Philpot Curran. 6439-6
Cushla-ma-chree. John Philpot Curran. 6820-0
Cushlamochree. Frances Wright Turner. 6799-9
Cushman, Ralph Spaulding
    Christmas prayer. 6337-3
    I will not hurry. 6337-3
    The parson's prayer. 6337-3
    The secret. 6337-3
"**Cushy** cow bonny, let down thy milk". Mother Goose. 6363-2, 6452-3
"**Cushy** cow bonny, let down thy milk". Unknown. 6904-5
Cusses. Muriel F. Hochdorf. 6850-2
Cust, Henry
    Non nobis. 6204-0,6437-X
Cust, Robert Needham
    A day in Palestine. 6848-0
    Hiram's tomb. 6848-0
    Scene in Lebanon. 6848-0
Cust, Robert Needham (tr.)
    From the Persian. Unknown, 6848-0
Custance, Olive
    Oh! do you hear the rain. 6301-2
    The parting hour. 6656-9
    Primrose hill. 6172-9,6292-X,6292-X,6172-9
    'Quelque part une enfance tres douce doit mourir'. 6785-9
    Twilight. 6274-1,6292-X
    The waking of sring. 6656-9
Custard and mustard. Unknown. 6937-1
Custer. Edmund Clarence Stedman. 6946-0
Custer lives in Humboldt County. Janet Campbell Hale. 7005-1
Custer must have learned to dance. Elizabeth Woody. 7005-1
Custer's last charge. Frederick Whittaker. 6913-4
Custer's last charge. Frederick Whittaker. 6706-9,6088-9
Custice, Louise C.
    In the doorway. 6078-1
"**Customs** change and nations fall". The first tooth. Edgar A. Guest. 6869-3
"**Cut** a little opening". Buttonholes. Hazel Hall. 6880-4
"**Cut** off by the soul's refusal". To-day. Gertrude Huntington McGiffert. 6838-3

"**Cut** the cables". Robert Burns Wilson. 6741-X
"**Cut** through the green wilderness...". The old state road. Benjamin Franklin Taylor. 6815-4
Cuthbertson, James Lister
    The bush. 6784-0
    Corona inutilis. 6784-0
    Wattle and myrtle. 6784-0
Cutler, Elbridge Jefferson
    Calvary song. 6008-0
    The drum-call in 1861. 6344-6
    Law and liberty. 6964-9
    The regiment's return. 6344-6,6411-6
    The rising of the people. 6678-X
    The volunteer. 6286-5,6113-3,6735-2,6340-3,6471-X
Cutler, H.S.
    The Son of God goes forth to war. 6304-7
Cutler, Julian S.
    Do something for somebody. 6109-5
    The old clipper days. 6798-0
    Roger and I. 7008-6
    Wild thorn blossoms. 6049-8
Cutler, George W.
    E pluribus unum. 6909-6
    E pluribus unum. 6304-7,6294-6
    The miser. 6409-4
    Song of steam. 6385-3,6406-X
    Song of the lightning. 6302-0,6385-3
Cutler, J.S.
    Knitting. 6672-0
Cutter, Walter A.
    Loyalties. 6143-5
Cuttin' rushes. Moira (Nesta Higginson Skrine) O'Neill. 6090-0,6423-X,6174-5,6019-6
Cutting. Fitz-Greene Halleck. 6121-4
Cutting corn in Vermont. Daniel L. Cady. 6988-6
The **cutting** of the cake, fr. The white house ballads. Eugene Field. 6949-5
Cutting pigs. Karl Elder. 6860-X
Cutting, Mary Steward
    The unseen trail. 7007-8
Cutting, Sewall S.
    Tribute to Burlington. 7030-2
Cutts, Mary H.
    Solomon's prayer. 7030-2
Cutts; Baron Cutts, John
    Only tell her that I love. 6563-5
    Song ("Only tell her"). 6201-8
The **cutty** wren. Unknown. 6380-2
Cwm farm near Capel Curig. Huw Menai. 6360-8
Cybele drawn by lions, fr. Endymion. John Keats. 6545-7
Cycle. Sean Jennett. 6666-6
"A **cycle** was closed and rounded". Bennington. W.H. Babcock. 6946-0
The **cycle's** rim, sels. Olive Tilford Dargan. 6300-4
The **cycle**. Robinson Jeffers. 6619-4
Cyclical night. Jorge Luis Borges. 6803-0
Cycling to Dublin. Robert Greacen. 6930-4
"The **cyclone-cellar's** open wide". The return. Walter Trumbull. 6995-9
The **cyclone**. Stewart Brisby. 6870-7
"The **Cyclops** blinks - his eye glows red". Traffic. Harold Willard Gleason. 6750-6
A **Cyclops'** philosophy, fr. Cyclops. Euripides. 6435-3
Cyclops' song. Thomas Dekker. 6334-9
The **Cyclops**. Theocritus. 7039-6
The **cygney** finds the water, fr. Aurora Leigh. Elizabeth Barrett Browning. 6934-7
Cymbeline. William Shakespeare. 6188-5
Cymbeline, sel. William Shakespeare. 6958-4
Cymbeline, sels. William Shakespeare. 6154-0,6232-6,6073-0, 6108-7,6122-2,6182 ,6198-2,6208-3,6240-7,6289-X,6332-2,6334 ,6339-X,6395-0,6423-X,6473-6,6623-2,6239 , 6436-3,6645-3,6301-2,6560-0,6430-2,6192-3,6472-8, 6250-4
Cymochles and Phaedria, fr. The faerie queene. Edmund Spenser. 6436-1
Cymon and Iphigenia. Giovanni Boccaccio. 6970-3
Cynara. Ernest Dowson. 6427-2,6102-8
Cynddylan's hall. Unknown (Welsh) 6528-7
Cynwulf

Christ tells of his passion. 6489-2
Christ, sels. 6489-2
The Christ, sels. Margaret Williams (tr.). 6282-2
Death of Saint Guthlac. 6022-6
Heaven ("for the happy"). 6489-2
The human race comes to be judged. 6489-2
A maiden ring-adorned, fr. Christ. 6489-2
A maiden ring-adorned, fr. The Christ. Margaret Williams (tr.). 6282-2
Cynic. Tomi Caroly Tinsley. 6178-8
The cynic in the woods. Arthur Patchett Martin. 6768-9
"A cynic of much savoir-faire". Limerick:"A cynic of much savoir-faire". Mrs. Charles Harris. 6811-1
The cynic of the woods. Arthur Patchett Martin. 6591-0, 6592-9,6656-9
The cynic. Clair [pseud]. 6817-0
The cynic. Theodosia Garrison. 6441-8,6019-6
Cynical ode to an ultra-cynical public. Charles Mackay. 6089-7
Cynics. Ralph Cheyney. 6542-2
Cynicus to W. Shakespeare. James Kenneth Stephen. 6089-7, 6722-0
Cynthia. Sir Edward Dyer. 6436-1,6191-5
Cynthia. Fulke Greville; 1st Baron Brooke. 6436-1
Cynthia. Edmund Spenser. 6935-5
Cynthia Ann. Walter Stanley ("Stanley Vestal") Campbell. 6397-7
Cynthia's bridal evening. John Keats. 6543-0
Cynthia's revels, sels. Ben Jonson. 6179-6,6378-0,6239-3, 6208-3,6301-2,6645
Cypress. John Peter. 6788-3
The cypress curtain of the night. Thomas Campion. 6315-2, 6328-4,6533-3
The cypress wreath. Sir Walter Scott. 6980-0
"A cypress-bough, and a rose-wreath sweet". Thomas Lovell Beddoes. 6980-0
The cypress-tree. Grace Blackburn. 6115-X
Cypria
  Flowery garments. Cecil Maurice Bowra (tr.). 6435-3
Cyprian woman: Greek folk song. Margaret Widdemer. 6029-3
Cyprus. Sergeant N. Boodson. 6468-X
Cyrano to his chiding friends. Edmond Rostand. 6351-9
Cyrano's presentation of cadets. Brian Hooker. 6250-4
Cyrene. Pindar. 6435-3
"Cyriack, this three years' day these eyes". John Milton. 6122-2
"Cyriack, whose Grandsire on the Royal Bench". John Milton. 6562-7
"Cyriack, whose grandsire". Sonnet ("Cyriack"). John Milton. 6315-2
Cyriadis. C.G. Poore. 6038-2
"Cythere the Bithynian...". Antipater of Thessalonica. 6251-2
Czechenherzu, Arn. Czech z
  The return. Paul Selver (tr.). 6763-8

D'Addio, Carmelita K.
  To thee...O foolish youth. 6799-9
D'Alcamo, Cielo (Ciullo)
  Dialogue: lover and lady. Dante Gabriel Rossetti (tr.). 6325-X
D'Alfonso, Antonio
  Perseverance. 6767-0
D'Alton, John (tr.)
  My wishes. Patrick Healy, 6930-4
  Why, liquor of life! Turlogh O'Carolan, 6858-8
  Why, liquor of life? Turlough Carolan, 6930-4
D'Amici, Ruggieri
  Canzone: of distance. John Heath-Stubbs (tr.). 6325-X
D'Anduze, Claire
  "They may blame thy tenderness". ? Costello (tr.). 6226-1
D'Angelo, Pascal
  Light. 6776-X
  Midday. 6776-X
  Midday. 6036-6
  Song of light. 6036-6

To some modern poets. 6036-6
D'Anne qui luy jecta de la neige. Clement Marot. 6106-0
D'Aquino, Rinaldo
  Lament for the sailing of the crusade. T.G. Bergin (tr.). 6325-X
D'Arcy, Hugh Antoine
  The face on the bar-room floor. 6303-9,6732-8,6167-2
  The face upon the floor. 6736-0
D'Artagnan's ride. Gouverneur Morris. 6732-8
D'Auria, Gemma
  Design for ashes. 6839-1
  Equilibrium. 6839-1
D'Avalos' prayer. John Masefield. 6732-8,6214-8,6508-2
D'Avenant, Sir William
  Gondibert, sels. 6208-3
  "The lark now leaves his watry nest". 6208-3
  Song ("Wake all"). 6315-2
  To the Queen, entertain'd at night. 6208-3
D'Sola, Otto
  Before the coming of the planes that burn the cities. Angel Flores (tr.). 6759-X
  Last song to a girl of the waterfront. Angel Flores (tr.). 6759-X
  Plentitude. Angel Flores (tr.). 6759-X
D'Urfey, Thomas
  "Born with the vices of my kind". 6933-9
  "Bright was the morning, and cool the air". 6933-9
  Chloe divine. 6317-9
  The fisherman's song. 6026-9
  The marriage-hates match'd, sels. 6562-7
  Sawney was tall. 6430-2
  Scotch song. 6152-4
  "A shepherd kept sheep on a high so high". 6157-5
  Solon's song. 6152-4
  Song ("I'll sail"). 6179-6
  "Tantivee, tivee...", fr. The marriage-hates match'd. 6562-7
The d'rection post. William Barnes. 6018-8
"D'ye see that peculiar object there". An idiot's gallantry. John F. Nicholls. 6921-5
D-dawn -- June 6, 1944. Margaret McGarvey. 6839-1
D-Y bar. James Welch. 7005-1
D.,C.
  St. Rooseveltius. 6995-9
D.,E. E.
  Elijah on Mount Carmel. 6848-0
D.,E.T.
  Promenading onthology. 6118-4
  Promenading ontology. 6118-4
D.,F.
  Lay of the grateful patient. 7021-3
  Song of travel. 6817-0
D.,F.M.H.
  Spring. 6846-4
D.,F.W.
  Only a private. 6074-9
D.,G.
  The same. 6116-8
D.,L.W.
  Loon river anthology. 6817-0
D.,M.A.
  Willie and the apple. 6131-1
D.,M.H.F.
  A dream about the old nursery rhymes. 6131-1
D.,M.P.
  Little mother. 6449-3
D.,R.
  The last spring. 6118-4
D.,S.
  Jacob's dream. 6848-0
D.,S.E.
  The shepherd's dump. 6383-7
D.,W.J.
  Song of the motorist. 6817-0
D.O.M.. Sir Henry Wotton. 6931-2
The D.T.'s. Unknown. 6983-5
Da Lentini, Jacopo
  Sonnet: of his lady in heaven. Dante Gabriel Rossetti (tr.). 6325-X
Da boy from Rome. Thomas Augustine Daly. 6310-1

Da capo. Henry Cuyler Bunner. 6441-8,6735-2
Da faith of Aunta Rosa. Thomas Augustine Daly. 6303-9
Da greata baseball. Thomas Augustine Daly. 6717-4
Da leetla boy. Thomas Augustine Daly. 6096-X,6162-1,6303-9, 6310-1,6476-0,6732-8,6710-7,6161-3,6393-4
Da pup een da show. Thomas Augustine Daly. 6510-4
Da strit pianna. Wallace Irwin. 6280-6
Da Thief. Thomas Augustine Daly. 6338-1
Dabbling in the dew. Unknown. 6490-6,6732-8
Dabbs, James McBride
   Miriam Beata. 6761-1
Dabney, Janice
   Preparing to climb. 6822-7
   Tones. 6857-X
Dabydeen, Cyril
   Farewell. 6767-0
   Folklore. 6790-5
   Lives. 6790-5
   Posterity. 6790-5
   Rehearsal. 6790-5
   Rhapsodies. 6790-5
Dacey, Philip
   Edward Weston in Mexico City. 6966-5
DaCosta, John Chalmers
   The army of despair. 6482-5
Dacre, Lady (tr.)
   "O my own Italy! though words are vain". Francesco Petrarch, 6325-X
Dad. William Edward Ross. 6889-8
Dad discusses clothes. Edgar A. Guest. 6748-4
"Dad never had much to say". Dad. William Edward Ross. 6889-8
Dad o' mine. E.F. Wilkinson. 6715-8
Dad of mine. Mary M. Jones. 6799-9
Dad's letters. Unknown. 6589-9
Dad's little fiddle. Fred Warner Sibley. 6680-1
Dad's old breeches. Unknown. 6889-8
Dada. Phillipe Soupault. 6351-9
Daddy ("Alone I sit in my den tonight.") Unknown. 6715-8
Daddy John. Jorge de Lima. 6759-X
Daddy knows. James William Foley. 6889-8
"Daddy rides the rodeo, while pride rides...". Childs memory. Terri Meyette Wilkins. 6870-7
"Daddy says he used to stare". The cry of the children. Neil Bell. 6804-9
Daddy worthless. Lizzie W. Champney. 6913-4
Daddy's little girl. Lindamichellebaron. 6899-5
Daddy's sentinel. Mary Farrar. 6715-8
Daedalus. Roselle Mercier Montgomery. 6039-0
Daedalus. John Sterling. 6271-7,6438-8
Daedalus in Crete. Angelos Sikelianos. 6352-7
Daedalus sings in the dusk. Virginia Taylor McCormick. 6326-8
Daemon and lectern and a life-size mirror. Horace Gregory. 6527-9
The daemon lover. Unknown. 6133-8,6134-6,6518-X,6547-3, 6613-5,6067
The daemon of the world, sel. Percy Bysshe Shelley. 6958-4
Daffadowndilly. Christina Georgina Rossetti. 6558-9
Daffodil. Michael Drayton. 6194-X,6191-5
Daffodil ("The dainty lady daffodil..."). Mary E. Sharpe. 6049-8
The daffodil fields, sels. John Masefield. 6634-8
Daffodil time. Clinton Scollard. 6441-8,6368-3
Daffodil time. William Shakespeare. 6634-8
Daffodils. Ruth Guthrie Harding. 6338-1,6653-4
Daffodils. Robert Herrick. 6302-0,6385-3,6018-8,6219-9
Daffodils. James Abraham Martling. 6952-5
Daffodils. Lizette Woodworth Reese. 6226-0,6347-0
Daffodils. Lady Margaret Sackville. 6781-6
Daffodils. William Shakespeare. 6114-1
Daffodils. William Wordsworth. 6047-1,6102-8,6136-2,6232-6, 6236-9,6240 ,6246-6,6337-3,6478-7,6481-7,6501-5,6529 ,6271-7,6302-0,6385-3,6328-4,6339-X,6401 ,6291-1, 6332-2,6600-3,6634-8,6134-6,6142 ,6498-1,6503-1,6512-0,6558-9,6597-X,6239 ,6732-8,6456-6,6543-0,6737-9, 6668-2,6464 ,6639-9,6219-9,6585-6,6304-7,6114-1,6153 ,6135-4,6192-3,6560-0,6104-4,6438-8,6458
Daffodils ("O daffodils, come out, I pray.") Unknown. 6720-4

"The daffodils are on the lea". Villanelle. May Probyn. 6770-0
The daffodils of old Saint Paul's. Lizette Woodworth Reese. 6331-4,6439-6
Daffodils over night. David Morton. 6466-3,6653-4
The daffodils. Emory Pottle. 6817-0
Daffy-down-dilly. Mother Goose. 6049-8,6363-2,6529-5
Daffy-down-dilly. Anna B. Warner. 6519-8,6601-1,6639-9, 6638-0,6456-6
The daft days. Robert Fergusson. 6198-2,6086-2,6195-0,6152-4
Daft Jean. Sydney Dobell. 6518-X
Dafydd ap Gwilym
   To the lark. 6102-8
   The woodland mass. Gwyn Williams (tr.). 6528-7
Dagger. Mikhail Lermontov. 7039-6
A dagger of the mind, fr. Macbeth. William Shakespeare. 6385-3
The dagger scene. William Shakespeare. 6570-8
Daggett, Rollin M.
   My New Year's guests. 6241-5
Dagmar. Elna Harwood. 6690-9
The dagmar cross. Unknown. 6409-4
Dagonet
   Kate Maloney. 6411-6
Dagonet makes a song for the king. J. Corson Miller. 6037-4
Dagonet's conzonet. Ernest Rhys. 6732-8,6102-8,6250-4
The daguerreotype. William Vaughn Moody. 6006-4;6310-1;6627-5
The daguerrotype. Eva Wilder McGlasson. 6576-7
Dahl, Borghild
   To my father, P. M. Dahl. 6342-X
Dahle, Helen Jenswold
   Lake Superior fishermen. 6342-X
Dahlgren, Frederik August
   The sun-parasol. Charles Wharton Stork (tr.). 6045-5
Dahlias. D.M. Holland. 6232-6
Dahomean song for the dead. Unknown. 6879-0
"A daie, a night, an houe of sweete content". Canto quinto. Thomas Campion. 6794-8
Daihaku, Princess
   "How will you manage". Arthur Waley (tr.). 7039-6
Daiken, Leslie
   Bohernabreena. 6930-4
   Larch hill. 6930-4
   Lines written in a country parson's orchard. 6930-4
   Shamrocks for Mayakovsky. 6895-2
   Spring, St. Stephen's green. 6930-4
Dailies. Jean Pellerin. 6351-9
The Daily --. Idris Davies. 6895-2
"Daily I dream of some ideal life". Life ideal. John Edward Magraw. 6800-6
Daily bread. Wilfred Wilson Gibson. 6301-2
Daily bread. Unknown. 6065-4
The daily burden. Alfred Lord Tennyson. 6461-2
Daily cross. Earl Bigelow Brown. 6144-3
Daily dying. Unknown. 6915-0
A daily motto. Unknown. 6889-8
Daily trials. Oliver Wendell Holmes. 6753-0
"Daily walked the fair and lovely". The azra. Heinrich Heine. 7039-6
"Daily, in the cool of evening". The Asra. Heinrich Heine. 6842-1
The daimyo's pond. Edmund Blunden. 6071-4
Dain do eimhir, sels. Sorley Maclean. 6379-9
Dain eile, sels. Sorley Maclean. 6379-9
Daini No Sammi
   "As fickle as the mountain gusts". William N. Porter (tr.). 6852-9
Dains, Ruth
   What the acorn said. 6249-0
Dainty daughter. Stanley Wood. 6836-7
A dainty fop. Danske Carolina Dandridge. 7041-8
"A dainty hand my darling has". Hands. Thompson Seiser Westcott. 6936-3
"Dainty is the frock I wear". Unknown. 6050-1
"Dainty little dandelions", sels. Unknown. 6601-1
"Dainty little stockings". Christmas ("Dainty little stockings"). Unknown. 6745-X

DAINTY

"Dainty maid, fair maid, your name I fain...". A mystery. ? Metcalfe. 7021-3
A dainty sang. Allan Ramsay. 6831-6
"Dainty shell in my window lying". Sea-born. Agnes K. Gibbs. 6836-7
A dainty song. Allan Ramsay. 6932-0
"Dainty sweet bird, who art incaged there" Unknown. 6380-2
"A dainty thing's the villanelle". Villanelle ("A dainty"). William Ernest Henley. 6289-X,6724-7,6646-1,6770-0
The dainty young heiress. Charles Sackville; 6th Earl of Dorset. 6092-7
"A dainty young heiressour slave." Charles Sackville; 6th Earl of Dorset. 6250-4
Dainty, fine, sweet nymph. Thomas Morley. 6328-4
Dairy charm. Unknown. 6466-3
A 'dairy' maid. Unknown. 6247-4
Dairy-maid song. E.J.H. Goodfellow. 6173-7
The daises. George Edward Woodberry. 6309-8
Daisies. Bliss Carman. 6374-8,6467-1,6102-8,6337-3,6497-3, 6076-5,6396-6,6423-X
Daisies. Geoffrey Chaucer. 6659-3
Daisies. Hilda Conkling. 6393-4
Daisies. Thomas Buchanan Read. 6529-5
Daisies. Frank Dempster Sherman. 6311-X,6132-X,6338-1,6639-9,6638-0
Daisies ("She was a little Irish maid"). Unknown. 6745-X
The daisies. James Stephens. 6527-9
Daisy. Francis Thompson. 6233-4,6246-6,6437-X,6473-6,6477-9,6634 ,6726-3,6507-4,6655-0,6656-9,6383-7,6023 , 6102-8,6508-2,6301-2
Daisy. Emily Warren. 7022-1
The daisy ("Daisies, bright daisies keep nodding...") Mrs. B.C. Rude. 6049-8
"Daisy and Lily/Lazy and silly". Slyph's song, fr. Facade. Edith Sitwell. 7000-0
The daisy and the flood. Thomas Lovell Beddoes. 6545-7
The daisy elf. Dora Adele Shoemaker. 6249-0
The daisy follows soft the sun. Emily Dickinson. 6321-7, 6429-9
Daisy Fraser. Edgar Lee Masters. 6897-9
"The daisy is fine and fair". A nosegay. Mary N. Prescott. 6965-7
Daisy time. Fleta Forrester. 6137-0
Daisy time. Marjorie L.C. Pickthall. 6797-2
Daisy's dimples. Joseph Ashby Sterry. 6658-5
Daisy's faith. Joanna H. Mathews. 6165-6,6411-6,6571-6
The daisy's song, sels. John Keats. 6047-1
The daisy's song. John Keats. 6519-8
Daisy's Thanksgiving. Unknown. 6699-2
Daisy's valentines. Austin Dobson. 6772-7
Daisy, sels. Francis Thompson. 6232-6,6427-2
The daisy, sels. William Wordsworth. 6545-7
The daisy.. Unknown. 6373-X,6452-3,6466-3
The daisy. Gertrude Alger. 6798-0
The daisy. Geoffrey Chaucer. 6240-7
The daisy. John Leyden. 6302-0;6385-3
The daisy. James Montgomery. 6302-0;6385-3;6597-X;6373-X
The daisy. Charles Phillips. 6529-5
The daisy. James Rennell Rodd; 1st Baron Rennell. 6937-1
The daisy. Virna Sheard. 6115-X
The daisy. Alfred Lord Tennyson. 6437-X,6655-0,6624-0,6656-9
The daisy. Unknown. 6049-8
The daisy. William Wordsworth. 6018-8
The daisy. Marya Alexandrovna Zaturenska. 6984-3
Dakin, Irene
    Moon blooms. 6818-9
    The phantom composer. 6818-9
Dakota. Joel Benton. 6484-1
Dakota land. Unknown. 6003-X
A Dakota wheatfield. Hamlin Garland. 6336-5
"Dakyns, when I am dead". Epistola ad Dakyns. Thomas Edward Brown. 6809-X
Dale, Edward Everett
    The prairie schooner. 6265-2
Dale, T.
    Regulus. 6911-8
    Regulus. 6167-2
Dalecarlian march. Erik Axel Karlfeldt. 6045-5

Daley, Edith
    His last words. 6995-9
    The little words. 6076-5,6102-8
    Miracle. 6076-5,6102-8
    Praise ("What do they know of penitence"). 6359-4
Daley, Helen S.
    Spelling-class. 6715-8
Daley, Victor
    A-roving. 6784-0
    Day and night. 6784-0
    The muses of Australia. 6784-0
    Romance. 6591-0,6592-9
Dali fantasy. Countess W. Twitty. 6178-8
Dallas, Mary Kyle
    At the altar. 6671-2
    Aurelia's valentine. 6671-2
    Bessie's dilemma. 6671-2
    Broken dreams. 6671-2
    dream ("Was it a dream or not.") 6671-2
    Father Paul. 6671-2
    A great man. 6671-2
    Her heart was false and mine was broken. 6671-2
    Knitting. 6680-1
    Love's reminiscences. 6671-2
    Miaouletta. 6671-2
    'N' for Nannie and 'B' for Ben. 6671-2
    The old, old story. 6671-2
    The statue's story. 6671-2
    The toast. 6915-0
    The toast. 6617-8,6685-2
    What the crickets said. 6671-2
The dalliance of the eagles. Walt Whitman. 6208-3
Dalliba, Gerda
    To a child. 6076-5,6102-8
Dalmon, Charles
    A caterpillar's apology for eating a favorite gladiolus. 6510-4
    A caterpillar's apology for eating a favorite... 6861-8
    A cow at Sullington. 6510-4
    Early morning meadow song. 6026-9
    Much in little. 6778-6
    O what if the fowler. 6861-8
Dalton, Annie Charlotte
    The call of the Carillon. 6224-5
    Listening in, sels. 6843-X
    Lycosa the spider. 6021-8
    The praying-mantis. 6081-1
    To the young man Jesus. 6021-8
Dalton, Henry
    Short story. 6979-7
Dalton, Moray
    A dead airman. 6542-2
    Rupert Brooke (in memoriam). 7026-4
    To Italy. 7027-2
    To some who have fallen. 7027-2
Dalton, Power
    Changeling. 6036-6
    Words. 6036-6
    Zenith. 6036-6
Dalven, Rae (tr.)
    Acheloos. Angelos Sikelianos, 6352-7
    The almond tree. Georgios Drossinis, 6352-7
    Altar of liberty. Sophia Mavroidi Papadaky, 6352-7
    Athanase Diakos. Aristote Valaoritis, 6352-7
    Athens. Nicephorus Vrettakos, 6352-7
    Athens. Kostas Kariotakis, 6352-7
    Athens. Rita Boumy Pappas, 6352-7
    Awaiting the barbarians. Constantine P. Cavafy, 6352-7
    The ballad of Andrew. Kostas Varnalis, 6352-7
    Battarias. Miltiades Malakassis, 6352-7
    Body remembered. Constantine P. Cavafy, 6352-7
    Chess knight. Michalis Stasinopoulos, 6352-7
    Child of the wind with harmonica. Nicephorus Vrettakos, 6352-7
    The cistern. Georgios Seferis, 6352-7
    The city. Constantine P. Cavafy, 6352-7
    The clown. Tefcros Anthias, 6352-7
    Comrades in death. Yiannis Griparis, 6352-7
    The creeping vine. Aristote Valaoritis, 6352-7
    The cretan. Dionysios Solomos, 6352-7

Daedalus in Crete. Angelos Sikelianos, 6352-7
A dead maiden's complaint. Gerasimos Markoras, 6352-7
The dead youth. Kostes Palamas, 6352-7
The destruction of Psara. Dionysios Solomos, 6352-7
Diakos. Kostas Kariotakis, 6352-7
Doomed. Kostas Varnalis, 6352-7
The dream. Dionysios Solomos, 6352-7
The dream. Georgios Vizinos, 6352-7
Dynasty of chimeras. Kassaris Emmanuel, 6352-7
Dynasty of the chimeras. Kassaris Emmanuel, 6352-7
Easter day. Dionysios Solomos, 6352-7
Elegy on the grave of a small fighter. Nicephorus Vrettakos, 6352-7
The embroidery on the kerchief. Kostas Krystallis, 6352-7
Epigram. Lambros Porphyras, 6352-7
Epilogue. Tefcros Anthias, 6352-7
The execution of the Klepht. Julius Typaldos, 6352-7
The fathers. Kostes Palamas, 6352-7
For Ammonis who died at 29 at 610 Constantine P. Cavafy, 6352-7
The forest. Miltiades Malakassis, 6352-7
Four years. Nicholas Pappas, 6352-7
Girl from Roumely. Alexandros Pallis, 6352-7
God forsakes Anthony. Constantine P. Cavafy, 6352-7
The 'good' people. Kostas Varnalis, 6352-7
Granny Tassia. Markos Avgeris, 6352-7
The grave. Kostes Palamas, 6352-7
Greek earth. Georgios Drossinis, 6352-7
Hands thrust in pockets. Tefcros Anthias, 6352-7
The haunted ship. Kassaris Emmanuel, 6352-7
Helen. Odysseus Elytis, 6352-7
The hidden sorrow. Georgios Vizinos, 6352-7
Hymn to liberty. Dionysios Solomos, 6352-7
Hymn to passion. Kostes Palamas, 6352-7
I walked the road of the dawn. Dionysios Solomos, 6352-7
I would love to be a shepherd. Kostas Krystallis, 6352-7
In silence. Lorenzo Mavilis, 6352-7
Innocent fears. Gerasimos Markoras, 6352-7
Ionian song. Constantine P. Cavafy, 6352-7
It is raining again. Apostolos Melachrinos, 6352-7
Itahaca. Constantine P. Cavafy, 6352-7
Jesus. Joseph Eliyia, 6352-7
Just one more spring. Nicephorus Vrettakos, 6352-7
Kanaris. Alexandros Pallis, 6352-7
Kera Phrosini. Aristote Valaoritis, 6352-7
Kleisoura. Angelos Sikelianos, 6352-7
The laborer. Galatea Kazantzakis, 6352-7
Laborers. Kostes Palamas, 6352-7
Lacrimae rerum. Lambros Porphyras, 6352-7
The last fairy-tale. Lambros Porphyras, 6352-7
Let the boat go. Kostes Hatzopoulos, 6352-7
Lethe. Lorenzo Mavilis, 6352-7
Letter from the front. Angelos Sikelianos, 6352-7
The little servant. Sophia Mavroidi Papadaky, 6352-7
Love song. Sophia Mavroidi Papadaky, 6352-7
The lover of his country. Andreas Calvos, 6352-7
The mad pomegranate tree. Odysseus Elytis, 6352-7
Magic refrains. Apostolos Melachrinos, 6352-7
Manuel Komninos. Constantine P. Cavafy, 6352-7
March of the spirit. Angelos Sikelianos, 6352-7
Maria's dream. Dionysios Solomos, 6352-7
Maria's prayer. Dionysios Solomos, 6352-7
Marigo. Zacharios Papandoniou, 6352-7
Marina of the rocks. Odysseus Elytis, 6352-7
Michael. Kostas Kariotakis, 6352-7
Militarism. Joseph Eliyia, 6352-7
Morning sea. Constantine P. Cavafy, 6352-7
The mother of Christ. Kostas Varnalis, 6352-7
Mount Rhodope. Yiannis Griparis, 6352-7
Noble parentage. Lorenzo Mavilis, 6352-7
The ocean. Andreas Calvos, 6352-7
Of the ship. Constantine P. Cavafy, 6352-7
The old shepherd. Zacharios Papandoniou, 6352-7
Olive tree. Lorenzo Mavilis, 6352-7
One of the Jews (50 A.D.) Constantine P. Cavafy, 6352-7
Our Torah. Joseph Eliyia, 6352-7
The pains of the Virgin Mary. Kostas Varnalis, 6352-7
Photinos. Aristote Valaoritis, 6352-7
Photinos the plowman. Aristotelis Valoritis, 6352-7
Playing the lyre. Apostolos Melachrinos, 6352-7
Plebian song. Markos Avgeris, 6352-7
Post-war roll call. Nicholas Pappas, 6352-7
The prayer of the humble. Zacharios Papandoniou, 6352-7
Prayer to God. Kostas Ouranis, 6352-7
Prevesa. Kostas Kariotakis, 6352-7
Resistance. Angelos Sikelianos, 6352-7
Return. Constantine P. Cavafy, 6352-7
Reveille for the dead. Yiannis Griparis, 6352-7
Rose-fragrance. Kostes Palamas, 6352-7
The sacred way. Angelos Sikelianos, 6352-7
Sad sunsets. Zacharios Papandoniou, 6352-7
Satrapy. Constantine P. Cavafy, 6352-7
The satyr or the song of nudity. Kostes Palamas, 6352-7
Serenade at the window of the wise men. Zacharios Papandoniou, 6352-7
Since nine o'clock. Constantine P. Cavafy, 6352-7
Sinner. Galatea Kazantzakis, 6352-7
Sleep. Kostas Kariotakis, 6352-7
The song of freedom and the sea. Yiannis Sphakianakis, 6352-7
The song of the vanquished. Nicholas Karvounis, 6352-7
Song to my sister. Yannis Ritsos, 6352-7
Spring. Yiannis Vilaras, 6352-7
Spring night, sels. Gerasimos Markoras, 6352-7
Spring storm. Miltiades Malakassis, 6352-7
Spring symphony. Yannis Ritsos, 6352-7
The Stygian oath. Angelos Sikelianos, 6352-7
Sweet Athens. Sotiris Skipis, 6352-7
Sweet death. Lorenzo Mavilis, 6352-7
Takis Plumis. Miltiades Malakassis, 6352-7
Temptation. Dionysios Solomos, 6352-7
Thirty three days. Nicephorus Vrettakos, 6352-7
To a mother. Sophia Mavroidi Papadaky, 6352-7
To Francesca Frazer. Dionysios Solomos, 6352-7
To my mother. Petros Vlastos, 6352-7
To the imperial eagle. Kostas Krystallis, 6352-7
To the sacred battalion. Andreas Calvos, 6352-7
The trip. Lambros Porphyras, 6352-7
Trojans. Constantine P. Cavafy, 6352-7
The twelve songs of the gypsy. Kostes Palamas, 6352-7
Two. Gerasimos Markoras, 6352-7
Very seldom. Constantine P. Cavafy, 6352-7
Vespers. Georgios Drossinis, 6352-7
Vestal virgins. Yiannis Griparis, 6352-7
The village of love. Petros Vlastos, 6352-7
The vintage. Kostas Krystallis, 6352-7
Walls. Constantine P. Cavafy, 6352-7
War hymn. Rhigas Pheraios, 6352-7
Woman from Samos. Alexandros Pallis, 6352-7
Women of Suli. Theoni ("Myrtiotissa") Dracopoulu, 6352-7
You will remember me. Sotiris Skipis, 6352-7
The young provincial. Michalis Stasinopoulos, 6352-7

Daly, James J.
In coventry. 6096 X
The Latin tongue. 6096 X
Nox ignatiana. 6292-X
October of the angels. 6543-0

Daly, John
A toast to the flag. 6476-0,6143-5,6076-5,6102-8

Daly, June
The captive lion. 6625-9
The kraals. 6625-9

Daly, May Palmer
The rose and the waif. 6965-7

Daly, Thomas Augustin
At home. 6875-8
Mistletoe and holly. 6875-8

Daly, Thomas Augustine
A ballade of brides. 6875-8
Ballade of the tempting book. 6875-8
Ballade to the women. 6875-8
Between two loves. 6089-7,6320-9,6653-4,6464-7
The blossomy barrow. 6338-1,6307-1
Carlotta mia. 6707-7
A child's Christmas song. 6431-0
Chrees'mas time. 6807-3

DALY

Da boy from Rome. 6310-1
Da faith of Aunta Rosa. 6303-9
Da greata baseball. 6717-4
Da leetla boy. 6096-X,6162-1,6303-9,6310-1,6476-0,6732-8,6710-7,6161-3,6393-4
Da pup een da show. 6510-4
Da Thief. 6338-1
Deesa greata holiday Fourth-July. 6721-2
Een Napoli. 6266-0,6396-9
For goodness' sak. 6887-1
For old lovers. 6431-0
Irish bachelor. 6714-X
John Keats. 6464-7
Kiss her. 6702-6
Kitty's graduation. 6718-2
Leetla Giorgio Washeenton. 6891-X
Leetla Joe. 6486-8
Mia Carlotta. 6722-0,6732-8,6102-8,6458-2,6300-4,6076-5,6464-7
Mistletoe and holly. 6807-3
The mother. 6300-4
Mrs. Maguire - a Christmas gift. 6807-3
October. 6172-9,6292-X
On the road to Arden. 6307-1
The ould apple woman. 6162-1,6607-0
Pasquale passes, fr. Madrigali. 6849-9
Perennial May. 6161-3,6161-3,6393-4
The poet. 6172-9,6292-X,6172-9
Rosa's curiosity. 6887-1
Song for August. 6320-9
A song for October. 6274-1
The song of the thrush. 6266-0,6478-7,6486-8,6102-8,6076-5
The spoiled child. 6702-6
The tides of love. 6722-0,6736-0
To a bereaved mother. 6303-9
To a plain sweetheart. 6172-9,6292-X
To a robin. 6172-9,6292-X
To a thrush. 6096-X,6292-X,6172-9,6327-6
To the minstrel girl. 6089-7
Two 'mericana men. 6162-1
Two days. 6307-1
W'en spreeng ees com' 6162-1,6607-0

Daly, Tom
On the road to Arden. 6548-1

Dam Neck, Virginia. Richard Eberhart. 6666-6

Dam, Henry J.W.
Theosophic marriage. 6714-X

Damaetas. George Gordon, 6th Baron Byron. 6945-2
Damaetas' jig in praise of his love. Sir John Wotton. 6189-3
Damages, two hundred pounds. William Makepeace Thackeray. 6996-7

Damagetus
A wife's grave. R.A. Furness (tr.). 6435-3

Damaris. Alice Cary. 6865-0;6969-X
Damaris Brown. Unknown. 6137-0
Damascene, St. John. See John of Damascus,St.

Damascius
"In body alone was Zosime". F.L. Lucas (tr.). 6251-2
A slave girl. J.A. Pott (tr.). 6435-3

Damascus. Edna Holroyd Yelland. 6120-4
A damascus nightingale. Stephen Crombie. 6073-0
The Damascus road. Daniel Hughes. 6144-3
Damascus, John of. See John of Damascus,Saint
"The damask meadows and the crawling streams". Country dreams. Richard Corbet. 6935-5
Dame Duck's first lecture on education. Unknown. 6127-3, 6502-3
Dame Fredegonde. William Edmonstoune Aytoun. 6278-4
Dame Hickory. Walter De La Mare. 6596-1
"Dame of the night of hair". A song for Marna. Bliss Carman and Richard Hovey. 6890-1
The dame school. Henry Kirke White. 6543-0
Dame Trot and her cat. Unknown. 6699-2
Dame Wiggins of Lee. Unknown. 6120-6
Dame Wiggins of Lee, and her seven wonderful cats. Mary E. Sharpe. 6459-0
The dame's garden, fr. The schoolk mistress. William Shenstone. 6649-6

"Dame, get up and bake your pies". Unknown. 6904-5
"Dame, what makes your ducks to die?" Unknown. 6904-5
Damelus' song to his Diaphenia. Henry Chettle. 6436-1
Damelus' song to his Diaphenia. Henry Constable. 6198-2, 6208-3,6191-5
"The dames of France are fond and free". The girl I left behind me. Thomas Osborne Davis. 6930-4

Daming, Mrs. H.A.
Life. 6260-1,6273-3

"Damis the Nysaean of a little bark...". Antipater. 6251-2
The damnation of Byron. A.D. Hope. 6349-7
The damned. Manuel Moreno Jimeno. 6759-X

Damocharis the Grammarian
The cat and the partridge. William Bedell Stanford (tr.). 6511-2

Damon and Cupid. John Gay. 6733-6
Damon and Pythias. Johann C. Friedrich von Schiller. 6606-2
Damon and Pythias, sels. John Banim. 6148-6
Damon and Pythias; or, true friendship. William Peter. 6402-7
"Damon died young; no bell was tolled for him". Toll the bell for Damon. Maxwell Anderson. 6817-0
Damon the mower. Andrew Marvell. 6191-5
Damon to the Syracusans. John Banim. 6406-X,6606-2
"Damon! Come drive thy flocks this way!". Clorinda and Damon. Andrew Marvell. 6935-5
Damon's lament. William Drummond of Hawthornden. 6191-5

Damon, S. Foster
Burning bush. 6506-6
Epilogue. 6506-6
Epitaph on a philosopher. 7014-0
Fete. 6037-4
Greeks. 6506-6
Jonathan's lullaby. 6761-1
Last supper: Jesus to Judas. 6619-4

"Damon, if thou wilt believe me". Charles Sackville; 6th Earl of Dorset. 6544-9
The damozel of doom. Tom McInnes. 6115-X

Damrosch, Alice Blaine
Swimming by night. 6300-4

"The damsel donned her kirtle sheen". Christmas, fr. Marmion. Sir Walter Scott. 6466-3
The damsel of Peru. William Cullen Bryant. 6412-4
The damsel of the plain. Theodore Watts-Dunton. 7015-9
A damsel possessed of great beauty. Unknown. 6058-7
"A damsel sweet in Colchester". Unknown. 6059-5
Dan and Dimple and how they quarreled. Alice Cary. 6060-9
Dan Collins. James L. Duff. 6761-1
Dan McGann declares himself. Edgar A. Guest. 7033-7
Dan's wife. Kate Tannatt Woods. 6273-3,6416-7

Dana, Julia M.
Lost Tommy. 6743-3
Tommy Day's Easter eggs. 6720-4

Dana, Mary S.B.
Flee as a bird. 6304-7
Passing under the rod. 6219-9,6913-4,6260-1
Under the rod. 6001-3

Dana, Mrs. J.M.
Alphabet of summer. 6715-8

Dana, P.
A cenotaph. 7021-3

Dana, Richard Henry
And fare thee well, my own green, quiet vale. 6752-2
Appearance of the spectre horse and the burning ship.. 6752-2
The constancy of nature contrasted with...human life. 6752-2
Daybreak. 6752-2
The death of sin and the life of holiness. 6752-2
Description of the quiet island, fr. The buccaneer. 6752-2
The dying raven. 6752-2
The early spring brook. 6077-3
Effect of the ocean...on the mind of the buccaneer... 6752-2
Epistle written while recovering from a severe illness. 6752-2
He knoweth our frame, He remembereth we are dust. 6752-2

The husband's and wife's grave. 6302-0;6385-3
I saw her once. 6077-3
Immortality. 6240-7
Intimations of immortality. 6014-5
The island. 6385-3,6600-3
The life of god in the soul of man. 6752-2
The little beach bird. 6121-4,6219-9,6300-4,6309-8,6176-1,6006-4,6385-3,6597-X,6073-0
The pleasure-boat. 6302-0,6385-3,6142-7,6302-9
Power of the soul. 6752-2
Proem to The buccaneer. 6121-4
Return of the buccaneer. 6752-2
The soul. 6302-0;6385-3
"A sound is in the Pyrennes!", fr. The bucanneer. 6752-2
The spectre horse. 6600-3
The third and last appearance of the spectre horse... 6752-2
Danae. Simonides. 6435-3
Danae. Simonides. 6271-7
Dance. Alice Corbin. 6628-3
Dance. Mary Carolyn Davies. 6959-2
Dance. Raymond Peckham Holden. 6959-2
Dance. Alfred Kreymborg. 6959-2
Dance. Sadi [or Saadi] (Mushlih-ud-Din) 6448-5
Dance. Lynne Sukenick. 6792-1
Dance. Jaime Torres Bodet. 6759-X
The dance at McDougall's. Thomas O'Hagan. 6115-X
The dance at the little Gila ranch. Unknown. 6274-1
The dance at the little gila ranch. James Barton Adams. 6959-2
Dance at Uncle Bob's. Ernest McGaffey. 6711-5
The dance by the roadside. Gustaf Froding. 6045-5
A dance chant. Unknown (Osage Indians) 6730-1
A dance chante. Unknown (Iroquois Indian) 6730-1
Dance figure. Ezra Pound. 6897-9,6959-2
Dance finale. Samuel E. Boyd. 6178-8
Dance for me. David Casapit. 6899-5
A dance for rain. Witter Bynner. 6619-4,6581-3,6265-2
"The dance goes on in merry guise". Dance music. M. A. B. Evans. 6959-2
A dance hall. John Hall Wheelock. 6959-2
A dance in the palace of Vulcan. Homer. 6959-2
A dance in the palace of Alcinous. Homer. 6959-2
The dance in the steerage. Joseph Warren Beach. 6959-2
Dance instructions for a young girl. Kimiko Hahn. 6790-5
"The dance is on the bridge of death". The bridge of death. Unknown (French). 6771-9
Dance motive. Percy MacKaye. 6959-2
Dance music. M. A. B. Evans. 6959-2
Dance of a Nautch girl. Unknown. 6959-2
The dance of death. Austin Dobson. 6123-0
The dance of death. Sir Walter Scott. 6087-0,6578-3
The dance of death. Austin Dobson. 6770-0
The dance of death. Unknown (Greek) 7042-6
The dance of delight. Unknown. 6959-2
The dance of love. Sir John Davies. 6182-6
The dance of old age. Unknown (Algonquin Indian) 6864-2
The dance of the daisies. Sarah Morgan Bryan Piatt. 6049-8
Dance of the dead. Johann Wolfgang von Goethe. 6696-8
The dance of the graces, fr. The faerie queene. Edmund Spenser. 6436-1
Dance of the leaves. Louise Abney. 6143-5
Dance of the lost key. Jacinto Fombona Pachano. 6642-9
Dance of the lost key. Jacinto Fombona Pachano. 6642-9
The dance of the merry damsels. John Keats. 6959-2
The dance of the milkmaids. Unknown. 6959-2
Dance of the months. Unknown. 6373-X
The dance of the muses. Hesiod. 6959-2
The dance of the nuns. Angel Guimera. 6959-2
The dance of the seven deadly sins. William Dunbar. 6200-8, 6102-8
Dance of the snowflakes. Alice E. Allen. 6147-8
The dance of the sunbeams. Bliss Carman. 6959-2
"The dance of the sword". Taylor, Tom. Unknown (Breton). 6665-8
The dance of the sword. Unknown. 6873-1
Dance of women. Dante Gabriel Rossetti. 6959-2
The dance on the terrace. Li-Tai-Pe. 6959-2
"Dance on, dance on to your flute's song". A girl dancing on the shore. Henry C. Thomas. 6959-2
"Dance on; we would not touch you". The dance. John Cowper Powys. 6959-2
Dance song. Angelo Poliziano. 6325-X
Dance song. Unknown. 6959-2
Dance song. Unknown. 6959-2
Dance the romaika. Thomas Moore. 6959-2
Dance time. Josephine Preston Peabody. 6652-6
"Dance to your daddy." Mother Goose. 6452-3
Dance to your shadow. Kenneth Macleod. 6873-1
"Dance! dance!". Summer. Unknown. 6720-4
"The dance! the dance!". The dance. Roden Noel. 6873-1
"Dance, and let tired eyes, weary of seeing...". Isadora Duncan dancing. Joel Elias Springarn. 6959-2
"Dance, dance, and visit now the shadowes...". A song and dance triumphant of the maskers. Thomas Campion. 6794-8
"Dance, dance, baby". A little song. L. Alma Tadema. 6937-1
The dance, fr. The witch's ballad. William Bell Scott. 6600-3
"Dance, little baby, dance up high." Mother Goose. 6452-3
Dance, my children. Norman Macleod. 6959-2
Dance, my heart! Rabindranath Tagore. 6959-2
"Dance, Thumbkin, dance". Unknown. 6904-5
"Dance, my heart! dance today with joy". Dance, my heart! Rabindranath Tagore. 6959-2
"Dance, yellows and whites and reds",fr. Parleyings. Robert Browning. 6123-0
"Dance-music - trap-drum - blaring saxophone". Mariana and the radio. Phyllis Megroz. 6782-4
Dance-music, fr. Music. Henry Van Dyke. 6961-4
"The dance-the dance-with wild and whirling...". A dance hall. John Hall Wheelock. 6959-2
The dance. Thomas Campion. 6794-8,6182-6
The dance. Paul Fort. 6490-6
The dance. Stella Gibbons. 6893-6
The dance. Horace Holley. 6959-2
The dance. Grace Denio Litchfield. 6959-2
The dance. George Mason and John Earsden. 6315-2
The dance. E. de Masters. 6684-4
The dance. Edna St. Vincent Millay. 6959-2
The dance. David Nash. 6818-9
The dance. Roden Noel. 6873-1
The dance. John Cowper Powys. 6959-2
The dance. William Somervile. 6959-2
The dance. James Stevens. 6959-2
The dance. Arthur Symons. 6959-2
The dance. Unknown. 6946-0,6753-0
The dance. Unknown. 6015-3
The dance. Unknown. 6753-0
The dance. William Carlos Williams. 6516-3
Dancer. Vincent Starrett. 6300-4
The dancer in the shrine. Amanda Benjamin Hall. 6538-4, 6034-X
The dancer in the wood. John Russell McCarthy. 6959-2
Dancer, John
"Ha! now you think you've cheated me. Oh, no!" 6317-9
The dancer, fr. the Bustan. Sadi [or Saadi] (Mushlih-ud-Din) 7039-6
A dancer. Cale Young Rice. 6959-2
The dancer. Joseph ("Seosamh MacCathmhaoil") Campbell. 6959-2,6244-X
The dancer. Madison Cawein. 6959-2
The dancer. Mary Carolyn Davies. 6959-2
the dancer. Arthur Davison Ficke. 6959-2
The dancer. Helen Hoyt. 6959-2
The dancer. Ibn Kharuf. 6362-4
The dancer. Jeremiah. 6959-2
The dancer. Rudolph Chambers Lehmann. 6959-2
The dancer. Grace Fallow Norton. 6959-2
The dancer. James Stephens. 6959-2
Dancers. Scudder Middleton. 6039-0
Dancers. James Oppenheim. 6959-2
The dancers. Michael (Katherine Bradley & Edith Cooper) Field. 6656-9
The dancers. John Freeman. 6070-4
The dancers. Joseph Freeman. 6880-4
The dancers. Richard Watson Gilder. 6959-2
The dancers. Alexander Gray. 6269-5

DANCERS

The **dancers**. Margaret Widdemer. 6959-2
Dancey, E. Pearl
    At parting. 6750-6
    Cry of a lonely heart. 6750-6
    A father's dilemma. 6750-6
    To J. 6750-6
Dancing. Sir John Davies. 6959-2
Dancing Adairs. Conrad Aiken. 6897-9
Dancing boys. James Oppenheim. 6959-2
The **dancing** days. Arthur Stringer. 6959-2
The **dancing** fern. Marian Storm. 6036-6
The **dancing** friar. Unknown. 6959-2
A **dancing** girl. Frances Sargent Osgood. 6004-8
The **dancing** girl. James Weldon Johnson. 6959-2
Dancing girls. Arthur Peterson. 6959-2
Dancing in the flat creek quarters. John Alfred Macon. 6675-5
Dancing in the meadow. Aristophanes. 6959-2
Dancing of the air. Sir John Davies. 6959-2
The **dancing** sea, fr. Orchestra. Sir John Davies. 6125-7
The **dancing** seal. Wilfred Wilson Gibson. 6668-2
Dancing the minuet. F.E.E. Hamilton. 6116-8
Dandelion. Kate Louise Brown. 6373-X,6639-9,6638-0
Dandelion. Hilda Conkling. 6538-4
Dandelion. Nellie M. Garabrant. 6137-0,6373-X,6459-0,6456-6,6964-9
Dandelion. Lida Wilson Turner. 6841-3
Dandelion. Unknown. 6312-8
The **dandelion** ("O dandelion, eellow as gold"). Unknown. 6623-2
"The **dandelion** is your neighbor's boy". Dandelion. Lida Wilson Turner. 6841-3
"The **dandelion** to the daisy said". Argument. Edgar A. Guest. 6748-4
Dandelion's hair. Unknown. 6312-8
Dandelion, what do you do? Unknown. 6937-1
Dandelion-first up. Unknown. 6529-5
The **dandelion**.. John Banister Tabb. 6473-6,6396-9
The **dandelion**. Gertrude Alger. 6798-0
The **dandelion**. Martha E. Cunningham. 6750-6
The **dandelion**. Vachel Lindsay. 6228-8;6338-1
The **dandelion**. Katharine Pyle. 6820-0
The **dandelion**. Unknown. 6049-8,6466-3
Dandelions. E.L. Benedict. 6529-5
Dandelions. Virginia Taylor McCormick. 6585-6
Dandelions. Albert Durrant Watson. 6797-2
The **dandelions**. Helen Gray Cone. 7041-8
The **dandelions**. Helen Gray Cone. 6047-1,6519-8,6597-X,6374-8,6632-1,6421-3
The **dandelions**. Unknown. 6674-7
Dandie Dinmonts. William Henry Ogilvie. 7008-6
Dandridge, Danske
    O God of battles. 6088-9
    On the eve of the war. 6471-X
    The spirit of the fall. 6309-8
Dandridge, Danske Carolina
    A dainty fop. 7041-8
    Pegasus. 7041-8
The **dandy** cat. Laura E. Richards. 6120-6
The **dandy** fifth. Frank H. Gassaway. 6917-7
The **dandy** fifth. Frank H. Gassaway. 6277-6,6451-5,6706-9
A **dandy** lion. M.E. B. 6965-7
The **dandy** O. Unknown. 6157-5
A **dandy**. William Shakespeare. 6228-8
Dane, Barry. See Logan, John Edward
Dane, Clemence
    Him I follow, fr. Will Shakespeare. 6532-5
    Salute to Greece. 6761-1
    Will Shakespeare, sels. 6532-5
The **danes**.. George Walter Thornbury. 6290-3
Danger. Susan Frances ("Seranus") Harrison. 6115-X
Danger. Helen Hunt Jackson. 7041-8
Danger. Helen Hunt Jackson. 6754-9
"**Danger** is not in action, but in sloth". Tyrannicide. Walter Savage Landor. 7009-4
"The **danger** is over, the battle is past". Song after a wedding. Thomas Southerne. 6874-X
The **danger** signal. S. Blair McBeath. 6672-0
The **danger**. Norman Gale. 6872-3
Dangerfield, Clinton
    The traveller. 7012-4
A **dangerous** music. Michael Knoll. 6870-7
Dangerous sport. Elizabeth Turner. 6018-8
Daniel. Vachel Lindsay. 6602-X,6125-7
Daniel. Hannah More. 6848-0
Daniel. Richard Wilton. 6848-0
Daniel Boone. Arthur Guiterman. 6891-X
Daniel Boone's last look westward. Cale Young Rice. 7017-5
Daniel Boone's last look westward. Cale Young Rice. 6326-8
Daniel Boone, fr. Don Juan. George Gordon, 6th Baron Byron. 6302-0;6385-3
Daniel Defoe. Walter Savage Landor. 6380-2
Daniel Gray. Josiah Gilbert Holland. 6300-4
Daniel Periton's ride. Albion W. Tourgee. 6922-3
Daniel Periton's ride. Albion W. Tourgee. 6744-1
Daniel Webster. Oliver Wendell Holmes. 6385-3
Daniel Webster's horses. Elizabeth J. Coatsworth. 6218-0
Daniel Webster's plow. Benjamin Franklin Taylor. 6815-4
Daniel, Arnaut
    Bel m'es quan lo vens m'alena. Harriet Waters Preston (tr.). 7039-6
Daniel, George
    The robin. 6933-9
Daniel, Samuel
    Are they shadows that we see? 6182-6,6733-6,6315-2
    "Beauty, sweet love, is like the morning dew" 6182-6, 6436-1
    Beauty, time, and love, sels. 6317-9,6102-8
    "But love whilst that thou may'st be loved again" 6182-6,6436-1
    Care-charmer sleep. 6737-9,6315-2,6182-6,6187-7,6246-5, 6436-1,6536-8,6634-8,6533-3,6102-8,6153-2
    Chorus (Behold what furies still"). 6315-2
    Chrous, fr. Cleopatra. 6436-1
    Chrous, fr. Philotas. 6436-1
    The civil wars, sels. 6194-X
    The complaint of Rosamond, sels. 6198-2
    The complaint of Rosamond. 6430-2
    Constancy. 6436-1
    Delia. 6186-9
    Delia, sels. 6208-3,6194-X,6645-3
    A description of beauty, translated out of Marino. 6436-1
    Early love. 6429-9,6226-1,6321-7
    Eidola, fr. Tethys' festival. 6317-9
    English poetry. 6436-1
    Enjoy the April now. 6182-6
    Epistle to the Lady Margaret, Countess of Cumberland. 6198-2,6634-8
    Eyes, hide my love. 6182-6
    "Fair is my Love, and cruel as she's fair" 6182-6,6436-1
    From an epistle to the Countess of Cumberland. 6600-3
    Had sorrow ever fitter place. 6182-6
    Henry's lament. 6436-1
    Humaner letters. 6935-5
    Hymen's triumph, sels. 6827-8
    "I must not grieve my Love, whose eyes would read" 6182-6
    Justice. 6935-5
    Knowing the heart of man is set to be. 6438-8
    "Let others sing of knights and paladins" 6182-6,6436-1
    Lonely beauty. 6436-1
    "Look, Delia, how we esteem the half-blown rose". 6182-6,6436-1,6726-3
    Love. 6438-8
    Love. 6830-8
    Love is a sickness. 6092-7
    "Love is a sickness full of woes." 6513-9,6430-2,6219-9, 6737-9,6385-3,6317-9,6315-2,6436-1,6182-6,6302-2
    Love's birth and becoming. 6189-3
    Musophilus, sels. 6198-2
    O blessed letters, fr. Musophilus. 6934-7
    Ode ("Now each creature"). 6436-1,6315-2,6182-6
    An ode. 6191-5
    A pastoral ("O happy"). 6191-5
    Pastoral of Daniel. 6436-1
    A pastoral. 6191-5
    Poet and critic. 6436-1
    The poet's audience. 6935-5

Prayer to sleep. 6202-4
Quand vous serez bien vieille. 6202-4
Reminiscence. 6935-5
Rosamond's appeal. 6436-1
"Sacred religion! Mother of form and fear!" 6935-5
Secrecy. 6436-1
Shadows. 6436-1
Song ("Are they"). 6189-3
Sonnet ("Care-charmer sleep"). 6189-3,6150-8
Sonnet ("If this be love"). 6436-1
Sonnet ("My cares"). 6436-1
Sonnet ("My spotless love"). 6436-1
Sonnet ("The star"). 6436-1
Sonnet ("These plaintive verse"). 6436-1
Sonnet ("Thou canst die"). 6436-1
Sonnet ("Time, cruel"). 6436-1
Sonnet ("Unto the boundless"). 6436-1
Sonnet ("When winter"). 6436-1
Sonnet on sleep. 6219-9
Sonnets to Delia. 6436-1,6189-3,6660-7
Sonnets to Delia, sels. 6198-2,6430-2
Sorrow. 6436-1
Suave mari magno. 6935-5
A supplication. 6830-8
Tethys' festival, sels. 6317-9
To Delia. 6315-2,5250-4,6645-3,6646-1
To Delia, sels. 6301-2
To his reader. 6436-1
To Sir Thomas Egerton. 6436-1
To the Countess of Cumberland, sels. 6208-3
To the Lady Lucy, countess of Bedford. 6436-1
To the Lady Margaret, countess of Cumberland. 6315-2, 6436-1,6219-9,6194-X
Ulysses and the Siren. 6182-6,6258-X,6315-2,6436-1,6536-8
"When men shall find thy flower, thy glory". 6187-7, 6182-6,6436-1
Daniell, Edith
Inspect us. 6089-7
Daniell, J.F.
The jubilee of Melbourne. 6768-9
Daniells, Roy
"I never swung a staff and deep, oh deep". 6446-9
Daniels, Earl
Small apocalypse. 6979-7
Daniels, Francis Potter
An epitaph. 6841-3
Funeral ode on Marvin McTyeire Parks. 6841-3
With a funeral wreath. 6841-3
A **Danish** barrow. Francis Turner Palgrave. 6656-9
Dannebrog. B.S. Ingemann. 6555-4
Danny Deever. Rudyard Kipling. 6150-8,6371-3,6569-0,6723-9, 6560-0,6289-X,6332-2,6396-3,6656-9,6301-2,6491
'**Danny** Deever' up to date. Unknown. 6247-4
Danowsky, Roberta Santlofer
A friend's death. 6857-X
Her husband's death. 6857-X
"**Dans** ce cabriolet de place j'examine" Charles Augustin Sainte-Beuve. 6801-4
"**Dans** des terrains cendreux, calcines, sans...". La beatrice. Charles Baudelaire. 6801-4
"**Dans** les ravins la route oblique". Soir. Victor Hugo. 6801-4
Danse macabre. Edwin Meade Robinson. 6959-2
Danse macabre. Antonia Y. Schwab. 6218-0
Dante. Giovanni Boccaccio. 6624-0
Dante. William Cullen Bryant. 6483-3
Dante. Richard Garnett. 7015-9
Dante. Henry Wadsworth Longfellow. 6077-3,6333-0,6536-8, 6288-1,6126-5,6371
Dante. Michelangelo Buonarroti. 7039-6
Dante. Michelangelo Buonarroti. 6325-X
Dante Alighieri
Ballata: He will gaze upon Beatrice. Dante Gabriel Rossetti (tr.). 7039-6
Beatrice. 6679-8
Francesca of Rimini, fr. The divine comedy. George Gordon, 6th Baron Byron (tr.). 6945-2
Her helpfulness. 6321-7
His lady's praise. 6321-7
I felt a spirit of love begin to stir. Dante Gabriel Rossetti (tr.). 6527-9
The inferno, sels. 6732-8
La vita nuova, sels. Dante Gabriel Rossetti (tr.). 7039-6
Nimrod and the monsters of hell. Leigh Hunt (tr.). 6102-8
Of Beatrice de Portinari. Dante Gabriel Rossetti (tr.). 6102-8
Paolo and Francesca. 6102-8
Paolo and Francesca, fr. The divine comedy. 6256-3
Paolo and Francesca, sels. Stephen Phillips (tr.). 6046-3,6541-4
Paradise, sels. Henry F. Cary (tr.). 6428-0
Paulo and Francesca, fr. Inferno. Leigh Hunt (tr.). 6659-3
Purgatory, sels. Henry F. Cary (tr.). 6428-0
St. Bernard's hymn to the Virgin. 6734-4
Sestina: Of the lady Pietra degli Scrovigni. Dante Gabriel Rossetti (tr.). 7039-6
Sonnet: Of Beatrice d' Portinari, on All Saints' Day. Dante Gabriel Rossetti (tr.). 7039-6
Sonnet: Of beauty and duty. Dante Gabriel Rossetti (tr.). 7039-6
Sonnet: To Guido Cavalcanti. Percy Bysshe Shelley (tr.). 7039-6
To death. Charles Eliot Norton (tr.). 6879-0
Dante Alighieri. Dante Gabriel Rossetti. 6424-8
"**Dante Alighieri in Becchina's praise**". Sonnet: He rails against Dante. Cecco Angiolieri da Siena. 7039-6
"**Dante Alighieri, a dark oracle**". Sonnet: Inscription for a portrait of Dante. Giovanni Boccaccio. 7039-6
Dante and Ariosto. Thomas Edward Brown. 6809-9
Dante at Verona. Dante Gabriel Rossetti. 6484-1
Dante Gabriel Rossetti: Simple Simon. Charles Powell. 6982-7
"**Dante** was naif although he had an inkling". Leonard Bacon. 6619-4
Dante's angels. Patrick Lane. 6767-2
Dante, sels. Dante Gabriel Rossetti. 6122-2,6198-2
Dante, Shakespeare, Milton, fr. Balder. Sydney Dobell. 6656-9
Danube and the Euxine. William Edmonstoune Aytoun. 6948-7
The **Danube** river. Hamilton Aide. 6656-9
"The **Danube** to the Severn gave", fr. In memoriam. Alfred Lord Tennyson. 6867-7
"**Danube,** Danube! wherefore com'st thou". Danube and the Euxine. William Edmonstoune Aytoun. 6948-7
Daphnaida. Edmund Spenser. 6908-8
Daphnaida, sels. Edmund Spenser. 6879-0
Daphnaida, sels. Edmund Spenser. 6189-3,6472-8
Daphne. Bliss Carman. 6423-X,6250-4
Daphne. Hildegarde Flanner. 6509-0,6037-4
Daphne. Ann Louise Hayes. 6515-5
Daphne. Thomas S. Jones Jr. 6253-9
Daphne. John Lyly. 6182-6
Daphne. Edna St. Vincent Millay. 6850-2
Daphne. Edith Sitwell. 7000-0
Daphne. Edith Sitwell. 6777-8
Daphne and Apollo. George Jester. 6817-0
"'**Daphne** with her thighs in bark". Her majesty's ship. Gene Fowler. 6792-1
Daphnis and Chloe. John Gay. 6972-X
"**Daphnis** is mute, and hidden nymphs complain". Theocritus. Maurice Francis Egan. 7041-8
"**Daphnis** stood pensive in the shade". Daphnis and Chloe. John Gay. 6972-X
"**Daphnis** the fair, that with the Doric strains". An offering to Pan. Theocritus. 6962-2
Daphnis to Ganymede. Richard Barnfield. 6182-6
Dapple-grey. Unknown. 6937-1
Dappledun. Phoebe Cary. 6060-9
"**Dar** islands of the Orient". The celebes. John Boyle O'Reilly. 7041-8
"**Dar's** bressing in baptizing drops". Daddy worthless. Lizzie W. Champney. 6913-4
Darby and Joan. St. John Honeywood. 6307-1
Darby and Joan. Unknown. 6260-1
Darby and Joan. Frederic Edward Weatherley. 6656-9
The **darby** ra. Unknown. 6058-7

DARE

Dare quam accipere. Mathilde Blind. 6437-X,6730-1
"Dare to be true". George Herbert. 6623-2
"Dare to be true, nothing can need a lie". Jottings for sportsmen. George Herbert. 6861-8
Dare to stand alone. Unknown. 6617-8
"Dare you haunt our hallowed green?". The fairies' dance. Unknown. 6959-2
Dare, Ella
   Only one kind word. 6682-8
Dare, Shirley
   Lullaby ("A song for the baby"). 6131-1
Darest thou now, O soul. Algernon Charles Swinburne. 6289-X
Darest thou now, O soul, fr. Whispers of heavenly death. Walt Whitman. 6006-4,6007-2,6154-0,6337-3,6730-1, 6121
Darest thou, now O soul, fr. Whispers of heavenly death. Walt Whitman. 6300-4,6396-9,6288-1,6431-0,6560-0, 6126-5,6153-2
Dargai ridge. Theodore Goodridge Roberts. 6224-5,6591-0, 6502-9
Dargan, Olive Tilford
   Beyond the war. 6029-3
   The cycle's rim, sels. 6300-4
   Defiance. 6184-2
   Evvie's mother. 6326-8
   Far bugles. 6039-0,6071-4
   Fatherland. 6031-5
   The game. 6266-0
   "Girl I love." 6581-3
   Home. 6880-4
   In the black country. 6036-6
   The inquisitor. 6037-4
   Interferin' 7038-8
   It will be a hard winter. 6619-4
   Lute and furrow. 6619-4,6326-8
   The master. 6037-4
   On Clingman dome. 6326-8,6653-4
   Path Flower. 6556-2,6102-8,6076-5,6161-3
   Path Flower. 6393-4
   The path-flower. 6028-5,6076-5,6161-3,6393-4
   Sal's gap. 6326-8
   There's Rosemary. 6310-1
   To a Texas primrose. 6033-1,6326-8
   To William Blake. 6037-4
   "To-day I went among the mountain folk" 6019-6
   Twilight. 6326-8
   We creators. 6326-8
   Ye who are to sing. 6327-6
Darien. Sir Edwin Arnold. 6946-0
The daring prince, fr. A session with... James Whitcomb Riley. 6091-9
Dario, Ruben
   Greeting to the American eagle. 6102-8
Darius Green and his flying machine. John Townsend Trowbridge. 6142-7,6279-2,6392-6,6498-1,6732-8,6089-7,6739-5,6181-4,6736-0,6706-9,6566
"Dark accurate plunger down the successive...". The subway. Allen Tate. 6808-1
"Dark all without it knits: within". The forest-naturalist. Andrew Marvell. 6943-6
"Dark all without it knits; within". In a forest. Andrew Marvell. 6935-5
"Dark and lugubrious, his eyes". The condor. Michael Hogan. 6870-7
Dark angel. Elizabeth Bartlett. 6388-8
The dark angel, sels. Lionel Johnson. 6317-9
The dark angel. Lionel Johnson. 6022-6,6096-X,6489-2,6244-X,6735-3,6292,6172-9,6508-2,6655-1
"A dark apocalypse of grief". Gethsemane. William White. 6868-5
"Dark as the clouds of even". The black regiment. George Henry Boker. 6946-0
"Dark as wells, his eyes". Long person. Gladys Cardiff. 7005-1
Dark bamboos. Clifford Franklin Gessler. 6039-0
Dark blessing. Jessie Farnham. 6750-6
The dark breed. Frederick Robert Higgins. 6072-2
"Dark burned the sunset." Stefan George. 6160-5
The dark cavalier. Margaret Widdemer. 6556-2.6467-1,6250-4, 6393-4
The dark chamber. Ethel Romig Fuller. 6979-7
The dark chamber. Louis Untermeyer. 6619-4,6726-3,6011-0
The dark champion. Roy Campbell. 6800-6
The dark chateau. Walter De La Mare. 6508-2
"Dark chieftain of the heath and height!". The brigand leader and his wife. Felicia Dorothea Hemans. 6973-8
The dark cup, sels. Sara Teasdale. 6531-7
Dark Ellen. Julia Johnson Davis. 6072-2
"Dark days, cold nights, the hosts of ill afoot". Promotion. Charles Whitby. 6994-0
Dark encounter. Ralph Cheyney. 6039-0
"Dark eyebrows swim like turtles" Robert Bly. 6803-0
"Dark fell the night, the watch was set". Alfred the harper. John Sterling. 6980-0
"Dark forests clothe the mountain-side". Ballad ("Dark forests"). Raffi. 6050-1
Dark garden. Leonora Speyer. 6232-6,6649-6
'The dark girl' by the 'holy well'. John Keegan. 6090-0, 6174-5
The dark glass, fr. The house of life. Dante Gabriel Rossetti. 6110-9,6199-0,6250-4
The dark glass. Dante Gabriel Rossetti. 6828-6
"The dark green summer, with its massive hues". Sonnet ("The dark green"). Hartley Coleridge. 6545-7
Dark hands. Nannie M. Travis. 6178-8
The dark heart. Pamela Travers. 6985-1
Dark heritage. Marcus B. Christian. 6178-8
The dark hills. Edwin Arlington Robinson. 6289-X,6619-4, 6161-3,6726-3,6345-4
Dark hotel. Alfred Dorn. 6218-0
Dark house in autumn. Conrad Pendleton. 6218-0
"Dark house, by which once more I stand", fr Memoriam. Alfred Lord Tennyson. 6536-8,6645-3
Dark house, by which once more I stand, fr. In memoriam. Alfred Lord Tennyson. 6867-7
The dark house. Francis Carey ("Jan van Avond") Slater. 6800-6
"Dark hurrying shapes beset my path that night". Night-shapes. W.R. Titterton. 6884-7
The dark inanimate. Eric Wilson Barker. 6648-8
"Dark is the mind's deep dwelling". Poetry and the subconscious. Martin Armstrong. 6776-X
"Dark is the night! How dark! No light,no fire". The gambler's wife. Reynell Coates. 6916-9
"Dark Ithaca rises from the waters". Song for Telemachus. Edward Ashcroft. 6782-4
Dark love. David Wadsworth Cannon Jr. 6178-8
The dark man. Lida Bell. 6906-1
The dark man. Nora Hopper. 6873-1
The dark memory. John Hall Wheelock. 6039-0,6071-4
The dark morning. Thomas Merton. 6108-7
The dark night, sels. May Sinclair. 6320-9
The dark palace. Alice Milligan. 6174-5
"The dark road journeys to the darkening sky". Reverie. Edwin Muir. 6777-8
The dark room. Richard Watson Gilder. 7041-8
The dark room. Edmund Wilson. 6042-0
Dark Rosaleen. ? Costello. 6244-X
Dark Rosaleen. James Clarence Mangan. 6844-8
Dark Rosaleen. James Clarence Mangan. 6090-0,6096-X,6174-5, 6732-8,6317-9,6292-X,6022-6,6560-0,6656-9,6250-4, 6172-9,6383-7,6102-8,6301-2
Dark Rosaleen. Hugh O'Donnell (atr) 7039-6
The dark side. Adelaide Anne Procter. 6957-6
"The dark sofst languages are being silenced". Cave series, sel. Margaret Atwood. 6767-0
Dark song. Edith Sitwell. 6210-5
The dark song. Shirley Brownrigg. 6850-2
"Dark voiced and deeply passioned". A question. Max Eastman. 6036-6
"Dark was de night an' cool was de groun'." Unknown. 6375-6
"Dark was the sky that Christmas eve". How the Christ-flower bloomed. Nora Archibald Smith. 6807-3
"Dark was the wintry sky above". The pilgrim's pot of clams. Thomas N. Stone. 6798-0
"Dark waters into crystalline brilliance...". Troopship, fr. In war time. Wilfred Wilson Gibson. 6884-7
The dark way. Joseph Mary Plunkett. 6872-3

"Dark were the skies, deep groaned the sea". Eggert
   Olafsson. Matthias Jochumsson. 6854-5
Dark wings. James Stephens. 6897-9
Dark winter is going. James Munro. 6180-X
Dark Yuggoth. Lin Carter. 6218-0
Dark, and the shells are falling. Unknown. 6589-9
"Dark, dark was the day when we looked...". Culloden.
   Andrew Lang. 6793-9
"Dark, dark, precious and volatile hour". Winter dawn in a
   country kitchen. Fannie Stearns Davis. 6761-1
Dark, dark, the seas and lands. Herbert Trench. 6877-4
"Dark, deep, and cold the current flows". The land which
   no one knows. Ebenezer Elliott. 6934-7
"Dark, eternal boulders soar proudly to the...". On the
   river Vardar. Vojislav Ilic. 6765-4
"Dark, languours, with heavy lidded eyes". New Orleans.
   Berton Braley. 6853-7
The dark, to be read to a child. Laura Spencer Portor.
   6039-0
The dark-eyed gentleman. Thomas Hardy. 6733-6
The dark-eyed sailor. Unknown. 6057-9
The dark-eyed sailor. Unknown. 6057-9
"Dark-eyed/O woman of my dreams". Dance figure. Ezra
   Pound. 6897-9,6959-2
The dark-jut stone. Marguerite A. Brewster. 6857-X
"Dark-shadowed dawn/Grey fingers in the east". Dawn.
   Kingsley Fairbridge. 6800-6
The dark. George (Mary Ann Cross) Eliot. 6656-9
The darkened mind. James Russell Lowell. 6333-0
Darkest Africa. Hollis Russell. 6397-7
Darkey fisherman's rainy day. Paul Laurence Dunbar. 6719-0
The darkling thrush. Thomas Hardy. 6073-0,6477-9,6536-8,
   6634-8,6657-7,6437,6507-4,6430-2,6666-6,6655-0,6250-
   4,6199 ,6328-5,6645-3,6723-9
"Darkly the cloud of night comes rolling on". Keene; or,
   lament of an Irish mother over her son. Felicia
   Dorothea Hemans. 6973-8
"Darkly their glibs o'erhang". The fate of King Dathi.
   Thomas Osborne Davis. 6930-4
"Darkly thou glidest onward". The subterranean stream.
   Felicia Dorothea Hemans. 6973-8
Darkness. George Gordon, 6th Baron Byron. 6102-8,6392-6,
   6110-9,6430-2,6199-0
Darkness. Robert Loveman. 6941-X
"Darkness and death? Nay, Pioneer, for thee". Walt
   Whitman. Francis Howard Williams. 6820-0
"Darkness and the boiler". The truth about the incident.
   Kyu-dong Kim. 6775-1
"The darkness and the dread and the despair". Protection.
   Wathen Mark Wilks Call. 7009-4
Darkness before dawn. Gelett Burgess. 6880-4
"The darkness brings no quiet here, the light". The
   railway station. Archibald Lampman. 7041-8
"Darkness fell on the mud village". In a Sudan village.
   Isabel Anderson. 6894-4
The darkness gathers. Hjalmar Soderberg. 6045-5
Darkness is thinning. Saint Gregory the Great. 6271-7,6302-
   0,6385-3
Darkness music. Muriel Rukeyser. 6391-8
The darkness of the Crucifixion. Felicia Dorothea Hemans.
   6973-8
"Darkness refuses the amnesia". Night crackles. Elizabeth
   Woody. 7005-1
"The darkness steals the forms of all...queens". Grief.
   David Herbert Lawrence. 6897-9
"The darkness throbbed that night with...heat". The
   assignation. Herbert Edwin Clarke. 7015-9
"Darkness, blind darkness every way". Light and darkness.
   Alice Cary. 6969-X
The darkness. Lionel Johnson. 6507-4
The darktown nine. Edward Wilbur Mason. 6118-4
Darley Dale. Clinton Scollard. 6441-8
Darley, George
   The call of the morning. 6930-4
   The call. 6219-9
   Chorus of spirits. 6930-4
   Chorus of spirits, fr. Sylvia. 6656-9
   Declivities of heaven, fr. Nepenthe. 6545-7
   Dirge. 6873-1
   Dreams of flying. 6648-8
   Eagles. 6943-6
   The enchanted lyre. 6317-9
   The enchanted spring. 6545-7
   Errors of ecstasoe, sel. 6930-4
   Ethelstan, sels. 6980-0
   Ethelstan: Runilda's chant, sels. 6258-X
   The fairies. 6980-0
   The fallen star. 6090-0,6102-8
   The flower of beauty. 6656-9
   The gambols of children. 6302-0,6385-3,6219-9
   Have you not oft, in the still wind. 6648-8
   The hoopoe. 6943-6
   I've been roaming. 6658-5
   "It is not beauty I demand". 6187-7,6046-3
   It is not beauty I demand, sels. 6545-7
   Last night. 6244-X
   Lay of the forlorn. 6930-4
   The loveliness of love. 6246-5
   The lure, fr. It is not beauty I demand. 6545-7
   May day. 6658-5
   The mermaidens' vesper hymn, fr. Syren songs. 6208-3,
      6258-X,6315-2,6334-9,6545-7
   Morning-song, fr. Sylvia. 6656-9
   Nepenthe. 6208-3
   Nepenthe, sels. 6246-5,6125-7
   Nephon's song, fr. Sylvia. 6656-9
   O blest unfabled incense tree. 6187-7,6244-X
   O'er the wild gannet's bath. 6125-7
   On the death of a recluse. 6244-X
   Osme's song. 6191-5
   Peasant song, fr. Sylvia. 6334-9,6490-6
   The peasant's chorus, fr. Sylvia, or the May queen.
      6191-5
   The peasants' chorus. 6191-5
   The phoenix, fr. Nepenthe. 6125-7,6315-2
   The phoenix. 6315-2,6545-7,6125-7
   Robin's cross. 6930-4
   Robin's cross. 6018-8
   Romanzo to Sylvia, fr. Sylvia. 6656-9
   Runilda's chant. 6930-4
   A rural retreat. 6980-0
   The sea ritual. 6930-4
   The sea-ritual, fr. Syren songs. 6090-0,6334-9
   Serenade. 6658-5
   Serenade of a loyal martyr. 6930-4
   Siren chorus. 6244-X
   Song ("Down"). 6930-4
   Song ("Sweet in her green dell"). 6186-9,6246-5,6317-9
   Song of the bluebells. 6334-9
   Song of the graces, fr. Sylvia. 6334-9,6490-6
   The song of the mermaids. 6125-7
   A song of the phoenix. 6153-2
   Song of the summer winds. 6302-0,6385-3,6219-9
   Song, fr. Ethelstan. 6980-0
   Suicide. 6980-0
   Summer winds. 6656-9
   Sunset, fr. Harvest home. 6545-7
   Sylvia's song. 6658-5
   Sylvia, or the May queen, sels. 6334-9,6656-9
   Sylvia, sels. 6301-2
   Syren songs, sels. 6334-9
   To my Egeria, sels. 6545-7
   To poets. 6545
   True loneliness. 6094-3
   The unicorn, fr. Nepenthe. 6125-7
   A village blacksmith. 6980-0
   Wherefore, unlaurelled boy. 6934-7
Darling. Unknown. 6312-8
The darling birds. Unknown. 6452-3
The darling of the year. Unknown. 6171-0
Darling old stick. Unknown. 6057-9
"'darling one!'- pleaded Pierre". Pierre. James Abraham
   Martling. 6952-5
Darling, Elsie L.
   Three wonderful things. 6713-1
Darling, Gertrude
   White birch. 6764-6
"Darling, I am growing old!". Ballade of a backslider.
   Edwin Meade Robinson. 6875-8
Darling, Margaret Stanion

DARLING

Country lane. 6218-0
Darling, Sheldon
Life's mystery. 6818-9
"Darling, while the tender moon". On the river. Phoebe Cary. 6865-0;6969-X
Darlington, Andrew
Occasionally Paul Eluard. 6998-3
Darlow, David John
Drought. 6800-6
Khama, sels. 6800-6
Darmesteter, Agnes. See Robinson, Agnes
Darnell, H.F.
The maple. 6433-7,6591-0,6592-9
Dart, Izella Willis
Our trees. 6342-X
"A darting dragon-fly - but lo!" Kikaku. 6850-2
Dartmoor. Felicia Dorothea Hemans. 6973-8
Dartmoor: sunset at Chagford: Homo loqvitvr. Thomas Edward Brown. 6809-X
Dartmoor: sunset at Chagford: Respondent dhmioyptoe. Thomas Edward Brown. 6809-X
Dartmouth's winter camps. Unknown. 7035-3
Dartside. Charles Kingsley. 6793-X
The **Darweesh..** Sadi [or Saadi] (Mushlih-ud-Din) 6448-5
Darwin. Mortimer Collins. 6385-3
Darwin. Eugene Myers. 6793-X
Darwin J. Flakoll (tr.)
Flowers from the volcano. Claribel Alegria, 7036-1
I'm a mirror. Claribel Alegria, 7036-1
Little cambric tamales. Claribel Alegria, 7036-1
Darwin, Erasmus
The botanic garden, sels. 6482-5
Destruciton of Sennacherib's army by a... 6848-0
Fuseli's 'Nightmare,' fr. The loves of the plants. 6545-7
Immortal nature. 6879-0
Immortal nature, fr. The economy of vegetation. 6932-0
Loves of the plants. 6240-7
Moses concealed on the Nile. 6848-0
Of good and evil, sels. 6482-5
The Papyrus, fr. The botanic garden. 6934-7
Song to May. 6219-9
Steel, fr. The botanic garden. 6934-7
Vegetable loves, fr. The loves of plaints. 6932-0
Darwinian ballad. Unknown. 6089-7
Darwinism. Agnes Mary F. ("Madame Duclaux") Robinson. 6656-9
Darwinism in the kitchen. Unknown. 6273-3
Darwinity. Herman Charles Merivale. 6089-7
Das ewig-weibliche. James Russell Lowell. 6641-0
Das kleine kind. George V. Hobet. 6249-0
Das licht des auges. Johann C. Friedrich von Schiller. 6621-6
Das Zahlenlied. Muriel F. Hochdorf. 6850-2
Dash away. John Martin. 6496-5
The **dash** for the colors. Frederick G. Webb. 6670-4
"A **dash** of yellow sand". Erie waters. Emily Pauline ("Tekahionwake") Johnson. 6837-5
"**Dashing** thro' the snow". Jingle bells. Unknown. 7035-3
Dashing through the snow. David MacClene. 6272-5
The **dashing** white sergeant. John Burgoyne. 6328-4
Daskam, Josephine Dodge
A Christmas hymn for children. 6608-9
Motherhood ("The night throbs on..."). 6097-8,6260-1
The prince. 6310-1,6102-8,6026-5,6076-5,6102-8,6310-1
Dat ol' mare o' mine. Paul Laurence Dunbar. 6510-4
Dat yaller gown. Charles H. Turner. 6139-7
Dat's my lil' boy. Unknown. 6721-2
Dat's right, ain't it? Ben King. 6274-1
Date oblym bellesario. Francis Hopkinson. 6753-0
Dates. Unknown (Arabic) 7039-6
Datta, Roby
Good and bad thoughts. 6591-0,6592-9
On Tibet. 6591-0,6592-9
Songs of Ind. 6591-0,6592-9
Datur hora quieti. Sir Walter Scott. 6246-6,6371-3
Daubeny, Charles
Verses on a cat. 6120-6
The **dauber** rounds Cape Horn. John Masefield. 6473-6,6107-9
Dauber, sels. John Masefield. 6506-6,6538-4,6726-3,6646-1

Daubler, Theodor
The arc-lamps. Babette Deutsch (tr.). 6160-5
Daudet, Alphonse
The French ensign, sels. 6695-X
Dauenhauer, Richard
Driving in a snowstorm, King Salmon to Naknek. 6855-3
Lukanin beach I. 6855-3
"Night flight, Fort Yukon-Fairbanks" 6855-3
Russian Easter, 1981 6855-3
Daughter. Kimiko Hahn. 6790-5
Daughter at arithmetic. Dorothy McFarlane. 6750-6
A **daughter** of Admetus. Thomas Sturge Moore. 6210-5
"The **daughter** of a Saxon king, to womanhood..". The ride of death. Eugene J. Hall. 6686-0,6167-2,6924-X
"**Daughter** of Egypt, veil thine eyes!". Song ("Daughter of Egypt"). Bayard Taylor. 6309-8
"The **daughter** of Ira". Requiescat. Frances Fletcher. 7030-2
"**Daughter** of Jove, relentless power". Hymn to adversity. Thomas Gray. 6975-4
"**Daughter** of Paeon, queen of every joy". Air, fr. The art of preserving health. John Armstrong. 6968-1
"**Daughter** of Psyche, pledge of that wild night". Prelude, fr. Music. Henry Van Dyke. 6961-4
The **daughter** of debate. Elizabeth I; Queen of England. 6436-1
A **daughter** of Eve. Christina Georgina Rossetti. 6655-0
The **daughter** of Herodias. Unknown. 6683-6
A **daughter** of Israel. Robert Burns Wilson. 6848-0
The **daughter** of Jairus Beatrice Redpath. 6115-X
Daughter of Pan. Nancy Telfair. 6841-1
Daughter of Philistia, fr. Olrig grange. Walter Chalmers Smith. 6656-9
"**Daughter** of th' Italian heaven!". Corinne at the capitol. Felicia Dorothea Hemans. 6973-8
"**Daughter** of the ancient Eve". The after woman. Francis Thompson. 6828-6
"The **daughter** of the Lesbian king". Pisidice. Andrew Lang. 6987-8
"**Daughter** of Zion, from the dust". The restoration of Israel. James Montgomery. 6848-0
The **daughter** of the desert. James Clarence Harvey. 6688-7
A **daughter** of the leech. Robert Browning. 6094-3
A **daughter** of the north. Gelett Burgess. 6875-8
The **daughter** of the regiment. Clinton Scollard. 6074-9
A **daughter** of the revolution. Unknown. 6274-1
The **daughter** of the snow. Madison Cawein. 7035-3
"The **daughter** sits in the parlor". The modern belle. Unknown. 6911-8
Daughter to mother. Walter De La Mare. 6905-3
"**Daughter** to that good earl, once president". Sonnet 010 ("Daughter to that good earl..."). John Milton. 6933-9
The **daughter's** rebellion. Francis Hopkinson. 6946-0
"**Daughter, daughter, marry no man**". The king's son. Richard Hovey. 7006-X
"**Daughter,** little daughter with the wide...". Experience. Helen Cowles Le Cron. 7038-8
"**Daughter,** thou art come to die". A very old song. William Laird. 6897-9
The **daughter.** Alice Cary. 6969-X
The **daughters** of Asopus. Corinna [pseud]. 6435-3
The **daughters** of Atlas. Aeschylus. 6435-3
"**Daughters** of Eve! your mother did not well".
Remonstrance. Jean Ingelow. 6980-0
"**Daughters** of Eve, draw near-I would behold..". To a black gin. J. Brunton Stephens. 6768-9
Daughters of Jephtha. Louis Untermeyer. 6036-6
Daughters of joy. Herbert Trench. 6877-4
The **daunce** of the daughters of delight. Edmund Spenser. 6959-2
The **daunce** of the shepheards. Edmund Spenser. 6959-2
Dauntless. Frank D. Swaney. 7001-9
Dauntless. Arthur Weir. 6681-X
"**Dauntless** as the pioneers/That pressed...". Hymn of progress. Byrdie L. Martin. 6799-9
Dauthendey, Max
August, fr. Love's calendar. Babette Deutsch (tr.). 6160-5
Deep in the nosegay. Babette Deutsch (tr.). 6160-5

Every leaf tends earthward. Babette Deutsch (tr.). 6160-5
July, fr. Love's calendar. Babette Deutsch (tr.). 6160-5
Love's calendar, sels. Babette Deutsch (tr.). 6160-5
March, fr. Love's calendar. Babette Deutsch (tr.). 6160-5
The moon is a fiery rose. Babette Deutsch (tr.). 6160-5
November, fr. Love's calendar. Babette Deutsch (tr.). 6160-5
The rain seems possessed. Babette Deutsch (tr.). 6160-5
"We walk by the sea." Babette Deutsch (tr.). 6160-5

Dave. James Logie ("Hugh Haliburton") Robertson. 6819-7
Dave (sc. Daphnis). James Logie ("Hugh Haliburton") Robertson. 6180-X
Dave Lilly. Joyce Kilmer. 6292-X, 6300-4
Davenant, Sir William
Aubade. 6186-9
Ballad, fr. The rivals. 6867-7
Character and love of Birtha, fr. Gondibert. 6867-7
Christians reply to the phylosopher. 6341-1
Conscience. 6867-7
Cursed jealousy. 6867-7
Epitaph. 6022-6
For the Lady Olivia Porter; a present upon a Newyears day. 6341-1
For the Lady Olivia Porter;a present upon New-years day. 6933-9
Gondibert: an heroick poem, sels. 6562-7, 6152-4, 6194-X
"The lark now leaves his watery nest". 6187-7, 6198-2, 6562-7, 6726-3
The law against lovers, sels. 6472-8
Life and death. 6933-9
Lover and philosopher. 6022-6
Morning. 6022-6
Morning song. 6250-4, 6301-2
News from Plymouth, sel. 6958-4
"O thou that sleep'st like pig in straw". 6187-7
On a soldier going to the wars. 6867-7
On the captivity of the Countess of Anglesey. 6867-7
The philosopher and the lover; to a mistress dying. 6317-9
The philosopher and the lover. 6208-3
Platonic lovers. 6867-7
Praise and prayer. 6198-2, 6250-4, 6122-2, 6198-2
"She ne'er saw courts, yet courts could have undone". 6934-7
Sir Francis Drake reviv'd. 6547-3
The soldier going to the field. 6092-7
The soldier going to the wars. 6830-8
Song ("Before"). 6562-7, 6341-1
Song ("O thou"). 6562-7
Song ("The lark now leaves his wintry nest"). 6933-9
Song ("The lark now leaves"). 6219-9, 6431-1
Stray selections. 6867-7
"This cursed jealousy, what is't?" 6317-9
To a mistress dying. 6472-8
"To Streets (The People's region...", fr. Gondibert... 6562-7
To the qveene, entertain'd at night... 6562-7, 6341-1
Wake, all the dead. 6830-8
"Weep no more for what is past", fr. The cruel brother. 6867-7

Davenport, Delle Bloss
Which shall I choose? 6818-9
Davenport, Henry
A lover without arms. 6702-6, 6505-8
Davenport, Robert
A requiem. 6189-3
Davenport, W.E.
The avatar. 7001-9
Davey, Norman
The sestina of the minor poet. 6875-8
David. John Stuart Blackie. 6848-0
David. Guy Butler. 6788-3
David. Edmund Vance Cooke. 6619-4, 6039-0
David. Mary Carolyn Davies. 6033-1, 6478-7
David. Charles and Mary Lamb. 6295-4
David. James Abraham Martling. 6952-5
David. Marian Storm. 6037-4

"**David** Cassidy picks me on the Dating Game". David Cassidy then. Dennis Cooper. 7003-5
David and Abigail. William Henry Venable. 6848-0
David and Bathshua. Charles William Cayzer. 6848-0
David and Goliah. Michael Drayton. 6848-0
David and Goliath. Hannah More. 6848-0
David and Goliath. Herbert Edward Palmer. 6625-9
David and Saul. George Crabbe. 6848-0
David Cassidy then. Dennis Cooper. 7003-5
David enamoured of Bethsabe. George Peele. 6848-0
David Garrick, fr. Retaliation. Oliver Goldsmith. 6250-4
David Gwyn. Sir Lewis Morris. 6290-3
David in heaven. Richard Lawson Gales. 6950-9
David in the cave of Adullam. Charles and Mary Lamb. 6295-4
The **David** jazz. Edwin Meade Robinson. 6102-8, 6076-5
David Livingstone. Unknown. 6337-3, 6625-9
David Shaw, hero. David Buckham. 7022-1
"**David** read Greek with me in college.- Black". David. James Abraham Martling. 6952-5
David today. Alexander Laing. 6979-7
David's epitaph on Jonathan. Francis Quarles. 6023-4
David's grief for his child. Nathaniel Parker Willis. 6848-0
David's journey after comforting Saul. Robert Browning. 7020-5
David's lament. Unknown. 6490-6
David's lament for Jonathan. Bible. 6084-6
David's lament over Absalom. Nathaniel Parker Willis. 6889-8
David's lament over Absalom. Nathaniel Parker Willis. 6294-6, 6425-6
David's lament, fr. Book of Samuel. Bible. 6125-7, 6143-5
David's poem. Ben Hiatt. 6792-1, 6998-3
David's song before Saul. Robert Browning. 6179-6
David's Thanksgiving. George Wither. 6848-0
David's three mighty ones. Henry Francis Lyte. 6848-0
David, aged four. Unknown. 6337-3
Davideis, sels. Abraham Cowley. 6562-7
Davidman, Joy
The dead partisan. 6561-9
Dirge for the suicides. 6561-9
Elegy for Garcia Lorca. 6561-9
For the Nazis. 6561-9
Jews of no man's land. 6761-1
New spiritual. 6561-9
Noel. 6764-6
Office windows. 6761-1
Spartacus 1938. 6561-9
Trojan women. 6561-9
Davidman, Joy (tr.)
Prayer (Lord, let"). Julian [or Juljan] Tuwim, 6068-4
Prayer for wilderness. Julian [or Juljan] Tuwim, 6068-4
Davidson, Alexander Mackenzie
Cortege. 6269-5
The fourth shepherd. 6269-5
The great lover. 6269-5
Mole ruit sua. 6269-5
Davidson, Donald
Afternoon call. 6326-8
Andrew Jackson, fr. The tall men. 7017-5
Avalon. 6326-8
Drums and brass. 6037-4
Ecclesiasticus. 6037-4, 6326-8
Epithalamion. 6619-4
Fire on Belmont Street, fr. The tall men. 7017-5
Jasper. 6039-0
John Darrow. 6037-4
John Sevier, fr. The tall men. 7017-5
Lee in the mountains. 7017-5
Lines for a tomb. 6072-2
The long street. 6808-1
An outland piper. 6326-8
Pavana. 6076-5, 6102-8
Pavane. 6076-5, 6102-8
Redivivus. 7017-5
Southward returning. 7017-5
Spoken at a castle gate. 6039-0
The tall men, sels. 7017-5
Utterance. 6619-4

DAVIDSON

The wolf. 6326-8
Davidson, Edward
Judas. 6393-4
Davidson, Gustav
Ambushed by angels. 6218-0
Downgoing. 6218-0
From nothing strange. 6218-0
The golden leopard. 6979-7
Imperatrix. 6619-4
Mortal hunger. 6979-7
Somewhere I chanced to read. 6619-4
Wailing Wall. 6761-1
Davidson, Harriet Miller
A song for the hot winds. 6273-3
Davidson, Irene Maryl
The little towns. 6265-2
Davidson, John
Annie Smith. 6383-7
Bacchus and Ariadne, fr. Scaramouch in Naxos. 6819-7
A ballad of a nun. 6102-8,6250-4,6301-2
A ballad of an artist's wife. 6274-1
A ballad of heaven. 6655-0,6507-4,6656-9,6371-3,6648-8,6102-8
A ballad of hell. 6518-X,6726-3,6153-2,6655-0
The battle of Bannockburn, fr. Bruce. 6819-7
Butterflies. 6301-2
The Chilterns. 6655-0
Christmas eve. 6608-9
A Cinque port. 6228-8,6477-9,6541-4,6639-9
Epping Forest. 6161-3
Fleet Street Eclogues. 6954-1
Fleet Street eclogues, sels. 6232-6,6301-2
For lovers, sels. 6819-7
Good counsel. 6793-X
Grub street, sels. 6819-7
Harvest home song. 6820-0
Harvest-home song. 6274-1,6056-9
Holiday at Hampton Court. 6102-8
In a music hall, sels. 6819-7
In Romney marsh. 6873-1
In Romney marsh. 6246-5,6258-X,6477-9,6501-5
Is love worth learning? 6819-7
The last journey, fr. The testament of John Davidson. 6845-6
The last journey. 7012-4
London. 6477-9,6656-9
Love at first sight, fr. Smith: a tragedy. 6819-7
Man as God. 6102-8
The man forbid. 6954-1
The merchantman. 6507-4
Midsummer day. 6785-9
Noon, fr. For lovers. 6819-7
A northern suburb. 6102-8
Piper, play. 6274-1,6656-9,6102-8
Poem 006. ("Some said"). 6274-1
A prescription for a spring morning. 6114-1
Proem. 6274-1
The Rev. Habakkuk McGruther of Cape Wrath, in 1879. 6819-7
Rondel. 6819-7
Roundeau ("My love, my wife..."), fr. Grub street. 6819-7
A runnable stag. 6079-X,6253-9
St. George's day, sels. 6102-8
St. George's Day, sels. 6954-1
Selene Eden, fr. In a music hall. 6819-7
Shakespeare's flower. 7020-5
Song ("The boat is chafing"). 6102-8,6252-0
Song of a train. 6334-9
Spring song. 6102-8
Summer. 6232-6
The testament of John Davidson, sels. 6301-2
Thirty bob a week. 6210-5,6659-3
To the new men. 6199-0,6371-3
Transformation song, fr. Scaramouch in Naxos. 6819-7
An unhistorical pastoral, sels. 6232-6
The vengeance of the duchess. 6655-0
Villanelle, fr. Grub street. 6819-7
Davidson, John Nelson
Boks of the Bible. 6274-1,6714-X

Our twenty-six Presidents in rhyme. 6274-1
Davidson, Lucretia Maria
The fear of madness. 6752-2
The song at twilight. 6752-2
To a star. 6752-2
Davidson, Margaret
The storm. 6385-3
Davidson, Robert
Elijah. 6848-0
Davidson, T.W.
Rules of descent in the United States. 6878-2
Davidson, Thomas
The auld ash tree. 6960-6
Love's last suit. 6960-6
Lullaby ("Hush thee, sweet baby"). 7022-1
On the Cheviots: a reverie at the end of summer. 6960-6
Davidson, Winifred
April afternoon, Point Loma (1769). 6039-0
Evening slippers. 6039-0
Juan Cabrillo. 6039-0
Mission beach. 6039-0
Old Spanish 'light'. 6039-0
Point Loma sonnets, sels. 6038-2
Davie Gellatley's song, fr. Waverley. Sir Walter Scott. 6518-X
Davie, G.S. (tr.)
The good wife. Sadi [or Saadi] (Mushlih-ud-Din), 6448-5
Davies of Hereford, John
The author loving these homely meats... 6182-6
"It is as true as strange, else trial feigns" 6182-6
"So shoots a star as doth my mistress glide" 6182-6
To our English Terence, Mr. Will. Shakespeare. 6483-3
Davies, Benjamin D.
Way down south on the old S'wannee. 6799-9
World peace hymn. 6799-9
Davies, Blodwen
Ministering. 6461-2
Davies, Charles
Portrait of several selves. 6360-8
There is a poem everywhere. 6360-8
Davies, Constance
The French polisher. 6360-8
New triads. 6360-8
Rhaiadr. 6360-8
Davies, Ernest E.
On Armistice Day. 6542-2
Davies, Helen Wolfe
My father. 6750-6
Davies, Idris
Come down. 6895-2
The Daily --. 6895-2
The day is come. 6895-2
"From Ammanford to Fleur-de-lys." 6360-8
'Gawlia deserta,' sels. 6360-8
Hywel and Blodwen. 6360-8
In Cheltenham. 6895-2
Interlude. 6360-8
The lay preacher ponders. 6210-5
Marx and Heine and Dowlais. 6895-2
Renaissance. 6360-8
Sonnet ("I tossed"). 6360-8
Summer holiday. 6895-2
William Morris. 6360-8
The year of victory. 6895-2
Davies, John
Buttered pippin-pies. 6125-7
Davies, Julia Johnson
De gospel train. 6778-6
Davies, Leland
The mandrake. 6076-5,6102-8
Davies, Lin
The bugler. 6542-2
Davies, Mary Carolyn
Aeroplane factory. 7038-8
After all and after all. 6031-5
Armistice Day. 6051-X
Be different to trees. 6232-6,6184-2
The blood-stained cross. 6032-3
By an iris-shadowed pool. 6619-4
California. 6241-5

California poppies. 6241-5
A casualty list. 6032-3
Cloistered. 6300-4
Comrades of the trail. 6374-8
Dance. 6959-2
The dancer. 6959-2
David. 6033-1,6478-7
The day before April. 6556-2,6250-4,6300-4
The dead make rules. 6250-4
Door-mats. 6076-5,6250-4,6736-0
The door. 6501-5
The dream-bearer. 6102-8,6250-4
Even Eve 'n' Adam. 6750-6
Feet. 6031-5
For poets. 6880-4
A girl's songs. 6031-5,6556-2
The gown. 6250-4
The gymnastic clock. 6638-0
Heaven. 6750-6
Honeymoon. 6441-8
Hunger. 6979-7
Leading. 6461-2
Let me be a giver. 6461-2
Let's have a picnic out-of-doors. 6466-3
Lindbergh. 7019-1
Love song. 6019-6
Men are the devil. 6736-0
Of roses. 6441-8
On a windy night..., fr. Tree songs. 6184-2
On becoming a book. 6979-7
Out of the earth. 6232-6
The peak. 6476-0,6490-6
A prayer for every day. 6750-6
Red yews, fr. Tree songs. 6184-2
Reminiscences. 6250-4
The rulers. 6954-1
Rust. 6102-8,6250-4
The Saturdays' party in fairyland. 6638-0
Sea-gull. 6073-0
Sea-gull song. 6607-0
Smith, of the third Oregon, dies. 6556-2
Song ("Because I love"). 6619-4
Song ("We cannot die"). 6619-4
Songs of a girl. 6897-9
Spring sows her seeds: nineteen eighteen. 6032-3,6393-4
The terrible dead. 6324-1
They who laugh. 7038-8
To an outgoing tenant. 6880-4
To other Marys. 6034-X
Traps. 6032-3
Tree songs, sels. 6184-2
Tree-taught, fr. Tree songs. 6184-2
We two and marriage. 7038-8
What the Christmas tree thinks. 6466-3
Youth builds. 6143-5

Davies, Rhys
Louvre. 6360-8
Seine. 6360-8

Davies, Sir John
An acclamation. 6584-8
Acrostic ("Earth"). 6724-7
Affliction. 6436-1
The answer to the objection. 6584-8
Apprehension: fantasy: memory. 6584-8
Contention between four maids... 6584-8
A contention betwixt a wife, a widow, and a maid. 6436-1,6584-8
The dance of love. 6182-6
Dancing. 6959-2
Dancing of the air. 6959-2
The dancing sea, fr. Orchestra. 6125-7
Dedications, sels. 6584-8
Drawn from the desire of knowledge. 6584-8
Drawn from the motion of the soul. 6584-8
Erroneous opinions of the creation of souls. 6584-8
Feeling. 6584-8
The folly of knowledge, fr. The immortality of the soul. 6934-7
From contempt of death in the better sort of spirits. 6584-8
From the fear of death in the wicked souls. 6584-8
From the general desire of immortality. 6584-8
From the very doubt and disputation of immortality. 6584-8
The general consent of all. 6584-8
A gulling sonnet. 6182-6
Hearing. 6584-8
How the soul doth exercise her powers in the body. 6584-8
I know myself a man, fr. Nosce teipsum. 6125-7
In what manner the soul is united to the body. 6584-8
The intellectual memory. 6584-8
The intellectual powers of the soul. 6584-8
Knowledge and reason. 6436-1
Man [or I knew myself a man]. 6182-6,6108-2,6737-9
The mariner's song. 6436-1
Much knowledge, little reason, fr. Nosce teipsum. 6125-7
The muse reviving. 6584-8
Nosce teipsum. 6369-1,6584-8
Nosce teipsum!, sels. 6198-2,6194-X
"O Light!...," fr. Nosce teipsum!. 6198-2
Objection: that the soul is ex traduce. 6584-8
Objections against the immortality of the soul. 6584-8
Of Homer's Odyssey. 6187-7
Of human knowledge. 6584-8
Of the soul of man and the immortality thereof. 6584-8
On a pair of garters. 6187-7,6584-8
Orchestra. 6258-X,6436-1,6584-8
Orchestra, a poem of dancing, sels. 6317-9,6208-3
The passions of sense. 6584-8
The power of sense. 6584-8
Reasons drawn from divinity. 6584-8
Reasons drawn from nature. 6584-8
The sea danceth. 6833-2
Sight. 6584-8
Smelling. 6584-8
Sonnet ("If you would"). 6584-8
Sonnet ("Oft did I hear"). 6584-8
Sonnet ("Once did my Philomel"). 6584-8
Sonnet ("Sickness"). 6584-8
Sonnets to Philomel. 6584-8
The soul and the body. 6436-1
The soul compared to a river. 6584-8
The soul. 6600-3
Taste. 6584-8
That it cannot be a body. 6584-8
That the soul cannot be destroyed. 6584-8
That the soul is a spirit. 6584-8
That the soul is a thing subsisting itself... 6584-8
That the soul is created immediately by God. 6584-8
That the soul is immortal, and cannot die. 6584-8
That the soul is more than a perfection or reflection.. 6584-8
That the soul springs from the blend of..body's humours. 6584-8
Three kinds of life answerable to...soul. 6584-8
To his lady. 6584-8
To his very friend, Master Richard Martin. 6584-8
To my most gracious dread sovereign. 6584-8
To Queen Elizabeth. 6436-1
To the prince. 6584-8
To the right noble..Prince Henry,Earl of Northumberland. 6584-8
To the rose. 6436-1,6189-3
To the spring. 6182-6
The vegetative or quickening power. 6584-8
What the soul is. 6584-8
Which is a proud, and yet a wretched thing. 6726-3
Why the soul is united to the body. 6584-8

Davies, Trefor
Song of an old sailor. 6258-X

Davies, William Henry
Advice. 6334-9
Ale. 6501-5
All nature danceth. 6935-5
April's charms. 6253-9
April's lambs. 6884-7
The bell. 6491-4
The best frend. 6607-0

Bird and brook. 6884-7
The bird of paradise. 6234-2
The birds of steel. 7029-9
Born of tears. 6246-5
The child and the mariner. 6234-2,6478-7,6458-2,6508-2
A child's pet. 6476-0,6510-4
Come, come, my love. 6320-9
Crowns. 6072-2
Day's black star. 6943-6
Days that have been. 6477-9,6528-7
Days too short, fr. Songs of joy. 6234-2,6253-9,6393-4
A dream of winter. 6253-9
Dreams of the sea. 6258-X
Early morn. 6477-9
Early spring. 6250-4
The elements. 6508-2
The example. 6134-6,6232-6,6726-3,6250-4,6508-2,6102-8
Fancy's home. 6508-2
A fleeting passion. 6234-2
The force of love. 6884-7
Forgiveness. 6861-8
A great time. 6234-2,6339-X,6726-3,6250-4,6102-8
A greeting. 6266-0,6102-8,6506-6
Happy wind. 6374-8,6466-3,6250-4
The hawk ("Thou dost not fly..."). 6073-0,6234-2
The heap of rags, fr. Songs of joy. 6234-2
In May, fr. Songs of joy. 6234-2,6253-9
In spring-time. 6374-8
In the country. 6102-8
Joy. 6508-2
The kingfisher. 6073-0,6044-7,66234-2,6246-5,6395-0, 6253-9,6250-4
Leisure. 6464-7, 6508-2,6427-1,6477-9,6501-5,6726-3, 6102-8,6250-4,6668-2,6371-3,6421-3,6639-9
The likeness. 6339-X
"Little flower, I hold you here" 7020-5
Love lights the fire. 6781-6
Love's plans. 6779-4
A lovely woman. 6210-5
The mind's liberty. 6234-2
The moon. 6234-2,6023-4,6253-9,6250-4,6668-2
"My love could walk in richer hues." 6317-9
My youth. 6266-0
Nature's friend. 6510-4,6161-3,6102-8,6393-4,6510-4, 6232-6,6465-5,6476-0,6509-0,6607-0
No master. 6508-2
No place or time. 6782-4
Old autumn. 6780-8
On what sweet banks. 6184-2
One poet visits another. 6210-5
Our Sussex Downs. 6776-X
Passion's hounds. 6884-7
The poet. 6778-6
The rabbit. 6861-8
The rabbit. 6421-3
Rain. 6338-1,6466-3,6371-3,6393-4
The rainbow. 6777-8
Raptures. 6668-2
Re-union. 6778-6
Rogues. 6070-6
Sadness and joy. 6134-6,6501-5
The sailor to his parrot. 6833-2
The sea ("Her cheeks were white..."). 6258-X
See where young love. 6777-8
Self-ignorance. 6935-5
Sheep. 6659-3,6102-8,6044-7,6290-3,6528-7,6538-4,6510-4
The sleepers. 6506-6,6102-8,6464-7,6508-2
Songs of joy. 6501-5
Songs of joy, sels. 6234-2
Space. 6072-2
Sweet stay-at-home. 6234-2,6320-9,6250-4,6320-9,6508-2
A thought. 6844-8
A thought. 6250-4
Thunderstorms. 6625-9,6250-4
Time's justice. 7014-0
To sparrows fighting. 6659-3
The truth. 6210-5
The two children. 6250-4
The two flocks. 6723-9
Venus. 6778-6

The villain. 6726-3,6581-3,6491-4
Wasted hours. 6581-3
The ways of time. 6338-1
When on a summer's morn. 6234-2
The white cascade. 6253-9

Davin, Nicholas Flood
Illusion. 6433-7
A prairie year, fr. Eos: a prairie dream. 6795-6

Davis, Addie F.
A sermon in flowers. 6927-4

Davis, Alfred J.
John Lind. 6342-X

Davis, Allen
Song ("The water-thrushes play.") 6039-0

Davis, Ben Wood
After the opera. 6927-4
After the waltz. 6928-2
Barcarolle. 6927-4
Childless. 6918-5
Columbus. 6925-8
Decoration ode. 6927-4
The schoolmaster's sleep. 6408-6

Davis, Bertha Gerneaux
My dolls. 6417-5

Davis, Charles S.
Washington's birthday. 6394-2

Davis, Dorothy
Dream. 6750-6
Mother love. 6750-6

Davis, Dorothy Marie
Old women trees. 6750-6

Davis, Edith Ella
Inscription for a prayer book. 6214-8
Nobility. 6214-8
Summons. 6214-8

Davis, Edna Ethel
Lore. 6144-3

Davis, Edward P.
"Good night, beloved, in the west". 6983-5
The mountains. 6983-5

Davis, Edward Parker
Woodrow Wilson. 7001-9

Davis, Emily
A song of winter. 6528-7

Davis, Esther Eugenia
Language of music. 6799-9

Davis, Ethel Mary
Our poets. 6342-X

Davis, Eugene
The vesper bell. 6674-7

Davis, F.T.
A sailor's yarn. 6681-X

Davis, Fannie Stearns
Afternoon. 6607-0,6476-0
Ancient beautiful things. 6556-2,6688-7,6019-6,6102-8, 6026-5
As in a picture-book. 6619-4
Celestial Rhymes. 7038-8
The circus. 6466-3
Comrades. 6019-6,6327-6
Day. 6266-0,6478-7
Evening song. 6653-4
For a child. 6891-X
Gipsy feet. 6374-8
Good-bye! 6076-5
Hill-fantasy. 6887-1
Hill-fantasy. 6762-X
Home. 6266-0
'I sing no more'. 6607-0
The lost dream. 7038-8
Love has shining eyes. 6320-9
The moods. 6762-X
Moon folly. 6393-4,6497-3
The narrow doors. 6556-2
An old song. 6019-6
Profits. 6007-2
Profits. 6897-9
The pupil returns to his master. 6619-4,6467-1
A sea spell. 6653-4
The song-sparrow. 6887-1

Souls. 6310-1,6509-0
The turn of the road. 6184-2
Uncle Frazar. 6538-4
Up a hill and a hill. 6338-1,6393-4,6653-4,6374-8
Wait for me. 7038-8
Water fantasy. 6310-1
Winter dawn in a country kitchen. 6761-1
You shall not wear velvet. 6538-4,6421-3
Davis, Florence Boyce
The legend of the Christmas rose. 6449-3
An old orchard in winter. 7030-2
Davis, Francis
The fishermsn's song. 6219-9
Kathleen ban adair. 6409-4
Nanny. 6858-8
Davis, Frank Marshall
Miss Samantha Wilson. 6178-8
Peace is a fragile cup. 6178-8
Davis, H.L.
Dog-fennel. 6037-4
A hill come out of the sea. 6071-4
Davis, Harold Lenoir
Proud riders. 6020-X
Davis, Helen Bayley
Jack Frost. 6891-X
Davis, Hope Harding
Our knight. 7019-1
Davis, J.
The sun. 6902-9
Davis, John Francis (tr.)
"The affairs of the world are all hurry and trouble..." Unknown (Chinese), 6545-7
"By the side of the Hoongtide bridge..." Unknown (Chinese), 6545-7
"I throw on my clothes, and wait for the moon." Unknown (Chinese), 6545-7
"The .last month of the winter was the for the most part..." Unknown (Chinese), 6545-7
"See how the gently falling rain." Unknown (Chinese), 6545-7
"Their slender shadows fill the enclosure..." Unknown (Chinese), 6545-7
"To the front of yon old peaked hill..." Unknown (Chinese), 6545-7
Davis, Julia Johnson
Ballad of Jack Jouett. 6042-0
Dark Ellen. 6072-2
De gospel train. 6039-0
Ef I needs de money. 6761-1
John. 6979-7
Loss. 6037-4
My books. 6036-6
She sews fine linen. 6037-4
To an ass. 6979-7
Davis, Kate A.
The tale of the titles told. 6928-2
Davis, Leland
The ballad of Adam's first. 6037-4
A ballad of jealousy. 6880-4
A ghetto catch. 6037-4
Davis, Mary T.
A message of the ocean. 6764-6
Davis, Mary [or Mollie] Evelyn Moore
The blind beggar. 7021-3
Counsel. 6632-1
Lee at the wilderness. 6074-9
Davis, Milton Ben (tr.)
The art of poetry. Vicente Huidobro, 6759-X
Dead poets. Enrique Pena Barrenechea, 6759-X
Elegy for Becquer. Enrique Pena Barrenechea, 6759-X
The game. Conrado Nale Roxlo, 6759-X
Las Sierpes Street. Oliverio Girondo, 6759-X
Nocturne. Conrado Nale Roxlo, 6759-X
The unforeseen. Conrado Nale Roxlo, 6759-X
Davis, Noah
Jesse Seligman. 6848-0
Davis, Ozora S.
Our opportunity, today. 6461-2
Davis, Robert
Fertility rite. 6855-3
Fragment of a legend. 6855-3
Game. 6855-3
The man who loved knots. 6855-3
Taking the night trail. 6855-3
Davis, Robert H.
"He came from out the void" 6995-9
Roosevelt. 6449-3
Davis, Robert Meacham
Mabel's way. 6118-4
Davis, Roy
Retrospect. 6722-0
Thoughts. 6722-0
Davis, Samuel
The lines around Petersburg. 6074-9
Davis, Sarah F.
"In the marsh...", sels. 6601-1
Davis, Slack
The holiday. 6530-9
Davis, Thomas Osborne
Annie, dear. 6858-8
The banks of the Lee. 6302-0;6385-3
The battle eve of the brigade. 6930-4
Battle of Fontenoy. 6404-3,6630-5
The battle-eve of the brigade. 6046-3
Boatman of Kinsale. 6656-9
Celts and Saxons. 6714-X
Clare's dragoons. 6930-4
The fate of King Dathi. 6930-4
The flower of finae. 6302-0;6385-3
Fontenoy. 6344-6, 6219-9
The Geraldines. 6858-8
The girl I left behind me. 6930-4
The green above the red. 7009-4
The Irish hurrah. 6930-4
Lament for the death of Eoghan Ruadh (Owen Roe) O'Neil. 6858-8
Lament for the death of Eoghan Ruadh O'Neill. 6244-X
Lament for the Milesians. 6858-8
Love's longings. 6858-8
Maire Bhan Astor. 6302-0;6385-3
My grave. 6930-4
My land. 6858-8
My land. 6135-4
My land. 6858-8
A nation once again. 7009-4
Native swords. 6858-8,7009-4,6858-8,7009-4
Our own again. 6858-8
The sack of Baltimore. 6302-0,6385-3,6656-9
A song for the Irish militia. 7009-4
Song of the volunteers of 1782. 6858-8
Tone's grave. 6930-4
The welcome. 6014-5,6302-0,6385-3,6219-9,6409-4,6656-9
The west's asleep. 6930-4
Davis, William Virgil
Mine disaster. 6803-0
Davis, Winifred
Nellie's decorations. 6684-4
Davison, Edward
Any boy to his first love. 6779-4
The enchanted heart. 6777-8
The enchanted heart. 6102-8
The girl remembers her dead lover. 6072-2
The lovers. 6317-9
The snare. 6232-6,6102-8
Sonnet ("Now that the moonlight"). 6250-4
Sonnet ("O thou"). 6250-4
Sonnet to N. in sickness. 6761-1
The undying heart. 6320-9
Davison, Francis
"Ah Cupid, I mistook thee". 6187-7
"Are lovers full of fire". 6187-7
Are women fair? 6089-7
Bought. 6379-0
Epitaph ("Lovely"). 6436-1
Epitaph ("Thou alive"). 6436-1
Epitaph ("Wit's"). 6436-1
Her commendation. 6436-1
His farewell to his unkind and unconstant mistress. 6182-6,6436-1
"In health and ease am I". 6187-

"Like to the seely fly". 6187-7
"Love, if a god thou art". 6187-7
Madrigal ("Some there are fair to see to") 6182-6
Madrigal ("The sound of thy sweet name...") 6182-6
My only star. 6182-6
Song ("Lady"). 6182-6
"Sorrow seldom killeth any". 6187-7
To Cupid. 6436-1
Davison, Francis (tr.)
Psalm 013. Bible, 6271-7
Davison, Heloise
Absence. 6847-2
Vale. 6847-2
Where? 6847-2
Davison, W.
A dialogue between him and his heart. 6935-5
Davison, Walter
At her fair hands. 6182-5,6436-1,6726-3,6317-9
To his lady, who had vowed virginity. 6436-1
"Davus, I detest/Orient display". 'Persicos odi' Austin Dobson. 6875-8
Davy and Goliar. William Edward Penney. 6923-1
Davy the teamster. Estelle Thomson. 6409-4
'Davy'. Louise Imogen Guiney. 7008-6
Davy, Sir Humphry
The eagles. 6980-0
The fire-flies. 6980-0
Fontainbleu. 6980-0
A fragment. 6980-0
Life. 6980-0
Mont Blanc. 6980-0
On the death of Lord Byron. 6980-0
The sybil's temple. 6980-0
The tempest. 6219-9
Thought. 6980-0
Written after recovery from a dangerous illness. 6600-3
"Davy, her knight, her dear, was dead". 'Davy' Louise Imogen Guiney. 7008-6
"The daw/The rook and magpie to the grey...". Summer, fr. The seasons. James Thomson. 6958-4
Dawendine. Emily Pauline ("Tekahionwake") Johnson. 6837-5
Dawes, Robert G.
Transportation corps march. 6237-7
Dawes, Rufus
The buried love. 6752-2
Dawless, Smith
Conversation piece. 6527-9
Dawn. Richard Aldington. 6393-4
Dawn. George Lawrence Andrews. 6037-4
Dawn. Gordon Bottomley. 6897-9
Dawn. Ilse Brem. 6769-7
Dawn. Struthers Burt. 6253-9
Dawn. Isabel Butchart. 6653-4
Dawn. Geoffrey Chaucer. 6153-2
Dawn. Helena Coleman. 6591-0,6592-2
Dawn. Frances Cornford. 6019-6
Dawn. Miriam LeFevre Crouse. 6144-3
Dawn. Louis Dudek. 6446-9
Dawn. Kingsley Fairbridge. 6800-6
Dawn. John Ford. 6533-3
Dawn. Richard Watson Gilder. 6240-7,6600-3,6385-3,6597-X
Dawn. Daniel Henderson. 6386-1,6420-5,6542-2
Dawn. Ibn Billita. 6362-4
Dawn. Ibn Muqana. 6362-4
Dawn. Francis Ledwidge. 6812-X
Dawn. P.S. M. 6332-2
Dawn. P.S. M. 7031-0
Dawn. James McCarroll. 6433-7
Dawn. Roselle Mercier Montgomery. 6326-8
Dawn. George William ("A.E.") Russell. 6253-9
Dawn. Martin Schutze. 6320-9
Dawn. Frederick George Scott. 6021-8,6337-3,6433-7,6115-X, 6648-8
Dawn. William Shakespeare. 6438-8
Dawn. Tanikado. 6027-7
Dawn. Woodson Tyree. 6397-7
Dawn. Unknown. 6959-2
Dawn. Unknown. 6436-1
Dawn. Nathaniel Parker Willis. 6752-2
Dawn after Christmas. Elias Lieberman. 6954-1

"Dawn after dawn as I look up to the woods". Winter cordwood. Raymond Fuller Fuller. 6761-1
Dawn and a woman. John Logan. 6803-0
Dawn and dark. Norman Gale. 6102-8
Dawn and dusk. Frank Dempster Sherman. 7041-8
Dawn at Beaumont Hamel. Rosamund Marriott ("Graham R. Tomson") Watson. 6650-X
Dawn at Kinloch. Louis B. Wehle. 6253-9
Dawn at Lexington. Katharine Lee Bates. 6039-0
Dawn at Liverpool. Archibald T. Strong. 6784-0
Dawn at Venice. Martha Gilbert Dickinson. 6624-0
Dawn broke today. Amory Hare. 6347-0
"The dawn came out of the navel of night". The coming of the sons of god. Herman Fetzer. 7007-8
"Dawn came suddenly on wings!". Morning vow. Jane Dunning Rounds. 6799-9
"Dawn cross-hatches the sheets with cancer". Occasionally Paul Eluard. Andrew Darlington. 6998-3
"The dawn has left a rosy light". The early morning ride. Dorothea Gilroy. 7010-8
Dawn in an Alexandria garden. Lucy Leone Marsch. 6342-X
Dawn in Argua. Lloyd Mifflin. 6631-3
Dawn in besieged Leningrad. Vera Inber. 6546-5
Dawn in Inishtrahull. Daniel James O'Sullivan. 6930-4
Dawn in London. Nikolai Ushakov. 6546-5
Dawn in my garden. Marguerite Wilkinson. 6232-6,6338-1
Dawn in the desert. Clinton Scollard. 6266-0,6476-0
Dawn in the Everglades. Halle W. Warlow. 6073-0
"The dawn is a pale, cold nun". Moods. Nellie Burget Miller. 6836-7
"The dawn is ever lovelier that the day". Infancy. Edith Colby Banfield. 6836-7
"The dawn is overcast, the morning lowers". Ode to St. Swithin. Thomas Hood. 6974-6
"The dawn is smiling on the dew that covers". The genesis of butterflies. Victor Hugo. 6771-9,7039-6
"Dawn of a pleasant morning in May". Lee to the rear. John Reuben Thompson. 7017-5
Dawn of day. William Browne. 6182-6
The dawn of freedom. Alfred Lord Tennyson. 6793-X
The dawn of love. James I; King of Scotland. 6180-X
"The dawn of new ages is breaking". The banner that welcomes the world. Hezekiah Butterworth. 6451-5, 6926-6
"The dawn of peace is breaking! breaking!". The dawn of the centennial. Sarah Louise Oberholtzer. 6912-6
The dawn of peace. Alfred Noyes. 6337-3;6473-6;6532-5
The dawn of peace. Alice Cary. 6969-X
The dawn of the centennial. Sarah Louise Oberholtzer. 6912-6
"The dawn of the everlasting day". Prayer ("The dawn"), fr. The image in the sand. Edward Frederick Benson. 6501-5
"Dawn off the foreland -the young flood making". The mine-sweepers. Rudyard Kipling. 7026-4
Dawn on Chateaugay. Constance Deming Lewis. 6841-3
Dawn on mid-ocean. John Hall Wheelock. 6331-4,6631-3
Dawn on the Alps. Percy Bysshe Shelley. 6252-0
Dawn on the east coast. Alun Lewis. 6209-1
Dawn on the Irish coast. John Locke. 6671-2
Dawn on the night-journey. Dante Gabriel Rossetti. 6380-2
"The dawn passed long ago, the milkman too". Boy waking. Roberta Holloway. 6808-1
The dawn patrol. Paul Bewsher. 7026-4
"Dawn peered through the pines as we dashed...". Riding with Kilpatrick. Clinton Scollard. 6946-0
"Dawn shudders white again, and homeward...". Reprieve. Eden Phillpotts. 7014-0
Dawn song. Ibn Sa'id (of Alcala La Real) 6362-4
Dawn song. Linwood Daggette Smith Jr. 7024-8
"Dawn the sun steadily now". The one who is within. Nia Francisco. 7005-1
"Dawn turned on her purple pillow". A December day, fr. Berkshire notes. Sara Teasdale. 6778-6
Dawn unfolds. Velimir Rajic. 6765-4
"The dawn was apple-green". Green. David Herbert Lawrence. 6897-9
The dawn wind. Rudyard Kipling. 6476-0,6607-0
Dawn winds. Vera Nicolson. 6253-9
"Dawn! and over the peaks, over the...wall". The vigil of

Padre Junipero. Hermann Hagedorn. 6944-4
Dawn, L.M.
    The funeral dirge. 6524-4
"**Dawn**, and at length the land". The new continent. Robert Haven Schauffler. 6847-2
Dawn, fr. A song of the south. Joaquin Miller. 6753-0
Dawn, fr. Ion. Euripides. 6435-3
Dawn, fr. My beautiful lady. Thomas Woolner. 6934-7
Dawn, noon and dewfall. James Whitcomb Riley. 6993-2
Dawn-angels. Agnes Mary F. ("Madame Duclaux") Robinson. 6656-9
"**Dawn-early** though it was,they found much work". Snow moment. Estelle Rooks. 6850-2
The **dawn**.. Lady Jane F. ("Speranza") Wilde. 6174-5
The **dawn**. Robert Loveman. 6941-X
Dawning. Gulielma Day Orr. 6906-1
The **dawning** o' the year. Mary Elizabeth Blake. 6309-8
The **dawning** of the day. Unknown. 6057-9
The **dawning** of the day. Unknown. 6930-4
The **dawning** of the day. Unknown. 6635-6
The **dawning**. Henry Vaughan. 6931-1
"The **dawns** have brought a distinct...". Dawn. Unknown. 6959-2
Dawson's woman. W. Miller. 6697-6
Dawson, A.M.P.
    Twinkle, twinkle, little star! 6804-9
Dawson, Arthur
    Bumbers, Squire Jones. 6858-8
Dawson, Daniel L.
    The seeker in the marshes. 7041-8
Dawson, Emma Frances
    Old glory. 6241-5
Dawson, Eric P.
    When the war's at an end. 6542-2
Dawson, Grace Strickler
    Casually this cup. 6042-0
    This day. 6779-4
Dawson, James
    By the Alma. 6577-5
    The frames of space. 6640-2
    Leaves on the Capitol grass. 6640-2
    Memorial sonnet. 6640-2
    Metaphysical verses. 6640-2
    Michael, lying awake to think his thoughts. 6640-2
Dawson, Lois
    Wonder. 6850-2
Dawson, Lulu Brunt
    Douleur. 6750-6
Dawson, M. Phelps
    After the Fourth of July. 6580-5,6820-0
Dawson, Miles M.
    Nobleman. 6076-5,6102-8
    The thistle. 6338-1
Dawson, William James
    The angel at the ford. 6656-9
    Bird's song at morning. 6656-9
    A child's protrait. 6656-9
    Ideal memory. 6656-9
    To a desolate friend. 6656-9
Dawtrey, Hannah J.
    For vanity. 6510-4
Day. Owen Barfield. 6777-8
Day. Robert Browning. 6625-9
Day. Fannie Stearns Davis. 6266-0,6478-7
Day. William McLennan. 6433-7
Day. Arthur L. Phelps. 6433-7
Day Lewis, Cecil
    The album. 6208-3
    All gone. 6209-1
    "As one who wanders into old workings." 6209-1
    The assertion. 6391-8
    Bombers. 6491-4
    Children look down upon the morning-gray. 6491-4
    The Christmas tree. 6246-5
    The conflict. 6209-1
    Consider these, for we have condemned them. 6375-6
    Dedicatory stanzas. 6390-X
    Departure in the dark. 6391-8
    The ecstatic. 6625-9
    The flight, sels. 6209-1

From feathers to iron. 6150-8
A hard frost. 6257-1
Hornpipe. 6491-4
In the heart of contemplation. 6209-1
In these our winter days. 6625-9
Is it far to go? 6246-5
"It is the true star" 6072-2
"Live you by love confined." 6317-9,6354-3
The magnetic mountain (21). 6985-1
The magnetic mountain (24). 6985-1
The magnetic mountain (3). 6985-1
The magnetic mountain, sels. 6258-X,6532-5
Maple and sumach. 6209-1
Moving in. 6536-8
The Nabara. 6257-1
Nearing again the legendary isle. 6357-8,6210-5
Newsreel. 6052-8
Now she is like the white tree-rose. 6210-5
Now to be with you, elate, unshared. 6491-4
One and one. 6391-8
Poem ("A forward child..."). 6783-2
Reconciliation. 6391-8
"."Rest from loving and be living. 6536-8
Sing we the two lieutenants. 6625-9
The sitting. 6209-1
Tempt me no more. 6375-6
A time to dance, sels. 6879-0
A time to dance. 6209-1,6354-3
War poem. 6390-X
Word over all. 6391-8
"You that love England." 6209-1
"**Day** after day after day". The prison guard. J.J. Maloney. 6870-7
"**Day** after day I have come and sat". The dead boy's portrait and his dog. Gerald Massey. 7008-6
"**Day** after day it raged:". The storm in the valley. Sylvester Baxter. 6798-0
"**Day** after day no gun had spoken". Alfred Gordon. 6796-4
"**Day** after day the treeless street was baked". August. Muna Lee. 6038-2
"**Day** after day they caught rain in the...". Two animals, one flood. Diane Glancy. 7005-1
"**Day** after day, beside a drying brook". The faith that waits. John R. Webb. 6818-9
"**Day** after day/I while away". Looking for a happy smile. Jesse Sill. 6799-9
The **day** after tomorrow. Margarethe Herzele. 6769-7
The **day** after Trinity. Richard Oyama. 6790-5
A **day** after. Bedros Tourian. 6050-1
Day and dark. George Cabot Lodge. 6754-9
Day and night. Thomas Campion. 6189-3
Day and night. Helena Coleman. 6115-X
Day and night. Victor Daley. 6784-0
Day and night. William ("Fiona Macleod") Sharp. 6253-9
Day and night. Henry Van Dyke. 6961-4
Day and night. Peter Paul Wiplinger. 6769-7
Day and night songs. William Allingham. 6656-9
Day and night up-country. Lance Fallaw. 6800-6
The **day** and the work. Edwin Markham. 6449-3
A **day** as a wage. Keene Wallis. 6880-4
day at Laguerre's/A. May Folwell Hoisington. 7038-8
The **day** before April. Mary Carolyn Davies. 6556-2,6250-4, 6300-4
The **day** before Thanksgiving. Frank S. Pixley. 6675-5
The **day** breaks. Thomas Curtis Clark. 6144-3
Day by day. Julia Harris May. 6337-3
Day by day. Frank Dempster Sherman. 6109-5
"**Day** by day the organ-builder in his lonely...". The legend of the organ builder. Julia C.R. Dorr. 6917-7
"The **day** closed in a wrath of cloud. The gale". The auxiliary cruiser. N.M.F. Corbett. 7027-2
The **day** closes. Carlton Talbott. 6026-9
Day dawn. Emily Pauline ("Tekahionwake") Johnson. 6837-5
Day dawn of the heart. Mary T. Lathrop [or Lathrap]. 6144-3;6335-7
"**Day** dawned on old Miletus. Castle wall". The departure of Paul. Charles W. Denison. 6755-7
"**Day** dawned, and Hannah look'd upon her boy". Hannah and Samuel. Nathaniel Parker Willis. 6848-0
"**Da** departs this upper air". Song ("Day departs...").

DAY

Edward Coote Pinkney. 7017-5
A day dream's reflection. William Allingham. 6997-5
A day dream. Emily Bronte. 6648-8
A day dream. Phoebe Cary. 6969-X
A day dream. Nelly Miller Seely. 6799-9
Day dreams. Anna Tozier. 6260-1
"Day droops while hovering night". Lament ("Day droops..."). Francis Carey ("Jan van Avond") Slater. 6800-6
The day ended, fr. The pilgrimage of Festus. Conrad Aiken. 6984-3
"Day follows night, and night returns to day". Thoughts of home, fr. Sonnets from a prison camp. Archibald Allan Bowman. 6785-9
A day for wandering. Clinton Scollard. 6161-3
"Day glimmered and I went, a gentle breeze". The lake of Geneva. Samuel Rogers. 6749-2
"Day goes faltering toward the tumbled west". Exit. David Morton. 6778-6
"Day goeth bold in cloth of gold". Day and night. Victor Daley. 6784-0
"Day had awakened all things that be". Daybreak. Percy Bysshe Shelley. 6239-3,6623-2
"The day had been a day of wind and storm". After a tempest. William Cullen Bryant. 6752-2
"The day had come, the day of many years". First evening. Bayard Taylor. 6976-2
"Day hangs its light between two dusks...". In the dusk. Francis Ledwidge. 6812-X
"The day has a secret it warily keeps". Weather wisdom. Vivian Heyerdahl. 6799-9
"Day has barred her windows close...". East coast lullaby. Lady Anne Lindsay. 6833-2
"The day hath gone to God". Philip James Bailey. 6238-5
A day in a long hot summer. Yuri Kageyama. 6790-5
A day in Ireland. Unknown. 6244-X
A day in June. James Russell Lowell. 6242-3,6265-2,6464-7
A day in June. Alice Choate Perkins. 6053-6
A day in June. Henry Stevenson Washburn. 6456-6
A day in March. Dayton Thomas Gould. 6818-9
A day in March. Bayard Taylor. 6976-2
A day in Palestine. Robert Needham Cust. 6848-0
A day in spring. Kristinn Stefansson. 6854-5
A day in Sussex. Wilfrid Scawen Blunt. 6331-4,6477-9
A day in the Pamfili Doria. Harriet Beecher Stowe. 6302-0;6385-3
A day in winter. L.C. Whiton. 6965-7
"Day in, day out,/The line of corner boys". Corner boys. Bryan MacMahon. 6930-4
"The day is blond with sun and hot as summer". Augury. Josephine Jacobsen. 6839-1
The day is brief. Thomas Curtis Clark. 6461-2
"The day is cold, and dark, and dreary". The rainy day. Henry Wadsworth Longfellow. 6260-1,6176-1,6499-X, 6554-6,6583-X,6337,6373-X,6632-1,6457-4,6565-1,6219-9,6212,6008-0,6560-0,6964-9,6018-8,6126-5,6121-4, 6288-1,6008-0,6491
The day is come. Idris Davies. 6895-2
The day is coming. William Morris. 6188-5,6657-7,6730-1, 6110-9,6430-2,6102-8,6508-2,6655-0
"The day is dark". Sehnsucht; or what you will. Corinna [pseud].. 6817-0
Day is dead. Augusta Webster. 6656-9
"The day is done". Phoebe Cary. 6802-2,6440-X,6089-7
"The day is done". Gertrude Elliott Dodge. 6764-6
"The day is done; and, lo! the shades". Epilogue. Horace. 6949-5
"The day is done". A wasted day. John Buckham. 6889-8
The day is done. Henry Wadsworth Longfellow. 6934-7
The day is done. Henry Wadsworth Longfellow. 6102-8,6457-4, 6654-2,6219-9,6300-4,6513,6183-4,6176-1,6014-5,6243-1,6332-2,6498,6260-1,6735-2,6337-3,6373-X,6374-8, 6527,6610-0,6632-1,6304-7,6639-9,6575-9,6457
The day is done. Henry Wadsworth Longfellow. 6934-7
The day is done. Henry Wadsworth Longfellow. 6008-0,6461-2, 6560-0,6250-4,6976-5,6104-6,6126-5,6288-1,6723-9, 6585-6
The day is done. Percy Bysshe Shelley. 6075-7
Day is dying. George (Mary Ann Cross) Eliot. 6240-7
"Day is dying in the west". The hush of eventide. Leona Lakeman. 6894-4
The day is dying in the west. Mary Artemisia Lathbury. 6418-3
The day is gone. John Keats. 6086-2
"Day is here! Day is here, is here!". Daylight. Unknown (Pawnee Indian). 6891-X
"The day is passing,/Long purple shadows". The end. Byron Haverly Blackford. 6818-9
"Day is past!". Good night. Felicia Dorothea Hemans. 6973-8
"The day is set, the ladies met". The quilting. Anna Bache. 6910-X
"The day is spent in labor". The night is mine, fr. Working gang poems. Byron Herbert Reece. 6761-1
"The day is still so young, it cannot be". Together at dawn. Dorothy Randolph Byard. 6761-1
"The day is tired with idleness and awe". Solstice. Charles Weekes. 6930-4
Day light. Tim Dlugos. 7003-5
"The day love came I did not know his face". The day love came. Anna Spencer Twitchell. 6836-7
"The day of brightest dawn(day soonest flown!)". The shortest day. Walter Savage Landor. 6874-X
The day of coming days. Lionel Johnson. 6508-2
"The day of crystal now is gone". Night is here. Robert P. Tristram Coffin. 7040-X
"The day of Gettysburg had set". Brotherhood. Josiah Gilbert Holland. 6911-8
The day of days. Unknown. 6272-5
The day of days. William Morris. 6604-6,6110-9
The day of doom, sels. Michael Wigglesworth. 6753-0
The day of doom, sels. Michael Wigglesworth. 6008-0
The day of doom, sels. Michael Wigglesworth. 6753-0
The day of flowers. Felicia Dorothea Hemans. 6973-8
The day of Inverlochy. John (Iain Lom) MacDonald. 6845-6
"Day of glory! Welcome day!". The Fourth of July. John Pierpont. 6946-0,6465-5,6820-0
"The day of Roncesvalles was a dismal..for you". The admiral Guarinos. Unknown (Spanish). 6757-3
The day of judgement. Jonathan Swift. 6208-3,6152-4,6278-4
The day of judgement. Isaac Watts. 6102-8,6186-9,6198-2, 6315-2,6641-0,6150
The day of judgement. Isaac Watts. 6152-4
The day of judgement. Edward Young. 6931-2
The day of judgmen. Wentworth Dillon, Earl of Roscommon. 6641-0
The day of judgment. Unknown (Gaelic) 6845-6
The day of judgment. Henry Vaughan. 6830-8
The day of liberty, fr. Prometheus unbound. Percy Bysshe Shelley. 6199-0
The day of love, fr. Prometheus unbound. Percy Bysshe Shelley. 6199-0
The day of my profession. Sister Mary Christina. 6285-7
A day of notes (that fit into the puzzle of a poem) J. Charles Green. 6870-7
The day of peace. John E. Barrett. 6840-5
Day of rain. Doris Trahagen De Aragon. 6906-1
The day of remembrance. Alfred Noyes. 6151-6
The day of Resurrection. Saint John of Damascus. 6337-3
A day of snow. Speer Strahan. 6096-X
A day of sun. Adelaide Davis Reynolds. 7030-2
The day of the battle. Alfred Edward Housman. 6665-8
A day of the Indian summer. Sarah Helen Whitman. 6618-6
The day of the Lord. Charles Kingsley. 6271-7,6102-8,6660-7
Day of the parade. Alan Chong Lau. 6790-5
Day of these days. Laurie Lee. 6209-1
"A day of torpor in the sullen heat". August. James Whitcomb Riley. 6993-2
The day of victory. Rachel Capen Schauffler. 6177-X
The day old bet was sold. Frank H. Gassaway. 6370-5
Day on a hill. Oliver Jenkins. 6764-6
A day on the hills. James Herbert Morse. 6006-4
"The day retires as o'er the plain". Ben Hafed. William Whitehead. 6917-7
"The day returns by which we date our years". Christmas tears. Henry Van Dyke. 6961-4
"The day returns, my bosom burns." Robert Burns. 6302-0, 6385-3,6250-4,6737-9
"The day returns, my natal day" Walter Savage Landor. 6828-

The day returns, my natal day. Walter Savage Landor. 6110-9,6086-2
"The day rides forth on robes of cobalt blue". Daybreak. Beulah Vick Bickley. 6789-1
The day shall yet be fair. Celia Thaxter. 6337-3
The day that autumn came. John Gould Fletcher. 6345-4
"The day the winds went underground I...". The day the winds. Josephine Miles. 6792-1,6998-3,6792-1,6998-3
A day this is boundless. Laurence Binyon. 6233-4
A day to come. Alice Meynell. 7015-9
The day to the night. Alice Meynell. 6955-X
"Day unto day". The candle. Walter De La Mare. 6905-3
"The day was breaking in crumbletown". The crumps of crumbletown. Carolyn Wells. 6882-0
"The day was breaking over Persia's realm". The golden scepter. Mabel S. Merrill. 6926-6
"The day was ill, turbid, under an opaque sky". The clock. Jovan Ducic. 6765-4
"The day was not long". Accomplishment. Jackson Holland Patterson. 6841-3
The day we do not celebrate. Robert J. Burdette. 6588-0
"The day we offer Him all our best." Stanley Schell. 6713-1
A day well spent. Unknown. 6930-0
"A day when April willows fringed the pool". The willow whistle, sels. Edward William Thomson. 6796-4
"A day when I can not". Poem. James Lewisohn. 6870-7
"The day when we are freemen all...". The coming day. William James Linton. 7009-4
"A day will come, in not undreamed of years". New vistas. Thomas Curtis Clark. 6954-1
The day will come. Marion Strobel. 6619-4
"The day will soon be gone". Fujiwara no Michinbou. 7039-6
"The day with cold gray feet clung shiveringly". Claribel's prayer. Lynde Palmer. 6889-8
The day you are born. Cathy Song. 6790-5
The day you came. Lizette Woodworth Reese. 6320-9
"The day you died, my share of all". She to him. Geoffrey Dearmer. 6884-7
The day you went. Beatrice Ravenel. 6102-8,6076-5
A day'dream's reflection. William Allingham. 7015-9
Day's affirmation. Herbert Read. 6210-5
"The day's at hand, the young, the gay". St. Valentine's day. Leigh Hunt. 6787-5
Day's black star. William Henry Davies. 6943-6
The day's demand. Josiah Gilbert Holland. 6337-3
Day's end. Laurence Binyon. 6437-X
Day's end. Helen Hoyt. 6777-8
Day's end. Toyohiko Kagawa. 6337-3
A day's end. Allan Updegraff. 6327-6
"The day's grown old; the fainting sun". Charles Cotton. 6187-7
"Day's hosts have passed down yonder". Night. Benedikt Grondal. 6854-5
"The day's long splendour dies". The lark in autumn. Alfred Hayes. 6785-9
The day's march. Robert Nichols. 6872-3,7026-4
The day's oration is in flowers. E.L. Hall. 6171-0
"Day's rain is done. The rainy mist of night" Alexander Pushkin. 6103-4
The day's ration. Ralph Waldo Emerson. 6077-3,6288-1,6126-5
The day's result. Unknown. 6461-2
A day's run. Jorge Luis Borges. 6642-9
Day, Alice Booth
  Beauty. 6750-6
Day, Beth
  Selling the farm. 6572-4
  Three gates. 6654-2
Day, Carlos
  My kinsman. 6995-9
Day, Clarence
  And/or. 6722-0
  Marco Polo. 6089-7
  Menelaus. 6089-7
  Our friend the egg. 6089-7
Day, Dorothea
  My captain. 6065-X
Day, G.P.
  A problem. 6117-6
Day, Herbert Ernest
  A paradox ("'Tis a curious fact..."). 6117-6
Day, Holman F.
  Aunt Shaw's pet jug. 7025-6
  Cure for homesickness. 7025-6
  Feedin' the stock. 6510-4
  Grampy sings a song. 6089-7
  I've got them calves to veal. 6510-4
  The mother. 6183-4
  The stock in the tie-up. 6510-4
  Story of a kicker. 6701-8
  Tale of the Kennebec mariner. 7025-6
  Uncle Tascus and the deed. 7025-6
  With love-from mother. 6097-8,6260-1
Day, Jeffery
  'On the wings of the morning' 7029-9
Day, John
  A ditty ("Peace, peace, peace, make no noise") 6182-6
Day, Lionel
  Cosmos. 6850-2
  On seeing the 175th Infantry memorial. 6850-2
  The rum ship. 6850-2
  To new year revellers. 6850-2
  To the clipper ship, Benjamin F. Packard. 6850-2
  To the passing of sail. 6850-2
  When you went back. 6850-2
Day, Lloyd
  The explorer. 6750-6
Day, Mary E.
  The parting lovers. 6565-1
  The parting lovers. 6917-7
Day, Miles Jeffrey Game
  To my brother. 7027-2,6650-X
Day, S.M.
  Mistakes. 6303-9
Day, Sarah J.
  Crocus. 6891-X
Day, Thomas Fleming
  The clipper. 6833-2
  The coasters. 6006-4
  The main-sheet song. 6833-2,7012-4
  Making land. 6833-2
  The sailor of the sail. 7012-4
  Warning. 7012-4
Day, William
  Mount Vernon, the home of Washington. 6465-5
"Day, in melting purple dying". Song ("Day, in melting"). Maria Gowen Brooks. 6271-7,6219-9
"Day, in melting purple dying." Maria Gowen Brooks. 6302-0;6385-3
"The day, quite overcome with heat". Summer afternoon. May Howard McEachern. 6750-6
"The day, with a cold, dead color". Hagen Walder. Alice Cary. 6969-X
"The day, with its sandals dipped in dew". Memory's wildwood. Unknown. 6910-X
Day-break. James Abraham Martling. 6952-5
The day-dream, sels. Alfred Lord Tennyson. 6676-3
A day-dream. Samuel Taylor Coleridge. 6543-0
The day-dream. Alfred Lord Tennyson. 6271-7,6429-9,6614-3, 6321-7
"The day-long cold hard rain drove". Surviving. James Welch. 7005-1
The day-star in the east. Helen Hunt Jackson. 6162-1
"Day-stars! that ope your eyes at morn". Hymn to the flowers. Horace Smith. 6910-X
Day: a pastoral. John Cunningham. 6932-0
A day: an epistle to John Wilkes, of Aylesbury, Esq. John Armstrong. 6968-1
A day. Emily Dickinson. 6473-8,6509-0,6519-8
A day. Verner von Heidenstam. 6045-5
The day. Witter Bynner. 6542-2
The day. Helen Pearce. 6808-1
The day. Theodore Spencer. 6491-4
Daybreak. Beulah Vick Bickley. 6789-1
Daybreak. Richard Henry Dana. 6752-2
Daybreak. Ibn Burd. 6362-4
Daybreak. Richard Jefferies. 6253-9
Daybreak. Henry Wadsworth Longfellow. 6134-8,6302-,6385-3,

DAYBREAK

    6490-6,6502-3,6597 ,6623-2,6126-5,6421-3
Daybreak. Phillip Yellowhawk Minthorn. 7005-1
Daybreak. Hazel May Oyler. 6799-9
Daybreak. Emma Peirce. 6818-9
Daybreak. Percy Bysshe Shelley. 6239-3,6623-2
Daybreak. Stephen Spender. 6390-X
Daybreak. Unknown. 6135-4
Daybreak. Louis Untermeyer. 6033-1,6393-4,6542-2
Daybreak in February. William Caldwell Roscoe. 7015-9
Daybreak in the city, fr. Hecale. Callimachus. 6435-3
Daybreak over the hall of fame. Leon Loiselle. 6799-9
Daybreak song. Unknown (American Indian) 6396-9
"**Daybreak** upon the hills!". Peace. Adeline Dutton (Train) Whitney. 6946-0
Daylight. Unknown (Pawnee Indian) 6891-X
"The **daylight** gains upon the night". The fireside chairs. William Barnes. 6980-0
"The **daylight** is dying". The garden of Kama: Kama the Indian Eros. Laurence (Adele Florence Nicolson) Hope. 6856-1
Daylight saving. Edward Steese. 6071-4
"**Daylong** a craven cry goes up". 'Is there any word from the Lord?' John Vance Cheney. 6848-0
Dayre, Sydney
    Cherry time. 6137-0
    The Chickadee. 6578-3
    The dead kitten. 6965-7,6699-2
    Frowns or smiles. 6137-0
    Getting acquainted. 6249-0
    Good-night. Eudora S. Bumstead (tr.). 6373-X
    Grandma's angel. 6682-8
    A lesson for Mama. 6105-2,6242-3,6713-1
    A letter to Mother Nature. 6690-9
    Remorse. 6820-0
Dayrise and sunset. George Walter Thornbury. 6658-5
Days. Karle Wilson Baker. 6250-4,6556-2
Days. Ralph Waldo Emerson. 6288-1,6560-0,6008-0,6431-0, 6153-2,6252 ,6309-8,6467-1,6300-4,6737-9,6126-5,6076 ,6396-9,6464-7,6006-4,6102-8,6176-1,6473-6,6536-8, 6488 ,6501-5,6726-3,6735-2,6723-9,6250-4,6646
Days. William White. 6868-9
Days ago. Dianne Hai-Jew. 6790-5
Days and nights. Thomas Sturge Moore. 6266-0
The **days** are done. George Gordon, 6th Baron Byron. 6945-2
"The **days** are hot, the nights are warm". Drought. Walter ("Old Saltbush") Smith. 6768-9
Days at sea. May Lewis. 6979-7
The **days** gone by. James Whitcomb Riley. 6260-1,6632-1
"The **days** grow drear...". December mourn. Estelle Lenore Silverman. 6847-2
"The **days** have slain the days, and the...". The half of life gone. William Morris. 6828-6
Days in the months. Unknown. 6724-7
Days like these. Ella Elizabeth Egbert. 6374-8
"The **days** may wear, the weeks may spend". To one waering arbutus. Edward Sandford Burgess. 6847-2
Days of absence. Jean Jacques Rousseau. 6744-1
Days of birth. Unknown. 6105-2,6724-7
'The **days** of forty-nine'. Unknown. 6946-0
The **days** of forty-nine. Unknown. 6281-4
"**Days** of manufacture". October, fr. Calendar. Frances Abbot. 6764-6
"**Days** of my youth". Resignation. St. George Tucker. 7017-5
Days of my youth. St. George Tucker. 6214-8
The">"**days** of our happiness gliding away. Unknown. 6874-X
"The **days** of our mourning were many below". A song in heaven. Charles W. Denison. 6755-7
"The **days** of Rabbi Ben Ephraim". Rabbi Ben Ephraim's treasure. Owen (Edward Bulwer-Lytton, Earl Lytton) Meredith. 6848-0
The **days** of our youth. Unknown (Arabic) 7039-6
"**Days** of sudden green". April, fr. Calendar. Frances Abbot. 6764-6
Days of the month. Mother Goose. 6135-4
The **days** of the month. Unknown. 6105-2,6479-5
Days that are gone. A.W. Curtis. 6523-6
The **days** that are no more. Unknown. 6273-3
The **days** that are no more. Alfred Lord Tennyson. 6271-7, 6219-9
Days that come and go. John Vance Cheney. 6006-4,609-8

Days that have been. William Henry Davies. 6477-9,6528-7
The **days** that never were. Julia C.R. Dorr. 7030-2
The **days** that were. William Morris. 6110-9
Days too short, fr. Songs of joy. William Henry Davies. 6234-2,6253-9,6393-4
"The **days** were at their longest". Dobbs his ferry. William Allen Butler. 6903-7
The **daytime** moon. C.E. Lawrence. 6069-2
Daytime naps. Burges Johnson. 6715-8
Daytime slumber. Nam-jo Kim. 6775-1
Dayton, A. Alphonse
    Why he wouldn't sell the farm. 6565-1
Dayton, Eldorous
    The harpist of Ur. 6818-9
Dazey, Charles Turner
    February rain. 6456-6
Dazzled. Arthur Sze. 6790-5
"**Dazzled** thus with the height of place". Upon the sudden restraint of the Earl of Somerset... Sir Henry Wotton. 6933-9
Dazzler in Grand Central. Frank E. Palmer. 6761-1
Dazzling moment. Louis Ginsberg. 6042-0
"The **dazzling** whiteness of Hawaiian skies". Memories of Hawaii. Clarence L. Haynie. 6841-3
Ddhree shkaders. Unknown. 6823-5
De Amicitiis. Eugene Field. 6274-1
De Aragon, Doris Trahagen
    Day of rain. 6906-1
    Fantasy. 6906-1
    Frozen enchantment. 6906-1
    Rain. 6906-1
    Smoke. 6906-1
De Arango, Camen
    Peace. 6761-1
De Bary, Anna Bunston
    As rivers of water in a dry place. 6776-X,6253-9
De Beranger, Pierre Jean
    The king of Yvetot. William Makepeace Thackeray (tr.). 6996-7
De Bolt, William Walter
    Spring opened her purse today. 6857-X
De Brown, Jere
    Thet boy ov ourn. 6139-7
De Butts, Brenda
    Full moon. 6253-9
De Camp, E.O.
    The cloud across the moon. 6906-1
    Distance. 6906-1
    The first peep. 6906-1
    The lost day. 6906-1
    The wind. 6906-1
    Your eyes. 6906-1
De Casseres, Benjamin
    The closed room. 7007-8
    Moth-terror. 6556-2
    Yogi. 6076-5,6102-8
De Coeur, Belle
    Une petite chanson de lamentation a ma mere. 6818-9
De Condres, Rhea
    The queer one. 6249-0
De Ford, Miriam Allen
    Homage to Charles Lindbergh. 7019-1
De Forest, J.W.
    The phantom ship. 6833-2
    The sea-maiden. 6833-2
De Forest, John William
    In Louisiana. 6016-2
De France
    Just between friends. 6818-9
De Guerin, Maurice
    The shamrock. 6820-0
De Guildford, Nicholas
    The owl and the nightingale. 6198-2
De Hales, Thomas
    A luve ron. 6198-2
De Hampole, Richard Rolle
    The prickle of conscience. 6198-2
De Jong, David Cornel
    Pleasant street. 6017-8
De Kay, Charles

Arcana sylvarum. 7041-8
'Barnaval,' sel. 7041-8
'Barnaval,' sel. 7041-8
The draft riot. 6946-0
Invocation. 7041-8
Peace. 6597-X
Serenade. 7041-8
Surrender. 7041-8
The tornado. 6833-2
The tornado. 7041-8
Ulf in Ireland. 6716-6
Ulf in Ireland. 7041-8
De La Fontaine, Jean. See La Fontaine, Jean de
De La Mare, Joseph
    Trees. 6134-6
De La Mare, Walter
    A-tishoo. 6596-1
    Absence. 6905-3
    Alas, alack. 6538-4,6454-X
    All but blind. 6102-8
    '...All gone...' 6905-3
    All that's past. 6477-9,6250-4,6150-8,6464-7,6726-3, 6508-2
    Alone. 6125-7
    Alulvan. 6596-1
    Arabia, fr. The listeners. 6234-2,6726-3,6250-4,6668-2
    Are you so lovely? 6905-3
    Arithmetic. 6905-3
    As Lucy went a-walking. 6596-1
    Astray. 6905-3
    Autumn. 6246-5
    >The ballad of Christmas. 6746-8
    The barber's. 6466-3
    The bees' song. 6722-0
    Before dawn. 6216-4
    The birth of Venus. 6905-3
    Bluebells. 6596-1
    The Bourne. 6905-3
    Bread and cherries. 6937-1
    The buckle. 6421-3,6596-1
    Bunches of grapes. 6089-7,6459-0,6114-1,6596-1,6454-X, 6018-8
    The candle. 6905-3
    Captain Lean. 6596-1
    Cecil. 6596-1
    The challenge. 6905-3
    The child in the story awakes. 6596-1
    The child in the story goes to bed. 6459-0,6596-1
    The Chinese pot. 6905-3
    The Christening. 6596-1
    The cupboard. 6466-3,6262-8,6454-X
    Dame Hickory. 6596-1
    The dark chateau. 6508-2
    Daughter to mother. 6905-3
    De profundis. 6905-3
    Deadalive. 6905-3
    The death-dream. 6958-4
    The disguise. 6905-3
    Down-adown-derry. 6596-1
    Dr Mole. 6905-3
    Dreams, sels. 6648-8
    The dwarf. 6596-1
    Earth folk. 6253-9
    Echo. 6905-3
    Echoes. 6780-8
    The empty chariot. 6042-0
    The end. 6905-3
    England. 6905-3
    England ("No lovelier hills than thine have laid"). 6331-4,6631-3,6439-6
    The Englishman. 6596-1
    The enigma. 6905-3
    Envoy ("Child, do you love the flower.") 6596-1
    Epilogue. 6905-3
    Epitaph on one whole played Ariel in his youth. 6778-6
    An epitaph. 6315-2,6477-9,6250-4,6153-2,6301-2
    Evening. 6253-9
    The fairies dancing. 6596-1
    Fare well. 6179-6,6246-5
    The feckless dinner party. 6210-5

    Fey. 6905-3
    A fiddler. 6905-3
    The fiddlers. 6596-1
    Five eyes. 6511-2
    The fly. 6339-X,6808-1,6596-1
    The fool rings his bells. 7026-4
    For a child. 6905-3
    Foreboding. 6905-3
    From amid the shadows. 6905-3
    Full moon. 6044-7
    The funeral. 6596-1
    The gage. 6596-1
    The galliass. 6210-5
    The ghost. 6250-1,6257-1,6354-3
    Good-bye. 6184-2,6506-6
    The grey wolf. 6596-1
    "Happy, happy, it is to be" 6253-9,6656-9
    Hard labour. 6905-3
    The hare. 6596-1
    Haunted. 6596-1
    Have done! 6905-3
    The horn. 6253-9,6596-1
    Horse in a field. 6776-X
    'How sleep the brave'. 7026-4
    The huntsmen. 6527-9
    I am. 6905-3
    I met at eve. 6423-X,6808-1,6596-1,6421-3
    I saw three witches. 6254-7,6596-1
    Immanent. 6905-3
    In a churchyard. 6905-3
    Intermittent fever. 6905-3
    Intruder. 6905-3
    The isle of lone. 6596-1
    "It is a wraith - no mortal haunts my way". 6905-3
    Jenny. 6905-3
    Jenny Wren. 6395-0
    Jim Jay. 6162-1,6393-4
    John Mouldy. 6596-1
    The journey 6628-3
    Joy. 6761-1
    Kings and queens. 6334-9
    The lamplighter. 6596-1
    Lethe. 6905-3
    "Life lives on life". 6905-3
    The linnet. 6250-4,6073-0,6315-2,6102-8,6250-4
    The listeners, sels. 6234-2,6102-8
    The listeners. 6653-4,6464-7,6639-9,6723-9,6234-2,6246-5,6339-X,6395-0,6427-2,6477-9,6107-9,6375-6,6150-8, 6153-2,6301-2,6371-3,6648-8,6653-4,6693-4,6490-6, 6527-9,6488-4,6726-3,6648-8
    The little bird. 6421-3
    The little green orchard. 6508-2
    The little old Cupid. 6649-6
    The little salamander. 6102-8
    Lob lie-by-the-fire. 6162-1
    Lovelocks. 6596-1
    Lullaby ("Sleep, sleep"). 6596-1
    Martha. 6477-9
    The miller and his son. 6596-1
    The miracle. 6250-4
    Miss Loo, fr. The listeners. 6234-2,6653-4,6393-4,6639-9
    Miss T. 6538-4,6545-X
    The missing word. 6905-3
    The moth. 6659-3
    The mother bird. 6596-1,6510-4
    Motley. 7029-9
    The mountains. 6253-9
    The mourner. 6905-3
    Music. 6465-5,6250-4,6653-4
    Napoleon. 6427-2,6210-5
    Never more, sailor. 6258-X
    Never yet. 6905-3
    Nicholas Nye. 6510-4
    The night-swans. 6596-1
    No, no, no! 6905-3
    Nocturne. 6320-9
    Nod. 6044-7,6162-1,6477-9,6464-7,6653-4,6044-7,6162-1, 6477-9
    Now. 6905-3

O dear me! 6596-1
O lovely England. 6905-3
Off the ground. 6079-X
The ogre. 6596-1
The old angler. 6508-2
An old cannon. 6905-3
Old Susan. 6465-5,6476-0,6464-7,6653-4,6723-9,6465-5, 6476-0,6464-7,6653-4,6723-9
One swallow. 6905-3
Outcasts. 6905-3
The owl. 6905-3
The pedlar. 6596-1,6422-1,6596-1
The phantom ("Upstairs in the large closet, child"). 6596-1
The phantom. 6596-1
The pilgrim. 6596-1
The pilgrim. 6596-1
Poor Henry. 6538-4
The portrait of a warrior. 6596-1
Puss. 6905-3
Queen Djenira. 6301-2,6102-8
The rainbow. 6596-1
Rats. 6905-3
The raven's tomb. 6596-1
The reawakening. 7029-9
The reflection. 6905-3
Reflections. 6905-3
Rejected. 6905-3
Reunion. 6905-3
Reverie. 6596-1
The ride-by-nights. 6334-9
A robin. 6125-7
Sam's three wishes; or, life's little whirligig. 6228-8, 6458-2,6079-X
The scarecrow. 6477-9
The scribe. 6477-9
The seas of England. 6793-X
Second childhood. 6905-3
Second thoughts. 6905-3
She. 6905-3
The ship of Rio. 6833-2
Silver. 6161-3,6393-4,6162-1,6395-0,6509-0,6464-7,6396-9
The silver penny. 6596-1
Sleep. 6958-4
The sleeper, fr. The listeners. 6234-2,6506-6
Sleephead. 6596-1
Sleeping beauty. 6478-7,6596-1
So it would seem. 6905-3
Some one. 6368-3
Song ("O for a moon"). 6596-1
A song of enchantment. 6250-4
The song of shadows. 6354-3,6581-3
A song of soldiers. 6395-0
The song of the mad prince. 6044-7,6508-2
The song of the mad prince. 6872-3
The spectre. 6722-0
Spring. 6905-3
St Andrews. 6905-3
The storm. 6783-2
The strange spirit. 6985-1
The stranger. 6250-4
Sunk Lyonesse. 6331-4
The sunken garden. 6232-6,6477-9,6250-4,6649-6
The supper. 6018-8,6596-1,6018-8
Suppose. 6506-6
The tailor. 6653-4
Tarbury Steep. 6905-3
Tartary. 6478-7,6102-8,6596-1,6161-3,6396-9,6501-5,6454-X
Then. 6421-3
There blooms no bud in May. 6253-9
Thou art my long-lost peace. 6761-1
The three beggars. 6596-1
The three cherry trees. 6338-1,6628-3
The three strangers. 6477-9
'The thrush'. 6905-3
Tired Tim. 6937-1,6861-8,6026-9,6102-8
Tit for tat. 6510-4
Titmouse. 6510-4

To a candle. 6246-5
To E.T.: 1917. 7029-9
To K.M. 6985-1
The truth of things. 6905-3
The tryst. 6905-3
Ulladare. 6905-3
Uncircumventible. 6905-3
The vacant farmhouse. 6257-1
The vision. 6783-2
The visitant. 6648-8
Voices. 6421-3
Wanderers. 6161-3,6581-3
We who have watched. 6905-3
When love flies in. 6905-3
'Why, the come in...' 6905-3
The widow. 6069-2
Winter. 6125-7
Winter dusk, fr. The listeners. 6234-2,6320-9,6648-8, 6723-9
Wireless. 6905-3
De La Selva, Saloman
Tropical town. 6076-5,6102-8
De Ligouri, Saint Adolphus
Madonna's lullaby. James J. Galvin (tr.). 6282-2
De Long, Juanita
My hereafter. 6303-9
De Luca, Angela
A midnight serenade for her perfumed majesty. 6818-9
De Luca, Angelo
Expiation. 6818-9
De Mary, Elizabeth
Pioneer woman. 6270-9
De Maupassant, Guy. See Maupassant, Guy de
De Medici, Lorenzo. See Medici, Lorenzo de'
De Menocal, Esmee
What I love. 6042-0
De Mille
The Indian names of Canada. 6134-6
De Mille (atr).
The Indian names of Acadia. 6795-6
De Quincey, Thomas
Charles Lamb, fr. Literary reminiscences. 6958-4
Dreaming, sel. 6958-4
de Silva, C. Celeste
My shattered dreams. 6799-9
De Stein, Edward. See Stein, Edward de
De Tabley, John B.L. Warren, 3d Baron
Anticipation. 6246-5
At the council. 6046-3
An autumn serenade. 7020-5
The churchyard on the sands, sels. 6246-5
The churchyard on the sands. 6315-2,6153-2
Circe. 6656-9
A cradle song. 6233-4
Fortune's wheel. 6656-9
A frosty day. 6315-2
Hymn to Astarte, sels. 6301-2
A hymn to Aphrodite. 6046-3
The knight in the wood. 6380-2
Misrepresentation. 6046-3
Nuptial song. 6046-3
The ocean wood. 6785-9
An ode. 6785-9
Orestes. 6102-8
Orestes, sels. 6301-2
The royal aspects of the earth. 7020-5
The second madrigal. 6658-5
A song of faith forsworn. 6656-9
A song of the rolling wind. 6246-5
The study of a spider. 6102-8,6747-6
The study of a spider. 7020-5
The two old kings. 6656-9
A winter sketch. 6658-5
A woodland grave. 6656-9
De Tabley, John B.L. Warrne, 3d Baron
A simple maid. 6656-9
De Vega, Lope
The good shepherd ("Shepherd! that with thine..."). Henry Wadsworth Longfellow (tr.). 6065-X
Tommorrow. Henry Wadsworth Longfellow (tr.). 6102-8

De Vere, Aubrey Thomas
   Aeschylus. 7015-9
   Cardinal Manning. 6172-9,6292-X,6656-9
   The cathedral of Milan. 6631-3
   A character. 6980-0
   Columbus. 6678-X
   Dirge of Rory O'More. 6858-8
   Early friendship. 6302-0,6385-3,6543-0
   An Epicurean's epitaph. 6656-9
   Epitaph. 6090-0
   Flowers I would bring. 6656-9
   Friends of youth. 6084-6
   Genoa. 6631-3
   Giotto's Campanile. 6631-3
   A girl's song. 6246-5
   Glengariff. 6086-2
   Gougane barra. 6086-2
   Happy are they who kiss thee. 6066-8
   Her beauty. 7015-9
   Her shadow. 6302-0
   Horn Head, county of Donegal. 6096-X
   Human life. 6172-9,6292-X,6656-9
   Hymn for the feast of the Annunciation. 6282-2
   Le recit d'une soeur. 6046-3
   Lines ("The sights"). 6102-8
   The little black rose. 6930-4
   The little black rose. 6022-6
   Love's spite. 6656-9
   Lycius. 6980-0
   Mater amabilis. 6282-2
   Mont Blanc. 6749-2
   National apostacy. 7015-9
   The queen's vespers. 6656-9
   The sacraments of nature. 6022-6
   Sad is our youth. 6046-3,6543-0
   Saint Patrick and the impostor. 6674-4
   Scene in a madhouse. 6930-4
   The setting of the moon near Corinth. 7015-9,6997-5, 7015-9
   The sisters. 6980-0
   Song. 6737-9,6656-9,6658-5
   Song ("Give me back my heart..."). 6980-0
   Song ("Seek not"). 6096-,6172-9
   Song ("Sing the old song..."). 6934-7
   Song ("When I was young"). 6693-3,6246-5
   Sonnet ("Sad is our youth"). 6219-9
   Sorrow. 7015-9,60 0-0,6303-9,6214-8,6292-X,6199-0,6250-4,6172-9,6371-3,6656-9
   Spring. 6096 X
   Stanzas ("All things"). 6980-0
   The sun god. 6090-0,6096-X
   The sun-god. 6022-8,6102-8,6383-7
   They leave the land of gems. 6747-6
   To a flower on the skirts of Mont Blanc. 6749-2
   Venice by day. 6631-3
   Venice in the evening. 6631-3
   "A wayward child, scarce knowing what he wanted". 6980-0
   The wedding of the clans. 6858-8
   A year of sorrow. 6022-6
De Vere, Aubrey Thomas (tr.)
   Stabat mater. Jacopone da Todi (Jacobus de Benedictus), 6282-2
de Vere, Edward. See Oxford, Earl of
De Vere, Mary Ainge ("Madeline Bridges")
   Children. 6274-1
   God keep you. 6337-3
   Her perfect lover. 6576-7
   Life's mirror. 6303-9,6337-3,6654-2,6109-5
   Poet and lark. 6096-X
   The saint and the sinner. 6451-5
   There are loyal hearts. 6260-1
   The third proposition. 6089-7
   "Wid thady's pipe beside the door". 6292-X
   A woman's gifts. 6620-8
De Vere, Sir Aubrey
   The children band. 6233-4,6086-2
   A Christmas carol ("They leave the land of gems..."). 6145-1
   The cliffs, fr. Atlantic coast scenery. 6997-5
   "Have I not felt the longing". 6997-5
   Jerusalem. 7015-9
   'Judah's hallowed bards.' 6848-0
   Malbay sands, fr. Atlantic coast scenery. 6997-5
   The "motion/Of waves, the breezes fragrant from the sea" 6997-5
   The opening of the tomb of Charlemagne. 6086-2
   The right use of prayer. 6086-2
   The rock of Cashel. 6086-2
   Saint Peter's by moonlight. 6331-4,6631-3,6439-6
   The sisters. 6600-3
   The solitudes of Malbay, fr. Atlantic coast scenery. 6997-5
   Spanish point. 6086-2
   The true basis of power. 7015-9
   Waterloo. 6086-2
   Zoe, an Athenian child. 6233-4
De Vere, William
   'Walk, damn you, walk!' 7012-4
De Vito, Ethel Barnett
   Sophisticate. 6750-6
De Yriarte, Tomaso
   The musical ass. 6724-7
De amore et spinis. Unknown (Latin) 6948-7
De appile tree. Joel Chandler Harris. 6605-4,6281-4
De baby show. Wilson MacDonald. 6722-0
De ballit of de boll weevil. Unknown. 6281-4
De belle ob Ebonville. Henry Davis Middleton. 6274-1
De big Bethel Church. Joel Chandler Harris. 6300-4
"De black cat crossed his luck." James D. Carrothers. 6120-6,6692-2
De blue tail fly. Unknown. 6594-5
De circus turkey. Unknown. 6280-6
'De conjure man.' Charles C. Jones. 6692-5
De Cushville hop. Ben King. 6166-4
De flagello myrteo, sels. Richard Garnett. 6317-9
De fust banjo. Irwin Russell. 6076-5,6281-4,6300-4
De glory road. Clement Wood. 6736-0,6467-1,6102-8,6607-0, 6732-8,6076-5,6281-4
De gospel train. Julia Johnson Davies. 6778-6
De gospel train. Julia Johnson Davis. 6039-0
De Guiana, Carmen epicum. George Chapman. 6436-1
De gustibus. Robert Browning. 6043-6,6199-0,6110-9,6541-4, 6430-2,6655 ,6123-0,6154-0,6473-6,6624-0,6657-7,6656
De gustibus. John Erskine. 6118-4,6619-4
De gustibus, sels. Robert Browning. 6464-7
De Gustibus-- St. John Hankin. 6760-3
De instituto authoris. Thomas Campion. 6794-8
"De la depouille de nos bois". La chute des feuilles. Charles Millevoye. 6801-4
De libris. Cosmo Monkhouse. 6297-0
De lil' brack sheep. Unknown. 6719-0
'De Lord am coming'. Ellen Murray. 6926-6
De lunatico. George A. Baker. 6004-8
De massa ob de sheepfol'. Sarah Pratt McLean Greene. 6102-8,6310-1,6552-X,6632-1,6476-0,6076
De massa ob de sheepfol'. Unknown. 6260-1
De Monfort: a tragedy. Joanna Baillie. 6813-8
De morte. Sir Henry Wotton. 6933-9
De naevo in facie faustinae. Thomas Bastard. 6317-9
De nice leetle Canadienne. William Henry Drummond. 6692-5, 6591-0,6592-9,6115-X
De ol' man. Alonzo W. Combs. 6281-4
De ole elder's mistake. Ellen Murray. 6927-4
De Partu Virginis, sels. Sincerus Sannazarius. 6282-2
De prodjeckin' son. Booth Lowrey. 6281-4
De profundis. Walter De La Mare. 6905-3
De profundis. Jovan Ducic. 6765-4
De profundis. George Macdonald. 6199-0
De profundis. James Abraham Martling. 6952-5
De profundis. Christina Georgina Rossetti. 6655-0
De profundis. Alfred Lord Tennyson. 6977-0
De profundis. Katharine (Hinkson) Tynan. 6656-9
De profundis. Unknown. 6730-1
De profundis. Charles Whitby. 6994-0
De profundis, fr. Psalm 130. Bible. 6337-3
De promise lan' John Richard Moreland. 6083-8,6281-4
De Quincy's deed. Hoer Greene. 6923-1

DE   384

De Quincy's deed. Homer Greene. 6610-0
De regimine principum (on Chaucer). Thomas Hoccleve. 6198-2
De Roberval, sels. John Hunter-Duvar. 6656-9
"De room wha'r de squire's co't sat was packed". Why uncle Ben back-slid. Ralph Bingham. 6926-6
De rosis hibernis. Sir Edmund Gosse. 6656-9
De sheepfol'. Sarah Pratt McLean Greene. 6007-2,6083-8, 6153-2,6006-4,6737-9,6502
De stove pipe hole. William Henry Drummond. 6281-4
De sunflower ain't de daisy. Unknown. 6291-1
De te. Adam Lindsay Gordon. 6951-7
De tea fabula. Sir Arthur Quiller-Couch. 6440-X
De tired pickaninny's star-song. Mary Bailie. 6692-5
De trop. L. W. 7021-3
De union growin' strong. Charles Langford. 6149-4
De wood hants. Anne Virginia Culbertson. 6696-8
De yaller Chinee. Unknown. 6139-7
"The de'il cam' fiddling through the town". The exciseman. Robert Burns. 6845-6
De'sperience be de reb'rend Quacko Strong. Unknown. 6414-0
The deabting society. Eugene J. Hall. 6921-5
Deacon Adams to his son. Unknown. 6692-5
The deacon and his daughter. Isabella Valancy Crawford. 6591-0,6592-2
Deacon Hezekiah. Unknown. 6910-X
Deacon Jones's grievance. Paul Laurence Dunbar. 6675-5
Deacon Stokes. Thomas Quilp. 6403-5
The deacon's confession. N.S. Emerson. 6683-6
The deacon's courtship. Mrs. L.D.A. Stuttle. 6414-0
The deacon's daughter. Unknown. 6061-7
The deacon's masterpiece. Oliver Wendell Holmes. 6176-1, 6332-2,6499-X,6600-3,6735-2,6089 ,6307-1,6431-0,6438-8,6008-0,6288-1,6121 ,6505-8,6467-1,6491-1,6219-9, 6739-5,6281 ,6307-1,6431-0,6438-8,6008-0,6288-1,6121 ,6505-8,6467-1,6491-1,6219-9,6739-5,6281 ,6076-5, 6126-5
The deacon's prayer. William O. Stoddart. 6412-4
The deacon's story. N.S. Emerson. 6294-6
The deacon's story. N.S. Emerson. 6910-X
The deacon's Thanksgiving. Willis Hawkins. 6703-4
The deacon, me and him. Louis Eisenbeis. 6923-1
Dead. Rhoda Coghill. 6930-4
Dead. Hazel Fern Craytor. 6799-9
Dead. William Dean Howells. 7041-8
Dead. Lionel Johnson. 6208-3,6246-6
Dead. James Abraham Martling. 6952-5
Dead. John J. Procter. 6433-7
Dead 'Wessex,' the dog, to the household. Thomas Hardy. 6488-4,6536-8
The dead ("Blow out, you bugles"), fr. 1914. Rupert Brooke. 6250-4
The dead ("These hearts were woven"), fr. 1914. Rupert Brooke. 6250-4
A dead airman. Moray Dalton. 6542-2
The dead alive. Pierre Jean de Beranger. 6787-5
Dead and alive. Alice Cary. 6969-X
"Dead and gone truth's faltering lisper". The mingling of nations. Benjamin Franklin Taylor. 6815-4
"Dead and gone, the days we had together". Past days. Algernon Charles Swinburne. 6875-8
"The dead are in their silent graves". The forsaken. Thomas Hood. 6974-6
"The dead are with us everywhere". The dead. A.E. Murray. 7031-0,7027-2
A dead astronomer. Francis Thompson. 6655-0
The dead at Clonmacnois. Angus O'Gillan. 6930-4
The dead at Clonmacnois. Angus O'Gillan. 6437-X,6472-8
The dead at Clonmacnois. Thomas William Rolleston. 6873-1
The dead aviator. Francis Hackett. 6292-X,6300-4
The dead babe. Eugene Field. 6318-7
The dead babe. Eugene Field. 6949-5
A dead baby. Dinah Maria Mulock Craik. 6980-0
Dead before death. Christina Georgina Rossetti. 6828-6
The dead bird. Emma Celia & Lizzie J. Rook. 6137-0
Dead birds and Easter. May Riley Smith. 6720-4,6510-4
Dead boy. John Crowe Ransom. 6357-8,6326-8,6491-4
The dead boy's portrait and his dog. Gerald Massey. 7008-6
The dead broncho-buster. Berton Braley. 6853-7
The dead brother. Unknown. 6829-4

Dead calm at sea. Samuel Taylor Coleridge. 6304-7
Dead calm in the tropics. Samuel Taylor Coleridge. 6543-0
The dead cannoneer. James Ryder Randall. 6113-3
A dead chameleon. Arthur Shearly Cripps. 6800-6
"The dead child lay in the shroud". The gift of the sea. Rudyard Kipling. 6810-3
The dead child. George Barlow. 6274-1,6437-X,6656-9
A dead child. Lucian. 6435-3
The dead child. Charles W. Denison. 6755-7
The dead Christ. Julia Ward Howe. 6271-7
The dead church. Charles Kingsley. 6568-6
Dead Cleopatra. Conrad Aiken. 6897-9
The dead coach. Katharine (Hinkson) Tynan. 6656-9
The dead comrade. Edward Carpenter. 6542-2
The dead comrade. Richard Watson Gilder. 6820-0
The dead comrade. dichard Watson Gilder. 6340-3,6424-8
The dead crab. Andrew Young. 6315-2,6210-5,6659-3
A dead craftsman. Frederick Robert Higgins. 6779-4
The dead Czar Nicholas. Dinah Maria Mulock Craik. 6302-0;6385-3
The dead dancer. Snow Longley Hough. 6316-0
The dead doll. Unknown. 6165-6,6167-2
The dead doll. Margaret (Janvier) Vandegrift. 6271-7,6131-7
Dead Dundee, fr. The burial march of Dundee. William Edmonstoune Aytoun. 6934-7
The dead elm on the hilltop. George Dillon. 6984-3
The dead faith. Fanny Heaslip Lea. 6730-1
The dead feel not. Theognis. 6435-3
The dead fowler. Mnasalcas. 6435-3
The dead fox-hunter. Robert Graves. 7029-9
Dead friend. Isabel Fiske Conant. 6850-2
A dead friend. Edgar Fawcett. 6632-1
A dead friend. Norman Gale. 6656-9
The dead friend. Robert Southey. 6085-4
The dead friend. Alfred Lord Tennyson. 6302-0;6385-3
Dead gods. Erik Blomberg. 6045-5
The dead grenadier. Benjamin Franklin Taylor. 6815-4,7002-7
The dead grenadier. Pedro Juan Vignale. 6759-X
A dead harvest. Alice Meynell. 6044-7;6477-9
Dead Hector. James Abraham Martling. 6952-5
'Dead heroes' Karoniaktatie. 7005-1
The dead heroes. Isaac Rosenberg. 6641-0
The dead host's welcome. John Fletcher. 6563-5,6230-X
The dead house. James Russell Lowell. 6126-5
The dead in frock coats. Carlos Drummond de Andrade. 6758-1
Dead in his bed. A.L. Ballou. 6273-3
Dead in the Sierras. Joaquin Miller. 6424-8,6467-1,6102-8, 6732-8,6076-5,6300-4,6484-1
"Dead in the battle,-dead on the field". The soldier's dirge. Elizabeth Harman. 6820-0
Dead in the street. Unknown. 6909-6
"Dead is the air, and still!...". August. Bayard Taylor. 6976-2
"Dead is the famous Nancy,/One time Queen...". In memory of Nancy Hanks. William J. Lampton. 7010-8
"Dead is the roll of the drums". Abraham Lincoln. Henry Howard Brownell. 6113-3,6239-3,6709-3,6305-5,6524-4
"Dead kings and queens, give up your gold!". The loot of Luxor. Laurence Housman. 6778-6
The dead kings. Francis Ledwidge. 6812-X
The dead kitten. Unknown. 6277-6
The dead kitten. Sydney Dayre. 6965-7,6699-2
The dead knight. John Masefield. 6395-0
Dead languages. Jay Macpherson. 6767-0
The dead leader. I. Edgar Jones. 6924-X
"The dead leaves strew the forest walk". Stanzas ("The dead leaves"). John Gardiner Calkins Brainard. 6077-3
The dead leaves strew the forest-walk. John Gardiner Calkins Brainard. 6752-2
Dead leaves, fr. In Tuscany. Cora Fabri. 6876-6
Dead letter office. William Rose Benet. 6217-2
The dead letter, sels. Austin Dobson. 6649-6
A dead letter. Austin Dobson. 6676-3,6094-3,6508-2,6656-9
The dead Liebnecht. Rudolf Leonhardt. 6160-5
A dead locust. Aristodicus. 6435-3
"Dead lonely night and all streets quiet now". December.

William Morris. 7020-5
Dead love. Phoebe Cary. 6969-X
Dead love. Unknown. 6675-5
A dead maiden's complaint. Gerasimos Markoras. 6352-7
The dead make rules. Mary Carolyn Davies. 6250-4
The dead man ariseth and singeth a hymn to the sun. Unknown (Egyptian) 7039-6
Dead man's cottage. J.H. Knight-Adkin. 7027-2
Dead man's dump. Isaac Rosenburg. 6209-1,6666-6
Dead man's glory. David Martin. 6895-2
Dead man's morrice. Alfred Noyes. 6151-6
The dead man's song. Young Ewing Allison. 6300-4
A dead march. May C. ([Mary] Gillington) Byron. 7037-X
A dead march. Cosmo Monkhouse. 6215-6,6656-9
The dead march. Mary T. Lathrop. 7002-7
Dead marine. Louis O. Coxe. 6666-6
The dead mariner. Charles W. Denison. 6755-7
Dead men. Lizette Woodworth Reese. 6037-4
Dead men laugh. Hollis Russell. 6397-7
"Dead men of 'ninety-two". Sonnet ("Dead men"). Arthur Rimbaud. 6665-8
Dead men tell no tales. Haniel Long. 6032-3;6289-X;6332-2;6501-5
Dead men, to a metaphysician. Hervey Allen. 6036-6
The dead minstrel. John E. Barrett. 6840-5
The dead miser. Gotthold Ephraim Lessing. 6278-4
A dead mole. Andrew Young. 6659-3
The dead mother. Robert Buchanan. 6819-7
The dead mother. Edith (Bland) Nesbit. 7037-X
The dead musician. Charles L. O'Donnell. 6292-X,6172-9
The dead Napoleon. William Makepeace Thackeray. 6478-7,6552-X
The dead nereid. Eugenio Florit. 6642-9
The dead nymph. Charles Henry Luders. 7041-8
Dead of night. Manuel Bandeira. 6759-X
The dead Pan. Elizabeth Barrett Browning. 6657-7
"'Dead on the field of honor' - now at last". Woodrow Wilson. John Jordan Douglass. 7001-9
"Dead Petra in her hill-tomb sleeps". 'The rock' in El Ghor. John Greenleaf Whittier. 6848-0
The dead partisan. Joy Davidman. 6561-9
A dead past. Adelaide Anne Procter. 6957-6
Dead poet. Josephine Pinckney. 6038-2
The dead poet. Lord Alfred Bruce Douglas. 6483-3,6102-8,6301-2
The dead poet. John Gawsworth. 6893-6
Dead poets. Enrique Pena Barrenechea. 6759-X
Dead poets. Rosamund Marriott ("Graham R. Tomson") Watson. 6875-8
The dead politician. Francis Bret Harte. 6219-9
Dead ponies. Brenda Chamberlain. 6379-9
The dead president. Edward Rowland Sill. 6524-4
"Dead princess, living power, if that...". Dedicatory poem to the Princess Alice. Alfred Lord Tennyson. 6867-7,6977-0
The dead pussy cat. Unknown. 6249-0,6274-1,6691-7,6578-3
The dead pussy cat. Marion Short. 6963-0
The dead pussy-cat. John Bennett. 6120-6
The dead quire. Thomas Hardy. 6430-2
The dead ride fast. Richard P. Blackmur. 6390-X
The dead room. Sara V. Prueser. 6906-1
A dead rose. Elizabeth Barrett Browning. 6123-0,6383-7,6543-0
"Dead roses and dying" Alexander Blok. 6103-6
The dead rover. Berton Braley. 6853-7
A dead seaman speaks. Sara Himlinsky. 7019-1
The dead ship of Harpswell. John Greenleaf Whittier. 6126-5
The dead ship of Harpswell. John Greenleaf Whittier. 6833-2
The dead singer. Allen Eastman Cross. 6848-0
Dead snake. William Jay Smith. 6388-8
Dead soldier. Nicolas Guillen. 6759-X
Dead soldier. Frantisek Halas. 6068-4
The dead soldier-boy. William Mason Turner. 6414-0
The dead soldier-poet. Albert J. Heil. 6799-9
The dead soldier. Sydney Oswald. 6474-4
The dead Solomon. John Aylmer Dorgan. 6848-0
A dead song-writer. Lucilius. 6435-3
The dead sparrow. William Cartwright. 6861-8

The dead stowaway. Will Carleton. 6155-9
The dead student. Will Carleton. 6412-4
A dead summer. Mary Elizabeth Blake. 7041-8
The dead to the living. Laurence Binyon. 6476-0
The dead tribune. Denis Florence MacCarthy. 6174-5,6022-6
The dead village. Edwin Arlington Robinson. 6723-9
Dead volcano. Helen Louise Stapleford. 6799-9
A dead warrior. Laurence Housman. 6069-2
Dead waters. John French Wilson. 7007-8
The dead who have died in the Lord. James Glassford. 6600-3
"A dead woman stands". On the banks of the Chang. Margarethe Herzele. 6769-7
The dead words. Vernon Watkins. 6360-8
"A dead year is clasped by a dead December". New Year resolve. Ella Wheeler Wilcox. 6863-4
A dead year. Jean Ingelow. 6940-1
"Dead you shall lie, for ever...". Sappho. 6251-2
The dead youth. Kostes Palamas. 6352-7
"Dead! Is it possible? He, the bold rider". Custer's last charge. Frederick Whittaker. 6913-4
'Dead! name unknown'. Horace B. Durant. 6921-5
"The dead! the glorious dead!...". The magic glass. Felicia Dorothea Hemans. 6973-8
"Dead!- Time and death, ye cruel and....". Dead. James Abraham Martling. 6952-5
"Dead!/The one word sped". My kinsman. Carlos Day. 6995-9
"Dead!/What nobler shroud was ever spun". Woodrow Wilson dead. Norman H. Crowell. 7001-9
The dead, fr. The town. David Morton. 6531-7,6030-7
The dead, I. Rupert Brooke. 6224-5,6332-2,6653-4
The dead, II. Rupert Brooke. 6224-5,6332-2,6161-3,6653-4
"Dead, with their eyes to the foe". Melville and Coghill. Andrew Lang. 6793-X
The dead-beat. Wilfred Owen. 6542-2
The dead-house. Alice Cary. 6865-0;6969-X
Dead-sea fruit. Hilton Brown. 6269-5
The dead.. Violet Gillespie. 6474-4
The dead. Mathilde Blind. 6199-0,6383-7
The dead. John Le Gay Brereton. 6784-0
The dead. Rupert Brooke. 6214-8,6491-4,6301-2,6542-2,6371-3,6464 ,6044-7,6051-X,6465-5,6477-9,6427-2,6393
The dead. Robert J. Crot. 6337-3
The dead. George Dyre Eldridge. 6327-6
The dead. John Langhorne. 6600-3
The dead. A.E. Murray. 7031-0,7027-2
The dead. Semonides. 6435-3
The dead. Charles Hamilton Sorley. 7027-2
The dead. Victor Starbuck. 6326-8
The dead. Sigourney Thayer. 7027-2
The dead. Jones Very. 6288-1,6300-4
The dead. John Williams. 6388-8
Deadalive. Walter De La Mare. 6905-3
The deadly cup. Unknown. 6684-4,6685-2
Deadly kisses. Pierre de Ronsard. 6771-9
A deadly weapon. George Robert Sims. 6921-5
"Deadness of English winter, dreariness". Rhapsody in a third-class carriage. Richard Aldington. 6985-1
Deads. Alison Bundy. 6900-2
Deadwood. Walter Stanley ("Stanley Vestal") Campbell. 6628-3
Deaf. Margaret Deland. 6847-2
Deaf and dumb. Robert Browning. 6337-3
Deaf men. Merrill Moore. 6482-5
"Deaf to God, who calls and walks". Doomsday morning. Genevieve Taggard. 6817-0
"Deaf to the hurly-burly of the street". Israelite graveyard. Cesar Tiempo. 6759-X
The deaf woman's courtship. Unknown. 6549-X
Deaf-mute in the pear tree. P.K. Page. 6767-0
The deaf-mute sermon. Francis Carlin. 6032-3
The deaf. Seymour Gordden Link. 6979-7
Deahl, James
    The passing. 6767-0
Deakin Brown's way. George Horton. 6923-1
"Deal gently with me, O my friends". Love, the best monument. Unknown. 6919-3
"Deal gently with my garden". Vale. Heloise Davison. 6847-2
"Deal gently with us, ye who read!" Oliver Wendell Holmes.

6238-5
A deal in real estate. Arthur Guiterman. 6773-5
Deal, Ada B.
    Night. 6818-9
Deal, C.E.
    The mystery. 6799-9
Deal, Edwin E.
    Solitude. 6799-9
    Wisdom. 6799-9
Dean Antony. Ruth Weiss. 6901-0
The **dean's** lady. George Crabbe. 6315-2
Dean, Elmer
    The stallion. 6979-7
Dean, Emma Marlatt
    To the hardy ones. 6042-0
Dean, Eva
    Buried treasure. 6486-8
Dean, Harry M.
    Have you? 6374-8
    Mother's rocking-chair. 6097-8
Dean, John M.
    Introspection. 7001-9
Deane, Anthony C.
    The ballad of the Billycock. 6026-9,6102-8
    The beauties of nature. 6996-7
    Bo-peep. 6440-X
    A certain cure. 6996-7
    Contributed by Mr. Andrew Lang. 6875-8
    The cult of the Celtic. 6440-X
    Here is the tale. 6089-7
    Imitation. 6089-7
    Imitation ("Calm and implacable"). 6089-7,6440-X
    Jack and Jill ("Here is the tale..."). 6440-X
    John Jenkins. 6996-7
    Little Jack Horner. 6440-X
    An ode ("I sing a song"). 6440-X
    Rural bliss. 6089-7
    The three mice. 6440-X
Deane, Gladys Verville
    Deserted swing. 6764-6
    On having a son. 6764-6
Deane, Leila Chamberlain
    I would that I were like a tree. 6799-9
The **deaprted.** John Banister Tabb. 7017-5
"Dear Agnes, gleam'd with joy and...with tears". Birthday lines to Agnes Baillie. Joanna Baillie. 6980-4
"Dear Aldrich, now Novermber's mellow days". Thomas Bailey Aldrich: Birthday verses, 1906. Henry Van Dyke. 6961-4
"Dear Anna - between friend and friend". A poetical epistle to Lady Austen. William Cowper. 6814-6
Dear Carrigaline. Michael Joseph Barry. 6858-8
"Dear architect of fine Chateaux en l'air". To William Hayley, Esq. in reply to his solicitation. William Cowper. 6814-6
"Dear are some hidden things". Free will. Alice Meynell. 6955-X
"Dear are the days of youth! Age dwells". The death of Calmar and Orla. George Gordon, 6th Baron Byron. 6945-2
"Dear bard and prophet, that thy rest". To Emma Lazarus- 1905 Richard Watson Gilder. 6848-0
"Dear bard and prophet, that thy rest is deep". To Emma Lazarus- 1905 Richard Watson Gilder. 6848-0
"Dear Becher, you tell me to mix with mankind". Lines addressed to the Rev. J.T. Becher. George Gordon, 6th Baron Byron. 6945-2
"Dear Bell - I enclose what you ask in..letter". Credat Judaeus Apella, fr. Hippodromania. Adam Lindsay Gordon. 6951-7
"Dear Betty! come give me sweet kisses". A ballad ("Dear Betty"). Sir Charles Hanbury Williams. 6230-X
"Dear boy, let us think of the pleasures...". Holiday hours. Felicia Dorothea Hemans. 6973-8
"Dear charming nymph, neglected and decried". Farewell to poetry, fr. The deserted village. Oliver Goldsmith. 6932-0
"Dear child divine". To the child Jesus. W. Roche. 6937-1
"Dear child of nature". To a young lady. William Wordsworth. 6122-2,6250-4,6086-2,6110-9

"Dear Chloe, while the busy crowd". A paradise below, fr. The fireside. Nathaniel Cotton. 6934-7
"Dear comrade, arise, from slumber awake". Aristophanes. 6435-3
Dear country mine. Richard Watson Gilder. 6386-1,6304-7
"Dear Cynthia, though thou bear'st the name". Sir Francis Kynaston. 6187-7
"Dear Cypris, if thou savest those at sea". Unknown. 6435-3
"Dear countrymen, whate'er is left to us". Dedication, fr. Fo'c's'le yarns: 2d series. Thomas Edward Brown. 6809-X
Dear dandelion. Laura D. Nichols. 6049-8
Dear dark head. William Rooney. 6022-6
Dear dark head. Unknown. 6244-X
"Dear Earth, within Thy bosom grant rest...". Unknown. 6251-2
"Dear doctor of St. Mary's". A song upon Miss Harriet Hanbury, addressed to the... Sir Charles H. Williams. 6874-X
"Dear doctor, I have read your play". Epistle from Mr. Murray to Dr. Polidori. George Gordon, 6th Baron Byron. 6945-2
"Dear doctor, whose blandly invincible pen". To O.W. Holmes. Paul Hamilton Hayne. 6820-0
"Dear dog that seems to stand and gravely...". Rhapsody on a dog's intelligence. Burges Johnson. 7008-6
"Dear dragger of the heavy books". To my seatmate. Unknown. 6847-2
"Dear earth, remembering his long toil on thee". The old husbandman. Unknown (Greek). 6879-0
"Dear Erin, how sweetly thy green bosom rises". Cushla-ma-chree. John Philpot Curran. 6820-0
"Dear Erin, how sweetly thy green bosom rises!". Cuisle mo chroidhe. John Philpot Curran. 6858-8
"Dear Eustatio, I write that you may write...". Amours de voyage. Arthur Hugh Clough. 6828-6
"Dear elm, it is of thee" Unknown. 6049-8
"Dear exile from the hurrying crowd". Aforetime. Thomas Sturge Moore. 6884-7
Dear father. Unknown. 6715-8
"Dear father and dear mother: Let me crave". Erotion. Martial. 7039-6
"Dear fool, be true to me!". To sleep. Alice Meynell. 6955-X
"Dear Frederick:/Your letter was received". Susie to her ex-young man. Ethel M. Kelley. 6817-0
"Dear frens, I'se glad ter see yo' heah". Sable sermon. I. Edgar Jones. 6922-3
"Dear friend, I know this world is kin". Death. George Frederick Cameron. 7041-8
"Dear friend, I never more shall hear". My best Kentucky reel. James Buckham. 6798-0
"Dear friend:- you ask me to inspect". 'Our poets' beauties' James Abraham Martling. 6952-5
A dear friend. Algernon Charles Swinburne. 6085-4
"'Dear friends and gentle hearts,' he wrote". To Stephen Collins Foster. Eleanore Randall Lamkin. 6750-6
Dear ghost. Gulielma Day Orr. 6906-1
"Dear god! were I fisher and". Nelly of the top-knots. Douglas Hyde. 6873-1
"Dear God, if I should die and then". Prayer ("Dear God"). Adelaide Foerch Schinzel. 6270-9
"Dear God, on far horizons". A prayer. Magdalene C. Stephens. 6799-9
"Dear God, please walk beside me". Prayer. Fannie H. Goslin. 6799-9
"Dear God, still presence from my infant days". In extremis. Mildred D. Harding. 6857-X
"Dear God, such strangeness comes o'er me". Forest phantasy. Jaroslav Vrchlicky. 6886-3
"Dear God, the light is come". A prayer ("Dear God, the light is come"). Unknown. 6359-4
"Dear God, you seem so near, so close to me". Divine informality. Madeline Slade. 6750-6
"'Dear God,' she used to pray...". The answer. Isabella Bryans Longfellow. 6750-6
"Dear God/I wonder if you've time". Prayer from a working girl. Elsie Robinson. 6750-6
"The dear good angel of the spring". Sappho. 6435-3

"Dear gracious Lord, if that thy pain". Supplication. Alice Cary. 6865-0;6969-X
"Dear Graham, whilst the busy crowd". Ode to Mr. Graham, the aeronaut. Thomas Hood. 6974-6
Dear harp of my country. Thomas Moore. 6174-5,6086-2,6430-2
Dear heart. Christine Park Hankinson. 6841-3
The dear Irish boy. Unknown. 6858-8
"Dear heart, come closer, while the light". Between the lights. Unknown. 6889-8
"Dear heart, could it be so". Nocturne. Gertrude Huntington McGiffert. 6838-3
"Dear heart, have you not learned". Do you not know? Katherine Ruggles. 6818-9
"Dear heart, when thus I stroke your aching...". The sickbed. Hermann Hagedorn. 6944-4
"Dear hearts, whose love has been so sweet...". Last words. Helen Hunt Jackson. 6836-7
"Dear hope! earth's dowry, and heavn's debt!". M. Crashaws answer for hope. Richard Crashaw. 6933-9
"Dear is my inlaid sword; across the border". Song of Taj Mahomed. Laurence (Adele Florence Nicolson) Hope. 6856-1
"Dear Jock, ye're higher up the brae". Hughie's advice to his younger brother John. James Logie ("Hugh Haliburton") Robertson. 6819-7
"Dear Joseph - five and twenty years ago". An epistle to Joseph Hill, Esq. William Cowper. 6814-6
"Dear Joseph- five and twenty years ago". An epistle to Joseph Hill, esq. William Cowper. 6874-X
"Dear Kate, I do not swear and rave". A love song. Eliza Cook. 6980-0
Dear is my little native vale. Samuel Rogers. 6328-4,6543-0,6668-2
Dear Islay! Thomas Pattison. 6180-X
Dear Jack. William Makepeace Thackeray. 6802-2
Dear lads and lassies. Unknown. 6629-1
"Dear lady, I don't mind admitting to you". Negation. Berton Braley. 6853-7
"Dear lady, when thou frownest". Robert Bridges. 6487-6
"Dear laird, ye're comin' up the brae". To the laird. James Logie ("Hugh Haliburton") Robertson. 6819-7
Dear land. Sliabh Cuilinn. 6858-8
Dear land of all my love, r. The centennial ode. Sidney Lanier. 6239-3;6386-1
"Dear Laura, when you were a flirting young miss". Unknown. 6407-8
"Dear lass whose influence dale and height". A wish. Sigurdur Julius Johannesson. 6854-5
"Dear laws, come to my breast!". The laws of verse. Alice Meynell. 6955-X
"Dear lilac, how enchanting". Quince to lilac. Bliss Carman and Richard Hovey. 6890-1
"Dear Lillian, all I wished is won!". In Italy. Bayard Taylor. 6976-2
"Dear little child, just lent to me". Culmination. Marion Hendrick Ray. 6764-6
"Dear little Dorothy, she is no more!". Dorothy. Rose Hawthorne Lathrop. 7041-8
"Dear little fellow—you are fast". By his bedside. Fern Mary Munsell. 6799-9
"Dear little flag in the window there". The service flag. William Herschell. 6443-4,6449-3,6964-9,6846-4
"Dear little glass spheres, I send them". Marbles. John Harolde. 7016-7
Dear little goose. Mary Mapes Dodge. 6713-1
Dear little heads in the pew. Margaret Elizabeth Sangster. 6889-8
"Dear little home, I see you now among the...". Lost cabin. Delphine Harris Coy. 6836-7
Dear little lady. Pauline Kunderd Manly. 6799-9
"The dear little maiden was sorrowful. Word". Griselda in pound - A.D. 1760. Margaret Junkin Preston. 6965-7
"Dear little one." Issa. 6027-7
"Dear little prince, so merry and wise". A May-day garland. Richard Lawson Gales. 6950-9
"A dear little squirrel sat under a tree". The squirrel. Unknown. 6937-1
"Dear little violet". Calling the violet. Lucy Larcom. 6891-X

"Dear Long, in the sequestered scene". To Edward Noel Long, Esq. George Gordon, 6th Baron Byron. 6945-2
"Dear Lord, accept a sinful heart". Self-acquaintance. William Cowper. 6814-6
"Dear Lord, I must not leave this earth". No time to die. Sudie Stuart Hager. 6750-6
"Dear Lord, I'm not complaining". A small girl's prayer. Beryl Scouten Holgren. 6750-6
"Dear Lord, in the battle that goes on...". Prayer of a sportsman. Berton Braley. 6853-7
"Dear Lord, to preserve my sanity". Prayer for laughter. Madeline Slade. 6750-6
"Dear Lord/The brightness of this day". A prayer. Minnie Elizabeth Otto. 6799-9
Dear little violets. John Moultrie. 6519-8
Dear lord and father of mankind, fr.The brewing of Soma. John Greenleaf Whittier. 6337-3,6527-9
"The dear Lord's best interpreters." John Greenleaf Whittier. 6225-3
Dear Lord, who sought at dawn. Harry Webb Farrington. 6337-3
The dear love of comrades, fr. 'Calamus' Walt Whitman. 6954-1
"Dear love, where the red lilies blossomed...". Bleak weather. Ella Wheeler Wilcox. 6956-8
Dear lovely death. Langston Hughes. 6879-0
"Dear ma'am - we seldom take the pen". To Mrs. Barnes, fr. Croaker papers. Fitz-Greene Halleck and Joseph Rodman Drake. 6753-0
"Dear Ma,/You write". Pin money. Jana Harris. 6901-0
"Dear maiden whom I love, I wish you you". My wish for you. Anna Vernon. 6789-1
"Dear master, help me along life's way". When evening comes. Della Sowers. 6799-9
"Dear Master: I've no palms to strew upon...". Palm Sunday. May Hammond Witters. 6799-9
"Dear me". Harriet Nutty. 6130-3
Dear Minna. Maxwell Bodenheim. 6036-6
"Dear me, you're so red! cried the white rose". The white rose and the poppy. Anna [or Annie] L. Hannah. 6924-X,6167-2
"Dear mistress, our master summons us". To our Virginia. Louis J. Magee. 7004-3
"Dear Mom:/Today, I found God!". Letter from Alice. Iris Jamieson. 6750-6
"Dear Mother Abbess, leave we pray". Argenteuil, 1128. George Moore. 6779-4
"Dear Mother Goose! most motherly and dear". Mother Goose. James Whitcomb Riley. 6965-7
"Dear mother Earth, within your breast". Unknown. 6435-3
'Dear mother, I've come home to die'. Edgar Bowers. 6074-9
Dear Mr. President. Langston Hughes. 6561-9
The dear mystery. John Hall Wheelock. 6619-4
"Dear native brook! wild streamlet of the west". Sonnet to the river Otter. Samuel Taylor Coleridge. 6967-3
"Dear native regions, I foretell". Extract from the conclusion of a poem...leaving school. William Wordsworth. 6828-6
Dear night, this world's defeat. Henry Vaughan. 6337-3
"Dear object of defeated care!". Lines written beneath a picture. George Gordon, 6th Baron Byron. 6945-2
Dear old Flo. S.J. Stone. 6131-1
Dear old grandma. Mrs. G. M. Winslow. 6130-3
Dear old granite state. Annie Bartlett Shepard. 6764-6
Dear old London. Eugene Field. 6735-2
Dear old mothers. Charles S. Ross. 6461-2
The dear old toiling one. David Gray. 6656-9
"Dear one, I love thine eyes, amazed" Feodor Ivanovich Tyutchev. 6103-6
"Dear one, with aching heart, I know". Consolation. Robert Paul Turbeville. 7016-7
"Dear Palmer, just a year ago...Carlsbad cure". Carlsbad. Eugene Field. 6949-2
"Dear parents and friends, we greet you tonight". Unknown. 66601-1
"Dear parents, grieve no more for me". The spirit's song of consolatifn. F.W.P. Greenwood. 6752-2
"Dear president, whose art sublime". To Sir Joshua Reynolds. William Cowper. 6814-6
"Dear Quirister, who from those shadows sends". Dear

DEAR

Quirister... William Drummond of Hawthornden. 6943-6
"Dear R.L.S., whose books each night". To R.L.S. Christopher Morley. 6875-8
"Dear Saviour! when thy weary feet". Suffering with Christ. Charles W. Denison. 6755-7
The dear president. John James Piatt. 6524-4
Dear Quirister... William Drummond of Hawthornden. 6943-6
Dear reader. Ernest Radford. 6875-8,6770-0
"Dear silent one". Query. Elizabeth Stanton Lay. 6750-6
"Dear singer of our fathers' day". To John Greenleaf Whittier. William Hayes Ward. 6820-0
"Dear sir of late delighted with the sight". To her most honoured father, Thomas Dudley Esq. Anne Bradstreet. 6753-0
"Dear Sir, - Your letter came to han'.". Mr. Hosea Bigelow to the editor..., fr. Bigelow papers. James Russell Lowell. 6753-0
"Dear Sir, You wish to know my notions". Letter from a candidate, fr. Bigelow papers. James Russell Lowell. 6787-5
"Dear sir: your astonishment's odd". Limerick:"Dear sir: your astonishment's odd." Unknown. 6308-X
"Dear Sirs:/Of course I'll come. I've...". In response to executive order 9066... Dwight Okita. 6790-5
"Dear Smith, the sleest, paukie thief". Epitaph to James Smith. Robert Burns. 6932-0
"Dear son of Aegeus, to the gods alone". Sophocles. 6435-3
"Dear son of mine, the baby days are over". A mother's dedication. Margaret Peterson. 7026-4
"Dear son/have you received the papers back". A letter from home. John Paul Minarik. 6870-7
Dear things and queer things. Louisa Cooke Don-Carlos. 6818-9
"Dear to my soul! then leave me not forsaken!" Henry Constable. 6182-6,6586-4
Dear Tom, this brown jug. Francis Fawkes. 6328-4
"Dear to my soul, then me not forsaken!". Sonnet ("Dear to my soul"). Henry Constable. 6436-1
"Dear tranquil habit, with her silent hands". Tranquil habit. Auguste Angellier. 6961-4
"Dear Uncle Sam has many girls". Nicknames of the states. H.U. Johnson. 6923-1
"Dear uplands, Chester's favorite fields". Clover. Sidney Lanier. 6753-0
"Dear urge no more that killing cause". To one that pleaded her own want of merit. Thomas Stanley. 6933-9
"Dear was he whose body this is". Dear was he, fr. Life of St. Cellach of Killala. Unknown. 6930-4
The dear white hand. Henry Van Dyke. 6983-5
"Dear Zeus, at thy ways I wonder...". Theognis. 6251-2
"Dear woods, of cherished memories". The old woods. Estelle Geraldine Griffen. 6799-9
"Dear youth, too early lost, who now art laid". On the death of a young and favorite slave. Martial. 7039-6
"Dear, dear! I wonder what's got in de men?". Lixey. Unknown. 6824-3
"Dear, dear! what can the matter be?" Unknown. 6452-3
"Dear, dear, dear". The thrush's song. W. Macgillivray. 7022-1
"Dear, dear, dear,/In the rocky glen". The thrush's song. W. Macgillivray. 6873-1
"Dear, do not your fair beauty wrong". Thomas May. 6187-7
"Dear, I could weep, but that my brain is dry." Thomas Lovell Beddoes. 6317-9
"Dear, faithful beasts who went before". My dead dogs. Rowland Thirlmere. 6875-8
"Dear, from thine arms". Song ("Dear, from thine arms.") John Wilmot, 2d Earl of Rochester. 6189-3
"Dear, gentle faith! on the sheltered porch". Faith. Phoebe Cary. 6865-0;6969-X
"Dear, had the world in it's caprice". Respectability. Robert Browning. 6828-6
"Dear, heavn-designing soul!". To a young gentle-woman. Richard Crashaw. 6933-9
"Dear, I tried to write you such a letter". A letter. Adelaide Anne Procter. 6957-6
"Dear, if you change! I'll never choose again." Unknown. 6181-8,6182-6,6317-9
"Dear, it you change, I'll never choose again". Song ("Dear, if you change"). Unknown. 6436-1
"Dear, let me dream of love". A prayer ("Dear, let me dream"). Selwyn Image. 6274-1,6656-9
"Dear, near and true,- no truer time himself". A dedication. Alfred Lord Tennyson. 6828-6
"Dear, noble friend! a virgin cask". An invitation to Maecenas. Horace. 6949-5
"Dear, set the casement open". A chaplet of flowers. Adelaide Anne Procter. 6957-6
"Dear, simple girl, those flattering arts". Answer to Lines written in Rousseau's Letters of...nun. George Gordon, 6th Baron Byron. 6945-2
Dear, they have poached the eyes you loved so well. Rupert Brooke. 6722-0
"Dear, when I did from you remove". Madrigal. Edward Herbert, 1st Baron Herbert of Cherbury. 6182-6
"Dear, why should you command me to my rest". Michael Drayton. 6182-6,6187-7
"Dear, why should you command me to my rest". Sonnet ("Dear, why should"). Michael Drayton. 6436-1
Dearborn Observatory, Chicago. Benjamin Franklin Taylor. 6815-4
"Deare if I with guile would guild a true intent" Thomas Campion. 6794-8,6380-2
"Deare love, for nothing less than thee". John Donne. 6187-7
"Deare Venus, if thou wilt bee kinde." Unknown. 6563-5
"Dearest all faire is in your browne." Unknown. 6563-5
"Dearest and best! Light of my way!". Fides amantis. Robert Buchanan. 6819-7
The dearest friends are the auldest friends. Robert Louis Stevenson. 6085-4
Dearest little one. Ernest Rhys. 6097-8
Dearest love! believe me. Thomas Pringle. 6226-1
The dearest poets. Leigh Hunt. 6102-8
Dearest spot. W.R. Wrighton. 6304-7
"Dearest wife, I've raised thy pillow". Answer to 'I am dying'. William Laurie. 6910-X
"Dearest, do not you delay me". Serenade, fr. The Spanish curate. John Fletcher. 6827-8
Dearest, do not you delay me. John Fletcher. 6563-5
"Dearest, how hard it is to say". The peace of Christmas-time. Eugene Field. 6949-5
"Dearest, we have no time to sing of love". But sing your love. Helen Bryant. 6761-1
The dearest. John Sterling. 6980-0
Dearmer, Geoffrey
From 'W' beach. 7029-9
Nous autres. 6884-7
Pavlova. 6777-8
She to him. 6884-7
The tailor. 6506-6
The Turkish trench dog. 6477-9,6510-4
Dearness, William
The first eight verses of chapter seventeen of the... 6848-0
The pledges given at Sinai. 6848-0
Dearness, William (tr.)
Psalm 137. Bible. 6848-0
Dearth. Virginia Richards Casabona. 6799-9
Deas, Fannie M.P.
That boy John. 6690-9
DeBoe, Ruby Price
Our angels. 6799-9
Snow clad. 6799-9
"Deat Santa, lean your ear this way". A word to Santa Claus. Unknown. 6807-3
Death. Aeschylus. 6987-8,6879-0
Death. Maltbie Davenport Babcock. 6303-9,6337-3,6730-1
Death. Evgeni Baratynsky. 6103-6
Death. Mary Helen Barbie. 7016-7
Death. Maxwell Bodenheim. 6102-8,6348-9,6076-5,6467-1
Death. Emily Bronte. 6023-4
Death. Emily Bronte. 6123-0
Death. Rupert Brooke. 6730-1
Death. George Frederick Cameron. 7041-8
Death. Agnes Lindsay Carnegie. 6180-X
Death. William Croswell Doane. 6177-X
Death. John Donne. 6371-3
Death. Thomas Flatman. 6563-5

Death. Foster Harris. 6397-7
Death. George Herbert. 6563-5
Death. Thomas Hood. 6980-0
Death. Thomas Hood. 7015-9
Death. Thomas Hood. 6980-0
Death. Thomas Hood. 7015-9
Death. Walter Savage Landor. 6250-4
Death. George Cabot Lodge. 7007-8
Death. Lucretius. 6102-8
Death. Henry Luttrell. 6874-X
Death. John Bruce MacCallum. 6482-5
Death. Alan Mackintosh. 6542-2
Death. Alan Mackintosh. 6872-3
Death. James Abraham Martling. 6952-5
Death. Robert Nicoll. 6960-6
Death. James Oppenheim. 6730-1
Death. Katherine Philips. 6023-4
Death. Katherine Phillips. 6668-2
Death. Beilby Porteus. 6934-7
Death. Percy Bysshe Shelley. 6828-6
Death. Horace Smith. 6606-2
Death. Edmund Spenser. 6337-3
Death. Unknown. 6436-1
Death. Unknown (Arabic) 7039-6
Death. Unknown (Greek) 6435-3
Death. Unknown (Indian) 6337-3
Death. William Walsh. 6198-2
Death. Charles Wesley. 6271-7
Death. Walt Whitman. 6659-3
Death. William Carlos Williams. 6482-5
Death. William Butler Yeats. 6246-6,6339-X,6472-8
Death. Edward Young. 6294-6
Death ("Like other tyrants"). Unknown. 6294-6
Death ("O death"). Unknown. 6436-1
Death - diviniation. Charles Wharton Stork. 6374-8,6556-2
Death - what is it? James Newton Matthews. 6482-5
Death a sonnet. William Walsh. 6563-5
Death alone. Pablo (Neftali Ricardo Reyes Basualto) Neruda. 6759-X
Death and a rose. Claribel Weeks Avery. 6764-6
Death and birth. Algernon Charles Swinburne. 6123-0
The death and burial of Cock Robin. Unknown. 6452-3,6135-4
Death and Cupid. John Godfrey Saxe. 6302-0;6385-3
Death and despair. Walter James Turner. 6472-8
Death and Doctor Hornbook. Robert Burns. 6180-X
The death and dying words of poor Mailie,... Robert Burns. 6198-2
"Death and famine on every side". Famine song. Laurence (Adele Florence Nicolson) Hope. 6856-1
"Death and I/On a hill so high". The vision of life. Frances Anne Kemble. 6980-0
The death and last confession of Wandering Peter. Hilaire Belloc. 6339-X,6427-2
Death and life. Herbert Edward Clarke. 6793-X
Death and life. Confucius. 6732-8
Death and life. William Croswell Doane. 6461-2
Death and love. Elizabeth Barrett Browning. 6383-7
Death and resurrection. George Croly. 6730-1
Death and return in January. Roger Lipsey. 6821-9
Death and Roosevelt. Ernest Harold Baynes. 6995-9
Death and sleep. Percy Bysshe Shelley. 6980-0
Death and the drunkard. Unknown. 6410-8
Death and the fairies. Patrick MacGill. 6872-3
Death and the flowers. Eden Phillpotts. 7031-0
Death and the lord. Hermann Hagedorn. 6944-4
Death and the ruffians, fr. The Canterbury tales. Geoffrey Chaucer. 6102-8
Death and the warrior. Felicia Dorothea Hemans. 6973-8
Death and the youth. Letitia Elizabeth ("L.E.L.") Landon. 6385-3;6600-3
Death and transfiguration. Norman Rosten. 6561-9
Death and transfiguration. Marya Alexandrovna Zaturenska. 6532-5
Death as the fool. Frank T. Marzials. 6656-9
Death as the teacher of love-lore. Frank T. Marzials. 6656-9
Death at the camp. Keiho Soga. 6981-9
"Death at the headlands, Hesiod, long ago". Hesiod, 1908. Alexander Mair. 6845-6
"Death be not proud". Sonnet ("Death be not proud"). John Donne. 6109-3,6341-1,6430-2
The death bed. Thomas Hood. 6102-8,6278-4,6513-9,6560-0, 6656-9,6046-3,6214-8,6219-9,6332-2,6604-6,6186-9, 6240-7,6246-6,6271 ,6337-3,6392-6,6437-X,6481-7,6660-7,6737
Death by rarity. Marguerite Young. 6391-8
Death by water, fr. The waste land. Thomas Stearns Eliot. 6879-0
Death by water, fr. The waste land. Thomas Stearns Eliot. 6258-X,6531-7,6472-8
"Death came tonight and set my sorrows free". Out of bondage. Melba Williams. 6906-1
"Death canot yet extinquish that entyre." Unknown. 6563-5
Death carol, fr. President Lincoln's burial hymn. Walt Whitman. 6271-7,6337-3,6309-8,6646-1
"Death chose a fitting time". Monody for S. A. Douglas! James Abraham Martling. 6952-5
Death comes riding, fr. Governor Lenhard. Einar Hjorleifsson Kvaran. 6283-0
"Death deep in me". Without thinking. Ernst Nowak. 6769-7
Death deposed. William Allingham. 6930-4
"Death doth not wait as most things wait". Life without death. Stephen Teets. 6799-9
"Death found him as he faced his foes". Woodrow Wilson. Nelson Robins. 7001-9
"Death found strange beauty on that cherub...". Death of an infant. Lydia Huntley Sigourney. 6752-2
"Death had no terrors, life no joys". Fujiwara No Yoshitaka. 6852-9
"Death has come bridegroom unto many a bride". The lost love. Edward Farquhar. 6939-8
'Death has crowned him a martyr.' Ella Wheeler Wilcox. 6692-5
Death house. Miriam Wolfson. 6850-2
"Death in an ancient country was a...passport". Elegy on the pilot. Reuel Denney. 6978-9
Death in battle, fr. The battle of Maldon. Unknown. 6489-2
Death in bed, fr. The life of Guthlac. Unknown. 6489-2
Death in Harlem. Langston Hughes. 6042-0
Death in love, fr. The house of life. Dante Gabriel Rossetti. 6110-9,6250-4
Death in the arctic. Robert Service. 6159-1
Death in the bush. Margaret Thomas. 6591-0,6592-9
Death in the corn. Detlev von Liliencron. 6665-8
The death in the desert, sels. Robert Browning. 6144-3
A death in the desert. Robert Browning. 6931-2
A death in the desert. Robert Browning. 6245-8
A death in the desert. Robert Browning. 6931-2
Death in the kitchen. Thomas Hood. 6974-6
A death in the streets. Mario Petaccia. 6870-7
Death in the sun. Eugenio Florit. 6642-9
Death invoked. Philip Massinger. 6022-6
"Death is a cool, bronze swallow". Death. Mary Helen Barbie. 7016-7
"Death is a dream". Song ("Death is a dream"). Alfred Noyes. 6169-9
Death is a little thing. George Abbe. 6218-0
Death is a second cousin dining with us tonight. Geraldine Kudaka. 6790-5
"'Death is a voyage', I heard it lightly told". O mariners! Archibald Rutledge. 6833-2
"Death is another life; we bow our heads". Philip James Bailey. 6238-5
Death is before me to-day. Unknown (Egyptian) 6337-3
Death is but death. Will Dyson. 6349-7
"Death is but usher to a change". Gain by death. William White. 6868-5
Death is great. Rainer Maria Rilke. 6643-7
Death is not without but within him, fr Cino da Pistoia. Dante Gabriel Rossetti. 6123-0
"Death is so dark to youth". So dark, so dear. Robert Loveman. 6941-X
"Death is stronger than all the governments...". Death snips proud men. Carl Sandburg. 6879-0
Death is swallowed up in victory. Henry Kirke White. 6214-8
Death lament of John O'Mahony. Douglas Hyde. 6174-5
"Death lies in wait for you, you wild thing...". Sonnet ("Death lies in wait"). John Masefield. 6879-0
"Death loved thee o, that when...day was done". Woodrow

DEATH

Wilson. W.E.P. French. 7001-9
Death makes all men brothers. Louise S. Upham. 6913-4
"**Death** may leap on a sunny day" Raymond Thompson. 6870-7
Death means freedom. William Croswell Doane. 6720-4
The **death** of a beautiful girl. Virginia Moore. 6039-0
Death of a beautiful wife. Henry King. 6302-0;6385-3
The **death** of a dandy. John Peale Bishop. 6036-6
The **death** of a great man. Alfred Noyes. 6151-6
Death of a hero. Paul Scott. 6475-2
Death of a hornet. D.G. Jones. 6446-9
The **death** of a horse. Jodi Ann Johnson. 6900-2
Death of a jazz music in. William Jay Smith. 6388-8
The **death** of a Romish lady. Unknown. 6003-X
The **death** of a snake. William Plomer. 6985-1
Death of a sunflower. Raymond Souster. 6767-0
Death of a teacher. L.F. Gerlach. 6515-5
The **death** of a Zulu. William Plomer. 6788-3
The **death** of Adam. Unknown. 6848-0
The **death** of Admiral Benbow. Unknown. 6157-5,6547-3,6732-8
The **death** of Admiral Blake. Sir Henry Newbolt. 6844-8
The **death** of Ahad. Richard Wilton. 6848-0
The **death** of Ailill. Francis Ledwidge. 6812-X
The **death** of Ailill. Francis Ledwidge. 6930-4
The **death** of Ajax, fr. Metamorphosis. Ovid. 6424-8
Death of Alexander III. Unknown. 6323-3
Death of an actress. Louis MacNeice. 6389-6
Death of an inebriate. Unknown. 6045-1
Death of an infant. Lydia Huntley Sigourney. 6752-2
Death of an infant. Dirk Smits. 6127-3
The **death** of an old squid. Unknown. 6167-2
The **death** of Anaxagoras. William Canton. 6250-4
The **death** of Arnkel. Sir Edmund Gosse. 6661-5,6683-6
The **death** of Artemidora. Walter Savage Landor. 6122-2,6196-6,6199-0,6656-9,6543-0
Death of Arthur. Alfred Lord Tennyson. 6302-0;6385-3
The **death** of Baladeadro, fr. The story of Baladeadro. George Gordon McCrae. 6768-9
The **death** of Bertram. Sir Walter Scott. 6606-2
The **death** of Bryant. Edmund Clarence Stedman. 7041-8
The **death** of Byron. Ralph S. Thompson. 6983-5
The **death** of Calmar and Orla. George Gordon, 6th Baron Byron. 6945-2
The **death** of Carus. Count Platen. 6842-1
The **death** of Charles I. Andrew Marvell. 6188-5
Death of Christ. Arthur R. MacDougall Jr. 6144-3
The **death** of Chrysaor, fr. The hellenics. Walter Savage Landor. 6828-6
The **death** of Clanronald. Felicia Dorothea Hemans. 6973-8
The **death** of Cleopatra. Horace. 6676-3
The **death** of Cleopatra. Unknown. 6690-9
The **death** of cock robin. Gerda Fay. 6249-0,6502-3
Death of Coleridge. Charles Lamb. 6304-7
The **death** of Colman. Thomas Frost. 6946-0
The **death** of Columba. John Stuart Blackie. 6819-7
The **death** of Conradin. Felicia Dorothea Hemans. 6973-8
Death of Cuchalain. Eleanor Rogers Cox. 6712-9,6292-X
The **death** of Cuchulain. William Butler Yeats. 6125-7m,6245-8
The **death** of Daphnis. Theocritus. 7039-6
The **death** of Don Pedro. Unknown (Spanish) 6757-3
The **death** of Dr. Morrison. Unknown. 6278-4
The **death** of Eve. William Vaughn Moody. 6753-0
The **death** of flowers. William Cullen Bryant. 6239-3,6271-7,6303-9,6486-8,6600-3,6632-
The **death** of friends. Edward Young. 6084-6
Death of Gaudentis. Harriet Annie. 6910-X
Death of General Grant. Benjamin Franklin Taylor. 6815-4
The **death** of General Pike. Laughton Osborn. 6946-0
The **death** of geography. Eve Merriam. 6783-2
The **death** of Goody Nurse. Rose Terry Cooke. 6946-0
The **death** of Grant. Ambrose Bierce. 6076-5,6102-8,6340-3
The **death** of Guinevere. Harry Lyman Koopman. 6682-8
The **death** of Hamlet. John E. Barrett. 6840-5
The **death** of Hampden. Pakenham Beatty. 6656-9
Death of Harold Hardrada. Unknown. 6323-3
Death of Harrison. Nathaniel Parker Willis. 6678-X
The **death** of Hector, fr. The Iliad. Homer. 6933-9
The **death** of Hercules. John Gay. 6972-X
The **death** of Herminius, fr. The battle...Lake Regillus. Thomas Babington Macaulay, 1st Baron Macaulay. 6427-2,6610-0
The **death** of Hoel. Thomas Gray. 6975-4
The **death** of Hofer. Julius Mosen. 6914-2
The **death** of Jacob. Mary L. Clough. 6848-0
The **death** of Jefferson. Hezekiah Butterworth. 6946-0
The **death** of Jefferson. Unknown. 7002-7
The **death** of Jezebel. Unknown. 6848-0
Death of John Q. Adams. I.E. Holmes. 6402-7
The **death** of Kais. Nizami. 6448-5
Death of King Conor Macnessa. Timothy Daniel [or Donill] Sullivan. 6415-9
The **death** of King Edmund. Lydia Huntley Sigourney. 6685-2
The **death** of King Edward I. Unknown. 6881-2
The **death** of Klondike Jack. Unknown. 6817-0
Death of Lara. George Gordon, 6th Baron Byron. 6980-0
The **death** of Leag, Cuchulain's charioteer. Francis Ledwidge. 6812-X
The **death** of Lenin. Vladimir Mayakovsky. 6546-5
The **death** of Leonidas. George Croly. 6302-0,6385-3,6344-6,6606-2
The **death** of Liali. Nizami. 6448-5
Death of Lincoln. Charles G. ("Miles O'Reilly") Halpine. 6708-5
Death of Lincoln despotism. Unknown. 6946-0
The **death** of Lincoln. William Cullen Bryant. 6008-0,6288-1,6077-3,6176-1,6289-X,6265-2,6524-4,6126
The **death** of little Jim. Unknown. 6392-6
Death of little Nell, fr. 'Old Curiosity Shop'. Charles Dickens. 6724-7,6167-2
The **death** of Lyon. Henry Peterson. 6074-9
The **death** of Lyon. Unknown. 6113-3
The **death** of Marie Toro. Robert Service. 6159-1
The **death** of Marlborough. George Walter Thornbury. 6980-0
The **death** of Marlborough. George Walter Thornbury. 6656-9
The **death** of Marmion. Sir Walter Scott. 6014-5,6606-2,6610-0,6661-5,6543-0
The **death** of master Tommy Rook. Eliza Cook. 6242-3,6502-3,6808-1
The **death** of Meleager, fr. Atalanta in Calydon. Algernon Charles Swinburne. 6437-X,6655-0,6102-8,6110-9
The **death** of Mirandola, 1494. Andrew Lang. 6771-9
The **death** of Mora-Mora, fr. The story of Baladeadro. George Gordon McCrae. 6768-9
The **death** of Moses. George Eliot. 6848-0
The **death** of Moses. Jessie G. McCartee. 6408-6
The **death** of Moses. James Montgomery. 6848-0
The **death** of Moses. Richard Henry Stoddard. 6848-0
Death of Mother Jones. Unknown. 6149-4
The **death** of Napolean. Isaac McClellan. 6102-8,6479-5,6076-5
The **death** of Napoleon. Isaac McLellan Jr. 6752-2
The **death** of Ned Kelly. John Streeter Manifold. 6895-2
The **death** of Nelson. Matthew Arnold. 6502-3
The **death** of Nelson. Adam Lindsay Gordon. 6951-7
The **death** of Nessus the centaur. John Gay. 6972-X
The **death** of Oberon. George Walter Thornbury. 6254-7,6114-1,6424-8
The **death** of Oenone. Alfred Lord Tennyson. 6527-9
The **death** of old Joe Yazzie. Ronald Rogers. 7005-1
The **death** of Parcy Reed. Unknown. 6055-2,6185-0,6067-9
The **death** of Paris. William Morris. 6196-6
The **death** of Patroclus, fr. The Iliad. Homer. 6435-3
The **death** of peace. Ronald Ross. 7026-4
The **death** of Philarete. William Browne. 6191-5
The **death** of Polybius Jubb. Roy Campbell. 6722-0
The **death** of Puck. Eugene Lee-Hamilton. 6473-6
The **death** of Queen Blache. Unknown (Spanish) 6757-3
The **death** of Queen Jane. Unknown. 6185-0,6518-X
Death of Queen Katharine. William Shakespeare. 6214-8
The **death** of Rhesus, fr. Rhesus. Euripides. 6435-3
The **death** of Richard Wagner. Algernon Charles Swinburne. 6315-2
The **death** of Robin Hood. William Rose Benet. 6781-6
The **death** of Robin Hood. Eugene Field. 6949-5
The **death** of Roland the knight. Robert Buchanan. 6134-6
The **death** of Roland. Robert Buchanan. 6669-0
The **death** of Roland. Unknown (French). 6573-2
The **death** of Roosevelt. Theresa Virginia Beard. 6995-9
The **death** of Ruth. George Crabbe. 6980-0
Death of Saint Guthlac. Cynewulf. 6022-6

The death of Sampson, fr. Samson Agonistes. John Milton. 6358-6,6125-7
The death of Santa Claus. Vincent Starrett. 6218-0
The death of Shallum. Lucy A. Randall. 6848-0
The death of sin and the life of holiness. Richard Henry Dana. 6752-2
The death of slavery. William Cullen Bryant. 6340-3,6403-5
The death of Sohrab. Matthew Arnold. 6322-5
Death of Stonewall Jackson. Henry Lynden Flash. 6113-3, 6016-0
The death of Stonewall Jackson. Stephen Vincent Benet. 6879-0
The death of Sualtem. Francis Ledwidge. 6812-X
Death of Taluta. Unknown (American Indian) 6396-9
The death of the ball-turret gunner. Randall Jarrell. 6666-6,6665-8
The death of the bee. John Russell Hayes. 6936-3
Death of the beloved. Rainer Maria Rilke. 6648-8
Death of the bull. Roy Campbell. 6210-5
The death of the craneman. Alfred Hayes. 6390-X,6375-6, 6666-6
Death of the day. Walter Savage Landor. 6641-0
The death of the first-born. Samuel Rogers. 6848-0
The death of the flowers. William Cullen Bryant. 6121-4, 6309-8,6396-X,6438-8,6219-9,6304 ,6560-0,6639-9,6232-6,6240-7,6302-0,6385-3,6288-1,6431
Death of the grandmother. Gwendolen Haste. 6979-7
The death of the hired man. Robert Frost. 6153-2,6029-3, 6121-4,6628-3,6645-3,6077-3,6527-9,6732-8,6646-1, 6458-2
Death of the King of Babylon, fr. Isaiah XIV. Bible. 6472-8
The death of the Loch Ness monster. Gwendolyn Macewen. 6767-0
The death of the minuet. Catherine Maria Fanshaw. 6959-2
The death of the old clock. Charles Capron Marsh. 6116-8
The death of the old squire. Unknown. 6914-9
the death of the old squire. Unknown. 7010-8
The death of the old year. Alfred Lord Tennyson. 6302-0, 6385-3,6479-5,6456-6,6438-8,6747-6,6219-9,6394-2, 6571-6
The death of the old [or, owd] squire. Unknown. 6744-1, 6155-9,6571-6
The death of the poet. Rainer Maria Rilke. 6879-0
The death of the reveller. W.A. Eaton. 6412-4,6617-8
Death of the virtuous. Anna Letitia Barbauld. 6219-9,6271-7,6600-3
The death of the wilderness, sels. Chaim Nachman Bialik. 7039-6
The death of Themistocles, sels. John Nichol. 6819-7
The death of Virgil. Angelo di Costanzo. 6325-X
The death of Wallace. Robert Southey. 6188-5
The death of Warren. Epes Sargent. 6946-0
The death of Wolfe. Unknown. 6753-0
The death of Wolfe. Unknown. 6946-0
The death of Wyatt. Henry Howard, Earl of Surrey. 6584-8
The death of Yajnadatta, fr. The Ramayana. Unknown (Sanskrit) 6372-1
"The death of your child". Correspondence. Susan Rea. 6822-7
A death on Easter day. Algernon Charles Swinburne. 6123-0
Death over the air. Jacinto Fombona Pachano. 6759-X
The death penalty. Ross Laurse. 6792-1
Death ray. Lola Ridge. 6619-4
The death ride. Gerald Massey. 6424-8
Death row. Charles Culhane. 6870-7
A death scene. Emily Bronte. 7037-X,6832-4
"Death shall be death forever unto thee". Forever dead. Sappho. 7039-6
Death snips proud men. Carl Sandburg. 6879-0
Death song. Robert Stephen Hawker. 6437-X
Death song. Alonzo Lewis. 6946-0
The death song of Go-ge-we-osh. Unknown (American Indian) 6396-9
The death song, sels. Richard Hovey. 6501-5
A death song. William Morris. 6123-0,6655-0,6656-9
A death song. William Morris. 7009-4
Death stands above me. Walter Savage Landor. 6289-X,6337-3, 6339-X,6086-2,6396-9,6153 ,6052-8,6086-2,6023-4,6199-0,6110-9,6110 ,6396-9,6668-2,6430-2

"Death stands there in the background, but...". Instructions on how to wind a watch. Julio Cortazar. 6758-1
"Death stately came to a young man, and said". Death deposed. William Allingham. 6930-4
Death stirs the arras. Eleanor Sands Smith. 6979-7
Death the conqueror. James Shirley. 6301-2
Death the enemy, fr. Alcestis. Euripides. 6435-3
Death the leveller. Anyte. 6435-3
Death the leveller. Shirley James. 6600-3
Death the leveller, fr The contention of Ajax & Ulysses. James Shirley. 6246-6,6337-3,6732-8,6075-7,6138-9, 6186 ,6315-2,6339-X,6395-0,6489-2,6427-2,6302 ,6385-3,6102-8,6737-9,6659-3,6150-8,6153
Death the peacemaker. Ellen H. Flagg. 6074-9,6340-3
"'Death to the aristocrats' the people roar'd". A slave's triumph. Ebenezer Jones. 7009-4
"Death touched the winter's arm, and spoke". Death and the lord. Hermann Hagedorn. 6944-4
The death vow of Don Alonzo of Aguilar. Unknown (Spanish) 6757-3
"Death walks through the mind's dark woods". Poem ("Death walks"). Henry Treece. 6379-9
"Death! that struck when I was most confiding". Death. Emily Bronte. 6123-0
Death's alchemy. William Sidney Walker. 6656-9
Death's blunder. Helen Angele Goodwin. 6414-0
Death's carriage stops the way. John Whitaker Watson. 6774-3
Death's choice. George Halse. 6916-9
Death's conqueror, fr. Corinthians. Bible. 6337-3
Death's dolls are we. Charles Norman. 6780-8
Death's emissaries. James Shirley. 6315-2
Death's final conquest. James Shirley. 6646-1,6543-0,6271-7,6605-2,6438-8,6219-9,6424-8
Death's guerdon. Lizette Woodworth Reese. 6274-1
Death's heritage. Humbert Wolfe. 6072-2
Death's jest book. Thomas Lovell Beddoes. 6545-7
Death's jest book, sel. Thomas Lovell Beddoes. 6958-4
Death's jest book, sel. Thomas Lovell Beddoes. 6958-4
Death's jest book, sels. Thomas Lovell Beddoes. 6472-8, 6198-2,6317-9,6378-0,6482-5,6199-0,6656
"Death's nobility again". In battle. Wallace Stevens. 6897-9
"Death's pale cold orb has turned to...eclipse". Avalon. Thomas Holley Chivers. 6754-9
Death's pale play-thing. Susan Miles. 6985-1
Death's ramble. Thomas Hood. 6089-7,6278-4
Death's silence. William Elijah Hunter. 6800-6
Death's summons. Thomas Nashe. 6198-2,6189-3
Death's summons, sel. Thomas Nashe. 6153-2
Death's valley. Walt Whitman. 6126-5
"Death, a light outshining life, bids...". The ballad of Melicertes. Algernon Charles Swinburne. 6875-8
"Death, I say, my heart is bowed". The shroud. Edna St. Vincent Millay. 6897-9,6986-X
"Death, be not proud, though some have called thee" John Donne. 6182-6,6488-4,6473-6,6389-1,6634-8,6536-8, 6315-2,6726-3,6194-X,6250-4,6125-7,6153-2,6214-8, 6737-9,6645-3
Death, fr. Continuation of Lucan. Thomas May. 6337-3
Death, fr. Songs of farewell. Dora Greenwell. 7037-X
Death, fr. The Bhagavad-gita. Unknown (Sanskrit) 6337-3
Death, fr. The giaour. George Gordon, 6th Baron Byron. 6302-0;6385-3
Death, fr. The house of night. Philip Freneau. 6399-3
Death, life, fear. Lilla Cabot Perry. 6501-5
"Death, of thee do I make my moan". To death, of his lady. Dante Gabriel Rossetti. 6875-8
"Death, on a solemn night of state". The court of death. John Gay. 6972-X
Death, sels. John Clare. 6472-8,6545-7
"Death, the black wizard of the center". The turnaround for higherground. Pancho Aguila. 6870-7
"Death, the open gateway to life". The gateway. Margaret McNeish. 6906-1
"Death, though already in the world, as". The legend of the dead lambs. Owen (Edward Bulwer-Lytton, Earl Lytton) Meredith. 6848-0
"Death, why hast thou made life so hard...". Canzone: Of

DEATH,

his dead lady. Giacomino Pugliesi. 7039-6
"Death, why so cruel? What! no other way". Bacon's epitaph, made by his man. John Cotton (atr). 6946-0
"Death, why so cruel? What! No other way", made by his man. Unknown. 7017-5
A death-bed lament. Robert Greene. 6543-0
The death-bed of Benedict Arnold. Unknown. 6451-5
Death-bed of Bomba, King of Naples. Unknown. 6302-0;6385-3
A death-bed. James Aldrich. 6214-8,6219-9,6271-7,6737-9, 6911-8,6309-8
A death-bed. Francis Turner Palgrave. 6980-0
The death-bridge of the Tay. Will Carleton. 6550-3,6919-3
Death-chant for the sultan Mahmoud. Bartholomew Simmons. 6980-0
Death-chant of the centaurs, sels. Stephen Vincent Benet. 6300-4
The death-child. William ("Fiona Macleod") Sharp. 6656-9
The death-dream. Walter De La Mare. 6958-4
The death-going of Scyld, fr. Beowulf. Unknown. 6102-8
Death-in-love. Dante Gabriel Rossetti. 6828-6
The death-ride.. John Westland Marston. 6407-8
A death-scene. Emily Bronte. 6828-6
The death-song of Alcestis. Felicia Dorothea Hemans. 6973-8
The death-song of Chi-wee-moo. A.H. Chandler. 7041-8
The death-song of Ossian. Unknown. 6873-1
The death-song of Turann. John Todhunter. 6174-5
The deathbed.. Leonard Feeney. 6096 X
Deathless. William Douw Lighthall. 6796-4
"Deathless principle, arise". Augustus Montague Toplady. 6931-2
The deathless tale. Charles Hanson Towne. 6144-3,6335-7, 6608-9
Deaths. Hjalmar Jonsson. 6854-5
Deaths. Dan Propper. 6901-0
Deaths and entrances. Dylan Thomas. 6391-8
The deaths of Antoiny and Cleopatra. William Shakespeare. 6153-2
The deaths of Myron and Klydone, fr. In a day. Augusta Webster. 6656-9
Deathwatch. Al Masarik. 6901-0
The debate in the sennit. James Russell Lowell. 6946-0
The debate of the body and the soul, sels. Unknown. 6102-8
The debate of the gods. John Gay. 6972-X
Debauch. Ibn Rashiq. 6362-4
Deborah. W.W. Christman. 6662-3
Deborah Lee. Unknown. 6302-0;6385-3
Deborah Lee-- a parody. Unknown. 6045-1
Deborah's triumphant song. Laurence Howell. 6848-0
Debris. Lola Ridge. 6102-8,6076-5
Debs, Eugene V.
    Jesus ("The martyred Christ of the working class...") 6144-3
DeBurgh, H.J.
    Half hours with the classics. 6089-7,6724-7
Debt. Henry William Parsons. 6490-6
Debt. Sara Teasdale. 6077-3,6300-4
Debt in two costumes. Wood Levette Wilson. 7021-3
The debt unpayable. Francis William Bourdillon. 6542-2
The debt.. Edward Verrall Lucas. 6474-4
The debt. Theodosia Garrison. 6449-3
Debt[s].. Jessie B. Rittenhouse. 6102-8,6019-6,6076-5,6300-4,6250-4
Debut of spring. Jeannette Carter Brautigan. 6789-1
A debutante's boquets. M.D. Hatch. 7021-3
The debutante. Guy Wetmore Carryl. 6266-0,6476-0,6732-8
The debutante. Eugene Field. 6949-5
The debutante. Henry Tyrrell. 7041-8
Debutantrum. William Rose Benet. 6307-1
Dec. 4-8 Daniel Diamond. 7003-5
Decade of rain. Richard Solly. 6857-X
A decade. Amy Lowell. 6488-4,6536-8
Decadent. E. Merrill Root. 6039-0
"Decadent ships of brash display-". The ships of Glou'ster. Ruth Hornbrook. 6818-9
The decameron, sels. Giovanni Boccaccio. 6325-X
A decanter of Madeira, aged 86, to George Bancroft... Silas Weir Mitchell. 6300-4,6307-1,6431-0
Decatur's toast. Arthur Guiterman. 6773-5
Decay. George Herbert. 6378-0

The decay of a people. William Gilmore Simms. 7017-5
The decay of Venice. Silas Weir Mitchell. 6624-0
A decayed monastery. Thomas Dermody. 6930-4
The deceased. Keith Douglas. 6210-5
Deceit. Joanna Baillie. 6294-6
The deceit of appearances. William Shakespeare. 6543-0
Deceitful hope. Julius Polyaenus. 6435-3
The deceitful mistress. Thomas Lodge. 6827-8
The deceitfulness of love. Unknown. 6271-7
The deceived lover sueth only for liberty. Sir Thomas Wyatt. 6302-0;6385-3
Deceivers. Hugh Orange. 6072-2
December. Alice Arnold. 6807-3
December. Elizabeth V. Auvache. 6799-9
December. Joel Benton. 6006-4,6597-X
December. Harriet F. Blodgett. 6145-1
December. Luman R. Bowdish. 6799-9
December. Henry S. Cornwell. 6632-1
December. William Croswell Doane. 6674-4
December. Heloise M.B. Hawkins. 6836-7
December. John Keats. 6239-3
December. Maurice Kenny. 7005-1
December. William Morris. 7020-5
December. Andrew Murray. 6821-9
December. Eden Phillpotts. 6071-4
December. Christina Georgina Rossetti. 6747-6
December. Frank Dempster Sherman. 6311-X
December. Edmund Spenser. 6191-5
December. Bayard Taylor. 6976-2
December 31. Samuel Ellsworth Kiser. 6291-1
December and May. Thomas Hood. 6974-6
December child. Virginia Wuerfel Slayton. 6906-1
A December day, fr. Berkshire notes. Sara Teasdale. 6778-6
A December day. Robert Fuller Murray. 6180-X
A December day. Sara Teasdale. 6465-5
"December days are dark and gray". December. Elizabeth V. Auvache. 6799-9
December in Arnold wood. Merrill Moore. 6037-4
December mourn. Estelle Lenore Silverman. 6847-2
A December prayer. G.C. Wing Jr. 6118-4
December twenty-fourth. Eleanor Slater. 6144-5,6337-3
December's thrush. Unknown. 7020-5
December, fr. Sonnets of the months. Folgore da San Gemignano. 6325-X
"A decent distance from the mercy seat". Not a swarrow falleth. Philip Littell. 6880-4
Deception. Cora Fabri. 6876-6
"Deck thee with jewels from the Indian mine". To Viola. Alfred Henry Haynes Bell. 6800-6
"Deck thyself, maiden". Estonian bridal song. Johann Gottfried von Herder. 7039-6
Deck, James G.
    The king in his beauty. 6065-X
Deckar
    "The best of men". 6238-5
Decker, Jean
    To a daguerreotype. 6850-2
DeClue, Charlotte
    Ijajee's story. 7005-1
    In memory of the moon.(A killing.) 7005-1
    Morning song. 7005-1
    Place-of-many-swans. 7005-1
The deckhands. Unknown. 7012-5
Declaration. Amanda Benjamin Hall. 6761-1
A declaration of belief. Walter Russell Bowie. 6532-5
"A declaration on the plaintiff's part". The orderly parts of pleading. S.D. Sibbet. 6878-2
The declaration. Nathaniel Parker Willis. 6089-7,6404-3, 6278-4
Declaring the male. Sam Bradley. 6803-0
Declivities of heaven, fr. Nepenthe. George Darley. 6545-7
Decoramenta. Henry S. Ely. 6118-4
Decoration. Thomas Wentworth Higginson. 6263-6,6431-0
Decoration Day. Susie M. Best. 7022-1
Decoration Day. Hezekiah Butterworth. 7022-1
"Decoration Day--and graves of soldiers". Memorial. Dale Gahl. 6799-9
Decoration day. Edgar Fawcett. 7041-8
Decoration Day. Francis Miles Finch. 6424-8
Decoration day. Richard Watson Gilder. 7041-8

Decoration Day. Richard Watson Gilder. 6340-3
Decoration Day. Henry Wadsworth Longfellow. 6340-3,6574-0
Decoration Day. Louis Stoddard. 6761-1
Decoration Day. Benjamin Franklin Taylor. 6815-4
Decoration Day. Ella Wheeler Wilcox. 6672-0
Decoration day at Charleston. Henry Timrod. 6240-7
Decoration Day on the place. James Whitcomb Riley. 6892-8
Decoration ode. Ben Wood Davis. 6927-4
The decorative mania. Unknown. 6215-6
A decoy partridge. Simias. 6435-3
Decrease, release: dum morior orior. Robert Southwell. 6380-2,6586-4
"A decrepit old gasman, named Peter". Limerick:"A decrepit old gasman, named Peter." Unknown. 6308-X
Decried. J. Roy Zeiss. 6039-0
Dectera of the Dun. Alice Milligan. 6628-3
Dedicare. Eugene Richard White. 7007-8
Dedicated to Major Bowes. Margaret Elizabeth Sangster. 6654-2
Dedicated to Mrs. E.R. Jones. L. Lillian Strain. 6270-9
Dedication. Drummond Allison. 6210-5
Dedication. Louis FitzGerald Benson. 6337-3,6525-2
Dedication. Pauline Florence Brower. 6327-6
Dedication. Lucy Wilson Buxton. 7016-7
Dedication. Holger Drachmann. 6555-4
Dedication. John Erskine. 6501-5
Dedication. Eugenius III. 6282-2
Dedication. John Galsworthy. 6888-X
Dedication. Alfred Gordon. 6115-X
Dedication. Ralph Gustafson. 6021-8
Dedication. Piet Hein. 6555-4
Dedication. Helen Hunt Jackson. 7041-8
Dedication. Henry Wadsworth Longfellow. 6333-0
Dedication. Patrick MacGill. 6930-4
Dedication. Czeslaw Milosz. 6758-1
Dedication. Alfred Noyes. 6151-6;6169-9
Dedication. Francis Reginald Scott. 6021-8
Dedication. Algernon Charles Swinburne. 6828-6
Dedication. Ethel Arnold Tilden. 6337-3
Dedication. Charles Wesley. 6337-3
A dedication ("Dear, near and true...") Alfred Lord Tennyson. 6110-9
Dedication ("We dedicate a church today"). William Cullen Bryant. 6525-2
Dedication for a book of Conning Tower contributions. Lee Wilson Dodd. 6817-0
Dedication for a home. John Oxenham. 6144-3;6335-7
Dedication for a spear. Simonides. 6435-3
Dedication hymn. Nathaniel Parker Willis. 6752-2
Dedication hymn ("O thou"). John Pierpont. 6752-2
Dedication hymn ("With trump"). John Pierpont. 6752-2
The dedication in Don Juan. George Gordon, 6th Baron Byron. 6200-8,6110-9
Dedication of a municipal rose garden. Martha England Murphey. 6799-9
Dedication of the chronicles of England and France. Robert Fabyan. 6282-2
Dedication of the designs to Blair's 'Grave'. William Blake. 6086-2
Dedication to a book of stories selected..Irish novelists. William Butler Yeats. 6375-6
Dedication to a first book. William Rose Benet. 6320-9
A dedication to Athene. Archias. 6435-3
Dedication to Leigh Hunt, Esq. John Keats. 6250-4
Dedication to Mary Angela. Alfred Noyes. 6298-9
Dedication to poems and ballads. Algernon Charles Swinburne. 6657-7
A dedication to the author of Holmby house. Adam Lindsay Gordon. 6951-7
Dedication to Wilfird and Alive Meynell. Francis Thompson. 6942-8
A dedication, fr. Aylmer's field. Alfred Lord Tennyson. 6655-0
Dedication, fr. Barrack room ballads. Rudyard Kipling. 6810-3
Dedication, fr. Fo'c's'le yarns: 1st series. Thomas Edward Brown. 6809-X
Dedication, fr. Fo'c's'le yarns: 2d series. Thomas Edward Brown. 6809-X
Dedication, fr. Idylls of the king. Alfred Lord Tennyson.
6154-0,6199-0,6219-9
Dedication, fr. In war time. John Greenleaf Whittier. 6735-2
Dedication, fr. Second book of verse. Eugene Field. 6949-5
Dedication, fr. Sonnets of the months. Folgore da San Gemignano. 6325-X
Dedication, fr. The dream. Caroline Elizabeth Sarah Sheridan Norton. 6980-0
Dedication, fr. The revolt of Islam. Percy Bysshe Shelley. 6980-0
Dedication, fr. The town. David Morton. 6531-7
Dedication, to Poems and ballads, 1st series. Algernon Charles Swinburne. 6110-9,6655-0
A dedication. Sara Coleridge. 6233-4
A dedication. Adam Lindsay Gordon. 6793-X,6784-0
A dedication. Rudyard Kipling. 6337-3,6437-X,6102-8
A dedication. Alfred Lord Tennyson. 6828-6
The dedication. George Herbert. 6430-2
Dedications, sels. Sir John Davies. 6584-8
Dedicatory ode, sels. Hilaire Belloc. 6477-9
Dedicatory poem to the Princess Alice. Alfred Lord Tennyson. 6867-7,6977-0
Dedicatory sonnet. Christina Georgina Rossetti. 6655-0
Dedicatory stanzas. Cecil Day Lewis. 6390-X
Dedinac, Milan
    How silent they who die. Mae Lloyd Parker Ruzich (tr.). 6068-4
Deduction. Mark Van Doren. 6076-5
A deed and a word. Charles Mackay. 6273-3;6481-7;6669-0
A deed and a word. Charles Mackay. 6889-8
The deed is the man. James C. McNally. 6889-8
The deed of Lieutenant Miles. Clinton Scollard. 6946-0
"Deedle, deedle dumpling, my son John". Unknown. 6363-2
Deeds. Unknown. 6861-8
"Deeds not words: I say so too!". Facta non verba. Henry Van Dyke. 6961-4
The deeds of anger. Edgar A. Guest. 7033-7
Deeds of kindness. F. P. 6452-3
Deeds of kindness. Epes Sargent. 6135-4
The deeds of King Olaf, sels. Charles Whitby. 6994-0
Deeds of valor at Santiago. Clinton Scollard. 6946-0
Deeds undone. Gamaliel Bradford. 6072-2
Deeds versus creeds. Annie I. Muzzey. 6045-1
Deeds, not heredity. Sadi [or Saadi] (Mushlih-ud-Din) 6889-8
Deeds, not words. Unknown. 6294-6
"Deem as ye list, upon good cause." Sir Thomas Wyatt. 6584-8
"Deem not devoid of elegance the sage". Thomas Warton Jr. 6122-2
"Deem not, devoid of elegance, the sage". Written in a blank leaf of Dudgale's Monasticon. Thomas Warton Jr.. 6831-6
Deems, Charles F.
    "The world is wide". 6109-5
Deen, Geryl
    Whose son? 7019-1
"A deep and a mighty shadow". Bryan Waller ("Barry Cornwall") Procter. 6980-0
Deep and dark blue ocean, fr. Childe Harold. George Gordon, 6th Baron Byron. 6125-7
"The deep and lordly Danube". The wayside dream. Bayard Taylor. 6976-2
The deep blue sea. Mrs. Thomas B. Upchurch. 6270-9
"Deep bosomed, buxom, at first glance, mature". Chicago. Berton Braley. 6853-7
"Deep buried 'neath Assyria's barren plains". An ancient grievance. Unknown. 6936-3
"The deep divine dark dayshine of the sea". Algernon Charles Swinburne. 6997-5
Deep down. James Stuart Montgomery. 6374-8
Deep dusk. Ellen M. Carroll. 7016-7
"Deep garden/of dark-green leaves". Garden. Andreas Okopenko. 6769-7
"Deep in a distant bay, and deeply hidden". The lonely isle. Claudian. 7039-6
"Deep in a vale where rocks on every side". Sonnet ("Deep in a vale"). Gustav Rosenhane. 7039-6
"Deep in a vale, a stranger now to arms". The American soldier. Philip Freneau. 6753-0

DEEP

"Deep in my heart is a fountain of love". Fountain. Marie Louise Allen. 6906-1
Deep in my soul. George Gordon, 6th Baron Byron. 6328-4
"'Deep in the ages', you said...". In memory of Vachel Lindsay. Sara Teasdale. 6782-4
"Deep in the heart of the forest the lily...". The lily of Yorrow. Henry Van Dyke. 6961-4
Deep in the heavens. Ricarda Huch. 6643-7
"Deep in the northern lands". In the battell hemlocks. Frederick Lewis Pattee. 7030-2
Deep in the nosegay. Max Dauthendey. 6160-5
"Deep in the shady sadness of a vale". The fall of the Titans, fr. Hyperion. John Keats. 6935-5
"Deep in the Siberian mine". Message to Siberia. Alexander Pushkin. 7039-6
"Deep in the shady sadness of a vale", fr. Hyperion. John Keats. 6122-2,6289-X
"Deep in the silent forest shades of...". Song of the St. Lawrence. Lily Alice Lefevre. 6797-2
"Deep in the warm vale...", fr. The saint's tragedy. Charles Kingsley. 6123-0
"Deep in the woods this distillate of snow". A winter's tail. W.M. Bronk. 6764-6
"Deep lines of honour all can hit". The portrait. Anne Finch, Countess of Winchilsea. 6932-0
"Deep locked in the ocean the secret lies". The pilots bride. George M. Vickers. 6922-3
Deep longing. Detlev von Liliencron. 6160-5
"Deep loving, well knowing". Our Colonel. Arthur Guiterman. 6995-9
"Deep loving, well knowing/His world and...". Our colonel. Arthur Guiterman. 6773-5
"The deep mid-ocean waters perpetually". Agnes Mary F. ("Madame Duclaux") Robinson. 6997-5
"Deep on the convent-roof the snows". Saint Agnes' eve. Alfred Lord Tennyson. 6828-6
Deep peace. Josephine Royle. 6076-5
A deep revenge. Thornton W. Burgess. 6798-0
A deep sea dream. Mary Artemisia Lathbury. 6965-7
Deep sea soundings. Sarah Williams. 6730-1,6214-8
"Deep sighs, records of my unpitied grief". Ditty. Edward Herbert, 1st Baron Herbert of Cherbury. 6908-8
Deep sleep. Gabriela (Lucila Godoy Alcayaga) Mistral. 6759-X
"Deep solitude I sought. There was a dell". Solitude. Lydia Huntley Sigourney. 6752-2
Deep stuff. Keith Preston. 6722-0
Deep unto deep. John Banister Tabb. 6850-2
"Deep was the furrow in the royal brow". Saul and David. James Grahame. 6848-0
"Deep within my heart of hearts, dear". Two loves. Adelaide Anne Procter. 6957-6
"Deep within the jungle's darkness". The black panther. James Mooney. 6850-2
"A deep, delicious hush in earth and sky". A noon interval. James Whitcomb Riley. 6993-2
"Deep, fiery clouds o'ercast the sky". The thunder-storm. Felicia Dorothea Hemans. 6973-8
The deep, sels. Gladys Cromwell. 6501-5
"A deep-bassed, thunder-rolling psalm". Creation's psalm. Swithin Saint Swithaine. 6848-0
"The deep-mouth'd sea". William Shakespeare. 6997-5
The deep-sea cables. Rudyard Kipling. 6331-4
Deep-sea calm. Hardwicke Drummond Rawnsley. 6997-5
The deep-sea peril. Edith M. Thomas. 6019-6
A deep-sworn vow. William Butler Yeats. 6244-X
"A deep-toned lyre hung murmuring". The lyre's lament. Felicia Dorothea Hemans. 6973-8
The deep-water man. James Stuart Montgomery. 6374-8
"The deep/All down the sand". Alfred Lord Tennyson. 6997-5
The deep. John Gardiner Calkins Brainard. 6385-3
"A deeper crimson in the rose". Dorothea. Henry Van Dyke. 6961-4
The deeper seas. Henry Bellamann. 6833-2
"Deeper than all sense of seeing". Right living. Unknown. 6923-1
"Deeper than the narwhal sinketh". The sea-deeps. Thomas Miller. 6018-8,6833-2
"Deeper, deeper, let us toil". Unknown. 6601-1
Deeply gone. Jon Silkin. 6218-0

"Deeply have I slept". Death's jest book, sel. Thomas Lovell Beddoes. 6958-4
"The deeps have music soft and low". Where corals lie. Richard Garnett. 6997-5
Deer. John Drinkwater. 6253-9
Deer. Chun-myung No. 6775-1
Deer. Herbert Zand. 6769-7
Deer in Mooreland. William Rose Benet. 6782-4
"The deer may leap within the glade". Little John and the red friar. William Edmonstoune Aytoun. 6948-7
The deer of Ireland. Padraic Colum. 6069-2
The deer's cry. Saint Patrick. 6730-1
"Deer, lightning, bluebird, toad". Beneath the mound. R. T. Smith. 7005-1
"Deer-hoof dint and moccasin print". Minetta water. Arthur Guiterman. 6773-5
The deer-trapper. Francis Sterne Palmer. 6510-4
The deer. Virginia Wilson Lachicotte. 7016-7
"Deere my deere why are you cruell." Unknown. 6563-5
"Deere turne awaye thyne eyes soe bright." Unknown. 6563-5
Deesa greata holiday Fourth-July. Thomas Augustine Daly. 6721-2
Deeves, M.
    Stonewall's requiem. 6074-9
The deevil's waltz. Sidney Goodsir Smith. 6210-5
Defeat. Witter Bynner. 6979-7
Defeat. James A. Emanuel. 6178-8
Defeat. Tom MacInnes. 6021-8
Defeat. Countess W. Twitty. 6178-8
Defeat. Tanya Tyler. 6899-5
Defeat and victory. Wallace Rice. 6946-0
Defeat of the rebels. Robert Graves. 6666-6
The defeat of the Spanish armada. William Warner. 6547-3
The defeated years. Kirke Meechem. 6037-4
The defeated. Alun Lewis. 6528-7,6360-8
The defence of Guenevere. William Morris. 6186-9,6657-7, 6526-0,6110-9,6430-2,6655
The defence of Lucknow. Alfred Lord Tennyson. 6412-4,6240-7,6110-9,6419-1
The defence of the Alamo. Joaquin Miller. 6946-0
The defence of the Alamo. Joaquin Miller. 6471-X,6300-4, 6419-1
A defence of Xantippe. Unknown. 6919-3
Defenceless. Grace Holbrook Blood. 6764-6
The defenders.. John Drinkwater. 6477-9
Defense against the dark. Louis Ginsberg. 6648-8
The defense of Lawrence. Richard Realf. 6062-5
Defenses. Lucile Enlow. 6841-3
Defiance. John W. Boldyreff. 6818-9
Defiance. Robert Burns. 6322-5
Defiance. Olive Tilford Dargan. 6184-2
Defiance. Sir Walter Scott. 6438-8
Defiance. Percy Bysshe Shelley. 6087-0
The defiance of Hector and Ajax. Homer. 6424-8
Defiance to false gods. Bernice Lesbia Kenyon. 6619-4
Defiance, fr. Childe Harold's pilgrimage. George Gordon, 6th Baron Byron. 6545-7
The defiance. Thomas Flatman. 6933-9
The defiance. Thomas Flatman. 6023-4,6152-4
The defiance. Thomas Flatman. 6933-9
Defiant, cold and brave. Ben H. Smith. 6662-3
Defile of Gondo, fr. The prelude. William Wordsworth. 6832-4
Defiled. Medora Clarke. 6920-7
Defiled is my name. Anne Bolelyn. 6328-4
The defiled sanctuary. William Blake. 6191-5
Definace to love. Michael Drayton. 6827-8
Definition. Robert D. Calhoun. 6017-X
Definition. Grace Noll Crowell. 6365-9
Definition. Josephine Miles. 6640-2
Definition. Edwin Rolfe. 6375-6
The definition of beauty. Robert Herrick. 6378-0
Definition of creativeness. Boris Pasternak. 6546-5
The definition of love. Andrew Marvell. 6208-3,6315-2,6562-7,6563-5,6726-3,6430-2,6431-1,6150-8
Definition of my brother. William Sydney Graham. 6210-5, 6379-9
Definitions. William James Linton. 6600-3
Definitions of the word gout. Tina Koyama. 6790-5
Definitive things. Michael Benedikt. 6803-0

Deflowered. John Galsworthy. 6888-X
Defoe, Daniel
    The English race. 6932-0
    A hymn to the Pillory, sels. 6380-2
    Introduction to the true-born Englishman. 6200-8
    'The true-born Englishman', sels. 6733-6
    The true-born Englishman, sels. 6831-6
    The true-born Englishman, sels. 6152-4
    The true-born Englishman, sels. 6831-6
    "Wherever God erects a house of prayer". 6238-5
DeFoe, Ina Draper
    Prayer for a girl no longer young. 6750-6
    Return to earth. 6750-6
    Song of the hop fields. 6750-6
DeFord, Miriam Allen
    The musicmaker's child. 6029-3
    Running water. 6880-4
    Traveller's duty. 6037-4
DeFosset, Theressa M.
    Clocks. 6906-1
    On the beach. 6906-1
    She said to me. 6906-1
    To ignorance. 6906-1
    When winter stalks across the hills. 6906-1
DeFrees, Madeline
    Atlas of Oregon. 7032-9
The **deformed** transformed: a drama. George Gordon, 6th Baron Byron. 6945-2
The **deformity** lover. Felice Picano. 7003-5
Degen and R. Eberhart, Jessie (tr.)
    Happy are those who have died. Charles Peguy, 6665-8
    Shadow. Guillaume Apollinaire, 6665-8
    War. Guillaume Apollinaire, 6665-8
The **degeneracy** of Greece. George Gordon, 6th Baron Byron. 6606-2
The **degenerate** bees. John Gay. 6972-X
A **degenerate** of the pink family. Mary E. Hough. 6764-6
Degnan, Bryan
    Having clung so hard. 6761-1
DeGraff, Marjorie
    Coup d'etat. 6850-2
    Fire. 6850-2
    Late chrysanthemums. 6850-2
    Thoughts on taking an anaesthetic. 6850-2
Dehmel, Richard
    Before the storm. Ludwig Lewisohn (tr.). 7039-6
    great carousel<The. Babette Deutsch (tr.). 6160-5
    The great carousel. Babette Deutsch (tr.). 6160-5
    The harp. Babette Deutsch (tr.). 6160-5
    Harvest song. Ludwig Lewisohn (tr.). 7039-6
    The laborer. Jethro Bithell (tr.). 7039-6
    Mountain psalm. Babette Deutsch (tr.). 6160-5
    Song before night. Babette Deutsch (tr.). 6160-5
    Song to my son. Babette Deutsch (tr.). 6160-5
    The swimmer. Babette Deutsch (tr.). 6160-5
    Vigil. Ludwig Lewisohn (tr.). 7039-6
    Welcome. Babette Deutsch (tr.). 6160-5
    The workingman. Babette Deutsch (tr.). 6160-5
Dehn, Paul
    At the dark hour. 6666-6
    Government official. 6666-6
    Lament for a sailor. 6666-6
Dei gratia. William Wilkins. 6174-5
Deianira's wooing, fr. Trachiniae. Sophocles. 6435-3
Deid folks' ferry. Rosamund Marriott ("Graham R. Tomson") Watson. 6656-9
Deidre and Conchobar. Eugene O'Curry. 6582-1
Deidre looks back at Scotland. Sean O'Faolain. 6582-1
Deidre wedded. Herbert Trench. 6877-4
Deidre's lament over Naoisi. Whitley Stokes. 6582-1
"**Deigne** at my hands this crown of prayer...". La Corona. John Donne. 6933-7
The **deil's** awa' wi' the exciseman. Robert Burns. 6328-4, 6430-2
Deirdre. James Stephens. 6234-2,6244-X,6581-3,6513-9,6301-2,6393
Deirdre. William Butler Yeats. 6541-4
Deirdre dancing. Herbert Trench. 6090-0
Deirdre is dead. William ("Fiona Macleod") Sharp. 6655-0
Deirdre wedded, sels. Herbert Trench. 6174-5
Deirdre's farewell to Alba. John Todhunter. 6174-5
Deirdre's farewell to Alba. Unknown. 6930-4
Deirdre's farewell to Scotland. Unknown. 6930-4
Deirdre's great lamentation for the sons of Usnach. John Todhunter. 6174-5
Deirdre's lament. Unknown. 6930-4
Deirdre's lament for the sons of Usnach. Unknown. 6873-1
Deirdre's lament for the sons of Usnach. Unknown. 6244-X
Deissler, Mary Louise
    Man of Galilee. 6065-X
Deitsche advertisement. C. Toler Wolfe. 6791-3,6823-5
Deitz, Howard
    On the rising generation. 6026-9
DeJong, David Cornel
    Pleasant streetster days. 6017-X
Dejection. Robert Bridges. 6487-6
Dejection. James Gorham. 6850-2
Dejection: an ode. Samuel Taylor Coleridge. 6828-6
Dejection: an ode. Samuel Taylor Coleridge. 6315-2,6430-2,6199-0,6271-7,6378-0,6086-2,6110-9,6208-3,6536-8
Dekins, Stephen Taylor
    The persecuted Jew. 6848-0
Dekker (atr), Thomas
    The old and young courtier. 6301-2
Dekker, Thomas
    "Art thou poor, yet hast thou golden slumbers". 6187-7, 6198-2,6430-2
    A basket-maker's song. 6436-1
    Beauty, arise! 6182-6
    A bridal song. 6436-1
    A catch. 6153-2
    "Cold's the wind,...", fr. The shoemaker's holiday. 6198-2,6383-7
    Content. 6423-X,6189-3,6396-9
    Country glee. 6436-1,6150-8,6191-5
    A cradle song. 6436-1
    Cyclops' song. 6334-9
    The first true gentleman. 6102-8
    Fortune. 6436-1
    Fortune and virtue. 6245-8
    Fortune smiles. 6383-7
    The gifts of Fortune and Cupid. 6189-3
    Golden slumbers kiss your eyes. 6228-8,6490-6
    The happy heart. 6134-6,6737-9,6301-2,6246-5,6291-1, 6302-0,6385-3,6339-X
    Haymakers, rakers, reapers and mowers. 6383-7
    The honest whore, sels. 6317-9,6301-2
    Horace concocting an ode. 6996-7
    The invitation, fr. The sun's darling. 6827-8
    Lullaby. 6634-8,6634-8,6131-1,6189-3,6219-9,6737-9
    Lullaby ("Golden slumbers"). 6179-6,6233-4,6182-6,6315-2,6533-3,6633-X,6194-X
    May. 6436-1
    The merry month of May. 6189-3,6383-7
    O sorrow, sorrow. 6194-X
    O sweet content. 6473-6,6634-8,6197-4,6153-2,6191-5, 6194-X,6660-7
    Oh, the month of May! 6182-6
    Old fortunatus, sels. 6198-2
    The patient Grissel. 6250-4
    Patient Grissill, sels. 6198-2
    A portrait. 6230-X
    A portrait. 6230-X
    Saint Hugh. 6436-1
    The shoemaker's holiday, sels. 6198-2
    Song ("Virtue's branches"). 6182-6,6726-3
    The song of the Cyclops. 6179-6,6378-0,6808-1
    Song, fr. Patinet grissill. 6958-4
    Sweet content. 6543-0,6252-0,6219-9,6513-9,6182-6,6186-9,6315-2,6427-2,6726-3,6315-2,6258-4,6639-9,6513-9, 6252-0
    Troll the bowl! 6182-6,6189-3
    Troynovant. 6315-2,6436-1,6125-7
    "Virtue smiles: cry holiday,", fr. Old fortunatus. 6198-2
Del Guidice, Carol
    After man's massacre. 6883-9
    "The winter family" 6883-9
Del Picchia, Menotti
    Bay of Guanabara. Dudley Poore (tr.). 6759-X

DEL

The narrow street. Dudley Poore (tr.). 6759-X
Delamain, Jacques
  Spring night. 7020-5
DeLan, Surville J.
  Timber line. 6920-7
Deland, Margaret
  The bluebell. 6652-6
  Bossy and the daisy. 6937-1
  The Christmas silence. 6145-1,6608-9,6373-X,6519-8
  The clover. 6441-8
  Deaf. 6847-2
  Easter music. 6144-3,6465-5
  The fairies' shopping. 6519-8
  The first best Christmas night. 6608-9
  The golden-rod. 6338-1
  Life. 7041-8
  The old garden. 6847-2
  The succory. 6424-8
  Summer. 7041-8
  The waits. 6145-1
  While shepherds watched their flocks by night. 6145-1, 6239-3
  While shepherds watched their flocks by night. 7041-8
  Words, words, words. 6652-6
Delano on saturday night. Margaret Horsch Stevens. 6342-X
Delavan, Maude Smith
  Charmaid. 6750-6
Delavigne
  Sunshine. 6424-8
  Three days in the life of Columbus. 6425-6
Delavigne, Casimir
  La devastation du musee et des monuments. 6801-4
  La villa Adrienne. 6801-4
Delavigne, Casimir (tr.)
  Three days in the life of Columbus. Unknown, 6606-2
A **Delaware** youth and his uncle. Unknown (Algonquin Indian) 6864-2
The **delayer**. A.C. Shead. 6397-7
Delcomyn, Marion
  Song ("Like the south").. 6327-6
The **delectable** ballad of the waller lot. Eugene Field. 6318-7
Delia. Samuel Daniel. 6186-9
Delia's pocket-handkerchief. Robert Southey. 6787-5
Delia, sels. Samuel Daniel. 6208-3,6194-X,6645-3
"**Delia**, th' unkindest girl on earth". William Cowper. 6814-6
Delicate cluster. Walt Whitman. 6126-5,6288-1
"The **delicate** silver gates are closed". Love song. George Brandon Saul. 6038-2,6619-4
"**Delicately**, as a flurry of snow in November". Telling tall tales. Joseph Joel Keith. 6761-1
Delicatessen. Joyce Kilmer. 6498-1
Deliciae sapientiae de amore. Coventry Patmore. 6096 X
"**Delicious** beauty, that loth lie". Song ("Delicious beauty"). John Marston. 6182-6
A **delicious** interruption. James Whitcomb Riley. 6128-1
Delight in disorder. Robert Herrick. 6099-4,6208-3,6271-7, 6315-2,6339-X,6481-,6488-4,6536-8,6562-7,6563-5,6726-3,6732-8,6543-0,6723-9,6645-3,6219-9,6301-2,6026-9, 6659-3,6430-2,6189-3,6092-7,6250-4,6646-1
Delight in God only. Francis Quarles. 6102-8,6271-7,6385-3, 6337-3,6219-9,6737
The **delight** song of Tsoai-Talee. N. Scott Momaday. 7005-1
"A **delightful** change from the town's abode". Barnyard melodies. Fred Emerson Brooks. 6921-5,6695-X
"**Delightful** hour of sweet repose". Sabbath evening twilight. Unknown. 6752-2
"**Delightful** to be on the hill of Howth". Columcille's greeting to Ireland. Columcille (atr.). 6930-4
"**Delightful** would it be to me to be in Uchd Ailiun". Unknown. 6258-X
"**Delightful** would it be to me to be in...". Columcille fecit. Unknown. 6873-1
Delights of camp life. Unknown. 6273-3
The **delights** of Christmas. Unknown. 6608-9
Delilah. Adam Lindsay Gordon. 6951-7
Delilah. Virginia Lyne Tunstall. 6039-0
Delilah. Ella Wheeler Wilcox. 6956-8
Delilah poem. George Barker. 6390-X

Delinquent rabbit. Wilbur Dick Nesbit. 6720-4
Delirium. Betty Myers. 6841-3
Delius, Anthony
  Chameleon. 6788-3
  The coming. 6788-3
  The explorer. 6788-3
  The gamblers. 6788-3
  The great divide, sels. 6788-3
  The pilgrims. 6788-3
"**Deliver** me, o Lord, my God". Psalm 059. Bible. 6848-0
Deliverance. John Kendrick Bangs. 6654-2
The **deliverance** of Jehovah, fr. Psalm 27. Bible. 6730-1
The **deliverer**, fr. Samson Agonistes. John Milton. 6933-9
Dell and I. Ella Wheeler Wilcox. 6863-4
Dell, Floyd
  A birthday sonnet. 6880-4
  Cupid's holiday. 6039-0
  Sonnet ("Can you not"). 6880-4
  Sonnet ("One thing"). 6880-4
  To Edna St. Vincent Millay. 6880-4
  Two sonnets. 6880-4
The **dell**. Samuel Taylor Coleridge. 6935-5
The **Della** Cruscans. William Gifford. 6932-0
Deloney, Thomas
  A joyful new ballad. 6157-5
  The shoe-makers' song, fr. The gentle craft. 6334-9
  The winning of Cales. 6157-5
  Would God that it were holiday! 6182-6
Delos. Callimachus. 6435-3
Delos. Lawrence Durrell. 6379-9
Delos. Pindar. 6435-3
Delos. Bernard Spencer. 6209-1
Delphi humoresque. William Alexander Percy. 6039-0
"The **Delphian** oracle is dumb". Unknown. 6902-9
Delphic Oracle
  The army of Xerxes. Alfred Dennis Godley (tr.). 6435-3
  The fallen shrine. Sir William Marris (tr.). 6435-3
  Neutral Argos. Alfred Dennis Godley (tr.). 6435-3
  The power of an oath. Alfred Dennis Godley (tr.). 6453-4
  The wooden walls of Athens. Alfred Dennis Godley (tr.). 6435-3
DeLuca, M. Florence
  On my life's design. 6894-4
Delphiniums. Anne Lloyd. 6232-6
Delsarte girl. Alice E. Ives. 6698-4
The **delta** autumn. William Alexander Percy. 6037-4,6326-8
The **deluge**. Unknown. 6193-1
Delusion. Hattie Horner Louthan. 6836-7
A **delusion** of reference. R.A.D. Ford. 6446-9
Delusions 004. Charles Madge. 6209-1
Delusions 006. Charles Madge. 6379-9
Delusions 008. Charles Madge. 6788-3
"**Delusions** of the days that once have been". Prologue, fr. Giles Corey of the Salem farms. Henry Wadsworth Longfellow. 6946-0
Delzell, Frances Belle
  Rest. 6799-9
The **demagogue**. William Falconer. 6971-1
Dementia vernalis. John V.A. Weaver. 6538-4
Demeter. Robert Bridges. 6487-6
Demeter at Elusis. Unknown (Greek) 6435-3
Demeterius enters Athens. Hermocles. 6435-3
Demetrius. Constance Faunt LeRoy Runcie. 6670-4
The **demi-gods**. Anthony Bertram. 6781-6
Deming, Mrs. H.A.
  A curious life poem. 6410-8
  "Why all this toil...", fr. A curious life poem. 6410-8
Demirjian, Derenik
  The Eve of Ascension Day. 6050-1
Demirjibashian, Elia
  The song of the vulture. 6050-1
The **demise** of Doe and Roe. Unknown. 6878-2
Demmy Jake. David Law ("Pegleg Arkwright") Proudfit. 6247-4
The **demobilized** soldier, fr. The prelude. William Wordsworth. 6545-7
Democracy. Alfred Kreymborg. 6012-9
Democracy downtrodden. William Michael Rossetti. 7015-9
"A **democrat** I have never been". The mob is an awful bunch

of cattle. Milan Curcin. 6765-4
Democritus. Robert Bridges. 6487-6
Demodocus
    The snake it was that died. John Hermann Merivale (tr.). 6435-3
Demogorgon's speech. Percy Bysshe Shelley. 6315-2
The **demolished** farce; or, who is the author? Richard Harris ("Thomas Ingoldsby") Barham. 6802-2
Demon. Alexander Blok. 6103-6
Demon. Alfred Mombert. 6160-5
The **demon** kittens. Unknown. 6682-8
The **demon** lover. Unknown. 6056-0,6075-7,6180-X,6558-9,6687-9
Demon lovers. Elinor Wylie. 6399-3,6036-6
The **demon** of our land. Edward R. Huxley. 6885-5
The **demon** of the Gibbet. Fitz-James O'Brien. 6518-X
The **demon** of the mirror. Bayard Taylor. 6670-4
The **demon** ship. Thomas Hood. 6554-6
A **demon's** false description of his race... James Abraham Hillhouse. 6752-2
The **demon-ship.** Thomas Hood. 6911-8
"**Demonic** Yankee who could taste". Emily Dickinson. Paul Engle. 6761-1
The **demons** of opium, fr. Sir Eustace Gray. George Crabbe. 6545-7
The **demons** of the cities. Georg Heym. 6160-5
Demos. Edwin Arlington Robinson. 6033-1
Dempsey, H. Frances
    Pledge and prayer. 6717-4
Denham, Sir John
    Cooper's hill. 6208-3,6152-4,6562-7
    Cooper's hill, sels. 6198-2,6194-X
    "My eye, descending...", fr. Cooper's Hill. 6198-2
    Natura naturata. 6380-2,6152-4
    O could I flow. 6250-4
    On Mr. Abraham Cowley's death and burial amongst... 6198-2,6483-3
    On the Earl of Strafford's trial and death. 6315-2
    The Thames from Cooper's Hill, fr. Cooper's Hill. 6933-9
    The Thames, fr. Cooper's hill. 6150-8,6102-8
    To the five members of the honourable house of commons. 6380-2
Denial. George Herbert. 6208-3,6315-2
Denial. Lancaster Pollard. 6374-8
"**Denial** past, life comes to thee". Too late. Gertrude Huntington McGiffert. 6838-3
A **denial.** Elizabeth Barrett Browning. 6301-2
Denison, Charles W.
    The American village. 6755-7
    The anniversary deaths. 6755-7
    At sea on the sabbath. 6755-7
    The burial of Knowles. 6755-7
    The buried boy to his mother. 6755-7
    Children's temperance song. 6755-7
    The current coin of heaven. 6755-7
    The dead child. 6755-7
    The dead mariner. 6755-7
    The departure of Paul. 6755-7
    The drunkard's dream. 6911-8
    The dying convict. 6755-7
    The dying missionary. 6755-7
    The dying student. 6755-7
    The early dead. 6755-7
    The factory girl. 6755-7
    Family clusters. 6755-7
    The first rose of summer. 6755-7
    Genesis 1:2. 6755-7
    The grave. 6755-7
    Heaven's own child. 6755-7
    The husband to his sick wife. 6755-7
    The Indian chief. 6755-7
    Infant's funeral hymn. 6755-7
    Invocation, fr. The American village. 6755-7
    The lesson of the grave. 6755-7
    The light of life. 6755-7
    The missionary's home. 6755-7
    The missionary's song. 6755-7
    Morus-multicaulis; a satire...American silk speculators. 6755-7
    Moses writing in the wilderness. 6755-7
    Parting at sea. 6755-7
    The pilgrim's rest. 6755-7
    The poisoner and his victim. 6755-7
    The presence of God. 6755-7
    Reply of the harp. 6755-7
    The rumseller's song. 6414-0
    The sailor. 6755-7
    A song in heaven. 6755-7
    The spirit-hand and voice. 6755-7
    Stanzas ("How oft, in my tear-flowing..."). 6755-7
    The step-mother. 6755-7
    The storm spirit's tale of The Lexington. 6755-7
    The stormy petrel. 6755-7
    Suffering with Christ. 6755-7
    Swiss boy's adieu to the Rhone. 6755-7
    To Clarence. 6755-7
    To one in heaven. 6755-7
    To the flakes of snow. 6755-7
    The vacant chairs. 6755-7
    The voices of the seas. 6755-7
    The woodland chapel. 6755-7
    The wreck. 6755-7
Denison, Eldredge
    Her garden ("This was her dearest walk last year..."). 6338-1
Denison, Elizabeth W.
    Willie's mishap. 6965-7
Denison, Henry
    Life. 7030-2
Denison, J.P.
    Wing tee wee. 6089-7
Denison, Mary A.
    Beautiful grandmamma. 6131-1
    Grandfather's rose. 6139-7
    Mary O'Connor, the volunteer's wife. 6139-7
    Poor Katy. 6131-1
Denlinger, H.
    My dog Jerry. 6799-9
Denman, Annie
    For his sake. 6065-X
Denman, Sir John (tr.)
    Harmodius and Aristogeiton. Callistratus, 6271-1
Denmark song. Johannes V. Jensen. 6555-4
Denmark speaks. Soren Hallar. 6555-4
Dennen, Grace Atherton
    The coming of dawn. 6374-8,6607-0
    The frost. 6036-6
    Gold-of-Ophir roses. 6241-5
    The riding of Peaceful Henry. 6037-4
    Winding the clock. 6036-6
Denner's old woman. Vincent Bourne. 6814-6
Denney, Reuel
    A boxer called Panther. 6527-9
    Elegy on the pilot. 6978-9
    The hammer-throw. 6527-9,6640-2
    Invocation. 6640-2
    The knowers. 6516-3
    Norwich Hill. 6640-2
    Sequel to Van Winkle. 6761-1
    Song ("You are"). 6640-2
Denning, J. Renton
    Saransar. 6793-X
Dennis, C.J.
    The intro. 6722-0
    Pilot cove. 6722-0
Dennis, O.M.
    Rispetto. 6850-2
Dennison, E.W.
    Little maid and the speckled hen. 6688-7
Dennison, George A.
    Transformation. 6226-1
Dennison, Mary A.
    A Christmas ballad. 6572-4
    The volunteer's wife. 6344-6
Denny, Ernest
    Julian the apostate. 6532-5
Denny, Mary P.
    The Christmas radio. 6799-9
    Ode to America. 6799-9

DENNY

Radio chime. 6799-9
Denny, Sir Edward
    Hope of our hearts. 6065-X
Dennys, John
    The angler's song. 6182-6
Dennys, Richard Molesworth
    Better far to pass away. 6650-X
Denouement. Elizabeth Lou Sellers. 6750-6
"Densely wrapp'd in shades". Abraham at Machpelah. Lydia Huntley Sigourney. 6848-0
Densmore, Frances (tr.)
    Epitaph on Sitting Bull. Unknown (American Indian), 6396-9
    Message of a rejected suitor. Unknown (American Indian), 6396-9
    On hearing the cry of an ominous raven. Unknown (American Indian), 6396-9
    Song of an Indian Warrior. Unknown (American Indian), 6396-9
    A song of parting. Unknown (American Indian), 6396-9
    A war scout dreams of home. Unknown (American Indian), 6396-9
    A warrior warns the foe. Unknown (American Indian), 6396-9
A **dentist**.. Unknown. 6722-0
Denton, Clara J.
    Like Washington. 6712-3
    Pat and the 'specimens'. 6203-2
    Playing 'grown up'. 6313-6
    The pumpkins. 6203-2
    Something better. 6712-3
    Something to be thankful for. 6618-6
Denton, Emily R.
    Snow pattern. 6799-9
dePender, Rene Albourne
    Rhapsody. 6818-9
DeQuincey, Thomas
    Fairies' song. 6249-0
Deny yourself, fr. Translations from the Chinese. Christopher Morley. 6307-1,6736-0
"Deo gracias, Anglia". A carol of Agincourt. Unknown. 6001-2
Deo opt. max. George Sandys. 6933-9
Deo optimo maximo. Louise Imogen Guiney. 6007-2
"Depart, depart, depart!" Alexander Scott. 6317-9
Departed. John Banister Tabb. 6300-4
Departed. William Wordsworth. 6438-8
The **departed** friend. Robert Louis Stevenson. 6486-8
The **departed** friend. Salvador Novo. 6759-X
Departed friends. Samuel Rogers. 6085-4
Departed friends. Henry Vaughan. 6337-3,6604-6,6660-7
The **departed**. Paul Eldridge. 6397-7
The **departed**. Felicia Dorothea Hemans. 6973-8
The **departed**. John Banister Tabb. 7017-5
The **departing** boat. Yong-chul Park. 6775-1
The **departing** of Clote Scarp. Sir Charles George Douglas Roberts. 6795-6
"Departing sumer hath assumed". The poet growing old. William Wordsworth. 6935-5
A **department** store ditty. Unknown. 6280-6
Departmental. Robert Frost. 6399-3,6637-2
Departure. Al-Hadrami. 6362-4
Departure. Ylessa Dubonee. 6178-8
Departure. J. Charles Green. 6870-7
Departure. Hermann Hagedorn. 6310-1,6300-4,6509-0
Departure. Muriel F. Hochdorf. 6850-2
Departure. Ibn Mujbar. 6362-4
Departure. Genny Lim. 6790-5
Departure. Edna St. Vincent Millay. 6034-X
Departure. Jessie Young Norton. 6841-3
Departure. Jalal [or Jelal] ed-din Rumi. 6448-5
Departure. Leonard Alfred George Strong. 6257-1
Departure. Henry Van Dyke. 6961-4
Departure. John Hall Wheelock. 6027-7,6320-9
Departure ("It was not like your great..."). Coventry Patmore. 6250-4,6508-2,6022-6,6292-X,6102-8,6513, 6317-9,6246-6,6489-2,6301-2,6172-9,6655
Departure from home. H. Von Fallersleben. 6952-5
The **departure** from paradise. John Milton. 6848-0
The **departure** from Phaeacia. Andrew Lang. 6771-9

Departure in the dark. Cecil Day Lewis. 6391-8
The **departure** of King Sebastian. Unknown (Spanish) 6757-3
The **departure** of Paul. Charles W. Denison. 6755-7
The **departure** of Proserpine. Francis Ledwidge. 6812-X
The **departure** of summer. Thomas Hood. 6423-X
The **departure** of the good daemon. Robert Herrick. 6378-0
The **departure** of the nightingale. Charlotte Smith. 6219-9
Departure of the pioneer. John Gardiner Calkins Brainard. 6752-2
The **departure** of the swallow. William Howitt. 6302-0,6385-3,6600-3,6656-9
Departure of the swallows. Theophile Gautier. 6302-0,6358-6
Departure platform. Kenneth Allott. 6379-9
Departure's girlfriend. W. S. Merwin. 6803-0
The **departure**, fr. The day dream. Alfred Lord Tennyson. 6240-7,6260-1,6676-3,6585-6
The **departure**. Carl Christian Bagger. 6555-4
Dependence. William Cowper. 6438-8
Dependence on God. Francis Quarles. 6337-3
Deported. Kathryn White Ryan. 6034-X
Deposition and death of Edward II. Christopher Marlowe. 6323-3
A **deposition** from beauty. Thomas Stanley. 6092-7
A **deposition** from love. Thomas Carew. 6341-1,6378-0,6430-2, 6194-X,6150-8,6933
Deprecating parrots. Beulah May. 6833-2
Depression. Morris Rosenfeld. 7011-6
"Depressions, wars - spring from greed". Free to choose. Gertrude Shisler Dupper. 6203-2
Depth, fr. Once again the Eden. Noel Hudson Stearn. 6789-1
"The **depths** of infinite shade". A prairie year, fr. Eos: a prairie dream. Nicholas Flood Davin. 6795-6
The **deputy**. Kenneth C. Kaufman. 6397-7
Der baby. Unknown. 6791-3
Der baby. Unknown. 6407-8,6742-5
Der coming man. Charles Follen Adams. 6565-1,6921-5
Der Deutscher's maxim. Charles Follen Adams. 6923-1
Der dog and der lobster. Unknown. 6277-6
'Der dog und der lobster'. Saul Sertrew. 6791-3,6823-5, 6175-3
Der drummer. Charles Follen Adams. 6791-3,6823-5,7041-8
Der fischer. Johann Wolfgang von Goethe. 6252-0
Der frohe wandersmann. Count Joseph von Eichendorff. 6252-0
Der good lookin schnow. Unknown. 6791-3
Der gute kamerad. Johann Ludwig Uhland. 6252-0
Der heilige mantel von aachen. Benjamin Francis Musser. 6282-2
"Der lived a king inta da aste". Unknown. 6111-7
Der mai ist gekommen. Emanuel Geibel. 6252-0
Der mann im Keller. Unknown (German) 6949-5
Der moon. Wade Whipple. 6791-3
Der mule. Unknown. 6175-3
Der mule shtood on der steamboad deck. James S. Burdett. 6791-3,6823-5
Der mule shtood on der steamboad deck. Unknown. 6277-6
Der nighd pehind Grisdmas. Sidney W. Wetmore. 6791-3,6823-5
"Der night vas dark as anydhing". Zwei lager. Charles Follen Adams. 6791-3,6823-5
"Der noble Ritter Hugo". Ballad of the mermaid. Charles Godfrey Leland. 7025-6,6760-3
Der oak und der vine. Charles Follen Adams. 6505-8,7920-7
Der schleighride. Wade Whipple. 6791-3
Der shoemaker's poy. Unknown. 6175-3
Der spider and der fly. Charles Follen Adams. 6924-X
Der vater-mill. Charles Follen Adams. 6920-7,7041-8
'Der wreck of der Hezberus' before Longfellow. Esse Phoster. 6791-3,6823-5
Derby day. Fanny Foster Clark. 6695-X
Derby, Carol Florence
    Bedtime. 6249-0
    My child. 6249-0
Derby, Edward G.S. Stanley, 14th Earl of (tr.)
    "Achilles then within his tent...", fr. The Iliad. Homer, 6435-3
    Achilles' prayer, fr. The Iliad. Homer, 6435-3
    "And thus they fought...", fr. The Iliad. Homer, 6435-3
    Apollo destros his horses, fr. The Iliad. Homer, 6435-

3
"He said: and on his horses...", fr. The Iliad. Homer, 6435-3
The horses of Achilles, fr. The Iliad. Homer, 6435-3
The Iliad, sels. Homer, 6289-X
"Dere never was a man on earth". The notion of rastus. Edgar A. Guest. 6862-6
"Dere now bemoany to de ouder air". Aristophanes. 6435-3
"Dere's somet'ing stirrin' ma blood to-night". The voyageur. William Henry Drummond. 7035-3
Derelict. Young Ewing Allison. 6107-9
Derelict. Henry Johnson. 6870-7
A **derelict.** Robert Loveman. 6941-X
The **derelict.** Rudyard Kipling. 6810-3
The **derelict.** Robert L. Munger. 6300-4
The **derelict.** Herbert Scott. 6803-0
Dereliction. Edward Shillito. 6144-3,6335-7
Dereme, Tristan
Pelops. 6351-9
Pelops. Joseph T. Shipley (tr.). 6351-9
We are still. 6351-9
Derennes, Charles
Persephone. Joseph T. Shipley (tr.). 6351-9
Persephone, sels. 6351-9
Derham, Enid
Farewell. 6784-0
The mountain road. 6784-0
O city, look the eastward way. 6784-0
The suburbs. 6784-0
Derleth, August
Brook sound at evening. 6783-2
The fine April weather. 6761-1
Lost child. 6979-7
Moon and fog. 6218-0
Place-ghost. 6218-0
Wild apples. 6979-7
Dermody, Thomas
A decayed monastery. 6930-4
John Baynham's epitaph. 6930-4
An ode to myself. 6930-4
The shepherd's despair. 6930-4
Songs. 6858-8
Dermot O'Dowd. Samuel Lover. 6825-1
Dermot's parting. Unknown. 6910-X
Derozio, Henry Louis Vivian
On the abolition of Suttee. 6591-0,6592-9
Derricotte, Toi
The distrust of logic. 7032-9
Derry, Selma
Heritage. 6039-0
The **dervish.** Edwin Chamberlin. 6906-1
Derwent, Lord
Which music? 6783-2
Derwentwater. Unknown. 6859-6
Derwentwater's farewell. Unknown. 6859-6
Derwood, Gene
In the proscenium. 6390-X
The innocent. 6666-6
It's the other boys who live afraid. 6391-8
N.B. Symmetrians. 6390-X
Rides. 6389-6
With God conversing. 6389-6
Derzhavin, Gabriel Romanovitch
God. Sir John Bowring (tr.). 6385-3,6964-9,6392-6,6404-3
Ode to the deity. Sir John Bowring (tr.). 6568-6
Des morgens. Friedrich Holderlin. 6253-9
Desaugiers, M.A.M.
Pro and contra. Henry Carrington (tr.). 6025-0
Desbordes-Valmore, Marceline
L'attente. 6801-4
Parted. 6429-9
Parted ("Do not write..."). 6321-7,6429-9
"Descend from heav'n Urania, by that name". Invocation to Urania, fr. Paradise lost. John Milton. 6933-9
"Descend from heaven, Urania, by that name". His invocation to the muse: the poem half finished. John Milton. 6935-5
Descend, fair sun! George Chapman. 6182-6
Descend, ye nine, fr. 'Ode on St. Cecilia's Day'. Alexander Pope. 6239-3
"**Descended** of an ancient line". Ode ("Descended"). Horace. 6152-4
Descent. Jalal [or Jelal] ed-din Rumi. 6448-5
Descent from the cross. Michael (Katherine Bradley & Edith Cooper) Field. 6096 X
Descent from the cross, sels. Christina Georgina Rossetti. 6144-3
The **descent** of Odin. Thomas Gray. 6152-4,6195-0
The **descent** of the child. Susan L. Mitchell. 6244-X
The **descent** of the Ganges, fr. The Ramayana. Unknown (Sanskrit) 6372-1
The **descent** of the vulture. Marya Alexandrovna Zaturenska. 6389-6
The **descent** on Middlesex. Peter St. John. 6946-0
The **descent** to Hela. William Herbert; Earl of Pembroke. 6980-0
"**Descent/You'll** grant, is not alone nobility". Pride of rank. James Sheridan Knowles. 6980-0
The **descent.** Michael Guttenbrunner. 6769-7
The **descent.** Samuel Rogers. 6302-0;6385-3
The **descent.** Mary Dixon Thayer. 7007-8
Deschamps, Emile
A quelques poetes. 6801-4
Nizza. 6801-4
Deschamps, Eustache
Virelay ("Am I beautiful?"). Ralph Nixon Currey (tr.). 6227-X
"'**Describe** the borough',though our idle tribe". The borough, sels. George Crabbe. 6831-6
Description and praise of his love Geraldine. Henry Howard, Earl of Surrey. 6198-2,6586-4,6430-2
A **description** of a city shower, sels. Jonathan Swift. 6120-6
A **description** of a city shower. Jonathan Swift. 6315-2, 6733-6,6152-4
A **description** of a city shower. Jonathan Swift. 6930-4
A **description** of a city shower. Jonathan Swift. 6278-4
Description of a convent. Richard Crashaw. 6285-7
The **description** of a maske on S. Stephens night. Thomas Campion. 6794-8
The **description** of a maske presented before the... Thomas Campion. 6794-8
Description of a medieval schoolboy. John Lydgate. 6186-9
A **description** of a musical consort of birds. William Browne. 6191-5
Description of a New England country dance. Thomas Green Fessenden. 7030-2
Description of a ninety-gun ship. William Falconer. 6971-1
A **description** of a strange (and miraculous) fish. Martin Parker. 6157-5
Description of a sultry summer's noon. Carlos Wilcox. 6752-2
The **description** of an enuious and naughtie neighbour. Thomas Tusser. 6586-4
The **description** of an impertinent. Horace. 6814-6
The **description** of an Irish feast. Hugh MacGowran. 6930-4
A **description** of beauty, translated out of Marino. Samuel Daniel. 6436-1
Description of Castara. William Habington. 6099-4
The **description** of Elizium. Michael Drayton. 6191-5
Description of his prison garden. fr. The king's quair. James I; King of Scotland. 6649-6
A **description** of his ugly lady. Thomas Hoccleve. 6881-2
A **description** of love. Sir Walter Raleigh. 6436-1,6026-9
Description of Marmion, fr. Marmion. Sir Walter Scott. 6552-X
Description of mist opening in the hills, fr. Excursion. William Wordsworth. 6867-7
The **description** of Sir Geoffrey Chaucer. Robert Greene. 6436-1
Description of spring, wherein each thing renews. Henry Howard, Earl of Surrey. 6198-2,6586-4,6232-6,6271-7, 6182-6,6586 ,6315-2,6646-1,6219-9,6192-3,6194-X,6430 ,6192-8,6315-2,6491-4,6198-2
A **description** of such a one as he would love. Sir Thomas Wyatt. 6198-2,6600-3,6543-0,6192-3
Description of the contrarious passions in a lover. Sir Thomas Wyatt. 6430-2
A **description** of the country's rereations. Sir Henry

DESCRIPTION

Wotton. 6191-5
Description of the lists built by Theseus for the...
   Geoffrey Chaucer. 6935-5
A description of the morning. Jonathan Swift. 6208-3,6733-6,6152-4,6195-0
Description of the quiet island, fr. The buccaneer,
   Richard Henry Dana. 6752-2
The description of the shepherd and his wife. Robert
   Greene. 6191-5
A description of the spring. Sir Henry Wotton. 6563-5,6668-2
Description of vertue. Nicholas Grimald. 6586-4
A description of Wallace. Henry the Minstrel ("Blind
   Harry") 6180-X
Description of Wyoming. Thomas Campbell. 6980-0
Description, speeches, and songs of the Lords Maske.
   Thomas Campion. 6794-8
Desdemona's song, fr. Othello. William Shakespeare. 6315-2,
   6732-8,6102-8
Dese bones gwine to rise again. Unknown. 6594-5
"Deseo". Americo Casiano. 6898-7
Desert. Arthur Crew Inman. 6037-4
Desert. Josephine Miles. 6640-2
"Desert and camels, ocean and pine". On entering
   Palestine. H.S. Gulliver. 6841-3
Desert dangers. Jakob Thorarensen. 6283-0
The desert disillusion. Berton Braley. 6853-7
Desert drift, sels. Alice Corbin. 6628-3
Desert flowers. Keith Douglas. 6210-5
Desert hymn to the sun. Bayard Taylor. 6976-2
"The desert is parched in the burning sun". Reverie of
   Mahomed Akram at the Tamarind tank. Laurence (Adele
   Florence Nicolson) Hope. 6856-1
Desert love song. Hattie Horner Louthan. 6836-7
Desert night. Helen Hartmann. 6850-2
The desert of Maine. Robert P. Tristram Coffin. 6628-3
Desert picture. Elida Merriam Green. 6799-9
The desert remembers her reasons. Genevieve Taggard. 6619-4
"The desert sands are heated, parched & dreary". The
   garden by the bridge. Laurence (Adele Florence
   Nicolson) Hope. 6856-1
"The desert stretches long and wide" Jovan Ducic. 6765-4
The desert travellers. Laurence David Lerner. 6788-3
Desert wanderings. Thomas Curtis Clark. 6144-3
Desert warfare. Signalman G. Harker. 6468-X
"Desert/your body". Flight. Lisa Rydeski. 6883-9
The desert. M. St.J. Wilmoth. 6468-X
The desert. Charles Erskine Scott Wood. 6102-8,6076-5
Deserted. Madison Cawein. 6332-2,6336-5
Deserted. Unknown. 6273-3
The deserted barn. Arthur Crew Inman. 6037-4
Deserted buildings. Frances Archer Walls. 6906-1
The deserted city, sels. Francis Sherman. 6021-8
The deserted city. Edwin Chamberlin. 6906-1
The deserted city. Sir Charles George Douglas Roberts.
   6102-8
A deserted cottage. James H. Fitzpatrick. 6894-4
A deserted farm. Ethel Aldrich Girardet. 6764-6
A deserted farm. George Sterling. 6778-6
The deserted garden. Alasdair Alpin MacGregor. 6477-9
The deserted garden. Pai Ta-Shun. 6338-1
The deserted garden. Elizabeth Barrett Browning. 6232-6,
   6302-0,6655-0,6649-6
Deserted gipsy's song: hillside camp. Laurence (Adele
   Florence Nicolson) Hope. 6856-1
A deserted home. Sidney Royse Lysaght. 6477-9
The deserted homestead. Benjamin Franklin Taylor. 6815-4
The deserted house· Mary Elizabeth Coleridge. 6512-0
The deserted house. Felicia Dorothea Hemans. 6973-9
The deserted house. Alfred Lord Tennyson. 6980-0
The deserted house. Alfred Lord Tennyson. 6250-4,6438-8
The deserted house. Alfred Lord Tennyson. 6980-0
The deserted lover consoleth himself... Sir Thomas Wyatt.
   6198-2
The deserted mill. August Schnezler. 6165-6,6409-4
The deserted mountain way. William White. 6868-5
The deserted pasture. Bliss Carman. 6053-6,6374-8
"Deserted pedestals and void recess". The realm of unholy
   lovers, fr. Tree of time. Gertrude Huntington

McGiffert. 6838-3
The deserted plantation. Paul Laurence Dunbar. 6281-4
Deserted roads. Berton Braley. 7012-4
Deserted swing. Gladys Verville Deane. 6764-6
Deserted village. Peter Wellington Clark. 6178-8
The deserted village, sel. Oliver Goldsmith. 6954-1
The deserted village, sels. Oliver Goldsmith. 6024-2,6102-8,6208-3,6395-0,6410-8,6527,6600-3,6365-9,6174-5,
   6654-2,6301-2
The deserted village. Oliver Goldsmith. 6101-X,6087-0,6198-2,6332-2,6473-6,6122,6271-7,6302-0,6385-3,6315-2,
   6459-0,6504,6604-6,6732-8,6668-2,6197-4,6219-9,6660,6195-0,6250-4,6245-8,6543-0,6152-4,6192,6086-2,
   6102-8,6430-2
A deserted wife. William Wordsworth. 6980-0
The deserter from the cause. Gerald Massey. 6656-9
The deserter's meditaton. John Philpot Curran. 6086-2,6545-7
The deserter.. Edward Rowland Sill. 6211-3
The deserter. John Philpot Curran. 6322-5
The deserter. Alfred Edward Housman. 6733-6,6508-2
The deserter. John Streeter Manifold. 6895-2
The deserter. John Streeter Manifold. 6666-6
The desertion of beauty. Unknown. 6022-6
Deserts. Ann [or Annie E.] Hamilton. 6337-3
Deshoulieres, Antoinette
   Grisette dines. 6120-6
Desideratum. Elena Vossen Greenfield. 6841-3
Desideravi. Theodore Maynard. 6320-9
Desideria. Lionel Johnson. 6655-0
Desideria. William Wordsworth. 6246-6
Desiderium. Phineas Fletcher. 6933-9
Desiderium. Richard Le Gallienne. 6027-7,6581-3
Desiderium indesideratum. Francis Thompson. 6641-0
Desiderium: in memoriam, S.F.A. Andrew Lang. 6987-8
Design. Robert Frost. 6010-2
Design and performance. Felicia Dorothea Hemans. 6973-9
Design for a garden. Bertye Young Williams. 6906-1
Design for a list of pictures. Arthur Symons. 6210-5
Design for a perfect world. Louis Untermeyer. 6880-4
Design for ashes. Gemma D'Auria. 6839-1
Design for heaven, 1941. Lewis Thomas. 6761-1
Design for mediaeval tapestry. Abraham M. Klein. 6021-8
Designation. Thomas Moore. 6294-6
Desire. Matthew Arnold. 6730-1
Desire. William Cornish. 6436-1
Desire. Hafiz. 6448-5
Desire. Selma Hamann. 6906-1
Desire. Frances S. Larkin. 6799-9
Desire. Georgiana Livinston. 6906-1
Desire. [James] Pittendrigh Macgillivray. 6269-5
Desire. Emma Hicks McDonald. 6799-9
Desire. Oreon Marie McKee. 6799-9
Desire. Constance Nichols. 6178-8
Desire. George William ("A.E.") Russell. 6244-X
Desire. William ("Fiona Macleod") Sharp. 7014-0
Desire. Sir Philip Sidney. 6436-1,6584-8,6383-7
Desire. Edith Haskell Tappan. 6764-6
Desire. Thomas Traherne. 6931-2
Desire and disillusion, fr. Childe Harold's pilgrimage.
   George Gordon, 6th Baron Byron. 6199-0
The desire for hermitage. Sean O'Faolain. 6582-1
Desire in spring. Francis Ledwidge. 6506-6,6161-3,6393-4,
   6653-4
Desire of knowledge. Christopher Marlowe. 6935-5
"The desire of love, joy". Desire. William ("Fiona
   Macleod") Sharp. 7014-0
"The desire of man being infinite" William Blake. 7014-0
The desire of nations. Edwin Markham. 6386-1,6420-5,6542-2
'Desire to depart', sels. Barbara Millar. 6269-5
Desire under the pines. Tim Dlugos. 7003-5
Desire we past illusions to recall. William Wordsworth.
   6199-0,6828-6
Desire's government. A. W. 6182-6
A desire. Adelaide Anne Procter. 6424-8
A desire. Adelaide Anne Procter. 6957-6
The desire. Katharine (Hinkson) Tynan. 6233-4,6102-8,6301-2
The desired swan-song. Samuel Taylor Coleridge. 6722-0
Desires. Guy de Maupassant. 6732-8

Desires of men and women. John Berryman. 6389-6
Desiring to love. Charles Wesley. 6271-7
Desmet, Idaho, March 1969 Janet Campbell Hale. 7005-1
The Desmond. Thomas Moore. 6090-0
Desnos, Robert
    At world's end. X.J. Kennedy (tr.). 6803-0
Desolate. James Abraham Martling. 6952-5
The desolate city. Wordsworthshaw 6328tint. 6437-X,6172-9, 6292-X
"Desolate is my station...". Unknown. 6251-2
"A desolate shore." William Ernest Henley. 6508-2
The desolate valley, sels. Thomas Pringle. 6788-3
"Desolate winter has fled from the woods...". Winter gone. Sir John Collings ("Solomon Eagle") Squire. 6782-4
Desolation. Ann Louise Hayes. 6515-5
Desolation. Kao Shih. 6732-8
Desolation. Thomas Masson. 6166-4;6440-X
Desolation. Ella Wheeler Wilcox. 6956-8
"The desolation and the agony". Burial of an emigrant's child in the forest. Felicia Dorothea Hemans. 6973-8
The desolation of Veii. Bessie Rayner Parkes. 6624-0
Despair. Fulke Greville; 1st Baron Brooke. 6436-1
Despair. Muriel F. Hochdorf. 6850-2
Despair. James Abraham Martling. 6952-5
Despair. James Abraham Martling. 6952-5
Despair. Marian Osborne. 6115-X
Despair. Morris Rosenfeld. 7011-6
Despair. Alfred Lord Tennyson. 6573-2
Despair. Alfred Lord Tennyson. 6977-0
Despair is never quite despair. Felicia Dorothea Hemans. 6567-8
The despair of Troilus. Geoffrey Chaucer. 6315-2
Despair, fr. The faerie queene. Edmund Spenser. 6378-0
"Despairing beside a clear stream". Colin's complaint. Nicholas Rowe. 6932-0,6867-7
The despairing lover. William Walsh. 6024-2,6102-8,6733-6, 6026-9,6152-4,6652
The despairing lover. William Hamilton. 6874-X
The despairing lover. William Walsh. 6932-0
The despairing shepherd. John Gay. 6972-X
Desperate. Cino da Pistoia. 6325-X
The desperate lover. Thomas Flatman. 6830-8
Desperato's banquet. William Strode. 6328-4
Despise the world. Unknown. 6881-2
Despised and rejected. Christina Georgina Rossetti. 6337-3
"Despised by the world and unblest with a wife". Peter Lockpocket. Unknown. 6916-9
Despite all that. Ann Stanford. 6792-1,6998-3
"Despite of a little fear lurking". Crossing the Rubicon. Unknown. 6878-2
Despoiled. George E. Bowen. 6274-1
Despondency. Letitia Elizabeth ("L.E.L.") Landon. 6980-0
Despondency and aspiration. Felicia Dorothea Hemans. 6973-8
Despondency rebuked. Arthur Hugh Clough. 6271-7
The desponding soul's wish. John Byrom. 6932-0
Desportes, Philippe
    A sonnet ("Icarus"). 6978-9
Desposed. Unknown. 6697-6
Despotism tempered by dynamite. James ("B.V.") Thomson. 7009-4
Despotisms. Louise Imogen Guiney. 7027-2
Despotisms. Virginia Stait. 6039-0
Desprez, F.
    Lasca. 6392-6,6414-0
DesSins, Evon
    Sea gems. 6818-9
The dessert. Charles and Mary Lamb. 6295-4
Dessus, Ronald James
    The difference between a lie and the truth. 6870-7
    Geronimo: old man lives on. 6870-7
    "Imagine a world of people whose motto is" 6870-7
    "Surrounded by walls am I" 6870-7
    "Ta wa nee ta wa nee- I softly call into the..." 6870-7
The destined maid: a prayer. Richard Le Gallienne. 6875-8
"Destined to war from very infancy". Epitaph ("Destined"). Gabriello Chiabrera. 7039-6
Destinie. Abraham Cowley. 6341-1
Destiny. Matthew Arnold. 6250-4
Destiny. Sir Edwin Arnold. 6337-3,6226-1

Destiny. Jessie Tarbox Beals. 6232-6
Destiny. Geoffrey Chaucer. 6438-8
Destiny. Ralph Waldo Emerson. 6250-4,6288-1
Destiny. Edgar A. Guest. 6869-3
Destiny. Helen A. Saxe. 6270-9
Destiny. Thomas Stanley. 6315-2
Destiny. Arthur Stringer. 6115-X
"Destiny knocked at the door". America at St. Paul's. Margaretta Byrde. 7031-0,7027-2
The destiny of dreams. S. Charles Jellicoe. 6174-5
Destiny uncertain. Walter Savage Landor. 6874-X
Destiny, fr. Raphael. John Greenleaf Whittier. 6337-3
Destiny, fr. Upon an honest man's fortune. John Fletcher. 6337-3
Destitute. Mary Elizabeth Mahnkey. 6662-3
Destroy a day. Alfred Kreymborg. 6781-6
The destroyer of destroyers. Wallace Rice. 6946-0
Destroyer song. Unknown. 6237-7
"Destroyer! what do you here...". Good-night. Frederick Greenwood. 6772-7
The destroyer. James Abraham Martling. 6952-5
Destroyers. Sir Henry Head. 7027-2
Destroyers. Klaxon (John Graham Bower) 7029-9,6846-4
Destroyers off Jutland. Reginald McIntosh Cleveland. 7026-4
The destroyers, sels. Archibald Fleming. 6375-6
The destroyers. Rudyard Kipling. 6810-3
The destroying angel. Abraham Cowley. 6848-0
"Destroying obstacles for the benefit of this world". Unknown (Newari) 7013-2
Destruciton of Sennacherib's army by a... Erasmus Darwin. 6848-0
The destruction of Babylon. Unknown. 6848-0
Destruction of Jerusalem. Robert Southey. 6848-0
The destruction of Jerusalem. Johnson Pierson. 6848-0
The destruction of Pharaoh. John Ruskin. 6848-0
The destruction of Psara. Dionysios Solomos. 6352-7
The destruction of Sennacherib, sels. George Gordon, 6th Baron Byron. 6395-0,6419-1
The destruction of Sennacherib. George Gordon, 6th Baron Byron. 6075-7,6101-X,6183-4,6289-X,6478-7,6504-,6102-8,6239-3,6323-2,6271-7,6339-X,6479-,6473-6,6481-7, 6490-6,6512-0,6527-9,6600-,6606-2,6732-8,6438-8,6114-1,6219-9,6267 ,6263-3,6192-3,6430-2,6560-0,6104-4, 6212 ,6131-1,6214-8,6304-7,6018-8,6424-8,6723 ,6543-0,6737-9,6421-3,6086-2,6110-9,6547 ,6639-9
Destruction of the house. Ann L. Zoller. 6857-X
The destruction of the Pequods, fr. Greenfield hill. Timothy Dwight. 6753-0
Destruction of the Philistines. John Milton. 6606-2
The destuction of Troy, sels. Unknown. 6258-X
"A desultory dog once met..discontented donkey". The donkey and his company. J.G. Francis. 6786-7
A desultory poem, written on the Christmas eve of 1794 Samuel Taylor Coleridge. 6828-6
"Detached from his command". General Ira Allen: founder of the state... Daniel L. Cady. 6989-4
"Detah for you was eiderdown of rest". An epitaph. George Chamalian. 6850-2
Deter, Francis H.
    The buttercups. 6906-1
    Fallen riches. 6906-1
    Reflection. 6906-1
Determination. Edgar A. Guest. 6869-3
"Determined with one sally to erase". Francesco Petrarch. 6325-X
Dethall, S.A.
    Invocation. 6542-2
Detty, O.M.L.
    Winter - pro and con. 6750-6
Deuell, Dorothy Jane
    Angry admonition. 6750-6
Deus absconditus. Anne Ridler. 6209-1
Deus, quis similis. Bible. 6830-8
Deutero, fr. Isaiah. Bible. 6143-5
Deutsch and Avrahm Yarmolinsky, Babette (tr.)
    The amphora. Fedor Sologub, 7039-6
    Flax. Ivan Bunin, 7039-6
    The holy rose. Vyacheslav Ivanov, 7039-6

DEUTSCH

The pear-tree. Iwan [or Yvan] Goll, 6160-6
Phantasus, sels. Arno Holz, 6160-6
Pieta ("So once more, Jesus, I behold your feet"). Rainer Maria Rilke, 6160-6
The poet to his beloved. Wilhelm Klemm, 6160-6
Project for a new world. Alfred Mombert, 6160-6
The prophet. Alexander Pushkin, 7039-6
Quai du Rosaire. Rainer Maria Rilke, 6160-6
Radiant ranks of seraphim. Valery Bryusov, 7039-6
Russia. Alexander Blok, 7039-6
The Scythians. Aleksandr Blok, 6546-5
The sons of our sons. Ilya Ehrenburg, 6879-0
Work. Alexander Pushkin, 7039-6

Deutsch, Babette
Anna. 6959-2
Apocrypha. 6777-8
Aprocrypha. 6037-4
Archaeology. 7014-0
Avatars. 6037-4
Bacchanal. 6959-2
Candles. 6653-4
Colloque metaphysique. 6037-4
Dialogue. 6071-4
Distance. 6653-4
Earliness at the cape. 6388-8
Flight. 6783-2
The flight. 7019-1
A girl. 6076-5,6102-8,6396-9
The hound. 6374-8
In durance. 6070-6
Marriage. 6019-6
Maternity ("I must go all my days"). 6097-8,6619-4
Megalosaurus. 6069-2
Memory. 6761-1
Morning workout. 6388-8
Old women. 6619-4,6076-5,6102-8
On a night of rain. 6778-6
Pausa. 6217-2
Penreb's tomb. 6035-8
Petrograd. 6880-4
Pity. 6726-3,6619-4
The pledge of Benjamin. 6038-2
Poet. 6038-2
Portraits. 6035-8
Severance. 6880-4
Soiree. 6780-8
Soliloquy. 7038-8
Solitude. 6076-5,6102-8
Thoughts at the year's end. 6506-6,6531-7
"Tuppence coloured." 6467-1

Deutsch, Babette (tr.)
Acherontic chill. Detlev von Liliencron, 6160-5
After partridge shooting. Detlev von Liliencron, 6160-5
All is gold. Anna Akhmatova, 6546-5,6160-5
Along the noisy streets. Alexander Pushkin, 6879-0
Amen. Georg Trakl, 6160-5
The arc-lamps. Theodor Daubler, 6160-5
Ares. Albert Ehrenstein, 6160-5
At midnight. Kurt Heynicke, 6160-5
August, fr. Love's calendar. Max Dauthendey, 6160-5
Autumn. Rainer Maria Rilke, 6160-5
Ballad of our dear lady of the railway carriage. Rene Schickele, 6160-5
Ballad of the followers. Franz Werfel, 6160-5
The battle of the Marne. Wilhelm Klemm, 6160-5
"Be not afraid, God." Rainer Maria Rilke, 6160-5
The birch tree. Detlev von Liliencron, 6160-5
The bird of sadness. Christian Morgenstern, 6160-5
"Black as a nun." Christian Morgenstern, 6160-5
Blue hydrangeas. Rainer Maria Rilke, 6160-5
Caravan of longing. Iwan [or Yvan] Goll, 6160-5
The carousel. Rainer Maria Rilke, 6160-5
The children's crusade. Johannes R. Becher, 6160-5
Cloud fantasies: I. Christian Morgenstern, 6160-5
"Come to the park." Stefan George, 6160-5
"Dark burned the sunset." Stefan George, 6160-5
The dead Liebnecht. Rudolf Leonhardt, 6160-5
Deep in the nosegay. Max Dauthendey, 6160-5
Deep longing. Detlev von Liliencron, 6160-5
Demon. Alfred Mombert, 6160-5

The demons of the cities. Georg Heym, 6160-5
The divine door-keeper. Franz Werfel, 6160-5
Early spring at the woods' edge. Detlev von Liliencron, 6160-5
End of the world. Else Lasker-Schuler, 6160-5
Eternal shipwreck. Iwan [or Yvan] Goll, 6160-5
Evening. Georg Heym, 6160-5
Every leaf tends earthward. Max Dauthendey, 6160-5
Exaltation. Kurt Heynicke, 6160-5
Fever. Klabund, 6160-5
First snow. Christian Morgenstern, 6160-5
Fog. Alfred Lichtenstein, 6160-5
For I am yet a child. Franz Werfel, 6160-5
Fourteen stations of love, sels. Paul Mayer, 6160-5
"From nether dark." Stefan George, 6160-5
From out of the glow. Stefan George, 6160-5
"From the creator's throne God fell." Alfred Mombert, 6160-5
Gethsemane. Kurt Heynicke, 6160-5
Goldfish on the writing desk. Max Brod, 6160-5
great carousel<The. Richard Dehmel, 6160-5
The great carousel. Richard Dehmel, 6160-5
The harp. Richard Dehmel, 6160-5
The head. Armin T. Wegner, 6160-5
Heavenly father at evening. Franz Werfel, 6160-5
Home-coming. Albert Ehrenstein, 6160-5
Homer. Albert Ehrenstein, 6160-5
The hunt. Adolf von Hatzfeld, 6160-5
In the morning. Ernst Stadler, 6160-5
"In the temple's midst." Alfred Mombert, 6160-5
Journey from Copenhagen to Skodsborg. Klabund, 6160-5
July, fr. Love's calendar. Max Dauthendey, 6160-5
Legend of the bewitched nunnery. Max Herrmann-Neisse, 6160-5
Love's calendar, sels. Max Dauthendey, 6160-5
Machinery. Paul Zech, 6160-5
Man and woman go through the cancer ward. Gottfried Benn, 6160-5
The man in the mirror. Franz Werfel, 6160-5
March, fr. Love's calendar. Max Dauthendey, 6160-5
Memories in hospital. Alfred Vagts, 6160-5
mistaking, The. Stefan George, 6160-5
The mistaking. Stefan George, 6160-5
"The monarchs of the world." Rainer Maria Rilke, 6160-5
Moon. Georg Heym, 6160-5
The moon is a fiery rose. Max Dauthendey, 6160-5
Moon song of a girl. Franz Werfel, 6160-5
Moon tableaux: IV. Christian Morgenstern, 6160-5
Moonrise. Christian Morgenstern, 6160-5
Morgue. Gottfried Benn, 6160-5
Mountain psalm. Richard Dehmel, 6160-5
My love song. Else Lasker-Schuler, 6160-5
My people. Else Lasker-Schuler, 6160-5
Necessity. Christian Morgenstern, 6160-5
Night. Wilhelm Klemm, 6160-5
Night song of the fish. Christian Morgenstern, 6160-5
Not made by hands. Piotr Oreshin, 6546-5
November, fr. Love's calendar. Max Dauthendey, 6160-5
The novice, sels. Mikhail Lermontov, 6879-0
Now I am filled with death. Franz Werfel, 6160-5
"O world, let me behold." Christian Morgenstern, 6160-5
Observation post. Kurt Heynicke, 6160-5
An old woman passes. Franz Werfel, 6160-5
The old woman. Rainer Maria Rilke, 6160-5
"On the staircase." Christian Morgenstern, 6160-5
"On the stairs leading to my marble halls." Alfred Mombert, 6160-5
Palm song. Else Lasker-Schuler, 6160-5
The pear tree. Iwan [or Yvan] Goll, 6160-5
Phantasus, sels. Arno Holz, 6160-5
Pieta. Rainer Maria Rilke, 6160-5
The poet to his beloved. Claire Studer-Goll, 6160-5
The poet to his beloved. Klabund, 6160-5
<u>Prayer. Claire Studer-Goll, 6160-5</u>
"Project for a new world." Alfred Mombert, 6160-5
Put out my eyes, and I can see you still. Rainer Maria Rilke, 6337-3,6160-5
Quai du Rosaire. Rainer Maria Rilke, 6160-5
The rain seems possessed. Max Dauthendey, 6160-5
Reconciliation. Else Lasker-Schuler, 6160-5

Reflections. Wilhelm Klemm, 6160-5
Song before night. Richard Dehmel, 6160-5
Song to my son. Richard Dehmel, 6160-5
Songs. Gottfried Benn, 6160-5
Spanish dancer. Rainer Maria Rilke, 6160-5
Sphinx. Else Lasker-Schuler, 6160-5
Sphinx among the roses. Detlev von Liliencron, 6160-5
Storm. Detlev von Liliencron, 6160-5
Suffering. Albert Ehrenstein, 6160-5
Summer. Adolf von Hatzfeld, 6160-5
The swimmer. Richard Dehmel, 6160-5
Thersites. Paul Mayer, 6160-5
Time. Detlev von Liliencron, 6160-5
To you. Else Lasker-Schuler, 6160-5
Torso. Iwan [or Yvan] Goll, 6160-5
"We are all workmen." Rainer Maria Rilke, 6160-5
"We walk by the sea." Max Dauthendey, 6160-5
"We wander up and down." Stefan George, 6160-5
Welcome. Richard Dehmel, 6160-5
"What will you do, God?" Rainer Maria Rilke, 6160-5
"When my hot lips." Stefan George, 6160-5
The widow at the bed of her son. Franz Werfel, 6160-5
The wind strode wildly. Klabund, 6160-5
window at the bed of her son<The. Franz Werfel, 6160-5
Winter. Paul Mayer, 6160-5
Winter scene. Detlev von Liliencron, 6160-5
The wooden fence. Christian Morgenstern, 6160-5
The workingman. Richard Dehmel, 6160-5
You are the future. Rainer Maria Rilke, 6337-3
"You know not who I am." Stefan George, 6160-5
"You, neighbor God." Rainer Maria Rilke, 6160-5
Deutsch, Karl W. (tr.)
 Epitaph. Jiri Wolker, 6665-8
 On this my sickbed beats the world. Jiri Wolker, 6665-8
"Deux vieux marins des mers du nord". Au nord. Emile Verhaeren. 6801-4
Devaney, James
 The evening gleam. 6349-7
 Winter westerlies. 6349-7
Development. Robert Browning. 6110-9
Development. Samuel Weldon. 6717-4
The development of man, fr. Paracelsus. Robert Browning. 6199-0
Dever, Joseph
 Queen of horizons. 6282-2
Devere, William
 'Cepting Ike. 6690-9
Devereux, Robert. See Essex, Earl of
DeVilliers-Hertzler, E.
 Faith. 6818-9
 Life. 6818-9
Device. Herbert Read. 6985-1
Deviceless darkness. Arthur Mizener. 6017-X
Devil. Unknown. 6609-7
The devil and St. Donat. Hermann Hagedorn. 6944-4
The devil and the lawyers. Unknown. 6294-6
The devil and the lawyers. Unknown. 6878-2
The devil at home, fr. The devil's progress. Thomas Kibble Hervey. 6996-7
"The devil came up to the earth one day". A deadly weapon. George Robert Sims. 6921-5
Devil doll. Lisa Grenelle. 6218-0
"The devil hath made him a ship". The devil and St. Donat. Hermann Hagedorn. 6944-4
"The devil he came to his house one day". Unknown. 6059-5
The devil in search of a wife. Annie Porter. 6370-5
The devil is dying. Willard Wattles. 6441-8
The devil prompts a sonnet. Ronald Walker Barr. 6906-1
"Devil returned to hell by two", fr. The Devil's drive. George Gordon, 6th Baron Byron. 6996-7
"The devil returned to hell by two". The devil's drive. George Gordon, 6th Baron Byron. 6945-2
"The devil sits in his easy chair". The devil at home, fr. The devil's progress. Thomas Kibble Hervey. 6996-7
"The devil was bored with the whole affair". Ballad of the lady in hell. Annette Patton Cornell. 6750-6
The devil's auction. Charles Erskine Scott Wood. 6102-8,6076-5
The devil's bag. James Stephens. 6506-6
Devil's cauldron. Monk Gibbon. 6257-1

The devil's complaint. Sana'i. 6448-5
The devil's drive. George Gordon, 6th Baron Byron. 6945-2
Devil's edge, fr. Fires, book III. Wilfred Wilson Gibson. 6234-2
The devil's meditation. Michael Sweany. 6337-3
The devil's stepping-stones. Arthur Guiterman. 6773-5
The devil's thoughts. Samuel Taylor Coleridge. 6271-7,6092-7,6219-9
The devil's walk on earth. Robert Southey. 6089-7,6278-4
The devil's walk, sels. Robert Southey. 6867-7
The devil's walk. Robert Southey and Samuel Taylor Coleridge. 6200-8
The devil's walk. Richard Porson. 6787-5
The devil-dancers. William Plomer. 6788-3
"Devilish squirmy spider,/Whose traffic cop...". The irate bee. Ida L. Padleford. 6818-9
Devils. Alexander Pushkin. 6103-6
Devior molluscule. Francis Reginald Scott. 6021-8
Devlin, Denis
 Encounter. 6930-4
 The statue and the perturbed burghers. 6930-4
Devlin, James H.
 Sweet blooms at dusk. 6799-9
"Devoid of title, distinction or gold". Abraham Lincoln. Edward R. Huxley. 6885-5
The Devon maid. John Keats. 6086-2
Devon men. Unknown. 7031-0
The Devon sage. John Galsworthy. 6331-4
Devon to me! John Galsworthy. 6888-X
A Devonshire Christmas. Alfred Noyes. 6151-6
The Devonshire lane. Aohn Marriott. 6089-7;6331-4
The Devonshire lane. Unknown. 6787-5
The Devonshire mother. Marjorie Wilson. 7027-2
A Devonshire rhyme. Unknown. 6891-X
A Devonshire song. Alfred Noyes. 6151-6
A Devonshire song. Unknown. 6933-9
Devoore, Anne
 My saint. 6274-1
"A devotee, with bloody knife". To Calvin L. Porter. James Abraham Martling. 6952-5
Devotion. Robert Burns. 6322-5
Devotion. Thomas Campion. 6186-9,6102-8,6737-9
Devotion. Sylvia Storla Clarke. 6789-1
Devotion. Berta G. McGuirk. 6750-6
Devotion. Unknown. 6434-5
Devotion to duty. Siegfried Sassoon. 6357-8
Devotional incitements. William Wordsworth. 6142-7,6232-6
The devourers.. Rose Macaulay. 6477-9
"Devouring time, blunt thou the lion's paws." William Shakespeare. 6187-7,6726-3,6383-7,6125-7
"Devouring time, blunt thou the lion's paws". Sonnet 019 ("Devouring time"). William Shakespeare. 6436-1
A devout lover. Thomas Randolph. 6733-6,6102-8
The devout man prays to his relations. William Herbert; Earl of Pembroke. 6881-2
A devout prayer of the passion. Unknown. 6881-2
Dew. Thomas Ekenhead Mayne. 6174-5
Dew. Frank S. Williamson. 6784-0
"A dew diamond". Betrothal. Estelle Rooks. 6850-2
"The dew falls fast and the night is dark". King's bridge. Frederick William Faber. 6980-0
"The dew is gleaming in the grass". Clouds. Archibald Lampman. 6795-6
"The dew is on the summer's greenest grass". Death. Robert Nicoll. 6960-6
"The dew no more will weep". Sorrow. Richard Crashaw. 6935-5
"Dew upon the robin as he lilts there...". Dew. Frank S. Williamson. 6784-0
Dew yu know. Bill Bissett. 6767-0
"The dew, - the storm/Did alike proceed". Musings near Aquapendente, sels. William Wordsworth. 6867-7
Dew, Mary Jane
 A leafy welcome. 6818-9
The dew-drop. H.F. Amiel. 6424-8
Dew-drops. Rene Francois Armand Sully-Prudhomme. 6876-6
"Dew-drops in the grass". El Dorado, fr. Glimpses. Russell M. Spear. 6850-2
"Dew-fed am I/With drops from the sky". The song of the highland river. John Stuart Blackie. 6819-7

Dew-plants. Ernest G. Moll. 6384-5
Dew-we? (Dewey). T.E. Roach. 6589-9
The dew. Unknown. 6373-X
Dewart, Edward Hartley
    Divine guidance. 6796-4
Dewdney, Christopher
    The lateshow diorama. 6767-0
    Winter central. 6767-0
Dewdrop, wind and sun. Joseph Skipsey. 6437-X
A dewdrop. Frank Dempster Sherman. 6311-X,6452-3
The dewdrop. Joseph Skipsey. 6656-9
The dewdrop. Richard Chenevix Trench. 6424-8
Dewdrops. Bertha Merena Mauermann. 6789-1
Dewey and his men. Wallace Rice. 6946-0
Dewey at Manila. Robert Underwood Johnson. 6062-5,6741-X
Dewey in Manila Bay. R.V. Risley. 6741-X
Dewey, E.H. Graham
    Her wish. 7021-3
Dewey, Orville
    Labor. 6449-3
Dewey, Thomas Emmet
    Kansas. 6615-1
DeWitt, Samuel A.
    Quatrains for a bank cashier. 6979-7
Dewey, admiral. Frank A. Marshall. 6741-X
The dews.. John Banister Tabb. 6338-1
Dewson, F.A.
    Prophecy. 6542-2
    Wheat. 6818-9
The dewy dens of Darrow. Unknown. 6061-7
Dewy garlands. Asclepiades. 6819-7
Dexter, Eleazar
    Adam and Eve. 7030-2
Dexter, Henry M. (tr.)
    Shepherd of eager youth, sels. Clement of Alexandria, 6337-3
Dextera excelsi. A. Souby. 6818-9
"Dhere vas vat you call a maxim". Der Deutscher's maxim. Charles Follen Adams. 6923-1
"Dhere vasn't someding haf so schweed". Der schleighride. Wade Whipple. 6791-3
The Dhoon. Thomas Edward Brown. 6508-2
The dhoon. Thomas Edward Brown. 6809-X
Dhoulkarnain. Koran. 6679-8
The dhows. Francis Brett Young. 6833-2
Dhree shkaders. Unknown. 6791-3,6823-5
"Dhree skaders vent ofer mit Central Park". Ddhree shkaders. Unknown. 6823-5
Di Michelle, Mary
    My hands in Purdah. 6767-0
Diaduminius. Pierre Benoit. 6351-9
Diagonals. Aline Kilmer. 6019-6
Diakos. Kostas Kariotakis. 6352-7
The dial of flowers. Felicia Dorothea Hemans. 6973-8
Dial-hands. Saint-Paul Roux. 6351-9
Dialectics of flight. John Hall Wheelock. 6388-8
Dialogue. Walter Conrad Arensberg. 6897-9
Dialogue. Babette Deutsch. 6071-4
Dialogue. Florence Kiper Frank. 6037-4
Dialogue. George Herbert. 6933-9
Dialogue. Ibn Munakhkhal. 6362-4
Dialogue. Jules Laforgue. 6801-4
Dialogue. Thomas Moore. 6278-4
Dialogue. Jay G. Sigmund. 6042-0
A dialogue ("Mars Cupid, I hear thou..."). Sir Charles Sedley. 6544-9
Dialogue before sunrise. Jules Laforgue. 6351-9
Dialogue between a proud young mother and a neighbor. Jane Gray Ward. 6850-2
Dialogue between Hector and Andromache, fr. The Iliad. Horace. 6975-4
A dialogue between him and his heart. W. Davison. 6935-5
A dialogue between himself and Mistress Eliza... Robert Herrick. 6874-X
A dialogue between Hom-Veg and Ballure's river. Thomas Edward Brown. 6809-X
Dialogue between the resolved soul & created pleasure. Andrew Marvell. 6933-9
A dialogue between the resolved soul and created pleasure. Andrew Marvell. 6341-1

A dialogue between the soul and body. Andrew Marvell. 6562-7,6341-1,6150-8
A dialogue between the soul and the body. A. W. 6189-3
A dialogue between Thyrsis and Dorinda. Andrew Marvell. 6191-5
A dialogue betwixt God and the soul. Sir Henry (atr. to, after Horace) Wotton. 6341-1
A dialogue betwixt God and the soul. Sir Henry Wotton. 6931-2,6933-9
A dialogue betwixt time and a pilgrime. Aurelian Townsend. 6378-0,6562-7,6150-8
A dialogue from Plato. Austin Dobson. 6089-7
A dialogue of self and soul. William Butler Yeats. 6209-1, 6354-3
Dialogue of the body with the soul, leading it... Jacopone da Todi. 6325-X
Dialogue of the horses. Will Carleton. 6510-4
Dialogue on the panning of Zelda Sayre Fitzgerald. Kaye McDonough. 6901-0
A dialogue sung the first night, the king... Thomas Campion. 6794-8
Dialogue with the dead, fr. Epigrams. Callimachus. 6435-3
Dialogue: lover and lady. Cielo (Ciullo) D'Alcamo. 6325-X
A dialogue. George Herbert. 6935-5
A dialogue. Gertrude Huntington McGiffert. 6838-3
A dialogue. A. W. 6935-5
"The dials of these honeyed clocks". Sunflowers. Robert P. Tristram Coffin. 7040-X,6781-6
The dials.. Arthur Wallace Peach. 6338-1
Diamond. Douglas V. Le Pan. 6761-1
Diamond cut diamond. Emma Dunning Banks. 6426-4
The diamond flood. Unknown. 6149-4
The diamond wedding. Edmund Clarence Stedman. 6996-7
The diamond wedding. Unknown. 6410-8,6744-1
Diamond, Daniel
    Dec. 4-8 7003-5
Diamond, Lucy
    The raindrops' message. 6937-1
A diamond. Robert Loveman. 6941-X
The diamond. Allen Upward. 6897-9
The diamond. James John Garth Wilkinson. 6385-3,6438-8
Diana. John Keats. 6102-8
Diana. Sir Walter Raleigh. 6436-1
Diana. Ernest Rhys. 6437-X,6656-9
Diana. James Maurice Thompson. 7041-8
"Diana Fitzpatrick Mauleverer James". Miss James. Alan Alexander Milne. 6891-X
"Diana from her frozen height". Snow at evening. William Roehrick. 6850-2
Diana remembers Actaeon. Jessie Lemont. 6979-7
Diana's lament. Juanita Havill. 6857-X
"Diana, naked in the shadowy pool". Francesco Petrarch. 6325-X
Diaper, William
    Sea eclogue. 6315-2
Diaphenia. Henry Chettle. 6187-7,6181-8
Diaphenia. Henry Constable. 6182-6,6328-4,6228-8,6246-5, 6634-8,6317
Diavolina. Fielding H. Garrison. 6482-5
Diaz Loyola, Carlos. See "Rokha, Pablo de"
Diaz, A.M.
    Willie wee. 6965-7
Diaz, Abby (Morton)
    Two little rogues. 6915-0,6167-2
"A Dibdin properly displayed". The collector's discontent. Eugene Field. 6949-5
Dibdin's ghost. Eugene Field. 6735-2,6431-0
Dibdin, Charles
    Blow high, blow low. 6086-2,6383-7
    Constancy. 6322-5
    Heaving of the lead. 6302-0
    The high-mettled racer. 6219-9
    Jack at the opera. 7025-6
    Jack's fidelity. 6833-2
    Let us all be unhappy together. 6996-7
    Lovely Nan. 6543-0
    Nongtongpaw. 6909-6
    Nongtongpaw. 6089-7
    The perfect sailor. 6322-5
    Poor Jack. 6219-9,6258-X

Poor Tom Bowling. 6153-2
The sailor's consolation. 6105-2,6290-3,6240-7,6107-9
The sailor's consolation. 6639-9
Sir Sidney Smith. 6302-0
The skater's march. 7035-3
tar for all weathers. 6543-0
Tom Bowling. 6134-6,6186-9,6385-3,6547-3,6219-9,6737, 6543-0
Tom Bowling's epitaph. 6024-2,6086-2
Dibdin, Thomas
All's well. 6302-0;6385-3
A child that has a cold. 6125-7
The snug little island. 6302-0;6385-3
Dic. Jonathan Swift. 6278-4
The **dice** were loaded. Mary Gilmore. 6349-7
Dichter, Griswald
The Maine. 6741-X
Dicing. Agathias Scholasticus. 6435-3
The **Dick** Johnson reel. Jake Falstaff. 6722-0
Dick King. Lance Fallaw. 6800-6
"**Dick** Whittington, the scullion lad". A ballad of Dick Whittington. Richard Lawson Gales. 6950-9
Dick o the cow. Unknown. 6185-0
Dick Powell. Ronald Koertge. 6792-1, 6998-3
Dick Turpin and the lawyer. Unknown. 6057-9
Dick Turpin's ride. Alfred Noyes. 6169-9
Dick's family. Ella Wheeler Wilcox. 6863-4
Dick, Cotsford
Ballade of belief. 6770-0
Ballade of burial. 6770-0
Triolet ("Plague"). 6770-0
Triolets ("Away from"). 6770-0
Triolets ("How nice"). 6770-0
Triolets for 'The twelfth,' sels. 6770-0
A vacation villanelle. 6770-0
Dickenga, I.E.
Heavenward. 6921-5
Dickens. Phoebe Cary. 6865-0,6969-X
The **Dickens** gallery. M.J. Farrah. 6417-5
Dickens in camp. Francis Bret Harte. 6385-3,6240-7,6406-X, 6465-5,6478-7,6632 ,6600-3,6707-7,6309-8,6300-4,6304-7,6291 ,6250-4,6188-1,7041-8
Dickens, Charles
Anniversary ode. 6168-0
The children. 6260-1
A Christmas carol, fr. Pickwick papers. 6145-1
'The cricket on the hearth', sels. 6724-7
Death of little Nell, fr. 'Old Curiosity Shop'. 6724-7, 6167-2
The fine old English gentleman. 6157-5
The ivy green. 6049-8,6240-7,6302-0,6385-3,6479-5,6889, 6486-8,6250-4,6639-9,6219-9,6457-4,6658 ,6934-7
Little Nell's funeral, fr. Old curiosity shop. 6909-6
Merry autumn days. 6466-3
Merry Christmas. 6449-3
Mr. Wardle's carol. 6747-6
"Oh, a dainty plant is the ivy green", sels. 6601-1
Old curiosity shop, sels. 6724-7
The Pickwick papers, sels.eman. 6145-1
Round. 7022-1
Song ("Love is not"). 6066-8
Song of the kettle, fr. 'The cricket on the hearth'. 6724-7
Things that never die. 6303-9,6461-2
The village coquettes. 6959-2
Dickenson, John
A pastoral catch. 6189-3
Tityrus to his fair Phyllis. 6182-6
Dickerson-Watkins, L.
Do you like butter? 6937-1
"**Dickery**, dickery dare". Unknown. 6363-2
Dickey, Roger C.
In Provincetown bay. 6798-0
The **dickey-bird.** Emma Celia & Lizzie J. Rook. 6137-0
Dickie, E.P.
"If I be lifted up" 6144-3
Dickie-bird! Dickie-bird! Unknown. 6629-1
Dickinson, Charles M.
The children. 6385-3,6404-3,6742-5,6219-9,7041-8
Dickinson, Emily

Afraid? Of whom am I afraid? 6177-X
After great pain a formal feeling comes. 6491-4
Alter? when the hills do. 6006-4,6646-1
Apparently with no surprise. 6754-9
April. 6374-8
As if the sea should part. 6154-0
Autumn. 6307-1,6421-3,6723-9,6374-8,6466-3,6250-4,6253-9,6307-1
Beauty crowds me. 6300-4
"Because I could not stop for death." 6348-9,6491-4
"The bee is not afraid of me". 6299-7,6239-3
"Bereaved of all, I went abroad". 6348-9
Betrayal. 6179-6
"A bird came down the walk". 6348-9,6454-X,6513-9
The bluebird ("Before you thought of spring"). 6073-0
A book. 6478-7
Bring me the sunset in a cup. 6374-8
The bustle in a house. 6288-1
Called back. 6102-8
A cemetery. 6153-2
Chartless. 6239-3,6303-9,6331-4,6418-3,6102-8,6096-5, 6309-8,6107-9,6396-9,6250-4,6439-6,6214-8,6300-4
The children. 6076-5,6102-8
Choice. 6019-6,6250-4,6309-8
"The clock stopped-not the mantel's". 6348-9,6380-2
Colloquy. 6076-5,6102-8
Constant. 6620-8,6300-4
"The cricket sang". 6348-9
The daisy follows soft the sun. 6321-7,6429-9
A day. 6473-8,6509-0,6519-8
Disenchantment. 6121-4
Dying. 6754-9
The eclat of death. 6879-0
Edelweiss. 6578-3
Emigrants. 6121-4
Eternity. 6300-4
Evening. 6236-9
Except that heaven had come so near. 6908-8
Exclusion. 6076-5,6102-8
Exultation. 6253-9
"Exultation is the going". 6380-2
The first lesson. 6321-7
Forever cherished be the tree. 6153-9
Friendship. 6396-9
Fringed gentian. 6121-4
The gentian. 6253-9
"The grass so little has to do". 6047-1,6239-3,6373-X, 6481-7
"Grief is a mouse". 6399-3
'Have you got a brook in your little heart?'. 6429-9, 6321-7
The heart asks pleasure first. 6288-1
Heart, we will forget him. 6006-4,6300-4
The hemlock. 6253-9
Her 'last poems'/Poets ended. 6483-3
Hope. 6121-4
Hope is the thing with feathers. 6236-9,6246-5,6513-9
"I asked no other thing". 6339-X,6646-1
I can wade grief. 6908-8
"I cannot live with you". 6399-3
I died for beauty. 6726-3,6008-0,6348-9,6380-2,6488-4, 6527-9,6536-8,6726-
I dreaded that first robin so. 6288-1
"I felt a funeral in my brain". 6348-9
I found the phrase. 6754-9
I had no time to hate. 6288-1
"I have a king who does not speak". 6348-9
"I heard a fly buzz when I died". 6348-9,6536-8
"I held a jewel in my fingers". 6726-3
I know that he exists. 6754-9
"I like a look of agony". 6380-2
"I like to see it lap the miles". 6536-8,6464-7,6491-4
I meant to have but modest needs. 6288-1
I measure every grief I meet. 6908-8
"I never hear the word 'escape'". 6380-2
I never saw a moor. 6473-6,6723-9
I shall not live in vain. 6303-9
"I started early, took my dog". 6380-2
I taste a liquor never brewed. 6332-2,6488-4,6399-3, 491-4

DICKINSON

"I'll tell you how the sun rose". 6299-7,6288-1
"I'm nobody! Who are you". 6380-2,6501-5,6726-3,6107-9,
    6736-0,6396-9
"I've seen a dying eye". 6348-9
If. 6473-6
If anybody's friend be dead. 6288-1
If I can stop one heart from breaking. 6006-4,6162-1
"If I shouldn't be alive". 6348-9,6513-9
"If you were coming in the fall". 6299-7,6429-9,6321-7
Immortality. 6179-6
In the garden. 6232-6,6008-0,6649-6
"In winter, in my room." 6348-9
Indian summer. 6374-8,6253-9,6646-1
Intoxication. 6076-5,6102-8
"It is an honourable thought". 6187-7,6348-9
"It was not death, for I stoop up". 6348-9
"The last night that she lived". 6246-5
Life. 6006-4,6077-3,6300-4
"The lightning is a yellow fork". 6399-3
The locomotive. 6891-X
The lonely house. 6467-1
"A long, long sleep, a famous sleep". 6380-2
The lost jewel. 6121-4
Love. 6077-3
The lovers. 6008-0
The martyrs. 6121-4
Morning. 6861-8
Morning. 6501-5
The morns are meeker than they were. 6534-1
The mountain sat. 6374-8
Much madness is divinest sense. 6121-4
"My life closed twice before its close." 6187-7,6317-9,
    6339-X,63448-9,6726-3
My nosegays are for captives. 6501-5
"My triumph lasted till the drums." 6665-8
Mysteries. 6153-2
"A narrow fellow in the grass". 6246-5,6348-9
No time to hate. 6076-5,6102-8,6321-7
"Not any sunny tone". 6348-9
Not what we did shall be the test. 6154-0
"Not with a club the heart is broken". 6726-3
O course, I prayed. 6536-8
"Of all the souls that stand create". 6246-5
"Of all the sounds despatched abroad". 6348-9
"Of bronze and blaze". 6348-9
One dignity for all. 6879-0
The ones that disappeared are back. 6253-9
Pain has an element of blank. 6908-8
Parting. 6102-8,6250-4,6006-4,6019-6,6076-5,6467-1,6309-
    8,6300-4
The past. 6121-4
Peace. 6250-4
Peace. 6250-4,6309-8
Pedigree. 6250-4,6736-0,6250-4,6503-1
The pedigree of honey. 6534-1
Post-mortem. 6076-5,6102-8
Precious words. 6107-9
A precious, mouldering pleasure 'tis. 6162-1
Presentiment. 6076-5,6102-8,6076-5,6102-8,6208-3
Proof. 6320-9
The railway train. 6332-2,6473-6,6421-3,6723-9
"Rearrange a wife's affection." 6399-3
The robin. 6073-0,6374-8,6473-6
"Safe in their alabaster chambers". 6187-7,6348-9
"The show is not the show". 6339-X
Simplicity. 6501-5,6008-0,6250-4
The sky is low. 6491-4
The snake. 6332-2,6214-8
Some keep Sunday going to churcn. 6418-3
"The soul selects her own society". 6726-3,6153-2
Success. 6332-2
"Success is counted sweetest." 6513-9,6665-8
Summer shower. 6373-X
Sunset and sunrise. 6368-3
Suspense. 6102-8,6250-4,6309-8
"Sweet is the swamp with its secrets". 6348-9
A tempest. 6332-2
"There came a wind like a bugle". 6315-2,6348-9,6288-1
There is no frigate like a book. 6154-0,6162-1,6289-X,
    6107-9

"There's a certain slant of light". 6536-8,6491-4
"There's been a death in the opposite house". 6380-2
"They might not need me; but they might". 6889-8
They say that 'time assuages' 6908-8
They say that 'time assuages'. 6879-0
"This quiet dust was gentlemen and ladies". 6187-7,6733-
    6,6289-X,6288-1,6464-7
A thought went up my mind. 6754-9
Time and eternity: XXVII. 6879-0
Time's healing. 6121-4
To fight aloud is very brave. 6008-0
To hear an oriole. 6754-9
To make a prairie it takes clover and one bee. 6534-1
"To my quick ear the leaves conferred". 6246-5,6348-9
To the beloved. 6320-9
Twenty-one lyrics from 'Life.' 6431-0
Two voyagers. 6473-6
Vanished. 6076-5,6102-8
The waking year. 6177-X,6307-1
The way I read a letter's this. 6008-0
"We never knew how high we are". 6162-1
"While we were fearing it, it came". 6380-2
Who robbed the woods? 6473-6
"A wife at daybreak I shall be". 6399-3
A wife at daybreak I shall be. 6288-1
The wife. 6320-9
Wild Eden. 6006-4
Wild nights. 6006-4
The wind. 6754-9
'A word is dead' 6861-8
A wounded deer leaps highest. 7039-6
You left me, sweet. 6908-8

Dickinson, G. Lowes (tr.)
    Sine amore nil est jucundum. Mimnermus, 6435-3
Dickinson, John
    "Come join hand in hand, brave Americans all". 6753-0
    The liberty song. 6008-0
Dickinson, Martha Gilbert
    Dawn at Venice. 6624-0
Dickinson, Mary Lowe
    Jerry. 6414-0,6706-9,6574-0
Dickinson, Patric
    "I am no pet who can set." 6317-9
    Lament for the great yachts. 6257-1
    The redwing. 6257-1
Dickson, David
    The new Jerusalem. 6302-0;6385-3
Dickson, George
    Fat cattle in trucks near the Fairfield crane (Glasgow)
    6778-6
Dickson, Margarette Ball
    Song of the crow wing. 6342-X
Dickson, Samuel Henry
    I sigh for the land of the cypress and pine. 7017-5
Dickson, Virginia
    Rain fell last night. 6750-6
Dicky of Ballyman. Unknown. 6613-5
Dictionary. Samuel Marshak. 6546-5
"Dictionary needs redoing". Library note. Eve Merriam.
    6761-1
Dictum sapienti. Charles Henry ("John Paul") Webb. 6004-8,
    6026-9
"Did Cytherea to the skies". On a bath. Plato. 6814-6
"Did any bird come flying". Christina Georgina Rossetti.
    6187-7
"Did ever swain a nymph adore". Robin's complaint.
    Unknown. 6874-X
"Did I dream? Was't a fancy". A nightmare. Eugene Field.
    6949-5
"'Did I exist before my birth?'". Life's past and future.
    William Hankins Chitwood. 6799-9
"Did I know convict Joe? Yes, I knew him". Convict Joe.
    Alexander G. Murdoch. 6921-5
"Did I seek life? Not so; its weight was...". A song of
    life. Anne Reeve Aldrich. 7041-8
Did not. Thomas Moore. 6026-9
"Did not my muse (what can she less?).". An apology for
    not showing her what I had wrote. William Cowper.
    6814-6
Did not pass. Mary E. Burnett. 6629-1

"Did not the heavenly rhetoric of thine eye". Perjury excused, fr. Love's labour's lost. William Shakespeare. 6827-8
"Did not thy reason and thy sense". An attempt at the manner of Waller. William Cowper. 6814-6
"Did the wild blast of battle sound". Trebarrow. Robert Stephen Hawker. 6873-1
"Did they dare...to slay Owen Roe O'Neil?". Lament for the death of Eoghan Ruadh (Owen Roe) O'Neil. Thomas Osborne Davis. 6858-8
"Did ya hear about lil' Johnny Castro?". Did ya hear? Yasmeen Jamal. 6870-7
"Did ye ever hear o guid Earl o Bran". Unknown. 6111-7
Did you - will you? Unknown. 6689-5
"Did you ask dulcet rhymes from me," fr. Drum-taps. Walt Whitman. 6934-7
"Did you ever carry water". Garden relief. Margaret Pitcairn Strachan. 6750-6
"Did you ever go a-walking". Fairy antics. Ethel M. Brainerd. 6906-1
"Did you ever go back to the woman you used...". The woman you used to love. Unknown. 6750-6
"Did you ever have a chipmunk for a friend?" Jessie Orton Jones. 6999-1
"Did you ever hear of Dives..lived..Palestine". Dives and Lazarus. Ernest Bilton. 7009-4
"Did you ever hear of Editor Whedon". Daisy Fraser. Edgar Lee Masters. 6897-9
"Did you ever hear of the drummer boy...". The drummer boy of Mission Ridge. Unknown. 6963-0
"Did you ever hear tell of old Timothy Tuff". Tim Tuff. Edward Capern. 6909-6
"Did you ever hear the old fifer play". The old fifer. Norman W. Gilbert. 7030-2
"Did you ever in the springtime". Ruts. Nellie E. Warren. 6799-9
"Did you ever meet laugh-and-be-jolly?". Laugh and be jolly. Nancy Byrd Turner. 6861-8
"Did you ever see an alligator". Arlo Will. Edgar Lee Masters. 6897-9
"Did you ever see mah ponay--". The race at Petit Cote. William Edward Baubie. 7035-3
"Did you ever see our pet?". Two faces under a hood. M.E. B.. 6965-7
"Did you ever/Swing in my swing". Backyard swing. Janet Campbell Hale. 7005-1
"Did you feel our hands on your hands as...". Lindbergh. Mary Carolyn Davies. 7019-1
"Did you get your hair from strings of harps?". Wonder. Lois Dawson. 6850-2
"Did you hear about the crocodile and Tommy...". Tommy and the crocodile. Robert C.V. Meyers. 6927-4
"Did you know, little child". The welcome. Nettie Palmer. 6784-0
Did you not see. Alex Kuo. 6790-5
"Did you say you wished to see me, sir?". Poor house Nan. Lucy Marion Blinn. 6451-5,7022-1
"Did you see Paidin,/Paidin, the besom-man". The besom-man. Joseph ("Seosamh MacCathmhaoil") Campbell. 6930-4
"Did you see my wife...". Unknown. 6363-2
"Did you tackle the trouble that came your way". How did you die? Edmund Vance Cooke. 6732-8,6337-3,6964-9, 6291-1,6337-3,6260-1,6274-1
"Did you think I could forget it". The silver wedding. Mrs. C.M. Stowe. 6910-X
"Did you think you heard the wind". The wind. E.O. De Camp. 6906-1
The didactic poem. Richard Garnett. 6656-9
Diddle diddle dumpling. Mother Goose. 6466-3
"Diddledy, diddledy, dumpty". Unknown. 6363-2
Didn't thing. Unknown. 6312-8
"Didn't think of losin' him." Frank Lebby Stanton. 6687-9
Dido. Grant S. Hough. 6316-0
Dido. Richard Porson. 6089-7
Dido among the shades, fr. Aeneid. Vergil. 6933-9
"Dido my dear, alas, is dead," fr. Shepeardes calendar. Edmund Spenser. 6125-7
"Dido was the carthage queene". A ballad. Thomas Campion. 6794-8

"Dido with the driven hair". The beaten path. Anne Goodwin Winslow. 6778-6
Dido's hunting. Henry Howard, Earl of Surrey. 6436-1
Dido, on the departure of Aeneas. Helen Pinkerton. 6515-5
"'Didst ever see a hanging?' 'No, not one'.". The phantoms of St. Sepulchre. Charles Mackay. 6912-6
"Die down, O dismal day!". Sonnet ("Die down"). David Gray. 6271-7
"Die down, O dismay day." David Gray. 6302-0,6385-3,6543-0
Die kuche. Alfred Kreymborg. 6010-2
Die lorelei. Heinrich Heine. 6527-9
Die lorelei. Heinrich Heine. 6527-9
Die nacht. Count Joseph von Eichendorff. 6252-0
Die not, fond man. Unknown. 6182-6
Die rose, die lilie, die taube, die sonne. Heinrich Heine. 7039-6
Die walkuere. Flaccus [pseud]. 6817-0
"Died last night at twelve o'clock". August lilies. Benjamin Franklin Taylor. 6815-4
Died of his wounds. Sir Henry Head. 6482-5
Died young. Cora Fabri. 6876-6
Diefenbach, Jean
    Another beetle. 6262-8
Diego Ordas in El Dorado. Unknown. 6385-3
Diekenga, I.E.
    Blacksmith's song (no. 1). 6711-5
Dieppe. Joyce Rowe. 6895-2
Diers, Theodore C.
    My Nebraska. 6465-5
Dierx, Leon
    Adieu. 6351-9
    Home from the party. 6351-9
    Journee d'hiver. 6801-4
Dies irae. Thomas de Celano. 6385-3
Dies irae. Abraham Coles. 6302-0
Dies irae. James Leo Duff. 6144-3
Dies irae. Sir Walter Scott. 6337-3,6291-9
Dies irae. Thomas of Celano. 6219-9,6543-0
Dies irae. Thomas of Celano. 6730-1
Dies irae. Thomas of Celano. 6219-9
Dies irae. Thomas of Celano. 6219-9
Dies irae. Unknown. 6741-X
Dies irae. B.H. W. 7031-0
Dies irae - dies pacis. John Oxenham. 6337-3
Dies ultima. Frank Dempster Sherman. 6309-8
Diet, fr. The art of preserving health. John Armstrong. 6968-1
Dietz, Ella
    The first snow. 6695-X
Dieudonne. William Henry Drummond. 6843-X
Difference. Helen Hoyt. 6628-3
Difference. Sarah N. Pulsifer. 6789-1
Difference. William Reohrick. 6850-2
The difference between a lie and the truth. Ronald James Dessus. 6870-7
The difference.. Benjamin Franklin. 6722-0
The difference. Annie I. Muzzey. 6583-X
The difference.. Laura E. Richards. 6078-1,6452-3
The difference.. Robert Louis Stevenson. 6429-9,6321-7
The difference. Edgar A. Guest. 6748-4
The difference. Laura E. Richards. 6937-1
The difference. Mary Louise Ritter. 6385-3
The difference. Susan Shogren. 6883-9
The difference. John Banister Tabb. 6102-8,6076-5
Differences. Charles Mackay. 6219-9
Differences. Valerie Tarver. 7024-8
Different graces. Walter Savage Landor. 6233-4
Different minds. Richard Chenevix Trench. 6219-9
Different points of view. Unknown. 6600-3
Different tastes. James Beattie. 6402-7
A different way. Esther Lloyd Hagg. 6144-3
Different winter. Louise Townsend Nicholl. 6388-8
Differentia. Emily Porter St. John. 6316-0
"Difficult as it is, she sits". Daughter at arithmetic. Dorothy McFarlane. 6750-6
Difficult love-making. Will Carleton. 6671-2
A difficult problem. Charlotte W. Thurston. 7022-1
Difficulties. Edgar A. Guest. 6869-3
Difficulties of a statesman. Thomas Stearns Eliot. 6399-3
The difficulties of translation, fr. Aeneid. Vergil. 6845-

DIFFICULTIES

6
The **difficulty** of rhyming. Unknown. 6913-4
The **difficulty** of riming. Unknown. 6277-6,6565-1
The **difficulty**.. James Freeman Clarke. 6429-9
The **difficulty**. James Freeman Clarke. 6321-7
The **difficulty**. Heinrich Heine. 6226-1
Diffidence. Unknown. 6915-0
Diffidence. Unknown. 6139-7,6167-2
Diffugere vives. Horace. 6252-0
"**Dig** into mother earth, deep toward her heart".
    Skyscraper. Genevieve Gray Rawson. 6906-1
Digby, Sir Kenelm
    On his late espoused saint. 6022-6
Digby; Earl of Bristol, John
    Grieve not, dear love. 6879-0
Digdog. Ruth Pitter. 6985-1
A **digest** of Lord's ---'s evidence. G. J. 6878-2
The **digger's** grave. Sarah Welch. 6274-1,6656-9
The **digger's** song. Amy Sutherland. 6591-0,6592-9
The **diggers**. Paula R. Sharp. 6900-2
Digges, Leonard
    "If, of a wretched state and all forlorn." 6317-9,6562-7
Digging out the roots. Duane Niatum. 7005-1
Digging potaters in Vermont. Daniel L. Cady. 6988-6
"**Diggory** diggory delvet!". The mole. Beatrix Potter. 6937-1
Dighton is engaged. Gelett Burg ss. 6089-7,6441-8,6732-8
Dignified courtship. Unknown. 6922-3
"A **dignified** deer, with sprangling horns". The polite deer. Carolyn Wells. 6882-0
The **dignity** of labor. Robert Bersohn. 6722-0
The **dignity** of man-Lesson #1 Walter H. Kerr. 6388-8
A **digression** to hospitalitie. Thomas Tusser. 6586-4
Digue dondaine, digue dondon. Yvor Winters. 6808-1
Dildido, dildido. Robert Greene. 6383-7
Dilemma. Orrick Johns. 6031-5,6556-2,6300-4
Dilemma. Viola Brothers Shore. 6817-0
The **dilemma**.. Oliver Wendell Holmes. 6441-8,6683-6,6735-2
A **dilemma**. Unknown. 6732-8
"A **dillar**, a dollar". Mother Goose. 6363-2
Dillard, Gavin
    "First time he" 7003-5
    Magic. 7003-5
    The sighting. 7003-5
Dillenbach, John D.
    Colorado. 6836-7
Dillerville, Humphrey
    Sixteenth century. 6037-4
Dilley, Edgar Meck
    Hail, Pennsylvania! 6936-3
Dillman, Will
    Old Young. 6686-0
Dillmore, Richard Casper
    Cupid peeped in through the blinds. 6927-4
Dillon, George
    Address to the doomed, fr. The flowering stone. 6979-7
    April's amazing meaning. 6619-4,6581-3,6071-4
    Autumn wind. 6253-9
    Boy in the wind. 6619-4,6779-4
    Compliment to mariners. 6619-4
    The dead elm on the hilltop. 6984-3
    Elegy. 6808-1
    The humble horse. 6039-0
    I think Delilah had a heart. 6039-0
    In two months now. 6232-6
    Legend. 6039-0
    Memory of Lake Superior. 6396-9
    The noise of leaves. 6374-8,6217-2
    Pigeons. 6073-0
    Spring articulate. 6039-0
    Twilight in a tower. 6808-1
Dillon, Wentworth (tr.)
    Dies irae. Thomas of Celano, 6730-1
Dillon, Wentworth. See Roscommon
The **dilly** and the d's. Unknown. 6278-4
"A **dim** and mighty minster of old time". Cathedral hymn. Felicia Dorothea Hemans. 6973-8
"**Dim** as the borrow'd beams of moon..",fr.Religio laici. John Dryden. 6831-6

"**Dim** as the borrowed beams of moon and stars". Reason and religion, fr. Religio laici. John Dryden. 6867-7
Dim beauty. Unknown. 7007-8
"The **dim** blue-laced veins on either brow". Rachel, fr. Joseph and his breathen. Charles Jeremiah Wells. 6934-7
"**Dim** child of darkness and faint-echoing space". Fear. Hartley Coleridge. 6980-0
"**Dim** hour! that sleep'st on pillowing clouds afar". The hour when we shall meet again. Samuel Taylor Coleridge. 6967-3
"**Dim** miles of smoke behind - I look before". London. John Nichol. 7015-9
"The **dim** rays through the water bring me up". Whale poem. Andy Roberts. 6883-9
"**Dim** shadows gather thickly round...". The golden gate. Adelaide Anne Procter. 6957-6
"The **dim** star of the ocean lieth cool". Robert Buchanan. 6997-5
"A **dim** voice calls/From a distant field". Haze. Gon-kang Yun. 6775-1
The **dim** waters of uncertainty. Mary Pauline Richardson. 6789-1
"**Dim**, as the borrow'd beams of moon and stars". Reason and revelation, fr. Religio laici. John Dryden. 6933-9
"**Dim**, gradual thinning of the shapeless gloom". The troops. Siegfried Sassoon. 7027-2
"**Dimbled** scheeks, mit eyes off plue".eMine vamily. Charles Follen Adams. 6572-4,6917-7,6572-4
Dimensions. Berton Braley. 6853-7
Dimes and dollars. Henry Mills. 6912-6
Dimes for turnips blood. Unknown. 6689-5
Diminuendo. Tom Kristensen. 6555-4
Diminution. Harry Kemp. 6042-0
Diminutive ululans. Francis Macnamara. 6090-0
"**Dimmed** are the flowers now". Night piece. A.R. Ubsdell. 6781-6
Dimmette, Celia
    The goblets. 6789-1
Dimmick, Joanne
    Line in the morning. 6761-1
    Rehearsal for a wedding. 6761-1
Dimness. John Keble. 6980-0
Dimond, William
    The mariner's dream. 6302-0;6385-3,6302-0,6385-3,6219-9
    The sailor-boy's dream. 6410-8,6131-1,6606-2,6742-5
Dimout in Harlem. Langston Hughes. 6561-9
Dinah. Norman Gale. 6510-4
Dinah kneading dough. Paul Laurence Dunbar. 6441-8
The **diners** in the kitchen, fr. A session with... James Whitcomb Riley. 6091-9
Ding dong. Unknown. 6182-6
"**Ding** dong didero,/Blow big bellows". Smith's song. George Sigerson. 6930-4
"'**Ding dong!' quoth the bell**". The rape of the bell. Augusta Moore. 6925-8
Ding, dong, bell. Mother Goose. 6363-2,6452-3,6699-2
"**Ding**, dong, darrow". Unknown. 6363-2
"**Dingty**, diddlety, my mammy's maid". Unknown. 6363-2
Dingwall, Mary K.D.
    Washington's day. 6712-3
"A **dingy** donkey, formal and unchanged". A fable. John Hookham Frere. 6802-2
"A **dingy** picture: others passed it by". In the Louvre. John Todhunter. 7015-9
The **dining** room. Francis Jammes. 6351-9
Dining-room mirror. Jorge Carrera Andrade. 6642-9
Dining-room mirror. Jorge Carrera Andrade. 6642-9
Dining-room tea. Rupert Brooke. 6234-2
Dinkel, Terry B.
    The iconoclasts. 6906-1
    In an old garden. 6906-1
    Lady moon. 6906-1
The **dinkey-bird**. Eugene Field. 6089-7,6732-8,6265-2,6318-7,6467-1
"**Dinna** ask me." John Dunlop. 6302-0,6385-3,6226-1,6737-9
Dinna chide the mither. Margaret Elizabeth Sangster. 6414-0
Dinneen and T. O'Donoghue, P.S. (tr.)
    The Geraldine's daughter. Egan O'Rahilly, 6930-4

More power to Cromwell. Egan O'Rahilly, 6930-4
On a cock which was stolen from a good priest. Egan
    O'Rahilly, 6930-4
On a pair of shes presented to him, sels. Egan
    O'Rahilly, 6930-4
The storm. Egan O'Rahilly, 6930-4
The **dinner** hour, fr. Lucille. Owen (Edward Bulwer-Lytton,
    Earl Lytton) Meredith. 6732-8
The **dinner** party. William Cowper. 6186-9
The **dinner-hour**, fr. Lucile. Owen (Edward Bulwer-Lytton,
    Earl Lytton) Meredith. 6656-9
Dinner-time. Edgar A. Guest. 6862-6
Dinner-time (Sloane Street). Douglas Goldring. 6506-6
Dinnis Kilboo's sanatarium. Charles T. Catlin. 6451-5
Dinnis, Enid
    The cherub-folk. 6096 X
    A ditty of creation. 6096 X
    To my mother church. 6096 X
Dinnshenchas, sels. Unknown. 6930-4
Dinogad's petticoat, fr. Book of Aneirin. Unknown (Welsh)
    6528-7
"The **dinosaur's** fluid neck". Steam shovel, fr. Industrial
    poems. A.M. Sullivan. 6839-1
The **dinosaur**. Bert Leston Taylor. 6307-1
Dinsmore, Silas
    The churning song. 6273-3
Diocletian. Edward Farquhar. 6939-8
Diogenes. Max Eastman. 6897-9
Diogenes dresses down a proud monarch. Lucian. 6637-2
Dion. William Wordsworth. 6438-8
Dion of Syracuse. Plato. 6435-3
Dion of Tarsus. Unknown. 6850-2
Dion of Tarsus. Unknown (Greek) 7039-6
"**Dion** of Tarsus, here I lie". Unknown (Greek) 6637-2
Dione. A pastoral tragedy. John Gay. 6972-X
Dionysians in a bad time. Irving Layton. 6767-0
"**Dionysius**, of Tarsus, here doth rot". Unknown. 6251-2
Dionysus. Gertrude Huntington McGiffert. 6838-3
"**Dionysus!** Dionysus! Dionysus!". Young Bacchante's hymn.
    Salomon de la Selva. 6959-2
Dioscorides
    A faithful servant. R.A. Furness (tr.). 6435-3
    "A Lydian I, a Lydian slave...". F.L. Lucas (tr.). 6251-2
    A young mother. George Allen (tr.). 6435-3
Diotimus
    The cow herd. R.A. Furness (tr.). 6435-3
"**Dip** down upon the northern shore". The months. Alfred
    Lord Tennyson. 7020-5
"**Diplomats** in China". To Mrs. J.B.J. Louis J. Magee. 7004-3
The **diplomats**. Alfred Noyes. 6337-3
Dipping candles in Vermont. Daniel L. Cady. 6988-6
"**Dipping** oars in the shining water". Forgetting. Unknown.
    6983-5
Dipsychus. Arthur Hugh Clough. 6828-6
Dipsychus, sels. Arthur Hugh Clough. 6331-4,6102-8,6199-0,
    6430-2
Dirce. Walter Savage Landor. 6430-2,6150-8,6102-8,6301-2,
    6656-9,6086-2,6092-7,6122-2;6208-3;6315-2;6339-
    X;6722-3;6726
"**Dire** rebel though he was". Character of Artevelde, fr.
    Philip Van Artevelde. Henry Taylor. 6980-0
Directions for a rebel. William Robert Rodgers. 6391-8
Directions for cultivating a hop-garden. Thomas Tusser.
    6649-6
Directions for the reading-class. F. Ursula Payne. 6718-2
The **director**. Edward Farquhar. 6939-8
The **direful** tale of horror. Berton Braley. 6853-7
Dirge. Thomas Bailey Aldrich. 6431-0
Dirge. Thomas Lovell Beddoes. 6217-7,6302-0,6656-9
Dirge. Thomas Lovell Beddoes. 6908-8
Dirge. Thomas Lovell Beddoes. 6317-7,6328-4
Dirge. Thomas Lovell Beddoes. 6641-0
Dirge. Thomas Lovell Beddoes. 6315-2,6437-X,6383-7
Dirge. Madison Cawein. 6431-0
Dirge. William Collins. 6639-9
Dirge. Georgia H. Cooper. 6850-2
Dirge. Adelaide Crapsey. 6019-6,6102-8,6431-0,6581-3,6076-
    5,6300-4,6653-4,6030-7,6019-6,6102-8,6431-0,6581-3,
    6076-5,6300-4,6653-4
Dirge. George Croly. 6271-7,6214-8
Dirge. George Darley. 6873-1
Dirge. Charles Gamage Eastman. 6910-X,6219-9
Dirge. Ralph Waldo Emerson. 6250-4,6431-0
Dirge. Kenneth Fearing. 6324-1,6375-6
Dirge. John Fletcher. 6198-2,6189-3
Dirge. John Ford. 6315-2,6383-7
Dirge. Howard Gilbert. 6304-7
Dirge. Felicia Dorothea Hemans. 6973-8,6271-7
Dirge. Maurice Hewlett. 6872-3
Dirge. Muriel F. Hochdorf. 6850-2
Dirge. Leigh Hunt. 6934-7
Dirge. Leigh Hunt. 6250-4
Dirge. Leigh Hunt. 6934-7
Dirge. Alfred Kreymborg. 6010-2
Dirge. Theodore Maynard. 6884-7
Dirge. Anthony Munday. 6436-1
Dirge. Thomas William Parsons. 6431-0
Dirge. George Peele. 6182-6
Dirge. Edith Lovejoy Pierce. 6337-3
Dirge. William Stanley Roscoe. 6271-7
Dirge. Johann C. Friedrich von Schiller. 6438-8
Dirge. William Shakespeare. 6737-9
Dirge. James Shirley. 6604-6
Dirge. Robert Calverley Trevelyan. 6234-2
Dirge. Unknown. 6724-7
Dirge. John Webster. 6533-3
Dirge ("Fear no more"). William Shakespeare. 6179-6,6334-9,
    6604-6
Dirge (To the memory of Miss Ellen Gree, of Kew...).
    Unknown. 6089-7
Dirge at sea. Felicia Dorothea Hemans. 6973-8
A **dirge** concerning the late lamented king of..cannibal.
    William Augustus Croffut. 6089-7
A **dirge** for a righteout cat. Vachel Lindsay. 6120-6;6334-9
Dirge for a soldier. George Henry Boker. 6946-0,6309-8,
    6470-1,6121-4,6288-1,6291-9,6300-4,6396-9,6113-3,
    6240-7,6271-7,6302-0,6385-3,6437-,6471-X,6473-6,6481-
    7,6486-8,6490-6,6552-,6600-3,6732-8,6737-7,6665-8,
    6431-0,6304
Dirge for a young girl. James Thomas Fields. 6271-7,6302-0,
    6385-3
Dirge for Aoine. Nora Hopper. 6174-5
Dirge for Ashby. Josephine Junkin Preston. 6946-0
Dirge for civilization. Ruth Lechlitner. 6490-6
Dirge for Fidele. William Collins. 6092-7
Dirge for fidele, fr. Songs. William Shakespeare. 6600-3
A dirge for King Niall of the nine hostages. Unknown. 6090-0
Dirge for love. William Shakespeare. 6153-2
A **dirge** for McPherson. Herman Melville. 6074-9
Dirge for one who fell in battle. Thomas William Parsons.
    6239-3,6459-0,6732-8,6309-8,6304-7,6006
A **dirge** for Phyllip Sparowe, sels. John Skelton. 6198-2
Dirge for Robin Hood. Anthony Munday. 6641-0
A dirge for summer. Sebastion Evans. 6656-9
Dirge for the barrel-organ of the new barbarism. Louis
    Aragon. 6665-8
"A **dirge** for the brave old pioneer". The old pioneer.
    Theodore O'Hara. 7017-5
A dirge for the deep-sea trawler. Thomas Ekenhead Mayne.
    6174-5
Dirge for the suicides. Joy Davidman. 6561-9
Dirge for the year. Percy Bysshe Shelley. 6239-3,6271-7,
    6737-9,6250-4,6747-6
Dirge for two veterans. Walt Whitman. 6288-1
Dirge for Wolfram, fr. Death's jest book. Thomas Lovell
    Beddoes. 6832-4
Dirge in Cymbeline. William Collins. 6291-9,6543-0,6250-4,
    6600-3,6271-7,6604-6,6153-2,6086-2,6438
Dirge in woods. George Meredith. 6198-2,6052-8,6315-2,6726-
    3,6199-0,6508 ,6199-0,6430-2,6023-4,6491-4,6046-3,
    6102-8,6430-2,6153-2,6655-0
Dirge of a child. Felicia Dorothea Hemans. 6772-7
Dirge of Alaric the Visgoth. Edward Everett. 6385-3
The **dirge** of Alaric, king of the Visigoths. Unknown. 6889-8
Dirge of Imogen. William Shakespeare. 6271-7
The **dirge** of Jephtah's daughter. Robert Herrick. 6848-0

DIRGE

The **dirge** of Jephthah's daughter. Robert Herrick. 6271-7, 6334-9
Dirge of O'Sullivan Bear. Unknown (Irish) 6858-8
Dirge of Outalissi. Thomas Campbell. 6980-0
Dirge of Rachel. William Knox. 6848-0
Dirge of Rory O'More. Aubrey Thomas De Vere. 6858-8
Dirge of the dead sisters. Rudyard Kipling. 6810-3
The **dirge** of the drinker. William Edmonstoune Aytoun. 6278-4
Dirge of the highland chief in Waverley. Felicia Dorothea Hemans. 6973-8
The **dirge** of the householder. Richard Stillman Powell. 7021-3
Dirge of the moola of Kotal. George Thomas Lanigan. 6089-7
Dirge of the munster forest. Emily Lawless. 6244-X
Dirge of the satyrs and wood nymphs. Thomas Nashe. 6334-9
A **dirge** of victory. Edward John Plunkett, 18th Baron Dunsany. 7029-9
Dirge without music. Edna St. Vincent Millay. 6317-9,6602-X,6513-9
Dirge, fr. Cymbeline. William Shakespeare. 6668-2
The **dirge**, fr. Cymbeline. William Shakespeare. 6423-X,6153-2,6291-9,6371-3
Dirge, fr. Lilith. George Sterling. 6347-0
Dirge, fr. Supplices. Euripides. 6435-3
Dirge, fr. The contention of Ajax and Ulysses. James Shirley. 6108-7,6022-6
A **dirge**, fr. The white divel. John Webster. 6023-4
A **dirge**, sels. Ralph Waldo Emerson. 6934-7
A **dirge**.. Felicia Dorothea Hemans. 6198-2,6108-2,6214-8
A **dirge**.. Percy Bysshe Shelley. 6102-8,6332-2,6250-4,6125-7,6110-9
A **dirge**.. Richard Henry Stoddard. 6113-3
Dirge: 1-2-3 was the number... Edward Estlin Cummings. 6637-2
A **dirge**. Francis Beaumont and John Fletcher. 6383-7
A **dirge**. Thomas Lovell Beddoes. 6879-0
A **dirge**. Thomas Lovell Beddoes. 6908-8
A **dirge**. William Browne. 6191-5
A **dirge**. George Croly. 6980-0,6407-8
A **dirge**. Felicia Dorothea Hemans. 6973-8
A **dirge**. Felicia Dorothea Hemans. 6087-0
A **dirge**. Felicia Dorothea Hemans. 6934-7
A **dirge**. Felicia Dorothea Hemans. 6973-8
A **dirge**. Henry King. 6934-7
A **dirge**. Robert Nicoll. 6960-6
A **dirge**. Victor Perowne. 6846-4
A **dirge**. Christina Georgina Rossetti. 6315-2,6657-7
A **dirge**. Christina Georgina Rossetti. 6125-7
A **dirge**. Mokichi Saito. 6482-5
A **dirge**. Percy Bysshe Shelley. 6430-2,6560-0,6545-7,6122-2,6473-6,6527-9,6726-3,6199-0
A **dirge**. James Shirley. 6189-3
A **dirge**. Sir Philip Sidney. 6099-4,6186-9,6383-7,6250-4,6301-2
A **dirge**. Alfred Lord Tennyson. 6271-7
A **dirge**. John Webster. 6182-6,6276-3,6533-3
A **dirge**. John Webster. 6328-4,6194-X,6153-2,6291-9,6301-2,6102
A **dirge**. Frank S. Williamson. 6784-0
The **dirge**. Robert Stephen Hawker. 6023-4
The **dirge**. Henry King. 6302-0,6385-3,6250-4
The **dirt** doctor. Melvin Douglass Brown. 6870-7
"**Dirt** road on the left, if laid much steeper". Passing. Charles Malam. 6761-1
Dirt song. Irving Brickman. 6237-7
"**Dirt** sticks under fingernails". Pulling weeds. Eric Chock. 6790-5
Dirty Gertie from Bizerte. Unknown. 6237-7
The **dirty** hand. Carlos Drummond de Andrade. 6758-1
Dirty Jim. Jane Taylor. 6233-4,6242-3,6459-0
Dirty kitty-cat. Stanley Schell. 6699-2
The **dirty** old man. William Allingham. 6358-6,6512-0,6927-4
"**Dirty** water reflects too/like". Momma's not Gods image. Noah Mitchell. 6870-7
'**Dis** den I'll dink of dou. Unknown. 6175-3
Dis what de union done. George Jones. 6149-4
"A **dis**, a dis, a green grass". Unknown. 6317-9,6334-9
Disabled. Wilfred Owen. 6375-6,6666-6
Disabled-Armistice Day. Catherine Parmenter. 6449-3

A **disagreeable** feature. Edwin Meade Robinson. 6102-8,6076-5
The **disagreeable** man. Sir William Schwenck Gilbert. 6280-6,6026-9
Disappointed. Paul Laurence Dunbar. 6861-8
Disappointed hopes. Thomas Moore. 6543-0
The **disappointed** lover. Algernon Charles Swinburne. 6302-0;6385-3
The **disappointed** lover. Unknown. 6826-X
The **disappointed** snow-flakes. Unknown. 6373-X
The **disappointed**.. Ella Wheeler Wilcox. 6291-1
Disappointment. Maria Gowen Brooks. 6385-3
Disappointment. James Russell Lowell. 6304-7
Disappointment. John Boyle O'Reilly. 6930-4
Disappointment. John Boyle O'Reilly. 6022-6
Disappointment. Coventry Patmore. 6092-7
Disappointment. William Roehrick. 6850-2
Disappointment of a thrall, fr. Two gentlemen in bonds. John Crowe Ransom. 6011-0
<u>**Disappointment**, fr. A pastoral ballad. William Shenstone. 6024-2</u>
"**Disarm** this beautiful machine". The ghost, fr. Space of breath. Harold Lewis Cook. 6780-8
Disarmament. John McCrae. 7014-0
Disarmament. John Greenleaf Whittier. 6051-X,6087-0,6420-5,6542-2
Disaster. Charles Stuart Calverley. 6440-X,6089-7
Discard. Zola Monk. 6906-1
The **discardment**. Alan Paton. 6788-3
Disch, Tom
    The prospect behind us. 6803-0
"**Discharged** again! Yes, I am free". Warden, keep a place for me. David Law ("Pegleg Arkwright") Proudfit. 6915-0
Discharged, fr. In hospital. William Ernest Henley. 6655-0, 6508-2
The **disciple**. John Berryman. 6391-8
The **disciple**. Dwight Bradley. 6144-3
The **disciple**. Catulle Mendes. 6102-8
Discipline. Alice Van Leer Carrick. 6130-3
Discipline. George Herbert. 6339-X,6562-7,6634-8,6732-8,6315-2,6737 ,6250-4,6513 9,6341-1
Discipline. Unknown. 6415-9
The **discipline** of wisdom. George Meredith. 6828-6
The **discipline** of wisdom. George Meredith. 6199-0
Disciplinin' sistah Brown. James E. Campbell. 6710-7
Discipulo discedenti. Heathcote William Garrod. 6785-9
Disclosed. George Herbert Fullerton. 6818-9
Disco Chinatown. Yuri Kageyama. 6790-5
"A **disconnected** connection". March water songs I. Jacqueline J. Johnson. 6899-5
"**Disconsolate** and sad". Platonick love. Edward Herbert, 1st Baron Herbert of Cherbury. 6933-9
Discontent. Sarah Orne Jewett. 6519-8,6049-8,6131-1,6639-9,6638-0
<u>**Discontent**. Unknown. 6312-8</u>
Discontent. Sarah ("Susan Coolidge") Woolsey. 6373-X
Discontent, fr. The road to Avernus. Adam Lindsay Gordon. 6951-7
The **discontented** buttercup. Sarah Orne Jewett. 6742-5
A **discontented** fir-tree. Rosamund Livingstone McNaught. 6807-3
A **discontented** sugar broker. Sir William Schwenck Gilbert. 6512-0
The **discontented** yew tree. William Brighty Rands. 6131-1
Discontents in Devon. Robert Herrick. 6562-7,6430-2
Discontinuity. Ulalume Gonzalez de Leon. 7036-1
"**Discord** and plots, which have undone our age". To the University of Oxford. John Dryden. 6970-3
Discordants. Conrad Aiken. 6513-9
Discouraged. Adelaide Anne Procter. 6957-6
The **discouraged** cherry tree. Kathleen Millay. 6449-3
Discouragement. Phillip A. M. Villiers de l'isle-Adam. 6873-1
discouraging model. James Whitcomb Riley. 6992-4
Discourse with Cupid. Ben Jonson. 6271-7
"**Discourse**, bruised heart, on trivial things". Burrs and brambles. Robert Graves. 6778-6
"**Discourteous** death, of clemency the foe". To death. Dante Alighieri. 6879-0

"Discover thou what is". Song to the wind. Taliesin. 6873-1
Discovered. Paul Laurence Dunbar. 6274-1,6300-4,6505-8
Discovered. Cecil E.C. Hodgson. 6316-0
Discovered. Unknown. 6983-5
The discoverer of the North Cape. Henry Wadsworth Longfellow. 6176-1,6531-4,6396-9,6322-5,6808-1
The discoverer. Edmund Clarence Stedman. 6889-8
The discoverer. Edmund Clarence Stedman. 6240-7,6243-1, 6177-X
Discoveries. Vernon Watkins. 6391-8,6666-6
Discovery. John Bracken. 6761-1
Discovery. Ethel M. Feuerlicht. 6847-2
Discovery. Hildegarde Flanner. 6619-4
Discovery. Hermann Hagedorn. 6266-0,6501-5
Discovery. Richard Hovey. 7006-X
Discovery. Carol Phillips. 6750-6
Discovery. Phyllis Reid. 6659-3
Discovery. Dorothy Sigmund. 6750-6
Discovery. Unknown. 7007-8
Discovery ("On this March day the ferns in milk-green") Maxwell Bodenheim. 6561-9
Discovery and conquest of America. James Montgomery. 6980-0
Discovery of Madeira. William Lisle Bowles. 6980-0
A discovery of no importance. Willard Wattles. 6441-8
Discovery of San Francisco Bay. Richard Edward White. 6946-0
Discovery of San Francisco Bay. Richard Edward White. 6921-5
Discovery of this time. Archibald MacLeish. 6389-6,6666-6
The discovery of tobacco. Unknown. 6453-1
Discovery, fr. Once again the Eden. Noel Hudson Stearn. 6789-1
A discovery. Gertrude Huntington McGiffert. 6838-3
The discovery. Monk Gibbon. 6930-4
The discovery. Stanley Snaith. 6317-9
The discreet collector. Eugene Field. 6949-5
The discriminations: virtuous amusements and wicked... Jim Bogan. 6966-5
Disdain. Agnes MacCarthy Hickey. 6818-9
Disdain me still. William Herbert; Earl of Pembroke. 6182-6
"Disdain not, snow, my humble verse to hear". A panegyrical to Mr. Thomas Snow. John Gay. 6972-X
Disdain returned. Thomas Carew. 6562-7,6099-4,6271-7,6563-5,6604-6,6250 ,6189-3,6194-X,6092-7,6438-8,6291-9, 6660
"Disdaine me not sweet loue though I be ould." Unknown. 6563-5
The disdainful shepherdess. Unknown. 6436-1
Disenchanted. Phoebe Cary. 6969-X
Disenchantment. Emily Dickinson. 6121-4
Disenchantment. Louis Untermeyer. 6011-0
"The disenchantment of distance". Out of sight. Virginia Russ. 6799-9
The disenthralled. John Greenleaf Whittier. 6617-8
The disgraced courtier's lament. Sir Walter Raleigh. 6935-5
Disguise. Evana Llynn. 6906-1
The disguise. Walter De La Mare. 6905-3
The disguised maiden. Francis Beaumont and John Fletcher. 6385-3
Disguises. Thomas Edward Brown. 6730-1
The dishonest cat. Mrs. Frederick W. Pender. 6692-2
The dishonest miller. Unknown. 6058-7
"Dishonoured rock and ruin! that, by law". Eagles. George Darley. 6943-6
Disillusion. Rubye Arnold. 7016-7
Disillusioned. Thomas Curtis Clark. 6144-3
Disillusionment of ten o'clock. Wallace Stevens. 6808-1
The disimbodied spirit. William Oliver Bourne Peabody. 6752-2
Disinherited. J. Patrick Byrne. 6761-1
The disinterment. Bartholomew Simmons. 6980-0
"'Disloyal'". Tule Lake internment camp. Muin Ozaki. 6981-9
"A dismal day of sullen rain; each tree". Cardinal. Avis H. Grant. 6906-1
The dismal dole of the doodledoo. Eugene Field. 6949-5

"Dismayed/I waited by a pool". Prayer ("Dismayed"). Julia Ross Alden. 6906-1
Dismissal. Thomas Campion. 6436-1
Dismond, H. Binga
 The dominicaine. 6178-8
 Revolt in the South. 6178-8
 To the men of the Soviet army. 6178-8
Disobedience. Elizabeth Turner. 6018-8
"Disown me not, O! patient mother earth!". Epitaph ("Disown"). Lady Margaret Sackville. 6777-8
The dispensary, sels. Sir Samuel Garth. 6198-2,6482-5,6152-4
A displeasure against loue, fr. Melancholic humors. Nicholas Breton. 6586-4
Dispossessed poet. Monk Gibbon. 6930-4
Dispraise of love. Unknown. 6830-8
Dispraise of love and lovers' follies. A. W. 6182-6,6436-1
Dispraises of a courtly life. Sir Philip Sidney. 6315-2, 6586-4,6430-2
Disproving a legend. Ethel Lynn Beers. 6155-9
The disputants. William Carlos Williams. 6808-1
Disquiet of reason. Gene Frumkin. 6803-0
Disraeli; Earl of Beaconsfield, Benjamin
 Popanilla on man. 6200-8
 Wellington. 6199-0
Dissatisfied with a Log for King, the frogs get a crane. Jean de La Fontaine. 6637-2
Dissecting room. John Fallon. 6482-5
The dissemblers. Thomas Hardy. 6655-0
The dissenter. Lilliam M. Swenson. 6144-3
The dissolution. John Donne. 6430-2
"Distaff, the spinner's friend, gift of Athena". Theocritus. 6435-3
A distaff. Erinna. 6435-3
Distance. E.O. De Camp. 6906-1
Distance. Babette Deutsch. 6653-4
Distance. John Boyle O'Reilly. 7041-8
Distance and peace. Robert Francis. 6783-2
Distance lends enchantment. Unknown. 6589-9
Distance the enchantress. Unknown. 6260-1
The distant Alps. Florence Smith. 6749-2
"Distant and long have I waited without going". To Mackinnon of Strath. John (Iain Lom) MacDonald. 6845-6
Distant as the Duchess of Savoy. Unknown. 6881-2
Distant footsteps. Cesar Vallejo. 6642-9
"A distant note disturbs the peaceful night". The midnight storm. John E. Barrett. 6840-5
Distant point. David Martin. 6895-2
The distant ship. Felicia Dorothea Hemans. 6973-8
Distant song. Henry Spiess. 6351-9
Distant sound of the sea at evening. Felicia Dorothea Hemans. 6997-9
Distant sound of the sea at evening. Felicia Dorothea Hemans. 6973-8
Distant star. Eleanor Jordan Houston. 6316-0
Distant view of a provincial town. Sir John Betjeman. 6633-X
Distant voices. Alfred Noyes. 6151-6
Distant voices. Dora Sigerson Shorter. 6785-9
Distemper. Vera B. Thomson. 6316-0
Distichs. John Hay. 6089-7
Distichs and saws. Samuel Butler. 6543-0
Distillation. Bliss Carman and Richard Hovey. 6890-1
"Distinguish god in your imaginings". Unknown. 6435-3
Distinguo. Lizinka Campbell Turner. 6880-4
Distinquished baby. Eva Lovett Carson. 6312-8
Distinquished madmen. Joseph Freeman. 6880-4
"Distracted with care". The despairing lover. William Walsh. 6932-0
The distraction.. Helen Parry Eden. 6096-X
The distress'd wife. John Gay. 6972-X
The distressed sailor's garland. Unknown. 6547-3
The distressed travellers; or, labour in vain. William Cowper. 6814-6
District no. 9. Frank Morgan Imbrie. 6681-X
"A district school not far away". The smack in school. William Pitt Palmer. 6505-8,6565-1,6706-9,6889-0, 6219-9,6142-7,6064-1,6302-0,6402-7,6385-3
"The district school-master was sitting...". The

schoolmaster's guests. Will Carleton. 6281-4,6914-2
The **distrust** of logic. Toi Derricotte. 7032-9
"**Disturb** the sanctuary". Paperweight escape. Stephen Todd Booker. 6870-7
A **disturbed** reverie. Unknown. 6744-1
"The **disvnited** Scithians when they sought". To the most puisand and gratious Iames king of great. Thomas Campion. 6794-8
"'**Dites**, la jeune belle!". Barcarolle. Theophile Gautier. 6801-4
Dithridge, Rachel Lewis
    Swinging under the apple trees. 6715-8
Dithyramb for death. Philip Horton. 6640-2
Dithyramb of the worlds. Otakar Brezina. 6763-8
Ditlevsen, Tove
    Mother fear. Charles Wharton Stork (tr.). 6555-4
    My heart. Charles Wharton Stork (tr.). 6555-4
    The snake in paradise. Charles Wharton Stork (tr.). 6555-4
Ditty. Edward Herbert, 1st Baron Herbert of Cherbury. 6908-8
Ditty. Ted Robinson. 6337-3
Ditty. Sir Philip Sidney. 6246-6,6429-9,6465-5,6481-7,6732-8,6429-9,6652-6,6192-3,6560-0,6321-7,6371-3,6737-9
Ditty. Robert Louis Stevenson. 6655-0
Ditty ("If this town should tumble down.") Audrey Beecham. 6472-8
  ditty A"My true love hath my heart"). Sir Philip Sidney. 6226-1
Ditty ("O holy Love, religious saint!") Sir Robert Chester. 6182-6
A **ditty** ("Peace, peace, peace, make no noise") John Day. 6182-6
The **ditty** ("Young Colin Clout, a lad..."). John Gay. 6315-2
Ditty in imitation of the Spanish entre tanto... Edward Herbert, 1st Baron Herbert of Cherbury. 6562-7,6182-6
A **ditty** of creation. Enid Dinnis. 6096 X
The **ditty** of six virgins. Thomas Watson. 6436-1
The **ditty** the city sang, fr. Old and new New York. Alfred Kreymborg. 6012-9
The **divagator.** Gamaliel Bradford. 6032-3
Divall, Edith Hickman
    Friendship. 6461-2
The **divan.** Richard Henry Stoddard. 6004-8,6753-0
The **dive.** Ted Robins. 6527-9
The **diver.** Felicia Dorothea Hemans. 6973-8
The **diver.** E.L. Mayo. 6751-4
The **diver.** Leslie Nutting. 6767-0
The **diver.** Theobald Purcell-Buret. 6258-X
The **diver.** W.W. Eustace Ross. 6446-9
The **diver.** Johann C. Friedrich von Schiller. 6842-1
The **diver.** Johann C. Friedrich von Schiller. 6344-6,6370-5,6409-4
The **diver.** Johann C. Friedrich von Schiller. 6842-1
The **diver.** Edward Sydney Tylee. 6018-8
Divergence, fr. Once again the Eden. Noel Hudson Stearn. 6789-1
Divers. Robert Haven Schauffler. 6619-4
"**Divers** doth use [as I have heard and know].". Sonnet ("Divers doth"). Sir Thomas Wyatt. 6584-8
Divers doth use, as I have heard and know. Sir Thomas Wyatt. 6430-2
The **divers.** Peter Quennell. 6985-1
Diversions of the re-echo club. Carolyn Wells. 6089-7
Diversities of fortune. Thomas Hood. 6302-0;6385-3
Diversities of judgment. Alexander Pope. 6409-4
Diversity. Frank Ernest Hill. 6619-4
Diversity. Everard V. Thompson. 6065-X
Diversity of gifts. Sappho. 6435-3
Diversity of gifts. Solon. 6435-3
A **diverted** tragedy. James Whitcomb Riley. 6091-9
The **diverting** history of John Gilpin. William Cowper. 6014-5,6271-7,6484-1,6371-3,6131-1,6291 ,6024-2,6396-9, 6152-4,6518-X,6086-2,6739 ,6105-2,6239-3,6486-8,6089-7,6154-0,6242
Dives and Lazarus. Ernest Bilton. 7009-4
Dives and Lazarus. Unknown. 6185-0
Dives asking a drop. Richard Crshaw. 6023-4

Dives in torment. Robert Norwood. 6115-X
Dives in torment, sels. Robert Norwood. 6843-X
Divided. David Gray. 7041-8
Divided. Jean Ingelow. 6271-7,6385-3,6438-8,6066-8,6304-7
Divided destinies. Rudyard Kipling. 6089-7
Dividends. Hubert Creekmore. 6666-6
Dividing the spoils. Al Masarik. 6901-0
Divina commedia. Henry Wadsworth Longfellow. 6302-0,6385-3, 6483-3,6488-4,6008-0,6461 ,6641-0,6309-8,6126-5,6121-4,6104-4,6250 ,6560-0,6288-1,6371-3,6723-9,6737-9, 6513
Divina commedia, sels. Henry Wadsworth Longfellow. 6536-8
Divination by a daffadill. Robert Herrick. 6562-7,6194-X, 6189-3
Divine astrology. J. Lewis Milligan. 7014-0
Divine awe. George Edward Woodberry. 6250-4,6309-8
A **divine** barrier. George F. Savage-Armstrong. 6631-3
The **divine** call. Sister Mary Genevieve. 6285-7
Divine care. Francis Quarles. 6337-3
The **divine** comedy, sels. George Kett. 6800-6
Divine compassion. John Greenleaf Whittier. 6333-0,6641-0
The **divine** door-keeper. Franz Werfel. 6160-5
The **divine** door-keeper. Franz Werfel. 6160-5
Divine drama. Bess Foster Smith. 6799-9
Divine ejaculation. John Quarles. 6271-7
The **divine** fantasy, sels. John Hall Wheelock. 6300-4
The **divine** forest. Charles R. Murphy. 6762-X
Divine guidance. Edward Hartley Dewart. 6796-4
A **divine** image. William Blake. 6024-2,6086-2,6152-4,6250-4, 6430-2,6150 ,6125-7,6208-3,6337-3,6339-X,6526-8,6730
Divine informality. Madeline Slade. 6750-6
Divine justice amiable. Madame De la Mothe Guion. 6814-6
Divine love. Richard Crashaw. 6337-3
Divine love. Gerhard Tersteegen. 6271-7,6438-8
Divine love. Charles Wesley. 6730-1,6214-8
Divine love endures no rival. Madame De la Mothe Guion. 6814-6
The **divine** lullaby. Eugene Field. 6949-5
The **divine** philosopher. Empedocles. 6435-3
Divine poems, sels. John Donne. 6472-8
Divine providence. Sadi [or Saadi] (Mushlih-ud-Din) 6448-5
The **divine** rebel. George Scheftel. 6144-3
Divine rhythm. Henry Meade Bland. 6303-9
The **divine** strategy. Edwin Markham. 6607-0
Divine, Charles
    The garden I love. 6232-6
    Let's go dancing. 6959-9
    Little senorita. 6891-X
    Never will you hold me. 6441-8,6619-4
    Psychoneuroses. 6542-2
    Spanish song. 6331-4
    Toward another dawn. 7019-1
    When Private Mugrums parley vous. 6846-4
Divine, Eric
    If Robert Herrick had been Dorothy Parker. 6850-2
"**Divinest** poesy! without thy wings". Poesy. Edward Moxon. 6980-0
Diving for pearls. Traise Yamamoto. 6790-5
Diving the field. William Aberg. 6870-7
The **divinity.** Matthew Arnold. 6199-0
The **division..** Thomas Hardy. 6186-9
Divisions on a ground--No.II. Arthur Symons. 6507-4
Divisions on a ground--No.III. Arthur Symons. 6507-4
The **divorce.** Adrianne Marcus. 6792-1
The **divorce.** Thomas Stanley. 6317-9,6341-1
Divorced. Richard Monckton Milnes; 1st Baron Houghton. 6085-4
The **diwan** of Hafiz, sels. Hafiz. 6732-8
Dix, Edward A.
    A fragment. 6983-5
Dix, Fred Keller
    Grandma's movie show. 6906-1
    Pardoned. 6906-1
    A seashell. 6906-1
    Where are all the common people? 6906-1
    Who finds a sonnet. 6906-1
Dix, John A. (tr.)
    Dies irae. Thomas de Celano, 6385-3
    Dies irae. Thomas of Celano, 6219-9
Dix, W. C.

Silver lamps. 6065-X
Dix, William F.
   Solitude. 6983-5
Dixey, H.G.
   Limerick:"..young man of Lugano". 6811-1
   Limerick:"A foolish young anarchist". 6811-1
   Limerick:"A menagerie came to our place". 6811-1
   Limerick:"A railway official at Crewe". 6811-1
   Limerick:"A traveller once, to his sorrow". 6811-1
   Limerick:"I had a young pupil called Ned". 6811-1
   Limerick:"I once knew a gard'ner whose aunt". 6811-1
   Limerick:"I said to a man of Norwich". 6811-1
   Limerick:"There was a young hopeful called Daniel". 6811-1
   Limerick:"With railways not being content". 6811-1
Dixey, Wolstan
   Christmas questions. 6147-8
   The Christmas star. 6523-6
   The light-ship. 6523-6
   Merry Christmas. 6523-6
   A New Year's dream. 6394-2
   The teacher's tale. 6523-6
   Wintry weather. 6394-2
   A wonderful cure in Barley town. 6523-6
Dixie. Daniel Emmett. 6074-9,6088-9,6736-0,6121-4,6267-9
Dixie. Daisy Arnold Maude. 6841-3
Dixie. Albert Pike. 6015-3,6340-3,6707-7,6732-8,6735-2, 6459-0,6008-0,6267-9,6300-4
Dixie Brown. Unknown. 6057-9
A **Dixie** lullaby. Strickland Gillilan. 6307-1
The **Dixie** miner's rally. Davie Robb. 6149-4
'**Dixie**'. (Alfred) Damon Runyon. 6836-7
Dixie's isle. Unknown. 6057-9
Dixit, et in mensam-. Charles William Shirley Brooks. 6092-7
Dixon (or Robert Farrell), George Washington
   Turkey in the straw. 6736-0
Dixon, James Main
   The bard of auld lang syne. 6476-0
Dixon, Richard Watson
   Both less and more. 6315-2
   Dream ("With camel's hair I clothed my skin"). 6315-2
   Humanity. 6199-0
   Love's consolation, sels. 6317-9
   Mano: a poetical history, sels. 6656-9
   O ubi? Nusquam. 6317-9
   Ode on advancing age. 6844-8
   Ode on conflicting claims. 6656-9
   Of a vision of hell, which a monk had, fr. Mano. 6656-9
   Of temperence in fortune, fr. Mano. 6656-9
   skylark, fr. Mano. 6656-9
   Song ("The feathers of the willow"). 6246-5,6315-2,6253-9
   Song ("Why fadest"). 6125-7
   Sonnet ("Give me"). 6317-9
   To fancy. 6844-8
   Winter will follow. 6246-5
   The wizard's funeral. 6246-5,6315-2
Dixon, Ruth Collins
   A-helpin' save with Hoover. 6681-X
Dixon, Sarah A.
   Cape Cod. 6798-0
   Cape Cod pines. 6798-0
   The cape in June. 6798-0
   The clam digger. 6798-0
   The cranberry bog. 6798-0
   Cummaquid. 6798-0
   Fishing. 6798-0
   The May flower. 6798-0
   The old scow. 6798-0
   Paradise. 6798-0
Dixon, W. Macneile
   To fellow-travellers in Greece. 7026-4
   When the traveller returns. 6395-0
"**Dixon,** a Choctaw, twenty years of age". A savage. John Boyle O'Reilly. 6861-8,7041-8
The **dizzy** girl. Elizabeth Turner. 6105-2
The **djinns.** Victor Hugo. 6732-8
Dlugos, Tim
   Close. 7003-5

Day light. 7003-5
Desire under the pines. 7003-5
New hope. 7003-5
Dnyanodaya
   Wait on. 6461-2
"Do all the good you can". John Wesley's rule. Unknown. 6260-1,6466-3
"Do all the good you can". John Wesley. 6109-5
"Do angels wear white dresses, say?". Questions of the hour. Sarah Morgan Bryan Piatt. 6772-7
"Do anything you wish". But don't be humble, fr. Working gang poems. Byron Herbert Reece. 6761-1
"Do I love you?". You. Celestin Pierre Cambiaire. 6826-X
Do good. Unknown. 6629-1
Do I love thee? John Godfrey Saxe. 6226-1
Do it now. Berton Braley. 6853-7
Do lovers' tongues. Grace Baer Hollowell. 6750-6
"Do me a courtest". The errand. James Herbert Morse. 7041-8
Do me right, and do me reason. Thomas Lodge. 6827-8
"Do men grow wholly old". Age. Arthur Seymour John Tessimond. 6893-6
"Do noble things, not dream them all day long." Charles Kingsley. 6225-3
Do not ask. Laurence Whistler. 6475-2
"Do not believe in my verses and rhymes". Do not believe... Aleksa Santic. 6765-4
"Do not believe Tithonus wished to go". I anonymous. Eve Merriam. 6761-1
Do not believe... Aleksa Santic. 6765-4
"Do not conceal thy radiant eyes". Sir Francis Kynaston. 6187-7
"Do not curse me". Mutum est pictura poema. Horace Gregory. 6761-1
"Do not despair". For Johnny. John Pudney. 6895-2
"Do not despair, my sister, of a brother's...". Under our own wings. Nellie Wong. 6790-5
"Do not despise too much the clumsy fingers". Honor to the eagle. Helene Mullins. 7019-1
Do not disturb. Richard Armour. 6761-1
"Do not do what is untoward, oh lord of my life". Unknown (Newari) 7013-2
Do not embrace your mind's new Negro friend. William Meredith. 6666-6
"Do not erect cold tombstones over my grave". Epitaph among sunflowers. Hyung-soo Ham. 6775-1
Do not fear. Bryllion Fagin. 6789-1
"Do not fear to put thy feet". Song ("Do not fear"). John Fletcher. 6052-8,6182-6
Do not fear, my love. Louis Untermeyer. 6026-9
Do not forget, my dear. Mary Elizabeth Mahnkey. 6662-3
Do not grieve. Louise Chandler Moulton. 6006-4
"Do not hinder me now who would". Woman. Eleanor S. Jewell. 6764-6
"Do not hinder me today, Lord Gopala! I am going..." Unknown (Newari) 7013-2
"Do not keep me at home, oh amaju!...". Unknown (Newari) 7013-2
"Do not keep me here, sir, making me suffer". Unknown (Newari) 7013-2
"Do not lift him from the bracken". The widow of Glencoe, sels. William Edmonstoune Aytoun. 6934-7
"Do not look for wrong and evil". Alice Cary. 6969-X
Do not love me now. Viola Cornett. 6750-6
Do not pity the young. John Holmes. 6761-1
"Do not reproach me, that I am not true". Extenuation. Jamie Sexton Holme. 6836-7
"Do not rustle, rye" Alexey Koltsov. 6103-6
"Do not salute me, I am not your friend". The ghost. Cu Chonnacht O Cleirigh. 6244-X
Do not sing that song again. H.F. McDermott. 6916-9
"Do not suppose that I confess". The contessa to her judges. Cale Young Rice. 7017-5
"Do not take me to your breast". Poet. Babette Deutsch. 6038-2
"Do not take your piece". Bio-poetic statement: instruction to warriors on... Carroll Arnett Gogisgi. 7005-1
Do not tell him. Roselle Mercier Montgomery. 6039-0
"Do not torure the moment longer for..meaning". Green

vine. Dorothy E. Reid. 6906-1
"Do not touch him - do not wake him!". Warning. Johann Wolfgang von Goethe. 6948-7
"Do not trust black eyes, but fear them". Avetis Isahakian. 6050-1
Do not wait. Lumilla Claire Clark. 6109-5
"Do not, I do not prise thy beauty at too high". Song ("Do not, O do not prise"). Unknown. 6436-1
"Do not, O do not prize thy beauty at too high". Unknown. 6187-7
"Do not,O do not prize thy beauty at too high a rate". Unknown. 6181-8,6182-6
Do right. Unknown. 6743-3
Do something. Lucy Larcom. 6273-3
Do something. Unknown. 6530-9,6743-3,6654-2
Do something for somebody. Julian S. Cutler. 6109-5
"Do tell me, sister Marian, that's a dear". Cross purposes. S.A. (Sarah Annie Shield) Frost. 6851-0
Do texans kiss after sex? David Emerson Smith. 7003-5
"Do the duty that lies nearest to thee". Johann Wolfgang von Goethe. 6623-2
"Do the tears that arise in the heat of the strife ". The purpose of life. Frank Putnam. 6583-X,6274-1
Do the work that's nearest. Charles Kingsley. 6337-3
Do they mean me? D. Hercules Armstrong. 6761-1
Do thy day's work. Unknown. 6260-1,6449-3
"Do thy duty, that is best." Henry Wadsworth Longfellow. 6225-3
"Do we have many accidents here, sir?". The bridge keeper's story. W.A. Eaton. 6922-3
"Do we indeed desire the dead", fr. In memoriam. Alfred Lord Tennyson. 6867-7
"Do we not say, forgive us, Lord". Vain repentance. Phoebe Cary. 6969-X
"Do we weep for the heroes who died for us". C.S.A. Abram Joseph Ryan. 7041-8
"Do ye hear the children weeping, o my...". The bitter cry of the children. Elizabeth Barrett Browning. 6954-1
"Do ye ken John Peel with his coat so gay". John Peel. Mark Andrews. 7008-1
Do ye think of the days that are gone? Unknown. 6486-8
Do you. Wilmot Schoff. 6249-0
"Do you also hear the silence between us?". A resonant silence. David Llorens. 7024-8
"Do you ask what the birds say?" Samuel Taylor Coleridge. 6793-X
Do you blame her? Phoebe Cary. 6969-X
"Do you call to mind the scriptural tale". The prodigal son. Ira South. 7007-8
"Do you ever think of me? you who died". Unforgotten. Laurence (Adele Florence Nicolson) Hope. 6856-1
Do you fear the force of the wind? Hamlin Garland. 6332-2
Do you fear the wind? Hamlin Garland. 6101-X,6102-8,6356-X, 6374-8,6501-5,6396-9,6368-3,6421-3,6464-7,6250-4, 6431-0,6102-8,6736-0,6076-5,6309-8
"Do you feel that the moment of truth...". On automation. Andy Warhol. 6803-0
"Do you find no burden in singing?". Blackbird. Ronald Bottrall. 6985-1
"Do you give thanks for this? - or that?". Gratitude. Henry Van Dyke. 6961-4
"Do you grieve no costly offering". A love token. Adelaide Anne Procter. 6957-6
Do you guess it is I? Eliza Lee Follen. 6452-3
"Do you hear the cry as the pack goes by?". Wind-wolves. William D. Sargent. 6891-X
Do you know him? M.E. B. 6965-7
"Do you know how it feels to be black, to do". It hurts! Makeda Zulu. 6883-9
Do you know how many stars? Unknown. 6743-3
Do you know how many stars? Unknown (German) 6452-3
"Do you know how the people of all the land". From Potomac to Merrimac. Edward Everett Hale. 6946-0
"Do you know my children". A message from Reverend Fat Back made possible by... Melvin Douglass Brown. 6870-7
Do you know that distant country? Suk-jung Shin. 6775-1
"Do you know that your soul is of my soul...". To my son. Margaret Johnstone Graflin. 6889-8
"Do you know what it is to be vagrant born?". A waif.
Bliss Carman. 7006-X
"Do you know what it is to dance?". The dancing girl. James Weldon Johnson. 6959-2
"Do you know what tree I love best?" Jessie Orton Jones. 6999-1
"Do you know where good ends/And just where...". Wisdom. Edwin E. Deal. 6799-9
"Do you know where the rainbow ends?". Quiet. Helen Corlett. 6799-9
"Do you know Yancey's? Where the". Roosevelt in Wyoming. Robert Bridges. 6995-9
"Do you know you have asked for the costliest". A woman's question. Elizabeth Barrett Browning. 6889-8
"Do you know, I have often had a dream". Bishop Blougram's apology, sel. Robert Browning. 6958-4
"Do you know, daughter of the Persians". Mihyar al-Dailami. 6766-2
Do you like butter? L. Dickerson-Watkins. 6937-1
"Do you like secrets?" Jessie Orton Jones. 6999-1
"Do you love me as much as you did, dear Jack?". Unkind. Unknown. 6983-5
"'Do you love me, dear?' he cried". Modern. Evelyne Love Cooper. 6850-2
"Do you love me, little children?". The children. Richard Realf. 6772-7
"Do you not hear the Aziola cry?". The Aziola. Percy Bysshe Shelley. 6383-7
Do you not know? Katherine Ruggles. 6818-9
"Do you not see, beloved?" Vladimir Solovyev. 6103-6
"Do you pray for the sinful souls of the world". Prayer ("Do you do pray..."). Bernice E. Carter. 6894-4
"Do you recall what now is living only". The old times. Letitia Elizabeth ("L.E.L.") Landon. 6980-0
Do you remember. Don Marquis. 6732-8
Do you remember. William Wetmore Story. 6004-8
"Do you remember a June morning years ago...". Sierra memory. Elizabeth Grey Stewart. 6761-1
"Do you remember all the sunny places". Recollections. Caroline Elizabeth Sarah Sheridan Norton. 6980-0
"Do you remember how together" Mikhail Lermontov. 6103-6
"Do you remember how we played". Chess. John Robert Moses. 6936-3
"Do you remember how, one autumn night". Estrangement. F.G. Scott. 7041-8
"Do you remember Mechlin chimes". Honeymoon. Anna Wickham. 6893-6
"Do you remember me? or are you proud?" Walter Savage Landor. 6246-6,6086-2,6110-9
Do you remember once. Alan Seeger. 6320-9
"Do you remember that careless band". Fairyland. Anne Glenny Wilson. 6784-0
Do you remember that night? Unknown. 6930-4
Do you remember that night? Unknown. 6244-X
"Do you remember the blizzard, brother?...". Memories of pioneer days. Lucy Burgman. 6799-9
"Do you remember the dark pool at Nimes". The pool. Alice Corbin. 6897-9
"Do you remember the name I wore". Little queen. Ella Wheeler Wilcox. 6956-8
"Do you remember, Mary." Alexey Tolstoy. 6103-6
"Do you remember, chum of mine". I wish that I could run away. John Whitaker Watson. 6774-3
"Do you remember, O Delphic Apollo". Webster Ford. Edgar Lee Masters. 6897-9
"Do you remember, sister". In the garden. Pai Ta-Shun. 6338-1
Do you remember? John E. Barrett. 6840-5
"Do you seek to bind me, ye gods". The sword of Tethra. William Larminie. 6930-4
"Do you sigh for the power you dream of". Notus ignoto. Bayard Taylor. 6976-2
"Do you swing with the tide little boat...". Boat song. Adelaide Cilley Waldron. 6764-6
Do you think of me? Elizabeth Barrett Browning. 6085-4
"Do you think old people should be put away". Question. Grace Paley. 6803-0
"Do you think we are crushed out of living...". The two Johns. Benjamin Franklin Taylor. 6815-4
"Do you wish to give yourself to me...". Exaltation of elementary materials. Xavier Abril. 6759-X

Do you? Edgar A. Guest. 6862-6
Do your all. Edgar A. Guest. 6846-4
Do your best. Unknown. 6314-4,6744-1,6167-2
"'Do your bit!' How cheap and trite". Do your all. Edgar A. Guest. 6846-4
"Do'st see how unregarded now". Sonnet ("Do'st see"). Sir John Suckling. 6378-0
Do, re, mi, fa, sol, la, si. Unknown. 6698-4
DOA in Dulse. Diane Burns. 7005-1
Do-in
How sad and gloomy is the world. William N. Porter (tr.). 6852-9
Doak, H.L.
The bathers. 6506-6
The scarecrow. 6930-4
Doane, Emma M.
The Coast Guard of Cape Cod. 6798-0
Doane, George Washington
The banner of the cross. 6065-X
Bishop Doane on his dog. 6107-9
Bishop Doane's tribute to his dog Cluny. 6510-4
Bishop Ravenscroft. 6752-2
Christ, the way. 6065-X
Evening. 6006-4,6735-2
Robin redbreast. 6820-0
The sculptor. 6424-8
Softly now the light of day. 6001-3,6461-2,6304-7
Doane, Heman
The prence pear tree. 6798-0
Doane, Jerry. See Morse, Katharine Duncan
Doane, William Croswell
'Cluny' 7008-6
Death. 6177-X
Death and life. 6461-2
Death means freedom. 6720-4
December. 6674-4
The modern baby. 6736-0
Dobbin. Alfred Noyes. 6169-9
Dobbs his ferry. William Allen Butler. 6903-7
Dobell, Sydney
The absent soldier's son. 6302-0,6385-3,6627-5
America. 6198-2,6473-6,6656-9,6102-8,6250-4,6607
America, sels. 6199-0
The army surgeon, fr. Sonnets. 6380-2
Balder, sels. 6102-8
The ballad of Keith of Ravelston. 6046-3,6301-2
Basking. 6240-7
Chamouni. 6832-4
A chanted calendar. 6236-9
The common grave, fr. Sonnets. 6380-2
Daft Jean. 6518-X
Dante, Shakespeare, Milton, fr. Balder. 6656-9
England, fr. Balder. 6832-4
Epigram on the death of Edward Forbes. 6656-9
For charity's sake. 6980-0
Fragment of a sleep-song. 6656-9
Home in war-time. 6656-9
Home, wounded. 6302-0;6385-3
How's my boy? 6097-8,6136-2,6239-3,6302-0,6385-3,6627-5, 6656-9,6543-0,6102-8,6424-8
How's my boy? 6833-2,6910-X
How's my boy?. 6097-8,6344-6
In wartime, a prayer of the understanding. 6198-2
Keith of Ravelston. 6600-3,6660-7,6383-7,6518-X,6250-4
Market-wife's song. 6385-3
Men say, Columbia, fr. America. 6199-0
The milkmaid's song. 6302-0,6385-3,6014-5
Monk's song. 6102-8
Nor force nor fraud, fr. America. 6199-0
A nuptial eve. 6656-9
On the death of Mrs. Browning. 6656-9
The orphan's song. 6246-5,6301-2
The procession of flowers. 6239-3
The procession of the flowers. 6239-3
The procession of the flowers. 6820-0
"Ravelston, Ravelston/The stile beneath the tree." 6317-9
Return. 6317-9
Sea ballad, fr. Balder. 6656-9
"She touches a sad string of soft recall." 6385-3

Sonnets, sels. 6380-2
Spring's procession. 6114-1
The swallow. 6943-6
Tommy's dead. 6014-5,6302-0,6385-3,6656-9,6219-9,6219-9, 6543-0,6578-3
A vision of battle. 6344-6
Dobson, Austin
Advice. 6652-6
After Watteau. 6875-8
Angelus song. 6240-7
Ars victrix. 6527-9,6102-8,6508-2,6655-0,6656-9
At the convent gate. 6655-09
A ballad of antiquaries. 6508-2
The ballad of Beau Brocade. 6046-3
A ballad of heroes. 6289-X,6340-3,6465-5,6476-0
The ballad of imitation. 6770-0
The ballad of imitation. 6655-0
A ballad of prose and rhym. 6508-2
The ballad of prose and rhym. 6301-2
The ballad of the bore. 6655-0
Ballad of the Spanish armada. 6610-0,6322-5
A ballad to Queen Elizabeth. 6123-0,6258-X,6026-9,6639-9
Ballade of the thrush. 6073-0,6424-8
Before Sedan. 6915-0
Before Sedan. 6240-7,6046-3,6424-8,6660-7
"Below, the Doctor's garden lay", fr. The drama. 6123-0
The book-plate's petition. 6297-0
Carver and the caliph. 6694-1
The child-musician. 6239-3,6424-8,6543-0
Circe, fr. Rose-leaves. 6770-0
Clean hands. 6051-X
The cradle. 6123-0,6240-7,6656-9
Cupid's alley. 6688-7
The cure's progress. 6230-X
Daisy's valentines. 6772-7
The dance of death. 6123-0
The dance of death. 6770-0
The dead letter, sels. 6649-6
A dead letter. 6676-3,6094-3,6508-2,6656-9
A dialogue from Plato. 6089-7
Don Quixote. 6501-5
Dora versus Rose. 6089-7,6026-9
The drama of the doctor's window, sels. 6123-0
The dying of Tanneguy du Bois. 6660-7
Envoy ("Where are the secrets it knew?) 6659-3
A fairy tale. 6123-0,6476-0
Fame is a food that dead men eat. 6879-0
'Fame is a food that dead men eat' 7012-4
"Fame is a silence where hath been no sound". 6844-8
A fancy from Fontenelle. 6046-3
A final word. 6297-0
For a charity annual. 6250-4
For a closing page. 7014-0
For a copy of Herrick. 6483-3,6655-0
For a copy of Theocritus. 6123-0,6483-3,6655-0,6250-4, 6656-9
For a copy of Theocritus. 6770-0
The forgotten grave. 6656-9
A gage d'amour. 6656-9
A garden song. 6232-6,6423-X,6649-6,6301-2,6508-2,6655-0,6649-6,6301-2,6315-2
A gentleman of the old school. 6423-X,6508-2,6660-7
"Good-night, Babette!" 6543-0,6102-8,6508-2,6046-3,6656-9
A Greek gift, fr. Rose-leaves. 6770-0
A greeting. 6250-4
Growing gray. 6123-0,6385-3
Henry Wadsworth Longfellow. 6820-0
Henry Wadsworth Longfellow. 6250-4
Household art. 6123-0,6655-0
"I intended an ode", fr. Rose-leaves. 6850-2
In after days. 6301-2,6655-0,6653-4,6646-1,6123-0,6289-X,6476-0,6656-9,6250-4,6508-2,6046-3,6102-8,6153-2, 6301-2
In the Royal Academy. 6683-6
In town. 6652-6
'In vain to-day' 6770-0
Jocosa lyra. 6089-7,6289-X,6724-7
July. 6770-0

A kiss, fr. Rose-leaves. 6770-0
A kiss. 6289-X,6026-9,6153-2,6646-1
The ladies of Saint James's. 6331-4,6639-9,6658-5,6458-2,6301-2,6508-2,6655-0,6656-9
The last despatch. 6760-3
"Le Roman de la rose." 6652-6
Little blue ribbons. 6669-0
The lost elixir. 6123-0
Love's quest. 7014-0
The love-letter. 6996-7
A lovers' quarrel. 6481-7
The milkmaid. 6123-0,6473-6,6658-5
Molly Trefusis. 6331-4
My books. 6297-0
New and old. 6655-0
A nightingale in Kensington gardens. 6123-0
Notes of a honeymoon. 6677-1
"O fons banduslae." 6656-9
O navis. 6123-0,6656-9
"O Poet, then, forbear". 6289-X
"Old books, old wine, old Nankin blue" 6084-6
The old sedan-chair. 6669-0,6652-6
An old-fashioned garden, fr The dead letter. 6649-6
On a fan that belonged to the Marquise de Pompadour. 6026-9,6230-X,6659-3
On a nankin plate. 6770-0
On a nankin plate. 6875-8
On London stones. 6488-4
On the future of poetry. 6655-0
The paradox of time. 6655-0,6481-7
'Persicos odi' 6875-8
The poet and the critics. 6996-7
The pompadour's fan. 6481-7
A postscript to Retaliation. 6508-2
Pot-pourri. 6508-2
The prodigals. 6289-X
The romaunt of the rose. 6213-0
A rondeau to Ethel. 6770-0
A rondeau to Ethel. 6123-0,6656-9
The rondeau. 6724-7
The rose and the gardener. 6424-8
Rose kissed me to-day. 6371-3
Rose-leaves. 6655-0
Rose-leaves, sels. 6770-0
The sick man and the birds. 7014-0
Song of angiola in heaven. 6240-7
A song of the four seasons. 6102-8,6508-2,6123-0,6320-9,6652-6,6655-0,6102-8
The song of the sea wind. 6250-4
The squire at Vauxhall. 6186-9
The story of Rosina. 6677-1
The street singer. 6770-0
The sun-dial. 6680-1
A tear, fr. Rose-leaves. 6770-0
The tiolet ("I intended an ode,"). 6724-7,6301-2
To a child. 6233-4
To a Greek girl. 6123-0,6331-4,6655-0,6656-9
To a June rose. 6770-0
To a missal of the thirteenth century. 6508-2
To Brander Matthews. 6026-9
To daffodils. 6875-8
To Lord de Tabley. 6046-3
To Lydia Languish. 6652-6
To Q.H.F. 6483-3,6219-9
To Quoque. 6089-7
Triolet ("Oh, love"). 6770-0
'Tu ne quaesieris' 6770-0
Tu quoque. 6887-1
The two painters. 7014-0
Two sermons. 6655-0
Urceus exit, fr. Rose-leaves. 6770-0,6527-9,6250-4
The virgin with the bells. 6673-9
A virtuoso. 6219-9
Vitas Hinnuleo. 6123-0,6289-X
"A voice in the scented night" 6875-8
The wanderer. 6123-0,6289-X,6226-1,6737-9
We hope to win. 7031-0
When Burbage played. 6473-6
'When finis comes' 6875-8
When I saw you last, Rose. 6770-0,6289-X,6473-6,6488-4,6153-2,6652-6
When there is peace. 6051-X,6123-0
"When this old world was new." 6655-0
With pipe and flute. 6123-0,6501-5
'With pipe and flute' 6875-8
Dobson, Austin (tr.)
Extremum tanain. Horace, 7039-6
'O fong banduslae.' Horace, 6624-0
A paradox of time. Pierre de Ronsard, 7039-6
The paradox of time. Pierre de Ronsard, 6513-9
Persicos odi. Horace, 6732-8
To Chloe. Horace, 7039-6
To Monsieur De La Mothe Le Vayer. Moliere (Jean Baptiste Poquelin), 6879-0,7039-6
Vitas hinnuleo. Horace, 6732-8
Dobson, Henry Austin. See Dobson, Austin
Dobson, Rosemary
Cockerel sun. 6349-7
In a convex mirror. 6349-7
The missal. 6349-7
Doc Hill. Edgar Lee Masters. 6102-8,6732-8,6076-5
The **dock** dreamer. Harvey McKenzie. 6750-6
Dock rats. Marianne Moore. 6751-4
Dockstader, Lew
The Negro funeral. 6109-5
Doctor and clergyman. John Johnson Bolton. 6694-1
The **doctor** and his apples. Unknown. 6910-X
The **doctor** and his patients. Sir Charles Sedley. 6544-9
The **doctor** and the lampreys. Horace Smith. 6416-7
Dr. Birch and his young friends, sels. William Makepeace Thackeray. 6239-3
Dr. Buttonhook. K.N. B. 6130-3
Dr. Coppelius. Wrey Gardiner. 6379-9
Dr. Delany's villa. Thomas Sheridan. 6996-7,6874-X
Doctor Faustus. Christopher Marlowe. 6179-6
"Doctor Faustus was a good man". Mother Goose. 6363-2
Doctor Faustus, sels. Christopher Marlowe. 6541-4,6250-4,6125-7,6204-0,6289-X,6369-1,6378-0,6634-8
Doctor Fell. Thomas (Tom) Brown. 6152-7,6464-7
Doctor Foster. Unknown. 6466-3
"Doctor Foster went to Gloucester". Mother Goose. 6363-2
Dr. Goodcheer's remedy. Nixon Waterman. 6260-1,6583-X
Doctor Hilaire, sels. William Henry Drummond. 6482-5
The **doctor** in love. A. McFarland. 6240-7
Doctor in physicke. Thomas Campion. 6794-8
Doctor Johnson, fr. An island in the moon. William Blake. 6545-7
Dr. Jonson's picture cow. Edgar A. Guest. 6401-9,6135-4
Dr. Jotham Tindale's cue a cure. William Watson Turnbull. 6415-9
Dr. Levett. Samuel Johnson. 6087-0
Doctor lobster. James Russell Lowell. 6787-5
Doctor of billiards. Edwin Arlington Robinson. 6808-1
The **doctor** of music, fr. The Canterbury tales. Geoffrey Chaucer. 6934-7
Doctor Rabelais. Eugene Field. 6949-5
Dr. Sam. Eugene Field. 6949-5
Dr. Siegfried Iseman. Edgar Lee Masters. 6628-3
Dr. Swift to Mr. Pope. Jonathan Swift. 6024-2
Doctor Tom Mew. Unknown. 6692-2
The **doctor's** choice. Alice M. Ball. 6611-9
The **doctor's** dream, sels. William Snowden Battles. 6482-5
The **doctor's** first query. Edgar A. Guest. 6748-4
The **doctor's** life, sels. Isaac N. Himes. 6482-5
Doctor's waiting room. Edgar A. Guest. 6869-3
The **doctor**, sels. George W. Caldwell. 6482-5
Doctor-. Robert Browning. 6848-0
The **doctor**. Thomas Edward Brown. 6809-X
The **doctor**. E.O. Laughlin. 6482-5
Doctors. Eugene Field. 6949-5
The **doctrine** of categories. Hans Magnus Enzensberger. 7032-9
Dodd, Elizabeth
Dream of spring. 6821-9
Dodd, Lee Wilson
The comrade. 6897-9
Dedication for a book of Conning Tower contributions. 6817-0
The escape. 6501-5
Finally. 6042-0

The flower. 6619-4
In memoriam. 6817-0
Lament of a New England art student. 6506-6
A little grimy-fingered girl. 6846-4
More life...more! 6501-5
The paring. 6032-3
The parting. 6032-3
Publicity. 6041-2
Secular ode. 6184-2
The temple. 6076-5,6102-8
To a neo-pagan. 6031-5
To Jonathan Swift. 6782-4
To the younger generation. 6817-0
Vacuum. 6070-6

Doddridge, Pearl V.
west, The. 6799-9

Doddridge, Philip
"Amazing, beauteous change!" 6302-0;6385-3
Awake, my soul! 6214-8
The Christian life. 6411-6
Dum vivimus, vivamus. 6385-3,6291-9
"Eternal source of every joy!" 6302-0
For New-Year's Day. 6219-9
God the everlasting light of the saints above. 6024-2, 6545-7
Hark, the glad sound! 6219-9,6747-6
Hear us, in this thy house. 6065-X
Hymn ("Ye golden lamps of heav'n, farewell") 6152-4
Jesus, I love thy charming name. 6065-X
"'Live while you live', the epicure would say". 6931-2
"O happy day that fixed my choice." 6302-0
Ye golden lamps of Heaven, farewell! 6600-3,6219-9

Dodds, E.R.
When the ecstatic body grips. 6244-X

Dodds, E.R. (tr.)
Patroculus' body saved, fr. The Iliad. Homer, 6435-3, 6665-8
"So they carried the dead man...", fr. The Iliad. Homer, 6435-3

Dodds, Eric
The moon worshippers. 6244-X

Dodge, Corinne B.
The dream shall live. 6316-0

Dodge, Gertrude E.
The wise old crow. 6894-4

Dodge, Gertrude Elliott
"The day is done". 6764-6

Dodge, H.C.
Bait of the average fisherman. 6724-7,6505-8
The funny small boy. 6530-9
A graduating essay. 6682-8
How Columbus found America. 6922-3
If. 6089-7,6652-6
Nobody knows but mother. 6772-7
Signs of the times. 6505-8
A splendid fellow. 6089-7
That 'fellow' who came on Sunday. 6505-5
What vacation is. 6690-9

Dodge, Henry Nehemiah
Spirit of freedom, thou dost love the sea. 6833-2
Thrustararorum. 6833-2

Dodge, Ida Flood
I too hate war. 6799-9

Dodge, Louis
Her garden. 6338-1
Syrian song: No. III. 6072-2

Dodge, Mary Abigail ("Gail Hamilton")
Both sides. 6120-6

Dodge, Mary Barker
The army of spring. 6965-7
The chimney nest. 6273-3,6373-X

Dodge, Mary E.
Learning to pray. 6045-1
A stranger in the pew. 6912-6

Dodge, Mary Mapes
Among the animals. 6131-1
Birdies with broken wings. 6519-8,6135-4
Christmas eve. 6608-9
Dear little goose. 6713-1
Emerson. 6465-5
The frost king. 6820-0
Home and mother. 6089-7
Jane's rescue. 6249-0
Jeannette and Jo. 6131-1
Letting the old cat die. 6131-1
Life in laconics. 6089-7
Little words. 6004-8
The mayor of Scuttleton. 6739-5
The minuet. 6889-8,6712-3,6102-8,6076-5,6652-8,6964-9, 6004
Mother. 6097-8
Mother's darling. 6772-7
Nearly ready. 6519-8
Night and day. 6519-8
Now the noisy winds are still. 6519-8
An offertory. 6145-1,6519-8
One and one. 6135-4
Over the way. 6089-7,6004-8
Pussy's class. 6131-1
Snowflakes. 6519-8,6135-4
Spring. 6049-8
Stocking song on Christmas eve. 6806-5
Two mysteries. 6240-7,6303-9
The two mysteries. 6424-8
Umpires. 6429-9,6321-7,6429-9
The way to do it. 6743-3
The zealless xylographer. 6089-7,6724-7

Dodge, Ruth-Ellen
Come, let us choose. 6764-6
Tombstones. 6764-6

Dodgin' trouble. Joseph Morris. 6211-3

Dodgson, Charles Lutwidge ("Lewis Carroll")
A-sitting on a gate. 6179-6
An acrostic ("A boat"). 6724-7
Acrostic ("Are you deaf"). 6724-7
After Mary Howitt. 6739-5
The aged aged man. 6150-8
Alice in Wonderland, sels. 6523-6
Atalanta in Camden-town. 6440-X
The baker's tale. 6371-3,6861-8
The bat. 6440-X
Beautiful soup. 6802-2
Betty's song to her doll. 6249-0
Brother and sister. 6125-7
Butter and something. 6249-0
Child to a rose. 6249-0
The crocodile. 6440-X
Echoes. 6724-7
Fame's penny trumpet. 6996-7
Father William. 6132-X,6089-7,6479-5,6501-5,6440-X
Father William questioned, fr. Alice in Wonderland. 6523-6
A game of fives. 6652-6
The ghost's confession, fr. Phantasmagoria. 6254-7
He thought he saw. 6236-9,6356-X
Hiawatha's photographing. 6802-2
Hiawatha's photographing. 6290-3
How doth the little crocodile. 6722-0,6527-9
Humpty Dumpty recitation. 6089-7,6125-7
The hunting of the snark, sels. 6656-9
The hunting of the snark. 6722-0,6089-7,6732-8
It is my own invention. 6732-8
Jabberwocky. 6732-8,6089-7,6488-4,6527-9,6534-1,6375-6, 6026-9,6301-2,6656-9,6723-9
Little birds. 6722-0
The lobster quadrille. 6334-9,6440-X,6466-3,6334-9,6132-X,6519-8,6134-6
The looking-glass world. 6368-3
The mad gardener's song. 6554-X
Maggie's visit to Oxford, sel. 6120-6
The manlet. 6440-X
The mice. 6724-7
The mock turtle's song. 6125-7
Of Alice in wonderland. 6656-9
One piecee thing. 6722-0
Phantasmagoria, sels. 6254-7
Poeta fit, non nascitur. 6501-5
A sea dirge. 6258-X
She's all my fancy painted him. 6026-9,6902-9
Some hallucinations. 6089-7

DODGSON

A song of love. 6239-3
Sylvie and Bruno. 6902-9
Sylvie and Bruno, sels. 6339-X
The tale of a mouse. 6724-7
Tema con variazioni. 6724-7
The three voices. 6633-X
Through the looking-glass, sels. 6332-2
Tis the voice of the lobster. 6802-2
Turtle soup. 6334-9,6334-9,6440-X
Twinkle, twinkle, little bat. 6802-2
Twinkle, twinkle, little bat! 6722-0
A valentine. 6652-6
The voice of the lobster. 6440-X
The walrus and the carpenter. 6102-8,6639-9,6638-0,6239-3,6290-3,6332-2,6732-8,6089-7,6416-7,6356-X,6421-3, 6454-X
Ways and means. 6089-7
The white knight's ballad. 6554-X
The whiting and the snail. 6861-8
Ye carpette knyghte. 6724-7
You are old, Father William. 6134-6,6290-3,6722-0,6732-8,6179-6,6092-7,6104-4,6464-7

Dodington; Lord Melcombe, George Bubb
Ode: Love thy country, wish it well. 6152-4

The dodo. Hilaire Belloc. 6125-7

Dodochian, C.A.
The wandering Armenian to the swallow. Alice Stone Blackwell (tr.). 6050-1

Dodoism, fr. The paradise of birds. William John Courthope. 6427-2

Dodsley, Robert
The kings of Europe. 6152-4
Song ("Man's a poor"). 6152-4

Dodson, Owen
Metaphor for a Negro woman: Mary Paschall. 6017-X

Doe not, O doe not prize thy beauty at too high a rate. Thomas Campion (atr.) 6378-0
"Doe you not wonder at the strange rare sound." Unknown. 6563-5
The doe. Sara E. Smith. 6761-1
Doer and dreamer. E.E. Bowen. 6793-X

Doerf, Edmund
Good intentions. 6799-9
Thought. 6799-9

"Does all of life's routine". Life's booklet. Edward R. Huxley. 6885-5
"Does all the shining endless sea". Question. Georgianna Livinston. 6906-1
"Does anyone build covered bridges now?". Covered bridges. Jennie Pendleton Hall. 6750-6
"Does April weep because of March...". Family shame. Fannie Williams. 6850-2
"Does Charidas beneath thee lie?". Epitaph on Charidas of Cyrene. Callimachus. 6879-0
"Does haughty Gaul invasion threat?" Robert Burns. 6830-8
"Does he belong here?" fr. Sonnets to Orpheus. Rainer Maria Rilke. 6068-4
"Does he belong here?," fr. Sonnets to Orpheus. Rainer Maria Rilke. 6068-4
"Does he hunt with the great Orion" Katharine Lee Bates. 6995-9
Does it ever make a difference. Jacqueline J. Johnson. 6899-5
Does it matter? Siegfried Sassoon. 6490-6,6732-8,6542-2, 6464-7,6102-8,6666
"Does it pay?". Ella Wheeler Wilcox. 6583-X
Does spring come to a lost land. Sang-hwa Lee. 6775-1
"Does the harsh-toned voice of the crow". Who knows where beauty lies? Agnes Stewart Beck. 6799-9
"Does the poet understand what the nightingale". The poet. Cora Fabri. 6876-6
Does the road wind uphill. Christina Georgina Rossetti. 6187-7,6328-4
"Does the snow fall at sea?". A snow-song. Henry Van Dyke. 6961-4
"Does your gift from heaven give you...". Gift from heaven. Edgar A. Guest. 6869-3
"Does your heart go back to Galway....". Blue Peter. Stanislaus Lynch. 6930-4
"Doesn't seem much chance to doubt it". Enough. Berton Braley. 6995-9
"Doff thy new spectacles". A Boston lullaby. Unknown. 7021-3
Dog. Charles R. Murphy. 6072-2
"A dog and a cat went out". Mother Goose. 6363-2,6466-3
Dog and cat. Unknown. 6699-2
Dog and gun. Unknown. 6058-7
The dog and the cat, and the duck and the rat. Unknown. 6120-6
The dog and the fox. To a lawyer. John Gay. 6972-X
The dog and the tramp. Eva Best. 6923-1
The dog and the water-lily. William Cowper. 6175-7,6133-8, 6430-2
The dog and the water-lily. William Cowper. 6814-6
The dog Argos, fr. The Odyssey. Homer. 6435-3
Dog at night. Louis Untermeyer. 6464-7
The dog beneath the skin, sels. Wystan Hugh Auden. 6375-6
Dog conscious. Edward Farquhar. 6939-8
'The dog I loved you so' Zitella Cocke. 7008-6
The dog in the river. Phaedrus. 7039-6
Dog is mine. Emma C. Dowd. 6710-7
The dog kindergarden. Unknown. 6928-2
The dog of reflection. Jeffreys Taylor. 6459-0
The dog of St. Bernard's. Miss Fry. 6131-1
The dog sale. Fred Emerson Brooks. 6701-8
"The dog that is beat has a right to complain". On Sir Henry Clinton's recall. Unknown. 6946-0
Dog that never had a chance. Myrtle B. Carpenter. 6715-8
"A dog there was, Petronius by name". Petronius. Frederic P. Ladd. 7008-6
Dog trainer. Edgar A. Guest. 6748-4
Dog wanted. Margaret Mackprang Mackay. 6750-6
The dog's confession. Frederic Edward Weatherley. 6684-4
A dog's grave. Winifred M. Letts. 6510-4
The dog-days. James Vincent Cunningham. 6640-2
Dog-fennel. H.L. Davis. 6037-4
Dog-grel verses, by a poor blind. Thomas Hood. 7008-6
"The dog-rose and the marguerite". About the second-last rose of summer. Charles Plumb. 7020-5
The dog-star pup. Henry Herbert Knibbs. 7008-6
A dog. Josephine Preston Peabody. 6030-X
The dog. Edgar A. Guest. 6869-3
The dog. George Sterling. 6510-4
Dogdog. Richard Lyons. 6803-0
Doggie, go away. Unknown. 6706-9
Dogmatic philosophy. Robert J. Burdette. 6588-0
The dogs at the homestead, fr. Idyll xxv. Theocritus. 6435-3
"Dogs in the garden, catch 'em Towser". Unknown. 6363-2
The dogs of Bethlehem. Katharine Lee Bates. 6162-1
"The dogs of war have slipped the leash". 'Woodrow Wilson'. Celia P. McGowan. 7001-9
The dogs of war. Nora Archibald Smith. 6510-4
"The dogs were shining;they sensed too well". The light-o'-love. Howard Vigne Sutherland. 6836-7
Dogwood blossoms. Peter Blue Cloud. 7005-1
The dogwood tree. Christopher Morley. 6217-2

Doherty, Lillian
Stella matutina. 6543-0

Doing chores in Vermont. Daniel L. Cady. 6989-4
Doing for others. E. Schaeffer. 6304-7
Doing its best. Unknown. 6529-5
Doing nothing. Unknown. 6629-1
The doings of Delsarte. Eugene Field. 6949-5
A doketor's drubbles. George M. Warren. 6912-6

Doktor, Harriet
Sagacity. 6850-2
Sleep. 6850-2

Doku-Ho
Love's island. Ian Oliver (tr.). 6032-3

Dolan, Dorothy Lowry
Cinerarias. 6789-1
The good ship. 6789-1
Rendezvous. 6789-1

Dolben, Digby Mackworth
"Come to me, beloved". 6931-2
He would have his lady sing. 6844-8
"I asked for peace". 6931-2
The shrine. 6844-8
Song ("The world"). 6315-2

Dolce far niente. Laman Blanchard. 6874-X
Dolce far niente. Charles G. ("Miles O'Reilly") Halpine. 6273-3
Dolcino to Margaret. Charles Kingsley. 6123-0,6620-8
Dole, Catherine A.
    New Hampshire song. 6764-6
Dole, Nathan Haskell
    Amateur photography. 6670-4
    Larks and nightingales. 6505-8
    A legend. 6144-3
    Lincoln's birthday. 6524-4
    Man's hidden side. 6076-5
    The mirage. 6029-3
    Our native birds. 6089-7
    The vision of peace. 6266-0
Dole, Nathan Haskell (tr.)
    A legend. Unknown, 6337-3
The **dole**. Sir Walter Scott. 6383-7
The **dole**. John Webster. 6383-7
The **doleful** lay of the wife of Asan Aga. Johann Wolfgang von Goethe. 6948-7
Doll drill. Emma Celia & Lizzie J. Rook. 6173-7
Doll Rosy's bath. Unknown. 6314-4
The **doll** show. Unknown. 6740-9
Doll Topsy. Unknown. 6713-1
The **doll's** lullaby. Unknown. 6684-4
The **doll's** wooing. Eugene Field. 6949-5
Doll-baby show. George Cooper. 6131-1
The **doll-baby** show. George Cooper. 6137-0
The **doll**.. Agnes Lee. 6031-5
Dolladine. William Brighty Rands. 6519-8,6135-4
Dollar a day. Unknown. 6312-8
Dollard, James B.
    At dead o' the night, Alanna. 6115-X
    Ballad of the banshee. 6115-X
    The battle-line. 6846-4
    The fairy harpers. 6115-X
    The fairy piper. 6797-2
    The haunted Hazel. 6115-X
    Meelin mountain. 6797-2
    Ould Kilkinny. 6115-X
    The passing of the sidhe. 6115-X
    Rupert Brooke. 6115-X
    The silver anvils. 6797-2
    Song of the little villages. 6331-4,6292-X,6172-9
    The sons of Patrick. 6172-9,6292-X
    The soul of Karnaghan Buidhe. 6096-X,6292-X,6172-9
    To the aviators of Leaside and Armour Heights. 6796-4
Dollear, Pearl G.
    Hoping. 6799-9
Dollie. Samuel Minturn Peck. 7041-8
Dollie. Samuel Minturn Peck. 6083-8,6505-8
Dolliver, Clara
    No baby in the house. 6078-1
    Pardon complete. 6917-7
Dolloff, Amy J.
    At Easter. 6764-6
    Elm trees. 6764-6
Dolls. Robert Service. 6159-1
Dolls' wedding. Unknown. 6713-1
The **dolls**. William Butler Yeats. 6645-3
A **dolly** dialogue. Carolyn Wells. 6882-0
Dolly Varden. Francis Bret Harte. 6004-8
"**Dolly** knows what is the matter- Dolly and I". Homesick. Anna F. Burnham. 6965-7
Dolly's christening. Unknown. 6772-7
Dolly's mamma. Unknown. 6713-1
The **dolly's** mother. James Whitcomb Riley. 6091-9
Dolly's wedding. Unknown. 6684-4
The **Dolmens**. Gonzalo Escudero. 6759-X
Dolor oogo. Sir Arthur Quiller-Couch. 6258-X,6547-3
Dolores. Algernon Charles Swinburne. 6657-7,6732-8,6655-0, 6508-2
The **dolphin-walk**. Milton Acorn. 6767-0
Dolphins in blue water. Amy Lowell. 6299-7
The **dolphins**. Hamish Maclaren. 6833-2
Dombashawa. Peter Jackson. 6788-3
The **dome** of Sunday. Karl Shapiro. 6391-8,6666-6
"**Dome** up, O heaven! yet higher o'er my head!" George Macdonald. 6238-5

Domer, Harry Tennyson
    A hearth song. 6799-9
The **domestic** affections. Felicia Dorothea Hemans. 6973-8
Domestic asides; or, truth in parenthesis. Thomas Hood. 6974-6
Domestic birds, fr. The seasons. James Thomson. 6102-8, 6302-0,6385-3
Domestic bliss. Charles Rann Kennedy. 6980-0
Domestic didactics, sels. Thomas Hood. 6974-6
Domestic economy. Unknown. 6214-4
A **domestic** episode. Unknown. 6680-1
A **domestic** event. F. Fertiault. 6297-0
Domestic love. George Croly. 6543-0
Domestic peace. Samuel Taylor Coleridge. 6543-0
Domestic poems. Thomas Hood. 6278-4
A **domestic** scene, fr. The legend of Florence. Leigh Hunt. 6980-0
A **domestic** tempest. Unknown. 6411-6
A **domestic** tragedy. Robert Service. 6159-1
The **domestic** tutor's position. Joseph Hall. 6200-8
The **domesticated** artillery men. Unknown. 6237-7
Domesticity. Eleanor Goodson Mitchell. 6750-6
Domett, Alfred
    Amohia's flight. 6591-0,6592-9
    The calm and silent night. 6747-6
    A Christmas hymn. 6820-0
    A Christmas hymn. 6145-1,6239-3,6543-0,6639-9,6219-9, 6424-8,6656-9,6102-8
    A glee for winter. 6658-5,6597-X,6656-9
    The haunted mountain, fr. Ranolf and Amohia. 6768-9
    The island. 6591-0,6592-9
    A kiss. 6658-5
    The legend of Tawhaki, fr. Ranolf and Amohia. 6768-9
    The legend of the Tawhaki. 6591-0,6592-9
    The Nativity. 6046-3
    The pink terraces, N.Z., fr. Ranolf and Amohia. 6768-9
    The prelude to Ranolf and Amohia. 6768-9
    Ranolf and Amohia, sels. 6768-9
    The storm. 6591-0,6592-9
    Tangi. 6591-0,6592-9
The **domicile** erected by John. Unknown. 6279-2
The **domicile** of John. Alexander Pope. 6440-X
The **dominant** sea. Frank Moore Jeffery. 6789-1
Domination of black. Wallace Stevens. 6348-9
Domine probasti. Bible. 6830-8
Domine quo vadis? Sir William Watson. 6255-5,6730-1
Domine, audivi. Bible. 6830-8
Domine, cui sunt Pleiades curae. Sir Charles George Douglas Roberts. 6656-9
Domine, quo vadis? Unknown. 6022-6
Dominguez, Delia
    The blue bottles. Marjorie Agosin (tr.) 7036-1
    I read fortunes in dreams. Marjorie Agosin (tr.). 7036-1
    The sun looks back. Marjorie Agosin (tr.). 7036-1
Domini est terra. Bible. 6830-8
The **dominicaine**. H. Binga Dismond. 6178-8
Dominion. John Drinkwater. 6607-0
Dominion. Jean Ingelow. 6543-0
Dominion Day. Fidelis [pseud]. 6795-6
Dominion day. Agnes Maule Machar. 6591-0,6592-9
Dominion day. John Reade. 7041-8
The **dominion** of Australia. James Brunton Stephens. 6591-0, 6656-9,6592-9
"**Domino** players on the yard". Vivisection. Gene Fowler. 6792-1
Dominus illuminatio mea. Richard Doddridge Blackmore. 6337-3,6437-X,6303-9,6723-9
Dommet, Alfred
    A Christmas chant. 6915-0
Domus caedet arborem. Charlotte Mew. 6985-1
Don Crambo. Robert C.V. Meyers. 6921-5
Don Durk of Dow Dee. Mildred Plew Meigs. 6143-5
Don Garzia. Samuel Rogers. 6980-0
Don Juan. George Gordon, 6th Baron Byron. 6198-2,6959-2
Don Juan. Theophile Gautier. 6801-4
Don Juan adolescent. George Gordon, 6th Baron Byron. 6633-X
Don Juan in hell. Charles Baudelaire. 6343-8
Don Juan in Portugal. Florence Wilkinson. 6619-4

DON

Don Juan's arrival in England. George Gordon, 6th Baron Byron. 6633-X
Don Juan's nightmare. Catulle Mendes. 6351-9
Don Juan, sels. George Gordon, 6th Baron Byron. 6102-8, 6154-0,6282-2,6302-0,6315-2,6332-,6385-3,6395-0,6483-3,6527-9,6604-0,6726-,6732-8,6733-6,6332-1,6196-6, 6430-2,6250 ,6560-0,6472-8,6199-0,6659-3,6660-7,6110
Don Pedro and fair Inez. Robert C.V. Meyers. 6923-1
Don Quixote. Austin Dobson. 6501-5
Don Quixote. Arthur Davison Ficke. 6250-4
Don Ramiro. Heinrich Heine. 6842-1
Don [pseud].
 To be continued. 6817-0
"Don autumn with his magic sley". The weaver. Mabel W. Arnold. 6894-4
'Don'd feel too big'. Unknown. 6791-3
Don's asleep. Mrs. L.S. Richards. 6764-6
Don't. Emma Celia Rook. 6744-1
Don't. Nixon Waterman. 6687-9
Don't ask for a kiss. George A.C. MacKinlay. 6395-0
"Don't ask me to read a long poem". Poetry. O.E. Enfield. 6799-9
Don't be down-hearted. Berton Braley. 6853-7
Don't be foolish pray. Unknown. 6157-5
Don't be in a hurry. Unknown. 6744-1
Don't be sorrowful, darling. Rembrandt Peale. 6240-7
"Don't bow down before the little box". The enemies of the little box. Vasko Popa. 6758-1
Don't cheer. Robert Service. 6159-1
Don't come around but if you do... Charles Bukowski. 6998-3
Don't cut the string. George David Stewart. 6482-5
"Don't drive like hell through God's country". A sunday sermon. Fred Pfister. 6860-X
Don't envy other folks. Unknown. 6583-X
Don't fret. Robert J. Burdette. 6588-0
Don't give up. Phoebe Cary. 6060-9,6183-4,6456-6
'Don't give up the ship'. Benjamin Franklin Taylor. 6815-4
Don't go down in the mine. J.R. Lincoln. 6149-4
Don't go in. Mary A. Kidder. 6527-9,6685-2
"Don't grow old too fast, my sweet". Mother's song. Unknown. 6078-1
Don't kill the birds. Daniel Clement Colesworthy. 6356-X, 6373-X,6456-6
Don't kill yourself. Carlos Drummond de Andrade. 6758-1
"Don't let the song go out of your life". Kate R. Stiles. 6109-5
"Don't offend/the fullbloods". Song of the breed. Carroll Arnett Gogisgi. 7005-1
"Don't open the little box". The craftsmen of the little box. Vasko Popa. 6758-1
"--Don't pay me for singing". Cantaliso in a bar. Nicolas Guillen. 6759-X
"Don't praise yourself, lest others doubt...". Of bragging, fr. Proverbs. Arthur Guiterman. 6861-2
"Don't say that you think me courageous...". Hunting a madman. John F. Nicholls. 6924-X
"Don't sit around and feel blue". Can do. Everett C. Richmond. 6799-9
Don't stop at the station despair. Joaquin Miller. 6583-X
"Don't take on so, Hiram". Always right. Eugene Field. 6949-5
"Don't talk of September! - a lady". The hunting season. Thomas Haynes Bayly. 7025-6
"Don't talk to me of parties, Nan...". The dead kitten. Sydney Dayre. 6965-7,6699-2
Don't tell. Eva Best. 6137-0
Don't tell all you know. Unknown. 6466-3
"Don't tell me of buds and blossoms". Answer to pauper. Thomas Hood. 6974-6
Don't trouble trouble. Mark Guy Pearse. 6337-3;6583-X
Don't wait. Samuel Ellsworth Kiser. 6109-5
"Don't wake him. Let him sleep a little longer". Boy sleeping. Robert Francis. 6761-1
Don't want to work for nothing. Richard Lawson. 6149-4
""Don't wear that snake"". The rattlesnake band. Robert J. Conley. 7005-1
"Don't wish the wind would fall!". The wind. Nancy Byrd Turner. 6861-2
Don't worry. Ripley Dunlap Saunders. 6109-5
Don't worry, little girl. Edgar A. Guest. 6862-6
"Don't you hear the scholars thrumming". School time Benjamin Franklin Taylor. 6815-4
"Don't you hear them coming, tramping down...". Glasier's men. H.A. Cody. 6797-2
Don't you know. Edgar A. Guest. 6862-6
Don't you see? Katharine Lee Bates. 6274-1
"Don't you smell fire?" Thomas Hood. 6974-6
"Don't you take no sail off 'er...". What the old man said. Cicely Fox Smith. 6833-2
Don't you think so, Bill? Fred Emerson Brooks. 6579-1
Don't!. Kate Field. 6721-2
"Don't".. James Jeffrey Roche. 6652-6
The don't-believeres. Edgar A. Guest. 6862-6
Don-Carlos, Louisa Cooke
 Dear things and queer things. 6818-9
Donaghty, William A.
 Tantum ergo. 6839-1
Donaghy, Lyle
 A Leitrim woman. 6930-4
 Linota Rufescens. 6930-4
 Not by the shore. 6782-4
Donaghy, William A.
 Fourth station ("This afternoon in loud Jerusalem"). 6282-2
 The stations of the cross, sels. 6532-5
 Thirteenth station. 6282-2
Donahoe, D.J.
 The angelic chorus. 6172-9,6292-X
Donahue, Ralph J.
 Migrant wings. 6750-6
 Small boy's resignation. 6750-6
Donal Kenny. John Keegan Casey. 6090-0
"Donal o'dreams has no bed for his sleeping". The fiddler. Edna Valentine Trapnell. 7007-8
Donald D. Walsh (tr.)
 "Give me back my world" Rita Geada, 7036-1
 On the witches' sabbath. Rita Geada, 7036-1
 So that they will burn. Rita Geada, 7036-1
Donald and the stag. Robert Browning. 6669-0
Donald Caird. Sir Walter Scott. 6830-8
Donald Evans. Witter Bynner. 6036-6
Donald Macgilavry. Unknown. 6859-6
Donald Munro. Unknown. 6057-9
"Donald's gane up the hill hard and hungry". Donald Macgilavry. Unknown. 6859-6
Donald's return to Glencoe. Unknown. 6057-9
Donald's wife. Charles Keen Taylor. 6936-3
Donaldson, Jeffrey
 An old map of somewhere. 6767-0
Donaldson, Robert
 In some wide place. 6836-7
 To those who shout for hate. 6836-7
 Tribute. 6836-7
Donaldson, Robert A.
 Night road. 6542-2
 Roosevelt dead. 6995-9
Donaldson, Thomas Blaine
 Champagne. 6936-3
Donall oge. Unknown (Irish) 6244-X
"Done is a battell on the dragon blak!". A hymn of the Resurrection. William Dunbar. 6881-2
The Doneraile litany. Patrick O'Kelly. 6724-7
Doney, May
 Ruth. 6250-4
"Dong - dong - the bells rang out". The fire-bell's story. George L. Catlin. 6916-9
The dong with a luminous nose. Edward Lear. 6290-3,6125-7
Dong, Molly
 The elderly. 6883-9
 Running... 6883-9
Donkey. Alfred Kreymborg. 6012-9
The donkey and his company. J.G. Francis. 6786-7
The donkey and his panniers. Thomas Moore. 6278-4
The donkey and his panniers. Thomas Moore. 6787-5
The donkey and the mocking-bird. Jose Rosas. 6614-3
"Donkey whose talent for burden was wond'rous". The donkey and his panniers. Thomas Moore. 6787-5
"A donkey/ascending a mountain". Proletarians. Luis Munoz Martin. 6759-X

The **donkey**. Gilbert Keith Chesterton. 6044-7,6337-3,6730-1,
    6102-8,6153-2,6250 ,6477-9,6510-4,6668-2,6532-5,6228-
    8,6246 ,6465-5,6476-0,6509-0
Donn, Dora
    Be kind. 6529-5
Donn, M.H.F.
    A model tea party. 6137-0
"**Donna** Clara! Donna Clara!". Don Ramiro. Heinrich Heine.
    6842-1
Donna Julia's letter, fr. Don Juan. George Gordon, 6th
    Baron Byron. 6832-4
Donna Vera. John Nichol. 6819-7
Donne, John
    Absence. 6250-4,6301-2
    Aire and angels. 6106-0,6341-1
    An anatomy of the world. 6378-0,6369-1
    The anniversary. 6150-8,6341-1,6023-4,6430-2,6186-9,
        6562-7,6536-8,6634-8,6317-9
    Annunciation ("Salvation to all that will is nigh") .
        6282-2
    The apparition. 6315-2,6562-7
    "As due by many titles I resigne". 6562-7
    Ascension. 6933-9
    "At the round earth's imagined corners, blow". 6369-1,
        6536-8,6562-7,6315-2,6179-6
    "At the round earth's imagined corners, blow." 6645-3
    Autumnal beauty. 6935-5
    The autumnall. 6378-0,6562-7
    The bait. 6536-8,6722-0,6092-7,6430-2,6191-5,6191-5
    "Batter my heart, three peron'd God; for, you". 6562-7,
        6634-8,6150-8
    Bequests, fr. The will. 6324-1
    The blossome. 6562-7,6189-3,6341-1
    Blow your trumpets, angels. 6125-7
    Break of day. 6182-6,6634-8,6491-4
    A burnt ship. 6665-8
    "Busie old fool, unruly Sun". 6187-7
    The calm. 6315-2,6547-3,6562-7
    The canonization. 6182-6,6189-2,6315-2,6562-7,6494-1
    The character of the bore. 6200-8
    Commendatory verses upon Mr. Thomas Coryat's crudities.
        6198-2
    The computation. 6198-2,6430-2
    Crucifying. 6933-9
    The curse. 6430-2
    "Deare love, for nothing less than thee". 6187-7
    Death. 6371-3
    "Death, be not proud, though some have called thee"
        6182-6,6488-4,6473-6,6389-1,6634-8,6536-8,6315-2,
        6726-3,6194-X,6250-4,6125-7,6153-2,6214-8,6737-9,
        6645-3
    The dissolution. 6430-2
    Divine poems, sels. 6472-8
    Doth not a tenarif, fr. Anatomy of the world. 6125-7
    The dream. 6182-6-6198-2,6315-2,6317-9,6562-7,6150-8,
        6723-9,6430-2,6250-4,6341-1,6301-2
    The ecstacy, sels. 6317-9,6339-X
    The ecstasy. 6186-9,6315-2,6536-8,6438-8
    Elegie 010, The dreame. 6958-4
    Elegie on the Lady Marckham, sels. 6472-8
    Elegie: his parting from her. 6933-9
    Elegie: On his mistris. 6341-1
    Elegies, sels. 6106-0
    Elegy on his mistress. 6315-2,6369-1
    Elegy on Miss Elizabeth Drury. 6438-8
    An elegy upon the death of the Lady Markham. 6660-7
    Elegy, the autumnal. 6369-1,6430-2
    Elegy: death, sels. 6106-0
    Elegy: his picture. 6208-3,6341-1
    Epithalamiom, sels. 6301-2
    Epithalamion made at Lincolnes inne. 6933-9
    The expiration. 6182-6,6341-1
    The extasie. 6154-0,6208-3,6562-7,6341-1
    A fever. 6369-1
    The first anniversary. 6562-7
    The flea. 6488-4,6536-8,6733-6
    For forgiveness. 6214-8
    Foreknowledge. 6935-5
    Forget. 6198-2,6726-3
    "From being anxious, or secure", fr. The litany. 6931-2

"From needing danger, to be good", fr. The litany. 6931-
    2
The funeral. 6562-7,6189-3,6341-1,645-3,6301-2,6198-2,
    6317-9,6536-8,6488-4,6154-0
"Go and catch a falling star". 6536-8,6634-8,6092-7,
    6371-3,6723-9
God. 6219-9
Good Friday, 1613. Riding westward. 6536-8,6562-7,6341-
    1
The good-morrow. 6562-7,6250-4,6383-7,6341-1,6150-8,
    6182-6,6208-3,6536-8,6315-2,6339-X,6491-4,6301-2,
    6645-3,6723-9,6378-0
Hail Bishop Valentine, fr. An epithalamium... 6125-7
"Hear us O hear us O Lord, to thee", fr. The litany.
    6931-2
His picture. 6378-0,6562-7
Holy sonnet X. 6527-9,6491-1
Holy sonnets. 6208-3,6378-0
Holy sonnets, sels. 6645-3,6430-2
A hymn to Christ, at the author's last going...Germany.
    6931-2
"A hymn to Christ, at the avthors last going...". 6562-
    7,6430-2
A hymn to Christ. 6208-3,6438-8
A hymn to God the father. 6192-3,6341-1,6154-0,6189-3,
    6645-3,6660-7,6737-9,6198-2,6418-3,6634-8,6315-2,
    6527-9,6562-7
Hymn to God, my God, in my sickness. 6315-2,6438-8,6425-
    7,6150-8,6438-8
Hymne to God my God, in my sicknesse. 6208-3,6562-7,
    6430-2,6341-1
"I am a little world made cunningly". 6369-1,6562-7
"I can love both faire and brown". 6187-7
"I wonder, by my troth, what thou and I". 6187-7
"I'll undo the world by dying." 6637-2
The idea realised. 6935-5
"If faithfull soules be alike glorifi'd". 6562-7
If men be worlds. 6438-8
If poisonous minerals..., fr. Holy sonnets. 6154-0,
    6324-1
"If, as I have, you also do" 6935-5
The indifferent. 6198-2,6430-2,6194-X
La Corona. 6933-9
A lame beggar. 6491-4
A lecture upon the shadow. 6562-7
Letter to Sir H. Wotton at his going
    ambassador..Venice. 6933-9
The litany, sels. 6214-8
Little think'st thou, poor flower. 6317-9
Love. 6438-8
Love's alchemy. 6430-2
Love's deity. 6182-6,6198-2,6339-X,6369-1,6527-9,6430-2,
    6726-3
"Love's progress", sels. 6733-6
Lovers infinitenesse. 6208-3,6562-7,6182-6,6341-1,6194-
    X
Loves deitie. 6562-7
Loves growth. 6378-0
Loves usury. 6562-7
The message. 6182-6,6726-3,6341-1,6543-0
"Must I grow you fixt subject, because you are true?"
    6637-2
Nativitie. 6933-9
A nocturnall upon S. Lucies Day. 6106-0,6208-3,6536-8,
    6562-7,6341-1
"O might those sighes and teares returne againe". 6562-
    7
"O my black soul! now thou art summoned". 6369-1
The obsequies of the Lord Harrington. 6369-1
Obsequies to the Lord Harrington, sel. 6958-4
Ode ("Absence"). 6182-6,6189-3
Of the progress of the soul. 6369-1,6472-8
Oh, how feeble is man's power. 6438-8
On his mistress. 6378-0,6536-8,6562-7
On the sacrament. 6192-3
The paradox. 6430-2
The progress of the soul, sels. 6125-7
The prohibition. 6182-6,6189-3,6182-6,6341-1
The recluse hermit. 6438-8
The relic. 6182-6,6369-1,6315-2,6726--3,6562-7,6430-2,

6341-1,6723-9
Resurrection. 6933-9
"The revenous earth..." fr. Elegie:death. 6106-0
Satire. 6341-1
Satire I ("Away thou fondling motley humorist") 6430-2
Satire III. 6562-7
Satire IIII. 6562-7
Satire on religion III, sels. 6378-0
Satires, sels. 6194-X
The second anniversarie, sels. 6208-3,6150-8
The second anniversary, sels. 6194-X
The second anniversary. 6562-7
Send back my long-stray'd eyes to me. 6652-6
"Show me deare Christ, thy spouse, so bright...". 6562-7
"Since she whome I lovd, hath payd her last debt". 6562-7
"So, so, break off this last lamenting kiss". 6187-7
Song. 6645-3
Song ("Go and catch a falling star."). 6646-1,6102-8, 6301-2,6341-1,6089-7,6182-6,6527-9,6187-7,6562-7, 6733-6,6198-2,6315-2,6726-1,6430-2
Song ("Sweetest love"). 6430-2,6150-8,6184-3,6182-6, 6536-8,6562-7,6341-1,6153-2
Sonnet ("At the round"). 6341-1,6472-8,6430-2
Sonnet ("Batter my heart"). 6341-1,6430-2
Sonnet ("Death be not proud"). 6109-3,6341-1,6430-2
Sonnet ("Show me deare Christ"). 6341-1,6430-2
Sonnet ("Since she whom"). 6430-2,6472-8
Sonnet ("This is my playes"). 6430-2,6431-1
Sonnet ("Thou hast made"). 6430-2,6431-1
Sonnet ("What if"). 6430-2,6431-1
Sonnet 010: On death. 6660-7
Sonnet on the Nativity. 6746-8,6747-6
Soothsay. 6935-5
"Spit in my face you Jewes, and pierce my side". 6562-7
Stanzas from a litany. 6186-9
The storm ("England, to whom we owe..."). 6547-3
The storm ("Then like two mighty kings..."), sels. 6258-X
The storme. 6562-7
The sun rising. 6315-2,6634-8,6733-6,6562-7,6733-6
"Sweetest love, I do not go". 6187-7,6208-3
"Take heed of loving me". 6187-7
Temple. 6933-9
"That we may change to evenness", fr. The litany. 6931-2
This is my body. 6144-3
"This is my play's last scene, here Heavens appoint". 6315-2,6369-1,6562-7
"Thou hast made me, and shall thy work decay". 6187-7, 6378-0,6562-7
Thoughts on death. 6935-5
"'Tis ture 'tis day; what though it be." 6187-7
To his love. 6935-5
To his mistress. 6935-5
To his mistress going to bed. 6733-6
To Sir H.W. at his going ambassador to Venice. 6562-7, 6341-1
To Sir Henry Goodyere. 6186-9,6562-7
To the countesse of Bedford on New-Yeares Day. 6562-7, 6341-1
"Tomorrow when thou leav'st, what wilt thou say?" 6637-2
The triple fool. 6430-2
"Twice or thrice had I loved thee". 6187-7
Twickenham garden. 6315-2,6562-7,6341-1
Twickhnam garden. 6933-9
The undertaking. 6562-7,6438-8,6250-4
A valediction forbidding mourning. 6341-1,6383-7,6189-3, 6491-4,6301-2,6660-7,6342-2,6194-X,6250-4,6536-8, 6208-3,6378-0,6562-7,6340-2
A valediction: of the booke. 6378-0
A valediction: of weeping. 6187-7,6341-1
Verses to Sir Henry Wotton, sels. 6543-0
Vision. 6186-9
The whale, fr. The progress of the soul. 6125-7
"What if this present were the worlds last night". 6562-7
The will. 6562-7,6430-2

"Wilt thou forgive that sin where I begun". 6187-7
Womans constancy. 6562-7
Donnelly, Eleanor C.
A contrast. 6918-5,6579-9
The fate of Charlotte Russe. 6919-3
Gualbero's victory. 6915-0
Gualbero's victory. 6610-0
Ladye Chapel at Eden Hall. 6172-9
Mary Immaculate. 6172-9
The old surgeon's story. 6916-9
The vision of the monk Gabriel. 6910-X
Donnelly, Francis P.
Machree. 6320-9
The victory. 6096 X
Donnelly, Susan
Rilke speaks of angels. 6966-5
The rooms. 6822-7
Donner, Herman Montagu
Guardian of thy land. 6995-9
Jetsam. 6327-6
The **donnybrook** jig. Wentworth Dillon, Earl of Roscommon. 6089-7
Donohue, James J.
Last antiphon: to Mary. 6282-2
Donovan, Anne
Lyttleton. 7018-3
Songs for the virgin, sels. 7018-3
Strangers, fr. Songs for the virgin. 7018-3
Women have their idols goldplated... 7018-3
Donovan, J.W.
The granger's wife. 6409-4
Land poor. 6408-6
Mill river ride. 6408-6
Donovan, Lawrence Kyrle
Paddy's content. 6260-1
Donovan, Lois
'We' 7019-1
Doodridge, Philip
"Awake, my soul, stretch every nerve." 6001-3
The Christian life. 6606-2
Dooher, Muredach J.
Renascence. 6930-4
The woman with child. 6930-4
Doolittle, Hilda ("H.D.")
Acon. 6331-4
Adonis. 6077-3,6619-4
"Again," fr. Morpheus. 6012-9
All mountains. 6253-9
"And turn," fr. Myrtle bough. 6012-9
Antipater of Sidon. 7014-0
At Baia. 6348-9
At Eleusis. 6070-6
At Ithaca. 6069-2
"Bring fluted asphodel," fr. Songs from Cyprus. 6011-0
"Bring myrrh and myrtle bud," fr. Songs from Cyprus. 6011-0
Cassandra. 6037-4
Centaur song. 6069-2
Chance meeting. 6354-3
Chorus, fr. Morpheus. 6209-1
Cities. 6808-1
Egypt. 6184-2
Evadne. 6348-9,6019-6
Evening. 6315-2,6209-1
"For I must find," fr Myrtle bough. 6012-9
"For you are graved indelibly," fr Myrtle bough. 6012-9
Fourth song from Cyprus. 6250-4
The garden. 6531-7,6348-9,6531-7
"Gather for festival," fr. Songs from Cyprus. 6011-0
"Give me your poppies/mightier priestly state," fr.Morpheus. 6012-9
"Give me your poppies/red with rare white," fr Morpheus. 6012-9
Halcyon, sels. 6012-9
Heat. 6556-2,6726-3,6076-5,6102-8
Helen. 6777-8
Helen. 6077-3,6527-9
Heliodora. 6010-2
Hermes of the way. 6897-9
Hermes Trismegistus. 6210-5

Hippolytus temporizes. 6036-6
Hippolytus temporizes, sels. 6072-2
Holy satyr. 6010-2
"I live," fr. Morpheus. 6012-9
"I say I am quite done," fr. Let Zeus record. 6011-0
"I would forego," fr. Morpheus. 6354-3
"I would forgo." 6317-9
"I'm not here," fr. Halcyon. 6012-9
The islands. 6619-4,6217-2,6019-6,6034-X,6513-9
Keeper of the orchards. 6232-6,6076-5,6102-8,6076-5
Lais. 6010-2
Let Zeus record, sels. 6011-0
Lethe. 6536-8,6726-3,6513-9,6153-2
Loss. 6250-4
"Men cannot mar you," fr. Let Zeus record. 6011-0
Moonrise. 6531-7
Morpheus, sels. 6012-9
Myrtle bough, sels. 6012-9
"No, it isn't true," fr Halcyon. 6012-9
"None watched with me," fr. Let Zeus record. 6011-0
'Not honey'. 6348-9
"Now the house shakes," fr Halcyon. 6012-9
"O for you," fr. Halcyon. 6012-9
Orchard. 6556-2
Oread. 6289-X,6102-8,6464-7,6076-5,6488-4,6509-0
"Perhaps they said," fr. Halcyon. 6012-9
"Perhaps, they said", fr. Halcyon. 6012-9
Phaedra rebukes Hoppolyta. 6035-8
Phaedra remembers Crete. 6035-8
Phrygian and oriental, fr. Morpheus. 6012-9
"Phrygian and oriental," fr Morpheus. 6012-9
The pool. 6491-4,6531-7,6491-4
Priapus. 63004-4,6300-4
Pygmalion. 6020-X
Sea gods. 6161-3,6393-4
Sea iris. 6029-3
Sea rose. 6209-1
Sheltered garden. 6506-6,6649-6,6513-9
The shrine. 6348-9
Simaetha. 6348-9
"So give me poppies," fr Morpheus. 6012-9
"So having died," fr. Morpheus. 6012-9
" Sometimes I chide the manner of your dress," fr. Let Zeus. 6011-0
Song ("Where is the nightingale.") 6153-2
Song ("You are"). 6348-9
Songs from Cyprus, sels. 6011-0
"Stars wheel in purple," fr. Let Zeus record. 6011-0
Storm. 6531-7
Swiftly relight the flame. 6210-5
"That's life," fr. Halcyon. 6012-9
Thetis. 6037-4
Toward the Piraeus. 6619-4,6010-2
"Well then, never come again," fr Halcyon. 6012-9
"When blight lay," fr. Let Zeus record. 6011-0
"Where is the nightingale," fr. Songs from Cyprus. 6011-0
Where love is king. 6076-5,6102-8
"While we shouted," fr. 6581-3
"White rose, O white," fr. Songs from Cyprus. 6011-0
The wind sleepers. 6531-7
"Would you prefer myrrh-flower," fr. Let Zeus record. 6011-0
"You are armed," fr. Myrtle bough." 6012-9
"You say, 'Lie still,'"fr Halcyon. 6012-9
"You're impatient, unkind," fr Halcyon. 6012-9
"You're very dear," fr. Halcyon. 6012-9
"Your hands," fr. Myrtle bough. 6012-9
"Yourself in myself," fr Myrtle bough. 6012-9
Doom. Arthur O'Shaughnessy. 6437-X
Doom in bloom. Laura Riding. 6354-3
The doom of beauty. Michelangelo Buonarroti. 7039-6
The doom of Constance. Sir Walter Scott. 6094-3
The doom of Devorgoil, sels. Sir Walter Scott. 6828-6
The doom of Hippolytus. Euripides. 6435-3
The doom of King Acrisius, sels. William Morris. 6997-5
"Doom'd as I am in solitude to waste". On the death of Sir W. Russell. William Cowper. 6814-6
Doom's day. George Herbert. 6378-0
The doom-bar. Alice E. Gillington. 6541-4

Doom-devoted. Louis Golding. 6776-X
The doom-well of St. Madron. Robert Stephen Hawker. 6518-X
Doomed. Kostas Varnalis. 6352-7
The doomed man. Joseph Addison Alexander. 6337-3
'Doomed.'. Unknown. 6120-6,6610-4
A dooms-day thought. Thomas Flatman. 6152-4
Doomsday. Hans Magnus Enzensberger. 7032-9
Doomsday morning. Genevieve Taggard. 6817-0
The door and the window. Henry Reed. 6379-9
The door at the end of our garden. Frederic Edward Weatherley. 6368-3
"The door can open". Passage to the end. Eduardo Anguita. 6759-X
"The door closed/& we were there". The sweat. Nila NorthSun. 7005-1
"The door has closed between you now and me". The closed door. Thekla N. Berstecher. 6906-1
"'The door in the kitchen,' said Mrs...". 'Mind the paint' Berton Braley. 6853-7
The door is now shut. Claribel Weeks Avery. 6789-1
The door is open. Kate Douglas Wiggin. 6654-2
The door of death. William Blake. 6125-7,6461-2
"The door of Heaven open seemed". Unknown. 6050-1
"The door of many a maiden's heart". A safe attachment. S. St. G. Lawrence. 7021-3
The door of spring. Ethelwyn Wetherald. 6797-2
Door open. Jeannette Sewell. 6847-2
The door to memory's hall. Mrs. J.M. Winton. 6412-4
Door-mats. Mary Carolyn Davies. 6076-5,6250-4,6736-0
The door. Mary Carolyn Davies. 6501-5
The door. Florence Hinds. 6799-9
The door. Orrick Johns. 6320-9,6619-4
Doors. Zona Gale. 6320-9
Doors. Hermann Hagedorn. 6102-8,6467-1,6102-8,6076-5,6153-2,6506-6,6250-4,6431-0,6556-2
Doors. Ruby McDonald. 6799-9
Doors of daring. Henry Van Dyke. 6961-4
The doors of heaven. Robert Nathan. 6761-1
Doors of the temple. Aldous Huxley. 6532-5,6250-4
The doors. Lloyd Mifflin. 6300-4
The doorstep, fr. The homestead. Gertrude Huntington McGiffert. 6838-3
The doorstep. Edmund Clarence Stedman. 6302-0,6385-3,6441-8,6321-7,6585-6,6408-6,6429-9,6600-3,6632-1,6486-8, 6260 ,6121-4,6226-1,6307-1,6505-8
Dora. Thomas Edward Brown. 6395-9,6536-8,6250-4,6508-2
Dora. Alfred Lord Tennyson. 6045-1,6133-8,6255-5,6605-4, 6655-0,6110-9,6568-6
Dora versus Rose. Austin Dobson. 6089-7,6026-9
Dora, fr. Clevedon verses. Thomas Edward Brown. 6809-X
Doralicia's song. Robert Greene. 6315-2,6436-1,6191-5
Doran's ass. Unknown. 6057-9
Doran, Louise A.
    The ship. 6833-2
The Dorchester giant. Oliver Wendell Holmes. 6614-3,6484-1
Dordan, Agnes
    Evening. 6850-2
Doremus, Helen
    For Phillip who would be six years old today. 6750-6
    "Tongue in his cheek, youth climbs the path." 6750-6
Dorgan, John Aylmer
    The dead Solomon. 6848-0
    Fate. 6600-3
Doria. Ezra Pound. 6300-4
Doria. Ezra Pound. 6897-9
Doricha. Poseidippus. 7039-6,6879-0
Dorinda. Charles Sackville; 6th Earl of Dorset. 6092-7
"Dorinda's sparkling wit, and eyes". Song ("Dorinda's sparkling"). Charles Sackville; 6th Earl of Dorset. 6544-9,6562-7,6152-4
"Dorinda's youthful spouse". The widow. Christian Furchtegott Gellert. 6916-9
"Dorinda, since you must decay". Timely advice to Dorinda. Anne Finch, Countess of Winchilsea. 6831-6
Doris. Clarence S. Harper. 6118-4,6274-1
Doris. Arthur J. Munby. 6240-7
"Doris, see the amorous flame." Unknown. 6563-5
Dorlan's home-walk. Arthur Guiterman. 6628-3
Dorman, Samuel
    The dream of the Spanish general. 6741-X

DORMOUSE 424

The **dormouse** and the doctor. Alan Alexander Milne. 6722-0
The **dormouse.** Rose Fyleman. 6262-8
Dorn, Alfred
    Dark hotel. 6218-0
    Invisible painter. 6218-0
    Reversions. 6218-0
Dorn, Edward
    Los mineros. 6803-0
Dornin, Nova
    I ask but this. 6750-6
    "I don't know how it happened: All I know." 6750-6
Doro, Edward
    The boar and the shibboleth. 6250-4
Doron's description of Samela. Robert Greene. 6315-2,6586-4
Doron's eclogue joined with Camela's. Robert Greene. 6191-5
Dorothea. Sarah N. Cleghorn. 7030-2
Dorothea. Henry Van Dyke. 6961-4
Dorothy. Alfred Kreymborg. 6034-X
Dorothy. Rose Hawthorne Lathrop. 7041-8
Dorothy. Wallace Rice. 6459-0
Dorothy dances. Louis Untermeyer. 6036-6
Dorothy in the garret. John Townsend Trowbridge. 6302-0, 6385-3,6344-8
Dorothy Q. Oliver Wendell Holmes. 6176-1,6473-6,6600-3, 6652-6,6265-2,6438 ,6004-8,6288-1,6431-0,6126-5,6723-9
Dorothy's dower. Phoebe Cary. 6865-0;6969-X
Dorothy's mustn'ts. Ella Wheeler Wilcox. 6166-4
Dorothy's room, fr. Dorothy. Arthur J. Munby. 6656-9
Dorothy: a country story, sels. Arthur J. Munby. 6656-9
Dorr, Henry R.
    Comrades. 6946-0
Dorr, Julia C.R.
    The armorer's errand. 7030-2
    The armorer's errand. 6673-9
    Awakening. 6327-6
    "The buttercups, bright-eyed and bold", sels. 6601-1
    The days that never were. 7030-2
    Elsie's child. 6416-7
    The fallow field. 6414-0,6673-9
    Forshadowings. 6578-3
    Four o'clocks. 6338-1
    Homesick. 6338-1,6374-8
    Knowing. 6632-1
    The legend of the organ builder. 6917-7
    The legend of the organ-builder. 6486-8,6610-0
    Outgrown. 6240-7,6385-3,6438-8
    St. John's eve. 7030-2
    Santa Claus. 6147-8
    Somewhere. 6461-2
    "The stately lilies stand", sels. 6601-1
    A summer song. 6529-5
    Thornless roses. 6066-8
    The three ships. 6385-3
    To a late-comer. 6006-4,6019-0,6309-8
    Twenty-one. 6219-9
    Vashti. 6413-2
    Vermont. 7030-2
    When dreams depart. 7030-2
    Wonderland. 6529-5
Dorrie, Charles H.
    The recompense. 6741-X
Dorris' spinning. Margaret Junkin Preston. 6965-7
"**Dorset!** whose early steps with mine...strayed". To the Duke of Dorset. George Gordon, 6th Baron Byron. 6945-2
Dorset, E.
    To pansy. 6039-0
Dorsey, A.H.
    O'Connell's heart. 6408-6
Dorus to Pamela. Sir Philip Sidney. 6191-5
Dorus's song. Sir Philip Sidney. 6315-2
Dorypha, fr. Far west. Blaise Cendrars. 6351-9
Dos Passos, John
    Jardin des Tuileries. 6649-6
Dos Passos, John (tr.)
    Poem ("A frail sound"). Antonio Machado, 7039-6
    Poem ("Figures in the fields..."). Antonio Machado, 7039-6
A **dos't** o' blues. James Whitcomb Riley. 6892-8
"**Dose** efening clouds vas sedding fast". Shoo flies. Unknown. 6791-3,6823-5
"**Dost** live? Then thou immortal art". Immortality. Gertrude Huntington McGiffert. 6838-3
"**Dost** thou believe that we from nothing came". Belivest thou this? William C. Paris. 6764-6
"**Dost** thou know what it was?...". Prelude. Fr. Sekanina. 6763-8
"**Dost** thou know, Bianca". The usurer. Henry Hart Milman. 6980-0
Dost thou look back? Alfred Lord Tennyson. 6087-0,6424-8
"**Dost** thou not know God's country...". God's country. O.C. Auringer. 6920-7
"**Dost** thou not tire, Isaura, of this play?". Isaura. Ella Wheeler Wilcox. 6956-8
Dost thou remember. Thomas Moore. 6226-1
"**Dost** thou remember how we lived at home". Childhood. Frederick William Faber. 6980-0
Dostal-Lutinov, Karel
    The swans. Paul Selver (tr.). 6763-8
Dot. Joseph Ashby Sterry. 6770-0
Dot and Dolly. Minnie W. Patterson. 6167-2,6924-X
"**Dot** and her father saw a yacht". Dot's query. Carolyn Wells. 6882-0
Dot baby off mine. Charles Follen Adams. 6175-3,6505-8, 6573-2
Dot Dutchman in der moon. E. Carson Thorpe. 6577-5
"**Dot** dog he vas dot kind of dog". 'Der dog und der lobster'. Saul Sertrew. 6791-3,6823-5,6175-3
'**Dot** funny leetle baby'. Unknown. 6791-3,6823-5
Dot lambs vot Mary haf got. Charles Follen Adams. 6175-3
Dot lambs vot Mary haf got. Unknown. 6791-3,6823-5
Dot lambs vot Mary haf got. Unknown. 6277-6,6568-6
Dot leedle boy. James Whitcomb Riley. 6277-6
'**Dot** leedle Loweeza'. Charles Follen Adams. 6791-3
Dot loaf of bread. Carl Pretzel [pseud]. 6791-3
Dot long-handled dipper. Charles Follen Adams. 6247-4,6505-8
Dot shly leedle raskel. Unknown. 6791-3
Dot young viddow Clara. Carl Pretzel [pseud]. 6791-3,6175-3
Dot's Christmas; or, the sober hat. Emma Dunning Banks. 6426-4
Dot's query. Carolyn Wells. 6882-0
Dot's version of the text. Anita M. Kellogg. 6670-4
"**Dot-dash/The** signals light". Morse code. Miriam Wolfson. 6850-2
Doten, Elizabeth
    The kingdom. 6344-6
    A song of the north. 6219-9
Doten, Janice M. Goodrich
    A little while. 7030-2
Doth not a tenarif, fr. Anatomy of the world. John Donne. 6125-7
"**Doth** some one say that there be gods above?". Kings. Euripides. 6954-1
"**Doth** the hawk fly by thy widom, and stretch" Bible. 7020-5
"**Doth** then the world go thus, doth all thus move?". William Drummond of Hawthornden. 6246-5
"**Doth** thy heart stir within thee at the sight". Orchard-blossoms. Felicia Dorothea Hemans. 6973-8
"**Dotted** about the prairies". Dry farms. Jean Milne Gower. 6836-7
Dotten, Milton C.
    Twilight. 6818-9
Doty, Walter G.
    The best firm. 6861-8
    The best firm. 6135-4
Douberly, Ralph
    A fool speaks his mind. 6841-3
    Graveyard. 6841-3
    Love disappointed. 6841-3
    My dreams go with you always. 6841-3
    Seek me, life. 6841-3
    The sunrise is a greeting. 6841-3
Double acrostic ("Unite and untie are the same..."). Unknown. 6724-7

A double ballad of August. Algernon Charles Swinburne. 6875-8
A double ballad of good counsel. Algernon Charles Swinburne. 6875-8
Double ballad of the singers of the time. John Payne. 6875-8
Double ballad. Of the singers of the time. John Payne. 6770-0
Double ballade of life and fate. William Ernest Henley. 6770-0,6875-8
Double ballade of primitive man. Andrew Lang. 6089-7;6732-8
Double ballade of the nothingness of things. William Ernest Henley. 6770-0,6875-8
Double blessedness. Thomas Hood. 6302-0
"The double cherry trees, which grew". Lady Ise. 6852-9
The double conquest. William Whitehead. 6867-7
The double crown. John E. Barrett. 6840-5
Double duty. W.E. Farbstein. 6722-0
The double fortress. Alfred Noyes. 6169-9
The double knock. Thomas Hood. 6724-7
Double red daisies. Robert Graves. 6466-3
The double rock. Henry King. 6378-0
The double shame. Theodore Spencer. 6389-6
The double skein. Alice Cary. 6865-0;6969-X
The double sunflower. Celia Thaxter. 6612-7
The double transformation. Oliver Goldsmith. 6787-5
The double-faced creed. Unknown. 6724-7
Double-focus. Al Purdy. 6767-0
The double-headed snake of Newbury. John Greenleaf Whittier. 6753-0
The double-headed snake of Newbury. John Greenleaf Whittier. 6484-1
The double-headed snake of Newbury. John Greenleaf Whittier. 6753-0
Doubleday, Thomas
　Angling. 7015-9
　The sea cave. 7015-9,6997-5,7015-9,6997-5
Doubt. Isabel M. Fleming. 6799-9
Doubt. Fernand Gregh. 6351-9,6730-1
Doubt. Helen Hunt Jackson. 6303-9,6730-1
Doubt. L. Stauffer Oliver. 6936-3
Doubt. Sara Teasdale. 6317-9
Doubt and prayer. Alfred Lord Tennyson. 6199-0
A doubt of martyrdom. Sir John Suckling. 6122-2,6198-2
"The doubt which ye misdeem, fair love, is vain". Sonnet 065 ("The doubt"), fr. Amoretti. Edmund Spenser. 6271-7,6219-9
Doubt you to whom my muse. Sir Philip Sidney. 6250-4
"Doubt you to whom my muse these notes entendeth" Sir Philip Sidney. 6935-5
Doubt, fr. In memoriam. Alfred Lord Tennyson. 6600-3,6730-1
A doubt. Henry Alford. 6980-0
A doubt. Richard Hughes. 6302-0,6385-3
The doubt. Elizabeth I; Queen of England. 6301-2
The doubter's prayer. Anne Bronte. 6337-3,6730-1,6214-8
The doubter.. John Troland. 6583-X
A doubtful choice. Edward de Vere, 17th Earl of Oxford. 6182-6
Doubtful dreams. Adam Lindsay Gordon. 6951-7
Doubting. G.M. Downey. 6304-7
Doubting. Virginia Taylor McCormick. 6326-8
A doubting heart. Adelaide Anne Procter. 6096-X,6014-5, 6302-0,6385-3,6291-9,6575-9
Doubting Thomas. Lillian F. Hodges. 6750-6
"Doubtless, sweet girl! the hissing lead". Lines addressed to a young lady. George Gordon, 6th Baron Byron. 6945-2
Doubts, fr. Measure for measure. William Shakespeare. 6337-3
Douce, F. (tr.)
　Anglo-Norman carol. Unknown, 6756-5
Doudney, Sarah
　The children's gardens. 6772-7
　Children's joys. 6772-7
　"The children's world is full of sweet surprises". 6238-5
　Cleopatra to Antony. 6273-3
　Farewell to the old year. 6456-6
　The hardest time of all. 6273-3,6303-9
　"It is thy voice that floats above the din". 6238-5
　"O piety! O heavenly piety!" 6238-5
　Pansies. 6273-3
　The water mill. 6964-9
　The water-mill. 6273-3
　What life hath. 6273-3
The doughboy and the gob. C. A. 6817-0
Dougher, Jan
　Budding author's behest. 6857-X
Dougherty, Lynn
　Soundness. 6900-2
Doughlas, Keith
　Mersa. 6209-1
Doughnuts and cider. Edgar A. Guest. 6862-6
Doughty, Charles M.
　The Gauls sacrifice. 6210-5
　Hymn to the sun. 6210-5
　A Roman officer writes. 6210-5
Doughty, Le Garde S.
　And day is done. 6042-0
Doughty, Mulford
　Somewhere in France. 6542-2
Douglas. Dinah Maria Mulock Craik. 6732-8,6437-X
Douglas Gordon. Frederic Edward Weatherley. 6656-9
The Douglas tragedy. Unknown. 6055-2,6056-0,6098-6,6180-X, 6271-7,6197,6067-6
Douglas' account of himself. John Home. 6304-7
Douglas' complaint. Unknown. 6524-4
The Douglas' dream. Unknown. 6958-4
Douglas, Archibald
　To a modern girl. 7021-3
Douglas, Douglas, tender and true. Dinah Maria Mulock Craik. 6481-7,6109-6,6102-8,6543-0,6304-7
Douglas, Elroy
　This day. 6178-8
Douglas, Evelyn. See Barlas, John
Douglas, Gavin
　May. 6861-8
Douglas, Gavin [or Gawain]
　Buk of Eneados, sels. 6193-1
　Prologue to the Aenid, sels. 6931-2
　Song to the sun. 6134-6
　Welcome to the sun. 6022-6
Douglas, Gavin [or Gawain] (tr.)
　The difficulties of translation, fr. Aeneid. Vergil, 6845-6
　The entrance to hell, fr. Aeneid. Vergil, 6845-6
Douglas, Gilean
　While yet the green leaf. 6761-1
Douglas, Harold
　In memoriam: John Cookson. 6761-1
Douglas, Jesse
　Warning. 6722-0
Douglas, Keith
　Canoe. 6379-9
　The deceased. 6210-5
　Desert flowers. 6210-5
　Enfidaville. 6257-1
　Leukothea. 6379-9
　The offensive. 6379-9
　On a return from Egypt. 6379-9
　Poem ("These grasses"). 6379-9
　Remember me. 6379-9
　A round number. 6379-9
　Time eating. 6209-1,6379-9
Douglas, Lady John Scott and William
　Annie Laurie. 6289-X,6737-9
Douglas, Letitia Virginia
　The keepers of the light. 6417-5
　The wizard's spell. 6923-1
Douglas, Lord Alfred Bruce
　The city of the soul. 6102-8
　The dead poet. 6483-3,6102-8,6301-2
　Each new hour's passage is the acolyte. 6726-3
　The green river. 6096-X
　Impression du nuit: London. 6439-6
　In excelsis. 6778-6
　Of a dead poet. 6292-X
　Prayer ("Often the western"). 6292-X

DOUGLAS

Rejected. 6785-9
Song ("Steal from the meadows"). 6292-X
Sonnet on the sonnet. 6785-9
A summer storm. 6292-X
To Olive. 6096-X,6269-5

Douglas, Lord Alfred Bruce (tr.)
Harmonie du soir. Charles Baudelaire, 7039-6
"If he should come again..." Maurice Maeterlinck, 6343-8
La beaute. Charles Baudelaire, 7039-6
Sois sage o ma douleur. Charles Baudelaire, 7039-6

Douglas, Malcolm
A family drum corps. 6672-0
Teddy O'Rourke. 6672-0

Douglas, Marian (Annie D.G. Robinson)
Catching the colt. 6249-0,6574-0
Chimney-tops. 6131-1
The country child. 6127-3
The first parting. 6407-8
Freedom's flower. 6049-8
A good Thanksgiving. 6638-0
Kitty. 6127-3,6131-1,6424-8
Little sorrow. 6127-3,6639-9,6638-0
The motherless turkeys. 6131-1,6127-3,6621-6,6742-5
Mrs. Piper. 6695-X
My winter friend. 6131-1
Naming the baby. 6131-1
Picture poems for young folks. 6004-8
The puritan lovers. 6385-3,6600-3
The song of the bee. 6373-X,6131-1,6368-3
The song of the busy bee. 6456-6
Two pictures. 6385-3,6673-9,6131-1
Waiting for the may. 6131-1
The white kitten. 6684-4

Douglas, Marjory Stoneman
Martin Tabert of North Dakota. 7038-8

Douglas, Sir George
The antiquity of art. 6819-7
Elegy on Thomas Tod Stoddart, the angler-poet. 6819-7
A night-piece. 6819-7

Douglas, Stephen A.
Bury me in the morning. 6889-8

Douglas, Wayne
Going home in the morning. 6273-3,6670-4

Douglas, William
Annie Laurie. 6104-4,6486-8,6289-X,6396-9,6250-4,6066-8, 6239-3,6240-7,6136-2,6332-2,6479-5

Douglas, Winfred (tr.)
Alma redemptoris mater. Hermanus Contractus, 6282-2
Ave regina coelorum. Unknown, 6282-2
Regina coeli. Unknown, 6282-2
Salve regina. Hermanus Contractus, 6282-2

Douglas, sels. John Home. 6911-8

Douglass, Benjamin Wallace
Corn song. 6662-3

Douglass, Douglass Burns
Westward. 6118-4
Wind of the southland. 6118-4

Douglass, George
In memoriam. 6995-9

Douglass, John Jordan
Woodrow Wilson. 7001-9

Douglass, Marjorie Stoneman
These bones gonna rise again. 6037-4

Douleur. Lulu Brunt Dawson. 6750-6
Dove. Myra A. Shattuck. 6715-8
"A dove flew with an olive branch". The olive branch. George Meredith. 7014-0
The dove of Dacca. Rudyard Kipling. 6239-3
The dove of thought. Verner von Hnidenstam. 6045-5
"The dove says, 'Coo, coo, what shall I do?". Mother Goose. 6363-2,6466-3
"The dove shall be a hawk in kind". Love's constancy. John Clare. 6943-6

Dove, Rita
The Afghani nomad coat (part V) 7032-9

The dove. Abul Hasan (of Seville) 6362-4
The dove. John Keats. 6424-8
Dovecott mill. Phoebe Cary. 6865-0;6969-X
Dover. Joseph Ashby Sterry. 6770-0

Dover beach. Matthew Arnold. 6052-8,6208-3,6337-3,6178-0, 6437-X,6604 ,6371-3,6192-3,6250-4,6301-2,6439-6,6650 ,6023-4,6046-3,6102-8,6150-8,6110-9,6199 ,6153-2, 6196-6,6430-2,6560-0,6659-3,6646 ,6513-9,6645-3,6723-9,6660-7,6491-4,6656 ,6585-6
'Dover Beach'- a note to that poem. Archibald MacLeish. 6536-8
Dover beach, sels. Matthew Arnold. 6589-9
Dover cliff. F. Wyville Home. 6656-9
Dover cliffs. William Lisle Bowles. 6543-0
Dover cliffs, fr. King Lear. William Shakespeare. 6302-0, 6385-3,6484-1,6597-X,6438-8
Dover road - midnight. John Starie. 6764-6
Dover watch. Ruth Forbes Sherry. 6316-0
Doves. Louise Imogen Guiney. 6073-0,6501-5
Doves' eyes. Phoebe Cary. 6969-X
The doves. William Cowper. 6543-0
The doves. Katharine (Hinkson) Tynan. 7039-6

Doveton, F.P.
Some day. 6440-X

Dovrak, Xaver
Astray. Paul Selver (tr.). 6763-8

Dow's flat. Francis Bret Harte. 6302-0,6385-3,6735-2,6566-X,6281-4,6121

Dow, Dorothy
Field magic. 6039-0
Things. 6619-4
To Atalanta. 6776-X
Where no seeds grow. 6619-4

Dow, Enoch C.
Farmer. 6662-3

Dow, Henrietta M.
The Allagash Falls. 6894-4

Dow, Sabrina H. (tr.)
The hundred Louis d'Or. Unknown (French), 6166-4

Dowd, Alice M.
Seaweed. 6799-9

Dowd, Constance R.
Trailer. 6750-6

Dowd, Emma C.
Boy's Washington composition. 6712-3
Cicely croak. 6249-0
Dog is mine. 6710-7
Giving concerts. 6130-3
"Shortest month of all." 6712-3
A smile and a frown. 6579-1
Thanksgiving. 6715-8

Dowd, Mabel C.
Jamie, the gentleman. 6965-7

Dowden, Edward
Autumn song. 6930-4
Awakening. 7015-9
Brother death. 7015-9
Burdens. 6383-7
Communion. 6214-8
Evening, near the sea. 7015-9
Evening, near the sea. 6997-5
Evening, near the sea. 7015-9
Evening, near the sea. 6997-5
Finding God. 6303-9
In the cathedral close. 6244-X
An interior. 7015-9
Lady Margaret's song. 6090-0
Leonardo's Monna Lisa. 6656-9
Mona Lisa. 6930-4
Renunciants. 6244-X,6656-9
Song ("Girls"). 6244-X
Two infinities. 6656-9
Vision ("We by no shining Galilean lake") 6144-3
"Wide ocean amorosly/Spreads to the sun..." 6997-5

Dowden, Elizabeth. See West, Elizabeth D.

Dowden, Ernest
"But thou are terrible, with the unrevealed". 6997-5

Dowding, Walter
I'r hen iaith a'i chaneuon. 6360-8
Wales: a mourning. 6360-8

Dowe, Jennie E.T.
Larry kisses the right way. 6702-6

A dower for my daughter. Peggy Pond Church. 6585-6
The dowie dens o' Yarrow. Henry Scott Riddell. 6180-X

The **dowie** dens o' Yarrow. Unknown. 6271-7,6395-0,6328-4, 6518-X
The **dowie** houms of Yarrow. Unknown. 6180-X,6186-9,6419-1, 6067-6,6153-2,6219
Dowland (atr), John
    Lullaby ("Weep you no more"). 6153-2
Dowland, John
    Behold a wonder here. 6026-9
    Come away, sweet love. 6315-2
    Fine knacks for ladies. 6315-2
    "My merry mates! to Neptune's praise". 6258-X
    Praise blindness! 6328-4
    Sleep. 6302-0;6385-3
    Weep you no more. 6315-2
Dowlin, Jessie M.
    He came on wings. 6761-1
Dowling, Allan D.
    The arrow's death. 6979-7
Dowling, Bartholomew
    The battle of Fontenoy. 6219-9
    Indian revelry. 6219-9
    "The Irish brigade" at Fontenoy. 6404-3
    Our last toast. 6736-0,6273-3
    The revel. 7012-4,6930-4
    The revel. 6656-9
    Revelry in India. 6996-7
    The song of the dying. 6045-1
"**Down** 'ob'n sir? Circus, bank, bank!". A huproar. Ernest Radford. 6875-8,6770-0
"**Down** a broad river of the western wilds". Indian woman's death-song, fr. Records of woman. Felicia Dorothea Hemans. 6973-8
Down a down, fr. Rosalynde. Thomas Lodge. 6328-4
Down among the dead men. William Morris. 6828-6
Down among the dead men. Unknown. 6328-4
Down among the wharves. Eleanore Myers Jewett. 6833-2
Down around the river. James Whitcomb Riley. 6993-2,6990-8
"**Down** at the docks on his lonesome beat". The dock dreamer. Harvey McKenzie. 6750-6
"**Down** by one green and shady grove". Unknown. 6059-5
"**Down** by the bridge/They sit and wait". Water-front. Cecil French Salkeld. 6930-4
"**Down** by the edge of the cold pink sea". The D.T.'s. Unknown. 6983-5
Down by the old garden gate. James Abraham Martling. 6952-5
Down by the riverside. Brian Turner. 7018-3
Down by the salley gardens. William Butler Yeats. 6508-2, 6655-0,6660-7,6246-6,6244-X,6477-9,6437-X,6513-9
"**Down** by the waters, Ulladare". Ulladare. Walter De La Mare. 6905-3
"**Down** by the well she stood, a shadow-girl". The shadow girl. Cullen Gouldsbury. 6800-6
"**Down** by yon weeping willow". Unknown. 6059-5
"'**Down** cellar', said the cricket". The potatoes' dance. Vachel Lindsay. 6891-X
Down channel. A.G. Prys-Jones. 6648-8
"**Down** down across the open sea to Shikoku". Ancestors' graves in Kurakawa. Joy Kogawa. 6790-5
"The **down** drop of the blackbird". Three spring notations on bipeds. Carl Sandburg. 7039-6
"**Down** drops the red sun; through the gloaming". On the cliffs, sels. Adam Lindsay Gordon. 6997-5
Down east and up along. Edwin Osgood Grover. 6374-8
Down Fifth Avenue. John Curtis Underwood. 6393-4
"**Down** from her dainty head". The lily princess. Unknown (Japanese). 6891-X
"**Down** from her high estate she stept". Sophie Perovskaya. Joaquin Miller. 7009-4
The **down** grade. Thomas R. Thompson. 6617-8
"**Down** grassy lanes where cottonwood and peach". Negro settlement. Anderson M. Scruggs. 6782-4
Down hall, sels. Matthew Prior. 6369-1
Down here. Rene Francois Armand Sully-Prudhomme. 6351-9
Down here the hawthorn. Thomas Moult. 6884-7
Down home. Randolph Outlaw. 6870-7
Down in a coal mine. Unknown. 6149-4
"**Down** in a dark dungeon I saw a brave knight." Unknown. 6452-3
Down in a garden. Unknown. 6562-7,6563-5,6026-9

"**Down** in a green and shady bed". The violet. Ann and Jane Taylor. 7028-0
"**Down** in a little back garden". Mud pies. Florence A. Jones. 6889-8
Down in a valley. William Browne. 6527-9
Down in a wine vault. Don Marquis. 6722-0
Down in Salley's gardens. Unknown. 6061-7
"**Down** in dear old Indiana". The everlasting hills. Bessie Williams Osman. 6799-9
"**Down** in our cellar on a Monday and a Tuesday". Old Ellen Sullivan. Winifred Welles. 6891-X
Down in the clover. Mary E. (Freeman) Wilkins. 6965-7
"**Down** in the dell I wandered". Bayard Taylor. 6976-2
"**Down** in the depths". The ocean's dead. S.V.R. Ford. 6922-3
"**Down** in the depths of a jungle glade". A friend in need. Carolyn Wells. 6882-6
"**Down** in the fens of Lincolnshire a bird". Day. Owen Barfield. 6777-8
"**Down** in the old French quarter". Dr. Sam. Eugene Field. 6949-5
"**Down** in the south, by the waste without sail". Beyond Kerguelen. Henry Clarence Kendall. 6784-0
Down in the strawberry bed. Clinton Scollard. 7022-1
Down in the strawberry bed. Unknown. 6674-4
"**Down** in the underground are the shovel hands". Niggers. Stanley Kimmel. 6781-6
"**Down** in the valley". Sweet Evelena. Unknown. 6826-X
Down in the valley. William Fred Sachs. 6906-1
Down in yonder meadow. Unknown. 6861-8
Down in yonder meadow. Unknown. 6228-8,6732-8
"**Down** in yonder meadow where the green...". Down in yonder meadow. Unknown. 6861-8
"**Down** lay in a nook". Song ("Down lay"). Sir Henry Taylor. 6271-7
"**Down** London Lanes, with swinging lanes". Mosby at Hamilton. Madison Cawein. 6946-0
"**Down** on the beach when the tide is out". Treasures. Mary Dixon Thayer. 6891-X
"**Down** on the pampas of Argentina". The old cowpuncher speaks. Berton Braley. 6853-7
"**Down** on the wild Mustard river". Unknown. 6059-5
"**Down** on your knees, boys, holystone the decks". Cleaning ship. Charles Augustus Keeler. 6833-2
"**Down** south there is a curio-shop". The discreet collector. Eugene Field. 6949-5
"**Down** the air, everywhere". Rain song. Frederick Jackson. 6937-1
Down the bayou. Mary Ashley Townsend. 7041-8
Down the bayou. Mary Ashley Townsend. 6300-4
"**Down** the blue chasm of the street". The street of peacocks. Alice Mabel Alder. 6800-6
"**Down** the broad, imperial Danube". The torture-chamber at Ratisbon. William Allen Butler. 6903-7
Down the burn, Davie. Robert Crawford. 6086-2,6180-X
"**Down** the court thudding hard though the...". Basketball. James Lewisohn. 6870-7
"**Down** the dimpled green-sward dancing". Song ("Down"). George Darley. 6930-4
"**Down** the glutted river's throat". The floating island. Ruth Miller. 6788-3
"**Down** the highways and byways of yesteryears". Mother. Robert W. James. 6799-9
"**Down** the hill the waters cascade". Unknown. 6364-0
Down the Little Big Horn. Francis Brooks. 6062-5
Down the Mississippi. John Gould Fletcher. 6299-7,6336-5
Down the Mississippi: night landing. John Gould Fletcher. 6506-6
"**Down** the lanes of boyhood, let me go once...". The lanes of boyhood. Edgar A. Guest. 6862-6
"**Down** the long street he limps...anxious eye". The enterprise. Wilfred Wilson Gibson. 6781-6
"**Down** the peach-tree slid". In vain. Alice Cary. 6969-X
Down the rain falls. Elizabeth J. Coatsworth. 6554-X
"**Down** the rippling, dancing river". On the river. Howard W. Long. 6919-3
Down the rivuh, down, boys. Unknown. 6609-7
Down the road. Wilfred Wilson Gibson. 6779-4
"**Down** the road rides a German lad". The three lads. Elizabeth Chandler Forman. 7031-0

DOWN

"Down the Savoy valleys sounding". The church of Brou. Matthew Arnold. 6947-9,6828-6
"Down the St. Lawrence winter storms begin". Songs of the Canadian winter. James K. Liston. 7035-3
Down the road to Sally's. Charles Capron Marsh. 6116-8
Down the Simplon pass, fr. The prelude. William Wordsworth. 6199-0
Down the slope. Charlotte P. Hawes. 6600-3
Down the Songo. Richard Hovey. 7006-X
"Down the street, with a lilting swing". The crutches' tune. Elizabeth R. Stoner. 6846-4
Down the wood-path. John Henry Hopkins Jr. 7030-2
"Down through the deep deep grey-green seas...". A dream of burial in mid-ocean. John Addington Symonds. 6997-5,7015-9
"Down through the snow-drifts in the street". The boy. Eugene Field. 6949-5,6902-9
Down to sleep. Helen Hunt Jackson. 6239-3,6212-1,6456-6
Down to St. Ives. Unknown. 6699-2
Down to the capital. James Whitcomb Riley. 6694-1
"Down to the stream they flying go". Shibboleth. E.H.J. Cleveland. 6909-6
"Down toward the deep-blue water...". Your lad, and my lad. Randall Parrish. 6443-4,6846-4
"Down Wessex way, when spring's a-shine". The spring call. Thomas Hardy. 7020-5
Down went McGinty. Joseph Flynn. 6736-0
Down with the rosemary and bays. Robert Herrick. 6747-6
Down with the traffic. Dwight Williams. 6916-9
Down with the tyrants. Unknown. 6149-4
Down world. Mark Van Doren. 6391-8
Down, wanton, down! Robert Graves. 6733-6,6210-5
Down-adown-derry. Walter De La Mare. 6596-1
The down-and-out. Clarence Leonard Hay. 7007-8
Down-hall. Matthew Prior. 6152-4
Down-setting. Rosalie Moore. 6761-1
The down. Ibn Rashiq. 6362-4
"Downe downe afflicted soule and paie thy due." Unknown. 6563-5
"Downe in a dale satt a nimph weeping." Unknown. 6563-5
"Downe in a vale there satt a shepherdesse." Unknown. 6563-5
"Downe in the depth of mine iniquity". Sonnet 099 ("Downe in the depth of mine iniquity"). Fulke Greville; 1st Baron Brooke. 6933-9
"Downe too farre unsurping day." Unknown. 6563-5
"Downe, downe proud minde..." Unknown. 6378-0
Downen, Viola
  Prayer while dusting. 6750-6
Downer, Mary Thomasine
  Comparison. 6818-9
Downer, W.B.
  Children's praise song. 6049-8
Downey, Charles Julian
  The, sels bridegroom. 6836-7
  The maestro. 6836-7
  The other side of the world. 6836-7
Downey, G.M.
  Doubting. 6304-7
Downey, Harris
  Exhibition. 6017-X
The downfall of piracy. Benjamin Franklin (atr) 6946-0
Downfall of Poland. Thomas Campbell. 6240-7
The downfall of the Gael. Fearflatha O'Gnive. 6930-4,7039-6
Downgoing. Gustav Davidson. 6218-0
Downing, Abbotte McKinnon
  Inspiration. 6799-9
Downing, Andrew
  Vi et Armis. 6274-1
Downing, Edward Collins
  To the Minnesota river. 6342-X
Downing, Eleanor
  Mary. 6172-9,6292-X
  On the Feast of Assumption. 6172-9,6292-X
  On the feast of the assumption. 6096 X
  The pilgrim. 6172-9,6292-X
  The pilgrim. 6172-9
  Transmutation. 6096 X
Downing, Ellen Mary
  A dream of other years. 6858-8
  To-day. 6858-8
Downing, Ellen Mary Patrick
  The old church at Lismore. 6046-3
  Were I but his own wife. 6656-9
Downing, Fanny
  The old story. 6486-8
  Prometheus vinctus. 6113-3
Downing, Mary
  The grave of Macaura. 6219-9
Downman, Hugh
  Infancy. 6482-5
The downright country-man, or The faithful dairy maid. Unknown. 6157-5
Downs, Annie S.
  Washington's kiss. 6691-7
The downs.. Robert Bridges. 6395-0,6423-X,6487-6,6477-9,6541-4
The downs.. John Galsworthy. 6477-9
"Downstairs I laugh, I sport and jest with all". L. E. L. Christina Georgina Rossetti. 6828-6
Downton, Henry
  Brave and true. 6743-3,6167-2
"Downwind the lion catches scent". The sleeping gypsy-a painting by Rousseau. Nick Johnson. 6966-5
<u>Downy flakes and children. Blanche Elliott. 6906-1</u>
The downy owl. Edith Willis Linn. 6073-0
The downy woodpecker. John Burroughs. 6073-0
Dowsley, Norah Lilian D'Altera
  Bait. 6800-6
  Rain in the night. 6800-6
Dowson, Ernest
  Ad domnulam suam. 6513-9
  Amor profanus. 6507-4,6648-8,6655-0
  April love. 6513-9
  Beata solitudo. 6508-2
  Benedictio domini. 6507-4,6292-X,6508-2,6172-9
  Brief life. 6274-1
  Carthusians. 6096-X,6507-4,6292-X,6172-9
  Cynara. 6427-2,6102-8
  Dregs. 6380-2,6507-4,6102-8,6301-2,6508-2,6655-0
  Epigram. 6022-6
  Exile. 6507-4
  Extreme unction. 6785-9
  Extreme unction. 6507-4,6172-9,6383-7,6655-0,6301-2,6508-2,6022-6
  Faith. 6096 X
  The garden of shadow. 6232-6
  Had you waited. 6274-1
  Impenitentia ultima. 6507-4,6508-2,6655-0
  In tempore senectutis. 6250-4
  A last word. 6507-4,6655-0,6507-4
  Libera me. 6507-4
  My lady April. 6655-0
  A New Zealand Christmas. 6096 X
  Non sum qualis eram bonae sub regno Cynarae. 6785-9
  Non sum qualis eram bonae sub regno cynarae. 6246-5,6317-9,6507-4,6250-4,6513-9,6301-2,6508-2,6655-0
  Non sum qualis eram bonae sub regno Cynarae. 6785-9
  Nuns of the perpetual adoration. 6507-4
  O mors! quam amara est memoria tua homini pacem habenti... 6508-2,6513-9,6655-0
  The one in bedlam. 6096 X
  Quarantana. 6096-X
  Rondeau. 6507-4
  Rondeau. 6875-8
  St. Peter. 6096 X
  Sapientia lunae. 6508-2
  Seraphita. 6659-3
  Spleen. 6380-2,6507-4
  They are not long. 6250-4
  To one in bedlam. 6785-9
  To one in bedlam. 6507-4,6726-3,6022-6
  Vain resolves. 6507-4,6250-4,6655-0
  Venite descendamus. 6508-2
  Villanelle of Acheron. 6875-8
  Villanelle of his lady's treasures. 6652-6
  Villanelle of Marguerites. 6508-2
  Villanelle of sunset. 6958-4,6875-8
  Villanelle of the poet's road. 6875-8

Vitae summa brevis spem nos vetat incohare longam. 6508-2,6655-0,6315-2,6507-4,6726-3,6125-7,6153-2
You would have understood me. 6507-4
Yvonne of Brittany. 6507-4
Dowson, Ernest (tr.)
Il pleut doucement sur la ville. Paul Verlaine, 6513-9
Il pleut doucement sur la ville. Paul Verlaine, 7039-6
Spleen. Paul Verlaine, 7039-6
Doxology for peace. R.B.Y. Scott. 6337-3
Doyle, Albert
The man and the park. 6799-9
This be for death. 6839-1
Doyle, Camilla
Cuckoos, larks, and sparrows. 6506-6
The town rabbit in the country. 6069-2
Doyle, Edward
The Nubian, Greek and Jew. 6848-0
Doyle, Francis
The fusiliers' dog. 6510-4
Doyle, Joseph Nevin
The snowshoers song. 7035-3
Doyle, Lynn
An ulsterman. 6930-4
Doyle, Marion
Letter to Saint Peter. 6750-6
Manhattan malady. 6750-6
Message to my father. 6750-6
November memory. 6042-0
October. 6654-2
Reply to advice to youth. 6750-6
Saint and sinner. 6750-6
Splendidly dead. 6654-2
Doyle, Sir Arthur Conan
The blind archer. 6702-6
Corporal Dick's promotion. 6580-5
The frontier line. 6793-X
The groom's story. 6707-7
The guards came through. 6088-9
The guns in Sussex. 7031-0,7027-2
The homecoming of the Eurydice. 6793-X
Master. 6274-1,6692-5
Mind and matter. 6482-5
The song of the bow. 6134-6,6290-3,6332-2,6478-7
Doyle, Sir Francis Hastings
The Epicurean. 6199-0
The loss of the Birkenhead. 6242-3,6233-6,6656-9
The old cavalier. 6188-5
The private of the buffs. 6289-X,6290-3,6302-0,6385-3, 6656-9,6322-5,6102-8,6660-7,6262-6,6250-4,6271
The red thread of honor. 6107-9,6242-3,6427-2,6504-X, 6322-5
The return of the guards. 6980-0
Rizpah, daughter of Aiah. 6980-0
To the memory of Captain Arthur Watkin Williams Wynn. 6980-0
Dr Mole. Walter De La Mare. 6905-3
"The drab/concrete walls". 'Temporary escape' Leonard Keller. 6792-1
Drachenfels. George Gordon, 6th Baron Byron. 6331-4,6439-6, 6631-3
Drachman, Julia M.
You too? 6037-4
Drachmann, Holger
Amber. Charles Wharton Stork (tr.). 6555-4
Dedication. Charles Wharton Stork (tr.). 6555-4
Drink the sweet scent! Charles Wharton Stork (tr.). 6555-4
I sit as I have always sat. Charles Wharton Stork (tr.). 6555-4
Parting in autumn. Charles Wharton Stork (tr.). 6555-4
The wild red wine. Charles Wharton Stork (tr.). 6555-4
Dracopoulu, Theoni ("Myrtiotissa")
Women of Suli. Rae Dalven (tr.). 6352-7
The draft riot. Charles De Kay. 6946-0
Drafted. Helen Louise Barron Bostwick. 6045-1
The drafted man. Charles Badger Clark Jr. 6032-3
Dragnet. Joseph Auslander. 6393-4
Dragon. Jeannette Marks. 6762-X
The dragon drink. Ellen Murray. 6685-2
Dragon flies. Walter James Turner. 6246-6

The dragon fly. Walter Savage Landor. 6092-7
The dragon of the seas. Thomas Nelson Page. 6946-0
The dragon of Wantley. Unknown. 6133-8,6271-7,6328-4
Dragon-fly love. William Plomer. 6985-1
The dragon-fly, fr. The two voices. Alfred Lord Tennyson. 6597-X
The dragon-fly. Mary Howitt. 6131-1
The dragon-fly. Jessie B. Rittenhouse. 6476-0,6510-4
Dragonette, Rita M.
Party. 6750-6
Dragonfly. Estella M. Williamson. 6316-0
Dragons. Edward Lovelle Stewart. 6482-5
Dragut, the corsair. Unknown (Spanish) 6757-3
Draherin O Machree. Michael Hogan. 6090-0
Drake. Alfred Noyes. 6151-6
Drake. Unknown. 6934-7
Drake's drum. Sir Henry Newbolt. 6087-0,6323-3,6138-9,6188-5,6332-2,6473 ,6547-3,6732-8,6104-4,6301-2,6153-2, 6668 ,6224-5,6437-X,6258-X,6290-3,6331-4,6339 ,6427-2,6477-9,6490-6,6634-8,6639-9
Drake's spirits. John Galsworthy. 6888-X
Drake, Alexander
Kensal green. 6632-1
Drake, Alice
Mammy's treasuh. 6249-0
Drake, Geoffrey
The hero. 6258-X
Drake, Gustave V.
An astral romance. 7021-3
Drake, Joseph Rodman
The American flag, sels. 6239-3
The American flag. 6077-3,6176-1,6240-7,6302-0,6385-3, 6402-7,6425-6,6473,6486-8,6600-3,6735-2,6401-9, 6606-2,6639-9,6424-8,6396-9,6457-9,6309-8,6219-9, 6304-7,6135-4,6223-7,6228-1,6442-6,6431-1,6212-1, 6265-2,6470-1,6131-1,6212-1,6470-1,6131-1,6121-4, 6102-8,6076-5,6396-9,6457-9,6309-8,6219-9,6304-7, 6135-4,6223-7,6228-1,6442-6,6431-1,6212-1,6265-2, 6470-1,6131-1,6212-1,6470-1,6131-1,6121-4,6102-8, 6076-5,6300-4
The culprit fay, sels. 6008-0,6135-4
The culprit fay. 6121-4,6219-9,6467-1,6102-8,6076-5, 6484-1,6077-3,6239-3,6302-0,6385-3,6673-9
An elfin knight. 6639-9
Elfin song. 6431-0
A fairy in armor. 6519-8,6135-4
The fay's sentence, fr. The culprit fay. 6300-4
Inconstancy. 6441-8
The king of the doctors, sels. 6482-5
Th man who frets at worldly strife. 6291-1,6004-8,6121-4,6291-1
Meeting. 6648-8
The mocking-bird's song. 6373-X
Song of the fays, fr. The culprit fay. 6334-9
To a friend. 6753-0
To a friend. 6288-1
To a friend. 6753-0
To a lady. 6004-2
To the defenders of New Orleans. 6946-0
To the surgeon general of the state of New York. 6121-4
Drake, Joseph Rodman. See also Halleck, F-G
Drake, Leah Bodine
Fantasy in a forest. 6783-2
Figures in a nightmare. 6648-8
The gods of the Dana. 6218-0
The middle ages: two views. 6388-8
On a night of stars. 6648-8
The pool. 6218-0
The rider. 6388-8
Terror by night. 6648-8
A warning to skeptics. 6218-0
The witches. 6218-0
The woods grow darker. 6218-0
The word of willow. 6218-0
Drake, William A.
The guardsman. 6537-6
Renunciation. 6071-4
Drake, sels. Charles Fitz-Geffrey. 6483-3
Drake, sels. Alfred Noyes. 6541-4
The drake. Ruth Manning-Sanders. 776-X

DRALEY

Draley, George
   Nephon's song. 6490-6
Drama. William Hart-Smith. 6384-5
The **drama** of the doctor's window, sels. Austin Dobson. 6123-0
A **drama** of three. Unknown. 6917-7
Drane, Augusta T.
   Maris Stella. 6172-9,6292-X
Dransfield, Jane
   Eight doves. 6979-7
   The great square. 6979-7
The **draped** charter. Tom James. 6149-4
"**Draped** in festoons of cobwebs gray". Little brown trunk. Gussie Ross Jobe. 6906-1
Draper, A.S.
   We's aridin' on de honeymoon train. 6799-9
Draper, Jane
   I look into the stars. 6037-4
Draper, John W.
   Ballet russe. 6959-2
Draper, William H.
   "Call him the child of God" 6995-9
   Hush, all ye sounds of war. 6144-3
   The red Christmas. 7027-2
Dratt, Florence Evelyn
   A Christmas song. 6608-9
Draw a pail of water. Unknown. 6114-1
"Draw a pail of water". Unknown. 6904-5
"Draw closer, O ye trees". Lloyd Mifflin. 6338-1
"Draw me nere". The magician and the baron's daughter. Unknown. 6881-2
"Draw me not!Let your laurels round me wreathe". Inscription for the scabbard of a sword of honour. Herbert Trench. 6877-4
Draw me, savior, after thee. Charles Wesley. 6065-X
Draw near, o son of God. Charles Wesley. 6065-X
"Draw near, young men, and learn of me". Unknown. 6059-5
"Draw oop dem bapers, lawyer...". Baitsy and I are oudt. George M. Warren. 6918-5
"Draw oud der bapers, lawyer". Betsey und I hafe bust ub. James S. Burdett. 6791-3,6823-5
"Draw the shades across the window". Mourning. Willa Blake. 6750-6
Draw the sword, O republic. Edgar Lee Masters. 6051-X,6393-4
The **draw-bridge** keeper. Henry Abbey. 6909-6
The **drawback**. Edgar A. Guest. 6869-3
Drawing. Sergei Mikhalkov. 6546-5
Drawing near the light. William Morris. 6604-6,6660-7,6110-9
Drawing water. Phoebe Cary. 6969-X
Drawings by children. Lisel Mueller. 6966-5
"**Drawn** from the bubbling fountain, filled...". Drought. May C. (Mary) Gillington) Byron. 6800-6
Drawn from the desire of knowledge. Sir John Davies. 6584-8
Drawn from the motion of the soul. Sir John Davies. 6584-8
"Drawn in the crimson of a battle-plain". Address delivered at...new theatre at Richmond. Henry Timrod. 6753-0
The **dray**. Laurence Binyon. 6507-4
Drayton, Grace
   Mother love. 6249-0
   The suffragette. 6249-0
Drayton, H.S.
   Grace Vernon Bussell. 6920-7
Drayton, Michael
   Agincourt. 6659-3,6371-3,6419-1,6332-2,6179-6,6182-6, 6186-9,6228-8,6323-3,6726-3,6733-6,6473-6,6301-2, 6660-7
   Agincourt, sels. 6339-X,6322-5
   The arming of Pigwiggen, fr. 'Nymphidia'. 6239-3
   "As other Men, so I my selfe doe Muse," 6586-4
   "Away yee barb'rous woods", fr. Polyolbion. 6933-9
   Ballad of Agincourt. 6303-2,6331-4,6385-3,6504-X,6536-8, 6536-8,6634-8,6634-8,6331-4,6023-4,6197-4,6102-8, 6219-9,6302-0;6385-3
   The ballad of Agincourt. 6263-6
   The ballad of Dowsabell. 6315-2
   The baron's wars, sels. 6194-X

   Batte's song. 6315-2
   Battle of Agincourt. 6188-5,6239-3,6808-1,6424-8,6543-0
   The beggar. 6383-7
   Birds in the fens, fr. Polyolbion. 6125-7
   "Blacke pytchy Night, companyon of my woe." 6586-4
   "Bright starre of Beauty, on whose eye-lids sit" 6586-4
   "Calling to minde since first my Loue begun," 6586-4
   Cassamen and Dowsabell. 6436-1,6191-5
   Christopher Marlowe, fr. To Henry Reynolds. 6125-7
   Cloris and Mertilla. 6315-2
   "Come, let us kisse and parte." 6302-0;6385-3
   A contest. 6191-5
   The court of fairy, fr. Nymphidia. 6198-2,6378-0
   The crier. 6182-6,6473-6,6722-0,6562-7,6092-7,6153, 6430-2
   "Cupid, I hate thee, which I'd have thee know." 6317-9
   Daffodil. 6194-X,6191-5
   David and Goliah. 6848-0
   "Dear, why should you command me to my rest". 6182-6, 6187-7
   Definace to love. 6827-8
   The description of Elizium. 6191-5
   The Earl of Surrey to Geraldine. 6436-1
   "The Earle Douglas for this day", fr. Polyolbion. 6933-9
   Ecologue. 6436-1
   Endymion's convoy. 6436-1
   England's heroical epistles. 6198-2
   "An evil spirit, your beauty haunts me still." 6182-6, 6586-4
   Fame and fortune. 6436-1
   A fine day. 6239-3,6466-3,6018-8
   Fools gaze at painted courts, fr. Polyolbion. 6125-7
   Give me my self. 6317-9
   Gorbo and Batte. 6315-2
   The harp. 6438-8
   The heart. 6562-7
   His ballad of Agincourt. 6194-X
   "How many paltry, foolish, painted things" 6182-6,6586-4
   I give thee eternity. 6737-9
   "I hear some say, 'This man is not in love.'" 6317-9
   Idea, sels. 7039-6
   Idea, sels. 6879-0
   Idea, sels. 6198-2,6317-9,6378-0,6194-X,6430-2
   Ideas mirrour, sel. 6958-4
   Ideas mirrour, sels. 6378-0
   "If chaste and pure deoution of my youth." 6586-4
   Immortality in song. 6092-7,6250-4,6102-8
   "In pride of wit, when high desire of fame." 6586-4
   "Into these loues, who but for passion lookes." 6586-4
   King Henry as Rosamond. 6436-1
   King Henry to fair Rosamond. 6543-0
   "Like an adventurous seafarer am I". 6258-X,6586-4
   Lines ("Clear had the day"). 6315-2
   Love banished heaven. 6543-0
   Love's farewell. 6246-5,6560-0,6226-1,6543-0,6737-9
   Love's parting. 6153-2
   Madrigal. 6908-8
   "Many there be excelling in this kind," 6586-4
   Marlowe. 6250-4
   "Me thinkes I see some crooked Mimicke ieere." 6586-4
   Morning birds in spring. 6935-5
   "My hart imprisoned in a hopeles ile." 6586-4
   "My hayre, looke from those turrets of thine eyes." 6586-4
   "My native country then...," fr. Polyolbion... 6562-7
   "Neare to the silver Trent," fr. The shepheards sirena. 6562-7
   Nimphidia, the court of fayrie. 6378-0,6473-6,6562-7
   The ninth eclogue. 6430-2
   Nymphidia, sels. 6198-2,6239-3,6473-6,6634-8,6194-X
   Ode 012 ("Fair stood"). 6198-2
   Ode to the Cambro-Britons and their harp... 6645-3
   An ode written in the peake. 6933-9
   "Of all the beasts", fr. Polyolbion. 6933-9
   "Our flouds-queen Thames, for ships and swans..." 6586-4
   Paraphrase. 6848-0
   Paraphrase from Isaiah. 6848-0

The parting. 6186-9,6240-7,6339-X,6427-2,6102-8,6301
Phoebe on Latmus. 6436-1
Pigwiggin in arms himself. 6134-6
A play with proverbs. 6202-4
Pogwiggin arms himself. 6134-6
Polyolbion, sels. 6125-7,6194-X
Polyolbion, the thirteenth song, sels. 6562-7,6194-X
The prayer of Mardocheus. 6848-0
A prayer of Tobias. 6848-0
Queen Mab sets out, fr. Nymphidia. 6634-8
Queen Mab's visit to Pigwiggin, fr. Nymphidia. 6306-3, 6466-3
The queen's chariot. 6933-9
The quest of Cynthia. 6543-0
A remonstrance. 6830-8
roundelay ("Tell me, thou skilful shepherd's swain"). 6182-6
Rowland's rhyme. 6436-1
The sacrifice to Apollo. 6933-9
The sacrifice to Apollo. 6562-7
The Severn, fr. The baron's war. 6125-7
The shepheards sirena, sels. 6562-7
The shepherd's daffodil. 6134-6,6182-6,6208-3
The shepherd's garland, sels. 6228-8,6317-9,6378-0
"Since ther's no helpe, come let vs kisse and part." 6645-3,6723-9,6182-6,6187-7,6289-X,6317-9,6473-6, 6586 ,6634-8,6723-8,6646-1,6192-X,6250-4,6371
Sirena. 6191-5,6383-7
The sixt nimphall, sels. 6933-9
Some atheist in love. 6250-4
"Some men there be, which like my method well." 6586-4
"Some misbeleeuing, and prophane in loue." 6586-4
Song to Beta. 6436-1
Sonnet. 6429-9
Sonnet ("An evil spirit"). 6315-2,6436-1
Sonnet ("Black pitchy"). 6315-2,6436-1
Sonnet ("Calling to mind"). 6436-1
Sonnet ("Dear, why should"). 6436-1
Sonnet ("How many paltry"). 6315-2,6436-1
Sonnet ("If chaste"). 6436-1
Sonnet ("My fair"). 6436-1
Sonnet ("My heart"). 6436-1
Sonnet ("Read here"). 6436-1
Sonnet ("Since there's no help"). 6321-7,6150-8,6315-2, 6436-1,6023-4,6189-3,6197-4,6219
Sonnet ("Stay"). 6436-1,6586-4
Sonnet ("The glorious sun"). 6436-1
Sonnet ("To nothing"). 6436-1
Sonnet ("Whilst thus"). 6436-1
Sonnet ("Why should your"). 6436-1
Sonnet 061 6660-7
Sonnet-- To the critic. 6315-2
Sonnet: To the Lady L.S. 6189-3
Sonnet: To the river Ankor. 6189-3
Sonnets to idea. 6436-1
A summer's eve. 6935-5
A summer's eve. 6250-4,6383-7
"Sweet secrecie, what tongue can tell thy worth?" 6586-4
Sylvia. 6315-2
"There's nothing grieues me, but that age..." 6586-4
To Cupid ("Maidens, why spare ye?") 6182-6
To himselfe and the harpe. 6933-9
To his coy love. 6182-6,6317-9,6562-7,6092-7,6543-0
To my most dearly-loved friend, Henry Reynolds... 6483-3,6502-7,6430-2
To my worthy friend Mr. George Chapman and...Hesiod. 6483-3
"To nothing fitter can I thee compare" 6182-6,6586-4
To the Cambro-Britans, and their harpe... 6562-7,6192-3, 6430-2,6189-3
To the Virginian voyage. 6933-9
To the Virginian voyage. 6198-2,6323-3,6334-9,6547-3, 6562-7,6484
"To those, the gentle south", fr. Polyolbion. 6933-9
Valediction. 6830-8
The Virginian voyage. 6315-2,6430-2,6150-8
"Vouchsafe to grace these rude vnpolish'd tymes," 6586-4
A Warwickshire morning. 6943-6

"When Phoebus lifts his head", fr. Polyolbion. 6933-9
"Whilst thus my Pen striues to eternize thee," 6586-4
"A witlesse gallant, a young wench that woo'd." 6586-4
"A world of mighty kings and princes", fr. Polyolbion. 6933-9
Dread. Rosa Mulholland; Lady Gilbert. 6096 X
Dread aloe. Hildegarde Flanner. 6808-1
"**Dread** color! sign of royalty and sin". Purple. Daisy Arnold Maude. 6841-3
"**Dread** force, in whom of old we loved to see". To nature (II). Emily Ffeiffer. 7015-9
"**Dread** Potter, in thy hands we lay". A pagan's baptism. Arthur Shearly Cripps. 6788-3
The **dread** of height. Francis Thompson. 6292-X,6507-4,6172-9,6655-0
"**Dread**, desolate mount!". Vesuvius ("Dread"). Christopher Pearse Cranch. 6624-0
The **dreadful** boy. Unknown. 6530-9
"**dreadful** days go up and up, to fall". Prison. Horace Shipp. 6884-7
"The **dreadful** hour is sighing for a moon". All-Hallows eve. Francis Ledwidge. 6812-X
A **dreadful** mistake. Unknown. 6713-1
The **dreadful** story about Harriet and the matches. Heinrich Hoffmann. 6242-3
dreadful story of Pauline and the matches. August Heinrich Hoffman. 6120-6
Dream. Ellen M. Acton. 6818-9
Dream. Anna Hempstead Branch. 6007-2,6556-2
Dream. Dorothy Davis. 6750-6
Dream. Rolfe Humphries. 6071-4
Dream. Mikhail Lermontov. 6103-6
Dream. Robert Haven Schauffler. 6184-2
dream ("Was it a dream or not.") Mary Kyle Dallas. 6671-2
Dream ("With camel's hair I clothed my skin"). Richard Watson Dixon. 6315-2
Dream about me. Nathaniel I. Twitt. 6178-8
A **dream** about the old nursery rhymes. M.H.F. D. 6131-1
Dream after touring the Tokyo Tokei. Joy Kogawa. 6790-5
Dream and deed. Matthew Richey Knight. 7041-9
The **dream** and the blood. Louis Untermeyer. 6070-6
Dream baby. Joseph Morris. 6078-1
The **dream** called life. Pedro Calderon de la Barca. 7039-6
A **dream** child. Don Marquis. 6732-8
A **dream** dance. Francis Ledwidge. 6812-X
The **dream** days. Edgar A. Guest. 6862-6
The **dream** fairy. J. Walker. 6804-9
Dream fantasy. William ("Fiona Macleod") Sharp. 6730-1
Dream garden. Rosalie Maher. 6850-2
A **dream** garden. Geoffrey Chaucer. 6649-6,6153-2
"The **dream** has spilled its genial plentitude". Eurydice. Margaret Allonby. 6788-3
"A **dream** I had - a dream as blue and brave". King of a king. Mary Belden James. 6847-2
"A **dream** I had in the dead of night". Tiger bay. Robert Buchanan. 6926-6
A **dream** in May morning. Geoffrey Chaucer. 6935-5
"The **dream** is the babe in the lovelit nest". The deed is the man. James C. McNally. 6889-8
"A **dream** it was in which I found myself". The dream called life. Pedro Calderon de la Barca. 7039-6
Dream lake. Robert W. Chambers. 6654-2
Dream land. Frances Anne Kemble. 6437-X
A **dream** lesson. Carolyn Wells. 6132-X
Dream love. Ruth E.J. Sarver. 6178-8
A **dream** maiden. Harriet Eleanor Hamiliton (Baille) King. 6543-0
"**Dream** me no city in the crystal sky". A summer paradise. William Dudley Foulke. 6879-0
Dream moments. Alletha Goss Hargrave. 6799-9
"**Dream** not of swords and guns galore". Discovery. Unknown. 7007-8
A **dream** observed. Anne Ridler. 6379-9
A **dream** of a blessed spirit. William Butler Yeats. 6477-9
The **dream** of a boy who lived at nine-elms. William Brighty Rands. 6452-3
The **dream** of a dreamer. Unknown. 6274-1
The **dream** of a girl who lived ar seven-oaks. William Brighty Rands. 6452-3
The **dream** of Aengus Og. Eleanor Rogers Cox. 6556-2

DREAM

A dream of Artemis. Francis Ledwidge. 6812-X
A dream of beauty. Clark Ashton Smith. 6648-8
A dream of burial in mid-ocean. John Addington Symonds. 6997-5,7015-9
Dream of Clarence, fr. King Richard III. William Shakespeare. 6188-5,6302-0,6385-3,6304-7,6648-8
The dream of Dakiki. Firdusi] (Abul Kasin Mansur) Firdausi [or Firdawsi. 6730-1
A dream of death. William Butler Yeats. 6477-9
A dream of defeated beauty. George William ("A.E.")_ Russell. 6070-6,6250-4
Dream of dying. Thomas Lovell Beddoes. 6958-4
Dream of dying, sels. Thomas Lovell Beddoes. 6545-7
A dream of Egypt. John Todhunter. 7015-9
A dream of England. Charles Wharton Stork. 6033-1
The dream of Eugene Aram. Thomas Hood. 6133-8,6271-7,6661-5,6732-8,6302-0,6385,6102-8,6291-9,6518-X,6656-9,6648-8
A dream of fair woman, sels. Alfred Lord Tennyson. 6997-5
A dream of fair women, sel. Alfred Lord Tennyson. 6958-4
A dream of fair women. Alfred Lord Tennyson. 6483-3
A dream of fair women. Alfred Lord Tennyson. 6122-2,6198-2, 6655-0,6657-7,6110-9,6250
The dream of fixing things. Arthur Smith. 6792-1
The dream of Gerontius, sels. John Henry, Cardinal Newman. 6934-7
The dream of Gerontius, sels. John Henry, Cardinal Newman. 6046-3
The dream of Gerontius, sels. John Henry, Cardinal Newman. 6934-7
The dream of Gerontius. John Henry, Cardinal Newman. 6022-6
Dream of his lady ("Fair eyes, ye mortal..."). Giovanni Battista Guarini. 6325-X
Dream of his lady ("O eyes, you mortal stars"). Giovanni Battista Guarini. 6325-X
A dream of home. Alice Cary. 6969-X
A dream of immortality. William Drummond of Hawthornden. 6935-5
The dream of John Macdonnell. Unknown (Irish) 6858-8
A dream of life. John Morris. 6583-X
A dream of mountaineering. Po Chu-I. 6958-4
A dream of November. Sir Edmund Gosse. 6507-4
"The dream of my life has been shattered". My shattered dreams. C. Celeste de Silva. 6799-9
A dream of one dead. A. Bernard Miall. 6785-9
A dream of other years. Ellen Mary Downing. 6858-8
A dream of Sappho. Richard Hovey. 6121-4
The dream of Schiller. William Cullen Bryant. 6648-8
The dream of Sister Agnes. Unknown. 6695-X
Dream of spring. Elizabeth Dodd. 6821-9
A dream of spring. Samuel Taylor Coleridge. 6654-2
A dream of spring. Percy Bysshe Shelley. 6935-5
A dream of springtime. Eugene Field. 6949-5
A dream of summer. Mary N. Prescott. 6131-1
A dream of summer. John Greenleaf Whittier. 6049-8
Dream of the beggar-woman. Maurice Reidy. 6761-1
The dream of the boats. Helen Isabel Walbridge. 6118-4
The dream of the condemned. George Crabbe. 6980-0
The dream of the future. Denis Florence McCarthy. 6858-8
The dream of the multi-millionaire. Charles Whitby. 6994-0
The dream of the reveller. Charles Mackay. 6617-8
The dream of the romaunt of the rose. Geoffrey Chaucer. 6315-2
The dream of the rood, sels. Unknown. 6489-2
The dream of the rood. Unknown. 6022-6
The dream of the ropemaker's son. Rhys Carpenter. 6037-4
A dream of the south wind. Paul Hamilton Hayne. 6006-4
The dream of the Spanish general. Samuel Dorman. 6741-X
A dream of the unknown. Percy Bysshe Shelley. 6246-6,6302-0,6543-0
The dream of the world without death, fr. The book of Orum. Robert Buchanan. 6656-9
A dream of winter. William Henry Davies. 6253-9
A dream of wrecks, fr. Richard III. William Shakespeare. 6125-7
A dream of youth. Lionel Johnson. 6655-0
The dream path. Eugene Crombie. 6650-X
Dream people. Isabel Ecclestone-Mackay. 6433-7,6648-8
Dream rambles. I. Edgar Jones. 6927-4

A dream realized. Jesse L. Bernheisel. 6654-2
Dream roses. Heloise M.B. Hawkins. 6836-7
Dream scars. Kateri Lanthier. 6767-0
The dream shall live. Corinne B. Dodge. 6316-0
Dream ship. Mary E. Hill. 6799-9
Dream song. Richard Middleton. 6421-3
The dream that cracked a whip. Frances Airth. 6750-6
Dream the greatest dream. Florence Earle Coates. 6653-4
Dream tryst. Richard Le Gallienne. 6879-0
Dream variation. Langston Hughes. 6102-8,6076-5,6628-3
A dream within a dream, sels. Edgar Allan Poe. 6545-7
A dream within a dream. Edgar Allan Poe. 6126-5,6648-8, 6176-1,6732-8,6250-4,6288-1,6125-7
Dream!. Jens Peter Jacobsen. 6555-4
'Dream'.. James Whitcomb Riley. 6992-4
"Dream'st thou of heaven?". Dreams of heaven. Felicia Dorothea Hemans. 6973-8
A dream, after reading Dante's episode of Paolo... John Keats. 6483-3
Dream, dream, dream! Eugene Field. 6949-5
"Dream, dream, thou flesh of me!". Lullaby ("Dream"). Patience Worth [pseud.]. 6030-7
The dream, fr. The book of the duchesse. Geoffrey Chaucer. 6958-4
A dream, sels. Thomas Campbell. 6648-8
The dream, sels. Geoffrey Chaucer. 6301-2
The dream, sels. Caroline Elizabeth Sarah Sheridan Norton. 6980-0
The dream-bearer. Mary Carolyn Davies. 6102-8,6250-4
The dream-child invitation. Alfred Noyes. 6151-6
A dream-child. Dinah Maria Mulock Craik. 6772-7
The dream-daemon. Lin Carter. 6218-0
Dream-drowned. Phyllis Megroz. 6779-4
Dream-faces. Horace Rublee. 7030-2
A dream-garden.. Ella Young. 6090-0,6174-5,6558-9,6628-3
"Dream-haunted face". The disguise. Walter De La Mare. 6905-3
Dream-land. Edgar Allan Poe. 6753-0
Dream-land. Christina Georgina Rossetti. 6271-7,6655-0, 6186-9,6657-7,6250-4,6508
Dream-land, fr. In Tuscany. Cora Fabri. 6876-6
Dream-life. Adelaide Anne Procter. 6957-6
Dream-love. Samuel Minturn Peck. 6226-1
Dream-love. Christina Georgina Rossetti. 6123-0,6246-6
Dream-march. James Whitcomb Riley. 6091-9
Dream-pedlary. Thomas Lovell Beddoes. 6186-9,6198-2,6315-2, 6427-2,6437-X,6482-,6199-0,6301-2,6102-8,6512-0,6533-3,6732 ,6656-9,6658-5,6668-2,6737-7
A dream-poem.. Antoinette De Coursey Patterson. 6038-2
The dream-seller man. Eugenia Stoutenburgh. 6032-3
The dream-ship. Miriam Rees Edmondson. 6118-4
The dream-ship. Eugene Field. 6692-5,6579-1
The dream-teller. Padraic Gregory. 6930-4
Dream-tryst. Francis Thompson. 6828-6
Dream-tryst. Francis Thompson. 6250-4
Dream-tryst. Francis Thompson. 6942-8
Dream-valley. Albert Durrant Watson. 6115-X
A dream.. Antoinette De Coursey Patterson. 6338-1
A dream.. Unknown. 6436-1,6529-5
"Dream/You are too much". The dream that cracked a whip. Frances Airth. 6750-6
The dream: a tragedy. Joanna Baillie. 6813-8
A dream. Gertrude Alger. 6798-0
A dream. William Allingham. 6090-0,6102-8,6383-7,6153-2, 6656-9,6648
A dream. Matthew Arnold. 6947-9
A dream. William Blake. 6134-6,6378-0,6479-5,6454-X,6638-0, 6639 ,6086-2,6195-0,6378-0
A dream. Robert Bridges. 6487-6
A dream. Julia Brinckerhoff. 6686-0
A dream. Alice Cary. 6969-X
A dream. Patrick Reginald Chalmers. 6506-6
A dream. F. W. Faber. 6958-4
A dream. John Galsworthy. 6888-X
A dream. Helen Hunt Jackson. 6754-9
A dream. William Langland. 6150-8
A dream. Philip Bourke Marston. 7015-9
A dream. James Abraham Martling. 6952-5
A dream. Gertrude Huntington McGiffert. 6838-3
A dream. Edward Moxon. 6980-0

A dream. Stephen Phillips. 6337-3,6102-8,6464-7
A dream. Edgar Allan Poe. 6288-1
A dream. Adelaide Anne Procter. 6219-9
A dream. Mary Enola Rudolph. 6799-9
A dream. Percy Bysshe Shelley. 6793-X
A dream. Roy Nance Smethers. 6818-9
A dream. Edward Thomas. 6958-4
A dream. Theodore Watts-Dunton. 7015-9
The dream. George Gordon, 6th Baron Byron. 6102-8,6271-7, 6302-0,6385-3,6291-9
The dream. John Donne. 6182-6-6198-2,6315-2,6317-9,6562-7, 6150-8,6723-9,6430-2,6250-4,6341-1,6301-2
The dream. Richard Eberhart. 6390-X
The dream. Maud Morrison Huey. 6818-9
The dream. Edna St. Vincent Millay. 6986-X
The dream. Gladys Marie Parker. 6178-8
The dream. Siegfried Sassoon. 7014-0
The dream. Smpad Shahaziz. 6050-1
The dream. John Sheffield; Duke of Buckingham. 6544-9
The dream. Dionysios Solomos. 6352-7
The dream. Gaspara Stampa. 6325-X
The dream. Johann Ludwig Uhland. 6948-7
The dream. Georgios Vizinos. 6352-7
"The dreamdog". Walther Nowotny. 6769-7
The dreame. Ben Jonson. 6958-4
The dreamer and reaper. J.H. Ecob. 6049-8
"A dreamer he, one fed on cloud and star". The poet. Gertrude Huntington McGiffert. 6838-3
"Dreamer of mighty dreams, wherein there lie". Dauntless. Frank D. Swaney. 7001-9
"The dreamer turns". Street cries. Josephine Pinckney. 7017-5
"Dreamer! and wouldst thou know". A thought of the future. Felicia Dorothea Hemans. 6973-8
The dreamer's pipe. Unknown. 6453-1
Dreamer, dreamer. John Travers Moore. 6906-1
The dreamer.. Vachel Lindsay. 6310-1,6250-4
A dreamer. Arthur Guiterman. 6773-5
A dreamer. Robert Loveman. 6941-X
The dreamer. Hugh Francis Blunt. 6954-1
The dreamer. Felicia Dorothea Hemans. 6973-8
The dreamer. Josephine A. Meyer. 6847-2
The dreamer. Beatrice Payne Morgan. 6841-3
The dreamer. Daphne Muir. 6800-6
The dreamer. Thomas O'Hagan. 6796-4
The dreamer. John Harsen Rhoades. 6789-1
The dreamer. David MacDonald Ross. 6784-0
The dreamer. Robert Service. 6159-1
The dreamer. Gunnar Mascoll Silfverstolpe. 6045-5
The dreamer. Unknown. 6302-0;6385-3
Dreamers. Isabel Fiske Conant. 6461-2
Dreamers. Joaquin Miller. 6240-7
Dreamers. Siegfried Sassoon. 6332-2,6464-7,6653-4,6542-2
Dreamers pf dreams. William Herbert Carruth. 6104-4,6337-3
"Dreamers, drinkers, rebel youth". 'King Pandion, he is dead' Don Marquis. 6875-8
"The dreamers, drowned in their uncharted seas". Dream-drowned. Phyllis Megroz. 6779-4
The dreamers. William Wilfred Campbell. 6115-X
The dreamers. Martha Haskell Clark. 6653-4
The dreamers. Theodosia Garrison. 6101-X,6497-3,6503-1, 6653-4,6431-0
The dreamers. Sydney Jephcott. 6784-0
The dreamers. Walter Adolphe Roberts. 6034-X
Dreames. Robert Herrick. 6562-7
Dreamhurst. Elizabeth Roberts MacDonald. 6115-X
Dreaming. Edgar A. Guest. 6862-6
Dreaming. George McCalla Spears. 6799-9
Dreaming. Unknown. 6116-8
"Dreaming I watch the silver limpid dew". Dew-drops. Rene Francois Armand Sully-Prudhomme. 6876-6
The dreaming child. Felicia Dorothea Hemans. 6973-8
Dreaming in the trenches. William Gordon McCabe. 7017-5
"Dreaming my dingy dreams to-day I trod". A dead chameleon. Arthur Shearly Cripps. 6800-6
Dreaming oaks. John Keats. 6793-X
Dreaming of cities dead. Eleanor Rogers Cox. 6096-X,6292-X, 6172-9
Dreaming spires. Roy Campbell. 6788-3
Dreaming that I went with Li and Yu to visit Yuan Chen. Po Chu-I. 6958-4
"Dreaming you say thank you". Voices that have filled my day. Fay Chiang. 6790-5
Dreaming, sel. Thomas De Quincey. 6958-4
Dreamland. Helen Bosanquet. 7042-6
Dreamland. Josie McNamara Lydon. 6836-7
Dreamland. Edgar Allan Poe. 6176-1,6732-8,6250-4,6288-1, 6126-5,6648
Dreams. Cecil Frances Alexander. 6930-4
Dreams. Cecil Frances Alexander. 6090-0
Dreams. Auguste Angellier. 6961-4
Dreams. Gamaliel Bradford. 6039-0
Dreams. Thomas Edward Brown. 6655-0
Dreams. Thomas Edward Brown. 6809-X
Dreams. Alice Cary. 6865-0;6969-X
Dreams. John Dryden. 6250-4
Dreams. Reginald C. Eva. 6461-2
Dreams. Edgar A. Guest. 6748-4
Dreams. Ruth Landon. 6396-9
Dreams. Andrew Lang. 6771-9
Dreams. Winifred M. Letts. 6090-0
Dreams. Robert Loveman. 6941-X
Dreams. Virginia Taylor McCormick. 6039-0
Dreams. Edgar Allan Poe. 6288-1
Dreams. Lizette Woodworth Reese. 6039-0
Dreams. Edwin L. Sabin. 6097-8
Dreams. Sir Walter Scott. 6438-8
Dreams. Virna Sheard. 6115-X
Dreams. Frank Dempster Sherman. 6311-X
Dreams. S. Virginia Sherwood. 6510-4
Dreams. Charles Weekes. 6873-1
Dreams ("The night hours wane, the bleak winds ..."). Unknown. 6273-3
The dreams ahead. Edwin Carlisle Litsey. 6211-3;6260-1
Dreams and deeds. John Hunter. 6144-3,6337-3
Dreams and life. Erik Axel Karlfeldt. 6045-5
Dreams and realities. Phoebe Cary. 6865-0;6969-X,6385-3
Dreams and realities, sels. Phoebe Cary. 6337-3
Dreams are best. Robert Service. 6159-1
"The dreams are old before you". It is finished. Barney Bush. 7005-1
Dreams are so pale. Katharine Beverly. 6178-8
"Dreams are the mists of thoughts". Dreaming. George McCalla Spears. 6799-9
"Dreams are they-but they are God's dreams". God's dreams. Thomas Curtis Clark. 6954-1
"The dreams I dream will all come true". If I am sitting close to you. Jessie Downs Belknap. 6799-9
Dreams come true, fr. Electra. Sophocles. 6435-3
Dreams for sale. S. Walter Norris. 6670-4
Dreams in Hades. Gustaf Froding. 6045-5
Dreams in progress. Richard Oyama. 6790-5
Dreams in Rome. Arthur Symons. 6624-0
Dreams of flying. George Darley. 6648-8
Dreams of heaven. Felicia Dorothea Hemans. 6973-8
Dreams of lost Atlantis. Alejandro Murguia. 6792-1
"The dreams of my heart", fr. The dark cup. Sara Teasdale. 6531-7
Dreams of my youth, sels. Edward Kenealy. 6545-7
Dreams of the dead. Felicia Dorothea Hemans. 6973-8
Dreams of the sea. William Henry Davies. 6258-X
Dreams of youth. William Lisle Bowles. 6980-0
"The dreams of youth are fairest". The dreams of youth. Edgar A. Guest. 6862-6
Dreams old and nascent. David Herbert Lawrence. 6730-1
"The dreams our son dreams now are dreams...". Just war. Maria Jacobs. 6767-0
Dreams to sell. Thomas Lovell Beddoes. 6114-1
"Dreams, books, are each a world...". Books, fr. Personal talk. William Wordsworth. 6934-7
"Dreams, like children hand in hand". Dreams. Robert Loveman. 6941-X
Dreams, sels. Walter De La Mare. 6648-8
"Dreams, your time hasn't come" Herbert Zand. 6769-7
"Dreams/prayers". Alois Hergouth. 6769-7
The dreams. Eugene Field. 6949-5
"The dreamy crags with raucous voices croon". Hymn to the sunrise. Unknown. 6902-9
The dreamy dog. Joshua Freeman Crowell. 6130-3
"Drear and sullen skies". Melancholy. John Travers Moore.

DREAR

6906-1
"Drear we were and dull". The guest. Gertrude Huntington McGiffert. 6838-3
"Dreary and forsaken/The weatherbeaten...". Bright intervals. Jessie Haefner. 6799-9
The dreary black hills. Unknown. 6003-X,6281-4
"A dreary mansion, large beyond all need", fr. The prelude. William Wordsworth. 6958-4
"A dreary place would be this earth". The little people. Nathaniel Parker Willis. 6772-7
A dreary song. Shirley Brooks. 6440-X
"Drecker, the draw-bridge keeper, opened wide". The draw-bridge keeper. Henry Abbey. 6909-6
The dree night. Unknown. 6125-7
Dregs. Ernest Dowson. 6380-2,6507-4,6102-8,6301-2,6508-2, 6655-0
Dregs. Cesar Vallejo. 6759-X
Dreiser, Theodore
    Evening - mountains. 6979-7
The dreme, sels. Sir David Lindsay. 6180-X
The dreme, sels. Sir David Lyndsay. 6180-X
Drennan, J.
    Faith and virtue. 6717-4
Drennan, William
    The battle of Beal-an-atha-buidhe. 6858-8
    Eire. 6930-4
    Erin. 6714-X
    Erin, sels. 6439-6
    Wake of William Orr. 6244-X,6102-8,6076-5
Dresbach, Glenn Ward
    Autumn crickets. 6850-2
    Bat chimney. 6789-1
    Boy in a coal car. 6761-1
    Cattle before the storm. 6510-4
    Empty corral. 6490-6
    A fawn's first snow. 6396-9
    Ghostly battles. 6619-4
    Hurdy-gurdy. 6750-6
    If scars are worth the keeping. 6619-4
    The island. 6761-1
    The last cowboy. 6265-2
    Late for chores. 6761-1
    Let there be kites again. 6761-1
    Lost valley. 6750-6
    The marsh. 6510-4
    Old barns in the rain. 6761-1
    The old sailor. 6833-2
    Range cattle. 6761-1
    Sent for water. 6750-6
    Since youth is all for gladness. 6076-5,6102-8
    Songs I-III. 6039-0
    The tamed drake. 6662-3
    To a scarlet tanager. 6073-0,6102-8,6076-5
    The white cane. 6750-6
    Yucca in the moonlight. 6265-2
A Dresden shepherdess. A.B. Houghton. 6116-8
Dresia, William
    God laughs. 6397-7
    November night. 6397-7
    Orientale. 6397-7
    Saucy goose. 6397-7
    Time. 6397-7
Dress model. Douglas B. Krantzor. 6083-8
The dress reformer. Unknown. 6702-6
"The dress that my brother has put on is thin". Lady Otomo no Sakanoy. 7039-6
"Dressed and adorned as though for her wedding". Cortege. Leopoldo Marechal. 6759-X
"Dressed in his clumsy, stiff, aquatic clothes". The diver. E.L. Mayo. 6751-4
The dressed turkey. Unknown. 6745-X
Dresser, Paul
    On the banks of the Wabash, far away. 6465-5
The dresser. Walt Whitman. 6753-0,6300-4
Dressing the doll. William Brighty Rands. 6519-8,6656-9
Dressing up. Edgar A. Guest. 6748-4
Drew, Benjamin
    Bartholomew Gosnold's dream. 6798-0
Drew, Edwin
    The super's story. 6045-1

Drew, Iva H.
    The old sampler. 6764-6
Dreyer, Cora Wilcox
    Country-bred. 6490-6
Dreyfus. Edwin Markham. 6848-0
"A dried blowfish crumbling now, a pocket". Only one-after a painting by Georgian O'Keeffe. Ralph Burns. 6966-5
Dried out. Gwendolen Haste. 6880-4,6750-6
"The drift is in the hollow of the hill". The flowers to come, fr. English Stornelli. Augusta Webster. 7037-X
Drifted out to sea. Rose Hartwick Thorpe. 6273-3
The drifter. Percy W. Reynolds. 7007-8
Drifting. Thomas Buchanan Read. 6142-7,6239-3,6402-7,6554-6,6331-4,6240 ,6271-7,6302-0,6385-3,6473-6,6481-7, 6484 ,6632-1,6300-4,6309-8,6431-0,6291-9,6252
Drifting among the thousand islands. Agnes Maule Machar. 7041-8
Drifting away. Charles Kingsley. 6123-0
Drifting away, sels. Charles Kingsley. 6931-2
"Drifting in pattern the snowflakes appear". Snow ghosts. Joyce Lancaster. 6850-2
Drifting thoughts. Ellen Otis. 6798-0
Driftwood. Richard Cheever Dunning. 6071-4
Driftwood. Winifred Welles. 6607-0
Drige ("I reached the middle of the mount"). Ralph Waldo Emerson. 6753-0
Drill man blues. George Sizemore. 6149-4
Drill song. Unknown. 6237-7
The drill. Harry Brown. 6665-8
Drimin donn dilis. John Walsh. 6174-5
Drimin dubh. Unknown (Irish) 6858-8
Drinan, Adam
    Love Song. 6379-9
Drink. Bertel Gripenberg. 6045-5
"Drink and be merry, for what of tomorrow?". The brief present. Unknown (Greek). 6879-0
"Drink and be merry, merry, merry boyes". Song ("Drink and be merry...") Thomas Morton. 6753-0,6288-1
"Drink and be merry: there is no man knows". Unknown. 6435-3
Drink and drown sorrow, fr. The bloody brother. Francis Beaumont and John Fletcher. 6934-7
"Drink and sing, eat and laugh". Song ("Drink and sing"). Thomas Love Peacock. 6472-8
"Drink deep when the winejar's opened...". Hesiod. 6251-2
"Drink deep, O soul, of hours that swiftly...". Soul thirst. Helen Oderkirk O'Rourke. 6799-9
The drink from a jack-boot. Pfarrius. 6842-1
"Drink if you will to happy days". Lone wolf lament. Tom MacInnes. 6797-2
"Drink on, love on, not always lover..." Strato. 6251-2
Drink the sweet scent! Holger Drachmann. 6555-4
Drink to her. Thomas Moore. 6543-0
"Drink to me only with thine eyes." Ben Jonson. 6328-4, 6187-7,6289-X,6536-8,6208-3,6645
"Drink to me only with thine eyes." Philostratus. 6302-0;6385-3
"Drink to-day, and drown all sorrow". Drink and drown sorrow, fr. The bloody brother. Francis Beaumont and John Fletcher. 6934-7
Drink today and drown all sorrow. John Fletcher and Philip Massinger. 6430-2
A drink with something in it. Ogden Nash. 6628-3
Drink! Drink! Drink! Louise S. Upham. 6408-6
"Drink! Why wait for lamps? The day". Alcaeus. 6435-3
Drink's doings. Unknown. 6617-8
"Drink, drink, Asclepiades...". Asclepiades. 6251-2
Drinke to day...", fr. The tragedy of Rollo... John Fletcher. 6198-2,6562-7,6189-3
Drinker. Patrick Anderson. 6446-9
Drinking. Anacreon. 6271-7
Drinking. Abraham Cowley. 6186-9,6315-2,6427-2,6722-0,6092-7,6250-4,6513-9
"Drinking a potion of forgetfulness". Rhythm of the palms: Kandy, Ceylon - symphony. Winifred Huff Gill. 6789-1
Drinking song. William Cartwright. 6563-5
Drinking song. John Fletcher. 6182-6
Drinking song. Theodore Maynard. 7012-4
Drinking song. Thomas Randolph. 6563-5
Drinking song. Richard Brinsley Sheridan. 6086-2

Drinking song. Unknown. 6116-8,6563-5
Drinking song ("A house well supplied.") Avenzoar. 6362-4
Drinking song ("Hasten hither, saki mine.") Ubada. 6362-4
Drinking song ("The pleasures of love..."). Sir George Etherege. 6544-9
Drinking song for present-day gatherings. Morris Bishop. 6026-9
Drinking song of Munich. Thomas Campbell. 6934-7
A drinking song, fr. Antony and Cleopatra. William Shakespeare. 6436-1
A drinking song. William Shakespeare. 6436-1
A drinking song. Eugene Field. 6949-5
A drinking song. Bryan Waller ("Barry Cornwall") Procter. 6658-5
Drinking time. Daniel James O'Sullivan. 6930-4
The drinking-house over the way. M.L. Nutting. 6925-8
Drinking-song. Ellen Glasgow. 7038-8
Drinkwater, John
    Anthony Crundle. 6506-6
    At Grafton. 6477-9
    Birthright. 6726-3
    Blackbird. 6073-0,6477-9,6639-9,6668-2
    Burning bush, sels. 6320-9
    The carver in stone. 6234-2
    The Christ child at Christmas. 6532-5
    The city. 7014-0
    Cotswold love. 6331-4,6476-0
    The crowning of dreaming Jim. 6228-8
    Deer. 6253-9
    The defenders. 6477-9
    Dominion. 6607-0
    Earth love. 6875-8
    Fairford nightingales. 6073-0
    The Feckenham men. 6236-9,6161-3,6639-9
    The fires of God, fr. Poems of love and earth. 6234-2
    The fires of God, sel. 6954-1
    For thee they died. 6051-X,6224-5
    From generation to generation. 7029-9
    The garden. 6649-6
    A ghost speaks on the Styx. 6320-9
    Holiness. 6161-3
    In Lady Street. 6336-5,6668-2
    Invocation. 6250-4
    Last confessional. 6250-4
    A lesson to my ghost. 6184-2
    Malediction. 6884-7
    Mamble. 6477-9
    A man's daughter. 6301-2
    May garden. 6649-6
    Moonlit apples. 6477-9
    Mrs. Willow. 6668-2
    Of Greatham. 6234-2
    Old Crow. 6668-2
    Olton pools. 6477-9
    A prayer ("Lord, not"). 6303-9,6532-5,6108-2,6214-8, 6337-3,6359
    Reciprocity. 6506-6,6581-3
    Riddles, R.F.C. 7027-2
    Roundels of the year. 6875-8
    The ships of grief. 7029-9
    Spectral. 6884-7
    Sunrise on Rydal water. 6236-9,6331-4,6393-4
    Symbols. 6102-8,6393-4
    Thrift. 6607-0
    To the lovers that come after us. 6879-0
    The toll-gate house. 6395-0
    A town window. 6044-7,6234-2,6476-0,6477-9
    Vocation. 6102-8
    Votive. 6776-X
    We mothers know. 6542-2
    We willed it not. 7026-4
    The witch ball. 6071-4
The drip of the Irish rain. Margaret M. Halvey. 6249-0
"Drip, drip, the rain comes falling". Waiting in the rain. James Herbert Morse. 7041-8
Dripps, R.D.
    The early snow. 6983-5
    Triolet. 6983-5
Driscoll, Louise
    The blue jay. 6073-0,6232-6,6653-4

Bulbs. 6232-6
The child of god. 6031-5
Dust of a dancer. 6396-9
Emancipated. 7038-8
Epitaph. 6031-5,6393-4
Experience. 7038-8
God's pity. 6501-5
The good hour. 6619-4
Grace for gardens. 6338-1,6374-8
Green leaf. 7038-8
Harbury. 6300-4,6476-0,6509-0,6556-2,6102-8,6076-5
Harvest in Flanders. 6443-4
Hold fast your dreams. 6478-7,6607-0
The idol. 6076-5,6102-8
Indifference. 6510-4
Late plowing. 6607-0
Lost gardens. 6649-6
Marigolds. 6300-4
Old gardens. 6649-6
Spring market. 6374-8
Their Thanksgiving day. 6466-3
Two old men. 6374-8
A weed. 6184-2
Driscoll, Marjorie Charles
    The song of Thomas the rhymer. 6241-5
Driscoll, Louise
    The humming bird. 7038-8
"Drive a Ford or a Packard six". Road law. Berton Braley. 6853-7
A drive to lone ranger. Ray A. Young Bear. 7032-9
A drive. Otto Gelsted. 6555-4
Driven. Mary V. Traeger. 6857-X
"Driven wild with rum, he turned into..street". The drunkard's death. I. Edgar Jones. 6916-9
Driving. John Newlove. 6767-0
Driving home the cows. Kate Putnam Osgood. 6113-3,6402-7, 6273-3,6340-3,6471-X,6479 ,6600-3,6621-6,6632-1,6302-0,6385-3,6016 ,6104-4,6300-4,6304-7
Driving in a snowstorm, King Salmon to Naknek. Richard Dauenhauer. 6855-3
Driving oxen in Vermont. Daniel L. Cady. 6989-4
Driving saw logs on the Plover. Unknown. 6281-4
Driving sheep. Rose Macaulay. 6477-9
Driving through Oregon (December 1973) John Haines. 6855-3
"A droll conversation I once heard". A baby show. H. H.. 6965-7
The dromedary.. Hilaire Belloc. 6722-0
The dromedary. Archibald Young Campbell. 6510-4,6044-7
Dromgoole, William Allen
    Building the bridge for him. 6303-9
    Sea-weed. 6576-7
"The drone of war-plane neared,and dimmed away". Immanent. Walter De La Mare. 6905-3
The drones of the community. Percy Bysshe Shelley. 6606-2
"Droo as I leave, most every day". 'Dot funny leetle baby'. Unknown. 6791-3,6823-5
"Droop not, my brothers! I hear a glad strain". The song of hope. Felicia Dorothea Hemans. 6973-8
"Drooping were the violets and the roses...". Day's end. Helen Hoyt. 6777-8
"Drop golden showers...", fr. The courageous Turke. Thomas Goffe. 6562-7,6563-5
"Drop me the seed, that I, even in my brain". Sonnet ("Drop me the seed"). John Masefield. 6338-1
A drop of brine. Kristinn Stefansson. 6854-5
A drop of dew. Andrew Marvell. 6302-0,6385-3,6334-9,6438-8, 6383-7,6543
The drop of water. Harry Stackpole. 7022-1
"Drop, drop, slow tears". A hymne ("Drop, drop, slow tears"). Phineas Fletcher. 6933-9
"Drop, drop, slow tears." Phineas Fletcher. 6302-0,6385-3, 6737-9,6189-3
The drop. James Abraham Martling. 6952-5
The dropped stitch. Unknown. 6461-2
"Dropping roses from her hand". The word of summer. Elsa Barker. 7030-2
"Dropping words of larks, the sweetest tongue". The broken tryst. Francis Ledwidge. 6812-X
Drossinis, Georgios
    The almond tree. Rae Dalven (tr.). 6352-7

DROSSINIS

Greek earth. Rae Dalven (tr.). 6352-7
Vespers. Rae Dalven (tr.). 6352-7
"**Drough** der streeds of Frederickdown". Parody on Barbara Frietchie. Unknown. 6791-3
Drought. Christine Busta. 6769-7
Drought. May C. ([Mary] Gillington) Byron. 6800-6
Drought. David John Darlow. 6800-6
Drought. Robert Gessner. 6761-1
Drought. Geoffrey Johnson. 6257-1
Drought. Denys Lefebvre. 6800-6
Drought. Edith Mirick. 6979-7
Drought. William Henry Ogilvie. 6793-X,6784-0
Drought. Harold Fehrsen Sampson. 6800-6
Drought. Walter ("Old Saltbush") Smith. 6768-9
Drought. Katharine (Hinkson) Tynan. 6244-X
Drought and doctrine. J. Brunton Stephens. 6768-9
Drought harvest. Alta Booth Dunn. 6662-3
Drought, Kathryn L.
　Papier-mache. 6750-6
"The **drouping** night thus creepeth on them fast". The faerie queene. Edmund Spenser. 6958-4
Drouth. Ella Wheeler Wilcox. 6956-8
A **drover**. Padraic Colum. 6872-3
The **drovers**. John Greenleaf Whittier. 6457-4
Drowned. Unknown. 6873-1
"The **drowned** descend with distance in...eyes". Elegy for the drowned men who return. Roberto Ibanez. 6759-X
Drowned in harbour. Antipater of Thessalonica. 6435-3
The **drowned** lady. Unknown. 6125-7
The **drowned** lover. Lady Margaret Sackville. 6777-8
The **drowned** lover. Lady Margaret Sackville. 6019-6
The **drowned** lovers. Unknown. 6518-X,6438-8
A **drowned** soldier. Cyril Tourneur. 6087-0
Drowned woman. Elinor Wylie. 6619-4,6036-6
Drowned!. John Whitaker Watson. 6774-3
Drowning. John Ransom Palmer. 6482-5
The **drowning** ducks. Thomas Hood. 6974-6
The **drowning** lady. Unknown. 6061-7
The **drowning** of Conaing. Frank (Michael O'Donovan) O'Connor. 6582-1
The **drowning** singer. Unknown. 6889-8
The **drowning** singer. Unknown. 6744-1
Drows, Ruth L.
　Spring. 6799-9
"**Drowsy** huts kneel like white nuns in a row". At the sign of the golden key, fr. Suite Belgique. Gertrude Huntington McGiffert. 6838-3
"**Drowsy** light of November wings". Late afternoon doves. Jutta Schutting. 6769-7
"A **drowsy** music drifts across the dusk". Autumn crickets. Glenn Ward Dresbach. 6850-2
"**Drowsy** old summer, with nothing to do". Summer dreams. Edgar A. Guest. 7033-7
The **drowsy** sleeper. Unknown. 6058-7,6003-X
"The **drowzy** night hir wings has spred." Unknown. 6563-5
"The **drudging** world looks up and smiles at him". The aviator. Dorothy Alyea. 7019-1
The **drug** clerk. Eunice Tietjens. 6619-4
Drug store. John V.A. Weaver. 6736-0
The **drug-store**. Muna Lee. 6397-7
The **druggist**. Larry Rubin. 6218-0
Drugstore. John V.A. Weaver. 6464-7
"The **Druid** Urien had daughters seven". A ballad ("The Druid Urien"). Sir Walter Scott. 6087-0
Druid chorus on the landing of the Romans. Felicia Dorothea Hemans. 6973-8
The **druid** Christmas, fr. my lady, dancer... Vachel Lindsay. 6206-7
The **druid-harp**, fr. My lady, dancer for the universe. Vachel Lindsay. 6206-7
The **druid**. Douglas Hyde. 6174-5
Druidic gums. T. Inglis Moore. 6349-7
Drum. Langston Hughes. 6879-0
A **drum** for Ben Boyd, sels. Francis Webb. 6384-5
Drum taps. Walt Whitman. 6753-0
Drum taps to heaven. James Church Alvord. 6542-2
"**Drum**, drum, drum, der-um, drum, drum". The drummer of company C. Robert C.V. Meyers. 6925-8
The **drum-call** in 1861. Elbridge Jefferson Cutler. 6344-6
"The **drum/whips** up steam" H. C. Artmann. 6769-7

A **drum**. Stanley Waterloo. 6923-1
The **drum**. Eugene Field. 6318-7
The **drum**. Otto Laaber. 6769-7
The **drum**. Joseph Johnston Lee. 6846-4
The **drum**. John Scott (of Amwell) 6932-0
The **drum**. Edith Sitwell. 6106-0,6506-6,6210-5
The **drum**. Edward Forre Sutton. 6336-5
The **drummer** boy of Mission Ridge. Unknown. 6963-0
The **drummer** boy of Missouri Ridge. Kate Brownlee Sherwood. 6672-0
Drummer boy of the Rappahannock. Fred Emerson Brooks. 6707-7
The **drummer** boy of Waterloo. Unknown. 6058-7,6674-7
The **drummer** boy. Thomas Chalmers. 6404-3
Drummer hodge. Thomas Hardy. 6507-4,6657-7
The **drummer** of company C. Robert C.V. Meyers. 6925-8
The **drummer's** bride. Unknown. 6407-8
The **drummer-boy** and the shepherdess. William Brighty Rands. 6114-1
The **drummer-boy's** burial. Unknown. 6302-0;6385-3
The **drummer-boy**. Unknown. 6621-6,6304-7
Drummond de Andrade, Carlos
　Childhood. Dudley Poore (tr.). 6759-X
　Fantasia. Dudley Poore (tr.). 6759-X
　Garden in Liberty Square. Dudley Poore (tr.). 6759-X
Drummond of Hawthornden, William
　"Alexis, here she stayed; among these pines" 6182-6
　The angels for the nativity of our Lord. 6931-2
　The angels. 6145-1,6239-3,6438-8,6746-8
　"As in a duskie and tempestuous night". 6208-3
　The ascension of Christ. 6302-0
　Beauty fades. 6219-9
　The book of nature. 6934-7
　The book. 6332-2
　The bubble. 6737-9
　Change should breed change. 6931-2
　Damon's lament. 6191-5
　Dear Quirister... 6943-6
　"Doth then the world go thus, doth all thus move?". 6246-5
　A dream of immortality. 6935-5
　The end of life. 6385-3
　For the baptist. 6315-2,6562-7
　For the Baptiste. 6933-9
　For the Magdalene. 6315-2
　For the nativity of our Lord. 6334-9
　A good that never satisfies the mind. 6543-0
　The greatest wonder. 6746-8
　"How that vast heaven intitled first is rolled." 6182-6
　Human frailty. 6304-7
　An hymne of the ascension. 6933-9
　"I fear not henceforth death." 6317-9
　I know that all beneath the moon decays. 6194-X,6250-4
　If crossed with all mishaps be my poor life. 6194-X
　Invocation. 6301-2
　A kiss ("Hark, happy lovers, hark!") 6182-6
　Lament ("Chaste maids which haunt..."). 6315-2
　A lament. 6737-9
　The lessons of nature. 6246-5,6246-5,6250-4,6543-0
　Life a bubble. 6935-5
　'Like the Idalian Queene'. 6208-3,6182-6,6562-7,6153-2, 6737-9,6092
　Love which is here a care. 6931-2
　Madrigal. 6246-5,6315-2,6250-4
　Madrigal ("My thoughts hold mortal strife") 6182-6
　Madrigal ("Sweet rose, whence is this hue."). 6189-3
　Madrigal ("The beauty and the life") 6182-6
　Madrigal ("The ivory, coral, gold") 6182-6
　Madrigal ("This life, which seems so fair."). 6189-3
　Madrigal 001 ("This life which seemes so fair"). 6933-9
　Madrigal 003 ("Like the Idalian queene"). 6933-9
　Madrigal 005 ("My thoughts hold mortall strife"). 6933-9
　Madrigal 007 ("Unhappie light"). 6933-9
　Madrigal I ("This life, which seems so fair,"). 6198-2, 6182-6
　Madrigal: love vagabonding. 6315-2
　"My lute, be as thou wast when thou didst grow". 6182-6, 6187-7
　My thoughts hold mortal strife. 6934-7

The nativitie. 6933-9
No trust in time. 6315-2
"Now while the night her sable veil hath spread." 6187-7
Of Phyllis. 6182-6
On his royal patron. 6935-5
On sleep. 6660-7
Phoebus arise. 6845-6
Phoebus, arise! 6182-6,6194-X,6250-4,6315-2
Phoebus, arise. 6182-6,6194-X,6198-2,6250-4,6315-2,6562-7,6634-8
Phyllis ("In petticoat of green"). 6239-3
The praise of the solitary life. 6194-X,6219-9
The praise of a solitary life. 6194-X,6219-9
Primitiae. 6202-4
Saint John Baptist. 6246-5,6634-8,6737-9,6153-2
Sextain I ("The heaven doth not contain so many..."). 6198-2
The shepherds. 6145-1,6438-8
The shepherds. 6747-6
Sleep ("Sleep, silence' child,sweet father ..."). 6182-6,6634-8,6194-X,6737-9
A solitary life. 6933-9
Solitude. 6250-4
Song ("Phoebus, arise.") 6102-8,6189-3
Song 002 ("It autumne was..."). 6933-9
Sonnet ("A good"). 6302-0,6219-9
Sonnet ("A passing glance"). 6198-2
Sonnet ("I fear"). 6380-2
Sonnet ("I know that"). 6301-2
Sonnet ("My lute"). 6315-2
Sonnet ("What doth"). 6879-0,6908-8
Sonnet ("Alexis"). 6908-8
Sonnet ("Are these"). 6908-8
Sonnet ("How many times"). 6908-8
Sonnet ("Mine eyes"). 6908-8
Sonnet ("Sweet soul"). 6908-8
Sonnet 007 ("That learned Graecian..."). 6933-9
Sonnet 008 ("My lute be as thou..."). 6933-9
Sonnet 009 ("Sleepe, silence child..."). 6933-9
Sonnet 012 ("As in a duskie and tempestuous night"). 6933-9
Sonnet 024 ("In minds pure glasse..."). 6933-9
Sonnet 046 ("Alexis, here shee stay'd..."). 6933-9
Sonnet: On solitude. 6189-3
Sonnet: Posting time. 6189-3
Sonnet: Repent, repent! 6189-3,6250-4
Sonnet: Spring. 6189-3
Sonnet: Sweet bird. 6189-3
Sonnet: To Sir W. Alexander. 6189-3
Sonnet: To the nightingale. 6189-3
Spring bereaved. 6317-9
Summons to love. 6246-5,6543-0
Sweet bird... 6943-6
"Sweet nymphs, if, as ye stray". 6187-7
"Sweet spring, thou turn'st...". 6182-6,6208-3
"That learned Graecian (who did so excell)". 6562-7
"This life, which seems so fair." 6187-7,6246-5
"Thrice happy he,...", fr. Urania. 6198-2,6252-0
The thrush. 6302-0;6385-3
To a nightingale. 6933-9
To a nightingale. 6219-9
To a nightingale. 6933-9
To Chloris. 6194-X
To his lute. 6246-5,6250-4,6219-9
To Sir William Alexander. 6933-9
To Sir W[illiam] A[lexander]. 6562-7
To the nightingale. 6317-9,6219-9
Urania, sels. 6198-2
"What doth it serve to see sun's burning face" 6182-6
The world a game. 6668-2,6194-X
The world a hunt. 6933-9,6150-8,6933-9
"The world a hunting is". 6208-3
The world a hunting is. 6934-7
The world. 6933-9
Drummond, F.L.
    A sonnet ("The leafless trees"). 6983-5
Drummond, Hamilton
    The silence of love. 6273-3
Drummond, William Henry
    The cure of Calumette. 6591-0,6592-2
    De nice leetle Canadienne. 6692-5,6591-0,6592-9,6115-X
    De stove pipe hole. 6281-4
    Dieudonne. 6843-X
    Doctor Hilaire, sels. 6482-5
    The habitant's jubilee ode. 6591-0,6592-2
    The habitant's summer. 6793-X
    The habitant. 6433-7
    How Bateese came home. 6692-5,6281-4
    Johnnie Courteau. 6433-7,6115-X,6446-9,6591-0,6592-9
    Johnnie's first moose. 6161-3
    The last portage. 6433-7
    Le docteur Fiset. 6591-0,6592-2
    Leetle Bateese. 6266-0,6433-7,6476-0,6719-0,6102-8,6591,6592-9,6964-9
    Little Lac Grenier. 6266-0,6433-7,6252-0
    M'sieu Smit'; the adventures of an Englishman in...Canadian 6633-X
    Madeleine Vercheres. 6115-X
    The old pine tree. 7035-3
    The voyageur. 7035-3
    When Madam Albani sings. 6537-6
    The wreck of the 'Julie Plante'. 6021-8,6089-7,6274-1, 6433-7,6722-0,6274 ,6115-X,6161-3,6739-5,6646-9
    "Yass, dat is de way my Victorian...jubilee". 6796-4
Drummossie Muir. James Hogg. 6859-6
"Drums and battle-cries". True peace, fr. 'Casa guidi windows' Elizabeth Barrett Browning. 6954-1
Drums and brass. Donald Davidson. 6037-4
The drums. Berton Braley. 6853-7
The drums. Berton Braley. 6732-8
Drunina, Yulia
    The rye unharvested. Jack Lindsay (tr.). 6546-5
"Drunk in the kitchen, I ring God". Telephoning God. Gary Soto. 6792-1, 6998-3
"Drunk with delight, the rose I gave her dreams". Sonnet ("Drunk with delight"). Robert Loveman. 6941-X
Drunk: on crutches. Raymond Souster. 6446-9
Drunkard. J.O. Rockwell. 6304-7
The drunkard and his daughter, or please Mr. Barkeeper. Unknown. 6826-X
The drunkard and his wife. Jean de La Fontaine. 6064-1
A drunkard to his bottle. Joseph Sheridan Le Fanu. 6930-4
A drunkard's address to a bottle of whiskey. Joseph Sheridan Le Fanu. 6090-0
A drunkard's address to a bottle of whiskey. Joseph Sheridan Le Fanu. 6090-0
The drunkard's conceit. Unknown (German) 6787-5
The drunkard's death. I. Edgar Jones. 6916-9
The drunkard's dream. Unknown. 6058-7,6685-2
The drunkard's dream. Charles W. Denison. 6911-8
The drunkard's dream. Francis S. Smith. 6409-4
The drunkard's thirst. Unknown. 6919-3
The drunkard's wife. Ruth Cooper. 6919-3
The drunkard, fr. Metropolitan. Edith Sitwell. 7000-0
Drunken beauty. Ibn Billita. 6362-4
Drunken boat. Arthur Rimbaud. 6351-9
The drunken boat. Arthur Rimbaud. 6343-8
The drunken captain. Unknown. 6826-X
Drunken girl. Muriel Rukeyser. 6391-8
A drunken man on Highgate Hill. Paul Hasluck. 6349-7
A drunken satyr from Newton County tells how he met... Michael Burns. 6860-X
"Drunken with dew, a bandit bee". The freebooter. Robert Loveman. 6941-X
Drunkeness. ? Randolph. 6294-6
Drury Lane hstings. James Smith. 6802-2
Drury's dirge. Horace Smith. 6278-4
Drury's dirge. Horace Smith. 6802-2
Drury, Henry
    Over the thresholds of my library. 6297-0
Dry be that tear. Richard Brinsley Sheridan. 6174-5,6086-2
"The dry death-rattle of the streets". Good-bye to you, old town. Talbot Mundy. 7007-8
"The dry earth cracked-men turned away-afraid". Anniversary for armistice. Muriel F. Hochdorf. 6850-2
Dry farms. Jean Milne Gower. 6836-7
The dry heart. Alan Porter. 6782-4
The dry salvages, sels. Thomas Stearns Eliot. 6258-X,6210-

DRY

"Dry those fair, those crystal eyes". Against weeping. Henry King. 6935-5
"Dry-eyed she sat up waiting through the night". Mother's grief. Hildegard Ott Russell. 6799-9
"Dryad of the willow tree has flowing...hair". Dryads. Marie Louise Allen. 6906-1
"DThus having past all peril, I was come". The temple of Venus. Edmund Spenser. 6935-5
Dryad song. Margaret Fuller. 6730-1
Dryads. Marie Louise Allen. 6906-1
Dryads. Siegfried Sassoon. 6253-9
Dryburgh abbey. Charles Swain. 6219-9
Dryden (atr), John (tr.)
    The te deum. Unknown (Latin), 7039-6
Dryden et al., John
    The plea of the woodman, Arbor Day sels. 6376-4
Dryden, John
    Absalom and Achitophel. 6562-7,6152-4,6430-2
    Absalom and Achitophel, sels. 6637-2,6195-0,6250-4,6024-2,6179-6,6198-2,6208-3,6726-3,6733
    Achitophel, fr. Absalom and Achitophel. 6660-7,6102-8
    Against the fear of death. 6472-8
    Ah fading joy. 6315-2,6125-7
    Ah, how sweet! 6302-0,6385-3,6219-9,6301-2
    "Alas! what stay is there in human state". 6867-7
    Albion and Albanius, sels. 6208-3
    Alexander's feast, sels. 6427-2
    Alexander's feast; or, the power of music. 6102-8,6189-3,6322-5,6660-7,6560-0,6152 ,6438-8,6022-6,6023-4, 6197-4,6430-2,6195 ,6424-8,6491-4,6543-0,6154-0,6246-5,6473-6,6562-7,6198-2,6315 ,6239-3,6302-0,6385-3, 6726-3,6646-1,6219
    All for love, or the world well lost, sels. 6106-0
    "All, all of a piece throughout." 6125-7
    Almanzor and Almahide, sels. 6562-7
    "And could we choose the time and choose aright". 6867-7
    "And welcome now (great monarch) to your own". 6933-9
    Annus Mirabilis. 6208-3
    Annus Mirabilis, sels. 6198-2,6562-7,6195-0
    Anthony Ashley Cooper, Earl of Shaftesbury, fr. Absalom. 6934-7
    Astraea redux. 6152-4
    Astraea redux, sels. 6933-9
    Astraea redux, sels. 6106-0,6198-2,6195-0
    Aureng-Zebe, sels. 6562-7,6152-4,6195-0
    Ave atque vale, fr. Sigismonda and Guiscardo. 6933-9
    Beauty and youth. 6867-7
    "The birch, the myrtle, and the bay", sels. 6601-1
    Boccace, sels. 6562-7
    Britannia rediviva;..the birth of James Prince of Wales. 6970-3
    "Can life be a blessing". 6562-7
    The Catholic Church, fr. The hind & the panther. 6933-9
    Character of a good parson. 6600-3,6543-0
    Character of Buckingham. 6634-8
    Character of the Earl of Shaftesbury. 6543-0
    Character of Villiers, Duke of Buckingham. 6543-0
    A charm. 6125-7
    The Church of England, fr. The hind & the panther. 6933-9
    The church's testimony. 6022-6
    The churches of Rome and of England. 6022-6
    Come, if you dare, our trumpets sound, fr. King Arthur. 6970-3
    The conquest of Granada, sels. 6152-4
    Conversion. 6489-2,6022-6
    "Dim as the borrow'd beams of moon..",fr.Religio laici. 6831-6
    Dreams. 6250-4
    The Duke of Buckingham. 6150-8
    Eleanora; a panegyrical poem. 6970-3
    Elegy on the death of Mr. Oldham, sels. 6472-8
    Eleonora. 6302-0;6385-3
    Eleonora, sels. 6867-7
    Epigram on Milton. 6154-0,6483-3,6717-4
    An epilogue. 6970-3
    Epilogue for the King's House. 6970-3
    Epilogue intended to have been spoken..Lady Wentworth. 6970-3
    Epilogue spoken at Oxford by Mrs. Marshall. 6152-4
    Epilogue spoken at Oxford, by Mrs. Marshall. 6970-3
    Epilogue spoken at the acting of The silent woman. 6970-3
    Epilogue to Albion and Albanius. 6970-3
    Epilogue to All for love. 6970-3
    Epilogue to Amboyna. 6970-3
    Epilogue to Henry II, by Mr. Mountfort. 6970-3
    Epilogue to Mithridates, King of Pontius, by Mr. N. Lee. 6970-3
    Epilogue to Oedipus. 6970-3
    Epilogue to The husband his own cuckold. 6970-3
    Epilogue to The Indian emperor. 6970-3
    Epilogue to The Indian queen. 6970-3
    Epilogue to The man of mode, by Sir George Etherege. 6970-3
    Epilogue to The pilgrim. 6970-3
    Epilogue to the second part of The conquest of Granada. 6970-3
    Epilogue to The wild gallant, when revived. 6970-3
    Epistle to the Whigs. 6200-8
    Epistles, sels. 6970-3
    Epitaph intended for his wife. 6089-7,6527-9
    Epitaph on his wife. 6722-0
    Epitaph on Mrs. Margaret Paston. 6970-3
    Epitaph on Mrs. Margaret Paston of Burningham... 6908-8
    An evening's love, sels. 6208-3
    The fair stranger. 6970-3
    "Fair, sweet and young, receive a prize". 6562-7
    "Farewell ungratefull traytor". 6562-7,6195-0
    "Farewell, fair Armida, my joy and my grief". 6970-3
    The fear of death. 6315-2
    Fife and drum. 6424-8
    Finite reason. 6315-2
    The fire of London. 6323-3,6125-7
    "For truth has such a face and such a mien". 6867-7
    Fortune. 6874-X
    Fortune. 6092-7
    The fourth day's battle, fr. Annus mirabilis: 1666. 6933-9
    Freedom of the savage. 6543-0
    George Villiers, Duke of Buckingham, fr. Absalom... 6934-7
    "Go tell Amynta, gentle swain". 6970-3
    The great London fire, fr Annus mirabilis. 6195-0
    "Great wits are sure to madness", fr. Absalon... 6867-7
    Grief ("Oh! nothing now can please me"). 6294-6
    The happy man. 6396-9
    "He who writ this...", fr. Secret-love. 6562-7
    The heavenly gift of poesy, fr. To...Anne Killigrew. 6934-7
    Heroic stanzas. 6152-4
    Heroic stanzas, sels. 6195-0
    "High state and honours to others impart". 6970-3
    The hind and the panther, sels. 6024-2,6198-2,6562-7, 6152-4,6195-0
    The hind and the panther. 6970-3
    "How happy the lover". 6315-2,6562-7
    "How I loved/Witness, ye days and nights..." 6317-9
    Human life. 6543-0
    Hunting song. 6195-0
    "I am a monarch, the king of trees". 6376-4
    "I feed a flame within, which so torments me." 6317-9, 6150-8
    "I'm weary of my part". 6238-5
    Imitation of Horace. 6654-2
    In friendship false, implacable in hate," fr. Absalom. 6637-2
    Incantation. 6195-0
    Indian emperor, sels. 6208-3
    The infant, fr. Lucretius. 6867-7
    Jacob Tonson, his publisher. 6125-7
    Jealousy, the tyrant of the mind. 6219-9
    King Arthur, sels. 6970-3
    King James II. 6022-6
    The lady's song. 6315-2,6191-5
    The laureate of dulness. 6150-8
    A letter to Sir George Etherege. 6970-3
    Life a cheat. 6102-8,6250-4

Limit of fate. 6867-7
Lines printed under the engraved portrait of Milton. 6152-4
Lines written under the portrait of John Milton. 6198-2, 6302-0,6385-3,6129-9
"Long betwixt love and fear Phillis tormented". 6562-7
Lord Shaftesbury. 6315-2
Love triumphant, sels. 6970-3
Love's despair. 6022-6
Mac Flecknoe. 6200-8,6483-3,6536-8,6562-7,6660-7,6645, 6152-4,6192-3,6430-2,6195-0,6491-4,6637
Mac Flecknoe, sels. 6733-6,6197-4,6646-1
The maiden queen, sels. 6970-3
The malcontents, fr. Absalom and Achitophel. 6933-9
Mankind. 6250-4
May morning in the palace garden, fr Palamon & Arcite. 6649-6
The May queen. 6970-3
The medal. 6152-4
Men, fr. All for love. 6867-7
Mercury's song to Phaedra. 6152-4
Midnight. 6022-6
"A milk white Hind...", fr. The hind and the panther. 6562-7
Mithridates, King of Pontus, sels. 6430-2
"My soul lies hid is shades of grief", fr.Rival ladies. 6867-7
The new London, fr. Annus mirabilis: 1666. 6933-9
No, no, poor suff'ring heart. 6315-2,6152-4,6195-0
"Now with a general peace the world was blest". 6933-9
O souls, in whom no heavenly fire. 6250-4
The oak. 6047-1
Ode for St. Cecilia's day. 6610-0
The ode on St. Cecilia's Day, sels. 6239-3
Ode to Anne Killigrew. 6315-2
Ode to the memory of Mrs. Annie Killigrew. 6543-0
Ode to the pious memory of the accomplished young ... 6024-2
An ode to the pious memory..., sels. 6726-3
Oedipus, sel. 6958-4
Oedipus, sels. 6472-8
Of a scholar and his mistress. 6970-3
"Of these the false Achitophel...", fr. Absalom... 6726-3
Og. 6385-3
"Oh, sight! the mother of desires", fr. King Arthur. 6970-3
The old age of the temperate. 6867-7
Oliver Cromwell. 6385-3
On Milton. 6250-4
On Mrs. Margaret Paston. 6659-3
On Shadwell. 6996-7
On Sir Palmes Fairbone's tomb in Westminster Abbey. 6970-3
On the death of a very young gentleman. 6908-8,6970-3
On the death of Amyntas. 6970-3
On the death of Mr. Purcell. 6659-3
On the death of the Earl of Dundee. 6970-3
On the Duke of Buckingham. 6228-8
On the Lady Whitmore. 6970-3
On the monument of Miss Mary Frampton. 6970-3
On the monumentof the Marquis of Winchester. 6970-3
On the young statesman. 6970-3
On young master Rogers. 6970-3
"One in herself not rent...", fr. The hind...panther. 6562-7
"Our author by experience finds...", fr. Aureng-Zebe. 6562-7
Ovid's metamorphoses, sel. 6958-4
A pair well matched. 6092-7
Palamon and Arcite. 6195-8
Palamon and Arcite, sels. 6649-6,6195-0
Phillis unwilling. 6874-X
The plea of the trees - a medley. 6601-1
Poem on Milton. William Cowper (tr.). 6814-6
The popish plot. 6022-6
Portents and prodigies..., fr. All for love. 6106-0
The portrait of Milton. 6022-6,6022-X,6302-9
The power of love, fr. Cymon and Iphigenia. 6933-9
The power of music. 6250-4

Presbyterians, fr. The hind & the panther. 6933-9
"A pretty task, and so I told you...," fr. Aureng-Zebe. 6562-7
Priestcraft and private judgement, fr. Religio laici. 6933-9
The primacy of dullness, fr. MacFlecknoe. 6933-9
Private judgement condemned, fr. The hind & the panther. 6933-9
Prolgue to The tempest. 6970-3
Prologue. 6970-3
Prologue spoken at the opening of the New House...1674. 6970-3
Prologue spoken the first day of the king's house... 6970-3
Prologue to Albion and Albanius. 6970-3
Prologue to Albumazar. 6970-3
Prologue to Amboyna. 6970-3
Prologue to Arviragus and Philica revived. 6970-3
Prologue to Aureng-Zebe. 6733-6
Prologue to Aureng-Zebe, 1675. 6933-9
Prologue to Aurengezebe. 6970-3
Prologue to Caesar Borgia. 6970-3
Prologue to Crice. 6970-3
Prologue to Don Sebastian. 6970-3
Prologue to King Arthur. 6970-3
Prologue to Limberham. 6970-3
Prologue to Nahum Tate's The loyal general. 6152-4
Prologue to Oedipus. 6970-3
Prologue to Sir Martin Marr-all. 6970-3
Prologue to Sophonisba. 6970-3
Prologue to The Earl of Sussex, by Mr. Banks. 6970-3
Prologue to The Indian queen. 6970-3
Prologue to The loyal brother, by Mr. Southern. 6970-3
Prologue to The mistakes. 6970-3
Prologue to The pilgrim, revived.. our author's benefit. 6970-3
Prologue to The prophetess, by Beaumont and Fletcher. 6970-3
Prologue to The rival ladies. 6970-3
Prologue to the University of Oxford, 1673... 6933-9
Prologue to Troilus and Cressida. 6970-3
Prologue to Tyrannic love. 6970-3
Prologue, fr. Aureng-zebe. 6152-4,6195-8
Prologue, fr. Troilus and Cressida. 6152-4
A Puritan sheriff. 6733-6
Ravenna ("Of all the cities in the Romanian lands"). 6624-0
Reason. 6600-3,6634-8
Reason and religion, fr. Religio laici. 6867-7
Reason and revelation. 6489-2
Reason and revelation, fr. Religio laici. 6933-9
Religio laici. 6562-7
Religio laici, sels. 6198-2
Rondelay ("Chloe found Amyntas lying"). 6562-7
Roundelay. 6026-9
The rude militia. 6150-8
St. Cecilia's day. 6438-8
Satire on the Dutch. 6200-8
The scriptures, fr. Religio laici. 6933-9
The sea fight, fr. Amboyna. 6970-3
The second part of Absalom and Achitopel, sels. 6562-7
Secret-love, sels. 6562-7
The sects. Private judgment, fr. The hind and the panther. 6543-0
The secular masque. 6562-7
Shadwell, fr. Mac Flecknoe. 6197-4
Shadwell, fr. Mac Flecknoe. 6867-7
Shaftesbury, fr. Absalom and Achitophel. 6933-9
A simile. 6867-7
"Since every man who lives is born to die". 6407-8
Song ("After"). 6430-2
Song ("Ah fading joy"). 6187-3,6430-2
Song ("Calm was the even"). 6152-4,6430-2
Song ("Can life be a blessing"). 6733-6,6152-4
A song ("Fair, sweet and young, receive a prize"). 6933-9
Song ("Farewell ungratefull traytor"). 6933-9
Song ("Farewell, ungrateful traitor.") 6102-8,6301-2
Song ("Hear, ye sullen"), fr. Oedipus. 6472-8
Song ("I feed a flame"). 6195-0

DRYDEN

Song ("Why should a foolish"). 6152-4,6430-2
Song ("You charmed"). 6024-2,6152-4
Song ("Your hay"). 6152-4
Song for Saint Cecilia's day, 1687. 6334-9,6473-6,6489-2,6527-9,6562-7,6600 ,6154-0,6186-9,6198-2,6208-3, 6246-5,6302 ,6385-3,6634-8,6679-8,6152-4,6430-2,6192 ,6250-4,6560-0,6143-5,6150-8,6189-3,6219 ,6491-4, 6543-0,6660-7,6153-2,6102-8
A song from the Italian. 6152-4
Song of Venus. 6315-2,6733-6
Song to a fair, young lady going out of the town... 6562-7,6250-4,6023-4
Song, fr. King Arthur. 6189-3
The Spanish fryar, sels. 6208-3
The Spanish galleons seen by an Aztec. 6258-X
Stanzas on Oliver Cromwell, sels. 6198-2
Stray lines. 6867-7
The swallow. 6943-6
Sylvia the fair. 6733-6
Theodore and Honoria, fr. Boccace. 6562-7
Thomas Shadwell the poet, fr. Absolom and Achitopel. 6125-7
"Three poets, in three distant ages born". 6562-7
Threnodia Augustalis: a funeral pindaric ode. 6970-3
Time's whiter series, fr. Astraea redux. 6106-0
To a fair young lady, going out of the town in spring. 6970-3
To Britannia, fr. King Arthur. 6970-3
To Henry Higden, on his translation of...Juvenal. 6970-3
To her royal highness the Duchess of York. 6970-3
To his friend, John Hoddesdon on his divine epigrams. 6970-3
To his royal highness,...appearance at Duke's theatre. 6970-3
To his sacred majesty Charles the Second. 6970-3
To his sacred majesty, a panegyrick...1661, sels. 6933-9
To Mr. Congreve. 6659-3
To Mr. Granville, afterwards Lord Lansdowne. 6970-3
To Mr. Lee, on his tragedy of Alexander the Great. 6970-3
To Mr. Motteux,on his tragedy called Beauty in distress. 6970-3
To Mr. Southern, on his comedy called The wives' excuse. 6970-3
To my dear friend, Mr. Congreve. 6024-2,6483-3,6562-7, 6152-4,6195-0
To my friend Mr. J. Northleigh. 6970-3
To my friend, Mr. Congreve, 1693. 6186-9
To my honour'd friend Dr. Charleton... 6562-7,6152-4
To my honour'd kinsman John Driden... 6562-7
To my honoured friend Sir Robert Howard. 6970-3
To Sir Godfrey Kneller, principal painter... 6970-3
To the Countess of Abingdon. 6084-6
To the Duchess of Ormond, fr. Tales from Chaucer. 6970-3
To the Duchess of York, on her return from Scotland. 6970-3
To the Earl of Roscommon, on his essay of trans. verse. 6970-3
To the king and queen, upon the union..two companies. 6970-3
To the Lady Castlemain -afterwards Duchess of Cleveland. 6970-3
To the Lord Chancellor Edward Hyde, Earl of Clarendon. 6970-3
To the memory of Mr. Oldham. 6024-2,6208-3,6315-2,6483-3,6562-7,6733 ,6152-4,6150-8
To the me7ory of Mrs. Anne Killigrew. 6152-4,6195-0, 6250-4
To the pious memory of the accomplisht young lady... 6562-7
To the pious memory of...Mrs. Anne Killigrew. 6483-3
To the University of Oxford. 6970-3
To the University of Oxford (2). 6970-3
To the University of Oxford, 1674 6208-3
To the University of Oxford, 1674. 6970-3
To the University of Oxford, 1681. 6970-3
To the University of Oxford,...The silent woman. 6970-3
"To this the Panther...", fr. The hind and the panther. 6562-7
Tradition ("Oh but, says one, Tradition set aside"). 6489-2,6543-0
Tradition, fr. Religio laici. 6867-7
Troilus and Cressida, sel. 6958-4
Troilus and Cressida, sels. 6152-4
Two daughters of this aged stream are we,fr.King Arthur. 6970-3
Tyrannick love, sel. 6958-4
Tyrannick love, sels. 6208-3,6430-2,6659-3
Under Milton's picture. 6600-3,6543-0,6660-7
Under the portrait of Milton. 6726-3,6438-8,6102-8,6301-2,6424-8
The unity of the Catholic church. 6543-0
Upon the death of Lord Hastings. 6152-4
Upon the death of the Earl of Dundee. 6022-6
Veni creator spiritus. 6543-0,6219-9
Vox populi, fr. The medall. 6933-9
The war with Holland, fr Annus mirablils. 6195-0
"When in mid-air...", fr. An ode to the pious... 6726-3
The world well lost. 6489-2
The zambra dance. 6733-6,6152-4,6430-2
Zimri. 6186-9,6302-0,6385-3,6102-8

Dryden, John (tr.)
Against the fear of death. Lucretius, 7039-6
Ars amatoria, sels. Ovid, 6637-2
Battle of Actium, fr. Aeneid. Vergil, 6933-9
Baucis and Philemon, fr. Metamorphoses. Ovid, 7039-6
The character of a good parson. Geoffrey Chaucer, 6970-3
The cock and the fox; or, the tale of the nun's priest. Geoffrey Chaucer, 6970-3
Cymon and Iphigenia. Giovanni Boccaccio, 6970-3
Dido among the shades, fr. Aeneid. Vergil, 6933-9
The flood, fr. Metamorphoses. Ovid, 6125-7
The flower and the leaf; or, the lady in the arbour. Geoffrey Chaucer, 6970-3
Incantation, fr. Oedipus. Sophocles, 6189-3
Marcellus, fr. Aeneid. Vergil, 6933-9
"Meantime when thoughts of death disturb thy head". Lucretius, 6879-0
The messiah. Vergil, 7039-6
Ode ("Descended"). Horace, 6152-4
Ode to Maecenas, sels. Horace, 6879-0
On the nature of things, sels. Lucretius, 6879-0
Ovid offers the would-be rake a variety of devices... Ovid, 6637-2
Palamon and Arcite. Geoffrey Chaucer, 6679-8
Palamon and Arcite; or, the knight's tale. Geoffrey Chaucer, 6970-3
The phoenix self-born, fr. Metamorphoses. Ovid, 6125-7
Plutarch. Agathias, 7039-6
"Rang'd on the line opposed, Antonius brings," fr. Aeneid. Vergil, 6665-8
A sacred grove. Theocritus, 6232-6
Selections. Homer, 6195-0
Sigismonda and Guiscardo. Giovanni Boccaccio, 6970-3
Tales from Chaucer, sels. Geoffrey Chaucer, 6970-3
Theodore and Honoria. Giovanni Boccaccio, 6970-3
"Thus having said, brave Hector...", fr. The Iliad. Homer, 6562-7
To Maecenas. Horace, 7039-6
To Thaliarchus. Horace, 7039-6
To Thaliarchus. Horace, 6527-9,
Veni creator spiritus. Charlemagne (atr.), 6214-8,6730-1
Veni creator spiritus. Unknown, 6152-4,6219-9
Veni creator spiritus. Unknown (Latin), 7039-6
Veni, creator spiritus. Unknown (Latin), 6337-3
"What has this bugbear death to frighten man". Lucretius, 6879-0
The wife of Bath. Geoffrey Chaucer, 6970-3

The **Drynan** Dhun. Robert Dwyer Joyce. 6090-0,6174-5
The **Drynan** dhun. Unknown. 6174-5

Du Bellay, Joachim
Epitaph on a pet cat. Ralph Nixon Currey (tr.). 6227-X, 6511-2
Epitaph on a pet dog. Ralph Nixon Currey (tr.). 6227-X
Hymn to the winds. Andrew Lang (tr.). 6253-9

Hymn to the winds. Andrew Lang (tr.). 6771-9
Rome. Ezra Pound (tr.). 7039-6
The ruins of Rome. 6631-3
Sonnet ("Happy as Ulysses"). Ralph Nixon Currey (tr.). 6227-X
Sonnet ("He who would like"). Ralph Nixon Currey (tr.). 6227-X
Sonnet ("I hate"). Ralph Nixon Currey (tr.). 6227-X
Sonnet ("Newcomer"). Ralph Nixon Currey (tr.). 6227-X
A sonnet to heavenly beauty. Andrew Lang (tr.). 7039-6, 6771-9
Sonnet to heavenly beauty. 6214-8
To his friend in Elysium. Andrew Lang (tr.). 6771-9, 6039-7
A vow to heavenly Venus. Andrew Lang (tr.). 6771-9
A winnower of wheat to the winds. Ralph Nixon Currey (tr.). 6227-X

Du Bridge, Elizabeth Brown
The crimson cross. 6846-4

Du Maurier, George
Limerick:"A young man from Madere arose". Langford Reed (tr.). 6811-1
Limerick:"Il etait un homme de Madere". 6811-1,6811-1, 6308-X
"A little work, a little play". 6109-5
A little. 6889-8
We can do so little. 6684-4

Du bist wie eine blume. Heinrich Heine. 6732-8,6226-1
"Du bois de Ker-Melo jusqu'au moulin de Teir". Marie. Auguste Brizeux. 6801-4
Du sublime au ridicule. Felix E. Schelling. 6936-3
"Du temps que j'etais ecolier". La nuit de Decembre. Alfred de Musset. 6801-4
Du wacher wald. Rainer Maria Rilke. 6253-9
Dualisms. Alfred Lord Tennyson. 6977-0

Duan, Jon
The rout of Belgravia. 6440-X

DuBois, F.R.
The ballad of the overconfident pollywog. 6118-4

DuBois, Rochelle
No. 6 6898-7
No. 8 6898-7
'A palette' 6898-7

Dubiety. Robert Browning. 6123-0,6657-7
A dubious "old Kriss" James Whitcomb Riley. 6091-9
"A dubious, strange, uncomprehended life". A character - and a question. James Ashcroft Noble. 7015-9
"Dubius is such a scrupulous good man". The uncertain man. William Cowper. 6996-7
Dublin afternoon. Richard Eberhart. 6017-X
Dublin bay. Helen Selina Sheridan; Lady Dufferin. 6090-0

Dubonee, Ylessa
Departure. 6178-8
Nocturne. 6178-8

Dubrovnik's wine. Jovan Ducic. 6765-4
Ducal palace. George Gordon, 6th Baron Byron. 6624-0

Ducas, Dorothy
The atheist's wail. 6532-5

Duchess. Lilian Bowes Lyon. 6257-1
Duchess May. Elizabeth Barrett Browning. 6669-0
The duchess of Malfi, sels. John Webster. 6179-6,6369-1, 6125-7,6102-8,6472-8
The duchess of Malfi. John Webster. 6186-9,6208-3
The duchess's white cats. Rafael Mendez Dorich. 6759-X
Duchesse Blanche. Geoffrey Chaucer. 6438-8

Ducic, Jovan
The acquaintaceship. 6765-4
The clock. 6765-4
De profundis. 6765-4
"The desert stretches long and wide" 6765-4
Dubrovnik's wine. 6765-4
The envoy from Dubrovnik. 6765-4
Epitaph in Dubrovnik. 6765-4
The little princess. 6765-4
Madrigal from Dubrovnik. 6765-4
The meeting. 6765-4
My poetry. 6765-4
The poplars. 6765-4
The sea willow. 6765-4
The sun. 6765-4
Twilight. 6765-4

The duck and the kangaroo. Edward Lear. 6459-0,6454-X
The duck and the nightingale. William Ellery Leonard. 6887-1
"The duck flies low over the trees". Food for thought. Carol Spelius. 6857-X
A duck for dinner, fr. Owl's clover. Wallace Stevens. 6751-4
The duck.. Ogden Nash. 6722-0
Ducks. Norman Ault. 6937-1
Ducks. Frederick W. Harvey. 6477-9
Ducks. Clinton Scollard. 6368-3
Ducks and heron. Agnes Kendrick Gray. 6850-2
Ducks' ditty. Kenneth Grahame. 6466-3
Ducks, sels. Frederick W. Harvey. 6395-0,6501-5,6532-5
The ducks. Unknown. 6312-8

Duclo, Estelle
O nations! 6979-7

A dude. Joseph Bert Smiley. 6924-X
The dude. Unknown. 6616-X

Dudek, Louis
Dawn. 6446-9
Europe, sels. 6446-9
The jungle. 6446-9
Mouths. 6446-9
The pomegranate. 6446-9
To a young woman. 6767-0

Dudgeon, William
The maid that tends the goats. 6086-2

Dudley, Anita
Westminster bells. 6331-4

Dudley, Anna May
The sophisticates. 6799-9

Dudley, Dorothy
La Rue de la Montagne Sainte-Genevieve. 6897-9

Dudley, E.L.
The mucker's love song. 6118-4

Dudley, Helen
Song ("I have seen..."). 6897-9
To one unknown. 6019-6

Dudley, Thomas
Lines written at the approach of death. 6008-0
A New England gentleman's epitaph. 6077-3,6176-1

Due north. Benjamin R.C. Low. 6833-2
Due north. Benjamin R.C. Low. 6266-0
Duel. Stepan Shepipachov. 6546-5
The duel.. Theodore Maynard. 6096 X
The duel. Eugene Field. 6135-4,6318-7,6368-3,6735-2,6479-5, 6497-3,6401-9,6692-2,6104
The duel. Thomas Hood. 6183-4
The duel. Harold Trowbridge Pulsifer. 6036-6
Dueling. William Cowper. 6302-0;6385-3
The duelist. Muna Lee. 6397-7
The duenna, sels. Richard Brinsley Sheridan. 6174-5

Duer, Caroline
An international episode. 6274-1
An international episode. 6946-0
A portrait. 6431-0
A vignette. 6652-6

Duer, Caroline and Alice
How like a woman. 6441-8,6652-6

Duet. Erik Blomberg. 6045-5
Duet. Charles Lotin Hildreth. 6441-8
Duet (I sing with myself). Leonora Speyer. 6102-8,6501-5, 6732-8,6076-5,6250-4,6037
Duet from Becket, fr. Locksley Hall. Alfred Lord Tennyson. 6867-7
The duet.. Ella Wheeler Wilcox. 6453-1,6732-8
A duet. Thomas Sturge Moore. 6301-2

Duff, James L.
Dan Collins. 6761-1

Duff, James Leo
Cradle song. 6282-2
Dies irae. 6144-3
The loan of a stall. 6282-2
Mater dolorosa. 6241-5
Refrain for the seasons. 6839-1
To a wood-rat. 6510-4
Upon this rock. 6292-X

Dufferin, Frederick Temple Blackwood, Baron

DUFFERIN

    The black death of Bergen. 6580-5
Dufferin, Lady. See Sheridan, Helen Selina
Duffey, Mrs. E. B.
    Two ways of telling the same thing. 6611-9
Duffield, Pitts
    For sale. 7021-3
Duffield, Samuel Willoughby
    The sabbath eve. 6848-0
    Three good doctors. 6743-3
    Two of a trade. 6373-X
Duffin, Celia
    God's fool. 6090-0
Duffin, Ruth
    The woman's toll. 7031-0
Duffus, R.L.
    Lincoln memorial. 6143-5
Duffy, Grace Imogen
    Love. 6818-9
Duffy, John
    To a child singing by himself. 6839-1
    To the Holy Ghost. 6839-1
    Wall crucifix. 6839-1
    "We have minted her beauty in multitude...medallions". 6839-1
Duffy, Sir Charles Gavan
    Fag an bealach. 6858-8
    Inishowen. 6858-8
    The Irish rapparees. 6858-8
    The Irish rapparees. 6656-9
    The Irish rapparees. 6858-8
    The muster of the north. 6858-8
    The patriot's bride. 6240-7
"Duffy-down-dilly has come to town." Mother Goose. 6739-5
The dug-out.. Siegfried Sassoon. 6332-2,6634-8,6666-6,6665-8
Dugall Quin. Unknown. 6185-0
Dugan, Alan
    From a story in The New York Sunday Times travel... 7032-9
    Pro-nuke blues. 7032-9
Dugan, Caro A.
    An old ship's figure-head. 6798-0
Dugan, Eileen
    Pilgrimage ("Now are the bells..."). 6043-9
    Post war. 6043-9
Duganne, Augustine Joseph Hickey
    Bethel. 6015-3,6113-3,6062-5,6678-X
    Caractacus. 6924-X
    Lament of the widowed inebriate. 6685-2
    On to freedom. 6404-3
Dugas, Marie
    Knute Nelson. 6342-X
Dugdale
    "In the middle part of Britain there is a hideous fen" 7020-5
Duggan, Eileen
    After the Annunciation. 6282-2
    Epiphany. 6282-2
    The name. 6282-2
    St. Peter. 65543-0
Duhamel, Georges
    Ballad of Florentin. 6351-9
    It was a May morning. 6351-9
Duke Jr., R.T.W.
    What the clay said unto the potter. 6184-2
The duke and the tinker. Unknown. 6787-5
"The duke is the lad to frighten a lass". The duke is the lad. Thomas Moore. 6930-4
The duke of Athole's nurse. Unknown. 6185-0
The Duke of Benevento. Sir John Henry Moore. 6152-4
The Duke of Buckingham, fr. Of the ueses of riches. Alexander Pope. 6932-0
The Duke of Buckingham. John Dryden. 6150-8
The Duke of Gloster on his deformity. William Shakespeare. 6543-0
The duke of Gordon's daughter. Unknown. 6055-2,6185-0,6067-6
The Duke of Grafton. Unknown. 6125-7
The duke of Plaza-Toro. Sir William Schwenck Gilbert. 6512-0,6026-9

Duke see the tie pile. Unknown. 6609-7
The duke's layde. Hermann Hagedorn. 6944-4
The dukite snake. John Boyle O'Reilly. 6554-6,6570-8
The Dukite snake. John Boyle O'Reilly. 6915-0
Dulaney, Emma C.
    Honey-bug baby. 6711-5
Dulce et decorum. T.P. Cameron ("Tipcuca") Wilson. 6653-4
Dulce et decorum est. Wilfred Owen. 6357-8,6491-4,6542-2,6666-6,6210-5
Dulceet decorum. E.W. Hornung. 6793-X
Dulcina. Sir Walter Raleigh. 6026-9
Dulciora. Henry Van Dyke. 6961-4
Dulcis memoria. Henry Van Dyke. 6961-4
Dulcken, H.W. (tr.)
    Barbarossa. Friedrich Ruckert, 6614-3
    The Nibelungen treasure. Unknown (German), 6614-3
    The richest prince. Andreas Kerner, 6614-3
"The dule's i' this bonnet o' mine." Edwin Waugh. 6271-7,6302-0,6385-3,6656-9,6219-9
"The dull gray paint of war". The armed liner. H. Smalley Sarson. 7031-0,6846-4
A dull life. Berton Braley. 6853-7
"Dull thunders moan around the temple rock". Champions of the truth. John Keble. 6980-0
"The dull, gray clouds which overhung..earth". Snow. William White. 6868-5
Dull, wretched worms. Henry Vaughan. 6934-7
Dullness. George Herbert. 6641-0
"Duly with knees that feign to quake". Rimmon. Rudyard Kipling. 6810-3
Dum vivimus vigilamus. Charles Henry ("John Paul") Webb. 6004-8,6300-4
Dum vivimus, vivamus. Philip Doddridge. 6385-3,6291-9
Dum-Dum. See Kendall, J.K.
Dumain's rhymes, fr. Love's labour's lost. William Shakespeare. 6436-1
A dumb appear. Jessie Pope. 7010-8
The dumb child. Unknown. 6913-4
The dumb child. Unknown. 6219-9
The dumb soldier. Robert Louis Stevenson. 6401-9,6135-4
Dumb, dumb, dumb. Unknown. 6930-4
Dumbarton's drums. Allan Ramsay. 6328-4
Dumbleton, E. C.
    The Tamil maid. 6591-0,6592-9
Dumbrille, Dorothy
    Christmas, 1940. 6224-5
DuMont, Neva
    Idle hands. 6799-9
Dumfounded. Unknown. 6661-5
The dummy line. Unknown. 6594-5
Dumpy ducky. Lucy Larcom. 6129-X
The dun snake. Harry Noyes Pratt. 66628-3
Duna. Marjorie L.C. Pickthall. 6332-2,6476-0,6732-8,6653-4,6102-8
Dunbar (atr), William
    "Jerusalem, rejoice for joy". 6636-4
    On the resurrection of Christ. 6489-2,6636-4
Dunbar's lament when he was sick. William Dunbar. 6830-8
Dunbar, Mark T.
    Red in tooth. 6900-2
Dunbar, Paul Laurence
    Accountability. 6736-0
    Angelina ("When de fiddle gits to singing..."). 6274-1,6653-4
    At candle-lightin' time. 6254-7,6696-8,6281-4
    A banjo song. 6274-1
    The boogah man. 6653-4
    Chrismus on the plantation. 6281-4
    The colored band. 6891-X
    Columbian ode. 6465-5
    Compensation. 6309-8
    A corn-song. 6431-0
    Corn-stalk fiddle. 6711-5
    Darkey fisherman's rainy day. 6719-0
    Dat ol' mare o' mine. 6510-4
    Deacon Jones's grievance. 6675-5
    The deserted plantation. 6281-4
    Dinah kneading dough. 6441-8
    Disappointed. 6861-8
    Discovered. 6274-1,6300-4,6505-8

Encouragement. 6694-1,6964-9
Get somebody else. 6721-2
"Grave Lincoln bade the raging tempest cease." 6709-3
Harriet Beecher Stowe. 6820-0
How Lucy backslid. 6692-5
Hymn. 6653-4
Hymn ("O li'l' lamb out in de col'). 6266-0,6076-5,6102-8
In the morning. 6714-X
Itching heels. 6714-X
Keep a-plugging away. 6332-2
Lincoln. 6305-5
Little brown baby. 6078-1,6694-1,6505-8
Lonesome. 6465-5
Lullaby. 6006-4,6309-8,6653-4
Lullaby ("Bedtime's come"). 6891-X
Lullaby ("Kiver up"). 6580-5
A Negro love song. 6006-4
Negro lullaby. 7025-6
Ode for Memorial Day. 6340-3
The ol' tunes. 6927-4
The photograph. 6700-X
Po' little lamb. 6700-X
The poet and his song. 6465-5
Rise up early in de mawnin'. 6687-9
The rivals. 6281-4
Signs of the times. 6703-4
Song of summer. 6006-4,6332-2,6653-4
The spellin' bee. 6887-1
Spring song. 6820-0
Time to tinker 'roun'! 6006-4,6691-7
The turning of the babies in the bed. 6365-9
Wadin' in de crick. 6537-6
When all is done. 6889-8,6303-9
When de co'n pone's hot. 6006-4,6365-9,6580-5
When Malindy sings. 6332-2,6707-7,6653-4

Dunbar, Wallace
It's vera weel. 6139-7

Dunbar, William
Ave, fr. Ane Ballat of our Lady. 6324-1
The ballad of Kind Kittok. 6636-4
Ballad of our lady. 6282-2,6022-6
The dance of the seven deadly sins. 6200-8,6102-8
Dunbar's lament when he was sick. 6830-8
The fear of death confounds me. 6881-2
Follows how Dunbar was desyrd to be ane freir. 6430-2
The golden targe, sels. 6378-0,6193-1
The goldyn targe. 6586-4
A hymn of the Resurrection. 6881-2
A hymn to Mary. 6881-2
In honour of the city of London. 6331-4,6150-8,6439-6
Kynd Kittock in heaven. 6733-6
The lament for the Makaris quhen he was seik, sels. 6934-7
Lament for the Makaris... 6150-8,6586-4,6022-6,6430-2, 6472-8,6125-9,6023
London. 6934-7
The man of valour to his lady fair. 6881-2
Meditation in winter. 6380-2
Mirth of May. 6943-6
O reverend Chaucer! rose of rhetoris all. 6301-2,6383-7
On the navitity of Christ. 6931-2
Rorate celi desuper. 6153-2
Sanct Salvatour, send silver sorrow. 6193-1
A song for the hour. 6741-X
Song of the rose. 6383-7
"Sweet rose of virtue and gentilness". 6187-7
The thrissill and the rois. 6198-2
Timor mortis conturbat me, fr. The lament...Makaris... 6934-7
To a lady. 6430-2,6659-3
To the city of London. 6125-7
The tretis of the tua mariit wemen and the edo. 6845-6
Vanitas vanitatum. 6830-8
Welcome to Margaret Tudor. 6088-9

Duncan Campbell. Unknown. 6057-9
Duncan Gray. Robert Burns. 6154-0,6180-X,6198-2,6246-6, 6332-2,6634-,6302-0,6328-4,6385-3,6560-0,6291-9,6737

Duncan, E.A.
The old soldier's story. 6913-4

Duncan, Henry
Curling song. 7035-3

Duncan, J.C.M.
Winter in Canada. 6433-7

Duncan, John Gray
The soul of felicity. 6799-9

Duncan, Lindsay
The Chirstmas guests. 6924-X
Christmas guests. 6676-3

Duncan, Lindsay (Cloud)
Christmas guests. 6768-9

Duncan, Mary Lundie
A child evening prayer. 6137-0
Evening hymn. 6131-1
Jesus, tender shepherd, hear me. 6466-3
The snow-shower. 6373-X

Duncan, Nora M.
The tyrant. 6799-9

Duncan, Thomas
The strolling girls. 6324-1

Duncan, William J.
Right building. 6927-4

Duncan-Clark, S.J.
Victory! 6846-4

The **dunciad** - the description of dullness. Alexander Pope. 6200-8
The **dunciad**, sel. Alexander Pope. 6958-4
The **Dunciad**, sels. Alexander Pope. 6152-4,6195-0,6197-4
The **dunciad**. Alexander Pope. 6198-2;6200-8
Duncton Hill. Hilaire Belloc. 6250-4
A **dune** sonnet. Max Eastman. 6031-5
Dunedin in the gloaming. Jessie MacKay. 6784-0
"**Dunedin** nights are often cold". A small ode on mixed flatting. James Baxter. 7018-3
The **dunes**.. Harry Kemp. 6038-2

Dunetz, Lora
The ailing parent. 6388-8
All that summer. 6388-8
Black cat. 6388-8

The **dungeon**, fr. Osorio, Act V. Samuel Taylor Coleridge. 6332-2

Dunham, Ethel Love
To four mothers. 6799-9

Dunham, Sarah M.
Shut in. 6889-8

Dunievitz, Samuel
The child's soul ward. 6799-9
Walt Whitman. 6799-9

The **dunker's** daughter. James Abraham Martling. 6952-5

Dunkerfoodle (pseud.), Hans von
Hold dot fort, for ve vos coming. 6471-X

Dunkerqure-Paris line. Naomi Mitchison. 6782-4
Dunkirk. Robert Nathan. 6783-2
Dunkirk. Edwin John Pratt. 6224-5
Dunkirk. Laura E. Richards. 6224-5
Dunkirk ("Will came back from school that day"). Robert Nathan. 6224-5
Dunkirk, 1940. Tom Farnol. 6895-2

Dunklee, Mary Vaughn
Sabbath. 6490-6

Dunlang O'Hartigan. Patrick Joseph McCall. 6174-5

Dunlop, John
"Dinna ask me." 6302-0,6385-3,6226-1,6737-9
Oh! dinna ask me gin I lo'e thee. 6086-2,6960-6
The year that's awa'. 6086-2

Dunlop, Lane (tr.)
The butterfly. Francis Ponge. 6803-0
Le parti pris des choses, sels. Francis Ponge. 6803-0
The mollusc. Francis Ponge. 6803-0

Dunmore. Charles Malam. 7030-2

Dunn, Alta Booth
After drought. 6662-3
Drought harvest. 6662-3
Legacy. 6662-3
Prairie earth. 6662-3
Rocky Mountains. 6662-3
Song of summer. 6662-3
Spring climbs high. 6662-3

Dunn, Charles Francis
In olden time. 6983-5

DUNN

A song of the sea. 6983-5
Dunn, Edward S.
    In Pennsylvania's praise. 6936-3
Dunn, Elizabeth Bemis
    Evening. 6799-9
    His presence. 6799-9
Dunn, J. Allan
    Land-fettered. 7007-8
Dunn, Joseph (tr.)
    The combat of Ferdiad an Cuchulain. Unknown, 6930-4
Dunn, Julia Mills
    Carmelita. 6682-8
Dunn, Marietta Hoover
    Our martyred hero, Lincoln. 6708-5
Dunn, S.B.
    Bring laurel. 6709-3
Dunn, William Ashenhurst
    The four voices. 6983-5
Dunning, Ralph Cheever
    Bitter sweet, fr. The four winds. 6531-7
    The four winds, sels. 6531-7
    In the snow, fr. The four winds. 6531-7
    My garden, fr. The four winds. 6531-7
Dunning, Richard Cheever
    Driftwood. 6071-4
    Shadows. 6071-4
Dunoon. Thomas Edward Brown. 6809-X
Duns Scotus's Oxford. Gerard Manley Hopkins. 6052-8,6641-0, 6375-6
Dunsany, Edward John Plunkett, 18th Baron
    A call to the wild. 6930-4
    A dirge of victory. 7029-9
    The great guns of England. 7031-0
    A heterodoxy. 6930-4
    A heterodoxy. 6648-8
    The return of song. 6873-1
    Song from an evil wood. 6872-3
    A song of wandering. 6777-8
    A song of wandering. 6102-8
    Songs from an evil wood. 7027-2
    To a lost spirit. 6648-8
    To a spirit seen in a dream. 6648-8
    To Keats. 6184-2
    To the outermost planet. 6782-4
Dunstan on the death of his mother, fr. Edward the fair. Henry Taylor. 6980-0
Dunstan's account of his temptations,fr.Edward the fair. Henry Taylor. 6980-0
Dunstone hill. Robert Bridges. 6487-6
Duntley, Wilbur
    The turkey of life. 6703-4
Dunton
    The elusive motif. 6817-0
The **duomo..** Edith M. Thomas. 6624-0
Duovir. John Finley. 6184-2
Duplicity. David Ray. 6761-1
The **duplicity** of women. John Lydgate. 6881-2
Dupper, Gertrude Shisler
    Free to choose. 6750-6
Durand. Johann Ludwig Uhland. 6948-7
Durand of Blonden. Johann Ludwig Uhland. 7039-6
Durant, Augusta
    Martial music. 6691-7
Durant, Horace B.
    Christ calming the tempest. 6923-1
    'Dead! name unknown'. 6921-5
    Hugh Gordon's iron mill. 6922-3
    Make room in heaven. 6923-1
    The only true life. 6921-5
    The party caucus. 6417-5
    A shadow from an insane asylum. 6924-X
    A trip to the stars. 6925-8
    What the diver saw. 6921-5
Durban revisited. Ralph Nixon Currey. 6788-3
Durbin, Eliza W.
    Our Washington. 6712-3,6449-3
Durbin, Harriet Whitney
    A little Dutch garden. 6368-3
Durer painting the saviour's head. Jan Svatopluk Machar. 6886-3
Durer's Melancholia. Sir William Watson. 6153-2
Durer's piece of turf. Norbert Krapf. 6966-5
Durfee, Harriet E.
    Four pictures. 6926-6
    Under the old oak tree - Agarland. 6927-4
Durfey, Thomas
    The praise of Christmas. 6143-5
<u>**Durham** field. Unknown. 6185-0,6067-6</u>
The **Durham** lock-out. Unknown. 6157-5
During a chorale by Cesar Franck, fr. To Celia. Witter Bynner. 6897-9
During darkness. Jean Starr Untermeyer. 6345-4
During lambing season. Keidrych Rhys. 6360-8
During music. J.B.B. Nichols. 6230-x
During music. Arthur Symons. 6656-9
During sickness. Mabel V. Irvine. 6269-5
During the day. Paul Celan. 6769-7
"**During** the high noon of time". Translation from a lost language. Minna Gellert. 6979-7
During the quarrel. Unknown. 6116-8
Durisdeer. Lady John Scott. 6180-X
Durivage, Francis A.
    All. 6481-7,6693-3
    The cavalry charge ("With bray of trumpet"). 6113-3, 6016-2,6566-X
    The Christian maiden and the lion. 6412-4
Durkin, Douglas Leader
    A little philosophy. 6796-4
Durnford, Delova
    But I don't know. 6750-6
Durrell, Lawrence
    A ballad of the good Lord Nelson. 6733-6
    Carol on Corfu. 6339-X
    Coptiac poems. 6209-1
    Delos. 6379-9
    Eight aspects of Melissa. 6379-9
    Green coconuts. 6209-1
    In Arcadia. 6209-1
    Nemea. 6210-5
    On Ithaca standing. 6210-5
    Swans. 6209-1
    This unimportant morning. 6379-9
    A water-colour of Venice. 6209-1
"**Durst** thou again say life and soul has lifted." Thomas Lovell Beddoes. 6317-9
Durward, Bernard Isaac
    Good night. 6292-X
    To my firstborn. 6292-X
    To Ping-ku, asleep. 6379-9
Durward, John T.
    Missed again. 6292-X
Duryea, William Rankin
    A song for the 'heart and home.' 6302-0;6385-3
Duryee, Mary Ballard
    And the days were accomplished. 6979-7
    Season of the heart. 6761-1
Dusk. Mabel Crehore Greene. 6841-3
Dusk. DuBose Heyward. 6619-4,6036-6,6326-8
Dusk. Yannis Ritsos. 6758-1
Dusk. Theodore Spencer. 6389-6,6666-6
Dusk. Feodor Ivanovich Tyutchev. 6622-4
Dusk at sea. Thomas S. Jones Jr. 6556-2,6102-8,6431-0,6076-5,6607-0
"**Dusk** fills the room/She sits with the others". My friend in the nursing home. Nancy Woodbury. 6857-X
Dusk from a train window. Cale Young Rice. 6326-8
"**Dusk** gathers. On the seaward hedge". Stranded. E.H. Visiak. 6884-7
Dusk in the desert. Mary Sylvester Paden. 6836-7
Dusk in the low country. DuBose Heyward. 6102-8,6076-5
Dusk thoughts. Countess W. Twitty. 6178-8
"**Dusk,** purpling twilight". Dusk. Mabel Crehore Greene. 6841-3
"**Dusk,** when the heavy clouds are low with rain". The eastern plain. Marion Muir Richardson. 6836-7
Dusk-memories. Ellen M. Carroll. 6039-0
Dusky answer. Jack Conroy. 6906-1
"The **dusky** handwork of the night". Heirloom lace. Lola Greenfield Lawrence. 6799-9
The **dusky** night rides down the sky, fr. Don Quixote...

Henry Fielding. 6328-4
"Dusky skies are fading under nature's stare". Down in the valley. William Fred Sachs. 6906-1
"The dusky sky fades into blue". A paean to the dawn. Bayard Taylor. 6976-2
"The dusky sound/Of a heifer's bell". Little poem for evening. Frances Frost. 7030-2
"The dusky star-set blue of Southern night". The merchant of Venice. Helen Gray Cone. 6848-0
Dust. Dorothy Anderson. 6034-X
Dust. Rupert Brooke. 6234-2,6437-X,6026-9
Dust. Elizabeth Hollister Frost. 6979-7
Dust. Ethel Romig Fuller. 6039-0
Dust. Sister Mary Angelita. 6096-X,6292-X
Dust. Eden Phillpotts. 7014-0
Dust. George William ("A.E.") Russell. 6730-1,6102-8
Dust. William Soutar. 6782-4
Dust. Celia Thaxter. 6612-7
"Dust as we are, the immortal spirit grows". Apparition on the lake, fr. The prelude. William Wordsworth. 6832-4
The dust dethroned. George Sterling. 6102-8,6310-1,6076-5
"The dust flies fast through the murky air". A hot wind reverie, in November. Unknown. 6787-5
"Dust it floats upon the light". The atophier. Eric Silvernale. 6883-9
"The dust of Carthage and the dust". Ballade of dead cities. Andrew Lang. 6875-8
Dust of a dancer. Louise Driscoll. 6396-9
The dust of Timas. Sappho. 7039-6
Dust of time. Virginia Scott. 6799-9
Dust storm. David Morton. 6783-2
"The dust trails on the lonely road". Moravian landscape. S. Prochazka. 6763-8
"'Dust undt dust?' No spirit unto spirit". Shelley. George Frederick Cameron. 7041-8
The dust will settle. Luci Tapahonso. 7005-1
Dust, corpse of time. Jorge Carrera Andrade. 6642-9
Dust, corpse of time. Jorge Carrera Andrade. 6642-9
"Dust-laden, languid flowers droop and fade". In memoriam. Louis J. Magee. 7004-3
Dust-song. Winifred Virginia Jackson. 6037-4
The dust. Nathalia Crane. 56012-9
The dust. Gertrude Hall. 6431-0
The dust. Lizette Woodworth Reese. 6077-3,6653-4
Dustin, Agnes Bardin
   The hill farms. 6764-6
Dustin, May E.
   Could I have borne it?. 6617-8
Dusting. Viola Meynell. 6096 X
The dustman. Unknown. 6018-8
The dustman. Frederic Edward Weatherley. 6135-4
Dusty end. Sir William Watson. 6396-9
The dusty hour-glass. Amy Lowell. 6338-1
"Dusty light falls through windows". Cities behind glass. Linda Hogan. 7005-1
"Dusty moth, your satin wing". Glass. Lucile Enlow. 6841-3
"The dusty records of the bye-gone days". Invocation, fr. The American village. Charles W. Denison. 6755-7
Dutch graves in Bucks County. Wallace Stevens. 6391-8
Dutch in the Medway, fr. Last instructions to a painter. Andrew Marvell. 6933-9
Dutch lullaby. Eugene Field. 6089-7,6105-2,6373-X,6166-4, 6456-6
Dutch lullaby. Howard A. Plummer. 6118-4
A Dutch lullaby. Eugene Field. 7041-8
The Dutch patrol. Edmund Clarence Stedman. 6431-0
A Dutch picture. Henry Wadsworth Longfellow. 6006-4,6105-2, 6732-8,6322-5,6467-1,6004-8,6431-0,6114-1
A Dutch proverb. Matthew Prior. 6092-7,6152-4
The Dutch room. David D. Nolta. 6900-2
Dutch slumber song. Viola Chittenden White. 6653-4
The Dutchess of Monmouth's lamentation for the loss... Unknown. 6157-5
The Dutchman and the raven. Unknown. 6791-3
Dutchman's breeches. Arthur Guiterman. 6773-5
A Dutchman's dog story. J.T. Brown. 6505-8
The Dutchman's family. Unknown. 6175-3
Dutchman's quirk. Arthur Guiterman. 6773-5
The Dutchman's serenade. Unknown. 6277-6,6412-4,6567-8

The Dutchman's serenade. Unknown. 6791-3
Dutchman, Dutchman, won't you marry me? Unknown. 6003-X
The duteous heart. Robert Bridges. 6487-6
"A duteous squire was Fridolin". The walk to the forges. Johann C. Friedrich von Schiller. 6842-1
A dutiful parent. J.G. Francis. 6786-7
Dutt, Romesh (tr.)
   Pushan, god of pasture. Unknown (Sanskrit), 7039-6
Dutt, Tom (tr.)
   The cedars of Lebanon. Alphonse Marie Louis de Lamartine, 7039-6
Dutt, Toru
   Our casurina tree. 6656-9
Dutton, Geoffrey
   The mountain. 6349-7
Dutton, Maude Barrows
   Genius to her poet. 6118-4
Duty. Robert Browning. 6964-9
Duty. Arthur Hugh Clough. 6828-6
Duty. Ralph Waldo Emerson. 6239-3,6250-4,6736-0,6421-3, 6424-8,6585
Duty. L.B. Fritts. 6397-7
Duty. Ellen Sturgis Hooper. 6461-2
Duty. Richard Chenevix Trench. 6793-X
Duty. Unknown. 6385-3
Duty ("When Duty comes a-knocking at your gate"). Edwin Markham. 6291-1
Duty and kindness. Julia Fletch Carney. 6135-4
Duty to death, LD. Dick Roberts. 6666-6
Duty to one's country. Hannah Moore. 6606-2
Duty's reward. Unknown. 6273-3
"Duty- that's to say, complying". Duty. Arthur Hugh Clough. 6828-6
Duvar, John Hunter
   Brown on England's lay. 7041-8
   From Enamorado. 7041-8
   Song from Enamorado. 7041-8
   Twilight song, fr. De Roberval. 7041-8
Duyn, Mona Van
   A Christmas card, after the assassination. 6803-0
Dwarf and giant. William Allen Butler. 6903-7
"A dwarf hops on the rack" Hermann Gail. 6769-7
Dwarf of disintegration. Oscar Williams. 6391-8
The dwarf.. W. Wesley Trimpi. 6515-5
The dwarf. Walter De La Mare. 6596-1
"The dwedrops quiver on the cobweb tents". Sunrise. Robert P. Tristram Coffin. 7040-X
Dwellers of a tide pool. M. Florence Hay. 6316-0
Dwelling in the heart. Tu Fu. 6102-8
The dwelling place. Henry Vaughan. 6337-3,6730-1,6214-8, 6341-1
The dwelling-place. Henry Vaughan. 6931-2
Dwells a maiden. Thomas Noel Wrenn. 6983-5
"Dwells within the soul of every artist". Unexpressed. Adelaide Anne Procter. 6957-6
Dwight, John S. (tr.)
   The landlady's daughter. Johann Ludwig Uhland, 6302-0
   Prometheus. Johann Wolfgang von Goethe, 7039-6,6879-0
Dwight, John Sullivan
   "Sweet is the pleasure." 6302-0
   True rest. 6385-3,6486-8,6737-9
Dwight, Timothy
   The assault on the fortress. 6946-0
   The battle of Ai. 6077-3
   Columbia. 6015-3,6077-3,6302-0,6385-3,6471-X,6286 ,6121-4,6568-6,6288-1,6444-2
   The conquest of Canaan, sels. 6077-3,6008-0
   The destruction of the Pequods, fr. Greenfield hill. 6753-0
   Farmer's advice to the villagers, fr. Greenfield hill. 6753-0
   The glory of Washington. 6449-3
   God bless our native land. 6304-7
   Greenfield hill, sels. 6753-0
   Greenfield Hill, sels. 6008-0,6288-1
   Greenfield hill, sels. 6753-0
   I love thy kingdom, Lord. 6288-1,6219-9
   Love to the church. 6735-2
   Psalm 137. 6121-4
   The smooth divine. 630-4

To the federal convention. 6946-0
The triumph of infidelity, sels. 6288-1
Dwight, Timothy (tr.)
Psalm 137. Bible, 6121-4
Dybek, Stuart
Homage to Giacometti. 6803-0
The **Dyckman** house. Arthur Guiterman. 6773-5
Dye, Robert
Alma mater. 6527-9
Dyer, E.P.
The spelling class. 6915-0
Dyer, John
British commerce. 6932-0
The country walk. 6528-7
English weather. 6150-8
The enquiry. 6932-0
An epistle to a friend in town. 6968-1
The fleece, sels. 6198-2
The fleece, sels. 6932-0
The fleece. 6968-1
Grongar hill. 6024-2,6302-0,6315-2,6385-3,6600-3,6634,
6195-0,6152-4,6129-9,6245-8,6125-7
Grongar hill, sels. 6198-2,6208-3,6150-8
The inquiry. 6968-1
A nation's wealth. 6932-0
The ruins of Rome. 6932-0
The ruins of Rome. 6968-1
To Aaron Hill, Esq., on his poem called Gideon. 6968-1
To Aurelia. 6302-0;6385-3
To his son. 6024-2,6528-7
To Mr Savage, son of the late Earl Rivers. 6968-1
The wool trade. 6932-0
The yellow barn, fr. The country walk. 6545-7
Dyer, Sidney
Work, for the night is coming. 6304-7
Dyer, Sir Edward
Another of the same..., fr. The Phoenix Nest. 6586-4
Contentment. 6134-6,6242-3,6479-5
Corydon to his Phyllis. 6182-6
Cynthia. 6436-1,6191-5
Kingdom. 6315-2,6436-1
'The lowest trees have tops'. 6208-3
A modest love. 6436-1
My mind to me a kindgon is. 6198-2,6332-2,6182-6,6385-3,
6543-0,6102 6250-4,6214-8,6189-3,6230-X,6023-4,6513
,6639-9
Natural comparisons with perfect love. 6334-9
To Phillis the fair shepherdess. 6543-0
The trees ("Behold the trees unnumbered rise"). 6601-1
Dyer, Susan
Zamboanga. 6327-6
The **dyer**. Unknown. 6125-7
Dying. Emily Dickinson. 6754-9
Dying. Jessie Holt. 6144-3
Dying. Roden Noel. 6656-9
Dying. Jiri Wolker. 6068-4
The **dying** actor. Edgar Fawcett. 6410-8
The **dying** Adrian to his soul. Matthew Prior. 6250-4
Dying airman to nature. Frederick Victor Branford. 7014-0
"The **dying** at last of these splendors away". A vision of
Mont Blanc. Thomas Moore. 6749-2
The **dying** bard's prophecy. Felicia Dorothea Hemans. 6973-8
The **dying** bard. Sir Walter Scott. 6438-8
The **dying** beauty, sels. Thomas Holley Chivers. 6482-5
The **dying** boy to the sloe blossom. Ebenezer Elliott. 6980-0
The **dying** boy. John B. Gough. 6744-1,6167-2
The **dying** boy. Unknown. 6045-1
The **dying** boys on the raft. George Gordon, 6th Baron
Byron. 6543-0
The **dying** brigand. Unknown. 6045-1
The **dying** Californian. Unknown. 6058-7,6003-X
The **dying** chief. William Sawyer. 6927-4
The **dying** child. John Clare. 6934-7
The **dying** child. John Clare. 6380-2
The **dying** child. John Clare. 6934-7
The **dying** child. Dora Greenwell. 6502-3
The **dying** child. Unknown. 6752-2
The **dying** child. George M. Vickers. 6918-5
The **dying** child. Carlos Wilcox. 6752-2

The **dying** Christian to his soul. Emperor Hadrian. 7039-6
The **dying** Christian to his soul. Alexander Pope. 6186-9,
6240-7,6337-3,6425-6,6606-2,6692 ,6214-8,6219-9,6301-
2,6543-0,6565-1,6737
The **dying** Christian. Alexander Pope. 6914-2
The **dying** convict. Charles W. Denison. 6755-7
The **dying** cowboy. Unknown. 6057-9,6058-7,6527-9,6732-8,
6003-X,6003-X
The **dying** damsel's doelful destiny: or, true love...
Unknown. 6562-7
A **dying** fall. Thomas Campion. 6935-5
The **dying** favorite speaks. Snow Longley Hough. 6316-0
The **dying** fire. Walter Savage Landor. 6186-9
The **dying** fireman. Walt Whitman. 6322-5
The **dying** Gertrude to Waldegrave. Thomas Campbell. 6302-
0;6385-3
The **dying** girl and flowers. Felicia Dorothea Hemans. 6973-8
The **dying** girl to her lover. Winthrop Mackworth Praed.
6046-3
The **dying** girl. Richard Dalton Williams. 6174-5
The **dying** girl. Unknown. 6752-2
The **dying** gladiator. George Gordon, 6th Baron Byron. 6138-
9,6402-7,6602-2,6424-8,6304-7
The **dying** gypsy's dirge. Sir Walter Scott. 6087-0
The **dying** Hebrew. Thomas Kibble Hervey. 6848-0
Dying heroes. Walt Whitman. 6087-0
The **dying** hogger. Unknown. 6281-4
A **dying** hymn. Alice Cary. 6240-7,6385-3,6407-8,6007-2,6969-X
The **dying** improvisatore. Felicia Dorothea Hemans. 6980-0,
6973-8
Dying in harness. John Boyle O'Reilly. 7041-8
Dying in harness. John Boyle O'Reilly. 6632-1
The **dying** Kafir. George Blair. 6800-6
The **dying** king. Alexander Smith. 6424-8
Dying leaves. Preston Paine Foster. 6906-1
The **dying** lover. Richard Henry Stoddard. 6102-8,6732-8,
6076-5
The **dying** man in his garden. George Sewell. 6246-6,6219-9
The **dying** man speaks. Milton S. Rose. 6836-7
Dying men, fr. King Richard II. William Shakespeare. 6337-3
The **dying** mine brakeman. Orville J. Jenks. 6149-4
The **dying** missionary. Charles W. Denison. 6755-7
"A **dying** mother gave to you". To Mary Field French. Eugene
Field. 6949-5
The **dying** newsboy. Emily Thornton. 6964-9
The **dying** nun. John Vance Cheney. 6327-6
The **dying** of Tanneguy du Bois. Austin Dobson. 6660-7
Dying old and dying young. Susan L. Williams. 6857-X
The **dying** patriot. James Elroy Flecker. 6653-4,6044-7,6224-5,6234-2,6477-9,6393-4
The **dying** pioneer. Brian ("Korongo") Brooke. 6938-X
The **dying** raven. Richard Henry Dana. 6752-2
The **dying** reservist. Maurice Baring. 6785-9
The **dying** saviour. Paul Gerhardt. 6014-5,6302-0,6385-3
Dying scout. William Lawrence Chittenden. 6702-6
"'**Dying** so young, may I retain of youth'". Field burial.
Carroll Carstairs. 6818-9
The **dying** soldier boy. A.B. Cunningham. 6074-9
The **dying** soldier of Joshua. Alexander S. Arnold. 6848-0
The **dying** soldier. Richard Coe. 6403-5
The **dying** soldier. Unknown. 6826-X
The **dying** soldier. John Whitaker Watson. 6774-3
Dying speech of Marino Faliero. George Gordon, 6th Baron
Byron. 6606-2
"The **dying** splendors of the ancient day". Time and the
minstrels. Edward Farquhar. 6939-8
The **dying** street Arab. Matthias Bark. 6407-8
The **dying** student. Charles W. Denison. 6755-7
Dying summer. Virginia Lee. 6764-9
"The **dying** sun/slides over the tiger teeth". Prison
graveyard. Etheridge Knight. 6870-7
The **dying** swan, sels. Alfred Lord Tennyson. 6369-1
The **dying** swan. Thomas Sturge Moore. 6179-6;6246-2
The **dying** swan. Alfred Lord Tennyson. 6977-0,6828-6
The **dying** swan. Unknown. 6125-7
Dying that I might live. Charles Wesley. 6065-X
Dying town. Leslie McDonald. 6799-9

Dying wish. Velimir Rajic. 6765-4
The dying words of Stonewall Jackson. Sidney Lanier. 6753-0,6946-0
Dying words of Warwick. William Shakespeare. 6543-0
"The dying year! the dying year!". Autumn. William Oliver Bourne Peabody. 6752-2
The dying year. Clyde Walton Hill. 6449-3
The dying-day of death. Ronald Campbell Macfie. 6180-X
"Dying? I am not dying. Are you mad?". His youth. Ella Wheeler Wilcox. 6863-4
The dyke-builder. Henry Treece. 6666-6
The dykes. Rudyard Kipling. 6810-3
Dykstra, Helen
    Forgotten wounds. 6662-3
Dyment, Clifford
    Air raid. 6475-2
    "As a boy with a richness of needs I wandered" 6257-1
    Fox. 6257-1
    Hedgehog in air raid. 6475-2
    Man and beast. 6475-2
    News of suffering. 6475-2
    A switch cut in April. 6354-3
    The temple. 6783-2
    The temple. 6475-2
    "To London the train gallops, its shrill steel hooves" 6257-1
The dynamiter's daughter. E. Stanway Jackson. 6922-3
The dynamiter's daughter. E. Stanway Jackson. 6744-1
The dynamo's song. Louis J. Magee. 7004-3
Dynastic tiff. Geoffrey Hellman. 6026-9
The dynasts, sel. Thomas Hardy. 7014-0
The dynasts, sels. Thomas Hardy. 6726-3,6665-8
Dynasty of chimeras. Kassaris Emmanuel. 6352-7
Dynasty of the chimeras. Kassaris Emmanuel. 6352-7
Dyson, Edward
    Peter Simson's farm. 6784-0
    The worked-out mine. 6784-0
Dyson, Will
    Death is but death. 6349-7
    Planet moon. 6349-7
    Planet moon, sels. 6349-7
"Dyvers thy death doo dyverslye bemone" Henry Howard, Earl of Surrey. 6380-2
Dzadourian, Alexander
    The Armenian poet's prayer. 6050-1

E pluribus unum. George W. Cutter. 6909-6
E pluribus unum. George W. Cutter. 6304-7,6294-6
E pluribus unum. R. Priestley Hayes. 6936-3
E tenebris. Oscar Wilde. 6292-X,6144-3,6335-7,6337-3,6489-2,6214
"'E was warned agin 'er". The sergeant's weddin'. Rudyard Kipling. 6810-3
"E'en as all waters seek the sea". Seeking waters. Doris R. Beck. 6799-9
"E'en as the flowers do wither". Song ("E'en as the flowers"). Unknown. 6436-1
"E'en as the flowers do wither". Unknown. 6187-7
"E'en like two little bank-dividing brooks". The lover and the beloved. Francis Quarles. 6830-8
"E'er I begin, I must premise". The vultur, the sparrow, and other birds. John Gay. 6972-X
"E'er the foundations of the world were laid". A thought on eternity. John Gay. 6972-X
"E'ev now, where alpine solitudes ascend". The Alps. Oliver Goldsmith. 6749-2
"'E's a sportsman is our padre". The padre. C.W. Blackall. 6846-4
E. See Fullerton, Mary
E.,A.
    The breath of light. 6873-1
    Mystery. 6873-1
E.,A.L.O.
    Beware of the wolf. 6131-1
    Knights of the cross. 6131-1
    Nature's voice. 6131-1
    The new doll. 6131-1

E.,E.
    In sano corpore. 6817-0
    Who'll tend baby? 6273-3
E.,E.J.
    Toeing the line. 6936-3
E.,G.
    Upon the threshold. 6273-3
E.,K.N.
    A beautiful legend. 6294-6
E.,M.
    What they dreamed and said. 6273-3
E.,N.S.
    My town, sels. 6798-0
E.,R.M.
    "Little lichen, fondly clinging", sels. 6601-1
E.,S.X.
    The bell of old north. 6983-5
E.A.P. - a portrait. Delmore Schwartz. 6850-2
E.B.B.. James ("B.V.") Thomson. 6483-3,6655-0
E.B.B., 1861. James ("B.V.") Thomson. 6046-3
"E.L.M.! the woods as sovereign own thee!". Acrostic ("E.L.M."). James Abraham Martling. 6952-5
E.e. and thee and me. Alex Fraser. 6857-X
E.G. de R. James Russell Lowell. 6230-X
E.P. ode pour l'election de son sepulchre. Ezra Pound. 6527-9,6209-1
E.P.A.. Pancho Aguila. 6870-7
Each and all. Ralph Waldo Emerson. 6006-4,6332-2,6385-3, 6457-4,6501-5,6600 ,6008-0,6250-4,6265-2,6428-8,6288-1,6431 ,6610-0,6730-1,6212-1,6126-5,6121-4,6219 , 6252-0
Each and all. William Shakespeare. 6438-8
"Each beast can choose his fere according to his mind" Henry Howard, Earl of Surrey. 6584-8
"Each city, each/village offers the customary". Postcards. Gerry Shikatani. 6767-0
"Each creation/drawn from the deep hot kiln". Afterbirth (sculpture #4-bronze). Beryle Williams. 6966-5
Each day a life. Robert Service. 6159-1
"Each day when the glow of sunset". Are the children at home? Unknown. 6910-X
"Each dying day, life comes to some new end". Farewell. J. Howard Flower. 7030-2
"Each fearful storm that o'er us rolls". Substance. Alice Cary. 6969-X
"Each for himself is still the rule". In the great metropolis. Arthur Hugh Clough. 6828-6
"Each gesture 'speaks,' light pressing like...". History. Donald Britton. 7003-5
"Each in his hidden sphere of joy or woe". Caroline Leslie. 6238-5
Each in his own tongue. William Herbert Carruth. 6889-8, 6006-4,6076-5,6541-1,6250-4,6107-9,6241 ,6266-0,6104-4,6309-8,6646-1,6104-4,6464 ,6303-9,6161-3,6473-6, 6476-0,6509-0,6615
Each in his separate way. Mary Swain Paxton. 6397-7
"Each in the self-same field we glean". L'envoi to E.W.G. Andrew Lang. 6987-8
"Each man me telleth I change most my devise". Sonnet ("Each man"). Sir Thomas Wyatt. 6584-8
"Each moment/rises up screaming into life". Wind and impulse. Duane Big Eagle. 7005-1
"Each monument holy is". Richard Watson Gilder. 6007-2
"Each morn I wake, each morn I wake". The death-song of Chi-wee-moo. A.H. Chandler. 7041-8
Each morn a thousand roses brings, fr. Rubaiyat. Omar Khayyam. 7039-9
"Each morning there were lambs with bloody...". Foxes among the lambs. Ernest G. Moll. 6761-1
"Each morning when thy waking eyes first see", sels. Anna Maria Wells. 6601-1,6376-4
"Each morning, faces, faces, faces". Faces. Cyprus R. Mitchell. 6954-1
Each new hour's passage is the acolyte. Lord Alfred Bruce Douglas. 6726-3
"Each night before I sleep". To my terrier Rex. Agnes Kendrick Gray. 6841-3
"Each night we hear the sound". Sounds. Paul David Ashley. 6870-7
"Each night when I behold my bed". Secuturus, fr. Clevedon

EACH
448

verses. Thomas Edward Brown. 6809-X
"Each night, each night, as on my bed I lie". The secrets of the clerk. Unknown. 6873-1
"Each night/I take your name". When you're away. Mary Lanigan Healy. 6750-6
"Each of my mothers was beautiful". Flesh of the furies. Minna Gellert. 6979-7
"Each on his own strict line we move". Too late. Matthew Arnold. 6947-9
"Each poem finely chiseled on a page". For the publication of 'The poets' pack'. Estelle Rooks. 6850-2
Each root to separate dwellings led, fr. Tree of time. Gertrude Huntington McGiffert. 6838-3
"Each sabbath eve, as the streets grow dim". In the candle light. Golda M. Goldman. 6847-2
Each satisfied with himself, the animals criticize... Jean de La Fontaine. 6637-2
"Each second that passes, ever within..places". Thus sang the burning stars. Otakar Brezina. 6763-8
"Each tender phrase you whisper". Desideratum. Elena Vossen Greenfield. 6841-3
"Each thin hand resting on a grave". One in blue and one in gray. Unknown. 6912-6
"Each this gem of thought should heed". Kindly deeds. Edward R. Huxley. 6885-5
"Each time I go to her house". Guest. Ruth Eckman. 6750-6
"Each time I return to Johannesburg it is summer". David Wright. 6788-3
"Each time we love". Alexander Smith. 6238-5
"Each time" Edgar Anawrok. 6855-3
"Each wave came on a glittering rippled hill". William Morris. 6997-5
Each year's song. Walter Benton. 6761-1
"Each, after all, learns only what he can". Johann Wolfgang von Goethe. 6238-5
Eades, Frances
    The sheepshearing man. 6799-9
Eager spring. Gordon Bottomley. 6161-3,6430-2
Eager, Cora M.
    The ruined merchant. 6909-6
    Where is papa to-night. 6569-4
    Will the new year come to-night, mamma? 6403-5,6565-1
Eagle. Myra A. Shattuck. 6715-8
Eagle. James B. Thomas. 6073-0
The eagle ("How the eagle does:—"). Timothy Otis Paine. 6274-1
The eagle and the lion. George Frederick. 6274-1
The eagle and the mole. Elinor Wylie. 6393-4,6464-7,6506-6, 6726-3,6250-4,6513-9,6153-2
The eagle and the vulture. Thomas Buchanan Read. 6946-0
Eagle dance. Witter Bynner. 6628-3
"The eagle has passed on!...into the blue". On the death of Woodrow Wilson. Roselle Mercier Montgomery. 7001-9
"The eagle hearts of all the north". The battle-flag of Sigurd. William Motherwell. 6960-6
The eagle hen. Vachel Lindsay. 6206-7
The eagle hunter. Rose O'Neill. 6619-4
"The eagle is my power". The eagle-feather fan. N. Scott Momaday. 7005-1
"An eagle marching on a line". Unknown. 6364-0
"The eagle nestles near the sun". A song of content. John James Piatt. 7041-8
The eagle of Corinth. Henry Howard Brownell. 6062-5
The eagle of song. Bacchylides. 6435-3
The eagle screams. Unknown. 6417-5
Eagle sonnets. Clement Wood. 6036-6
Eagle sonnets, sels. Clement Wood. 6250-4
The eagle swift. Adam of St. Victor. 6065-X
The eagle that ts forgotten. Vachel Lindsay. 6102-8,6076-5, 6581-3,6288-1,6161-3,6121 ,6289-X,6310-1,6602-X,6726-3,6732-8,6300 ,6464-7,6467-1
The eagle trail. Hamlin Garland. 6102-8,6076-5
Eagle valor, chicken mind. Robinson Jeffers. 6666-6
Eagle youth. Karle Wilson Baker. 6051-X
"Eagle! this is not thy sphere!". The wounded eagle. Felicia Dorothea Hemans. 6973-8
"Eagle! why soarest thou above that tomb". Unknown. 6435-3
"Eagle! why soarest thou above that tomb?". Spirit of Plato. Unknown (Greek). 7039-6,6850-2,6648-8

The eagle's journey. Owen (Edward Bulwer-Lytton, Earl Lytton) Meredith. 6943-6
The eagle's love. Shushanik Gourghinian. 6050-1
The eagle's rock. Unknown. 6407-8,6567-8
The eagle's song. Mary Austin. 6979-7
The eagle's song. Richard Mansfield. 6340-3,6358-6,6741-X, 6277-6
The eagle, and the assembly of animals. John Gay. 6972-X
The eagle, sels. Alfred Lord Tennyson. 6239-3
The eagle-feather fan. N. Scott Momaday. 7005-1
The eagle.. Arthur Guiterman. 6532-5
The eagle.. Khanlari. 6448-5
The eagle. Bible. 7020-5
The eagle. Caroline Russell Bispham. 6995-9
The eagle. James Gates Percival. 6820-0
The eagle. Alfred Lord Tennyson. 6110-9,6150-8,6655-0,6421-3,6250-4,6430 ,6153-2,6143-5,6424-8,6464-7,6723-9, 6510 ,6138-9,6083-8,6657-7,6597-X,6073-0,6187 ,6154-0,6558-9,6385-3,6732-8,6438-8,6102 ,6339-X,6369-1, 6623-2,6246-6,6512-0,6466
The eagle. Alice C. Weitz. 7038-8
Eagles. George Darley. 6943-6
Eagles. Elizabeth Woody. 7005-1
Eagles and snails. Stanton A. Coblentz. 6071-4
The eagles of discontent. Antonin Sova. 6763-8
Eagles, fr. Songs of the voices of birds. Jean Ingelow. 6105-2
"Eagles, leave your sky". Broadcast to the scholars in the eyrie. David Ross. 6979-7
"Eagles, that wheel above our crests". The cedars of Lebanon. Alphonse Marie Louis de Lamartine. 7039-6
The eagles. Sir Humphry Davy. 6980-0
The eaglet. Amanda Benjamin Hall. 7019-1
Eamonn an Chnuic. Unknown. 6090-0
"The ear is waked when music plays". Conclusion. Tom Boggs. 6761-1
Earine. Ben Jonson. 6191-5
Earl Bothwell. Unknown. 6185-0
Earl Brand. Unknown. 6057-9,6058-7,6185-0
Earl Crawford. Unknown. 6185-0
"Earl Douglas, brace thine helmet on". The Bruce's locket. ? Strachwitz. 6842-1
Earl Hakon's doom, fr. The deeds of King Olaf. Charles Whitby. 6994-0
Earl Haldan's daughter. Charles Kingsley. 6980-0
Earl Haldan's daughter. Charles Kingsley. 6613-5
Earl Haldan's daughter. Charles Kingsley. 6980-0
Earl Mar's daughter. Unknown. 6055-2,6228-8,6239-3,6558-9, 6067-2,6613
Earl March look'd on his dying child. Thomas Campbell. 6737-9
Earl Norman and John Truman. Charles Mackay. 6656-9
Earl o' quarterdeck. George Macdonald. 6385-3,6438-8,6319-5
The earl of Aboyne. Unknown. 6185-0
The earl of Errol. Unknown. 6185-0
The earl of Mar's daughter. Unknown. 6185-0,6518-X
Earl of Murray. Unknown. 6061-7
The Earl of Surrey to Geraldine. Michael Drayton. 6436-1
The earl of Westmoreland. Unknown. 6185-0
"Earl Richard once upon a day". Unknown. 6518-X
Earl Rothes. Unknown. 6185-0
Earl Sigurd's Christmas Eve. Hjalmar Hjorth Boyesen. 6578-3
Earl Walter. Gottfried A. Berger. 6842-1
Earl, Ellen
    Pickaninny. 6750-6
Earl, Mrs.
    On the death of Mrs. Holland. 6046-3
"The Earle Douglas for this day", fr. Polyolbion. Michael Drayton. 6933-9
Earle, John Charles
    Lo, I am with you always. 6144-3
    Rest. 7015-9
Earle, Octavia
    Our tea-party. 6715-8
Earle, Pliny
    What is it to die? 6482-5
Earle, Virginia
    Time: twentieth century. 6839-1

Earliest Christian hymn. Clement of Alexandria. 6730-1
"The earliest ray of opening day". Early candle writing in Vermont. Daniel L. Cady. 6989-4
Earliest sea song. Unknown. 6732-8
Earliest spring. William Dean Howells. 6007-2,6437-X
Earliness at the cape. Babette Deutsch. 6388-8
Earls, Michael
    An autumn rose-tree. 6096-X,6172-9,6292-X
    The road beyond the town. 6762-X
    To a Carmelite postulant. 6172-9,6292-X
Early. Leonora Speyer. 6780-8
Early adieux. Adam Lindsay Gordon. 6951-7
Early and late. S. Marie Talbot. 6836-7
Early bells. Marjorie Meeker. 6808-1
The early blue-bird. Lydia Huntley Sigourney. 6219-9
Early candle writing in Vermont. Daniel L. Cady. 6989-4
An early Christian. Robert Barnabas Brough. 6437-X
Early chronology. Siegfried Sassoon. 6210-5
Early days in Vermont. Daniel L. Cady. 6988-6
The early dead. Charles W. Denison. 6755-7
Early death. Hartley Coleridge. 6337-3
Early death and fame. Matthew Arnold. 6641-0
Early evening quarrel. Langston Hughes. 6751-4
"An early fire". 'What lack we?', sels. Gudmundur Fridjonsson. 6854-5
"Early I rose". Love song. Unknown (Papago Indian). 7039-6
Early friendship. Aubrey Thomas De Vere. 6302-0,6385-3, 6543-0
The early gods. Witter Bynner. 6338-1
An early Illinois winter. Alex Kuo. 6790-5
Early impression. Andreas Okopenko. 6769-7
Early in the mornin' Unknown. 6609-7
"Early in the morning, when the dawn is..roofs". The milkman. Christopher Morley. 6891-X
"Early in the spring,with the wind on my cheek". The wise frogs. Ethelwyn Wetherald. 6797-2
Early influences. Mark Akenside. 6932-0
Early Irish triads. Unknown. 6090-0
Early love. Samuel Daniel. 6429-9,6226-1,6321-7
Early love of the country and of poetry. William Cowper. 6543-0
Early May in New England. Percy MacKaye. 6006-4
Early moon. Carl Sandburg. 6299-7,6513-9
Early morn. William Henry Davies. 6477-9
Early morning. Kenneth Neal. 6475-2
Early morning at Bargis. Hermann Hagedorn. 6374-8
Early morning meadow song. Charles Dalmon. 6026-9
The early morning ride. Dorothea Gilroy. 7010-8
Early morning test light over Nevada, 1955 Robert Vasquez. 6900-2
"Early morning./Small birds drop from the...". Ojisan after the stroke: three notes to himself. Tina Koyama. 6790-5
The early morning. Hilaire Belloc. 6044-7,6292-X,6246-6, 6423-X,6301-2,6172 ,6102-8
Early news. Anna Maria Pratt. 6368-3
Early nightfall. Scharmel Iris. 6897-9
"An early nourris sits and sings". Unknown. 6111-7
"Early on a Lammas morning". Cumha Ghriogair Mhic Griogair. Unknown. 6873-1
"Early one morning". Unknown. 6328-4,6125-7
"Early one summer morning". Mother. Mary Mapes Dodge. 6097-8
Early piety. Reginald Heber. 6219-9
Early piety. James Abraham Martling. 6952-5
Early pleasure. Ibn Hamdis. 6362-4
Early poems. Arthur Hugh Clough. 6123-0
Early poems, sels. Arthur Hugh Clough. 6123-0
Early rising. Lady Flora Hastings. 6242-3,6131-1,6242-3
Early rising. Carsten Hauch. 6555-4
Early rising. John Godfrey Saxe. 6089-7,6183-4,6255-5,6302-0,6294-6,6404 ,6176-1,6441-8,6610-0,6722-0,6735-2, 6739 ,6300-4,6505-8,6004-8
"The early settler/Stopped to chat". Our busy street. Clara T. Brown. 6906-1
"The early settlers 'round these parts". Vermont stone wall. Daniel L. Cady. 6989-4
Early snow. Ken Etheridge. 6360-8
The early snow. R.D. Dripps. 6983-5
Early spring. William Henry Davies. 6250-4

Early spring. Johann Wolfgang von Goethe. 6948-7
Early spring. Sidney Keyes. 6209-1
Early spring. Edith Sitwell. 7000-0
Early spring. Alfred Lord Tennyson. 6374-8,6597-X,6250-4
Early spring at the woods' edge. Detlev von Liliencron. 6160-5
The early spring brook. Richard Henry Dana. 6077-3
Early spring in Vermont. Daniel L. Cady. 6988-6
Early spring: adagio, fr. Time is a dream. Lillian V. Inke. 6640-2
"Early th fires of life burned fierce and...". To Muffet. Alma Tatum Garner. 6799-9
"Early they took Dun-Edin's road". The camp, fr. Marmion. Sir Walter Scott. 6832-4
"Early this morning, dawn laggard and drear". The bugler. Ernest Rhys. 6783-2
Early thoughts. William Edward Hartpole Lecky. 6174-5
Early to bed. Alfarata Hilton. 6466-3
The early worm. Walter Clarke Rodman. 6936-3
Early, Bruce
    Church. 6750-6
Early, early in the spring. Unknown. 6826-X
"Early, oh very early in the dawn-dusk". Autumn dawn. Helen L. Bayley. 6798-0
"Early/the sun rising over West Virginia hills". The miner. Fritz Hamilton. 6998-3
An earnest cry. Frances Dana Barker ("Aunt Fanny") Gage. 6617-8
An earnest suit. Sir Thomas Wyatt. 6302-0,6385-3,6189-3
Earnestness. Ella Wheeler Wilcox. 6956-9
Earning a dinner. Matthew Prior. 6278-4
Ears in the turrets hear. Dylan Thomas. 6210-5
"Ears that have hearkened to hammers...thunder". Song of the dew. Alexander Alan Steinbach. 6789-1
"Ears to which alone belong". To V-- (2). Louis J. Magee. 7004-3
Earth. John Gould Fletcher. 6033-1
Earth. Alfonso Gutierrez Hermosillo. 6759-X
Earth. Oliver Herford. 6104-4,6583-X
Earth. Laura Riding. 6354-3
Earth. William Caldwell Roscoe. 6656-9
Earth. Unknown. 6724-7
Earth. Brian Vrepont. 6384-5
Earth. John Hall Wheelock. 6031-5,6232-6,6289-X,6338-1, 6565-2,6250-4,6336-5,6161-3,6393-4,6646-1
Earth and air. Frank Ernest Hill. 6038-2
Earth and her birds. Alfred Noyes. 6151-6
Earth and man. George Meredith. 6657-7
The earth and man. Stopford Augustus Brooke. 6090-0,6250-4, 6478-7
Earth and sea. Oliver St. John Gogarty. 6069-2
Earth and sky. Hovhannes Toumanian. 6050-1
"Earth and sky and ocean held their breath". Sir Joseph Noel Paton. 6997-5
Earth and sky, fr. Chrysippus. Euripides. 6435-3
Earth angel. Barbara Young. 6076-5
"Earth bare the long-ridged mountains...". Hesiod. 6251-2
"Earth born they spurn the skies- and soon...". The waters. James Abraham Martling. 6952-5
Earth bows to the new bomb. Aline Badger Carter. 6144-3
The earth cycle dream. Phillip Yellowhawk Minthorn. 7005-1
Earth folk. Walter De La Mare. 6253-9
The earth for all. Gerald Massey. 7009-4
"Earth gets its price for what earth gives us". June. James Russell Lowell. 6240-7,6260-1,6385-3,6465-5, 6479-5,6250-4,6107-9,6104-4,6421-3,6456-6,6481-7, 6575-9,6585-6
"The earth grows white with harvest; all day..". The harvest of the sea. John McCrae. 6833-2
"The earth had put on a green robe". Ibn Sahl. 6766-2
"The earth has blossomed, and far and near". June. Emanuel Leseticky z Lesehradu. 6763-8
"The earth has fallen cold and deep". The burial. Unknown. 6752-2
"Earth has not anything to show more fair". Calm. William Wordsworth. 7020-5
"Earth has not anything to show more fair". William Wordsworth. 6187-7,6255-5,6726-3
"The earth holds out her arms, serene & strong". Polarity. Zola Monk. 6906-1

EARTH

Earth is enough. Edwin Markham. 6335-7;6337-3
"The earth is fair around us". To-day. Ellen Mary Downing. 6858-8
The earth is full of God's goodness. James Montgomery. 6337-3
"The earth is full of brightness". Rocking baby by the fire. Unknown. 6772-7
"The earth is the Lord's , and the fulness...". Domini est terra. Bible. 6830-8
"Earth is the Lord's!". Psalm 024. Bible. 6848-0
"Earth is the Lord's, and the fulness thereof". Psalm 024, fr. The book of psalms. Bible. 7039-6
"The earth is the Lord's..", fr. The Bible. Unknown. 6527-9
"Earth is the spirit's rayless call". 'I would not live always'. B.B. Thatcher. 6752-2
"Earth is too hot and sweet to sleep tonight". Fireflies. Robert P. Tristram Coffin. 7040-X
Earth like a mother. Ethel Johnston McNaught. 6662-3
Earth love. John Drinkwater. 6875-8
Earth love. Beatrice Redpath. 6115-X
Earth lover. Harold Vinal. 6036-6
"Earth now is green". Acrostic ("Earth"). Sir John Davies. 6724-7
"Earth o'erflows with nectared gladness". Wool is up. Garnet Walch. 6768-9,6591-0,6592-9
Earth out of earth. Unknown. 6881-2
"Earth seems as peaceful and as bright". A good day. Phoebe Cary. 6969-X
Earth song. David McKee Wright. 6051-X
Earth speaks. Ethel Case Cook. 6799-9
The earth speaks. Lilian Sauter. 7023-8
Earth to earth. Phoebe Cary. 6969-X,6639-9
Earth to earth. Michael (Katherine Bradley & Edith Cooper) Field. 6274-1,6656-9
Earth to Earth. Unknown. 6134-6
"'Earth to earth, and dust to dust'.". A dirge. George Croly. 6980-0,6407-8
"Earth travails". At harvest. Joseph ("Seosamh MacCathmhaoil") Campbell. 6897-9
Earth voices. Bliss Carman. 6115-X,6843-X
"The earth was a vision of beauty divine". The gift of a rose. John Robert Henderson. 6836-7
"The earth was but a platform for thy power". Newton. Richard Hengist Horne. 7014-0
"Earth was not earth before her sons appeared". Appreciation. George Meredith. 6828-6
"Earth was too small to hold him long". Woodrow Wilson. Harry Noyes Pratt. 7001-9
Earth watch. Louis Hasley. 6017-X
"The earth will stay the same" Frank Ernest Hill. 7014-0
Earth wisdom. Alfred Kreymborg. 6030-7
"The earth with thunder torn, with fire blasted". Fulke Greville; 1st Baron Brooke. 6181-8
The earth worshiped! Catherine Cate Coblentz. 6144-3
"Earth yawned/Really!. Good morning, spring. Mary Morrison. 6750-6
"Earth! guard what here we lay in holy trust". Monumental inscription. Felicia Dorothea Hemans. 6973-8
Earth's angels. Unknown. 6918-5
Earth's breast. Elizabeth Barbara Canaday. 6039-0
Earth's burdens. Ernest Charles Jones. 6656-9
Earth's common things. Minot Judson Savage. 6303-9,6337-3, 6461-2,6585-6
"Earth's crammed with beauty." Robert Browning. 6225-3
Earth's dear vanities. Unknown. 7007-8
Earth's Easter. Robert Haven Schauffler. 6556-2,6177-X
Earth's greatest charms. Unknown. 6097-8
Earth's immortalities. Robert Browning. 6110-9,6383-7
Earth's immortalities, sels. Robert Browning. 6655-0
Earth's joys. Edward R. Huxley. 6885-5
Earth's lyric. Bliss Carman and Richard Hovey. 6890-1
Earth's noblemen. Unknown. 6413-2
Earth's secret. George Meredith. 6828-6
Earth's secret. George Meredith. 6199-0
"Earth's shadow crosses the full-moon". Lunar eclipse. Diane Glancy. 7005-1
Earth's silences. Ethelwyn Wetherald. 6115-X
Earth's victories. James Shirley. 6830-8
The earth's vigil. Gilbert Keith Chesterton. 7014-0

"The earth, all light and loveliness...". Heaven. Unknown. 6752-2
The earth, fr. Nightfall. Lady Margaret Sackville. 6785-9
"The earth, late chok'd with showers". Thomas Lodge. 6181-8;6182-6;6586-4
"Earth, ocean, air, beloved brotherhood!". Alastor; or, the spirit of solitude. Percy Bysshe Shelley. 6138-9, 6110-9,6430-2,6250-4
"Earth, ocean, air...", fr. Alastor. Percy Bysshe Shelley. 6726-3
"Earth, stepmother of the wind". Stepmother of the wind. Preston Paine Foster. 6906-1
"The earth, still drowsy from its hibernation". Spring planting. William Roehrick. 6850-2
"The earth, still heavy and warm...". Nocturne. Archibald MacLeish. 6779-4
"The earth, the sky, the land and sea". The musician. Robert Loveman. 6941-X
Earth, with her thousand voices, praises God. Henry Wadsworth Longfellow. 6752-2
"The earth, with its bright and glorious things." Henry Nutcombe Oxenham. 6046-3
"Earth, with its dark and dreadful ills". A dying hymn. Alice Cary. 6240-7,6385-3,6407-8,6007-2,6969-X
"Earth, you have had great lovers in your hour". Poets. Hortense Flexner. 6776-X
Earth-born. Robert E. Howard. 6218-0
Earth-born. Odell Shepard. 6030-7,6431-0
The earth-born saint, fr. Our sweet singer J.A. Oliver Wendell Holmes. 6934-7
Earth-bound. Theodore Maynard. 6532-5
Earth-breaths. Winifred Virginia Jackson. 6038-2
The earth-child. Gerald Gould. 6423-X
"Earth-loving elms of grace that vie". Octette (004). Edward Sandford Burgess. 6847-2
The earth-mother. John Sandes. 6784-0
The earth-spirit.. William Ellery Channing. 6176-1
The earth-spirit. William Ellery Channing. 6438-8
Earth-wonder. Lucretius. 6102-8
The earth.. Leonard Mann. 6384-5
"Earth/Air/Fire/& water". Mount Tamalpais. Geoffrey Cook. 6792-1
"Earth/tell any child who runs you in...spring". Tell any child. Frances Frost. 6761-1
Earth: the passing of a dancer. Rhys Carpenter. 6959-2
The earth. Edward R. Huxley. 6885-5
The earth. Leonard Mann. 6349-7
Earth?. Otakar Brezina. 6886-3
"An earthen shadow lay on men's endeavors". The flight. Babette Deutsch. 7019-1
Earthen urn. Kathryn White Ryan. 6037-4
"Earthlings will yet do noble things". Through rivers of blood. Sara Adler Rosalsky. 6750-6
The earthly house. Phoebe Cary. 6865-0;6969-X
"An earthly nurrice sits an' sings". The silkie o' Sule Skerrie. Unknown. 6833-2
The earthly paradise, sels. William Morris. 6122-2,6123-0, 6186-9,6287-7,6208-3,6526 ,6199-0,6659-3,6383-7,6110-9,6046-3,6427-2,6656-9,6655-0
An earthly paradise. Percy Bysshe Shelley. 6935-5
The earthly paradise. William Morris. 6198-2,6657-8,6315-2, 6508-2,6543-0
The earthly paradise. W.R. Moses. 6640-2
"The earthly roses at God's call have made". On the death of a pious lady. Olof Wexionius. 7039-6
Earthward. Muriel F. Hochdorf. 6850-2
Earthward. Sarah N. Pulsifer. 6789-1
Ease in writing. Alexander Pope. 6153-2
"Ease is the weary merchant's pray'r". Ode ("Ease is the weary..."). Horace. 6814-6
Easel picture: Decoration Day. Amy Lowell. 6069-2
"Easily as a child that plays...", fr. The Iliad. Homer. 6251-2
Easily given. Unknown. 6418-3
"Easily to th old". Exit. Wilson MacDonald. 6779-4
The East a-callin', fr. Ave Imperatrix. Oscar Wilde. 6427-2
East and west. Matthew Arnold. 6110-9
East and west. Hilaire Belloc. 6723-9
East Anglian bathe. Sir John Betjeman. 6246-6

East Anglian seas and shores, sels. George Crabbe. 6258-X
East coast lullaby. Lady Anne Lindsay. 6833-2
East Coker. Thomas Stearns Eliot. 6209-1
East London. Matthew Arnold. 6337-3,6730-1,6660-7,6655-0, 6430-2,6250 ,6102-8,6110-9,6199-0
East River. Padraic Colum. 6764-6
East Side kites. Berenice Van Slyke. 6808-1
"The east if full of singing". Pilgrimage. Mildred Focht. 6847-2
East wind. Abbie Farwell Brown. 6331-4
"The east wind is blowing". A poem ("The east wind"). Li Po. 6649-6
The east wind. Charles Buxton Going. 6309-8
An east-end coffee-stall. Alfred Noyes. 6151-6
Eastburn (atr.), James Wallis
   Icarus. 6752-2
   Song, fr. Yamoyden. 6752-2
   Yamoyden, sels. 6752-2
Eastburn, James Wallis
   The blind man's lament. 6752-2
   Part of the 19th Psalm. 6752-2
   The restoration of Israel. 6752-2
   The temple of Theseus. 6752-2
   To Pneuma. 6752-2
The eastcoat.. Christian Morgenstern. 6643-7
Easter. Thornton W. Burgess. 6798-0
Easter. Myles Connolly. 6096-X
Easter. Richard Watson Gilder. 6820-0
Easter. Edgar A. Guest. 6862-6
Easter. George Herbert. 6271-7,6328-4,6558-9,6641-0,6438-8, 6177 ,6301-2
Easter. Genevieve M.J Irons. 6177-X
Easter. Emily Pauline ("Tekahionwake") Johnson. 6837-5
Easter. Joyce Kilmer. 6850-2,6897-9,6891-X
Easter. Martin Luther. 6177-X
Easter. Miyoshi. 6027-7
Easter. John G. Neihardt. 6217-2
Easter. John G. Neihardt. 6789-1
Easter. Edwin L. Sabin. 6465-5
Easter. Edwin L. Sabin. 6820-0
Easter. Edmund Spenser. 6186-9,6328-4,6150-8
Easter. John Banister Tabb. 6473-6
Easter. Benjamin Franklin Taylor. 6815-4
Easter. Charles Hanson Towne. 6144-3,6335-7
Easter ("I got me flowers to strew Thy way"). George Herbert. 6466-3
Easter ("Rise heart; thy Lord is risen..."). George Herbert. 6562-7
Easter ("Today unnumbered church bells ring") John Van Brakle. 6144-3
Easter ("With song and sun-burst...") Robert Whitaker. 6144-3
Easter - 1947. Gladys McKee. 6839-1
Easter 1916. William Butler Yeats. 6244-X,6150-8,6209-1
Easter altar-cloth. Julia H. Thayer. 6720-4
Easter angels. Phillips Brooks. 6225-3
An Easter anthem. William White. 6868-5
Easter at Ypres: 1915. W.S.S. Lyon. 7027-2
Easter bells. Ninette M. Lowater. 6171-0
Easter bridal song. Alice Cary. 6720-4
Easter buds. Wood Levette Wilson. 7021-3
An Easter canticle, sels. Charles Hanson Towne. 6337-3
An Easter canticle. Charles Hanson Towne. 6144-3,6266-0, 6303-9,6490-6,6532-5
Easter carol. George Newell Lovejoy. 6144-3,6177-X
An Easter carol ("Flash forth, thou sun"). Christina Georgina Rossetti. 6337-3,6465-5,6466-3,6641-0,6177-X,6143
An Easter carol ("Spring bursts today"). Christina Georgina Rossetti. 6891-X
The Easter children. Elsa Barker. 6954-1
Easter chimes. Virginia Donaghe McClurg. 6836-7
Easter chorus, fr. Faust. Johann Wolfgang von Goethe. 6214-8,6730-1
Easter chorus, fr. Faust. Johann Wolfgang von Goethe. 6337-3
Easter dawn. Frances Ridley Havergal. 6177-X
Easter day. Arthur Hugh Clough. 6198-2
Easter day. Richard Crashaw. 6489-2
Easter day. Josephine Rice Creelman. 6177-X
Easter day. John Keble. 6177-X
Easter day. Dionysios Solomos. 6352-7
Easter day. Edmund Spenser. 6383-7
Easter day. Charles Wesley. 6177-X
Easter day. William White. 6868-5
Easter day. Oscar Wilde. 6624-0
Easter Day in Rome. Oscar Wilde. 6177-X
Easter day, II. Arthur Hugh Clough. 6110-9,6199-0,6430-2, 6655-0
Easter day: Naples, 1849. Arthur Hugh Clough. 6046-3,6102-8,6430-2,6655-0
The Easter day. Martha Snell Nicholson. 6065-X
Easter eucharist. Unknown. 6337-3
Easter eve. Henry Alford. 7015-9
Easter eve. James Branch Cabell. 6337-3
Easter eve. Albert E.S. Smythe. 6796-4
Easter eve at Kerak-Moab. Clinton Scollard. 6578-3
Easter even. Margaret French Patton. 6177-X
Easter even. Christina Georgina Rossetti. 6820-0
Easter flower. Claude McKay. 6880-4
Easter flowers. Unknown. 6225-3
Easter girl. Unknown. 6720-4
Easter gloves ("The rose is red, the violet blue"). Unknown. 6466-3
Easter greeting. Unknown. 6629-1
Easter hymn. Alfred Edward Housman. 6337-3,6536-8,6641-0
Easter hymn. Saint John of Damascus. 6065-X
Easter hymn. Ernest Jones. 7009-4
Easter hymn. Henry Vaughan. 6641-0
Easter hymn. Charles Wesley. 6225-3,6337-3,6214-8
Easter hymn, sels., fr. Faust. Johann Wolfgang von Goethe. 6144-3
An easter hymn. Thomas Blackburn. 6271-7,6429-9
Easter in wartime. Richard Lawson Gales. 6950-9
Easter Island. Frederick George Scott. 6433-7
Easter joy. Daisy Conway Price. 6144-3;6335-7
Easter light. Ida Norton Munson. 6144-3
Easter lilies. George W. Crofts. 6225-3
Easter lilies. Sarah ("Susan Coolidge") Woolsey. 6177-X
"Easter lilies freshly bloom". Mary's Easter. Marie Mason. 6820-0
"Easter Sunday, the children". Dream of spring. Elizabeth Dodd. 6821-9
Easter message. John Van Brakle. 6144-3
Easter morn. Giles (the Younger) Fletcher. 6182-6
Easter morning. Louise Abney. 6143-5
Easter morning. George A. Baker. 6187-7
Easter morning. Phillips Brooks. 6337-3
Easter morning. Winfred Ernest Garrison. 6144-3
Easter morning. Frances Laughton Mace. 6177-X
Easter morning. Louise Chandler Moulton. 6171-0
Easter morning. Edna Dean Proctor. 7041-8
Easter morning. Lilian Sauter. 7023-X
Easter morning. Edmund Spenser. 6337-3,6177-X
Easter music. Margaret Deland. 6144-3,6465-5
Easter must be reclaimed. George W. Wiseman. 6337-3
Easter night. Alice Meynell. 6144-3,6335-7,6668-2
Easter ode, 1915. Alfred Gordon. 6115-X
Easter offerings. Emily Henderson. 6720-4
An Easter phantasy. W.T. McIntyre. 6118-4
Easter poem. John Prichard. 6360-8
An Easter poem for all the year. Herbert Edward Palmer. 6777-8
An Easter poem. Herbert Edward Palmer. 6532-5
An Easter poem. Marion Riche. 6921-5
An Easter reveille. John R. Slater. 6337-3
Easter revelation. Clara Emelia Ullman. 6818-9
Easter rhyme. Unknown. 6312-8
Easter road. Henry Van Dyke. 6961-4
Easter sacraments. Henry Park Schauffler. 6335-7,6177-X
Easter song. Mary Artemisia Lathbury. 6143-5
Easter song. Stuart Merrill. 6607-0
An Easter song. T.W. Handford. 6629-1
An Easter song. Sarah ("Susan Coolidge") Woolsey. 6177-X
"Easter thaws no overwintered mind". Autumn love. John Crowe Ransom. 7017-5
Easter thought. Sister Mary Benvenuta. 6096 X
Easter week. Charles Kingsley. 6123-0,6177-X
Easter week. Unknown. 6930-4
Easter wings. George Herbert. 6527-9,6562-7,6430-2,6341-1,

EASTER

Easter, 1923. John G. Neihardt. 6777-8
Easter, sels. George Herbert. 6208-3
Easter-day in a mountain churchyard. Felicia Dorothea
    Hemans. 6973-8
Easter-eggs. Reginald Wright Kauffman. 6846-4
Easter-tide. Evangeline Robinson. 6764-6
An Easter-tide deliverance. Maria H. Bulfinch. 6177-X
Eastern cry. Mary McNeil Fenollosa. 7038-8
Eastern dancers. Sarojini Chattopadhyay. 6507-4
An eastern evening. Robert Southey. 6980-0
An eastern legend. Grace Duffield Goodwin. 6684-4
An eastern legend. Margaret L. Woods. 6648-8
Eastern morn. William White. 6868-5
The eastern plain. Marion Muir Richardson. 6836-7
An eastern question. H.M. Paull. 6089-7
Eastern shore. Charles Bruce. 6446-9
"The eastern sky is streaked with red". Morning song.
    Eugene Field. 6949-5
An eastern song. Victor F. Murray. 6269-5
The eastern star. Marie L. Marshall. 6799-9
Eastly, Jean J.
    Autumn. 6799-9
Eastman, Barrett
    Chiquita: a legend of the western seas. 6274-1
    How we burned the "Philadelphia". 6062-5,6274-1
    When my turn comes. 6274-1
Eastman, Charles A. (tr.)
    Death of Taluta. Unknown (American Indian). 6396-9
Eastman, Charles Gamage
    The afternoon nap. 6127-3
    Dirge. 6910-X,6219-9
    Evening in summer. 7030-2
    The farmer sat in his easy chair. 6240-7,6632-1
    Of love and wine. 7030-2
    A picture ("The farmer sat in his easy chair"). 6131-1,
        6219-9
    A picture. 6219-9
    A snow-storm. 6302-0,6385-3,6407-8
Eastman, Elaine Goodale
    Ashes of roses. 6431-0
    A countrywoman of mine. 6431-0
    Madonna. 6097-8
Eastman, Mabel Hillyer
    There will be dreams again. 6846-4
Eastman, Max
    At the aquarium. 6102-8,6506-6,6730-1,6076-5,6300-4
    The battle-fields. 6037-4
    Coming to port. 6509-0,6393-4
    Diogenes. 6897-9
    A dune sonnet. 6031-5
    Fire and water. 6880-4
    Hours. 6880-4
    A hymn to God in time of stress. 6532-5
    In March. 6897-9
    In my room. 6880-4
    Invocation. 6102-8,6730-1,6393-4,6076-5,6161-3
    Isadora Duncan. 6880-4
    Isadora Duncan. 6959-2
    Kansas. 6880-4
    Little fishes. 6880-4
    The lonely bather. 6880-4
    A modern messiah. 6880-4
    A praiseful complaint. 6880-4
    A question. 6036-6
    A question. 6036-6
    Rainy song. 6032-2
    Those you dined with. 6880-4
    To a dancing partner. 6036-6
    To a tawny thrush. 6300-4
    To Nicolai Lenin. 6880-4
    X rays. 6880-4
Eastman, Max (tr.)
    Dagger. Mikhail Lermontov. 7039-6
    Message to Siberia. Alexander Pushkin. 7039-6
    The mountain. Mikhail Lermontov. 7039-6
    A sail. Mikhail Lermontov. 7039-6
Eastman, S.A.
    The story of a little red hen. 6690-9
Eastman, Sophie E.
    6177-X
    The little teacher. 6684-4
    A spool of thread. 6678-X
Easton, Alexander N.
    Mad Anthony's charge. 6922-3
Easton, F.T.
    An echo from the 17th. 6505-8
    No wonder. 6505-8
Eastward. Algernon Charles Swinburne. 6153-2
Eastward bound. Sir Charles George Douglas Roberts. 6396-9
"Eastward our ark of government is gone". Into the
    sunrise. Percy MacKaye. 7001-9
"Eastward the valley of my soul was lit". Evensong. T. E.
    Brown. 7020-5
Eastway, Edward. See Thomas, Edward
Eastwick, E.B. (tr.)
    Guardians. Sadi [or Saadi] (Mushlih-ud-Din), 6448-5
Easy. Rudolph Chambers Lehmann. 6155-9
Easy is the triolet. William Ernest Henley. 6527-9
"Easy is the triolet,/If you really learn...". Triolet,
    after Catullus. William Ernest Henley. 6770-0
Easy lessons. Phoebe Cary. 6060-9
The easy wife. Unknown. 6415-9
"Easy, Ned, easy, go soft...". Aristophanes. 6435-3
"Eat! they are cates for a lady's lip". Slave-produce.
    Elizabeth M. Chandler. 7009-4
"Eat, birds, eat and make no waste". Unknown. 6904-5
"Eater weaper, chimbley-sweeper". Nursery rhyme ("Eaper
    weaper"). Unknown. 6179-6
The 'eathen. Rudyard Kipling. 6810-3
Eather, Josephine
    Reno, symbol of the West. 6799-9
Eating. Stephen Crane. 6102-8,6076-5
"Eating alone/I shuffle a magazine". The Bluebird cafe. Jo
    McDougall. 6860-X
Eating lechon, with my brothers and sisters. Luis
    Cabalquinto. 6790-5
Eating song. Sir Walter Raleigh. 6722-0
Eating soup. Unknown. 6278-4
Eaton
    Shadowed. 6218-0
Eaton or Phillip King, Sir John Eaton
    Song ("Tell me not"). 6563-5
Eaton, Arthur Wentworth Hamilton
    At grandmother's. 7041-8
    Ballad of the Gaspereau. 6797-2
    The bridge. 6115-X
    Flood tide. 7041-8
    I watch the ships. 6115-X
    L'Ile Sainte Croix. 6115-X,6591-0,6592-2
    L'ordre de bon temps. 7041-8
    The legend of Glooscap. 7041-8,6797-2
    The lotus of the Nile. 6115-X
    Love-letters. 7041-8
    Old wharves, Halifax, Nova Scotia. 6591-0,6592-2
    The phantom light of the Baie des Chaleurs. 6115-X
    The phantom light of Baie des Chaleurs. 6115-X
    Port Royal. 6591-0,6592-2
    Pray for the dead. 6465-5
    Puritan planters. 6591-0,6592-2
    The re-settlement of Acadia. 6795-6
    The resettlement of Acadia. 7041-8
    Sometime. 7041-8
    The voyage of sleep. 7041-8
    The whaling town. 7041-8
Eaton, Burnham
    Inbound. 6218-0
    Lost voice on this hill. 6218-0
    The unexplored. 6218-0
Eaton, Charles Edward
    American landscape. 6761-1
    The oarsman. 6803-0
    These are the things of youth. 6761-1
    The tree stands tenser. 6761-1
    Tropes of one season. 6218-0
Eaton, Dorothy Burnham
    Essence. 6750-6
Eaton, Earle H.
    When Nelly hangs her stocking up. 7021-3
Eaton, Isaac F.
    Farmer John's Thanksgiving. 6618-6,6703-4

Eaton, Robert J.
    Indian legend. 6249-0
Eaton, Virginia
    Leaf burning. 6750-6
    This day. 6461-2
    The unknown soldier. 6088-9
Eaton, W.A.
    The bridge keeper's story. 6922-3
    The death of the reveller. 6412-4,6617-8
    The fireman's wedding. 6922-3
    The haunted smithy. 6416-7,6167-2
    How I won my wife. 6417-5
    Last token. 6710-7
    My first recital. 6925-8
    My first recital. 6744-1
    A slave's auction. 6690-9
    To my love. 6919-3
    Touch it not. 6617-8
Eaton, Walter Prichard
    The lilac. 6762-X
    Skis. 7035-3
    The willows. 6891-X
The **eavesdropper**. Bliss Carman. 6102-8,6076-5
Ebb and flow. George William Curtis. 6300-4,6309-8,6431-0
The **ebb** and flow. Edward Taylor. 6176-1
"**Ebb** on with me across the sunset tide". Song, fr. Flesh: a Gregorian ode. Edward J. O'Brien. 6762-X
Ebb tide at noon. Gelett Burgess. 6241-5
"**Ebb** tide to me as of the sea!". The old woman of Beare. Unknown. 6930-4
"**Ebb** tide to me!/My life drifts downward...". The old woman of Beare. Eleanor Hull. 6873-1
Ebb-tide. Phoebe Cary. 6969-X
Ebb-tide. Robert Southey. 6302-0
"**Ebbed** and flowed the muddy Pei-Ho...". Blood is thicker than water. Wallace Rice. 6946-0
Ebbtide at sundown. Michael (Katherine Bradley & Edith Cooper) Field. 6844-8
Eben Picken, bookseller. William Douw Lighthall. 6433-7
"**Ebenezer** Eastman, of Gilmanton, is dead". Mary Butler's ride. Benjamin Franklin Taylor. 6815-4
Eberhardt, John J.
    Prepetual motion. 6040-0
Eberhart, Gilbert L.
    The fife. 6924-X
Eberhart, Joanna
    Spring in the Rockies. 6799-9
Eberhart, Richard
    Dam Neck, Virginia. 6666-6
    The dream. 6390-X
    Dublin afternoon. 6017-X
    The fury of aerial bombardment. 6666-6
    The groundhog. 6399-3,6389-6,6666-6,6209-1
    Hand-view. 6390-X
    In the garden. 6388-8
    Iowa summer. 6803-0
    Ives. 6803-0
    Kafka's America. 6390-X
    The largess. 6390-X
    The lost children. 6388-8
    A meditation. 6389-6
    of truth: the protagonist speaking. 6391-8
    The preacher sought to find out acceptable words. 6666-6
    The soul longs to return whence it came. 6641-0,6389-6
    Speech from a play. 6391-8
    A stone. 6388-8
    Testimony. 7032-9
    Trying to read through my writing. 6803-0
    Trying to sleep late on a saturday morning in November. 6803-0
    World War. 6666-6
Eberhart, Richard (tr.)
    On the Lacedaemonian dead at Plataea. Simonides, 6665-8
    The Thermopylae ode. Simonides, 6665-8
Eberstein, Myrtle
    Song of a woman with twins. 6034-X
Ebert, ?
    Schwerting the Saxon. Elizabeth Craigmyle (tr.). 6842-1
Ebo. A.C. Gordon. 6675-5

Ebony and ivory. Ibn Hamdin. 6362-4
Ebony rhythm. Hood C. Butler. 6178-8
Ebright, Frederick
    Checkmate. 6017-X
    Letter from exile. 6761-1
    Memorial to the great big...self-sacrificing advertisers. 6666-6
"**ecce** autem duro fumans sub vomere taurus". One shall be taken. Vergil. 7020-5
Ecce domisti. Bible. 6830-8
Ecce homo. John Ackerson. 6337-3
Ecce homo. Witter Bynner. 6730-1
Ecce homo. David Gascoyne. 6210-5,6379-9
Ecce homo! Edith Albert. 6847-2
Ecce in deserto. Henry Augustin Beers. 6431-0
Ecce puer. James Joyce. 6536-8
Eccentric. Unknown. 6936-3
Eccentric ballet. Marya Alexandrovna Zaturenska. 6761-1
"An **eccentric** old lady of Rhyl". Limerick:"An eccentric old lady of Rhyl". Unknown. 6811-1
"An **eccentric** old person of Slough". Limerick:"An eccentric old person of Slough". George Robey. 6811-1
Eccles, Walter
    Not understood. 6461-2
Ecclesiastes. Morris Bishop. 6036-6
Ecclesiastes. Thomas Edward Brown. 6809-X
Ecclesiastes in the metre of Omar. William Byron Forbush. 6848-0
Ecclesiastes, sels. Bible. 6282-2,6490-6,6143-5
Ecclesiastical sonnets, sels. William Wordsworth. 6867-7
Ecclesiasticus. Donald Davidson. 6037-4,6326-8
Ecclesiasticus, sels. Bible. 6252-0
Ecclesiaticus, sels. Unknown. 6282-2
Ecclestone-Mackay, Isabel
    Dream people. 6433-7,6648-8
Ecco il santo. Katharine Lee Bates. 6532-5
Echetlos. Robert Browning. 6657-7,6110-9
Echo. Archias. 6435-3
Echo. Dorothy F. Blackwell. 6178-8
Echo. Walter De La Mare. 6905-3
Echo. Louise Fischer. 6850-2
Echo. L.V. Hall. 6049-8
Echo. John Milton. 6150-8
Echo. Thomas Moore. 6174-5,6244-X,6086-2
Echo. Christina Georgina Rossetti. 6226-1,6508-2,6655-0, 6246-6,6315-2,6328-4,6526-0,6641-0,6657
Echo. John Godfrey Saxe. 6089-7,6277-6,6302-0,6385-3,6613-2,6732-,6724-7,6964-9
Echo. Sir Philip Sidney. 6584-8
Echo and silence. Sir Samuel Egerton Brydges. 6240-7,6086-2,6291-9
Echo and the ferry. Jean Ingelow. 6183-4,6669-0,6574-0, 6114-1
Echo and the lover. Unknown. 6385-3
An **echo** from the 17th. F.T. Easton. 6505-8
An **echo** from Willowwood. Christina Georgina Rossetti. 6656-9
The **echo** in the heart. Henry Van Dyke. 6961-4
The **echo** of a song. James William Foley. 6889-8
Echo of an agon. Mark White. 6893-6
"The **echo** of the whole sea's speech". Dante Gabriel Rossetti. 6997-5
The **echo** of Victor Hugo, sels. Francis Thompson. 6339-X
Echo turned to stone. Vasko Popa. 6758-1
Echo's dirge for Narcissus. Ben Jonson. 6153-2
Echo's lament for NArcissus. Ben Jonson. 6737-9,6189-3
Echo's secret. Unknown. 6116-8
Echo's song. Ben Jonson. 6099-4,6315-2
Echo, fr. Comus. John Milton. 6933-9
Echo-song. Felicia Dorothea Hemans. 6973-8
An **echo**. Sir William Alexander; Earl of Stirling. 6134-6
An **echo**. Jonathan Swift. 6278-4
An **echo**. Grace Hyde Trine. 6076-5
Echoed music. Ruth Peiter. 6906-1
Echoes. Walter De La Mare. 6780-8
Echoes. Charles Lutwidge ("Lewis Carroll") Dodgson. 6724-7
Echoes. William Ernest Henley. 6315-2,6250-4
Echoes. Ruth Lambert Jones. 6762-X
Echoes. Thomas Moore. 6302-0;6385-3;6246-6

Echoes. Adelaide Anne Procter. 6957-6
Echoes. Mary Ellen Tanner. 6270-9
Echoes from camp Upton. Irving Brenner. 7007-8
Echoes from the Sabine farm. Eugene and Roswell Martin Field. 6949-5
"The echoes of Sumter had thrilled...land". O'Branigan's drill. William W. Fink. 6918-5
Echoes of a silver flute. Zola Monk. 6906-1
Echoes of Jesus. Lucille Coleman. 6144-3
Echoes of love's house. William Morris. 6844-8
Echoes of New York. Anna Elizabeth Hedman. 6764-6
Echoes of Philae. H. Thompson Rich. 6039-0
Echoes, sels. William Ernest Henley. 6123-0,6258-X,6508-2
The echoing green. William Blake. 6086-2,6454-X,6371-3, 6491-4,6195-0,6152 ,6018-8,6138-9,6179-6,6228-8,6236-9,6466
Eckel, Elizabeth
    The tired missionary. 6761-1
Eckman, Ruth
    Guest. 6750-6
    Puddles. 6750-6
The eclat of death. Emily Dickinson. 6879-0
Eclipse. Al-Ghassani. 6362-4
Eclipse. Gene Seville Cook. 6799-9
Eclipse. William Carson Fagg. 6870-7
Eclipse. Edward Farquhar. 6939-8
Eclipse. Edgar A. Guest. 6869-3
Eclipse. Jessie Haefner. 6799-9
Eclipse. Frances Montague. 6316-0
An eclipse. Pindar. 6435-3
The eclipse. James Abraham Martling. 6952-5
The ecliptic: cancer, or, the crab, sels. Joseph Gordon Macleod. 6379-9
Eclogue. John Crowe Ransom. 6039-0,6071-4
Eclogue. George Wither. 6191-5
Eclogue by a five-barred gate. Louis MacNeice. 6536-8,6354-3
An eclogue for Christmas. Louis MacNeice. 6209-1,6645-3
Eclogue of the liberal and the poet. Allen Tate. 6389-6
An eclogue to Mr. Johnson. Thomas Randolph. 6562-7
Eclogue: a man, a woman, Sir Roger. Thomas Chatterton. 6086-2
Eclogue: Elinoure and Juga. Thomas Chatterton. 6086-2
Eclogue: Robert and Raufe. Thomas Chatterton. 6086-2
Eclogues. John Gay. 6972-X
The eco. Unknown. 6312-8
Ecob, J.H.
    The dreamer and reaper. 6049-8
Ecologue. Michael Drayton. 6436-1
Ecologue. Jaroslav Vrchlicky. 6763-8
Ecologue 015, sels. Luis de Camoens [or Camoes]. 6973-8
Ecologue of Virgil. Nahum Tate. 6867-7
An ecologue. Vergil. 6949-5
An economical man. Sam Walter Foss. 6702-6
Economics. Steve Semler. 6883-9
Economy. John ("Peter Pindar") Wolcott. 6278-4
"Economy's a very useful broom". Overdone economy. John ("Peter Pindar") Wolcott. 6926-6
"Ecoutez la chanson bien douce" Paul Verlaine. 6801-4
Ecrit en exil. Victor Hugo. 6801-4
The ecstacy, sels. John Donne. 6317-9,6339-X
"Ecstasie, rash production of the thoughts". Errors of ecstasoe, sel. George Darley. 6930-4
Ecstasy. Mrs. H.H.A. Beach. 6764-6
Ecstasy. Matthias Jochumsson. 6283-0
Ecstasy. Eric Mackay. 6656-9
Ecstasy. Frances Dell Moore. 6799-9
Ecstasy. Sarojini Naidu. 6019-6
Ecstasy. Harold Trowbridge Pulsifer. 6102-8,6501-5,6076-5
Ecstasy. Rachel Annand Taylor. 6269-5
Ecstasy. Walter James Turner. 6477-9
The ecstasy. John Donne. 6186-9,6315-2,6536-8,6438-8
Ecstatic ode on vision. Richard Hughes. 6250-4
The ecstatic. Cecil Day Lewis. 6625-9
Ed. Eugene Field. 6949-5
Ed and Sid and Bernard. Edward MacDuff. 6290-3
"Ed was a man that played for keeps". Ed. Eugene Field. 6949-5
Ed's boots. Brad Gooch. 7003-5
Eddi's service Rudyard Kipling. 6655-0

Eddie visits the barber. Emma Celia & Lizzie J. Rook. 6137-0
"The eddies swirl in the treacherous ford". The pony express. Arthur Chapman. 7010-8
Eddy and Davy have teeth and teeth. Ann Buddy. 6249-0
Eddy, Roy
    To Father Lucien Galtier. 6799-9
Edelweiss. Emily Dickinson. 6578-3
Edelweiss. Warren Pease. 6274-1
Edelweiss. Count Carl Snoilsky. 6045-5
The edelweiss. John E. Barrett. 6840-5
Eden. Nathaniel Burt. 6761-1
Eden. Thomas Traherne. 6536-8
Eden bower. Dante Gabriel Rossetti. 6828-6
Eden remembered. Robert Browning. 7020-5
"Eden's smile my vineyard wore". Unknown. 6050-1
Eden, Guy
    Camp fire musings. 6591-0,6592-9
    The stockrider. 6591-0,6592-9
    The water-bellow. 6591-0,6592-9
Eden, Helen Parry
    The admonition: to Betsey. 7029-9
    An afterthought on apples. 6096-X
    The ascent. 6785-9
    The confessional. 6172-9,6292-X
    The distraction. 6096-X
    An elegy. 6172-9,6292-X
    A parley with grief. 6096-X
    A purpose of amendment. 6172-9,6292-X,6172-9
    Put up again thy sword into its place. 6339-X
    Sir bat-ears. 6510-4
    Sorrow. 6172-9,6292-X
    To Betsey-Jane, on her desiring to go incontinently... 6044-7
    An upland station. 6421-3
Eden-hunger. Sir William Watson. 6338-1
Eden: or one view of it. Theodore Spencer. 6390-X
Edgar A. Guest. Louis Untermeyer. 6527-9
Edgar Allan Poe. Robert H. Barlow. 6218-0
Edgar Allan Poe. DuBose Heyward. 6036-6
Edgar Allan Poe. Clifford Lanier. 6465-5
Edgar Allen Poe: Little Miss Muffet. Charles Powell. 6982-7
Edgar's defiance of Edmund. William Shakespeare. 6543-0
Edgar's wife. Phoebe Cary. 6865-0;6969-X
Edgar, J.D. (tr.)
    Saguenay. Louis Frechette, 6795-6
Edgar, Sir James
    This Canada of ours. 6224-5
    Canadian camping song. 6591-0,6592-2
    The Canadian song-sparrow. 6795-6
    The Canadian whitethroat. 6591-0,6592-2
    The white-throated sparrow. 6793-X
Edge. Charlotte Farrington Babcock. 6253-9
The edge of doom. Alice Cary. 6865-0;6969-X
Edge of the mountain. Ilse Aichinger. 6769-7
The edge of the swamp. William Gilmore Simms. 7017-5
The edge of the world, fr. Orithyia. Sophocles. 6435-3
The edge of the world. Mary Fanny Youngs. 6368-3
The edge of words. Peter Handke. 6769-7
Edge, Mary Allen
    Beginnings. 6037-4
Edge, Maude Brannon
    A passing thought. 6270-9
The edge. Ken Norris. 6767-0
The edge. Lola Ridge. 6930-4
The edgecumbe group. Arthur A. Greve. 6857-X
Edged tools. Edmund Clarence Stedman. 6735-2,6652-6
"Edgehill, red sun on stubble, steel blades ...". Alfred Noyes. 6298-9
Edgerton, James Arthur
    The coming race. 6836-7
    My creed. 6836-7
    Old-fashioned philosophy. 6109-5
    The poet. 6836-7
    When Lincoln died. 6708-5
Edgett, Edwin Francis
    For Belgium, fr. Masquerades. 6032-3
    Masquerades, sels. 6032-3
    Old books for new. 6032-3,6476-0

Thus spake the prophet Isaiah, fr. Masquerades. 6032-3
"Edi be thu, hevene queene". In praise of Mary. Unknown. 6881-2
Edifying reflections of a tobacco smoker. Unknown. 6453-1
Edinburgh. Arthur Guiterman. 6331-4,6722-0
Edinburgh. Alfred Noyes. 6151-6,6331-4,6439-6,6631-3
Edinburgh. Alexander Smith. 6180-X
Edinburgh after Flodden. William Edmonstoune Aytoun. 6219-9,6370-5,6263-6
Edinburgh in autumn. Christine Orr. 6269-5
The Edinburgh reviewers. James and Horace Smith. 6760-3
Edith alseep. Sara Coleridge. 6233-4
Edith and Harold. Arthur Gray Butler. 6437-X
Edith Cavell. Laurence Binyon. 7026-4
Edith Cavell. McLandburgh Wilson. 6846-4
Edith Cavell. George Edward Woodberry. 6030-7
Edith's lesson. Margaret Sangster. 6965-7
Edith's secret. J.K. Ludlum. 6314-4
Edith, fr. Records of woman. Felicia Dorothea Hemans. 6973-8
"Edith, it seems to me life is so brief". To Edith. Cora Fabri. 6876-6
Editor. Glenna Luschei. 6792-1, 6998-3
Editor Whedon. Edgar Lee Masters. 6897-9
"Editor ate too much; the editor ate too long". A vision. Jessie T. Craig. 6925-8
"An editor in Kankakee". 'Yours fraternally'. Eugene Field. 6949-5
An editor's first-born. George Washington Cable. 6004-8
The editor's wooing. Robert Henry ("Orpheus C. Kerr") Newell. 6089-7
Edlesborough. Anne Ridler. 6379-9
Edman, Irwin
    Eternity. 6879-0
    Gentlemen, be abolished! 6761-1
    Intermission, please! 6722-0
    A little bow to books on how to. 6722-0
    Lux aeterna. 6619-4
    To Henry David Thoreau. 6722-0
Edmeston, James
    An evening blessing. 6065-X
    Prayer to the Trinity. 6656-9
    Saviour, breathe an evening blessing. 6461-2
Edminson, V.L.
    Temper in October. 6477-9
Edmison, Lillian M.
    Possessions. 6270-9
Edmonds, J.M. (tr.)
    Best days. Unknown (Greek), 6435-3
    Blind man's bluff. Unknown (Greek), 6435-3
    For the sheaf. Unknown (Greek), 6435-3
    Here we go gathering. Unknown (Greek), 6435-3
    "I go a-hunting a Copper Fly". Unknown, 6435-3
    Immortality conferred in vain. Theognis, 6435-3
    Leave a kiss within the cup. Agathias Scholasticus, 6435-3
    Night. Sappho, 6435-3
    "A sheaf, a sheaf, send, send a great sheaf". Unknown, 6435-3
    Tortoise in the shell. Unknown (Greek), 6435-3
    "Turtle-tortle, what dost thou there". Unknown, 6435-3
    "Two days are the best of a man's wedded life". Unknown, 6435-3
    "Where are my roses, where are my violets". Unknown, 6435-3
Edmonds, Paul
    Elizabeth O'Grady. 6937-1
    A farmer went to market. 6937-1
    Little Tommy Tiddler. 6937-1
    Sleepy-head. 6937-1
Edmondson, Miriam Rees
    The dream-ship. 6118-4
Edmondston, J.
    Forgiveness. 6049-8
Edmund Burke's attack on Warren Hastings. John ("Peter Pindar") Walcott. 6278-4
Edmund Burke, fr. Retaliation. Oliver Goldsmith. 6188-5, 6250-4,6150-8
Edmund Clarence Stedman. Henry Van Dyke. 6961-4
Edmund Pollard. Edgar Lee Masters. 6754-9,6879-0

"Edmund! thy grave with aching eye I scan". Lines to a friend who died of a frenzy fever. Samuel Taylor Coleridge. 6967-3
Edmund' song, fr. Rokeby. Sir Walter Scott. 6604-6,6660-7
Edmund, Father C.P. See Hill, Benjamin D.
Edmunds, Maurice
    The porter's story. 6451-5
Edmunds, Murrell
    Epitaphs. 6042-0
Edna's birthday. Emma Celia & Lizzie J. Rook. 6137-0
Edom o' Gordon. Unknown. 6055-2,6056-0,6180-X,6600-3,6067-6
Edsall, Florence Small
    To a cat purring. 6120-6
Edson, C. L.
    Ravin's of piute poet Poe. 7007-8
    Young Mark Twain. 7007-8
Edson, C.L.
    April on the half moon mountain. 6615-1
    Butchering day. 6615-1
    The farmer. 6615-1
    In idol-smashing land. 6615-1
    My sage-brush girl. 6615-1
    The prairie pioneers. 6615-1
    The promise of bread. 6615-1
    The real foreign invasion. 6615-1
    A regular dry spell. 6615-1
    Sunflowers. 6615-1
    Threshing time. 6615-1
Edson, Charles S.
    Ravin's of Piute poet Poe. 6464-7
Edson, George T. and C.L.
    Out of the Kansas dust. 6615-1
Edson, J.B.
    It will be a Kansas year. 6615-1
    Joy in the corn belt. 6615-1
Educated. Unknown. 6983-5
Education. Arthur Guiterman. 6337-3
Education. Virginia Woods Mackall. 6037-4
Education. Angela Morgan. 6184-2
The education of nature. William Wordsworth. 6246-6,6302-0, 6385-3,6634-8
Education's martyr. May Kendall. 7037-X
Educational courtship. Unknown. 6919-3
Educational courtship. Unknown. 6167-2
Edward. Unknown. 6052-8,6058-7,6154-0,6185-0,6180-X,6488 , 6646-1,6153-2,6150-8,6430-2,6193-1,6645 ,6458-2,6491-4
Edward ("How came this blood on your sleeve.") Unknown. 6061-7
Edward ballad. Unknown. 6061-7
Edward Graves. Andrew Nelson Lytle. 6039-0
Edward Gray. Alfred Lord Tennyson. 6437-X,6165-6
The Edward Hopper retrospective. Tony Quagliano. 6966-5
Edward II. Christopher Marlowe. 6679-8
Edward II, sels. Christopher Marlowe. 6189-9;6369-1
Edward Millington. Richard Church. 6257-1
Edward the Third, sels. Unknown. 6317-9
Edward Weston in Mexico City. Philip Dacey. 6966-5
Edward, Edward. Unknown. 6055-2,6056-0,6271-7,6328-4,6395-0,6634 ,6726-3,6518-4,6107-9,6067-0,6219-9
Edwardes, Richard
    Amantium irae amoris redintegratio. 6436-1,6383-7,6301-2
    May. 6334-9,6436-1,6334-9,6383-7
Edwardine, Sister M.
    Ad Mariam. 6543-0
    Madonna remembers. 6543-0
Edwardine, Sister Mary
    For a novice. 6761-1
    Possessions. 6761-1
Edwards, Amelia Blandford
    "Give me three grains of corn, mother." 6302-0,6385-3, 6403-5
Edwards, Archie
    What though the dark! 6065-X
Edwards, B.M.
    God, make my life a little light. 6303-9
Edwards, Donald Earl
    The cross. 6144-3

EDWARDS

Faith. 6144-3
Edwards, E. Evans
    The modern Cain. 6403-5
Edwards, Eli
    The Harlem dancer. 6032-3
    The Harlem dancer. 6959-2
    Invocation ("Ancestral Spirit, hidden from my sight") 6032-3
Edwards, Emilia
    'Fill that cookie jar, ma'. 6894-4
Edwards, Ethel Ashton
    The return. 6648-8
    The return. 6778-6
    To my beloved dead. 6777-8
Edwards, H.L.R.
    From knees up, Muvver Brown. 6360-8
    Lugano, August 1937. 6360-8
    Museum portico. 6360-8
Edwards, H.S.
    The old canteen. 6576-7
Edwards, John
    Clouds. 6799-9
Edwards, John R.
    The war: A-Z. 6089-7
Edwards, Jonathan, D.D.
    "When a man can live apart". 6238-5
Edwards, Mary Stella
    The choice. 6070-6
    Vanished. 6780-8
Edwards, Matilda C.
    My mother at the gate. 6914-2
    My mother at the gate. 6097-8
Edwards, Oliver
    The cat and the man. 6511-2
Edwards, Richard
    Amantium irae amoris..., fr. The paradise of dainty... 6182-6,6315-2,6586-4
    The falling out of faithful friends. 6934-7
    Of women. 6182-6
Edwards, Thomas
    Sonnet: On a family picture. 6152-4
"**Edwin** Robinson is dead". Edwin Arlington Robinson. Robert Paul Turbeville. 7016-7
Edwin and Angelina. Oliver Goldsmith. 6142-7,6152-4,6543-0
Edwin and Emma. David Mallet [or Malloch]. 6543-0
Edwin and Paulinus. Unknown. 6385-3
Edwin Arlington Robinson. Harry Elmore Hurd. 6042-0
Edwin Arlington Robinson. Edwin Carty Ranck. 6033-1
Edwin Arlington Robinson. Robert Paul Turbeville. 7016-7
Edwin Morris; or, the lake. Alfred Lord Tennyson. 6977-0
Edwin the fair, sels. Henry Taylor. 6980-0
Edwin the Fair, sels. Sir Henry Taylor. 6656-9
Eede, Ruth
    For Rhodo. 6906-1
    The lanthorn. 6906-1
    Now I have lost you. 6906-1
    Portrait of a fruitless prophet. 6906-1
    Quest. 6906-1
Eedes, Richard
    Of man and wife. 6182-6
The **eemis-stane**. Christopher M. ("Hugh MacDiarmid") Grieve. 6379-9
Een Napoli. Thomas Augustine Daly. 6266-0,6396-9
Ef I needs de money. Julia Johnson Davis. 6761-1
"**Ef** here ain't a terbaker spit...". An old woman's complaint. R.L. Roys. 6918-5
The **effect** of example. John Keble. 6337-3,6478-7
Effect of oratory upon a multitude. George Croly. 6980-0
Effect of the ocean...on the mind of the buccaneer... Richard Henry Dana. 6752-2
The **effect**. Siegfried Sassoon. 6542-2
An **effective** narration. Unknown. 6929-0
The **effects** of age. Walter Savage Landor. 6874-X
Effects of spring. J. Wilson. 6049-8
Efficiency. Felix E. Schelling. 6443-4
Efficiency expert. Lloyd Stone. 6750-6
Effie's reasons. Phoebe Cary. 6060-9
The **effigies**. Felicia Dorothea Hemans. 6973-8
The **effigy**. Guido Cavalcanti. 6325-X
Effusion. William Wordsworth. 6331-4
Effusion by a cigar smoker. Horace Smith. 6453-1
Effusion upon the death of James Hogg, sels. William Wordsworth. 6867-7
"**Eftsoones** they heard...", fr. The faerie queen. Edmund Spenser. 6726-3
"**Eftsoons** the priest had made his say". Passing of the compliment, fr. The white house ballads. Eugene Field. 6949-5
"**Egalton's** hills are sunny". Hugh Thorndyke. Alice Cary. 6969-X
Egan, Maurice Francis
    He made us free. 6172-9,6292-X
    Madonna of the empty arms. 6282-2
    Maurice de Guerin. 7041-8
    Maurice de Guerin. 6096-X,6292-X,6172-9,6300-4,6096 X
    Of flowers. 7041-8
    The old violin. 7041-8
    The old violin. 6172-9,6292-X
    Theocritus. 7041-8
    Theocritus. 6632-1
    Vigil of the Immaculate Conception. 6172-9,6292-X
Egan, Maurice Francis (tr.)
    Canticle of the sun. Saint Francis of Assisi, 6730-1
Egar, J.H.
    Sing, sing for Christmas. 6806-5
Egbert, Alice Edith
    The charm. 6118-4
Egbert, Ella Elizabeth
    Days like these. 6374-8
Egbert, Grace Louise
    Moon song. 6847-2
    An offering. 6847-2
    Words for music. 6847-2
Egbert, Marion Thornton
    The blue-bird. 6274-1
Egemo, Constance
    The great wave of Kanagwa. 6966-5
Egerton ms. 2711, British museum, sels. Sir Thomas Wyatt. 6586-4
Egerton, Helen Merrill
    Bluebirds. 6796-4
    In autumn fields. 6797-2
    Sandpipers. 6797-2
    "When crimson tinges the maple buds". 6797-2
"An **egg** a chicken! don't tell me". The miracle of the egg. Unknown. 6926-6
An **egg** a chicken. Unknown. 6314-4
The **egg**. Jean Follain. 6758-1
The **egg**. Jean Follain. 6803-0
The **egg**. Laura E. Richards. 6891-X
Eggebrecht, Jurgen
    Gestaltwandel. 6253-9
Eggert Olafsson. Matthias Jochumsson. 6854-5
Eggleston, Edward
    Street cries. 6247-4,6413-2
Eggs and birds. William Brighty Rands. 6502-3
Eggs and birds. Unknown. 6629-1
The **eggs** and the horses. R.S. S. 6302-0
The **eggs** and the horses. Unknown. 6302-0;6385-3
"**Eggs**, butter, bread". Unknown. 6904-5
The **eggs**. Tomaso de Yriarte. 6278-4
An **eggstravagance**. Oliver Wendell Holmes. 6512-0
An **eggstravagance**. Oliver Wendell Holmes. 6861-8
Egidio of Coimbra. Thomas Walsh. 6292-X,6172-9
Egilsrud, Johan S.
    Seen near Brainerd. 6342-X
Eglinton, Charles
    Arrival and departure. 6788-3
    Cheetah. 6788-3
    Meeting. 6788-3
    The vanquished. 6788-3
Eglinton, John. See Magee, William K.
Eglinton, Marie L.
    Gone is Ulysses. 6995-9
The **ego** cries itself. Leonora Speyer. 7038-8
Ego et Echo. John Godfrey Saxe. 7022-1
Ego flos campi. Bible. 6830-8
"An **ego** pressed onward". Neal Cassady. Charles Plymell. 6998-3
Ego'sdream. Alfred Kreymborg. 6348-9

Egoism. W. Craddle. 6722-0
The egoist. Anna Wickham. 6210-5
Egotism. William Cunningham. 6397-7
Egotism. May Frank. 6397-7
Egotism. Anna Wickham. 6893-6
Egotist. John Bruce MacCallum. 6482-5
"Egrets rise with white wings". Waipahu to Waialua. Alvin Suzuki. 6900-2
Eguren, Jose Maria
    The girl with the blue lamp. Donald Devenish Walsh (tr.). 6759-X
    Lied V. Donald Devenish Walsh (tr.). 6759-X
    Marginal. Donald Devenish Walsh (tr.). 6759-X
Egypt. Hilda ("H.D.") Doolittle. 6184-2
Egypt. Edward Farquhar. 6939-8
Egypt. Mary Brent Whiteside. 6841-3,6781-6
"Egypt and pharoah and the Nile". Cleopatra. Robert Loveman. 6941-X
"Egypt's might is tumbled down". Mary Elizabeth Coleridge. 6395-0,6186-9,6339-X
An Egyptian love charm. Gertrude Huntington McGiffert. 6838-3
Egyptian love song. Unknown. 6732-8
The Egyptian princess. Sir Edwin Arnold. 6980-0
Egyptian serenade. George William Curtis. 6240-7,6735-2
The Egyptian sphynx. James Abraham Martling. 6952-5
"Eh! qui m'emportera sur des flots..." Alphonse Marie Louis de Lamartine. 6801-4
"Eh? Why am I keeping that old crippled mare?". Bess. Alfred T. Chandler. 6768-5
Eheu fugaces. Richard Harris ("Thomas Ingoldsby") Barham. 6092-7,6278-4
Eheu! Fugaces. Walter Learned. 7041-8
Eheu! fugaces. Walter Learned. 6004-8
Ehrenburg, Ilya
    Our children's children will marvelk. Jeannette Eyre (tr.). 6665-8
    The sons of our sons. Babette Deutsch and Avrahm Yarmolinsky (tr.). 6879-0
    The sons of our sons. Jack Lindsay (tr.). 6546-5
Ehrensberger, Irma Louise
    Tasks. 6750-6
Ehrenstein, Albert
    Ares. Babette Deutsch (tr.). 6160-5
    Home-coming. Babette Deutsch (tr.). 6160-5
    Homer. Babette Deutsch (tr.). 6160-5
    Suffering. Babette Deutsch (tr.). 6160-5
Ehrmann, Max
    Peace shall live. 6542-2
    A prayer ("Let me do my work each day"). 6750-6
    Willie won. 6707-7
Ei Jesus hodie natus est de virgine. Unknown. 6756-5
Eia, martyr Stephane. Unknown. 6756-5
Eichberg, Anna Ph.
    Meteors. 6273-3
Eichendorff, Count Joseph von
    Abschied. 6252-0
    Der frohe wandersmann. 6252-0
    Die nacht. 6252-0
    Fruhlingsgruss. 6252-0
    Lockung. 6252-0
    Mondnacht. 6252-0
    Morgengebet. 6252-0
    On the death of my child. 6648-8
    The robber-brothers. Elizabeth Craigmyle (tr.). 6842-1
    Wanderschaft. 6252-0
    War's dunkle, ich lag im walde. 6252-0
Eidola, fr. Tethys' festival. Samuel Daniel. 6317-9
"Eies look off theires no beeholdinge." Francis Beaumont (atr) 6563-5
Eiger, Monch, and Jungfrau. Nathaniel Langdon Frothingham. 6749-2
8/1.. John Campbell. 7032-9
8/19.. John Campbell. 7032-9
8/2.. John Campbell. 7032-9
8/24 (The farmhouse finally speaks). John Campbell. 7032-9
8 a.m. Tom Mitchelson. 6899-5
Eight aspects of Melissa. Lawrence Durrell. 6379-5
Eight bells. Unknown. 6549-X
The VIII Eight canto. Vnperfite, fr. Two Cantos... Edmund Spenser. 6586-4
"Eight centuries unheeded by the west!". With Fitzgerald's 'Omar Khayyam' Gleeson White. 6875-8
Eight doves. Jane Dransfield. 6979-7
"Eight fingers, ten toes". The difference. Laura E. Richards. 6937-1
"Eight live brown voices". Fear of the dark. Terri Jewell. 6899-5
Eight months old, fr. Songs for Sally. Marion Strobel. 6778-6
Eight o'clock. Richard K. Arnold. 6515-5
Eight o'clock. Alfred Edward Housman. 6315-2
Eight o'clock. Margaret E. Johnson. 6965-7
Eight oars and a coxswain. Arthur Guiterman. 6773-5
Eight of S. Barnards verses,... Thomas Tusser. 6586-4
Eight poems. Edward Estlin Cummings. 6391-8
Eight secular elegies. George Barker. 6391-8
"Eight times the clock has struck". Eight o'clock. Margaret E. Johnson. 6965-7
Eight volunteers. Lansing C. Bailey. 6741-X
"Eight years have fled since,in the wilderness". The last bison. Charles Mair. 6795-6
The eight-day clock. Alfred Cochrane. 6230-X
Eighteen. Sister Mary Honora. 6388-8
018.. Cesar Vallejo. 6642-9
Eighteen forty-nine. Unknown. 6630-5
Eighteen sixty-one. Walt Whitman. 6126-5,6288-1
Eighteen sixty-one's call to arms, sels. Edward J. Wheeler. 6714-X
1802.Eighteen. Robert Graves. 6257-1
Eighteenth century despises the gardens of the seventeenth. Richard Graves. 6649-6
"The eighteenth of October". Unknown. 6111-7
An eighteenth-century fan. Raymond W. Walker. 6118-4
The eighth month. Edmund Spenser. 6793-X
The eighth ode of the second book of Horace imitated. Thomas Warton (the Elder) 6962-X
The eighth ode of the second book of Horace. Sir Charles Sedley. 6544-9
Eighth Passus, fr. Pier's Plowman's vision. William Langland. 6200-8
"The eighth was August, being rich arrayed". The eighth month. Edmund Spenser. 6793-X
An eightsome reel. William H. Hamilton. 6269-5
"Eighty and nine with their captain". The charge by the ford. Thomas Dunn English. 6916-9
"Eighty years beside Loch Goil". The idiot. Frederick Victor Branford. 6778-6
Eikamp, Helen
    Because. 6857-X
Eileen Aroon. Thomas Furlong. 6086-2
Eileen Aroon. Gerald Griffin. 6090-0,6096-X,6174-5,6437-X, 6512-0,6732
Eileen Aroon. Carroll O'Daly. 6930-4
"Eilidh, Eilidh, Eilidh, heart of me, dear...". The closing doors. William ("Fiona Macleod") Sharp. 6873-1
Ein Deutches lied. Unknown. 6175-3
Ein Deutsches lied. Unknown. 6791-3,6823-5
Ein fichtenbaum steht einsam. Heinrich Heine. 7039-6
Ein tag. Carl Friedrich Kayser. 6847-2
Ein traumbild. C.W. Yeomans. 6116-8
Einkehr. Johann Ludwig Uhland. 6252-0
Einmal vor manchem Jahre. Ricarda Hugh. 6253-9
Einsamkeit. Rainer Maria Rilke. 6253-9
Einsiedeln Abbey. William Wordsworth. 6749-2
Einstein. Archibald MacLeish. 6754-9
Einstein among the coffee-cups. Louis Untermeyer. 6722-0
Eire. William Drennan. 6930-4
Eire a ruin. Sliabh Cuilinn. 6858-8
Eire a ruin. John O'Hagan. 6174-5
Eire's awakening. Cathal O'Byrne. 6174-5
Eisele, Albert
    Crest in the kitchen. 6799-9
    Flaming towns. 6042-0
Eiseman et al., Alfred
    The army mule, the navy goat & the kick of the kangaroo. 6237-7
Eisenbeis, Loui
    Are you ready? 6927-4

Christmas a hundred years to come. 6923-1
The church fair. 6920-7
The church in Lucre Hollow. 6925-8
The church kitten. 6924-X
The deacon, me and him. 6923-1
Joner swallerin' a whale. 6417-5
Matildy goes to meetin'. 6925-8
The meetin'-house is split. 6926-6
Our church sociable. 6417-5
Our ranks are getting thin. 6927-4
The parson's vacation. 6921-5
Eisenberg, Emanuel
Reflections in a hospital. 6026-9
Eisenberg, Phil
Incised to change. 6857-X
"Either he is an excellent critic". Little roach poem. C.W. Truesdale. 6966-5
Eivlin a ruin. George Sigerson. 6174-5
Ek, Karin
An eye. Charles Wharton Stork (tr.). 6045-5
Ekelof, Gunnar
Monologue with its wife. Robert Bly (tr.). 6803-0
El Aghir. Norman Cameron. 6210-5
El barrio bondage. Arthur T. Wilson. 6899-5
El Camilo. Minna Irving. 6670-4
El Canalo. Bayard Taylor. 6670-4,6241-5
El Cid, sels. Unknown (Spanish) 6484-1
El desdichado. Gerard de Nerval. 6801-4
El desdichado. Gerard de Nerval. 6317-9
El Dorado, fr. Glimpses. Russell M. Spear. 6850-2
El Dorado: a song. Charles Mill Gayley. 6241-5
El Emplazado. William Henry Venable. 6946-0
El Gallo. Witter Bynner. 6072-2
El Greco. E.L. Mayo. 6324-1
El hijo del mar. Charles Howard Shinn. 7010-8
El Khalil. Bayard Taylor. 6976-2
El Mahdi to the tribes of the Soudan. Edna Dean Proctor. 7041-8
El minerito. Eduardo Gallegos. 6149-4
El monte- hymn. James Abraham Martling. 6952-5
El poniente. Ruth Comfort Mitchell. 6241-5,6464-7
El vaquero. Lucius Harwood Foote. 6241-5
El-azrek. Bayard Taylor. 7010-8
Elaine. Edna St. Vincent Millay. 6033-1,6102-8,6619-4,6019-6,6076-5,6464-7,6300-4_
Elaine's love song. Alfred Lord Tennyson. 6320-9
Elaine's song (Lancelot and Elaine). Alfred Lord Tennyson. 6110-9
Elaine, fr. Idyls of the king. Alfred Lord Tennyson. 6669-0,6046-3
Elaine, sels. Alfred Lord Tennyson. 6541-4
Elam Chase's fiddle. Robert Clarkson Tongue. 6924-X
Elam, William C.
The Mecklenburg declaration. 6946-0
The elden tree. Joanna Baillie. 6813-8
The elder brother, sels. Francis Beaumont and John Fletcher. 6369-1
The elder brother, sels. John Fletcher. 6562-7
Elder Lamb's donation. Will Carleton. 6505-8,6672-0
The elder scripture. John Keble. 6271-7
The elder tree. Unknown. 6125-7
"The elder's bridal in July". Scherzo. Clara Shanafelt. 6897-9
The elder's rebuke. Emily Bronte. 6123-0
The elder's warning. William Edmonstoune Aytoun. 6948-7
Elder, Karl
Cutting pigs. 6860-X
Elder, Lilla Thomas
Uncle Sam's young army. 6715-8
Elderberry flute song. Peter Blue Cloud. 7005-1
The elderly gentleman. George Canning. 6089-7,6440-X
The elderly. Molly Dong. 6883-9
"Eldest of things, divine equality!". The hymn of liberated nations. Percy Bysshe Shelley. 7009-4
"The eldest son bestrides him". The undertaker's horse. Rudyard Kipling. 7010-8
"Eldest-born of pow'rs divine!". To health. Unknown (Greek). 6814-6
Eldorado. Edgar Allan Poe. 6464-7,6121-4,6077-3,6176-1, 6299-7,6255-5,6498-1,6732 ,6008-0,6250-4,6288-1,6126-5,6424-8

Eldred, Mrs. L.C.
The single head of wheat. 6413-2
Eldridge, C.S.
Medical tyro waiting for patients. 6274-1,6714-X
Eldridge, George Dyre
The dead. 6327-6
Eldridge, Jay Glover
Centennial Hymn. 6799-9
Eldridge, L. Eugene
My home. 6798-0
Eldridge, Paul
The departed. 6397-7
Emperor T'Ang, skeptic. 6069-2
Gray roadster. 6397-7
Of China and her wisdom. 6464-7
Sonnets of an Indian heiress. 6397-7
Turning the cheek. 6071-4
Wang Peng, famous sociologist. 6464-7
Eldrige, Denison
To - ("'Twas at a ball"). 7021-3
Eleanor. Unknown. 6983-5
Eleanor [pseud].
Annotation. 6817-0
Eleanora; a panegyrical poem. John Dryden. 6970-3
Eleanore. Alfred Lord Tennyson. 6977-0
Eleanore, Sister M.
Mother. 6543-0
A question of sacrifice. 6543-0
Eleanore, sels. Alfred Lord Tennyson. 6997-5
Eleazar Wheelock. Richard Hovey. 6722-0
Election day. Margaret Boyce Bonnell. 6995-9
Election handbill of green. Jorge Carrera Andrade. 6642-9
Election handbill of green. Jorge Carrera Andrade. 6642-9
The election: a comedy. Joanna Baillie. 6813-8
Electra and Orestes, fr. Electra. Euripides. 6435-3
Electra, sels. Euripides. 6541-4
Electra, sels. Euripides. 6541-4
Electra, sels. Sophocles. 6621-6
Electric storm. Michael C. Martin. 6666-6
The electrician's valentine. Unknown. 6385-3
The electrician. Berton Braley. 7014-0
Electrocution script. P.L. Jacobs. 6870-7
Electronic art. E.M. Bennett. 7018-3
"Electronic baby born to be". Dream after touring the Tokyo Tokei. Joy Kogawa. 6790-5
Elegiac. Henr6 Wadsworth Longfellow. 6077-3
Elegiac. James Gates Percival. 6340-3,6300-4,6309-8
An elegiac epistle to a friend. John Gay. 6972-X
Elegiac mood. Gordon Bottomley. 6897-9
Elegiac mood. Gordon Bottomley. 6872-3
Elegiac musings, sels. William Wordsworth. 6867-7
Elegiac sonnet. Charlotte Smith. 6208-3
Elegiac stanzas. William Wordsworth. 6110-9,6199-0,6291-9, 6122-2,6289-X,6369-1,6196-6,6430-2
Elegiac stanzas on the death of Sir Peter Paerker, Bart. George Gordon, 6th Baron Byron. 6945-2
Elegiacs. Alfred Lord Tennyson. 6977-0
Elegiarvm liber (in Latin) Thomas Campion. 6794-8
Elegie. Jean Moreas. 6801-4
Elegie 010, The dreame. John Donne. 6958-4
Elegie Americaine. John V.A. Weaver. 6732-8
Elegie on the Lady Marckham, sels. John Donne. 6472-8
Elegie upon Anacreon. Abraham Cowley. 6483-3
An elegie upon the death of the dean of Pauls, Dr.John Donne. Thomas Carew. 6341-1,6562-7
Elegie: his parting from her. John Donne. 6933-9
Elegie: On his mistris. John Donne. 6341-1
Elegies on George Talbot, esq. William Habington. 6935-5
Elegies over John Reed. Marya Alexandrovna Zaturenska. 6076-5,6102-8,6076-5
Elegies, sels. John Donne. 6106-0
Elegies, sels. Sextus Propertius. 6088-9
Elegy. Alfred Austin. 6102-8
Elegy. George Barker. 6390-X
Elegy. Duane Big Eagle. 7005-1
Elegy. Robert ("Droch") Bridges. 6508-2
Elegy. Margaret E. Bruner. 6120-6
Elegy. George Gordon, 6th Baron Byron. 6246-5
Elegy. George Dillon. 6808-1

Elegy. George S. Fraser. 6379-9
Elegy. Thomas Gray. 6486-8
Elegy. Arthur Guiterman. 6089-7
Elegy. William H. Hamilton. 6269-5
Elegy. R.G. Howarth. 6349-7
Elegy. Anne Hunter. 6908-8
Elegy. Thomas S. Jones Jr. 6347-0
Elegy. Karoniaktatie. 7005-1
Elegy. Sidney Keyes. 6209-1,6666-6
Elegy. Henry King. 6600-3,6250-4
Elegy. Edna St. Vincent Millay. 6102-8,6289-X,6076-5,6396-9
Elegy. Clark Mills. 6640-2
Elegy. Charles Norman. 6042-0
Elegy. Ovid. 6814-6
Elegy. Alexander Pope. 6250-4
Elegy. Frederic Prokosch. 6389-6
Elegy. Alexander Pushkin. 6103-6
Elegy. Norman Rosten. 6561-9
Elegy. Salomon de la Selva. 6759-X
Elegy. Chidiock Tichborne. 6436-1,6315-2,6436-1,6181-8, 6187-7,6125
Elegy. W. Wesley Trimpi. 6515-5
Elegy ("A white nymph"). Andre Chenier. 7039-6
Elegy ("Among"). Robert Bridges. 6487-6
Elegy ("Assemble"). Robert Bridges. 6487-6
Elegy ("Clear"). Robert Bridges. 6487-6,6250-4,6430-2
Elegy ("Every man"). Andre Chenier. 7039-6
Elegy ("How well"). Robert Bridges. 6487-6
An elegy ("Since you"). Ben Jonson. 6315-2
Elegy ("The wood"). Robert Bridges. 6154-0,6487-6,6507-4, 6250-4,6430-2
An elegy ("Though beauty"). Ben Jonson. 6186-9
Elegy (In memoriam-- June 1941, R. R.). David Gascoyne. 6475-2,6210-5
Elegy - the summer house on the mound. Robert Bridges. 6186-9,6245-8,6487-6
Elegy 001: To Charles Deodati. John Milton. 6814-6
Elegy 002: On the death of the university beadle... John Milton. 6814-6
Elegy 003: On the death of the bishop of Winchester. John Milton. 6814-6
Elegy 004: To his tutor, Thomas Young, chaplain... John Milton. 6814-6
Elegy 005: On the approach of spring. John Milton. 6814-6
Elegy 006: To Charles Deodati. John Milton. 6814-6
Elegy 007 ("As yet a stranger..."). John Milton. 6814-6
Elegy 008. William Bell. 6210-5
Elegy 012. William Bell. 6210-5
elegy address'd to his Excellency Governour Belcher, sels. Mather Byles. 6008-0
Elegy before death. Edna St. Vincent Millay. 6034-X,6431-0
Elegy by Green for Byle's cat. Joseph Green. 6120-6
Elegy for a dead king. Al-Kutandi. 6362-4
Elegy for a dead soldier. Karl Shapiro. 6399-3,6665-8,6666-6
Elegy for a lost continent. Margaret R. Richter. 6979-7
Elegy for all ages. Pablo de (Carlos Diaz Loyola) Rokha. 6642-9
Elegy for Becquer. Enrique Pena Barrenechea. 6759-X
An elegy for D.H. Lawrence. William Carlos Williams. 6483-3,6641-0
Elegy for Garcia Lorca. Joy Davidman. 6561-9
Elegy for Margaret. VI. Stephen Spender. 6208-3
Elegy for minor poets. Louis MacNeice. 6257-1
Elegy for Mr. Goodbe. Osbert Sitwell. 6250-4
Elegy for N.N. Czeslaw Milosz. 6758-1
Elegy for our dead. Edwin Rolfe. 6666-6
Elegy for the drowned men who return. Roberto Ibanez. 6759-X
Elegy for the face at your elbow. John Ciardi. 6751-4
Elegy for the forgotten oldsmobile. Adrian C. Louis. 7005-1
Elegy for the Irish poet Francis Ledwidge. Grace Hazard Conkling. 6653-4
Elegy for two banjos. Karl Shapiro. 6391-8,6666-6
Elegy for William Soutar. William Montgomerie. 6379-9
Elegy for your absence. Eugenio Florit. 6642-9
Elegy in a country churchyard. Gilbert Keith Chesterton. 6722-0

Elegy in a country churchyard. Gilbert Keith Chesterton. 6884-7
Elegy in memory of Joseph Rodman Drake. Halleck Fitz-Greene. 6088-9,6396-9
Elegy in spring. Nathaniel A. Benson. 6021-8
An elegy of a woman's heart. Sir Henry Wotton. 6198-2
Elegy of the Duke of Marmalade. Luis Pales Matos. 6759-X
Elegy on a dead mermaid washed ashore at Plymouth Rock. Robert Hillyer. 6036-6
Elegy on a lady, whom grief...killed. Robert Bridges. 6437-X,6477-9,6508-2,6301-2
An elegy on a lap-dog. John Gay. 6024-2,6092-7
Elegy on a pet dove that was killed by a dog. Alexander ("Nether Lochaber") Stewart. 6180-X
Elegy on a young airdale bitch lost two years since... Yvor Winters. 6628-3
The elegy on Addison, sels. Thomas Tickell. 6198-2
Elegy on Albert Edward the peacemaker. Unknown. 6157-5
Elegy on an empty skyscraper. John Gould Fletcher. 6782-4
An elegy on an infant. Thomas Warton (the Elder) 6962-2
An elegy on Ben Jonson. John Cleveland. 6933-9
An elegy on Ben Jonson. John Cleveland. 6341-1
An elegy on Ben Jonson. John Donne. 6933-9
Elegy on Captain Matthew Henderson. Robert Burns. 6271-7, 6385-3,6423-X,6600-3,6291-9
Elegy on David Laing, Esq. Thomas Hood. 6974-6
Elegy on De Marsay. James Kenneth Stephen. 6046-3
Elegy on dead fashion, fr. Three variations on a theme. Edith Sitwell. 7000-0
Elegy on his mistress. John Donne. 6315-2,6369-1
Elegy on Jefferson Davis. Allen Tate. 6641-0
Elegy on Madam Blaize. Oliver Goldsmith. 6102-8,6198-2, 6486-8,6385-3,6722-0,6304
Elegy on Madame Blaize. Oliver Goldsmith. 6086-2
Elegy on Maggie Johnston. Allan Ramsay. 6086-2
Elegy on Miss Elizabeth Drury. John Donne. 6438-8
Elegy on Mr. William Shakespeare. William Basse. 6483-3, 6250-4
An elegy on Mrs. Mary Blaize. Oliver Goldsmith. 6152-4
Elegy on Newstead abbey. George Gordon, 6th Baron Byron. 6945-2
An elegy on parting. James Thomson. 6816-2
Elegy on partridge. Jonathan Swift. 6200-8
Elegy on Shakespeare. William Basse. 6933-9
Elegy on the abrogation of the birth-night ball... Catherine Maria Fanshawe. 6874-X
Elegy on the death of a mad dog. Oliver Goldsmith. 6075-7, 6134-6,6239-3,6244-X,6271-7,6290 ,6291-9,6131-1,6152-4,6430-2,6739-5,6026 ,6385-3,6425-6,6486-8,6552-X, 6732-8,6105 ,6424-8,6668-2,6464-7,6518-X,6086-2,6104 ,6498-1,6332-2,6089-7,6133-8,6240-7,6165 ,6104-4, 6491-4
Elegy on the death of an unfortunate lady. Alexander Pope. 6543-0
Elegy on the death of an unfortunate lady, sels. Alexander Pope. 6472-8
Elegy on the death of Dr. Channing, sels. James Russell Lowell. 6337-3
Elegy on the death of John Keats. Percy Bysshe Shelley. 6935-5
Elegy on the death of Mme. Anna Pavlova. Edward Harry William Meyerstein. 6781-6
Elegy on the death of Mr. Oldham, sels. John Dryden. 6472-8
Elegy on the death of Scots music. Robert Fergusson. 6086-2
Elegy on the death of Thomas Shepard, sels. Urian Oakes. 6077-3,6008-0
Elegy on the eve. George Barker. 6665-8
An elegy on the glory of her sex, Mrs. Mary Blaize. Oliver Goldsmith. 6089-7,6271-7,6304-2,6732-8
Elegy on the grave of a small fighter. Nicephorus Vrettakos. 6352-7
Elegy on the heroine of childhood. Vernon Watkins. 6391-8
Elegy on the pilot. Reuel Denney. 6978-9
Elegy on Thomas Tod Stoddart, the angler-poet. Sir George Douglas. 6819-7
Elegy on Thryza. George Gordon, 6th Baron Byron. 6246-5
Elegy on William Cobbett. Ebenezer Elliot. 6656-9
Elegy over a tomb. Edward Herbert, 1st Baron Herbert of

ELEGY

Cherbury. 6562-7,6208-3,6182-6,6641-0,6341-0
The elegy to spring, sels. Michael Bruce. 6960-6
Elegy to the invented woman. Xavier Abril. 6759-X
Elegy to the lost and already blurred by time. Xavier Abril. 6759-X
Elegy to the memory of an unfortunate lady. Alexander Pope. 6317-9,6604-6,6641-0,6150-8,6291-9,6022-6,6660-7
Elegy to the memory of my beloved friend, Mr. Thomas Godfrey. Nathaniel Evans. 6288-1
Elegy under the stars. Anne Morrow Lindbergh. 6979-7
An elegy upon James Therburn. James Thomson. 6816-2
An elegy upon the death of Doctor Donne, dean of Paul's. Thomas Carew. 6483-3
An elegy upon the death of the Lady Markham. John Donne. 6660-7
An elegy upon..incomparable King Charles the First,sels. Henry King. 6933-9
Elegy V. George Barker. 6210-5
Elegy written in a college library. George Ellis. 6802-2
Elegy written in a country churchyard. Thomas Gray. 6024-2, 6246-6,6075-7,6101-X,6102-8,6142 ,6645-3,6723-9,6631-3,6668-2,6491-4,6639 ,6138-9,6302-0,6358-6,6385-3, 6552-X,6208 ,6301-2,6304-7,6150-8,6153-2,6104-4,6197 ,6154-0,6186-9,6198-2,6239-3,6240-7,6060 ,6245-4, 6291-9,6250-4,6430-2,6424-8,6560 ,6271-7,6289-X,6315-2,6332-2,6337-3,6369 ,6646-1,6192-3,6543-0,6195-0, 6660-7,6152 ,6407-8,6457-4,6459-0,6473-6,6479-5,6484 ,6086-2,6023-4,6438-8,6439-6,6488-4,6504-X,6527-9, 6536-8,6600-3,6604 ,6634-8,6641-0,6726-3,6732-8,6122-2
Elegy written in a country churchyard, sels. Thomas Gray. 6179-6,6087-0,6317-9,6339-X
Elegy written in a railway station. Unknown. 6278-4
Elegy written in spring. Michael Bruce. 6086-2
Elegy written in the Temple gardens. Unknown. 6878-2
Elegy wrote in the tower, 1554 Sir John Harington. 6182-6
Elegy XI. William Shenstone. 6152-4
Elegy, sels. Thomas Chatterton. 6545-7
Elegy, sels. Louise Labe. 6227-X
Elegy, the autumnal. John Donne. 6369-1,6430-2
Elegy. He complains how soon...life is over. William Shenstone. 6932-0
Elegy: death, sels. John Donne. 6106-0
Elegy: He complains how soon...life is over. William Shenstone. 6831-6
Elegy: his picture. John Donne. 6208-3,6341-1
Elegy: The poet expatiates on the beauty..Delia's hair. Robert Southey. 6802-2
Elegy: The poet invokes the spirits of the elements... Robert Southey. 6802-2
Elegy: The poet relates how he obtained...hand-kerchief. Robert Southey. 6802-2
Elegy: The poet relates how he stole a lock of...hair. Robert Southey. 6802-2
An elegy: to an old woman. Thomas Parnell. 6152-4
An elegy. William Browne. 6230-X
An elegy. William Browne. 6908-8
An elegy. Helen Parry Eden. 6172-9,6292-X
An elegy. David Gascoyne. 6210-5
An elegy. Ben Jonson. 6194-X
Element. Patricia K. Page. 6446-9
An elementary school classroom. Stephen Spender. 6209-1
Elements. John Henry, Cardinal Newman. 6656-9
"Elements-structures/1 wind tower". Berlin masque. John Hejduk. 6803-0
The elements. William Henry Davies. 6508-2
The elements. John Henry, Cardinal Newman. 6383-7
The elements. Oscar Williams. 6375-6
Elena's song. Sir Henry Taylor. 6437-X,6301-2
Elena's song, fr. Philip van Artevelde. Sir Henry Taylor. 6934-7
Eleonora. John Dryden. 6302-0;6385-3
Eleonora, sels. John Dryden. 6867-7
Elephant. Noel Harry Brettell. 6788-3
The elephant and the bookseller. John Gay. 6315-2
The elephant is slow to mate. David Herbert Lawrence. 6375-6
The elephant juggler. J.G. Francis. 6786-7
"An elephant sat on some kegs". An elephant. Joseph G. Francis. 6891-X
"The elephant seemed a trifle sad...". A gratified ambition. Carolyn Wells. 6882-0
The elephant tries to rescue the jackass. Marshal E. Grover. 6799-9
The elephant, or the force of habit. Alfred Edward Housman. 6722-0
An elephant. Joseph G. Francis. 6891-X
The elephant. Carlos Drummond de Andrade. 6758-1
Elephants. Marianne Moore. 6209-1
Elessde. Unknown. 6787-5
Eletephony. Laura E. Richards. 6736-0
Eleusis. Gertrude Huntington McGiffert. 6331-4
Eleven. Archibald MacLeish. 6649-6
Eleven poems, sels. Yannis Ritsos. 6803-0
Eleven saved. Ruth Manning-Sanders. 6072-2
Eleventh Armored. L.E. Perry & J.R. Bogue. 6237-7
Eleventh floor view. Patricia M. Johnson. 6857-X
The eleventh hour. Francis St. Vincent Morris. 6650-X
The eleventh hour. Anna L. Ruth. 6910-X
Eleventh song. Sir Philip Sidney. 6198-2,6586-4
The 11th Eleventh: and last book of the ocean... Sir Walter Raleigh. 6380-2
The elf and the doormouse. Oliver Herford. 6401-9,6466-3, 6132-X,6519-8,6545-X,6368-3,6639-9,6638-0
The elf and the dormouse. Oliver Herford. 6135-4
Elf night. Ronald Rogers. 7005-1
The elf's lament. Daniel Martin Karcher. 6936-3
The elf-child. James Whitcomb Riley. 6696-8,6505-8
The elf-stroke. Unknown (Danish) 6948-7
The elfin artist. Alfred Noyes. 6151-6;6162-1;6607-0
An elfin cruise. J. 6116-8
Elfin dancer. Bernard Gilbert. 6959-2
The elfin knight. Unknown. 6056-0,6058-7,6180-X,6185-0
An elfin knight. Joseph Rodman Drake. 6639-9
Elfin lamps. Frank Dempster Sherman. 6311-X
Elfin music. Percy Bysshe Shelley. 6328-4
Elfin skates. Eugene Lee-Hamilton. 6473-6
Elfin song. Joseph Rodman Drake. 6431-0
An elfin summons. Eugene Field. 6949-5
The elfin valley. Mary Webb. 6253-9
The elfman. Grace Ruthenburg. 6039-0
Elgin cathedral epitaph. Unknown. 6339-X
Eli and Samuel. Edward Everett Hale. 6848-0
Elia. E.J. McPhelim. 6481-7
Eliab Eliezer. James Roann Reed. 6273-3,6924-X
Elijah. Robert Davidson. 6848-0
Elijah. Abraham M. Klein. 6042-0
Elijah. James Abraham Martling. 6952-5
Elijah Brown. Unknown. 6688-7
Elijah fed by ravens. James Grahame. 6848-0
Elijah in Horeb. John Keble. 6848-0
Elijah in the wilderness. James Montgomery. 6848-0
Elijah on Mount Carmel. E. E. D. 6848-0
Elijah's interview. Thomas Campbell. 6848-0
Elinda's glove. Richard Lovelace. 6933-9
Eliot Jr., Henry W.
    His sentence. 6118-4
    Life in the chem lab. 6118-4
Eliot to Wilson. Percy MacKaye. 7001-9
Eliot, Charles W.
    The sunny side. 6552-X
Eliot, George
    The death of Moses. 6848-0
    The legend of Jubal. 6848-0
Eliot, George (Mary Ann Cross)
    "Alas! how bitter are the wrongs of love!" 6238-5
    Arion. 7037-X
    Brother and sister. 6772-7
    Brother and sister. 6233-4,6239-3,6424-8,6321-7,6429-9, 6429-9
    Brother and sister, sels. 6543-0
    The choir invisible. 6260-1,6303-9,6479-5,6304-7,6424-8
    The dark. 6656-9
    Day is dying. 6240-7
    "Give me no light, great heaven, but such as turns." 6238-5
    The hermit. 6424-8
    How Lisa loved the king. 6679-8
    I am lonely, fr. The Spanish Gypsy. 6239-3

I think we had the chief of all love's joys. 6066-8
Lisa's message to the king. 6543-0
O, may I join. 6238-5,6486-8,6600-3,6730-1,6560-0,6199,
    6301-2,6543-0,6660-7,6102-8,6214-8,6656
O, may I join the choir invisible. 6240-7
Our mother. 6365-9
Presentiment of better things, sel. 6954-1
Presentiment of better things, sels. 6359-4
"The sense of vastness, when at night". 6997-5
Song of the Zincali. 6656-9
'The Spanish gypsy', sels. 6239-3
Spring song. 6519-8
"There, speak in whispers, fold me to thy heart". 6238-5
The tide of faith. 6730-1
Two lovers. 6260-1,6481-7,6543-0,6429-9,6321-7,6250,
    6066-8,6429-9
You may count that day. 6291-1

Eliot, Henrietta R.
Contents of a boy's pockets. 6715-8

Eliot, Thomas Stearns
Ash Wednesday I. 6645-3
Ash Wednesday, sels. 6317-9,6315-2
Ash-Wednesday VI. 6208-3
The Boston Evening Transcript. 6399-3
The burial of the dead, fr. The waste land. 6531-7
Burnt Norton. 6645-3
Chorus I, fr. The rock. 6532-5
Chorus VI, fr. The rock. 6532-5
Chorus X, fr. The rock. 6532-5
Cousin Nancy. 6491-4
Death by water, fr. The waste land. 6879-0
Death by water, fr. The waste land. 6258-X,6531-7,6472-8
Difficulties of a statesman. 6399-3
The dry salvages, sels. 6258-X,6210-5
East Coker. 6209-1
"Eyes that last I saw in tears". 6011-0
The fire sermon, fr. the waste land. 6531-7
A game of chess, fr. The waste land. 6531-7
Gerontion. 6208-3,6315-2,6348-9,6375-6,6150-8
The hippopotamus. 6733-6,6375-6,6637-2
The hollow men, sels. 6246-5
The hollow men. 6077-3,6348-9,6527-9,6645-3,6375-6,6071
    ,6354-3,6659-3,6491-4
Journey of the Magi. 6179-6,6246-5,6536-8,6641-0,6734-3,
    6209,6645-3
La figlia che piange. 6527-9,6393-4,6210-5
La la, fr. The waste land. 6531-7
Lines for an old man. 6399-3,6210-5
Little Gidding. 6208-3
The love song of J. Alfred Prufrock. 6102-8,6076-5,6488-
    4,6399-3,6527-9,6348-9,6536-8,6150,6300-4,6491-4
Macavity: the mystery cat. 6290-3,6339-X,6257-1,6511-2
Marina. 6246-5,6536-8,6354-3,6150-8,6209-1
Morning at the window. 6808-1,7039-6
Mr. Eliot's Sunday morning service. 6733-6
New Hampshire. 6315-2
Part IV, fr. The dry salvages. 6282-2
Portrait of a lady. 6076-5,6102-8,6348-9,6635-8,6619-4,
    6645
Portrait of a lady. 6897-9
Portrait of a lady. 6076-5,6020-X,6348-9
Prelude ("The winter evening"). 6236-9
Prelude 002. 6808-1
Prelude 003. 6808-1
Prelude 004. 6808-1
Preludes. 6077-3,6020-X,6077-3
Rannoch by Glencoe. 6208-3
Rhapsody on a windy night. 6052-8
The rock, sels. 6532-5,6375-6
A song for Simeon. 6931-2
The soul of man must quicken. 6354-3
Sweeney among the nightingales. 6348-9,6536-8,6645-3,
    6250-4,6150-8,6209
"This is the dead hour". 6011-0
Three dream songs. 6011-0
Triumphal march. 6052-8,6665-8
The waste land, sels. 6527-9,6531-7
The waste land. 6536-8,209-1

What the thunder said, fr. The waste land. 6531-7
Whispers of immortality. 6339-X,6348-9,6150-8,6483-9
"The wind sprang up at four o'clock". 6011-0

Eliot, Thomas Stearns (tr.)
Anabasis, sels. St.-J. (Alexis Saint-Leger Leger) Perse,
    6343-8

Elisa. Edmund Spenser. 6436-1
"Elisha Ben Abuja, deeply skilled". Turn again! Sabine
    Baring-Gould. 6848-0
Elisha's chamber. Richard Wilton. 6848-0
The elixir of life. William McGill. 6674-4
The elixir. George Herbert. 6239-3,6466-3,6102-8,6179-6,
    6337-3,6418-3,6660-7,6668-2,6194-X,6383-7,6604-6,
    6730-1,6197-4,6291-9,6438-8,6023-4
The elixir. Unknown. 7007-8

Eliyia, Joseph
Jesus. Rae Dalven (tr.). 6352-7
Militarism. Rae Dalven (tr.). 6352-7
Our Torah. Rae Dalven (tr.). 6352-7

Eliza, queen of the shepherds. Edmund Spenser. 6228-8
"Eliza, what fools are the Musselman sect". To Eliza.
    George Gordon, 6th Baron Byron. 6945-2
Elizabeth. Lizette Woodworth Reese. 6632-1
Elizabeth. George Brandon Saul. 6036-6,6250-4

Elizabeth I; Queen of England
The daughter of debate. 6436-1
The doubt. 6301-2
"I grieve, and dare not show my discontent." 6317-9
Importune me no more. 6182-6
On the sacrament. 6934-7
Youth and Cupid. 6436-1

Elizabeth at Tilbury. Francis Turner Palgrave. 6424-8
Elizabeth Barrett Browning. Norma Bright Carson. 6486-8
Elizabeth Barrett Browning: Where are you going to...
    Charles Powell. 6982-7
Elizabeth O'Grady. Paul Edmonds. 6937-1
Elizabeth of Bohemia. Sir Henry Wotton. 6075-7,6186-9,6102-
    8,6246-6,6395-0,6422,6301-2,6250-4,6737-9,6438-8
Elizabeth, aged nine. Margaret Elizabeth Sangster. 6424-8
"Elizabeth, Elspeth, Betsy, and Bess". Unknown. 6904-5
"Elizabeth, frigidly stretched". Recollection in autumn.
    Valentin Iremonger. 6930-4

Elkins, Jean
Hill life. 6764-6
Wind songs. 6764-6

The Elkridge hunt club. D.S. G. 7010-8
Ella Wheeler Wilcox: Little Tom Tucker. Charles Powell.
    6982-7
"Elle est la terre, elle est la plaine...". La terre:
    hymne. Victor Hugo. 6801-4
"Elle etait belle, si la nuit". Sur une morte. Alfred de
    Musset. 6801-4
"Elle me dit: quelque chose". La coccinelle. Victor Hugo.
    6801-4
Ellen hanging clothes. Lizette Woodworth Reese. 6653-4,
    6032-3,6464-7
Ellen Irwin; or the braes of Kirtle. William Wordsworth.
    6518-X
Ellen M'Jones Aberdeen. Sir William Schwenck Gilbert. 6512-
    0,6732-8
Ellen McJones Aberdeen. Sir William Schwenck Gilbert. 6918-5
Ellen Terry. Anna Gannon. 6230-X
Ellen the fair. Unknown. 6057-9
Ellen's song. Sir Walter Scott. 6138-9

Ellerbe, Cecilia
On lonely coasts. 6039-0

Ellerton, John
Again to thy dear name. 6304-7
The God of the living. 6730-1
Living unto Thee. 6303-9
Now the labourer's task is o'er. 6730-1,6214-8
Saviour, again to thy dear name. 6304-7

Ellingwood, Lena B.
Old sidewalks. 6764-6

Ellingwood, Marion G.
To Mount Washington. 6764-6

Elliot, Charlotte
Just as I am. 6219-9
Let me be with thee. 6656-9

ELLIOT

O thou, the contrite sinner's hand. 6219-9
Thy will be done. 6219-9
Elliot, Ebenezer
The builders. 6656-9
Elegy on William Cobbett. 6656-9
An excursion to the mountains. 6543-0
The happy lot. 6543-0
Love strong in death. 6543-0
Song. 6543-0
Elliot, Gabrielle
Pierrot goes to war. 7027-2
Elliot, Jane [or Jean]
The flowers of the forest. 6180-X,6198-2,6323-3,6086-2, 6219-9
Lament for Flodden. 6188-5,6246-5,6600-3
Elliot, Lady Charlotte
My soul shall cling to thee. 6065-X
The wife of Loki. 6656-9
Elliot, Lydia Landon
Lincoln. 6524-4
Elliot, M.L.
My doggy. 6937-1
Elliot, Roberta Kerr
Chrysanthemums. 6576-7
Elliot, Samuel R.
The burden of night. 6632-1
Elliot, Sir Gilbert
Amyata. 6219-9
My sheep I neglected. 6180-X
Elliot, William Foster
A critic. 6506-6
A critic. 6817-0
Elliot, Winnifred
No room. 6799-9
Elliott, Blanche
Downy flakes and children. 6906-1
Musicale. 6906-1
Pavlowa. 6906-1
Sewer tree. 6906-1
Tiny quail. 6906-1
Elliott, Ebenezer
Battle song. 6102-8,6323-8,6383-7,6322-5
Bothwell. 6980-0
The bramble flower. 6127-3
Burns. 6302-0,6385-3
Come and gone. 6980-0
Corn-law hymn. 6102-8,6600-3
The dying boy to the sloe blossom. 6980-0
England. 6605-2
Flowers for the heart. 6980-0
Forest worship. 6600-3
Fountains abbey. 7015-9
A ghost at noon. 6600-3
Hymn ("Nurse of the pilgrim sires..."). 6980-0
The land which no one knows. 6934-7
Marching song. 6102-8
O Lord, how long. 6323-3
On seeing Audubon's Birds of America. 6980-0
The people's anthem. 6102-8
The Pilgrim fathers. 6980-0
Plaint. 6186-9,6641-0,6543-0,6660-7
Plaint ("Dark, deep, and cold the current flows"). 6186-9
A poet's epitaph. 6660-7,6102-8,6302-0,6385-3,6102-8, 6656-9,6543 ,6102-8,6271-7,6302-9
A poet's prayer. 6934-7
The press. 6605-2
Reform. 7009-4
The revolution of 1832. 7009-4
Ribbledin; or the christening. 6980-0
Sleep. 6980-0
Song ("Child is thy father dead?"). 6102-8
Song ("Let idlers despair"). 7009-4
Spring. 6302-0,6385-3
Thomas. 6980-0
The three Marys at Castle Howard, in 1812 and 1837. 6832-4
The wonders of the lane. 6980-0
Elliott, Ellen Coit
Prima donna of the Negro jazz orchestra. 6036-

Song of the waiting land. 6037-4
Elliott, Henry Rutherford
A recipe for sanity. 6274-1,6109-5
Elliott, Herbert
New England coast. 6761-1
Elliott, Jorge (tr.)
Vices of the modern world. Nicanor Parra, 6803-0
Elliott, Lydia Lando
Lincoln. 6524-4
Elliott, Madge
No kiss. 6919-3
Said tulip, 'That is so.' 6373-X
Elliott, Mary
The crocus. 6135-4
Elliott, Sir Gilbert
Amynta. 6934-7
Elliott, William Foster
Beauty. 6071-4
In repudiation. 6070-6
Elliott, William Yandell
Black man. 6071-4,6039-0
Roundhead and cavalier. 6037-4
Elliott, Winnifred
Ore shippers' song. 6342-X
Ellis Park. Helen Hoyt. 6101-X,6374-8,6476-0,6497-3,6556-2, 6336-5,6653-4,6628-3,6497-3,6556-2,6101-X,6374-8, 6476-0,6497-3,6556-2
Ellis, Colin
Against publishing satires. 6339-X
Bishop Spaniel's sermons. 6339-X
Ellis, F.S. (tr.)
The garden, fr. The romance of the rose. Guillaume de Lorris, 6649-6
The romaunt of the rose, sels. Guillaume de Lorris, 6649-6
Ellis, G.
Simon de Montfort. 6323-3
Ellis, George
Elegy written in a college library. 6802-2
The races. 6652-6
Rondeau. 6932-0
Ellis, H.F.
Message to General Montgomery. 6722-0
Ellis, Havelock
The gospel of consolation. 6482-5
In the Strand. 6482-5
The revelation. 6482-5
Ellis, Havelock (tr.)
Song ("If the sea were one..."). Unknown (Spanish), 7039-6
Song ("Let the rich man..."). Unknown (Spanish), 7039-6
Song ("To love with no return"). Unknown (Spanish), 7039-6
Ellis, James Tandy
Ten Broeck. 7010-8
Ellis, Joseph
Silence. 7015-9
Ellis, Kenneth M. (tr.)
Cagobens village. Unknown (American Indian), 6396-9
The death song of Go-ge-we-osh. Unknown (American Indian), 6396-9
Lament ("The Sioux are singing songs"). Unknown (American Indian), 6396-9
Thunder medicine. Unknown (American Indian), 6396-9
The Wahpeton Sioux. Unknown (American Indian), 6396-9
Ellis, Virginia
My bug Amos. 6750-6
Ellison, Henry
London, after midnight. 7015-9
Sunset. 7015-9
A sunset thought. 7015-9
Elliston, George
April morning. 6374-8
Color of air. 6861-8
End of summer. 7038-8
End of summer. 6039-0
End of the world. 7038-8
End of the world. 6039-0
Friend who understands. 6585-6
Friendly house. 6039-0

From a trundle bed. 6906-1
Going to sleep. 6861-8
Guess. 6906-1
How beautiful. 6585-6
Sound. 6039-0
Talk. 6906-1
Touch. 6906-1
Youth. 6906-1
Ellsworth. Unknown. 6946-0
Ellsworth, Clarice
Intemperance. 6397-7
Ellsworth, D.A.
Gwine to marry Jim. 6710-7
Pa's soft spot. 6929-0
Piller fights. 6964-9
Shindig in the country. 6274-1
Ellsworth, Erastus W.
The Mayflower. 6678-X
What is the use? 6600-3
Ellsworth, W.W.
Nightfall. 6413-2,6521-X
Ellwood, Thomas
Prayer ("Oh! that mine"). 6730-1
Prayer ("Unto the glory"). 6600-3
The **elm** and the vine. Jose Rosas. 6614-3
Elm angel. Harold Monro. 6209-1
The **elm** beetle. Andrew Young. 6315-2
Elm blossom. Unknown. 6049-8
Elm trees. Amy J. Dolloff. 6764-6
Elm versus apple. May Riley Smith. 6049-8
The **elm**. Hilaire Belloc. 6844-8
Elmer Brown. James Whitcomb Riley. 6091-9,6702-6,6702-6
Elmer Jr., Franklin D.
Christmas blessing. 6144-3
The lost Christ ("Where have we laid him now") 6144-3
Tale of one hill. 6144-3
The unlikely rebel. 6144-3
Elmo
Now and then. 6014-5
Our Ernest. 6014-5
Speak to us, O lord. 6014-5
"**Elms** of the Mohawk, all the way". Octette (003). Edward Sandford Burgess. 6847-2
The **elocution** lesson. Frances Nash. 6578-3
The **elocutionist's** curfew. Wilbur Dick Nesbit. 6277-6
Eloisa to Abelard. Alexander Pope. 6024-2,6315-2,6536-8, 6152-4,6430-2
Eloisa to Abelard, sels. Alexander Pope. 6198-2,6195-0
Eloisa, fr. Eloisa to Abelard. Alexander Pope. 6932-0
Eloquence. Amelia B. Coppuck Welby. 6294-6
Eloquence that persuades. Johann Wolfgang von Goethe. 6414-0
Eloquent rags. Vincent Godfrey Burns. 6042-0
"**elowers** that in thy garden rise". Song ("The flowers that in thy garden"). Sir Henry Newbolt. 6210-5
Elsa. Hilda Conkling. 6776-X
Elsa's eyes. Louis Aragon. 6343-8
"'**Else**'./Young & subtle charm thou wert slain". When years have passed shall I still bewail thee. Stanislav Karel Neumann. 6763-8
"**Elsie** Marley is grown so fine". Unknown. 6904-5
Elsie's child. Julia C.R. Dorr. 6416-7
Elsie's house. Stanley McNail. 6218-0
Elsinore. B.A. Gould Jr. 6116-8
Elsinore. Lucy H. Hooper. 6451-5
Elspeth (Elspeth MacDuffie O'Hallowran)
It's a fib. 6026-9
Sentimental journey. 6722-0
Elspeth's ballad, fr. The antiquary. Sir Walter Scott. 6518-X
Elspie and Philip, fr. The bothie of Tober-na-vuolich. Arthur Hugh Clough. 6832-4
Elster, Evelyn
Beauty builds. 6342-X
Elswitha. Mary Barry. 6273-3
Elton, Charles Abraham
Landscape of my heart, fr. The brothers. 6545-7
Elton, Charles Abraham (tr.)
Hannibal's [assage of the Alps. Silius Italicus, 6749-2
Lament for Bion. Moschus, 6385-3

Elton, Godfrey
Lugete o veneres cupidinesque. 6541-4
News. 6541-4
Elton, Oliver
Ballade des enfants sans souci. 6875-8
Elton, Oliver (tr.)
"All, all that once was mine is mine for ever" Afanasi Fet, 6103-6
Girls' song. Alexander Pushkin, 6103-6
Home. Nikolay Nekrasov, 6103-6
"Storm in the skies in the evening" Afanasi Fet, 6103-6
Tatyana's letter. Alexander Pushkin, 6103-6
To the stars that have gone out. Afanasi Fet, 6103-6
Eluard, Paul
Absences. 6351-9
Between the two poles of politeness. Ira Sadoff (tr.). 6803-0
The Gertrude Hoffman girls. 6351-9
Les malheurs des immortels, sels. Ira Sadoff (tr.). 6803-0
Max Ernst. George Reavey (tr.). 6343-8
The modesty well in view. Ira Sadoff (tr.). 6803-0
Pablo Picasso. Clement Greenberg (tr.). 6068-4
Such a woman. Ruthven Todd (tr.). 6343-8
Universe-solitude. Samuel Beckett (tr.). 6343-8
The **elusive** motif. Dunton. 6817-0
Elusive nature. Henry Timrod. 6597-X
The **elves'** dance. Thomas Ravenscroft. 6891-X
The **elves'** dance. Unknown. 6959-2
The **elves'** dance. Unknown. 6189-3
The **elves**. Charles Marie Leconte de Lisle. 6351-9
Elwes. Richard
These faithful verses. 6339-X
Ely, Henry S.
Decoramenta. 6118-4
Elys, Edmund
My mind keeps out of the host of sin. 6380-2
Elysian trail. Katharine Brown Burt. 6799-9
Elysium. Arthur Guiterman. 6320-9
Elysium. Felicia Dorothea Hemans. 6567-8
Elysium. Felicia Dorothea Hemans. 6973-8
Elysium. Agnes Mary F. ("Madame Duclaux") Robinson. 6648-8
Elytis, Odysseus
Helen. Rae Dalven (tr.). 6352-7
The mad pomegranate tree. Rae Dalven (tr.). 6352-7
Marina of the rocks. Rae Dalven (tr.). 6352-7
Emancipated. Louise Driscoll. 7038-8
Emancipation. Robert Loveman. 6941-X
Emancipation from British dependence. Philip Freneau. 6015-3,6286-5
The **emancipation** group. John Greenleaf Whittier. 6305-5, 6524-4
The **emancipation** of man. Unknown. 6744-1
The **emancipation** of the press. John Jeffrey. 7009-4
The **emancipators.** Randall Jarrell. 6666-6
The **emanglom.** Henri Michaux. 6758-1
The **emanglons**, sels. Henri Michaux. 6758-1
Emans, Elaine V.
Exception. 6750-6
Lines written for a wife. 6750-6
To a young girl. 6750-6
When larks have sung. 6342-X
Emanuel, James A.
Defeat. 6178-8
Emaricdulfe. E. C. 6182-6
The **embankment.** T.E. Hulme. 6209-1
Embarcation. Thomas Hardy. 6323-3
The **embargo**, sels. William Cullen Bryant. 6008-0
The **embargo.** Josiah Quincy. 6610-0
Embarkation song. Geoffrey Matthews. 6895-2
The **embarkation**, fr. Evangeline. Henry Wadsworth Longfellow. 6946-0
"'**Embarquons-nous!**' I seem to go". After Watteau. Austin Dobson. 6875-8
The **embarrassed** amorist. Louis Untermeyer. 6441-8
The **embarrassing** episode of Little Miss Muffet. Guy Wetmore Carryl. 6732-8
An **ember** picture. James Russell Lowell. 6691-7,6288-1,6004-8,6230-X,126-5
Emblem. Francis Quarles. 6315-2

EMBLEM

"An emblem of freedom, stern, haughty, and high". ?
    Street. 6601-1
An emblem of peace. Unknown. 6917-7
Emblem to be cut on a lonely rock at sea. T.O. Beachcroft.
    6781-6
An emblem. Alice Cary. 6865-0;6969-X
Emblems. Richard Coe. 6910-X
Emblems of conduct. Hart Crane. 6375-6
Emblems of Easter. Unknown. 6720-4
"Embodied in this clay and fixed by fire". At the ceramic
    exhibition. Harriet Stanton Place. 6789-1
"Embracing the woman I love". Prelude ("Embracing").
    Edmund McKenna. 6028-5
The embroidery on the kerchief. Kostas Krystallis. 6352-7
Embry, Jacqueline
    Bonnet sonnet. 6039-0
    Tea. 6736-0
    Unregenerate. 6036-6
Embryo. Mary Ashley Townsend. 6006-4
Embury, Emma C.
    On the death of Duke of Reichstadt. 6385-3
The emerald hill. Marie d'Autremont Gerry. 6342-X
An emerald is as green as grass. Christina Georgina
    Rossetti. 6623-2
"An emerald is as green as grass". A flint. Christina
    Georgina Rossetti. 7028-0
Emerald lake. James Rose. 6799-9
"Emerges Florence, with earth-smell of death". Out of the
    darkness, fr. A Florentine cycle. Gertrude
    Huntington McGiffert. 6838-3
Emerson. Amos Bronson Alcott. 6431-0
Emerson. Craven Langstroth Betts. 6820-0
Emerson. Mary Mapes Dodge. 6465-5
Emerson, Claire
    Portrait. 6799-9
Emerson, Edward Bliss
    The last farewell. 6438-8
Emerson, G.R.
    The baby's kiss. 6412-4,6572-4
Emerson, N.S.
    The deacon's confession. 6683-6
    The deacon's story. 6294-6
    The deacon's story. 6910-X
    Why Liab and I parted. 6690-9
Emerson, O.F.
    To Wordsworth. 6049-8
Emerson, Ralph Waldo
    Abraham Lincoln. 6449-3
    The Adirondacs, sels. 6484-1
    The amulet. 6429-9,6321-7
    The apology. 6077-3,6176-1,6600-3,6126-5,6288-1,6008 ,
        6121-4,6431-0
    April and May, fr. 'May-Day'. 6239-3
    Art. 6753-0
    "As the sunbeams stream...", fr. Woodnotes. 6047-1
    Bacchus. 6077-3,6176-1,6250-4,6300-4,6309-8
    The battle of Lexington, sels. 6601-1
    Blight. 6077-3,6288-1
    The Bohemian hymn. 6730-1,6126-5,6214-8,6250-4,6288-1,
        6467
    Borrowing. 6302-0,6385-3,6722-0,6735-2
    Boston. 6267-9,6470-1
    Boston hymn. 6014-5,6113-3,6299-7,6302-0,6385-3,6473 ,
        6600-3,6730-1,6288-1,6126-5
    Boston hymn, sel. 6954-1
    Boston hymn, sels. 6102-8,6076-5
    Brahma. 6006-4,6077-3,6102-8,6176-1,6186-9,6246 ,6302-0,
        6385-3,6399-X,6726-3,6730-1,6732 ,6735-2,6088-0,6250-
        4,6560-0,6126-5,6396 ,6288-1,6431-0,6153-2,6467-1,
        6300-4,6309-8,6252-0,6121-4,6076
    Character. 6753-0
    Character. 6252-0,6288-1
    Character. 6753-0
    Chickadee. 6466-3
    "Come learn with me," fr. Woodnotes, II. 6250-4
    Compensation. 6753-0
    Compensation. 6288-1
    Compensation. 6753-0
    The Concord fight. 6601-1,6552-X,6263-6
    Concord hymn. 6449-3,6639-9,6665-8,6739-9,6267-9,6265 ,
        6223-7,6250-4,6560-0,6135-4,6288-1,6107 ,6104-4,6470-
        1,6736-0,6126-5,6153-2,6121 ,6300-4,6396-9,6421-3,
        6006-4,6208-3,6239-3,6240-7,6289-X,6332 ,6457-4,6641-
        0,6473-6,6732-8,6735-2,6723
    Concord momument hymn. 6385-3
    The day's ration. 6077-3,6288-1,6126-5
    Days. 6288-1,6560-0,6008-0,6431-0,6153-2,6252 ,6309-8,
        6467-1,6300-4,6737-9,6126-5,6076 ,6396-9,6464-7,6006-
        4,6102-8,6176-1,6473-6,6536-8,6488 ,6501-5,6726-3,
        6735-2,6723-9,6250-4,6646
    Destiny. 6250-4,6288-1
    Dirge. 6250-4,6431-0
    A dirge, sels. 6934-7
    Drige ("I reached the middle of the mount"). 6753-0
    Duty. 6239-3,6250-4,6736-0,6421-3,6424-8,6585
    Each and all. 6006-4,6332-2,6385-3,6457-4,6501-5,6600 ,
        6008-0,6250-4,6265-2,6428-8,6288-1,6431 ,6610-0,6730-
        1,6212-1,6126-5,6121-4,6219 ,6252-0
    The enchanter. 6126-5,6288-1,6265-2
    Eros. 6429-9,6-66-8,6250-4,6288-1,6126-5,6321
    Etienne de La Boece. 6753-0
    Etienne de la boece. 6252-0
    Etienne de La Boece. 6753-0
    "Ever find me dim regards". 6753-0
    Experience. 6176-1,6288-1,6126-5
    Fable. 6505-8
    Fable ("The mountain and the squirrel"). 6356-X,6519-8,
        6176-1,6089-7,6735-2,6288 ,6092-7,6421-3,6126-5,6736-
        0,6723-9
    Faith, fr. Sacrifice. 6427-2
    Fate. 6006-4,6077-3,6176-1
    Flower chorus. 6374-8,6466-3
    "For nature beats in perfect tune", sels. 6047-1
    "For thought, and not praise". 6753-0
    "For what need I of book or priest". 6753-0
    Forbearance. 6102-8,6176-1,6239-3,6299-7,6332-2,6465 ,
        6076-5,6300-4,6008-0,6288-1,6421-3,6723 ,6527-9,6730-
        1,6006-4,6126-5,6121-4,6252
    Forerunners. 6250-4,6288-1,6431-0
    Fragments on nature and life. 6126-5
    Fragments on the poet. 6232-6,6126-5
    Freedom. 7014-0
    Friendship. 6429-9
    Friendship ("A ruddy drop of manly blood"). 6085-4,6006-
        4,6385-3,6252-0,6429-9,6126 ,6066-8,6250-4,6288-1,
        6321-7,6585-6
    Give all to love. 6006-4,6102-8,6176-1,6320-9,6732-8,
        6317 ,6396-9,6300-4,6464-7,6288-1,6350-4,6560 ,6208-
        3,6076-5,6066-8,6126-5,6464-7,6754-9
    God's message to men. 6964-9
    Good-bye. 6076-5,6300-4,6250-4,6288-1,6252-0,6464 ,6102-
        8,6176-1,6374-8,6385-3,6732-8,6730 ,6396-9,6126-5,
        6219-9,6008-0,6461-2,6431
    Grace. 6288-1
    Guy. 6252-0
    Hamatreya. 6077-3,6208-3,6399-3,6288-1,6121-4,6126
    "The hand that rounded Peter's dome", sels. 6601-1
    "He planted where the deluge ploughed". 6753-0
    Heri, cras, hodie. 6302-0,6385-3,6735-2
    The hero. 6176-1
    Heroism. 6102-8,6302-0,6385-3,6399-3,6732-8,6252 ,6076-
        5
    "His instant thought a poet spoke". 6753-0
    History. 6176-1,6107-9
    "Hold of the maker, not the made". 6753-0
    Holidays. 6753-0
    Holidays. 6126-5,6288-1
    Holidays. 6753-0
    The humble-bee. 6006-4,6102-8,6239-3,6299-7,6473-6,6597
        ,6076-5,6153-2,6121-4,6510-4,6265-2,6126 ,6486-8,
        6632-1,6732-8,6735-2,6396-9,6723 ,6219-9,6288-1,6431-
        0,6004-8,6307-1,6250 ,6008-0
    Hymn ("By the rude bridge that arched the flood.") 6102-
        8,6176-1,6286-5,6632-1,6503-1,6076 ,6442-6
    Hymn sung at the completion of the Concord monument.
        6008-0
    "I have no brothers and no peers". 6753-0
    Illusion. 7014-0
    In an age of fops and toys, fr. Voluntaries. 6212-1
    In the woods 6253-9

The informing spirit. 6730-1,6288-1,6126-5
Justice. 6302-0,6385-3
"Let man serve law for man" 6954-1
Let me go where'er I will. 6374-8,6252-0
"Let me go where'er I will". 6753-0
Letters. 6302-0;6385-3
Lines to Ellen. 6126-5,6288-1
Love reigns forever. 6461-2
'Make tomorrow a new morn!' 6954-1
May-Day, sels. 6239-3,6510-4
Merlin. 6753-0
Merlin. 6126-5,6250-4,6288-1
Merlin. 6753-0
Merops. 6208-3,6288-1,6126-5
Mithridates. 6176-1,6399-3
Monadnoc, sels. 6077-3,6431-0,6484-1
Monadnock from afar. 6461-2
The mountain and the squirrel. 6105-2,6290-3,6299-7, 6049-8,6134-6,6136 ,6127-3,6424-8,6456-6,6401-9,6501-5,6552
Music. 6176-1,6730-1,6126-5
Musketaquid. 6232-6,6288-1,6126-5
My garden. 6232-6,6288-1,6649-6,6126-5
"My half-day's work is done". 6238-5
A nation's strength. 6954-1
Nature. 6236-9,6288-1,6126-5
No great nor small. 6461-2
"No profit goes where is no pleasure taken". 6238-5
Northman. 6302-0;6385-3
Ode ("O tenderly"). 6102-8,6286-5,6465-5,6486-8
Ode ("Though loath"). 6176-1,6399-3
Ode inscribed to W.H. Channing. 6126-5,6288-1
Ode sung in the town hall, Concord, July 4, 1857. 6239-3,6300-4,6126-5,6102-8,6076-5,6288
Ode to beauty. 6126-5,6288-1
Pan. 6126-5,6288-1,6288-1
Philosopher. 6250-4
Philosopher ("Philosophers are lined with eyes within") 6250-4
philosopher's camp, fr. The Adirondacs. 6252-0
The philosopher's cat. 6252-0
Philosophy. 7014-0
Poet. 6302-0,6385-3,6735-2,6302-9
The poet, sels. 6753-0
Politics. 6753-0
Politics. 6121-4
Politics. 6753-0
Politics ("Gold and iron are good"). 6121-4
The problem, sels. 6934-7
The problem, sels. 6077-3,6219-9,6426-0
The problem. 6431-0,6126-5,6219-9,6300-4,6309-8,6647 , 6007-2,6009-0,6112-4,6008-0,6250-4,6560-0,6076-5, 6288-1,6121 ,6102-8,6285-3,6479-5,6600-3,6730-1,6735
Public servant of the gods. 6954-1
Quatrains. 6153-2
Quatrains and fragments. 6302-0,6385-3
Quatrains and translations. 6126-5
Quatrains, fr. Voluntaries. 6153-2
Rebuke. 6232-6
Responses. 6240-7
The rhodora, sels. 6289-X
The rhodora. 6049-8,6077-3,6374-8,6176-1,6239-3,6737 , 6332-2,6302-0,6385-3,6726-3,6473-6,6585 ,6008-8,6212-1,6735-2,6047-1,6102-8,6232 ,6250-4,6288-1,6431-0, 6214-8,6219-9,6121 ,6300-4,6265-2,6076-5,6126-5,6104-4,6396 ,6639-9,6964-9,6250-4,6288-1,6431-0,6214-8, 6219-9,6121 ,6300-4,6265-2,6076-5,6126-5,6104-4,6396
The river. 6126-5
The romany girl. 6077-3
Saadi. 6126-5,6288-1,6250-4
Saadi, sels. 6300-4
Sacrifice. 6735-2,6250-4,6263-6
Sacrifice, sels. 6427-2
"The sea tosses and foams to find". 6997-5
The sea. 6302-0;6385-3
Seashore. 6753-0
Seashore. 6126-5,6288-1,6431-0
Seashore. 6753-0
Shakespeare. 6735-2
"Shun passion, fold the hands of thrift". 6753-0

The snow-storm. 6491-4,6008-0,6250-4,6288-1,6396-9,6121-4,6484 ,6076-5,6126-5,6008-0,6250-4,6288-1,6396-9, 6121-4,6484 ,6076-5,6126-5,6077-3,6102-8,6136-2,6246-6,6289-X,6239 ,6176-1,6299-7,6473-6,6302-0,6385-3, 6399 ,6673-9,6466-3,6723-9,6300-4,6431-0,6464
"So night is grandeur to our dust", sels. 6601-1
Something sings. 6396-9
Song of nature. 6597-X
The soul's prophecy. 6600-3
"Speak not thy speech," fr. Woodnotes. 6250-4
The sphinx. 6126-5,6288-1,6288-1
The summons. 6252-0
"The sun set, but set not his hope". 6753-0
Sursum corda. 6250-4
Suum cuique. 6659-3
"Teach me your mood, O patient stars!" 6753-0
Terminus. 6176-1,6399-3,6008-8,6250-4,6288-1,6659
The test. 6102-8,6076-5,6250-4
Thanksgiving. 6466-3
"That book is good". 6753-0
There always, alway something sings. 6250-4
These halcyons. 6253-9
Thine eyes still shone. 6600-3,6288-1,6126-5
"Thou wert the morning star among the living", sels. 6601-1
Thought. 6126-5,6288-1
Threnody. 6177-X,6288-1,6250-4
The titmouse. 6073-0,6519-8,6288-1,6126-5,6510-4
To Ellen. 6126-5,6288-1
To Ellen at the South. 6299-7,6126-5
To Eva. 6934-7
To Eva. 6600-3,6735-2,6250-4,6291-9
To J.W. 6126-5,6288-1
To Rhea. 6250-4
To the humble-bee. 6302-0;6385-3
Two rivers. 6176-1,6126-5,6219-9,6723-9,6288-1,6431-0
Uriel. 6176-1,6250-4,6288-1,6126-5,6467-1
Voluntaries. 6126-5,6288-1,6396-9
Voluntaries, sels. 6730-1,6008-8,6212-1,6464-7
Waldeinsamkeit. 6126-5,6252-0,6006-4,6597-X,6730-1,6250-4,6288-1,6431
Walden. 6649-6
We are never old. 6465-5
We thank thee. 6618-6
Wealth. 6077-3,6176-1
Webster. 6753-0
Webster. 6126-5
Webster. 6753-0
"Who ne'er his bread in sorrow ate". 6238-5
A wood-note. 6134-6
Woodnotes. 6077-3,6288-1,6126-5,6121-4,6252-0
Woodnotes, sels. 6047-1,6730-1,6431-0,6008-0,6250-4
"The word unto the prophet spoken", sels. 6601-1
The world-soul, sels. 6934-7
The world-soul. 6753-0
The world-soul. 6126-5,6288-1,6250-4
The world-soul. 6753-0
Worship. 6753-0
Worship. 6288-1,6252-0
Worship. 6753-0
Written at Rome. 6753-0
Written at Rome. 6126-5,6288-1
Written at Rome. 6753-0
Written in a volume of Goethe. 6126-5,6288-1,6396-9
Written in Naples. 6753-0
Written in Naples. 6126-5,6288-1
Written in Naples. 6753-0
The youth's reply to duty. 6552-X

Emerson, Ralph Waldo (tr.)
Make friends. Ali Ben Abu Taleb, 6337-3

Emerson, fr. A fable for critics. James Russell Lowell. 6399-3

Emery, Clark
Father. 6761-1

Emery, George D.
The heroic dead. 6471-X

Emery, Gilbert
Soldier-dead. 6649-3

Emery, Steuart M.
Poiu. 6846-4

EMIGRANT
466

The emigrant lassie. John Stuart Mackie. 6656-9
The emigrant mother. Unknown. 6858-8
"An emigrant ship with a world aboard". God knows. Unknown. 6918-5
"An emigrant ship with a world abroad". 'God knows'. Benjamin Franklin Taylor. 6815-4
Emigrant to America. Vicente Huidobro. 6642-9
The emigrant's farewell. Thomas Pringle. 6180-X
The emigrant's funeral. R.J. McGeorge. 6433-7
Emigrant's song. Thomas Pringle. 6625-9
Emigrant's song. Thomas Pringle. 6800-6
The emigrant's wish. Unknown. 6385-3
The emigrant. Unknown. 6859-6
Emigrants. Emily Dickinson. 6121-4
The emigrants in the Bermudas. Andrew Marvell. 6219-9
The emigrants. Thomas Pringle. 6788-3
Emigration. William Michael Rossetti. 7015-9,6793-X
The emigration of the fairies, sels. John Hunter-Duvar. 6795-6
Emigravit. Helen Hunt Jackson. 6431-0
Emilia. Sarah N. Cleghorn. 6467-1
Emilia, sels. Robinson Jeffers. 6649-6
Emilia, sels. Unknown. 6562-7
Emily. Lizette Woodworth Reese. 7038-8
Emily Bronte. Robert Bridges. 6487-6
Emily Dickinson. Melville Crane. 6464-7
Emily Dickinson. Paul Engle. 6483-3
Emily Dickinson. Paul Engle. 6761-1
Emily Dickinson. Robert Allison Evans. 6761-1
Emily Dickinson. Mae Winkler Goodman. 6979-7
Emily Hardcastle, spinster. John Crowe Ransom. 6070-6,6326-8,6393-4
"Emily Mayfield all the day". Little Cyrus. Alice Cary. 6969-X
Emily, John, James, and I. Sir William Schwenck Gilbert. 6722-0
"The eminent Rsi Bhavabhuti came to give away..." Unknown (Newari) 7013-2
The Emir's game of chess. Unknown. 6255-5,6580-5
Emma and Eginhard. Henry Wadsworth Longfellow. 6255-5
Emma Lazarus. Richard Watson Gilder. 6848-0
Emmanuel, Kassaris
    Dynasty of chimeras. Rae Dalven (tr.). 6352-7
    Dynasty of the chimeras. Rae Dalven (tr.). 6352-7
    The haunted ship. Rae Dalven (tr.). 6352-7
Emmanuel, Sister M. (tr.)
    Psalter of the blessed virgin Mary. Saint Bonaventure, 6282-2
Emmett's epitaph. Robert Southey. 6385-3
Emmett, Daniel
    Dixie. 6074-9,6088-9,6736-0,6121-4,6267-9
    Old Dan Tucker. 6594-5
Emmett, Will
    Winnie's welcome. 6139-7,6155-9
Emmonsail's heath in winter. John Clare. 6208-3
Emmonsail's heath in winter. John Clare. 6943-6
Emmy. Arthur Symons. 6437-X,6507-4,6732-8,6508-2,6655-0
Emory, William Closson
    Be still. 6464-7
Emotions. Imogene Bland. 6857-X
Empedocles
    The blood-guilty. T.F. Higham (tr.). 6435-3
    The divine philosopher. William Ellery Leonard (tr.). 6435-3
    The limitations of knowledge. T.F. Higham (tr.). 6435-3
    Nature the artist. T.F. Higham (tr.). 6435-3
    Transmigration. Frances Cornford (tr.). 6435-3
Empedocles on Etna. Matthew Arnold. 6250-4,6947-9
Empedocles on Etna, sels. Matthew Arnold. 6934-7
Empedocles on Etna, sels. Matthew Arnold. 6102-8,6199-0, 6301-2,6378-0.6430-2,6656
Empedocles on Etna, sels. Matthew Arnold. 6879-0
Empedocles' song, fr. Empedocles on Etnaa. Matthew Arnold. 6828-6
The emperor and the rabbi. George Croly. 6848-0
Emperor evermore. Emily Henrietta Hickey. 6046-3
The emperor of ice-cream. Wallace Stevens. 6324-1,6209-1, 6217-2
"The emperor of sax, two eunuch tenors". Program. John Ciardi. 6751-4

The emperor of the east, sels. Philip Massinger. 6533-3, 6562-7
Emperor T'Ang, skeptic. Paul Eldridge. 6069-2
The emperor's bird's-nest. Henry Wadsworth Longfellow. 6502-3
An emperor's daughter stands alone. Geoffrey Chaucer. 6481-7
"The emperors of fourteen dynasties". The Middle Kingdom. Allen Upward. 6897-9
The emperors' bird's-nest. Henry Wadsworth Longfellow. 6502-3,6614-3
The emperors' garden. Amy Lowell. 6649-6
Empire (Persepolis). William ("Fiona Macleod") Sharp. 6102-8
Empire and victory. Percy Bysshe Shelley. 6186-9
The empire answers. Verna Loveday Harden. 6224-5
The empire builder. John Jerome Rooney. 6022-6,6172-9
Empire builders. Archibald MacLeish. 6628-3
Empire first. John T. Lesperance. 6433-7
Empire first. John ("Laclede") Talon-Lesperance. 6795-6
The empire of China is crumbling down. Vachel Lindsay. 6033-1
The empire ship. Nixon Waterman. 6260-1
The Empire State Building. Florence Estelle Bryant. 6799-9
The empire state. Lucy Burgman. 6799-9
"An empire to be lost or won". Whitman's ride for Oregon. Hezekiah Butterworth. 6946-0
Empire, fr. Old and new New York. Alfred Kreymborg. 6012-9
Emplem flowers. Christina Georgina Rossetti. 6123-0
Employment. George Herbert. 6302-0
Employment. Jane Taylor. 6452-3,6135-4
"The express night hath jewels rare". Night. Robert Loveman. 6941-X
Empson, William
    Arachne. 6985-1
    Aubade. 6210-5,6391-8
    Bacchus. 6390-X
    Camping out. 6209-1
    Homage to the British Museum. 6209-1,6391-8
    Invitation to Juno. 6209-1
    Just a smack at Auden. 6210-5
    Legal fiction. 6150-8,6354-3,6391-8
    Missing dates. 6208-3,6389-6,6209-1
    "Not wrongly moved by this dismaying scene" 6527-9,6666-6
    Note on local flora. 6209-1
    This last pain. 6209-1,6391-8
    To an old lady. 6150-8,6210-5
    Villanelle. 6985-1
"Emptied and pearly skulls". The statue and the perturbed burghers. Denis Devlin. 6930-4
Emptiness. John Ransom Palmer. 6482-5
Empty. Berton Braley. 6732-8
"Empty and cold is the night without". The reflection. Walter De La Mare. 6905-3
"An empty bar room". Be yourself. Julia A. Booth. 6883-9
Empty barn, dead farm, fr. Blue Juanita. Malcolm Cowley. 6531-7
The empty bottle. William Edmonstoune Aytoun. 6278-4
"The empty buildings stood in spectral stone". Deserted buildings. Frances Archer Walls. 6906-1
The empty chariot. Walter De La Mare. 6042-0
Empty corral. Glenn Ward Dresbach. 6490-6
The empty cup. Thomas Edward Brown. 6809-X
The empty cup. W.W. Christman. 6662-3
Empty house. Rosario Castellanos. 7036-1
Empty house. Elizabeth J. Coatsworth. 6218-0
The empty house. Hans Magnus Enzensberger. 7032-9
Empty houses. Mary Colborne-Veel. 6784-0
Empty kettle. Louis (LittleCoon) Oliver. 7005-1
"An empty laugh, I heard it on the road". The laugh. Thomas Edward Brown. 6809-X
The empty life, fr. Macbeth. William Shakespeare. 6337-3
An empty little bed. Audrey Lee Kirkman. 6799-9
"The empty marvel of a splendid cage". The body fair. Mark Andre Raffalovitch. 7015-9
The empty nest. Elizabeth York Case. 6565-1
The empty pocket. Charles F. Lummis. 6670-4
The empty quatrain. Henry Van Dyke. 6961-4
Empy shells. Margaret Crosland. 6475-2

The empty sleeve. J.R. Bagby. 6074-9
The empty soul. Walter Russell Bowie. 6337-3
The empty stocking. Unknown. 6807-3
Empty the haunted air. Arthur Mizener. 6761-1
Empty vessel. Christopher M. ("Hugh MacDiarmid") Grieve. 6210-5
"Empty". Gerhard Ruhm. 6769-7
"Empty, idle tube of wood!". The pipe. Edward Farquhar. 6939-8
"En avant! partez, camarades". Le vieux caporal. Pierre Jean de Beranger. 6801-4
"En ce temps dedaigneux, la Rime". Ballade de Victor Hugo. Theodore de Banville. 6801-4
En famille. Edith Sitwell. 6985-1
En famille. Edith Sitwell. 7000-0
En garde. W.T. McIntyre. 6118-4
En garde! William T. MacIntyre. 6983-5
En garde, messieurs. William Lindsey. 6798-0
En garde, messieurs. William Lindsey. 6300-4
"En garde, messieurs, too long have I endured". En garde, messieurs. William Lindsey. 6798-0
En masque. Io Sloan Therme. 6270-9
"En paix sous les ombrages/Du palaid d'Adrien". La villa Adrienne. Casimir Delavigne. 6801-4
"En Puerto Rico her sea rinsed". Tearing down the foundation. Catherine Sanders. 6898-7
En roulant ma Boule. William McLennan. 6433-7
En roulant ma boule. Unknown (French Canadian) 6795-6
En route. Arthur H. Clough. 6484-1
En route. Brander Matthews. 6770-0
En route, fr. Amours de voyage. Arthur Hugh Clough. 6110-9
"En voyage". Caroline Atherton Mason. 6273-3,6654-2
Enamored architect of airy rhyme. Thomas Bailey Aldrich. 6309-8,6431-0
"Enamour'd, artless, young, on foreign ground". Sonnet ("Enamour'd"). John Milton. 6814-6
"Encased in mud, and breathing valley steam". The buffalo. Herbert Price. 6800-6
The enchanted castle. Amy Lowell. 6184-2
The enchanted fawn, fr. 'Dinnshenchas' Unknown. 6930-4
Enchanted forest. Muriel F. Hochdorf. 6850-2
The enchanted heart. Edward Davison. 6777-8
The enchanted heart. Edward Davison. 6102-8
The enchanted island. Alfred Noyes. 6151-6
The enchanted lyre. George Darley. 6317-9
The enchanted mistress. Egan O'Rahilly. 6244-X
The enchanted oak. Oliver Herford. 6677-1
The enchanted princess. George Reston Malloch. 6269-5
The enchanted sheepfold. Josephine Preston Peabody. 6102-8, 6556-2,6019-6,6076-5
The enchanted shirt. John Hay. 6089-7,6486-8,6239-3,6277-6, 6290-3,6415 ,6107-9,6808-1,6739-5,6134-6,6242-3,6249-0,6614-3,6696-8
The enchanted spring. George Darley. 6545-7
The enchanted traveller. Bliss Carman. 6631-3,6331-4
The enchanted vest. John E. Barrett. 6840-5
The enchanter. Ralph Waldo Emerson. 6126-5,6288-1,6265-2
"Enchanting vision stirred a weary heart". The afterglow. Marianne Clarke. 6799-X
Enchantment. Phoebe Cary. 6969-X
Enchantment. Georgia Holloway Jones. 6178-8
The enchantment.. Thomas Otway. 6198-2;6317-9;6563-5
The enchantment. Thomas Otway. 6092-7
Enchantments. Alice Cary. 6385-3
Enchantments of the middle age. David Cecil. 6070-6
Enchantress. Al-Munfatil. 6362-4
"Enchantress, farewell! who so oft..decoy'd me". Farewell to the muse. Sir Walter Scott. 6980-0
"Encinctur'd with a twine of leaves". Fragment ("Encinctur'd"). Samuel Taylor Coleridge. 6545-7
"Enclosed the lacquered, coiling snake". The zoo in the city. Sara Van Alstyne Allen. 6979-7
"Enclosed within, a ribald find". The red and blue. Arthur Spayd Brooke. 6936-1
An encomium on tobacco. Unknown. 6453-1
Encore. Unknown. 6273-3,6576-2
Encore! encore! Unknown. 6924-X
Encounter. John Peale Bishop. 6979-7
Encounter. Denis Devlin. 6930-4
Encounter. Ida Graves. 6780-8

Encounter. William Griffith. 6102-8,6076-5
Encounter. Marion Strobel. 6782-4
The encounter. Charlotte Brown. 6396-9
Encouragement. Emily Bronte. 6123-0
Encouragement. Paul Laurence Dunbar. 6694-1,6964-9
Encouragement. Elizabeth Phelps Rounsevell. 6274-1
Encouragement to exile. Petronius Arbiter. 7039-6
Encouragements to a lover. Sir John Suckling. 6246-6,6732-8,6104-2
End. Peter Paul Wiplinger. 6769-7
End and beginning. Amelia Josephine Burr. 6030-7
The end of a leave. Roy Fuller. 6379-9
End of a world. William Robert Rodgers. 6390-X
The end of all. Edward Fitzgerald. 6090-0
End of another home holiday. David Herbert Lawrence. 6209-1
The end of aodh-of-the-songs. William ("Fiona Macleod") Sharp. 6872-3
The end of being. Seneca. 6730-1
The end of being. Seneca. 6337-3
An end of dancing. Sir Owen Seaman. 6959-2
The end of David. Unknown. 6848-0
The end of desire. Hugh McCrae. 6349-7
The end of Dr. Faustus, fr. The tragical history of... Christopher Marlowe. 6659-3
End of farce. James Rorty. 6979-7
End of Humpty Dumpty. Eleanor Glenn Wallis. 6324-1
The end of it all. Frank Putnam. 6303-9
The end of it all. Frank Putnam. 6889-8
The end of life, fr. The grave. Robert Blair. 6934-7
The end of life. Philip James Bailey. 6543-0
The end of life. William Drummond of Hawthornden. 6385-3
End of season. Robert Penn Warren. 6390-X
End of summer. George Elliston. 7038-8
End of summer. George Elliston. 6039-0
The end of summer. Edna St. Vincent Millay. 6338-1,6649-6
The end of the armada. Algernon Charles Swinburne. 6323-3
The end of the day. Duncan Campbell Scott. 6433-7,6274-1, 6656-9
The end of the drought. Peter McArthur. 6115-X
The end of the episode. Thomas Hardy. 6186-9,6317-9
The end of the first part, fr. Three stages. Christina Georgina Rossetti. 6828-6
The end of the last fight of the Revenge, sels. Gervase Markham. 6547-3
The end of the performance. Yannis Ritsos. 6803-0
The end of the play. William Makepeace Thackeray. 6102-8, 6424-8,6543-0,6656-9,6145-1,6732-8,6239-3,6122-2, 6240-7,6271 ,6302-0,6385-3,6660-7,6197-4,6219-9,6301
The end of the quest. Dorothy Stott Shaw. 6836-7
The end of the road. Norah M. Holland. 6796-4
The end of the season. W.G. Tinckom-Fernandez. 7012-4,7008-6
The end of the story. Terence Tiller. 6379-9
The end of the suitors, fr. The Odyssey. Homer. 6933-9
The end of the war. Herbert Read. 6666-4
The end of the way. Unknown. 6918-5
End of the world. George Elliston. 7038-8
End of the world. George Elliston. 6039-0
End of the world. Else Lasker-Schuler. 6160-5
The end of the world, fr. Chambers of imagery. Gordon Bottomley. 6234-2,6393-4
The end of the world. Archibald MacLeish. 6324-1,6039-0, 6645-3
An end of travel. Robert Louis Stevenson. 6655-0
The end of Troy, fr. Troades. Euripides. 6435-3
An end to idling, sel. Peter Handke. 6769-7
An end, fr. Pictures of autumn. Sara Teasdale. 6011-0,6393-4
"An end, the end is come...". Finis venit. Bible. 6830-8
An end.. Christina Georgina Rossetti. 6186-9
An end. Sara Teasdale. 6778-6
The end. Henry Glassford Bell. 6960-6
The end. Byron Haverly Blackford. 6818-9
The end. Walter De La Mare. 6905-3
The end. William Ernest Henley. 6230-X
The end. C. Hilton-Turvey. 6327-6
The end. Walter Savage Landor. 6328-4
The end. Wilfred Owen. 6879-0
The end. Stella Reinhardt. 6397-7

The end. Marguerite Wilkinson. 6033-1
Ending. Maxwell Bodenheim. 6034-X
Endings. Daniel Whitehead Hicky. 6841-3
The endless army. Gretchen O. Warren. 7027-2
The endless battle. Berton Braley. 6853-7
"An endless journey by foot" Friederike Mayrocker. 6769-7
The endless procession. Unknown. 6415-9
The endless song. Ruth McEnery Stuart. 6089-7
Endorsement to the deed of separation, in...1816. George Gordon, 6th Baron Byron. 6945-2
Endpiece. Olga Berggolts. 6546-5
Endrezze-Danielson, Anita
    Blue horses: west winds. 7005-1
    Night Mare. 7005-1
    Song-maker. 7005-1
    There are three bones in the human ear. 7005-1
    Why stone does not sing by itself. 7005-1
Endurance. Elizabeth Akers Allen. 6219-9
Endurance. Isa Blagden. 7037-X
Endurance. Edgar A. Guest. 6862-6
The enduring music. Harold Vinal. 6833-2
The enduring people. L.E.S. Cotterell. 6468-X
The enduring word. Audrey Wurdemann. 6532-5
The enduring. John Gould Fletcher. 6619-4,6010-2
The enduring. John Holmes. 6761-1
Endyion. Witter Bynner. 6780-8
Endymion. John Keats. 6186-9,6527-9,6543-0
Endymion. Henry Wadsworth Longfellow. 6006-4,6735-2,6288-1,6126-5
Endymion. Marion M. Miller. 6983-5
Endymion. Oscar Wilde. 6174-5,6655-0
Endymion and Diana. Philip Ayres. 6023-4
Endymion's convoy. Michael Drayton. 6436-1
Endymion, sels. John Keats. 6122-2,6198-2,6332-2,6369-1,6732-8,6513,6110-9,6430-2,6196-6,6250-4,6199-0
Enemies. R.N.D. Wilson. 6244-X
The enemies of the little box. Vasko Popa. 6758-1
The enemies.. Dora Sigerson Shorter. 6174-5
Enemy. Carleton Ford Shaw. 6761-1
Enemy conscript. Robert Service. 6159-1
"The enemy of life, decayer of all kind". Epigram ("The enemy"). Sir Thomas Wyatt. 6584-8
'The energy of light.' John Hay. 6388-8
"Enfants, on vous dira plus tard que le...". Premier Janvier. Victor Hugo. 6801-4
Enfidaville. Keith Douglas. 6257-1
Enfield, O.E.
    Contrast. 6799-9
    Poetry. 6799-9
"Enfors we us with all our might". A carol of St. George. Unknown. 6881-2
The enfranchised labourer. Wathen Mark Wilks Call. 7009-4
The enfranchised slaves and their benefactress. Elizabeth M. Chandler. 7009-4
Engaged. F.H. Curtiss. 6682-8
Engaged. J.L. Pennypacker. 6413-2
Engelberg, the hill of angels. William Wordsworth. 6749-2,6884-1
Engels, Norbert
    Ex Maria virgine. 6282-2
The engine driver's story. W. Wilkins. 6922-3,6744-1
Engine failure. Timothy Corsellis. 6666-6
Engineer O.C.S. song. Harry A. Schauffler. 6237-7
The engineer's last run. Unknown. 6450-7
The engineer's murder. Henry Morford. 6412-4
The engineer's ride. James Abraham Martling. 6952-7
The engineer's signal. Francis Bret Harte. 6632-1
Engineer's song. Unknown. 6237-7
"An 'Engineer's story', in form regulation". How an engineer won his bride. James Noel Johnston. 6924-X
The engineer's story. Eugene J. Hall. 6139-7,6964-9
The engineer's story. Rose Hartwick Thorpe. 6277-6,6370-5
The engineer's story. Unknown. 6910-X
Engineer's Yell. Unknown. 6722-0
The engineer. John E. Barrett. 6840-5
Engineers making love. Robert J. Burdette. 6415-9
England. Laurence Binyon. 6477-9
England. William Wilfred Campbell. 6224-5,6433-7,6115-X
England. Arthur Hugh Clough. 6383-7
England. William Cowper. 6150-8

England. Walter De La Mare. 6905-3
England. Ebenezer Elliott. 6605-2
England. John Hanmer, Baron Hanmer. 7015-9,6793-X,6793-X
England. Andrew Lang. 6819-7
England. James Lincoln. 6188-5
England. Joaquin Miller. 6753-0
England. John Henry, Cardinal Newman. 6172-9,6022-6,6292-X,6656-9
England. William Shakespeare. 6459-0,6631-3
England. Unknown. 6563-5
England ("Let it flame or fade, and the war roll..."). Alfred Lord Tennyson. 6087-0
England ("No lovelier hills than thine have laid"). Walter De La Mare. 6331-4,6631-3,6439-6
England ("Shoulders of upland brown laid dark..."). Edith (Bland) Nesbit. 6423-X
England ("Who would not live for her"). Harold Begbie. 6224-5
England ("Whoever lives true life will love true love") Elizabeth Barrett Browning. 6123-0
England after the civil wars. Andrew Marvell. 6935-5
England and America. Florence Taber Holt. 7026-4
England and America in 1782. Alfred Lord Tennyson. 6123-0,6655-0,6110-9,6199-0
England and America in 1782. Alfred Lord Tennyson. 6946-0
England and her colonies. Sir William Watson. 6793-X
England and Spain; or, valour and patriotism. Felicia Dorothea Hemans. 6973-2
England and Switzerland, 1802. William Wordsworth. 6246-6,6332-2,6501-5,6732-8,6737-9
England beseiged. Elizabeth Browne. 6789-1
"England his heart; his corpse the waters have". Richard Barnfield. 6258-X
England in 1819. Percy Bysshe Shelley. 6323-3,6199-0,6150-8
England my mother. Sir William Watson. 6793-X
England my mother, sels. Sir William Watson. 6289-X
England stands alone. Theodore Watts-Dunton. 6323-3
England to America. Alfred Austin. 6084-6
England to Denmark. Herbert Warren. 6474-4
England to France. Alfred Gordon. 6115-X
England to free men. John Galsworthy. 7026-4
England to India. Robert Bridges. 6487-6
"England wears not the mask of hate". England's way. Charles Whitby. 6994-0
"England will keep her dearest...". Robert Bridges. 6487-6
"England! awake! awake! awake!" William Blake. 6138-9
"England! once Europs envye now her scorne." Unknown. 6563-5
"England! that thou was faint of heart". Sonnet ("England"). Grace E. Tollemache. 6474-4
"England! the time is come when..shouldst wean". Sonnet ("England"). William Wordsworth. 6867-7
"England! where the sacred flame". The vigil. Sir Henry Newbolt. 7026-4
England's answer. Rudyard Kipling. 6810-3
England's darling, or Great Britain's joy and hope... Unknown. 6157-5
England's dead. Felicia Dorothea Hemans. 6250-4
England's dead. Felicia Dorothea Hemans. 6973-8
England's dead. Frank Taylor. 6474-4
England's fields. Lloyd Roberts. 6115-X
England's heroical epistles. Michael Drayton. 6198-2
England's sorrow. Unknown. 6524-4
England's standard, fr. The armada. Thomas Babington Macaulay, 1st Baron Macaulay. 6427-2
England's triumph, or The subject's joy. Unknown. 6157-5
England's way. Charles Whitby. 6994-0
England, 1802. William Wordsworth. 6102-8,6186-9,6240-7,6483-3,6301-2,6464
England, 1941. Edward Thompson. 6783-2
England, George Allan
    Into the battalions of death. 7007-8
England, Merrie
    The Roman nose. 6724-7
England, arise! Edward Carpenter. 6954-1,7009-4
England, fr. Balder. Sydney Dobell. 6832-4
England, fr. Richard II. William Shakespeare. 6634-8
England, fr. The return. Rudyard Kipling. 6427-2
England, my England. William Ernest Henley. 6242-3,6395-0,

6224-5,6290-3,6123-0,6331 ,6102-8,6439-6,6437-X
"England, of all the debts we owe to thee". Gratitude. B. Worsley-Gough. 6776-X
"England, on every sea thy navy rides". A monition. John Kells Ingram. 6793-X
"England, queen of the waves". Epilogue ("England"). Algernon Charles Swinburne. 6323-3
England, queen of the waves. Algernon Charles Swinburne. 6473-6,6322-5
England, unprepared for war. Mark Akenside. 6932-0
England, with all thy faults, I love thee still. William Cowper. 6188-5
England: an ode. Algernon Charles Swinburne. 6657-7
Engle, and Ellen King, H. E.
  The West Virginia hills. 6465-5
Engle, Evelyn
  What is this thing called time? 6761-1
Engle, Paul
  America remembers, sels. 6375-6
  Emily Dickinson. 6483-3
  Emily Dickinson. 6761-1
  February. 6761-1
  The last whiskey cup. 6736-0
  Mary. 6250-4
Engle, Ruth Enck
  Even as the grass. 6750-6
The English and the sea, fr. A war with Spain. Edmund Waller. 6934-7
English bards and Scotch reviewers. George Gordon, 6th Baron Byron. 6196-6
English bards and Scotch reviewers, sels. George Gordon, 6th Baron Byron. 6934-7,6102-8,6483-3,6198-2
The English boy. Felicia Dorothea Hemans. 6973-8
The English captains. Charles Fitz-Geffrey. 6547-3
English Channel. William Wordsworth. 6438-8
"An English clergyman came spick and span", fr. Mari. Arthur Hugh Clough. 6123-0
English epitaph on Queen Elizabeth, wife of Henry VII. Unknown. 6378-0
The English flag. Rudyard Kipling. 6473-6,6479-5
An English girl. F. Wyville Home. 6656-9
The English girl. Jane Taylor. 6233-4
The English graves. Gilbert Keith Chesterton. 7029-9
English hills ("O that I were"). John Freeman. 6331-4
English history in rhyme. Unknown. 6629-1
English horn. Laurence McKinney. 6722-0
English irregular: '99-'02. Rudyard Kipling. 6138-9,6153-2
The English language, sels. William Wetmore Story. 6239-3
The English martyrs. Felicia Dorothea Hemans. 6973-8
"The English men had their bows...". Unknown. 6518-X
The English metres. Alice Meynell. 6096 X
An English mother. Robert Underwood Johnson. 6097-8,6627-5
"An English muse shall close the solemn scene". To her majesty Caroline on her accession to the throne. Thomas Warton (the Elder). 6962-2
An English padlock. Matthew Prior. 6208-3,6152-4
English poetry. Samuel Daniel. 6436-1
The English race. Daniel Defoe. 6932-0
The English robin. Harrison Weir. 6302-0;6385-3
The English schoolboy. John Heywood. 6022-6
An English sheel. Arthur Christopher Benson. 6656-9
English soldier's song of memory. Felicia Dorothea Hemans. 6973-8
"A English sparrow, pert and free". A card of invitation to Mr. Gibbon...1781. William Hayley. 6932-0
The English sparrow. Mary Isabella Forsyth. 6597-X
English Stornelli, sels. Augusta Webster. 7037-X
The English tongue. Lewis Worthington Smith. 6473-6
English verse. Edmund Waller. 6250-4
An English village. William Cobbett. 7020-5
English war song. Alfred Lord Tennyson. 6977-0
The English war. Dorothy L. Sayers. 6783-2
English weather. John Dyer. 6150-8
English, D.
  Butterfly. 6804-9
English, Ivy
  The angelic song. 6745-X
English, Thomas Dunn
  Arnold at Stillwater. 6062-5,6674-4,6419-1
  Assunpink and Princeton. 6946-0
  At seventy-two, sels. 6482-5
  The ballad of the colors. 6451-5,6576-7
  The bankrupt's visitor. 6411-6
  The battle of Monmouth. 6946-0
  The battle of New Orleans. 6267-9,6470-1
  The battle of New Orleans. 6946-0
  The battle of the Cowpens. 6678-X,6470-1
  The battle of the king's mill. 6946-0
  Ben Bolt. 6085-4,6451-5,6632-1,6732-8,6744-1,6723 ,6300-4,6431-0,6121-4
  Betty Zane. 6946-0
  The Browns. 6912-6
  The burning of Jamestown. 6946-0
  The charge by the ford. 6916-9
  The charge by the ford. 6015-3,6113-3,6062-5
  Come back. 6410-8
  The fall of Maubila. 6946-0
  The game Knut played. 6915-0
  Johnny Bartholomew. 6062-5,6406-X
  Kate Vane. 6004-8
  The legend of Ogre castle. 6672-0
  Maple ("That was a day of delight"). 6049-8
  The old mill. 6936-3
  Out in the streets. 6909-6
  The quarrel of the wheels. 6416-7
  The rescue of Albret. 6924-X
  The sack of Deerfield. 6946-0
  The shoemaker's daughter. 6414-0
English, William
  Cashel of Munster. Sir Samuel Ferguson (tr.). 6930-4
The Englishman in Italy. Robert Browning. 6484-1,6655-0, 6657-7
An Englishman's sea-dirge. Unknown. 6416-7
The Englishman.. Gilbert Keith Chesterton. 6722-0
The Englishman. Eliza Cook. 6302-0
The Englishman. Walter De La Mare. 6596-1
Englyn. Unknown (Welsh) 6528-7
Englynion. Unknown. 6528-7
Englynion to his love. David Jones. 6528-7
Engraved on the collar of a dog. Alexander Pope. 6125-7
"Engrossed, the abandoned crickets sing". At the grave of Cecil Rhodes. Peter Jackson. 6788-3
Enid's song. Alfred Lord Tennyson. 6304-7
Enid's song (marriage of Geraint). Alfred Lord Tennyson. 6110-9
Enid, fr. Idyls of the king. Alfred Lord Tennyson. 6669-0
Enid, sels, fr. Idyls of the king. Alfred Lord Tennyson. 6484-1
Enigma. Joseph Auslander. 6778-6
Enigma. Ingeborg Bachmann. 6769-7
Enigma. Hugh McCrae. 6349-7
Enigma. Matthew Prior. 6278-7
Enigma. Katherine Reeves. 6218-0
Enigma. Mae Berry Rogers. 6799-9
Enigma in Altman's. Phyllis McGinley. 6722-0
Enigma on cod. Unknown. 6724-7
Enigma on the letter H. Catherine Maria Fanshawe. 6089-7, 6724-7,6302-0,6385-5,6092-7
Enigma on the letter I. Catherine Maria Fanshawe. 6724-7
The enigma. Walter De La Mare. 6905-3
Enithamon's song, fr. Vala. William Blake. 6125-7
Enixa est puerpera. Unknown. 6756-5
Enj'ying poor health. George Horton. 6675-5
Enjoy the April now. Samuel Daniel. 6182-6
"Enjoy the sweets of life's luxuriant May". Garcilaso de la Vega. 6973-8
Enjoyment of the present. Richard Chenevix Trench. 6915-0
Enlargement. Helena Coleman. 6115-X
"Enlightened as you are, you all must know". An address, fr. Croaker papers. Fitz-Greene Halleck and Joseph Rodman Drake. 6753-0
Enlisted. Eliza Calvert Hall. 6340-3,6741-X
Enlisted today. Unknown. 6074-9,6113-3
Enlow, Lucile
  Chrysalis. 6841-3
  Defenses. 6841-3
  Glass. 6841-3
  Lottery. 6841-3
  Reflections. 6841-3
  Repentance of a love-miser. 6841-3

Second sight. 6841-3
Ennius
"Like a shower of rain," fr. Annales. John Wight (tr.). 6665-8
Ennodius
How of the virgin mother shall I sing? 6282-2
Hymnus sanctae Mariae, sels. 6282-2
Ennui. Henry Thornton Craven. 6936-3
Ennui. Frances Fuerst Quick. 6799-9
"**Eno**, eno, Juan Coqueno". Unknown. 6364-0
Enoch Arden. Alfred Lord Tennyson. 6679-8,6084-6,6655-0
Enoch Arden at the window. Alfred Lord Tennyson. 6302-0;6385-3
Enoch Arden, sels. Alfred Lord Tennyson. 6066-8
Enoch the immortal. Unknown. 6848-0
"The **enormous** head of a bison". The head on the table. John Haines. 6855-3
Enough. Berton Braley. 6995-9
"**Enough** for me to realize". Eternity. Grace Griswold Bisby. 6818-9
"**Enough** has been said about roses". To Hilda of her roses. Grace Hazard Conkling. 6762-X
"**Enough** of air. A desert subject now". Diet, fr. The art of preserving health. John Armstrong. 6968-1
"**Enough** of Grongar, and the shady dales". The ruins of Rome. John Dyer. 6968-1
Enough of thought, philosopher. Emily Bronte. 6380-2
"**Enough** of thought, philosopher!". The philosopher. Emily Bronte. 6828-6
"**Enough** that you must turn your days to discs". Quatrains for a bank cashier. Samuel A. DeWitt. 6979-7
Enough!. John Bunyan. 6461-2
"**Enough**, enough; all this we knew before". Advice: a satire. Tobias George Smollett. 6975-4
"**Enough:** and leave the rest to fame." Andrew Marvell. 6317-9
"**Enough:** you have the dream, the flame". Due north. Benjamin R.C. Low. 6833-2
"**Enough;** and leave the rest to fame!". An epitaph. Andrew Marvell. 6102-8
The **enquiring** soul. Thomas Traherne. 6337-3
The **enquiry.** John Dyer. 6932-0
Enright, D.J.
'The black' country. 6257-1
The **ensign** bearer. Unknown. 6964-9
The **ensign** breaker. Unknown. 6408-6
Enslaved, sels. John Masefield. 6320-9,6541-0
Ensor, R.C.K. (tr.)
Nicoteles, fr. Epigrams. Callimachus. 6435-3
The **entail.** Horace Walpole; 4th Earl of Orford. 6874-X
"**Entangling** is the snare, clustered is...". The tercets of Llywarc'h. Llywarc's Hen. 6873-1
"**Enter** and learn the story of the rulers". Inscriptions at the city of brass, fr. 1000 & 1 nights. Unknown (Arabian). 6879-0
Enter these enchanted woods. George Meredith. 6252-9
"**Enter** this cavern, stranger! here, awhile". Inscription for a cavern that overlooks the river Avon. Robert Southey. 6867-7
The **entered** apprentices' song. Matthew Birkhead. 6328-4
Entering by his door. Richard Baxter. 6065-X
Entering the room. Roger Pfingston. 6966-5
Enterprise and Boxer. Unknown. 6946-0
The **enterprise.** Wilfred Wilson Gibson. 6781-6
Entertaining sister's beau. Francis Bret Harte. 6014-5, 6451-5,6155-9
The **enthusiast..** Herman Melville. 6333-0
The **enthusiast:** an ode. William Whitehead. 6086-2
The **enthusiast:** or, the lover of nature, sels. Joseph Warton. 6208-3,6152-4
The **enthusiast.** Joseph Warton. 6831-6
Enthusiasts. Lionel Johnson. 6174-5
The **entire** surrender. Madame De la Mothe Guion. 6814-6
Entirely. Louis MacNeice. 6357-8
"**Entombed** within a nation's reverent love". Edward Crapsey. 6238-5
Entrance into heaven. Sara Henderson Hay. 6144-3
The **entrance** into the ark. Jean Ingelow. 6848-0
Entrance of Columbus into Barcelona. Grenville Mellen. 6438-8

The **entrance** to hell, fr. Aeneid. Vergil. 6845-6
"**Entranced** they gaze, and o'er the...track". St. Oran, sels. Mathilde Blind. 6997-5
Entre nous. Sophie ("Ellen Burroughs") Jewett. 6620-8
Entre Paris et Saint-Denis. Unknown (French Canadian) 6795-6
"'**Entreat** me not. Let Orpah go'". Ruth's choice. Mrs. Mackay. 6848-0
Entreaty. Walter G. Arnold. 6178-8
Entreaty. Irene M. Ward. 6782-4
An **entreaty** for peace. Edward R. Huxley. 6885-5
Entropy. Roy G. Pearce. 6482-5
Entry to the desert. James Rorty. 6619-4
The **enviable** isles. Herman Melville. 6333-0,6253-9,6300-4
The **envious** wren. Phoebe Cary. 6060-9
Envoi. John Barton. 6767-0
Envoi. Cecil Chesterton. 6096 X
Envoi. Arthur Shearly Cripps. 6800-6
Envoi. Walter Savage Landor. 6208-3
Envoi. John G. Neihardt. 6291-1
Envoi. Josephine Preston Peabody. 6556-2
Envoi. Ezra Pound. 6339-X
Envoi. Kathleen Raine. 6379-9
Envoi. Edward de Stein. 7029-9
Envoi. Algernon Charles Swinburne. 6123-0
Envoi. Randall Swingler. 6895-2
Envoi. William Roscoe Thayer. 6762-X
Envoi. J. Ernest Whitney. 6836-7
Envoi. Anna Wickham. 6581-3
Envoi. Thomas L. Work. 6768-9
Envoi ("O ye"). Nizami. 6448-5
Envoi ("Prince"). Edmund Clerihew Bentley. 6659-3
Envoi (1919). Ezra Pound. 6619-4,6354-3
Envoi, fr. Amours de voyage. Arthur Hugh Clough. 6110-9
Envoi, fr. Hugh Selwyn Mauberley. Ezra Pound. 6399-3
Envoy. Henry Cuyler Bunner. 6307-1
Envoy. William Canton. 6233-4
Envoy. Bliss Carman. 6301-2,6501-5,6732-8
Envoy. DuBose Heyward. 6393-4
Envoy. Richard Hovey. 6250-4,6431-0
Envoy. James Whitcomb Riley. 6990-8
Envoy. Robert Louis Stevenson. 6339-X,6465-5,6250-4
Envoy. Unknown. 6145-1
Envoy ("Child, do you love the flower.") Walter De La Mare. 6596-1
Envoy ("Go, songs, for ended is our brief, sweet play") Francis Thompson. 6250-4,6508-2,6426-0,6477-9,6490-6, 6527-9,6655-0
Envoy ("The God who made denial"). Gerald Gould. 6532-5
Envoy ("Where are the secrets it knew?) Austin Dobson. 6659-3
The **envoy** from Dubrovnik. Jovan Ducic. 6765-4
An **envoy** to an American lady. Richard Monckton Milnes; 1st Baron Houghton. 6656-9
Envoy to Fo'c's'le yarns: Go back! Thomas Edward Brown. 6809-X
Envoy, fr. A lover's diary. Gilbert Parker. 6656-9
Envoy, fr. More songs from Vagabondia. Richard Hovey. 6300-4
Envy. Edgar A. Guest. 6748-4
Envy. Edgar A. Guest. 6862-6
Envy. Arthur Guiterman. 6503-1,6583-X
Envy. Jacqueline Hoyt. 6850-2
Envy. Seumas (James Starkey) O'Sullivan. 6174-5
Envy. Adelaide Anne Procter. 6686-0
Envy. Benjamin Rosenbaum. 6038-2
Envy. Charles Wells. 6102-8
Envy. Winifred White. 6764-6
Envy and avarice. Victor Hugo. 6610-0
Envy goes groping. R.D. FitzGerald. 6349-7
Enzensberger, Hans Magnus
Countdown. Reinhold Grimm, Felix Pollak (tr.). 7032-9
The doctrine of categories. Reinhold Grimm, Felix Pollak (tr.). 7032-9
Doomsday. Reinhold Grimm, Felix Pollak (tr.). 7032-9
The empty house. Reinhold Grimm, Felix Pollak (tr.). 7032-9
Peace conference. Reinhold Grimm, Felix Pollak (tr.). 7032-9
Eoiae, sels. Hesiod. 6435-3

The eolian harp. Samuel Taylor Coleridge. 6828-6
The Eolian harp. Samuel Taylor Coleridge. 6545-7
Ephemera. Hazel Hall. 6037-4
Ephemerae for Bruska. Keidrych Rhys. 6360-8
Ephesians, sels. Bible. 6143-5
Ephraim repenting. William Cowper. 6814-6
Ephraim repenting. William Cowper. 6848-0
Ephraim's storm lullaby. C. Minton H. Collester. 6118-4
Ephrem, Saint
    Christmas hymn, sels. W.H. Kent (tr.). 6282-2
    Virgin truly full of wonder. W.H. Kent (tr.). 6282-2
An epic for Kansas. Willard Wattles. 6615-1
An epic of Gotham. Lester. 6817-0
The epic of Hades. Sir Lewis Morris. 6046-3
Epic of the Yser. Grace Blackburn. 6115-X
Epic of women, fr. Bisclaveret. Arthur O'Shaughnessy. 6832-4
The epic. Mary F. Lerch. 7019-1
The epic. Alfred Lord Tennyson. 6604-6,6655-0,6660-7
Epicedium. J. Corson Miller. 6033-1
Epicedium - going or gone. Charles Lamb. 6802-2
Epicedium: William Cullen Bryant. Bayard Taylor. 6976-2
Epicharmus
    On pedigree. William Cowper (tr.). 6814-6
Epicoene, sels. Ben Jonson. 6083-8
"An epicure dining at Crewe". Limerick:"An epicure dining at Crewe." Unknown. 6308-X,6811-1
"An epicure, dining at Crewe". Unknown. 6722-0
"An epicure, dining at Crewe". Limerick:"An epicure, dining at Crewe". Unknown. 6811-1
The epicure. Sung by one in the habit of a town... Unknown. 6562-7
The epicure. Abraham Cowley. 6513-9,6482-5,6733-6
An Epicurean ode. John Hall. 6562-7,6341-1
Epicurean reminiscences of a sentimentalist. Thomas Hood. 6219-9
An Epicurean's epitaph. Aubrey Thomas De Vere. 6656-9
The Epicurean. Sir Francis Hastings Doyle. 6199-0
Epigram. Iola M. Brister. 6178-8
Epigram. Samuel Taylor Coleridge. 6219-9
Epigram. Francis Coutts. 6785-9
Epigram. William Cowper. 6814-6
Epigram. Ernest Dowson. 6022-6
Epigram. Edwin Essex. 6096-X
Epigram. Philip Freneau. 6753-0
Epigram. Richard Garnett. 6437-X
Epigram. Louis Gilmore. 6070-6,6250-4
Epigram. Charles G. ("Miles O'Reilly") Halpine. 6505-8
Epigram. Robert Hillyer. 6722-0
Epigram. Thomas Hood. 7025-6
Epigram. Ben Jonson. 6438-8
Epigram. Walter Savage Landor. 6230-X
Epigram. Lambros Porphyras. 6352-7
Epigram. Francis Quarles. 6315-2
Epigram. John Wilmot, 2d Earl of Rochester. 6424-8
Epigram. Rulhieres. 6945-2
Epigram. Robert Haven Schauffler. 6047-1
Epigram. Unknown. 6436-1
Epigram. Sir William Watson. 6730-1,6102-8
Epigram. Sir William Watson. 6861-8
Epigram ("A face"). Sir Thomas Wyatt. 6436-1
Epigram ("Frank carves"). Matthew Prior. 6152-4
Epigram ("He who bends"). William Blake. 6179-6
Epigram ("I give"). William Blake. 6179-6
Epigram ("Lux"). Sir Thomas Wyatt. 6584-8
Epigram ("My lord"). Matthew Prior. 6633-X
Epigram ("Quote Satan to Arnold..."). Unknown. 6946-0
Epigram ("Rudely forced"). Unknown. 6946-0
Epigram ("Scarus hates"). Unknown. 7017-5
Epigram ("Sighs"). Sir Thomas Wyatt. 6584-8
Epigram ("The enemy"). Sir Thomas Wyatt. 6584-8
Epigram ("The fruit"). Sir Thomas Wyatt. 6584-8
Epigram ("The sword"). William Blake. 6179-6
Epigram ("To John"). Matthew Prior. 6092-7,6152-4,6934-7
Epigram ("Who hath heard"). Sir Thomas Wyatt. 6584-8
Epigram ("Yes, every poet"). Matthew Prior. 6152-4
Epigram (Lord Pam"). Jonathan Swift. 6380-2
Epigram (on Colley Cibber) Samuel Johnson. 6092-7
Epigram 101. Ben Jonson. 6369-1
Epigram II. Alexander Pope. 6152-4

"An epigram is but a feeble thing". William Cowper. 6814-6
An epigram of Martial, imitated. Sir Charles Hanbury Williams. 6932-0
Epigram on an academic visit to the continent. Richard Porson. 6722-0
Epigram on Drake. Abraham Cowley. 6438-8
Epigram on Drake. William Cowley. 6438-8
Epigram on Francis Drake. Abraham Cowley. 6867-7
Epigram on George II and Colley Cibber, Esq. Samuel Johnson. 6975-4
Epigram on Handel and Bononcini. John Byrom. 6932-0
Epigram on his garden shed (1). William Cowper. 6814-6
Epigram on his garden shed (2). William Cowper. 6814-6
Epigram on Milton. John Dryden. 6154-0,6483-3,6717-4
Epigram on Miltonicks. Samuel Wesley. 6932-0
Epigram on my wedding day. George Gordon, 6th Baron Byron. 6945-2
Epigram on Sir Francis Drake. Ben Jonson. 6219-9,6424-8
Epigram on the braziers' company having resolved... George Gordon, 6th Baron Byron. 6945-2
Epigram on the death of Edward Forbes. Sydney Dobell. 6656-9
Epigram on the feuds between Handel and Bononcini. John Byrom. 6152-4
Epigram on the passing of Christmas. Edgar Bowers. 6515-5
Epigram on the poor of Boston employed..paving streets. Unknown. 6722-0
Epigram on the refusal of Oxford to subscribe... William Cowper. 6814-6
Epigram on the toasts of the Kit-Kat club, anno 1716. Alexander Pope. 6152-4
An epigram on..L. Echard's & G. Burnet's histories. Matthew Green. 6968-1
An epigram to King Charles. Ben Jonson. 6430-2
An epigram upon his majestie's great ship... Thomas Heywood. 6547-3
Epigram, fr. Tom Paine. George Gordon, 6th Baron Byron. 6945-2
Epigram, The road to Rome. Robin Flower. 7014-0
Epigram: fatum supremum. Unknown. 6933-9
Epigram: on the Sir Francis Drake. Unknown. 6933-9
An epigram. Thomas Campion. 6794-8
Epigramma. Thomas Campion. 6794-8
Epigrammatvm (in Latin) Thomas Campion. 6794-8
Epigrams. Samuel Taylor Coleridge. 6385-3
Epigrams. James Vincent Cunningham. 6017-X
Epigrams. John Heywood. 6022-6
Epigrams. Ben Jonson. 6430-2
Epigrams. John ("Peter Pindar") Walcott. 6278-4
Epigrams. Sir William Watson. 6656-9
Epigrams ("On our lady of Blachernae"). Unknown. 6282-2
Epigrams ("On the Annunciation"). Unknown. 6282-2
Epigrams ("Treason doth never prosper;..."). Sir John Harington. 6427-2
Epigrams ("When I am dead..."). Hilaire Belloc. 6427-2
Epigrams ("'I hardly ever ope my lips,'"). Richard Garnett. 6427-2
Epigrams of art, life, and nature, sels. Sir William Watson. 6723-9
Epigrams on Castlereagh. George Gordon, 6th Baron Byron. 6733-6,6945-2
Epigrams("To the most holy mother of God"). Unknown. 6282-2
Epigrams, sels. John Milton. 6814-6
Epigrams, sels. Steingrimur Thorsteinsson. 6854-5
Epigrams, sels. Sir William Watson. 6301-2
Epigrams, sels. Steingrimur Thorsteinsson. 6283-0
Epilog, fr. The North Sea. Heinrich Heine. 7039-6
Epilogue. Lascelles Abercrombie. 6250-4,6393-4,6437-X
Epilogue. Maxwell Anderson. 6039-0
Epilogue. Tefcros Anthias. 6352-7
Epilogue. Edwina Stanton Babcock. 6331-4
Epilogue. Robert Browning. 6437-X,6657-7,6656-9,6655-0, 6464-7,6214 ,6102-8,6214-8,6250-4,6199-0
Epilogue. S. Foster Damon. 6506-6
Epilogue. Walter De La Mare. 6905-3
Epilogue. William Ernest Henley. 6508-2
Epilogue. Horace. 6949-5
Epilogue. Philip Horton. 6640-2
Epilogue. Langston Hughes. 6628-3

Epilogue. William Alexander Percy. 7014-0
Epilogue. William Alexander Percy. 6326-8
Epilogue. George William ("A.E.") Russell. 6785-9
Epilogue. Allan Seager. 6042-0
Epilogue. Francis Carey ("Jan van Avond") Slater. 6625-9
Epilogue ("At the midnight"). Robert Browning. 6473-6,6196-6
Epilogue ("England"). Algernon Charles Swinburne. 6323-3
Epilogue ("If we shadows"). William Shakespeare. 6436-1
Epilogue ("Now the hungry"). William Shakespeare. 6436-1
Epilogue , fr. Midsummer night's dream. William Shakespeare. 6315-2,6732-8,6102-8
Epilogue for a school performance. Unknown. 6064-1
Epilogue for the King's House. John Dryden. 6970-3
Epilogue in Berlin. Gerald Bisinger. 6769-7
Epilogue intended to have been spoken by a lady... Samuel Johnson. 6975-4
Epilogue intended to have been spoken..Lady Wentworth. John Dryden. 6970-3
Epilogue spoken at Oxford by Mrs. Marshall. John Dryden. 6152-4
Epilogue spoken at Oxford, by Mrs. Marshall. John Dryden. 6970-3
Epilogue spoken at the acting of The silent woman. John Dryden. 6970-3
Epilogue to 'A judgment in heaven' Francis Thompson. 6828-6
Epilogue to a judgment in heaven, sel. Francis Thompson. 7014-0
Epilogue to Albion and Albanius. John Dryden. 6970-3
Epilogue to All for love. John Dryden. 6970-3
Epilogue to Alun Mabon. Ceirog. 6528-7
Epilogue to Amboyna. John Dryden. 6970-3
Epilogue to Asolando. Robert Browning. 6123-0,6154-0,6198-2,6208-3,6337-3,6501 ,6023-4,6110-9,6301-2,6660-7, 6723-9,6737 ,6604-6,6657-7
Epilogue to Henry II, by Mr. Mountfort. John Dryden. 6970-3
Epilogue to Lessing's 'Laocoon'. Matthew Arnold. 6250-4
Epilogue to Mithridates, King of Pontius, by Mr. N. Lee. John Dryden. 6970-3
Epilogue to Oedipus. John Dryden. 6970-3
An epilogue to Polycrates. Ibycus. 6435-3
Epilogue to the accuser who is the God of this world. William Blake. 6378-0
Epilogue to the Breakfast-table series. Oliver Wendell Holmes. 6126-5
Epilogue to The husband his own cuckold. John Dryden. 6970-3
Epilogue to The Indian emperor. John Dryden. 6970-3
Epilogue to The Indian queen. John Dryden. 6970-3
Epilogue to The man of mode, by Sir George Etherege. John Dryden. 6970-3
Epilogue to the Pacchiarotto volume. Robert Browning. 6110-9
Epilogue to The pilgrim. John Dryden. 6970-3
Epilogue to the poet's sitter. Francis Thompson. 6942-8
Epilogue to the Satires. Alexander Pope. 6152-4
Epilogue to the second part of The conquest of Granada. John Dryden. 6970-3
Epilogue to The wild gallant, when revived. John Dryden. 6970-3
Epilogue, fr. A judgment in heaven. Francis Thompson. 6477-9,6489-2,6661-5
Epilogue, fr. Dramatis personae. Robert Browning. 6144-3, 6110-9
Epilogue, fr. Pacchiarotto volume. Robert Browning. 6110-9
Epilogue, fr. The everlasting mercy. John Masefield. 6581-3
Epilogue, fr. The golden journey to Samarkand. James Elroy Flecker. 6508-2
Epilogue, fr. The strength of the hills. Enid Bliss Kiernan. 6764-6
Epilogue, sels. Robert Browning. 6144-3
The epilogue, sels. Alfred Lord Tennyson. 6198-2
Epilogue, to Joanna Baillie's Family legend. Henry Mackenzie. 6813-8
Epilogue: Credo. Arthur Symons. 6507-4
An epilogue. John Dryden. 6970-3
An epilogue. Wilfred Wilson Gibson. 6069-2

An epilogue. Alfred Noyes. 6169-9,6250-4
The epilogue. Unknown. 6753-0
Epiphany. Eileen Duggan. 6282-2
Epiphany. Reginald Heber. 6271-7,6465-5,6291-9,6424-8
The epiphany of Apollo. Callimachus. 6435-3
Epiphany vision (in the ward). Mary Adair-Macdonald. 7031-0
Epipsychidion. Percy Bysshe Shelley. 6828-6,6086-2,6199-0
Epipsychidion, sels. Percy Bysshe Shelley. 6317-9,6378-0, 6102-8,6198-2,6258-X,6282 ,6427-2,6110-9,6196-6,6649-6
Episode in a library. Zbigniew Herbert. 6758-1
The episode of Nisus and Euryalus. George Gordon, 6th Baron Byron. 6945-2
An episode.. John Addington Symonds. 6624-0,6656-9
An episode. Muriel Early Sheppard. 6281-4
Episodes of haying time. Holger Christensen. 6799-9
Epistle. Robert Nathan. 6337-3
Epistle ("Good Poets, who are so full of pain"). Philip Freneau. 6399-3
An epistle addressed to Sir Thomas Hanmer, sels. William Collins. 6195-0
An epistle containing the strange medical experience... Robert Browning. 6655-0
An epistle frmo Mount Tmolous. Bayard Taylor. 6976-2
Epistle from Algiers. Thomas Campbell. 6092-7
Epistle from Lord Borington to Lord Granville. George Canning. 6200-8,6086-2
Epistle from Mr. Murray to Dr. Polidori. George Gordon, 6th Baron Byron. 6945-2
An epistle from Thomas Hearn. Joseph Warton. 6024-2
Epistle I, fr. Moral essays. Alexander Pope. 6152-4
Epistle II, sels. Alexander Pope. 6198-2
An epistle in June. Helen Gray Cone. 6847-2
Epistle of condolence. Thomas Moore. 6930-4
An epistle of Kaeshish. Robert Browning. 6199-0
An epistle to a friend in town. John Dyer. 6968-1
Epistle to a friend to persuade hiim to the wars. Ben Jonson. 6438-8
Epistle to a friend, in answer to some lines...cheerful. George Gordon, 6th Baron Byron. 6945-2
An epistle to a friend. Samuel Rogers. 6543-0
Epistle to a German. Allen Kanfer. 6042-0
An epistle to a lady. John Gay. 6972-X
An epistle to a Protestant lady in France. William Cowper. 6814-6
Epistle to a student of dead languages. Philip Freneau. 6753-0
Epistle to a young friend. Robert Burns. 6260-1,6332-2, 6370-5,6543-0
Epistle to Augusta. George Gordon, 6th Baron Byron. 6110-9, 6828-6,6945-2,6945-2
Epistle to Charles Cowden Clarke. John Keats. 6943-6,6828-6
Epistle to Davie, a brother poet. Robert Burns. 6180-X
Epistle to Dr. Arbuthnot. Alexander Pope. 6024-2,6198-2, 6536-8,6152-4,6195-0,6197-4,6430-2,6726-3,6733-6
Epistle to Dr. Arbuthnot, sels. Alexander Pope. 6483-3, 6604-6,6102-8,6122-2,6315-2,6637
Epistle to Dr. Blacklock. Robert Burns. 6932-0
An epistle to Dr. Guibbons, a celebrated physician. Thomas Warton (the Elder) 6962-2
Epistle to Dr. Young upon his poem on the lsdt laft day. Thomas Warton (the Elder) 6962-2
Epistle to Elizabeth, countess of Rutland, sels. Ben Jonson. 6726-3
Epistle to George Felton Mathew. John Keats. 6828-6
An epistle to her grace, Henrietta. John Gay. 6972-X
Epistle to J.H. Reynolds. John Keats. 6092-7
Epistle to John Lapraik, an old Scottish bard. Robert Burns. 6430-2,6152-4,6150-8
Epistle to John Lapraik, sels. Robert Burns. 6332-2,6195-0
An epistle to Joseph Hill, Esq. William Cowper. 6814-6
An epistle to Joseph Hill, esq. William Cowper. 6874-X
An epistle to Joseph Hill. William Cowper. 6153-2,6370-5
An epistle to Lady Rutland. Ben Jonson. 6208-3
Epistle to Martha Blount on her leaving the town... Alexander Pope. 6152-4
Epistle to Mr. Addison, sels. Alexander Pope. 6560-0
Epistle to Mr. Murray. George Gordon, 6th Baron Byron.

Epistle to Mrs. Blount. Alexander Pope. 6153-2
Epistle to my brother George. John Keats. 6828-6
Epistle to Pope, sels. Edward Young. 6102-8
Epistle to Reynolds, fr. On imagination. John Keats. 6199-0
An epistle to Robert Lloyd, Esq. William Cowper. 6814-6
Epistle to Robert, Earl of Oxford. Alexander Pope. 6302-0
An epistle to Sir Edward Sackville, now Earl of Dorset. Ben Jonson. 6380-2
Epistle to Sir R. Walpole. Henry Fielding. 6092-7
Epistle to Sir Robert Walpole, 1730. Henry Fielding. 6086-2
Epistle to Sir Robert Walpole, 1731. Henry Fielding. 6086-2
Epistle to the Earl of Dorset. Ambrose Philips. 6831-6
Epistle to the Lady Margaret, Countess of Cumberland. Samuel Daniel. 6198-2,6634-8
An epistle to the most learned doctor w--d----d. John Gay. 6972-X
Epistle to the Rev. John M'Math. Robert Burns. 6831-6
Epistle to the right honourable Paul Methuen, Esq. John Gay. 6024-2
An epistle to the right honourable the Earl of... John Gay. 6972-X
An epistle to the right honourable William Pulteney. John Gay. 6972-X
Epistle to the Whigs. John Dryden. 6200-8
Epistle to Thomas Moore, sels. George Gordon, 6th Baron Byron. 6945-2
Epistle written while recovering from a severe illness. Richard Henry Dana. 6752-2
An epistle, sels. Matthew Green. 6315-2
An epistle.. Robert Browning. 6657-7
An epistle. Robert Browning. 6828-6
An epistle. Ben Jonson. 6430-2
Epistles, sels. John Dryden. 6970-3
Epistola ad Dakyns. Thomas Edward Brown. 6809-X
Epitaph. Lascelles Abercrombie. 6023-4
Epitaph. Thomas Lovell Beddoes. 6908-8
Epitaph. William Browne. 6189-3
Epitaph. William Browne. 6198-2,6512-0
Epitaph. Thomas Carew. 6301-2
Epitaph. Samuel Taylor Coleridge. 6828-6
Epitaph. Samuel Taylor Coleridge. 6199-0
Epitaph. Alfred Edgar Coppard. 6072-2
Epitaph. Tristan Corbiere. 6351-9
Epitaph. Sir William Davenant. 6022-6
Epitaph. Aubrey Thomas De Vere. 6090-0
Epitaph. Louise Driscoll. 6031-5,6393-4
Epitaph. Hermann Hagedorn. 6944-4
Epitaph. Robert Herrick. 6018-8
Epitaph. Thomas Kibble Hervey. 6600-3
Epitaph. Robert Hillyer. 6037-4
Epitaph. Victor Hugo. 6876-6
Epitaph. Iraj. 6448-5
Epitaph. Thomas Jordan. 6563-5
Epitaph. Amy Levy. 6872-3
Epitaph. John Bruce MacCallum. 6482-5
Epitaph. George Macdonald. 6730-1,6337-3
Epitaph. Josephine A. Meyer. 6847-2
Epitaph. Matthew Prior. 6934-7
Epitaph. Sir Walter Raleigh. 6436-1
Epitaph. George Steele Seymour. 6789-1
Epitaph. Simonides. 6438-8
Epitaph. Robert Southey. 6867-7,6980-0
Epitaph. Leonard Alfred George Strong. 6244-X
Epitaph. Sara Teasdale. 6038-2
Epitaph. Mark (Samuel Langhorne Clemens) Twain. 6889-8
Epitaph. Unknown. 6935-5
Epitaph. Francois Villon. 6227-X
Epitaph. John Francis Waller. 6475-2
Epitaph. Rosamund Marriott ("Graham R. Tomson") Watson. 6507-4
Epitaph. Robert Wilde. 6102-8
Epitaph. Jiri Wolker. 6665-8
Epitaph. Sir Henry Wotton. 6179-6
Epitaph. Elinor Wylie. 6036-6
An epitaph ("Alanus calvus"). Unknown. 6881-2
An epitaph ("At three-score..."). Unknown (Greek) 6814-6

Epitaph ("Destined"). Gabriello Chiabrera. 7039-6
Epitaph ("Disown"). Lady Margaret Sackville. 6777-8
An epitaph ("Gaily I lived..."). Unknown. 6733-6
Epitaph ("Here lie I, Martin Elginbrodde.") Unknown. 6337-3
Epitaph ("Here lies my wife"). Unknown. 6052-8
Epitaph ("Here lies the body of William Jones.") Unknown. 6472-8
Epitaph ("Joy"). Lady Margaret Sackville. 6778-6
Epitaph ("Let no cold marble"). Unknown. 6453-1
Epitaph ("Lovely"). Francis Davison. 6436-1
Epitaph ("My light"). Lady Margaret Sackville. 6777-8
An epitaph ("My name"). Unknown (Greek) 6814-6
Epitaph ("Not without"). Gabriello Chiabrera. 7039-6
Epitaph ("O thou"). Gabriello Chiabrera. 7039-6
An epitaph ("Painter"). Unknown (Greek) 6814-6
An epitaph ("Take to thy bosom"). Unknown (Greek) 6814-6
Epitaph ("There never"). Gabriello Chiabrera. 7039-6
Epitaph ("Thou alive"). Francis Davison. 6436-1
Epitaph ("Underneath this sable"). Ben Jonson. 6438-8
Epitaph ("Underneath this stone"). Ben Jonson. 6438-8
Epitaph ("Weep not"). Gabriello Chiabrera. 7039-6
Epitaph ("Wit's"). Francis Davison. 6436-1
EpitaPh (Levi Lincoln Thaxter). Robert Browning. 6656-9
Epitaph (O! Rose-red"). Lady Margaret Sackville. 6777-8
An epitaph (on a pointer) William Cowper. 6092-7
An epitaph (to F.F.). Gertrude Huntington McGiffert. 6838-3
The epitaph - and the reader. Paulus Silentiarius. 6879-0
The epitaph acrostick on Robert Blake. George Harrison. 6547-3
Epitaph among sunflowers. Hyung-soo Ham. 6775-1
Epitaph extempore. Matthew Prior. 6219-9
Epitaph for a bigot. Dorothy Vena Johnson. 6178-8
Epitaph for a cat. Margaret E. Bruner. 6120-6
Epitaph for a deserving lady. Edward Anthony. 6875-8
Epitaph for a friend living in London. Wayne McNeil. 7003-5
An epitaph for a godly man's tomb. Robert Wild. 6563-5, 6125-7
An epitaph for a godly man's tomb. Robert Wilde. 6023-4
Epitaph for a hospital nurse. Edmund Wilson. 6880-4
Epitaph for a man from Virginia City. Kenneth W. Porter. 6388-8
Epitaph for a poet. DuBose Heyward. 6501-5,6326-8
Epitaph for a sailor buried ashore. Sir Charles George Douglas Roberts. 6433-7,6656-9
Epitaph for a voyageur. Theodore Goodridge Roberts. 6433-7
Epitaph for a wooden soldier. Grant H. Code. 6218-0
Epitaph for a young German. Edmund Wilson. 6880-4
Epitaph for any New Yorker. Christopher Morley. 6501-5
Epitaph for Cimantha Proctor. Unknown. 6527-9
Epitaph for James Smith. Robert Burns. 6026-9
Epitaph for Joseph Blackett, late poet and shoemaker. George Gordon, 6th Baron Byron. 6945-2
Epitaph for liberal poets. Louis MacNeice. 6391-8
Epitaph for Mr Hogarth. Samuel Johnson. 6975-4
Epitaph for my tomb. Alfonsina Storni. 6759-X
Epitaph for one who would not be buried in Westminster Abbey. Alexander Pope. 6022-6
Epitaph for Susie Clemens. Robert Richardson. 6396-9
Epitaph for the poet. Arthur Davison Ficke. 6076-5
Epitaph for the poet, sels. Arthur Davison Ficke. 6102-8, 6076-5
Epitaph for the town gossip. Ralph Friedrich. 6761-1
Epitaph for the unknown soldier. Annette Kohn. 6846-4
Epitaph for William Pitt. George Gordon, 6th Baron Byron. 6945-2
Epitaph in a minor key, fr. Gather these bones. Lewis Turco. 6218-0
Epitaph in anticipation. Leonard Bacon. 6722-0
Epitaph in ballade form. Richard Aldington. 6875-8
Epitaph in Croyland Abbey. Unknown. 6874-X
Epitaph in Dubrovnik. Jovan Ducic. 6765-4
Epitaph in Fahan churchyard. William Alexander. 6046-3
The epitaph in form of a ballad. Algernon Charles Swinburne. 6770-0,6875-8
Epitaph in Hales-Owen churchyard, on Miss Anne Powell. William Shenstone. 6772-7
Epitaph in old mode. Sir John Collings ("Solomon Eagle")

EPITAPH

Squire. 6581-3
Epitaph in the cathedral of Derry. William Alexander. 6046-3
Epitaph intended for his wife. John Dryden. 6089-7,6527-9
Epitaph of Constantine Kanaris. Wilhelm Muller. 6948-7
Epitaph of Dionysia. Unknown. 6437-X
The epitaph of graunde amoure, fr. The palace of pleasure. Stephen Hawes. 6125-7
The epitaph of graunde amoure. Stephen Hawes. 6198-2,6427-2,6436-1
The epitaph of Habbie Simpson. Robert Sempill of Beltrees. 6180-X
An epitaph of his grandfather. Thomas Shipman. 6563-5
The epitaph of Hubert Van Eyck. William Bell Scott. 6819-7
Epitaph of Sir Thomas Gravener. Sir Thomas Wyatt. 6436-1, 6584-8
An epitaph of the death of Nicholas Grimald. Barnaby Googe. 6641-0
Epitaph of the Earl of Leicester. Sir Walter Raleigh. 6584-8
Epitaph on a beautiful child. Mabel P.segate. 6906-1
Epitaph on a bombing victim. Roy Fuller. 6379-9
Epitaph on a candle. Unknown. 6278-4
Epitaph on a free but tame redbreast. William Cowper. 6814-6
Epitaph on a friend. Robert Burns. 6337-3
Epitaph on a friend. George Gordon, 6th Baron Byron. 6945-2
Epitaph on a hare. William Cowper. 6134-6,6175-7,6133-8, 6092-7,6086-2,6131 ,6084-6,6543-0,6668-2,6228-8,6290-3,6634
Epitaph on a Jacobite. Thomas Babington Macaulay, 1st Baron Macaulay. 6138-9,6732-8,6046-3,6656-9
Epitaph on a living author. Abraham Cowley. 6219-9
Epitaph on a locomotive. Unknown. 6278-4
Epitaph on a madman's grave. Morris Gilbert. 6033-1,6736-0
Epitaph on a pessimist. Thomas Hardy. 6633-X
Epitaph on a pet cat. Joachim Du Bellay. 6227-X,6511-2
Epitaph on a pet dog. Joachim Du Bellay. 6227-X
Epitaph on a philosopher. S. Foster Damon. 7014-0
Epitaph on a poet in a Welsh courtyard. Walter Savage Landor. 6980-0
An epitaph on a robin-redbreast. Samuel Rogers. 6133-8, 6808-1,6383-7,6250-4,6424-8
Epitaph on a soldier. Cyril Tourneur. 6182-6
Epitaph on a talkative old maid. Benjamin Franklin. 6722-0
Epitaph on a tuft-hunter. Thomas Moore. 6760-3
Epitaph on a vagabond. Alexander Gray. 6069-2
"Epitaph on a virgin". Robert Herrick. 6187-7,6383-7,6737-9
Epitaph on an army of mercenaries. Alfred Edward Housman. 6477-9,6665-8,6102-8,6150-8,6723-9
Epitaph on an early settler. Hereward K. Cockin. 7041-8
Epitaph on an infant. Samuel Taylor Coleridge. 6967-3
Epitaph on an infant. Samuel Taylor Coleridge. 6365-9
Epitaph on an infant. Samuel Taylor Coleridge. 6772-7
Epitaph on an unfortunate artist. Robert Graves. 6722-0
Epitaph on Argalus and Parthenia. Sir Philip Sidney. 6086-2,6250-4
Epitaph on Castlereagh. George Gordon, 6th Baron Byron. 6945-2
Epitaph on Charidas of Cyrene. Callimachus. 6879-0
Epitaph on Charles II. John Wilmot, 2d Earl of Rochester. 6198-2,6188-5,6527-9,6722-0,6562-7,6092-7,6250-4, 6150-8,6668-2
Epitaph on Claude Phillips. Samuel Johnson. 6975-4
Epitaph on Dr. Johnson. William Cowper. 6483-3
Epitaph on Dr. Johnson. William Cowper. 6814-6
Epitaph on Dr. Parnell. Oliver Goldsmith. 6483-3
Epitaph on Drake. Thomas Beedome. 6339-X
Epitaph on Eleanor Freeman, who died A.D. 1650, aged 21 Unknown. 6908-8
Epitaph on Elizabeth, L. H. Ben Jonson. 6122-2,6271-7,6186-9,6600-3,6182-6,6198 ,6194-X,6250-4,6291-0,6562-7, 6726-3
Epitaph on erotion. Martial. 6732-8
Epitaph on Fop, a dog belonging to Lady Throckmorton. William Cowper. 6814-6
Epitaph on Gay in Westminster Abbey. Alexander Pope. 6934-7

Epitaph on Heraclitus. Callimachus. 6102-8
Epitaph on himself. Aeschylus. 6102-8
Epitaph on himself. Samuel Taylor Coleridge. 6102-8,6301-2, 6337-3,6931-2
Epitaph on himself. Matthew Prior. 6092-7,6301-2
An epitaph on his deceased friend. Robert Fletcher. 6563-5
An epitaph on his most honored friend, Richard, Earl... Henry King. 6908-8
Epitaph on his wife. John Dryden. 6722-0
Epitaph on Holy Willie. Robert Burns. 6200-8,6278-4
Epitaph on John Adams, of Southwell. George Gordon, 6th Baron Byron. 6945-2
Epitaph on John Knox. Unknown. 6125-7
Epitaph on King Charles I. James Graham; Marquess of Montrose. 6933-9
Epitaph on Lady Mary Villiers (I) Thomas Carew. 6908-8
Epitaph on Lady Mary Villiers (II) Thomas Carew. 6908-8
Epitaph on Lady Ossory's bullfinch. Horace Walpole; 4th Earl of Orford. 6125-7
Epitaph on Margaret Ratcliffe. Ben Jonson. 6867-7
Epitaph on Master Philip Gray, fr. Underwoods. Ben Jonson. 6867-7
Epitaph on Miss Elizabeth Stanley. James Thomson. 6816-2
An epitaph on Mistress Mary Prideaux. George Morley. 6563-5
Epitaph on Mr. Chester, of Chicheley. William Cowper. 6814-6
Epitaph on Mrs Jane Clarke. Thomas Gray. 6975-4
An epitaph on Mrs. El: Y. William Browne. 6908-8
Epitaph on Mrs. M. Higgins, of Weston. William Cowper. 6814-6
Epitaph on Mrs. Margaret Paston. John Dryden. 6970-3
Epitaph on Mrs. Margaret Paston of Burningham... John Dryden. 6908-8
Epitaph on my father. Robert Burns. 6337-3
Epitaph on my first daughter. Ben Jonson. 6867-7
Epitaph on Newton. Alexander Pope. 6850-2
Epitaph on one whole played Ariel in his youth. Walter De La Mare. 6778-6
Epitaph on Peter Staggs. John ("Peter Pindar") Walcott. 6278-4
Epitaph on Rabelais. Pierre de Ronsard. 6227-X
Epitaph on Salathiel Pavy. Ben Jonson. 6092-7
Epitaph on Shakespeare. John Milton. 6558-9,6737-9,6438-8
Epitaph on Sir Philip Sidney. Fulke Greville; 1st Baron Brooke. 6315-2,6436-1,6483-3,6438-8
Epitaph on Sir Philip Sidney. Sir Walter Raleigh. 6584-8, 6219-9
Epitaph on Sir Philip Sidney lying in St. Paul's. Edward Herbert, 1st Baron Herbert of Cherbury. 6562-7
Epitaph on Sir Thomas Hanmer, Bart. Samuel Johnson. 6975-4
Epitaph on Sir William Williams. Thomas Gray. 6641-0
Epitaph on Sitting Bull. Unknown (American Indian) 6396-9
Epitaph on Southey. Thomas Moore. 6278-4
Epitaph on S[alomon] P[avy], a child... Ben Jonson. 6315-2, 6122-2,6737-9,6645-3,6320-X,6291 ,6430-2,6150-8,6153-2,6562-7,6181-8,6182-6,6208-3,6052-8,6198
An epitaph on the admirable dramatic poet... John Milton. 6102-8,6291-9
Epitaph on the Athenian dead at Plataea. Simonides. 6879-0
Epitaph on the countess dowager of Pembroke. William Browne. 6315-2,6189-3,6250-4,6150-8,6301-2
Epitaph on the Countess of Pembroke. William Browne. 6250-4
Epitaph on the Countess of Pembroke. Ben Jonson. 6102-8, 6302-0,6385-3,6369-1,6291-9,6737
Epitaph on the Duchess of Maine's cat. Francois La Mothe Le Vayer. 6511-2
Epitaph on the Earl of Strafford. John Cleveland. 6933-9
Epitaph on the Earl of Strafford. John Cleveland. 6472-8
Epitaph on the Earl of Strafford. John Cleveland. 6933-9
Epitaph on the Lady Mary Villers. Thomas Carew. 6562-7, 6563-5,6430-2,6194-X,6189-3
An epitaph on the Marchioness of Winchester. John Milton. 6641-0
Epitaph on the tombstone erected over the Marquis...leg. George Canning. 6219-9
Epitaph on Thomas Clere. Henry Howard, Earl of Surrey. 6584-8
Epitaph on Tom D'urfey. Unknown. 6024-2

Epitaph on Virgil and Tibullus. Domitius Marsus. 6945-2
Epitaph on W--. Robert Burns. 6278-4
Epitaph on Washington. Unknown. 6158-3,6449-3,6712-3
Epitaph over the grave of two brothers. Felicia Dorothea Hemans. 6973-8
Epitaph placed on his daughters tomb by Mark Twain. Robert Richardson. 6337-3
Epitaph to a man. Robert Reedburg. 7024-8
Epitaph to James Smith. Robert Burns. 6932-0
Epitaph to William Northcot. Charles Unwin. 6814-6
An epitaph upon ---. Andrew Marvell. 6315-2;6563-5
Epitaph upon a child that died. Robert Herrick. 6186-9, 6337-3,6153-2,6396-9,6737-9
An epitaph upon a young married couple dead. Richard Crashaw. 6726-3,6563-5,6430-2,6562-7,6179-6
An epitaph upon husand and wife who died & were buried. Richard Crashaw. 6317-9,6052-8,6337-3,6291-9,6214-8
An epitaph upon Mr. Ashton a comfortable citizen. Richard Crashaw. 6933-9
An epitaph upon the celebrated Claudy Philips..musician. Samuel Johnson. 6932-0
An epitaph upon the right honourable Sir Phillip...(I) Edmund Spenser. 6908-8
An epitaph upon the right honourable Sir Phillip...(II) Edmund Spenser. 6908-8
Epitaph upon the year 1806. William Robert Spencer. 6086-2
Epitaph V. On Mrs. Corbet,who dyed of a cancer on her breast. Alexander Pope. 6152-4
An epitaph vpon the right honorable... Sir Walter Raleigh. 6586-4
Epitaph written in the snow. Jessie Wilmore Murton. 6979-7
Epitaph XI. On Mr. Gay. In Westminster Abbey, 1732 Alexander Pope. 6152-4
Epitaph XII. Intended for Sir Isaac Newton... Alexander Pope. 6152-4
Epitaph" on Sir Walter Rawleigh at his execution. Unknown. 6933-9
Epitaph, for the tombstone erected...Marquis of Angelsea... George Canning. 6086-2
Epitaph, found somewhere in space. Hugh Wilgus Ramsaur. 6337-3
Epitaph, intended for himself. James Beattie. 6086-2,6180-X,6641-0
An epitaph, or punning run mad. Unknown. 6787-5
Epitaph: for a mouthy woman. Countee Cullen. 6071-4
Epitaph: in obitum M.S. X Maij, 1614. William Browne. 6933-9
Epitaph: on Sir Walter Raleigh at his execution. Unknown. 6879-0
An epitaph. William Basse. 6102-8
An epitaph. James Beattie. 6339-X
An epitaph. Thomas Carew. 6198-2
An epitaph. George John Cayley. 6092-7
An epitaph. George John Cayley. 6089-7
An epitaph. George Chamalian. 6850-2
An epitaph. William Cowper. 6814-6
An epitaph. Francis Potter Daniels. 6841-3
An epitaph. Walter De La Mare. 6315-2,6477-9,6250-4,6153-2, 6301-2
An epitaph. John Gay. 6228-8
An epitaph. Stephen Hawes. 6186-9
An epitaph. Stephen Hawes. 6022-6
An epitaph. Alfred Edward Housman. 6733-6
An epitaph. Edwin Markham. 6303-9;6337-3
An epitaph. Andrew Marvell. 6102-8
An epitaph of man. Andrew Marvell. 6250-4
An epitaph. Richard Kendall Munkittrick. 6274-1
An epitaph. Matthew Prior. 6089-7,6633-X
An epitaph. Matthew Prior. 6152-4
An epitaph. Bryan Waller ("Barry Cornwall") Procter. 6980-0
An epitaph. Sir John Collings ("Solomon Eagle") Squire. 6430-2,6431-1
An epitaph. Sir William Watson. 6396-9
The epitaph. John Alexander Bouquet. 6337-3
The epitaph. Thomas Gray. 6634-8,6732-8
The epitaph. Thomas Gray. 6214-8
The epitaph. Robert C.V. Meyers. 6417-5
The epitaph. Katharine (Hinkson) Tynan. 6730-1,6374-8
Epitaphium alterum. William Cowper. 6814-6

Epitaphium citharistriae. Victor Plarr. 6581-3
Epitaphium Citharistriae. Victor Plarr. 6507-4,6301-2,6102-8
Epitaphium felis. John Jortin. 6511-2
An epitaphn upon Thomas, Lord Fairfax. George Villiers, 2d Duke of Buckingham. 6934-7
Epitaphs. Murrell Edmunds. 6042-0
Epitaphs ("Here lies a lady"). Marjorie Allen Seiffert. 6031-5
Epitaphs for a bad girl. A.D. F. 6817-0
Epitaphs for aviators. Shane Leslie. 6506-6
Epitaphs for the speed age. Leonard H. Robbins. 6396-9
Epithalamion, sels. John Donne. 6301-2
Epithalamion. Donald Davidson. 6619-4
Epithalamion. James Elroy Flecker. 6508-2
Epithalamion. Nigel Heseltine. 6360-8
Epithalamion. Robert Kelly. 6803-0
Epithalamion. Edmund Spenser. 6102-8,6122-2,6182-6,6186-9, 6271-7,6385 ,6436-1,6586-4,6430-2,6189-3,6023-4,6301
Epithalamion for Amaryllis. John Chipman Farrar. 6441-8
Epithalamion made at Lincolnes inne. John Donne. 6933-9
Epithalamion of a peach, fr. Two gentlemen in bonds. John Crowe Ransom. 6011-0
Epithalamion teratos. George Chapman. 6182-6,6315-2
Epithalamion, sels. Edmund Spenser. 6154-0,6198-2,6317-9, 6600-3,6634-8,6726 ,6150-8
Epithalamium. John Gardiner Calkins Brainard. 6271-7,6600-3,6291-9
Epithalamium. Alice Cary. 6865-0;6969-X
Epithalamium. Sir Edmund Gosse. 6437-X
Epithalamium. Edward Sandford Martin. 6652-6
Epithalamium. Samuel Sheppard. 6189-3
Epithalamium. Sir Philip Sidney. 6584-8,6194-X
Epithalamium. Arthur Symons. 6210-5
Epithalamium. Unknown. 6563-5
Epithalamium and elegy. Witter Bynner. 6619-4
Epithalamium for cavorting ghosts. Dachine Rainer. 6388-8
Epithalamium for Mary Stuart and the Dauphin of France. George Buchanan. 6845-6
Epithalamium, sels. Walter James Turner. 6324-1
An epithalamium, sels. Ben Jonson. 6301-2
Epithalamy. Ben Jonson. 6830-8
Epitome. Joseph Mary Plunkett. 6628-3
The epoch. Nikolai Tikhonov. 6546-5
Epode. Ben Jonson. 6194-X
Eppert, Josie
    Mid-March. 6906-1
    Ode to October. 6906-1
    To a warbling vireo. 6906-1
Eppie Morrie. Unknown. 6185-0,6518-X
Epping Forest. John Davidson. 6161-3
Epping hunt. Thomas Hood. 6974-6
Epstein's "Christ" John Cournos. 6069-2
Epting, Mrs. T. B.
    Guide us. 6818-9
An epytaphe of the death of Nicholas Grimald. Barnaby Googe. 6586-4
Equal rights. Edward R. Huxley. 6885-5
"Equal to Jove that youth must be". Ad lesbiam. Caius Catallus. 6945-2
Equal troth, fr. The house of life. Dante Gabriel Rossetti. 6110-9
Equality. Eva Caminsky. 6818-9
Equality. Phoebe Cary. 6969-X
Equality. Herman L. McMillan. 7024-8
Equality of man. Edward R. Huxley. 6885-5
Equestrian courtship. Thomas Hood. 6621-6
The equestrian statue of Washington. William Allen Butler. 6903-7
Equestrienne. Joan Colby. 6966-5
The equilibrists. John Crowe Ransom. 6326-8
Equilibrium. Gemma D'Auria. 6839-1
Equinoctial. Adeline Dutton (Train) Whitney. 6240-7
The equinox, fr. Seaweed. Henry Wadsworth Longfellow. 6833-2
The equinox. DuBose Heyward. 6102-8,6628-3
"The equinoxes pass". The dark heart. Pamela Travers. 6985-1
"Equipoise: becalmed". Evening in Connecticut. Louis MacNeice. 6783-2

EQUITY

"The **Equity** chorus sent me here". The italics are George Macdonald's. Marc Connelly. 6817-0
Equivocal verses. Unknown. 6724-7
The **equi**vocation. John Gay. 6972-X
ERA. Christine Christian. 6857-X
"**Er**- dear, and all that sort of rot". In the king's english. Berton Braley. 6853-7
"**Er-Heb** beyond the hills of Ao-Safai". The sacrifice of Er-Heb. Rudyard Kipling. 6810-3
Erasistratus forbear, sels. George L. Walton. 6482-5
Erasmus Wilson. James Whitcomb Riley. 6892-8
Erasmus, Desiderius
    Votive ode. J.T. Walford (tr.). 6282-2
Erat hora. Ezra Pound. 6879-0
Erben, Karel Jaromir
    The willow. Paul Selver (tr.). 6763-8
Erda. Vera Bishop Konrick. 6218-0
Erdgewalt. Rudolf G. Bidding. 6253-9
"**Ere** Cabot's prow was westward turned". City Hall park. Arthur Guiterman. 6773-5
"**Ere** five score years have run their..rounds". A prophecy. Arthur Lee (atr) 6946-0
"**Ere** God had built the mountains". Wisdom. William Cowper. 6814-6
"**Ere** long they come where that same wicked...". The cave of despair. Edmund Spenser. 6935-5
"**Ere** Murfreesboro's thunders rent the air". The battle of Murfreesboro. Kinahan Cornwallis. 6946-0
"**Ere** sin could blight or sorrow fade". Epitaph on an infant. Samuel Taylor Coleridge. 6967-3
"**Ere** the daughter of Brunswick is cold...grave". The Irish avatar. George Gordon, 6th Baron Byron. 6945-2
Ere the golden bowl is broken. Anna Hempstead Branch. 6348-9,6217-2
Ere the sun went down. George Weatherly. 6920-7
"**Ere** we Gomera cleared, a coward cried". Sonnet ("Ere we Gomera"). Sidney Lanier. 6753-0
Ere with cold beads of midnight dew, sels. William Wordsworth. 6867-7
"**Ere** yet my heart was sweet love's tomb". Love, pride, and forgetfulness. Alfred Lord Tennyson. 6977-0
"**Ere** yet the sun is high". Iris. Unknown (Japanese). 6891-X
"**Erect** like the hollyhocks they tended". Perennials. Ruth J. Barrett. 6764-6
Eremites. Palladas. 6435-3
The **Eretrian** dead. Plato. 6435-3
The **Eretrian** dead. Plato. 6435-3
Erhard, Betty Alice
    June. 6662-3
Eric and Axel. Bayard Taylor. 6976-2
"**Eric** of Marka holds the knife". Mary of Marka. Bliss Carman and Richard Hovey. 6890-1
Ericksen, Mabel Natalie
    Bargain. 6750-6
    Reservation school. 6342-X
Erickson, Lois J. (tr.)
    "Above white clouds I hear sweet." Kyoroku, 6027-7
    "All day/The bird sits in his cage." Isas, 6027-7
    Autumn. Nagata, 6027-7
    Azaleas. Muda, 6027-7
    "A band of beggars out to view." Kohei, 6027-7
    "Birds sit and sing among the flowers." Shou, 6027-7
    "The butterflies can scarcely find." Kyoshi, 6027-7
    The carpenter. Gumpei Yamamuro, 6027-7
    "Cherry flowers." Issa, 6027-7
    A child of prayer. Unknown (Japanese), 6027-7
    Christ liveth in me. Toyohiko Kagawa, 6027-7
    Chrysanthemums. Unknown (Japanese), 6027-7
    Clinging to thee. Unknown (Japanese), 6027-7
    Comfort. Miyauchi, 6027-7
    "The cunning fireflies." Ryoto, 6027-7
    Dawn. Tanikado, 6027-7
    Day's end. Toyohiko Kagawa, 6337-3
    "Dear little one." Issa, 6027-7
    Easter. Miyoshi, 6027-7
    "Even the rocks of Futami." Basho (Matsuo Basho), 6027-7
    "Far beyond/White lilies, wild around my feet." Kyoko, 6027-7
    "The fireflies massed upon the palm fronds." Buson, 6027-7
    "A firefly/Flitted by." Ryoto, 6027-7
    Flood. Tamiko Yamamuro, 6027-7
    "Flying birds/Beware!" Shiko, 6027-7
    "For lack of rain." Rakuten, 6027-7
    Gethsemane. Unknown (Japanese), 6027-7
    Glorying. Miyauchi, 6027-7
    God's justice. Nagata, 6027-7
    God's plan. Miyoshi, 6027-7
    God's word. Takayoshi Matsuyama, 6027-7
    The goodness of God. Nagata, 6027-7
    "He is so little, and the way is dim." Okura, 6027-7
    Heaven. Takamoto, 6027-7
    "High noon." Shiki, 6027-7
    The hills of God. Takamoto, 6027-7
    His grace. Ishii, 6027-7
    His will. Kanda, 6027-7
    A homeless beggar. Izan, 6027-7
    "How can I tell you, dear." Soseki, 6027-7
    "I breathe but, Oh!" Moritake, 6027-7
    I call the swallows. Toyohiko Kagawa, 6027-7
    "I gathered in my rod and line." Toyo, 6027-7
    "I sit alone and listen." Kijo, 6027-7
    "I thought I saw a fallen flower." Moritake, 6027-7
    "I thought my net was full of shining fish." Oto, 6027-7
    "I thrilled to hear the heavenly." Yaha, 6027-7
    "I've not the heart to pick the violets." Naojo, 6027-7
    In all things, victory. Nagata, 6027-7
    In prison. Tamiko Yamamuro, 6027-7
    "An island etched on a silver sky." Basho (Matsuo Basho), 6027-7
    Japan can teach. Toyohiko Kagawa, 6027-7
    The kingdom of God is within in. Toyohiko Kagawa, 6027-7
    Leading. Nagata, 6027-7
    "Lightly, lightly/Summer breezes playing." Bokujin, 6027-7
    The living Christ. Toyohiko Kagawa, 6027-7
    "Look! On the great great bronze bell." Buson, 6027-7
    Looking up. Hiromi, 6027-7
    Lotus. Unknown (Japanese), 6027-7
    Love means adventure. Toyohiko Kagawa, 6027-7
    Loveliness. Unknown (Japanese), 6027-7
    Lovely things. Unknown (Japanese), 6027-7
    Mirrors. Toyohiko Kagawa, 6027-7
    The moon and the dewdrop. Unknown (Japanese), 6027-7
    Morning prayer. Utako Hayashi, 6027-7
    My all. Takamoto, 6027-7
    My flowers. Shizumoki, 6027-7
    My road. Handa, 6027-7
    My task. Utako Hayashi, 6027-7
    My violets. Unknown (Japanese), 6027-7
    New year. Fujita, 6027-7
    A new year bride. Tamiko Yamamuro, 6027-7
    The new year. Tsurue Miyauchi, 6027-7
    Night. Tamiko Yamamuro, 6027-7
    "Night/And a doorway left ajar." Yakamochi, 6027-7
    "Nightfall/And I all lone." Unknown (Japanese), 6027-7
    "A nightingale sat singing out his heart." Torin, 6027-7
    Not alone. Utako Hayashi, 6027-7
    "Now autumn comes to me." Shiko, 6027-7
    "O little insects in my autumn garden." Miyamori, 6027-7
    O skylarks, teach Japan to sing. Toyohiko Kagawa, 6027-7
    One with the universe. Toyohiko Kagawa, 6027-7
    Perfume of plum upon the air. Basho (Matsuo Basho), 6027-7
    Prayer ("Oh, make my heart"). Utsunomiya, 6027-7
    Prayer reaches him. Nagata, 6027-7
    "Pure, and fragile and pale". Kiyowara, 6027-7
    Silence. Toyohiko Kagawa, 6027-7
    The simple life. Toyohiko Kagawa, 6027-7
    "Small tendrils of a morning glory..." Chiyo Ni, 6027-7
    "Smiles on my lips, while quick tears blind my eyes." Chiyo Ni, 6027-7
    So cold. Tamiko Yamamuro, 6027-7

"Some ears are tuned to catch the insects' songs." Wafu, 6027-7
A song of daily life. Utako Hayashi, 6027-7
The soul like iron. Unknown (Japanese), 6027-7
Spring. Toyohiko Kagawa, 6027-7
"Still chirp the crickets." Basho (Matsuo Basho), 6027-7
"Storehouse burned." Masahide, 6027-7
"A summer night/With breezes sweet." Buson, 6027-7
Sunset. Unknown (Japanese), 6027-7
Sunshine. Fujita, 6027-7
Suprise. Unknown (Japanese), 6027-7
"There are no gloomy days." Kyohaku, 6027-7
"These cherry flowers." Issa, 6027-7
"This, then, the end of a dream of power." Basho (Matsuo Basho), 6027-7
The thorn. Unknown (Japanese), 6027-7
Thou art. Kawabuchi, 6027-7
Thoughfulness. Yamaguchi, 6027-7
The thought of God. Nagata, 6027-7
To one in heaven. Nagata, 6027-7
"The tree will soon be hewn." Issa, 6027-7
True love. Unknown (Japanese), 6027-7
"Two little boats sail side by side." Hochi, 6027-7
"Two slender stalks of black bamboo." She-ei, 6027-7
Waiting for the dawn. Toyohiko Kagawa, 6027-7
"The waving ripe fields glow with gold." Basho (Matsuo Basho), 6027-7
"What kind of men are these?" Shiki, 6027-7
"White of the first light snow." Basho (Matsuo Basho), 6027-7
"White plum tree, where can my loved one be?" Fujiwara, 6027-7
Work. Toyohiko Kagawa, 6027-7
Your death. Takamoto, 6027-7

Ericson, Ethel May
Afar in Tuna. 6847-2
The little streets. 6847-2
O hana san to the wistarias. 6847-2

The Erie Canal. Unknown. 6281-4
Erie waters. Emily Pauline ("Tekahionwake") Johnson. 6837-5
Erin. William Drennan. 6714-X
Erin's flag. Abram Joseph Ryan. 6406-X,6630-5
Erin's lovely home. Unknown. 6057-9
Erin's plea. S. Charles Jellicoe. 6174-5
Erin, sels. William Drennan. 6439-6

Erinna
All passes into dust save deathless art alone. 6102-8
Baucis. Sir William Marris (tr.). 6435-3
A distaff. Cecil Maurice Bowra (tr.). 6435-3

Erinna. Anitpater of Sidon. 6879-0
Erinna. Meleager. 6102-8
Erinna, sels. Antipater of Sidon. 6435-3

Erksine, Thomas, Lord
French and English. 6278-4

The Erl King-Goethe. James Abraham Martling. 6952-5
The Erl-king. Johann Wolfgang von Goethe. 6695-X,6580-5, 6585-6
The erl-king. Johann Wolfgang von Goethe. 6842-1
The Erl-king. Johann Wolfgang von Goethe. 6254-7,6732-8, 6328-4,6358-6,6102-8,6613
The erl-king. Johann Wolfgang von Goethe. 7039-6

Erlingsson, Porsteinn
Evening. Jakobina Johnson (tr.). 6854-5
The heritage. Vilhjalmur Stefansson (tr.). 6854-5
My nest. Gudmund J. Gislason (tr.). 6854-5
The shrike. Runolfur Fjeldsted (tr.). 6854-5
The terms. Jakobina Johnson (tr.). 6854-5

Erlingsson, Thorsteinn
The snow-bunting. Runolfur Fjeldsted (tr.). 6283-0
The terms. Jakobina Johnson (tr.). 6283-0

Erlinton. Unknown. 6185-0,6067-6

Erman, Don
The artist speaks. 6789-1

Ernle, George (tr.)
The appeal of the phoenix, fr. The Iliad. Homer, 6435-3
"Conquer the proud spirit...", fr. The Iliad. Homer, 6435-3

Ernst, Marguerite Franziska

The water lily fairy. 6818-9
Eros. Robert Bridges. 6317-9
Eros. Florence Earle Coates. 6320-9
Eros. Ralph Waldo Emerson. 6429-9,6-66-8,6250-4,6288-1, 6126-5,6321
Eros. Edward Farquhar. 6939-8
Eros. Amy S. Jennings. 6039-0,6072-2
Eros and his mother. Apollonius Rhodius. 6435-3
Eros and Psyche. Lucius Apuleius. 6487-6
The Eros chorus in Antigone. Sophocles. 6094-3
Eros does not always smite. Michael (Katherine Bradley & Edith Cooper) Field. 6872-3
"Eros is the god of love". Song of Eros. Bion. 6949-5
"Eros of the flying mists!". An idyl. Henry Hunter Welsh. 6936-3
Eros turannos. Edwin Arlington Robinson. 6333-0,6348-9, 6399-3
"Eros! wherefore do I see thee, with the glass". Love's hour-glass. Johann Wolfgang von Goethe. 6948-7
Erotion. Martial. 7039-6
Erotion. Algernon Charles Swinburne. 6204-0
"Err shall they not, who resolve explore". Parody of a translation from the Medea of Euripides. Samuel Johnson. 6975-4
The errand imperious. Edwin Markham. 6386-1
An errand.. Jane Barlow. 6090-0
The errand. James Herbert Morse. 7041-8
Errantry. John Galsworthy. 6888-X
Erratic. Paul Celan. 6769-7
Erroneous opinions of the creation of souls. Sir John Davies. 6584-8
Error and loss. William Morris. 6110-9
Errors of ecstasoe, sel. George Darley. 6930-4
Ersatz. Raymond Souster. 6446-9
The ersatz bread. Slater Brown. 6761-1

Erskine, Andrew
How sweet this lone vale. 6180-X

Erskine, John
Acateon. 6253-9
Achilles and the maiden. 6184-2
Apparition. 6034-X
Ash Wednesday. 6393-4
De gustibus. 6118-4,6619-4
Dedication. 6501-5
'Love that never told can be.' 6118-4
Modern ode to the modern school. 6736-0
The sea-gull. 6327-6
The shepherd speaks. 6144-3
The sons of Metaneira. 6031-5
To George Edward Woodberry. 6118-4
Valentine to one's wife. 6102-8,6441-8,6619-4,6732-8, 6250-4,6071 ,6076-5
Whip-poor-will. 6253-9
Winter-song for Pan. 6118-4

Erskine, Ralph
The Indian weed. 6230-X

Erskine, Sir Henry
In the garb of old Gaul. 6180-X

Erskine, William
This house where once a lawyer dwelt. 6722-0

Erskine; Earl of Rosslyn, Francis R.S.
Among my books. 6297-0
Bed-time. 6519-8,6656-9,6092-7,6627-5,6078-1

Erskine; Earl of Rossn, Francis R.S.
Memory. 6656-9

"Erstwhile he lay in state". The first Easter dawn. William White. 6868-5

Ervin, Daisy Lee
Far fields. 6906-1
Hard metals. 6906-1
I hwove a colored altar cloth. 6906-1
To a diarist. 6906-1
To dream. 6906-1
Wings. 6906-1

Erwpιov axoos apoupns [Etosian achthos aroures]. Robert ("Droch") Bridges. 6210-5

Erycius of Thessaly
A shepherd's death. 6102-8

Eryri Wen. Felicia Dorothea Hemans. 6973-8
Erysichthon. Callimachus. 6435-3

Erzingatzi, Hovhannes
    "Like an ocean is this world". 6050-1
"Es fallen lesier hier sussen musik klange". Choric song
    of the lotos eaters. Alfred Lord Tennyson. 6847-2
Es fallt ein stern herunter. Heinrich Heine. 7039-6
Es stehen unbeweglich. Heinrich Heine. 7039-6
Esbensen, Barbara J.
    Postcard from Zamboanga. 6966-5
Escapade. Kenneth Leslie. 6833-2
Escape. Caroline Giltinan. 6037-4
Escape. Jamie Sexton Holme. 6836-7
Escape. Gwennie James. 6042-0
Escape. Georgia Douglas Johnson. 6039-0
Escape. Lionel Johnson. 6655-0
Escape. Andrew McCord Jones. 6870-7
Escape. Leonard Mann. 6384-5
Escape. Alfred Noyes. 6781-6
Escape. Maye DeWeese Porter. 6906-1
Escape. James Rorty. 6501-5
Escape. Lilian White Spencer. 6836-7
Escape. Paul (J.h. Clemenceau Le Clerq) Tanaquil. 6037-4
Escape. Unknown. 6337-3
Escape. Elinor Wylie. 6236-9,6619-4,6257-9,6467-1
Escape at bedtime. Robert Louis Stevenson. 6466-3,6368-3,
    6421-3,6454-X,6655-0
Escape at moonrise. Josephine Pinckney. 6326-8
"Escape blossomed in the car". Vivisection, sels. Gene
    Fowler. 6870-7
Escape from winter. James Gates Percival. 6752-2
The escape of Count Fernan Gonzalez. Unknown (Spanish)
    6757-3
The escape of Gayferos. Unknown (Spanish) 6757-3
The escape. Lee Wilson Dodd. 6501-5
The escape. Edwin Muir. 6666-9
"Escaped from London, now four moons and more". A day: an
    epistle to John Wilkes, of Aylesbury, Esq. John
    Armstrong. 6968-1
"Escaped the gloom of mortal life, a soul". His own
    epitaph. James Beattie. 6960-6
Eschatology. Morris Bishop. 6722-0
Eschenbach, Sir Wolfram von
    His own true wife. Jethro Bithell (tr.). 7039-6
The escort of the yellowstone. John Steven McGroarty. 6995-
    9
"Escorted by obstinate memories, I take...". Old poem.
    Octavio Paz. 6758-1
Escudero, Gonzalo
    The Dolmens. Dudley Fitts (tr.). 6759-X
    God. Dudley Fitts (tr.). 6759-X
    Zoo. Richard O'Connell (tr.). 6759-X
The escurial. Theophile Gautier. 6424-8
Esdaile, G. Arundell (tr.)
    "From Sparta to Apollo we", fr. Lost at sea. Simonides,
    6435-3
    Lost at sea. Simonides, 6435-3
Esenin, Sergei
    Confession of a hooligan. Jack Lindsay (tr.). 6546-5
    The herd of horses. Cecil Maurice Bowra (tr.). 6103-6
    Not vain the winds. Jack Lindsay (tr.). 6546-5
    "O fields of corn, o fields of corn" R.M. Hewitt (tr.).
    6103-6
    Wake me tomorrow. Jack Lindsay (tr.). 6546-5
    "Where, my childhood's home, art thou". Cecil Maurice
    Bowra (tr.). 6103-6
An Eskimelodrama.. Unknown. 6274-1
An Eskimelodrama; or the eskapade of an Eskamaid. Unknown.
    6118-4
Eskmeals. Hardwicke Drummond Rawnsley. 6997-5
Esling, Charles H.A.
    Barge song on the Schuylkill River. 6936-3
"Esmeh, the favourtie wife of Shah-Zarar". The sorceress.
    Edgar Fawcett. 7041-8
Esoeris. Lydia Gibson. 6880-4
Esolen, Tony
    Christmas vacation. 6900-2
Espaliers. Mary Atwater Taylor. 6232-6
"Especially when the October wind". Poem ("Especially
    when"). Dylan Thomas. 6379-9,6360-8
Especially when the October wind. Dylan Thomas. 6488-4
Espied. James A. Mackereth. 6071-4

The esplanade method. August Strindberg. 6045-5
The espousal. John Gay. 6972-X
Esprit, Jacques
    The man in the moon and I. 6247-4
An essay for promoting psalmody, sels. Nahum Tate. 6867-7
An essay on criticism, sels. Alexander Pope. 6195-0,6250-4,
    6560-4,6491-4,6543-0,6102-8,6289-X,6198-2,6208-3,
    6527-9,6726
An essay on criticism. Alexander Pope. 6122-2,6152-4,6192-
    3,6430-2
Essay on deity. Elder Olson. 6250-4
Essay on man. Alexander Pope. 7014-0
An essay on man, sels. Alexander Pope. 6024-2,6102-8,6198-
    2,6730-1,6301-2,6732 ,6491-4,6245-8,6195-0,6250-4,
    6560-0
'Essay on man,' sels. Alexander Pope. 6943-6
An essay on man. Alexander Pope. 6152-4,6192-3,6430-2
Essay on memory. R.D. FitzGerald. 6349-7
An essay on the fleet riding in the downes. Unknown. 6157-
    5
An essay on the understanding. Unknown. 6278-4
An essay on translated verse, sels. Wentworth Dillon, Earl
    of Roscommon. 6198-2
Essayan, Zabelle
    "The incense at the altar slowly burns". 6050-1
Essence. Dorothy Burnham Eaton. 6750-6
Essence. Raine Stryder. 6857-X
Essence. Ethel Arnold Tilden. 6038-2
Essence of opera. Unknown. 6271-7
Essential. Berton Braley. 6853-7
Essential requirements. Edward R. Huxley. 6885-5
Essentials. Sister Mary St. Virginia. 6761-1
Essentials. Charles Russell Wakeley. 6461-2
Essex. Arthur Shearly Cripps. 6477-9
Essex. George Cabot Lodge. 6762-X
Essex regiment march. George Edward Woodberry. 6946-0
Essex salt-marsh. Andrew Young. 6324-1
Essex, Edwin
    Epigram. 6096-X
    Loneliness. 6096-X,6292-X
Essex, Robert Devereux, 2d Earl of
    Change. 6436-1
    Change thy mind since she doth change. 6182-6
    Content. 6436-1
    Happy were he. 6182-6
    A passion of my Lord of Essex. 6189-3
    A passion. 6189-3
    "There is none." 6230-X
    A wish. 6737-4
Essie smiles. Warren Ariail. 7016-7
Esson, Louis
    Brogan's lane. 6784-0
    Cradle song. 6784-0
    The old black billy an' me. 6784-0
    The shearer's wife. 6784-0
Est, est. Wilhelm Muller. 6842-1
Established. Rose O'Neill. 6019-6
"Estates go to the issue". Canons of descent. Unknown.
    6878-2
Esteem and love. Steingrimur Thorsteinsson. 6854-5
Estes, Laurence E.
    As the wind. 6342-X
Estevan, Saskatchewan. E.W. Mandel. 6446-9
Esther. Helen Hunt Jackson. 6848-0
Esther. J.R. Robinson. 6848-0
Esther, sels. Wilfrid Scawen Blunt. 6301-2
Esthetique du mal, sels. Wallace Stevens. 6209-1
Estonian bridal song. Johann Gottfried von Herder. 7039-6
Estrada, Genaro
    Lament for lost love. Donald Devenish Walsh (tr.). 6759-
    X
    Little song in the air. Donald Devenish Walsh (tr.).
    6759-X
    Paraphrase of Horace. Donald Devenish Walsh (tr.). 6759-
    X
Estrada, Rafael
    Mexican soldiers. Donald Devenish Walsh (tr.). 6759-X
    Traces. Donald Devenish Walsh (tr.). 6759-X
    Twilight. Donald Devenish Walsh (tr.). 6759-X
Estranged. Blanche Waltrip Rose. 6906-1

Estrangement. Edward Harry William Meyerstein. 6893-6
Estrangement. Wade Oliver. 6482-5
Estrangement. John Peter. 6788-3
Estrangement. F.G. Scott. 7041-8
Estrangement. Sir William Watson. 6477-9
Estray. John McClure. 6397-7
The estray. Harry Bache Smith. 6721-2
Estrello, Francisco E.
    Hands of Christ. 6144-3
Estrildis. Kenneth Hare. 6070-6
The estuary. Allen Upward. 6897-9
Estunt the griff. Rudyard Kipling. 6440-X
Esyllt. Glyn Jones. 6360-8
Et dona ferentes. Rudyard Kipling. 6810-3
Et nunc et semper. Laura Helena Brower. 7001-9
Et sa pauvre chair. Alec Brock Stevenson. 6037-4
Et sunt commercia coeli. Herbert P. Horne. 6844-8
Etc etc etc. Dorothy C. Parrish. 7024-8
Etching. Dennis Murphy. 6076-5
Etching at dusk. Frederic Prokosch. 6073-0
"Etching in a leap". Antelope with cattle. Robert McBlair. 6850-2
Etenim res creatae exerto capite observantes... Henry Vaughan. 6935-5
Eteocles and Polynices, fr. Phoenissae. Euripides. 6435-3
"Etereal minstrel". To a skylark ("Ethereal minstrel!"). William Wordsworth. 6073-0,6086-2,6110-9,6219-9,6453-0
Eternal Christmas. Elizabeth Stuart Phelps. 6144-3;6335-7;6337-3
"Eternal God omnipotent! The one". Invocation. Caelius Sedulius. 6930-4
Eternal desire. William Lorenzo Morrison. 6178-8
Eternal dream. Morris Hurley. 6799-9
The eternal endurance of friendship. Cristoph George Ludwig Meister. 6952-5
Eternal Father, strong to save. William Whiting. 6337-3
Eternal God whose searching eye doth scan. Edwin McNeill Poteat. 6337-3
Eternal God, whose power upholds. Henry Hallam Tweedy. 6337-3
The eternal goodness, sels. John Greenleaf Whittier. 6008-0,6288-1,6309-8,6007-2,6102-8,6076-5,6431-0,6121-4
The eternal goodness. John Greenleaf Whittier. 6753-0
The eternal goodness. John Greenleaf Whittier. 6300-4
The eternal goodness. John Greenleaf Whittier. 6753-0
The eternal Helen. Witter Bynner. 6070-6
Eternal hope. Unknown. 6337-3
Eternal justice. Charles Mackay. 6912-6
Eternal light. William H. Furness. 6600-3
Eternal light! Thomas Binney. 6337-3,6730-1
Eternal London. Thomas Moore. 6278-4
Eternal love. Sir Philip Sidney. 6383-7
Eternal magic. Gertrude W. Robinson. 6906-1
Eternal masculine. William Rose Benet. 6012-9
"Eternal mind! creation's light and lord". Hymn 005, fr. Hymns of a hermit. John Sterling. 6980-0
"Eternal mother, when my race is run". Where my treasure is. Eden Phillpotts. 6793-X
"Eternal mover, whose diffused glory". D.O.M. Sir Henry Wotton. 6931-2
The eternal play. Richard Le Gallienne. 6030-7
An eternal poem. Samuel Taylor Coleridge. 6278-4,6089-7
The eternal quest, fr. Job. Bible. 6337-3
Eternal recurrence. Rolfe Humphries. 6880-4
Eternal rhyme. William Shakespeare. 6383-7
Eternal shipwreck. Iwan [or Yvan] Goll. 6160-5
Eternal snows. Lilian Sauter. 7023-X
"Eternal source of every joy!" Philip Doddridge. 6302-0
Eternal spirit of the chainless mind. George Gordon, 6th Baron Byron. 6240-7
Eternal spirit, evermore creating. Henry B. Robins. 6337-3
Eternal spring. Edgar A. Guest. 6748-4
The eternal spring. John Milton. 6239-3
"Eternal time, that wastest without waste". To time. A. W.. 6934-7,6879-0,6182-6
Eternal truth. Oliver Wendell Holmes. 6461-2
"Eternal truth, almighty, infinite", fr. Caelica. Fulke Greville; 1st Baron Brooke. 6931-2
Eternal unrest. Antonin Sova. 6886-3

Eternal vigil. Edmond Gore Alexander Holmes. 6090-0
The eternal way. Richard Le Gallienne. 6289-X
"The eternal word of God is ever now". The exhaustless word. William White. 6868-5
The eternal word. Henry Wadsworth Longfellow. 6144-3;6335-7
The eternal years. Frederick William Faber. 6014-5
The eternal young. Edgar A. Guest. 6401-9
Eternal youth. A. Judson Hanna. 7007-8
The eternal. Percy Bysshe Shelley. 6240-7
The eternal. Esaias Tegner. 6045-5
"Eternall truth, almighty, infinite". Sonnet 097 ("Eternall truth"). Fulke Greville; 1st Baron Brooke. 6933-9
Eternities. Winifred Johnston. 6397-7
Eternity. Grace Griswold Bisby. 6818-9
Eternity. Emily Dickinson. 6300-4
Eternity. Irwin Edman. 6879-0
Eternity. Robert Herrick. 6563-5,6641-0,6726-3
Eternity. Thomas Meyer. 7003-5
Eternity. Edmund Spenser. 6935-5
Eternity. William Sydney Thayer. 7014-0
Eternity ("He who bends to himself a Joy"). William Blake. 6315-2,6339-X
Eternity and the tooth. Christopher Morley. 6532-5
Eternity of love protested. Thomas Carew. 6341-1,6933-9
The eternity of love. William Ernest Henley. 6396-9
Ethan Allen. Rufus Wilmot Griswold. 7030-2
Ethan Allen, sels. George Lansing Raymond. 6695-X
Ethelstan, sels. George Darley. 6980-0
Ethelstan: Runilda's chant, sels. George Darley. 6258-X
"Ethereal minstrel...", fr. To a skylark. William Wordsworth. 6529-5
"Ethereal race, inhabitants of air". An ode on Aeolus's harp. James Thomson. 6816-2
Etherege, Sir George
    Carpe diem. 6092-7
    Catch. 6544-9
    "Chloris, 'tis not in your power". 6933-9
    Drinking song ("The pleasures of love..."). 6544-9
    The forsaken mistress. 6544-9
    "From hunting whores, and hanting play". 6544-9
    Gatty's song. 6544-9
    If she be not as kind as fair. 6563-5
    Lines to a lady: who asked of him how long... 6187-7
    She wou'd if she cou'd, sels. 6562-7,6563-5
    Silvia. 6544-9,6563-5
    "Since Love and verse, as well as Wine". 6544-9
    Sir Joslin's song. 6544-9
    Song ("If she be not"). 6544-9,6733-6,6152-4
    Song ("Ladies"). 6544-9
    Song ("The pleasures of love"). 6152-4
    Song ("When first Amintas"). 6544-9
    Song ("When Phillis watch'd"). 6544-9
    A song ("Ye happy swains"). 6544-9
    Song of Bassett. 6544-9
    To a lady, asking him how long he would love her. 6315-2,6317-9,6544-9,6563-5,6152-4,6195
    To a very young lady. 6544-9,6563-5,6152-4
    To little or no purpose I spent many days. 6562-7,6563-5
    Ye happy swains, whose hearts are free. 6934-7
    "Ye happy swains, whose hearts are free" 6874-X
Etherege, Sir John
    "Ladies, though to your conquering eyes." 6317-9
Etheridge, Ken
    Annunciation. 6360-8
    Carnations. 6360-8
    Early snow. 6360-8
    Mask. 6360-8
    An old collier. 6360-8
    Spring fragment. 6360-8
Ethick, fr. The testament of beauty. Robert Bridges. 6487-6
Ethics. George R. Wallace. 6983-5
Ethinthus, queen of waters, fr. Europe. William Blake. 6125-7,6545-7
Ethiopia saluting the colours. Walt Whitman. 6126-5,6659-3,6179-6,6113-3,6077-3,6246-6,6288-1
Ethnogenesis&. Henry Timrod. 6333-0

Ethwald: a tragedy. Joanna Baillie. 6813-8
Etienne de La Boece. Ralph Waldo Emerson. 6753-0
Etienne de la boece. Ralph Waldo Emerson. 6252-0
Etienne de La Boece. Ralph Waldo Emerson. 6753-0
Etin the forester. Unknown. 6055-2,6056-2
Etiquette. Sir William Schwenck Gilbert. 6089-7,6079-X, 6291-9,6646-1,6633-X
Etiquette. Unknown. 6412-4
"An Eton stripling training for the law". Modern logic. Unknown. 6787-5
An Etruscan song. John William Mackail. 6656-9
Etruscan tombs. Agnes Mary F. ("Madame Duclaux") Robinson. 6331-4,6726-3
Etruscan vase. Jean Nuchtern. 6857-X
Etsi omnes, ego non. Ernest Myers. 6656-9
Etter, Dale
    Sonnets for Ellen. 6799-9
The ettin o' Sillarwood. William Motherwell. 6960-6
Ettrick Shepherd, The. See Hogg, James
Ettrick banks. Unknown. 6180-X
Etude. Carlos Pellicer. 6759-X
Etude geographique. Stoddard King. 6722-0,6218-4
Etude realiste. Algernon Charles Swinburne. 6102-8,6560-0, 6110-9,6656-9,6078-1,6122-2,6198-2,6239-3,6732-8
Etude realiste. Algernon Charles Sqinburne. 6875-8
"Eu'ry dame affects good fame, what ere her doings be" Thomas Campion. 6794-8
Eubulus
    Love is not winged. T.F. Higham (tr.). 6435-3
"The eucalyptus-blooms are sweet". The flying mouse..., fr. Australian transcripts. William ("Fiona Macleod") Sharp. 6768-9
Eucharist. E. Merrill Root. 6144-3
Euchenor chorus, fr. The city. Arthur Upson. 6310-1
Euchred!. J.G. Francis. 6786-7
Euclid. Vachel Lindsay. 6375-6,6736-0
Euclid. Edna St. Vincent Millay. 6102-8,6076-5
Euclid alone. Edna St. Vincent Millay. 6153-2
"Euclid alone has looked on beauty bare". Sonnet 022 ("Euclid alone"). Edna St. Vincent Millay. 6808-1
Euclid alone has looked on beauty nare. Edna St. Vincent Millay. 6339-X,6488-4,6527-9,6536-8,6619-4,6726 , 6250-4,6101-2
"Euclid alone looked on beauty bare". Sonnet ("Euclid alone"). Edna St. Vincent Millay. 6154-0,6121-4,6161-3
Eudy, Mary Cummings
    Crystals and flame. 6850-2
    Oxen. 6850-2,6979-7
    Three lonely women. 6850-2
Euenus
    A swallow. William Cowper (tr.). 6435-3
    The vine and the goat. Henry Van Dyke (tr.). 6961-4
    The vine to the goat. Sir William Marris (tr.). 6435-3
Eugenia. George Chapman. 6208-3
Eugenics. Theognis. 6435-3
Eugenics. Anna Wickham. 6880-4
Eugenie. James Abraham Martling. 6952-5
Eugenius III
    Dedication. Raymond F. Roseliep (tr.). 6282-2
"Eulalie!- such thy name to mortal men". Acrostic ("Eulalie"). James Abraham Martling. 6952-5
Eulalie; a song. Edgar Allan Poe. 6255-5,6126-5
Eulert, Don
    The transformation. 6792-1
Eulogistic snatches. Kuno Meyer. 6582-1
Eulogium on rum. Joseph Smith. 6083-8,6307-1
Eulogy. Charles Edward Butler. 6640-2
Eulogy. Leonard G. Foster. 6820-0
Eulogy. Edgar A. Guest. 6748-4
Eulogy for a tough guy. Daniel L. Klauck. 6870-7
Eulogy of my horse. Siegfried Sassoon. 6357-8
Eulogy on laughing. Jonathan Mitchell Sewall. 6787-5
Eulogy on the times. Thomas Green Fessenden. 7030-2
Eumaeus the swineherd. Homer. 6435-3
Eumares. Asclepiades. 7039-6
Eunice. Robert C.V. Meyers. 6921-5
Eupepsia. Edward Farquhar. 6939-8
"Euphemia studies law, Aminta". Song 003, fr. Songs for puritans. Richard Aldington. 6985-1

Euphoron. Bayard Taylor. 6976-2
Euphranor, sels. Unknown. 6423-X
Euphrosyne. Matthew Arnold. 6219-9,6250-4,6560-0
Eupolis
    Pericles. T.F. Higham (tr.). 6435-3
Eureka. Josiah Gilbert Holland. 6066-8,6581-3
Eureka. Arthur T. Merrill. 6818-9
Eureka [pseud].
    "A pure devotion is a cleansing fire". 6800-6
Euripides
    The Aftermath, fr. Iphigenia in Aulis. Richard Lattimore (tr.). 6665-8
    Agamemnon's children, fr. Iphigenia in Tauris. Gilbert Murray (tr.). 6435-3
    Alcestis, sels. Gilbert Murray (tr.). 6879-0
    Andromeda. John Addington Symonds (tr.). 6435-3
    Apollo the betrayer, fr. Ion. Cecil Maurice Bowra (tr.). 6435-3
    Bacchae, sel. 7014-0
    The bacchae, sels. Gilbert Murray (tr.). 6334-9
    Bacchanal, fr. Baccae. T.F. Higham (tr.). 6435-3
    The beginning of day, fr. Phaethon. 6435-3
    Bereavement, fr. Alcestis. Cecil Maurice Bowra (tr.). 6435-3
    Bird of the sea, fr. Iphigenia in Taurus. Gilbert Murray (tr.). 6435-3
    The birds of god, fr. Hippolytus. Gilbert Murray (tr.). 6435-3
    Children, fr. Danae. T.F. Higham (tr.). 6435-3
    Chivalry, fr. Supplices. Cecil Maurice Bowra (tr.). 6435-3
    Chorus of captive Greek women, fr. Iphigenia in Tauris. Gilbert Murray (tr.). 6334-9
    Chorus of satyrs, driving their goats, fr. The cyclops. Percy Bysshe Shelley (tr.). 7039-6
    Chorus, fr. Alcestis. Alfred Edward Housman (tr.). 7039-6
    Chorus, fr. Hippolytus. 6252-0
    Chorus, fr. Hippolytus. Gilbert Murray (tr.). 7039-6
    Chorus, fr. The Bacchae. 6252-0
    Chorus, fr. The Bacchae. Gilbert Murray (tr.). 6334-9, 6102-8
    Chorus, fr. The Trojan women. Gilbert Murray (tr.). 6334-9
    Chorus: The kings of Troy, fr. Andromache. George Allen (tr.). 6665-8
    A chrous, fr. Hecuba. Thomas Warton (the Elder) (tr.). 6962-2
    Criticism of life, fr. Hippolytus. Andrew Lang (tr.). 6987-8
    A Cyclops' philosophy, fr. Cyclops. Percy Bysshe Shelley (tr.). 6435-3
    Dawn, fr. Ion. Cecil Maurice Bowra (tr.). 6435-3
    The death of Rhesus, fr. Rhesus. Gilbert Murray (tr.). 6435-3
    Death the enemy, fr. Alcestis. Robert Browning (tr.). 6435-3
    Dirge, fr. Supplices. George Allen (tr.). 6435-3
    The doom of Hippolytus. Cecil Maurice Bowra (tr.). 6435-3
    Earth and sky, fr. Chrysippus. Cecil Maurice Bowra (tr.). 6435-3
    Electra and Orestes, fr. Electra. George Allen (tr.). 6435-3
    Electra, sels. Gilbert Murray (tr.). 6541-4
    Electra, sels. Gilbert Murray (tr.). 6541-4
    The end of Troy, fr. Troades. Gilbert Murray (tr.). 6435-3
    Eteocles and Polynices, fr. Phoenissae. George Allen (tr.). 6435-3
    The furies, fr. Orestes. George Allen (tr.). 6435-3
    The garland, fr. Hippolytus. Cecil Maurice Bowra (tr.). 6435-3
    Hippolytus to Artemis. 7020-5
    Hippolytus, sels. Gilbert Murray (tr.). 6879-0
    Hippolytus, sels. Gilbert Murray (tr.). 6541-4
    Hippolytus, sels. Gilbert Murray (tr.). 6541-4
    His death, fr. Hippolytus. George Allen (tr.). 6435-3
    Hospitality, fr. Alcestis. Robert Browning (tr.). 6435-3

"In the elm-woods and the oaken". Gilbert Murray (tr.). 6395-0
The Ipighenia in tauris, sels. Gilbert Murray (tr.). 6334-9
The joy of life. 6102-8
The joy of life. Gilbert Murray (tr.). 6732-8
Kings. John Addington Symonds (tr.). 6954-1
The kings of Troy, fr. Andromache. George Allen (tr.). 6435-3
Last chorus, fr. Medea. Nicholas Rowe (tr.). 6867-7
The long, long dances. 6959-2
Love is idle, fr. Danae. Cecil Maurice Bowra (tr.). 6435-3
Love song, fr. The cyclops. Percy Bysshe Shelley (tr.). 7039-6
Medea's resolve, fr. Medea. F.L. Lucas (tr.). 6435-3
Medea, sels. George Gordon, 6th Baron Byron (tr.). 6945-2
Mocaria and Iolaus, fr. Heraclidae. George Allen (tr.). 6435-3
Night watch, fr. Rhesus. Gilbert Murray (tr.). 6435-3
O Bacchanals, come! 6959-2
Old age, fr. Erechtheus. Cecil Maurice Bowra (tr.). 6435-3
The old men, fr. Aeolus. Cecil Maurice Bowra (tr.). 6435-3
On Cithaeron, fr. Bacchae. Gilbert Murray (tr.). 6435-3
Orestes and Electra, fr. Orestes. John Addington Symonds (tr.). 6435-3
Phaedra's song, fr. Hippolytus. Gilbert Murray (tr.). 6253-9
Phaedra's song. Gilbert Murray (tr.). 6253-9
Polyxena, fr. Hecuba. George Allen (tr.). 6435-3
Pure love, fr. Theseus. Cecil Maurice Bowra (tr.). 6435-3
Pylades, fr. Iphigenia in Tauris. Gilbert Murray (tr.). 6435-3
Shifting fortune, fr. Medea. F.L. Lucas (tr.). 6435-3
Siren-spirits, fr. Helena. J.T. Sheppard (tr.). 6435-3
Six letters, fr. Theseus. Cecil Maurice Bowra (tr.). 6435-3
Song of the initiated, fr. Cretenses. Gilbert Murray (tr.). 6435-3
Take life as it comes, fr. Hypsipyle. Walter Headlam (tr.). 6435-3
There are no gods, fr. Bellerophon. John Addington Symonds (tr.). 6435-3
Thou shall not die, fr. Hercules furens. Cecil Maurice Bowra (tr.). 6435-3
To Alcestis, fr. Alcestis. Richard Aldington (tr.). 6435-3
To Artemis, fr. Hippolytus. Andrew Lang (tr.). 6987-8
The Trojan women, sels. Gilbert Murray (tr.). 6334-9
Troy, fr. Hecuba. J.T. Sheppard (tr.). 6435-3
Troy, fr. Troades. Gilbert Murray (tr.). 6435-3
Vanity of vanities, fr. Meleager. 6435-3
Vengeance, fr. Medea. F.L. Lucas (tr.). 6435-3
Watch before dawn, fr. Iphigenia in Aulis. F. Melian Stawell (tr.). 6435-3
What is life?, fr. Phrixus. John Addington Symonds (tr.). 6435-3
What is life?, fr. Polyidus. Cecil Maurice Bowra (tr.). 6435-3
Where shall wisdom be found?, fr. Baccahe. Gilbert Murray (tr.). 6435-3
Whither away?, fr. Hecuba. T.F. Higham (tr.). 6435-3
The worst horror. John Addington Symonds (tr.). 6435-3
Youth, fr. Hercules Furens. George Allen (tr.). 6435-3
Euripides. Alexander Aetolus. 6435-3
Euripides. Edward Bulwer-Lytton; Baron Lytton. 6980-0
Euripides. Thucydides. 6435-3
Euripides, sels. Thomas Warton Jr. 6867-7
Euroclydon. Thomas Edward Brown. 6809-X
Europa and the bull. Moschus. 6435-3
Europe. Walt Whitman. 6121-4,6288-1
Europe, sels. Louis Dudek. 6446-9
European recognition. James Abraham Martling. 6952-5
Eurydice. Margaret Allonby. 6788-3
Eurydice. Francis William Bourdillon. 6250-4
Eurydice to Orpheus. Robert Browning. 6641-0,6199-0

Eurymachus's fancy. Robert Greene. 6436-1
Eusden, Lawrence
    The courtier. 6867-7
    George II. 6867-7
    On the Spectator's critique of Milton. 6867-7
    A poem on the happy succession...King George II. 6867-7
    To Mr. --. 6867-7
    To the Reverend Dr. Bentley. 6867-7
Eusebius of Tyre
    "All power is in essence poetical" 7014-0
"Eustace K. Bonehead, of Chicago, in Il".
    Limerick:"Eustace K. Bonehead...". Langford Reed. 6811-1
Eustace, John C. (tr.)
    Celestial queen, fr. De partu virginis. Sincerus Sannazarius, 6282-2
    De Partu Virginis, sels. Sincerus Sannazarius, 6282-2
Eutaw springs. Philip Freneau. 6015-3
Euterpe. Alfred Noyes. 6169-9
Euthanasia. George Gordon, 6th Baron Byron. 6543-0
Euthanasia. Henry More. 6385-3,6438-8
Euthanasia. Margaret Junkin Preston. 7022-1
Euthanasia. John Todhunter. 6507-4
Euthanasia. Edward Winship. 6274-1
Euthanasia; or, the happy death. Richard Crashaw. 6250-4, 6543-0
Euthanasy. R.H. Law. 7031-0
Eutopia. Francis Turner Palgrave. 6980-0
Euwer, Anthony
    Cats and humans - all the same. 6120-6
    Gettin' born. 6722-0
    Limeratomy. 6861-8
    Mistress McGrether. 6710-7
    My face. 6722-0
    "No matter how grouchy you're feeling". 6722-0
    Then give us wings. 6443-4
Ev'n like two little bank-dividing brooks. Francis Quarles. 6641-0.6341-1
"Ev'n like two little bank-dividing brooks". My beloved is mine, and I am his. Francis Quarles. 6933-9
"Ev'n on the tenderest hour of love". Foreboding. Walter De La Mare. 6905-3
"Ev-er-y child who has the use". Some geese. Oliver Herford. 6902-9
Eva. Charles Godfrey Leland. 6004-8
Eva. Rainer Maria Rilke. 6643-7
Eva, Reginald C.
    Dreams. 6461-2
    The password. 6144-3
Evacuation of New York by the British. Unknown. 6946-0
"Evading its obsidian eyes". Opossum road-kill. Gary Nelson. 6900-2
Evadne. Hilda ("H.D.") Doolittle. 6348-9,6019-6
Evadne and her son. Pindar. 6435-3
Evagene Baker - who was dyin' of dred consumption... James Whitcomb Riley. 6892-8
Evald, Johannes
    King Christian. Henry Wadsworth Longfellow (tr.). 7039-6
Evalina. Unknown. 6003-X
Evanescence. Mary Swain Paxton. 6397-7
Evanescence. Shitago. 6102-8
Evanescent love. Eugene Redmond. 7024-8
Evangel. Clarence Monteith Workman. 6799-9
"Evangelical vicar in want". Limerick:"Evangelical vicar in want". Ronald Knox. 6811-1,6811-1,6308-X
Evangeline. Henry Wadsworth Longfellow. 6503-1,6673-9,6250-4,6126-5,6094-3
Evangeline in the prairie. Henry Wadsworth Longfellow. 6302-0;6385-3
The Evangeline trail. Ostie Vernona Betts. 6265-2
Evangeline, sels. Henry Wadsworth Longfellow. 6753-0,6208-3,6066-8,6008-0,6288-1,6431-0,6288-1,6484-1,6395-0, 6365-9,6732-8,6550-3,6077-3,6289-X
An evangelist's wife. Edwin Arlington Robinson. 6052-8
Evans, Abbie Huston
    Cock-crow. 6076-5
    Hill-born. 6037-4
    Salvage. 6253-9
    Says life of youth. 6069-2

EVANS

Sea fog. 6253-9,6036-6
The servant of the prophet. 6532-5,6037-4
Wild apples. 6036-6
'—Will he give him a stone?' 6532-5
Evans, Abel
A fat man. 6228-8
For Sir John Vanbrugh, architect. 6722-0
On Blenheim house. 6932-0
On Sir John Vanbrugh. 6932-0
Evans, C. Ethel
The princess. 6653-4
Evans, David
Poem ("Screamlight streams"). 6360-8
Poem ("The cotton-still"). 6360-8
Poem I ("The cotton-still spire.") 6360-8
Sona dialect. 6360-8
Synthesis. 6360-8
This political time-plotted day. 6360-8
Evans, Donald
With death the uncouth. 6030-7
Evans, Essex
'To the Irish dead'. 6846-4
Evans, Evan
Verses to Mr. Vaughan of Hengwrt. 6528-7
Evans, Florence Wilkinson
The flower factory. 6501-5,6607-0,6161-3,6265-2,6501-5, 6607-0
The fugitives. 6954-1
Our lady of idleness, sels. 6954-1
A Roman garden. 6338-1
Students. 6331-4
Tarantella. 6331-4
Evans, George Essex
An Australian symphony. 6784-0
The women of the west. 6591-0,6592-9
Evans, George Ewart
At the seaside. 6360-8
Poem ("Progress"). 6360-8
Winter 1939. 6360-8
Evans, Hugh J.
My love Karin. 6591-0,6592-9
Evans, Hugh John
The veld. 6800-6
Evans, J.E.
In service. 6443-4
The service flag. 6846-4
Evans, Jean
The uknown soldier meditates. 6799-9
Evans, Lucille
The composer. 6316-0
Penelope. 6316-0
Evans, M. A. B.
Dance music. 6959-2
Evans, Mrs.
Night in Eden. 6415-9
Evans, Nathaniel
Elegy to the memory of my beloved friend, Mr. Thomas Godfrey. 6288-1
Ode to my ingenious friend, Mr. Thomas Godfrey. 6004-8, 6288-1
Evans, Nellie H.
The Black Hills. 6799-9
Toiling children. 6799-9
Evans, Patrick
At morning an iris. 6379-9
Green grass growing. 6379-9
Evans, Robert Allison
Emily Dickinson. 6761-1
Requiem of the air. 6761-1
Evans, Ruth
For 1941. 6761-1
Evans, Sebastian
Shadows. 6528-7
Evans, Sebastion
A dirge for summer. 6656-9
The seven fiddlers. 6518-X
What the trumpeter said. 6656-9
Evans, Selma Saari
At Burntside lake. 6342-X
Evans, Virginia Moran
The vision. 6648-8
Evaporation. Rosalie Maher. 6850-2
Evarra and his gods. Rudyard Kipling. 6810-3
Evasion. Alice B. Craig. 6799-9
Eve. Oliver Herford. 6736-0
Eve. Ralph Hodgson. 6232-6,6236-9,6246-6,6427-2,6733-6, 6464 ,6026-9,6153-2,6210-5,6102-8,6199-0,6250
Eve. Christina Georgina Rossetti. 6378-0
Eve. Christina Georgina Rossetti. 6848-0
Eve. Lydia Huntley Sigourney. 6848-0
Eve. Francis Ernley Walrond. 6800-6
Eve at the fountain. John Kebble Hervey. 6848-0
The **Eve of Ascension Day.** Derenik Demirjian. 6050-1
The **eve of Bannockburn.** John Barbour. 6180-X
The **eve of battle, 1645.** Silas Weir Mitchell. 6936-3
The **eve of Bunker Hill.** Clinton Scollard. 6946-0
The **eve of Crecy.** William Morris. 6383-7,6659-3,6657-7, 6046-3,6508-2,6110-9,6639-9,6655
The **eve of election, sels.** John Greenleaf Whittier. 6623-2
The **eve of Quatre Bras.** George Gordon, 6th Baron Byron. 6793-X
Eve of St. Agnes. Alfred Lord Tennyson. 6046-3
Eve of St. Agnes, sels. John Keats. 6289-X,6501-5,6317-9
The **eve of St. Agnes, sels.** John Keats. 6301-2
The **eve of St. Agnes.** John Keats. 6052-8,6600-3,6198-2, 6369-1,6473-6,6536 ,6291-9,6646-1,6660-7,6199-0,6196- 6,6430 ,6122-2,6154-0,6271-7,6302-0,6385-3,6488 , 6560-0,6192-3,6250-4,6102-8,6245-8,6153 ,6527-9,6604- 6,6726-3,6732-8,6723-9,6645 ,6023-4,6086-2,6110-9, 6371-3
The **eve of St. Agnes.** John Keats. 6828-6
The **eve of St. Bartolomew.** George Walter Thornbury. 6424-8
The **eve of St. John.** Sir Walter Scott. 6199-0,6518-X,6075- 7,6086-2,6110-9,6419-1,6613-5
The **eve of St. Mark.** John Keats. 6186-9,6378-0,6726-3,6086- 2,6110-9
"The **eve of mystery and holy charm".** Christmas eve in the Karoo. Ethelreda Lewis. 6800-6
The **eve of the election.** John Greenleaf Whittier. 6385-3, 6709-3,6600-3,6709-3,6291-9
The **eve of Waterloo, fr. Childe Harold.** George Gordon, 6th Baron Byron. 6188-5,6242-3,6375-5,6427-2,6479-5,6552- ,6114-1,6107-9,6621-6,6263-6,6267-9,6964
Eve penitent, fr. Paradise lost. John Milton. 6933-9
Eve speaks. Myra Clark. 6761-1
Eve speaks. Louis Untermeyer. 6030-7
Eve speaks to Adam, fr. Paradise lost. John Milton. 6125-7
Eve to Adam. John Milton. 6138-9;6634-8
Eve's blood. Anatole France. 6351-9
Eve's conjugal love. John Milton. 6543-0
Eve's daughter. Edward Rowland Sill. 6243-1,6429-9,6004-8, 6505-8,6321-7
Eve's lament. John Milton. 6848-0
Eve's lament. Sean O'Faolain. 6582-1
Eve's lament. Unknown. 6930-4
Eve's lamentation, fr. Paradise lost. John Milton. 6049-8
Eve's mirror. John Milton. 6679-8
Eve's recollections. John Milton. 6543-0
"Eve's/Leaves". The antiquity of fashions. Mary J.J. Wrinn. 6850-2
Eve, Maria Louisa
Conquered at last. 6273-3
The new Dixie. 6074-9
Eve, fr. Paradise lost. John Milton. 6933-9
Eve, sels. Charles Peguy. 6343-8
"Eve, with her warm lips redder". Water mocassin. Laura Lourene LeGear. 6979-7
Eve-song. Mary Gilmore. 6349-7
Eveleen's bower. Thomas Moore. 6980-0
Eveleth, Alice Towne
Public opinion. 6764-6
Evelyn. Unknown. 6826-X
Evelyn Hope. Robert Browning. 6014-5,6123-0,6198-2,6240-7, 6271-7,6302-,6301-2,6291-9,6110-9,6046-3,6560-0,6655 ,6303-9,6370-5,6385-3,6473-6,6486-8,6600-,6023-4, 6102-8,6383-7,6543-0,6655-0,6656 ,6657-7
Evelyn Ray. Amy Lowell. 6531-7
"Even after all these years there comes..dream". Sonnet ("Even after all"). John Masefield. 6879-0
"Even along the railway platform it was spring". We'll all

feel gay. Winfield Townley Scott. 6761-1
"Even among the deformed". Beauty. Paul David Ashley. 6870-7
"Even as a child too well she knew". The only ornament. Phoebe Cary. 6969-X
"Even as a snail am I, who in the dark". Humble smile. Ruth Pitter. 6893-6
"Even as I used to rumble his gray hair". My father. Helen Wolfe Davies. 6750-6
"Even as his who on some midnight hears". Philip Bourke Marston. 6997-5
"Even as one voice the great sea sang.From out". The song of the sea. Sir William Watson. 6997-5
Even as the bird. E. Merrill Root. 6144-3
Even as the grass. Ruth Enck Engle. 6750-6
Even Eve 'n' Adam. Mary Carolyn Davies. 6750-6
"Even as the seed of the marigold". The marigold. Allen Upward. 6897-9
"Even before our dinner was quite done". New England afternoon. E. Merrill Root. 6880-4
"Even Eros/stops". Ten love notes. Thomas Meyer. 7003-5
"Even for the short time" Sojin Takei. 6981-9
"Even if words are inadequate for expression". Like a boy. Joseph Joel Keith. 6761-1
Even in a palace. Marcus Aurelius Antoninus. 6424-8
Even in death. Helen Corinne Bergen. 6686-0
"Even in death they prosper, even in the death". Necropolis. Karl Shapiro. 6751-4
"Even is come; and from the dark, park, hark!". A nocturnal sketch. Thomas Hood. 6916-9
Even me. James Abraham Martling. 6952-5
"Even now she sometimes". Pomegranate. Gail N. Harada. 6790-5
" .Even now, mad girl, dost ape..painted Briton,"fr. Elegies. Sextus Propertius. 6088-9
"Even smoke/Which is bitter". Smoke. Doris Trahagen De Aragon. 6906-1
Even so. Dante Gabriel Rossetti. 6828-6,7020-5
Even such is time. Sir Walter Raleigh. 6182-6,6188-5,6584-8,6726-3,6187-7,6395 ,6125-7,6189-3,6192-3,6639-3
"Even such is time, that takes in trust". To-day a man, to-morrow none. Sir Walter Raleigh. 6879-0
"Even such is time, which takes in trust". Epitaph. Sir Walter Raleigh. 6436-1
Even tavern-musicke. Sir Thomas Browne. 6230-X
Even the best. Gary Allan Kizer. 6870-7
Even the bitter and difficult. Robin Lampson. 6042-0
"Even the clump of soil on coffin lid". The window. Ella Brody. 6750-6
'Even the least of these'. Ada M. Roberts. 6607-0
"Even the rocks of Futami." Basho (Matsuo Basho) 6027-7
"Even the sea dies, Lorca said at a weak...". Guernica. James Lewisohn. 6870-7
Even this shall pass. Unknown. 6166-4
Even this shall pass away. Theodore Tilton. 6255-5,6255-5, 6337-3,6583-X,6730-1
'Even this shall pass away'. Theodore Tilton. 6889-8
Even to the dead. Whitney Montgomery. 6648-8
"The even weave of the canvas". Painted passages. Gail N. Harada. 6790-5
Even-song. George Herbert. 6208-3
Even-song. Benjamin R.C. Low. 6607-0
Even-star. Richard Garnett. 6785-9
Evenen in the village. William Barnes. 6423-X,6660-7
Evening. Clara M. Beede. 6799-9
Evening. William Blake. 6487-6
Evening. Sylvia Hortense Bliss. 7030-2
Evening. William Lisle Bowles. 6543-0
Evening. Robert J. Burdette. 6588-0
Evening. Elizabeth J. Coatsworth. 6069-2
Evening. Hilda Conkling. 6538-4
Evening. George Croly. 6304-7
Evening. Walter De La Mare. 6253-9
Evening. Emily Dickinson. 6236-9
Evening. George Washington Doane. 6006-4,6735-2
Evening. Hilda ("H.D.") Doolittle. 6315-2,6209-1
Evening. Agnes Dordan. 6850-2
Evening. Elizabeth Bemis Dunn. 6799-9
Evening. Porsteinn Erlingsson. 6854-5
Evening. John Fletcher. 6133-8

Evening. Edith L. Fraser. 7016-7
Evening. Wendell Phillips Garrison. 6627-5
Evening. Georg Heym. 6160-5
Evening. Oliver Wendell Holmes. 6302-00
Evening. Frances Anne Kemble. 6046-3
Evening. Kikaku. 6102-8
Evening. Owen (Edward Bulwer-Lytton, Earl Lytton) Meredith. 7015-9
Evening. John Milton. 6935-5
Evening. Silas Weir Mitchell. 6250-4,6309-8
Evening. Harold Monro. 6210-5
Evening. Marjorie L.C. Pickthall. 6433-7
Evening. Edward Pollock. 6241-5
Evening. Victoria Mary Sackville-West. 6083-8
Evening. Charles Sangster. 6433-7
Evening. Sappho. 6435-3
Evening. Sir Walter Scott. 6075-7,6457-4,6459-0,6457-4, 6086-2
Evening. Percy Bysshe Shelley. 6331-4,6484-1
Evening. Robert Southey. 6980-0
Evening. Stephan G. Stephansson. 6854-5
Evening. Stephan G. Stephansson. 6283-0
Evening. Charles Strong. 7015-9
Evening. Alfred Lord Tennyson. 6271-7
Evening. Annie Edgerly Thayer. 6764-6
Evening. Jamie Tobias. 6883-9
Evening. Walter James Turner. 6331-4
Evening. Unknown. 6271-7
Evening. William Wordsworth. 6543-0
Evening (Nahant), fr. Places. Sara Teasdale. 6010-2
Evening - mountains. Theodore Dreiser. 6979-7
Evening after manure hauling. Byron Herbert Reece. 6761-1
Evening among the Alps. Felicia Dorothea Hemans. 6749-2
Evening at home. Theodore R. Nathan. 6850-2
Evening at Palermo. John Addington Symonds. 6252-0
An evening at sea. John Press. 6258-X
An evening at Skolje. Aleksa Santic. 6765-4
Evening at the abbey, fr. Pollio. William Julius Mickle. 6545-7
Evening at the farm. John Townsend Trowbridge. 6239-3,6142-7,6392-6,6554-6,6565-1
"The evening bends upon a stubborn day". Sonnet ("The evening bends"). Pearce Young. 6515-5
"The evening blazes an alien sun". Studies in heat, 1983 Terri Jewell. 6899-5
An evening blessing. James Edmeston. 6065-X
Evening brings us home. Unknown. 6916-9
Evening brings us home. Unknown. 6304-7
Evening by the Thames. William Wordsworth. 6980-0
Evening chant. Adelaide Anne Procter. 6957-6
The evening cloud. Christopher (John Wilson) North. 6219-9, 6385-3,6600-3,6543-0
Evening clouds. Francis Ledwidge. 6812-X
Evening clouds. Francis Ledwidge. 7027-2
"Evening colours her amber breasts". Woman made of stars. Earle Thompson. 7005-7
"Evening comes on: arising from the stream". An eastern evening. Robert Southey. 6980-0
"Evening comes/between astral". Freeze tag. Gordon Henry. 7005-1
The evening company. James Whitcomb Riley. 6128-1
"The evening darkens over". Robert Bridges. 6487-6,6508-2
An evening doze. Albert E. Hunt. 6417-5
"The evening fog of resignation, creeping". Maturescence, fr. Once again the Eden. Noel Hudson Stearn. 6789-1
"The evening found us whom the day had fled". The father. Muriel Stuart. 6884-7
The evening gleam. James Devaney. 6349-7
An evening guest. Dinah Maria Mulock Craik. 6980-0
Evening hymn. Matilda Barbara Betham-Edwards. 6636-9
Evening hymn. Sir Thomas Browne. 6600-3,6291-9,6737-9,6337-3
Evening hymn. Mary Lundie Duncan. 6131-1
Evening hymn. Frederick William Faber. 6219-9
Evening hymn. John Keble. 6065-X,6337-3,6291-9
Evening hymn. Thomas Ken. 6302-0,6337-3
Evening hymn. Adelaide Anne Procter. 6957-6
Evening hymn. George Wither. 6219-9
Evening hymn of the Alpine shepherds. William Beattie. 6219-9

EVENING

'The evening hymn.' Joseph Crosby Lincoln. 6119-2
The evening hymn. Unknown. 6629-1
An evening idyll. Unknown. 6280-6,6413-2
Evening in camp. Patricia Ledward. 6666-6
Evening in Connecticut. Louis MacNeice. 6783-2
Evening in England. Francis Ledwidge. 6332-2,6102-8,6439-6
Evening in February. Francis Ledwidge. 6812-X
Evening in Glloucester harbor. Epes Sargent. 6833-2
Evening in May. Francis Ledwidge. 6812-X
Evening in paradise. John Milton. 6302-0,6315-2,6385-3, 6239-3,6424-8,6543 ,6302-0;6315-2;6385-3;6239-3
Evening in summer. Charles Gamage Eastman. 7030-2
Evening in the desert. Henry Birch-Reynardson. 7029-9
Evening in the great Smokies. DuBose Heyward. 6326-8
Evening in Tyringham valley. Richard Watson Gilder. 6374-8, 6484-1
"Evening kisses the sea". For my darling. James Abraham Martling. 6952-5
The evening knell. John Fletcher. 6182-6,6533-3
The evening land. David Herbert Lawrence. 6069-2
"Evening like laden fruit trees hang immanent". Autumn evening. Francis Scarfe. 6895-2
"The evening meal being past, I turn and climb". Room with a view, sels. Alistair Paterson. 7018-3
Evening meal in the twentieth century. John Holmes. 6527-9
Evening meal in the twentieth century. John Holmes. 6761-1
Evening music of the angels. James Abraham Hillhouse. 6752-2
Evening near ragged mountain. Joseph Hood Barnes. 6764-6
"Evening now, from purple wings". Evening: an ode (1). Samuel Johnson. 6975-4
The evening of the visitation. Thomas Merton. 6282-2
Evening on Calais beach. William Wordsworth. 6533-3,6439-6
Evening on the harbour. Virginia Lyne Tunstall. 6036-6
Evening on the marshes. Barry Straton. 6795-6
Evening on the Potomac. Richard Hovey. 7006-X
Evening over the forest. Beatrice Mayor. 6477-9
"The evening passes fast away". Self-interrogation. Emily Bronte. 6828-6
Evening pastimes. Alice Cary. 6969-X
An evening prayer ("If I have done an unkind act..."). Bess Kine Baker. 6303-9
An evening prayer ("The day is ended. Ere I sink..."). Harriet McEwen Kimball. 6303-9
Evening prayer, at a girls' school. Felicia Dorothea Hemans. 6973-8
An evening prayer. Bernard Barton. 6127-3
An evening prayer. C. Maude Battersby. 6525-2,6461-2
An evening prayer. Unknown. 6337-X
Evening primrose. John Clare. 6545-7
The evening primrose. Emily Bronte. 6253-9
The evening primrose. John Langhorne. 6932-0
The evening primrose. Timothy Otis Paine. 6274-1
The evening primrose. Dorothy Parker. 6232-6,6026-9
Evening quatrains. Charles Cotton. 6315-2,6378-0,6125-7, 6023-4
Evening rambles. Thomas Pringle. 6800-6
Evening recollections of the exile. Felicia Dorothea Hemans. 6543-0
"Evening red and morning gray". Unknown. 7028-0
"Evening red and morning gray." Unknown. 6452-3
The evening rest. Unknown. 6118-4
An evening revery. William Cullen Bryant. 6431-0
Evening rift. Alan Creighton. 6021-8
"Evening robes herself all °estal". The heart of evening. Lucy H. King Smith. 6906-1
Evening scene. E.J. Scovell. 6209-1
An evening scene. Coventry Patmore. 6123-0
"The evening shadows lengthen on the lawn". Inscription, tr the mistress of Cedarcroft. Bayard Taylor. 6976-2
Evening sigh. Emil Aasrestrup. 6555-4
Evening sky. Leonie Adams. 6012-9
"The evening sky is all aglow". The pasture bars. Charles H. Stone. 7030-2
"The evening sky was as green as jade". Feroza. Laurence (Adele Florence Nicolson) Hope. 6856-1
Evening slippers. Winifred Davidson. 6039-0
Evening smoke. Edgar A. Guest. 6869-3
Evening song. Cecil Frances Alexander. 6638-0
Evening song. Fannie Stearns Davis. 6653-4

Evening Song. John Fletcher. 6239-3,6668-2
Evening song. Emma Gertrude Jaeck. 6799-9
Evening song. Sidney Lanier. 6102-8,6126-5,6250-4,6288-1, 6431-0,6300 ,6240-7,6243-1,6320-9,6481-7,6726-3,6513 ,6066-8,6102-8,6076-5,6309-8,6464-7
Evening song. Thomas Miller. 6600-3
Evening song. Unknown. 6952-5
Evening song of maidens. Henry Hart Milman. 6980-0
Evening song of Senlin. Conrad Aiken. 6628-3
Evening song of the Tyrolese peasants. Felicia Dorothea Hemans. 6749-2,6973-8
Evening song of the weary. Felicia Dorothea Hemans. 6973-8
Evening song on the plantation. John Alfred Macon. 6139-7
Evening star. Edgar Allan Poe. 6333-0
"The evening star trembles and hides from him". The evening star. Richard Watson Gilder. 7041-8
The evening star. Grace Blackburn. 6115-X
The evening star. Thomas Campbell. 6302-0;6385-3
The evening star. John Clare. 6125-7
The evening star. Richard Watson Gilder. 7041-8
The evening star. Harold Seton. 6846-4
The evening star. Unknown. 6936-3
The evening star. William Wordsworth. 6438-8
Evening thoughts. Eliza Lee Follen. 6530-9
"An evening towards the end of March. A gentle". Spring night. Jacques Delamain. 7020-5
"Evening traffic homeward burns". Before disaster. Yvor Winters. 6751-4
Evening twilight, fr. The North Sea. Heinrich Heine. 7039-6
Evening voluntaries, sels. William Wordsworth. 6867-7
Evening voluntary. William Wordsworth. 6832-4
An evening walk in spring. Arthur Hugh Clough. 6655-0
An evening walk, sels. William Wordsworth. 6484-1,6196-6, 6199-0,6545-7
An evening walk. John Clare. 6659-3
An evening walk. William Wordsworth. 6828-6
The evening walk. Henry Kirke White. 6085-4
"Evening was brown and misty/The window...". Andante for autumn. Herman Salinger. 7039-6
The evening watch. Henry Vaughan. 6177-X
Evening wind. Un-kyo Kang. 6775-1
The evening wind. William Cullen Bryant. 6753-0
The evening wind. William Cullen Bryant. 6077-3,6102-8, 6240-7,6271-7,6299-7,6291 ,6076-5,6126-5,6304-7,6008-1,6288-1,6302-0,6385-3
The evening wind. James Abraham Martling. 6952-5
An evening's love, sels. John Dryden. 6208-3
"The evening's thrush has three small songs". The three songs. Robert P. Tristram Coffin. 7040-X
Evening, and maidens. William Barnes. 6437-X
"Evening, as slow thy placid shades descend". Sonnet ("Evening, as slow"). William Lisle Bowles. 6152-4
Evening, by a tailor. Oliver Wendell Holmes. 6278-4
Evening, fr. Don Juan. George Gordon, 6th Baron Byron. 6302-0;6385-3
Evening, fr. In a day. Augusta Webster. 7037-X
Evening, fr. Parted love. William Bell Scott. 6819-7
Evening, fr. Sea-pictures. Christopher Pearse Cranch. 6997-5
Evening, fr. Summer by the lakeside. John Greenleaf Whittier. 6008-0
Evening, fr. Syr Martyn. William Julius Mickle. 6545-7
Evening, fr. The task. William Cowper. 6932-0
Evening, fr. The task. William Cowper. 6934-7
Evening, fr. The task. William Cowper. 6932-0
Evening, fr. The task. William Cowper. 6934-7
Evening, near the sea. Edward Dowden. 7015-9
Evening, near the sea. Edward Dowden. 6997-5
Evening, near the sea. Edward Dowden. 7015-9
Evening, near the sea. Edward Dowden. 6997-5
"The evening, the heather". Poem ("The evening...") Laurie Lee. 6783-2
Evening: an ode (1). Samuel Johnson. 6975-4
Evening: an ode (2). Samuel Johnson. 6975-4
Evening: Ponte a Mare, Pisa. Percy Bysshe Shelley. 6631-3
Evening: Spain. Walter James Turner. 6631-3
Evening: the motors. Robert Penn Warren. 6072-2
Evening: zero weather. Thomas Merton. 6839-1
The evening. Unknown. 6952-5

"The evenings bury themselves". Erratic. Paul Celan. 6769-7
"Evenings, when the thyme is sizzled in". Romiosini, sel. Yannis Ritsos. 6803-0
"Evenings, your back is thick with blood". The man who loved knots. Robert Davis. 6855-3
"Evenings/When the house is quiet". Setting the table. Dorothy Aldis. 6891-X
Evens, Jonathan
 It is finished. 6065-X
Evensong. Conrad Aiken. 6030-7,6513-9
Evensong. T. E. Brown. 7020-5
Evensong. Thomas Edward Brown. 6809-X
Evensong. Josephine Norfolk Carr. 6799-9
Evensong. Norreys Jephson O'Conor. 6762-X
Evensong. James Whitcomb Riley. 6091-9
Evensong. Robert Louis Stevenson. 6337-3,6473-6,6732-8, 6102-8,6655-0,6214
Evensong. (Frederick) Ridgely Torrence. 6310-1,6431-0,6300-4
An event. Tom Masson. 6889-8
Eventail. Edith Sitwell. 6884-7
Eventide. Thomas Burbidge. 6600-3,6656-9
Eventide. Caroline Atherton Mason. 6337-3
Eventide at Muizenberg. Francis Watermeyer. 6800-6
Eventide in winter. M. Adelaide Griffin. 6764-6
Events. George O'Neil. 6037-4,6069-2
Eventual birth of thought. B.J. Morse. 6360-8
"Ever been lost? Well, I have, and I know". Lost. George A. Scarborough. 6761-1
"Ever before no hand save mine". In hospital. Gertrude Huntington McGiffert. 6838-3
"Ever find me dim regards". Ralph Waldo Emerson. 6753-0
"Ever just over the top of the next brown rise". On the road. Sir Charles George Douglas Roberts. 6843-X
"Ever let the fancy roam". Fancy. John Keats. 6828-6
"Ever my step must return". Chant for the salt marsh. Katharine Brown Burt. 6789-1
Ever pressing forward. Mary Rosalie Stolz. 6717-4
"Ever seeking, not believing". The iconoclasts. Terry B. Dinkel. 6906-1
"Ever since ending of the summer weather". The silence. Emile Verhaeren. 6785-9
"Ever since the great planes were murdered...". Domus caedet arborem. Charlotte Mew. 6985-1
'Ever so long ago'. T.P. Sanborn. 6116-8
"Ever the ocean tides, slipping between...". Low country. Josephine Johnson. 6979-7
Ever the same. Josephine Preston Peabody. 6338-1
Ever true. Unknown. 6889-8
Ever watchful. Ta' Abbata Sharra. 7039-6
"The ever-lustrous name of patriot". The true patriotism. Sir William Watson. 6793-X
The ever-saved. William White. 6868-5
Everest. Horace Shipp. 6257-1
Everest, Charles W.
 Pass along 'Oh, be joyful.' 6685-2
Everest, Clare
 Sister Madeleine. 6273-3
Everett. Thomas William Parsons. 6820-0
Everett, Alexander H.
 Versification of the beginning of..last book of Martyrs. 6752-2
Everett, David
 You'd scarce expect. 6710-7
Everett, Edward
 Dirge of Alaric the Visgoth. 6385-3
Everett, Elizabeth Abbey
 Friendship town. 6799-9
Everett, Grace Wilson
 Ye who mourn- 6818-9
Everett, Laura Bell
 Faith. 6303-9
 The skein of grievous war. 6542-2
 World-winter. 6542-2
Everett, Leolyn Louise
 Buddhist song. 6785-9
Everett, M.E.H.
 Mother is her name. 6715-8
 Rebekah. 6118-4

Everett, Olivia
 Grandma's house. 6857-X
Evergreens. Edward Coate Pinkney. 6077-3,6752-2
"The evergreens stand proudly now". Undaunted evergreens. Mary Jane Carr. 6799-9
The evergreens. William White. 6868-5
"Everie bush new springing" Unknown. 6380-2
The everlasting arms, fr. Psalm 91. Bible. 6730-1
The everlasting arms. A.G. Prys-Jones. 7031-0
Everlasting farewells. Alice Meynell. 6955-X
The everlasting flowers. Edgar A. Guest. 6869-3
The everlasting gospel, sels. William Blake. 6931-2
The everlasting gospel, sels. William Blake. 6191-5
The everlasting gospel, sels. William Blake. 6931-2
"An everlasting hill was torn". Goldau. John Neal. 6749-2
The everlasting hills. Bessie Williams Osman. 6799-9
The everlasting memorial. Horatius Bonar. 6417-5,6304-7
The everlasting mercy, sels. John Masefield. 6236-9,6532-5, 6732-8,6730-1,6581-3
The everlasting oblivion. John Marston. 6436-1
The everlasting return. Lola Ridge. 6033-1
Everlasting to everlasting, sels. Namdev. 6337-3
"The everlasting universe of things". Mont Blanc. Percy Bysshe Shelley. 6749-2
The everlasting voices. William Butler Yeats. 6659-3
"Evermore/Her eyelids droop'd...". A deserted wife. William Wordsworth. 6980-0
Everson, William
 The poet is dead. 6792-1, 6998-3
Everts, Lillian
 Rainbow-room. 6750-6
 Secrets. 6750-6
Evertson, Frances
 The ship o' dreams. 6799-9
"Every afternoon/when the rush-hour traffic". The fire breather, Mexico City. Jaime Jacinto. 6790-5
"Every age/Through being beheld too close...". A simile, fr. Aurora Leigh. Elizabeth Barrett Browning. 6832-4
"'Every angel is terrible'". Rilke speaks of angels. Susan Donnelly. 6966-5
Every bird of nature. Leonie Adams. 6012-9
"Every boy knows what it's like". What every boy knows. Antler. 7003-5
"Every country has its troubles". The cochero and the horse. Norbert Lyons. 7010-8
Every day. Felix Mendelssohn. 6466-3
"Every day hath its night". Song ("Every day hath its night"). Alfred Lord Tennyson. 6977-0
"Every day is a fresh begining". Unknown. 6109-5
Every day shaggy man mushroom. Mary Norbert Korte. 6792-1
"Every duty we omit...". John Ruskin. 6623-2
Every earthly creature. John Malcolm Brinnin. 6391-8
"Every evening baby goes." Mary Frances Butts. 6452-3
"Every evening, after tea". Teeny-weeny. Eugene Field. 6949-2
"Every gentle breeze that's blowing is a...". The tempters. Edgar A. Guest. 6862-6
Every leaf tends earthward. Max Dauthendey. 6160-5
"Every letter I write is". At their place. Paul Mariah. 6870-7
Every little helps. Unknown. 6529-5,6629-1,6131-1
"Every little while they tell use that the...". The passing of the horse. Samuel Ellsworth Kiser. 7010-8
"Every man has his sorrows; yet each still". Elegy ("Every man"). Andre Chenier. 7039-6
Every man in his humour, Act I. Ben Jonson. 6186-9
Every man is inner dark. Tom Boggs. 6761-1
Every man take a glass in his hand. Unknown. 6328-4
"Every morn at break of day". Guest. Evelyne Love Cooper. 6850-2
"Every mornin' I useta watch and wonder". 'The pigeon-scarer'. John V.A. Weaver. 6817-0
"Every morning, while hurrying along...to work". Light. Pascal D'Angelo. 6776-X
Every mother's love the best. Unknown. 6692-2
"Every night at Currabwee". At Currabwee. Francis Ledwidge. 6812-X
"Every night when you are giving". The silent speak for you. Jeffery Beam. 7003-5
"Every once in a while". Not macho, just macho. Gene

EVERY

Fowler. 6998-3
"Every one of you won the war". You and you. Edith Wharton. 6963-0
Every one sang. Siegfried Sassoon. 6051-X,6228-8,6395-0, 6477-9,6509-0,6634 ,6607-0,6607-0,6153-2,6161-3,6581-3,6666-6,6542
"Every passion play". Judas. Gerhard Fritsch. 6769-7
Every soul is a circus. Vachel Lindsay. 6206-7
Every Thanksgiving Day. Harriet Prescott Spofford. 6449-3
Every thing. Harold Monro. 6393-4
"Every thing from you is accepted". Baha' al-Din Zuhair. 6766-2
Every time I see a ship. Harry Kemp. 6798-0
"Every way she opposes me, even with arms". A domestic scene, fr. The legend of Florence. Leigh Hunt. 6980-0
Every year. Albert Pike. 6916-9
Every-day heroes. Bertrand Shadwell. 6274-1
Everybody has to go home sometime. Marsha Elaine Kash. 6998-3
"Everybody loved Chick Lorimer in our town". Gone. Carl Sandburg. 6754-9
"Everyday I sit at a table". The August second syndrome. J.A. Hines. 6870-7
Everyday alchemy. Genevieve Taggard. 6464-7
Everyman. Unknown. 6194-X
"Everything blooms:/frost-blossom". Hoarfrost. Christine Busta. 6769-7
Everything decays, fr. Oedipus coloneous. Sophocles. 6435-3
"Everything in the world has been photographed". Hold my hand. Edmund Pennant. 6966-5
Everything is dark. Pierre Reverdy. 6343-8
"Everything is in flight now, trees and men". Flight. Babette Deutsch. 6783-2
"Everything is only a reflection" Ernst Schonwiese. 6769-7
"Everything pleased my neighbor Jim". 'My neighbor Jim'. Unknown. 6889-8
"Everything would have been better if I hadnot". I have seen the mountains. Horace Gregory. 6761-1
"Everywhere is our wilderness everywhere" George Barker. 6379-9
"Everywhere the sad autumn drops like maple...". Boy. Dong-ju Yun. 6775-1
Everywhere, everywhere Christmas tonight. Phillips Brooks. 6465-5,6747-6
"Everywhere/I come across stark camel bones...". The bushed burned with fire. Judah M. Turkat. 6839-1
Evicted. Beatrice M. Murphy. 7024-8
Evidence. Brother X (pseud.) 6662-3
Evidence. Thomas Curtis Clark. 6337-3

'Exactly so.' Lady T. Hastings. 6089-7
Exaggeration. Elizabeth Barrett Browning. 6965-7
Exaltation. Kurt Heynicke. 6160-5
Exaltation. Paul Shivell. 6266-0
Exaltation of elementary materials. Xavier Abril. 6759-X
Examinations. Howard Mumford Jones. 6506-6
Example. Annie D. Hanks. 6632-1
Example. John Keble. 6303-9,6385-3
Example.Unknown128406Terminated
EXILE'S

The exile's dirge. Felicia Dorothea Hemans. 6973-8
An exile's farewell. Adam Lindsay Gordon. 6951-7,6768-9
An exile's garden. Sophie ("Ellen Burroughs") Jewett. 6338-1
Exile's letter. Ezra Pound. 6209-9
An exile's mother. Emily Lawless. 6174-5
The or dawn on the Irish coast exile's return. John Locke. 7007-8
The exile's song. Robert Gilfillan. 6219-9
Exile, a sequence, sels. Ralph Nixon Currey. 6783-2
The exile. Berton Braley. 6853-7
The exile. John Clare. 6545-7
The exile. Robert Graves. 6354-3
The exile. Thomas Hood. 6974-4
The exile. Katharine (Hinkson) Tynan. 6793-X
The exile. Anna Wickham. 6893-6
Exiled. Mary McGuire. 6926-6
Exiled. Edna St. Vincent Millay. 6034-X,6431-0

Evolution. Emily Pfeiffer. 7015-9
Evolution. Harry Thurston Peck. 6274-1
Evolution. Emily Pfeiffer. 7037-X
Evolution. Langdon Smith. 6102-8,6732-8,6088-9,6076-5,6736-0
Evolution. John Banister Tabb. 6076-5,6431-0,6300-4,6464-7, 6006-4,6102-8,6732-8,6266-0,6303-9,6337 ,6532-5,6467-1,6646-1,6653-4,6309-8
Evolution. Frances Beatrice Taylor. 7019-1
The evolution of a 'name'. Charles Battell Loomis. 6996-7
Evolution of man. Edward R. Huxley. 6885-5
Evvie's mother. Olive Tilford Dargan. 6326-8
Ewald, Johannes
  Little Gunver. Charles Wharton Stork (tr.). 6555-4
  The three Valkries. Charles Wharton Stork (tr.). 6555-4
Ewart, Gavin
  The Bofors A.A. gun. 6666-6
  Cigarette for the bambino. 6666-6
  "For whom the bell tolls" 6666-6
  Miss Twye. 6379-9
  Poem ("To go"). 6379-9
  Sonnet ("The point"). 6666-6
  When a beau goes in. 6666-6
Ewe-boughts, Marion. Unknown. 6180-X
The ewe-buchtin's bonnie. Lady Grisell [or Grizel] Baillie. 6086-2
The ewe-buchtin's bonnie. Thomas Pringle. 6180-X
Ewen, John
  The boatie rows. 6180-X,6086-2,6219-9
Ewer, W.H.
  Five souls. 6051-X,6542-2
Ewer, W.N.
  The chosen people. 6026-9
The ewer. Milan Rakic. 6765-4
The ewie wi' the crookit horn. John Skinner. 6180-X
Ewing Jr., Thomas
  Jonathan. 6848-0
Ewing, Annemarie
  Fisherman's blunder off New Bedford, Massachusetts. 6388-8
  If the heart be homeless. 6388-8
  The man within. 6388-8
  Prayer ("For still indulging this unruly child"). 6750-6
Ewing, Gertrude
  Sobersides. 6799-9
Ewing, Jeannie Pendleton
  How Larry sang the 'Angus'. 6928-2
  How we played King William. 6928-2
  An inventor's wifinterface/SPTO: 12828 Terminated
EXILE'S

Execution of Major Andre. Nathaniel Parker Willis. 6088-9
The execution of Montrose. William Edmonstoune Aytoun. 6370-5,6552-X,6167-2,6291-9,6263-6,6424 ,6656-9
The execution of Montrose. William Edmonstoune Aytoun. 6948-7
The execution of the Klepht. Julius Typaldos. 6352-7
The execution. Richard Harris ("Thomas Ingoldsby") Barham. 6219-9,6579-1

Experience. John Boyle O'Reilly. 6437-X,6022-6
Experience. Dorothy Parker. 6722-0
Experience. Eden Phillpotts. 6872-3
Experience. Edna Davis Romig. 6836-7
Experience. William Bell Scott. 7015-9
Experience. Unknown. 6116-8
An experience and a moral. Frederick Swartwout Cozzens. 6385-3,6486-8
Experience with a refractory cow. Unknown. 6744-1
Experience, fr. Saint Paul. Frederick W.H. Myers. 6337-3
"Experience, like a pale musician, holds". Perplexed music. Elizabeth Barrett Browning. 7037-X
Experto crede. Ernest Hartley Coleridge. 6084-6,6085-4
Expiation. Angelo De Luca. 6818-9
The expiration. John Donne. 6182-6,6341-1
Explain please. Lucille Schmedtje. 6850-2
Explaining the bitterness of the wind. Richard Kirk. 6039-0

'Exactly so.' Lady T. Hastings. 6089-7
Exaggeration. Elizabeth Barrett Browning. 6965-7
Exaltation. Kurt Heynicke. 6160-5
Exaltation. Paul Shivell. 6266-0
Exaltation of elementary materials. Xavier Abril. 6759-X
Examinations. Howard Mumford Jones. 6506-6
Example. Annie D. Hanks. 6632-1
Example. John Keble. 6303-9,6385-3
Example. Unknown. 6406-X
The example of Christ. Isaac Watts. 6271-7
The example. William Henry Davies. 6134-6,6232-6,6726-3, 6250-4,6508-2,6102-8
An exceeding great army. Ethan Ayer. 6218-0
Excellence. Amos Bronson Alcott. 6288-1
Excellence. Robert Francis. 6761-1
Excellency of Christ, fr. C^{s}rist's victorie... Giles (the Younger) Fletcher. 6337-3,6065-X,6730-4
The excellency of wine. Roger Boyle, Earl of Orrery. 6563-5
"Excellent Manxman, Scotia gave you birth". In memoriam: J. Macmeikin. Thomas Edward Brown. 6809-X
An excellent ballad of charity. Thomas Chatterton. 6732-8, 6102-8,6086-2,6195-0,6152-4,6245
Excellent Jane. Elizabeth Turner. 6018-8
"Excellent mistress faierer yn ye moone." Unknown. 6563-5
An excellent new ballad. James Graham; Marquess of Montrose. 6230-X
An excellent new song on a seditious pamphlet. Jonathan Swift. 6157-5
An excellent new song on the rebellion. Unknown. 6859-6
The excellent way. Robert Bridges. 6487-6
Excelsior. Henry Wadsworth Longfellow. 6014-5,6211-3,6402-7,6498-1,6735-2,6964,6304-7,6566-X,6291-9,6126-5, 6560-0,6457-4,6212-1,6135-4,6288-1,6457-4
Excelsior. Unknown. 6440-X
Except I love. Robert Parry. 6182-6
Except that heaven had come so near. Emily Dickinson. 6908-8
"Except ye repent" J. Franklin Pineo. 6144-3
Except...sometimes. Victoria Adelaide Harvey. 6750-6
Exception. Elaine V. Emans. 6750-6
The exception. Phocylides. 6435-3
Excerpts from 'Riffs' (a work in progress) Dennis Lee. 6767-0
The excesses of God. Robinson Jeffers. 6337-3,6532-5
Excessive modesty. William Cowper. 6294-6
Exchange. Hafsa. 6362-4
An exchange of fortune. Statyllius Flaccus. 6435-3
The exchange.. Samuel Taylor Coleridge. 6722-0
The exchange. Samuel Taylor Coleridge. 6828-6
The exchange. Samuel Taylor Coleridge. 6092-7,6430-2
The exciseman. Robert Burns. 6845-6
"An exclamation point/Is a soldier on review". Punctuation language. Olga Edith Gunkle. 6750-6
Exclamatory. Unknown. 6279-2
Exclusion. Emily Dickinson. 6076-5,6102-8
The exclusive's broken idol. Unknown. 6278-4
The excommunication of the Cid. Unknown (Spanish) 6757-3
Exculpation. Johann Wolfgang von Goethe. 6948-7
An excursion to the mountains. Ebenezer Elliot. 6543-0
The excursion, sels. William Wordsworth. 6134-8,6730-1
The excursion. Tu Fu. 7039-6
The excusacyon of the auctore. Stephen Hawes. 6198-2,6586-4
Excuse. Matthew Arnold. 6271-7,6321-7
An excuse for Lalage. Horace. 6949-5
Excuse me if I cry into my handkerchief. Vachel Lindsay. 6206-7
"Excuse me if I don't weep". Funeral song for Mamie Eisenhower. Nellie Wong. 6790-5
EExcuse me, madam, if amidst your tears". An epistle to her grace, Henrietta. John Gay. 6972-X
Excuse the harshness excuse the grime but... A.D. Winans. 6998-3, 6901-0
The excuse. Robert Heath. 6563-5
The excuse. Sir Walter Raleigh. 6584-8
Excuses. Al-Asamm. 6362-4
The execution of Hugo. George Gordon, 6th Baron Byron. 6980-0
Execution of Major Andre. nna Seward. 6088-9

Execution of Major Andre. Nathaniel Parker Willis. 6088-9
The execution of Montrose. William Edmonstoune Aytoun. 6370-5,6552-X,6167-2,6291-9,6263-6,6424,6656-9
The execution of Montrose. William Edmonstoune Aytoun. 6948-7
The execution of the Klepht. Julius Typaldos. 6352-7
The execution. Richard Harris ("Thomas Ingoldsby") Barham. 6219-9,6579-1
The execution. George Gordon, 6th Baron Byron. 6438-8
Exegi monumentum. Alexander Pushkin. 6622-4
Exempt. Amelia Josephine Burr. 6847-2
Exempt. Christopher Morley. 6538-4
"Exempt from every grief, 'twas mine to live". Sonnet 278 ("Exempt from every grief"). Luis de Camoens [or Camoes]. 6973-8
Exemption. Evangeline Robinson. 6764-6
The exequies. Thomas Stanley. 6341-1,6562-7,6563-5
Exequy on his wife. Henry King. 6102-8,6250-4
The exequy to his matchlesse never to be forgotten... Henry King. 6908-8
The exequy, sels. Henry King. 6317-9
The exequy.. Henry King. 6208-3,6102-8,6562-7,6317-9,6271-7,6315,6341-1,6150-8,6023-4,6563-5,6726-3
Exercise in logic. Amy Lowell. 6070-6
Exercise in m$_n$notony. William M. Galbraith. 6761-1
An exercise recitation. Emma Celia & Lizzie J. Rook. 6137-0
Exercise, fr. The art of preserving health. John Armstrong. 6968-1
Exercises. Jack Lindsay. 6895-2
"Exert thy voice, sweet harbinger of spring". To the nightingale. Anne Finch, Countess of Winchilsea. 6831-6
"Exert thy voice, sweet harbinger of spring!". The poet to the nightingale. Anne Finch, Countess of Winchilsea. 6935-5
Exeunt, fr. The road to Avernus. Adam Lindsay Gordon. 6951-7
"Exhale your grief upon the scented air". Inscription for a garden gate (2). Ruth H. Hausman. 6850-2
The exhaustless word. William White. 6868-5
Exhibition. Harris Downey. 6017-X
Exhilaration. Joyce Lancaster. 6850-2
Exhortacion to learne by others trouble. Henry Howard, Earl of Surrey. 6586-4
Exhortation. Rafael Jesus Gonzalez. 6792-1,6998-3
Exhortation. Pearce Young. 6515-5
Exhortation to prayer. William Cowper. 6814-6
Exhortation to prayer. Margaret Mercer. 6304-7
Exhortation to the Greeks. George Gordon, 6th Baron Byron. 6610-0
Exhortation to youth. Geoffrey Chaucer. 6489-2
An exhortation. Wilfrid Scawen Blunt. 7015-9
Exile. Conrad Aiken. 6778-6
Exile. Ingeborg Bachmann. 6769-7
Exile. Audrey Beecham. 6379-9
Exile. Thomas Edward Brown. 6809-X
Exile. Ernest Dowson. 6507-X
Exile. Theodore Maynard. 6096 X
Exile. Susan L. Mitchell. 6174-5
Exile. Alejandra Pizarnik. 7036-1
Exile. Kathryn White Ryan. 6619-4
Exile. Virna Sheard. 6446-9
Exile. Arthur Stringer. 6797-2
Exile. Winifred Welles. 6034-X
Exile and return. Edward Farquhar. 6939-8
Exile from God. John Hall Wheelock. 6007-2,6032-7,6556-2, 6730-1
"The exile from his native land". The exiled heart. Josephine Johnson. 6839-1
"The exile has never a friend of loyal...". Theognis. 6251-2
Exile in August. Arthur Shearly Cripps. 6625-9
Exile of Erin. Thomas Campbell. 6198-2,6300-2,6385-3,6543-0,6291-9,6457-4,6744-1
The exile of the Acadians. Henry Wadsworth Longfellow. 6552-X
The exile to his country. Unknown. 6859-6
The exile to his wife. Joseph Brennan. 6219-9,6407-8
The exile's devotion. Thomas D'Arcy McGee. 6656-9

EXILE'S

The **exile's** dirge. Felicia Dorothea Hemans. 6973-8
An **exile's** farewell. Adam Lindsay Gordon. 6951-7,6768-9
An **exile's** garden. Sophie ("Ellen Burroughs") Jewett. 6338-1
Exile's letter. Ezra Pound. 6209-1
An **exile's** mother. Emily Lawless. 6174-5
The or dawn on the Irish coast **exile's** return. John Locke. 7007-8
The **exile's** song. Robert Gilfillan. 6219-9
Exile, a sequence, sels. Ralph Nixon Currey. 6783-2
The **exile**. Berton Braley. 6853-7
The **exile**. John Clare. 6545-7
The **exile**. Robert Graves. 6354-3
The **exile**. Thomas Hood. 6974-6
The **exile**. Katharine (Hinkson) Tynan. 6793-X
The **exile**. Anna Wickham. 6893-6
Exiled. Mary McGuire. 6926-6
Exiled. Edna St. Vincent Millay. 6034-X,6431-0
Exiled. Robert Louis Stevenson. 6793-X
Exiled. Myra Wadsworth. 6270-9
The **exiled** heart. Josephine Johnson. 6839-1
Exiles. Gail French. 6659-3
Exiles. Edith Matilda Thomas. 7041-8
The **exiles** speak to Ireland. Shane Leslie. 6174-5
The **exiles**.. Ellen M.H. Gates. 6273-3
The **exiles**.. John Milton. 6186-9
The **exiles**. Oliver Goldsmith. 6543-0
Exit. John Gould Fletcher. 6289-X,6345-4
Exit. Wilson MacDonald. 6021-8
Exit. Wilson MacDonald. 6779-4
Exit. David Morton. 6778-6
Exit. David Morton. 6070-6
Exit. Sir William Watson. 6656-9
Exit God. Gamaliel Bradford. 6032-3,6337-3,6532-5
Exit holiday. Morris Rosenfeld. 7011-6
Exodus 15. Bible. 6732-8
Exodus for Oregon. Joaquin Miller. 6288-1
Exodus for Oregon, sels. Joaquin Miller. 6102-8,6076-5
The **exodus**.. Lady Jane F. ("Speranza") Wilde. 6174-5
The **exodus**. James Abraham Martling. 6952-5
Exorcism. Bayard Taylor. 6976-2
Exorcism. Edith M. Thomas. 6121-4
Exorcism of the straight/man/demon. Aaron Shurin. 7003-5
The **exorcism**. Norman Moser. 6998-3
Exordium. George Cabot Lodge. 6310-1
Exortum est in love and lysse. Unknown. 6756-5
"**Exotic** lady!/Shimmering silver star dust". Evening. Annie Edgerly Thayer. 6764-6
"**Expect** great things from God." Henry Carey. 6225-3
Expectans expectavi. Charles Hamilton Sorley. 6337-3,6532-5,6607-0,6730-1
"**Expectant** but free and lovely to see". Canada. Guttormur J. Guttormsson. 6854-5
Expectation. Gladys Brierly Ashour. 6750-6
Expectation. Sir Edmund Gosse. 6770-0
Expectation. Adelaide Anne Procter. 6957-6
Expectation. Thomas Stanley. 6562-7,6563-5
Expectation. Theodore Wratislaw. 6270-9
Expectation of death. Unknown (Greek) 6435-3
The **expectation**. Frederick William Faber. 6022-6
The **expectation**. Richard Lawson Gales. 6747-6
Expecting the barbarians. Constantine P. Cavafy. 6068-4
Expectoration the second. Samuel Taylor Coleridge. 6278-4
An **expectoration**. Samuel Taylor Coleridge. 6278-4
Expedition. David Morton. 6850-2
Expedition to Wessagusset, fr. The courtship..Standish. Henry Wadsworth Longfellow. 6946-0
Expeditional. C.W. Brodribb. 7027-2
"The **expense** of spirit in a waste of shame". William Shakespeare. 6138-9,6317-9,6186-9,6726-3,6181-8,6536
"The **expense** of spirit in a waste of shame". Sonnet 129 e ("The expense of spirit"). William Shakespeare. 6189-3,6560-0,6208-3,6315-2,6427-2,6436-1,6250-4
Expenses. Adelaide Crapsey. 6897-9
Experience. Louise Driscoll. 7038-8
Experience. Ralph Waldo Emerson. 6176-1,6288-1,6126-5
Experience. William Dean Howells. 6006-4
Experience. Letitia Elizabeth ("L.E.L.") Landon. 6980-0
Experience. Helen Cowles Le Cron. 7038-8
Experiece. Eldon George McLean. 6178-8

Experience. John Boyle O'Reilly. 6437-X,6022-6
Experience. Dorothy Parker. 6722-0
Experience. Eden Phillpotts. 6872-3
Experience. Edna Davis Romig. 6836-7
Experience. William Bell Scott. 7015-9
Experience. Unknown. 6116-8
An **experience** and a moral. Frederick Swartwout Cozzens. 6385-3,6486-8
Experience with a refractory cow. Unknown. 6744-1
Experience, fr. Saint Paul. Frederick W.H. Myers. 6337-3
"**Experience**, like a pale musician, holds". Perplexed music. Elizabeth Barrett Browning. 7037-X
Experto crede. Ernest Hartley Coleridge. 6084-6,6085-4
Expiation. Angelo De Luca. 6818-9
The **expiration**. John Donne. 6182-6,6341-1
Explain please. Lucille Schmedtje. 6850-2
Explaining the bitterness of the wind. Richard Kirk. 6039-0
Explanation. Valerie Tarver. 7024-8
An **explanation**.. Walter Learned. 6273-3,6026-9
An **explanation**. Arthur Guiterman. 6817-0
The **explanation**. Gene Frumkin. 6803-0
The **explanation**. Rudyard Kipling. 6810-3
An **explanaton** of the grasshopper. Vachel Lindsay. 6466-3,6554-X
An **explication**. John Frederick Nims. 6803-0
Exploit of Hector. Homer. 6304-7
Exploration by air. Fleming MacLeish. 6978-9
Explorer. Clarence L. Haynie. 6841-3
The **explorer's** message. Mrs. Hubert ("Australie") Heron. 6768-9
The **explorer's** wooing. Eugene Field. 6949-5
The **explorer**. Lloyd Day. 6750-6
The **explorer**. Anthony Delius. 6788-3
The **explorer**. Rudyard Kipling. 6887-1
The **explorer**. Rudyard Kipling. 6507-4,6726-3,6396-9
The **explorer**. William Plomer. 6788-3
The **explorers**. Martin Armstrong. 7014-0
"**Exploring** the cold night of the lateshow...". The lateshow diorama. Christopher Dewdney. 6767-0
Exportulation. Edward Farquhar. 6939-8
Exposition of the contents of a cab, fr. Pecksniffiana. Wallace Stevens. 6531-7
Expostulation. William Cowper. 6814-6
Expostulation. John Greenleaf Whittier. 6753-0
Expostulation. John Greenleaf Whittier. 6126-5,6288-1
Expostulation. John Greenleaf Whittier. 6753-0
Expostulation and reply. William Wordsworth. 6304-7,6660-7, 6430-2,6199-0,6142-7,6198-2,6604-6,6086-2,6196-9
Expostulation and reply, sels. William Wordsworth. 6867-7
An **expostulation**. Isaac Bickerstaffe. 6092-7
The **expostulation**. Thomas Shadwell. 6430-2
Exposure. Ibn al-Zaqqaq. 6362-4
Exposure. Wilfred Owen. 6209-1,6666-6
The **express**. Stephen Spender. 6228-8,6536-8,6625-9,6491-4,6375-6,6107
Expression. Annie B. Alguire. 6789-1
Expulsion from paradise, fr. Paradise lost. John Milton. 6125-7
Exquisite lady. Mary Elizabeth Osborn. 6388-8
"The **exquisite** painter Ko-tsu". The windmill. Allen Upward. 6897-9
"**Exquisite** world, powerful, joyous, spendid". To the natural world: at 37. Genevieve Taggard. 6879-0
Expecto resurrectionem. Charlotte Mew. 6317-9
The **extasie**. John Donne. 6154-0,6208-3,6562-7,6341-1
Extempore effusion upon the death of James Hogg. William Wordsworth. 6369-1,6483-3,6641-0,6110-9,6472-8
Extempore verses ("God bless"). John Byrom. 6932-0
Extempore verses ("Long was"). John Byrom. 6831-6
Ext mpore verses upon a trial of skill...Figg & Sutton. John Byrom. 6932-0
Extended invitation. Jesse Stuart. 6218-0
Extenuation. Jamie Sexton Holme. 6836-7
Extermination. Richard D'Alton Williams. 6930-4
Extinct monsters. Eugene Field. 6949-5
Extinguish the hyacinth. Walter Buchebner. 6769-7
Extract from the conclusion of a poem...leaving school. William Wordsworth. 6828-6
Extract from the dedicatory ode..Gettysburg Nat'l

Cemetery. Bayard Taylor. 6403-5
Extracts from addresses to the Academy of Fine Arts. Wallace Stevens. 6389-6
Extracts from the Rubaiyat of Omar Cayenne. Gelett Burgess. 6089-7
An **extravaganza**. Victor Hugo. 6066-8
Extreme unction. Ernest Dowson. 6785-9
Extreme unction. Ernest Dowson. 6507-4,6172-9,6383-7,6655-0,6301-2,6508-2,6022-6
Extreme unction. James Russell Lowell. 6632-1
Extremes. James Whitcomb Riley. 6091-9,6452-3,6466-3
Extremities. Alice Cary. 6969-X
Extremum tanain. Horace. 7039-6
Exultant. Pauline Catena. 6396-9,6288-1
Exultation. Emily Dickinson. 6253-9
Exultation. Shaemas O'Sheel. 6501-5
Exultation. John Hall Wheelock. 6036-6
"**Exultation** is the going". Emily Dickinson. 6380-2
"**Exulting**, the lark to the heaven is soaring". Spring song. Jaroslav Vrchlicky. 6763-8
Eye and heart. Ibn al-Batti. 6362-4
"'The **eye** for an eye' was the law". Out of darkness, a star. L. Paul Roberts. 6799-9
The **eye** in the rock. John Haines. 6855-3
"The **eye** must be dark that...long has been dim". To Mary. Thomas Kibble Hervey. 6980-0
"**Eye** of stone". Angelus. Carmen Alicia Cadilla. 6759-X
The **eye** of the beholder. James Lionel Michael. 6784-0
The **eye** of the beholder. Idabel Williams. 6906-1
"An **eye** whose magic wakes the hidden springs". Osler. William Sydney Thayer. 7014-0
"An **eye** with the piercing eagle's fire". Thaddeus Stevens. Phoebe Cary. 6865-0,6969-X,6946-0
"The **eye**, it cannot choose but see". Expostulation and reply, sels. William Wordsworth. 6867-7
The **eye-mote**. Sylvia Plath. 6803-0
Eye-witness. (Frederick) Ridgely Torrence. 6250-4,6161-3, 6393-4,6467-1,6007-2,6031-5,6102-8,6556-2,6076-5
An **eye**. Joseph Auslander. 6779-4
An **eye**. Karin Ek. 6045-5
The **eye**. Robinson Jeffers. 6666-6,6208-3
Eyelashes. Ibn al-Hammara. 6362-4
Eyeless and limbless and shattered. Cecil Roberts. 6102-8
Eyeless at Gaza. John Milton. 6322-5
Eyes. Rubye Arnold. 7016-7
Eyes. Charles and Mary Lamb. 6295-4
Eyes and lips. Auguste Angellier. 6961-4
Eyes and tears. Andrew Marvell. 6380-2
Eyes are lit up. Robert P. Tristram Coffin. 6984-3
"**Eyes** are queer windows looking in, not out". Blank verse. Muriel F. Hochdorf. 6850-2
Eyes calm. Robert Browning. 6723-9
"**Eyes** gaze no more as yet you may." Unknown. 6563-5
The **eyes** have it. William Stephens. 6375-6
"**Eyes** lie awake in hope of happy seinge." Unknown. 6563-5
"The **eyes** like gimlet holes upon the dark". I remember the block party. Oscar Williams. 6761-1,6389-6
"**Eyes** not down-dropped nor over-bright,but fed". Isabel. Alfred Lord Tennyson. 6977-0
Eyes of black and eyes of blue, fr. The viceroy. Harry B. Smith. 6652-6
The **eyes** of children at the brinkof the sea's grasp. Josephine Jacobsen. 6388-8
The **eyes** of God. Hermann Hagedorn. 6347-0,6506-6,6619-4
The **eyes** of God. Gabriel (Thomas Nicoll Hepburn) Setoun. 6452-3
"The **eyes** of Queen Esther and how they conquered..." Vachel Lindsay. 6032-3
The **eyes** of the Christ. Norma Bright Carson. 6486-8
"The **eyes** of the Yogin sitting on the phalica..." Unknown (Newari) 7013-2
The **eyes** of war. Chart Pitt. 6443-4
"**Eyes** ravished with rapture, celestially...". Indian dancers. Sarojini Naidu. 6959-2
"**Eyes** so eagerly seeking truth". Eyes. Rubye Arnold. 7016-7
Eyes so tristful. Diego de Saldana. 7039-6
"**Eyes** that are closed in the stillness...death". Now. Robert S. Bailey. 7016-7
"**Eye** that last I saw in tears". Thomas Stearns Eliot.
6011-0
"**Eyes** that without a tongue can speak to me". Angelo Poliziano. 6325-X
Eyes, hide my love. Samuel Daniel. 6182-6
Eyre, Jeannette (tr.)
How could we, beforehand, live in quiet. Nikolai Gumilev, 6665-8
Our children's children will marvelk. Ilya Ehrenburg, 6665-8
Eysteinn of Asgrimsson
Author's entreaty for his lay, fr. Lilya. Eirikur Magnusson (tr.). 6282-2
Eytinge, Margaret
An acquaintance declined. 6965-7
Baby Louise. 6385-3,6219-9
The countersign was Mary. 6273-3,6451-5
If not quite true, it ought to be. 6713-1
Indignant Polly Wog. 6670-4
Mrs. Bee explains. 6965-7
A puzzle. 6576-7
The weed's mission. 6965-7
Why the dog's nose is cold. 7008-6
Ezekiel. Thomas S. Jones Jr. 6532-5
Ezekiel. Barbara Miller Macandrew. 6848-0
Ezekiel. John Greenleaf Whittier. 6848-0
"**Ezekiel** saw the wheel". Negro spiritual ("Ezekiel saw the wheel"). Unknown. 6176-1
Ezra House. James Whitcomb Riley. 6892-8

F I was er horse!?' Burges Johnson. 6510-4
F.,A.D.
Epitaphs for a bad girl. 6817-0
F.,A.J.
November. 6118-4
F.,C.W.
Running a race. 6680-1
F.,E.S.
Blood-root. 6597-X
F.,E.T.
Lilith. 6433-7
F.,H.G.
Sestina of the fliv. 6817-0
F.,M.E.
A birthday greeting. 6273-3
F.B.C.; Chancellorsville, May 3, 1863. William Allen Butler. 6903-7
F.C.. Mildred Kleinschmidt. 6397-7
"**Fa, Fi, Fo, Fum!**". Unknown. 6363-2
Fa, la, la! Unknown. 6383-7
Fabbri, Cora
In Florence. 6331-4,6631-3
Layde Maude. 6682-8
Peace. 6486-8
Tuscan hills. 6624-0
Faber, F. W.
A dream. 6958-4
Faber, Frederick William
6980-0
Angelic songs are swelling. 6304-7
Bamberg, sels. 6046-3
Childhood. 6980-0
The eternal years. 6014-5
Evening hymn. 6219-9
The expectation. 6022-6
Faith of our fathers. 6337-3,6723-9
The flight of the wild swans. 6046-3
Genoa. 6046-3
The glimpse. 6980-0
The god of my childhood. 6127-3,6242-3,6131-1
God our father. 6730-1
God's mercy. 6337-3
"Good is that darkening of our lives." 6225-3
Grandeur of Mary. 6022-6,6172-9,6292-X
Hark, hark, my soul!. 6723-9
He satisfies. 6065-X
The heart of the eternal. 6303-9,6214-8
The heart's home. 6214-8

FABER

Heaven. 6502-3
Herodotus. 6096-X
How wonderful thou art! 6461-2
Jesus, child and Lord. 6065-X
Jesus, my God and my all. 6065-X
King's bridge. 6980-0
The land beyond the sea. 6271-7
Mundus morosus. 6022-6
The nearest friend. 6127-3,6131-1
O paradise! O paradise! 6730-1
On tne ramparts at Angouleme. 7015-9
Our lady in the middle ages. 6282-2,6022-6
Paradise. 6219-9
Past friends. 6046-3,6040-3
The perplexity. 6980-0
The pilgrims of the night. 6219-9
Preface. 6046-3
Preface ("Blame not my verse..."). 6046-3
Regina coeli. 6282-2
Right must win, fr. On the field. 6219-9,6656-9,6543-0, 6172-9,6014-5,6022-6,6337-3,6385-3,6600-3,6292
The shadow of the rock. 6096-X,6046-3
Socrates. 7015-9
Therapia. 6046-3
"There's a wideness in God's mercy". 6238-5,6654-2
To a lake party. 6046-3
To-day. 6543-0
The will of God. 6337-3,6600-3,6219-9,6656-9
The world morose. 6437-X
Written in a little lady's little album. 6934-7
Written in Conway castle. 6046-3

Faber, Robert C.
Tenth point of law. 6042-0

Fable. Ralph Waldo Emerson. 6505-8
Fable. Alfred Jarry. 6343-8
Fable. George O'Neil. 6253-9
Fable. Dorothy Parker. 6026-9
Fable. Frederic Prokosch. 6666-6
A fable ("I know not what the sly little fairy.") Unknown. 6373-X
A fable ("Some cawing Crows..."). Ella Wheeler Wilcox. 6630-5
Fable ("The mountain and the squirrel"). Ralph Waldo Emerson. 6356-X,6519-8,6176-1,6089-7,6735-2,6288 , 6092-7,6421-3,6126-5,6176-1,6288-1,6126-5
A fable for critics, sels. James Russell Lowell. 6959-2
A fable for critics, sels. James Russell Lowell. 6753-0
A fable for critics, sels. James Russell Lowell. 6008-0, 6121-4,6399-3,6483-5,6176-1,6288-1,6126-5
A fable for five years old. John Hookham Frere. 6092-7
A fable for poets. Berton Braley. 6853-7
A fable of cloud-land. Alice Cary. 6865-0;6969-X
Fable of lost succession. Ellen Tifft. 6783-2
The fable of the magnet and the churn, fr. Patience. Sir William Schwenck Gilbert. 6891-X
Fable of the wood rose and the laurel. Unknown. 6752-2
Fable XXXVII. John Gay. 6024-2
A fable, for Henricus D., Esq., Jr. Thomas Edward Brown. 6809-X
Fable, related by a beau to Aesop. Sir John Vanbrugh. 6874-X
A fable: the mice and felis. John Kendrick. 6120-6
A fable. William Cowper. 6814-6
A fable. John Hookham Frere. 6802-2
A fable. David Garrick. 6733-6
A fable. James Abraham Martling. 6952-5
A fable. David Matthews. 6753-0
Fables. John Gay. 6972-X
Fables. John Gay. 6814-6
Fables for the ladies, sels. Edward Moore. 6152-4
Fables, sels. John Gay. 6152-4
Fabliau of Florida, fr. Pecksniffiana. Wallace Stevens. 6531-7

Fabri, Cora
Absence. 6876-6
Anita, fr. In Tuscany. 6876-6
Autumn, fr. Thistledown. 6876-6
Dead leaves, fr. In Tuscany. 6876-6
Deception. 6876-6
Died young. 6876-6
Dream-land, fr. In Tuscany. 6876-6
Heart songs. 6876-6
'I have no spring', she saith. 6876-6
Idyl, fr. In Tuscany. 6876-6
If. 6876-6
In Tuscany, sels. 6876-6
InFlorence, fr. In Tuscany. 6876-6
Ladye Maude. 6876-6
Little hand. 6876-6
May. 6876-6
Memoria in eterna. 6876-6
Minor note 001, fr. In Tuscany. 6876-6
Minor note 002, fr. In Tuscany. 6876-6
Minor note 003, fr. In Tuscany. 6876-6
Minor note 004, fr. In Tuscany. 6876-6
Minor note 005, fr. In Tuscany. 6876-6
Minor note 006, fr. In Tuscany. 6876-6
Minor note 007, fr. In Tuscany. 6876-6
Minor note 008, fr. In Tuscany. 6876-6
Minor note 009, fr. In Tuscany. 6876-6
Minor note 010, fr. In Tuscany. 6876-6
Minor note 011, fr. In Tuscany. 6876-6
Minor note 012, fr. In Tuscany. 6876-6
Misconception. 6876-6
Moon-shadows. 6876-6
Moonlight. 6876-6
Mors et vita. 6876-6
Mystery. 6876-6
Ode to a nightingale. 6876-6
Old letters. 6876-6
An old maid. 6876-6
Peace, fr. In Tuscany. 6876-6
The poet. 6876-6
A portrait. 6876-6
'Rose et noir'. 6876-6
Sea-breeze, fr. In Tuscany. 6876-6
A sea-spell, fr. In Tuscany. 6876-6
Snow-flakes, fr. In Tuscany. 6876-6
Song ("If the bird"). 6876-6
Sonnet ("A poet wrote"). 6876-6
The spirit of spring. 6876-6
Spring, fr. Thistledown. 6876-6
Stornelli and Strambotti, fr. In Tuscany. 6876-6
Summer, fr. Thistledown. 6876-6
Sunrise. 6876-6
Thistledown. 6876-6
A thought. 6876-6
To Edith. 6876-6
Triolet 001, fr. Thistledown. 6876-6
Triolet 002, fr. Thistledown. 6876-6
Triolet 003, fr. Thistledown. 6876-6
Triolet 004, fr. Thistledown. 6876-6
Triolet 005, fr. Thistledown. 6876-6
Triolet 006, fr. Thistledown. 6876-6
Triolet 007, fr. Thistledown. 6876-6
Triolet 008, fr. Thistledown. 6876-6
Tuscan hills, fr. In Tuscany. 6876-6
White clover, fr. In Tuscany. 6876-6
White roses. 6876-6
Who knows? 6876-6
A winter piece. 6876-6
Winter, fr. Thistledown. 6876-6
Winter-time. 6876-6
With the linnets. 6876-6
Woman's way. 6876-6

Fabri, Cora (tr.)
"All the stars, gold-footed, wander". Heinrich Heine, 6876-6
"As the moon's reflection trembleth". Heinrich Heine, 6876-6
Dew-drops. Rene Francois Armand Sully-Prudhomme, 6876-6
Epitaph. Victor Hugo, 6876-6
Here below. Rene Francois Armand Sully-Prudhomme, 6876-6
"I saw a small, white sea-gull". Heinrich Heine, 6876-6
"I wander and weep in the forest". Heinrich Heine, 6876-6
"In my life, so dark and dreary". Heinrich Heine, 6876-6
"In the golde summer morning". Heinrich Heine, 6876-6

Meditation. Theophile Gautier, 6876-6
"My soul and I will steep so softly". Heinrich Heine, 6876-6
"The rare red rose loves the butterfly". Heinrich Heine, 6876-6
"Shadow-kisses, shadow passion". Heinrich Heine, 6876-6
"So you forget, and have forgotten all". Heinrich Heine, 6876-6
"Sweetly float upon my heart". Heinrich Heine, 6876-6
"The troubles crowd, and the bells are ringing". Heinrich Heine, 6876-6
The **fabric**. Gamaliel Bradford. 6036-6
Fabula. Unknown. 6120-6
Fabyan, Robert
    Dedication of the chronicles of England and France. 6282-2
Facade. Edith Sitwell. 7000-0
"**Face** and figure of a child". A portrait ("Face"). Elizabeth Barrett Browning. 6934-7
The **face** divine. Ethelyn Alice Stoddard. 6836-7
Face in a mirror. Jack L. Anderson. 6870-7
A **face** in the tongs. Lucy Larcom. 6129-X
"A **face** more vivid than he dreamed who drew". Esther. Helen Hunt Jackson. 6848-0
The **face** of all the world is changed, I think. Elizabeth Barrett Browning. 6199-0,6430-2
The **face** of Jesus Christ. Christina Georgina Rossetti. 6065-X,6335-7
"The **face** of all the world is changed, I think". Sonnet ("The face of all"). Elizabeth Barrett Browning. 6934-7
The **face** of the waters. R.D. FitzGerald. 6349-7
"**Face** on face in the city, and when will...". City comradeship. Anna Louise Strong. 6954-1
The **face** on the bar-room floor. Hugh Antoine D'Arcy. 6303-9,6732-8,6167-2
"A **face** so near". Feminine resistance. Unknown. 6983-5
"A **face** that should content me wonders well". Epigram ("A face"). Sir Thomas Wyatt. 6436-1
"A **face** that should content me wondrous well". The one he would love. Thomas Sir Wyat. 6874-X
The **face** upon the floor. Hugh Antoine D'Arcy. 6736-0
"The **face**, oh Lord, why dost thou hide". Psalm 010. Bible. 6848-0
Face-tapping. Unknown. 6078-1
The **face**.... Karoniaktatie. 7005-1
A **face**.. Robert Browning. 6123-0,6110-9,6655-0,6543-0,6656-9
A **face**.. Ella Wheeler Wilcox. 6078-1
A **face**.. William T. Washburn. 6066-8
The **face**. Ebenezer Jones. 6656-9
The **face**. Frederic Manning. 7027-2
The **face**. Edwin Muir. 6209-1
The **faceless** man. Robert Service. 6159-1
Faces. Jack L. Anderson. 6870-7
Faces. Lenora K. Hilliard. 6799-9
Faces. Cyprus R. Mitchell. 6954-1
Faces. Harold Trowbridge Pulsifer. 6034-X
"**Faces** I have seen as numerous as raindrops". Psalm. Benjamin Rosenbaum. 6038-2
"The **faces** of the men are black as they enter". Mine disaster. William Virgil Davis. 6803-0
"The **faces** that we see in dreams". Dream-faces. Horace Rublee. 7030-2
The **faces** we meet. Allie Wellington. 6913-4
"**Faces**, faces everywhere/Glad faces, sad faces". Faces. Lenora K. Hilliard. 6799-9
Faces, sels. Walt Whitman. 6008-0
The **facetious** story of John Gilpin. William Cowper. 6279-2
Facilis descensus. Unknown. 6183-4
Facility. Robert Service. 6159-1
Facing my portrait. Yolanda Bedregal de Conitzer. 6759-X
Facing the dawn. William Hiram Foulkes. 6461-2
"**Facing** the guns, he jokes as well". Thomas of the light heart. Sir Owen Seaman. 6861-8,7026-4
Facing the wall. R.A. Medlam. 6799-9
Facing west from California's shores. Walt Whitman. 6399-3, 6288-1,6126-5
Fact. Mildred Solwan. 6850-2
Facta non verb. Henry Van Dyke. 6961-4

The **factor's** song. Unknown. 6061-7
Factories. Margaret Widdemer. 6012-8,6162-1,6303-9,6476-0, 6501-5,6732 ,6337-3,6300-4,6102-8,6076-5,6464-7
Factories, fr. Old and new New York. Alfred Kreymborg. 6012-9
Factory children. Richard Burton. 6337-3
"A **factory** girl with smudges on her cheek". Pittsburgh. Berton Braley. 6853-7
The **factory** girl's last day. Michael Thomas Sadler. 7009-4
The **factory** girl's last day. Unknown. 6406-X
A **factory** girl. C.J. Buell. 6097-8
The **factory** girl. Charles W. Denison. 6755-7
Factory whistles. Alexey Gastev. 7014-0
Factory windows are always broken. Vachel Lindsay. 6375-6
The **factory**. Letitia Elizabeth ("L.E.L.") Landon. 6102-8
The **factory**. Letitia Elizabeth ("L.E.L.") Landon. 6980-0
Facts. William A. Norris. 6777-8
Faculty meeting. David Morton. 6880-4
Faculty recital. Benjamin Albert Botkin. 6397-7
The **fad** obsolete. Maude Andrews. 7021-3
Fade, flowers, fade. Edmund Waller. 6733-6
Fade, then-die, depart, and come no more. Conrad Aiken. 6779-4
"**Faded** and fair, in an old arm-chair". Grandmother Gray. Mary Keeley Boutelle. 6915-0
Faded coat of blue. Unknown. 6260-1
The **faded** coat of blue. J.H. McNaughton. 6074-9
Faded flowers. Ida M. Buxton. 6919-3
Faded flowers. James Abraham Martling. 6952-5
Faded leaves. Alice Cary. 6969-X
Faded pictures. William Vaughn Moody. 6431-0
The **faded** violet. Unknown. 6014-5
The **faded** violet. Thomas Bailey Aldrich. 6121-4
Fading away. Jessica Sybrant. 6883-9
Fading beauty. Unknown. 6562-7,6563-5
Fading notes. Garey D. Frierson. 6898-7
A **fading** of the sun. Wallace Stevens. 6751-4
Fading summer. Thomas Nashe. 6189-3
Fading-leaf and fallen-leaf. Richard Garnett. 6437-X
The **faerie** queen. Sir Walter Raleigh. 6301-2
The **faerie** queene, sels. Edmund Spenser. 6049-8,6102-8, 6186-9,6369-1,6732-8,6634 ,6122-2,6208-3,6289-X,6527-9,6726-3,6154 ,6179-6,6378-0,6483-3,6604-6,6501-5, 6239 ,6192-3,6430-2,6194-X,6472-8,6659-3,6649 ,6197-4,6491-4,6660-7
The **faerie** queene. Edmund Spenser. 6198-2,6501-5
The **faerie** queene. Edmund Spenser. 6958-4
The **faerie's** child. Thomas Caulfield Irwin. 6174-5
The **faerie's** child. Thomas Caulfield Irwin. 6930-4
Faeries' song. William Butler Yeats. 6252-0
The **faery** earl. Rosa Mulholland; Lady Gilbert. 6174-5
The **faery** foster-mother. Robert Buchanan. 6656-9
The **faery** queene, sels. Edmund Spenser. 6935-5
The **faery** reaper. Robert Buchanan. 6437-X
A **faery** song. Madeleine Nightingale. 6477-9,6639-9
A **faery** song. William Butler Yeats. 6138-9,6236-9,6334-9
Fag an bealach. Sir Charles Gavan Duffy. 6858-8
Fagg, William Carson
    The book. 6870-7
    Eclipse. 6870-7
    The leaf. 6870-7
    Portraits. 6870-7
    Reaching. 6870-7
Fagin, Bryllion
    Do not fear. 6789-1
    Tragedienne. 6042-0
    We are the the first. 6789-1
Fagin, N. Bryllion
    The grass grows far. 6039-0
Fagon, Louis
    Young love is like a rosebud. 6347-0
Fahnstock, Elizabeth
    A prayer for strength. 6303-9
Fahy, Francis A.
    Killiney far away. 6858-8
    Killiney far away. 6873-1
    Little Mary Cassidy. 6090-0
    The old plaid shawl. 6858-8
    The ould plaid shawl. 6292-X
    A rebel heart. 7009-4

Fail-yet rejoice..."..." Adelaide Anne Procter. 6402-7
Fai land. Thomas Edward Brown. 6809-X
Failure. Orrick Johns. 6506-6
Failure. Mary Sinton Leitch. 6144-3;6335-7
Failure. Jean Nuchtern. 6857-X
Failure. Charles Quiet. 6617-8
Failure. Unknown. 6273-3
The failure. Merle Kulow Sherrill. 6818-9
Failures. Lucia Trent. 6954-1
Failures. Arthur Upson. 6730-1
The failures.. Theodosia Garrison. 6211-3
The failures. Berton Braley. 6853-7
Fain I would. Unknown. 6182-6,6189-3
"Fain we ask Erinn". The incantation. Amergin (atr.). 6930-4
"Fain were I from tradition free". Heredity. Johann Wolfgang von Goethe. 7042-9
"Fain would I be sleeping, dreaming". The plaint of the wife. Unknown (Russian). 7039-6
"Fain would I change that note". Madrigal. Unknown. 6138-9
Fain would I change that note. Tobias Hume. 6204-0,6150-8
Fain would I change that note. Unknown. 6181-8,6182-6,6187-7,6659-3,6383-7
"Fain would I change that note." Unknown. 6317-9
Fain would I hve a prettie thing to give unto my ladie. Unknown. 6157-5
"Fain would I pass from all the pain". A wish. Charles Dent Bell. 6770-0
"Fain would I ride with thee". Eileen Aroon. Carroll O'Daly. 6930-4
"Fain would I sing of wars and things". Little interlopers. James C. Melody. 6761-1
"Fain would I wake you sweet, but fear". Wake, gently wake, fr. Wit at several weapons. Francis Beaumont and John Fletcher. 6827-8
Fain would I wed. Thomas Campion. 6733-6
Fain would I, but I dare not. Sir Walter Raleigh. 6830-8
Fain would my thoughts. John Austin. 6931-2
"Faine would I chang my maiden life." Unknown. 6563-5
"Faine would I Cloris (ere I dye)." Unknown. 6563-5
"Faine would I my loue disclose" Thomas Campion. 6794-8
"Faine would I wed a faire yong man that day and..." Thomas Campion. 6794-8
"Faint against the twilight, dim...the evening". Old women. Klaxon (John Graham Bower). 7031-0
"Faint are the flowers, for the sunbeams...". Tellocha's delight. Stanley Wood. 6836-7
"Faint as the far-down tone". The voice of thought. Thomas Holley Chivers. 7017-5
"Faint as the sighing winds which fret". Sassafras. Robert McIntyre. 6836-7
"A faint blue cloud of smoke". Roasting corn. Clara Doty Bates. 6965-7
"Faint flush to rose, that lady tree, pink...". Pink avatar-cornus Florida rubra. Ruth Stewart Schenley. 6857-X
"Faint is the sea's voice for so vast a thing". Silence. George Sterling. 6779-4
"Faint on Rephaim's sultr side". David's three mighty ones. Henry Francis Lyte. 6848-0
"Faint preludings on a flute". Isadora Duncan dancing. Louis Untermeyer. 6959-2
"Faint trailing wisps of clouds". Dream moments. Alletha Goss Hargrave. 6799-9
"Faint with the heat, a murmur on the calm...". A mood. Otakar Brezina. 6886-3
"A faint wound of sound". Withdrawal. Jack Lindsay. 6895-2
Faint yet pursuing. Coventry Patmore. 6931-2
Faint, yet pursuing. William White. 6868-5
"Fainter and fainter grows". An October nightfall. Herbert Tucker. 6800-6
"Fainter and fainter may fall on my ear". Faithful. Phoebe Cary. 6865-0;6969-X
"Fainter her slow step falls from day to day". The child of earth. Caroline Elizabeth Sarah Sheridan Norton. 6980-0,6911-8
"Fair Albion, smiling, sees her son depart". Lines in the traveller's book at Orchomenus. George Gordon, 6th Baron Byron. 6945-2
Fair Amoret. William Congreve. 6733-6

"Fair Amoret is gone astray" William Congreve. 6874-X
"Fair am I, mortals, as a stone-carved dream". La beaute. Charles Baudelaire. 7039-6
"Fair Amaryllis, wil thou never peep". Amaryllis, fr. Idylls. Theocritus. 6987-8
"Fair Amoret is gone astray". A hue and cry after fair Amoret. William Congreve. 6932-0
"Fair and fair and twice so fair". Oenone's song: Cupid's curse. George Peele. 6934-7
Fair and fair, and twice so fair. George Peele. 6383-7
"Fair and fair, and twice so fair". George Peele. 6132-2, 6181-8;6182-6;6328-4;6634-8;6536-8
Fair Annie. Sir Walter Scott. 6438-8
Fair Annie. Unknown. 6055-2,6056-0,6180-X,6185-0,6518-X, 6067
Fair Annie of Lochroyan. Unknown. 6055-2,6219-9
Fair Anny of Roch-royal. Unknown. 6613-5
"Fair angels pass'd by next in seemly bands". The annunciation, fr. Davideis. Abraham Cowley. 6931-2
"Fair are the flowers and the children...". Richard Realf. 6238-5
"Fair are the flowers the tardy spring". The wild rose. Eliza Scudder. 6798-0
"Fair art thou as a flower". Song: Du bist wie eine blume. Heinrich Heine. 6961-4
"Fair as the night - when all the astral fires". 'A similitude'. Charles Harpur. 6784-0
The fair at windgap. Austin Clarke. 6930-4
The fair brass. Robert Bridges. 6186-9,6487-6
"The fair breeze blew, the white foam flew". The silent sea. Samuel Taylor Coleridge. 7020-5
"Fair Burlington! I bring a song to thee". Tribute to Burlington. Sewall S. Cutting. 7030-2
The fair but cruel girl. Unknown. 6328-4
Fair Charlotte. Unknown. 6058-7
The fair Circassian. Richard Garnett. 6437-X,6656-9
The fair copyholder. Charles H. Crandall. 6620-8
"Fair Daffodils, we weep to see". Robert Herrick. 6187-7
"Fair cousin mine! the golden days". Chivalry at a discount. Edward Fitzgerald. 6874-X
"Fair Ellayne, she walked by Welland river". Welland river. William Morris. 7034-5
"Fair Ellen was long the delight of the young". The paint king. Washington Allston. 6752-2
Fair day. Lillie Hall. 7016-7
Fair days. Robert Herrick. 6369-1
The fair Dorothy. Charles Baudelaire. 6343-8
Fair Eleanor. William Blake. 6518-X
Fair Eleanor. Phoebe Cary. 6865-0;6969-X
"Fair enchantress, gaily kind". To hope. Felicia Dorothea Hemans. 6973-8
A fair enthusiast. Unknown. 6925-8
A fair exchange. George Birdseye. 6505-8
Fair Fanny Moore. Unknown. 6003-X
The fair flower of Northumberland. Unknown. 6185-0,6319-5
"Fair flower of fifteen springs, that still". To his young mistress. Pierre de Ronsard. 6771-9
A fair foe. George Sigerson. 6174-5
Fayr Greece! sad relic of departed worth. George Gordon, 6th Baron Byron. 6240-7
Fair Harvard. Samuel Gilman. 6289-X
Fair Hebe. John West; Earl de la Warr. 6086-2
Fair Hebe and reason. John West; Earl de la Warr. 6092-7.6086-2
Fair Helen. Sir Walter Scott. 6438-8
Fair Helen of Kirconnel. Felicia Dorothea Hemans. 6973-8
Fair Helen of Kirkconnell. Unknown. 6180-X,6246-6,6271-7, 6289-X,6302-0,6385 ,6661-5,6687-9,6518-4
"The fair frail blooms which loved the sun". True. Elizabeth Akers Allen. 6889-8
"Fair friend, 'tis true, your beauties move". Halfway in love. Ben Jonson. 6935-5
"Fair girl, the light of whose morning keeps". Morning and afternoon. Phoebe Cary. 6969-X
"Fair gratitude! in strain sublime". Christmas carol. Felicia Dorothea Hemans. 6973-8
"Fair Helen to the Scaean portals came". Helen on the walls, fr. The Iliad. Homer. 6987-8
The fair hills of Eire. Padraic Colum. 6331-4
The fair hills of Eire; O! James Clarence Mangan. 6174-5

The fair hills of Eire. Padraic Colum. 6161-3
The fair hills of Ireland. Sir Samuel Ferguson. 6437-X, 6439-6,6383-7
The fair hills of Ireland. Unknown. 6244-X
Fair Ines. Thomas Hood. 6122-2,6271-7,6437-X,6732-8,6219-9, 6102-8,6250-4,6543-0,6301-2,6656-9
"Fair images of sleep". The sculptured children. Felicia Dorothea Hemans. 6973-8
"Fair insect, that, with thread-like legs...". To a musquito. Unknown. 6752-2
"Fair is her body, bright her eye". Song ("Fair is her body..."). Unknown (French). 7039-6
Fair is my love. Robert Greene. 6182-6
"Fair is my love that feeds among the lilies". Bartholomew Griffin. 6102-8,6182-6,6187-7,6586-4
"Fair is my Love, and cruel as she's fair" Samuel Daniel. 6182-6,6436-1
"Fair is my Love, when her fair golden hair heares" Edmund Spenser. 6182-6
"Fair is my love, when her fair golden hairs". Sonnet 081 ("Fair is my love"), fr. Amoretti. Edmund Spenser. 6491-4
"Fair is my love...", fr. The passionate pilgrim. William Shakespeare. 6182-6
"Fair is our lot - O goodly is our heritage!". A song of the English. Rudyard Kipling. 6810-3
"Fair is Port Royal river". A ballad of Port Royal. Jamesuis Hannay. 7041-8
"Fair is the castle up on the hill". Lullaby ("Fair is"). Eugene Field. 7041-8
"Fair is the castle upon the hill". Hushaby, sweet my own. Eugene Field. 6834-0;6949-5
"Fair is the majesty of all thy works". The lake of Zurich. Friedrich Gottlieb Klopstock. 6749-2
"Fair is the night and fair the day". William Morris. 6187-7
"Fair is the rising morn when o'er the sky". Sonnet 001 ("Fair is the rising morn..."). Robert Southey. 6867-7
Fair is the rose. Unknown. 6182-6,6187-7
"Fair is the sea;and fair the sea-borne billow". Stella Maris, sels. John Addington Symonds. 6997-5
"Fair is the world...", fr. The glittering plain. William Morris. 6123-0
"Fair is their fame who stand in earth's...". Heroes. Laurence Housman. 6861-8
"Fair isle, that from the fairest of all...". Sonnet to Zante. Edgar Allan Poe. 6753-0
The fair isle. Felicia Dorothea Hemans. 6973-8
Fair Janet. Unknown. 6185-0,6067-6,6518-4
"Fair lady Isabel sits in her bower sewing". Unknown. 6111-7,6518-X
Fair Lucy. Unknown. 6061-7
"Fair lady! whose harmonious name the Rhine". Sonnet ("Fair lady"). John Milton. 6814-6
"Fair lady, mourn the memory". Culloden day. Unknown. 6859-6
"Fair lake, thy lovely and thy haunted shore". The castle of Chillon. Letitia Elizabeth ("L.E.L.") Landon. 6749-2
"Fair Locarno smiles". Locarno. William Wordsworth. 6749-2
The fair maid and eth sun. Arthur O'Shaughnessy. 6656-9
The fair maid of the west. Unknown. 6157-5
"The fair maid who, on the first day of May". May day. Unknown. 6466-3
"The fair maid who, the first of May". Unknown. 6904-5
The fair maid's choice or the seaman's renown. Unknown. 6547-3
"Fair maid, through hours of endless constancy". Sonnet ("Fair maid"). Harriet Meyer. 6850-2
"Fair maid, we need not take the hint". Robert Burns. 6104-4
"Fair maiden! when I look at thee". To a fair maiden. Walter Savage Landor. 6874-X
Fair maiden!. Adam Gottlob Oehlenschlager. 6555-4
Fair maiden, who is this bairn? Unknown. 6282-2
Fair maidens' beauty will soon fade away. Robert Dwyer Joyce. 6244-X
Fair Margaret and sweet William. Unknown. 6185-0,6057-9, 6058-7,6098-6,6185-0,6067-6,6518

Fair Margaret's misfortunes. Unknown. 6055-2
Fair Mary of Livingston. Unknown. 6907-X
Fair Mary of Wallington. Unknown. 6185-0
"Fair marble tell to future days". On twin-sisters. Unknown. 6874-X
The fair millinger. Frederick Wadsworth Loring. 6089-7
Fair Oriana. Robert Jones. 6328-4
"Fair mother earth lay on her back last night". Ode to the spirit of earth in autumn. George Meredith. 6828-6
"Fair pearl crown'd nymph, whose gushing". An invocation to a water-nymph. Thomas Warton (the Elder). 6962-2
The fair penitent, sels. Nicholas Rowe. 6867-7
Fair places. Mabel Hall Goltra. 6789-1
"Fair pleedges of a fruitful tree." Robert Herrick. 6302-0
Fair Rohtraut. Eduard Friedrich Morike. 6842-1
Fair Rosalynd. Thomas Lodge. 6250-4
Fair Rosamond. Unknown. 6098-6
"Fair queen, away! To thy charger speak". The queen of Prussia's ride. A.L. Smith. 6744-1,6917-7
"Fa r Roslin Chapel, how divine". Roslin and Hawthornden. Henry Van Dyke. 6961-4
"Fair Salamis, the billow's roar". Chorus, fr. Ajax. Sophocles. 7039-6
"Fair seed-time had my soul", fr. The prelude. William Wordsworth. 6867-7
The fair shepherdess. Thomas Lodge. 6383-7
"Fair ship, that from the Italian shore", fr Memoriam. Alfred Lord Tennyson. 6536-8
The fair singer, sels. Andrew Marvell. 6317-9
The fair singer. Andrew Marvell. 6187-7,6339-X,6563-5,6733-6,6250-4,6341
"Fair soul, who in this faltering age did show". In memory of F.C.C. Francis Turner Palgrave. 7015-9
The fair spectator. Robert E. Rinehart. 6983-5
"Fair star of evening, splendour of the west". William Wordsworth. 7015-9
"Fair stood the wind for France". Ode 012 ("Fair stood"). Michael Drayton. 6198-2
The fair stranger. John Dryden. 6970-3
Fair summer droops. Thomas Nashe. 6182-6
"Fair summer is here, glad summer is here!". The nightingale to the workman. Morris Rosenfeld. 7011-6
"Fair sun, if you would have me praise your light." Henry Constable. 6586-4,6181-1
"Fair Sylvia, cease to blame my youth". Unknown. 6933-9
"Fair sun, if you would have me praise your light". Sonnet ("Fair sun"). Henry Constable. 6436-1
"Fair Tajo! thou whose calmly-flowing tide". Sonnet 108 ("Fair Tajo"). Luis de Camoens [or Camoes]. 6973-8
"Fair the gift to Merlin given". Merlin's apple trees. Thomas Love Peacock. 7020-5
The fair thief. Sir Charles Wyndham; Earl of Egremont. 6092-7,6250-4
Fair tree, fr. The tree. Anne Finch, Countess of Winchilsea. 6049-8
Fair virtue, the mistress of Philarete, sels. George Wither. 6198-2,6194-X
"Fair vision! thou'rt from sunny skies". To a picture of the Madonna. Felicia Dorothea Hemans. 6973-8
"Fair was her young and girlish face". The April fool. Eugene Field. 6949-5
"Fair wert thou in the dreams". Elysium. Felicia Dorothea Hemans. 6973-8
"Fair white bird, what song art thou singing". A ballad of departure. Unknown (Greek). 6771-9
The fair young wife. Helen Adam. 6218-0
"Fair youth, too timid to lift your eyes". Lovers and sweethearts. Phoebe Cary. 6969-X
"Fair, and soft, and gay, and young". Song ("Fair, and soft"). Robert Gould. 6563-5,6152-4
The fair, fair maid. Unknown. 6134-6
Fair, if you expect admiring. Thomas Campion. 6328-4
"Fair, joyous child, with wondrous eyes". To Alice--my namesake. Alice Polk Hill. 6836-7
"Fair, kind, true; a treasure each alone". On the Lady Whitmore. John Dryden. 6970-3
Fair, rich, and young. Sir John Harington. 6182-6
"Fair, sweet and young, receive a prize". A song ("Fair, sweet and young, receive a prize"). John Dryden. 6933-9

FAIR,

"Fair, sweet and young, receive a prize". John Dryden. 6562-7
The fair-haired girl. Unknown. 6930-4
The fair. Eden Phillpotts. 6069-2
Fairbairn, Helen
    The winter spirit. 6795-6
Fairbanks under the solstice. John Haines. 6855-3
Fairbridge, Kingsley
    The bastard. 6591-0,6592-9
    Bongwi. 6800-6
    Bongwi. 6625-9
    Burial. 6800-6
    Burial ("Yowe, yowe, mwanango duku!"). 6625-9
    Dawn. 6800-6
    Fear. 6591-0,6592-9
    The hunting of Shumba. 6591-0,6592-9
    The hunting of Shumba. 6800-6
    Naming song of Kusawa Afa. 6625-9
    The pioneer. 6591-0,6592-9
    The puff-adder. 6800-6
    The red cloud. 6800-6
    The song maker. 6788-3
    Song of the Africander woman. 6591-0,6592-9
    The song-maker. 6625-9
    Umfeti. 6625-9,6591-0,6592-9
    Yellow eyes. 6800-6
    Yellow eyes. 6625-9
Fairbridge, W.S.
    Consecration of the house. 6384-5
Fairclough, Henry Rushton (tr.)
    A garden is a goodly thing. Aulus Septimius Serenus, 6649-6
"Faire Archibella to thine eyes." Unknown. 6563-5
"Faire, if you expect admiring". A booke of Ayres (XI). Thomas Campion. 6794-8
Fairer than fairest. Unknown. 6562-7,6563-5
"Fairer than thee." Unknown. 6302-0;6385-3
"Fairest and loveliest of created things". Woman. William Herbert; Earl of Pembroke. 6980-0
Fairest between Lincoln and Lindsey. Unknown. 6881-2
"Fairest flower, all flowers excelling". To a child of five years old. Nathaniel Cotton. 6772-7
The fairest flower. Johann Wolfgang von Goethe. 6677-1
The fairest he. Horatius Bonar. 6065-X
The fairest hues, sels. William Wordsworth. 6867-7
Fairest Lord Jesus. Unknown (German) 6730-1
Fairest of freedom's daughters. Jeremiah Eames Rankin. 6946-0
The fairest of her days. Unknown. 6182-6
"Fairest Theina let me know." Unknown. 6563-5
"Fairest of lands! Sole home of liberty!". London bridge; or, capital and labor. James Abraham Martling. 6952-5
"Fairest of morning lights appear". Psalm for Christmas day. Thomas Pestel. 6747-6,6931-2
"Fairest of morning lights, appear". For Christmas day. Thomas Pestel. 6756-5
"Fairest of virgins, daughter of a god". To the muse. Edward Moxon. 6980-0
"The fairest thing in all the world". Moonshine. W.S. Moody Jr.. 7021-3
"The fairest thing in mortal eyes." Charles, Duc d' Orleans. 6302-0;6385-3;6271-7
Fairfax, Edward
    Pluto's council. 6436-1
    A prayer brings rain. 6436-1
Fairfax, Edward (tr.)
    Armida's garden, fr. Jerusalem delivered. Torquato Tasso, 6649-6
    Jerusalem delivered, sels. Torquato Tasso, 6649-6
Fairfax, J. Griffyth
    The forest of the dead. 7029-9
    Mesopotamia. 7029-9
    Sir Stanley Maude. 7029-9
Fairfax, Thomas, Baron
    Upon a patch of face. 6563-5
    Upon the new-built house at Appleton. 6563-5
"Fairfax, the valiant! and the only he". An epitaphn upon Thomas, Lord Fairfax. George Villiers, 2d Duke of Buckingham. 6934-7

"Fairfax, whose name in armes through Europe". On the Lord Gen. Fairfax at the siege of Colchester. John Milton. 6933-9
Fairford nightingales. John Drinkwater. 6073-0
Fairies. Hilda Conkling. 6368-3,6538-4
Fairies. Kikaku. 6891-X
Fairies. Francis Ledwidge. 6812-X
Fairies. Margaret McNeish. 6906-1
Fairies - or fireflies? Sarah Morgan Bryan Piatt. 6965-7
Fairies and flowers. Celestin Pierre Cambiaire. 6826-X
"The fairies are a charming folk...". The fairies. John G. Herndon. 6891-X
The fairies dancing. Walter De La Mare. 6596-1
'The fairies have never a penny to spend'. Rose Fyleman. 6478-7,6607-0,6639-9,6723-9,6421-3,6253-9,6368-3
The fairies have never a penny to spend. Rose Fyleman. 6891-X
The fairies in New Ross. Unknown. 6930-4
The fairies in Prince Edward Island. John Hunter-Duvar. 6795-6
The fairies of the caldon low. Mary Howitt. 6127-3,6132-X, 6242-3,6271-7,6356-X,6496-5,6424-8,6131-1,6219-9, 6456-6,6639-9,6638-0,6249-0,6502-3,6519-8,6614-3, 6623-2
The fairies' Christmas. Mary A. Benson. 6684-4
The fairies' dance. Frank Dempster Sherman. 6311-X
The fairies' dance. Unknown. 6134-6,6189-3
The fairies' dance. Unknown. 6959-2
The fairies' farewell, sels. Richard Corbet. 6427-2
The fairies' farewell. Richard Corbet. 6052-8,6563-5,6194-X,6271-7
The fairies' farewell. Marjorie L.C. Pickthall. 6797-2
The fairies' flitting. Ethel Talbot. 6804-9
The fairies' lullaby, fr. A midsummer night's dream. William Shakespeare. 6052-8,6328-4,6302-0,6385-3
The fairies' lullaby. Eleanor Hull. 6090-0
The fairies' passage. James Clarence Mangan. 6090-0
Fairies' recall. Felicia Dorothea Hemans. 6973-8
The fairies' shopping. Margaret Deland. 6519-8
The fairies' siege. Rudyard Kipling. 6427-2,6655-0
Fairies' song. Thomas DeQuincey. 6249-0
Fairies' song. Leigh Hunt. 6198-2,6302-0,6385-3,6026-9
Fairies' song. Thomas Randolph. 6302-0;6385-3
Fairies' song. Unknown. 6271-7
The fairies' song ("You spotted snakes"). William Shakespeare. 6315-2
Fairies' song, fr. A midsummer-night's dream. William Shakespeare. 6083-8
The fairies' tea. Unknown. 6707-7,6277-6
Fairies' work. Isaac Bassett Choate. 6394-2
Fairies, fr. Kensington garden. Thomas Ticknell. 6932-0
"The fairies, it is said". Fairies. Kikaku. 6891-X
The fairies. William Allingham. 6301-2,6421-3,6454-X,6543-0,6638-0,6090-0,6133-8,6271-7,6328-4,6437-X,6534 , 6131-1,6219-9,6135-4,6125-7,6383-7,6639 ,6102-8,6104-4,6114-1,6252-0,6656-9
The fairies. George Darley. 6980-0
The fairies. Rose Fyleman. 6254-7,6639-9,6638-0
The fairies. John G. Herndon. 6891-X
The fairies. Robert Herrick. 6562-7,6252-0
The fairies. Sybil Morford. 6465-5,6639-9,6638-0
The fairies. Thomas Warton Jr. 6438-8
Fairless, Michael
    Out of the shadow. 6746-8,6447-6
Fairy. unknown. 6156-7
Fairy and child. Eugene Field. 6421-3
The fairy and Ianthe's soul. Percy Bysshe Shelley. 6543-0
Fairy antics. Ethel M. Brainerd. 6906-1
The fairy artist. Nellie M. Garrabrant. 6466-3
A fairy banquet, fr. Britannia's pastorals. William Browne. 6194-X
The fairy beam upon you. Ben Jonson. 6189-3
Fairy bell. Marion Short. 6675-5
The fairy book. Norman Gale. 6242-3,6639-9,6638-0
The fairy boy. Samuel Lover. 6174-5,6459-0
The fairy boy. Unknown. 6614-3
Fairy bread. Robert Louis Stevenson. 6252-0
The fairy child. John Anster. 6271-7
The fairy circus. Vachel Lindsay. 6265-2
Fairy dances. Unknown. 182-6

FAITH

Fairy faces. Unknown. 6145-1,6273-3
Fairy favors. Felicia Dorothea Hemans. 6973-8
Fairy folk. Alice Cary. 6546-6,6060-9
Fairy folk. Louise Imogen Guiney. 6965-7
The fairy folk. William Allingham. 6368-3,6424-8,6456-6, 6614-3
The fairy folk. Robert Bird. 6132-X,6519-8,6135-4,6639-9, 6638-0
Fairy foot. May Folwell Hoisington. 6039-0
The fairy fort. Abbie Farwell Brown. 6029-3
The fairy frolic. John Lyly. 6134-6,6466-3,6383-7,6301-2
The fairy harpers. James B. Dollard. 6115-X
'Fairy hill'. David Stefansson fra Fagraskogi. 6854-5
The fairy host. Unknown. 6090-0
A fairy in armor. Joseph Rodman Drake. 6519-8,6135-4
The fairy in the meadow. Rose Fyleman. 6253-9
Fairy jewels. Frank Dempster Sherman. 6311-X
The fairy knowe. Margaret Winefride Simpson. 6269-5
Fairy land. Elizabeth York Case. 6569-4
Fairy land. Andrew Lang. 6771-9
Fairy land. William Shakespeare. 6102-8,6236-9
The fairy life. William Shakespeare. 6732-8
"Fairy lines of tracery/From the reaches of...". Seaweed. Alice M. Dowd. 6799-9
The fairy lough. Moira (Nesta Higginson Skrine) O'Neill. 6331-4,6437-X,6439-6,6639-9
Fairy lullaby. William Shakespeare. 6143-5
A fairy lullaby. Eugene Field. 6949-5
The fairy Midir's invitation to Etain. Sean O'Faolain. 6582-1
Fairy music. Rose Fyleman. 6421-3
The fairy music. Nora Hopper. 6174-5
The fairy nurse. Edward Walsh. 6930-4
The fairy of them dell. Alice Cary. 6673-9
The fairy piper. James B. Dollard. 6797-2
The fairy queen Proserpina. Thomas Campion. 6733-6
The fairy queen. Unknown. 6219-9,6368-3,6454-X,6134-6,6466-3,6271-7,6385-3,6512-0,6614
Fairy revels. John Lyly. 6198-2,6189-3
The fairy ring. Andrew Young. 6125-7
A fairy scene, fr. Endymion. John Keats. 6980-0
The fairy ship. Gabriel (Thomas Nicoll Hepburn) Setoun. 6466-3
Fairy shipwreck. Frank Dempster Sherman. 6311-X
Fairy song. Felicia Dorothea Hemans. 6973-8
Fairy song. Winthrop Mackworth Praed. 6301-2
Fairy song. William Shakespeare. 6138-9,6134-6
Fairy song ("Shed no tear! O shed no tear!"). John Keats. 6254-7,6271-7,6302-0,6385-3,6479-5,6291 ,6219-9,6424-8,6737-9
Fairy song ("When daisies close and poppies nod"). Elinor Sweetman. 6090-0,6174-5
Fairy song, fr. A midsummer night's dream. William Shakespeare. 6512-0
Fairy song, fr. The land of heart's desire. William Butler Yeats. 6930-4
A fairy song. John Lyly. 6436-1
A fairy song. Unknown. 6105-2
Fairy songs. William Shakespeare. 6436-1,6737-9
A fairy story. Frank Dempster Sherman. 6311-X
The fairy tailor. Rose Fyleman. 6638-0
A fairy tale in the ancient English style. Thomas Parnell. 6975-4
A fairy tale. Austin Dobson. 6123-0,6476-0
A fairy tale. Thomas Hood. 6974-6
A fairy tale. Henry Van Dyke. 6961-4
The fairy temple, or Oberon's chapel, sels. Robert Herrick. 6194-X
The fairy tempter. Samuel Lover. 6613-5
The fairy thorn. Sir Samuel Ferguson. 6090-0,6518-X,6244-X, 6613-5,6153-2,6656
The fairy thrall. May C. ([Mary] Gillington) Byron. 6274-1
The fairy to Puck, fr. Songs. William Shakespeare. 6600-3, 6424-8
Fairy toil. Isabella Valancy Crawford. 6021-8
A fairy voyage. Unknown. 6466-3
"A fairy went a walk one day". The snail and the fairy. F. Hoatson. 6937-1
A fairy went a-marketing. Rose Fyleman. 6639-9
The fairy wood. Robin Flower. 6253-9

Fairy workers. Patrick MacGill. 6873-1
A fairy's life, fr. The tempest. William Shakespeare. 6466-3
A fairy's song. William Shakespeare. 6502-3
The fairy's spell. Frederick W. Poole. 6818-9
Fairy-land. Edgar Allan Poe. 6288-1
The fairy. Charles and Mary Lamb. 6295-4
The fairy. Unknown. 6132-X,6542-3
Fairyland. Doris V. Lecky. 6850-2
Fairyland. John R. Reid. 6799-9
Fairyland. Anne Glenny Wilson. 6784-0
Fairyland. Mrs. J.G. ("Austral") Wilson. 6768-9
"Fairyland has let me in/For a dear brief...". Junior public library. Lilian White Spencer. 6836-7
Fairyland, fr. Midsummer-night's dream. William Shakespeare. 6239-3
Fairytales. Peter Hellings. 6360-8
Fait accompli, fr. Two gentlemen in bonds. John Crowe Ransom. 6011-0
Faith. Philip James Bailey. 6980-0
Faith. John Kendrick Bangs. 6214-8
Faith. Sarah Knowles Bolton. 6303-9,6525-2
Faith. Grace Evelyn Brown. 6818-9
Faith. Robert Browning. 6214-8
Faith. Emma Carleton. 6337-3
Faith. Phoebe Cary. 6865-0;6969-X
Faith. Thomas Chatterton. 6481-7
Faith. Thomas Holley Chivers. 7017-5
Faith. Preston Clark. 6337-3
Faith. E. DeVilliers-Hertzler. 6818-9
Faith. Ernest Dowson. 6096 X
Faith. Donald Earl Edwards. 6144-3
Faith. Laura Bell Everett. 6303-9
Faith. Gertrude Fitzpatrick. 6789-1
Faith. Hortense Flexner. 6607-0,6253-9,6653-4
Faith. Gene Frumkin. 6803-0
Faith. William Dean Howells. 6337-3,6730-1
Faith. Victor Hugo. 6351-9
Faith. Hugh O. Isbell. 6144-3
Faith. Maud Frazer Jackson. 6337-3
Faith. Frances Anne Kemble. 6385-3,6437-X,6600-3,6438-8, 6219-9,6303-9,6656-9
Faith. Charles S. Kinnison. 6303-9
Faith. Samuel Ellsworth Kiser. 6291-1
Faith. Robert Loveman. 6941-X
Faith. John Richard Moreland. 6144-3,6039-0,6326-8
Faith. John Oxenham. 6337-3,6461-2
Faith. Ray Palmer. 6006-4;6735-2
Faith. Alexander Pope. 6730-1,6214-8
Faith. Edwin McNeill Poteat. 6144-3,6337-3
Faith. Sir Walter Raleigh. 6532-5
Faith. Carolyn Renfrew. 6789-1
Faith. George Santayana. 6006-4,6418-3,6589-9,6730-1,6431-0,6464
Faith. Robert Service. 6159-1
Faith. Edward Rowland Sill. 6291-1
Faith. G.A. Studdert-Kennedy. 6337-3
Faith. John Banister Tabb. 6266-0,6730-1,6303-9
Faith. John Greenleaf Whittier. 6730-1,6461-2
Faith. Ella Wheeler Wilcox. 6337-3,6461-2
Faith and despondency. Emily Bronte. 6828-6
Faith and fate. Richard Hovey. 6753-0
Faith and fate. Richard Hovey. 6735-2
Faith and freedom. William Wordsworth. 6239-3
Faith and hope. Rembrandt Peale. 6385-3
Faith and knowledge fight the dragon, fr The purple island. Phineas Fletcher. 6194-X
Faith and reason. Elizabeth York Case. 6568-6
Faith and reason. Lizzie York Case. 6913-4
Faith and sight. Mary Gardner Brainard. 6337-3
Faith and virtue. J. Drennan. 6717-4
Faith and works. Alice Cary. 6407-8,6969-X
Faith and works. William Howard Montgomery. 6166-4
Faith and works. Unknown. 6410-8
"Faith be noe longer coy." Unknown. 6563-5
"Faith has its centre fixed in God". The abiding three. William White. 6868-5
Faith in God. F. Lister Hawks. 6502-3,6131-1
"Faith is a grasping of almighty power." Ann [or Annie E.] Hamilton. 6225-3

FAITH

"Faith is a higher faculty than reason". Faith. Philip James Bailey. 6980-0
"Faith is not merely praying". Faith. Samuel Ellsworth Kiser. 6291-1
"Faith is the flower that blooms unseen". Faith. Thomas Holley Chivers. 7017-5
The faith of Christ's freemen. Thomas Curtis Clark. 6144-3
Faith of closed doors. Unknown. 6461-2
The faith of love. Felicia Dorothea Hemans. 6973-8
Faith of our fathers. Frederick William Faber. 6337-3,6723-9
Faith of our mothers. Arthur B. Patten. 6337-3
The faith of the poet. Victor Hugo. 6102-8
A faith on trial, sels. George Meredith. 6730-1
Faith shall build a fairer throne. Oliver Wendell Holmes. 6337-3,6214-8
The faith that waits. John R. Webb. 6818-9
A faith that will not shrink. William Hiley Bathurst. 6461-2
Faith's surrender. Rossiter Johnson. 7041-8
Faith's victory. William White. 6868-5
Faith, Mary
  My very dear. 6249-0
Faith, fr. Sacrifice. Ralph Waldo Emerson. 6427-2
Faith, fr. The ancient sage. Alfred Lord Tennyson. 6337-3, 6123-0,6214-8
Faith, fr. The excursion. William Wordsworth. 6337-3
Faith, hope and charity. Isabella Valancy Crawford. 6796-4
Faith, I wish I were a leprechaun. Margaret Tod Ritter. 6490-6
Faith, love, and death. Dowell O'Reilly. 6784-0
Faithful. Phoebe Cary. 6865-0;6969-X
Faithful. Sarah ("Susan Coolidge") Woolsey. 6461-2
Faithful among the faithless, fr. Paradise lost. John Milton. 6934-7
The faithful bird. William Cowper. 6133-8,6808-1
The faithful comrade. P.J. Fisher. 7031-0
A faithful dog. Richard Burton. 6476-0,6510-4
The faithful farmers. Cap Waller. 6799-9
Faithful follower, gentle friend. Richard Burton. 7008-6
A faithful friend. Unknown. 6085-4
The faithful friend. William Cowper. 6085-4
The faithful friend. William Cowper. 6814-6
The faithful lovers. Unknown. 6385-3
The faithful lovers. Unknown. 6910-X
A faithful picture of an ordinary society. William Cowper. 6996-7
"Faithful reports of them have reached me oft!". The isles: an ode. Sir Charles George Douglas Roberts. 7041-8
A faithful servant. Dioscorides. 6435-3
The faithful servant. Richard R. Kirk. 6326-8
the faithful servant. S. P. Koon. 6818-9
The faithful shepherd, sels. Giovanni Battista Guarini. 6325-X
The faithful shepherdess, sel. John Fletcher. 6958-4
The faithful shepherdess, sels. John Gould Fletcher. 6543-0
The faithful shepherdess, sels. John Fletcher. 6317-9,6562-7,6383-7
The faithful shepherdess. Francis Beaumont and John Fletcher. 6369-1
The faithful shepherdress, sel. John Fletcher. 6958-4
"The faithful sky in lake and light repeats". On Lake Llanquihue. Wilberto L. Canton. 6759-X
The faithful soldier. Unknown. 6523-6
Faithful unto death. Clifford Harrison. 6661-5,6683-6
Faithful unto death. Richard Handfield Titherington. 6946-0
Faithless. Alice Cary. 6969-X
The faithless flowers. Margaret Widdemer. 6232-6,6338-1
A faithless friend. Theognis. 6435-3
'A faithless generation asked a sign' Molly Anderson Haley. 7019-1
The faithless knight. William Allingham. 6518-X
The faithless lover. Unknown. 6934-7
Faithless Nellie Gray. Thomas Hood. 6014-5,6089-7,6271-7, 6289-X,6302-0,6486 ,6092-7,6212-1,6219-9,6278-4,6808-1,6739 ,6614-3,6732-8,6518-X
Faithless Sally Brown. Thomas Hood. 6089-7,6271-7,6302-0, 6385-3,6518-X,6808-1,6219-9
"Faithless the watch that I kept: now I...". The sleepy sentinel. Rudyard Kipling. 6958-4
"Faithless, perverse, and blind". Unbelief. Phoebe Cary. 6865-0;6969-X
"Faithlesse and fond mortality!". Upon the death of a gentleman. Richard Crashaw. 6908-8
The Fakenham ghost. Robert Bloomfield. 6105-2,6079-X
"Falce loue awaye, & all my sighes send back." Unknown. 6563-5
The falcon and the dove. Herbert Read. 6209-1
The falcon hath borne my mate away. Unknown. 6558-9,6153-2
The falcon. Wilfrid Scawen Blunt. 6022-6
The falcon. Unknown. 6931-2
The falcon. Unknown. 6022-6
The falcon. Unknown. 6931-2
The falconer of God. William Rose Benet. 6007-2,6102-8, 6162-1,6347-0,6476-0,6501 ,6076-5,6161-3,6012-9,6250-4,6513-9,6300 ,6007-2,6730-1,6732-8,6337-3,6393-4, 6236-9,6506-6,6509-0,6532-5,6556-2,6607
Falconer, Edmund. See O'Rourke, Edmund
Falconer, William
  Address to Miranda. 6971-1
  All hands unmoor! 6833-2
  "As the proud horse...", fr. The shipwreck. 6547-3
  The demagogue. 6971-1
  Description of a ninety-gun ship. 6971-1
  "Foams the wild beach below with maddening rage". 6997-5
  The fond lover. 6971-1
  "The ghost of day yet haunts the troubled west". 6997-5
  "The glassy ocean hushed forgets to roar". 6997-5
  High o'er the poop the audacious seas aspire. 6833-2
  Ode on the Duke of York's second departure from England. 6971-1
  On the uncommon scarcity of poetry. 6971-1
  A poem, sacred to the memory..Feredric Prince of Wales. 6971-1
  The shipwreck, sels. 6258-X,6547-3,6195-0
  The shipwreck. 6971-1
  The shipwreck. 6302-0,6385-3,6245-8
  Shortening sail. 6833-2
  "The tired ocean crawls along the beach". 6997-5
Falke, Gustav
  God's harp. Ludwig Lewisohn (tr.). 7039-6
  When I die. Margarete A. Munsterberg (tr.). 6879-0
Falkenbury, Francis E.
  South Street. 6467-1
Falkner, William Howard
  Her answer. 6936-3
Falkowski, E.
  Mine song. 6954-1
Fall. Aleksa Santic. 6765-4
Fall fashions. Edith M. Thomas. 6745-X
"The fall has come, the trembling leaves". Autumn leaves. Celestin Pierre Cambiaire. 6826-X
Fall in. Frank S. Brown. 6650-X
Fall in. Kate Brownlee Sherwood. 6577-5
Fall in! Amelia Josephine Burr. 6031-5
Fall in! Frank N. Scott. 6741-X
Fall leaves. Josephine Franco. 6850-2
The fall of a soul. John Addington Symonds. 6656-9
Fall of angels and of man, fr. Genesis. Caedmon. 6489-2
The fall of Corydon. W.B. A. 7021-3
The fall of D'Assas. Felicia Dorothea Hemans. 6610-0
The fall of D'Assas. Felicia Dorothea Hemans. 6973-8
The fall of Eve. Unknown. 6724-7
The fall of Greece. George Gordon, 6th Baron Byron. 6240-7
The fall of heroes. Sir William Watson. 6396-9
The fall of hyperion, a dream. John Keats. 6958-4
The fall of Icarus. Ovid. 6978-9
The fall of J.W. Beane. Oliver Herford. 7021-3
The fall of Jerusalem. Henry Hart Milman. 6848-0
The fall of Jerusalem. Alfred Lord Tennyson. 6848-0
The fall of Jock Gillespie. Rudyard Kipling. 6518-X
"The fall of kings/The rage of nations...". Love of nature, fr. The seasons (Autumnm). James Thomson. 6932-0
The fall of man and the early ages of the earth. Hesiod. 6251-2
The fall of man. Caedmon. 6848-0

The **fall** of Maubila. Thomas Dunn English. 6946-0
The **fall** of Niagara. John Gardiner Calkins Brainard. 6385-3,6600-3,6632-1
The **fall** of Poland. Thomas Campbell. 6980-0
The **fall** of princes, sels. John Lydgate. 6483-3
The **fall** of Richmond. Herman Melville. 6946-0
The **fall** of Satan, fr. The flaming terrapin. Roy Campbell. 6788-3
A **fall** of snow. James Thomson. 6793-X
Fall of Tecumseh. Unknown. 6752-2
The **fall** of Tecumseh. Unknown. 6946-0
The **fall** of the Aar. William Wordsworth. 6749-2
The **fall** of the city. Archibald MacLeish. 6265-2
The **fall** of the deer. Thomas Hood. 6974-6
The **fall** of the House of Usher, sels. Edgar Allan Poe. 6176-1
The **fall** of the leaf. Henry David Thoreau. 6243-1
The **fall** of the leaves. Henry Van Dyke. 6961-4
The **fall** of the mighty. Brian ("Korongo") Brooke. 6938-X
The **fall** of the Titans, fr. Hyperion. John Keats. 6935-5
Fall of Warsaw, 1794 Thomas Campbell. 6606-2,6425-6
Fall of Wolsey. William Shakespeare. 6304-7
Fall song ("The ash-berry clusters..."). Unknown. 6049-8
"The **fall** that she turned fifty". The one who grew to be a wolf. Patricia Monaghan. 6966-5
Fall time down in Georgia. Maybelle Mayne Porter. 6841-3
The **fall** wind. John S. Thomson. 6274-1
Fall'n is thy throne. Thomas Moore. 6543-0
"**Fall'n**, fall'n, a silent heap; her heroes all". The ruins of Rome. John Dyer. 6932-0
Fall, Lucius M.
    Silence. 6799-9
    Sublimity. 6799-9
"**Fall**, fall, fall". Snow. Unknown. 6983-5
Fall, leaves, fall. Emily Bronte. 6246-6,6315-2
A **fall-crick** view of the earthquake. James Whitcomb Riley. 6247-4
The **fall**. Sir Richard Fanshawe. 6933-9
The **fall**. Thomas Hood. 6974-6
The **fall**. Eden Phillpotts. 6884-7
The **fall**. Nathaniel Wanley. 6562-7
Fallacy. Ricardo Weeks. 6178-8
Fallaw, Lance
    A Cape homestead. 6800-6
    Day and night up-country. 6800-6
    Dick King. 6800-6
    The navigators. 6800-6
    Old St. Thomas' churchyard, Durban. 6800-6
    Simon Van der Stel. 6800-6
    Simon van der Stel. 6625-9
    The spirit of hidden places. 6591-0,6592-9
    The spirit of hidden places. 6800-6
    Two homelands. 6800-6
Fallen. W. Kersley Holmes. 7027-2
Fallen. William J. Lampton. 6698-4
Fallen. George Edgar Montgomery. 6273-3
The **fallen** angels. John Milton. 6138-9,6543-0
Fallen cities. Gerald Gould. 6250-4
Fallen fences. Winifred Virginia Jackson. 6762-X
Fallen is thy throne. Thomas Moore. 6848-0
The **fallen** leaves. Caroline Elizabeth Sarah Sheridan Norton. 6980-0
The **fallen** lime-tree. Felicia Dorothea Hemans. 6973-8
Fallen majesty. William Butler Yeats. 6464-7
The **fallen** pharoah. Leonard Van Noppen. 6327-X
Fallen riches. Francis H. Deter. 6906-1
The **fallen** shrine. Delphic Oracle. 6435-3
The **fallen** star. George Darley. 6090-0,6102-8
A **fallen** star. Albert Chevalier. 6701-8
The **fallen** subaltern. Herbert Asquith. 7026-4
"**Fallen** that mighty form, silent the voice". Phillips Brooks. John Hall Ingham. 6820-0
The **fallen** tower of Siloam. Robert Graves. 6666-6
"**Fallen** was the house of Giafar; and its name". The mourner for the Barmecides. Felicia Dorothea Hemans. 6973-8
"**Fallen** with autumn's falling leaf". On the death of President Garfield. Oliver Wendell Holmes. 6946-0
A **fallen** yew. Francis Thompson. 6828-6
A **fallen** yew. Francis Thompson. 6655-0

A **fallen** yew. Francis Thompson. 6942-8
The **fallen**.. Duncan Campbell Scott. 6051-X
"**Fallen**? How fallen? States and empires fall". On the defeat of Henry Clay. William Wilberforce Lord. 6946-0
Faller, Harold
    Killarkey. 6042-0
    A stop by the brook at high noon. 6042-0
"**Falleth** now from off a tree". Emblems. Richard Coe. 6910-X
"**Falling** all the night-time". Snowflakes. John Vance Cheney. 7041-8
Falling asleep. Margaret S. Hosmer. 6316-0
Falling asleep. Siegfried Sassoon. 6332-2
"**Falling** asleep while I dreamed of fragrance". Fragrance. Amy Parkinson. 6796-4
The **falling** bowlder. James Abraham Martling. 6952-5
Falling day. Christy MacKaye. 6799-9
Falling down to bed. Nila NorthSun. 7005-1
Falling in and falling out. Elmer Ruan Coates. 6921-5
The **falling** leaf. James Montgomery. 6250-4
"The **falling** leaves seem pitiful to see". Autumn. Edgar A. Guest. 6869-3
"**Falling** of dust is the ticking of time...". Relics. Laurence Pratt. 6761-1
The **falling** of thrones. Ella Wheeler Wilcox. 6863-4
The **falling** out of faithful friends. Richard Edwards. 6934-7
Falling petals. Ji-hoon Cho. 6775-1
Falling snow. Amy Lowell. 6897-9
Falling snow. Unknown. 6529-5,6745-X
The **falling** star. Sara Teasdale. 6554-X
Falling to sleep. Unknown. 6127-3
"**Falling** upon the frozen world last night". Winter rain. Ella Wheeler Wilcox. 7041-8
"**Falling**, never upward, why, oh why". The awakening. Rubye Arnold. 7016-7
Fallon, David
    Nature's cathedrals. 6478-7
    Nature's miracle. 6476-0
    Spring symphony. 6478-7
Fallon, John
    Dissecting room. 6482-5
    Inscription for an old well. 6482-5
Fallon, Padraic
    Virgin. 6930-4
    Wisdom. 6930-4
Fallout. P.J. (Polly) Holt. 6883-9
Fallow. Charles Mackay. 6980-0
The **fallow** deer at the lonely house. Thomas Hardy. 6488-4
The **fallow** field. Julia C.R. Dorr. 6414-0,6673-9
Fallow land. Eunice Clark. 6375-6
The **fallow** mind. Dorothy Livesay. 6021-8
The **falls** of Terni. George Gordon, 6th Baron Byron. 6624-0
Falls of the Mohawk. Thomas Moore. 6484-1
The **falls** of the Passaic. Washington Irving. 6484-1
Fallstrom, Daniel
    Oh, never ask! Charles Wharton Stork (tr.). 6045-5
    Stockholm in white. Charles Wharton Stork (tr.). 6045-5
    To a sea-gull in the steamer's wake. Charles Wharton Stork (tr.). 6045-5
The **Falmouth** bell. Katharine Lee Bates. 6798-0
False. Ella Wheeler Wilcox. 6863-4
False alarms. Adelaide O'Keefe. 6614-3
False alarms. Ann and Jane Taylor. 6105-2
"**False** and fickle, or fair and sweet". The Lady Jacqueline. Phoebe Cary. 6969-X
False and true. Unknown. 6273-3
False bay. Frank Templeton Prince. 6788-3
The **false** firecracker. Carolyn Wells. 6882-0
The **false** fox. Unknown. 6125-7
False friend. Al-Hajjam. 6362-4
False friends. Edmund Spenser. 6084-6
False friends-like. William Barnes. 6133-8,6134-6
The **false** friends. Dorothy Parker. 6441-8
A **false** gallop of analogies. W. St. Leger. 6722-0
A **false** genius. Adelaide Anne Procter. 6957-6
False gods. Katharine (Hinkson) Tynan. 6785-9
The **false** gods. Edwin Arlington Robinson. 6161-3
False &kindness. Unknown. 6699-2

FALSE

The **false** knight on the road. Unknown. 6061-7
The **false** knight. Unknown. 6003-X
"**False** lamkin was as good a mason". Unknown. 6059-5
False love. John Lilliat. 6436-1
False love. Sir Walter Raleigh. 6436-1,6584-8
False love and true logic. Laman Blanchard. 6089-7
The **false** lover won back. Unknown. 6185-0
False nightmare. Allen Tate. 6389-6
False poets and true. Thomas Hood. 6974-6
False spring. Louise Owen. 6764-6
A **false** step. Elizabeth Barrett Browning. 6732-8,6655-0
"**False** though she be to me and love". Song ("False though she be to me and love"). William Congreve. 6932-0
False though she be to me and love. William Congreve. 6226-1
"**False** though she be to me and love". William Congreve. 6024-2,6208-3
"**False** world, thou ly'st: Thou canst not lend". Francis Quarles. 6562-7
"**False** world, thou ly'st: thou canst not lend". Wilt thou set thine eyes upon that which is not? Francis Quarles. 6933-9
"**False**! Good God, I am dreaming!". False. Ella Wheeler Wilcox. 6863-4
"**False**, cruel, disappointed, stung to...heart". In seditionem horrendam. William Cowper. 6814-6
False, fickle man! Unknown. 6670-6
The **false-hearted** knight. Unknown. 6061-7
Falsehood "corrected". Elizabeth Turner. 6105-2
Falstaff fights against a hundred or so..., fr Henry IV. William Shakespeare. 6637-2
Falstaff's sister. Dorothy Margaret Stuart. 6779-4
Falstaff's song. Edmund Clarence Stedman. 6102-8,6076-5, 6431-0,6309-8
Falstaff, Jake
   The Dick Johnson reel. 6722-0
   Paradise lost. 6817-0
"**Famam**, posteritas quam dedit orpheo". De instituto authoris. Thomas Campion. 6794-8
Fame. Leonard Bacon. 6464-7
Fame. Alice Cary. 6865-0;6969-X
Fame. Edgar A. Guest. 6748-4
Fame. Ben Jonson. 6438-8
Fame. Gertrude Huntington McGiffert. 6838-3
Fame. James Herbert Morse. 6996-7
Fame. Alexander Pope. 6302-0,6365-3,6543-0
Fame. Lady Margaret Sackville. 6778-6
Fame. Johann C. Friedrich von Schiller. 6240-7
Fame. John Banister Tabb. 6102-8,6067-5,6646-1
Fame. Sir Thomas Noon Talfourd. 6980-0
Fame. Unknown. 6118-4,6274-1
Fame and envy, fr. Epistle to Pope. Edward Young. 6102-0
Fame and fate. Edmund Vance Cooke. 6280-6
Fame and fortune. Michael Drayton. 6436-1
"**Fame** guards the wreath we call a crown". Fame. Alice Cary. 6865-0;6969-X
Fame is a food that dead men eat. Austin Dobson. 6879-0
'**Fame** is a food that dead men eat' Austin Dobson. 7012-4
"**Fame** is a silence where hath been no sound". Austin Dobson. 6844-8
The **fame** of Lincoln. A. Dallas Williams. 6524-4
"The **fame** of those pure bards whose faces lie". To the memory of poets. Sir Thomas Noon Talfourd. 6980-0
"**Fame** pays no heed to birth or place". Fame. Edgar A. Guest. 6748-4
Fame vs. riches. Horace. 6949-5
Fame's penny trumpet. Charles Lutwidge ("Lewis Carroll") Dodgson. 6996-7
"**Fame's** trumpet blows a silver note". Lincoln. John E. Barrett. 6840-5
Fame, V.
   The chintz-birds. 6804-9
Fame, fr. Earth's immortalities. Robert Browning. 6655-0
"**Fame**, wisdom, love, and power were mine". 'All is vanity, saith the preacher'. George Gordon, 6th Baron Byron. 6945-2
Fame—fame—fame. W. Livingston Larned. 6274-1
"The **famed** Italian muse, whose rhymes advance". To the University of Oxford, 1681. John Dryden. 6970-3
A amiliar letter to several correspondents. Oliver Wendell Holmes. 6089-7
Familiar lines. Unknown. 6277-6
"**Familiar** of the sky, you have known". For a British flyer. Katherine Garrison Chapin. 6761-1
Familiar sheets. Ulalume Gonzalez de Leon. 7036-1
A **familiar** spirit. Wendell Phillips Stafford. 7030-2
Familiar things. Brother X (pseud.) 6662-3
Familiarity dangerous. Vincent Bourne. 6814-6,6511-2
"**Families**, when a child is born". On the birth of his son. Su Tung-p'o. 7039-6
Family affair. Unknown. 6713-1
Family album. Lonny Kaneko. 6790-5
Family album. Louis Stoddard. 6761-1
The **family** Bible. Felicia Dorothea Hemans. 6097-8
The **family** cat. Unknown. 6529-5,6692-2
Family clusters. Charles W. Denison. 6755-7
The **family** dinner-party. Menander. 6435-3
Family doctor. Dorothy Bladin Hill. 6750-6
A **family** drum corps. Malcolm Douglas. 6672-0
A **family** favorite. Louis J. Magee. 7004-3
Family financiering. Unknown. 6451-5
Family financiering. Unknown. 6889-8
The **family** fool. Sir William Schwenck Gilbert. 6026-9
"The **family** is like a book". The family. Unknown. 6889-8
Family legend. Joanna Baillie. 6813-8
The **family** meeting. Charles Sprague. 6240-7,6385-3,6600-3, 6219-9
The **family** meeting. Charles Sprague. 6889-8
The **family** name. Charles Lamb. 6980-0
The **family** of nations. Willard Wattles. 6946-0
The **family** party. Edgar A. Guest. 6862-6
Family poetry. Richard Harris ("Thomas Ingoldsby") Barham. 6278-4
Family portrait. Leonard Feeney. 6282-2
Family portrait: a measure of subway bones. Arthur T. Wilson. 6899-5
The **Family** prayer for difficult days. Edgar A. Guest. 6869-3
Family pride. Marguerite Merington. 6130-3
Family quarrels. John Godfrey Saxe. 6278-4
A **family** row. Edgar A. Guest. 7033-7
Family shame. Fannie Williams. 6850-2
Family tree. Ibn al-Qaffun. 6362-4
Family trees. Douglas Malloch. 6338-1,6478-7,6449-3
The **family**. Unknown. 6889-8
Famine in a besieged city, fr. Philip Van Artevelde. Henry Taylor. 6980-0
Famine on a schedule. Helen Hardman. 6750-6
"**Famine** once we had". New England's growth, fr. New England. William Bradford. 6946-0
Famine song. Laurence (Adele Florence Nicolson) Hope. 6856-1
The **famine** year. Lady Jane F. ("Speranza") Wilde. 6174-5
The **famine**, fr. The song of Hiawatha. Henry Wadsworth Longfellow. 6077-3,6616-X,6142-7,6554-6,6370-5,6008-0,6288-1,6567-8,6402-7
"The **famished** maw of couchant caninery". Thomas Hardy: Old Mother Hubbard. Charles Powell. 6982-7
"**Famished**, the lions were in their". The lions. Victor Hugo. 6848-0
"**Famous** animals/spoke here". Holiday Inn at Bemidji. Gerald Vizenor. 7005-1
The **famous** ballad of the jubilee cup. Sir Arthur Quiller-Couch. 6722-0,6732-8
The **famous** fight at Malago. Unknown. 6157-5,6547-3
The **famous** flower of servingmen. Unknown. 6185-0,6613-5
Famous men, fr. Ecclesiasticus. Bible. 6179-5
The **famous** Mulligan Ball. Frank Lebby Stanton. 6583-X
A **famous** riddle. Unknown. 6724-7
A **famous** sea fight between Captain Ward and the Rainbow. Unknown. 6547-3
A **famous** sea-fight. John Looke. 6157-5
Fan. Walter Lew. 6790-5
A **fan**. Jonathan Swift. 6278-4
The **fan**. John Gay. 6198-2
The **fan**. John Gay. 6972-X
The **fan**. Rene Francois Armand Sully-Prudhomme. 6351-9
The **fan**. Wilfrid Thorley. 6071-4
The **fan**. Elizabeth Turner. 6018-8
Fanchon the cricket. Eugene Field. 6949-5

Fancies. John Ford. 6240-7
Fancies in Filigree. James Branch Cabell. 6875-8
Fancies in the firelight. Thomas Buchanan Read. 6749-2
Fancy. Laurence (Adele Florence Nicolson) Hope. 6856-1
Fancy. Leigh Hunt. 6980-0
Fancy. John Keats. 6271-7,6315-2,6486-8,6501-5,6219-9,6199,6086-2,6110-9,6196-6,6230-X
Fancy. John Keats. 6828-6
Fancy and desire. Edward de Vere, 17th Earl of Oxford. 6191-5,6383-7
The fancy concert. Leigh Hunt. 6358-6
Fancy fishing. James L. Weil. 6218-0
A fancy from Fontenelle. Austin Dobson. 6046-3
Fancy in Nubibus. Samuel Taylor Coleridge. 7015-9
Fancy in Nubibus. Samuel Taylor Coleridge. 6219-9,6250-4
Fancy in Nubibus. Samuel Taylor Coleridge. 7015-9
Fancy in Nubibus. Samuel Taylor Coleridge. 6302-0;6385-3
The fancy people. Marshall Schacht. 6389-6
The fancy shot. Charles Dawson Shanly. 6113-3,6471-X,6735-2
The fancy work maiden. Sam Walter Foss. 6744-1
Fancy's home. William Henry Davies. 6508-2
Fancy's knell. Alfred Edward Housman. 6187-7,6102-8,6508-2
"Fancy's the wealth of wealth...". Fancy. Leigh Hunt. 6980-0
"Fancy, and I, last evening walkt". To Amoret gone from him. Henry Vaughan. 6933-9
Fancy, fr. The merchant of Venice. William Shakespeare. 6134-6,6228-8,6302-0,6385-3,6114-1
A fancy. Thomas Lodge. 6182-6;6436-1;6315-2;6436-1
Fand yields Cuchulainn to Emer. Sean O'Faolain. 6582-1
'Fand', sels. William Larminie. 6174-5
Fandango. Walter Stanley ("Stanley Vestal") Campbell. 6281-4
Fandel, John
    Summertime is credo. 6839-1
Fandel, Peter
    Roosevelt. 6449-3
Fane, Julian Henry
    Ad matrem. 6097-8,6627-5
Fane, Mildmay. See Westmoreland, 2d Earl of
Fane, Sir Francis
    "Cupid, I scorn to beg...", fr. Love in the dark. 6562-7,6563-5
    Love in the dark, sels. 6562-7,6563-5
Fane; Baroness Currie, Violet
    Afterwards. 6656-9,6046-3
    Forbidden love. 7037-X
    A foreboding. 6656-9
    In green old gardens. 6656-9,6649-6
    A May song. 6656-9
    Rest. 7037-X
    To a new sundial. 6338-1
    A wife's confession. 6675-5
Fanning, Ella Augusta
    The summer cat. 6120-6
Fanny. Anne Reeve Aldrich. 6004-8
Fanny Fales. See Frances E. Swift
    6798-0
Fanny's edu|ation, fr. Fanny. Fitz-Greene Halleck. 6753-0
Fanny's mud pies. Elizabeth Sill. 6629-1
Fanny, Aunt. See Gage, Frances Dana Barker
"Fanny, beware of flattery". Flattery. Sir Charles Hanbury Williams. 6787-5
Fanny, sels. Fitz-Greene Halleck. 6753-0
Fanny, sels. Fitz-Greene Halleck. 6077-3
Fanny; or, the beauty and the bee. Charles Mackay. 6652-6
Fanshaw, Catherine Maria
    The death of the minuet. 6959-2
Fanshawe, Catherine Maria
    Elegy on the abrogation of the birth-night ball... 6874-X
    Enigma on the letter H. 6089-7,6724-7,6302-0,6385-5,6092-7
    Enigma on the letter I. 6724-7
    Fragment in imitation of Wordsworth. 6440-X
    An imitation of Wordsworth. 6089-7
    The letter H. 6416-7
    Ode ("Lo! where the gaily vestur'd throng"). 6802-2
    Riddle. 6102-8,6239-3,6125-7

    A riddle on the letter H. 6874-X
Fanshawe, Sir Richard
    The fall. 6933-9
    Hope. 6933-9
    Now war is all the world about. 6315-2
    Ode, upon occasion of His Majesties proclamation..1630 6933-9
    Of beauty. 6908-8
    Of time. 6563-5
    A rose. 6562-7,6563-5
    "Thou blushing rose, within whose virgin leaves" 6935-5
Fanshawe, Sir Richard (tr.)
    The faithful shepherd, sels. Giovanni Battista Guarini, 6325-X
    The golden age, fr. The faithful shepherd. Giovanni Battista Guarini, 6325-X
Fantaisie. Gerard de Nerval. 6801-4
Fantasia. Carlos Drummond de Andrade. 6759-X
Fantasia. Joseph Freeman. 6880-4
Fantasia in E minor. Elizabeth Bush. 6799-9
Fantasia on claviers at night. Herbert Trench. 6877-4
Fantasy. Doris Trahagen De Aragon. 6906-1
Fantasy. Ben Jonson. 6385-3,6438-8
Fantasy. Hugh McCrae. 6349-7
Fantasy. Ruth Mathest Skidmore. 6396-9
Fantasy ("A bird ran up the onyx steps of night") Louis Untermeyer. 6032-3
Fantasy in a forest. Leah Bodine Drake. 6783-2
Fantasy in purple. Langston Hughes. 6619-4
"Far above us where a jay". Morning on the Lievre. Archibald Lampman. 6797-2
Far and wide she went. Caedmon. 6833-2
"Far are the wings of intellect astray". Prayer continued. Felicia Dorothea Hemans. 6973-8
"Far as man can see". Song of the rain chant. Unknown (Navaho Indian). 7039-6
"Far at sea and west of Spain". The land of Cokaygne. Unknown. 6930-4
The far awa lan'. Unknown. 6411-6
Far away. Felicia Dorothea Hemans. 6973-8
Far away. Maud Lindsay. 6304-7
"Far away across the seas". Those we left behind. Celestin Pierre Cambiaire. 6826-X
"Far away from the hill-side, the lake...". Departure of the pioneer. John Gardiner Calkins Brainard. 6752-2
"Far away in the twilight time". The double-headed snake of Newbury. John Greenleaf Whittier. 6753-0
Far away the camp fires burn. Unknown. 6304-7
"Far away, very far in the north". The woman and the serpent. Unknown (Algonquin Indian). 6864-2
"Far back in the shadowy regions of the past". Old Yarmouth. Mary Matthews Bray. 6798-0
"Far back, in my musings, my thoughts have...cast". The old kitchen floor. Unknown. 6964-9
"Far be the bookish muses! Let them find". Invocation to the African muse, fr.The flaming terrapin. Roy Campbell. 6788-3
"Far behind him crept blackness and...". The song of the spirits. Joseph Sheridan Le Fanu. 6930-4
"Far beneath/Sleepeth the glassy ocean like a sheet". Robert Buchanan. 6997-5
"Far better in its place the lowliest bird". Wrong seraph and right bird. Jean Ingelow. 6943-6
"Far beyond the desert". On the train. Muin Ozaki. 6981-9
"Far beyond/White lilies, wild around my feet." Kyoko. 6027-X
Far bugles. Olive Tilford Dargan. 6039-0,6071-4
A far country. Alister Mackenzie. 6781-6
A far cry to heaven. Edith M. Thomas. 6467-1,6730-1
"Far distant friends will drop a tear". Unknown. 6059-5
"Far down in the meadow the wheat grows green". Alice's supper. Laura E. Richards. 6891-X
"Far down the dark avenue of trees". Night solitude. Louise Louis. 6750-6
"Far down the road of song, the wind and rain". Sonnet 003, fr. Sonnet sequence. Isabel Alden Kidder. 6764-6
"Far fall the day when England's realm...". Sonnet ("Far fall the day"). George Edward Woodberry. 7026-4
Far fields. Daisy Lee Ervin. 6906-1
"Far from my dearest friend, 'tis mine to rove". An

evening walk. William Wordsworth. 6828-6
"Far from our garden at the edge of a gulf". The gulf. Denise Levertov. 6803-0
"Far from the deep roar of the Aegean main". Farewell. Plato. 7039-6
"Far from the earth the deep-descended day". A ballade of the night. Margaret L. Woods. 6875-8
"Far from the glorious light of day". The prisoner of the Bastile. Mrs. J.O. Warner. 6925-8
"Far from the heart of culture". Wystan Hugh Auden. 6665-8
"Far from the land of the sunlight". The valley of rest. Carl [pseud]. 6983-5
Far from the madding crowd. Nixon Waterman. 6374-8
"Far from the rustlings of the poplar-bough". To the sky. Felicia Dorothea Hemans. 6973-8
"Far from the sea in his grey later days". 'Cap'n'. Arthur Wallace Peach. 6833-2
"Far from the sun and summer gale", fr.Progress..poesy. Thomas Gray. 6793-X
"Far from the sun and summer-gale". The progress of poesy, sels. Thomas Gray. 6934-7
"Far from the turmoil and the dust of trade". The dancers. Joseph Freeman. 6880-4
"Far from this foreign Easter damp and chilly". Easter flower. Claude McKay. 6880-4
"Far from thy dearest self, the scope". To his mistress in absense. Torquato Tasso. 7039-6
"Far from you now, in this unfriendly town". Swift, in absence. Gilbert Maxwell. 6761-1
"The far green westward heavens are bland". Heartsease country. Algernon Charles Swinburne. 6875-8
"Far happier are the dead, methinks, than they". Anticipation. Lucilius. 6850-2
"Far happier are the dead, methinks, than they". Unknown. 6435-3
"Far have I clamber'd in my mind". Hymn to charity and humility. Henry More. 6931-2
"Far have you come, my lady, from the town" Robert Louis Stevenson. 6875-8
"Far in a western brookland." Alfred Edward Housman. 6246-6,6374-8,6430-2,6250-4,6199-0,6508-2,6723-9,6645-3
"Far in the depths of a sombre wood". Ballade ("Far in the depths"). Unknown. 6118-4
"Far in the further east the skilful craftsman". Fancy. Laurence (Adele Florence Nicolson) Hope. 6856-1
"Far in the glass of the Aegean sea". Homer. William Edmonstoune Aytoun. 6948-7
"Far in the west the dead day's pyre". The skaters. Charles Gordon Rogers. 7035-3
"Far in the wilds of Araby". Petra. Anna R-.. 6848-0
The far land. John Hall Wheelock. 6730-1
"Far lone amang the highland hills". The lass o' Arranteenie. Robert Tannahill. 6960-6
"Far o'er the mountain summit lies". Musk gully, Dromana. J. Steele Robertson. 6768-9
Far o'er the ocean. Felicia Dorothea Hemans. 6973-8
"Far off the old snows ever new". Simmenthal. Frederick W.H. Myers. 6749-2
"Far off, the silent sea gloomed cold and gray". Alfred Austin. 6997-5
"Far on its rocky knoll descried". Stanzas composed at Carnac. Matthew Arnold. 6947-9
"Far on its rocky knoll descried", fr. Stanzas..Carnac. Matthew Arnold. 6997-5
"Far out upon the veld, a slender tree". The camp-fire. Charles Claybrook Woollacott. 6800-6
"Far over the billows unresting forever". Thalatta. William Boyd Allen. 6833-2
Far over yonder. Rafael Maya. 6759-X
"Far richer than a thornless rose". Thorn and rose. Henry Van Dyke. 6961-4
"Far spread, below". The story of Vinland, fr. Psalm of the west. Sidney Lanier. 6946-0
"Far swept from Lundy, spanned from side..side". M.T.W. Thomas Edward Brown. 6809-X
"Far the gray loch runs". Schiehallion. Herbert Trench. 6877-4
"Far through the Delphian shades". The storm of Delphi. Felicia Dorothea Hemans. 6973-8
Far to the bridge. Mabel W. Phillips. 6316-0

"Far town-ward sounds a distant tread". The buccaneer, fr. Rokeby. Sir Walter Scott. 6832-4
"Far travel the gleams of her glory". Woman. Lilian Sauter. 7023-X
"Far up at Glorian the wind is sighing". Memories. Edward Hilton Young. 7027-2
"Far up the ancient trading path he dwelt". The Indian trader. Chapman J. Milling. 7016-7
"Far weightier cares and wider scenes expand". The bird-boy. Robert Bloomfield. 6980-0
Far west. Arthur James Marshall Smith. 6446-9
Far west, sels. Blaise Cendrars. 6351-9
Far, and yet near. Elizabeth Barrett Browning. 6429-9,6321-7
"Far, far away, I see a long trail". Lief's trail. Celestin Pierre Cambiaire. 6826-X
"Far, far beyond yon eastern steeps". Song of the clouds. Eugene Field. 6949-5
"Far, through the quiet night, my loved one...". The return. Ethel Ashton Edwards. 6778-6
Far-away. George Sigerson. 6292-X
Far-far-away. Alfred Lord Tennyson. 6123-0,6110-9,6371-3,6199-0,6655-0,6657
The far-farers.. Robert Louis Stevenson. 6625-9
"Far-fetched and dear bought, as the...". A singing lesson. Algernon Charles Swinburne. 6770-0
"Far-off he heard upon the truce of night". Paris. George Sterling. 6979-7
Fara diddle dyno. Unknown. 6182-6,6315-2,6733-6
Farber, Norma
    Parkinson and the octopus. 6218-0
    Unicorns at Harvard. 6218-0
    Witching hour. 6218-0
Farbstein, W.E.
    Double duty. 6722-0
Fare for a gipsy heart. Louis Ragg. 6750-6
"Fare thee weel, my native cot". Lenachan's farewell. Unknown. 6859-6
"Fare thee well". The farewell. Thomas Hood. 6974-6
"Fare thee well! and if forever." George Gordon, 6th Baron Byron. 6219-9,6302-0,6486-8,6543-0,6438-8,6086-2,6110
Fare thee well, fr. Henry IV. William Shakespeare. 6908-8
"Fare thee well, great heart!", fr. King Henry IV. William Shakespeare. 6879-0
Fare thee well, thou lovely one. Thomas Moore. 6226-1
Fare well. Walter De La Mare. 6179-6,6246-5
Fare ye well, Inniskillen. Unknown. 6058-7
"Fare-thee-well, our last and fairest". Wee Willie. David Macbeth Moir. 6980-0
Fareweel. Alexander Maclagan. 6014-5
Farewell. Bernard Barton. 6980-0
Farewell. Cyril Dabydeen. 6767-0
Farewell. Enid Derham. 6784-0
Farewell. J. Howard Flower. 7030-2
Farewell. Reginald Heber. 6980-0
Farewell. William Herbert; Earl of Pembroke. 6980-0
Farewell. Laurence (Adele Florence Nicolson) Hope. 6856-1
Farewell. Harry Kemp. 6374-8
Farewell. Mikhail Lermontov. 6622-4
Farewell. Gertrude Huntington McGiffert. 6838-3
Farewell. Sir Henry Newbolt. 7031-0
Farewell. Robert Nichols. 7029-9
Farewell. Plato. 7039-6
Farewell. Sir Walter Scott. 6322-5
Farewell. Algernon Charles Swinburne. 6240-7
Farewell. John Addington Symonds. 6437-X,6513-9,6656-9
Farewell. Bert Leston Taylor. 6089-7
Farewell. James Maurice Thompson. 6632-1
Farewell. Katharine (Hinkson) Tynan. 6096-X,6374-8,6477-9,6653-4
Farewell. Sir Thomas Wyatt. 6317-9,6436-1,6150-8
A farewell ("Flow down, cold rivulet, to the sea"). Alfred Lord Tennyson. 6383-7,6110-9,6543-0,6737-9,6122-2,6597-X,6457-4,6123-0,6254-7
A farewell ("With all my will, but much against..."). Coventry Patmore. 6096-X,6204-0,6208-3,6317-9,6339-X,6508-2,6022-6
Farewell advice. Charles Kingsley. 6424-8
"Farewell all future hopes yt guide ye course." Unknown.

FAREWELL!

"'Farewell and adieu' was the burden...". At sea. Algernon Charles Swinburne. 6875-8
'Farewell and adieu'. Unknown. 6732-8
"Farewell Carjola!/I pray thee look thou giv'st..." John Webster. 6317-9
"Farewell awhile, my bonnie darling!". The test. Bayard Taylor. 6976-2
Farewell dance. Maye DeWeese Porter. 6906-1
"Farewell fair saint, may not the seas & wind". On his mistresse going to sea. Thomas Cary. 6933-9
Farewell frost, sels. Robert Herrick. 6558-9
"Farewell has long been said; I have". After a parting. Alice Meynell. 6955-X
A farewell hymn to the valley of Irwan. John Langhorne. 6251-4
Farewell in February. Sylvia Lynd. 6776-X
Farewell of a Virginia slave mother to her daughters sold. John Greenleaf Whittier. 6300-4,6126-5
The farewell of Arthur, fr. Guinevere, fr. The idylls.. Alfred Lord Tennyson. 6867-7
The farewell of Clarimonde. Ella Wheeler Wilcox. 6956-8
Farewell of the birds. H.K. P. 6743-3
Farewell peace. Unknown. 6946-0
"Farewell rewards and fairies". A proper new ballad, intituled The fairies faredwell.. Richard Corbet. 6933-9
A farewell song of white clouds. Li Po. 6253-9
The farewell song. Thomas Campion. 6794-8
"Farewell the reign of cruelty." Sir Thomas Wyatt. 6584-8
"Farewell the tea-board, with..gaudy equipage". A lady's adieu to her tea-table. Unknown. 6753-0
"F rewell Titan, Gorgon, Typhon". Monstrum horrendum. Edward Farquhar. 6939-8
A farewell to a fondling. Thomas Churchyard. 6182-6
A farewell to Abbotsford. Felicia Dorothea Hemans. 6973-8
A farewell to Agassiz. Oliver Wendell Holmes. 6753-0
"Farewell to a' our Scottish fame". Such a parcel of rogues in a nation. Unknown. 6859-6
Farewell to all beautiful places. Arthur MacGillivray. 6761-1
Farewell to all my greatness. William Shakespeare. 6102-8
A farewell to America. Richard Henry Wilde. 7017-5
Farewell to Anzac. Cicely Fox Smith. 7029-9
Farewell to Anzac. Cicely Fox Smith. 7031-0
Farewell to Anzac. Cicely Fox Smith. 7027-2
A farewell to arms. George Peele. 6187-7,6198-2,6186-9, 6339-X,6150-8,6153-2,6189-3,6301-2,6737-9
"Farewell to barn and stack and tree." Alfred Edward Housman. 6430-2
Farewell to brother Jonathan. Caroline (pseud.) 6753-0
Farewell to brother Jonathan. Unknown. 6589-9
"Farewell to cold winter, adieu to white frost". Unknown. 6059-5
Farewell to Cupid. Fulke Greville; 1st Baron Brooke. 6436-1
Farewell to earth. Lady Mary Wortley Montagu. 6152-4
"Farewell to fair Alba, high house of the sun". Deirdre's farewell to Alba. Unknown. 6930-4
"Farewell to Lochaber, farewell to the glen". 'Lochaber no more!' Neil Munro. 7027-2
A farewell to false love. Sir Walter Raleigh. 6182-6
A farewell to Far. Gerald Nugent. 6930-4
Farewell to Fiunary. Norman Macleod (the Elder) 6180-X
Farewell to fiunary. Norman Macleod. 6873-1
The farewell to folly, sels. Robert Greene. 6122-2
Farewell to France. Marie Stuart. 6227-X
Farewell to Glen-Shalloch. James Hogg. 6859-6
A farewell to Glenarbac. Arthur Henry Hallam. 6980-0
Farewell to Ireland. Colum-Cille (atr) 7039-6
Farewell to Italy ("I leave thee, beauteous Italy..."). Walter Savage Landor. 6624-0,6656-9,6110-9,6086-2
Farewell to Italy ("We lingered at Domo d'Ossola-"). Robert Underwood Johnson. 6624-0
A farewell to land. George Gordon, 6th Baron Byron. 6136-2
A farewell to London in the year 1715. Alexander Pope. 6733-6,6152-4
The farewell to love. Francis Beaumont and John Fletcher. 6641-0
Farewell to Mackenzie. Sir Walter Scott. 6543-0

Farewell to Malta. George Gordon, 6th Baron Byron. 6092-7, 6945-2
Farewell to mathematics. Frederick Victor Branford. 6884-7
Farewell to my lyre. Esaias Tegner. 6045-5
Farewell to Nancy. Robert Burns. 6024-2,6271-7,6219-9,6560-0,6094-3,6543
A farewell to Patrick Sarsfield. James Clarence Mangan. 6090-0
Farewell to place of comfort. J.B.B. Nichols. 6477-9
"Farewell to pleasant Dilston hall". Derwentwater's farewell. Unknown. 6859-6
"Farewell to Sliev Morna". Lay of the forlorn. George Darley. 6930-4
Farewell to poetry, fr. The deserted village. Oliver Goldsmith. 6932-0
A farewell to poetry. Thomas Warton (the Elder) 6962-2
A farewell to Pope. John R. Thompson. 6753-0
Farewell to school days. Minerva Birch. 6717-4
A farewell to Sir John Norris and Sir Francis Drake. George Peele. 6436-1
Farewell to summer. George Arnold. 6820-0
A farewell to the borderland. Thomas Pringle. 6960-6
"Farewell to the cot 'mong the whins...bracken". The crofter's farewell. Robert Bird. 7009-4
Farewell to the court. Sir Walter Raleigh. 6208-3,6436-1, 6584-8
The farewell to the dead, fr. Lays of many lands. Felicia Dorothea Hemans. 6973-8
Farewell to the dolls. Lida Wilson Turner. 6841-3
Farewell to the fairies. Richard Cobbett. 6385-3
Farewell to the fairies. Richard Corbet. 6114-1,6301-2, 6383-7,6134-6,6600-3
Farewell to the farm. Robert Louis Stevenson. 6132-X,6334-9,6808-1
"Farewell to the feast-day! the pray'r book...". Exit holiday. Morris Rosenfeld. 7011-6
Farewell to the glen. Dante Gabriel Rossetti. 6110-9
A farewell to the most famous generals..." George Peele. 6547-3
Farewell to the muse. George Gordon, 6th Baron Byron. 6945-2
Farewell to the muse. Sir Walter Scott. 6980-0
Farewell to the old year. Sarah Doudney. 6456-6
Farewell to the Pilgrims. Th. M. Bakke. 6818-9
Farewell to the tranquil mind, fr. Othello. William Shakespeare. 6934-7
Farewell to the world of Richard Bishop. Unknown. 6157-5
"Farewell to thee and to our dreams farewell". In a graveyard. Theodore Watts-Dunton. 7015-9,6785-9
"Farewell to thee, Araby's daughter." Thomas Moore. 6302-0, 6385-3,6219-9
A farewell to tobacco, sels. Charles Lamb. 6934-7
A farewell to tobacco. Charles Lamb. 6092-7,6219-9,6278-4, 6089-7;6200-8;6453-1;6302-0;6385-3;6732
Farewell to town, sels. Nicholas Breton. 6934-7
A farewell to town. Nicholas Breton. 6092-7
Farewell to Tuscany. John Addington Symonds. 6624-0
A farewell to Wales. Felicia Dorothea Hemans. 6973-8
A farewell to wives. Unknown. 6563-5
"Farewell to you then, once dearest". The last love. Edward Farquhar. 6939-8
"Farewell ungratefull traytor". Song ("Farewell ungratefull traytor"). John Dryden. 6933-9
"Farewell ungratefull traytor". John Dryden. 6562-7,6195-0
Farewell!. C.H. Van Housen. 6995-9
"Farewell - but not forever, hope replies". Epitaph to William Northcot. Charles Unwin. 6814-6
"Farewell! a long farewell, to all my greatness". Wolsey's farewell to his greatness, fr. King Henry VII. William Shakespeare. 6964-9
"Farewell! a long farewell, to all my", fr. Henry VIII. William Shakespeare. 6323-3
Farewell! Advent. James Ryman. 6881-2
"Farewell! all good wishes go with him to-day". Lines sung at the dinner given to Charles Kemble... J. Hamilton Reynolds. 6874-X
"Farewell! but whenever you welcome the hour". Thomas Moore. 6085-4,6198-2,6486-8,6102-8,6385-3,6430-2, 6219-9,6543-0,6424-8
"Farewell! endued will that could engage". Lines composed

FAREWELL!

for a memorial of Ashley Cowper, Esq. William Cowper. 6814-6
"'Farewell! Farewell, great heart!'". Farewell! C.H. Van Housen. 6995-9
Farewell! farewell!, fr. The pirate. Sir Walter Scott. 6180-X
"Farewell! for now a stormy morn and dark". Outward bound. Edward Sydney Tylee. 6946-0
"Farewell! if ever fondest prayer." George Gordon, 6th Baron Byron. 6302-0,6543 0,6737-9,6828-6
"Farewell! since never more". Epitaph. Thomas Kibble Hervey. 6600-3
"Farewell! the village leaning to the hill". On a troopship, 1915. Herbert Asquith. 7027-2
"Farewell! thou art too dear for my possessing". William Shakespeare. 6246-6,6302-0,6385-3,6182-6,6204-0
"Farewell! thou art too dear for my possessing". Sonnet 087 ("Farewell! thou art too dear"). William Shakespeare. 6052-8,6271-7,6328-4,6436-1,6250-4
"Farewell! thou glorious Tishbite seer". The ascension of Elijah. James Stephenson. 6848-0
"Farewell! we must part; we have turned...". Farewell to brother Jonathan. Caroline (pseud.). 6753-0
'Farewell'.. Unknown. 6260-1
"Farewell, adieu, that court-life life!". Song ("Farewell, adieu"), fr. Horestes. John Pickering. 6182-6
"Farewell, Aziz, it was not mine to fold you". Farewell. Laurence (Adele Florence Nicolson) Hope. 6856-1
"Farewell, adieu, that court-like life!". John Pickering. 6181-8
"Farewell, all my welfare!" Sir Thomas Wyatt. 6584-8
Farewell, dear love! Unknown. 6430-2
Farewell, dear love! Since thou wilt needs be gone. Unknown. 6182-6
"Farewell, dear love, since thou wilt needs". Song ("Farewell, dear love"). Unknown. 6436-1
"Farewell, dear scenes, for ever closed to me". Lines written on a window-shutter at Weston. William Cowper. 6814-6
"Farewell, fair Armida, my joy and my grief". John Dryden. 6970-3
"Farewell, false hearts! whose best affections". The valediction. William Cowper. 6814-6
Farewell, false love! John Fletcher. 6641-0
"Farewell, farewell to my mother's own...". The water peri's song. Thomas Hood. 6874-X
"Farewell, farewell! Her vans the vessel tries" Arthur Hugh Clough. 6828-6
Farewell, farewell, fond love. Unknown. 6328-4
"Farewell, farewell, my sweet Suzanne". Autumn song. Conrad Orton Milliken. 6936-3
Farewell, farewell, old year. Clinton Scollard. 6875-8
"Farewell, farewell, to my mother's...daughter". The water peri's song. Thomas Hood. 6802-2
Farewell, friend. William Roehrick. 6850-2
"Farewell, life!" Thomas Hood. 6302-0,6385-3,6199-0,6219-9
"Farewell, love, and all thy laws forever". Sonnet ("Farewell, love"). Sir Thomas Wyatt. 6584-8
"Farewell, Macready, since to-night we part". Sonnet to William Charles Macready. Alfred Lord Tennyson. 6977-0
Farewell, lovely Polly. Unknown. 6826-X
Farewell, Manchester. Arthur O'Shaughnessy. 6793-X
"Farewell, my more than fatherland!". A farewell to America. Richard Henry Wilde. 7017-5
"Farewell, my sweet, until I come". To Chloris. Charles Cotton. 6934-7
"Farewell, O dream of mine!". A farewell. Adelaide Anne Procter. 6957-6
"Farewell, now, Hope and Fortune...". Unknown. 6251-2
Farewell, o Patrick Sarsfield. Unknown. 6930-4
"Farewell, oh little son of mine!". Farewell. Gertrude Huntington McGiffert. 6838-3
Farewell, old year. Florence L Sidley. 6270-9
Farewell, rewards and fairies. Richard Corbet. 6092-7,6315-2
The farewell, sels. Robert Burns. 6472-8
"Farewell, sweet Boy, complain not of my truth" Fulke Greville; 1st Baron Brooke. 6380-2
Farewell, sweet Mary. Unknown. 6058-7

502

Farewell, this world. Unknown. 6881-2
"Farewell, thou child of my right hand, my joy". On his first sonne. Ben Jonson. 6933-9
Farewell, thou lovely wood. H. Hoffman Von Fallersleben. 6952-5
"Farewell, ungrateful traitor". Song ("Farewell, ungrateful traitor.") John Dryden. 6102-8,6301-2
Farewell, unkist. Sir Thomas Wyatt. 6315-2
"Farewell, whose like on earth I shallnot find". In memoriam: W.G. Ward. Alfred Lord Tennyson. 6867-7
"Farewell. My blessing with you:", fr. Hamlet. William Shakespeare. 6610-0
A farewell.. William Shakespeare. 6087-0
"Farewell/Shadows and scenes...". The farewell. Letitia Elizabeth ("L.E.L.") Landon. 6980-0
A farewell. George Arnold. 6066-8
A farewell. Matthew Arnold. 6947-9
A farewell. Robert Burns. 6075-7,6228-8,6246-6,6737-9
A farewell. George Gascoigne. 6315-0,6436-1
A farewell. Charles Kingsley. 6479-5,6737-9,6461-2,6656-9, 6304-7,6046-3,6102-8,6135-4,6219-9,6131-1,6658 ,6240-7,6670-4,6123-0,6239-3,6473-6,6429 ,6623-2,6242-3, 6249-0,6459-0,6732-8
A farewell. E.R.R. Linklater. 6269-5
A farewell. Harriet Monroe. 6102-8,6320-9,6019-6,6076-5, 6309-8
A farewell. Alexander Montgomerie. 6830-8
A farewell. Plato. 6850-2
A farewell. Adelaide Anne Procter. 6957-6
A farewell. George William ("A.E.") Russell. 6437-X
A farewell. Sir Philip Sidney. 6436-1,6586-4,6482-6,6436-4, 6584-8,6153
A farewell. Duchess of Sutherland. 6661-5
A farewell. William Wordsworth. 6232-6,6649-6
The farewell. Charles Churchill. 6152-4
The farewell. Felicia Dorothea Hemans. 6973-8
The farewell. Charles Fenno Hoffman. 6226-1
The farewell. Thomas Hood. 6974-6
The farewell. Winifred Virginia Jackson. 6762-X
The farewell. Letitia Elizabeth ("L.E.L.") Landon. 6980-0
The farewell. Sir Walter Scott. 6134-6
The farewell. Unknown. 6752-2
The farewell. Unknown. 6138-9,6680-1
The farewell. John Greenleaf Whittier. 6302-0,6365-9,6385-3
"Farewell? O no! it may not be". The resolution of Ruth. Unknown. 6752-2
"Farewell? Oh, no! It may not be". Ruth and Naomi. William Oliver Bourne Peabody. 6848-0
Farewells from paradise. Elizabeth Barrett Browning. 6437-X
"'Farewells!' O what a word!". Everlasting farewells. Alice Meynell. 6955-X

Farfone, Frances
Goose and the gander. 6750-6

Fargue, Leon Paul
Aeternae memoriae patris. Eugene Jolas (tr.). 6343-8
On the thread of the pale hour. W.J. Strachan (tr.). 6343-8

Farjeon, Eleanor
Argus. 6236-9
A carol for Christmas Eve. 6143-5
The carol singer. 6339-X
Child's carol. 6421-3
The chocolate bus. 6804-9
Circus. 6891-X
Coach. 6554-X
Country vegetables. 6466-3
The flower seller. 6466-3
For a cock. 6554-X
For a dewdrop. 6778-6
Friday Street. 6937-1
The gypsy. 6236-9
Heigh-ho, April!. 6554-X
Jessica dances. 6959-2
Kingcups. 6236-9
Light the lamps up, lamplighter! 6421-3
Marble Arch. 6937-1
Meeting Mary. 6421-3,6581-3
Nearly. 6249-0

The night will never stay. 6250-4
Now every child. 6143-5
The old man's toes. 6554-X
Our mother's tunes. 6891-X
Picking up sticks. 6466-3
Sailor. 6554-X
St. Valentine's way. 6339-X
Shall I to the byre go down. 6608-9
The shopman. 6466-3
Six green singers. 6216-4,6608-9,6143-5,6421-3
Song-birds for sale. 6943-6
Thanksgiving carol. 6143-5
When Hannibal crossed the alps. 6334-9
White horses. 6554-X
William I - 1066. 6107-9
The wind. 6639-9

Farley, Corinne
Soul-feeding hyacinths. 6144-3

Farley, Henry
The bounty of our age. 6563-5

Farm ballads, sels. Will Carleton. 6155-9
Farm boy. Alexander Mertes. 6750-6
Farm boy. Mary Sloane. 6761-1
Farm boy at school. Eleanor Alletta Chaffee. 6042-0
The farm boys' song. Emma Celia & Lizzie J. Rook. 6741-7
The farm drudge. Angela Morgan. 7038-8
The farm hand. Edgar A. Guest. 6862-6
"The farm lay along the slope of a mountain". The mountain farm. Walter Hard. 7030-2
The farm on the links. Rosamund Marriott ("Graham R. Tomson") Watson. 6437-X,6656-9
A farm picture. Walt Whitman. 6288-1
Farm woman. Bernice Carey Fitch. 6750-6
The farm, sels. Archibald MacLeish. 6581-3
Farm-circle. Frank Ernest Hill. 6038-2
"The farm-lad quarried from the mow". Going to court. Alice Cary. 6865-0;6969-X
Farm-yard song. John Townsend Trowbridge. 6127-3,6404-3, 6479-5,6104-4,6131-1,6456
The farm. Jane Taylor. 6018-8

Farmar, Constance
The actor. 6777-8

Farmer. Enoch C. Dow. 6662-3
"The farmer 'moves right up the line'.". Cutting corn in Vermont. Daniel L. Cady. 6988-6
Farmer and sailor. Plato. 6435-X
The farmer and the counsellor. Horace Smith. 6064-1
The farmer and the counsellor. Unknown. 6878-2
The farmer and the counsellor. Unknown. 6403-5
The farmer and the counsellor. Unknown. 6878-2,6787-5
Farmer and wheel; or, the new Lochinvar. Will Carleton. 6919-3
Farmer Ben's theory. Unknown. 6414-0
Farmer Brown. John Whitaker Watson. 6774-3
"The farmer came in from the field one day". The farmer's wife. Unknown. 6915-0
Farmer dying. Ben H. Smith. 6662-3
Farmer Gray. Unknown. 6294-6
"The farmer he hitched his hog to the plow". Unknown. 6059-5
"A farmer he lived in the west country". Folk song. Unknown. 6179-6
"The farmer hid in his cornfield". A robber of the night. Gladys Tracy Hornbeck. 6799-9
The farmer in deep thought. William Carlos Williams. 6070-6
Farmer John. John Townsend Trowbridge. 6014-5
Farmer John. Unknown. 6451-5
Farmer John's Thanksgiving. Isaac F. Eaton. 6618-6,6703-4
Farmer John's thanksgiving. Unknown. 6272-5
A farmer muses. Glenister Hoskins. 6662-3
Farmer Nick's scarecrow. Nora E. Crosby. 6314-4
The farmer of Westerha' James Logie ("Hugh Haliburton") Robertson. 6476-0
The farmer one hundred years ago. Benjamin Franklin Taylor. 6815-4
"The farmer ploughs into the ground". Seed. Herman Charles Bosman. 6788-3
A farmer remember Lincoln. Witter Bynner. 6102-8,6076-5
The farmer remembers the Somme Vance Palmer. 6349-7

The farmer sat in his easy chair. Charles Gamage Eastman. 6240-7,6632-1
Farmer Stebbins at football. Will Carleton. 6926-6
Farmer Stebbins at Ocean Grove. Will Carleton. 6917-7,6155-9
Farmer Stebbins on rollers. Will Carleton. 6416-7
"The farmer sat there milking Bess". The baby's footprint. Mary E. (Freeman) Wilkins. 6965-7
The farmer talks. Edgar A. Guest. 6862-6
"The farmer turns for home". Pastoral ("The farmer"). Muriel Lewis. 6349-7
A farmer went riding. Mother Goose. 6132-X
A farmer went to market. Paul Edmonds. 6937-1
"A farmer went trotting." Mother Goose. 6363-2,6452-3
Farmer Whipple - bachelor. James Whitcomb Riley. 6992-4
"A farmer went trotting". Bumpety bump. Unknown. 6937-1
Farmer's advice to the villagers, fr. Greenfield hill. Timothy Dwight. 6753-0
The farmer's blunder. William E. Miller. 6402-7
Farmer's borderland. Edward Farquhar. 6939-8
Farmer's boy. Unknown. 6339-X,6518-X,6003-X
The farmer's boy, sels. Robert Bloomfield. 6302-0,6385-3
The farmer's bride. Charlotte Mew. 6250-4,6506-6,6102-8, 6250-4
"The farmer's cradlers rock the field of wheat". The farmer one hundred years ago. Benjamin Franklin Taylor. 6815-4
The farmer's curst wife. Unknown. 6057-9,6061-7,6185-0
The farmer's daughter Cherry. Isabella Valancy Crawford. 6591-0,6592-2
The farmer's daughter. Alice Cary. 6969-X
"The farmer's goose, who in the stubble". The progress of poetry. Jonathan Swift. 6930-4
The farmer's gun. Andrew Young. 6339-X,6659-3
The farmer's ingle. Robert Fergusson. 6152-4
The farmer's invitation. William Barnes. 6747-6
"A farmer's lease contain'd a flaw". The pig in a poke. Unknown. 6787-5
The farmer's life. George P. Beard. 6571-6
A farmer's prayer. Roselle Mercier Montgomery. 6326-8
The farmer's round. Unknown. 6105-2
The farmer's song bird. George Horton. 6927-4
The farmer's song-friend. George Horton. 6680-1
The farmer's well. Unknown. 6929-0
Farmer's wife. Bianca Bradbury. 6979-7
The farmer's wife and the raven. John Gay. 6972-X
The farmer's wife. Lois Arnold Bolton. 6761-1
The farmer's wife. Berton Braley. 6853-7
The farmer's wife. Martha Ostenso. 6019-6
The farmer's wife. Unknown. 6915-0
A farmer's woman. John Reed. 6880-4
The farmer's year, sels. Hesiod. 6435-3

Farmer, Edward
Little Jim. 6772-7

Farmer, John
You pretty flowers. 6328-4

"Farmer, neighbor, friend, Walt". 'But, Walt, it may not hold' Joel Cox. 6860-X
The farmer. C.L. Edson. 6615-1
The farmer. Emma Celia & Lizzie J. Rook. 6137-0
The farmer. E. Merrill Root. 6880-4
The farmer. Unknown. 6744-1,6167-2
Farmers. Helene Mullins. 6782-4
Farmers. William Alexander Percy. 6303-9,6337-3,6730-1, 6034-X
Farmers. Unknown. 6427-2
The farmers outlaw weeds. Vincent Godfrey Burns. 6542-2
Farmers' teas in Vermont. Daniel L. Cady. 6989-4
'Farming it' in Vermont. Daniel L. Cady. 6988-6

Farnell-Bond, Genevieve
The faun. 6327-6

The Farnese Hercules. Sacheverell Sitwell. 6209-1

Farnham, Jessie
Dark blessing. 6750-6
Fragments ("The way"). 6750-6
Proposed pact. 6750-6

Farningham, Marianne
"And soon, when this life with its waiting is over". 6407-8
Consider the lilies. 6918-5

The joy of doing good. 6523-6
The last hymn. 6486-8,6569-4
The last hymn. 6914-2
Let us give thanks. 6449-3
The morning psalm. 6414-0
Thou knowest best. 6416-7
Farnol, Tom
Dunkirk, 1940. 6895-2
Farnum, C.G.
Let me live for a time way back from the road. 6482-5
Farolita. Mei-mei Berssenbrugge. 6790-5
Farquhar, Edward
Adam's choice. 6939-8
Another poem. 6939-8
The arbiter. 6939-8
At worst. 6939-8
The backlog. 6939-8
Balance. 6939-8
The beauty of the Unakas. 6939-8
Bethesda. 6939-8
Chatham, in seventy-eight. 6939-8
Christianity. 6939-8
Christianity in the apostles. 6939-8
Citadel. 6939-8
City of the dead. 6939-8
The cliff and the cataract. 6939-8
Clouds and dawn. 6939-8
Clouds and moon. 6939-8
The coming. 6939-8
Commencing monk. 6939-8
The confidant. 6939-8
Consecration. 6939-8
The cross. 6939-8
Diocletian. 6939-8
The director. 6939-8
Dog conscious. 6939-8
Eclipse. 6939-8
Egypt. 6939-8
Eros. 6939-8
Eupepsia. 6939-8
Exile and return. 6939-8
Exportulation. 6939-8
Farmer's borderland. 6939-8
Forward. 6939-8
The fulness of days. 6939-8
Grain life. 6939-8
Grasshopper's last word. 6939-8
The great and the greatest. 6939-8
Harbor. 6939-8
The haunting of Olaf. 6939-8
Her reclamation. 6939-8
Heredity. 6939-8
The home of Adalbert. 6939-8
Hope of the Moor. 6939-8
Jehanne. 6939-8
Job. 6939-8
Julian. 6939-8
Jungle. 6939-8
The last love. 6939-8
The latest nun. 6939-8
Leadership. 6939-8
Leaf and limb. 6939-8
Lesson of history. 6939-8
Libyssa. 6939-8
The lost love. 6939-8
Lover's walk. 6939-8
Mary. 6939-8
Master and slave. 6939-8
Mediterranean. 6939-8
Microcosm. 6939-8
Militant. 6939-8
Mission. 6939-8
Monstrum horrendum. 6939-8
Morning and afternoon. 6939-8
My faithful. 6939-8
Mystery of King Herod. 6939-8
Napoleon in regeneration. 6939-8
The oak of Saint Boniface. 6939-8
On the study table. 6939-8
Only a shadow. 6939-8
Painting. 6939-8
The passing of poesy. 6939-8
Pavilion. 6939-8
Pentholatry. 6939-8
Permanence. 6939-8
The pipe. 6939-8
Prospect from Gilboa. 6939-8
Pure to the pure. 6939-8
The radical. 6939-8
The rape of virtue. 6939-8
The real ghost. 6939-8
Regeneration. 6939-8
Saint Adelaide. 6939-8
Search for the world. 6939-8
Shadow market. 6939-8
Silver and gold. 6939-8
Spain's own story. 6939-8
Speech of angels. 6939-8
The spy. 6939-8
Success at last. 6939-8
A tale of loves. 6939-8
The tenant. 6939-8
Time and the minstrels. 6939-8
Tourist's guide. 6939-8
Transient and permanent. 6939-8
A truant. 6939-8
The unregarded. 6939-8
Urania. 6939-8
Wolfe. 6939-8
The wooing. 6939-8
Yesterday. 6939-8
Youth. 6939-8
Farquhar, George
Song ("How blest"). 6563-5
Farquhar, Hilda Shutts
The common little things. 6799-9
Farragut. William Tuckey Meredith. 6062-5,6243-1,6471-X, 6340-3,6641-0,6424
Farragut, David Glasscoe
Through fire in Mobile bay. 6074-9
Farrah, M.J.
The Dickens gallery. 6417-5
Farran, Don
Gold coin. 6039-0
Farrar, Canon
Who are the free? 6523-6
Farrar, John
Ancients of New England. 7030-2
Hymn to Lucifer. 7030-2
Squaw. 6778-6
Farrar, John Chipman
Alone. 6607-0
The ambitious mouse. 6466-3,6368-3
A barge wife. 6619-4
Brest left behind. 6051-X,6452-2
Bundles. 6466-3
Chanticleer. 6466-3
A comparison. 6421-3,6368-3
Epithalamion for Amaryllis. 6441-8
A hill-woman. 6619-4
A hillside farmer. 6607-0
Magic. 6300-4
Moral song. 6368-3
Parenthood. 6509-0
Prayer. 6465-5,6608-9
Prayer ("Last night"). 6746-8
Shops. 6466-3
Song for a forgotten shrine to Pan. 6102-8,6076-5
When Amaryllis bowls. 6441-8,6300-4
Wish. 6509-0
Farrar, Mary
Daddy's sentinel. 6715-8
Farrar, Rosemary
The cocks have crowed. 6761-1,6979-7
Leisure. 6761-1
Misfit. 6761-1
Rustic paradox. 6799-9
Twilight snow. 6761-1
"Farre have I clambred in my min". An hymne in honour of...charitie and humilitie. Henry More. 6933-9

Farrell (or George Washington Dixon), Robert
    Turkey in the straw. 6736-0
Farrell, Eleanor Knox
    Christ in Crete. 6761-1
Farren, Robert
    Immolation. 6930-4
    Joy's peak. 6282-2
    Mary ("Thou art God's sky"). 6282-2
    The mason. 6930-4
    To the bell-ringer. 6930-4
Farries, Mary
    Floodtime in Minnesota. 6342-X
Farrington, E.I.
    Mother knows. 6097-8
Farrington, Harry Webb
    The airmen's hymn. 6337-3
    As he walked with us. 6144-3
    Dear Lord, who sought at dawn. 6337-3
    Our Christ. 6065-X,6337-3,6532-5
Farrow, G.E.
    The converted cannibals. 6089-7
    The retired pork-butcher and the spook. 6089-7
Farrukhi
    The branding. E.G. Browne (tr.). 6448-5
Farther north. M. Travis Lane. 6767-0
Farther on. Lucy Larcom. 6129-X
Farther sight. Howard McKinley Corning. 6042-0
"The farthest country is Tierra del Fuego". Remote. Robert Hillyer. 6984-3
Fashion. Arthur Guiterman. 6441-8
Fashion. Horace Twiss. 6802-2
Fashion in Vermont. Daniel L. Cady. 6989-4
"The fashion is to sneer at them, to mock...". Old stuff. Berton Braley. 6853-7
"Fashion the feel of it". Fog horn at night. Helen Mitchel. 6750-6
Fashionable call. Blanche Elizabeth Wade. 6714-X
A fashionable lady. Clara Doty Bates. 6965-7
A fashionable novel. Thomas Haynes Bayly. 6874-X
"Fashioned of dreams and strung moonbeams". Vanity. Mary Lovell Cope. 6841-3
Fashions. Alfred Noyes. 6151-6
"The fashions change,for change is dear to men". Metaboah. Thomas Edward Brown. 6809-X
Fashions for fascists. Arthur Guiterman. 6761-1
"Fast by the Trent". Avaro, a tale. Thomas Warton (the Elder). 6962-2
"Fast from yon icile's inverted spire". Icicle drops. Arthur John Lockhart. 6795-6
"Fast in your heart, o rondeau rare". An acrostical valentine. Frank Dempster Sherman. 6770-0
The fast mail and the stage. John H. Yates. 6912-6
Fast or slow time. Sarah A. Athearn. 6764-6
"Fast-rooted, with no sound, no stir". Native forest. George Rostrevor Hamilton. 6781-6
"Fasten your souls so high, that constantly". Elizabeth Barrett Browning. 6238-5
Fastidious. Harriet B. Sterling. 6137-0
The fastidious serpent. Henry Johnstone. 6089-7,645-3
Fasting. Emily Pauline ("Tekahionwake") Johnson. 6837-5
"A fastinge supper call you this." Unknown. 6563-5
"The fasts are done; the Aves said". Easter morning. Edna Dean Proctor. 7041-8
Fat cattle in trucks near the Fairfield crane (Glasgow) George Dickson. 6778-6
"Fat green candle on a shelf alone". Bayberry candle. Muriel F. Hochdord. 6850-2
"The fat light clings upon my skin". The spider, fr. Metropolitan. Edith Sitwell. 7000-0
A fat man. Abel Evans. 6228-8
"Fat, pamper'd Porus, eating for renown". The glutton. Thomas Warton (the Elder). 6962-2
The fat-buttocked bushmen. Earnest A. Hooton. 6722-0
Fata morgana. Kathleen Raine. 6354-3
A fatal acquaintance. Unknown. 6058-7
The fatal arrow. Unknown. 6680-1
The fatal glass. Laura U. Case. 6912-6
Fatal interview, sels. Edna St. Vincent Millay. 6154-0
Fatal love. Matthew Prior. 6633-X
The fatal passion. Leigh Hunt. 6980-0

The fatal rose. Lillian Mack. 6799-9
The fatal sisters. Thomas Gray. 6052-8,6122-2,6154-0,6545-7,6152-4,6195 ,6430-2
The fatal snowstorm. Unknown. 6057-9
The fatal vision, fr. The two spirits. Percy Bysshe Shelley. 6545-7
The fatal wedding. Unknown. 6003-X
Fatalism, fr. The Rubaiyat. Omar Khayyam. 6337-3
Fate. Ethel M. Brainerd. 6906-1
Fate. Richard Burton. 6029-3
Fate. John White Chadwick. 6321-7
Fate. John Aylmer Dorgan. 6600-3
Fate. Ralph Waldo Emerson. 6006-4,6077-3,6176-1
Fate. Leslie Harrison. 6118-4
Fate. Francis Bret Harte. 6102-8,6414-0,6076-5,6212-1,6219-9,6424
Fate. Clara Keck Heflebower. 6906-1
Fate. Ibn Abdun. 6362-4
Fate. Francis Ledwidge. 6812-X
Fate. Harold Monro. 6776-X
Fate. Richard Kendall Munkittrick. 6083-8
Fate. Susan Marr Spalding. 6320-9,6481-7,6585-6,6107-9, 6309-8,6094-3,6255-5,6632-1,6681-X
Fate. Susan Marr Spaulding. 6889-8
Fate. Algernon Charles Swinburne. 6828-6
Fate. Unknown. 6271-7,6417-5
Fate. Unknown. 6273-3
Fate. Willoughby Weaving. 6184-2
Fate. J. P. Zimmerman. 6861-8
Fate ("A face of a summer ago"). Merle St. Croix Wright. 6429-9,6321-7
Fate ("All unconscious I beheld her"). John White Chadwick. 6429-9
Fate - graduation. Unknown. 6718-2
Fate and the younger generation. David Herbert Lawrence. 6722-0
Fate defied. Adelaide Crapsey. 6393-4
Fate knows no tears. Laurence (Adele Florence Nicolson) Hope. 6856-1
The fate of a broom: an anticipation. Thomas Love Peacock. 6874-X
The fate of a Cuban spy. James W. Stanistreet. 6249-0
The fate of Amy, sels. John Clare. 6934-7
The fate of beauty. George Gordon, 6th Baron Byron. 6980-0
Fate of Charles the Twelfth. Samuel Johnson. 6605-2
The fate of Charlie. Unknown. 6859-6
The fate of Charlotte Russe. Eleanor C. Donnelly. 6919-3
The fate of Jack Burgoyne. Unknown. 6946-0
The fate of John Burgoyne. Unknown. 6015-3,6121-4
The fate of King Dathi. Thomas Osborne Davis. 6930-4
The fate of MacGregor. James Hogg. 6344-6,6415-9
The fate of Mackay. Noah Little. 6695-X
The fate of Narcissus. William Warner. 6436-1
The fate of Nassan. Unknown. 6724-7
The fate of pious Dan. Sam Walter Foss. 6996-7
The fate of Sergeant Thin. Henry Glassford Bell. 6787-5
The fate of Sin Foo. Samuel Minturn Peck. 6745-X
The fate of the glorious devil. Unknown. 6724-7
The fate of the Hessian. Arthur Guiterman. 6773-5
The fate of the prophets, fr. The divine tragedy. Henry Wadsworth Longfellow. 6730-1
Fate of Virginia. Thomas Babington Macaulay, 1st Baron Macaulay. 6706-9,6304-7
The fate of Virginia. Unknown. 6606-2
"Fate wafts us from the pygmies' shore". Gods of war. George William ("A.E.") Russell. 7027-2
"Fate! fortune! chance! whose blindness". Death. Horace Smith. 6606-2
Fate's malignity. Ibn Wahbun. 6362-4
Fate, fr. Atalanta in Calydon. Algernon Charles Swinburne. 6110-9
"The fateful hour, when death stood by". The father. Bayard Taylor. 6976-2
"The fateful line of level light". The rune of the sea. Gertrude Huntington McGiffert. 6838-3
The fates. Stephen Spender. 6390-X,6645-3
Father. Clark Emery. 6761-1
Father. Trang Thai. 6883-9
Father. Unknown. 6715-8
Father ("Oh Father- if Thou wouldstindeed"). Arthur

FATHER

Davison Ficke. 6532-5
Father Abbey's will. John Seccomb. 6077-3,6176-1
Father Abraham Lincoln. Edward William Thomson. 6524-4
Father an child. Richard Watson Gilder. 7041-8
"A father and a son that ne'er before". On Romain beach. Douglas Mackintosh. 7016-7
"Father and I went down to camp". The Yankee's return from camp. Edward Bangs. 6946-0
Father and daughter. Jean Follain. 6758-1
The father and jupiter. John Gay. 6972-X
"Father and mother, many a year". The children. Harriet Eleanor Hamiliton (Baille) King. 6772-7
Father and son. Gudmundur Fridjonsson. 6854-5
Father and son. Frederick Robert Higgins. 6985-1
Father and son. Delmore Schwartz. 6389-6
Father and son. William Shakespeare. 6087-0
Father and son. Calvin Dill Wilson. 6443-4
Father at play. Hannah More Johnson. 6131-1
Father Christmas. Norman Gale. 6579-1
Father Christmas' message. J.A. Atkinson. 6147-8
Father Couture. Susan ("Seranus") Frances. 6797-2
Father Coyote. George Sterling. 6083-8,6121-4
Father Damien. John Banister Tabb. 6022-6,6292-X,6121-4, 6250-4,6172-9
"Father calls me William, sister calls me Will". Jest 'fore Christmas. Eugene Field. 6834-0;6949-5,6891-X, 6820-0
A father does his best. Elwyn Brooks White. 6722-0,6026-9
Father doesn't. Unknown. 6715-8
Father for theory, mother for action. Unknown. 6715-8
Father Francis. Walter Herries Pollock. 6656-9
Father Gerard Hopkins, S.J. Joyce Kilmer. 6483-3
Father Gilligan. William Butler Yeats. 6518-X
Father Goose. L. Frank Baum. 6274-1
Father Grumble. Unknown. 6058-7,6003-X
Father in heaven. William Ashbury. 6566-X
"Father in heaven! from whom..simplest flower". A prayer ("Father in heaven!..."). Felicia Dorothea Hemans. 6973-8
Father is coming. Mary Howitt. 6078-1,6127-3,6459-0,6131-1
Father John. Unknown. 6273-3
Father land and mother tongue. Samuel Lover. 6165-6,6302-0, 6385-3
A father lost, a husband won. William Shakespeare. 6094-3
Father Malloy. Edgar Lee Masters. 6897-9
Father Mapple's hymn, fr. Moby Dick. Herman Melville. 6176-1;6399-3,6399-3
Father Mapple's hymn, fr. Moby Dick. Herman Melville. 6833-2
Father Molloy. Samuel Lover. 6089-7
Father Molloy. Samuel Lover. 6825-1,6915-0
Father O'Flynn. Alfred Perceval Graves. 6174-5,6732-8,6808-1
Father O'Flynn. Unknown. 6090-0
Father O'Shea. Amelia Josephine Burr. 6032-3
Father of all. Unknown. 6715-8
"Father of all, my soul defent". Psalm XVI. Unknown. 6848-0
"Father of earth and heaven". A Thanksgiving hymn. Henry Ware Jr.. 6752-2
"Father of earth and heaven!". Battle hymn. Karl [or Charles] Theodore Korner. 6606-2
Father of heaven. Francesco Petrarch. 6214-8
"Father of heaven and earth". Evening song of the weary. Felicia Dorothea Hemans. 6973-8
"The Father of heaven his own son he sent". A new year, a new year, a child was yborn. Unknown. 6756-5
"'Father of lakes!' thy waters bend". Lake Superior. Samuel G. Goodrich. 6752-2
"Father of light! great God of heaven". The prayer of nature. George Gordon, 6th Baron Byron. 6213-8,6945-2
"Father of mercies, God of love". Psalm 051, stanzas suggested by. Bible. 6848-0
"Father of nations! Help of the feeble hand". Collect for Dominion Day. Sir Charles George Douglas Roberts. 6795-6
"Father of nations! Help of the feeble hand!". collect for Dominion day. Sir Charles George Douglas Roberts. 7041-8

Father of our country. Mrs. Madrid H. Smith. 6270-9
The father of the bride. Edgar A. Guest. 6748-4
The father of the forest. W. Watson. 6323-3
The father of the groom. Edgar A. Guest. 6748-4
Father of the man. Granville Paul Smith. 6761-1
A father of women. Alice Meynell. 6955-X
Father Paul. Mary Kyle Dallas. 6671-2
"The father of worlds took thought". To Addie. Louis J. Magee. 7004-3
The father reading the Bible. Felicia Dorothea Hemans. 6973-8
Father Roach. Samuel Lover. 6825-1,6914-2
"Father rockered by the fireplace". I remember homestead Sundays. Lola Beall Graham. 6857-X
"A father said unto his hopeful son". Pass. Eugene Fitch Ware. 7025-6
"A father sat by the chimney-post". Good and better. Unknown. 6915-0
"' Father sent me here a-courting". Unknown. 6059-5
A father speaks. Louis Untermeyer. 6875-8
"Father takes to the road and lets his hair down" Alan Chong Lau. 6790-5
Father to mother. Robert ("Droch") Bridges. 6006-4
Father William. Charles Lutwidge ("Lewis Carroll") Dodgson. 6132-X,6089-7,6479-5,6501-5,6440-X
Father William. Robert Southey. 6502-3
Father William. Unknown. 6089-7
Father William questioned, fr. Alice in Wonderland. Charles Lutwidge ("Lewis Carroll") Dodgson. 6523-6
"Father who art in heaven, pray". Not for bishops. Robert L. Wolf. 6880-4
"Father! guide me! day declines". The traveller's evening song. Felicia Dorothea Hemans. 6973-8
"Father! that in the olive shade". Hymn, by the sick-bed of a mother. Felicia Dorothea Hemans. 6973-8
"The father".. George F. Savage-Armstrong. 6656-9
'A father's advice'. Brian ("Korongo") Brooke. 6938-X
A father's advice. Brian ("Korongo") Brooke. 6650-X
A father's blessing. Richard Corbet. 6737-9
The father's choice. S.B. Parsons. 6417-5
The father's counsel. Ellen Murray. 6920-7
The father's curse. Victor Hugo. 6610-0
A father's dilemma. E. Pearl Dancey. 6750-6
A father's fury. William Shakespeare. 6102-8
"Father's in the woodshed". At the summer cottage. Edgar A. Guest. 6862-6
A father's job. Edgar A. Guest. 6869-3
Father's letter. Eugene Field. 6281-4
A father's prayer. Mouzon W. Brabbham. 6525-2
Father's problem. Edgar A. Guest. 6869-3
Father's story. Elizabeth Madox Roberts. 6891-X
Father's voice. Unknown. 6451-5
Father's way. Eugene Field. 6672-0
A father's wish. Edgar A. Guest. 7033-7
"Father, I cry to thee!". Battle prayer. Karl [or Charles] Theodore Korner. 6949-5
"Father, I know that all my life". Psalm 031:15. My times are in thy hand. Bible. 6848-0
"Father, I scarcely dare to pray". A last prayer. Helen Hunt Jackson. 7041-8
Father, into thy hands. Thomas B. Pollock. 6065-X
Father, lead on. Unknown. 6912-6
"Father, oh, my dear father". Father. Trang Thai. 6883-9
"Father, sitting on the side of your...bed". D-dawn -- June 6, 1944. Margaret McGarvey. 6839-1
Father, take my hand. Samuel Dowse Robbins. 6303-9
"Father, take my hand". Henry N. Cobb. 6409-4
Father, Thy will be done. Sarah Flower Adams. 6219-9
"Father, thy name is dear to me". My father. William White. 6868-5
"Father, thy word is past,man shall find grace". The atonement, fr. Paradise lost. John Milton. 6933-9
"Father, we come into thy presence singing". Baccalaureate hymn. Winifred H. Phillips. 6847-2
Father, we thank thee. Rebecca J. Weston. 6337-3
"Father, what can you want of me...mother...". Never blood. Tooni Gordi. 6799-9
"Father, what colour are God's eyes". God's eyes. George Herbert Clarke. 6797-2
Father, whate'er of earthly bliss. Anne Steele. 6303-9,

6304-7
Father, where do the wild swans go?. Ludvig Holstein. 6555-4
"Father, who travels the road so late?". The candidate. Unknown. 6928-2
Father, whose will is life and good. Hardwicke Drummond Rawnsley. 6337-3
"Father- to thee anew I consecrate". Sonnet. James Abraham Martling. 6952-5
"Father:/The way is hard, and I am torn..doubt". A tired prayer. Elsie Robinson. 6750-6
The father. Dorothy Scott Ballard. 6144-3
The father. Wilfred Wilson Gibson. 6393-4
The father. Richard Lattimore. 6388-8
The father. Muriel Stuart. 6884-7
The father. Bayard Taylor. 6976-2
Fatherhood. Henry Charles Beeching. 6477-9
Fatherland. Olive Tilford Dargan. 6031-5
Fatherland. Eloise Robinson. 6033-1
The fatherland. James Russell Lowell. 6087-0,6239-3,6337-3, 6386-1,6420-5,6465-5,6143-5
"Fathers and the mothers on..certain happy day". At the school exercises. Edgar A. Guest. 6869-3
The fathers of New England. Charles Sprague. 6678-X
The fathers. Kostes Palamas. 6352-7
Fathoming brains. Stockton Bates. 6923-1
"Fathoms deep beneath the wave". Mermaids and mermen. Sir Walter Scott. 6833-2
Fati valet hora benigni. Samuel Bishop. 6086-2
Fatigatus ex Itinere. Janet Erskine Stuart. 6096-X
Fatigue attacks the nerves, the brain. John Ransom Palmer. 6482-5
Fatigue call. Unknown. 6237-7
Fatigued. Hilaire Belloc. 6633-X
Fatima. Alfred Lord Tennyson. 6317-9,6378-0
Fatima and Raduan. William Cullen Bryant. 6302-0;6385-3
The fatted calf. Henry Duncan Chisholm. 6761-1
The fatties. Ann Menebroker. 6998-3
Fatum Supremum. Unknown. 6563-5
Fauconshawe. Adam Lindsay Gordon. 6951-7
Faulds, Lena E.
    The American flag. 6529-5,6684-4
Faulkner, Mrs. R.A.
    Frost on the window. 6433-7
Faulkner, Mrs. S.E. Sherwood
    Sunrise on the ocean. 6591-0,6592-2
Faulkner, Sanford C.
    The Arkansas traveler. 6465-5
Faulkner, William
    The lilacs. 6039-0
'Faultless'.. Mrs. Herrick Johnson. 6925-8
A faun in Wall Street. John Myers O'Hara. 6310-1,6250-4
A faun song. Edward H. Butler. 6983-5
A faun's song. Bliss Carman and Richard Hovey. 6890-1
The faun, sels. Richard Hovey. 6047-1,6252-0,6047-1
Faun-taken. Rose O'Neill. 6300-4
The faun. Genevieve Farnell-Bond. 6327-6
The faun. Richard Hovey. 6374-8
The faun. Thomas Sturge Moore. 6210-5
The faun. Ezra Pound. 6210-5
The faun. Sara King Wiley. 6253-9,6431-0
Fauntleroy. Benjamin F. Butler Jr. 6417-5
"Faunus! who lov'st the flying nymphs to chase". To Faunus, fr. Ode 018. Horace. 6973-8
"Faur oot i the sea-faem a wee bird keepit". Unknown. 6325-X
Fause Foodrage. Unknown. 6185-0
The fause knight upon the road. Unknown. 6185-0,6395-0
The fause lover. Unknown. 6098-6,6518-X
Fauset, Jessie Redmond
    Christmas eve in France. 6032-3
    Oriflamme. 6365-9
Faust in Iowa. Charles Brown Nelson. 6042-0
Faust, Frederick
    The secret. 6031-5
Faust, Henri
    Sonnets for lost divinities. 6039-0
    Voyagers. 6039-0
Faust, sels. Johann Wolfgang von Goethe. 6144-3
Faust, sels. Johann Wolfgang von Goethe. 6732-8

"Faustina hath the fairer face". Song ("Faustina hath the fairer face.") Unknown. 6436-1
"Faustina hath the fairer face". Unknown. 6181-8
Faustine. Algernon Charles Swinburne. 6655-0,6657-7
Faustus last speech on earth. Christopher Marlowe. 6686-0
Faustus to Helen. Christopher Marlowe. 6094-3
Faustus' dying soliloquy, fr. Faustus. Christopher Marlowe. 6934-7
Favete Linguis. Aline Kilmer. 6096 X
Favored. Phoebe Cary. 6969-X
A favoring wind. Unknown. 6983-5
The favorite.. Mildred Whitney Stillman. 6078-1
The favour. Henry Vaughan. 6935-5
Favourites. Ibn Abd Rabbihi. 6362-4
Fawcett's fame. Campbell Rae-Brown. 6681-X
Fawcett, Edgar
    Baby's dreams. 6632-1
    Bird of passage. 6240-7
    Chorus of Anglomaniacs. 6505-8
    Cleopatra. 6131-1
    A dead friend. 6632-1
    Decoration day. 7041-8
    The dying actor. 6410-8
    Fiat justitia. 7041-8
    Fireflies. 6102-8,6076-5,6309-8
    Gold. 7041-8
    Grass. 6049-8
    The house on the hill. 6370-5
    A humming bird. 6073-0
    The iceberg. 6358-6
    Imperfection. 7041-8
    Ivy. 7041-8
    March. 6965-7
    Master and slave. 7041-8
    The meeting. 7041-8
    The moon in the city. 7041-8
    The old beau. 6632-1
    The other side of the moon. 6358-6
    Pipes and beer. 6358-6,6453-1
    A prayer ("God bless"). 6078-1
    The punishment. 7041-8
    Roses. 6049-8
    The sorceress. 7041-8
    Still water. 7041-8
    A straggler. 7041-8
    The tears of Tulla. 6683-6
    To an oriole. 6073-0,6597-X,6300-4,6250-4,6309-8
    To an oriole. 7041-8
    To the evening star. 6431-0
    A toad. 6597-X,6632-1
    A white camellia. 6597-X
    Wild roses. 6632-1
    The young Samson. 6848-0
Fawcett, James Waldo
    Macabre. 6036-6
Fawcett, John
    Blest be the ties that bind. 6304-7
Fawkes, Francis
    The brown jug. 6385-3
    Dear Tom, this brown jug. 6328-4
Fawkes, Francis (tr.)
    When I drain the rosy bowl. Anacreon, 6328-4
Fawley, Alice
    Lines upon hearing a political convention... 6662-3
The fawn in the snow. William Rose Benet. 6011-0
A fawn's first snow. Glenn Ward Dresbach. 6396-9
The fawn.. Edna St. Vincent Millay. 6299-7
The fawn. Virginia Wilson Lachicotte. 7016-7
The fawn. Thomas Moore. 6134-6
Fawnia. Robert Greene. 6436-1,6189-3,6737-9
Faxton, E.
    Lighthouse May. 6571-6
Fay. Thomas Ashe. 6772-7
The fay's sentence, fr. The culprit fay. Joseph Rodman Drake. 6300-4
Fay, Anna Maria
    Rondel. 6770-0
Fay, Gerda
    The death of cock robin. 6249-0,6502-3
Fay, Julia Douglas

The battle of Bennington. 7030-2
Fealy, Nellie E.
  The waters of the lake. 6799-9
Fear. Samuel Butler. 6278-4
Fear. Hartley Coleridge. 6980-0
Fear. Kingsley Fairbridge. 6591-0,6592-9
Fear. Edgar A. Guest. 6869-3
Fear. Langdon Elwyn ("John Philip Varley") Mitchell. 6441-8
Fear. Edward Hersey Richards. 6178-8
Fear. Hollis Russell. 6397-7
Fear. Percy Bysshe Shelley. 6294-6
"**Fear** death?-to feel the fog in my throat". Prospice. Robert Browning. 6001-3,6123-0,6154-0,6208-3,6289-X, 6291 ,6328-4,6332-2,6337-3,6437-X,6473-6,6479 ,6501-5,6604-6,6655-0,6657-7,6730-1,6732 ,6102-8,6110-9, 6196-6,6199-0,6301-2,6737 ,6023-4,6214-8,6371-3,6560-0,6656-9,6660 ,6107-9,6212-5,6250-4,6430-2,6723-9, 6820 ,6001-3,6123-0,6154-0,6208-3,6289-X,6291 ,6328-4,6332-2,6337-3,6437-X,6473-6,6479 ,6501-5,6604-6, 6655-0,6657-7,6730-1,6732 ,6102-8,6110-9,6196-6,6199-0,6301-2,6737 ,6023-4,6214-8,6371-3,6560-0,6656-9, 6660 ,6107-9,6212-5,6250-4,6430-2,6723-9
"**Fear** no more the heat o' the sun". Dirge ("Fear no more"). William Shakespeare. 6179-6,6334-9,6604-6
"**Fear** no more the heat o' the sun", fr. Cymbeline. William Shakespeare. 6879-0
"**Fear** no more the heat o' the sun," fr. Cymbeline. William Shakespeare. 6491-4,6646-1,6189-3,6197-4,6125-7,6250 ,6194-X,6438-8,6023-4,6192-3,6052-8,6228-8,6641-0, 6154-0,6187-7,6726 ,6339-X,6302-0,6385-3,6328-4,6536-8,6645 ,6733-6,6395-0,6315-2,6122-2,6182-6,6334
"**Fear** no unlicensed entry". Sleep on. Sir William Schwenck Gilbert. 6996-7
Fear not. Gertrude Huntington McGiffert. 6838-3
"**Fear** not that my music seems". Secret treasure. Sara Teasdale. 6781-6
"**Fear** not, O maidens, shivering". The little ghost who died for love. Edith Sitwell. 7000-0
Fear not, O soul. Mary Eleanor Roberts. 6327-6
Fear not: for behold, I bring..good tidings, fr. St. Luke. Bible. 6747-6
The **fear** of Bo-talee. N. Scott Momaday. 7005-1
The **fear** of death confounds me. William Dunbar. 6881-2
The **fear** of death. John Dryden. 6315-2
The **fear** of death. Sir Edmund Gosse. 6250-4
The **fear** of death. John Keats. 6737-9
The **fear** of death. William Shakespeare. 6150-8,6543-0
The **fear** of madness. Lucretia Maria Davidson. 6752-2
Fear of the dark. Terri Jewell. 6899-5
Fear of the earth. Alex Comfort. 6379-9,6475-2
"The **fear** was on the cattle, for the gale..sea". Mulholland's contract. Rudyard Kipling. 6810-3
"**Fear** was within the tossing bark". Christ stilling the tempest. Felicia Dorothea Hemans. 6973-8
The **fear**, fr. Battle. Wilfred Wilson Gibson. 6897-9
A **fear**. Francis Ledwidge. 6812-X
The **fear**. Robert Frost. 6348-9,6506-6,6375-6
The **fear**. Andrew Young. 6246-6
Fearful death. Unknown. 6881-2
A **fearful** operation. R.W. Payne. 6260-1
"**Fearfully** and mournfully". Pysche borne by zephyrs to the island of pleasure. Felicia Dorothea Hemans. 6973-8
Fearing, Kenneth
  Aphrodite metropolis (1). 6751-4
  Confession overheard in the subway. 6666-6
  Continuous performanc. 6751-4
  Cultural notes. 6751-4
  Dirge. 6324-1,6375-6
  Minnie and Mrs. Hoyne. 6324-1
  Obituary. 6324-1
  Portrait II. 6399-3
  Portrait II ("The clear brown eyes..."). 6399-3
  Public life. 6751-4
  Requiem. 6641-0
  St. Agnes' eve. 6751-4
  Scheherezade. 6751-4
  These are the live. 6375-6
  They liked it. 6751-4
Fearing, Lillian Blanche
  What have I done? 6303-9
"**Fearless** fellow, thou sad soul". Song ("Fearless follow"). Unknown. 6563-5
"A **fearless** journeyer o'er the mountain-snow". Louise Schelper (1). Felicia Dorothea Hemans. 6973-8
Fearon, Paul
  Night piece to another Julia. 6120-6
  Serenade. 6120-6
Fears and scruples. Robert Browning. 6110-9
Fears in solitude. Samuel Taylor Coleridge. 6828-6
Fears in solitude, sels. Samuel Taylor Coleridge. 6527-9.6052-8,6369-1
Fearwell love and all thy lawes for ever. Sir Thomas Wyatt. 6491-4
Feast. Edna St. Vincent Millay. 6102-8,6102-8,6726-3,6076-5
The **feast** day. Amy McDonall. 6466-3
A **feast** during the plague. Alexander Pushkin. 6622-4
The **feast** in the wilderness. John Milton. 6634-8
"The **feast** is o'er! Now brimming wine". The knight's toast. Sir Walter Scott. 6365-9,6512-0,6614-3,6304-7, 6964-9
"The **feast** is spread through England". The lesson of the war, 1855. Adelaide Anne Procter. 6957-6
Feast o' St. Stephen. Ruth Sawyer. 6806-5
The **feast** of Dian, fr. Endymion. John Keats. 6086-2,6110-9
The **feast** of freedom. Victor Hugo. 6102-8
The **feast** of harvest. Edmund Clarence Stedman. 6618-6
A **feast** of lanterns. Yuan Mei. 6649-6
The **feast** of life. Letitia Elizabeth ("L.E.L.") Landon. 6980-0
The **feast** of lights. Emma Lazarus. 6214-8
The **feast** of lights. Morris Rosenfeld. 7011-6
The **feast** of Mondamin. Unknown. 6205-9
"A **feast** of moon and men and barking hounds". Georgia dusk. Jean Toomer. 6880-4
Feast of our lady, help of christians. Unknown. 6282-2
The **feast** of Padre Chala. Thomas Walsh. 6039-0
The **feast** of roses. Thomas Moore. 6679-8
The **feast** of Saint Brigid of Kildare. St. (atr.) Brigid. 6930-4
The **feast** of the dead. Charlotte Becker. 6274-1
The **feast** of the doll. Nora Archibald Smith. 6452-3
Feast of the epiphany. Marion Couthouy Smith. 6995-9
The **feast** of the Eucharist. William White. 6868-5
The **feast** of victory. Johann C. Friedrich von Schiller. 6842-1
Feast on wine or fast on water. Gilbert Keith Chesterton. 6026-9
"The **feast** prepared, the spelndor round". The Chinese dinner. Unknown. 6912-6
The **feast** time of the year. Dora Read Goodale. 6703-4
"A **feast** was spread in the baron's hall". The elden tree. Joanna Baillie. 6813-8
The **feast**. Raymond Kresensky. 6017-X
The **feast**. Henry Vaughan. 6271-7
Feasting, I watch. Richard Garnett. 6328-4
The **feather** litter of the cold, sels. Sacheverell Sitwell. 6106-0
"The **feather** whence the pen". Ecclesiastical sonnets, sels. William Wordsworth. 6867-7
"A **feather**, a fish and a flatiron". A weighty matter. Carolyn Wells. 6882-0
The **feather**. Vernon Watkins. 6210-5
Feathers. Phoebe Cary. 6060-9
Feathers. Olive Hopegood. 6349-7
Feathers. Walter Savage Landor. 6874-X
"The **feathers** in a fan". Man. Humbert Wolfe. 6779-4
"The **feathers** of the willow". Song ("The feathers of the willow"). Richard Watson Dixon. 6246-5,6315-2,6253-9
Featherstone's doom. Robert Stephen Hawker. 6656-9
"The **feathery** fern-trees make a screen". In the fern, fr. Australian transcripts. William ("Fiona Macleod") Sharp. 6768-9
Features of creatures, fr. Two gentlemen in bonds. John Crowe Ransom. 6011-0
Februarie, fr. The shepheardes calendar. Edmund Spenser. 6122-2
February. JamesBerry Bensel. 6456-6
February. Henry S. Cornwell. 6632-1

February. Paul Engle. 6761-1
February. Anna Neil Gilmore. 6820-0
February. Ann Louise Hayes. 6515-5
February. William Morris. 6657-7
February. Frank Dempster Sherman. 6466-3,6311-X
February. Francis Thompson. 6044-7
February. Karel Toman. 6886-3
February. Unknown. 6134-6,6248-2,6312-8,6466-3
February. Francis Brett Young. 6044-7,6558-9
"February - fortnights, two". February. Frank Dempster Sherman. 6466-3,6311-X
February 3, 1924. Katharine Lee Bates. 7001-9
February afternoon. Edward Thomas. 6357-8
February bathed in rain. Ann Hope. 6841-3
A February friend. Jean Graham. 6797-2
February in Rome. Sir Edmund Gosse. 7015-9
February in the Pyrenees, fr. Jonas Fisher. James Carnegie; Earl of Southesk. 6819-7
February letter to Jack Spicer. Helen Luster. 6792-1
February night. Wyn Griffith. 6360-8
February rain. Charles Turner Dazey. 6456-6
February speaks. Denis Aloysius McCarthy. 6478-7
February speaks. Unknown. 6158-3
February thaw. Kenneth Slade Alling. 6036-6
February twelfth. Mary F. Hepburn. 6466-3
February twilight. Virginia Lyne Tunstall. 6779-4
February twilight, fr. Berkshire notes. Sara Teasdale. 6778-6
February, 1896. Louis J. Magee. 7004-3
February, 1897. Louis J. Magee. 7004-3
February, 1898. Louis J. Magee. 7004-3
"February, tall and trim, straight of form...". February. Anna Neil Gilmore. 6820-0
The Feckenham men. John Drinkwater. 6236-9,6161-3,6639-9
The feckless dinner party. Walter De La Mare. 6210-5
Fecundi calices. Bacchylides. 6435-3
Fedele's song. Anthony Munday. 6436-1
The Federal Constitution. William Milns. 6946-0
The federal convention. Unknown. 6946-0
The federation of the world, fr. Locksley hall. Alfred Lord Tennyson. 6337-3,6465-5
Fee, Chester Anders
    Spirit. 6799-9
"Fee, faw, fum! bubble and squeak!". Holy-cross day. Robert Browning. 6848-0
"The feeble sea-birds, blinded in the storms". The stability of science. Oliver Wendell Holmes. 7014-0
"Feeble, shadowy, shallow?" Alfred Austin. 6997-5
Feed. Raymond Knister. 6021-8,6446-9
Feed my sheep. Unknown. 6916-9
Feed still thyself. Sir Walter Raleigh. 6380-2
Feedin' the stock. Holman F. Day. 6510-4
Feeding the fairies. Unknown. 6452-3
A feel in the Christmas air. James Whitcomb Riley. 6807-3
"The feel of it/a wailing baby". Heartbreak. Sheila Hertel. 6883-9
Feeling. Sir John Davies. 6584-8
Feeling big in Vermont. Daniel L. Cady. 6989-4
Feelings of the Tyrolese. William Wordsworth. 6543-0
Feeney, Leonard
    The altar boy. 6543-0
    And still. 6214-8
    Because of her who flowered..., fr. Song for a listener. 6282-2
    The deathbed. 6096 X
    Family portrait. 6282-2
    A fledgling robin. 6022-6,6292-X
    A gift of flowers. 6543-0
    The little flower. 6285-7
    The lonely crib. 6543-0
    Nails. 6543-0
    Noel. 6532-5
    Song for a listener, sels. 6282-2
    The way of the cross. 6543-0
    The welcome. 6543-0
Feeney, Thomas Butler
    The lonely man. 6761-1
Feet. Mary Carolyn Davies. 6031-5
"'Feet just like ice' say". By now. Ralph Salisbury. 7005-1

"The feet of dancers/Shine with laughter". They who dance. Marjorie Allen Seiffert. 6959-2
The feet of the young men. Rudyard Kipling. 6465-5,6236-9, 6427-2,6732-8
"Feet on the hills and heads in the sky". A springtime pilgrimage. Arthur Guiterman. 6773-5
Feigned courage. Charles and Mary Lamb. 6233-4;6239-3;6105-2
Feigned courage. Mary Lamb. 6772-7
The feilure of Adamnan. Unknown. 6090-0
Fein, Cheri
    Lullaby ("Night time"). 6822-7
Feineman, Betty Ann
    Reason dethroned. 6799-9
Feineman, Zenobia Crutcher
    Two generations. 6799-9
Feinstein, Martin
    In memoriam. 6531-7
Feist, Bertha E.
    The first game of the season. 6585-6
Feldman, Helen Consuelo
    I'd give my love. 6847-2
Felicia Hemans. Letitia Elizabeth ("L.E.L.") Landon. 6046-3
Felicity. Isaac Watts. 6931-2
'Felicity. Enquire within' William Ernest Henley. 6770-0
Feline anyway. Eden Phillpotts. 6102-8
The felire of Adamnan. Patrick Joseph McCall. 6090-0
Felise. Algernon Charles Swinburne. 6828-6
Felix Randal. Gerard Manley Hopkins. 6208-3,6246-6,6657-7, 6209-1,6375-6,6430
Fell from aloft. Brandon Thomas. 6661-5
The felled tree. Alice Cary. 6969-X
A feller's hat. Edgar A. Guest. 7033-7
"A fellow all his life lived hoarding gold". The miser. Edward Fitzgerald. 6996-7
"A fellow can't help hearing". Gossip. Edgar A. Guest. 6862-6
"A fellow in a market town". The razor seller. John ("Peter Pindar") Wolcott. 6909-6
The fellow in greasy jeans. Charles F. Lummis. 6686-0
"A fellow near Kentucky's clime". John Thompson's daughter. Phoebe Cary. 6089-7,6440-X,6964-9
"A fellow prisoner" Keiho Soga. 6981-9
A fellow slave. Morris Rosenfeld. 7011-6
The fellow that looks like me. Unknown. 6057-9
Fellow travelers. John Hancock. 6894-4
The fellow who can whistle. Sidney Warren Mase. 6583-X
Fellow who had done his best. Frank Lebby Stanton. 6211-3
Fellow who is game. Unknown. 6715-8
"fellow who lisped went to Merthyr". Limerick:"A fellow who lisped went to Merthyr". Unknown. 6811-1
A fellow's mother. Unknown. 6690-9
Fellow, Henry C.
    Paint me a picture. 6799-9
    A revealing prayer. 6799-9
Fellow-citizens. Verner von Heidenstam. 6045-5
"Fellow-women, I am hene to-night to discuss..". Priscilla Prim's views on woman's rights. Unknown. 6920-7
"Fellows in arms! whose bliss, whose...good". Cato's address to his troops in Lybia, fr. Pharsalia. Lucan. 6932-0
Fellows, Marguerite
    Troubadour's song. 6118-4
Fellowship. Michael (Katherine Bradley & Edith Cooper) Field. 6096-X
Fellowship. Edith Harriet Jones. 6799-9
Fellowship. Elinor Lennen. 6144-3
The fellowship of books. Edgar A. Guest. 7033-7
The fellowship of prayer. Nancy Byrd Turner. 6065-X
Fellowship with all. Walter Rauschenbusch. 6954-1
The fellowship. Katharine Lee Bates. 6006-4
Fells, Sir Patrick
    Bloom, beauteous blossoms. 6724-7
Felltham, Owen
    The sympathy. 6317-9,6563-5
    Upon a rare voice. 6563-5
    "When, dearest, I but think on thee". 6933-9,6562-7, 6563-5
Felo-de-se. James Elroy Flecker. 6872-3

FELONS

The felons. John T. Campion. 6858-8
Fels, Ethel Emily
    The candle. 6906-1
    On looking at your picture. 6906-1
    Redbud. 6906-1
    To Gertrude. 6906-1
    To M.L.A. 6906-1
    Your eyes. 6906-1
Felshin, Simon
    Karl Radek. 6880-4
    My mother. 6506-6
Felstiner, John (tr.)
    "Goddam the empty sky" Violeta Parra, 7036-1
Felton, Henry
    In ancient Greece. 6934-7
Felton, Mary
    Two baby feet. 6078-1
Female characters of scripture: sonnets, sels. Felicia Dorothea Hemans. 6973-8
The female convict. Letitia Elizabeth ("L.E.L.") Landon. 6302-0;6385-3
Female glory. Richard Lovelace. 6369-1
The female god. Isaac Rosenberg. 6210-5
The female husband, who had been married... Unknown. 6157-5
The female martyr. John Greenleaf Whittier. 6285-7
The female of the species. Rudyard Kipling. 6083-8,6427-2, 6655-6
The female Phaeton. Matthew Prior. 6092-7
Female rain. Laura Tohe. 7005-1
Female tenderness. Douglas Jerrold. 6279-2
The female warrior. Unknown. 6058-7
Feminine. Henry Cuyler Bunner. 6441-8,6735-2
Feminine arithmetic. Charles G. ("Miles O'Reilly") Halpine. 6089-7,6441-8,6652-8,6505-8,6278-4,6004
Feminine resistance. Unknown. 6983-5
Feminine signs. Edgar A. Guest. 6748-4
The feminine touch. Edgar A. Guest. 6748-4
Femme et chatte. Paul Verlaine. 7039-6
Femme fatale. Vincent Starrett. 6218-0
A fence or an ambulance. Joseph Malins. 6963-0
A fence. Carl Sandburg. 6289-X
Fendt, Gene
    Bennington lake. 6857-X
Fenelon's Prayer. Virginia B. Harrison. 6578-3
The Fenian men. Michael Scanlan. 6858-8,7009-4
The Fenian song. Unknown. 6057-9
Fenians all. Brian O'Riordan. 6767-0
Fenisong, Ruth
    Religion. 6818-9
Fenner, Cornelius George
    Gulf-weed. 6271-7,6302-0,6385-3,6219-9
Fenner, Edward
    Signs of rain. 6724-7
Fenollosa, Mary McNeil
    The birth of the flowers. 6338-1
    Eastern cry. 7038-8
    Flying fish. 6431-0
    The great bronze buddha at Kamakura. 7038-8
    Iris flowers. 6338-1
    The juggler. 7038-8
    The mischievous morning glory. 6510-4
    The proud vegetables. 6232-6,6338-1,6338-1
    The seed. 6510-4
Fenstermaker, Vesle
    Almost. 6857-X
Fenton, Cora D.
    The call. 6374-8
Fenton, Elijah
    Olivia. 6023-4
    To a lady. 6932-0
Fentress, John W.
    Abraham Lincoln. 6178-8
    Booker T. Washington. 6178-8
Fenwick, Frances de Wolfe
    One girl and three views. 6702-6
"Fer forty year and better you have been...". To my old friend, William Leachman. James Whitcomb Riley. 6892-8
Ferd Herold blues. Unknown. 6609-7

Ferdinando and Elvira. Sir William Schwenck Gilbert. 6089-7,6501-5
Ferdinando and Elvira, or the gentle pieman. Sir William Schwenck Gilbert. 6902-9
Ferguson's cat. Unknown. 6385-3,6523-6
Ferguson, Dugald
    The upper darling. 6591-0,6592-9
Ferguson, Elizabeth Graeme
    The country parson. 6004-8
Ferguson, James
    Auld daddy darkness. 6132-X,6466-3,6519-8,6627-5,6690-9, 6368
Ferguson, John
    A broken-down actor. 6269-5
    The circus clown. 6269-5
    A cock crowing in a poulterer's shop. 6269-5
    From a sanatorium. 6269-5
    The optimist. 6506-6
Ferguson, Marion Lockwood
    The last frontiersman. 7019-1
Ferguson, Sir Samuel
    The burial of King Cormac. 6244-X,6639-9
    Cashel of Munster. 6437-X
    Cean dubh deelish. 6437-X,6383-7
    The Coolum. 6090-0
    The fair hills of Ireland. 6437-X,6439-6,6383-7
    The fairy thorn. 6090-0,6518-X,6244-X,6613-5,6153-2, 6656
    The forging of the anchor. 6917-7
    The forging of the anchor. 6302-0,6385-3,6183-4,6271-7, 6600-3,6438 ,6219-9,6639-0,6543-0
    The giant walker. 6090-0
    Lament for the death of Thomas Davis. 6930-4
    Lament for Thomas Davis. 6090-0,6244-X
    The lapful of nuts. 6668-2
    The legend of Fergus Leideson. 6090-0
    Molly Asthore. 6873-1
    Pastheen Finn. 6090-0,6174-5
    The pretty girl of Loch Dan. 6302-0,6385-3,6174-5,6302-9
    The washer of the ford. 6090-0
    The Welshman of Tirawley. 6437-X
    Westminster Abbey. 6793-X
Ferguson, Sir Samuel (tr.)
    Boatman's hymn. Andrew Magrath, 6930-4
    Cashel of Munster. William English, 6930-4
    Cashel of munster. Unknown, 6244-X
    the coolun. Maurice O'Dugan, 6930-4
    The cup of O'Hara. Turlough Carolan, 6930-4
    Dear dark head. Unknown, 6244-X
    Deirdre's farewell to Alba. Unknown, 6930-4
    Deirdre's lament for the sons of Usnach. Unknown, 6244-X
    The downfall of the Gael. Fearflatha O'Gnive, 6930-4, 7039-6
    Drimin dubh. Unknown (Irish), 6858-8
    The fair hills of Ireland. Unknown, 6244-X
    The fair-haired girl. Unknown, 6930-4
    Lament for Corc and Niall of the nine hostages. Torna (atr.), 6930-4
    The lapful of nuts. Unknown, 6244-X
    O'Byrne's bard to the clans of Wicklow. Unknown (Irish), 6858-8
    Song of the boatman (duan an bhadora). Unknown (Irish), 6858-8
    The story of Macha, fr. 'Dinnshenchas' Unknown, 6930-4
    Youghall harbor. Unknown, 6930-4
Ferguson, William P.F.
    We miss him so! 6995-9
Fergusson, Elizabeth
    The heart. 6541-4
Fergusson, Robert
    Braid claith. 6180-X,6086-2,6195-0,6152-4,6383-7
    Caller water, sels. 6198-2,6086-2
    The daft days. 6198-2,6086-2,6195-0,6152-4
    Elegy on the death of Scots music. 6086-2
    The farmer's ingle. 6152-4
    The lea rig. 6960-6
    Leith races. 6086-2
    Ode to the gowdspink. 6086-,6195-0

The sitting of the session. 6086-2
To the tron-kirk bell. 6086-2
Fergusson, W.
A mother's gift-the Bible. 6097-8
Feri dead. Frances Cornford. 7014-0
Fericano, Paul
The after. 6901-0
Borderline. 6901-0
Collage of us in May windows. 6901-0
San Francisco pier poems. 6901-0
Upstairs in c ward. 6998-3
Fericano, Paul F.
Clockwork. 6792-1
Katherine. 6792-1
Ferishtah's fancies, sels. Robert Browning. 6110-9
Ferlinghetti, Lawrence
The general song of humanity. 6792-1, 6998-3
Political poem. 6803-0
Fermoy. See Pigott, John Edward
The **fern** and the moss. Eliza Cook. 6927-4
The **fern** called: 'the grasshopper's grandma'. Vachel Lindsay. 6206-7
Fern hill. Dylan Thomas. 6208-3,6246-6,6357-8,6528-7
"**Fern** seed, hemp seed, water of the well". Hallowe'en charm. Arthur Guiterman. 6773-5
Fern song. John Banister Tabb. 6136-2,6519-8,6421-3
Fern, Fanny
Romance at home. 6742-5
Fern-seed. Celia Thaxter. 6612-7
Fernald, C.A.
A rose to a friend. 'Every year'. 6260-1
Fernandez, Raymond Ringo
Cell-rap #27 6870-7
For Mulatto. 6870-7
"Lies and gossip" 6870-7
Poem for the conguero in d-yard. 6870-7
Real deal revelation. 6870-7
"**Fernando**, King of Aragon, before Granada lies". The death vow of Don Alonzo of Aguilar. Unknown (Spanish). 6757-3
Ferns and pharisees. Alfred Noyes. 6169-9
The **ferns** and the flakes. Emma E. Browne. 6965-7
"The **ferns** love the mountains". Quatrain. C.G. Thompson. 7016-7
Fero, Gracia L.
Sharing his cross. 6065-X
Feroza. Laurence (Adele Florence Nicolson) Hope. 6856-1
Ferrer, Jose Miguel
Nocturne of sin and its accusation. Richard O'Connell (tr.). 6759-X
Ferriar, John
The bibliomania. 6297-0
Ferrier, Susan
The laird o'cockpen (additional stanzas) 6760-3
Ferril, Thomas Hornsby
The arrow of acestes. 7019-1
Basic communication. 6388-8
Calico, cantle, scythe and snath, fr. Inner song... 6751-4
Ghost town. 6490-6
Harper's Ferry floating away. 6761-1
Inner song while watching a song dance, sels. 6751-4
January. 6836-7
Judging from the tracks. 6836-7
Kochia. 6388-8
Lincoln Memorial. 6781-6
Lost ships. 6833-2
The man who thought he was a horse. 6388-8
Nothing is long ago. 6761-1
Portraits. 6836-7
Postscript to a song. 6836-7
A rhyme of prejudice. 6836-7
Second lullaby. 6836-7
This foreman. 6531-7
What trinkets?. 6388-8
Winter lake. 6836-7
Ferris, G.T.
Chickamauga. 6340-3,6741-X
Ferris, Haviland
For C.P. Cavafy. 7003-5

Ferris, Jessie Storrs
Spirit bridal. 6274-1
Ferriter, Pierce
He charges her to lay aside her weapons. Earl of Longford (tr.). 6930-4
The **ferry** boat and the passenger. Yong-woon Han. 6775-1
The **ferry** for Shadowtown. Unknown. 6929-0
The **ferry** for Shadowtown. Unknown. 6373-X
Ferry Hinksey. Laurence Binyon. 6138-9
Ferry me across the water. Christina Georgina Rossetti. 6125-7
The **ferry** of Gallaway. Alice Cary. 6969-X
A **ferry** tale. Charles Edward Carryl. 6724-7
The **ferry** to nowhere. Charles Edward Carryl. 6732-8
Ferry, David
The antagonist. 6388-8
On the way to the island. 6388-8
Out of that sea. 6388-8
Poem about walking. 6388-8
The unawkward singers. 6388-8
The **ferry.** George Henry Boker. 6431-0
The **ferry.** Johann Ludwig Uhland. 6842-1
"**Ferryman** that rowest the barge...". Zonas. 6251-2
The **ferryman.** Unknown. 6610-0
Fertiault, F.
A domestic event. Andrew Lang (tr.). 6297-0
A traitor. Andrew Lang (tr.). 6297-0
Fertile dawn. Ellen M. Carroll. 7016-7
Fertility. James Maurice Thompson. 6243-1
Fertility rite. Robert Davis. 6855-3
"The **fervid** breath of our flushed southern May". Evening on the Potomac. Richard Hovey. 7006-X
Fessenden, Thomas Green
Description of a New England country dance. 7030-2
Eulogy on the times. 7030-2
Ye sons of Columbia. 6946-0
Fessenden, Thomas W.
Mother. 6365-9
My mother. 6097-8
To mother. 6337-3
The **festal** hour. Felicia Dorothea Hemans. 6973-8
Festal song. William Pierson Merrill. 6730-1
Feste's songs, fr. Twelfth night. William Shakespeare. 6436-1,6026-9,6150-8
A **festial** response. Unknown. 6490-6
Festina lente. Robert J. Burdette. 6588-0
Festival. Louise Louis. 6799-9
The **festival** of the year. Edith Willis Linn. 6268-7
The **festival.** Frederic Prokosch. 6389-6,6666-6
The **festive-time..** Unknown. 6272-5
Festus describes his friend, fr. Festus. Philip James Bailey. 6980-0
Festus, sels. Philip James Bailey. 6198-2,6225-3,6238-5, 6337-3,6317-9,6693 ,6656-9
Fet, Afanasi
"All, all that once was mine is mine for ever" Oliver Elton (tr.). 6103-6
"For long I stood motionless, watching" Vivian de Sola Pinto (tr.). 6103-6
Never. Cecil Maurice Bowra (tr.). 6103-6
The prisoner. Cecil Maurice Bowra (tr.). 6103-6
"Storm in the skies in the evening" Oliver Elton (tr.). 6103-6
Swallows. 6103-6
To the stars that have gone out. Oliver Elton (tr.). 6103-6
"What an evening! Streamlets run" Cecil Maurice Bowra (tr.). 6103-6
"Whispering. A timid sigh" R.W. Hewitt (tr.). 6103-6
"**Fetch** the candles! Make a light!". All Souls night. F.L. Montgomery. 6850-2
Fetching water from the well. Unknown. 6302-0,6344-6,6385-3,6413-2
Fete. S. Foster Damon. 6037-4
The **fete** champetre. Sir John Betjeman. 6733-6
Fetter, George Griffith
Mother. 6097-8,6260-1
Fetzer, Herman
The coming of the sons of god. 7007-8
Feud. Lew Sarett. 6619-4,6039-0

FEUD:

The **feud**: a ballad. Adam Lindsay Gordon. 6951-7
The **feud**. Frederick George Scott. 6115-X,6450-2
Feuerlicht, Ethel M.
    Discovery. 6847-2
    Kirman weaves the first prayer-rug. 6847-2
    Living waters. 6847-2
'**Feuerzauber**'.. Louis Untermeyer. 6556-2,6250-4
Fever. Klabund. 6160-5
The **fever** in my blood has died. George Henry Boker. 6288-1
"The **fever's** hue hath left thy cheek, beloved". The painter's last work. Felicia Dorothea Hemans. 6973-8
A **fever**. John Donne. 6369-1
"A **few** clouds float across the grand blue sky". Horse-bathing parade. W. Kersley Holmes. 7027-2
"**Few** in joy's sweet riot/Able are to listen". Triolet ("Few"). George Macdonald. 6770-0
"**Few** know of life's beginnings - men behold". Success alone seen. Letitia Elizabeth ("L.E.L.") Landon. 6980-0
A **few** left. Berton Braley. 6853-7
A **few** lines from a hard-workin' man to his dear old un. Louis J. Magee. 7004-3
A **few** lines on completing forty-seven, fr. Domestic... Thomas Hood. 6974-6
A **few** lines on completing forty-seven. Thomas Hood. 6633-X
"A **few** more years, and the will drag my bones". Brooding. Jan Svatopluk Machar. 6886-3
A **few** old proverbs. Unknown. 6049-8
"**Few** roads and far to grey Glencar". Glencar. Stephen Lucius Gwynn. 6872-3
"A **few** sdeps, a few sdeps". The charge of de 'Dutch brigade'. Charles M. Connolly. 6155-9,6791-3
"A **few** short rolling years have fled". Cantata, sels. John Howell. 6768-9
A **few** stray sunbeams. Eliza Sproat Turner. 6131-1
Few there be. Unknown (Greek) 6435-3
"**Few** to good-breeding make a just pretence". The modern maid, fr. Characters of women. Edward Young. 6932-0
"The **few** to whom the law hath given the earth.". A coming cry. Ebenezer Jones. 7009-4
Few wholly faithful. Unknown. 6065-X
"**Few** years have passed since thou and I". To a youthful friend. George Gordon, 6th Baron Byron. 6945-2
"A **few** years since, at some provincial college". Retaliation. Unknown. 6787-5
Few, Marguerite
    A song of service. 6461-2
"**Few**, few were they whose swords of old", sels. William Cullen Bryant. 66601-1
Fewell, Curry
    This I regret. 6750-6
Fey. Walter De La Mare. 6905-3
Fey Joan. Alfred Noyes. 6169-9
Fey, Harold E.
    To a revolutionist. 6144-3
Fey, fr. The Battle of Otterbourne. Unknown. 6427-2
Feyman's fate. Hjalmar Jonsson. 6854-5
Fezandie, Hector
    The cannibal and the skeleton. 6361-6
"**Ffaine** I would but O i dare not." Unknown. 6563-5
"**Ffaire** and scornefull doe thy worst." Unknown. 6563-5
"**Ffaire** eyes regard my loue soe truelie tryed." Unknown. 6563-5
"**Ffaire** will you then that I shall dye." Unknown. 6563-5
"**Ffarewell** deere infante sucke ffrom my pensive brest" Unknown. 6563-5
Ffeiffer, Emily
    Evolution. 7015-9
    To nature (II). 7015-9
    To nature (III). 7015-9
Ffrench, Yvonne
    The Amazons. 6782-4
    Underworld. 6782-4
Fi-fi in bed. Robert Service. 6159-1
Fiametta, sels. Agnes Mary F. ("Madame Duclaux") Robinson. 6770-0
Fiammetta. Dante Gabriel Rossetti. 6655-0
The **Fian** banners. Unknown. 6873-1
Fiat justitia. Edgar Fawcett. 7041-8
Fiat lux. Lloyd Mifflin. 6310-1,6467-1

Ficke, Arthur Davison
    Absolution. 6217-2
    Among shadows. 6897-9
    And if he die? 6879-0
    Attic. 6880-4
    Beauty in exile, sels. 6320-9
    Come forth! For spring is singing in the boughs. 6619-4
    "Come forth." 6581-3
    the dancer. 6959-2
    Don Quixote. 6250-4
    Epitaph for the poet. 6076-5
    Epitaph for the poet, sels. 6102-8,6076-5
    Father ("Oh Father- if Thou wouldst indeed"). 6532-5
    Five serenades, sels. 6069-2
    The granite heart. 6761-1
    Harvard Phi Beta Kappa poem, fr. Nocturne in a library. 6051-X
    The headland. 6031-5
    Her hands. 6037-4
    I am in love with high far-seeing places. 6509-0,6556-2, 6431-0,6393-4
    "I am in love with high far-seeing places", fr.Sonnets. 6897-9
    I am weary of being bitter. 6374-8,6509-0,6723-9
    I renounce the dream. 6879-0
    Immortals in exile. 6467-1
    In this hour. 6761-1
    Kisa-gotami. 6327-6
    Like him whose spirit. 6897-9
    Long and lovely. 6979-7
    Marcia. 6037-4
    Meeting. 6897-9
    My love and I. 6118-4
    Nocturne in a library, sels. 6051-X
    Not till the temples of our secret trust. 6347-0
    November dusk. 6648-8
    November night. 6253-9
    The oracle. 6431-0
    Poet accepting a laurel wreath. 6817-0
    Portrait of a stranger. 6037-4
    Portrait of an old woman. 6076-5,6501-5,6102-8,6076-5, 6102-8
    Rain in the desert, fr. Arizona poems. 6897-9
    The revolt of uncle Peter. 6761-1
    Rue des Vents, sels. 6648-8
    Ruth. 6037-4
    The secret. 6042-0
    Serenade at noonday. 6037-4,6069-2
    Sonnet ("In the fair picture.") 6250-4
    Sonnet ("This is the burden"). 6347-0,6250-4
    Sonnet 049: Tumultuous shore. 6532-5
    Sonnet, fr. Beauty in exile. 6320-9
    Sonnets of a portrait painter. 6506-6
    Sonnets of a portrait painter, sels. 6897-9
    Sonnets of a portrait-painter, sels. 6300-4
    "There are strange shadows fostered of the moon". 6897-9
    "There are strange shadows fostered of the moon" 6393-4
    There stretch between us wonder-woven bonds. 6619-4
    This day is all a greyness of dim rain. 6347-0
    Three sisters. 6556-2,6581-3,6300-4
    To a child - twenty years hence. 6347-0
    To an old friend. 6300-4
    To the harpies. 6431-0
    View from the heights. 6347-0
    The waterfall. 6648-8
    What if some lover in a far-off spring. 6619-4
    Winter day. 6253-9
    The yard in December. 6118-4
Ficken, Dorothy
    Nonsense rhymes. 6130-3
"**Fickle** custom! Nothing stays!". The spinning wheel. Felix Carmen. 7021-3
The **fickle** day. Phoebe Cary. 6865-0;6969-X
The **fickle** m b, fr. Coriolanus. Wilbiam Shakespeare. 6302-0
"**Fickle** of choice is memory". St Andrews. Walter De La Mare. 6905-3
Ficklen, Edward B.
    Winter song for the foolish heart. 6017-X

Fickleness. Harry Kemp. 6441-8
A **fiction** how Cupid made a nymph wound herself... A. W. 6191-5
The **fiddle** and the bow. Humbert Wolfe. 6393-4
Fiddle, faddle, feedle. Unknown. 6937-1
"**Fiddle-de-dee**, fiddle-de-dee". Unknown. 6904-5
Fiddle-dee-dee. Eugene Field. 6486-8
"**Fiddle-heads** of ferns, first violin or bass". Prelude, fr. Program notes. Sarah A. Athearn. 6764-6
Fiddler Jones. Edgar Lee Masters. 6628-3
The **fiddler** of Berlin. Hermann Hagedorn. 6542-2
The **fiddler** of Dooney. William Butler Yeats. 6044-7,6331-4, 6477-9,6423-X,6437-X,6509
The **fiddler's** farewell. Alfred Noyes. 6151-6
A **fiddler**. Walter De La Mare. 6905-3
The **fiddler**. A.W. Bellaw. 6675-5
The **fiddler**. Edna Valentine Trapnell. 7007-8
"The **fiddlers** were scraping so cheerily, O". The Christmas ball. Mary E. (Freeman) Wilkins. 6965-7
The **fiddlers**. Walter De La Mare. 6596-1
The **fiddling** lad. Adelaide Crapsey. 6374-8
Fidele's dirge. William Collins. 6102-8,6383-7,6301-2
Fidele's dirge, fr. Cymbeline. William Shakespeare. 6436-1, 6150-8
Fidele's grassy tomb. Sir Henry Newbolt. 6255-5
Fidele, fr. Cymbeline. William Shakespeare. 6075-7,6099-4, 6102-8,6186-9,6246-6,6732 ,6332-2,6560-0
Fidelis. Adelaide Anne Procter. 6226-1
Fidelis [pseud].
   Dominion Day. 6795-6
   An Indian summer carol. 6795-6
Fidelity. Ibn Zaidun. 6362-4
Fidelity. Thomas Lodge. 6436-1
Fidelity. William Wordsworth. 6438-8,6510-4,6133-8,6271-7, 6369-1,6457-4,6579-5
Fides. Emma Playter Seabury. 6836-7
Fides amantis. Robert Buchanan. 6819-7
Fides probata coronat. William White. 6868-5
Fidessa, sels. Bartholomew Griffin. 6378-0
Fidler, Eva
   My song. 6847-2
"**Fie!** moping still by the sleepy brook?". Pussy willow and the south wind. Emily A. Braddock. 6965-7
"**Fie**, fie on blind fancy!" Robert Greene. 6181-8,6182-6
Fie, pleasure, fie! George Gascoigne. 6182-6
"**Fie**, satire, fie!...," fr. The scourge of villainy. John Marston. 6198-2
Field ambulance in retreat. May Sinclair. 6474-4,6542-2
Field burial. Carroll Carstairs. 6818-9
Field flowers. Thomas Campbell. 6543-0
Field flowers. Unknown. 6373-X
"The **field** is filled with fragrance". Song ("The field is filled"). Willoughby Weaving. 6506-6
Field left fallow. Ben Belitt. 6640-2
Field lilies. Unknown. 6304-7
The **field** lillies. L.C. Whiton Stone. 6529-5
Field magic. Dorothy Dow. 6039-0
The **field** marshal. Ernst Moritz Arndt. 6952-5
The **field** mouse. William ("Fiona Macleod") Sharp. 6236-9, 6421-3
The **field** of Gilboa. William Knox. 6848-0
The **field** of glory. Edwin Arlington Robinson. 6027-7,6619-4
"A **field** of golden wheat there grows". Harvest song. Richard Dehmel. 7039-6
Field of honor. Sara Henderson Hay. 6750-6
The **field** of Talavera. Thomas Hardy. 6323-3
"A **field** of spacious buttercups I spy". The buttercups. Francis H. Deter. 6906-1
The **field** of the grounded arms. Fitz-Greene Halleck. 6753-0
The **field** of the world. James Montgomery. 6980-0
The **field** of Waterloo. George Gordon, 6th Baron Byron. 6294-6,6402-7
The **field** of Waterloo. Sir Walter Scott. 6188-5
Field plowing. William Roehrick. 6850-2
'**Field** preaching'. Phoebe Cary. 6969-X,6600-3
Field sports. Alexander Pope. 6932-0
The **field** sweet-brier. Alice Cary. 6969-X
Fieldwireless. Benjamin Albert Botkin. 6397-7

The **field's** retention. Jose Y. Teran Jr. 6870-7
Field, A.N.
   The challenge of the guns. 7026-4
Field, Anne P.L.
   At singing time. 6097-8
   The Christmas fires. 6145-1
   A Christmas insurrection. 6145-1
   Maternity ("Within the crib that stands..."). 6097-8, 6627-5
   The night after Christmas. 6145-1
   On a seventeenth birthday. 6097-8
   When the stars of morning sang. 6145-1
Field, Annie P.L.
   A prayer at Bethlehem. 6145-1
Field, Arthur Gordon
   Perpetual Christmas. 6463-9
Field, Ben
   Chinese slippers. 6316-0
   Old gloves. 6316-0
Field, Charles K.
   A California Easter mass. 6241-5
   The years. 6241-5
Field, Charles Kellogg
   The prof.'s little girl. 6117-6
Field, Edward
   Stars in my eyes. 6803-0
Field, Elliot
   Vinco. 6144-3
Field, Eugene
   Abu Midran. 6949-5
   After reading Trollope's History of Florence. 6949-5
   Ailsie, my bairn. 6949-5
   The akhoond of swat. 6949-5
   Always right. 6949-5
   Apple-pie and cheese. 6004-8,6307-1
   The April fool. 6949-5
   The Armenian mother. 6949-5
   Ashes on the slide. 6949-5
   At Cheyenne. 6949-5
   At play. 6949-5
   At the door. 6772-7
   At the door. 6834-0;6949-5
   Bachelor hall. 6949-5
   A ballad of ancient oaths. 6949-5
   Ballad of the jelly-cake. 6949-5
   The ballad of the Taylor pup. 6949-5
   Ballad of women I love. 6949-5
   Ballade of women I love. 6875-8
   Balow, my bonnie. 6949-5
   Bambino (Corsican lullaby). 6949-5
   Barbara. 6949-5
   A battle in Yellowstone Park. 6949-5
   Be my sweetheart. 6949-5
   Beard and baby. 6078-1,6318-7
   The bell-flower tree. 6949-5
   The bells of Notre Dame. 6949-5
   Ben Apfelgarten. 6949-5
   The bench-legged fyce. 6949-5
   Bethlehem town. 6949-5
   Bethlehem-town. 6007-2
   Yhe bibliomaniac's bride. 6949-5
   The bibliomaniac's prayer. 6735-2
   Big Thursday. 6949-5
   Bill's tenor and my bass. 6085-4
   Boccaccio. 6949-5
   The Boltons, 22. 6949-5
   'Booh!' 6078-1,6318-7
   The bottle and the bird. 6949-5
   The bottle tree. 6318-7
   The bow-leg boy. 6949-5
   The boy. 6949-5,6902-9
   The broken ring. 6949-5
   A brook song. 6273-3
   The brook. 6949-5
   The bugaboo. 6949-5
   Buttercup, poppy, forget-me-not. 6684-4
   The Cafe Molineau. 6949-5
   Carlsbad. 6949-5
   Casey's tabble dote. 6694-1
   Chicago weather. 6949-5

FIELD

Child and mother. 6834-0;6949-5,6891-X
Child and mother. 6097-8,6365-9,6627-5,6682-8,6368-3, 6576
Christmas. 6949-5
Christmas eve. 6242-3,6147-8
Christmas hymn. 6147-8
Christmas morning. 6949-5
Christmas treasures. 6273-3,6670-4,6608-9,6747-6
A Christmas wish. 6368-3
Chrystmasse of olde. 6949-5
Clare market. 6949-5
The clink of the ice. 6949-5
Cobbler and stork. 6834-0;6949-5
Cold consolation. 6949-5
The collector's discontent. 6949-5
Contentment. 6114-1
The convalescent gripster. 6949-5
The conversazzhyony. 6949-5
Coquetry. 6949-5
Corinthian Hall. 6949-5
Cradle song. 6949-5
Croodlin' doo. 6949-5
Crumpets and tea. 6949-5
The cunnin' little thing. 6949-5
The cutting of the cake, fr. The white house ballads. 6949-5
De Amicitiis. 6274-1
The dead babe. 6318-7
The dead babe. 6949-5
Dear old London. 6735-2
The death of Robin Hood. 6949-5
The debutante. 6949-5
Dedication, fr. Second book of verse. 6949-5
The delectable ballad of the waller lot. 6318-7
Dibdin's ghost. 6735-2,6431-0
The dinkey-bird. 6089-7,6732-8,6265-2,6318-7,6467-1
The discreet collector. 6949-5
The dismal dole of the doodledoo. 6949-5
The divine lullaby. 6949-5
Doctor Rabelais. 6949-5
Dr. Sam. 6949-5
Doctors. 6949-5
The doings of Delsarte. 6949-5
The doll's wooing. 6949-5
A dream of springtime. 6949-5
Dream, dream, dream! 6949-5
The dream-ship. 6692-5,6579-1
The dreams. 6949-5
A drinking song. 6949-5
The drum. 6318-7
The duel. 6135-4,6318-7,6368-3,6735-2,6479-5,6497-3, 6401-9,6692-2,6104
Dutch lullaby. 6089-7,6105-2,6373-X,6166-4,6456-6
A Dutch lullaby. 7041-8
Ed. 6949-5
An elfin summons. 6949-5
The explorer's wooing. 6949-5
Extinct monsters. 6949-5
Fairy and child. 6421-3
A fairy lullaby. 6949-5
Fanchon the cricket. 6949-5
Father's letter. 6281-4
Father's way. 6672-0
Fiddle-dee-dee. 6486-8
The fire-hangbird's nest. 6949-5
Fisherman Jim's kids. 6949-5
The fisherman's feast. 6949-5
The 5th of July. 6949-5
The fly-away horse. 6949-5
The fool. 6949-5
For the charming Miss I.F.'s album. 6949-5
The French must go. 6949-5
From the Rubaiyat of Omar Khayyam. 6949-5
From the same canteen. 6949-5
Ganderfeather's gift. 6834-0;6949-5
Garden and cradle. 6318-7
'Gee swee Zamericane'. 6949-5
Gettin' on. 6949-5
Gettysburg. 6949-5
Goggly-goo. 6318-7

Gold and love for dearie (Cornish lullaby). 6834-0;6949-5
Good children street. 6318-7
A good man's sorror. 6949-5
'Good-by - and God bless you!' 6949-5
Gosling stew. 6949-5
Grandma's bombazine. 6949-5
Grandma's prayer. 6735-2
The grandsire. 6949-5
Grant. 6949-5
The great journalist in Spain. 6949-5
'Guess'. 6949-5
The happy household. 6078-1
The happy household. 6318-7
The happy household. 6949-5
The Hawthorn children. 6949-5
Heigho, my dearie (Orkney lullaby). 6949-5
Her fairy feet. 6949-5
Hi-spy. 6785-9,6834-0;6949-5
A hint for 1884. 6949-5
His lordship, the chief justice. 6949-5
Holly and ivy. 6147-8
Horace I. 6026-9
Horace to Pyrrha. 6307-1
How Flaherty kept the bridge. 6949-5
How Salty win out. 6949-5
Human nature. 6949-5
Humanity. 6949-5
The humming top. 6835-9,6949-5
Hushaby, sweet my own. 6834-0;6949-5
A hushaby. 6949-5
Hymn" midnight hour. 6949-5
Ill requited. 6949-5
An imitation of Dr. Watts. 6949-5
In Amsterdam. 6735-2
In Flanders. 6949-5
In Holland. 6949-5
In New Orleans. 6949-5
In praise of pie. 6949-5
In praise of truth and simplicity in song. 6949-5
In the firelight. 6949-5
In the firelight. 6273-3,6303-9
The Indian and the trout. 6949-5
Inscription for my little son's silver plate. 6452-3
Inter-mintry. 6834-0;6949-5
An invitation to sleep. 6949-5
Ipswich. 6949-5
The Jaffa and Jerusalem railway. 6949-5
Japanese lullaby. 6373-X,6529-5,6627-5,6683-6,6421-3, 6456
Jennie. 6949-5
Jessie. 6949-5
Jest 'fore Christmas. 6834-0;6949-5,6891-X,6820-0
Jest 'fore Christmas. 6534-1,6486-8,6356-X,6739-5,6318-7,6608
Jewish lullaby. 6949-5,6848-0
John Smith. 6949-5
King Grover craves pie, fr. The white house ballads. 6949-5
The kissing of the bride, fr. The white house ballads. 6949-5
Kissing time. 6318-7
Krinken. 6479-5,6104-4
Lady button-eyes. 6949-5
Lament of a neglected boss. 6949-5
A leap-year episode. 6652-6
A leap-year lament. 6949-5
The limitations of youth. 6949-5
Little all-aloney. 6949-5
Little blue pigeon. 6639-9
Little Boy Blue. 6006-4,6101-X,6102-8,6242-3,6303-9, 6365 ,6653-4,6723-9,6288-1,6309-8,6304-7,6464 ,6401-9,6486-8,6501-5,6509-0,6512-0,6534 ,6161-3,6431-0, 6104-4,6076-5,6632-1,6732
Little Homer's slate. 6834-0;6949-5
Little Mack. 6949-5
Little Miss Bragg. 6834-0;6949-5
Little Miss Dandy. 6949-5
Little Mistress Sans-Merci. 6949-5
The little peach. 6273-3,6735-2,6089-7,6732-8

A little woman. 6451-5
Little-of-dear. 6949-5
Little-oh-dear. 6835-9
Lizzie. 6949-5
Long ago. 6004-8
Longings. 6949-5
Lover's lane, Saint Jo. 6441-8
Lullaby ("Fair is"). 7041-8
A lullaby ("The stars are twinkling..."). 6949-5
Lydia Dick. 6735-2
Lydia Dick. 6949-5
Lyman, Frederick, and Jim. 6949-5
The Lyttel boy. 6300-4
Madge: ye hoyden. 6949-5
Make-believe land. 6368-3
The man with the hoe. 6077-3
Marcus Varro. 6949-5
Marsh song - sunrise. 6247-4
Marthy's younkit. 6686-0
Mary Smith. 6949-5
Mediaeval eventide song. 6949-5
Mein faeder bed. 6949-5
The modern martyr. 6949-5
Modjesky as cameel. 6949-5
Morning song. 6949-5
Mother and child. 6949-5
Mother and I. 6114-1
Mr. Billings of Louisville. 6949-5
Mr. Dana, of the New York Sun. 6949-5
Mr. Holman's farewell. 6949-5
Mrs. Reilly's peaches. 6949-5
My garden. 6949-5
My mother's faith. 6365-9
My playmates. 6949-5
My Sabine farm. 6949-5
Mysterious doings. 6887-1,6949-5
The mystery of Pasadene. 6949-5
The naughty doll. 6529-5
Nellie. 6949-5
The new tenor. 6698-4
New-Year's eve. 6949-5
The night wind. 6497-3,6691-7,6318-7,6456-6
Nightfall in Dordrecht. 6331-4,6484-1,6519-8,6431-0, 6439-6,6631
Nightfall in Dordrecht. 6834-0;6949-5
A nightmare. 6949-5
Norse lullaby. 7041-8
Norse lullaby. 6373-X,6456-6
Norse lullaby. 6891-X
November. 6949-5
Now I lay me down to sleep. 6312-8
O'Connor's iloquint spache. 6949-5
Of blessed memory. 6949-5
The official explanation. 6949-5
Oglesby (1884). 6949-5
Oh, little child (Sicilian lullaby). 6949-5
An Ohio ditty. 6949-5
An Ohio idyl. 6949-5
'The old homestead'. 6949-5
The old sexton. 6949-5
Old times, old friends, old love. 6004-8
One day I got a missive. 6949-5
The onion tart. 6949-5
Our biggest fish. 6834-0;6949-5
Our flag. 6835-9
Our lady of the mine. 6949-5
Our two opinions. 7041-8
Our two opinions. 6429-9,6085-4,6732-8,6467-1,6281-4, 6161-3,6321 ,6429-9
Our whippings. 6949-5
Over the hills and far away. 6949-5
An overworked word. 6949-5
Pan liveth. 6949-5
A paraphrase. 6652-6
Parlez-vous Francais? 6949-5
The partridge. 6949-5
Passing of the compliment, fr. The white house ballads. 6949-5
A patriot's triumph. 6949-5
The peace of Christmas-time. 6949-5

The peter-bird. 6949-5
A piazza tragedy. 6724-7
Picnic-time. 6318-7
Picnic-time. 6949-5
Pike's Peak. 6949-5
A piteous plaint. 6949-5
Pittypat and tipptoe. 6834-0;6949-5
Plaint of the Missouri 'coon..Berlin Zoological Gardens. 6949-5
A play on words. 6722-0
A plea for the classics. 6949-5
The pneumogastric nerve. 6949-5
A poem in three cantos. 6949-5
Poet and king. 6949-5
The poet's return. 6949-5
The political Maud. 6949-5
The preference declared. 6735-2
The Princess Ming. 6949-5
Prof. Vere de Blaw. 6949-5
A proper trewe idyll of Camelot. 6949-5
Providence and the dog. 6949-5
'Puritan' - 'Genesta'. 6949-5
Rare roast beef. 6949-5
Red. 6949-5
The red, red west. 6949-5
The remorseful cakes. 6629-1
The ride to bumpville. 6835-9
The ride to Bumpville. 6949-5
The rock-a-by lady. 6421-3,6456-6,6097-8,6466-3,6242-3, 6534-1,6707-7,6318
Romance of a 'cuss-word'. 6949-5
A romance. 6273-3
The rose and the iceberg. 6949-5
Sag Harbor. 6949-5
The 'St. Jo Gazette'. 6949-5
St. Martin's Lane. 6949-5
A scherzo. 6949-5
The schnellest zug. 6949-5
The secret of the sphinx. 6949-5
Seein' things. 6254-7,6696-8,6739-5
A Shoshone legend. 6949-5
Shuffle-shoon and amber-locks. 6834-0;6949-5
The shut-eye train. 6835-9,6834-0;6949-5
Singing in God's acre. 6686-0
Sister Rose's suspicions, fr. The white house ballads. 6949-5
Sister's cake. 6744-1
The sleeping child. 6949-5
The snakes. 6949-5
So, so, rock-a-by so! 6318-7
Soldier, maiden, and flower. 6949-5
Soldiers with Brutus. 6719-0
Some time. 6429-9,6097-8,6321-7,6429-9
Song ("Why do bells"). 6466-3,6216-4
Song ("Why do the bells..."). 6949-5
Song for the departed. 6949-5
The song of Luddy-dud. 6318-7
Song of the all-wool shirt. 6949-5
A song of the Christmas wind. 6949-5
Song of the clouds. 6949-5
The song of the mugwump. 6949-5
Spelling reform. 6724-7
Spirit Lake. 6949-5
Spring blew open the door. 6887-1
Star of the east. 6216-4,6465-5
The Stoddards. 6834-0;6949-5
The stork. 6078-1,6318-7
Stoves and sunshine. 6887-1
Stoves and sunshine. 6949-5
The straw hat. 6949-5
The straw parlor. 6949-5
The sugar plum tree. 6249-0,6466-3,6097-8,6135-4,6368-3
Suppose. 6949-5
The susceptible widow. 6949-5
Swing high and swing low. 6949-5
The tea gown. 6632-1,6735-2,6652-6
Teeny-weeny. 6949-5
Telka. 6949-5
Telling the bees. 6949-5
That sugar-plum tree. 6576-7

FIELD

Thirty-nine. 6004-8
Thomas A. Hendricks's appeal. 6949-5
Three days in springtime. 6949-5
The three kings of Cologne. 6614-3,6608-9
The three kings. 6239-3
The three tailors. 6949-5
The three-cent stamp. 6949-5
The tin bank. 6949-5
To a little brook. 6949-5
To a sleeping baby's eyes. 6949-5
To a soubrette. 6949-5
To a usurper. 6834-0;6949-5
To Denman Thompson. 6949-5
To Emma Abbott. 6949-5
To Mary Field French. 6949-5
To mistress Pyrrha. 6441-8,6652-6
To my mother ("How fair you are..."). 6097-8
To Pyrrha. 6733-6
To Robin Goodfellow. 6949-5
To the Lady Julia. 6949-5
To the passing saint. 6949-5
To Ward H. Lamon, asleep on his library floor. 6949-5
The truth about Horace. 6949-5
The truth about Horace. 6089-7,6289-X,6732-8,6307-1, 6505-8
Twin idols. 6949-5
The two coffins. 6949-5
Two little skeezucks. 6772-7
The two little skeezucks. 6949-5
The two little skeezucks. 6891-X
Two opinions. 6682-8,6576-7
Two valentines. 6949-5
The tying of the tie, fr. The white house ballads. 6949-5
Uncle Eph. 6949-5
A valentine to my wife. 6949-5
A valentine. 6465-5
A very weary actor. 6949-5
The vineyard. 6949-5
The violet's love story. 6949-5
A Virgilian picnic. 6949-5
The wanderer ("Upon a mountain height..."). 6273-3
The wanderer. 6639-9
A war-song. 6949-5
The wedding-day, fr. The white house ballads. 6949-5
A western boy's lament. 6949-5
When I was a boy. 6578-3
When Stedman comes to town. 6949-5
The white house ballads, sels. 6949-5
Why do bells of Christmas ring? 6519-8
The wind. 6949-5
Winfreda. 6949-5
With Brutus in St. Jo. 6949-5
With trumpet and drum. 6772-7,6835-9
With two spoons for two spoons. 6949-5
The wooing of the southland (Alaskan ballad). 6949-5
Wynken, Blynken, and Nod. 6464-7,6639-9,6638-0,6653-4, 6454-X,6006-4,6627-5,6466-3,6501-5,6078-1,6102 ,6132-X,6134-6,6242-3,6479-5,6486-8,6519 ,6732-8,6135-4, 6300-4,6309-8,6114-1,6076
'Yours fraternally'. 6949-5
Yvytot. 6949-5
A zephyr from Zululand. 6949-5

Field, Eugene (tr.)
Battle prayer. Karl [or Charles] Theodore Korner, 6949-5
Broken fiddle. Pierre Jean de Beranger, 6949-5
Catullus to Lesbia. Catullus, 6949-5
Chapel. Johann Ludwig Uhland, 6949-5
Child at play. Victor Hugo, 6949-5
Consistency. Horace, 6949-5
Der mann im Keller. Unknown (German), 6949-5
An ecologue. Vergil, 6949-5
Epilogue. Horace, 6949-5
Fame vs. riches. Horace, 6949-5
Flower to butterfly. Victor Hugo, 6949-5
The happy isles. Horace, 6949-5
Hymn ("O heart of mine..."). Martin Luther, 6949-5
Idyl (1). Bion, 6949-5
Idyl (2). Bion, 6949-5
In praise of contentment. Horace, 6949-5
In the springtime (1). Horace, 6949-5
An invitation to Maecenas. Horace, 6949-5
Let us have peace. Horace, 6949-5
Lost Cupid. Moschus, 6949-5
Love song. Heinrich Heine, 6949-5
Lyric intermezzo. Heinrich Heine, 6949-5
The lyric muse. Horace, 6949-5
Ma vocation. Pierre Jean de Beranger, 6949-5
Mother and sphinx. Unknown (Egyptian), 6949-5
My last song perhaps. Pierre Jean de Beranger, 6949-5
An ode to fortune. Horace, 6949-5
Old Spanish song. Unknown (Spanish), 6949-5
The poet's metamorphosis. Horace, 6949-5
Pool in the forest. Victor Hugo, 6949-5
The preference declared. Horace, 6949-5
Quitting again. Horace, 6949-5
The reconciliation (1). Horace, 6949-5
A Rhine-land drinking song. Unknown (German), 6949-5
A Roman winter-piece (1). Horace, 6949-5
Sailor and shade. Horace, 6949-5
Song of Eros. Bion, 6949-5
A spring poem. Bion, 6949-5
A tardy aplogy (2). Horace, 6949-5
Three cavaliers. Johann Ludwig Uhland, 6949-5
To a bully. Horace, 6949-5
To a jar of wine. Horace, 6949-5
To Albuis Tibullus (1). Horace, 6949-5
To Aristius Fuscus. Horace, 6949-5
To Chloe (2). Horace, 6949-5
To Chloe (3). Horace, 6949-5
To Chloe (4). Horace, 6949-5
To his lute. Horace, 6949-5
To Leuconoe (2). Horace, 6949-5
To Ligurinus (2). Horace, 6949-5
To Lydia. Horace, 6949-5
To Lydia (1). Horace, 6949-5
To M.L. Gray. Horace, 6949-5
To Maecenas. Horace, 6949-5
To Melopomene. Horace, 6949-5
To Mistress Pyrrha (1). Horace, 6949-5
To Mother Venus. Horace, 6949-5
To my old coat. Pierre Jean de Beranger, 6949-5
To Phyllis (1). Horace, 6949-5
To Pompeius Varus. Horace, 6949-5
To Quintus Dellius. Horace, 6949-5
To Quintus Hirpinus. Horace, 6949-5
To the fountain of Bandusia. Horace, 7039-6
To the fountain of Bandusia (1). Horace, 6949-5
To Venus. Horace, 6949-5
White stag. Johann Ludwig Uhland, 6949-5
The white stag. Johann Ludwig Uhland, 6614-3
Widow or daughter? Heinrich Heine, 6949-5
Wine, women, and song. Horace, 6949-5

Field, Eugene and Roswell Martin
Echoes from the Sabine farm. 6949-5

Field, Grace Stone
A surprise. 6130-3

Field, Henry Lionel
The wind on the heath. 6650-X

Field, Kate
Don't! 6721-2
Heads, not hearts, are trumps. 6682-8

Field, Mary
Names. 6880-4

Field, Mary H.
Grandfather's story. 6928-2

Field, Michael (Katherine Bradley & Edith Cooper)
Across a gaudy room. 6507-4
An Aeolian harp. 6656-9
Aridity. 6931-2
Beloved, my glory. 6250-4
The burial of Robert Browning. 6656-9
Bury her at even. 6844-8
Callirhoe, sels. 6477-9
Canute the Dane. 6188-5
Canute the Great, sels. 6656-9
The dancers. 6656-9
Descent from the cross. 6096 X
Earth to earth. 674-1,6656-9

Ebbtide at sundown. 6844-8
Eros does not always smite. 6872-3
Fellowship. 6096-X
A flaw. 6073-0
Gold. 6250-4
Iris. 6656-9
Let us wreathe the mighty cup. 6658-5
Lettice. 6274-1,6656-9
Mete me out my loneliness. 6507-4
Nests in elms. 6073-0
Renewal. 6437-X
Shepherd Apollo. 6477-9
Song, fr. Callirrhoe ("I dance and dance!..."). 6477-9
A summer wind. 6096 X
The tragic Mary Queen of Scots. 6507-4
'Where the blessed feet have trod'. 6931-2
Where winds abound. 6658-5
Wind of summer. 6656-9
Winds to-day are large and free. 6658-5
The woods are still. 6437-X

Field, Mildred Fowler
Prone on the grass. 7038-8
Purple veins. 6040-4

Field, Nathaniel
Rise, lady mistress, rise! 6182-6
Song ("Rise lady mistresse, rise"). 6933-9

Field, Rachel (Lyman)
At the theater. 6891-X
Gypsies. 6554-X
The music box from Munich. 6761-1
New England gothic. 6532-5
Old gardener time. 6236-9
The piper. 6454-X,6554-X
The playhouse key. 6891-X
The pointed people. 6891-X
Taxis. 6554-X

Field, Richard H.
"When you go to a store in Ascutney". 6722-0

Field, Roswell
An old man's soliloquy. 6451-5

Field, Roswell Martin (tr.)
An appeal to Lyce. Horace, 6949-5
At the ball game. Horace, 6949-5
Chloris properly rebuked. Horace, 6949-5
A counterblast against garlic. Horace, 6949-5
An excuse for Lalage. Horace, 6949-5
In the springtime (2). Horace, 6949-5
Poking fun at Xanthias. Horace, 6949-5
The reconciliation (2). Horace, 6949-5
The roasting of Lydia. Horace, 6949-5
A Roman winter-piece (2). Horace, 6949-5
A tardy aplogy (1). Horace, 6949-5
To Albuis Tibullus (2). Horace, 6949-5
To Barine. Horace, 6949-5
To Chloe (1). Horace, 6949-5
To Diana. Horace, 6949-5
To Glycera. Horace, 6949-5
To his book. Horace, 6949-5
To Leuconoe (1). Horace, 6949-5
To Ligurinus (1). Horace, 6949-5
To Lydia (2). Horace, 6949-5
To Maecenas. Horace, 6949-5
To Mistress Pyrrha (2). Horace, 6949-5
To Neobule. Horace, 6949-5
To Phyllis (2). Horace, 6949-5
To Postumus. Horace, 6949-5
To the fountain of Bandusia (2). Horace, 6949-5
To the ship of state. Horace, 6949-5

Field, Sara Bard
Contemporary. 6144-3,6532-5
Could you not watch with me one little hour?. 6628-3
I had a fair young son. 6628-3
My city. 6039-0
Never to know. 6880-4,6879-0
Not a single little one. 6880-4
October holiday. 6628-3
The pale woman. 6217-2,6040-4,6217-2
To a young son. 6071-4
We whom the dead have not forgiven. 6628-3
Winter revery. 6464-7

Field, Walter Taylor
Flag of the free. 6478-7

Field, Wright
The present battle-field. 6846-4
The stranger. 6750-6
To a skull. 6036-6

Field-Marshal Earl Roberts. Sir Owen Seaman. 7029-9
The field-path. Charles Swain. 6437-X

Fielding, Anna M.
Conscripts. 7010-8
Music's many moods. 6789-1

Fielding, Henry
A-hunting we will go. 6385-3,6398-5,6153-2
The author and the statesman. 6278-X
The dusky night rides down the sky, fr. Don Quixote... 6328-4
An epistle to Sir R. Walpole. 6092-7
Epistle to Sir Robert Walpole, 1730. 6086-2
Epistle to Sir Robert Walpole, 1731. 6086-2
Hunting song. 6334-9,6152-4
A letter to Sir Robert Walpole. 6152-4
The maiden's choice. John Mason Neale (tr.). 6302-0;6385-3
On a halfpenny. 6230-X
The roast beef of old England. 6152-4
Song written in the year 1732 6152-4
To Celia. 6086-2,6092-7
To Sir R. Walpole. 6092-7
Written at Mr. Pope's house at Twickenham. 6152-4
Written extempore on a halfpenny. 6086-2

The **fields** abroad with spangled flowers. Unknown. 6125-7
"**Fields** and a vacant house and barns". Homestead reclaimed. Marie Emilie Gilchrist. 6906-1
"**Fields** are chill; the sparse rain has stopped". Clearing at dawn. Li T'ai-po. 7039-6
"The **fields** are full of poppies...". 'In the early, pearly morning': song by Valgovind. Laurence (Adele Florence Nicolson) Hope. 6856-1
The **fields** are full. Edward Shanks. 6102-8
"The **fields** are ravaged, forests burned...". Permanency. Louisa Carroll Thomas. 6789-1
The **fields** are spread. Elizabeth J. Coatsworth. 6554-X
Fields at evening. David Morton. 6250-4
"The **fields** fold in silence the ripened...". Waiting. John Vance Cheney. 7041-8
The **fields** from Islington to Marybone. William Blake. 6125-7
The **fields** o' Ballyclare. Denis Aloysius McCarthy. 6162-1
The **fields** of Coleraine, fr. Hippodromania. Adam Lindsay Gordon. 6951-7
The **fields** of dawn, sels. Lloyd Mifflin. 6597-X
The **fields** of the Marne. Frank Carbaugh. 6589-9,6650-X
Fields of thought. Charles R. Murphy. 6038-2
The **fields** of war. Isaac McLellan Jr. 6678-X
"The **fields** sing every morning". Approach. Sister Mary Ada. 6839-1

Fields, Annie
Cedar Mountain. 6946-0
Climbing. 6600-3
A memory of Interlaken. 6749-2
Theocritus. 6309-8

Fields, James Thomas
The alarmed skipper. 6089-7,6279-2,6307-1,6736-0
Ballad of the tempest. 6271-7,6412-4,6219-9
Ballad of the wicked nephew. 6575-9
The captain's daughter. 6356-X,6052-8,6479-5,6127-3, 6614-3,6131 ,6214-8
Courtesy. 6654-2
Dirge for a young girl. 6271-7,6302-0,6385-3
In a strange land. 6240-7
Jupiter and ten. 6344-6,6575-9
Lot Skinner's elegy. 6505-8
The lucky horseshoe. 6414-0
Mabel, in New Hampshire. 6441-8,6652-6,6004-8
The Nantucket skipper. 6045-1,6240-7,6523-6,6385-3,6219-9
The owl-critic. 6089-7,6411-6,6744-1,6183-4,6732-8,6739 ,6505-8,6736-0,6464-7,6571-6
Patient Mercy Jones. 6413-2
Rover's petition. 6572-4

FIELDS
518

  The search. 6004-8
  The stars and stripes. 6015-3,6223-7
  The tempest. 6486-8,6632-1,6240-7,6302-0,6385-3
  To the old year. 6394-2
  The turtle and the flamingo. 6089-7,6239-3
  Wordsworth. 6600-3
Fields, R. McLain
  Cheerfulness. 6109-5
"The fields, Teruko-san, are threshed. A good". The Hibakusha's letter. David Mura. 6790-5
The fields. Witter Bynner. 6509-0,6556-2
"The fierce confederate storm". William Wordsworth. 6238-5
"Fierce is the flame of the vengeance of Erin". O'Neill's war song. Michael Hogan. 6930-4
"The fierce queen wearied, and she smote...". Ballade of the hanging gardens of Babylon. Richard Le Gallienne. 6875-8
"A fierce storm raged and black winds blew". The drunken captain. Unknown. 6826-X
"Fierce tyrant, death, who in thy wrath...". The tragedy of Croesus. Sir William Alexander; Earl of Stirling. 6908-8
"Fierce was the glare of Cashmere's". Alexander at the gates of paradise. Richard Chenevix Trench. 6848-0
"Fierce was the wild billow". Peace. Saint Antolius. 6214-8
Fierce was the wind billow. Saint Anatolius. 6337-3
"Fiercely, methinks, will he rage in his heart...". Aristophanes. 6435-3
The fiery birth of the hills. Robert Buchanan. 6819-7
"The fiery bright yellow". A flame. Mark Coady. 6883-9
Fiery cross of clan Alpine. Sir Walter Scott. 6302-0,6543-0
"The fiery javelins of heaven are hurled". Storm in Hawaii. Maurice Hill. 6799-9
The fiery ordeal. Unknown. 6683-6
"A fiery red comes out of the east like a...". It's day in Hopi-land. Jean Allard Jeancon. 6836-7
A Fiesolan idyl. Walter Savage Landor. 6198-2,6086-2,6110-9,6196-6,6430-2,6543-0,6656-9
Fiesta, fr. Desert drift. Alice Corbin. 6628-3
Fiester, S.F.
  The rarest pearl. 6921-5
  The under-current. 6580-5
Fife and drum. John Dryden. 6424-8
Fife tune. John Streeter Manifold. 6666-6,6733-6,6665-8
Fife, H.B.
  To the Spirit of St. Louis. 7019-1
The fife. Gilbert L. Eberhart. 6924-X
Fifer, H.N.
  He lived a life. 6214-8
The fifieth birthday of Agassiz. Henry Wadsworth Longfellow. 6233-4,6385-3,6431-0,6126-5,6585-6
Fifine at the fair, sels. Robert Browning. 6997-5
Fifine at the fair, sels. Robert Browning. 6110-9
Fifine at the fair, sels. Robert Browning. 6997-5
'The fift' ward j'int debate.' Joseph Crosby Lincoln. 6119-2
1536-1936.Fift. Emyr Humphries. 6360-8
Fifteen. Hermann Hagedorn. 6347-0
The fifteen acres. James Stephens. 6236-9
Fifteen and fifty. Alice Cary. 6969-X
Fifteen epitaphs, sels. Louise Imogen Guiney. 6096 X
"Fifteen years will reconstruct and span". The old place. Joseph Joel Keith. 6761-1
The fifteenth of April. Duncan Campbell Scott. 6433-7
Fifteenth Sunday after Trinity. John Keble. 6543-0
Fifth Avenue at noon. Eve Merriam. 6761-1
Fifth avenue, 1915 Hermann Hagedorn. 6954-1
Fifth day. R.D. FitzGerald. 6349-7
Fifth elegy. Alex Comfort. 6209-1
"The fifth from the north wall". Cross of gold. David Gray. 7041-8
Fifth philosopher's song. Aldous Huxley. 6633-X
The fifth-floor window. Lola Ridge. 6531-7
Fiftieth milestone of class. Mrs. Keyes-Becker. 6717-4
"Fifty and more" Sojin Takei. 6981-9
Fifty sonnets. William Shakespeare. 6436-1
Fifty years apart. Unknown. 6273-3
Fifty years spent. Struthers Burt. 6556-2

"Fifty-nine's a lovely age". A brithday greeting. Helen Bosanquet. 7042-6
"A fig for St. Denis of France". St. Patrick. William Maginn. 6820-0
"A fig for St. Dennis of France". Saint Patrick. William Maginn. 6787-5
"A fig for those by law protected!". Chorus, fr. The jolly beggars. Robert Burns. 7009-4
Figgis, Darrell
  Anach. 6090-0
  Coire dubh linn. 6090-0
  Inisgallun. 6930-4
  Multum in parvo. 6785-9
Fight. Percy MacKaye. 6419-1
The fight at Dajo. Alfred E. Wood. 6946-0
The fight at Fort Sumter. Unknown. 6074-9
The fight at Sumter. Unknown. 6946-0
The fight at the bridge, fr. Horatius. Thomas Babington Macaulay, 1st Baron Macaulay. 6427-2
The fight at the San Jacinto. John Williamson Palmer. 6274-1,6735-2,6062-5,6300-4
The fight in the centre, fr.The battle...Lake Regillus. Thomas Babington Macaulay, 1st Baron Macaulay. 6427-2
The fight of Lookout. Richard L. Cary Jr. 6678-X
The fight of Paso del Mar. Bayard Taylor. 6670-4,6008-0
The fight of Paso del Mar. Bayard Taylor. 6976-2
The fight of the "Armstrong" privateer. James Jeffrey Roche. 6062-5,6610-0
The fight over the body of Keitt. Unknown. 6946-0
Fight the good fight. John Samuel Bewley Monsell. 6337-3
"Fight well, my comrades...". Robert Bridges. 6487-6
Fight with a water-spirit. Norman Cameron. 6257-1
The fight with self. Edgar A. Guest. 6862-6
The fight with the dragon. Johann C. Friedrich von Schiller. 6842-1
The fight with the dragoon. Unknown. 6022-6
The fight with the snapping turtle. William Edmonstoune Aytoun. 6948-7
"The fight worth while on this good old earth". The fight worth while. Edgar A. Guest. 6862-6
The fight. Jack Mitford. 6547-3
The fighter.. Samuel Ellsworth Kiser. 6291-1
The fighter. Edgar A. Guest. 6869-3
Fightin fire. Margaret H. Lawless. 6924-X
The fighting failure. Everard Jack Appleton. 6736-0
'Fighting Mac'. Robert Service. 6159-1
The fighting parson. Henry Ames Blood. 6286-5
The fighting race. Joseph I.C. Clarke. 6274-1,6732-8,6102-8,6307-1,6467-1,6732-8,6736-0
The fighting scribe of Iona. Hermann Hagedorn. 6944-4
Fighting south of the castle. Unknown. 6527-9,6665-8
Fighting south of the castle. Unknown (Chinese) 7039-6
Fighting stock. Daniel Henderson. 6995-9
The fighting Temeraire. Sir Henry Newbolt. 6334-9,6046-3
The fighting word. Berton Braley. 6853-7
Fighting words. Dorothy Parker. 6375-5
A fighting-man. Joseph ("Seosamh MacCathmhaoil") Campbell. 6930-4
Figs of thistles. Phoebe Cary. 6969-X
Figueroa, Rudolfo
  Surgical art versus beauty. Margaret Allison (tr.). 6482-5
A figurative description of...procedure of divine love. Madame De la Mothe Guion. 6814-6
Figure. George Brandon Saul. 6036-6
Figure from Genesis. Nancy Byrd Turner. 6761-1
"Figure this out". Facts. William A. Norris. 6777-8
The figure-head. Crosbie Garstin. 6833-2
Figurehead. Dorothy Paul. 6833-2
Figures in a nightmare. Leah Bodine Drake. 6648-8
"Figures in the fields against the sky!". Poem ("Figures in the fields..."). Antonio Machado. 7039-6
Figuring it all up. Unknown. 6274-1
File Three. Unknown. 6443-4
Files on parade. Rudyard Kipling. 6683-6
"Files/The files/Office files!". The files. Rudyard Kipling. 6810-3
Fili mi, custodi. Bible. 6830-8
Filia patri. Helen Pinkerton. 6515-5

Filial deity. Francis Carlin. 6839-1
Filial greeting. Charles Whitby. 6994-0
Filial love. George Gordon, 6th Baron Byron. 6302-0;6385-3
Filial piety of David. Lydia Huntley Sigourney. 6848-0
Filicaja, Vincenzo da
   "Italia! thou, by lavish nature graced". Felicia
      Dorothea Hemans (tr.). 6973-8
   "When from the mountain's brow the gathering shades".
      Felicia Dorothea Hemans (tr.). 6973-8
Filiolae dulcissimae. Henry Alford. 6046-3
Filip, Raymond
   Watching whales watching us. 6767-0
Filippo Baldinucci on the privilege of burial. Robert
   Browning. 6848-0
Filippo, Rustico di
   Sonnet: Of the making of Master Messerin. Dante Gabriel
      Rossetti (tr.). 7039-6
"Fill a glass with golden wine," fr. Echoes. William
   Ernest Henley. 6508-2
"Fill fill ye bowele ye lusty wyne will dye." Unknown.
   6563-5
"Fill high the blue hirlas, that shines...wave". The
   hirlas horn. Felicia Dorothea Hemans. 6973-8
"Fill high the bowl, and spice it well, and pour". John
   Keble. 6931-2
Fill high to-night. William Pembroke Mulchinock. 6174-5
"Fill joy's room with the sweet incense of...". Three
   guests. Ethel Skipton Barringer. 6799-9
Fill me, boys, as deep a draught. Thomas Moore. 6328-4
'Fill that cookie jar, ma'. Emilia Edwards. 6894-4
Fill the baskets. Unknown. 6272-5
"Fill the bowl and praise the wine". Drinking-song. Ellen
   Glasgow. 7038-4
Fill the bowl with rosy wine. Abraham Cowley. 6934-7
Fill the bowl, butler! Unknown. 6881-2
Fill the goblet again. George Gordon, 6th Baron Byron.
   6092-7
"Fill up the glass! - but let it be". To absent friends.
   Unknown. 6928-2
"Fill, fill the goblet full with sack!". Song in a siege.
   Robert Heath. 6933-9
"Filled with delight they mingled with Mohan". The dance
   of the milkmaids. Unknown. 6959-2
Fillmore, Ronald W.
   Cobwebs. 6894-4
"A filmy western sky of smoky red". Canadian twilight.
   Lucy Maud Montgomery. 6797-2
Filson, Mrs. A.J. ("Ricketty Kate")
   Affinity. 6349-7
Fin. Helmut Zenker. 6769-7
Fin de fete. Charlotte Mew. 6985-1
Fin de siecle. Newton Mackintosh. 6902-9
Fin de siecle. Unknown. 6089-7
The fin-de-siecle angel. Unknown. 7021-3
Final autumn. Josephine Johnson. 6375-6
Final burning. Karen Osborn. 6860-X
Final chorus, fr. Atalanta in Calydon. Algernon Charles
   Swinburne. 6110-9
Final chorus, fr. Love is enough. William Morris. 6110-9
The final conflagration. Unknown (Greek) 6435-3
Final confrontation. Sheila Martindale. 6767-0
A final cry. Anne Morrow Lindbergh. 6761-1
A final day dialogue. William J. Lampton. 7021-3
Final hour. Yannis Ritsos. 6758-1
Final judgment. Edgar A. Guest. 6748-4
The final lesson. Arthur Stringer. 6337-3,6115-X
The final mystery. Sir Henry Newbolt. 6477-9
A final spring. Frederick Herbert Adler. 6906-1
The final struggle, fr. The new world. Louis James Block.
   6946-0
The final triumph of hope. Thomas Campbell. 6543-0
A final word. Austin Dobson. 6297-0
The final word. Dom Moraes. 6339-X
Finale. William Ernest Henley. 6653-4
Finale. Josephine A. Meyer. 6847-2
Finale. Beatrice Payne Morgan. 6841-3
Finale. William Shakespeare. 6102-8
Finale. Lilian White Spencer. 6836-7
Finale. Unknown. 6064-1
Finale ("So GLORIED all the night. Each trundle-bed").

James Whitcomb Riley. 6128-1
Finale of Christus. Henry Wadsworth Longfellow. 6126-5
Finalities. Maxwell Bodenheim. 6776-X
Finality. Winifred Virginia Jackson. 6076-5
Finality. Alexander Pope. 6541-4
Finally. Lee Wilson Dodd. 6042-0
"Finally/they confront me". Final confrontation. Sheila
   Martindale. 6767-0
Finch, Anne. See Winchilsea, Countess of
Finch, Francis Miles
   The blue and the gray. 6263-6,6300-4,6121-4,6102-8,6076-
      5,6309 ,6304-7,6642-2,6104-1,6449-3,6470-1,6396-3,
      6442-6,6565 ,6045-1,6344-6,6014-5,6600-3,6215-6,6610
      ,6136-2,6240-7,6271-7,6340-3,6385-3,6478 ,6273-3,
      6113-3,6486-8,6006-4,6053-6,6101 ,6512-0,6589-9,6732-
      8,6016-2,6431-0,6288 ,6706-9,6074-9,6102-8,6451-5,
      6457-4,6471
   Decoration Day. 6424-8
   Memorial Day. 6143-5
   Nathan Hale. 6396-9,6424-8,6015-3,6457-4,6478-7,6471-X,
      6481-7,6470
   The patriot spy, fr. Nathan Hale. 6442-2
   Storm - the king. 6673-9
   The storm king, sels. 6049-8
Finch, Julia Neely
   The unborn. 6097-8
Finch, Robert
   Alone. 6021-8,6446-9
   The flying fish. 6021-8
   Jardin de la Chapelle Expiatoire. 6446-9
   The reticent phrase. 6021-8
   Scroll-section. 6446-9
   Train window. 6021-8,6446-9
   Window-piece. 6021-8
Find a way. John Godfrey Saxe. 6449-3,6498-1
"Find me a lonely cave". Song ("Find me a lonely cave").
   Unknown. 6563-5
"Find me a sky of softest grey". An order. C.F. McClumpha.
   6983-5
Find the favorite. James Whitcomb Riley. 6091-9
Find your level. I. Edgar Jones. 6921-5
The find.. Charles Kingsley. 6423-X
The find. Francis Ledwidge. 6812-X
Finding. Rupert Brooke. 6320-9
Finding God. Edward Dowden. 6303-9
The finding of Jamie. John G. Neihardt. 6473-6
The finding of Moses. James Grahame. 6848-0
The finding of the cross. Jessie H. Brown. 6575-9
The finding of the lyre. James Russell Lowell. 6457-4,6503-
   1,6212-1,6457-4,6639-9,6964
"Finding the city below me like a flame". Twilight in a
   tower. George Dillon. 6808-1
Finding the sunset. Unknown. 6917-7
The fine April weather. August Derleth. 6761-1
"The fine art of forming friendships". Making friends.
   L.M. Zimmerman. 6799-9
Fine clay. Winifred Shaw. 6349-7
A fine day on Lough Swilly. William Alexander. 6090-0
A fine day. Michael Drayton. 6239-3,6466-3,6018-8
Fine flowers in the valley. Unknown. 6055-2,6056-0,6518-X,
   6153-2
"Fine knacks for ladies". Song ("Fine knacks"). Unknown.
   6436-1
Fine knacks for ladies. John Dowland. 6315-2
"Fine knacks for ladies,cheap,choice,brave and new".
   Unknown. 6181-8
"Fine merry franions". Epicedium - going or gone. Charles
   Lamb. 6802-2
The fine nature. Edmund Blunden. 6783-2
A fine new ballad of Cawsand Bay. Hamilton Moore. 6501-5
A fine night in winter. Sylvia Lynd. 6779-4
The fine old Dutch gentleman. Unknown. 6791-3
The fine old English gentleman. Charles Dickens. 6157-5
"A fine one is the cluricaun". The cluricaun. Marc
   Connelly. 6817-0
"The fine rays of the setting sun will...". It's not yet
   time to light the candles. Suk-jung Shin. 6775-1
The fine song for singing. Robert Louis Stevenson. 6339-X
"Fine violets! Fresh violets! Come buy!". Spring voices.
   Ernest Radford. 6875-8

FINE   520

"Fine violets! frest violets! come but!". Spring voices.
    Ernest Radford. 6770-0
"Fine young folly, though you wear". William Habington.
    6933-9
"Fine-wrought as when from deft Cellini's hand". An old
    silver bowl. Gertrude Huntington McGiffert. 6838-3
Finerty, John F.
    May-day at sea. 6833-2
Finesse. Ruby E. Bolton. 6750-6
"The finest bolt or hasp or clasp". Our Vermont pie-safe
    button. Daniel L. Cady. 6989-4
The finest day of one's life. Jacques Baron. 6351-9
Fingal and Ros-crana. Unknown. 6873-1
Fingal's cave. John Keats. 6484-1
Fingal's weeping. Neil Munro. 6873-1
A finger and a huge, thick thumb. James Norman Hall. 7027-
    2
Finger play. Unknown. 6937-1
Finger play. Unknown. 6937-1
Finger, Charles J.
    The cowboy's dream. 6281-4
    Saing Giles's bowl. 7007-8
"Finger-prints on the window". Children. Bernard Raymund.
    6880-4
"The fingers of the air caress your face". Susan. David
    Gascoyne. 6985-1
Finis. Robert J. Burdette. 6588-0
Finis. Le Baron Cooke. 6039-0
Finis. Robin Flower. 6582-1,6641-0
Finis. Walter Savage Landor. 6102-8,6102-8,6560-0,6501-5
Finis. James Abraham Martling. 6952-5
Finis. John McClure. 6326-8
Finis. Eden Phillpotts. 6872-3
Finis. Unknown. 6244-X
Finis. Rosamund Marriott ("Graham R. Tomson") Watson. 6019-
    6
Finis exoptatus, fr. Ye wearie wayfarer. Adam Lindsay
    Gordon. 6951-7
Finis venit. Bible. 6830-8
"Finish, good lady...", fr. Antony and Cleopatra. William
    Shakespeare. 6339-X
The finished course. Saint Joseph of the Stadium. 6730-1
Finistere. Robert Service. 6159-1
Finite reason. John Dryden. 6315-2
Fink, Jane M.
    Bone county. 6900-2
    Litany. 6900-2
Fink, William W.
    Larrie O'Dee. 6089-7,6416-7,6167-2,6505-8,6573-2
    Leadville Jim. 6920-7
    Little tee-hee. 6416-7
    Marry me, darling, to-night. 6505-8
    O'Branigan's drill. 6918-5
Finkel, Donald
    The lotus eaters. 6803-0
    Why we didn't rent the cabin. 6860-X
Finland love-song. Unknown. 6116-8
Finland love-song. Unknown (Finnish) 6370-5
Finletter, Thomas Dickson
    All-Hallowe'en. 6936-3
    At the King of Prussia. 6936-3
    Sleigh-bells. 6936-3
Finley, Catherine L.
    Icicles on trees. 6178-8
    Perception. 6178-8
Finley, John
    And to such as play only the bass viol. 6607-0
    Bachelor's hall. 6302-0,6385-3,6219-9
    A birthnight candle. 6476-0,6607-0
    Duovir. 6184-2
Finley, John E.
    The Red Cross spirit speaks. 6449-3
Finley, John Huston
    'H.H.'. 6102-8
    The poor poet's lullaby. 6076-5,6102-8
    The Red Cross spirit speaks. 6509-0,6088-9
    The road to Dieppe. 6332-2
    The sepulcher in the garden. 6144-3
    The three wise men. 6144-3
    The valley of the blue shrouds. 7027-2

'Via Die'. 6331-4
Finneen O'Driscoll the rover. Robert Dwyer Joyce. 6174-5,
    6292-X
Finnegan to Flannigan. Unknown. 6260-1
Finnegan, Frank X.
    The guardsman. 6471-X
Finney, Bernard
    The genesis. 6898-7
    A one-winged bird. 6898-7
    A woman dressed in black. 6898-7
Finney, Ross L.
    O Lincoln. 6708-5
Finnigan's wake. Unknown. 6058-7,6399-3
Finnigin to Flannigan. Strickland Gillilan. 6211-3,6732-8,
    6694-1,6605-4,6089-7,6277 ,6736-0,6579-1
Finovar. Ella Young. 6628-3
Fionn, Flann (atr.)
    Aldfrid's itinerary through Ireland. James Clarence
        Mangan (tr.). 6930-4
    Aldfrid's itinerary through Ireland. John O' Donovan
        (tr.). 6930-4
"The fir tree snuggles in winter clothes". Winter - pro
    and con. O.M.L Detty. 6750-6
The fir tree. Luella Clark. 6049-8
"The fir trees taper into twigs...", fr. Summer images.
    John Clare. 6187-7
The fir woods. Sir Charles George Douglas Roberts. 6795-6
The fir-tree and the brook. Helen Hunt Jackson. 7041-8
"A fir-tree standeth lonely". Song: Ein fichtenbaum.
    Heinrich Heine. 6961-4
"A fir-tree stood, 'mid ice and snow". A discontented fir-
    tree. Rosamund Livingstone McNaught. 6807-3
The fir-tree.. Edith M. Thomas. 6623-2
Firdausi [or Firdawsi,Firdusi] (Abul Kasin Mansur)
    Alas for youth. R.A. Nicholson (tr.). 7039-6
    The birth of Rustem. J. Champion (tr.). 6448-5
    The dream of Dakiki. A.V. Williams Jackson (tr.). 6730-
        1
    Kiumers. J. Champion (tr.). 6448-5
    Rustem and Akwan Dev. E.H. Palmer (tr.). 6448-5
    Rustem slays Sohrab. James Atkinson (tr.). 6448-5
    Satire on Mahmud. J. Champion (tr.). 6448-5
    The Shah-nameh, sels. S. Robinson (tr.). 6372-1
    Sohrab is born. James Atkinson (tr.). 6448-5
Fire. Diane Bliss. 6900-2
Fire. Stanton A. Coblentz. 6039-0
Fire. Marjorie DeGraff. 6850-2
Fire. Ibn Sara. 6362-4
Fire. Emma Reed Shoaff. 6270-9
Fire. Eunice Tietjens. 6036-6
Fire and ale. Horace Smith. 6802-2
Fire and glass. William Rose Benet. 6011-0
Fire and ice. Robert Frost. 6726-3,6250-4,6288-1,6010-2,
    6491-4
Fire and snow. Mark Turbyfill. 6037-4
Fire and water. Max Eastman. 6880-4
Fire and water. Benjamin Franklin Taylor. 6815-4
"The fire blazed bright till deep midnight". Lord John of
    the east. Joanna Baillie. 6813-8
The fire breather, Mexico City. Jaime Jacinto. 6790-5
The fire bringer, sels. William Vaughn Moody. 6077-3;6501-
    5;6532-5;6730-1
The fire by the sea. Alice Cary. 6385-3
The fire by the sea. Phoebe Cary. 6001-3
Fire castles. Arvia MacKaye. 6029-3
The fire dancer. Lewis Worthington Smith. 6959-2
The fire drill. Stanley Schell. 6684-4
"The fire flits ont the walls". Alone. Phillips Stewart.
    7041-8
Fire for the alien. Laura Veach Clark. 6799-9
Fire in New Orleans: December 2, 1972, sels. Norman Simms.
    7018-3
Fire in the heavens. Christopher J. Brennan. 6384-5,6349-7
The fire in the noose. Nikolai Tikhonov. 6546-5
Fire in the woods; or, the old settler's story. Andrew
    McLachlan. 6795-6
Fire is in the flint, fr. Ferishtah's fancies. Robert
    Browning. 6655-0
Fire laddies we. Stanley Schell. 6715-8
Fire of apple-wood. M.A. DeWolfe Howe. 6051-X

The fire of driftwood. Henry Wadsworth Longfellow. 6243-1, 6333-0,6085-4,6288-1,6309-8
The fire of Frendraught. Unknown. 6185-0,6518-4
The fire of heaven, fr. Balin and Balan. Alfred Lord Tennyson. 6199-0
"Fire of heaven, whose starry arrow". Robert Bridges. 6487-6
The fire of London. John Dryden. 6323-3,6125-7
The fire of love. Charles Sackville; 6th Earl of Dorset. 6302-0;6385-3
The fire of the frost. Elizabeth Roberts MacDonald. 6115-X
Fire on Belmont Street, fr. The tall men. Donald Davidson. 7017-5
Fire on the hills. Robinson Jeffers. 6628-3
Fire pictures. Emma Rounds. 6891-X
The fire sermon, fr. the waste land. Thomas Stearns Eliot. 6531-7
The fire side: a pastoral soliloquy. Isaac Hawkins Browne. 6932-0
The fire tenders. Grace Noll Crowell. 6449-3
"The fire that filled my heart of old". James ("B.V.") Thomson. 6508-2
"Fire that must flame is with apt fuell fed" Thomas Campion. 6794-8
"The fire upon the hearth is low". In the firelight. Eugene Field. 6949-5
Fire!. Sydney Flowers. 6929-0
Fire, fire! Henry Bold. 6328-4
Fire, fire! Thomas Campion. 6328-4
"Fire, she burn, this old spirit". Fire. Diane Bliss. 6900-2
"The fire, the dusky waterlily edge on the...". To Helen Frankenthaler of Circe, 1974 Anne Cherner. 6966-3
The fire-bell's story. George L. Catlin. 6916-9
Fire-bells. M.R. Johnson. 6680-1
The fire-fiend. C.D. Gardette. 6403-5
The fire-fiend. Jessie Glenn. 6411-6,6744-1
The fire-flies, sels. Charles Mair. 6797-2
The fire-flies. Sir Humphry Davy. 6980-0
Fire-flowers. Emily Pauline ("Tekahionwake") Johnson. 6837-5
Fire-fly city. Henry Van Dyke. 6961-4
The fire-fly. Sarah ("Susan Coolidge") Woolsey. 6621-6
The fire-hangbird's nest. Eugene Field. 6949-5
Fire-logs. Carl Sandburg. 6102-8,6076-5
"A fire-mist and a planet". Each in his own tongue. William Herbert Carruth. 6889-8,6006-4,6076-5,6541-1, 6250-4,6107-9,6241 ,6266-0,6104-4,6309-8,6646-1,6104-4,6464 ,6303-9,6161-3,6473-6,6476-0,6509-0,6615
The fire-worshippers, fr. Lalla Rookh. Thomas Moore. 6198-2;6102-8
The fire. Hugh F. McDermott. 6568-6
The fire. John Greenleaf Whittier. 6230-X
The fired pot. Anna Wickham. 6210-5
Fireflies. Gertrude Alger. 6798-0
Fireflies. Robert P. Tristram Coffin. 7040-X
Fireflies. Edgar Fawcett. 6102-8,6076-5,6309-8
Fireflies. W.H. McCreary. 6253-9
Fireflies. Antoinette De Coursey Patterson. 6338-1
Fireflies. A.C. S. 6629-1
Fireflies ("Little lamps of the dusk"). Carolyn Hall. 6466-3,6498-1
Fireflies in a graveyard. Robert P. Tristram Coffin. 6984-3
Fireflies in the corn. David Herbert Lawrence. 6393-4
Fireflies in the corn. David Herbert Lawrence. 6897-9
Fireflies in the garden. Robert Frost. 6464-7
"The fireflies massed upon the palm fronds." Buson. 6027-7
Firefly. Elizabeth Madox Roberts. 6326-8
Firefly. George Uba. 6790-5
Firefly ("I didn't mean to hurt you, firefly"). Edna D. Wood. 6466-3
"The firefly haunts were lighted yet". In the morning. Patrick MacGill. 7027-2
The firefly.. Ogden Nash. 6722-0
"A firefly/Flitted by." Ryoto. 6027-7
Firelight. R. H. 6118-4
Firelight. Heinrich Heine. 6120-6
Firelight. Edwin Arlington Robinson. 6289-X
Firelight. Margaret Rush. 6750-6

"Firelight danced along the uneven walls". Attic. Arthur Davison Ficke. 6880-4
"The firelight danced and wavered". The silken shoe. Paul Hamilton Hayne. 6965-7
"Firelight on stemmed glasses". Winter-piece. Robert P. Tristram Coffin. 7040-X
Fireman O'Rafferty. Joseph Crosby Lincoln. 6119-2
The fireman's prize. Unknown. 6417-5,6675-5
The fireman's story. Unknown. 6964-9
The fireman's wedding. W.A. Eaton. 6922-3
The fireman. Robert T. Conrad. 6671-2,6744-1
The fireman. Robert T. Conrad. 6909-6
The fireman. Stephen Phillips. 7014-0
Fires. Joseph ("Seosamh MacCathmhaoil") Campbell. 6069-2
Fires. Wilfred Wilson Gibson. 6506-6,6199-0
"Fires grew pale on Rome's deserted shrines". The last Constantine. Felicia Dorothea Hemans. 6973-8
Fires in Illinois. John James Piatt. 7041-8
The fires of God, fr. Poems of love and earth. John Drinkwater. 6234-2
The fires of God, sel. John Drinkwater. 6954-1
"The fires that burn on all the hills". Khan Zada's song on the hillside. Laurence (Adele Florence Nicolson) Hope. 6856-1
The fires that glow. Della Hudmon Willien. 6789-1
Fires, sels. Wilfred Wilson Gibson. 6234-2
The fireside chairs. William Barnes. 6980-0
The fireside kitten. Elizabeth J. Coatsworth. 6120-6
The fireside. Nathaniel Cotton. 6219-9,6385-3,6271-7,6620-8
Firestone, Clark B.
  A buccaneer chorus. 7007-8
  Coasts. 7007-8
The firetail's nest. John Clare. 6943-6
Firewood. Raymond Holden. 6037-4
Fireworks in Vermont. Daniel L. Cady. 6989-4
Fireworks, fr. Marine. Edith Sitwell. 7000-0
"The firing ceased: and like a wounded foe". Hialmar and the Aasvogel. Roy Campbell. 6800-6
Firkins, Chester
  On a subway express. 6102-8,6310-1,6501-5,6532-5,6732-8, 6467 ,6250-4,6336-5,6736-0,6396-9,6076-5,6484 ,6102-8,6310-1,6501-5,6532-5,6732-8,6467 ,6250-4,6336-5, 6736-0,6396-9,6076-5,6484
  On the way home. 6274-1
Firkins, O.W.
  To a Greek bootblack. 6473-6
  To America in war time. 7027-2
"A firm and sure foundation stone". Ode. Ibbie McColm Wilson. 6848-0
"Firm be thy soul! - serene in power". To Delius, fr. Ode 003. Horace. 6973-8
The firm of happiness, limited. Norman Cameron. 6210-5
Firmilian. William Edmonstoune Aytoun. 6948-7
Firmness. William Shakespeare. 6438-8
First. Unknown. 6158-3
"The first 'big man' I ever knew". Jericho, Vermont. Daniel L. Cady. 6988-6
"First a little dirt on my mouth and slowly...". Billy the kid. Shuntaro Tanikawa. 6803-0
First aid. Peter Hopegood. 6384-5
The first American Congress. Joel Barlow. 6946-0
First American ode. George Barker. 6389-6
The first American sailors. Wallace Rice. 6478-7
First and last. Algernon Charles Swinburne. 6123-0
First and last. Unknown. 6271-7
"The first and the last time". Two for blueford redman. Haydn Sloan. 6860-X
The first and the last. Horatius Bonar. 6065-X
The first anniversary. John Donne. 6562-7
First appearance in type. Oliver Wendell Holmes. 6910-X
First appearance in type. Unknown. 6294-6
The first appearance of Orion, fr. Orion. Richard Hengist Horne. 6980-0
First attempt at a sonnet. Roberta Werdinger. 6857-X
First auction. David Baker. 6860-X
The first autumn. Marshall Schacht. 6478-7
The first banjo. Irwin Russell. 6307-1
The first banjo. Unknown. 6915-0
The first bath of ablution. Morris Rosenfeld. 7011-6

FIRST

The first battle of the revolution. Unknown. 6621-6
The first battle of Ypres. Margaret L. Woods. 6474-4
The first best Christmas night. Margaret Deland. 6608-9
The first bird o' spring. Henry Van Dyke. 6961-4
The first birthday. Hartley Coleridge. 6233-4
The first bluebird. James Whitcomb Riley. 6162-1,6266-0, 6478-7
The first bluebirds. Katharine Lee Bates. 6510-4
First born. Frances O'Connell Corridan. 6292-X
"First born of chaos, who so fair didst come". Hymn: to light. Abraham Cowley. 6933-9
First born of chaos...", fr. Verses written... Abraham Cowley. 6562-7
The first bud o' the year. Charles G. Blanden. 6274-1
"First by Andromache the women's...", fr. The Iliad. Homer. 6251-2
"The first came in was the scarlet red". Unknown. 6059-5
"First came the primrose, on the bank high". The procession of the flowers. Sydney Dobell. 6820-0
The first chantey. Rudyard Kipling. 6810-3
The first child. Rudolph Chambers Lehmann. 6233-4
The first Christmas eve. William White. 6868-5
First Christmas night of all. Nancy Byrd Turner. 6449-3
The first Christmas, fr. St. Luke. Bible. 6465-5
The first Christmas-tree. Myra A. Goodwin. 6927-4
The first Christmas. Anne Emilie Poullson. 6466-3,6623-2, 6608-9
The first Christmas. Unknown. 6078-1
The first client. Irwin Russell. 6878-2
The first client. Irwin Russell. 6410-8,6744-1
The first cloud. Unknown. 6918-5
"First come down was dressed in red". Lord Daniel. Unknown. 6826-X
"First comes Tom Baynes among these...quills". Prelude, fr. Fo'c's'le yarns: 3d series. Thomas Edward Brown. 6809-X
The first concert. Antonin Sova. 6886-3
"The first concoction perfited." Unknown. 6563-5
First Corinthians, sels. Bible. 6107-9
First Corinthians, sels. Bible. 6143-5,6527-9
The first dandelion. Walt Whitman. 6047-1,6126-5,6153-2
First day in England. Francis Carey ("Jan van Avond") Slater. 6800-6
"The first day of Christmas my true love sent...". Unknown. 6334-9
The first day of creation. John Milton. 6931-2
"The first day of spring in the year...". Reynard the fox. Unknown. 6930-4
"The first day of the month of May". Rondel ("The first day"). Charles, Duc d' Orleans. 6227-X
"The first day of Yule have we in mind". Make we mirth for Christmas birth, and sing... Unknown. 6756-5
"The first day when Christ was born". Nowell, el, el, el, el I thank a maiden every deal. Unknown. 6756-5
The first day. Christina Georgina Rossetti. 6198-2
"First did I feare, when first my love began," Giles (the Elder) Fletcher. 6586-4
The First Division marches. Grantland Rice. 6736-0
The first Easter dawn. William White. 6868-5
The first eight verses of chapter seventeen of the... William Dearness. 6848-0
First epilogue to Oenia. Allen Tate. 6038-2
The first epistle of the second book of Horace. Alexander Pope. 6483-3
First evening. Bayard Taylor. 6976-2
The first fathers. Robert Stephen Hawker. 6437-X
"The first few days back at the Indian school". Cat or stomp. Laura Tohe. 7005-1
First fig. Edna St. Vincent Millay. 6501-5
The first fledgling. Emma Tuttle. 6772-7
First flight. Elford Caughey. 6761-1
The first flight. Bible. 7020-5
The first flowers. John Greenleaf Whittier. 6049-8
The first food. George Sterling. 6556-2
First footsteps. Algernon Charles Swinburne. 6828-6
First footsteps. Algernon Charles Swinburne. 6424-8
The first frost. Thornton W. Burgess. 6798-0
The first frost. Edith H. Shank. 6270-9
The first game of the season. Bertha E. Feist. 6585-6
The first gray hair. Thomas Haynes Bayly. 6980-0,6543-0

"First halt. They heard within a sugar patch". The fairies in Prince Edward Island. John Hunter-Duvar. 6795-6
"First he made the door, a walk". Four pictures by Juan, age 5. David McKain. 6966-5
"First I walked with pride, but". Fellow travelers. John Hancock. 6894-4
The first historical ballad: a martyrdom of Santa Eulalia. Federico Garcia Lorca. 6068-4
"First I want to be happy" Konrad Bayer. 6769-7
First ice. Kenneth Slade Alling. 6036-6
A 'first impression': Tokyo. Edmund Blunden. 6778-6
"The first inuentor of musicke (most sacred...". To the flowre of princes, Charles, Prince of Great... Thomas Campion. 6794-8
The first inuocation in a full song ("Powerfull...") Thomas Campion. 6794-8
The first julep. Bliss Carman and Richard Hovey. 6890-1
First kiss. Christie Lund. 6750-6
The first kiss of love. George Gordon, 6th Baron Byron. 6945-2
The first kiss. Thomas Campbell. 6226-1,6302-0;6385-3
The first kiss. Theodore Watts-Dunton. 6656-9,6737-9
First lady. Edna L. Harrison. 6178-8
First landing of the pilgrims. Robert Southey. 6484-1
The first lay of Gudrun. Unknown (Icelandic) 7039-6
The first lesson. Emily Dickinson. 6321-7
The first letter. Unknown. 6314-4
First look at the baby. Edgar A. Guest. 6748-4
First love. George Gordon, 6th Baron Byron. 6240-7,6385-3, 6092-7
First love. Charles Stuart Calverley. 6633-X,6518-X,6089-7, 6732-8
First love. John Clare. 6125-7
First love. Johann Wolfgang von Goethe. 6732-8
First love. Christopher M. ("Hugh MacDiarmid") Grieve. 6893-6
First love. Isabel Ecclestone Mackay. 6021-8
First love. Lizette Woodworth Reese. 6274-1
First love. George William ("A.E.") Russell. 6781-6,6782-4
First love remembered. Dante Gabriel Rossetti. 6110-9
The first lover. Laurence (Adele Florence Nicolson) Hope. 6856-1
First loves. Jean Stephen Johnston. 6750-6
The first maple. Maybelle McLaurin Kinsey. 7016-7
First maternity. Katharine Brown Burt. 6750-6
The first meeting. Christina Georgina Rossetti. 6429-9, 6226-1,6321-7
The First Minnesota at Gettysburg. MacKinlay Kantor. 6628-3
"The first morn of April, so balmy and fair". April's fools. Mrs. A. Giddings Park. 7022-1
First mother. Vivian Yeiser. 6365-9
First news from Villafranca. Elizabeth Barrett Browning. 6123-0
"The first night we slept in a Nissen hut". Exercises. Jack Lindsay. 6895-2
The first night. Isolde Kurz. 6643-7
The first Nowell the angel did say. Unknown. 6756-5
The first Nowell. Unknown. 6105-2,6608-9,6746-8
First O songs for a prelude. Walt Whitman. 6340-3
The first of April ("Today the swards of heaven..."). Geoffrey Johnson. 6465-5
The first of April ("When indoor young ones club..."). William Hone. 6465-5,6018-8
The first of April, sels. Thomas Warton Jr. 6195-0
The first of April, sels. Thomas Warton Jr. 6867-7
The first of April. Mortimer Collins. 6047-1,6274-1
The first of April. Geoffrey Johnson. 6783-2
First of March. Frederick Tennyson. 6980-0
First of May. William Wordsworth. 6438-8
The first of May. Unknown. 6105-2
"First of the men of state". Wilson. Edmund Vance Cooke. 7001-9
"First old Minna, bent and lowly". Measuring the graves. Morris Rosenfeld. 7011-9
"First on the list is Washington...". Our presidents - a memory rhyme. Isabel Ambler Gilman. 6964-9
"The first one he loved-an accident". The deformity lover. Felice Picano. 7003-5
First or last. Thomas Hardy. 6655-0

First or last?. Margaret Veley. 6656-9
The first pager. Guy Lee. 6995-9
The first parting. Marian (Annie D.G. Robinson) Douglas. 6407-8
The first party. Josephine Pollard. 6572-4,6914-2
The first peep. E.O. De Camp. 6906-1
First philosopher's song. Aldous Huxley. 7039-6
The first prayer. Charles Swain. 6980-0
The first proclamation of Miles Standish. Margaret Junkin Preston. 6736-0
The first quarrel. Alfred Lord Tennyson. 6677-1
The first rainbow. Bible. 7020-5
"The first roof we ever knew". Home. Evelyn Grace Flynn. 6847-2
The first rose of summer. Charles W. Denison. 6755-7
"The first rose on my tree-rose". Edna St. Vincent Millay. 6986-X
"The first rough month that ends the...time". George Odger. Sir Edmund Gosse. 6793-X
The first sabbath. James Grahame. 6848-0
"First saw you in the bottom drawer". Marilyn Monroe. Al Masarik. 6901-0
The first sestiad, fr. Hero and Leander. Christopher Marlowe. 6430-2
The first sestiad, sels. Christopher Marlowe. 6122-2;6198-2
The first settler's story. Will Carleton. 6281-4,7041-8, 6413-2,6550-3,6706-9
First sex. Dennis Cooper. 7003-5
"First shall the heavens want starry light". Thomas Lodge. 6181-8;6328-4
"First shall the heavens want starry light". A lover's vow. Thomas Lodge. 6830-8
The first ship. Dugald Moore. 6873-1
First sight. Anna Hempstead Branch. 6266-0
First sight. Sir Edmund Gosse. 6770-0
First sight. Philip Larkin. 6339-X
First sight. Christopher Marlowe. 6150-8
First sight of spring. John Clare. 7015-9
The first six verses of the ninetieth psalm. Bible. 6848-0
The first skylark of spring. Sir William Watson. 6660-7, 6656-9
First snow. Christian Morgenstern. 6160-5
First snow. Martha Ostenso. 6037-4
First snow. John ("Laclede") Talon-Lesperance. 6795-6
First snow. Charles Erskine Scott Wood. 6619-4,6628-3
The first snow fall. James Russell Lowell. 6459-0,6632-1, 6219-9,6288-1,6560-0,6104-4,6126-5,6302-0,6385-3, 6078-1,6332-2,6127-3
The first snow in Vermont. Daniel L. Cady. 6989-4
First snow on the hills. Leonora Speyer. 6421-3
The first snow. Ella Dietz. 6695-X
The first snow. Alice Meynell. 6955-X
The first snow. Ada Cassell Sell. 6799-9
The first snow. Unknown. 6373-X,6529-5
The first snow. Angie W. Wray. 6394-2
First snowfall. David Brokken. 6857-X
The first snowfall. Charles Warren Stoddard. 6285-7
The first song of Esai. George Wither. 6848-0
First song, fr. Astrophel and Stella. Sir Philip Sidney. 6586-4
The first song-sparrow. Unknown. 6466-3
The first sorrow. Adelaide Anne Procter. 6957-6
First spring flowers. Mary Woolsey Howland. 6385-3
First spring morning. Robert Bridges. 6242-3,6334-9,6487-6
The first squire (1). Thomas Campion. 6794-8
The first squire (2). Thomas Campion. 6794-8
The first St. Martin's summer. Emma E. Brown. 6965-7
First stand on the mainland. Muin Ozaki. 6981-9
The first step ("My little one begins his feet to try") Andrew Bice Saxton. 6078-1
The first steps ("Last night I held my arms to you"). Edgar A. Guest. 6078-1
First Sunday after Epiphany. John Keble. 6046-3
First Sunday after Trinity. John Keble. 6046-3
The first swallow. Charlotte Smith. 6133-8,6808-1
The first te deum. Margaret Junkin Preston. 6413-2
The first temptation, fr. Paradise regained. John Milton. 6931-2
The first Thanksgiving day. Alice Williams Brotherton. 6618-6
The first Thanksgiving day. Margaret Junkin Preston. 6614-3
The first Thanksgiving day. Margaret Junkin Preston. 7041-8
The first Thanksgiving: Boston, 1631. Arthur Guiterman. 6618-6
The first Thanksgiving. Hezekiah Butterworth. 7002-7
The first Thanksgiving. Clinton Scollard. 6946-0
The first Thanksgiving. Unknown. 6703-4
"First the whole universe avails us not". Stanzas ("First the whole"). Jaroslav Vrchlicky. 6886-3
"First there were two of us, then..three of us". The storm. Walter De La Mare. 6783-2
"The first thing that I remember was Carlo...". Asleep at the switch. George Hoey. 6915-0
First things first. Wystan Hugh Auden. 6388-8
The first three. Clinton Scollard. 6946-0
"First time he kiss'd me, he but only kiss'd." Elizabeth Barrett Browning. 6560-0
"First time he" Gavin Dillard. 7003-5
First time I kissed Sary. Nixon Waterman. 6719-0
"The first time his grandfather beat him". Gorky's childhood. Lorna Crozier. 6767-0
"The first time that I saw the sea". My sea. Susan N. Pulsifer. 6789-1
"The first time the emperor Han heard". The word. Allen Upward. 6897-9
The first time. James L. White. 7003-5
"The first to climb the parapet". The cricketers of Flanders. James Norman Hall. 7026-4
The first tooth. William Brighty Rands. 6078-1
The first tooth. Edgar A. Guest. 6869-3
First travels of Max. John Crowe Ransom. 6108-7
"The first truckload/jars sleep loose". Day of the parade. Alan Chong Lau. 6790-5
The first true gentleman. Thomas Dekker. 6102-8
First variation on a theme by George Peele. Sacheverell Sitwell. 6985-1
The first violet. Marie B. Williams. 6240-7
The first voyage of John Cabot. Unknown. 6188-5
The first voyage of John Cabot. Katharine Lee Bates. 6162-1
The first voyage of John Cabot. Unknown. 6946-0
The first watch. Edgar A. Guest. 6748-4
First winter. Gail N. Harada. 6790-5
First winter song. Unknown. 6090-0
The first word. Leila Jones. 6761-1
"The first words spoken". Periods of adjustment. Shawn Wong. 6790-5
The first year. E.J. Scovell. 6209-1
"First you ask/me to walk". I don't know what you want. Lyn Lifshin. 6998-3
"First you see fixt in this huge mirror blue". All nature danceth. William Henry Davies. 6935-5
The first, best country, fr. The traveller. Oliver Goldsmith. 6239-3
"First, from each brother's hoard a part...". Reporters. George Crabbe. 6996-7
"First' O songs, for a prelude". Drum taps. Walt Whitman. 6753-0
"First, of the Heliconian Muses be my song". Hesiod. 6251-2
First, second, third. Elizabeth Barrett Browning. 6429-9, 6321-7
"First, see the land which thou intend'st..buy". The purchasing of land. Unknown. 6878-2
"First, taking one of the branch". To my wife in time of war. Michael Dennis Browne. 7032-9
"First, worship God; he that forgets to pray". Precepts. Thomas Randolph. 6915-0
"First-born and final relic of the night". Even-star. Richard Garnett. 6785-9
First-day thoughts. John Greenleaf Whittier. 6527-9,6288-1, 6126-3
The first-lieutenant - old style. Unknown. 6589-9
The firstborn.. John Arthur Goodchild. 6078-1,6233-4,6627-5
The firste moevere of...fr. The Knigtes tale. Geoffrey Chaucer. 6908-8

FIRSTFRUITS

Firstfruits in 1812. Wallace Rice. 6946-0
Firth
    Britannia rules of orthography. 6722-0
Firth, Jelen M.
    Shadowy outline. 6750-6
Firzgerald, Edward
    Old song. 6437-X
    The three arrows. 6437-X
Fischer, Louise
    Echo. 6850-2
    Rondel of yellow. 6850-2
    Sea fantasy. 6850-2
Fischer, William J.
    In the cloister. 6285-7
Fischerknabe singt im kahn. Johann C. Friedrich von Schiller. 6252-0
Fish. W.W. Eustace Ross. 6446-9
Fish. Sydney Smith. 6230-X
Fish food. John Wheelwright. 6399-3
Fish have their times to bite. Unknown. 6802-2
"The fish hit water nymphs, breaking surface". Late spring in the nuclear age. Andrew Hudgins. 7032-9
Fish poem. Joy Kogawa. 6767-0
Fish story. P.L. Jacobs. 6870-7
A fish story. Henry Augustin Beers. 6089-7,6723-9
The fish's wish. Carolyn Wells. 6882-0
Fish, F.W.
    Then and now, 1776-1876. 6912-6
Fish, Lisbeth G.
    Ode to Longs Peak. 6836-7
Fish, W.W. Blair
    Lavender. 6338-1
The fish, the man, and the spirit, sels. Leigh Hunt. 6258-X,6199-0,6545-7
The fish, the man, and the spirit. Leigh Hunt. 6125-7
Fish-day. Mazie V. Caruthers. 6120-6
The fish-hawk. John Hall Wheelock. 6464-7,6723-9,6073-0, 6395-0,6506-2,6037-4,6393-4
Fish-women at Calais. Unknown. 6142-7
The fish. Elizabeth Bishop. 6399-3
The fish. Benjamin Albert Botkin. 6397-7
The fish. Rupert Brooke. 6234-2,6510-4
The fish. Marianne Moore. 6399-3,6491-4
Fishback, Margaret
    Brooklynese champion. 6722-0
    I stand corrected. 6722-0
    I take 'em and like 'em. 6722-0
    On viewing a florist's whimsy at fifty-ninth and... 6722-0
    Out of the woods. 6654-2
    Per contra. 6144-3,6076-5,6102-8
    Poem for Mother's Day. 6287-3
    Queen of the mayhem. 6628-3
    Sprig fever. 6089-7
    A strange interlude. 6089-7
    This way out. 6026-9
    Triolet on a downhill road. 6722-0
    Unrequited love on the back piazza. 6120-6
    Wanted: one cave man with club. 6722-0
Fishburn, Josephine Redmond
    Child poems. 6033-1
Fisher Jamie. John Buchan. 6269-5,6331-4
"The fisher lad stooped from his skiff-side". Delusion. Hattie Horner Louthan. 6836-7
Fisher song. John Greenleaf Whittier. 6424-8
A fisher's apology. Arthur Johnstone. 6845-6
The Fisher's boy. Henry David Thoreau. 6125-7,6431-0
"The fisher's clothes, though cheap, withstand". Impu Mon-in No Osuke. 6852-9
The fisher's cottage. Heinrich Heine. 6302-0
The fisher's cottage. Heinrich Heine. 6271-7
The fisher's cottage. Charles Godfrey Leland. 6302-0
The fisher's life. Unknown. 6125-7
The fisher's widow. Arthur Symons. 6793-X
Fisher, A. Hugh
    The old Cossack. 6777-8
Fisher, Aileen
    A coffeepot face. 6891-X
    Rich. 6891-X
Fisher, Charles
    Preoccupation with death. 6360-8
    Some prodigies. 6360-8
Fisher, Ella Warner
    Go to sleep. 7030-2
Fisher, Hazel Grant
    When mother quilted. 6799-9
Fisher, Helen Dwight
    The immigrant Madonna. 6954-1
Fisher, Helen Field
    The new leaf. 6337-3
Fisher, Jasper
    Fuimus troes, sels. 6562-7
    A morisco. 6334-9,6563-5,6563-5
    "The Skie is glad...", fr. Fuimus troes. 6562-7
    "So the Siluer-feathered...", fr. Fuimus troes. 6562-7
    Song ("At the spring.") 6334-9
    Song to a viol. 6317-9,6563-5
Fisher, Lala
    The reaper. 6591-0,6592-9
Fisher, Lenore Eversole
    Anatomical observation. 6750-6
    Mistake. 6750-6
    "When the last person/Here is dead." 6750-6
Fisher, Lori
    Pentimento for an art student. 6966-5
Fisher, Mahlon Leonard
    Afterwards. 6556-2
    If one should come. 6029-3
    In cool, green haunts. 6510-4
    July. 6029-3
    Love of children. 6032-3
    My mother. 6393-4
    My song, be silent. 6032-3
    November. 6027-7,6102-8
    Old amaze. 6556-2
    The old plough-horse. 6510-4,6509-0
    Oxen. 6032-3,6510-4
    Per contra. 6144-3,6076-5,6102-8,6337-3
    A poet to his father. 6393-4
    Stairways. 6032-3
    When I am ended. 6979-7
Fisher, P.J.
    The faithful comrade. 7031-0
Fisher, Phil J.
    'I die daily.' 6337-3
Fisher, Robert
    New Hampshire. 6662-3
Fisher, Rubye Mae
    Monody. 6850-2
    Rival. 6850-2
    Spring song. 6850-2
    To a stray cat. 6850-2
The fisher-boat. Eliza Cook. 7037-X
Fisher-boy in the boat, fr. Songs of Lucerne. Johann C. Friedrich von Schiller. 6749-2
A fisher-folk legend of Picardie. Gertrude Huntington McGiffert. 6838-3
The fisher-lad.. J.A. Nicklin. 6474-4
The fisher. Johann Wolfgang von Goethe. 6302-0;6385-3
Fisherman. Harry Kemp. 6798-0
"A fisherman bold was Peterkin Spray". The wonderful fishing of Peterkin Spray. Isabel Ecclestone Mackay. 6797-2
"The fisherman goes out at dawn". The fisherman. Abbie Farwell Brown. 6833-7
Fisherman husband. Brenda Chamberlain. 6528-7
Fisherman Jim's kids. Eugene Field. 6949-5
Fisherman Job. James Roann Reed. 6273-3
"A fisherman in Provincetown". The small earth. Samuel L. Schierloh. 6799-9
Fisherman of the moon. Jose Gorostiza. 6642-9
"The fisherman sitteth by the ke". The ke. James Abraham Martling. 6952-5
A fisherman speaks. Scharmel Iris. 6144-3,6335-7
"The fisherman stood all day by the beach". Old Huldah. Elisha Norman Gunnison. 6914-2
"The fisherman wades in the surges". Squandered lives. Bayard Taylor. 6976-2
Fisherman' blunder off New Bedford, Massachusetts. Annemarie Ewing. 6388-8

The fisherman's boy. Unknown. 6058-7
The fisherman's chant. Sir Francis Cowley Burnard. 6089-7, 6724-7
The fisherman's feast. Eugene Field. 6949-5
The fisherman's funeral. Unknown. 6600-3
The fisherman's girl. Unknown. 6058-7
The fisherman's hut. Charles Timothy Brooks. 7022-1
The fisherman's hymn. Alexander Wilson. 6833-2,6300-4
The fisherman's light. Susanna Strickland Moodie. 6591-0, 6592-9
Fisherman's luck. Wilfred Wilson Gibson. 6833-2
Fisherman's solitude. Edgar A. Guest. 6748-4
Fisherman's song. Joanna Baillie. 6180-X
The fisherman's song. Thomas D'Urfey. 6026-9
The fisherman's summons. Unknown. 6600-3
The fisherman's summons. Unknown. 6911-8
The fisherman's tax. Grace Shoup. 6509-0
The fisherman's tomb. Leonidas of Tarentum. 6819-7
The fisherman's wife. Alice Cary. 6572-4
The fisherman's wife. Unknown. 6671-2
The fisherman.. Charles Kingsley. 6165-6,6271-7,6302-0, 6737-9
The fisherman. Abbie Farwell Brown. 6833-2
The fisherman. Jay Macpherson. 6446-9
The fisherman. Bryan Waller ("Barry Cornwall") Procter. 6133-8
The fisherman. William V.V. Stephens. 6841-3
"Fishermen say fifty years ago, instead of...". Watching whales watching us. Raymond Filip. 6767-0
"The fishermen say, when your catch is done". The sea wolf. Violet McDougal. 6891-X
The fishermen sing. Mary Belden James. 6847-2
"Fishermen will relate that in the south". The lord of the isle. Stefan George. 7039-6
The fishermen's hut. Theocritus. 6435-3
Fishermen's weather. Unknown. 6466-9
The fishermen. John Greenleaf Whittier. 6165-6,6808-1,6639-9
The fishermsn's song. Francis Davis. 6219-9
Fishers. Albert Reginald Gold. 6144-3,6335-7
Fishers. Edwin Meade Robinson. 6307-1
Fishers. Ted Robinson. 6732-8
Fishers in the night. Beulah May. 6144-3
Fishers of men. Alfred Noyes. 6151-6
Fishers of men. Adelaide Anne Procter. 6957-6
The fishers.. Herbert H. Longfellow. 6038-2
The fishers. Brian Vrepont. 6349-7
The fishers. Albert Durrant Watson. 6591-0,6592-9
Fishes. Unknown. 6937-1
Fishin'-hunger. Edgar A. Guest. 6862-6
Fishin'.. Louise Ayres Garnett. 6036-6
Fishing. George A. Baker. 6187-7
Fishing. Sarah A. Dixon. 6798-0
Fishing. Edgar A. Guest. 6374-8
Fishing. Unknown. 6132-X
Fishing. Ella Wheeler Wilcox. 6695-X
The fishing fleet. Lincoln Colcord. 6653-4
Fishing for water buckets in the cistern. A.M. Fleming. 6799-9
Fishing in the Australian alps. Ernest G. Moll. 6722-0
The fishing party. James Whitcomb Riley. 6993-2
Fishing song. Rose Terry Cooke. 6240-7,6271-7
Fishing song. Conrad Orton Milliken. 6936-3
"Fishing this morning at the mouth of the...". Fort Macon. Bruce Jenkins. 6900-2
A fishing village. Lionel Stevenson. 6843-X
"The fishing-boats are tossed about". Ne-yoshi-tada. 6852-9
Fisk, Perrin Bachellor
    Camel's hump. 7030-2
Fiske, Horace Spencer
    The home express. 6274-1
    The liberator. 6524-4
    Olympian victors. 6274-1
    St. Gauden's Lincoln statue, Chicago. 6708-5
    Skater's song at night. 7035-3
    The song of the light canoe. 6274-1,6478-7
    A song to Illinois. 6818-9
    Toboggan song. 7035-3
    Winter speeding. 7035-3

Fiske, Isabella Howe
    If. 6130-3
A fit of rime against rime. Ben Jonson. 6378-0
Fit only for Apollo. Francis Beaumont. 6125-7
Fit remembrance. I.L. Salomon. 6979-7
Fitch, Amoretta
    If I were you. 6906-1
    In memory. 6906-1
    Resurrection. 6906-1
    A thrill in my heart. 6906-1
Fitch, Anita
    Grace before meat. 6036-6
Fitch, Arden S.
    Bill and Belle. 6682-8
Fitch, Bernice Carey
    Farm woman. 6750-6
    To one born dead. 6750-6
Fitch, W.R.
    I shall not pass again. 6303-9
Fitts & R. Fitzgerald, Dudley (tr.)
    Thebes of the seven gables, fr. Antigone. Sophocles, 6665-8
Fitts, Dudley
    Imaginary dialogue. 6641-0
Fitts, Dudley (tr.)
    Angel-nocturne. Xavier Villaurrutia, 6759-X
    Angelus. Carmen Alicia Cadilla, 6759-X
    Church. Gilberto Gonzalez y Contreras, 6759-X
    Cortege. Leopoldo Marechal, 6759-X
    The Dolmens. Gonzalo Escudero, 6759-X
    Earth. Alfonso Gutierrez Hermosillo, 6759-X
    Fugue. Alfonso Gutierrez Hermosillo, 6759-X
    God. Gonzalo Escudero, 6759-X
    A good year. Alejandro Carrion, 6759-X
    Gulf of Mexico. Alfonso Reyes, 6759-X
    Heat. Gilberto Gonzalez y Contreras, 6759-X
    Island. Wilberto L. Canton, 6759-X
    Liturgy of my legs. Pablo (Neftali Ricardo Reyes Basualto) Neruda, 6759-X
    Lone gentleman. Pablo (Neftali Ricardo Reyes Basualto) Neruda, 6759-X
    My poem to the children killed in the war in Spain. Jose Ramon Heredia, 6759-X
    Nanigo to heaven. Luis Pales Matos, 6759-X
    Nature vive. Vicente Huidobro, 6759-X
    Nocturne in which death speaks. Xavier Villaurrutia, 6759-X
    November 7: Ode to a day of victories. Pablo (Neftali Ricardo Reyes Basualto) Neruda, 6759-X
    Number 017. Constantino Suasnavar, 6759-X
    Number 021. Constantino Suasnavar, 6759-X
    Number 043. Constantino Suasnavar, 6759-X
    Oblivion. Octavio Paz, 6759-X
    The perfect life. Jorge Carrera Andrade, 6759-X
    Praise of Saccarello Street. H. Sanchez Quell, 6759-X
    Prayer for each awakening. Luis Cane, 6759-X
    Recollection of love. Efrain Huerta, 6759-X
    Responsories. Carmen Alicia Cadilla, 6759-X
    Responsory for Garcia Lorca. Oscar Castro Z., 6759-X
    Sad air. Carmen Alicia Cadilla, 6759-X
    She. Vicente Huidobro, 6759-X
    Sleepless Palinurus. Silvina Ocampo, 6759-X
    The sounds of dawn. Efrain Huerta, 6759-X
    The sower. R. Olovares Figueroa, 6759-X
    Sunday. Carlos Pellicer, 6759-X
    Third time. Carlos Pellicer, 6759-X
    Tomorrow. Regino Pedroso, 6759-X
    Training. Demetrio Herrera S., 6759-X
    Visit to a tenement. Nicolas Guillen, 6759-X
    The wall. Octavio Paz, 6759-X
Fitz Travers' song. Sir Walter Scott. 6438-8
Fitz-Geffrey, Charles
    The bee. 6182-6
    Drake, sels. 6483-3
    The English captains. 6547-3
    The last voyage of Sir Francis Drake, and Sir John... 6547-3
    On Sir Francis Drake. 6547-3
    Take frankincense, O God, fr. Holy transportations. 6125-7

Fitz-Greene Halleck. John Greenleaf Whittier. 6385-3
Fitz-Greene, Halleck
   Elegy in memory of Joseph Rodman Drake. 6088-9,6396-9
Fitz-James and Roderick Dhu, fr. The lady of the lake. Sir Walter Scott. 6198-2,6543-0
Fitz-Patrick, Nan
   Pond Brothers, Minneapolis. 6342-X
   Pond brothers, Minneapolis, 1834. 6342-X
Fitz-Patrick, Natalie
   Lake of the woods. 6342-X
Fitzgerald, Dr.
   A rhyme for Tipperary. 6724-7
Fitzgerald, Edward
   Alas that spring should vanish with the rose. 6090-0
   Because. 6652-6
   "A book of Verses underneath the Bough". 6187-7
   Chivalry at a discount. 6874-X
   The end of all. 6090-0
   For a New Year's Eve. 6747-6
   Good-night. 6874-X
   "I sometimes think that never blows so red". 6187-7
   The meadows in spring. 6423-X,6250-4,6230-X
   The miser. 6996-7
   "The Moving Finger writes, and, having writ". 6187-7
   "Myself when young did eagerly frequent". 6187-7
   Old song. 6239-3
   Omar's lament. 6844-8
   Rubaiyat of Omar Khayyam of Naishapur. 6828-6
   Song of the year. 6793-X
   Teacher of dramatics. 6042-0
   "They say the lion and the lizzard keep". 6844-8
Fitzgerald, Edward (tr.)
   Ah love! could you and I with him conspire,fr. Rubaiyat. Omar Khayyam, 7039-6
   Ah, make the most of what we yet may spend, fr.Rubaiyat. Omar Khayyam, 7039-6
   Ah, my beloved, fill the cup that clears, fr. Rubaiyat. Omar Khayyam, 7039-6
   Ah, with the grape my fading life provided,fr. Rubaiyat. Omar Khayyam, 7039-6
   And that inverted bowl they call the sky, fr. Rubaiyat. Omar Khayyam, 7039-6
   And this reviving herb whose tender green, fr. Rubaiyat. Omar Khayyam, 7039-6
   And we, that now make merry in the room, fr. Rubaiyat. Omar Khayyam, 7039-6
   And when like her, Oh Saki, fr. Rubaiyat. Omar Khayyam, 7039-6
   And, as the cock crew, those who stood..., fr.Rubaiyat. Omar Khayyam, 7039-6
   Before the phantom of false morning died, fr. Rubaiyat. Omar Khayyam, 7039-6
   "A book of verses beneath the bough," fr. Rubaiyat. Omar Khayyam, 6232-6
   A book of verses underneath the bough, fr. Rubaiyat. Omar Khayyam, 7039-6
   But helpless pieces of the game he plays, fr. Rubaiyat. Omar Khayyam, 7039-6
   Come, fill the cup, and in the fire..spring, fr.Rubaiyat. Omar Khayyam, 7039-6
   The dream called life. Pedro Calderon de la Barca, 7039-6
   Each morn a thousand roses brings, fr. Rubaiyat. Omar Khayyam, 7039-6
   Fatalism, fr. The Rubaiyat. Omar Khayyam, 6337-3
   For 'is' and 'is-not', fr. Rubaiyat. Omar Khayyam, 7039-6
   For some we loved, the loveliest, fr. Rubaiyat. Omar Khayyam, 7039-6
   Heaven and hell, fr. The Rubaiyat. Omar Khayyam, 6337-3
   Heaven but the vision of fufilled desire, fr. Rubaiyat. Omar Khayyam, 7039-6
   I sent my soul through the invisible, fr. Rubaiyat. Omar Khayyam, 7039-6
   "I sometimes think that never blows so red"fr.Rubaiyat. Omar Khayyam, 6317-9
   I sometimes think that never blows so red, fr. Rubaiyat. Omar Khayyam, 7039-6
   If it be destined. Francesco Petrarch, 7039-6
   Indeed the idols I have loved so long, fr. Rubaiyat. Omar Khayyam, 7039-6
   Into this universe, and why not knowing, fr. Rubaiyat. Omar Khayyam, 7039-6
   Lokk to the blowing rose about us, fr. Rubaiyat. Omar Khayyam, 7039-6
   The moving finger writes, and, having writ, fr.Rubaiyat. Omar Khayyam, 7039-6
   Oh, threats of hell and hopes of paradise, fr. Rubaiyat. Omar Khayyam, 7039-6
   The revelations of devout and learned, fr. Rubaiyat. Omar Khayyam, 7039-6
   Rubaiyat of Omar Khayyam of Naishapur. Omar Khayyam, 6186-9,6501-5,6427-2,6657-7,6536-8,6246 ,6726-3,6655-0,6732-8
   Rubaiyat of Omar Khayyam of Naishapur, sels. Omar Khayyam, 6198-2,6289-X,6315-2,6339-X,6527-9,6437 ,6730-1,6448-5,6153-2,6301-2,6046-3,6125 ,6094-3,6660-7,6659-3,6560-0,6199-0,6649 ,6102-8,6250-4,6656-9, 6491-4
   Salaman and Absal. Jami, 6448-5
   Some for the glories of this world, fr. Rubaiyat. Omar Khayyam, 7039-6
   Strange, it is not?, fr. Rubaiyat. Omar Khayyam, 7039-6
   That even my buried ashes such a snare, fr. Rubaiyat. Omar Khayyam, 7039-6
   There was the door to which I found no key, fr.Rubaiyat. Omar Khayyam, 7039-6
   They say the lion and the lizard keep, fr. Rubaiyat. Omar Khayyam, 7039-6
   Tis but a tent where takes..one day's rest, fr.Rubaiyat. Omar Khayyam, 7039-6
   Up from earth's center through..seventh gate, fr.Rubaiya. Omar Khayyam, 7039-6
   "Wake! For the sun", fr. Rubaiyat. Omar Khayyam, 7039-6
   Waste not your hour, fr. Rubaiyat. Omar Khayyam, 7039-6
   We are not other than a moving row, fr. Rubaiyat. Omar Khayyam, 7039-6
   Well, let it take them!, fr. Rubaiyat. Omar Khayyam, 7039-6
   What, without asking, hither hurried whence, fr.Rubaiyat. Omar Khayyam, 7039-6
   Whether at Naishapur or Babylon, fr. Rubaiyat. Omar Khayyam, 7039-6
   Why, if the soul can fling the dust aisde, fr. Rubaiyat. Omar Khayyam, 7039-6
   With me along the strip of herbage strown, fr. Rubaiyat. Omar Khayyam, 7039-6
   Wordly wisdom, fr. The Rubaiyat. Omar Khayyam, 6337-3
   Would but some winged angel ere too late, fr. Rubaiyat. Omar Khayyam, 7039-6
   Would but the desert of the fountain yield,fr. Rubaiyat. Omar Khayyam, 7039-6
   Yet ah, that spring should vanish, fr. Rubaiyat. Omar Khayyam, 7039-6
   Yon rising moon that looks for us again, fr. Rubaiyat. Omar Khayyam, 7039-6
   You know, my friends, with..brave carouse, fr. Rubaiyat. Omar Khayyam, 7039-6
Fitzgerald, F. Scott
   Obit on Parnassus. 6722-0
Fitzgerald, Gerald M.C. ("A. Page")
   Sister and nun. 6285-7
   A sister. 6285-7
Fitzgerald, Kim
   Cowardliness is a dull black. 6883-9
Fitzgerald, Mary S.
   Homing. 6789-1
FitzGerald, R.D.
   Envy goes groping. 6349-7
   Essay on memory. 6349-7
   The face of the waters. 6349-7
   Fifth day. 6349-7
FitzHugh, Sallie P.
   The little path. 6799-9
Fitzgerald, Robert Stuart (tr.)
   Houses like angels. Jorge Luis Borges, 6759-X
   Love's priority. Jorge Luis Borges, 6759-X
   The night they kept vigil in the south. Jorge Luis Borges, 6759-X
   Patio. Jorge Luis Borges, 6759-X

Sepulchral inscription. Jorge Luis Borges, 6759-X
To Rafael Cansinos Assens. Jorge Luis Borges, 6759-X
Fitzgerald, W. (tr.)
Lays of tom-cat Hiddigeigei. J.V. Scheffel, 6511-2
Fitzpatrick, Brian
Centoaph songs. 6349-7
Fitzpatrick, Gertrude
Christmas tree. 6789-1
Faith. 6789-1
Heaven. 6789-1
The lesson of the rose. 6789-1
Moratorium. 6789-1
Travail. 6789-1
Fitzpatrick, James H.
A deserted cottage. 6894-4
Fitzpatrick, John
Mater dolorosa. 6292-X,6172-9
The 5th of July. Eugene Field. 6949-5
The **five** ages. Hesiod. 6435-3
"**Five** and forty paddle steamers sailing up...". Dunkirk, 1940. Tom Farnol. 6895-2
"**Five** and twenty years ago". Our silver wedding day. Benjamin Franklin Taylor. 6815-4
Five bells. Kenneth Slessor. 6349-7
Five carols for Christmastide. Louise Imogen Guiney. 6282-2
Five criticisms. Alfred Noyes. 6151-6
Five days and nights. Vera Inber. 6546-5
Five degrees south. Francis Brett Young. 6833-2
"**Five** elms as solid underneath as ever". New Hampshire. Rosemary Thomas. 6979-7
Five epigrams. Donald Hall. 6388-8
Five eyes. Walter De La Mare. 6511-2
Five frivolous songs, sels. Robert Service. 6159-1
Five great odes, sels. Paul Claudel. 6351-9
Five inconsequential charms. Elizabeth J. Coatsworth. 6036-6
The **five** joys of Mary. Unknown. 6881-2
The **five** joys. Unknown. 6756-5
Five kernels of corn. Hezekiah Butterworth. 6703-4
Five kitty cats. Unknown. 6692-2
Five knacks for ladies. Unknown. 6182-6
Five little brothers. Unknown. 6690-9
Five little chickens. Unknown. 6530-9,6695-X
The **five** little fairies. Maud Burnham. 6452-3,6466-3
"**Five** little pussy cats". cats' tea-party<The. Frederic Edward Weatherley. 6937-1
Five little wandersongs. Berton Braley. 6853-7
Five little white heads. Walter Learned. 6552-X;6632-1
Five lives. Edward Rowland Sill. 7041-8
Five lives. Edward Rowland Sill. 6505-8,6399-3
Five lyrics from 'Drought'. Francis Carey ("Jan van Avond") Slater. 6625-9
Five men. Zbigniew Herbert. 6758-1
"**Five** mites of monads dwelt in a round drop". Five lives. Edward Rowland Sill. 7041-8
The **five** musicians. Edith Sitwell. 7000-0
Five o'clock. Richard K. Arnold. 6515-5
"The **five** o'clock bell rang out with a...". Herman. Brian Ruona. 6883-9
Five o'clock hour. Mildred Boie. 6761-1
"**Five** of us are sitting on the deck of a ship". On a ship. Veljko Petrovic. 6765-4
"**Five** oxen, grazing in a flowery mead". On a seal. Plato. 7039-6
Five prayers. Blanche Edith Baughan. 6784-0
Five questions. Betty A. Mitchell. 6857-X
Five sacred elegies. George Barker. 6391-8
The **five** seals in the sky, sels. Vachel Lindsay. 6206-7
Five serenades, sels. Arthur Davison Ficke. 6069-2
Five serpents. Charles Burgess. 6388-8
Five sisters. Kate Greenaway. 6262-8
Five songs. Edith Sitwell. 7000-0
Five sonnets. Conrad Aiken. 6783-2
Five souls. W.H. Ewer. 6051-X,6542-2
"**Five** strong dtectives are in a cell...". Third degree. Michael Gold. 6880-4
Five toes. Unknown. 6937-1
Five trees. Louis Untermeyer. 6037-4
The **five** unmistakable marks. David Jones. 6360-8

Five visions of Captain Cook, sels. Kenneth Slessor. 6384-5
Five war epitaphs. Rudyard Kipling. 6210-5
Five wines. Robert Herrick. 6089-7,6724-7
"**Five** withered years, held in a prison camp!". Wisteria scent. Eddie-Lou Cole. 6857-X
"**Five** years have passed, five summers". Lines ("Five years"). William Wordsworth. 6634-8
Five-per-cent. Robert Service. 6159-1
Fives'-court. Thomas Edward Brown. 6809-X
"**Fix** thine eyes upon the sea". The longest day, sels. William Wordsworth. 6867-7
Fixing over the barns in Vermont. Daniel L. Cady. 6989-4
Fizer, Gustav P.
Th two locks of hair. Henry Wadsworth Longfellow (tr.). 6066-8
Fjeldsted, Runolfur (tr.)
By the sea. Steingrimur Thorsteinsson, 6854-5
The cataract. Kristjan Jonsson, 6854-5
Gunnar's holm. Jonas Hallgrimsson, 6854-5
The kiss. Einar Hjorleifsson Kvaran, 6854-5
The shrike. Porsteinn Erlingsson, 6854-5
The snow-bunting. Thorsteinn Erlingsson, 6283-0
The waterfall (Dettifoss). Kristjan Jonsson, 6283-0
Flaccus [pseud].
A ballad of the great war. 6817-0
Die walkuere. 6817-0
The study hour. 6817-0
Thais. 6817-0
Flaccus, Kimball
To Alfred Kreymborg. 6979-7
Flaccus, Quintus Horatius
Non omnis moriar. 6621-6
Flaceus, William Kimball
J'aspire. 6396-9
Flag. Chi-hwan Yu. 6775-1
Flag and cross. Alfred J. Hough. 6223-7
The **flag** at Gettysburg. John E. Barrett. 6840-5
The **flag** at half-mast. Helen M. Cooke. 6695-X
The **flag** at Shenandoah. Joaquin Miller. 6576-7
Flag Day. Martha Burr Banks. 6684-4
Flag everlasting. A.G. Riddoch. 6846-4
The **flag** goes by. Henry Holcomb Bennett. 6239-3,6479-5, 6457-4,6356-X,6465-5,6478 ,6223-7,6107-9,6736-0,6300-4,6449-3,6654 ,6503-1,6512-0,6579-1,6639-9
The **flag** goes by. Unknown. 6471-X
The **flag** of England. Rudyard Kipling. 6322-5
The **flag** of freedom. Unknown. 6529-5
Flag of liberty and light. George Sanford Holmes. 6836-7
"**Flag** of our faith: lead on". Flag everlasting. A.G. Riddoch. 6846-4
The **flag** of our union. George Pope Morris. 6171-0,6718-2, 6223-7
The **flag** of peace. Charlotte Perkins Stetson Gilman. 6461-2
The **flag** of stars. Grace Ellery Channing-Stetson. 6223-7
The **flag** of the Constellation. Thomas Buchanan Read. 6223-7
Flag of the free. Walter Taylor Field. 6478-7
Flag of the rainbow. Unknown. 6924-X
Flag of then free. Francis T. Smith. 6846-4
Flag of truce. Amanda T. Jones. 6113-3
The **flag** of Washington. F.W. Gillett. 6171-0
Flag song. Harriet Prescott Spofford. 6223-7
Flag song. Avery Coonley Ward. 6465-5
Flag song. Lydia Avery Coonley Ward. 6891-X
Flag song for Washington's birthday. Annie E. Chase. 6712-3
The **flag** speaks. Walter E. Peck. 6846-4
The **flag** that has never known defeat. Charles L. Benjamin and George D. Sutton. 6471-X
'**Flag** the train'. William B. Chisholm. 6923-1
The **flag's** message. Unknown. 6158-3
flag, The. M.W. S. 6471-X
The **flag**; an incident of Strain's expedition. James Jeffrey Roche. 6946-0
The **flag**. George Henry Boker. 6223-7
The **flag**. Henry Lynden Flash. 6471-X,6223-7
The **flag**. Edgar A. Guest. 6356-X
The **flag**. Gertrude E. Heat. 6714-X

FLAG

The flag. Edward A. Horton. 6846-4
The flag. Julia Ward Howe. 6223-7,6438-8
The flag. Lucy Larcom. 6820-0
The flag. Arthur Macy. 6260-1
The flag. Henry C. Potter. 6223-7
The flag. M.W. S. 6223-7
The flag. Felix E. Schelling. 6443-4
The flag. Benjamin Franklin Taylor. 6815-4
The flag. Unknown. 6156-7
Flagg and Julian Street, James Montgomery
    Said Opie Read. 6089-7
Flagg, Ellen H.
    The Blue and the Gray. 6304-7
    Death the peacemaker. 6074-9,6340-3
Flagg, James Montgomery
    Limerick:"Said the Reverend Jabez McCotton." 6308-X
Flagg, Wilson
    The O'Lincoln family. 6385-3,6597-X,6742-5
The flagon.. Pannard. 6724-7
Flagrante bello. K.C. Spiers. 7031-0
Flags. Unknown. 6937-1
"The flags below the shadowy fern". Summer's ending.
    Andrew Lang. 6771-9
The flags on Fifth Avenue. Christopher Morley. 6653-4
Flaherty, Gunner P. J.
    ...But not forgotten. 6468-X
Flaischlen, Casar
    Most quietly at times. Jethro Bithell (tr.). 7039-6
"Flak, shrapnel crackles. Lurk in murkier lair". Berneval.
    Jack Lindsay. 6895-2
"Flakes of foam are flown from the ebb". The sea-shore.
    William Bell Scott. 6997-5
"Flakes of foam are flown from the ebb". William Bell
    Scott. 6793-X
Flamborough Head. Thomas Moult. 6331-4
Flamboyant. Minnie Elizabeth Otto. 6799-9
Flame. Hermann Ford Martin. 6038-2
Flame. Elizabetth Greene Streator. 6270-9
Flame. E.L.F. Van Dyke. 6750-6
Flame and gray. Elizabeth Ball. 6397-7
"A flame drawn from the depths of slumber". Bronze law. Je-
    chun Park. 6775-1
Flame from ice. Mabel Wing Castle. 6316-0
The flame tree, fr. Australian transcripts. William
    ("Fiona Macleod") Sharp. 6768-9
"Flame-heart, take back your love. Swift,sure". Fire and
    water. Max Eastman. 6880-2
"Flame/rising the sooner to die". Dance. Jaime Torres
    Bodet. 6759-X
A flame. Mark Coady. 6883-9
The flame. Elise Jean Jacobs. 6847-2
The flame. Michelle Lee. 6883-9
The flame. Robert Paul Turbeville. 7016-7
"The flames of God are in the streets". Vision. Thomas
    Curtis Clark. 6954-1
The flaming circle. Louis Untermeyer. 6010-2
The flaming heart, sels. Richard Crashaw. 6933-9
The flaming heart, sels. Richard Crashaw. 6562-7
The flaming heart. Richard Crashaw. 6315-2,6726-3,6285-7,
    6563-5,6189-3,6194
"A flaming ostrich fan of red". I'd give my love. Helen
    Consuelo Feldman. 6847-2
Flaming towns. Albert Eisele. 6042-0
A flamingo's egg. Terence Heywood. 6788-3
The flamingo. Lewis Gaylord Clark. 6902-9
The flamingo. Lewis Gaylord Clarke. 6089-7
Flamingoes. Harriet Sennett. 6073-0
"Flamingos/with a one leg stance". Catalysis. Ann
    Menebroker. 6792-1
Flammer, Mary
    Liza Ann's lament. 6675-5
Flammonde. Edwin Arlington Robinson. 6029-3,6393-4,6431-0,
    6288-1,6102-8,6348-9,6556-2,6250-4,6076-5
Flanagan, Dorothy Belle
    Blind Boone. 6396-9
Flanary, Robert Bryan
    Lest we forget. 6799-9
Flanders. Frederick Victor Branford. 6269-5
Flanders 1915. Lady Margaret Sackville. 7031-0
A flanders grave. Nathaniel Nathanson. 6476-0

Flanders poppies. Ian Colvin. 6051-X
Flanders roses. Nikolai Ushakov. 6546-5
Flanders, Helen Hartness
    Committal. 7030-2
Flanders, Isadore Elizabeth
    In Kew Gardens. 6789-1
Flanders, Jane
    The house that fear built: Warsaw, 1943 6803-0
Flanders, O house of plenty. Karel van Woestijne. 6068-4
Flannan isle. Wilfred Wilson Gibson. 6258-X,6395-0,6458-2,
    6437-X
Flanner, Hildegarde
    A bird sings at night. 6808-1
    A bird sings at night. 6073-0
    Daphne. 6509-0,6037-4
    Discovery. 6619-4
    Dread aloe. 6808-1
    Flowers of Apollo. 6619-4
    God pity them. 6808-1
    High stream's end. 6628-3
    Hill over Rincon. 6628-3
    <u>Illusive month. 6628-3</u>
    Of old sat freedom on the heights? 6761-1
    The owl ("The sweet and ghostly laughter"). 6073-0
    Philippian. 6038-2,6505-6
    Poem for use. 6761-1
    Pray ("With him who sets the lily on the stem"). 6393-4
    Prayer ("With him"). 6393-4
    Prelude ("He speaks"). 6035-8
    The rain. 6628-3
    St. Augustine. 6037-4
    This land is America. 6042-0
    To a tree in bloom. 6506-6,6509-0
    Twelve o'clock freight. 6628-3
"Flap, flap, the captive bird in the cage". The scholar in
    the narrow street. Tso Ssu. 7039-6
Flash. Stephen Todd Booker. 6870-7
Flash. Hazel Hall. 6007-2,6619-4
The flash frigate. Unknown. 6547-3
"The flash of blue wings 'cross the sky". The pageant.
    Sylvia Clark. 6764-6
"Flash of jewelled sunlight". To an April child. Hilda
    Mary Hooke. 6797-2
"A flash of lightning petrified, austere". The Washington
    Monument. Kathryn White Ryan. 7001-9
"Flash of my coming hours illuminate...". Legend of secret
    guilt. Otakar Brezina. 6886-3
Flash, Henry Lynden
    Death of Stonewall Jackson. 6113-3,6016-0
    The flag. 6471-X,6223-7
    The gallant fifty-one. 6946-0
    The legion of honor. 6074-9
    Stonewall Jackson. 6820-0,6946-0
    <u>Zollicoffer. 6074-9</u>
Flash-lights. Mary Aldis. 6076-5,6102-8
Flash: The fireman's story. Will Carleton. 6465-5,6451-5,
    6497-3,6107-9,6574-0
"The flashing of an arc that bright & briefly". Flying
    fish. Katherine Kelley Taylor. 6833-2
Flat waters of the west in Kansas. Carl Sandburg. 6778-6
A 'flat' contradiction. S. Jennie Smith. 6927-4
Flatman, Thomas
    The bachelor's song. 6152-4
    Death. 6563-5
    The defiance. 6933-9
    The defiance. 6023-4,6152-4
    The defiance. 6933-9
    The desperate lover. 6830-8
    A dooms-day thought. 6152-4
    O, the sad day. 6830-8
    On marriage. 6722-0,6092-7
    Pastoral dialogue: Castara and Parthenia. 6152-4
    Pastoral dilogue: Castara and Parthemia. 6152-4
    The sad day. 6328-4
    The slight. 6317-9,6563-5
    A thought of death. 6933-9
    A thought of death. 6152-4
    A thought of death. 6933-9
    unconcerned<The. 6152-4
    The wish. 6563-5

The **flatter's** lament. Unknown. 6274-1
Flatterers. Edgar A. Guest. 6748-4
Flattery. Sir Charles Hanbury Williams. 6278-4
Flattery. Sir Charles Hanbury Williams. 6787-5
The **flatting** mill. William Cowper. 6814-6
Flavia. William Shenstone. 6086-2
"**Flavia's** wit, has too much sense to pray". Characters of women: Flavia, Atossa, and Cloe. Alexander Pope. 6932-0
Flavius Claudius Julianus Imperator
    Beer. T.F. Higham (tr.). 6435-3
A **flaw.** Michael (Katherine Bradley & Edith Cooper) Field. 6073-0
"A **flawless** cup: how delicate and fine". The empty quatrain. Henry Van Dyke. 6961-4
Flawless his heart. James Russell Lowell. 6946-0
Flax. Ivan Bunin. 7039-6
The **flax** flower. Mary Howitt. 6373-X,6519-8
The **flax-beater.** Alice Cary. 6865-0;6969-X
"A **flea** and a fly in a flue,". Unknown. 6083-8,6498-1,6722-0
"A **flea** and a fly in a flue". Limerick:"A flea and a fly in a flue." Unknown. 6308-X
The **flea** market. Patricia M. Johnson. 6857-X
The **flea..** Roland Young. 6722-0
The **flea.** John Donne. 6488-4,6536-8,6733-6
Flechette, Louis
    'La decouverte du Mississipi' 7041-8
Flecker, James Elroy
    Ballad of Camden Town. 6371-3
    The ballad of Hampstead Heath. 6079-X
    Ballade. 7014-0
    Brumana. 6044-7,6477-9,6659-3,6508-2
    The dying patriot. 6653-4,6044-7,6224-5,6234-2,6477-9, 6393-4
    Epilogue, fr. The golden journey to Samarkand. 6508-2
    Epithalamion. 6508-2
    Felo-de-se. 6872-3
    Forty-two poems, sels. 6234-2
    A fragment. 6234-2
    Gates of Damascus. 6234-2,6508-2
    The golden journey to Samarkand. 6395-0,6427-2,6509-0, 6541-4,6161-3,6508-2
    The Hammam name. 6210-5
    Hassan, sels. 6427-2
    In hospital. 7014-0
    In Phaeacia. 6250-4,6541-4
    Joseph and Mary, fr. Forty-two poems. 6234-2
    Last love. 6320-9
    'A linnet who had lost her way' 7007-8
    Lord Arnaldos. 7007-8
    No coward's song. 6659-3
    November eves. 6044-7,6653-4
    Oak and olive. 6331-4,6477-9,6508-2
    The old ships. 6138-9,6234-2,6331-4,6427-2,6477-9,6246-, 6246-6,6508-2,6723-9,6653-4,6258-X,6501-5,6726-3, 6371-3,6464-7,6138-9,6234-2,6331-4,6427-2,6477-9, 6246-,6246-6,6508-2,6723-9,6653-4,6258-X,6501-5,6726-3,6371-3,6464-7
    The parrot. 6073-0,6210-5
    Prologue, fr. The golden journey to Samarkand. 6508-2
    The queen's song, fr. Fory-two poems. 6234-2,6508-2
    Riouperoux. 6437-X
    Santorin. 6234-2,6258-X,6210-5
    A ship, an isle, a sickle moon. 6258-X,6395-0,6477-9, 6421-3,6250-4
    Stillness. 6246-6,6581-3,6508-2
    "Tenebris interlucentem" 6102-8,6723-9
    To a poet a thousand years hence. 6250-4,6339-X,6476-0, 6506-6,6625-9,6508-2,6125-7,6301-2,6581-3,6102-8, 6541-4
    The war song of the Saracens. 6395-0,6427-2,6437-X,6477-9,6508-2
    The Welsh sea. 6331-4
    Yasmin. 6234-2
Flecker, James Elroy (tr.)
    Don Juan in hell. Charles Baudelaire, 6343-8
    The gate of the armies. Henri de Regnier, 6343-8
    Mignon. Johann Wolfgang von Goethe, 7039-6
    Opportunity. Niccolo Machiavelli, 7039-6
    Philomel. Paul Fort, 6343-8
    Stances, sels. Jean Moreas, 6343-8
Fleckno, an English priest at Rome. Andrew Marvell. 6562-7
Flecknoe, Richard
    Invocation of silence. 6563-5
    Noble love. 6022-6
    On Mary, Duchess of Richmond. 6563-5
"**Fled** are those times, when..harmonous strains". Truth in poetry, fr. The village. George Crabbe. 6932-0
"**Fled** now the sullen murmurs of the north". The farmer's boy, sels. Robert Bloomfield. 6302-0,6385-3
A **fledgling** robin. Leonard Feeney. 6022-6,6292-X
Flee as a bird. Mary S.B. Dana. 6304-7
Flee fro' the press. Matthew Arnold. 6322-5
Flee from the press. Geoffrey Chaucer. 6328-4
"**Flee** from the press, and dwell...". Truth. Geoffrey Chaucer. 6489-2
The **fleece,** sels. John Dyer. 6198-2
The **fleece,** sels. John Dyer. 6932-0
The **fleece.** John Dyer. 6968-1
Fleecing time. Edith Sitwell. 7000-0
"The **fleecy** flakes come fallin' down". Trackin' rabbits. Unknown. 7035-3
The **fleet** at Santiago. Charles E. Russell. 6946-0
Fleet Street. Arthur Adams. 6784-0
Fleet Street. Louis Howland. 6793-X
Fleet Street. Shane Leslie. 6096-X,6477-9,6439-6
Fleet Street Eclogues. John Davidson. 6954-1
Fleet Street eclogues, sels. John Davidson. 6232-6,6301-2
"A **fleet** of schooners slowly respond". Wooden wheels. Lowell C. Ballard. 6799-9
The **fleet** under sail. Sir Franklin Lushington. 6046-3
"A **fleet** with flags arrayed". A ballad of the French fleet. Henry Wadsworth Longfellow. 6946-0
A **fleeting** passion. William Henry Davies. 6234-2
"A **fleeting** rose-bud crave eternal life". Ambition. Gertrude Huntington McGiffert. 6838-3
The **fleeting** visitant. Unknown. 6274-1
The **fleets..** M.G. Meugens. 6474-4
Fleisher, Bernice
    The perfectionist. 6966-5
Fleming, A.M.
    Fishing for water buckets in the cistern. 6799-9
    In memoriam. 6799-9
Fleming, Archibald
    The destroyers, sels. 6375-6
    The ghost of the clerk. 6761-1
    The jungle, sels. 6375-6
    Report, fr. The jungle. 6375-6
    Speech of the first sentry, fr. The destroyers. 6375-6
Fleming, Beatrice
    "We thought we'd ignore/The sudden sweet madness." 6750-6
Fleming, Elizabeth
    The chain of Princes Street. 6331-4,6466-3,6631-3
    Pear kin and apple kin. 6262-8
    Pearkin and applekin. 6262-8
    The spoon. 6937-1
Fleming, Isabel M.
    Doubt. 6799-9
Fleming, L.
    The war horse. 6846-4
Fleming, Leonard
    The wind at dawn. 6625-9,6800-6
Fleming, Marie H.
    Recall. 6799-9
Fleming, Marjorie
    Here lies sweet Isabell. 6179-6
    Sonnet to a monkey. 6228-8,6339-X,6026-9
Fleming, Mary
    Two kisses. 6022-6,6292-X
Fleming, Paul
    "I thought to work for Him. "Master!" I said". 6238-5
    To my soul. 6424-8
    "Why shouldst thou fill to-day with sorrow." 6225-3, 6238-5
A **Flemish** madonna. Charles Wharton Stork. 6102-8,6607-0, 6076-5
A **Flemish** village. H. A. 6589-9,6846-4
A **Flemish** village. Herbert Asquith. 7027-2

FLESH

The flesh and the dream. John Hall Wheelock. 6007-2
The flesh and the spirit. Anne Bradstreet. 6333-0,6288-1
"Flesh is sad, alas! and all the books..read". Sea-wind. Stephane Mallarme. 7039-6
Flesh of the furies. Minna Gellert. 6979-7
Flesh, I have knocked at many a dusty door. John Masefield. 6301-2
Fletcher
    Sweet musick. 6134-6
Fletcher and Philip Massinger, John
    Beauty clear and fair. 6430-2
    Drink today and drown all sorrow. 6430-2
Fletcher or William Rowley, John
    Come follow me, you country lasses. 6563-5
Fletcher or William Strode, John
    Hence, all you vain delights. 6563-5
Fletcher, Alice Cunningham (tr.)
    Invocation to the morning star. Unknown (American Indian), 6396-9
    Song to the mountains. Unknown (Pawnee Indian), 7039-6
Fletcher, Frances
    Requiescat. 7030-2
Fletcher, Frank
    O son of man. 6337-3
Fletcher, Giles (the Elder)
    "First did I feare, when first my love began," 6586-4
    "I live (sweetie love) whereas the gentle winde," 6586-4
    "In tyme the strong and statelie turrets fall," 6586-4
    The lady of vain delight. 6679-8
    Licia, sels. 6181-8
    Licia: sonnet XLVII. 6198-2
    "Like Memnon's rock, touched with the rising sun" 6182-6
    "Love is the blossom where there blows." 6317-9
    "Lyke Memnons rocke toucht, with the rising Sunne," 6181-8,6586-4
    An ode, sels. 6198-2
    Panglory's wooing song. 6271-7,6219-9
    "Saddle all alone, not long I musing satte," 6586-4
    "Seven are the lights, that wander in the skies," 6586-4
    Time. 6436-1
    "Twice had Diana bent...", fr. Christs victorie... 6562-7
Fletcher, Giles (the Younger)
    The celestial city. 6933-9
    Christ's triumph after death. 6186-9
    Christ's triumph over death, sels. 6315-2,6144-X
    Christ's victorie and triumph in heaven..., sels. 6144-3,6337-3
    Christs victorie on earth, sels. 6562-7
    Easter morn. 6182-6
    Excellency of Christ, fr. Christ's victorie... 6337-3, 6065-X,6730-4
    The heavenly Jerusalem. 6931-2
    In Gethsemane. 6337-3
    On the crucifixion. 6931-2
    Who can forget? 6747-6
    Wooing song. 6182-6
Fletcher, Iain (tr.)
    La giostra, simonetta. Angelo Poliziano, 6325-X
Fletcher, Ian
    Adolescents in the dusk. 6209-1
Fletcher, J.S.
    Out at sea. 6695-X,6923-1
Fletcher, John
    Amoret, sels. 6935-5
    Aspatia's song. 6102-8,6186-9
    Aspatia's song, fr. The maid's tragedy. 6102-8,6186-9, 6328-4,6153-2,6396-9
    "Away, delights! go seek some other dwelling." 6317-9, 6182-6
    Battle song ("Arm, arm..."). 6334-9
    Battle song, fr. The mad lover. 6334-9
    Beauty clear and fair. 6198-2,6563-5,6317-9,6562-7,6189-3
    Bridal song. 6733-6,6153-2
    Britons, strike home!, fr. Bonduca. 6328-4
    Care-charming sleep. 6194-X,6052-,6501-5,6737-9,6430-2, 6383-7
    Cast your caps and cares away. 6328-4
    The charm. 6198-2,6189-3
    "Come hither, you that love, and hear me sing". 6187-7, 6733-6
    Come, shepherds, come! 6182-6,6187-7
    "Come, sleep, and with thy sweet deceiving." 6187-7, 6533-3
    Come, you whose loves are dead. 6182-6
    The dead host's welcome. 6563-5,6230-X
    Dearest, do not you delay me. 6563-5
    Destiny, fr. Upon an honest man's fortune. 6337-3
    Dirge. 6198-2,6189-3
    Drinke to day...", fr. The tragedy of Rollo... 6198-2, 6562-7,6189-3
    Drinking song. 6182-6
    The elder brother, sels. 6562-7
    Evening. 6133-8
    The evening knell. 6182-6,6533-3
    Evening Song. 6239-3,6668-2
    The faithful shepherdess, sel. 6958-4
    The faithful shepherdess, sels. 6317-9,6562-7,6383-7
    The faithful shepherdress, sel. 6958-4
    Farewell, false love! 6641-0
    Folding the flocks. 6634-8
    Funeral song. 6334-9,6125-7
    God Lyaeus. 6634-8,6250-4,6301-2
    The god of sheep. 6052-8,6182-6
    Hear, ye ladies. 6186-9,6733-6,6182-6,6430-2,6092-7, 6076-5,6737-9
    "Hence, all you vain delights" 6935-5
    Hence, all you vain delights, fr. The nice valour. 6934-7
    "Hold back thy hours, dark night, till we have". 6187-7
    Hymn to Pan. 6102-8,6191-5
    In praise of melancholy. 6830-8
    Invocation to sleep. 6198-2,6533-3,6726-3,6189-3
    Jack, thou'rt a toper. 6328-4
    Lay a garland on my hearse. 6052-8,6182-6,6726-3,6181-3
    The library a glorious court, fr. The elder brother. 6934-7
    Love's emblems. 6182-6,6198-2,6733-6,6189-3,6301-2
    The lover's progress, sels. 6908-8
    Lovers, rejoice! 6182-6
    Marriage hymn. 6198-2,6189-3
    Marriage song, fr. The two noble kinsmen. 6334-9
    Melancholy. 6102-8,6186-9,6246-6,6737-9,6301-2,6246-6, 6219-9
    Merrythough's song (1). 6933-9
    Merrythough's song (2). 6933-9
    Mine host's song. 6328-4
    Morning song. 6935-5
    "Now the lusty spring is seen", fr. Valentinian. 6187-7, 6092-7,6562-7
    O lead me to some peaceful gloom, fr. Bonduca. 6328-4
    Orpehus with his lute. 6328-4,6125-7
    Orpheus. 6182-6,6150-X
    Orpheus I am, come from the deeps below. 6641-0
    The passionate man's song. 6933-9
    Pastoral evening hymn. 6190-7
    Pastoral morning hymn. 6190-7
    Pastoral reveille. 6190-7
    Prayer to Venus. 6563-5
    The priest's chant. 6933-9
    The priest's evening song. 6191-5
    The priest's morning song. 6191-5
    The river god. 6935-5
    The river-god'song. 6634-8
    "Roses, their sharp spines being gone" 6935-5
    The satyr's farewell. 6933-9
    Satyr's song. 6933-9
    The satyr. 6935-5
    Serenade, fr. The Spanish curate. 6827-8
    "Sing his praises that doth keep". 6187-7,6562-7
    Sleep ("Care-charming sleep, thou easer of all woes"). 6634-8
    Sleep ("Come, Sleep, and with thy sweet deceiving") 6501-5
    The sleeping mistress. 6198-2
    Song ("Beauty clear and fair"). 6933-9

Song ("Do not fear"). 6052-8,6182-6
Song ("Let the bells ring..."). 6933-9
Song ("Oh fair sweet face..."). 6933-9
Song for the sick emperor, fr. Valentinian. 6334-9
Song in the wood. 6182-6
A song of bridal. 6830-8
Song of the priest of Pan, fr. The faithful shepherdess. 6604-6,6660-7
Song to Bacchus. 6198-2,6189-3
Song to Pan, fr. The faithful sheperdess. 6604-6,6018-8,6660-7
Song, fr. Valentinian. 6102-8
Songs of the shepherds, fr. The faithful shepherdess. 6334-9
Sound, fame, thy brazen trumpet! 6328-4
Spring time and love, fr. Valentinian. 6827-8
Sweetest melancholy. 6198-2,6250-4,6189-3
"Tell me, dearest, what is love?" 6181-8,6182-6,6383-7
To Angelina, fr. The elder brother. 6827-8
To my mistress's eyes, fr. Women pleased. 6827-8
To the blest Evanthe. 6563-5
The tragedy of Rollo Duke of Normandy, sels. 6562-7
True in death. 6634-8
Vain tears. 6935-5
Valentinian, sels. 6102-8
Weep no more. 6182-6,6198-2,6641-0,6219-9,6189-3
What shall I do to show? 6328-4
"Who hath restored my sense, given me new breath." 6317-9
The woodlands, fr. The faithful Shepherdess. 7020-5

Fletcher, John Gould
Advent. 6337-3,6345-3
Arizona. 6509-0
Arizona poems: Mexican quarter. 6506-6
At sunrise. 6345-4
Autumnal clouds. 6348-9
The beggar's holiday. 6194-X
The black rock. 7017-5
The black rock. 6034-X
Blake. 6289-X,6345-4
Blue symphony. 6348-9
Blue water. 6776-X
Blue water. 6010-2
Branches of Adam, sels. 6012-9
Broadway's canyon. 6289-X
Building of the Hudson River Bridge. 6781-6
Channel sunset. 7027-2
Chinese poet among barbarians. 6010-2
Clipper ships. 6161-3
Creation and fall, fr. Branches of Adam. 6012-9
The day that autumn came. 6345-4
Down the Mississippi. 6299-7,6336-5
Down the Mississippi: night landing. 6506-6
Earth. 6033-1
Elegy on an empty skyscraper. 6782-4
The enduring. 6619-4,6010-2
Exit. 6289-X,6345-4
The faithful shepherdess, sels. 65 3-0
The future. 6010-2
Green symphony. 6348-9,6029-3,6253-9
The groundswell. 6619-4
Hence, all you vain delights. 6194-X,6430-2
The home-coming. 6345-4
The hoopskirt. 6299-7
The house to the man. 7017-5
Impromptu. 6010-2
Irradiations. 6299-7,6348-9
Irradiations, sels. 6300-4
Jason at Corinth. 6072-2
The joy of battle. 6322-5
Kingdoms. 6345-4
The last rally. 7027-2
Lazarus, sels. 6011-0
Lincoln. 6299-7,6556-2,6465-5,6458-2,6653-4,6030
The man beneath the mountain. 6042-0
Man his own star. 6250-4
Memorial for 1940. 6783-2
The month of May, fr. The knight of the burning pestle. 6125-7
My father's watch. 6641-0

The nice valour, sels. 6543-0
Night of stars. 6102-8,6331-4,6076-5
The night wind. 6490-6,6143-5
Noon. 6345-4
On the verandah. 6607-0
Our acts our angels are. 6424-8
Over the rooftops, fr. Irradiations. 6467-1
Painted women. 6011-0
Pan. 6668-2
Prayers. 6069-2
Prayers for wind. 6010-2,6010-2,6069-2
Prayers, sels. 6069-2
Prelude and ode. 6184-2
The priest's evening song. 6191-5
The priest's morning song. 6191-5
The queen of Corinth, sels. 6543-0
A rebel. 6010-2
Renewal time. 6979-7
The road. 6345-4
The rock. 6010-2
Russia invades Poland. 6761-1
St. Paul's Chapel, New York. 6070-6
The satyr's service. 6191-5
Satyr's song, fr. The faithful shepherdess. 6383-7
The second walk in the garden. 6348-9
Shepherds all and maidens fair. 6194-X
The skaters. 6850-2
The skaters. 6467-1
The skaters. 6850-2
Sleep. 6250-4
Snowy mountains. 6010-2
Song ("Care, charming sleep.") 6102-8
Spring. 6467-1,6338-1,6509-0,6556-2,6393-4,6030-7
The star. 6345-4
The stone place. 6345-4
Sunset. 6345-4
The swan. 7017-5
The swan. 6217-2,6250-4,6345-4
Tide of storms. 6984-3
To a survivor of the flood. 6011-0
To almighty God. 6072-2
To Columbus. 6071-4
To his sleeping mistress. 6189-3
Towards the north star. 6299-7
The tower. 6345-4
Upon the hill. 6010-2
Vision. 6619-4,6300-4
Whirlpools of purple, fr. Irradiations. 6984-3
White symphony. 6348-9
Windmills. 6393-4
Women's longing. 6092-7

Fletcher, Mary
The legend of St. Christopher. 6416-7,6669-0

Fletcher, Phineas
Canto 001, fr. The locvsts, or apollyonists. 6562-7
Chromis. 6315-2
Desiderium. 6933-9
"Drop, drop, slow tears." 6302-0,6385-3,6737-9,6189-3
Faith and knowledge fight the dragon, fr The purple island. 6194-X
The great consult of Satan and his peers. 6186-9
Hymn ("Drop, drop, slow tears") 6182-6,6271-7,6315-2, 6106-0,6562-7,6150-8,6219-9,6315-2,6106-0,6562-7
A hymne ("Drop, drop, slow tears"). 6933-9
Koila, fr. The purple island. 6194-X
Lines written at Cambridge, to W.R., Esquire. 6182-6
A litany. 6931-2
The locvsts, or apolyonists, sels. 6562-7
The overthrow of Lucifer. 6933-9
The purple island, sels. 6194-X
The purple island. 6194-X
The shepherd's life, fr. The purple island. 6194-X
The shepherd's life. 6191-5
Sin, despair, and Lucifer. 6933-9
Song ("Fond men"). 6182-6
Stella and Mira. 6191-5
To my soul in its blindness. 6563-5
Woman's inconstancy. 6182-6

Fletcher, Robert
An epitaph on his deceased friend. 6563-5

FLETCHER,

"Fletcher, though some call it thy fault...". Upon the dramatick poems of Mr. John Fletcher. William Cartwright. 6933-9
Fleur de lys. Rayner Heppenstall. 6666-6
Fleur de lys. Corinne Huntington Jackson. 6799-9
Fleurange [pseud].
    The spirit of the carnival. 6795-6
Fleurette. Robert Service. 6159-1,6509-0,6336-5,6419-1
Flexner, Hortense
    Breaking the molds. 6954-1
    Breaking the moulds. 7038-8
    Faith. 6607-0,6253-9,6653-4
    French clock. 6777-8
    Futility. 6506-6
    Holiday crowd. 6808-1
    Judgment. 6069-2
    Masks. 6506-6
    Poets. 6776-X
    Poets. 6076-5,6036-6,6102-8
    Poets ("Earth, you have had great lovers..."). 6036-6, 6076-5,6102-8
    Purchase. 6035-8
    Snuff-boxes. 6653-4
    Street of good fortune--Pompeii. 6331-4,6631-3
    The wakeful dark. 6607-0
Flexner, James
    In the hours of darkness. 6891-X
Flibbertygibbet and me. May R. Mackenzie. 6426-4
The flicker on the fence. S.M. McManus. 6929-0
A flicker went free. Robert P. Tristram Coffin. 6761-1
"The flickering lights men live by in the dark". Pieties. David Morton. 6979-7
Flickinger, Gertrude S.
    To my foster son. 6799-9
The flies: an eclogue. Thomas Parnell. 6975-4
The flies. Matthew Prior. 6278-4
Flight. Charles Stuart Calverley. 6652-6
Flight. Babette Deutsch. 6783-2
Flight. Mabel Christian Forbes. 6269-5
Flight. Muriel F. Hochdorf. 6850-2
Flight. Grant S. Hough. 6316-0
Flight. Lisa Rydeski. 6883-9
Flight. Unknown. 6396-9
Flight. Harold Vinal. 6218-0
Flight. Margaret Widdemer. 7038-8
Flight. Florence Glenn Zipf. 6270-9
Flight Commander Stork. Marian Osborne. 6797-2
The flight for life. William Sawyer. 6744-1
The flight for life. William Sawyer. 6916-9
The flight from Granada. Unknown (Spanish) 6757-3
Flight into darkness. Ralph Gustafson. 6446-9
The flight into Egypt. Emile Cammaerts. 6785-9
The flight into Egypt. Francis Sylvester ("Father Prout") Mahony. 6385-3
Flight of crows. William Ellery Leonard. 6184-2
The flight of crows. Emily Pauline ("Tekahionwake") Johnson. 6837-5
A flight of fancy. Frances Sargent Osgood. 6878-2
The flight of fondest hopes. Thomas Moore. 6102-8
Flight of kisses. Gamaliel Bradford. 6070-6
The flight of Lindbergh. Agnes Kendrick Gray. 7019-1
The flight of love. Percy Bysshe Shelley. 6246-6,6543-0, 6737-9
The flight of Nicolete. Rosamund Marriott ("Graham R. Tomson") Watson. 6875-8
The flight of Satan. John Milton. 6978-9
"A flight of mallards". Intermezzo. Clem Portman. 6857-X
The flight of the Argonauts. William Morris. 6186-9
The flight of the birds. Edmund Clarence Stedman. 6239-3
The flight of the bucket. Rudyard Kipling. 6440-X
The flight of the duchess, sels. Robert Browning. 6123-0
The flight of the duchess. Robert Browning. 6271-7,6655-0
The flight of the flyer. Cy Warman. 6836-7
The flight of the geese. Sir Charles George Douglas Roberts. 6597-X,6446-9,6073-0,6656-9
The flight of the goddess. Thomas Bailey Aldrich. 6309-8
The flight of the Gods. Adelaide Biddles. 6411-6
Flight of the roller-coaster. Raymond Souster. 6446-9
Flight of the spirit. Felicia Dorothea Hemans. 6648-8
Flight of the spirit. Felicia Dorotea Hemans. 6973-8

532

Flight of the spirit, fr. Thoughts during sickness. Felicia Dorothea Hemans. 6980-0
Flight of the swallow. Frederick Tennyson. 6785-9
The flight of the wild geese. William Ellery Channing. 6438-8,6467-1
The flight of the wild swans. Frederick William Faber. 6046-3
The flight of the Xerxes. Maria Jane Jewsbury. 6410-8
A flight of wild geese. Harold Stewart. 6349-7
The flight of youth. Richard Henry Stoddard. 6006-4,6243-1, 6735-2,6102-8,6337-3,6732 ,6431-0,6288-1,6121-4,6076-5,6300-4,6309-8,6737-9,6250-4
A flight shot. James Maurice Thompson. 6431-0,6861-8
Flight, Claude
    The confidant. 6804-9
The flight, sels. Cecil Day Lewis. 6209-1
The flight. Richard Church. 6778-6
The flight. Babette Deutsch. 7019-1
The flight. John Keats. 6543-0
The flight. Lloyd Mifflin. 6243-1,6310-1,6300-4,6646-1, 6737-9
The flight. Sara Teasdale. 6011-0,6076-5,6300-4,6038-2, 6102-8,6602-X,6619-4,6726-3
The flight. Tessa Sweazy Webb. 6906-1
The flight. George Edward Woodberry. 6393-4
Flights. Adelia Brownell. 7019-1
"Fling forth a lie among the crowd". Unknown. 6238-5
"Fling forth the proud banner of Leon again". Ancient battle-song. Felicia Dorothea Hemans. 6973-8
"Fling it from mast and steeple". Our flag. Margaret Elizabeth Sangster. 6449-3,6646-1
"Fling out our banner to the breeze". Fourth of July, 1876. W.F. Fox. 6913-4
"Fling out the flaunting banners". The spirit of the carnival. Lily Alice Lefevre. 7035-3
"Fling out the red banner!it fiery front under". Song of the red republican. Gerald Massey. 7009-4
"Fling the stones and let them all". Isadora Duncan dancing. Louis Untermeyer. 6959-2
"Fling your red scarf faster and faster...". Mask. Carl Sandburg. 6959-2
"Fling yourself here...". Unknown. 6251-2
Flinn, Patricia Burns
    Nocturne. 6818-9
Flint, Annie Johnson
    Carpenter's son. 6065-X
    Christ - and we. 6337-3
    "A glorious end". 6097-8
    He giveth more. 6461-2
    'He that believeth'. 6303-9
    I look not back. 6065-X
    The name of Jesus. 6065-X
    No other hands but ours. 6461-2
    What God hath promised. 6337-3,6654-2
Flint, Francis Stewart
    Fragment ("That night"). 6320-9
    London. 6872-3
    Poems in unrhymed cadence. 6897-9
    Prayer ("As I walk"). 6161-3,6393-4
Flint, Francis Stewart (tr.)
    Cleopatra. Albert Samain, 6343-8
Flint, Larry
    Sons of the ten. 6042-0
Flint, M.
    Mounds on the western rivers. 6752-2
Flint, Micah P.
    Lines on passing the grave of my sister. 6752-2
A flint. Christina Georgina Rossetti. 7028-0
"A flirt is she, so debonair". 'Beware'. John C. Mathis. 6983-5
Flirtation. Edgar A. Guest. 6748-4
Flirtation. Helen Hoyt. 6628-3
Flirtation. Ibn Zaidun. 6362-4
Flirtation. Claude McKay. 6880-4
Flirtation. Unknown. 6919-3
"A flirted fan of blade and gold". A flirted fan. William Ernest Henley. 6770-0
Flirting with a fan. Eugene J. Hall. 6707-7
The flitch of Dunmow. James Carnegie; Earl of Southesk. 6656-9

Flitting. James Abraham Martling. 6952-5
The flitting, sels. John Clare. 6545-7
The flitting. John Clare. 7020-5
"Float thou majestically". Flag of then free. Francis T. Smith. 6846-4
"Floating and soaring, capturing the wind". My rainbow balloon. Marla Temanson. 6883-9
The floating barque. Unknown (Ukrainian) 6115-X
Floating cloud. Marianne J. Cornell. 6249-0
The floating island. Ruth Miller. 6788-3
"Floating up from the slimy swamp". Swamp mist. Mary Lovell Cope. 6841-3
"Floating!/Floating - and all the stillness". Down the Songo. Richard Hovey. 7006-X
The flock at evening. Odell Shepard. 6032-3,6431-0
A flock of birds. Annie Chase. 6049-8
"A flock of black birds" Sojin Takei. 6981-9
"Flock of crows high from the northland flies". Autumn. Detlev von Liliencron. 7039-6
The flock of doves. Celia Thaxter. 6612-7
"A flock of swallows whirl". The adventurer. Royall Snow. 6906-1
"Flocks of days dark on the sky". Das Zahlenlied. Muriel F. Hochdorf. 6850-2
Flodden. Sir Walter Scott. 6087-0,6323-3,6378-0,6188-5, 6240-7,6621 ,6322-5
Flodden field. David Macbeth Moir. 6980-0
Flodden field. Unknown. 6098-6,6185-0
Flogged child. Joseph Joel Keith. 6218-0
Flohr, Natalie
    The martyr. 6144-3
Flood. Ethel Anderson. 6384-5
Flood. Tamiko Yamamuro. 6027-7
Flood control. Louis Stoddard. 6750-6
Flood legend. Marian L. Brown. 6857-X
The flood of years. William Cullen Bryant. 6385-3,6304-7, 6569-4,6288-1,6126-5,6265
Flood tide. Stephen Vincent Benet. 6467-1
Flood tide. Arthur Wentworth Hamilton Eaton. 7041-8
Flood tide. Hermann Hagedorn. 6501-5
Flood tide. Marjorie Alice Miller. 6374-8
The flood, fr. Metamorphoses. Ovid. 6125-7
Flood-tide. Margaret Junkin Preston. 6798-0
Flood-tide of flowers in Holland. Henry Van Dyke. 6961-4
"Flooded are the brakes and dell". To the moon. Johann Wolfgang von Goethe. 6948-7
Floods. Ella Wheeler Wilcox. 6956-8
Floodtime in Minnesota. Mary Farries. 6342-X
"Flooer o the cypress-tree". Unknown. 6325-X
The floorless room. Gelett Burgess. 6534-1
Flora's lament. Unknown. 6859-6
Flora's lamentable passion. Unknown. 6157-5
"Flora, the nymph, is dead". The dead nymph. Charles Henry Luders. 7041-8
A floral birthday greeting. E. Maude Jackson. 6661-5
Floral offerings. Unknown. 6744-1
Florence. Samuel Taylor Coleridge. 6624-0
Florence Nightingale. Henry Wadsworth Longfellow. 6793-X
Florence Vane. Philip Pendleton Cooke. 6008-0,6302-0,6385-3,6271-9,6008-0,6219-9,6735
Florence, Denis
    The Irish wolf-hound. 6090-0
Florence, Ward M.
    The Roman sentinel. 6744-1,6167-2
    The Roman sentinel. 6917-7
    The sneezing man. 6407-8
"Florence, then, no more". Exile and return. Edward Farquhar. 6939-8
Florence: design for a city. Elizabeth Jennings. 6257-1
A Florentine cycle. Gertrude Huntington McGiffert. 6838-3
A Florentine Juliet. Sarah ("Susan Coolidge") Woolsey. 6697-6,6567-8
Flores, Angel (tr.)
    Almeria. Pablo (Neftali Ricardo Reyes Basualto) Neruda, 6665-8
    The battle of Jarama. Pablo (Neftali Ricardo Reyes Basualto) Neruda, 6665-8
    Before the coming of the planes that burn the cities. Otto D'Sola, 6759-X
    Burial in the east. Pablo (Neftali Ricardo Reyes Basualto) Neruda, 6759-X
    Death alone. Pablo (Neftali Ricardo Reyes Basualto) Neruda, 6759-X
    Death over the air. Jacinto Fombona Pachano, 6759-X
    The International Brigade arrives at Madrid. Pablo (Neftali Ricardo Reyes Basualto) Neruda, 6665-8
    Last song to a girl of the waterfront. Otto D'Sola, 6759-X
    Nocturnal collection. Pablo (Neftali Ricardo Reyes Basualto) Neruda, 6759-X
    Plentitude. Otto D'Sola, 6759-X
    Sonata and destruction. Pablo (Neftali Ricardo Reyes Basualto) Neruda, 6759-X
    A warning for Abraham Lincoln. Jacinto Fombona Pachano, 6759-X
    While I sang my song. Jacinto Fombona Pachano, 6759-X
Floretty's musical contribution. James Whitcomb Riley. 6128-1
Florian, Jean Pierre Claris de
    The flying-fish. 6424-8
Florida. Jennifer M. Armstrong. 6900-2
The Florida ibis. Hezekiah Butterworth. 7041-8
"The Florida pelican/Is a doleful old bird". Ode to the pelican. Minnie Elizabeth Otto. 6799-9
Florida song. Samuel A. Hamilton. 6719-0
Florine. Thomas Campbell. 6934-7
Florio, John
    Immortality in books. 6934-7
    Of books. 6182-6
The florist's story. Edgar A. Guest. 6748-4
Florit, Eugenio
    Aquarium. H.R. Hays (tr.). 6642-9
    Atlantic. H.R. Hays (tr.). 6642-9
    The baby girl. Donald Devenish Walsh (tr.). 6759-X
    The dead nereid. H.R. Hays (tr.). 6642-9
    Death in the sun. H.R. Hays (tr.). 6642-9
    Elegy for your absence. H.R. Hays (tr.). 6642-9
    The martyrdom of Saint Sebastian. Donald Devenish Walsh (tr.). 6759-X
    Nocturne. H.R. Hays (tr.). 6642-9
    On someone's death. Muna Lee (tr.). 6759-X
    The present evening. H.R. Hays (tr.). 6642-9
    The signal. H.R. Hays (tr.). 6642-9
    Strophes to a statue. Donald Devenish Walsh (tr.). 6759-X
    To the dead butterfly. Richard O'Connell (tr.). 6759-X
Florizel in love. Louis Gilmore. 6071-4
Flos aevorum. Richard Le Gallienne. 6232-6,6266-0,6102-8, 6250-4,6309-8,6320
Flos Virginum. Maurice Hewlett. 6102-8,6301-2
Flossie. L.R. Hamberlin. 6680-1
Flossie Lane's marriage. Emma Dunning Banks. 6426-4
Flotsam. Ricardo Weeks. 6178-8
Flotsam and jetsam. Unknown. 6273-3,6385-3
Flour fritters. Isaac Taylor Headland. 6466-3
"Flour of England, fruit of Spain." Mother Goose. 6452-3
"Flourishing vine, whose kindling clusters glow". Fragment ("Flourishing vine"). Percy Bysshe Shelley. 6545-7
Flow. Michelle Schutts. 6883-9
Flow. Unknown. 6563-5
Flow and ebb. Ibn Safar. 6362-4
"Flow down, cold rivulet, to the sea." Alfred Lord Tennyson. 6138-9
Flow gently, sweet Afton. Robert Burns. 6183-4,6198-2,6706-9,6219-9,6304-7
Flow my teares fau from yor springs. Unknown. 6563-5
"Flow not so fast, ye fountains!". John Dowland's the third and last book of songs...,sels. Unknown. 6908-8
The flow of eternal light and power. Mary Mullis Hinricks. 6857-X
"Flow on forever, in thy glorious robe". Niagra. Lydia Huntley Sigourney. 6889-8
"Flow on forever, in thy glorious robe". Lydia Huntley Sigourney. 6238-5
"Flow on, noble rivers! Flow on, flow on". A song of Canadian rivers. Thomas O'Hagan. 6797-2
"Flow on, rejoice, make music". The stream set free. Felicia Dorothea Hemans. 6973-8
Flow on, thou shining river. Thomas Moore. 6328-4

FLOW'RY

A flow'ry offering, fr. Hortorum. Rene Rapin. 6649-6
Flow, O my tears! Unknown. 6182-6
"Flow, flow the waves hated". Illusion. Ralph Waldo Emerson. 7014-0
"Flow, my tears! fall from your springs". John Dowland's the second book of songs or airs, sels. Unknown. 6908-8
"Flow, Rio Verde!". The Rio Verde song. Felicia Dorothea Hemans. 6973-8
The flower ("Once in a golden hour..."). Alfred Lord Tennyson. 6049-8,6110-9,6199-0,6371-3,6655-0,6123-0, 6656-9
Flower and fruit. Julian Huxley. 6781-6
The flower and the leaf; or, the lady in the arbour. Geoffrey Chaucer. 6970-3
The flower and the leaf. Rosamund Marriott ("Graham R. Tomson") Watson. 6785-9
The flower bed. Unknown. 6373-X
Flower chorus. Ralph Waldo Emerson. 6374-8,6466-3
Flower courage. Edgar A. Guest. 6869-3
Flower dances. Unknown (German) 6373-X
The flower factory. Florence Wilkinson Evans. 6501-5,6607-0,6161-3,6265-2,6501-5,6607-0
The flower factory. Florence Wilkinson. 6393-4
The flower folk. Christina Georgina Rossetti. 6456-6
A flower from the Catskills. E. W. 6273-3
Flower game. Unknown. 6706-9
A flower garden. William Wordsworth. 6649-6
The flower girl. Unknown. 6530-9
The flower girl. Edith Wordsworth. 6925-8
A flower in the city street. Arthur S. Bourinot. 6115-X
Flower in the crannied wall. Alfred Lord Tennyson. 6154-0, 6303-9,6332-2,6497-3,6501-5,6657 ,6232-6,6289-X,6123-0,6623-2,6337-3,6655 ,6527-9,6730-1,6723-9,6464-7, 6424-8,6656 ,6421-3,6371-3,6737-9,6560-0,6107-9,6250 ,6102-8,6110-9
A flower is looking through the ground. Harold Monro. 6872-3
"The flower is repeated". Windflower leaf. Carl Sandburg. 6776-X
The flower mission. Unknown. 6049-8
The flower o' Dumblane. Robert Tannahill. 6302-0,6385-3, 6543-0
The flower of beauty. George Darley. 6656-9
The flower of finae. Thomas Osborne Davis. 6302-0;6385-3
The flower of flowers, fr. The mistress of Philarete. George Wither. 6934-7
Flower of hemp. Louise Ayres Garnett. 6393-4
The flower of Jesse. John Awdlay (atr) 6756-1
The flower of Levern side. Robert Tannahill. 6960-6
Flower of liberty. Oliver Wendell Holmes. 6498-1,6049-8, 6465-5,6707-7,6223-7,6964
The flower of liberty. Oliver Wendell Holmes. 6914-2
Flower of love. Oscar Wilde. 6732-8
The flower of love lies bleeding. Richard Henry Stoddard. 6753-0,6004-8
The flower of love, fr. Melincourt. Thomas Love Peacock, 6832-4
The flower of mending. Vachel Lindsay. 6556-2,6431-0,6300-4
A flower of Mullein. Lizette Woodworth Reese. 6121-4
The flower of nut-brown maids. Eleanor Hull. 6090-0
Flower of quince. Virginia Taylor McCormick. 6038-2,6102-8, 6076-5
"Flower of starry clearness bright!". To the blue anemone. Felicia Dorothea Hemans. 6973-8
"Flower of the autumn bright". Goldenrod. Ethel M. Funkhouser. 6818-9
"Flower of the deep red zone". Sermons in stones. Alice Cary. 6969-X
The flower of the desert. Felicia Dorothea Hemans. 6049-8
"Flower of the dust am I". Sonnet ("Flower"). Clement Wood. 6250-4
"Flower of the mountain by the wanderer's hand". On a forget-me-not. Frances Anne Kemble. 6980-0
Flower of the world. Robert Buchanan. 6873-1
"The flower of virtue is the heart's content". Sonnet: Of virtue. Folgore da San Geminiano. 7039-6
The flower of virtue. George Wither. 6189-3
Flower of youth. Katharine (Hinkson) Tynan. 709-9

"Flower petals fall". From summer hours. Emile Verhaeren. 7039-6
Flower petals on the sleeves. Ji-hoon Cho. 6775-1
Flower play. Gerhard Ruhm. 6769-7
The flower seller. Eleanor Farjeon. 6466-3
Flower show. Isabel Fiske Conant. 6232-6
The flower spider. Alice Cary. 6060-9
The flower spirit. Unknown. 6752-2
"The flower that of all the rest". The chrysanthemum. Unknown. 6983-5
Flower to butterfly. Victor Hugo. 6949-5
The flower vendor. Luis Cabalquinto. 6790-5
Flower woman. Blanche Waltrip Rose. 6906-1
The flower's helpers. Malana A. Harris. 6048-X
The flower's knowledge. Sarah ("Susan Coolidge") Woolsey. 6523-6
The flower's lesson. Unknown. 6529-5
The flower's name, fr. Garden fancies. Robert Browning. 6321-7
The flower's name. Robert Browning. 6123-0,6232-6,6246-6, 6302-0,6385-3,6677-,6199-0,6250-4,6429-9,6655-0,6585-6
Flower, Elliott
 In poverty street. 6274-1
 The larceny. 6274-1
 Queen of her heart. 6274-1
 The soldier's wife. 6274-1
Flower, J. Howard
 Farewell. 7030-2
 A requiem. 7030-2
Flower, Norman
 A creed in a garden. 6337-3
Flower, Robin
 Epigram, The road to Rome. 7014-0
 The fairy wood. 6253-9
 Finis. 6582-1,6641-0
 The great Blasket. 6070-6
 In tuaim inbhir. 6641-0
 The open-air scriptorium. 6582-1
 Saint Ite. 6285-7
 Say not that beauty. 6250-4
 September. 6071-4
 Tir na n-og. 6253-9
 The wanderer. 6070-6
Flower, Robin (tr.)
 At Mass. Unknown, 6244-X
 Finis. Unknown, 6244-X
 In Tuaim Inbhir. Unknown, 6244-X
 My Christ ever faithful. Unknown, 6244-X
 Over my head the forest wall. Unknown, 6244-X
 Pangur ban. Unknown, 6930-4
 Pangur Ban. Unknown (Irish), 6511-2
 Saint Ita's fosterling. Saint (atr.) Ita, 6930-4
 We will not die, these lovers say. Richard Burke, 6244-X
Flower, Sarah. See Adams, Sarah Flower
The flower, fr. Pastoral poesy. John Clare. 6545-7
The flower, sels. George Herbert. 6102-8,6232-6
Flower, tree, and bird. Hermann Hesse. 6643-7
Flower-beds in the Tuileries. Grace Ellery Channing-Stetson. 7027-2
The flower-boat. Robert Frost. 6012-9
"The flower-born Blodueda". Song ("The flower-born Blodueda.") Richard Hovey. 6431-0
The flower-fed buffaloes. Vachel Lindsay. 6315-2,6011-0, 6125-7
Flower-girls. Lucy Larcom. 6129-X
Flower-market, Copenhagen. Robert Hillyer. 6331-4
Flower-pieces. Algernon Charles Swinburne. 6875-8
Flower-quiet in the rush-strewn sheiling. Austin Clarke. 6096 X
Flower-quiet in the rush-strewn sheiling. Austin Clarke. 6244-X
The flower-school.. Rabindranath Tagore. 6338-1,6421-3
Flower-songs, sels. Erik Axel Karlfeldt. 6045-5
Flower-strewn graves. Samuel Francis Smith. 6337-3
"A flower/is a flower/is a tower". Dean Antony. Ruth Weiss. 6901-0
The flower. Lee Wilson Dodd. 6619-4
The flower. William Hamilton. 6800-6

The **flower**. George Herbert. 6933-9
The **flower**. George Herbert. 6438-8,6219-9,6271-7,6208-3, 6378-0,6600-3,6641-0
The **flower**. Thomas Hood. 6092-7
The **flower**. Samuel Speed. 6563-5
Flowerdew, Anne
    Fountain of mercy! God of love! 6219-9
"**Flowered** the dusky shadows". Moon blooms. Irene Dakin. 6818-9
The **flowering** cacti. Gene Fowler. 6792-1
Flowering quince: for Rosa. L.R. Lind. 6325-X
The **flowering** rod. Beulah Vick Bickley. 6789-1
Flowering shrubs, fr. The task. William Cowper. 6545-7
The **flowering** tree. Robert Bridges. 6487-6
The **flowering** urn. Laura Riding. 6209-1
The **flowerphone**.. Abbie Farwell Brown. 6338-1
Flowers. Sir Edwin Arnold. 6980-0
Flowers. Ethel Mae Artz. 6799-9
Flowers. Clara T. Brown. 6906-1
Flowers. Anna B. Coughlin. 6249-0
Flowers. Felicia Dorothea Hemans. 6973-8
Flowers. Florence Taber Holt. 6034-X
Flowers. Thomas Hood. 6302-0,6385-3,6656-9
Flowers. Leigh Hunt. 6502-3
Flowers. John Keble. 6219-9
Flowers. James Abraham Martling. 6952-5
Flowers. Bryan Waller ("Barry Cornwall") Procter. 6980-0
Flowers. H. W. Sloan. 6818-9
Flowers. Benjamin Franklin Taylor. 6815-4
The **flowers** ("All the names I know from nurse"). Robert Louis Stevenson. 6123-0
Flowers ("Spake full well, in language..."). Henry Wadsworth Longfellow. 6047-1,6049-8,6577-5,6219-9
Flowers akin to humanity. Unknown. 6720-4
"**Flowers** always know what they should do". Jessie Orton Jones. 6999-1
Flowers and love, fr. The decameron. Giovanni Boccaccio. 6325-X
Flowers and music in a room of sickness. Felicia Dorothea Hemans. 6973-8
Flowers and spice, fr. Narva and Mored. Thomas Chatterton. 6545-7
Flowers and vegetables, fr. Syr Martyn. William Julius Mickle. 6545-7
"The **flowers** are dying since you left". To one departed. Lee Hingston. 6817-0
"The **flowers** are loved, the weeds are spurned". Weeds and flowers. John Vance Cheney. 6820-0
Flowers at the cave of Staffa. William Wordsworth. 6438-8
Flowers beloved of Christ. Unknown. 6720-4
"**Flowers** bloom bloom/In the hills". Flowers on the hills. So-wol Kim. 6775-1
"**Flowers** bloom in Christ's sermon...". Flowers. Benjamin Franklin Taylor. 6815-4
"**Flowers** by the wayside growing". Wayside blossoms. Mary Matthews Bray. 6798-0
"**Flowers** every night". Jalal [or Jelal] ed-din Rumi. 6448-5
Flowers for Lycidas. John Milton. 6634-8
Flowers for Memorial Day. Charles Phillips. 6529-5
Flowers for the brave. E.W. Chapman. 6304-7
Flowers for the brave. Celia Thaxter. 6215-6
Flowers for the graces. Sappho. 6435-3
Flowers for the heart. Ebenezer Elliott. 6980-0
"**Flowers** for the loved,the lost! Bring flowers". On a dear child. William Peter. 6980-0
Flowers for the sick. James Abraham Martling. 6952-5
Flowers from the volcano. Claribel Alegria. 7036-1
Flowers I would bring. Aubrey Thomas De Vere. 6656-9
"**Flowers** hast thou in thyself, and foliage". Sonnet: To his lady Joan, of Florence. Guido Cavalcanti. 7039-6
"The **flowers** have faded I received from thee". Faded flowers. James Abraham Martling. 6952-5
Flowers in ashes. James Matthewes Leagre. 7017-5
Flowers in the dark. Sarah Orne Jewett. 6338-1
Flowers o' the spring. William Shakespeare. 6558-9
Flowers of Apollo. Hildegarde Flanner. 6619-4
The **flowers** of June. James Terry White. 6338-1
The **flowers** of the field. John Keble. 6980-0
The **flowers** of the forest. Alison Rutherford Cockburn. 6383-7
The **flowers** of the forest. Mrs. Cockburn. 6134-6
The **flowers** of the forest. Jane [or Jean] Elliot. 6180-X, 6198-2,6323-3,6086-2,6219-9
The **flowers** of the forest. Alison Rutherford. 6180-X
Flowers of the May. Unknown. 6049-8
Flowers on the hills. So-wol Kim. 6775-1
"**Flowers** perfume under our feet". Zoo. Gary Langford. 7018-3
"**Flowers** sing to everyone". Flowers. Clara T. Brown. 6906-1
"**Flowers** sleep in the eastern glow". Life. Xavier de Magellon. 6351-9
"**Flowers** that died in the buried years". Elijah. James Abraham Martling. 6952-5
"The **flowers** the sultry summer kills". The fate of Amy, sels. John Clare. 6934-7
The **flowers** to come, fr. English Stornelli. Augusta Webster. 7037-X
Flowers without fruit. John Henry, Cardinal Newman. 6271-7, 6199-0
"**Flowers**! when the saviour's calm...eye". The lilies of the field. Felicia Dorothea Hemans. 6973-8
"**Flowers**! winter flowers! - the child is dead". Flowers for the heart. Ebenezer Elliott. 6980-0
"**Flowers**". Josef Mayer-Limberg. 6769-7
The **flowers**' ball. Unknown. 6249-0
Flowers, Sarah L.
    My daughter Jane. 6916-9
Flowers, Sydney
    Fire! 6929-0
Flowers, fr. Jubilate Agno. Christopher Smart. 6545-7
Flowers, fr. Thoughts during sickness. Felicia Dorothea Hemans. 6980-0
Flowers, fr. Winter night's tale. William Shakespeare. 6597-X,6438-8
Flowers, sels. William Beans Magruder. 6482-5
The **flowers**.. Rudyard Kipling. 6224-5,6477-9,6437-X
The **flowers**. John Galsworthy. 6888-X
The **flowers**. William Brighty Rands. 6437-X
Flowery garments. Cypria. 6435-3
The **flowery** path of life. Clara Degman Hook. 6906-1
"The **flowery** spring-I heard her, coming upon her way". Alcaeus of Mytilene. 6251-2
Flowing stream. Ibn Hamdis. 6362-4
The **flowing** tide, fr. English Stornelli. Augusta Webster. 7037-X
The **flowing** tide. Godfrey Fox Bradby. 6639-9
The **flowing** tide. Augusta Webster. 6997-5
Flown birds. Edith M. Thomas. 6121-4
The **flown** soul. George Parsons Lathrop. 6632-1
Flues, Gilmore
    Unfaltering. 7019-1
"**Flung** on my pillow does the last night's wine". Catiline, sels. George Croly. 6980-0
"A **flurried** scud of sunlit sails". The change of flags. Arthur Guiterman. 6773-5
Flush or faunus. Elizabeth Barrett Browning. 6934-7
The **flute** of krishna. James B. Thomas. 6073-0
Flute song. Unknown (Greek) 6435-3
"The **flute** that melts beneath...fingers". The pastoral. Pierre Louys. 6351-9
The **flute**. Wilfred Wilson Gibson. 6458-2
The **flute**. Jose Maria de Heredia. 6180-X
The **flute**. Pierre Louys. 6351-9
The **flute**. Amy Lowell. 6033-1,6538-4
The **flute**. Dorothy O'Gara. 6764-6
Fluttered wings. Christina Georgina Rossetti. 6656-9
"**Fluttering** spread thy purple pinions". Lines by a person of quality. Alexander Pope. 6902-9
Fly a clean flag. Edgar A. Guest. 6443-4
"A **fly** and a flea in a flue". Limerick:"A fly and a flea in a flue". Unknown. 6811-1
"**Fly away!** thou heavenly one!". On a dead babe. James Whitcomb Riley. 6892-8
"**Fly away**, bark". The empty cup. Thomas Edward Brown. 6809-X
"**Fly away**, birdie, birdie!". Release. Mary Artemisia Lathbury. 6965-7
Fly back to Christ. Charles Wesley. 6065-X

FLY

"Fly back where melodies like lilies grow". To music. Maude Gordon-Roby. 6762-X
"Fly from the world, o Bessy, to me" Thomas Moore. 6874-X
"Fly hence, shadows". Song ("Fly hence"). John Ford. 6315-2
Fly hence, shadows. John Ford. 6563-5
The fly in church. Jocelyn C. Lea. 6249-0
"Fly madly, on time, fly fast and fly free". Retort to time. Shyrlee Kohn. 6850-2
Fly not yet. Thomas Moore. 6328-4,6543-0
"Fly out, o rosy banner, on the breeze!". Song from Enamorado. John Hunter Duvar. 7041-8
Fly soft, ye gentle hours. Unknown. 6563-5
Fly to Jesus. Charles Wesley. 6065-X
"Fly to the desert, fly with me." 6homas Moore. 6302-0, 6385-3,6244-X,6600-3,6253-9
"Fly to the mountain! Fly!". Conemaugh. Elizabeth Stuart Phelps Ward. 6946-0
"Fly westward, westward, gentle wind". Ballade of Exmoor. F.S. P.. 6770-0
"Fly, envious time, till thou run out thy race" John Milton. 6935-5
"Fly, fly! The foe advances fast". Charles Cotton. 6187-7
Fly, little letter. W.C. C. 6116-8
"Fly, Love, that art so sprightly" Unknown. 6380-2
The fly-away horse. Eugene Field. 6949-5
The fly. Michael Bruce. 6131-1
The fly. Walter De La Mare. 6339-X,6808-1,6596-1
The fly. Miroslav Holub. 6758-1
The fly. B.R. M. 6937-1
The fly. William Oldys. 6271-7,6088-9
The fly. Karl Shapiro. 6390-X
The fly. Theodore Tilton. 6131-1
The flycat. Grace May North. 6130-3
Flycatchers. Robert Bridges. 6487-6
"Flye to her heart, houer about her heart," Bartholomew Griffin. 6586-4
"Flye, flye, flye from the world, O fly,..." Unknown. 6380-2
"Flying birds/Beware!" Shiko. 6027-7
The flying cloud. Unknown. 6281-4,6057-9,6281-4
Flying crooked. Robert Graves. 6209-1
The flying dead. Rose O'Neill. 6619-4
The flying Dutchman of the Tappan Zee. Arthur Guiterman. 6161-3
The flying Dutchman, sels. E.M. Clerke. 6997-5
The flying dutchman. Edwin Arlington Robinson. 6033-1
The Flying Dutchman. A.M. Sullivan. 6833-2
The flying Dutchman. Charles Whitby. 6994-0
Flying fish. Mary McNeil Fenollosa. 6431-0
Flying fish. J. Corson Miller. 6833-2
Flying fish. Katherine Kelley Taylor. 6833-2
The flying fish. Robert Finch. 6021-8
The flying fish. John Gray. 6315-2,6547-3,6125-7
The flying heralds. Benjamin Franklin Taylor. 6815-4
Flying home. Maude S. Rea. 6799-9
The flying house. Carolyn Wells. 6882-0
Flying Jim's last leap. Emma Dunning Banks. 6412-4,6426-4, 6964-9
Flying kite. Frank Dempster Sherman. 6311-X
The flying mist. Edwin Markham. 6597-X
The flying mouse..., fr. Australian transcripts. William ("Fiona Macleod") Sharp. 6768-9
The flying papooses are boys and girls with wings. Vachel Lindsay. 6206-7
The flying squirrel. Mary E. Burt. 6479-5
The flying tailor. James Hogg. 6802-2
Flying the beam. Frances Greenleaf Jensen. 6342-X
The flying wheel. Katharine (Hinkson) Tynan. 6730-1
The flying years. Unknown. 7007-8
Flying-fish: an ode. Charles Wharton Stork. 6031-5
The flying-fish. Jean Pierre Claris de Florian. 6424-8
Flynn of Virginia. Francis Bret Harte. 6481-7
Flynn, Claire Wallace
  The gift-bearer. 7019-1
Flynn, Clarence E.
  His epitaph. 6510-4
Flynn, Evelyn Grace
  Home. 6847-2
  n an evil time. 6847-2

In Mott Street. 6847-2
Lilacs. 6847-2
The teacup. 6847-2
Flynn, Joseph
  Down went McGinty. 6736-0
Flynn, Mary A.
  Jamaica pond at night. 6894-4
Foal. Vernon Watkins. 6209-1
Foam and fangs. Walter Parke. 6089-7;6440-X
Foam flakes. Standish O'Grady. 6090-0
"Foam flies white over rocks of black". Ballad of Pentyre town. Rosamond Marriott ("Graham R. Tomson") Watson. 6997-5
Foam stray. Joseph Auslander. 6039-0
"Foams the wild beach below with maddening rage". William Falconer. 6997-5
Foch. Frederick George Scott. 6797-2
Focht, Mildred
  The angel. 6847-2
  Four trees. 6847-2
  Four trees. 6478-7
  Incognito. 6847-2
  Pilgrimage. 6847-2
The focus of that face. Edwin McNeill Poteat. 6144-3
The foe at the gates. John Dickson Bruns. 6113-3
The foe within. Henry Wadsworth Longfellow. 6337-3
"The foes of Zion quake for fright". Psalm 053 Bible. 6848-0
Foetal song. Joyce Carol Oates. 6803-0
Fog. Sylvia Adelman. 6850-2
Fog. Joseph Auslander. 6071-4
Fog. Laurence Binyon. 6507-4
Fog. Ina Ladd Brown. 6799-9
Fog. Rex George Fuller. 6037-4
Fog. Robinson Jeffers. 6619-4
Fog. Alfred Lichtenstein. 6160-5
Fog. John Reed. 6347-0
Fog. Lizette Woodworth Reese. 6653-4
Fog. Carl Sandburg. 6464-7,6653-4,6491-4,6454-X,6723-9, 6052-8,6077-3,6102-8,6299-7,6332-2,6509 ,6536-8,6076-5,6153-2,6161-3,6393-4,6628
Fog - Spanish phantasy. Agnes Kendrick Gray. 6841-3
Fog at the isles of shoals. Marguerite Emilio Buxton. 6764-6
"The fog had made a twilight on the water". From this the strength. Fred Lape. 6761-1
"The fog has bandaged my eyes. I am blinded". The Dolmens. Gonzalo Escudero. 6759-X
Fog horn at night. Helen Mitchel. 6750-6
Fog horns on Lake Superior. Meda G. Casler. 6342-X
"The fog inrolling, dark and still". Where they sleep. Gretchen O. Warren. 6762-X
Fog off Brunswick Sound. Daniel Whitehead Hicky. 6783-2
"The fog settles over us/a brooding". Prairie schooner poem. Glenna Luschei. 6792-1
The fog-girl. Elisabeth Kuskulis. 6836-7
Fog-land. Edward R. Huxley. 6885-5
The fog-sea. George Sterling. 6777-8
Fog: in time of war. Charles Hanson Towne. 6761-1
The fog. Robert P. Tristram Coffin. 6527-9
The fog. Frederick R. McCreary. 6102-8,6076-5
The fog. Unknown. 6373-X
"A foggy bottom night". Folsom. Ben Hiatt. 6792-1, 6998-3
The foggy dew. Unknown. 6157-5
Fogy themes. Edward R. Huxley. 6885-5
"Foin des mecontents!/Comme bayayeuse...". Le petit homme rouge. Pierre Jean de Beranger. 6801-4
"Fold back the sun-baright hair; kiss the...". Grief and faith. Amelie ("Princess Pierre Troubetzkoy") Rives. 7041-8
"Fold now thine arms, and hang the head". To Myrrha, hard-hearted. Robert Herrick. 6830-8
Fold the banners, fr. High tide at Gettysburg. Will Henry Thompson. 6088-9
Fold your pale hands. Kathleen Close. 6253-9
The fold. Mabel Christian Forbes. 6269-5
The fold. Alice Meynell. 6955-X
The folded flock. Wilfrid Meynell. 6096 X
The folded flock. Wilfrid Meynell. 6172-9,6292-X
Folded power. Gladys Cromwell. 6032-3

Folding a shirt. Denise Levertov. 6379-9
Folding the flocks. Francis Beaumont and John Fletcher. 6271-7,6302-0,6385-3,6219-9,6424-8,6737
Folding the flocks. John Fletcher. 6634-8
Folds of a white dress/shaft of light. Deborah Keenan. 6966-5
Foley, David W.
   Within the gates. 6337-3
Foley, F.W.
   Greetings for two. 6887-1
Foley, Henel
   Youth's sleep. 6958-4
Foley, James William
   Chums. 6964-9
   Daddy knows. 6889-8
   The echo of a song. 6889-8
   A friend went then. 6085-4
   Good-morning. 6889-8
   Graduation time. 6718-2
   Greetings for two. 6085-4,6281-4
   A hymn to happiness. 6291-1
   Jim Brady's big brother. 6964-9
   Lullaby ("Sleepy little"). 6964-9
   Nemesis. 6089-7
   North Dakota hymn. 6465-5
   Old Hallowe'en friends. 6696-8
   One of these days. 6291-1
   Passamquoddy's apple toddy. 6307-1
   Plain Bob and a job. 6963-0
   Present for little boy blue. 6715-8
   Scientific proof. 6089-7
   Song of endeavor. 6291-1
   Sterlized country school. 6693-3
   Stubbed his toe. 6303-9
   A toast to merriment. 6291-1
   Undismayed. 6291-1
   Value of smiles. 6713-1
Foley, Leo T.
   For a nun. 6799-9
Folge, Leroy
   The homecoming. 6846-4
Foliage. Felicia Dorothea Hemans. 6973-8
The **Folk** of the air. William Butler Yeats. 6656-9
Folk song. Unknown. 6179-6
Folk song. Unknown. 6179-6
Folk song. Unknown. 6179-6
Folk song. Unknown. 6179-6
Folk song. Unknown. 6179-6
Folk song. Unknown. 6466-3
Folk song. Unknown. 6179-6
Folk song. Unknown. 6179-6
Folk song (1). Robert Hillyer. 6984-3
Folk song (2). Robert Hillyer. 6984-3
Folk song - from the Danish. Antoinette De Coursey Patterson. 6036-6
Folk tale. Linda Pastan. 6803-0
Folk-lore. Edward R. Huxley. 6885-5
Folklore. Cyril Dabydeen. 6790-5
"**Folks** are gettin' most too distant". Where are all the common people? Fred Keller Dix. 6906-1
"**Folks** are queer as they can be". Always saying 'don't'. Edgar A. Guest. 7033-7
Folks need a lot of loving. Strickland Gillilan. 6337-3
"**Folks** up here at Roseville got up a lectur'..". The Rossville lectur' course. James Whitcomb Riley. 6892-8
"The **folks** up here, as I conclude". Setting the table in Vermont. Daniel L. Cady. 6989-4
Follain, Jean
   Age. William Stanley Merwin (tr.). 6803-0
   Asia. 6758-1
   Asia. William Stanley Merwin (tr.). 6803-0
   The barn owl. 6758-1
   Black meat. 6758-1
   The egg. 6758-1
   The egg. William Stanley Merwin (tr.). 6803-0
   Father and daughter. 6758-1
   Housewives. 6758-1
   Signs. 6758-1
Follansbee, Mitchell D.
   I like to quote. 6722-0
Follen, Eliza Lee
   Annie's garden. 6452-3,6135-4
   The baby's birthday. 6452-3
   Charley and his father. 6131-1
   Do you guess it is I? 6452-3
   Evening thoughts. 6530-9
   Follow me! 6452-3
   The good moolly cow. 6452-3
   Good-night. 6131-1
   Kitty in the basket. 6502-3,6131-1,6456-6
   The little boy's goodnight. 6135-4
   The moon. 6132-X,6114-1
   The new moon. 6368-3,6639-9,6452-3,6502-3,6127-3,6249-0, 6373-X,6684-,6684-4,6131-1,6456-6,6638-0
   Oh! look at the moon. 6131-1,6135-4
   Runaway brook. 6456-6
   Stop, stop, pretty water. 6127-3,6373-X,6629-1,6131-1
   "Where are you going". 6132-X
"**Follow** a shadow, it still flies you". Song ("Follow a shadow"). Ben Jonson. 6219-9
"**Follow** a shadow, it still flies you." Ben Jonson. 6385-3, 6328-4,6026-9
Follow me. John Oxenham. 6144-3,6335-7,6337-3,6461-2
Follow me. Abram Joseph Ryan. 6240-7
'**Follow** me 'ome'. Rudyard Kipling. 6810-3
Follow me! Eliza Lee Follen. 6452-3
Follow me! Sheldon Shepard. 6144-3
Follow the Christ. Alfred Lord Tennyson. 6337-3
Follow the gleam, fr. Merlin and the gleam. Alfred Lord Tennyson. 6337-3,6465-5,6107-9
"**Follow** the ribs of my thought, lines". Cactus. Terence Heywood. 6788-3
"**Follow** the star. The unseen sighing wings". In excelsis. Lord Alfred Bruce Douglas. 6778-6
"**Follow** the trickroutes/homewardbound in...". Auras on the interstates. Gerald Vizenor. 7005-1
Follow thou me. Christina Georgina Rossetti. 6303-9
"**Follow** thy fair sun, unhappy shadow". Song ("Follow thy fair sun"). Thomas Campion. 6436-1
"**Follow** thy fair sun, unhappy shadow." Thomas Campion. 6317-9,6328-4,6430-2,6250-4,6383-7,6315 ,6194-X,6182-6
"**Follow** your saint, follow with accents sweet". Thomas Campion. 6182-6,6181-8,6204-0,6328-4,6301-2,6383 , 6023-4,6250-4,6189-3,6187-7,6317-9,6536
"**Follow** your saint, follow with accents sweet". Song ("Follow your saint"). Thomas Campion. 6436-1
"**Follow** your saint, follow with accents sweet!". A dying fall. Thomas Campion. 6935-5
Follow! follow! follow! James Stephens. 6253-9
A **follower.** Daisy Conway Price. 6144-3;6335-7
The **followers.** Ethelwyn Wetherald. 6115-X
Following. Gene Frumkin. 6803-0
Following Van Gogh (Avignon, 1982) Marla Puziss. 6966-5
"The **following** communication". An effective narration. Unknown. 6929-0
"The **following** fact is true". A charge to the poets, sels. William Whitehead. 6867-7
Followis how Dunbar was desyrd to be ane freir. William Dunbar. 6430-2
Folly. Unknown. 6787-5
Folly. Vivian Yeiser. 6038-2;6374-8
The **folly** of being comforted. William Butler Yeats. 6477-9, 6320-9,6659-3
The **folly** of knowledge, fr. The immortality of the soul. Sir John Davies. 6934-7
Folsom. Ben Hiatt. 6792-1, 6998-3
Folsom, August 11th: a question of races. Pancho Aguila. 6792-1, 6998-3
Folsom, Elizabeth K.
   In West Yarmouth. 6798-0
Folsom, Florence
   Linette. 6688-7
Folsom, M.M.
   Whip poor will. 6183-4
"**Fom** the hills of the west, as the sun's". The hebrew minstrel's lament. Unknown. 6848-0
Fombona Pachano, Jacinto
   America, my sweet. H.R. Hays (tr.). 6642-9

The clouds have already told me. H.R. Hays (tr.). 6642-9
The coca tree. H.R. Hays (tr.). 6642-9
The complaint. H.R. Hays (tr.). 6642-9
Dance of the lost key. H.R. Hays (tr.). 6642-9
Death over the air. Angel Flores (tr.). 6759-X
I announce the kingdom of the stars. H.R. Hays (tr.). 6642-9
The puddle. H.R. Hays (tr.). 6642-9
Since tomorrow is Sunday. H.R. Hays (tr.). 6642-9
A warning for Abraham Lincoln. Angel Flores (tr.). 6759-X
While I sang my song. Angel Flores (tr.). 6759-X
"Fond affection, hence, and leave me!". Song ("Fond affection"). Robert Parry. 6182-6
Fond love, no more. Thomas Ford. 6563-5
The fond lover. William Falconer. 6971-1
Fond maydes, take warninge while you may. Unknown. 6563-5
"Fond me! whose wretched care". Song ("Fond men"). Phineas Fletcher. 6182-6
"Fond of funerals? Yes, rather.". A grave undertaking. P.. 6983-5
"Fond youth! who dream'st that hoarded gold". Menander. 6814-6
Fonss, Otto C.
  Shooting stars. Charles Wharton Stork (tr.). 6555-4
Fontainbleu. Sir Humphry Davy. 6980-0
Fontainbleu (autumn). Sara Teasdale. 6039-0
Fontaine, Jean de la. See La Fontaine, Jean de
Fontaine, Lamar
  All quiet along the Potomac tonight. 6074-9
Fontainebleau. Sara Teasdale. 6538-4,6641-0,6011-0
Fontenoy. Thomas Osborne Davis. 6344-6, 6219-9
Fontenoy 1745. Emily Lawless. 6090-0;6174-5
Fontenoy, 1745, I. Emily Lawless. 6090-0
Fontenoy, 1745, II. Emily Lawless. 6090-0
"Foo, the little peach-bloom dog". To a roof-tile horse. William Roehrick. 6850-2
Food and drink, sels. Louis Untermeyer. 6527-9
"Food and raiment, health and fire". Luxury. Edgar A. Guest. 6748-4
Food for thought. Carol Spelius. 6857-X
"Food o' moon's beams". Patience Worth [pseud.]. 6030-7
Food of love. Harry Romaine. 7021-3
The food riots. Marguerite Wilkinson. 6880-4
Food, clothes and drink. Edgar A. Guest. 6862-6
Fool and false. Unknown (Sanskrit) 7039-6
The fool and the poet. Alexander Pope. 6089-7,6278-4
Fool and wise. Coventry Patmore. 6501-5
The fool hath said in his heart. Humbert Wolfe. 6532-5
Fool moralizing on time, fr. As you like it. William Shakespeare. 6302-0
"The fool of nature, stood with stupid eyes". The power of love, fr. Cymon and Iphigenia. John Dryden. 6933-9
The Fool reads Lear a lesson on parting..., fr. Lear. William Shakespeare. 6637-2
The fool rings his bells. Walter De La Mare. 7026-4
A fool speaks his mind. Ralph Douberly. 6841-3
"Fool! I mean not". Suicide. George Darley. 6980-0
Fool's gold. Rhys Pasley. 7018-3
Fool's gold. Clyde Robertson. 6799-9
Fool's paradise. Josephine Johnson. 6038-2
The fool's paradise. Charles Whitby. 6994-0
The fool's prayer. Unknown. 6165-6,6412-4
The fool's prayer. Edward Rowland Sill. 6277-6,6243-1,6273-3,6486-4,6706-9,6303 ,6337-3,6358-6,6459-0,6478-7,6481-7,6550 ,6358-6,6735-2,6101-X,6102-8,6232-6,6260 ,6621-6,6730-1,6732-8,6578-3,6467-1,6419 ,6309-8,6396-9,6300-4,6121-4,6431-0,6214 ,6307-1,6288-1,6102-8,6076-5,6250-4,6513
The fool's prayer. Edward Rowland Sill. 6861-8
The fool's revenge. Tom Taylor. 6656-9
Fool's songs in a windmill. Hamish Maclaren. 6780-8
"A fool, a fool! I met a fool i' the forest". Unknown. 6392-6
"A fool, when plagued by fleas at night". The fool. Eugene Field. 6949-5
Fool-youngens. James Whitcomb Riley. 6091-9
The fool. Henry Baerlein. 6541-4
The fool. Eugene Field. 6949-5

The fool. Padraic Pearse. 6930-4
The fool. Padraic Pearse. 6873-1
The fool. Robert Service. 6159-1
A fooles tounge. John Heywood. 6586-4
Foolish boy forbeare and flee. Unknown. 6563-5
The foolish boys. Unknown. 6248-2
The foolish elm. Ella Wheeler Wilcox. 6863-4
The foolish fir-tree. Henry Van Dyke. 6961-4
The foolish harebell. George Macdonald. 6743-3
The foolish little girl. George Phillips. 6130-3
"A foolish little maiden bought a foolish..bonnet". What the choir sang about the new bonnet. M.T, Morrison. 6964-9
A foolish little maiden. Unknown. 6416-7
Foolish little robin. Unknown. 6049-8
The foolish little shadow. Emily K. Solliday. 6249-0
The foolish virgins. Alfred Lord Tennyson. 6385-3
"A foolish young anarchist". Limerick:"A foolish young anarchist". H.G. Dixey. 6811-1
Foolishness. Lucille Schmedtje. 6850-2
Fools. Ben Jonson. 6182-6
Fools. Unknown. 6787-5
Fools gaze at painted courts, fr. Polyolbion. Michael Drayton. 6125-7
"Fools may pine, and sots may swill". Double ballade of life and fate. William Ernest Henley. 6770-0,6875-8
"The fools that are wealthy are sure of a...". On the marriage act. Unknown. 6874-X
Fools, knaves - flowers and trees. John Greenleaf Whittier. 6232-6
"Fools, which each man meets in his dish...". Prologue to Sir Martin Marr-all. John Dryden. 6970-3
Foot note to Eden. Annette Patton Cornell. 6750-6
A foot of earth. Sara V. Prueser. 6906-1
The foot prints and the wave. Lucy Wilson Buxton. 7016-7
Foot soldier. John Banister Tabb. 6452-3
Foot soldier. Rhea Tregebov. 6767-0
Foot, Henry Martyn
  Shadow. 6591-0,6592-0
The foot-hills, fr. Desert drift. Alice Corbin. 6628-3
Foot-note for idyls. James Branch Cabell. 6875-8
The foot-path way. Unknown. 7007-8
The foot-path. James Russell Lowell. 6126-5
The football Casabianca. Wilbur Dick Nesbit. 6274-1
Football field: evening. J.A.R. McKellar. 6384-5
The football girl. Raymond W. Walker. 6118-4
Football hero. Strickland Gillilan. 6717-4
The football maiden. Unknown. 6118-4
A football player. Edward Cracroft Lefroy. 6396-9
Foote, Agnes C.
  Annunciation to all women. 6144-3
Foote, Inez
  I love my fellow man. 6799-9
Foote, Lucius Harwood
  El vaquero. 6241-5
"The footfalls of the parting Myrmidons". Briseis. Charles Williams. 6884-7
The footfalls. Robert P. Tristram Coffin. 7040-X
Footman Joe. G. Hebert. 6787-5
A footnote. Stephen Spender. 6210-5
Footprints. Ludvig Bodtcher. 6555-4
Footprints in the snow. Alice Campbell. 6764-6
Footprints in the snow. Frank Dempster Sherman. 6597-X, 6252-0
Footprints of decay. Unknown. 6911-8
Footsloggers. Ford Madox (Hueffer) Ford. 6250-4
"The footsteps of a hundred years". The founders of Ohio. William Henry Venable. 6946-0
Footsteps of angels. Henry Wadsworth Longfellow. 6302-0, 6303-9,6735-2,6121-4,6219-9,6126-5,6288-1,6304-7
Footsteps on the other side. Unknown. 6909-6
Fop. William Shakespeare. 6438-8
For 'is' and 'is-no$_t$', fr. Rubaiyat. Omar Khayyam. 7039-6
For 'Mother's Day' Eugene Dimon Preston. 6836-7
For 'Our lady of the rocks.' Dante Gabriel Rossetti. 6378-0
For 'The wine of Circe'. Dante Gabriel Rossetti. 6655-0
For 1941. Ruth Evans. 6761-1
For a birthday. Christopher Morley. 6875-8
For a book of tales. Alfred Noyes. 6151-6

For a British flyer. Katherine Garrison Chapin. 6761-1
"For a cap and bells our life we pay". June. James Russell
    Lowell. 6820-0
For a certain beloved gentleman. Margaret E. Bruner. 6799-
    9
For a certain young poet. Halley W. Groesbeck. 6906-1
For a charity annual. Austin Dobson. 6250-4
For a child. Fannie Stearns Davis. 6891-X
For a child. Walter De La Mare. 6905-3
For a child. Eleanor Vinton. 6764-6
For a child. Charles Wesley. 6732-8
For a child expected. Anne Ridler. 6391-8,6379-9
For a child named Katharine. Louise Townsend Nicholl. 6032-
    3
For a child who died. Joseph G.E. Hopkins. 6761-1
For a closing page. Austin Dobson. 7014-0
For a cock. Eleanor Farjeon. 6554-X
For a copy of Herrick. Austin Dobson. 6483-3,6655-0
For a copy of Theocritus. Austin Dobson. 6123-0,6483-3,
    6655-0,6250-4,6656-9
For a copy of Theocritus. Austin Dobson. 6770-0
For a crippled girl. Isaac Benjamin. 6249-0
For a dancer. Josephine Jacobsen. 6979-7
For a dead kitten. Sara Henderson Hay. 6120-6,6076-5
For a dead lady. Edwin Arlington Robinson. 6288-1,6464-7,
    6723-9,6333-0,6208-3,6246-6,6726-3,6333-0,6348
For a design of a butterfly resting on a skull. Felicia
    Dorothea Hemans. 6973-8
For a dewdrop. Eleanor Farjeon. 6778-6
For a fallen star. Marie de L. Welch. 6506-6
For a fan. Richard Watson Gilder. 6652-6
For a flag-waving business man. Henry Stephens. 6850-2
For a forest walker. William Ellery Leonard. 6253-9
For a fountain. Bryan Waller ("Barry Cornwall") Procter.
    6253-9
For a gravestone in Spain. Walter Savage Landor. 6641-0
For a grotto. Mark Akenside. 6831-6
For a little bird that bludered into church. Sara
    Henderson Hay. 6076-5
For a little brown dog. Unknown. 6510-4
"For a long time I have been staring...". Liturgy of my
    legs. Pablo (Neftali Ricardo Reyes Basualto) Neruda.
    6759-X
"For a long time I watched the crows flying". The crows.
    Milutin Bojic. 6765-4
"For a man that is almost blind". Mock medicine. Unknown.
    6881-2
For a materialist. Adelaide Love. 6337-3
For a modernist sermon. Kenneth Burke. 6532-5
"...For a month now there has been no rain". Letter from
    exile. Frederick Ebright. 6761-1
For a musician. George Wither. 6933-9
For a nativity. Lisel Mueller. 6388-8
"For a naughty nabob of Nigeria". Limerick:"For a naughty
    nabob of Nigeria". Unknown. 6811-1
For a new world. John Oxenham. 6335-7
For a new year. Leonard Hinton. 6396-9
For a New Year's Eve. Edward Fitzgerald. 6747-6
For a November afternoon. Barton Hills. 6042-0
For a novice. Sister Mary Edwardine. 6761-1
For a nun. Leo T. Foley. 6799-9
For a pessimist. Countee Cullen. 6850-2
For a pessimist. Countee Cullen. 6464-7
For a pessimist. Countee Cullen. 6850-2
For a picture of St. Cecilia attended by angels. Felicia
    Dorothea Hemans. 6973-8
"For a piece of the earth". The earth cycle dream. Phillip
    Yellowhawk Minthorn. 7005-1
For a poet growing old. Lawrence Lee. 6619-4
For a poet's bride. Daniel Whitehead Hicky. 6841-3
For a poetry reading to which no one came. Larry Rubin.
    6218-0
For a quick eye for beauty. Sarah N. Cleghorn. 6861-8
'For a scrap of paper'. Paul Hyacinth Loyson. 7031-0
For a shy lover. Genevieve Taggard. 6036-4
For a silent poet. Jessica Powers. 6761-1
For a valentine ("If you could look into my heart"). Mary
    Elizabeth Newell. 6466-3
For a Venetian pastoral. Dante Gabriel Rossetti. 6110-9,
    6196-6,6655-0

For a wayside inscription. Stark Young. 6038-2
For a widower or widow. George Wither. 6271-7
For a woman near her travail. Charles Wesley. 6198-2
For a word. William Alexander Percy. 6777-8
For a young lady... Aleksa Santic. 6765-4
For a' that and a' that. Robert Burns. 6024-2,6102-8,6157-
    5,6186-9,6457-4,6479-,6102-8,6153-2,6394-2,6453-0,
    6737-9,6464 ,6302-0,6332-2,6385-3,6395-0,6732-8,6560
    ,6104-4,6152-4,6197-4,6430-2
For a'that and a'that. Charles William Shirley Brooks.
    6802-2
"For ages, wild and restless waves had cast". The jubilee
    of Melbourne. J.F. Daniell. 6768-9
For all I knew. Thomas Lynn. 6857-X
For all ladies of Shalott. Aline Kilmer. 6619-4
For all my grandmothers. Beth Brant. 7005-1
"For all of us the world's a stage". For Phillip who would
    be six years old today. Helen Doremus. 6750-6
"For all that I am of this mortal world". Credo. Thomas
    Lynn. 6857-X
"For all that I am wrong". Sonnet ("For all"). Charles L.
    Buchanan. 6327-6
"For all that laugh, and all that weep". Song ("For all
    that laugh..."), fr. The ancient sage. Alfred Lord
    Tennyson. 6867-7
For all the saints. William Walsham How. 6337-3
For all these. Juliet Wilbor Tompkins. 6260-1,6481-7
"For all this I considered in my heart...". Omnia haec.
    Bible. 6830-8
For all we have and are. Rudyard Kipling. 6224-5,6289-X,
    6290-3
For all who need. Unknown. 6337-3
For Ammonis who died at 29 at 610 Constantine P. Cavafy.
    6352-7
For an 'Homage to Rimbaud' Eugenio Montale. 6803-0
For an altar to independence. Robert Burns. 6793-X
For an autograph. James Russell Lowell. 6289-X,6337-3,6126-
    5
For an autograph, sels. James Russell Lowell. 6332-2
"For an empty crown is a bauble". Lucy Larcom. 6109-5
For an epitaph at Fiesole. Walter Savage Landor. 6110-9,
    6086-2,6624-0,6656-9
For an open mind. Vera White. 6750-6
For an unborn child. Willard Maas. 6042-0
For Annabel Lee. Edgar Allan Poe. 6121-4
For Anne Gregory. William Butler Yeats. 6315-2,6733-6,6209-
    1
For Annie. Edgar Allan Poe. 6250-4,6288-1,6126-5,6121-4,
    6077-3,6176-1,6317-9,6302-0,6365-3
For anniversary marriage days. George Wither. 6214-8,6250-
    4
For any Catholic girl. Daniel J. Honan. 6839-1
For any January first. Lilian White Spencer. 6490-6,6143-5
For any lady's birthday. Lawrence Lee. 6619-4
For apathy. Ruth H. Hausman. 6850-2
For Arl in her sixth month. Al Young. 6792-1
For Avi killed in Lebanon. Mark Osaki. 6790-5
For Barbara. Andrew Brooks. 6767-0
"For authorities whose hopes". The paper nautilus.
    Marianne Moore. 6783-2
"For awhile I too was haunted by". Amnesiac. Mark Osaki.
    6790-5
"For beauty I am not a star,". Unknown. 6083-8,6498-1
"For beauty lost and loved my spirit grieved". Recovery.
    Archibald Rutledge. 7016-7
For beauty, we thank thee. John Oxenham. 6461-2
For Belgium, fr. Masquerades. Edwin Francis Edgett. 6032-3
For believers. Charles Wesley. 6271-7
For Berenice. Pierre Benoit. 6351-9
For Betalo. Irma Brandies. 6847-2
"For better, for worse". Ellen Thorneycroft Fowler. 6620-8
For Billie Holiday. Langston Hughes. 6178-8
For Bob: a dog. David Morton. 6478-7
For boldness. Hortense Laudauer. 6640-2
For C.P. Cavafy. Haviland Ferris. 7003-5
"For brides who grace these passing days". A ballade of
    brides. Thomas Augustine Daly. 6875-8
"For Britons, chief/It was reserv'd...". British commerce,
    fr. Liberty. James Thomson. 6932-0
For charity's sake. Sydney Dobell. 6980-0

FOR 540

"For Charlie's sake." John Williamson Palmer. 6302-0;6385-3
For Chicle & Justina. Diana Bickston. 6870-7
For Christ's sake. Carl Sandburg. 6345-4
For Christmas day. Hezekiah Butterworth. 6673-9
For Christmas day. Bishop Hall. 6756-5
For Christmas day. Francis Kinwelmersh. 6328-4
For Christmas day. Francis Kinwelmersh. 6756-5
For Christmas day. Thomas Pestel. 6756-5
For Christmas day. Charles Wesley. 6152-4
For Cleo Wright. Corrine Hales. 6900-2
"For Crethis the teller of stories..." Callimachus. 6251-2
For Cuba. Robert Mowry Bell. 6471-X
"For Death we all are nurtured...". Palladas. 6251-2
For Decoration Day. Rupert Hughes. 6340-3
"For days and nights I did not sing". My dormant lyre. Januario Puruganan. 6906-1
"For days before, the wild-dove cooed for rain". Third evening. Bayard Taylor. 6976-2
"For days, along the highway, the people knelt". Before Orleans. Katherine Kelley Taylor. 6906-1
For decoration day. S.M. Kniel. 6314-4
For Decoration Day. Charles Phillips. 6684-4
For Decoration Day. Unknown. 6171-0
For Dinah, the Adeneys' cat. Anne Wilkinson. 6446-9
"For dedy liif, my livy deth I wite". Come, death - my lady is dead. Charles, Duc d' Orleans. 6881-2
"For Demerara bound with cod she flies". Escapade. Kenneth Leslie. 6833-2
For dissection. Jerome Meyers. 6482-5
For Easter day. Charles Wesley. 6152-4
"For down this path has April come again". Old April. Virginia Lyne Tunstall. 6778-6
"For each new mornitg with its light". Thanksgiving. Ralph Waldo Emerson. 6466-3
"For England when with favoring gale". Heaving the lead. J. Pearce. 6833-2,6385-3
"For easy things that may be got at will". Edmund Spenser. 6623-2
For eight-days-old. Lilian White Spencer. 6490-6
For Emily Dickinson. Hortense Laudauer. 6640-2
For England. J.D. Burns. 6784-0
For England when with favouring gale. William Pearce. 6934-7
"For England's sake men give their lives. Winifred M. Letts. 6301-2
For England's sake, sels. William Ernest Henley. 6123-0
For Ernie Marshall if he's still around. William Wantling. 6998-3
"For ever gone! the world is growing old!". A vision of the stars. Thomas Kibble Hervey. 6980-0
"For ever, fortune, wilt thou prove". To fortune. James Thomson. 6816-2
"For ever, fortune, wilt thou prove". James Thomson. 6246-6,6086-2
"For every evil under the sun". Simple rule. Unknown. 6861-8
"For every evil under the sun". Mother Goose. 6363-2
"For every ill beneath the sun". Mother Goose. 6452-3
For Exmoor. Jean Ingelow. 6437-X
"For every one". Wood-folk lore. Bliss Carman and Richard Hovey. 6890-1
"For every shaft that Cupid aims". Eros. Edward Farquhar. 6939-8
For fasting days. Muriel Stuart. 6269-5
"For fertile brain and facile tongue". Epitaph for the town gossip. Ralph Friedrich. 6761-1
For forgiveness. John Donne. 6214-8
For France. Florence Earle Coates. 6443-4
For Frances Ledwidge. Norreys Jephson O'Conor. 6483-3
For Frank. Kaye McDonough. 6901-0
"For forms of government let fooIls contest". Charity, fr. An essay on man. Alexander Pope. 6932-0
"For forty years the meetinghouse at Riverdale". The obstinate music-box. S.V.R. Ford. 6921-5
"For four months the guards sabotaged". Getting back to work (in solitary confinement) Leon Baker. 6870-7
"For France and liberty he set apart". Napoleon. Gamaliel Bradford. 7027-2
For freckle-faced Gerald. Etheridge Knight. 6870-7

For Freda. Margery Smith. 6475-2
For freedom. Edna Dean Proctor. 6678-X
For friends of Peter Pan. Laura Wright. 6249-0
For G. Wilfred Wilson Gibson. 6317-9
For General Arana Osorio of Guatemala. Wayne Miller. 6901-0
"For gentlest uses, oftimes nature takes". Engelberg, the hill of angels. William Wordsworth. 6749-2,6884-1
"For giving me desire". Desire. Thomas Traherne. 6931-2
"For God, our God, is a gallant foe". Ballad for gloom. Ezra Pound. 6897-9
"For giving me desire." Thomas Traherne. 6317-9
For God so loved the world. Georgia Harkness. 6144-3
For good luck. Juliana Horatia Ewing. 6519-8,6135-4,6368-0
For goodness' sak. Thomas Augustine Daly. 6887-1
For Gwenhwyfar and Blodeuwedd. Davies Aberpennar. 6360-8
For Hank Williams. Kell Robertson. 6998-3, 6901-0
For Harry and June. Ray Matthew. 6384-5
For he was Scotch, and so was she. Jean Blewett. 6115-X
For healing. Arthur James Marshall Smith. 6021-8
"For heaven's skae, let us sit upon the ground". Kingship. William Shakespeare. 6935-5
"For her gait, if she be walking". Song ("For her gait"). William Browne. 6102-8,6186-9
For her heart only. Unknown. 6182-6
For her on the first day out. Robert Bagg. 6388-8
"For her the proud stars bend, she sees". Fruitage. William Kean Seymour. 6884-7
"For hills and woods and streams unsung". By Faughan. Francis Ledwidge. 6812-9
"For him I built a palace underground". Building of the palace of Poseidon, fr. Orion. Richard Hengist Horne. 6980-0
"For him who sought his country's good". Washington's monument. Unknown. 6946-0
"For him, who, lost to ev'ry hope of life". Apology for vagrants, fr. The country justice. John Langhorne. 6932-0
For hire. Morris Rosenfeld. 7011-6
For his father. Lionel Wiggam. 6640-2
"For his love that bought us all dear". Sing we all, for time it is. Unknown. 6756-5
For his sake. Annie Denman. 6065-X
"For hours I've waited for the sun". Vigil. Michael Knoll. 6870-7
"For human nature hope remains alone". Hope. Theognis. 7039-6
"For I dipt into the future, far as human...". Locksley hall, sel. Alfred Lord Tennyson. 7014-0
"For I dipt into the future...". A poet's prophecy, fr. Locksley Hall. Alfred Lord Tennyson. 6930-0
"For I must (nor let it grieve thee).". A farewell to tobacco, sels. Charles Lamb. 6934-7
"For I was a gaunt, grave councillor". La fraisne. Ezra Pound. 6897-9
"For I was reared/In the great city, pent...". Town and country. Samuel Taylor Coleridge. 7020-5
For hymn reading. Thomas Hastings. 6001-3
"For I am not without authority...", fr. Jubilate agno. Christopher Smart. 6380-2
For I am sad. Don Marquis. 6089-7
For I am yet a child. Franz Werfel. 6160-5
"For I dip into the future", fr. Locksley Hall. Alfred Lord Tennyson. 6123-0
"For I must find," fr Myrtle bough. Hilda ("H.D.") Doolittle. 6012-9
"For I would walk alone", fr. The prelude. William Wordsworth. 6867-7
For inspiration. Michelangelo Buonarroti. 6214-8
For inspiration. Michelangelo Buonarroti. 6730-1;6418-3
For instance. Robert McAlmon. 6072-2
"For is there aught in sleep can charm the...". Summer, fr. The seasons. James Thomson. 6958-4
"For it is the Archer Apollo, and the Muses...". Hesiod. 6251-2
For James Earl Carter. Todd S.J. Lawson. 6901-0
For Jane. Charles Bukowski. 6792-1
For Johnny. John Pudney. 6257-1
For Johnny. John Pudney. 6895-2
For Josephina. Wayne Miller. 6792-1,6998-3, 6901-0

"For it was winter now". Short story. Henry Dalton. 6979-7
"For Jillian of Berry, she dwells on a hill". Merrythough's song (2). John Fletcher. 6933-9
"For Kirke/who understands the amusement...". For Kirke on his 34th birthday. Kaye McDonough. 6792-1
For joy. Florence Earle Coates. 6461-2,6232-6
For June. Joshua Freeman Crowell. 6798-0
For just a second. Tanya Tyler. 6899-5
For Katrina's sun-dial. Henry Van Dyke. 6961-4
For Katrina's window. Henry Van Dyke. 6961-4
For Kirke on his 34th birthday. Kaye McDonough. 6792-1
"For know, by lot from jove I am the power". The genius of the wood. John Milton. 6935-5
For lack of gold. Adam Austin. 6180-X,6086-2
"For lack of rain." Rakuten. 6027-7
For life and death. Unknown. 6273-3
For life, with all its yields of joy or woe. Robert Browning. 6066-8
"For light and life, for strength and work". I thank thee, God. Elaine M. Livingston. 6799-9
"For listening and instructional purposes". A drive to lone ranger. Ray A. Young Bear. 7032-9
"For long I stood motionless, watching" Afanasi Fet. 6103-6
"For long years on a fragile bark". God forgives, but men do not. Celestin Pierre Cambiaire. 6826-X
For love. Unknown. 6912-6
"For love of the roving foot". A good-bye. Bliss Carman and Richard Hovey. 6890-1
For love's sake. Ben Jonson. 6328-4
For love's sake. Margaret Junkin Preston. 6917-7
"For love's sake, kiss me once again". Of kissing. Ben Jonson. 6935-5
"For love's sweet sake." Bryan Waller ("Barry Cornwall") Procter. 6302-0;6385-3
For lovers, sels. John Davidson. 6819-7
For Maister Geoffrey Chaucer. Robert Hillyer. 6483-3,6036-6
For man to act, fr. Christian ethics. Thomas Traherne. 6931-2
"For many a winter in Billiter Lane". Christmas out of town. James Smith. 6996-7
"For many a winter in Billiter lane". Christmas out of town. James Smith. 6874-X
"For many thousand ages". Es stehen unbeweglich. Heinrich Heine. 7039-6
"For many years/androgynous with truth". Minerals from stone. Joy Kogawa. 6767-0
For me. Unknown. 6144-3
"For me my spear is kneaded bread...". Archilochus. 6251-2
For me the blithe ballade. Clinton Scollard. 6770-0,6875-8
"For me the jasmine buds unfllod". Song ("For me the jasmine"). Florence Earle Coates. 6310-1,6393-4
"For me, one silly task is like another". Cassandra. Louise Bogan. 7038-8
For memory's sake. Floyd W. Jefferson. 6118-4
"For mercy, courage, kindness, mirth". Song ("For mercy"). Laurence Binyon. 6102-8,6161-3,6250-4
"For mercy, courage, kindness, mirth." Laurence Binyon. 6138-9,6501-5
"For metaphors of man we search...". Sir William Watson. 6289-X
For Monique Graham. Wayne Miller. 6998-3, 6901-0
For Mulatto. Raymond Ringo Fernandez. 6870-7
"For miles the Illawarra range". The flame tree, fr. Australian transcripts. William ("Fiona Macleod") Sharp. 6768-9
For music. George Gordon, 6th Baron Byron. 6086-2
For music. Thomas Gray. 6975-4
For music. William Alexander Percy. 7014-0
For music. Bryan Waller ("Barry Cornwall") Procter. 6543-0
"For music (which is earnest of a heaven", fr.Pauline. Robert Browning. 6123-0
"For my 25th birthday in 1941 John Ciardi. 6666-6
"For my beloved daughter, now away". I would ask this. Alise Williams Whitelaw. 6789-1
For my brother and sister southwestern indian poets. Geary Hobson. 7005-1
For my darling. James Abraham Martling. 6952-5
For my father. Paul Potts. 6210-5

For my father. Paul Potts. 6895-2
For my funeral. Alfred Edward Housman. 6536-8
For my own monument. Matthew Prior. 6315-2,6634-8,6092-7, 6152-4
For my pupils in the war years. John Malcolm Brinnin. 6391-8
For my sister on her 5th wedding anniversary. Terry Kennedy. 6998-3
For my son. Muriel Rukeyser. 6803-0
For my son. Elizabeth Grey Stewart. 6750-6
For my son on his twelfth birthday. Frances Frost. 6761-1
For my students, returning to college. John Williams. 6388-8
For my wife. Julian Symons. 6666-6,6379-9
For myself. J.A. Hines. 6870-7
"For nature beats in perfect tune", sels. Ralph Waldo Emerson. 6047-1
"For nature daily through her grand design." Frederick Goddard Tuckerman. 6333-0
For New Englanders and others. Louise Owen. 6761-1
For New-Year's Day. Philip Doddridge. 6219-9
"' For nine days then we were...", fr. The Odyssey. Homer. 6251-2
For Ninette. Mimi [pseud]. 6817-0
For Noel. Beulah Allyne Bell. 6799-9
"For nobler minds, the worst of miseries". Poverty. Theognis. 7039-6
"For not in quiet English fields". Oscar Wilde. 6238-5
"For now are wider ways, profounder tides". The deeper seas. Henry Bellamann. 6833-2
For old lovers. Thomas Augustine Daly. 6431-0
For Omar. Humbert Wolfe. 6483-3
"For once the zephyrs have removed the cold". Spring-time, fr. Tristia. Ovid. 6948-7
For once, then, something. Robert Frost. 6288-1
"For one carved instant as they flew". Sea gulls. Edwin John Pratt. 6833-2
"For one long term, or e'er her trial came". Inscription. George Canning and John Hookham Frere. 6802-2
"For Orford and for Waldegrave". To Mr. Murray ("For Orford"). George Gordon, 6th Baron Byron. 6945-2
"For Priscilla". Poem ("For Priscilla"). Nicholas Moore. 6475-2
For one of Gian Bellini's Little Angels. John Addington Symonds. 6631-3
For one that hears himself much praised. George Wither. 6600-3
For one who was lovely. Bertye Young Williams. 6750-6
For one who will remember. Laura Riding. 6071-4
For one who would not be buried in Westminster Abbey. Alexander Pope. 6022-6
For one who would not take his life in his hands. Delmore Schwartz. 6375-6,6666-6
For others-and his wife. Edgar A. Guest. 6862-6
For our children. Carrie Welch. 6149-4
For our dead. Clinton Scollard. 6340-3
For our lady of sorrow. H. Boner. 6779-4
For Paddy O'Sullivan. A.D. Winans. 6792-1
For perfect peace. Charles Wesley. 6065-X
For Phillip who would be six years old today. Helen Doremus. 6750-6
For pity, pretty eyes, surcease. Thomas Lodge. 6182-6
For poets. Mary Carolyn Davies. 6880-4
For poets slain in war. Walter Adolphe Roberts. 6033-1, 6102-8,6076-5
For prosperity. Kathleen Raine. 6379-9
"For quite a long time I have worshipped Bhimasea Deva. Unknown (Newari) 7013-2
For remembrance. Amelia Josephine Burr. 6320-9
For remembrance. Duncan Campbell Scott. 6433-7
For remembrance. Edward Shanks. 6872-3
For Rhodo. Ruth Eede. 6906-1
For Roy Campbell. David Wright. 6788-3
"For round about the walls yclothed were". The house of Cupid. Edmund Spenser. 6935-5
For sale. Pitts Duffield. 7021-3
For Saundra. Nikki Giovanni. 7024-8
"For sale: a very fine line of hearts". Bargains in hearts. Maud Hosford. 7021-3
For self-help. Alice Cary. 6969-X

FOR

For service. Berton Braley. 6853-7
"For seven years my mother has been...". Visits. Daniel L. Klauck. 6870-7
"For seventy years had Israel worn the". Belshazzar. Edward Maturin. 6848-0
"For shame deny that thou bear'st love to any". Sonnet 010 ("For shame deny"). William Shakespeare. 6447-7
"For she is a vapour", fr. Wisdom. Unknown. 6282-2
For Sheila. Margaret Allonby. 6788-3
For Sir John Vanbrugh, architect. Abel Evans. 6722-0
For sleep when overtired or worried. Sarah N. Cleghorn. 6501-5
For sleeping now. Alex Comfort. 6475-2
For soldiers. Humphrey Gifford. 6641-0,6182-6
"For some of us" Michael Lally. 7003-5
"For some of us/this is where the world". Centertown. Judith Neeld. 6821-9
For some we loved, the loveliest, fr. Rubaiyat. Omar Khayyam. 7039-6
'For somehow a green earth's growing'. Mary C.T. McGuinness. 6847-2
For St. Bartholomew's eve. Malcolm Cowley. 6375-6
For Steve. Earle Birney. 6666-6
"For songs divine, half heard and half...". L'envoi. Sir Henry Howarth Bashford. 7007-8
"For spring is a boisterous child laughing...". Seasons. Mary Elizabeth Schwartz. 6906-1
"For still indulging this unruly child". Prayer ("For still indulging this unruly child"). Annemarie Ewing. 6750-6
"For still the new transcends the old...". A nobler order. Stanton Coit. 6954-1
"For Sudek, this is sex". Instead of features. Jim Moore. 6966-5
"For summer rain, and winter's sun". A thanksgiving. John Kendrick Bangs. 6303-9,6337-3
For summer time. George Wither. 6099-4
For sustenance. Coe Botkin. 6799-9
"'For that brave sun the father of the day". Dancing of the air. Sir John Davies. 6959-2
"For that first shy kiss I gave thee, love". Love's witchery. Josephine Hancock Logan. 6789-1
For that he looked not upon her. George Gascoigne. 6182-6
"For that small heart that beats beneath my...". I ask but this. Nova Dornin. 6750-6
"For that thy face is fair I love thee not". Love's reaon. Henry Van Dyke. 6961-4
For the baptist. William Drummond of Hawthornden. 6315-2, 6562-9
For the Baptiste. William Drummond of Hawthornden. 6933-9
For the beauty of the earth. Folliott Sandford Pierpoint. 6337-3
For the bed at Kelmscott. William Morris. 6828-6
"For the blessings of the field". Unknown. 66601-1
For the Burns centennial celebration. Oliver Wendell Holmes. 6126-5
For the charming Miss I.F.'s album. Eugene Field. 6949-5
For the crowning of the king, sels. Tom MacInnes. 6224-5
"For the dead and for the dying". Pro mortuis. Henry Ames Blood. 7041-8
For the dead on the mountains. David Brock. 6761-1
For the dedication of a toy theatre. Benjamin R.C. Low. 6029-3
For the depressed. Julian Symons. 6666-6
"For the dream unfinished". Plain chant for America. Katherine Garrison Chapin. 6761-1
For the eighth of December. George Meason Whicher. 6034-X
For the eightieth birthday of George Meredith. Alfred Noyes. 6151-6
For the fallen. Laurence Binyon. 6224-5,6289-X,6337-3,6477-9,6639-9
For the feast of Giordano Bruno. Algernon Charles Swinburne. 6657-7
For the feast of St. Genevieve and Joan of Arc, sels. Charles Peguy. 6351-9
For the field. Eric Chock. 6790-5
"For the finer spirits of (the world) there...". Two dwelling places, fr. 'Above the battle' Romaine Rolland. 6954-1
"For the first time a lovely scene". Eve. Lydia Huntley Sigourney. 6848-0
For the friends at Hurstmont. Henry Van Dyke. 6961-4
For the frozen girl, Jean Hilliard, and Wally Nelson... Joy Howard. 6900-2
For the future. Adelaide Anne Procter. 6957-6
For the g5fts of the spirit. Edward Rowland Sill. 6490-6, 6143-5
"For the Greek and Latin...". fr. Jubilate agno. Christopher Smart. 6380-2
"For the growing youth/What soul was his...". A youthful poet contemplating nature. William Wordsworth. 6980-0
"For the hay and the corn". Thanksgiving. Unknown. 6703-4
"For the heart, willing and not willing". Poem ("For the heart"). Jean Garrigue. 6017-X
For the hour after love. Anne Singleton. 6808-1
For the ides of March. George Meason Whicher. 6039-0
For the Lady Olivia Porter; a present upon a Newyears day. Sir William Davenant. 6341-1
For the Lady Olivia Porter;a present upon New-years day. Sir William Davenant. 6933-9
"For the immortal moment of a passionate dance". The dance. Arthur Symons. 6959-2
"For the joy of cool, green places". Prayer of the poor. Thomas Curtis Clark. 6954-1
"For the last time I risk caresses" Alexander Pushkin. 6103-6
"For the last time, maybe, upon the knoll". Farewell. Robert Nichols. 7029-9
"For the Lord's portion is his people...". The first flight. Bible. 7020-5
For the love of Jean. Unknown. 6180-X
For the Magdalene. William Drummond of Hawthornden. 6315-2
"For the man/Who, in this spirit..", fr. The excursion. William Wordsworth. 6867-7
For the marriage of Faustus and Helen, sels. Hart Crane. 6209-1
For the master's sake. Minnie Mason Beebe. 6818-9
For the meeting of the Burns Club. Oliver Wendell Holmes. 6126-5
For the meeting ¡f the national sanitary associaiton. Oliver Wendell Holmes. 7014-0
For the Moore centennial celebration. Oliver Wendell Holmes. 6240-7
"For the mountain air I'd die". Unknown. 6050-1
For the nativity of our Lord. William Drummond of Hawthornden. 6334-9
For the Nazis. Joy Davidman. 6561-9
For the new age. Richard Warner Borst. 6954-1
For the new year. John S. Hoyland. 6490-6
For the new year. Norman Nicholson. 6379-9
For the peace of Jerusalem. John Wesley. 6065-X
For the people. James Jeffrey Roche. 7009-4
For the picture, the last of England. Ford Madox Brown. 6656-9
For the poor. William Cowper. 6814-6
"For the poor body that I own". Garadh. Padraic Colum. 6930-4
For the proud-hearted. Unknown. 6747-6
For the publication of 'The poets' pack'. Estelle Rooks. 6850-2
For the Red Cross. Sir Owen Seaman. 7031-0
'For the sake of a joke'. Brian ("Korongo") Brooke. 6938-X
"For the sharp conflicts I have had with sin". Thanksgiving. Alice Cary. 6969-X
For the sheaf. Unknown (Greek) 6435-3
For the signboards. Vladimir Mayakovsky. 6546-5
"For the strength of the hills we bless thee". Hymn of the Vaudois moutaineers in times of persecution. Felicia Dorothea Hemans. 6973-8
"For the structure that we raise." Henry Wadsworth Longfellow. 6225-3
"For the tender beech and the sapling oak". The beech and the sapling oak, fr. Maid Marian. Thomas Love Peacock. 6934-7
For the undefeated. Eleanor Wells. 6761-1,6783-2
"For the union: a young true-blue". Winslow Homer, prisoners from the front. Roger Blakely. 6966-5
"For the unrecorded, for the unsaid". Once more, ye laurels... Sara Henderson Hay. 6761-1

For the wanderer. Edwin Waugh. 6747-6
For the youngest. Charles Wesley. 6198-2
"For thee I shall not die". I shall not die for thee. Douglas Hyde. 6873-1
"For thee soft crowns in thine untrambled mead". To Artemis, fr. Hippolytus. Euripides. 6987-8
For thee they died. John Drinkwater. 6051-X,6224-5
"For thee thine own self grows to be". The playmate. Winifred Lucas. 6785-9
"For thee this woven garland from a mead". Hippolytus to Artemis. Euripides. 7020-5
"For thee, Ausonia! nature's bounteous hand". Sonnet to Italy. Felicia Dorothea Hemans. 6973-8
"For thee, St. Joseph, thou most beautiful". The dunker's daughter. James Abraham Martling. 6952-5
"For them no glory as of eagles' wings". The peacemakers. Emily Vivian. 6799-9
For them that died in battle. William Alexander Percy. 6326-8
"For there are spun". Ruth, sels. William Wordsworth. 6867-7
"For there are two heavens, sweet". A heaven upon earth. Leigh Hunt. 6980-0
"For there are two heavens, sweet." Leigh Hunt. 6066-8
For these. Edward Thomas. 6232-6,6338-1
For they a,one have need of sorrow. Mary Clemmer. 6066-8
"For things we never mention". The broken men. Rudyard Kipling. 6810-3
"For thirdly he works it...", fr. Jubilate agno. Christopher Smart. 6380-2
"For thirty year, come herrin'-time". The skipper-hermit. Hiram Rich. 6833-2
"For this and that and various things". Committee meetings. Edgar A. Guest. 7033-7
"For this true nobleness I seek in vain". James Russell Lowell. 6753-0
"'For this were ye made', the king saith". War march. Margaret Widdemer. 6880-4
For this world. Walter Rauschenbusch. 6490-6
"For tho' the years their golden round". Francis Turner Palgrave. 6712-3
"For those who come to live within my sight". Epilogue, fr. The strength of the hills. Enid Bliss Kiernan. 6764-6
For those who fail. Joaquin Miller. 6260-1,6337-3,6478-7, 6499-X,6501-5,6104-4,6114-1
For those who fail. Joaquin Miller. 6861-8
For those who follow. Bertye Young Williams. 6906-1
"For those who work" Muin Ozaki. 6981-9
"For thou wert born of woman! thou didst come". Ode, to the saviour. Henry Hart Milman. 6980-0
"For thou, a holy shepherdess and kind". Louise Schelper (2). Felicia Dorothea Hemans. 6973-8
"For though the caves were rabitted". Henry David Thoreau. 6208-3
"For though the judge,conscience makes no show". Conscience. Sir William Davenant. 6867-7
"For thought, and not praise". Ralph Waldo Emerson. 6753-0
For thoughts. Celia Thaxter. 6066-8
"For three years...", fr. Hugh Selwyn Mauberley. Ezra Pound. 6399-3
"For time is like a fashionable", fr. Troilus... William Shakespeare. 6481-7
For to admire. Rudyard Kipling. 6395-0
"For too much love 'tis soothly said". Rondeau. Robert Bridges. 6875-8
"For truth and wisdom, foremost of the brave." Percy Bysshe Shelley. 6712-3
"For truth has such a face and such a mien". John Dryden. 6867-7
"For two hours/I sit with seven writers". The edgecumbe group. Arthur A. Greve. 6857-X
"For us, the dead, though young". The unreturning. Clinton Scollard. 6946-0
For vanity. Hannah J. Dawtrey. 6510-4
For W.A. Mozart. Edgar Bowers. 6515-5
"For want of a nail the show was lost". Mother Goose. 6363-2,6452-3
"For want of a nail, the shoe was lost". Unknown. 6904-5
"For weeks he tried to interest her". Small boy's resignation. Ralph J. Donahue. 6750-6
"For what is life, if measured by the space". A Pindaric ode, sels. Ben Jonson. 6879-0
For what is life? Ben Jonson. 6087-0
"For what is life? At best a brief delight". Unknown. 6407-8,6087-0
"For what need I of book or priest". Ralph Waldo Emerson. 6753-0
"For what of splendor or of fame". Sic transit gloria. William Talbot Allison. 6796-4
"For what the world admires I'll wish no more". The resolve. Mary Lee, Lady Chudleigh. 6932-0
For where is she so fair? Bertha Dean Foss. 6750-6
For Whitsunday, fr. The Paradise of Dainty Devices. M. Kindlemarsh. 6586-4
For Whittier's seventieth birthday. Oliver Wendell Holmes. 6126-5
"For who what is shall measure by what seems". The unremitting voice, sels. William Wordsworth. 6867-7
"For who would bear the whips and scorns of time". William Shakespeare. 6238-5
"For whom the bell tolls" Gavin Ewart. 6666-6
For Wooly. Leigh Hanes. 6761-1
"For years I was doomed to worship a...". The viper. Nicanor Parra. 6758-1
"For years, it seems, I've only plowed". Sad harvest. Clara S. Hoff. 6750-6
"For you alone how shall I write". Rondeau, to Elaine. Gareth Marsh Stanton. 6875-8
"For you I knit these lines, and on their ends". To Lord Dunsany. Francis Ledwidge. 6812-X
"For you are graved indelibly," fr Myrtle bough. Hilda ("H.D.") Doolittle. 6012-9
For you O democracy. Walt Whitman. 6126-5,6288-1
For Zorro. Diana Bickston. 6870-7
For 'Pages inedites'. Robert Bridges. 6487-6
"For you the open seas, the world's highway". Two lives. Gertrude Huntington McGiffert. 6838-3
"For you the warm and glowing hearth". Vagabond. Jamie Sexton Holme. 6836-7
For, Lord, the crowded cities be. Rainer Maria Rilke. 7039-6
"For, lo, the winter is past". Spring. Unknown. 6466-3
Foran, Ethel Ursula
The land of fancy. 6789-1
Ocean waves. 6789-1
Foran, Joseph K.
Rosh-Hashanah. 6848-0
The foray of Con O'Donnell A.D. 1495, sel. Denis Florence MacCarthy. 6930-4
The foray. Sir Walter Scott. 6395-0
"Forbear from pride of publishing, my child". Young poet, fr. Poetical sketches. Robert Hillyer. 6761-1
Forbearance. Ralph Waldo Emerson. 6102-8,6176-1,6239-3, 6299-7,6332-2,6465 ,6076-5,6300-4,6008-0,6288-1,6421-3,6723 ,6527-9,6730-1,6006-4,6126-5,6121-4,6252
Forbearance. Owen (Edward Bulwer-Lytton, Earl Lytton) Meredith. 6512-0
Forbes, Arthur
Care I for roses so? 6761-1
Forbes, Eleanor Bichnell
In the silence. 6799-9
Forbes, Giralda
'No man can set a limit to the march of a nation'. 6761-1
Forbes, Mabel Christian
Flight. 6269-5
The fold. 6269-5
The harbour-mouth. 6269-5
Love-music. 6269-5
Visible and invisible. 6269-5
Forbidden drink. Robert Lovett. 6722-0
The forbidden fire. Tristan Tzara. 6343-8
Forbidden love. Violet Fane; Baroness Currie. 7037-X
Forbidden love. Bryan Waller ("Barry Cornwall") Procter. 6980-0
The forbidden rose. Charles Wharton Stork. 6036-6
Forbush, William Byron
Ecclesiastes in the metre of Omar. 6848-0
Forby utherland. George Gordon McCrae. 6274-1,6656-9

FORC'D 544

"Forc'd from home, and all its pleasures". The morning dream. William Cowper. 6814-6
The **force** of habit. Charles and Mary Lamb. 6295-4
The **force** of habit. Unknown. 6410-8
The **force** of love. William Henry Davies. 6884-7
The **force** of prayer, sels. William Wordsworth. 6867-7
The **force** of prayer, sels. William Wordsworth. 6337-3
The **force** of prayer. William Wordsworth. 6134-6,6518-X
"The **force** that through the green fuse drives", Poem ("The force"). Dylan Thomas. 6379-9
The **forced** recruit. Elizabeth Barrett Browning. 6219-9, 6196-6
Forcing a way. Unknown. 6902-9
Ford (atr), John
    "Can you paint a thought? or number." 6317-9
Ford (atr), Thomas
    There is a lady sweet and kind. 6153-2
Ford o' Kabul river. Rudyard Kipling. 6210-5,6508-2
The **Ford** Sunday evening hour. Henry Rago. 6761-1
Ford, Anna M.
    Fox and geese. 6167-2
Ford, Corey
    The up-set. 6722-0
Ford, Daniel Barker
    A lay of Cape Cod. 6798-0
Ford, Edward Baunton
    "Mother most dear, long is the path but plain". 6800-6
    Tiphaine La Fee. 6800-6
Ford, Ford Madox (Hueffer)
    Antwerp. 6897-9
    Clair de lune. 6102-8
    Footsloggers. 6250-4
    Gray matter. 6541-4
    The great view. 6793-X
    The gypsy and the snowman. 6228-8
    The iron music. 6393-4
    The old houses of Flanders. 6331-4,6509-0,6393-4,6464-7, 6653-4
    The sanctuary. 6320-9
    Sidera cadentia. 6793-X
    The silver music. 6785-9
    To Petronella at sea. 6320-9
    What the orderly dog saw. 6785-9
Ford, Ford Madox (Hueffer) (tr.)
    The posy ring. Clement Marot, 7039-6
Ford, Francis Alan
    Song of the gulf stream. 6833-2
Ford, Grace D.
    Highest education. 6764-6
Ford, Gregory J.
    Bits and pieces. 7024-8
Ford, Harriet
    His sister, his cousin, and his pants. 6719-0
Ford, Horatio
    Fringed gentian. 6118-4
Ford, Janice
    My rose. 6799-9
Ford, John
    The broken heart, sels. 6198-2,6562-7,6472-8,6186-9
    A broken heart. 6830-8
    The broken heart. 6934-7
    Calantha's dirge. 6189-3
    Can you paint a thought. 6430-2
    Dawn. 6533-3
    Dirge. 6315-2,6383-7
    Fancies. 6240-7
    Fly hence, shadows. 6563-5
    Lines to John Webster. 6369-1
    Love and death. 6219-9
    The lover's melancholy, sels. 6198-2,6369-1,6472-8
    The musical duel. 6385-3
    Now love dies. 6563-5
    "Oh, no more, no more, too late." 6315-2,6317-9,6562-7
    Penthea's dying song. 6189-3
    Perkin Warbeck. 6188-1
    Song ("Fly hence"). 6315-2
    A song ("Glories, pleasures, pomps..."). 6933-9
    A song ("Oh no more, no more, too late"). 6933-9
    'Tis a pity she's a whore, sels. 6472-8
Ford, K.B.
    A baby kangaroo. 6530-9
Ford, Mary A.
    A hundred years from now. 6215-6
    A hundred years from now. 6914-2
Ford, R.A.D.
    A delusion of reference. 6446-9
    Roadside near Moscow. 6446-9
Ford, Richard Clyde
    Forest boat song. 6281-4
Ford, Robert
    The bonniest bairn in a' the warl'. 6239-3
Ford, S.V.R.
    Inasmuch. 6417-5,6964-9
    The obstinate music-box. 6921-5
    The ocean's dead. 6922-3
    Shouting Jane. 6921-5
Ford, Thomas
    Fond love, no more. 6563-5
    Since first I saw your face. 6328-4
    "There is a lady sweet and kind". 6933-9
"The **fore-royal** furled, I pause and I stand". Making land. Thomas Fleming Day. 6833-2
"**Forebear** the public to abuse". To a certain voluminous scribler. Thomas Warton (the Elder). 6962-2
Forebearance. William Cowper. 6337-3
Forebeare fond swaine I cannot love. Unknown. 6563-5
Foreboding. Don Blanding. 6143-5
Foreboding. Grant H. Code. 6218-0
Foreboding. Walter De La Mare. 6905-3
Foreboding. Alexander Pushkin. 6103-6
"**Foreboding** sudden of untoward change". By the Conemaugh. Florence Earle Coates. 6946-0
A **foreboding**.. James Russell Lowell. 6429-9,6226-1,6321-7
A **foreboding**. Violet Fane; Baroness Currie. 6656-9
The **foreboding**. Robert Graves. 6246-6
Forecast. Philip James Bailey. 6438-8
Forecast. Geoffrey Chaucer. 6438-8
Forecast. Elspeth Macduffie O'Halloran. 6441-8
Forecast. Sydney King Russell. 6218-0
The **foreclosure** of the mortgage. Mrs. E.T. Corbett. 6916-9
Forefather's hymn. Leonard Bacon. 6473-6
Forefather's song. Unknown. 6176-1
The **forefather**. Richard Burton. 6431-0
Foreground and background. Albert Teodor Gellerstedt. 6045-5
Foreign children. Robert Louis Stevenson. 6132-X,6456-6
The **foreign** land. Coventry Patmore. 6186-9
Foreign lands. Robert Louis Stevenson. 6456-6,6047-1,6466-3,6639-9,6638-0,6656-9
Foreign lands. Unknown. 6049-8
Foreign missions in battle array. Vachel Lindsay. 6337-3;6532-5
Foreign soil. Dianne Hai-Jew. 6790-5
Foreign travel. Samuel Rogers. 6484-1,6519-8
Foreign views of the statue. Fred Emerson Brooks. 6451-5, 6687-9,6920-7
The **foreigner**.. Francis Sherman. 6433-7
Foreigners at the fair. Fred Emerson Brooks. 6691-7
Foreknowledge. John Donne. 6935-5
Foreknown. Doris Kenyon. 6648-8
Foreknown. Sara Teasdale. 6070-6,6250-4
The **foreman's** wife. Jeff Tagami. 6790-5
Foreman, Paul
    Yevtushenko! 6792-1
Forerunner to rain. Virginia Moore. 6232-6
Forerunner to rain. Virginia Moore. 6780-8
The **forerunner**. Marion Thornton. 7019-1
Forerunners. Ralph Waldo Emerson. 6250-4,6288-1,6431-0
"**Foresake** me not thus, Adam, witness heav'n". Eve penitent, fr. Paradise lost. John Milton. 6933-9
Foreshadowings. Theodore Watts-Dunton. 7015-9
The **foreshore**. George Crabbe. 6150-8
Foresight. William Shakespeare. 6438-8
Foresight saga. William Roehrick. 6850-2
Forest. Jean Garrigue. 6390-X
The **forest** at dusk. Genevieve Gray Rawson. 6906-1
The **forest** bird. Walter James Turner. 6625-9
Forest boat song. Richard Clyde Ford. 6281-4
Forest couplets. Clarence Urmy. 6241-5
"The **forest** falls asleep and dreams". Nocturne. Conrado

Nale Roxlo. 6759-X
The forest fire. Sir Charles George Douglas Roberts. 6591-0,6592-9
The forest glade. Charles Tennyson Turner. 6656-9
The forest guardian. Sylvia Clark. 6764-6
"A forest has small privacy". Committal. Helen Hartness Flanders. 7030-2
"The forest has spells to enchant me". Saguenay. Louis Frechette. 6795-6
A forest hymn, sels. William Cullen Bryant. 6102-8,6076-5, 6126-5
A forest hymn. William Cullen Bryant. 6014-5,6047-1,6049-8, 6407-8,6473-6,6735-,6008-0,6288-1,6431-0,6076-5,6121-4,6214 ,6302-0,6385-3,6457-4,6673-9,6304-7
The forest in winter. Robert Southey. 6793-X
Forest leaves in autumn. John Keble. 6980-0
The forest maid. William Cullen Bryant. 6437-4
The forest of the dead. J. Griffyth Fairfax. 7029-9
The forest of Tiveden, sels. Verner von Heidenstam. 6045-5
A forest path in winter. Archibald Lampman. 7035-3
Forest phantasy. Jaroslav Vrchlicky. 6886-3
The forest pine. Laurence Binyon. 6253-9
Forest primeval park. Date Thomson Curial. 6342-X
Forest rainstorm. Elizabeth Voss. 6906-1
"The forest rears no tombstone for its dead". Memorial. Stanton A. Coblentz. 6750-6
A forest rendezvous. William Griffith. 6034-X
The forest sanctuary. Felicia Dorothea Hemans. 6973-8
A forest scene. Edith May. 6049-8
Forest song. William Henry Venable. 6449-3
A forest song. Alfred Noyes. 6250-4,6151-6
Forest tragedy. Helena Coleman. 6591-0,6592-2
Forest trees. Unknown. 6373-X
The forest trees. Eliza Cook. 6049-8
The forest wedding. Christian Richardt. 6555-4
Forest worship. Ebenezer Elliott. 6600-3
The forest, sels. Ben Jonson. 6301-2
Forest-fire. Mary B. Sanford. 6670-4
Forest-mirrors, fr. My lady, dancer for the universe. Vachel Lindsay. 6206-7
The forest-naturalist. Andrew Marvell. 6943-6
A forest. Percy Bysshe Shelley. 6935-5
The forest. John Keats. 6102-8
The forest. Miltiades Malakassis. 6352-7
The forest. Dorothy Quick. 6218-0
Forestalled. Unknown. 6721-2
Forester's song. Alfred Edgar Coppard. 6891-X
Forester's song. Alfred Edward Coppard. 6780-8
The foresters.. Alfred Lord Tennyson. 6123-0
"Forests may glow like a wave of fire". Mirages. Arlen Oberson. 6818-9
"The forests that were fired by men, return". Renewal time. John Gould Fletcher. 6979-7
"Forests/around a plush-covered table". Opium. Max Holzer. 6769-7
A foretaste of spring. George Herbert Clarke. 6274-1
Forethought. Josephine Preston Peabody. 6441-8
Forever. John Boyle O'Reilly. 6240-7,6337-3,6730-1,6461-2
Forever. John Boyle O'Reilly. 6920-7
Forever. Unknown. 6273-3
Forever. Jack Wilson. 6850-2
Forever and a day. Thomas Bailey Aldrich. 6307-1
Forever and forever. C.C. Converse. 6304-7
Forever cherished be the tree. Emily Dickinson. 6153-9
Forever dead. Sappho. 7039-6
"Forever man questions life's meaning...". Questioning. Edgar A. Guest. 6748-4
Forever on Thanksgiving day. Wilbur Dick Nesbit. 6449-3
Forever our own. Sarah ("Susan Coolidge") Woolsey. 6461-2
Forever the sun is pouring his gold. Unknown. 6461-2
"Forever unappeased, bereft they pace". The sanctuary of young mothers, fr. Tree of time. Gertrude Huntington McGiffert. 6838-3
Forever with the Lord. James Montgomery. 6385-3,6600-3, 6219-9
"'Forever' is not much nor all". Forever. Jack Wilson. 6850-2
'Forever'.. Charles Stuart Calverley. 6722-0,6026-9
Forever?. Sylvester Baxter. 6798-0
Foreward. Melrose Pitman. 6906-1

Forewarned. Alice Brown. 6441-8
Foreword. Francis Paxton. 6397-7
Foreword. Robert Service. 6159-1
Forfeits. Henry Cuyler Bunner. 6004-8
The forgers. Duncan Campbell Scott. 6115-X
Forget. Rubye Arnold. 7016-7
Forget. John Donne. 6198-2,6726-3
"Forget NeR Hampshire? By her cliffs...". The hills are home. Edna Dean Proctor. 6764-6
Forget it. Unknown. 6583-X
Forget it. Unknown. 6889-8
Forget it. Unknown. 6889-8
Forget it, soldier! C.F. R. 6443-4
Forget me not. Amelia Opie. 6219-9
Forget not the field. Thomas Moore. 7009-4
Forget not yet the tried intent. Sir Thomas Wyatt. 6250-4, 6430-2
"Forget not yet the tried intent." Sir Thomas Wyatt. 6182-6,6186-9,6584-8,6189-3
"Forget six counties overhung with smoke". Prologue. William Morris. 6427-2,6199-0,6660-7
Forget thee. John Moultrie. 6620-8
Forget thee, --no, never!. Alaric A. Watts. 6226-1
Forget thee? John Moultrie. 6889-8
"Forget them not! though now their name". The memory of the dead. Felicia Dorothea Hemans. 6973-8
"Forget, forget the tyranny of sleep". The magic hour. Everest Lewin. 6779-4
"Forget, forget!". Sleep song, fr. Music. Henry Van Dyke. 6961-4
Forget-me-not. Unknown. 6049-8,6373-X,6529-5,6456-6
"Forget-me-not! It is the cry of clay". A bunch of forget-me-nots. Thomas Hood. 6974-6
Forgetful number. Vasko Popa. 6758-1
Forgetful Pa. Edgar A. Guest. 6465-5,6281-4
Forgetfulness. Maxwell Bodenheim. 6348-9
Forgetfulness. Harold Monro. 6581-3
Forgetfulness. R.A. Thorpe. 7015-9
Forgetting. Unknown. 6983-5
The forging of the anchor. Sir Samuel Ferguson. 6917-7
The forging of the anchor. Sir Samuel Ferguson. 6302-0, 6385-3,6183-4,6271-7,6600-3,6438 ,6219-9,6639-0,6543-0
Forgive. Lalia Mitchell Thornton. 6065-X
Forgive. John Greenleaf Whittier. 6303-9,6335-7,6337-3
"Forgive and forget! why the world would be lonely". Charles Swain. 6980-0
Forgive me! Hazel M. Olson. 6461-2
"Forgive me, rose and nightingale". Repentance for political activity. Edward Thompson. 6782-4
"Forgive me, that, by sordid cares compelled". To beauty. Charles Whitby. 6994-0
"Forgive my wooden tongue". From a line by Cyril Dabydeen. Martin Singelton. 6767-0
"'Forgive, O God, the occidental anger.'". A half-caste prays. Gordon LeClaire. 6750-f
Forgiven. Helen Hunt Jackson. 6066-8
Forgiven?. Jeannette Bliss Gillespy. 6118-4
Forgiveness. Al-Jaziri. 6362-4
Forgiveness. Alice Cary. 6865-0;6969-X
Forgiveness. William Henry Davies. 6861-8
Forgiveness. J. Edmondston. 6049-8
Forgiveness. Henry Francis Lyte. 6065-X
Forgiveness. Charles L. O'Donnell. 6030-7,6096-X,6619-4, 6300-4
Forgiveness. George William ("A.E.") Russell. 6090-0
Forgiveness. Sadi [or Saadi] (Mushlih-ud-Din) 6448-5
Forgiveness. Will Smallwood. 6178-8
Forgiveness. Unknown. 6606-2
Forgiveness. John Greenleaf Whittier. 6126-5,6211-3,6260-1, 6337-3,6288-1
A forgiveness, sels. Robert Browning. 6541-4
"Forgot winged words mid foldings of the hills". Dionysus. Gertrude Huntington McGiffert. 6838-3
Forgotten. Paul Hamilton Hayne. 6121-4
Forgotten. Thomas S. Jones Jr. 6347-0
Forgotten. Sappho. 6435-3
Forgotten acres. N. Gordon Le Ber. 6042-0
The forgotten books. Thomas S. Collier. 6297-0
Forgotten boyhood. Edgar A. Guest. 7033-7

FORGOTTEN

Forgotten children. Estelle Rooks. 6850-2
The forgotten city. William Carlos Williams. 6389-6
The forgotten grave. Austin Dobson. 6656-9
"Forgotten in a sleepy western town". Sonnets for Ellen. Dale Etter. 6799-9
"Forgotten playground, grave". Elegy. W. Wesley Trimpi. 6515-5
"Forgotten seers of lost repute". A ballad of forgotten tunes. Agnes Mary F. ("Madame Duclaux") Robinson. 6770-0
"Forgotten soldier, in the winter grass". Trooper Temple Pulvermacher. William Branford. 6788-3
The forgotten soul. Margaret Widdemer. 6327-6
Forgotten wounds. Helen Dykstra. 6662-3
The fork. Charles Simic. 6803-0
Forker, Greg
    And the gas chamber drones in the distance. 6870-7
    And the winner is. 6870-7
    Christ. 6870-7
    Reasons to go home. 6870-7
    A test of competence. 6870-7
    The torch. 6870-7
Forlorn. William Dean Howells. 7041-8
Forlorn hope. William Shakespeare. 6935-5
A forlorn hope. Unknown. 6701-8
The forlorn one. Richard Harris ("Thomas Ingoldsby") Barham. 6089-7
The forlorn shepherd's complaint. Thomas Hood. 6385-3
"Forlorn!- forlorn! Nor land nor succor...". Despair. James Abraham Martling. 6952-5
Form. Eva Gore-Booth. 6337-3,6641-0
'Form fours'. Frank Sidgwick. 6474-4,6722-0
"The form's divinity, the heart's best grace". Epitaph. Thomas Lovell Beddoes. 6908-8
"The form, the form alone is eloquent!". Sonnet to a coquette (2). Alfred Lord Tennyson. 6977-0
Forma bonum fragile. Matthew Prior. 6278-4
Formal lyric. Walter James Turner. 6210-5
Forman, Elizabeth Chandler
    The three lads. 7031-0
Formation. Frank Ernest Hill. 7014-0
Formation flight. John Milton. 6978-9
"Formed long ago, yet made to-day". Unknown. 6904-5
Former barn lot. Mark Van Doren. 6039-0
Former beauties, fr. At Casterbridge fair. Thomas Hardy. 6828-6
The former glory. Wilfred Rowland Childe. 6096 X
Formosae puellae. Herbert P. Horne. 6656-9
Formula. Carolyn J. Ogletree. 7024-8
Forrest, M.
    The heroes. 7027-2
    The lonely woman. 6784-0
Forrest, William
    The marigold. 6489-2,6022-6
Forrester, Alfred A. ("Alfred Crowquill")
    To my nose. 6385-3,6089-2,6724-7
Forrester, Ellen
    The Irish widow to her son. 6927-4
    Irish widow's message to her son in America. 6090-0
Forrester, Fleta
    Daisy time. 6137-0
Forrester, Frances
    Much in a name. 6721-2
    The story of a picture. 6577-5
Forrestt, Ann Draper
    Four Aprils. 6761-1
Forsaken. Margaret Forst. 6906-1
Forsaken. Unknown. 6732-8
The forsaken bride. Unknown. 6246-6
A forsaken garden. Algernon Charles Swinburne. 6723-9,6656-9,6655-0,6199-0,6001-3,6232-6,6110-9,6250-4,6196-9, 6649 ,6052-8,6122-2,6154-0,6208-3,6246-6,6271 ,6289-X,6315-2,6437-X,6634-8,6657-7,6726
The forsaken hearth. Felicia Dorothea Hemans. 6973-8
Forsaken homes and graves. H.H. Blackham. 6768-9
"Forsaken hulk! Its rotting timbers lie". The wreck. Charles W. Denison. 6755-7
The forsaken maid. Richard Brome. 6328-4
The forsaken maid. Unknown (Irish) 6858-8
The forsaken merman. Matthew Arnold. 6046-3,6102-8,6153-2, 6196-6,6199-0,6558 ,6114-1,6110-9,6197-4,6252-0,6430-2,6558 ,6319-5,6424-8,6371-3,6383-7,6656-9,6723 , 6646-1,6639-9,6828-6,6133-8,6271-7,6437-X,6512-0, 6655-0
The forsaken mistress. Sir George Etherege. 6544-9
The forsaken. Hamilton Aide. 6656-9
The forsaken. Thomas Hood. 6974-6
The forsaken. Duncan Campbell Scott. 6433-7
Forsete, John of
    Cuckoo song. 6527-9
    Summer is a-coming in. 6466-3
Forshadowings. Julia C.R. Dorr. 6578-3
Forsslund, Karl Erik
    Hay-making. Charles Wharton Stork (tr.). 6045-5
Forst, Margaret
    Alarm. 6906-1
    Forsaken. 6906-1
    Memories. 6906-1
    Mona Lisa. 6906-1
    Self-pity. 6906-1
    Twilit street. 6906-1
    Winter robin. 6906-1
Forsyth, James
    Artillery shoot. 6666-6
    Soldier's dove. 6666-6
    To my wife. 6666-6
Forsyth, Mary Isabella
    The English sparrow. 6597-X
Forsyth, Sheila C.
    Blizzard, April 6, 1982 6857-X
    Shellbound. 6857-X
Forsythia. Doris V. Lecky. 6850-2
Fort Bowyer. Charles L.S. Jones. 6946-0
Fort Dearborn, Chicago. Benjamin Franklin Taylor. 6815-4
Fort Donelson. Thomas Hunter. 6847-2
Fort Duquesne. Florus B. Plimpton. 6946-0
Fort Macon. Bruce Jenkins. 6900-2
Fort McHenry. Unknown. 6946-0
"Fort Stanwix guns are dumb. No longer death". The battle of Oriskany. Benjamin Franklin Taylor. 6815-4
"Fort Wagner! that is a place for us". The hero of Fort Wagner. Phoebe Cary. 6969-X
The fort of Rathangan. ? Berchan. 6125-7
The fort of Rathangan. Unknown. 6244-X
The fort of Rathangan. Unknown (Irish) 6125-7
A fort on the river, fr. The Indian stone. George Steele Seymour. 6789-1
Fort Sill internment camp. Muin Ozaki. 6981-9
Fort Snelling. W.D. Frye. 6342-X
Fort town. Kathleen Sutton. 6761-1
Fort Tryon. Arthur Guiterman. 6773-5
Fort, John N.
    'Swore off'. 6923-1
Fort, Paul
    Ballad of the bells, sels. 6351-9
    Ballade. Frederick York Powell (tr.). 7039-6
    Ballades. 6801-4
    Bell of dawn. 6607-0
    The bond of love. 6351-9
    Chant du soir. 6253-9
    The dance. 6490-6
    The harmonious vision of the earth. Vernon Watkins (tr.). 6343-8
    Hymn IX, fr. In the spring. 6351-9
    In the spring, sels. 6351-9
    In the wheat. 6351-9
    L'emoi forestier. 6253-9
    La grande ivresse. 6253-9
    La ronde. 6134-6
    The lad's return. 6490-6
    Light. 6351-9
    Pan and the cherries. 6351-9
    Philomel. James Elroy Flecker (tr.). 6343-8
    <u>This maiden. 6351-9</u>
    Vision du crepuscule. 6801-4
"Forth from the curtain of clouds...". The wedding day, fr. The courtship of Miles Standish. Henry Wadsworth Longfellow. 6753-0
"Forth sped the gallant sailors, blithe & free". Gloriana's England. Archibald T. Strong. 6784-0

"Forth start the boys in buttons & their best". Old-
    fashioned declamation. Benjamin Franklin Taylor.
    6815-4
Forth, my gallant honey-bees!. Ludvig Holstein. 6555-4
Fortitude. Edna Davis Romig. 6836-7
Fortitude. Unknown. 6303-9
Fortitude amid trials. Unknown. 6605-2
"A fortnight ago, a thief plundered my zinnias". Requital.
    Ruth Inscho. 6750-6
"Fortunate are the feet of the swallow," fr. The glade.
    Edward Shanks. 6317-9
The fortunate dead. Algernon Charles Swinburne. 6828-6
The fortunate islands. Andrew Lang. 6987-8
The fortunate isles. Joaquin Miller. 6730-1,6964-9,6889-8
Fortunate love. Sir Edmund Gosse. 6875-8
Fortunati nimium. Thomas Campion. 6604-6,6192-3,6660-7
Fortunatus (Venantius Honorius Clementianus)
    "Hail, days of days! in peals of praise". 6065-X
    O glory of virgins. Sister Maura (tr.). 6282-2
    Passion Sunday. 6271-7
    Vexilla regis. 6543-0
    Vexilla regis. John Mason Neale (tr.). 6385-3
    Welcome, happy morning. 6177-X
Fortunatus et ille. Vergil. 6252-0
Fortunatus nimium. Robert Bridges. 6482-5,6487-6
Fortune. Thomas Dekker. 6436-1
Fortune. John Dryden. 6874-X
Fortune. John Dryden. 6092-7
Fortune. Fitz-Greene Halleck. 6302-0;6385-3
Fortune. Sir John Harington. 6385-3
Fortune. Charles Madge. 6357-8
Fortune. Alfred Lord Tennyson. 6087-0,6134-4
Fortune. Sir Thomas Wyatt. 6436-1
Fortune ("Eye-flattering fortune, look thou never...").
    Sir Thomas More. 6489-2
Fortune ("The lady fortune is both friend and foe").
    Unknown. 6022-6
Fortune - Enid's song. Alfred Lord Tennyson. 6385-3
"Fortune and glory may be lost and woone". To the most
    high and mighty. Thomas Campion. 6794-8
Fortune and virtue. Thomas Dekker. 6245-8
Fortune from God. Unknown. 6233-4
"Fortune has brought me down - her wonted way". His
    children. Hittan of Tayyi. 7039-6
The fortune in the daisy. Phoebe Cary. 6865-0;6969-X
Fortune is like the moon. Sophocles. 6435-3
Fortune my foe. Alfred Perceval Graves. 6273-3
Fortune smiles. Thomas Dekker. 6383-7
The fortune teller. John Holmes. 6388-8
"Fortune! I thank thee: gentle goodness!thanks". Verses
    written at Bath on finding the heel of a shoe.
    William Cowper. 6814-6
"Fortune! why thus, where'er my footsteps tread". Pietro
    Metastasio. 6973-8
Fortune's wheel. John B.L. Warren, 3d Baron De Tabley.
    6656-9
"Fortune, impartial to each dog". Ye juvenile offender.
    Unknown. 6878-2
"Fortune, that, with malicious joy". Fortune. John Dryden.
    6874-X
Fortune-teller and maiden. Mary L. Gaddess. 6671-2
Fortune-teller, fr. Comedy of errors. William Shakespeare.
    6302-0
The fortune-teller. Matthew Prior. 6152-4
Forty singing seamen. Alfred Noyes. 6162-1,6236-9,6473-6,
    6478-7,6732-8,6102-8,6107-9,6458-2,6393-4,6396-9
Forty to twenty. Unknown. 6914-2
Forty to-day. George Henry Miles. 6096 X
Forty years after. H.H. Porter. 6089-7,7021-3
Forty years ago. Francis Huston. 6085-4
Forty years ago. Unknown. 6142-7,6260-1,6294-6,6565-1
"Forty years back, when much had place". George Meredith.
    Thomas Hardy. 6828-4
Forty years on. Edward Bowen. 6046-3
044.. Cesar Vallejo. 6642-9
'49.. Joaquin Miller. 6077-3
Forty-two poems, sels. James Elroy Flecker. 6234-2
Forward. Edward Farquhar. 6939-8
Forward. Alfred Noyes. 6151-6
Forward. Sarah ("Susan Coolidge") Woolsey. 6211-3
Forward. Sarah ("Susan Coolidge") Woolsey. 6918-5
"A forward child, a sullen child". Poem ("A forward
    child..."). Cecil Day Lewis. 6783-2
"Forward I now in duties go". Job 23: 8-10 Charles Wesley.
    6848-0
"Forward through the dark blue night". The flight into
    Egypt. Emile Cammaerts. 6785-9
"The forward violet thus did I chide". William
    Shakespeare. 6122-2,6187-7,6198-2,6302-0,6385-3
"The forward violet thus did I chide". Sonnet 099 ("The
    forward violet"). William Shakespeare. 6271-7,6436-1,
    6250-4
"'Forward!' the brave old captain said". The battle of
    Inkerman. George W. Bungay. 6919-3
"Forward!/'On to the front!' the order ran". Going and
    coming. Mary Elizabeth Blake. 7041-8
Forward, march! Unknown. 6049-8
Fosdick, Harry Emerson
    An autumn leaf. 6118-4
    God of grace and God of glory. 6337-3
    O God, in restless living. 6337-3
    The Prince of peace. 6337-3
    A prince of peace. 6420-5
Fosdick, William Whiteman
    The maize. 6302-0,6385-3
Foshay tower. Nancy Coose. 6342-X
Foss, Bertha Dean
    For where is she so fair? 6750-6
Foss, Fanya
    May is this new May. 6042-0
Foss, Sam Walter
    Abraham and Ephraim. 6505-8
    An art critic. 6690-9
    The auctioneer's gift. 6923-1
    The awakening of Uncle Sam. 6741-X
    The bloodless sportsman. 6510-4
    Boston. 6088-9
    The buster. 6926-6
    The calf-path. 6162-1,6486-8
    The coming American, sels. 6337-3
    The coming American. 6107-9
    A cosmopolitan woman. 6682-8
    An economical man. 6702-6
    The fancy work maiden. 6744-1
    The fate of pious Dan. 6996-7
    He didn't amount to shucks. 6924-X
    He wanted to know. 6687-9
    He worried about it. 6260-1,6694-1,6964-9
    He'd had no show. 6481-7
    The higher catechism. 6730-1
    The higher fellowship. 6303-9
    The house by the side of the road. 6101-X,6291-1,6102-8,
        6162-1,6266-0,6337-,6337-3,6104-4,6076-5,6418-3,6476-
        0,6730-1,6732-8
    Hullo! 6085-4,6260-1,6707-7,6964-9
    Husband and heather. 6089-7
    I dunno and I knowit. 6312-8
    "I'm the little red stamp." 6712-3
    The ideal husband to his wife. 6089-7
    The jest of fate. 6688-7
    Jim Bowker. 6580-5
    Keep on just the same. 6280-6
    Land on your feet. 6692-2
    Large eternal fellows. 6303-9
    A life story. 6097-8
    The meeting of the Clabberhuses. 6089-7,6691-7,6089-7,
        6691-7,6505-8
    A modern martyrdom. 6652-6
    A mother's martyrdom. 6505-8
    No hope for literature. 6247-4
    O'Flaherty and John Stubbs. 6926-6
    1898 and 1562. 6741-X
    The origin of sin. 6996-7
    A philosopher. 6505-8,6089-7
    A prayer for Cyrus Brown. 6089-7,6505-8,6307-1
    The prayer of Cyrus Brown. 6089-7,6307-1,6505-8
    The prayer of Cyrus Brown. 7025-6
    Quartets' anthem. 6698-4
    Sambo's prayer. 6721-2
    The shaving of Jacob. 6280-6

FOSS 548

Foster, Stephen Collins (cont.)
The song of Dewey's guns. 6741-X
The song of the cannon. 6286-5,6471-X
The song that Silas sung. 6682-8
Spring cleaning, fr. The Yankee blade. 6047-1
Tellin' what the baby did. 6772-7
Then ag'in. 6089-7,6102-8,6732-8,6076-5
Two gods. 6303-9,6337-3
Uncle Sam's spring cleaning. 6471-X
The volunteer organist. 6923-1
The volunteer organist. 6166-4,6260-1,6486-8,6964-9
War. 6340-3,6471-X
When a man's out of a job. 6274-1
The young musician. 6929-0
Fossett, P.C.
Abner's second wife. 6922-3
Fossils. James Stephens. 6930-4
Foster, Agness Greene
'You' 6818-9
Foster, David Skaats
The game of chess. 6441-8
Foster, Edith
I had a dream. 6799-9
Foster, Edna A.
Cat convention. 6692-2
Foster, Fanny
Tom's little star. 6411-6
Foster, Francis M.
Hunger. 6178-8
A lover's lament. 6178-8
Foster, George T.
The church steps. 6273-3
Foster, H.A.
Christmas eve. 6408-6
Foster, Jeanne Robert
The awakening. 6320-9
The backslider. 6607-0
The bitter herb. 6556-2
John Butler Yeats. 6036-6
The King o' Spain's daughter. 6102-8,6076-5
Moth-flowers. 6338-1
The rains of Arran. 6331-4
Scotch Arran. 6331-4
Song of Ballyshannon. 6331-4,6374-8
"Tell me, what is poetry" 6476-0,6607-0
Wild cherry. 6619-4
The William P. Frye. 6946-0,7026-4
Foster, Leonard G.
Eulogy. 6820-0
Foster, Leonard G. (tr.)
The wedding gift. Unknown, 6929-0
Foster, Madeline B.
Impressions of Bermuda. 6799-9
Foster, Margaret Haynes
The honest bargain. 7016-7
A love that was. 7016-7
Pedagogy. 7016-7
Priedieu. 7016-7
Rebel. 7016-7
Sound. 7016-7
To a lost idol. 7016-7
Foster, Mary Salinda
Treaty of Traverse Des Sioux. 6342-X
Foster, Preston Paine
Dying leaves. 6906-1
Men in the park. 6906-1
Moan on, Mississippi. 6906-1
Stepmother of the wind. 6906-1
Foster, Stephen Collins
Massa's in the cold, cold ground. 6632-1,6706-9,6732-8, 6723-9,6396-9,6431-0,6281-4,6300-4
My old Kentucky home. 6006-4,6706-9,6136-2,6240-7,6385-3,6479-5,6632-1,6732-8,6486-8
My old Knetucky home. 6465-5,6288-1,6431-0,6121-4,6300-4,6723-9,6396-9,6484-1,6464-7
Nelly was a lady. 6077-3
O, boys, carry me 'long. 6632-1
Old black Joe. 6706-9,6281-4
Old dog tray. 7008-6
Old folks at home. 6077-3,6136-2,6240-7,6289-X,6479-5, 6632-1,6288-1,6431-0,6121-4,6219-9,6732-8,6006-4,

6365-9,6300-4,6723-9,6077-3,6136-2,6240-7,6289-X, 6479-5,6632-1,6288-1,6431-0,6121-4,6219-9,6732-8, 6006-4,6365-9,6300-4,6723-9
Swanee river. 6465-5
Foster, William A.
The bonny Tweed for me. 6180-X
Foster, William Prescott
Icebergs. 6833-2
The sea's voice. 6833-2,7041-8
The silence of the hills. 7041-8
"The wind and the stars and the sea" 7041-8
The **foster-mother's** tale. Samuel Taylor Coleridge. 6967-3
Fothergill, George A.
The master of the horse. 7010-8
Fought and won. M.A. Maitland. 6685-2
"Foul vermin they". Rats. Walter De La Mare. 6905-3
Foulke, William Dudley
Ad patriam, sel. 6954-1
The city's crown. 6954-1
The city's crown. 6337-3,6730-1
Justice for womankind. 6954-1
Life's evening. 6730-1
"Lo! He would lift the burden" 6995-9
Our lost captain. 6995-9
A summer paradise. 6879-0
Foulkes, William Hiram
Facing the dawn. 6461-2
Found. Josephine Preston Peabody. 6019-6
Found by the shepherd. Unknown. 6260-1
Found on an English sun dial. Unknown. 6861-8
Found out. Edgar A. Guest. 6862-6
Found, fr. Sonnets for pictures. Dante Gabriel Rossetti. 6526-0,6655-0
Foundation. Frances Minturn Howard. 6979-7
Foundations. Martha M. Schultze. 6922-3
The **founder** of the almshouse. George Crabbe. 6543-0
Founder's day. Robert Bridges. 6437-X,6487-5
Foundering of the Dolphin. C.E. Reed. 6744-1
Foundering of the Dolphin. C.E. Reed. 6918-5
The **founders** of Ohio. William Henry Venable. 6946-0
The **foundry**. Richard Scrace (pseud.) 6433-7
The **fount** of Castaly. Joseph O'Connor. 6481-7
"Fount of the woods! thou art hid no more". Our Lady's well. Felicia Dorothea Hemans. 6973-8
"A **fount** there is, doth overfling". At the fountain. Marcabrun. 7039-6
Fountain. Marie Louise Allen. 6906-1
The **fountain** at the tomb. Nicias. 7039-6
The **fountain** at Vaucluse. Sir William Jones. 6484-1
"The **fountain** in its source". Living water. Madame De la Mothe Guion. 6814-6
The **fountain** in the rain. Katharine R. Siegert. 6270-9
"A **fountain** issuing into light". Recluse. James Montgomery. 6980-0
The **fountain** of Egeria. George Gordon, 6th Baron Byron. 6543-0
The **fountain** of Marah. Felicia Dorothea Hemans. 6973-8
Fountain of mercy! God of love! Anne Flowerdew. 6219-9
The **fountain** of oblivion. Felicia Dorothea Hemans. 6980-0
The **fountain** of oblivion. Felicia Dorothea Hemans. 6973-8
The **fountain** of pity. Henry Bataille. 6351-9
"Fountain of sweets! Eternal dove!". Whit Sunday. Joseph Beaumont. 6931-2
The **fountain** of tears. Arthur O'Shaughnessy. 6383-7
The **fountain** of tears. William O'Shaughnessy. 6437-X
The **Fountain** of Trevi. Bayard Taylor. 6331-4,6439-6
The **fountain** of youth, sels. Hezekiah Butterworth. 6614-3, 6484-1
The fountain of youth: a dream of Ponce de Leon. Hezekiah Butterworth. 6552-X
The **fountain** song. Eugene O'Neill. 6490-6,6143-5
A **fountain**, a bottle, a donkey's ears, and some books. Robert Frost. 6070-4
The **fountain**, sels. William Cullen Bryant. 6049-8
The **fountain**, sels. William Wordsworth. 6369-1
The **fountain**.. Harry Kemp. 6338-1,6347-0
The **fountain**.. Sara Teasdale. 6338-1,6509-0,6649-6,6653-4
The **fountain**. William Cullen Bryant. 6673-9
The **fountain**. Herbert S. Gorman. 6393-4
The **fountain**. Ibn al-Ra'i'a. 662-4

The fountain. James Russell Lowell. 6519-8,6466-3,6623-2,
    6077-3,6133-8,6134-6,6135-4,6131-1,6424-8,6639-9,
    6136-2,6356-X,6692-5
The fountain. Mu'tamid. 7039-6
The fountain. Lynn Riggs. 6808-1
The fountain. Samuel Rogers. 6980-0
The fountain. Henry Longan Stuart. 6244-X
The fountain. Sara Teasdale. 6649-6
The fountain. William Wordsworth. 6246-6,6271-7,6086-2,
    6560-0,6110-9
Fountains. Sacheverell Sitwell. 6872-3
Fountains abbey. Ebenezer Elliott. 7015-9
"Fountains that frisk and sprinkle". Ballade made in the
    hot weather. William Ernest Henley. 6770-0
The founts of song. William ("Fiona Macleod") Sharp. 6730-
    1,6628-3
"4 a.m. and rain since dark, rain dropping". Waiting for
    trains at Col d'Aubisque. Robert Hedin. 6855-3
"4egin/let's begin/let's all begin again". Again and
    again. Doris Muhringer. 6769-7
4 1/2 point 5 Ed Lipman. 6870-7
The four ages of man. Anne Bradstreet. 6673-9
The four ages. William Cowper. 6814-6
Four and a half. John Holmes. 6761-1,6783-2
Four and eight. Ffrida Wolfe. 6937-1
Four and eight. Ffrida Wolfe. 6368-3
"Four and twenty bonny boys". Unknown. 6518-X
"Four and twenty taylors went to kill a snail". Mother
    Goose. 6363-2
The four appearances. Conrad Aiken. 6389-6
Four Aprils. Ann Draper Forrestt. 6761-1
"Four arms, two necks, one wreathing". Song ("Four arms").
    Unknown. 6182-6
"Four be the elements". Song for punch-drinkers. Johann C.
    Friedrich von Schiller. 6787-5
The four best things. Unknown (Greek) 6435-3
Four birds. Unknown. 6125-7
The four bridges. Jean Ingelow. 6940-1
The four brothers, sel. Carl Sandburg. 6954-1
Four Capri impromptus. William Alexander Percy. 6037-4
Four celebrated characters. Unknown. 6744-1
Four children. Robert Graves. 6779-4
Four Choctaw songs. Jim Barnes. 7005-1
"Four children on a rumbling cart". Tinker's moon. Ewart
    Milne. 6930-4
"Four chubby angels, like adult cherubim". An old map of
    somewhere. Jeffrey Donaldson. 6767-0
Four classes of men. Unknown. 6523-6
Four corners of the prism. Oscar Williams. 6390-X
Four country poems. Jessie Stuart. 6761-1
Four crimson violets. Rachel Annand Taylor. 6628-3
Four distiches, sels. J. St. Joe Strachey. 6069-2
Four ducks on a pond. William Allingham. 6052-8,6090-0,
    6102-8,6368-3,6396-9,6660
Four elegies. Edith Sitwell. 7000-0
Four epigrams. John Owen. 6528-7
The four eras. Samuel Rogers. 6980-0
"Four farms over it looked like a braid of...". Tornado.
    Robert Hedin. 6855-3
The four flies. E.D. Pierson. 6247-4
Four footprints. Thomas Hardy. 6102-8
Four fountains after Respighi. Jessica Carr. 6762-X
Four III. Edward Estlin Cummings. 6354-3
"Four gallant ships from England came". The battle of
    Stonington on the seaboard of Connecticut. Philip

"Four greveseather 6946e0upon the wooded crest". Sleepy
    Hollow, Concord. John Clair Minot. 6762-X
"A .410 gauge pistol made from plumbing...". Pipe dreams.
    Diana Bickston. 6870-7
"Four hundred years have glided by". Christopher Columbus.
    Edward R. Huxley. 6885-5
Four in the morning, fr. Facade. Edith Sitwell. 7000-0
The four kisses. George M. Vickers. 6927-4
The four knights. Robert C.V. Meyers. 6919-3
"Four lamps were burning o'er two mighty grave".
    Jerusalem. John Gardiner Calkins Brainard. 6752-2
A four leaf clover. Unknown. 6211-3
"Four little birds in a nest too small". Birds of no
    feather. Maggie B. Peeke. 6965-7

Four little foxes. Lew Sarett. 6102-8,6490-6,6506-6,6512-0,
    6602-0,6619 ,6510-4,6464-7,6396-9,6393-4,6217-2,6250-
    4,6253-9,6076-5
"Four little sunbeams came earthward one day". The four
    sunbeams. Unknown. 6926-6
"Four Scotchmen, bu the name of Adams". On some
    encroachments on the river. Unknown. 6874-X
Four lives. Garnet B. Freeman. 6912-6
Four lyrics. Arthur K. Sabin. 6884-7
The four Marys. Unknown. 6061-7
Four men. Jeanette H. Yeatman. 6648-8
The four misfortunes. John Godfrey Saxe. 6165-6
The four monarchyes, sels. Anne Bradstreet. 6008-0
Four mottoes. Alice Freeman Palmer. 6926-6
Four natural women. William Wordsworth. 7020-5
Four o'clocks. Julia C.R. Dorr. 6338-1
Four pets. Christina Georgina Rossetti. 6452-3
Four pictures. Harriet E. Durfee. 6926-6
Four pictures by Juan, age 5. David McKain. 6966-5
Four poems for April. Louis Adeane. 6379-9
Four poems to a wave. H. Stuart. 6071-4
The four points. E.L. Benedict. 6530-9
Four prayers. Unknown. 6930-4
Four preludes on playthings of the wind. Carl Sandburg.
    6506-6,6602-X
The four princesses at Wilna. Henry Wadsworth Longfellow.
    6320-9
Four scenes. Millie C. Pomeroy. 6411-6
"Four seasons fill the measure of the year". The seasons
    of man. John Keats. 7020-5
The four seasons of the year, sels. Anne Bradstreet. 6008-
    0
The four seasons. Unknown. 6385-3,6131-1
Four sisters. Charles Cotton. 6733-6
The four sisters. Unknown. 6049-8
Four songs. Edith Jabson. 6039-0
Four songs, after Verlaine, sels. Alfred Noyes. 6151-6
Four sonnets. Thomas S. Jones Jr. 6556-2
Four sonnets. Hazel S. Marshall. 6761-1
Four speeches from a play. Delmore Schwartz. 6390-X
The four sunbeams. M.K. B. 6638-0
The four sunbeams. Unknown. 6926-6
The four sweet months. Robert Herrick. 6114-1
Four things. Unknown. 6337-3
Four things. Henry Van Dyke. 6337-3,6512-0,6107-9,6104-4,
    6421-3
Four things Choctaw. Jim Barnes. 7005-1
Four things make us happy here. Robert Herrick. 6558-9
"Four things the wise man knew not to declare". Jealousy.
    William Herbert; Earl of Pembroke. 6980-0
"Four times the sun had risen and set...". The embarkation,
    fr. Evangeline. Henry Wadsworth Longfellow. 6946-0
Four track news, sels. W.H. Wilson. 6109-5
Four trees. Mildred Focht. 6847-2
Four trees. Mildred Focht. 6478-7
Four tunes. Helen Gross Hume. 6847-2
The four voices. William Ashenhurst Dunn. 6983-5
Four winds. Sara Teasdale. 6310-1,6441-8,6300-4
Four winds. Unknown. 6018-8,6262-8,6131-1
The four winds, fr. The song of Hiawatha. Henry Wadsworth
    Longfellow. 6623-2
The four winds, sels. Ralph Cheever Dunning. 6531-7
The four winds. Unknown. 6105-2,6466-3
The four winds. Shane Leslie. 6930-4
The four winds. Charles Henry Luders. 6006-4,6243-1,6431-0,

The four6918d$,6508m8 Dempster Sherman. 6311-X,6373-X,6623-
    2,6639-9,6638-0
Four wolves. Stan Rice. 6901-0
Four words. Elizabeth Akers Allen. 6066-8, 6226-1
Four years. Dinah Maria Mulock Craik. 6046-3
Four years. Nicholas Pappas. 6352-7
Four years old. Benjamin Franklin Taylor. 6815-4
Four years old. Unknown. 6706-9
"Four young men, of a Monday morn". The prize of the
    Margaretta. Will Carelton. 6946-0
The four zoas, sels. William Blake. 6106-0
"Four-and-eighty years are o'er me". The battle of
    Monmouth. Thomas Dunn English. 6946-0
The four-cornered tower: Llaynbri. Nigel Heseltine. 6360-8

FOUR-LEAF
550

Four-leaf clover. Ella Higginson. 6047-1,6476-0,6529-5, 6274-1,6498-1
Four-leaf clover. George Houghton. 6066-8
Four-leaf clover. Richard Monckton Milnes; 1st Baron Houghton. 6226-1
A four-line philosophy. Joseph Anthony. 6396-9
"The four-way winds of the world have blown". Strike the blow. Unknown. 6946-0
A four-year old. Unknown. 6684-4
The four. Geoffrey Grigson. 6666-6
The foure PP. John Heywood. 6193-1
14 July 1956. Laurence David Lerner. 6788-3
Fourteen stations of love, sels. Paul Mayer. 6160-5
"Fourteen volcanoes rise/in my remembered...". Flowers from the volcano. Claribel Alegria. 7036-1
Fourteenth birthday. Phyllis McGinley. 6388-8
Fourth act. Robinson Jeffers. 6666-6
The fourth day's battle, fr. Annus mirabilis: 1666. John Dryden. 6933-9
Fourth declamation (police of the dead day) Jean Garrigue. 6803-0
Fourth dimension. Gelett Burgess. 6817-0
Fourth dimension. Jessie Young Norton. 6841-3
The fourth dimension. Robert Bridges. 6487-6
The fourth eclogue. Vergil. 6734-4
The fourth of August. Laurence Binyon. 7029-9
Fourth of July. George Washington Bethune. 6414-0,6678-X
Fourth of July. Unknown. 6693-3
The fourth of July ("Let the herds..."). Charles Leonard Moore. 6286-5
The fourth of July ("To the sages who spoke..."). Charles Sprague. 6286-5
Fourth of July at 'The Corners'. Benjamin Franklin Taylor. 6815-4
Fourth of July at Ripton. Eugene J. Hall. 6927-4
Fourth of July in Vermont. Daniel L. Cady. 6988-6
Fourth of July ode. James Russell Lowell. 6465-5
A Fourth of July record. Lilian Dynevor Rice. 6745-X
Fourth of July wish. Frank Walcott Hutt. 6715-8
The Fourth of July, 1776. Maurice Hewlett. 7027-2
Fourth of July, 1876. W.F. Fox. 6913-4
"Fourth of July, they say, sir". Young America. Carolyn Wells. 6820-0
The fourth of July. Frances Dana Barker ("Aunt Fanny") Gage. 6130-2
The Fourth of July. John Pierpont. 6946-0,6465-5,6820-0
The Fourth of July. Charles Sprague. 6820-0
Fourth of June at Eton. Robert Bridges. 6487-6
The fourth shepherd. Alexander Mackenzie Davidson. 6269-5
Fourth song from Cyprus. Hilda ("H.D.") Doolittle. 6250-4
Fourth song, fr. Astrophel and Stella. Sir Philip Sidney. 6586-4
The fourth squire. Thomas Campion. 6794-8
Fourth station ("Mothers who have seen him die...") Paul Claudel. 6282-2
Fourth station ("They say this is his mother—"). Ruth Shaumanm. 6282-2
Fourth station ("This afternoon in loud Jerusalem"). William A. Donaghy. 6282-2
Fourth station (Jesus his Mother meets"). Padraic Colum. 6282-2
Fourwheeling to the gravel pit. Nita Bourbon. 6857-X
"Foweles in the frith". I live in great sorrow. Unknown. 6881-2
Fowle, William B.
    Katie's answer. 6280-6
    Vat you please. 6403-5
Fowler, Ellen Thorneycroft
    "For better, for worse". 6620-8
    Wishing. 6291-1
Fowler, Elsie M.
    Little Christ child. 6465-5
Fowler, Gene
    The flowering cacti. 6792-1
    Her majesty's ship. 6792-1
    Hunting song. 6792-1
    The Jervis Bay goes down. 6224-5
    The last ancestor. 6792-1
    Not macho, just macho. 6998-3
    Venus' return to the sea. 6792-1

Vivisection. 6792-1
Vivisection, sels. 6870-7
Fowler, Wibur Humphrey
    Prayer ("Purge me"). 6337-3
Fowler, William
    If when I die. 6182-6
    In Orknay. 6845-6
    Ship-broken men whom stormy seas sore toss. 6845-6
The fowler. Wilfred Wilson Gibson. 6102-8
The fowler. Wilfred Wilson Gibson. 6778-6
Fowls in the frith. Unknown. 6380-2
The fowls. Madeleine Nightingale. 6368-3
Fox. Edward Bulwer-Lytton; Baron Lytton. 6046-3
Fox. Clifford Dyment. 6257-1
Fox and H. Orenstein, Edward
    Quartermaster song. 6237-7
Fox and cock. Geoffrey Chaucer. 6438-8
Fox and geese. Anna M. Ford. 6167-2
"The fox and his wife they had a great strife". Unknown. 6363-2
The fox and the cat. James Vincent Cunningham. 6133-8
The fox and the crow. Jane Taylor. 6424-8
The fox and the farmer. Unknown. 6079-X
The fox at the point of death. John Gay. 6133-8,6183-4, 6195-0
The fox hoaxes the raven out of his cheese. Jean de La Fontaine. 6637-2
The fox hunt. John Masefield. 6150-8
The fox in the well. John Townsend Trowbridge. 6165-6,6742-5
"A fox one night when the moon shone bright". Unknown. 6059-5
Fox race. Roy Helton. 6628-3
"The fox ran up into the mill". Unknown. 6050-1
The fox sparrow. W.W. Christman. 6073-0
The fox went through the town, Oh! Unknown. 6594-5
Fox, Annie
    The voiceless chimes. 6921-5
Fox, Charles A.
    The morning sea. 6997-5
    Sea voices. 6997-5
Fox, Charles James
    To Mrs. Crewe. 6874-X
Fox, George (tr.)
    The county of Mayo. Unknown, See Lavelle, Thomas
    The county of Mayo. Thomas Lavelle, 6858-8,6858-8,6244-X
Fox, Hugh
    Sicktime. 6998-3
Fox, Moireen
    Liadain to Curithir. 6897-9
    To the mountain Ben Bulben. 6090-0
Fox, Sybil Lavinia
    Nights and days. 6118-4
Fox, W.F.
    Beneath the surface. 6408-6
    Fourth of July, 1876. 6913-4
    My love. 6413-2
    A name. 6407-8
    Our sweet unexpressed. 6912-6
    A psalm of hope. 6911-8
    Reply to 'The welcome'. 6409-4
    To-morrow. 6410-8
Fox, W.J. (tr.)
    The martyrs' hymn. Martin Luther, 6302-0;6385-3
Fox, William Johnson
    The barons bold. 6188-5,6656-9
    Praise to the heroes. 7009-4
A fox, a fox, up gallants. Unknown. 6328-4
"The fox, the ape, the humble-bee". Song ("The fox, the ape"). William Shakespeare. 6134-6
Fox-Smith, Cicely. See Smith, Cicely Fox
The fox.. Unknown. 6058-7,6132-X
The fox. Kahlil Gibran. 6393-4
The fox. Phoebe Hesketh. 6257-1
The fox. Francis Maguire. 6761-1
The fox. R. Williams Parry. 6528-7
The fox. Edith Sitwell. 7000-0
Foxcroft, Frank
    Jericho. 6848-0

Foxes among the lambs. Ernest G. Moll. 6761-1
"The foxglove by the cottage door". Four and eight. Ffrida Wolfe. 6937-1
"The foxglove I know". Up and down. B.R. M.. 6937-1
The foxhunter's dream. G. C. Scheu. 7010-8
Foxton, E. See Palfrey, Sarah E.
Foxworthy, J.L.
　'Consider the birds'. 6269-5
　A waterfall. 6269-5
Foy-month. David Atwood Wasson. 6597-X
The Foys of the road. Bliss Carman. 6597-X
"Fra bank to bank, fra wood to wood I rin". Cupid and Venus. Mark Alexander Boyd. 6845-6
"Fra cruachan tae aberdeen". Ballade of the forest in summer. Patrick Reginald Chalmers. 6875-8
Fra fonti. Robert C.V. Meyers. 6416-7
Fra Giacomo. Robert Buchanan. 6918-5
Fra Giacomo. Robert Buchanan. 6385-3
Fra Lippo Lippi. Robert Browning. 6154-0,6198-2,6427-2, 6488-4,6536-8,6657-,6196-6,6430-2,6110-9,6199-0,6655-0,6723
Fra Lippo Lippi. Robert Browning. 6828-6
Fra Luigi's marriage. Helen Hunt Jackson. 6676-3
Fra moreale. S.B. R. 6116-8
"Fra whaur ye hing, my cauldrife frien'.". Hughie's winter excuse for a dram. James Logie ("Hugh Haliburton") Robertson. 6819-7
Fracastorius
　To Baptista Turriano, on the death of his sons. Thomas Warton (the Elder) (tr.). 6962-2
A fragile thing is beauty. Arthur Stringer. 6779-4
Fragility. James Edgar Smith. 6178-8
Fragment. William Cowper. 6730-1
Fragment. Gerard Manley Hopkins. 6375-6
Fragment. Amy Lowell. 6730-1
Fragment. Edwin Arlington Robinson. 6348-9
Fragment. Sappho. 6219-9
Fragment. Clark Ashton Smith. 6648-8
Fragment. Henry Vaughan. 6730-1
Fragment. Anne Finch, Countess of Winchilsea. 6641-0
Fragment ("Amid the shining swords"). Sharaf al-Din. 6362-4
Fragment ("And what of"). Jan z Wojkowicz. 6763-8
Fragment ("As balmy"). Dante Gabriel Rossetti. 6545-7
A fragment ("Boast not these titles..."). Ben Jonson. 6867-7
A fragment ("Could I remount"). George Gordon, 6th Baron Byron. 6945-2
Fragment ("Encinctur'd"). Samuel Taylor Coleridge. 6545-7
Fragment ("Flourishing vine"). Percy Bysshe Shelley. 6545-7
Fragment ("Give me"). Edmund John. 6102-8
Fragment ("He came to me..."). William Cowper. 6814-6
Fragment ("I had a dream..."). Thomas Hood. 6974-6
Fragment ("I sleep..."). Herbert Trench. 6877-4
Fragment ("I went"). Percy Bysshe Shelley. 6958-4,6545-7
A fragment ("It was a sandy..."). Alice Cary. 6865-0;6969-X
A fragment ("Noble warrior"). John Kells Ingram. 6174-5
Fragment ("Or I will burst"). Thomas Lovell Beddoes. 6545-7
Fragment ("Praise not"). Ibn al-Missisi. 6362-4
A fragment ("Rest on your battle-fields..."). Felicia Dorothea Hemans. 6973-8
Fragment ("Spirit"). William Blake. 6545-7
Fragment ("That night"). Francis Stewart Flint. 6320-9
Fragment ("The hedgerow"). John Clare. 6545-7
A fragment ("They say that poison..."). Adam Lindsay Gordon. 6951-7
Fragment ("Walking by moonlight on the golden margin"). Frances Anne Kemble. 6980-0
Fragment ("Walking by moonlight"). Frances Anne Kemble. 6980-0
A fragment ("Were I the sun..."). Louis J. Magee. 7004-3
Fragment ("When soft winds"). Percy Bysshe Shelley. 6828-6
fragment ("When, to their airy"). George Gordon, 6th Baron Byron. 6945-2
A fragment ("Where is the giant..."). Alfred Lord Tennyson. 6977-0
A fragment ("Yon bird..."). Thomas Edwar Brown. 6809-X

Fragment from a ballad. Alexander Smith. 6102-8
A fragment from Saint Gregory Nazianzen. John Henry, Cardinal Newman. 6285-7
Fragment in imitation of Wordsworth. Catherine Maria Fanshawe. 6440-X
Fragment of a chorus of 'Dejaneira'. Matthew Arnold. 6250-4
Fragment of a chorus of a Dejaneira. Matthew Arnold. 6947-9
Fragment of a legend. Robert Davis. 6855-3
Fragment of a poem on the world before the flood. Reginald Heber. 6848-0
A fragment of a satire. Thomas Warton (the Elder) 6962-2
Fragment of a sleep-song. Sydney Dobell. 6656-9
Fragment of a sonnet. Pierre de Ronsard. 6102-8
Fragment of a sonnet. Pierre de Ronsard. 7039-6
Fragment of an 'Antigone'. Matthew Arnold. 6947-9
Fragment of an anti-Papist ballad. Unknown. 6157-5
Fragment of an ode to Maia. John Keats. 6086-2,6250-4,6430-2
Fragment of an ode to Maia, written on May Day, 1818 John Keats. 6828-6
Fragment of an ode to the moon. Henry Kirke White. 6086-2
Fragment of an oration. George Canning. 6874-X
Fragment of an oratorio. Thomas Campbell. 6848-0
A fragment of Empedocles. Frances Cornford. 6581-3
"A fragment of moon that shines". Vespers. Luis Carlos Lopez. 6759-X
A fragment of science, fr. Hudibras. Samuel Butler. 6787-5
Fragment on Keats. Percy Bysshe Shelley. 6250-4
Fragment written shortly after the marriage...Chaworth. George Gordon, 6th Baron Byron. 6945-2
Fragment, fr. the Bahristan of Jami. Unknown. 6120-6
A fragment, sels. Percy Bysshe Shelley. 6369-1
A fragment.. James Elroy Flecker. 6234-2
A fragment: The woodman and the nightingale. Percy Bysshe Shelley. 6828-6
A fragment: To music. Percy Bysshe Shelley. 6250-4
Fragment: Wedded souls. Percy Bysshe Shelley. 6250-4
A fragment. Madison Cawein. 6102-8,6076-5
A fragment. Allan Cunningham. 6960-6
A fragment. Sir Humphry Davy. 6980-0
A fragment. Edward A. Dix. 6983-5
A fragment. John Gay. 6092-5
A fragment. Christopher Marlowe. 6436-1
A fragment. George Outram. 6878-2
A fragment. Unknown. 6089-7,6312-8
Fragmenta. Martha Champion. 6640-2
Fragmentary blue. Robert Frost. 6345-4
Fragments. John Masefield. 6477-9
Fragments. Mary Brent Whiteside. 6039-0
Fragments ("The sun"). Elizabeth Rachel Muller. 6818-9
Fragments ("The way"). Jessie Farnham. 6750-6
Fragments from other poems. Alexander Pope. 6102-8
Fragments of Irish songs. Unknown. 6058-7
Fragments on nature and life. Ralph Waldo Emerson. 6126-5
Fragments on the poet. Ralph Waldo Emerson. 6232-6,6126-5
Fragments: To Charley Walker (1). Adam Lindsay Gordon. 6951-7
Fragments: To Charley Walker (2). Adam Lindsay Gordon. 6951-7
Fragments: To Charley Walker (3). Adam Lindsay Gordon. 6951-7
Fragments: To Charley Walker (4). Adam Lindsay Gordon. 6951-7
Fragrance. Amy Parkinson. 6796-4
"The fragrance of a baby's breath". Infinitude. Hattie Meyers. 6799-9
A fragrant grove. William Browne. 6935-5
"The fragrant petals of a faded rose". A summer souvenir. Aidna Van Orden. 6847-2
"A fragrant prayer upon the air". A poem to be said on hearing the birds sing. Unknown (Irish). 7039-6
"A fragrant sag of fruit distinctly grouped". Sonnet 015 (A fragrant sag"). Edward Estlin Cummings. 6808-1
The fragrant timber of her fan. Henry Hanby Hay. 7022-1
Frail flame. Isabel Fiske Conant. 6071-4
Frail hands. Lucia Trent. 6218-0
"Frail life! in which, through mists...". Life and death. Sir William Davenant. 6933-9

FRAIL

"A frail sound of a tunic trailing". Poem ("A frail sound"). Antonio Machado. 7039-6
Frail strength. Louis Ginsberg. 6072-2
The frailtie and hurtfulnes of beautie. Henry Howard, Earl of Surrey. 6586-4
Frailty. George Herbert. 6931-2
The frailty of beauty. J. C. 6182-6
"Framed in its shadow-rectangle". Facing my portrait. Yolanda Bedregal de Conitzer. 6759-X
"Framed in the cavernous fireplace sits a boy". An old thought. Charles Henry Luders. 6936-3
"Framed in the sedan windows, the tall...faces". Giraffes. Noel Harry Brettell. 6788-3
The frames of space. James Dawson. 6640-2
The framework-knitters lamentation. Unknown. 6157-5
The framework-knitters petition. Unknown. 6157-5
France. Cecil Chesterton. 7026-4
France. Oliver Goldsmith. 6932-0
France. Percy MacKaye. 6102-8,6076-5,6250-4,6300-4
France. Phelps Morane. 6761-1
France. Elliott Napier. 6784-0
France. Armentier Ohanian. 6846-4
France. Walt Whitman. 6121-4
France 1870. George Meredith. 6122-2
France and England. William Wordsworth. 6543-0
"France is planting her gardens". Flower-beds in the Tuileries. Grace Ellery Channing-Stetson. 7027-2
"France must have dogwood, too". Le printemps empoissone. Frances Westgate Butterfield. 6979-7
"France your country, as we know". Colinette. Andrew Lang. 6771-9
"France!/It is I answering". Republic to republic. Witter Bynner. 6946-0
France, Anatole
    The bad workman. 6351-9
    Eve's blood. 6351-9
    A Roman senator. 6351-9
    The venusberg. 6351-9
France, Marie de
    Song from Chartivel. Arthur O'Shaughnessy (tr.). 7039-6
    Would I might go far over sea. Arthur O'Shaughnessy (tr.). 7039-6
"France, a l'heure ou tu te prosternes" Victor Hugo. 6801-4
France, sels. Samuel Taylor Coleridge. 6198-2
France: an ode. Samuel Taylor Coleridge. 6828-6
France: an ode. Samuel Taylor Coleridge. 6192-3,6196-6, 6430-2,6071-4
"Franceline rose in the dawning gray". Vive la France! Charlotte Holmes Crawford. 6030-7,6088-9,6419-1,6846-4,6476-0,6509
Frances E. Willard. May Preston Slosson. 6685-2
'Frances'. Richard Wightman. 7008-6
Frances, Harrison S.
    Petite Ste. Rosalie. 6115-X
Frances, Susan ("Seranus")
    At Lac Labelle. 6797-2
    At St. Jerome. 6797-2
    Father Couture. 6797-2
Francesca. H. Savile Clark. 6681-X
Francesca. Ezra Pound. 6581-3
Francesca da Rimini. William Edmonstoune Aytoun. 6278-4
Francesca da Rimini, fr. Dante. Dante Gabriel Rossetti. 6122-2,6198-2,6199-0
Francesca of Rimini, fr. The divine comedy. Dante Alighieri. 6945-2
Francie. Rose Hawthorne Lathrop. 7041-8
Francis. Earl B. Marlatt. 6143-5
Francis Davidson (tr.)
    Psalm 013. Bible, 6848-0
Francis keeps her promise. Ann and Jane Taylor. 6105-2
Francis Ledwidge. Grace Hazard Conkling. 6556-2
Francis Thompson: Hush-a-bye, baby. Charles Powell. 6982-7
Francis of Assisi, Saint
    The canticle of brother sun. Mona Swann (tr.). 6334-9
    Canticle of the creatures (or, Canticle of the sun). Matthew Arnold (tr.). 6337-3
    Canticle of the sun. Maurice Francis Egan (tr.). 6730-1
    The canticle of the sun. 6143-5,6252-0
    Hymn of love. 6543-0
    Our Lord Christ: of order. Dante Gabriel Rossetti (tr.). 7039-6
    Praise of cleated things. 6236-9
    St. Francis' prayer. 6337-3
Francis Raphael, Mother
    A nun's beloved. 6285-7
Francis Xavier, Saint
    Hymn ("My God, I love thee, not because.") 6730-1
    "My God, I love thee." Edward Caswall (tr.). 6302-0, 6385-3,6271-7,6337-3
Francis, Ann
    The song of songs. 6848-0
Francis, J.G.
    6786-7
    The bald eagle and the barber. 6786-7
    The bicycle ride. 6786-7
    A case of highway robbery. 6786-7
    The cat and the cream. 6786-7
    The cat-o'-nine-tails. 6786-7
    Coasting cats. 6786-7
    The donkey and his company. 6786-7
    A dutiful parent. 6786-7
    The elephant juggler. 6786-7
    Euchred! 6786-7
    The genial grimalkin. 6786-7
    The giraffe ride. 6786-7
    A happy new year. 6786-7
    Late! 6786-7
    The lion in the barber-shop. 6786-7
    Maternal counsel. 6786-7
    A medical opinion. 6786-7
    A musical evening. 6120-6
    A needless apprehension. 6786-7
    Pictures with a moral for boys and dogs. 6786-7
    The prickly pig, the pug and pard. 6786-7
    A queer barber-shop. 6786-7
    Quits. 6786-7
    The reformed lion. 6786-7
    A sea change. 6786-7
    "Some cat-land fancies, drawn and dressed". 6786-7
    Some fun with a toy spider. 6786-7
    The spring curtain. 6786-7
    Story of the catnip ball. 6786-7
    Study of hedgehog stealing apple. 6786-7
    "'T is a perfect picnic day!" 6786-7
    "A Tam o'shanter dog". 6786-7
    The tea-party. 6786-7
    "They didn't have a penny". 6786-7
    A very happy family. 6120-6
    Ye joyful owl. 6786-7
Francis, J.W.D.
    Pilate's monologue. 6720-4
Francis, Joseph G.
    An elephant. 6891-X
    A lion. 6891-X
    A musical evening. 6786-7
Francis, Martha Jeanette
    A prayer ("More than lure"). 6270-9
Francis, Phillip (tr.)
    The sabine farm. Horace, 6624-0
Francis, Robert
    Boy riding forward backward. 6388-8
    Boy sleeping. 6761-1
    Cold. 6388-8
    Distance and peace. 6783-2
    Excellence. 6761-1
    I am not flattered. 6761-1
    Roots. 6042-0
    The seed-eaters. 6388-8
A Franciscan prayer. Arthur Shearly Cripps. 6625-9,6800-6
Francisco, Nia
    Awee. 7005-1
    Men tell and talk. 7005-1
    Morning and myself. 7005-1
    The one who is within. 7005-1
    Story tellers summer, 1980 7005-1
Franck, Johann
    Peace and joy in Jesus Christ. 6065-X
Franco, Josephine
    Fall leaves. 6850-2

In memoriam. 6850-2
Franco, Luis L.
   Goat-pen. Muna Lee (tr.). 6759-X
Francois Villon, 1450. Andrew Lang. 6771-9
Francois Villon, sels. Dante Gabriel Rossetti. 6123-0,6198-2
Frangipanni. Unknown. 6902-9
Frank Fidd. Unknown. 6057-9
Frank Hayman. Benjamin Franklin Taylor. 6924-X
"**Frank** carves very ill, yet will palm all the meats".
    Epigram ("Frank carves"). Matthew Prior. 6152-4
Frank, A.L.
   The rose beyond the wall. 6303-9
Frank, Edgar
   Goshen! 6337-3
   My town is a cathedral. 6954-1
Frank, Florence Kiper
   Dialogue. 6037-4
   A girl strike-leader. 6954-1
   The Jew to Jesus. 6144-3,6337-3,6730-1,6393-4
   The Jewish conscript. 6532-5,6542-2
   The movies. 6052-8,6476-0
   You. 6897-9
Frank, J.M.
   Observation. 6857-X
Frank, Julia Hazel
   A birthday greeting. 6847-2
   When Azrael comes knocking. 6847-2
   Your letter. 6847-2
Frank, May
   Concession. 6397-7
   Egotism. 6397-7
   Free verse. 6397-7
   Mississippi mist. 6397-7
   The road to faeryland. 6397-7
Frank, Waldo
   Plaint. 6069-2
Frank, the fireman. Thomas Frost. 6681-X
Frankau, Gilbert
   Ammunition column. 7027-2
   Gun-teams. 6510-4
   Headquarters. 7026-4
   Mother and mate. 7027-2
   The voice of the guns. 7027-2
Franke, Carl Ludwig
   Resignation. James Abraham Martling (tr.). 6952-5
Frankenburg, Lloyd
   Hide in the heart. 6389-6
Frankicense. Ibn al-Zaqqaq. 6362-4
Frankie Baker. Unknown. 6826-X
Frankie's trade. Rudyard Kipling. 6833-2
Franklin (atr), Benjamin
   The downfall of piracy. 6946-0
The **franklin's** prologue, fr. the Canterbury tales.
    Geoffrey Chaucer. 6430-2
The **franklin's** tale, fr. The Canterbury tales. Geoffrey
    Chaucer. 6430-2
The **franklin's** tale, sels. Geoffrey Chaucer. 6649-6
The **franklin's** tale, sels. Geoffrey Chaucer. 6232-6
Franklin, Benjamin
   The difference. 6722-0
     Epitaph on a talkative old maid. 6722-0
   "Here Skugg lies snug". 6722-0
   Jack and Roger. 6125-7
   Metaphorical papers. 6914-2
   The mother country. 6946-0
   Paper. 6385-3,6673-9,6307-1,6004-8
   Poor Richard's opinion. 6878-2
   Quatrain. 6722-0
Franklin, Jean Dwight
   Optimism. 6109-5
Franklin, Richard
   Rendezvous. 6857-X
Franklin, William ("Wild Bill")
   The captive. 6870-7
   'Gotta' smoke?' 6870-7
   Hunger striker. 6870-7
   Lawn order. 6870-7
   My street baby's lament. 6870-7
   Paper words. 6870-7

Frankness between friends. Berton Braley. 6085-4
Franz, Willis Walton
   A lullaby ("Close to the heart"). 6097-8
Franzen, Franz Mikael
   Champagne. Charles Wharton Stork (tr.). 6045-5
Fraser Jr., John A.
   Nancy. 6014-5
   A reporter's prayer. 6680-1
Fraser, Alex
   E.e. and thee and me. 6857-X
Fraser, Alexander Louis
   A gloaming call. 6433-7
   'Kin unknown'. 6796-4
   November. 6433-7
Fraser, C. Lovat
   The wind. 6850-2
Fraser, Edith L.
   Evening. 7016-7
   The lowlands. 7016-7
   My red geranium. 7016-7
   Old rice-fields. 7016-7
   Sand dunes. 7016-7
   These common things. 7016-7
Fraser, George S.
   A bought embrace. 6666-6
   Crisis. 6379-9
   Elegy. 6379-9
   Lean street. 6379-9
   Nilotic elegy. 6666-6
   On a memory of beauty. 6209-1,6379-9
   A poem about love. 6379-9
   Rostov. 6666-6
   S.S. city of Benares. 6379-9
   Sonnet ("My simple heart"). 6379-9
   Summer and winter. 6209-1
   The time. 6666-6
Fraser, George S. (tr.)
   "Beauty of ladies of compassionate heart". Guido
     Cavalcanti, 6325-X
   Last song: from exile. Guido Cavalcanti, 6325-X
   "There in a woodland, to my thought more bright". Guido
     Cavalcanti, 6325-X
   The virgin, bright and beautiful to-day. Stephane
     Mallarme, 6343-8
   "Who's this that comes, as each man looks at her".
     Guido Cavalcanti, 6325-X
   "You have in you the flowers and the green grass".
     Guido Cavalcanti, 6325-X
Fraser, J.A.
   The veteran. 6795-6
Fraser, James Anderson
   Apprehension. 6337-3
Fraser, Kathleen
   One of the chapters. 6792-1
Fraser, Marjorie Frost
   America. 6042-0
Fraser, Sir James (tr.)
   'For a scrap of paper'. Paul Hyacinth Loyson, 7031-0
Fraser-Tytler, C.C. See Liddell, Catherine C.
The **Frasers** in the correl. James Hogg. 6859-6
Frasier, Scottie McKenzie
   Hills. 6037-4
   The peacock ("In the cold blue haze of a January day").
     6036-6
   The peacock. 6036-6
Frater ave atque vale. Alfred Lord Tennyson. 6110-9,6125-7,
   6199-0,6655-0,6483-3,6657-7,6122-2,6624-0,6331-4
Fraternity. Victor Hugo. 6351-9
Fraternity. John Banister Tabb. 6250-4
Fraterville mine explosion. C.L. Luallen. 6149-4
Fratri Dilectissimo. John Buchan. 6427-2
"**Fraught** with flame, and clad in crimson...". Lost in the
    Mallee. Charles Allan Sherard. 6768-9
Fraunces' tavern. Arthur Guiterman. 6773-5
The **fray** o' suport. Unknown. 6055-2
Fray Serra. Lilian White Spencer. 6102-8,6076-5
"**Frayed** on the jagged cornice, the rope parted". For the
    dead on the mountains. David Brock. 6761-1
Frazee-Bower, Helen
   Alien. 6777-8

Courage. 6347-0
On reading a volume of poetry. 6042-0
Poet's hunting song. 6750-6
Tears are but spindrift. 6750-6
This is the tragedy. 6337-3
Three sisters. 6036-6
Two married. 6037-4
When death shall come. 6337-3
Frazer, J.D.
The gathering of the nation. 6858-8
Frazer, John de Jean
The holy wells. 6858-8
The prisoner at the bar. 7009-4
Song for July 12th, 1843. 6090-0
Frazer, M.W.
Come, sign the pledge. 6417-5
Freaks of the frost. Hannah Flagg Gould. 6621-6
Frear, Mary Dillingham
If only. 6799-9
Our Roosevelt. 6995-9
Frechette, Louis
'Le drapeau anglais' 7041-8
Saguenay. J.D. Edgar (tr.). 6795-6
'Saint-Malo' 7041-8
"Freckles/tickle your nose". Bits and pieces. Gregory J. Ford. 7024-8
Fred Apollus at Fava's. Nicholas Moore. 6379-9
Fred's store. Ben H. Smith. 6662-3
Freddie and the cherry-tree. Unknown. 6502-3
Freddy and the cherry-tree. Ann ("Aunt Effie") Hawkshawe. 6018-8,6135-4
"Frederick Knieps, physician...". The big mystical circus. Jorge de Lima. 6759-X
Frederick, George
The eagle and the lion. 6274-1
Fredericks, Aaron W.
Uncle Ike's roosters. 6415-9
Fredericksburg. Thomas Bailey Aldrich. 6076-5,6102-8,6271-7,6470-1,6737-9,6442 ,6121-4,6467-1
Fredericksburg. James Abraham Martling. 6952-5
Fredericksburg. W.F. W. 6016-2
Fredman's epistles, sels. Karl Mikael Bellman. 6045-5
Fredugis - lament for Alcuin. Helen Waddell. 6641-0
Free. Louis Untermeyer. 6345-4
Free America. Joseph Warren (atr.) 6015-3
"Free are the muses, and where freedom is". Breath on the oat. Joseph Russell Taylor. 6946-0
"The free canary warbles". The canary. Morris Rosenfeld. 7011-6
Free enterprise. Clyde McGee. 6144-3
Free fantasia on Japanese themes. Amy Lowell. 6032-3,6538-4
The free flag. Unknown. 6223-7
Free from the world. Sir Matthew Hale. 6793-X
"Free is my heart from every weight". On the lake. Johann Wolfgang von Goethe. 6948-7
Free little chilluns on de flo'. John McMaster. 6249-0
"Free love - free field - we love...". Songs, fr. The last tournament, fr. The idylls... Alfred Lord Tennyson. 6867-7
The free mind. William Lloyd Garrison. 6632-1
A free nation. Edwin Markham. 6337-3
'A free puff'. Arthur Irving Gray. 6453-1
Free to choose. Gertrude Shisler Dupper. 6750-6
Free verse. May Frank. 6397-7
Free verse. Robert Graves. 6506-6
Free will. Alice Meynell. 6955-X
Free wine on communion day. Linwood Daggette Smith Jr. 7024-8
A free woman. James Rorty. 6780-8
The free woman. Theodosia Garrison. 6102-8,6076-5
Free, Spencer Michael
The human touch. 6337-3,6482-5
The old=time family doctor. 6482-5
Free-will and predestination. Maurice Hare. 6339-X
The free. Eliza Cook. 6980-0
The freebooter. Robert Loveman. 6941-X
The freed bird. Felicia Dorothea Hemans. 6973-8
The freedman. Viola Gerard Garvin. 7007-8
Freedom. John Babour. 6180-X,6250-4,6383-7

Freedom. Joel Barlow. 6176-1
Freedom. K. von K. Bruns. 6799-9
Freedom. Ralph Chaplin. 6880-4
Freedom. William Cowper. 7009-4,6793-X
Freedom. Ralph Waldo Emerson. 7014-0
Freedom. J. Charles Green. 6870-7
Freedom. Mabel Crehore Greene. 6841-3
Freedom. Sylvia Lee. 6818-9
Freedom. Eve Lott. 6880-4
Freedom. James Russell Lowell. 6176-1,6250-4
Freedom. Thomas Paine. 6143-5
Freedom. Palladas. 6435-3
Freedom. Phillips Stewart. 6433-7
Freedom. Alfred Lord Tennyson. 6337-3,6655-0
Freedom. Aidna Van Orden. 6847-2
Freedom ("Are we, then, wholly fallen?"). James Russell Lowell. 6486-8
Freedom ("I am not strong till Thou hast clasped..."). Unknown. 6335-7
Freedom ("I tell you a poet must be free"). Leonard Mann. 6384-5
Freedom ("We are not free: Freedom doth not consist"). James Russell Lowell. 6087-0
Freedom and love. Thomas Campbell. 6543-0,6246-5
"Freedom arriving bleeding". Nightmare no. 37 Richard George-Murray. 7003-5
"Freedom called them - up they rose". The gallant fifty-one. Henry Lynden Flash. 6946-0
Freedom considered. Harriet Sampson. 6979-7
Freedom for the mind. William Lloyd Garrison. 6735-2
"Freedom from world-old tyrannies I see". Freedom. Aidna Van Orden. 6847-2
Freedom in America. Walter Crane. 7009-4
Freedom in dress. Ben Jonson. 6302-0,6385-3,6737-9,6438-8
Freedom is lonely. Gertrude Scott Jewell. 6662-3
Freedom of nature. James Thomson. 6240-7
The freedom of the hills. Robert Bird. 7009-4
Freedom of the savage. John Dryden. 6543-0
Freedom of the will. Robert Southey. 6867-7
Freedom the goddess. Arthur W. Jose. 6784-0
"Freedom! sweet freedom! our voices resound", sels. Oliver Wendell Holmes. 66601-1
Freedom's ahead. Robert Buchanan. 6001-3
Freedom's dawning. James Abraham Martling. 6952-5
"Freedom's first champion in our fettered land". Garrison. Amos Bronson Alcott. 6431-0,6820-0
Freedom's flower. Marian (Annie D.G. Robinson) Douglas. 6049-8
Freedom's gathering. William H. Burleigh. 6709-3
Freedom's hero, fr. The prisoner of Chillon. George Gordon, 6th Baron Byron. 6337-3
Freedom's natal day. Elizabeth M. Griswold. 6820-0
Freedom's snare. Ed Lee. 6178-8
Freedom's Thanksgiving day. Thomas Chalmers Harbaugh. 6703-4
Freedom's true heroes. George Gordon, 6th Baron Byron. 6543-0
Freedom's voice. Joshua Freeman Crowell. 6798-0
Freedom, our queen. Oliver Wendell Holmes. 6449-3
"Freedom, yes, but a freedom combed and curled". Distinguo. Lizinka Campbell Turner. 6880-4
Freedoms. Gerald Gould. 6884-7
Freeland, William
In prospect of death. 7015-9
The new-comers. 6078-1
Freeman, Garnet B.
Four lives. 6912-6
Retrospection. 6273-3
Freeman, Gladys McCain
The hills are like a woman. 6799-9
Freeman, John
Adam. 6777-8
The alde. 6477-9
Caterpillars. 6250-4
The dancers. 6070-6
English hills ("O that I were"). 6331-4
Happy is England now. 6477-9
Let me be like a tree. 6461-2
The murdered face. 6776-X
Music comes. 7014-0

Old Testament. 6778-6
Old Testament. 6071-4
The physician. 7014-0
The return. 7026-4,7029-9
Rhymeless. 6354-3
The searchlight. 7014-0
The stars in their courses. 7027-2
To my mother. 6320-9
Unconquarable. 6779-4
The visit. 6506-6
The waxworks. 6072-2
Freeman, Joseph
Be still to-day. 6778-6
The dancers. 6880-4
Distinquished madmen. 6880-4
Fantasia. 6880-4
A girl's song. 6880-4
Freeman, Mary E. See Wilkins, Mary E.
Freeman, Olivia
An old stone god. 6648-8
Freeman, Robert
Beyond the horizon. 6337-3
God bless our home. 6337-3
In my father's house. 6461-2
Peace on earth. 6542-2,6420-5
Prayer ("White captain"). 6144-3,6461-2,6542-2,6420-5, 6337-3
Freeman, W.H.
Vat have I got to pay? 6910-X
Freeman, Walter
Mother church. 6482-5
The **freeman**. William Cowper. 6302-0;6385-3
The **Freer** gallery, Washington, D.C. Vachel Lindsay. 6012-9
Freer, Mabel Stevens
The mother. 6303-9
The **freesia** flower. Albert Durrant Watson. 6797-2
Freethought. Edward H. Guillaume. 7009-4
Freeze tag. Gordon Henry. 7005-1
"**Freeze**, freeze, thou bitter sky", fr. As you like it. William Shakespeare. 6395-0
Freight boats. James S. Tippett. 6891-X
"A **freight** train rolls". The journey. Henry Johnson. 6870-7
The **freight** yards. Phoebe Hoffman. 7007-8
Freightbells in Oregon. Conrad Pendleton. 6783-2
"**Freighted** with passengers of every sort". Address to a steam-vessel. Joanna Baillie. 6813-8
Freiligrath, Ferdinand
Hurra, Germania! Elizabeth Craigmyle (tr.). 6842-1
The lion's ride. 6271-7
Mount Nebo. J. Gostick (tr.). 6848-0
The scheik of Sinai in 1830. William Edmonstoune Aytoun (tr.). 6948-7
The traveler's vision. 6385-3
"Were I before the gates of Mecca!" Elizabeth Craigmyle (tr.). 6842-1
Fremont, John C.
On recrossing the Rocky Mountains in winter,... 6600-3
French adage. Unknown. 6724-7
French and English. Thomas, Lord Erskine. 6278-4
French and English. Thomas Hood. 6018-8
The **French** and Spanish guerrillas. William Wordsworth. 6665-8
French clock. Hortense Flexner. 6777-8
The **French** ensign, sels. Alphonse Daudet. 6695-X
French in the trenches. William J. Robinson. 6846-4
The **French** market. W.P. J. 6676-3
The **French** must go. Eugene Field. 6949-5
"A **French** once - so runs a certain ditty". The Frenchman and the flea powder. Unknown. 6909-6
French peasants. Monk Gibbon. 6257-1
The **French** polisher. Constance Davies. 6360-8
The **French** revolution, fr. The prelude. William Wordsworth. 6110-9,6545-7
The **French** row. James Hearst. 6491-4
The **French** tambour. Heinrich Heine. 6084-6
"**French** were the first to use..mental might". Chant royal on the fixed forms. Jane Gray Ward. 6850-2
French with a master. Theodore Tilton. 6273-3,6280-6,6670-4,6652-6

French, Avis Turner
I fear not life. 6764-6
October came again. 6750-6
A vagabond's wish. 6764-6
French, Cecil
What is worth the singing? 6244-X
French, Gail
Before the glass. 6659-3
Exiles. 6659-3
French, Herbert
The soldier's song. 6274-1
French, Julia A.
To an adored one. 6750-6
French, Nora May
"I must not yield." 6019-6
The mission graves. 6102-8
The outer gate. 6310-1
French, R.C.
Xerxes at the Hellespont. 6744-1
French, Virginia L.
'Our father who art'. 6532-5
The palmetto and the pine. 6694-1,6074-9,6486-8,6570-8
The palmetto and the pine. 6913-4
French, W.E.P.
Courting and proverbs. 6707-7
'Taps'. 7001-9
Woodrow Wilson. 7001-9
French, Walter Lyman
Your sanctuary. 6337-3
'**Frenchie**'.. Frank C. McCarthy. 7008-6
The **Frenchman** and the flea powder. Unknown. 6823-5
The **Frenchman** and the flea powder. Unknown. 6909-6
The **Frenchman** and the flea-powder. Unknown. 6142-7
The **Frenchman** and the mosquitos. Unknown. 6823-5
A **Frenchman** and the rats. Unknown. 6823-5
The **Frenchman** and the rats. Unknown. 6279-2
The **Frenchman** and the rats. Unknown. 6910-X
The **Frenchman** and the sheep'd trotters. Unknown. 6823-5
Frenchman on the English language. Edmund Vance Cooke. 6702-6
"A **Frenchman** once - so runs a certain ditty". The Frenchman and the flea powder. Unknown. 6823-5
"A **Frenchman** once, who was a merry wight", A Frenchman and the rats. Unknown. 6823-5
"A **Frenchman** went up to St. John's". Limerick:"A Frenchman went up to St. John's". M. Strickland. 6811-1
A **Frenchman's** dinner. Unknown. 6136-2
Freneau, Philip
America independent. 6753-0
American liberty. 6753-0
The American soldier. 6753-0
An ancient prophecy. 6015-3
Arnold's departure. 6753-0
Arnold's departure. 6121-4
Arnold's departure. 6753-0
Barney's invitation. 6946-0
Barney's invitation. 6288-1
The battle of Lake Champlain. 6946-0
The battle of Stonington on the seaboard of Connecticut. 6946-0
The beauties of Santa Crux, sels. 6008-0,6288-1
The beauties of Santa Cruz. 6333-0
The Bonhomme Richard and Serapis. 6946-0
The British prison ship, sels. 6753-0
The British prison ship, sels. 6008-0,6288-1
The British prison ship, sels. 6753-0
Columbus in chains. 6946-0
Columbus to Ferdinand. 6946-0
Congress hall, N.Y. 6753-0
Death, fr. The house of night. 6399-3
Emancipation from British dependence. 6015-3,6286-5
Epigram. 6753-0
Epistle ("Good Poets, who are so full of pain"). 6399-3
Epistle to a student of dead languages. 6753-0
Eutaw springs. 6015-3
George the Third's soliloquy. 6753-0
The honey bee. 6265-2
The house of night, sels. 6176-1,6399-3
The house of night, sels. 6008-0,6288-1
The house of night. 6121-4

FRENEAU 556

The hurricane. 6121-4
The Indian burying gound. 6396-9,6008-0,6288-1,6431-0,
    6121-4,6077-3,6176-1,6333-0,6641-0,6309-8,6648-8,
    6008-0,6288-1,6431-0,6121-4
The Indian burying ground. 6265-2
Indian death-song. 6302-0
Libera nos, domine. 6589-9
Literary importation. 6753-0
Literary importation. 6288-1
Literary importation. 6753-0
May to April. 6049-8
The midnight consultation, sels. 6753-0
A newman's address (1784). 6753-0
A newman's address (1786). 6753-0
The northern soldier. 6121-4
Occasioned by General Washington's arrival in Phila.
    6946-0
Occasioned by General Washington's arrival in Phila.
    6946-0
Ode ("God save"). 6589-9,6265-2,6288-1,6121-4
Ode on the frigate Constitution. 6753-0
On a honey bee. 6006-4,6008-0,6288-1,6121-4
On observing a large red-streak apple. 6176-1
On retirement. 6753-0
On the anniversary of the storming of the Bastille.
    6121-4,6288-1
On the British commercial depredations. 6753-0
On the British invasion. 6946-0
On the capture of the Guerriere. 6946-0
On the death of Benjamin Franklin. 6820-0
On the death of Captain Nicholas Biddle. 6946-0
On the death of Dr. Benjamin Franklin. 6077-3,6176-1,
    6088-9
On the departure of the British from Charleston. 6946-0
On the emigration to America and peopling the western..
    6946-0
On the king's speech recommending peace with..American.
    6946-0
On the memorable victory. 6288-1
On the memorable victory of Paul Jones. 6753-0
On the prospect of a revolution in France. 6753-0
On the prospect of a revolution in France. 6288-1
On the prospect of a revolution in France. 6753-0
On the religion of nature. 6333-0
On the ruins of a country inn. 6004-8
On the sleep of plants. 6288-1
The parting glass. 6004-8,6288-1,6307-1,6004-8,6288-1
The political balance, sels. 6008-0,6288-1
The political balance. 6753-0
The political balance. 6288-1
The political balance. 6753-0
A political litany. 6753-0
A political litany. 6288-1
A political litany. 6753-0
A political litany. 6288-1
The political weathercock. 6753-0
The power of fancy. 6753-0
The power of fancy. 6288-1
The power of fancy. 6753-0
The power of fancy. 6288-1
The progress of balloons. 6753-0
THe progress of balloons. 6288-1
The progress of baloons. 6288-1
Prologue to a theatrical entertainment in Philadelphia.
    6753-0
A prophecy. 6753-0
A prophecy. 6589-9
The republican genius of Europe. 6008-0
Retirement. 6288-1,6431-0
The royal adventurer. 6015-3
Seventeen hundred and ninety-one. 6753-0
Sir Henry Clinton's invitation to the refugees. 6946-0
Song of Thyrsis. 6176-1,6441-8,6300-4,6309-8
Song on Captain Barney's victory over ship General
    Monk. 6946-0
Stanzas ("Where now"). 6176-1
Stanzas occasioned by the ruins of a country inn. 6288-
    1
To a caty-did. 6307-1,6597-X,6732-8,6004-8,6008-0,6288-
    1

To a honey bee. 6102-8,6176-1,6076-5,6736-0,6300-4
To an author. 6333-0
To Cynthia. 6121-4
To my book. 6753-0
To my book. 6288-1
To my book. 6753-0
To Sir Toby. 6753-0
To the Americans of the United States. 6753-0
To the memory of the brave Americans. 6121-4,6589-9,
    6641-0,6008-0,6288-1,6470-1,6121-
To the public. 6753-0
The wild honeysuckle. 6076-5,6121-4,6008-0,6288-1,6265-
    2,6300-4,6646-1,6006-4,6077-3,6102-8,6232-6,6333-0
Frere, John Hookham
The boy and the wolf. 6401-9,6135-4
The course of time. 6802-2
A fable for five years old. 6092-7
A fable. 6802-2
The monks and the giants, sels. 6832-4
Proem to a national work, by Wm. & Robt. Whistlecraft.
    6980-0
Sir Gawain. 6980-0
Frere, John Hookham (tr.)
El Cid, sels. Unknown (Spanish), 6484-1
Hope. Theognis, 7039-6
Life of men, fr. The birds. Aristophanes, 6545-7
Poverty. Theognis, 7039-6
The yacht. Caius Catallus, 7039-6
Frere, John Hookham. See Canning, G. jt.atr.
Frere; George Canning & George Ellis, John H.
The loves of the triangles. 6802-2
Fresco-sonnet to Christian Sethe (1). Heinrich Heine. 7039-
    6
Fresco-sonnet to Christian Sethe (2). Heinrich Heine. 7039-
    6
Frescoes for Mr. Rockefeller's city. Archibald MacLeish.
    6536-8
Frescoes for Mr. Rockefeller's city, sels. Archibald
    MacLeish. 6645-3
"Fresh as of old the breeze of morn". Gwendydd's song, fr.
    Merlin. John Veitch. 6819-7
A fresh beginning. Sarah ("Susan Coolidge") Woolsey. 6461-
    2
Fresh fields. Oliver St. John Gogarty. 6581-3
"Fresh from his fastnesses", fr. Rhymes and rhythms.
    William Ernest Henley. 6473-6,6507-4
"Fresh from the dewy hill, the merry year". Song ("Fresh
    from the dewy hill"). William Blake. 6086-2
"Fresh glides the brook and blows the gale". The sabbath.
    Edward Bulwer-Lytton; Baron Lytton. 6980-0
"Fresh mists of Roman dawn". Four fountains after
    Respighi. Jessica Carr. 6762-X
"Fresh morning gusts have blown away all fear". Sonnet.
    John Keats. 6828-6
"Fresh palms for the Old Dominion!". The battle of
    Charlestown. Henry Howard Brownell. 6946-0
"Fresh spring, the herald of love's mighty king." Edmund
    Spenser. 6181-8,6182-6,6125-7
"Fresh spring, the herald of love's mighty king". Sonnet
    070 ("Fresh spring"), fr. Amoretti. Edmund Spenser.
    6301-2
"Fresh the breeze, the morning bright!". Skating song.
    H.H. Furness Jr.. 7035-3
"Fresh trees he fell'd and wove". Orion's extirpation of
    the beasts from Chios, fr.Orion. Richard Hengist
    Horne. 6980-0
Fresh vistas. Jud Lyon. 6764-6
"Fresh wet wind and the wide glittering light". The heron.
    Geoffrey Johnson. 6782-4
"The fresh, bright bloom of the daffodils". April
    fantasie. Ellen Mackay Hutchinson Cortissoz. 6820-0
"Freshest breeze I caught", fr. Epistle to my brother.
    John Keats. 6997-5
A freshet. Antiphilus of Byzantium. 6435-3
Freshman's bold plunge. Unknown. 6719-0
Freshman, Esther
It is enough. 6750-6
Fresno notebook. Neeli Cherkovski. 6792-1
"Fret not, nor ask, Leuconoe". To Leuconoe. Dorothy Vera
    Miller. 6847-2

"Fret not, poor soul: while doubt and fear". Confido et conquiesco. Adelaide Anne Procter. 6957-6
The fret of Father Carty. Joseph I.C. Clarke. 6076-5
"Fret on fond Cupid, curse thy feeble bow." Unknown. 6563-5
"The fretful stir". William Wordsworth. 6238-5
The fretful thermometer. Leila Lyon Topping. 6130-3
Fretting Jennie. Unknown. 6304-7
Freud. Nathalia Crane. 6012-9
Freud in New England. Anchusa [pseud]. 6817-0
Frey, Carol A.
 The child was asleep. 6857-X
Freya's spinning wheel. Adam Gottlob Oehlenschlager. 6555-4
A friar complains. Thomas Phillips (atr) 6881-2
The friar in the well. Unknown. 6185-0
Friar Jerome's beautiful book. Thomas Bailey Aldrich. 6396-9,6614-3
The friar of Genoa. Scharmel Iris. 6292-X,6172-9
Friar of order gray. Sir Walter Scott. 6438-8
The friar of orders gray, fr. Percy's Reliques. Unknown. 6502-3,6022-6
The friar of orders gray. John O'Keefe. 6089-7
The friar of orders gray. John O'Keefe. 6930-4
The friar of orders gray. Thomas Percy. 6102-8,6600-3,6732-8,6302-0,6385-3,6152-9,6219-9,6518-X
Friar Philip. Unknown. 6406-X
Friar Servetus. Clifford Lanier. 6674-7
Friar Tuck. Sidford F. Hamp. 6926-6
Friar's enormities. Unknown. 6881-2
The friar's song. Thomas Love Peacock. 6122-2
The friar's tale, fr. The Canterbury tales. Geoffrey Chaucer. 6102-8
The friar. Julian de Casal. 6543-0
The friars of Dijon. Thomas Campbell. 6787-5
The friction of the fractions. Jean Graham. 6797-2
Friday afternoon at the Boston Symphony Hall. Faulkner Armytage. 6996-7
"Friday came and the circus was there". The circus. Elizabeth Madox Roberts. 6891-X
Friday evening meetings. Joseph Crosby Lincoln. 6119-2
"Friday is always sweeping-day." Stanley Schell. 6713-1
Friday night. Evelyn Underhill. 6285-7
Friday night's dream. Unknown. 6904-5
Friday Street. Eleanor Farjeon. 6937-1
Friday, fr. The shepherd's week. John Gay. 6152-4
"Friday, the 17th, was Carrie's birthday". The Seddons. P. W.. 6817-0
Friday; or, the dirge. John Gay. 6972-X
Fridjonsson, Gudmundur
 Father and son. Skuli Johnson (tr). 6854-5
 'What lack we?', sels. Jakobina Johnson (tr.). 6854-5
 'What lack we?' Jakobina Johnson (tr.). 6283-0
Fridolon's pleasure-garden, sels. Erik Axel Karlfeldt. 6045-5
Fried egg. N.M. Hoffman. 6857-X
Fried, Erich
 Advantages of nudism. Milne Holton and Herbert Kuhner (tr.). 6769-7
 Copyright. Milne Holton and Herbert Kuhner (tr.). 6769-7
 Soap bubbles. Milne Holton and Herbert Kuhner (tr.). 6769-7
 Speechless. Milne Holton and Herbert Kuhner (tr.). 6769-7
Friedlaender, Violet Helen
 Passover. 6474-4
 Road makers. 6337-3
 To a blue tit. 6073-0
 To my hockey stick. 7035-3
Friedlander, Esther
 Summer day at Minnetonka. 6342-X
Friedrich, Ralph
 Epitaph for the town gossip. 6761-1
 From a photograph album. 6761-1
 In this gray season. 6761-1
 Of poems. 6979-7
 Plea for stillness. 6042-0
 Psalm for today. 6761-1
 Words in a perilous time. 6783-2

Friend. Marjorie Dugdale Ashe. 6799-9
Friend after friend departs. James Montgomery. 6085-4,6461-2,6219-9
"Friend and foe are lying here". Graveyard. Ralph Douberly. 6841-3
Friend death, fr. Thoughts on birth, life and death. Stockton Bates. 6928-2
"A friend drops me at Indian cemetary". The Hemingway syndrome. Adrian C. Louis. 7005-1
Friend forest-horse. Vachel Lindsay. 6206-7
A friend in heaven. Lucy Larcom. 6085-4
A friend in need. Jack Burroughs. 6510-4
A friend in need. Carolyn Wells. 6882-0
A friend in the garden. Juliana Horatia Ewing. 6018-8
Friend of all. Charles Wesley. 6271-7
A friend of Carlyle. Alfred Noyes. 6151-6
The friend of friends. Richard Hengist Horne. 7015-9
The friend of humanity and the knife grinder. George Canning and John Hookham Frere. 6152-4,6733-6
Friend of humanity and the knife-grinder. George Canning. 6385-3,6271-7,6438-8,6086-2,6219-9
The friend of humanity and the knife-grinder. Unknown. 6200-8,6278-4
The friend of humanity and the knife-grinder. Unknown. 6874-X
"A friend of mind said yesterday...". The rewards of industry. Edgar A. Guest. 6862-6
A friend of mine. John E. Barrett. 6840-5
"Friend of my soul, forever true". Rondel of perfect friendship. Gelett Burgess. 6875-8
"Friend of my youth! when young we roved". To the Earl of Clare. George Gordon, 6th Baron Byron. 6945-2
"Friend of my youth, companion of my later days". Unknown. 6453-1
"Friend of my youth, shedd'st thou the...". An elegiac epistle to a friend. John Gay. 6972-X
Friend of sinners. Richard Burnham. 6065-X
Friend of souls. Unknown. 6065-X
"Friend of the people, purposeful and". Vision. Corinne Roosevelt Robinson. 6995-9
"Friend of the steadfast heart". In the heart of the hills, sels. Albert Durrant Watson. 6796-4
Friend or foe? Frederic Edward Weatherley. 6273-3
Friend sorrow. Adelaide Anne Procter. 6600-3
A friend that's true. Unknown. 6085-4
A friend went then. James William Foley. 6085-4
"The friend who holds a mirror to my face". Unknown. 6238-5
Friend who understands. George Elliston. 6585-6
The friend's burial, sels. John Greenleaf Whittier. 6337-3
The friend's burial. John Greenleaf Whittier. 6437-X
A friend's death. Roberta Santlofer Danowsky. 6857-X
A friend's grave. Simonides. 6435-3
A friend's greeting. Edgar A. Guest. 6085-4
A friend's greeting. Bayard Taylor. 6240-7
A friend's lament for Simoisius. Louise Imogen Guiney. 6467-1
A friend's wish. Bliss Carman and Richard Hovey. 6890-1
Friend, Robert
 Unemployed. 6761-1
"Friend, am I silent? know that here". Sea and roses. Francis Macnamara. 6985-1
"Friend, by the way you hump yourself...". Plaint of the Missouri 'coon..Berlin Zoological Gardens. Eugene Field. 6949-5
"Friend, come thou like a friend". Address to the new year. Dinah Maria Mulock Craik. 6449-3,6820-0
"Friend, farly nocht; na caus is to complene". Prologue to the Aenid, sels. Gavin [or Gawain] Douglas. 6931-2
"Friend, I give you this consolation". In which a toal eclipse of the moon is eclipsed by... John Morgan. 6855-3
"Friend, I have wished you here these...days". To J.N. Lilian Sauter. 7023-X
"Friend, if the mute and shrouded dead". Love and death. Caius Catallus. 7039-6
"Friend, the old man that was last year". Mau than, sel. John Balaban. 6803-0
"Friend, those delights of ours". Birch and paddle. Sir Charles George Douglas Roberts. 6795-6

FRIEND,

"Friend, you seem thoughtful...". A sea dialogue. Oliver Wendell Holmes. 6833-2
A friend. Gertrude Alger. 6798-0
A friend. Countess of Blessington. 6787-5
A friend. Nicholas Grimwoald. 6084-6
A friend. Lionel Johnson. 6292-X,6477-9,6655-0,6172-9,6250-4,6022-6,6477-9
A friend. Lucy Larcom. 6066-8
The friend. Nicholas Grimwoald. 6085-4
The friend. Edgar A. Guest. 6869-3
"Friendless; the world is, friendless...". Vision. James Abraham Martling. 6952-5
A friendly address to Mrs. Frey, in Newgate. Thomas Hood. 6974-6
A friendly hand. Unknown. 6675-5
Friendly house. George Elliston. 6039-0
Friendly obstacles. Unknown. 6337-3
Friendly people. John G. Herndon. 6891-X
Friendly zephyr. Hafiz. 6448-5
Friends. Carri Caswell. 6883-9
Friends. Thomas Curtis Clark. 6461-2
Friends. Mary Goose. 7005-1
Friends. Anna Hansen Hayes. 6836-7
Friends. Lionel Johnson. 6507-4
Friends. Walter Savage Landor. 6832-4
Friends. Bea Myers. 6750-6
Friends. Esther Bergman Narey. 6799-9
Friends. L.G. Warner. 6623-2
Friends ("I have a friend whose stillness rests me so") Vlyn Johnson. 6607-0
"Friends are taked from my sight". Deaths. Hjalmar Jonsson. 6854-5
Friends beyond. Thomas Hardy. 6186-9,6437-X,6477-9,6472-8, 6508-2
Friends beyond. Frederick L. Hosmer. 6337-3
Friends departed. Henry Vaughan. 6385-3,6102-8,6341-1
Friends departed, sels. Henry Vaughan. 6102-8
Friends far away. Horace Twiss. 6302-0
Friends in death. William Shakespeare. 6085-4
Friends in need. Estelle Taylor. 6270-9
Friends in paradise. Henry Vaughan. 6737-9
"Friends of human progress, give a cheer!". Discovery. John Bracken. 6761-1
Friends of youth. Aubrey Thomas De Vere. 6084-6
"Friends to freedom! is't not time". An invitation. James Clarence Mangan. 7009-4
"Friends whom one fine day gave life". Dead poets. Enrique Pena Barrenechea. 6759-X
"Friends! hear the words my wandering...". On Southey's death. Walter Savage Landor. 6874-X
"Friends, hear the words my wandering thoughts". On Southey's death. Walter Savage Landor. 6832-4
"Friends, in this world of hurry." Charles Kingsley. 6225-3
"Friends, Romans, countrymen...", fr. Julius Caesar. William Shakespeare. 6606-2,6610-0,6726-3
"Friends, let us slight no pleasant spring". The living present. Alice Cary. 6969-X
"Friends, push round the bottle...". Song, for a venison dinner. Joseph Stansbury. 6753-0
"Friends, the hour in which we live, and in...". Les miserables, sel. Victor Hugo. 6954-1
"Friends, what's the matter with me?". Lines on reading D.H. Lawrence, Sherwood Anderson,et al. John Haynes Holmes. 6817-0
"'Friends,' listen to the Annals of". The tale of the titles told. Kate A. Davis. 6928-2
"Friends...old friends". William Ernest Henley. 6085-4, 6084-6
"Friends: as long as there is food and drink..." Unknown (Newari) 7013-2
Friendship. George Gordon, 6th Baron Byron. 6322-5
Friendship. Emily Dickinson. 6396-9
Friendship. Edith Hickman Divall. 6461-2
Friendship. Ralph Waldo Emerson. 6429-9
Friendship. John L. Hobson. 6764-6
Friendship. Edward R. Huxley. 6885-5
Friendship. Samuel Johnson. 6543-0
Friendship. Mildred Jones Keefe. 6143-5
Friendshp. Alfred Lord Tennyson. 6669-0

Friendship. Ella Wheeler Wilcox. 6085-4,6066-8
Friendship ("A ruddy drop of manly blood"). Ralph Waldo Emerson. 6085-4,6006-4,6385-3,6252-0,6429-9,6126 , 6066-8,6250-4,6288-1,6321-7,6585-6
Friendship ("Friendship needs no studied phrases"). Unknown. 6085-4,6273-3
Friendship ("Friendship, peculiar boon of heav'n"). Samuel Johnson. 6085-4
Friendship ("In deep distress one sees..."). Jean Marot. 6085-4
Friendship ("What virtue or what mental grace"). William Cowper. 6085-4
Friendship after love. Ella Wheeler Wilcox. 6536-8,6019-6
Friendship and love. John Lyly. 6085-4
"Friendship is a name". James Shirley. 6085-4
Friendship is not like love. Edward Lucas White. 6085-4
Friendship town. Elizabeth Abbey Everett. 6799-9
"Friendship unites with silken cord". Friendship. Edward R. Huxley. 6885-5
Friendship's end. Eda Lou Walton. 6072-2
"Friendship's like music". Francis Quarles. 6085-4
"Friendship's the privilege". The loyal general, sels. Nahum Tate. 6867-7
Friendship, fr. Christabel. Samuel Taylor Coleridge. 6332-2
Friendship, fr. Hamlet. William Shakespeare. 6302-0,6385-3, 6464-7
Friendship, fr. the Gulistan. Sadi [or Saadi] (Mushlih-ud-Din) 7039-6
Friendship, fr. The testament of beauty. Robert Bridges. 6337-3
Friendship, love and truth. Unknown. 6085-4,6273-3
"Friendship, peculiar boon of heaven". Friendship: an ode. Samuel Johnson. 6975-4
"Friendship, thou'rt false!". An acrostic ("Friendship"). Unknown. 6724-7
Friendship: an ode. Samuel Johnson. 6975-4
A friendship. Sophie ("Ellen Burroughs") Jewett. 6066-8
The friendship. Unknown. 7012-4
Frienship. William Cowper. 6814-6
Frierson, Garey D.
    Fading notes. 6898-7
    The rains of monsoon. 6898-7
The frigate pelican. Marianne Moore. 6978-9
Frightened. Helen Leah Reed. 6715-8
Frightened birds. Unknown. 6684-4
Frightening death. Charles Anson Ingraham. 6482-5
"A frightful face? Wal, yes, yer correct". The fireman's story. Unknown. 6964-9
Frik
    Reproaches. 6050-1
Frimaire. Amy Lowell. 6034-X
Friman, Alice R.
    Leda and the swan. 6966-5
A fringe of snow. Glennys Balske. 6342-X
Fringed gentian. Emily Dickinson. 6121-4
Fringed gentian. Horatio Ford. 6118-4
The fringed gentian. William Cullen Bryant. 6621-6
Fringed gentians. Amy Lowell. 6338-1
"Fringed gentians in the meadow". Gentians in October. Martha H. Hollinshead. 6799-9
Frisbie, A.L.
    John of Mt. Sinai. 6922-3
    Quosque tandem, O catiline? 6699-2
Frisbie, C.
    A castle in the air. 6752-2
Frisbie, L.
    The reverie. 6752-2
The Frisian wife. Unknown. 6193-1
"Frisky as a l¡mbkin". The lovable child. Anne Emilie Poulsson. 6891-X
"A frisky lamb". Song ("A frisky lamb.") Christina Georgina Rossetti. 6233-4
Frisselle, Carrie Corliss
    The palms. 6764-6
The frist friend. Rudyard Kipling. 6891-X
Frithiof's farewell. Esaias Tegner. 7039-6
Fritsch, Gerhard
    Afterward. Milne Holton and Herbert Kuhner (tr.). 6769-7

August moon. Milne Holton and Herbert Kuhner (tr.). 6769-7
In the forest. Milne Holton and Herbert Kuhner (tr.). 6769-7
Judas. Milne Holton and Herbert Kuhner (tr.). 6769-7
Fritts, L.B.
Duty. 6397-7
Fritz. Gotthold Ephraim Lessing. 6278-4
Fritz [pseud].
Confession. 6817-0
Fritz und I. Charles Follen Adams. 6791-3,6823-5
Fritz Valdher is made a mason. Fritz Hoofnagel. 6175-3
Fritz's education. Unknown. 6530-9
Fritz, Lyman A.
Never mind. 6799-9
The frivolous girl. Unknown. 6273-3
Fro you, mother. Hilda Conkling. 6538-4
Froding, Gustaf
"Behold, this dreamer cometh!" Charles Wharton Stork (tr.). 6045-5
The city lieutenant. Charles Wharton Stork (tr.). 6045-5
The dance by the roadside. Charles Wharton Stork (tr.). 6045-5
Dreams in Hades. Charles Wharton Stork (tr.). 6045-5
Home-coming. Charles Wharton Stork (tr.). 6045-5
Idealism and realism. Charles Wharton Stork (tr.). 6045-5
Little Joe-Johnny. Charles Wharton Stork (tr.). 6045-5
A love-song. Charles Wharton Stork (tr.). 6045-5
Mountain trolls. Charles Wharton Stork (tr.). 6045-5
The old mountain troll. Charles Wharton Stork (tr.). 6045-5
An old room. Charles Wharton Stork (tr.). 6045-5
Pastoral. Charles Wharton Stork (tr.). 6045-5
Pastoral ("Hark"). Charles Wharton Stork (tr.). 6045-5
A poor monk of Skara. Charles Wharton Stork (tr.). 6045-5
The poor monk of Skara. Charles Wharton Stork (tr.). 6045-5
A prayer-meeting. 6045-5
Prince Aladdin of the lamp. Charles Wharton Stork (tr.). 6045-5
"Sigh, sigh, rushes!" Charles Wharton Stork (tr.). 6045-5
A spring-time sweetheart. Charles Wharton Stork (tr.). 6045-5
Winter night. Charles Wharton Stork (tr.). 6045-5
The frog and the mouse. Unknown. 6058-7,6594-5
"The frog half fearful jumps across the path". Summer evening. John Clare. 6844-8
A frog he would a wooing go. Unknown. 6079-X,6057-9,6132-X, 6401-9,6363-2,6135-4,6131
A frog he would a wooing go. Unknown. 6135-4
A frog story. Unknown. 6682-8
"A frog vas a-singing von day in der brook". 'Don'd feel too big'. Unknown. 6791-3
"Frog went a-courtin, he did ride". Unknown. 6059-5,6281-4
The frog's good-bye. Unknown. 6373-X,6529-5
The frog's goodbye. Unknown. 6373-X
"The frog's idea of a joke is to seize the lion's mane" Unknown (Newari) 7013-2
The frog.. Unknown. 6722-0,6736-0
The frog. Hilaire Belloc. 6089-7,6232-6,6102-8,6464-7,6421-3
The frog. John Bunyan. 6179-6
"A froggie did a-courting go". Unknown. 6059-5
Frogs. Sir Charles George Douglas Roberts. 6795-6
Frogs at school. George Cooper. 6131-1
Frogs at school. Unknown. 6132-X,6165-6,6530-9,6684-4
The frogs' singing-school. E.T. Corbell. 6368-3
The frogs' song. Aristophanes. 6435-3
The frogs, sels. Aristophanes. 6337-3
The frogs. Archibald Lampman. 6433-7
Frolic. George William ("A.E.") Russell. 6478-7,6421-3
The frolic mariners of Devon. William Browne. 6125-7
Frolicher, John C.
Ghosts. 6490-6
"A frolicking fellow is time". Time. Julie Mathilde Lippmann. 7041-8

The frolicksome duke. Unknown. 6055-2,6613-5
The frolicksome farmer. Unknown. 6157-5
The frolicksome parson outwitted. Unknown. 6157-5
From '85. Barry Straton. 6795-6
From 'Lavater', fr. Borrowed thoughts. Adelaide Anne Procter. 6957-6
From 'Lost Alice', fr. Borrowed thoughts. Adelaide Anne Procter. 6957-6
From 'Phantastes', fr. Borrowed thoughts. Adelaide Anne Procter. 6957-6
From 'W' beach. Geoffrey Dearmer. 7029-9
From ****, fr. Borrowed thoughts. Adelaide Anne Procter. 6957-6
From a bus window. Irma M. Patch. 6342-X
From a car-window. Ruth Guthrie Harding. 6338-1,6019-6, 6653-4,6029-3
"From a chimney on the roof". Capers et caper. Eugene Fitch Ware. 7025-6
From a city street. Armond Carroll. 6327-6
From a copy of 'Les chants de maldoror' Alejandra Pizarnik. 7036-1
From a down-town skyscraper. Wilfred J. Funk. 6732-8
From a felucca. Cale Young Rice. 6331-4,6326-8
From a Flemish graveyard. Iolo Aneurin Williams. 6474-4
From a full heart. Alan Alexander Milne. 6089-7
"From a gull's oily breath/from a Greek letter". From all these, you. Harold Norse. 6792-1
From a high Manhattan window. Myrtle A. McDougal. 6397-7
From a high place. Unknown. 6732-8,6648-8
"From a high place I saw the city". The poems of West Ham, sels. Unknown. 6954-1
From a hill top. Angela Morgan. 6861-8
From a hilltop. David Morton. 6071-4
From a hint in the minor poets. Samuel Wesley. 6024-2
"From a junto that labour with absolute power". A political litany. Philip Freneau. 6753-0
"From a land of milk and honey". Weeping and singing. Cesar Tiempo. 6759-X
From a letter. Ben H. Smith. 6662-3
"From a letter thrown on the table a line...". The lines of the hand. Julio Cortazar. 6758-1
From a line by Cyril Dabydeen. Martin Singelton. 6767-0
"From a lofty alpine summit look down...". Monch and Jungfrau. Graf von Auersperg. 6749-2
From a lonely hearth. Anna Spencer Twitchell. 6836-7
From a lover. Jacqueline Hoyt. 6850-2
From a New York skyscraper. James Oppenheim. 6954-1
"From a mountain top a coet looked down". The poet. Seumas O'Brien. 6292-X
From a photograph album. Ralph Friedrich. 6761-1
From a pier. Jessie B. Rittenhouse. 6071-4
From a prisoner of war. John Buxton. 6761-1
From a railway carriage. Robert Louis Stevenson. 6334-9, 6459-0
"From a ruin thou art singing". The lonely bird. Felicia Dorothea Hemans. 6973-8
From a sanatorium. John Ferguson. 6269-5
From a sonnet sequence. Robert Hillyer. 6431-0
From a sonnet sequence. Bernard K. Kay. 6764-4
From a story in The New York Sunday Times travel... Alan Dugan. 7032-9
From a street corner. Eleanor Hammond. 6347-0
From a trench. Maud Anna Bell. 7027-2
From a tropical shore. Katherine Garrison Chapin. 6042-0
From a trundle bed. George Elliston. 6906-1
From a very little sphinx, sels. Edna St. Vincent Millay. 6011-0
From a vision. Ts'ao Chih. 6253-9
From a walk. Vojislav Ilic Jr. 6765-4
From Albert to Bapaume. Alec Waugh. 7029-9
"From a wife of small fortune, but yet...proud". The honest man's litany. Unknown. 6787-5
"From Africa he said he came". Our Jacko. Louis J. Magee. 7004-3
"From all division let our land be free". Australian federation. William Gay. 6784-0
"From all that dwell below the skies". Psalm 117. Bible. 6848-0
"From all that dwell." Isaac Watts. 6302-0
From all the fools who went before. Margaret Root Garvin.

6619-4
"From all the harvest of your words to me". Treasure. Mabel Crehore Greene. 6841-3
From all these events, from the slump, from the war... Stephen Spender. 6375-6
From all these, you. Harold Norse. 6792-1
"From all uneasie passions free". Song ("From all uneasie"). John Sheffield; Duke of Buckingham. 6544-9
"From Ashur's vales when proud Sennacherib...". Destruciton of Sennacherib's army by a... Erasmus Darwin. 6848-0
From all uneasy passions free. John Sheffield; Duke of Buckingham. 6328-4,6563-5
From America. Elizabeth Townsend Swift. 6474-4
From amid the shadows. Walter De La Mare. 6905-3
"From Ammanford to Fleur-de-lys." Idris Davies. 6360-8
From an address at an Icelandic celebration. Stephan G. Stephansson. 6854-5
From an Elizabethan lover to his lady. Mildred Solwan. 6850-2
From an epistle to the Countess of Cumberland. Samuel Daniel. 6600-3
From an ivory tower. Helen Frith Stickney. 6979-7
From an old boat. Edward H. Butler. 6983-5
From an old ritual. Bliss Carman. 6252-0
From Assisi. Helen J. Sanborn. 6624-0
'From battle, murder and sudden death, good lord...' John Moran. 6770-0,6875-8
"From beauteous Windsor's high & story'd halls". Verses written after facing Windsor Castle. Thomas Warton (the Elder). 6962-2
"From being anxious, or secure", fr. The litany. John Donne. 6931-2
From Bethlehem to Calvary. Meredith Nicholson. 6144-3;6335-7,6335-7
"From beneath her cotton 'kappie'.". Katrina. Denys Lefebvre. 6800-6
"From Bideford to Appledore the meadows lie...". Devon men. Unknown. 7031-0
From beyond. Lucia Trent. 6039-0
From birth to battlefield. Unknown. 6274-1
From Bosrah. Beatrice Allhusen. 7031-0
"From blown seeds of ecstasy memories grow". Moonlight sonata. Muriel F. Hochdorf. 6850-2
"From Bogie side to bog o' Gight". Bogie side; or, Huntly's raid. Unknown. 6859-6
From boy to man. Henry Howard, Earl of Surrey. 6134-6
From Boyaca in the country. Maria Mercedes Carranza. 7036-1
From Carcassonne. Osbert Sitwell. 6331-4
"From burning cell-blocks rose loud groans...". Pardoned. Fred Keller Dix. 6906-1
"From child to youth; from youth to arduous". The heart of the night, fr. The house of life. Dante Gabriel Rossetti. 6828-6
"From childhood's hour I have not been". Edgar Allan Poe. 6238-5
From Clee to heaven the beacon burns. Alfred Edward Housman. 6224-5
"From circuit to circuit although we may roam". Songs of the circuit. Unknown. 6878-2
"From cold east shore to warm west sea". The last Taschastas, sels. Joaquin Miller. 6753-0
"From conquest Jephtha came, with". Jephtha's vow. James Grahame. 6848-0
From contempt of death in the better sort of spirits. Sir John Davies. 6584-8
From Cornwall to the Hebrides. Alan Rook. 6475-2
"From country, from coast and from city". A ballade of bothers. Unknown. 6770-0
"From cove and harbour". The return of the fleet to Bretagne. Gertrude Huntington McGiffert. 6838-3
From dark to light. Silas Weir Mitchell. 6337-3
"From dawn to dark they stood". 'Our left'. Francis Orrery Ticknor. 6946-0
From dawn to dawn. Morris Rosenfeld. 7011-6
"From dawn to dusk, and from dusk to dawn". The day to the night. Alice Meynell. 6955-X
"From day to day came a heavy roar". Tilghman's ride from Yorktown to Philadelphia...1781. Howard Pyle. 6917-7
"From death's dark portals". The old year. Ethel Talbot. 6793-X
From deeper stillnesses. Marietta Thompson Sprague. 6316-0
"From depth of sin, and from a deep despair". Psalm 130. Paraphrase. Bible. 6848-0
"From deserts wild and many a pathless wood". To Sir Walter Scott. Thomas Pringle. 6800-6
From disciple to master. Monk Gibbon. 6072-2
From distant lands. Peter Hellings. 6360-8
From Dover. L.C. Nielsen. 6555-4
From dust thou art. Frances Waddle. 6750-6
From Enamorado. John Hunter Duvar. 7041-8
"From east to west they're burning, in...". The little fires. Henry Herbert Knibbs. 7012-4
"From east to west, from north to south...". To King George. Sirdar Daljit Singh. 7031-0
"From Eden's first good-morning...". Life's journey. John E. Barrett. 6840-5
"From Emmrick's court rides Anavalt". Legend from Cabell. Myrril [pseud].. 6817-0
"From England's gilded halls of state". Westminster Abbey. Sir Samuel Ferguson. 6793-X
"From eve to morn, from morn to parting night". On his own Agamemnon and Iphigeneia. Walter Savage Landor. 6828-6
"From every spire in London". Annis Vane - A.D. 1558. Margaret Junkin Preston. 6965-7
"From fairest creatures we desire increase". William Shakespeare. 6187-7
"From fairest creatures we desire increase". Sonnet 001 ("From fairest creatures"). William Shakespeare. 6208-3,6436-1,6732-8,6430-2
"From fall to spring, the russet acorn". Holidays. Ralph Waldo Emerson. 6753-0
From far. Alfred Edward Housman. 6339-X,6252-0
From far. Philip Bourke Marston. 6543-0
From far. Charles Pelham Mulvaney. 7041-8
From far away. William Morris. 6747-6
From far Japan. Robert Loveman. 6941-X
"From far away/Rice Lake loons". Waking on a greyhound. Gordon Henry. 7005-1
"From France, desponding and betray'd". On the British invasion. Philip Freneau. 6946-0
From feathers to iron. Cecil Day Lewis. 6150-8
From foreign lands. Robert Loveman. 6941-X
"From frozen climes,and endless tracks of snow". Epistle to the Earl of Dorset. Ambrose Philips. 6831-6
"From gab of jay and chatter of crake". A ballade of Philomela. Sir Charles George Douglas Roberts. 6770-0
From generation to generation. John Drinkwater. 7029-9
From generation to generation. William Dean Howells. 6467-1
From generation to generation. Sir Henry Newbolt. 6210-5
"From giant oaks, that wave their branches...". Vegetable loves, fr. The loves of plaints. Erasmus Darwin. 6932-0
"From Gilgal's camp went foth, at". The battle of Gibeon. Bernard Barton. 6848-0
From glory unto glory. Henry Van Dyke. 6961-4
'From God to God.' Vergil. 6337-3
From Gombor. Nikolai Ushakov. 6546-5
From Greenland's icy mountains. Reginald Heber. 6418-3, 6730-1,6086-2,6214-8,6304-7
"From gold-mosaic'd wave". The greengage tree. Edith Sitwell. 7000-0
"From gross der rifer, at broke of day". Schneider's ride. Unknown. 6791-3,6823-5
"From Halifax station a bully there came". Halifax station. Unknown. 6946-0
"From Hanover to Leipzig is but a little way". The schnellest zug. Eugene Field. 6949-5
From hand to mouth. Unknown. 6918-5
From haunts of beasts. Joseph Bernard Rethy. 6995-9
"From heart through mind into image". The past. William Oandasan. 7005-1
"From heaven was sent an angel of light". Now we should sing and say nowell. Unknown. 6756-5
"From heavy dreams fair Helen rose". Willia and Helen.

Sir Walter Scott. 6828-6
"From hedgerows where aromas fain would be". Despotisms. Louise Imogen Guiney. 7027-2
"From Hell Gate to Gold Gate". The overland train to California. Benjamin Franklin Taylor. 6815-4
"From her red veins the mother fashioned". Roosevelt, the leader. Mary Siegrist. 6995-9
"From here red veins the mother fashioned him". Roosevelt-the leader. Mary Siegrist. 7012-4
"From here upon the wind-bleached rocks...dark". To the passing of sail. Lionel Day. 6850-2
"From high endeavour/On his bright wings". High noon. Hamish Maclaren. 6893-6
"From high upon the deck/I see". Watching seasons. Betty A. Mitchell. 6857-X
"From hill and plain to the State of Maine". From the same canteen. Eugene Field. 6949-5
From his Canadian home. Unknown. 6281-4
"From his brimstone bed, at break of day". The devil's walk. Richard Porson. 6787-5
"From his flock stray'd Coridon". Robert Greene. 6187-7
"From his shoulder Hiawatha". Hiawatha's photographing. Charles Lutwidge ("Lewis Carroll") Dodgson. 6802-2
"From holy flower to holy flower". The study of a spider. John B.L. Warren, 3d Baron De Tabley. 7020-5
From home. Ewart Alan Mackintosh. 6650-X
"From hunting whores, and hanting play". Sir George Etherege. 6544-9
From India. William Cox Bennett. 6408-6
From inward shining. Robert Wayne. 6839-1
From Islington to Marybone. William Blake. 6641-0
From J. Haydn to Constanze Mozart (1791). Edgar Bowers. 6515-5
"From its scabbard, pure and bright". The sword of Robert Lee. Abram Joseph Ryan. 6753-0
"From Java, Sumatra, and old Cathay". A ship comes in. Oliver Jenkins. 6764-6
"From keel to fighting top, I love". Manilla Bay. Arthur Hale. 6946-0
"From Lewis, Monsieur Gerard came". Yankee Doodle's expedition to Rhode Island. Unknown. 6946-0
"From Lewis, Monsieur Gerard, came". Yankee doodle's expedition to Rhode Island. Unknown. 6753-0
From knees up, Muvver Brown. H.L.R. Edwards. 6360-8
From lightning and tempest. Adam Lindsay Gordon. 6951-7
From love and nature. Richard Monckton Milnes; 1st Baron Houghton. 6658-5
"From low to high doth dissolution climb". William Wordsworth. 6187-7,6150-8
"From masters I have ever kept apart". And sae came of it. Johann Wolfgang von Goethe. 7042-6
From memory. Yun-sung Kim. 6775-1
'From Mohock and from Hawkubite' John Gay. 6972-X
From Mount Mansfield. Bettie Margot Cassie. 6750-6
"From mill and mart to peace of God's...realm". Countryside in New England. Mabel A. Metcalf. 6894-4
"From misted mountain heights the road...". Sea level. Edith T. Newcomb. 6799-9
"From morn to eve they struggled-life & death". Life and death. Cosmo Monkhouse. 7015-9
"From morn to eve, Rome's iron tide". The last day of Jerusalem. George Croly. 6848-0
"From my chamber last night I looked out..sky". Dearborn Observatory, Chicago. Benjamin Franklin Taylor. 6815-4
From my diary, July 1914. Wilfred Owen. 6209-1
"From my grief on Fal's proud plain I sleep". 'My grief on Fal's proud plain,' sel. George Keating. 6930-4
From my loitering. Vernon Watkins. 6360-8
"From my pillow, looking forth by light". Memories of Cambridge, fr. The prelude. William Wordsworth. 6867-7
"From my sonorous city". Women. Jose Gorostiza. 6759-X
From my window. Mother M. Columba. 6543-0
From my window. N. Margaret Myers Lawrence. 6342-X
From my window. Elna L. Von Pingel. 6799-9
From Nazareth. Margaret Elizabeth Sangster. 6335-7
"From my window I can see". The open sea. Dorothea MacKellar. 6784-0
"From my window, facing south". The autumn house. George M. Brady. 6930-4
"From my window/I see you, old man". Neighbor. Madeline Hare. 6857-X
"From my youth upwards/My spirit walk'd not...". Manfred to the sorceress. George Gordon, 6th Baron Byron. 6980-0
"From Onathlamba in the west". A zephyr from Zululand. Eugene Field. 6949-5
"From needing danger, to be good", fr. The litany. John Donne. 6931-2
"From nether dark." Stefan George. 6160-5
"From night to night,through circling darkness whirled. Samuel Waddington. 7015-9
From nothing strange. Gustav Davidson. 6218-0
From ode. Richard Watson Gilder. 7014-0
From our ghostly enemy. Robert Graves. 6071-4
"From out his castle on the sand". The sea-king. L. Frank Tooker. 6833-2
"From out his grave the drummer". The spectre review. ? Zedlitz. 6842-1
"From out his heavenly sallyport". Mid-April in Vermont. Daniel L. Cady. 6988-6
"From out my deep, wide-bosomed west". Rejoice. Joaquin Miller. 6946-0
From out of the glow. Stefan George. 6160-5
"From out of the north-land his leaguer he led". Saint Leger. Clinton Scollard. 6946-0
"From out our crowded calendar". Memorial Day. McLandburgh Wilson. 6820-0
"From out the desolation of the north". A tryst. Celia Thaxter. 7041-8
"From out the dragging vastness of the sea". Convalescence. Amy Lowell. 7027-2
"From out the stately lexicon of sea". My friend. Fred W. Leu. 6906-1
"From out the Syrian sky an angel host". Come to him. Orville Lawrence Kuhn. 6799-9
"From out the west, where darkling storm-clouds". Rainfall. Emily Pauline ("Tekahionwake") Johnson. 6837-5,6785-9
"From out the year the choicest day". Labor Day. Edward R. Huxley. 6885-5
"From Pembroke's princely dome,where mimic art". Sonnet 005: Written after seeing Wilton House. Thomas Warton Jr.. 6867-7
"From Pembroke's princely dome,where minic art". Sonnet. Written after seeing Wilton-house. Thomas Warton Jr.. 6932-0,6219-9
"From pain and sorrow all around". Toshi-nari. 6852-9
From Paumanok starting I fly like a bird. Walt Whitman. 6126-5,6288-1
From Perugia. John Greenleaf Whittier. 6624-0
From Pisgah. William White. 6868-5
From Potomac to Marrimac. Edward Everett Hale. 6946-0
"From plains that reel to southward, dim". Heat. Archibald Lampman. 7041-8
"From Poremba, Dombrovsky Petr did fare". Peterswald. Petr Bezruc. 6763-8
"From Portugal to Finland now". Song ("From Portugal to Finland now"). Frederic Prokosch. 6761-1
"From proud Atlantic's surging waves". The starry flag. Stockton Bates. 6922-3
From psalm 137 (1). Bible. 6848-0
From psalm 137 (2). Bible. 6848-0
"From purest wells of English undefiled". James Russell Lowell. John Greenleaf Whittier. 6820-0
"From rebel veins my life I drew". A rebel heart. Francis A. Fahy. 7009-4
"From ridge to ridge". Joshua Freeman Crowell. 6130-3
"From rifted granite veins, far-hid and cool". The spring. George Meason Whicher. 6847-2
"From right to left, and to and fro". The maze. Vincent Bourne. 6814-6
From romances sans paroles. Arthur Symons. 6507-4
From Romany to Rome. Wallace Irwin. 6732-8
From Sacrifice. Margaret Elizabeth Sangster. 6144-3
From Sagesse. Paul Verlaine. 7039-6
From Sand Creek, sel. Simon J. Ortiz. 7005-1
From Selma. Langston Hughes. 6178-8
"From romp upon the autumn hills". Turning. Carrie E.

Bronson. 6927-4
"From Santiago, spurning the morrow". The destroyer of destroyers. Wallace Rice. 6946-0
"From scenes like these old Scotia's grandeur". Old Scotia's grandeur, fr. The cotter's Saturday night. Robert Burns. 6934-7
"From service freed he takes his last...rest". Woodrow Wilson. Edith Cherrington. 7001-9
"From Sinai's top the lightnings flashed". Mount Sinai. Horatius Bonar. 6848-0
From shadow - sun. Agnes L. Pratt. 6925-8
From Shannon to sea. Edmond Gore Alexander Holmes. 6090-0
From shore. Esther A. Whitmarsh. 6880-4
"From Sparta to Apollo we", fr. Lost at sea. Simonides. 6435-3
"From sky to sky the veld, vast, tawny, bare". The veld. Hugh John Evans. 6800-6
"From slimy swamps dismal with trailing moss". European recognition. James Abraham Martling. 6952-5
"From some far-distant place". Query. Florence Ralston Werum. 6906-1
"From song and dream for ever gone". Elegiac mood. Gordon Bottomley. 6897-9
"From song and dream forever gone". Elegiac mood. Gordon Bottomley. 6872-3
"From sound to stone and from the voice...". Second dream. Bernardo Ortiz de Montellano. 6759-X
"From spaded trench and wooded mountain side". The curse of Kishineff. Bertrand Shadwell. 6848-0
"From Stirling castle we have seen". Yarrow unvisited. William Wordsworth. 6110-9,6086-2,6219-9,6371-3,6543-0,6828 ,6122-2,6198-2,6246-6,6271-7,6075-7,6600
"From Strato's tower, forth flashed the". The destruction of Jerusalem. Johnson Pierson. 6848-0
From stone to steel. Edwin John Pratt. 6021-8,6446-9
"From street and square, from hill and glen". Heirs of time. Thomas Wentworth Higginson. 7009-4,6954-1
"From such romantic dreams, my soul, awake!". Lake Uri. William Wordsworth. 6749-2
From summer hours. Emile Verhaeren. 7039-6
From Tecumseh's soliloquy at the Thames. Charles Mair. 6796-4
'from Texas to Maine'. George Henry Preble. 6223-7
"From tall tree leafy tops". To a Cape canary. Francis Carey ("Jan van Avond") Slater. 6800-6
From tha rhyme of the great river. Joaquin Miller. 7041-8
"From that dejected brow in silence beaming". The setting of the moon near Corinth. Aubrey Thomas De Vere. 7015-9,6997-5,7015-9
"From the afterbirth of your bitterness". As all things pass. Diana Bickston. 6870-7
From the ageless soil. George Sanford Holmes. 6836-7
From the Arabic: an imitation. Percy Bysshe Shelley. 6830-8
"From the big horror of war's hoarse alarms". A poem, sacred to the memory..Feredric Prince of Wales. William Falconer. 6971-1
"From the bosom of the ocean I seek thee". Song ("From the bosom..."). Bayard Taylor. 6976-2
"From the bread of life" Hedwig Katscher. 6769-7
From the bridge. John Keats. 6466-3
From the bridge. Don Marquis. 6431-0
"From the bright stars, or from..viewless air". To a departed spirit. Felicia Dorothea Hemans. 6973-8
From the building of the bridge. Barry Straton. 7041-8
From the burren. Emily Lawless. 6090-0
"From the cabin window". On the ship to the mainland. Keiho Soga. 6981-9
From the cabrillo at Santa Barbara. Emily Wilson Sander. 6818-9
From the Clyde to Braidwood. Mrs. Hubert ("Australie") Heron. 6768-9
From the cold sod that's o'er you. Edward Walsh. 6174-5
"From the commander's quarters on Westchester". Aaron Burr's wooing. Edmund Clarence Stedman. 6946-0
"From the cool and dark-lipped furrows...". The breath of light. A. E.. 6873-1
"From the Cotswolds, from the Chilterns...". The ballad of London river. May C. ([Mary] Gillington) Byron. 6793-X

"From the creator's throne God fell." Alfred Mombert. 6160-5
"From the cupboard the mouse". Song for a late hour. Raymond Holden. 6808-1
"From the dark tower which is a ship's mast". Stroke of one. Jorge Carrera Andrade. 6759-X
"From the dawn of history onward". The gift of flight. Astra [pseud].. 7014-0
From the deep. John Gawsworth. 6893-6
"From the deep dank darkness through...door". The haunted house. Harriet Meyer. 6850-2
"From the deep shadow of the silent fir-grove". Chamouny at sunrise. Friederike Brunn. 6749-2
"From the distance, the mountains look...". River village. Yung-gul Lee. 6775-1
"From the distant violet-crowned Athens". The bride of Corinth. Johann Wolfgang von Goethe. 6842-1
"From the doors of...Trois Freres Provenceaux". The salle Montesqieu. William Allen Butler. 6903-7
"From the doorway, Manuela, in the sunny..morn". Manuela. Bayard Taylor. 6976-2
"From the drear north, a cold and cheerless...". The heritage. Edward Bliss Reed. 6833-2
"From the dull confines of the drooping west". A return to London. Robert Herrick. 6793-X
From the earth, a cry. John Boyle O'Reilly. 6542-2
From the east to the west. Andrew Lang. 6987-8
"From the echoes of the past". Song of the whetstone. Emma S. Tucker. 7030-2
From the fair Lavinian shore. William Shakespeare. 6328-4
From the fear of death in the wicked souls. Sir John Davies. 6584-8
"From the fierce aspect of this river...". The fall of the Aar. William Wordsworth. 6749-2
From the flats. Sidney Lanier. 6126-5,6288-1
"From the flow'rs and from the trees". An elfin summons. Eugene Field. 6949-5
From the fly-leaf of the Rowfant Montaigne. Frederick Locker-Lampson. 6297-0
From the French. Thomas Moore. 6278-4
"From the forests and highlands". The song of Pan. Percy Bysshe Shelley. 6830-8
From the general desire of immortality. Sir John Davies. 6584-8
"From the glowing southern regions". Caswallon's triumph. Felicia Dorothea Hemans. 6973-8
"From the grass a daisy looked". Who holdeth up the sky? Emilie Tolman. 6965-7
From the grave. Ella Wheeler Wilcox. 6956-8
From the Greek anthology. Leonard Alfred George Strong. 6722-0
"From the ground she knows". Preparing to climb. Janice Dabney. 6822-7
From the gulf. William Henry Ogilvie. 6784-0
"From the hag and hungry goblin". Loving mad Tom. Unknown. 6829-4
"From the hag and hungry goblin". Unknown. 6187-7,6562-7
"From the hall of our fathers in anguish we...". Hebrew melody. Mrs. James Gorden Brooks. 6848-0,6752-2
"From the Kei to Umzimkulu". Jim. Perceval Gibbon. 6788-3
From the highway. Grantland Rice. 6085-4
From the hills. Thomas S. Jones Jr. 6300-4
"From the hills of dream. William ("Fiona Macleod") Sharp. 6252-0
From the hon. Henry- to Lady Emma- Thomas Moore. 6874-X
From the innocent impostors. Thomas Shadwell. 6867-7
From the iron gate. Robert C.V. Meyers. 6924-X
From the Japanese. Unknown. 6274-1
"From the land of logs and peaches". A poem in three cantos. Eugene Field. 6949-5
"From the last hill that looks on thy...dome". On the day of the destruction of Jerusalem by Titus. George Gordon, 6th Baron Byron. 6945-2,6848-0
"From the laurel's fairest bough". The battle of Valparaiso. Unknown. 6946-0
"From the leafy maple ridges". The Canadian song-sparrow. Sir James Edgar. 6795-6
"From the long sleep of centuries". Arise! Roden Noel. 7009-4
"From the low sunless levels where body...". The future is

fair. Charles Whitby. 6994-0
"From the man whom I love though my heart...". Sng ("From the man..."). Tobias George Smollett. 6975-4
"From the mint two bright new pennies came". The two pennies. Unknown. 6924-X
"From the misty shores of midnight...". Tennyson. Henry Van Dyke. 6961-4
From the mountains to the Champaign. Thomas Carlyle. 6934-7
From the night of forebeing. Francis Thompson. 6437-X
From the north. James Abraham Martling. 6952-5
From the north. Bayard Taylor. 6976-2
"From the north I blow". Song ("From the north I blow"). James Gorham. 6850-2
"From the north the populated breeze". A book for Christmas. Margaret Allonby. 6788-3
"From the old squire's dwelling,gloomy & grand". The hFmestead, fr. Dovecote mill. Phoebe Cary. 6865-0;6969-X
"From the ominous vast of the city's deep". The surf of the slums. Unknown. 6954-1
From the other side. Alejandra Pizarnik. 7036-1
From the Parthenon I learn. Willard(Wattles. 6777-8
"From the Parthenon I learn". Willard Wattles. 6102-8,6076-5
From the Persian. Unknown. 6848-0
"From the outward world about us". Secret writing. Alice Cary. 6865-0;6969-X
"From the perilous, pale, silent snows". The spirit of spring. Cora Fabri. 6876-6
"From the plane". Third time. Carlos Pellicer. 6759-X
"From the puissance of the sea". To a sea-shell. William White. 6868-5
"From the quickened womb of primal gloom". Light. William Pitt Pammer. 6910-X
"From the recesses of a lowly spirit." Sir John Bowring. 6302-0,6385-3,6600-3,6656-9
From the Rubaiyat of Omar Khayyam. Eugene Field. 6949-5
"From the rim it trickles down". The hill-water. Duncan Ban MacIntyre. 6873-1
"From the river Euphrates, the river". The apple of life. Owen (Edward Bulwer-Lytton, Earl Lytton) Meredith. 6848-0
"From the river I yell". Childhood. Jean Nuchtern. 6857-X
From the sabine farm. Alfred Noyes. 6169-9
From the same canteen. Eugene Field. 6949-5
From the Santa-Fe trail. Vachel Lindsay. 6299-7
"From the shadow of the forest, where the...". Indian love song. Gertrude Alger. 6798-0
"From the shieling that stands by the lone...". War song of O'Driscoll. Gerald Griffin. 6930-4
From the shore. Gerd Aage Gilhoff. 6798-0
From the Somme. Leslie Coulson. 7029-9
"From the shore-line of the sea". Waifs from the sea. William White. 6868-5
"From the south they came, birds of war". War song ("From the south..."). Unknown (Ojibwa Indian). 7039-6
From the spire of Milan cathedral. Robert Haven Schauffler. 6331-4
From the state of love, sels. John Cleveland. 6324-1
"From the sun low in sky". The perfect thing. Lizette Woodworth Reese. 6781-6
"From the sunken road a rain frog croaks" Christine Lavant. 6769-7
"From the sunny climes of France". To Austin Dobson. Frank Dempster Sherman. 6770-0,6875-8
"From the taut hills, the austere pine". The aristocrat. Elizabeth Stanton Hardy. 6979-7
"From the temple torn asunder". The crucifixion. Thomas Holley Chivers. 7017-5
"From the tennis lawn you can hear the guns...". Peace. Rose Macaulay. 6884-7
"From the throne of command my mother said...". Malinche. Rosario Castellanos. 7036-1
"From the town of Bellinzona, several hundred". The judge of Bellinzona. J.J. Reithard. 6918-5
From the train. Eugenio Montale. 6803-0
From the train window. Grace Mansfield. 6750-6
"From the trees the wind is stripping". The home coming. May C. ([Mary) Gillington) Byron. 7037-X

From the triads of Ireland. Unknown. 6930-4
"From the undiscovered deep". The naval reserve. Evelyn Underhill. 7029-9,7031-0
"From the valley they say you are going". Red River valley. Unknown. 6826-X
"From the veranda I watch the jetsam". Turista. Mark Osaki. 6790-5
From the very doubt and disputation of immortality. Sir John Davies. 6584-8
"From the very tiptop of the town hall steeple". The weather-cock. Carolyn Wells. 6882-0
From the virgins. Katherine Mann Mann. 6180-X
From the Weehawken ferry. Blanche Shoemaker Wagstaff. 7038-8
"From the whistling reed of a shepherd lad". An old world melody. William Lindsey. 6798-0
From the wilderness. William Soutar. 6782-4
"From the window". Number 20. Doughtry ("Doc") Long Jr.. 7024-8
From the world beyond. Josef Holy. 6763-8
From the wreck. Adam Lindsay Gordon. 6591-0,6592-9,6744-1
From the wreck. Adam Lindsay Gordon. 6918-5
From the youth of all nations. H.C. Harwood. 6474-4,6542-2
From Theodore de Banville. Arthur Reed Ropes. 6875-8
"From there, after six days and seven...". Cities & desire 005. Italo Calvino. 6758-1
"From these high towers this noble issuing". Sonnet ("From these high"). Edmund Spenser. 6301-2
"From things consider'd with a stricter view". Last chorus, fr. Medea. Euripides. 6867-7
"From this appropriate court, renowned Lucerne". Lucerne. William Wordsworth. 6749-2
"From this distance the ships in the harbor". Two pen and ink studies for despair. Jordan Smith. 6803-0
"From this fair point of present bliss". A retrospect. Adelaide Anne Procter. 6957-6
"From this grey crag in ether islanded". The eagle's journey. Owen (Edward Bulwer-Lytton, Earl Lytton) Meredith. 6943-6
From this the strength. Fred Lape. 6761-1
"From thorny wilds a monster came". Self-love and truth incompatible. Madame De la Mothe Guion. 6814-6
"From thought to thought, from mountain-peak...". Francesco Petrarch. 6325-X
From three fly leaves. James Kenneth Stephen. 6652-6
From time to eternity. Henriette Roland Holst. 6068-4
"From torch reversed the flame". Girolamo Savonarola. 6238-5
"From Tuscane came my lady's worthy race." Henry Howard, Earl of Surrey. 6584-8,6645-3
From Venice was that afternoon. Jean Garrigue. 6390-X
"From unfinished night accidents". Dream scars. Kateri Lanthier. 6767-0
"From unremembered ages we". Chorus of spirits of the mind, fr. Prometheus unbound. Percy Bysshe Shelley. 6935-5
"From wastes of war, and weary maze of speech". The return of Botha. Ethelreda Lewis. 6800-6
"From what dripping cell, through what...". A drunkard to his bottle. Joseph Sheridan Le Fanu. 6930-4
"From whence, and why such impudence". The appearance of Cromwell's ghost..battle of Culloden. Unknown. 6859-6
"From where I sat and milked the cows...". Windows of color. Daniel Smythe. 6761-1
"From where the chaparrals uplift". Rough riders. Edwin L. Sabin. 6995-9
"From White's and Will's". Song ("From White's"). Ambrose Philips. 6024-2
From which war. Phillip Yellowhawk Minthorn. 7005-1
From William Grismond's downfall. Unknown. 6547-3
From winter's tree. Marjorie Allen Seiffert. 6076-5
"From within/Slight rain seems to purr". Rain on a cottage roof. Freda Laughton. 6930-4
"From Yorktown on the fourth of May". The gallant fighting 'Joe'. James Stevenson. 6946-0
"From you and home I sleep afar". Under the moon. Bayard Taylor. 6976-2
"From you I have been absent in the spring". Sonnet 098 ("From you"). William Shakespeare. 6271-7,6436-1,

FROM

        6430-2,6438-8,6250-4
"From you have I been absent in the spring". William
    Shakespeare. 6125-7,6186-9,6198-2,6187-7,6240-7,6122-
    6,6182
"From you r heaven of tender" Friederike Mayrocker. 6769-7
"From Zeus begin we, never nameless we". Aratus. 6435-3
Fron Altruria. Frances M. Milne. 6274-1
Front line. William Rose Benet. 6032-3,6051-X
Frontenac Inn. Nan M. Clark. 6342-X
The frontier line. Sir Arthur Conan Doyle. 6793-X
Frontier picture. Edward Singer. 6687-9
Frontiers. Mary Wickham Porcher. 7014-0
"Fronting amazed Cythera grows" Alexander Pushkin. 6103-6
Frost. Estelle Rooks. 6850-2
Frost. Laurence Alma Tadema. 6242-3
Frost. Alex Talmadge. 6850-2
Frost. Cyril G. Taylor. 6269-5
Frost. Edith M. Thomas. 6102-8,6076-5
Frost. Edith Matilda Thomas. 7041-8
Frost. Lionel Wiggam. 6640-2
Frost at midnight. Samuel Taylor Coleridge. 6208-3,6199-0,
    6430-2,6052-8,6378-0,6233-4,6315-2,6634-8
Frost at midnight, sels. Samuel Taylor Coleridge. 6395-0
Frost at night. James Thomson. 6150-4
The frost elves. Mary L. Wolverton. 6116-8
"The frost hath spread a shining net". The pixies. Samuel
    Minturn Peck. 6875-8,6770-0
Frost in harvest. Coventry Patmore. 6980-0
Frost in spring. Jessie B. Rittenhouse. 6393-4
"The frost is here". Winter. Alfred Lord Tennyson. 6623-2,
    6466-3,6456-6
The frost king. Mary Mapes Dodge. 6820-0
Frost on the window. Mrs. R.A. Faulkner. 6433-7
Frost pictures. Unknown. 6373-X,6456-6
Frost song. Marjorie L.C. Pickthall. 6591-0,6592-9
The frost spirit. John Greenleaf Whittier. 6077-3,6466-3,
    6018-8
"The frost that stings like fire upon my cheek". Winter
    uplands. Archibald Lampman. 7035-3
Frost to-night. Edith M. Thomas. 6509-0,6338-1,6332-2,6310-
    1,6266-0,6476 ,6512-0,6583-X,6393-4,6161-3
"The frost will bite us soon". Harvest home song. John
    Davidson. 6820-0
Frost, Barbara
    Possession ("They say I own the cottage on the hill").
    6040-4
Frost, Elizabeth Hollister
    Dust. 6979-7
    Had you been old. 6879-0
Frost, Frances
    Blue harvest. 6396-9
    For my son on his twelfth birthday. 6761-1
    Girl in a tree. 6374-8
    The hint beyond. 6750-6
    Hydrographic report. 6833-2
    Language. 7030-2
    Little poem for evening. 7030-2
    The mountain. 6764-6
    New England letter. 6761-1
    New England steeple. 6532-5
    New Hampshire once. 6764-6
    Old pasture. 6782-4
    Park Avenue cat. 6120-6
    Rainy woods. 7030-2
    Sea town. 6833-2
    Sounds. 6042-0
    Tell any child. 6761-1
    Tune for carrousels. 6761-1
    Words to a son. 6761-1
    Year's end. 6042-0
Frost, Frances M.
    Next door neighbor. 6750-6
Frost, Francis
    Purple grackles. 6073-0
Frost, Philip P.
    Morning and evening. 6118-4
Frost, Robert
    Acceptance. 6879-0
    Acquainted with the night. 6339-X,6125-7
    After apple-picking. 6399-3,6488-4,6536-8,6556-2,6602-X

    After the apple-picking. 6338-1,6300-4,6491-4,6723-9
    The aim was song. 6250-4
    Birches. 6029-3,6257-1,6288-1,6336-5,6396-9,6300-4,6646-
        1,6723-9,6265-2,6217-2,6161-3,6121-4,6162-1,6332-2,
        6348-9,6509-0,6527-9,6556-,6332-2,6467-1,6300-4,6646-
        1,6491-4
    The birthplace. 6012-9
    The black cottage, sels. 6052-8
    The black cottage. 6162-1,6399-3,6121-4
    Blue-butterfly day. 6076-5
    Bond and free. 6320-9
    The bonfire. 6031-5,6542-2
    A brook in the city. 6010-2,6510-4
    Brown's descent, or, The willy-nilly slide. 6162-1,6722-
        0,6393-4
    Christmas trees. 6746-8
    The code - heroics. 6897-9
    Come in. 6783-2
    Come in. 6339-X
    A considerable speck. 6722-0
    A correction. 6722-0
    Th cow in apple time. 6162-1,6393-4
    The death of the hired man. 6153-2,6029-3,6121-4,6628-3,
        6645-3,6077-3,6527-9,6732-8,6646-1,6458-2
    Departmental. 6399-3,6637-2
    Design. 6010-2
    The fear. 6348-9,6506-6,6375-6
    Fire and ice. 6726-3,6250-4,6288-1,6010-2,6491-4
    Fireflies in the garden. 6464-7
    The flower-boat. 6012-9
    For once, then, something. 6288-1
    A fountain, a bottle, a donkey's ears, and some books.
        6070-6
    Fragmentary blue. 6345-4
    The gift outright. 6208-3,6666-6
    Going for water. 6253-9
    Good hours. 6723-9
    Good-bye and keep cold. 6121-4,6431-0,6345-4
    The grindstone. 6010-2
    The gum gatherer. 6393-4
    The hardship of accounting. 6722-0
    The hill wife, sels. 6030-7,6102-8,6208-3,6076-5,6030-7
    The hill wife. 6556-2,6288-1
    A hillside thaw. 6288-1
    Home burial. 6348-9,6365-9
    Home, fr. The death of the hired hand. 6337-3
    House fear, fr. The Hill Wife. 6102-8
    A hundred collars. 6538-4,6736-4
    Hyla brook. 6348-9
    The impulse, fr. The hill wife. 6030-7
    The impulse. 6317-9,6030-7
    In the home stretch. 6030-7
    A late walk. 6338-1,6649-6
    A leaf-treader. 6042-0
    The lesson for today. 6391-8,6666-6
    The line-gang. 6421-3
    The lockless door. 6345-4
    Lodged. 6102-8,6232-6,6070-6,6012-9,6076-5
    Loneliness, fr. The Hill Wife. 6102-8,6208-3
    Mending wall. 6102-8,6154-0,6179-6,6228-8,6289-X,6299-7,
        6250-4,6288-1,6153-2,6076-5,6536-8,6161-3,6467-1,
        6723-9,6464-7,6332-2,6427-2,6476-0,6509-0,6527-9,
        6726-3,6732-8
    Mending wall, sels. 6337-3
    A minor bird. 6073-0
    Misgiving. 6619-4
    Moon compass. 6764-6
    The most of it. 6979-7
    The mountain. 6506-6
    Mowing. 6333-0,6250-4,6333-0
    My November guest. 6250-4,6431-0
    The need of being versed in country things. 6208-3
    Neither out far nor in deep. 6125-7
    Not to keep. 6031-5,6542-2
    Nothing gold can stay. 6726-3,6645-3
    October. 6333-0
    The oft-repeated dream, fr. The hill wife. 6030-7,6250-
        4,6513-9
    The oft-repeated dream. 6984-3
    An old man's winter night. 6393-4

Once by the Pacific. 6527-9
The onset. 6431-0,6607-0,6619-4,6288-1,6161-3,6506
Our hold on the planet. 6527-9
Out, out- 6527-9
The oven-bird. 6073-0,6348-9
Pan with us. 6236-9
The parlor joke. 6345-4
The passing glimpse. 6012-9,6040-4,6012-9
The pasture. 6154-0,6299-7,6338-1,6339-X,6538-4,6454-X,
   6355-1,6356-X,6480-9,6154-0,6299-7,6338-1,6339-X,
   6538-4,6454-X,6355-1,6356-X,6480-9
The peaceful shepherd. 6532-5
A peck of gold. 6299-7
Place for a third. 6034-X
Plowmen. 6345-4
A prayer in spring. 6266-0,6303-9,6337-3,6532-5,6214-8
Putting in the seed. 6208-3,6338-1
Reluctance. 6121-4,6246-6
The road no taken 6250-4,6513-9,6029-3,6125-7,6121-4
The road not taken 6300-4,6371-3
The road not taken. 6052-8,6101-X,6102-8,6162-1,6246-6,
   6527-9,6556-2,6348-9,6076-5,6431-0
The rose family. 6441-8
Rose pogonias. 6333-0
The runaway. 6332-2,6465-5,6246-6,6345-4,6257-1
Sand dunes. 6012-9
A semi-revolution. 6391-8
Snow. 6288-1
Snow dust. 6102-8,6607-0,6076-5
A soldier. 6641-0,6666-6,6665-8
The sound of the trees. 6348-9,6509-0,6393-4,6464-7,
   6467-1,6653-,6513-9
Spring pools. 6581-3
The star-splitter. 6777-8
Stars. 6333-0
Stopping by woods on a snowy evening. 6037-4,6253-9,
   6581-3,6153-2,6421-3,6464-7,6491-4,6121-4,6069-2,
   6421-3,6052-8,6512-0,6101-X,6228-8,6236-9,6488-,6503-
   1,6506-6,6527-9,6534-1,6619-4,6726-
Storm fear. 6421-3,6431-0
The telephone. 6431-0
A time to talk. 6299-7,6478-7
To a thinker. 6645-3
To E.T. 6034-X
To earthward. 6464-7,6317-9,6320-9,6399-3,6527-9,6619-4,
   6246-
To Edward Thomas. 6542-2
To the thawing wind. 6154-0
Tree at my window. 6208-3
A tuft of flowers. 6299-7,6536-8,6162-1,6266-0,6289-X,
   6501-
A tuft of flowers. 6628-3,6288-1
The tuft of flowers. 6850-2
Two look at two. 6320-9
Two tramps in mud time. 6375-6
The valley's singing day. 6607-0
The vantage point. 6333-0
West-running brook. 6536-8
The white-tailed hornet. 6488-4
The witch of Coos. 6776-X
The witch of Coos. 6531-7,6010-2
The wood-pile. 6333-0,6348-9
Frost, Robert (tr.)
   L'arret a la lisiere des bois par un soir de neige.
      Edouard Roditi, 6527-9
Frost, S.A. (Sarah Annie Shield)
   Country quiet. 6851-0
   Cross purposes. 6851-0
   It never rains, but it pours. 6851-0
   Morning calls. 6851-0
   The valentine. 6851-0
   Will you advertise? 6851-0
Frost, Thomas
   'Attempted suicide'. 6926-6
   The death of Colman. 6946-0
   Frank, the fireman. 6681-X
   Going away. 6670-4
   The guns in the grass. 6946-0
   The little tin cup. 6674-7
   Lydia's ride. 6576-7

The old fire-dog. 6675-5
Who's dead? 6721-2
Frost-bitten. George A. Baker. 6187-7
The frost-elf. Francis Saltus Saltus. 6965-7
"The frost-king sat on a throne of snow". Montreal
   carnival sports. George Martin. 7035-3
Frost-morning. William Alexander. 6090-0
Frost-work. Arthur John Lockhart. 7041-8
The frost. Grace Atherton Dennen. 6036-6
The frost. Hannah Flagg Gould. 6302-0,6385-3,6479-5,6132-X,
   6629-1,6373 ,6018-8,6131-1,6638-0,6639-9
The frosted pane. Sir Charles George Douglas Roberts. 6597-
   X,6301-2
A frosty day. John B.L. Warren, 3d Baron De Tabley. 6315-2
"The frosty fires of northern starlight". The Norseman's
   ride. Bayard Taylor. 6976-2
Frothingham, Nathaniel Langdon
   Eiger, Monch, and Jungfrau. 6749-2
Frothingham, Nathaniel Langdon (tr.)
   Solomon and the sower. Friedrich Ruckert, 6848-0
   Song of the Parcae. Johann Wolfgang von Goethe, 6438-8
Frowns and sneers. Unknown. 6629-1
Frowns or smiles. Sydney Dayre. 6137-0
Frozen enchantment. Doris Trahagen De Aragon. 6906-1
Frozen fire. Floris Clark McLaren. 6750-6
The frozen girl. Unknown. 6826-X
The frozen grail. Elsa Barker. 6300-4,6310-1,6732-8,6396-9
Frozen music. Adeline Rubin. 6397-7
"Frozen, rotting, dark leaves". Scene from a dream. Janet
   Campbell Hale. 7005-1
The frugal snail. Charles Lamb. 6529-5
Fruhlingsgruss. Count Joseph von Eichendorff. 6252-0
Fruit. Ruth Miller. 6788-3
The fruit garden path. Amy Lowell. 6338-1
Fruit gathering: XL. Rabindranath Tagore. 6879-0
"The fruit of all the service that I serve". Epigram ("The
   fruit"). Sir Thomas Wyatt. 6584-8
"The fruit of that beauty". Salome. Orrick Johns. 6959-2
Fruit of the flower. Countee Cullen. 6250-4
The fruit shop. Amy Lowell. 6029-3
Fruit tree. Ibn Qadi Mila. 6362-4
The fruit vendor. Frances Beatrice Taylor. 6797-2
The fruit-rancher. Lloyd Roberts. 6115-X
"Fruit-vender church". Sunday. Jorge Carrera Andrade. 6759-
   X
Fruitage. William Kean Seymour. 6884-7
Fruitionless. Ina D. Coolbrith. 6309-8
The fruits of a clear conscience. Joshua Sylvester. 6198-2
Frumkin, Gene
   Crises. 6803-0
   Disquiet of reason. 6803-0
   The explanation. 6803-0
   Faith. 6803-0
   Following. 6803-0
   A trick of memory. 6803-0
Frustra. William Shakespeare. 6732-8
Frustrate. Louis Untermeyer. 6736-0
The frustrate wave. Unknown. 7020-5
Frustration. Howard Hilles. 6789-1
Frustration. Anne Scott. 6750-6
Frustration, a heritage. Thelma Parker Cox. 7024-8
Frutta di mare. Geoffrey Scott. 6125-7
Fry, Miss
   The dog of St. Bernard's. 6131-1
Frye, E.F.
   'Saint Emily'. 6965-7
Frye, W.D.
   Fort Snelling. 6342-X
"Fu' yellow lie the corn-rigs". Rothesay bay. Dinah Maria
   Mulock Craik. 7037-X
The Fudge family in Paris, sels. Thomas Moore. 7025-6
The fudge family in Paris. Thomas Moore. 6959-2
Fugitive. David Morton. 6347-0
Fugitive. Blanche Waltrip Rose. 6906-1
Fugitive. George Steele Seymour. 6789-1
Fugitive. Ricardo Weeks. 6178-8
"A fugitive was I". Behind the waterfall. William Schroll.
   6857-X
The fugitive. Alice Meynell. 6955-X
The fugitives.. Percy Bysshe Shelley. 6183-4,6358-6,6466-3,

FUGITIVES.

6518-X
The fugitives.. Florence Wilkinson. 6310-1,6393-4
The fugitives; a tale of slavery. John E. Barrett. 6840-5
The fugitives. Florence Wilkins,in Evans. 6954-1
Fugue. Alfonso Gutierrez Hermosillo. 6759-X
Fugue. Marjorie L. Wolfe. 6818-9
Fugue of death. Paul Celan. 6758-1
Fuguet, Dallett
   The blithe mask. 6337-3
   Indian summer. 6936-3
   Moses took the river course. 6936-3
   Vespers. 6936-3
Fuimus troes, sels. Jasper Fisher. 6562-7
Fuimus!. Winthrop Mackworth Praed. 6543-0
Fuit ilium. Edmund Clarence Stedman. 6004-8
Fuite en Angleterre. Emile Cammaerts. 6785-9
Fujiawara no Toshiyuki
   "Although it is not plainly visible to the eye". Arthur Waley (tr.). 7039-6
Fujita
   New year. Lois J. Erickson (tr.). 6027-7
   Sunshine. Lois J. Erickson (tr.). 6027-7
Fujiwara
   "White plum tree, where can my loved one be?" Lois J. Erickson (tr.). 6027-7
Fujiwara Kore-tada (Prince Ken-toku)
   "I dare not hope my lady-love". William N. Porter (tr.). 6852-9
Fujiwara No Kiyosuke
   Time was when I despised my youth. William N. Porter (tr.). 6852-9
Fujiwara no Michinaga
   "The day will soon be gone". Arthur Waley (tr.). 7039-6
Fujiwara No Michinobu
   Although I know the gentle night. William N. Porter (tr.). 6852-9
Fujiwara No Mototoshi
   "It is a promise unfulfilled". William N. Porter (tr.). 6852-9
Fujiwara No Oki-kaze
   "Gone are my old familiar friends". William N. Porter (tr.). 6852-9
Fujiwara No Sanekata
   Though love, like blisters made from leaves. William N. Porter (tr.). 6852-9
Fujiwara No Toshi-yuki
   To-night on Sumi-no-ye beach. William N. Porter (tr.). 6852-9
Fujiwara No Yoshitaka
   "Death had no terrors, life no joys". William N. Porter (tr.). 6852-9
Fujiwara Sadakata
   "I hear thou art as modest as". William N. Porter (tr.). 6852-9
Fujiwara Sanseada (Go Tokudai-ji Sadajin)
   "The cuckoo's echo dies away". William N. Porter (tr.). 6852-9
Fujiwara Tadamichi
   "When rowing on the open sea". William N. Porter (tr.). 6852-9
Fulfil thy will. Christina Georgina Rossetti. 6303-9
Fulfilling. MacKnight Black. 6954-1
Fulfillment. Cathleen Keegan. 6648-8
Fulfillment. William Augustus Muhlenberg. 6730-1
Fulfillment. J.B.B. Nichols. 6477-9,6102-8
Fulfillment. Robert Nichols. 6542-2
Fulfillment. Orrin J. Richards Jr. 6342-X
Fulfillment. Viola Roseboro. 7014-0
Fulfillment. Unknown. 6687-9
Fulfillment. Gretchen O. Warren. 7027-2
Fulfilment. Gertrude Huntington McGiffert. 6838-3
Fulfilment. Robert Nichols. 7026-4
Full bloom. Ruth Klein. 6850-2
Full cycle. John White Chadwick. 6946-0
"A full day's ride from the nearest town". Wheel-tracks. Elliott C. Lincoln. 7007-8
"Full early in that dewy time of year". Text and moral. Alice Cary. 6865-0;6969-X
A full edition. Joseph Lilienthal. 6118-4;6274-1
Full fair. Hafiz. 6448-5

Full fathom five thy father lies, fr. The tempest. William Shakespeare. 6194-X,6438-8,6645-3,6099-4,6154-0,6187-7,6246-6,6258-X,6536 ,6122-2,6182-6,6395-0,6547-3, 6132-X,6328 ,6490-6,6726-2,6723-9,6252-0,6125-7,6189
"Full forty days he pass'd, whether on hill". The first temptation, fr. Paradise regained. John Milton. 6931-2
A full harvest. James Whitcomb Riley. 6993-2
Full heart. Glory E. Scott. 6799-9
The full heart. Robert Nichols. 6374-8,6301-2,6723-9
"Full in the splendor of this morning's hour". Ave Caesar! Rudolph Chambers Lehmann. 7008-6
"Full little knowest thou that hast not tried". What hell it is, fr. Mother Hubbard's tale. Edmund Spenser. 6934-7
"Full many a dreary hour have I past". Epistle to my brother George. John Keats. 6828-6
"Full many a fiend did haunt this house...". An imitation of Spencer. John Armstrong. 6968-1
"Full many a glorious morning I have seen". Sonnet 033 ("Full many a glorious"). William Shakespeare. 6645-3,6660-7,6491-4,6250-4,6301-2,6430-2,6560-0,6102-8, 6208-3,6315-2,6271-7,6108-7,6427-,6154-0,6436-1,6604-6,6732-8,6023-4,6189
"Full many a glorious morning have I seen". William Shakespeare. 6122-2,6182-6,6488-4,6187-7,6198-2,6597
"Full many a glorious morning have I seen." William Shakespeare. 6219-9,6371-3,6383-7,6371-3
"Full many a project that never was hatched". Humpty Dumpty. Adeline Dutton (Train) Whitney. 6917-7
Full moon. Brenda De Butts. 6253-9
Full moon. Walter De La Mare. 6044-7
Full moon. Robert Graves. 6208-3
Full moon. Galway Kinnell. 6388-8
Full moon. Victoria Mary Sackville-West. 6581-3
Full moon. Sappho. 7039-6
Full moon. Elinor Wylie. 6036-6
"The full moon from her cloudless skies". Robert Bridges. 6487-6,6655-0
"The full moon glimmers still and white". To Marian asleep. Sarah Morgan Bryan Piatt. 6772-7
"The full moon shines and shimmers". A rhyme of a cedar shell. William Lindsey. 6798-0
Full moon, Santa Barbara. Sara Teasdale. 6036-6,6010-2
"Full of faults, you say". Yone Noguchi. 6850-2
"Full of grief, the low winds sweep". Culloden moor. Amice Macdonell. 6873-1
Full of life now. Walt Whitman. 6126-5,6288-1
"Full oft the innocent sufferer sees". Longing for reunion with the dead. William Wordsworth. 6980-0
"Full often have I stod at close of day". Queen of night. Arthur J. Jenner. 6818-9
"Full often, when our fathers saw the red...". The green above the red. Thomas Osborne Davis. 7009-4
"Full on his forehead fell the expiring light". Benjamin Harrison. Charles E. Russell. 6820-0
Full seas. Bruce Souders. 6857-X
A full song. Thomas Campion. 6794-8
The full suite. ? Metcalf. 7021-3
"Full thirty foot she towered from waterline..". The three-decker. Rudyard Kipling. 6810-3
"Full thirty frosts since thou wert young". Upon a venerable rival. William Cowper. 6814-6
"Full thirty years of age art thou". The old dragoon to his cloak. Carl Von Holter. 6952-5
"A full tide rose with ground-swell". Alfred Lord Tennyson. 6793-X
"Full twenty summer-times ago". The deserted homestead. Benjamin Franklin Taylor. 6815-4
"Full twenty years and more,our laboring stage". Prologue to Albion and Albanius. John Dryden. 6970-3
Full valleys. Francis Reginald Scott. 6021-8
"Full well I know..." Hartley Coleridge. 6380-2
"Full well it may be seen." Sir Thomas Wyatt. 6584-8
Full-circle. Maxwell Anderson. 6034-X
"A full-tide/Rose with ground swell...". Sea-dreams, sels. Alfred Lord Tennyson. 6997-5
Fuller and Warren. Unknown. 6061-7,6003-X
Fuller, Charles H.
   Green things groing. 6049-8

Fuller, Ethel Romig
    Concerning boundaries. 6461-2
    The dark chamber. 6979-7
    Dust. 6039-0
    God hears prayer. 6532-5
    How wise are the flowers! 6750-6
    The pioneer mother. 6463-9
    Proof. 6337-3,6461-2,6654-2
    Wind is a cat. 6891-X
Fuller, Hector
    The peace he sought. 7001-9
Fuller, Howard Elsmere
    To Edgar Allan Poe. 6818-9
Fuller, Margaret
    Bestowal. 6006-4
    Dryad song. 6730-1
    The passion-flower. 6006-4
Fuller, Melville W.
    Grant. 6922-3
Fuller, Raymond Fuller
    Winter cordwood. 6761-1
Fuller, Rex George
    Fog. 6037-4
    The plowman. 6037-4
Fuller, Rez George
    The plowman ("Brown stubble turning across..."). 6037-4
Fuller, Roy
    Crustaceans. 6379-9
    The end of a leave. 6379-9
    Epitaph on a bombing victim. 6379-9
    The giraffes. 6379-9
    Good-bye for a long time. 6379-9
    The green hills of Africa. 6788-3
    The hero. 6209-1
    In Africa. 6788-3
    January 1940. 6666-6
    Letter to my wife. 6379-9
    Meditation. 6209-1
    Native working on the aerodome. 6379-9
    October 1942. 6666-6
    The petty officers' mess. 6124-9
    The plains. 6788-3
    Poem ("Pity"). 6379-9
    Sadness, glass, theory. 6666-6
    Spring 1942. 6379-9
    Spring 1943. 6666-6
    The tribes. 6788-3
    What is terrible. 6666-6
    Winter night. 6379-9
    A wry smile. 6666-6
Fuller, Violet
    Ring, joyful bells! 6449-3
Fullerton, Edward Grier
    Rondel. 6936-3
Fullerton, George Herbert
    Disclosed. 6818-9
Fullerton, Mary
    Comet. 6384-5
    The heart's not yet a neighbor. 6384-5
    Learning. 6384-5
    The selector's wife. 6349-7
    The skull. 6784-0
    War. 6384-5
Fullingim, Archer
    On a high red hill in southwest Texas. 6397-7
    Twilight. 6397-7
Fullmer, Merle
    Red river ox carts. 6342-X
Fullness of love. Elizabeth Barrett Browning. 6429-9,6226-1,6321-7
The **fulness** of days. Edward Farquhar. 6939-8
The **fulness** of time. James Stephens. 6339-X
Fult Faithorne. William Aspenwall Bradley. 6102-8,6076-5
Fulton, Alice
    The magistrate's escape. 6966-5
    Needfire, this low heaven. 6900-2
"**Fumant** a ma fenetre, en ete, chaque soir". Une aumone. Francois Coppee. 6801-4
Fun. Leroy F. Jackson. 6497-3
Fun. Douglas Malloch. 6401-9

"The **fun** is in the winning, not the spending". The real sport. Edgar A. Guest. 6748-4
Fun on grandpa's farm. Unknown. 6715-8
The **fun** that Adam missed. Carl Smith. 6929-0
Funaroff, Sol
    Of my deep hunger. 6375-6
The **fundamentalist.** Wilson MacDonald. 6021-8
Fundisi. Ruth Miller. 6788-3
Funeral. Schuyler B. Jackson. 6777-8
Funeral. Jay G. Sigmund. 6072-2
Funeral anthem. Henry Hart Milman. 6980-0
Funeral at high tide. Hervey Allen. 6326-8
Funeral custom in Egypt. Unknown. 6412-4
The **funeral** day of Sir Walter Scott. Felicia Dorothea Hemans. 6973-8
The **funeral** dirge. L.M. Dawn. 6524-4
Funeral elegies, sels. Francis Quarles. 6908-8
Funeral elegy on the death of...Mr. Michael Drayton. Sir Aston Cokayne. 6933-9
A **funeral** elegy upon the death of...John Cotton... John Norton. 6753-0
The **funeral** genius; an ancient statue. Felicia Dorothea Hemans. 6973-8
Funeral hymn. Phoebe A. Hanaford. 6524-4
Funeral hymn. William Walsham How. 6730-1
Funeral hymn. William Walsham Howe. 6214-8
Funeral hymn. Sir Walter Scott. 6214-8
Funeral hymn. Unknown. 6752-2
The **funeral** hymn. Phineas Densmore Gurley. 6524-4
Funeral ode on Marvin McTyeire Parks. Francis Potter Daniels. 6841-3
The **funeral** of Martin Luther King, Jr. Nikki Giovanni. 7024-8
Funeral of Napoleon I. Sir J.H. Hagarty. 6433-7
The **funeral** of Philip Sparrow. John Skelton. 6022-6
The **funeral** of the Count of Saldana. Unknown (Spanish) 6757-3
The **funeral** of the mountains. Fred Emerson Brooks. 6674-7
The **funeral** of youth: threnody. Rupert Brooke. 6210-5
Funeral on the death of the Princess Charlotte. Robert Southey. 6832-4
The **funeral** parlor. Henry Johnson. 6870-7
Funeral song. John Fletcher. 6334-9,6125-7
Funeral song. Unknown. 6334-9,6472-8
Funeral song for Mamie Eisenhower. Nellie Wong. 6790-5
Funeral song for the Indian chief Blackbird. Amy Lowell. 6345-4
Funeral song for the Princess Charlotte of Wales, sels. Robert Southey. 6867-7
A **funeral** song lamenting Sir Philip Sidney. Unknown. 6641-0
A **funeral** thought. Bayard Taylor. 6976-2
The **funeral** tree of the Sokokis. John Greenleaf Whittier. 6049-8,6484-1
A **funeral..** Frederic Lawrence ("R.L. Paget") Knowles. 6116-8
The **funeral..** Will Carleton. 6139-7
A **funeral.** Henry Alford. 6980-0
The **funeral.** Walter De La Mare. 6596-1
The **funeral.** John Donne. 6562-7,6189-3,6341-1,645-3,6301-2, 6198-2,6317-9,6536-8,6488-4,6154-0
The **funeral.** John Gay. 6972-X
The **funeral.** Stephen Spender. 6375-6
The **funeral.** Carolyn C. Wilson. 6033-1
The **funeral.** Marguerite Young. 6979-7
Fungi. Charles Wharton Stork. 6038-2
The **fungi.** W.M. Bronk. 6764-6
Funk. Robert Service. 6159-1
Funk, Marian Nevin
    Madman. 6037-4
Funk, Wilfred J.
    From a down-town skyscraper. 6732-8
    The insatiable sex. 6732-8
    Minors. 6232-6
Funkhouser, Ethel M.
    Goldenrod. 6818-9
Funnell, Alfred Jennings
    A hidden hand--somewhere. 6799-9
"The **funniest** story I ever heard". She would be a Mason. Unknown. 6911-8

FUNNIEST

The **funniest** thing in the world. James Whitcomb Riley. 6452-3,6368-3
"**Funny** (or not so)". The artist. Stewart Brisby. 6870-7
Funny bunny. Able Pleasant. 6130-3
A **funny** bunny. Carolyn Wells. 6882-0
"A **funny** creature is my clam". My new clam. Stephanie L. Binckli. 6750-6
A **funny** fellow. Frank Dempster Sherman. 6311-X
Funny folks. Harriet Nutty. 6130-3
The **funny** little fellow. James Whitcomb Riley. 6772-7,6990-8
A **funny** little girl. Carolyn Wells. 6882-0
The **funny** old clown. Robert J. Burdette. 6588-0
The **funny** small boy. H.C. Dodge. 6530-9
The **funny** story. Josephine Pollard. 6426-4
The **funny** story. Unknown. 6247-4
Funny, isn't it? Unknown. 6629-1
Funston. James J. Montague. 6615-1
The **fur** coat. James Stephens. 6102-8
The **fur** king. Samuel M. Baylis. 7035-3
The **fur**-backed skate fish. Vachel Lindsay. 6206-7
Furbee, Ruth
    Worship. 6337-3
The **furies**, fr. Orestes. Euripides. 6435-3
"The **furious** storm takes wing". A ballade of death. Hunter MacCulloch. 6770-1
"**Furl** your sail, my little boatie". 'Little boatie'. Henry Van Dyke. 6961-4
Furlong, Alice
    An awakening. 6090-0
    The betrayal. 6090-0
    I will forget. 6090-0,6096-X,6096 X
    My share of the world. 6437-X
    Yuletide. 6292-X,6172-9
Furlong, Eca Earll
    When mother is away. 6713-1
Furlong, Thomas
    Eileen Aroon. 6086-2
Furlong, Thomas (tr.)
    Roisin dubh. Unknown (Irish), 6858-8
Furlough. Ann Louise Hayes. 6515-5
"The **furnace** has wild hair of pipes". 1937 Robert Wallace. 6860-X
The **furnace** man. Amelia Josephine Burr. 6750-6
Furnace wharf. Geoffrey Johnson. 6761-1
The **furnance**. Homer. 6814-6
Furness Jr., H.H.
    Skating song. 7035-3
Furness, R.A. (tr.)
    Archeanassa. Asclepiades, 6435-3
    The blinding of Tiresias. Callimachus, 6435-3
    "Come, sit beneath". Unknown, 6435-3
    The cow herd. Diotimus, 6435-3
    The cup-bearer. Meleager, 6435-3
    "Dear mother Earth, within your breast". Unknown, 6435-3
    Delos. Callimachus, 6435-3
    The epiphany of Apollo. Callimachus, 6435-3
    A faithful servant. Dioscorides, 6435-3
    A gardener. Unknown (Greek), 6435-3
    Heliodora's wreath. Meleager, 6435-3
    "Here lies the son of Battus..." Callimachus, 6435-3
    Life a voyage. Palladas, 6435-3
    Love in spring. Meleager, 6435-3
    Love's capriciousness, fr. Epigrams. Callimachus, 6435-3
    The mosquito turned messenger. Meleager, 6435-3
    Odi profannum vulgus, fr. Epigrams. Callimachus, 6435-3
    On a stone at Corinth. Unknown (Greek), 6435-3
    "One single nymph all other nymphs above." Callimachus, 6435-3
    The poet's father. Callimachus, 6435-3
    Preface to Erinna's poems. Asclepiades, 6435-3
    "The rose's bloom is short..." Unknown, 6435-3
    "So this, my good Sabinus, is the one". Unknown, 6435-3
    A statue of Pan. Unknown (Greek), 6435-3
    There is no loving after death. Asclepiades, 6435-3
    To Aratus, fr. Epigrams. Callimachus, 6435-3
    Under a laurel. Anyte, 6435-3
    We are born every day. Palladas, 6435-3
    When the rose is dead. Unknown (Greek), 6435-3
    A wife's grave. Damagetus, 6435-3
Furness, William H.
    Eternal light. 6600-3
Furniture. Eve Merriam. 6017-X
The **furniture** of a woman's mind. Jonathan Swift. 6152-4
The **furrow** and the hearth. Padraic Colum. 6250-4,6393-4
"The **furrow's** long behind my plow". Ballade of the little things that count. Burges Johnson. 6875-8
The **furrow**.. Padraic Colum. 6338-1
"A **furry** coat has the bear to wear". The pig's tail. Norman Ault. 6937-1
Furry-day song. Unknown. 6328-4
Furse, Margaret Cecilia
    The lamp flower. 6477-9
    'She became what she beheld'. 6607-0
"**Further** and further we leave the scene". In war-time. Florence Earle Coates. 7026-4
Further document on the human brain. W.R. Moses. 6640-2
Further instructions. Ezra Pound. 6102-8,6076-5,6506-6
The **fury** of aerial bombardment. Richard Eberhart. 6666-6
Furze and broom. Unknown. 6134-6
Fuschia hedges in Connacht. Padraic Colum. 6096 X
"**Fuscus**, whoso to good inclines". To Aristius Fuscus. Horace. 6949-5
"The **fused** heat of words". Crystals and flame. Mary Cummings Eudy. 6850-2
Fuseli's 'Nightmare,' fr. The loves of the plants. Erasmus Darwin. 6545-7
The **fusiliers'** dog. Francis Doyle. 6510-4
"**Fusing** the blaze of the red and the gold". Incursio. Ruth H. Hausman. 6850-2
Fusion's last dodge. Unknown. 6709-3
Fussing place. Annie Willis McCullough. 6715-8
Fussy. Laura E. Richards. 6891-X
Futile errand. Byron Herbert Reece. 6761-1
The **futile**. Genevieve Taggard. 6347-0
Futility. Charlotte Blaising. 6750-6
Futility. Berton Braley. 6853-7
Futility. Hortense Flexner. 6506-6
Futility. Glycon. 6435-3
Futility. Mary S. Hawling. 6782-4
Futility. Wilfred Owen. 6052-8,6179-6,6246-6,6357-8,6317-9, 6354-3,6209-1
Futility. Claude George Wilson. 6799-9
Future full of cheer. Oscar Kuhns. 6717-4
Future generation. Nila NorthSun. 7005-1
"The **future** hides in it". Johann Wolfgang von Goethe. 6238-5
The **future** is fair. Charles Whitby. 6994-0
The **future** is not for us. Ronald Bottrall. 6354-3
The **future** life. William Cullen Bryant. 6240-7,6385-3,6735-2
The **future** of the classics. Unknown. 6089-7,6724-7
The **future** peace and glory of the church. William Cowper. 6271-7,6641-0
The **future** speaks. Louis K. Anspacher. 6799-9
"A **future** worthy of the dead". Good-will. Eden Phillpotts. 7014-0
The **future**.. Edward Rowland Sill. 6243-1,6303-9,6737-9
The **future**.. Unknown. 6583-X
The **future**. Matthew Arnold. 6177-X,6196-6,6430-2,6828-6
The **future**. George Frederick Cameron. 6433-7
The **future**. John Gould Fletcher. 6010-2
The **future**. Alexander Pope. 6302-0;6365-3;6732-8
The **future**. Unknown. 6889-8
Futurity. Elizabeth Barrett Browning. 6123-0
Futurity. Elizabeth Barrett Browning. 7037-X
Futurity. William Herbert; Earl of Pembroke. 6980-0
Fuzzy wuzzy leaves us. E.P. C. 6440-X
Fuzzy-wuzzy. Rudyard Kipling. 6162-1,6332-2,6079-X,6655-0, 6656-9
"**Fye** awaye fye what meane you by this." Unknown. 6563-5
Fyleman, Rose
    Alms in autumn. 6044-7,6374-8,6466-3,6253-9
    The attic. 6466-3
    The beech-tree. 6262-8
    The child next door. 6891-X
    The cuckoo. 6356-X
    The dormouse. 6262-8

'The fairies have never a penny to spend'. 6478-7,6607-0,6639-9,6723-9,6421-3,6253-9,6368-3
The fairies have never a penny to spend. 6891-X
The fairies. 6254-7,6639-9,6638-0
The fairy in the meadow. 6253-9
Fairy music. 6421-3
The fairy tailor. 6638-0
A fairy went a-marketing. 6639-9
I don't like beetles. 6044-7
Mice. 6891-X
Mother. 6891-X
Mr. Minnitt. 6466-3
Please. 6539-2
Please. 6891-X
Sometimes. 6861-8
Tadpoles. 6262-8
Tinker, tinker. 6262-8
Very lovely. 6368-3
Vision. 6466-3,6368-3
Wishes. 6044-7
Woman and professor. 6072-2
Yesterday in Oxford Street. 6331-4,6466-3,6466-3
"Fyll the cuppe, Phylyppe,". Unknown. 6198-2
Fynn, Arthur J.
The land where the columbines grow. 6836-7
Fynn, Penelope
The warrior tree. 6799-9

G. Hilaire Belloc. 6018-8
G.
On a summer's eve. 6116-8
G.,A.R.
"Ye shall find the babe." 6225-3
G.,D.S.
The Elkridge hunt club. 7010-8
G.,E.O.
My church. 6954-1
G.,E.R.
Solitude. 6118-4
G.,H.L.
Mother England. 6224-5
G.,M.
Camouflage. 6589-9
G.,M.E.W.
Old amontillado. 6116-8
G.,M.H.
Nothing but leaves. 6358-6
G.,S.E.
'Bide a wee, and dinna fret.' 6273-3
G.,T.H.
Hopes and fears. 6118-4
G.I. blues. Unknown. 6237-7
G.W.. Unknown. 6889-8
"Gabe first glanced Jewel". Cross rhythms. Renee Roper. 6899-5
Gabe's Christmas Eve. Robert C.V. Meyers. 6416-7
The Gaberlunzie man. James V; King of Scotland. 6328-4
The gaberlunzie man. Unknown. 6829-4
The gaberlunzie-man. Unknown. 6180-X
"The gabled roofs of old Malines". The bells of Malines. Henry Van Dyke. 6961-4
Gabriel. Bayard Taylor. 6976-2
Gabriel meets Satan, fr. Paradise Lost. John Milton. 6315-2
"Gabriel of high degree". Nova, nova: ave fit ex eva. Unknown. 6756-5
Gabriel's charge to Michael. Joost van den Vondel. 6102-8
Gabriel's trumpet. Unknown. 6609-7
"Gabriel, brighter than the sun". Make merry this new year, thanking God with...cheer. Unknown. 6756-5
"Gabriel, fram hevene king". The Annunciation. Unknown. 6881-2
"Gabriel, that angel bright". Regina celi, letare. Unknown. 6756-5
Gadbury, John
A ballad upon the popish plot. 6157-5
Gaddess, Mary L.

A bundle of loves. 6672-0
Fortune-teller and maiden. 6671-2
Highland lovers. 6711-5
Life's day. 6674-7
Old sweet song. 6711-5
The search for happiness. 6672-0
Stealing roses. 6680-1
Gadoshkibos. Diane Burns. 7005-1
Gadsdon, W.H.
The martyred nation. 7031-0
A **Gaelic** Christmas. Liam P. Clancy. 6282-2
The **Gaelic** litany to our lady. Unknown. 6282-2
Gaelic lullaby. Unknown. 6132-X
Gaelic speech; or "Auld Lang Syne" done up in Tartan. Unknown. 6440-X
Gaer, Yossef
Streets of San Francisco: Market Street and Pacific Avenue. 6071-4
Gaffer at the fair. Laurence Housman. 6506-6
Gaffer Gray. Thomas Holcroft. 6787-5
Gaffney, Francis A.
Our lady of the rosary. 6022-6
Gaffney, Sallie
Spring kisses. 6818-9
Youth. 6818-9
Gagakiu. Steve Richmond. 6792-1
Gagaku. Steve Richmond. 6792-1, 6998-3
A **gage** d'amour. Austin Dobson. 6656-9
Gage, Frances Dana Barker ("Aunt Fanny")
Back to mother's arms. 6097-8
Ben Fisher. 6407-8
An earnest cry. 6617-8
The fourth of July. 6130-3
God, free the drink captive. 6685-2
A home picture. 6910-X
The housekeeper's soliloquy. 6403-5
The rain upon the roof. 6273-3
"'What shall I do?' My boy, don't stand asking". 6238-5
The year that is to come. 6408-6
Gage, G.W.
The perfect light. 6654-2
The **gage.** Walter De La Mare. 6596-1
Gahl, Dale
Memorial. 6799-9
Gaiety of descendants. Douglas Newton. 6379-9
Gail, Hermann
"A dwarf hops on the rack" Milne Holton and Herbert Kuhner (tr.). 6769-7
"I too could inject gasoline" Milne Holton and Herbert Kuhner (tr.). 6769-7
"You don't even have feet" Milne Holton and Herbert Kuhner (tr.). 6769-7
"Your sentence" Milne Holton and Herbert Kuhner (tr.). 6769-7
"Gaily I lived as ease and nature taught" Unknown. 6874-X
"Gaily and greenly let my seasons run". Wishes of youth. Laman Blanchard. 7015-9
"Gaily I lived". An epitaph ("Gaily I lived..."). Unknown. 6733-6
'Gaily the troubadour'. Andrew Lang. 6802-2
Gain and loss. Peter Taylor. 6269-5
Gain by death. William White. 6868-5
Gain of loss. Horatius Bonar. 6304-7
The **gain.** Edgar A. Guest. 6748-4
Gaining ground. Ella Wheeler Wilcox. 6617-8
Gaining wings. Edna Dean Proctor. 6889-8
Galatea. Chard Powers Smith. 6039-0
Galatea. Elizabeth Stuart Phelps Ward. 7041-8
Galatea again. Genevieve Taggard. 6726-3
Galatea to Pygmalion. Roselle Mercier Montgomery. 7038-8
The **galaxy.** Robert Loveman. 6941-X
Galbraith, W. Campbell
Red poppies in the corn. 6476-0
Galbraith, William M.
Exercise in monotony. 6761-1
Galbreath, C.B.
In Flanders field: an answer. 6963-0
A **gale** of wind. Jack Mitford. 6547-3
Gale, Marion Perham
God's challengers. 6542-2

GALE

Gale, Martha Tyler
  Snow-flakes and snow-drifts. 6166-4
Gale, Norman
  The bad boy. 6242-3
  Bartholomew. 6078-1,6242-3
  The best friend. 6510-4
  A bird in hand. 6510-4
  The blue-tit. 6510-4
  Child of loneliness. 6730-1
  Content. 6656-9
  The country faith. 6656-9,6374-8,6437-X,6730-1,6114-1, 6808-1
  Cradle song. 6772-7
  A creed. 6102-8,6301-2
  The danger. 6872-3
  Dawn and dark. 6102-8
  A dead friend. 6656-9
  Dinah. 6510-4
  The fairy book. 6242-3,6639-9,6638-0
  Father Christmas. 6579-1
  The lost friend. 6105-2,6084-6
  A love-song. 6301-2
  Lullaby ("Sleep, my angels"). 6233-4
  Mustard and cress. 6105-2,6639-9,6638-0
  A neighbour. 6510-4
  Playing at paradise. 6772-7
  A poem for Prue. 6510-4
  A priest. 6656-9
  The second coming. 6337-3,6501-5
  The shaded pool. 6437-X
  A shilling each. 6785-9
  Song ("This peach"). 6656-9
  Song ("Wait"). 6656-9
  A song. 6658-5
  Spring. 6374-8
  Thanks. 6374-8
  To my brothers. 6656-9
  To sleep, sels. ("But thou, O Sleep, bend down...") 6501-5
  To the ideal. 6266-0
  To the sweetwilliam. 6338-1
  The voice. 6266-0
Gale, R.J.
  The teacher's 'if'. 6964-9
Gale, Zona
  Children of tomorrow. 6461-2
  Contours. 6007-2,6461-2
  Doors. 6320-9
  Half thought. 6007-2
  Light. 6007-2
  North star. 6102-8,6076-5,6300-4,6102-8
  The secret way. 6007-2
  The sky-goer. 6300-4
  Voice. 6954-1
  Woman. 6954-1
Gales, Ellen M. Huntington
  A little bird. 6510-4
Gales, Richard Lawson
  An Andalusian folk song. 6950-9
  As ghosts may walk. 6950-9
  Ascension day. 6950-9
  The ballad of Andrew Symington. 6950-9
  A ballad of Dick Whittington. 6950-9
  A ballad of Easter eve. 6950-9
  A ballad of Saint Christopher. 6950-9
  A ballad of St. Christopher. 6079-X
  A child's Christmas rhyme. 6950-9
  A childermas rhyme. 6216-4
  The chimes. 6950-9
  Cockadoodledoo. 6216-4
  Contentment. 6950-9
  David in heaven. 6950-9
  Easter in wartime. 6950-9
  The expectation. 6747-6
  The goose girl. 6950-9
  The guests. 6216-4
  The happy night. 6776-X
  Heartsease. 6950-9
  The heavenly noel. 6558-9
  The heavenly noel. 6950-9
  The holly hedge of paradise. 6950-9
  The house by Blavet. 6558-9
  The images. 6950-9
  In praesepio. 6216-4
  The last journey. 6950-9
  Litany of our lady. 6950-9
  A May-day garland. 6950-9
  The pilgrim. 6950-9
  A poet's bazaar. 6950-9
  The renewal. 6950-9
  "Search the flower people thro". 6950-9
  'Si le roy m'avait donne'. 6950-9
  The skylark. 6950-9
  The soul's passage. 6950-9
  The temptation of Saint Anthony. 6668-2
  Three Christmas songs. 6216-4
  The travellers. 6950-9
  Twelfth night. 6950-9
  Two sunsets. 6950-9
  The vagabonds. 6950-9
  Waiting for the kings. 6216-4,6608-9
Galesburg fire department. Joseph Bert Smiley. 6925-8
Galilean. Margielea Stonestreet. 6144-3
The **galiongee**. William Maginn. 6802-2
Gall, Richard
  Cradle song. 6180-X,6086-2
  The Hazlewood witch. 6180-X,6086-2
  My only Jo and dearie, o. 6180-X,6219-9
Gallagher, F. O'Neil
  The all alone tree. 6466-3
Gallagher, Francis
  To a river horse. 6799-9
Gallagher, James T.
  Cape Cod. 6798-0
Gallagher, William Davis
  August. 6597-X
  Autumn. 6385-3
  The cardinal bird. 6006-6,6073-0,6597-X,6265-2
  The laborer. 6344-6,6407-8,6632-1,6304-7
  The mothers of the west. 6946-0
  Move on the columns. 6113-3
"The **gallant** Count of Greiers". The Count of Greiers. Johann Ludwig Uhland. 6948-7
The **gallant** fifty-one. Henry Lynden Flash. 6946-0
The **gallant** fighting 'Joe'. James Stevenson. 6946-0
The **gallant** French serpent and Eve. Unknown. 6166-4
The **gallant** Grahams. Unknown. 6271-7
"The **gallant** figure of the past". Romance is gone. Joyce Lancaster. 6850-2
Gallant old splitter of rail. Unknown. 6709-3
The **gallant** seaman's resolution. Unknown. 6547-3
The **gallant** seaman's return from the Indies. Unknown. 6547-3
The **gallant** seaman's song at his meeting of Betty. Unknown. 6547-3
"The **gallant** ship went down at sea". A millon, all in gold! John Whitaker Watson. 6774-3
A **gallant** wescue. W. Sapte Jr. 6920-7
A **gallant** woman. Clara Shanafelt. 6897-9
Gallaudet, Herbert D.
  Holy places. 6337-3
  Young man in a Galilean doorway. 6144-3
Gallaudet, W.E.
  Lines to the western mummy. 6752-2
Gallegos, Eduardo
  El minerito. 6149-4
Gallery. Michael Spooner. 6822-7
The **gallery.** Andrew Marvell. 6562-7,6341-1
The **gallery.** Sir Thomas Wyatt. 6436-1
Galley slave. Vincent Starrett. 7007-8
The **galley-rowers.** John Masefield. 6334-9
The **galley-slave.** Rudyard Kipling. 7007-8
The **galley.** Ibn Hariq. 6362-4
The **galliass.** Walter De La Mare. 6210-5
Galligher, F. O'Neill
  The all alone tree. 6368-3
Gallipoli. Dorothy Margaret Stuart. 7029-9
The **Galloway** raid. Unknown. 6613-5
Gallows and crosses. J.E.H. MacDonald. 6021-8
The **gallows** tree. Frederick Robert Higgins. 6930-4

The gallows. Edward Thomas. 6179-6,6246-6,6102-8,6257-1
Galraith, W. Campbell
    Red poppies in the corn. 7031-0
Galsworthy, John
    Abandonment. 7008-6
    Acceptation. 6888-X
    Autumn. 6888-X
    Autumn by the sea. 6888-X
    The bells of peace. 6509-0
    'The birth of Venus'. 6888-X
    The cliff church. 6888-X
    Counting the stars. 6888-X
    Countryman's song. 6888-X
    Courage. 6888-X
    Courage. 6266-0
    Cuckoo song: Dartmoor. 6888-X
    The cup. 6888-X
    Dedication. 6888-X
    Deflowered. 6888-X
    The Devon sage. 6331-4
    Devon to me! 6888-X
    The downs. 6477-9
    Drake's spirits. 6888-X
    A dream. 6888-X
    England to free men. 7026-4
    Errantry. 6888-X
    The flowers. 6888-X
    Gaulzery moor. 6888-X
    Hetaira. 6888-X
    High spring. 6888-X
    I ask. 6888-X
    Land song of the west country. 6888-X
    Let. 6888-X
    Life? 6888-X
    Limerick:"An angry young husband called Bicket". 6811-1
    Love. 6888-X
    Magpie. 6888-X
    Memories. 7008-6
    A mood. 6888-X
    The moon at dawn. 6888-X
    The Moor grave. 6888-X
    Never get out! 6427-2
    Nightmare. 6888-X
    Old year. 6888-X
    On a soldier's funeral. 6888-X
    Past. 6888-X
    Peace in the world. 6427-2,6337-3,6337-3
    Persia - Moritura. 6888-X
    Pitiful. 6510-4
    Plymouth. 6888-X
    A prayer ("If on a spring"). 6532-5
    Promenade. 6888-X
    Question. 6888-X
    Rhyme after rain. 6888-X
    Rhyme of the land and sea. 6888-X
    The robin. 6888-X
    Rose and yew. 6888-X
    Russia - America. 7026-4
    The seeds of light. 6888-X
    Serenity. 6888-X
    Silver point. 6888-X
    Slum cry. 6888-X
    The soldier speaks. 7027-2
    The soul. 6888-X
    Straw in the street. 6888-X
    Street lamps. 6888-X
    Sweet oath in Mallorca. 6232-8
    Time. 6888-X
    Tittle-tattle. 6888-X
    To my dog. 6888-X
    To the spirit of our times, 1899. 6888-X
    Valley of the shadow. 6337-3,6532-5,6420-5
    Village sleep song. 6888-X
    When love is young. 6888-X
    Wind. 6374-8,6653-4
    Wonder. 6532-5
Galvin, James J.
    Lady of O. 6282-2
    Morning star. 6282-2
    Ox-borne madonna ("Once they minted Our Lady..."). 6282-2
Galvin, James J. (tr.)
    Madonna's lullaby. Saint Adolphus De Ligouri, 6282-2
Galway Bay. George Barker. 6209-1
Galway races. Unknown. 6244-X
'Gam ze ya'avor' James O'Neill. 6848-0
Gamaliel Bradford. Carl Edwin Burklund. 6761-1
Gamaliel of Jerusalem. M. E. B. 6848-0
Gambara, Veronica
    To the Emperor Charles V and to King Francis I... T.G. Bergin (tr.). 6325-X
Gamble. Iraqi. 6448-5
Gamble, William M.
    Antiquated volumes. 6983-5
Gamble, William Miller
    A.D. 1608. 6983-5
Gambler. G.A. Studdert-Kennedy. 6144-3,6337-3,6335-7
The gambler's last deal. Elliott Preston. 6415-9
The gambler's tale. Will Victor McGuire. 6923-1
The gambler's wife. Reynell Coates. 6916-9
The gambler's wife. Reynell Coates. 6568-6
The gambler. Unknown. 6003-X
The gamblers. Anthony Delius. 6788-3
The gambols of children. George Darley. 6302-0,6385-3,6219-9
Game. Robert Davis. 6855-3
Game. Allen Planz. 6803-0
The game Knut played. Thomas Dunn English. 6915-0
A game of chess, fr. The waste land. Thomas Stearns Eliot. 6531-7
A game of chess. Mortimer Collins. 6658-5
The game of chess. David Skaats Foster. 6441-8
A game of fives. Charles Lutwidge ("Lewis Carroll") Dodgson. 6652-6
A game of letters. Lizzie J. Rook. 6147-8
The game of life. John Godfrey Saxe. 6583-X
A game of marbles. Ruth Comfort Mitchell. 6576-7
A game of tag. Unknown. 6466-3,6684-4
Game of three, fr. Bread out of iron. Marjorie Allen Seiffert. 6531-7
"The game we played was strictly cat and mouse". Ultimate prerogative. John J. Haining. 6857-X
A game-rhyme. Unknown. 6328-4
The game.. Maxwell Bodenheim. 6561-9
The game.. Grantland Rice. 6291-1
The game. Olive Tilford Dargan. 6266-0
The game. Walker Gibson. 6388-8
The game. Conrado Nale Roxlo. 6759-X
The gamecock. Jay G. Sigmund. 6037-4
The gamekeeper. Edward Verrall Lucas. 6018-8
Games. Eleanor Noyes Johnson. 6764-6
The games. Edwin Ford Piper. 6032-3
Gamesters all. DuBose Heyward. 6326-8
Gamwell, Sara De Wolf
    What she said. 6924-X
Ganderfeather's gift. Eugene Field. 6834-0;6949-5
Gandhi. Angela Morgan. 6102-8,6076-5
Gandy, H.
    Lost spirits. 7035-3
    White worlds. 7035-3
"Gane were but the winter cauld". A fragment. Allan Cunningham. 6960-6
Gane were but the winter cauld. Allan Cunningham. 6271-7, 6219-9,6737-9
Ganesa. Unknown (Newari) 7013-2
Ganessa the god. H.W. Green. 6591-0,6592-9
The Ganges. Mary McGuire. 6920-7
Gannett, William Channing
    "A cheerful spirit gets on quick". 6623-2
    Consider the lilies. 6337-3,6730-1,6143-5
    The highway. 6730-1
    In twos. 6429-9,6066-8,6321-7
    Listening for God. 6600-3
    A mother's breast. 6097-8
    The old love song. 6429-9,6429-9,6321-7
    The stream of faith. 6730-1
Gannon, Anna
    Ellen Terry. 6230-X
Gannon, Marie Beatrice
    A toast. 6097-8

GANOOK,

Ganook, fr. The story of Balladeadro. George Gordon McCrae. 6768-9
Gant, Margaret
    May-time ("When May-time comes I love to feel"). 6466-3
"**Gaoler**" of the donjon deep". Ballade of the oubliette. Bert Leston Taylor. 6875-8
The **gaoler**.. Helen Gray Cone. 6473-6
The **gap** of the winds. Robert Notvest. 6818-9
Garabrant, Nellie M.
    Bly blue and his gun. 6699-2
    Dandelion. 6137-0,6373-X,6459-0,6456-6,6964-9
Garadh. Padraic Colum. 6930-4
Garage sale. Carol Kyle. 6821-9
"A **garbage** wagon, rolling/Along snowy...". After the holidays. Eliazbeth Guion Hess. 6799-9
Garbarini, Mary
    Alone. 6789-1
    Loom o' lights. 6789-1
    Rath-na-leen. 6789-1
Garbett, Thomas F.
    Willie Clark. 6416-7
Garci Perez de Vargas. Unknown (Spanish) 6757-3
Garcia Lorca. Aaron Kramer. 6561-9
Garcia Lorca, Federico
    Ballad of the summoning. Lloyd Mallan (tr.). 6068-4
    The bullfight. Lloyd Mallan (tr.). 6068-4
    The first historical ballad: a martyrdom of Santa Eulalia. Lloyd Mallan (tr.). 6068-4
    Night song of the Andalusian sailors. Edward Honig (tr.). 6068-4
    Poems, sels. 6068-4
    San Miguel. Lloyd Mallan (tr.). 6068-4
    Song of the rider. Edward Honig (tr.). 6068-4
Garcia Perez de Vargas. Unknown (Spanish) 6438-8,6126-5
Garcilaso de la Vega
    "Enjoy the sweets of life's luxuriant May". Felicia Dorothea Hemans (tr.). 6973-8
"**Garcon!** You, you". The hero of the commune. Margaret Junkin Preston. 6916-9
"The **gard'ner** rings the bell at close of day". Elegy written in the Temple gardens. Unknown. 6878-2
"A **gard'ner**, of peculiar taste". The gardener and the hog. John Gay. 6972-X
Gard, Lillian
    Her 'allowance'. 6474-4,6653-4
Gard, Walter S.
    When Old Glory came to stay. 6449-3
Gard, Wayne
    Hollyhocks. 6039-0
Garden. Andreas Okopenko. 6769-7
"A **garden** 'bed'; perhaps they call it so". Rejuvenation. Alice Louise Cary. 6799-9
Garden and cradle. Eugene Field. 6318-7
The **garden** and summer-house, fr. The story of Rimi. Leigh Hunt. 6649-6
The **garden** at Bemerton. Lizette Woodworth Reese. 6338-1, 6649-6
Garden at sunset. Marj Kuhl. 6362-4
"The **garden** beds I wandered by". A conservative. Charlotte Perkins Stetson Gilman. 6996-7
The **garden** by moonlight. Amy Lowell. 6647-X
The **garden** by the bridge. Laurence (Adele Florence Nicolson) Hope. 6856-1
A **garden** by the sea. William Morris. 6232-6,6102-8
A **garden** close. Lorenzo de' Medici. 6232-6
Garden days. Robert Louis Stevenson. 6123-0
Garden experience. Edgar A. Guest. 6869-3
Garden fairies. Philip Bourke Marston. 6656-9
Garden fairies. Unknown. 6368-3
Garden fancies, sels. Robert Browning. 6649-6
"The **garden** flew round with the angel". The pleasures of merely circulating. Wallace Stevens. 6751-4
A **garden** friend. Anna Catherine Markham. 6338-1
The **garden** gate. Unknown. 6058-7
The **garden** glorious, fr. The pastime of pleasure. Stephen Hawes. 6649-6
A **garden** homily. Richard Aldington. 6069-2
A **garden** hymn. Molly Anderson Haley. 6232-6
The **garden** I love. Charles Divine. 6232-6
The **garden** in August. Gertrude Huntington McGiffert. 6338-1,6649-6
Garden in Liberty Square. Carlos Drummond de Andrade. 6759-X
The **garden** in September. Robert Bridges. 6232-6,6487-6, 6649-6
The **garden** in september. Robert ("Droch") Bridges. 6649-6
A **garden** in the desert. Harriet Monroe. 6232-6
A **garden** in Venice. Dorothy Frances Gurney. 6338-1
Garden incident. George O'Neil. 6649-6
"The **garden** is a cool expanse of green". Forgotten children. Estelle Rooks. 6850-2
A **garden** is a goodly thing. Aulus Septimius Serenus. 6649-6
"The **garden** is steeped in moonlight". Summer night piece. Amy Lowell. 6984-3
Garden magic. Ernest Hartsock. 6649-6
The **garden** of Adonis, fr. The faerie queene. Edmund Spenser. 6378-0,6649-6
The **garden** of Alcinous, fr. The Odyssey. Homer. 6232-6
The **garden** of Alcinous, fr. The Odyssey. Homer. 6649-6
The **garden** of beauty. Edmund Spenser. 6543-0
The **garden** of Boccaccio. Samuel Taylor Coleridge. 6828-6
The **garden** of Boccaccio. Samuel Taylor Coleridge. 6086-2, 6110-9,6199-0
The **garden** of dreams. Bliss Carman. 6338-1,6320-9
The **garden** of Eden. Bible. 7020-5
The **garden** of Eden. John Milton. 6232-6,6649-6
The **garden** of Epicurus. George Meredith. 6199-0,6649-6
The **garden** of God. George William ("A.E.") Russell. 6730-1
The **garden** of Irem. Bayard Taylor. 6976-2
The **garden** of Kama: Kama the Indian Eros. Laurence (Adele Florence Nicolson) Hope. 6856-1
The **garden** of love. William Shakespeare. 6429-9,6321-7
The **garden** of love. William Blake. 6232-6,6271-7,6302-0, 6315-2,6317-9,6385-,6086-2,6195-0,6301-2,6430-2
The **garden** of Mnemosyne. Rosamund Marriott ("Graham R. Tomson") Watson. 6338-1
The **garden** of nations. Edwin Arlington Robinson. 6070-6
The **garden** of no-delight. Frances Shaw. 6232-6
The **garden** of peace. Alfred Noyes. 6151-6
A **garden** of posies. Georgia H. Cooper. 6850-2
The **garden** of Proserpine, sels. Algernon Charles Swinburne. 6208-3,6427-2,6543-0
The **garden** of Proserpine. Algernon Charles Swinburne. 6046-3,6102-8,6660-7,6150-8,6301-2,6508 ,6110-9,6199-0, 6723-9,6646-1,6655-0,6645 ,6154-0,6122-2,6232-6,6289-X,6536-8,6527 ,6198-2,6657-7,6726-3,6196-6,6250-4, 6430
The **garden** of Prosperina, fr. The faerie queene. Edmund Spenser. 6125-7
The **garden** of roses. Johann Ludwig Uhland. 6976-2
The **garden** of shadow. Ernest Dowson. 6232-6
The **garden** of sorrow. Hugh Wilgus Ramsaur. 6347-0
"The **garden** of the gods! its winswept drives". Gardens. Heloise M.B. Hawkins. 6836-7
The **garden** of the gods. William Allen Butler. 6903-7
The **garden** of the gods. Gertrude Huntington McGiffert. 6838-3
The **garden** of the holy souls. Harriet Eleanor Hamiliton (Baille) King. 6022-6,6292-X
Garden of the rose. Charles Buxton Going. 6266-0
The **garden** of years, sels. Guy Wetmore Carryl. 6320-9
The **garden** on the sands. Unknown. 6049-8
A **garden** path. May Justus. 6466-3
The **garden** path. Joseph Bert Smiley. 6928-2
A **garden** picture. Alfred Lord Tennyson. 6232-6
A **garden** piece. Sir Edmund Gosse. 6770-0
A **garden** prayer. Thomas Walsh. 6338-1
Garden relief. Margaret Pitcairn Strachan. 6750-6
Garden reverie. Edward Shanks. 6232-6
A **garden** rose. G. Leland Green. 6799-9
A **garden** rose. Thomas Thornely. 6780-8
The **garden** scene, fr. Romeo and Juliet. William Shakespeare. 6302-0,6543-0
The **garden** seat. Thomas Hardy. 6641-0
Garden song. James Branch Cabell. 6250-4
Garden song. Alfred Lord Tennyson. 6600-3
Garden song ("I wonder where I may gather ..."). Unknown. 6466-3
A **garden** song, fr. Lalla rookh. Thomas Moore. 6649-6

The garden song, fr. Maud. Alfred Lord Tennyson. 6438-8
A garden song. Austin Dobson. 6232-6,6423-X,6649-6,6301-2, 6508-2,6655-0,6649-6,6301-2,6315-2
The garden spider. Charles Mackay. 6510-4
"The garden that I love". Alfred Lord Tennyson. 6793-X
The garden that I love. Florence L. Henderson. 6214-8
The garden thermometer. Benjamin Franklin Taylor. 6815-4
"The garden trees are busy with the shower". Arthur Henry Hallam. 6980-0
Garden under lighting. Leonora Speyer. 6467-1
The garden vision. William ("Fiona Macleod") Sharp. 6232-6
A garden wall. David Morton. 6232-6,6034-X
"The garden was a frowsy mass". Late chrysanthemums. Ruth Klein. 6850-2
"The garden where dreams flower is far". Dream garden. Rosalie Maher. 6850-2
Garden wiles. Helen Philbrook Patten. 6764-6
The garden year. Sara Coleridge. 6466-3
The garden year. Sara Coleridge. 6649-6
The garden year. Unknown. 6452-3,6135-4
The garden's queen. John Reynolds. 6563-5
"The garden's quit with me: as yesterday". The garden. Joseph Beaumont. 6931-2,6933-9,6931-2,6933-9
A garden, fr. Moral essays. Alexander Pope. 6649-6
The garden, fr. The homestead. Gertrude Huntington McGiffert. 6838-3
The garden, fr. The romance of the rose. Guillaume de Lorris. 6649-6
A garden, fr. The story of Rimini. Leigh Hunt. 6198-2
The garden, fr. The task. William Cowper. 6814-6
The garden, sels. Abraham Cowley. 6232-6
The garden, sels. Andrew Marvell. 6228-8
Garden-fancies. Robert Browning. 6429-9,6092-7,6321-7,6652-6,6655-0
Garden-lion. Evelyn Hayes. 6125-7
The garden-maker.. L.D. Morsbach. 6274-1
A garden-piece.. Sir Edmund Gosse. 6338-1
"The garden-shadows are flecked with...light". Under deep apple boughs. Elizabeth Craigmyle. 7037-X
A garden. Sappho. 6435-3
A garden. Percy Bysshe Shelley. 6459-0
The garden. Al-Nashshar. 6362-4
The garden. Joseph Beaumont. 6931-2,6933-9,6931-2,6933-9
The garden. Joseph Beaumont. 6562-7,6563-5
The garden. Clara T. Brown. 6906-1
The garden. Abraham Cowley. 6271-7
The garden. Hilda ("H.D.") Doolittle. 6531-7,6348-9,6531-7
The garden. John Drinkwater. 6649-6
The garden. Caroline Giltinan. 6649-6,6037-4
The garden. Nicholas Grimald. 6489-2,6649-6
The garden. Andrew Marvell. 6023-4,6125-7,6668-2,6052-8, 6122-2,6198-2,6208-3,6423-X,6733 ,6250-4,6341-1,6150-8,6301-2,6645-3,6723 ,6315-2,6339-X,6563-5,6604-6, 6726-3,6430 ,6191-5,6152-4,6649-6,6194-6,6438-8,6660
The garden. Gertrude Huntington McGiffert. 6338-1,6653-4
The garden. Alice Meynell. 6338-1
The garden. Harold Monro. 6985-1
The garden. Charles Norman. 6039-0
The garden. Belle F. Owens. 6144-3
The garden. Rose Parkwood. 6730-1,6034-X
The garden. Lois Stanton Phillips. 6799-9
The garden. Ezra Pound. 6897-9
The garden. Henri de Regnier. 6649-6
The garden. Edwin Arlington Robinson. 6723-9
The garden. Mary Chisholm Seager. 6270-9
The garden. James Shirley. 6933-9
The garden. James Shirley. 6649-6
The garden. James Shirley. 6933-9
The garden. Jones Very. 6333-0
The garden. Gretchen O. Warren. 6649-6
The gardener and the hog. John Gay. 6972-X
"The gardener standing by." Unknown. 6317-9
"A gardener tended his plot". The gardener. Emalene Sherman. 6799-9
A gardener walks at evening. Ruth Crary Clough. 6789-1
Gardener's burial. Unknown. 6304-7
The gardener's burial. Henry Johnstone. 6046-3
The gardener's cat. Patrick Reginald Chalmers. 6120-6,6503-1,6510-4,6653-4
The gardener's daughter, sels. Alfred Lord Tennyson. 6066-8,6649-6
The gardener's daughter; or, the pictures. Alfred Lord Tennyson. 6977-0
The gardener's daughter. Alfred Lord Tennyson. 7020-5
The gardener's grandchild. Mrs. Hawtrey. 6131-1
The gardener's home, fr. Dovecote mill. Phoebe Cary. 6865-0;6969-X
Gardener's song. Sacheverell Sitwell. 6778-6
The gardener, fr. The land. Victoria Mary Sackville-West. 6649-6
"Gardener—We shall have to cut you down". The picture. Arthur B. Rhinow. 6799-9
The gardener.. Lucy Fitch Perkins. 6466-3
The gardener.. Unknown. 6055-2,6518-X,6056-0,6185-0
A gardener. Unknown (Greek) 6435-3
The gardener. Francis Ledwidge. 6812-X
The gardener. Edward Verrall Lucas. 6018-8
The gardener. Emalene Sherman. 6799-9
The gardener. Edith Sitwell. 6070-6
The gardener. Robert Louis Stevenson. 6649-6
The gardener. Arthur Symons. 6649-6
The gardener. Rabindranath Tagore. 7020-5
Gardening. John Kendrick Bangs. 6654-2
Gardening. Edgar A. Guest. 6862-6
Gardening. T.S. Wallace. 6857-X
"Gardening is hardening". Gardening. Edgar A. Guest. 6862-6
Gardens. Katharine Lee Bates. 6232-6
Gardens. Heloise M.B. Hawkins. 6836-7
The gardens at Versaille, fr. The gardens. Abbe de Lille. 6649-6
Gardens of Babylon. Laura Benet. 6880-4
The gardens of the Hesperides. John Milton. 6232-6,6649-6
Gardens of the Santee. Henry Bellamann. 6649-6
The gardens of the sea. George Sterling. 6833-2
gardens of Venus, frs garden, fr. King Richard the Second. Edmund Spenser. 6649-6
The gardens, sels. Abbe de Lille. 6649-6
Gardette, C.D.
  The fire-fiend. 6403-5
Gardiner, Celia E.
  "But oh! 'twas hard to have him go, -- to know." 6066-8, 6226-1
Gardiner, Evelyn Gail
  With gleaming sail. 6118-4,6274-1
Gardiner, James (tr.)
  A flow'ry offering, fr. Hortorum. Rene Rapin, 6649-6
  Hortorium, sels. Rene Rapin, 6649-6
Gardiner, Wrey
  Dr. Coppelius. 6379-9
  Our true beginnings. 6379-9
  Poetry is happiness. 6379-9
  Walking in London. 6379-9
Gardner, Bertha Lee
  A ballad of earth and sky. 7019-1
Gardner, Isabella
  Nursery rhymes for Vietnam. 6803-0
Gardner, J. Mae
  Roads in the snow. 6894-4
Gardner, James
  Cuba. 6471-X
Gardner, Jo
  "Let me lift Jesus, Lord". 6065-X
  Lilies of the valley. 6065-X
  The only one. 6065-X
Gardner, Kathleen
  Three wishes. 6750-6
Gardner, W.L.
  The princess and the rabbi. 6415-9
Gardyne, Mary Elkins
  Oup in ole Vermont. 7030-2
Garesche, Edward F.
  At the leap of the waters. 6172-9
  Niagara. 6172-9,6192-X,6022-6
  The nuns. 6285-7
  Sun-browned with toil. 6029-3
  To a holy innocent. 6096-X
  To a martyr. 6096 X
  The young priest to his hands. 6032-3
Gareth and Lynette. Alfred Lord Tennyson. 6473-6,6264-4,

6250-4
Gareth and Lynette, sels. Alfred Lord Tennyson. 6144-3
Gareth, fr. Garth and Lynette. Alfred Lord Tennyson. 7022-1
Garey, Hannah E.
    Thanksgiving. 6618-6
Garfield at Chattanooga. Unknown. 6314-4
Garfield's ride at Chickamauga. Hezekiah Butterworth. 6074-9
Garfield, James A.
    Golden grains. 6413-2
    Memory. 6142-7,6413-2
    "When the rough battle of the day is done". 6238-5
Gargan, Janet
    The caged squirrel. 6510-4
    The captured eagle. 6510-4
Gargantua. Hervey Allen. 6076-5,6102-8,6462-1.6464-2
The gargantuan flight. Lynn Riggs. 6808-1
Gargoyles. Gertrude Huntington McGiffert. 6331-4,6631-3
"Gargoyles frightened men toward heaven". Ptarmigan valley. Robert Hedin. 6855-3
Garibaldi in Piedmont. Phoebe Cary. 6969-X
Garibaldi's retirement. Richard Garnett. 7015-9
Garioch, Robert
    Ghaisties. 6379-9
"A garland I will weave of mountain flowers". The Alps in summer. John Addington Symonds. 6749-2
The garland for Debs. Louis Untermeyer. 6345-4
A garland for Heliodora. Meleager. 7039-6
A garland for Heliodora. Christopher (John Wilson) North. 6396-9
Garland for Mr. Pound. Norman Rosten. 6561-9
The garland I send thee. Thomas Moore. 6226-1
The garland of laurel, sels. John Skelton. 6378-0,6483-3, 6586-4
The garland of sleep. Auguste Angellier. 6961-4
The garland of the blessed Virgin Marie. B. I. 6563-5
Garland, Florence B.
    Puzzled. 6764-6
Garland, Hamlin
    August. 6396-9
    Collor in the wheat. 6964-9
    The cry of the age. 6730-1
    A Dakota wheatfield. 6336-5
    Do you fear the force of the wind? 6332-2
    Do you fear the wind? 6101-X,6102-8,6356-X,6374-8,6501-5,6396-9,6368-3,6421-3,6464-7,6250-4,6431-0,6102-8, 6736-0,6076-5,6309-8
    The eagle trail. 6102-8,6076-5
    The gift of water. 6484-1
    The gold-seekers. 6736-0,6431-0
    The herald crane. 6073-0,6597-X
    The herdsman. 6498-1
    In the days when the cattle ran. 6497-3
    In the grass. 6476-0,6309-8
    Line up, brave boys. 6597-X,6252-0
    Logan at Peach Tree Creek. 6946-0
    Magic. 6464-7
    The meadow-larks. 6006-4
    The mountains are a lonely folk. 6102-8,6476-0,6076-5, 6653-4
    My prairies. 6964-9
    Noon on the plain. 6484-1
    O the fierce delight. 6102-8,6076-5
    On the Mississippi. 6102-8,6076-5
    Pioneers. 6484-1
    Prairie fires. 6102-8,6076-5,6076-5,6102-8
    A ridge of corn. 6615-1
    A river gorge. 6850-2
    Sport. 6102-8,6076-5
    To a captive crane. 6102-8,6076-5,6250-4,6510-4
    The toil of the trail. 6006-4,6597-X,6374-8
    The ute lover. 6431-0
    The whistling Marmot. 6597-X
Garland, Robert
    A prayer in khaki. 6443-4
The garland, f . Hippolytus. Euripides. 6435-3
The garland. Matthew Prior. 6563-5,6092-7
"The garlands fade that spring so lately wove". Sonnet written at the close of spring. Charlote Smith.

6932-0
Garley, George
    The sea-ritual. 6641-0
The garmont of gude ladies. Robert Henryson. 6180-X,6383-7, 6022-6
"Garner innocent pleasures". Innocent pleasures. Edward R. Huxley. 6885-5
Garner, Alma Tatum
    My home. 6799-9
    To Muffet. 6799-9
Garnet, Jasper
    Give me back my boy. 6695-X
Garnett, Judith L.C.
    Tresspass! murder! 6799-9
Garnett, Louise Ayres
    Ballad of the doorstone. 6619-4
    The cow. 6130-3
    Fishin'. 6036-6
    Flower of hemp. 6393-4
    The glimpse. 6327-6
    Gwine up ter heab'n. 6036-6
    Hound at night. 6619-4
    Noah en de ark, sels. 6538-4
    The prodigal. 6034-X
    The rover. 6038-2
    Seekin'. 6777-8,6037-4
    The sisters. 6509-0,6036-6
    Song of liberty. 6386-1
    Soul at play. 6037-4
    The star splitter. 6038-2
    Young loveliness. 6037-4
Garnett, Richard
    Age. 7015-9
    Age. 6656-9
    Age. 7015-9
    "And constant shells that evermore retain". 6997-5
    "And the crest/Of every mounting wave..." 6997-5
    The ballad of the boat. 6138-8,6657-4,6481-7,6046-3, 6656-9
    Dante. 7015-9
    De flagello myrteo, sels. 6317-9
    The didactic poem. 6656-9
    Epigram. 6437-X
    Epigrams ("'I hardly ever ope my lips,'") 6427-2
    Even-star. 6785-9
    Fading-leaf and fallen-leaf. 6437-X
    The fair Circassian. 6437-X,6656-9
    Feasting, I watch. 6328-4
    Garibaldi's retirement. 7015-9
    The highwayman's ghost. 6518-X
    The island of shadows. 6656-9
    The lyrical poem. 6656-9
    Marigold. 6120-6
    The mermaid of Padstow. 6518-X
    Nausicaa. 6785-9
    The nix. 6133-8
    Nocturne. 6437-X
    On an urn. 6656-9
    Our master, Meleager. 6092-7
    The sicilian octave described and exemplified. 6770-0
    Sonnet: age. 6437-X
    To America. 6656-9
    The violet to the nightingale. 6943-6
    Where corals lie. 6997-5
Garnett, Richard (tr.)
    Die rose, die lilie, die taube, die sonne. Heinrich Heine, 7039-6
    Es fallt ein stern herunter. Heinrich Heine, 7039-6
    Eumares. Asclepiades, 7039-6
    Few there be. Unknown (Greek), 6435-3
    "Many the Bacchi that brandish the rod". Unknown, 6435-3
    Menodotis. Leonidas of Alexandria, 6850-2
    Menodotis. Leonidas of Alexandria, 7039-6
    Sag' mir wer einst die uhren erfund. Heinrich Heine, 7039-6
    Sonnet ("Leave me"). Luis de Camoens [or Camoes], 7039-6
    To Cincius. Marcus Argentarius, 6879-0
    Warum sind denn die rosen so blass. Heinrich Heine,

7039-6
Garnyvillo. Edward Lysaght. 6174-5
Garrabrant, Nellie M.
    The fairy artist. 6466-3
"A garret grows a human thing". The psalm book in the garret. Benjamin Franklin Taylor. 6815-4
Garret, Harriet
    The gift of love. 6799-9
The garret. Ezra Pound. 6102-8,6076-5
The garret. William Makepeace Thackeray. 6481-7,6732-8
Garretson, Mary Raymond
    A wise mouse. 6699-2
Garrett, Edmund H.
    How spring comes at Craigville. 6798-0
Garrett, Edward
    The unbolted door. 6409-4
Garrett, Elizabeth
    O, fair New Mexico. 6465-5
Garrett, F.E. (tr.)
    "I would I were a damask rose". Unknown, 6435-3
    Lais' mirror. Plato, 6435-3
    "O that a lovely lyre were I". Unknown, 6435-3
    Wishes. Unknown (Greek), 6435-3
    Would I were a rose. Unknown (Greek), 6435-3
Garrett, Fydell Edmund
    Inscriptions. 6224-5,6625-9,6800-6
    Inventory. 6800-6
    The last trek. 6800-6
Garrett, George
    Caedmon. 6388-8
    On reading the 'Metamorphoses' 6388-8
    Snapshot of a pedant. 6388-8
    Snapshot: ambassadress. 6388-8
    Snapshot: politician. 6388-8
    Tiresias. 6388-8
Garrick, David
    Advice to the Marquis of Rockingham. 6874-X
    Come, come, my good shepherds. 6086-2
    A fable. 6733-6
    Heart of oak. 6087-0,6547-3,6328-4,6732-8
    Let the gay ones and great. 6328-4
    On Quin the actor. 6396-9
    Shakespeare. 6484-1
    Song in connection with Shakespeare Jubilee, 1769. 6086-2
    To Mr. Gray on the publication of his odes. 6932-0
    Warwickshire. 6024-2
    "Ye fair married dames, who so often deplore" 6874-X
Garrigue, Jean
    The cage. 6390-X
    Forest. 6390-X
    Fourth declamation (police of the dead day) 6803-0
    From Venice was that afternoon. 6390-X
    Poem ("For the heart"). 6017-X
    The stranger. 6390-X
Garrison. Amos Bronson Alcott. 6431-0,6820-0
Garrison. John Greenleaf Whittier. 6126-5
The garrison of Cape Ann, sels. John Greenleaf Whittier. 6484-1
The garrison of Cape Ann. John Greenleaf Whittier. 6552-X, 6661-5,6288-1,6126-5
Garrison town. Emmanuel Litvinoff. 6666-6
Garrison, Fielding H.
    Diavolina. 6482-5
Garrison, Peggy
    To my poetry teacher. 6998-3
Garrison, Theodosia
    April. 6374-8,6478-7,6503-1,6653-4
    April 2nd. 6031-5
    As the larks rise. 7007-8
    At the sign of the cleft heart. 6166-4
    The ballad of the cross. 6509-0,6393-4
    Blighty. 6331-4
    A city voice. 6374-8,6653-4
    Compensation. 6211-3,6501-5
    Cupid-his mark. 6274-1
    The cynic. 6441-8,6019-6
    The debt. 6449-3
    The dreamers. 6101-X,6497-3,6503-1,6653-4,6431-0
    The failures. 6211-3
    The free woman. 6102-8,6076-5
    The great cross of mercy. 6449-3
    The green inn. 6006-4,6374-8,6253-9,6336-5
    The grief. 6320-9
    The gypsying. 6374-8,6653-4
    The hills. 6374-8
    Himself. 6083-8,6307-1
    The joy o'life. 6732-8
    The Kerry lads. 6331-4
    Knowledge. 6085-4
    The little Christian. 6732-8
    A love song. 6556-2,6431-0
    May flowers. 6653-4
    Memorial Day. 6449-3
    The mighty oak. 6995-9
    Monseigneur plays. 7038-8
    A morning. 6374-8,6252-0
    The neighbors. 6648-8
    Old friendship street. 6085-4,6266-0
    An old poet. 6184-2
    One fight more. 6291-1,6501-5
    The poplars. 6338-1,6465-5,6653-4,6338-1
    A prayer ("I do not pray"). 6291-1
    A prayer at planting time 6232-6 6649-6
    The Red Cross Christmas seal. 6449-3
    Resurgam. 6337-3
    The return. 7038-8
    The road's end. 6607-0
    Saint Jeanne. 6449-3
    Shade. 6337-3,6338-1,6509-0,6464-7
    The shepherd who stayed. 6478-7,6608-9
    A song in a garden. 6338-1,6374-8
    A song of Marco Polo. 7038-8
    A song to Belinda. 6338-1,6653-4
    The soul of Jeanne D'Arc. 7026-4
    Stains. 6300-4,6076-5,6102-8,6310-1,6337-3,6509-0,6730-1
    Storm in April. 6232-6
    The storm. 6347-0
    The tears of harlequin. 6310-1,6250-4
    "These shall prevail." 6396-9
    The two brothers. 6648-8
    Unconquered. 6211-3
    The vagabond. 6320-9
    The victor. 6648-8
    Villages. 6072-2
    The wife. 6266-0
    With the same pride. 6846-4
Garrison, Troy
    Spoken for many mouths. 6761-1
Garrison, Wendell Phillips
    Evening. 6627-5
    The vision of Abraham Lincoln. 6524-4
Garrison, William Lloyd
    "Church of the living God! in vain thy foes". 6238-5
    The free mind. 6632-1
    Freedom for the mind. 6735-2
    Hope for the enslaved. 7009-4
    Independence Day. 7009-4
    Liberty for all. 6286-5
    Sonnet ("High walls"). 6600-3
    Sonnet written in prison. 6385-3,6250-4
    To an eloquent advocate of Indian rights. 7009-4
    To the Hon. Theodore Frelinghuysen. 6752-2
    The triumph of freedom. 7009-4
Garrison, Winfred Ernest
    At Carcassonne. 6542-2
    Easter morning. 6144-3
    The quest. 6461-2
    Temptation. 6144-3,6335-7
    Thy sea so great. 6337-3,6214-8
Garrity, Mattie
    The rain. 6850-2
Garrod, Heathcote William
    A 'bump supper'. 6785-9
    Discipulo discedenti. 6785-9
    Invitation. 6785-9
    Revolt. 6506-6
Garrod, Heathcote William (tr.)
    Love and death. Caius Catallus, 7039-6

Garryowen. Unknown. 6858-8,6930-4
Garstin, Crosbie
    Callao. 6464-7
    Chemin des dames. 7029-9
    The figure-head. 6833-2
    Nocturne. 6253-9
    'Old soldiers.' 6541-4
    On the back veld. 6625-9
    'Spanish ledges.' 6541-4
    The transport rider. 6625-9
Garth, Sir Samuel
    The dispensary, sels. 6198-2,6482-5,6152-4
Gartman, Elias
    Lindbergh's lay. 7019-1
Garvey, Helen Irene
    Apostle of the helpless. 6342-X
Garvin, Amelia Beers. See "Hale, Katherine"
Garvin, J. L.
    A journalist's communion. 7020-5
Garvin, John W.
    Busy bee. 6797-2
    O Canada! 6797-2
    The sawmill. 6797-2
Garvin, Margaret Root
    From all the fools who went before. 6619-4
    To a poet. 6327-6
    To each his own. 6083-8
Garvin, Viola Gerard
    Au Clair de la lune. 6781-6
    Babylon. 7007-8
    The freedman. 7007-8
    The house of Caesar. 7007-8
    Prayer for Michaelmas. 6558-9
    September. 6780-8
Gary Gotow. George Uba. 6790-5
Gascoigne's good morrow. George Gascoigne. 6586-4,6641-0
Gascoigne's passion. George Gascoigne. 6380-2
Gascoigne, George
    'And if I did what then?'. 6182-6,6208-3,6380-2
    The arraignment of a louer. 6586-4
    A farewell. 6315-0,6436-1
    Fie, pleasure, fie! 6182-6
    For that he looked not upon her. 6182-6
    Gascoigne's good morrow. 6586-4,6641-0
    Gascoigne's passion. 6380-2
    Gascoygne's good night. 6586-4
    The grace of God. 6134-6
    I tell thee, priest. 6087-0
    Inscription in a garden. 6436-1
    Lines written on a garden seat. 6232-6,6649-6
    The looks of a lover enamoured. 6182-6
    A lover's lullaby. 6830-8
    The lullaby ("Sing lullabies"). 6383-7
    Lullaby of a lover. 6099-4,6182-6,6586-4,6189-3
    "Of all the birds that I do know". 6181-8
    "Sing lullaby, as women do". 6181-8
    The steel glass, sels. 6586-4,6194-X
    The steel glass. 6198-2
    A strange passion of a lover. 6122-2
Gascoyen, Morys (tr.)
    The song of the oaks. Anatole Le Braz, 6232-6
Gascoygne's good night. George Gascoigne. 6586-4
Gascoyne, David
    Ecce homo. 6210-5,6379-9
    Elegy (In memoriam-- June 1941, R. R.). 6475-2,6210-5
    An elegy. 6210-5
    The gravel-pit field. 6379-9
    In defense of humanism. 6391-8
    In perpetuum mobile. 6985-1
    Lachrymae. 6106-0
    Miserere. 6209-1,6379-9,6391-8
    Orpheus in the underworld. 6210-5,6354-3
    The sacred hearth. 6210-5
    September sun: 1947. 6209-1
    Slate. 6985-1
    Spring MCMXL. 6475-2
    The supposed being. 6391-8
    Susan. 6985-1
    The three stars. 6475-2
    The unattained. 6354-3

    The uncertain battle. 6475-2
    Walking at Whitsun. 6475-2
    A wartime dawn. 6391-8
    Winter garden. 6246-6
Gascoyne, David (tr.)
    The two witnesses. Pierre Jean Jouve, 6343-8
    Woman and earth. Pierre Jean Jouve, 6343-8
Gaselee, Sir Stephen
    On china blue. 6722-0
Gaslight. Kwang-kyun Kim. 6775-1
Gaspar Becerra. Henry Wadsworth Longfellow. 6126-5
The Gaspard tragedy. Unknown. 6057-9
Gasper, A. See Willson, Arabella M.
Gasquet, Joachim
    Primordial springs. 6351-9
    Primordial springs. Joseph T. Shipley (tr.). 6351-9
    Why do we live? 6351-9
Gass, Alice Dougan
    Of such... 6750-6
Gassaway, Frank H.
    'Advance.' 6673-9
    Bay Billy. 6370-5,6413-2,6521-X,6510-4,6639-9
    The dandy fifth. 6917-7
    The dandy fifth. 6277-6,6451-5,6706-9
    The day old bet was sold. 6370-5
    The "grand advance" 6621-6,6579-1
    The pride of Battery B. 6370-5,6426-4,6621-6,6964-9
Gassed. Rowland Thirlmere. 7027-2
Gastev, Alexey
    Factory whistles. 7014-0
"Gastibelza, l'homme a la carabine". Guitare. Victor Hugo. 6801-4
Gaston, William
    The old north state. 6465-5
The gastronaut. Jonathan Williams. 6803-0
Gate of Camelot. Alfred Lord Tennyson. 6438-8
"The gate of Horn are dull of hue". The gates of Horn. Rosamund Marriott ("Graham R. Tomson") Watson. 6875-8
The gate of departure. Joseph Johnston Lee. 6269-5
"The gate of paradise was shut". The music at the gate. Mary Lucretia Barker. 6789-1
The gate of the armies. Henri de Regnier. 6343-8
The gate of the year, sels. M. Louise Haskins. 6337-3
"The gate was thrown open, I rode out alone". How Salvator won. Ella Wheeler Wilcox. 6671-2,6964-9
The gate-posts, fr. The homestead. Gertrude Huntington McGiffert. 6838-3
The gate. Elizabeth J. Coatsworth. 6034-X
The gate. Eugene Crombie. 6650-X
The gate. Yasmeen Jamal. 6870-7
Gates. Margaret McNeish. 6906-1
Gates ajar. Anna L. Ruth. 6404-3
The gates ajar. Albert Bigelow Paine. 6615-1
Gates and doors. Joyce Kilmer. 6162-1,6236-9,6266-0,6478-7, 6532-5,6143-5,6214-8,6746-8,6653-4,6608-9
Gates of Damascus. James Elroy Flecker. 6234-2,6508-2
The gates of hell. Thomas Sackville; 1st Earl of Dorset. 6935-5
"The gates of horn are dull of hue". The gates of horn. Rosamund Marriott ("Graham R. Tomson") Watson. 6770-0
The gates of Horn. Rosamund Marriott ("Graham R. Tomson") Watson. 6875-8
The gates of paradise. William Blake. 6208-3
Gates, Barrington
    Wet night. 6072-2
Gates, Ellen M.H.
    The bars of fate. 6291-1
    Beautiful hands. 6097-8,6260-1
    The exiles. 6273-3
    Good-night. 6654-2
    "How many times, as through the rooms I hasten". 6238-5
    My mother's hands. 6273-3,6303-9
    My mother's picture ("How many times..."). 6097-8
    Sleep sweet. 6260-1,6337-3,6501-5
    Strength. 6211-3
    A vision. 6414-0
    Your mission. 6291-1,6260-1
Gates, Jessie Rose

Peace after sorrow. 6337-3
Gates, Robert
  Our trade. 6954-1
Gateway of the garden of the gods. J. Ernest Whitney. 6836-7
The gateway. Margaret McNeish. 6906-1
"Gather all the sweet of May". Song for youth. Dana Burnet. 6891-X
"Gather for festival," fr. Songs from Cyprus. Hilda ("H.D.") Doolittle. 6011-0
"Gather kittens while you may". Song ("Gather kittens"). Oliver Herford. 6440-X
"Gather or take fierce degree". A short poem for Armistice Day. Herbert Read. 6985-1
Gather round, all ye good men. Samuel M. Baylis. 7035-3
"Gather the garlands rare to-day". Memorial Day. Cy Warman. 6820-0
Gather the rose. Edmund Spenser. 6182-6
Gather these bones, sels. Lewis Turco. 6218-0
"Gather thy brightness, O sun". Sleeping. Burton Egbert Stevenson. 6983-5
"Gather together the nations! pooclaim the war". The gathering of the nations. Thomas D'Arcy McGee. 7009-4
Gather ye rosebuds, while ye may. Robert Herrick. 6560-0
"Gather your roses while you may". If Robert Herrick had been Dorothy Parker. Eric Divine. 6850-2
"Gathered under leaded/skies and packed...". Manomin. Phyllis Wolf. 7005-1
Gathering blackberries. Phoebe Cary. 6969-X
Gathering flowers. Unknown. 6629-1
Gathering grasses. Unknown. 6684-4
Gathering of Athol. Unknown. 6859-6
The gathering of the church. John Keble. 6046-3
The gathering of the clans, fr. A session with... James Whitcomb Riley. 6091-9
The gathering of the Hays. Unknown. 6859-6
Gathering of the Macdonalds. Unknown. 6859-6
The gathering of the nation. J.D. Frazer. 6858-8
The gathering of the nations. Thomas D'Arcy McGee. 7009-4
Gathering rant. Unknown. 6859-6
Gathering song of Donald the Black. Sir Walter Scott. 6228-8,6246-6,6302-0,6385-3,6153-2
Gathering song of Donald [or, Donui] Dhu. Sir Walter Scott. 6075-7,6479-5,6239-3,6242-2,6639-9
"Gathering the echoes of forgotten wisdom". Ode ("Gathering the echoes..."). George Santayana. 6754-9
"Gathering, tall, a wave in a vicious sea". Heart's desire. John Peter. 6788-3
The gathering. Herbert B. Swett. 6471-X
The gathering. Herbert B. Swett. 6946-0
"Gatigwanasti, Ayunini, Suate". Owl and rooster. Gladys Cardiff. 7005-1
Gatineau Point. Susan Frances ("Seranus") Harrison. 6115-X
Gatty's song. Sir George Etherege. 6544-9
Gaudeamus Igitur. Unknown. 6732-8,6102-8
Gaudeamus igitur. Unknown (Latin) 6879-0
Gaudeamus Igitur. Margaret L. Woods. 6477-9,6507-4
The Gauls sacrifice. Charles M. Doughty. 6210-5
Gaulzery moor. John Galsworthy. 6888-X
"Gaunt in the midst of the prairie". Chicago. John Boyle O'Reilly. 6946-0
"The gaunt trees black and naked stand". Ballade of Easter dawn. Edwin Meade Robinson. 6875-8
Gaunt's dying speech, fr. Richard II. William Shakespeare. 6138-9
"A gaunt-built woman and her son-in-law". Polonius and the ballad singers. Padraic Colum. 6897-9
Gautier, Helen Taylor
  My prayer. 6764-6
Gautier, Theophile
  Art. 6732-8
  Art. George Santayana (tr.). 7039-6,6879-0
  Barcarolle. 6801-4
  Choc de cavaliers. 6801-4
  Clairmonde. Lafcadio Hearn (tr.). 7039-6
  Clarimonde. 6732-8,6102-8,6468-8
  Departure of the swallows. 6302-0,6358-6
  Don Juan. 6801-4
  The escurial. Charlotte Fiske Bates (tr.). 6424-8
  An invitation. 6652-6
  La melodie et l'accompagnement. 6801-4
  The last sigh of the moor. Charlotte Fiske Bates (tr.). 6484-1
  Les matelots. 6253-9
  Love at sea. 6732-8
  Meditation. Cora Fabri (tr.). 6876-6
  Notre Dame. 6631-3
  Notre Dame. Eva M. Martin (tr.). 6331-4,6439-6
  Ribeira. 6801-4
  The spectre of the rose. 6676-3
  Variations sur le carnaval de Venise. 6801-4
  What the swallows say. 6102-8
Gavotte in D minor. Amy Lowell. 6034-X
Gavronsky, Serge (tr.)
  To New York. Leopold Sedar Senghor. 6803-0
Gaw, Ethelean Tyson
  Robbed. 6542-2
  voice of Francis Drake/The. 7038-8
  Woodrow Wilson returns from Versailles. 7001-9
'Gawlia deserta,' sels. Idris Davies. 6360-8
Gawsworth, John
  The bridge. 6893-6
  The dead poet. 6893-6
  From the deep. 6893-6
  Regret. 6893-6
  "So now September ends, and on the sea". 6893-6
  Turville mill. 6893-6
  W.H. Davies. 6783-2
"Gay Bacchus liking Estcourt's wine". Anacreontic (2). Thomas Parnell. 6975-4
"Gay daffodils". Daffodils. Lady Margaret Sackville. 6781-6
Gay girl to good girl. Muriel Stuart. 6269-5
"Gay go up and gay go down." Unknown. 6331-4,6452-3
The gay Gordons. Sir Henry Newbolt. 6395-0
The gay goss-hawk. Sir Walter Scott. 6438-8
The gay goss-hawk. Unknown. 6056-0,6134-6,6180-X,6185-0, 6239-3,6518,6067-6,6613-5
The gay green fairy. Dorcas Littlefield. 6249-0
Gay Jemmie, the miller. Unknown. 6594-5
The gay lady that went to church. Unknown. 6518-X
"A gay morning breeze". City dawn. Naomi Rogin. 6850-2
A gay people. Rolfe Humphries. 6761-1
"Gay Robin is seen no more". Robert Bridges. 6242-3,6487-6
"A gay Spanish maid at the age of sixteen". Unknown. 6059-5
The gay Spanish maid. Unknown. 6057-9
"The gay sea-plants fammiliar were to her". Sea-nurtured. Jean Ingelow. 6833-2
"Gay snowflakes took the town by storm". The snow storm. Mabel Hall Goltra. 6789-1
"Gay spring bonnets". Easter-tide. Evangeline Robinson. 6764-6
"A gay young spark, who long had sighed". The lawyer's stratagem. Unknown. 6878-2
Gay, John
  Achilles: an opera. 6972-X
  Acis and Galatea: an English pastoral opera. 6972-X, 6250-4
  Advertisement. 6972-X
  The ant in office. 6972-X
  The apotheosis of Hercules. 6972-X
  Araminta. 6972-X
  Arcadia. 6092-7
  The baboon and the poultry. 6972-X
  Ballad ("Of all the girls"). 6157-5
  A ballad on ale. 6972-X
  A ballad on quadrille. 6972-X
  A ballad on quadrille. 6092-7
  A ballad. 6191-5,6152-4,6219-9
  The banish'd beauty. 6972-X
  The barley-mow and the dunghill. 6972-X
  The bear in a boat. 6972-X
  "Before the barn-door crowing", fr. The beggar's opera. 6733-6
  The beggar's opera, sels. 6733-6,6637-2,6152-4,6491-4
  The beggar's opera. 6972-X
  The birth of the squire. 6972-X

GAY

Black-eyed Susan. 6250-4,6560-0,6092-7,6543-0,6198-2, 6328-4,6246-6,6302-0,6385-3,6502
Blouzelinda's funeral. 6932-0
Blouzelinda's funeral, fr. Shepherd's week. 6932-0
Book I, sels. 6198-2
The bull and the mastiff. 6972-X
The butterfly and the snail. 6133-8
Canto 002 6972-X
The captives. A tragedy. 6972-X
The cock-maid, the turnspit,and the ox. 6972-X
A contemplation of night. 6152-4
The coquet mother and coquet daughter. 6972-X
The council of horses. 6133-8,6239-3,6552-X
the countryman and jupiter. 6972-X
The court of death. 6972-X
The courtier and proteus. 6972-X
Cowards are cruel, but the brave. 6623-2
Cupid, hymen and plutus. 6972-X
The cur and the mastiff. 6972-X
The cur, the horse, and the shepherd's dog. 6972-X
Damon and Cupid. 6733-6
Daphnis and Chloe. 6972-X
The death of Hercules. 6972-X
The death of Nessus the centaur. 6972-X
The debate of the gods. 6972-X
The degenerate bees. 6972-X
The despairing shepherd. 6972-X
Dione. A pastoral tragedy. 6972-X
The distress'd wife. 6972-X
The ditty ("Young Colin Clout, a lad..."). 6315-2
The dog and the fox. To a lawyer. 6972-X
The eagle, and the assembly of animals. 6972-X
Eclogues. 6972-X
An elegiac epistle to a friend. 6972-X
An elegy on a lap-dog. 6024-2,6092-7
The elephant and the bookseller. 6315-2
An epistle to a lady. 6972-X
An epistle to her grace, Henrietta. 6972-X
An epistle to the most learned doctor w--d----d. 6972-X
Epistle to the right honourable Paul Methuen, Esq. 6024-2
An epistle to the right honourable the Earl of... 6972-X
An epistle to the right honourable William Pulteney. 6972-X
An epitaph. 6228-8
The equivocation. 6972-X
The espousal. 6972-X
Fable XXXVII. 6024-2
Fables. 6972-X
Fables. William Cowper (tr.). 6814-6
Fables, sels. 6152-4
The fan. 6198-2
The fan. 6972-X
The farmer's wife and the raven. 6972-X
The father and jupiter. 6972-X
The fox at the point of death. 6133-8,6183-4,6195-0
A fragment. 6092-7
Friday, fr. The shepherd's week. 6152-4
Friday; or, the dirge. 6972-X
'From Mohock and from Hawkubite' 6972-X
The funeral. 6972-X
The gardener and the hog. 6972-X
Go rose, my Chloe's bosom grace. 6192-3
The goat without a beard. 6972-X
The great frost. 6932-0
The great frost. 6932-0
The hare and many friends. 6198-2,6249-0,6385-3,6084-6, 6646-1
His own epitaph. 6527-9
Horace, epod. 004, imitated. 6972-X
the hound and the huntsman. 6972-X
"How happy could I be", fr. The beggar's opera. 6398-5
Iolaus restor'd to youth. 6972-X
The jackal, leopard, and other beasts. 6972-X
A journey to Exeter. 6398-5
The jugglers. 6972-X
The lady and the wasp. 6972-X
The lady's lamentation. 6024-2,6733-6,6092-7
"Life is a jest, and all things show it". 6289-X

Lines on a lap dog, sels. 6501-5
The lion and the cub. 6133-8,6239-3,6459-0,6424-8
'Love in her eyes sits playing'. 6208-3
The lyon, the fox, and the geese. 6972-X
The lyon, the tyger, and the traveller. 6972-X
Macheath and Polly. 6315-2
The mad-dog. 6972-X
The man and the flea. 6972-X
The man, the cat, the dog, and the fly. 6972-X
The man-mountain's answer to the lilliputian verses. 6972-X
Manuscript draft of part of the welcome to pope. 6972-X
The mastiff. 6972-X
The miser and plutus. 6972-X
A mohocks. A tragi-comical farce. 6972-X
Molly mog, or The fair maid of the inn. 6157-5,6152-4, 6633-X
Molly mog: or, the fair maid of the inn. 6972-X
Monday; or, the squabble. 6972-X
Monday; or, the squabble. 6191-5
The monkey who had seen the world. 6972-X
The mother, the nurse, and the fairy, sels. 6365-9
The mother, the nurse, and the fairy. 6972-X
A motto for the opera of mutius scaevola. 6972-X
Mr. Pope's welcome from Greece. 6932-0
Mr. Pope's welcome from Greece, sels. 6483-3
'My dear Belladine' 6972-X
My own epitaph. 6195-0
Nelly. 6972-X
A new song of new similes. 6787-5
A new song of new similies. 6972-X
A new song. 6089-7
Newgate's garland: being a new ballad. 6972-X
O, ruddier than the cherry. 6192-3
Of walking the streets by night. 6733-6
The old hen and the cock. 6972-X
The old woman and her cats. 6972-X
On a lap-dog. 6604-6,6278-4,6396-9,6660-7
On a miscellany of poems to Bernard Lintott. 6152-4
Ovid's metamorphoses, sels. 6972-X
The owl and the farmer. 6972-X
owl, the swan, the cock, the spider, the ass, and... 6972-X
The pack-horse and the carrier. 6972-X
The painter who pleased nobody and everybody. 6473-6, 6600-3,6604-6,6660-7
Pan and fortune. 6972-X
A panegyrical to Mr. Thomas Snow. 6972-X
Panthea. 6972-X
The peacock, the turkey and the goose. 6473-6
The peacock, the turkey, and the goose. 6473-6
The persian, the sun and the cloud. 6972-X
The Persian, the sun, and the cloud. 6543-0
The philospher and the pheasant. 6972-X
"Phyllida, that loved to dream" 6874-X
The pin and the needle. 6972-X
Plutus, cupid and time. 6972-X
'The poems from Gay's chair' 6972-X
The poet and the rose. 6972-X
Polly: an opera. 6972-X
Presentation inscription to Mr. Tommy Potter. 6972-X
Prologue. 6972-X
The prophecy of Themis. 6972-X
Pythagoras and the countryman. 6972-X
The Quidnunckis. 6200-8
The quidnunkies. 6186-9,6200-8
The ratcatcher and cats. 6120-6,6511-2
The ravens, the sexton, and the earth-worm, sels. 6378-0
A receipt for stewing veal. 6972-X
The rehearsal at Goatham. 6972-X
Rural sports. 6972-X
Rural sports. A Georgic inscribed to Mr. Pope. 6972-X
Saturday; or, the flights. 6972-X
The scold and the parrot. 6972-X
The setting-dog and the partridge. 6972-X
The shepherd and the philosopher. 6972-X
The shepherd's dog and the wolf. 6972-X
The shepherd's week, sels. 6024-2,6122-2,6195-0,6152-4
The shepherd's week. 6972-X

The sick man and the angel. 6996-7,6972-X
'Sleep, O sleep'. 6187-7,6208-3
Song ("At setting"). 6240-7
Song ("Can love"). 6315-2
Song ("O ruddier"). 6024-2,6488-4
Song ("Think of dress in ev'ry light"). 6932-0
Song ("Youth's the season"). 6024-2
Song, fr. Polly. 6958-4
The spaniel and the chameleon. 6972-X
The spell. 6254-7,6613-5
The spell. 6820-0
The squire and his cur. 6972-X
The story of Achelous and Hercules. 6972-X
The story of Arachne. 6972-X
The story of Chephisa. 6972-X
The story of Fiordispina. 6972-X
The story of Zerbin and Isabella. 6972-X
Sweet William's farewell to black-eyed Susan. 6219-9, 6024-2,6186-9,6271-7,6152-4,6195-0,6150
Tales. An answer to the Sompner's prologue to Chaucer. 6972-X
The tame stag. 6972-X
The tea-table. 6972-X
A thought on eternity. 6972-X
Three hours after marriage. 6972-X
Thursday, fr. The shepherd's week. 6024-2,6152-4,6646-1
Thursday; or the spell. 6972-X
Thursday; or, the spell. 6191-5
To a lady on her passion for old china. 6315-2
To a lady on her passion for old china. 6972-X
To a young lady, with some lampreys. 6972-X
To Bernard Lintott. 6972-X
To my ingenious and worthy friend W-L- 6972-X
To the learned ingenious author of Licentia poetica... 6972-X
To the most honourable the Earl of Oxford... 6972-X
The toilette. 6152-4
The transformation of Galanthis. 6972-X
transformation of Lychas into a rock. 6972-X
Translations from Ariosto. 6972-X
Trivia 001 6972-X
Trivia, sels. 6152-4,6195-0
Trivia. Book 001 6972-X
Trivia. Book 002 6972-X
Trivia. Book 003 6972-X
Trivia; or, the art of walking the streets of London. 6972-X
A true story of an apparition. 6972-X
Tuesday, fr. The shepherd's week. 6024-2
Tuesday; or, the ditty. 6972-X
The turkey and the ant. 6972-X
'Twas when the seas were roaring. 6219-9
The two monkeys. 6972-X
The two owls and the sparrow. 6972-X
The two roses. 6383-7
The universal apparition. 6972-X
"Virgins are like...", fr. The beggar's opera. 6733-6
The vultur, the sparrow, and other birds. 6972-X
A warning. 6105-2,6290-3
Wednesday; or the dumps. 6972-X
"Were I laid on Greenland's coast", fr. beggar's opera. 6733-6
The what d'ye call it: a tragi-comi-pastoral farce. 6972-X
The wife of Bath. 6972-X
The wild boar and the ram. 6972-X
Wine. 6278-4
Work for a cooper. 6972-X
Gay, Mrs. Charles
Hush-a-by twentieth century baby. 6711-5
Gay, William
Australia infelix. 6784-0
Australia, 1894. 6784-0
Australian federation. 6784-0
Communion hymn. 6144-3
The crazy world. 6784-0
A sonnet of battle. 6784-0
To M. 6784-0
"Gay, gay, gay, gay". Remember the day of judgment. Unknown. 6881-2

Gayheart, a story of defeat. Dana Burnet. 6029-3
Gayley, Charles Mill
El Dorado: a song. 6241-5
Gaylord, Willis
Lines written in an album. 6385-3
Gayoso girls are golden. Walter McClellan. 6037-4
"Gaze not on swans in whose soft breast." Henry Noel. 6317-9
"Gaze not on Youth; let age containe" Unknown. 6380-2
"Gaze not on swans, in whose soft breast". Beauty extoll'd. Unknown. 6689-5
"Gaze not on thy beauties pride". Good counsell to a young maid. Thomas Carew. 6933-9
Gaze of death. Otakar Brezina. 6886-3
"Gaze upon the lovely, green". Neysa McMein. 6850-2
Gazelle. Ibn al-Qabila. 6362-4
Gazelle and swan. Unknown. 6689-5
Gazelles and unicorn, fr. The long road. John Gray. 6125-7
"Gazing at the barracks" Taisanboku Mori. 6981-9
Gazzoletti, Antonio
Christopher Columbus. Adam Rondel (tr.). 6697-6
Geach, E.F.A.
Romance. 6421-3
Geada, Rita
"Give me back my world" Donald D. Walsh (tr.). 7036-1
On the witches' sabbath. Donald D. Walsh (tr.). 7036-1
So that they will burn. Donald D. Walsh (tr.). 7036-1
Gearhart, Edna
My cat and I. 6120-6
Geary, Eugene
Nathan Hale. 6744-1,6167-2
Gebir. Walter Savage Landor. 6208-3,6110-9
Geddes, Alexander
Alexander. 6929-0
Lewie Gordon. 6180-X,6086-2
Satire. 6022-6
Gee I like to think of dead. Edward Estlin Cummings. 6751-4
'Gee swee Zamericane'. Eugene Field. 6949-5
Gee-up dar, mules. Edwin Ford Piper. 6033-1,6736-0
"'Gee...haw'...the furrow's deep". Oxen. Mary Cummings Eudy. 6850-2,6979-7
Geehale, an Indian lament. Unknown. 6752-2
Geese. Oliver Herford. 6300-4
The geese of Athabasca. William Ellery Leonard. 6887-1
Gehazi. Rudyard Kipling. 6427-2
Geibel, Emanuel
Der mai ist gekommen. 6252-0
A Rhine legend. William W. Caldwell (tr.). 6484-1
To the silent one. 6226-1
Geijer, Erik Gustaf
The charcoal-burner's son. Charles Wharton Stork (tr.). 6045-5
A march. Charles Wharton Stork (tr.). 6045-5
Mignonette. Charles Wharton Stork (tr.). 6045-5
Music. Charles Wharton Stork (tr.). 6045-5
Geisler, Mary Hibbs
U.P. cafe. 6936-3
Geisslova, Irma
Song ("Lark, in the glow of eve"). Paul Selver (tr.). 6763-8
Geist's grave. Matthew Arnold. 6230-X,6604-6,6656-9,6660-7
Gelber, Julius
Steam shovel. 6850-2
Gelder, Francis
A ballad of 1941. 6475-2
Gelezumas, Clement
Just a mannish custom. 6799-9
Gellerstedt, Albert Teodor
Foreground and background. Charles Wharton Stork (tr.). 6045-5
Isolation. Charles Wharton Stork (tr.). 6045-5
My belief. Charles Wharton Stork (tr.). 6045-5
There is a laddie. Charles Wharton Stork (tr.). 6045-5
Gellert, Christian Furchtegott
Jesus lives, and so shall I. 6065-X
The widow. Charles Timothy Brooks (tr.). 6279-2
The widow. Henry Wadsworth Longfellow (tr.). 6916-9
Gellert, Leon
The cross. 6784-0

House-mates. 6349-7
The husband. 6784-0
In the trench. 6349-7
These men. 6349-7
Through a porthole. 6784-0
Gellert, Minna
    Flesh of the furies. 6979-7
    Translation from a lost language. 6979-7
Gelsted, Otto
    A drive. Charles Wharton Stork (tr.). 6555-4
    The ninth of April. Charles Wharton Stork (tr.). 6555-4
The gem and the flower, fr. Of the characters of men. Alexander Pope. 6932-0
"A gem in nature's genial bosom placed". The lake. Deborah Kleinert. 6847-2
A gem in tribute. Unknown. 6889-8
"Gem of all isthmuses and isles that lie". Sirmio. Caius Catallus. 7039-6
Gemignano, Folgore da San
    April, fr. Sonnets of the months. Dante Gabriel Rossetti (tr.). 6325-X
    Conclusion, fr. Sonnets of the months. Dante Gabriel Rossetti (tr.). 6325-X
    December, fr. Sonnets of the months. Dante Gabriel Rossetti (tr.). 6325-X
    Dedication, fr. Sonnets of the months. Dante Gabriel Rossetti (tr.). 6325-X
    January, fr. Sonnets of the months. Dante Gabriel Rossetti (tr.). 6325-X
    May, fr. Sonnets of the months. Dante Gabriel Rossetti (tr.). 6325-X
    October, fr. Sonnets of the months. Dante Gabriel Rossetti (tr.). 6325-X
    Sonnets of the months, sels. Dante Gabriel Rossetti (tr.). 6325-X
Gemini and virgo. Charles Stuart Calverley. 6722-0,6233-4
The gemless ring. Herbert Trench. 6877-4
"Gemmed with white daisies was the...world". To Tony (aged 3). Marjorie Wilson. 7027-2
Gems. Ethel Brodt Wilson. 6789-1
Gems of gold. Nora Perry. 6523-6
Gems on tendrils. Lucy Stout. 6270-9
"The gen'ral!one of those brave old commanders". The old general. Sir Charles Hanbury Williams. 6932-0
"Gene and James, Robert and Ray". Games. Eleanor Noyes Johnson. 6764-6
Genealogical reflection. Ogden Nash. 6026-9
Genee, Edythe Hope
    Haunted house. 6750-6
Geneology. Bob Kaufman. 6901-0
"The general 'eard the firin' on the flank". Stellenbosh. Rudyard Kipling. 6810-3
General Albert Sidney Johnston. Mary Jervey. 6113-3
The General Armstrong. Unknown. 6946-0
A general communion. Alice Meynell. 6172-9,6292-X
The general consent of all. Sir John Davies. 6584-8
General Dabney H. Maury. Rosewell Page. 6074-9
The general dance. Unknown. 6959-2
General Grant. James Russell Lowell. 6552-X
General Howe's letter. Unknown. 6946-0
General Ira Allen: founder of the state... Daniel L. Cady. 6989-4
General James B. Steedman at Chickamauga. Benjamin Franklin Taylor. 6815-4
General John. Sir William Schwenck Gilbert. 6902-9
General Joseph Reed... Edward C. Jones. 6402-7
General Joubert. Rudyard Kipling. 6810-3
General Lesly's march to Longmarston moor. Unknown. 6328-4
General Quiroga rides to death in a carriage. Jorge Luis Borges. 6642-9
General Quiroga rides to death in a crriage. Jorge Luis Borges. 6642-9
"The general has only e ghty men, and the...". Theme for a tapestry. Julio Cortazar. 6758-1
The general song of humanity. Lawrence Ferlinghetti. 6792-1, 6998-3
General summary. Rudyard Kipling. 6996-7
General William Booth enters into heaven. Vachel Lindsay. 6076-5,6102-8,6396-9,6464-7,6628-3,6730 ,6153-2,6209-1,6288-1,6300-4,6354-3,6431 ,6723-9,6399-3,6337-3, 6531-7,6077-3,6556-2,6732
General Xeres and the battle of Salamis, sels. Unknown. 6983-5
The general. Siegfried Sassoon. 6427-2,6733-6
Generation unto generation. Elisabeth Kuskulis. 6836-7
The generation. George M. Brady. 6930-4
"The generations of the virgin are tattoed...". Poem of any virgin. Jorge de Lima. 6759-X
Generosity. Steingrimur Thorsteinsson. 6854-5
Generosity, fr. Epigrams. Steingrimur Thorsteinsson. 6283-0
A generous creed. Elizabeth Stuart Phelps. 6730-1
"The generous sons of Erin, in manly virtue..". In praise of Grattan. Edward Lysaght. 7009-4
Genesis. Ronald Bottrall. 6150-8
Genesis. Ray Mathew. 6384-5
Genesis 024 Arthur Hugh Clough. 6848-0
Genesis 1:2. Charles W. Denison. 6755-7
The genesis of butterflies. Victor Hugo. 6771-9,7039-6
Genesis VI. Bible. 6732-8
Genesis, sels. Bible. 6282-2,6193-1
Genesis, sels. Caedmon. 6489-2
Genesis, sels. Delmore Schwartz. 6391-8
The genesis. Bernard Finney. 6898-7
Genevieve. Samuel Taylor Coleridge. 6302-0,6385-3,6543-0, 6102-8,6438-8,6219-9,6600-3
Genevieve, Sister Mary
    The divine call. 6285-7
Genevra. Emma Sophie Stilwell. 6140-0
The genial grimalkin. J.G. Francis. 6786-7
Genius. Alice Cary. 6865-0;6969-X
Genius. Elmer Ruan Coates. 6920-7
Genius. Felicia Dorothea Hemans. 6973-8
Genius. Richard Hengist Horne. 6656-9
Genius. Edward Lucas White. 6730-1
"Genius and poetry should still advance". Sonnet 010 ("Genius"). Thomas Gordon Hake. 7014-1
Genius in beauty. Dante Gabriel Rossetti. 6110-9,6371-3, 6430-2
Genius in beauty, fr. The house of life. Dante Gabriel Rossetti. 6828-6
Genius in beauty, fr. The house of life. Dante Gabriel Rossetti. 6508-2
Genius loci. Margaret L. Woods. 6437-X
"Genius of Albion, hear". Ode for the king's birthday, 1797, sels. Henry James Pye. 6867-7
The genius of Byron. Robert Pollok. 6543-0
"Genius of ancient Greece! whose faithful eyes". Invocation to the genius of Greece. Mark Akenside. 6932-0
"Genius of Raphael! if thy wings". A Jewish family. William Wordsworth. 6848-0
The genius of death. George Croly. 6302-0;6385-3
The genius of Greece. Walter Savage Landor. 6828-6
"The genius of th' Augustan age". On the author of Letters on literature. William Cowper. 6814-6
The genius of the wood. John Milton. 6935-5
Genius singing to love. Felicia Dorothea Hemans. 6973-8
Genius slumbering. James Gates Percival. 6752-2
Genius to her poet. Maude Barrows Dutton. 6118-4
Genius waking. James Gates Percival. 6752-2
A genius. James Noel Johnson. 6675-5
Genoa. Aubrey Thomas De Vere. 6631-3
Genoa. Frederick William Faber. 6046-3
Genoa ("Gently, as roses die, the day declines"). William Hamilton Gibson. 6624-0,6631-3
Genoa mia! Pastorini. 6973-8
Genseric. Owen (Edward Bulwer-Lytton, Earl Lytton) Meredith. 6114-1
Gentian. Kate Louise Brown. 6373-X
"Gentian blue as noon-lit sea". Coronal: a legend of the Annuciation. Ruth Forbes Sherry. 6979-7
"Gentian, I have found you out". The child and the gentian. Mary Frances Butts. 6965-7
The gentian. Emily Dickinson. 6253-9
Gentians in October. Martha H. Hollinshead. 6799-9
Gentility. Geoffrey Chaucer. 6438-8
Gentle Alice Brown. Sir William Schwenck Gilbert. 6089-7
Gentle Alice Brown. Sir William Schwenck Gilbert. 6902-9
Gentle Alice Brown. Sir William Schwenck Gilbert. 6911-8

"Gentle and generous, brave-hearted, kind". The comfort of the trees. Richard Watson Gilder. 6946-0,6820-0
"Gentle and lovely form". Woman on the field of battle. Felicia Dorothea Hemans. 6973-8
"Gentle and tender, sweet and true". She is. Robert Loveman. 6941-X
The gentle check. Joseph Beaumont. 6563-5
The gentle child. Unknown. 6684-4
A gentle echo on woman. Jonathan Swift. 6089-7,606-9
Gentle fatherland. Ramon Lopez Velarde. 6642-9
Gentle herdsman, tell to me. William Alexander Percy. 6134-6
Gentle Hugh Herries. Allan Cunningham. 6980-0
"Gentle Jesus, meek and mild". Charles Wesley. 6931-2
"A gentle knight was pricking on the plaine". Canto 001, fr. The faerie queene. Edmund Spenser. 6122-2
"Gentle Mary of the dairy". Gentle Mary. James Abraham Martling. 6952-5
Gentle love, this hour befriend me. Aaron Hill. 6328-4
Gentle Mary. James Abraham Martling. 6952-5
"Gentle moon that mov'st so stilly". To the moon. Unknown. 6952-5
"The gentle Mrs. Decimal". The friction of the fractions. Jean Graham. 6797-2
Gentle nymphs, be not refusing. William Browne. 6182-6
"The gentle presence that we knew". Tessie. John E. Barrett. 6840-5
A gentle reminder. Alice Wellington Rollins. 6147-8
Gentle river, gentle river. Unknown (Spanish) 7039-6
The gentle shepherd, sels. Allan Ramsay. 6239-3,6195-0
"The gentle touch" Barbara Reed Raschilla. 6857-X
The gentle traveller. Henry Van Dyke. 6961-4
Gentle words. Unknown. 6530-9
"Gentle ye fall, ye summer leaves". Magus Muir. William Edmonstoune Aytoun. 6948-7
Gentleman froggie. Unknown. 6061-7
"The gentleman got up betimes to shoot". A country house party. George Gordon, 6th Baron Byron. 6996-7
Gentleman in oils. Harold Vinal. 6218-0
Gentleman Jim. Daniel O'Connell. 6273-3
A gentleman living alone. Pablo (Neftali Ricardo Reyes Basualto) Neruda. 6803-0
A gentleman of fifty soliloquizes. Don Marquis. 6300-4
A gentleman of Somerset. W.G. Hole. 6793-X
A gentleman of the old school. Austin Dobson. 6423-X,6508-2,6660-7
A gentleman of the old school. Unknown. 6385-3
'A gentleman'.. Robert Barnabas Brough. 7009-4
A gentleman's meeting. Unknown. 6826-X
"The gentleman, when once we win". Gentlemen, be abolished! Irwin Edman. 6761-1
A gentleman.. William Shakespeare. 6294-6
A gentleman. Unknown. 6413-2
"Gentlemen adventurers with their past behind". Gentlemen adventures. Berton Bradley. 7007-8
The gentlemen of Oxford. Norah M. Holland. 6846-4
Gentlemen of the high command, fr. Heil, heilige nacht. Ogden Nash. 6337-3
Gentlemen, be abolished! Irwin Edman. 6761-1
Gentlemen-rankers. Rudyard Kipling, 6810-3
A gentlemen. Unknown. 7008-6
Gentleness, virtue, wisdom..", Percy Bysshe Shelley. 6793-X
"Gentleness, virtue, wisdom...", fr. Prometheus.. Percy Bysshe Shelley. 6879-0
"The gentler bord the maiden." Alfred Lord Tennyson. 6623-2
The gentlest lady. Dorothy Parker. 6282-2
"Gentlie, gently prethee tyme." Unknown. 6563-5
"Gently death came to him and bent". Close up the ranks! Edward Sims Van Zile. 6995-9,6449-3
"Gently dip, but not too deep". George Peele. 6181-8;6208-3
Gently he draweth. Unknown. 6065-X
"Gently it lifts--/And a world of surprise". Life's curtain. Emma Magin Bissell. 6799-9
"Gently o gently wthout fright." Unknown. 6563-5
"Gently supported by the ready aid". On ---. Richard Monckton Milnes; 1st Baron Houghton. 6980-0
"Gently!- gently!- down!- down!". Chorus of spirits.

George Darley. 6930-4
"Gently, most gently, on thy victim's head". To consumption. Henry Kirke White. 6980-0
Geo-politics. Alvaro Cardona-Hine. 6966-5
Geoffrey Barron. Katharine (Hinkson) Tynan. 6518-X
Geoffrey Keating to his letter. Geoffrey Keating. 6090-0
Geoffrey Keating to his letter. Unknown. 6090-0
Geoghegan, Arthur Gerald
    After Aughrim. 6090-0,6174-5,6088-9
    The battle of Ardnocher. 6518-X
    The mountain fern. 6174-5
Geographers. Alexander Barclay. 6022-6
A geographic question. Unknown. 6274-1
A geographical love song. Unknown. 6724-7
The geography demon. Unknown. 6925-8
The geography horse. W. Kersley Holmes. 6804-9
Geography of this time. Archibald MacLeish. 6391-8
Geography, sels. Edward Verrall Lucas. 6018-8
A geological madrigal. Francis Bret Harte. 6802-2
A geologist's epitaph. Jane W. Stedman. 6722-0
Geometry discredited. Elinor Lennen. 6316-0
The geometry of motion-crossing the Golden Gate bridge. Kaye McDonough. 6792-1
Geordie. Unknown. 6185-0
Geordie to his tobacco-pipe. George S. Phillips. 6453-1
The George Aloe and the sweepstake. Unknown. 6185-0
"George Gissing on a lovely day". Gissing's sixpenny miracle. Edgar A. Guest. 6748-4
George and the chimney-sweep. Ann and Jane Taylor. 6105-2
George and the chimney-sweeper. Adelaide O'Keefe. 6772-7
George Barnwell. James Smith. 6802-2
George be quiet! Evelyne Love Cooper. 6850-2
George Collins. Unknown. 6826-X
George Crabbe. Edwin Arlington Robinson. 6333-0,6375-6
George Eliot. John E. Barrett. 6840-5
George Gray, fr. Spoon river anthology. Edgar Lee Masters. 6289-X
George Herbert. Thomas S. Jones Jr. 6483-3
George II. Lawrence Eusden. 6867-7
George III. William Wordsworth. 6543-0
George Jones. Unknown. 6057-9
George Meredith. Thomas Hardy. 6828-6
George Meredith. Thomas Hardy. 6199-0
George Nidiver. E. H. 6062-5,6271-7,6502-3,6438-8,6263-6
George Odger. Sir Edmund Gosse. 6793-X
George Reilly. Unknown. 6058-7
"George lives in an apartment and". Radiator lions. Dorothy Aldis. 6891-X
"George Trustrum, ere the day be done". To G. Trustrum. Thomas Edward Brown. 6809-X
"George William Curtis met a lad". A patriot's triumph. Eugene Field. 6949-5
George the Third's soliloquy. Philip Freneau. 6753-0
George Villiers, Duke of Buckingham, fr. Absalom... John Dryden. 6934-7
George Washington. John Hall Ingham. 6946-0
George Washington. Unknown. 6337-3,6690-9,6708-5,6745-X, 6449-3,6690-9,6712-3
George Washington. Phillis Wheatley. 6712-3
George Washington ("By broad Potomac's silent shore.") Unknown. 6712-3
George Washington ("How did George Washington look...") Unknown. 6158-3
George Washington ("I saw him standing in the crowd.") Unknown. 6712-3
George Washington ("Oh, sweet Virginia hills!"). Francesca Falk Miller. 6158-3,6449-3
George Washington ("Only a baby, fair and small"). Unknown. 6158-3
George Washington was lucky! Unknown. 6158-3
George's cherry-tree. Amanda Waldron. 6712-3
George, Legare
    Song for a lost girl. 6761-1
George, Marguerite
    Brief biography. 6218-0
    Here I lie. 6218-0
    Paneled in pine. 6218-0
George, Roy
    The spirit of transportation. 6037-4
George, Stefan

After harvest, fr. The year of the soul. 6643-7
"Come to the park." Babette Deutsch (tr.). 6160-5
"Dark burned the sunset." Babette Deutsch (tr.). 6160-5
"From nether dark." Babette Deutsch (tr.). 6160-5
From out of the glow. Babette Deutsch (tr.). 6160-5
The lord of the isle. Ludwig Lewisohn (tr.). 7039-6
mistaking, The. Babette Deutsch (tr.). 6160-5
The mistaking. Babette Deutsch (tr.). 6160-5
Prelude. C.F. MacIntyre (tr.). 6665-8
Rapture. Ludwig Lewisohn (tr.). 7039-6
Stanzas concerning love. Ludwig Lewisohn (tr.). 7039-6
"The Star of the Covenant", sels. 6643-7
To a young leader of the first world war. E.B. Ashton (tr.). 6068-4,6665-8
"We wander up and down." Babette Deutsch (tr.). 6160-5
"When my hot lips." Babette Deutsch (tr.). 6160-5
The year of the soul, sels. 6643-7
"You know not who I am." Babette Deutsch (tr.). 6160-5
"George, son of lairds that awn'd the laund". Hobnobbing on the Ochils. James Logie ("Hugh Haliburton") Robertson. 6819-7
George-Murray, Richard
"If an apple seed" 7003-5
Mark's ring. 7003-5
Nightmare no. 37 7003-5
The Georges. Walter Savage Landor. 6125-7
Georgetown. G.A. Taylor. 6906-1
"Georgey Porgey, pudding and pie". Unknown. 6904-5
Georgia. Robert Loveman. 6465-5
Georgia dusk. Jean Toomer. 6880-4
A Georgia volunteer. Mary Ashley Townsend. 6074-9,6411-6, 6113-3,6340-3,6016-2
Georgia waters. Thomas Holley Chivers. 7017-5
Georgic IV, sels. Vergil. 6649-6
"Georgie never robbed a public highway". Unknown. 6059-5
"Georgie Porgie, pudding and pie". Mother Goose. 6363-2
Georgina Trevellyn to Louisa, fr. Amours de voyage. Arthur Hugh Clough. 6123-0
Georgns, Esther Valck
Time. 6799-9
Geraldine and I. Frederick Locker-Lampson. 6661-5
The Geraldine's daughter. Unknown. 6174-5
The Geraldine's daughter. Egan O'Rahilly. 6930-4
The Geraldines. Thomas Osborne Davis. 6858-8
Geraldy, Paul
Jealousy. 6351-9
A maid comes by. 6351-9
Meditation. 6351-9,6026-9
The mother. 6351-9
Romance. 6351-9
Stereoscope. 6351-9
Time. 6351-9
Geranium in the window. Elinor Gibney Kibbee. 6764-6
Geraniums. Wilfred Wilson Gibson. 6234-2,6023-4,6508-2
Gerard de Nerval. Andrew Lang. 6771-9
Gerhardt & J.W.Alexander, Paul (tr.)
O sacred head, now wounded. Arnulf Loewen (atr), 6337-3
Gerhardt, Paul
All my heart this night rejoices. Catherine Winkworth (tr.). 6337-3
Courage. John Wesley (tr.). 6730-1
The dying saviour. 6014-5,6302-0,6385-3
"O sacred head! now wounded". 6065-X
Gerlach, L.F.
Algebra of divorce. 6515-5
Death of a teacher. 6515-5
The misogynist. 6515-5
Seasonal moraine. 6515-5
Too early death. 6515-5
Germain, Andre
Pale song. 6351-9
To wounded France. 6351-9
The traveler. 6351-9
The German band. Earl Derr Biggers. 6274-1
The German fatherland. Ernst Moritz Arndt. 6484-1
German Jewess prays. Fania Kruger. 6042-0
German mother. Kaye Starbird. 6761-1
"The German people reared them". Shipbuilders. Arthur Stanwood Pier. 6762-X
German prisoners. Joseph Johnston Lee. 6337-3,6542-2,7031-0
"German retreat from Arras". War pictures. Ruth Lambert Jones. 6762-X
The German tower-keeper, fr. Jonas Fisher. James Carnegie; Earl of Southesk. 6819-7
The German watchman's song. Unknown. 6014-5
The German's fatherland. Unknown. 6240-7
German, Delia R.
The wood of Chancellorsville. 6402-7,6678-X,6385-3
The German-French campaign. Christina Georgina Rossetti. 6123-0
Germanakos, N.C. (tr.)
Romiosini, sel. Yannis Ritsos, 6803-0
"The Germans in Greek". On the Greek scholar Gottfried Hermann. Richard Porson. 6874-X
Germany. Josephine Miles. 6396-9
Germany, fr. Geography. Edward Verrall Lucas. 6018-8
Germs of greatness. Eliza Cook. 6923-1
Gernutus, the Jew of Venice. Unknown. 6079-X
Gerok, ?
The horses of Gravelotte. Elizabeth Craigmyle (tr.). 6842-1
Geron and Histor. Sir Philip Sidney. 6584-8
Geronimo. Ernest McGaffey. 6946-0
"Geronimo was a great indian chief who died...". Geronimo: old man lives on. Ronald James Dessus. 6870-7
Gerontion. Thomas Stearns Eliot. 6208-3,6315-2,6348-9,6375-6,6150-8
Gerry's rocks. Unknown. 6057-9
Gerry, C.F.
The bluebird ("'Tis early spring...") 6049-8
Gerry, Marie d'Autremont
The emerald hill. 6342-X
Gershwin, Ira
The babbitt and the bromide. 6026-9
"Gertrude - there's a good old scout!". Askew, we ask you. Melville Cane. 6979-7
"Gertrude and Gulielma, sister-twins". Frederick Goddard Tuckerman. 6333-0
The Gertrude Hoffman girls. Paul Eluard. 6351-9
Gertrude of Wyoming
"Clasp me a little longer, on the brink". 6973-8
Gertrude of Wyoming, sels. Thomas Campbell. 6980-0
Gertrude's prayer. Rudyard Kipling. 6208-3
Gertrude; or, fidelity till death, fr. Records of woman. Felicia Dorothea Hemans. 6973-8
Gervais. Margaret Adelaide Wilson. 7027-2
Gervais, Caroline H.
'In his blanket on the ground'. 6074-9
Gesnard, J.W.
An apostrophe to the oyster. 6919-3
Gesner
Morning song. Felicia Dorothea Hemans (tr.). 6973-8
Gessler, Clifford
Hawaiian blues. 6761-1
Siesta hour. 6979-7
Gessler, Clifford Franklin
Dark bamboos. 6039-0
Prayer ("O thou"). 6035-8
Star-dancers. 6038-2
Gessner, George
Song of praise. James Abraham Martling (tr.). 6952-5
Gessner, Robert
Drought. 6761-1
A gest of Robyn Hode. Unknown. 6185-0
The gest of Robyn Hode. Unknown. 6102-8
Gestaltwandel. Jurgen Eggebrecht. 6253-9
Gesture. Elisabeth Clarke. 6818-9
Gesture. Winifred Welles. 6102-8,6337-3,6076-5,6034-X
"Get all the good there is today". Optimism. Unknown. 6109-5
Get ivy and holly. Thomas Tusser. 6747-6
"Get ivy and hull, woman, deck up thine house". Christmas. Thomas Tusser. 6756-5
"Get leave to work". Elizabeth Barrett Browning. 6238-5
'Get out of my shop!' Jennie E. Munson. 6685-2
Get somebody else. Paul Laurence Dunbar. 6721-2
"Get thee behind me. Even as, heavy-curled". 'Retro me, sathana!' Dante Gabriel Rossetti. 6828-6,6110-9
"Get thee hence from my way". Thou and I. Petr Bezruc.

6763-8
"Get thee to the mountains". Birthing: 2000 Pancho Aguila. 6870-7
Get there if you can and see the land... Wystan Hugh Auden. 6375-6
"Get to understand the lad". Just a boy. Edgar A. Guest. 7033-7
Get up and bar the door. Unknown. 6056-0,6180-X,6185-5, 6228-8,6499-X,6558 ,6067-6,6491-4
Get up and go on. Strickland Gillilan. 6583-X
"Get up, get up for shame! The blooming morn". May-day. Robert Herrick. 6935-5
"Get up, get p for ushame! the blooming mourn". Going a-maying. Robert Herrick. 6820-0
"Get up, little sister, the morning is bright". Song of early rising. Lady Flora Hastings. 6772-7
"Get u , my liptle handmaid". The best judgment. Alice Cary. 6969-X
"'Get ye up from the wrath of God's". The cities of the plain. John Greenleaf Whittier. 6848-0
"Get you gone, you will undo me". Song ("Get you gone"). Sir Charles Sedley. 6544-9
"Get yourself elected". Comrade laughter. Paul Potts. 6895-2
Gethsemane. Matilda Barbara Betham-Edwards. 6065-X
Gethsemane. Kurt Heynicke. 6160-5
Gethsemane. Rudyard Kipling. 6210-5
Gethsemane. Edmund Leamy. 6172-9,6461-2,6292-X
Gethsemane. James Montgomery. 6219-9
Gethsemane. Unknown (Japanese) 6027-7
Gethsemane. William Walsh. 6096 X
Gethsemane. William White. 6868-5
Gethsemane. Ella Wheeler Wilcox. 6337-3,6240-7
Gethsemane's gift. Katherine Bregy. 6337-3
Gettin' born. Anthony Euwer. 6722-0
Gettin' on. Eugene Field. 6949-5
Gettin' ready to graduate. Unknown. 6718-2
Getting acquainted. Sydney Dayre. 6249-0
Getting back to work (in solitary confinement) Leon Baker. 6870-7
Getting even. Robert J. Burdette. 6588-0
Getting fired or 'Not being retained' Sandra Gilbert. 6792-1
Getting gray. William Green Brownson. 6482-5
Getting her a valentine. Edgar A. Guest. 6862-6
"Getting his pleasures, like his supper, cheap". MacCracken. Dante Gabriel Rossetti. 6802-2
Getting information out of pa. Unknown. 6715-8
"Getting off the metro on the way to work". Nelligan. Laurence Hutchman. 6767-0
Getting out. J.J. Maloney. 6870-7
Getting ready for school. Juliet Wilbor Tompkins. 6713-1
Getting ready to go to meeting in Vermont. Daniel L. Cady. 6989-4
Getting rid of the ego. Ken Wainio. 6998-3,6901-0
Getting set. Grantland Rice. 6583-X
Getting to be a man. Samuel Ellsworth Kiser. 6687-9
Getting up. Henry S. Leigh. 6920-7
Getting up. Jane Taylor. 6078-1,6627-5
Getting up the winter wood in Vermont. Daniel L. Cady. 6988-6
Getting well. Walt Mason. 6583-X
Gettysburg. Eugene Field. 6949-5
Gettysburg. James Jeffrey Roche. 6074-9
Gettysburg. Ernest Warburton Shurtleff. 6575-9
Gettysburg. Edmund Clarence Stedman. 6113-3,6016-2
The Gettysburg address. Abraham Lincoln. 6337-3;6503-1
Gettysburg ode. Bayard Taylor. 6976-2
The Gettysburg ode, sels. Bayard Taylor. 6305-5,6524-4
Ghaisties. Robert Garioch. 6379-9
Ghazal of Isa Akhun Zada. Edward Powys Mathers. 6513-9
Ghazal: Japanese paintbrush. Randy Mott. 6966-5
The ghazul, or oriental love-song. William Makepeace Thackeray. 6802-2
The gheber's bloody glen. Thomas Moore. 6414-0
Gheluvelt. Robert Bridges. 6487-6
Ghetto. Yvette Johnson. 7024-8
A ghetto catch. Leland Davis. 6037-4
The ghetto, sels. Lola Ridge. 6300-4
The ghetto. Lola Ridge. 6102-8,6076-5

Ghil, Rene
 The altruist order, sels. 6351-9
 The stars went out. 6351-9
Ghiselin, Brewster
 Waking. 6761-1
Ghoses. James D. Corrothers. 6696-8
Ghost. R.H. Grenville. 6218-0
Ghost. Agnes Miegel. 6643-7
Ghost. J. Corson Miller. 6648-8
Ghost. John V.A. Weaver. 6102-8,6732-8,6076-5
A ghost at noon. Ebenezer Elliott. 6600-3
Ghost fairies. Frank Dempster Sherman. 6311-X
The ghost in the cellarage. John Heath-Stubbs. 6379-9
Ghost night. Lizette Woodworth Reese. 6254-7
"The ghost of a wind came over the hill". Nancibel. Bliss Carman and Richard Hovey. 6890-1
The ghost of an old continental. Fred Emerson Brooks. 6920-7
Ghost of an old love. E. Vivian Prentice. 6721-2
"The ghost of day yet haunts the troubled west". William Falconer. 6997-5
The ghost of Fadon. Joanna Baillie. 6813-8
The ghost of Goshen. Unknown. 6167-2
The ghost of lone rock. Clara M. Howard. 6675-5
The ghost of Patroclus, fr. The Iliad. Homer. 6435-3
The ghost of Shakespeare. Alfred Noyes. 6151-6
The ghost of St. Anthony falls. Ada Clarke Carmichiel. 6342-X
Ghost of the beautiful past. Edmund Blunden. 6655-0
The ghost of the clerk. Archibald Fleming. 6761-1
a ghost out of Stratford. David Morton. 6331-4,6439-6
A ghost speaks on the Styx. John Drinkwater. 6320-9
Ghost stories. Flavia Rosser. 6696-8
Ghost to come. Margaret Widdemer. 6218-0
Ghost town. Thomas Hornsby Ferril. 6490-6
The ghost whose lips were warm. Edith Sitwell. 7000-0
The ghost's confession, fr. Phantasmagoria. Charles Lutwidge ("Lewis Carroll") Dodgson. 6254-7
The ghost, fr. Space of breath. Harold Lewis Cook. 6780-8
The ghost, sels. Charles Churchill. 6024-2
The ghost, sels. Charles Churchill. 6831-6
The ghost, sels. Charles Churchill. 6191-5
The ghost, sels. Charles Churchill. 6831-6
Ghost-town saloon: winter. Joseph Payne Brennan. 6218-0
The ghost. Richard Harris ("Thomas Ingoldsby") Barham. 6278-4
The ghost. Cu Chonnacht O Cleirigh. 6244-X
The ghost. Walter De La Mare. 6250-1,6257-1,6354-3
The ghost. Hermann Hagedorn. 6027-7,6347-0,6648-8
The ghost. Thomas Hood. 6974-6
The ghost. James Stephens. 6070-6
The ghost. Bayard Taylor. 6402-7
The ghost. Sara Teasdale. 6320-9
The ghost. Unknown. 6294-X,6568-6
The ghost. James Wright. 6218-0
Ghostesses. Unknown. 6125-7
Ghosties at the wedding. Eden Phillpotts. 6884-7
"Ghostly and livid, robed with shadow, see!". The hills on their thrones. Robert Buchanan. 6819-7
Ghostly battles. Glenn Ward Dresbach. 6619-4
The ghostly galley. Jessie B. Rittenhouse. 6102-8,6619-4, 6076-5
Ghostly reaper. Harold Vinal. 6218-0
Ghostly tree. Leonie Adams. 6012-9
"Ghostly, etheral, mystical form!". The lady of snows. C.N. Buzzard. 7035-3
Ghostries. H. Cholmondeley Pennell. 6120-6
Ghosts. Robert Bridges. 6487-6,6201-5
Ghosts. Marion Francis Brown. 6039-0
Ghosts. Winifred Adams Burr. 6218-0
Ghosts. Joseph ("Seosamh MacCathmhaoil") Campbell. 6090-0
Ghosts. John C. Frolicher. 6490-6
Ghosts. Charles Lotin Hildreth. 7041-8
Ghosts. Brian Hooker. 6467-1
Ghosts. Elizabeth Jennings. 6339-X
Ghosts. Marguerite Mooers Marshall. 6027-7
Ghosts. Virginia Taylor McCormick. 6585-6
Ghosts. Gertrude Huntington McGiffert. 6838-3
Ghosts. John Nerber. 6017-X
Ghosts. Alfred Noyes. 6151-6

GHOSTS 584

Ghosts. Harold Trowbridge Pulsifer. 6038-2;6347-0
Ghosts. Alastair Reid. 6218-0
Ghosts. Unknown. 6116-8
Ghosts. Marguerite Wilkinson. 6509-0,6161-3
Ghosts. Margaret L. Woods. 6648-8
Ghosts in the barn. Lu B. Cake. 6696-8
Ghosts of Indians. Witter Bynner. 6506-6,6431-0,6421-3, 6653-4,6464-7
The ghosts of Oxford. W. Snow. 7027-2
"Ghosts of dead soldiers in the battle slain". Guns of peace. Dinah Maria Mulock Craik. 7015-9
The ghosts of the buffaloes. Vachel Lindsay. 6490-6;6527-9
Ghosts of the conquest. Albert Edward Clements. 6542-2
Ghosts of the new world. Alfred Noyes. 6151-6;6509-0
The ghosts' moonshine. Thomas Lovell Beddoes. 6317-9,6378-0
The ghosts, fr. The song of Hiawatha. Henry Wadsworth Longfellow. 6254-7,6315-2,6696-8,6566-X
"Ghosts: they conjure". Translations. Wing Tek Lum. 6790-5
The ghosts. Helen Goldbaum. 6640-2
The ghosts. Robert Service. 6159-1
The ghyrlond of the blessed virgin Marie. Ben Jonson. 6282-2
GI. Raymond F. Roseliep. 6218-0
Gianoli, Paul
    Clay. 6860-X
Giant mushrooms. Dan Lemke. 6883-9
The giant pen. Eloise Wade Hackett. 6342-X
The giant puffball. Edmund Blunden. 6210-5
The giant walker. Sir Samuel Ferguson. 6090-0
The giant's ring: Ballylesson, near Belfast. Robinson Jeffers. 6879-0
The giant. Esaias Tegner. 6045-5
Giantess. Charles Baudelaire. 6343-8
Giants. R.C. Trevelyan. 6783-2
The giaour. George Gordon, 6th Baron Byron. 6250-4
Gibberish. Mary Elizabeth Coleridge. 6477-9
Gibbon, Monk
    The bees. 6930-4
    Being but men. 6780-8
    Devil's cauldron. 6257-1
    The discovery. 6930-4
    Dispossessed poet. 6930-4
    French peasants. 6257-1
    From disciple to master. 6072-2
    The house. 6072-2
Gibbon, Perceval
    An answer. 6793-X
    The green things. 6793-X
    Homeward bound. 6793-X
    Jim. 6788-3
    Komani. 6800-6
    Mimosa. 6800-6
    Sea-farers. 6793-X
    The veld. 6800-6
    The veldt. 6591-0,6592-9
    The Voorloopers. 6800-6
Gibbons, Bertha L.
    The holy crib. 6906-1
    The masked knight. 6906-1
    Pearls to wear. 6906-1
    Prayers I saw ascend. 6270-9
    Summer's tapestry. 6906-1
    Sweeping. 6906-1
    Treasure for the master. 6906-1
Gibbons, John Sloan
    Three hundred thousand more. 6121-4
    We are coming, Father Abraham. 6524-4
Gibbons, Orlando
    The silver swan. 6472-8
Gibbons, Stella
    The bell. 6893-6
    The dance. 6893-6
    Love. 6893-6
    Song ("Secretly turns the year"). 6893-6
    The two wishes. 6780-8
    The wakeful swans. 6781-6
    The withered thorn. 6893-6
Gibbons, Thomas
    Thy goodness, Lord, our souls confess. 6219-9

"The gibbous moon was in a wan decline". Approach of morning, fr. Philip Van Artevelde. Henry Taylor. 6980-0
Gibbs, Agnes K.
    Sea-born. 6836-7
Gibbs, Opal Leonore
    Interceding. 6065-X
Gibbs, R.E.
    All in the wind. 6118-4
Gibbs, R.M.
    Night and day. 6116-8
Giblin, Gayle
    Hotel. 6799-9
Gibney, Somerville
    In for it. 6652-6
Gibraltar. Wilfrid Scawen Blunt. 6096-X,6437-X,6484-1,6656-9,6439-6,6022
Gibraltar. Robert Browning. 6331-4
Gibraltar. Richard Chenevix Trench. 6437-X
Gibran, Kahlil
    The fox. 6393-4
    Love. 6979-7
    Night and the madman. 6102-8,6076-5
    On giving, fr. The prophet. 6337-3
    The prophet, sels. 6320-9,6648-0
    Said a blade of grass. 6393-4
    The sermon on the mount. 6143-5,
Gibson, Charles
    God, through his offspring nature, gave me love. 6762-X
Gibson, Douglas
    Air-raid warning. 6475-2
    Insensibility. 6475-2
    The secret dream. 6475-2
    "Surely the dreams". 6475-2
Gibson, Frances W.
    Gowans under her feet. 6918-5
Gibson, James Y.
    Sonnet on the sonnet. 6724-7
Gibson, Lydia
    Autumn song. 6880-4
    Esoeris. 6880-4
    Goats. 6880-4
    A handful of sand. 6880-4
    Jonah. 6880-4
    Paris. 6880-4
    A river in drouth. 6880-4
    The swimmer's song. 6880-4
    Vecchietta. 6880-4
Gibson, Walker
    Advice to travelers. 6388-8
    The game. 6388-8
    Love. 6388-8
Gibson, Wilfred Wilson
    Air-raid, fr. In war time. 6884-7
    All life moving to one measure. 6464-7
    "All night under the moon," fr. For G. 6317-9
    Angus Armstrong, fr. Casualties. 6653-4
    The anniversary. 6071-4
    Bacchanal, fr. In war time. 6884-7
    Back. 6337-3,6464-7,6542-2
    Battle. 7031-0
    Battle. 6897-9
    Battle: hit. 6332-2
    Before action. 6653-4
    Between the lines. 6332-2,6474-4,6542-2
    Black. 6102-8
    The blind rower. 6508-2
    The blind stranger. 6780-8
    Breakfast. 6393-4
    The brothers. 6628-3
    The cakewalk. 6959-2
    Casualties. 6653-4
    A catch for singing. 6266-0
    Color. 6897-9
    The conscript. 6337-3,6250-4,6464-7,6508-2
    Daily bread. 6301-2
    The dancing seal. 6668-2
    Devil's edge, fr. Fires, book III. 6234-2
    Down the road. 6779-4
    The enterprise. 6781-6

An epilogue. 6069-2
The father. 6393-4
The fear, fr. Battle. 6897-9
Fires. 6506-6,6199-0
Fires, sels. 6234-2
Fisherman's luck. 6833-2
Flannan isle. 6258-X,6395-0,6458-2,6437-X
The flute. 6458-2
For G. 6317-9
The fowler. 6102-8
The fowler. 6778-6
Geraniums. 6234-2,6023-4,6508-2
The going. 6234-2,6153-2
Gold. 6897-9
The golden room. 6072-2
The gorse. 6234-2
Gray's inn. 6779-4
Hands. 6653-4
The hare, fr. Fires. 6234-2
Henry Trumbull. 6210-5
Hill-born, fr. Battle. 6897-9
Hit, fr. Battle. 6897-9
Hoops. 6234-2
The housewife, fr. Battle. 6897-9
The ice, fr. Thoroughfares. 6199-0
The ice-cart. 6395-0,6476-0,6668-2
In a restaurant. 6464-7
In course of time. 6488-4
In the ambulance. 6732-8,6102-8,6542-2
In war-time, fr. In war time. 6884-7
Inspiration. 6730-1
John's wife. 6850-2
The joke, fr. Battle. 6897-9
Katherine Veitch. 6162-1
Lament. 6102-8
Lament ("We who are left, how shall we look again"). 6477-9,6542-2
The lark. 6488-4
Leave, fr. In war time. 6884-7
The lonely tree. 6228-8,6509-0,6723-9
Luck. 6258-X
The machine. 6458-2
Marriage. 6337-3
The messages. 6332-2,6393-4,6542-2
Noel Dark, fr. Casualties. 6653-4
Northumberland. 6723-9
Northumbrian duet: Ned Nixon and his Maggie. 6071-4
Oblivion. 6897-9
The old bed. 6393-4
Old man jobling. 6162-1
On Broadway. 6161-3
On Hampstead Heath, fr. Thoroughfares. 6199-0
On the embankment. 6208-2
The operation. 6161-3
The orphans. 6509-0,6161-3,6723-9
Otterburn. 6542-2
The ovens. 6646-1
The paisley shawl. 6653-4
The parrots. 6478-7,6395-0
Philip Dagg, fr. Casualties. 6508-2
The platelayer. 6508-2
Prelude ("As one"). 6289-X
Proem. 6872-3
Prometheus, fr. Thoroughfares. 6199-0
The question. 7029-9
The ragged stone. 6542-2
Ragtime. 6508-2
Ralph Straker, fr. Casualties. 6653-4
Retreat. 6542-2
The return. 6102-8
Roses. 6338-1
Rupert Brooke. 6483-3,6464-7,6508-2,6653-4
Sally Black and Geordie Green. 6778-6
Sight. 6102-8
Sight. 6861-3
Snug in my easy chair. 6228-2,6477-9
Song ("If once."). 6437-X
The stone. 6162-1,6336-5
Stow-on-the-Wold. 6542-2
Sweet as the breath of the whin. 6044-7
Tenants. 6581-3
Thoroughfares, sels. 6199-0
To the memory of Rupert Brooke. 6161-3
Troopship, fr. In war time. 6884-7
The vindictive staircase, or the reward of industry. 6508-2
The voice. 6162-1

Gibson, William Hamilton
Genoa ("Gently, as roses die, the day declines"). 6624-0,6631-3
Naples. 6624-0
Pisa. 6631-3
Virgil's tomb ("We seek, as twilight saddens..."). 6624-0

Giddings, Franklin H.
Ultimate hell. 6474-4

The giddy girl. Elizabeth Turner. 6105-2
The giddy girl. Ella Wheeler Wilcox. 6863-4
"Giddy girls, noisy boys". Unknown. 6363-2
"The giddy sun's kaleidoscope". Myself on the merry-go-round, fr. Marine. Edith Sitwell. 7000-0
"A giddy young fellow of Sparta". Limerick:"A giddy young fellow of Sparta". Unknown. 6811-1
"A giddy young maiden with nimble feet". The giddy girl. Ella Wheeler Wilcox. 6863-4

Gide, Andre
Pomegranate song. 6351-9
Pomegranate song. Joseph T. Shipley (tr.). 6351-9

Gidlow, Elsa
California orchard. 6628-3
Christ's pity. 6628-3
Midnight lake. 6628-3
Only one way. 6880-4
Rhythm. 6042-0
Songs, fr. Steel-flanked stallion. 6628-3
Steel-flanked stallions, sels. 6628-3
Twentieth century songs. 6628-3
Twentieth century songs, sels. 6527-9

"Gie me a soul, O God!". The poet's prayer. O.E. Sanden. 6799-9

Gielow, Martha S.
Mammy's luck charm fer de bride. 6696-8

Giep, Naomi W.
My darling. 6894-4

Gifford, Edwina Cushing
Bird song. 6894-4

Gifford, Fannie Stearns. See Davis, Fannie

Gifford, Humfrey
A prayer ("O mighty God"). 6931-2

Gifford, Humphrey
For soldiers. 6641-0,6182-6
Song ("A woman's face"). 6182-6

Gifford, Richard
Little ye, Sister-Nine, fr. Contemplation. 6934-7
To health, fr. Contemplation. 6934-7

Gifford, Will
Spelling down. 6913-4

Gifford, William
The Della Cruscans. 6932-0

"A gift for the fairest! No indian shawl". The rebel's hyena song. James Abraham Martling. 6952-5
Gift from heaven. Edgar A. Guest. 6869-3
"Gift from the cold and silent past!". The Norsemen. John Greenleaf Whittier. 6946-0
Gift of a mirror to a lady. David Wagoner. 6388-8
The gift of a rose. John Robert Henderson. 6836-7
The gift of a skull. John Skelton. 6022-6
The gift of empty hands. Sarah Morgan Bryan Piatt. 6212-1
The gift of flight. Astra [pseud]. 7014-0
A gift of flowers. Leonard Feeney. 6543-0
The gift of God. Edwin Arlington Robinson. 6348-9,6607-0, 6250-4,6121-4,6161-3
The gift of insight. Nora F. McCormick. 6799-9
The gift of Jesus. William White. 6868-5
The gift of love. Harriet Garret. 6799-9
The gift of rest. W.W. Christman. 6662-3
The gift of the king. Sabine Baring-Gould. 6848-0
The gift of the sea. Rudyard Kipling. 6810-3
The gift of Tritemius. John Greenleaf Whittier. 6478-7, 6639-9

GIFT

The gift of water. Hamlin Garland. 6484-1
A gift of wine. Leo W. Ward. 6761-1
The gift outright. Robert Frost. 6208-3,6666-6
The gift that none could see. Mary E. (Freeman) Wilkins. 6255-5,6672-0
The gift that none could see. Mary E. (Freeman) Wilkins. 6965-7
"The gift to King Amphion". Poem on the power of sound, sels. William Wordsworth. 6980-0
The gift-bearer. Claire Wallace Flynn. 7019-1
A gift.. Emily Henrietta Hickey. 6174-5
The gift.. Louis V. Ledoux. 6556-2
A gift. Berton Braley. 6853-7
A gift. Amy Lowell. 6300-4,6102-8
The gift. Abu Aiyub. 6362-4
The gift. Abul Arab. 6362-4
The gift. Leonie Adams. 6012-9
The gift. Elizabeth Barrett Browning. 6383-7
The gift. Dana Burnet. 6761-1
The gift. Oliver Goldsmith. 6732-8
The gift. Aline Kilmer. 6393-4,6161-3
The gift. Rose O'Neill. 6102-8,6076-5
The gift. Laura Spencer Portor. 6449-3
The gift. George William ("A.E.") Russell. 6301-2
The gift. Unknown. 6943-6
The gift. William Carlos Williams. 6388-8
The gift. Francis Brett Young. 7029-9
"Gifted of heaven! who hast, in days gone by". To Mrs. Siddons. Joanna Baillie. 6813-8
Gifts. Helen Wieand Cole. 6144-3
Gifts. Juliana Horatia Ewing. 6019-6,6189-3
Gifts. Lillian M. Hagar. 6818-9
Gifts. Emma Lazarus. 6702-6,6214-8,6424-8,6730-1
Gifts. Muna Lee. 6102-8,6076-5
Gifts. James Thomson. 7012-4
Gifts. James ("B.V.") Thomson. 6437-X,6107-9
Gifts. Blanche Shoemaker Wagstaff. 6607-0
Gifts. May Williams Ward. 6039-0,6071-4
Gifts. William White. 6868-5
Gifts and givers. Berton Braley. 6853-7
The gifts divine. John Kendrick Bangs. 6303-9
The gifts of Fortune and Cupid. Thomas Dekker. 6189-3
The gifts of God. George Herbert. 6291-1,6246-6,6302-0, 6385-3,6424-8
Gifts of peace. D. Isabelle Millar. 6799-9
The gifts of peace. Thomas S. Jones Jr. 6033-1,6607-0
Gifts of the dead. Rupert Brooke. 6650-X
Gifts of the dead. Habberton Lulham. 7031-0
Gifts returned. Walter Savage Landor. 6089-7,6092-7
"The gifts we longed and prayer for". Our ignorance in asking. Johann Wolfgang von Goethe. 7042-6
Gifts without season. Joseph Auslander. 6337-3
"Gigantic figure of a mighty age" Leon Huhner. 6995-9
"Gigantic phantom crags and ghostly trees". The rune of the fog. Gertrude Huntington McGiffert. 6838-3
The gigglety girl. Unknown. 6247-4
Gigha. William Sydney Graham. 6209-1,6379-9
Gil Brenton. Unknown. 6185-0
Gil Morice. Unknown. 6180-X
"Gil's history appears to me". An epigram on..L. Echard's & G. Burnet's histories. Matthew Green. 6968-1
The gila monster route. Unknown. 6399-3
Gilbert Keith Chesterton: Little Jack Horner. Charles Powell. 6982-7
Gilbert, A.H.
My lady on the links. 6118-4
Gilbert, Bernard
Elfin dancer. 6959-2
'I have no ring'. 6474-4
Gilbert, Creighton (tr.)
"He who created time, and out of nothing". Michelangelo Buonarroti, 6325-X
"I never used to think myself so fine". Michelangelo Buonarroti, 6325-X
"Lady, up to your high and shining crown". Michelangelo Buonarroti, 6325-X
"Led on through many years to my last hours". Michelangelo Buonarroti, 6325-X
"Though time may prod against me and insist". Michelangelo Buonarroti, 6325-X
"When life is running out in me thorugh time". Michelangelo Buonarroti, 6325-X
Gilbert, Ellen
Prodigal. 6337-3
Gilbert, F.M.
My boy. 6925-8
Gilbert, Frank M.
A stray sunbeam. 6451-5
A stray sunbeam. 6920-7
Gilbert, Helen
The plodder's petition. 6303-9
Gilbert, Howard
Dirge. 6304-7
Gilbert, L. Zack
Long, black line. 6178-8
Gilbert, Lady. See Mulholland, Rosa
Gilbert, Levi
Pump-handle shake. 6717-4
Gilbert, Morris
Epitaph on a madman's grave. 6033-1,6736-0
Gilbert, Norman W.
The old fifer. 7030-2
Gilbert, Paul
Your own version. 6337-3
Gilbert, Paul T.
Tiolet ("I love you, my lord!'). 6089-7,6724-7
Gilbert, Sandra
Getting fired or 'Not being retained' 6792-1
Gilbert, Sir William Schwenck
The aesthete. 6026-9
Anglicised Utopia. 6996-7
Annie Protheroe. 6410-8
The ape and the lady. 6280-6
Arac's song. 6722-0
Baines Carew, gentleman. 6878-2
The British tar. 6026-9
The bumboat woman's story. 6572-4,6219-9
Captain Reece of the mantlepiece. 6412-4,6732-8,6239-3, 6219-9
The contemplative sentry. 6026-9
The disagreeable man. 6280-6,6026-9
A discontented sugar broker. 6512-0
The duke of Plaza-Toro. 6512-0,6026-9
Ellen M'Jones Aberdeen. 6512-0,6732-8
Ellen McJones Aberdeen. 6918-5
Emily, John, James, and I. 6722-0
Etiquette. 6089-7,6079-X,6291-9,6646-1,6633-X
The fable of the magnet and the churn, fr. Patience. 6891-X
The family fool. 6026-9
Ferdinando and Elvira. 6089-7,6501-5
Ferdinando and Elvira, or the gentle pieman. 6902-9
General John. 6902-9
Gentle Alice Brown. 6089-7
Gentle Alice Brown. 6902-9
Gentle Alice Brown. 6911-8
H.M.S. Pinafore, sels. 6120-6,6732-8
Haunted. 6760-3
Heart-foam. 6902-9
The heavy dragoon. 6501-5
The humane mikado. 6026-9
Iolanthe, sels. 6732-8
It was the cat, fr. H.M.S. Pinafore. 6120-6
King goodheart. 6026-9
Ko-Ko's song. 6512-0,6108-7,6534-1
A lady and an ape. 6236-9
Limerick:"..old man of St. Bees". 6811-1
Limerick:"..young man of St. Bees." 6308-X
Limerick:"If you want a proud foe..." 6811-1
Little buttercup, fr. H.M.S. Pinafore. 6732-8
Lord Chancellor's song, fr. Iolanthe. 6512-0,6108-7, 6732-8
Lord high admiral's song, fr. H.M.S. Pinafore. 6732-8
Lost Mr. Blake. 6406-X
The mighty must. 6724-7,6089-7
Mikado's song, fr. The Mikado. 6732-8
The Mikado, sels. 6732-8
Mister William. 7025-6
The modern major-general. 6512-0,6534-1
The modest couple. 7025-6

Nightmare. 6150-8
Out of sorts. 6026-9
Patience. 6637-2
The perils of invisibility. 7025-6,6915-0
The played-out humorist. 6089-7
The policeman's lot. 6026-9
The practical joker. 6089-7
Pygmalion and Galatea. 6361-6
Pygmalion and Galatea, sels. 6656-9
The rival curates. 6633-X
The rover's apology. 6026-9
Sing for the garish eye. 6902-9,6089-7
Sir Bailey Barre. 6512-0
Sir Guy the crusader. 6089-7
Sir Roderic's song. 6236-9,6722-0
Sleep on. 6996-7
The story of Prince Agib. 6108-7,6089-7
The story of Prince Agib. 6902-9
The suicide's grave. 6722-0,6062-9
The susceptible chancellor. 6026-9
There lived a king. 6228-8,6722-0
"There was an old man of St. Bees." 6083-8,6724-7
Thomson Green and Harriet Hale. 6861-8
Three little maids from school. 6490-6
Titwillow, fr. The Mikado. 6732-8
To Phoebe. 6089-7,6652-6
To sit in solemn silence. 6722-0
To the stall-holders at a fancy fair. 6440-X
To the terrestrial globe. 6089-7,6722-0,6732-8,6610-0, 6083-8,6583 ,6385-3,6424-8,6301-2,6464-7,6371-3,6102
An unfortunate likeness. 6406-X
When I was a lad. 6527-9
Willow, titwillow! 6490-9,6288-1
The yarn of the 'Nancy Bell'. 6089-7,6706-9,6249-0,6552-X,6614-3,6258 ,6132-X,6497-3,6302-0,6385-3,6155-9, 6458 ,6661-5,6332-2,6583-X,6459-0,6232-X,6236 ,6732-8,6706-9,6512-0,6406-X,6277-6,6610 ,6107-9,6396-9, 6566-X,6464-7
The yeomen of the guard, sels. 6228-8

Gilbert, W.B.
Though others slept. 6995-9

Gilbert, Warren
The girl with bright hair. 6070-6
The joy ride. 6531-7,6071-4
Lyric. 6070-6

Gilbert, William B.
Profit or loss. 6954-1

Gilboa. William Knox. 6848-0

Gilchrist, Edward P.
Sky-boy. 6750-6

Gilchrist, Helen Ives
A moment. 7007-8
A sea song. 6070-6

Gilchrist, Marie Emilie
Acceptance. 6906-1
Autumnal. 6619-4
Barnyard symphony. 6906-1
Botanical. 6906-1
Burning haystack. 6906-1
Chance-fallen seed. 6102-8,6232-6,6076-5
Homestead reclaimed. 6906-1
The long dream. 6906-1
Part of autumn. 6040-4
Springtime theft. 6653-4
Winter orchard. 6906-1

Gilded gold. Francis Thompson. 6942-8

Gilder, Jeanette
My creed. 6730-1
The parting of the ways, sels. 6337-3

Gilder, Joseph B.
The parting of the ways. 6396-9

Gilder, Richard Watson
"After sorrow's night." 6370-5
After-song. 6066-8,6309-8
Ah, be not false. 6735-2
At four-score. 6429-9,6321-7
At Niagara. 6484-1
At night. 6243-1
At the president's grave. 6946-0,6820-0
"Beyond the branches of the pine" 7041-8

A birthday song. 6465-5
Builders of the state. 6465-5
The burial of Grant. 6340-3
Call me not dead. 6730-1
'Call me not dead' 7041-8
The celestial passion. 7041-8
The celestial passion. 6300-4,6431-0
Charleston. 6946-0
A Christmas hymn. 6337-3,6746-8
The Christmas tree in the nursery. 6806-5
The Christmas tree in the nursery. 6807-3
The comfort of the trees. 6946-0,6820-0
Cradle song ("In the embers shining bright"). 6623-2, 6424-8
The dancers. 6959-2
The dark room. 7041-8
Dawn. 6240-7,6600-3,6385-3,6597-X
The dead comrade. 6820-0
The dead comrade. 6340-3,6424-8
Dear country mine. 6386-1,6304-7
Decoration day. 7041-8
Decoration Day. 6340-3
"Each monument holy is". 6007-2
Easter. 6820-0
Emma Lazarus. 6848-0
Evening in Tyringham valley. 6374-8,6484-1
The evening star. 7041-8
Father an child. 7041-8
For a fan. 6652-6
From ode. 7014-0
Give me a theme. 6996-7
God the strong, God of the weak. 6337-3
"Great nature is an army gay". 6597-X
The great remembrance, sels. 7022-1
"Guardians of a holy trust" 6954-1
The heroic age. 6386-1,6735-2
Holy land. 6007-2
How to the singer comes the song? 6730-1
'I count my times by times that I meet thee'. 6429-9, 6431-0,6309-8,6321-7
If the Christ you mean. 6303-9
'In a night of midsumme.' 6177-X
Inauguration day. 6465-5
The invisible. 6730-1
Janet. 6652-6
John Paul Jones. 6465-5
Keats. 7041-8
Land that we love. 6386-1
'Live thou in nature' 6995-9
"Love me not, love, for that I first loved thee". 6429-9,6094-3,6321-7,6429-9
Love's jealousy. 7041-8
The master-poets. 7041-8
A memory of Rubenstein. 6848-0
A mid-summer song. 6476-0,6519-8,6004-8,6307-1
Motto for a tree-planting. 6465-5
Music and words. 6358-6
My love for thee doth march like armed men. 6429-9,6321-7
"My love for thee doth march like armed men" 7041-8
"Navies nor armies can exalt...". 6289-X
New York. 6088-9
Noel. 6735-2
North to the south. 6340-3
Not from the whole wide I choose thee. 6066-8
A November child. 6424-8
"Oh love is not a summer mood" 7041-8
"O silver river flowing toward the sea" 7041-8
Ode. 7041-8
Ode ("I am the spirit"). 6431-0
"Oh, love is not a summer mood". 6429-9,6620-8,6226-1, 6066-8,6321-7
On the life-mask of Abraham Lincoln. 6243-1,6465-5,6305-5,6524-4,6250-4,6431 ,6737-9
On the life-mask of Abraham Lincoln. 7041-8
Only once. 7041-8
The Parthenon by moonlight. 6331-4,6439-6
THe Parthenon by moonlight. 6439-6
The passing Christ, sels. 6335-7,6337-3
The poem, to the critic. 6996-7

The real Christ, fr. The passing Christ. 6335-7
Reform. 7041-8
Reform. 6735-2
A rhyme of Tyringham. 6484-1
The river inn. 6735-2
Sery. 6145-1
Sheridan. 6820-0
Sheridan. 7041-8
Sherman. 6340-3,6431-0
Sherman. 6820-0
The smile of her I love. 6066-8
A song ("If Jesus Christ"). 6102-8,6076-5
Song ("Not from the whole"). 6429-9,6309-8,6226-1,6321-7
Song ("Years"). 7041-8
Song ("Years have flown"). 6243-1,6309-8
The song of a heathen. 6065-X,6335-7,6102-8,6144-3,6337-3,6730 ,6076-5,6300-4
A song of early autumn. 6374-8,6597-X
The sonnet. 7041-8
The sonnet. 6632-1,6646-1
The sower. 6600-3
The sower. 7041-8
Sunset from the train. 7041-8
"There is nosthing new under the sun" 7041-8
To Emma Lazarus- 1905 6848-0
To Emma Lazarus- 1905 6848-0
To Lincoln's bust in bronze. 6708-5
To the spirit of Abraham Lincoln. 6708-5,6305-5,6524-4
The tool. 6996-7
A tragedy of to-day. 6848-0
A true love. 6226-1
The violin. 6465-5
The voice of the pine. 6047-1,6597-X,6252-0
Washington Square. 6484-1
'When the girls come to the old house.' 6006-4
'The white city'. 6946-0
The white tsar's people. 7041-8
White, pillared neck. 6652-6
Who love can never die. 6303-9
"Whose name was writ in water!..." 6083-8
A woman's thought. 6102-8,6243-1,6735-2,6066-8,6076-5
A woman's thought. 7041-8
"The woods that bring the sunset near". 6243-1,6632-1,6309-8
'woods that bring the sunset near' 7041-8
Gilderoy. Unknown. 6056-0
Gildersleeve, Basil L.
To the University of Virginia ("No summer rose..."). 6184-2
Giles and Abraham. Elmer Ruan Coates. 6910-X
Giles' hope. Samuel Taylor Coleridge. 6996-7
Giles's hope. Samuel Taylor Coleridge. 6089-7
Giles, Greg
Confederate wall. 6883-9
Giles, H.A. (tr.)
You will die. Unknown (Chinese), 7039-6
Gilfillan, Robert
Blue bonnets over the border. 6802-2
The exile's song. 6219-9
In the days o' Langsyne. 6543-0
O, why left I my hame? 6180-X
Gilhoff, Gerd Aage
Analogies. 6798-0
From the shore. 6798-0
Grotesque. 6798-0
Gilington, Alice E.
The rosy musk-mallow. 6274-1
Gilkey, John Augustus
The heroes of the Yukon. 6336-5
Gilkyson, Phoebe
The mother. 6214-8
Gill, Elsa
Spring in the subway. 6478-7
Gill, Frances Tyrrell
Beneath the wattle boughs. 6274-1,6656-9
Beneath the wattle boughs. 6768-9
Love's loyalty. 6768-9
Soeur fidele. 6285-7
Gill, Julia

Christ and the little ones. 6127-3
Hannah, the mother. 6304-7
I want to be an angel. 6131-1
"Suffer the little ones to come unto me". 6131-1
Gill, Mary Terry
To a nun. 6285-7
Gill, W. Walter
The stack-builder. 6134-6
Gill, William Henry (tr.)
"Hear us, O Lord, from Heaven...". Unknown, 6258-X
Gill, Winifred Huff
Rhythm of the palms. 6789-1
Rhythm of the palms: Kandy, Ceylon - prelude. 6789-1
Rhythm of the palms: Kandy, Ceylon - symphony. 6789-1
Rhythm of the palms: Plaza de Mayo (1). 6789-1
Rhythm of the palms: Plaza de Mayo (2). 6789-1
Rhythm of the palms: Rio de Janeiro - a lullaby. 6789-1
Rhythm of the palms: Rio de Janeiro - the minuet. 6789-1
Swing-rhythm of the palms. 6789-1
Gille Machree. Gerald Griffin. 6174-5
Gillespie. Sir Henry Newbolt. 6473-6,6079-X,6212-1
Gillespie, M. Pearl
My dream house. 6894-4
Gillespie, Violet
The dead. 6474-4
Gillespie, Yetza
Blue heron. 6979-7
Gillespy, Jeannette Bliss
The angel. 6118-4
Forgiven? 6118-4
Seaward. 6118-4
A valentine. 6118-4
Gillet, Mrs. A.D.
The peril of the passenger train. 6921-5
Gillett, F.W.
The flag of Washington. 6171-0
Gillette, L. Fidelia Woolley
Hallowe'en. 6696-8
Gillian. Unknown. 6089-7,6440-X
Gillies, Andrew
Two prayers. 6337-3
Gillies, Donald
Woodrow Wilson. 7001-9
Gillies, Erl. G. (tr.)
You women. Stefan fra Hvitadal, 6854-5
Gilliflower. Ibn al-Abbar. 6362-4
The gilliflower of gold. William Morris. 6536-3,6657-7, 6726-3,6732-8,6639-9,6110-9,6153-2,6656-9,6560-0, 6655-0,6508
Gillilan, Strickland
'Are you there?' 6303-9
As I on go my way. 6337-3
Becoming a man. 6211-3
A Dixie lullaby. 6307-1
Finnigin to Flannigan. 6211-3,6732-8,6694-1,6605-4,6089-7,6277 ,6736-0,6579-1
Folks need a lot of loving. 6337-3
Football hero. 6717-4
Get up and go on. 6583-X
Her great secret. 6449-3
'I'm going to, anyway'. 6889-8
Keep sweet. 6291-1
The kind lady's furs. 6510-4
'Kishinex' 6848-0
Lines on the antiquity of microbes. 6527-9
Modern medicine. 6280-6
The music that carries. 6583-X
On the antiquity of microbes. 6722-0
Patriotic remnants. 6280-6
The songs of men. 6583-X
Stair-step children. 6721-2
Watch yourself go by. 6211-3
When he goes to play with the. 6449-3
When the snow sifts through. 6605-4
Gilliland, Winona Montgomery
Spring cleaning. 6750-6
To a Chinese gong. 6750-6
Gillington, Alice E.
The doom-bar. 6541-4

Nocturnes: I. 7037-X
Nocturnes: II. 7037-X
The rosy musk-mallow. 6274-1,6656-9
The seven whistlers. 6656-9
To the west! 6997-5
A west-country love song! 7037-X
Gillington, Mary C. See Byron, May C.
Gillison, Lenora
Supremacy. 6178-8
Gillman, Frederick J.
God send us men. 6337-3,6386-1
Gillman, Richard
Moved by her music. 6388-8
Snow fell with a will. 6388-8
Gillmore, Anna H.
Work. 6764-6
The **gilly** of Christ. James Campbell. 6244-X
Gilman, C. L.
You're a dog. 7008-6
Gilman, Caroline
Annie in the grave-yard. 6271-7
Boy's complaint about butter. 6131-1
The child's wish in June. 6385-3,6127-3
Choice of occupations. 6131-1
The household woman. 6219-9
Not ready for school. 6131-1
To the Ursulines. 6285-7
Gilman, Charlotte Perkins Stetson
The bed of fleur-de-lys. 6241-5
The cattle train. 6510-4
Child labor. 6102-8,6076-5
A common inference. 6730-1,6303-9,6431-0
A conservative. 6431-0
A conservative. 6996-7
The contemptible neutral. 6274-1
The flag of peace. 6461-2
Give way! 6730-1
I resolve. 6260-1
It takes courage. 6583-X
The lion path. 6291-1
The living God. 6303-9,6730-1
"A man must live". 6473-6
"A man must live." 6337-3,6473-6
Mother to child. 6097-8
Mother, what is death? 6752-2
An obstacle. 6211-3,6431-0
Resolve. 6291-1,6730-1
The rock and the sea. 6580-5
She who is to come. 6954-1
Similar cases. 6505-8,6102-8,6490-6,6732-8
To labor. 6274-1
To labor. 6954-1
To the preacher, sels. 6337-3
Tree feelings. 6374-8,6510-4
Two prayers. 6730-1
Wedded bliss. 6505-8
The wolf at the door. 6954-1
Gilman, F.J.
God send us men. 6303-9
Gilman, Isabel Ambler
Our presidents - a memory rhyme. 6964-9
The sunset city. 6964-9
Gilman, Samuel
Fair Harvard. 6289-X
Gilmore, Anna Neil
February. 6820-0
Gilmore, G.W.
Slow. 6983-5
Gilmore, James Robert
Three days ("So much to do: so little done!"). 6583-X
Gilmore, Joseph H.
He leadeth me. 6337-3,6730-1
Gilmore, Louis
Epigram. 6070-6,6250-4
Florizel in love. 6071-4
Improvisation. 6070-6
To a goldfish. 6070-6
Gilmore, Mary
The dice were loaded. 6349-7
Eve-song. 6349-7

I saw the beauty go. 6384-5
Marri'd. 6784-0
Nationality. 6384-5
Never admit the pain. 6384-5
Of wonder. 6384-5
Supplication. 6818-9
Swans at night, sels. 6349-7
Sweethearts. 6784-0
They called her sunshine. 6384-5
Turn to the grass. 6349-7
The Waradgery tribe. 6384-5
Gilmore, Patrick S.
Columbia. 6411-6,6444-2
When Johnny comes marching home. 6121-4,6753-0
Gilpatrick, Naomi
Now. 6839-1
Gilroy, Dorothea
The early morning ride. 7010-8
Gilt. E. Ernest Murrell. 6042-0
"**Gilt** glitters in nap". Port Arthur riddle. Barbara Gravelle. 6901-0
Giltinan, Caroline
Alone in spring. 6619-4,6034-X,6326-8
The builder. 6619-4,6036-6,6328-8
Communion. 6292-X,6172-9
Consecration. 6037-4
Contrition across the waves. 6543-0
The courtyard pigeons. 6073-0,6029-3
The coward. 6031-5
Escape. 6037-4
The garden. 6649-6,6037-4
The hungry. 6954-1
The magician. 6038-2
Overnight, a rose. 6096-X,6266-0,6303-9,6556-2,6029-3, 6326
A portrait. 6039-0,6649-6
A portrait. 6039-0,6649-6
Respite. 6038-2
The revealer. 6032-3
The seeker. 6096-X,6039-0
The thirteenth station. 6096-X,6326-8
Transformed. 6036-6
Unborn. 6039-0
Gin by pailfuls. Sir Walter Scott. 6125-7
The **gin** friend. Charles Mackay. 6685-2
Gin I was God. Charles Murray. 6269-5
"**Gin** ye but kent the wecht o dule in prief". Unknown. 6325-X
Ginerva. Samuel Rogers. 6543-0,6219-9
Ginerva, fr. Italy. Samuel Rogers. 6302-0,6385-3,6744-1, 6486-8,6624-0
Ginerva, fr. Italy. Samuel Rogers. 6832-4
The **gingerbread** tree. Harriet Prescott Spofford. 6049-8
The **gingerbread.** Margaret Wheeler Ross. 6130-3
"**Gingerly** is good King Tarquin shaving". Tarquin and the augur. William Edmonstoune Aytoun. 6948-7
"**Ginsberg** had insight". Matrix III. Ed Lipman. 6870-7
Ginsberg, Allen
Some writing from a journal (1959, NY). 6803-0
Ginsberg, Louis
April. 6034-X
Cry of the dead. 6420-5
Curves. 6037-4
Dazzling moment. 6042-0
Defense against the dark. 6648-8
Frail strength. 6072-2
I know that any weed can tell. 6619-4
The internationalist. 6420-5,6542-2
Prayer for courage. 6761-1
A quiet street after rain. 6396-9
The room. 6648-8
Song ("Though your little"). 6619-4
Though man goes under. 6761-1
Waterfalls of stone. 6880-4,6808-1
When bombs on Barcelona burst. 6979-7
Ginther, Pemberton
Possession. 6799-9
Gioconda. Thomas McGreevy. 6930-4
Giotto's Campanile. Aubrey Thomas De Vere. 6631-3
Giotto's campanile. Thomas O'Hagan. 6292-X,6172-9

Giotto's tower. Henry Wadsworth Longfellow. 6624-0,6288-1, 6126-5,6309-8,6631-3
Giovanni Dupre. Robert Bridges. 6487-6
Giovanni, Nikki
    Black judgement. 7024-8
    For Saundra. 7024-8
    The funeral of Martin Luther King, Jr. 7024-8
    My poem. 7024-8
Giovanni, Norman Thomas di (tr.)
    Instinct. Cesare Pavese, 6803-0
Giovannitti, Arturo
    Anniversary. 6880-4
    May Day in Moscow. 6880-4
    Mea culpa. 6347-0
"The gipsies came to lord Cassilis' gate". Johnny Faa, the lord of little Egypt. Unknown. 6829-4
"The gipsies came to our good lord...". Unknown. 6518-X
"The gipsies came to the good squire's gate." Unknown. 6317-9
Gipsy. Robert Service. 6159-1
The gipsy bride. Emma Dunning Banks. 6686-0
The gipsy camp (in Epping Forest) John Clare. 6125-7
Gipsy children's song. Lucy Larcom. 6129-X
"The gipsy comes with his caravan". World wanderers. Charles C. Jones. 7007-8
Gipsy feet. Fannie Stearns Davis. 6374-8
The gipsy lass. Helen B. Cruickshank. 6269-5
Gipsy love. Arthur Symons. 6655-0
Gipsy song. Sara Hamilton Birchall. 6374-8
Gipsy songs. Ben Jonson. 6563-5
The gipsy trail. Rudyard Kipling. 6289-X,6374-8,6732-8, 6655-0
Gipsy vans. Rudyard Kipling. 6427-2,6655-0
The gipsy wedding. Sara Hamilton Birchall. 6374-8
Gipsy-heart. Amelia Josephine Burr. 7012-4
Gipsying. Witter Bynner. 6628-3
The giraffe ride. J.G. Francis. 6786-7
The giraffe. Marvin Solomon. 6388-8
Giraffes. Noel Harry Brettell. 6788-3
The giraffes. Roy Fuller. 6379-9
Girardet, Ethel Aldrich
    A deserted farm. 6764-6
"Gird on thy sword...", fr. A hymn of nature. Robert Bridges. 6487-6
"Gird up thy loins now like a man". Accinge sicut. Bible. 6830-8
The girdle of friendship. Oliver Wendell Holmes. 6014-5, 6126-5,6066-8
A girdle. Edmund Waller. 6240-7
"Girdled by Huron's throbbing and thunder". Manitou. William Wilfred Campbell. 6795-6,7041-8
Girdler, John
    Almost attained. 6836-7
    Old, old trees. 6836-7
    Prayer. 6836-7
Girelius, Charles Gustav
    Laborers. 6143-5
Th'girl 'at lives next door. Unknown. 6721-2
Girl and butterfly. Edith Sitwell. 6357-8
The girl and her fawn. Andrew Marvell. 6242-3
A girl combs her hair. Kimiko Hahn. 6790-5
A girl dancing on the shore. Henry C. Thomas. 6959-2
The girl describes her fawn. Andrew Marvell. 6018-8
A girl from Ireland. John E. Barrett. 6840-5
Girl from Roumely. Alexandros Pallis. 6352-7
The girl I left behind me. Thomas Osborne Davis. 6930-4
The girl I left on New River. Unknown. 6826-X
"Girl I love." Olive Tilford Dargan. 6581-3
The girl I love. Unknown (Irish) 6858-8,6930-4
"A girl in Savoie wrote to me". The answer. Geoffrey Matthews. 6895-2
Girl in a tree. Frances Frost. 6374-8
The girl in the laboratory thinks of her grandmother. Jane Brown. 7014-0
"The girl in the lane, that couldn't speak plain". Unknown. 6904-5
"A girl is standing with careless feet". Air castles. Clara H. Bradner. 6920-7
The girl of all periods. Coventry Patmore. 6123-0,6656-9
The girl of Cadiz. George Gordon, 6th Baron Byron. 6271-7, 6331-4,6439-6,6219-9
The girl of our town. R.R. K. 6118-4
A girl of Pompeii. Edward Sandford Martin. 6624-0
A girl of Pompeii. Harrison Smith Morris. 6431-0
A girl of the period. Unknown. 6919-3
Girl of the red mouth. Martin MacDermott. 6174-5,6292-X, 6930-4
The girl remembers her dead lover. Edward Davison. 6072-2
A girl shelling peas. Robert P. Tristram Coffin. 6761-1
"A girl sits next to me at school". Compensation. Ruth H. Hausman. 6850-2
A girl strike-leader. Florence Kiper Frank. 6954-1
'The girl takes her place among the mothers'. Marya Alexandrovna Zaturenska. 6777-8
The girl that I didn't get. Unknown. 6675-5
"The girl that lives in the looking-glass". Shadow and echo. Mary Frances Butts. 6965-7
Girl walking. Charles G. Bell. 6388-8
A girl was too reckless of grammar. Guy Wetmore Carryl. 6089-7
The girl who was drowned at Onslow. Unknown. 6057-9
"A girl who weighs many an oz". Limerick:"A girl who weighs many an oz". P.T. Mannock. 6811-1
The girl with bright hair. Warren Gilbert. 6070-6
"Girl with eyes like dying flowers". Lullaby ("Girl with eyes"). Max Harris. 6349-7
The girl with the blue lamp. Jose Maria Eguren. 6759-X
The girl with thirty-nine lovers. Unknown. 6676-3
A girl's a girl for a'that. Unknown. 6273-3
A girl's autumn reverie. Ella Wheeler Wilcox. 6863-4
A girl's idea. Unknown. 6248-2
A girl's mood. Lizette Woodworth Reese. 6581-3
Girl's song. Aleksey Surkov. 6546-5
A girl's song. Katharine (Hinkson) Tynan. 6474-4
A girl's song. Aubrey Thomas De Vere. 6246-5
A girl's song. Joseph Freeman. 6880-4
A girl's song. Thomas Moore. 6114-1
A girl's songs. Mary Carolyn Davies. 6031-5,6556-2
"Girl, a pearl, single, won". Unknown. 6364-0
Girl, cat and custard. Unknown. 6699-2
Girl-athletes. Haniel Long. 6038-2
A girl. Archilochus. 6435-3
A girl. Babette Deutsch. 6076-5,6102-8,6396-9
A girl. Ezra Pound. 6357-8
The girl. Scudder Middleton. 6033-1
Girls. Robert Louis Burgess. 6037-4
"Girls and boys, come out to play". Unknown. 6904-5
"Girls and boys, come out to play." Mother Goose. 6363-2, 6452-3
"Girls didn't wear a tailor-suit". In mamma's day. Curley (pseud).. 7021-3
Girls on the Yueh River. Li Po. 6125-7
"The girls they will for the young men plead". Unknown. 6059-5
The girls' lot. Agathias Scholasticus. 6435-3
Girls' song. Alexander Pushkin. 6103-6
"Girls, when I am gone away". Song ("Girls"). Edward Dowden. 6244-X
Girondo, Oliverio
    Las Sierpes Street. Milton Ben Davis (tr.). 6759-X
"Girt in my guiltless gown, as I sit here and sew." Henry Howard, Earl of Surrey. 6584-8
"Girt round with rugged mountains". Bregenz. Adelaide Anne Procter. 6749-2
"Girt with the river's silver zone". Two cities. William Allen Butler. 6903-7
A Girtonian funeral. Unknown. 6802-2
Gisborne, Thomas
    The worm. 6086-2
Gislason, Gudmund J. (tr.)
    Deaths. Hjalmar Jonsson, 6854-5
    Feyman's fate. Hjalmar Jonsson, 6854-5
    The grave. Kristjan Jonsson, 6854-5
    Iceland. Jonas Hallgrimsson, 6854-5
    My nest. Porsteinn Erlingsson, 6854-5
    Senility. Hjalmar Jonsson, 6854-5
    Silence broken. Hjalmar Jonsson, 6854-5
    Skarphedinn among the flames. Hannes Hafstein, 6854-5
    Tale of the wayside. Kristjan N. ("K.N.") Julius, 6854-5

Valagils-river. Hannes Hafstein, 6854-5
Gislason, Thorsteinn
    Spring. Skuli Johnson (tr.). 6854-5,6283-0
    Thorvaldur Thoroddsen. Jakobina Johnson (tr.). 6854-5
    Thorvaldur Thoroddsen. Jakobina Johnson (tr.). 6283-0
Gissing's sixpenny miracle. Edgar A. Guest. 6748-4
"Git yo' little fillies ready". The dance at the little gila ranch. James Barton Adams. 6959-2
Gitanjali, sels. Rabindranath Tagore. 6337-3,6730-1,6320-9
"Gitaut, the Norman marquis, sat in his...hall". The last banquet. Edward Renaud. 6915-0
Gittin' inter shape. Ben King. 6303-9
Gittings, Robert
    Parting. 6202-4
    Winter aconites. 6339-X
Give. Adelaide Anne Procter. 6957-6
Give a man a horse. James ("B.V."). Thomson. 6180-X,6328-4, 6660-7,6508-2,6655-0,6301-2,6383-7
"Give a man a horse he can ride". Gifts. James Thomson. 7012-4
Give a man a horse he can ride. Sir Edwin Arnold. 6301-2
Give a rouse. Robert Browning. 6198-2,6271-7,6328-4,6334-9, 6501-5,6732-,6110-9,6199-0,6430-2,6655-0,6656-9,6723 ,6271-7
Give all to love. Ralph Waldo Emerson. 6006-4,6102-8,6176-1,6320-9,6732-8,6317 ,6396-9,6300-4,6464-7,6288-1, 6350-4,6560 ,6208-3,6076-5,6066-8,6126-5,6464-7,6754-9
Give and take. R. Priestley Hayes. 6936-3
Give back my missing ones. James Abraham Martling. 6952-5
"Give beauty all her right". Song ("Give beauty"). Thomas Campion. 6436-1
Give beauty all her right. Thomas Campion. 6328-4,6383-7, 6794-8
"Give ear, ye British hearts of gold". Rodney's Glory. Owen Roe O'Sullivan. 6930-4
"Give goold their gold and knaves their power", sels. John Greenleaf Whittier. 6047-1
Give her but a least excuse, fr. Pippa passes. Robert Browning. 6199-0
Give him a lift. Unknown. 6109-5
"Give is a name to fill the mind". The name of France. Henry Van Dyke. 6961-4
"Give me a calm, a thankful heart". A little prayer. Anne Steele. 6889-8
"Give me a camp by the side of the swamp". Cummaquid. Sarah A. Dixon. 6798-0
Give me a cottage on some Cambrian wild. Henry Kirke White. 6086-2
"Give me a good digestion, Lord". Prayer ("Give me a good digestion"). Unknown. 6303-9
"Give me a hard, hard row to hoe". My prayer. Caroline McCarty. 6799-9
"Give me a land of brave retreats". Brave retreats. William O. Perkins Jr.. 6799-9
Give me a lass with a lump of land. Allan Ramsay. 6152-4
"Give me a mask, I'll join the masquerade". Fresco-sonnet to Christian Sethe (2). Heinrich Heine. 7039-6
"Give me a mattress...". Antiphilus. 6251-2
"Give me a penny, kind lady!". On Epsom Down. Ianthe Jerrold. 6776-X
Geve me a single day. Edgar A. Guest. 6862-6
"Give me a son. The blessing sent". The mother, the nurse, and the fairy. John Gay. 6972-X
Give me a theme. Richard Watson Gilder. 6996-7
Give me a wish. Rose Terry Cooke. 6502-3
Give me back my boy. Jasper Garnet. 6695-X
"Give me back my heart, fair child". Song ("Give me back my heart..."). Aubrey Thomas De Vere. 6980-0
"Give me back my world" Rita Geada. 7036-1
Give me back my youth again. Johann Wolfgang von Goethe. 6240-7
"Give me back the soul of youth once more!". My dead. Bayard Taylor. 6976-2
"Give me cool words, cool words to ease...". Green shadows. Helen Hoyt. 7030-2
Give me drink. John Whitaker Watson. 6774-3
Give me gay courage. Edith M. Smith. 6270-9
"Give me granite rock, New Hampshire". Granite state. Frances Ann Johnson. 6764-6

"Give me leave to rail at you". Song ("Give me leave"). John Wilmot, 2d Earl of Rochester. 6187-7
"Give me March winds and a dog at my heel". A vagabond's wish. Avis Turner French. 6764-6
"Give me more love or more disdain." Thomas Carew. 6302-0, 6385-3,6328-4,6226-1,6737-9
"'Give me my bow', said Robin Hood". The death of Robin Hood. Eugene Field. 6949-5
"Give me my burnished armor". Courage. Margaret Ridgely Partridge. 6861-8
"Give me my robe...", fr. Antony and Cleopatra. William Shakespeare. 6339-X
"Give me my scallop-shell of Quiet". Sir Walter Raleigh. 6181-8,6187-7
Give me my self. Michael Drayton. 6317-9
Give me my work. George Whetstone. 6182-6
"Give me my youth, and let me play". Une petite chanson de lamentation a ma mere. Belle De Coeur. 6818-9
"Give me no light, great heaven, but such as turns." George (Mary Ann Cross) Eliot. 6238-5
Give me no lover young with love. Lucia Trent. 6619-4
Give me rest. George Edgar Grisham. 6682-8
Give me rest. Unknown. 6273-3
"Give me room, a little room". Anna Wickham. 6893-6
"Give me the bible bards- I love them". Prelude. George Alexander Kohut. 6848-0
"Give me the crown of thorns; let fair and...". Renunciation. Fanny Bixby Spencer. 6954-1
"Give me the dance of your boughs, O tree". Song to a tree. Edwin Markham. 6891-X
"Give me the darkest corner of a cloud". Sonnet ("Give me"). Richard Watson Dixon. 6317-9
"Give me the earth, my mother, my mate". Moonstruck. Maurice Carpenter. 6895-2
Give me the eyes. Walter Savage Landor. 6110-9,6199-0
"Give me the eyes" Walter Savage Landor. 6828-6
Give me the hand. Goodman Barnaby. 6911-8
"Give me the honey of thy lips". The bee to the blossom. James Abraham Martling. 6952-5
"Give me the merchants of Indian mines." Christopher Marlowe. 6317-9
Give me the old. Robert Hinckley Messinger. 6632-1,6423-X, 6219-9,6438-8
"Give me the patience of the silent hills--". The patience of the hills. Blanche Shoemaker Wagstaff. 7038-8
"'Give me the prettiest valentine ...'". Getting her a valentine. Edgar A. Guest. 6862-6
"Give me the pulse of the tide again". Peace. Alfred Noyes. 6151-6
"Give me the spirit to live on life's ...". Frontiers. Mary Wickham Porcher. 7014-0
Give me the splendid silent sun. Walt Whitman. 6006-4,6431-0,6126-5,6309-8
"Give me the sweet old-fashioned spring". Old-fashioned spring. Benjamin Franklin Taylor. 6815-4
"Give me the white paper!". Columbus. Edward Everett Hale. 6946-0
"Give me this day, and all my days to come". Eupepsia. Edward Farquhar. 6939-8
"Give me those flowers there, Dorcas...". At a sheep-shearing. George Wither. 6935-5
"Give me three grains of corn, mother." Amelia Blandford Edwards. 6302-0,6385-3,6403-5
Give me thy heart. Adelaide Anne Procter. 6022-6
"Give me thy thoughts, my gentle maid". The eve of battle, 1645. Silas Weir Mitchell. 6936-3
"Give me to drink...", fr. Antony and Cleopatra. William Shakespeare. 6339-X
Give me your hand. Frederick Herbert Adler. 6906-1
Give me your hand. Gerhard Ruhm. 6769-7
"Give me your hand, old revolutionary". The centenarian's story. Walt Whitman. 6753-0
"Give me your hands". Fragment ("Give me"). Edmund John. 6102-8
"Give me your last aloha". A friend's wish. Bliss Carman and Richard Hovey. 6890-1
".Give me your poppies/mightier priestly state," fr.Morpheus. Hilda ("H.D.") Doolittle. 6012-9
"Give me your poppies/red with rare white," fr Morpheus. Hilda ("H.D." Doolittle. 6012-9

GIVE

Give me your whole heart, fr. The Bhagavad Gita. Unknown (Sanskrit) 6337-3
"Give me yourself one hour; I do not crave". Request. Laurence (Adele Florence Nicolson) Hope. 6856-1
Give me youth and the world is mine. Celestin Pierre Cambiaire. 6826-X
"Give me, full-handed, lilies, give me the rose". Matteo Maria Boiardo. 6325-X
"Give me, mot folded wings". Passing on. Aimee Paul Thomas. 6799-9
"Give me, ye weeping nine...". On the death of Mr. William Levinz. Thomas Warton (the Elder). 6962-2
Give not with your hands. MacKnight Black. 6039-0
Give o'er, foolish heart. Robert Veel. 6328-4
"Give one beautiful gift to me". A priceless gift. Mildred Maralyn Mercer. 6906-1
Give our conscience light. Aline Badger Carter. 6144-3
"Give pardon, blessed soul, to my bold cries". To Sir Philip Sidney's soul. Henry Constable. 6908-8
Give place. Adelaide Anne Procter. 6957-6
"Give place all ye that doth rejoice." Sir Thomas Wyatt. 6584-8
Give place, ye lovers. Henry Howard, Earl of Surrey. 6302-0,6385-3,6584-8,6250-4,6383-7,6543
"Give place, ye lovers, here before". In his lady's praise. Henry Howard, Earl of Surrey. 6830-8
Give something away. Unknown. 6669-0
Give thanks. Doane Robinson. 6703-4
Give thanks. Unknown. 6272-5
Give thanks for what? W.F. Croffut. 6618-6,6171-0,6744-1
Give thanks for what? W.F. Croffut. 6917-7
'Give thanks for what?' Unknown. 6273-3
"Give thanks, o heart, for the high souls". Conscripts of the dream. Edwin Markham. 6954-1
"Give the id a dog and you've furnished him...". A gift. Berton Braley. 6853-7
Give the little boys a chance. Unknown. 6629-1
Give them the flowers now. Leigh Mitchell Hodges. 6260-1, 6303-9,6964-9
"Give thy thoughts no tongue". William Shakespeare. 6238-5, 6291-1
"Give to barrows, trays and pans". 'Make tomorrow a new morn!' Ralph Waldo Emerson. 6954-1
"Give to the barrows, trays and pans". Art. Ralph Waldo Emerson. 6753-0
"Give unto the Lord, O ye mighty". Afferte domino. Bible. 6830-8
"Give up the dream that love may trick..fates". Transient. Don Marquis. 6879-0
Give us a call. Unknown. 6414-0
'Give us Barabbas'. Emily Pauline ("Tekahionwake") Johnson. 6837-3
"Give us a name to fill the mind". The name of France. Henry Van Dyke. 7026-4
"Give us from dawn to dark". The bush. James Lister Cuthbertson. 6784-0
Give us men. Josiah Gilbert Holland. 6887-1
Give us men. Unknown. 6416-7,6710-7
Give us men! Edward Henry Bickersteth. 6337-3
"'Give us the calf of gold', the people say". Woodrow Wilson returns from Versailles. Ethelean Tyson Gaw. 7001-9
Give us this day. Josephine Royle. 6076-5
"Give us this day our daily bread". Our daily bread. Rita Benton. 6954-1
'Give us this day our daily bread.' Maltbie Davenport Babcock. 6337-3
"Give water to a thirsty dog" Jutta Schutting. 6769-7
Give way! Charlotte Perkins Stetson Gilman. 6730-1
"Give words, kind words, to those who err". Lydia Huntley Sigourney. 6238-5
"Given the seriousness of these affairs". Textile mills and prison reform. George Rachow. 6870-7
Giver of all. Christopher Wordsworth. 6337-3
"Giver of glowing light!". Hymn to the sun. Thomas Hood. 6974-6
The giver of stars. Amy Lowell. 6320-9
The giver's reward. Unknown. 6411-6
Giving. William F. Kirk. 6337-3
Giving and taking. Hesiod. 6435-3

Giving concerts. Emma C. Dowd. 6130-3
Giving thanks. Unknown. 6171-0,6618-6,6449-3
Giving to God. Christopher Wordsworth. 6656-9
Giving up butterflies. Geraldine Kudaka. 6790-5
Gjellerup, Karl
    Love rides the lion. Charles Wharton Stork (tr.). 6555-4
    O, let me kiss. Charles Wharton Stork (tr.). 6555-4
    A pair. Charles Wharton Stork (tr.). 6555-4
The glacial flea. Vachel Lindsay. 6206-7
Glacier. Mary Sinton Leitch. 6102-8
The glacier, fr. Three Alpine sonnets. Henry Van Dyke. 6961-4
The glacier-bed. Emilia Aylmer Blake. 6167-2,6744-1
The glacier-bed. Emilia Aylmer Blake. 6925-8
"Glad and blithe mote ye be". A hymn of the incarnation. Unknown. 6881-2
Glad day. W. Graham Robertson. 6114-1
The glad evangel. Kate Douglas Wiggin. 6145-1
"Glad Message of the voice of Zeus". Sophocles. 6435-3
The glad new year. William Shattuck. 6274-1
The glad new year. Dinah Maria Mulock Craik. 6937-1
Glad sight, sels. William Wordsworth. 6867-7
The glad song. Joseph Morris. 6291-1
Glad tidings. William Wordsworth. 6188-5
Glad tidings from the King of kings. Charles Coffin. 6065-X
The glad young chamois. Burges Johnson. 6861-8
Gladden, Washington
    The baby over the way. 6078-1,6273-3
    "My bark is wafted to the strand," fr. My pilot. 6225-3
    O happy soul. 6337-3
    O master, let me walk with thee. 6335-7,6303-9,6337-3, 6418-3,6730-1
    The pastor's reverie. 6273-3
    Through dimness to truth. 6717-4
    Ultima veritas. 6303-9,6337-3,6473-6,6621-6
Gladding, Jody
    Letter to Michael from New York. 6900-2
Gladding, Mary High
    Subway. 6818-9
The glade. Edward Shanks. 6317-9
The gladiator. George Gordon, 6th Baron Byron. 6438-8
The gladiator. J.A. Jones. 6406-X
The gladiator. Unknown. 6744-1
Gladiolas. Edgar A. Guest. 6869-3
Gladioli. Ann Bryant. 6750-6
"Gladly they saw me sleeping on the shore". Sophocles. 6435-3
Gladness. Anna Hempstead Branch. 6266-0,6501-5
Gladness. Genevieve Taggard. 6393-4
The gladness of nature. William Cullen Bryant. 6047-1,6049-8,6127-3,6457-4,6597-X,6135
The gladness of the sea. Hardwicke Drummond Rawnsley. 6997-5
Gladsmuir. Unknown. 6859-6
"A gladsome girl—a summer's morn". Early and late. S. Marie Talbot. 6836-7
Gladstone. Stephen Phillips. 6723-9
Gladstone. Julian Symons. 6666-6
Gladstone, William Ewart (tr.)
    "As when the billow gathers...", fr. The Iliad. Homer, 6435-3
    The ship of state. Horace, 7039-6
    The two hosts, fr. The Iliad. Homer, 6435-3
Gladwin, William Z.
    April. 6529-5
    The spring of the year. 6529-5
Glaenzer, Richard Butler
    A ballad of Redhead's Day. 6946-0
    Colonel Roosevelt in Dominica. 6995-9
    The golden plover. 6030-7
    The harvest moon. 6880-4
    Man or manikin. 6291-1
    Sark of the leewards. 6033-1
    Star-magic. 6897-9
    Sure, it's fun! 6474-4,6029-3,6542-2
    To Edgar Lee Masters. 6029-3
    A west indian dance. 6959-2
"Glamorgan is in Wales, and in". The cobbler of Glamorgan.

Hermann Hagedorn. 6944-4
Glamour. Edith Colby Banfield. 6836-7
A **glance** at history. Walt Mason. 6211-3
A **glance** backward. Mary E. Blanchard. 6414-0,6686-0
"The **glance** that doth my neighbor doubt". Alice Cary. 6969-X
The **glance.** Ibn Iyad. 6362-4
Glances. [James] Pittendrigh Macgillivray. 6269-5
Glancy, Diane
    Looking for my old indian grandmother in the summer... 7005-1
    Lunar eclipse. 7005-1
    Mary Ackerman, 1938, Eugene Buechel photograph... 7005-1
    There won't be another. 7005-1
    Two animals, one flood. 7005-1
Glantz, Sharon
    "The sanity patrol is out to get you" 6857-X
Glanville, Irene McMillan
    I love to hear you whistle. 6583-X
Glapthorne, Henry
    Unclose those eyelids. 6563-5
Glasgerion. Unknown. 6055-2,6185-0,6076-5,6518-4
"**Glasgerion** was a king's own son". Unknown. 6518-X
Glasgow. Alexander Smith. 6180-X
Glasgow Peggie. Unknown. 6185-0
Glasgow, Alice
    Hulks. 6847-2
    Song for rain (001). 6847-2
    Song for rain (002). 6847-2
Glasgow, Ellen
    Drinking-song. 7038-8
Glasgow, G.R.
    Attila. 7031-0
    A lullaby ("Because some men"). 7031-0
Glasgow, Julia
    Perhaps. 6817-0
Glasier's men. H.A. Cody. 6797-2
Glasier, Jessie C.
    Somewhere ("'Tis always morning somewhere..."). 6109-5
Glass. Lucile Enlow. 6841-3
The **glass** blower. Eleanor Jordan Houston. 6316-0
Glass dialectic. Howard Nemerov. 6666-4
Glass houses. Edwin Arlington Robinson. 6038-2
"A **glass** is good, and a lass is good". John O'Keefe. 6453-1
A **glass** of beer. James Stephens. 6722-0
A **glass** of cold water. John B. Gough. 6403-5
The **glass** of time. George Sterling. 6031-5
The **glass** swan. W. Wesley Trimpi. 6515-5
Glass, Julia Daingerfield
    I shall go back. 6799-9
    To my grandmother's portrait. 6799-9
Glass, Simon
    Prescience. 6818-9
A **glass-ribbed** nest. Marianne Moore. 6389-6
The **glass..** Pannard. 6724-7
"The **glasses** are raised, the voices drift...". Pub. Julian Symons. 6761-1
Glassford, James
    The dead who have died in the Lord. 6600-3
"The **glassy** ocean hushed forgets to roar". William Falconer. 6997-5
"**Glassy** water, glassy water". Rio verde, rio verde, sels. Unknown. 6975-4
Glaucus
    Cenotaph. Walter Leaf (tr.). 6435-3
    An inscription by the sea. Edwin Arlington Robinson (tr.). 7039-6,6879-0
    "Nod a sod hath Erasippus...". F.L. Lucas (tr.). 6251-2
    "Now, all ye nymphs...". F.L. Lucas (tr.). 6251-2
    Pan and Daphnis. Walter Leaf (tr.). 6435-3
Glaucus. Sidney Keyes. 6209-1
Glayne, George
    Symphony music. 6818-9
Glazebrook, Harriet A.
    The lips that touch liqour shall never touch mine. 6617-8
    A story of Santa Claus. 6617-8
Glazier, William Belcher

Cape-cottage at sunset. 6271-7,6302-0,6385-3
"A **gleam** of gold in gloom and gray". Allegra agonistes. Grace Fallow Norton. 6897-9
The **gleaming** sea. Percy Bysshe Shelley. 6138-9
"**Gleams** of English orchards dance". St. Ouen in Picardy. Unknown. 7031-0
The **gleaner.** Jane Taylor. 6502-3
Gleaners. Helen Bosanquet. 7042-6
Gleason, Ethel E.
    Reverie. 6764-6
Gleason, Harold Willard
    If the kitten had flown. 7019-1
    Traffic. 6750-6
    Valedictory. 6761-1
    Vesta. 6761-1
A **glee** for February. Louis Untermeyer. 6490-6,6143-5
A **glee** for winter. Alfred Domett. 6658-5,6597-X,6656-9
The **gleeman.** Frederick Victor Branford. 6071-4
Glen Allen's daughter. Unknown. 6682-8
"The **glen** is mine". Charles Murray. 6800-6
The **glen** of silence. Christopher M. ("Hugh MacDiarmid") Grieve. 6379-9
"The **glen** was fair as some Arcadian dell". The sleeper. Bayard Taylor. 6976-2
Glen, William
    Wae's me for Prince Charlie. 6180-X,6271-7,6219-9
'**Glen,**' a sheep-dog. Hilton Brown. 6269-5
Glen-Almain, the narrow glen. William Wordsworth. 6850-2, 6935-5,6867-7
Glenara. Thomas Campbell. 6600-3,6606-2,6438-8,6613-5
Glenaradale. Walter Chalmers Smith. 6180-X,6437-X
Glencar. Stephen Lucius Gwynn. 6872-3
Glencoe. Gilbert Keith Chesterton. 6301-2
Glendinning, William
    Sing to me, mother. 6836-7
Glenfinishk. John O'Leary. 6858-8
Glenfinlas. Sir Walter Scott. 6245-8
Glenfinlas; or Lord Ronald's coronach. Sir Walter Scott. 6828-6
Glengariff. Aubrey Thomas De Vere. 6086-2
Glenkindie. William Bell Scott. 6656-9
Glenkindie. Unknown. 6180-X
Glenlogie. Unknown. 6055-2,6056-0,6239-3,6600-3,6185-0, 6067-6,6438-8,6219-9
Glenn, Jessie
    The fire-fiend. 6411-6,6744-1
Glens of Wicklow. George F. Savage-Armstrong. 6174-5
Glickman, Gary
    Inside you insdie me. 6857-X
Glickman, Susan
    Sassafras. 6767-0
Glide soft, ye silver floods. William Browne. 6182-6,6023-4
A **glimpse** of Pan. James Whitcomb Riley. 6993-2
"A **glimpse** of higher bridal". Anniversary. Heloise M.B. Hawkins. 6836-7
The **glimpse.** Frederick William Faber. 6980-0
The **glimpse.** Louise Ayres Garnett. 6327-6
The **glimpse.** Sir William Watson. 6737-9
Glimpses. Russell M. Spear. 6850-2
Glines, Ellen
    The mistress of the inn. 6072-2
    Noli me tangere. 6039-0
"**Glion!** - Ah, twenty, it cuts". Obermann once more. Matthew Arnold. 6110-9,6199-0,6749-2
Glimpse in autumn. Jean Starr Untermeyer. 6345-4
"**Glisk** o the burn". Unknown. 6325-X
"**Glistening** high in the midnight sun...". Dewey and his men. Wallace Rice. 6946-0
Glitter box. Jana Harris. 6901-0
"The **glittering** heaven's refulgent glow". Part of the 19th Psalm. James Wallis Eastburn. 6752-2
The **glittering** plain, sels. William Morris. 6123-0
A **gloaming** call. Alexander Louis Fraser. 6433-7
Gloire de Dijon. David Herbert Lawrence. 6872-3
"**Gloom** and the night...", fr. A hymn of nature. Robert Bridges. 6487-6
"**Gloom** is upon thy lonely hearth". The deserted house. Felicia Dorothea Hemans. 6973-8
"The **gloom** of death is on the raven's wing". The raven.

GLOOM

Nicarhus. 7039-6
"Gloom of the night, gloom of the night". Aristophanes. 6435-3
"Gloom!/An October like November". Antwerp. Ford Madox (Hueffer) Ford. 6897-9
"Gloom, the mute spinner, grief weaved...". The burden of eternity. Jirt Karascek ze Lvovic. 6763-8
"The gloomiest day hath gleams of light". Lights and shades. Felicia Dorothea Hemans. 6973-8
"Gloomy and black are the cypress-trees". A vision. Adelaide Anne Procter. 6957-6
A gloomy day. Norbert Krapf. 6966-5
The gloomy night is gathering fast. Robert Burns. 6180-X, 6332-2
Gloomy winter's now awa'. Robert Tannahill. 6180-X,6086-2
Gloria belli. William J. Benners Jr. 6923-1
Gloria in excelsis. Georgiana Kling,e ("George Klingle") Holmes. 6461-2
Gloria in excelsis. Unknown. 6730-1
Gloria in excelsis. Unknown. 6778-6
Gloria mundi. Siegfried Sassoon. 6357-8
Gloria patri. Harvey C. Grumbine. 6799-9
The gloria patri. John Heywood. 6022-6
Gloriana. Edmund Spenser. 6188-5
Gloriana's England. Archibald T. Strong. 6784-0
Glories. Nelson Antrim Crawford. 6032-3
Glories. Lionel Johnson. 6641-0,6250-4,6383-7
"The glories of our blood and state". James Shirley. 6933-9
"The glories of our blood and state". Dirge. James Shirley. 6604-6
The glories of our blood and state. James Shirley. 6250-4, 6513-9,665-8,6639-9,6668-2,6125-7,6187-7,6328-4,6562-7,6733-6,6023-4
The glories of the present. Edgar A. Guest. 6862-6
The glories of the world sink down in gloom. Joseph Mary Plunkett. 6096 X
"Glories, pleasures, pomps". Dirge. John Ford. 6315-2,6383-7
"Glories, pleasures, pomps, delights and ease". A broken heart. John Ford. 6830-8
"Glorious God had great pity". Sing we with mirth, joy and solace. Unknown. 6756-5
"A glorious end". Annie Johnson Flint. 6097-8
The glorious fool. Henry Herbert Knibbs. 7012-4
The glorious gift of God. Benjamin Beddome. 6065-X
"Glorious god in Trinity". Jesu, fili Dei. John Trouluffe & Richard Smert. 6756-5
"A glorious headland bare to sun and sky". E.H. Brodie. 6997-5
"Glorious is the blending/Of light affections". Obedience and humility. William Wordsworth. 6980-0
The glorious name. Amos R. Wells. 6065-X
The glorious song of old. Edmund Hamilton Sears. 6145-1, 6424-8
The glorious song. Edmund Hamilton Sears. 6747-6
The glorious stars of heaven. Joshua Sylvester. 6250-4
"A glorious sun has set. And lo". The eagle. Caroline Russell Bispham. 6995-9
"The glorious sun went blushing to his bed". Sonnet ("The glorious sun"). Michael Drayton. 6436-1
The glorious survivors. Alfred Edgar Coppard. 6210-5
"A glorious tale indeed is mine". Mystery of King Herod. Edward Farquhar. 6939-8
"Glorious the day when in arms at Assunpink". Assunpink and Princeton. Thomas Dunn English. 6946-0
"Glorious things of thee are spoken". Psalm 087. Bible. 6848-0
Glorious things of thee are spoken. John Newton. 6337-3, 6214-8
"A glorious tree is the old gray oak". The oak. George Hill. 6049-8,6820-0
The glorious victory of Navarino!. Unknown. 6157-5
"A glorious voice has ceased!". The funeral day of Sir Walter Scott. Felicia Dorothea Hemans. 6973-8
"Gloriously the morn awakened". 'De Lord am coming'. Ellen Murray. 6926-6
Glorny's weir. Winifred M. Letts. 6090-0
Glory. Estelle Rooks. 6850-2
"Glory and honor and fame and everlasting...". Sherma.

Richard Watson Gilder. 6820-0
"Glory and loveliness have passed away". To Leigh Hunt, esq. John Keats. 6828-6
"The glory and the ardour of stage". Elegy on the death of Mme. Anna Pavlova. Edward Harry William Meyerstein. 6781-6
"A glory apparels the corn". June. James Abraham Martling. 6952-5
"Glory be to God for dappled things." Gerard Manley Hopkins. 6187-7,
Glory hallelujah! Unknown. 6016-2
Glory hallelujah! or John Brown's body. Charles Sprague Hall. 6946-0,6753-0
Glory hallelujah, or new John Brown song. Unknown. 6753-0
Glory in the commonplace, fr. Aurora Leigh. Elizabeth Barrett Browning. 6337-3
Glory in the northwest. Robert J. Burdette. 6588-0
The glory of age. Edgar A. Guest. 6862-6
The glory of all England. Edward W. Bok. 6039-0
The glory of God in creation. Thomas Moore. 6337-3
Glory of God revealed in Jesus, fr. Second Corinthians. Bible. 6337-3
The glory of God, fr. Psalms. Bible. 6136-2
The glory of God. Helen L. Bayley. 6798-0
The glory of motion. Reginald St. John Tyrwhitt. 6271-7, 6656-9
The glory of ships. Henry Van Dyke. 6961-4
The glory of the game. William Hamilton Cline. 6274-1
The glory of the garden. Rudyard Kipling. 6655-0
The, fr. The Book of Job glory of the horse. Bible. 7010-8
Glory of the plains. Sarah D. Ulmer. 6799-9
The glory of the year. Ernest Whitney. 6770-0
The glory of the year. J. Ernest Whitney. 6836-7
The glory of Washington. Timothy Dwight. 6449-3
Glory of women. Siegfried Sassoon. 6542-2
"A glory shines across the coming years". The coming race. James Arthur Edgerton. 6836-7
"The glory that was Greece is dust". Permanence. Jamie Sexton Holme. 6836-7
"'glory that was Greece', I read". The missing word. Walter De La Mare. 6905-3
The glory that was Greece. George Gordon, 6th Baron Byron. 6198-2,6114-1,6322-5
Glory to God alone. Madame De la Mothe Guion. 6814-6
"Glory to God on high, and jolly mirth". A Christmas carol. Francis Quarles. 6756-5
Glory to the king of kings. Charles Wesley. 6732-8
"Glory to the name of Jesus". Albert Benjamin Simpson. 6065-X
Glory to thee this night. Thomas Ken. 6065-X
Glory to them. Anderson M. Scruggs. 6780-8,6841-3,6337-3
The glory trail. Charles Badger Clark Jr. 6281-4,6161-3, 6464-7,6594-5
Glorying. Miyauchi. 6027-7
Gloucester moors. William Vaughn Moody. 6006-4,6310-1,6473-6,6726-3,6735-2,6288-1,6431-0,6467-1,6468-1,6491-4, 6723
Gloucester moors, sel. William Vaughn Moody. 6954-1
Gloucester moors, sels. William Vaughn Moody. 6102-8,6730-1,6076-5
The glove and the lions. Leigh Hunt. 6543-0,6571-6,6131-1, 6458-2,6219-9,6419-1,6424-8,6543-0,6571-6,6131-1, 6458-2,6219-9,6419-1,6424-8,6087-0,6105-2,6136-2, 6165-6,6198-2,6211-,6134-6,6302-0,6385-3,6527-9,6552-X,6614-,6239-3,6242-3,6407-8,6479-5,6499-X,6512-
The glove. Robert Browning. 6271-7,6527-9,6458-2,6419-1, 6655-0
The glove. Ben Jonson. 6182-6
The glove. Richard Lovelace. 6187-7,6026-9
The glove. Johann C. Friedrich von Schiller. 6842-1
The glove. Johann C. Friedrich von Schiller. 6606-2
The glove. Johann C. Friedrich von Schiller. 6732-8
Glover, C.W.
   The song my mother sang. 6097-8
Glover, Jean
   O'er the muir amang the heather. 6180-X,6086-2,6383-7
Glover, Richard
   Address of Leonidas. 6344-6
   Ballad of Admiral Hosier's ghost. 6086-2
Glover, Terrot Reaveley (tr.)

To his wife. Decimus Magnus Ausonius, 7039-6
The glow within. Berton Braley. 6761-1
The glow-worm. Vincent Bourne. 6814-6
The glow-worm. Edward Shanks. 6726-3
The glow-worm. William Wordsworth. 6134-6,6317-9,6545-7, 6383-7
Gloryrying in the cross. Isaac Watts. 6219-9
Glug-glug in salt sea. Robert Clairmont. 6751-4
Gluggity glug. Unknown. 6302-0
Gluggity-glug. George Colman the Younger. 6385-3,6240-7
"Glum and remote in the failing light range...". Suburbia. Charles Whitby. 6994-0
"GM, 27, 5'8", 135". Poetry reading. Duncan Mitchel. 7003-5
A glut on the market. Patrick Kavanagh. 6930-4
The glutton. Al-Sumaisir. 6362-4
The glutton. William Langland. 6022-6
The glutton. Thomas Warton (the Elder) 6962-2
Gluttony. William Langland. 6150-8
Glycine's song. Samuel Taylor Coleridge. 6383-7,6395-0
Glycine's song, fr. Zapolya. Samuel Taylor Coleridge. 6828-6
Glycon
   "All's dust, all's laughter...". F.L. Lucas (tr.). 6251-2
   Futility. J.A. Pott (tr.). 6435-3
Glyndon, Howard (Laura C. Redden Searing)
   The battle of Gettysburg. 6402-4
   Mazzini. 6240-7,6385-3
   The president's proclamation. 6524-4
   Which is best. 6066-8
Glyndon, Howard. See Redden, Laura C.
Glynn, John Francis
   Judge Not. 6954-1
   Unfettered. 6954-1
"The gnarled magnolia let a fragrant flower". Magnolia. Mary Helen Barbie. 7016-7
"A gnarled old tree trunk with shoots". The hanging tree. G. Perle Schmidt. 6799-9
Gnarled roots. Ethel H. Kleppinger. 6857-X
Gnass, Frances Marvel
   Unmasked. 6799-9
The gnat. Joseph Beaumont. 6315-2
Gnosis. Christopher Pearse Cranch. 6288-1,6309-8
The gnu. Hilaire Belloc. 6102-8
"Go & choose wt sport you will." Unknown. 6563-5
"Go 'way fiddle! - folks is tired o' hearin'..". The first banjo. Unknown. 6915-0
"Go 'way, fiddle! Folks is tired o' hearing...". The origin of the banjo. Irwin Russell. 7025-6
"Go - thou art all unfit to share". On a mischievous bull. William Cowper. 6814-6
"Go and catch a falling star". Song ("Go and catch a falling star."). John Donne. 6646-1,6102-8,6301-2, 6341-1,6089-7,6182-6,6527-9,6187-7,6562-7,6733-6, 6198-2,6315-2,6726-1,6430-2
"Go and catch a falling star". John Donne. 6536-8,6634-8, 6092-7,6371-3,6723-9
"'Go back, go back,' cries Andrew Battan...". Unknown. 6059-5
"Go book, go songs,and with your rhymes I send". To Mrs. C-S. Louis J. Magee. 7004-3
"Go bow thy head in gentle spirit". To a lily. James Matthewes Leagre. 7017-5
"Go bring the captive, he shall die". Ortiz. Hezekiah Butterworth. 6946-2
Go dark year: 1939. David Ross. 6761-1
Go down to Kew in lilac-time. Alfred Noyes. 6338-1,6499-X, 6649-6
Go down, death. James Weldon Johnson. 6337-3,6464-7,6628-3
Go down, Moses. Sally Bruce Kinsolving. 6979-7
Go down, Moses. Unknown. 6527-9,7017-5
'Go down, Moses!' Marcus B. Christian. 6178-8
"Go far enough away from anything". Distance and peace. Robert Francis. 6783-2
Go fetch me a pint o' wine. Robert Burns. 6198-2,6328-4
"Go for a sail this mornin'?". In the harbor. George Robert Sims. 6917-7
Go forth to the mount. Thomas Moore. 6848-0
"Go forth with precious seed". The missionary's song. Charles W. Denison. 6755-7
"Go forth! for she is gone!". The bird's release, fr. Lays of many lands. Felicia Dorothea Hemans. 6973-8
"Go forth, sad fragments of a broken strain". Introduction, fr. Yamoyden. Robert C. Sands. 6752-2
"Go forth, thou man of force!". The high-priest to Alexander. Alfred Lord Tennyson. 6848-0
Go forward. Ellen Murray. 6925-8
"Go foth to the mount- bring the olive". Go forth to the mount. Thomas Moore. 6848-0
Go from me. Elizabeth Barrett Browning. 6339-X,6019-6,6199-0,6250-4
"Go from me. Yet I feel that I shall stand". Sonnet ("Go from me"). Elizabeth Barrett Browning. 6236-9,6604-6, 6226-1
"Go home, boat people" Arlene E. Paul. 6857-X
Go it alone. John Godfrey Saxe. 6566-X
"Go make your mark far above me". Nearer my God and thee. Cy Warman. 6836-7
"Go not far in the land of light!". Wait. Alice Cary. 6969-X
"Go not, happy day". Song ("Go not"). Alfred Lord Tennyson. .437-X
"Go not, happy day", fr. Maud. Alfred Lord Tennyson. 6122-2,6110-9,6383-7
Go now, my song. Andrew Young. 6125-7
"Go on! go on!". A sermon at Clevedon. Thomas Edward Brown. 6809-X
Go rose, my Chloe's bosom grace. John Gay. 6192-3
"Go seek in the wild glen". Gentle Hugh Herries. Allan Cunningham. 6980-0
Go sleep, ma honey. Edward D. Barker. 6006-4
"Go softly, you whose careless feet". Boot hill. Sharlot M. Hall. 7012-4,7038-8
"Go tell Amynta, gentle swain". John Dryden. 6970-3
"Go tell old Nancy". Unknown. 6299-7
"Go tell the Spartans, thou that passeth by". Thermoplyae. Simonides. 7039-6
Go tell them that Jesus is living. Unknown. 6065-X
"Go thou and seek the house of prayer!". Written on a Sunday morning. Robert Southey. 6932-0
"Go thou thy way, and I go mine". Mizpah. Julia A. Baker. 6889-8
Go thou to Rome, fr. Adonais. Percy Bysshe Shelley. 6125-7
Go thou, that vainly dost mine eyes invite. Henry King. 6563-5
"Go thy waies since yu wilt goe." Unknown. 6563-5
Go to bed. Unknown. 6125-7
Go to bed early. Unknown. 6937-1
"Go to bed first." Unknown. 6363-2,6452-3
Go to dark Gethsemane. James Montgomery. 6144-3
"Go to now, ye rich men, weep and howl for...". 'Go to now, ye rich' Bible. 6954-1
Go to Saint Pether. Unknown. 6058-7
Go to sleep. Ella Warner Fisher. 7030-2
"Go to sleep, my baby". Unknown. 6364-0
Go to the barn with a lantern. Robert P. Tristram Coffin. 7040-X
"Go to the forest shade". The last wish. Felicia Dorothea Hemans. 6973-8
Go to thy rest, fair child. Unknown. 6302-0
"Go to thy rest, fair child." Lydia Huntley Sigourney. 6385-3
Go vay, Becky Miller, go vay! Unknown. 6791-3,6823-5,6823-5
Go vay, Becky Milley, go vay! Unknown. 6918-5
"Go where a foot hath never trod". Moses in the desert. James Montgomery. 6848-0
"Go where glory waits thee." Thomas Moore. 6302-0,6486-8, 6129-9,6543-0
"Go where the waters fall". The waterfall, sels. John Keble. 6832-4
"Go where the waves run rather Holborn-hilly". Lines to a lady. Thomas Hood. 6974-6
"Go you, O winds that blow from north to south" Alexander Craig. 6182-6
Go young man. M. Rosser Lunsford. 6857-X
"Go! Call them up from the sea, from the...". The call of the adventurers. Orrin K. Charles. 7007-8
Go! Forget me. Charles Wolf. 6174-5

Go! heart, hurt with adversity. Unknown. 6881-2
"Go! little bill, and command me hertely". She saw me in church. Unknown. 6881-2
"Go! little bill, and do me recommende". A love letter. Unknown. 6881-2
"Go! piteous hart, rased with dedly wo". Unfriendly fortune. John Skelton. 6881-2
"Go! trace th' unnumbered streams, o'er earth". The rivers. Felicia Dorothea Hemans. 6973-8
"Go, and look not back again". Discipulo discedenti. Heathcote William Garrod. 6785-9
Go, bird, and to the sky". Released. John Banister Tabb. 6785-9
"Go, boy, and light the torch! the night". The fisherman's hut. Charles Timothy Brooks. 7022-1
"Go, boy, and thy good mistress tell". Macbeth. James Smith. 6802-2
"Go, feel what I have felt." Unknown. 6302-0;6385-3
"Go, flag the train, boys, flag the train!". 'Flag the train'. William B. Chisholm. 6923-1
"Go, for they call you, shepherd, from the hill!" Matthew Arnold. 7020-5
"Go, for they call you, shepherd, from the...". The scholar gipsy. Matthew Arnold. 6208-3,6437-X,6655-0, 6023-4,6046-3,6301 ,6196-6,6420-3,6245-8,6250-4,6199-0,6125 ,6110-9,6150-8,6668-2,6828-6
"Go, happy fan, in all the land". With a fan from Rimmel's. William Ernest Henley. 6770-9
Go, heart. James Wedderburn. 6189-3
Go, heart, unto the lamp of licht. Unknown. 6845-6
"Go, in thy glory, o'er the ancient sea". The parting ship. Felicia Dorothea Hemans. 6973-8
"Go, little book, and find our friend". Lines sent to George Lyttelton. James Thomson. 6816-2
"Go, little poem, and present". Acrostic ("Go, little poem"). Charles Lamb. 6724-7
"Go, lovely boy! to yonder tow'r". Verses written during the war, 1756-1763. Thomas Osbert Mordaunt. 6932-0
Go, lovely rose. Edmund Waller. 6104-4,6646-1,6543-0,6371-3,6438-8,6732 ,6301-2,6203-4,6219-9,6396-9,6737-9, 6099-4,6102-8,6385-3,6187-7,6289-X,6733 ,6122-2,6154-0,6186-9,6246-6,6328-4,6339 ,6208-3,6152-4,6194-X, 6430-2,6026-9,6250 ,6481-7,6563-5,6726-3,6317-9,6198-2,6302
"Go, lovely rose!". Song ("Go, lovely rose!"). Edmund Waller. 6150-8,6189-3,6723-9,6052-8,6204-0,6315-2, 6562-7,6604-6
Go, ploughman, plough. Joseph ("Seosamh MacCathmhaoil") Campbell. 6891-X
Go, pretty birds! Thomas Heywood. 6198-2,6129-9
"Go, pytyous hart, rasyd with dedly wo" John Skelton. 6380-2
"Go, roam through the isle; view her...towers". Twydee. William Peter. 6980-0
Go, rose, go. William Beale. 6328-4
Go, sad complaint. Charles, Duc d' Orleans. 6881-2
Go, silly worm. Joshua Sylvester. 6182-6
"Go, silly worm, drudge, trudge, and travell". Omnia somnia. Joshua Sylvester. 6933-9
"Go, sit upon the lofty hill". The autumn. Elizabeth Barrett Browning. 6123-0
Go, song of mine. Dante Gabriel Rossetti. 6328-4
"Go, songs, for ended is our brief, sweet play". Francis Thompson. 6383-7
"Go, soul, the body's guest". Sir Walter Raleigh. 6181-8
"Go, spend your penny, beauty". Sonnet ("Go, spend"). John Masefield. 6023-4
"Go, take thine angle, and with practised line". Angling. Thomas Doubleday. 7015-9
"Go, thou gentle whispering wind". Love's errand. Thomas Carew. 6830-8
"Go, topless, Geraneia...", fr. Lost at sea. Simonides. 6435-3
"Go, travel 'mid the hills!...",fr.Seaside meditation. Elizabeth Barrett Browning. 6123-0
"Go, virgin kid, with lambent kiss". To a glove. Unknown. 6874-X
"Go- thou art free- thou that dist lift". The murderer. James Abraham Martling. 6952-5
Go-kyo-goku

"I'm sleeping all alone, and hear". William N. Porter (tr.). 6852-9
"A goal ahead, - dim -.". Your ambition. Annie B. Alguire. 6789-1
The goal and the way. John Oxenham. 6386-1
Goal far and near. Margaret Avison. 6767-0
The goal of life. Robert Burns. 6322-5
The goal.. Walt Mason. 6583-X
The goal. Frank W. Gunsaulus. 6337-3
The goal. Marie Tello Phillips. 6799-9
The goal. Ella Wheeler Wilcox. 6337-3
The goat and the swing. John Townsend Trowbridge. 6165-6
The goat paths. James Stephens. 6234-2,6244-X,6395-0,6726-3,6513-9,6581
The goat without a beard. John Gay. 6972-X
Goat-pen. Luis L. Franco. 6759-X
The goat.. Roland Young. 6722-0
The goat. Anyte. 6435-3
The goat. Carolyn Wells. 6882-0
Goats. Lydia Gibson. 6880-4
Goats. Charles Erskine Scott Wood. 6396-9
Gob-ny-ushtey (Water's mouth). Thomas Edward Brown. 6809-X
The goblets. Celia Dimmette. 6789-1
"Goblin and kobold and elf and gnome". The Lord of the Dunderberg. Arthur Guiterman. 6773-5
The goblin clock-maker. Constance M. Topping. 6042-0
Goblin feet. John Ronald Renel Tolkien. 6421-3
The goblin goose. Unknown. 6440-X
Goblin market. Christina Georgina Rossetti. 6614-3,6634-8, 6657-7,6655-0,6458-2,6430-2,6245-8
Goblin market, sels. Christina Georgina Rossetti. 6334-9, 6526-0
"A goblin trapped in netted skein". Ballade of fairy gold. Rosamund Marriott ("Graham R. Tomson") Watson. 6770-0
The goblin's song. James Telfer. 6125-7
Goblins. Unknown. 6696-8
God. Henry Bellamann. 6036-6
God. Sir John Bowring. 6240-7
God. Gamaliel Bradford. 6291-1,6303-9,6337-3,6532-5,6730-1
God. Gabriel Romanovitch Derzhavin. 6385-3,6964-9,6392-6, 6404-3
God. John Donne. 6219-9
God. Gonzalo Escudero. 6759-X
God. John Banister Tabb. 6337-3
God ("There is an Eye that never sleeps"). James Cowden Wallace. 6303-9,6730-1
"God almightie first planted a garden...". Of gardens. Sir Francis Bacon. 7020-5
God and man. S.A. Nagel. 6303-9,6337-3
God and man. Albert Durrant Watson. 6115-X
God and man, fr. Oedipus tyrannus. Sophocles. 6435-3
The god and the Bayadere. Johann Wolfgang von Goethe. 6842-1
The god and the schoolboy. William Canton. 6250-4
God and the strong ones. Margaret Widdemer. 6532-5,6542-2, 6265-2,6161-3,6029-3
God and the universe. Alfred Lord Tennyson. 6123-0,6214-8
"A god and yet a man". Wit wonders. Unknown. 6881-2
The god at play. Laurence Housman. 6507-4
God be in my head. Sarum Primer. 6337-3
God be in my head. Unknown. 6179-6,6489-2
"God be with the Irish host". O'Byrne's bard to the clans of Wicklow. Unknown (Irish). 6858-8
"God be with you in your need". Resurgat. Arthur Shearly Cripps. 6788-3
"God bless my little one! How fair!". A prayer ("God bless"). Edgar Fawcett. 6078-1
God bless our father-land. Oliver Wendell Holmes. 6014-5
"God bless our good prince,&..establish..crown". The German tower-keeper, fr. Jonas Fisher. James Carnegie; Earl of Southesk. 6819-7
God bless our home. Robert Freeman. 6337-3
"God bless our lord the king!". The king's anthem. Unknown. 6859-6
God bless our native land. Timothy Dwight. 6304-7
God bless our native land. Siegfried A. Mahlmann and William E. Hickson. 6337-3
God bless our native land. Unknown. 6623-2
God bless our school. Unknown. 6913-4

God bless our stars forever. Benjamin Franklin Taylor. 6815-4
God bless our union. G. Parker. 6149-4
"God bless the ancient Puritans", sels. Oliver Wendell Holmes. 66601-1
"God bless the day you took to livin'!". A few lines from a hard-workin' man to his dear old un. Louis J. Magee. 7004-3
God bless the flag. Unknown. 6465-5
"God bless the grey mountains of dark Donegal!". Inishowen. Sir Charles Gavan Duffy. 6858-8
"God bless the king, I mean...faith's defender". Extempore verses ("God bless"). John Byrom. 6932-0
"God bless the little children". The little children. Unknown. 6772-7
"God bless the man who first invented sleep". Sleep. John Godfrey Saxe. 6787-5
"God bless the master of this house". The singers in the snow. Unknown. 6806-5
God bless the master of this house. Unknown. 6904-5
God bless thee, boy. Eliza Cook. 6097-8
God bless us every one. James Whitcomb Riley. 6145-1
"God bless you all this Christmas day". A Christmas carol. Edgar A. Guest. 7033-7
God bless you, dear, to-day. John Bennett. 6274-1
"God bless you, lads!". Women to men. Unknown. 7031-0
"God bless you, parents of young lives gone...". To four mothers. Ethel Love Dunham. 6799-9
God bless your beautiful hand! John Whitaker Watson. 6774-3
God dawg my lousy soul. Unknown. 6609-7
"God did anoint thee with his odorous oil", sels. Elizabeth Barrett Browning. 6601-1
"God did not test him in the open space". The test. Edgar A. Guest. 6748-4
"God doth suffice! O thou, the patient one." Sir Edwin Arnold. 6225-3
"God drew the plan and flung these ramparts...". From the ageless soil. George Sanford Holmes. 6836-7
God everywhere in nature. Carlos Wilcox. 6385-3
A God for you, fr. Songs for Sally. Marion Strobel. 6778-6
A God for you. Marion Strobel. 6039-0
God forgives, but men do not. Celestin Pierre Cambiaire. 6826-X
God forsakes Anthony. Constantine P. Cavafy. 6352-7
"God from the first created diversely". Semonides. 6251-2
"God gave a gift to earth: a child". God's gifts. Adelaide Anne Procter. 6772-7,6957-6
"God gave all men all earth to love". Sussex. Rudyard Kipling. 6810-3
"God gave me thee, nor all the world's alarms". Possession. Unknown. 6889-8
God give me joy. Thomas Curtis Clark. 6461-2
God give us men! Josiah Gilbert Holland. 6260-1,6465-5, 6143-5
"God gives his mercies to be spent". Vanity of the world. William Cowper. 6814-6
"God gives not kings the style of gods in vain". Sonnet ("God gives not kings"). James I; King of Scotland. 6934-7
"God gives us love. Something to love". Lines to J.S., sels. Alfred Lord Tennyson. 6867-7
"God grant that all who watch to-day." Julia H. Thayer. 6225-3
"God has a house three streets away". The furnace man. Amelia Josephine Burr. 6750-6
"God has a library". God's library. J. Lewis Milligan. 6796-4
"God has builded a house with a low lintel". Sanctuary. Aline Kilmer. 6776-X
"God has not told us whither we are going:". A marching song for women. Margaret Widdemer. 7038-8
"God has painted varied scenes". Mirror paintings. Jessie Haefner. 6799-9
God hears prayer. Ethel Romig Fuller. 6532-5
"God help us! Who's ready? There's danger...". Who's ready? Edna Dean Proctor. 6753-0
"'God helping me', cried Columbus...". Columbia's banner. Edna Dean Proctor. 7022-1
"God helping me/I promise not to be an alcoholic". A resolve. Unknown. 6715-8
God hides his people. Madame De la Mothe Guion. 6814-6
God in a garden. Frances Stockwell Lovell. 7030-2
God in all. Unknown. 6461-2
God in nature. William Wordsworth. 6142-7
"God in the great assembly stands". Psalm 082. Bible. 6848-0
God incarnate. Ruth M. Williams. 6065-X
"God is a master workman. He". God's blunder. Clement Wood. 6880-4
"God is a proposition". The magnetic mountain (21). Cecil Day Lewis. 6985-1
God is at the anvil. Lew Sarett. 6337-3,6374-8,6730-1
God is at the organ. Joyce Kilmer. 6303-9
God is at the organ. Egbert Sandford. 6337-3
God is good. Unknown. 6752-2
God is here. Madeleine Aaron. 6337-3
God is love. Sir John Bowring. 6014-5,6219-9.6337-3
God is love. Alice Cary. 6969-X
God is love. Unknown. 6271-7,6312-8
'God is love'. Thomas Edward Brown. 6809-X
God is my strong salvation. James Montgomery. 6337-3
God is not dumb, fr. Bibliolatres. James Russell Lowell. 6337-3,6418-3,6730-1
God is nowhere. Unknown. 6912-6
God is one. Unknown (Indian) 6337-3
"God is our refuge and strength". Psalm 056. Bible. 6861-8
"God is praise and glory". Psalm of battle. Unknown (Arabic). 7039-6
"God is shaping the great future of the island". The islands of the sea. George Edward Woodberry. 6946-0
"God is too great to be merely wise". Greatness. Minerva Wright Rockwell. 6799-9
"God is with me! God is with me!". In a thunderstorm. Unknown. 6952-5
God keep you. Mary Ainge ("Madeline Bridges") De Vere. 6337-3
God knoweth. Mary Gardner Brainard. 6600-3
God knoweth. M.A. Bridgman. 6304-7
God knoweth best. William White. 6868-5
God knows. Unknown. 6918-5
God knows best. Caroline Atherton Mason. 6889-8
God knows best. Caroline Atherton Mason. 6337-3;6303-9
"God knows it, I am with you. If to prize". To a republican friend, 1848. Matthew Arnold. 6828-6,6199-0,6655-0
'God knows'. Benjamin Franklin Taylor. 6815-4
"God knows, it would be pleasanter to spend". The time of wheat. Bert Cooksley. 6761-1
God laughs. William Dresia. 6397-7
God leads the way. Cleanthes. 6435-3
"God let never so old a man". Unknown. 6518-X
God looketh on the heart. Unknown. 6720-4
"God loves an idle rainbow". Ralph Hodgson. 6897-9
God Lyaeus. John Fletcher. 6634-8,6250-4,6301-2
"God made a man to bear the brunt of hate". Abraham Lincoln. Harry Elmore Hurd. 6761-1
"God made a race of plowmen". Plowmen. Howard McKinley Corning. 6954-1
God made all things. Unknown. 6629-1
"God made my mother on an April day". My mother. Francis Ledwidge. 6812-X,6873-1
"God made our bodies of all the dust". Britons beyond the seas. Harold Begbie. 6793-X
"God made the night, and, marvelling how". Quatrain ("God made the night..."). Robert Loveman. 6941-X
God made this day for me. Edgar A. Guest. 6374-8
"God made you in his image, yet I saw". The sixth day. Horace Shipp. 6884-7
God makes a path. Roger Williams. 6337-3,6418-3,6730-1
"God makes a rime". Ben H. Smith. 6662-3
"God makes sech nights, all white an' still". The courtin'. James Russell Lowell. 6008-0,6083-8,6092-7, 6219-9,6265-2,6307 ,6121-4,6396-9,6281-4,6126-5,6288-1,6964 ,6823-5,6302-0,6385-3,6279-2,6089-4,6332-2, 6473 ,6600-3,6696-8,6732-8,6735-2,6176-1,6404 ,6610-0,6505-8,6438-8,6419-1,6431-0,6278
"God measures souls by their capacity". Ella Wheeler Wilcox. 6066-8
God moves in a mysterious way. William Cowper. 6304-7,6737-

GOD

9
God neither known nor loved by the world. Madame De la Mothe Guion. 6814-6
"God never meant that we should call this home". M.E.K. 6238-5
"God numbers them, his servants hoary hairs". Sonnet: for the hairs of your head are all numbered. William Kirby. 6796-4
"God o'er the sea has sent/What apparitions!". The, sels bridegroom. Charles Julian Downey. 6836-7
God of a universe within whose bounds. Katharine L. Aller. 6337-3
The God of Abraham praise. Thomas Olivers. 6219-9
God of all love and pity. Caroline M. Noel. 6303-9
God of grace and God of glory. Harry Emerson Fosdick. 6337-3
"The God of loue my shepherd is." Unknown. 6563-5
"The God of love my shepherd is". The twenty-third psalme. Bible. 6848-0
The god of love. John Payne. 6770-0
The god of music. Edith M. Thomas. 6479-5
The god of my childhood. Frederick William Faber. 6127-3, 6242-3,6131-1
"God of my life, to thee I call". Looking upward in a storm. William Cowper. 6814-6
"God of our father's rise". Birthday ode for the year 1800. Henry James Pye. 6867-7
"God of our fathers, see the strife—". Love divine. Isabelle Noyes. 6818-9
God of our life. Hugh Thomson Kerr. 6337-3
"God of our sires, who reigneth so unsteadily". Darkness before dawn. Gelett Burgess. 6880-4
The god of sheep. John Fletcher. 6052-8,6182-6
God of the earth, the sky, the sea. Samuel Longfellow. 6337-3
The God of the living. John Ellerton. 6730-1
God of the nations. Walter Russell Bowie. 6337-3
God of the nations. John Haynes Holmes. 6337-3
"God of the nations! thou whose hand". The birthday of Washington. Silas Weir Mitchell. 6936-3
God of the open air. Henry Van Dyke. 6961-4
God of the prophets. Denis Wortman. 6337-3
"God of the thunder! from whose cloudy seat". Jewish hymn in Babylon. Henry Hart Milman. 6980-0,6848-0
God of the young. William Rose Benet. 6761-1
"The god of war, money changer of dead bodies". Aeschylus. 6665-8
The god of war. Sophocles. 6435-3
The god of wealth. Timocreon. 6435-3
"God of winds, when thou art growne." Unknown. 6563-5
"God of years, thy love hath led us". Centennial Hymn. Jay Glover Eldridge. 6799-9
God our father. Frederick William Faber. 6730-1
God our help. Unknown. 6931-2
God our refuge. Richard Chenevix Trench. 6337-3
God our refuge, fr. Psalm 91. Bible. 6337-3
God pity them. Hildegarde Flanner. 6808-1
God prays. Angela Morgan. 6337-3,6730-1,6542-2
God provideth for the morrow. Unknown. 6049-8
God punishes. Archilochus. 6435-3
"God rest that Jewy woman". Song for the clatter-bones. Frederick Robert Higgins. 6930-4
God rest ye merry, gentlemen. Unknown. 6466-3,6746-8,6747-6
God rest ye, merry gentlemen. Dinah Maria Mulock Craik. 6145-1,6608-9
God rest you merry, gentlemen. Unknown. 6105-2,6145-1,6337-3
"God rest you, Chrysten gentil men". Chrystmasse of olde. Eugene Field. 6949-5
"God said, 'I am tired of kings'". Boston hymn, sel. Ralph Waldo Emerson. 6954-1
"God said, 'I am tired of kings'.". Remarks about kings. Henry Van Dyke. 6961-4
"God said, and frowned, as he looked...". John Masefield. Amy Sherman Bridgeman. 6762-X
"God said: I am tired of kings". God's message to men. Ralph Waldo Emerson. 6964-9
God save Ireland. Timothy Daniel [or Donill] Sullivan. 6930-4

598

God save Ireland. Timothy Daniel [or Donill] Sullivan. 6858-8
God save Ireland! Timothy Daniel [or Donill] Sullivan. 7009-4
"God save great George our king". A loyal song. Henry Carey. 6934-7
"God save me for thy holy name". Psalm 054. Bible. 6848-0
"God save old Scotland! Such a cry". The Rev. Habakkuk McGruther of Cape Wrath, in 1879. John Davidson. 6819-7
God save our gracious king. Unknown. 6337-3
God save our native land. Julius H. Seelye. 6578-3
God save our president. Francis De Haes Janvier. 6913-4
God save our president. Francis De Haes Janvier. 6946-0
God save the king. Henry Carey. 6219-9,6126-5,6240-7,6732-8
God save the king. Unknown. 6271-7,6289-X
God save the nation! Theodore Tilton. 6113-3
"God save the rights of man". Ode ("God save"). Philip Freneau. 6589-9,6265-2,6288-1,6121-4
God save the state. Charles Timothy Brooks. 6171-0
God scatters beauty. Walter Savage Landor. 6153-2,6199-0
"God scatters beauty as he scatters flowers" Walter Savage Landor. 6828-6
God sees. Unknown. 6629-1
God send us men. Frederick J. Gillman. 6337-3,6386-1
God send us men. F.J. Gilman. 6303-9
"God send us peace, and keep red strife away". At Fredericksburg - Dec. 13, 1862. John Boyle O'Reilly. 6917-7
"God sends his teachers unto every age", fr. Rhoecus. James Russell Lowell. 6934-7
"God sends us a little home". A prayer for a little home. Unknown. 6303-9,6964-9
"God sent him in a garden fair". Weariness. Edgar A. Guest. 6869-3
"God sowed a seed within your soul". Your work. Carolyn Renfrew. 6789-1
"God speaketh in the flowers. Each rosy...". Flowers. James Abraham Martling. 6952-5
God speaks in all religions. Thomas Lake Harris. 6102-8, 6337-3,6076-5
"God speed the horse on the fields of France". On the fields of France. Thomas H. Herndon. 7010-8
"God speed the year of jubilee". The triumph of freedom. William Lloyd Garrison. 7009-4
"God spoke to her, and so she fell asleep". Peace. Cora Fabbri. 6486-8
"God strengthen me to bear myself". Who shall deliver me. Christina Georgina Rossetti. 6931-2
God suffers. Georgia Harkness. 6532-5
God supreme. Wilhelm Hey. 6952-5
God the architect. Harry Kemp. 6303-9,6337-3,6730-1,6250-4, 6214-8
"God the creator! our father eternal". Come to our land. James Abraham Martling. 6952-5
"God the creator, with a pulseless hand". The measure. Elizabeth Barrett Browning. 6848-0
"God the dew". Prayer ("God the dew.") Maltbie Davenport Babcock. 6461-2
God the everlasting light of the saints above. Philip Doddridge. 6024-2,6545-7
God the life of nature. Mordecai Kaplan. 6532-5
God the strong, God of the weak. Richard Watson Gilder. 6337-3
God the true source of consolation. Thomas Moore. 6392-6
"God thought to give the sweetest thing". The mother. George Newell Lovejoy. 6097-8,6143-5
"God touched his eyes - he saw the...future". Woodrow Wilson. Marguerite Weed. 6847-2
God was otherwheres. Unknown. 6720-4
The God who hides. Francis Quarles. 6337-3
"God who made the great book of the world". The brothers, sels. William Wordsworth. 6867-7
"A god who makes/Swift clouds". An autumn god. Margaret W. Paradise. 7014-0
The god who waits. Leslie Coulson. 6650-X
"God will'd creation, but creation was not". Volition. Thomas Wade. 6980-0
God wills it. Gabriela (Lucila Godoy Alcayaga) Mistral.

6759-X
"God wills no man a slave. The man most meek". Washington. James Jeffrey Roche. 6946-0
God with us. Nancy Byrd Turner. 6144-3
God within yet above. Sir Lewis Morris. 6337-3
"God wrote his loveliest poem on the day". Silver poplars. Grace Noll Crowell. 6778-6
"God! do not let my loved one die". A prayer ("God! do not let"). James Russell Lowell. 6486-8
"God! scorched by battle-fires we stand". Hymn of the Polish exiles. Harriet Martineau. 7009-4
"God! what does it matter! Go!/What do I care?". Black frost. May Folwell Hoisington. 7038-8
God's acre. Conrad Aiken. 6011-0
God's acre. Blanche Edith Baughan. 6784-0
God's acre. Witter Bynner. 6556-2
God's acre. A. C. Stockman. 6952-5
God's anvil. Julius Sturm. 6911-8
God's barn. Winifred Welles. 6761-1
God's beverage. James S. Watkins. 6916-9
"God's blessing lead us, help us!". Hymn against pestilence. St. (atr.) Colmon. 6930-4
God's blessing on Munster. Saint Patrick (atr) 6930-4
God's blessings. William Cornish. 6153-2
God's blunder. Clement Wood. 6880-4
God's challengers. Marion Perham Gale. 6542-2
God's child. Roden Noel. 6772-7
God's concern. Palladas. 6435-2
God's controversy with New England, sels. Michael Wigglesworth. 6008-0
God's country. O.C. Auringer. 6920-7
God's creatures, fr. Hymn XIV. Christopher Smart. 6545-7
God's dark. John Martin. 6337-3
God's denunciation against Pharaoh-Hophra, or Apries. Alfred Lord Tennyson. 6848-0
God's dominion and decrees. Isaac Watts. 6152-4
God's dreams. Thomas Curtis Clark. 6532-5
God's dreams. Thomas Curtis Clark. 6954-1
God's eyes. George Herbert Clarke. 6797-2
God's father care. Unknown (German) 6373-X
God's ferns. J.H. Jowett. 6232-6
"God's fire-ball rolling smooth o'er heavens..". In deserto. Arthur Shearly Cripps. 6800-6
God's first temples. William Cullen Bryant. 6392-6,6521-X, 6376-4
God's fool. Celia Duffin. 6090-0
God's fools. William H. Hamilton. 6269-5
God's funeral. Thomas Hardy. 6532-5,6730-1
God's garden. Richard Burton. 6338-1,6632-1,6730-1
God's garden. Dorothy Frances Gurney. 6337-3,6654-2
God's gift. Ernest Howard Crosby. 6006-4
God's gift. Alfred Noyes. 6476-0
God's gift to man. Elizabeth B. Thompson. 6270-9
God's gifts. Adelaide Anne Procter. 6772-7,6957-6
God's gifts to the people. Unknown. 6149-4
God's grandeur. Gerard Manley Hopkins. 6246-6,6315-2,6489-2,6107-9,6655-0
God's handmaid. Hugh Francis Blunt. 6285-7
God's hands. Robert Liddell Lowe. 6640-2
God's harp. Gustav Falke. 7039-6
God's hills. William Noel Hodgson. 7027-2
God's hills. Edward Melbourne. 7031-0
God's in hiks heaven. Robert Browning. 6654-2
"God's in me when I dance./God, making spring". Dance. Mary Carolyn Davies. 6959-2
God's jewels. Estella Moul Miller. 6906-1
God's judgment on a wicked bishop. Robert Southey. 6614-3, 6458-2,6129-9,6419-1
God's judgment on Hatto. Robert Southey. 6302-0,6385-3, 6484-1
God's justice. Nagata. 6027-7
God's library. J. Lewis Milligan. 6796-4
God's likeness. John Banister Tabb. 6850-2
God's love. Unknown. 6049-8
God's mark on all things. Amelia Opie. 6629-1
God's masterpiece, us humans. Anna Jirak Krause. 6799-9
God's mercy. Frederick William Faber. 6337-3
God's message to men. Ralph Waldo Emerson. 6964-9
God's mother. Laurence Housman. 6282-2
God's mothers. Douglas Malloch. 6449-3

God's music. Frederic Edward Weatherley. 6417-5
"God's need for beauty must have been immense". Conception. Grace Phillips. 6750-6
God's omnipresent agency. Carlos Wilcox. 6752-2
God's own country. Arthur Shearly Cripps. 6625-9
God's pity. Louise Driscoll. 6501-5
God's plan. Miyoshi. 6027-7
God's plans. May Riley Smith. 6337-3
"God's power does here transmute our ill...". Transmutations. William White. 6868-5
God's providence. John Milton. 6935-5
God's ragamuffin army. George Lansing Taylor. 6686-0
God's remembrance. Francis Ledwidge. 6244-X
"God's son is born, his mother is a maid". Blessed be that lady bright. Unknown. 6756-5
God's sunshine. John Oxenham. 6654-2
God's support and guidance. Unknown. 6294-6
God's unspeakable gift. Macey P. Sealey. 6065-X
God's virtue. Barnabe Barnes. 6436-1
God's way. Horatius Bonar. 6337-3,6525-2
God's way. Dorothy Clarke Wilson. 6337-3
God's ways. Unknown. 6303-9,6337-3
God's will. Mildred Howells. 6337-3
God's will for you and me. Unknown. 6211-3
God's wisdom and power. Unknown. 6049-8
God's wonders. Eliza Lamb Maryln. 6925-8
God's word. Takayoshi Matsuyama. 6027-7
God's work. Gabriel (Thomas Nicoll Hepburn) Setoun. 6937-1
God's work. Ella Wheeler Wilcox. 6617-8
God's world. John Clifford. 6337-3
God's world. Edna St. Vincent Millay. 6102-8,6154-0,6303-9, 6332-2,6506-6,6538 ,6371-3,6253-9,6336-5,6104-4,6076-5,6121 ,6556-2,6374-8
God's world. Edna St. Vincent Millay. 6861-8
"God's world is bathed in beauty". Two worlds. Adelaide Anne Procter. 6957-6
God's-acre. Henry Wadsworth Longfellow. 6302-0,6385-3,6465-5,6486-8,6214-8,6304
"God, almighty, be thou praised". The ambrosian song of praise. Unknown. 6952-5
"God, dear God! Does she know her port". Gloucester moors, sel. William Vaughn Moody. 6954-1
"God, for the man who knew him face to face". Helen Hunt's grave. Virginia Donaghe McClurg. 6836-7
God, fr. Dawn. Harold Monro. 6730-1
God, free the drink captive. Frances Dana Barker ("Aunt Fanny") Gage. 6685-2
God, He's gwine to set dis world on fire. Unknown. 6594-5
"God, give me sympathy and sense". Prayer. Margaret Emerson Bailey. 6654-2
"God, let me write a rhyme so pure". Not thou. Robert Loveman. 6941-X
God, make me brave. Unknown. 6214-8
God, make my life a little light. B.M. Edwards. 6303-9
God, our dwelling place, fr. Psalm 90. Bible. 6337-3
"God, set our feet low and our forehead high", sels. Elizabeth Barrett Browning. 6601-1
"God, that heaven's seven climates hath...". Moses and the dervish. Owen (Edward Bulwer-Lytton, Earl Lytton) Meredith. 6848-0
"God, the eternal! Infinite!". Cain: a mystery. George Gordon, 6th Baron Byron. 6848-0,6945-2
"God, the master pilot". The great adventure. Kendall Banning. 6846-4
God, the omnipotent. Henry Fothergill Chorley and John Ellerton. 6337-3
God, the unplucked notes. Walta Borawski. 7003-5
God, thou art good. Philip Henry Savage. 6006-4
"God, though this life is but a wraith". Prayer ("God, though this life"). Louis Untermeyer. 6076-5,6250-4, 6732-8,6653-4,6723-9,6102-8,6211-3,6211-3,6337-3, 6501-5,6266-0,6730-1,6102
God, through his offspring nature, gave me love. Charles Gibson. 6762-X
"God, to thee we humbly bow". A battle hymn. George Henry Boker. 6753-0
God, when you thought of a pine tree. Unknown. 6374-8
"God, who created me from sodden clay" Fedor Sologub. 6103-6
God, you have been too good to me. Charles Wharton Stork.

GOD, 600

6007-2,6337-3,6509-0,6730-1,6393-4
God-bye, young man. Alfred Edward Housman. 6371-3
God-forgotten. Thomas Hardy. 6507-4,6655-0
The **god-maker,** man. Don Marquis. 6337-3,6532-5,6730-1,6431-0
God-seeking. Sir William Watson. 6730-1
"**God-speed,** and naught to stay me!". The unseen trail. Mary Steward Cutting. 7007-8
"**God**/For the gladness here where the sun...". Our prayer of thanks. Carl Sandburg. 6897-9
"**God**/They are so cold and still/They who die". Enigma. Mae Berry Rogers. 6799-9
"**Goddam** the empty sky" Violeta Parra. 7036-1
Goddard, Gloria
    Prunned trees. 6076-5
    To the commonplace. 6102-8,6076-5
Goddard, Gregg
    The airman. 6474-4
Goddard, Julia
    Hide and seek. 6913-4
Goddess. Amir Khusrau. 6448-5
The **goddess** of the hearth. Unknown (Greek) 6435-3
The **goddess.** Kathleen Raine. 6210-5
Goddesses three, sels. Unknown. 6427-2
Goddesses' glory. Unknown. 6563-5
"**Godes** son for the love of man". Make we merry in this feast. Unknown. 6756-5
Godfrey Gordon Gustavus Gore. William Brighty Rands. 6891-X,6861-8
Godfrey, Thomas
    Amyntor. 6288-1
    the court of fancy, sels. 6008-0
    The invitation. 6288-1,6072-2
    The prince of Parthia, a tragedy, sels. 6008-0
    The prince of Parthia, sels. 6008-0,6009-9
    A song ("Young Thyrsis"). 6288-1
    The wish. 6288-1
Godiva. Oliver Herford. 6440-X
Godiva. Alfred Lord Tennyson. 6331-4,6110-9,6464-1,6655-0
Godley, Alfred Dennis
    After Horace. 6089-7
    The motor-bus. 6633-X
    Pensees de Noel. 6089-7
    Penses de Noel. 6089-7,6287-3
Godley, Alfred Dennis (tr.)
    The army of Xerxes. Delphic Oracle, 6435-3
    "Hear, Epicydes' son: 'twere much to thy present". Unknown, 6435-3
    Neutral Argos. Delphic Oracle, 6435-3
    The power of an oath. Delphic Oracle, 6453-4
    The wooden walls of Athens. Delphic Oracle, 6435-3
Godly casuistry, fr. Hudibras. Samuel Butler. 6933-9
The **godly.** Samuel Butler. 6278-4
Godolphin Horne. Hilaire Belloc. 6228-8
Godolphin, Sidney
    Chorus. 6317-9
    Chorus ("Vain man, born to no happiness"). 6315-2
    "Cloris, it is not thy disdain". 6187-7
    "Lord when the wise men came from afar". 6933-9
    Lord when the wise men came from farr. 6341-1
    On Sir F. Carew. 6908-8
    Or love me less or love me more. 6563-5
    Quatrains. 6933-9
    Reply. 6933-9
    Song ("Cloris"). 6341-1
    Song ("Noe more"). 6341-1
    Song ("Or love mee lesse..."). 6933-9
    Song ("Or love mee"). 6562-7
    To Chloris. 6563-5
    Wise men and shepherds. 6931-2
Godoy Alcayaga, Lucila. See "Mistral, Gabriela"
Godric, Saint
    A cry to Mary. 6881-2
Gods. Walt Whitman. 7014-0
Gods and heores at the Gael. Eleanor Rogers Cox. 6172-9
The **gods** are dead. William Ernest Henley. 6770-0
The **gods** are dead. William Ernest Henley. 6875-8
"The **gods** are dead? Perhaps they are!...". The gods are dead. William Ernest Henley. 6770-0
"The **gods** are gone, the temples over-thrown". Sorrento. Bayard Taylor. 6976-2
"**Gods** are gone. In vain about their shoulders". In the Hebrites. F.L. Lucas. 6782-4
The **gods** are just. William Shakespeare. 6438-8
"The **gods** are not of Rome or Italy". On the south shore of Avernus, fr. Hannibal. John Nichol. 6819-7
"The **Gods** held me in Egypt...", fr. The Odyssey. Homer. 6251-2
Gods in the gutter. Robert Service. 6159-1
The **gods** laughed on high Olympus. Leonora Speyer. 6033-1
"The **gods** let slip that fiendish grip". The convalescent gripster. Eugene Field. 6949-5
The **gods** of the Dana. Leah Bodine Drake. 6218-0
Gods of War. George William ("A.E.") Russell. 6542-2
"The **gods** of vast Valhalla". A song of the new gods. Robert Norwood. 7014-0
Gods of war. George William ("A.E.") Russell. 7027-2
"The **gods** released a vision on a world...". The wings of lead. Nathalia Crane. 7019-1
"The **gods** they robbed me of my life...". On a niobe of Praxiteles. Unknown (Greek). 6879-0
"**Gods** who rule the earth are far removed," fr.Hannibal. John Nichol. 6819-7
The **gods'** children. Aeschylus. 6435-3
Godspeed. Harriet Prescott Spofford. 6833-2
Godspeed our work. Unknown. 6149-4
Godspeed to his book. James I; King of Scotland. 6659-3
Godwhen, A.
    "Now wolde I faine some merthes make." 6317-9,6636-4, 6187-7
"**Goe** & seeke some other love." Unknown. 6563-5
"**Goe** bidd the swan in silence dye." Unknown. 6563-5
"**Goe** empty joyes." Unknown. 6563-5
"**Goe** find some whispering shade neare Arne...". Caelum non animum. William Habington. 6793-X
"**Goe** thow my soule to thy desired rest." Unknown. 6563-5
"**Goe** thy waies and turne no more." Unknown. 6563-5
"**Goe!** hunt the whiter ermine! and present". For the Lady Olivia Porter;a present upon New-years day. Sir William Davenant. 6933-9
"**Goe,** little booke." James Russell Lowell. 6304-7
Goebel, Arthur
    Vision. 6850-2
Goedicke, Patricia
    The point of emptiness. 7032-9
Goethals, the prophet engineer. Percy MacKaye. 6102-8,6473-6,6465-5,6076-5,6464-7
Goethe. Bayard Taylor. 6976-2
Goethe (atr), Johann Wolfgang von
    "The shallows murmur/But the deeps are dumb". 6889-8
"**Goethe** in Weimar sleeps", fr. Memorial verses. Matthew Arnold. 6793-X
"**Goethe** in Weimar sleeps, and Greece". Memorial verses. Matthew Arnold. 6046-3,6102-8,6199-0,6250-4,6430-2, 6641 ,6655-0,6656-9,6645-3,6828-6
Goethe, Johann Wolfgang von
    An den mond. 6252-0
    And sae came of it. Bernard Bosanquet (tr.). 7042-6
    The artist's morning song. William Edmonstoune Aytoun (tr.). 6948-7
    As a man soweth. 6337-3
    Ballad of the harper. Thomas Carlyle (tr.). 6328-4
    Barkers, i.e. the critics, fr. Gedichte. Bernard Bosanquet (tr.). 7042-6
    The bride of Corinth. Elizabeth Craigmyle (tr.). 6842-1
    The brothers. William Edmonstoune Aytoun (tr.). 6948-7
    The cavalier's choice. 6676-3
    The cavalier's choice. William Edmonstoune Aytoun (tr.). 6948-7
    Character. 6109-5
    Chorus, fr. Walpurgis night. 6102-8
    Constancy, fr. Gedichte. Bernard Bosanquet (tr.). 7042-6
    Cupid as a landscape painter. William Edmonstoune Aytoun (tr.). 6948-7
    Dance of the dead. 6696-8
    Der fischer. 6252-0
    "Do the duty that lies nearest to thee". 6623-2
    The doleful lay of the wife of Asan Aga. William Edmonstoune Aytoun (tr.). 6948-7

"Each, after all, learns only what he can". 6238-5
Early spring. William Edmonstoune Aytoun (tr.). 6948-7
Easter chorus, fr. Faust. 6214-8,6730-1
Easter chorus, fr. Faust. Arthur Cleveland Coxe (tr.). 6337-3
Easter hymn, sels., fr. Faust. 6144-3
Eloquence that persuades. 6414-0
The Erl-king. 6695-X,6580-5,6585-6
The erl-king. Elizabeth Craigmyle (tr.). 6842-1
The Erl-king. Sir Walter Scott (tr.). 6254-7,6732-8, 6328-4,6358-6,6102-8,6613
The erl-king. Sir Walter Scott (tr.). 7039-6
Exculpation. William Edmonstoune Aytoun (tr.). 6948-7
The fairest flower. 6677-1
Faust, sels. 6144-3
Faust, sels. Bayard Taylor (tr.). 6732-8
First love. 6732-8
The fisher. Charles Timothy Brooks (tr.). 6302-0;6385-3
"The future hides in it". 6238-5
Give me back my youth again. 6240-7
The god and the Bayadere. Elizabeth Craigmyle (tr.). 6842-1
Good resolutions, fr. Gedichte. Bernard Bosanquet (tr.). 7042-6
Gypsy song. 6490-6
The happy pair. William Edmonstoune Aytoun (tr.). 6948-7
Hartz-journey in winter. Bayard Taylor (tr.). 6976-2
Haste not, rest not. 6337-3
Heredity. Bernard Bosanquet (tr.). 7042-6
Hermann and Dorothea. 6679-8
The higher shrewdness. Bernard Bosanquet (tr.). 7042-6
Holy family. William Edmonstoune Aytoun (tr.). 6948-7
"I live for those that love me". 6238-5
The king in Thule. William Edmonstoune Aytoun (tr.). 6948-7
The king of Thule. James Clarence Mangan (tr.). 7039-6
The king of Thule. Bayard Taylor (tr.). 6385-3
Knowest thou the land. Thomas Carlyle (tr.). 6328-4
Let us go on. 6461-2
Lili's park. William Edmonstoune Aytoun (tr.). 6948-7
Live each day. 6461-2
Longing. William Edmonstoune Aytoun (tr.). 6948-7
Longing. Thomas Carlyle (tr.). 6328-4
Love's hour-glass. William Ed·onstoune Aytoun (tr.). 6948-7
Love's nearness. Henry Van Dyke (tr.). 6961-4
The loved one ever near. 6066-8,6508-2
Mailied. 7020-5
Margaret's plea to the Virgin Mother. 6214-8
Marriage unequal. William Edmonstoune Aytoun (tr.). 6948-7
The master. Bernard Bosanquet (tr.). 7042-6
Mephistopheles to the student, fr. Faust. Bernard Bosanquet (tr.). 7042-6
Mignon. James Elroy Flecker (tr.). 7039-6
Mignon's song. 6481-7
Mignon's song. Felicia Dorothea Hemans (tr.). 6385-3
Mignon's song. Felicia Dorothea Hemans (tr.). 6973-8
The minstrel. James Clarence Mangan (tr.). 6271-7
The Musagetes. William Edmonstoune Aytoun (tr.). 6948-7
"O'er all the hill-tops", fr. Wanderer's night-songs. Henry Wadsworth Longfellow (tr.). 6289-X
On the lake. William Edmonstoune Aytoun (tr.). 6948-7
Our ignorance in asking. Bernard Bosanquet (tr.). 7042-6
The page and the maid of honor. 6676-3
The pariah. 6677-1
The pariah. William Edmonstoune Aytoun (tr.). 6948-7
Philistine mysticism. Bernard Bosanquet (tr.). 7042-6
Pink. 6049-8
Poesy. William Edmonstoune Aytoun (tr.). 6948-7
Prolog im himmel. 6253-9
Prologue in heaven, fr. Faust. Percy Bysshe Shelley (tr.). 7039-6,6102-8
Prometheus. John S. Dwight (tr.). 7039-6,6879-0
Psyche. William Edmonstoune Aytoun (tr.). 6948-7
The pupil of Merlin. 6787-5
The researcher, fr. Gedichte. Bernard Bosanquet (tr.). 7042-6

Rest. 6457-4
"Rest is not quitting." 6109-5
Sacred ground. William Edmonstoune Aytoun (tr.). 6948-7
Salvation, fr. Faust. Bernard Bosanquet (tr.). 7042-6
Second life. William Edmonstoune Aytoun (tr.). 6948-7
Selection, fr. Wilhelm Meister. 7014-0
Separation. William Edmonstoune Aytoun (tr.). 6948-7
The seven sleepers of Ephesus. 6676-3
The seven sleepers of Ephesus. William Edmonstoune Aytoun (tr.). 6948-7
The shepherd's lament. William Edmonstoune Aytoun (tr.). 6948-7
The shepherd's lament. Bayard Taylor (tr.). 6976-2
Sincerity the soul of eloquence. 6408-6,6605-2
Slumber and sleep. Arthur Hugh Clough (tr.). 6958-4
Soldier's song, fr. Faust. Bayard Taylor (tr.). 6976-2
A song from the Coptic. 6102-8
The song of Mignon. Bayard Taylor (tr.). 6976-2
Song of the Parcae. Nathaniel Langdon Frothingham (tr.). 6438-8
Sorrow. 6889-8
Sorrow. Gretchen O. Warren (tr.). 6337-3
Sorrow without consolation. William Edmonstoune Aytoun (tr.). 6948-7
"Thou that from the heavens...", fr. Wanderer's... Henry Wadsworth Longfellow (tr.). 6289-X
The thought eternal. Ludwig Lewisohn (tr.). 7039-6,6879-0
"'Tis no doubt pleasant". 6407-8
To a golden heart. William Edmonstoune Aytoun (tr.). 6948-7
To a golden heart, worn round his neck. Margaret Fuller Ossoli (tr.). 7039-6
To Lina. William Edmonstoune Aytoun (tr.). 6948-7
To Luna. William Edmonstoune Aytoun (tr.). 6948-7
To the moon. William Edmonstoune Aytoun (tr.). 6948-7
To the originals, fr. Gedichte. Bernard Bosanquet (tr.). 7042-6
To the parted one. Christopher Pearse Cranch (tr.). 7039-6
The treacherous maid of the mill. William Edmonstoune Aytoun (tr.). 6948-7
The treasure-seeker. William Edmonstoune Aytoun (tr.). 6948-7
The true life-passion. Bernard Bosanquet (tr.). 7042-6
True rest. 6260-1,6654-2,6337-3
Uber allen gipfein. 6252-0
Use well the moment. 6337-3
The violet. 6732-8
A voice from old Germany. Bernard Bosanquet (tr.). 7042-6
A voice from the invisible world. James Clarence Mangan (tr.). 7039-6
Wanderers nachtlied. 7020-5
Wanderer's night songs. Henry Wadsworth Longfellow (tr.). 6484-7
Wanderer's night songs, sels. Henry Wadsworth Longfellow (tr.). 6289-X
Wanderer's night-songs. Henry Wadsworth Longfellow (tr.). 7039-6
Warning. William Edmonstoune Aytoun (tr.). 6948-7
The wedding feast. William Edmonstoune Aytoun (tr.). 6948-7
"What I don't see". 6238-5
Who never ate with tears his bread. 6214-8
Who never ate with tears his bread. Farnsworth Wright (tr.). 6730-1
Who'll buy a cupid? William Edmonstoune Aytoun (tr.). 6948-7
The wild rose. 6732-8
Wilhelm Meister, sel. 7014-0
With a golden necklace. William Edmonstoune Aytoun (tr.). 6948-7
"Wouldst shape a noble life? Then cast". 6109-5
The wreaths. William Edmonstoune Aytoun (tr.). 6948-7
The youth and the mill-stream. William Edmonstoune Aytoun (tr.). 6948-7

Goetschius, Antoinette
Meditation. 6337-3
Goetz, Philip B.

Song of the choo-choo. 6130-3
Goff, Eris
　May. 6750-6
Goffe, Thomas
　The couragious Turke, sels. 6562-7
　"Drop golden showers...", fr. The couragious Turke. 6562-7,6563-5
Gog and Magog. Thomas Hood. 6974-6
Gogarty, Oliver St. John
　The apple tree. 6532-5
　Between Brielle and Manasquan. 6930-4
　The blackbird in the town. 6482-5
　The boon companion. 6427-2
　Earth and sea. 6069-2
　Fresh fields. 6581-3
　Golden stockings. 6096-X,6244-X
　Good luck. 6292-X,6096-X
　I tremble to think. 6482-5
　Leda and the swan. 6930-4
　Non dolet. 6102-8,6244-X
　On Troy. 6722-0
　Palinode. 6482-5
　A parable for poetasters. 6722-0
　Perfection. 6244-X
　The plum tree by the house. 6985-1
　Portrait. 6072-2
　Portrait: Jane W. 6072-2
　The ship ("A ship from Valparaiso came"). 6258-X
　Sunt apud infernos tot milia formosarum. 6070-6
　To a friend in the country. 6930-4
　To an old tenor. 6722-0
　To death. 6337-3
　To W.B. Yeats, to build a fountain to commemorate...victory . 6070-6
　Verse. 6317-9
　Verse ("What should we know"). 6022-6,6292-X
　The weathercock. 6071-4
　With a coin from Syracuse. 6985-1
Goggly-goo. Eugene Field. 6318-7
Gogisgi, Carroll Arnett
　Ayohu Kanogisdi death song. 7005-1
　Bio-poetic statement: instruction to warriors on... 7005-1
　Last May. 7005-1
　Look back. 7005-1
　The old man said. 7005-1
　Song of the breed. 7005-1
Goin' down to town. Unknown. 6594-5
Goin' home today. Will Carleton. 6155-9,6409-4
Goin' to walk all ovah God's heb'n. Unknown. 6265-2
Going. Polly Hardy. 6894-4
Going a nutting. Jennie D. Moore. 6529-5
Going a-maying. Robert Herrick. 6820-0
Going a-Maying. Robert Herrick. 6322-5
Going a-nutting. Edmund Clarence Stedman. 6239-3
Going and coming. Mary Elizabeth Blake. 7041-8
Going and coming. Edward A. Jenks. 6385-3
Going away. Thomas Frost. 6670-4
Going back. George Rachow. 6870-7
Going back at evening. Jim Thomas. 6860-X
Going back to school. Stephen Vincent Benet. 6299-7
Going blind. Rainer Maria Rilke. 6643-7
Going blind. John Banister Tabb. 6096 X
Going crosslots in Vermont. Daniel L. Cady. 6988-6
Going down hill on a bicycle. Henry Charles Beeching. 6423-X,6437-X,6107-9,6161-3
Going down in ships. Harry Kemp. 6374-8
Going for the cows. Eugene J Hall. 6575-9
Going for water. Robert Frost. 6253-9
The going forth. Conrad Aiken. 6761-1
Going home. Maurice Kenny. 7005-1
Going home. Robert Service. 6159-1
Going home. Benjamin Franklin Taylor. 6632-1
Going home. Nathaniel Parker Willis. 6424-8
Going home for Christmas. Unknown. 6807-3
Going home in the morning. Wayne Douglas. 6273-3,6670-4
Going into breeches. Charles and Mary Lamb. 6233-4;6242-3;6519-8;6105-2
Going into exile. Frederic Prokosch. 6761-1
Going north. Luis Salinas. 6792-1

The **going** of his feet. Harry Kemp. 6374-8,6532-5
The **going** of the battery. Thomas Hardy. 6793-X
Going on an errand. Unknown. 6701-8
Going on an errand. Unknown. 6923-1
Going out and coming in. Mollie E. Moore. 6909-6
"**Going** out to pain". Door open. Jeannette Sewell. 6847-2
Going softly. Unknown. 6273-3
Going to aunt Ruth's to tea. Unknown. 6629-1
Going to bed. Marian McMunn. 6750-6
Going to bed. Unknown. 6078-1
Going to church. Coventry Patmore. 6315-2,6066-8,6226-1
Going to court. Alice Cary. 6865-0;6969-X
Going to school. Unknown. 6314-4,6530-9
Going to sleep. George Elliston. 6861-8
Going to sleep. George Rostrevor Hamilton. 6339-X
Going to the fair. James Whitcomb Riley. 6281-4
Going to the front. Hardwicke Drummond Rawnsley. 7027-2
Going to the spelling school. Benjamin Franklin Taylor. 6815-4
Going to the store. Benjamin Albert Botkin. 6397-7
Going to the warres. Richard Lovelace. 6933-9
Going to the wars. Richard Lovelace. 6197-4,6322-5
Going to the water. Geary Hobson. 7005-1
Going too far. Mildred Howells. 6331-4,6496-5,6439-6
Going up the line. Martin Armstrong. 7029-9
Going up to London. Nancy Byrd Turner. 6478-7,6331-4,6501-5,6396-9,6421-4
Going west. Eleanor Jewett. 6846-4
Going with the flow. Traci Teas. 6883-9
Going, Charles Buxton
　Armistice. 6051-X,6309-8
　At the top of the road. 6274-1
　The blessed road. 6144-3,6335-7
　Columbus. 6653-4
　The east wind. 6309-8
　Garden of the rose. 6266-0
　If I were a fairy. 6338-1
　Joan of Arc at Domremy. 6653-4
　Landlocked. 6653-4
　The march of men. 6266-0
　My soul and I. 6303-9,6337-3
　Rain in the hills. 6653-4
　A schoolroom idyl. 6451-5
　A sleepy song. 6653-4
　The song of steel. 6006-4
　The spell of the road. 6006-4
　Spring in England. 6653-4
　To Arcady. 6441-8
　The wild rose. 6338-1
The **going**.. Thomas Hardy. 6204-0
The **going**. Wilfred Wilson Gibson. 6234-2,6153-2
Gold. Edgar Fawcett. 7041-8
Gold. Michael (Katherine Bradley & Edith Cooper) Field. 6250-4
Gold. Wilfred Wilson Gibson. 6897-9
Gold. Thomas Hood. 6917-7
Gold. Glyn Johns. 6379-9
Gold. Florence Luft. 6850-2
Gold. Helen M. Shuster. 6799-9
"**Gold** and all this werdis win". Crucified to the world. Unknown. 6881-2
"**Gold** and iron are good". Politics. Ralph Waldo Emerson. 6753-0
"**Gold** I've none, for use or show". Lyrick for legacies. Robert Herrick. 6933-9
Gold and love for dearie (Cornish lullaby). Eugene Field. 6834-0;6949-5
Gold beads. Maude Wheeler Pierce. 7030-2
Gold Coast customs. Edith Sitwell. 7000-0
Gold coin. Don Farran. 6039-0
The **gold** dust fire. Unknown. 6609-7
Gold fish. J. Corson Miller. 6039-0
Gold hair. William Morris. 6110-9
Gold in the mountain. Herman Melville. 6176-1
"The **gold** links lie so near the mill." Sarah N. Cleghorn. 6076-5,6102-8,6464-7
Gold locks and silver locks. Celia Thaxter. 6612-7
"The **gold** mountain men said". Chinatown talking story. Kitty Tsui. 6790-5
"The **gold** of the sunset illuminates the deep". Evening.

Porsteinn Erlingsson. 6854-5
"Gold of the tangled wilderness of wattle". Wattle and myrtle. James Lister Cuthbertson. 6784-0
"Gold or silver every day,/Dies to grey". Ballade of truisms. William Ernest Henley. 6770-0
"The gold rain of eve was descending". The cailin deas. George Sigerson. 6858-8
The gold room - an idyl. Bayard Taylor. 6652-6
Gold song. Nora Hopper. 6174-5
The gold star. Edgar A. Guest. 6846-4
Gold stripes. Florence A. Vicars. 7031-0
The gold thread, sels. Norman Macleod. 6242-3
"Gold weighed 'gainst honour is naught...". Told by a Brahmin. Friedrich Ruckert. 6842-1
"Gold wings across the sea". Song ("Gold wings"). William Morris. 6315-2
Gold!. Thomas Hood. 6302-0,6385-3,6337-3,6629-1,6732-8
"Gold! Gold! Have and hold!". Jonathan's lullaby. S. Foster Damon. 6761-1
Gold, Albert Reginald
Fishers. 6144-3,6335-7
Gold, Liz
Gringa. 6900-2
Gold, Michael
A strange funeral in Braddock. 6880-4
Third degree. 6880-4
Gold-of-Ophir roses. Grace Atherton Dennen. 6241-5
The gold-seekers. Hamlin Garland. 6736-0,6431-0
The gold-threaded coat. Tu Ch'ia-niang. 6491-4
Goldau. John Neal. 6749-2
Goldbaum, Helen
Analog for love. 6640-2
The crickets. 6640-2
The ghosts. 6640-2
Literary incident. 6640-2
"There will not be days like this forever" 6640-2
Goldbeck, Cecil
Waters of the sea. 6833-2
Goldberg, William
After reading a life of Mozart. 6585-6
Golden - of the Selkirks. Emily Pauline ("Tekahionwake") Johnson. 6837-5
The golden age, fr. The faithful shepherd. Giovanni Battista Guarini. 6325-X
The golden age. William Edmonstoune Aytoun. 6948-7
The golden apples, fr. The earthly paradise. William Morris. 6199-0
Golden autumn. Mrs. Hawtrey. 6529-5
"A golden bird in the sunset sky". Curing (2), fr. Songs from an invalid chair. Josephine A. Meyer. 6847-2
The golden bowl. Mary McMillan. 6338-1
"A golden cage of sunbeams". The bird of hope. Charles Swain. 6980-0
Golden city. Unknown. 6609-7
The golden city of St. Mary. John Masefield. 6332-2;6395-0
The golden city, sels. John ("Evelyn Douglas") Barlas. 7009-4
The golden city. Frederick Tennyson. 6669-0
"A golden cloud slept for her pleasure". The mountain. Mikhail Lermontov. 7039-6
The golden cockerel. Lynn Riggs. 6808-1
Golden Crown sparrow of Alaska. John Burroughs. 6597-X
"The golden dandelion stars". Dandelions. Albert Durrant Watson. 6797-2
The golden day. Arthur Wallace Peach. 6449-3
Golden days. Adelaide Anne Procter. 6957-6
Golden days. Robert Service. 6159-1
"The golden dreamboat's ready". Lullaby ("The golden dreamboat's ready"). Edgar A. Guest. 6401-9,6135-4
'Golden eyes'. Laurence (Adele Florence Nicolson) Hope. 6856-1
Golden falcon. Robert P. Tristram Coffin. 6073-0,6619-4
The golden farmer. John Collins. 6874-X
Golden fish. Titanomachia. 6435-3
"The golden foot-prints of departing day". Sunset. Henry Ellison. 7015-9
The golden garret. Alfred Noyes. 6169-9
The golden gate. Adelaide Anne Procter. 6957-6
"The golden gates are open now". A final day dialogue. William J. Lampton. 7021-3

"The golden gates of day in quiet close". Sunset. Dwight Williams. 6919-3
"The golden gates of sleep unbar" Percy Bysshe Shelley. 6935-5
"The golden gates of slumber unbar". A bridal song. Percy Bysshe Shelley. 6328-4
"The golden gift that nature did thee give." Henry Howard, Earl of Surrey. 6584-8
A golden girl. Bryan Waller ("Barry Cornwall") Procter. 6302-0;6385-3
The golden glove. Unknown. 6057-9,6518-X
The golden glove. Unknown. 6059-5
Golden glow. Abul Hasan (of Seville) 6362-4
Golden grains. James A. Garfield. 6413-2
Golden hair. F. Burge Smith. 6131-1
"The golden hair that Gulla wears". Bought locks. Martial. 7039-6
"Golden hair'd ally whose name is one...mine". To Alfred Tennyson, my grandson. Alfred Lord Tennyson. 6867-7
"Golden hair'd ally whose name...one with mine". To Alfred Tennyson, my grandson. Alfred Lord Tennyson. 6977-0
Golden hands. Unknown. 6501-5
The golden heart. Witter Bynner. 6031-5
The golden journey to Samarkand. James Elroy Flecker. 6395-0,6427-2,6509-0,6541-4,6161-3,6508-2
The golden jubilee, Hunter College, 1870-1920 E. Adelaide Hahn. 6847-2
Golden keys. Unknown. 6963-0
"Golden leaves" Kit Blomer. 6883-9
The golden legend, sels. Henry Wadsworth Longfellow. 6282-2
The golden leopard. Gustav Davidson. 6979-7
The golden locks of Anna. Robert Burns. 6830-8
The golden mean. Anacreon. 6435-3
The golden mean. Alice Cary. 6969-X
The golden mean. Henry Howard, Earl of Surrey. 6584-8
The golden mile-stone. Henry Wadsworth Longfellow. 6429-9, 6321-7,6659-3,6641-2
The golden nickel. Francis Carlin. 6037-4
Golden October. Walter E. Isenhour. 6799-9
The golden plover. Jonas Hallgrimsson. 6283-0
The golden plover. Richard Butler Glaenzer. 6030-7
Golden pulse. John Myers O'Hara. 6310-1
The golden ringlet. Amelia B. Coppuck Welby. 6385-3
Golden rod. Clara Doty Bates. 6529-5
Golden rod. Emma Celia & Lizzie J. Rook. 6137-0
The golden rod ("From the flying train, behold...") Unknown. 6049-8
The golden rod. Eva J. Beede. 6049-8
The golden rod. Hopestill Goodwin. 6049-8
The golden room. Wilfred Wilson Gibson. 6072-2
Golden Rowan. Bliss Carman. 6656-9
"Golden rose the house, in the portal I saw". Apparuit. Ezra Pound. 6754-9
"Golden rose the moon of March...". Easter eve. Albert E.S. Smythe. 6796-4
The golden rule ("Be you to others kind and true.") Unknown. 6424-8
The g lden rule ("To do to others as I would.") Unknown. 6424-8
Golden rules for the young. Unknown. 6105-2
The golden scepter. Mabel S. Merrill. 6926-6
Golden shoes. Unknown. 6045-1
The golden shoes. Josephine Preston Peabody. 6266-0,6252-0
The golden side. Unknown. 6273-3
The golden silence. William Winter. 6240-7
"Golden slumbers kiss your eyes". Lullaby ("Golden slumbers"). Thomas Dekker. 6179-6,6233-4,6182-6,6315-2,6533-3,6633-X,6194-X
Golden slumbers kiss your eyes. Thomas Dekker. 6228-8,6490-6
"Golden slumbers kisse your eyes". Song, fr. Patinet grissill. Thomas Dekker. 6958-4
The golden spider in the mind. Geoffrey Scott. 6985-1
Golden spurs. Virginia Scott Miner. 6465-5
Golden stars. Henry Van Dyke. 6961-4
Golden stockings. Oliver St. John Gogarty. 6096-X,6244-X
The golden stool. Gene Holmes. 6178-8
The golden street. William O. Stoddard. 6911-8
"Goldensun of evening". To the setting sun. A. B. Werner

GOLDEN

Geb. Welti. 6952-5
"The **golden** sun, in splendour likest heaven". The sun. John Milton. 6935-5
"A **golden** sunset clear and pale". The good ship. Dorothy Lowry Dolan. 6789-1
The **golden** sunset. Samuel Longfellow. 6600-3
The **golden** supper. Alfred Lord Tennyson. 6669-0
The **golden** targe, sels. William Dunbar. 6378-0,6193-1
The **golden** telegram. Grover I. Jacoby Jr. 6316-0
The **golden** text. George Frederick Cameron. 6656-9,6861-8
"A **golden** thing is friendship; holy is". Idas and Marpessa, sels. Howard Vigne Sutherland. 6836-7
"The **golden** throated frog turning liquidity...". Wisdom born of spring. Flora White. 6799-9
"**Golden** through the golden morning". The return. Eleanor Rogers Cox. 6946-0
The **golden** touch. Florence Randal Livesay. 6797-2
Golden turf. So-wol Kim. 6775-1
"The **golden** urns of life are broken now". At evening time it shall be light. William White. 6868-5
Golden vanitee. Unknown. 6518-X
The **golden** vanity. Unknown. 6228-8,6258-X,6547-3,6732-8
Golden wares. Patricia Peart. 6764-6
Golden wedding. William W. Pratt. 6337-3
A **golden** wedding. William Allen Butler. 6903-7
The **golden** wedding. David Gray. 6271-7
The **golden** wedding. James Abraham Martling. 6952-5
The **golden** willow tree. Unknown. 6594-5
Golden wings. William Morris. 6726-3
Golden wings, sels. William Morris. 6179-6
Golden words. Adelaide Anne Procter. 6957-6
"The **golden** year is nearly sped". A leap-year lament. Eugene Field. 6949-9
The **golden** year. Alfred Lord Tennyson. 6977-0
Golden, Bernette
Morning. 7024-8
There are seeds to sow. 7024-8
Words. 7024-8
"**Golden**, crimson, glows the sunset...". The explorer's message. Mrs. Hubert ("Australie") Heron. 6768-9
The **golden-crested** wren. Thomas Miller. 6018-8
"The **golden-lipped** buttercup of the day". Nocturnes: I. Alice E. Gillington. 7037-X
"The **golden-pinioned** breezes lift". Day-break. James Abraham Martling. 6952-5
Golden-rod. Elaine Goodale. 6049-8
Golden-rod. Frank Dempster Sherman. 6311-X
Golden-rod. John Banister Tabb. 6121-4
Golden-rod. Isabell Sherrick Wardell. 6836-7
The **golden-rod**.. Margaret Deland. 6338-1
"The **golden-throated** merle and mellow thrush". Flight of the swallow. Frederick Tennyson. 6785-9
Golden-throated pastoral horn. Grace Hazard Conkling. 6327-6
Golden-tressed Adelaide. Bryan Waller ("Barry Cornwall") Procter. 6233-4,6656-9,6219-9,6131-1
Goldenhair. James Joyce. 6125-7,6301-2
"The **goldening** peach on the orchard wall." David Gray. 6960-6
Goldenrod. Ethel M. Funkhouser. 6818-9
Goldenrod. Mrs. F.J. Lovejoy. 6373-X
Goldenrod. John Russell McCarthy. 6396-9
Goldenrod. Unknown. 6373-X
The **goldenrod**. Anschusa [pseud]. 6846-4
The **goldfinch**. Odell Shepard. 6073-0,6338-1
Goldfinches. John Keats. 6239-3
Goldfinches. Elisabeth Scollard. 6073-0
Goldfish. Lena Whittaker Blakeney. 6397-7
Goldfish on the writing desk. Max Brod. 6160-5
"The **goldfish** play". Aquarium. Jose Gorostiza. 6759-X
The **goldfish**. William F. Kirk. 6307-1
Goldilocks. Jean Ingelow. 6438-8
Golding, Arthur
Philemon and Baucis. 6436-1
Golding, Arthur (tr.)
The fall of Icarus. Ovid, 6978-9
"Now have I brought a work to end", fr. Metamorphoses. Ovid, 6879-0
Golding, Hazel
Grannys receipt. 6750-6

Golding, Louis
Bees in peach blossom. 6069-2
Broken bodies. 6337-3,6490-6
Doom-devoted. 6776-X
Greece remembered. 6779-4
Kindled from deep darkness. 6777-8
Second seeing. 6730-1
Shepherd singing ragtime. 6884-7
The singer of high state. 6884-7
South sun and brimming sea. 6778-6
Storm. 6782-4
Too much beauty, world. 6780-8
Tyrannies. 6761-1
Golding, Margaret
The sunset town. 6798-0
Goldman, Golda M.
In the candle light. 6847-2
Goldman, Samuel
To -. 6818-9
Goldmark, Susan
Snow storm. 6253-9
The white throat. 6253-9
Goldring, Douglas
Dinner-time (Sloane Street). 6506-6
The Spanish sailor. 6506-6
Voyages. 6897-9
West End lane. 6506-6
The **goldsmith's** daughter. Johann Ludwig Uhland. 6677-1
Goldsmith's whistle. Harriet Prescott Spofford. 7041-8
Goldsmith, Beatrice
Afternoon. 6640-2
Hour. 6640-2
Melancholia. 6640-2
9 to 10 p.m. 6640-2
Nineteenth birthday. 6640-2
Goldsmith, Goldwin
The monkey's glue. 6902-9
Goldsmith, Oliver
"Ah no. To distant climes, a dreary scene" 6935-5
The Alps. 6749-2
"And as a bird each fond endearment tries". 6238-5
Auburn, fr. The deserted village. 6932-0
Beau Tibbs, his character and family. 6200-8
The better country. 6240-7
British climate and freedom. 6935-5
Captivity. 6250-4
The captivity, sels. 6174-5
Character of the French. 6543-0
Character of the Italians. 6543-0
Character of the Swiss. 6543-0
The clown's reply. 6228-8
The common man, fr. The deserted village. 6337-3
The country parson. 6459-0
David Garrick, fr. Retaliation. 6250-4
The deserted village, sel. 6954-1
The deserted village, sels. 6024-2,6102-8,6208-3,6395-0, 6410-8,6527 ,6600-3,6365-9,6174-5,6654-2,6301-2
The deserted village. 6101-X,6087-0,6198-2,6332-2,6473-6,6122 ,6271-7,6302-0,6385-3,6315-2,6459-0,6504 , 6604-6,6732-8,6668-2,6197-4,6219-9,6660 ,6195-0,6250-4,6245-8,6543-0,6152-4,6192 ,6086-2,6102-8,6430-2
The double transformation. 6787-5
Edmund Burke, fr. Retaliation. 6188-5,6250-4,6150-8
Edwin and Angelina. 6142-7,6152-4,6543-0
Elegy on Madam Blaize. 6102-8,6198-2,6486-8,6385-3,6722-0,6304
Elegy on Madame Blaize. 6086-2
An elegy on Mrs. Mary Blaize. 6152-4
Elegy on the death of a mad dog. 6075-7,6134-6,6239-3, 6244-X,6271-7,6290 ,6291-9,6131-1,6152-4,6430-2,6739-5,6026 ,6385-3,6425-6,6486-8,6552-X,6732-8,6105 , 6424-8,6668-2,6464-7,6518-X,6086-2,6104 ,6498-1,6332-2,6089-7,6133-8,6240-7,6165 ,6104-4,6491-4
An elegy on the glory of her sex, Mrs. Mary Blaize. 6089-7,6271-7,6304-2,6732-8
Epitaph on Dr. Parnell. 6483-3
The exiles. 6543-0
Farewell to poetry, fr. The deserted village. 6932-0
The first, best country, fr. The traveller. 6239-3
France. 6932-0

The gift. 6732-8
Great Britain. 6302-0;6385-3
A great man. 6902-9
Happiness dependent on ourselves. 6932-0
The haunch of venison. 6092-7,6152-4
The hermit. 6271-7,6219-9,6518-X
His bedchamber. 6545-7
Holland. 6302-0;6385-3
Home. 6302-0;6385-3
Hope. 6932-0
Hope ("Hope, like a gleaming taper's light,"). 6174-5, 6337-3,6583-X
Hope, fr. Captivity. 6934-7
Hope, fr. the oratorio of The captivity. 6174-5
Italy and Switzerland. 6302-0
The logicians refuted. 6200-8
Man wants but little, fr. Edwin and Angelina. 6934-7
Memory. 6482-5
Memory, sels. 6174-5
Mrs. Mary Blaize. 6092-7
National decay. 6240-7
O memory! thou fond deceiver. 6086-2
On a beautiful youth struck blind with lightning. 6430-2
On the death of a mad dog. 6142-7
On woman. 6737-9
Parson Gray. 6089-7
The pastor, fr. The deserted village. 6174-5
The patriot's boast. 6793-X
The pitying heart. 6134-6,6466-3,6134-6
Real happiness. 6932-0
Recollections of home and infancy. 6543-0
Retaliation. 6200-8,6733-6,6093-7,6162-4,6430-2,6086
Retaliation, sels. 6024-2,6188-5,6122-2,6198-2,6195-0, 6250
The rising village, sels. 6446-9
The rose. 6328-4
The schoolmaster. 6499-X,6639-9
Sir Joshua Reynolds, fr. Retaliation. 6250-4
Song ("Ah, me!"). 6244-X
Song ("Let school-masters"). 6430-2
Song ("When lovely woman"). 6122-2,6198-2
Stanzas on woman, fr. The vicar of Wakefield. 6108-7, 6732-8,6174-5
"Sweet auburn! loveliest village of the plain". 6186-9
Switzerland. 6749-2
'Threnodia Augustalis', sels. 6174-5
The traveller, sels. 6934-7
The traveller, sels. 6239-3,6543-0
The traveller. 6087-0,6271-7,6219-9,6543-0,6430-2,6250 , 6152-4,6195-0
The vicar of Wakefield, sels. 6108-7,6332-2
The vicar of Wakefield. 6083-8
The village parson. 6730-1,6150-8
The village pastor. 6543-0
The village preacher, fr. The deserted village. 6244-X, 6337-3,6410-8,6610-0,6153-2,6304
The village schoolmaster and the village inn. 6543-0
The village schoolmaster. 6552-X,6610-0,6104-4,6153-2
The village. 6244-X
When lovely woman stoops to folly,fr.Vicar of Wakefield. 6560-0,6328-4,6289-X,6246-6,6086-2,6152-4, 6192
Woman. 6482-5,6301-2
The wretch, condemned with life to part. 6219-9
The goldsmith.. Rainer Maria Rilke. 6643-7
The goldyn targe. William Dunbar. 6586-4
Golf. Unknown. 6249-0
Golf and life. Samuel Ellsworth Kiser. 6274-1
The golf fiend. R.F. B. 7021-3
Golf luck. Edgar A. Guest. 7033-7
The golfer's Rubaiyat. H.W. Boynton. 6440-X
Golgotha. Gertrude May Lutz. 6979-7
Golgotha. Katherine Greenleaf Pedley. 6144-3
Golgotha. Siegfried Sassoon. 6491-4
Golgotha's cross. Raymond Kresensky. 6144-3
Goll, Claire
    The chaplinade, sels. 6351-9
    Songs for a Jewess. 6351-9
    To 'busno. 12 6351-9
    You. 6351-9
Goll, Iwan [or Yvan]
    Caravan of longing. Babette Deutsch (tr.). 6160-5
    Eternal shipwreck. Babette Deutsch (tr.). 6160-5
    John Landless leads the caravan. William Carlos Williams (tr.). 6068-4
    The pear tree. Babette Deutsch (tr.). 6160-5
    The pear-tree. Babette Deutsch and Avrahm Yarmolinsky (tr.). 6160-6
    River of lead. Galway Kinnell (tr.). 6803-0
    Torso. Babette Deutsch (tr.). 6160-5
Goll, Ralph E.
    Kokomo arraigned. 6880-4
Golomb, Mollie Rebecca
    I'd give my love. 6847-2
Goltra, Mabel Hall
    Fair places. 6789-1
    Pin Oak Hall. 6789-1
    The snow storm. 6789-1
    The world of tomorrow. 6789-1
Gomei
    Baby's hands. 6891-X
Gomersall, Robert
    Upon our vain flattery of ourselves. 6563-5
Gomez, Auguste
    Mary Magdalene. 6818-9
Gondibert, sels. Sir William D'Avenant. 6208-3
Gondibert: an heroick poem, sels. Sir William Davenant. 6562-7,6152-4,6194-X
Gondolieds. Helen Hunt Jackson. 6243-1
"The gondolier, in music clear". Barcarolle. Ben Wood Davis. 6927-4
Gondoline. Henry Kirke White. 6686-0
Gone. Mary Elizabeth Coleridge. 6437-X
Gone. Adam Lindsay Gordon. 6951-7,6784-0
Gone. William Dean Howells. 6066-8
Gone. Charles Mackay. 6620-8,6066-8
Gone. M.A. Mays. 6799-9
Gone. Ruby Clarke McIntyre. 6847-2
Gone. Marie Tello Phillips. 7038-8
Gone. Carl Sandburg. 6754-9
Gone. Unknown. 6273-3
Gone. John Greenleaf Whittier. 6304-7
"Gone are my old familiar friends". Fujiwara No Oki-kaze. 6852-9
"Gone are the glorious Greeks of old". The Greek boy. William Cullen Bryant. 6965-7
"Gone are the tales that once we read!". Ballade of dime novels. Arthur Guiterman. 6875-8
Gone before. Benjamin Franklin Taylor. 6392-6
Gone before. Benjamin Franklin Taylor. 6912-6
"Gone down in the flood, and gone out...flame". The sinking of the Merrimac. Lucy Larcom. 6946-0
"Gone down the tide". Walter Savage Landor. 6997-5
'Gone forward'. Margaret Junkin Preston. 6113-3
"Gone from this world of earth, air, sea & sky". Elegiac musings, sels. William Wordsworth. 6867-7
Gone in the wind. James Clarence Mangan. 6096-X,6174-5, 6t44-X,6337-3,6489-2,6022-6,6102-8,6383-7
"Gone is the bard, who, like a powreful spirit". On the death of Lord Byron. Sir Humphry Davy. 6980-0
"Gone is the joy,-gone is the thril of". The A.E.F. to T.R. Corinne Roosevelt Robinson. 6995-9
"Gone is the spire that slept for centuries". A Flemish village. H. A.. 6589-9,6846-4
"Gone is Ulysses! From his native". Gone is Ulysses. Marie L. Eglinton. 6995-9
Gone is the spring. Alan Rook. 6475-2
Gone is Ulysses. Marie L. Eglinton. 6995-9
"Gone the promise, pains and care". Second thoughts. Walter De La Mare. 6905-3
"Gone to be married? gone to swear a peace". Unknown. 6392-6
Gone to her head. Unknown. 6274-1
Gone to school. Unknown. 6097-8
Gone to war. Unknown (American Indian) 6396-9
"Gone were but the winter". Christina Georgina Rossetti. 6187-7
Gone with a handsomer man. Will Carleton. 6911-8
Gone!. George Houghton. 7041-8

GONE!

Gone!. Alfred Lord Tennyson. 6977-0
Gone! Gone! Forever gone. Gerald Griffin. 6930-4
The gone. Jesse Stuart. 6218-0
Gone?. Amelia Josephine Burr. 6847-2
Gonello: an Italian story. Unknown. 6677-1
Gongaware, Elizabeth D.
    Love. 6799-9
Gongora, Luis de
    Let me go warm. Henry Wadsworth Longfellow (tr.). 7039-6
Gonzales, Otto Paul
    The ugly girl wants to eat an apple. William T. Lawlor (tr.). 6898-7
Gonzalez de Leon, Ulalume
    Discontinuity. Sara Nelson (tr.). 7036-1
    Familiar sheets. Sara Nelson (tr.). 7036-1
    (Parentheses]. Eliot Weinberger (tr.). 7036-1
    Written garden. Eliot Weinberger (tr.). 7036-1
    Yellow butterfly. Sara Nelson (tr.). 7036-1
Gonzalez Martinez, Enrique
    Then twist the neck this delusive swan. John Peale Bishop (tr.). 6759-X
Gonzalez y Contreras, Gilberto
    Church. Dudley Fitts (tr.). 6759-X
    Heat. Dudley Fitts (tr.). 6759-X
Gonzalez, Otto Paul
    La Cubana. William T. Lawlor (tr.). 6898-7
    News of the neighborhoods. William T. Lawlor (tr.). 6898-7
Gonzalez, Rafael Jesus
    Exhortation. 6792-1,6998-3
Gooch, Brad
    Ed's boots. 7003-5
    Walk. 7003-5
    Words to be broadcast over eagle's nest sound system-I. 7003-5
Good 'postle Paul, fr. In merry mood. Nixon Waterman. 6260-1
Good advice. Emma Celia & Lizzie J. Rook. 6741-7
Good advice. Christina Georgina Rossetti. 6452-3
Good ale. John Still. 6271-7,6302-0,6385-3
Good and bad children. Robert Louis Stevenson. 6459-0,6629-1,6018-8,6655-0
Good and bad luck. John Hay. 6089-7,6629-1,6026-9
Good and bad thoughts. Roby Datta. 6591-0,6592-9
Good and bad wives. Unknown. 6157-5
Good and better. Unknown. 6915-0
Good and evil. Alice Cary. 6969-X
Good and evil. William Charles Scully. 6800-6
Good and fair. Ben Jonson. 6385-3
Good and great God! Ben Jonson. 6931-2
"Good and great God! How should I fear". No coming to God without Christ. Robert Herrick. 6931-2
The good angel of the household. Gertrude Huntington McGiffert. 6838-3
The good birds. Elinor Wylie. 6036-6
A good bishop. Unknown (German) 6730-1
A good boy. Robert Louis Stevenson. 6459-0
Good bye. Thomas Moore. 6620-8
Good bye. Unknown. 6312-8,6385-3
"'Good bye, darling'/From the lonely shadows". Across the years. Harriet Stanton Place. 6789-1
Good bye, old house. Millie C. Pomeroy. 6415-9
Good cheer. Charlotte Bronte. 6424-8
Good children street. Eugene Field. 6318-7
The good companion. Belle F. Owens. 6144-3
Good company. Karle Wilson Baker. 6374-8,6476-0,6556-2, 6730-1,6393-4,6421 ,6030-7,6265-2,6253-9,6509-0,6510-4,6653
Good company. Unknown. 6137-0
A good conscience. William Shakespeare. 6543-0
A good conscience. Unknown. 6142-7
Good counseil of Chaucer. Geoffrey Chaucer. 6102-8,6219-9, 6543-0
Good counsel. John Davidson. 6793-X
Good counsel. James I; King of Scotland. 6180-X
Good counsel. Carolyn Wells. 6739-5
Good counsell to a young maid. Thomas Carew. 6933-9
"Good creatures, do you love your lives,"fr.More poems. Alfred Edward Housman. 6828-6

"The good dame looked from her cottage". The leak in the dike. Phoebe Cary. 6451-5,6614-3,6569-4,6865-0,6969-X
"Good day, good day". In honour of Christmas. Unknown. 6881-2
"Good Deacon Roland - "may his tribe increase!"". Inasmuch. S.V.R. Ford. 6417-5,6964-9
Good day, good day. Unknown. 6756-5
A good day. Phoebe Cary. 6969-X
Good days and bad. Hesiod. 6435-3
"A good deed knows nor age nor winding-sheet". A good deed. Lizette Woodworth Reese. 6861-8
A good deed. Charles Mackay. 6523-6
A good deed. Lizette Woodworth Reese. 6861-8
Good deeds past. William Shakespeare. 6304-7
A good direction. Thomas Hood. 6974-6
Good dreams. Owen R. Washburn. 7030-2
Good dry lodgings. Francis Sylvester ("Father Prout") Mahony. 6760-3
"The good earth, sprawled in green". Summertime is credo. John Fandel. 6839-1
A good eating song. William Cartwright. 6563-5
Good English hospitality. William Blake. 6157-5
"Good editor Dana - God bless him, we say". The great journalist in Spain. Eugene Field. 6949-5
"Good Elnathan went from Slocum". A cenotaph. P. Dana. 7021-3
"Good Father John O'Hart/In penal days rode...". The priest of Coloony. William Butler Yeats. 6930-4
The good folks. Wilbur Dick Nesbit. 6303-9
Good friday. Edgar A. Guest. 6862-6
Good Friday. J. Willis Heber. 6799-9
Good Friday. Catherine F. Manning. 6799-9
Good Friday. Susan Miles. 6071-4
Good Friday. Christina Georgina Rossetti. 6144-3,6337-3, 6641-0
Good Friday. Arthur James Marshall Smith. 6021-8,6337-3
Good Friday. Lucy H. King Smith. 6270-9
Good Friday. Martha Provine Leach Turner. 6337-3
Good Friday ("'The Son of God am I,' he humbly said") Alice B. Jurica. 6144-3
Good Friday ("Gall is the taste of life when we") Vincent Holme. 6144-3
Good Friday ("I for thy sake was pierced...") Girolamo Savonarola. 6144-3,6424-8
Good Friday ("Peter and James and John"). Lizette Woodworth Reese. 6335-7
Good Friday ("You drove the nails in His white..."). Edgar Daniel Kramer. 6335-7
Good Friday (Gypsy song). Unknown. 6125-7
Good Friday - 1939. Rosamund Dargan Thomson. 6017-X
Good Friday 1327. Francesco Petrarch. 6325-X
Good Friday night. William Vaughn Moody. 6753-0
Good Friday night. William Vaughn Moody. 6153-2
Good Friday night. William Vaughn Moody. 6753-0
Good Friday song. Robert P. Tristram Coffin. 6532-5
Good Friday's hoopoe. Douglas Ainslie. 6180-X
Good Friday, 1613. Riding westward. John Donne. 6536-8, 6562-7,6341-1
"Good friend, for Jesus' sake, forbear". Unknown. 6850-2
"Good friend, if by a curious chance you burn". Poet accepting a laurel wreath. Arthur Davison Ficke. 6817-0
"Good friends, who meet in bookly cheer". Readers round table at Christmas. John Hooks. 6789-1
"Good God! Must I now meekly bend my head". The Kanawha striker. Unknown. 6880-4
"Good God, how sweet are all things here". The retirement, sels. Charles Cotton. 6934-7
'Good from a book'. Elizabeth Barrett Browning. 6465-5
The good girl. Elizabeth Turner. 6018-8
Good grease. Mary TallMountain. 7005-1
The good great man. Samuel Taylor Coleridge. 6302-0,6385-3, 6271-7,6604-6,6214-8,6660 ,6110-9,6199-0,6219-9,6304-7,6737-9,6605
The good heart. Robert Burns. 6438-8
The good hour. Louise Driscoll. 6619-4
Good hours. Robert Frost. 6723-9
Good in everything. William Shakespeare. 6461-2
Good intentions. Edmund Doerf. 6799-9

"Good is that darkening of our lives." Frederick William Faber. 6225-3
The good Joan. Lizette Woodworth Reese. 6543-0
"Good is the Saxon speech! clear,short..strong". Our Anglo-Saxon tongue. James Barron Hope. 7017-5
"Good Junipero the Padre". By the cross of Monterey. Richard Edward White. 6922-3
"Good Junipero the padre". Discovery of San Francisco Bay. Richard Edward White. 6921-5
"Good Junipero, the padre". Discovery of San Francisco Bay. Richard Edward White. 6946-0
"The good Lord Nann and his fair bride". The Lord Nann and the fairy. Unknown. 6873-1
"The good Lord understood us when he taught us". Learn to smile. Edgar A. Guest. 7033-7
A good joke on Maria. Unknown. 6417-5
Good King Wenceslas. John Mason Neale. 6746-8,6747-6
Good King Wenceslas. Unknown. 6014-5,6459-0,6614-3
Good king Wenceslas. Unknown. 6478-7
Good King Wenceslas. Unknown (Latin) 6608-9
Good King Wenceslaus. John Mason Neale. 6465-5,6639-9
A good knight in prison. William Morris. 6980-0
"Good ladies, ye that have your pleasure in exile." Henry Howard, Earl of Surrey. 6584-8
The good little boy. Edgar A. Guest. 7033-7
The good little sister. Phoebe Cary. 6060-9
The good live for ever, fr. Epigrams. Callimachus. 6435-3, 6046-3,6253-9
The good Lord Clifford. William Wordsworth. 6219-9
Good luck. Oliver St. John Gogarty. 6292-X,6096-X
Good luck and bad. Grantland Rice. 6583-X
The good man of Alloa. James Hogg. 6614-3
The good man's evening. James Abraham Martling. 6952-5
"A good man's love! Oh prithee stay". Yes or no? G. Weatherly. 6770-0
A good man's sorror. Eugene Field. 6949-5
The good man. Sir Henry Wotton. 6600-3
"Good manners may in seven words be found". Of courtesy, fr. Proverbs. Arthur Guiterman. 6861-8
"Good men and true! in this house who dwell". The croppy boy. Carroll Malone. 6858-8
"Good men, shew, if you can tell" Thomas Campion. 6794-8
The good moolly cow. Eliza Lee Follen. 6452-3
"Good mornin' til yez, yer honor!". The advertisement answered. Frank M. Thorn. 6916-9,6742-5
"Good morni ', sir,rMr. Printer". Makin' an editor outen o' him. Will Carleton. 6014-5,6913-4
"Good mornin'. My ma sent me". Borrowin' the baby. Wilbur Dick Nesbit. 6889-8
Good morning. Robert Browning. 6401-9,6519-8,6135-4,6424-8
Good morning, America!. Harry Kemp. 6449-3
"Good morning, madam". Portrait of a lady. Marjorie Allen Seiffert. 6035-8
"Good morning, sir. Give us your paw". Billy K. Simes. Elmer Ruan Coates. 6920-7
Good morning, spring. Mary Morrison. 6750-6
Good morning, Stalingrad. Langston Hughes. 6561-9
Good morrow. Thomas Heywood. 6490-6,6604-6,6099-4,6600-3, 6026-9,6660 ,6153-2,6197-4,6219-9
"Good morrow to the golden morning". Birthday verses. Thomas Hood. 6974-6
Good morrow, 'tis Saint Valentine's day. Unknown. 6328-4
Good morrow, 'tis St. Valentine's day. Song ("Good morrow"), fr. Hamlet. William Shakespeare. 6820-0
"Good mother, what quaint legend are..reading". Revolutionary story. Alice Cary. 6969-X
"Good muse, rock me asleep" Nicholas Breton. 6935-5
Good name in man and woman. William Shakespeare. 6457-4, 6503-1,6291-1,6238-5,6102-8,6424
A good name mo e desirable than riches. Louis B. Coley. 6690-9
"Good name was dear to all. Without it, none". Reputation. Robert Pollock. 6980-0
Good name, fr. Othello. William Shakespeare. 6101-4
Good neighbors. Willard Wattles. 6036-6
Good news. Arthur Guiterman. 6503-1
Good news. Tertius Van Dyke. 6954-1
Good news from Georgia. Unknown. 6274-1
Good night. William Barnes. 6546-7
Good night. George Godon, 6th Baron Byron. 6732-8

Good night. Bernard Isaac Durward. 6292-X
Good night. Guttormur J. Guttormsson. 6854-5
Good night. Felicia Dorothea Hemans. 6973-8
Good night. Victor Hugo. 6109-5,6466-3,6623-2,6424-8
Good night. Karl [or Charles] Theodore Korner. 6302-0;6385-3
Good night. Silas Weir Mitchell. 6337-3
Good night. Joan Nichol. 6437-X
Good night. Sana'i. 6448-5
Good night. Robert Tannahill. 6086-2
Good night. Unknown. 6632-1,6131-1,6226-1,6219-9
Good night. Mark Van Doren. 6076-5
Good night, and joy be wi' you a' Sir Alexander Boswell. 6383-7
"Good night, beloved, in the west". Edward P. Davis. 6983-5
Good night, my love. Charles Cotton. 6328-4
'Good night, papa.' Unknown. 6744-1
"Good night, pretty sleepers of mine". Last words over a little bed at night. Sarah Morgan Bryan Piatt. 6772-7
"Good night. Ensured release". Alta quies, fr. More poems. Alfred Edward Housman. 6828-6
The good of it. Dinah Maria Mulock Craik. 6001-3
"Good old days - dear old days". New-Year's eve. Eugene Field. 6949-5
"The good old man is gone!". Bishop Ravenscroft. George Washington Doane. 6752-2
The good old plough. Unknown. 6302-0
Good old souls. James Carnegie; Earl of Southesk. 6661-5
Good old things. John Collins. 6874-X
"'Good old times'-all times when old are good". The age of bronze. George Gordon, 6th Baron Byron. 6945-2
The good old times. Benjamin Thompson. 6176-1
The good old times. Robert J. Burdette. 6712-3
The good old way. Unknown. 6414-0,6486-8
A good old world. Edgar S. Nye. 6583-X
Good omens. William Shakespeare. 6438-8
Good or bad. Unknown. 6937-1
The good parson, fr. The Canterbury tales. Geoffrey Chaucer. 6337-3,6730-1
"Good peasant, we are strangers here". The felons. John T. Campion. 6858-8
A good play. Robert Louis Stevenson. 6132-X,6183-4,6456-6, 6655-0
"Good plays are scarce". On Moore's last operatic farce, or farcical opera. George Gordon, 6th Baron Byron. 6945-2
"Good Rabbi Nathan had rejoiced to spend". The two friends. John Godfrey Saxe. 6848-0
"Good Saint Marcarius, full of grace". Saint Macarius of the desert. Phoebe Cary. 6865-0;6969-X
The good provider's wife. Julia Clay Barron Webb. 6750-6
Good reasons. Keith Preston. 6722-0
Good resolutions, fr. Gedichte. Johann Wolfgang von Goethe. 7042-6
The good rich man. Caspar Friedrich Loffins. 6952-5
A good rule. Unknown. 6158-3,6484-4,6131-1
A good rule. Alice Cary. 6060-9
The good samaritan. Orville Lawrence Kuhn. 6799-9
The good shepherd ("I know mine own..."). J. Harold Gwynne. 6065-X
The good shepherd ("Shepherd! that with thine..."). Lope De Vega. 6065-X
The good shepherd with the kid. Matthew Arnold. 6102-8
The good shepherd. D.N. Howe. 6964-9
The good shepherd. Keidrych Rhys. 6379-9
The good shepherd. Christina Georgina Rossetti. 6144-3
The good shepherd. Clyde Edwin Tuck. 6065-X
The good ship alma mater. Helen Gray Cone. 6847-2
Good ship, alma mater. Unknown. 6718-2
The good ship. Dorothy Lowry Dolan. 6789-1
A good sight of Andromeda. Milton Acorn. 6767-0
"The good sir Griflet did not die". Curing, fr. Songs from an invalid chair. Josephine A. Meyer. 6847-2
"Good sir, whose powers are these?", fr. Hamlet. William Shakespeare. 6665-8
The good sister. Christina Georgina Rossetti. 6429-9,6321-7
"Good Susan be as secrett as you can." Unknown. 6563-5

GOOD

Good temper. Charles and Mary Lamb. 6295-4
A good Thanksgiving. Marian (Annie D.G. Robinson) Douglas. 6638-0
"A good that never satisfies the mind". Sonnet ("A good"). William Drummond of Hawthornden. 6302-0,6219-9
A good that never satisfies the mind. William Drummond of Hawthornden. 6543-0
The good thief. John Banister Tabb. 6096 X
Good tidings. Unknown. 6105-2,6466-3
Good tidings to Zion. Thomas Kelly. 6848-0
'Good tidings unto the meek' Bible. 6954-1
Good tidings, fr. Luke. Bible. 6337-3
A good time coming. Oliver Wendell Holmes. 6271-7
The good time coming. Charles Mackay. 6219-9
Good times. Unknown. 6109-5
Good wife. Thomas Campion. 6194-X
The good wife's ale. Ben Jonson. 6733-6
"Good wife, what are you singing for?". We've always been provided for. Unknown. 6917-7
The good wife. Sadi [or Saadi] (Mushlih-ud-Din) 6448-5
The good wife. Unknown. 6279-2
The good will, fr. Pharsalia. Lucan. 7042-6
"Good wine's the greatest boon on earth!". Martin Luther's song. Unknown. 6936-3
The good woman made welcome in heaven. Richard Crashaw. 6114-1
"Good woman/Don't love the man". Parasite. Alfred Kreymborg. 6897-9
A good woman. Jean Blewett. 6591-0,6592-2
A good world after all. Margaret Elizabeth Sangster. 6583-X
Good writing. Samuel Butler. 6278-4
A good year. Alejandro Carrion. 6759-X
The 'good' people. Kostas Varnalis. 6352-7
Good, John Mason (tr.)
    Concerning the nature of things, sels. Titus Lucretius Carus, 6482-5
Good, Ruth
    Mountains and other outdoor things. 6966-5
The good, great man. Samuel Taylor Coleridge. 6828-6
A good, great name. Frances E. Willard. 6685-2
"Good, kindly Mother Nature plays". Mother Nature. Edgar A. Guest. 6862-6
The good, old-fashioned people. James Whitcomb Riley. 6091-9
"The good, the brave/Whose mighty dust in glory sleeps" Andrew Coles. 6712-3
"Good, to forgive;/Best, to forget!". La Saisiaz. Robert Browning. 6828-6
Good-by. Robert Loveman. 6941-X
Good-by. Christina Georgina Rossetti. 6656-9
Good-by ("We say it for an hour or for years"). Grace Denio Litchfield. 6273-3,6085-4
'Good-by - and God bless you!' Eugene Field. 6949-5
'Good-by but not farewell.' Edith Putnam Painton. 6718-2
'Good-by' (valedictory poem). Unknown. 6718-2
"Good-by', fond hearts, good-by!". Bon voyage. William White. 6868-5
"Good-by, old stamp; it's nasty luck". The three-cent stamp. Eugene Field. 6949-5
Good-by, sweetheart. Mary Clemmer. 6066-8
"Good-by, the tears are in my eyes". Rondel. Francois Villon. 7039-6
Good-by, winter. C.S. Stone. 6049-8
Good-bye. May C. ([Mary] Gillington) Byron. 6800-6
Good-bye. Eliza Cook. 6085-4
Good-bye. Walter De La Mare. 6184-2,6506-6
Good-bye. Ralph Waldo Emerson. 6076-5,6300-4,6250-4,6288-1, 6252-0,6464 ,6102-8,6176-1,6374-8,6385-3,6732-8,6730 ,6396-9,6126-5,6219-9,6008-0,6461-2,6431
Good-bye. Emily Pauline ("Tekahionwake") Johnson. 6837-5
Good-bye. Andrew Lang. 6771-9
Good-bye. E.O. Peck. 6314-4
Good-bye. Maimie A. Richardson. 6269-5
"Good-bye - yes, I am going". Answered. Ella Wheeler Wilcox. 6956-8,6863-4
Good-bye acrostic. Unknown. 6715-8
"Good-bye and fare ye well, for we'll sail...". Shipmates. Cicely Fox Smith. 7012-4
Good-bye an how-d'ye-do. William R. Spencer. 6874-X

Good-bye and keep cold. Robert Frost. 6121-4,6431-0,6345-4
Good-bye for a long time. Roy Fuller. 6379-9
Good-bye my fancy! Walt Whitman. 6300-4,6431-0,6333-0,6008-0,6288-1,6121-4,6126-5
Good-bye to dolly. Unknown. 6684-4
"Good-bye to the town!- good-bye!". July. Austin Dobson. 6770-2
Good-bye to you, old town. Talbot Mundy. 7007-8
Good-bye!. Fannie Stearns Davis. 6076-5
"Good-bye! Forget the days of wane" Nikolay Nekrasov. 6103-6
"Good-bye! The tears are in my eyes". Rondel (Francois Villon) Andrew Lang. 6875-8
"Good-bye! the tears are in my eyes". Rondel. Francois Villon. 6771-9
'Good-bye'.. Unknown. 6260-1
Good-bye, little boy. Isabel Richey. 6702-6
Good-bye, little cabin. Robert Service. 6159-1
Good-bye, little flowers. Kate Louise Brown. 6529-5
Good-bye, old church. Millie C. Pomeroy. 6921-5
"Good-bye, old friend." Unknown. 6510-4
"Good-bye, schoolhouse! Good-by, books!". Camp chums. Rose Waldo. 6891-X
"Good-bye. Yes, I am going". Answered. Ella Wheeler Wilcox. 7041-8
A good-bye. Bliss Carman and Richard Hovey. 6890-1
The good-for-nothing cat. Unknown. 6699-2
Good-morning. James William Foley. 6889-8
Good-morning. Unknown. 6312-8
Good-morning to God. Mary T. Hamlin. 6131-1
"Good-morning, Karlene. It's a very". Karlene (2). Bliss Carman and Richard Hovey. 6890-1
"Good-morning, Mr. What-d'ye-call!...". The china-mender. Thomas Hood. 6974-6
"Good-morrow to you, Valentine!". Unknown. 6466-3
"Good-morrow, neighbour! Hast thou heard...". Gossip. Mildred Plew Merryman. 6782-4
A good-morrow. Thomas Shadwell. 6563-5
The good-morrow. John Donne. 6562-7,6250-4,6383-7,6341-1, 6150-8,6182-6,6208-3,6536-8,6315-2,6339-X,6491-4, 6301-2,6645-3,6723-9,6378-0
Good-night. Hester A. Benedict. 6085-4,6273-3
Good-night. Sydney Dayre. 6373-X
Good-night. Edward Fitzgerald. 6874-X
Good-night. Eliza Lee Follen. 6131-1
Good-night. Ellen M.H. Gates. 6654-2
Good-night. Frederick Greenwood. 6772-7
Good-night. Thomas Hood. 6278-4
Good-night. Robert C. Sands. 6219-9
Good-night. Percy Bysshe Shelley. 6092-7
Good-night. Margaret A. Sinclair. 6274-1
Good-night. Jane Taylor. 6078-1,6242-3,6452-3,6459-0,6627-5,6114
Good-night. Unknown. 6132-X,6629-1
Good-night and good-morning. Richard Monckton Milnes; 1st Baron Houghton. 6242-3,6127-3,6314-4,6373-X,6385-3, 6629 ,6638-0,6135-4,6131-1,6424-8,6639-9,6519-8,6543-0
Good-night in Hopi-land. Jean Allard Jeancon. 6836-7
Good-night in the porch, sels. Owen (Edward Bulwer-Lytton, Earl Lytton) Meredith. 6046-3
"Good-night is the word, good-night to the...". The four brothers, sel. Carl Sandburg. 6954-1
The good-night or blessing. Robert Herrick. 6026-9
Good-night prayer for a little child. Henry Johnstone. 6452-3
Good-night to the season. Winthrop Mackworth Praed. 6026-9, 6092-7
"Good-night to thee, lady! tho' many". Good-night. Edward Fitzgerald. 6874-X
"Good-night! I have to say good-night". Palabras carinosas. Thomas Bailey Aldrich. 6226-1,6309-8,6321-7,7041-8,6429-4
"'Good-night', he said, and he held her hand". A challenge. James Clarence Harvey. 6923-1
"Good-night, Babette!" Austin Dobson. 6543-0,6102-8,6508-2, 6046-3,6656-9
Good-night, good-by. Dora Greenwell. 6502-3
Good-night, good-morning. Charles Synge Bowen, Baron Bowen. 6046-3

Good-night, little star. Unknown. 6629-1
"**Good-night,** sweetheart! It can't be ten...". The parting lovers. Mary E. Day. 6917-7
"**Good-night,** the day has slipped to sleep". Serenade. Robert Loveman. 6941-X
A **good-night.** Francis Quarles. 6933-9
A **good-night.** Francis Quarles. 6052-8
Good-will. Eden Phillpotts. 7014-0
Good-will and God's peace. Sylvester Baxter. 6798-0
The **good.** James Abraham Martling. 6952-5
The **good.** John Boyle O'Reilly. 6923-1
Goodale, Dora Read
    April! April! are you here? 6964-9
    Bob white. 6073-0,6272-5
    Clematis. 6049-8
    "Clustered lilies in the shadows", sels. 6601-1
    "The cricket pipes his song again", sels. 6601-1
    "Crimson clover I discover", sels. 6601-1
    The feast time of the year. 6703-4
    The grumbler. 6530-9,6314-4
    Hail, bonny September! 6691-7
    High and low. 6519-8
    "I love the fair lilies and roses so gay", sels. 6601-1
    The judgment. 6300-4
    The May basket. 6466-3
    Ripe grain. 6240-7
    Strawberry blossom. 6529-5
    "When the fields are wet with clover", sels. 6601-1
    "Where the woodland streamlets flow", sels. 6601-1
Goodale, Elaine
    Arbutus. 6049-8
    Ashes of roses. 6240-7
    Baby. 6429-9,6321-7
    Could she have guessed. 6770-0
    Golden-rod. 6049-8
    Mother. 6429-9,6321-7
    "The starry, fragile wind-flower", sels. 6601-1
Goodall, W.
    Three jolly beggars. 6804-9
Goodburne, Marjorie
    Sonnet ("See how your world"). 6662-3
Goodbye ("Goodbye to tree and tower"). Norreys Jephson O'Conor. 6031-5;6556-2
Goodbye - to my mother. Margaret Larkin. 6093-5
A **goodbye** from the ship. Witter Bynner. 6776-X
Goodchild, John Arthur
    The firstborn. 6078-1,6233-4,6627-5
    Schone Rothraut. 6274-1,6656-9
Goodchild, Keighley
    While the billy boils. 6768-9
Goode, J.B.
    Who ne'er has suffered. 6260-1
Goodell Jr., Abner Cheney
    Hymn ("O Thou who givest life.") 6524-4
Goodenough, Arthur Henry
    The cry of the uncreated. 7030-2
    The lips of April. 7030-2
    My Thanksgiving. 6703-4
    The world goes by. 6887-1
The **goodest** mother. Unknown. 6097-8,6273-3
Goodfellow, E.J.H.
    Books. 6137-0
    Dairy-maid song. 6173-7
    The old and new year. 6268-7
The **goodhue** state-house. Jessie Welborn Smith. 7038-8
Goodhue, Isabel Seely
    A modern youth. 6929-0
Goodhue, Yelees
    Morning voices. 6694-1
Goodier, Sharon
    Unicorn. 6767-0
"**Goodly** it is to seek the woodland knoll". The knoll, fr. The homestead. Gertrude Huntington McGiffert. 6838-3
Goodlye doctrine and instruction. John Halle. 6482-5
Goodman, Edward H.
    Sheldon Church, South Carolina. 6799-9
Goodman, J.T.
    Abraham Lincoln. 6524-4
Goodman, Kenneth S.
    A Norse love song. 6983-5
Goodman, Mae Winkler
    Emily Dickinson. 6979-7
Goodman, Richard
    Poem with cowslips. 6985-1
    Poem, 1933. 6985-1
Goodman, Ryah Tumarkin
    They know. 6218-0
Goodmorning with light. John Ciardi. 6666-6
The **goodness** of God. Bible. 6396-9
The **goodness** of God. Nagata. 6027-7
"The **goodness** of the heart is shown in deeds". Calmness of the sublime. Philip James Bailey. 6980-0
Goodrich, Orrin
    Borrioboola gha. 6344-6,6406-X
Goodrich, Samuel G.
    Lake Superior. 6752-2
    The river. 6373-X
Goodson, Louise
    On our street. 6750-6
Goodwin, Grace Duffield
    Aucassin et Nicolete. 6274-1
    An eastern legend. 6684-4
Goodwin, Helen Angele
    Death's blunder. 6414-0
Goodwin, Hopestill
    The golden rod. 6049-8
    The May flower. 6049-8
Goodwin, J. Cheever
    Awkward. 6416-7
Goodwin, James
    Her satin fan. 6116-8
Goodwin, Lavinia S.
    The mortal life. 7030-2
Goodwin, Myra A.
    The first Christmas-tree. 6927-4
    The lightkeeper's daughter. 6410-8,6744-1,6744-1
Goodwin, Ruby Berkle
    Guilty. 6178-8
    If this be good-bye. 6178-8
    New Year's prayer. 6178-8
    We launched a ship. 6178-8
Goody Blake and Harry Gill. William Wordsworth. 6133-8, 6304-7,6918-5
"**Goody** Bull and her daughter together fell out". The world turned upside down. Unknown. 6946-0
Goodyear, Rosalie
    Remembering the dar. 6750-6
Googe, Barnaby
    Coming homeward out of Spain. 6182-6
    An epitaph of the death of Nicholas Grimald. 6641-0
    An epytaphe of the death of Nicholas Grimald. 6586-4
    Goyng towardes Spayne. 6586-4
    Oculi augent dolorem. 6586-4
    Of money. 6182-6
    "Once musing as I sat." 6317-9
    Out of sight, out of mind. 6182-6,6089-7,6724-7
    To M. Henrye Cobham of the most blessed state of lyfe. 6586-4
    A twelfth-night superstition. 6747-6
    The uncertayntie of lyfe. 6586-4
Goold, Elisabeth
    Spring night. 6750-6
Goonetillake, S. Helen
    A Sanskrit stanza. 6591-0,6592-9
Goop rhymes. Gelett Burgess. 6861-8
Goose a la mode. Elizabeth Cavazza. 6440-X
Goose and gander. Unknown. 6125-7
Goose and the gander. Frances Farfone. 6750-6
The **goose** girl. Richard Lawson Gales. 6950-9
Goose, Mary
    Cornfield myth. 7005-1
    Friends. 7005-1
    Insight. 7005-1
    Just an old man. 7005-1
    Last night in Sisseton, S.D. 7005-1
"**Goose,** if I had you upon Sarum-plain." William Shakespeare. 6484-1
The **goose.** Alfred Lord Tennyson. 6089-7,6239-6,6092-7
The **gooseberry** bush. Idella Purnell. 6039-0
Goosegirl's song. Unknown. 6466-3

GOOSEY,

"Goosey, goosey, gander." Mother Goose. 6363-2,6452-3
Gorakhanatha and Lokanatha. Unknown (Newari) 7013-2
Gorbo and Batte. Michael Drayton. 6315-2
The **gorcock**. James Grahame Marquesse of Montrose. 6943-6
Gordi, Tooni
    Never blood. 6799-9
The **Gordian** knot. Thomas Tomkis. 6182-6
Gordon. Ernest Myers. 6656-9
Gordon (I). Sir William Watson. 7015-9
Gordon (II). Sir William Watson. 7015-9
Gordon (atr), Adam Lindsay
    A voice from the bush. 6951-7
Gordon, A.C.
    Before the party. 6686-0
    Ebo. 6675-5
    Kyarlina Jim. 6139-7
    Law at our boarding-house. 6878-2
Gordon, Adam Lindsay
    After the quarrel. 6437-X
    After the quarrel, fr. The road to Avernus. 6951-7
    Argemone. 6951-7
    Ars longa. 6951-7
    Ashtaroth: a dramatic lyric. 6951-7
    Banker's dream, fr. Hippdromania. 6951-7
    A basket of flowers. 6951-7
    Bellona. 6951-7
    Borrowed plumes. 6951-7
    By flood and field, fr. Ye wearie wayfarer. 6951-7
    By wood and wold. 6784-0
    By wood and wole, fr. Ye wearie wayfarer. 6951-7
    The chase and the race, fr. Ye wearie wayfarer. 6427-2
    Cito pede preterit aetas, fr. Ye wearie wayfarer. 6951-7
    Confiteor. 6951-7
    Credat Judaeus Apella, fr. Hippodromania. 6951-7
    Cui bono. 6951-7
    De te. 6951-7
    The death of Nelson. 6951-7
    A dedication to the author of Holmby house. 6951-7
    A dedication. 6793-X,6784-0
    Delilah. 6951-7
    Discontent, fr. The road to Avernus. 6951-7
    Doubtful dreams. 6951-7
    Early adieux. 6951-7
    Exeunt, fr. The road to Avernus. 6951-7
    An exile's farewell. 6951-7,6768-9
    Fauconshawe. 6951-7
    The feud: a ballad. 6951-7
    The fields of Coleraine, fr. Hippodromania. 6951-7
    Finis exoptatus, fr. Ye wearie wayfarer. 6951-7
    A fragment ("They say that poison..."). 6951-7
    Fragments: To Charley Walker (1). 6951-7
    Fragments: To Charley Walker (2). 6951-7
    Fragments: To Charley Walker (3). 6951-7
    Fragments: To Charley Walker (4). 6951-7
    From lightning and tempest. 6951-7
    From the wreck. 6591-0,6592-9,6744-1
    From the wreck. 6918-5
    Gone. 6951-7,6784-0
    Hippodromania; or, whiffs from the pipe. 6951-7
    How we beat the favourite. 6427-2,6518-X,6656-9,6681-X
    A hunting rhyme. 6951-7
    A hunting song. 6951-7
    In the garden, fr. The road to Avernus. 6951-7
    In utrumque paratus, fr. Ye wearie wayfarer. 6951-7
    "Jones plays the deuce wuth is grammar." 6951-7
    The last leap. 6951-7,6784-0
    Laudamus. 6951-7
    Lex talionis, fr. Ye wearie wayfarer. 6951-7
    Man's testament. 6427-2
    No name. 6951-7
    'The old leaven'. 6951-7
    On the cliffs, sels. 6997-5
    The patrol [Gordon] and the gold-digger. 6951-7
    Podas okus. 6951-7
    Potters' clay, fr. Ye wearie wayfarer. 6951-7
    Quare fatigasti [or, Whither bound]. 6951-7
    The rhyme of joyous garde. 6951-7
    Rippling water. 6951-7
    The risks of the game, fr. Ye wearie wayfarer. 6427-2

    The road to Avernus, sels. 6951-7
    The roll of the kettledrum; or, the lay of..last charger. 6951-7
    The romance of Britomarte. 6661-5
    The sick stock-rider. 6656-9
    The sick stockrider, sels. 6427-2,6437-X,6046-3
    The sick stockrider. 6591-0,6592-9
    The sick stockrider. 6951-7
    The sick stock-rider. 6768-9
    A song of autumn. 6951-7,6784-0
    The song of the surf. 6997-5
    The song of the surf. 6951-7
    Sunlight on the sea. 6951-7
    The swimmer. 6997-5,6951-7,7012-4
    Ten paces off, fr. The road to Avernus. 6951-7
    To A. Patchen Martin. 6951-7
    To my sister. 6951-7
    To my soul. 6951-7
    'Twixt the cup and the lip, fr. Hippodromania. 6951-7
    Two exhortations, fr. The road to Avernus. 6951-7
    An unfinished poem. 6951-7
    Unshriven. 6951-7
    Valecdictory. 6656-9
    Valedictory poem. 6951-7
    Visions in the smoke, fr. Hippodramania. 6951-7
    "Whenever you meet with a man from home". 6951-7
    Whisperings in wattle-boughs. 6437-X
    Whisperings in Whattle Boughs. 6591-0,6592-9
    Wolf and hound. 6591-0,6592-9
    Wormwood and nightshade. 6951-7
    Ye wearie wayfarer. 6951-7
    Ye wearie wayfarer, sels. 6427-2
    Zu der edlen jagd, fr. Ye wearie wayfarer. 6951-7
Gordon, Adam Lindsay (tr.)
    A legend of Madrid. Unknown (Spanish), 6951-7
    Pastor cum. Horace, 6951-7
    The three friends. Unknown (French), 6951-7
Gordon, Alexander Gordon, 4th Duke of
    Cauld kail in Aberdeen. 6180-X
Gordon, Alfred
    "Day after day no gun had spoken". 6796-4
    Dedication. 6115-X
    Easter ode, 1915. 6115-X
    England to France. 6115-X
Gordon, Angela
    Loch Fiodiag. 6253-9
Gordon, Armistead Churchill
    The University of Virginia. 6184-2
Gordon, Bertha Frances
    Song at the brink of death. 6006-4
    To a violin. 6274-1
Gordon, Clara
    In memory of my father. 6799-9
Gordon, Daniel
    Misogyny. 6818-9
Gordon, Don
    Laocoon. 6665-8
    Sea. 6833-2
    The shadow of the swan. 6779-4
Gordon, Grace
    Mattie's wants and wishes. 6744-1,6167-2
Gordon, Guanetta
    Phantom. 6750-6
Gordon, H.E.
    The house not made with hands. 6925-8
Gordon, H.L.
    On reading President Lincoln's letter. 6524-4
Gordon, James Lindsay
    At the concert. 6682-8
    Remembered. 6741-X
    Wheeler at Santiago. 6946-0
Gordon, Jessie
    Only. 6416-7
Gordon, John H.
    When the swallows homeward fly. 6304-7
Gordon, John Warren
    The pleasures of an angler. 7030-2
Gordon, Mark
    The meeting. 6767-0
Gordon, R.K. (tr.)

Beowulf, sels. Unknown, 6179-6
Gordon, William Steward
    A hymn for the new age. 6337-3
Gordon-Roby, Maude
    To music. 6762-X
Gore, James F.
    Plato and Diogenes. 6926-6
Gore-Booth, Eva
    Aspiration. 6174-5
    The cross. 6144-3,6337-3
    Crucifixion. 6337-3
    Form. 6337-3,6641-0
    Harvest. 6161-3
    In the pinewoods. 6174-5
    The little waves of Breffny. 6090-0,6174-5,6331-4,6266-0,6090-0,6476 ,6161-3,6639-9
    The lost traveller's dream. 7029-9
    A moment's insight. 6090-0,6174-5
    The perilous light. 6374-8
    The perilous night. 6374-8
    The quest. 6337-3
    There is no age. 6266-0
    To Maeve. 6174-5
    The travellers. 6320-9
    The waves of Breffny. 6374-8,6102-8,6253-9
    The weaver. 6090-0
Gorell, Ronald Gorell Barnes, Lord
    London to Paris. 6723-9
    London to Paris by air. 6228-8,6723-9
    To the British Expeditionary Force. 7029-9
    Ypres. 7027-2
"The **gorgeous** blossoms of that magic tree". To a Persian boy in the bazaar at Smyrna. Bayard Taylor. 6976-2
A **gorgeous** day. Estelle Webb Thomas. 6799-9
gorgeous gallery. Unknown. 6586-4
The **gorgeous** giraffe. Carolyn Wells. 6882-0
Gorgio lad. Amelia Josephine Burr. 6102-8,6076-5,6253-9
Gorgo and Praxinoa, fr. Idyll xv. Theocritus. 6435-3
Gorham, James
    Counterfeit. 6850-2
    Dejection. 6850-2
    The message. 6850-2
    Song ("From the north I blow"). 6850-2
    To H.B.S. 6850-2
Gorham, Myrtle Campbell
    Service, please. 6178-8
The **gorilla.**. Unknown. 6277-6
Gorky's childhood. Lorna Crozier. 6767-0
Gorman, Herbert S.
    The birds ("I thought to shoulder time"). 6073-0,6619-4
    The burning bush. 6032-3
    Chimaera in taffeta. 6217-2
    The fountain. 6393-4
    I cannot put you away. 6034-X
    The last fire. 6036-6,6250-4
    Lese-majeste. 6102-8,6076-5,6037-4
    Lilith, Lilith. 6034-X
    The lost heart. 6033-1,6880-4
    The satyrs and the moon. 6467-1
    A tartar horse. 6619-4
    Trance. 6037-4
    Viaticum. 6619-4
Gormley, John J.
    Old pipe of mine. 6453-1
Gorostiza, Jose
    Aquarium. Donald Devenish Walsh (tr.). 6759-X
    Autumn. H.R. Hays (tr.). 6642-9
    The bloom hoists its banner. H.R. Hays (tr.). 6642-9
    Fisherman of the moon. H.R. Hays (tr.). 6642-9
    Pauses. H.R. Hays (tr.). 6642-9
    Pauses II. H.R. Hays (tr.). 6642-9
    A poor little conscience. Donald Devenish Walsh (tr.). 6759-X
    Prelude. H.R. Hays (tr.). 6642-9
    Who is it? H.R. Hays (tr.). 6642-9
    Who will buy me an orange? H.R. Hays (tr.). 6642-9
    Women. Donald Devenish Walsh (tr.). 6759-X
Gorse. Nigel Heseltine. 6360-8
Gorse. Alfred Noyes. 6151-6
The **gorse.**. Wilfred Wilson Gibson. 6234-2

Gorsuch, Anna Lovelace
    Biography. 6750-6
The **gorwynion**. Llywarc's Hen. 6873-1
'The **goshdern** words.' John Edward Hazzard. 6714-X
Goshen!. Edgar Frank. 6337-3
Goslin, Fannie H.
    Prayer. 6799-9
Gosling stew. Eugene Field. 6949-5
Gospel according to St. Luke, sels. Bible. 6243-5
Gospel according to St. Matthew, sels. Bible. 6143-5
The **gospel** for the poor. Benjamin Franklin Taylor. 6815-4
The **gospel** of consolation. Havelock Ellis. 6482-5
The **gospel** of labor. Henry Van Dyke. 6730-1
The **gospel** of peace. James Jeffrey Roche. 6946-0
The **gospel** of Saint Matthew. Bible. 6958-4
Gospel of the fields. Arthur Upson. 6374-8
The **gospel** of the oak. Benjamin Franklin Taylor. 6815-4
The **gospel** train. Unknown. 6466-3
Goss, William Thompson
    Man to man. 6178-8
    Variety. 6178-8
Gossamer. Virginia Moore. 6761-1
Gosse, Sir Edmund
    Alcyone. 7015-9
    Ballade of dead cities. 6473-6,6732-8,6102-8
    By the well. 6770-0
    The charcoal-burner. 6437-X,6046-3
    De rosis hibernis. 6656-9
    The death of Arnkel. 6661-5,6683-6
    A dream of November. 6507-4
    Epithalamium. 6437-X
    Expectation. 6770-0
    The fear of death. 6250-4
    February in Rome. 7015-9
    First sight. 6770-0
    Fortunate love. 6875-8
    A garden piece. 6770-0
    A garden-piece. 6338-1
    George Odger. 6793-X
    Hans Christian Anderson, 1805-1875 6656-9
    Happy children. 6233-4
    If love should faint. 6770-0
    Impression. 6507-4,6732-8,6102-8,6301-2
    In the grass. 6770-0
    Labour and love. 7014-0
    The land of France. 6331-4
    Lovers' quarrel. 6770-0
    Lying in the grass. 6186-9,6477-9,6437-X,6656-9,6543-0
    Madrigal. 6483-3
    On a lute found in a sarcophagus. 6656-9
    Philomel in London. 6477-9,6476-0
    The pipe-player. 6656-9
    The praise of Dionysus (1). 6770-0,6875-8
    The praise of Dionysus (2). 6959-2
    The return of the swallows. 6543-0
    Revelation. 6437-X,6102-8,6250-4
    Rondeau. 6875-8
    Rondel. 6770-0
    Rondel (After Anyte of Tegea). 6875-8
    Sestina. 6770-0,6289-X
    Song for music. 6656-9
    Song for the lute. 6658-5
    The sultan of my books. 6297-0
    Theocritus. 6483-3,6656-9
    Theodore de Banville. 6875-8
    To a traveler. 6396-9
    To Austin Dobson. 6301-2
    To my daughter. 6233-4
    The tomb of Sophocles. 7015-9
    Triolet, after Catullus. 6875-8,6770-0
    Villanelle ("Little"). 6770-0,6875-8
    Villanelle ("Wouldst thou"). 6770-0,6875-8
    The voice of D.G.R. 6656-9
    Wanderer, linger here awhile. 6253-9
    With a copy of Herrick. 6483-3,6558-9,6656-9,6668-2
    "Wouldst thou not be content to die". 6850-2
    The wounded gull. 6510-4
Gosse, Sir Edmund (tr.)
    The boy and the flute. Bjornstjerne Bjornson, 7039-6
    Cicero. Martial, 6297-0

GOSSE

Epitaph on the Duchess of Maine's cat. Francois La Mothe Le Vayer, 6511-2
In the orchard. Henrik Ibsen, 7039-6
Love and books. K.D. of Wirsin (Swedish), 6297-0
On the death of a pious lady. Olof Wexionius, 7039-6
Sonnet ("And then I sat"). Gustav Rosenhane, 7039-6
Sonnet ("Deep in a vale"). Gustav Rosenhane, 7039-6
Virgil. Martial, 6297-0
The wall-flower. Henrik Arnold Thaulov Wergeland, 7039-6

Gossip. Edgar A. Guest. 6862-6
Gossip. Mildred Plew Merryman. 6782-4
Gossip. Unknown. 6294-6
Gossip at Bow Mills. Gerald Chittenden. 6039-0
Gossip Joan. Unknown. 6134-6
Gossip mine. Unknown. 6186-9
The **gossip** of the nuts. Unknown. 6703-4
The **gossip.** Lucy Malleson. 6804-9
The **gossip.** John Richard Moreland. 6441-8
Gossipers. Edward R. Huxley. 6885-5
Gossips. Mary Elizabeth Schwartz. 6906-1
The **gossips.** Ella Wheeler Wilcox. 6745-X
Gostick, J. (tr.)
Mount Nebo. Ferdinand Freiligrath, 6848-0
"Got a ride south of Galesburg". 20 years of irreversible brain damage. George Tsongas. 6998-3, 6901-0
"'Got any boys?' the marshal said". The puzzled census-taker. John Godfrey Saxe. 6889-8
Got my name on de record. Cleveland Perry. 6149-4
"Got one? Don't say so! Which did you get?". The best sewing-machine. Unknown. 6917-7
"Got your note today and I'm glad you wrote". A letter to Peter. Fay Chiang. 6790-5
Gotham, sels. Charles Churchill. 6024-2
A **gothamite** in Camelot. Berton Braley. 6853-7
"The **Gothic** looks solemn". On Oxford. John Keats. 6802-2
The **Gothic** rose. Wilfred Rowland Childe. 6096 X
Gotoba [or Toba II], Emperor
"How I regret my fallen friends". William N. Porter (tr.). 6852-9
"Gotta go for day-break walk". Sena. Ruth Weiss. 6998-3, 6901-0
'Gotta' smoke?' William ("Wild Bill") Franklin. 6870-7
Gotterdammerung. Ernest Hartsock. 6420-5,6542-2
Gottheil, Gustav
Yom Kippur. 6214-8
Gotthold, Arthur F.
The grind's dream. 6118-4
The **Gottinger** barber. J.E. Carpenter. 6918-5
Gottschalk, Laura Riding. See Riding, Laura
Gougane barra. Aubrey Thomas De Vere. 6086-2
Gougaune Barra. Jeremiah [or James] Joseph Callanan. 6302-0,6385-3,6409-4,6858-6
Gough, Jacob
A plea for Castles in the air. 6273-3
Gough, John B.
The dying boy. 6744-1,6167-2
A glass of cold water. 6403-5
The pilot. 6165-6
Plea for 'castles in the air'. 6273-3
The power of habit. 6165-6,6567-8,6304-7
The power of heart. 6165-6
Goulard, Stanley
Range riding. 6396-9
Gould and S.R. Hadsell, C.N.
The trail. 6397-7
Gould Jr., B.A.
Candida. 6116-8
Elsinore. 6116-8
Gould's signal. Francis Bret Harte. 6744-1,6424-8
Gould, C.C.
Come carol, make carol. 6339-X
Gould, Dayton Thomas
A day in March. 6818-9
Gould, Elizabeth
Miss tabby cat's reception. 6692-2
When time comes creeping. 6889-8
Gould, Gerald
Beauty the pilgrim. 6625-9
The companion. 6335-7

Compensation. 6776-X
The earth-child. 6423-X
Envoy ("The God who made denial"). 6532-5
Fallen cities. 6250-4
Freedoms. 6884-7
The happy tree. 6730-1
The little things. 6844-8
Morning. 6423-X
Obligato. 6780-8
Ode 002. 6532-5
Portrait. 6506-6
The sea-captain. 6833-2
'Tis but a week. 6477-9,6639-9
Wander-thirst. 6396-9,6421-3,6083-8,6423-X,6476-0,6374-8,6639-9,6102
Wanderlust. 6274-1
You walk in a strange way. 6872-3
Gould, Hannah Flagg
The blind boy. 6131-1
The crocus's soliloquy. 6373-X
Freaks of the frost. 6621-6
The frost. 6302-0,6385-3,6479-5,6132-X,6629-1,6373 , 6018-8,6131-1,6638-0,6639-9
The ground laurel. 6373-X
It snows. 6131-1
Jack Frost. 6127-3,6519-8,6456-6
A name in the sand. 6303-9,6479-5,6214-8
A name in the sand. 6912-6
Peach blossoms. 6049-8
The pebble and the acorn. 6049-8
The snow-flake. 6459-0
The storm in the forest. 6049-8
"...though often told/The story of thy deeds..." 6712-3
The wild violet. 6049-8
Gould, Larry
All day rain. 6750-6
Gould, Nellie Eldora
Home. 6764-6
Gould, Robert
Celia has a thousand charms. 6328-4
The hopeless comfort. 6152-4
Song ("Fair, and soft"). 6563-5,6152-4
Gould, Sabine Baring
Hadad. 6848-0
Gould, T.H.
A rhapsody. 6118-4
Gould, Wallace
"Across the heights the June",fr. Children of the sun. 6031-5
Children of the sun, sels. 6031-5
The **goulden** vanitee. Unknown. 6547-3
Gouldsbury, Cullen
The councillor. 6788-3
The pace of the ox. 6625-9,6591-0,6592-9
The pace of the ox. 6800-6
The shadow girl. 6800-6
Goulette, Christina
Until then. 6894-4
The **gourd** and the palm. Unknown. 6614-3,6424-8
The **gourd** dancer. N. Scott Momaday. 7005-1
"The **gourd** has still its bitter leaves". I wait my lord. Unknown (Chinese). 7039-6
The **gourd-heads.** William D. Barney. 6218-0
Gourghinian, Shushanik
The eagle's love. 6050-1
Gourley, William B.
Cushing vs. Blake. 6878-2
Kuhn et al. vs. Jewett, receiver. 6878-2
Gourmont, Remy de
Jeanne. 6351-9
Le houx. 6253-9
Litanies of the rose. 6351-9
Simone. 6351-9
The **gouty** merchant and the stranger. Horace Smith. 6089-7, 6385-3,6606-2,6403-5
The **gouty** merchant and the stranger. Unknown. 6787-5
Government official. Paul Dehn. 6666-6
Governor Lenhard, sels. Einar Hjorleifsson Kvaran. 6283-0
Gow, Winnie M.
Baby in churc. 6450-7

The gowan glitters on the sward. Joanna Baillie. 6600-3
Gowans under her feet. Frances W. Gibson. 6918-5
Gower, George
    The story of Ulysses. 6547-3
Gower, Jean Milne
    Blind. 6836-7
    Children of the loom. 6836-7
    Dry farms. 6836-7
    Grey day. 6836-7
    In happy canon. 6836-7
    Inspiration point. 6836-7
    A potsherd. 6836-7
    Sky-line drive. 6836-7
    Sport. 6836-7
    Sun worshippers. 6836-7
    To a vagabond. 6836-7
    A vision. 6836-7
    The way of the moon. 6836-7
Gower, John
    The cave of sleep, fr. Confession amantis. 6958-4
    Confession Amantis (Medea and Eson). 6198-2,6193-1
    Jason and Medea. 6022-6
    Nebuchadnezzar. 6438-8
    Richard the Redeless. 6186-9
    Somnolence, fr. Confessio amantis. 6958-4
    The story of Phoebus and Daphne. 6186-9
    The tale of Rosiphelee. 6050-1
The Gowk.. Violet Jacob. 6477-9
The gowk. William Soutar. 6379-9
"A gown of haze hung round the sleepy sun". The potter's field. George M. Vickers. 6918-5
The gown. Mary Carolyn Davies. 6250-4
Gowns of gossamer. Lucy Larcom. 6129-X
Gowper, M.G.
    Poet and peasant. 6782-4
Goyng towardes Spayne. Barnaby Googe. 6586-4
Graber, Edwin C.
    Butterfly parade. 6799-9
Grace. Ralph Waldo Emerson. 6288-1
Grace and Dolly. Emma Celia & Lizzie J. Rook. 6137-0
Grace and her friends. Lucy Larcom. 6127-3,6639-9
Grace and love. George Meredith. 6828-6
Grace and providence. William Cowper. 6814-6
Grace at evening. Edwin McNeill Poteat. 6144-3
Grace at table. Edgar A. Guest. 6869-3
Grace be with them all that love. Shelley Jones. 7003-5
Grace before eating. Robert Burns. 6303-9,6214-8
Grace before meat. Anita Fitch. 6036-6
Grace before meat. Robert Herrick. 6125-7
A grace before reading. Helen Coale Crew. 6030-7
"Grace comes only after the long study of...". Prelude. Traise Yamamoto. 6790-5
Grace darling. Unknown. 6919-3
Grace for a child. Robert Herrick. 6189-3,6321-7,6430-2, 6429-9
Grace for a spring morning. Frances Stoakley Lankford. 6839-1
Grace for children. Robert Herrick. 6931-2
Grace for gardens. Louise Driscoll. 6338-1,6374-8
Grace for light. Moira (Nesta Higginson Skrine) O'Neill. 6538-4,6161-3,6654-X,6727-1
"Grace full of grace, though in these verses here". Sonnet ("Grace full of grace"). Henry Constable. 6436-1
The grace of God. George Gascoigne. 6134-6
The grace of her beauty. Unknown. 6189-3
Grace of the way. Francis Thompson. 6828-6
Grace Vernon Bussell. H.S. Drayton. 6920-7
"The grace wife of Keith'. Alice Cary. 6969-X
Grace's choice. Charles Battell Loomis. 7021-3
Grace's friends. Lucy Larcom. 6129-X
"Grace, triumphant in the throne". Not of works. William Cowper. 6814-6
A grace. Robert Herrick. 6179-6
"Gracefully shy is yon gazelle". Destiny uncertain. Walter Savage Landor. 6874-X
Gracia. Ella Wheeler Wilcox. 6956-8
Gracie. Phoebe Cary. 6969-X
Gracie of Alabama. Francis Orrery Ticknor. 6062-5
Gracie Og Machree. John Keegan Casey. 6873-1
Gracie's fancies. Brenda Aubert. 6965-7

"Gracile peacock, you are a handsome bird!". The peacock. Beatrice Payne Morgan. 6841-3
"Gracious Lord, our children see". Prayer for children. William Cowper. 6814-6
The gracious answer. Henry N. Cobb. 6409-4
The gracious past. James Russell Lowell. 6085-4
Gracious saviour born of Mary. Edmund Hamilton Sears. 6608-9
The gracious time, fr. Hamlet. William Shakespeare. 6239-3
"Gracious, Diune, and most omnipotent." Barnabe Barnes. 6586-4
Gradatim. Josiah Gilbert Holland. 6101-X,6260-1,6291-1, 6610-0,6730-1,6240 ,6337-3,6499-X,6570-8,6214-8,6309-8
The gradgerratum' of Joe. William Allen White. 6615-1
"Graduates in economics,/Doctors in divinity". The black trout. Eugenio Montale. 6803-0
A graduating essay. H.C. Dodge. 6682-8
Graduation. Unknown. 6294-6,6131-1
Graduation and two years later. Unknown. 6698-4
Graduation ode, to the class of 1861, of St. Louis... James Abraham Martling. 6952-5
Graduation time. James William Foley. 6718-2
Graeme and Bewick. Sir Walter Scott. 6438-8
Graeme and Bewick. Unknown. 6134-6,6518-X
Graf Zeppelin. Harriet Monroe. 6628-3
Graff, Dorothy E.
    W. H. C. Folsom. 6342-X
Graffiti in a university rest;room: 'killing people...' Jim Mitsui. 6790-5
Graflin, Margaret Johnstone
    To my son. 6889-8
Grafton Street. James Stephens. 6331-4
Graham of Gartmore. See Graham, Robt (Cunningham)
Graham, Al
    Theme song for a songwriters' union. 6722-0
Graham, David
    Worcester, next nine exits. 6900-2
Graham, Dougal
    The turnimspike. 6180-X
Graham, Harry
    A portrait. 6995-9
Graham, Harry ("Col. D. Streamer")
    Aunt Eliza. 6722-0,6026-9,6125-7,6026-9,6125-7
    A border ballad. 6724-7
    Common sense. 6427-2
    Compensation. 6633-X
    The conversational reformer. 6736-0
    Grandpapa. 6722-0
    Impetutous Samuel. 6902-9
    Indifference. 6633-X
    Misfortunes never come singly. 6902-9
    Patience. 6722-0
    Presence of mind. 6722-0,6269-5
    The stern parent. 6125-7
    Tact. 6026-9
    Tender-heartedness. 6026-9
    Winter sports. 6633-X
Graham, Jean
    A February friend. 6797-2
    The friction of the fractions. 6797-2
    The tonsil's coming-out party. 6797-2
    Where dreams are sold. 6433-7
    Woodrow Wilson. 7001-9
Graham, Joyce A. Maxtone. See "Struther, Jan"
Graham, Lola Beall
    I remember homestead Sundays. 6857-X
    Richard Armour-the great word-magician. 6857-X
Graham, Muriel Elsie
    An October birthday. 6269-5
Graham, Neile
    Map of Vancouver island. 6767-0
Graham, R.P.
    'Tis spring-time. 6314-4
Graham, Ramona
    The circling year. 6964-9
Graham, Robert (Cunningham)
    Cavalier's song. 6086-2
    "If doughty deeds my lady please." 6302-0,6385-3,6246-6, 6328-4,6639-9,6732

GRAHAM

Graham (cont.)
    My lady's pleasure. 6094-3
    O tell me how to woo thee. 6180-X
    Oh, tell me how to woo thee. 6652-6
    Tell me how to woo thee. 6219-9
    To his lady. 6322-5
Graham, Rosa
    Peggy's doubt. 6965-7
Graham, S.
    A home everywhere. 6752-2
Graham, William Sydney
    At whose sheltering shall the day sea. 6209-1
    The children of Greenock. 6210-5
    Definition of my brother. 6210-5,6379-9
    Gigha. 6209-1,6379-9
    Listen, put on morning. 6210-5
    Love poem. 6209-1
    The name like a river. 6210-5
    Night's fall unlocks the dirge of the sea. 6209-1,6379-9
    Poem ("O gentle queen"). 6379-9
    To my father. 6210-5
Graham; Marquess of Montrose, James
    Epitaph on King Charles I. 6933-9
    An excellent new ballad. 6230-X
    "He either fears his fate too much". 6238-5
    Heroic love. 6322-5
    I'll never love thee more. 6429-9,6600-3,6321-7,6737-9, 6429-9,6180-X,6438-8
    Lines on the execution of Charles I. 6845-6
    Montrose to his mistress. 6315-2
    Montrose's love. 6226-1
    My dear and only love. 6219-9,6302-0,6385-3,6563-5,6150-8,6023-4,6189
    My dear and only love, sels. 6427-2
    On himself, upon hearing what was his sentence. 6933-9
    A proper new ballad. 6317-9
    The sabbath. 6302-0,6385-3
    The touch, fr. My dear and only love. 6427-2
    Upon the death of King Charles I. 6935-5
    Verses completed on the eve of his execution. 6180-X
Grahame Marquesse of Montrose, James
    The gorcock. 6943-6
    The redbreast's haunt. 6943-6
Grahame, James
    Elijah fed by ravens. 6848-0
    The finding of Moses. 6848-0
    The first sabbath. 6848-0
    Jacob and Pharaoh. 6848-0
    Jephtha's vow. 6848-0
    The jubilee. 6848-0
    Saul and David. 6848-0
Grahame, Jenny
    The wayward wife. 6383-7
Grahame, Kenneth
    Carol. 6478-7
    Christmas carol. 6891-X
    Ducks' ditty. 6466-3
Graih my chree. Hall Claine. 6873-1
The grail. Sidney Keyes. 6210-5
The grail. Nellie Burget Miller. 6836-7
Grain life. Edward Farquhar. 6939-8
A grain of corn. Unknown. 6049-8
A grain of rice. Francis Reginald Scott. 6446-9
A grain of salt. Wallace Irwin. 6089-7,6722-0
A grain of truth. George M. Vickers. 6921-5
Grain treasury. Lilian Osborn. 6342-X
Grainger, James
    Solitude. 6152-4
    Solitude, sels. 6482-5
Grainne. Cathal O'Byrne. 6174-5
Grammachree. Charles Wolfe. 6383-7
Grammar as taught in fairyland. Margaret Morrison. 6713-1
"The grammar has a rule absurd". No rule to be afraid of. Berton Braley. 6853-7
A grammar lesson. Helen W. Grove. 6925-8
Grammar-rules. Sir Philip Sidney. 6092-7
A grammarian's funeral, sels. Robert Browning. 6123-0
A grammarian's funeral. Robert Browning. 6198-2,6315-2, 6337-3,6358-6,6657-1,6730-,6102-8,6196-6,6430-2,6046-3,6110-9,6199 ,6250-4,6301-2,6655-0

A grammarian's funeral. Robert Browning. 6828-6
"The grammars and the spellers". Vacation time. Margaret Elizabeth Sangster. 6820-0
The gramophone at Fond-du-lac. Robert Service. 6159-1
Grampy sings a song. Holman F. Day. 6089-7
'Gran' Boule'; a seaman's tale of the sea. Henry Van Dyke. 6961-4
Gran'ma al'us does. Unknown. 6273-3
Granada. Mikhail Arkadyevich Svetlov. 6546-5
Granadilla. Amy Lowell. 6345-4
The "grand advance" Frank H. Gassaway. 6621-6,6579-1
"Grand aisle of elms! your graceful arms". McCosh walk. Edward J. Patterson. 6983-5
"Grand are the days we celebrate". Unknown. 6205-9
"A grand attempt some Amazonian dames". On a fortification at Boston begun by women. Benjamin Tompson. 6946-0
Grand ballet. Frances Cornford. 6354-3
Grand Canyon. Lilian White Spencer. 6836-7
The Grand Canyon. Adelaide Crapsey. 6464-7
The Grand Canyon. Henry Van Dyke. 6961-4
The grand cortege. Christopher J. Brennan. 6349-7
Grand finale. Sara King Carleton. 6218-0
The grand match. Moira (Nesta Higginson Skrine) O'Neill. 6083-8,6090-0,6102-8
The grand question debated. Jonathan Swift. 6092-7
Grand scheme of emigration. Unknown. 6743-3
"Grand the expanse of the heavens...". God's wonders. Eliza Lamb Maryln. 6925-8
Grand-pere. Robert Service. 6159-1,6419-1
Grandad. Robert Service. 6159-1
The grandame. Charles Lamb. 6086-2
"Granddad sat outside the door". Granddad's polka. Robert C.V. Meyers. 6922-3
The grandest boast. Dean Settoon Mernagh. 6750-6
"The grandest charge of cavalary". The hero of New Hamburg. Benjamin Franklin Taylor. 6815-4
Grandeur. Winifred M. Letts. 6266-0,6102-8
"Grandeur and truth, infinite grace". Emancipation. Robert Loveman. 6941-X
Grandeur of ghosts. Siegfried Sassoon. 6257-1
Grandeur of Mary. Frederick William Faber. 6022-6,6172-9, 6292-X
Grandfather. Christopher La Farge. 6761-1
Grandfather. Andrew Murray. 6821-9
"Grandfather has three sparks". Akawense. Phyllis Wolf. 7005-1
Grandfather shows the spirit of '76. Unknown. 6715-8
Grandfather Squeers. James Whitcomb Riley. 6990-8
Grandfather Watts's private fourth. Henry Cuyler Bunner. 6105-2,6166-4
"Grandfather went himself. His eye was good". Ladders. Loton Rogers Pitts. 6761-1
Grandfather's barn. Eben Eugene Rexford. 6215-6
Grandfather's barn. Unknown. 6745-X
Grandfather's clock. Robert C.V. Meyers. 6925-8
Grandfather's clock. Unknown. 6889-8
Grandfather's clock. Henry C. Work. 6964-9
"Grandfather's come to see baby to-day". Two of them. Lucy Marion Blinn. 6965-7
Grandfather's ghost. Joseph Payne Brennan. 6218-0
Grandfather's house. Mary McGuire. 6918-5
Grandfather's love. Sara Teasdale. 6266-0
Grandfather's rose. Mary A. Denison. 6139-7
Grandfather's story. Mary H. Field. 6928-2
The grandfather. John Jay Chapman. 6036-6
Grandfathers. Dennis Shady. 6870-7
Grandma. William Roehrick. 6850-2
Grandma. Unknown. 6451-5
Grandma Robbin's temperance mission. Emma Dunning Banks. 6426-4
"Grandma didn't snore". Eclipse. William Carson Fagg. 6870-7
"Grandma said never tell a lie because". The difference between a lie and the truth. Ronald James Dessus. 6870-7
A Grandma that's just splendor. Emma A. Opper. 6684-4
"Grandma told me all about it". The minuet. Mary Mapes Dodge. 6889-8,6712-3,6102-8,6076-5,6652-8,6964-9, 6004
"Grandma was nodding, I rather think". A rogue. Mary L.

Wyatt. 6965-7
Grandma'a radio. Florence Hascall Butler. 6249-0
Grandma's advice. Dixie Wolcott. 6675-5
Grandma's angel. Sydney Dayre. 6682-8
Grandma's angel. Unknown. 6314-4
Grandma's Bible. Leafa Dorne Seibert. 6270-9
Grandma's bombazine. Eugene Field. 6949-5
Grandma's garden. Unknown. 6672-0
Grandma's house. Olivia Everett. 6857-X
Grandma's house is the house. Unknown. 6715-8
Grandma's movie show. Fred Keller Dix. 6906-1
Grandma's posy-bowl. Delia Hart Stone. 6713-1
Grandma's prayer. Eugene Field. 6735-2
Grandma's shamrocks. E.A. Sutton. 6920-7
Grandma's surprise. Unknown. 6927-4
Grandma's wedding-day. Thomas Chalmers Harbaugh. 6675-5
Grandma's wedding-day. Unknown. 6744-1
Grandma's wedding-day. Unknown. 6925-8
Grandma, that's just splendid. Unknown. 6312-8
"Grandmamma made a cooky-cat". The career of the cooky-cat. Carolyn Wells. 6882-0
Grandmamma's fan. Edith Sessions Tupper. 6682-8,6692-5
Grandmamma's valentine. Adeline Dutton (Train) Whitney. 6965-7
"Grandmither, think not I forget." Willa Sibert Cather. 6310-1,6019-6,6393-4
Grandmother. Paula Gunn Allen. 7005-1
Grandmother. Ray A. Young Bear. 7005-1
Grandmother. Gary Beck. 6900-2
Grandmother. John Paul Minarik. 6870-7
Grandmother. May Probyn. 6770-0
Grandmother Gray. Mary Keeley Boutelle. 6742-5
Grandmother Gray. Mary Keeley Boutelle. 6915-0
"Grandmother counted linens". Acquisition. Clara Hyde. 6750-6
"Grandmother Davis made a red & white coverlet". Autobiography. Mary Willis Shuey. 6761-1
Grandmother is getting tired. Karen Sagsetter. 6821-9
Grandmother poems. Marilyn Chin. 6790-5
Grandmother Steele's sampler. Rachel Mack Wilson. 6906-1
Grandmother to her grandson. Celia Thaxter. 6612-7
Grandmother' polly. Grace Marie Stanistreet. 6249-0
The grandmother's apology. Alfred Lord Tennyson. 6574-0
Grandmother's bible. Hattie A. Cooley. 6415-9
Grandmother's cap. Mary E.N. Hatheway. 6965-7
'Grandmother's gathering boneset'. Edith M. Thomas. 6338-1
Grandmother's quilt. Unknown. 6964-9
Grandmother's sermon. Ellen A. Jewett. 6414-0
Grandmother's story of Bunker Hill battle. Oliver Wendell Holmes. 6249-0,6288-1,6442-6,6470-1,6126-5
Grandmother's valentine. Minna Irving. 6274-1
The grandmother. Elizabeth Madox Roberts. 6891-X
The grandmother. Alfred Lord Tennyson. 6977-0
Grandmothers. Unknown. 6121-1,6304-7
Grandpa. Dinah Maria Mulock Craik. 6684-4,6502-3
Grandpa. Edgar A. Guest. 6401-9,6135-4
Grandpa and baby. Unknown. 6928-2
Grandpa's 'summer sweets.' Joseph Crosby Lincoln. 6119-2
Grandpa's Christmas. Ella Wheeler Wilcox. 6863-4
Grandpa's courtship. Helen Whitney Clark. 6139-7
Grandpapa. Harry ("Col. D. Streamer") Graham. 6722-0
Grandpapa's spectacles. Mrs. M.L. Rayne. 6772-7
Grandpapa's spectacles. Elizabeth Sill. 6131-1
Grandpapa's spectacles. Unknown. 6743-3
Grandser. Abbie Farwell Brown. 6102-8,6076-5,6037-4
The grandsire. Eugene Field. 6949-5
Granducci, Josephine B.
    I cannot grieve. 6906-1
    Through eternity. 6906-1
    Throw wide the doors. 6906-1
Grange, Olrig
    "But all through life I see a cross". 6238-5
The granger and the gambler. W. H. 6451-5
The granger's wife. J.W. Donovan. 6409-4
Granich, Irwin
    The little children. 6337-3
Granite. Lew Sarett. 6076-5
"A granite cliff on either shore". The Brooklyn Bridge. Edna Dean Proctor. 6946-0
The granite heart. Arthur Davison Ficke. 6761-1

Granite man - a prayer. Benjamin Rosenbaum. 6037-4
The granite mountain. Lew Sarett. 6033-1
Granite state. Frances Ann Johnson. 6764-6
Granland, Sten
    Snow at Christmas. Charles Wharton Stork (tr.). 6045-5
Granma's words. Ted D. Palmanteer. 7005-1
Grannis, Anita
    The poet. 6037-4
Granniss, Anna Jane
    My guest. 6260-1
    The old red cradle. 6930-0
    Talk. 6761-1
Granny. Walter J. Healy. 6799-9
Granny Tassia. Markos Avgeris. 6352-7
Granny's little flock. Charles J. Hanford. 6274-1
Granny's receipt. Hazel Golding. 6750-6
Granny's story. Emily Huntington Miller. 6618-6
Granny's trust. Unknown. 6554-6
Grano, Paul
    A word for the innkeeper. 6349-7
"Granpa,/he was a warrior". Pass it on grandson. Ted D. Palmanteer. 7005-1
Grant. Eugene Field. 6949-5
Grant. Melville W. Fuller. 6922-3
Grant. Benjamin Franklin Taylor. 6815-4
Grant - dying. Thomas Chalmers Harbaugh. 6701-8
Grant at rest. John James Meehan. 6820-0
"Grant me an humble, childlike mind". The blessed trail. Thomas B. Livingston. 6799-9
"Grant me the muse, ye gods! whose...flight". Lines, fr. a letter to C.P. Esq., ill with rheumatism. William Cowper. 6814-6
"Grant me, O God, if but a moment's space". A prayer in war-time. J. Redwood Anderson. 6783-2
'Grant that we die young.' Verner von Heidenstam. 6045-5
"Grant us grace that we may greet him". Our Roosevelt. Mary Dillingham Frear. 6995-9
Grant, Anne (Mrs. Grant of Laggan)
    Could I find a bonnie glen. 6086-2
    "O where, tell me where." 6180-X
    On a sprig of heath. 6219-9
Grant, Avis H.
    April. 6906-1
    Cardinal. 6906-1
    Hope. 6906-1
    I hear a call. 6906-1
    Memories. 6906-1
    Question. 6906-1
Grant, Charles
    Little Willie. 6518-X
Grant, Elizabeth (Mrs. Grant of Carron)
    Roy's wife of Aldivalloch. 6180-X,6086-2
Grant, Gordon
    The last Gloucesterman. 6833-2
    The old quartermaster. 6833-2
Grant, John Cameron
    Ballade. 6770-0
    Ballade-Lilith. 6770-0
    A coward still. 6770-0
    John Greenleaf Whittier. 6820-0
    Rondel. 6770-0
Grant, M.M.
    The brownies. 6715-8
Grant, Mary
    Harriet Ames. 6850-2
"Grant, O regal in bounty, a subtle...largess". Hymn to the sea. Sir William Watson. 6833-2
Grant, Peter
    When the bloom is on the heather. 7022-1
Grant, Robert (tr.)
    Psalm 071. Bible, 6848-0
Grant, Sir Robert
    The brooklet. 6302-0;6385-3
    A cultured mind! Before I speak. 6770-0
    Hymn ("When gathering clouds"). 6271-7
    Litany. 6271-7,6385-3,6219-9
    The majesty and mercy of God. 6730-1
    O savior! Whose mercy. 6600-3
    A pedigree! Ah, lovely jade! 6770-0
    Popping the question. 6358-6

GRANT

A pot of gold! O mistress fair. 6770-0
A pretty face! O maid divine. 6770-0
A rondeau a la Baltimore, fr. Roundeaux of cities. 6850-2
A rondeau a la Boston, fr. Roundeaux of cities. 6850-2
A rondeau a la New York, fr. Roundeaux of cities. 6850-2
A rondeau a la Philadelphia, fr. Roundeaux of cities. 6850-2
Rondeaux of cities. 6850-2
Rondeaux of cities. 6875-8
The superman. 7026-4
"When gathering clouds around I view." 6302-0,6337-3, 6219-9

Grant, Susan
June. 6118-4
The stupid grown ups. 6118-4

Grant, Ulysses S.
"I intend to fight it out on this line". 6623-2

Granville, Charles
Traveller's hope. 6437-X

Granville-Barker, Helen
The captive butterfly. 6510-4
The owls. 6510-4

Granville; Baron Lansdowne, George
Adieu l'amour. 6024-2
Cloe. 6562-7
The happiest mortals once we were. 6563-5
I'll tell her. 6563-5
Impatient with desire. 6563-5
The she-gallants. 6083-8
Song ("I'll tell her"). 6562-7
Song: to Myra. 6152-4
Thoughtful nights. 6328-4
To Myra. 6152-4

Grape daiquiri. Tina Koyama. 6790-5
The grape-vine swing. William Gilmore Simms. 6006-4,6302-0, 6385-3
Grapes. Yuk-sa Lee. 6775-1
"Grapes of gold on silver stems". Star-fancies. James Buckham. 7030-2
The grapes of wrath. Christopher Morley. 6722-0
The grapevine swing. Samuel Minturn Peck. 6476-0;6682-8;6498-1
Grasp it like a man! Aaron Hill. 6861-8
Grass. Edgar Fawcett. 6049-8
Grass. Carl Sandburg. 6121-4,6107-9,6646-1,6464-7,6077-3, 6162-1,6232-6,6332-2,6337-3,6420 ,6536-8,6602-X,6619-4,6726-3,6665-8,6542
"The grass around my limbs in deep and sweet". An interior. Edward Dowden. 7015-9
The grass grows far. N. Bryllion Fagin. 6039-0
"The grass has come alive". Caterpillar. Helen Burlin. 6979-7
Grass heritage. Helen Molyneaux Salisbury. 6782-4
"Grass is tougher than steel". Pilgrim. A.M. Sullivan. 6839-1
"The grass lies flat beneath the wind". The lamp on the prairie. Phoebe Cary. 6969-X
"Grass of levity". An inscription ("Grass of levity") Unknown. 6182-6
Grass of the field. Mary Neal Copeland. 6894-4
The grass on the mountain. Unknown (Paiute Indian) 7039-6, 6602-X
"The grass so litle has to do". Emily Dickinson. 6047-1, 6239-3,6373-X,6481-7
The grass. May Lewis. 6979-7,6039-0
The grass. Walt Whitman. 6374-8,6473-6
Grasses. Scudder Middleton. 6393-2
The grasshopper and cricket. John Keats. 6198-2,6232-6, 6302-0,6385-3,6304-7,6102-8,6639-9
The grasshopper and the cricket. Leigh Hunt. 6850-2
The grasshopper and the cricket. Leigh Hunt. 6250-4
The grasshopper and the cricket. Leigh Hunt. 6850-2
Grasshopper green. Unknown. 6132-X,6466-3,6368-3,6639-9, 6638-0
Grasshopper's last word. Edward Farquhar. 6939-8
The grasshopper, sels. Richard Lovelace. 6198-2
"Grasshopper, your fairy song". Earth. John Hall Wheelock. 6031-5,6232-6,6289-X,6338-1,6565-2,6250-4,336-5,

6161-3,6393-4,6646-1
The grasshopper.. Edith M. Thomas. 6006-4,6597-X
The grasshopper. Anacreon (atr) 7039-6,6271-7
The grasshopper. Wilfred Rowland Childe. 6510-4
The grasshopper. Abraham Cowley. 6133-8,6604-6,6396-9,6660-7
The grasshopper. Richard Lovelace. 6933-9
The grasshopper. Richard Lovelace. 6052-8,6099-4,6563-5, 6438-8,6341-1,6315-7,6562-7,6733-3,6208-3
The grasshopper. Alfred Lord Tennyson. 6977-0
The grasshopper. Unknown. 6373-X
"Grassy field, the lambs, the nibbling sheep". Hallam's church, fr. Clevedon verses. Thomas Edward Brown. 6809-X
The grate fire. Edgar A. Guest. 7033-7
Grateful are the songs we sing. Lettie E. Sterling. 6703-4
"The grateful heart for all things blesses" Walter Savage Landor. 6874-X
Grateful Lucy. Elizabeth Turner. 6018-8
The grateful preacher. John Godfrey Saxe. 6914-2
The grateful swan. Alice Cary. 6060-9
A grateful tribute. William White. 6868-5
Gratiana dancing. Richard Lovelace. 6959-2
Gratiana dancing and singing. Richard Lovelace. 6315-2, 6565-7,6092-7,6430-2,6341-1,6230 ,6563-5
Gratiana dauncing and singing. Richard Lovelace. 6933-9
"Gratias ago." Geoffrey Howard. 6374-8
A gratified ambition. Carolyn Wells. 6882-0
Gratitude. Arturo [pseud.]. 6817-0
Gratitude. William Cornish. 6436-1
Gratitude. William Cowper. 6092-7
Gratitude. Polly Hunter. 6249-0
Gratitude. Mikhail Lermontov. 6103-6
Gratitude. Margaret Elizabeth Sangster. 6337-3
Gratitude. Henry Van Dyke. 6961-4
Gratitude. B. Worsley-Gough. 6776-X
Gratitude and love to God. Madame De la Mothe Guion. 6814-6
Gratitude down South. Edwina Wood Whiteside. 6270-9
Gratitude, fr. King Henry VI. William Shakespeare. 6337-3
Gratulatory to Mr. Ben. Johnson for his adopting of him. Thomas Randolph. 6933-9

Grauch, Bessie Irons
No, never. 6799-9

"Grave Dante loved it, watched it as...built". 'By that way pass the gods', fr. A Florentine cycle. Gertrude Huntington McGiffert. 6838-3
The grave and the rose. Victor Hugo. 6771-9,7039-6
The grave by the lake. John Greenleaf Whittier. 6600-3
The grave by the sorrowful sea. L.M. Laning Bayley. 6923-1
Grave gallantry. James Branch Cabell. 6875-8
"Grave history walks again the earth". Unknown. 6902-9
"Grave hour and solemn choice - bare is..sword". To America in war time. O.W. Firkins. 7027-2
A grave in Flanders. Robert O.A. Crewe-Milnes, Marquess of Crewe. 7031-0
The grave in the Busentius. Count Platen. 6842-1
The grave in the Matopos. Robert Alexander Nelson. 6800-6
A grave in winter. Chard Powers Smith. 6039-0
"Grave Lincoln bade the raging tempest cease." Paul Laurence Dunbar. 6709-3
Grave of Albert Sidney Johnston. J.B. Synnott. 6074-9
The grave of Charles Dickens. Unknown. 6909-6
The grave of Colonus, fr. Oedipis coloneus. Sophocles. 6435-3
The grave of Hipponax. Theocritus. 7039-6
Grave of Keats. Percy Bysshe Shelley. 6331-4,6439-6
The grave of Keats ("Fair little city ..."). Silas Weir Mitchell. 6624-0
The grave of Keats. Oscar Wilde. 6624-0,6631-3
The grave of King Arthur. Thomas Warton Jr. 6122-2,6152-4
The grave of Korner. Felicia Dorothea Hemans. 6973-8
The grave of Lincoln. Edna Dean Proctor. 6524-4
The grave of love. Thomas Love Peacock. 6830-8
The grave of love. Thomas Love Peacock. 6102-8;6246-6
The grave of Macaura. Mary Downing. 6219-9
The grave of Roosevelt. Snow Longley Hough. 6995-9
The grave of Rury. Thomas William Rolleston. 6174-5,6244-X
The grave of Shelley. Oscar Wilde. 6624-0
A grave on Ossa. Aeschylus. 6435-3

"The grave said to the rose". The grave and the rose. Victor Hugo. 6771-9,7039-6
A grave undertaking. P. 6983-5
Grave, John
 A song of Sion, sels. 6008-0
A grave, fr. Tegea. Simonides. 6435-3
The grave, sels. Robert Blair. 6198-2,6294-6,6195-0,6152-4
The grave, sels. Unknown. 6102-8
The grave, sels. Robert Blair. 6831-6
Grave-digger's song, fr. Prince Lucifer. Alfred Austin. 6656-9
The grave-yard in the song. Jaroslav Vrchlicky. 6763-8
A grave. Winifred Lucas. 6785-9
A grave. Marianne Moore. 6208-3,6531-7,6217-2
A grave. John Richard Moreland. 6036-6
The grave. Robert Blair. 6086-2
The grave. Charles W. Denison. 6755-7
The grave. Kristjan Jonsson. 6854-5
The grave. James Montgomery. 6302-0,6219-7
The grave. Kostes Palamas. 6352-7
The grave. Unknown. 6022-6,6125-7
The gravedigger. Bliss Carman. 6161-3,6309-8,6433-7,6509-0
The gravedigger. Unknown. 6787-5
Gravel. Paul Mariah. 6870-7
The gravel path. Laurence Alma Tadema. 6452-3
The gravel-pit field. David Gascoyne. 6379-9
Gravelle, Barbara
 Moon into capricorn. 6998-3
 Moon into capricorn. 6901-0
 My daddy read Luke Short, baby. 6901-0
 Port Arthur riddle. 6901-0
"Graven and shapely with the silk of granite". Burns monument. John Singer. 6895-2
Graven on the palms of his hands. Charles Wesley. 6065-X
Graven thoughts. Sir Philip Sidney. 6584-8
"The graver by Apollo's shrine". Cameos. Andrew Lang. 6987-8
Graves. Carl Sandburg. 6628-3
Graves at Christiania. Katharine Lee Bates. 6331-4
The graves of a household. Felicia Dorothea Hemans. 6165-6,6383-7,6250-4,6543-0,6129-9,6133-8,6240-7,6385-3,6502-3,6127-3,6964
The graves of Gallipoli. L. L. 6846-4
Graves of infants. John Clare. 6383-7,6437-X
The graves of martyrs. Felicia Dorothea Hemans. 6973-8
The graves of the patriots. James Gates Percival. 6340-3;6406-X
Graves, Alfred Perceval
 Brothers in arms. 6474-4
 Changing her mind. 6692-5
 Father O'Flynn. 6174-5,6732-8,6808-1
 Fortune my foe. 6273-3
 Herring is king. 6873-1
 An Irish lullaby. 6078-1,6442-3
 The Irish spinning-wheel. 6174-5,6255-5
 Johnny Cox. 6518-X
 My proud dark-eyed sailor. 6072-2
 The rose of Kenmare. 6255-5
 The sailor girl. 6518-X
 Shamrock leaves. 6793-X
 The song of the Exmoor hunt. 6518-X
 The song of the ghost. 6518-X
 The song of the Pratee. 6873-1
 Uiseo mo leanb. 6776-X
 The white blossom's off the bog. 6174-5,6656-9
 The wreck of the 'Aideen'. 6174-5,6046-3
Graves, Charles Larcom
 Adieu to Argyll. 6760-3
Graves, Etta M.
 Autumn's altar. 6764-6
 Creative. 6764-6
Graves, Grace M.
 Prayer for a dampened spirit. 6750-6
Graves, Ida
 Encounter. 6780-8
Graves, John Woodcock
 John Peel. 6732-8
Graves, Richard
 Eighteenth century despises the gardens of the seventeenth. 6649-6

Graves, Robert
 The assault heroic. 6393-4
 At best, poets. 6339-X
 At the games. 6070-6
 The bards. 6209-1
 A boy in church. 6634-8
 Burrs and brambles. 6778-6
 Careers. 6506-6
 Children of darkness. 6069-2
 The cool web. 6246-6
 The corner-knot. 6072-2
 The dead fox-hunter. 7029-9
 Defeat of the rebels. 6666-6
 Double red daisies. 6466-3
 Down, wanton, down! 6733-6,6210-5
 1802.Eighteen. 6257-1
 Epitaph on an unfortunate artist. 6722-0
 The exile. 6354-3
 The fallen tower of Siloam. 6666-6
 Flying crooked. 6209-1
 The foreboding. 6246-6
 Four children. 6779-4
 Free verse. 6506-6
 From our ghostly enemy. 6071-4
 Full moon. 6208-3
 I'd love to a fairy's child. 6368-3
 In broken images. 6150-8,6354-3
 In the wilderness. 6246-6,6634-8
 In time. 6339-X
 Interruption. 6391-8
 It's a queer time. 6332-2,6102-8,6542-2
 Lament for Pasiphae. 6210-5
 The last post. 7027-2
 The laureate. 6210-5
 The legs. 6257-1,6354-3,6391-8
 Lollocks. 6125-7
 The lord-chamberlain tells of a famous meeting. 6069-2
 Lost acres. 6209-1
 Lost love. 6339-X
 A love story. 6210-5
 Love without hope. 6125-7
 Mid-winter waking. 6150-8
 Mirror, mirror. 6776-X
 Never such love. 6208-3
 Not dead. 6301-2
 O love in me. 6209-1
 Ogres and pygmies. 6733-6,6391-8,6209-1
 On portents. 6209-1
 A pinch of salt. 6607-0
 A pinch of salt. 6872-3
 The poets ("Any honest housewife would sort them out"). 6357-8
 The poets. 6625-9
 The presence. 6071-4,6071-4,6124-9
 Pure death. 6472-8
 Pygmalion to Galatea. 6513-9
 Quayside. 6209-1
 Recalling war. 6666-6
 Reproach. 6844-8
 The return. 6069-2
 She is no liar. 6339-X
 She tells her love while half asleep. 6210-5
 Sick love. 6150-8
 Star-talk. 6044-7,6421-3,6668-2
 Sullen moods. 6872-3
 Time. 6150-8,6209-1,6354-3
 To bring the dead to life. 6209-1
 To Juan at the winter solstice. 6209-1
 To walk on hills. 6354-3
 To whom else-. 6209-1
 Twin souls. 6777-8
 Two fusiliers. 7029-9
 Ulysses. 6210-5
 Vanity. 6150-8
 The wretch. 6354-3
The gravestone. Amy Lowell. 6779-4
Gravestones ("Betwixt the stirrop...") Unknown. 6427-2
Gravestones ("Here lie I, Martin Elginbrodde;") George Macdonald. 6427-2
Gravestones ("Here lies wise..") John Cleveland. 6427-2

GRAVEYARD

Graveyard. Ralph Douberly. 6841-3
The graveyard at West Point. William Allen Butler. 6903-7
The graveyard rabbit. Frank Lebby Stanton. 6307-1,6006-4
Gravid. Helen Hoyt. 6038-2
Gray. Frederick R. McCreary. 6619-4
Gray. Oscar Williams. 6374-8
Gray (atr), William
    The hunt is up! 6153-2
"Gray bird...no gallant omens in the sky". The gray bird. Lorraine Wing. 7019-1
"The gray cloak of motherhood". Ballad of a gray cloak. Elizabeth Buell. 6799-9
The gray day. Robert J. Burdette. 6610-0
"Gray days, you knew, and beat of rain...". Saga-men. Virginia Stacey. 7019-1
"Gray distance hid each shining sail". Jubilate. George Arnold. 6833-2
The gray dove's answer. Frederic Edward Weatherley. 6639-9, 6638-0
The gray forest eagle. Alfred Billings Street. 6344-6,6678-X
"The gray fox for the mountains". Of foxes. Bertye Young Williams. 6979-7
Gray gauntlet. Elmina Atkinson. 7031-0
Gray geese flying. Frederic Prokosch. 6073-0
Gray gull. Louise Goodson Tennyson. 6316-0
Gray hair in youth. Edith M. Thomas. 6632-1
"Gray hair soft, smoothly parting". An old maid. Cora Fabri. 6876-6
The gray heralds. Archibald Rutledge. 7016-7
"Gray hills, low rocks, blurred sea...". Trevone. Song I: Minor key. Lilian Sauter. 7023-X
"Gray is the pall of the sky" Roger Sterrett. 6995-9
The gray kitten. Jane Campbell. 6510-4
The gray man. William Hervey Woods. 6327-6
Gray matter. Ford Madox (Hueffer) Ford. 6541-4
A gray moth. Marjorie Allen Seiffert. 6628-3
"Gray mother of mighty nations". A chant of empire. James Rhoades. 7031-0
The gray norns. Edwin Markham. 6347-0;6490-6
"The gray of the morning". Eve. Francis Ernley Walrond. 6800-4
Gray on himself. Thomas Gray. 6975-4
Gray roadster. Paul Eldridge. 6397-7
"The gray sea and the long black land". Meeting at night. Robert Browning. 6828-6
Gray shore. James Rorty. 6833-2
"The gray stems rise, the branches braid". Sylvan spirits. Bayard Taylor. 6976-2
"Gray stubble, wisecrack light". Mr. Pete Totten. Gerald Cable. 6855-3
"A gray Thanskgiving morning". Cousin John. C.T. B.. 6889-8
The gray swan. Alice Cary. 6127-3,6406-X,6239-3,6497-3, 6964-9
"Gray woods within whose silent shade". The ocean wood. John B.L. Warren, 3d Baron De Tabley. 6785-9
Gray's elegy on Horace Walpole's cat. Thomas Gray. 6699-2
Gray's inn. Wilfred Wilson Gibson. 6779-4
"Gray's Inn-a shadowy room and smouldering there". Alfred Noyes. 6298-9
Gray, ?
    The hunt is up. 6328-4
Gray, A.P.
    The tree, the serpent, and the star. 6074-9
Gray, Agnes Kendrick
    Amber from Egypt. 6478-7
    Ducks and heron. 6850-2
    The flight of Lindbergh. 7019-1
    Fog - Spanish phantasy. 6841-3
    The hermit thrush. 6841-3
    An Italian donkey. 6841-3
    The little crooked garden. 6232-6
    A road to Firenze. 6619-4
    The shepherd to the poet. 6102-8,6476-0,6030-7,6076-5
    To a certain shop girl. 6039-0
    To my terrier Rex. 6841-3
    To my terrier Rex. 6619-4
Gray, Alexander
    The dancers. 6269-5
    Epitaph on a vagabond. 6069-2
    Heaven. 6269-5
    The kings from the east. 6845-6
    Lassie, what mair wad ye ha'e? 6845-6
    On a cat, ageing. 6269-5,6511-2
    Scotland ("Here in the uplands"). 6269-5
Gray, Alexander (tr.)
    Selections. Heinrich Heine, 6845-6
Gray, Alma L.
    High water mark. 6750-6
Gray, Arthur Irving
    'A free puff'. 6453-1
Gray, Barry
    Ships at sea. 6344-6
Gray, Blakeney
    The philosophic beggar. 6486-8
    Reverie of a batchelor. 6714-X
Gray, Charles
    The social cup. 6960-6
Gray, David
    The corn-crake. 6180-X
    Cross of gold. 7041-8
    The dear old toiling one. 6656-9
    "Die down, O dismay day." 6302-0,6385-3,6543-0
    Divided. 7041-8
    The golden wedding. 6271-7
    "The goldening peach on the orchard wall." 6960-6
    His epitaph. 6960-6
    Homesick. 6097-8,6302-0,6385-3,6543-0
    I die, being young. 6656-9
    In the shadows. 6102-8
    In the shadows, sels. 6960-6
    The luggie, sels. 7035-3
    My epitaph. 6337-3,6437-X,6656-9
    "O winter, wilt thou never, never go?" 6302-0;6385-3
    Rest. 7041-8
    Sir John Franklin and his crew. 7041-8
    Sonnet ("Die down"). 6271-7
    Sonnet ("If it must be"). 6180-X
    The thrush's song. 7015-9
    To a friend. 7015-9
    To J.H. (Col. John Hay) 7041-8
Gray, Eleanor
    "We walk alone through all life's various ways". 6238-5
Gray, Elliot
    Triolets. 6116-8
Gray, Frances Angevine
    Colloquy on a hill top. 6789-1
    Otherwhere. 6218-0
    Tapers. 6218-0
    Tenant. 6218-0
Gray, Francis C. (tr.)
    Dante. Giovanni Boccaccio, 6624-0
    Sonnet 108. Giovanni Boccaccio, 6484-1
Gray, John
    Charleville. 6507-4
    The flying fish. 6315-2,6547-3,6125-7
    Gazelles and unicorn, fr. The long road. 6125-7
    Lord, if Thou art not present. 6096 X
    The night nurse goes her round. 6315-2
    The ox. 6236-9
    The tree of knowledge. 6096 X
    Wings in the dark. 6507-4,6547-3
Gray, Leonard
    Intangible influence. 6764-6
Gray, Maxwell
    Rondel. 6066-8
Gray, Mrs. J.L.
    Morn. 6912-6
Gray, Thomas
    The alliance of education and government. 6152-4
    The bard, sels. 6258-X
    The bard. 6543-0,6322-5,6660-7,6438-8,6086-2,6087-0, 6075-7,6246-6,6271-7,6323-3,6122 ,6198-2,6604-6,6192-3,6195-0,6430-2,6219
    "The boast of heraldry, the pomp of power". 6238-5
    The curse upon Edward. 6102-8
    The death of Hoel. 6975-4
    The descent of Odin. 6152-4,6195-0
    Elegy. 6486-8

Elegy written in a country churchyard. 6024-2,6246-6,
    6075-7,6101-X,6102-8,6142 ,6645-3,6723-9,6631-3,6668-
    2,6491-4,6639 ,6138-9,6302-0,6358-6,6385-3,6552-X,
    6208 ,6301-2,6304-7,6150-8,6153-2,6104-4,6197 ,6154-
    0,6186-9,6198-2,6239-3,6240-7,6060 ,6245-6,6291-9,
    6250-4,6430-2,6424-8,6560 ,6271-7,6289-X,6315-2,6332-
    2,6337-3,6369 ,6646-1,6192-3,6543-0,6510-5,6660-7,
    6152 ,6407-8,6457-4,6459-0,6473-6,6479-5,6484 ,6086-
    2,6023-4,6438-8,6439-6,6488-4,6504-X,6527-9,6536-8,
    6600-3,6604 ,6634-8,6641-0,6726-3,6732-8,6122-2
Elegy written in a country churchyard, sels. 6179-6,
    6087-0,6317-9,6339-X
Epitaph on Mrs Jane Clarke. 6975-4
Epitaph on Sir William Williams. 6641-0
The epitaph. 6634-8,6732-8
The epitaph. 6214-8
"Far from the sun and summer gale", fr.Progress..poesy.
    6793-X
The fatal sisters. 6052-8,6122-2,6154-0,6545-7,6152-4,
    6195 ,6430-2
For music. 6975-4
Gray on himself. 6975-4
Gray's elegy on Horace Walpole's cat. 6699-2
Hymn to adversity. 6975-4
Hymn to adversity. 6246-6,6122-2,6732-8,6543-0,6086-2,
    6152 ,6195-0,6150-8,6219-9
Hymn to adversity, sels. 6934-7
Impromptu. 6369-1,6380-2
A long story. 6092-7
Now the golden morn aloft. 6328-4
An ode from the Norse tongue. 6198-2
Ode of a favourite cat, drowned in a tub of goldfishes.
    6246-6
Ode on a distant prospect of Eton college. 6102-8,6246-
    6,6600-3,6604-6,6198-2,6271 ,6645-3,6219-9,6631-3,
    6660-7,6385-3,6438 ,6122-26250-4,6291-9,6430-2,6195-
    0,6543
Ode on the death of a favourite cat. 6092-7
Ode on the pleasure arising from vicissitude. 6152-4,
    6195-0,6246-6,6086-2
Ode on the spring. 6152-4,6195-0,6250-4,6246-6,6198-2,
    6219-9,6152-4,6543-0
Ode to the spring. 6934-7
On a distant prospect of Eton College. 6086-2
On a favorite cat, drowned in a tub of goldfishes. 6239-
    3,6332-2,6732-8,6236-9,6133-8,6024 ,6511-2,6668-2,
    6808-1,6086-2,6024-2,6238-4,6634-8,6228-8,6552-X,
    6120-6,6733 ,6552-X,6558-9,6239-3,6332-2,6732-8,6236-
    9,6133-8,6024 ,6511-2,6668-2,6808-1,6086-2,6024-2,
    6238-4,6634-8,6228-8,6552-X,6120-6,6733 ,6552-X,6558-
    9
On the death of a favourite cat. 6278-4,6723-9
On the death of Richard West. 6152-4,6195-0,6430-2
On the spring. 6086-2
Opening paradise. 6291-1
The progress of poesy, sels. 6934-7
The progress of poesy, sels. 6102-8,648303,6301-2
The progress of poesy, sels. 6934-7
The progress of poesy. 6543-0,6152-4,6195-0,6086-2,6430-
    2,6250-4,6219 ,6024-2,6198-2,6122-2,6246-6,6659-3,
    6153 ,6543-0,6152-4,6195-0,6086-2,6430-2,6250-4,6219
    ,6024-2,6198-2,6122-2,6246-6,6659-3,6153
The rape of Helen, fr. Agrippina. 6545-7
Sketch of his own character. 6152-4,6195-0
Song ("Thyrsis, when we parted"). 6430-2
Song to an old air. 6383-7
Sonnet ("In vain"). 6024-2
Sonnet written on the death of Richard West. 6122-2,
    6488-4,6383-7,6491-4
Spring. 6302-0;6385-3
Stanzas suggested by a view of the seat...Kent, 1766.
    6975-4
To Richard Bentley. 6935-5
Tophet. 6369-1,6380-2
The triumphs of Owen, sels. 6152-4
The triumps of Owen. 6831-6
The truimph of Owen, sels. 6975-4
Where ignorance is bliss. 6211-3
William Shakespeare to Mrs. Anne, regular servant...
    6152-4

Gray, Thomas (tr.)
    "Third in the labours of the disc came on". Publius
        Papinius Statius, 6975-4
    The triumphs of Owen. Gwalchmai, 6528-7
"Gray, gray if Abbey Asaroe, by...". Abbey Asaroe. William
    Allingham. 6930-4
"A gray, slow-moving, dust-powered wave,". Sheep-herding.
    Sharlot M. Hall. 7008-6
"Gray-robed wanderer in sleep - wanderer". Meeting. Arthur
    Davison Ficke. 6897-9
"A graying stranger blinks at me". Reflections. Sylvia
    Storla Clarke. 6789-1
Grays Peak in winter. Josie McNamara Lydon. 6836-7
Graziano, Frank
    The potato eaters. 6966-5
"Grazing cows/upon a hill". Peace. Betty A. Mitchell. 6857-
    X
Greacen, Robert
    The bird. 6475-2
    Cycling to Dublin. 6930-4
    Night-piece. 6475-2
    To a faithless lover. 6930-4
Greasing boots in Vermont. Daniel L. Cady. 6988-6
Greasy Mary. Arthur T. Wilson. 6899-5
Greasy Wops and Yankee boys. Unknown. 6237-7
Great A, little a. Unknown. 6904-5
The great adventure. Kendall Banning. 6846-4
The great adventure. Berton Braley. 6853-7
The great adventure. Brian ("Korongo") Brooke. 6938-X
The great adventure. Henry David Thoreau. 6437-X
The great adventurer. Unknown. 6134-6,6246-6,6732-8,6250-4,
    6189-3
"The great almighty spake, and thus said he". The ten
    commandments. George Wither. 6848-0
"Great altars of the world, high snows serene". Eternal
    snows. Lilian Sauter. 7023-X
The great and the greatest. Edward Farquhar. 6939-8
"Great and understanding nation". To America in 1876.
    Martin Farquhar Tupper. 6913-4
"Great arch! Through which kings pass alone". Sovereignty.
    Lilian Sauter. 7023-X
"Great are the myths". Walt Whitman. 6271-7
"Great are thy works...", fr. Paradise lost. John Milton.
    6334-9
The great armistice. Robert Haven Schauffler. 6051-X
"Great art thou, O Lord." Saint Augustine. 6337-3
The great auk's ghost. Ralph Hodgson. 6722-0,6723-9
The great bell of Pekin. Jessie F. O'Donnell. 6680-1
The great bell Roland. Theodore Tilton. 6554-6,6302-0,6402-
    7
"Great big dog". The tale of a dog and a bee. Unknown.
    6937-7
The great black crow. Philip James Bailey. 6089-7
The great Blasket. Robin Flower. 6070-6
The great blue heron. Victoria Saffelle Johnson. 6979-7
The great blue heron. Celia Thaxter. 6612-7
The great breath. George William ("A.E.") Russell. 6726-3,
    6730-1,6656-9,6252-0,6153-2,6199-0,6659-3
Great Brit in. Oliver Goldsmith. 6302-0₀6385-3
The great bronze buddha at Kamakura. Mary McNeil
    Fenollosa. 7038-8
The great brown owl. Ann ("Aunt Effie") Hawkshawe. 6018-8
"The great buck-wagon, our 'desert ship'.". A song of the
    wagon-whip. Samuel Cron Cronwright-Schreiner. 6800-6
great carousel<The. Richard Dehmel. 6160-5
The great carousel. Richard Dehmel. 6160-5
The great change. James I; King of Scotland. 6186-9
Great city. Harold Monro. 6897-9
The great city. Walt Whitman. 6102-8,6076-5
The great company. Alys Fane Trotter. 7029-9
The great consult of Satan and his peers. Phineas
    Fletcher. 6186-9
"Great coral hips mid leaves of last June's...". November.
    Grace Bentley Beach. 6847-2
The great critics. Charles Mackay. 6996-7
The great cross of mercy. Theodosia Garrison. 6449-3
Great Diocletian. Abraham Cowley. 6125-7
"A great dim barn with the fragrant hay". The old barn.
    Benjamin Franklin Taylor. 6815-4
"Great Earl of Bath, your reign is o'er". An ode to the

GREAT

Earl of Bath. Sir Charles H. Williams. 6874-X
Great distance. Harold Monro. 6072-2
The great divide, sels. Anthony Delius. 6788-3
The great divide. Lew Sarett. 6102-8,6607-0,6076-5,6253-9
The great elm. Robert Bridges. 6487-6
Great events. E. S. 6130-3
"Great famous wit! whose rich and easy vein". To a bad poet. Samuel Butler. 6760-3
"Great father Alighier, if from the skies". To Dante. Vittorio Alfieri. 7039-6
A great fight. Robert Henry ("Orpheus C. Kerr") Newell. 6089-7,6744-1
Great fleas. Unknown. 6722-0,6026-9
"Great fortune is an hungry thing". Chorus, fr. Agamemnon. Aeschylus. 7039-6
"Great Garibaldi, through the streets one day". Respect the burden. Dinah Maria Mulock Craik. 6914-2
Great friend. Henry David Thoreau. 6333-0
The great frost. John Gay. 6932-0
The great frost. John Gay. 6932-0
"Great God! I'd rather be". William Wordsworth. 6238-5
Great God, I ask thee for no meaner pelf. Henry David Thoreau. 6333-0
"The great god fear grinned back at me". Fear. Edgar A. Guest. 6869-3
"Great God to whom the right belongs". Psalm 094. Bible. 6848-0
"Great God! at whose 'creative word'.". Hymn ("Great God!..."). Felicia Dorothea Hemans. 6973-8
"Great God, I ask thee for no meaner pelf". A prayer ("Great God"). Henry David Thoreau. 6337-3,6288-1
"Great God, that bowest sky and star". Hymn for the church militant. Gilbert Keith Chesterton. 6931-2
The great grandfather. Charles and Mary Lamb. 6295-4
The great grey plain. Henry Lawson. 6784-0
The great grey water. E.J. Brady. 6784-0
"Great guardians of our freedom, we pursue". American liberty. Philip Freneau. 6753-0
The great guns of England. Edward John Plunkett, 18th Baron Dunsany. 7031-0
Great heart. Rudyard Kipling. 6732-8
Great heart. John Oxenham. 6337-3
"Great heart, who taught thee so to dye?". Epitaph" on Sir Walter Rawleigh at his execution. Unknown. 6933-9
"Great heav'n! how frail thy creature man...". Love and reason. Matthew Prior. 6932-0
The great hunt. Carl Sandburg. 6556-2
The great immortal Washington. W.S. Hyde. 6712-3
Great is Diana of the mannahattoes! Arthur Guiterman. 6773-5
"Great is justice!, fr. 'Leaves of grass'" Walt Whitman. 6954-1
Great is our our grief. Nina Jones. 6995-9
"Great is the Lord, and greatly he". Psalm 048 Bible. 6848-0
"Great Jehovah, king of glory". Guide us. Mrs. T. B. Epting. 6818-9
"Great Jove, to whose almighty throne". Prometheus vinctus, sels. Aeschylus. 6945-2
Great is to-day. John Vance Cheney. 6006-4
Great is to-day. John Vance Cheney. 7041-8
The great journalist in Spain. Eugene Field. 6949-5
The great journey, fr. Maha-Bharata. Unknown (Sanskrit) 6372-1
"Great Julius was a cuckold & may I." Unknown. 6563-5
The great London fire, fr Annus mirabilis. John Dryden. 6195-0
"Great Lords, that keep the dignities of Thebes". Sophocles. 6435-3
"Great king, thne sov'raigne ruler of...land". To his late majesty, concerning...English poetry. Sir John Beaumont. 6933-9
"Great lady, were you Helen long ago?". Helen - old. Isabel Ecclestone Mackay. 6843-X
"Great laureate of England, mighty voice". Towers of remembrance. Robert Underwood Johnson. 7001-9
"Great Lord of all things! Pow'r divine!". David and Goliath. Hannah More. 6848-0
The great lover, sels. Rupert Brooke. 6491-4
The great lover. Rupert Brooke. 6044-7,6234-2,6332-2,6477-

9,6732-8,6538 ,6154-0,6320-9,6476-0,6506-6,6464-7, 6666 ,6508-2,6653-4
The great lover. Rupert Brooke. 6102-8
The great lover. Alexander Mackenzie Davidson. 6269-5
The great lover. Glenn W. Rainey. 6841-3
"The great machines go whirling around". At the workers' benches. Raymond Kresensky. 6954-1
The great magician. John Godfrey Saxe. 7030-2
"The great man down, you mark his favorite flies". William Shakespeare. 6238-5
"Great man, humanity full-orbed wert thou". In memoriam: James Abram Garfield. William White. 6868-5
The great man. Eunice Tietjens. 6607-0,6730-1,6653-4
A great man. Mary Kyle Dallas. 6671-2
A great man. Oliver Goldsmith. 6902-9
A great man. Owen (Edward Bulwer-Lytton, Earl Lytton) Meredith. 6793-X
The great man. Eunice Tietjens. 6019-6
The great mariage..., fr. The pastime of pleasure. Stephen Hawes. 6198-2
"A great mart's majestic arterial beat". The heroes and the flowers. Benjamin Franklin Taylor. 6815-4
"Great master of our mother-tongue". At Stratford. Louis J. Magee. 7004-3
"Great master of the poet's art!". John Greenleaf Whittier. Phoebe Cary. 6969-X,6820-0
"Great Merlin of old had a magical trick". The pupil of Merlin. Johann Wolfgang von Goethe. 6787-5
"Great men have been among us; hands that penned". William Wordsworth. 6323-3,6110-9,6250-4,6543-0
The great minimun. Gilbert Keith Chesterton. 6732-8
The great misgiving. Sir William Watson. 6437-X,6660-7
"Great mother! we have wondered that thy sons". Wahonomin (Indian hymn to the queen). Frederick George Scott. 6795-6
The great musical critic. Unknown. 6606-2
"Great nature clothes the soul, which is..thin". The soul's garment. Margaret Cavendish; Duchess of Newcastle. 6931-2
"Great nature had a million words". The pipes o' Pan. Henry Van Dyke. 6961-4
"Great nature is an army gay". Richard Watson Gilder. 6597-X
"Great nature's inmost heart". Philistine mysticism. Johann Wolfgang von Goethe. 7042-6
"Great nature's inmost heart". Haller. 7042-6
"Great nature's watchful eye, the sun". The almanack for 1743, sels. Nathaniel Ames. 6753-0
"Great night of darkness, holding me in void". World enough, sels. Jesse Stuart. 6783-2
"The great Pacific journey I have done". A cockney wail. Unknown. 6911-8
"The great Pacific railway". The railroad cars are coming. Unknown. 6891-X
The great north road. Alfred Noyes. 6151-6
"Great our need, but greater far." Frances Ridley Havergal. 6225-3
The great outdoors. Maud Russell. 6374-8
The great Panjandrum himself. Unknown. 6722-0
The great physician the doctor- Pasteur. Isabel Fiske Conant. 7014-0
The great physician. Charles Kingsley. 6337-3
The great question. Alice Cary. 6969-X
The great redeemer lives. Anne Steele. 6065-X
The great refusal. Thomas S. Jones Jr. 6532-5
The great remembrance, sels. Richard Watson Gilder. 7022-1
"A great ring/pure endless light". Inside and out. Romina Morse. 6883-9
"Great Sassacus fled from the eastern shores". Death song. Alonzo Lewis. 6946-0
The great river. Henry Van Dyke. 6007-2
The great Saint Bernard. Samuel Rogers. 6749-2
"Great sea-dog, fighter in the great old way!". Hawke. Archibald T. Strong. 6784-0
The great seducer. Cale Young Rice. 6619-4
A great shame. Rose Terry Cooke. 6965-X
Great shepherd of the sheep. Charles Wesley. 6065-X
"Great shining disc of burnished brass...". To a Chinese gong. Winona Montgomery Gilliland. 6750-6
"The great ship spreads her wings...". Godspeed. Harriet

Prescott Spofford. 6833-2
The great silkie of Sule Skerry. Unknown. 6185-0,6547-3, 6125-7
A great singer. Carolyn Wells. 6882-0
"Great soul, to all brave souls akin". The star. Marion Couthouy Smith. 6946-0,6995-9
"Great Spitz's ghost! Have you come back". To a stray cat. Rubye Mae Fisher. 6850-2
"Great Table Mountain, which I daily scan". 'Out of the strong came forth sweetness'. Frederick Charles Kolbe. 6800-6
Great spirits now on earth are sojourning. John Keats. 6110-9,6086-2
The great square. Jane Dransfield. 6979-7
The great St. Bernard. Samuel Rogers. 6302-0,6385-3,6481-4
The great swamp fight. Caroline Hazard. 6946-0
The great teacher. Frances Ridley Havergal. 6461-2
"A great tempest rages on the Plain of Ler...". Song of the sea. Rumann (atr.) MacColmain. 6930-4
Great things. Thomas Hardy. 6186-9
"Great things are done when men and mountains meet." William Blake. 6501-5
"Great things haver pass'd the last...year". Seventeen hundred and ninety-one. Philip Freneau. 6753-0
Great thoughts. Philip James Bailey. 6980-0,6543-0
A great time. William Henry Davies. 6234-2,6339-X,6726-3, 6250-4,6102-8
"The great unequal conflict passed". Occasioned by General Washington's arrival in Phila. Philip Freneau. 6946-0
"The great unequal conflict past". Occasioned by General Washington's arrival in Phila. Philip Freneau. 6946-0
"The great unheeded walk amid". Hidden great. James Abraham Martling. 6952-5
The great view. Ford Madox (Hueffer) Ford. 6793-X
"The great voice of great streams". Pastoral ("The great voice".). Louis Aragon. 6351-9
The great voice. Clinton Scollard. 6266-0,6337-3
The great wager. G.A. Studdert-Kennedy. 6335-7
The great wave of Kanagwa. Constance Egemo. 6966-5
"Great were the hearts and strong the minds". Washington. William Cullen Bryant. 6964-9,6820-0
"A great while ago- it is no matter when". A story by somebody. James Abraham Martling. 6952-5
The great white owl. Celia Thaxter. 6612-4
"Great wits are sure to madness", fr. Absalon... John Dryden. 6867-7
"Great word, that fill'st my mind with calm...". Freethought. Edward H. Guillaume. 7009-4
"The great world stretched its arms to me...". In Irish rain. Martha Haskell Clark. 6762-X
"Great, good and just, could I but rate". Epitaph on King Charles I. James Graham; Marquess of Montrose. 6933-9
"Great, good, and just! Could I but rate". Upon the death of King Charles I. James Graham; Marquess of Montrose. 6935-5
"Great, good, just, could I but rate". Lines on the execution of Charles I. James Graham; Marquess of Montrose. 6845-6
"The great, wild, free soul" J.A. H. 6995-9
Great-granddad. Jack Lampert. 6594-5
"Great-grandfathers, blessed by great...". Geneology. Bob Kaufman. 6901-0
Great-grandmother's garden. M.J. Jacques. 6373-X
Great-heart. Rudyard Kipling. 6995-9
The greater birth. Hermann Hagedorn. 6266-0,6648-8
"The greater cats with golden eyes." Victoria Mary Sackville-West. 6317-9,6246-6,6511-2,6354-3
The greater glory. Myra Brooks Welch. 6337-3
The greater guilt. G.A. Studdert-Kennedy. 6144-3
Greater love. Antipater of Sidon. 6435-3
Greater love. Wilfred Owen. 6317-9,6666-6,6375-6,6209-1, 6665-8,6542
The greater moment. Helen L. Bayley. 6798-0
The greater music. Theodore Weiss. 6388-8
The greater mystery. John Myers O'Hara. 6619-4
Greater than. Margaretta Schuyler. 6880-4
The greatest battle that ever was fought. Joaquin Miller. 6337-3
The greatest city. Walt Whitman. 6134-6
The greatest gift. Blanche Edith Baughan. 6784-0
The greatest gift. Annie J. Teem. 6270-9
The greatest loss. Frances Brown. 6337-3
The greatest of these. Walter Rauschenbusch. 6420-5
The greatest tribute. Philemon. 6435-3
The greatest wonder. William Drummond of Hawthornden. 6746-8
The greatest work. Ray M. Johnson. 6337-3
The greatest. Marion Brown Shelton. 6337-3
Greatness. Alexander Pope. 6302-0,6365-3,6102-8
Greatness. Minerva Wright Rockwell. 6799-9
Greatness. Unknown. 6933-9
Greatness and success. Sir Henry Taylor. 6543-0
Greatness and success, fr. Philip Van Artevelde. Henry Taylor. 6980-0
Greatness in littleness, fr. Ode to Sir Lucius Cary... Ben Jonson. 6102-8
The greatness of love, fr. First Corinthians. Bible. 6337-3
The greatness of the soul. Alfred Lord Tennyson. 6291-1
Greatness, fr. Llyn-y-dreiddiad-vrawd, the pool of... Thomas Love Peacock. 6427-2
A Grecian fable. Unknown. 6742-5
Grecian kindness: a song. John Wilmot, 2d Earl of Rochester. 6544-9
Grecian lamp unearthed near Sparta. Mary J.J. Wrinn. 6979-7
The Grecian temples at Paestum. Rossiter W. Raymond. 6302-0;6385-3
"The Grecian wits, who satire first began". To Henry Higden, on his translation of...Juvenal. John Dryden. 6970-3
Gredler, Kate Crichton
   October. 6799-9
Greece. George Gordon, 6th Baron Byron. 6424-8
Greece remembered. Louis Golding. 6779-4
"Greece was; Greece is no more". 'The white city'. Richard Watson Gilder. 6946-0
Greece, fr. Childe Harold. George Gordon, 6th Baron Byron. 6302-0,6385-3,6196-6,6304-7
Greece, fr. Cleon. Robert Browning. 6427-2
Greece, fr. The giaour. George Gordon, 6th Baron Byron. 6302-0;6385-3
Greece, part 002, fr. Liberty. James Thomson. 6816-2
Greediness punished. Friedrich Ruckert. 6127-3,6614-3
The greedy boy. Elizabeth Turner. 6105-2
The greedy fox. Unknown. 6165-6
Greedy Richard. Ann and Jane Taylor. 6105-2
Greef, Wilhelm
   The lilies in the field. James Abraham Martling (tr.). 6952-5
"A Greek Islander, being taken to the Vale...". Where is the sea? Felicia Dorothea Hemans. 6833-2
The Greek and Turkman. George Croly. 6606-2
The Greek at Constantinople. Richard Monckton Milnes; 1st Baron Houghton. 6046-3
The Greek boy. William Cullen Bryant. 6965-7
Greek children's song. Unknown. 6623-2
The Greek club. Unknown. 6936-3
The Greek dead at Thermopylae. Simonides. 6435-3
Greek earth. Georgios Drossinis. 6352-7
Greek epitaph. Unknown. 6861-8
The Greek fathers. John Henry, Cardinal Newman. 6172-9, 6292-X
Greek folk song. Margaret Widdemer. 6250-4
Greek folk song: a Cyprian woman. Margaret Widdemer. 6393-4
Greek folk song: remembrance. Margaret Widdemer. 6393-4
Greek funeral chant, or myriologue, fr. Lays... Felicia Dorothea Hemans. 6973-8
A Greek gift, fr. Rose-leaves. Austin Dobson. 6770-0
A Greek idyl. Mortimer Collins. 6656-9
The Greek partisan. William Cullen Bryant. 7009-4
Greek songs, sels. Felicia Dorothea Hemans. 6973-8
Greek sonnet. Jean Richepin. 6351-9
Greek temples. Irwin [pseud]. 6817-0
Greek war-song. Unknown (Greek) 6945-2
A Greek youth. Halley W. Groesbeck. 6906-1

GREEKS

Greeks. S. Foster Damon. 6506-6
"The Greeks had genius, 'twas a gift". Fame vs. riches. Horace. 6949-5
The Greeks' return from battle. Felicia Dorothea Hemans. 6606-2
Green. David Herbert Lawrence. 6897-9
Green. David Herbert Lawrence. 6354-3
The green above the red. Thomas Osborne Davis. 7009-4
"Green afternoon serene and bright". A city afternoon. Edith Wyatt. 6897-9
"Green aisles of pines stir something deep...". Pine aisles. Edith Haskell Tappan. 6764-6
Green and black. Sir Charles Scott Sherrington. 6482-5
Green and gold. Sir John Ernest Adamson. 6800-6
"A green and silent spot amid the hills". The dell. Samuel Taylor Coleridge. 6935-5
"A green and silent spot, amid the hills". Fears in solitude. Samuel Taylor Coleridge. 6828-6
A green and silent spot. Samuel Taylor Coleridge. 6793-X
Green apple time. Edgar A. Guest. 7033-7
"Green be the graves where her martyrs are...", sels. Oliver Wendell Holmes. 66601-1
Green be the turf. Fitz-Greene Halleck. 6304-7
The green bed. Unknown. 6058-7
Green beds. Unknown. 6057-9
The green bird seeth Iseult. William Alexander Percy. 6036-6
Green branches. Joan Ramsay. 6337-3
Green broom. Unknown. 6228-8,6290-3,6518-X,6026-9,6319-5
Green candles. Humbert Wolfe. 6393-4
Green cherries, sels. William Bell Scott. 6526-0
Green coconuts. Lawrence Durrell. 6209-1
The green corn dance. Alice Corbin. 6076-5,6102-8,6628-3
A green cornfield. Christina Georgina Rossetti. 6123-0
Green crosses. Abbie Farwell Brown. 6162-1,6607-0
The green dove and the raven. Robert Dwyer Joyce. 6518-X
The green fields and meadows. Unknown. 6058-7
Green fields of England. Arthur Hugh Clough. 6934-7
"Green fields of England!" Arthur Hugh Clough. 6828-6
Green fields of England!, fr. Songs in abscence. Arthur Hugh Clough. 6110-9,6430-2,6655-0
"Green fields of England!...", fr. Songs in absence. Arthur Hugh Clough. 6123-0,6240-7
Green fire. Charles Wharton Stork. 6776-X
The green gnome. Robert Buchanan. 6136-2,62424-3,6271-7, 6302-0,6600-3
Green golden door. Jeannette Marks. 6034-X
Green grass. Unknown. 6228-8,6334-9
Green grass growing. Patrick Evans. 6379-9
The green grass growing all around. Unknown. 6891-X
Green grass under the snow. Anna A. Preston. 6583-X;6723-3
"Green grasses grow between the broken flag". The cloister. Katharine R. Hegeman. 6799-9
Green gravel. Unknown. 6134-6
Green grow the rashes. Robert Burns. 6180-X,6302-0,6385-3, 6726-6,6732-8,6646 ,6026-9,6152-4,6086-2,6301-2,6195-0,6659 ,6491-4,6737-9
'Green grow the rushes O.' William Edward Penney. 6702-6
Green growing bush. Helen Pinkerton. 6515-5
"Green grows the laurel on the bank". Life's incongruities. Egbert Phelps. 6240-7,7030-2
Green haven halls. Charles Culhane. 6870-7
The green hill far away. Unknown. 6629-1
The green hills of Africa. Roy Fuller. 6788-3
Green in December. Marya Alexandrovna Zaturenska. 6042-0
"Green in light are the hills, and a calm wind". The reawakening. Walter De La Mare. 7029-9
The green inn. Theodosia Garrison. 6006-4,6374-8,6253-9, 6336-5
The green isles of ocean. Felicia Dorothea Hemans. 6973-8
Green leaf. Louise Driscoll. 7038-8
Green leaves. Basho (Matsuo Basho) 6510-4
The green leaves all turn yellow. James Kenney. 6174-5
"Green leaves of the forest". Color. Jeannette Sewell. 6847-2
The green linnet. William Wordsworth. 6110-9,6196-6,6250-2, 6199-0,6668-2,6246-6,6395-0,6423-X,6808-1,6023-4, 6086
The green little shamrock of Ireland. Andrew Cherry. 6858-8

The green little shamrock of Ireland. Andrew Cherry. 6465-5
"Green little vaulter in the sunny grass". The grasshopper and the cricket. Leigh Hunt. 6850-2
The green man. Alfred Noyes. 6151-6
The green mossy banks of the lea. Unknown. 6057-9
The Green Mountain Boys. William Cullen Bryant. 6267-9
The Green Mountain justice. Henry Reeves. 6963-0
The green mountain justice. Unknown. 6279-2,6392-6,6570-8
The Green Mountain justice. Unknown. 6889-8,6910-X
The green navies. John Prichard. 6360-8
The green o' the spring. Denis Aloysius McCarthy. 6476-0, 6490-6,6338-1
Green rain. Mary Webb. 6228-8
Green River. William Cullen Bryant. 6523-6,6288-1,6126-5, 6121-4,6484-1,6376
"Green ripples singing down the corn". Spring and autumn. Francis Ledwidge. 6812-X
The green river. Lord Alfred Bruce Douglas. 6096-X
"The green seas wave, and the woods are flooded". Ode ("The green seas"). Hugh Chisholm. 6389-6
Green shadows. Helen Hoyt. 7030-2
"Green shadows quiver, restless, here". The untrodden road. Joyce Lancaster. 6850-2
The green singer. John Shaw Neilson. 6784-0
Green song. Edith Sitwell. 6391-8
"Green spot of holy land". A thought of paradise. Felicia Dorothea Hemans. 6973-8
"Green sunny road that skirts the foot". The road to Appenzell. Henry Glassford Bell. 6749-2
Green symphony. John Gould Fletcher. 6348-9,6029-3,6253-9
Green things growing. Dinah Maria Mulock Craik. 6047-1, 6239-3,6597-X,6239-3,6135-4
Green things growing. Charles H. Fuller. 6049-8
The green things. Perceval Gibbon. 6793-X
The green tree in the fall. Jessie B. Rittenhouse. 6374-8
Green trees. Katharine (Hinkson) Tynan. 6781-6
Green upon the cape. Dion Boucicault. 6858-8
Green vine. Dorothy E. Reid. 6906-1
Green wall my grave. Martin Seymour-Smith. 6357-8
"Green water of waves". Little green Bermuda poem. Hilda Conkling. 6776-X
Green waters. Charles Ould. 6800-6,6625-9
"Green wave the oak for ever o'er thy rest". The grave of Korner. Felicia Dorothea Hemans. 6973-8
A green wave. William ("Fiona Macleod") Sharp. 6997-5,6793-X
"Green ways or gray/Labor or play." Unknown. 6225-3
Green weeds. James Stephens. 6628-3
Green weeds. James Stephens. 6776-X
The green willow. Unknown. 6436-1
"Green willows are for girls to study under". Heresy for a classroom. Rolfe Humphries. 6817-0
"Green wooden leaves clap right away". Springing Jack. Edith Sitwell. 7000-0
Green woods. Elizabeth J. Coatsworth. 6218-0
A green Yule. Charles Murray. 6180-X
Green, Alice Fidelia
    A song for mother. 6461-2
Green, Arthur Leslie
    Life's greeting. 6116-8
Green, Coroebus
    The ballad of Cassandra Brown. 6918-5
Green, Elida Merriam
    Desert picture. 6799-9
    Painted lady. 6799-9
Green, G. Leland
    A garden rose. 6799-9
Green, G.M. (tr.)
    The lake of Van. Raffi, 6050-1
Green, Godfrey
    The blind man. 6857-X
    A mystery. 6857-X
Green, H.M.
    Bush goblins. 6784-0
Green, H.W.
    Ganessa the god. 6591-0,6592-9
    The knuckles. 6591-0,6592-9
Green, Homer
    In the orchard path. 6260-1

Green, J. Charles
  A day of notes (that fit into the puzzle of a poem) 6870-7
  Departure. 6870-7
  Freedom. 6870-7
  Isolation cell poem. 6870-7
  Parole denial. 6870-7
Green, Joseph
  Elegy by Green for Byle's cat. 6120-6
  Poet's lament for the loss of his cat. 6699-2,6008-0
  The poet's lamentation for the loss of his cat. 6008-0
Green, Julia Boynton
  The bittern. 6039-0
  The cantaloupe. 6039-0
Green, Julian (tr.)
  The passion of our lady. Charles Peguy, 6282-2
Green, Kathleen Conyngham
  Old Joan. 6466-3
Green, Matthew
  A cure for the spleen, fr. The spleen. 6932-0
  An epigram on..L. Echard's & G. Burnet's histories. 6968-1
  An epistle, sels. 6315-2
  The grotto. 6968-1
  On Barclay's apology for the Quakers. 6968-1
  On even keel. 6150-8
  The seeker. 6831-6,6968-1
  The sparrow and diamond. 6831-6,6968-1,6943-6
  The spleen, sels. 6024-2,6152-4,6195-0
  The spleen, sels. 6831-6
  The spleen; an espistle to Mr Cuthbert Jackson. 6968-1
Green, Nevin
  The year. 6799-9
Green, R.M.
  A valentine. 6118-4
Green, Roy Farrell
  Jack's second trial. 6697-6
"Green, green, and green again, and greener". Sonnet ("Green"). Conrad Aiken. 6783-2
"The green, humped, wrinkled hills...". The green hills of Africa. Roy Fuller. 6788-3
"Green, rose and gold". Two sunsets. Richard Lawson Gales. 6950-9
The green-gown. Unknown. 6157-5
"The green-house is my summer seat". The faithful friend. William Cowper. 6814-6
"The green-tailed drake looks out of the coop". The drake. Ruth Manning-Sanders. 6776-X
Greenaway, Kate
  Around the world. 6452-3
  Ball. 6466-3
  Blue shoes. 6891-X
  The boat sails away. 6262-8
  The cats have come to tea. 6466-3
  Child's song ("The King and the Queen were riding"). 6466-3
  Five sisters. 6262-8
  A happy child. 6452-3,6135-4
  The lamb. 6452-3,6135-4
  The little wife. 6262-8
  Margery Brown. 6132-X
  On the bridge. 6368-3
  Prince Finikin. 6132-X
  Ring-a-ring. 6891-X
  Susan Blue. 6891-X
  A tea-party. 6452-3,6135-4,6368-3
  To baby. 6891-X
  When you and I grow up. 6466-3
Greenberg, Bob
  Politics. 6883-9
Greenberg, Clement (tr.)
  Pablo Picasso. Paul Eluard, 6068-4
Greencastle Jenny. Helen Gray Cone. 6419-1,6062-5
Greene's farewell to folly, sels. Robert Greene. 6586-4
Greene, Albert Gorton
  The baron's last banquet. 6425-6,6486-8,6552-X,6606-2, 6392-6,6909 ,6567-8,6219-9,6744-1
  Old Grimes. 6419-1,6505-8,6219-9,6300-4,6739-5,6889 , 6105-2,6486-8,6385-3,6089-7,6479-5,6632-1,6739-5, 6004-8,6571-6,6105-2,6486-8,63853,6089-7,6479-5, 6632-1,6739-5,6004-8,6571-6
  "Old Grimes is dead." 6583-X
Greene, Charlotte Louise
  The storm. 6798-0
Greene, Clara Marcelle
  A la mode. 6670-4
Greene, Emily Jane
  He's coming home at last. 6178-8
Greene, George Arthur
  Beyond? 6174-5,6507-4
  Inisfail. 6174-5
  Irish memories. 6090-0
  Mountain voices. 6174-5
  On great sugarloaf. 6090-0
  The past. 6174-5
  Song of the songsmiths. 6507-4
Greene, Graham
  A tramp finds himself inspected by an owl. 6071-4
Greene, Hiram Moe
  We need no marble shaft. 6995-9
Greene, Homer
  De Quincy's deed. 6923-1
  De Quincy's deed. 6610-0
  My daughter Louise. 6917-7
  My daughter Louise. 6273-3
  What my lover said. 6255-5,6373-3,6413-2
Greene, Kathleen Conyngham
  An animal song. 6510-4
Greene, Lorna
  An atom of celestial beauty. 7030-2
Greene, Mabel Crehore
  Dusk. 6841-3
  Freedom. 6841-3
  Lament for summer. 6841-3
  My love for you. 6841-3
  To my other self. 6841-3
  Treasure. 6841-3
Greene, Richard
  Contentment. 6737-9
Greene, Richard L.
  Autolycus' song (in basic English). 6722-0
  Song to Imogen (in basic English). 6722-0
Greene, Robert
  "Ah! were she pitiful as she is fair". 6181-8,6187-7
  "Ah! what is love? It is a pretty thing". 6181-8,6187-7, 6302-0,6385-3,6122-2
  Arbasto's song, fr. Arbasto. 6934-7
  Arbasto, sels. 6586-4
  Beauty, alas, where wast thou born. 6182-6
  Content, fr. Farewell to folly. 6660-7,6385-3,6604-6, 6383-7,6191-5,6219-5
  Coridon and Phillis. 6436-1
  "Cupid abroad was 'lated in the night." 6099-4
  Cupid's ingratitude. 6827-8
  A death-bed lament. 6543-0
  The description of Sir Geoffrey Chaucer. 6436-1
  The description of the shepherd and his wife. 6191-5
  Dildido, dildido. 6383-7
  Doralicia's song. 6315-2,6436-1,6191-5
  Doron's description of Samela. 6315-2,6586-4
  Doron's eclogue joined with Camela's. 6191-5
  Eurymachus's fancy. 6436-1
  Fair is my love. 6182-6
  The farewell to folly, sels. 6122-2
  Fawnia. 6436-1,6189-3,6737-9
  "Fie, fie on blind fancy!" 6181-8,6182-6
  "From his flock stray'd Coridon". 6187-7
  Greene's farewell to folly, sels. 6586-4
  Happy as a shepherd. 6793-X
  Happy as a shepherd. 6874-X
  Hexametra alexis in laudem rosamundi. 6182-6
  Infida's song. 6436-1
  James IV. 6186-9
  A jig. 6182-6
  Lamilia's song. 6436-1
  Love and jealousy. 6182-6
  Love in Arcady. 6830-8
  Lullaby ("Weep not"). 6078-1
  Maesia's song. 6436-1,6668-2
  Mars and Venus. 6436-1

GREENE

Menaphon's ditty. 6436-1
Menaphon's roundelay. 6668-2
Menaphon's song. 6198-2,6315-2,6436-1
Menaphon, sels. 6122-2
A mind content. 6182-6
The mourning garment, sels. 6122-2
Of his mistress ("Tune on my pipe the praises...") 6182-6
Of his mistress ("Tune on"). 6182-6
A palinode. 6436-1
The palmer's ode. 6436-1,6586-4
The penitent palmer's ode. 6315-2,6436-1
Philomel'a second ode. 6191-5
Philomela's ode. 6198-2,6271-7,6189-3,6194-X
Philomela's ode ("Sitting by a river side"). 6194-X, 6198-2
Philomela's ode in her arbour. 6436-1
Philomela's ode that she sung in her arbour. 6586-4
Philomela's ode, fr. Philomela. 6436-1,6586-4,6191-5
Philomela's song. 6189-6
Philomela, sels. 6122-2
Samela. 6182-6,6385-3,6436-1,6250-4,6383-7
Sephestia's cradle song. 6634-8
Sephestia's lullaby. 6533-3,6627-5,6301-2
Sephestia's song. 6233-4,6436-1
Sephestia's song to her child. 6198-2,6315-2,6586-4, 6189-3
The shepherd's ode. 6436-1
The shepherd's wife's song. 6250-4,6194-X,6513-9,6150-8, 6191-5,6219-9,6315-2,6182-6,6586-4,6198-2,6436-1, 6733-6,6436-1
"Sitting by a river's side", fr. Philomela. 6122-2,6317-9
"Some say Love", fr. Menaphon. 6122-2
Song ("Sweet are the thoughts"). 6198-2,6271-7
Song of the shepherd's wife. 6385-3
Sonnet or dittie ("Mars in a fury gainst..."). 6315-2
"Sweet Adon', dar'st not glance thine eye?" Alan Conder (tr.). 6317-9
"Sweet are the thoughts that savour of content". 6181-8, 6187-7,6122-2,6194-X,6723-9
Sweet content. 6099-4
"Weep not, my wanton...", fr. Menaphon. 6122-2,6182-6, 6181-8,6739-9
"What meant the poets in invective verse." 6317-9
What thing is love?, fr. Menaphon. 6934-7
Whereat erewhile I wept, I laugh. 6182-6
Greene, Roy
  A rural philosopher. 6548-1
Greene, Roy Farrell
  In the choir. 7021-3
  My sister has a beau. 7022-1
  A post-nuptial reverie. 7021-3
Greene, Sarah Pratt McLean
  De massa ob de sheepfol'. 6102-8,6310-1,6552-X,6632-1, 6476-0,6076
  De sheepfol'. 6007-2,6083-8,6153-2,6006-4,6737-9,6502
Greene, William Chase
  The surf at Chatham. 6798-0
  Vignette. 6798-0
"Greener than Arden Forest is my city square..". Roofs. Anne McClure. 6808-1
Greenfield hill, sels. Timothy Dwight. 6753-0
Greenfield hill, sels. Timothy Dwight. 6008-0,6288-1
Greenfield hill, sels. Timothy Dwight. 6753-0
Greenfield, Elena Vossen
  Desideratum. 6841-3
  Love. 6841-3
  The mermaid. 6841-3
  Migration. 6841-3
  My grief. 6841-3
Greenfield, Ethel
  Melodies unsung. 6850-2
  Reflections on the moon. 6850-2
  To an heirloom. 6850-2
  Villanelle to my dad. 6850-2
Greenfield, Fay Slobod
  Captive. 6799-9
The greengage tree. Edith Sitwell. 7000-0
Greenhood, David

Bread winners. 6042-0
The hungry. 6808-1
Liberty. 6808-1
A greenhouse, fr. The task. William Cowper. 6649-6
The Greenland fishery. Unknown. 6258-X
Greenland whale fishery. Unknown. 6518-X
Greenland, George
  Pretty ringtime. 6804-9
  The soldier of the south. 7031-0
Greenleaf, Lawrence M.
  The temple of living masons. 6923-1
Greenleaf, Mrs. J.T.
  A mistake. 6137-0
Greenleaf, Thorpe
  Patriotic sentiments, fr. The American rural home. 6171-0
Greenleaf, Thrope
  The American rural home, sels. 6171-0
Greenough, C.P.
  Commonwealth vs. McAfee. 6878-2
  Luther vs. Worcester. 6878-2
  Opinion of justices. 6878-2
Greenough, Emma Pomeroy
  Chalcedony. 6273-3
Greentree, R.
  Malacca. 6591-0,6592-9
Greenwell, Dora
  The battle-flag of Sigurd. 6437-X
  Content. 6461-2
  Death, fr. Songs of farewell. 7037-X
  The dying child. 6502-3
  Good-night, good-by. 6502-3
  His name. 6144-3,6335-7
  Home. 6066-8
  The little girl's lament. 6502-3
  The man with three friends. 6437-X
  A song of farewell. 6656-9
  A story by the fire. 6127-3,6502-3
  The sunflower. 6600-3
  To Christina Rossetti. 6656-9
  Vespers. 6600-3
"Greenwich Village your sicilian streets...". The last of the Bohemians. Jack Micheline. 6901-0
The Greenwich pensioner. Unknown. 6290-3,6547-3,6114-1
Greenwood cemetery. Crammond Kennedy. 6302-0;6385-3
Greenwood cemetery. Francis Scott Key. 6302-0;6385-3
Greenwood cemetery. William Wallace. 6916-9
Greenwood greetings. Unknown. 6171-0
The greenwood shrift. Caroline Anne Bowles and Robert Southey. 6302-0,6385-3,6408-6,6271-7
The greenwood tree, fr. As you like it. William Shakespeare. 6623-2,6424-8
The greenwood tree. Thomas Love Peacock. 6186-9
Greenwood, F.W.P.
  The spirit's song of consolation. 6752-2
Greenwood, Frederick
  Good-night. 6772-7
Greenwood, Grace. See Lippincott, Sara J.
The greenwood. William Lisle Bowles. 6085-4,6271-7,6302-0, 6385-3,6428-8
Greepe, Thomas
  The taking of Cartagna. 6547-3
Greer, Edith Borden
  The Christmas fir. 6799-9
Greer, Hilton Ross
  The road of midnight pageants. 6265-2
  To a bird on a downtown wire. 6073-0
Greer, Roslyn
  Triangle. 7024-8
"Greet all the company for me". Rondel ("Greet all"). Charles, Duc d' Orleans. 6227-X
Greeting. Joan Coster. 6262-8
Greeting. Unknown. 6466-3,6167-2
Greeting from England. Unknown. 6741-X
Greeting from England. Unknown. 6946-0
Greeting from far away. Friedrich Ruckert. 6226-1
The greeting of Kynast. Friedrich Ruckert. 6613-5
Greeting to the American eagle. Ruben Dario. 6102-8
Greeting to the George Griswold. Unknown. 638-8
A greeting.. Jonas Hallgrimsson. 6283-0

A greeting.. Joseph Twyman. 6274-1
A greeting. William Henry Davies. 6266-0,6102-8,6506-6
A greeting. Austin Dobson. 6250-4
A greeting. Jonas Hallgrimsson. 6854-5
A greeting. Philip Bourke Marston. 6656-9
Greetings. Mary McKinley Cobb. 6841-3
Greetings for two. F.W. Foley. 6887-1
Greetings for two. James William Foley. 6085-4,6281-4
Greetings to my love. Thomas Heywood. 6827-8
Greetings to Norway. Johann Sigurjonsson. 6283-0
Greeves-Carpenter, E.M.
    Seen on a war-shrine in Pennsylvania. 6542-2
Greg, Walter Wilson
    On the tomb of Guidarello Guidarelli at Ravenna. 6046-3
Gregan, Paul
    Mother of mothers. 6174-5
    Nature and man. 6174-5
    Queens in tir-na-n'og. 6778-6
Gregg, Frances
    So as you touch me I dream. 6327-6
Gregg, Laura M.
    The reconciliation. 6818-9
Gregg, Robert Etheridge
    Love and the sea. 6116-8
Gregh, Fernand
    Doubt. 6351-9,6730-1
    To the unknown God. 6351-9
Gregory of Narek, Saint
    "The lips of the Christ-child are like to twin leaves". Alice Stone Blackwell (tr.). 6050-1
Gregory the Great, Saint
    Darkness is thinning. John Mason Neale (tr.). 6271-7, 6302-0,6385-3
    Morning hymn. 6214-8
    Morning hymn. Edward Caswall (tr.). 6730-1
Gregory, Allebe
    Litany. 6846-4
Gregory, Augusta Gregory, Lady
    The old woman remembers. 6070-6
    The old woman remembers. 6930-4
Gregory, Augusta Gregory, Lady (tr.)
    Donall oge. Unknown (Irish), 6244-X
    The enchanted mistress. Egan O'Rahilly, 6244-X
    The grief of a girl's heart. Unknown (Irish), 6125-7
    I am Ireland. Padraic Pearse, 6244-X
    A lament for Ireland ("I do not know of anything...") Shemus Cartan, 6244-X
    Mary Hynes. Anthony Raftery, 6244-X
Gregory, Charles Noble
    Two men. 6925-8
Gregory, Horace
    A boy of twenty. 6393-4
    Daemon and lectern and a life-size mirror. 6527-9
    I have seen the mountains. 6761-1
    Mutum est pictura poema. 6761-1
    O mors aeterna. 6780-8
    The passion of M'Phail, sels. 6389-6
    Poem for my daughter. 6782-4
    Police sergeant Malone and the six dead drinkers. 6017-X
    Praise to John Skelton. 6483-3
    The sailor. 6751-4
    Salvos for Randolph Bourne. 6375-6
    Stanzas for my daughter. 6641-0
    "Through streets where crooked Wicklow flows." 6250-4, 6464-7
    Tombstone with cherubim. 6375-6
    Two letters from Europe. 6389-6
    Voices of heroes. 6390-X
    The well. 6516-3
    The woman who disapproved of music at the bar. 6390-X
Gregory, Padraic
    The ballad of the Lady Lorraine. 6541-4
    A bard's lament over his children. 6090-0
    The dream-teller. 6930-4
    Padric the fiddler. 6090-0
    Shaun O'Neill. 6249-0
    'They're only weans'. 6090-0
Gregory, V. Valiska
    The weaving. 6821-9

Gregory, Warren Fenno
    The broken banjo. 6116-8
    Tit for tat. 6116-8
Gregson, John Stanley
    Virginia tobacco. 6453-1
"Greife com away and doe not thou refuse." Unknown. 6563-5
Grelle, Leone Rice
    Auction. 6750-6
Grenada. Mikhail Arkadyevich Svetlov. 6665-8
Grenadier. Alfred Edward Housman. 6187-7,6538-4
The grenadiers. Heinrich Heine. 6732-8,6102-8
Grendel's mother, fr. Beowulf. Unknown. 6372-1
"Grene groweth the holy". Love ever green. Henry VIII; King of England (atr). 6881-2
Grenelle, Lisa
    Devil doll. 6218-0
Grenfell, Gerald Wilson
    To John. 6650-X
Grenfell, Julian
    He is dead who will not fight. 7031-0
    The hills. 6650-X
    Into battle. 6044-7,6224-5,6315-2,6427-2,6474-4,6477-9, 6650-X,6665-8
    To a black greyhound. 6427-2,6477-9
Grenstone. Witter Bynner. 6031-5
A Grenstone elm. Witter Bynner. 6653-4
Grenstone Falls. Witter Bynner. 6628-3
Grenstone river. Witter Bynner. 6467-1
Grenville, R.H.
    Borderline. 6218-0
    Ghost. 6218-0
    Intuition. 6218-0
    Nightmare. 6218-0
Gresham, Walter J.
    Let me walk with the men in the road. 6964-9
"The gret big church wuz crowded full...". The volunteer organist. Sam Walter Foss. 6166-4,6260-1,6486-8,6964-9
"The gret big church wuz crowded...". The volunteer organist. Sam Walter Foss. 6923-1
Gretchen. Unknown. 6740-9
Greve, Arthur A.
    After the rain. 6857-X
    The edgecumbe group. 6857-X
Greville, Fanny Macartney
    Prayer for indifference. 6024-2,6086-2,6315-2
    Prayer for indifference, sels. 6317-9
Greville, Frances
    Prayer for indifference. 6024-2,6315-2,6317-9,6086-2
Greville; 1st Baron Brooke, Fulke
    Absence and presence. 6436-1
    "Absence, the noble truce" 6380-2
    Caelica. 6186-9,6380-2,6436-1
    Caelica and Philocell. 6436-1,6195-5
    Caelica, sels. 6931-2,6378-0,6317-9,6586-4,6931-2
    Change. 6436-1,6150-8
    Chorus of priests. 6935-5
    Chorus primus - Of time: eternitie. 6933-9
    Chorus Quintus- Tartarorum. 6933-9
    Chorus sacerdotum. 6208-3,6194-X,6150-8
    "Cupid, thou naughtie Boy, when thou wert loathed" 6380-2
    Cynthia. 6436-1
    Despair. 6436-1
    "The earth with thunder torn, with fire blasted". 6181-8
    Epitaph on Sir Philip Sidney. 6315-2,6436-1,6483-3,6438-8
    "Eternal truth, almighty, infinite", fr. Caelica. 6931-2
    Farewell to Cupid. 6436-1
    "Farewell, sweet Boy, complain not of my truth" 6380-2
    His lady's eyes. 6436-1
    "I offer wrong to my beloved saint". 6380-2
    "I, with whose colours Myra dress'd her head". 6181-8, 6187-7
    An inqvisition vpon fame and honovr. 6586-4
    "Juno, that on her head loves liverie carried". 6380-2
    Love and fortune. 6436-1
    Love and honour. 6436-1

GREVILLE;

Love beyond change. 6194-X
"Love is the peace whereto all thoughts do strive". 6181-8
Love's glory. 6436-1
"Merlin, they say, an English prophet borne" 6380-2
More than most fair. 6182-6
Mustapha, sels. 6378-0
Myra. 6182-6,6186-9,6194-X,6150-8,6315-2,6436-1
Myra's fickleness. 6191-5
"The nurse-life Wheat within his greene huske growing" 6380-2
"O false and treacherous probability", fr. Caelica. 6931-2
"O wearisome condition of humanity". 6187-7
Of his Cynthia. 6182-6
Of human learning. 6933-9
Pomp a futile mask for tyranny. 6194-X
"Sathan, no Woman, yet a wandring spirit" 6380-2
Sion lays waste. 6641-0
"Sion lies waste, and thy Jerusalem", fr. Caelica. 6931-2
Sonnet ("When as mans"). 6472-8
Sonnet 087 ("When as man's life..."). 6933-9
Sonnet 088 ("Man, dreame no more..."). 6933-9
Sonnet 094 ("Men, that delight"). 6933-9
Sonnet 097 ("Eternall truth"). 6933-9
Sonnet 099 ("Downe in the depth of mine iniquity"). 6933-9
Sonnet 103 ("O false and treacherous"). 6933-9
Sonnet 105 ("Three things"). 6933-9
Time and eternity. 6436-1
To her eyes. 6827-8
To his lady. 6436-1
A treatie of humane learning, sels. 6586-4
True knowledge and its use. 6935-5
True monarch. 6194-X
Whenas man's life, the light of human lust, fr. Caelica. 6931-2
"Who ever sailes neere to Bermuda coast" 6380-2
"Wrapp'd up, O Lord, in man's degeneration",fr.Caelica. 6931-2
You little stars that live in skies. 6182-6
Youth and maturity. 6436-1
"Grevus is my sorow". Unkindness has killed me. Unknown. 6881-2
Grey. Karle Wilson Baker. 6326-8
Grey. Fray Angelico Chavez. 6761-1
Grey. Archibald T. Strong. 6784-0
"Grey and crooked, cloying". War. Julia A. Booth. 6883-9
The grey cock, or, Saw you my father? Unknown. 6185-0
The grey company. Jessie MacKay. 6784-0
"Grey dawn - and lucent star that slowly paled". Faith, love, and death. Dowell O'Reilly. 6784-0
"A grey dawn sky,and bleak grey-gleaming sands". Bait. Norah Lilian D'Altera Dowsley. 6800-6
Grey day. Jean Milne Gower. 6836-7
A grey day. William Vaughn Moody. 6431-0
The grey dusk. Seumas (James Starkey) O'Sullivan. 6174-5
The grey friar. Thomas Love Peacock. 6026-9
Grey Galloway. Thomas S. Cairncross. 6269-5
Grey goose and gander. Unknown. 6904-5
Grey hair. Rufinus. 6435-3
Grey him. Paul Mariah. 6870-7
The grey horse troop. Robert W. Chambers. 7012-4
The 'grey horse' troop. Robert W. Chambers. 6946-0
"Grey is the color of time". Morning song. Charlotte DeClue. 7005-1
Grey knitting. Katherine (Amelia Beers Warnock Garvin) Hale. 6115-X
The grey linnet. James McCarroll. 6433-7
The grey monk, sels. William Blake. 6301-2
The grey monk. William Blake. 6250-4
Grey owl's poem. Gwendolyn Macewen. 6767-0
The grey plume. Francis Carlin. 6619-4
Grey rocks and greyer sea. Sir Charles George Douglas Roberts. 6310-1,6374-8,6433-7
"The grey sea and the long black land". Robert Browning. 6997-5
The grey spring. Alfred Noyes. 6169-9
The grey squirrels. William Howitt. 6638-0

"A grey suit at midnight". Black hole in space. Clem Portman. 6857-X
"Grey towers make me think of thee". Looking backward. Rose Hawthorne Lathrop. 7041-8
"Grey winter hath gone, like a wearisome guest". September in Australia. Henry Clarence Kendall. 6768-9,6437-X, 6656-9
The grey wolf. Walter De La Mare. 6596-1
The grey wolf. Arthur Symons. 6210-5
Grey Zimbabwe. Peter Jackson. 6788-3
Grey, Cynthia
    Her senior smile your Waterloo. 6718-2
Grey, Herbert
    'Cause he'd nothing else to do. 6692-5
Grey, Lillian
    His riches. 6703-4
    His riches. 6921-5
Grey, Margery Berridge
    To a skylark. 6433-7
Grey, Pamela
    Moon magic. 6466-3
"Grey-black harp strings of the sapling forest". Harmonies. Melrose Pitman. 6906-1
"Grey-glimmering thro' the dusky air". The incoming tide. William ("Fiona Macleod") Sharp. 6997-5
A Greyport legend. Francis Bret Harte. 6239-3,6424-8
Gribble, L.R.
    I saw three ships. 6490-6
Gribble, R.T. (tr.)
    Everlasting to everlasting, sels. Namdev, 6337-3
Gridley, Carol
    I know there will be peace. 6662-3
Gridley, Inez George
    Barely possible. 6750-6
    By earth restored. 6662-3
    Warning to whodunit fans. 6750-6
Grief. Elizabeth Barrett Browning. 6246-6,6315-2,6437-X, 6657-7,6737-9,6383 ,6214-8,6543-0
Grief. David Herbert Lawrence. 6897-9
Grief. Thomas Moore. 6294-6
Grief. Angela Morgan. 6291-1;6501-5
Grief. Adelaide Anne Procter. 6957-6
Grief. William Thomas Walsh. 6761-1
Grief. Christine Hamilton Watson. 6799-9
Grief ("Oh! nothing now can please me"). John Dryden. 6294-6
Grief and faith. Amelie ("Princess Pierre Troubetzkoy") Rives. 7041-8
Grief and God. Stephen Phillips. 6730-1
Grief and joy. Frederic Lawrence ("R.L. Paget") Knowles. 6889-8
Grief for the dead. Unknown. 6302-0;6385-3
"Grief is a mouse". Emily Dickinson. 6399-3
The grief of a girl's heart. Unknown (Irish) 6125-7
"Grief on the death, it has blackened my heart". A woman of the mountain keens her son. Padraic Pearse. 6879-0
"Grief should be". Unknown. 6238-5
"The grief that is but feigning". The valley of vain verses. Henry Van Dyke. 6961-4
"Grief! that in my soul com'st stealing". Melancholy serenade 005. Jaroslav Vrchlicky. 6763-8
Grief, fr. Hamlet. William Shakespeare. 6302-0;6385-3
"Grief, keep within and scorn to show but...". Mrs. M. E. her funeral teares for the death of her... Unknown. 6908-8
The grief. Theodosia Garrison. 6320-9
"The griefs of a little boy are forever". Four and a half. John Holmes. 6761-1,6783-2
Grier, Eldon
    In memory Garcia Lorca. 6446-9
    The minotaur. 6446-9
    Quebec. 6446-9
Grierson, Herbert J.C. (tr.)
    The flute. Jose Maria de Heredia, 6180-X
    On the passing of my little daughter. Joost van den Vondel, 6180-X
Gries, Walter F.
    The Cornish miner. 6281-4
The griesly wife. John Streeter Manifold. 6108-7

A **grievance..** James Kenneth Stephen. 6440-X
Grieve not for beauty. Witter Bynner. 6336-5,6393-4
Grieve not, dear love. John Digby, 1st Earl of Bristol. 6563-5
Grieve not, dear love. John Digby; Earl of Bristol. 6879-0
Grieve not, ladies. Anna Hempstead Branch. 6102-8,6310-1, 6441-8,6732-8,6076-5,6300
"**Grieve** not, my Albius". To Albuis Tibullus (2). Horace. 6949-5
Grieve, Christopher M. ("Hugh MacDiarmid")
At the cenotaph. 6375-6
The bonnie broukit bairn. 6845-6
Cattle show. 6845-6
Crowdieknowe. 6269-5
The eemis-stane. 6379-9
Empty vessel. 6210-5
First love. 6893-6
The glen of silence. 6379-9
A herd of does. 6269-5
Hymn to Sophia: the wisdom of God. 6641-0
"If there are any bounds to any man". 6893-6
In the hedgeback. 6379-9
The man in the moon. 6379-9
Milk-wort and bog cotton. 6379-9
Munestruck. 6379-9
O wha's been here afore me, lass. 6210-5
On the ocean floor. 6893-6
Parley of beasts. 6317-9
Perfect. 6379-9
Reflections in an ironworks. 6375-6
Scunner. 6210-5
The skelton of the future (at Lenin's tomb). 6845-6
Somersault. 6269-5
The two parents. 6210-5
Water music. 6845-6
The watergaw. 6269-5,6379-9
"Wheesht, wheesht, my foolish hert." 6317-9
With a lifting of the head. 6893-6
Grieve, Christopher M. ("Hugh MacDiarmid") (tr.)
Birlinn Chlann-raghnaill. Alexander (Alasdair MacMhaighstir A.) Macdonald, 6845-6
The day of Inverlochy. John (Iain Lom) MacDonald, 6845-6
Ireland weeping. William Livinston, 6845-6
Message to the bard. William Livinston, 6845-6
The praise of Ben Dorain. Duncan Ban MacIntyre, 6845-6
To Mackinnon of Strath. John (Iain Lom) MacDonald, 6845-6
The **grievings** of a proud spirit. George Croly. 6980-0
Grievous words. Suzanne Lehman. 6249-0
Griffen, Estelle Geraldine
Jesus is calling. 6799-9
The old woods. 6799-9
Griffin, Amos J.
Salute to the tan Yanks. 6178-8
Griffin, B.F.
Springtime. 6118-4
Griffin, Bartholomew
"Arraign'd poore captiue at the barre I stand," 6586-4
"Care-charmer sleepe, sweet ease in restles miserie," 6586-4
"Compare me to the child that plaies with fire," 6586-4
"Fair is my love that feeds among the lilies". 6102-8, 6182-6,6187-7,6586-4
Fidessa, sels. 6378-0
"Flye to her heart, houer about her heart," 6586-4
"I have not spent the April of my time" 6182-6,6586-4
Sleep ("Care-charmer sleep, sweet ease in restless...") 6436-1
"Worke worke apace you blessed Sisters three," 6586-4
Youth ("I have not spent the April of my time"). 6436-1
Griffin, Blanche H.
Nature's balm. 6894-4
Griffin, Gerald
Aileen aroon. 6930-4
The bridal of Malahide. 6174-5,6518-X,6576-7
Cead Mile Failte, Elim!, fr. 'The invasion'. 6174-5
Eileen Aroon. 6090-0,6096-X,6174-5,6437-X,6512-0,6732
Gille Machree. 6174-5
Gone! Gone! Forever gone. 6930-4
Hy-Brasail--the isle of the blest. 6090-0,6174-5,6244-X
I love my love in the morning. 6096-X,6022-6
'The invasion', sels. 6174-5
Keep them rolling. 6237-7
Know ye not that lovely river. 6930-4
Lines addressed to a seagull. 6930-4
Lines to a seagull. 6174-5
Love's song. 6226-1
The nightingale. 6292-X,6172-9
Nocturne. 6656-9
O Brazil, the isle of the blest. 6022-6
Orange and green. 6174-5,6451-5
A place in thy memory. 6656-9
The sister of charity. 6285-7,6451-5
The sister of charity. 6912-6
Sleep that like the couched dove. 6930-4
To the blessed Virgin Mary. 6930-4
War song of O'Driscol. 6930-4
Griffin, Howard
After being discharged. 6839-1
Griffin, Jonathan (tr.)
I am tired. Fernando Pessoa, 6758-1
Griffin, M. Adelaide
Eventide in winter. 6764-6
Griffith, D.E.
The abandoned mine. 6149-4
Griffith, E.M.
The old cradle. 6672-0
Griffith, George Bancroft
Before it is too late. 6097-8,6274-1
Our fallen heroes. 6271-7
The trusty boy. 6530-9
Griffith, William
Aloha. 6478-7,6607-0
August song. 6347-0
Autumn song. 6102-8,6076-5
Canticle. 6161-3,6073-0,6347-0,6509-0,6253-9,6393-4
Encounter. 6102-8,6076-5
A forest rendezvous. 6034-X
A hermit thrush in the catskills. 6073-0
"I, who fade with the lilacs". 6102-8,6076-5,6034-X
I, who laughed my youth away. 6034-X
Interlude. 6232-6,6029-3
My dog. 6510-4
Novitiate. 6232-6
Novitiate. 6782-4
Origins. 6184-2
Pierette in memory. 6076-5,6102-8
Pierrette in memory. 6102-8,6556-2,6076-5
Pierrot makes a song. 6441-8
The reproach. 7008-6
Sappho to Atthis. 6232-6
Serenade. 6029-3
Shadow. 6102-8,6076-5
Spring blew open the door. 6184-2
Spring song. 6029-3,6073-0,6102-8,6338-1,6556-2,6076-5
Two poems of Pierrot. 6581-3
The year is changing its name. 6232-6
Griffith, Wyn
All saints. 6360-8
Branwen, sels. 6360-8
February night. 6360-8
Madame rumour. 6360-8
New Year's Eve. 6360-8
Poem ("If there be time"). 6360-8
Silver jubilee. 6360-8
Griffiths, Ciwa
Sunset. 6799-9
Griffiths, Jennie Scott
Liberty. 6799-9
Griffiths, Jessie Stearns
The passing of a friend. 6270-9
Griffiths, Nora
The wykhamist. 6474-4
Grigg, Joseph
Ashamed of Jesus. 6065-X
Griggs, Helen Byrom
Lindbergh. 7019-1
Griggsby's staion. James Whitcomb Riley. 6732-8
Grigson Geoffrey

GRIGSON

The four. 6666-6
June in Wiltshire. 6666-6
The landscape of the heart. 6666-6
Meeting by the Gjulika meadow. 6666-6
Uccello on the heath. 6666-6
Under the cliff. 6666-6
Grill room. Jesse F. Patterson. 6178-8
Grilley, Charles T.
    Before and after. 6277-6
    Miss Amelia's colored Lochinvar. 6701-8
    My chips. 6714-X
    Play ball. 6717-4
    The stuttering auctioneer. 6280-6
    When mah lady yawns. 6277-6
Grillo, Maximiano
    Oh, Selva! 6253-9
"Grim cloisters/Where miracles are wrought". Interlude. Lilian White Spencer. 6836-7
"Grim death took little Jerry,". Unknown. 6722-0
"Grim is the face that looks into the night". Mother and sphinx. Unknown (Egyptian). 6949-5
The grimace of death. Josephine Hancock Logan. 6789-1
Grimald, Nicholas
    Description of vertue. 6586-4
    The garden. 6489-2,6649-6
    Mans life after Possidonius, or crates. 6586-4
    Metrodorus minde to the contrarie. 6586-4
    Of frendship. 6586-4
    A true love ("What sweet relief...") 6182-6
    A truelove. 6436-1
    Virtue. 6436-1
Grime. Anne Harley Avila. 6750-6
Grimes, E.B.
    No other word. 6097-8
Grimes, Marie
    Kitten and firefly. 6120-6
Grimm, Reinhold (tr.)
    Prewar. Thomas Brasch, 7032-9
Grimstone, J.
    Love on the Cross. 6636-4
    Mater Dolorosa. 6636-4
Grimwoald, Nicholas
    A friend. 6084-6
    The friend. 6085-4
Grin. Robert Service. 6159-1
The grind's dream. Arthur F. Gotthold. 6118-4
"Grind, mill, grind". Unknown. 6435-3
The grindstone. Robert P. Tristram Coffin. 7040-X
The grindstone. Robert Frost. 6010-2
Grinfield, T.
    How kindly hast thou led me! 6219-9
Gringa. Liz Gold. 6900-2
Griparis, Yiannis
    Comrades in death. Rae Dalven (tr.). 6352-7
    Mount Rhodope. Rae Dalven (tr.). 6352-7
    Reveille for the dead. Rae Dalven (tr.). 6352-7
    Vestal virgins. Rae Dalven (tr.). 6352-7
Gripenberg, Bertel
    At the end of play. Charles Wharton Stork (tr.). 6045-5
    Drink. Charles Wharton Stork (tr.). 6045-5
    Youth. Charles Wharton Stork (tr.). 6045-5
Griper Greg. Unknown. 6406-X,6742-5
Grisaille. Terence Heywood. 6788-3
Grisaille with a spot of red. Samuel Yellen. 6388-8
Griscom, Arthur
    Skating song. 7035-3
    The sleigh ride. 7035-3
Griselda. Geoffrey Chaucer. 6438-8
Griselda goose. Phoebe Cary. 6060-9
Griselda in pound - A.D. 1760. Margaret Junkin Preston. 6965-7
Grisette dines. Antoinette Deshoulieres. 6120-6
Grisham, George Edgar
    Give me rest. 6682-8
Grissom, Arthur
    Ballade of forgotten loves. 7021-3
    Ballade of forgotten loves. 6089-7
Grissom, Irene Welsh
    A pioneer woman. 6270-9
Griswold, Caroline
    The beautiful snow. 6909-6
Griswold, Elizabeth M.
    Freedom's natal day. 6820-0
Griswold, Hattie Tyng
    'The Birkenhead.' 6686-0
    Gwendolen. 6690-9
    Under the daisies. 6240-7
Griswold, Rufus Wilmot
    Ethan Allen. 7030-2
    To Jane. 7030-2
Grizzly. Ann Chandonnet. 6855-3
Grizzly. Francis Bret Harte. 6006-4,6597-X,6431-0,6424-8, 6510-4
The groaning board. Pink [pseud]. 6817-0
Groaning earth. Martha Millet. 6561-9
The groans of wounded souls. Sadi [or Saadi] (Mushlih-ud-Din) 6954-1
The grocery store cat. Margaret E. Bruner. 6120-6
Groesbeck, Halley W.
    For a certain young poet. 6906-1
    A Greek youth. 6906-1
    A soliloquy of Elizabeth Tudor. 6906-1
    Sonnet ("I have no need"). 6906-1
    To Mary Stuart. 6906-1
    Understanding. 6906-1
Groesbeck, Kenneth
    Armistice, 1928 6542-2
Grondal, Benedikt
    In absence. Watson Kirkconnell (tr.). 6283-0
    Night. Skuli Johnson (tr.). 6854-5
    Regret. Jakobina Johnson (tr.). 6283-0
    Regret. Jakobina Johnson (tr.). 6854-5
Grongar hill. John Dyer. 6024-2,6302-0,6315-2,6385-3,6600-3,6634 ,6195-0,6152-4,6129-9,6245-8,6125-7
Grongar hill, sels. John Dyer. 6198-2,6208-3,6150-8
The groom's story. Sir Arthur Conan Doyle. 6707-7
The groomsman to his mistress. Thomas William Parsons. 6385-3,6441-8,6219-9
Groping. Ella Orndorff Hunt. 6906-1
Gros temps la nuit. Victor Hugo. 6801-4
Grosebeck, Amy
    The brothers. 6218-0
Gross, Adeline E.
    The singer and the child. 6919-3
Gross, Daniel I.
    London Bridge. 6799-9
Gross, Lila Clair
    Storm at Minnetonka. 6342-X
"Gross, with protruding ears". Commercial. Laurence Binyon. 6884-7
Grosseteste, Robert
    A little song. F.M. Capes (tr.). 6282-2
Grossmith, George
    He told me so. 6661-5
    The wife who sat up. 6280-6
Grotesque. Gerd Aage Gilhoff. 6798-0
A grotesque love-letter. Unknown. 6881-2
Groth, Klaus
    The submerged town. Elizabeth Craigmyle (tr.). 6842-1
The grotto of Egeria. Thomas Kibble Hervey. 6102-8
The grotto of Egeria. William Sotheby. 6980-0
Grotto of the nativity. Katharine Lee Bates. 6331-4
The grotto. Matthew Green. 6968-1
The grotto. Francis Scarfe. 6379-9
Ground hog. Unknown. 6594-5
Ground instruction, fr. Exploration by air. Fleming MacLeish. 6978-9
The ground laurel. Hannah Flagg Gould. 6373-X
The ground squirrel. Paul Hamilton Hayne. 6965-7
Ground swell. G. Stanley Koehler. 6388-8
"The groundflame of the crocus breaks the mold". The progress of spring, fr. The promise of May. Alfred Lord Tennyson. 6867-7
The groundhog. Richard Eberhart. 6399-3,6389-6,6666-6,6209-1
Grounds of the terrible. Harold Begbie. 6481-7
The groundswell. John Gould Fletcher. 6619-4
"Group after group are gathering...". The Sunday school. Lydia Huntley Sigourney. 6752-2
A group of gipsies. George Crabbe. 690-0

"A **group** of topers at a table sat". The toper and the flies. John ("Peter Pindar") Wolcott. 6787-5
"**Groups** of me/dressed in brown clothing". State prison 4:00 p.m. Thomas G. Nickens. 6870-7
Grove, Eliza
   A cat to her kittens. 6459-0
Grove, Helen W.
   A grammar lesson. 6925-8
Grove, Matthew
   In praise of his lady. 6182-6
A **grove**. Samuel Taylor Coleridge. 6793-X
The **grove**. Edwin Muir. 6391-8
Grover Cleveland. Joel Benton. 6946-0
Grover, Edwin Osgood
   Banquet song. 6441-8
   Down east and up along. 6374-8
   Southward bound. 6421-3
   Spring's answer. 6374-8
   Though the miles divide us. 6097-8
   To a mocking bird. 6073-0
Grover, Marshal E.
   The elephant tries to rescue the jackass. 6799-9
The **groves** of Blarney. Richard Alfred Milliken. 6174-5, 6244-X,6092-7,6086-2,6219-9,6918
"The **groves** of Eden, vanish'd now so long". Windsor forest, sels. Alexander Pope. 6831-6
"The **groves** were God's first temples", sels. William Cullen Bryant. 6047-1
The **groves**. William Cullen Bryant. 6629-1
'**Grow** in hope and grace'. Barbara Anne Baker. 7024-8
"**Grow** not too high". Sonnet ("Grow not"). Edna St. Vincent Millay. 6012-9
Grow old along with me. Robert Browning. 6654-2
"**Grow** weary if you will, let me be sad". Lesbia. Richard Aldington. 6897-9
Growing. Unknown. 6312-8,6337-3
Growing gray. Austin Dobson. 6123-0,6385-3
The **growing** of the Christmas tree. John E. Barrett. 6840-5
Growing old. Annie B. Alguire. 6789-1
Growing old. Matthew Arnold. 6110-9,6828-6
Growing old. Karle Wilson Baker. 6585-6
Growing old. Mrs. M.W. Chase. 6929-0
Growing old. Marc Eugene ("Vandyke Brown") Cook. 6441-8, 6004-8
Growing old. Walter Learned. 6083-8,6300-4
Growing old. Francis Ledwidge. 6090-0,6301-2
Growing old. Margaret Elizabeth Sangster. 6273-3
Growing old. Unknown. 6713-1
Growing old. Unknown. 6918-5
Growing old. Rollin J. Wells. 6303-9
Growing rich. Alice Cary. 6969-X
"**Growing** to full manhood now". In memoriam: those killed in the north-west, 1885. Frederick George Scott. 6795-6
Growing up. Edgar A. Guest. 6748-4
"**Grown** old in courts, thou art not surely one". Adriano, sels. Pietro Mestastio. 6975-4
"**Grown** sick of war, and war's alarms". On the king's speech recommending peace with..American. Philip Freneau. 6946-0
Grown-up land. Unknown. 6215-6
"The **grown-ups**".. Cesar Vallejo. 6759-X
Growth. Emily J. Bugbee. 6049-8
Growth. John Lee Higgins. 6232-6
Growth. John Richard Moreland. 6036-6
Growth. Stella Reinhardt. 6397-7
Growth. William White. 6868-5
Growth. Sarah Williams. 7037-X
The **growth** of Lorraine. Edwin Arlington Robinson. 6897-9
The **growth** of love, sels. Robert Bridges. 6154-0
The **growth** of love. Robert Bridges. 6487-6
The **growth** of love. James Sheridan Knowles. 6980-0
The **growth** of love. Sir Charles Sedley. 6543-0
The **growth** of Perseus. W. Wesley Trimpi. 6515-5
Growth of the soul. Edward R. Huxley. 6885-2
A **Grub** street recessional. Christopher Morley. 6817-0
Grub street, sels. John Davidson. 6819-7
Gruber, Edmund L.
   The caissons go rolling along. 6237-7
A **grudg** against Boston. Charles Potts. 6998-3

Grueninger, Irene Davis
   Hans' dog, Pete. 6906-1
   I wonder why. 6906-1
   A kite. 6906-1
   Self-judgment. 6906-1
   The wren. 6906-1
Grufydd's feast. Felicia Dorothea Hemans. 6973-8
Grumbine, Harvey C.
   Gloria patri. 6799-9
   Praise be to Noah. 6799-9
   Rx. 6799-9
   Your fecund breath. 6799-9
Grumble corner and thanksgiving street. Unknown. 6923-1
The **grumble** family. Unknown. 6583-X
The **grumbler**. Dora Read Goodale. 6530-9,6314-4
The **grumbling** hive: or, knaves turn'd honest. Bernard Mandeville. 6152-4
The **grumbling** soldier. Edgar A. Guest. 6869-3
Grundtvig, Nicolai F.S.
   Niels Ebbesen. Charles Wharton Stork (tr.). 6555-4
   Sabbath morn. 6177-X
Grundy, George B. (tr.)
   Epitaph on Charidas of Cyrene. Callimachus. 6879-0
   His son. Asclepiades, 7039-6
   His son. Callimachus, 6879-0
   Life's journey. Unknown (Greek), 6879-0
   The new-made grave. Heraclitus, 6879-0
   On a grave at Meroe. Unknown (Greek), 6879-0
   On a niobe of Praxiteles. Unknown (Greek), 6879-0
   The poet's friend. Simonides, 6435-3
   The Spartans at Thermopylae. Simonides, 6879-0
Gualbero's victory. Eleanor C. Donnelly. 6915-0
Gualberto's victory. Eleanor C. Donnelly. 6610-0
Guard. Michael C. Martin. 6666-6
Guard. Catherine Ready. 7019-1
Guard of the eastern gate. Emily Pauline ("Tekahionwake") Johnson. 6433-7
A **guard** of the sepulcher. Edwin Markham. 6335-7;6730-1
"**Guard** well the temple of the mind". The sanctum sanctorum. Robert Loveman. 6941-X
The **guard's** story. Unknown. 6911-8
Guard, R. Lee
   November. 6818-9
The **guarded** wound. Adelaide Crapsey. 6393-4
The **guardian** angel. Robert Browning. 6484-1,6604-6,6624-0, 6110-9,6660-7
The **guardian** angel. Thomas S. Jones Jr. 6648-8
Guardian angels, fr. The faerie queene. Edmund Spenser. 6436-1
Guardian of thy land. Herman Montagu Donner. 6995-9
Guardians. Sadi [or Saadi] (Mushlih-ud-Din) 6448-5
"**Guardians** of a holy trust" Richard Watson Gilder. 6954-1
The **guardians**. Ibn Sa'id (of Alcala La Real) 6362-4
"**Guarding** her hungry brood of helpless young". Bird neighbors. Arlyle Mansfield. 6799-9
"**Guarding** the cattle on my native hill". The sling. Roy Campbell. 6788-3
The **guards** came through. Sir Arthur Conan Doyle. 6088-9
The **guardsman**. William A. Drake. 6537-6
The **guardsman**. Frank X. Finnegan. 6471-X
Guarini, Giovanni Battista
   Dream of his lady ("Fair eyes, ye mortal..."). Philip Ayres (tr.). 6325-X
   Dream of his lady ("O eyes, you mortal stars"). Ronald Bottrall (tr.). 6325-X
   The faithful shepherd, sels. Sir Richard Fanshawe (tr.). 6325-X
   The golden age, fr. The faithful shepherd. Sir Richard Fanshawe (tr.). 6325-X
   Madrigals. John Wilbye (tr.). 6317-9
   Spring. Leigh Hunt (tr.). 7039-6
   "This saith my Cloris bright." John Wilbye (tr.). 6317-9
The **gude** gaun game o' curlin' James A. Sidey. 7035-3
The **gude** greye katt. James Hogg. 6802-2
Gude Wallace. Unknown. 6185-0
Gude'en to you, Kimmer. Robert Burns. 6633-X
Gudgen, H.T.
   On a daughter'sbirthday anniversary. 6799-9
Gudmundsson, Gudmundur

GUDMUNDSSON

Lament ("Snows cloaked"). Watson Kirkconnell (tr.). 6283-0
Peace on earth, sels. Jakobina Johnson (tr.). 6283-0
Peace on earth, sels. Jakobina Johnson (tr.). 6854-5
Prologue, fr. Peace on earth. Jakobina Johnson (tr.). 6283-0
The rose. Jakobina Johnson (tr.). 6283-0

"Gudrun of old days". The first lay of Gudrun. Unknown (Icelandic). 7039-6

Guenther, Charles (tr.)
The library is on fire. Rene Char, 6803-0

Guerard, Vera Elizabeth
At sea. 7024-8
Spring of joy. 7024-8

Guerdon. Lena L. Jennings. 6799-9
The guerdon of the son. George Sterling. 6607-0
The guerilla leader's vow. Felicia Dorothea Hemans. 6973-8
Guerilla song, founded on...Spanish patriot Mina. Felicia Dorothea Hemans. 6973-8
The guerillas. S. Teackle Wallis. 6016-2

Guerin, Charles
In my old verses. 6351-9
"Le sombre ciel lacte se voute en forme d'arche" 6801-4
Night of shadows. 6351-9
Out of the deep. Wilfrid Thorley (tr.). 6607-0
To Francis Jammes. 6351-9

Guernica. Aaron Kramer. 6561-9
Guernica. James Lewisohn. 6870-7
Guess. George Elliston. 6906-1
"Guess I've never told you, sonny...". Tale of the Kennebec mariner. Holman F. Day. 7025-6
Guess what's in my pocket. Unknown. 6740-9
Guess who. Nellie R. Cameron. 6713-1
Guess who? Berton Braley. 6995-9
'Guess'.. Eugene Field. 6949-5
Guessing song. Henry Johnstone. 6519-8,6368-4
Guest. Evelyne Love Cooper. 6850-2
Guest. Ruth Eckman. 6750-6
Guest. Beresford Richard. 6541-4
A guest speaks. Aline Kilmer. 6478-7

Guest, Barbara
Lunch at Helen Frankenthaler's. 6803-0

Guest, Edgar A.
About children. 6869-3
Absence. 6748-4
The absentee. 6748-4
Achievement. 6869-3
After a proposal. 6862-6
The after-dinner smoke. 6862-6
Afterwards. 6748-4
The age of ink. 7033-7
Age talks to youth. 6748-4
All for the best. 7033-7
All I know. 6748-4
All in a lifetime. 6748-4
All in the day's work. 6748-4
Always saying 'don't'. 7033-7
Apple tree. 6869-3
The apple vendor. 6869-3
Argument. 6748-4
Ask your mother. 6748-4
At her wedding. 6869-3
At the cottage. 6862-6
At the school exercises. 6869-3
At the summer cottage. 6862-6
Autumn. 6869-3
Autumn. 6862-6
Autumn evenings. 7033-7
Autumn scene. 6869-3
The average man. 6862-6
Aw gee whiz! 7033-7
Baby's got a tooth. 6078-1
A baby's love. 6862-6
Back to school. 6862-6
The bad axe fair. 6723-9
Ballad of a careless man. 6748-4
The bank clerk. 6862-6
The bank roll. 6862-6
Bbeubaytt6748f4Belleau Wood. 6846-4

Beauty. 6869-3
Because he lived. 6869-3
Bedtime. 7033-7
The beggar. 6748-4
The benefit of trouble. 6862-6
Best of all meals. 6748-4
The better job. 7033-7
Bi-focal trouble. 6869-3
Big dog. 6748-4
The birch tree. 6869-3
The black sheep. 6869-3
The blue spruce. 6869-3
Boarding the birds. 6748-4
Bob white. 6510-4
The book of memory. 7033-7
A bookkeeper's son. 6748-4
A boy and his dad. 7033-7
A boy and his dog. 6510-4
A boy and his stomach. 6401-9,6135-4
The boy and the flag. 6135-4
the boy mind. 6862-6
Boy o' mine. 7033-7
Boyhood ambitions. 6748-4
The bread line. 6869-3
The bright side. 6862-6
Brothers all. 7033-7
Buckle in. 6862-6
Burning candle. 6748-4
The busines of an uncle. 6869-3
Business. 6862-6
The call of the woods. 7033-7
The call. 6374-8
Can't. 6291-1
The card club's first meeting. 6862-6
Careless. 6869-3
'Carry on'. 7033-7
The carver. 6869-3
Castor oil. 6548-1
Change of mind. 6869-3
Charms. 6862-6
Cherry pie. 6748-4
Childhood. 6748-4
The chip on your shoulder. 7033-7
The choice. 6869-3
The choir at Pixley. 6862-6
A Christmas bit. 6869-3
A Christmas carol. 7033-7
Christmas eve. 6862-6
The Christmas gift for mother. 7033-7
The Christmas spirit. 6862-6
Chums. 6862-6
Circus memories. 6869-3
City pigeons. 6748-4
City-weary. 6374-8
Cleaning the furnace. 7033-7
Club presidents. 6748-4
Columbus. 6748-4
Committee meetings. 7033-7
Comradeship. 6862-6
Consolation. 6862-6
The contented man. 6862-6
Contradictin' Joe. 7033-7
The cookie jar. 7033-7
The cost of praise. 6862-6
Couldn't live without you. 7033-7
Courage. 6869-3
Courtesy on departure. 6748-4
Courtship's end. 6748-4
A creed. 6449-3
Cure for the sulks. 6869-3
The cure for weariness. 7033-7
Dad discusses clothes. 6748-4
Dan McGann declares himself. 7033-7
The deeds of anger. 7033-7
Destiny. 6869-3
Determination. 6869-3
The difference. 6748-4
Difficulties. 6869-3
Donnen?t6862-6862-6

Do your all. 6846-4
Dr. Jonson's picture cow. 6401-9,6135-4
The doctor's first query. 6748-4
Doctor's waiting room. 6869-3
Dog trainer. 6748-4
The dog. 6869-3
Don't worry, little girl. 6862-6
Don't you know. 6862-6
The don't-believeres. 6862-6
Doughnuts and cider. 6862-6
The drawback. 6869-3
The dream days. 6862-6
Dreaming. 6862-6
Dreams. 6748-4
The dreams of youth. 6862-6
Dressing up. 6748-4
Easter. 6862-6
Eclipse. 6869-3
Endurance. 6862-6
Envy. 6748-4
Envy. 6862-6
Eternal spring. 6748-4
The eternal young. 6401-9
Eulogy. 6748-4
Evening smoke. 6869-3
The everlasting flowers. 6869-3
Fame. 6748-4
The family party. 6862-6
The Family prayer for difficult days. 6869-3
A family row. 7033-7
The farm hand. 6869-3
The farmer talks. 6862-6
The father of the bride. 6748-4
The father of the groom. 6748-4
A father's job. 6869-3
Father's problem. 6869-3
A father's wish. 7033-7
Fear. 6869-3
A feller's hat. 7033-7
The fellowship of books. 7033-7
Feminine signs. 6748-4
The feminine touch. 6748-4
The fight with self. 6862-6
The fight worth while. 6862-6
The fighter. 6869-3
Final judgment. 6748-4
First look at the baby. 6748-4
The first steps ("Last night I held my arms to you"). 6078-1
The first tooth. 6869-3
The first watch. 6748-4
Fisherman's solitude. 6748-4
Fishin'-hunger. 6862-6
Fishing. 6374-8
The flag. 6356-X
Flatterers. 6748-4
Flirtation. 6748-4
The florist's story. 6748-4
Flower courage. 6869-3
Fly a clean flag. 6443-4
Food, clothes and drink. 6862-6
For others—and his wife. 6862-6
Forgetful Pa. 6465-5,6281-4
Forgotten boyhood. 7033-7
Found out. 6862-6
A friend's greeting. 6085-4
The friend. 6869-3
The gain. 6748-4
Garden experience. 6869-3
Gardening. 6862-6
Getting her a valentine. 6862-6
Gift from heaven. 6869-3
Gissing's sixpenny miracle. 6748-4
Give me a single day. 6862-6
Gladiolas. 6869-3
The glories of the present. 6862-6
The glory of age. 6862-6
God made this day for me. 6374-8
The gold star. 6846-4
Golf luck. 7033-7

Good friday. 6862-6
The good little boy. 7033-7
Gossip. 6862-6
Grace at table. 6869-3
Grandpa. 6401-9,6135-4
The grate fire. 7033-7
Green apple time. 7033-7
Growing up. 6748-4
The grumbling soldier. 6869-3
The gullible fishermen. 6748-4
Gypsy blood. 6748-4
Hail and farewell. 6748-4
Hand-painted china days. 6748-4
Happiness. 6869-3
The happy man. 7033-7
The happy toad. 6869-3
He's taken out his papers. 7033-7
A heart to heart talk. 6862-6
Hello, tulips. 6869-3
His chance. 6862-6
His first long trousers. 6862-6
His philosophy. 6862-6
Home. 6736-0
Home. 6732-8,6964-9
Home and office. 7033-7
Home ingredients. 6748-4
Home-makers. 6869-3
The homecomer's song. 6862-6
The homely man. 7033-7
The homes of joy. 6862-6
Honor. 6748-4
How did you tackle your work? 6291-1
How do you buy your money? 7033-7
The human alarm clock. 6869-3
The humble throng. 6748-4
Husbands. 6748-4
I ain't dead yet. 7033-7
I go home for lunch. 6748-4
I volunteer. 6748-4
'I want to better myself.' 6748-4
I'd rather be a failure. 7033-7
If I had youth. 6476-0
If I were Santa Claus. 6862-6
If this were all. 7033-7
The ill-tempered man. 6748-4
Incident. 6869-3
Incident at Bethlehem. 6748-4
Indebted. 6869-3
Independence day. 6862-6
The influence of woman. 6862-6
Innocence. 6869-3
Is there a Santa Claus? 6862-6
It couldn't be done. 6291-1,6736-0
Jimmy. 6862-6
Joseph of Arimathea. 6869-3
The joys of earth. 6862-6
The joys of home. 7033-7
The joys we miss. 7033-7
Just a boy. 7033-7
Keep to the right. 6862-6
The kick under the table. 7033-7
The killing pace. 6862-6
The kindergarten miss. 6862-6
The kindly neighbor, sels. 6337-3
The kindly neighbor. 6461-2
The king. 6748-4
Knowledge and doubt. 6748-4
Laddies. 6509-0
Landlord and tenant. 6869-3
The lanes of boyhood. 6862-6
The layman. 6869-3
Leader of the gang. 7033-7
Learn to smile. 7033-7
Let's be brave. 6211-3
Life. 6862-6
Life. 6748-4
life and hereafter. 6862-6
Life is what we make it. 7033-7
Life's highway. 6869-3
Life's single standard. 703-7

GUEST

The lilacs. 6862-6
Lillian's reading. 6862-6
The limitations of greatness. 6862-6
Linen and lace. 6869-3
Literary mother. 6862-6
Little battered legs grows up. 6748-4
Little by little. 6748-4
The little country drug store. 6869-3
Little girl. 6862-6
Little girls. 6135-4
Little girls are best. 7033-7
Little lady riches. 6869-3
Little miss six o'clock. 6862-6
The little old-fashioned church. 6862-6
The little sick girl. 6748-4
The little streets. 6748-4
A little the best of it. 6862-6
Little wrangles. 7033-7
Lonely. 7033-7
The lonely garden. 6846-4
The lonely man. 6748-4
Looking back. 7033-7
Looking back. 6862-6
Looking forward. 6748-4
Loss. 6748-4
Love. 6862-6
Love affair. 6748-4
Love of beauty. 6869-3
The lovely smile. 6869-3
The lucky man. 7033-7
Lullaby ("The golden dreamboat's ready"). 6401-9,6135-4
Luxury. 6748-4
Magazine girls. 6862-6
The making of friends. 6085-4
Making the best of it. 6869-3
Man. 6748-4
The man I'm for. 6862-6
A man must want. 6211-3
The man of his word. 6862-6
The man who is good to a boy. 6748-4
Man's experience. 6862-6
Man's name. 6748-4
Mark Twain. 6862-6
Marriages. 6869-3
The Martins. 6869-3
Masculine signs. 6748-4
The master. 6748-4
Me and ouija board. 7033-7
A meal-time reactionary. 6748-4
The meaning of loss. 6748-4
Memorial Day. 7033-7
Memorial day. 6862-6
Memory. 6748-4
Men and the dreamers. 6862-6
Men she could have married. 6748-4
Mice, absolutely free! 6869-3
Money. 6862-6
Mother. 6862-6
Mother Nature. 6862-6
The mother on the sidewalk. 6443-4
A mother thought. 6449-3
The mother watch. 6097-8
Mother's Day. 6097-8
Mother's glasses. 6097-8
Mother's knee. 6365-9
Mother's party dress. 6862-6
The mother. 6748-4
The mothers at the windows. 6748-4
My Bible. 6337-3
My choice. 6748-4
My creed. 6337-3
My paw said so. 6401-9
My plan. 6862-6
My religion. 7033-7
My word! 6862-6
Myself. 6337-3
Neighboring. 6869-3
The neighbors. 6862-6
New method of thinking. 6748-4
The New Year's caller. 6862-6

A new year's wish. 6862-6
The next generation. 6748-4
No better land than this. 7033-7
No children! 7033-7
No room for hate. 7033-7
No use signin'. 7033-7
Noisy place. 6869-3
Not a man's job. 6748-4
Not so fast! 6748-4
Nothing to laugh at. 7033-7
Nothing unusual. 6862-6
The notion of rastus. 6862-6
November. 6869-3
An ode to Nellie. 6862-6
Of such stuff is memory. 6748-4
The old and the new way. 6869-3
The old days 6862-6
An old employer talks. 6748-4
Old friends. 6085-4
Old gray-beard annuals. 6748-4
The old hot-dog wagon. 6748-4
Old mister laughter. 7033-7
Old years and new. 7033-7
The old-fashioned cooks. 6862-6
The old-time sitting room. 6748-4
On lying down. 6748-4
On station farewells. 6862-6
On traveling. 6631-3
One kindly deed. 6869-3
The ordinary folks. 6869-3
The ordinary man's adventure. 6748-4
Orphans of the living. 6748-4
Other's success. 6862-6
Our house. 6135-4
Our little needs. 6862-6
Out in the open. 6862-6
Out of the day. 6862-6
Pa and the monthly bills. 7033-7
Pack peddler. 6748-4
Paging Mr. McGregor. 6401-9
Paid in advance. 6869-3
Parental pride. 6869-3
Parents. 6748-4
The path to home. 6359-4
Patience. 6869-3
The pay envelope. 6748-4
The peaks of valor. 7033-7
Permanent. 6748-4
Pixley folks. 6862-6
A place at the top. 6862-6
The plain road. 6869-3
Plant a garden. 6869-3
Plato in a taxi. 6748-4
Playing father. 6869-3
Practicing time. 6249-0
Prayer ("Strengthen us"). 6869-3
Prayer for strength. 6748-4
Prayer for the home, sels. 6337-3
A prayer. 6862-6
Preparations for departure. 6748-4
Pretending not to see. 7033-7
Prisoner at the bar. 6869-3
The prodigal's return. 6869-3
Progress. 6748-4
The proof of a golfer. 6869-3
The proud pheasant. 6869-3
The pup. 6510-4
Questioning. 6748-4
The quitter. 6748-4
A rabbit moves in. 6748-4
Rabbits. 6869-3
Radio. 6869-3
The radio. 6449-3
The railroad engineer. 6748-4
Rather stay home. 6862-6
Real people. 6869-3
The real sport. 6748-4
The reason for work. 6862-6
Reputation. 6748-4
Results and roses. 6232-6,6338-1

Reunited. 6862-6
The rewards of industry. 6862-6
The rich man's woes. 6862-6
The right family. 6862-6
Ripe old age. 6748-4
Roadside table. 6748-4
Roses, birds and some men. 6862-6
The runaway. 6748-4
Runner McGee. 6846-4
Safe at home. 7033-7
The safe golfer. 6869-3
St. Valentine. 6869-3
The salesman. 6748-4
Satisfied with life. 7033-7
The score. 6869-3
See it through. 6291-1
Self-importance. 6869-3
Self-respect. 6748-4
September. 6862-6
Sermons we see. 6337-3
Service. 6869-3
She mothered five. 7033-7
She powders her nose. 7033-7
The sidewalks of life. 6748-4
The simple things. 7033-7
Since I have done my best. 6862-6
Sittin' on the porch. 7033-7
Sleeping child. 6869-3
Sleigh bells. 6748-4
Some day. 6862-6
Some other time. 6748-4
Somebody spoke a cheering word. 6862-6
The song of the builder. 7033-7
A song. 6862-6
A song. 6862-6
Songs of gloom. 6862-6
The songs of night. 6862-6
The spendthrift. 6862-6
The spoiler. 7033-7
Starting out. 6869-3
Stick to it. 6211-3
Street scene. 6748-4
Strength. 6748-4
Success. 6862-6
A successful dad. 6862-6
The summer argument. 6862-6
Summer dreams. 7033-7
The summer girl. 6862-6
Sunday in the country. 6862-6
Sunrise. 6374-8
Supper's ready. 6869-3
The sweetest soul I ever knew. 6862-6
Sympathy. 6862-6
Talk over there. 6748-4
Tea and toast. 6748-4
The tempters. 6862-6
The temptress. 6869-3
Ten-year-pld. 6869-3
The test. 6748-4
Thanksgiving Day. 6748-4
There will always be something to do. 6291-1
They didn't know. 6748-4
They're coming back. 6862-6
They're lsughing now. 6748-4
The things eternal. 6748-4
The things that haven't been done before. 6291-1
The things you can't forget. 7033-7
Think happy thoughts. 6862-6
This he asked. 6748-4
Those candid pictures. 6748-4
Those duty calls. 6869-3
Those first long trousers. 6869-3
Thought for the brave. 6869-3
The three me's. 7033-7
Thumbing through life. 6748-4
The tinsmith goes above. 6869-3
To a little girl. 7033-7
To a young man. 6291-1
To all parents. 6748-4
To an old friend. 7033-7

To the failures. 6862-6
To the father. 6748-4
Today. 6862-6
Too big a price. 7033-7
The town of nothing-to-do. 6862-6
the tragedy of age. 6862-6
The trick. 6748-4
The trickster. 6748-4
Trophies. 6869-3
Trouble being friends. 7033-7
The troublesome boy. 6748-4
True delight. 6869-3
The true man. 7033-7
Tuffy. 6869-3
Twenty-five years. 6869-3
Two sentimentalists. 6869-3
The two side. 6748-4
Two sources of wealth. 6748-4
Two viewpoints. 6862-6
Two windows. 6748-4
An uncle. 6862-6
Under a tree. 6862-6
Undoing a college education. 6748-4
Unpurchasable. 6748-4
Up and down the lanes of love. 6862-6
Upsy-daisy. 6748-4
The vagabond. 6374-8
Valentine. 6748-4
A valentine. 6862-6
A vanished joy. 7033-7
Victim of fear. 6869-3
Victory. 6748-4
"Wait till your pa comes home". 7033-7
Walking the boy. 6748-4
Warning to children. 6869-3
Washington. 6869-3
The way of the world. 6862-6
The way to do. 6862-6
The way to make friends. 6862-6
The wayward. 6869-3
We're dreamers all. 7033-7
Weariness. 6869-3
Wedding plans. 6869-3
Weeds. 6748-4
Weight gainer. 6401-9
What a baby costs. 6078-1
What a sick woman does. 6862-6
What father knows. 6102-8,6076-5,6102-8
What home's intended for. 7033-7
What I call living. 7033-7
What I want. 6748-4
What is success? 7033-7
What makes an artist. 7033-7
What makes the game. 6869-3
What matters it? 6748-4
What to do. 6862-6
What we need. 7033-7
What's in it for me? 6869-3
When day is done. 7033-7
When father played baseball. 6449-3
When friends drop in. 7033-7
When I sing. 6748-4
When life is done. 6337-3
When ma wants something new. 7033-7
When mother's sewing buttons on. 7033-7
When Pa gets back. 6862-6
When sorrow comes. 7033-7
When the baby arrives. 6869-3
When the dressmaker comes. 6862-6
When the minister calls. 7033-7
When we play the fool. 7033-7
When we understand the plan. 7033-7
When we were kids. 6862-6
When we're all alike. 7033-7
Where children play. 7033-7
'Where's mamma?'. 7033-7
Why I'm glad. 6862-6
The wide outdoors. 7033-7
The willing horse. 7033-7
Winds of the morning. 6862-6

Winter. 6748-4
Winter in the garden. 6748-4
Wisdom. 6869-3
A wish. 6862-6
With dog and gun. 7033-7
Wives. 6748-4
Woman and her mirror. 6748-4
A woman's love. 6862-6
A woman's ways. 6862-6
Women. 6748-4
A wonderful world. 6862-6
Wondering. 6748-4
Woodrow Wilson. 7001-9
The work of summer. 6869-3
The world and Bud. 7033-7
The world is against me. 6291-1
The worry-chaser. 6862-6
The wrist watch man. 6443-4
X-ray pictures of two men. 6748-4
The yellow dog. 6510-4
You and your boy. 6862-6
The youngest child. 6748-4
Zinnias. 6869-3
The guest. Thomas Ashe. 6094-3
The guest. Jorge Carrera Andrade. 6759-X
The guest. Harriet McEwen Kimball. 6680-1
The guest. Gertrude Huntington McGiffert. 6838-3
The guest. Emma Celia & Lizzie J. Rook. 6137-0
The guest. Unknown. 6337-3,6150-8,6563-5
Guests. David Morton. 6850-2
Guests. Unknown. 6427-2,6153-2
The guests of night. Bayard Taylor. 6976-2
The guests. Richard Lawson Gales. 6216-4
Guhyakali. Unknown (Newari) 7013-2
Guidance. Alanson Tucker Schumann. 6266-0
Guidance. William Shakespeare. 6438-8
"The guidance of the human race". Thought. Edward R. Huxley. 6885-5
"Guide me through the day, dear father". Prayer ("Guide me"). Lutie Price Leslie. 6270-9
Guide me, O thou great Jehovah! W. Williams. 6521-X
Guide me, O thou great Jehovah! William Williams. 6219-9
The guide post. Unknown. 6924-X
Guide us. Mrs. T. B. Epting. 6818-9
Guido and Marina. Thomas Hood. 6974-6
Guido Ferranti. Oscar Wilde. 6672-0
"Guido, I would that Lapo, thou, and I". Sonnet: To Guido Cavalcanti. Dante Alighieri. 7039-6
Guild, Marion Pelton
   Hear, O America! 7001-9
   The perfect love. 6006-4
   The perfect lyric. 6006-4
   The ultimate love. 6006-4
Guild, Thatcher H.
   My rose and hers. 6118-4
The guileless witness. Unknown. 6294-6
Guilielmus rex. Thomas Bailey Aldrich. 6439-6,6484-1
Guillaume, Edward H.
   Freethought. 7009-4
Guillen, Jorge
   Terrestial sphere. Frances Avery Pleak (tr.). 6068-4
   Terrestrial sphere. Francis Avery Pleak (tr.). 6068-4
Guillen, Nicolas
   Ballad of the Guije. H.R. Hays (tr.). 6642-9
   Ballad of the two grandfathers. H.R. Hays (tr.). 6642-9
   Big-lipped Negro. H.R. Hays (tr.). 6642-9
   Cantaliso in a bar. Langston Hughes (tr.). 6759-X
   Dead soldier. Langston Hughes (tr.). 6759-X
   Reveille at daybreak. H.R. Hays (tr.). 6642-9
   Sensemaya. H.R. Hays (tr.). 6642-9
   "Solder, I can't figure why". H.R. Hays (tr.). 6759-X
   Two children. H.R. Hays (tr.). 6759-X
   Visit to a tenement. Dudley Fitts (tr.). 6759-X
   Wake for Papa Montero. Langston Hughes (tr.). 6759-X
   Yellow Girl. H.R. Hays (tr.). 6642-9
Guilo. Ella Wheeler Wilcox. 6956-8
Guilt in solitude. Arthur John Lockhart. 7041-8
Guilty. Ruby Berkle Goodwin. 6178-8
Guilty. Frederick George Scott. 6021-8
Guilty. Irene Waage. 6799-9

Guilty. Marguerite Wilkinson. 6337-3
"Guilty before thee,/Helpless, undone". The petition. James Abraham Martling. 6952-5
Guilty conscience. William Shakespeare. 6102-8
Guilty or not guilty. Unknown. 6408-6,6523-6,6621-6,6744-1, 6742-5,6273-
Guimera, Angel
   The dance of the nuns. 6959-2
Guinea. Jacques Roumain. 6759-X
Guinea fowl. Winifred M. Letts. 6421-3
The guinea pig. Unknown. 6902-9
Guinevere to Lancelot. Robert Batson. 6385-3
Guinevere, fr. Idyls of the king. Alfred Lord Tennyson. 6669-0,6110-9,6199-0,6655-0
Guinevere, sels. Alfred Lord Tennyson. 6122-2
Guiney (atr.), Louise Imogen
   Out in the fields with God. 6337-3
Guiney, Louise Imogen
   After the storm. 7041-8
   Arboricide. 6096 X
   Athassel abbey. 6431-0
   Beati mortui. 6309-8
   Carol. 6437-X
   Carol ("The ox he openeth wide the doore.") 6746-8
   A carol ("Vines branching stilly.") 6746-8
   Cobwebs. 6338-1
   'Davy' 7008-6
   Deo optimo maximo. 6007-2
   Despotisms. 7027-2
   Doves. 6073-0,6501-5
   Fairy folk. 6965-7
   Fifteen epitaphs, sels. 6096 X
   Five carols for Christmastide. 6282-2
   A friend's lament for Simoisius. 6467-1
   In Leinster. 6437-X,6467-1
   Irish peasant song. 6310-1,6331-4,6431-0
   John Brown: a paradox. 6946-0
   The kings. 6464-7,6431-0,6250-4,6336-5,6026-5,6243-1, 6266-0,6501-5
   The knight errant. 6096 X
   Leinster. 6022-6,6292-X
   The light of the house. 7041-8
   Lover loquitur. 6441-8
   Memorial Day. 6820-0
   Memorial Day. 6340-3
   Nam semen est verbum dei. 6532-5
   Ode for a master mariner ashore. 6292-X,6172-9
   Of Joan's youth. 6096-X,6310-1,6300-4
   Open, time. 6431-0
   Out in the fields with God. 6374-8,6418-3,6730-1
   A passing song. 7041-8
   The poet. 7041-8
   Private theatricals. 6441-8
   Rooks! new college gardens. 6073-0
   Sanctuary. 6007-2,6309-8
   Song: In Leinster. 6467-1
   A talisman. 6161-3
   Tarpeia. 6688-7
   Tarpeia. 7041-8
   To a dog's memory. 6096-X,6431-0
   Tryst noel. 6300-4,6310-1,6437-X,6608-9,6292-X,6172-9
   Two epitaphs. 6431-0
   When on the marge of evening. 6096-X,6431-0
   "When on the marge of evening." 6019-6
   The wild ride. 6006-4,6303-9,6336-5,6102-8,6501-5,6732-8,6476-0,6161-3,6393-4,6292-X,6153-2,6076-5,6431-0, 6172-9,6467-1
Guinicelli, Guido
   Canzone: He perceives his rashness in love... Dante Gabriel Rossetti (tr.). 7039-6
   Canzone: of the gentle heart. Dante Gabriel Rossetti (tr.). 6325-X
   He will praise his lady. 6102-8
   Sonnet: Of moderation and tolerance. Dante Gabriel Rossetti (tr.). 7039-6
Guion, Madame De la Mothe
   The acquiescence of pure love. William Cowper (tr.). 6814-6
   Aspirations of the soul after God. William Cowper (tr.). 6814-6

A child of God longing to see him beloved. William Cowper (tr.). 6814-6
Divine justice amiable. William Cowper (tr.). 6814-6
Divine love endures no rival. William Cowper (tr.). 6814-6
The entire surrender. William Cowper (tr.). 6814-6
A figurative description of...procedure of divine love. William Cowper (tr.). 6814-6
Glory to God alone. William Cowper (tr.). 6814-6
God hides his people. William Cowper (tr.). 6814-6
God neither known nor loved by the world. William Cowper (tr.). 6814-6
Gratitude and love to God. William Cowper (tr.). 6814-6
Happy solitude - unhappy men. William Cowper (tr.). 6814-6
Joy in martyrdom. William Cowper (tr.). 6814-6
The joy of the cross. William Cowper (tr.). 6814-6
Living water. William Cowper (tr.). 6814-6
Love faithful in the absence of the beloved. William Cowper (tr.). 6814-6
Love increased by suffering. William Cowper (tr.). 6814-6
The love of God the end of life. William Cowper (tr.). 6814-6
Love pure and fervent. William Cowper (tr.). 6814-6
The Nativity. William Cowper (tr.). 6814-6
The necessity of self-abasement. William Cowper (tr.). 6814-6
The perfect sacrifice. William Cowper (tr.). 6814-6
Repose in God. William Cowper (tr.). 6814-6
Scenes favourable to meditation. William Cowper (tr.). 6814-6
The secrets of divine love are to be kept. William Cowper (tr.). 6814-6
Self-diffidence. William Cowper (tr.). 6814-6
Self-love and truth incompatible. William Cowper (tr.). 6814-6
Simple trust. William Cowper (tr.). 6814-6
The soul that loves God finds him every where. William Cowper (tr.). 6814-6
The swallow. William Cowper (tr.). 6814-6
The testimony of divine adoption. William Cowper (tr.). 6814-6
The triumph of heavenly love desired. William Cowper (tr.). 6814-6
Truth and devine love rejecyed by the world. William Cowper (tr.). 6814-6
The vicissitudes experienced in the Christian life. William Cowper (tr.). 6814-6
Watching unto God in the night season. William Cowper (tr.). 6814-6
Watching unto God in the night season (2). William Cowper (tr.). 6814-6
Watching unto God in the night season (3). William Cowper (tr.). 6814-6

Guirk, Berta G.
Lines to a philanderer. 6750-6

Guitar. Iosif Utkin. 6546-5
Guitare. Victor Hugo. 6677-1
Guitare. Victor Hugo. 6801-4

Guiterman, Arthur
Anthologistics. 6722-0
Apology. 6875-8
An April romance. 6773-5
The ballad of John Paul Jones. 6773-5
Ballade of caution. 6875-8
Ballade of dime novels. 6875-8
Barcarole. 6331-4,6439-6
A bill from Cupid. 6320-9
Blessing on little boys. 6619-4
The block-house in the park. 6773-5
The blue hen's chickens. 6817-0
The book line. 6773-5
Borger Joris's hammer. 6773-5
Bowling green. 6773-5
A boy and his pup. 6510-4
Buttermilk channel. 6773-5
Call to the colors. 6274-1
The cardinal-bird. 6338-1
The change of flags. 6773-5
Chums. 6891-X
A city garden. 6773-5
City Hall park. 6773-5
The 'clermont' 6773-5
Columbines. 6232-6,6338-1
The coming of the trees. 6449-3
The country dance. 6959-2
The critics. 6773-5
Daniel Boone. 6891-X
A deal in real estate. 6773-5
Decatur's toast. 6773-5
The devil's stepping-stones. 6773-5
Dorlan's home-walk. 6628-3
A dreamer. 6773-5
Dutchman's breeches. 6773-5
Dutchman's quirk. 6773-5
The Dyckman house. 6773-5
The eagle. 6532-5
Edinburgh. 6331-4,6722-0
Education. 6337-3
Eight oars and a coxswain. 6773-5
Elegy. 6089-7
Elysium. 6320-9
Envy. 6503-1,6583-X
An explanation. 6817-0
Fashion. 6441-8
Fashions for fascists. 6761-1
The fate of the Hessian. 6773-5
The first Thanksgiving: Boston, 1631. 6618-6
The flying Dutchman of the Tappan Zee. 6161-3
Fort Tryon. 6773-5
Fraunces' tavern. 6773-5
Good news. 6503-1
Great is Diana of the mannahattoes! 6773-5
Haarlem heights. 6946-0
Haarlem Heights. 6773-5
The hall of fame. 6773-5
Hallowe'en charm. 6773-5
Hills. 6101-X,6102-8,6266-0,6337-3,6374-8,6653-4,6029-3, 6076-5,6464-7,6476-0,6732-8
House blessing. 6337-3,6654-2
The house of blazes. 6773-5
How are you? 6722-0
How Pearl street was paved. 6773-5
Hudson. 6773-5
Hudson's voyage. 6503-1
The idol-maker prays. 6556-2,6250-4
In the hospital. 6027-7,6303-9,6337-3,6556-2,6607-0, 6653-4,6730-1
Independence Square, Christmas 1783 6449-3
The inn: an old epitaph. 6773-5
The irreverent Brahmin. 6303-9,6307-1
Kissing bridge. 6773-5
Ku Klux. 6817-0
A legend of Maiden Lane. 6773-5
The legend of the Bronx. 6773-5
The legend of the first cam-u-el. 6089-7,6102-8,6076-5, 6026-9,6464-7
A lilt in fall. 6773-5
Little lost pup. 6512-0,6107-9,6510-4
The London Bobby. 6331-4,6439-6
The Lord of the Dunderberg. 6773-5
Mary Murray of Murray Hill. 6773-5
A mascot. 6510-4
Mavrone. 6089-7
A melancholy beaver. 6509-0
Messire Geoffrey Chaucer to his editor. 6464-7
Mexican serenade. 6089-7
Minetta water. 6773-5
Montgomery's return. 6773-5
A New Mexican bo-peep. 6628-3
New York. 6773-5
Of bragging, fr. Proverbs. 6861-8
Of courtesy, fr. Proverbs. 6861-8
Of courtesy, fr. Proverbs. 6861-8
Of explanations, fr. Proverbs. 6861-8
Of flowers and bees, fr. Proverbs. 6861-8
Of giving, fr. Proverbs. 6861-8
Of indomitability. 6861-8
Of industry, fr. Proverbs. 6861-8

GUITERMAN

Of magnanimity, fr. Proverbs. 6861-8
Of order, fr. Proverbs. 6861-8
Of packs and burdens. 6861-8
Of persistence. 6861-8
Of quarrels, fr. Proverbs. 6861-8
Of sportsmanship. 6861-8
Of vigor. 6861-8
Off Fire Island. 6773-5
The old 'constitution' 6773-5
An old road. 6773-5
Old trinity. 6773-5
On the Harlem. 6773-5
On the vanity of earthly greatness. 6722-0,6375-6
The Oregon Trail. 6891-X
Our colonel. 6465-5
Our colonel. 6773-5
Our Colonel. 6995-9
The palisades. 6773-5
Parable. 6875-8
Passion. 6441-8
The Pilgrims' Thanksgiving feast. 6722-0
The pioneer. 6861-8
The pioneer. 6478-7
The pirate's spuke. 6773-5
A plea. 6441-8
The poem on spring. 6307-1
A poet's proverb. 6337-3
Polly Cortelyou. 6773-5
Possession. 6773-5
Proverbs, sels. 6861-8
A pure mathematician. 6460-4
Pussy-willows. 6653-4
The quest of the Ribband. 6628-3
Quivira. 6614-3
The rag dolly's valentine. 6249-0
Ragnarok: the twilight of the gods. 6846-4
A raid of the neutral ground. 6773-5
Rambout Van Dam. 6773-5
The rattle-watch of New Amsterdam. 6773-5
The river. 6773-5
The road. 6773-5
The rough riders. 6995-9
The rush of the Oregon. 6274-1
Saxon harvest health. 6773-5
A scandal in New Amsterdam. 6773-5
A sea charm. 6773-5
Sea-chill. 6374-8
The Shakesperean bear. 6089-7
The silver canoe. 6619-4
A skater's valentine. 7035-3
A sketch from life. 6089-7
Sleepy hollow. 6773-5
A song in June. 6773-5
A springtime pilgrimage. 6773-5
The storm ship. 6773-5
Storm signals. 6773-5
The storming of Stony Point. 6946-0,6773-5
Strictly germ proof. 6089-7,6102-8,6488-4,6497-3,6501-5, 6583-
Strictly germ-proof. 6732-8,6464-7,6396-9,6736-0,6076-5
Than God for a man! 6995-9
The thank-offering. 6773-5
Theodore Roosevelt's letters to his children. 6995-9
This is she. 6441-8,6307-1
Thunder-storm. 6773-5
To Commodore Matthew Calbraith Perry. 6761-1
A tract for autos. 6497-3,6628-3
A trial in New Amsterdam. 6773-5
Tubby Hook. 6773-5
Tulips. 6338-1
Uncle Sam to John Bull. 6773-5
Under the Christmas tree. 6147-8
Under the goal posts. 6107-9
Under the Palisades. 6773-5
The vizier's apology. 6464-7
The voice unto pharaoh. 6954-1
Voorrede. 6773-5
Washington in Wall Street. 6773-5
What the gray cat sings. 6465-5
William the testy. 6773-5

Wind-in-the-hair and rain-in-the-face. 6476-0,6607-0
Wizard's well. 6773-5
Young Washington. 6891-X
Zenger the printer. 6773-5
Guiterman, Eleanor
Class song. 6847-2
Gulchin
The curtain fell. A.J. Arberry (tr.). 6448-5
Gulf lightning. Jules Laforgue. 6351-9
Gulf of Mexico. Alfonso Reyes. 6759-X
Gulf stream. Sarah ("Susan Coolidge") Woolsey. 6833-2
The **gulf** stream. Henry Bellamann. 6833-2
Gulf-weed. Cornelius George Fenner. 6271-7,6302-0,6385-3, 6219-9
The **gulf**. Denise Levertov. 6803-0
Gulistan, sels. Sadi [or Saadi] (Mushlih-ud-Din) 7039-6
Gull. Glyn Jones. 6360-8
Gull lake. Marjorie Mills. 6342-X
Gull passage by moonlight. Milton Acorn. 6767-0
"The **gull** shall whistle in his wake, the...". The voortrekker. Rudyard Kipling. 7012-4
"The **gull-flight** his—the long flight...". Lindbergh. Helen Byrom Griggs. 7019-1
A **gull**.. Robert Hillyer. 6331-4
Gulla lullaby. Josephine Pinckney. 6039-0
The **gullah** cry. Eleanor Fox Ponder. 6750-6
The **gullible** fishermen. Edgar A. Guest. 6748-4
Gullickson, Orpha
Autumn tumbleweeds. 6342-X
A **gulling** sonnet. Sir John Davies. 6182-6
Gulliver, H.S.
The crystal. 6841-3
On entering Palestine. 6841-3
Out of the bog. 6841-3
To Martigny. 6841-3
Gulls. George Kuttner. 6900-2
Gulls. Jean Starr Untermeyer. 6072-2
Gulls. William Carlos Williams. 6208-3
Gulls in an aery morrice. William Ernest Henley. 6655-0
Gulls over Great Salt Lake. Ross Sutphen. 6073-0
Gulls: summer. Louise Owen. 6761-1
The **gulls**. Anna Lee Tomkins. 6799-9
The **gully**, sels. Frank ("Furnley Maurice") Wilmot. 6384-5
"**Gulping** air, two of them". Why don't they go back to Transylvania? Robert Peters. 6792-1, 6998-3
The **gum** gatherer. Robert Frost. 6393-4
Gumilev, Nikolai
The captains. Cecil Maurice Bowra (tr.). 6103-6
How could we, beforehand, live in quiet. Jeannette Eyre (tr.). 6665-8
I and you. Vivian de Sola Pinto (tr.). 6103-6
Loneliness. Cecil Maurice Bowra (tr.). 6103-6
"A **gun** is heard at the dead of night". A race for life. James Lyman Molloy. 6924-X
Gun-teams. Gilbert Frankau. 6510-4
Gundry, Arthur W.
My cigar. 6453-1
Gunga Din. Rudyard Kipling. 6211-3,6162-1,6332-2,6451-5, 6499-X,6107-9,6396-9,6964-9
Gunkle, Olga Edith
Punctuation language. 6750-6
Gunn's leg. Unknown. 6744-1,6167-2
Gunnar's holm. Jonas Hallgrimsson. 6854-5
The **gunner** and the bird. Emma Celia & Lizzie J. Rook. 6137-0
The **gunners**. Gertrude Bartlett. 6115-X
Gunning off clapboard. K.G. Huntress. 6761-1
Gunnison, Elisha Norman
Betty Lee. 6167-2,6569-4
Old Huldah. 6914-2
Guns above the song. I.D. Perry. 6316-0
"**Guns** and knives aren't enough". Circled by a housefly. Helen G. Quigless. 7024-8
Guns as keys: and the great gate swings. Amy Lowell. 6031-5
The **guns** in Sussex. Sir Arthur Conan Doyle. 7031-0,7027-2
The **guns** in the grass. Thomas Frost. 6946-0
Guns of peace. Dinah Maria Mulock Craik. 7015-9
Guns of Verdun. Patrick Reginald Chalmers. 6224-5
"**Guns/he** kept his". My daddy read Luke Short, baby.

Barbara Gravelle. 6901-0
The **guns**. Stephen Vincent Benet. 6542-2
Gunsaulus, Frank W.
   Be sure. 6889-8
   The goal. 6337-3
Gunslinger. Dennis Kelly. 7003-5
Gurley, James M.
   One hour into my watch Camp Lejeune. 6900-2
Gurley, Phineas Densmore
   The funeral hymn. 6524-4
Gurney, Arthur
   Come, ye lofty. 6219-9
Gurney, Dorothy Frances
   A garden in Venice. 6338-1
   God's garden. 6337-3,6654-2
   'The Lord God planted a garden'. 6338-1,6730-1
   O perfect love. 6337-3
Gurney, Ivor
   To the poet before battle. 6250-4
Gurney, J.H.
   William Tell. 6131-1
The **Guru** Granth, sels. Puran Singh. 6732-8
Gustaf of Leopold, Karl
   A legacy. Charles Wharton Stork (tr.). 6045-5
Gustafson, Ralph
   Anatomy of melancholy. 6767-0
   Biography. 6021-8
   The broken pianola. 6767-0
   Dedication. 6021-8
   Flight into darkness. 6446-9
   Mythos. 6446-9
   "On such a wet and blustery night." 6446-9
   On the Struma massacre. 6979-7
   Quebec sugarbush. 6021-8
   "S.S.R., lost at sea." 6446-9
   Seascape. 6021-8
   Thaw. 6021-8
   A window, a table, on the north. 6446-9
Gustam, Ella Gertrude
   She got it. 6702-6
A **gustatory** achievement. James Whitcomb Riley. 6091-9
"**Gustavo** Adolfo Becquer, who in...slumber". Elegy for Becquer. Enrique Pena Barrenechea. 6759-X
"**Gustavo** said,/'Your poems are like samba'". What the rooster does before mounting. Cyn. Zarco. 6790-5
Gustavus II (G. Adolphus); King of Sweden
   Battle hymn. Catherine Winkworth (tr.). 6730-1
"**Gusts** of the sun race on the approaching sea". Of Thomas Traherne and the pebble outside. Sidney Clouts. 6788-3
"**Gusty** and raw was the morning". The fight of Paso del Mar. Bayard Taylor. 6976-2
Guta's song. Charles Kingsley. 6541-4
Gutersloh, Albert Paris
   Alexandra's fourteenth birthday. Milne Holton and Herbert Kuhner (tr.). 6769-7
   August of life. Milne Holton and Herbert Kuhner (tr.). 6769-7
   The boy awakens. Milne Holton and Herbert Kuhner (tr.). 6769-7
   Intuition. Milne Holton and Herbert Kuhner (tr.). 6769-7
   Preface. Milne Holton and Herbert Kuhner (tr.). 6769-7
Gutherie, Thomas Anstey ("F. Anstey")
   Burglar Bill. 6633-X
Guthrey, E. Bell
   'He done his damdest' 7012-4
Guthrie, James
   Last song. 6269-5
   Of Eden. 6269-5
   Those pinafore girls. 6269-5
Guthrie, Kenneth Sylvan
   The robber. 6102-8
Guthrie, Ramon (tr.)
   After the flood. Arthur Rimbaud. 6343-8
Gutierrez Hermosillo, Alfonso
   Earth. Dudley Fitts (tr.). 6759-X
   Fugue. Dudley Fitts (tr.). 6759-X
The **guts** of the army. Unknown. 6237-7
Guttenbrunner, Michael
   The descent. Milne Holton and Herbert Kuhner (tr.). 6769-7
   Hitler and the generals. Milne Holton and Herbert Kuhner (tr.). 6769-7
   Homecoming. Milne Holton and Herbert Kuhner (tr.). 6769-7
   The patient. Milne Holton and Herbert Kuhner (tr.). 6769-7
   Val d'Annivier. Milne Holton and Herbert Kuhner (tr.). 6769-7
Gutter rats. Eldon George McLean. 6178-8
Gutteridge, Bernard
   Burma hills. 6666-6
   Namkwin Pul. 6666-6
   Patrol: Buonamary. 6666-6
Guttormsson, Guttormur J.
   Canada. Jakobina Johnson (tr.). 6854-5
   Good night. Jakobina Johnson (tr.). 6854-5
   The soul of the house. Skuli Johnson (tr.). 6854-5
"**Guvener** B. is a sensible man". What Mr. Robinson thinks. James Russell Lowell. 6760-3
Guy. Ralph Waldo Emerson. 6252-0
Guy Faux's night. William Barnes. 6018-8
Guy Fawkes. Unknown. 6385-3,6003-X
Guyon, Jeanne Marie Bouvier de la Motte
   Adoration. 6730-1
   By thy life I live. 6337-3
   A little bird I am. 6730-1,6214-8
   A prisoner's song. 6337-3
   Since God is there. William Cowper (tr.). 6337-3
Gwalchmai
   The triumphs of Owen. Thomas Gray (tr.). 6528-7
Gwendolen. Hattie Tyng Griswold. 6690-9
Gwendoline. Bayard Taylor. 6440-X
Gwendydd's song, fr. Merlin. John Veitch. 6819-7
Gwilym, Dafydd Ab
   The summer. 6873-1
Gwilym, Davydd Ab
   To the lark. 6873-1
Gwine to marry Jim. D.A. Ellsworth. 6710-7
Gwine up ter heab'n. Louise Ayres Garnett. 6036-6
Gwylym, David Ap
   The mass of the birds. 6943-6
Gwynn, Edward (tr.)
   The enchanted fawn, fr. 'Dinnshenchas' Unknown, 6930-4
   Tara, fr. 'Dinnshenchas' Unknown, 6930-4
Gwynn, Stephen (tr.)
   The woman of Beare. Unknown, 6244-X
Gwynn, Stephen Lucius
   The captive polar bear. 6510-4
   Cowslips. 6174-5
   Glencar. 6872-3
   Inscription for a fountain. 6244-X
   Ireland. 6090-0,6174-5
   Mater severa. 6793-X
   Out in the dark. 6174-5
   A song of defeat. 6090-0
   The woman of Beare. 6174-5
Gwynne, J. Harold
   The good shepherd ("I know mine own..."). 6065-X
Gwynneth, John
   My love that mourneth for me. 6756-5
Gyda of Varsland. Anne Virginia Culbertson. 6680-1
The **gymnastic** clock. Mary Carolyn Davies. 6638-0
Gymnastic game. Unknown. 6706-9
Gyoson
   "In lonely solitude I dwell". William N. Porter (tr.). 6852-9
Gypsies. Robert Browning. 6466-3
Gypsies. Rachel (Lyman) Field. 6554-X
Gypsies. Elizabeth Voss. 6906-1
The **gypsies'** road. Dora Sigerson Shorter. 6437-X,6507-4
The **gypsies**.. Daniel Corkery. 6096 X
The **gypsies**. Sir Henry Howarth Bashford. 6490-6
Gypsy. Vojislav Ilic. 6765-4
The **gypsy** and the snowman. Ford Madox (Hueffer) Ford. 6228-8
Gypsy blood. Edgar A. Guest. 6748-4
The **gypsy** flower girl. Edward L. McDowell. 6695-X
The **gypsy** girl. Ralph Hodgson. 6332-2,66464-7

GYPSY

The **gypsy** heart. Harry Noyes Pratt. 6102-8,6476-0,6076-5
The **gypsy** heart. Aidna Van Orden. 6847-2
The **gypsy** laddie. Unknown. 6058-7,6185-0
The **gypsy** laddie. Unknown. 6826-X
Gypsy nights, sels. Jake Zeitlin. 6072-2
Gypsy song. Johann Wolfgang von Goethe. 6490-6
A **gypsy** song. Unknown. 6274-1
Gypsy tapestry. Selma Hamann. 6906-1
Gypsy's violin. Ida Steele Osgood. 6799-9
The **gypsy's** wedding day. Unknown. 6058-7
Gypsy-heart. Katharine Lee Bates. 6266-0,6476-0,6374-8
The **gypsy**.. Eleanor Farjeon. 6236-9
The **gypsy**. Henry Bellaman. 6778-6
The **gypsy**. Langston Hughes. 6628-3
The **gypsy**. Alfred Noyes. 6151-6
The **gypsy**. Wilfrid Thorley. 6778-6
The **gypsying**. Theodosia Garrison. 6374-8,6653-4

"H'it's h'easy to be 'appy". Don't you know. Edgar A. Guest. 6862-6
H.
   A message. 6116-8
   Pure and true and tender. 6226-1
H. and Whitley Stokes and John Stracah, K. (tr.)
   The scribe. Unknown. 6930-4
H.,B.
   Anacreon to the sophist. 6817-0
   Lines on the death of baby. 6486-8
H.,D. See Doolittle, Hilda
H.,E.
   George Nidiver. 6062-5,6271-7,6502-3,6438-8,6263-6
   To be continued. 6817-0
H.,E.S.
   The chimney sweep. 6438-8
   The nobly born. 6385-3,6438-8,6424-8
   Wayfarers. 6438-8
   The wood fire. 6438-8
H.,F.C. (tr.)
   The drunkard's conceit. Unknown (German), 6787-5
H.,G.
   Malapropos. 6770-0
H.,H.
   A baby show. 6965-7
H.,H. See Jackson, Helen Hunt
H.,H.M.
   Not blind. 6116-8
H.,J.
   Acrostic. 6453-1
   Today. 6889-8
H.,J.A.
   "The great, wild, free soul" 6995-9
H.,J.B.
   The inventin'est man. 6281-4
H.,J.L.
   1945. 6761-1
H.,J.V.
   Them was the nights. 6817-0
H.,L.J.
   Baby's complaint. 6131-1
H.,L.L.
   Advice. 7021-3
H.,M.J.
   War prayer. 6741-X
H.,M.K.
   Prayer hymn. 6144-3,6335-7,6144-3
H.,N.G.
   Any soldier son to his mother. 7031-0
H.,O.W.
   Crossing the ford. 6752-2
H.,P.
   Li'l pickaninny coon. 6118-4
H.,R.
   The battle of Monmouth. 6946-0
   Firelight. 6118-4
H.,R.D.
   Lullaby ("Hush thee, hush.") 6118-4
H.,T.S. (atr).

   Our own. 6568-6
H.,W.
   The granger and the gambler. 6451-5
   Happy shepherds, sit and see. 6122-2
H.,W.J.
   A college rowing song. 6116-8
'H.H.'.. John Huston Finley. 6102-8
H.M.S. Glory at Sydney. Charles Causley. 6258-X
H.M.S. Pinafore, sels. Sir William Schwenck Gilbert. 6120-6,6732-8
H.W.L.. John Nichol. 6656-9
"Ha de! May the goddess Sarasvati, whom I invoked..". Unknown (Newari) 7013-2
"Ha de, you nine Nagas and Indra..." Unknown (Newari) 7013-2
"Ha ha! ha ha! this world doth pass." Unknown. 6181-8,6317-9
"Ha! ha! I've found you out at last!". Meat on Friday. James Abraham Martling. 6952-5
"Ha! now you think you've cheated me. Oh, no!" John Dancer. 6317-9
Ha! Posanes, by my loss of peace tis shee! Unknown. 6563-5
"Ha, little one!". Failand. Thomas Edward Brown. 6809-X
Haaland, Erma
   1938 bonnets. 6799-9
Haarlem heights. Arthur Guiterman. 6946-0
Haarlem Heights. Arthur Guiterman. 6773-5
Haase, Emma Zinke
   'Tis laudable and honorable. 6799-9
Habakkuk
   Wall street, 600 B.C. 6954-1
Habakkuk III
   The prayer of Habakkuk. 6087-0
Habakkuk's prayer. William Broome. 6848-0
Habeas corpus. Helen Hunt Jackson. 7041-8
Habeas corpus. Helen Hunt Jackson. 6102-8,6730-1,6431-0, 6300-4,6076-5
Haberle, Betty
   My mother. 6548-1
Habet. Brian Hooker. 6118-4
Habib
   The wine-bearer. A.J. Arberry (tr.). 6362-4
Habington's sky. W. Habington. 7020-5
Habington, William
   Against them who lay unchastity to the sex of woman. 6562-7
   Caelum non animum. 6793-X
   Castara. 6271-7,6302-0,6385-5,6219-9
   Cognitabo pro peccato meo. 6189-3
   The compliment. 6022-6
   Description of Castara. 6099-4
   Elegies on George Talbot, esq. 6935-5
   "Fine young folly, though you wear". 6933-9
   Melancholy. 6315-2
   Night. 6271-7,6219-9
   Nox nocti indicat scientiam. 6194-X,6341-1,6189-3,6022-6,6150-8,6198-2,6315-2,6489-2,6563-5,6641-0
   Nox nocti indicat scientiam (David). 6933-9
   The queene of Arragon, sels. 6208-3
   Quoniam ego in flagella paratus sum. 6022-6,6022-X
   Recogitabo tibi omnes annos meos. 6022-6
   The reward of innocent love. 6022-6,6194-X
   Swift in thy watery chariot. 6328-4
   "Time! where didst thou those years inter". 6931-2
   To Castara. 6315-2,6189-3
   To Cupid, upon a dimple in Castara's cheek. 6827-8
   To roses in the bosom of Castara. 6315-2,6563-5,6562-7,6491-4,6194-X,6092-7,6341-1
   To the moment last past. 6189-3
   Upon Castara's departure. 6563-5
   Upon the thought of age and death. 6023-4
   Upon thought Castara may die. 6022-6
   We saw and woo'd each other's eyes. 6737-9
   "Welcome, thou safe retreat". 6931-2
   'Welcome, thou safe retreat'. 6489-2
   What am I who dare. 6489-2
   "When I survey the bright celestial sphere". 6934-7
   "When I survey the bright". 6931-2
Habit. Edward R. Huxley. 6885-5
Habit is a cable; we weave a thread of it every". Horace

Mann. 6623-2
The habit of perfection. Gerard Manley Hopkins. 6292-X, 6096-X,6172-9,6655-0
The habitant's jubilee ode. William Henry Drummond. 6591-0, 6592-2
The habitant's summer. William Henry Drummond. 6793-X
The habitant. William Henry Drummond. 6433-7
The habitation of those who failed, fr. Tree of time. Gertrude Huntington McGiffert. 6838-3
Hachi no ki, sels. Seami. 6106-0
Hack and hew. Bliss Carman. 6656-9,6433-7,6732-8
Hackett, Eloise Wade
    Conventionality. 6337-3
    The giant pen. 6342-X
Hackett, Francis
    The dead aviator. 6292-X,6300-4
    Harry Hawker. 6033-1
Hackley, B.
    Po' little Jude. 6682-8
"Had Adam stood in innocence till now". The almanack for 1738, sels. Nathaniel Ames. 6753-0
"Had Botticelli painted thee...". An epitaph (to F.F.). Gertrude Huntington McGiffert. 6838-3
Had Cain been Scot. John Cleveland. 6092-7
Had Christ not lived and died. Edith Lynwood Winn. 6335-7
"Had God no other heart but this". The jelly-fish. Robert P. Tristram Coffin. 7040-X
"Had I but known". The poet. Boris Pasternak. 6068-4
"Had I but the torrent's might". The death of Hoel. Thomas Gray. 6975-4
"Had I no revelation but thy voice". Bartimeus to the bird. John Banister Tabb. 6943-6
"Had I not cradled you in my arms". Pocahontas to her English husband, John Rolfe. Paula Gunn Allen. 7005-1
"Had I that fabled herb". The battle of the bight. Sir William Watson. 7027-2
"Had I the power to choose one priceless gift". The gift of love. Harriet Garret. 6799-9
"Had he and I...", fr. The dynasts. Thomas Hardy. 6726-3
Had I a cave. Robert Burns. 6302-0
Had I a golden pound. Francis Ledwidge. 6812-X,6292-X,6812-X
Had I a heart for falsehood framed. Richard Brinsley Sheridan. 6600-3
"Had I a heart for falsehood framed", fr. The duenna. Richard Brinsley Sheridan. 6934-7
"Had I a trumpet, and that trumpet fames." Thomas Carew (atr.) 6563-5
Had I but served my god. William Shakespeare. 6214-8
Had I not loved before. Ralph Cheyney. 6441-8
Had I some magic power. Christian Winther. 6555-4
Had I the choice. Walt Whitman. 6374-8
Had I wist. Algernon Charles Swinburne. 6424-8
"Had not the Lord, may Israel say". Psalm 124 Bible. 6848-0
Had sorrow ever fitter place. Samuel Daniel. 6182-6
Had there been peace. Edith Lovejoy Pierce. 6144-3
"Had this effulgence disappeared". Composed upon an evening of extraordinary splendor. William Wordsworth. 6110-9,6199-0,6828-6
"Had this fair figure which this frame display". On seeing a bust of Mrs Montague. Samuel Johnson. 6975-4
Had we but known. C.B. McAllister. 7001-9
"Had we but world enough, and time". Andrew Marvell. 6187-7
"Had we known then the years that lay ahead". Rime of retrospection. Walter M. Bastian. 6761-1
Had you been old. Elizabeth Hollister Frost. 6879-0
"Had you but herd her sing." Unknown. 6563-5
"Had you loved me". No, no, no! Walter De La Mare. 6905-3
"Had you taken Rom of story, you had taken...". The taking of Bagdad. Kadra Maysi. 7007-8
Had you waited. Ernest Dowson. 6274-1
Hadad. Sabine Baring Gould. 6848-0
Hadad. James Abraham Hillhouse. 6848-0
Hadad's description of the city of David. James Abraham Hillhouse. 6752-2
Hadad's description of the city of David. James Abraham Hillhouse. 6848-0

Hadad, sels. James Abraham Hillhouse. 6752-2
Hadasseh of Tiberias. M. E. B. 6848-0
Haddden, Florence English
    Pipestone national monument. 6342-X
Haddox, Dorothy
    Sonnet ("Once more"). 6316-0
    A white hound leaping. 6316-0
    Wolf. 6316-0
"Hades laid hand upon me...". Unknown. 6251-2
The Hades of science. Edward Willard Watson. 6482-5
Hadley, Clara Boynton
    To Beethoven. 6799-9
Hadley, Lizzie M.
    Christmas folk and the children. 6268-7
    His mother's cooking. 6426-4
    His mother's cooking. 6921-5
    Historical trees--told in rhyme. 6049-8
    Kittens and babies. 6921-5
    Kittens and babies. 6426-4
    The laurel wreath. 6268-7
    The months and holidays. 6268-7
    The months. 6745-X
    The rainbow fairies. 6638-0
    Resurrexit. 6268-7
    The Russian Santa Claus. 6147-8
    The story of Thanksgiving. 6268-7
    Thanksgiving exercise. 6178-0,6618-6
Hadley, Lzzie M.
    Kittens and babies. 6426-4
Hadley, Martha J.
    Hope. 6274-1
Hadramaut. Bayard Taylor. 6440-X
Hadrian Emperor (P. Aelius Hadrianus)
    Poor little, pretty, fluttering thing. Matthew Prior (tr.). 6289-X
    Troy restored. Sir William Marris (tr.). 6435-3
"Hadrian dead? Then thrust a bodkin straight". Pasquino on the death of Pope Hadrian VI. Jan Svatopluk Machar. 6886-3
Hadrian, Emperor
    The dying Christian to his soul. Alexander Pope (tr.). 7039-6
Hadsell, S.R. See Gould, C.N., jt. auth.
"Hadst thou stayed, I must have fled!". The legend beautiful. Henry Wadsworth Longfellow. 6661-5,6706-9, 6419-1,6114-1,6964-9
'Haec olim meminisse invabit'. Smeed [pseud]. 6817-0
Haefner, Jessie
    Bright intervals. 6799-9
    Eclipse. 6799-9
    Mirror paintings. 6799-9
"Haek! 'Tis the rush of the horses". The call. Francis William Bourdillon. 7027-2
Haenigsen, H.W.
    Listen, pigeon, bend an ear. 6722-0
"Haf you seen mine leedle Shonny?". Shonny Schwartz. Charles Follen Adams. 6175-3,6791-3
Hafiz
    Abou Ishak. 6102-8
    The beloved. R.A. Nicholson (tr.). 6448-5
    Comfort. Gertrude Bell (tr.). 6448-5
    Comrades, the morning breaks. Richard Le Gallienne (tr.). 6253-9
    Desire. Gertrude Bell (tr.). 6448-5
    The diwan of Hafiz, sels. G. L. Bell (tr.). 6732-8
    Friendly zephyr. J. Nott (tr.). 6448-5
    Full fair. John Payne (tr.). 6448-5
    Harvest. Richard Le Gallienne (tr.). 6448-5
    Lawful wine. Walter Leaf (tr.). 6448-5
    The lesson of the flowers. E.H. Palmer (tr.). 6448-5
    Love and wine. J. Richardson (tr.). 6448-5
    Love's language. Richard Le Gallienne (tr.). 6448-5
    My bosom grac'd. T. Law (tr.). 6448-5
    Nostalgia. Richard Le Gallienne (tr.). 6102-8
    Ode 006. Gertrude Lowthian Bell (tr.). 7039-6
    Ode 011. John Hindley (tr.). 7039-6
    A Persian sing. 6428-0
    A Persian song. Sir William Jones (tr.). 6528-7,6543-0
    A Persian song. T. Law (tr.). 6448-5
    Red rose. John Payne (tr.). 6448-

Revelation. R.A. Nicholson (tr.). 6448-5
Rose bloom. Gertrude Bell (tr.). 6448-5
Slave. J.H. Hindley (tr.). 6448-5
Strife. R.A. Nicholson (tr.). 6448-5
Swimming. Walter Leaf (tr.). 6448-5
Tidings of union. Gertrude Bell (tr.). 6448-5
To his departed mistress. 6102-8
Wild deer. A.J. Arberry (tr.). 6448-5

Hafsa
Exchange. A.J. Arberry (tr.). 6362-4
The shield. A.J. Arberry (tr.). 6362-4

Hafstein, Hannes
Nearing cold-dale. Jakobina Johnson (tr.). 6283-0
Nearing Cold-dale. Jakobina Johnson (tr.). 6854-5
Skarphedinn among the flames. Gudmund J. Gislason (tr.). 6854-5
Spring. Jakobina Johnson (tr.). 6283-0
The storm. Skuli Johnson (tr.). 6854-5
Valagils-river. Gudmund J. Gislason (tr.). 6854-5

The **hag** of Beare. Sean O'Faolain. 6582-1
"**Hag-haunted** men who stare too long at rivers". Dawn after Christmas. Elias Lieberman. 6954-1
The **hag**. Robert Herrick. 6604-6,6219-9,6660-7,6136-2,6228-8,6271-7,6334-9,6562-7
Hagar. Hartley Coleridge. 6848-0
Hagar. Sarah Hammond Kelly. 6880-4
Hagar. Eliza Poitevent Nicholson. 6683-6,6577-5
Hagar departed. Edward Everett Hale. 6848-0
Hagar in the desert. Mary Tighe. 6848-0
Hagar in the wilderness. Nathaniel Parker Willis. 6917-7, 6752-2,6848-0
Hagar's farewell. Augusta Moore. 6925-8,6848-0

Hagar, Lillian M.
Gifts. 6818-9

Hagarty, Sir J.H.
Funeral of Napoleon I. 6433-7
The sea. 6433-7

Hagedorn, Hermann
Abdiel-the-Syrian's chant of the kiss. 6944-4
Anniversary. 6347-0
Arab song. 6944-4
The boy and his mother. 6944-4
The boy in armor. 6490-6,6542-2
Broadway. 6250-4
The cabaret dancer. 6959-2
A chant on the terrible highway. 6944-4
The chasm. 6347-0
The cobbler of Glamorgan. 6944-4
Converse of angels. 6944-4
The crier in the night. 6944-4
Death and the lord. 6944-4
Departure. 6310-1,6300-4,6509-0
The devil and St. Donat. 6944-4
Discovery. 6266-0,6501-5
Doors. 6102-8,6467-1,6102-8,6076-5,6153-2,6506-6,6250-4, 6431-0,6556-2
The duke's layde. 6944-4
Early morning at Bargis. 6374-8
Epitaph. 6944-4
The eyes of God. 6347-0,6506-6,6619-4
The fiddler of Berlin. 6542-2
Fifteen. 6347-0
Fifth avenue, 1915 6954-1
The fighting scribe of Iona. 6944-4
Flood tide. 6501-5
The ghost. 6027-7,6347-0,6648-8
The greater birth. 6266-0,6648-8
The heart of youth, sels. 6532-5
Holiday. 6944-4
How spring came to New York. 6032-3
The hummingbird. 6338-1
Hymn for the victorious dead. 6051-X,6449-3
The infidel. 6944-4
The keepers of the nation. 6944-4
L'envoi (To-night on Madagascan..."). 6944-4
Ladders through the blue. 6501-5
Laneer. 6944-4
The last faring. 6944-4
The last Wabanaki. 6944-4
Lift upthe curtain, fr. The heart of youth. 6532-5

Light. 6761-1
The marketplace in Pievenick. 6944-4
Memory. 6944-4
The merciful ensign. 6327-6
Monna Vita. 6944-4
The mother in the house. 6097-8,6607-0,6365-9,6465-5, 6490-6
Music at twilight. 6944-4
An ode of dedication. 6031-5
On the senate's repudiation of an honorable compact. 6944-4
"Out of this cage my body". 6944-4
The peddler. 6944-4,7007-8
Pirates of Tortuga. 6599-6
Prayer during battle. 6476-0,6556-2,6653-4,6476-0
Prayer for the times. 6954-1
Prologue to morning. 6337-3
The pyres. 6474-4,6029-3,6336-5,6542-2
Rest at noon. 6338-1
Resurrection. 6542-2
The rhapsody of Abdiel-the Syrian for his beloved. 6944-4
The riders. 6443-4
Roosevelt. 6995-9
Shipwreck. 6944-4
The sickbed. 6944-4
Song ("There is a music..."). 6944-4
Song after rain. 6944-4
Song at ending day. 6944-4
Song is so old. 6310-1,6396-9
Song of the grail seekers. 6653-4
Starry night. 6337-3
The three false women of Llanlar. 6944-4
To the makers of song! 6031-5
'A traveler from a distant land'. 6031-5
The troop of the guard. 6499-X,6717-4,6714-4
The vigil of Padre Junipero. 6944-4
Warriors of the dream. 6347-0,6039-0
"The wild rose." 6467-1
Wings. 6944-4
The wool gatherer. 6944-4
"You who love beauty." 6039-0

Hagedorn, Jessica
Ming the merciless. 6790-5
Motown/Smokey Robinson. 6790-5
Song for my father. 6790-5
"The woman who thought she was more than a Samba" 6790-5

Hageman, Miller
The birds' convention. 6682-8
The cobra. 6166-4
The little white angel of Connemaugh. 6686-0
Periton's ride. 6682-8
The skylark. 6670-4

Hagen Walder. Alice Cary. 6969-X

Hagenau, Sir Reinmar von
A childish game. Jethro Bithell (tr.). 7039-6

Hager, Levi Lewis
Anniversary of the birth of Abraham Lincoln. 6524-4

Hager, Sudie Stuart
No time to die. 6750-6

Hagert, Charles Howard
Three strikes - out. 6936-3

Hagesichora. Alcman. 6435-3

Hagg, Esther Lloyd
A different way. 6144-3
His garments. 6144-3
They saw and believed. 6144-3

"**Haggard** faces and trembling knees". Ballade of misery and iron. George Carter. 6954-1
The **haggis** of Private McPhee. Robert Service. 6159-1
Hagiograph. Rayner Heppenstall. 6379-9

Hagthorpe, John
To time. 6563-5

Hahn, E. Adelaide
Ballade. 6847-2
The golden jubilee, Hunter College, 1870-1920 6847-2
The original slacker. 6847-2
Persicos odi, puer, apparatus. 6847-2
Propempticon. 6847-2

Student self-government. 6847-2
Hahn, Kimiko
   Dance instructions for a young girl. 6790-5
   Daughter. 6790-5
   A girl combs her hair. 6790-5
   When you leave. 6790-5
Hai-Jew, Dianne
   Days ago. 6790-5
   Foreign soil. 6790-5
   Thirst of the dragon. 6790-5
   This night. 6790-5
Haidee and Juan, fr. Don Juan. George Gordon, 6th Baron Byron. 6832-4
Haidee, fr. Canto II. George Gordon, 6th Baron Byron. 6110-9
Haight, Dorothy
   What Bobbie dreamed. 6039-0
Haight, Sylvia M.
   Montana. 6662-3
Haiku. Louis Cuneo. 6792-1
Haiku. Georgia Kunz. 6899-5
"Hail and farewell". Ships that sail in the night. Dysart McMullen. 6846-4
Hail and farewell. George Gordon, 6th Baron Byron. 6322-5
Hail and farewell. Edgar A. Guest. 6748-4
Hail Bishop Valentine, fr. An epithalamium... John Donne. 6125-7
"Hail and farewell to those who fought & died". The dead. John Le Gay Brereton. 6784-0
"Hail and farewell! Lo, I am the last...". The last Gloucesterman. Gordon Grant. 6833-2
"Hail and farewell, across the clash of swords". Sir Stanley Maude. J. Griffyth Fairfax. 7029-9
"The hail falls pitterpat". Hail on the pine trees. Basho (Matsuo Basho). 6891-X
Hail fellow, well met. Albert Hardy. 6451-5
"Hail happy land, whose fertile grounds". The man, the cat, the dog, and the fly. John Gay. 6972-X
"Hail him- whom every world obeys!". Mishawake. James Abraham Martling. 6952-5
"Hail holy light, offspring...", fr. Paradise lost. John Milton. 6315-2;6240-7;6562-7;6726-3
Hail Lincoln's birthday. Ida Scott Taylor. 6709-3
"Hail holy light,ofspring of heav'n first-born". Light, fr. Paradise lost. John Milton. 6933-9
"Hail May, with fair queen and May-pole". May. Unknown. 6049-8
Hail man! Angela Morgan. 6730-1
Hail Mary, full of grace, mother in virginity. Unknown. 6756-5
"Hail native language, that by sinews weak". At a vacation exercise. John Milton. 6933-9
Hail on the pine trees. Basho (Matsuo Basho) 6891-X
"Hail sons of generous valor". To the defenders of New Orleans. Joseph Rodman Drake. 6946-0
Hail the eight-hour day. Sir Walter Scott. 6149-4
"Hail the flower whose early bridal". Arbutus. Elaine Goodale. 6049-8
"Hail the glorious Golden City". The city of the light. Felix Adler. 6954-1
"Hail thou, my native soil! Thou blessed plot" William Browne. 6935-5
Hail to mud!. Frances V. Stegeman. 6662-3
Hail to the chief who in triump advances,fr.The lady... Sir Walter Scott. 6828-6
Hail to the chief who in triumph advances! Sir Walter Scott. 6086-2,6110-9,6102-8
Hail to the Lord's anointed! James Montgomery. 6214-8
"Hail to the chief who in triumph advances!". Hail to the chief who in triump advances,fr.The lady... Sir Walter Scott. 6828-6
"'Hail to the chief' of bright renown". Grant. Benjamin Franklin Taylor. 6815-4
"Hail to the hero of the Arctic dare". To the top of the world. Edwin Markham. 7014-0
"Hail to the king!/Inge, the boy-king...". Inge, the boy king, sels. Hjalmar Hjorth Boyesen. 7002-7
Hail to the major. Melville Cane. 6654-2
"Hail to the merry autumn days...". Round. Charles Dickens. 7022-1

"Hail to the rosy morn, whose ray". Ode for his majesty's birthday, June 4, 1765. William Whitehead. 6867-7
Hail to thee, blithe spirit. Laura Simmons. 6076-5
"Hail to thee, boy, mighty one". Unknown. 6435-3
"Hail to thee, gallant foe!". Cervera. Bertrand Shadwell. 6946-0
"Hail to thee, hoary warder of this grove". The oak of Saint Boniface. Edward Farquhar. 6939-8
"Hail to thee, monarch of African mountains". Kilimandjaro. Bayard Taylor. 6976-2
Hail! Minnesota! Arthur Upson and Truman E. Rickard. 6465-5
Hail! South Dakota. Deecort Hammitt. 6465-5
"Hail! fairy queen, adorned with flowers". Song: the return of May. Felicia Dorothea Hemans. 6973-8
"Hail! hallowed spot! to names immortal dear!". The missionary's home. Charles W. Denison. 6755-7
"Hail! King I call thee". A lyric from a play. Unknown. 6881-2
"Hail! lake of the woodlands, with waters...". Long pond. Daniel Wing. 6798-0
"Hail! morning sun, thus early bright". Morning song. Gesner. 6973-8
"Hail! Power divine, whose sole command". Hymn on the power of God. James Thomson. 6816-2
"Hail! pretty emblem of my fate!". To the sunflower. Horace Walpole; 4th Earl of Orford. 6874-X
"Hail! seventy-four cut down! Hail,top and lop". To a decayed seaman. Thomas Hood. 6974-6
Hail! the glorious golden city. Felix Adler. 6730-1
Hail! to the veterans. N.K. Richardson. 6402-7
Hail, America. Frederic Lawrence ("R.L. Paget") Knowles. 6471-X,6223-7
"Hail, adamantine steel! magnetic lord". Steel, fr. The botanic garden. Erasmus Darwin. 6934-7
Hail, arbor day. Lizzie D. Roosa. 6049-8
"Hail, banner of our holy faith". The cross and the flag. William Henry, Cardinal O'Connell. 6846-4
"Hail, Father! whose creating call". Hymn to God the father. Samuel Wesley. 6931-2
Hail, bonny September! Dora Read Goodale. 6691-7
Hail, Columbia. Joseph Hopkinson. 6936-3,6015-3,6077-3, 6156-7,6176-1,6457-4,6471 ,6304-7,6449-3,6267-9,6300-4,6736-0,6121 ,6015-3,6077-3,6156-7,6176-1,6457-4, 6471
Hail, comely and clean. Unknown. 6756-5
"Hail, days of days! in peals of praise". Fortunatus (Venantius Honorius Clemantianus) 6065-X
Hail, fair morning, fr. Life of St. Cellach of Killala. Unknown. 6930-4
"Hail, gentle dawn! Mild blushing goddess...". The chace, sels. William Somervile. 6831-6
"Hail, glorious edifice, stupendous work!". Loyal effusion. Horace Smith. 6802-2
"Hail, great Apollo! guide my feeble pen". The British lyon roused. Stephen Tilden. 6946-0
"Hail, happy Britain, freedom's blest retreat". 'Prophecy'. Gulian Verplanck. 6946-0
Hail, holiest liberty. Thomas Cooper. 7009-4
Hail, holy cross! William White. 6868-5
Hail, maiden root. Caelius Sedulius. 6282-2
"Hail, meeek'd maiden, clad in sober grey". Ode to evening. Joseph Warton. 6831-6
"Hail, mildly pleasing solitude". Hymn on solitude. James Thomson. 6152-4,6816-2
"Hail, Pilot! lifting high". Pilot! Rita Berman. 7019-1
"Hail, noble prince of France!", fr. King John. William Shakespeare. 6323-3
"Hail, old patrician trees so great and good!" Alice B. Neal. 6049-8
Hail, old patrician...", fr. Several discourses... Abraham Cowley. 6562-7
Hail, Pennsylvania! Edgar Meck Dilley. 6936-3
"Hail, queen of plants,pride of Elsyian bowers". The tea table, fr. Panacea. Nahum Tate. 6867-7
"Hail, red hail". Glug-glug in salt sea. Robert Clairmont. 6751-4
"Hail, Roadian! hail, colossus! who dost stand". Ode to Mr. M'Adam. Thomas Hood. 6974-6
"Hail, St. Michael with the long spear!". A satire on the

HAIL,

people of Kildare. Unknown. 6930-4
"Hail, sword of Carroll! Oft hast thou been...". The song of Carroll's sword. Dallan (atr.) MacMore. 6930-4
"Hail, the quiet cattle!". Joan and Jesus. Ralph Cheyney. 6880-4
Hail, thou head! Saint Bernard of Clairvaux. 6065-X
"Hail, thou most sacred, venerable thing!". To darkness. John Norris. 6934-7
Hail, thou once despised Jesus. John Bakewell. 6065-X,6219-9,6065-X
"Hail, thou who shinest from the moon". He establisheth his triumph. Unknown (Egyptian). 7039-6
Hail, twilight, sels. William Wordsworth. 6867-7
Hail, vacation! Unknown. 6717-4
Hail, Vermont! Josephine Hovey Perry. 6465-5
Hail, wedlock! William Livingston. 6719-0
"Haile wedded love, mysterious law,true source". Wedded love, fr. Paradise lost. John Milton. 6933-9
"Haile! sterne superne. Haile! in eterne". A hymn to Mary. William Dunbar. 6881-2
Haile, Iris Lee
    Perhaps this time... 6750-6
'Hailing the doctor' in Vermont. Daniel L. Cady. 6988-6
"Haill! Quene of heven and steren of blis". A little hymn to Mary. Unknown. 6881-2
Haines, John
    Circles and squares. 6855-3
    Driving through Oregon (December 1973) 6855-3
    The eye in the rock. 6855-3
    Fairbanks under the solstice. 6855-3
    The head on the table. 6855-3
    If the owl calls again. 6855-3
    Listening in October. 6855-3
    Missoula in a dusty light. 6855-3
    On a skull carved in crystal. 6855-3
    Paul Klee. 6803-0
    The stone harp. 6803-0
    The stone harp. 6855-3
Haining, John J.
    Indian summer. 6857-X
    Ultimate prerogative. 6857-X
"Hair like to be melted midnight". Her. Robert Loveman. 6941-X
"Hair splayed on the pillow. I think: a...". Biting through. Traise Yamamoto. 6790-5
The hair's-breadth. Nicholas Moore. 6379-9
"Hair, wax, rouge, honey, teeth, you buy". On a battered beauty. Unknown (Greek). 6814-6
Haircut. Hiroshi Kashiwagi. 6998-3
"A hairnet covered her head". For all my grandmothers. Beth Brant. 7005-1
"The hairs about his muzzle tipp'd with wet". The hunting of Shumba. Kingsley Fairbridge. 6800-6
Hairst. James (1827-1888) Thomson. 6960-6
Haiti. Kathryn White Ryan. 6096 X
Hakanson, Esther
    His gloves. 6750-6
Hake, Thomas Gordon
    Old souls. 6656-9
    Our bookshelves. 6297-0
    The painter, sels. 6997-5
    The sibyl. 6656-9
    Sonnet 010 ("Genius"). 7014-0
    Sonnet 032 ("The thousand volumes"). 7014-0
Hakluyt and the English voyages. Catherine Cate Coblentz. 6979-7
Hakluyt unpurchased. Franklin McDuffee. 6833-2,7007-8
Hakutsu
    "O pine-tree standing". Arthur Waley (tr.). 7039-6
Hal's birthday. Lucy Larcom. 6129-X
Halas, Frantisek
    Dead soldier. Ewald Osers (tr,). 6068-4
    It is time. Ewald Osers (tr.). 6068-4
Halcyon, sels. Hilda ("H.D.") Doolittle. 6012-9
"Hale and hearty, and sixty-three". Wanted--a wife. Jesse Sill. 6799-9
"Hale the Yule-log in!". The Yule-log. Clinton Scollard. 7035-3
Hale, Arthur
    The cruise of the Fair American. 6946-0

Manilla Bay. 6946-0
    The Yankee privateer. 6946-0
Hale, Edward Everett
    Adrian Block's song. 6946-0
    Anne Hutchinson's exile. 6946-0
    The ballad of Bunker Hill. 6946-0
    Columbus. 6946-0
    Eli and Samuel. 6848-0
    From Potomac to Merrimac. 6946-0
    Hagar departed. 6848-0
    The heart's door. 6109-5
    Jehovah liveth. 6848-0
    The lamentable ballad of the bloody brook. 6946-0
    Lend a hand. 6337-3
    "Look up and not down". 6109-5,6225-3,6211-3
    The marching song of Stark's men. 6946-0
    The nameless saints. 6337-3,6418-3,6730-1
    New England's Chevy Chase. 6465-5,6573-2,6736-0
    Omnipresence. 6730-1
    Put it through. 6946-0
    Send me. 6461-2
    "To look up and not down". 6623-2
Hale, H.D.
    Semper idem. 6116-8
Hale, Janet Campbell
    Backyard swing. 7005-1
    Custer lives in Humboldt County. 7005-1
    Desmet, Idaho, March 1969 7005-1
    Scene from a dream. 7005-1
    Walls of ice. 7005-1
    Where have all the indians gone? 7005-1
Hale, Katherine (Amelia Beers Warnock Garvin)
    The answer. 6115-X
    At noon. 6115-X
    Ballad of Jasper road. 6797-2
    Cun-ne-wa-bum. 6843-X
    Grey knitting. 6115-X
    I used to wear a gown of green. 6115-X
    In the trenches. 6115-X
    Miracles. 6797-2
    Song of roses. 6433-7
    To Peter Pan in winter. 6797-2,6115-X
    When you return. 6115-X
    You who have gayly left us. 6224-5,6115-X
Hale, Mrs.
    The light of home. 6752-2
    The silk-worm. 6752-2
Hale, Sara Josepha
    Books. 6294-6
    Mary's lamb. 6502-3,6456-6
    Teachings of nature. 6294-6
Hale, Sir Matthew
    Free from the world. 6793-X
    "A sabbath well spent brings a week of content". 6238-5
Hale, Y. M. C. A. Kenneth Neal. 6475-2
Halek, Viteslav
    "Like to a spreading tree am I", fr. Songs of evening. Paul Selver (tr.). 6763-8
    "The moon is up amidst the stars", fr. Songs of evening. Paul Selver (tr.). 6763-8
    "Now all is sleeping in the world",fr.Songs of evening. Paul Selver (tr.). 6763-8
    "O God, within this soul of mine", fr.Songs of evening. Paul Selver (tr.). 6763-8
    "Pale moon in the skies doth rest",fr.Songs of evening. Paul Selver (tr.). 6763-8
    Songs of evening, sels. Paul Selver (tr.). 6763-8
    "Springtime is wafted from afar", fr. Songs of evening. Paul Selver (tr.). 6763-8
    "The stars up yonder in the sky", fr. Songs of evening. Paul Selver (tr.). 6763-8
    "Thou art still but a flower-bud",fr. Songs of evening. Paul Selver (tr.). 6763-8
    "The trees are rustling softly", fr. Songs of evening. Paul Selver (tr.). 6763-8
Hales, Corrine
    For Cleo Wright. 6900-2
    Power. 6900-2
Halevi, Jehuda [or Judah]
    Hymn for Pentecost. 6214-8

To Zion. Maurice Samuel (tr.). 7039-6
Haley, Molly Anderson
    The architect. 6144-3,6335-7
    'A faithless generation asked a sign' 7019-1
    A garden hymn. 6232-6
    He knew the land. 6083-8
    Intolerance. 6337-3
    "Not to destroy but to fulfill". 6420-5
    A prayer for Christian unity. 6144-3
    A river of grace. 6144-3,6335-7
    Vacant lots. 6102-8,6076-5
    "We have seen his star in the east". 6144-3,6335-7
Haley, Russell
    Corona death-trap hotel, fr. On the fault line. 7018-3
    The lore of diminishing returns, fr. On the fault line. 7018-3
    On the fault line, sels. 7018-3
'Half a crop' in Vermont. Daniel L. Cady. 6988-6
Half a score o' sailormen. Cicely Fox Smith. 7031-0
"Half a score of gutter-snipes...". Helping. P. B.. 7031-0
Half an hour before supper. Francis Bret Harte. 6911-8
"Half an hour till train time, sir". Bill Mason's bride. Francis Bret Harte. 6910-X
Half and half again. Beau Beausoleil. 6901-0
Half asleep. Gertrude Huntington McGiffert. 6838-3
"A half baked potato, named Sue". Limerick:"A half baked potato, named Sue." George Libaire. 6308-X
Half deity. Marianne Moore. 6733-6
Half hours with the classics. H.J. DeBurgh. 6089-7,6724-7
"Half lost in the liquid azure bloom of...sea". Alfred Lord Tennyson. 6997-5
The half of life gone. William Morris. 6828-6
"Half raised upon the dying couch, his hand". The boy's last request. Unknown. 6911-8
"A half score years have sped away". Youth and maiden, fr. Dovecote mill. Phoebe Cary. 6865-0;6969-X
Half stun'd I look around. Sir Ronald Ross. 6482-5
"Half the horizon is the sea". Sunrise: Maine coast. Robert P. Tristram Coffin. 7040-X
Half thought. Zona Gale. 6007-2
Half truth. Richard Monckton Milnes; 1st Baron Houghton. 6226-1
Half way stone. Karle Wilson Baker. 6585-6
Half-ballad of Waterval. Rudyard Kipling. 6810-3
The half-breed girl. Duncan Campbell Scott. 6021-8,6591-0, 6115-X,6433-7
A half-caste prays. Gordon LeClaire. 6750-6
The half-door. Seumas (James Starkey) O'Sullivan. 6628-3
The half-hitch. Unknown. 6061-7
Half-mast. Lloyd Mifflin. 6946-0
Half-mast the flag. Samuel Valentine Cole. 6995-9
"Half-mast the flag by sweet St. Mary's shore". In memoriam. Thomas Edward Brown. 6809-X
"Half-mast the flag, ad let the bell be". Half-mast the flag. Samuel Valentine Cole. 6995-9
Half-waking. William Allingham. 6660-7
Half-way doin's. Irwin Russell. 6412-4
Half-wisdom. Frederic Prokosch. 6781-6
"The half-world's width divides us; where...". Divided. David Gray. 7041-8
Halfway in love. Ben Jonson. 6935-5
Haliburton, Hugh. See Robertson, James Logie
Halibut cover harvest. Kenneth Leslie. 6021-8
Halifax station. Unknown. 6946-0
Halket, George
    Logie o' Buchan. 6086-2
Halkett, Elizabeth. See Wardlaw, Lady
The hall of Cynddylan. Felicia Dorothea Hemans. 6973-8
The hall of Cynddylan. Unknown. 6732-8
The hall of fame. Arthur Guiterman. 6773-5
"The hall of harps is lone to-night". The dying bard's prophecy. Felicia Dorothea Hemans. 6973-8
Hall of primates. Robert Clairmont. 6751-4
The hall of shadows. Alexander McLachlan. 6795-6
The hall of sleep. Theodora Bates. 6118-4
Hall, Abby Mary
    The rose's mite. 6116-8
Hall, Ada E.
    Angling. 6818-9
Hall, Amanda Benjamin
    The ballad of Mean Marks. 6039-0
    The ballad of the three sons. 6531-7,6039-0
    The dancer in the shrine. 6538-4,6034-X
    Declaration. 6761-1
    The eaglet. 7019-1
    Harpsichord. 6783-2
    'I venerate a carpenter' 7038-8
    Idyl. 6607-0
    Instant out of time. 6979-7
    Ironin' day. 6538-4
    Lament. 7038-8
    Mary. 6037-4
    Overture. 6037-4
    Portrait. 6042-0
    Portrait. 6042-0
    The school boy learns to fly. 6979-7
    Sven. 6038-2
    Testament. 7038-8
    Too many songs. 6619-4
    Too soon. 6102-8,6076-5,6777-8,6619-4
    Valse triste. 6037-4
Hall, Anne
    Arbutus. 6049-8
Hall, Arthur Howard
    Where Columbia stands. 6741-X
Hall, Arthur Vine
    The brothers. 6800-6
    In the gardens. 6800-6
    Round the camp fire, sels. 6800-6
    Singsingetjie. 6800-6
    Table mountain, sels. 6800-6
    Thomas Pringle. 6625-9
Hall, Bishop
    For Christmas day. 6756-5
Hall, Bolton
    Laugh it off. 6880-4
Hall, C.W.
    The prairie fire. 7022-1
Hall, Carlyle B.
    I wake up screaming. 6178-8
    Malevolence. 6178-8
    Solitude. 6178-8
Hall, Carolyn
    Fireflies ("Little lamps of the dusk"). 6466-3,6498-1
Hall, Charles S.
    John Brown's body. 6088-9
Hall, Charles Sprague
    Glory hallelujah! or John Brown's body. 6946-0,6753-0
Hall, Charles Winslow
    Who marches next Memorial Day? 6889-8
Hall, Christopher Newman
    My times are in thy hand. 6656-9
Hall, Clarissa
    Brief pledge. 6789-1
    Butterfly in the Boston Athenaeum. 6789-1
Hall, Constance Ann
    'Humoresque.' 6750-6
Hall, Covington
    The rifle. 6542-2
Hall, Donald
    The beautiful horses. 6388-8
    Five epigrams. 6388-8
    Laocoon. 6388-8
    The morning porches. 6388-8
Hall, E.L.
    The day's oration is in flowers. 6171-0
Hall, E.S.
    Ideal beauty. 6768-9
Hall, Eliza Calvert
    Enlisted. 6340-3,6741-X
    A lesson in mythology. 6273-3
    A modern Psyche. 7021-3
Hall, Eugene J
    Going for the cows. 6575-9
Hall, Eugene J.
    Abraham Lincoln. 6524-4
    Annie Pickens. 6921-5
    Big Ben Bolton. 6414-0
    The deabting society. 6921-5
    The engineer's story. 6139-7,6964-9

HALL

Hall, [continued]
    Flirting with a fan. 6707-7
    Fourth of July at Ripton. 6927-4
    The highway cow. 6273-3
    Jesus, lover of my soul. 6417-5
    Kate Shelly. 6917-7
    Kate Shelly. 6142-7,6451-5,6478-7
    The king and the child. 6743-3,6964-9
    Only a chicken. 6314-4
    The ride of death. 6686-0,6167-2,6924-X
    Victoria Grey. 6682-8

Hall, Florence Foster
    Young Daedalus. 7019-1

Hall, Frances
    Chinese sunset. 6782-4
    Winter midnight. 6750-6

Hall, Gertrude
    Blind-man's-bluff. 6672-0
    The dust. 6431-0
    How dreary looks the ivied cot. 6431-0
    How shall we tell an angel. 6431-0
    In a dark hour. 6097-8
    In the art museum. 6431-0
    A king's daughter. 6431-0
    Les Papillottes. 6652-6
    Mrs. Golightly. 6441-8
    My old counselor. 6431-0
    One distant April. 6309-8
    Rather, o falcon eyes. 7038-8
    The rival. 6102-8,6076-5
    To a weed. 6338-1,6431-0

Hall, H. Duncan
    Night. 6784-0

Hall, Hallie
    In an old southern garden. 6799-9

Hall, Hazel
    At the corner. 6628-3
    Audience to poet. 6038-2
    Before quiet, fr. Songs of farewell. 6778-6
    Blossom-time. 7038-8
    Buttonholes. 6880-4
    Crossed heart. 6038-2
    Ephemera. 6037-4
    Flash. 6007-2,6619-4
    He walks with his chin in the air. 6036-6
    Hearsay, fr. Songs of farewell. 6778-6
    Here comes the thief. 6037-4,6070-6
    Incidental. 6036-6
    Maker of the songs. 6037-4
    A man goes by. 6036-6
    Maturity. 6036-6
    Measurements. 6880-4
    Middle-aged. 6628-3
    My song. 6619-4
    Night. 6071-4
    On the street. 6538-4
    One by one, one by one. 6347-0
    Passers. 6036-6
    Passers, the patrician. 6036-6
    Protest, fr. Songs of farewell. 6778-6
    Puzzled stitches. 6880-4
    The room upstairs. 6880-4
    The sea. 6037-4
    Shawled. 6538-4
    Sleep charm, fr. Songs of farewell. 6778-6
    Slow death. 6038-2
    Songs of farewell, sels. 6778-6
    The still return. 6880-4
    Submergence. 6038-2
    Submergence, fr. Songs of farewell. 6778-6
    Sunlight through a window. 6007-2
    They will come. 6777-8
    The thin door. 6007-2
    Three girls. 6102-8,6347-0,6076-5,6034-X
    Two sewing. 6979-7
    Walkers. 6034-X
    A whistler in the night. 6628-3
    Words for weeping. 6037-4

Hall, Helen
    Here comes the thief. 6506-6

Hall, J.C.
    The crack. 6257-1
    Responsibilties. 6257-1
    Spring offensive. 6783-2
    The telescope. 6257-1
    War. 6257-1

Hall, James Norman
    The cricketers of Flanders. 7026-4
    A finger and a huge, thick thumb. 7027-2
    In Flanders. 6420-5
    Out of Flanders. 6443-4,6452-2
    Tour de L'Ile. 6761-1

Hall, Jennie Pendleton
    Covered bridges. 6750-6

Hall, John
    The call. 6317-9,6208-3,6563-5,6341-1,6023-4
    The call. 6933-9
    An Epicurean ode. 6562-7,6341-1
    "Happy choristers of air". 6187-7,6334-9
    Home travell. 6023-4
    Love was the worm. 6475-2
    The lure, sels. 6317-9
    Metropolis. 6475-2
    The morning star. 6563-5
    Of beauty. 6317-9
    On a houre-glasse. 6341-1
    On an hour-glass, sels. 6317-9
    Pastoral hymn. 6931-2
    A pastoral hymn. 6563-5,6641-0,6378-0,6341-1
    A pastoral hymne. 6933-9
    The personal passion. 6475-2
    The point of battle. 6475-2
    "Since that this thing we call the world". 6187-7
    To his tutor. 6187-7
    Walking to Westminster. 6475-2
    "What need I travel, since I may". 6187-7

Hall, John Leslie (tr.)
    Beowulf, sels. Unknown, 6646-1
    Grendel's mother, fr. Beowulf. Unknown, 6372-1

Hall, Joseph
    Anthem. 6830-8
    Book I, satire III (With some pot-fury,...). 6198-2
    The domestic tutor's position. 6200-8
    Immortal babe, who this dear day. 6747-6
    The impecunious fop. 6200-8
    The olden days. 6436-1
    On simony. 6200-8
    Satire XII ("Great is the folly of a feeble braine,"). 6208-3
    Virgidemiarum libri sex, sels. 6194-X

Hall, L.V.
    Echo. 6049-8

Hall, Lena
    Levels. 6039-0
    Perspective. 6039-0
    Sea nurtured. 6038-2
    The way of water. 6038-2

Hall, Lillie
    Beggar maid. 7016-7
    Fair day. 7016-7
    Lesson. 7016-7
    Pleasure. 7016-7
    Rebuke to Ceres. 7016-7
    Watcher. 7016-7

Hall, Mabel Kinney
    "Within the torrent's onward whirl" 6995-9

Hall, Mary Lee
    Turn again to life. 6337-3

Hall, Newton M.
    Shadow ships. 6116-8

Hall, Norman Shannon
    Old Jim. 6846-4
    Woodrow Wilson. 7001-9

Hall, Sharlot M.
    Arizona. 6946-0
    Boot hill. 7012-4,7038-8
    The range rider. 7010-8
    A saddle-song. 7010-8
    Sheep-herding. 7008-0
    The trail of death. 7010-8
    Two-bits. 7010-8

Hall, Thomas Franklin
    A Cape Cod home, sels. 6798-0
    Sovereign, sels. 6798-0
Hall, Thomas Winthrop
    Teaching a girl to skate. 7035-3
Hall, Tom
    A bachelor's views. 6453-1
    My cigarette ("Ma pauvre petite"). 6453-1
Hallam's church, fr. Clevedon verses. Thomas Edward Brown. 6809-X
Hallam, Arthur Henry
    A farewell to Glenarbac. 6980-0
    "The garden trees are busy with the shower". 6980-0
    "Lady, I bid thee to a sunny dome". 6980-0
    "A melancholy thought had laid me low". 6980-0
    My bosom friend. 6085-4
    A scene in summer. 6980-0
    "Speed ye, warm hours, along th' appointed path". 6980-0
    To my mother. 6980-0,6934-7
    When barren doubt. 6097-8
    "When gentle fingers cease to touch the string". 6980-0
    "Why throbbest thou, my heart, why thickly breathest?" 6980-0
    Written at Caudebec in Normandy. 6980-0
    Written in Edinburgh. 6484-1,6656-9
Hallar, Soren
    Denmark speaks. Charles Wharton Stork (tr.). 6555-4
Hallberg, Richard
    On spring poems. 6850-2
    Resolution. 6850-2
    To a plaster owl. 6850-2
    To Robert Frost. 6850-2
Halle, John
    Anatomye, sels. 6482-5
    Goodlye doctrine and instruction. 6482-5
Halleck and Joseph Rodman Drake, Fitz-Greene
    Abstract of the surgeon-general's report, fr. Croaker. 6753-0
    An address, fr. Croaker papers. 6753-0
    Croaker papers, sels. 6753-0
    The man who frets at wordly strife, fr. Croaker papers. 6753-0
    The national painting, fr. Croaker papers. 6753-0
    To Captain Seaman Weeks, fr. Croaker papers. 6753-0
    To Croaker, Junior, fr. Croaker papers. 6753-0
    To E. Simpson, Esq., fr. Croaker papers. 6753-0
    To Mr. Simpson, fr. Croaker papers. 6753-0
    To Mrs. Barnes, fr. Croaker papers. 6753-0
    To XXXX, esquire, fr. Croaker papers. 6753-0
Halleck, Fitz-Greene
    Alnwick castle. 6302-0-6385-3,6735-2,6288-1,6219-9
    American culture, fr. Fanny. 6753-0
    The ballad of Ishmael day. 6402-7
    Burns. 6302-0,6385-3,6600-3,6735-2,6219-9
    Connecticut. 6735-2
    Cutting. 6121-4
    Fanny's education, fr. Fanny. 6753-0
    Fanny, sels. 6753-0
    Fanny, sels. 6077-3
    The field of the grounded arms. 6753-0
    Fortune. 6302-0;6385-3
    Green be the turf. 6304-7
    The iron grays. 6753-0
    Joseph Rodman Drake. 6240-7,6486-8,6302-0,6385-3,6076-5
    Marco Bozzaris. 6102-8,6142-7,6732-8,6239-3,6271-7,6302 ,6008-0,6431-0,6560-0,6076-5,6288-1,6121 ,6385-3, 6392-6,6401-9,6402-7,6425-6,6459 ,6219-9,6267-9,6263-6,6300-4,6304-7,6419 ,6479-5,6486-8,6552-X,6606-2, 6610-0,6621 ,6424-8,6467-1,6571-6
    Ode to fortune. 6004-8
    On a portrait of a red jacket. 6385-3,6600-3
    On the death of Joseph Rodman Drake. 6085-4,6243-1,6732-8,6437-X,6077-3,6102 ,6291-9,6121-4,6076-5,6288-1, 6431-0,6219 ,6176-1,6309-8,6176-1,6271-7,6337-3,6632-1,6735-2
    The patriots' death. 6240-7
    Red jacket. 6735-2,6288-1
    Song of the decanter. 6402-7
    Success in New York, fr. Fanny. 6753-0
    "There is an evening twilight of the heart". 6238-5
    To a portrait of a red jacket. 6678-X
    Weehawken. 6077-3,6302-0,6385-3
    Woman. 6441-8,6004-8
    "Woman! with that word". 6238-5
    Wyoming. 6752-2
Halleck, Fitz-Greene (tr.)
    Psalm 137. Bible, 6848-0
A **hallelujah** chorus, fr. Psalm 248. Bible. 6337-3
"**Hallelujah!/Praise** Jehovah, o my soul!". Psalm 146. Bible. 6848-0
"**Hallelujah!/Praise**, ye servants of Jehovah". Psalm 135. Bible. 6848-0
Hallelujah, I'm a bum. Unknown. 6237-7
Hallelujah, sels. George Wither. 6122-2,6198-2
Haller
    "Great nature's inmost heart". Bernard Bosanquet (tr.). 7042-6
Haller, Malville
    A boy's tent. 6038-2
    Old Mr. So-and-So. 6393-4
Hallet, Mary
    Calvary ("A dying figure against the sky") 6144-3
    My saviour. 6144-3
    Portrait. 6042-0
    Portrait. 6042-0
    The rhythm of his life 6144-3,6335-7
    The singing of yourself in me. 6042-0
Hallett, Samuel W.
    The bayberry candle. 6798-0
    An ode to Cape Cod. 6798-0
Hallgrimsson, Jonas
    The golden plover. Watson Kirkconnell (tr.). 6283-0
    A greeting. Jakobina Johnson (tr.) 6283-0
    A greeting. Jakobina Johnson (tr.). 6854-5
    Gunnar's holm. Runolfur Fjeldsted (tr.). 6854-5
    Iceland. Gudmund J. Gislason (tr.). 6854-5
Halliburton, Hugh. See Robertson, James Logie
Halliburton, Maurine
    Incarnation. 6648-8
Halliday, A.E.
    Limerick:"Lady Astor, M.P., for sobriety". 6811-1
Hallo, my fancy. Unknown. 6385-3
"**Halloo!** upon the bookman's flinty road". On reading Books alive by Vincent Starrett. Rachel Albright. 6789-1
Hallow even. Carrie Ward Lyon. 6254-7
Hallow my fancie, sels. William Cleland et al. 6179-6
Halloway, John Wesley
    Calling the doctor. 6281-4
Hallowe'en. Harry Behn. 6236-9
Hallowe'en. Madison Cawein. 6696-8
Hallowe'en. Arthur Cleveland Coxe. 6820-0
Hallowe'en. L. Fidelia Woolley Gillette. 6696-8
Hallowe'en. Nora Hopper. 6820-0
Hallowe'en. John Mayne. 6086-2
Hallowe'en. Grace Rowe. 6243-5
Hallowe'en. Carrie Stern. 6696-8
Hallowe'en ("Bolt and bar the front door"). Molly Capes. 6254-7
Hallowe'en ("Pixie, kobold, elf, and sprite"). Joel Benton. 6254-7,6465-5
Hallowe'en ("Upon that night, when fairies light"). Robert Burns. 6254-7
Hallowe'en charm. Arthur Guiterman. 6773-5
Hallowe'en cheer. Unknown. 6696-8
A **Hallowe'en** memory. Christopher Morley. 6254-7,6307-1
"**Hallowed** by thy name - halleluiah!". The human cry. Alfred Lord Tennyson. 6977-0
Hallowed ground. Thomas Campbell. 6302-0,6385-3,6271-7, 6337-3,6219-9,6404 ,6250-4
The **hallowed** season, fr. Hamlet. William Shakespeare. 6337-3
Halloween ("Walk into the dark room"). Carrie Ward Lyon. 6254-7
The **hallowing** of the fleet. William Johnson Cory. 6793-X
"The **halls** that were loud with the merry tread". The new school. Joyce Kilmer. 7027-2
Halls, Leo

Ports of call. 6599-6
Hallstrom, Per
   Inspiration. Charles Wharton Stork (tr.). 6045-5
Hallucination. Eugene Jolas. 6351-9
Hallucination: I. Arthur Symons. 6655-0
Hallucinations?. Beverly Randolph Tucker. 6482-5
"Hallway staris, reserved for my emotions". Masochistic tendencies (/a caustic bastard) Carolyn Baxter. 6870-7
Halm, Karl von
   A question. H.I.D Ryder (tr.). 6066-8,6226-1
"A halo glorious crowns the sight". The shrine. Lucy H. King Smith. 6906-1
Halpine, Charles G. ("Miles O'Reilly")
   The ancient Abe. 6524-4
   Baron Renfrew's ball. 6946-0
   The canteen. 6412-4
   Comrades known in marches many. 6113-3,6340-3
   Death of Lincoln. 6708-5
   Dolce far niente. 6273-3
   Epigram. 6505-8
   Feminine arithmetic. 6089-7,6441-8,6652-8,6505-8,6278-4,6004
   The hill of Killenarden. 6858-8
   Irish astronomy. 6302-0,6165-6,6505-8
   Janette's hair. 6240-7
   The last resort. 6278-4
   Lecompton's black brigade. 6946-0
   'Mr. Johnson's policy of reconstruction'. 6946-0
   The mushroom hunt. 6278-4
   The night ride of ancient Abe. 6524-4
   Not a star from the flag shall fade. 6459-0
   O lady of Kinsa. 6858-8
   Quakerdom - the formal call. 6302-0,6385-3
   Quakerdom: the formal call. 6004-8
   Song of Sherman's army. 6113-3,6402-7,6470-1
   Song of the soldiers. 6470-1
   The thousand and thirty-seven. 6113-3,6735-2
   The trooper to his mare. 6219-9
   Widow-ology. 6441-8
Halse, George
   Death's choice. 6916-9
Halsham, John
   My last terrier. 6230-X
The halt in the garden. Robert Hillyer. 6506-6,6039-0
"Halt! Shoulder arms! Recover! As you were!". Sonnet to Britain. William Edmonstoune Aytoun. 6948-7
A **halt**. Zbigniew Herbert. 6758-1
The **halt**. Edward Shanks. 7029-9
Haltersick's song. John Pikeryng. 6436-1
Halverson, Martin
   Highway buttons. 6342-X
Halvey, Margaret M.
   The drip of the Irish rain. 6249-0
Halvey, Marie Shields
   At parting. 6654-X
The **halycons**. Alcman. 6435-3
Ham, Hyung-soo
   Epitaph among sunflowers. 6775-1
Ham, Marion Franklin
   A hymn for Mother's Day. 6143-5
   A hymn of Thanksgiving. 6143-5
   O Lord of life, thy kingdom is at hand. 6337-3
   The soarin' o' the eagle. 6741-X
The **Hamadryad**, fr. The hellenics. Walter Savage Landor. 6828-6
The **Hamadryad**. Walter Savage Landor. 6153-2,6196-6,6199-0
Hamann, Selma
   Desire. 6906-1
   Gypsy tapestry. 6906-1
   Inevitable. 6906-1
   Liceat me ministrare. 6818-9
   An old man's lamentations. 6906-1
   Ships and hearthstones. 6906-1
   Silver lining. 6906-1
   Then keeps gypsy his fast days. 6906-1
Hamatreya. Ralph Waldo Emerson. 6077-3,6208-3,6399-3,6288-1,6121-4,6126
Hamberlin, L.R.
   Flossie. 6680-1

Hambleton, Ronald
   Slow movement: adagio. 6021-8
   Sockeye salmon. 6446-9
Hamburger Mary's. Todd S.J. Lawson. 6792-1, 6998-3
Hamda
   Beside a stream. A.J. Arberry (tr.). 6362-4
   Revenge. A.J. Arberry (tr.). 6362-4
Hamden Provision co. Barbara Hughes. 6792-1
"Hame came our goodman". Unknown. 6111-7
Hame, hame, hame. Allan Cunningham. 6732-8,6180-X,6271-7, 6383-7,6737-9,6317
"Hamelin town's in Brunswick". The pied piper of Hamelin. Robert Browning. 6089-7,6179-6,6302-0,6358-3,6484-1,6614 ,6105-2,6127-3,6133-8,6239-3,6290-3,6427 ,6136-2,6242-3,6271-7,6401-9,6504-X,6732 ,6304-7,6131-1,6135-4,6107-9,6102-8,6110 ,6219-9,6421-3,6371-3,6668-2,6419-1,6639 ,6304-7,6131-1,6135-4,6107-9,6102-8,6110 ,6219-9,6421-3,6371-3,6668-2,6419-1,6639 ,6861-8,6828-6
Hamersley, J. Hooker
   The countersign. 6451-5
   Yellow roses. 6451-5,6682-8
Hamerton, Philip Gilbert
   The sanyassi. 6656-9
   The wild huntsman. 6656-9
Hamilcar Barca. Sir Roger Casement. 6096 X
Hamilton. Marie E.J. Pitt. 6784-0
Hamilton trees. Lucia M. Mooney. 6684-4
Hamilton, A. Charles
   His majesty the baby. 6772-7
Hamilton, Ann [or Annie E.]
   Brother Rugino. 6037-4
   Chanson d'or. 6037-4
   Chanson noir. 6037-4
   Christ's giving. 6144-3,6225-3
   Deserts. 6337-3
   "Faith is a grasping of almighty power." 6225-3
   "If thou art blest." 6225-3
   Inscription. 6037-4
   Pause. 6776-X
   Peter. 6036-6
   Song overheard on the highway. 6038-2
   Sonnet ("When I was far"). 6036-6
   Susie. 6036-6
   There might be glory in the night. 6782-4
   Two songs. 6039-0
   We long to see Jesus. 6065-X
Hamilton, Charles Granville
   Contrast ("And it was in the winter") 6144-3,6335-7
Hamilton, Charles Grenville
   Business. 6954-1
Hamilton, Cicely
   Non-combatant. 6474-4
Hamilton, David Osborne
   The idiot. 6036-6
   Once more the moon. 6069-2
   To men unborn. 6449-3
Hamilton, Edwin
   My wooing. 6652-6
Hamilton, Elizabeth
   My ain fireside. 6219-9
Hamilton, Eloise
   How shall they sleep? 6224-5
Hamilton, Eugene Lee. See Lee-Hamilton,Eugene
Hamilton, F.E.E.
   Dancing the minuet. 6116-8
Hamilton, Flora Brent (tr.)
   The garden. Henri de Regnier, 6649-6
Hamilton, Florence
   April. 6076-5
   Conjecture. 6076-5
   If a man die. 6337-3
   Note. 6017-X
   Song ("Love gave"). 6324-1
Hamilton, Fritz
   The miner. 6998-3
Hamilton, Gail
   Archie Dean. 6914-2
   Archie Dean. 6554-6,6569-4
   battle song for freedom. 6165-6

Both sides. 6742-5
Hamilton, George Rostrevor
 The cell. 6253-9
 A cross in Flanders. 7031-0,7026-4
 Going to sleep. 6339-X
 Invocation ("O Thou, Creator from original chaos"). 6532-5
 The library, Greatham. 6783-2
 Multiplicity. 6250-4
 Native forest. 6781-6
 On the Albert Memorial. 6072-2
 Tunny-fish. 6782-4
 The unknown traveller. 6339-X
Hamilton, H.J.
 Requiem to the dinosaurs and mastodons. 6799-9
Hamilton, Ian
 The ballad of Hadji and the boar. 7010-8
Hamilton, Janet
 A ballade of memorie. 7037-X
Hamilton, John
 Up in the mornin' early. 6180-X
Hamilton, John Alan
 Love's disguise. 6116-8
Hamilton, John Allen
 Three triolets. 6116-8
Hamilton, Kate W.
 Which general? 6529-5,6691-7
Hamilton, Marion Ethel
 Children on a hill. 6979-7
Hamilton, Mary Gertrude
 The voice in the spring. 6762-X
Hamilton, Robert Browning
 Pleasure and sorrow. 6337-3
Hamilton, Samuel A.
 Florida song. 6719-0
Hamilton, Sir William Rowan
 O brooding spirit. 6244-X
 Spirit of wisdom and of love. 7015-9
 To death. 7015-9
Hamilton, Venetia
 To a mother. 6461-2
Hamilton, William
 The despairing lover. 6874-X
 The flower. 6800-6
 The song of an exile. 6650-X
 The song of an exile. 6800-6
Hamilton, William (of Bangour)
 The braes of Yarrow. 6180-X,6152-4,6240-7,6271-7,6600-3, 6086-2,6219-9,6438
 A soliloquy, imitation of Hamlet. 6198-2
Hamilton, William (of Gilbertfield)
 The last dying words of Bonnie Heck. 6180-X
 Willie was a wanton wag. 6180-X
Hamilton, William H.
 The carpenter. 6269-5
 An eightsome reel. 6269-5
 Elegy. 6269-5
 God's fools. 6269-5
 Hymn for harvest-time. 6269-5
 Immortality. 6269-5
 The spirit. 6269-5
 To the master of harmonies. 6269-5
Hamilton-King, H.E.
 The ballad of the midnight sun. 6518-X
'—a scotch terrier Hamish'. C. Hilton Brown. 7008-6
Hamlet. Vachel Lindsay. 6345-4
Hamlet at the Boston. Julia Ward Howe. 6358-6
Hamlet contemplates death, fr. Hamlet. William Shakespeare. 6337-3
Hamlet insults Polonius, baits Rosencrantz...,fr Hamlet. William Shakespeare. 6637-2
The Hamlet of A. MacLeish, sels. Archibald MacLeish. 6527-9
Hamlet parodies Osric's Euphuisms..., fr. William Shakespeare. 6637-2
Hamlet reproaching the queen, fr. Hamlet. William Shakespeare. 6302-0
Hamlet to the players. William Shakespeare. 6304-7
Hamlet's address to his father's ghost. William Shakespeare. 6543-0

Hamlet's esteem for Horatio. William Shakespeare. 6543-0
Hamlet's ghost. William Shakespeare. 6565-1
Hamlet's soliloquy on death. William Shakespeare. 6014-5, 6543-0
Hamlet's soliloquy, fr. Hamlet. William Shakespeare. 6294-6,6732-8,6566-X,6438-8,6102-8
Hamlet, Frances Crosby
 Prayer. 6144-3
 Prayer ("Thou who didst multiply"). 6144-3
Hamlet, sel. William Shakespeare. 7014-0
Hamlet, sels. William Shakespeare. 6104-4,6301-2,6144-3, 6148-6,6198-2,6260-1,6289-X,6339 ,6148-6,6294-6,6369-1,6378-0,6085-4,6102 ,6392-6,6402-7,6406-X,6479-5, 6481-7,6512 ,6527-9,6601-1,6605-2,6606-2,6610-0,6637 ,6726-3,6732-8,6239-3,6250-4,6560-0,6107
The hamlet, sels. Thomas Warton Jr. 6867-7
Hamlin, Mary T.
 Good-morning to God. 6131-1
Hamm, Margherita Arlina
 Ancient seminary maid. 6718-2
 Saviour rose to-day. 6720-4
The Hammam name. James Elroy Flecker. 6210-5
Hammer and anvil. Samuel Valentine Cole. 6266-0,6303-9
Hammer and nails. Kenneth W. Porter. 6954-1
The hammer, fr. Chicago poems. Carl Sandburg. 6531-7
The hammer-throw. Reuel Denney. 6527-9,6640-2
The hammers. Ralph Hodgson. 6488-4
Hammitt, Deecort
 Hail! South Dakota. 6465-5
Hammond (atr), Miss
 What the choir sang about the new bonnet. 6131-1
Hammond, Basil C.
 Consideration. 6799-9
Hammond, Eleanor
 From a street corner. 6347-0
 The magic window. 6891-X
Hammond, Emily Vanderbilt
 Legends for trees. 6585-6
Hammond, Emma Hally
 Living. 6799-9
Hammond, Hala Jean
 Hate. 6542-2
Hammond, James
 Love elegies, sels. 6152-4
Hammond, Maria Johns
 A composite cat. 6699-2
 A multitudinous me. 6799-9
Hammond, William
 The cruel mistress. 6563-5
 Husbandry. 6563-5
 To his sister, Mrs. S.: man's life. 6933-9
 To his sister, Mrs. S.: the rose. 6933-9
Hamp, Sidford F.
 Friar Tuck. 6926-6
Hampl, Patricia
 An artist draws a peach. 6966-5
Hampton beach. John Greenleaf Whittier. 6271-7,6302-0,6385-3,6126-5
Hampton hymn. Edgar Warren. 6764-6
Hampton, Edgar Lloyd
 The peace call. 6449-3
"Han'som, stranger? Yes, she's purty an' ez peart..". The engineer's story. Eugene J. Hall. 6139-7,6964-9
Han, Ha-woon
 Blue birds. 6775-1
 Reed flute. 6775-1
Han, Yong-woon
 The ferry boat and the passenger. 6775-1
 I do not know. 6775-1
 Love's silence. 6775-1
 Obedience. 6775-1
Hanaford, Phoebe A.
 Funeral hymn. 6524-4
Hanback, Nelson
 Pathetique. 6799-9
Hancock, John
 Fellow travelers. 6894-4
Hancock, Le Touche
 Looking on the bright side. 6109-5
Hancock, Nellie Davis

A sonnet to you. 6799-9
Hancock, Sallie J.
   A response to "Beautiful snow". 6403-5
The hand and foot. Jones Very. 6333-0
Hand in hand. James Russell Lowell. 6304-7
"Hand me the sweet cup...". Zonas. 6251-2
"The hand of death was upon him. There he lay". The poisoner and his victim. Charles W. Denison. 6755-7
"The hand of him here torpid lies". Epitaph for Mr Hogarth. Samuel Johnson. 6975-4
Hand of labor. Lilburn H. Townsend. 6449-3
The hand of Lincoln. Edmund Clarence Stedman. 6014-5,6708-5,6524-4
The hand of Lincoln. Edmund Clarence Stedman. 7041-8
"The hand of my lady is soft and white". God bless your beautiful hand! John Whitaker Watson. 6774-3
The hand of nature, fr.The pleasures of the imagination. Mark Akenside. 6934-7
"The hand of the Lord was upon me, and...". The book of Ezekiel. Bible. 6958-4
"The hand of the Lord was upon me..." Bible. 6958-4
"The hand of the reaper". Sir Walter Scott. 6238-5
"The hand of time was heavy on the brow". The story of Rebekah. Thomas M. Armstrong. 6921-5
Hand over hand. Unknown. 6547-3
"The hand that rounded Peter's dome", sels. Ralph Waldo Emerson. 6601-1
"The hand that ruled the helm was yours". On the Harlem. Arthur Guiterman. 6773-5
The hand that signed the paper felled a city. Dylan Thomas. 6339-X,6354-3,6666-6,6257-1
"The hand that wields the knife". Alfred Noyes. 6298-9
A hand-mirror.. Walt Whitman. 6333-0
The hand-organ ball. Joseph Crosby Lincoln. 6119-2
Hand-organ man's little girl. Unknown. 6312-8
Hand-painted china days. Edgar A. Guest. 6748-4
Hand-view. Richard Eberhart. 6390-X
A hand. Bernard Spencer. 6379-9
The hand. Dorothy Berry Hughes. 6979-7
The hand. Ebenezer Jones. 6437-X
Handa
   My road. Lois J. Erickson (tr.). 6027-7
Handford, T.W.
   Bessie Bo Peep of Engle Steepe. 6629-1
   An Easter song. 6629-1
   Leaves from fatherland. 6629-1
   On grandpapa's knee. 6629-1
"A handful cams to Seicheprey". Seicheprey. Unknown. 6946-0
"A handful of blacks drawn up on the". Colonel Roosevelt in Dominica. Richard Butler Glaenzer. 6995-9
A handful of dust. James Oppenheim. 6102-8,6076-5,6300-4
A handful of sand. Lydia Gibson. 6880-4
Handfuls. Carl Sandburg. 6897-9
Handgrenades in my grapefuit. Douglas Blazek. 6998-3
The handiwork of Flora. George Peele. 6191-5
Handke, Peter
   The edge of words. Milne Holton and Herbert Kuhner (tr.). 6769-7
   An end to idling, sel. Milne Holton and Herbert Kuhner (tr.). 6769-7
Handkerchief song. Evana Llynn. 6906-1
Hands. Anita Scott Coleman. 6178-8
Hands. Wilfred Wilson Gibson. 6653-4
Hands. Mary K. Hanley. 6530-9
Hands. Helen Hoyt. 6628-3
Hands. Winifred Virginia Jackson. 6038-2
Hands. Alexander Javitz. 6778-6
Hands. Robinson Jeffers. 6628-3
Hands. Cyprus R. Mitchell. 6038-2
Hands. William Morris. 6110-9
Hands. Henry Spiess. 6351-9
Hands. Louis Untermeyer. 6032-3
Hands. Thompson Seiser Westcott. 6936-3
Hands across the sea. Edward Verrall Lucas. 6018-8
Hands all round. Alfred Lord Tennyson. 6110-9
Hands and fingers. Unknown. 6314-4
hands drop off. A.F. Kent Bradley. 6925-8
Hands of Christ. Francisco E. Estrello. 6144-3
The hands of Christ. Leslie Savage Clark. 61443,6337-3

Hands off China. Vladimir Mayakovsky. 6068-4
Hands on a card-table. Polly Chase. 6039-0
"The hands that catch a gleaming day". To a diarist. Daisy Lee Ervin. 6906-1
Hands thrust in pockets. Tefcros Anthias. 6352-7
"Hands".. Frederick Cloud. 6299-7
"The hands". Walther Nowotny. 6769-7
The hands, sels. Anna Spencer Twitchell. 6836-7
The handsel ring. George Houghton. 7041-8
The handsome knight. Al-Mu'tamid. 6362-4
The handsomest man in the room. William Macquorn Rankine. 6652-6
Handwover coverlets. John Maher Murphy. 6761-1
Handy spandy. Mother Goose. 6363-2,6466-3,6262-8
Handy spandy. Unknown. 6937-1
Hanes, Leigh
   For Wooly. 6761-1
   Moon magic. 6979-7
   Screech owls. 6979-7
Hanes, Leigh Buckner
   Late acquaintance. 6042-0
   Mountains in twilight. 6490-6
   Old pine trees. 6083-8
Hanford, Charles J.
   Granny's little flock. 6274-1
"Hang garlands on the bathroom door". The bath. Rudolph Chambers Lehmann. 7008-6
Hang me among your winds. Lew Sarett. 6337-3
"Hang not the full weight of your hope on me:". The future speaks. Louis K. Anspacher. 6799-9
Hang out the flag. Stafford King. 6342-X
"Hang sorrow, cast away care". Song ("Hang sorrow, cast away care"). Unknown. 6933-9
"Hang thee, vile north easter". Another ode to the northeast wind. Unknown. 6802-2
Hang up his harp; he'll wake no more. Eliza Cook. 6102-8
"Hang up his harp; he'll wake no more." Eliza Cook. 6302-0;6385-3
Hang up the baby's stocking. Unknown. 6145-1,6684-4,6131-1
"Hange golden sleepe vppon hir eye-lids faire." Unknown. 6563-5
The hanged thing. Walter H. Kerr. 6218-0
Hangford, G. W.
   Speak gently. 6629-1
"Hangin' on." Frank Lebby Stanton. 6691-7
Hanging Johnny. Unknown. 6547-3
The hanging limb. Unknown. 6281-4
The hanging of the crane. Henry Wadsworth Longfellow. 6288-1
Hanging scroll. Gerald Stern. 6966-5
The hanging tree. G. Perle Schmidt. 6799-9
The hangman's ballad. Unknown. 6602-X
The hangman's song. Unknown. 6003-X
The hangman's song. Unknown. 6826-X
The hangman's wife. Hertha Kraftner. 6769-7
"Hangman, hangman, slack up your rope". The hangman's song. Unknown. 6826-X
Hangover. Philip H. Rhinelander. 6722-0
Hankey, Donald
   Lord of us all. 6337-3
Hankey, Kate
   The old, old story. 6131-1
Hankin, St. John
   De Gustibus-- 6760-3
Hankinson, Christine Park
   Alchemy. 6841-3
   Battle. 6841-3
   Dear heart. 6841-3
   Nuptials. 6841-3
   The sea. 6841-3
Hanks, Annie D.
   Example. 6632-1
Hanley, Mary K.
   Hands. 6530-9
Hanline, Maurice A.
   A song of Pierrot. 6300-4
Hanly, Elizabeth
   November eleventh. 6846-4
Hanmer, John Hanmer, Baron
   England. 7015-9,6793-X,6793-X

Mycenae. 7015-9
The old fisher. 7015-9
The pine woods. 6656-9
To the fountain at Frascati. 6624-0
Hanna, A. Judson
    Eternal youth. 7007-8
Hanna, Edward Judson
    Three gifts. 6144-3
Hanna, Hazel
    My garden. 6799-9
    Nature. 6799-9
    Ressurection. 6799-9
Hanna, Isaac
    The company store. 6149-4
Hannah and Samuel. Nathaniel Parker Willis. 6848-0
Hannah Armstrong. Edgar Lee Masters. 6029-3
Hannah Bantry in the pantry. Unknown. 6904-5
Hannah binding shoes. Lucy Larcom. 6240-7,6344-6,6408-6, 6239-3,6459-0,6735 ,6219-9,6304-7,6424-8,6484-1,6571-6,6744
Hannah Healy, the pride of Howth. Unknown. 6858-8
Hannah Jane. D.R. ("Petroleum V. Nasby") Locke. 6889-8
Hannah, Anna [or Annie] L.
    The white rose and the poppy. 6924-X,6167-2
Hannah, the mother. Julia Gill. 6304-7
Hannay, Jamesuis
    A ballad of Port Royal. 7041-8
Hannay, Patrick
    A maid me loved. 6563-5,6026-9
    Song ("Now do the birds"). 6563-5
    When as I wake. 6958-4
Hannele, sels. Gerhart Hauptmann. 6681-X
Hannibal's [assage of the Alps. Silius Italicus. 6749-2
Hannibal, sels. John Nichol. 6819-7
Hannon, Rose A.
    A legend. 6894-4
Hanover winter song. Richard Hovey. 7035-3
Hanover, John
    The miner's death. 6554-6
"Hans Breitmann choined de Toorners". Hans Breitmann and the Turners. Charles Godfrey Leland. 6791-3,6823-5
Hans and Fritz. Charles Follen Adams. 6791-3,6823-5,6914-2
Hans and Fritz. Unknown. 6451-5,6569-4
Hans Bleimer's mool. Isaac Hinton Brown. 6014-5
Hans Breitmann and the Turners. Charles Godfrey Leland. 6791-3,6823-5
Hans Breitmann's party. Charles Godfrey Leland. 6089-7, 6240-7,6302-0,6300-4,6307-1,6092-7,6155-9,6505-8
Hans Christian Anderson, 1805-1875 Sir Edmund Gosse. 6656-9
Hans in a fix. Unknown. 6279-2
Hans in a fix. Unknown. 6791-3,6823-5
Hans Vogel. Robert Buchanan. 6672-0
Hans' dog, Pete. Irene Davis Grueninger. 6906-1
Hans' midnight excuses. Unknown. 6791-3
Hanscom, Beatrice
    The old collector. 6441-8,6652-6
    Procrustes' bed. 6274-1
    Procrustes's bed. 6274-1
Hansen, Alfred M.
    Spring. 6799-9
Hansen, Katherine
    White as snow. 6799-9
Hansom cabbies. Wilfrid Thorley. 6776-X
Hanson, Dorothy
    Milky Way. 6764-6
Hanson, Frances
    Bugles in the dawning. 6224-5
Hanson, Gertrude
    The heart is Bethlehem. 6144-3
    I must light a candle. 6144-3
    Lac qui parle. 6342-X
    This holy night. 6144-3
Hanson, Joseph Mills
    Cowboy song. 6889-8,7007-8
    The little dreams. 6589-9
    Poppies. 6846-4
Hansson, Ola
    Songs of home, sels. Charles Wharton Stork (tr.). 6045-5

Hap. Thomas Hardy. 6186-9,6657-7
Hapless doom of woman. Alfred Lord Tennyson. 6655-0
"Haply some rajah first in ages gone". An ancient chess king. Jean Ingelow. 7015-9,7037-X,7015-9,7037-X
The happening. Mary Aldis. 6037-4
Happiest days. Unknown. 6226-1
The happiest girl in the world. Augusta Webster. 6429-9, 6321-7
The happiest heart. John Vance Cheney. 6310-1,6476-0,6102-8,6337-3,6730-1,6076-5,6250-4,6431-0,6300-4
The happiest land. Henry Wadsworth Longfellow. 6424-8
The happiest mortals once we were. George Granville; Baron Lansdowne. 6563-5
The happiest time of a woman's life. Frances H. Lee. 6889-8
Happiness. Earl Alonzo Brininstool. 6274-1
Happiness. Robert Burns. 6654-2
Happiness. Edgar A. Guest. 6869-3
Happiness. Grethe Helberg. 6555-4
Happiness. Ben Jonson. 6867-7
Happiness. John Keble. 6014-5,6424-8
Happiness. Virginia Wilson Lachicotte. 7016-7
Happiness. Richard Monckton Milnes; 1st Baron Houghton. 7015-9
Happiness. Alexander Pope. 6294-6,6302-0,6365-3,6600-3, 6304-7
Happiness. Bryan Waller ("Barry Cornwall") Procter. 6980-0
Happiness. Arschag Tchobanian. 6050-1
Happiness. Mary Dixon Thayer. 6037-4
Happiness an art. Edward Young. 6932-0
Happiness dependent on ourselves. Oliver Goldsmith. 6932-0
The happiness fairy. Emily K. Solliday. 6249-0
The happiness of America, sels. David Humphreys. 6008-0
"Happiness, pain,/Laughter, tears". The span of life. J. Talbott. 6818-9
Happy 'tis, thou blind, for thee. Douglas Hyde. 6090-0
"Happy and free, securely bless'd". The fair stranger. John Dryden. 6970-3
Happy are they who kiss thee. Aubrey Thomas De Vere. 6066-8
"Happy are those who can relieve". Ode ("Happy are those"). Herbert Read. 6532-5
Happy are those who have died. Charles Peguy. 6665-8
"Happy as Ulysses, his voyage done". Sonnet ("Happy as Ulysses"). Joachim Du Bellay. 6227-X
Happy as a king. Gabriel (Thomas Nicoll Hepburn) Setoun. 6639-9
Happy as a shepherd. Robert Greene. 6793-X
Happy as a shepherd. Robert Greene. 6874-X
The happy beggarman. Unknown. 6930-4
The happy bird. John Clare. 7015-9
The happy bird. Unknown. 6373-X
Happy Britannia, fr. The seasons (Summer). James Thomson. 6932-0
"Happy boy, happy boy". Youth in arms. Harold Monro. 6897-9
The happy change. William Cowper. 6152-4
The happy child. William Brighty Rands. 6429-9,6321-7
A happy child. Kate Greenaway. 6452-3,6135-4
Happy children. Sir Edmund Gosse. 6233-9
Happy children. Robert Louis Stevenson. 6530-9
"Happy choristers of air". Pastoral hymn. John Hall. 6931-2
"Happy choristers of air". John Hall. 6187-7,6334-9
"Happy choristers of aire". A pastorall hymne. John Hall. 6933-9
A happy couple. H. Elliott McBride. 6920-7
The happy dancer. Aristophanes. 6959-2
A happy day. Unknown. 6583-X
A happy day. Unknown. 6889-8
Happy days. Robert E. Bernhard. 6894-4
Happy ending. Wystan Hugh Auden. 6645-3
The happy ending. Alice Mary Kimball. 6880-4
Happy ghosts. Vincent B. Brecht. 6936-3
Happy greetings. Unknown. 6272-5
Happy he. Unknown. 6182-6
Happy he with such a mother. Alfred Lord Tennyson. 6097-8
The happy heart. Thomas Dekker. 6134-6,6737-9,6301-2,6246-5,6291-1,6302-0,6385-3,6339-X
Ae happy hour. Alexander Laing. 6180-X

HAPPY

The happy hour. Mary Frances Butts. 6097-8
The happy hour. Sylvia Lynd. 6320-9
The happy household. Eugene Field. 6078-1
The happy household. Eugene Field. 6318-7
The happy household. Eugene Field. 6949-5
The happy hunting grounds. Emily Pauline ("Tekahionwake") Johnson. 6837-5
The happy husband. Samuel Taylor Coleridge. 6543-0
The happy husbandman, or Country innocence. Unknown. 6157-5
The happy hyena. Carolyn Wells. 6466-3
"Happy in love was the bold Venetian sailor". Innamorata. William Force Stead. 6780-8
"Happy insect! what can be". The grasshopper. Anacreon (atr). 7039-6,6271-7
Happy insensibility. John Keats. 6246-6,6429-9,6321-7
Happy is England. John Keats. 6934-7
Happy is England now. John Freeman. 6477-9
Happy is he. Leonora Speyer. 6073-0,6217-2
"Happy is he, who, caring not for Pope". Calais, 1802, sels. William Wordsworth. 6867-7
"Happy is the country life". Unknown. 6933-9
The happy islands. Isabel Maude Peacocke. 6784-0
The happy isle, fr. The faerie queene. Edmund Spenser. 6436-1
The happy isles. Horace. 6949-5
Happy it is. Douglas Hyde. 6174-5
The happy land. William James Linton. 7009-4
The happy land. Unknown. 6193-1
Happy landing. W.G. & K.J.F. Schauffler & Jack S. Miner. 6237-7
The happy life of a country parson. Alexander Pope. 6092-7
The happy life. Henry Howard, Earl of Surrey. 6659-3,6584-8
The happy life. Mary Webb. 6421-3
The happy life. Sir Henry Wotton. 6240-7,6369-1,6479-5, 6302-0,6385-3,6271,6730-1,6214-8,6438-8,6134-6
The happy little cripple. James Whitcomb Riley. 6990-8
The happy little wife. Phoebe Cary. 6060-9
The happy lot. Ebenezer Elliot. 6543-0
Happy love. Charles Mackay. 6226-1
"'Happy love'! When shall that be?". The enigma. Walter De La Mare. 6905-3
"A happy lover who has come", fr. In memoriam. Alfred Lord Tennyson. 6867-7
A happy man. Carphyllides. 7039-6
The happy man. William Cowper. 6302-0;6385-3
The happy man. John Dryden. 6396-9
The happy man. Edgar A. Guest. 7033-7
The happy man. Annie M.L. Hawes. 7021-3
The happy man. Gilles Menage. 6089-7
A happy marriage. Thomas Campion. 6659-3
The happy marriage. Edward Moore. 6219-9
The happy miner. Unknown. 6281-4
"The happy mortal, who these treasures shares". The island of the blest, fr. Odes. Pindar. 6932-0
A happy new year! Thomas Hood. 6974-6
A happy new year. J.G. Francis. 6786-7
Happy night and happy silence. Edward Thring. 6747-6
The happy night. Richard Lawson Gales. 6776-X
The happy night. Sir John Collings ("Solomon Eagle") Squire. 6102-8
The happy pair. Johann Wolfgang von Goethe. 6948-7
The happy passing. William Ernest Henley. 6793-X
The happy piper. William Blake. 6114-1
The happy savage. Unknown. 6831-6
The happy sheep. Wilfrid Thorley. 6466-3,6262-8
The happy sheep. Wilfrid Thorley. 6368-3
Happy shepherds. Lady Anne Lindsay. 6747-6
Happy shepherds, sit and see. W. H. 6122-2
Happy shepherds, sit and see. William Hunnis. 6198-2
The happy smoking-ground. Richard Le Gallienne. 6453-1
Happy solitude - unhappy men. Madame De la Mothe Guion. 6814-6
"Happy songster! perch'd above". On the grasshopper. Unknown (Greek). 6814-6
"Happy soon we'll meet again". My brother and sister, in the country. Felicia Dorothea Hemans. 6973-8
The happy swain. Ambrose Philips. 6086-2
Happy Thanksgiving day. Lettie E. Sterling. 6703-4

"Happy the man who free from cares and strife". The second epode of Horace imitated. Thomas Warton (the Elder). 6962-2
"Happy the man who sees a god employed." William Cowper. 6225-3
"Happy the man whose wish and care". The contented man. Alexander Pope. 6874-X
"Happy the man, and happy he alone". Ode to Maecenas, sels. Horace. 6879-0
Happy the man, fr. Ode on solitude. Alexander Pope. 6187-7;6337-3
"Happy the man, who his whole time doth bound". The old man of Verona. Claudian. 7039-6
"Happy the nation whose God...", fr. The Bible. Unknown. 6606-2
Happy thought. Gertrude Pahlow. 6817-0
Happy thought. Robert Louis Stevenson. 6105-2,6122-2,6655-0,6723-9,6368-3
"The happy time when dreams have power to...". To J.H. (Col. John Hay) David Gray. 7041-8
The happy toad. Edgar A. Guest. 6869-3
The happy townland. William Butler Yeats. 6174-5,6179-6
The happy tree. Gerald Gould. 6730-1
The happy trio. Robert Burns. 6830-8
The happy valley. Pall Olafsson. 6283-0
A happy Vermonter. Daniel L. Cady. 6989-4
The happy wanderer. Percy ("Percy Hemingway") Addleshaw. 6437-X
A happy warrior. John Greenleaf Whittier. 6499-X
The happy warrior. Thomas Curtis Clark. 6995-9
The happy warrior. William Wordsworth. 6087-0,6589-9,6263-6,6438-8
"Happy was I". Jalal [or Jelal] ed-din Rumi. 6448-5
Happy were he. Robert Devereux, 2d Earl of Essex. 6182-6
"Happy were he could finish forth his fate". 'A passion of my lord of Essex' Unknown. 6935-5
"Happy were they, the mothers, in whose sight". The children whom Jesus blessed. Felicia Dorothea Hemans. 6973-8
"The happy white-throat on the swaying bough". The happy bird. John Clare. 7015-9
Happy wind. William Henry Davies. 6374-8,6466-3,6250-4
The happy wind. Ninette M. Lowater. 6130-3
Happy women. Phoebe Cary. 6969-X,6006-4
The happy world. William Brighty Rands. 6452-3,6466-3
"Happy ye leaves! when as those lily hands". Sonnet 001 ("Happy ye leaves"), fr. Amoretti. Edmund Spenser. 6315-2
"Happy, happier far than thou." Felicia Dorothea Hemans. 6066-8
Happy, happy country swains. Unknown. 6563-5
"Happy, happy, it is to be" Walter De La Mare. 6253-9,6656-9
"Happy, my life, the love you proffer". Triolet, after Catullus. Sir Edmund Gosse. 6875-8,6770-0
"Happy, oh, happy, so happy, so happy!". Verse ("Happy"). Unknown. 6118-4
"Happy, thrice happy times in silver age!". Desiderium. Phineas Fletcher. 6933-9

Harada, Gail N.
    First winter. 6790-5
    New year. 6790-5
    Painted passages. 6790-5
    Pomegranate. 6790-5

Harangue on the death of Chayim Nachman Bialik. Cesar Tiempo. 6759-X

Harbaugh, Henry
    Through death to life. 6909-6

Harbaugh, Thomas Chalmers
    Adam never was a boy. 6926-6
    Adam never was a boy. 6701-8
    The banner Betsey made. 6444-2
    Freedom's Thanksgiving day. 6703-4
    Grandma's wedding-day. 6675-5
    Grant - dying. 6701-8
    Not too old to fight. 6846-4
    Trouble in the 'amen corner.' 6414-0,6451-5,6964-9

"A harbinger of spring". The wren. Irene Davis Grueninger. 6906-1

Harbingers. Louella C. Poole. 6478-7

Harbor. Edward Farquhar. 6939-8
"A harbor in a sunny, southern city". Columbus. Helen L. Smith. 6964-9
The harbor longs for shouting. George Abbe. 6764-6
The harbor mine. F. McK. 6471-X
Harbor water, fr. Tidewater. Beatrice Ravenel. 6326-8
The harbor. Josephine Pinckney. 6037-4
The harbor. Carl Sandburg. 6154-0,6531-7,6527-9,6491-4
The harbor. Robert Southey. 6484-1
Harborless. Leslie Nelson Jennings. 6880-4
'Harbors only entered in the night' Felix Riesenberg. 7007-8
The harbour-mouth. Mabel Christian Forbes. 6269-5
The harbour. Winifred M. Letts. 6887-1
Harbury. Louise Driscoll. 6300-4,6476-0,6509-0,6556-2,6102-8,6076-5
Harby, Lee C.
    A legend of three missions. 6674-7
Harcourt, T.A.
    An ideal future. 6273-3
    What a Christmas carol did. 6917-7
"Hard above all things mortal is". Love's fragility. Alan Porter. 6780-8
"Hard aport! Now close to shore sail!". Adrian Block's song. Edward Everett Hale. 6946-0
"Hard as hurdle arms, with a broth of...". Harry Ploughman. Gerard Manley Hopkins. 6828-6
Hard by a crystal fountain. Thomas Morley. 6328-4
"Hard by the bower that held the maid". Mora-Mora, fr. The story of Baladeadro. George Gordon McCrae. 6768-9
"Hard by the eastern gate of hell". The descent to Hela. William Herbert; Earl of Pembroke. 6980-0
"Hard by the Indian lodges, where the bush". The corn husker. Emily Pauline ("Tekahionwake") Johnson. 6837-5
"A hard con/locking in the cell". Mask of stone. Henry Johnson. 6870-7
"Hard fate, that I should banished be". O my king. Unknown. 6859-6
A hard frost. Cecil Day Lewis. 6257-1
"Hard hatred faire, if thou wilt not consent." Unknown. 6563-5
"Hard is the fate of him who loves". Song ("Hard"). James Thomson. 6816-2
"Hard Rock/was/'known not to take no shit". Hard Rock returns to prison from the hospital for... Etheridge Knight. 6870-7
Hard labour. Walter De La Mare. 6905-3
Hard metals. Daisy Lee Ervin. 6906-1
Hard Rock returns to prison from the hospital for... Etheridge Knight. 6870-7
"The hard sand breaks". Hermes of the way. Hilda ("H.D.") Doolittle. 6897-9
"Hard seeds of hate I planted". Blight. Edna St. Vincent Millay. 6986-X
Hard times. Unknown. 6109-5,6651-8,6687-9
"Hard times, hard times...for White-face!". White-face. James Rorty. 6781-6
"Hard toil can roughen form and face". Sir Walter Scott. 6407-8
Hard weather. George Meredith. 6828-6
Hard weather. George Meredith. 6199-0
A hard word. Unknown. 6684-4
The hard working miner. Unknown. 6149-4
Hard, Walter
    Medical aid. 6722-0
    The mountain farm. 7030-2
"A hard, stern man upon a sick bed lay". God is nowhere. Unknown. 6912-6
"Hard-headed, hard-souled men walked here". A tale. Robert Henigan. 6860-X
Hard-toed shoes. Albert Smith. 6149-4
"Harden now thy tyred hart, with more then flinty..." Thomas Campion. 6380-2,6794-8
Harden, Verna Loveday
    The empire answers. 6224-5
The harder task. Unknown. 6337-3
"The hardest thing in bringing up". Managing Vermont boys. Daniel L. Cady. 6989-4
The hardest time of all. Sarah Doudney. 6273-3,6303-9

"The hardest work in all the year". 'Shopping' in Vermont. Daniel L. Cady. 6988-6
Hardin, Floyd
    Onward, Christian soldier. 6542-2
    To my baby. 6880-4
Harding, Edward
    A morning meditation. 6174-5
    Nightfall. 6174-5
Harding, Eugenie B.
    Cuba's maiden martyr. 6686-0
Harding, Mildred D.
    In extremis. 6857-X
Harding, Philip M.
    The internationalists. 6542-2
    White feather. 6542-2
Harding, Ruth Guthrie
    At the old ladies' home. 6030-7
    The call of the Scot. 6088-9
    Daffodils. 6338-1,6653-4
    From a car-window. 6338-1,6019-6,6653-4,6029-3
    "I heard her whisper." 6648-8
    In a forgotten burying-ground. 6027-7
    A lark went singing. 6648-8
    The Madonna of the carpenter shop. 6608-9
    On a fly-leaf of Schopenhauer's Immortality. 6337-3
    Song ("Today I have fled"). 6029-3
    Threnody. 6083-8,6102-8,6076-5
    You. 6556-2
Harding, Samuel
    Of Death. 6563-5
Hardinge, William M. (tr.)
    Not such your burden. Agathias, 7039-6
    Pastoral. Theocritus, 6102-8
    Pastoral. Meleager, 6253-9
    Spring. Meleager, 7039-6
    To a locust. Meleager, 6253-9
    Vanity of vanities. Palladas, 7039-6
"Hardly a hermit thrush had stirred". Novitiate. William Griffith. 6782-4
"Hardly we breathe, although the air be free". The sea cave. Thomas Doubleday. 7015-9,6997-5,7015-9,6997-5
Hardman, Helen
    Famine on a schedule. 6750-6
The hardship of accounting. Robert Frost. 6722-0
Hardships of a boy. Unknown. 6715-8
Hardwick arras. Wilfred Rowland Childe. 6780-8
The hardy soldier. Isaac Watts. 6934-7
Hardy, Albert
    Hail fellow, well met. 6451-5
    Sam. 6451-5
Hardy, Arthur Sherburne
    Iter supermum. 6309-8
Hardy, Elizabeth Clark
    Some time at eve. 6085-4
Hardy, Elizabeth Stanton
    The aristocrat. 6979-7
    Sea shell. 6337-3
    Signature upon rock. 6979-7
Hardy, Irene
    A wedding-day gallop. 6241-5
Hardy, Lizzie Clark
    The hole in the floor. 6916-9
    Some time at eve. 6303-9
    Tommy Brown. 6687-9
    When I sail away. 6337-3
Hardy, Polly
    Going. 6894-4
Hardy, R. Wayne
    The lone biker. 6870-7
    Meeting halfway. 6870-7
    October hill. 6870-7
    Poem written before Mother's day for Mrs. Lopez from... 6870-7
    A wintering moon. 6870-7
Hardy, Thomas
    After a journey. 6208-3,6246-6,6150-8
    After reading Psalms XXXIX, XL, etc. 6378-0
    After the club-dance, fr. At Casterbridge fair. 6828-6
    After the fair, fr. At Casterbridge fair. 6828-6
    After the visit. 6208-3,6246-6

Afterwards. 6655-0,6208-3,6541-4,6375-6,6125-7,6653-4, 6723
"Ah, are you digging on my grave?" 6506-6,6527-9
An ancient to ancients. 6776-X
An ancient to ancients. 6641-0,6102-8,6023-4,6659-3
'And there was a great calm.' 6125-7
Angosto Theo. 6730-1
At a house in Hampstead. 6828-6
At Casterbridge fair, sels. 6828-6
At Casterbridge fair: former beauties. 6208-3
At Castle Boterel. 6208-3,6246-6,6150-8
At Lulworth cove a century back. 6659-3
At tea. 6491-4
At the draper's. 6637-2
At the pyramid of Cestius near the graves of Shelley... 6331-4
An August midnight. 6828-6
Autumn in the park. 7020-5
The ballad singer. 6186-9,6317-9
Beeny cliff. 6645-3
Before marching, and after. 6051-X
The blinded bird. 6102-8
A broken appointment. 6506-6,6657-7,6150-8
Budmouth dears. 6733-6
By the earth's corpse. 6657-7
The carrier. 6102-8
Channel firing. 6665-8
Chorus ("Yea, the coneys are scared"). 6315-2
Choruses on the eve of Waterloo. 6334-9
A Christmas ghost-story. 6828-6
A church romance. 6210-5
Compassion. 6510-4
The convergence of the twain. 6210-5
The dark-eyed gentleman. 6733-6
The darkling thrush. 6073-0,6477-9,6536-8,6634-8,6657-7, 6437 ,6507-4,6430-2,6666-6,6655-0,6250-4,6199 ,6508-2,6645-3,6723-9
Dead 'Wessex,' the dog, to the household. 6488-4,6536-8
The dead quire. 6430-2
The dissemblers. 6655-0
The division. 6186-9
Drummer hodge. 6507-4,6657-7
The dynasts, sel. 7014-0
The dynasts, sels. 6726-3,6665-8
Embarcation. 6323-3
The end of the episode. 6186-9,6317-9
Epitaph on a pessimist. 6633-X
The fallow deer at the lonely house. 6488-4
The field of Talavera. 6323-3
First or last. 6655-0
Former beauties, fr. At Casterbridge fair. 6828-6
Four footprints. 6102-8
Friends beyond. 6186-9,6437-X,6477-9,6472-8,6508-2
The garden seat. 6641-0
George Meredith. 6828-6
George Meredith. 6199-0
God's funeral. 6532-5,6730-1
God-forgotten. 6507-4,6655-0
The going of the battery. 6793-X
The going. 6204-0
Great things. 6186-9
"Had he and I...", fr. The dynasts. 6726-3
Hap. 6186-9,6657-7
The haunter. 6246-6
He abjures love. 6378-0
Her dilemma. 6828-6
Her immortality. 6655-0
Her initials. 6828-6
His education. 6186-9
"I found her out there." 6317-9
I look into my glass. 6210-5
"I look into my glass". 6187-7,6317-9
I met a man. 7014-0
"I need not go". 6187-7,6437-X
'I said to love'. 6657-7
"I said to love." 6655-0
The impercipient. 6337-3,6657-7,6730-1,6430-2,6508-2
In a cathedral city. 6908-8
In a waiting-room. 6331-4
In a wood. 6289-X,6430-2,6508-2

In church. 6637-2,6491-4
In Tenebris. 6208-3,6657-7,6491-4
In the days of crinoline. 6722-0
In the moonlight. 6154-0,6102-8,6301-2
In the servants' quarters. 6506-6,6532-5
In time of 'the breaking of nations'. 6844-8
In time of 'The breaking of nations'. 6315-2,6659-3, 6581-3,6102-8,6153-2,6655 ,6625-9,6052-8,6186-9,6634-8
The inquiry, fr. At Casterbridge fair. 6828-6
Lament. 6879-0
Last chorus, fr. The dynasts. 7014-0
Last words to a dumb friend. 6511-2
Lausanne. 6641-0,6657-7,6210-5
Let me enjoy. 6655-0
"Let's meet again to-night, my Fair", fr. Queen. 6634-8
The man he killed. 6154-0,6589-9,6301-2,6464-7,6102-8, 6542-X,6655-0
Marching song. 6334-9
The market-girl, fr. At Casterbridge fair. 6828-6
Men who march away. 6186-9,6477-9,6474-4,6634-8
The minute before meeting. 6378-0
The missed train. 6070-6
Moments of vision. 7014-0
Mute opinion. 6657-7
Nature's questioning. 6657-7,6199-0
Near Lanivet. 6315-2
Neutral tones. 6108-7,6150-8,6655-0,6491-4
New year's eve. 6527-9,6508-2
The night of Trafalgar. 6179-6,6258-X,6541-4,6125-7
On a midsummer eve. 6186-9,6210-5,6655-0
On an invitation to the United States. 7039-6
On Sturminster foot-bridge. 6430-2
On the departure platform. 6317-9
On the portrait of a woman about to be hanged. 6069-2, 6659-3
On the portrait of a woman about to be hanged. 6777-8
1967. 6879-0
Outside the window. 6491-4
The oxen. 6636-9,6044-7,6186-9,6216-4,6303-9,6477-9, 6532 ,6508-2,6655-0,6723-9,6608-9,6668-2,6421 ,6625-9,6634-8,6337-3,6476-0,6581-3,6430 ,6746-8,6153-2, 6645-3
Paths of former time. 6908-8
The phantom horsewoman. 6186-9,6317-9,6186-9
The pity of it. 6666-6
The pity of it. 7031-0
A poet. 6655-0
The puzzled game-birds. 6510-4
The queen of Cornwall, sels. 6634-8
Rain on a grave. 6828-6
Rain on a grave. 6430-2
"Regret not me." 6179-6,6246-6,6317-9,6733-6
The reminder. 6488-4
Revulsion. 6828-6
The robin. 6943-6
The Roman road. 7014-0
The roman road. 7020-5
Rome. 6828-6
The ruined maid. 6733-6,6633-X
The sacrilege. 6655-0
The second night. 6655-0
The self-unseeing. 6208-3,6246-6
Semi-choruses and chorus from "The Dynasts". 6607-0
The seven times. 6655-0
She hears the storm. 6154-0,6102-8
She, to him. 6186-9,6437-X
The sheep fair. 6393-4
Shelley's skylark. 6655-0,6331-4,6483-3,6625-9,6634-8, 6250-4,6439
Shut out that moon, sels. 6472-8
The sigh. 6655-0
A singer asleep. 6483-3,6430-2,6508-2
The sleep-worker. 6186-9
Snow in the suburbs. 6655-0
Song of the soldiers. 7031-0
The spring call. 7020-5
The Statue of Liberty. 6199-0
The subalterns. 6507-4
Surview: cogitavi vias meas. 6317-9

Tess's lament. 6210-5
Then and now. 7026-4
This summer and the last. 6908-8
A thought in two moods. 6199-0
To an unborn pauper child. 6186-9
To life. 6828-6
To Lizbie Brown. 6317-9
To Shakespeare. 6483-3,6655-0
To the moon. 6125-7
Transformations. 6393-4
The two houses. 6336-5
The two Rosalinds. 6184-2
Under the waterfall. 6506-6
"Upon a pet's page I wrote". 6289-X
The voice. 6208-3,6320-9,6150-8
Wagtail and baby. 6510-4
Waiting - both. 6538-4,6726-3
Waiting both. 7014-0
Weathers. 6138-9,6726-3,6138-9,6179-6,6339-X,6427 ,6506-6,6026-9,6153-2,6655-0
Wessex heights. 6208-3
When I set out for Lyonnesse. 6331-4,6657-6,6439-6
"When the present has latched its postern". 6187-7
"When we lay where Budmouth Beach is." 6317-9
'Why do I?' 6908-8
A wife waits, fr. At Casterbridge fair. 6828-6
The wind blew words. 6199-0,6393-4
Without ceremony. 6879-0,6908-8
Wives in the Sere. 6655-0
The woman in the rye. 6655-0
The year's awakening. 6266-0,6374-8,6478-7,6253-9
Hardy, Thomas (tr.)
Forgotten. Sappho. 6435-3
Hardyknute. Lady Wardlaw; Elizabeth Halkett. 6960-6,6086-2
The hare and many friends. John Gay. 6198-2,6249-0,6385-3, 6084-6,6646-1
Hare drummer. Edgar Lee Masters. 6431-0
Hare, A.W.
Italy. 6600-3,6631-3
Hare, Amory
All will be well. 6619-4
Ancestors. 7038-8
The crown. 6979-7
Dawn broke today. 6347-0
How swiftly the bright coins of thought. 6347-0
Humility. 7038-8
I sometimes wonder. 6347-0
Life. 6347-0
My love was born when stars were dancing. 6347-0
The olympians. 6038-2
The theft. 6037-4
To one I love. 6347-0,6607-0
Walking at night. 6374-8
'What if we made our senses so astute'. 6607-0
Hare, Kenneth
Estrildis. 6070-6
Puritan ("Through life's sweet..."). 6070-6
The puritan. 6070-6
Stad Damme. 6893-6
Hare, Madeline
Neighbor. 6857-X
Hare, Maurice
Byway in biography. 6339-X
Free-will and predestination. 6339-X
Hare, Thomas Truxtun
A Bohemian drinking song. 6936-3
To one I love. 6936-3
The **hare**, fr. Fires. Wilfred Wilson Gibson. 6234-2
Hare-hunting, fr. The chace. William Somervile. 6932-0
The **hare**. Walter De La Mare. 6596-1
The **hare**. Stanley Snaith. 6257-1
The **hare**. William Wordsworth. 6134-6
Harebell and pansy. Laurence Binyon. 7020-5
A **harebell**. Lucy Larcom. 6129-X
The **harebell**. Muriel Stuart. 6269-5
Harebells. Emily Henrietta Hickey. 7037-X,6046-3
Harford, Lesbia
Beauty and terror. 6349-7
I have golden shoes. 6349-7
Harger, Charles Moreau
The prairie schooner. 6615-1
Hargrave, Alletha Goss
Dream moments. 6799-9
Hargrave, Ivan
Let the warm air condense on the window. 6475-2
Nocturne. 6475-2
There will be music. 6475-2
Hargreaves, W.
Song of the drunkard. 6404-3
Haring, Fay Goode
Satisfied. 6799-9
Harington, George
Song ("Trust the form"). 6563-5
Harington, Sir John
Angelica and the ork. 6436-1
Elegy wrote in the tower, 1554 6182-6
Epigrams ("Treason doth never prosper;...") 6427-2
Fair, rich, and young. 6182-6
Fortune. 6385-3
I see my plaint. 6182-6
Of a certain man. 6089-7,6089-7,6385-3
Of a certaine man. 6385-3
Of a precise tailor. 6089-7
Of the warres in Ireland. 6385-3
Of treason. 6102-8,6385-3,6733-6
Of writers that carp at other men's books. 6385-3
Orlando furioso, book XXXIV, sels. 6586-4
A sonnet made on Isabella Markham... 6182-6,6436-1
Harington, Sir John (tr.)
Bought locks. Martial, 7039-6
Harjo, Joy
Anchorage. 7005-1
Crossing the border into Canada. 7005-1
New Orleans. 7005-1
Remember. 7005-1
"She had some horses" 7005-1
"Hark - to the sound!". The rising of the north. Bryan Waller ("Barry Cornwall") Procter. 6980-0
"Hark hark how Bellona thunders." Unknown. 6563-5
"Hark how the lyrick choristers o' th' wood". To Clarastella on St. Valentines day morning. Robert Heath. 6933-9
Hark jolly shepherds. Thomas Morley. 6328-4
Hark the herald angels sing. Charles Wesley. 6466-3,6747-6, 6304-7,6608-9
"Hark the horn!". Kane to the king. Unknown. 6859-6
"Hark the voice of every nation". The roll-call of the ages. James Leigh Joynes. 7009-4
"Hark to the cowbells". Pastoral ("Hark"). Gustaf Froding. 6045-5
"Hark to the long resilient surge o'...tide". The sea in bondage. William ("Fiona Macleod") Sharp. 6997-5
Hark to the merry birds. Robert Bridges. 6266-0,6478-7, 6487-6
"Hark to the rattle's discordant swell!". The rattle-watch of New Amsterdam. Arthur Guiterman. 6773-5
Hark to the shouting wind. Henry Timrod. 6374-8
"Hark to the solemn bell". Unknown. 6238-5
Hark!. Rose Terry Cooke. 6155-9
"Hark! 'tis freedom that calls, come...". A song ("Hark! 'tis freedom..."). Unknown. 6946-0
"Hark! 'tis the bluebird's venturous strain". The bluebird. Thomas Bailey Aldrich. 6820-0
"Hark! 'tis the prophet of the skies". Redemption. William Bingham Tappan. 6752-2
"Hark! 'Tis the rush of the horses". The call. Francis William Bourdillon. 7031-0
"Hark! 'tis the rushing of a wind that sweeps". Percy Bysshe Shelley. 6997-5
"Hark! 'tis the twanging horn o'er...bridge". The winter evening, fr. The task. William Cowper. 6814-6
"Hark! 'tis the voice of the mountain". The battle of Eutaw. William Gilmore Simms. 6946-0
"Hark! do I hear again the roar". Columbus dying. Edna Dean Proctor. 6946-0
"Hark! from the right bursts forth a trumpet's". Battle of Maclodio [or Macalo], fr. Conte di Carmagnola. Vittorio Alfieri. 6973-8
"Hark! from yon covert, where those...oaks". Hare-hunting, fr. The chace. William Somervile. 6932-0

Hark! hark! Leonora Speyer. 6102-8,6374-8,6076-5
"Hark! hark! down the century's long...slope". Yorktown centennial lyric. Paul Hamilton Hayne. 6946-0
"Hark! hark! the lark at heaven's gate sings". William Shakespeare. 6723-9,6660-7,6737-9,6543-0,6639-9,6424,6189-3,6197-4,6371-3,6125-7,6153-2,6192-3,6252-0,6099-4,6052-8,6558-9,6232-6,6187-7,6726 ,6395-0,6073-0,6182-6,6240-7,6289-X,6132 ,6315-2,6328-4,6604-6,6481-7,6122-2,6154 ,6743-6,6302-0,6385-3,6536-8,6438-8,6194
Hark! hark! the nightingale. Tony Shepherd. 6383-7
"Hark! hark! the sweet vibrating lyre". Ode on music. Francis Hopkinson. 6753-0
"Hark! hark! they're come! those merry bells". The welcome home. Caroline Anne Bowles Southey. 6980-0
"Hark! heard you not those hoofs of dreadful note?". Unknown. 6240-7
Hark! how all the welkin rings. Charles Wesley. 6219-9
"Hark! in the still night. Who goes there?". Sixteen dead men. Dora Sigerson Shorter. 6930-4
"Hark! now everything is still". John Webster. 6182-6,6315-2,6536-8,6641-0,6194-X,6189
"Hark! see'st thou not the torrent's flash". Unknown. 6902-9
"Hark! that's the nightingale". Pain or joy. Christina Georgina Rossetti. 6943-6
Hark! the convent bells are ringing. Thomas Haynes Bayly. 6543-0
"Hark! the heavenly chords resounding". The advent. William White. 6868-5
Hark! the herald angels sing. Charles Wesley and George Whitefield. 6337-3
"Hark! What spirit...", fr. A hymn of nature. Robert Bridges. 6487-6
"Hark! the hours are softly calling". Spring. Adelaide Anne Procter. 6957-6
"Hark! the rattling roll of the musketeers". The cavalry charge. Benjamin Franklin Taylor. 6113-3,6471-X,6016-2,6304-7,6580-5
"Hark! The wandering prairie spirit chants". The rune of the prairie. Gertrude Huntington McGiffert. 6838-3
"Hark! the wind!". Wings. Hermann Hagedorn. 6944-4
"Hark! Young democracy from sleep". Young democracy. Bernard O'Dowd. 6784-0
"Hark!.../What booming". Arcana sylvarum. Charles De Kay. 7041-8
"Hark!/An idea/Is like a tiny spark". An idea. Januario Puruganan. 6799-9,6906-1
"Hark, 'tis a mother singing to her child". A mother singing. Edward Moxon. 6980-0
"Hark, 'tis freedom that calls, come, patriots". A song ("Hark,'tis freedom"). Unknown. 6589-9
"Hark, all you ladies that do sleep." Thomas Campion. 6182-6,6181-8,6430-2
"Hark, hark the trumpets blowing, Hussars". The field marshal. Ernst Moritz Arndt. 6952-5
Hark, hark! The dogs do bark. Unknown. 6466-3
"Hark, hark! the lark at heaven's gate sings". To Imogen, fr. Cymbeline. William Shakespeare. 6827-8
"Hark, hark". Unknown. 6363-2
Hark, hark, my soul!. Frederick William Faber. 6723-9
"Hark, how the surges dash". Where are the ships of Tyre? Clinton Scollard. 6850-2,6770-0,6875-8
Hark, my soul. John Austin. 6931-2
"Hark, my soul it is the Lord". William Cowper. 6065-X
"Hark, now everything is still". Dirge. John Webster. 6533-3
"Hark, the cock crows, and yon bright star". The new year: to Mr. W.T. Charles Cotton. 6933-9
Hark, the glad sound! Philip Doddridge. 6219-9,6747-6
"Hark, the robins sweetly sing". Spring song. Jessie Young Norton. 6049-8
"Hark, the soft and silvery note". Autumn glow. Joshua Freeman Crowell. 6798-0
Hark, where the trumpet now calls. Unknown. 6328-4
"Harke how ye nightingale displayes." Unknown. 6563-5
"Harke this lesson." Unknown. 6563-5
"Harke, harke, me thinkes I heer Loue Saye." Unknown. 6563-5
"Harken, o Lord, unto the right". Psalm 017. Bible. 6848-0

Harker, Signalman G.
  Desert warfare. 6468-X
Harkness, Georgia
  The agony of God. 6337-3
  For God so loved the world. 6144-3
  God suffers. 6532-5
  Simon of Cyrene. 6144-3
  Swinging toward the light. 6337-3
  The understanding heart. 6337-3
Harlan, Raymond A.
  When feelin' sad and blue. 6583-X
Harland, Marion
  A sunset prophecy. 6688-7
Harlaw. Sir Walter Scott. 6395-0
Harlem. Jean Brierre. 6178-8
The Harlem dancer. Eli Edwards. 6032-3
The Harlem dancer. Eli Edwards. 6959-2
Harlem, Montana: just off the reservation. James Welch. 7005-1
Harley's rose. David Lang. 6857-X
Harley, T.
  'Limpy Tim.' 6744-1
Harlot's catch. Robert Nichols. 6210-5
The harlot's house. Oscar Wilde. 6959-2
The harlot's house. Oscar Wilde. 6301-2
Harlow, Parr
  Arbor day ode. 6049-8
  Invocation ("We, children of the free"). 6049-8
  Invocation (for Arbor Day). 6171-0
Harlow, S. Ralph
  Church triumphant. 6337-3
  O young and fearless prophet. 6337-3
  Who is so low. 6337-3
Harlowe, Beatrice
  Ring loud, O Easter bells. 6720-4
  A snow-shoe tramp. 7035-3
  Storm fiends. 6714-X
Harman, Elizabeth
  The soldier's dirge. 6820-0
The harmless luxury. Phoebe Cary. 6969-X
Harmodius and Aristogeiton. Callistratus. 6271-1
Harmodius and Aristogeiton. Unknown (Greek) 6435-3
Harmonie du soir. Charles Baudelaire. 7039-6
Harmonies. Melrose Pitman. 6906-1
"Harmonious din, thee only that hour brings". Tidal music. E.H. Brodie. 6997-5
The harmonious heedlessness of Little Boy Blue. Guy Wetmore Carryl. 6891-X
The harmonious vision of the earth. Paul Fort. 6343-8
"Harmony - the only heaven". Harmony is heaven. Edward R. Huxley. 6885-5
Harmony in unlikeness. Charles Lamb. 6086-2
Harmony is heaven. Edward R. Huxley. 6885-5
The harmony of love. Thomas Lodge. 6189-3
Harmosan. Count Platen. 6842-1
Harmosan. Richard Chenevix Trench. 6219-9,6271-7,6344-6,6045-1,6614-3,6302-0,6385 ,6370-5,6552-X,6424-8,6639-9
The harnet and the bittle. J.Y. Akerman. 6125-7
Harney, W.E.
  West of Alice. 6384-5
Harney, Will Wallace
  Jimmy's wooing. 6620-8
  Running the blockade. 6113-3
  The stab. 6406-X,6104-4
Harney, Will Walllace
  Adonais. 7041-8
Haro. Henry Cuyler Bunner. 6721-2
"Haro of the north". Song ("Haro of the north,") fr. The lady of the lake. Sir Walter Scott. 6199-0
"Haro! Haro!/Judge now betwixt this woman...". The appeal to Harold. Henry Cuyler Bunner. 7041-8
Harold. Alfred Lord Tennyson. 6188-5
Harold P. Wright (tr.)
  Billy the kid. Shuntaro Tanikawa, 6803-0
  Cliffs. Rin Ishigaki, 6803-0
  Living. Rin Ishigaki, 6803-0
Harold and Tostig. Unknown. 6323-3
Harold the dauntless. Sir Walter Scott. 6049-8
Harold the dauntless, sels. Sir Walter Scott. 6047-1

Harold the wanderer, fr. Chile Harold's Pilgrimage. George
    Gordon, 6th Baron Byron. 6832-4
Harold's song. Sir Walter Scott. 6519-X
Harold's song to Rosabelle, fr.Lay of the last minstrel.
    Sir Walter Scott. 6604-6,6660-7
Harold, sels. Alfred Lord Tennyson. 6066-8
Harolde, John
    Marbles. 7016-7
    Moving deep. 7016-7
    The raveling venture, sels. 7016-7
    To die. 7016-7
Haroun Al Raschid. Henry Wadsworth Longfellow. 6934-7
"Haroun the Just! - yet once that name". The Barmecides.
    Richard Chenevix Trench. 6980-0
Haroun's favorite song. Unknown (Arabian) 6232-6
Harp in the rigging. Hamish Maclaren. 6833-2
"The harp is hushed, in Kedron's vale". Mount Carmel. John
    Kebble Hervey. 6848-0
The harp of a thousand strings. Joshua S. Morris. 6277-6
The harp of Ossian. James Hogg. 7009-4
The harp of sorrow. Ethel Clifford. 6730-1
"Harp of the mountain-land! sound forth again". The harp
    of Wales. Felicia Dorothea Hemans. 6973-8
"The harp of Zion sleepeth". The harp of Zion. James
    Willis. 6848-0
"The harp of Zion's psalmist now is still". The silent
    harp. Unknown. 6913-4
"Harp of Zion, pure and holy". Harp of Zion. William Knox.
    6848-0
Harp of the north. Sir Walter Scott. 6087-0,6110-9,6371-3
Harp of the north, farewell! Sir Walter Scott. 6086-2
The harp of the wind. Frances Shaw. 6509-0
The harp of Wales. Felicia Dorothea Hemans. 6973-8
Harp of wind and dream-like strain. Emily Bronte. 6655-0
Harp of Zion. William Knox. 6848-0
The harp of Zion. James Willis. 6848-0
Harp song of the Dane women. Rudyard Kipling. 6208-3
The harp that once through Tara's halls. Thomas Moore.
    6014-5,6328-4,6732-8,6438-8,6660-7,6737 ,6022-6,6086-
    2,6430-2,6560-2,6196-6,6104 ,6122-2,6244-X,6604-6,
    6484-1,6459-0,6481 ,6199-0,6250-4,6219-9,6513-9,6543-
    0,6964 ,6198-2,6239-3,6479-5,6302-0,6385-3,6102
The harp the monarch minstrel swept. George Gordon, 6th
    Baron Byron. 6848-0,6543-0
The harp.. Jakob Johannesson Smari. 6283-0
The harp: an ode. Bayard Taylor. 6976-2
The harp. Richard Dehmel. 6160-5
The harp. Michael Drayton. 6438-8
The harp. George Houghton. 7041-8
The harp. Virna Sheard. 6115-X
Harpagon and Valere talk..., fr. The miser. Moliere (Jean
    Baptiste Poquelin) 6637-2
Harpagon decides on a husband for his daughter,fr Miser.
    Moliere (Jean Baptiste Poquelin) 6637-2
Harpalus' complaint of Phillida's love. Unknown. 6436-1
Harpalus' complaint of Phillida's love bestowed on
    Corin... . Henry Howard, Earl of Surrey. 6191-5
The harper of Chao. Po Chu-I. 6357-8
Harper's Ferry. Carl John Bostelmann. 6979-7
Harper's Ferry floating away. Thomas Hornsby Ferril. 6761-
    1
Harper, C.F.
    Song of the battle-ships. 6471-X
Harper, Charles
    An Aboriginal mother's lament. 6627-5,6656-9,6768-9
    The cloud. 6768-9
    The creek of the four graves. 6768-9
    A storm on the mountains. 6768-9
Harper, Clarence S.
    Doris. 6118-4,6274-1
Harper, Isabel Westcott
    Highland night. 7027-2
Harper, John Warren
    He never took a vacation. 6631-3
Harper, Oliver
    The international band. 6926-6
The harper. Thomas Campbell. 6380-2
The harper. Helene Mullins. 6619-4
The harpist of Ur. Eldorous Dayton. 6818-9
Harpocrates. Bayar Taylor. 6976-2

Harps hung up in Babylon. Arthur Colton. 6310-1,6102-8,
    6730-1,6076-5,6467-1
Harps in Babylon. Arthur Colton. 6467-1
Harpsichord. Amanda Benjamin Hall. 6783-2
Harpur, Charles
    A midsummer noon in the Australian forest. 6384-5,6656-
    9
    'A similitude'. 6784-0
    Sonnet ("She loves me"). 6784-0
    Words. 6784-0
The harpy. Robert Service. 6159-1
Harrell, Kelly
    Away out on the mountain. 6179-6
Harriet Ames. Mary Grant. 6850-2
Harriet Beecher Stowe. Paul Laurence Dunbar. 6820-0
Harrigan, Ned
    "It glistened like silver, so sparkling and bright".
    6149-4
Harriman, Mrs. E.A.
    The rain. 6131-1
Harrington, Sir John
    Against writers that carp at other men's books. 6092-7
    Lines on Isabella Markham. 6219-9
    Of a certain man. 6996-7
    Of treason. 6934-7,6102-8
    A precise tailor. 6996-7
Harris (fr. Moorish), Walter (tr.)
    The garden of Alcinous, fr. The Odyssey. Homer, 6232-6
Harris and E.I. Williams, William
    The paratrooper's lament. 6231-8
Harris, C.M. (tr.)
    God's father care. Unknown (German), 6373-X
Harris, Foster
    Death. 6397-7
    Sundown. 6397-7
Harris, G.W.
    The coat of faded gray. 6074-9
Harris, Hazel Harper
    The hot tamale man. 6265-2
    Point of view. 6249-0
    A sailor's song. 6833-2
Harris, Helen C.
    I heard your heart's soft tears. 6178-8
    Spin me a dream. 6178-8
    To the singer. 6178-8
Harris, Isabella
    Hyannis by the sea. 6798-0
    The wind. 6798-0
Harris, Jana
    Glitter box. 6901-0
    The lady analyst & the little green room. 6901-0
    Pin money. 6901-0
Harris, Joel Chandler
    "Come along, true believer!". 6303-9
    De appile tree. 6605-4,6281-4
    De big Bethel Church. 6300-4
    My honey, my love. 6732-8
    Ol' Joshway an' de sun. 6280-6
    Plantation play song. 6332-2
    Plantation play-songs. 6332-2
    The plough-hand's song. 6096-X,6307-1
    Revival hymn. 6332-2
    Time goes by turns. 6281-4
    A wishing song. 6006-4
Harris, Kenneth
    The rocky hill. 6889-8
Harris, Louise Dyer
    Crossing Boston Common. 6722-0
    Review of a cook book. 6722-0
    Valley town. 6764-6
    What do you keep? 6764-6
Harris, M. Coleman
    A journey. 6654-2
Harris, Malana A.
    Chestnut time. 6529-5
    The flower's helpers. 6048-X
    Story of the apple. 6048-X
Harris, Max
    Lullaby ("Girl with eyes"). 6349-7
    Mad Jasper. 6349-7

HARRIS

Harris, Mrs. Charles
    Limerick:"..man with a fad". 6811-1
    Limerick:"..old lady who said". 6811-1
    Limerick:"..old man of Wisbeach". 6811-1
    Limerick:"..young lady of Luton". 6811-1
    Limerick:"A cynic of much savoir-faire". 6811-1
    Limerick:"A thoughtful old man of Lahore". 6811-1
Harris, Oralee Brown
    I am brown. 6750-6
Harris, Robert
    Three sailormen were drowned at sea. 6397-7
Harris, S. Taylor
    Peggy leg. 6290-3
    The plank. 6290-3
Harris, Thaddeus Mason
    The little orator. 6314-4,6673-9
Harris, Thomas Lake
    God speaks in all religions. 6102-8,6337-3,6076-5
    Sentences of wisdom, sels. 6102-8,6076-5
    Silent tongue, sels. 6102-8,6076-5
Harrison, Anthony
    The tinker and the glazier. 6064-1
Harrison, Belle R.
    Life. 6274-1
Harrison, Clifford
    The benediction ("In the year eighteen and nine..."). 6661-5
    The cabala. 6848-0
    Faithful unto death. 6661-5,6683-6
Harrison, Edna L.
    First lady. 6178-8
Harrison, George
    The epitaph acrostick on Robert Blake. 6547-3
Harrison, Henry
    Pride. 6954-1
    Warrior without a shield. 6042-0
Harrison, J.C.
    May. 6118-4
Harrison, Karl C.
    We make iron in Birmingham. 6954-1
Harrison, Kendall
    His share. 6031-5
    To a dead soldier. 6030-7
Harrison, Leslie
    Fate. 6118-4
Harrison, Richard
    Verrocchio. 6767-0
Harrison, Susan Frances ("Seranus")
    Benedict Brosse. 6115-X
    Catharine Plouffe. 6115-X
    Chateau Papineau. 6656-9
    Danger. 6115-X
    Gatineau Point. 6115-X
    In March. 6115-X
    Les chantiers. 6115-X
    The mother. 6474-4
    "O it were good, it were sweet". 6796-4
    The old regime, fr. Song of welcome. 6795-6
    Petite Ste. Rosalie. 6115-X,6081-1
    Rose Latulippe. 6795-6
    St. Jean B'ptiste. 6115-X
    September. 6656-9
    The voyageur. 6115-X
Harrison, Virginia B.
    Fenelon's Prayer. 6578-3
Harrison, William
    The tinker and the glazier. 6787-5
    The water cure. 6787-5
Harrold, William
    Time of apocalypse. 6998-3
Harrow and Flanders. Robert O.A. Crewe-Milnes, Marquess of Crewe. 6477-9
A Harrow grave in Flanders. Robert O.A. Crewe-Milnes, Marquess of Crewe. 6250-4
The harrowing of hell. Unknown. 6022-6
"Harry Ashland, one of my lovers." Unknown. 6385-3
Harry Carey's reply. Henry Carey. 6230-X
Harry Hawker. Francis Hackett. 6033-1
Harry Kemp. Willard Wattles. 6615-1
Harry Ploughman. Gerard Manley Hopkins. 6828-6

Harry Ploughman. Gerard Manley Hopkins. 6209-1
Harry Williams. Edgar Lee Masters. 6121-4
"Harry is a spender; brings me gifts of...". Gifts and givers. Berton Braley. 6853-7
"Harry whose tuneful and well measur'd song". Sonnet 013: To Mr. H. Lawes, on his aires. John Milton. 6933-9
Harry's arithmetic. Unknown. 6314-4
Harry's dog. Emma Celia & Lizzie J. Rook. 6137-0
Harry's mistake. Unknown. 6314-4
Harsen, Una W.
    Prayer before meat. 6144-3
    Sacrament. 6144-3
    To Mary, mother of Christ. 6144-3
"The harsh bray and hollow". Two kitchen songs. Edith Sitwell. 7000-0
"The hart he loves the high wood". Unknown. 6904-5
The hart of Mossfennan. John Veitch. 6819-7
Hart, Bessie G.
    A boy's mercy. 6670-4
Hart, Elizabeth
    Quest. 6042-0
Hart, F.W.
    Trysting. 6116-8
Hart, Henry Hersch (tr.)
    Nature and man. Wang Wei, 6482-5
Hart, Jerome A.
    Phantom of the rose. 6273-3
    The phantom of the rose. 6273-3
Hart, Joanne
    I walk on the river at dawn. 6966-5
Hart, Joel T.
    The captive humming bird. 6273-3
Hart, M.T.
    Tom. 6699-2
Hart, Richard
    An inhibited person. 6120-6
    The mill. 6039-0
    A mother with young kittens. 6120-6
Hart-Smith, William
    Columbus goes west. 6384-5
    Drama. 6384-5
    Space. 6349-7
Hart-leap well. William Wordsworth. 6133-8,6369-1,6219-9
Hart-leap well, sels. William Wordsworth. 6867-7
Harte, Francis Bret
    After the accident. 6565-1
    The aged stranger. 6889-8
    The aged stranger. 6732-8,6307-1,6572-4
    The angelus. 6241-5
    An Arctic vision. 6946-0
    At the hacienda. 6431-0
    The babes in the woods. 6077-3
    The ballad of the Emeu. 6089-7
    Battle bunny-- Malverne hill. 6743-3,6808-1
    Bill Mason's bride. 6910-X
    Caldwell of Springfield. 6742-5,6444-2
    Chicago. 6820-0
    Chicago: October 10, 1871 6212-1,6438-8
    The chimney's melody. 6573-2
    Chiquita. 6281-4,6467-1,6438-8,6255-5,6165-6,6271-7, 6498-1,6302-0,6735
    Concha. 6600-3
    Coyote. 6006-4,6134-6
    Crotalus. 6467-1
    The dead politician. 6219-9
    Dickens in camp. 6385-3,6240-7,6406-X,6465-5,6478-7, 6632 ,6600-3,6707-7,6309-8,6300-4,6304-7,6291 ,6250-4,6188-1,7041-8
    Dolly Varden. 6004-8
    Dow's flat. 6302-0,6385-3,6735-2,6566-X,6281-4,6121
    The engineer's signal. 6632-1
    Entertaining sister's beau. 6014-5,6451-5,6155-9
    Fate. 6102-8,6414-0,6076-5,6212-1,6219-9,6424
    Flynn of Virginia. 6481-7
    A geological madrigal. 6802-2
    Gould's signal. 6744-1,6424-8
    A Greyport legend. 6239-3,6424-8
    Grizzly. 6006-4,6597-X,6431-0,6424-8,6510-4
    Half an hour before supper. 6911-8
    The hawk's nest 6077-3

The heathen Chinee. 6102-8,6732-8,6302-0,6076-5
Her letter. 6370-5,6165-6,6289-X,6409-4,6499-X,6630 ,
   6004-8,6652-6,6219-9,6438-8,7041-8,6732-8,6385-3,
   6706-9
His answer to her letter. 6438-8
'How are you, sanitary?' 6113-3,6340-3,6016-2,6470-4
'I was with Grant.' 6406-X,6552-X
In the tunnel. 6062-5
Jessie. 6239-3
Jim. 6385-3,6404-3,6279-2,6722-0,6089-7,6735 ,6288-1,
   6300-4
John Burns of Gettysburg. 6062-5,6113-3,6392-6,6404-3,
   6471-X,6552 ,6470-1,6442-6,6016-2,6307-1,6267-9,6808
   ,6472-5
Madrono. 6431-0
Master Johnnie's next-door neighbor. 6260-1,6412-4,6572-4
Master Johnny's next door neighbor. 6155-9
Midd Edith helps things along. 6249-0,6486-8,6167-2,
   6570-8
Miss Blanche says. 6004-8
Miss Edith comforts brother Jack. 6713-1
Miss Edith's modest request. 6692-2
Mrs. Judge Jenkins. 6077-3,6289-X,6722-0
"Not yet, O friend! not yet". 6238-5
The old camp-fire. 6252-0
On a cone of the big trees. 6484-1
Our priviledge. 6113-3
The personified sentimental. 6902-9
Plain language from truthful James. 6092-7,6219-9,6438-
   8,6288-1,6307-1,6431-0,6736-0,6467-1,6505 ,6486-8,
   6735-2,6121-4,6300-4,6723-9,6464 ,6089-7,6271-7,6583-
   X,6722-0,6077-3,6385
Presidio de San Francisco 1800 6484-1
Ramon. 6385-3
Relieving guard. 6104-4,6250-4,6309-8
The return of Belisarius. 6281-4
The reveille. 6328-4,6113-3,6074-9,6239-3,6427-2,,6465-
   1,6471-X,6328-4,6113-3,6074-9,6239-3,6427-2,6465 ,
   6016-2,6322-5,6241-5,6639-9,6471-X
San Francisco. 6732-8
San Francisco, sels. 6289-X
Second review of the grand army. 6113-3,6074-9,6340-3
The society upon the Stanislaus. 6089-7,6270-7,6735-2,
   6102-8,6385-3,6481 ,6300-4,6219-9,6076-5,6121-4,6396-
   9,6089-7,6270-7,6735-2,6102-8,6385-3,6481
Swiss air. 6902-9
The throes of science. 6279-2
To a sea-bird. 6073-0,6597-X,6309-8
To the Piocene skull. 6302-0,6385-3,6089-7,6505-8
Truthful James, sels. 6077-3
The two ships. 6337-3
What Miss Edith saw from her window. 6578-3
What the bullet sang. 6322-5,6340-3,6437-X,6646-1,6467-
   1,6241-5,6300
What the chimney sang. 6132-X,6104-4
What the drums say. 6579-1
What the engines said. 6735-2
What the wolf really said to Little Red Riding-hood.
   6620-8,6004-8
The willows. 6089-7
The wonderful spring of San Joaquin. 6484-1
Harte, Walter
   A soliloquy. 6271-7,6302-0,6385-3
Hartich, Alice
   Remembering. 6464-7
Hartley, John
   To a daisy. 6274-1,6656-9
Hartley, Susan
   Holly. 6373-X
   Marigolds. 6373-X
   A winter song. 6215-6
Hartman, Helen M.
   Moving day. 6465-5
Hartman, Marcella
   Rejection slip. 6761-1
Hartman, Mary R.
   Rugged faces. 6818-9
Hartmann, Helen
   Desert night. 6850-2

Hartnoll, Phyllis
   The carpenter ("Silent at Joseph's side he stood").
      6144-3,6335-7,6532-5
Hartridge, Emelyn Battersby
   Song ("There are days"). 6116-8
Hartshorne, M.C.
   Reality. 6397-7
Hartsock, Ernest
   Armistice Day, 1928 6542-2
   Christ at eight. 6542-2
   Garden magic. 6649-6
   Gotterdammerung. 6420-5,6542-2
   Madonna in Flanders. 6542-2
   Okefenokee swamp. 6396-9
   Second coming. 6781-6
   Strange splendour. 6780-8
Hartswick, F.C.
   Somewhere-in-Europe-wodky. 6089-7
Hartswick, Jennie Betts
   To St. Valentine. 6820-0
Hartwick, Rose A.
   Curfew must not ring to-night. 6392-6
Hartwig, Gustav
   The last string. 6670-4
Hartz-journey in winter. Johann Wolfgang von Goethe. 6976-2
Hartzell, Ruth A.
   I love life. 6799-9
Harumichi No Tsuraki
   "The stormy winds of yesterday". William N. Porter
      (tr.). 6852-9
The Harvard commemoration ode, sels. James Russell Lowell.
   6340-3,6305-5,65244,6467-1
Harvard declares war. Brent Dow Allinson. 6542-2
Harvard Phi Beta Kappa poem, fr. Nocturne in a library.
   Arthur Davison Ficke. 6051-X
"Harvard, by that old man emeritus". Eliot to Wilson.
   Percy MacKaye. 7001-9
Harvest. Eva Gore Booth. 6730-1
Harvest. Dana Burnet. 6029-3
Harvest. Everett Cameron. 6761-1
Harvest. Ellen Mackay Hutchinson Cortissoz. 6271-7
Harvest. Eva Gore-Booth. 6161-3
Harvest. Hafiz. 6448-5
Harvest. Edith Heilman. 6042-0
Harvest. Mary Hoxie Jones. 6979-7
Harvest. Joyce Lancaster. 6850-2
Harvest. Elinor Lennen. 6316-0
Harvest. Thomas Nashe. 6436-1
Harvest. Alice Wellington Rollins. 6529-5
Harvest. Robert Haven Schauffler. 6501-5
The harvest circle. Melissa Cunningham Southworth. 6900-2
Harvest home. Henry Alford. 6214-8,6337-3,6730-1
Harvest home. George Villiers, 2d Duke of Buckingham. 6071-4
Harvest home. Frederick Tennyson. 6437-X
Harvest home. (Frederick) Ridgely Torrence. 6979-7
Harvest home song. John Davidson. 6820-0
The harvest home. Edward Hovell-Thurlow; 2d Baron Thurlow.
   7015-9
Harvest hwome: second part. William Barnes. 6659-3
Harvest hwome: the vu'st part. William Barnes. 6659-3
Harvest hymn. Felicia Dorothea Hemans. 6973-8
Harvest hymn. Charles Sangster. 6115-X
Harvest hymn. John Greenleaf Whittier. 6465-5,6618-6
Harvest in Flanders. Louise Driscoll. 6443-4
Harvest moon. Josephine Preston Peabody. 6542-2
Harvest moon. Josephine Preston Peabody. 7026-4
"A harvest moon rose gracefully...". Song of the hop
   fields. Ina Draper DeFoe. 6750-6
The harvest moon. Henry Wadsworth Longfellow. 6239-3;6333-0
Harvest moon: 1914. Josephine Preston Peabody. 6029-3
Harvest moon: 1916. Josephine Preston Peabody. 6030-7
The harvest moon. Richard Butler Glaenzer. 6880-4
The harvest of the sea. John McCrae. 6833-2
The harvest of time. Harold Trowbridge Pulsifer. 6777-8
The harvest of time. Harold Trowbridge Pulsifer. 6037-4
Harvest season. Oran Raber. 6761-1
Harvest song. ichard Dehmel. 7039-6

Harvest song. Heinrich Holty. 6820-0
Harvest song. Gertrude Huntington McGiffert. 6838-3
A harvest song. Edwin Markham. 6449-3
A harvest stiff comes back to town. Keene Wallis. 6880-4
Harvest time. Emily Pauline ("Tekahionwake") Johnson. 6433-7,6591-0
Harvest time in Vermont. Daniel L. Cady. 6988-6
The harvest wind. Arthur S. Bourinot. 6115-X
Harvest-home. Robert Bloomfield. 6980-0
Harvest-home. John McClure. 6039-0
Harvest-home. Charles Tennyson Turner. 6980-0
Harvest-home song. John Davidson. 6274-1,6056-9
The harvest. William Aberg. 6870-7
The harvest. Arthur Milton Pope. 6799-9
The harvest. Unknown. 6923-1
Harvesters. Margaret Perkins Briggs. 7038-8
The harvesters' song. George Peele. 6191-5
Harvesting wheat. Norbert Krapf. 6966-5
Harvestmen a-singing, fr. The old wives' tale. George Peele. 6122-2,6198-2,6189-3
Harvests of roses and grapes. Antonin Sova. 6886-3
Harvey, Alexander
With me in paradise. 6144-3,6335-7
Harvey, Christopher
Comfort in extremity. 6931-2
Harvey, Frederick W.
The bugler. 6477-9,6102-8
Ducks. 6477-9
Ducks, sels. 6395-0,6501-5,6532-5
If we return. 7029-9
On Painswick beacon. 6070-6
Stars. 6777-8
Harvey, Gabriel
To the learned shepheard. 6483-3
Harvey, James Clarence
At the stage door. 6923-1
The bicycle ride. 6923-1
A challenge. 6578-3
A challenge. 6923-1
The daughter of the desert. 6688-7
Laddie's long sleep. 7008-6
The nameless guest. 6920-7
The rabbi and the prince. 6614-3,6674-7
A Roman legend. 6417-5
The whistling regiment. 6450-7
The whistling regiment. 6923-1
Harvey, Margaret
Phantasy. 6836-7
Wayworn. 6836-7
Harvey, Victoria Adelaide
Except...sometimes. 6750-6
Not even a memory. 6750-6
Harvey, William
The boy with the little bare toes. 6368-3
Harwick mine disaster. Harry Mosley. 6149-4
Harwood, Charles W.
The color guard. 6223-7
Harwood, Elna
Dagmar. 6690-9
Harwood, H.C.
From the youth of all nations. 6474-4,6542-2
Harwood, Ruth
The shoe factory. 6776-X,6478-7
Haryngton, John
A heart of stone. 6827-8
"Has a love of adventure, a promise of gold". The whaleman's song. Unknown. 6833-2
The has and the are. Unknown. 6714-X
"Has any one seen my fair". Cressid. Nora Perry. 7041-8
"Has any one supposed it lucky to be born". Algernon Charles Swinburne. 6289-X
"Has anybody seen a little midget". Midget's bedtime. Unknown. 6965-7
"Has god, thou fool! work'd solely for thy...". 'Essay on man,' sels. Alexander Pope. 6943-6
"Has Nelson heard?". On the sinking of the Victoria. Thomas Edward Brown. 6809-X
"Has no one seen my heart of you". Thomas Lovell Beddoes. 6187-7
"Has not since been heard of". Unknown. 6742-5

"Has our government quite lost its wits". Limerick:"Has our government quite lost its wits". Unknown. 6811-1
Has she forgotten? James Whitcomb Riley. 6992-4
Has sorrow thy young days shaded? Thomas Moore. 6244-X, 6129-1,6543-0
"Has summer come without the rose". Song ("Has summer come"). Arthur O'Shaughnessy. 6232-6,6250-4,6226-1, 6301-2,6655-0
Has summer come without the rose? Arthur O'Shaughnessy. 6122-2,6094-3,6656-9
"Has the Marquis La Fayette". A new song. Joseph Stansbury. 6946-0
"Has the Marquis of Lafayette". A pasquinade. Joseph Stansbury. 6753-0
"Has the spring come back, my darling". In the dark (1). Alice Cary. 6969-X
The has-beens.. Walt Mason. 6291-1
Hasbrouck and the rose. Phelps Putnam. 6217-2
Haseesh. Victor Robinson. 6482-5
Haseloff, Charles
America. 6998-3
Haskell, Thomas Nelson
King Konkaput's apostrophe upon Pike'a Peak. 6836-7
Haskin, Leslie L.
Christ the carpenter. 6065-X
Haskins, H. Stanley
Indestructible. 6750-6
Haskins, M. Louise
The gate of the year, sels. 6337-3
Hasleden, Percy
Crooked corner. 6804-9
Hasley, Louis
Earth watch. 6017-X
Home is where. 6761-1
Hasluck, Paul
A drunken man on Highgate Hill. 6349-7
Hass, K. O.
Louisiana. 8818-9
Hassall, Christopher
"I heard a voice say 'Look...," fr. Penthesperon. 6317-9
Penthesperon, sels. 6317-9
Solilioquy to Imogen, fr. Penthesperon. 6317-9
Hassan Ben Hassan. James Abraham Martling. 6952-5
"Hassan Ben Khaled, singing in the streets". The temptation of Hassan Ben Khaled. Bayard Taylor. 6976-2
Hassan to his mare. Bayard Taylor. 6510-4
Hassan, sels. James Elroy Flecker. 6427-2
Hassler, C.C.
Story of Lincoln. 6708-5
"Hast thou a charm to stay the morning-star". Before sunrise, in the vale of Chamouni. Samuel Taylor Coleridge. 6749-2
"Hast thou a friend? Thou hast indeed". On a true friend. Unknown (Greek). 6814-6
"Hast thou been in the woods with honey-bee?". The child's return from the woodlands. Felicia Dorothea Hemans. 6973-8
"Hast thou come with the heart of..childhood..". The return. Felicia Dorothea Hemans. 6973-8
"Hast thou entered into the treasures of the snow?" Bible. 7020-5
"Hast thou entered...", fr. The Bible. Unknown. 6106-0
"Hast thou ever known the feeling". The belfry of Ghent. Robert Maguire. 6554-6,6912-6
"Hast thou given the horse strength?) hast...". The, fr. The Book of Job glory of the horse. Bible. 7010-8
Hast thou given the horse strength?, fr. Book of Job. Bible. 6125-7
"Hast thou indeed flown, marvellous boy". To Gustav Hamel. Charles Whitby. 6994-0
"Hast thou not seen an aged rifted tower". Hartley Coleridge. 6980-0
"Hast thou not seen an aged rofted tower". Sonnet ("Hast thou not"). Hartley Coleridge. 6545-7
"Hast thou o'er the clear heaven of thy soul". Comfort. Adelaide Anne Procter. 6957-6
"Hast thou seen the down in the air". A song ("Hast thou seen"). Sir John Suckling. 6562-7

"Hast thou seen with flash incessant." William Wordsworth. 6110-9
"Hast thou then wrapped us in thy shadow,death". To death. Sir William Rowan Hamilton. 7015-9
Hast thous seen the down in the air. Sir John Suckling. 6250-4
Haste not, rest not. Johann Wolfgang von Goethe. 6337-3
"Haste on, my joys! your treasure lies". Robert Bridges. 6487-6
Haste thee, nymph. John Milton. 6959-2
"Haste thee, nymph, and bring with thee". L'allegro, sels. John Milton. 6934-7
Haste, Gwendolen
    Cinema. 6808-1
    Death of the grandmother. 6979-7
    Dried out. 6880-4,6750-6
    Hollyhocks. 6232-6
    Horizons, fr. Montana wives. 6076-5
    The little theatre. 6037-4
    Montana wives. 6776-X
    Montana wives. 6538-4
    Montana wives, sels. 6076-5
    Montana wives: horizons. 6506-6
    Nostalgia. 6038-2
    Ophida. 6979-7
    Prayer of the homesteader. 6396-9
    'Rolands flame-hearted' 7019-1
"Haste, with your torches, haste!". Scene in a Dalecarlian mine. Felicia Dorothea Hemans. 6973-8
Hasten spring. William Sawyer. 6841-3
Hastings. John Reade. 6433-7
Hastings mill. Cicely Fox Smith. 6478-7
Hastings Mill. Cicely Fox Smith. 7012-4
"Hastings! I knew thee young, and of a mind". To Warren Hastings, Esq. William Cowper. 6814-6
Hastings' sonnets. Sir Egerton Brydges. 6980-0
Hastings, Cristel
    Things I love. 6750-6
Hastings, E.H.
    Over the hill. 6688-7
Hastings, Fanny de Groot
    Coral lizard. 6979-7
    Time table. 6799-9
Hastings, Frank
    Cripple Tim. 6689-5
Hastings, Lady Flora
    Early rising. 6242-3,6131-1,6242-3
    Song of early rising. 6772-7
    To a butterfly. 6772-7
Hastings, Lady T.
    'Exactly so.' 6089-7
Hastings, Mary Wilhelmina
    A lover to his lady-love. 6118-4
Hastings, Thomas
    For hymn reading. 6001-3
    In sorrow. 6735-2,6219-9
    The latter day. 6735-2
The hasty pudding, sels. Joel Barlow. 6008-0,6121-4,6399-3
The hasty pudding: canto III. Joel Barlow. 6077-3
The hasty pudding. Joel Barlow. 6753-0
The hasty pudding. Joel Barlow. 6288-1
The hasty pudding. Joel Barlow. 6753-0
The hat given to the poet by Li-Chien. Po Chu-I. 6106-0
A hat trimmed by a mad woman. Ruth Mason Rice. 6039-0
Hat vs. wig. Thomas Moore. 6878-2
The hat.. Unknown. 6415-9
Hatch, Edwin
    Breathe on me, breath of God. 6337-3
    Heaven. 6337-3
    Immortality ("For me--to have made one soul"). 6303-9
Hatch, Francis Whiting
    He laughed last. 6722-0
    So this is middle age! 6722-0
Hatch, M.D.
    A debutante's boquets. 7021-3
The hatchet.. Unknown. 6158-3
Hate. Hala Jean Hammond. 6542-2
Hate. James Stephens. 6437-X,6102-8,6250-4,6464-7
"Hate and love, hate and love; circles still..". Triangle. Roslyn Greer. 7024-8

Hate and revenge. William Shakespeare. 6294-6
Hate of the bowl. Unknown. 6392-6,6403-5
"Hate whom ye list, for I care not." Sir Thomas Wyatt. 6584-8
"The hated dog sits". In memory of the moon.(A killing.) Charlotte DeClue. 7005-1
"Hath any loved you well, down there". Song from Chartivel. Marie de France. 7039-6
"Hath the heart not alms for its palsied hours". Charity. Gertrude Huntington McGiffert. 6838-3
"Hath the pearl less whiteness", sels. Thomas Moore. 6601-1
"Hath the summer's breath, on the south wind..". The seabird flying inland. Felicia Dorothea Hemans. 6973-8
Hathaway, Baxter (tr.)
    Hell's purgatory, sels. Edoardo Sanguineti, 6803-0
Hatheway, Mary E.N.
    Grandmother's cap. 6965-7
    The seasons. 6049-8
    Two visits. 6744-1
Hatred. William Shakespeare. 6294-6
Hatred of sin. William Cowper. 6814-6
"'Hats off' in the crowd...". A farewell to Pope. John R. Thompson. 6753-0
Hattie's views on housecleaning. Unknown. 6744-1,6167-2
Hatton, J.W.
    Not guilty. 6414-0,6744-1
Hatzfeld, Adolf von
    The hunt. Babette Deutsch (tr.). 6160-5
    Summer. Babette Deutsch (tr.). 6160-5
Hatzopoulos, Kostes
    Let the boat go. Rae Dalven (tr.). 6352-7
Haubold, Edith Chandler
    Strange harbors. 6750-6
Hauch, Carsten
    Early rising. Charles Wharton Stork (tr.). 6555-4
    When o'er the fields. Charles Wharton Stork (tr.). 6555-4
"Haue I watcht the winters nyght." Unknown. 6563-5
The haug-eye man. Opie Read. 6088-9
Haugh, Irene
    In Donegal. 6782-4
Haughey, Mary C.
    The chapel road. 6750-6
The haughs of Cromdale. Unknown. 6859-6
The haughty aspen. Nora Archibald Smith. 6608-9
"Haughty words, oh girl, do not use these words..." Unknown (Newari) 7013-2
Haul away O. Unknown. 6547-3
"Haul on the rope. Make the high bell lean". To the bell-ringer. Robert Farren. 6930-4
Haul the bowline. Unknown. 6547-3
Haulage. E.E. Nott-Bower. 6722-0
Hauman, Ruth H.
    Spring. 6850-2
The haunch of venison. Oliver Goldsmith. 6092-7,6152-4
The haunt of Grendel, fr. Beowulf. Unknown. 6102-8
The haunt of the deer, fr. Ben Dorain. Duncan Ban MacIntyre. 6180-X
The haunt of the sorcerer, fr. Comus. John Milton. 6102-8;6385-3
Haunted. Walter De La Mare. 6596-1
Haunted. Sir William Schwenck Gilbert. 6760-3
Haunted. Aline Kilmer. 6250-4
Haunted. Helen Lanyon. 6244-X
Haunted. Renee Roper. 6899-5
Haunted. Virginia Wuerfel Slayton. 6906-1
Haunted. Wilbert Snow. 6509-0
Haunted. Lilian White Spencer. 6490-6
Haunted. Louis Untermeyer. 6649-6
Haunted chambers. Unknown. 6273-3
Haunted country. Robinson Jeffers. 6808-1
Haunted earth. John Hall Wheelock. 6007-2,6037-4
A haunted garden. Louis Untermeyer. 6338-1
The haunted garden. Henry Treece. 6379-9
Haunted ground. Felicia Dorothea Hemans. 6973-8
The haunted Hazel. James B. Dollard. 6115-X
The haunted heart. Jessie B. Rittenhouse. 6019-6
Haunted house. Edythe Hope Genee. 6750-6
Haunted house. Edwin Arlington Robinson 6011-0

HAUNTED

The **haunted** house, sels. Thomas Hood. 6369-1,6545-7,6648-8, 6046-3
A **haunted** house. Harriet Eleanor Hamilton (Baille) King. 6543-0
The **haunted** house. Edmund Blunden. 6648-8
The **haunted** house. Felicia Dorothea Hemans. 6973-8
The **haunted** house. Thomas Hood. 6744-1,6102-8,6167-2,6567-8
The **haunted** house. Rubin Kane. 6799-9
The **haunted** house. Harriet Meyer. 6850-2
The **haunted** house. Unknown. 6490-6
Haunted in old Japan. Alfred Noyes. 6301-2
The **haunted** mountain, fr. Ranolf and Amohia. Alfred Domett. 6768-9
The **haunted** palace. Edgar Allan Poe. 6102-8,6399-3,6076-5, 6008-0,6250-4,6560 ,6288-1,6431-0,6126-5,6464-7,6125-7,6243-1,6134-6,6332-6,6333-0,6735-2,6176 ,6153-2, 6219-9,6467-1
A **haunted** room. John Myers O'Hara. 6102-8,6076-5
The **haunted** room. Hedwig W.D. Hilker. 6847-2
The **haunted** ship. Kassaris Emmanuel. 6352-7
The **haunted** shore. Wathen Mark Wilks Call. 7015-9
The **haunted** smithy. W.A. Eaton. 6416-7,6167-2
"A **haunted** soul put under ban". Bongwi. Kingsley Fairbridge. 6800-6
The **haunted** spring. Samuel Lover. 6502-3
Haunted village. Sarah N. Cleghorn. 6030-7
"**Haunted**? Ay, in a social way". Haunted. Sir William Schwenck Gilbert. 6760-3
The **haunter**. Thomas Hardy. 6246-6
Haunting eyes. Caroline Elizabeth Sarah Sheridan Norton. 6226-1
The **haunting** face. Robert Underwood Johnson. 6029-3
The **haunting** of Olaf. Edward Farquhar. 6939-8
The **haunts** of the halcyon. Charles Henry Luders. 6936-3
Haupt, James C.
   Peace, be still. 6799-9
Hauptmann, Gerhart
   Hannele, sels. William Archer (tr.). 6681-X
Hausgen, Mattie Lee
   Her favorites. 6466-3
Haushofer, Albrecht
   In chains, fr. Sonnets from Moabite prison. 6643-7
   The rats, fr. Sonnets from Moabite prison. 6643-7
   Sonnets from Moabite prison, sels. 6643-7
Hausman, Rita H.
   Word quest. 6850-2
Hausman, Ruth H.
   Chance. 6850-2
   City autumn. 6850-2
   Compensation. 6850-2
   For apathy. 6850-2
   Incursio. 6850-2
   Inscription for a garden gate. 6850-2
   Inscription for a garden gate (2). 6850-2
   Monticello. 6850-2
   New quarters. 6850-2
   On finishing the day's Latin. 6850-2
   The only poet. 6850-2
   Poem. 6850-2
   Rondel for light words. 6850-2
   Rondel to the untiring voice. 6850-2
   To an idle god. 6850-2
   To the wind in the leaves. 6850-2
Hausted, Peter
   "Have pity, grief; I cannot pay". 6187-7,6563-5,6562-7
   Have you a desire. 6830-8
   "Have you a desire to see". 6187-7,6737-9
   Of his mistress. 6563-5
Hauster, Peter
   The rival friends, sels. 6562-7
Haute couture of poetry. Wilhelm Szabo. 6769-7
Haute politique. Granville Trace. 6542-2
Have a care of life. Theocritus. 6102-8
"**Have** a heart, lady, don't evermore flout me". By request. Berton Braley. 6853-7
Have charity. Unknown. 6406-X
"**Have** courage, O my conradry of dreamers!". The dreamers. Sydney Jephcott. 6784-0
Have courage, my boy, to say no. Unknown. 6889-8

Have done! Walter De La Mare. 6905-3
"**Have** ever you sat by a midnight shore". Musings. Michael J. Campione. 6799-9
"**Have** I nocht made ane honest shift". Ane satire of the three estaitis, sels. Sir David Lyndsay. 6845-6
"**Have** I now found an angel in unrest". The force of love. William Henry Davies. 6884-7
Have faith. Edward Carpenter. 6730-1
Have I found her? Unknown. 6182-6
"**Have** I not felt the longing". Sir Aubrey De Vere. 6997-5
"**Have** love! not love alone for one." Johann C. Friedrich von Schiller. 6225-3
"**Have** mercie Lord, for man hath sought". Psalm 056. Bible. 6848-0
"**Have** my friends in the town,...gay busy town". An epistle to a friend in town. John Dyer. 6968-1
"**Have** pity, grief; I cannot pay". Peter Hausted. 6187-7, 6563-5,6562-7
"**Have** the elder races halted". Pioneers! O pioneers!, sel. Walt Whitman. 6954-1
"**Have** the trusts devoured your pay?". Laugh it off. Bolton Hall. 6880-4
Have thou no fear. Seumas (James Starkey) O'Sullivan. 6506-6,6628-3
"'**Have** we not earned our rest?' O, hear...". Non tali auxilio. Helen Bosanquet. 7042-6
Have you a desire. Peter Hausted. 6830-8
"**Have** you a desire to see". Peter Hausted. 6187-7,6737-9
"**Have** you a friend (look round and spy)". the countryman and jupiter. John Gay. 6972-X
"**Have** you a religion". Pebble, song and water fall. Alfred Kreymborg. 6887-1
Have you an eye? Edwin Ford Piper. 6032-3;6556-2
"**Have** you been in our wild west country? then". The west country. Alice Cary. 6865-0;6969-X
"**Have** you brought my boots, Jemima?". Getting up. Henry S. Leigh. 6920-7
"**Have** you come then, O my darling...". Theocritus. 6251-2
"**Have** you come/To lead me". New love. Evangeline Robinson. 6764-6
"**Have** you ever been down to my countree". The land where I was born. John Shaw Neilson. 6784-0
"**Have** you ever been on a warm sunny day". Valagils-river. Hannes Hafstein. 6854-5
"**Have** you ever known the wonder of a June...". Phantasy. Margaret Harvey. 6836-7
"**Have** you ever made a just man?" Stephen Crane. 6996-7
"**Have** you ever seen the capeland". For June. Joshua Freeman Crowell. 6798-0
"**Have** you ever seen the carnival, at Paris...". The carnival of 1848. William Allen Butler. 6903-7
"**Have** you ever stooped in the frosty morn". A northern trappers trail. George Weldon. 7035-3
"**Have** you ever waked up in the middle of the night?" Jessie Orton Jones. 6999-1
"**Have** you felt the master's touch". The master's touch. Alice Louise Cary. 6799-9
Have you forgotten that juggler - fate. William Lindsey. 6347-0
"**Have** you forgotten yet?". Aftermath. Siegfried Sassoon. 6850-2
'**Have** you got a brook in your little heart?'. Emily Dickinson. 6429-9,6321-7
"**Have** you got the jellies made, mother?". The debutante. Eugene Field. 6949-5
"**Have** you heard how a girl saved the...express". Kate Shelly. Eugene J. Hall. 6917-7
"**Have** you heard of Mistress Whitby?". A case of pedigree. Unknown. 6921-5
"**Have** you heard of Philip Slingsby". The fight with the snapping turtle. William Edmonstoune Aytoun. 6948-7
"**Have** you heard of the maly turning taken...". The day of Inverlochy. John (Iain Lom) MacDonald. 6845-6
"**Have** you heard the story of Deacon Brown". The story of Deacon Brown. Unknown. 6915-0
"**Have** you heard the tale of the aloe plant". Through death to life. Henry Harbaugh. 6909-6
"**Have** you heard the tiny trumpets". The freesia flower. Albert Durrant Watson. 6797-2
"**Have** you heakened the eagle scream over...". The Irish

hurrah. Thomas Osborne Davis. 6930-4
"Have you learnt the sorrow of windy nights". Ballade of windy nights. William Henry Ogilvie. 6875-8
"Have you lost your Christ, my brother". The lost Christ. Estella Moul Miller. 6906-1
"Have you never heard of Jimmy O'Neil?". Jimmy O'Neil. James Abraham Martling. 6952-5
"Have you not heard the poets tell". Baby Bell. Thomas Bailey Aldrich. 6219-9,6889-8
"Have you not noted, in some family". The birth-bond. Dante Gabriel Rossetti. 6828-6
Have you not noted, in some family. Dante Gabriel Rossetti. 6560-0
Have you not oft, in the still wind. George Darley. 6648-8
Have you not seen the timid tear. Thomas Moore. 6543-0
"Have you noticed that the splendid dreams,the". Crow's-foot. H.M. Leys. 6804-9
"Have you observ'd the wretch in the street". Unknown. 6933-9
"Have you read in any book, heard anybody tell". Kelly's Ferry. Benjamin Franklin Taylor. 6815-4
"Have you rested some night in the mountains". The call of Colorado. Eugene Dimon Preston. 6836-7
"Have you seen but a bright lily grow". Unspotted from the world. Ben Jonson. 7020-5
"Have you seen but a bright lily grow". Ben Jonson. 6187-7, 6339-X
"Have you seen him". Farm boy. Alexander Mertes. 6750-6
"Have you seen that strange insect...'walkingstick'?". Jessie Orton Jones. 6999-1
"Have you seen the garden of Irem?". The garden of Irem. Bayard Taylor. 6976-2
"Have you seen walking through the village". Ollie McGee. Edgar Lee Masters. 6897-9
Have you thought? Unknown. 6583-X
"Have you worked for a tinker, mistris". Unknown. 6933-9
Have you written to mother?. Jane Ronalson. 6097-8,6260-1
Have you? Harry M. Dean. 6374-3
Have you? Gretta M. McOmber. 6249-0
Havelock. S. Brooks. 6323-3
Havelock. Unknown. 6793-X
Haven. Harold Trowbridge Pulsifer. 6036-6
"A haven of rest to soul and to eye". The garden. Lois Stanton Phillips. 6799-2
"The haven roars, and o the haven roars...". Credhe's lament. Unknown. 6873-1
"Haven't been to one in almost three years". Powwow 79, durango. Paula Gunn Allen. 7005-1
Haven, Albert Roland
    Spain's hour of doom. 6741-X
Haven, Alice B.
    Ask and ye shall receive. 6260-1
    Bull Run. 6678-X
The haven, fr. A tiny trip. Joseph Ashby Sterry. 6770-0
Havens, Theodore F.
    Told at the tavern. 6273-3
Havergal, Frances Ridley
    'Be quiet: fear not.' 6461-2
    Behold your king! 6065-X
    Bells across the snows. 6145-1,6147-8
    Bonnie wee Eric. 7002-7
    The Col de Balm. 6749-2
    The common offering. 6225-3
    Easter dawn. 6177-X
    "Great our need, but greater far." 6225-3
    The great teacher. 6461-2
    "He is near to help and bless." 6225-3
    I gave my life for thee. 6656-9
    Lord, speak to me, that I may speak. 6337-3,6461-2
    "Master! to do great work for thee, my hand". 6238-5
    The message of an aeolian harp, sels. 6066-8
    'Now!' 6914-2
    "Oh, let me know." 6225-3
    Reality. 6065-X,6730-1
    Take my life. 6337-3
    Thanksgiving. 6618-6
    "That's not the way at sea." 6304-7
    "Then hush! oh, hush! for the Father knows..." 6225-3
    Thou art coming. 6730-1
    Thy presence. 6337-3
    "Tune for thyself the music of my days." 6225-3
    "We cannot love too much." 6066-8
    "We worship Thee, we bless Thee." 6225-3
    Who is on the Lord's side. 6337-3
    A worker's prayer. 6303-9
Haverhill, 1640-1890. John Greenleaf Whittier. 6333-0
Havez, Jean
    Tanksgibbin turkey. 6703-4
Havill, Juanita
    Diana's lament. 6857-X
    Presence. 6857-X
"Having assembled, the Gopis went to the forest..." Unknown (Newari) 7013-2
Having climbed the topmost peak of the incense-burner... Po Chu-I. 6253-9
"Having climbed with morning between...trees". New England letter. Frances Frost. 6761-1
Having clung so hard. Bryan Degnan. 6761-1
"Having known other seasons, other faces". Prayer in an artic season. Marguerite Janvrin Adams. 6979-7
"Having no blessed candle, Nikral took". Nikral II. Margaret Larkin. 6808-1
"Having put off this expedition ten, maybe...". Garage sale. Carol Kyle. 6821-9
"Having put on/their sailor suits again". Afterward. Gerhard Fritsch. 6769-7
"Having reached my boiling point". Ghetto. Yvette Johnson. 7024-8
"Having so rich a treasury, so fine a hoard". The daisy. Marya Alexandrovna Zaturenska. 6984-3
'Having the thrashers' in Vermont. Daniel L. Cady. 6988-6
"Having this day my horse, my hand, my lance". Sonnet ("Having this day"). Sir Philip Sidney. 6219-9
"Having this day my horse, my hand, my". Sir Philip Sidney. 6187-7
"Having worshipped the Ganesa..." Unknown (Newari) 7013-2
Haw-blossoms. James Matthewes Leagre. 7017-5
Hawaiian blues. Clifford Gessler. 6761-1
Hawaiian hurricane. Genevieve Taggard. 6347-0
Hawaiian sunset. Clarence L. Haynie. 6841-3
Hawarden. B. Paul Neuman. 6793-X
Haweis, Thomas
    Come and welcome. 6065-X
    O thou from whom all goodness flows. 6219-9
    Remember me! 6065-X
Hawes, Annie M.L.
    The happy man. 7021-3
    The last Tudor. 6926-6
    Love tapped upon my lattice. 7021-3
Hawes, Charlotte P.
    Down the slope. 6600-3
Hawes, Stephen
    The belles ryngeth to evensonge. 6733-6
    The epitaph of graunde amoure, fr. The palace of pleasure. 6125-7
    The epitaph of graunde amoure. 6198-2,6427-2,6436-1
    An epitaph. 6186-9
    An epitaph. 6022-6
    The excusacyon of the auctore. 6198-2,6586-4
    The garden glorious, fr. The pastime of pleasure. 6649-6
    The great mariage..., fr. The pastime of pleasure. 6198-2
    Here begynneth the passe tyme of pleasure. 6586-4
    His epitaph. 6102-8,6641-0,6153-2,6301-2
    How graunde amoure was recyved of La Belle Pucell. 6193-1
    Howe remembraunce made his epytaphy on his grave. 6193-1
    A pair of wings. 6881-2
    The pastime of pleasure, sels. 6193-1,6369-1,6586-4, 6649-6,6193-1
    The pastime of pleasure. 6369-1,6641-0
    The true knight. 6022-6
Hawick's crossing. Jane Stuart. 6218-0
Hawk. Clinton Scollard. 6073-0
The hawk ("The hawk slipped out of the pine..."). Arthur Christopher Benson. 6073-0,6395-0
The hak ("Thou dost not fly..."). William Henry Davies. 6073-0,6234-2

HAWK

Hawk afield. Evelyn Scott. 6073-0
"The hawk broods earthward". The hawk. Sidney Clouts. 6788-3
"The Hawk said to the Dove...". Unknown. 6050-1
Hawk shadow. Florence Wilkinson. 6619-4
Hawk! hawk! the lark!, fr. Songs. William Shakespeare. 6600-3
The hawk's nest. Francis Bret Harte. 6077-3
A hawk's thoughts. Alexey Koltsov. 6103-6
Hawk's way. Ted Olson. 6324-1
The hawk. Sidney Clouts. 6788-3
The hawk. Ibn al-Qabturnu. 6362-4
The hawkbit.. Sir Charles George Douglas Roberts. 6597-X
Hawke. Sir Henry Newbolt. 6323-3,6107-9
Hawke. Archibald T. Strong. 6784-0
Hawker, Robert Stephen
    Aishah Schechinah. 6096-X,6378-0,6282-2,6323-3,6022-6
    And shall Trelawny die? 6427-2,6102-8,6668-2
    Angels of the spring. 6374-8
    Are they not all ministering spirits. 6199-0
    Aunt Mary. 6292-X,6172-9
    A Christ-cross rhyme. 6022-6
    A Cornish carol. 6747-6
    The Cornish emigrant's song. 6018-8
    The cuckoo's wit. 6105-2
    Death song. 6437-X
    The dirge. 6023-4
    The doom-well of St. Madron. 6518-X
    Featherstone's doom. 6656-9
    The first fathers. 6437-X
    The holly. 6105-2
    King Arthur's waes-hael. 6022-6,6282-2,6096-X,6437-X, 6172-9,6608 ,6292-X
    Mawgan of Melhuach. 6199-0
    Modryb Marya - Aunt Mary; a Christmas chant. 6756-5
    Morwennae Statio. 6096 X
    The mystic magi. 6125-7
    Pater vester pascit illa. 6656-9
    The quest of the Sangraal, sels. 6201-6
    The silent tower of Bottreau. 6473-6,6656-9
    Sir Beville. 6018-8
    Song of the Cornish men. 6271-7,6263-6
    The song of the western men. 6134-6,6437-X,6732-8,6188-5,6481-7,6639 ,6138-9,6105-2,6138-9,6136-2,6096-X, 6499 ,6023-4,6383-7,6322-5,6656-9,6660-7
    The southern cross. 6931-7
    To Alfred Tennyson. 6656-9
    Trebarrow. 6873-1
    Trelawney. 6228-8
    The wail of the Cornish mother. 6772-7
The hawker. Unknown. 6383-7
Hawkes, Charles
    Bilin' sap. 6497-3
Hawkes, Clarence
    Bilin' sap. 7035-3
    Christmas still lives. 6065-X
Hawkes, Henry Warburton
    "Thy kingdom come! O Lord." 6337-3
Hawkesyard. Sister Mary Benvenuta. 6096-X,6292-X
Hawkeye, Burlington
    The champion snorer. 6294-6
Hawking for the partridge. Unknown. 6380-2
Hawkins, Ethel Wallace
    The shadow of the end. 6118-4
Hawkins, Heloise M.B.
    Anniversary. 6836-7
    December. 6836-7
    Dream roses. 6836-7
    Gardens. 6836-7
    The joy of service. 6836-7
    Mine eyes have seen the glory. 6836-7
    Rainbow. 6836-7
Hawkins, Henry
    The bee. 6022-6
    Hoc cygno vinces. 6022-6
Hawkins, Milan E.
    What is the sonnet? 6799-9
Hawkins, S.S.
    The world is waiting for you. 6260-1
Hawkins, Sir Anthony. See "Hope, Anthony"

Hawkins, W.S.
    More cruel than war. 6964-9,6925-8
    Your letter, lady, came too late. 6074-9,6260-1
Hawkins, Willis
    The deacon's Thanksgiving. 6703-4
Hawks. James Stephens. 6102-8
Hawks, F. Lister
    The blind boy. 6131-1
    Faith in God. 6502-3,6131-1
Hawkshawe, Ann ("Aunt Effie")
    The carpenter's shop. 6018-8
    The clucking hen. 6937-1
    A cobweb made to order. 6131-1
    Cuckoo poem. 6018-8
    Freddy and the cherry-tree. 6018-8,6135-4
    The great brown owl. 6018-8
    The little boy and the stars. 6131-1
    The little hare. 6018-8
    The little raindrops. 6018-8,6937-1
    The old kitchen clock. 6135-4,6937-1
    Pussy-cat. 6459-0
    The water-mill. 6937-1,6018-8
    waves on the seashore. 6131-1
Hawley, Hudson
    Just thinkin'. 6443-4,6589-9
    Just thinking. 6846-4
Hawling, Mary S.
    Futility. 6782-4
Haworth churchyard. Matthew Arnold. 6655-0
Hawthorn. Unknown. 6273-3,6125-7
Hawthorn and lavender. William Ernest Henley. 6123-0
Hawthorn and lavender, sels. William Ernest Henley. 6507-4
The Hawthorn children. Eugene Field. 6949-5
Hawthorn for hope. Doris V. Lecky. 6850-2
"The hawthorn in the Devon lanes". The hawthorn. Jessie B. Rittenhouse. 6979-7
The hawthorn tree. Willa Sibert Cather. 6019-6
The hawthorn tree. Roberta Teale Swartz. 6619-4
Hawthorn, Kate
    Spring song ("Now the lovely spring has come..."). 6049-8
Hawthorn-time. Robert Crawford. 6269-5
The hawthorn. Jessie B. Rittenhouse. 6979-7
Hawthorne. Amos Bronson Alcott. 6820-0
Hawthorne. Henry Wadsworth Longfellow. 6126-5,6385-3,6600-3,6333-0,6600-3,6380-2,6385-3,6288-1,6304 ,6641-0
Hawthorne, Alice
    What is home without a mother? 6097-8,6449-3
Hawthorne, Julian
    Monarch and mendicant. 6327-6
Hawthorne, Nathaniel
    Brook farm. 6484-1
    Niagara. 6484-1
    The star of Calvary. 6006-4
Hawtrey, Edward Craven
    Helen seeks for her brothers. 6153-2
Hawtrey, Mrs.
    Autumn. 6131-1
    Boy's play and girl's play. 6127-3,6502-3
    Boys' play and girls' play. 6131-1
    Christmas. 6131-1
    The gardener's grandchild. 6131-1
    Golden autumn. 6529-5
Hay. Unknown. 6552-X
Hay fever. Unknown. 6411-6,6443-4
The hay field. Ethelwyn Wetherald. 6115-X
Hay wagon. Helen Frith Stickney. 6042-0
"Hay! hay! by this day". The scholar complains. Unknown. 6881-2
Hay's wharf. Richard Church. 6257-1
Hay, Clarence Leonard
    The down-and-out. 7007-8
Hay, Colonel John
    How it happened. 7041-8
    Regardant. 7041-8
Hay, Edwin B.
    Postively the last performance. 7022-1
    Two colors. 7022-1
Hay, F.W. Littleton
    The latest convert. 6453-1

Hay, Henry Hanby
   The fragrant timber of her fan. 7022-1
   A hymn for Arbor Day. 6047-1
Hay, John
   Aboriginal sin. 6388-8
   And grow. 6666-6
   Banty Tim. 6385-3,6550-3
   Bird song. 6388-8
   The chickadees. 6388-8
   The curse of Hungary. 6610-0
   Distichs. 6089-7
   The enchanted shirt. 6089-7,6486-8,6239-3,6277-6,6290-3,
      6415 ,6107-9,6808-1,6739-5,6134-6,6242-3,6249-0,6614-
      3,6696-8
   'The energy of light.' 6388-8
   Good and bad luck. 6089-7,6629-1,6026-9
   How it happened. 6620-8,6004-8
   Hymn of the Knights Templars. 6735-2
   Invocation ("Lord, from far several climes we come").
      6486-8
   Israel. 6848-0
   Jim Bludso. 6014-5,6052-8,6062-5,6077-3,6089-7,6134 ,
      6431-0,6281-4,6396-9,6076-5,6121-4,6736 ,6211-3,6260-
      1,6358-6,6370-5,6481-7,6486 ,6107-9,626502,6300-4,
      6464-7,6467-1,6332-3,6358-6,6451-5,6503-1,6605-4,
      6550 ,6497-3,6687-9,6732-8,6735-2,6512-0,6102
   Kilvany. 6424-8
   Liberty. 7022-1
   The light of love. 6226-1
   Little breeches. 6014-5,6089-7,6302-0,6481-7,6583-X,
      6605 ,6431-0,6214-8,6505-8,6260-1,6732-8,6294
   Love's prayer. 6066-8
   Miles Keogh's horse. 6510-4,6155-9
   The mystery of Gilgal. 6735-2
   Not in dumb resignation. 6337-3,6418-3,6730-1
   Old man of Tennessee. 6388-8
   On the bluff. 6484-1
   The pledge at Spunky Point. 6484-1
   The pledge of Spunkey Point. 6505-8
   The prairie. 6484-1
   Railway station. 6666-6
   Religion and doctrine. 6337-3,6730-1,6431-0
   Religion and doctrine. 6913-4
   Sister Saint Luke. 6285-7
   The stirrup cup. 6260-1,6605-4,6309-8
   Thy will be done. 6461-2
   To Theodore Roosevelt. 6995-9
   A triumph of order. 6406-X
   A winter night. 6785-9
   A woman's love. 6240-7,6385-3,6600-3
Hay, John (tr.)
   Amor mysticus. Sister Marcela de Carpio de San Felix,
      7039-6
   The azra. Heinrich Heine, 7039-6
Hay, M. Florence
   Artistry. 6316-0
   Dwellers of a tide pool. 6316-0
   Sea reverie. 6316-0
Hay, Peronnean D.
   The phantom bust. 6074-9
Hay, Sara Henderson
   The beasts. 6979-7
   Child on the beach. 6979-7
   Cordial soul. 6076-5
   Entrance into heaven. 6144-3
   Field of honor. 6750-6
   For a dead kitten. 6120-6,6076-5
   For a little bird that bludered into church. 6076-5
   Heresy indeed. 6532-5
   "Love suffereth long" 6144-3
   Mary. 6076-5
   Once more, ye laurels... 6761-1
   Prayer in April. 6337-3
   Reflections on an ideal existence. 6120-6
   The search. 6337-3
   The shape God wears. 6532-5
   Text ("Because I heard His ways were just"). 6532-5
   To my small son, in church. 6491-4
   Upon discovering one's own intolerance. 6337-3
   Warning. 6337-3

Hay, Sarah Henderson
   3 a.m. 6750-6
Hay, W. (tr.)
   On Ibycus. Unknown, 6624-0
Hay, fr. The bard of the Dimbovitza. Unknown. 6552-X
Hay-making. Karl Erik Forsslund. 6045-5
Hayashi, Utako
   Morning prayer. Lois J. Erickson (tr.). 6027-7
   My task. Lois J. Erickson (tr.). 6027-7
   Not alone. Lois J. Erickson (tr.). 6027-7
   A song of daily life. Lois J. Erickson (tr.). 6027-7
Hayden, Joe
   A hot time in the old time. 6736-0
Hayden, Lou Boyce
   Trials of a school-girl. 6710-7
   Young school reformer. 6713-1
Hayden, William Jr.
   Song for the barnstable celebration, 1839 6798-0
Hayes, Alfred
   The city of beggers. 6666-6
   The death of the craneman. 6390-X,6375-6,6666-6
   The hotel room. 6390-X
   Illusion. 6785-9
   The imitation of Faust. 6389-6
   In a coffee pot. 6640-2
   The lark in autumn. 6785-9
   Pasteur's grave. 7014-0
   Singleman. 6390-X
   Underground. 6640-2
Hayes, Ann Louise
   Alien. 6515-5
   Autumnal. 6515-5
   Daphne. 6515-5
   Desolation. 6515-5
   February. 6515-5
   Furlough. 6515-5
   In description. 6515-5
   Poem ("Here poppies"). 6515-5
   Poem ("Take thy silent"). 6515-5
   Prayer ("They will not"). 6515-5
   Query. 6515-5
   Sonnet for a marriage. 6515-5
Hayes, Anna Hansen
   Friends. 6836-7
   Homecoming. 6836-7
   Mother. 6836-7
   Renunciation. 6836-7
   The road in the sage. 6836-7
   Spring symphony. 6836-7
   Tapestries. 6836-7
Hayes, Evelyn
   Garden-lion. 6125-7
Hayes, Frank J.
   Little Jim. 6149-4
   We're coming, Colorado. 6149-4
Hayes, James M.
   A bleeding heart aflame. 6285-7
   But two I love. 6285-7
   The mother of the rose. 6172-9,6292-X
   Mother Saint Urban. 6285-7
   Old nuns. 6172-9,6285-7,6292-X
   Our lady of the skies. 6282-2
   Sister Mary Philomena. 6285-7
   Transfiguration. 6292-X,6172-9
Hayes, John Russell
   The death of the bee. 6936-3
   The library dove. 6510-4
   The old-fashioned garden. 6338-1
   Poppies. 6338-1
   The Quaker-lady. 6936-3
   White violets. 6936-3
Hayes, R. Priestley
   E pluribus unum. 6936-3
   Give and take. 6936-3
   The raving. 6936-3
Hayes, Will S.
   Contentment. 6273-3
Hayford, James
   Horn. 6388-8
   In closed universe. 6388-8

HAYFORD

    Under all this slate. 6388-8
Haying. John Fredericrick Herbin. 6446-9
'Haying the oats' in Vermont. Daniel L. Cady. 6988-6
Haying time in Vermont. Daniel L. Cady. 6988-6
Haying, Vermont and ginger drink coordinated. Daniel L. Cady. 6988-6
Hayley, William
    A card of invitation to Mr. Gibbon...1781. 6932-0
"Hayley, thy tenderness fraternal shown". To William Hayley, Esq. William Cowper. 6814-6
"Hayll, comly and clene". Unknown. 6106-0
"Hayll, derlyng dere". Unknown. 6106-0
"Hayll, sufferan Savyoure". Unknown. 6106-0
The **hayloft**. Robert Louis Stevenson. 6401-9,6466-3,6135-4
The **haymaker's** song. Alfred Austin. 6656-9
Haymakers, rakers, reapers and mowers. Thomas Dekker. 6383-7
Haynard, Virginia May
    If we knew. 6925-8
Hayne, Paul Hamilton
    After the tornado. 7041-8
    "And we, poor waifs, whose life term seems". 6238-5
    Ariel. 7041-8
    Artie's "amen". 6745-X,6155-9,6917-7
    Aspects of the pines. 7017-5,6753-0,6265-2,6288-1
    At last. 6177-X
    The battle of Charleston harbor. 6113-3,6062-5,6340-3, 6016-2
    Beauregard's appeal. 7041-8
    Between the sunken sun and the new moon. 6300-4,6121-4
    Beyond the Potomac. 6074-9,6113-3
    The bombardment of Vicksburg. 6552-X
    Bryant dead. 6820-0
    Butler's proclamation. 6946-0
    By the autumn sea. 6219-9
    Cambyses and the Macrobian bow. 6411-6
    Charleston. 6074-9
    A dream of the south wind. 6006-4
    Forgotten. 6121-4
    The ground squirrel. 6965-7
    Heroes of the south. 6113-3,6340-3
    In degree. 6889-8
    In harbor. 6102-8,6076-5,6288-1,6309-8,6464-7
    In the wheat-field. 6006-4
    Laocoon. 6121-4
    Little Lottie's grievance. 6965-7
    Little Nellie in the prison. 6413-2
    "A little while I fain would linger yet". 6753-0
    A little while I fain would linger yet. 7017-5,6008-0, 6288-1,6431-0
    Love scorns degrees. 6240-7,6385-3,6066-8
    Love's autumn. 6620-8
    Lyric of action. 6211-3,6577-5
    Macdonald's raid. 6411-6
    Midsummer in the south. 6121-4
    The mocking bird: at night. 6396-9
    The mocking bird. 6006-4,6077-3,6008-0,6121-4
    My study. 6753-0,7017-5
    The new sister. 6965-7
    The pine's mystery. 7017-5
    Praying for shoes. 6416-7
    Pre-existence. 7041-8
    Pre-existence. 6240-7,6600-3,6385-3,6219-9,6648-8,6219-9,6240-7
    The red lily. 7041-8
    The rose and thorn. 7041-8
    Shelley. 7017-5
    The silken shoe. 6965-7
    The snow-messengers. 6753-0
    The snow-messengers. 7017-5
    Sonnet-poets. 6753-0
    South Carolina to the states of the north. 6946-0
    A storm in the distance. 6265-2,6431-0
    The story of an ambuscade. 6673-9
    The stricken south to the north. 6946-0
    Sweetheart, good-bye! 6121-4
    To Longfellow. 7017-5
    To O.W. Holmes. 6820-0
    To W.H.H. 7017-5
    Tristram of the wood. 7041-8

    The true heaven. 6730-1
    Two epochs. 6066-8
    Under the pine. 6753-0
    Under the pine. 6121-4
    Under the pine. 6753-0
    The union of blue and gray. 6444-2
    Unveiled. 6753-0
    Upward and onward. 7002-7
    Vicksburg. 6074-9,6340-3,6678-X
    The will and the wing. 6753-0
    Yorktown centennial lyric. 6946-0
Hayne, William Hamilton
    Cavalry song. 6580-5
    The charge at Santiago. 6062-5
    Into the silence. 6995-9
    Loneliness. 6632-1
    Oliver Wendell Holmes. 6820-0
    Pine needles. 6047-1,6466-3,6049-9
    The red bird. 6695-X
    A sea lyric. 6833-2
    To my father. 7017-5
    Vernal solace. 6225-3
Haynes, Carol
    Aunt Selina. 6036-6
Haynes, Helen
    The cabin at the end of the road. 6799-9
Haynes, Louise
    Sometimes this happens. 6750-6
Haynes, Samuel A.
    The challenge. 6178-8
    Warning. 6178-8
Haynie, Clarence L.
    Counterfeit. 6841-3
    Explorer. 6841-3
    Hawaiian sunset. 6841-3
    Immunity of beauty. 6841-3
    Imperfect beauty. 6841-3
    Love's Hallowe'en. 6841-3
    Memories of Hawaii. 6841-3
    Surrender of beauty. 6841-3
Hays, Ednah Proctor (Clarke)
    The humming bird ("Dancer of air"). 6073-0,6597-X
    Mockingbird in a garden. 6232-6
    A Salem witch. 6946-0
Hays, H.R. (tr.)
    Alberto Rojas Jimenez comes flying. Pablo (Neftali Ricardo Reyes Basualto) Neruda, 6642-9
    Allegory of torment. Pablo de (Carlos Diaz Loyola) Rokha, 6759-X
    America, my sweet. Jacinto Fombona Pachano, 6642-9
    America, my sweet. Jacinto Fombona Pachano, 6642-9
    The angel and the rose. Carlos Oquendo de Amat, 6759-X
    Anger. Cesar Vallejo, 6642-9
    Anonymous speech. Ramon Lopez Velarde, 6642-9
    Anonymous speech. Jorge Carrera Andrade, 6642-9
    Aquarium. Eugenio Florit, 6642-9
    As time goes on. Emilio Adolfo von Westphalen, 6759-X
    The Ascension and the Assumption. Ramon Lopez Velarde, 6642-9
    Atlantic. Eugenio Florit, 6642-9
    Autumn. Jose Gorostiza, 6642-9
    Ballad of the Guije. Nicolas Guillen, 6642-9
    Ballad of the two grandfathers. Nicolas Guillen, 6642-9
    Benares. Jorge Luis Borges, 6642-9
    Big-lipped Negro. Nicolas Guillen, 6642-9
    Biography. Jorge Carrera Andrade, 6642-9
    Biography. Jorge Carrera Andrade, 6642-9
    The Black Messengers. Cesar Vallejo, 6642-9
    The bloom hoists its banner. Jose Gorostiza, 6642-9
    Bulletin of bad weather. Jorge Carrera Andrade, 6642-9
    Bulletin of bad weather. Jorge Carrera Andrade, 6642-9
    Butcher shop. Jorge Luis Borges, 6642-9
    The clouds have already told me. Jacinto Fombona Pachano, 6642-9
    The clouds have already told me. Jacinto Fombona Pachano, 6642-9
    The coca tree. Jacinto Fombona Pachano, 6642-9
    The coca tree. Jacinto Fombona Pachano, 6642-9
    The complaint. Jacinto Fombona Pachano, 6642-9
    The complaint. Jacinto Fombona Pachano, 6642-9

The damned. Manuel Moreno Jimeno, 6759-X
Dance of the lost key. Jacinto Fombona Pachano, 6642-9
Dance of the lost key. Jacinto Fombona Pachano, 6642-9
A day's run. Jorge Luis Borges, 6642-9
The dead nereid. Eugenio Florit, 6642-9
Death in the sun. Eugenio Florit, 6642-9
Dining-room mirror. Jorge Carrera Andrade, 6642-9
Dining-room mirror. Jorge Carrera Andrade, 6642-9
Distant footsteps. Cesar Vallejo, 6642-9
Dust, corpse of time. Jorge Carrera Andrade, 6642-9
Dust, corpse of time. Jorge Carrera Andrade, 6642-9
018. Cesar Vallejo, 6642-9
Election handbill of green. Jorge Carrera Andrade, 6642-9
Election handbill of green. Jorge Carrera Andrade, 6642-9
Elegy for all ages. Pablo de (Carlos Diaz Loyola) Rokha, 6642-9
Elegy for your absence. Eugenio Florit, 6642-9
Emigrant to America. Vicente Huidobro, 6642-9
Etude. Carlos Pellicer, 6759-X
Exaltation of elementary materials. Xavier Abril, 6759-X
Fisherman of the moon. Jose Gorostiza, 6642-9
044. Cesar Vallejo, 6642-9
General Quiroga rides to death in a crriage. Jorge Luis Borges, 6642-9
General Quiroga rides to death in a carriage. Jorge Luis Borges, 6642-9
Gentle fatherland. Ramon Lopez Velarde, 6642-9
Hydrographic poem. Jorge Carrera Andrade, 6642-9
Hydrographic poem. Jorge Carrera Andrade, 6642-9
I announce the kingdom of the star. Jacinto Fombona Pachano, 6642-9
I announce the kingdom of the stars. Jacinto Fombona Pachano, 6642-9
In. Vicente Huidobro, 6642-9
Indian rbellion. Jorge Carrera Andrade, 6642-9
Indian rebellion. Jorge Carrera Andrade, 6642-9
Journey. Salvador Novo, 6759-X
July avenue. Jorge Luis Borges, 6642-9
Lament. Pablo de (Carlos Diaz Loyola) Rokha, 6642-9
Lightless suburb. Pablo (Neftali Ricardo Reyes Basualto) Neruda, 6642-9
Little responsory for a republican hero. Cesar Vallejo, 6642-9
Madhouse poem. Carlos Oquendo de Amat, 6759-X
Masses. Cesar Vallejo, 6642-9
The mayor. Luis Carlos Lopez, 6642-9
The mayor. Luis Carlos Lopez, 6642-9
The miners. Cesar Vallejo, 6642-9
Mother. Carlos Oquendo de Amat, 6759-X
My cousin Agueda. Ramon Lopez Velarde, 6642-9
Nameless islands. Jorge Carrera Andrade, 6642-9
Nameless islands. Jorge Carrera Andrade, 6642-9
Natural flow of memory. Jorge Luis Borges, 6642-9
Nature vive. Vicente Huidobro, 6642-9
The nine monsters. Cesar Vallejo, 6642-9
The nine monsters. Pablo (Neftali Ricardo Reyes Basualto) Neruda, 6642-9
No. XVII. Pablo (Neftali Ricardo Reyes Basualto) Neruda, 6642-9
Nocturne. Eugenio Florit, 6642-9
Nocturne. Xavier Abril, 6759-X
Nothing belongs to us. Jorge Carrera Andrade, 6642-9
Nothing belongs to us. Jorge Carrera Andrade, 6642-9
Ode of the sun to the people's army. Pablo (Neftali Ricardo Reyes Basualto) Neruda, 6642-9
Ode with a lament. Pablo (Neftali Ricardo Reyes Basualto) Neruda, 6642-9
Old maids. Luis Carlos Lopez, 6642-9
Old maids. Luis Carlos Lopez, 6642-9
Our lives are pendulums. Ramon Lopez Velarde, 6642-9
The pale conquerors. Pablo de (Carlos Diaz Loyola) Rokha, 6642-9
A patio. Jorge Luis Borges, 6642-9
Pauses. Jose Gorostiza, 6642-9
Pauses II. Jose Gorostiza, 6642-9
Pedro Rojas. Cesar Vallejo, 6642-9
Prelude. Jose Gorostiza, 6642-9
Prelude to hope. Vicente Huidobro, 6642-9
The present evening. Eugenio Florit, 6642-9
The puddle. Jacinto Fombona Pachano, 6642-9
The puddle. Jacinto Fombona Pachano, 6642-9
The Recoleta. Jorge Luis Borges, 6642-9
Reveille at daybreak. Nicolas Guillen, 6642-9
Rubbish VII. Luis Carlos Lopez, 6642-9
Rubbish, IV. Luis Carlos Lopez, 6642-9
Rubbish, IV. Luis Carlos Lopez, 6642-9
Rubbish, VII. Luis Carlos Lopez, 6642-9
Savor. Pablo (Neftali Ricardo Reyes Basualto) Neruda, 6642-9
Seafaring towns. Pablo de (Carlos Diaz Loyola) Rokha, 6642-9
Sensemaya. Nicolas Guillen, 6642-9
Serenade of laughing life. Vicente Huidobro, 6642-9
Sexual water. Pablo (Neftali Ricardo Reyes Basualto) Neruda, 6642-9
The signal. Eugenio Florit, 6642-9
Since tomorrow is Sunday. Jacinto Fombona Pachano, 6642-9
"Solder, I can't figure why". Nicolas Guillen, 6759-X
Song of Thomas, departed. Winett de Rokha, 6759-X
The spider. Cesar Vallejo, 6642-9
The stranger. Jorge Carrera Andrade, 6642-9
Subterranean days and nights. Pablo de (Carlos Diaz Loyola) Rokha, 6642-9
Surrealist poem of the elephant and the song. Carlos Oquendo de Amat, 6759-X
Time of waiting. Vicente Huidobro, 6642-9
To a dog. Luis Carlos Lopez, 6642-9
To my native city. Luis Carlos Lopez, 6642-9
To Satan. Luis Carlos Lopez, 6642-9
Tribal lay. Pablo de (Carlos Diaz Loyola) Rokha, 6642-9
028. Cesar Vallejo, 6642-9
Two children. Nicolas Guillen, 6759-X
Walking around. Pablo (Neftali Ricardo Reyes Basualto) Neruda, 6759-X
Waltz in Yungay Square. Winett de Rokha, 6759-X
Who is it? Jose Gorostiza, 6642-9
Who will buy me an orange? Jose Gorostiza, 6642-9
Windy weather. Jorge Carrera Andrade, 6642-9
Yellow Girl. Nicolas Guillen, 6642-9
You come in the night with the fabulous smoke of..hair. Cesar Moro, 6759-X

Hays, Will S.
O'Grady's goat. 6964-9
The **hayseed's** impression of the snap shot man. Unknown. 6689-5
The **haystack** in the flood. William Morris. 6108-7,6315-2, 6526-0,6536-8,6657-7,6726 ,6023-4,6102-8,6371-3,6508-2,6419-1,6655 ,6110-9,6199-0,6430-2
The **Hayswater** boat. Matthew Arnold. 6947-9
Hayward, Emeroy
Cakes and pies. 6684-4
Haywood. Harold LaMont Otey. 6870-7
Haywood, Delia A.
A teetotaler's story. 6923-1
The **hazard** of loving the creatures. Isaac Watts. 6152-4
Hazard, Caroline
All hail to Thee, child Jesus, fr. Hymns and anthems... 6762-X
The great swamp fight. 6946-0
Hymns and anthems sung at Wellesley College, sels. 6762-X
Mount Carmel, fr. Hymns and anthems... 6762-X
The ninth hour. 6144-3,6335-7
O slow of heart, fr. Hymns and anthems... 6762-X
This is that bread, fr. Hymns and anthems... 6762-X
Vesper hymn, fr. Hymns and anthems... 6762-X
Waken, shepherds, fr. Hymns and anthems... 6762-X
The wilderness. 6144-3,6335-7
The wine-press, fr. Hymns and anthems... 6762-X
The **hazard**. John Kendrick Bangs. 6441-8
Haze. Debbie Balsaitis. 6883-9
Haze. Henry David Thoreau. 6176-1,6399-3,6438-8
Haze. Gon-kang Yun. 6775-1
Haze gold. Carl Sandburg. 6253-9
"The **haze** of white". Haze. Debbie Balsaitis. 6883-9
"A **haze** on the far horizon". Autumn; each in his own

tongue. William Herbert Carruth. 6891-X
Hazel Dorn. Bernard Sleigh. 6254-7
The hazel path. Jaroslav Vrchlicky. 6886-3
Hazelton, Ruth
    The thunderstorm. 6764-6
Hazelwood, Margaret
    Christmas burial. 6799-9
Hazen, Ella M.
    Unknown. 6478-7
Hazen, Jeanette Marshall
    Miss Blueberry. 6764-6
    Old shoes. 6764-6
Hazewell, Edward Wentworth
    Veteran and recruit. 6271-7
Hazlett, Mrs. S.C.
    Her lover. 6670-4
The Hazlewood witch. Richard Gall. 6180-X,6086-2
Hazlewood, Charlotte
    Reunion. 6789-1
    Token. 6789-1
"hazy landscape like the firmament hem". Indian summer. Mary Louisa Hellings. 6799-9
Hazzard, John Edward
    Ain't it awful, Mabel? 6089-7
    'The goshdern words.' 6714-X
    Jes' only her. 6707-7
He. Richard Stillman Powell. 7021-3
He 'digesteth harde yron'. Marianne Moore. 6390-X
He abjures love. Thomas Hardy. 6378-0
He advances his modest boast to fame. Horace. 6637-2
"He aint much of a dog to look at". Jack. Unknown. 6928-2
He and I. James Whitcomb Riley. 6992-4,6993-2
He and she. Christina Georgina Rossetti. 6655-0
He and she. Eugene Fitch Ware. 6736-0,6089-7
'He and she.' Sir Edwin Arnold. 6370-5,6102-8,6066-8
"He and the wilder part of earth". The hint beyond. Frances Frost. 6750-6
"He answered and said unto them, when it is...". Prophecy. Bible. 7020-5
He approacheth the hall of judgment. Unknown (Egyptian) 7039-6
"He arrived at the funeral parlor". The funeral parlor. Henry Johnson. 6870-7
"He ask'd me had I yet forgot". The lay of Elena. Henry Taylor. 6980-0
"He asked but bread of the world". Et nunc et semper. Laura Helena Brower. 7001-9
"He awoke this morning from a strange dream". Chief Leschi of the Nisqually. Duane Niatum. 7005-1
"He bare him up, he bare him down". Lully, lully...the falcon hath borne my make away. Unknown. 6756-5
He beats his women. Charles Bukowski. 6998-3
He bids adieu to his mistress. Alexander Montgomerie. 6317-9
"He broke down at last". Inevitable. Unknown. 6983-5
"He brought me here, told me to love". God, the unplucked notes. Walta Borawski. 7003-5
"He brought our savior to the western side". Rome. John Milton. 6624-0
"He builded his happiness out of these". Happiness. Edgar A. Guest. 6869-3
"He burst from bed/At whistle of day". Boy's day. Ruth Evelyn Henderson. 6861-8
He called her in. James Whitcomb Riley. 6992-4
"He came across the meadow-pass". An ancient rhyme. John O'Hagan. 6858-8
"He came all so still." Unknown. 6216-4
"He came coarse-cloaked, grotesque as...Pan". Socrates. Thomas S. Jones Jr.. 6850-2
"He came from out the void" Robert H. Davis. 6995-9
"He came in busy hours". The triumph of Cupid. Geraldine Meyrick. 7021-3
"He came in just at 5:15.". Finesse. Ruby E. Bolton. 6750-6
"He came in the glory of summer; in the...". Lawrence. Rossiter Johnson. 7041-8
"He came into a world that was not ready". The Messiah. Mabel W. Arnold. 6799-9
"He came into the camp of creed". Rabbi Isaac M. Wise. Walter Hurt. 6848-0

He came on wings. Jessie M. Dowlin. 6761-1
"He came to me in his swift course". Sweeney the mad, sels. Unknown. 6930-4
"He came to me in the extasy of pray'r". Fragment ("He came to me..."). William Cowper. 6814-6
"He came to my desk with quivering lip". A new leaf. Carrie Shaw Rice. 6964-9
He came to pay. Parmenas Mix. 6089-7,6506-8
"He came to the door with a wink in his eye". The salesman. Edgar A. Guest. 6748-4
"He came to town one winter day". Leadville Jim. William W. Fink. 6920-7
He came too late. Elizabeth Bogart. 6219-9
He came too late! Unknown. 6413-2
"He came unlook'd for, undesir'd". Song ("He came"). Sara Coleridge. 6437-X
"He came, her hero crowned". Home. Olive Tilford Dargan. 6880-4
"He came/When the 60's went from flowers to...". Who needs Charlie Manson? Raymond Thompson. 6870-7
"He can have my old revolver". When Teddy hits the west. Thaddeus C. Histed. 6995-9
"He cannot help it that his only eye". The photographer whose shutter died. William Meissner. 6966-5
He cares. Kabir. 6337-3
"He catches a mood". Poetaster. Muriel F. Hochdorf. 6850-2
"He ceased; and Satan stayed...", fr. Paradise lost. John Milton. 6726-9
He charges her to lay aside her weapons. Pierce Ferriter. 6930-4
"'He chases shadows',sneered the British tars". The first voyage of John Cabot. Unknown. 6946-0
"He climbed the mountain; and behold!". The death of Moses. James Montgomery. 6848-0
"He climbs his lady's tower, where sail". Song ("He climbs"). Eleanor Alexander. 6090-0
'He collected his thoughts' Edward Anthony. 6875-8
He come, he comes, the hero comes. Unknown. 6859-6
He comes. Jalal [or Jelal] ed-din Rumi. 6448-5
"He comes and sees a face divine". Love at first sigh. Alfred Henry Haynes Bell. 6800-6
"He comes in the night! he comes in the night!". Santa Claus. Unknown. 6772-7
"He comes in the spring". Shaman: for Malcolm. Erika Mumford. 6966-5
"He comes with conqueror's pace". Triumphal entry. Charles Norman. 6761-1
"He comes with herald clouds of dust". Unknown. 6902-9
He cometh forth into the day. Unknown (Egyptian) 7039-6
"He cometh, he cometh, the Lord passeth by". The still, small voice. McComb. 6848-0
He complaineth to his heart. Sir Thomas Wyatt. 6194-X
He complains how soon the pleasing novelty of life is over. William Shenstone. 6545-7
"He cooked cornbread". Ned Christie. Robert J. Conley. 7005-1
"He could not die when trees were green". The dying child. John Clare. 6934-7
"He could not separate the thought". Country church. Robert P. Tristram Coffin. 6984-3
"He could not specialize, because the ills". The country doctor. L. Ashton Thorp. 6764-6
"He could not walk a road of stained...earth". Portrait of a fruitless prophet. Ruth Eede. 6906-1
He counts winter stars. Emma Crobaugh. 6857-X
"He craves a bird's career". The school boy learns to fly. Amanda Benjamin Hall. 6979-7
"He curled there quiescent". Snake. Jessie Lemont. 6782-4
"He cut a sappy sucker from the...tree". The whistle. Charles Murray. 6800-6
"He did not die amidst the mocking glare". The death of Byron. Ralph S. Thompson. 6983-5
He did not know. Harry Kemp. 6730-1,6034-X
"He did not know that I was in the woodshed...". A father's dilemma. E. Pearl Dancey. 6750-6
"He did not wear his scarlet coat". The ballad of reading gaol. Oscar Wilde. 6930-4
He didn't amount to shucks. Sam Walter Foss. 6924-X
'He didn't oughter...' Si Alan Patrick Herbert. 6026-9
He didn't think. Phoebe Cary. 6529-5

He didn't want the 'scription. Unknown. 6155-9
"He died a poor man, so they say". The spendthrift. Edgar A. Guest. 6862-6
"He died at dawn in the land of snows". Riel: the rebel. Joaquin Miller. 7009-4
He died for me. George Washington Bethune. 6065-X
"He died, and left the world behind!". An epitaph. Bryan Waller ("Barry Cornwall") Procter. 6980-0
"He died, as soldiers die, amid the strife". Field-Marshal Earl Roberts. Sir Owen Seaman. 7029-9
"He does his job without a single thrill". Such stuff as dreams are made on. Berton Braley. 6853-7
"He does not die who can bequeath". 'He does not die' Hilaire Belloc. 7012-4
"He does the things a real man should". The worst thing you can say to him is I love you. Harold Norse. 6998-3
He doesth his alms to be seen of men. Unknown. 6911-8
He doeth all things well. Anne Bronte. 6303-9, 6337-3
'He done his damdest' E. Bell Guthrey. 7012-4
"He either fears his fate too much". James Graham; Marquess of Montrose. 6238-5
"He ended, and they both descend...", fr. Paradise... John Milton. 6562-7
He entereth America by the front door, fr. The Teddysee. Wallace Irwin. 6995-9
He establisheth his triumph. Unknown (Egyptian) 7039-6
"He far away behld the sea". William Morris. 6997-5
"He feared so much the growing old". Victim of fear. Edgar A. Guest. 6869-3
He fell among thieves. Sir Henry Newbolt. 6395-X, 6477-9, 6634-8, 6506-6, 6107-9, 6458, 6395-X, 6477-9, 6634-8, 6506-6, 6161-3, 6371
"He fell off the wheel of souls". DOA in Dulse. Diane Burns. 7005-1
"He felt the wild beast in him between-whiles" George Meredith. 6828-6
"He felt the wild beast in him...", fr. Modern love. George Meredith. 6659-3, 6508-2
"He figured life a house of mystic rooms". Sonnet in memory of John Keats (2). Helen Gray Cone. 6847-2
"He first deceased; she for a little tried". Upon the death of Sir Albertus Morton's wife. Sir Henry Wotton. 6935-5
"He fishes in the night of deep sea pools". Poets and poets. Thomas Edward Brown. 6809-X
"He flays the shaggy hide of earth". The farmer. E. Merrill Root. 6880-4
"He flew alone; and yet with him there went". The spirit of St. Louis. Althea Todd Alderson. 7019-1
"He flies the drifting dreams of men". Toy balloons. Anne Singleton. 6808-1
He for God only, she for God in him, fr. Paradise lost. John Milton. 6934-7
"He found a woman in the cave". Thalaba, sels. Robert Southey. 6832-4
"He found her by the ocean's moaning verge". George Meredith. 6508-2
"He found her by the ocean's moaning verge" George Meredith. 6828-6
He found it. Unknown. 6260-1
"He found us like the deathly thief". Second coming. Ernest Hartsock. 6781-6
"He frightened me when Ben and I first came". Strange tenderness. Frances Rogers Upton. 6750-6
"He gather'd blue forget-me-nots". Lovers. Unknown. 6429-9, 6321-7
"He gave his life for those he loved". Woodrow Wilson. Edward Parker Davis. 7001-9
He gets dhere shust der same! Charles Follen Adams. 7041-8
"He gets here and we drink and smoke". Paul. Dennis Saleh. 6792-1, 6998-3
He gives his beloved certain rhymes. William Butler Yeats. 6187-7
He gives nothing, fr. The vision of Sir Launfal. James Russell Lowell. 6337-3
He giveth his beloved sleep. Elizabeth Barrett Browning. 6304-7, 6424-8, 6569-4
He giveth his beloved sleep. Thomas H. Jones Jr. 6320-9
He gveth his loved ones sleep. Unknown. 6416-7

He giveth more. Annie Johnson Flint. 6461-2
"He glided in the doorway/In stillness of...". Why? Edla Park Peck. 6836-7
He goads himself. Louis Untermeyer. 6036-6
"He grasped his ponderous hammer...". The blacksmith of Limerick. Robert Dwyer Joyce. 6858-8
"He grew where waves ride nine feet high". In memoriam: Roy Campbell. Ralph Nixon Currey. 6788-3
"He had a falcon on his wrist". 'Love me, love my dog' Isabella Valancy Crawford. 6797-2
"He had been born a destined work to do". Tom Taylor. 6238-5
"He had done with fleets and squadrons...". Admiral dugout. Cicely Fox Smith. 7031-0
"He had drunk rōm founts of pleasure". Drawing water. Phoebe Cary. 6969-X
"He had found joy in these wide-reaching trees". The grave of Roosevelt. Snow Longley Hough. 6995-9
"He had no light nor printed chart". Columbus. Edgar A. Guest. 6748-4
"He had no times of study, and no place". Festus describes his friend, fr. Festus. Philip James Bailey. 6980-0
"He had the quietest face". A friend's death. Roberta Santlofer Danowsky. 6857-X
"He had wit and he was clever". The trickster. Edgar A. Guest. 6748-4
"He hadn't been there for fifteen years". When grandfather went to town. Robert C.V. Meyers. 6924-X
"He has a beautiful paste of sacred ashes...". Siva. Unknown (Newari). 7013-2
He has been there himself. Welby Walker. 6116-8
"He has comrades eight or ten for the gsmes...". To the father. Edgar A. Guest. 6748-4
"He has gone at last; yet I could not see". Hidden sorrow. Phoebe Cary. 6969-X
"He has gone to his God; he has gone...home". Funeral hymn. Unknown. 6752-2
"He has gone! he is gone!". The forsaken maid. Unknown (Irish). 6858-8
"He has granted thee, in little". Microcosm. Edward Farquhar. 6939-8
"He has grown in love". Of an old con. Geroge Mosby Jr.. 6870-7
"He has hard work who has nothing...", fr. The bible. Unknown. 6623-2
"He has hung his ridle over the door". Old hunter. William Sawyer. 6841-3
"He has outsoared the shadow of our night". Elegy on the death of John Keats. Percy Bysshe Shelley. 6935-5
"He has outsoared the shadow of our night", fr. Adonais. Percy Bysshe Shelley. 6934-7
"He has shaved off his whiskers...". 'Love with a witness', fr. Bailey ballads. Thomas Hood. 6974-6
"He has ta'en some twenty gentlemen...". The Cid and the leper. Unknown (Spanish). 6757-3
"He has taken his lovely music with him". Requiem (for Arthur Darley). Katharine (Hinkson) Tynan. 6780-8
He hated sham. John W. Low. 6995-9
"He hath garnished the excellent...", fr. The bible. Unknown. 6334-9
"He hath masted the flag of the crimson bars". The ballad of John Paul Jones. Arthur Guiterman. 6773-5
"He hath wronged his queen...". Sardanapalus: a tragedy. George Gordon, 6th Baron Byron. 6945-2
He heard her sing, sels. James Thomson. 6656-9
He held her hands. Unknown. 6690-9
"He held no dream worth waking; so he said". On the death of Robert Browning. Algernon Charles Swinburne. 6828-6
He holdeth fast to the memory of his identity. Unknown (Egyptian) 7039-6
"He hung around the corners then". The miner. Dai Alexander. 6895-2
He insisted/on being laid down. Lee Mallory. 6792-1
"He is a bird round which a trap closes". The holy man. Unknown. 6930-4
"He is a cynic, a slow smile". The cynic. Clair [pseud].. 6817-0
"He is a dreamer, let him pass". A dreamer. Robert Loveman. 6941-X

"He is a very dark brunette". Rondel. Edward Grier
    Fullerton. 6936-3
"He is a writer, a fantasist". Astounding tales. Jack
    Anderson. 7003-5
'He is all ours' Wendell Phillips Stafford. 6995-9
"He is blind and nevermore". Gassed. Rowland Thirlmere.
    7027-2
He is dead who will not fight. Julian Grenfell. 7031-0
He is declared true of word. Unknown (Egyptian) 7039-6
"He is flying over the sea/In a shell alone!". Lindbergh.
    Harriet Monroe. 7019-1
"He is gone - is dust". Dirge. Johann C. Friedrich von
    Schiller. 6438-8
"He is gone on the mountain". Coronach, fr. The lady of
    the lake. Sir Walter Scott. 6180-X,6087-0,6134-6,
    6228-8,6246-6,6271 ,6289-X,6512-0,6600-3,6634-8,6732-
    8,6385 ,6726-3,6424-8,6304-7,6371-3,6219-9,6110 ,
    6438-8,6086-2,6196-6,6458-2
"He is gone,--is dust!" Johann C. Friedrich von Schiller.
    6606-2
"He is gone. Heaven's will is best". Havelock. Unknown.
    6793-X
He is like the lotus. Unknown (Egyptian) 7039-6
He is my poet. William Perrier. 6316-0
"He is near to help and bless." Frances Ridley Havergal.
    6225-3
"He is never in a bunker, and...in the rough". The safe
    golfer. Edgar A. Guest. 6869-3
"He is no friend who in thine hour of pride". Friendship,
    fr. the Gulistan. Sadi [or Saadi] (Mushlih-ud-Din).
    7039-6
"He is not dead whose song survives". The dead minstrel.
    John E. Barrett. 6840-5
H is not dead, fr. Adonais. Percy Bysshe Shelley. 6337-3
"He is not dead, this friend". Conviction. N. R. A.
    Becker. 6818-9
He is not desecrate. David Morton. 6817-0
He is not old. Robert Loveman. 6941-X
He is not risen. W.S. Handley Jones. 6337-3
"He is one in whom the gypsy gods delight". Trails to the
    grey emperors. Iris Lora Thorpe. 6750-6
He is risen. Cecil Frances Alexander. 6177-X
He is risen. John Oxenham. 6144-3
He is risen. Charles Wesley. 6720-4
He is risen, sels. Joseph Auslander. 6337-3
"He is sleeping, calmly sleeping". At rest in the National
    Cathedral. C.N. Lund. 7001-9
"He is so little, and the way is dim." Okura. 6027-7
"He is so old;/ He sits against the further...". At the
    dance. Arthur Crew Inman. 6959-2
"He is so palsied by his dreams". Tyrannies. Louis
    Golding. 6761-1
"He is so very peculiar". The peculiar neighbor. Harriet
    M. Spalding. 6918-5
"He is the best beast, our friend, the mule". Unknown.
    6149-4
"He is the despots' despot.". The dance of death. Austin
    Dobson. 6770-0
He is the lonely greatness. Madeleine Caron Rock. 6144-3,
    6477-9
"He is the poet of the air. He writes". Lindbergh. E.R.
    Coe. 7019-1
He is the way. Wystan Hugh Auden. 6337-3
'He is to weet a melancholy earle". Stanzas on Charles
    Armitage Brown. John Keats. 6802-2
"He jests at scars, that never felt a wound". William
    Shakespeare. 6934-7
"He jostled her a little in the crowd". The white cane.
    Glenn Ward Dresbach. 6750-6
"He journeys o'er the ocean's foam". Fleet Street. Louis
    Howland. 6793-X
"He kept for his own joy all things of..worth". Miser.
    Joel Kendler. 6850-2
He kissed me. Unknown. 6670-4
"He knelt - the Saviour knelt and prayed". Christ's agony
    in the garden. Felicia Dorothea Hemans. 6973-8
"He knew my soul, he knew she was in". Ezekiel. Barbara
    Miller Macandrew. 6848-0
"He knew no music; but he liked to hear". Old ballads.
    Margaret Widdemer. 6764-6
He knew the land. Molly Anderson Haley. 6083-8
"He knew the mask of principle to wear". A statesman.
    Bayard Taylor. 6976-2
"He knew what mortals know when tried". Cowper's
    consolation. Phoebe Cary. 6969-X
"He knoweth not that the dead are thine." Mary Elizabeth
    Coleridge. 6507-4
He knoweth our frame, He remembereth we are dust. Richard
    Henry Dana. 6752-2
He knoweth the souls of the west. Unknown (Egyptian) 7039-
    6
"He knows the safe ways and unsafe". Pan. Francis
    Ledwidge. 6812-X,6861-8
He laments to no purpose. William Thomas Walsh. 6761-1
He laughed last. Francis Whiting Hatch. 6722-0
"He launched his boat where...dark waves flow". The
    wanderer of Africa. Alonzo Lewis. 6752-2
"He lay as one who lies and dreams". The ballad of reading
    gaol, sel. Oscar Wilde. 6958-4
"He lay at my side ont he eastern hill". My sailor. James
    Berry Bensel. 7041-8
"He lay. His propped-up countenance severe". The death of
    the poet. Rainer Maria Rilke. 6879-0
He leadeth me. Joseph H. Gilmore. 6337-3,6730-1
He leads. Elisabeth Scollard. 6337-3
"He leans far out and watches: down below". The mountain
    still. Madison Cawein. 7017-5
"He leant at the door/In his priest's clothes". The
    unfrocked priest. Joseph ("Seosamh MacCathmhaoil")
    Campbell. 6930-4
"He led her to the altar". Eliza Cook. 6980-0
"He left a load of anthracite". What was his creed?
    Unknown. 6889-8
"He left the upla d bawns and serene air". Milton. Ernest
    Myers. 7015-9
"He lies here. See the bush". His epitaph. Frederick
    William Ophel. 6784-0
"He lies on his back, the idling smith". The poet's forge.
    Helen Hunt Jackson. 7041-8
"He lifted from the dust". Helen Rogers Smith. 6065-X
"He like best watching tv". The artist. Peter Meinke. 6966-
    5
"He limps along the city street". Invalided. Edward
    Shillito. 7027-2
He lived a life. H.N. Fifer. 6214-8
"He lived amidst th' untrodden ways". Hartley Coleridge.
    6802-2
"He lived in a cave by the seas". Ballade of primitive
    man. Andrew Lang. 6770-0,6875-8
"He lived one hundrd and five,". Unknown. 6722-0
"He lived, bu as a ripple on the sea". Epitaph. George
    Steele Seymour. 6789-1
"He lives who lives to God alone". Stanzas printed on
    bills of mortality: 1793. William Cowper. 6814-6
He lives! he lives!. Irene Rutherford McLeod. 6653-4
"He lives, ever lives in the hearts of the free." Alfred
    Lord Tennyson. 6712-3
"He lives, he wakes-'tis death is dead, not he". Adonais,
    sels. Percy Bysshe Shelley. 6980-0
He liveth long who liveth well. Horatius Bonar. 6238-5,
    6294-6
"He look't and saw what numbers numberless". The Parthians,
    fr. Paradise regained. John Milton. 6933-9
"He lost it one night". The illumination of George Jr.
    Gerald Cable. 6855-3
"He loꞷ d". At the last. Will H. Hendrickson. 7007-8
"He loved peculiar plants and rare". Education's martyr.
    May Kendall. 7037-X
"He loved the plant with a keen delight". Story by Lalla-
    ji, the priest. Laurence (Adele Florence Nicolson)
    Hope. 6856-1
"He loves me". Unknown. 6363-2
'He loves me, he loves me not'. Unknown. 6116-8
"He loves not well whose love is bold!". My queen. William
    Winter. 7041-8
"He lurks among the reeds, beside the marsh". Malaria.
    Laurence (Adele Florence Nicolson) Hope. 6856-1
"He lying spilt like water from a bowl". Poem ("He
    lying"). Alison Boodson. 6379-9
He made the stars also. Lloyd Mifflin. 6243-1

He made us free. Maurice Francis Egan. 6172-9,6292-X
"He makes himself comfortable". The pronouns-a collection of 40 dances-for the, sels. Jackson MacLow. 6803-0
He maketh himself one with the only god... Unknown (Egyptian) 7039-6
"He many a creature did anatomize", fr. The virtuoso. Mark Akenside. 6934-7
"He may be fearfully clever, he may be...". Immutable. Berton Braley. 6853-7
"He may be lame". Unknown. 6364-0
"He measures eggs and butter, milk and flour". The baker. Lida Wilson Turner. 6841-3
'He must be a committeeman.' Unknown. 6707-7
"He must be holpen; yet how help shall I". The taming of Themistocles, sels. Bayard Taylor. 6802-2
"He must have smiled a little, I suppose". 'Humoresque.' Constance Ann Hall. 6750-6
"He must needs come along this hollow pass". The road to Kussnacht. Johann C. Friedrich von Schiller. 6749-2
"He need but crook his finger". Haute couture of poetry. Wilhelm Szabo. 6769-7
"He needs must leave the trapping & the chase". The Indian corn planter. Emily Pauline ("Tekahionwake") Johnson. 6796-4,6837-5
"He never gave me a chance to speak". After the quarrel, fr. The road to Avernus. Adam Lindsay Gordon. 6951-7
"He never had a problem, and he never...a care". Paid in advance. Edgar A. Guest. 6869-3
He never said he loved me. Alaric A. Watts. 6226-1
He never smiled again, fr. Lays of many lands. Felicia Dorothea Hemans. 6973-8
"He never thought it stepping down". The master. Edgar A. Guest. 6748-4
He never told a lie. Unknown. 6410-8
He never took a vacation. John Warren Harper. 6631-3
"He of the ocean is, its thunderous waves". A memory of Rubenstein. Richard Watson Gilder. 6848-0
"He offered me a glass of holy water". Two radio interview. Maurice Kenny. 7003-5
"He or she". Song ("He or she"). Unknown. 6563-5
"He or she that hopes to gain" Unknown. 6935-5
"He owned with a grin". The devil's walk, sels. Robert Southey. 6867-7
"He owns the bird-songs of the hills". James Whitcomb Riley. 6990-8
"He pass'd thro' life's tempestuous night". On Robert Burns. James Montgomery. 6874-X
"He passed from earth". The song of penitence, sels. Felicia Dorothea Hemans. 6973-8
"He passed the sea". William Morris. 6997-5
"He passes my window every day". The vegetable man. Edwin Chamberlin. 6906-1
"He paused without surprise/Upon the verge". The bird bath. Edith Harriet Jones. 6799-9
"He peeps in through the key-hole". The sand-man. George Cooper. 6922-3
"He placed fair Eleanor by hsi right". Unknown. 6059-5
"He planted where the deluge ploughed". Ralph Waldo Emerson. 6753-0
"He played by the river when he was young". Washington. Nancy Byrd Turner. 6891-X
"He pleases to reside on the top of...mountain". Cobhara-Lokesvara. Unknown (Newari). 7013-2
He prayed. Winifred M. Letts. 7031-0
"He prayeth best who loveth best". Samuel Taylor Coleridge. 6466-3,6479-5,6238-5,6337-3,6502-3,6456-9,6507-4
"'He profits most who serves us best!'". To serve is to gain. Charles H. Mackintosh. 6846-4
"He put it thus: "My Mary, dear". Unknown. 6407-8
"He puts footnotes on the paintings". The perfectionist. Bernice Fleisher. 6966-5
"He raised the cup to his pure, sweet lips". The fatal glass. Laura U. Case. 6912-6
"He raised up and raised high, and built". Matran. 6766-2
"He ran up the candlestick". Chinese nursery rhyme. Isaac Taylor Headland. 6937-1,6638-0
"He reads of the deeds of mighty men". The paralytic. Robert Loveman. 6941-X
He remembered. Florence Crocker Comfort. 6789-1
He remembers forgotten beauty. William Butler Yeats. 6320-9,6507-4
He respondeth. Unknown. 6453-1
"He rests. The world-weight of the years..past". Wilson. Dixon Merritt. 7001-9
"He rides in the eye of danger". The engineer. John E. Barrett. 6840-5
"He rides the wind, this indian brave of mine". Rider of the wind. Ida Crane Walker. 6857-X
"He riseth alone, - alone and proud". Mount Pilate. Sir Edwin Arnold. 6484-1,6749-2
"He rose like a sleepwalker just". Durer's piece of turf. Norbert Krapf. 6966-5
"He rose, and singing passed from sight". The lark. John Banister Tabb. 6943-6
He ruleth not through he raigne... Sir Thomas Wyatt. 6586-4,6194-X
"He runs like a mad rat seeking". Mazeworks. Elias Hruska Cortes. 6792-1
"He said he would 'climb up to God', believing". Climb up to God. Jessie Corrigan Pegis. 6761-1
He said that he was not our brother. John Banim. 6930-4
"He said unto the Lord:- 'shall I ne'er be...". Moses. Alfred de Vigny. 6848-0
"He said, 'Good-night, my heart is light'.". Premonition. Bliss Carman and Richard Hovey. 6890-1
"He said, and urged him...", fr. The Odyssey. Homer. 6435-3
"He said, the China on the shelf". Art's martyr. Andrew Lang. 6987-8
He said: 'If in his image I was made'. Trumbull Stickney. 6754-9
"He said: 'Thou petty people, let me pass'.". The kaiser and Belgium. Stephen Phillips. 7026-4
"He said: and on his horses...", fr. The Iliad. Homer. 6435-3
"He sailed upon the misted sea". The return. Elizabeth S. Noble. 6750-6
"He sang above the vineyards of the world". The singing man, sel. Josephine Preston Peabody. 6954-1
"He sang of God - the mighty source". A song to David, sels. Christopher Smart. 6934-7
"He sang of God, the mighty source". The song of David. Christopher Sharp. 6848-0
He sang out of his soul what he found there. Henry Bernard Carpenter. 6066-8
"He sang so wildly". Mother's love. Thomas Burbidge. 6097-8,6271-7,6656-9
"He sat all alone in his dark little room". The weaver's dream. Alice Cary. 6969-X
"He sat among his bags, and, with a look". Pollock. 6238-5
"He sat at the dinner table". Just like a man. Unknown. 6928-2
"He sat at the dinner table there". His mother's cooking. Lizzie M. Hadley. 6921-5
"He sat beside a blackboard tall...". A youthful martyr. M.E. B.. 6965-7
"He sat in silence on the ground". Ivan the csar. Felicia Dorothea Hemans. 6973-8
"He sat in the cool morning". The new warden. Jimmy Santiago Baca. 6870-7
"He sat in the parlor with Ray". An interrupted proposal. Robert C.V. Meyers. 6924-X
"He sat on the banks of his own native shore". Swiss boy's adieu to the Rhone. Charles W. Denison. 6755-7
He satisfies. Frederick William Faber. 6065-X
"He saved his land, but did not lay his soldier..." Eliza Cook. 6712-3
He saw far in the concave green of the sea. John Keats. 6833-2
He saw her home. Mikhail Isakovsky. 6546-5
"He saw his error/All men do when age". Ippolito di Este, sels. Walter Savage Landor. 6980-0
He saw my heart's woe. Charlotte Bronte. 6641-0
"He saw the noonday sun". Blind. June Lucas. 6954-1
"He says it's just another fence to mend". The keeper of the wall. Frederick W. Branch. 6764-6
"He scarce had ceas't when the superior fiend". Satan and the fallen angels, fr. Paradise lost. John Milton. 6933-9
"He searches and searches". March moon-night. Margarethe

Herzele. 6769-7
"He seemed so plump, furry, plunked down...". The underground pressure. John Tagliabue. 6803-0
"He seemed to know the harbour". The shark. Edwin John Pratt. 6797-2
"He sees the wife, from slim young comeliness". The wife. Anna Spencer Twitchell. 6836-7
"He sees through stone" Etheridge Knight. 6870-7
He serves his country best. Sarah ("Susan Coolidge") Woolsey. 6461-2
"He serveth the servant". The world-soul, sels. Ralph Waldo Emerson. 6934-7
"He set the world aflame". Jalal [or Jelal] ed-din Rumi. 6448-5
"He shall not dread misfortune's angry mien". Pietro Metastasio. 6973-8
"He shall not get me". Sleep. Harriet Doktor. 6850-2
He shall speak peace unto the nations. Lila V. Walters. 6065-X
"He showed up in the springtime, when the...". The old-timer. Arthur Chapman. 7010-8
He singeth in the underworld. Robert Hillyer. 6037-4
He singeth in the underworld. Unknown (Egyptian) 7039-6
"He sings to his mate when twilight falls". The vesper sparrow. Maude Freeman Osburne. 6836-7
"He sits all day where the waters play". In Provincetown bay. Roger C. Dickey. 6798-0
"He sits on the darkest bench". Child molester. Jay Meek. 6803-0
"He sits, cross-legged, 'neath a palm". The dervish. Edwin Chamberlin. 6906-1
"He sleeps as should sleep - among the great". The grave of Charles Dickens. Unknown. 6909-6
"He sleeps at last, and all the grief". The death of Hamlet. John E. Barrett. 6840-5
"He sleeps, forgetful of his once bright fame". Genius slumbering. James Gates Percival. 6752-2
"He sought the sea; his footsteps press the...". Christ quiets the tempest. Caelius Sedulius. 6930-4
"He spake not truth, however wise, who said". Dreams. Andrew Lang. 6771-9
"He spake, to whom I...", fr. The Odyssey. Homer. 6435-3
"He speaks a kind of truth who has the love...". A ballad for May Day, sels. Paul Potts. 6895-2
"He speaks/Open your eyes". Prelude ("He speaks"). Hildegarde Flanner. 6035-8
"He spends his days in clouds of soapy steam". Chinese laundryman. Jessie Young Norton. 6841-3
"He spends so much/of his time thinking". The diver. Leslie Nutting. 6767-0
"He spoils his house and throws his pains away". Alice Cary. 6969-X
He spoke of Burns, fr. An incident in a railroad car. James Russell Lowell. 6934-7
"He stands at the door of the church peeping". Little Pat and the parson. Unknown. 6914-2
"He stands at the kerb and sings". The street singer. Austin Dobson. 6770-0
"He stands before negation". The American. James Bertolino. 7032-9
"He stands with trmbling form". Coward. Delphia L. Hopper. 6906-1
"He stands, his hand extended to guide...". Woodrow Wilson. Virginia Taylor McCormick. 7001-9
".He stood alone within the spacious square", fr. The city.. James ("B.V.") Thomson. 6508-2
"He stood and call'd", fr. Paradise lost. John Milton. 6726-3
"He stood before his plate-glass door". The convict clerk. James Abraham Martling. 6952-5
"He stood before the Sanhedrin". Religion and doctrine. John Hay. 6913-4
"He stood beside a bush that burned". The bush that burned. Lois Moyes. 6799-9
"He stood in the station, she at his side". Our railroads. Unknown. 6917-7
"He stood upon the curbing and he waved...". Thumbing through life. Edgar A. Guest. 6748-4
"He stood, a worn-out city clerk". Peace: a study. Charles Stuart Calverley. 6996-7

"He stoopt Pierea...", fr. The Odyssey. Homer. 6435-3
"He stopped at last,/And a mild look of...". The destroying angel. Abraham Cowley. 6848-0
"He stumbled hom from Clifden fair". High and low. James H. Cousins. 6930-4
"He suffers; but his mournful days are crowned". The poet. Marion Muir Richardson. 6836-7
He sugges s having some fun while he'er still able. Horace. 6637-2
"He sways on the highest twig, wing deep". Memory. Joseph Hood Barnes. 6764-6
"He swept like fire the Italian hills & plains". Success at last. Edward Farquhar. 6939-8
"He swore he 'loved her dearly'.". Verse ("He swore"). Unknown. 6118-4
He swore he'd drink old England dry. Unknown. 6328-4
He takes my grief. William White. 6868-5
"He takes the road men call an endless track". Toward another dawn. Charles Divine. 7019-1
"He talked about the origin". The origin of sin. Sam Walter Foss. 6996-7
"He talked, and as he talked". The story teller. Mark Van Doren. 6780-8
He taunts an aging siren on the loss of her charms. Horace. 6637-2
He teaches her to kiss. Ben Jonson. 6659-3
He teases Xanthias about his new girl friend. Horace. 6637-2
He tells a matron to be her age. Horace. 6637-2
"He tells us that". Haiku. Louis Cuneo. 6792-1
He thanks heaven that he has gotten past... Horace. 6637-2
'He that believeth'. Annie Johnson Flint. 6303-9
'He that doeth the will', fr. Christus. Henry Wadsworth Longfellow. 6144-3;6335-7
"He that dwelleth in the secret place of...". Psalm 091 Bible. 6861-8
"He that from dust of worldly tumults flies". Of true liberty. Sir John Beaumont. 6933-9
"He that has grown to wisdom hurries not". Sonnet: Of moderation and tolerance. Guido Guinicelli. 7039-6
He that has kept clean. Florence A. Jones. 6109-5
"He that has left hereunder". Hic jacet qui in hoc saeculo fideliter militavit. Sir Henry Newbolt. 7027-2
He that has light within, fr. Comus. John Milton. 6337-3
"He that has sail'd...", fr. Childe Harold's... George Gordon, 6th Baron Byron. 6547-3
"He that hath such acuteness, and such wit". On Mr. Francis Beaumont (then newly dead). Richard Corbet. 6933-9
"He that in venturous barks hath been". The ocean. Felicia Dorothea Hemans. 6973-8
"He that is by Mooni now". Mooni, sels. Henry Clarence Kendall. 6768-9
"He that is down need fear no fall". Song ("He that is down"). John Bunyan. 6481-7
"He that is down needs fear no fall". The shepherd's song. John Bunyan. 6931-2
"He that is down, needs fear no fall". John Bunyan. 6562-7
"He that is my soul's repose". Jalal [or Jelal] ed-din Rumi. 6448-5
"He that is slow to anger...", fr. Bible, Proverbs. Unknown. 6496-5
"He that lacks time to mourn, lacks time to mend". Sir Henry Taylor. 6238-5
"He that lacks time to mourn, lacks time..mend". Repentance and improvement, fr. Philip Van Artevelde. Henry Taylor. 6980-0
"He that leadeth men must be just", fr. The Bible. Unknown. 6466-3
He that looks still on your eyes. William Browne. 6934-7
He that loves a rosy cheek. Thomas Carew. 6600-3,6328-4, 6668-2,6543-0,6302-0,6385-3,6187-7
He that loves a rosy cheek. Sir Heinrich von Rugge. 7039-6
He that marries a merry lass. Unknown. 6328-4,6026-9
"He that of such a height hath built his mind". Suave mari magno. Samuel Daniel. 6935-5
"He that was dead rose up and spoke - He spoke". The raising of the widow's son. Felicia Dorothea Hemans. 6973-8
"He that will be a lovr in every wise". Three things

Jeame lacks. Unknown. 6881-2
"He that would catch and catching hold." Unknown. 6563-5
"He that would thrive." Unknown. 6363-2,6452-3
"He that wrongs his friend." Alfred Lord Tennyson. 6225-3
"He the gay garden round about doth fly". The butterfly. Edmund Spenser. 6935-5
"He there does now enjoy eternal rest",fr.Faerie queen. Edmund Spenser. 6879-0
"He thinks not deep who hears the strain". 'The loves of every day' Witter Bynner. 6875-8
"He thought he kept the universe alone". The most of it. Robert Frost. 6979-7
He thought he saw. Charles Lutwidge ("Lewis Carroll") Dodgson. 6236-9,6356-X
"He thought he saw a banker's clerk". Sylvie and Bruno. Charles Lutwidge ("Lewis Carroll") Dodgson. 6902-9
"He thought that he could never smile again". Heart's-ease. Arthur William Beer. 6789-1
"He thought to quell the stubborn hearts...oak". Bonaparte. Alfred Lord Tennyson. 6977-0
"He threw his crutched stick down: there came". Old men complaining. Padraic Colum. 6897-9
"He told me he had seen a ruined garden". The garden. Harold Monro. 6985-1
He told me so. George Grossmith. 6661-5
"He took her fancy when he came". Unknown. 6407-8
"He took his pack upon his back". Pack peddler. Edgar A. Guest. 6748-4
He took my place. Horatius Bonar. 6065-X
"He took off his hat to the woman next door". For others-and his wife. Edgar A. Guest. 6862-6
"He tossed it on a rubbish heap". The meaning of loss. Edgar A. Guest. 6748-4
"He touched her hand, and the fever left her". The master's touch. Unknown. 6928-2
"He trembled for us". O Theophilus. Margaret Allonby. 6788-3
"He trudged on/Gainsaying nought". His legacy. Clara T. Brown. 6906-1
"He turned your lance, o death". Death and Roosevelt. Ernest Harold Baynes. 6995-9
He understood. Anne Virginia Culbertson. 6579-1
"He unto whom thou art so partial". Martial, lib. I, epig. I. George Gordon, 6th Baron Byron. 6945-2
"He used to talk of ships, and I remember". Inland. Joan Dareth Prosper. 7038-8
He vas dhinkin'. Unknown. 6175-3
He visits a hospital. Rolfe Humphries. 6619-4
"He wagged his tail to the very last". Laddie's long sleep. James Clarence Harvey. 7008-6
"He walked upon our garden wall". The thin cat. Florence Hoatson. 6937-1
He walketh by day. Unknown (Egyptian) 7039-6
"He walks amid the worldly". The poet. William Rooney. 6022-6
"He walks with God upon the hills!". The poet. Ina D. Coolbrith. 7041-8
He walks with his chin in the air. Hazel Hall. 6036-6
"He wanders round the garden wild". God's child. Roden Noel. 6772-7
"He wanted a velocipede". Teddy the teazer. M.E. B.. 6965-7
He wanted to know. Sam Walter Foss. 6687-9
"He was a bold Theosophist". An astral romance. Gustave V. Drake. 7021-3
"He was a boy of April beauty; one". Riddles, R.F.C. John Drinkwater. 7027-2
"He was a boy when first we met". Love returned. Bayard Taylor. 6976-2
"He was a French Boy Scout - a little lad". Two viewpoints. Amelia Josephine Burr. 6846-4
"He was a fellow brown of hue". Unknown. 6258-X
He was a friend indeed. William Hunter Brickhead. 6066-8
He was a gambler too... G.A. Studdert-Kennedy. 6532-5
"He was a gash an' faithfu' tyke". Luath, fr. 'The twa dogs' Robert Burns. 7008-6
"He was a king for an hour or tw ". The difference. Edgar A. Guest. 6748-4
"He was a lowly missionary". Rev. Oleus Bacon, D.D. - in memoriam. Unknown. 6912-6

"He was a many-sided man, but four-square". Theodore Roosevelt. Leonard Wood. 6995-9
"He was a mountain man, a weathered fellow". The round barn. Minnie Hite Moody. 6841-3
"He was a sculptor and wise in stones". Stone-cutter. William Sawyer. 6841-3
"He was a sentimental man. He'd...shed a tear". Two sentimentalists. Edgar A. Guest. 6869-3
"He was a stranger, but he wept". Sympathy. Warren Ariail. 7016-7
"He was a worthy citizen of the town". Fire on Belmont Street, fr. The tall men. Donald Davidson. 7017-5
"He was a-weary; but he fought his fight". Richard Realf. 6238-5
"He was born on the shores of the Ionean...". The sun. Jovan Ducic. 6765-4
"He was called tractor". Tractor. John L. Seller. 6870-7
"He was dozing, blanket half pulled". Ogden as Texas traveller. Guy R. Beining. 6998-3
"He was evil and ruined everything". Hitler and the generals. Michael Guttenbrunner. 6769-7
"He was hauled-hung". Lynched. Stephen Todd Booker. 6870-7
"He was in logick a great critick". Presbyterian knight and independent squire,fr. Hudibras. Samuel Butler. 6933-9
"He was in love with truth and knew her near". Walt Whitman. Harrison Smith Morris. 6820-0
"He was just a dog, mister—that's all". Just our dog. Unknown. 7008-6
"He was lost!—Not a shade of doubt of that". Little lost pup. Unknown. 7008-6
"He was no good; he was too young; but he...". Caravaggio and his models. Rene Ricard. 7003-5
"He was not all unhappy. His resolve". Alfred Lord Tennyson. 6238-5
He was of the forest. Robert P. Tristram Coffin. 7040-X
"He was one who followed". Sailor man. H. Sewall Bailey. 6833-2
"He was one/Of many thousand...". Greatness and success, fr. Philip Van Artevelde. Henry Taylor. 6980-0
"He was only a dog, but he went to war". The war dog. Unknown. 7008-6
"He was only a little lad". Sent for water. Glenn Ward Dresbach. 6750-6
"He was our noblest, he was our bravest & best". F.B.C.; Chancellorsville, May 3, 1863. William Allen Butler. 6903-7
"He was screaming in the cemetary long...". Long after midnight. Jack Micheline. 6998-3
"He was serving a life sentence". Mule-train. John L. Seller. 6870-7
"He was sitting alone with his beer". Ten o'clock at the town pump. Stanley Ward. 7003-5
"He was sitting on a doorstep as I went...". The road to Vagabondia. Dana Burnet. 7008-6
"He was sitting there on a stone". Elderberry flute song. Peter Blue Cloud. 7005-1
"He was so smiling and so debonair". So long. Nell Griffith Wilson. 6750-6
"He was standing on the corner". A Christmas-tide shadow. Norman Howard. 6925-8
"He was the boy of the house, you know". The boy of the house. Jean Blewett. 7022-1
"He was the fourth his mother bore". Sixty cubic feet. Randall Swingler. 6895-2
"He was the mutual mother when we cursed". Sonnet ("He was the mutual mother"). Herbert Corby. 6895-2
"He was the soul of goodness". William Shakespeare. 6238-5
"He was the word that spake it". On the sacrament. Elizabeth I; Queen of England. 6934-7
"He was warned against the womern". On a spelndud match. James Whitcomb Riley. 6892-8
"He was wrong to marry from the mill". He was of the forest. Robert P. Tristram Coffin. 7040-X
"He wasn't obliged to do it; a man had..paid". The ringer of the chimes. Jeannie Pendleton Ewing. 6926-6
"He watched her breathing." Thomas Hood. 6302-0,6385-3, 6291-9
"He wears a little ruff, your soul". To my husband. Unknown. 6880-4

"He wears a long and solemn face". Forgotten boyhood. Edgar A. Guest. 7033-7
"He went amid these glorious things of earth". Setting sail. James Gates Percival. 6752-2
He went for a soldier. Ruth Comfort Mitchell. 6474-4,6336-5
"He went his way and never knew". One kindly deed. Edgar A. Guest. 6869-3
"He went to sea on the long patrol". On patrol. Unknown. 7031-0
He whistled. Frank Lebby Stanton. 6211-3
"He who ascends to mountain-tops". Ambition ("He who ascends"). George Gordon, 6th Baron Byron. 6294-6, 6610-0
He who aspires. Robert Browning. 6303-9
"He who bends to himself a joy". Epigram ("He who bends"). William Blake. 6179-6
"He who binds to himself a joy." William Blake. 6187-7, 6317-9
"He who could view the book of destiny". On the death of a very young gentleman. John Dryden. 6908-8,6970-3
"He who created time, and out of nothing". Michelangelo Buonarroti. 6325-X
He who died at Azan. Sir Edwin Arnold. 6271-7
He who for love hath undergone. Richard Monckton Milnes; 1st Baron Houghton. 6320-9
He who forsakes the clerkly life, fr. 'Life of St....' Unknown. 6930-4
He who has known a river. Mary Sinton Leitch. 6619-4
"He who has strength for the task". Strength. Edgar A. Guest. 6748-4
He who has vision. Folger McKinsey. 6964-9
"He who in impious times undaunted stood". On the monumentore the Marquis of Winchester. John Dryden. 6970-3
He who in spring's rebirth. Robert Hillyer. 6984-3
He who loves the ocean. Mary Sinton Leitch. 6979-7
"He who marries beauty". For poets. Mary Carolyn Davies. 6880-4
"He who plants a tree". Who plants a tree. Lucy Larcom. 7022-1
"He who plants a tree, plants a hope". Plant a tree. Lucy Larcom. 6820-0
"He who possesses virtue at its best". Twin-born. Ella Wheeler Wilcox. 6956-8
"He who proclaims that love is light and vain". Sonnet 205 ("He who proclaims"). Luis de Camoens [or Camoes]. 6973-8
"He who sees the infinite" William Blake. 7014-0
"He who sits from day to day". Lines on a bill of mortality, 1790. William Cowper. 6931-2
"He who sublime in epic numbers rolled". Epitaph on Virgil and Tibullus. Domitius Marsus. 6945-2
"He who takes his hunger to the things". There is no help in bees. Robert P. Tristram Coffin. 7040-X
"He who thinks too much of the thorns knows". Symmetry. Nelle McCullough. 6799-9
"He who walks motionless through time with...". Identity card. Yannis Ritsos. 6803-0
"He who was born by a river". The prodigals. Joseph Joel Keith. 6761-1
"He who was driven into the wilderness". From the wilderness. William Soutar. 6782-4
"He who would be reborn must seek." Frances Crawford. 6515-5
"He who would like". Sonnet ("He who would like"). Joachim Du Bellay. 6227-X
"He who writ this...", fr. Secret-love. John Dryden. 6562-7
"He whom I praise? One young but as...". Young Daedalus. Florence Foster Hall. 7019-1
He whom a dream hath possessed. Shaemas O'Sheel. 6007-2, 6292-X,6476-0,6253-9,6076-5,6327-6,6102-8,6250-4, 6172-9,6336-5,6096-X,6310-1,6291-1,6102-8,6337-3, 6732 ,6602-X;6730-1
"He whose talk is of oxen will probably...". Dreaming, sel. Thomas De Quincey. 6958-4
"He will come straight...", fr. Hamlet. William Shakespeare. 6392-6
"He will not come, and still I wait". A little boy in the morning. Francis Ledwidge. 6930-4
"He will not come, the gallant flying boy". The ongoing. Mary Siegrist. 6995-9
He will praise his lady. Guido Guinicelli. 6102-8
"He will watch the hawk". Stephen Spender. 6536-8
He winna be guidit by me. Unknown. 6859-6
"He woke: the clank and racket of the train". Blighty. Siegfried Sassoon. 6846-4
"He wore a brace of pistols the night...". The bandit's fate. Unknown. 6787-5
He wore a crown of thorns. Alice Mortenson. 6065-X
"He wore a piece of purple towel". Hep-cat. John L. Seller. 6870-7
"He wore his coffin for a hat". For a pessimist. Countee Cullen. 6850-2
"He wore the day in his belt". Responsory for Garcia Lorca. Oscar Castro Z.. 6759-X
He worked. J.N. Scholes. 6144-3,6335-7
He worried about it. Lyman Abbott. 6744-1
He worried about it. Sam Walter Foss. 6260-1,6694-1,6964-9
He would have his lady sing. Digby Mackworth Dolben. 6844-8
"He would need the exact/knowledge of death". On a skull carved in crystal. John Haines. 6855-3
"He wrote and wrote, but could not make a name". Still water. Edgar Fawcett. 7041-8
"He wrote it, sitting with his back against". His last letter. Esther Weakley. 6750-6
"He wrote of those who laugh & those who moan". Charles Dickens. Arthur Hobson Quinn. 6936-3
"He yelled count finished! The machinery". A typical 6:00 p.m. in the fun house. Daniel Berrigan. 6870-7
"He'd even have his joke". The joke, fr. Battle. Wilfred Wilson Gibson. 6897-9
He'd had no show. Sam Walter Foss. 6481-7
"He'd made a fortune out of stocks, he...". Money. Edgar A. Guest. 6862-6
"He'll see it when he wakes." Frank Lee. 6113-3,6340-3
"He's 19 years old". 29 reasons I luv him. Walt Curtis. 7003-5
"He's a target for warnings and slogans of...". The jay walker. Berton Braley. 6853-7
"He's aff the kintra at a spang!". Hughie's indignation at the conduct of the...elder. James Logie ("Hugh Haliburton") Robertson. 6819-7
"He's an old American aristocrat who gives...". Watercolors. Scott Tucker. 7003-5
"He's cocksure in all his opinions". Sure he will. Berton Braley. 6853-7
He's come! The saviour has come! Alice Mortenson. 6065-X
He's coming here. Unknown. 6859-6
He's coming home at last. Emily Jane Greene. 6178-8
"He's dead and gone! He's dead and gone!". Ranger's grave. Caroline Anne Bowles Southey. 7008-8
"He's gane, he's gane!". Robert Burns. 6085-4,6438-8
He's just a dog. Joseph M. Anderson. 7008-6
"He's just plain yellow: no 'blue-ribbon'...". Just plain yellow. Anna Hadley Middlemas. 7008-6
"He's married well, you say? I see". Past and future. Joyce Lancaster. 6850-2
"He's not a witty boy, nor wise". A boy I know. Unknown. 6889-8
"He's not the happy man, to whom is given". To Dodington. James Thomson. 6816-2
He's ower the hills that I lo'e weel. Carolina Oliphant, Baroness Nairne. 6086-2
"He's seventy/running the country". The difference. Susan Shogren. 6883-9
"He's so vulnerable. That complexion". Fish story. P.L. Jacobs. 6870-7
He's taken out his papers. Edgar A. Guest. 7033-7
"He's worth a million dollars and you think...". The rich man's woes. Edgar A. Guest. 6862-6
"He, above the rest". John Milton. 6289-X
"He, making speedy way through spersed air". The house of Morpheus. Edmund Spenser. 6935-2
"He, the great world-musician at whose stroke". The master-poets. Richard Watson Gilder. 7041-8
He, too, loved beauty. Edwin McNeill Poteat. 6144-3,6335-7
"He, who with journey well begun". A November night's

traveller. Joanna Baillie. 6813-8
He—they—we. John Oxenham. 6144-3;6335-7
"'A he-man?' demands Gertrude Stein, not...". Declaring
    the male. Sam Bradley. 6803-0
The **head** and the heart. John Godfrey Saxe. 6575-9
The **head** of Bran. George Meredith. 6322-5
The **head** of Memnon. Horace Smith. 6980-0
The **head** of wisdom. Randall Jarrell. 6751-4
The **head** on the table. John Haines. 6855-3
"The **head** that oft this pillow press'd". The pillow. James
    Montgomery. 6980-0
Head, Nancy
    London tube station. 6761-1
Head, Sir Edmund (tr.)
    Selections. Sextus Propertius, 6046-3,6253-9
Head, Sir Henry
    Destroyers. 7027-2
    Died of his wounds. 6482-5
    Seedtime and harvest. 6482-5
    Songs of la mouche. 6482-5
"The **head**, once crowned with locks so fair". Charles F.
    Smith. 6254-7
The **head-stone**. William Barnes. 6437-X
The **head**. Armin T. Wegner. 6160-5
The **headache**. Robert Herrick. 6092-7
Headin' home. E.W. Patten. 6104-4
Heading upstate holding a child's book of autographs. Lee
    Upton. 6900-2
Headlam, Walter (tr.)
    Bound for harvest-home, Idyll vii. Theocritus, 6435-3
    A cicada ("Chirruping grasshopper, drunken...").
       Meleager, 6435-3
    "Could we but see men as they are". Unknown, 6435-3
    The crab and the snake. Unknown (Greek), 6435-3
    Epitaph on the Athenian dead at Plataea. Simonides,
       6879-0
    The grave of Colonus, fr. Oedipis coloneus. Sophocles,
       6435-3
    In the spring. Ibycus, 6435-3
    Io. Aeschylus, 6435-3
    Life after death. Pindar, 6435-3
    Moonlight. Philodemus of Gadara, 6435-3
    "My reverend Elders, worthy...", fr. Agamemnon.
       Aeschylus, 6435-3
    "Said the Crab unto the Serpent". Unknown, 6435-3
    "Stranger, where thy feet now rest". Sophocles, 6435-3
    Suave mari magno, fr. Tympanistae. Sophocles, 6435-3
    Take her, break her. Anacreon, 6435-3
    Take life as it comes, fr. Hypsipyle. Euripides, 6435-3
    "There is the sea...", fr. Agamemnon. Aeschylus, 6435-3
    To a bride. Sappho, 6435-3
    "What courier could arrive...", fr. Agamemnon.
       Aeschylus, 6435-3
    A window in the breast. Unknown (Greek), 6435-3
Headland orchards. (Frederick) Ridgely Torrence. 6007-2
Headland, Isaac Taylor
    Chinese nursery rhyme. 6937-1,6638-0
    Flour fritters. 6466-3
    The mouse. 6466-3
    Old Chang, the crab. 6466-3
    Old Mother Wind. 6466-3
    The rice seller. 6466-3
    The snail. 6466-3
The **headland**.. Arthur Davison Ficke. 6031-5
"**Headlands** and hills and a world of rocks". The valley of
    rocks. Gertrude Huntington McGiffert. 6838-3
"**Headlands** stood out into the moon-lit deep". Matthew
    Arnold. 6997-5
Headline history. William Plomer. 6633-X
The **headliner** and the breadwinner. Robert Service. 6159-1
Headlines. Foster Robertson. 6792-1
"The **headlines** screamed at me". Strontium cornflakes 1979
    Rebecca Minnich. 6883-9
Headquarters. Gilbert Frankau. 7026-4
Heads and tails. Claudia Lars. 6759-X
Heads, hearts, and hands. George W. Bungay. 6273-3
Heads, not hearts, are trumps. Kate Field. 6682-8
Heady, James Paul
    Adoration. 6894-4
    The queen of municipal hall. 6894-4

"**Heal** us, Emmanuel, here we are". Jehovah-Rophi. William
    Cowper. 6814-6
The **healer**, sels. John Greenleaf Whittier. 6335-7
The **healer**. John Greenleaf Whittier. 6337-3
The **healers**. Laurence Binyon. 6542-2
Healey, Evelyn H.
    Journey's end. 6337-3
Healing beauty. Ethel B. Cheney. 6662-3
The **healing** hands. Victor Robinson. 6482-5
The **healing** ministry of Jesus. Mabelle Fay Koonsen. 6799-9
The **healing** of the leper. Vernon Watkins. 6210-5
The **healing** of the wood. Clinton Scollard. 6510-4
Health alphabet. Unknown. 6629-1
Health and wealth. Richard Hovey. 6717-4
Health and wealth. Thomas William Parsons. 6004-8
Health and wealth. Unknown. 6964-9
"**Health** from the lover of the country, me". To Fuscus
    Aristus. Horace. 7039-1
"**Health** is the best that Heaven sends". Simonides. 6251-2
"**Health** is the first good lent to man". Unknown. 6435-3
Health of body dependent on soul. Jones Very. 6730-1
A **health** to the birds. Seumas MacManus. 6073-0,6510-4
"A **health** to you, Teddy". San Juan. George Macdonald
    Moore. 6995-9
A **health** unto his majesty. Jeremy Saville. 6125-7
"**Health**, highest visitant from heaven". The song of
    health. Ariphron of Sicyon. 6879-0
Health, sels. Nathaniel Cotton. 6482-5
"**Health**, strength, and beauty, who would...". On one in
    illness. Walter Savage Landor. 6874-X
"**Health**, success, adventure,...rainbow fortune".
    Inventory. Fydell Edmund Garrett. 6800-6
Health: an eclogue. Thomas Parnell. 6975-4
A **health**. Edward Coate Pinkney. 6102-3,6176-1,6243-1,6473-
    6,6600-3,6121-4,6219-9,6226-1,6008-0,6250-4,6289-X,
    6441-8,6732-8,6302-0,6365-3,6004-8,6076-5,6735-2,
    6288-1,6309-8
Healy, Cahir
    In the lap o' the bog. 6174-5
    Th'song o' th' say. 6174-5
Healy, Mary Lanigan
    Chasm. 6750-6
    When you're away. 6750-6
Healy, Patrick
    My wishes. John D'Alton (tr.). 6930-4
Healy, Walter J.
    Granny. 6799-9
"**Heap** cassia...", fr. Paracelsus. Robert Browning. 6726-3,
    6110-9,6196-6
"**Heap** high the coals until the fire". Love's sacrifice.
    Unknown. 7021-3
"**Heap** high the farmer's wintry board,"fr.The corn song.
    John Greenleaf Whittier. 6618-6,6703-4
The **heap** of rags, fr. Songs of joy. William Henry Davies.
    6234-2
"A **heap** of rocks marks the abandoned mine". The abandoned
    mine. Charles Claybrook Woollacott. 6800-6,6625-9
"**Heaped** be the fagots high". Twelfth night song. Clinton
    Scollard. 7035-3
"**Hear** a word that Jesus spake". The toiling of Felix.
    Henry Van Dyke. 6961-4
"**Hear** a word, a word in season...". All for the cause.
    William Morris. 6879-0
"**Hear** an ancient indian legend told in many a". The
    palisades. Arthur Guiterman. 6773-5
"**Hear** me as if thy eares had palate, Jack". An ode in the
    praise of Sack. Unknown. 6933-9
Hear me yet. Unknown. 6182-6
Hear me, O God. Ben Jonson. 6732-8
"**Hear** me, and I'll sing to you". The dynamo's song. Louis
    J. Magee. 7004-3
"**Hear** me, Brama, bending lowly!". The pariah. Johann
    Wolfgang von Goethe. 6948-7
Hear my prayer, O heavenly Father. Harriet T. Parr. 6219-9
"**Hear** my voice, birds of war!". War song ("Hear my
    voice..."). Unknown (Ojibwa Indian). 7039-6
"**Hear** now a curious dream I dreamed last night". My dream.
    Christina Georgina Rossetti. 6958-4
"**Hear** now the song of the dead...". The song of the dead.
    Rudyard Kipling. 6810-3

HEAR

"Hear the blackbird's travelogue". The blackbird troubadour. Mary Josephine Benson. 6797-2
"Hear the clatter of those feet". The telegraph boy. Louis J. Magee. 7004-3
"Hear the geysirs in the highlands". Iceland's song. Grimur Thomsen. 6854-5
"Hear the guns, hear the guns!". The song of the guns. Herbert Kaufman. 6846-4
Hear the voice. William Blake. 6086-2
"Hear the voice of the Bard!". William Blake. 6186-9,6246-6
"Hear the word of the Lord, ye rulers of...". 'You hands are full of blood' Bible. 6954-1
"Hear through the morning drums and ...". Jackson at New Orleans. Wallace Rice. 6820-0
"Hear through the morning drums and trumpets". Jackson at New Orleans. Wallace Rice. 6946-0
"Hear us O hear us O Lord, to thee", fr. The litany. John Donne. 6931-2
Hear us, in this thy house. Philip Doddridge. 6065-X
"Hear us, O Lord, from Heaven...". Unknown. 6258-X
"Hear what God the Lord hath spoken". Isaiah 060: 15-20 William Cowper. 6848-0
"Hear what Hesiod says". An inscription for all council-chambers, fr. Eth. Nic. Aristotle. 7042-6
"Hear what the desolate Rizpah said". Rizpah. William Cullen Bryant. 6848-0
Hear ye his voice. Robert Kirkland Kerrighan. 6796-4
"Hear, Epicydes' son: 'twere much to thy present". Unknown. 6435-3
"Hear, Lord, the song of praise and pray'r". Hymn for the use of the Sunday school at Olney. William Cowper. 6814-6
Hear, O America! Marion Pelton Guild. 7001-9
"Hear, o my people, I will tell". Psalm 078. Bible. 6848-0
Hear, o ye nations. Frederick L. Homer. 6386-1
"Hear, oh king sni-Bhimasena, grant me a boon!". Bhimasena. Unknown (Newari). 7013-2
"Hear, sweet spirit". Song ("Hear, sweet spirit"). Samuel Taylor Coleridge. 6086-2,6271-7,6545-7
"Hear, sweet spirit, hear the spell". An invocation, fr. Remorse. Samuel Taylor Coleridge. 6828-6
"Hear, ye ladies. John Fletcher. 6186-9,6733-6,6182-6,6430-2,6092-7,6076-5,6737-9
"Hear, ye sullen pow'rs below". Song ("Hear, ye sullen"), fr. Oedipus. John Dryden. 6472-8
Heard are the voices. Thomas Carlyle. 6240-7
"Heard of Contradictin' Joe?". Contradictin' Joe. Edgar A. Guest. 7033-7
"Heard ye how the bold McClellan". How McClellan took Manassas. Unknown. 6946-0
"Heard ye of Nimrud? cities fell before him". Nimrud and the gnat. Sir Edwin Arnold. 6848-0
"Heard ye that thrilling word". Dirge for Ashby. Josephine Junkin Preston. 6946-0
"Heard ye the blast whose sullen roar". Ode for the king's birthday, 1792, sels. Henry James Pye. 6867-7
"Heard ye the Gothic trumpet's blast". Alaric in Italy. Felicia Dorothea Hemans. 6973-8
"Heard'st thou that dying moan of...breath". Icarus. James Wallis Eastburn (atr.). 6752-2
The heare. William Barnes. 6656-9
"Heares non but onelie I." Unknown. 6563-5
Hearin' things at night. Mary Campbell Monroe. 6710-7
Hearing. Sir John Davies. 6584-8
Hearing Heaney read. Gregory Betts. 6767-0
Hearing of harvests rotting in the valleys. Wystan Hugh Auden. 6641-0
Hearing, I saw. P.D. Cummins. 6339-X
"Hearing, in the hollow wind of autumn". Nocturne. Thomas McGrath. 6761-1
"Hearke, now every thing is still". John Webster. 6933-9
"Hearken the stirring story". The fall of Maubila. Thomas Dunn English. 6946-0
"Hearken then awile to me". Song ("Hearken then"). William Browne. 6250-4
"Hearken to me, ye mothers of my tent". The song of Lamech. Arthur Hugh Clough. 6980-0,6848-0
Hearken to the hammers! Laurence Binyon. 6777-8
"Hearken to yon pine-warbler". A dirge, sels. Ralph Waldo Emerson. 6934-7
"Hearken, masters, to our singing". Watchman's call. Unknown. 6952-5
"Hearken, my chant, 'tis". A corymbus for autumn. Francis Thompson. 6942-8
"Hearken, the feet of the destroyed tread". Sonnet ("Hearken, the feet"). George Edward Woodberry. 7026-4
"Hearkene ye and heede me welle". The fairy's spell. Frederick W. Poole. 6818-9
Hearn, Lafcadio (tr.)
  Clairmonde. Theophile Gautier, 7039-6
Hearn, Marianne Farningham
  Consecration. 6337-3
  The last hymn. 6303-9
"Hears not my Phillis, how the birds". Song ("Hears not my Phillis"). Sir Charles Sedley. 6544-9,6562-7
"Hears the low plash of wave o'erwhelming". Sir Henry Taylor. 6997-5
Hearsay, fr. Songs of farewell. Hazel Hall. 6778-6
The hearse song. Unknown. 6237-7
The hearse-horse. Bliss Carman and Richard Hovey. 6890-1
Hearst, James
  Barns in November. 6491-4
  The French row. 6491-4
Heart and mind. Edith Sitwell. 6246-6,6210-5,6150-8
The heart and nature. Owen (Edward Bulwer-Lytton, Earl Lytton) Meredith. 6543-0
The heart and nature. Owen (Edward Bulwer-Lytton, Earl Lytton) Meredith. 6844-8
"The heart and service to you proffer'd." Sir Thomas Wyatt. 6584-8
Heart and soul. Sir Philip Sidney. 6099-4
The heart and the hambone. Edith Sitwell. 7000-0
The heart and the liver. John Godfrey Saxe. 6004-8
Heart and will. William James Linton. 7009-4
The heart asks pleasure first. Emily Dickinson. 6288-1
The heart entire. William Herbert; Earl of Pembroke. 6328-4
Heart exchange. Sir Philip Sidney. 6315-2,6473-6
A heart for every one. Charles Swain. 6226-1
"A heart full of thankfulness". A happy day. Unknown. 6889-8
The heart healed and changed by mercy. William Cowper. 6814-6
The heart is Bethlehem. Gertrude Hanson. 6144-3
"The heart is a garden, and never a seed". Thoughts. Rose Hartwick Thorpe. 6929-0
The heart knoweth its own bitterness. Aline Kilmer. 6153-2, 6300-X
The heart knoweth its own bitterness. Christina Georgina Rossetti. 6828-6
"The heart leaps with the pride of their story". The fleet at Santiago. Charles E. Russell. 6946-0
The heart lies fallow. Ruth Forbes Sherry. 6316-9
Heart o' the north. Robert Service. 6159-1
"The heart of a bird that comes north in...". Quest. Dorothy Choate Herriman. 6797-2
The heart of a bird. Dorothea MacKellar. 6510-4
The heart of a maid. Dora Sigerson Shorter. 6174-5
"Heart of a man is shaped quite like a heart". Moan on, Mississippi. Preston Paine Foster. 6906-1
"Heart of France for a hundred years". Victor Hugo. Henry Van Dyke. 6961-4
The heart of a woman. William Butler Yeats. 6844-8
Heart of all the world. Marion Couthouy Smith. 6474-4
The heart of Bruce in Melrose Abbey. Felicia Dorothea Hemans. 6973-8
The heart of Canada. Alfred Noyes. 6151-6
The heart of evening. Lucy H. King Smith. 6906-1
The heart of friendship. Unknown. 6889-8
The heart of God. W.E. Littlewood. 6065-X
Heart of gold. Rosamund Marriott ("Graham R. Tomson") Watson. 6785-9
"A heart of gold the daisy shows". A heart of gold. Virginia Donaghe McClurg. 6836-7
The heart of gold. Witter Bynner. 6320-9
The heart of light. Winifred Welles. 6217-2
The heart of Louisiana. Harriet Stanton. 6008-0,6753-0
"The heart of man, walk t which way it will". Repose of

the heart, fr. Philip Van Artevelde. Henry Taylor. 6980-0
"The heart of me is like a railroad bum". Fare for a gipsy heart. Louis Ragg. 6750-6
"Heart of my heart, when you pick up my paper". Restoration, fr. Matrimonial melodies. Berton Braley. 6853-7
Heart of oak. David Garrick. 6087-0,6547-3,6328-4,6732-8
A heart of stone. John Haryngton. 6827-8
The heart of the Bruce. William Edmonstoune Aytoun. 6370-5, 6613-5,6263-6
The heart of the bugle. Meredith Nicholson. 6509-0
The heart of the eternal. Frederick William Faber. 6303-9, 6214-8
Heart of the gael. Marie Mancino. 6799-9
The heart of the hills. Sir John Ernest Adamson. 6800-6
The heart of the lakes. William Wilfred Campbell. 6795-6
The heart of the night, fr. The house of life. Dante Gabriel Rossetti. 6828-6
The heart of the night, fr. The house of life. Dante Gabriel Rossetti. 6110-9,6199-0
The heart of the road. Anna Hempstead Branch. 7012-4
The heart of the sourdough. Robert Service. 6159-1
The heart of the tree. Henry Cuyler Bunner. 6047-1,6143-5
The heart of the war. Josiah Gilbert Holland. 6113-3,6402-7,6129-9
The heart of the woods. Florence Wilkinson. 6253-9
The heart of youth, sels. Hermann Hagedorn. 6532-5
The heart of youth. Unknown. 6073-0
"Heart oppress'd with desperate thought." Sir Thomas Wyatt. 6584-8
The heart recalcitrant. Leonora Speyer. 6513-9
A heart song. Elizabeth Rial Sargent. 6270-9
Heart songs. Cora Fabri. 6876-6
The heart that's young to love hath yold. W. H. Tourjee. 6818-9
The heart to carry on. Bertram Warr. 6446-9
A heart to heart talk. Edgar A. Guest. 6862-6
"Heart to heart!". In silence. Bliss Carman and Richard Hovey. 6890-1
The heart upon the sleeve. Elinor Wylie. 6531-7
Heart ventures. Unknown. 6414-0
"Heart! that didst press forward still". The heart of Bruce in Melrose Abbey. Felicia Dorothea Hemans. 6973-8
The heart's call. Edith M. Thomas. 6620-8,6066-8,6226-1
The heart's charity. Eliza Cook. 6918-5
Heart's compass, fr. The house of life. Dante Gabriel Rossetti. 6726-3,6110-9,6199-0,6655-0
The heart's country. Florence Wilkinson. 6310-1,6019-6
Heart's desire. John Peter. 6788-3
The heart's door. Edward Everett Hale. 6109-5
"Heart's ease! One could look for half a day..." Mary Howitt. 6049-8
Heart's garden. Norreys Jephson O'Conor. 6338-1
Heart's haven. Kendall Banning. 6337-3
Heart's haven, fr. The house of life. Dante Gabriel Rossetti. 6199-0,6430-2,6828-6
The heart's home. Frederick William Faber. 6214-8
Heart's hope, fr. The house of life. Dante Gabriel Rossetti. 6110-9,6199-0,6250-4,6828-6
The heart's journey (1). Siegfried Sassoon. 6985-1
The heart's journey (2). Siegfried Sassoon. 6985-1
The heart's journey (3). Siegfried Sassoon. 6985-1
The heart's journey. Siegfried Sassoon. 6150-8
The heart's not yet a neighbor. Mary Fullerton. 6384-5
The heart's proof. James Buckham. 6461-2
The heart's question. Cale Young Rice. 6607-0
The heart's return. Edwin Markham. 6241-9
The heart's sacredness. Richard Chenevix Trench. 7015-9
The heart's song. Arthur Cleveland Coxe. 6219-9
The heart's summer. Epes Sargent. 6085-4
Heart's tide. Ethel M. Hewitt. 6027-7
The heart's venture. William Browne. 6935-5
The heart's wild geese. Henry Treece. 6666-6
Heart's wild-flower. William Vaughn Moody. 6320-9,6300-4
Heart's-ease. Arthur William Beer. 6789-1
Heart's-ease. Walter Savage Landor. 6086-2,6110-9,6396-9
Heart's-ease. Unknown. 6273-3,6670-4
The heart's-ease. Fannie Williams. 6924-X

The heart, defenseless of shield. Milicent Laubenheimer. 6640-2
"Heart, my heart, with cares past curing thou...". Archilochus. 6251-2
"Heart, sad heart, for hwat are you pleading?". Heart, sad heart: a rondel. Louise Chandler Moulton. 7041-8
Heart, we will forget him. Emily Dickinson. 6006-4,6300-4
The heart-beat, fr. The song of my fiftieth birthday. Vachel Lindsay. 6206-7
The heart-cry of the duchess. John Webster. 6102-8
The heart-cry. Francis William Bourdillon. 6476-0
Heart-foam. Sir William Schwenck Gilbert. 6902-9
The heart-II. Francis Thompson. 6655-0
Heart-lighted. Lilian Sauter. 7023-X
Heart-rest. Sir Henry Taylor. 6211-3
"Heart-sick from hindrance and faint from...". In the city. Hattie Horner Louthan. 6836-7
"Heart-sick, homeless, weak, and weary". The edge of doom. Alice Cary. 6865-0;6969-X
"Heart-strings are delicately strung". Living. Daisy Covin Walker. 6799-9
Heart-summoned. Jesse Stuart. 6218-0
The heart. Michael Drayton. 6562-7
The heart. Elizabeth Fergusson. 6541-4
The heart. Francis Thompson. 6339-X
The heart. Unknown. 6312-8
Heartbreak. Sheila Hertel. 6883-9
Heartbreak. Howard Mumford Jones. 6326-8
Heartbreak hill. Celia Thaxter. 6484-1
Heartbreak hill. Celia Thaxter. 6912-6
Heartbreak road. Helen Gray Cone. 6076-5,6102-8
The heartening. Winifred Webb. 6964-9
Hearth. Peggy Bacon. 6891-X
"The hearth is warm". Abandoned woman's lament. Jackson Holland Patterson. 6841-3
The hearth of Urien. Unknown (Welsh) 6125-7
A hearth song. Harry Tennyson Domer. 6799-9
The hearth, fr. The homestead. Gertrude Huntington McGiffert. 6838-3
"The hearth, the hearth is desolate!...". The forsaken hearth. Felicia Dorothea Hemans. 6973-8
Hearth-song. Robert Underwood Johnson. 6266-0
Hearthstone and highway. Helen Coale Crew. 6327-6
Heartless. W.H. Smith. 6116-8
Hearts. Adelaide Anne Procter. 6957-6
Hearts and hearths. Benjamin Franklin Taylor. 6815-4
Hearts and lace paper. Unknown. 6466-3
"Hearts and ribbons in the wind!". Invitation. Lucille Schmedtje. 6850-2
"Hearts are tied with tiny threads". Triolets. Pax P. Hibben. 6983-5
Hearts courageous. John Oxenham. 6337-3
"Hearts good and true". Written in a little lady's little album. Frederick William Faber. 6934-7
Hearts of gold. Helen T. Clarke. 6965-7
Hearts of gold. William Henry Ogilvie. 6591-0,6592-9
Hearts of gold. Unknown. 6215-6
"Hearts of oak that have bravely deliver'd...". Stanzas on the battle of Navarino, 1827. Thomas Campbell. 7009-4
"The hearts of the mountains were void". Return. Frederick Victor Branford. 6884-7
"Hearts only thrive on varied good". Josiah Gilbert Holland. 6109-5
Hearts shall ever linger. Unknown. 6717-4
"Hearts that are great." Unknown. 6461-2
Hearts were made to give away. Annette Wynne. 6465-5
"Hearts, beat no more! Earth's sleep has come!". Requiem of archangels for the world. Herbert Trench. 6877-4
"Hearts, like apples, are hard and sour". Josiah Gilbert Holland. 6238-5
"Hearts, like doors, will ope with ease". Rules of courtesy. Unknown. 6861-8
"Hearts, like doors, will ope with ease." Unknown. 6452-3
Heartsease. Richard Lawson Gales. 6950-9
Heartsease coantry. Algernon Charles Swinburne. 6875-8
Heartsick!. Mary Elizabeth Blake. 7041-8
Heartstrong south and headstrong north, fr. Psalm... Sidney Lanier. 6753-0
Heat. Hilda ("H.D.") Doolittle. 6556-2,726-3,6076-5,6102-

HEAT

Heat. 8
Heat. Gilberto Gonzalez y Contreras. 6759-X
Heat. Archibald Lampman. 6021-8,6433-7,6115-X,5446-9,6656-9
Heat. Archibald Lampman. 7041-8
Heat lightning. James Whitcomb Riley. 6128-1
"Heat of the sun that maketh all men black". Daphne. Edith Sitwell. 7000-0
"The heat uncovers the window and attic-fan". Looking for my old indian grandmother in the summer... Diane Glancy. 7005-1
"The heat wave sweeps along the street". A ballade of midsummer. Brander Matthews. 6770-0,6875-8
"Heat, all pervading, crinkles up the soil". Drought. Denys Lefebvre. 6800-6
"The heat/Was like a huge". Summer heat. Roslyn Sollisch. 6850-2
Heater, Lo Amy
   Ivy poem. 6717-4
"The heath lies far & wide bestrewn with snow". Winter evening. Karel V. Rais. 6763-8
"The heath this night must be my bed." Sir Walter Scott. 6302-0,6385-3,6737-9
The heath this night must be my bed. Sir Walter Scott. 6219-9
"The heath this night". Song ("The heath this night"). Sir Walter Scott. 6271-7
Heath, (?)
   Women. 6436-1
Heath, Bertha
   The yesterdays and tomorrows. 6799-9
Heath, Blanche Trennor
   The other little girl. 6130-3,6713-1
   Polly dolly. 6130-3
Heath, Ella Crosby
   Poetry. 6607-0,6730-1
Heath, Gertrude E.
   The flag. 6714-X
Heath, Lilian M.
   Lift the Prohibition banner. 6685-2
Heath, Pricilla
   Lyric. 6764-6
   Lyric ("I am a Puritan"). 6764-6
   Lyric ("I stared"). 6764-6
Heath, Robert
   Clarastella distrusting. 6563-5
   The excuse. 6563-5
   On Clarastella singing. 6933-9
   On Clarastella, walking in her garden. 6563-5
   On the unusual cold and rainie weather in..summer,1648. 6933-9
   The sceptical lady. 6659-3
   Song in a siege. 6933-9
   To Clarastella on St. Valentines day morning. 6933-9
   To her at departure. 6908-8
Heath, Sir Robert
   Seeing her dancing. 6562-7
Heath-Stubbs, John
   Beggar's serenade. 6379-9
   The ghost in the cellarage. 6379-9
   Maria Aegyptiaca. 6209-1
   The mermaid at Zennor. 6209-1
   Two men in armour. 6379-9
   Virgin and unicorn. 6379-9
Heath-Stubbs, John (tr.)
   Canzone: of distance. Ruggieri D'Amici, 6325-X
   Dance song. Angelo Poliziano, 6325-X
"The heath-cock crawled o'er muir an' dale". The heath-cock. Unknown. 6859-6
The heath-cock. Joanna Baillie. 6302-0;6385-3
The heath-cock. Unknown. 6859-6
The heath. Thomas Boyd. 6930-4
"The heathen chinee's" reply. Unknown. 6404-3
The heathen Chinee. Francis Bret Harte. 6102-8,6732-8,6302-0,6076-5
A heathen hymn. Sir Lewis Morris. 6337-3
The heathen pass-ee. Arthur Clement Hilton. 6440-X,6092-7
Heather. William Henry Ogilvie. 6269-5
Heather. Marguerite Wilkinson. 6331-4,6439-6,6631-3
Heather ale. Robert Louis Stevenson. 6122-2,6290-3,6518-X, 6656-9,6458-2

The heather glen. George Sigerson. 6090-0
"The heather was blooming, the meadows were...". The heather was blooming. Robert Burns. 6943-6
The heather. Steen Steensen Blicher. 6555-4
The heather. Neil Munro. 6180-X
Heaton, John Langdon
   I tol' yer so. 6277-6
   The inconsistent sex. 6632-1
"Heau'n & beautye are aly'de." Unknown. 6563-5
"Heauen sinc thou art the only place of rest." Unknown. 6563-5
"Heave, mighty ocean, heave". A home everywhere. S. Graham. 6752-2
"The heave, the wave, and bend" John Neal. 6049-8
Heavely aid, fr. The faery queene. Edmund Spenser. 6337-3
Heaven. Rupert Brooke. 6199-0
Heaven. Bliss Carman. 6232-6,6649-6
Heaven. Mary Carolyn Davies. 6750-6
Heaven. Frederick William Faber. 6502-3
Heaven. Gertrude Fitzpatrick. 6789-1
Heaven. Alexander Gray. 6269-5
Heaven. Edwin Hatch. 6337-3
Heaven. George Herbert. 6334-9,6558-9
Heaven. M. Sophie Holmes. 6909-6
Heaven. Nancy Amelia Woodbury Priest. 6385-3
Heaven. Nina Dudley Staples. 6270-9
Heaven. Takamoto. 6027-7
Heaven. Jeremy Taylor. 6302-0;6385-3
Heaven. Katharine Haviland Taylor. 6750-6
Heaven. Unknown. 6752-2
Heaven. Unknown. 6302-0,6461-2
Heaven. Nancy Amelia Woodbury Priest Wakefield. 6240-7
Heaven. Willard Wattles. 6320-9
Heaven. Isaac Watts. 6730-1
Heaven ("Fish fly-replete, in depth of June"). Rupert Brooke. 6234-2,6426-6,6339-X,6730-1,6733-6,6199
Heaven ("for the happy"). Cynewulf. 6489-2
Heaven ("Life changes all our thoughts of heaven:"). Unknown. 6303-9
Heaven ("This world is all a fleeting show,"). Thomas Moore. 6303-9
Heaven and earth. James I; King of Scotland. 6125-7
"Heaven and earth, and all that hear me plain." Sir Thomas Wyatt. 6584-8
Heaven and earth: a mystery. George Gordon, 6th Baron Byron. 6945-2,6848-0
Heaven and hell. Sir William Watson. 6532-5
"Heaven and hell are one with fools". A fool speaks his mind. Ralph Douberly. 6841-1
Heaven and hell, fr. The marriage of heaven and hell. William Blake. 6545-7
Heaven and hell, fr. The Rubaiyat. Omar Khayyam. 6337-3
Heaven but the vision of fufilled desire, fr. Rubaiyat. Omar Khayyam. 7039-6
Heaven for horses. Lew Sarett. 6887-1
"Heaven has lit her level fields". Sunset - North Carolina. Ruth Vail. 6789-1
"Heaven help me! I'm in love again". Intermittent fever. Walter De La Mare. 6905-3
"Heaven is bare of God and earth is full". Nineteen-eighteen. Jeannette Sewell. 6847-2
"Heaven is not far, tho' far the sky". Christina Georgina Rossetti. 6931-2
Heaven lies about us in our infancy. William Wordsworth. 6078-1
The heaven of love. Frederick George Scott. 6433-7
Heaven overarches. Christina Georgina Rossetti. 6123-0, 6250-4,6508-2
"Heaven sang through me today". Rejuvenation. Gertrude Joan Buckman. 6850-2
The heaven that was. Theodore Watts-Dunton. 7015-9
The heaven that's here. Alice Cary. 6969-X
A heaven upon earth. Leigh Hunt. 6980-0
"Heaven weeps above the earth all night...". The tears of heaven. Alfred Lord Tennyson. 6977-0
"Heaven! 'tis delight to see how fair". Song ("Heaven!"). Charles, Duc d' Orleans. 6226-1
"Heaven's gates are not so highly arch'd." John Webster. 6225-3

Heaven's glory shone. Emily Bronte. 6828-6
Heaven's hour. William Winter. 6300-4
Heaven's last best work, fr. Of the characters of women. Alexander Pope. 6932-0
The heaven's mould. William Cavendish; Duke of Newcastle. 6317-9
"Heaven's not gained by a single bound." Josiah Gilbert Holland. 6225-3,6479-5
Heaven's own child. Charles W. Denison. 6755-7
Heaven, fr. Paradise lost. John Milton. 6933-9
Heaven-haven. Gerard Manley Hopkins. 6828-6
Heaven-haven. Gerard Manley Hopkins. 6022-6,6354-3,6430-2, 6508-2
The heavenly banquet. Sean O'Faolain. 6582-1
"The heavenly bay, ringed round with cliffs...". In guernsey. Algernon Charles Swinburne. 6770-0
The heavenly breeze. George Burgess. 6065-X
The heavenly Canaan. Isaac Watts. 6271-7
The heavenly city. Stevie Smith. 6210-5
The heavenly city. Unknown. 6153-2
The heavenly dove. Frederika Bremer. 6424-8
Heavenly father at evening. Franz Werfel. 6160-5
A heavenly friend. Paul Tucker. 6065-X
The heavenly gift of poesy, fr. To...Anne Killigrew. John Dryden. 6934-7
The heavenly guest. Leo Tolstoy. 7002-7
The heavenly hills of Holland. Henry Van Dyke. 6439-6
The heavenly Jerusalem. Giles (the Younger) Fletcher. 6931-2
The heavenly Jerusalem. F.B. P. 6934-7
The heavenly land. Isaac Watts. 6600-3
The heavenly noel. Richard Lawson Gales. 6558-9
The heavenly noel. Richard Lawson Gales. 6950-9
The heavenly pilot. Cormac. 6930-4
"The heavenly rider passed". Jalal [or Jelal] ed-din Rumi. 6448-5
The heavenly runaway. John Daniel Logan. 6797-2
"A heavenly song, I dare well say". This day. Unknown. 6756-5
"A heavenly town is Provincetown". The heavenly town. Alma Martin. 6798-0
"A heavenly vision, born of love and faith". Woodrow Wilson. Thomas Curtis Clark. 7001-9
The heavens above and the law within, fr. Psalm 19, Bible. 6730-1
"The heavens declare the glory of God", fr. The bible. Unknown. 6289-X
The heavens declare the glory of God, fr. Psalm 19 Bible. 6337-3
"The heavens declare the glory of God". Psalm 019, fr. The book of psalms. Bible. 7039-6
"The heavens declare thy glory, Lord!" Isaac Watts. 6302-0
"The heavens have cried their golden tears". The song of the heavens, the stars, Schumann & my wife. Hunus Jelinek. 6763-8
"The heavens spread a cloth of blue". Nuptials. Christine Park Hankinson. 6841-3
"The heavens themselves, the planets and...". On degree. William Shakespeare. 6935-5
"Heavens! how my heart beat rapture to behold". Poem on visiting the Academy of Philadelphia, June 1753 William Smith. 6936-3
"Heavens! what a goodly prospect spreads...". Happy Britannia, fr. The seasons (Summer). James Thomson. 6932-0
The heavens, fr. Psalm 19 Bible. 6125-7
The heavens. Walt Whitman. 6253-9
Heavenward. I.E. Dickenga. 6921-5
Heavenward. Carolina Oliphant, Baroness Nairne. 6086-2
Heavier the cross. B. Schmolke. 6910-X
Heavier the cross. Benjamin Schmolke. 6065-X
The heaviest cross of all. Katherine Eleanor Conway. 6172-9
Heaving of the lead. Charles Dibdin. 6302-0
Heaving the lead. J. Pearce. 6833-2,6385-3
The heavy bear. Delmore Schwartz. 6389-6
"The heavy clouds at length are scattering" Alexander Pushkin. 6103-6
The heavy dragoon. Sir William Schwenck Gilbert. 6501-5
"The heavy hand of afternon weighs down". Siesta hour. Clifford Gessler. 6979-7
"A heavy spot the forest looks at first". The Ravenna pine forest. Leigh Hunt. 6980-0
"The heavy teams go lumbering by". The MacDowell Colony. Agnes Ryan. 6764-6
Heavy water blues. Bob Kaufman. 6792-1
Heavy water blues. Bob Kaufman. 6998-3
Heavy with thought. Sir Cecil Spring-Rice. 6477-9
"Heavy, and hot, and gray". A symbol. Bayard Taylor. 6976-2

Heavysege, Charles
Count Filippo, sels. 6646-9
Hell's road. 6102-8
Night. 6433-7
Saul's faithfulness. 6102-8
Saul, sels. 6646-9
Self-examination. 6433-7
Song, fr. Count Filippo. 6646-9
"The stars are glittering in the frosty sky." 6646-9
Twilight. 6656-9
Winter night. 6433-7

Hebblethwaite, James
Perdita. 6784-0
The symbol. 6784-0
Wanderers. 6384-5,6253-9

Hebe. James Russell Lowell. 6243-1,6732-8,6288-1,6126-5
Hebe. Unknown. 6682-8

Hebel, Johann
Sunday morning. 6127-3

Heber, J. Willis
Good Friday. 6799-9

Heber, Reginald
Before the sacrament. 6086-2
A bow-meeting song. 6102-8
Bread of the world. 6337-3
Brightest and best of the sons of the morning. 6337-3, 6730-1,6304-7,6214-8,6608-9
The British bow. 6980-0
By cool Siloam's shady rill. 6337-3,6519-8,6086-2,6304-7
Christmas day. 6747-6
Christmas hymn. 6980-0
Early piety. 6219-9
Epiphany. 6271-7,6465-5,6291-9,6424-8
Farewell. 6980-0
Fragment of a poem on the world before the flood. 6848-0
From Greenland's icy mountains. 6418-3,6730-1,6086-2, 6214-8,6304-7
The holy trinity. 6219-9
Holy, holy, holy. 6337-3,6304-7,6732-8
Hymn for epiphany. 6747-6
If thou wert by my side. 6271-7,6600-3,6620-8,6302-0, 6385-3,6438
Lines written to his wife. 6219-9
Missionary hymn. 6219-9
Palestine. 6848-0
The passage of the Red Sea. 6848-0
Pitt. 6087-0
Providence. 6239-3
The son of God goes forth to war. 6337-3,6473-6
Song ("There is, they say, a secret well"). 6980-0
Sons of the morning. 6145-1
Stanzas on the death of a friend. 6219-9
Sympathy. 6089-7,6092-7,6573-2
Sympathy. 6919-3
"Thou art gone to the grave." 6271-7,6302-0,6214-8
Thrice holy. 6730-1,6214-8
To a Welsh air. 6934-7
Verses to Mrs. Heber. 6980-0
Who follows in his train? 6730-1
The widow of Nain. 6980-0

Hebert, G.
Footman Joe. 6787-5

An hebraic lamentation. Swithin Saint Swithaine. 6848-0
The hebrew bard. Isaac Watts. 6848-0
Hebrew dirge. Lydia Huntley Sigourney. 6848-0
The Hebrew father's prayer. William Wilfred Campbell. 6848-0
Hebrew hymn. Sir Walter Scott. 6014-5

HEBREW

"A Hebrew knelt, in the dying light". The dying Hebrew. Thomas Kibble Hervey. 6848-0
Hebrew melodies, sels. George Gordon, 6th Baron Byron. 6945-2
Hebrew melody. Mrs. James Gorden Brooks. 6848-0,6752-2
Hebrew melody. G. R. Smith. 6848-0
The hebrew minstrel's lament. Unknown. 6848-0
The Hebrew mother. Felicia Dorothea Hemans. 6409-4
The Hebrew mother. Barbara Miller Macandrew. 6848-0
A Hebrew tale. Lydia Huntley Sigourney. 6407-8
A hebrew tale. Lydia Huntley Sigourney. 6848-0
Hebrews. James Oppenheim. 6619-4,6010-2
Hebridean sea-prayer. Unknown (Gaelic) 6334-9
The Hebrides.. Louis MacNeice. 6536-8
Hecate, fr. Rhizotomi. Sophocles. 6435-3
Heckman, Ruth
    My mother's stories. 6249-0
Hector and Achilles. Homer. 6621-6
Hector and Andromache, fr. The Iliad. Homer. 6932-0
Hector in Hades. Robert ("Droch") Bridges. 6143-2
"Hector Protector was dressed all in green". Unknown. 6904-5
Hector to Astyanax. John Clark. 6800-6
Hector's farewell. Johann C. Friedrich von Schiller. 6842-1
"A hedge of trees surrounds me". The scribe. Unknown. 6930-4
Hedge, Frederic Henry
    Questionings. 6438-8
Hedge, Frederick Henry (tr.)
    Hymn ("A mighty"). Martin Luther, 6418-3,6730-1
    "A mighty fortress is our God." Martin Luther, 6302-0, 6385-3,6337-3
Hedge, T.H.
    Via crucis, via lucis. 6065-X
The hedge-rose opens. Alfred Noyes. 6151-6
Hedgehog in air raid. Clifford Dyment. 6475-2
The hedgehog. Laura Benet. 6464-7
The hedgehog. Beatrix Potter. 6937-1
"The hedgerow hips to glossy scarlet turn". Fragment ("The hedgerow"). John Clare. 6545-7
Hedges, Ada Hastings
    Solus. 6039-0
Hedges, John
    The will. 6302-0
Hedin, Robert
    Houdini. 6855-3
    Ptarmigan valley. 6855-3
    Sitka spruce. 6855-3
    The snow country. 6855-3
    Tornado. 6855-3
    Waiting for trains at Col d'Aubisque. 6855-3
    The wreck of the Great Northern. 6855-3
Hedman, Anna Elizabeth
    Echoes of New York. 6764-6
Hedrich, Ida M.
    Welcome for school entertainment. 6167-2
Hedrick, Addie M.
    Two crosses. 6144-3
"Hee ended, or I heard no more, for now". Paradise lost, sel. John Milton. 6958-4
"Heed not the folk who sing or say". Ballade of the optimist. Rosamund Marriott ("Graham R. Tomson") Watson. 6770-0
"Heed not the taunts of the other lads". To my foster son. Gertrude S. Flickinger. 6799-9
"Heed thou the doorstep, threshold to..world". The doorstep, fr. The homestead. Gertrude Huntington McGiffert. 6838-3
Heedless cruelty. William Cowper. 6102-8
Heedless o' my love. William Barnes. 6545-7
The heedless rake. Carolyn Wells. 6882-0
Heels over head with life. Maria Mercedes Carranza. 7036-1
Heermans, Mary A.
    Arbor Day song. 6047-1
    Tribute to nature. 6049-8
Heflebower, Clara Keck
    Fate. 6906-1
    I march with you! 6906-1
    Queries. 6906-1
    Shattered dreams. 6906-1
    The suicide. 6906-1
Hegeman, Katharine R.
    The cloister. 6799-9
Hegi, Nora Byrnes
    The Hinckley fire. 6342-X
Heidenstam, Verner von
    Alone by the lake. Charles Wharton Stork (tr.). 6045-5
    At the end of the way. Charles Wharton Stork (tr.). 6045-5
    The burial of Gustaf Froding. Charles Wharton Stork (tr.). 6045-5
    A day. Charles Wharton Stork (tr.). 6045-5
    The dove of thought. Charles Wharton Stork (tr.). 6045-5
    Fellow-citizens. Charles Wharton Stork (tr.). 6045-5
    The forest of Tiveden, sels. Charles Wharton Stork (tr.). 6045-5
    'Grant that we die young.' Charles Wharton Stork (tr.). 6045-5
    Home. Charles Wharton Stork (tr.). 6045-5
    Home-land. Charles Wharton Stork (tr.). 6045-5
    "How easily men's cheeks are hot with wrath!." Charles Wharton Stork (tr.). 6045-5
    Invocation and promise. Charles Wharton Stork (tr.). 6045-5
    A man's last word to a woman. Charles Wharton Stork (tr.). 6045-5
    Moonlight. Charles Wharton Stork (tr.). 6045-5
    My life. Charles Wharton Stork (tr.). 6045-5
    Nameless and immortal. Charles Wharton Stork (tr.). 6045-5
    Prayer amid flames. Charles Wharton Stork (tr.). 6045-5
    Prayer and flames. Charles Wharton Stork (tr.). 6045-5
    Starting on the journey. Charles Wharton Stork (tr.). 6045-5
    Sweden. Charles Wharton Stork (tr.). 6045-5
    Thoughts in loneliness, sels. Charles Wharton Stork (tr.). 6045-5
"The heifer shelters by a wall". The sighing mystery. Leonard Alfred George Strong. 6781-6
Heigh ho! Margaret Ashworth. 6937-1
Heigh-ho! daisies and buttercups. Jean Ingelow. 6304-7
Heigh-ho, April!. Eleanor Farjeon. 6554-X
Heigho, my dearie (Orkney lullaby). Eugene Field. 6949-5
The height of the ridiculous. Oliver Wendell Holmes. 6102-8,6385-3,6732-8,6288-1,6307-1,6739 ,6102-8,6385-3, 6732-8,6265-2,6300-4,6464 ,6176-1,6290-3,6332-2,6486-8,6722-0,6089 ,6076-5,6026-9,6107-9,6736-0,6126-5, 6121 ,6505-8,6964-9,6278-4
Heights and depths. William Canton. 6477-9
"The heights beckoned! I climbed". Ambition. Maybelle McLaurin Kinsey. 7016-7
"The heights by great men reached and kept". Henry Wadsworth Longfellow. 6238-5;6260-1;6601-1
The heights of Alma. Unknown. 6057-9
The heights. Edwin W. Bonta. 7019-9
"'Heil Fuehrer,' resounded from glen to glen". So big. Alberta M. Paris. 6750-6
Heil, Albert J.
    The dead soldier-poet. 6799-9
Heilman, Edith
    Harvest. 6042-0
Heimdall. Harold Vinal. 6218-0
Hein, Donald M.
    Winter road to Elgin. 6342-X
Hein, Piet
    Dedication. Charles Wharton Stork (tr.). 6555-4
Heine. Matthew Arnold. 6439-6
Heine. George Sylvester Viereck. 6848-0
Heine's grave. Matthew Arnold. 6848-0,6828-6,6250-4
Heine's grave, sels. Matthew Arnold. 6110-9
Heine, Heinrich
    Ad finem. Elizabeth Barrett Browning (tr.). 7039-6
    "All the stars, gold-footed, wander". Cora Fabri (tr.). 6876-6
    Almansor. Charles Godfrey Leland (tr.). 6484-1
    Anno 1829. Charles Stuart Calverley (tr.). 7039-6
    "As the moon's reflection trembleth". Cora Fabri (tr.). 6876-6

The Asra. Elizabeth Craigmyle (tr.). 6842-1
The azra. John Hay (tr.). 7039-6
Belshazzar. 6732-8
Belshazzar's downfall. 6415-9
Book of songs, sonnets, Dresden poetry, sels. 6439-6
The bridal. Elizabeth Craigmyle (tr.). 6842-1
The coffin. Louis Untermeyer (tr.). 7039-6
Die lorelei. Alexander Macmillan (tr.). 6527-9
Die lorelei. Louis Untermeyer (tr.). 6527-9
Die rose, die lilie, die taube, die sonne. Richard Garnett (tr.). 7039-6
The difficulty. 6226-1
Don Ramiro. Elizabeth Craigmyle (tr.). 6842-1
Du bist wie eine blume. 6732-8,6226-1
Ein fichtenbaum steht einsam. James Thomson (tr.). 7039-6
Epilog, fr. The North Sea. Louis Untermeyer (tr.). 7039-6
Es fallt ein stern herunter. Richard Garnett (tr.). 7039-6
Es stehen unbeweglich. James Thomson (tr.). 7039-6
Evening twilight, fr. The North Sea. John Todhunter (tr.). 7039-6
Firelight. Sir Theodore Martin (tr.). 6120-6
The fisher's cottage. 6302-0
The fisher's cottage. Charles Godfrey Leland (tr.). 6271-7
The French tambour. 6084-6
Fresco-sonnet to Christian Sethe (1). John Todhunter (tr.). 7039-6
Fresco-sonnet to Christian Sethe (2). John Todhunter (tr.). 7039-6
The grenadiers. 6732-8,6102-8
"I saw a small, white sea-gull". Cora Fabri (tr.). 6876-6
"I wander and weep in the forest". Cora Fabri (tr.). 6876-6
I'm black and blue. John Todhunter (tr.). 7039-6
The ilse. L.H. Humphrey (tr.). 6484-1
In a dream. Elizabeth Craigmyle (tr.). 6842-1
"In my life, so dark and dreary". Cora Fabri (tr.). 6876-6
"In the golden summer morning". Cora Fabri (tr.). 6876-6
The kings from the east. 6125-7
"The letter which you wrote me." Merle St. Croix Wright (tr.). 6226-1
The Lorelei. 6484-1,6102-8
The Lorelei. Emilie K. Baker (tr.). 6805-7
The Lorelei. Christopher Pearse Cranch (tr.). 6271-7
Loreley. 6732-8
Love song. Eugene Field (tr.). 6949-5
Love's burial. Elizabeth Craigmyle (tr.). 6842-1
Lyric intermezzo. Eugene Field (tr.). 6949-5
Madchen mit dem rothen mundchen. Sir Theodore Martin (tr.). 7039-6
A maiden in her chamber. Louis Untermeyer (tr.). 7039-6
Meergruss. 6252-0
Mein kind, wir waren kinder. Elizabeth Barrett Browning (tr.). 7039-6
Mein liebchen, wir sassen zusammen. James Thomson (tr.). 7039-6
Mir traumte wieder der alte traum. James Thomson (tr.). 7039-6
My songs are poisoned. Louis Untermeyer (tr.). 7039-6
"My soul and I will steep so softly". Cora Fabri (tr.). 6876-6
Never despair. 6523-6
Oh lovely fishermaiden. Louis Untermeyer (tr.). 7039-6
An old song. Edgar Alfred Bowring (tr.). 6879-0
On song's bright pinions. Merle St. Croix Wright (tr.). 6285-6
The pilgrimage to Kevlaar. Elizabeth Craigmyle (tr.). 6842-1
The pilgrimage to Kevlar. 6676-3
The pine tree. 6446-3,6102-8
Questions. Vernon Watkins (tr.). 6258-X
"The rare red rose loves the butterfly". Cora Fabri (tr.). 6876-6
Sag' mir wer einst die uhren erfund. Richard Garnett (tr.). 7039-6
The sea hath its pearls. Henry Wadsworth Longfellow (tr.). 7039-6
Selections. Elizabeth Barrett Browning (tr.). 6123-0
Selections. Alexander Gray (tr.). 6845-6
Selections. Merle St. Croix Wright (tr.). 6429-9,6321-7
"Shadow-kisses, shadow passion". Cora Fabri (tr.). 6876-6
"So you forget, and have forgotten all". Cora Fabri (tr.). 6876-6
Song ("In the Rhine"). Edgar Alfred Bowring (tr.). 6484-1
Song: Du bist wie eine blume. Henry Van Dyke (tr.). 6961-4
Song: Ein fichtenbaum. Henry Van Dyke (tr.). 6961-4
Sonnet to a cat. 6120-6
The story of a night. Elizabeth Craigmyle (tr.). 6842-1
Submission. Edgar Alfred Bowring (tr.). 6097-8
"Sweetly float upon my heart". Cora Fabri (tr.). 6876-6
Thine eyes. 6226-1
"The troubles crowd, and the bells are ringing". Cora Fabri (tr.). 6876-6
Warum sind denn die rosen so blass. Richard Garnett (tr.). 7039-6
The water fay. Charles Godfrey Leland (tr.). 6271-7, 6302-0
We once were children. 6084-6
Weavers. 6102-8
Weavers. 6954-1
When two are parted. Louis Untermeyer (tr.). 7039-6
Widow or daughter? Eugene Field (tr.). 6949-5
Heinelet. Gamaliel Bradford. 6032-3,6291-1
Heinrich, A.
 I am the plow. 6662-3
The heir of Linne. Unknown. 6185-0,6271-7,6438-8,6067-6, 6131-1,6219
The heir. Phoebe Cary. 6865-0;6969-X
"An heiress of Abergravenny". Limerick:"An heiress of Abergravenny". Unknown. 6811-1
Heirloom. Abraham M. Klein. 6042-0,6446-9
Heirloom lace. Lola Greenfield Lawrence. 6799-9
Heirmos, sels. Unknown. 6282-2
Heirs of time. Thomas Wentworth Higginson. 7009-4,6954-1
Heirs of twilight. Buteau Shock. 6799-9
Hejduk, John
 Berlin masque. 6803-0
Hektor and Andromache, fr. The Iliad. Homer. 6435-3
Hektor to Andromache, fr. The Iliad. Homer. 6665-8
"Hektor turn'd", fr. The Iliad. Homer. 6435-3
Helas. Oscar Wilde. 6301-2,6646-1,6244-X,6732-8,6102-8, 6250-4,6655-0
Helberg, Grethe
 Happiness. Charles Wharton Stork (tr.). 6555-4
Helburn, Theresa
 Mother. 6310-1
 Youth. 6467-1
Held fast. Sadi [or Saadi] (Mushlih-ud-Din) 6448-5
Helen. Hilda ("H.D.") Doolittle. 6777-8
Helen. Hilda ("H.D.") Doolittle. 6077-3,6527-9
Helen. Odysseus Elytis. 6352-7
Helen. Carr Liggett. 7007-8
Helen. Laurent Tailhede. 6351-9
Helen - old. Isabel Ecclestone Mackay. 6843-X
Helen and Corythos. Walter Savage Landor. 6315-2
Helen and Modus. Sheridan Knowles. 6382-9
Helen and Thetis. Alcaeus. 6435-3
Helen at the Scaean gates, fr. The Iliad. Homer. 6372-1
Helen Hunt's grave. Virginia Donaghe McClurg. 6836-7
Helen in Argos. Frederick Mortimer Clapp. 6118-4
Helen in hades. Harry Kemp. 6347-0
Helen of Kirkconnell. Unknown. 6056-0,6102-8,6138-9,6186-9, 6228-8,6604 ,6098-6,6136-2,6179-6,6204-0,6301-2,6322 ,6315-2,6339-X,6634-8,6075-5,6395-0,6055 ,6153-2, 6094-3,6250-4,6192-3,6067-6,6660-7,6668-2
Helen of Troy. Christopher Marlowe. 6150-8
Helen on the walls of Troy. Homer. 6102-8
Helen on the walls, fr. The Iliad. Homer. 6987-8
Helen seeks for her brothers. Edward Craven Hawtrey. 6153-2
Helen's face a book. Gelett Burgess. 6652-6

HELEN'S

Helen's tower. Robert Browning. 7015-9
Helen's tower. George F. Savage-Armstrong. 6174-5
Helen, fr. The Iliad. Homer. 6435-3
Helen, fr. The life and death of Dr. Faustus. Christopher Marlowe. 6732-8,6102-8,6726-3
"Helen, it is not you they have desired". To Helen of Troy. Helen Hoyt. 6781-6
Helen, the sad queen. Paul Valery. 7039-6
"Helen, thy beauty is to me". Edgar Allan Poe. 6187-7
Helena and Hermia, fr. 'A Midsummer-night's dream'. William Shakespeare. 6239-3
Helga. Carl Sandburg. 6345-4
Helicon. Alfred Noyes. 6169-9
Helicon and Cithaeron. Corinna [pseud]. 6435-3
"The helicopter bee fines down". Honey. Ruth Miller. 6788-3
Helidore dead. Meleager. 6732-8,6102-8
Heliodora. Hilda ("H.D.") Doolittle. 6010-2
Heliodora. Meleager. 6435-3
Heliodora's wreath. Meleager. 6435-3
Heliodore fled. John Daniel Logan. 6433-7
Heliodorus in the temple. Felicia Dorothea Hemans. 6848-0
Heliodorus in the temple. Felicia Dorothea Hemans. 6973-8
Heliotrope. Harry Thurston Peck. 6274-1,6441-8,6300-4,6652-6
Heliotrope. Unknown. 6271-7,6273-3
Hell a la mode. Vincent Godfrey Burns. 6542-2
Hell and hate. Robert Bridges. 6487-6
Hell gate. Alfred Edward Housman. 6536-8
Hell's half acre. J. Edgar Middleton. 6115-X
Hell's piper. Riccardo Stephens. 6873-1
Hell's purgatory, sels. Edoardo Sanguineti. 6803-0
Hell's road. Charles Heavysege. 6102-8
Hell, fr. Davideis. Abraham Cowley. 6931-2
Hell, fr. Paradise lost. John Milton. 6933-9
The hell-gate of Soissons. Herbert Kaufman. 6474-4,6419-1
The hell-gate of Soissons. Herbert Kaufman. 7026-4
The hell-god. Louise Morgan Sill. 6542-2
Hellas. Percy Bysshe Shelley. 6102-8,6086-2,6301-2
Hellas, sels. Percy Bysshe Shelley. 6110-9,6430-2,6250-4, 6199-6,6125-7,6154-0,6122-2,6198-2,6334-9,6208-3, 6369
Hellenica, I. Edward J. O'Brien. 6033-1
Hellenica, II. Edward J. O'Brien. 6033-1
Hellenistics. Robinson Jeffers. 6399-3
Heller, Liane
   Coma. 6767-0
The Hellespont. George Gordon, 6th Baron Byron. 6543-0
Hellings, Mary Louisa
   Indian summer. 6799-9
Hellings, Peter
   Fairytales. 6360-8
   From distant lands. 6360-8
   Study: for Ezra Pound. 6360-8
   Swansea market. 6360-8
   Synthesis, above Swansea. 6360-8
Hellman, Geoffrey
   Dynastic tiff. 6026-9
Hellman, George S.
   Sonnet: to the Hudson. 6118-4
"Hello, Teddy! All th' west is watchin'". Ready for Teddy. Unknown. 6995-9
Hello, tulips. Edgar A. Guest. 6869-3
A helluvan engineer. Unknown. 6237-7
Helmer, Charles D.
   The battle of Oriskany. 6946-0
Helmer, William
   O-h-h-hm he fiddled. 6662-3
Helmore, Thomas
   Christmas carol. 6806-5
The helmsman. M.A. DeWolfe Howe. 6051-X
Heloise to Abelard. Margaret Clyde Robertson. 6836-7
The Helot, sel. Isabella Valancy Crawford. 6021-8
The helot, sels. Isabella Valancy Crawford. 6115-X
"Help for a patriot distressed...". 'Cleared'. Rudyard Kipling. 6810-2
"Help me across, papa." Unknown. 6744-1,6167-2
Help one another. G.F. Hunting. 6466-3
Help one another. Unknown. 6373-X
"Help, Lord, because the godly man". Psalm 012 Bible. 6848-0
Help, fr. the Gulistan. Sadi [or Saadi] (Mushlih-ud-Din) 7039-6
Help, good shepherd. Ruth Pitter. 6931-2
Help, sure help, fr. Dipsychus. Arthur Hugh Clough. 6655-0
The help-givers. Laurence Housman. 6337-3
"Helpe O helpe kinde Abraham & send." Unknown. 6563-5
The helpful fairy. Sally Johnson. 6249-0
A helpful touch. Unknown. 6109-5
Helpin' out. William Judson Kibby. 6291-1
Helping. P. B. 7031-0
A helping hand. Ella Higginson. 6682-8
Helping lame dogs. Charles Kingsley. 6303-9
Helping mamma. Jennie D. Moore. 6529-5
Helping mamma. Emma Celia & Lizzie J. Rook. 6137-0
Helping mamma. Unknown. 6684-4
Helpless. Phoebe Cary. 6865-0;6969-X
"Helpless before the cross I lay". The sinner at the cross. Phoebe Cary. 6865-0;6969-X
The helpless gray head. Douglas Jerrold. 6411-6
A helpmate. A. Melville Bell. 6279-2
A helpmate. A. Melville Bell. 6912-6
Helps in Vermont haying. Daniel L. Cady. 6989-4
Helston, John
   'Advance, America'. 7027-2
   Kitchener. 7026-4
   Missel thrush. 6069-2
Helton, Roy
   Fox race. 6628-3
   "I walked out once by moonlight." 6037-4
   Lonesome water. 6628-3
   Miracles. 6337-3
   Old Christmas morning. 6072-2
   The song of dark waters. 6501-5,6281-4
   South song. 6039-0
   A street car symphony. 6038-2,6501-5
Helvellyn. Sir Walter Scott. 6438-8,6808-1,6131-1,6129-9, 6014-5,6087-0,6302-0,6385-3,6552-X
Helvellyn. William Wordsworth. 6134-6,6302-0,6385-3,6383-7
Helwig, Maggie
   Columbus at night. 6767-0
Hem and haw. Bliss Carman. 6337-3,6458-2,6890-1,6996-7
Hemans and Luis de Camoens, Felicia Dorothea (tr.) Psalm 137, sels. Bible, 6848-0
Hemans, Felicia Dorothea
   The Abencerrage, sels. 6439-6
   The Abencerrage. 6973-8
   Address to fancy. 6973-8
   Address to music. 6973-8
   Address to thought. 6973-8
   The adopted child. 6973-8
   The adopted child. 6271-7
   The aged Indian. 6973-8
   Alaric in Italy. 6973-8
   The Alpine horn. 6973-8
   The Alpine shepherd. 6973-8
   The American forest girl, fr. Records of woman. 6973-8, 6980-0,6929-0
   The ancestral song. 6973-8
   Ancient battle-song. 6973-8
   Ancient Greek song of exile, fr. Lays of many lands. 6973-8
   Ancient song of victory. 6973-8
   And I too in Arcadia. 6973-8
   The angel of the sun. 6973-8
   Angel visits. 6973-8
   The angels' call. 6973-8
   The angler. 6973-8
   The annunciation. 6973-8
   Antique Greek lament. 6973-8
   The antique sepulchre. 6973-8
   The April morn. 6973-8
   Arabella Stuart, fr. Records of woman. 6973-8
   Attraction of the east. 6980-0
   Attractions of the east. 6973-8
   A ballad of Roncesvalles. 6832-4
   The bards. 6973-8
   The battle of Morgarten. 6744-1,6575-9,6267-9,6749-2
   The battle-field. 6973-8
   The bee. 6973-8

The beings of the mind. 6973-8
The bell at sea. 6973-8
Belshazzar's feast. 6973-8
The bended bow, fr. Lays of many lands. 6973-8
Bernardo del Carpio. 6973-8
Bernardo del Carpio. 6134-6,6302-0,6706-9,6744-1,6014-5, 6142 ,6242-3,6392-6,6606-2,6661-5,6403-5,6419 ,6294-6,6419-1
The better land. 6502-3,6219-9,6131-1
The Bible in harmony with temperance. 6404-3
The bird at sea. 6973-8
Bird that art singing on Ebro's side. 6973-8
The bird's release, fr. Lays of many lands. 6973-8
Birds in summer. 6049-8
The birds of passage. 6973-8
The birds of the air. 6973-8
The birds. 6973-8
Books and flowers. 6973-8
The boon of memory. 6973-8
The bowl of liberty. 6973-8
Brandenburgh harvest-song. 6973-8
"The breaking waves dashed high." 6001-3
Breathings of spring. 6049-8
The breeze from shore. 6973-8
The bridal day. 6973-8
The bride of the Greek isle. 6554-6,6569-4
The bride's farewell. 6980-0
The brigand leader and his wife. 6973-8
Brightly thou hast fled. 6973-8
Bring flowers. 6973-8,6049-8
The broken chain. 6973-8
The broken flower. 6973-8
The broken lute. 6973-8
The brother's dirge. 6973-8
The burial in the desert. 6973-8
Burial of an emigrant's child in the forest. 6973-8
By a mountain-stream at rest. 6973-8
The call to battle. 6973-8
"Calm on the bosom of thy God." 6302-0
The Cambrian in America. 6973-8
The caravan in the desert. 6973-8
Carolan's prophecy. 6973-8
Casabianca. 6133-8,6211-3,6271-7,6459-0,6496-5,6502 , 6302-0,6404-3,6267-9,6263-6,6219-9,6322 ,6459-0,6102-8,6424-8,6639-9,6479-5,6134-6,6602-2,6732-8,6527-9, 6623
Caswallon's triumph. 6973-8
Cathedral hymn. 6973-8
The cavern of the three Tells, fr. Lays of many lands. 6973-8
The cavern of the three Tells, Grutli. 6749-2
The chamois hunter's love. 6973-8
Chant of the bards before their massacre by Edward I. 6973-8
The charmed picture. 6973-8
The chieftain's son. 6973-8
The child and dove. 6973-8
The child of the forests. 6973-8
The child reading the Bible. 6973-8
The child's first grief. 6772-7,6973-8
The child's last sleep. 6772-7
The child's last sleep. 6973-8
The child's return from the woodlands. 6973-8
The childe's destiny. 6600-3
The children whom Jesus blessed. 6973-8
Christ stilling the tempest. 6973-8
Christ's agony in the garden. 6973-8
Christmas. 6973-8
Christmas carol. 6424-8
Christmas carol. 6973-8
Christmas carol. 6973-8
The Cid's deathbed. 6973-8
The Cid's departure into exile. 6973-8
The Cid's funeral procession. 6973-8
The Cid's rising. 6973-8
The cliffs of Dover. 6973-8
Coeur de Lion at the bier of his father. 6302-0
Come away. 6973-8
Come home. 6543-0
Come to me, dreams of heaven! 6973-8

Come to me, gentle sleep. 6973-8
Communings with thought. 6973-8
The conqueror's sleep. 6973-8
The contadina. 6973-8
Corinne at the capitol. 6973-8
The coronation of Inez de Castro. 6302-0
Costanza, fr. Records of woman. 6973-8
The cottage girl. 6973-8
The cross in the wilderness. 6973-8
The cross of the south. 6973-8
The Crusader's return. 6973-8
The Crusader's war-song. 6973-8
The darkness of the Crucifixion. 6973-8
Dartmoor. 6973-8
The day of flowers. 6973-8
Death and the warrior. 6973-8
The death of Clanronald. 6973-8
The death of Conradin. 6973-8
The death-song of Alcestis. 6973-8
The departed. 6973-8
The deserted house. 6973-8
Design and performance. 6973-8
Despair is never quite despair. 6567-8
Despondency and aspiration. 6973-8
The dial of flowers. 6973-8
Dirge. 6973-8,6271-7
Dirge at sea. 6973-8
Dirge of a child. 6772-7
Dirge of the highland chief in Waverley. 6973-8
A dirge. 6198-2,6108-2,6214-8
A dirge. 6973-8
A dirge. 6087-0
A dirge. 6934-7
A dirge. 6973-8
The distant ship. 6973-8
Distant sound of the sea at evening. 6997-5
Distant sound of the sea at evening. 6973-8
The diver. 6973-8
The domestic affections. 6973-8·
The dreamer. 6973-8
The dreaming child. 6973-8
Dreams of heaven. 6973-8
Dreams of the dead. 6973-8
Druid chorus on the landing of the Romans. 6973-8
The dying bard's prophecy. 6973-8
The dying girl and flowers. 6973-8
The dying improvisatore. 6980-0,6973-8
Easter-day in a mountain churchyard. 6973-8
Echo-song. 6973-8
Edith, fr. Records of woman. 6973-8
The effigies. 6973-8
Elysium. 6567-8
Elysium. 6973-8
England and Spain; or, valour and patriotism. 6973-8
England's dead. 6250-4
England's dead. 6973-8
The English boy. 6973-8
The English martyrs. 6973-8
English soldier's song of memory. 6973-8
Epitaph over the grave of two brothers. 6973-8
Eryri Wen. 6973-8
Evening among the Alps. 6749-2
Evening prayer, at a girls' school. 6973-8
Evening recollections of the exile. 6543-0
Evening song of the Tyrolese peasants. 6749-2,6973-8
Evening song of the weary. 6973-8
The exile's dirge. 6973-8
Fair Helen of Kirconnel. 6973-8
The fair isle. 6973-8
Fairies' recall. 6973-8
Fairy favors. 6973-8
Fairy song. 6973-8
The faith of love. 6973-8
The fall of D'Assas. 6610-0
The fall of D'Assas. 6973-8
The fallen lime-tree. 6973-8
The family Bible. 6097-8
Far away. 6973-8
Far o'er the ocean. 6973-8
A farewell to Abbotsford. 6973-8

The farewell to the dead, fr. Lays of many lands. 6973-8
A farewell to Wales. 6973-8
The farewell. 6973-8
The father reading the Bible. 6973-8
Female characters of scripture: sonnets, sels. 6973-8
The festal hour. 6973-8
Flight of the spirit. 6648-8
Flight of the spirit. 6973-8
Flight of the spirit, fr. Thoughts during sickness. 6980-0
The flower of the desert. 6049-8
Flowers. 6973-8
Flowers and music in a room of sickness. 6973-8
Flowers, fr. Thoughts during sickness. 6980-0
Foliage. 6973-8
For a design of a butterfly resting on a skull. 6973-8
For a picture of St. Cecilia attended by angels. 6973-8
The forest sanctuary. 6973-8
The forsaken hearth. 6973-8
The fountain of Marah. 6973-8
The fountain of oblivion. 6980-0
The fountain of oblivion. 6973-8
A fragment ("Rest on your battle-fields..."). 6973-8
The freed bird. 6973-8
The funeral day of Sir Walter Scott. 6973-8
The funeral genius; an ancient statue. 6973-8
Genius. 6973-8
Genius singing to love. 6973-8
Gertrude; or, fidelity till death, fr. Records of woman. 6973-8
Good night. 6973-8
The grave of Korner. 6973-8
The graves of a household. 6165-6,6383-7,6250-4,6543-0, 6129-9,6133-8,6240-7,6385-3,6502-3,6127-3,6964
The graves of martyrs. 6973-8
Greek funeral chant, or myriologue, fr. Lays... 6973-8
Greek songs, sels. 6973-8
The Greeks' return from battle. 6606-2
The green isles of ocean. 6973-8
Grufydd's feast. 6973-8
The guerilla leader's vow. 6973-8
Guerilla song, founded on...Spanish patriot Mina. 6973-8
The hall of Cynddylan. 6973-8
"Happy, happier far than thou." 6066-8
The harp of Wales. 6973-8
Harvest hymn. 6973-8
Haunted ground. 6973-8
The haunted house. 6973-8
He never smiled again, fr. Lays of many lands. 6973-8
The heart of Bruce in Melrose Abbey. 6973-8
The Hebrew mother. 6409-4
Heliodorus in the temple. 6848-0
Heliodorus in the temple. 6973-8
The hero's death. 6973-8
The hirlas horn. 6973-8
Holiday hours. 6973-8
The home of love. 6973-8
The homes of England. 6198-2,6479-5,6732-8,6133-8,6302-0,6385 ,6543-0,6129-9,6502-3
Hope of future communion with nature. 6973-8
The hour of death. 6240-7,6315-2,6129-9,6403-5
The hour of prayer. 6219-9,6304-7
The hour of prayer. 6973-8
An hour of romance. 6973-8
How can that love so deep, so lone. 6973-8
Howel's song. 6973-8
The Huguenot's farewell. 6973-8
Hymn ("Great God!..."). 6973-8
Hymn ("O God of mercy!..."). 6973-8
Hymn for Christmas. 6145-1,6239-3
Hymn of the mountain Christian. 6014-5
Hymn of the traveller's household on his return. 6973-8
Hymn of the Vaudois moutaineers in times of persecution. 6973-8
Hymn, by the sick-bed of a mother. 6973-8
Hymns for childhood, sels. 6973-8
I come, I come, ye have called me long. 6304-7
I dream of all things free. 6973-8
I go, sweet friends. 6973-8
I go, sweet friends! 6085-4
I would we had not met again. 6973-8
If thou hast crushed a flower. 6973-8
The illuminated city. 6973-8
The image in lava. 6973-8
The image in the heart. 6973-8
Images of patriarchal life. 6973-8
Imelda, fr. Records of woman. 6973-8
The Indian city, fr. Records of woman. 6973-8
The Indian with his dead child. 6973-8
Indian woman's death-song, fr. Records of woman. 6973-8
The Indian's revenge. 6973-8
Inscription for a hermitage. 6973-8
Intellectual powers. 6973-8
Intellectual powers, fr. Thoughts during sickness. 6980-0
Intorduction, fr. Songs of captivity. 6973-8
Introductory verses, fr. Hymns for childhood. 6973-8
Invocation. 6973-8
Invocation ("Answer me, burning stars of night!...") 6606-2
Invocation, fr. Female characters of scripture. 6973-8
The invocation. 6973-8
Is there some spirit sighing? 6973-8
The isle of Founts, fr. Lays of many lands. 6973-8
The Italian girl's hymn to the Virgin. 6973-8
Ivan the csar. 6973-8
Ivan the Czar. 6928-2
Ivy song. 6973-8
The ivy-song. 6973-8
Joan of Arc in Rheims, fr. Records of woman. 6973-8
Joan of Arc, in Rheims. 6980-0
Juana, fr. Records of woman. 6973-8
The kaiser's feast. 6973-8
Keene; or, lament of an Irish mother over her son. 6973-8
Kindred hearts. 6385-3,6600-3,6084-6
The king of Arragon's lament for his brother. 6973-8
The lady of Provence. 6973-8
The lady of the castle, fr. Portrait gallery. 6973-8
The lament of Llywarch Hen [Llywarch the Aged]. 6973-8
The land of dreams. 6973-8
Landing of the pilgrim fathers. 6014-5,6452-4,6240-7, 6239-3,6260-1,6486 ,6457-4,6424-8,6263-6,6304-7,6219-9,6131 ,6271-7,6504-X,6049-8,6337-3,6552-X,6198 , 6088-9,6267-9,6438-8,6102-8,6323-3,6465-5,6478-7, 6479-5,6623-2,6732 ,6473-6,6498-1,6466-3,6302-0,6385-3,6459
The last banquet of Antony and Cleopatra. 6973-8
The last Constantine. 6973-8
Last rites. 6973-8
The last song of Sappho. 6973-8
The last tree of the forest. 6973-8
The last wish. 6973-8
Lays of many lands, sels. 6973-8
The league of the Alps; or..meeting on field of Grutli. 6973-8
Leave me not yet. 6973-8
"Leave me not yet, through rosy skies from far". 6980-0
"Leaves have their time to fall". 6238-5
Let her depart. 6973-8
Let us depart. 6848-0
Let us depart! 6973-8
Liberty. 6973-8
Lights and shades. 6409-4
Lights and shades. 6973-8
The lilies of the field. 6973-8
The lily of the vale. 6973-8
Lines written for the album at Rosanna. 6973-8
Lines written in a hermitage on the seashore. 6973-8
Lines written in memory of Elizabeth Smith. 6973-8
"Listen! in my breezy moan", sels. 6601-1
The lonely bird. 6973-8
Look on me with thy cloudless eyes. 6973-8
The lost pleiad. 6980-0
The lost Pleiad. 6973-8
Louise Schelper (1). 6973-8
Louise Schelper (2). 6973-8
The lyre and flower. 6973-8

The lyre's lament. 6973-8
Madeline, fr. Records of woman. 6973-8
The magic glass. 6973-8
The Maremma. 6973-8
Marguerite of France. 6414-0,6661-5
Marguerite of France. 6973-8
Marius among the ruins of Carthage. 6973-8
Marshal Schwerin's grave. 6973-8
Mary at the feet of Crhist. 6973-8
Mary Magdalene at the sepulchre. 6973-8
Mary Magdalene bearing tidings of the resurrection. 6973-8
The meeting of the bards. 6973-8
The meeting of the brothers. 6973-8
The meeting of the ships. 6165-6,6302-0,6385-3
Melancholy. 6973-8
Memorial of a conversation. 6973-8
The memorial of Mary. 6973-8
The memorial pillar, fr. Records of woman. 6973-8
The memory of the dead. 6973-8
The message to the dead. 6973-8
The messenger bird, fr. Lays of many lands. 6973-8
The minster. 6973-8
The minstrel bard. 6973-8
The minstrel to his harp. 6973-8
The mirror in the deserted hall. 6973-8
Modern Greece. 6973-8
A monarch's deathbed. 6973-8
Monumental inscription. 6973-8
Moorish bridal song, fr. Lays of many lands. 6973-8
Moorish gathering song. 6973-8
Morning. 6973-8
Mother! oh, sing me to rest. 6973-8
A mother's heart. 6097-8
Mother's litany by the sick-bed of a child. 6973-8,6014-5
The mountain fires. 6973-8
Mountain sanctuaries. 6973-8
The mourner for the Barmecides. 6973-8
Mozart's requiem. 6980-0
Mozart's requiem. 6973-8
The muffled drum, sels. 6934-7
The muffled drum. 6973-8
Music at a deathbed. 6973-8
Music from shore. 6973-8
The music of St. Patrick's. 6973-8
Music of yesterday. 6973-8
My brother and sister, in the country. 6973-8
The myrtle-bough. 6973-8
The name of England. 6973-8
Naples. 6973-8
Nature's farewell. 6973-8
Near thee, still near thee. 6973-8
The necromancer. 6973-8
Night hymn at sea. 6973-8
Night-blowing flowers. 6973-8
Night-scene in Genoa. 6973-8
The nightingale's death-song. 6973-8
The nightingale; child's evening hymn. 6973-8
No more. 6973-8
The northern spring. 6973-8
O love and death. 6066-8
O lovely voices of the sky. 6747-6
O thou breeze of spring! 6973-8
O ye hours! 6973-8
O ye voices! 6973-8
O'Connor's child. 6973-8
O'er the far blue mountains. 6973-8
The ocean. 6973-8
Ode to mirth. 6973-8
"Oh! cast thou not". 6238-5
Oh! droop thou not. 6973-8
Oh! skylark, for thy wing. 6973-8
Old church in an English park. 6973-8
Old Norway. 6973-8
The olive tree. 6049-8
The olive tree. 6973-8
On a flower from the field of Grutli. 6749-2
On a flower from the field of Grutli. 6973-8
On a leaf from the tomb of Virgil. 6973-8
On a picture of Christ bearing the cross. 6973-8
On a remembered picture of Christ. 6973-8
On a rose. 6973-8
On a scene in the Dargle. 6973-8
On my mother's birthday. 6973-8
On reading Coleridge's epitaph, written by himself. 6973-8
On reading Paul and Virginia in childhood. 6973-8
On records of immature genius. 6973-8
On Retzsch's design of the angel of death. 6973-8
On the datura arborea. 6973-8
On the death of Princess Charlotte. 6973-8
On watching the flight of a sky-lark. 6973-8
The orange bough. 6973-8
Orchard blossoms. 6049-8
Orchard-blossoms. 6973-8
Our daily paths. 6973-8
Our Lady's well. 6973-8
Owen Glyndwr's war-song. 6973-8
The painter's last work. 6973-8
The palm tree. 6980-0
The palm-tree. 6973-8
The palmer. 6973-8
Paraphrase of Psalm 148. 6973-8
The parting of summer. 6973-8
The parting ship. 6973-8
The parting song, fr. Lays of many lands. 6973-8
A parting song. 6980-0
A parting song. 6973-8
Parting words. 6392-6
Parting words. 6973-8
Passing away. 6973-8
Pauline, fr. Records of woman. 6973-8
The peasant girl of the Rhone, fr. Records of woman. 6973-8
The penitent anointing Christ's feet. 6973-8
The penitent's offering. 6973-8
A penitent's return. 6973-8
The petition of the red-breast. 6973-8
Picture of the infant Christ with flowers. 6973-8
The Pilgrim fathers. 6322-5,6422-1,6621-6,6605-4,6322-5, 6543-0,6322-5,6422
Pilgrim's song to the evening star. 6973-8
Pity; an allegory, versified. 6973-8
Places of worship. 6973-8
A poet's dying hymn. 6973-8
The poetry of the Psalms. 6973-8
Portrait gallery, sels. 6973-8
A prayer ("Father in heaven!..."). 6973-8
A prayer ("O God"). 6973-8
Prayer at sea after victory. 6973-8
Prayer continued. 6973-8
The prayer for life. 6973-8
The prayer in the wilderness. 6973-8
A prayer of affection. 6973-8
Prayer of the lonely student. 6973-8
Prince Madoc's farewell. 6973-8
Prisoner's evening song, fr. Prisoner's evening service. 6973-8
Prisoners' evening service; scene of French Revolution. 6973-8
The procession. 6973-8
Prologue, fr. The tragedy of Fiesco. 6973-8
Properzia Rossi, fr. Records of woman. 6973-8
Pysche borne by zephyrs to the island of pleasure. 6973-8
The queen of Prussia's tomb, fr. Records of woman. 6973-8
Raimond released, fr. The vespers of Palermo. 6382-9
The rainbow. 6973-8
The raising of the widow's son. 6973-8
Records of the autumn of 1834, sels. 6973-8
Records of the spring of 1834, sels. 6973-8
Records of woman, sels. 6973-8,6980-0,6929-0
Recovery. 6973-8
Recovery, fr. Thoughts during sickness. 6980-0
The release of Tasso. 6973-8
A remembrance of Grasmere. 6973-8
Remembrance of nature. 6973-8
Remembrance of nature, fr. Thoughts during sickness.

HEMANS

6980-0
The reply of the Shunamite woman. 6848-0
The reply of the Shunamite woman. 6973-8
Repose of a holy family. 6973-8
The requiem of genius. 6973-8
The restoration of the works of art to Italy. 6973-8
The return of May. 6049-8
The return to poetry. 6973-8
The return. 6973-8
Retzsch's design, fr. Thoughts during sickness. 6980-0
The revellers. 6973-8
Rhine song of the German soldiers after victory. 6973-8
The Rio Verde song. 6973-8
The river Clwyd in north Wales. 6973-8
The rivers. 6973-8
The rock beside the sea. 6973-8
The rock of Cader Idris. 6973-8
Rocks of my country. 6606-2
Roman girl's song. 6302-0
The ruin and its flowers. 6973-8
The ruin. 6973-8
The ruined castle. 6973-8
Rural walks. 6973-8
Ruth. 6848-0
Ruth. 6973-8
Sabbath sonnet. 6973-8
Sadness and mirth. 6973-8
The scared harp. 6973-8
Scene in a Dalecarlian mine. 6973-8
The sceptic. 6973-8
The sculptured children. 6973-8
Sea piece. 6973-8
Sea piece by moonlight. 6973-8
The sea-bird flying inland. 6973-8
The sea-song of Gafran. 6973-8
Sebastian of Portugal; a dramatic fragment. 6973-8
Second sight. 6973-8
Seek by the silvery Darro. 6973-8
The shade of Thesueus. 6973-8
The shadow of a flower. 6929-0,6973-8
Shakespeare. 6973-8
The shepherd-poet of the Alps. 6973-8
The Sicilian captive. 6674-4
Sickness like night. 6973-8
Sickness like night, fr. Thoughts during sickness. 6980-0
The siege of Valencia. 6973-8
The silent multitude. 6973-8
The silver locks. 6973-8
Sing to me, gondolier. 6973-8
Sister! since I met thee last. 6973-8
The sisters of Bethany after the death of Lazarus. 6973-8
The sisters of Scio. 6973-8
The sisters' dream. 6973-8
The sisters. 6973-8
The sky-lark. 6973-8
The sleeper of Marathon. 6973-8
The sleeper. 6973-8
The soldier's deathbed. 6973-8
Song ("Oh! bear me..."). 6973-8
Song ("Oh! ye voices..."). 6973-8
Song ("Say, does calm contentment dwell"). 6973-8
Song for an air by Hummel. 6973-8
The song of Miriam. 6848-0
The song of a seraph. 6973-8
Song of a wood nymph. 6973-8
A song of Delos. 6973-8
Song of emigration. 6973-8
The song of hope. 6973-8
The song of Mina's soldiers. 6973-8
The song of Miriam. 6973-8
The song of night. 6973-8
The song of our fathers. 6973-8
The song of penitence, sels. 6973-8
Song of the battle of Morgarten. 6973-8
A song of the rose. 6973-8
Song of the Spanish wanderer. 6973-8
The song of the Virgin. 6973-8
Song of Zephyrus. 6973-8

Song, founded on an Arabian anecdote. 6973-8
Song: the return of May. 6973-8
Songs of a guardian spirit, sels. 6973-8
Songs of captivity, sels. 6973-8
The songs of our fathers. 6543-0
Songs of Spain, sels. 6973-8
Songs of the affections, sels. 6973-8
Songs of the Cid, sels. 6973-8
Sonnet ("'Tis sweet to think..."). 6973-8
Sonnet ("Ah! now farewell"). 6973-8
Sonnet ("I love to hail"). 6973-8
Sonnet ("Where nature's grand"). 6973-8
Sonnet to Italy. 6973-8
Sonnet to my mother. 6973-8
The sound of the sea. 6973-8
The Spanish chapel. 6973-8
Spanish evening hymn. 6973-8
The Spartan's march. 6973-8
The spartan's march. 6606-2
The spells of home. 6973-8
The spirit's mysteries. 6973-8
The spirit's return. 6973-8
Stanzas to the memory of —. 6973-8
Stanzas to the memory of George the Third. 6973-8
The stars. 6973-8
The storm of Delphi. 6578-3
The storm of Delphi. 6973-8
The storm-painter in his dungeon. 6973-8
The stranger in Louisiana, fr. Lays of many lands. 6973-8
The stranger in Louisiana. 6980-0
The stranger on earth. 6973-8
The stranger's heart. 6973-8
The stream set free. 6973-8
The streams. 6973-8
The subterranean stream. 6973-8
The Suliote mother, fr. Lays of many lands. 6973-8
The summer's call. 6973-8
The sun. 6973-8
The sunbeam. 6049-8
The swan and the skylark. 6973-8
Swiss song, fr. Lays of many lands. 6973-8
The Switzer's wife, fr. Records of woman. 6973-8
The sword of the tomb, fr. Lays of many lands. 6973-8
A tale of the fourteenth century, sels. 6973-8
A tale of the secret tribunal. 6973-8
Taliesin's prophecy. 6973-8
Tasso and his sister. 6973-8
Tasso's coronation. 6973-8
Thekla at her lover's grave. 6973-8
The themes of song. 6973-8
There are sounds in the dark Roncesvalles. 6973-8
A thought at sunset. 6973-8
Thought from an Italian poet. 6973-8
A thought of home at sea. 6973-8
A thought of paradise. 6973-8
A thought of the future. 6973-8
A thought of the rose. 6973-8
A thought of the sea. 6973-8
Thoughts connected with trees (1). 6973-8
Thoughts connected with trees (2). 6973-8
Thoughts during sickness. 6980-0
Thoughts during sickness, sels. 6973-8
The thunder-storm. 6973-8
To a butterfly. 6973-8
To a departed spirit. 6973-8
To a distant scene. 6973-8
To a dying exotic. 6973-8
To a family Bible. 6980-0,6973-8
To a picture of the Madonna. 6973-8
To a wandering female singer. 6973-8
To Agnes. 6973-8
To an aged friend. 6973-8
To an infant. 6973-8
To fancy. 6973-8
To hope. 6973-8
To Miss F.A.L. on her birthday. 6973-8
To Miss F.A.L. on the death of her mother. 6973-8
To Mr. Edwards, the harper of Conway. 6973-8
To my mother. 6973-8

To my mother ("If e'er for human bliss or woe"). 6097-8
To my own portrait. 6973-8
To my younger brother...after the battle of Corunna. 6973-8
To one of the author's children on his birthday. 6973-8
To resignation. 6973-8
To Silvio Pellico, on reading his Prigione. 6973-8
To Silvio Pellico, released. 6973-8
To the blue anemone. 6973-8
To the eye. 6973-8
To the memory of General Sir Edward Pakenham. 6973-8
To the memory of Heber. 6973-8
To the memory of Sir Henry Ellis, who fell...Waterloo. 6973-8
To the mountain winds. 6973-8
To the muse of pity. 6973-8
To the sky. 6973-8
To Wordsworth. 6385-3
The tomb of Madame Langhans. 6973-8
The tombs of Plataea. 6973-8
The traveller at the source of the Nile. 6980-0
The traveller at the source of the Nile. 6973-8
The traveller's evening song. 6973-8
The treasures of the deep. 6302-0,6385-3,6219-9,6543-0
Triumphant music. 6973-8
The troubadour and Richard Coeur de Lion. 6973-8
Troubadour song. 6973-8
Troubadour song. 6973-8
The trumpet. 6973-8
The two homes. 6752-2
The two homes. 6606-2
The two monuments. 6973-8
The two voices. 6973-8
Ulla; or, the adjuration. 6973-8
The urn and sword. 6973-8
Valkyriur song, fr. Lays of many lands. 6973-8
The vassal's lament for the fallen tree, fr. Lays... 6973-8
The Vaudois valley. 6973-8
The Vaudois wife. 6973-8
A vernal thought. 6973-8
The vespers of Palermo. 6973-8
The victor. 6973-8
The view from Castri. 6973-8
The vigil of Rizpah. 6848-0
The vigil of arms. 6973-8
The vigil of Rizpah. 6973-8
The voice of God. 6973-8
The voice of home to the prodigal. 6973-8
The voice of music. 6973-8
The voice of Scio. 6973-8
Voice of spring. 6392-6,6720-4,6479-5,6529-5,6018-8, 6304 ,6543-0,6964-9
The voice of the waves. 6973-8
The voice of the wind. 6973-8
The voices of home. 6543-0
A voyager's dream of land. 6973-8
The wakening. 6973-8
Wallace's invocation to Bruce. 6973-8
The wanderer and the night-flowers. 6973-8
The wandering child. 6271-7
The wandering wind. 6973-8
War and peace, 1808. 6973-8
War song of the Spanish patriots. 6973-8
Washington's statue. 6980-0
Water-lilies. 6973-8
The water-lily. 6973-8
We return no more! 6973-8
The welcome to death. 6973-8
Welsh melodies, sels. 6973-8
Where is the sea? 6973-8
Where is the sea? 6833-2
The widow of Crescentius. 6973-8
The wife of Asdrubal. 6973-8
The wild hunstman, fr. Lays of many lands. 6973-8
Willow song. 6271-7
The wings of the dove. 6973-8
The wish. 6973-8
Woman and fame. 6973-8
Woman on the fild of battle. 6973-8

The women of Jerusalem at the cross. 6973-8
Wood walk and hymn. 6973-8
The world in the open air. 6973-8
The wounded eagle. 6973-8
The wreck. 6973-8
Written after visiting a tomb. 6973-8
Written in north Wales. 6973-8
Written in the first leaf of the album of Miss F.A.L. 6973-8
Written on the sea-shore. 6973-8
Ye are not missed, fair flowers! 6973-8
Youth. 6973-8
The Zegri mind. 6973-8

Hemans, Felicia Dorothea (tr.)
"Ah! cease - those fruitless tears restrain". Pietro Metastasio, 6973-8
Alcestis. Vittorio Alfieri, 6973-8
The basvigliana. Vincenzo Monti, 6973-8
Battle of Maclodio [or Macalo], fr. Conte di Carmagnola. Vittorio Alfieri, 6973-8
Caius Gracchus. Vincenzo Monti, 6973-8
Ecologue 015, sels. Luis de Camoens [or Camoes], 6973-8
"Enjoy the sweets of life's luxuriant May". Garcilaso de la Vega, 6973-8
"Fortune! why thus, where'er my footsteps tread". Pietro Metastasio, 6973-8
Genoa mia! Pastorini, 6973-8
"He shall not dread misfortune's angry mien". Pietro Metastasio, 6973-8
"I cry aloud, and ye shall hear my call". Carlo Maria Maggi, 6973-8
"If to the sighing breeze of summer-hours". Francesco Petrarch, 6973-8
"In tears, the heart opprest with grief". Pietro Metastasio, 6973-8
"Italia! oh, no more Italia now!" Alessandro Marchetti, 6973-8
"Italia! thou, by lavish nature graced". Vincenzo da Filicaja, 6973-8
"Let the vain courier waste his days". Lope de Vega Carpio, 6973-8
"Listen, fair maid, my song shall tell". Unknown (German), 6973-8
Mignon's song. Johann Wolfgang von Goethe, 6385-3
Mignon's song. Johann Wolfgang von Goethe, 6973-8
Morning song. Gesner, 6973-8
"No searching eye can pierce the veil". Luis de Camoens [or Camoes], 6973-8
Ode on the defeat of King Sebastian of Portugal. Ferdinand de Herrera, 6973-8
"Oh! those alone whose severed hearts". Pietro Metastasio, 6973-8
On ascending a hill leading to a convent. Francisco Manuel, 6973-8
On the Hebe of Canova. Pindemonte, 6973-8
Paraphrase of psalm 148. Bible, 6848-0
Rome buried in her own ruins. Francisco de Quevedo y Villegas, 6973-8
"The sainted spirit which, from bliss on high". Il Marchese Cornelio Bentivoglio, 6973-8
"She that cast down the empires of the world". Alessandro Pegolotti, 6973-8
The shore of Africa. Francesco Maria de Conti, 6973-8
Sonnet ("How strange a fate"). Luis de Camoens [or Camoes], 6973-8
Sonnet 019. ("Spirit beloved"). Luis de Camoens [or Camoes], 6973-8
Sonnet 023: to a lady who died at sea. Luis de Camoens [or Camoes], 6973-8
Sonnet 058 ("Should love"). Luis de Camoens [or Camoes], 6973-8
Sonnet 070 ("High in the glowing"). Luis de Camoens [or Camoes], 6973-8
Sonnet 080 ("Saved from the perils"). Luis de Camoens [or Camoes], 6973-8
Sonnet 108 ("Fair Tajo"). Luis de Camoens [or Camoes], 6973-8
Sonnet 128 ("There blooms"). Luis de Camoens [or Camoes], 6973-8
Sonnet 133 ("Waves of Mondego"). Luis de Camoens [or

HEMANS

Camoes], 6973-8
Sonnet 178 ("Oft have I sung"). Luis de Camoens [or Camoes], 6973-8
Sonnet 181. ("Where shall I find"). Luis de Camoens [or Camoes], 6973-8
Sonnet 186 ("Those eyes"). Luis de Camoens [or Camoes], 6973-8
Sonnet 205 ("He who proclaims"). Luis de Camoens [or Camoes], 6973-8
Sonnet 239 ("Beside the stream"), fr. Psalm 137. Luis de Camoens [or Camoes], 6973-8
Sonnet 271 ("This mountain"). Luis de Camoens [or Camoes], 6973-8
Sonnet 278 ("Exempt from every grief"). Luis de Camoens [or Camoes], 6973-8
So neb 282 (Wrapt in sad"), fr. Psalm 137. Luis de Camoens [or Camoes], 6973-8
"Sweet rose! whose tender foliage to expand". Pietro Metastasio, 6973-8
Swiss home-sickness. Unknown (Swiss), 6973-8
"Sylph of the breeze! whose dewy pinions light". Francesco Lorenzini, 6973-8
Thekla's song; or, the voice of the spirit. Johann C. Friedrich von Schiller, 6973-8
"This green recess, where through the bowery gloom". Bernardo Tasso, 6973-8
"Thou grot, whence flows this limpid spring". Chaulieu, 6973-8
"Thou in thy morn wert like a glowing rose". Torquato Tasso, 6973-8
"Thou that wouldst mark, in form of human birth". Francesco Petrarch, 6973-8
"Thou, the stern monarch of dismay". Pietro Bembo, 6973-8
"Thou, who hast fled from life's enchanted bowers". Juan de Tarsis, 6973-8
To Delius, fr. Ode 003. Horace, 6973-8
To Faunus, fr. Ode 018. Horace, 6973-8
To his attendant, fr. Ode 038. Horace, 6973-8
To the fountain of Bandusia, fr. Ode 013. Horace, 6973-8
To Venus, fr. Ode 030. Horace, 6973-8
"The torrent-wave, that breaks with force". Pietro Metastasio, 6973-8
"Unbending 'midst the wintry skies". Pietro Metastasio, 6973-8
Venice. Della Casa, 6973-8
Violets. Lorenzo de' Medici, 6973-8
The wanderer. Schmidt von Lubeck, 6973-8
"When from the mountain's brow the gathering shades". Vincenzo da Filicaja, 6973-8
"Wouldst thou to love of danger speak?" Pietro Metastasio, 6973-8
Hemenway, Abby Maria
    Annunciation night, fr. Mary of Nazareth. 6282-2
    Mary of Nazareth, sels. 6282-2
The Hemingwa syndrome. Adrian C. Louis. 7005-1
Hemingway, Ernest
    Chapter heading. 6069-2
Hemingway, Percy. See Addleshaw, Percy
"The hemisphere/Of magic fiction...", fr. The prelude. William Wordsworth. 6867-7
"The hemlock cup for Socrates". Idealists. Katharine Lee Bates. 7001-9
The hemlock tree. Henry Wadsworth Longfellow. 6049-8
The hemlock. Emily Dickinson. 6253-9
"Hemmed in by the hosts of the Austrians". Garibaldi in Piedmont. Phoebe Cary. 6969-X
Hemmer, Jarl
    Above the dark. Charles Wharton Stork (tr.). 6045-5
Hemminger, Graham Lee
    Tobacco. 6722-0
"Hemocratia nam'd - save only one". On Hermocratia. Unknown (Greek). 6814-6
The hemorrhage. Stanley J. Kunitz. 6666-6
The hemp. Stephen Vincent Benet. 6030-7
Hemphrey, Malcolm
    Hills of home. 7026-4
"The hen to herself said one beautiful day...". Unknown. 6059-5

"Hen-Cock, cock I have la-a-a-yed". Unknown. 6363-2
The hen-roost man. Ruth McEnery Stuart. 6089-7
The hen. Matthias Claudius. 6089-7,6996-7
The hen. Oliver Herford. 6902-9
"Hence all you vain delights". The passionate man's song. John Fletcher. 6933-9
"Hence care, & let me steep my drooping spirit". Solace derived from books. Edward Moxon. 6980-0
"Hence childish boy too long haue I." Unknown. 6563-5
"Hence flattring hopes. Cease longing and giue ore." Unknown. 6563-5
Hence hairt. Alexander Scott. 6180-X,6023-4
"Hence my epistle - skim the deep - fly o'er". Elegy 004: To his tutor, Thomas Young, chaplain... John Milton. 6814-6
"Hence vaine delights beegone, tempte mee noe more." Unknown. 6563-5
Hence with passion, sighs and tears. Thomas Heywood. 6563-5
"Hence with passion, sighs, and tears". Love's ecstasy. Thomas Heywood. 6827-8
"Hence with the lover who sighs o'er his wine". Volunteer boys. Unknown. 6753-0
"Hence! home, you idle...", fr. Julius Caesar. William Shakespeare. 6183-4
"Hence! thou unvarying song of varied loves". Childish recollections (2). George Gordon, 6th Baron Byron. 6945-2
"Hence, all ye vain delights." Francis Beaumont and John Fletcher. 6271-7,6302-0,6385-3
"Hence, all you vain delights". In praise of melancholy. John Fletcher. 6830-8
Hence, all you vain delights. John Fletcher or William Strode. 6563-5
Hence, all you vain delights. John Gould Fletcher. 6194-X, 6430-2
"Hence, all you vain delights" John Fletcher. 6935-5
Hence, all you vain delights, fr. The nice valour. John Fletcher. 6934-7
"Hence, avaunt! ('tis holy ground).". For music. Thomas Gray. 6975-4
"Hence, away, nor dare intrude!". Inscription opn a grot. Samuel Rogers. 6932-0
Hence, away, you sirens! George Wither. 6182-6
"'Hence, hie ye to the eastern hills!". The curse and the blessing. Unknown. 6848-0
"Hence, loath'd vulgarity". Fashion. Horace Twiss. 6802-2
"A henchman sworn of Ares, Lord God of wat, I live". Archilochus. 6251-2
The henchman. John Greenleaf Whittier. 6441-8,6437-X,6004-8,6652-6
Hendecasyllabies. Alfred Lord Tennyson. 6092-7
Henderson, Alice C. See Corbin, Alice
Henderson, Barbara
    Lohengrin. 7019-1
Henderson, Barbara (tr.)
    A hymn of hate against England, sels. Ernest Lissauer, 6427-2
Henderson, Bert
    Revealment. 6750-6
    This lonely acre. 6750-6
Henderson, Brian
    Nightfall by the river. 6767-0
Henderson, Daniel
    Consider, Lord, our clerk. 6979-7
    Dawn. 6386-1,6420-5,6542-2
    Fighting stock. 6995-9
    The homing heart. 6607-0
    Hymn for a household. 6144-3,6335-7,6337-3
    The lilies of the field. 6335-7,6337-3
    Love's legend. 6320-9
    Men of blood and mire. 6846-4,6589-9
    Nantucket whalers. 6396-9
    A nature-lover passes. 6034-X
    Opium clippers. 6833-2
    The road to France. 6946-0
    The road to France. 6846-4
    St. Swithin. 6396-9
    Sea mist. 6038-2
    The searchlight. 6331-4

Sleep. 6039-0
The stranger. 6232-6,6619-4,6037-4
The tea trader. 6750-6
Henderson, Emily
Easter offerings. 6720-4
Henderson, Florence L.
The garden that I love. 6214-8
Henderson, Fred
To Lucy. 6226-1
The voice of freedom. 7009-4
Henderson, John Robert
The gift of a rose. 6836-7
Remembrance. 6836-7
Shadow. 6836-7
She touched the strings. 6836-7
Henderson, Le Roy C,.
Somewhere in France. 6846-4
Henderson, M.
The outlaw. 6920-7
Henderson, M.L.
The king's daughter. 6505-8
Henderson, Mary
Love. 6750-6
Henderson, Rose
An abondoned abode. 6653-4
An outdoor theatre. 7038-8
The pagan. 6033-1
The patio. 6653-4
Rewa corn-dance. 6959-2
Henderson, Ruth Evelyn
Boy's day. 6861-8
Lesson in poetry. 6038-2
Henderson, William J.
On a hymn-book. 6441-8,6652-6
Hendricks, Walter
Beggar Bill. 6542-2
John Christian. 6542-2
Sheep. 6542-2
Hendrickson, Margaret E.
On thoughts. 6818-9
Hendrickson, Will H.
At the last. 7007-8
Hendry, J.F.
The constant north. 6379-9
Inverberg. 6379-9
Orpheus. 6379-9
The ship. 6379-9
Tir-nan-og. 6379-9
Hendry, James
The aftermath. 6273-3
Heney, Thomas
The boundary rider. 6784-0
To the poet. 6784-0
Henigan, Robert
A tale. 6860-X
Henisch, Peter
"But the flesh" Milne Holton and Herbert Kuhner (tr.). 6769-7
"One came" Milne Holton and Herbert Kuhner (tr.). 6769-7
"Visiting a friend in one of the best asylums in" Milne Holton and Herbert Kuhner (tr.). 6769-7
"What was in the beginning" Milne Holton and Herbert Kuhner (tr.). 6769-7
Henjo (Munesada Yoshimune)
"Oh stormy winds, bring up the clouds". William N. Porter (tr.). 6852-9
Henley, Lloyd
Mint Springs cemetery; Dougals County, Missouri. 6860-X
Polio memoir. 6860-X
Henley, William Ernest
After, fr. In hospital. 6250-4
'And lightly, like the flowers' 6770-0
Apparition. 6186-9,6659-3,6250-4,6508-2
"The April sky sags low and drear", fr. Hawthorn. 6123-0
Ave, Caesar!, fr. In hospital. 6508-2
Ballade made in the hot weather. 6770-0
Ballade of antique dances. 6770-0
Ballade of aspiration. 6770-0

Ballade of spring. 6770-0
Ballade of truisms. 6770-0
Ballade. 6724-7
Ballade made in the hot weather. 6508-2
Ballade of a Toyokuni colour print. 6875-8
Ballade of antique dances. 6875-8
Ballade of aspiration. 6875-8
Ballade of dead actors. 6875-8
Ballade of dead actors. 6026-9
Ballade of June. 6320-9,6473-6,6652-6
Ballade of ladies' names. 6652-6
Ballade of midsummer days and nights. 6123-0
Ballade of spring. 6875-8
Ballade of truisms. 6123-0
Ballade of youth and age. 6123-0
Barmaid, fr. London types. 6507-4
Before, fr. In hospital. 6102-8,6250-4,6659-3
Beside the idle summer sea, fr. Bric-a-brac. 6123-0
"Between the dusk of a summer night", fr. Hawthorn. 6123-0
The blackbird ("The nightingale has a lyre of gold"). 6073-0,6464-7,6104-4,6102-8
Bric-a-brac, sels. 6123-0
By the swinging seas. 6429-9,6321-7
'The chief,' fr. In hospital. 6250-4
"A child," fr. Echoes. 6508-2
The Christian slave. 6732-8
Collige rosas. 6437-X,6513-9
Culture in the slums. 6770-0
Culture in the slums. 6089-7,6440-X
"A desolate shore." 6508-2
Discharged, fr. In hospital. 6655-0, 6508-2
Double ballade of life and fate. 6770-0
Double ballade of the nothingness of things. 6770-0
Double ballade of life and fate. 6875-8
Double ballade of the nothingness of things. 6875-8
Easy is the triolet. 6527-9
Echoes. 6315-2,6250-4
Echoes, sels. 6123-0,6258-X,6508-2
The end. 6230-X
England, my England. 6242-3,6395-0,6224-5,6290-3,6123-0, 6331 ,6102-8,6439-6,6437-X
Epilogue. 6508-2
The eternity of love. 6396-9
'Felicity. Enquire within' 6770-0
"Fill a glass with golden wine," fr. Echoes. 6508-2
Finale. 6653-4
A flirted fan. 6770-0
For England's sake, sels. 6123-0
"Fresh from his fastnesses", fr. Rhymes and rhythms. 6473-6,6507-4
"Friends...old friends". 6085-4,6084-6
The gods are dead. 6770-0
The gods are dead. 6875-8
Gulls in an aery morrice. 6655-0
The happy passing. 6793-X
Hawthorn and lavender. 6123-0
Hawthorn and lavender, sels. 6507-4
Her little feet. 6089-7
"Hither, this solemn eventide", fr. Hawthorne and... 6507-4
Home. 6136-2,6239-3
I met a maiden to-day. 6226-1
I.M. Margaritae Sororis. 6653-4
If I were king. 6423-X,6453-1
In Fisherrow. 6250-4,6653-4
In hospital, sels. 6250-4
In hospital-music. 6123-0
In rotten row. 6453-1
In the year that's come and gone. 6429-9,6226-1,6321-7
Inter solades. 6230-X
Invictus. 6289-X,6427-2,6481-7,6732-8,6123-0,6291 ,6153-2,6161-3,6102-8,6560-0,6461-2,6250 ,6332-2,6337-3, 6437-X,6476-0,6498-1,6501 ,6104-4,6107-9,6214-8,6301-2,6371-3,6396 ,6503-1,6507-4,6512-0,6534-1,6589-9, 6726 ,6464-7,6655-0,6737-9,6723-9,6653-4
Is it good-bye? 6226-1
Lady-probationer, fr. In hospital. 6250-4
A late lark twitters. 6123-0,6073-0,6473-6,6301-2,6508-2,6655

HENLEY

    The leaves are sere. 6770-0
    "Life in her creaking shoes," fr. Echoes. 6508-2
    London types, sels. 6507-4
    London voluntaries. 6507-4
    London voluntaries, sels. 6301-2
    "Look down, dear eyes, look down", fr Hawthorn. 6123-0
    Love notes. 6066-8
    Madam life's a piece in bloom. 6655-0
    Made in the hot weather. 6239-3
    The man in the street, fr. For England's sake. 6123-0
    Margaritae sorori. 6186-9,6236-9,6289-X,6332-2,6726-3,
      6730 ,6371-3,6250-4,6161-3,6102-8,6214-8,6491
    Matri dilectissimae, fr. Echoes. 6123-0
    The men of Gotham. 6084-6
    Midsummer days and nights. 6732-8
    My love to me. 6770-0
    The night cat. 6102-8
    "The nightingale has a lyre of gold," 6508-2
    "Not to the staring day." 6508-2
    "O, Falmouth is a fine town." 6476-0,6655-0
    O, gather me the rose. 6396-9
    On the way to Kew. 6437-X,6250-4,6655-0,6123-0
    Or ever the knightly years were gone. 6102-8
    "Out of the night that covers me." 6199-0,6646-1
    Over the hills and far away. 6723-9
    A pleasant song. 6429-9,6321-7,6321-7,6429-9
    "Poplar and lime and chestnut," fr. Hawthorn. 6123-0
    Praise the generous gods for giving. 6291-1,6123-0,6291-1
    The pretty washer-maiden. 6473-X
    The pretty washermaider, fr. Echoes. 6423-X,6123-0
    Pro rege nostro. 6653-4
    R.T. Hamilton Bruce. 6508-2
    Rhymes and rhythms, sels. 6507-4,5608-2
    Romance. 6289-X,6396-9,6508-2,6723-9
    Rondel. 6770-0
    Rondel. 6875-8
    St. Margaret's bells. 6484-1
    Scherzando, fr. London voluntaries. 6508-2
    Scrubber, fr. In hospital. 6250-4
    "Sing to me, sing, and sing again", fr. Hawthorne...
      6507-4
    So be my passing, fr. In memoriam Margaritae Sorori.
      6337-3
    "Some starlit garden gray with dew." 6508-2
    Song. 6660-7
    Song of the sward. 6732-8
    "Space and dread and the dark", fr. Rhymes and rhythms.
      6507-4,6726-3,6655-0
    Staff nurse: new style. 6123-0
    Staff-nurse: old style, fr. In hospital. 6250-4
    'Sweet girl graduates, golden-haired' 6770-0
    Thick is the darkness. 6291-1
    "This is the moon of roses", fr. Hawthorn. 6123-0
    To A.D., fr. Echoes. 6123-0,6653-4
    To H.B.M.W. 6660-7
    To my wife. 6850-2
    To R.A.M.S. 6230-X
    To R.L.S. 6653-4
    To R.T.H.B. 6660-7
    To W.A., fr. Echoes. 6123-0
    Triolet, after Catullus. 6770-0
    The triolet. 6089-7,6427-7
    Unconquered. 6418-3
    "Under a stagnant sky", fr. Rhymes and rhythms. 6507-4
    Variations. 6875-8
    Vigil. 6315-2,6508-2
    Villanelle ("A dainty"). 6289-X,6724-7,6646-1,6770-0
    Villanelle ("In the clatter"). 6875-8
    Villanelle ("Where's the use"). 6770-0
    Villon's straight tip to all cross coves. 6770-0
    Villon's straight tip to all cross coves. 6089-7,6733-6
    Waiting. 6655-0
    The ways of death. 6052-8
    'We'll to the woods and gather may' 6770-0
    "The west a glimmering lake of light", fr. Echoes. 6123-0
    What is to come we know not. 6123-0,6204-0,6491-4
    When you are old. 6211-3,6429-9,6321-7,6429-9
    "When, in what other lie", fr. Hawthorne and lavender.

      6507-4
    Where forlorn sunsets. 6655-0
    While the west is paling. 6655-0
    The wind on the wold. 6653-4
    A window in Princes Street, sels. 6484-1
    With a fan from Rimmel's. 6770-0
    With strawberries. 6429-9,6476-0,6321-7,6429-9
Henley, William Ernest (tr.)
    Alons au bois le may cueillir. Charles, Duc d' Orleans,
      6850-2,7039-6
    And ligh'ly, like the flowers. Pierre de Ronsard, 6732-8
"Henley, what mark you in the sunset glare?". To W.E.
    Henley. Thomas Edward Brown. 6809-X
Henline, Mae Baker
    A prayer for great men of the nations. 6270-9
Henly, Anthony
    Song ("No, no, no, no"). 6563-5
Henly, William Ernest
    My love to me. 6875-8
Henneberger, May Allard
    Plants in an attic apartment. 6750-6
Hennell, Thomas
    A mermaiden. 6210-5
    Queen Anne's musicians. 6210-5
    Shepherd and shepherdess. 6210-5
Hennessey, W.M.
    The spear of Keltar. 6090-0
Hennessy, Doyle
    Liberty bell. 6839-1
    Nuclear fission. 6839-1
Hennessy, Roland Burke
    Lament of the players. 7001-9
Henri. George Sterling. 7027-2
"'Henri Heine'- 'tis here!". Heine's grave. Matthew
    Arnold. 6848-0,6828-6,6250-4
Henry Benjamin Whipple. Florence Gibbs Keenan. 6342-X
Henry C. Calhoun. Edgar Lee Masters. 6897-9
Henry Ditch. Edgar Lee Masters. 6300-4
Henry Hastings Sibley. Genevieve R. Breen. 6342-X
Henry Hudson's last voyage. Henry Van Dyke. 6484-1
Henry Hudson's quest. Burton Egbert Stevenson. 6484-1
Henry IV's soliloquy on sleep. William Shakespeare. 6639-9
Henry IV, part 001, sel. William Shakespeare. 6958-4
Henry IV, part 002 William Shakespeare. 6958-4
Henry Jr., Daniel
    Bobby Shafto, fr. Under a fool's cap. 6605-4
    Under a fool's cap, sels. 6605-4
    Violet's blue. 6605-4
Henry King. Hilaire Belloc. 6861-8
Henry Martyn. Unknown. 6057-9,6058-7,6185-0,6547-3
"Henry and King Pedro clasping". The death of Don Pedro.
    Unknown (Spanish). 6757-3
Henry of Navarre. Thomas Babington Macaulay, 1st Baron
    Macaulay. 6543-0
Henry St. John, Viscount Bolinbrooke, fr. An essay..man.
    Alexander Pope. 6932-0
Henry Trumbull. Wilfred Wilson Gibson. 6210-5
Henry V at Harfleur. William Shakespeare. 6294-6
Henry V before Harfleur. William Shakespeare. 6639-9
Henry V encouraging his soldiers. William Shakespeare.
    6424-8
Henry V, sel. William Shakespeare. 6958-4
Henry Vaughan. Thomas S. Jones Jr. 6483-3
Henry VI's pastoral wish. William Shakespeare. 6423-X
Henry W. Longfellow's funniest poem. Henry Wadsworth
    Longfellow. 6889-8
Henry Wadsworth Longfellow. Austin Dobson. 6820-0
Henry Wadsworth Longfellow. Austin Dobson. 6250-4
Henry Ward Beecher. Charles Henry Phelps. 6820-0
Henry Ward Beecher. Unknown. 6125-7
Henry the Minstrel ("Blind Harry")
    A description of Wallace. 6180-X
    Wallace's lament for the Graham. 6180-X
    War summons the lover. 6180-X
Henry VIII; King of England
    Alas! what shall I do for love? 6328-4,6528-7
    The holly. 6436-1
    The kynge's balade. 6328-4
    O my heart! 6328-4

Pastime. 6436-1
Pastime with good company. 6528-7,6383-7
To his lady. 6436-1
Henry VIII; King of England (atr)
Love ever green. 6881-2
Henry's address to his army, fr. King Henry V. William Shakespeare. 6934-7
Henry's audience of French ambassadors. William Shakespeare. 6438-8
Henry's lament. Samuel Daniel. 6436-1
Henry's soliloquy on sleep. William Shakespeare. 6543-0
Henry, Edna G.
Trees walking. 6036-6
Henry, Gordon
Freeze tag. 7005-1
Leaving smoke's. 7005-1
Outside white earth. 7005-1
Pine point, you are: 7005-1
Waking on a greyhound. 7005-1
Henry, James
The old story over again. 6620-8
Henry, Mrs. S.M.I.
The surrender. 6617-8
Henry, Nat
Poet. 6462-0
Henry, Re.
Lady Maud's oath. 6923-1
Henry, Thomas
The hut on the flat. 6768-9
Henryson, Robert
The bludy serk. 6180-X
The bludy serk. 6931-2
Cresseid's complaint against fortune. 6881-2
Cresseid's lament. 6150-8
The garmont of gude ladies. 6180-X,6383-7,6022-6
The mouse and the paddock. 6198-2
Robin and Makyne. 6180-X,6186-9,6430-2,6189-3
The testament of Cresseid, sels. 6378-0,6193-1
The testament of Cresseid. 6845-6
To Our Lady. 6022-6
The **hens.** Elizabeth Madox Roberts. 6464-7
Hensel, Luise
Prayer ("I am weary"). Margarete A. Munsterberg (tr.). 6259-8
Henshaw, Mrs. H.E.
Sleep, sleep! 6078-1
Hensley, Almon
Somewhere in France, 1918. 6846-4
Hensley, Lewis
Thy kingdom come, O God! 6641-0
Hensley, Sophie M.
There is no God. 7041-8
Triumph. 7041-8
Henson, Lance
At chadwicks bar and grill. 7005-1
Buffalo marrow on black. 7005-1
North. 7005-1
Poem near midway truck stop. 7005-1
Vision song (cheyenne) 7005-1
Hep-cat. John L. Seller. 6870-7
Hepatica. Alice Wellington Rollins. 6529-5
Hepburn, Elizabeth Newport
Machines- or men? 7014-0
Hepburn, Mary F.
February twelfth. 6466-3
Hepburn, Thomas N. See "Setoun, Gabriel"
Heppenstall, Rayner
Actaeon. 6210-5
Consolation in July. 6379-9
Fleur de lys. 6666-6
Hagiograph. 6379-9
Spring song. 6379-9
Tammuz. 6666-6
Heppler, Hazel S.
Twilight reverie. 6799-9
The **heptalogia.** Algernon Charles Swinburne. 6430-2
Hepzibah of the cent shop. Virginia Taylor McCormick. 6037-4,6326-8
Her. Robert Loveman. 6941-X
Her $ shoes. Unknown. 7021-3

Her 'allowance'. Lillian Gard. 6474-4,6653-4
Her 'last poems'/Poets ended. Emily Dickinson. 6483-3
Her 'no.' Unknown. 6702-6
"Her ankle is neat". A favoring wind. Unknown. 6983-5
Her answer. William Howard Falkner. 6936-3
Her answer. Sir Charles Sedley. 6544-9
Her answer. Unknown. 6166-4,6576-7
Her answer to his verses. Raymond Burnham. 6118-4
Her beautiful eyes. James Whitcomb Riley. 6992-4
Her beauty. Aubrey Thomas De Vere. 7015-9
Her beauty. William Shakespeare. 6423-X
"Her black eyes are made of beads". The old doll. Wilhelmina Seegmiller. 6891-X
Her bonnet. Mary E. (Freeman) Wilkins. 6632-1,6652-6
Her bonnie black e'e. William Laidlaw. 6960-6
Her brother's cigarette. Unknown. 6453-1
"Her brown hair plainly put away". A picture. Phoebe Cary. 6865-0;6969-X
"Her captains for the Baltic bound". The hallowing of the fleet. William Johnson Cory. 6793-X
"Her casement like a watchful eye". Balder's wife. Alice Cary. 6969-X
"Her chariot ready straight is made". The queen's chariot. Michael Drayton. 6933-9
"Her cheek was wan- her dress was worn". Give back my missing ones. James Abraham Martling. 6952-5
Her china cup. Frank Dempster Sherman. 6770-0
"Her clothes were what". Cousin Florrie. Muriel F. Hochdorf. 6850-2
Her coming. George Chapman. 6189-3,6250-4
Her commendation. Francis Davison. 6436-1
Her confirmation. Selwyn Image. 6656-9
Her conquest. Irwin Russell. 7041-8
"Her court was pure; her life serene". To Queen Victoria. Alfred Lord Tennyson. 6934-7
"Her cup of life with joy is full". Enchantment. Phoebe Cary. 6969-X
Her dairy. Peter Newell. 6466-3
Her day is over. D.P. McGuire. 6780-8
Her death. Margaret Radford. 6778-6
Her death (Miss Kilmansegg) Thomas Hood. 6656-9
Her dilemma. Thomas Hardy. 6828-6
Her dilemma. Paul B. McVey. 6118-4
Her dwelling place. Ada Foster Murray. 6300-4
Her epitaph. Thomas William Parsons. 6243-1;6735-2
Her epitaph. Francis Quarles. 6908-8
Her explanation. Edward Rowland Sill. 6431-0
"Her eyes are like the evening air". Hesper. Henry Van Dyke. 6961-4
"Her eyes are sunlit hazel". Portrait of a lady. Sarah N. Cleghorn. 6034-X,6161-3
Her eyes are wild. William Wordsworth. 6271-7
"Her eyes that shine with tender light". A brief description. Harry Romaine. 7021-3
"Her eyes the glow-worm lend thee". Serenade. Robert Herrick. 6935-5
Her face and brow. James Whitcomb Riley. 6992-4
"Her face is fair and smooth and fine". A vivid girl. Clara Shanafelt. 6897-9
"Her fairness, wedded to a star". Edward J. O'Brien. 6292-X,6096-X
Her fairy feet. Eugene Field. 6949-5
"Her father's telescope". In memory of Jean Rhys. Bill Olsen. 6900-2
Her faults. Harry Bache Smith. 6441-8,6652-6
Her favorites. Mattie Lee Hausgen. 6466-3
"Her fayre inflaming eyes" Thomas Campion. 6794-8
"Her feet beneath her petticoat". At a wedding. Sir John Suckling. 6959-2
Her fifteen minutes. Thomas Masson. 6277-6;6671-2
Her first bouquet. Clement Scott. 6714-X
Her first husband. Joseph Crosby Lincoln. 6707-7
Her first train. A.E. Watrous. 6632-1
Her first-born. Charles Tennyson Turner. 6097-8,6656-9, 6737-9,6627-5
Her fittest triumph is to show that good"." James Russell Lowell. 6226-1
Her flower. George Albert Soper. 6116-8
Her garden. Louis Dodge. 6338-1
Her garden. John Richard Moreland. 6037-4

HER

Her garden ("This was her dearest walk last year..."). Eldredge Denison. 6338-1
"Her gentlewomen...", fr. Antony and Cleopatra. William Shakespeare. 6339-X
Her gifts, fr. The house of life. Dante Gabriel Rossetti. 6526-0,6110-9,6250-4,6656-9
Her going. Agnes Lee. 6897-9
Her graduation rhyme. Unknown. 6718-2
Her grandpa. Charles D. Stewart. 7022-1
"Her gray cat yawned and stretched...". Night comes to an old lady. Estelle Rooks. 6850-2
Her great secret. Strickland Gillilan. 6449-3
Her hair. Sir Robert Chester. 6182-6
Her hair. James Whitcomb Riley. 6992-4
"Her hair the net of golden wire". Unknown. 6187-7
"Her hair was a waving bronze and her eyes". Disappointment. John Boyle O'Reilly. 6930-4
"Her hand a goblet bore for him". The two. Hugo von Hofmannsthal. 7039-6
"Her hand was still on her sword-hilt...". The young queen. Rudyard Kipling. 6810-3
Her hands. Anna Hempstead Branch. 6101-X
Her hands. Arthur Davison Ficke. 6037-4
"Her hands were clasped downward and doubled". Charity. Joaquin Miller. 7041-8
"Her hands were clasped, her dark eyes raised". Gertrude; or, fidelity till death, fr. Records of woman. Felicia Dorothea Hemans. 6973-8
"Her harp is of the newest make". The fin-de-siecle angel. Unknown. 7021-3
Her hat. Annabelle Lee. 6799-9
Her heards be thousand fishes. Edmund Spenser. 6125-7
Her heart. John Masefield. 6102-8
"Her heart she locked". The secret combination. Ellis Parker Butler. 7021-3
Her heart was false and mine was broken. Mary Kyle Dallas. 6671-2
"Her heart was light as human heart can be". Love's recompense. Phoebe Cary. 6969-X
"Her heart, born eager, generous and just". Epitaphs for a bad girl. A.D. F.. 6817-0
Her helpfulness. Dante Alighieri. 6321-7
"Her home is far, oh! far away!". Let her depart. Felicia Dorothea Hemans. 6973-8
Her house. Frank Ernest Hill. 6037-4
"Her house is banked against the stone walls". Skin of silence, smell of snow. Regina de Cormier-Shekerjian. 6821-9
"Her housetop rocks with bursting bombs". His mother. Honor Arundel. 6895-2
"Her husband died before her babe was born". Ex ore infantis. Thomas Edward Brown. 6809-X
Her husband's death. Roberta Santlofer Danowsky. 6857-X
Her ideal. Kate Masterson. 6417-5
Her immortality. Thomas Hardy. 6655-0
Her initials. Thomas Hardy. 6828-6
Her king. Unknown. 6983-5
Her laddie's picture. Mary Beale Brainerd. 6575-9
Her last letter. Ella Wheeler Wilcox. 6863-4
Her last lines. Emily Bronte. 6656-9
Her last poem. Alice Cary. 6600-3
Her last verses. Alice Cary. 6219-9
Her last words at parting. Thomas Moore. 6226-1
Her laugh in four fits. Unknown. 6670-4
Her Lenten sacrifice. Unknown. 6721-2
"Her laughter!/Moonlight - her pedestal...". The marble nymph. Gertrude Huntington McGiffert. 6838-3
Her lesson. Jean Blewett. 6797-2
Her letter. Francis Bret Harte. 6370-5,6165-6,6289-X,6409-4,6499-X,6630 ,6004-8,6652-6,6219-9,6438-8,7041-8, 6732-8,6385-3,6706-9
Her letter. Robert Service. 6159-1
Her letters. Lloyd Thomas. 6589-9
Her likeness. Dinah Maria Mulock Craik. 6302-0;6385-3
Her lips. Walter Savage Landor. 6874-X
"Her lips were so near". In explanation. Walter Learned. 6875-8
Her little boy. Unknown. 6260-1,6449-3
Her little feet. William Ernest Henley. 6089-7
"Her love she vowed was mine fore'er". Meleager. 6637-2

"Her love was the dew". Triolet 002, fr. Thistledown. Cora Fabri. 6876-6
Her lover. Mrs. S.C. Hazlett. 6670-4
"Her lover died. Away from her", fr. The minstrel girl. John Greenleaf Whittier. 6752-2
Her lovers. Unknown. 6166-4
"Her lute hangs shadowed in the apple-tree". A sea-spell. Dante Gabriel Rossetti. 6997-5
Her majesty. Edgar Wade Abbott. 7022-1
Her majesty. Robert Loveman. 6941-X
"Her majesty comes when the sun goes down". Her majesty. Edgar Wade Abbott. 7022-1
Her majesty's ship. Gene Fowler. 6792-1
Her man. Leetha Journey Probst. 6042-0
Her man described by her own dictamen. Ben Jonson. 6378-0, 6194-X
Her moral (Miss Kilmansey). Thomas Hood. 6481-7,6656-9
Her mother, fr. An order for a picture. Alice Cary. 6097-8
"Her mouth is carmine and her cheeks too red". New York. Berton Braley. 6853-7
"Her mouth was shaped to happy tunes". Affinity. Leonora Speyer. 6984-3
Her name. Anna F. Burnham. 6426-4
Her name. Victor Hugo. 6732-8
Her name. Edmund Spenser. 6383-7
Her name. Unknown. 6078-1,6273-3,6682-8,6449-3
"Her name a byword, and her life a shame". The Magdalene. John E. Barrett. 6840-5
"Her name it was Medora". The jewel of a nose. James Abraham Martling. 6952-5
"Her name was quite familiar to the Hottentots". Only a woman. Tom Masson. 6924-X
"Her name was Skinny Dynamite. She was a...". Skinny Dynamite. Jack Micheline. 6998-3
Her names. Unknown. 6924-X
Her old-time song. Emma M. Johnston. 6097-8
Her only flaw. Rufinus. 6435-3
Her opinion of the play. Marc Eugene ("Vandyke Brown") Cook. 6735-2,6004-8
Her own. Mayme C. Wyant. 6270-9
"Her pen drops eloquence as sweet". On a letter of Miss Fanshawe. William Cowper. 6814-6
Her perfect lover. Mary Ainge ("Madeline Bridges") De Vere. 6576-7
Her perfect praise. Robert Browning. 6429-9,6321-7
"Her perfume floats upon me in a perfect...". Lady Lilac. Robert Kirkland Kernighan. 6797-2
Her photograph. Frank McHale. 6578-3
Her picture. Ellen Mackay Hutchinson Cortissoz. 6309-8
Her pity. Philip Bourke Marston. 6656-9
Her portrait. Francis Thompson. 6942-8
Her praises ("She, like the morning...") Anthony Scoloker. 6182-6
Her prayer-for him. Egbert Sandford. 6474-4
Her preference. Unknown. 6671-2
Her programme of dance. Alfred L. Spencer. 6116-8
"Her prudence was a white fence". Curve ahead. Rosa Zagnoni Marinoni. 6750-6
Her rambling. Thomas Lodge. 6315-2;6436-1
Her reasons. Unknown. 6130-3,6713-1
Her reclamation. Edward Farquhar. 6939-8
Her refrain. John Boyle O'Reilly. 6320-9
Her reverie. Francis Carlin. 6250-4
Her right name. Matthew Prior. 6874-X
Her right name. Matthew Prior. 6092-7
"Her robes are of purple and scarlet". Babylon. James Jeffrey Roche. 7041-8
"Her roguish little eyes are blue". Triolet. R.D. Dripps. 6983-5
"Her rosie cheekes, her euer smiling eyes" Thomas Campion. 6794-8
Her rosy cheeks. Thomas Campion. 6328-4
"Her sails are strong and yellow as the sand". The clipper. Thomas Fleming Day. 6833-2
"Her sails are wove of the fogs that flee". The storm ship. Arthur Guiterman. 6773-5
Her satin fan. James Goodwin. 6116-8
"Her scuttle hatt is wondrous wide". An old rondo. Frank Dempster Sherman. 6770-0
Her seasons. Davd Wevill. 6767-0

Her senior smile your Waterloo. Cynthia Grey. 6718-2
Her shadow. Aubrey Thomas De Vere. 6302-0
"Her silver lamp half-filled with oil". Many mansions. Phoebe Cary. 6969-X
"Her skies, of whom I sing, are hung". The harmless luxury. Phoebe Cary. 6969-X
"Her slim white fingers run along the pod". A girl shelling peas. Robert P. Tristram Coffin. 6761-1
Her sofa. M.E. W. 7021-3
"Her soul from earth to heaven lies". Scala Jacobi portaque eburnea. Francis Thompson. 6942-8
"Her soul has dwelt in shadow now so long". The mourner. Mary H. Cabaniss. 6841-3
Her soul is pure. Robert Loveman. 6941-X
Her spinning-wheel. Carolyn Wells. 6875-8
"Her strong enchantments failing." Alfred Edward Housman. 6138-9,6150-8,6210-5
"Her suffering ended with the day". A death-bed. James Aldrich. 6214-8,6219-9,6271-7,6737-9,6911-8,6309-8
"Her supple breast thrills out". Philomela. Richard Crashaw. 6934-7
"Her supple breasts thrills out" Richard Crashaw. 6935-5
"Her thoughts were quiet mysteries". Flower woman. Blanche Waltrip Rose. 6906-1
"Her touch heals/in the great sip". Sarah: Cherokee doctor. Wendy Rose. 7005-1
"Her tragedies she always keeps alive". Resignation. Emily Ann Coffman. 6750-6
Her triumph, fr. A celebration of Charis... Ben Jonson. 6182-7,6562-7,6645-3
Her triumph, fr. Underwoods. Ben Jonson. 6023-4
"Her uncle and the squire rode out one summer's day". Unknown. 6059-5
Her valentine. Richard Hovey. 6652-6
Her veins are lit with strange desire. Annette Wynne. 6880-4
Her very tree, fr. Bread out of iron. Marjorie Allen Seiffert. 6531-7
Her vision. Unknown. 6923-1
Her voice. Martha Martin. 6585-6
Her voice. Gertrude Huntington McGiffert. 6838-3
"Her voice was so charming, so heart-felt...". The shrike. Porsteinn Erlingsson. 6854-5
"Her voice was tender as a lullaby". The farmer's daughter. Alice Cary. 6969-X
Her waiting face. James Whitcomb Riley. 6992-4
Her way. William Rose Benet. 6034-X,6607-0
Her wedding. Unknown. 6921-5
Her wedding eve. Virginia Frazer Boyle. 6686-0
Her window. Richard Leigh. 6562-7,6563-5
Her wish. E.H. Graham Dewey. 7021-3
Her wishes. Annie Campbell Huestis. 6796-4
Her words. Anna Hempstead Branch. 6509-0,6393-4,6723-9
Her words and prayers. John Pierpont. 6097-8
"Her words are buds". Scandal monger. Frederick Herbert Adler. 6906-1
"Her words to no one". Coming home from camp. Lonny Kaneko. 6790-5
Her world. Emily Huntington Miller. 6255-5
"Her, my own sad love divine". A song ("Her, my own..."). Herbert Trench. 6877-4
Heracles and Meleager. Bacchylides. 6435-3
Heracles, fr. Trachiniae. Sophocles. 6435-3
Heraclides
   "In Cnidus born, the consort I became". William Cowper (tr.). 6814-6
Heraclitus
   The new-made grave. George B. Grundy (tr.). 6879-0
Heraclitus, fr. Epigrams. Callimachus. 6435-3,6046-3,6253-9,6879-0,6230-x,6396 ,6052-8,6437-X,6668-2,6250-4, 6301-2,6246-5,6512-0,6186-9,6246-5,6639-9,6656
The herald crane. Hamlin Garland. 6073-0,6597-X
"Heralded into a belly swelling bladder...". On meeting the clergy of the Holy Catholic Church... Joy Kogawa. 6790-5
Herb of grace. Amelia Josephine Burr. 6338-1
The herb rosemary. Henry Kirke White. 6383-7
The herb-leech. Joseph ("Seosamh MacCathmhaoil") Campbell. 6930-4
Herber, Reginald
   Brightest and best of the sons of the morning. 6239-3
   Providence. 6239-3
Herbert of Cherbury, Edward Herbert, 1st Baron
   Another sonnet to black it self. 6562-7
   "Black beauty, which above that common light". 6106-0
   Celinda. 6438-8,6600-3
   Ditty. 6908-8
   Ditty in imitation of the Spanish entre tanto... 6562-7, 6182-6
   Elegy over a tomb. 6562-7,6208-3,6182-6,6641-0,6341-0
   Epitaph on Sir Philip Sidney lying in St. Paul's. 6562-7
   Judge not the preacher, fr. The church porch. 6934-7
   Love's eternity. 6189-3
   Madrigal. 6182-6
   Now that April of youth adorns. 6092-7
   Ode upon a question moved, whether love should continue. 6198-2,6317-9,6341-1,6150-8,6562-7
   Parted souls. 6908-8
   Platonick love. 6933-9
   Sonnet ("Innumerable beauties"). 6106-0
   Sonnet of black beauty. 6562-7,6563-5
   "Tears, flow no more, or if you needs must flow". 6562-7,6182-6
   The thought. 6563-5,6562-7
   To a lady who did sing excellently. 6933-9
   To her eyes. 6933-9
   To her hair. 6562-7
   Upon combing her hair. 6562-7
Herbert, Annie
   Mulligan's gospel. 6912-6
   The rift of the rock. 6914-2
   We shall know. 6408-6
   When the mists have rolled away. 6304-7
Herbert, Edward. See Herbert of Cherbury
Herbert, George
   Aaron. 6430-2,6431-1,6933-9
   Affliction. 6315-2,6378-0,6150-8,6341-1,6438-8
   The agonie. 6378-0
   The altar. 6491-4
   Antiphon. 6138-9,6527-9,6334-9
   Assurance. 6931-2
   "Awake, sad heart, whom sorrow ever drowns" 6935-5
   "Be useful where thou livest, that they may". 6239-3, 6242-3,6623-2
   Bitter-sweet. 6931-2
   "By all means, use sometime to be alone". 6238-5
   The call. 6271-7
   Christmas. 6138-9,6641-0,6746-8
   The church porch, sels. 6639-9
   The church porch. 6385-3,6194-X
   The church windows. 6933-9
   The church-floore. 6933-9
   The church-floore. 6341-1
   The church-floore. 6933-9
   Church-monuments. 6641-0
   Church-music. 6634-8
   the collar, sels. 6501-5
   The collar. 6341-1,6214-8,6660-7,6189-3,6723-9,6198-2, 6208-3,6052-8,6122-2,6315-2,6337 ,6339-X,6378-0,6527-9,6562-7,6563-5,6604 ,6726-3,6194-4,6430-2,6250-4, 6150-8,6645
   Complaining. 6219-9
   Conscience. 6378-0
   Constancy. 6138-9,6438-8
   Courage. 6512-0
   "Dare to be true". 6623-2
   Death. 6563-5
   Decay. 6378-0
   The dedication. 6430-2
   Denial. 6208-3,6315-2
   Dialogue. 6933-9
   A dialogue. 6935-5
   Discipline. 6339-X,6562-7,6634-8,6732-8,6315-2,6737 , 6250-4,6513-9,6341-1
   Doom's day. 6378-0
   Dullness. 6641-0
   Easter. 6271-7,6328-4,6558-9,6641-0,6438-8,6177 ,6301-2
   Easter ("I got me flowers to strew Thy way"). 6466-3
   Easter ("Rise heart; thy Lord is risen..."). 6562-7

HERBERT

Easter wings. 6527-9,6562-7,6430-2,6341-1,6177-X
Easter, sels. 6208-3
The elixir. 6239-3,6466-3,6102-8,6179-6,6337-3,6418-3,
    6660-7,6668-2,6194-X,6383-7,6604-6,6730-1,6197-4,
    6291-9,6438-8,6023-4
Employment. 6302-0
Even-song. 6208-3
The flower, sels. 6102-8,6232-6
The flower. 6933-9
The flower. 6438-8,6219-9,6271-7,6208-3,6378-0,6600-3,
    6641-0
Frailty. 6931-2
The gifts of God. 6291-1,6246-6,6302-0,6385-3,6424-8
Heaven. 6334-9,6558-9
Holy Christmas. 6747-6
"I got me flowers to straw thy way". 6187-7
Iesu. 6933-9
"Immortal love, author of this great frame." 6645-3
The invitation. 6641-0
Jesu. 6341-1
Jordan. 6208-3,6528-7,6641-0,6431-1,6150-8,6208-3,6528-
    7,6641-0
Jordan [1]. 6562-7
Jordan [2]. 6562-7
Jottings for sportsmen. 6861-8
Jottings for sportsmen. 6861-8
Life. 6302-0,6385-3,6563-5,6733-6,6341-1,6219-9,6438-8
Life. 6014-5,6562-7
Love. 6198-2,6187-7,6341-1,6125-7,6150-8,6153-2,6189-3,
    6737-9,6335-7,6208-3,6317-9,6337-3,6488-4,6563-,6562-
    7,6339-X,6726-3,6473-6,6625-9,6122-
Man. 6271-7,6438-8,6430-2,6214-8
Man's medley. 6018-8
Matins. 6138-9
Maxims. 6138-9
Mememto mori. 6322-5
Mortification. 6430-2,6472-8
"My God, where is that ancient heat towards thee". 6562-
    7
Nature. 6430-2
The odor. 6271-7
The odour. 6933-9
On worship, fr. The church porch. 6337-3
Our prayer. 6337-3
Paradise. 6558-9
A parodie. 6933-9
Peace. 6125-7,6613-5,6438-8,6194-X,6562-7
The pearl. 6208-3,6194-X
Pilgrimage ("I travell'd on, seeing the hill where lay)
    6125-7
The pilgrimage. 6125-7
Praise. 6302-0,6385-3
Prayer. 6052-8
Prayer ("Prayer the churches banquet..."). 6933-9
Prayer ("Prayer the churches"). 6933-9,6634-8
The pulley. 6052-8,6102-8,6122-2,6737-9,6337-3,6339-X,
    6488-4,6186-9,6371-3,6494-1,6491-4,6660-7,6383-7,
    6219-9,6473-6,6536-8,6634-8,6150-8,6430-2,6214-8,
    6250-4,6527-9,6562-7,6563-5,6645-3,6604-6,6726-3,
    6438-8,6194-X,6153-2,6052-8,6102-8,6122-2,6737-9,
    6337-3,6339-X,6488-4,6186-9,6371-3,6494-1,6491-4,
    6660-7,6383-7,6219-9,6473-6,6536-8,6634-8,6150-8,
    6430-2,6214-8,6250-4,6527-9,6562-7,6563-5,6645-3,
    6604-6,6726-3,6438-8,6194-X,6153-2
The quiddity. 6934-7
The quip. 6122-2,6134-6,6562-7,6122-2,6134-6,6562-1,
    6438-8,6430-2,6250-4,6562-1,6438-8,6122-2,6134-6,
    6562-1,6438-8,6430-2,6250-4,6562-1,6438-8
Redemption. 6562-7,6341-1
Repentance. 6430-2
Rest. 6600-3
The resurrection, or Easter-day. 6177-X
Revival. 6385-3
"Rise, heart; thy lord is risen. Sing his praise." 6014-
    5
"Said I not so?" 6302-0;6385-3
The second thanksgiving, or the reprisal. 6430-2
"Shine like the sun in every corner". 6623-2
Sin. 6102-2,6219-9,6737-9
Sins' round. 6315-2

"Sum up at night what thou hast done by day". 6238-5
Sunday ("Oh day most calme, most bright"). 6562-7,6219-
    9,6737-9
"Sundays the pillars are". 6238-5
"Sweet day! so cool, so calm, so bright". 6238-5,6187-7,
    6302-0
Sweet life. 6134-6
"Sweetest saviour, if my soul." 6302-0
The temper. 6563-5,6726-3
"Throw away thy rod". 6187-7
Time. 6563-5
To keep a true Lent. 6424-8
A true hymn. 6931-2
The twenty-third psalme. 6491-4
Virtue ("Sweet day, so cool, so calm, so bright"). 6250-
    4,6194-X,6341-1,6192-3,6177-X,6383-7,6150-8,6153-2,
    6197-4,6189-3,6219-9,6301-2,6304-7,6424-8,6371-3,
    6424-8,6645-3,6639-9,6491-4,6543-0,6250-4,6194-X,
    6341-1,6192-3,6177-X,6383-7,6150-8,6153-2,6197-4,
    6189-3,6219-9,6301-2,6304-7,6424-8,6371-3,6424-8,
    6645-3,6639-9,6491-4,6543-0,6102-8,6179-6,6186-9,
    6228-8,6232-6,6271-,6122-2,6208-3,6240-7,6604-6,6562-
    7,6052-,6315-2,6563-5,6600-3,6726-3,6730-1,6198-,
    6473-6,6634-8,6438-8,6660-7,6438-8
Virtue immortal. 6385-3,6481-7,6737-9
"Who could have thought my shrivell'd heart". 6187-7,
    6317-9
The windows. 6430-2,6341-1
The world. 6933-9
The world. 6122-2,6562-7,6563-5
Herbert, George (tr.)
    The twenty-third psalme. Bible, 6848-0
Herbert, Mary Sidney. See Pembroke, Countess
Herbert, Nellie C. T.
    A may-pole song. 6130-3
    When the circus comes. 6130-3
Herbert, Sir Alan Patrick
    Bacon and eggs. 6722-0
    Ballade of incipient lunacy. 6875-8
    The bowline. 6722-0
    The chameleon. 6512-0
    Coals of fire. 6637-2,6026-9
    Come to Britain. 6722-0
    'He didn't oughter...' 6026-9
    I can't think what he sees in her. 6637-2,6633-X
    Mrs. Mole. 6633-X
    The racing-man. 6722-0
    Recipe, fr. Two gentlemen of Soho. 6722-0
    The tide. 7029-9
    Tomato juice. 6722-0
    'Twas at the pictures, child, we met. 6722-0
    Two gentlemen of Soho, sels. 6722-0
Herbert, Zbigniew
    Arion. 6758-1
    Episode in a library. 6758-1
    Five men. 6758-1
    A halt. 6758-1
    Naked town. 6758-1
    Rosy ear. 6758-1
    The seventh angel. 6758-1
    Study of the object. 6758-1
    Wooden die. 6758-1
Herbert; Earl of Pembroke, William
    Aetius the unbeliever. 6980-0
    The battle field. 6980-0
    The descent to Hela. 6980-0
    The devout man prays to his relations. 6881-2
    Disdain me still. 6182-6
    Farewell. 6980-0
    Futurity. 6980-0
    The heart entire. 6328-4
    Hymn to death. 6980-0
    Jealousy. 6980-0
    The knight strained from battle. 6881-2
    The mother's plea. 6980-0
    A Palm-Sunday hymn. 6881-2
    A paradox. 6182-6
    The phantom fight. 6980-0
    Solitude. 6980-0
    Song ("Soules joy"). 6933-9

Washington. 6980-0
Woman. 6980-0
Herbin, John Fredericrick
    Haying. 6446-9
Herbs. Lizette Woodworth Reese. 6619-4
Herbs and simples. Martha Keller. 6218-0
Herbst, Stephanie
    City boy. 6883-9
    Pittsburgh. 6883-9
The **herd** boy. Haniel Long. 6509-0
The **herd** boy. Lu Yu. 6125-7
The **herd** laddie. Alexander Smart. 6180-X
A **herd** of does. Christopher M. ("Hugh MacDiarmid") Grieve. 6269-5
The **herd** of horses. Sergei Esenin. 6103-6
The **herd-boy** in the rain. May C. ([Mary] Gillington) Byron. 6800-6
Herder, Johann Gottfried von
    The children of sorrow. Elizabeth Craigmyle (tr.). 6842-1
    Estonian bridal song. William Taylor (tr.). 7039-6
    Moses and the worm. 6848-0
    Sir Olaf. Elizabeth Craigmyle (tr.). 6842-1,7039-6
"The **herdman** wandering by the lonely rills". The graves of Gallipoli. L. L.. 6846-4
The **herdman's** happy life, fr. M. Bird's set songs. M. Bird. 6198-2
The **herdman's** happy life. Unknown. 6122-2
The **herdmen**.. Unknown. 6436-1
Herdsman of the mountain, fr. Songs of Lucerne. Johann C. Friedrich von Schiller. 6749-2
The **herdsman**.. Hamlin Garland. 6498-1
"**Here** - in a garden overgrown". They held the wood. John Lomax. 6800-6
"**Here** - where last night she came...". A dream. Philip Bourke Marston. 7015-9
Here a little child I stand. Robert Herrick. 6187-7
Here a nit-wit lies. Patrick Barrington. 6722-0
"**Here** a pretty baby lies". Another. Robert Herrick. 6879-0
"**Here** again I stand". A soliloquy of Leolf, fr. Edward the fair. Henry Taylor. 6980-0
"**Here** along the shiny beach". On the beach. William White. 6868-5
"**Here** am I stretched, in careless ase". The bushman. A.C. Smith. 6768-9
"**Here** am I yet, another twelvemonth spent". 'Blank misgivings of a creature moving about in...' Arthur Hugh Clough. 6828-6
"**Here** am I, little Jumping Joan". Mother Goose. 6363-2
"**Here** Ananias lies because he lied". F.W. MacVeagh. 6722-0
Here and there. Alice Cary. 6969-X
Here and there. William White. 6868-5
"**Here** are cakes for thy body". The other world. Unknown (Egyptian). 7039-6
"**Here** are my old pants". Songs to a tramp. Harmon C. Wade. 7007-5
"**Here** are my thoughts, alive within this fold". The poet and his book. Alice Meynell. 6776-X
"**Here** are my thoughts, alive within this form". The poet and his book. Alice Meynell. 6955-X
Here are sands, ignoble things. Menander. 6435-3
"**Here** are the edge of the foam I watch him...". Child on the beach. Sara Henderson Hay. 6979-7
"**Here** are the faces of women/Young women". China town, San Francisco. D. Maitland Bushby. 6954-1
"**Here** are the flexing branches". Elegy. Clark Mills. 6640-2
"**Here** are the houses of the dead. Here youth". Greenwood cemetery. William Wallace. 6916-9
Here at Verdun. Chester M. Wright. 6846-4
"**Here** at original source, in water meadows". The Thames near its source. John Pudney. 6985-1
"**Here** at the village crossing". The call. Daniel Corkery. 6930-4
Here awa', there awa'. Unknown. 6180-X
"**Here** be the fairest homes the land can show". Colonus, fr. Oedipus. Sophocles. 6987-8
Here begynneth the passe tyme of pleasure. Stephen Hawes. 6586-4
Here below. Rene Francois Armand Sully-Prudhomme. 6876-6

"**Here** Brotachus of Gortyna, a Cretan born, is laid". Simonides. 6251-2
"**Here** blew winter once with the snowstorms...". The enchanted heart. Edward Davison. 6777-8
"**Here** by the baring bough". Autumn in the park. Thomas Hardy. 7020-5
"**Here** by the grapevine is the altar stone". The grindstone. Robert P. Tristram Coffin. 7040-X
"**Here** Byron and here Shelley slept". Hotel de l'Ancre, Ouchy. Joan Ramsay. 6782-4
"**Here** came no cry to tell..lone soul's passing". Requiem for a gull. Patricia Peart. 6764-6
"**Here** Cleita sleeps. You ask her life and race". The monument of Cleita. Theocritus. 7039-6,6879-0
"**Here** comes a lusty wooer". Unknown. 6317-9,6334-9
"**Here** comes holly that is so gent". Alleluai, alleluai, alleluai, now sing we. Unknown. 6756-5
"**Here** comes old Father Christmas". Christmas. Rose Terry Cooke. 6145-1
"**Here** comes the holy legate", fr. King John. William Shakespeare. 6323-3
"**Here** comes the marshal". The proclamation, fr. John Endicott. Henry Wadsworth Longfellow. 6946-0
Here comes the thief. Hazel Hall. 6037-4,6070-6
Here comes the thief. Helen Hall. 6506-6
Here dead lie we. Alfred Edward Housman. 6427-2
"**Here** dead we lie". An epitaph. Alfred Edward Housman. 6733-6
"**Here** death is born among flowers". A song in praise of the chiefs. Unknown (Aztec). 6803-0
"**Here** died a robin in the spring". The violet's love story. Eugene Field. 6949-5
"**Here** do we sit by yule-log fire". Christmas song. Felix E. Schelling. 6936-3
"**Here** dwells the soul of Plato for one while". Afternoon class. Isabel Alden Kidder. 6764-6
Here endeth the first lesson. Belle Turnbull. 6039-0
"**Here** even sunbeams stumble as they thread". In an old garden forgotten. Arthur Wallace Peach. 7030-2
"**Here** falls to-day love's equinoctial rain". Arlington Heights. Benjamin Franklin Taylor. 6815-4
"**Here** far away, seen from the topmost cliff". The lover's tale. Alfred Lord Tennyson. 6977-0
"**Here** find we peace and tumult, hepe, despair". On the fly-leaf. Robert Loveman. 6941-X
Here followeth the songe of the death of Mr Thewlis. Unknown. 6157-5
Here I lie. Marguerite George. 6218-0
"**Here** I lie at the chancel door,". Unknown. 6083-8
"**Here** I lie dead, and here I wait for thee". Unknown. 6435-3
Here I shall wait. Flossie Deane Craig. 6662-3
Here I sit alone. Unknown. 6931-2
"**Here** I stand, the gravestone...". Unknown. 6251-2
"**Here** from the brow of the hill I look". The old mill. Thomas Dunn English. 6936-3
"**Here** from the field's edge we survey". Highway: Michigan. Theodore Roethke. 6761-1
"**Here** gran'ma, here's a present...". Grandma's shamrocks. E.A. Sutton. 6920-7
"**Here** he, your law, vociferous wits". A village blacksmith. George Darley. 6980-0
"**Here** I am". Little jumping Joan. Unknown. 6937-1
"**Here** I am again, and what do I see?". Song amid the holly berries. Margaret Sidney. 6965-7
"**Here** I am at fourteen with". Photo. Don Coles. 6767-0
"**Here** I come, to my trade!". Deflowered. John Galsworthy. 6888-X
"**Here** I lie under the sands". Loon river anthology. L.W. D.. 6817-0
"**Here** I lie, Martin Elginbrodde". Epitaph. George Macdonald. 6730-1,6337-3
"**Here** I rest, says Alfonsina, here I lie". Epitaph for my tomb. Alfonsina Storni. 6759-X
"**Here** I sit, a blooming outlaw, with my rifle". The outlaw: or, a night on the German border. Brian ("Korongo") Brooke. 6938-X
"**Here** I stand beneath the mountains...". Beneath the mountains. Ruzena Jesenka. 6763-8
"**Here** I'm sitting, stitching, darning". 'In the garret are

HERE

our boys'. Unknown. 6915-0
"Here in America nothing is long ago". Nothing is long ago. Thomas Hornsby Ferril. 6761-1
"Here in happy England the fields are...quiet". The casualty list. W. L.. 7031-0
"Here in my curving hands I cup". This query dust. John Hall Wheelock. 6778-6
"Here in my sanatorium on the heights". Letter from a sanatorium: To K.J. Charles Whitby. 6994-0
"Here in solitude/My soul was nurst...". Childhood of Joan of Arc. Robert Southey. 6980-0
"Here in the long white ward I stand". The nurse. Unknown. 7031-0,6846-4
Here in the marshes. Elisabeth G. Palmer. 6662-3
"Here in the marshland, past..battered bridge". A grave in Flanders. Robert O.A. Crewe-Milnes, Marquess of Crewe. 7031-0
"Here in the Pentecostal woods are seen". Stanzas on poetry. Herbert Trench. 6877-4
"Here in the sanctuary of my dreams". Sonnet ("Here in the sanctuary"). Florence Kilpatrick Mixter. 6347-0
"Here in the sentient stillness of the hills". Poet at night in the hills. Milton S. Rose. 6836-7
"Here in this casket you may behold". Baby's letter. Louise E.V. Boyd. 6965-7
"Here in this fair and favored land". Thanksgiving chimes. John E. Barrett. 6840-5
"Here in this great house in the barrack sq.". The heart and the hambone. Edith Sitwell. 7000-0
"Here in thy home we await thy tread". Aristophanes. 6435-3
"Here interposing, as the goddess paused". The prospect, part 005, fr. Liberty. James Thomson. 6816-2
"Here is a flower that will not bloom by sun". Night-blooming cereus. Anderson M. Scruggs. 6841-3
"Here is a friend who proves his worth". He's just a dog. Joseph M. Anderson. 7008-6
"Here is a lily and here is a rose". Decoration Day. Susie M. Best. 7022-1
"Here is a nut shell, cinctured fine". A nut shell. Anna Hempstead Branch. 6861-8
"Here is a question I do ask...". Who killed Christ. Sheloh Khall. 6894-4
"Here is a world from other worlds apart". Plantation. Minnie Hite Moody. 6841-3
"Here is Bohemia, forest and river...". The home of Adalbert. Edward Farquhar. 6939-8
"Here is a wound that never will heal, I know. Edna St. Vincent Millay. 6010-2
"Here is cruel Psamtek, see". The story of cruel Psamtek. Unknown. 6902-9
"Here is her toilet-case-a crust". A belle of praeneste. Margaret Junkin Preston. 7041-8
"Here is his little cambric frock". My son. Ada Tyrell. 7031-0
"Here is little Effie's head". Portrait. Edward Estlin Cummings. 6020-X,6324-1
Here is music, dark and still. Geoffrey Scott. 6649-6
"Here is my cup; a fairy bell". The cup. John Galsworthy. 6888-X
"Here is my last good-bye". Before exile. Louise Mack. 6784-0
"Here is my tail now but we lose them". Tail, fr. 100 chameleons. Dennis Saleh. 6792-1
"Here is no easy fate, nor may you rest". The house to the man. John Gould Fletcher. 7017-5
"Here is no wealth of laden apple trees". City autumn. Ruth H. Hausman. 6850-2
"Here is nothing new nor aught unprroven". The old issue. Rudyard Kipling. 6810-3
"Here is proof the long dream is over". The long dream. Marie Emilie Gilchrist. 6906-1
"Here is the day delivered from time's waters". Promise of joy. Jessica Powers. 6761-1
"Here is the long-bided hour". Work. Alexander Pushkin. 7039-6
"Here is the old church. Now I see it all". Pictures of memory. John Reade. 7041-8
Here is the place where loveliness keeps house. Madison Cawein. 6300-4,6467-1,6310-1

694

"Here is the sorrow, the sighing". Here and there. Alice Cary. 6969-X
"Here is the sweetest grass-plot for a bed". On the hillside. Antonin Sova. 6886-3
Here is the tale. Anthony C. Deane. 6089-7
"Here is the valley, unsearched and cool". Bethesda. Edward Farquhar. 6939-8
"Here is the will of Cathaeir Mor". The testament of Cathaeir Mor. Unknown. 6930-4
Here is the world. Raymond Holden. 6761-1
"Here is the yoke, with arrow and share near..". The laborer. Jose Maria de Heredia. 7039-6
"Here is where silence grows". In the desert. Joseph Joel Keith. 6783-2
"Here Johnson lies - a sage, by all allow'd". Epitaph on Dr. Johnson. William Cowper. 6814-6
"Here it was once Leander crossed...". Antipater of Thessalonica. 6251-2
"Here lapped in hallowed slumber Saon lies". Saon of Acanthus. Callimachus. 6850-2
"Here let my Lord hang up his conquering lance". The celestial city. Giles (the Younger) Fletcher. 6933-9
"Here lie I, Martin Elginbrodde". Unknown. 6850-2
"Here lie I, Timon...". Timon's epitaph. Herodotus. 6850-2
"Here lie I, Timon; who...all...men did hate". Timon's epitaph. Asclepiades. 7039-6
"Here lie the kingdoms of the world, my sons". Song for three sons. Annette Patton Cornell. 6750-6
"Here lies a bard, Hipponax - honored name!". The grave of Hipponax. Theocritus. 7039-6
"Here lies a bee, the victim of his faith". Evidence. Keith Thomas. 6761-1
"Here lies a brave crusader, spent with grief". The crusader. Thomas Curtis Clark. 7001-9
"Here lies a cat of local fame". A family favorite. Louis J. Magee. 7004-3
"Here lies a clerk who half his life had spent". Volunteer. Herbert Asquith. 7031-0
Here lies a lady. John Crowe Ransom. 6250-4,6375-6,6488-4, 6536-8,6619-4,6037-4,6581-3
"Here lies a little boy who made believe". A dreamer. Arthur Guiterman. 6773-5
"Here lies a piece of Christ". Epitaph. Robert Wilde. 6102-8
"Here lies a piece of Christ,--a star in dust,". Unknown. 6083-8
Here lies Bill. Oliver Herford. 6722-0
"Here lies I and my three daughters,". Unknown. 6722-0
"Here lies I, Martin Elmrod;". Unknown. 6083-8
"Here lies John Auricular,". Unknown. 6722-0
"Here lies John Hill, a man of skill,". Unknown. 6722-0
"Here lies Johnny Cuncapod". Unknown. 6722-0
"Here lies Johnny Pidgeon". Robert Burns. 6289-X
"Here lies a poor gluttonous sinner". Suggested epitaph for the tomb of a glutton. Langford Reed. 6811-1
"Here lies in this small chamber". Epitaph. Francois Villon. 6227-X
"Here lies my gude and gracious Auntie". Unknown. 6722-0
"Here lies my wife". Epitaph ("Here lies my wife"). Unknown. 6052-2
"Here lies old John Magee, late the landlord..". An epitaph, or punning run mad. Unknown. 6787-5
"Here lies one box within another." Ben Jonson. 6722-0
"Here lies one that made shipwreck...". Theodoridas [or Theodorides]. 6251-2
"Here lies one who for medicine would not give". Unknown. 6722-0
"Here lies one who hearkens still". Phyllis Megroz. 6777-8
"Here lies one whose name was writ in water." John Keats. 6083-8
"Here lies one, who never drew". An epitaph. William Cowper. 6814-6
"Here lies our sovereign lord the king". John Wilmot, 2d Earl of Rochester. 6850-2,6289-X
Here lies Pierrot. Richard Burton. 6027-7
"Here lies poor stingy Timmy Wyatt". Unknown. 6722-0
"Here lies returned to clay". Unknown. 6722-0
Here lies sweet Isabell. Marjorie Fleming. 6179-6
"Here lies the body of Ann Mann,". Unknown. 6722-0
"Here lies the body of Jonathan Near". Unknown. 6722-0

"Here lies the body of Jonathan Stout". Unknown. 6722-0
Here lies the body of May Wilson Preston. May Wilson
    Preston. 6850-2
"Here lies the body of Sarah Sexton,". Unknown. 6722-0
"Here lies the body of William Jones". Epitaph ("Here lies
    the body of William Jones.") Unknown. 6472-8
"Here lies the country, alas!...". Prelude, fr. The
    daughter of Slava. Jan Kollar. 6763-8
"Here lies the flesh that tried". Epitaph. Louise
    Driscoll. 6031-5,6393-4
"Here lies the harvest at your feet". What it takes.
    Dorothy F. Rand. 6799-9
"Here lies the land to which all hearts may...". Cape Cod,
    sels. Joshua Freeman Crowell. 6798-0
"Here lies the man Richard". Unknown. 6722-0
"Here lies the mother of children seven". Unknown. 6722-0
"Here lies the son of Battus..." Callimachus. 6435-3
"Here lies the woven garb he wore". The robe of grass.
    John Le Gay Brereton. 6784-0
"Here lies wise and valiant dust". Epitaph on the Earl of
    Strafford. John Cleveland. 6933-9
"Here lies, to each her parents ruth". Epitaph on my first
    daughter. Ben Jonson. 6867-7
"Here lieth Hercules the second". John Baynham's epitaph.
    Thomas Dermody. 6930-4
Here lieth love. Thomas Watson. 6182-6
"Here lieth one whose name was writ on water". On Keats
    who desired that on his tomb should..inscribed.
    Percy Bysshe Shelley. 6934-7
"Here lyes Charles ye first ye great." Unknown. 6563-5
"Here may the band, that now in triumph shines". The
    heavenly Jerusalem. Giles (the Younger) Fletcher.
    6931-2
"Here melting mixed with air the ideal forms". Rome, part
    003, fr. Liberty. James Thomson. 6816-2
"Here might I pause & bend in reverence", fr. The prelude.
    William Wordsworth. 6867-7
"Here nature holds as in a hollowed hand". The skylark's
    nest. R.H. Long. 6784-0
"Here night is a magician, careless...". Egypt. Mary Brent
    Whiteside. 6841-3,6781-6
"Here no spring breaks". Emblem to be cut on a lonely rock
    at sea. T.O. Beachcroft. 6781-6
"Here now I stand, upon life's outer verge". Close to
    ninety. John Howard Bryant. 7022-1
"Here now, forevermore, our lives must part". What shall
    be do? Ella Wheeler Wilcox. 6956-8
"Here on the prairie wide what can I find". Thirst. Pearl
    Riggs Crouch. 6836-7
"Here on this hilltop, I renounce the dream". I renounce
    the dream. Arthur Davison Ficke. 6879-0
"Here once engaged the stranger's view". On revisiting
    Harrow. George Gordon, 6th Baron Byron. 6945-2
"Here pause: the poet claims at least this praise" William
    Wordsworth. 6110-9,6199-0,6828-6
"Here poppies move beneath the sun". Poem ("Here
    poppies"). Ann Louise Hayes. 6515-5
"Here rage the furies that...shaped the world". Land's end
    (Point Lobos, California). Stanton A. Coblentz. 6833-2
"Here rest, my soul, from meteor dreams". Mont Blanc.
    Aubrey Thomas De Vere. 6749-2
"Here rests his head upon the lap". The epitaph. Thomas
    Gray. 6634-8,6732-8
"'Here rests in honored glory'". The uknown soldier
    meditates. Jean Evans. 6799-9
"Here Rogers sat, and here for ever dwell". Over a covered
    seat in the flower-garden at Holland... Lord
    Holland. 6874-X
"Here room and kingly silence keep". By the Pacific Ocean.
    Joaquin Miller. 6753-0
"Here roots a glebe of rough mesquite". Requiem to the
    dinosaurs and mastodons. H.J. Hamilton. 6799-9
"Here shall rest unmoved...waning seasons". Elegy. Thomas
    S. Jones Jr.. 6347-0
"Here shalt thou rest/Upon this holy bank...". The
    faithful stepherdess, sel. John Fletcher. 6958-4
Here she goes - and there she goes. Unknown. 6403-5
"Here she goes and there she goes. James Nack. 6089-7,6064-1,6279-2

Here she goes, and there she goes. James Nack. 6889-8
"Here she is, in the gaze now empty...". On someone's
    death. Eugenio Florit. 6759-X
"Here she lies and takes her rest". Requiescat. Charles
    Whitby. 6994-0
"Here she lies, in bed of spice". Upon a maid. Robert
    Herrick. 6879-0
"Here she was wont to go! and here! and here!". Lines, fr.
    The sad shepherd. Ben Jonson. 6867-7
"Here she will sleep, for the day is over". Her day is
    over. D.P. McGuire. 6780-8
"Here sits the Lord Mayor". Mother Goose. 6363-2,6452-3
"Here Skugg lies snug". Benjamin Franklin. 6722-0
"Here sits the lord mayor". Chippety chin. Unknown. 6937-1
"Here slacken rein; here let the dusty mules". The summer
    camp. Bayard Taylor. 6976-2
"Here sombre death 'neath darksome mountains..". 'Neath
    'darksome fells'. Jon Thoroddsen. 6854-5
"Here sparrows build upon the trees". My early home. John
    Clare. 6934-9
"Here spreads the salt marsh, here the...". Elysian trail.
    Katharine Brown Burt. 6799-9
"Here stand I". The cliff church. John Galsworthy. 6888-X
"Here stands a good apple tree". Unknown. 6105-2
Here stands a post. Unknown. 6904-5
"Here the dunes end". Beyond the dunes. Muriel F.
    Hochdorf. 6850-2
"Here the great heart of France". A shrine in the
    Pantheon. Henry Van Dyke. 6961-4
"Here the high houses push up thin and pale". People in
    high houses. Robert P. Tristram Coffin. 7040-X
"Here the human past is dim and feeble...". Haunted
    country. Robinson Jeffers. 6808-1
"Here the mountain curves fade back and back". Black rock.
    William Roehrick. 6850-2
"Here the wind and I have met". Wind songs. Jean Elkins.
    6764-6
"Here they are. Think of it". Women open cautiously.
    Deborah Lee. 6790-5
"Here they are: the escapists...". Library. Harold Vinal.
    6761-1
"Here through this deep defile...", fr. William Tell.
    Johann C. Friedrich von Schiller. 6606-2
"Here to your testing, polished in the sun". Airman's
    certificate, fr. Exploration by air. Fleming
    MacLeish. 6978-9
"Here under the porch's grey bow". Home's a nest. William
    Barnes. 6980-0
"Here upon earth eternity is won". Quatrain XI. Thomas S.
    Jones Jr. 6850-2
"Here was I with my arm and heart". Too late. Robert
    Browning. 6828-6
"Here was the gate. The broken paling". Run wild. Bayard
    Taylor. 6976-2
Here we are. Unknown. 6312-8
"Here we are riding the rail". En route. Brander Matthews.
    6770-0
"Here we come a-wassailing". The wassailer's carol.
    Unknown. 6756-5
Here we come a-whistling. Unknown. 6756-5
Here we go gathering. Unknown (Greek) 6435-3
"Here we go up, up, up". Unknown. 7028-0
"Here we have a little pullet". Unknown. 6364-0
Here we have Idaho. Harry A. Powell. 6465-5
"Here we stan' on the Constitution....". The debate in the
    sennit. James Russell Lowell. 6946-0
"Here where Frank Judson lived...eighty years". Sonnet of
    strange vegetables. Louise Owen. 6764-6
"Here where old sea-trails". Shadow on the sand. Dedie
    Huffman Wilson. 6750-6
"Here where the grey rhenoster clothes...hill". The puff-
    adder. Kingsley Fairbridge. 6800-6
"Here with a handful of faded flowers..Ophelia". Ophelia.
    Frank Kendon. 6785-9
"Here you are/asking me again". The well-intentioned
    question. Wendy Rose. 7005-1
"Here's a bent tree". The golden spider in the mind.
    Geoffrey Scott. 6985-1
"Here's a flower for your grave". Triolet ("Here's a
    flower"). Justin Huntly McCarthy. 6770-0

"Here's a guy no different from me". Lindbergh. I.J. Kapstein. 7019-1
"Here's a half-dozen flies". A bunch of trout-flies. Henry Van Dyke. 6961-4
"Here's a happy new year! but with reason". On my wedding day. George Gordon, 6th Baron Byron. 6945-2
Here's a health. Jeremy Saville. 6328-4
Here's a health to Ane. Robert Burns. 6271-7
Here's a health to King Charles. Sir Walter Scott. 6110-9, 6723-9
Here's a health to King Charles, fr. Woodstock. Sir Walter Scott. 6828-6
"Here's a health to all brave English lads". The clans are coming. Unknown. 6859-6
"Here's a health to every sportsman...". A hunting song. Adam Lindsay Gordon. 6951-7
"Here's a health to the king whom the crown...". A toast. Unknown. 6859-6
"Here's a health to the valiant Swede". Unknown. 6859-6
Here's a health to them that's awa. Robert Burns. 6271-7
"Here's a health to them that's away". The Jacobite's pledge. Allan Ramsay. 6859-6
"Here's a health to them that's away." Unknown. 6138-9
"Here's a letter from John in th' city". The farmer talks. Edgar A. Guest. 6862-6
"Here's a letter from Robin, father". The ship-boy's letter. Unknown. 6928-2
Here's a little mouse. Edward Estlin Cummings. 6506-6
"Here's a little red song to the god of guts". The little red god. Unknown. 7012-4
"Here's a present for Rose". A Greek gift, fr. Rose-leaves. Austin Dobson. 6770-0
"Here's a sailor come home from the Guineas". The stranger. Sir Henry Howarth Bashford. 6778-6
"Here's a song for the dawn, for the noon...". A hearth song. Harry Tennyson Domer. 6799-9
"Here's adieu to my father...". Unknown. 6059-5
"Here's flowers for you". Shakespeare's lists. William Shakespeare. 7020-5
Here's his health in water. Unknown. 6859-6
Here's hopin'. Frank Lebby Stanton. 6291-1
Here's the bower. Thomas Moore. 6543-0
Here's the end of dreamland. Horatio Winslow. 6732-8
"Here's the first image of me, as a boy". Grandfather. Christopher La Farge. 6761-1
"Here's the tender coming". Unknown. 6258-X
"Here's to Maine, whose beauty has no dearth". A toast to Maine. Carrie Tolman. 6894-4
'Here's to Nelson's memory'. Robert Browning. 6657-7
"Here's to the blue of the wind-swept north". The blue and the gray in France. George M. Mayo. 6846-4
"Here's to the heart of friendship,tried &true". The heart of friendship. Unknown. 6889-8
"Here's to the home thast was never,never ours". Song of the dirft weed. Jessie MacKay. 6784-0
"Here's to the maiden of bashful fifteen". Song ("Here's to the maiden"). Richard Brinsley Sheridan. 6241-5, 6464-7
Here's to the maiden, fr. The school for scandal. Richard Brinsley Sheridan. 6174-5,6328-4,6026-9
"Here's to the mice that scares the lions". Mice. Vachel Lindsay. 6880-4
"Here's to the plow that furrowed". Saxon harvest health. Arthur Guiterman. 6773-5
"Here's to the world for a dwelling!". A Bohemian drinking song. Thomas Truxtun Hare. 6936-3
"Here's to thee". Unknown. 6334-9
Here's to thee, my Scottish lassie. John Moultrie. 6219-9
"Here's to thee, old apple tree". Unknown. 6105-2
"Here's to you, Arthur! You and I". Across the table. Bliss Carman and Richard Hovey. 6890-1
"Here, a maiden of bronze, I stand on Midas' grave." Cleobulus of Lindus. 6251-2
"Here, as the vesper chant". Notre Dame de Rouen. William Allen Butler. 6903-7
"Here, by God's kindly grace". Home coming. R.G.T. Coventry. 7029-9
"Here, by the shore, we go out each morning". Diving for pearls. Traise Yamamoto. 6790-5
"Here, by this sea, I waked - how long ago!". Bacchus and Ariadne, fr. Scaramouch in Naxos. John Davidson. 6819-7
"Here, free from riot's hated noise". Inscription for a moss-house in the shrubbery at Weston. William Cowper. 6814-6
"Here, here among the reeds he stands". Blue heron. Yetza Gillespie. 6979-7
"Here, here she lies, a budding rose". Epitaph in Hales-Owen churchyard, on Miss Anne Powell. William Shenstone. 6772-7
"Here, in my rude log cabin". The battle of New Orleans. Thomas Dunn English. 6946-0
"Here, in the field, last year". Compensation. Gerald Gould. 6776-X
"Here, in the hidden palm of the Pajaro Valley", Stonehouse. Jeff Tagami. 6790-5
"Here, in the red heart of sunset lying". Frogs. Sir Charles George Douglas Roberts. 6795-6
"Here, in this leafy place". Before Sedan. Austin Dobson. 6915-0
"Here, it is here - the close of the year". On a spiteful letter. Alfred Lord Tennyson. 6977-0
"Here, let me pause, and breathe awhile...". Percy's Masque, sels. James Abraham Hillhouse. 6752-2
"Here, my Amanda, let us seat ourselves". The beauties of nature. Anthony C. Deane. 6996-7
"Here, not so long ago, the grass grew rank". City growth. Naomi Rogin. 6850-2
"Here, o lily-white lady mine". The handsel ring. George Houghton. 7041-8
"Here, on our native soil, we breathe once". Composed in the valley near Dover, on the day of... William Wordsworth. 6828-6
"Here, Pedro, while I quench these candles". Murillo's trance. Margaret Junkin Preston. 6912-6
"Here, sifting between the reaches of stone". Between reaches of stone. Roberta Holloway. 6808-1
"Here, Stanley, rest! escaped this mortal...". Epitaph on Miss Elizabeth Stanley. James Thomson. 6816-2
"Here, time that was dim years away". The closed room. Mary Peaslee Root. 6750-6
"Here, wandering lone, amid these...fields". Aldborough, fr. The village. George Crabbe. 6934-7
"Here, where I dwell, I waste to skin and bone". Psalm 137. By the waters of Babylon. Bible. 6848-0
"Here, where my fresh-turned furrows run". The settler. Rudyard Kipling. 6810-3
"Here, where of old they sowed...mustard-seed". The ascent. Helen Parry Eden. 6785-9
"Here, where old Nankin glitters". The palace of bric-a-brac. Andrew Lang. 6802-2,6987-8
"Here, where the pale grass struggles with...". A decayed monastery. Thomas Dermody. 6930-4
"Here, where three counties join hands in...". Ivinghow hill. George Robins. 7020-5
"Here, where your garden fenced about and...is". The call of the city. Amy Levy. 6793-X
"Here,/ With my beer" George Arnold. 7041-8
Hereafter. Ronald Lewis Carton. 7027-2
Hereafter. Harriet Prescott Spofford. 6240-7,6600-3
Hereafter. Rosamund Marriott ("Graham R. Tomson") Watson. 6732-8,6656-9
Heredia, Jose Maria de
  Antoine et Cleopatre. 6801-4
  The conquerors. 6351-9
  The flute. Herbert J.C. Grierson (tr.). 6180-X
  In "The Book of loves". 6351-9
  The laborer. Wilfrid Thorley (tr.). 7039-6
  Le lit. 6801-4
  Niagara. 6752-2
  On the cydnus. 6351-9
  Slave. 6351-9
  Sunset. 6351-9,6102-8
  Vision of Khem. 6102-8
Heredia, Jose Ramon
  My poem for the children killed in the war in Spain. Dudley Fitts (tr.). 6759-X
Heredity. Thomas Bailey Aldrich. 6300-4
Heredity. Edward Farquhar. 6939-8
Heredity. Johann Wolfgang von Goethe. 7042-6

Heredity. William Dean Howells. 6102-8,6732-8,6076-5
Heredity. Theda Kenyon. 6732-8
Heredity. Frederick Peterson. 6482-5
Heredity. Lydia Avery Coonley Ward. 6214-8
Herein is love. Susie M. Best. 6066-8
Herendeen, Anne
    Mother. 6097-8
    Revolution. 6880-4
    The stranger. 6880-4
    A true poem. 6880-4
"Heres a jolly couple O the jolly jolly couple." Unknown. 6563-5
Heresy for a class room. Rolfe Humphries. 6527-9
Heresy for a classroom. Rolfe Humphries. 6817-0
Heresy indeed. Sara Henderson Hay. 6532-5
The heretic's tragedy. Robert Browning. 6378-0
The heretic, sels. Louis Untermeyer. 6083-8
The heretic. Bliss Carman. 6730-1
The heretics. William Ellery Leonard. 6880-4
Herford, Beatrice
    The old man. 6449-3
Herford, Oliver
    The audacious kitten. 6699-2
    The bachelor girl. 6652-6
    A bunny romance. 6018-8
    A butterfly of fashion. 6996-7
    The catfish. 6089-7
    Child's natural history. 6861-8
    The chimpanzee. 6501-5
    The cloud. 6089-7
    The cow. 6902-9
    Earth. 6104-4,6583-X
    The elf and the doormouse. 6401-9,6466-3,6132-X,6519-8, 6545-X,6368-3,6639-9,6638-0
    The elf and the dormouse. 6135-4
    The enchanted oak. 6677-1
    Eve. 6736-0
    The fall of J.W. Beane. 7021-3
    Geese. 6300-4
    Godiva. 6440-X
    The hen. 6902-9
    Here lies Bill. 6722-0
    A hopeless case. 6739-5
    Japanesque. 6724-7
    Kitten's night thoughts. 6891-X
    The laughing willow. 6089-7
    Limerick:"..so emlearned M.D.'s. 6308-X,6724-7
    Limerick:"..young lady of Twickenham." 6308-X,6722-0
    Mark Twain: a pipe dream. 6089-7
    Metaphysics. 6902-9
    The milk jug. 6466-3
    A mirror cat. 6699-2
    A modern dialogue. 6652-6
    The mon-goos. 6300-4
    Phylis Lee. 6089-7
    Phyllis Lee. 6089-7
    The platypus. 6902-9
    The poet's proposal. 6641-8,6652-6,6441-8
    Prince Pompom. 6861-8
    The silver question. 6902-9
    The snail's dream. 6466-3
    Some geese. 6902-9
    Song ("Gather kittens"). 6440-X
    A song ("Upon a time"). 6441-8
    A song of a heart. 6440-X
    Stairs. 6722-0
    The strike. 6739-5
    Tell-tale. 6232-6,6338-1
    A Thanksgiving fable. 6401-9,6618-6,6401-9,6519-8,6135-4
    Truth. 6652-6
    War relief. 6089-7
    Why ye blossome cometh before ye leafe. 6047-1
Herford, Will
    That God made. 6880-4
    That God made. 6532-5
    Welfare song. 6880-4
Hergouth, Alois
    "Dreams/prayers" Milne Holton and Herbert Kuhner (tr.). 6769-7

    "Night/has buried the wolves" Milne Holton and Herbert Kuhner (tr.). 6769-7
    "White/is the deeper shade of silence" Milne Holton and Herbert Kuhner (tr.). 6769-7
Heri, cras, hodie. Ralph Waldo Emerson. 6302-0,6385-3,6735-2
Heribert, William
    'Behold thy mother and they brother.' 6636-4
Heritage. Theresa Virginia Beard. 6029-3
Heritage. Laura Helena Brower. 6542-2
Heritage. Naomi E. Buford. 6178-8
Heritage. Douglas Clinton. 6178-8
Heritage. Countee Cullen. 6506-6,6619-4,6039-0
Heritage. Selma Derry. 6039-0
Heritage. Winifred Virginia Jackson. 6036-6
Heritage. Kathleen Merrick. 6258-X
Heritage. Dorothy Paul. 6653-4
Heritage. Josephine Preston Peabody. 6542-2
Heritage. Nancy Byrd Turner. 7038-8
Heritage, sels. Theodore Spencer. 6879-0
The heritage. Abbie Farwell Brown. 6266-0,6473-6
The heritage. Porsteinn Erlingsson. 6854-5
The heritage. James Russell Lowell. 6457-4,6499-X,6219-9, 6304-7,6457-4,6481-7,6407-8,6486-8,6600-3,6732-8, 6964
The heritage. Edward Bliss Reed. 6833-2
Herlozsohn, Carl
    A love test. 6652-6
Herman. Brian Ruona. 6883-9
Hermann and Dorothea. Johann Wolfgang von Goethe. 6679-8
Hermann and Thusnelda. Friedrich Gottlieb Klopstock. 6302-0;6385-3
Hermes genetic. Ben Belitt. 6640-2
Hermes of the lonely hill. Unknown (Greek) 6435-3
Hermes of the playground. Nicias. 6435-3
Hermes of the way. Hilda ("H.D.") Doolittle. 6897-9
Hermes Trismegistus. Hilda ("H.D.") Doolittle. 6210-5
Hermes Trismegistus. Henry Wadsworth Longfellow. 6431-0
Hermia and Helena. William Shakespeare. 6084-6
Hermione. Robert Buchanan. 6219-9
"A hermit (or if 'chance you hold).". The moralizer corrected. William Cowper. 6814-6
The hermit and the king. Sean O'Faolain. 6582-1
"Hermit hoar, in solemn cell". Imitation of the style of [Percy]. Samuel Johnson. 6975-4
The hermit of Niagara. James Abraham Martling. 6952-5
"The hermit on his pillar top". Twin souls. Robert Graves. 6777-8
Hermit thrush. Edna St. Vincent Millay. 6076-5
Hermit thrush. Marie Tudor. 6607-0
A hermit thrush in the catskills. William Griffith. 6073-0
Hermit thrush, fr. Seven movements. Alfred Kreymborg. 6011-0
The hermit thrush. Nelly Hart Woodworth. 6597-X
The hermit thrush. Agnes Kendrick Gray. 6841-3
The hermit thrush. Henry Van Dyke. 6961-4
Hermit's holiday. Molly C. Rodman. 6316-0
"A hermit's house beside a stream". On retirement. Philip Freneau. 6753-0
The hermit's song. Unknown. 6930-4
The hermit.. Sir Walter Raleigh. 6436-1
The hermit. James Beattie. 6219-9,6271-7,6302-0,6385-3, 6600-3
The hermit. George (Mary Ann Cross) Eliot. 6424-8
The hermit. Oliver Goldsmith. 6271-7,6219-9,6518-X
The hermit. Thomas Parnell. 6219-9
The hermit. George William ("A.E.") Russell. 6253-9
The Hermitage, sels. Edward Rowland Sill. 6484-1
A hermitage. John Henry, Cardinal Newman. 6980-0
The Hermitage. Edmund Spenser. 6543-0
Hermocles
    Demeterius enters Athens. John Addington Symonds (tr.). 6435-3
    "See how the mightiest gods, and best-beloved". John Addington Symonds (tr.). 6435-3
Hermocreon
    Water-nymphs. Sir William Marris (tr.). 6435-3
Hermotimus. William Edmonstoune Aytoun. 6437-X
"The hern flew east, the hern flew west". The heron. Unknown. 6829-4

Herndon. Silas Weir Mitchell. 6946-0
Herndon, John G.
   The fairies. 6891-X
   Friendly people. 6891-X
Herndon, Thomas H.
   On the fields of France. 7010-8
Herne, Robert
   Clipped is fancy's wing. 6480-4
Hero and Leander. Thomas Hood. 6974-6
Hero and Leander. Leigh Hunt. 6410-8
Hero and Leander. Christopher Marlowe. 6186-9,6436-1,6536-8,6122-2,6198-2,6250
Hero and Leander. Musaeus. 6251-2
Hero and Leander, sels. George Chapman. 6378-0
Hero and Leander, sels. Christopher Marlowe. 6102-8,6208-3, 6315-2,6586-4,6726-3,6250-4,6430-2,6194-X
Hero entombed, sels. Peter Quennell. 6209-1
A hero in despair. John Milton. 6087-0
A hero in the land of dough. Robert Clairmont. 6722-0
A hero in the land of dough. Robert Clairmont. 6751-4
A hero new. James Russell Lowell. 6708-5
The hero of Bridgewater. Charles L.S. Jones. 6946-0
The hero of Fort Wagner. Phoebe Cary. 6969-X
Hero of his village. Nigel Heseltine. 6360-8
The hero of New Hamburg. Benjamin Franklin Taylor. 6815-4
The hero of the commune. Margaret Junkin Preston. 6916-9
The hero of the commune. Margaret Junkin Preston. 6431-0
The hero of the gun. Margaret Junkin Preston. 6062-5
A hero of the mine. John E. Barrett. 6840-5
The hero of the rank and file. Michael Scanlan. 6680-1
"The hero of the world has ever been". The great physician the doctor- Pasteur. Isabel Fiske Conant. 7014-0
"The hero of/Affairs of love". Quitting again. Horace. 6949-5
"The hero said; and with the torture stung". transformation of Lychas into a rock. John Gay. 6972-X
Hero to Leander. Alfred Lord Tennyson. 6302-0,6385-3,6438-8
Hero wanted. Berton Braley. 6853-7
The hero's death. Felicia Dorothea Hemans. 6973-8
Hero's epitaph. William Shakespeare. 6641-0
Hero's invocation to death. Margaret Tod Ritter. 6619-4
Hero-worship. Juline W. Comstock. 7019-1
Hero-worship. William Bell Scott. 6656-9
A hero.. Florence Earle Coates. 6291-1
The hero.. Ralph Waldo Emerson. 6176-1
A hero. Carolyn Wells. 6882-0
The hero. Ambrose Bierce. 6465-5
The hero. Edmund Vance Cooke. 7019-1
The hero. Geoffrey Drake. 6258-X
The hero. Roy Fuller. 6209-1
The hero. Robert Nicoll. 6656-9
The hero. Sir Henry Taylor. 6669-0,6656-9
Herod. Alice Brooks. 6576-7
Herod and Mariamne. Amelie ("Princess Pierre Troubetzkoy") Rives. 6848-0
"Herod that was both wild and wode". Worship we this holy day, that all innocents for us... Unknown. 6756-5
Herod's lament for Mariamne. George Gordon, 6th Baron Byron. 6945-2,6848-0
Herod, sels. Stephen Phillips. 6046-3,6253-9
Herod, sels. Stephen Phillips. 6501-5
Herodas
   A low trade, fr. Mime. Gilbert Highet (tr.). 6435-3
Herodiade. Stephane Mallarme. 6351-9
Herodiade. Edith Sitwell. 7000-0
Herodias. Arthur O'Shaughnessy. 6250-4
Herodotus
   Timon's epitaph. William Shakespeare (tr.). 6850-2
Herodotus. Frederick William Faber. 6096-X
Heroes. Berton Braley. 6478-7
Heroes. Laurence Housman. 6861-8
Heroes. Edna Dean Proctor. 7041-8
Heroes. Edna Dean Proctor. 6639-9
Heroes. Frances A. Shaw. 6917-7
The heroes and the flowers. Benjamin Franklin Taylor. 6815-4
Heroes of Greece. George Gordon, 6th Baron Byron. 6406-X
"The heroes of Wexford have burst through...". The Wexford insurgent. Unknown (Irish). 6858-8
Heroes of the mines. I. Edgar Jones. 6411-6
Heroes of the south. Paul Hamilton Hayne. 6113-3,6340-3
Heroes of the Titanic. Henry Van Dyke. 6961-4
The heroes of the Yukon. John Augustus Gilkey. 6336-5
The heroes. M. Forrest. 7027-2
The heroes. Frederic Prokosch. 6761-1
The(heroes, Frederic Prokosch. 6783-2
The heroic age. Richard Watson Gilder. 6386-1,6735-2
Heroic ballad 1976. Will Irwin. 6817-0,6732-8
The heroic dead. George D. Emery. 6471-X
The heroic dead. Alfred Noyes. 6151-6
"Heroic good, target for which the young". Faint yet pursuing. Coventry Patmore. 6931-2
Heroic love. James Graham; Marquess of Montrose. 6322-5
A heroic poem, sels. Lynette Roberts. 6360-8
"Heroic spirits! take your rest!". Unknown. 6238-5
Heroic stanzas. John Dryden. 6152-4
Heroic stanzas, sels. John Dryden. 6195-0
Heroic vengeance, fr. Samson Agonistes. John Milton. 6933-9
Heroics. Elinor Wylie. 6036-6
Heroism. William Cowper. 6814-6
Heroism. William Cowper. 6385-3
Heroism. Ralph Waldo Emerson. 6102-8,6302-0,6385-3,6399-3, 6732-8,6252 ,6076-5
Heroism. Thomas Ken. 6337-3
Heroism. Theodore Roosevelt. 6654-2
Heroism. Johann C. Friedrich von Schiller. 6438-8
Heroism ("Whether we climb, whether we plod,") Lizette Woodworth Reese. 6266-0,6337-3,6501-5,6326-8,6214-8
Herold, A.-Ferdinand
   Marozie. 6351-9
   Winter dusk. 6351-9
"Heron is harsh with despair". Song ("Heron is harsh"). Brenda Chamberlain. 6379-9
Heron, Herbert
   To William Vaughn Moody. 6241-5
Heron, Mrs. Hubert ("Australie")
   The explorer's message. 6768-9
   From the Clyde to Braidwood. 6768-9
The heron. Madison Cawein. 7041-8
The heron. Edward Hovell-Thurlow; 2d Baron Thurlow. 6073-0, 6086-2
The heron. Mary Howitt. 6639-9
The heron. Geoffrey Johnson. 6782-4
The heron. Unknown. 6829-4
The heron. Brian Vrepont. 6349-7
Herons. Marie W. Reddy. 6841-3
The herons on Bo Island. Elizabeth Shane. 6073-0
The herons. Francis Ledwidge. 6930-4,6812-X
The herons. Francis Ledwidge. 6253-9,6022-6
The herons. Francis Ledwidge. 6812-X
"Herr Schnitzerl make a philosopede". Schnitzerl's philosopede. Charles Godfrey Leland. 6791-3,6823-5
Herrera S., Demetrio
   Training. Dudley Fitts (tr.). 6759-X
Herrera, Ferdinand de
   Ode on the defeat of King Sebastian of Portugal. Felicia Dorothea Hemans (tr.). 6973-8
Herrick hospital, fifth floor. Al Young. 6792-1
Herrick, Jean
   Time. 6083-8
Herrick, P.E.
   The clerk of the weather. 6290-3
Herrick, Richard
   Miracle, fr. Credo. 6324-1
Herrick, Robert
   The amber bead. 6125-7
   Anacre oink verse. 6732-8
   Anacreontic. 6189-3,6430-2
   Another. 6879-0
   Another grace for a child. 6562-7,6645-3,6194-X
   Another on her. 6194-X
   The apparition of his mistress calling him to Elysium. 6369-1,6733-6
   The argument of his book. 6562-7,6726-3
   The argument of the Hesperides. 6189-3,6543-0
   Argument to Hesperides. 6604-6
   Art above nature. 6827-8

"Attempt the end and never stand to doubt". 6623-2
A Bacchanalian toast. 6724-7
The bad season makes the poet sad. 6430-2
The bag of the bee. 6194-X,6430-2
Bashfulness. 6194-X
The bell-man. 6228-8,6254-7,6512-0,6194-X
The bracelet: to Julia. 6488-4,6194-X,6092-7,6652-6
"But here's the sunset of a tedious day.". 6083-8
The captive bee. 6219-9
Ceremonies for Candlemasse eve. 6334-9,6562-7,6430-2
Ceremonies for Christmas. 6145-1,6239-3,6734-4,6230-X
Ceremonies to the maids. 6747-6
A ceremony for Candlemas day. 6465-5
A charm. 6228-8,6125-7
Charol and Philomel. 6943-6
The cheat of Cupid: or the ungentle guest. 6733-6,6513-9,6383-7
Cherry ripe. 6228-8,6732-8,6198-2,6536-8,6383-7,6189-3, 6197-4,6219-9,6491-4,6723-9
Cherry-pit. 6430-2
Cherry-ripe. 6250-4
"Cherry-ripe, ripe, ripe, I cry". 6187-7
A child's grace. 6533-3
A child's present. 6114-1
Chop-cherry. 6369-1,6562-7,6026-9,6659-3
Christ and we. 6144-3
Christmas carol ("What sweeter music can we bring"). 6334-2,6623-2
A Christmas carol. 6216-4,6334-9,6441-0,6473-6,6143-5, 6747-6,6746-8,6114-1
Christmas echoes. 6272-5
The Christmas pie. 6747-6
Clothes do but cheat and cozen us. 6026-9
Come, bring with a noise. 6747-6,6608-9
Comfort. 6250-4
Comfort to a youth that had lost his love. 6935-5
Comfort to a youth that had lost his love. 6908-8
A conjuration, to Electra. 6194-X
Connubii flores, sels. 6334-9
Corinna's going a-maying. 6052-8,6527-9,6562-7,6732-8, 6102-8,6122-,6154-0,6186-9,6198-2,6385-3,6473-6,6536-,6604-6,6726-3,6733-6,6099-4,6465-5,6723-9,6291-9, 6660-7,6191-5,6197-4,6153-2,6472-8,6250-4,6560-0, 6430-2,6301-2,6194-X,6438-8,6371-3,6646-1,6723-9, 6291-9,6660-7,6191-5,6197-4,6153-2,6472-8,6250-4, 6560-0,6430-2,6301-2,6194-X,6438-8,6371-3,6646-1
Counsel to girls. 6246-6,6737-9
Counsel to virgins. 6481-7
A country life, sel. 6958-4
The country life. 6369-1,6385-3,6194-X,6438-8
Daffodils. 6302-0,6385-3,6018-8,6219-9
The definition of beauty. 6378-0
Delight in disorder. 6099-4,6208-3,6271-7,6315-2,6339-X, 6481-,6488-4,6536-8,6562-7,6563-5,6726-3,6732-8,6543-0,6723-9,6645-3,6219-9,6301-2,6026-9,6659-3,6430-2, 6189-3,6092-7,6250-4,6646-1
The departure of the good daemon. 6378-0
A dialogue between himself and Mistress Eliza... 6874-X
The dirge of Jephthah's daughter. 6848-0
The dirge of Jephthah's daughter. 6271-7,6334-9
Discontents in Devon. 6562-7,6430-2
Divination by a daffadill. 6562-7,6194-X,6189-3
Down with the rosemary and bays. 6747-6
Dreames. 6562-7
Epitaph. 6018-8
"Epitaph on a virgin". 6187-7,6383-7,6737-9
Epitaph upon a child that died. 6186-9,6337-3,6153-2, 6396-9,6737-9
Eternity. 6563-5,6641-0,6726-3
"Fair Daffodils, we weep to see". 6187-7
Fair days. 6369-1
"Fair pleedges of a fruitful tree." 6302-0
The fairies. 6562-7,6252-0
The fairy temple, or Oberon's chapel, sels. 6194-X
Farewell frost, sels. 6558-9
Five wines. 6089-7,6724-7
The four sweet months. 6114-1
Four things make us happy here. 6558-9
Gather ye rosebuds, while ye may. 6560-0
Going a-maying. 6820-0

Going a-Maying. 6322-5
The good-night or blessing. 6026-9
Grace before meat. 6125-7
Grace for a child. 6189-3,6321-7,6430-2,6429-9
Grace for children. 6931-2
A grace. 6179-6
The hag. 6604-6,6219-9,6660-7,6136-2,6228-8,6271-7,6334-9,6562-7
The headache. 6092-7
Here a little child I stand. 6187-7
Hesperides. 6369-1,6723-9
His content in the country. 6562-7
His creed. 6641-0
His desire. 6430-2
His farewell to sack. 6430-2
His grange; or, private wealth. 6105-2,6134-6,6562-7, 6430-2,6194-X
His lachrimae or mirth, turn'd to mourning. 6562-7
His litany to the Holy Spirit. 6194-X,6430-2,6214-8, 6102-8,6562-7,6488-4,6563-5
His parting with Mrs. Dorothy Kennedy. 6369-1
His poetry his pillar. 6208-3,6315-2,6562-7,6369-1,6563-5,6150
His poets. 6297-0
His prayer for absolution. 6931-2,6102-8,6122-2,6198-2, 6337-3
His prayer to Ben Jonson. 6483-3,6562-7,6092-7,6430-2, 6668-2,6189-3
His request to Julia. 6562-7
His returne to London. 6562-7
His tears to Thamesis. 6430-2
His theme. 6250-4,6301-2
His winding-sheet. 6194-X
His wish to God. 6931-2
The hock-cart or harvest home. 6191-5
The hock-cart, or harvest home... 6328-4,6562-7,6194-X, 6430-2
The holy spirit. 6302-0;6385-3
How marigolds came yellow. 6125-7
How roses came red. 6198-2,6125-7,6723-9
How springs came first. 6092-7
How violets came blue. 6194-X
Humility. 6623-2,6424-8
I call and I call. 6125-7
"I dare not ask a kiss". 6187-7
In the hour of my distress. 6337-3
Instead of neat inclosures, fr. An ode of the birth..Saviour. 6125-7
The invitation. 6430-2
Julia. 6240-7
Julia's bed. 6092-7
The kiss. 6302-0,6385-3,6737-9
Kissing and bussing. 6430-2
Lacon and Thyrsis. 6191-5
A lady dying in childbed. 6187-7
Litany to the holy spirit. 6186-9,6271-7,6641-0,6438-8, 6371-3
The litany. 6189-3,6250-4
Loss from the least. 6198-2
Love me little, love me long. 6732-8
Love what it is. 6874-X
Lovers how they come and part. 6317-9
The lyric argument. 6383-7
Lyrick for legacies. 6933-9
The mad maid's song. 6187-7,6634-8,6315-2,6563-5,6562-7, 6164-X,6383-7,6543-0,6668-2,6723-9
The maiden blush. 6874-X
May-day. 6935-5
A meditation for his mistress. 6488-4,6250-4
Moderation. 6194-X
Morning prayer. 6737-9
Mrs. Eliz. Wheeler. 6271-7
Music. 7014-0
Need. 6874-X
The New-Yeere's gift. 6421-3
Night piece. 6271-7,6385-3,6250-4,6189-3,6197-4
The night-piece, to Julia. 6315-2,6187-7,6512-0,6562-7, 6563-5,6726 ,6732-8,6186-9,6102-8,6228-8,6194-X,6102-8,6219-9,6150-8,6645-3,6092-7,6430-2,6301-2,6438-8, 6383-7,6152-3,6543-0,6737-9,6723-9

No coming to God without Christ. 6931-2
No fault in women. 6083-8,6089-7
Noble numbers, sels. 6369-1
Not every day fit for verse. 6562-7,6438-3
Not to love. 6430-2
O years. 6558-9
Oberon's feast. 6634-8,6808-1,6092-7,6430-2
An ode for Ben Jonson. 6122-2,6562-7,6187-7,6315-2,6483-3,6527,6153-2,6189-3,6438-8,6250-4,6645-3
An ode on the birth of our Saviour. 6239-3,6216-4,6145-1,6747-6
Of her breath. 6187-7
The old wives' prayer. 6334-9
On Chloris walking in the snow. 6827-8
On himself. 6641-0,6125-7,6737-9
On Julia's clothes. 6473-6
"Only a little more". 6187-7
A pastoral upon the birth of Prince Charles. 6164-8,6191-5
The pillar of fame. 6732-8
The poet loves a mistress but not to marry. 6026-9
The poetry of dress, sels. 6246-8,6438-8
The poetry of dress. 6246-6,6438-8,6737-9,6560-0
Pray and prosper. 6558-9
Prayer to Ben Jonson. 6385-3,6659-3,6438-8,6023-4
Preface. 6490-6,6143-5
The primrose. 6328-4,6385-3,6219-9,6250-4,6438-8,6092-7,6737-9,6018-8,6271-7,6219-9
A return to London. 6793-X
A ring presented to Julia. 6092-7
The rock of rubies. 6827-8
Serenade. 6935-5
"Shew me that world of stars, and whence". 6532-5
Soft musick. 6562-7
A song to the maskers. 6959-2
The star song. 6239-3,6438-8,6421-3,6558-9
The star-song: a carol to the king. 6931-2
The succession of the four sweet months. 6466-3,6623-2
"A sweet disorder in the dress." 6228-8,6187-7,6302-0,6385-3
"Sweet, be not proud of those two eyes". 6187-7,6302-0,6385-3
Sweetness in sacrifice. 6378-0
ternarie of littles, upom a pipkin of jellies sent... 6092-7,6194-X
A ternarie of littles, upon a pipkin of jellie sent... 6105-2,6722-0,6732-8,6089-7,6369-1
A thankful heart. 6461-2
A thanksgiving to God for his house, sels. 6337-3
A thanksgiving to God for his house. 6543-0,6668-2,6424-8,6219-9,6125-7,6253-9,6808-1,6214-8,6301-2,6023-4,6122-2,6385-3,6102-8,6198-2,6473-6,6634-,6337-3,6488-4,6423-X,6562-7,6418-8,6730-
"Though clock". 6187-7
Time. 6302-0;6385-3
To a child. 6187-7
To a gentlewoman objecting to him his gray hairs. 6369-1
To Anthea. 6378-0,6189-3,6197-4,6226-1
To Anthea ("If deare Anthea, my hard fate it be"). 6562-7
To Anthea ("Now is the time, when all the lights..."). 6562-7
To Anthea, who may command him anything. 6194-X,6430-2,6250-4,6430-2,6301-2,6322-5,6371-3,6094-3,6645-3,6301-2,6099-4,6154-0,6186-9,6246-6,6562-7,6563-,6315-2,6328-4
To be merry. 6383-7
To Ben Jonson. 6102-8,6230-X,6301-2
To blossoms. 6737-9,6189-3,6219-9,6153-2,6438-8,6250-4,6543,6075-7,6187-7,6246-6,6271-7,6315-2,6385,6488-4,6562-7,6563-5,6597-X,6600-3,6733
To carnations. 6092-7
To daffodils. 6737-9,6660-7,6668-2,6645-3,6543-0,6396-9,6639-9,6301-2,6371-3,6152-3,6189-3,6114-1,6150-8,6458-2,6430-2,6250-4,6563-5,6192-3,6194-X,6438-8,6075-7,6134-6,6208-3,6562-7,6099-4,6563-,6099-4,6102-8,6122-2,6133-8,6154-0,6179-,6186-9,6198-2,6228-8,6232-6,6236-9,6239-,6242-3,6246-6,6271-7,6315-2,6328-4,6423-,6459-0,6473-6,6490-6,6536-8,6558-9,6600-,6634-8,6726-3,6732-8,6604-6,6563-5
To daisies. 6099-4,6187-7,6562-7,6737-9,6250-4,6383-
To daisies, not to shut too soon. 6830-8
To death. 6737-9
To Dianeme. 6723-9,6226-1,6219-9,6092-7,6396-9,6250-4,6737-9,6189-3,6083-8,6102-8,6208-3,6246-6,6315-2,6395-,6562-7,6620-8,6634-8
To Electra. 6659-3,6026-9,6092-7,6052-8,6315-2,6733-6,6646-1,6189-3
To finde God. 6730-1
To fortune. 6732-8
To God. 6730-1
To God, on his sickness. 6931-2
To his booke. 6297-0
To his conscience. 6931-2
To his conscience. 6737-9
To his conscience. 6931-2
To his dear god. 6668-2
To his dying brother, Master William Herrick. 6430-2,6472-8
To his honoured kinsman, Sir William Soame. 6106-0
To his lovely mistresses. 6641-0,6430-2
To his maid Prew. 6933-9
To his mistress. 6830-8
To his mistress objecting to his age. 6328-4,6092-7,6737-9
To his muse. 6430-2
To his peculiar friend, Mr. John Wicks. 6092-7
To his saviour, a child; a present by a child. 6216-4,6519-8,6634-8,6734-4,6230-X,6421-
To his sweet saviour. 6194-X
To Julia. 6099-4
To keep a true Lent. 6198-2,6337-3,6600-3,6194-X,6219-9
To Larr. 6106-0
To laurels. 6733-6
To live merrily and to trust to good verses. 6189-3,6194-X,6472-8,6438-8,6230-X,6315-2,6369-1,6562-7,6733-6
To M. Henry Lawes, the excellent composer, of his lyrics. 6430-2
To meadows. 6301-2,6250-4,6383-7,6152-3,6114-1,6023-4,6092-7,6189-3,6668-2,6099-4,6138-9,6179-6,6186-9,6187-7,6232-,6271-7,6315-2,6563-,6563-5,6208-3
To music ("Charm me asleep, and melt me so"). 6122-2
To music, to becalm his fever. 6187-7,6328-4,6562-5,6150-8,6250-4
To musick, to becalme a sweet-sick-youth. 6958-4
To Myrrha, hard-hearted. 6830-8
To Oenone. 6092-7
To Perilla. 6271-7,6536-8,6562-7,6737-9,6194-X
To Phyllis, to love and live with him. 6536-8,6430-2,6191-5,6252-0,6491-4
To primroses filled with morning dew. 6737-9,6660-7,6543-0,6219-9,6018-8,6014-5,6102-8,6423-X,6563-5,6604-6,6187-7,6271-7,6385-3,6562-7
To robin red-brest. 6562-7
To the lark. 6073-0
To the reverend shade of his religious father. 6562-7,
To the rose. 6099-4,6250-4,6189-3,6737-9
To the sour reader. 6430-2
To the virgins, to make much of time. 6430-2,6092-7,6250-4,6513-9,6026-9,6660-7,6723-9,6491-4,6652-6,6646-1,6645-3,6321-7,6396-9,6219-9,6301-2,6226-1,6189-3,6152-3,6194-X,6125-7,6371-3,6052-8,6385-3,6122-2,6315-2,6726-3,6099-,6154-0,6186-9,6198-2,6208-3,6289-X,6339-,6395-0,6429-9,6527-9,6536-8,6562-7,6563-,6604-6,6634-8,6732-8,6187-7
To the water nymphs drinking at the fountain. 6187-7
To the western wind. 6562-7
To the willow tree. 6830-8
To violets. 6186-9,6187-7,6271-7,6369-1,6395-0,6623-,6250-4,6189-3,6424-8
To virgins. 6092-7
A true Lent. 6302-0,6385-3,6465-6,6737-9
Two epitaphs on a child that dies. 6153-2
Upon a child. 6189-3
Upon a child that died. 6189-3,6396-9,6808-1,6250-4,6491-4,6396-9,6808-1,6250-4,6491-4,6228-8,6315-2,6488-4,6533-3,6562-7,6189
Upon a lady that died in child-bed, and left a... 6874-

X
- Upon a maid. 6879-0
- Upon a maid. 6562-7,6125-7,6491-4
- Upon Ben Jonson. 6483-3,6430-2
- Upon her weeping. 6733-6
- Upon himself. 6562-7
- Upon his departure hence. 6052-8,6512-0,6527-9
- Upon his sister in law, mistresse Elizab: Herrick. 6562-7
- Upon his spaniel Tracie. 6733-6,6230-X
- Upon Julia's clothes. 6321-7,6125-7,6150-8,6430-2,6189-3,6194 ,6023-4,6092-7,6491-4,6723-9,6052-8,6122-2, 6154-0,6315-2,6429-9,6488 ,6536-8,6562-7,6732-8,6429-9,6371-3,6645
- Upon Julia's hair filled with dew. 6187-7,6194-X
- Upon Julia's voice. 6106-0,6369-1,6563-5,6733-6,6194-X
- Upon Master Fletchers incomparavle playes. 6483-3
- Upon Mistress Susanna Southwell her feet. 6108-7
- Upon Mr. Ben Jonson. 6430-2
- Upon Prew [or Prue] his maid. 6562-7,6430-2,6197-4,6396-9
- Upon Prudence Baldwin and her sickness. 6430-2
- Upon Sappho sweetly playing and sweetly singing. 6827-8
- Upon Sneape. 6194-X
- Upon some women. 6491-4
- Upon the loss of his mistresses. 6198-2,6378-0,6562-7, 6430-2,6194-X,6189
- Upon time. 6933-9
- The vine. 6733-6
- Violets. 6240-7,6302-0,6385-3
- The Virgin Mary. 6378-0
- The vision to Electra. 6026-9
- The wake. 6194-X
- The wassaile. 6334-9
- The watch. 6491-4
- Weigh me the fire. 6179-6
- When he would have his verses read. 6378-0,6562-7,6430-2
- "Whenas in silks my Julia goes." 6102-8,6187-7,6302-0, 6733-6,6383-7,6250 ,6301-2,6737-9
- The white island. 6271-7,6562-7,6563-5,6737-9,6438-8, 6125 ,6125-7,6197-4
- "White though ye be, yet, lilies, know". 6187-7
- "Why I tie about thy wrist". 6187-7
- The willow garland. 6430-2
- The witch. 6541-4
- "You say I love not, 'cause I do not play". 6187-7

Herrick, Robert (tr.)
- The cheat of Cupid. Anacreon, 6271-7
- The four best things. Unknown (Greek), 6435-3
- "Health is the first good lent to man". Unknown, 6435-3

Herrick, Roy B.
- The bad lands. 6799-9

Herriman, Dorothy Choate
- Orange elf-cups. 6797-2
- Quest. 6797-2
- The spruce tree. 6797-2

Herring is king. Alfred Perceval Graves. 6873-1
Herring is king. Unknown. 6090-0
The herring weir. Sir Charles George Douglas Roberts. 6446-9

Herring, Robert
- Chelsea crypt. 6360-8
- No nice girl's song. 6360-8
- Poem of quietness - 2. 6360-8
- Poem of quietness - 3. 6360-8
- Poem of quietness, sels. 6360-8
- Siege conditions. 6360-8

The herring. Sir Walter Scott. 6089-7
Herrings, fr. Verses made for women who cry apples... Jonathan Swift. 6380-2

Herrmann-Neisse, Max
- Legend of the bewitched nunnery. Babette Deutsch (tr.). 6160-5

Herron, Carl Vinton
- I know a road. 6335-7

Herron, George D.
- Make the world a home. 6335-7

Herschberger, Ruth
- The body. 6390-X
- Coup d'Etat. 6390-X
- Hymn to texture. 6390-X
- Nature poem. 6390-X
- Page torn from a note-book. 6390-X
- Promise. 6390-X
- Promise ("Promise has turned its back..."). 6390-X

Herschell, William
- The kid has gone to the colors. 6846-4,6443-4
- The old gang on the corner. 6846-4
- <u>The service flag.</u> 6443-4,6449-3,6964-9,6846-4
- The soldier of the silences. 6449-3

"Hersel pe highland shentleman". The turnimspike. Unknown. 6859-6
<u>Herself a rose who bore the rose.</u> Christina Georgina Rossetti. 6282-2
Herself and him. Patrick Joseph McCall. 6090-0;6714-X
Herself and myself. Patrick J. MacCall. 6090-0

Hersey, F.W.C.
- Triolet. 6118-4

Hersey, Marie Louise
- Country road. 6798-0
- Country road. 6762-X

Hershberger, L. L.
- Beauty. 6818-9

Herskovits, Frances (tr.)
- Dahomean song for the dead. Unknown, 6879-0

Hertel, Sheila
- Heartbreak. 6883-9
- Tomorrow's dream. 6883-9
- "Yellow light" 6883-9

Hertha. Algernon Charles Swinburne. 6110-9,6196-6,6102-8, 6655-0,6656-9,6122-2,6657-7,6199-0,6430-2,6560-0, 6508
Hertha, sels. Algernon Charles Swinburne. 6198-2,6543-0
Herve Riel. Robert Browning. 6183-4,6228-8,6239-3,6271-7, 6294-6,6331-,6110-9,6424-8,6419-1,6371-3,6322-5,6267 ,6332-2,6344-6,6370-5,6385-3,6395-0,6406-,6155-9, 6192-3,6250-4,6421-3,6573-2,6219 ,6427-2,6473-6,6478-7,6479-5,6504-X,6550-,6552-X,6621-6

Hervey, John Kebble
- Eve at the fountain. 6848-0
- Jerusalem. 6848-0
- Mount Carmel. 6848-0

Hervey, Thomas Kibble
- "Adieu, adieu! our dream of love." 6302-0;6385-3
- Cleopatra at Actium. 6424-8
- Cleopatra embarking on the Cydnus. 6102-8
- The convict ship. 6980-0
- The devil at home, fr. The devil's progress. 6996-7
- The dying Hebrew. 6848-0
- Epitaph. 6600-3
- The grotto of Egeria. 6102-8
- Homes and graves. 6980-0
- Hope. 6980-0
- "I am all alone and the visions that play". 6980-0
- I think of thee. 6656-9
- Love. 6302-0;6385-3
- "Slumber lie soft on thy beautiful eye". 6980-0
- Stanzas to a lady. 6980-0
- The temple of Jupiter Olympius, at Athens. 6980-0
- To Mary. 6980-0
- To Myra. 6980-0
- A vision of the stars. 6980-0

Herzberg, Max J.
- The midnight ferry. 6327-6

Herzel, Catherine Williams
- Sacrament. 6335-7

Herzele, Margarethe
- The day after tomorrow. Milne Holton and Herbert Kuhner (tr.). 6769-7
- The last snowflake. Milne Holton and Herbert Kuhner (tr.). 6769-7
- March moon-night. Milne Holton and Herbert Kuhner (tr.). 6769-7
- Mother chaos. Milne Holton and Herbert Kuhner (tr.). 6769-7
- On the banks of the Chang. Milne Holton and Herbert Kuhner (tr.). 6769-7

Herzing, Albert (tr.)
- Vultures, sel. Joyce Mansour, 6803-0

Heseltine, Nigel
    At first. 6360-8
    Barter our northern darkness. 6360-8
    Epithalamion. 6360-8
    The four-cornered tower: Llaynbri. 6360-8
    Gorse. 6360-8
    Hero of his village. 6360-8
    Microcosmos, sels. 6379-9
    Wanderer's night song. 6360-8

Hesiod
    The ages of man. Sir William Marris (tr.). 6435-3
    "And by her side went Eros, and Passion...". F.L. Lucas (tr.). 6251-2
    Autumn. F.L. Lucas (tr.). 6251-2
    Autumn ploughing. F.L. Lucas (tr.). 6251-2
    "Bid him to dine that loves thee, leave him...". F.L. Lucas (tr.). 6251-2
    Cicada days, fr. The farmer's year. T.F. Higham (tr.). 6435-3
    Combat of Heracles and Cycnus. Sir William Marris (tr.). 6435-3
    The dance of the muses. 6959-2
    "Drink deep when the winejar's opened...". F.L. Lucas (tr.). 6251-2
    "Earth bare the long-ridged mountains...". F.L. Lucas (tr.). 6251-2
    Eoiae, sels. 6435-3
    "Evil to choose is easy, of her thou canst find...". F.L. Lucas (tr.). 6251-2
    The fall of man and the early ages of the earth. F.L. Lucas (tr.). 6251-2
    The farmer's year, sels. 6435-3
    "First, of the Heliconian Muses be my song". F.L. Lucas (tr.). 6251-2
    The five ages. Jack Lindsay (tr.). 6435-3
    "For it is the Archer Apollo, and the Muses...". F.L. Lucas (tr.). 6251-2
    Giving and taking. Sir William Marris (tr.). 6435-3
    Good days and bad. Sir William Marris (tr.). 6435-3
    Length of life. Sir William Marris (tr.). 6435-3
    Light-footed Iphiclus. Sir William Marris (tr.). 6435-3
    Marriage. Jack Lindsay (tr.). 6435-3
    Might and right. Sir William Marris (tr.). 6435-3
    The muses' gift. Jack Lindsay (tr.). 6435-3
    Neighbours and kinsfolk. Sir William Marris (tr.). 6435-3
    "One carpenter hates another, potter hates potter...". F.L. Lucas (tr.). 6251-2
    Pandora. Jack Lindsay (tr.). 6435-3
    Plain living. Sir William Marris (tr.). 6435-3
    Precepts of Chiron, sels. Sir William Marris (tr.). 6435-3
    Sailing weather, fr. The farmer's year. Samuel Butler (tr.). 6435-3
    Shame. Sir William Marris (tr.). 6435-3
    The sign of the pleiads, fr. The farmer's year. T.F. Higham (tr.). 6435-3
    "A small ship-thou mayst praise her...". F.L. Lucas (tr.). 6251-2
    Spending and sparing. Sir William Marris (tr.). 6435-3
    The spring called parthenius. Sir William Marris (tr.). 6435-3
    Spring plowing. F.L. Lucas (tr.). 6251-2
    Summer. F.L. Lucas (tr.). 6251-2
    "Take care to keep thy name untouched of ill report". F.L. Lucas (tr.). 6251-2
    Theogony, sels. 6435-3
    "To spirits thrice ten thousand by God's will...". F.L. Lucas (tr.). 6251-2
    A visitation. Sir William Marris (tr.). 6435-3
    "Wed, above all, a woman that dwells not far away". F.L. Lucas (tr.). 6251-2
    When the crane flies south, fr. The farmer's year. Jack Lindsay (tr.). 6435-3
    When the snail climbs, fr. The farmer's year. Samuel Butler (tr.). 6435-3
    Wholesome strife. Sir William Marris (tr.). 6435-3
    Winter. F.L. Lucas (tr.). 6251-2
    Winter, fr. The farmer's year. T.F. Higham (tr.). 6435-3
    Works and days, sels. 6435-3
    Zeus and the titans. Jack Lindsay (tr.). 6435-3

Hesiod, 1908. Alexander Mair. 6845-6
Hesiod, sels. Homer. 6435-3
Hesiod; or, the rise of woman. Thomas Parnell. 6975-4
The **hesitant** heart. Winifred Welles. 6653-4
Hesitation. William Shakespeare. 6438-8
Hesketh, Phoebe
    The fox. 6257-1
Hesper. Henry Van Dyke. 6961-4
"**Hesper**, thou golden light...". Bion. 6251-2
Hesperia. John Payne. 7015-9
Hesperia. Algernon Charles Swinburne. 6437-X,6732-8,6656-9
Hesperia, sels. Richard Henry Wilde. 6077-3
Hesperides. Thomas Bailey Aldrich. 6121-4
Hesperides. Robert Herrick. 6369-1,6723-9
Hesperides. Harry Kemp. 6374-8
Hesperothen. Andrew Lang. 6771-9
Hesperus. George Gordon, 6th Baron Byron. 6153-2
Hesperus. Charles Sangster. 6433-7
Hesperus. James Stephens. 6244-X,6253-9
Hesperus. William Wordsworth. 6383-7
Hesperus sings, fr. The bride's tragedy. Thomas Lovell Beddoes. 6656-9
Hesperus the bringer. Sappho. 7039-6
Hesperus' song, fr. Cynthia's revels. Ben Jonson. 6239-3
Hesperus's hymn to Cynthia. Ben Jonson. 6315-2
Hesperus, fr. Lyra Modulata. Sir Ronald Ross. 6234-2
Hess, Eliazbeth Guion
    After the holidays. 6799-9
Hess, M. Whitcomb
    The vision of St. Bernard. 6282-2
Hess, Naomi Reynolds
    Story time. 6750-6
Hess. M. Whitcomb
    Odyssey, sixth book. 6839-1
Hesse, Hermann
    Alone. 6643-7
    Books. 6643-7
    Flower, tree, and bird. 6643-7
    Night. 6643-7
    Spring day. 6643-7
    Spring song. Ludwig Lewisohn (tr.). 7039-6
    There are times. 6643-7
    Transition. 6643-7
    Youth's flight. 6643-7
Hester. Charles Lamb. 6385-3,6246-6,6315-2,6600-3,6250-4, 6301-2,6092-7,6086-2,6737-9,6641-0
Hester. Lizette Woodworth Reese. 6653-4
Hester, William
    The lost. 6017-X
    Ode for daybreak. 6761-1
Hester, sels. Charles Lamb. 6317-9
"**Hestia, wherever homes shelter**...". Homer. 6435-3
Hetaira. John Galsworthy. 6888-X
A **heterodoxy**. Edward John Plunkett, 18th Baron Dunsany. 6930-4
A **heterodoxy**. Edward John Plunkett, 18th Baron Dunsany. 6648-8
Hetherington, B.H.M.
    The clerk. 6846-4
    The clerk. 6589-9
Hetty and the fairies. Matthias Barr. 6131-1
Hetty McEwen; or, the brave woman of Nashville. Lucy H. Hooper. 6403-5
"**Heu inimicitias quoties parit aemula forma**". Idem Latine redditum. William Cowper. 6814-6
Heu! quam remotus. William Cowper. 6814-6
"**Heureux** adolescents dont le coeur s'ouvre...". Don Juan. Theophile Gautier. 6801-4
'**Heureux** qui comme Ulysse...' John Streeter Manifold. 6666-6,6665-8
"**Hew** hard the marble from the mountain's heart". John Ford. Algernon Charles Swinburne. 7015-9
"'**Hew me'**, quoth he, 'a bowl'.". The bowl. Walter Clarke Rodman. 6936-3
The **hewel**, or woodpecker, fr. Upon Arlington house. Andrew Marvell. 6125-7
Hewins, Caroline M.
    The troll-man. 6921-5

Hewitt, Andrew
   Sailor's will. 6750-6
Hewitt, Arthur Wentworth
   The men of Windsor. 7030-2
Hewitt, Ethel M.
   Bois-etoile. 7027-2
   Heart's tide. 6027-7
Hewitt, John
   The creation of man. 6920-7
   Load. 6930-4
   The prayer in battle. 6920-7
Hewitt, Kathleen
   Intrusion. 6659-3
Hewitt, Luisa
   Secrets. 6466-3
Hewitt, Mary E.
   A yarn. 6911-8
Hewitt, R.M. (tr.)
   "Do you not see, beloved?" Vladimir Solovyev, 6103-6
   "Fronting amazed Cythera grows" Alexander Pushkin, 6103-6
   Lullaby in undertones. Fedor Sologub, 6103-6
   "O fields of corn, o fields of corn" Sergei Esenin, 6103-6
   "Once in the misty dawn with timid foot" Vladimir Solovyev, 6103-6
   Remembrances. Alexander Pushkin, 6103-6
   Silentium. Feodor Ivanovich Tyutchev, 6103-6
Hewitt, R.W. (tr.)
   "Whispering. A timid sigh" Afanasi Fet, 6103-6
Hewlett, Maurice
   Dirge. 6872-3
   Flos Virginum. 6102-8,6301-2
   The Fourth of July, 1776. 7027-2
   In the trenches. 7026-4
   Night-errantry. 6102-8
   Rosa nascosa. 6437-X
   Soldier, soldier. 6474-4
Hewlett, Maurice (tr.)
   The Achilles' reply to the embassy. Homer, 6435-3
   Hektor and Andromache, fr. The Iliad. Homer, 6435-3
   "Hektor turn'd", fr. The Iliad. Homer, 6435-3
   "Not then", fr. The Iliad. Homer, 6435-3
   "Now all sat down", fr. The Iliad. Homer, 6435-3
   Sarpedon and Glaucus, fr. The Iliad. Homer, 6435-3
   "Then swift Achilles answer'd...", fr. The Iliad. Homer, 6435-3
   Thersites, fr. The Iliad. Homer, 6435-3
Hexameter and Pentameter. Unknown. 6125-7
Hexameters, sels. Samuel Taylor Coleridge. 6395-0
Hexametra alexis in laudem rosamundi. Robert Greene. 6182-6
Hext, Marion J.
   The jewels. 6799-9
"'Hey c-9758'/'what'/". Inside a prison cell at count time. Daniel L. Klauck. 6870-7
"Hey diddle, dinkety, pottery, pet." Unknown. 6452-3
"Hey girl, how long you been here?". Motown/Smokey Robinson. Jessica Hagedorn. 6790-5
Hey nonny no! Unknown. 6182-6,6187-7,6315-0,6733-6,6189-3, 6328-4,6125-7
"Hey! diddle diddle/The cat and the fiddle." Mother Goose. 6363-2,6452-3,6466-3
"Hey! Jock, are ye glad ye listed?" Neil Munro. 7031-0
"Hey! little evergreens". The little fir-trees. Evaleen Stein. 6964-9
"Hey! my little yellow-bird". The yellow-bird. James Whitcomb Riley. 6993-2
"Hey! now the day daws". Aubade. Alexander Montgomerie. 6830-8
"Hey! now, now, now". Welcome! our messiah. Unknown. 6881-2
Hey, Wilhelm
   God supreme. James Abraham Martling (tr.). 6952-5
Hey, boy! Alexander Young. 6178-8
"Hey, hain't ye heerd o' thet Sp'it o' St...". St. Louie. L.S. Cooper. 7019-1
Hey, hey, hey, hey, the boar's head is armed gay. Unknown. 6756-5
"Hey, ho, dance away,/Dance away!". Maliseet indian dance-song. Unknown. 6959-2
"Hey, I've found some moneywort". Kids. Witter Bynner. 6891-X,6887-1
"Hey, laddie, hark to the merry, merry lark!". The skylark's song. John Bennett. 6820-0
Hey, lads. Viktor Klebnikov. 6546-5
"Hey, my kitten, my kitten." Mother Goose. 6452-3
Hey, nonny! Charles Kingsley. 6437-X
"Hey, old midsummer! are you here again". An old friend. James Whitcomb Riley. 6993-2
Hey, the dusty miller. Robert Burns. 6805-7
"Hey, there! Are you selectman Brown?". Walton's Vermont register. Daniel L. Cady. 6989-4
"Hey, Walt, you/should see these lilacs. Wild". Late spring, sur coast. Naomi Clark. 6792-1, 6998-3
Heydt, Herman A.
   The twain. 6799-9
Heyduk, Adolf
   New gypsy melodies, sels. Paul Selver (tr.). 6763-8
Heyerdahl, Vivian
   Weather wisdom. 6799-9
Heyl, Friedrika
   At sundown. 6253-9
Heym, Georg
   The demons of the cities. Babette Deutsch (tr.). 6160-5
   Evening. Babette Deutsch (tr.). 6160-5
   Moon. Babette Deutsch (tr.). 6160-5
Heynicke, Kurt
   At midnight. Babette Deutsch (tr.). 6160-5
   Exaltation. Babette Deutsch (tr.). 6160-5
   Gethsemane. Babette Deutsch (tr.). 6160-5
   Observation post. Babette Deutsch (tr.). 6160-5
Heyst-sur-mer. Richard Middleton. 6102-8,6301-2
Heyward, DuBose
   Alternatives. 6038-2
   Black Christmas. 6038-2,6326-8
   The blockader. 6326-8
   Dusk. 6619-4,6036-6,6326-8
   Dusk in the low country. 6102-8,6076-5
   Edgar Allan Poe. 6036-6
   Envoy. 6393-4
   Epitaph for a poet. 6501-5,6326-8
   The equinox. 6102-8,6628-3
   Evening in the great Smokies. 6326-8
   Gamesters all. 6326-8
   I stumbled upon happiness. 6326-8
   The mountain girl. 6326-8,6393-4
   The mountain graveyard. 6036-6
   The mountain town. 6037-4
   The mountain woman. 6619-4,6326-8
   New England landscape. 6038-2
   Pirate legend. 6038-2
   Prodigal. 7017-5
   A yoke of steers. 6506-6,6619-4,6518-4,6326-8
   Your gifts. 6538-4,6326-8
Heyward, Janie Screven
   Autumn leaves. 6036-6
Heywood, Delia A.
   A-soak in 'wum barrels'. 6927-4
   As seen in later years. 6927-4
   What would I be. 6684-4
Heywood, Jasper
   "If thou in surety safe wilt sit". 6181-8
   Look ere you leap. 6182-6,6328-4
   Who mindes to bring..., fr. The Paradise of Dainty... 6586-4
Heywood, John
   "Alas! by what mean may I make ye to know" 6182-6
   "Art thou Heywood with the mad mery wit" 6380-2
   Biyng a pyg. 6586-4
   Cardinal Fisher. 6022-6
   The cuckoo's voice. 6105-2
   The English schoolboy. 6022-6
   Epigrams. 6022-6
   A fooles tounge. 6586-4
   The foure PP. 6193-1
   The gloria patri. 6022-6
   How God will not do for vs. 6586-4
   If love, for love of long time had. 6182-6
   Of a cattes looke. 6586-4

HEYWOOD

Of a sheepes iye. 6586-4
Of byrdes and byrders. 6586-4
Of common medlers. 6586-4
Of enough and a feast. 6586-4
Of Heywood. 6586-4
Of louing a dog. 6586-4
Of nothing and althing. 6586-4
On the Princess Mary. 6436-1
The palmer. 6022-6
The portrait. 6438-8
A praise of his lady. 6182-6,6586-4,6092-7,6092-7,6182-6
A praise of Princess Mary, sels. 6188-5
A praise of Princess Mary. 6188-5
Tyburn and Westminster. 6022-6
Wedding and hanging. 6586-4

Heywood, Terence
By an ant-heap. 6788-3
Cactus. 6788-3
A flamingo's egg. 6788-3
Grisaille. 6788-3
Mantis. 6788-3
Notes for a bestiary. 6389-6

Heywood, Thomas
Annan water. 6134-6
The author to his booke. 6933-9
A challenge for beauty, sels. 6317-9
The cherubim, sels. 6730-1
The cries of Rome, fr. The rape of Lucrece. 6334-9
An epigram upon his majestie's great ship... 6547-3
Go, pretty birds! 6198-2,6129-9
Good morrow. 6490-6,6604-6,6099-4,6600-3,6026-9,6660 , 6153-2,6197-4,6219-9
Greetings to my love. 6827-8
Hence with passion, sighs and tears. 6563-5
Hierarchie of the Blessed Angel. 6730-1
Hymn to Diana ("Hail, beauteous Dian, queen of shades") 6182-6
Love's ecstasy. 6827-8
Matin song. 6339-X,6625-9
The message. 6328-4,6092-4,6649-6
Morning. 6075-7,6639-9
A morning song. 6134-6
The nations. 6092-7
Pack, clouds, away. 6073-0,6182-6,6302-0,6385-3,6620-8, 6271 ,6250-4,6189-3,6194-X,6189-3,6252-0,6371 ,6073-0,6423-X,6182-6,6726-3,6328-4,6395 ,6652-6,6668-2, 6737-9,6181-8,6187-7,6228-8,6246-6,6597-X,6732
The passing bell. 6563-5
Phillis. 6191-5
Praise of Ceres. 6182-6,6182-6,6306-3
The princes in the tower. 6188-5
Psyche. 6250-4
The rape of Lucrece, sels. 6317-9,6378-0,6726-3
The search for God. 6271-7,6385-3,6600-3,6337-3
"She that denies me, I would have." 6317-9
Song of Ceres, Proserpine, swains & country wenches. 6334-9
Song of the bell. 6189-3
To Phyllis. 6099-4
Ye little birds that sit and sing. 6182-6,6250-4,6383-7, 6153-2

Hezekiah's art. Joseph Crosby Lincoln. 6119-2
Hezekiah's Thanksgiving. George Wither. 6848-0
"Hi and whoop-hooray, boys!". On the sunny side. James Whitcomb Riley. 6993-2,6990-8
"Hi! another one! What's all the world about?". What Santa Claus thinks. Unknown. 6807-3
"Hi-ho, hi-ho!/Off to war we go." Unknown. 6237-7
Hi-spy. Eugene Field. 6785-9,6834-0;6949-5
"Hi-yo, the boatsmen row". Unknown. 6299-7
Hialmar and the Aasvogel. Roy Campbell. 6800-6

Hiatt, Ben
David's poem. 6792-1, 6998-3
Folsom. 6792-1, 6998-3

Hiatus. Lionel Wiggam. 6640-2
Hiawatha and Mudjekeewis, fr. The song of Hiawatha. Henry Wadsworth Longfellow. 6288-1
Hiawatha and the pearl-feather, fr. The song of Hiawatha. Henry Wadsworth Longfellow. 6018-8
Hiawatha's brothers. Henry Wadsworth Longfellow. 6466-3, 6510-4
Hiawatha's chickens. Henry Wadsworth Longfellow. 6466-3, 6510-4
Hiawatha's childhood. Unknown. 6134-6
Hiawatha's childhood, fr. The song of Hiawatha. Henry Wadsworth Longfellow. 6105-2,6127-3,6479-5,6132-X, 6242-3,6176 ,6008-0,6288-1,6121-4,6639-9,6454-X,6623
Hiawatha's departure, fr. The song of Hiawatha. Henry Wadsworth Longfellow. 6753-0
Hiawatha's departure, fr. The song of Hiawatha. Henry Wadsworth Longfellow. 6288-1
Hiawatha's departure, fr. The song of Hiawatha. Henry Wadsworth Longfellow. 6753-0
Hiawatha's fasting. Henry Wadsworth Longfellow. 6396-9
Hiawatha's fasting, fr. The song of Hiawatha. Henry Wadsworth Longfellow. 6753-0
Hiawatha's fishing, fr. The song of Hiawatha. Henry Wadsworth Longfellow. 6228-8,6496-5,6552-X,6008-0
Hiawatha's friends, fr. The song of Hiawatha. Henry Wadsworth Longfellow. 6496-5
Hiawatha's hunting. Unknown. 6134-6
Hiawatha's photographing. Charles Lutwidge ("Lewis Carroll") Dodgson. 6802-2
Hiawatha's photographing. Charles Lutwidge ("Lewis Carroll") Dodgson. 6290-3
Hiawatha's sailing. Unknown. 6134-6
Hiawatha's sailing, fr. The song of Hiawatha. Henry Wadsworth Longfellow. 6105-2,6466-3,6496-5,6623-2, 6288-1,6107-9,6121-4,6639-9
Hiawatha's wooing, fr. The song of Hiawatha. Henry Wadsworth Longfellow. 6014-5,6402-7,6585-6,6288-1, 6121-4
Hiawatha, sels. Henry Wadsworth Longfellow. 6077-3,6616-X, 6254-7,6289-X,6315-2,6484
Hiawathian. Unknown. 6700-X
The Hibakusha's letter. David Mura. 6790-5

Hibben, Pax P.
Ruy Blas. 6983-5
The song of the hammock. 6983-5
Triolets. 6983-5

"Hibiscus was red". Red. Charles Ould. 6800-6
"Hibiscus/In the basement my mother tended". Translations. Patricia Y. Ikeda. 6790-5
"Hic etiam jacet". Epitaphium alterum. William Cowper. 6814-6
Hic jacet. Louise Chandler Moulton. 7041-8
Hic jacet. Louise Chandler Moulton. 6300-4,6309-8,6431-0
Hic jacet qui in hoc saeculo fideliter militavit. Sir Henry Newbolt. 7027-2
"Hic vir, hic est". Charles Stuart Calverley. 6200-8,6092-7
"Hiccup, hiccup, go away!" Unknown. 6904-5
"Hiccup, snicup". Unknown. 6904-5

Hichens, R.S.
The sacrifice of genius. 6681-X

"Hick-a-more, hack-a-more". Unknown. 6904-5
"Hick-tee-dik!".. James Whitcomb Riley. 6091-9
"Hickety, pickety, my black hen". Mother Goose. 6363-2

Hickey, Agnes MacCarthy
Disdain. 6818-9
Journeys. 6818-9

Hickey, Emily Henrietta
A ballad of St. Swinthin's day. 6424-8
Beloved, it is morn. 6096-X,6292-X,6172-9,6656-9
Emperor evermore. 6046-3
A gift. 6174-5
Harebells. 7037-X,6046-3
His home and his own country. 6090-0
Madonna Della Vita. 7037-X
Per te ad lucem. 6174-5
A sea story. 6172-9,6518-X,6656-9,6292-X
The ship from Tirnanoge. 6090-0
Song ("Beloved"). 6437-X
To one stricken and smitten. 6174-5

Hickler, Rosalie
Prayer for any occasion. 6490-6
A prayer for love. 6461-2

Hickman, Mildred Evadne
Life goes on. 6799-9

Hickory, dickory, dock. Alethea Chaplin. 6937-1
"**Hickory**, dickory, dock/The mouse ran up the clock."
  Mother Goose. 6362-2,6452-3,6466-3
The **hickory-nut**. Grace O. Kyle. 6529-5
Hickox, Chauncey
  Killed at Fredericksburg. 6113-3
Hicks, Mabel
  Crosses. 6449-3
Hicks, Seymour
  Limerick:"..young lady of Zenda". 6811-1
Hicks, William
  Of his mistress grown old. 6563-5
Hickson, William Edward
  "Nor on this land alone." 6337-3
  Try again. 6356-X,6459-0,6497-3,6638-0
Hicky, Daniel Whitehead
  Endings. 6841-3
  Fog off Brunswick Sound. 6783-2
  For a poet's bride. 6841-3
  Inscription for a sundial. 6841-3,6780-8
  Little men. 6761-1
  Marsh twilight. 6841-3
  Only the living. 6761-1
  Prayer for a garden. 6649-6
  Rainy night. 6750-6
  Requiem for a young poet. 6782-4
  Say that he loved old ships. 6841-3,6833-2
  Silence. 6761-1
  Small song. 6337-3
  Snowstorm. 6396-9
  Song ("I have seen a thousand"). 6761-1
  The victors. 6782-4
  War has its day. 6761-1
  We with our vanities. 6841-3
  Wildflowers. 6042-0
Hicky, Daniel William
  Words before twilight. 6850-2
Hidden. S.T. Livingston. 6116-8
Hidden. Ffrida Wolfe. 6638-0
Hidden beauty. Isabelle Ruby Owen. 6799-9
Hidden brightness. Unknown. 6915-0
Hidden cities 001. Italo Calvino. 6758-1
Hidden great. James Abraham Martling. 6952-5
A **hidden** hand--somewhere. Alfred Jennings Funnell. 6799-9
Hidden joys. Laman Blanchard. 6656-9
Hidden joys. S.L. Blanchard. 6793-X
Hidden life. Louis J. Magee. 7004-3
The **hidden** life. William Cowper. 6814-6
The **hidden** love. Arthur Hugh Clough. 6110-9,6560-0
"**Hidden** lovers' woes". His own true wife. Sir Wolfram von Eschenbach. 7039-6
The **hidden** path; or, the Atlantic cable. Elizabeth H.J. Cleaveland. 6578-3
Hidden paths. Francis Carey ("Jan van Avond") Slater. 6800-6
The **hidden** place. Stephen Vincent Benet. 6253-9
The **hidden** purpose. Alfred Lord Tennyson. 6461-2
A **hidden** rhythm. Eda Lou Walton. 6038-2
The **hidden** rill. Unknown. 6523-6
The **hidden** songster. Unknown. 6373-X
Hidden sorrow. Phoebe Cary. 6969-X
The **hidden** sorrow. Georgios Vizinos. 6352-7
"**Hidden** springs were playing music and my day". Nature. Otakar Brezina. 6763-8
"A **hidden** strength/Which is heav'n gave it...". Chastity, fr. Comus. John Milton. 6933-9
The **hidden** tide. Roderick Quinn. 6784-0
Hidden treasure. Frank Oliver Call. 6797-2
The **hidden** weaver. Odell Shepard. 6730-1
The **hidden** years. Allen Eastman Cross. 6144-3
Hide and go seek. Henry Cuyler Bunner. 6260-1
Hide and seek. Alice Cary. 6060-9
Hide and seek. Julia Goddard. 6913-4
Hide and seek. Frank Dempster Sherman. 6311-X
Hide and seek. Henry Van Dyke. 6961-4
Hide in the heart. Lloyd Frankenburg. 6389-6
"**Hide** this one night thy crescent, kindly moon". To the moon. Pierre de Ronsard. 6771-9
"**Hide**, Absolon, thy gilte tresses clere". Ballade to his lady. Geoffrey Chaucer. 6830-8

The **hiders'** song, fr. John Brown's body. Stephen Vincent Benet. 6217-2
Hiding. Dorothy Aldis. 6891-X
"**Hiding** in the church of an abandoned stone". Confession to J. Edgar Hoover. James Wright. 6803-0
Hiding the skeleton, fr. Modern love. George Meredith. 6656-9
Hie away. Sir Walter Scott. 6086-2,6110-9,6421-3,6424-8, 6252-0,6242-3,6466-3,6512-0,6519-8,6623-2
"**Hie** upon the hielands". Ballad ("Hie upon hielands.") Unknown. 6179-6
"**Hie**, hie, says Anthony". Unknown. 6904-5
"**Hier** il m'a semble (sans doute j'etais ivre)". Choc de cavaliers. Theophile Gautier. 6801-4
Hierarchie of the Blessed Angel. Thomas Heywood. 6730-1
Hieroglyphica. Wallace Stevens. 6751-4
Hierusalem. Unknown. 6436-1
Higbee, Alma Robison
  Beyond. 6761-1
Higbee, F.F.
  Thy glory thou didst manifest. 6304-7
Higgins, Annie
  The acquired art. 6037-4
  Waking. 6880-4
Higgins, Frederick Robert
  The ballad of O'Bruadir. 6833-2
  The dark breed. 6072-2
  A dead craftsman. 6779-4
  Father and son. 6985-1
  The gallows tree. 6930-4
  Illan-na-gila. 6781-6
  Old Galway. 6096-X,6070-6,6096 X,6096-X,6070-6,6096 X
  The old jockey. 6246-6
  The old wine. 6785-9
  Padraic O'Conaire - Gaelic storyteller. 6483-3
  Radraic O'Conaire, Gaelic storyteller. 6483-3
  Song for the clatter bones. 6052-8,6324-1,6324-1
  Song for the clatter-bones. 6930-4
Higgins, Helen
  The birth of woman. 6396-9
Higgins, John
  Books. 6385-3
Higgins, John Lee
  Growth. 6232-6
Higginson, Ella
  Beggars. 6309-8
  Four-leaf clover. 6047-1,6476-0,6529-5,6274-1,6498-1
  A helping hand. 6682-8
  'Jest a-thinkin' o' you.' 6687-9
  The sweet low speech of the rain. 6374-8
Higginson, Mary Thacher
  Housed. 6097-8
  Inheritance. 6309-8
  The playmate hours. 6321-7
  Reprieve. 6097-8
Higginson, Mrs. Thomas Wentworth
  The playmate hours. 6321-7,6429-9
Higginson, Thomas Wentworth
  Autumn leaves. 6049-8
  Decoration. 6263-6,6431-0
  Heirs of time. 7009-4,6954-1
  The playmate hours. 6429-9
  Rabiah's defense. 6610-0
  'Since Cleopatra died.' 6431-0
  Sixty and six. 6424-8
  The snowing of the pines. 6047-1,6239-3,6253-9,6309-8
  Sonnet from Petrarch. 6429-9,6321-7
  Thankful for all. 6303-9,6461-2
  The trumpeter. 6386-1,6250-4,6309-8
  Two lessons. 6632-1
Higgleby, piggleby. Mother Goose. 6466-3,6262-8
"**Higgledy** piggledy". Unknown. 6904-5
Higgley Piggley. Unknown. 6904-5
"**High** above all a cloth of state...", fr. The...queen. Edmund Spenser. 6726-3
"**High** above hate I dreww:/O storms! farewell". Sanctuary. Lilla Cabot Perry. 6861-8
"**High** among the lonely hills",fr. The saint's tragedy. Charles Kingsley. 6123-0
"**High** and inscrutable...", fr. Don Juan. George Gordon,

HIGH

  6th Baron Byron. 6726-3
High and low. James H. Cousins. 6930-4
High and low. Dora Read Goodale. 6519-8
The high barbaree. Laura E. Richards. 6120-6
"High and low, high and low/Over the fields...". Plowers. Charlotte Leaming. 6799-9
"A high and naked square, a lonely palm". Rome. Arthur Symons. 6624-0
The high barbaree. Unknown. 6732-8
High Barbary. Howard Stables. 6650-X
"High beyond the granite portal arched across". A ballad of Sark. Algernon Charles Swinburne. 6770-0,6875-8
"A high bred young puppy from Skye". Tragedy. Unknown. 7008-6
The high countrie. Harry Noyes Pratt. 6478-7
"High diddle ding". Unknown. 6904-5
"High diddle doubt, my candle's out". Unknown. 6363-2
High flight. John Gillespie Magee Jr. 6337-3,6107-9,6224-5, 6532-5,6143-5,6491-4,6527-9
High fog. James Rorty. 6880-4
"High from the Ben a Hayich". Kishmul's galley. Marjory Kennedy-Fraser. 6873-1
"High grew the snow beneath the low-hung sky". Song of the axe. Isabella Valancy Crawford. 6795-6
High heart. Aline Kilmer. 6032-3
High heart. Edna Davis Romig. 6836-7
The high hill. Clinton Scollard. 6337-3,6214-8
The high hill. Lionel Wiggam. 6640-2
High house. Margaret Widdemer. 6979-7
High ideals not lost. Mary A. Burnell. 6718-2
"High in hills, beside a river". A deserted farm. Ethel Aldrich Girardet. 6764-6
"High in the air exposed the slave is hung". The slave trade. Robert Southey. 7009-4
"High in the apple bough jauntily swinging". The voice in the spring. Mary Gertrude Hamilton. 6762-X
"High in the breathless hall the minstrel sat". Song at the feast of Brougham castle. William Wordsworth. 6867-7
"High in the breathless hall the minstrel sate". Song at the feast of Brougham castle. William Wordsworth. 6828-6
"High in the glowing heavens, with cloudless..". Sonnet 070 ("High in the glowing"). Luis de Camoens [or Camoes]. 6973-8
"High in the gold-dredge tower". Treasure for the master. Bertha L. Gibbons. 6906-1
"High in the hemlock the cardinal calls". The fine April weather. August Derleth. 6761-1
"High in the midst, surrounded by his peers". Thoughts suggested by a college examination. George Gordon, 6th Baron Byron. 6945-2
"High in the palace a light burns at...night". The infidel. Hermann Hagedorn. 6944-4
"High is his perch, but humble is his home". The redbreast's haunt. James Grahame Marquesse of Montrose. 6943-2
"High life of a hunter! he meets, on the hill". The hunter. Christopher (John Wilson) North. 6980-0
"The high midnight was garlanding her head". Moonlight. Jacques Tahureau. 6771-9
"High name of poet! - sought in every age". On Moor Park - written at Paris, May 11, 1826. Sir Egerton Brydges. 6980-0
High noon. Hamish Maclaren. 6893-6
High noon at Los Alamos. Eleanor Wilner. 7032-9
High noon at midsummer on the campagna. William ("Fiona Macleod") Sharp. 6507-4
"High noon, and not a cloud in the sky". A voice from the bush. Mowbray Morris. 6951-7
"High noon, and not a cloud in the sky...". A voice from the bush. Unknown. 6768-9
"High noon." Shiki. 6027-7
High noon: Galveston beach. Stanley E. Babb. 6265-2
"High o'er his moldering castle walls". A voice from the invisible world. Johann Wolfgang von Goethe. 7039-6
"High o'er the clouds a sunbeam shone". The rape of the mist. Ella Wheeler Wilcox. 6863-4
"High o'er the din of these war-shocked days". The vision of Armageddon. J. Lewis Milligan. 7014-0

High o'er the poop the audacious seas aspire. William Falconer. 6833-2
"High on a granite boulder, huge in girth". Return of the fishing fleet, fr. The heather on fire. Mathilde Blind. 6997-5
High on a ridge of tiles. Maurice James Craig. 6511-2
"High on a shelf we keep the books you had". For a child who died. Joseph G.E. Hopkins. 6761-1
"High on a throne...", fr. Paradise lost. John Milton. 6562-7
"High on an oaken twig, apart". December's thrush. Unknown. 7020-5
"High on its hill the castle stands". Citadel. Edward Farquhar. 6939-8
"High on the crest of the blossoming grasses". Summer. Margaret Deland. 7041-8
"High on the loftiest mountain-tops, unfurl". A paraphrase on the 13th chapter of Isaiah. Thomas Warton (the Elder). 6962-2
"High on the mountain of sunrise...". He knoweth the souls of the west. Unknown (Egyptian). 7039-6
"High on the top of Ararat alone". Noah, fr. The flaming terrapin. Roy Campbell. 6788-3
High or low. Margaret Elizabeth Sangster. 6097-8
The high place at Marib. Grant H. Code. 6218-0
"A high rock face above Flathead lake". The eye in the rock. John Haines. 6855-3
High school basketball. Dennis Cooper. 7003-5
The high school girl. Unknown. 6215-6
The high seas. Sir Walter Scott. 6385-3
The high song. Humbert Wolfe. 6250-4,6541-4
High spring. John Galsworthy. 6888-X
"High state and honours to others impart". John Dryden. 6970-3
High stream's end. Hildegarde Flanner. 6628-3
High summer. Leonard Bacon. 6761-1
High summer. Ebenezer Jones. 6958-4,7015-9
High summer. George Reston Malloch. 6269-5
High summer. Katharine (Hinkson) Tynan. 7027-2
"High thoughts!They come and go". Thoughts of heaven. Robert Nicoll. 6960-6
High tide. George A. Mackenzie. 6433-7
High tide. Countess W. Twitty. 6178-8
High tide at Gettysburg. Will Henry Thompson. 6300-4,6467-1,6424-8,6309-8,6267-9,6008-0,6250-4,6088-9,6074-9, 6340-3,6473-6,6062-5,6678-X,6621
The high tide at Lincolnshire. Jean Ingelow. 6605-4,6239-3, 6427-2,6600-3,6134-6,6228-8,6250-4,6424-8,6102-8, 6438-8
High tide at midnight. Frederick W.H. Myers. 6997-5,7015-9
The high tide on the coast of Lincolnshire (1571). Jean Ingelow. 6656-9,6304-7,6219-9,6344-6,6246-6,6302-0, 6385-3,6518-X,6732-8,6179
"High tide, and the year at the ebb". A sea-glimpse. Lucy Larcom. 6997-5
High tide; or, the brides of Enderby (1571). Jean Ingelow. 6566-X,6964-9
The high tide. Unknown. 6742-5
"High up in the Vale of Cadore". Little Titian's palette. Margaret Junkin Preston. 6965-7
"High up the mountain-meadow...". Satyrus. 6251-2
"High up within yon gray old tower". The old church bell. Unknown. 6916-9
"High upon the gallows tree". God save Ireland! Timothy Daniel [or Donill] Sullivan. 7009-4
"High upon the gallows tree swung the...". God save Ireland. Timothy Daniel [or Donill] Sullivan. 6930-4
"High upon the gallows tree swung the...three". God save Ireland. Timothy Daniel [or Donill] Sullivan. 6858-8
"High upon the oak-tree bough". Robin chat. Margaret Whiting Spilhaus. 6800-6
The high wall. W.R. Titterton. 6884-7
"High walls and huge the body may confine". Sonnet ("High walls"). William Lloyd Garrison. 6600-3
High water mark. Alma L. Gray. 6750-6
A high way and a low. John Oxenham. 6461-2
High wind. Estelle Rooks. 6850-2
High wind at Spanish point. Katherine Garrison Chapin. 6042-0
The high wind. Unknown. 6125-7

The **high** words. Lynn Riggs. 6397-7
"**High,** pale, imperial palaces of snow cloud". Upper air. Frank Ernest Hill. 6808-1
"**High,** pale, imperial places of slow cloud". Upper air. Frank Ernest Hill. 7014-0
The **high-backed** chair. T.P. Sanborn. 6116-8
The **high-born** ladye. Thomas Moore. 6290-3;6518-X
High-chin Bob. Charles Badger Clark Jr. 7012-4
"**High-colored,** sparkling, very much alive". San Francisco. Berton Braley. 6853-7
The **high-mettled** racer. Charles Dibdin. 6219-9
The **high-priest** to Alexander. Alfred Lord Tennyson. 6848-0
A **high-school** national song. Vachel Lindsay. 6206-7
High-tide. Jean Starr Untermeyer. 6850-2
High-tide. Jean Starr Untermeyer. 6332-2
A **high-toned** old Christian woman. Wallace Stevens. 6036-6
"**High-yellow** of my heart, with breasts...". The peasant declares his love. Emile Roumer. 6759-X
Higham, T.F. (tr.)
    All things to all men. Theognis, 6435-3
    Artemis visits the Cyclopes. Callimachus, 6435-3
    "At once, she wen, and found the Cyclopes." Callimachus, 6435-3
    At the window. Praxilla, 6435-3
    The Athenian dead. Simonides, 6435-3
    Bacchanal, fr. Baccae. Euripides, 6435-3
    The bane of poverty. Theognis, 6435-3
    The battle of the books, fr. Aetia. Callimachus, 6435-3
    Beer. Flavius Claudius Julianus Imperator, 6435-3
    "Beware the lurking scorpion, friend". Unknown, 6435-3
    The blind old man. Unknown (Greek), 6435-3
    The blood-guilty. Empedocles, 6435-3
    "But Delos is pleasant, O Phoebus...". Homer, 6435-3
    A call to action. Callinus, 6435-3,6665-8
    The capture of Athens. Oracle of Serapis, 6435-3
    The cautious householder. Anaxilas, 6435-3
    A cenotaph, fr. Tegea. Simonides, 6435-3
    The childhood of Zeus. Moero, 6435-3
    Children, fr. Danae. Euripides, 6435-3
    The choirs of heaven. Unknown (Greek), 6435-3
    Cicada days, fr. The farmer's year. Hesiod, 6435-3
    "Clouds, ever drifting in air". Aristophanes, 6435-3
    The confident scientist. Alexis, 6435-3
    Country gods. Cometas, 6435-3
    Danae. Simonides, 6435-3
    Daybreak in the city, fr. Hecale. Callimachus, 6435-3
    The dead feel not. Theognis, 6435-3
    The dead fowler. Mnasalcas, 6435-3
    "Dear comrade, arise, from slumber awake". Aristophanes, 6435-3
    Dedication for a spear. Simonides, 6435-3
    "Distaff, the spinner's friend, gift of Athena". Theocritus, 6435-3
    "Distinguish god in your imaginings". Unknown, 6435-3
    Diversity of gifts. Sappho, 6435-3
    Diversity of gifts. Solon, 6435-3
    The eagle of song. Bacchylides, 6435-3
    "Easy, Ned, easy, go soft...". Aristophanes, 6435-3
    The Eretrian dead. Plato, 6435-3
    Erysichthon. Callimachus, 6435-3
    Eugenics. Theognis, 6435-3
    The exception. Phocylides, 6435-3
    An exchange of fortune. Statyllius Flaccus, 6435-3
    A faithless friend. Theognis, 6435-3
    Farmer and sailor. Plato, 6435-3
    The final conflagration. Unknown (Greek), 6435-3
    Flute song. Unknown (Greek), 6435-3
    The frogs' song. Aristophanes, 6435-3
    A garden. Sappho, 6435-3
    "Gloom of the night, gloom of the night". Aristophanes, 6435-3
    "Go, topless, Geraneia...", fr. Lost at sea. Simonides, 6435-3
    The god of wealth. Timocreon, 6435-3
    Golden fish. Titanomachia, 6435-3
    The golden mean. Anacreon, 6435-3
    A grave on Ossa. Aeschylus, 6435-3
    A grave, fr. Tegea. Simonides, 6435-3
    Greater love. Antipater of Sidon, 6435-3
    The Greek dead at Thermopylae. Simonides, 6435-3
    Her only flaw. Rufinus, 6435-3
    Here are sands, ignoble things. Menander, 6435-3
    Hermes of the lonely hill. Unknown (Greek), 6435-3
    How can man die better. Tyrtaeus, 6665-8,6435-3
    "How Hellas' youth". Aristophanes, 6435-3
    Human worms. Anaxilas, 6435-3
    "A hunter learns a soldier's trade". Unknown, 6435-3
    "I sing of Dionysus, an old story". Homer, 6435-3
    "I, Denys of Tarsus, lie dead". Unknown, 6435-3
    In praise of Bombyca. Theocritus, 6435-3
    In praise of hunting. Unknown (Greek), 6435-3
    Ionian holiday. Unknown (Greek), 6435-3
    The last journey, fr. Antigone. Sophocles, 6435-3
    The last request. Philetas, 6435-3
    The limitations of knowledge. Empedocles, 6435-3
    Lines written to accompany the gift of a distaff... Theocritus, 6435-3
    Linos. Unknown (Greek), 6435-3
    "Listen and learn what manner of god I am". Unknown, 6435-3
    The living god. Oracle of Serapis, 6435-3
    "Look, my countrymen". Sophocles, 6435-3
    Lost at sea. Simonides, 6435-3
    The lost world of Adonis. Praxilla, 6435-3
    Love. Anacreon, 6435-3
    Love is not winged. Eubulus, 6435-3
    A love song. Unknown, 6435-3
    A love song. Unknown (Greek), 6435-3
    Maidens' song. Unknown (Greek), 6435-3
    Mais ou est le preux Charlemagne? Unknown (Greek), 6435-3
    A mare. Mnasalcas, 6435-3
    Master of none. Titanomachia, 6435-3
    Master of none. Margites, 6435-3
    May I drink the blood of my enemies. Theognis, 6435-3
    Monuments perish. Simonides, 6435-3
    The moon. Sappho, 6435-3
    Mother, I cannot mind my wheel. Sappho, 6435-3
    A mountain glen. Unknown (Greek), 6435-3
    Nature the artist. Empedocles, 6435-3
    "Nine are we who enter...". Unknown, 6435-3
    Not dead, but gone before. Antiphanes, 6435-3
    "Not of my choosing, traveller, this desert...". Unknown, 6435-3
    "Now Apollo have mercy, and Artemis be thou kind". Homer, 6435-3
    "Now glorious Leto's child goes up...". Homer, 6435-3
    "Now hath the cast been made, and the net wide−". Unknown, 6435-3
    Nunc est bibendum. Anacreon, 6435-3
    "O Linos, pure music was given". Unknown, 6435-3
    Of the shade of Ajax, fr. The Odyssey. Homer, 6435-3
    Old age. Anacreon, 6435-3
    "Old pride and consequence, where lodge they now". Unknown, 6435-3
    "One Aeschylus, Athenian born". Aeschylus, 6435-3
    "Pallas, born by Triton side". Unknown, 6435-3
    "Pan, who hast to thy command". Unknown, 6435-3
    Pericles. Cratinus, 6435-3
    Pericles. Eupolis, 6435-3
    Picture of a physician. Leontius, 6435-3
    "Poor Virtue, she's but words...". Unknown, 6435-3
    The power of God. Unknown (Greek), 6435-3
    Pride of the flesh. Theognis, 6435-3
    The profession of flattery. Antiphanes, 6435-3
    Put money in thy purse. Theognis, 6435-3
    Reapers' song. Theocritus, 6435-3
    Refined gold. Theognis, 6435-3
    Reproach no man for poverty. Theognis, 6435-3
    The sailor's dedication. Macedonius, 6435-3
    A scorpion under every stone. Unknown (Greek), 6435-3
    Sentence of death. Palladas, 6435-3
    The sign of the pleiads, fr. The farmer's year. Hesiod, 6435-3
    "So I: when swift Achilles...", fr. The Odyssey. Homer, 6435-3
    The solace of art. Amphis, 6435-3
    Sophocles. Phrynichus, 6435-3
    "Sou'west blows the cloud together". Unknown, 6435-3
    "The sow pme acorn has". Unknown, 6435-3

HIGHAM

"Sow your wheat in muddy weather". Unknown, 6435-3
Sowing days. Unknown (Greek), 6435-3
Spartan three-choir festival. Unknown (Greek), 6435-3
Statue of a dog. Macedonius, 6435-3
"Swiftly through the forest brake". Unknown, 6435-3
Take thought. Plato, 6435-3
Thrasybulus. Pindar, 6435-3
Time the changer. Plato, 6435-3
"Time was, our hearts were young and". Unknown, 6435-3
Timomachus. Simonides, 6435-3
To Artemis ("To Artemis I kneel..."). Anacreon, 6435-3
To Athena. Unknown (Greek), 6435-3
To Athena. Alcaeus, 6435-3
To Cleobulus. Anacreon, 6435-3
To Dionysus. Unknown (Greek), 6435-3
To Dionysus ("Roving god, whose playfellows"). Anacreon, 6435-3
To Pan. Unknown (Greek), 6435-3
To virtue. Aristotle, 6435-3
The turn of a dragonfly's wing. Simonides, 6435-3
An unhappy man. Unknown (Greek), 6435-3
"Verily, verily that day shall come". Unknown, 6435-3
Virtue. Unknown (Greek), 6435-3
The way of knowledge. Parmenides, 6435-3
Wayward desire. Unknown (Greek), 6435-3
Weep for youth's passing. Theognis, 6435-3
"Wh-wh--wh-wh...where's". Aristophanes, 6435-3
"When Olympus Hera was given". Aristophanes, 6435-3
Whither away?, fr. Hecuba. Euripides, 6435-3
Who is free? Philemon, 6435-3
Wind and weather. Unknown (Greek), 6435-3
Wine and song. Nicaenetus, 6435-3
"Winter days and spring and summer still the yearly". Unknown, 6435-3
Winter, fr. The farmer's year. Hesiod, 6435-3
Zeus dances. Titanomachia, 6435-3
Highbaugh, Whitt
K.P. blues. 6237-7
Higher. Unknown. 6279-2,6440-X
The higher catechism. Sam Walter Foss. 6730-1
The higher command, fr. Antigone. Sophocles. 6337-3
The higher courage. Arthur Hugh Clough. 6655-0
The higher fellowship. Sam Walter Foss. 6303-9
The higher good. Theodore Parker. 6337-3
The higher loyalty, fr. Henry VIII. William Shakespeare. 6337-3
The higher pantheism in a nutshell. Algernon Charles Swinburne. 6089-7,6440-X,6657-7,6655-0
The higher pantheism. Alfred Lord Tennyson. 6198-2,6337-3, 6655-0,6657-7,6634-8,6731
The higher pantheism. Alfred Lord Tennyson. 6828-6
The higher pantheism. Alfred Lord Tennyson. 6110-9,6199-0, 6102-8,6214-8,6250-4,6560-0,6737-9
The higher shrewdness. Johann Wolfgang von Goethe. 7042-6
"Higher than a house, higher than a tree." Mother Goose. 6452-3
Highest education. Grace D. Ford. 6764-6
Highet and T.F. Higham, Gilbert (tr.)
"The blade I bear". Unknown, 6435-3
Harmodius and Aristogeiton. Unknown (Greek), 6435-3
Highet, Gilbert (tr.)
Advice to a lover, fr. Perikeiromene. Menander, 6435-3
An armoury. Alcaeus, 6435-3,6665-8
A boxer. Simonides, 6435-3
Charisius rebukes himself, fr. Epitrepontes. Menander. 6435-3
"Come, you seamen, deepwater mariners". Unknown, 6435-3
Crabbed age and youth. Theophilus, 6435-3
Hagesichora. Alcman, 6435-3
Hours. Unknown (Greek), 6435-3
Human imperfection. Simonides, 6435-3
The ichneumon. Oppian, 6435-3
The lawgiver's boast. Sappho, 6435-3
The lawgiver's boast. Solon, 6435-3
A low trade, fr. Mime. Herodas, 6435-3
A manifesto. Timotheus, 6435-3
A Nile chantey. Unknown (Greek), 6435-3
"Now I, the sinless saint, aiming at honour". Menander, 6435-3
"Now, Polemo, if the matter really is". Menander, 6435-3
"Old songs I will not sing". Timotheus, 6435-3
The protectress of Athens. Sappho, 6435-3
The protectress of Athens. Solon, 6435-3
A sea-fight, fr. Persae. Timotheus, 6435-3
Some women. Semonides, 6435-3
Temptation. Oppian, 6435-3
The voyage of love. Cercidas, 6435-3
"We spend six hours". Unknown, 6435-3
"When rebullient the brine". Timotheus, 6435-3
A winner of the pentathlon. Simonides, 6435-3
Highgate hill. Sir Henry Howarth Bashford. 7007-8
Highland cattle. Dinah Maria Mulock Craik. 6239-3
The **highland** chase. Sir Walter Scott. 6424-8
The **highland** emigrant's last farewell. Evan McColl. 6433-7
Highland fairies. J.B. Salmond. 6269-5
Highland Harry. Robert Burns. 6859-6
Highland Harry. Sutherland. 6859-6
Highland laddie. Unknown. 6859-6
The **highland** laddie. Allan Cunningham. 6859-6
The **highland** laddie. Allan Ramsay. 6195-0
Highland lovers. Mary L. Gaddess. 6711-5
Highland Mary. Robert Burns. 6102-8,6154-0,6180-X,6198-2, 6240-7,6246 ,6219-7,6723-9,6152-4,6430-2,6560-0,6195 ,6271-7,6289-X,6302-0,6385-3,6331-4,6473-,6023-4, 6104-4,6250-4,6301-2,6371-3,6439 ,6086-2,6226-1,6481-7,6486-8,6600-3,6732 ,6102-8,6197-4,6394-2,6631-3, 6543-0,6737
Highland new year's blessing. Unknown. 6134-6
Highland night. Isabel Westcott Harper. 7027-2
The **highland** shepherd. Joanna Baillie. 6543-0
The **highland** stranger. Sir Walter Scott. 6621-6
The **highland** stream, fr. The bothie of Tober-na-vuolich. Arthur Hugh Clough. 6832-4
The **highland** watch. James Hogg. 6328-4
The **highland** widow's lament. Robert Burns. 6383-7
The **highlander's** farewell. Unknown. 6859-6
The **highlander's** lament. Unknown. 6859-6
"The **highlandmen** came down the hill". Unknown. 6859-6
"**Highlands** of Hudson! ye saw them pass". The storming of Stony Point. Arthur Guiterman. 6946-0,6773-5
Highly evangelical osculation. Unknown. 6670-4
"**Highmindedness**, a jealousy for good". Addressed to Haydon. John Keats. 6828-6
Highmount. Louis Untermeyer. 6336-5
Highway 299 Gerald Cable. 6855-3
Highway buttons. Martin Halverson. 6342-X
The **highway** cow. Eugene J. Hall. 6273-3
A **highway** for freedom. James Clarence Mangan. 7009-4
"The **highway** of life is a bumpy road". The highway of life. Essie Bateman Sisk. 6799-9
Highway to nowhere. Grant H. Code. 6218-0
"**Highway,** since you my chief Parnassus be". Sir Philip Sidney. 6181-8,6182-6
The **highway..** Sir Philip Sidney. 6625-9
Highway: Michigan. Theodore Roethke. 6761-1
The **highway.** Manuel Bandeira. 6759-X
The **highway.** William Channing Gannett. 6730-1
The **highway.** William Colburne Husted. 6579-1
The **highwayman's** ghost. Richard Garnett. 6518-X
The **highwayman.** Alfred Noyes. 6101-X,6162-1,6289-X,6395-0, 6476-0,6503 ,6464-7,6419-1,6371-3,6396-9,6107-9,6102 ,6332-2,6499-X,6506-6,6512-0,6534-1,6538 ,6723-9, 6319-5,6161-3,6732-8
Highways. Leslie Nelson Jennings. 6031-5,6374-8
Hignite blues. Wesley J. Turner. 6149-4
Hiking up Hieizan with Alam Lau/Buddha's birthday 1974. Garrett Kaoru Hongo. 6790-5
Hilary of Arles, Saint
"Thou bounteous giver of the light". 6065-X
Hilburd, Mary Flagg
New Englanders. 6894-4
Hilda. Harry Noyes Pratt. 6628-3
Hilda. James H. Rayhill. 6450-7
Hilda's Christmas. M.A.L. Lane. 6623-2
Hilda's little hood. Hjalmar Hjorth Boyesen. 6577-5
Hilda, spinning. Unknown. 6745-X
Hilda, spinning. Unknown. 6917-7
Hildreth, Charles Lotin
The burden of time. 7041-8

Duet. 6441-8
Ghosts. 7041-8
Love. 7041-8
Song-the vigil. 7041-8
The tocsin. 7041-8
Hildreth, Fred
Our drummer boy. 6675-5
Hilker, Hedwig W.D.
The haunted room. 6847-2
The hill above the mine. Malcolm Cowley. 6375-6
Hill and vale. Lionel Johnson. 6253-9
A hill come out of the sea. H.L. Davis. 6071-4
Hill country April. Lida Wilson Turner. 6841-3
The hill farmer speaks. Ronald Stuart Thomas. 6257-1
The hill farms. Agnes Bardin Dustin. 6764-6
Hill hunger. Joseph Auslander. 6653-4
Hill hunger. Lillian Mayfield Roberts. 6347-0
A hill in Picardy. Clinton Scollard. 6542-2
Hill life. Jean Elkins. 6764-6
Hill magic. Estelle Rooks. 6850-2
The hill o' dreams. Helen Lanyon. 6090-0
The hill of Killenarden. Charles G. ("Miles O'Reilly") Halpine. 6858-8
The hill of vision, sels. James Stephens. 6234-2
Hill over Rincon. Hildegarde Flanner. 6628-3
The hill pines were sighing. Robert Bridges. 6187-7,6477-9, 6487-6,6430-2,6508-2
The hill place. Robert P. Tristram Coffin. 7040-X
A hill song. Richard Hovey. 7006-X
A hill song. Helen M. Merrill. 6115-X
The hill steps. Karle Wilson Baker. 6506-6
The hill summit, fr. The house of life. Dante Gabriel Rossetti. 6123-0,6110-9
The hill wife, sels. Robert Frost. 6030-7,6102-8,6208-3, 6076-5,6030-7
The hill wife. Robert Frost. 6556-2,6288-1
Hill's surrender; or, villany somewhere. Unknown. 6946-0
Hill, Aaron
"As lamps burn silent with unconscious light" 6874-X
Gentle love, this hour befriend me. 6328-4
Grasp it like a man! 6861-8
A retrospect. 6086-2
Song ("Oh! forbear"). 6086-2
Tender-handed stroke a nettle. 6934-7
A useful hint. 6086-2
Hill, Alice Polk
Christmas hymn. 6836-7
I am not ready yet. 6836-7
To Alice--my namesake. 6836-7
Hill, Benjamin Dionysius
Mother Mary Xavier. 6285-7
Our Lady's death. 6172-9,6292-X
Hill, Brian
Salonika in November. 7031-0
The vigil. 6070-6
Hill, Brian (tr.)
Ophelia. Arthur Rimbaud, 6125-7
Hill, Clyde Walton
The dying year. 6449-3
Lincoln. 6449-3
Hill, Dorothy Bladin
Family doctor. 6750-6
I saw Duluth. 6342-X
Hill, E.
When Polly buys a hat. 6242-3
Hill, Francis
Rich man, poor man. 6027-7
Hill, Frank Ernest
Autumn, forsake these hills. 6808-1
Diversity. 6619-4
Earth and air. 6038-2
"The earth will stay the same" 7014-0
Farm-circle. 6038-2
Formation. 7014-0
Her house. 6037-4
The lake of the fallen moon. 6039-0
Let you would be lovers. 6039-0
Lundy. 6037-4
Mirage. 6037-4
Snow water. 6619-4
Stone dust. 6039-0
Upper air. 6808-1
Upper air. 7014-0
Wing harbor. 7014-0
Hill, Frank Ernest (tr.)
Invocatio ad Mariam, fr. prologue to the 2nd nun's tale. Geoffrey Chaucer, 6282-2
Invocation, fr. the prologue of The prioress's tale. Geoffrey Chaucer, 6282-2
The Nun's priest's tale. Geoffrey Chaucer, 6637-2
The pardoner's tale, fr. The Canterbury tales. Geoffrey Chaucer, 6473-6
Hill, George
Leila. 6176-1
The oak. 6049-8,6820-0
Hill, Grace Livingston
Baking for the party. 6713-1
Hill, Graham
The snow man. 6772-7
Hill, Judyth
Paula's story. 6821-9
Hill, Julious C.
The wandering black-a-moor. 6799-9
Hill, Leslie Pinckney
My charge. 6337-3
Of greatness in teaching. 6337-3
The teacher. 6337-3
The teacher. 6818-9
Hill, M.B.
Lady sweet pea. 6710-7
Hill, Mabel
The miracle. 6799-9
Hill, Marguerite
The return. 6799-9
Hill, Marion
Lovelilts. 6089-7,6724-7
Hill, Mary E.
Dream ship. 6799-9
Hill, Mary Frances
Crowned. 6799-9
Hill, Maurice
Storm in Hawaii. 6799-9
Hill, Rudolph
'The spell' 6818-9
To April. 6397-7
The wind. 6397-7
Wisps of song. 6397-7
Hill, Sylvia
Prayer for spring. 6954-1
Hill, Thomas
The bobolink. 6271-7,6597-X,6529-5,6302-0;6385-3
Hill, William Earl
Prairie winds. 6818-9
"A hill, it always seems to me". Hills. Genevieve Gray Rawson. 6906-1
Hill-born. Abbie Huston Evans. 6037-4
Hill-born, fr. Battle. Wilfred Wilson Gibson. 6897-9
The hill-born. Struthers Burt. 6337-3,6501-5,6607-0
Hill-country. Aline Kilmer. 6250-4
Hill-fantasy. Fannie Stearns Davis. 6887-1
Hill-fantasy. Fannie Stearns Davis. 6762-X
The hill-flower. Alfred Noyes. 6151-6,6253-9
"Hill-folk, who long have lived among the...". Not the hushed grave. Vilda Sauvage Owens. 7038-8
Hill-side tree. Maxwell Bodenheim. 6348-9
Hill-top. Arvia MacKaye. 6327-4
Hill-top songs. Sir Charles George Douglas Roberts. 6161-3, 6115-X
The hill-water. Duncan Ban MacIntyre. 6873-1
A hill-woman. John Chipman Farrar. 6619-4
"A hill; a sled all painted red". Coasting. Wallace E. Mather. 6965-7
The hill. Rupert Brooke. 6153-2,6301-2,6659-3
The hill. Horace Holley. 6730-1
The hill. Edgar Lee Masters. 6897-9
The hill. Edgar Lee Masters. 6879-0
Hillcrest. Edwin Arlington Robinson. 6333-0,6208-3
Hiller, William Hurd
My master's face. 6337-3
Hilles, Howard

HILLES

Frustration. 6789-1
Horizons. 6789-1
When forests wear their Joseph's coats. 6789-1
Hillhouse, James Abraham
Close of the vision of judgment. 6752-2
A demon's false description of his race... 6752-2
Evening music of the angels. 6752-2
Hadad. 6848-0
Hadad's description of the city of David. 6752-2
Hadad's description of the city of David. 6848-0
Hadad, sels. 6752-2
"How aromatic evening grows," fr. Hadad. 6752-2
The last evening before eternity. 6752-2
Percy's Masque, sels. 6752-2
Poem written...opinions of a deaf and dumb child, sels. 6752-2
Roman Catholic chant, fr. Percy's Masque. 6752-2
The sage of Caucasus. 6752-2
"Trembling before thine awful throne." 6302-0
Hilliard, John Northern
A vagabond song. 6274-1
Hilliard, Lenora K.
Faces. 6799-9
Hillier, Arthur Cecil
In excelsis. 6507-4
Hillman, Carolyn
Wreaths. 6034-X
Wreaths. 6762-X
Hillman, Gordon Malherbe
'Is missus. 6032-3
Memphis. 6762-X
The tankers. 6034-X
A hillman. George William ("A.E.") Russell. 6071-4,6581-3
"Hilloo, hilloo, hilloo, hilloo!". Snowshoeing song. Arthur Weir. 7035-3
Hills. Hilda Conkling. 6253-9,6396-9,6421-3,6236-9
Hills. Scottie McKenzie Frasier. 6037-4
Hills. Arthur Guiterman. 6101-X,6102-8,6266-0,6337-3,6374-8,6653-4,6029-3,6076-5,6464-7,6476-0,6732-8
Hills. John Russell McCarthy. 6037-4
Hills. Genevieve Gray Rawson. 6906-1
The hills ahead. Douglas Malloch. 6654-2
"The hills all glowed with a festive light". The illuminated city. Felicia Dorothea Hemans. 6973-8
Hills and sea. Katharine Lee Bates. 6798-0
"Hills and valleys where April rallies his...". On the south coast. Algernon Charles Swinburne. 6828-6
"The hills are bare of verdure, the valleys...". The failures. Berton Braley. 6853-7
"The hills are bright with maples yet". Faded leaves. Alice Cary. 6969-X
"The hills are calling". Reveille. Dorothy O'Gara. 6764-6
"The hills are crying from the fields to me". The hills. Francis Ledwidge. 6812-X
The hills are home. Edna Dean Proctor. 6764-6
"The hills are like a woman...". The hills are like a woman. Gladys McCain Freeman. 6799-9
"The hills are misty with meadow-sweet". Resurgent moment. Luna Craven Osburn. 6764-6
"The hills are monkeys crouching". Chinese sunset. Frances Hall. 6782-4
"The hills are shadows, and they flow". Unknown. 6240-7
Hills brothers coffee. Luci Tapahonso. 7005-1
The hills in their sameness. Lalla Adams Stark. 7016-7
The hills keep holy ground. Hellene Seaman. 6337-3
"Hills of Annesley, black and barren". Fragment written shortly after the marriage...Chaworth. George Gordon, 6th Baron Byron. 6945-2
The hills of Carrara. John Ruskin. 6624-0
The hills of God. Takamoto. 6027-7
Hills of home. Witter Bynner. 6102-8,6556-2,6732-2,6076-2, 6431-0,6439
Hills of home. Malcolm Hemphrey. 7026-4
The hills of life, sels. Albert Durrant Watson. 6115-X
The hills of old Vermont. Daniel L. Cady. 6988-6
The hills of rest. Albert Bigelow Paine. 6006-4;6337-3;6476-0;6730-1
The hills of Ruel. William ("Fiona Macleod") Sharp. 6269-5
The hills of San Jose. Witter Bynner. 6628-3
The hills of the south country. Hilaire Belloc. 6084-6

Hills of tomorrow. Marian Buxton Clark. 6906-1
The hills of Tsa la gi. Robert J. Conley. 7005-1
The hills of youth. Alfred Noyes. 6169-9
The hills on their thrones. Robert Buchanan. 6819-7
"The hills slipped over each on each". Mountain twilight. William Renton. 6873-1
Hills surround me. Mok-wol Park. 6775-1
The hills were made for freedom. William Goldsmith Brown 6240-7
"Hills where once my love and I". A hill song. Richard Hovey. 7006-X
Hills, Barton
For a November afternoon. 6042-0
Hills, L.P.
Poetical courtship. 6921-5
Hills, William H.
The city sportsman. 6745-X
"The hills/were never closer". David's poem. Ben Hiatt. 6792-1, 6998-3
The hills. Berton Braley. 6336-5,6332-2,6336-5,6476-0
The hills. Theodosia Garrison. 6374-8
The hills. Julian Grenfell. 6650-X
The hills. Thomas S. Jones Jr. 6030-7
The hills. Francis Ledwidge. 6812-X
The hills. Harriet Plimpton. 6764-6
The hills. Daniel Smythe. 6761-1
The hillside cot. William Ellery Channing. 6438-8
A hillside farmer. John Chipman Farrar. 6607-0
A hillside thaw. Robert Frost. 6288-1
"The hillsides were of rushing, silvered water". Gioconda. Thomas McGreevy. 6930-4
Hilltops. Leslie Savage Clark. 6144-3
Hillyer, Robert
Aging poet, fr. Poetical sketches. 6761-1
Aging poetess, fr. Poetical sketches. 6761-1
Arabesque. 6649-6
Black magic. 6039-2
Christmas pastoral. 6337-3
Elegy on a dead mermaid washed ashore at Plymouth Rock. 6036-6
Epigram. 6722-0
Epitaph. 6037-4
Flower-market, Copenhagen. 6331-4
Folk song (1). 6984-3
Folk song (2). 6984-3
For Maister Geoffrey Chaucer. 6483-3,6036-6
From a sonnet sequence. 6431-0
A gull. 6331-4
The halt in the garden. 6506-6,6039-0
He singeth in the underworld. 6037-4
He who in spring's rebirth. 6984-3
In the tidal marshes. 6781-6
In time of mistrust, XIII. 6532-5
A letter to Robert Frost. 6483-3
Lost twilight. 6761-1
Lullaby ("The long canoe"). 6490-6
Mentis trist. 6619-4,6070-6
Midsummer moment. 6761-1
'The mirror of all ages are the eyes'. 6607-0
Moo! 6506-6,6722-0,6070-6
Night piece. 6042-0
The other world. 6037-4
Paths across the sea. 6036-6
Poetical sketches. 6761-1
Prelude. 6619-4
The recompense. 6320-9
Remote. 6984-3
Scherzo. 6490-6,6037-4
So ghostly then the girl came in. 6641-0,6648-8
Song ("Since only man..."). 6761-1
Thermopylae. 6347-0,6542-2
Thermopylae and Golgotha. 6033-1,6102-8,6337-3,6076-5
Threnody. 6036-6
To a Scarlatti passpied. 6250-4,6431-0,6653-4
To congress concerning...for universal military service. 6880-4
Young poet, fr. Poetical sketches. 6761-1
Hillyer, Robert (tr.)
Addition of the disk by King Akhnaten... Unknown (Egyptian), 7039-6

The dead man ariseth and singeth a hymn to the sun. Unknown (Egyptian), 7039-6
He approacheth the hall of judgment. Unknown (Egyptian), 7039-6
He cometh forth into the day. Unknown (Egyptian), 7039-6
He establisheth his triumph. Unknown (Egyptian), 7039-6
He holdeth fast to the memory of his identity. Unknown (Egyptian), 7039-6
He is declared true of word. Unknown (Egyptian), 7039-6
He is like the lotus. Unknown (Egyptian), 7039-6
He knoweth the souls of the west. Unknown (Egyptian), 7039-6
He maketh himself one with the only god... Unknown (Egyptian), 7039-6
He singeth in the underworld. Unknown (Egyptian), 7039-6
He walketh by day. Unknown (Egyptian), 7039-6
The other world. Unknown (Egyptian), 7039-6
There is a charming land. Adam Gottlob Oehlenschlager, 6331-4

Hilmer, William Hurd
The midnight mail. 6274-1
My master's face. 6144-3,6335-7

Hilton, Alfarata
A busy person. 6466-3
Early to bed. 6466-3
Nancy Etticoat. 6466-3

Hilton, Arthur Clement
The heathen pass-ee. 6440-X,6092-7
Octopus. 6802-2
"There was a young man of Sid. Sussex". 6722-0
The vulture and the husband-man. 6440-X

Hilton-Turvey, C.
The end. 6327-6

Him I follow, fr. Will Shakespeare. Clemence Dane. 6532-5
"Him I hold as happy as god in heaven". Sappho. 6251-2
"Him the almighty power", fr. Paradise lost. John Milton. 6726-3

Himes, Isaac N.
The doctor's life, sels. 6482-5

Himlinsky, Sara
A dead seaman speaks. 7019-1

Himmell, Sophie
But what of song? 6761-1
Sleep. 6979-7

Himself. Theodosia Garrison. 6083-8,6307-1
"Himself is least afraid". The poet. Mildred McNeal Sweeney. 6310-1

Hinchman, Anne
Winter. 6039-0

The Hinckley fire. Nora Byrnes Hegi. 6342-X

Hinckley, Abby S.
Motherhood ("She softly sings..."). 6097-8

Hinckley, Frederick A.
The common lot. 6798-0
A little girl. 6798-0
Watchman, what of the night. 6798-0

The hind and the panther, sels. John Dryden. 6024-2,6198-2, 6562-7,6152-4,6195-0
The hind and the panther. John Dryden. 6970-3
Hind etin. Unknown. 6185-0
Hind horn. Unknown. 6061-7,6154-0,6185-0,6198-2,6518-X
The hind's dance. James Logie ("Hugh Haliburton") Robertson. 6819-7
The hind.. Sir Thomas Wyatt. 6436-1

Hindley, J.H. (tr.)
Goddess. Amir Khusrau, 6448-5
Slave. Hafiz, 6448-5

Hindley, John (tr.)
Ode 011. Hafiz, 7039-6

A Hindoo died. Unknown. 6370-5
The Hindoo sceptic. Unknown. 6273-3
The Hindoo's death. George Birdseye. 6273-3
The hindoo's paradise. Unknown. 6414-0,6605-4
A hindoo's search for truth. Sir Alfred Comyn Lyall. 6240-7
"The hinds how blest, who ne'er beguiled". The hamlet, sels. Thomas Warton Jr.. 6867-7

Hinds, A.L.
Through toil. 6273-3

Hinds, Florence
The door. 6799-9

Hinds, John T.
Just tell them so. 6583-X

Hines, Herbert H.
A Christmas prayer. 6144-3,6337-3
The little street. 6214-8

Hines, J.A.
The August second syndrome. 6870-7
Cancel my subscription. 6870-7
For myself. 6870-7

Hingston, Lee
To one departed. 6817-0

"Hink, minx! the old witch winks". Unknown. 6904-5
Hinkson, Katherine. See Tynan, Katherine

Hinman, Addison H.
Longing for the old plantation. 6118-4
To the college idol. 6118-4

Hinricks, Mary Mullis
The flow of eternal light and power. 6857-X
The mortuary. 6857-X

The hint beyond. Frances Frost. 6750-6
A hint for 1884. Eugene Field. 6949-5
The Hint o' Hairst. Charles Murray. 6180-X
A hint to the wise. Pringle Barret. 6466-3
A hint.. Anna Maria Pratt. 6623-2
A hint.. Unknown. 6273-3
A hint. Unknown. 6921-5
A hinted wish. Martial. 7039-6

Hinton, Leonard
For a new year. 6396-9

Hinton, Lillian
Morning strolls. 6818-9

Hints. Alice Cary. 6969-X
Hints from Horace. George Gordon, 6th Baron Byron. 6945-2
The hipe. Patrick MacGill. 6653-4
"Hippity-hop to the barber shop". Unknown. 7028-0

Hipple, Mary A.
Blindness. 6249-0
The thinker dog. 6249-0

"Hippo, so dull of brain and skin". To a river horse. Francis Gallagher. 6799-9
Hippodromania; or, whiffs from the pipe. Adam Lindsay Gordon. 6951-7
Hippolytus temporizes. Hilda ("H.D.") Doolittle. 6036-6
Hippolytus temporizes, sels. Hilda ("H.D.") Doolittle. 6072-2
Hippolytus to Artemis. Euripides. 7020-5
Hippolytus, sels. Euripides. 6879-0
Hippolytus, sels. Euripides. 6541-4
Hippolytus, sels. Euripides. 6541-4
Hippolytus, sels. Gilbert Murray. 6477-9

Hipponax
"Out of the jug we drank...". F.L. Lucas (tr.). 6251-2
Take my overcoat and hold it..."..." F.L. Lucas (tr.). 6251-2
"Two days a woman's best...". F.L. Lucas (tr.). 6251-2
A visit from wealth. A.D. Knox (tr.). 6435-3

Hippopotamothalamion. John Hall Wheelock. 6388-8
The hippopotamus. Hilaire Belloc. 6179-6,6722-0
The hippopotamus. Thomas Stearns Eliot. 6733-6,6375-6,6637-2
Hips. Abu Hafs. 6362-4
Hira-Singh's farewell to Burmah. Laurence (Adele Florence Nicolson) Hope. 6856-1
Hiram Hover. Bayard Taylor. 6089-7,6440-X
Hiram Powers' Greek slave. Elizabeth Barrett Browning. 6102-8
Hiram Powers's Greek slave. Elizabeth Barrett Browning. 6934-7
Hiram's tomb. Robert Needham Cust. 6848-0
The hired man and Floretty. James Whitcomb Riley. 6128-1
"The hired man we knew of yore". The Vermont 'hired man'. Daniel L. Cady. 6988-6
The hireling Swiss regiment. Victor Hugo. 6344-6
The hirlas horn. Felicia Dorothea Hemans. 6973-8

Hiromi
Looking up. Lois J. Erickson (tr.). 6027-7

Hiroshima exit. Joy Kogawa. 6790-5

Hirsch, Edward
   Matisse. 6966-5
Hirsh, Edward L.
   What broken weapons. 6839-1
Hirshman, Jack
   Serronydion. 6792-1
Hirt auf dem berge. Johann C. Friedrich von Schiller. 6252-0
Hirtenlied. Richard Wagner. 6265-2
"His aged face". Street player. Sydney S. Abram. 6850-2
His ally. William Rose Benet. 6291-1,6501-5
His answer to her letter. Francis Bret Harte. 6438-8
His anthology. Meleager. 6435-3
"His awkward legs have not learned how". The roan colt. Keith Thomas. 6750-6
His ballad of Agincourt. Michael Drayton. 6194-X
His banner over me. Gerald Massey. 6303-9,6730-1,6656-9
"His bark/The daring mariner shall urge far..". Prophecy, fr. Il morgante maggiore. Luigi Pulci. 6946-0
His bedchamber. Oliver Goldsmith. 6545-7
His birthday. May Riley Smith. 6746-8
"His book is successful,he's steeped in renown". The poet of fashion. James Smith. 6996-7
His book's patron. Martial. 6297-0
His books. Robert Southey. 6102-8
His bookseller's address. Martial. 6297-0
His boys. Robert Service. 6159-1
His camel. Alqamah. 7039-6
His chance. Edgar A. Guest. 6862-6
His children. Hittan of Tayyi. 7039-6
"His classic studies...", fr. Don Juan. George Gordon, 6th Baron Byron. 6726-3
"His clumsy body is a golden fruit". Deaf-mute in the pear tree. P.K. Page. 6767-4
His code of honor. Zitella Cocke. 7008-6
His content in the country. Robert Herrick. 6562-7
"His country cowered under the mailed fist". The poltroon. Sarah N. Cleghorn. 6817-0
"His courtiers of the caliph crave". The spilt pearls. Richard Chenevix Trench. 6980-0
His creed. Robert Herrick. 6641-0
His dad. Earl Alonzo Brininstool. 6889-8
"His dark face kindled in the east". The Jew. George Alfred Townsend. 6848-4
His day. William Samuel Johnson. 6995-9
"His day was all sunshine, his young heart...". The kiss. Einar Hjorleifsson Kvaran. 6854-5
His death, fr. Hippolytus. Euripides. 6435-3
His deaths. Haniel Long. 6102-8
His desire. Robert Herrick. 6430-2
His despair. Thomas Beaumont. 6563-5
"His ear is ever open." Christina Muller. 6225-3
His education. Thomas Hardy. 6186-9
His enemy's honor. Unknown. 6382-9
His epitaph. Clarence E. Flynn. 6510-4
His epitaph. David Gray. 6760-6
His epitaph. Stephen Hawes. 6102-8,6641-0,6153-2,6301-2
His epitaph. Frederick William Ophel. 6784-0
His excuse for loving, fr. A celebration of Charis... Ben Jonson. 6562-7
His experience with the newspapers. Christopher Morley. 6538-4
His eye was sterm and wild. Unknown. 6909-6
"His eyes of clear and cloudless brown". His majesty the baby. A. Charles Hamilton. 6772-7
"His eyes were stars to follow". Finale. Lilian White Spencer. 6836-7
"His face was as the heavens...", fr. Antony and... William Shakespeare. 6339-X
"His face was glad as dawn to me". The songs of Ethlenn Stuart. William ("Fiona Macleod") Sharp. 6873-1
"His face was lean, and some-deal pined away". Misery, fr. The mirrour for magistrates. Thomas Sackville; 1st Earl of Dorset. 6934-7
His face was lit. W. Stewart Wallace. 6433-7
"His face was the oddest that ever was seen". The strange man. Unknown. 6891-X
"His falchion flashed along the Nile". Napoleon at rest. John Pierpont. 6752-2
His farewell to his unkind and unconstant mistress. Francis Davison. 6182-6,6436-1
His farewell to sack. Robert Herrick. 6430-2
"His father's sense, his mother's grace". On the birth of John William Rizzo Hoppner. George Gordon, 6th Baron Byron. 6945-2
"His fingers were sore and his face was black". A hero of the mine. John E. Barrett. 6840-5
His first Christmas tree. Unknown. 6710-7
His first day at school. Mary W. Slater. 6585-6
His first long trousers. Edgar A. Guest. 6862-6
His first love. Lizette Woodworth Reese. 6019-6
His flying machine. Unknown. 6744-1
"His foe is fire, fire, fire!". The fireman. Stephen Phillips. 7014-0
"His foe was folly and his weapon wit". Anthony (Sir Anthony Hope Hawkins) Hope. 6083-8
"His form is everywhere: all pervading in...". Vison of the sacred dance. Unknown. 6959-2
"His fourscore years and five". Whittier. Margaret Elizabeth Sangster. 6820-0
"His friend he loved". An epitaph. Sir William Watson. 6396-9
"His friend the watchman was still awake". A leave-taking. Arno Holz. 7039-6
"His friends he loved...". Sir William Watson. 6289-X
His garments. Esther Lloyd Hagg. 6144-3
"His gentle heart show through". Manong Benny. Virginia Cerenio. 6790-5
His glory tell. Horatius Bonar. 6065-X
His gloves. Esther Hakanson. 6750-6
"His golden locks time hath to silver turn'd". George Peele. 6181-8,6208-3,6182-6,6726-3,6315-2,6179
"His golden locks time hath to silver turned". An old soldier. George Peele. 6830-8
His good points. W. Livingston Larned. 7008-6
His grace. Ishii. 6027-7
His grange; or, private wealth. Robert Herrick. 6105-2, 6134-6,6562-7,6430-2,6194-X
His guiding star. Francis W. Moore. 6681-X
"His hair was so splendidly flaming". Bit by bitter. Ralph Cheyney. 6750-6
His hands. John Richard Moreland. 6144-3;6335-7;6337-3
"His hands with earthly work are done". Earth to earth. Phoebe Cary. 6969-X,6639-9
"His hazel eyes". Portrait. Georgia H. Cooper. 6850-2
"His head within my bosom lay". A woman's voice. George William ("A.E.") Russell. 6785-9
"His headstone said/Free at last, free at last". The funeral of Martin Luther King, Jr. Nikki Giovanni. 7024-8
His hirsute suit. Frank Sidgwick. 6722-0
His home and his own country. Emily Henrietta Hickey. 6090-0
"His honor's father yet remains". A response. Oliver Wendell Holmes. 6878-2
"His hope undone, now raves the impious king". Slaughter of the innocents by order of King Herod. Caelius Sedulius. 6930-4
His incomparable lady. Henry Howard, Earl of Surrey. 6436-1
"His instant thought a poet spoke". Ralph Waldo Emerson. 6753-0
His invocation to the muse: the poem half finished. John Milton. 6935-5
"His is the way" Thomas Curtis Clark. 6144-3
His lachrimae or mirth, turn'd to mourning. Robert Herrick. 6562-7
His lady of the sonnets. Robert Norwood. 6115-X
His lady's death. Pierre de Ronsard. 6771-9
His lady's eyes. Fulke Greville; 1st Baron Brooke. 6436-1
His lady's hand. Sir Thomas Wyatt. 6436-1
His lady's might. Unknown. 6436-1
His lady's praise. Dante Alighieri. 6321-7
His lady's tomb. Pierre de Ronsard. 6771-9,7039-6
His last letter. Esther Weakley. 6750-6
His last sonnet ("Bright star!"). John Keats. 6186-9,6315-2
His last verses. John Clare. 6219-9
His last victory. Samuel Valentine Cole. 6523-6
His last words. Edith Daley. 6995-9

His laureate. Joyce Kilmer. 6335-7
His legacy. Clara T. Brown. 6906-1
"His legs bestrid the ocean...", fr. Antony and... William Shakespeare. 6339-X
"His life was like white steel...". Lady Margaret Sackville. 6269-5
"His lips amid the flame outsent". Hugh Latimer. Henry Augustin Beers. 7041-8
"His lips purse a whistle". Riveter. Minnie Hite Moody. 6841-3
"His listening soul hears no echo of battle". Nellie Eugene Field. 6949-5
His litany to the Holy Spirit. Robert Herrick. 6194-X,6430-2,6214-8,6102-8,6562-7,6488-4,6563-5
"His little hopes, his little fears". Brother man. Eden Phillpotts. 7014-0
His lordship, the chief justice. Eugene Field. 6949-5
His love admits no rival. Sir Walter Raleigh. 6092-7
His majesty the baby. A. Charles Hamilton. 6772-7
His majesty's health. Unknown. 6563-5
His majesty's mine-sweepers. R. O'D. Ross-Lewin. 7031-0
His Matisses, 1938 Julia Keeler. 6767-0
"His master taken from his head". On the death of a minister. William Cowper. 6814-6
His messenger. Unknown. 6273-3
"His mind is a knife". Karl Radek. Simon Felshin. 6880-4
His mistress. Thomas Randolph. 6737-9
His mother. Honor Arundel. 6895-2
His mother. Wilbur Dick Nesbit. 6097-8
"His mother bids him go without a tear". The recruit. Isabel Ecclestone Mackay. 7027-2
"His mother did not think about". Misfit. Rosemary Farrar. 6761-1
His mother in her hood of blue. Lizette Woodworth Reese. 6282-2,6607-0
His mother speaks! Blanche Olin Twiss. 6032-3
His mother's cooking. Lizzie M. Hadley. 6426-4
His mother's cooking. Lizzie M. Hadley. 6921-5
His mother's face. Elizabeth Barrett Browning. 6097-8
His mother's kiss. Frank Lebby Stanton. 6097-8
His mother's service to our lady. Dante Gabriel Rossetti. 6875-8
His mother's song. Unknown. 6097-8,6964-9
His mother's song. Unknown. 7022-1
His mother's songs. Unknown. 6417-5
His mother's way. Frank Lebby Stanton. 6097-8
His mother's wedding-ring. George Crabbe. 6934-7
His mother-in-law. Walter Parke. 6089-7
His name. Pauline Frances Camp. 6995-9
His name. Dora Greenwell. 6144-3,6335-7
His name. Margaret Junkin Preston. 6062-5
"His name was Alexander Bartholomew McKay". The buster. Sam Walter Foss. 6926-6
His name was Bob. Mazie V. Caruthers. 6510-4
His name was Keko. Theo. Bridgman. 6799-9
"His name was William Mullins, and". Mullins the agnostic. A.T. Worden. 6927-4
His new brother. Joseph Crosby Lincoln. 6119-2;6166-4
His new brother. Unknown. 6078-1,6260-1
His new philosophy. Wilbur Dick Nesbit. 6583-x
His new suit. Samuel Ellsworth Kiser. 6340-3,6741-X
"His noise disturbed me - I could not abide". The loud silence. Susie M. Best. 6750-6
His only way. Habberton Lulham. 6474-4
"His or her's. Mother. Father. Time. Earth...". Nature, sels. David Meltzer. 6792-1
His own epitaph. James Beattie. 6960-6
His own epitaph. John Gay. 6527-9
His own epitaph, fr. Memorials of Thomas Hood. Thomas Hood. 6545-7
His own true wife. Sir Wolfram von Eschenbach. 7039-6
"His palms are black with India ink. The nails". Scrimshaw. Michael Hogan. 6870-7
His parting with Mrs. Dorothy Kennedy. Robert Herrick. 6369-1
His passion. George Conrad Pullman. 6144-3
His peace. William Alexander Percy. 6532-5
His petition to Queen Anne of Denmark (1618). Sir Walter Raleigh. 6584-8
"His petticoats now George cast off". George and the chimney-sweeper. Adelaide O'Keefe. 6772-7
His philosophy. Edgar A. Guest. 6862-6
His phoenix. William Butler Yeats. 6659-3
His picture. John Donne. 6378-0,6562-7
"His picture stands upon the shelf". Dust of time. Virginia Scott. 6799-9
His pilgrimage. Sir Walter Raleigh. 6122-2,6186-9,6198-2, 6501-5,6194-X,6250-4,6253-9,6301-2
His poem. Unknown. 6118-4
His poetry his pillar. Robert Herrick. 6208-3,6315-2,6562-7,6369-1,6563-5,6150
His poets. Robert Herrick. 6297-0
His poets. Leigh Hunt. 6297-0
'His poisoned shafts' Robert Bridges. 6770-0
"'His policy', do you say?". 'Mr. Johnson's policy of reconstruction'. Charles G. ("Miles O'Reilly") Halpine. 6946-0
"His port I love; he's in a proper mood". Douglas, sels. John Home. 6911-8
His prayer for absolution. Robert Herrick. 6931-2,6102-8, 6122-2,6198-2,6337-3
His prayer to Ben Jonson. Robert Herrick. 6483-3,6562-7, 6092-7,6430-2,6668-2,6189-3
His presence. Elizabeth Bemis Dunn. 6799-9
His presence. Mary Sidney Herbert, Countess of Pembroke. 6134-6
His promises. Martha Snell Nickolson. 6065-X
"His regiment came home today". The homecoming. Leroy Folge. 6846-4
His request to Julia. Robert Herrick. 6562-7
His returne to London. Robert Herrick. 6562-7
His reverie. Lily A. Long. 6620-8
His reward. Sir Thomas Wyatt. 6436-1
His riches. Lillian Grey. 6703-4
His riches. Lillian Grey. 6921-5
His rubies: told by Valgovind. Laurence (Adele Florence Nicolson) Hope. 6856-1
"His scanty raiment stained and rent". His code of honor. Zitella Cocke. 7008-6
"His scarred hand jcbs the starting lever". The musician. Honor Arundel. 6895-2
His sentence. Henry W. Eliot Jr. 6118-4
"His shagged head was like a red". The trustee. James Abraham Martling. 6952-5
His share. Kendall Harrison. 6031-5
"His sheep went idly over the hills". The rustic painter. Alice Cary. 6969-X
"His shoulder did I hold". Any saint. Francis Thompson. 6828-6
His sister, his cousin, and his pants. Harriet Ford. 6719-0
"His skin was cracked as leather, sunned...". The farm drudge. Angela Morgan. 7038-8
His son. Asclepiades. 7039-6
His son. Callimachus. 6879-0
His Sunday clothes. Unknown. 6247-4
"His songs were a little phrase". Of a poet patriot. Thomas MacDonagh. 6872-3,6930-4
"His soul fared forth (as from the deep...)". Samuel Taylor Coleridge. Dante Gabriel Rossetti. 6828-6
"His soul is like a secret room". Irony. Mary Frances Ward. 6818-9
"His soul stretched tight across the skies". Prelude 004. Thomas Stearns Eliot. 6808-1
"His soul to God! on a battle-psalm!". Albert Sidney Johnston. Francis Orrery Ticknor. 6946-0
His tapestry and mine. Margaret Elizabeth Sangster. 6654-2
His tears to Thamesis. Robert Herrick. 6430-2
His tender hands. Winnie Lynch Rockett. 6654-2
His Thanksgiving dream. Agnes M. Smith. 6703-4
"His the seat of honour at every celebration". Xenophanes. 6251-2
His theme. Robert Herrick. 6250-4,6301-2
His throne is with the outcast. James Russell Lowell. 6144-3,6335-7
"His tongue was touched with sacred fire". Henry Ward Beecher. Charles Henry Phelps. 6820-0
"His triumphs of a moment done". On the departure of the British from Charleston. Philip Freneau. 6946-0
"His valour passed beyond the Andes". Sepulchral

inscription. Jorge Luis Borges. 6759-X
His vanished master. John Jay Chapman. 7008-6
"His vertebrae, once needed much". Charles F. Smith. 6254-7
"His village neighbors vummed, no...dissenting". Valedictory. Harold Willard Gleason. 6761-1
"His voice above the crash of crumbling throne". Woodrow Wilson. Annah Robinson Watson. 7001-9
"His was another race than mine". Jesse Seligman. Noah Davis. 6848-0
"His was the cowards, not the hero's stance". Portrait of a friend. Francis King. 6475-2
"His was the sword that from its scabbard...". Grant. Eugene Field. 6949-5
His way. John Travers Moore. 6906-1
His wealth. Unknown. 6109-5
His widow. Cale Young Rice. 6441-8
His will. Kanda. 6027-7
His winding-sheet. Robert Herrick. 6194-X
His wisdom. Nicholas Breton. 6436-1,6026-9,6436-1
His wish. Unknown. 6130-3
His wish to God. Robert Herrick. 6931-2
"His woman is/Brown sand warrior". No. 6 Rochelle DuBois. 6898-7
"His words are bonds, his oaths are oracles". William Shakespeare. 6238-5
"His words seem'd oracles". Effect of oratory upon a multitude. George Croly. 6980-0
"His words were left after him". The stargazer's legacy. Vasko Popa. 6758-1
"His work is done, his toil is o'er". Faithful unto death. Richard Handfield Titherington. 6946-0
"His yoke-ox, growing feeble...". Addaeus. 6251-2
His youth. Ella Wheeler Wilcox. 6863-4
"Hist, oh hist". Thomas Lovell Beddoes. 6187-7
Histed, Thaddeus C.
    When Teddy hits the west. 6995-9
Historians ("They will say of this age"). Martha Millet. 6561-9
Historic episodes. Peter Wellingto Clark. 6178-8
Historic Oxford. Robert E. Sterling. 6650-X
"A historical painter, named Brown". Limerick:"A historical painter, named Brown". Dante Gabriel Rossetti. 6811-1
Historical trees--told in rhyme. Lizzie M. Hadley. 6049-8
History. Donald Britton. 7003-5
History. Malcolm Cowley. 6037-4
History. Ralph Waldo Emerson. 6176-1,6107-9
History. Haniel Long. 6039-0
History. Dorothy Reid. 6072-2
History. Robert Southey. 6219-9
History. Roberta Teale Swartz. 6039-0
History. Unknown. 6105-2
History. Sir William Watson. 6473-6,6102-8
History of a life. Bryan Waller ("Barry Cornwall") Procter. 6302-0
History of a moment. Carlos Bulosan. 6761-1
History of a pretty girl. Unknown. 6675-5
History of education. David McCord. 6722-0
The history of honey. Nathalia Crane. 6393-9
History of John Day. Thomas Hood. 6425-6
The history of the U.S. Winifred Sackville Stoner. 6736-0
History of two simple lovers. John Crowe Ransom. 6072-2
The history of weather. George Mattingly. 6792-1
A history. John Williams. 6388-8
Hit, fr. Battle. Wilfred Wilson Gibson. 6897-9
Hita, Juan Ruiz de
    Praise of little women. Henry Wadsworth Longfellow (tr.). 6279-2
    Praise of little women. 6279-2
The hitchen May-day song. Unknown. 6133-8,6242-3
Hitchens, E.L.
    Song of the drum. 6711-5
Hite, Vernon E.
    Malcolm X. 7024-8
    Trapped. 7024-8
"Hither haste, and gently strew". Song ("Hither haste"). Thomas Lovell Beddoes. 6187-7
"Hither thou com'st: the busy wind all night". The bird. Henry Vaughan. 6943-6

Hither turn the hearts of men, fr. A Florentine cycle. Gertrude Huntington McGiffert. 6838-3
"Hither, come hither, ye clouds renowned...". The cloud chorus. Aristophanes. 6987-8
Hither, meadow gossip, tell me! H. Prescott Beach. 6373-X
"Hither, o fragrant of Tmolus the golden". O Bacchanals, come! Euripides. 6959-2
"Hither, this solemn eventide", fr. Hawthorne and... William Ernest Henley. 6507-4
"Hither, where tangled thickets of the acacia". The babiaantje. Frank Templeton Prince. 6788-3
Hitler and the generals. Michael Guttenbrunner. 6769-7
Hitomaro
    On parting from his wife. 6732-8
    "When/Halting in front of it". Arthur Waley (tr.). 7039-6
Hitoshi
    "'Tis easier to hide the reeds". William N. Porter (tr.). 6852-9
Hittan of Tayyi
    His children. Sir Charles Lyall (tr.). 7039-6
Hives and homes. Phoebe Cary. 6060-9
Ho for noa noa. Berton Braley. 6853-7
"Ho! all you young Vermonters". Vacation hints for young Vermonters. Daniel L. Cady. 6988-6
Ho! boat ahoy! Emma Sophie Stilwell. 6575-9
Ho! Dancers. John Russell McCarthy. 6959-2
"Ho! burnish well, ye cunning hands". Song of the mariner's needle. C.R. Clarke. 6833-2
"Ho! for the blades of Harden!". The blades of Harden, fr. Whaup o' the rede. William Henry Ogilvie. 6845-6
"Ho! for the days of ice and snow". January. Irwin Shupp Jr.. 6936-3
"Ho! godless madmen at the helm". The slaver's wreck. William Cox Bennett. 7009-4
"Ho! Heimdal sounds the Gjallar-horn". Ragnarok: the twilight of the gods. Arthur Guiterman. 6846-4
"Ho! ho! the count was not one of those". The queen of Gothland. Herbert Trench. 6877-4
"Ho! ho! thrice ho! for the mistletoe". Christmas. Frank H. Sweet. 6807-3
"Ho! like an arrow I hurl myself". Swim song. Mary Lovell Cope. 6841-3
"Ho! madness/Of lover/Of mistress/Of harlot". Song of passion. J.G. Woods. 6799-9
"Ho! sing of your trout in the spring betimes". Ice-fishing in winter. John Harrington Keene. 7035-3
"Ho! There's a dance in the Ballahou!". A west indian dance. Richard Butler Glaenzer. 6959-2
"Ho! thou traveler on life's highway". Hold the light. Unknown. 6912-6
"Ho! to the top of the towering wall!". The bricklayers. G.H. Barnes. 6915-0,6167-2
"Ho! why dost thou shiver and shake". Gaffer Gray. Thomas Holcroft. 6787-5
"Ho! workers of the old time styled". The shoemakers. John Greenleaf Whittier. 6753-0
"Ho! ye watchmen of our Europe...". The emancipation of the press. John Jeffrey. 7009-4
"Ho! you chap of grit and sinew". The patrol [Gordon] and the gold-digger. Adam Lindsay Gordon. 6951-7
Ho, Chong Chi
    A world apart. 6732-8
"Ho, a song by the fire!". Hanover winter song. Richard Hovey. 7035-3
"Ho, brother Teague, dost hear de decree". Lillibulero. Unknown. 6858-8
"Ho, brother Teague, dost hear the decree?". Song ("Ho, brother Teague") Thomas Wharton, 1st Marquess of Wharton. 6179-6
"Ho, dancers! in your silken hose". Ho! Dancers. John Russell McCarthy. 6959-2
Ho, everyone that thirsteth, fr. Isaiah. Bible. 6337-3
Ho, for lubberland!. Unknown. 6547-3
"Ho, let her rip - with he royal clew a-quiver". In the trades. Cicely Fox Smith. 6833-2
"Ho, my bonnie boatie". A boat song. Unknown. 6873-1
"Ho, pretty bee, did you see my croodlin' doo?". Croodlin' doo. Eugene Field. 6949-5
"Ho, sailor of the sea!. How's my boy? Sydney Dobell.

6833-2,6910-X
"**Ho,** skipper on the sea-shore!". The troll-man. Caroline M. Hewins. 6921-5
"**Ho,** ST. Antoine!..thou quarter of the poor". The Jacobin of Paris. Viscount Strangford; George Sydney Smythe. 7009-4
"**Ho,** there! Fisherman, hold your hand!". The lost steamship. Fitz-James O'Brien. 6914-2
"**Ho,** woodsmen of the moutain-side!". A cry to arms. Henry Timrod. 6946-0
"**Ho,** ye slender youths in your top-boots clad". Kyjov. Petr Bezruc. 6763-8
"**Ho,** ye youthful swains, topbooted and lithe". Kijov. Petr Bezruc. 6886-3
Ho-ho of the golden belt. John Godfrey Saxe. 6787-5
"**Ho-hum!/Sakes!** I's all waked up". Morning. Pearl Boles. 6764-6
"**Ho-hum/There** goes the rooster". Morning soliloquy of one farmer. Helen Reed. 6750-6
Hoag, George Edward
    A hunter's dream. 6342-X
Hoag, Nina Pride
    Big Stone Lake. 6342-X
Hoagland, Clayton
    Two hungers. 6761-1
Hoagland, William
    The poem you write in sleep. 6900-2
Hoar, Constance Entwhistle
    The old hitching post. 6750-6
Hoar-frost. Amy Lowell. 6897-9
Hoar-frost. William White. 8868-5
"A **hoard** of rich treasure lay heaped...". Sole survivor. Beowulf. 6879-0
Hoard, Prescott
    Sky line. 6069-2
Hoarded joy. Dante Gabriel Rossetti. 6110-9
Hoare, Prince
    The Arethusa. 6328-4,6547-3,6322-5,6639-9,6086-2
Hoarfrost. Christine Busta. 6769-7
"The **hoary** dotard, aristocracy". A song of the people. Thomas Wade. 7009-4
"**Hoary** with age, upon his dying couch". The death of Jacob. Mary L. Clough. 6848-0
Hoatson, F.
    The bubble. 6937-1
    The snail and the fairy. 6937-1
    Yellow. 6937-1
    Yellow chicks. 6937-1
Hoatson, Florence
    Hyde Park. 6804-9
    The thin cat. 6937-1
Hob's love. Unknown. 6383-7
Hobart, Crea W.
    The lure of the road. 6906-1
    The Maine woods. 6906-1
    The old tree. 6906-1
    Rocky crest. 6906-1
Hobart, Ethel
    A valentine. 6118-4
Hobart, George V.
    I'm a lil' rough rider. 6721-2
    Jim. 6274-1
    Out sleighing with Sophia. 6692-5
Hobart, Mrs. Charles
    The changed cross. 6219-9
Hobart, Sarah D.
    The legend of St. Freda. 6922-3
"**Hobbes** clearly proves that every creature". A rhapsody on poetry, sel. Jonathan Swift. 6934-7
Hobbledy hops. Unknown. 6629-1
Hobbs, Mildred Ann
    Last night. 6662-3
    Winter settles down. 6662-3
the **hobby** horse. Unknown. 6466-3
Hobet, George V.
    Das kleine kind. 6249-0
Hobie Noble. Unknown. 6185-0
Hobnails in Eden. Robert Haven Schauffler. 6732-8
"**Hobnelia,** seated in a dreary vale". Thursday; or the spell. John Gay. 6972-X

Hobnobbing on the Ochils. James Logie ("Hugh Haliburton") Robertson. 6819-7
Hoboes. Berton Braley. 6853-7
Hobson and his men. Edward F. Burns. 6741-X
Hobson and his men. Robert Loveman. 6946-0
Hobson, Dorothy
    Awakening. 6979-7
    The snow comes silently. 6042-0
Hobson, Geary
    Barbara's land revisited-August 1978 7005-1
    For my brother and sister southwestern indian poets. 7005-1
    Going to the water. 7005-1
    Lonnie Kramer. 7005-1
    Tiger people. 7005-1
Hobson, John L.
    Friendship. 6764-6
Hobson, the cobbler. Unknown. 6061-7
Hoc cygno vinces. Henry Hawkins. 6022-6
Hoc est corpus. Alex Comfort. 6391-8
Hoccleve's humorous praise of his lady. Thomas Hoccleve. 6430-2
Hoccleve's lament for Chaucer and Gower. Thomas Hoccleve. 6430-2
Hoccleve, Thomas
    De regimine principum (on Chaucer). 6198-2
    A description of his ugly lady. 6881-2
    Hoccleve's humorous praise of his lady. 6430-2
    Hoccleve's lament for Chaucer and Gower. 6430-2
    Lament for Chaucer. 6483-3,6659-3
    Mi maister Chaucer. 6193-1
    To Sir John Oldcastle. 6198-2
Hoch! der Kaiser. Rodney Blake. 6089-7,6274-1
Hochdord, Muriel F.
    Bayberry candle. 6850-2
Hochdorf, Muriel
    To a campus oak. 6396-9
Hochdorf, Muriel F.
    Advice to red leaves. 6850-2
    Alas! 6850-2
    Anniversary for armistice. 6850-2
    Beyond the dunes. 6850-2
    Blank verse. 6850-2
    Commencement: June 1929. 6850-2
    Cousin Florrie. 6850-2
    Cousin Zetta. 6850-2
    Cusses. 6850-2
    Das Zahlenlied. 6850-2
    Departure. 6850-2
    Despair. 6850-2
    Dirge. 6850-2
    Earthward. 6850-2
    Enchanted forest. 6850-2
    Flight. 6850-2
    Hotel. 6850-2
    Marching song for the coming year. 6850-2
    Moonlight sonata. 6850-2
    Poetaster. 6850-2
    Rondel. 6850-2
    Schmerzen. 6850-2
    Secret. 6850-2
    Solitaire. 6850-2
    Sonnet ("Oh, you and I "). 6850-2
    The three sneezes. 6850-2
    Tribute - a year too late. 6850-2
    Triolet. 6850-2
    Unnamed sonnet. 6850-2
    When I am grown. 6850-2
    Wish. 6850-2
Hochi
    "Two little boats sail side by side." Lois J. Erickson (tr.). 6027-7
Hochsommernacht. Wilhelm Weigand. 6253-9
The **hock-cart** or harvest home. Robert Herrick. 6191-5
The **hock-cart,** or harvest home... Robert Herrick. 6328-4, 6562-7,6194-X,6430-2
Hockey. Unknown. 7035-3
The **hod-fellow.** Robert J. Burdette. 6588-0
Hodge. Robert Bridges. 6487-6
"**Hodge** held a farm, and smiled content". The case altered.

Hodge

Unknown. 6878-2,6787-5
Hodge, Alan
Waiting. 6317-9,6354-3
Hodge, Marie A.
Old man of the mountain. 6764-6
Hodge, the cat. Sarah ("Susan Coolidge") Woolsey. 6120-6, 6692-2
Hodges, Alida Dickerman
Marse Jesus - will it be long? 6764-6
Hodges, D.F.
Now is the time. 6085-4,6211-3
Hodges, Leigh Mitchell
Alone. 7019-1
Give them the flowers now. 6260-1,6303-9,6964-9
The optimist. 6583-X
Hodges, Lillian F.
Doubting Thomas. 6750-6
Hodgkins, Georgiana
The Colorado canyon. 6799-9
Lindbergh. 7019-1
Hodgkins, Louise Manning
Valiant-for-truth. 7001-9
Hodgson, Cecil E.C.
A caterpillar. 6316-0
Discovered. 6316-0
Lost lovely things. 6316-0
Hodgson, Ralph
"Babylon - where I go dreaming". 6897-9
The bells of heaven. 6102-8,6044-7,6427-2,6477-9,6532-5, 6634-8,6339 ,6501-5,6510-4,6668-2,6581-3,6723-9,6393
The bride. 6023-4
The bull. 6234-2,6726-3
Chuplet ("God loves a lovely rainbow.") 6102-8
Eve. 6232-6,6236-9,6246-6,6427-2,6733-6,6464 ,6026-9, 6153-2,6210-5,6102-8,6199-0,6250
"God loves an idle rainbow". 6897-9
The great auk's ghost. 6722-0,6723-9
The gypsy girl. 6332-2,66464-7
The hammers. 6488-4
Hymn to Moloch. 6943-6
The late, last rook. 6477-9
The missel thrush. 6943-6
The mystery. 6338-1,6477-9,6532-5,6337-3,6730-1,6723 , 6102-8,6301-2
Prometheus. 6199-0
"Reason has moons, but moons not hers". 6897-9
The riddle. 6722-0
The sedge warbler. 6253-9
The sedge-warbler. 7020-5
Silver wedding. 6184-2
Song ("There"). 6943-6
The song of honour, sels. 6317-9,6339-X
The song of honour. 6044-7,6332-2,6234-2,6427-2,6138-9, 6228 ,6161-3
Stupidity street. 6510-4,6464-7,6668-2,6723-9,6102-8, 6153 ,6044-7,6073-0,6228-8,6509-0,6732-8,6581
The swallow. 6872-3
Time, you old gipsy man. 6236-9,6339-X,6477-9,6512-0, 6634-8,6732 ,6506-6,6513-9,6464-7,6668-2
Hodgson, William Noel
Ave, mater--atque vale. 6477-9
Back to rest. 6477-9
Before action. 7026-4
Before action. 6337-3,6477-9,6501-5,6730-1,6650-X,6542
God's hills. 7027-2
Hoe your own row. Unknown. 6629-1
Hoe your roe. Frank Lebby Stanton. 6291-1
Hoebel, Kathleen
String of pearls. 6857-X
Sustenance. 6857-X
Hoefflin, Henry Samuel
The reach for immortality. 6799-9
Hoeing and praying. Unknown. 6928-2
Hoeing corn in Vermont. Daniel L. Cady. 6989-4
"The hoeing of day is done". A lullaby, fr. Kafir songs. Francis Carey ("Jan van Avond") Slater. 6800-6
Hoelty, Ludwig Heinrich Christoph
The old farmer to his son. James Abraham Martling (tr.). 6952-5
"Hoeredem (vt spes est) pariet nupta...". Epigramma.

Thomas Campion. 6794-8
Hoey, George
Asleep at the switch. 6915-0
Asleep at the switch. 6451-5
Hofeller, Leetha Journey
Prelude ("Cling now"). 6316-0
Hofer. William Wordsworth. 7009-4
Hoff, Clara S.
Sad harvest. 6750-6
Hoffenstein, Samuel
"After October, comes November". 6817-0
"Along the country roads there grow". 6817-0
Apologia. 6217-2
Breathes there a man. 6722-0
"I do not question woman's place". 6817-0
"I want to take a ship and go". 6817-0
"I'm tired of work, I'm tired of play". 6817-0
If you love me. 6026-9
Interlude, for a solitary flute, sels. 6532-5
Let our love be. 6441-8
A little while to love and rave. 6026-9
"Men in single state should tarry". 6817-0
"My heart is broken, my life is ended". 6817-0
"My luck with the proverbial sex". 6817-0
"Nothing from a straight line swerves". 6817-0
"Now, alas, it is too late". 6817-0
Observation. 6780-8
The ocean spills. 6026-9
"Oh, it is cruel and inhuman". 6817-0
"Only the wholesomest foods you eat". 6817-0
A poem intended to incite the utmost depression. 6089-7
Poems in praise of practically everything, sels. 6817-0
Poems in praise of practically nothing. 6089-7,6287-3, 6089-7
Poems in praise of practically nothing, sels. 6817-0
Poems of passion, carefully restrained.., sels. 6817-0
Poems of passion, carefully restrained... 6287-3
Primer. 6089-7
"Psychoanalyzed, I stand". 6817-0
"A queen as torrid as Sumatra". 6817-0
Some folks I know. 6026-9
"Some folks I know are always worried". 6817-0
Song of fairly utter despair. 6120-6
Songs about life and brighter things yet, sels. 6817-0
Songs of fairly utter despair, sels. 6817-0
Songs to break the tedium..., or heartbreak, sels. 6817-0
"This black predicament I sing". 6817-0
To a cat. 6120-6
To Claire. 6300-4
"When trouble drives me into rhyme". 6817-0
"When you're away, I'm restless, lonely". 6817-0
"Where primal instincts do not slumber". 6817-0
"You buy some flowers for your table". 6817-0
"You buy yourself a new suit of clothes". 6817-0
"You fall in love, it's a common habit". 6817-0
"You get a girl; and may you say you love her". 6817-0
"You have a most attractive pan". 6817-0
You hire a cook. 6722-0
"You leap out of bed; you start to get ready". 6817-0
"You practise every possible virtue". 6817-0
You work and work. 6722-0
"You work and work till your brain is weary". 6817-0
Your little hands. 6026-9
Hoffman Von Fallersleben, H.
Farewell, thou lovely wood. James Abraham Martling (tr.). 6952-5
The nightingale's reply. James Abraham Martling (tr.). 6952-5
Hoffman, August Heinrich
dreadful story of Pauline and the matches. 6120-6
Hoffman, Charles Fenno
The farewell. 6226-1
L'amour sans ailes. 6441-8
The mint julep. 6006-4,6735-2
Monterey. 6219-9,6267-9,6263-6,6300-4,6424-8,6470 ,6006-4,6015-3,6062-5,6271-7,6302-0,6385 ,6471-X,6552-X, 6632-1,6735-2,6309-8,6250
Rosalie Clare. 6004-8
Seek not to understand her. 6226-1

Sparkling and bright. 6077-3,6243-1,6085-4,6632-1,6271-7,6307 ,6004-8
Think of me, dearest. 6226-1
Thy name. 6226-1
Thy smiles. 6226-1
Hoffman, Charles Fenno (tr.)
Calling-one's own. Unknown (American Indian), 6393-4
Rio Bravo - a Mexican lament. Don Jose de Saltillo, 6946-0
Hoffman, George Edward
As it began to dawn. 6144-3
Hymn. 6337-3
Refreshment. 6144-3
Young warrior. 6144-3
Hoffman, Joseph
When we hold each other. 6799-9
Hoffman, N.M.
Fried egg. 6857-X
Hoffman, Phoebe
The cats of Baddeck. 6120-6
The civil engineers. 6034-X
The freight yards. 7007-8
Hoffmann, Heinrich
The dreadful story about Harriet and the matches. 6242-3
The story of Augustus who would not have any soup. 6614-3
The story of Augustus. 6401-9,6135-4
The story of little suck-a-thumb. 6105-2,6134-6,6242-3, 6459-0
Hoffmann, Thelma
Maturity. 6750-6
Hofford, M.L.
Jerusalem the beautiful. 6921-5
Hofman, Victor Victorovitch
A langorous waltz beside the river. 6959-2
Hofmannsthal, Hugo von
Ballad of the outer life. Jethro Bithell (tr.). 7039-6
Many indeed must perish in the keel. Jethro Bithell (tr.). 7039-6
The two. Ludwig Lewisohn (tr.). 7039-6
A Venetian night. Ludwig Lewisohn (tr.). 7039-6
The **hog-thorny** bear. Unknown. 6651-8
The **hog**. John Bunyan. 6179-6
Hogan, Linda
Black Hills survival gathering, 1980 7005-1
Blessing. 7005-1
Cities behind glass. 7005-1
Saint Coyote. 7005-1
Song for my name. 7005-1
Hogan, M.
Mannix the coiner. 6518-X
Hogan, Michael
Child of blue. 6870-7
The condor. 6870-7
Draherin O Machree. 6090-0
Lovely Maryanne. 6858-8
O'Neill's war song. 6930-4
Rust. 6870-7
Scrimshaw. 6870-7
Spring. 6870-7
Warriors. 6870-7
Hogben, John
"Somewhere in France". 7031-0
'Somewhere in France'. 7027-2
Truth and beauty. 7015-9
Hoge, Paton H.
A lost friend. 6085-4
Hogg, James
The Abbot M'Kinnon. 6219-9
Athol cummers. 6180-X
Bauldy Fraser. 6859-6
The boat race, fr. Queen Hynde. 6001-3
Bonnie Kilmeny gaed up the glen. 6845-6
Bonnie Prince Charlie. 6180-X,6395-0,6219-9,6267-9
A boy's song, sels. 6934-7
A boy's song. 6250-4,6114-1,6131-1,6301-2,6639-9,6454 , 6086-2,6638-0,6668-2,6543-0,6105-2,6373-X,6519-8, 6466-3,6479-5,6496 ,6242-3,6249-0,6401-9,6459-0,6552-X,6135 ,6623-2,6634-8,6075-7,6132-X,6134-6,6180

The broken heart. 6980-0
Callum-a-glen. 6859-6
Charlie is my darling. 6136-2,6219-9
The cherub. 6802-2
The curse of the laureate. 6802-2
Drumossie Muir. 6859-6
Farewell to Glen-Shalloch. 6859-6
The fate of MacGregor. 6344-6,6415-9
The flying tailor. 6802-2
The Frasers in the correl. 6859-6
The good man of Alloa. 6614-3
The gude greye katt. 6802-2
The harp of Ossian. 7009-4
The highland watch. 6328-4
Isabelle. 6802-2
Jock Johnstone, the tinkler. 6102-8,6302-0,6385-3,6577-5
The jolly curlers. 7035-3
Kilmeny. 6180-X,6302-0,6385-3,6271-7,6114-1,6219 ,6086-2,6438-8,6613-5
Kilmeny, sels. 6395-0,6427-2
The lament of Flora Macdonald. 6180-X,6088-9
The lark. 6271-7,6597-X,6629-1
The last cradle song. 6233-4
The liddel bower. 6086-2
Lock the door, Lariston. 6180-X,6395-0,6086-2
Love is like a dizziness. 6089-7,6240-7
McLean's welcome. 6180-X
Maclean's welcome. 6859-6
May of the Moril glen. 6613-5
The moon was a-waning. 6271-7
My love she's but a lassie yet, sels. 6934-7
Over the lea. 6793-X
Queen Mary's return to Scotland. 6980-0
The rapture of Kilmeny. 6600-3
The skylark. 6073-0,6239-3,6479-5,6180-X,6240-7,6240-7, 6304-7,6639-9,6424-8,6543-0,6242-3,6250-4,6114-1, 6219-9,6396-9,6086-2,6385-3,6395-0,6075-7
Turn the blue bonnet wha can. 6859-6
Walsinghame's song, fr. Wat o' the cleugh. 6802-2
The way for Billy and me. 6424-8
When Maggie gangs away. 6600-3,6710-7,6219-9
When the kye came home. 6180-X,6302-0,6385-3,6086-2, 6383-7,6219
The witch of Fife. 6102-8,6732-8,6438-8
Hogmanay. James (1827-1888) Thomson. 6960-6
Hoh-shuku-sei-ten. Gonnoske Komia. 6070-6
Hohenlinden. Thomas Campbell. 6014-5,6212-1,6104-4,6125-7, 6131-1,6737 ,6075-7,6102-8,6180-X,6271-7,6457-4,6484 ,6186-9,6192-3,6560-0,6196-6,6250-4,6543 ,6153-2, 6639-9,6660-7,6665-8,6219-9,6438 ,6198-2,6263-6,6267-9,6304-7,6726-3,6732 ,6086-2,6239-3,6240-7,6246-5, 6302-0,6385 ,6479-5,6504-X,6610-0
The **Hoidens**. James Branch Cabell. 6875-8
Hoikawa, Lady
"My doubt about his constancy". William N. Porter (tr.). 6852-9
Hoisington, May Folwell
Black frost. 7038-8
day at Laguerre's/A. 7038-8
Fairy foot. 6039-0
The hollow apple tree. 6102-8
Ramadan in the desert. 7038-8
A Surrey song. 6039-0
Travel's end. 6619-4
Hoist the flag! Oscar II; King of Sweden. 6045-5
Hoke, Thomas Gordon
The birth of Venus, sels. 6997-5
Hokusai's wave. Olga Cabral. 6966-5
Holbrook, E.A.
Child and tree. 6049-8
Children's arbor day march. 6049-8
Life in its spring-time. 6049-8
Song to the maple tree. 6049-8
Holcomb, Willard
A lost chord found. 6926-6
Holcombe, William H.
New Thanatopsis. 6045-1
Holcroft, Thomas
Gaffer Gray. 6787-5

HOLD

"Hold back thy hours, dark night, till we have". John Fletcher. 6187-7
"Hold back thy hours, dark night..". Wedding song, fr. The maid's tragedy. Francis Beaumont and John Fletcher. 6827-8
"Hold cruell love oh hold I yeild." Unknown. 6563-5
"Hold diligent coverse with thy children. Have them". Unknown. 6238-5
Hold dot fort, for ve vos coming. Hans von Dunkerfoodle (pseud.) 6471-X
Hold fast to the dear old sabbath. George M. Vickers. 6921-5
"Hold fast what I give you". Lily Warner. 6127-3,6131-1
Hold fast your dreams. Louise Driscoll. 6478-7,6607-0
"Hold hard, Ned! Lift me down once more". The sick stockrider. Adam Lindsay Gordon. 6951-7
"Hold hard, Ned! Lift me down once more...". The sick stock-rider. Adam Lindsay Gordon. 6768-9
Hold high the torch. Unknown. 6337-3
"Hold me upon thy faithful heart". Fair Helen of Kirconnel. Felicia Dorothea Hemans. 6973-8
Hold my hand. Edmund Pennant. 6966-5
"Hold not thy peace, God of my praise!". Psalm 109. Bible. 6848-0
"Hold of the maker, not the made". Ralph Waldo Emerson. 6753-0
"Hold the lantern aside, and shudder not so". Searching for the slain. Unknown. 6909-6
Hold the light. Unknown. 6912-6
"Hold them up reverently, let the light fall". Beads. Chapman J. Milling. 7016-7
Hold thou me fast. Christina Georgina Rossetti. 6065-X
"Hold up, hold up, you Jersey folk". Order of service. Merle Colby. 6780-8
"Hold.". Patrick Reginald Chalmers. 6510-4
Holden, Frances Viola
    The crown of womanhood. 6097-8
    A little girl in school. 6274-1
Holden, John Jarvis
    Look up! 6274-1
    Love, youth, song. 6274-1
    Mother and home. 6097-8
    Mother's love. 6097-8
    My Lady Anemone. 6274-1
    The orchard. 6274-1
    The touch of children's hands. 6274-1
Holden, Jonathan
    Politics. 6803-0
Holden, Marcia Nichols
    Convent. 6979-7
Holden, Marica Nichols
    Surf - Jones Beach. 6750-6
Holden, Raymond
    After the circus. 6037-4
    Awake under the stars. 6979-7
    Firewood. 6037-4
    Here is the world. 6761-1
    Midnight: Battery Park. 6808-1
    The mind has studied flight. 6979-7
    Song for a late hour. 6808-1
    Sugaring. 6034-X
    To nine who vanished long ago. 6037-4
    Wild honey. 6037-4
Holden, Raymond Peckham
    Dance. 6959-2
Holder, Phebe A.
    An hour with Whittier. 6924-X
    A woodland hymn. 6049-8
Holderlin's journey. Edwin Muir. 6483-3;6641-0
Holderlin, Friedrich
    Des morgens. 6253-9
    Life half lived. 6125-7
"Holding herself as if she had". A drunken satyr from Newton County tells how he met... Michael Burns. 6860-X
Holding town office in Vermont. Daniel L. Cady. 6989-4
Holdsworth, Philip J.
    My queen of dreams. 6768-9
    Station hunting on the Warrego. 6768-9
The hole in the floor. Lizzie Clark Hardy. 6916-9

The hole in the patch. Unknown. 6916-9
"A hole in the right front pocket". The challenge. Calvin Murry. 6870-7
Hole, W.G.
    A gentleman of Somerset. 6793-X
    Prayer before war. 7031-0
Holgren, Beryl Scouten
    A small girl's prayer. 6750-6
Holiday. Hermann Hagedorn. 6944-4
Holiday. Horace. 7039-6
Holiday. William Roehrick. 6850-2
Holiday. Edith Sitwell. 6150-8
Holiday. Marion Patton Waldron. 6032-3
Holiday. Gertrude Lee Wheeler. 6270-9
A holiday acrostic. Elizabeth Lloyd. 6268-7
Holiday at Hampton Court. John Davidson. 6102-8
The holiday convention. Emma Celia & Lizzie J. Rook. 6268-7
Holiday crowd. Hortense Flexner. 6808-1
Holiday home. Henry Cuyler Bunner. 6632-1
Holiday hours. Felicia Dorothea Hemans. 6973-8
Holiday Inn at Bemidji. Gerald Vizenor. 7005-1
A holiday task. Gilbert Abbott A Becket. 6902-9
A holiday. Lizette Woodworth Reese. 6431-0
The holiday. Slack Davis. 6530-9
Holidays. Ralph Waldo Emerson. 6753-0
Holidays. Ralph Waldo Emerson. 6126-5,6288-1
Holidays. Ralph Waldo Emerson. 6753-0
Holidays. Henry Wadsworth Longfellow. 6109-5,6429-9,6465-5, 6321-7
The holidays. Louise Pollock. 6048-X
The holidays. Schuyler E. Sears. 6906-1
The holidays. Jane Taylor. 6131-1
Holier night. Leslie Savage Clark. 6144-3
'The holiest among the mighty'. Jean Paul Richter. 6335-7, 6144-3
Holiness. John Drinkwater. 6161-3
"Holiness on the head". Aaron. George Herbert. 6430-2,6431-1,6933-9
Holland. Samuel Butler. 6278-4
Holland. Oliver Goldsmith. 6302-0;6385-3
Holland. Barbara Jane Provost. 6466-3
The Holland handkerchief. Unknown. 6061-7
Holland, D.M.
    Dahlias. 6232-6
Holland, George Jay
    The holy flame, 'menorah' 6848-0
Holland, Hugh
    Lament ("Lo, now he shineth yonder.") 6472-8
    Sonnet to Shakespeare. 6528-7
Holland, Josiah Gilbert
    Albert Durer's studio. 6331-4,6631-3
    "Are there not lofty moments when the soul". 6238-5
    Babyhood. 6481-7
    Bluebeard. 6413-2
    Brotherhood. 6911-8
    A Christmas carol ("There's a song in the air"). 6145-1, 6239-3,6006-4,6627-5,6304-7,6421
    A Christmas carol. 6820-0
    Cradle song. 6302-0,6385-3,6240-7,6512-0,6627-5,6078
    Daniel Gray. 6300-4
    The day's demand. 6337-3
    Eureka. 6066-8,6581-3
    Give us men. 6887-1
    God give us men! 6260-1,6465-5,6143-5
    Gradatim. 6101-X,6260-1,6291-1,6610-0,6730-1,6240 ,6337-3,6499-X,6570-8,6214-8,6309-8
    The heart of the war. 6113-3,6402-7,6129-9
    "Hearts only thrive on varied good". 6109-5
    "Hearts, like apples, are hard and sour". 6238-5
    "Heaven's not gained by a single bound." 6225-3,6479-5
    "I count this thing to be grandly true". 6238-5
    I have never known the winter's blast. 6238-5
    Katrina, sels. 6066-8
    The mistress of the manse, sels. 6066-8
    My children. 6053-6
    The need for men. 6386-1
    Old and blind. 6482-5
    The old clock of Prague. 6331-4
    On the Righi. 6749-2

The palmer's vision. 6183-4,6674-7
Rockaby, lullaby. 6519-8
Sleeping and dreaming. 6240-7
A song of doubt. 6730-1
A song of faith. 6730-1,6461-2
A Thanksgiving ode. 6629-1
There's a song in the air. 6144-3,6337-3,6747-6,6304-7
To my dog Blanco. 7008-6
A tribute. 6066-8
Wanted. 6101-X,6211-3,6482-5
The way to heaven. 6523-6,6304-7,6424-8
"We rise by things that are 'neath our feet". 6238-5
Where shall the baby's dimple be? 6078-1,6566-X
"A word and a stone once let go cannot be recalled". 6623-2
Holland, Lord
Over a covered seat in the flower-garden at Holland... 6874-X
Who seeks to please all men. 6337-3
Holland, Madeline
Night in the valley. 6800-6
Noontide. 6800-6
The pioneer. 6800-6
Holland, Norah M.
April in England. 6474-4
Captains adventurous. 7027-2
Cradle song. 6115-X
The end of the road. 6796-4
The gentlemen of Oxford. 6846-4
Home thoughts from abroad. 6115-X
The king of Erin's daughter. 6843-X,6115-X
The lost shoe. 6797-2
My dog and I. 6115-X,6510-4
The port o' missing ships. 6599-6
Sea song. 6115-X
Sea-gulls. 6332-2,6558-9
To W.B. Yeats. 6115-X
The unchristened child. 6115-X
Holland, Rupert Sargent
P's and Q's. 6540-6
Holland, fr. Geography. Edward Verrall Lucas. 6018-8
Hollander, Jean
Birthing. 6821-9
Hollands, H.T.
The wee-waw land. 6684-4
Holley, Horace
Cross patch. 6030-7
The dance. 6959-2
The hill. 6730-1
In a garden. 6338-1
Orchard. 6030-7
Holley, Marietta
The brothers. 6695-X
Summer. 6066-8
Holliday, Carl
Old "Prof" Dickson dies. 6038-2,6538-4
Holliday, Francia
Wanted wings. 6799-9
Holliday, Frank E.
How strange it will be. 6620-8
My little bo-peep. 6672-0
Hollingshead, John
What do you want at sixty-three? 7012-4
Hollinshead, Martha H.
Gentians in October. 6799-9
Hollo, my fancy! Unknown. 6563-5
Hollock, R.C.
'As a watch in the night'. 6983-5
The hollow apple tree. May Folwell Hoisington. 6102-8
The hollow bone. William Jeffrey. 6269-5
"The hollow dash of waves! the ceaseless roar!". A voyager's dream of land. Felicia Dorothea Hemans. 6973-8
The hollow land. William Morris. 6125-7
The hollow men, sels. Thomas Stearns Eliot. 6246-5
The hollow men. Thomas Stearns Eliot. 6077-3,6348-9,6527-9, 6645-3,6375-6,6071 ,6354-3,6659-3,6491-4
The hollow oak. Edward Bulwer-Lytton; Baron Lytton. 6543-0
"Hollow sea-shell which for years had stood". Sea-shell murmurs. Eugene Lee-Hamilton. 6997-5

"Hollow sea-shell which for years hath stood". Sea-shell murmurs. Eugene Lee-Hamilton. 7015-9
"A hollow, wan cocoon, each empty farm". God's barn. Winifred Welles. 6761-1
'Hollow-sounding and mysterious'. Christina Georgina Rossetti. 6473-6
Holloway, John Wesley
Black mammies. 6365-9
Holloway, Mark
To the Thames. 6475-2
Holloway, Roberta
After lovers. 6808-1
Between reaches of stone. 6808-1
Boy waking. 6808-1
City evening. 6808-1
Consolation for early September. 6808-1
Iris. 6628-3
Let us construct a god. 6072-2
A man who is at home within himself. 6628-3
A sailor's ballad. 6628-3
There lives a lady. 6628-3
Hollowell, Grace Baer
Do lovers' tongues. 6750-6
Holly. Susan Hartley. 6373-X
Holly against ivy. Unknown. 6881-2
Holly and ivy. Eugene Field. 6147-8
Holly and ivy made a great party. Unknown. 6756-5
The holly and the ivy. Unknown. 6134-6,6489-2,6216-4,6334-9,6641-0,6747 ,6150-8,125-7,6608-9,6636-4,6383-7, 6746,6756-5
The holly berry. Thomas Miller. 6747-6
Holly carol. Margaret Widdemer. 6746-8
The holly hedge of paradise. Richard Lawson Gales. 6950-9
Holly song. William Shakespeare. 6747-6
"Holly stands in the hall, fair to behold". A song on the ivy and the holly. Unknown. 6756-5
The holly tree. Robert Southey. 6086-2,6196-6,6219-9,6639-9,6543-0,6049-8,6147-1,6271-7,6302-0,6385-3,6601
The holly-tree. Bayard Taylor. 6976-2
The holly.. Robert Stephen Hawker. 6105-2
The holly. Eliza Cook. 6747-6
The holly. Henry VIII; King of England. 6436-1
The holly. Edith King. 6216-4
Hollyhock tea. Mary Elizabeth Mahnkey. 6662-3
A hollyhock. Frank Dempster Sherman. 6102-8,6047-1,6232-6, 6076-5
Hollyhocks. Wayne Gard. 6039-0
Hollyhocks. Gwendolen Haste. 6232-6
Hollyhocks. Lew Sarett. 6232-6
The hollyhocks. Ray Laurance. 6374-8
Hollywood. Don Blanding. 6736-0
Holm, Saxe. See Jackson, Helen Hunt
Holman, Frank Newton
In wreaths of smoke. 6453-1
Holman, Harriet
Angel wings. 7016-7
Beauty should not last forever. 7016-7
Candles. 7016-7
Lines to a dreamer. 7016-7
Longing. 7016-7
Holme, Jamie Sexton
Escape. 6836-7
Extenuation. 6836-7
The jester, to his audience. 6836-7
Permanence. 6836-7
The song unsung. 6836-7
Star-dust. 6836-7
Twilight. 6836-7
Vagabond. 6836-7
Holme, Vincent
Good Friday ("Gall is the taste of life when we") 6144-3
Holmes, C.E.L.
You put no flowers on my papa's grave. 6045-1,6142-7, 6565-1
You put no flowers on my papa's grave. 6964-9
Holmes, C.R.
Abandoned brothel. 6515-5
Hotel lobby. 6515-5
Impression at Reno. 6515-5

HOLMES

Holmes (cont.)
- Island battlefield. 6515-5
- Subway engineer. 6515-5
- To John Fiorini. 6515-5

Holmes, Daniel Henry
- Margery Daw. 6102-8,6076-5
- Turn, cheeses, turn. 6331-4

Holmes, Edmond Gore Alexander
- Amor fons amoris. 6090-0
- The creed of my heart. 6648-8
- Eternal vigil. 6090-0
- From Shannon to sea. 6090-0
- Immanence. 6337-3
- Light and shade. 6997-5
- Liscannor bay. 6997-5
- Loop head. 6997-5
- Night. 6997-5
- Sonnet ("Across the heaving"). 6331-4
- Sonnet 019 ("The hours are minutes..."). 6785-9
- Too deep for tears. 6090-0
- "Two walls of precipices black and steep". 6793-X
- The western sea. 6997-5

Holmes, Gene
- The golden stool. 6178-8

Holmes, George Sanford
- And yet fools say. 6464-7
- Flag of liberty and light. 6836-7
- From the ageless soil. 6836-7
- Mothers. 6836-7
- The spectral legion. 6836-7
- When labor marches. 6836-7

Holmes, Georgiana Klingle ("George Klingle")
- Be patient. 6461-2
- Gloria in excelis. 6461-2
- Palm Sunday hymn. 6144-3
- Patience with love. 6078-1,6413-2
- Shine out, o star. 6799-9
- While we may. 6303-9
- The wounded Christ-heart. 6420-5

Holmes, H.W.
- A valentine. 6118-4

Holmes, I.E.
- Death of John Q. Adams. 6402-7

Holmes, Jim
- Asshole poem. 7003-5
- Conversation piece. 7003-5
- TGG. 7003-5

Holmes, John
- Being young. 6265-2
- Boy reading. 6761-1
- Carry me back. 6388-8
- The chance. 6388-8
- Do not pity the young. 6761-1
- The enduring. 6761-1
- Evening meal in the twentieth century. 6527-9
- Evening meal in the twentieth century. 6761-1
- The fortune teller. 6388-8
- Four and a half. 6761-1,6783-2
- Legend and truth. 6042-0
- Man at work. 6722-0
- Table for one. 6722-0
- Testament. 6042-0
- Whose name was writ in water. 6042-0

Holmes, John A.
- A prologue for poems. 6780-8

Holmes, John F.
- Old New Hampshire. 6465-5

Holmes, John F.G.
- A blade of grass. 6764-6
- Life. 6764-6

Holmes, John Haynes
- All hail, the pageant of the years. 6337-3
- God of the nations. 6337-3
- Hymn of at-one-ment. 6337-3
- Lines on reading D.H. Lawrence, Sherwood Anderson,et al. 6817-0
- O Father, thou who givest all. 6337-3
- O God of field and city. 6337-3
- O God, whose love is over all. 6337-3
- O God, whose smile is in the sky. 6337-3
- Prayer for a world in arms. 6420-5
- The voice of God is calling. 6337-3

Holmes, M. Sophie
- Heaven. 6909-6

Holmes, Margaret
- Little Saint Caecilia. 6924-X
- Sister Veronica. 6285-7

Holmes, Oliver Wendell
- Additional verses to Hail Columbia. 6946-0
- Aestivation. 6089-7,6722-0,6724-7
- After a lecture om Wordsworth. 6126-5
- After a lecture on Keats. 6483-3,6431-0
- After a lecture on Shelley. 6126-5
- After the curfew. 6126-5,6288-1
- After the fire. 6946-0
- Album verses. 6121-4
- All here. 6753-0
- All here. 6126-5,6288-1
- All here. 6753-0
- "And where we love is home". 6109-5
- The archbishop and Gil Blas. 6413-2
- "As o'er the glacier's frozen sheet", sels. 6601-1
- At a meeting of friends. 6753-0
- At a meeting of friends. 6126-5
- At a meeting of friends. 6753-0
- At the pantomime. 6848-0
- At the Saturday Club. 6126-5,6288-1
- Aunt Tabitha. 6142-7,6249-0,6409-4,6661-5,6739-5
- The autocrat of the breakfast table, sels. 6332-2,6399-3
- Avis. 6127-3
- A ballad of the Boston tea party. 6323-3
- The ballad of the oysterman. 6126-5,6396-9,6419-1,6464-7,6136-2,6478-7,6497-3,6512-0,6610-0,6613 ,6165-6, 6176-1,6290-3,6332-2,6735-2,6089
- Before the curfew. 6632-1
- The 'best room'. 7022-1
- Bill and Joe. 6045-1,6085-4,6385-3,6512-0,6004-8,6288 , 6575-9,6126-5
- Birthday of Daniel Webster. 6126-5
- Birthday of Daniel Webster, sels. 6820-0
- Boston Common. 6484-1
- The boys. 6404-3,6610-0,6621-6,6565-1,6396-9,6304 ,6486-8,6521-X,6006-4,6102-8,6142-7,6260 ,6008-0,6288-1, 6076-5,6126-5,6121-4,6219 ,6265-2
- Broomstick train; or return of the witches. 6254-7,6698-8,6332-2,6126-5
- Brother Jonathan's lament for sister Caroline. 6015-3, 6113-3,6340-3,6471-X,6288-1,6126
- Bryant's seventieth birthday. 6753-0
- Bryant's seventieth birthday. 6126-5
- Bryant's seventieth birthday. 6753-0
- "Build thee more stately mansions, O my soul." 6225-3, 6238-5
- Cacoethes scribendi. 6089-7
- The chambered nautilus. 6176-1,6239-3,6243-1,6291-1, 6358-6,6473 ,6258-X,6260-3,6271-7,6337-3,6358-6,6385 ,6289-X,6601-1,6006-4,6077-3,6102-8,6183 ,6437-X, 6457-4,6459-0,6478-7,6481-7,6482 ,6479-5,6499-X,6600-3,6605-4,6735-2,6332 ,6512-0,6552-X,6632-1,6730-1, 6732-8,6560 ,6008-0,6250-4,6177-X,6076-5,6126-5,6121 ,6288-1,6431-0,6104-4,6304-7,6212-1,6214 ,6219-9, 6371-3,6300-4,6309-8,6421-3,6396-6,6639-9,6219-9, 6371-3,6300-4,6309-8,6421-3,6396-6,6639-9
- City and country. 6385-3
- City men in the country. 6606-2
- "The comet! he is on his way", sels. 66601-1
- The comet. 6302-0,6732-8,6008-0
- Contentment. 6089-7,6302-0,6385-3,6441-8,6498-1,6732 , 6745-X,6438-8,6288-1,6265-2,6230-X,6739 ,6004-8,6092-7
- The crooked footpath. 6260-1
- Daily trials. 6753-0
- Daniel Webster. 6385-3
- The deacon's masterpiece. 6176-1,6332-2,6499-X,6600-3, 6735-2,6089 ,6307-1,6431-0,6438-8,6008-0,6288-1,6121 ,6505-8,6467-1,6491-1,6219-9,6739-5,6281 ,6307-1, 6431-0,6438-8,6008-0,6288-1,6121 ,6505-8,6467-1,6491-1,6219-9,6739-5,6281 ,6076-5,6126-5
- "Deal gently with us, ye who read!" 6238-5
- The dilemma. 641-8,6683-6,6735-2

The Dorchester giant. 6614-3,6484-1
Dorothy Q. 6176-1,6473-6,6600-3,6652-6,6265-2,6438 ,
  6004-8,6288-1,6431-0,6126-5,6723-9
The earth-born saint, fr. Our sweet singer J.A. 6934-7
An eggstravagance. 6512-0
An eggstravagance. 6861-8
Epilogue to the Breakfast-table series. 6126-5
Eternal truth. 6461-2
Evening. 6302-00
Evening, by a tailor. 6278-4
Faith shall build a fairer throne. 6337-3,6214-8
A familiar letter to several correspondents. 6089-7
A farewell to Agassiz. 6753-0
First appearance in type. 6910-X
Flower of liberty. 6498-1,6049-8,6465-5,6707-7,6223-7,
  6964
The flower of liberty. 6914-2
For the Burns centennial celebration. 6126-5
For the meeting of the Burns Club. 6126-5
For the meeting of the national sanitary associaiton.
  7014-0
For the Moore centennial celebration. 6240-7
For Whittier's seventieth birthday. 6126-5
"Freedom! sweet freedom! our voices resound", sels.
  66601-1
Freedom, our queen. 6449-3
The girdle of friendship. 6014-5,6126-5,6066-8
God bless our father-land. 6014-5
"God bless the ancient Puritans", sels. 66601-1
A good time coming. 6271-7
Grandmother's story of Bunker Hill battle. 6249-0,6288-
  1,6442-6,6470-1,6126-5
"Green be the graves where her martyrs are...", sels.
  66601-1
The height of the ridiculous. 6102-8,6385-3,6732-8,6288-
  1,6307-1,6739 ,6102-8,6385-3,6732-8,6265-2,6300-4,
  6464 ,6176-1,6290-3,6332-2,6486-8,6722-0,6089 ,6076-
  5,6026-9,6107-9,6736-0,6126-5,6121 ,6505-8,6964-9,
  6278-4
"Hope, only Hope, of all that clings", sels. 6601-1
How the old horse won the bet. 6142-7,6392-6,6288-1,
  6126-5,6419-1,6288-1
The Hudson. 6126-5
Hymn ("O thou of soul and sense and breath.") 6305-5,
  6524-4
Hymn of peace. 6302-0
Hymn of trust. 6008-0,6126-5,6121-4,6007-2,6337-3,6303-
  9,6288-1,6723-9
"I love sweet features...", sels. 66601-1
"I love to hear thine earnest voice", sels. 66601-1
"I was sitting with my microsvope...", sels. 66601-1
In memory of Abraham Lincoln. 6871-5
In memory of John Greenleaf Whittier. 6126-5
Intramural aestivation. 6125-7
Introduction, fr. A rhymed lesson. 6753-0
Introduction, fr. Poetry. 6753-0
Invita Minerva. 6126-5
Iris, sels. 6317-9
The iron gate. 6411-6,6126-5
J.D.R. 6126-5,6288-1
James Russell Lowell, 1819-1891. 6126-5
James Russell Lowell, sels. 6820-0
Katydid. 6165-6,6302-0,6385-3,6629-1,6456-6,6565
L'inconnue. 6077-3,6092-7,6250-4,6126-5
La Grisette. 6126-5,6288-1
La maison d'or. 6126-5
The last leaf. 6753-0,6176-1,6243-1,6332-2,6473-6,6486-
  8,6583 ,6092-7,6250-4,6126-5,6723-9,6646-1,6424 ,
  6271-7,6289-X,6302-0,6385-3,6437-X,6441 ,6467-1,6304-
  7,6396-9,6300-4,6309-8,6219 ,6457-4,6459-0,6478-7,
  6481-7,6497-3,6610 ,6230-X,6126-5,6121-4,6265-2,6431-
  0,6560 ,6733-6,6735-2,6601-1,6077-3,6101-X,6142 ,
  6004-8,6307-1,6092-7,6008-0,6288-1,6732 ,6753-0
Latter day warnings. 6399-3,6512-0,6126-5,6288-1
Lexington. 6552-X,6735-2
Limerick:"The reverend Henry Ward Beecher". 6811-1
The living temple. 6473-6,6600-3,6730-1,6288-1,6121-4,
  6300 ,6304-7
The living temple. 6126-5
"Living, thou dost not live", sels. 6601-1

A logical story--the deacon's masterpiece... 6102-8,
  6076-5,6300-4
The Lord is my light. 6303-9
The lyre of Anacreon. 6126-5
Meeting of the alumni of Harvard College. 6753-0
The meeting of the dryads. 6049-8
Midsummer. 6597-X
The moral bully. 6753-0
The morning visit, sels. 6482-5
The mother's secret. 6365-9
The music grinders. 6610-0,6722-0,6632-1,6735-2,6505-8
The music-grinders. 6753-0
My annual. 6126-5
My aunt. 6278-4,6176-1,6332-2,6441-8,6735-2,6008-0,6121-
  4,6265-2,6505-8
My aviary. 6597-X
Nearing the snow-line. 6126-5
Never or now. 6113-3,6438-8,6016-2
New hail Columbia. 6304-7
No time like the old time. 6320-9
Non-resistance. 6753-0
"Not for him an earthly crown." 6712-3
Now or never. 6385-3
Nux postcoenatica. 7014-0
"O lady, there be many things." 6066-8
"O what are the prizes we perish to win", sels. 6601-1
Ode for a social meeting. 6302-0,6385-3,6083-8,6089-7
Ode for Washington's birthday. 6171-0
The old Constitution. 6424-8
Old Ironsides. 6006-4,6015-3,6136-2,6176-1,6211-3,6243 ,
  6396-9,6421-3,6639-9,6737-9,6121-4,6265 ,6260-1,6332-
  2,6385-3,6457-4,6465-5,6471 ,6438-8,6569-4,6470-1,
  6736-0,6104-0,6107 ,6401-9,6486-8,6126-5,6267-6,6304-
  7,6250 ,6008-0,6135-4,6560-0,6288-1,6442-1,6473-6,
  6478-7,6479-5,6496-5,6502-3,6552 ,6606-2,6610-0,6623-
  2,6632-1,6732-8,6239 ,6006-4,6015-3,6136-2,6176-1,
  6211-3,6243 ,6396-9,6421-3,6639-9,6737-9,6121-4,6265
  ,6260-1,6332-2,6385-3,6457-4,6465-5,6471 ,6438-8,
  6569-4,6470-1,6736-0,6104-0,6107 ,6401-9,6486-8,6126-
  5,6267-6,6304-7,6250 ,6008-0,6135-4,6560-0,6288-1,
  6442-1,6473-6,6478-7,6479-5,6496-5,6502-3,6552 ,6606-
  2,6610-0,6623-2,6632-1,6732-8,6239
The old man dreams. 6429-9,6321-7,6288-1,6126-5,6219-9,
  6964
On lending a punch bowl. 6632-1,6735-2,6092-7,6288-1,
  6004-8,6126 ,6121-4,6219-9
On the death of President Garfield. 6946-0
Once more. 6408-6
"One kindly deed may turn", sels. 6601-1
"One-hoss shay". 6102-8
The one-hoss shay. 6302-0,6385-3,6014-5,6279-2,6102-8
Our hymn. 6089-7
Our oldest friend. 6084-6
Our Yankee girls. 6126-5
Parson Turell's legacy. 6126-5,6435-3
Parting hymn. 6126-5,6435-3
The parting word. 6735-2
Perseverance. 6294-6
The philosopher to his love. 6735-2
The Pilgrim's vision. 6678-X
"The pleasures thou hast planned". 6601-1
The ploughman. 6219-9,6302-9
The plowman. 6219-9,6302-0,6385-3
Pluck and luck. 6260-1
Poesy. 6014-5
Poesy ("There breathes no being but has some pretense")
  6014-5
"Poor drudge of the city! how happy he feels," sels.
  6601-1
A portrait. 6753-0
Programme. 6126-5,6435-3
Prologue to Songs in many keys. 6126-5
Questions. 6510-4
Questions and answers. 6302-0,6304-7,6302-9
'Qui vive.' 6735-2
Reflections of a proud pedestrian. 6278-4
A response. 6878-2
A rhymed lesson, sels. 6601-1
Robinson of Leyden. 6484-1,6600-3
Rudolph the headsman. 6385-3,6498-1,6438-8

HOLMES

"Run if you like, but try to keep your breath." 6601-1
The school boy, sels. 6484-1
A sea dialogue. 6833-2
The September gale. 6165-6,6610-0,6964-9
The shadows. 6126-5
Shakespeare. 6753-0
Sherman's in Savannah. 6946-0
The silent melody. 6126-5
A song of other days, sels. 6601-1
Spring has come. 6623-2,6684-4
The stability of science. 7014-0
The star and the water-lily. 6735-2
The statesman's secret. 6753-0
The statesman's secret. 6126-5
The statesman's secret. 6753-0
The steamboat. 6271-7
The stethoscope song. 7014-0,6753-0
The stethoscope song. 6126-5
The stethoscope song. 6753-0
"Strive with the wanderer from the better path", sels. 6601-1
A Sun-day hymn. 6337-3,6473-6,6418-3,6730-1,6723-9,6126,6121-4
A sun-day lament. 6288-1
Tailor's soliloquy, sels. 6601-1
Then as to feasting. 6722-0
"They say that in his prime", fr. The last leaf. 6601-1
This is it. 6121-4
To a caged lion. 6510-4
To an English friend. 6126-5
To an insect. 6597-X,6092-7,6288-1,6004-8,6126-5
To Canaan. 6753-0
To George Peabody. 6438-8
To James Russell Lowell. 6126-5
To my readers. 6753-0
To my readers. 6126-5,6288-1
To my readers. 6753-0
To the portrait of "A gentleman". 6089-7
To the portrait of "A lady". 6735-2
To the portrait of a gentleman. 6278-4
The toadstool. 6621-6
Too young for love. 6320-9,6126-5
The two streams. 6523-6,6126-5,6424-8,6484-1
Under the violets. 6302-0,6600-3,6288-1,6126-5
Under the Washington elm, Cambridge. 6049-8,6735-2
Union and liberty. 6496-5,6610-0,6223-7,6136-5,6403-5
The union. 6001-3
Unsatisfied. 6176-1
Urania, sels. 6008-0
Veritas. 6126-5
"Virtue may flourish in an old cravat", sels. 6601-1
A voice of the loyal north. 6735-2
The voiceless. 6486-8,6600-3,6735-2,6102-8,6271-7,6250,6288-1,6076-5,6126-5,6121-4,6219-9
Voyage of the good ship Union. 6113-3,6126-5
Washington's birthday. 6449-3
Welcome to the nations. 6014-5,6286-5,6412-4
"What flower is this that greets the morn", sels. 6601-1
Where we love is home. 6066-8
Why they twinkle. 6001-3
The wonderful "one-hoss shay". 6049-8,6732-8,6736-0,6079-X,6808-1,6403
Words on language. 6521-X
"Youth fades; love droops...". 6238-5
Youth in our hearts. 6654-2

Holmes, W. Kersley
Fallen. 7027-2
The geography horse. 6804-9
Horse-bathing parade. 7027-2

Holst, Henriette Roland
From time to eternity. A.J. Barnouw (tr.). 6068-4

Holstein, Ludvig
Apple blossoms. Charles Wharton Stork (tr.). 6555-4
Father, where do the wild swans go?. Charles Wharton Stork (tr.). 6555-4
Forth, my gallant honey-bees!. Charles Wharton Stork (tr.). 6555-4
Thou lovely one far distant. Charles Wharton Stork (tr.). 6555-4

Holstenwall. Sidney Keyes. 6210-5

Holt, Florence Taber
England and America. 7026-4
Flowers. 6034-X

Holt, Isabella
Lament ("He is gone with his blue eyes.") 6030-7

Holt, Jessie
Dying. 6144-3
Judas. 6789-1

Holt, P.J. (Polly)
Afterward. 6883-9
Fallout. 6883-9

Holthusen, Hans Egon
It was my blood, fr. Lament for my brother. 6643-7
Lament for my brother, sels. 6643-7
Sacrifice. 6643-7

Holton and Herbert Kuhner, Milne (tr.)
Advantages of nudism. Erich Fried, 6769-7
Advertising. Ingeborg Bachmann, 6769-7
"After this flood" Ingeborg Bachmann, 6769-7
Afterward. Gerhard Fritsch, 6769-7
Again and again. Doris Muhringer, 6769-7
Alexandra's fourteenth birthday. Albert Paris Gutersloh, 6769-7
"Always birds/in the sky" H. C. Artmann, 6769-7
"An angel in black" Christine Busta, 6769-7
Ash Wednesday. Thomas Bernhard, 6769-7
August (1). Andreas Okopenko, 6769-7
August (2). Andreas Okopenko, 6769-7
August moon. Gerhard Fritsch, 6769-7
August of life. Albert Paris Gutersloh, 6769-7
Austrians. Josef Mayer-Limberg, 6769-7
"The balance sheet" Walther Nowotny, 6769-7
The beast that rode the unicorn. Conny Hannes Meyer, 6769-7
Before night. Hedwig Katscher, 6769-7
"Behind the back of our time" Christine Lavant, 6769-7
Belonging. Ilse Aichinger, 6769-7
"Biii bibibibibi." Friedrich Achleitner, 6769-7
"Bix/bum." Friedrich Achleitner, 6769-7
The boy awakens. Albert Paris Gutersloh, 6769-7
The boy. Hertha Kraftner, 6769-7
"But the flesh" Peter Henisch, 6769-7
Change. Helmut Zenker, 6769-7
Christ of Kazan. Wilhelm Szabo, 6769-7
Copyright. Erich Fried, 6769-7
Dawn. Ilse Brem, 6769-7
The day after tomorrow. Margarethe Herzele, 6769-7
Day and night. Peter Paul Wiplinger, 6769-7
Deer. Herbert Zand, 6769-7
The descent. Michael Guttenbrunner, 6769-7
"The dreamdog" Walther Nowotny, 6769-7
"Dreams, your time hasn't come" Herbert Zand, 6769-7
"Dreams/prayers" Alois Hergouth, 6769-7
Drought. Christine Busta, 6769-7
"The drum/whips up steam" H. C. Artmann, 6769-7
The drum. Otto Laaber, 6769-7
During the day. Paul Celan, 6769-7
"A dwarf hops on the rack" Hermann Gail, 6769-7
Early impression. Andreas Okopenko, 6769-7
Edge of the mountain. Ilse Aichinger, 6769-7
The edge of words. Peter Handke, 6769-7
"Empty" Gerhard Ruhm, 6769-7
End. Peter Paul Wiplinger, 6769-7
An end to idling, sel. Peter Handke, 6769-7
"An endless journey by foot" Friederike Mayrocker, 6769-7
Enigma. Ingeborg Bachmann, 6769-7
Epilogue in Berlin. Gerald Bisinger, 6769-7
Erratic. Paul Celan, 6769-7
"Everything is only a reflection" Ernst Schonwiese, 6769-7
Exile. Ingeborg Bachmann, 6769-7
Extinguish the hyacinth. Walter Buchebner, 6769-7
Fin. Helmut Zenker, 6769-7
"First I want to be happy" Konrad Bayer, 6769-7
Flower play. Gerhard Ruhm, 6769-7
"Flowers" Josef Mayer-Limberg, 6769-7
"From the bread of life" Hedwig Katscher, 6769-7
"From the sunken road a rain frog croaks" Christine

Lavant, 6769-7
"From you r heaven of tender" Friederike Mayrocker, 6769-7
Garden. Andreas Okopenko, 6769-7
Give me your hand. Gerhard Ruhm, 6769-7
"Give water to a thirsty dog" Jutta Schutting, 6769-7
"The hands" Walther Nowotny, 6769-7
The hangman's wife. Hertha Kraftner, 6769-7
Haute couture of poetry. Wilhelm Szabo, 6769-7
Hitler and the generals. Michael Guttenbrunner, 6769-7
Hoarfrost. Christine Busta, 6769-7
Homecoming. Michael Guttenbrunner, 6769-7
Hotel de la paix. Ingeborg Bachmann, 6769-7
The hour of death. Gunter Unger, 6769-7
"I and my body" Konrad Bayer, 6769-7
"I know it/as if I had been" Thomas Sessler, 6769-7
"I too could inject gasoline" Hermann Gail, 6769-7
"I'm a true child" Konrad Bayer, 6769-7
"I'm capable of loving" Walter Buchebner, 6769-7
"I'm nobody's fool" Josef Mayer-Limberg, 6769-7
"I've divided" Walther Nowotny, 6769-7
Imprisoned. Thomas Bernhard, 6769-7
In a hard shell. Otto Laaber, 6769-7
"In a tangled knot of humanity" Thomas Sessler, 6769-7
In the field. Otto Laaber, 6769-7
In the forest. Gerhard Fritsch, 6769-7
"In the slums" Friederike Mayrocker, 6769-7
Intangible. Max Holzer, 6769-7
Intermezzo: noon in the bazaar cafe. Gerald Bisinger, 6769-7
Intuition. Albert Paris Gutersloh, 6769-7
"It can't be understood" Alfred Kolleritsch, 6769-7
"It happened in the angel's shadow" Jutta Schutting, 6769-7
"It is no longer/that heaviness" Paul Celan, 6769-7
Judas. Gerhard Fritsch, 6769-7
The last snowflake. Margarethe Herzele, 6769-7
Late. Ilse Aichinger, 6769-7
Late afternoon doves. Jutta Schutting, 6769-7
Late days. Ilse Brem, 6769-7
Lenin in winter. Ernst Jandl, 6769-7
"Lenin" Josef Mayer-Limberg, 6769-7
"Let's travel" Doris Muhringer, 6769-7
Like the wind. Otto Laaber, 6769-7
Litany. Hertha Kraftner, 6769-7
March moon-night. Margarethe Herzele, 6769-7
Mattersburg/judengasse. Gunter Unger, 6769-7
Method a. Helmut Zenker, 6769-7
Miserere. Christine Busta, 6769-7
Mother chaos. Margarethe Herzele, 6769-7
My poem. Walter Buchebner, 6769-7
"My whole life long" Herbert Zand, 6769-7
"Ne pas se pencher en dehors" Walter Buchebner, 6769-7
"The night" Gerhard Ruhm, 6769-7
"Night/has buried the wolves" Alois Hergouth, 6769-7
Nightmare. Gunter Unger, 6769-7
No tree. Thomas Bernhard, 6769-7
"Nobody helps me" Konrad Bayer, 6769-7
Note. Helmut Zenker, 6769-7
"Occasionally you catch up with yourself" Alfred Kolleritsch, 6769-7
Of the beloved caravan. Conny Hannes Meyer, 6769-7
On the banks of the Chang. Margarethe Herzele, 6769-7
Once and now. Ernst Jandl, 6769-7
"One came" Peter Henisch, 6769-7
"One file" Josef Mayer-Limberg, 6769-7
One to another. Peter Paul Wiplinger, 6769-7
"Ooooooooooooooooooooo." Friedrich Achleitner, 6769-7
Opium. Max Holzer, 6769-7
Our child of pain. Christine Busta, 6769-7
"Out there in the night there are houses" Jutta Schutting, 6769-7
"A pair of wings writes" Max Holzer, 6769-7
"Paris is a game of roulette" Herbert Zand, 6769-7
Parting. Ernst Jandl, 6769-7
The patient. Michael Guttenbrunner, 6769-7
"Poate/Nu vom mai fi nici!" Gerald Bisinger, 6769-7
Preface. Albert Paris Gutersloh, 6769-7
"A rose/five roses/thirteen roses" H. C. Artmann, 6769-7

Roses. Ilse Brem, 6769-7
The sexton's assessment. Wilhelm Szabo, 6769-7
Situation. Reinhard Priessnitz, 6769-7
"The sky turned as yellow as cheap paper" Hertha Kraftner, 6769-7
"The smoke" Thomas Sessler, 6769-7
"A so." Friedrich Achleitner, 6769-7
Soap bubbles. Erich Fried, 6769-7
"Something dark/resembling a hand" Paul Celan, 6769-7
Sometimes. Ilse Brem, 6769-7
Speechless. Erich Fried, 6769-7
"The sun is a new house" H. C. Artmann, 6769-7
"Table. Table. Here" Max Holzer, 6769-7
Telegraph. Reinhard Priessnitz, 6769-7
"They've cut down/the sunflower" Christine Busta, 6769-7
This knife. Ernst Nowak, 6769-7
Thought out. Ilse Aichinger, 6769-7
"Through the bars of my heart" Friederike Mayrocker, 6769-7
"Through the steely air" Christine Lavant, 6769-7
Tired. Thomas Bernhard, 6769-7
"To live" Ernst Jandl, 6769-7
The tree. Hedwig Katscher, 6769-7
Turning on. Gunter Unger, 6769-7
Val d'Annivier. Michael Guttenbrunner, 6769-7
Variations on death. Kurt Klinger, 6769-7
"Visiting a friend in one of the best asylums in" Peter Henisch, 6769-7
"A water-blue tree/rises high" H. C. Artmann, 6769-7
We have lost. Peter Paul Wiplinger, 6769-7
"What good does the fact" Doris Muhringer, 6769-7
"What so strongly beats in your heart" Ernst Schonwiese, 6769-7
"What was in the beginning" Peter Henisch, 6769-7
"When I was a child" Doris Muhringer, 6769-7
"When one writes" Alfred Kolleritsch, 6769-7
"When someone dies" Ernst Schonwiese, 6769-7
"When the day" Thomas Sessler, 6769-7
"Where were you" Alfred Kolleritsch, 6769-7
"White/is the deeper shade of silence" Alois Hergouth, 6769-7
Who says. Otto Laaber, 6769-7
"Why do we call night" Ernst Schonwiese, 6769-7
With early cattails. Hertha Kraftner, 6769-7
Without thinking. Ernst Nowak, 6769-7
"You black, black/earth, mother" Paul Celan, 6769-7
"You don't even have feet" Hermann Gail, 6769-7
"You have taken me from all joy" Christine Lavant, 6769-7
You laugh-and balloons descend from the sky. Jutta Schutting, 6769-7
"You, my friend, reserve" Wilhelm Szabo, 6769-7
"Your candle of suffering" Hedwig Katscher, 6769-7
"Your sentence" Hermann Gail, 6769-7

Holton, Helen A.
Ring, Easter bells! 6720-4

Holty, Heinrich
Harvest song. 6820-0

Holty, Ludwig
Winter's snows. 6629-1

Holub, Miroslav
Cinderella. 6758-1
The fly. 6758-1
Man cursing the sea. 6758-1
Suffering. 6758-1
Zito the magician. 6758-1

Holway, Grace Bacon
Intelligent cat. 6699-2

"The **Holy** Ghost is to thee sent". Hail Mary, full of grace, mother in virginity. Unknown. 6756-5
"**Holy** Lord God! I love thy truth". Hatred of sin. William Cowper. 6814-6
The **holy** band. Jean Starr Untermeyer. 6345-4
Holy calm. William Wordsworth. 7020-5
The **holy** child. Charles Carroll Albertson. 6337-3
Holy Christmas. George Herbert. 6747-6
Holy church speaks. William Langland. 6489-2
The **holy** city. Frederic Edward Weatherley. 6486-8
The **holy** city. Walter Russell Bowie. 6337-3

HOLY

The **holy** city. Phyllis McGinley. 6734-4
Holy communion. Speer Strahan. 6172-9,6292-X,6172-9
The **holy** crib. Bertha L. Gibbons. 6906-1
Holy Cross. Unknown. 6022-6
Holy Cross day, sels. Robert Browning. 6046-3
The **holy** fair. Robert Burns. 6198-2,6430-2,6195-0,6152-4
Holy family. Johann Wolfgang von Goethe. 6948-7
The **holy** field. Henry Hart Milman. 6931-2
The **holy** flame, 'menorah' George Jay Holland. 6848-0
The **Holy** Grail, fr. Idylls of the King. Alfred Lord Tennyson. 6657-7,6655-0
Holy ground. John Banister Tabb. 6943-6
A **holy** hill. George William ("A.E.") Russell. 7039-6
Holy innocents. Christina Georgina Rossetti. 6078-1,6123-0, 6233-4,6214-8
Holy land. Richard Watson Gilder. 6007-2
The **holy** land of Walsingham. Benjamin Francis Musser. 6282-2
The **holy** land of Walsinghame. Unknown. 6829-4
"**Holy** maiden, blessed thou be". Singe we, singe we, regina celi, letare. Unknown. 6756-5
"**Holy** Moses, man of God, came to his...". Moses and the worm. Johann Gottfried von Herder. 6848-0
The **holy** man. Unknown. 6930-4
Holy matrimony. John Keble. 6337-3,6656-9
A **holy** nation. Richard Realf. 6481-7
The **holy** nativity of our Lord God. Richard Crashaw. 6473-6, 6730-1
The **holy** Nativity, sels. Richard Crashaw. 6194-X
The **holy** nunnery. Unknown. 6185-0
The **holy** of holies. Gilbert Keith Chesterton. 6730-1
The **holy** office. James Joyce. 6210-5
Holy places. Herbert D. Gallaudet. 6337-3
Holy poverty. Arthur Shearly Cripps. 6844-8
The **holy** rose. Vyacheslav Ivanov. 7039-6
Holy Saturday. John Banister Tabb. 6337-3
Holy satyr. Hilda ("H.D.") Doolittle. 6010-2
"The **holy** scriptures in cracked letters". Drought. Christine Busta. 6769-7
An **holy** sister. Abraham Cowley. 6760-3,6787-5
Holy sonnet X. John Donne. 6527-9,6491-1
Holy sonnets. John Donne. 6208-3,6378-0
Holy sonnets, sels. John Donne. 6645-3,6430-2
Holy spirit, dwell with me. Thomas Toke Lynch. 6337-3
The **holy** spirit. Harriet Auber. 6337-3
The **holy** spirit. Robert Herrick. 6302-0;6385-3
Holy spring. Dylan Thomas. 6666-6
The **holy** star. William Cullen Bryant. 6065-X
Holy Thursday. William Blake. 7009-4
Holy Thursday. William Blake. 6233-4,6339-X,6478-7,6536-8, 6634-8,6737,6086-2,6152-4,6214-8,6421-3,6430-2
Holy Thursday. Charles Edward Butler. 6640-2
"A **holy** stillness, beautiful and deep". A summer noon at sea. Epes Sargent. 6833-2
The **holy** tide. Frederick Tennyson. 6186-9,6437-X
"The **holy** touch of twilight fell". Los Angeles. James Abraham Martling. 6952-5
The **holy** trinity. Reginald Heber. 6219-9
Holy week. Robert Whitaker. 6144-3,6337-3
Holy week ("And having taken bread, he broke it"). Phoebe Smith Bachelder. 6144-3
The **holy** well. Unknown. 6931-2,6756-5
The **holy** wells. John de Jean Frazer. 6858-8
Holy Willie's prayer. Robert Burns. 6089-7,6180-X,6200-8, 6733-6,6438-8,6152,6278-4,6633-X,6637-2
The **holy** women. William Alexander Percy. 6326-8
Holy, Josef
    From the world beyond. Paul Selver (tr.). 6763-8
    Upon the waves. Paul Selver (tr.). 6763-8
Holy, holy, holy. Reginald Heber. 6337-3,6304-7,6732-8
Holy-cross day. Robert Browning. 6427-2
Holy-cross day. Robert Browning. 6848-0
Holyday, Barten
    Song ("O harmless feast") 6182-6
Holz, Arno
    A leave-taking. Jethro Bithell (tr.). 7039-6
    Phantasus. Ludwig Lewisohn (tr.). 7039-6
    Phantasus, sels. Babette Deutsch and Avrahm Yarmolinsky (tr.). 6160-6
    Phantasus, sels. Babette Deutsch (tr.). 6160-5

Holzer, Max
    Intangible. Milne Holton and Herbert Kuhner (tr.). 6769-7
    Opium. Milne Holton and Herbert Kuhner (tr.). 6769-7
    "A pair of wings writes" Milne Holton and Herbert Kuhner (tr.). 6769-7
    "Table. Table. Here" Milne Holton and Herbert Kuhner (tr.). 6769-7
Homage. Helen Hoyt. 6019-6,6393-4
The **homage** of beasts. Augusta Larned. 6510-4
Homage to Charles Lindbergh. Miriam Allen De Ford. 7019-1
Homage to Giacometti. Stuart Dybek. 6803-0
Homage to Hieronymus Bosch. Thomas McGreevy. 6930-4
Homage to literature. Muriel Rukeyser. 6375-6
Homage to our leaders. Julian Symons. 6379-9
Homage to Sextus Propertius: XII. Ezra Pound. 6209-1
Homage to the British Museum. William Empson. 6209-1,6391-8
"**Homage** to the venerable Buddha...". Buddha descends to Lumbini. Unknown (Newari). 7013-2
"**Homage** to thee, O Ra, at thy...arising!". The dead man ariseth and singeth a hymn to the sun. Unknown (Egyptian). 7039-6
Home. Esther J. Baum. 6847-2
Home. Joseph Beaumont. 6245-8
Home. Thekla N. Berstecher. 6906-1
Home. Olive Tilford Dargan. 6880-4
Home. Fannie Stearns Davis. 6266-0
Home. Evelyn Grace Flynn. 6847-2
Home. Oliver Goldsmith. 6302-0;6385-3
Home. Nellie Eldora Gould. 6764-6
Home. Dora Greenwell. 6066-8
Home. Edgar A. Guest. 6736-0
Home. Edgar A. Guest. 6732-8,6964-9
Home. Verner von Heidenstam. 6045-5
Home. William Ernest Henley. 6136-2,6239-3
Home. Edward R. Huxley. 6885-7
Home. Reginald Wright Kauffman. 6846-4
Home. Francis Ledwidge. 6812-X
Home. [James] Pittendrigh Macgillivray. 6269-5
Home. Hermann Ford Martin. 6037-4
Home. James Montgomery. 6543-0
Home. Nikolay Nekrasov. 6103-6
Home. John Henry, Cardinal Newman. 6383-7
Home. T.L. Paine. 6461-2
Home. William Alexander Percy. 6326-8
Home. Paulene Foster Ring. 6764-6
Home. Edward Rowland Sill. 6007-2,6255-5
Home. Ivan Swift. 6102-8
Home. Alfred Lord Tennyson. 6424-8
Home. Unknown. 6156-7,6744-1
Home. Unknown (Greek) 6385-3
Home. William Wordsworth. 6438-8
Home a different place. Arthur Chamberlain. 6715-8
Home again. M.S. Pike. 6304-7
Home again. Unknown. 6791-3,6823-5
The **home** altar. Sir Lewis Morris. 6543-0
Home and love. Robert Service. 6159-1
Home and mother. Mary Mapes Dodge. 6089-7
Home and mother. Unknown. 6629-1
Home and office. Edgar A. Guest. 7033-7
Home at last. Gilbert Keith Chesterton. 6730-1
Home at last. Adelaide Anne Procter. 6957-6
Home at last. G.J. Romanes. 6226-1
Home at night. James Whitcomb Riley. 6006-4
Home burial. Robert Frost. 6348-9,6365-9
A **home** by the warm southern sea. Mrs. B.C. Rude. 6049-8
Home comfort. Charles Kingsley. 6429-9,6321-7
Home coming. R.G.T. Coventry. 7029-9
The **home** coming. May C. ([Mary] Gillington) Byron. 7037-X
The **home** concert. Unknown. 6450-7,6576-7
Home defense. William Rose Benet. 6817-0
Home delights. Charles and Mary Lamb. 6295-4
Home economics. Rosario Castellanos. 7036-1
A **home** everywhere. S. Graham. 6752-2
The **home** express. Horace Spencer Fiske. 6274-1
'**Home** folks', sels. James Whitcomb Riley. 6239-3
Home for the holidays. Eliza Cook. 6242-3
Home from any war. Sarah N. Pulsifer. 6789-1
Home from the party. Leon Dierx. 6351-9

Home from town. Dorothy Wardell Boice. 6662-3
Home in war-time. Sydney Dobell. 6656-9
Home ingredients. Edgar A. Guest. 6748-4
"Home is the germ of earth's progress". Home. Edward R. Huxley. 6885-5
"Home is the place where the laughter should..". Home and office. Edgar A. Guest. 7033-7
Home is where. Louis Hasley. 6761-1
lome is where the heart is. Unknown. 6273-3
"Home is where the heart is, and my heart...". The widest hearthstone. Berton Braley. 6853-7
Home is where there's one to love us. Charles Swain. 6337-3,6407-8
The home keeper. Frank Lebby Stanton. 6097-8
Home lights. Harry Lee. 6320-9
Home means Nevada. Bertha Raffetto. 6465-5
A home mission prayer. William Cullen Bryant. 6525-2
"Home no more home to me". Robert Louis Stevenson. 6793-X
The home of Adalbert. Edward Farquhar. 6939-8
The home of Helen. Thomas Sturge Moore. 6331-4,6439-6
The home of Horace. George Meason Whicher. 6029-3
The home of love. Felicia Dorothea Hemans. 6973-8
Home of my thoughts. Marie Barton. 6525-2
The home of peace. Thomas Moore. 6413-2
The home of the Naiads, fr.The art of preserving health. John Armstrong. 6932-0
"Home of the free! Protector of the weak!". Persia - Moritura. John Galsworthy. 6888-X
"Home of the gifted! fare thee well". A farewell to Abbotsford. Felicia Dorothea Hemans. 6973-8
Home of the soul. Philip Phillips. 6577-5
"Home of the weary! I shall rest". The pilgrim's rest. Charles W. Denison. 6755-7
A home on the range. John A. Lomax. 6465-5
A home picture. Frances Dana Barker ("Aunt Fanny") Gage. 6910-X
Home sick baby. Elsie Malone McCollum. 6682-8
Home song. Henry Wadsworth Longfellow. 6239-3,6135-4,6570-8
Home song. Unknown. 6429-9,6321-7
A home song. Henry Van Dyke. 6478-7
Home sweet home with variations. Henry Cuyler Bunner. 6440-X
Home they brought her lap-dog dead. Charles Shirley Brooks. 7025-6
"Home they brought her warrior dead," fr. The princess. Alfred Lord Tennyson. 6655-0,6627-5,6560-0,6199-0,6383-7,6737 ,6078-1,6122-2,6087-0,6337-3,6302-0,6385 ,6301-2,6543-0,6110-9
"Home they brought him slain with spears". Song ("Home they brought him..."). Alfred Lord Tennyson. 6977-0
Home thoughts. Guy Butler. 6788-3
Home thoughts. Thomas D'Arcy McGee. 6096-X;6174-5
Home thoughts. Claude McKay. 6880-4
Home thoughts. Odell Shepard. 6478-7
Home thoughts. Unknown. 7029-9
Home thoughts from abroad. Robert Browning. 6047-1,6101-X,6123-0,6133-8,6134-4,6138-,6107-9,6110-9,6102-8,6046-3,6104-4,6196 ,6154-0,6186-9,6187-7,6198-2,6208-3,6232-,6430-2,6560-0,6250-4,6383-7,6199-0,6114 ,6331-4,6332-2,6339-X,6423-X,6427-2,6437-,6153-2,6301-2,6668-2,6396-9,6439-6,6646 ,6466-3,6473-6,6597-X,6604-6,6655-0,6657-,6464-7,6656-9,6586-6,6631-3,6660-7,6737 ,6723-9,6726-3,6828-6
Home thoughts from abroad. Norah M. Holland. 6115-X
Home thoughts in Bloomsbury. Roy Campbell. 6633-X
Home thoughts in Laventie. Edward Wyndham Tennant. 6044-7,6558-9,6477-9,6650-X
Home thoughts, from the sea. Robert Browning. 6123-0,6154-0,6198-2,6258-X,6395-0,6437 ,6196-6,6430-2,6114-1,6110-9,6322-5,6439 ,6473-6,6484-1,6655-0,6657-7
Home to mother. Unknown. 6097-8
Home travell. John Hall. 6023-4
Home truths from abroad. Unknown. 6440-X
Home with dawn. Arthur Shearly Cripps. 6625-9
Home wounded. Unknown. 6735-2
"Home! We welcome you home". S-51 John Jerome Rooney. 7014-0
Home's a nest. William Barnes. 6980-0
"Home's not merely four square walls". Unknown. 6238-5

Home, F. Wyville
    Dover cliff. 6656-9
    An English girl. 6656-9
    In a September night. 6656-9
Home, John
    Douglas' account of himself. 6304-7
    Douglas, sels. 6911-8
    Norval. 6385-3
Home, boys, home. Unknown. 6237-7
Home, can I forget thee. Unknown. 6304-7
"Home, for my heart still calls me". Homeward bound. Henry Van Dyke. 6961-4
Home, fr. Once again the Eden. Noel Hudson Stearn. 6789-1
Home, fr. The death of the hired hand. Robert Frost. 6337-3
The home, fr. The homestead. Gertrude Huntington McGiffert. 6838-3
"Home, home - where's my baby's home?". Anne Hutchinson's exile. Edward Everett Hale. 6946-0
Home, pup! William Johnson Cory. 6018-8
Home, rose, and home, Provence and La Palie. Arthur Hugh Clough. 6934-7
Home, sels. Katharine Lee Bates. 6798-0
Home, sweet home. John Howard Payne. 6077-3,6328-4,6706-9,6176-1,6240-7,6260 ,6121-4,6219-9,6300-4,6088-9,6135-4,6431 ,6260-1,6723-9,6585-6,6304-7,6424-8,6302-0,6337-3,6401-9,6732-8,6486-8,6457-4,6459-0,6479-5,6498-1,6632-1
Home, sweet home. C.C. Somerville. 6414-0
Home, wounded. Sydney Dobell. 6302-0;6385-3
Home-bound. Joseph Auslander. 6762-X
"The home-bound ship stood out to sea". The mystery of Croa-tan. Margaret Junkin Preston. 6946-0
Home-coming. Leonie Adams. 6253-9,6393-4
Home-coming. Albert Ehrenstein. 6160-5
Home-coming. Gustaf Froding. 6045-5
Home-coming. Unknown. 6273-3
Home-coming, fr. The Odyssey. Homer. 6435-3
The home-coming. Katharine Lee Bates. 6039-0
The home-coming. John Gould Fletcher. 6345-4
The home-coming. Robert Loveman. 6941-X
The home-coming. William Wordsworth. 6383-7
"Home-defence in our town!". Home defense. William Rose Benet. 6817-0
Home-land. Verner von Heidenstam. 6045-5
The home-land.. Witter Bynner. 6607-0
Home-longings. George F. Savage-Armstrong. 6174-5
A home-made fairy-tale. James Whitcomb Riley. 6990-8
Home-makers. Edgar A. Guest. 6869-3
Home-making. James Hurdis. 6943-6
Home-sickness. Henry Bellamann. 6776-X
Home-sickness. Justinus Kerner. 6484-8
Home-sickness. Adelaide Anne Procter. 6491-4
Home-thoughts from abroad. John Buchan. 6269-5
The home. Byrdie L. Martin. 6799-9
The homecomer's song. Edgar A. Guest. 6862-6
Homecoming. Michael Guttenbrunner. 6769-7
Homecoming. Anna Hansen Hayes. 6836-7
Homecoming. Sojin Takei. 6981-9
Homecoming in storm. Bernice Lesbia Kenyon. 6036-6
The homecoming of the Eurydice. Sir Arthur Conan Doyle. 6793-X
The homecoming of the sheep. Francis Ledwidge. 6331-4,6477-9,6478-7,6653-4
The homecoming. Leroy Folge. 6846-4
The homeland. Dana Burnet. 6478-7,6556-2
The homeland. Sir Cecil Spring-Rice. 6337-3
Homeless. Isabel Fiske Conant. 6850-2
Homeless. Susan L. Mitchell. 6174-5
Homeless. Adelaide Anne Procter. 6957-6
Homeless. Unknown. 6926-6
A homeless beggar. Izan. 6027-7
The homeless poor. Adelaide Anne Procter. 6957-6
The homely man. Edgar A. Guest. 7033-7
"A homely young heiress of Beccles". Limerick:"A homely young heiress of Beccles". Unknown. 6811-1
Homer
    Achilles and Lycaon, fr. The Iliad. Cecil Maurice Bowra (tr.). 6435-3
    Achilles and Patroclus, fr. The Iliad. Sir William

HOMER

Marris (tr.). 6435-3
Achilles and the Scamander, fr. The Iliad. Sir William Marris (tr.). 6435-3
Achilles and Thetis, fr. The Iliad. Sir William Marris (tr.). 6435-3
Achilles on the rampart, fr. The Iliad. Alfred Lord Tennyson (tr.). 6435-3
Achilles rallies the Greeks. 6102-8
Achilles shows himself in the battle by the ships. George Chapman (tr.). 6933-9
"Achilles then within his tent...", fr. The Iliad. Edward G.S. Stanley, 14th Earl of Derby (tr.). 6435-3
Achilles to Lycaon, fr. The Iliad. Richard Lattimore (tr.). 6665-8
Achilles' prayer, fr. The Iliad. Edward G.S. Stanley, 14th Earl of Derby (tr.). 6435-3
The Achilles' reply to the embassy. Maurice Hewlett (tr.). 6435-3
The advance of the Trojans, fr. The Iliad. William Cowper (tr.). 6435-3
After the chariot race, fr. The Iliad. Alexander Pope (tr.). 6435-3
Ajax in flight, fr. The Iliad. William Cowper (tr.). 6435-3
Ajax on the decks, fr. The Iliad. Andrew Lang et al. (tr.). 6435-3
"And Medon answer made...", fr. The Odyssey. John William Mackail (tr.). 6435-3
"And Nestor, the Geranian...", fr. The Odyssey. John William Mackail (tr.). 6435-3
"And now Cyllenian...", fr. The Odyssey. William Cowper (tr.). 6435-3
"And these all night...", fr. The Iliad. Alfred Lord Tennyson (tr.). 6435-3
"And thus they fought...", fr. The Iliad. Edward G.S. Stanley, 14th Earl of Derby (tr.). 6435-3
Andromache, fr. The Iliad. Samuel Butler (tr.). 6435-3
"Another part (a prospect differing...", fr. The Iliad. Alexander Pope (tr.). 6435-3
Apollo destroys his horses, fr. The Iliad. Edward G.S. Stanley, 14th Earl of Derby (tr.). 6435-3
"Apollo hearing this, passed quickly on". Percy Bysshe Shelley (tr.). 6435-3
The appeal of the phoenix, fr. The Iliad. George Ernle (tr.). 6435-3
"As when from his mountain-outlook...", fr. The Iliad. F.L. Lucas (tr.). 6251-2
"As when the billow gathers...", fr. The Iliad. William Ewart Gladstone (tr.). 6435-3
"As when the deep lies heaving...", fr. The Iliad. F.L. Lucas (tr.). 6251-2
"As when, high up...", fr. The Iliad. F.L. Lucas (tr.). 6251-2
At Pylos, fr. The Odyssey. John William Mackail (tr.). 6435-3
At Sparta, fr. The Odyssey. Samuel Butler (tr.). 6435-3
The beginning of the wrath, fr. The Iliad. Sir William Marris (tr.). 6435-3
The bending of the bow, fr. The Odyssey. William Cullen Bryant (tr.). 6372-1
"Beyond Ortygia there lies an isle", fr. The Odyssey. F.L. Lucas (tr.). 6251-2
"Bright as among the stars...", fr. The Iliad. William Cowper (tr.). 6606-2
"But about his house peered...", fr. The Odyssey. William Morris (tr.). 6435-3
"But Achilles, by the breakers...", fr. The Iliad. F.L. Lucas (tr.). 6251-2
"But Alcimus and Automedon...", fr. The Iliad. F.L. Lucas (tr.). 6251-2
"But as bees or supple-waisted...", fr. The Iliad. F.L. Lucas (tr.). 6251-2
"But as in a garden a poppy...", fr. The Iliad. F.L. Lucas (tr.). 6251-2
"But as o'er some parched mountain...", fr. The Iliad. F.L. Lucas (tr.). 6251-2
"But as on a day in winter...", fr. The Iliad. F.L. Lucas (tr.). 6251-2
"But as some star of bale...", fr. The Iliad. F.L. Lucas (tr.). 6251-2
"But s they talked, laid near...", fr. The Odyssey. F.L. Lucas (tr.). 6251-2
"But Delos is pleasant, O Phoebus...". T.F. Higham (tr.). 6435-3
"But Hector, when he saw...", fr. The Iliad. Sir William Marris (tr.). 6435-3
"But her knees at his words...", fr. The Odyssey. F.L. Lucas (tr.). 6251-2
"But now a herald...", fr. The Odyssey. F.L. Lucas (tr.). 6251-2
"But now Zeus throned in...", fr. The Iliad. F.L. Lucas (tr.). 6251-2
"But now-as ravening wolves...", fr. The Iliad. F.L. Lucas (tr.). 6251-2
"But the eternal father...", fr. The Iliad. William Cowper (tr.). 6435-3
"But this may not be. Age is shrouding you...". Jack Lindsay (tr.). 6435-3
"But to tell the white-armed...", fr. The Iliad. F.L. Lucas (tr.). 6251-2
"But when came early morning...", fr. The Odyssey. F.L Lucas (tr.). 6251-2
"But when her heart...", fr. The Odyssey. Sir William Marris (tr.). 6435-3
"But when the bands were mustered...", fr. The Iliad. F.L. Lucas (tr.). 6251-2
"But when the mother...", fr. The Odyssey. William Morris (tr.). 6435-3
"But when through Troy's wide...", fr. The Iliad. F.L. Lucas (tr.). 6251-2
"But when we were come...", fr. The Odyssey. F.L. Lucas (tr.). 6251-2
"But wise Telemachus...", fr. The Odyssey. John William Mackail (tr.). 6435-3
Calypso's island, fr. The Odyssey. George Chapman (tr.). 6435-3
"The clear-toned swan, to the beating of his wings". Jack Lindsay (tr.). 6435-3
Combat between Paris and Menelaus, fr. The Iliad. 6679-8
"Conquer the proud spirit...", fr. The Iliad. George Ernle (tr.). 6435-3
A dance in the palace of Vulcan. 6959-2
A dance in the palacle of Alcinous. 6959-2
The death of Hector, fr. The Iliad. George Chapman (tr.). 6933-9
The death of Patroclus, fr. The Iliad. Sir William Marris (tr.). 6435-3
The defiance of Hector and Ajax. Alexander Pope (tr.). 6424-8
The dog Argos, fr. The Odyssey. Thomas Edward ("Shaw") Lawrence (tr.). 6435-3
"Easily as a child that plays...", fr. The Iliad. F.L. Lucas (tr.). 6251-2
The end of the suitors, fr. The Odyssey. George Chapman (tr.). 6933-9
Eumaeus the swineherd. Samuel Butler (tr.). 6435-3
Exploit of Hector. 6304-7
"First by Andromache the women's...", fr. The Iliad. F.L. Lucas (tr.). 6251-2
"'For nine days then we were...", fr. The Odyssey. F.L. Lucas (tr.). 6251-2
The furnance. William Cowper (tr.). 6814-6
The garden of Alcinous, fr. The Odyssey. Walter Harris (fr. Moorish) (tr.). 6232-6
The garden of Alcinous, fr. The Odyssey. John William Mackail (tr.). 6649-6
The ghost of Patroclus, fr. The Iliad. William Cowper (tr.). 6435-3
"The Gods held me in Egypt...", fr. The Odyssey. F.L. Lucas (tr.). 6251-2
"He said, and urged him...", fr. The Odyssey. William Cowper (tr.). 6435-3
"He said: and on his horses...", fr. The Iliad. Edward G.S. Stanley, 14th Earl of Derby (tr.). 6435-3
"He spake, to whom I...", fr. The Odyssey. William Cowper (tr.). 6435-3
"He stoopt Pierea...", fr. The Odyssey. George Chapman (tr.). 6435-3

Hector and Achilles. 6621-6
Hector and Andromache, fr. The Iliad. Alexander Pope (tr.). 6932-0
Hektor and Andromache, fr. The Iliad. Maurice Hewlett (tr.). 6435-3
Hektor to Andromache, fr. The Iliad. Richard Lattimore (tr.). 6665-8
"Hektor turn'd", fr. The Iliad. Maurice Hewlett (tr.). 6435-3
Helen at the Scaean gates, fr. The Iliad. William Cullen Bryant (tr.). 6372-1
Helen on the walls of Troy. 6102-8
Helen on the walls, fr. The Iliad. Andrew Lang (tr.). 6987-8
Helen, fr. The Iliad. William Cowper (tr.). 6435-3
Hesiod, sels. 6435-3
"Hestia, wherever homes shelter...". Jack Lindsay (tr.). 6435-3
Home-coming, fr. The Odyssey. John William Mackail (tr.). 6435-3
The horses of Achilles, fr. The Iliad. Edward G.S. Stanley, 14th Earl of Derby (tr.). 6435-3
"I sing of Dionysus, an old story". T.F. Higham (tr.). 6435-3
Iliad, sel. Alexander Pope (tr.). 7014-0
The Iliad, sels. 6435-3,6605-2,6732-8,6679-8
The Iliad, sels. Robert Bridges (tr.). 6487-6
The Iliad, sels. William Cullen Bryant (tr.). 6372-1, 6610-0
The Iliad, sels. George Chapman (tr.). 6562-7,6194-X
The Iliad, sels. Edward G.S. Stanley, 14th Earl of Derby (tr.). 6289-X
The Iliad, sels. F.L. Lucas (tr.). 6251-2
The Iliad, sels. Alexander Pope (tr.). 6289-X,6543-0
The Iliad. Alexander Pope (tr.). 6198-2
"In haste the sons of Achaea...", fr. The Iliad. F.L. Lucas (tr.). 6251-2
"In meantime flew our ships...", fr. The Odyssey. George Chapman (tr.). 6547-3
"Indignantly he spoke...", fr. The Odyssey. Sir William Marris (tr.). 6435-3
Laertes, fr. The Odyssey. Sir William Marris (tr.). 6435-3
The lamentations, fr. The Iliad. Sir William Marris (tr.). 6435-3
The last fight, fr. The Iliad. Andrew Lang et al. (tr.). 6435-3
The last journey of the wooers, fr. The Odyssey. William Cowper (tr.). 6435-3
Menelaus and Odysseus, fr. The Iliad. William Cowper (tr.). 6435-3
Menelaus and Proteus, fr. The Odyssey. S.H. Butcher & Andrew Lang (tr.). 6435-3
"Muse, tell of Pan, the dear seed of Hermes...". Jack Lindsay (tr.). 6435-3
Nausicaa, fr. The Odyssey. George Chapman (tr.). 6933-9
Nausicaa, fr. The Odyssey. H.B. Cotterill (tr.). 6435-3
Nausicaa, fr. The Odyssey. Thomas Edward ("Shaw") Lawrence (tr.). 6435-3
"Next, ripe in yellow gold...", fr. The Iliad. Alexander Pope (tr.). 6435-3
Night before Troy. 6252-0
"Not then", fr. The Iliad. Maurice Hewlett (tr.). 6435-3
"Now all sat down", fr. The Iliad. Maurice Hewlett (tr.). 6435-3
"Now Apollo have mercy, and Artemis be thou kind". T.F. Higham (tr.). 6435-3
"Now glorious Leto's child goes up...". T.F. Higham (tr.). 6435-3
"Now Hermes of Cyllene...", fr. The Odyssey. F.L. Lucas (tr.). 6251-2
"Now marshall'd all beneath...", fr. The Iliad. William Cowper (tr.). 6435-3
"Now when at last...", fr. The Odyssey. H.B. Cotterill (tr.). 6435-3
"O father Zeus, if ev r among...", fr. The Iliad. F.L. Lucas (tr.). 6251-2
"O universal Mother, who dost keep". Percy Bysshe Shelley (tr.). 6435-3

Odysseus puts to sea, fr. The Odyssey. John William Mackail (tr.). 6435-3
The Odyssey, sels. 6435-3
The Odyssey, sels. William Cullen Bryant (tr.). 6372-1, 6484-1
The Odyssey, sels. George Chapman (tr.). 6527-9,6547-3
The Odyssey, sels. Andrew Lang (tr.). 6250-4
The Odyssey, sels. F.L. Lucas (tr.). 6251-2
The Odyssey, sels. Alexander Pope (tr.). 6527-9,6732-8
Of Circe, fr. The Odyssey. William Morris (tr.). 6435-3
Of Cyclops and the ram, fr. The Odssey. William Morris (tr.). 6435-3
"Of great Demeter here begins my lay". W.M.W. Call and T.F. Higham (tr.). 6435-3
Of his mother's shade, fr. The Odyssey. John William Mackail (tr.). 6435-3
Of Norman and Cyclops, fr. The Odyssey. William Morris (tr.). 6435-3
Of the laestrygones, fr. The Odyssey. Sir William Marris (tr.). 6435-3
Of the shade of Ajax, fr. The Odyssey. T.F. Higham (tr.). 6435-3
Of the shield of Achilles, fr. The Odyssey. William Cowper (tr.). 6435-3
"Of the wreath of the son...", fr. The Iliad. F.L. Lucas (tr.). 6251-2
"Of their lament...", fr. The Iliad. Sir William Marris (tr.). 6435-3
"Out of the lofty cavern wandering". Percy Bysshe Shelley (tr.). 6435-3
Palace of Alcinous, fr. The Odyssey. William Cullen Bryant (tr.). 6372-1
The parting of Hector and Andromache, fr. The Iliad. William Cullen Bryant (tr.). 6372-1,6102-8
Patroculus' body saved, fr. The Iliad. E.R. Dodds (tr.). 6435-3,6665-8
Penelope dreams, fr. The Odyssey. John William Mackail (tr.). 6435-3
Penelope dreams, fr. The Odyssey. Sir William Marris (tr.). 6435-3
Penelope forlorn, fr. The Odyssey. John William Mackail (tr.). 6435-3
Penelope makes trial of Odysseus, fr. The Odyssey. John William Mackail (tr.). 6435-3
Phaeacian nights - Demodocus, fr. The Odyssey. Thomas Edward ("Shaw") Lawrence (tr.). 6435-3
Phaeacian nights - Odysseus' tale, sels. 6435-3
Poetry and learning, fr. The Iliad. George Chapman (tr.). 6933-9
Praise of Homer, fr. The Odyssey. George Chapman (tr.). 6933-9
Priam and Achilles, fr. The Iliad. Robert Bridges (tr.). 6435-3
Priam and Achilles, fr. The Iliad. George Chapman (tr.). 6933-9
Priam and Achilles, fr. The Iliad. Alexander Pope (tr.). 6932-0
Priam appeals to Achilles. Leigh Hunt (tr.). 6102-8
"prudent chief with calm...," fr. The Iliad. Alexander Pope (tr.). 6435-3
The pursuit around the walls, fr. The Iliad. William Cowper (tr.). 6435-3
The pyre of Patroclus, fr. The Iliad. Alexander Pope (tr.). 6932-0
The rally, fr. The Iliad. Sir William Marris (tr.). 6435-3
"Round Achilles rose," fr. The Iliad. Sir William Marris (tr.). 6435-3
"The sacred keep of Ilion is rent." Andrew Lang (tr.). 6383-7
The sacrifice, fr. The Odyssey. George Chapman (tr.). 6933-9
Sarpedon and Glaucus, fr. The Iliad. Maurice Hewlett (tr.). 6435-3
Sarpedon to Glaukos, fr. The Iliad. Richard Lattimore (tr.). 6665-8
Sarpedonès speech, fr. The Iliad. George Chapman (tr.). 6933-9
"Sarpedon's words bit deep...", fr. The Iliad. Sir William Marris (tr.). 6435-3

HOMER

The scales of Zeus, fr. The Iliad. William Cowper (tr.). 6435-3
Scylla and Charybdis, fr. The Odyssey. George Chapman (tr.). 6933-9
Selections. John Dryden (tr.). 6195-0
"She called the famous smith...", fr. The Iliad. Sir William Marris (tr.). 6435-3
"She, with heavy heart". W.M.W. Call and T.F. Higham (tr.). 6435-3
"Sheer through his neck's...", fr. The Iliad. F.L. Lucas (tr.). 6251-2
The shield of Achilles, fr. The Iliad. Alexander Pope (tr.). 6435-3
The slaying, fr. The Odyssey. William Morris (tr.). 6435-3
The snow of stones, fr. The Iliad. Michael Balkwill (tr.). 6435-3
"So Ajax spoke and the others...", fr. The Iliad. F.L. Lucas (tr.). 6251-2
So did the son of Priam...", fr. The Iliad. Cecil Maurice Bowra (tr.). 6435-3
"So flashing-eyed Athene spoke...", fr. The Odyssey. F.L. Lucas (tr.). 6251-2
"So he spake, and all the wooers...", fr. The Odyssey. William Morris (tr.). 6435-3
"So Hector; and loud the Trojans...", fr. The Iliad. F.L. Lucas (tr.). 6251-2
"So hung the war in balance", fr. The Iliad. 6606-2
"So I spake, and he took...", fr. The Odyssey. William Morris (tr.). 6435-3
"So I: when swift Achilles...", fr. The Odyssey. T.F Higham (tr.). 6435-3
"So on both sides they battled...", fr. The Iliad. F.L. Lucas (tr.). 6251-2
"So round that sturdy ship...", fr. The Iliad. Sir William Marris (tr.). 6435-3
"So said he, and the crone...", fr. The Odyssey. John William Mackail (tr.). 6435-3
"So saying back to the dark...", fr. The Odyssey. John William Mackail (tr.). 6435-3
"So saying he passed from Thetis...", fr. The Iliad. F.L. Lucas (tr.). 6251-2
"So saying she came from her cavern...", fr. The Iliad. F.L. Lucas (tr.). 6251-2
"So saying, light-foot Iris...", fr. The Iliad. Alfred Lord Tennyson (tr.). 6435-3
"So saying, the goddess...", fr. The Iliad. William Cowper (tr.). 6435-3
"So saying, to Olympus with...", fr. The Iliad. F.L. Lucas (tr.). 6251-2
"So spake he, and the clouds...", fr. The Odyssey. John William Mackail (tr.). 6435-3
"So spoke Priam's noble son...", fr. The Iliad. F.L. Lucas (tr.). 6251-2
"So spoke the noble Achilles...". F.L. Lucas (tr.). 6251-2
"So Telemachus spoke. But Pallas...", fr. The Odyssey. F.L. Lucas (tr.). 6251-2
"So Telemachus spoke...gay", fr. The Odyssey. F.L. Lucas (tr.). 6251-2
"So the fugitives of the Trojans...", fr. The Iliad. F.L. Lucas (tr.). 6251-2
"So the noble Odysseus wakened...", fr. The Odyssey. F.L. Lucas (tr.). 6251-2
"So the old nurse took a basin...", fr. The Odyssey. F.L. Lucas (tr.). 6251-2
"So then the noble Odysseus...", fr. The Odyssey. F.L. Lucas (tr.). 6251-2
"So thence with heavy hearts...", fr. The Odyssey. F.L. Lucas (tr.). 6251-2
"So they carried the dead man...", fr. The Iliad. E.R. Dodds (tr.). 6435-3
"So was Menoetius' valiant son...", fr. The Iliad. William Cowper (tr.). 6435-3
"Soon of the shock of battle...", fr. The Iliad. F.L. Lucas (tr.). 6251-2
"The soul came to him...", fr. The Iliad. William Cowper (tr.). 6435-3
"Steadfast they stood, as mists...", fr. The Iliad. F.L. Lucas (tr.). 6251-2

The story of Bellerophon, fr. The Iliad. Alfred Tennyson and Arthur Henry Hallam (tr.). 6435-3
"Swiftly as dart the thoughts...", fr. The Iliad. F.L. Lucas (tr.). 6251-2
Tellemachus finds his father, fr. The Odyssey. William Cowper (tr.). 6435-3
"Then answer thus Antenor...", fr. The Iliad. William Cowper (tr.). 6435-3
"Then Aphrodite, the lover of laughter, was clad". Jack Lindsay (tr.). 6435-3
"Then close at hand came Athene...", fr. The Odyssey. F.L. Lucas (tr.). 6251-2
"Then first he form'd the immense...", fr. The Iliad. Alexander Pope (tr.). 6435-3
"Then hearkened the Argus-slayer...", fr. The Odyssey. F.L. Lucas (tr.). 6251-2
Then in the field the Trojans...", fr. The Iliad. F.L. Lucas (tr.). 6251-2
Then indeed had the sons...", fr. The Iliad. F.L. Lucas (tr.). 6251-2
"Then Menelaus, shaking...", fr. The Iliad. F.L. Lucas (tr.). 6251-2
"Then my well-greaved...", fr. The Odyssey. William Morris (tr.). 6435-3
"Then on his arm he settled...", fr. The Iliad. F.L. Lucas (tr.). 6251-2
"Then seeing him the noble Achilles...", fr. The Iliad. F.L. Lucas (tr.). 6251-2
"Then swift Achilles answer'd...", fr. The Iliad. Maurice Hewlett (tr.). 6435-3
"Then the white-armed goddess...", fr. The Iliad. F.L. Lucas (tr.). 6251-2
"Then up sprang storm-foot Iris...", fr. The Iliad. F.L. Lucas (tr.). 6251-2
"Thereat Laertes answered him...", fr. The Odyssey. Sir William Marris (tr.). 6435-3
"Therewith she left the cave...", fr. The Iliad. Sir William Marris (tr.). 6435-3
Thersites, fr. The Iliad. Maurice Hewlett (tr.). 6435-3
"These words were winged with his swift delight". Percy Bysshe Shelley (tr.). 6435-3
Thetis and Hephaetus, fr. The Iliad. Sir William Marris (tr.). 6435-3
"They found Odysseus dear...", fr. The Iliad. F.L. Lucas (tr.). 6251-2
"This said, he went to see", fr. The Iliad. George Chapman (tr.). 6562-7
"Thither when we came", fr. The Odyssey. Sir William Marris (tr.). 6435-3
"Thus having said, brave Hector...", fr. The Iliad. John Dryden (tr.). 6562-7
"Thus I revealed to my comrades...", fr. The Odyssey. F.L. Lucas (tr.). 6251-2
"Thus pondering he stood...", fr. The Iliad. William Cowper (tr.). 6435-3
"Thus sed-he, & Hermes hearing...", fr. The Iliad. Robert Bridges (tr.). 6487-6
"Thus shouting onward...", fr. The Iliad. Michael Balkwill (tr.). 6435-3
"Till sacred morn had brighten'd...", fr. The Iliad. William Cowper (tr.). 6435-3
"To censure me,...", fr. The Iliad. 6605-2
Translations, sels. Alexander Pope (tr.). 6195-0
The triumph of Hector, fr. The Iliad. William Mumford (tr.). 6679-8
The Trojan camp at night. Alfred Lord Tennyson (tr.). 6102-8
The Trojan camp-fires, fr. The Iliad. Alfred Lord Tennyson (tr.). 6435-3
The Trojans outside the walls, fr. The Iliad. George Chapman (tr.). 6933-9
"Two days and nights...", fr. The Odyssey. John William Mackail (tr.). 6435-3
The two hosts, fr. The Iliad. William Ewart Gladstone (tr.). 6435-3
Ulysses and Achilles, fr. The Odyssey. William Cullen Bryant (tr.). 6879-0
Ulysses and his dog, fr. The Odyssey. Alexander Pope (tr.). 6932-0
Ulysses in the waves, fr. The Odyssey. Gorge Chapman

(tr.). 6933-9
"Up leapt Achilles dear to Zeus...", fr. The Iliad.
    F.L. Lucas (tr.). 6251-2
The victory of Hector, fr. The Iliad. William Cullen
    Bryant (tr.). 6610-0
The vision of Theoclymenus, fr. The Odyssey. Thomas
    Edward ("Shaw") Lawrence (tr.). 6435-3
The wall, fr. The Iliad. William Cowper (tr.). 6435-3
The web, fr. The Odyssey. Sir William Marris (tr.).
    6435-3
"Who of the gods...", fr. The Iliad. Sir William Marris
    (tr.). 6435-3
"With that he gave...", fr. The Odyssey. Sir William
    Marris (tr.). 6435-3
"With these words Hermes sped...", fr. The Iliad.
    Robert Bridges (tr.). 6435-3
"Zeus spake; and storm-foot Iris...", fr. The Iliad.
    F.L. Lucas (tr.). 6251-2
Homer. William Edmonstoune Aytoun. 6948-7
Homer. Albert Ehrenstein. 6160-5
Homer. William Douw Lighthall. 7041-8
"Homer and Hesiod fathered on the Gods' divinity".
    Xenophanes. 6251-2
"Homer and Milton blind, Beethoven deaf". Unconquerable.
    John Freeman. 6779-4
Homer, Frederick L.
    Hear, o ye nations. 6386-1
"Homer-head, uplifted". A portra^{r}t. Gertrude Huntington
    McGiffert. 6838-3
Homeric hymn to Neptune. George Chapman. 6833-2
Homeric unities. Andrew Lang. 7015-9
Homeric unity. Andrew Lang. 6987-8
Homes. M.K. Westcott. 6937-1
Homes. Margaret Widdemer. 7027-2
Homes and graves. Thomas Kibble Hervey. 6980-0
The homes of England. Felicia Dorothea Hemans. 6198-2,6479-
    5,6732-8,6133-8,6302-0,6385,6543-0,6129-9,6502-3
The homes of joy. Edgar A. Guest. 6862-6
Homes of the cliff dwellers. Stanley Wood. 6836-7
Homesick. Anna F. Burnham. 6965-7
Homesick. Phoebe Cary. 6969-X
Homesick. Julia C.R. Dorr. 6338-1,6374-8
Homesick. David Gray. 6097-8,6302-0,6385-3,6543-0
Homesick. Dorothy Frances McCrae. 6784-0
Homesick. Joseph Ashby Sterry. 6770-0
Homesick. Unknown. 6743-3
Homesick. Howard Weeden. 6006-4
Homesick for the country. Unknown. 6302-0
Homesick in England. Robert Haven Schauffler. 6501-5
Homesickness. Henry Bellamann. 6037-4
Homestead reclaimed. Marie Emilie Gilchrist. 6906-1
The homestead strike. Unknown. 6149-4
The homestead, fr. Dovecote mill. Phoebe Cary. 6865-0;6969-
    X
The homestead. Gertrude Huntington McGiffert. 6838-3
Hometown. Luis Cabalquinto. 6790-5
Homeward. Gustave Kobbe. 6274-1
Homeward. Unknown. 6411-6
Homeward bound. William Allingham. 6660-7
Homeward bound. Perceval Gibbon. 6793-X
Homeward bound. William Edward Hartpole Lecky. 6250-4
Homeward bound. Adelaide Anne Procter. 6681-X
Homeward bound. D.H. Rogers. 6833-2
Homeward bound. B.S. S. 6274-1
Homeward bound. Robert Southey. 6833-2
Homeward bound. L. Frank Tooker. 6833-2
Homeward bound. Unknown. 6717-4
Homeward bound. Henry Van Dyke. 6961-4
The homeward bound (landfall). Bill Adams. 6833-2
"Homeward from earth's far ends thou art returned".
    Alcaeus of Mytilene. 6251-2
Homeward in Hokah. Edith Thompson. 6342-X
The homeward journey. Leonard [Lazarus] Aaronson. 6210-5
The homeward road. Charles Capron Marsh. 6116-8
Homeward! the evening comes. Arthur Hugh Clough. 6889-8
Homing. Mary S. Fitzgerald. 6789-1
The homing bee. Emily Pauline ("Tekahionwake") Johnson.
    6837-5
The homing heart. Daniel Henderson. 6607-0
Homo additus naturae. Rolfe Humphries. 6072-2

Homo natus de muliere. Bible. 6830-8
Homoeopathic soup. Unknown. 6089-7,6743-3
Homosexual lover seeks and finds shelter. Barry Southam.
    7018-3
"The homosexual young men and...amorous girls". Lone
    gentleman. Pablo (Neftali Ricardo Reyes Basualto)
    Neruda. 6759-X
Homunculus et la belle etoile, fr. Pecksniffiana. Wallace
    Stevens. 6531-7
Honan, Daniel J.
    For any Catholic girl. 6839-1
Hone, William
    The first of April ("When indoor young ones club...").
    6465-5,6018-8
Honecker, George J.
    Storybook fossils, sels. 6803-0
Honest Abe. Henry Howard Brownell. 6524-4
Honest Abe of the west. Edmund Clarence Stedman. 6708-5
"Honest and true, black and blue". Unknown. 7028-0
The honest bargain. Margaret Haynes Foster. 7016-7
An honest confession. Marc Eugene ("Vandyke Brown") Cook.
    6004-8
The honest deacon. Isaac Hinton Brown. 6014-5
The honest deacon. Unknown. 6412-6
Honest doubt. Robert Weston. 6337-3
Honest fame, fr. The temple of fame. Alexander Pope. 6932-
    0
"Honest little Peter Grey". Peter Grey. Alice Cary. 6969-X,
    6060-9
The honest little boy. Unknown. 6158-3
Honest lover. Sir John Suckling. 6328-4
The honest man's fortune, sels. Francis Beaumont and John
    Fletcher. 6369-1
The honest man's litany. Unknown. 6787-5
Honest poverty. Robert Burns. 6271-7,6438-8,6131-1
An honest rum-seller's advertisement. A. McWight. 6914-2
The honest whore, sels. Thomas Dekker. 6317-9,6301-2
Honesty. Sir Thomas Wyatt. 6436-1
Honey. Ruth Miller. 6788-3
The honey bee. Don Marquis. 6722-0
The honey bee. Philip Freneau. 6265-2
Honey boy. Billie Marie Crabb. 6750-6
'Honey' draws the line. Unknown. 6443-4
Honey-bee. Lucy Fitch Perkins. 6368-3
"The honey-bee that wanders all day long". James Sheridan
    Knowles. 6402-7
"The honey-bees on Mount Hymettus, long...ago". How the
    bees came by their sting. Carlotta Perry. 6923-1
Honey-bug baby. Emma C. Dulaney. 6711-5
Honeycomb. N.M. Bennet. 6799-9
Honeymoon. Mary Carolyn Davies. 6441-8
Honeymoon. Anna Wickham. 6893-6
The honeymoon, fr. Local lives. Millen Brand. 6803-0
The honeymoon. Walter Savage Landor. 6089-7
The honeymoon. John Tobin. 6676-3
The honeymoon. Unknown. 6874-X
"The honeysuckle embroiders". Elegy. George Barker. 6390-X
"Honeysuckle loves to crawl," sels. Sir Walter Scott. 6601-
    1
"The honeysuckle round the porch", sels. Alfred Lord
    Tennyson. 6601-1
The honeysuckle, fr. The house of life. Dante Gabriel
    Rossetti. 6123-0,6110-9,6655-0
Honeysuckles. Frank Dempster Sherman. 6006-4,6135-4
Honeywell, J.
    The menagerie. 6165-6,6279-2,6409-4
Honeywood, St. John
    Darby and Joan. 6307-1
    A radical song of 1786. 6946-0
Honez Joseph Unglesteiner. Unknown. 6175-3
Hongo, Garrett Kaoru
    Hiking up Hieizan with Alam Lau/Buddha's birthday 1974.
    6790-5
Honig, Edward (tr.)
    Night song of the Andalusian sailors. Federico Garcia
    Lorca, 6068-4
    Song of the rider. Federico Garcia Lorca, 6068-4
The honker. Berton Braley. 6853-7
Honky tonk in Cleveland, Ohio. Carl Sandburg. 6345-4
Honor. Samuel Butler. 6543-0

HONOR

Honor. Edgar A. Guest. 6748-4
Honor. William Wordsworth. 6385-3,6438-8
Honor to the eagle. Helene Mullins. 7019-1
"Honor to those whose words or deeds". Henry Wadsworth Longfellow. 6601-1
Honor Washington. Unknown. 6158-3
"Honor, with everything at stake". Honor. Edgar A. Guest. 6748-4
"The Honorable the City Clerk: Dear Sir". Letter to the city clerk. Frederick A. Wright. 6979-7,6751-4
"Honored be the hero evermore". The martyr of the arena. Epes Sargent. 6917-7
Honoria. Coventry Patmore. 6980-0
Honors I: A scholar is musing on his want of success. Jean Ingelow. 6940-1
Honors II: The answer. Jean Ingelow. 6940-1
Honors of war. John James Piatt. 6074-9
Honour. Ada Cambridge. 6784-0
Honour and desert, fr. The angel in the house. Coventry Patmore. 6250-4
"Honour and happiness unite". The Christian. William Cowper. 6814-6
Honour and shame. Alexander Pope. 6861-8
Honour in bud. Ben Jonson. 6322-5
"The honour o'er each hill". Ben Dorain. Duncan Ban MacIntyre. 6873-1
The honour of Bristol. Unknown. 6547-3,6322-5
"Honour the brave who sleep". Heroes of the Titanic. Henry Van Dyke. 6961-4
"Hoo daur ye blink upon the stooks". Auld fermer's address to the 'prodigal' sun. James Logie ("Hugh Haliburton") Robertson. 6819-7

Hoock, Harriet
    Answer. 6543-0

Hood Jr., Thomas
    The cannibal flea. 6440-X
    In memoriam technicam. 6089-7
    In memoriam technicam. 6802-2
    A letter of advice. 6652-6
    Muddled metaphors. 6902-9
    Poets and linnets. 6092-7
    Puss had three little kittens. 6699-2
    Ravings. 6802-2
    Takings. 6089-7
    The tea. 6440-X
    The wedding. 6802-2
    The wedding. 6089-7

Hood the Younger, Thomas. See Hood Jr., Thomas

Hood, Thomas
    Address to Mr. Cross, of Exeter Change... 6974-6
    An address to the steam washing company. 6974-6
    All in the downs. 6026-9
    Allegory. 6974-6
    The angler's farewell. 6974-6
    Answer to pauper. 6974-6
    Ariel and the suicide. 6980-0
    The art of book-keeping. 6606-2,6424-8,6219-9
    As it fell upon a day. 6974-6
    Autumn. 6018-8,6271-7,6272-5,6302-0,6385-3,6334-9,6512
    Autumnal ode, sels. 6395-0
    The bachelor's dream. 6089-7,6680-1,6219-9,6278-4
    Backing the favourite. 6974-6
    Bailey ballads, sels. 6974-6
    Ballad. 6656-9
    Ballad ("It was not in the winter"). 6271-7,6423-X
    Ballad ("She's up"). 6974-6
    Ballad ("Sigh on"). 6271-7
    Ballad ("Spring"). 6974-6
    Ben Bluff. 6089-7
    Bianca's dream. 6974-6
    Birthday verses. 6974-6
    Blank verse in rhyme. 6255-5
    A blow up. 6974-6
    The boy at the nore. 6760-3,6974-6
    The bridge of sighs. 6301-2,6122-2,6344-6,6014-5,6198-2, 6486-8,6246 ,6271-7,6289-X,6302-0,6385-3,6370-5,6402 ,6425-6,6437-X,6501-5,6604-6,6610-0,6661 ,6726-3, 6732-8,6660-7,6570-8,6646-1,6543 ,6102-8,6560-0,6513-9,6153-2,6192-9,6656
    The broken dish, fr. Domestic didactics. 6974-6
    The broken dish. 6092-7
    A bunch of forget-me-nots. 6974-6
    The burning of the love letter. 6874-X
    The burning of the love-letter. 6974-6
    A butcher. 6974-6
    By a lover. 6980-0
    The carelesse nurse mayd. 6724-7
    A charity sermon. 6974-6
    Child and mother. 6127-3,6424-8
    The china-mender. 6974-6
    The cigar. 6453-1
    Cockle v. Cackle. 6200-8
    Come with the ring. 6917-7
    The compass, with variations. 6974-6
    Conveyancing. 6974-6
    Craniology. 6974-6
    Death. 6980-0
    Death. 7015-9
    Death. 6980-0
    Death. 7015-9
    The death bed. 6102-8,6278-4,6513-9,6560-0,6656-9,6046-3,6214-8,6219-9,6332-2,6604-6,6186-9,6240-7,6246-6, 6271 ,6337-3,6392-6,6437-X,6481-7,6660-7,6737
    Death in the kitchen. 6974-6
    Death's ramble. 6089-7,6278-4
    December and May. 6974-6
    The demon ship. 6554-9
    The demon-ship. 6911-8
    The departure of summer. 6423-X
    Diversities of fortune. 6302-0;6385-3
    Dog-grel verses, by a poor blind. 7008-6
    Domestic asides; or, truth in parenthesis. 6974-6
    Domestic didactics, sels. 6974-6
    Domestic poems. 6278-4
    "Don't you smell fire?" 6974-6
    Double blessedness. 6302-0
    The double knock. 6724-7
    The dream of Eugene Aram. 6133-8,6271-7,6661-5,6732-8, 6302-0,6385 ,6102-8,6291-9,6518-X,6656-9,6648-8
    The drowning ducks. 6974-6
    The duel. 6183-4
    Elegy on David Laing, Esq. 6974-6
    Epicurean reminiscences of a sentimentalist. 6219-9
    Epigram. 7025-6
    Epping hunt. 6974-6
    Equestrian courtship. 6621-6
    The exile. 6974-6
    Fair Ines. 6122-2,6271-7,6437-X,6732-8,6219-9,6102-8, 6250-4,6543-0,6301-2,6656-9
    A fairy tale. 6974-6
    Faithless Nellie Gray. 6014-5,6089-7,6271-7,6289-X,6302-0,6486 ,6092-7,6212-1,6219-9,6278-4,6808-1,6739 , 6614-3,6732-8,6518-X
    Faithless Sally Brown. 6089-7,6271-7,6302-0,6385-3,6518-X,6808-1,6219-9
    The fall of the deer. 6974-6
    The fall. 6974-6
    False poets and true. 6974-6
    "Farewell, life!" 6302-0,6385-3,6199-0,6219-9
    The farewell. 6974-6
    A few lines on completing forty-seven, fr. Domestic... 6974-6
    A few lines on completing forty-seven. 6633-X
    The flower. 6092-7
    Flowers. 6302-0,6385-3,6656-9
    The forlorn shepherd's complaint. 6385-3
    The forsaken. 6974-6
    Fragment ("I had a dream..."). 6974-6
    French and English. 6018-3
    A friendly address to Mrs. Frey, in Newgate. 6974-6
    The ghost. 6974-6
    Gog and Magog. 6974-6
    Gold. 6917-7
    Gold! 6302-0,6385-3,6337-3,6629-1,6732-8
    A good direction. 6974-6
    Good-night. 6278-4
    Guido and Marina. 6974-6
    A happy new year! 6974-6
    The haunted house, sels. 6369-1,6545-7,6648-8,6046-3
    The haunted house. 6744-1,6102-8,6167-2,6567-8

"He watched her breathing." 6302-0,6385-3,6291-9
Her death (Miss Kilmansegg) 6656-9
Her moral (Miss Kilmanseg). 6481-7,6656-9
Hero and Leander. 6974-6
His own epitaph, fr. Memorials of Thomas Hood. 6545-7
History of John Day. 6425-6
Huggins and Duggins. 6802-2
Huggins and Duggins. 6974-6
Hymn to the sun. 6974-6
I love thee. 6328-4,6066-8,6226-1,6543-0
I remember, I remember. 6075-7,6481-7,6512-0,6127-3, 6233-4,6240 ,6192-3,6250-4,6104-4,6219-9,6658-5,6241-7,6328-4,6337-3,6369-1,6370-5,6457 ,6452-4,6639-9, 6424-8,6737-9,6302-0,6385-3,6459-0,6479-5,6486-8, 6504-X,6519-8,6583-X,6732
I remember, I remember, sels. 6601-1
'I'd be a parody', fr. Bailey ballads. 6974-6
I'm going to Bombay. 6974-6
I'm not a single man. 6680-1,6646-1
The Irish schoolmaster. 6802-2,6974-6
"It is not death, that sometime in a sigh". 6187-7
It was not in winter. 6737-9
It was the time of roses. 6250-4
Jack Hall. 6974-6
Jarvis and Mrs. Cope. 6974-6
John Day. 6974-6
John Trot. 6760-3
John Trot. 6974-6
The kangaroos. 6974-6
The lady at sea. 6271-7
The lady's dream. 6358-6,6219-9
The last man. 6378-0,6545-7
The last man. 6974-6
A lay of real life. 6408-6
A lay of real life. 6974-6
The lay of the laborer. 6656-9
The lay of the laborer. 6820-0
Lear. 6656-9
The lee shore. 6383-7
A legend of Navarre. 6974-6
Lieutenant Luff. 6974-6
Lines in a young lady's album. 6026-9
Lines on seeing my wife and two children sleeping... 6974-6
Lines to a friend at Cobham. 6974-6
Lines to a lady. 6974-6
Lines to Mary, fr. Bailey ballads. 6974-6
Literary and literal. 6974-6
Little Red Riding Hood. 6167-2
The logicians. 6974-6
The lost expedition. 6997-5
The lost heir. 6302-06385-3,6407-8,6279-2,6219-9
Love. 6980-0
Love. 6974-6
Love has not eyes. 6974-6
Love language of a merry young soldier. 6633-X
Love thy mother, little one. 6629-1
'Love with a witness', fr. Bailey ballads. 6974-6
Lycus, the centaur. 6974-6
Man and boy. 6383-7
"A man may cry church! church! at every word". 6238-5
Mary's ghost. 6974-6
The mermaid of Margate. 6974-6
Midnight. 6974-6
Miss Fanny's farewell flowers. 6974-6
Miss Kilmansegg and her precious leg. 6974-6
The monkey-martyr. 6974-6
Moral reflections on the cross of St. Paul's. 6974-6
More hullabaloo!. 6279-2
Morning meditations. 6302-0,6385-3,6600-3
My mother bids me spend my smiles. 6092-7
My son and heir. 6974-6
'Napoleon's midnight review'. 6974-6
No! 6302-0,6385-3,6089-7,6623-2,6724-7,6558 ,6092-7, 6125-7,6464-7,6278-4,6739-5
Nocturnal sketch. 6302-0,6385-3,6277-6,6724-7,6089-7, 6219-9,6633-X,6424-8
A nocturnal sketch. 6916-9
November. 6183-4,6239-3,6107-9,6424-8,6456-6
November in England. 6374-8,6597-X

"Now lay thine ear against this golden sand". 6997-5
"Now, lay thine ear against this golden sand". 6793-X
Number one. 6974-6
O lady, leave thy silken thread. 6328-4
Ode - autumn. 6974-6
Ode for St. Cecilia's eve. 6974-6
Ode for the ninth of November. 6974-6
Ode imitated from Horace. 6974-6
Ode on a distant prospect of Clapham academy. 6874-X
Ode on a distant prospect of Clapham Academy. 6092-7
Ode to Admiral Gambier, G.C.B. 6974-6
Ode to Edward Gibbon Wakefield, Esq. 6974-6
Ode to Joseph Grimaldi, Senior. 6974-6
Ode to Joseph Hume, Esq., M.P. 6974-6
Ode to M. Brunel. 6974-6
Ode to Madame Hengler. 6974-6
Ode to melancholy. 6974-6
An ode to melancholy, sels. 6980-0
Ode to Miss Kelly. 6974-6
Ode to Mr. Graham, the aeronaut. 6974-6
Ode to Mr. M°Adam. 6974-6
Ode to Mr. Malthus. 6974-6
Ode to Mr. Mathews. 6974-6
Ode to my little son. 6402-7,6219-9
Ode to my little son. 6889-8
Ode to N.A. Vigors, Esq. 6974-6
Ode to peace, fr. Domestic didactics. 6974-6
Ode to Perry. 6278-4
Ode to Rae Wilson, Esquire. 6302-0,6278-4
Ode to Richard Martin, Esquire. 6974-6
Ode to St. Swithin. 6974-6
Ode to the advocates for...removal of Smithfield market. 6974-6
Ode to the cameleopard. 6974-6
Ode to the great unknown. 6974-6
Ode to the late lord mayor. 6974-6
Ode to the moon. 6437-X
Ode to W. Jerdan, Esq. 6974-6
Ode to W. Kitchener, M.D. 6974-6
Ode-autumn. 6656-9
Ode: autumn, sels. 6934-7
Old ballad. 6974-6
The old house at home. 6629-1
On a picture of Hero and Leander. 6974-6
On Mistress Nicely, a pattern for housekeepers. 6974-6
On receiving a gift. 6974-6
On steam. 6974-6
On the art unions. 6278-4
On the death of the giraffe. 6974-6
On the removal of a menagerie. 6974-6
Our Village. 6092-7,6018-8
Pain in a pleasure boat. 6621-6
The painter puzzled. 6974-6
A parental ode to my son aged three years... 6089-7, 6233-4,6278-4
A Parthian glance. 6974-6
Past and present. 6134-6,6228-8,6246-6,6560-0,6464-7, 6668 ,6134-6,6228-8,6246-6
The pedlar and his trumpet. 6669-0
The pedler and his trumpet. 6669-0
A plain direction. 6639-9
Playing at soldiers. 6974-6
The plea of the midsummer fairies. 6974-6,7020-5
Please to ring the belle. 6092-7
"Please to ring the belle." 6092-7
The poet's portion, sels. 6545-7
The poet's portion. 6974-6
Pompey's ghost. 6358-6
The progress of art. 6974-6
A public dinner. 6974-6
Queen Mab ("A little fairy comes at night"). 6105-2, 6132-X,6242-3,6254-7,6452-3,6466 ,6692-5,6135-4,6424-8,6639-9,6638-0,6495
A recipe - for civilization. 6974-6
Reflections on a New Year's Day. 6974-6
Reminiscences of a sentimentalist. 6278-4
A report from below. 6974-6
A retrospective review. 6233-4
Rondeau. 6974-6
Rotterdam. 6484-1

HOOD

The ruling power. 6724-7
A rustic ode. 6980-0
Ruth. 6198-2,6239-3,6240-7,6271-7,6302-0,6385 ,6315-2,
    6423-X,6429-9,6437-X,6457-4,6499 ,6600-3,6732-8,6737-
    9,6668-2,6656-9,6543 ,6018-8,6250-4,6321-7,6199-0,
    6321-7,6383 ,6219-9,6424-8
A sailor's apology for bow-legs. 6974-6
A sailor's apology for bow-legs. 7025-6
A sailor's apology for bow-legs. 6833-2
Sally Simkin's lament. 6089-7,6258-X,6302-0
The sausage maker's ghost. 6916-9
The schoolmaster's motto. 6760-3
The schoolmaster's motto. 6974-6
Science. 6669-0
The sea of death, sels. 6545-7
The sea of death. 6208-3,6315-2,6648-8
Sea song. 6802-2,6974-6
The sea-spell. 6974-6
Serenade. 6737-9
Serenade ("Ah sweet, thou little knowest how"). 6271-7,
    6226-1,6278-4
A serenade ("Lullaby, oh lullaby"). 6416-7,6219-9
She is far from the land. 6974-6
Shooting pains. 6974-6
"Sigh on, sad heart, for love's eclipse". 6980-0
Silence. 6208-3,6102-8,6301-2,6737-9
Singing for the million. 6407-8
A singular expression at Somerset house. 6974-6
Song. 6543-0
Song ("A lake"). 6075-7,6271-7,6466-3,6421-3
Song ("My mother"). 6874-X
Song ("My mother bids me..."). 6974-6
Song ("O lady"). 6271-7,6600-3
Song ("The stars..."). 6974-6
Song for music. 6974-6
The song of the shirt. 6014-5,6198-2,6332-2,6401-9,6473-
    6,6486 ,6102-8,6383-7,6104-4,6560-0,6199-0,6250 ,
    6122-2,6134-6,6271-7,6302-0,6385-3,6437 ,6219-9,6301-
    2,6403-5,6656-9,6543-0,6723 ,6457-4,6459-0,6490-6,
    6512-0,6527-9,6600 ,6706-9,6732-8
Sonnet ("Along the Woodford road"). 6974-6
Sonnet ("By ev'ry sweet"). 6974-6
Sonnet ("It is not death"). 6315-2
Sonnet ("Love, dearest lady"). 6974-6
Sonnet ("Love, I am jealous"). 6974-6
Sonnet ("Love, see thy lover"). 6974-6
Sonnet ("The curse of Adam"). 6974-6
Sonnet ("The sky is glowing"). 6974-6
Sonnet ("Time was liked"). 6974-6
Sonnet ("Time was"). 6974-6
Sonnet for the 14tth of February. 6974-6
Sonnet on Mistress Nicely. 6378-0
Sonnet to Lord Wharncliffe on his game bill. 6974-6
Sonnet written in Keats' Endymion. 6974-6
Spring. 6278-4
The stag-eyed lady. 6974-6
The stage-struck hero. 6974-6
Stanzas. 6656-9
Stanzas ("We did not wear..."). 6974-6
Stanzas to Tom Woodgate, of Hastings. 6974-6
A storm at Hastings. 6974-6
The sub-marine. 6974-6
The Sunday question. 6278-4
The superiority of machinery. 6092-7
The supper superstition. 6974-6
Sweated labor, fr. The song of the shirt. 6337-3
The sylvan fairy. 6980-0
Symptoms of ossification. 6974-6
There's no romance in that! 6974-6
Those evening bells. 6802-2,6974-6
Tim Turpin. 6089-7
Time of roses. 6437-X,6513-9,6652-6
Time, hope, and memory. 6974-6
To - (composed at Rotterdam). 6092-7
To a bad rider. 6974-6
To a child embracing his mother. 6974-6
To a child embracing his mother. 6097-8,6233-4,6271-7,
    6627-5,6319-9
To a cold beauty. 6980-0,6974-6
To a critic. 6974-6

To a decayed seaman. 6974-6
To a false friend. 6974-6
To a Scotch girl, washing linen after her...fashion.
    6974-6
To a sleeping child. 6233-4
To an absentee. 6974-6
To an enthusiast. 6974-6
To Celia. 6974-6
To fancy. 6974-6
To Fanny. 6974-6
To Henrietta, on her departure for Calais. 6105-2
To hope. 6974-6
To Jane. 6974-6
To Mary housemaid on Valentine's Day, fr. Domestic...
    6974-6
To Minerva. 6874-X
To Minerva. 6092-7,6125-7,6230-X,6102-8
To Mr. Dymoke. 6974-6
To Mr. Wrench, at the English opera-house. 6974-6
To my daughter. 6271-7
To my infant son. 6302-0,6385-3
To my wife. 6974-6
To ocean. 6974-6
To Spencer Perceal, Esq., M.P. 6974-6
To Sylvanus Urban, Esq. 6974-6
To Thomas Bish, Esq. 6974-6
Tom Tatter's birthday ode. 6315-2,6733-6,6545-7
A true story. 6974-6
A true story. 6974-6
Truth in parentheses. 6404-3,6425-6,6779-2
The turtles. 6669-0
The two peacocks of Bedfont. 6974-6
The two swans. 6974-6
The undying one. 6974-6
A valentine. 6974-6
Verses in an album. 6250-4
The volunteer. 6974-6
The water lady. 6271-7,6302-0,6545-7,6656-9
The water peri's song. 6802-2
The water peri's song. 6874-X
"We me - 'twas in a crowd". 6802-2
"We watched her breathing thro' the night" 6935-5
The wee man. 6974-6
"What can an old man do but die." 6385-3
The widow. 6974-6
A winter nosegay. 6974-6
Written in a volume of Shakespeare. 6974-6
Written in a young lady's album. 6092-7

Hooded night. Robinson Jeffers. 6628-3
The **hoodoo**. James Whitcomb Riley. 7035-3
Hoofnagel, Fritz
    Fritz Valdher is made a mason. 6175-3
The **hoofs** of horses. William Henry Ogilvie. 6180-X
Hook, Clara Degman
    The flowery path of life. 6906-1
    The old-fashioned garden club. 6906-1
    To my mother in heaven. 6906-1
Hook, Theodore
    Cautionary verses. 6089-7
    Clubs. 6652-6
    Puns. 6018-8
Hooke, Hilda Mary
    Inspiration. 6796-4
    Iris. 6843-X
    Iris. 6797-2
    Misty moon. 6797-2
    October. 6797-2
    To an April child. 6797-2
    Vesper. 6797-2
Hooker's across. George Henry Boker. 6946-0
Hooker, Brian
    Ballade of farewell. 6875-8
    Ballade of the dreamland rose. 6338-1,6347-0,6250-4
    The city. 6030-7
    Cyrano's presentation of cadets. 6250-4
    Ghosts. 6467-1
    Habet. 6118-4
    Lilacs in the city. 6347-0
    The maker of images. 6029-3
    Offerings. 6347-0

Riverside. 6030-7
Song ("The skies are dimly"). 6347-0
To any woman. 6032-3
Hookes, N.
To Amanda walking in the garden. 6563-5
Hooks, John
Readers round table at Christmas. 6789-1
The torchlighter. 6789-1
Hooley, Teresa
Christ in Woolworth's. 6144-3,6335-7,6532-5
Scabious time. 6804-9
Sea fret. 6258-X
Sea-foam. 6044-7
"The hoop, the darling justly of the fair". On the hoop. James Thomson. 6816-2
The hoop-skirt. Unknown. 6247-4
Hooper, Ellen Sturgis
The chimney-sweep. 6502-3
Duty. 6461-2
Hooper, Helen
Memory. 6750-6
Hooper, Lucy H.
Elsinore. 6451-5
Hetty McEwen; or, the brave woman of Nashville. 6403-5
The king's ride. 6165-6
The three doves. 6385-3
Three visitors. 6673-9
Hooper, Lucy H. (tr.)
Civil war. Unknown (French), 6166-4
Civil war - an episode of the commune. Victor Hugo, 6924-X
The trumpeter's betrothed. Unknown, 6166-4
The hoopoe. George Darley. 6943-6
Hoops. Wilfred Wilson Gibson. 6234-2
The hoopskirt.. John Gould Fletcher. 6299-7
Hooray, I'm a millionaire. Davie Robb. 6149-4
Hoosier spring-poetry. James Whitcomb Riley. 6993-2
Hooton, Earnest A.
The fat-buttocked bushmen. 6722-0
Ode to a dental hygienist. 6722-0
Hope. Thomas Campbell. 6438-8
Hope. William Cowper. 6814-6
Hope. Emily Dickinson. 6121-4
Hope. Sir Richard Fanshawe. 6933-9
Hope. Oliver Goldsmith. 6932-0
Hope. Avis H. Grant. 6906-1
Hope. Martha J. Hadley. 6274-1
Hope. Thomas Kibble Hervey. 6980-0
Hope. William Dean Howells. 6431-0
Hope. John Langhorne. 6086-2
Hope. Mikhail Lermontov. 6103-6
Hope. Cecil R. Martin. 6799-9
Hope. Gertrude Huntington McGiffert. 6838-3
Hope. Anna Blake Mwzquida. 6337-3
Hope. Eden Phillpotts. 6782-4
Hope. Ernestine Renee Sellier. 6799-9
Hope. William Shenstone. 6385-3,6545-7,6191-6
Hope. Ben H. Smith. 6662-3
Hope. Phillips Stewart. 6433-7
Hope. Phillips Stewart. 7041-8
Hope. Theognis. 7039-6
Hope. Unknown. 6144-3,6291-1,6337-3
Hope. Unknown. 6889-8
Hope. Hortense Drucker Wagar. 6270-9
Hope. Anne Finch, Countess of Winchilsea. 6641-0
Hope ("And as, in sparkling majesty, a star"). John Keats. 6583-X
Hope ("He died!") Unknown. 6335-7
Hope ("Hope, like a gleaming taper's light,"). Oliver Goldsmith. 6174-5,6337-3,6583-X
Hope ("Hope, of all passions, most befriends us here."). Edward Young. 6211-3,6294-6
Hope ("When I was a little boy"). Gamaliel Bradford. 6607-0
Hope and fear. Thomas Campion. 6482-5
Hope and fear. Algernon Charles Swinburne. 6198-2,6110-9, 6196-6,6656-9,6199-0,6123
"Hope and mirth are gone. Beauty is departed". The cathedral. William G. Shakespeare. 7027-2
Hope and tears. John Vance Cheney. 6461-2

A hope carol. Christina Georgina Rossetti. 6123-0,6747-6
Hope deferred. Sir Lewis Morris. 7007-8
Hope deferred. Unknown. 6273-3
Hope deferred, fr. Outside the temple. William Bell Scott. 6819-7
Hope evermore and believe. Arthur Hugh Clough. 6198-2,6337-3,6730-1,6110-9,6196-6,6199-0,6560-0,6214-8
Hope for the enslaved. William Lloyd Garrison. 7009-4
Hope in him while thou livest. Kabir. 6337-3
"Hope in our hearts doth only stay". Alice Cary. 6969-X
Hope in the French Revolution. William Wordsworth. 6793-X
Hope is a tattered flag. Carl Sandburg. 6375-6
Hope is the thing with feathers. Emily Dickinson. 6236-9, 6246-5,6513-9
"Hope is the victor's armour, strong to bear". Hope. Gertrude Huntington McGiffert. 6838-3
"Hope no more for fatherland". Fag an bealach. Sir Charles Gavan Duffy. 6858-8
Hope of future communion with nature. Felicia Dorothea Hemans. 6973-8
Hope of our hearts. Sir Edward Denny. 6065-X
Hope of the Moor. Edward Farquhar. 6939-8
The hope of the resurrection. Frances Browne. 6177-X
The hope of the world. Sir William Watson. 6730-1
Hope overtaken. Dante Gabriel Rossetti. 6832-4
Hope sees a star. Robert G. Ingersoll. 6889-8
Hope springing up. John Wesley. 6065-X
Hope springs eternal. Alexander Pope. 6150-8
Hope the horn-blower. Sir Henry Newbolt. 6660-7
"Hope wafts my bark, and round my way". The prize. Phoebe Cary. 6969-X
Hope's song. Francis Carlin. 6607-0
Hope, A.D.
Australia. 6349-7
Conquistador. 6349-7
The damnation of Byron. 6349-7
The return from the Freudian islands. 6349-7
Hope, Alois
Winter. 6850-2
Hope, Ann
February bathed in rain. 6841-3
My rendezvous. 6841-3
Old woman. 6841-3
WHen I shall write. 6841-3
Why do you follow me to bed? 6841-3
Hope, Anthony (Sir Anthony Hope Hawkins)
"His foe was folly and his weapon wit". 6083-8
The perverseness of it. 6094-3
Hope, Henry
Now I have found a friend. 6065-X
Hope, James Barron
Cuba. 6471-X
John Smith's approach to Jamestown. 6946-0
Our Anglo-Saxon tongue. 7017-5
Hope, Laurence (Adele Florence Nicolson)
Adoration. 6856-1
Afridi love. 6856-1
The aloe. 6856-1
Ashore. 6102-8,6301-2
Back to the border. 6856-1
The cactus. 6338-1
Camp follower's song, Gomal River. 6856-1
Carpe Diem, fr. In the early, pearly morning. 6427-2
Deserted gipsy's song: hillside camp. 6856-1
Famine song. 6856-1
Fancy. 6856-1
Farewell. 6856-1
Fate knows no tears. 6856-1
Feroza. 6856-1
The first lover. 6856-1
The garden by the bridge. 6856-1
The garden of Kama: Kama the Indian Eros. 6856-1
'Golden eyes'. 6856-1
Hira-Singh's farewell to Burmah. 6856-1
His rubies: told by Valgovind. 6856-1
'In the early, pearly morning': song by Valgovind. 6856-1
Kashmiri song. 6732-8
Kashmiri song by Juma. 6856-1
Khan Zada's song on the hillside. 6856-1

HOPE

Kotri, by the river. 6856-1
Lalila, to the Ferengi lover. 6856-1
Less than the dust. 6732-8,6019-6
"Less than the dust". 6856-1
Lines by Taj Mahomed. 6856-1
'Lost delight', after the Hazara war. 6856-1
'Love lightly'. 6856-1
Mahomed Akram's appeal to the stars. 6856-1
Mahomed Akram's night watch. 6320-9
Malaria. 6856-1
Malay song. 6856-1
Marriage thoughts: by Morsellin Khan. 6856-1
Memory. 6856-1
No rival like the past. 6856-1
Ojira, to her lover. 6856-1
On the city wall. 6856-1
The orange garden. 6232-6,6649-6
Palm trees by the sea. 6856-1
The plains. 6856-1
Prayer ("You are all"). 6856-1
Protest: by Zahir-u-Din. 6856-1
The regret of the ranee in the hall of peacocks. 6856-1
Reminiscence of Mahomed Akram. 6856-1
Request. 6102-8
Request. 6856-1
Reverie of Mahomed Akram at the Tamarind tank. 6856-1
Reverie of Ormuz the Persian. 6856-1
Reverie: Zahir-u-Din. 6856-1
Sampan song. 6856-1
Sea song. 6019-6,6102-8,6856-1
The singer. 6856-1
Song by Gulbaz. 6856-1
Song by Sitara, of Kashmir. 6856-1
Song by Sitara, of Kashmir: the girl from Baltistan. 6856-1
Song of Faiz Ulla. 6856-1
Song of Khan Zada. 6856-1
Song of Taj Mahomed. 6856-1
Song of the colours: by Taj Mahomed. 6856-1
Song of the devoted slave. 6856-1
Song of Zahir-u-Din (1). 6856-1
Song of Zahir-u-Din (2). 6856-1
Song of Zahir-u-Din (3), written during fever. 6856-1
Starlight. 6856-1
Stars of the desert. 6320-9
Story by Lalla-ji, the priest. 6856-1
Story of Lilavanti. 6856-1
Story of Udaipore: told by Lalla-ji, the priest. 6856-1
Sunstroke. 6856-1
The teak forest, sels. 6427-2
The temple dancing girl. 6856-1
There is no breeze to cool the heat of love. 6856-1
This month almonds bloom at Kandahar. 6856-1
Thoughts: Mahomed Akram. 6856-1
Till I wake. 6856-1
To the hills! 6856-1
'To the unattainable'. 6856-1
To the unattainable: lament of Mahomed Akram. 6856-1
Unforgotten. 6856-1
Valgovind's boat song. 6856-1
Valgovind's song in the spring. 6856-1
Valgovind's song in the spring. 6732-8
Verse by Taj Mahomed. 6856-1
Verses ("You are my God"). 6856-1
Verses: Faiz Ulla. 6856-1
When love is over; song of Khan Zada. 6856-1
The window overlooking the harbour. 6856-1
Wisdom?, fr. The teak forest. 6427-2
Yasmini. 6856-1
Youth. 6856-1
Zira: in captivity. 6856-1

Hope, Margaret Lee
Prelude. 6799-9

Hope, Richard
A hymn of love. 7031-0

Hope, faith, love. Johann C. Friedrich von Schiller. 6240-7,6424-8
Hope, fr. Captivity. Oliver Goldsmith. 6934-7
Hope, fr. Essay on man. Alexander Pope. 6337-3
Hope, fr. The ballad of Reading gaol. Oscar Wilde. 6337-3
Hope, fr. the oratorio of The captivity. Oliver Goldsmith. 6174-5
"Hope, her starry vigil keeping". Burns' century song. Benjamin Franklin Taylor. 6815-4
"Hope, like the hyenna comming to be old." Henry Constable. 6586-4
"Hope, like the short-liv'd ray that gleams awhile". William Cowper. 6814-6
"Hope, only Hope, of all that clings", sels. Oliver Wendell Holmes. 6601-1
"Hope, peering from her fleecy car". Unknown. 6902-9
"Hope, though your sun is hid in gloom". Johann C. Friedrich von Schiller. 6238-5
"Hope,, like the hyena, coming to be old". Sonnet ("Hope"). Henry Constable. 6436-1
A hope.. Charles Kingsley. 6123-0
A hope. Anne Bronte. 6337-3
A hopeful brother. Frank Lebby Stanton. 6291-1
Hopefully waiting. Anson D.F. Randolph. 6302-0;6385-3

Hopegood, Olive
Feathers. 6349-7

Hopegood, Peter
First aid. 6384-5
The Nicorn's dower. 6349-7
The protagonist. 6349-7
There sleeps in the churchyard. 6349-7

A hopeless case. Oliver Herford. 6739-5
The hopeless comfort. Robert Gould. 6152-4
Hopeless desire soon withers and dies. A. W. 6436-1
"A hopeless flame did Corydon destroy". Ecologue of Virgil. Nahum Tate. 6867-7
The hopeless passion. Berton Braley. 6853-7
Hopes. Ibn al-Imam. 6362-4
Hopes and fears. T.H. G. 6118-4
Hopes in the wilderness. John Keble. 6848-0
The hopes of man. Joseph O'Connor. 6113-3
"Hopes what are they? Beads of morning". William Wordsworth. 6867-7
Hoping. Pearl G. Dollear. 6799-9

Hopkins Jr., John Henry
Down the wood-path. 7030-2
Three kings of Orient. 7030-2

Hopkins vs. W.P.R.R. Co. Unknown. 6878-2
Hopkins' last moments. Unknown. 6277-6

Hopkins, A.A.
It might have been. 6407-8

Hopkins, E.T.
To a dachshound. 7008-6

Hopkins, Ellice
Life in death. 7037-X
A vision of womanhood. 7037-X
A wave. 6997-5

Hopkins, Gerard Manley
Andromeda. 6209-1
"As kingfishers catch fire, dragonflies draw flame." 6209-1,6491-4
At the medding march. 6292-X,6489-2
Barnfloor and winepress. 6022-6
Binsey poplars (felled 1879). 6187-7,6491-4
The blessed Virgin compared to the air we breathe. 6282-2,6489-2
Brothers. 6430-2
The bugler's first communion. 6508-2
The candle indoors. 6828-6,6931-2
The candle indoors. 6209-1
The candle indoors. 6931-2
Carrion comfort. 6378-0,6489-2,6657-7,6354-3,6430-2, 6508
)Carrion comfort) 6828-6
Duns Scotus's Oxford. 6052-8,6641-0,6375-6
Felix Randal. 6208-3,6246-6,6657-7,6209-1,6375-6,6430
Fragment. 6375-6
"Glory be to God for dappled things." 6187-7,
God's grandeur. 6246-6,6315-2,6489-2,6107-9,6655-0
The habit of perfection. 6292-X,6096-X,6172-9,6655-0
Harry Ploughman. 6828-6
Harry Ploughman. 6209-1
Heaven-haven. 6828-6
Heaven-haven. 6022-6,6354-3,6430-2,6508-2
Hurrahing in harves. 6317-9,6354-3,6125-7

I have desired to go. 6258-X,6153-2
"I remember a house where all were good." 6187-7
"I wake and feel the fell of dark." 6536-8,6655-0,6430-2,6508-2,6645-3
Inversnaid. 6828-6
Inversnaid. 6022-6,6200-1,6253-9
Justus quidem tu es, domine. 6844-8
The lantern out of doors. 6931-2,6828-6
The leaden echo and the golden echo. 6246-6,6315-2,6334-9,6527-9,6536-8,6657 ,6655-0
"Manshape, that shone," fr. That nature is... 6106-0
Mary mother of divine grace... 6746-8
The May magnificat. 6282-2,6489-2,6641-0
"My own heart let me more have pity on; let." 6209-1
"No worse, there is none." 6315-2,6209-1,6655-0,6354-3
"Nothing is so beautiful as spring." 6187-7,6317-7
O deus ego amo te. 6489-2
Peace. 6246-6,6508-2
Pied beauty. 6228-8,6292-X,6209-1,6246-6,6337-3,6208 , 6339-X,6375-6,6150-8,6655-0,6645-3,6150 ,6418-3,6536-8,6641-0,6657-7,6491-4,6508
Rosa mystica. 6022-6
St. Winefred's well, sels. 6378-0
The sea and the skylard. 6508-2
The soldier. 6665-8
Sonnet ("I wake"). 6489-2
Sonnet ("Not, I'll not"). 6150-8,6208-3
Sonnet ("Thou art indeed"). 6150-8
Spelt from Sibyl's leaves. 6209-1,6150-8
Spring. 6292-X,6208-3,6489-2,6655-0,6172-9
Spring and fall. 6536-8,6645-3,6508-2,6150-8,6125-7, 6430
The starlight night. 6096-X,6022-6,6437-X,6172-9,6659-3, 6292
Surcease. 7007-8
That nature is a Heraclitean fire, sels. 6106-0
That nature is a Heraclitean fire... 6209-1
"Thou art indeed just, Lord, if I contend". 6931-2
Thou art just indeed, Lord. 6315-2,6655-0
To Oxford. 6378-0
To R.B. 6508-2
To what serves mortal beauty? 6378-0
Tom's garland. 6828-6
A vision of the mermaids. 6125-7
Wildness, fr. Inversnaid. 6427-2
The windhover. 6022-6,6096-X,6208-3,6315-2,6488-4,6536 , 6354-3,6655-0,6645-3,6491-4,6430-2,6292 ,6657-7,6292-X,6150-8,6659-3,6209-1,6508
Winter with the Gulf Stream. 6488-4
The woodlark. 6943-6
The wreck of the Deutschland. 6641-0,6150-8,6209-1
Hopkins, Henry Muller
On entering a new house. 6006-4
Hopkins, John (tr.)
Psalm 054. Bible, 6848-0
Psalm 058. Bible, 6848-0
Psalm 070. Bible, 6848-0
Psalm 079. Bible, 6848-0
Psalm 097. Bible, 6848-0
Hopkins, Joseph G.E.
For a child who died. 6761-1
To a baffled idealist. 6292-X,6337-3
Hopkins, Polly
A sonnet. 6799-9
Hopkins, Vera
Why Ben Schneider decides for prohibition. 6139-7,6416-7
Hopkinson, Francis
Advice to Amanda. 6753-0
American independence. 6946-0
The battle of the kegs. 6015-3,6176-1,6399-3,6008-0, 6288-1,6121-4,6265-2
The birds, the beasts, and the bat. 6753-0
Camp ballad. 6936-3
Date oblym bellesario. 6753-0
The daughter's rebellion. 6946-0
A hunting song. 6121-4
Jemmy the sailor. 6121-4
Louisbourg. 6753-0
A morning hymn. 6753-0

The new roof: a song for federal mechanics. 6265-2
The new roof; a song for federal mechanics. 6946-0
Ode on music. 6753-0
On the late successful expedition against Louisbourg. 6946-0
Political ballads, sels. 6753-0
Song ("My gen'rous heart"). 6527-9,6004-8,6121-4
Song ("See down Maria's blushing cheek"). 6936-3
To Celia on her wedding day. 6753-0
A toast to Washington. 6936-3
Verses inscribed to the officers of the 35th regiment. 6753-0
The wasp. 6753-0
Hopkinson, Joseph
Hail, Columbia. 6936-3,6015-3,6077-3,6156-7,6176-1,6457-4,6471 ,6304-7,6449-3,6267-9,6300-4,6736-0,6121 , 6015-3,6077-3,6156-7,6176-1,6457-4,6471
Hoppe, Anna
Consecration. 6065-X
Hopper's 'Nighthawks' (1942). Ira Sadoff. 6966-5
Hopper, Anna
Playing entertainment. 6687-9
Hopper, Delphia L.
A beautiful life. 6906-1
Beneath the apple tree. 6906-1
Coward. 6906-1
Hopper, Nora
April in Ireland. 6873-1
Beauty. 6507-4
The cold wind. 6174-5
A Connaught lament. 6872-3
The dark man. 6873-1
Dirge for Aoine. 6174-5
The fairy music. 6174-5
Gold song. 6174-5
Hallowe'en. 6820-0
June. 6396-9
The king of Ireland's son. 6244-X
Mo bouchaleen bwee. 6174-5
The sea. 6374-8
Soontree. 6785-9
The strangers. 6274-1
The vrigin's lullaby. 6807-3
The wind among the reeds. 6090-0,6244-X
Hoppin, William J.
Charlie Machree. 6911-8
Charlie Machree. 6142-7,6165-6,6344-6,6385-3,6392-6, 6451-5,6554-6,6567-8
'Hopping mad' in Vermont. Daniel L. Cady. 6988-6
Hopwood, Ronald A.
The king's messengers. 7029-9
The old way. 7029-9
Hora Christi. Alice Brown. 6007-2,6310-1,6337-3,6418-3, 6532-5,6730 ,6608-9,6746-8
Hora, Josef
Autumn. Ewald Osers (tr.). 6068-4
Horace
Ad leuconoen. Franklin Pierce Adams (tr.). 7039-6
Ad Pyrrha. Franklin Pierce Adams (tr.). 6732-8
Ad Xanthiam phoceum. Franklin Pierce Adams (tr.). 7039-6
An appeal to Lyce. Roswell Martin Field (tr.). 6949-5
At the ball game. Roswell Martin Field (tr.). 6949-5
Chloris properly rebuked. Roswell Martin Field (tr.). 6949-5
Consistency. Eugene Field (tr.). 6949-5
A counterblast against garlic. Roswell Martin Field (tr.). 6949-5
The death of Cleopatra. 6676-3
The description of an impertinent. William Cowper (tr.). 6814-6
Dialogue between Hector and Andromache, fr. The Iliad. 6975-4
Diffugere vives. 6252-0
Epilogue. Eugene Field (tr.). 6949-5
An excuse for Lalage. Roswell Martin Field (tr.). 6949-5
Extremum tanain. Austin Dobson (tr.). 7039-6
Fame vs. riches. Eugene Field (tr.). 6949-5
The happy isles. Eugene Field (tr.). 6949-5

HORACE

He advances his modest boast to fame. Franklin Pierce Adams (tr.). 6637-2
He suggests having some fun while we'er still able. Louis Untermeyer (tr.). 6637-2
He taunts an aging siren on the loss of her charms. Louis Untermeyer (tr.). 6637-2
He teases Xanthias about his new girl friend. Louis Untermeyer (tr.). 6637-2
He tells a matron to be her age. Louis Untermeyer (tr.). 6637-2
He thanks heaven that he has gotten past... Lewis Freeman Mott (tr.). 6637-2
Holiday. Louis Untermeyer (tr.). 7039-6
Horace and Lydia decide the old love's better. Louis Untermeyer (tr.). 6637-2
A humorous description of the author's journey... William Cowper (tr.). 6814-6
The immortality of verse. Alexander Pope (tr.). 7039-6
In praise of contentment. Eugene Field (tr.). 6949-5
In the springtime (1). Eugene Field (tr.). 6949-5
In the springtime (2). Roswell Martin Field (tr.). 6949-5
An invitation to Maecenas. Eugene Field (tr.). 6949-5
Invocation. Louis Untermeyer (tr.). 7039-6
Let us have peace. Eugene Field (tr.). 6949-5
The lyric muse. Eugene Field (tr.). 6949-5
"The man of firm and noble soul". George Gordon, 6th Baron Byron (tr.). 6945-2
Not altogether kindly, he reminds Lydia... Louis Untermeyer (tr.). 6637-2
'O fong banduslae.' Austin Dobson (tr.). 6624-0
Ode ("Boy! I detest..."). William Cowper (tr.). 6814-6
Ode ("Boy, I hate..."). William Cowper (tr.). 6814-6
Ode ("Descended"). John Dryden (tr.). 6152-4
Ode ("Ease is the weary..."). William Cowper (tr.). 6814-6
Ode ("See'st thou..."). William Cowper (tr.). 6814-6
Ode 002, sels. John Wight (tr.). 6665-8
Ode 003, sels. Gardner Taplin and R. Eberhart (tr.). 6665-8
Ode 007. Samuel Johnson (tr.). 6975-4
Ode 009, sels. 6975-4
Ode 022, sels. Samuel Johnson (tr.). 6975-4
An ode to fortune. Eugene Field (tr.). 6949-5
Ode to Maecenas, sels. John Dryden (tr.). 6879-0
Odes, sels. Samuel Johnson (tr.). 6641-0
Odes, sels. Thomas Warton (the Elder) (tr.). 6962-2
Odes, sels. 6637-2
On with the dance. 6959-2
Pastor cum. Adam Lindsay Gordon (tr.). 6951-7
Persian fopperies. William Cowper (tr.). 7039-6
Persicos odi. Austin Dobson (tr.). 6732-8
The poet's metamorphosis. Eugene Field (tr.). 6949-5
Poking fun at Xanthias. Roswell Martin Field (tr.). 6949-5
The preference declared. Eugene Field (tr.). 6949-5
Quitting again. Eugene Field (tr.). 6949-5
"Receive, dear friend, the truths I teach". William Cowper (tr.). 6230-X
The reconciliation (1). Eugene Field (tr.). 6949-5
The reconciliation (2). Roswell Martin Field (tr.). 6949-5
Regulus returns to Carthage. 7020-5
The roasting of Lydia. Roswell Martin Field (tr.). 6949-5
A Roman winter-piece (1). Eugene Field (tr.). 6949-5
A Roman winter-piece (2). Roswell Martin Field (tr.). 6949-5
The sabine farm. Phillip Francis (tr.). 6624-0
Sailor and shade. Eugene Field (tr.). 6949-5
Selections. W.B. Morrison (tr.). 6397-7
The ship of state. William Ewart Gladstone (tr.). 7039-6
A tardy aplogy (1). Roswell Martin Field (tr.). 6949-5
A tardy aplogy (2). Eugene Field (tr.). 6949-5
To a bully. Eugene Field (tr.). 6949-5
To a faun. 6959-2
To a jar of wine. Eugene Field (tr.). 6949-5
To Albuis Tibullus (1). Eugene Field (tr.). 6949-5
To Albuis Tibullus (2). Roswell Martin Field (tr.). 6949-5
To Aristius Fuscus. Eugene Field (tr.). 6949-5
To Barine. Roswell Martin Field (tr.). 6949-5
To Chloe. Austin Dobson (tr.). 7039-6
To Chloe (1). Roswell Martin Field (tr.). 6949-5
To Chloe (2). Eugene Field (tr.). 6949-5
To Chloe (3). Eugene Field (tr.). 6949-5
To Chloe (4). Eugene Field (tr.). 6949-5
To Chloris, sels. Franklin Pierce Adams (tr.). 6732-8
To Delius, fr. Ode 003. Felicia Dorothea Hemans (tr.). 6973-8
To Dellius. John Marshall (tr.). 6879-0
To Diana. Roswell Martin Field (tr.). 6949-5
To Faunus, fr. Ode 018. Felicia Dorothea Hemans (tr.). 6973-8
To Fuscus Aristus. Abraham Cowley (tr.). 7039-6
To Glycera. Roswell Martin Field (tr.). 6949-5
To his attendant, fr. Ode 038. Felicia Dorothea Hemans (tr.). 6973-8
To his book. Roswell Martin Field (tr.). 6949-5
To his book. Andrew Lang (tr.). 6297-0
To his lute. Eugene Field (tr.). 6949-5
To Leuconoe. 6102-8
To Leuconoe (1). Roswell Martin Field (tr.). 6949-5
To Leuconoe (2). Eugene Field (tr.). 6949-5
To Licinius. William Cowper (tr.). 7039-6
To Ligurinus (1). Roswell Martin Field (tr.). 6949-5
To Ligurinus (2). Eugene Field (tr.). 6949-5
To Lydia. Eugene Field (tr.). 6949-5
To Lydia (1). Eugene Field (tr.). 6949-5
To Lydia (2). Roswell Martin Field (tr.). 6949-5
To M.L. Gray. Eugene Field (tr.). 6949-5
To Maecenas. John Dryden (tr.). 7039-6
To Maecenas. Eugene Field (tr.). 6949-5
To Maecenas. Roswell Martin Field (tr.). 6949-5
To Melopomene. Eugene Field (tr.). 6949-5
To Mistress Pyrrha (1). Eugene Field (tr.). 6949-5
To Mistress Pyrrha (2). Roswell Martin Field (tr.). 6949-5
To Mother Venus. Eugene Field (tr.). 6949-5
To Neobule. Roswell Martin Field (tr.). 6949-5
To Phyllis (1). Eugene Field (tr.). 6949-5
To Phyllis (2). Roswell Martin Field (tr.). 6949-5
To Pompeius Varus. Eugene Field (tr.). 6949-5
To Postumus. Roswell Martin Field (tr.). 6949-5
To Pyrrha. John Milton (tr.). 7039-6
To Quintus Dellius. Eugene Field (tr.). 6949-5
To Quintus Hirpinus. Eugene Field (tr.). 6949-5
To Sally. John Quincy Adams (tr.). 7039-6
To Thaliarchus. John Dryden (tr.). 7039-6
To Thaliarchus. John Dryden (tr.). 6527-9,
To the fountain of Bandusia. Eugene Field (tr.). 7039-6
To the fountain of Bandusia (1). Eugene Field (tr.). 6949-5
To the fountain of Bandusia (2). Roswell Martin Field (tr.). 6949-5
To the fountain of Bandusia, fr. Ode 013. Felicia Dorothea Hemans (tr.). 6973-8
To the ship of state. Roswell Martin Field (tr.). 6949-5
To Venus. Eugene Field (tr.). 6949-5
To Venus, fr. Ode 030. Felicia Dorothea Hemans (tr.). 6973-8
True love is blind. 6084-6
Vitas hinnuleo. Austin Dobson (tr.). 6732-8
"Who, then, is free? The wise man." 6260-1
Wine, women, and song. Eugene Field (tr.). 6949-5
Horace and Lydia decide the old love's better. Horace. 6637-2
Horace concocting an ode. Thomas Dekker. 6996-7
Horace Greeley. Edmund Clarence Stedman. 6240-7
Horace I. Eugene Field. 6026-9
Horace in homspun, sels. James Logie ("Hugh Haliburton") Robertson. 6819-7
Horace paraphrased. Isaac Watts. 6315-2
Horace to Pyrrha. Eugene Field. 6307-1
Horace, Book II. Ode 010. William Cowper. 6814-6
Horace, Epistle VII. Book I. Imitated and addressed...Oxford. Jonathan Swift. 6152-4
Horace, epod. 004, imitated. John Gay. 6972-X

Horace, Lib. I, Epist IX, imitated. Matthew Prior. 6024-2
Horan, James Columbus
    Woodrow Wilson. 7001-9
The Horath and the Curiatii. T.D. Suplee. 6928-2
Horatian echo. Matthew Arnold. 6947-9
Horatian epode to the Duchess of Malfi. Allen Tate. 6209-1
Horatian ode upon Cromwell's return from Ireland. Andrew
    l Marvel . 6246-6,6323-3,6315-2,6562-7,6301-2,6150-8,
    6194-X,6219-9,6023-4
Horatian ode, sels. Andrew Marvell. 6179-6
An Horatian ode. Richard Henry Stoddard. 6305-5,6524-4
"Horatio, of ideal courage vain". Feigned courage. Mary
    Lamb. 6772-7
"Horatio, thou art i'en as just a man", fr. Hamlet.
    William Shakespeare. 6085-4
"Horatio- o day and night but this is...". Hamlet, sel.
    William Shakespeare. 7014-0
Horatius at the bridge. Thomas Babington Macaulay, 1st
    Baron Macaulay. 6142-7,6385-3,6554-6,6479-5,6732-8,
    6706 ,6403-5,6424-8,6304-7,6250-4,6102-8,6107 ,6425-
    6
Horatius, fr. Lays of ancient Rome. Thomas Babington
    Macaulay, 1st Baron Macaulay. 6504-X,6552-X,6332-2,
    6267-9,6114-1,6498 ,6263-6,6322-5,6219-9,6419-1,6572-
    4,6552-X,6014-5,6087-0,6242-3,6473-6
Horatius, sels. Thomas Babington Macaulay, 1st Baron
    Macaulay. 6427-2,6301-2
Horestes, sels. John Pickering. 6182-6
Horikawa, Lady
    "How can one e'er be sure". Arthur Waley (tr.). 7039-6
The horizon is definitely speaking. Diane Chang. 6790-5
Horizons. Struthers Burt. 6619-4
Horizons. Howard Hilles. 6789-1
Horizons. Blanche Mary Kelly. 6096-X
Horizons, fr. Montana wives. Gwendolen Haste. 6076-5
Horn. James Hayford. 6388-8
"The horn again! again!". Old Yule night. Alice M.
    Buckton. 6793-X
The horn blow. Jeff Tagami. 6790-5
Horn Head, county of Donegal. Aubrey Thomas De Vere. 6096-
    X
The horn of Egremont castle. William Wordsworth. 6290-3
The horn of the moon. Herbert Trench. 6877-4
Horn, Carl
    The angel. 6249-0
Horn, Edward N,.
    There was a tree of jade. 6751-4
Horn, Edward Traill
    The three wishes. 6611-9
The horn, fr. The song of Roland. Unknown (French) 6372-1
The horn. Leonie Adams. 6012-9
The horn. Walter De La Mare. 6253-9,6596-1
The horn. James Reaney. 6446-9
Hornbeck, Gladys Tracy
    A robber of the night. 6799-9
The hornbill. John Still. 6785-9
Hornbrook, Ruth
    The ships of Glou'ster. 6818-9
Horne, Cyril Morton
    Afterward. 6650-X
Horne, George Fox
    Codicil. 6042-0
Horne, Herbert P.
    Amico suo. 6274-1,6656-9
    Et sunt commercia coeli. 6844-8
    Formosae puellae. 6656-9
    "If she be made of white and red". 6656-9
    Nancy Dawson. 6656-9
    Nos exaudi, domine! 6747-6
    A song ("Be not"). 6301-2
    Sonnet ("If I could"). 6301-2
    Upon returning a silk handkerchief. 6301-2
Horne, J.G.
    "Alan-wart loon", sels. 6269-5
Horne, Richard Hengist
    Building of the palace of Poseidon, fr. Orion. 6980-0
    The first appearance of Orion, fr. Orion. 6980-0
    The friend of friends. 7015-9
    Genius. 6656-9
    In Berkshire. 6793-X

    Morning, fr. Orion. 6980-0
    Newton. 7014-0
    Orion's extirpation of the beasts from Chios, fr.Orion.
        6980-0
    Orion, an epic poem, sels. 6102-8,6656-9
    Orion, sels. 6980-0
    Pelters of pyramids. 6656-9,6732-8
    The plough. 6383-7,6437-X,6625-9,6656-9,6668-2
    Restoration of Orion, fr. Orion. 6980-0
    The slave. 6656-9
    Solitude and the lily. 6656-9
    Solitude and life. 6437-X
    Summer noon, fr. Orion. 6980-0
    The telegraph. 7014-0
    The telegraph. 7014-0
The horned owl. Bryan Waller ("Barry Cornwall") Procter.
    6073-0,6639-9
Hornpipe. Cecil Day Lewis. 6491-4
Hornpipe, fr. Facade. Edith Sitwell. 7000-0
The horns of elfland. Alfred Lord Tennyson. 6236-9,6252-0
"Horns to bulls wise nature lends". Beauty. Anacreon
    (atr). 7039-6
Hornung, E.W.
    Dulceet decorum. 6793-X
The horologe. Clark Ashton Smith. 6218-0
Horologium, sels. Unknown. 6282-2
"Horrible dens, sir, aren't they?". The magic wand. George
    Robert Sims. 6924-X,6661-5
A horrible example. Oliver Marble. 6274-1
"Horror-haunted Belgian plains riven by shot..". The
    superman. Sir Robert Grant. 7026-4
Horse. Elizabeth Madox Roberts. 6464-7
Horse & rider. Wey Robinson. 6722-0
"The horse and the dog had tamed a man...". Horse, dog,
    and man. Samuel Ellsworth Kiser. 7008-6
"The horse gallops where the wind is paved". Horse loose
    in city. Gary Langford. 7018-3
Horse in a field. Walter De La Mare. 6776-X
Horse loose in city. Gary Langford. 7018-3
The horse of Pete Lareau. Ivan Swift. 7010-8
The horse of Vevros. Schmidt-Phiseldeck. 6842-1
"The horse of poetry nibbles". The invitation. Donagh
    MacDonagh. 6930-4
The horse thief. William Rose Benet. 6861-8
The horse thief. William Rose Benet. 6030-2,6107-9,6253-9
A horse's epitaph. Robert Lowe; Viscount Sherbrooke. 6510-
    4
Horse, dog, and man. Samuel Ellsworth Kiser. 7008-6
Horse-bathing parade. W. Kersley Holmes. 7027-2
The horse-leech's daughter. Marjorie Allen Seiffert. 6038-
    2
Horse-thief Jim. Robert C.V. Meyers. 6928-2
The horse. Peter Parley. 6018-8
The horse. Francis Ponge. 6758-1
The horse. Ella Wheeler Wilcox. 6510-4
The horseback farmer. Arthur Chapman. 7012-4
The horseback ride. Sara J. ("Grace Greenwood")
    Lippincott. 6344-6
"The horseman rides in the valley's glow". The lake of
    Constance. Gustave Schwab. 6749-2
Horseman springing from the dark: A dream. Lilla Cabot
    Perry. 6501-5
The horseman. Idella Purnell. 6347-0
Horses. Edwin Muir. 6269-5,6070-6,6257-1
Horses. Dorothy Wellesley. 6071-4
The horses of Achilles, fr. The Iliad. Homer. 6435-3
The horses of Gravelotte. ? Gerok. 6842-1
Horses of the sea. Christina Georgina Rossetti. 6512-0,
    6454-X
Horses on the Camargue. Roy Campbell. 6625-9,6780-8,6985-1
"Horses, like men, ned a fair bit of schooling". The
    master of the horse. George A. Fothergill. 7010-8
The horses. Katharine Lee Bates. 6510-4
The horseshoes. Robert P. Tristram Coffin. 7040-X
Hort, G.M.
    Requiem for a courtesan. 6780-8
Hort, Gertrude M.
    A litany. 7012-4
Hortense. Frank John Urquart. 6116-8
Horton, Alice

Tale of a temptation. 6410-8
Horton, Edward A.
 The flag. 6846-4
Horton, George
 Deakin Brown's way. 6923-1
 Enj'ying poor health. 6675-5
 The farmer's song bird. 6927-4
 The farmer's song-friend. 6680-1
 The obstinate old man. 6672-0
Horton, Philip
 Antiphony for Thursday. 6640-2
 Dithyramb for death. 6640-2
 Epilogue. 6640-2
 On her chastity. 6640-2
Hortorium, sels. Rene Rapin. 6649-6
Horus. Gerard de Nerval. 6106-0
Hos ego versiculos. Francis Quarles. 6562-7
Hosanna! Joshua King. 6629-1
"**Hosanna!** hosanna! hosanna!". Waken, shepherds, fr. Hymns and anthems... Caroline Hazard. 6762-X
Hosea. Bible. 6143-5
Hosea Bigelow's lament. James Russell Lowell. 6438-8
Hosford, Maud
 Bargains in hearts. 7021-3
Hoshaw, Josephine
 The artist-eye. 6906-1
 Autumn. 6906-1
 The prairie. 6906-1
 Snowflakes. 6906-1
Hosier, Wiley G.
 The lotus. 6799-9
Hoskins, Glenister
 A farmer muses. 6662-3
Hoskins, John
 "Absence, hear thou my protestation." 6181-8,6182-6, 6187-7,6341-1
 To his little child Benjamin, from the tower. 6134-6
Hosmer, Frederick L.
 Cross and flag. 6223-7
 Friends beyond. 6337-3
 The indwelling God. 6007-2,6337-3,6730-1
 My dead. 6730-1
 O beautiful, my country. 6337-3
 Our country. 6386-1
 Thy kingdom come, O Lord. 6337-3,6730-1
Hosmer, Margaret S.
 The chrysalis. 6316-0
 Falling asleep. 6316-0
 The leonids. 6316-0
 Snowfall. 6316-0
Hosmer, William Henry Cuyler
 My own dark Genesee. 6484-1
 Song of Texas. 6946-0
Hospital. John Allen Wyeth. 6482-5
Hospital duties. Unknown. 6074-9
Hospital observation. Julian Symons. 6666-6
Hospital train. John Allen Wyeth. 6482-5
Hospital verses. Mokichi Saito. 6482-5
A **hospital.** Alfred Noyes. 6169-9
Hospitality. John Banister Tabb. 6452-3
Hospitality in ancient Ireland. Unknown. 6930-4
Hospitality, fr. Alcestis. Euripides. 6435-3
"The **hoss** he is a spelndud beast". The hoss. James Whitcomb Riley. 6892-8
The **host** of the air. William Butler Yeats. 6244-X,6153-2, 6419-1,6319-5,6628-3
The **hostage.** Helen Booth. 6920-7
The **hostage.** Johann C. Friedrich von Schiller. 6683-6
The **hostel,** or inn. Sir Walter Scott. 6543-0
The **hostess'** daughter. Johann Ludwig Uhland. 7039-6
"**Hostess**, a cup of wine, I pray". New gypsy melodies, sels. Adolf Heyduk. 6763-8
Hostrup, Jens Christian
 The woman of the north. Charles Wharton Stork (tr.). 6555-4
"The **hosts** of Don Rodrigo were scattered...". The lamentation of Don Roderick. Unknown (Spanish). 6757-3
"The **hosts** of Israel were journeying". Moses writing in the wilderness. Charles W. Denison. 6755-7

"The **hosts** of Israel were met. In ranks". The anniversary deaths. Charles W. Denison. 6755-7
The **hosts** of faery. Unknown. 6930-4
"**Hot** August noon - already on that day". King Arthur's tomb. William Morris. 7034-5
Hot afternoons have been in Montana. Eli Siegel. 6531-7, 6039-0
Hot cake. Shu Hsi. 6106-0
Hot cakes. Arthur Waley. 6506-6
"**Hot** hands that yearn to touch her...". By the well. Sir Edmund Gosse. 6770-0
"The **hot** mice feeding in red". Paul Klee. John Haines. 6803-0
"**Hot** noon; I sought the shaded gardens where". In the gardens. Arthur Vine Hall. 6800-6
Hot potatoes, fr. Counsel to those that eat. Edward Verrall Lucas. 6018-8
"The **hot** red rocks of Aden". Home thoughts. Unknown. 7029-9
"The **hot** September sun shone down on the...bay". The wide open spaces. Oscar H. Lear. 6817-0
Hot stuff. Edward Botwood. 6946-0
"**Hot** sun, cool fire, temper'd with sweet air". George Peele. 6181-8;6317-9
The **hot** tamale man. Hazel Harper Harris. 6265-2
A **hot** time in the old time. Joe Hayden. 6736-0
"**Hot** was the battle, and bloody the fight". The horses of Gravelotte. ? Gerok. 6842-1
"**Hot** weather? Yes; but really not". At ninety in the shade. James Whitcomb Riley. 6993-2
A **hot** wind reverie, in November. Unknown. 6787-5
"**Hot!/What!**". Radiator romping. Mary J.J. Wrinn. 6850-2
Hot-cross buns. Mother Goose. 6363-2,6466-3
"**Hot-cross** buns". Unknown. 7028-0
A **hot-weather** song. Don Marquis. 6488-4,6722-0,6736-0
Hotel. Gayle Giblin. 6799-9
Hotel. Muriel F. Hochdorf. 6850-2
Hotel Continental. William Jay Smith. 6666-6
Hotel de l'Ancre, Ouchy. Joan Ramsay. 6782-4
Hotel de la paix. Ingeborg Bachmann. 6769-7
A **hotel** in the storm. Julia Noyes Stickney. 6682-8
Hotel lobby. C.R. Holmes. 6515-5
Hotel lobby. Mildred Weston. 6722-0
The **hotel** room. Alfred Hayes. 6390-X
The **hotel.** Harriet Monroe. 6808-1
The **hotel.** Harriet Monroe. 6897-9
"**Hoth** doth the city sit solotary...". Quomodo sedet. Bible. 6830-8
The **hothouse** violet speaks. Robert ("Droch") Bridges. 6983-5
Hotspur. William Shakespeare. 6087-0,6438-8
Hotspur and the fop. William Shakespeare. 6304-7
Hotspur's defence. William Shakespeare. 6045-1
Hotspur's description of a fop, fr. King Henry IV. William Shakespeare. 6302-0;6385-3
Hotspur's quarrel with Henry IV. William Shakespeare. 6438-8
Hott, Mildred M.
 Stupidity. 6750-6
"The **hottest** seat in any state". Riding horse to cultivate in Vermont. Daniel L. Cady. 6988-6
Hotwells. Thomas Edward Brown. 6809-X
Houdini. Robert Hedin. 6855-3
Houfe, Charles A.
 The times to come. 7015-9
Hough, Alfred J.
 Flag and cross. 6223-7
 How they caught the panther. 6674-7
 Only the beautiful. 7030-2
 'We're building two a day!' 6919-3
Hough, E.
 My stout old heart and I. 6211-3,6260-1
Hough, Grant S.
 Dido. 6316-0
 Flight. 6316-0
 My rose. 6316-0
 Seneca to Paul. 6316-0
Hough, Mary E.
 A degenerate of the pink family. 6764-6
Hough, Snow Longley

The dead dancer. 6316-0
The dying favorite speaks. 6316-0
The grave of Roosevelt. 6995-9
Sonnet ("I dreamed"). 6501-5,6648-8,6214-8
Houghtaling, Esther
   Old Josiah predicts. 6799-9
Houghton Jr., Walter Edwards
   Chimes. 6038-2
Houghton, A.B.
   A Dresden shepherdess. 6116-8
   To Prue. 6116-8
Houghton, Claude
   To the fallen. 7027-2
Houghton, George
   Anniversary hymn. 7041-8
   Four-leaf clover. 6066-8
   Gone! 7041-8
   The handsel ring. 7041-8
   The harp. 7041-8
   The legend of Walbach tower. 6946-0
   The song. 7041-8
   Tapestries. 7041-8
Houghton, Lord. See Milnes, Richard Monckton
"**Hould** him up!". The christening. Thomas Edward Brown. 6809-X
"**Hould** on then, I tell ye! Do ye see...wall". A dialogue between Hom-Veg and Ballure's river. Thomas Edward Brown. 6809-X
Hound and hare. F.B. Sutherland. 6799-9
the **hound** and the huntsman. John Gay. 6972-X
Hound at night. Louise Ayres Garnett. 6619-4
The **hound** of heaven, sels. Francis Thompson. 6324-1
The **hound** of heaven. Francis Thompson. 6301-2,6655-0,6161-3,6214-8,6245-8,6153 ,6172-9,6430-2,6250-4,6292-X, 6102-8,6199 ,6096-X,6332-2,6427-2,6489-2,6022-6,6052 ,6315-2,6337-3,6418-3,6488-4,6507-4,6527 ,6726-3, 6730-1,6732-8,6723-9,6646-1,6508 ,6828-6
"The **hound** was cuffed, the hound was kicked". Song for The Jacquerie. Sidney Lanier. 7017-5
A **hound**. Simonides. 6435-3
The **hound**. Babette Deutsch. 6374-8
"The **hounds** of earth have chased their prey". Hound and hare. F.B. Sutherland. 6799-9
The **hounds** of spring. Algernon Charles Swinburne. 6102-8, 6252-0
Hour. Beatrice Goldsmith. 6640-2
Hour after dawn. Lynn Riggs. 6808-1
"**Hour** atter hour, deliberate stroke on stroke". Carpentry. Leslie Nelson Jennings. 6979-7
The **hour** before dawn. John Cowper Powys. 6102-8,6076-5
Hour before light. Josephine Johnson. 6761-1
The **hour** has come. Unknown. 6226-1
"**Hour** in which the grass grows". Childhood. Alejandra Pizarnik. 7036-1
"The **hour** is come: no more the joys". Consecration. Edward Farquhar. 6939-8
The **hour** is late. Ida Norton Munson. 6144-3
"The **hour** is past to fawn or crouch". Paddies evermore. Sliabh Cuilinn. 6858-8
"The **hour** of blood is past". Od on the deliverance of Europe, 1814. John Herman Merivale. 6980-0
The **hour** of death. Unknown. 6489-2
The **hour** of death. Felicia Dorothea Hemans. 6240-7,6315-2, 6129-9,6403-5
The **hour** of death. Gunter Unger. 6769-7
the **hour** of night. John Milton. 6558-9
The **hour** of peaceful rest. William Bingham Tappan. 6735-2
The **hour** of prayer. Felicia Dorothea Hemans. 6219-9,6304-7
The **hour** of prayer. Felicia Dorothea Hemans. 6973-8
An **hour** of romance. Felicia Dorothea Hemans. 6973-8
Hour of the lizard. Leslie Nelson Jennings. 6781-6
The **hour** of the morning-star. John Hall Wheelock. 6441-8
An **hour** of trial. Unknown. 6670-4
The **hour** when we shall meet again. Samuel Taylor Coleridge. 6967-3
An **hour** with thee. Richard Chenevix Trench. 6065-X
An **hour** with Whittier. Phebe A. Holder. 6924-X
An **hour** with you. Celestin Pierre Cambiaire. 6826-X
The **hour**.. Sara Teasdale. 6038-2
An **hour**. Dorothy Curran. 6750-6

An **hour**. Henry Van Dyke. 6961-4
The **hour**. Jessie B. Rittenhouse. 6102-8,6076-5
The **hour**. Edna Davis Romig. 6836-7
The **hour**. Sara Teasdale. 6777-8
The **hour**. Nancy Byrd Turner. 7019-1
Hours. Max Eastman. 6880-4
Hours. Adelaide Anne Procter. 6957-6
Hours. Unknown (Greek) 6435-3
"**Hours** are golden links, God's token". Adelaide Anne Procter. 6238-5
"The **hours** are minutes when we sit alone". Sonnet 019 ("The hours are minutes..."). Edmond Gore Alexander Holmes. 6785-9
"The **hours** are passing slow". Ballade of sleep. Andrew Lang. 6770-0
"**Hours** fly/Flowers die". For Katrina's sun-dial. Henry Van Dyke. 6961-4
"**Hours** I have known when color". Peace. Marguerite Wilkinson. 6102-8,6076-5
"The **hours** I spend". 'Sign of the times' Laura Kithen. 6857-X
Hours grey. Francis Viele-Griffin. 6343-8
Hours of idleness, sels. George Gordon, 6th Baron Byron. 6945-2
The **hours** of passion. Unknown. 6881-2
Hours of sleep. Unknown. 6724-7
The **hours** of sleepy night. Thomas Campion. 6182-6,6181-8
Hours of the passion. William of Shoreham. 6022-6
The **hours** of the planets, sels. Charles Madge. 6788-3
The **hours** of the planets. Charles Madge. 6209-1
"The **hours** passed by, a fleet confused crowd". Chant of the changing hours. Don Marquis. 6875-8
"The **hours** rise up putting off stars and it is". Impressions 004. Edward Estlin Cummings. 6808-1
"The **hours** were long with you away". Reunited. Edgar A. Guest. 6862-6
"**Hours** when I love you,are like tranquil pools". Hours. Max Eastman. 6880-4
The **hours**, fr. Prometheus. Percy Bysshe Shelley. 6980-0
The **hours**. John Peale Bishop. 6390-X
The **hours**. Matthew G. Lewis. 6874-X
The **hous** of fame, sels. Geoffrey Chaucer. 6483-3,6378-0
House. Robert Browning. 6527-9,6657-7,6110-9,6430-2,6655-0
"The **house** I lived in was a place". Boy reading. John Holmes. 6761-1
The **house** among the firs. Elizabeth Roberts MacDonald. 6115-X
House and home. Joseph Beaumont. 6933-9
House and home. Victor Hugo. 6337-3
House and home. Nixon Waterman. 6654-2
The **house** and the road. Josephine Preston Peabody. 6162-1, 6266-0,6509-0,6161-3,6393-4
House arrest. George Tsongas. 6792-1
The **house** at evening. William Rose Benet. 6034-X,6619-4
The **house** beautiful. Robert Louis Stevenson. 6138-9,6186-9, 6395-0,6477-9
The **house** beside the mill. Leroy F. Jackson. 6496-5
House blessing. Arthur Guiterman. 6337-3,6654-2
A **house** blessing. William Cartwright. 6125-7
The **house** by Blavet. Richard Lawson Gales. 6558-9
The **house** by the side of the road. Sam Walter Foss. 6101-X, 6291-1,6102-8,6162-1,6266-0,6337-,6337-3,6104-4,6076-5,6418-3,6476-0,6730-1,6732-8
The **house** carpenter. Unknown. 6003-X
The **house** desolate. Elinor Sweetman. 6174-5
House fear, fr. The Hill Wife. Robert Frost. 6102-8
The **house** full of wine. Johnson Barker. 6617-8
House hunting. Unknown. 6530-9
House in order. Edith Mirick. 6214-8
A **house** in Taos, sels. Langston Hughes. 6531-7
"A **house** in ruins. On the crannied walls". The sun-dial. Karel Toman. 6886-3
The **house** in the meadow. Louise Chandler Moulton. 6600-3
The **house** in the west. Austin Clarke. 6072-2
A **house** in war time. Richard Church. 6783-2
"The **house** is all in wooden rags". New England cottage. Leonora Speyer. 6984-3
"The **house** is burned, the trees around". The betrayal. Robert P. Tristram Coffin. 7040-X
The **house** is dark and dreary. Richard Henry Stoddard. 6219-

HOUSE

9
"The **house** is gambrel-roofed and gray with age". Sailor's snug harbor. Jessie Young Norton. 6841-3
"The **house** is low, soft green and gray". The village library. Helen L. Bayley. 6798-0
"The **house** lay snug as a robin's nest". Selfish sorrow. Alice Cary. 6865-0;6969-X
House long known. Amy Bonner. 6979-7
A **house** not made with hands. Earl Marble. 6410-8
The **house** not made with hands. H.E. Gordon. 6925-8
"**House** of a friend/touches her body". Fresno notebook. Neeli Cherkovski. 6792-1
The **house** of a hundred lights, sels. (Frederick) Ridgely Torrence. 6501-5
The **house** of Ate, fr. The faerie queene. Edmund Spenser. 6436-1
The **house** of beauty, fr. The deserted city. Francis Sherman. 6021-8
The **house** of blazes. Arthur Guiterman. 6773-5
House of Busyrane. Edmund Spenser. 6438-8
The **house** of Caesar. Viola Gerard Garvin. 7007-8
House of Calvin. Leonora Speyer. 6532-5
The **house** of cards. Christina Georgina Rossetti. 6466-3
The **house** of Christmas. Gilbert Keith Chesterton. 6532-5, 6473-6,6509-0,6337-3,6746-8
The **house** of clouds. Elizabeth Barrett Browning. 6682-8
The **House** of Commons in 1398. Richard the Redeless. 6186-9
The **house** of Cupid. Edmund Spenser. 6935-5
The **house** of death. Louise Chandler Moulton. 6076-5,6102-8, 6243-1,6431-2
The **house** of death. Louise Chandler Moulton. 7041-8
The **house** of death. A.T. Nankiwell. 7027-2
House of eyes. Robert P. Tristram Coffin. 7040-X
The **house** of fame, fr. Garlande of laurell. John Skelton. 6378-0
The **house** of fame, sels. Geoffrey Chaucer. 6193-1
The **house** of Hendra. Ernest Rhys. 6873-1
The **house** of Idiedaily. Bliss Carman. 7006-X
"**House** of five fires, you never raised me". In the Longhouse, Oneida museum. Roberta Hill Whiteman. 7005-1
House of life. Dorothy Quick. 6218-0
The **house** of life, sels. Dante Gabriel Rossetti. 6828-6
The **house** of life, sels. Dante Gabriel Rossetti. 6199-0, 6110-9,6196-6,6430-2,6108-2,6208-3,6122-2,6123-0, 6536-8,6526-0,6726-3,6123 ,6208-3,6656-9,6199-0,6108-2,6560-0,6250
The **house** of life. Madison Cawein. 6336-5
The **house** of life. Dante Gabriel Rossetti. 6657-7,6508-2
The **house** of Morpheus. Edmund Spenser. 6935-5
The **house** of night, sels. Philip Freneau. 6176-1,6399-3
The **house** of night, sels. Philip Freneau. 6008-0,6288-1
The **house** of night. Philip Freneau. 6121-4
The **house** of pain. Florence Earle Coates. 6214-8
The **house** of prayer. William Cowper. 6814-6
The **house** of pride. Edmund Spenser. 6935-5
The **house** of riches. Edmund Spenser. 6600-3
The **house** of Rimmon. Henry Van Dyke. 6961-4
House of straw, fr. These very stones. Marjorie Allen Seiffert. 6531-7
The **house** of the broken-hearted. Duncan Campbell Scott. 6433-7
The **house** of the heart. Siraj. 6362-4
The **house** of the trees. Ethelwyn Wetherald. 6374-8,6433-7, 6115-X,6252-0,6656-9
The **house** of time. William Cousins. 6178-8
The **house** of too much trouble. Albert Bigelow Paine. 6688-7
House of yesterday. Walter Shedlofsky. 6218-0
The **house** on Maple hill. Stanley McNail. 6218-0
The **house** on the hill. Edwin Arlington Robinson. 6299-7, 6726-3,6101-X,6102-8,6162-1,6509 ,6512-0,6076-5,6513-9,6581-3,6723-9,6491
The **house** on the hill. Edgar Fawcett. 6370-5
House spirits. Evelyn Scott. 6880-4
"A **house** stood here". Fin. Helmut Zenker. 6769-7
The **house** that fear built: Warsaw, 1943 Jane Flanders. 6803-0
The **house** that Jack built. Samuel Taylor Coleridge. 6440-X, 6089-7

740

The **house** that Jack built. Unknown. 6052-8,6401-9,6610-0, 6134-4
"A **house** that's built upon the sands". A man and his house. Matthew Biller. 6761-1
The **house** to the man. John Gould Fletcher. 7017-5
"The **house** was black as winds could dye it". One in a darkness. Robert P. Tristram Coffin. 7040-X
"The **house** was crammed from roof to". At the pantomime. Oliver Wendell Holmes. 6848-0
"The **house** was new". The new house. Caroline Salome Woodruff. 7030-2
"The **house** where I was born". The doves. Katharine (Hinkson) Tynan. 7039-6
The **house** where Lincoln died. Robert Mackay. 6524-4
The **house** with nobody in it. Joyce Kilmer. 6478-7,6497-3, 6964-9
The **house** with nobody in it. Joyce Kilmer. 6891-X
"A **house** without a suller wall". Banking up Vermont houses. Daniel L. Cady. 6988-6
House, Benjamin Davenport
  Appomattox. 6074-9
  The mother of Lincoln. 6524-4
House, Boyce
  Beauty is elsewhere. 6265-2
  Cities. 6265-2
House, Elizabeth
  My rejection slip is showing. 6857-X
  The rescued flower. 6857-X
House, Homer C.
  The price of peace. 6420-5
House-cleaning. Franklyn W. Lee. 6690-9
House-hunting. Alfred Noyes. 6151-6
House-mates. Leon Gellert. 6349-7
The **house-top..** Herman Melville. 6333-0;6380-2
A **house.** Sir John Collings ("Solomon Eagle") Squire. 6393-4
The **house.** Conrad Aiken. 6069-2
The **house.** Monk Gibbon. 6072-2
The **house.** Ibn al-Hammara. 6362-4
The **house.** T. Walking Eagle Marietta. 6870-7
The **house.** Arthur Symons. 6184-2
The **house.** Henry Treece. 6337-3
The **house.** Unknown. 6312-8
The **house.** Bennett Weaver. 6036-6
Housecleaning. Carrie W. Bronson. 6707-7,6711-5
Housecleaning day in Vermont. Daniel L. Cady. 6988-6
Housed. Mary Thacher Higginson. 6097-8
Household art. Austin Dobson. 6123-0,6655-0
Household gods. Walter Savage Landor. 6092-7
The **household** jewels. Unknown. 6412-4
The **household** sovereign. Henry Wadsworth Longfellow. 6385-3
Household thrush. Lillie E. Barr. 6711-5
The **household** woman. Caroline Gilman. 6219-9
The **householder.** Robert Browning. 6378-0
The **housekeeper's** soliloquy. Frances Dana Barker ("Aunt Fanny") Gage. 6403-5
A **housekeeper's** tragedy. Unknown. 6240-7
The **housekeeper.** Charles Lamb. 6302-0;6385-3;6498-1;6597-X;6600-3,6421-3,6424-8,6639-9,6457-4
Houselander, Caryll
  Litany to our lady. 6282-2
Houser, Jessie F.
  The woman healed. 6417-5
"The **houses are haunted**". Disillusionment of ten o'clock. Wallace Stevens. 6808-1
Houses at the edge of railway lines. Stephen Spender. 6391-8
"The **houses** jammed one on top of the other". Insignificant needs. Yannis Ritsos. 6758-1
Houses like angels. Jorge Luis Borges. 6759-X
"The **houses** of the village are, in great...". An English village. William Cobbett. 7020-5
Houses should have homes to live in. David Ross. 6513-9
A **housewife** speaks. Elizabeth Greene Thomas. 7016-7
The **housewife's** lament. Eloise Story. 6270-9
The **housewife's** prayer. Blanche Mary Kelly. 6292-X,6172-9, 6727-1,6096-X
The **housewife**, fr. Battle. Wilfred Wilson Gibson. 6897-9
The **housewife**: winter afternoon. Kale Wilson Baker. 6326-

8

The **housewife**. Catherine Cate Coblentz. 6144-3
Housewifery: I. Edward Taylor. 6176-1
Housewifery: II. Edward Taylor. 6176-1
Housewives. Jean Follain. 6758-1
Housh, Snow Longley. See Longley, Snow
Housman, Alfred Edward
  Along the field. 6508-2
  "Along the fields we came by." 6430-2
  Alta quies. 6536-8,6733-6
  Alta quies, fr. More poems. 6828-6
  Amelia mixed the mustard. 6722-0,6633-X
  "As I gird on for fighting," fr. Last poems. 6828-6
  "As through the wild green hills of Wyre." 6138-9
  Away with bloodshed. 6722-0
  "Be still, my soul, be still." 6102-8,6430-2,6508-2
  The blackbird ("When smoke stood up from Ludlow"). 6073-0
  Bredon hill. 6506-6,6538-4,6726-3,6508-2,6491-4
  The carpenter's son. 6536-8
  Cherry trees. 6625-9
  "The chestnut casts his flambeaux, and the flowers." 6187-7,6536-8,6508-2
  Chorus. 6102-8
  The cost of love. 6396-9
  "Could man be drunk for ever." 6187-7,6427-2
  Crossing alone the nighted ferry. 6472-8
  The day of the battle. 6665-8
  The deserter. 6733-6,6508-2
  Easter hymn. 6337-3,6536-8,6641-0
  Eight o'clock. 6315-2
  The elephant, or the force of habit. 6722-0
  Epitaph on an army of mercenaries. 6477-9,6665-8,6102-8, 6150-8,6723-9
  An epitaph. 6733-6
  Fancy's knell. 6187-7,6102-8,6508-2
  "Far in a western brookland." 6246-6,6374-8,6430-2,6250-4,6199-0,6508-2,6723-9,6645-3
  "Farewell to barn and stack and tree." 6430-2
  For my funeral. 6536-8
  From Clee to heaven the beacon burns. 6224-5
  From far. 6339-X,6252-0
  God-bye, young man. 6371-3
  "Good creatures, do you love your lives,"fr.More poems. 6828-6
  Grenadier. 6187-7,6538-4
  Hell gate. 6536-8
  "Her strong enchantments failing." 6138-9,6150-8,6210-5
  Here dead lie we. 6427-2
  Hugley Steeple. 6655-0
  "I hoed and trenched and weeded" 6828-6
  "I lay me down and slumber," fr. More poems. 6828-6
  If truth in hearts that perish. 6723-9
  The immortal part. 6508-2
  In haste. 6084-6
  "In my own shire, if I was sad" 6828-6
  In valleys green and still. 6210-5
  Infant innocence. 6722-0,6125-7
  Injustice. 6954-1
  "Into my heart an air that kills." 6138-9,6125-7,6508-2, 6723-9
  Is my team ploughing. 6872-3,6527-9,6536-8,6726-3,6513-9,6655-0
  The isle of Portland. 6491-4
  Lad, have you things to do? 6473-6
  The lads in their hundreds. 6527-9,6655-0,6491-4
  The land of Biscay. 6536-8
  Last poems, sels. 6828-6
  The laws of God, the laws of men. 6532-5
  The lent lily. 6465-5,6478-7
  "Loitering with a vacant eye" 6828-6
  A look into water. 6102-8
  Loveliest of trees. 6476-0,6534-1,6645-3,6723-9,6655-0, 6153-2,6125-7,6161-3,6253-9,6250-4,6396-9,6464-7, 6430-2,6581-3,6371-3,6102-8,6508-2
  The merry guide. 6850-2
  The merry guide. 6252-0
  The merry guide. 6850-2
  Methridates. 6732-8
  "The mill-stream, now that noises cease," fr.More poems. 6828-6
  More poems, sels. 6828-6
  Myself again. 6732-8
  The new mistress. 6538-4
  "Now dreary dawns the eastern light," fr. Last poems. 6828-6
  "Now hollow fires burn out to black". 6655-0
  "Now hollow fires burn out to black" 6828-6
  Oh fair enough are sky and plain. 6332-2,6396-9
  Oh stay at home, my lad and plough. 6538-4
  Oh who is that young sinner. 6210-5
  "Oh, see how thick!" 6274-1,6655-0
  "Oh, when I was in love with you". 6464-7
  "Oh, when I was in love with you" 6828-6
  "On moonlit heath and lonesome bank." 6536-8,6430-2, 6508-2,6655-0
  "On Wenlock edge the wood's in trouble." 6138-9,6179-6, 6339-X,6263-9,6508-2
  The oracles. 6508-2
  Others, I am not the first. 6375-6
  The power of malt. 6301-2
  The rain, it streams on stone and hillock. 6536-8
  Reveille. 6861-8
  Reveille. 6506-6,6102-8,6161-3,6430-2,6464-7,6252 ,6199-0,6508-2,6513-9,6723-9
  Say, lad, have you things to do?. 6723-9
  The shades of night. 6125-7
  A Shropshire lad, sels. 6828-6
  A Shropshire lad, sels. 6199-0,6301-2,6508-2,6154-0, 6332-2,6507-4,6657-7,6430-2,6154-0,6332-2,6507-4, 6657-7
  The sigh that heaves the grasses. 6508-2
  The stars have not dealt me. 6733-6
  Stars, I have seen them fall. 6125-7
  Summer time on Bredon. 6236-9
  "Tell me not here, it needs not saying." 6208-3,6246-6, 6102-8
  "Terence this is stupid stuff." 6726-3,6733-6,6430-2, 6375-6,6655-0
  There is Hallelujah Hannah. 6722-0
  "They say my verse is sad: no wonder," fr. More poems. 6828-6
  "Think no more, lad; laugh, be jolly" 6828-6
  "This time of year a twelve month past" 6828-6
  'Tis time, I think, by Wenlock time. 6872-3
  '"Tis time, I think, by Wenlock town". 6850-2
  To an athlete dying young. 6581-3,6473-6,6488-4,6527-9, 6536-8,6641-0,6726 ,6491-4,6508-2,6655-0,6723-9,6737-9,6396
  To his godson Gerald C.A. Jackson. 6722-0
  "To stand up straight and tread the turning" 6828-6
  "Twice a week the winter thorough". 6655-0
  A voice from the grave. 6102-8
  The Welsh marches. 6210-5
  Wenlock edge. 6150-8
  The west. 6508-2
  "Westward on the high hilled plains." 6332-2
  When Adam day by day. 6633-X
  "When first my way to fair I took," fr. Last poems. 6828-6
  When green buds hang in the elm. 6354-3
  "When I came last to Ludlow" 6828-6
  When I was one-and-twenty. 6426-3,6427-2,6488-4,6732-8, 6371-3,6464 ,6153-2,6655-0,6430-2,6513-9,6107-9,6102-8,6723-9,6737-9
  When I watch the living meet. 6726-3,6430-2
  "When I would muse in boyhood." 6138-9
  "When smoke stood up from Ludlow". 6655-0
  "White in the moon the long road lies" 6828-6
  "White in the moon the long road lies." 6536-8,6723-9, 6645-3
  With rue my heart is laden. 6506-6,6536-8,6732-8,6513-9, 6199-0,6250 ,6102-8,6430-2,6153-2,6508-2,6396-0,6301 ,6491-4,6655-0
  "Yonder see the morning blink," fr. Last poems. 6828-6
Housman, Alfred Edward (tr.)
  Chorus, fr. Alcestis. Euripides, 7039-6
  Chorus, fr. Seven against Thebes. Aeschylus, 7039-6
  Chrous, fr. Oedipus coloneus. Sophocles, 7039-6
  Old age, fr. Oedipus coloneus. Sophocles, 6435-3

"What man is he that yearneth". Sophocles, 6435-3
Housman, Laurence
    All fellows, sels. 6730-1
    "And the world was made flesh." 6337-3
    Annus Mirabilis (1902). 6477-9
    Badcombe Fair: night. 6069-2
    Bonds. 6337-3
    A Christmas carol. 6776-X
    A Christmas song. 6746-8
    The city of sleep. 6507-4
    The comforters. 6274-1
    The continuing city. 6730-1
    The crusader's tomb. 7029-9
    A dead warrior. 6069-2
    Gaffer at the fair. 6506-6
    The god at play. 6507-4
    God's mother. 6282-2
    The help-givers. 6337-3
    Heroes. 6861-8
    'Insets' in 'All fellows' 6102-8
    The loot of Luxor. 6778-6
    Love importunate. 6507-4
    A prayer for the healing of the wounds of Christ. 6337-3
    Resurrection, fr. Rue. 6337-3
    Separation. 6102-8
    The settlers. 6793-X
    The song of the builders. 6625-9
    Spikenard. 6581-3
    Summer night. 6884-7
    To Thomas Hardy. 6337-3
    The winners. 6793-X
    Young bloods. 6233-4
Houston street, N.Y. Carolyn Baxter. 6870-7
Houston, Eleanor Jordan
    Distant star. 6316-0
    The glass blower. 6316-0
Houston, Howard R.
    Two nocturnes. 6017-X
Houston, Margaret Bell
    Cerelle. 6396-9
    The poet in the market-place. 6327-6
    The poet in the market place. 6327-6
    Song from the traffic. 6490-6
    Tulips. 6326-8
Houston, Mark
    Among my books. 6118-4
Hovell-Thurlow; 2d Baron Thurlow, Edward
    Beauty. 6302-0,6385-3,6737-9
    The harvest home. 7015-9
    The heron. 6073-0,6086-2
    May. 6301-2
    Song to May. 6271-7,6086-2,6219-9
    Sonnet ("The crimson moon"). 6271-7
    Sonnet ("The nightingale"). 6271-7
    Sonnet ("Tis much"). 6271-7
    Sonnet ("Who best"). 6271-7
    Sonnet: summer. 6219-9
    Sonnet: to the moon. 6219-9
    The sylvan life. 6086-2
    To a bird. 6302-0,6385-3,6219-9,7015-9,6302-0,6385-3
"Hovering in mid-strema". The moonlit rock. Morton Marcus. 6792-1
Hovey, Richard
    Accident in art. 6527-9
    After business hours. 6753-0
    Again among the hills. 6374-8
    Among the hills. 6121-4
    At sea. 7006-X
    At the crossroads. 6161-3
    At the end of the day. 6224-5,6310-1,6473-6,6501-5,6735-2
    Ballad of the goodly fere. 6076-5
    Barney McGee. 6089-7,6732-8,6102-8,6076-2
    The battle of Manilla, sels. 6946-0
    Beethoven's third symphony. 7041-8
    The buccaneers. 7006-X
    The call of the bugles. 6753-0
    Comrades. 6310-1,6473-6,6476-0,6501-5,6464-7
    Comrades, sels. 6484-1
    Contemporaries. 7006-X
    The death song, sels. 6501-5
    Discovery. 7006-X
    Down the Songo. 7006-X
    A dream of Sappho. 6121-4
    Eleazar Wheelock. 6722-0
    Envoy. 6250-4,6431-0
    Envoy, fr. More songs from Vagabondia. 6300-4
    Evening on the Potomac. 7006-X
    Faith and fate. 6753-0
    Faith and fate. 6735-2
    The faun, sels. 6047-1,6252-0,6047-1
    The faun. 6374-8
    Hanover winter song. 7035-3
    Health and wealth. 6717-4
    Her valentine. 6652-6
    A hill song. 7006-X
    Hunting song. 6374-8,6121-4
    Hunting song, fr. King Arthur. 6890-1
    Immanence. 6730-1
    In the workshop. 7006-X
    Isabel. 7006-X
    The Kavanagh. 6307-1,6309-8
    King Arthur, sels. 6890-1
    The king's son. 7006-X
    Launa Dee. 6735-2
    Laurana's song. 7006-X
    Love in the winds. 6753-0
    Love in the winds. 6250-4,6300-4,6737-9
    Love in the winds. 6753-0
    The love of a boy-today. 6004-8
    The love of a boy. 6441-8
    Men of Dartmouth. 6121-4
    The mocking bird. 6073-0
    New York. 6006-4,6274-1
    The outlaw. 7006-X
    The sea gipsy. 6396-9,6252-2,6250-4,6431-0,6107-9,6336-5,6104-4,6300-4,6076-5,6114-1,6102-8,6236-9,6310-X,6331-4,6332-2,6423 ,6476-0,6509-0,6732-8,6535-2,6423-X,6646 ,6476-0,6509-0,6732-8,6535-2
    The sea. 6374-8
    Seaward. 6121-4
    Short beach. 6374-8
    Song ("The flower-born Blodueda.") 6431-0
    A song by the shore. 7006-X
    Spring. 6047-1,6374-8
    Spring, sels. 6007-2,6487-6
    The stein song. 6732-8,6161-3,6467-1
    Taliesin, sels. 6431-0
    The thought of her. 6310-1
    Three of a kind. 6890-1
    A toast. 6004-8
    Transcendence. 6007-2,6730-1
    Unforseen. 6441-8
    Unmanifest destiny. 6121-4,6467-1,6121-4,6431-0,6153-2,6396-9,6265-2,6121-4,6431-0,6153-2,6289-X,6337-3,6473-6,6730-1,6735-2
    Vagabondia. 6501-5
    Voices of unseen spirits. 6735-2
    The wander-lovers. 6423-X,6735-2,6431-0,6300-4
    The wanderer. 6252-0
    A winter thought of Dartmouth in Manhattan, sels. 6484-1
    The word of the Lord from Havanna. 6946-0
Hovhannessian, Hovhannes
    Araxes came devouringly. 6050-1
    "None await thy smiling rays." 6050-1
    The rock, sels. 6050-1
    The rock. 6050-1
"How". Thalaba, sels. Robert Southey. 6867-7
How – when – where. John Oxenham. 6337-3
How a cat was annoyed and a poet was booted. Guy Wetmore Carryl. 6120-6
How a man should be judged. Unknown. 6403-5
How a mathematician makes love. Unknown. 6721-2
How a witch sought to cajole the master. Unknown (Algonquin Indian) 6864-2
How a witch sought to cajole the master. Unknown (Algonquin Indian) 6864-2
How an angel looks. Unknown. 6690-9

How an engineer won his bride. James Noel Johnston. 6924-X
How and where. Alice Cary. 6969-X
"How are songs begot and bred?" Richard Henry Stoddard, 6753-0
How are thy servants b~est. Joseph Addison. 6931-2
"How are we living?". How and where. Alice Cary. 6969-X
"How are you hoeing your row, my boy?". The boy with the hoe. T.B. Weaver. 6964-9
'How are you, sanitary?' Francis Bret Harte. 6113-3,6340-3, 6016-2,6470-4
How are you? Arthur Guiterman. 6722-0
"How aromatic evening grows," fr. Hadad. James Abraham Hillhouse. 6752-2
How Barre, Vermont, was named. Daniel L. Cady. 6988-6
How Bateese came home. William Henry Drummond. 6692-5,6281-4
"How awful, how sublime this view". Written on the sea-shore. Felicia Dorothea Hemans. 6973-8
How beastly the bourgeois is. David Herbert Lawrence. 6125-7
How beautiful. George Elliston. 6585-6
"How beautiful a world were ours". Homes and graves. Thomas Kibble Hervey. 6980-0
"How beautiful and strange!The air that brings". Mission of song. Benjamin Franklin Taylor. 6815-4
"How beautiful appear on the mountains", fr. The Bible. Unknown. 6606-2
"How beautiful are thy feet with shoes...". Quam pulchri. Bible. 6830-8
"How beautiful beneath the bright blue sky". The sea. Robert Southey. 6867-7
How beautiful is night. Robert Southey. 6328-4
"How beautiful is night!". Night. Robert Southey. 6014-5, 6239-3
"How beautiful is youth! how bright it gleams". Henry Wadsworth Longfellow. 6238-5
"How beautiful the scene! The eye of day". The Indian chief. Charles W. Denison. 6755-7
"How beautiful the shiny turtle" Robert Bly. 6803-0
"How beautiful this night! the balmiest sigh". Night, fr. Queen Mab. Percy Bysshe Shelley. 6302-0,6385-3
How beautiful were once the roses. Ivan S. Turgenev. 6585-6
"How beautiful! - from his blue throne on high". The ocean. George Denison Prentice. 6833-2
How beauty came. J. Corson Miller. 6072-2
How Betsey and I made up. Will Carleton. 6045-1
"How beauty gleams within these emerald hills". The artist speaks. Don Erman. 6789-1
"How big is your heart?". To whom it may concern. Lola Aola Seery. 6750-6
"How black the barge of trailing pall". Montgomery's return. Arthur Guiterman. 6773-5
"How blest are lovers in disguise!". Song ("How blest"). George Farquhar. 6563-5
"How blest has my time been! what joys have...". The joys of wedlock. Edward Moore. 6874-X
"How blest he appears". Song ("How blest he appears"). Thomas Otway. 6563-5
"How blest the youth". William Cowper. 6814-6
"How blind the toil that burrows like the mole". Robert Browning. Henry Van Dyke. 6961-4
"How bravely autumn paints upon the sky". Written in a volume of Shakespeare. Thomas Hood. 6974-6
How brief a thing. David Morton. 6042-0
"How brief this drama of our life appears!" Unknown. 6238-5
How Brunhild was received at Worms, fr. Nibelungen lied. Unknown (German) 6372-1
How Burlington was saved. Charles Mair. 6166-4
"How bright these days still seem to glow". School-days. William White. 6868-5
"How bright this weird autumnal eve". Fires in Illinois. John James Piatt. 7041-8
"How brim-full of nothing's the life of a beau". The life of a beau. James Miller. 6932-0
"How call they old King Ringang's child?". Fair Rohtraut. Eduard Friedrich Morike. 6842-1
"How calm, how beauteous and how cool". Pool in the forest. Victor Hugo. 6949-5

"How calmly droops the dew on tree and plant". Suburban meadows. Edward Cracroft Lefroy. 7015-9
"How came that blood on thy coat-lap?". The dead brother. Unknown. 6829-4
"How came this troubled on to stray". Boy in the wind. George Dillon. 6619-4,6779-4
"How can I dread you, o portentous wise". The woman with the baby to the philosopher. Frances Cornford. 7014-0
"How can I laugh or dance as others do". When you are on the sea. Dora Sigerson Shorter. 6785-9
"How can I sing light-souled and fancy-free". A lyric. Lorenzo de' Medici. 7039-6
"How can I sing of my mistress's chiding?". The dirge of the householder. Richard Stillman Powell. 7021-3
How can I sing? Unknown. 6337-3
"How can I tell her/if she is in bed and...". For Monique Graham. Wayne Miller. 6998-3, 6901-0
"How can I tell them what it was I saw". Lincoln's dream. (Frederick) Ridgely Torrence. 6871-5
"How can I tell you what no words can tell?". Song without words. Dorothy E. Reid. 6906-1
"How can I tell you, dear." Soseki. 6027-7
"'How can I tell', Sir Edmund said". The standard-bearer. Henry Van Dyke. 6961-4
"How can I then return in happy plight". Sonnet 028 ("How can I"). William Shakespeare. 6436-1,6447-7
"How can I wait until you come to me?". Impatience. Ella Wheeler Wilcox. 6956-8
"How can I, that girl standing there". Politics. William Butler Yeats. 6761-1
"How can its clean and shiny stride be human". Automobile. Delmore Schwartz. 6850-2
How can man die better. Tyrtaeus. 6665-8,6435-3
"How can my muse want subject to invent". Sonnet 038 ("How can my muse"). William Shakespeare. 6447-7
"How can one e'er be sure". Lady Horikawa. 7039-6
"How can she catch the sunlight". Questions. Lord Thomson of Cardington. 6427-2
"How can that eye, with inspiration beaming". For a picture of St. Cecilia attended by angels. Felicia Dorothea Hemans. 6973-8
How can that love so deep, so lone. Felicia Dorothea Hemans. 6973-8
"How can that tree but withered be". Song ("How can that tree"). Unknown. 6182-6
How can the heart forget her? Unknown. 6513-9
How can the tree but waste? Thomas, 2nd Baron Vaux. 6328-4
How can they honor him. Anderson M. Scruggs. 6608-9
How Canada was saved (May 1660). George Murray. 6795-6
"How can they honour Him, the humble lad". Christmas 1930. Anderson M. Scruggs. 6781-6
"How can we hate enough to fight?". To a soap-box orator. Freda Kirchwey. 6880-4
"How can we manage with our brother". A brother gone. Gene Baker. 6995-9
"How can we reason still, how look afar". Meditation in June, 1917. Edward Shanks. 7029-9
"How can you speak to me so, Charlie!". The wife's Christmas. Phoebe Cary. 6969-X
"How careful was I, when I took my way". Sonnet 048 ("How careful was I"). William Shakespeare. 6447-7
"How certain the mule's step in the abyss". Rhapsody for the mule. Jose Lezama Lima. 6759-X
"How changed is nature from the time antique!". Something lost. Edward Cracroft Lefroy. 7015-9
How charming is divine philosophy. John Milton. 6543-0
How Christ came to a lonely child. Friedrich Ruckert. 6842-1
How clear she shines. Emily Bronte. 6655-0
How clear she shines, sels. Emily Bronte. 6123-0
"How clear tonight the far jang-jangling bells". Cattle bells. Lew Sarett. 6979-7
How clouds move. Barbara Hughes. 6792-1
How Columbus found America. H.C. Dodge. 6922-3
"How cold and hungry is the sea to-day". Trito Esuriens. Thomas Edward Brown. 6809-X
"How coldly I survey". The bitten grass. Edward Shanks. 6778-6
How ongress fought for Sheridan. Emma Dunning Banks. 6426-

HOW

4
"How cool and fair this cellar where". Der mann im Keller. Unknown (German). 6949-5
"How cool and wet the lowlands lie". The neighbor, fr. Studies for pictures. Bayard Taylor. 6976-2
"How cool the cattle seem!". Cattle. ? Banko. 6891-X
"How could God think of so many kinds of houses?" Jessie Orton Jones. 6999-1
"How could a man sleep otherwise than well". Handwover coverlets. John Maher Murphy. 6761-1
"How could her dim eyes". Recollection. Duane Big Eagle. 7005-1
How could we, beforehand, live in quiet. Nikolai Gumilev. 6665-8
How Cushing destroyed the Albemarle. Unknown. 6415-9
How Cyrus laid the cable. John Godfrey Saxe. 6946-0,6963-0
How Cyrus laid the cable. Unknown. 6743-3
"How could you be by halves". One of the chapters. Kathleen Fraser. 6792-1
"How dare I in thy courts appear". Hymn ("How dare I..."). Phoebe Cary. 6969-X
"How darkly o'er yon far-off mountain frowns". Sonnet 002 ("How darkly o'er yon..."). Robert Southey. 6867-7
"How dear to dis heart vas mine grandshild". 'Dot leedle Loweeza'. Charles Follen Adams. 6791-3
"How dear to my heart is the bank roll...". The bank roll. Edgar A. Guest. 6862-6
How death comes. Unknown. 6881-2
"How deep is granite?". City of granite. Eleanor Vinton. 6764-6
"How delightful, at sunset to lossen the boat!". The excursion. Tu Fu. 7039-6
"How desolate my former life". Yatsu-tada. 6852-9
"How desolate were nature, and how void". God's omnipresent agency. Carlos Wilcox. 6752-2
"How dessicate and right-angled". Measurements. Bartolo Cattafi. 6803-0
"How did he know, the young sky-rover". Wings. Blanche W. Schoonmaker. 7019-4
How did it happen? Emma Celia & Lizzie J. Rook. 6137-0
"How did the new baby get into the house?". The Christmas baby. Isabella Valancy Crawford. 6797-2
How did the party go? Hilaire Belloc. 6339-X
"How did this broken/Leaf ..". Autumn. Carol Stein. 6850-2
How did you die? Edmund Vance Cooke. 6732-8,6337-3,6964-9, 6291-1,6337-3,6260-1,6274-1
"How did you get there?". The man in the moon. Alethea Chaplin. 6937-1
"How did you picture her before the ages". To Isaias, seer. Sister Mary of the Visitation. 6839-1
How did you tackle your work? Edgar A. Guest. 6291-1
"How difficult it is for men". Taka (Gido-sanshi No Haha) 6852-9
"How difficult to teach these women love". The rapist speaks to himself. Herbert Scott. 6803-0
"How difficult, alas! to please mankind!". Praying for rain. John ("Peter Pindar") Wolcott. 6909-6
"How do I feel/Fine wrist to small feet?". Second nature. Diane Chang. 6790-5
"'How do I know there is no Death?'". No death. Mary Baggot. 6799-9
"How do I love thee? Let me count the ways." Elizabeth Barrett Browning. 6240-7,6289-X,6337-3,6465-5,6488-4, 6527 ,6199-0,6192-3,6513-9,6430-2,6560-0,6107 ,6019-6,6094-3,6250-4,6536-8,6620-8,6726 ,6464-7
"How do I love thee? Let me count the ways". Sonnet ("How do I love thee?"). Elizabeth Barrett Browning. 6154-0,6317-9,6604-6
"How do I love you, dear?". Lyric 025. Wendell Phillips Stafford. 7030-2
"How do I love you? Let me tell you, ducky". Revised editions of great poetry. Beatrice McElwee. 6750-6
"How do I say, in/between". Does it ever make a difference. Jacqueline J. Johnson. 6899-5
"How do the speeches". The cataract of T.R. Franklin Pierce Adams. 6995-9
"How do they live who never see the sky". How? Lee Spencer. 6954-1
"How do thy highways flow...". City of the dead. Edward Farquhar. 6939-8

"How do you buy your money? Edgar A. Guest. 7033-7
How do you do? Unknown. 6125-7
"How do you do?/No, I am not Chinese". Sure you can ask me a personal question. Diane Burns. 7005-1
"How do you know that May has come". May-day at sea. John F. Finerty. 6833-2
How do you spell 'missile'?: preliminary... George Uba. 6790-5
"How does life look behind the hill?". A young inquirer. Charlotte Mellen Packard. 6965-7
"How does love speak?". Love's language. Ella Wheeler Wilcox. 6956-8
How does love speak? Ella Wheeler Wilcox. 6863-4
"How does my garden grow?". Inscription for a garden gate. Ruth H. Hausman. 6850-2
How does the rain come? Charles Rollin Ballard. 7030-2
How doth the little busy bee. Isaac Watts. 6131-1,6639-9, 6242-3,6452-3,6459-0,6527-9,6638-0,6135-4
How doth the little crocodile. Charles Lutwidge ("Lewis Carroll") Dodgson. 6722-0,6527-9
How dreary looks the ivied cot. Gertrude Hall. 6431-0
"How dreary would the garden be" Alice Cary. 6049-8
"How eas'ly wert thou chained" Thomas Campion. 6794-8
"How easily men's cheeks are hot with wrath!." Verner von Heidenstam. 6045-5
"How excellent, o Lord, our Lord, thy". Psalm 008 Bible. 6848-0
"How fading are the joys we dote upon". Like angels' visits. John Norris. 6934-7
"How fair is the rose!". Arbutus. Isaac Watts. 6049-8
"How fair is the rose...", sels. Isaac Watts. 6601-1
"How falls it, oriole, thou hast come to fly". To an oriole. Edgar Fawcett. 7041-8
How far is it to Bethlehem? Frances Chesteron. 6746-8
How far is it to Bethlehem? Frances Chesterton. 6331-4, 6776-X
"How far that little candle throws his beams!". William Shakespeare. 6291-1
"How far thro' all the bloom and brake". Song ("How far thro'..."), fr. The ancient sage. Alfred Lord Tennyson. 6867-7
How far to Bethlehem? Madeleine Sweeny Miller. 6337-3,6654-2
"How far to Oaklands now, sir?". Sal Parker's ghost. Edwin Coller. 6918-5
"How far, how far are you faring...". April's daughter. Virginia Lyne Tunstall. 6979-7
"How far, how far, with unavailing eye". The sky, fr. Nightfall. Lady Margaret Sackville. 6785-9
'How far, o rich' Saint Ambrose. 6954-1
"How fare you, lady?". Penitence and death of Jane Shore. Nicholas Rowe. 6867-7
"How fast the rapid hours retire". Summer. William Oliver Bourne Peabody. 6752-2
"How fevered is the man, who cannot look". Two sonnets on fame. John Keats. 6828-6
"How few, of all the hearts that loved". The wanderer from the fold. Emily Bronte. 6828-6
"How fine it is/to wet one's pants". The derelict. Herbert Scott. 6803-0
How firm a foundation. K. 6337-3
How firm a foundation. Robert Keene (atr) 6730-1
How Flaherty kept the bridge. Eugene Field. 6949-5
"How flows thy being now?". To Silvio Pellico, released. Felicia Dorothea Hemans. 6973-8
"How fresh, O Lord, how sweet and clean". The flower. George Herbert. 6933-9
"How frightened you stood when the carriage...". Unknown. 6059-5
"How from the excavating tide they win". Henry Taylor. 6997-5
"How fruitless is each human hope, how vain". Lorenzo de' Medici. 6325-X
How Glooskap brought the summer. Frances Laughton Mace. 6053-6
How God answers. Unknown. 6337-3
How God was made. Kenneth Patchen. 6017-X
How God will not do for vs. John Heywood. 6586-4
"How funny 't is, when pretty lads and lasses". Description of a New England country dance. Thomas

Green Fessenden. 7030-2
"How gallantly, how merrily". The return of the admiral. Bryan Waller ("Barry Cornwall") Procter. 6980-0
"How gently rest they". God's acre. A. C. Stockman. 6952-5
"How glorious the earth in festal array!". Maytime. Emma Gertrude Jaeck. 6799-9
"How glows each patriot bosom...". The United States and Macedonian. Unknown. 6946-0
"How God-like is the human mind". Concepts. William White. 6868-5
How goes the night? Unknown (Chinese) 7039-6
How good are the poor. Victor Hugo. 6424-8
"How good the brief dusk is, & the long night". Requiescat. Barbara Young. 6781-6
"How grace this hallowed day?". Christmas. Henry Timrod. 6333-0
"How graceful Maria leads the dance!". On Maria dancing. Robert Burns. 6959-2
How grandpa proposed. Unknown. 6675-5
How graunde amoure was recyved of La Belle Pucell. Stephen Hawes. 6193-1
"How great a song in silence! When the ear". Relief. Walter John Coates. 6750-6
"How great are the blessings of government...". Charles II. Nahum Tate. 6867-7
"How great her travail, who went forth to find". To Madame Curie. Angela Morgan. 7014-0
"How green the earth, how blue the sky". The settlers. Laurence Housman. 6793-X
"How happens it, my cruel miss". To Chloe (3). Horace. 6949-5
"How happily shelter'd is he who reposes". On Samuel Rogers' seat in the garden at Holland house. Henry Luttrell. 6874-X
"How happj' art thou & I." Unknown. 6563-5
"How happy are the new-born race". The testimony of divine adoption. Madame De la Mothe Guion. 6814-6
"How happy could I be", fr. The beggar's opera. John Gay. 6398-5
How happy I'll be. Unknown. 6304-7
How happy is he born. Sir Henry Wotton. 6087-0
"How happy is the blameless vestal's lot?". Eloisa, fr. Eloisa to Abelard. Alexander Pope. 6932-0
"How happy the little birds. Unknown. 6930-4
"How happy the lover". John Dryden. 6315-2,6562-7
"How happy were my days, till now". Song ("How happy"). Isaac Bickerstaffe. 6932-0
How happy's that lover. Unknown. 6563-5
"How hard is my fortune". The convict of Clonmell. Unknown (Irish). 6244-X,6858-8
"How hardly doth the cold and careless world". Sara J. ("Grace Greenwood") Lippincott. 6996-7
"How has kind heav'n adorn'd the happy land". Italy and Britain. Joseph Addison. 6932-0
"How has the dragon lizard shrunken..this age". Coral lizard. Fanny de Groot Hastings. 6979-7
"How hast thou helped him that...without power". Cujus adjutor es. Bible. 6830-8
"How have I stammered, rendering thee & thine". Silver and gold. Edward Farquhar. 6939-8
"How have you managed to enter so, like a mist". Nocturne. Xavier Abril. 6759-X
"How he departed hence, you who stood by". Sophocles. 6435-3
How he saved St. Michael's. Mary Anna Phinney Stansbury. 6062-5
How he saved St. Michael's. Unknown. 6142-7,6408-6,6554-6, 6742-5,6263-6
How he turned out. Edwin Meade Robinson. 6458-2
"How healthily their feet upon the floor". Sonnet ("How healthily"). Edna St. Vincent Millay. 6161-3
"How heavy do I journey on the way". Sonnet 050 ("How heavy"). William Shakespeare. 6447-7
"How heavy do I journey on the way". William Shakespeare. 6204-0
"How Hellas' youth". Aristophanes. 6435-3
"How high yon lark is heavenward borne!". Song ("How high yon lark..."), fr. Phantasmion. Sara Coleridge. 7037-X
How his garments got turned. Unknown. 6919-3

How his garments got turned. Unknown. 6167-2
How I brought the good news from Aix to Ghent. Walter Carruthers Sellar and Julian Yeatman. 6633-X
How I brought the good news from Aix to Ghent. R.J. Yeatman and W.C. Sella. 6722-0
How I came to be a graduate student. Wendy Rose. 7005-1
How I kissed her. George M. Ritchie. 6675-5
How I love my books. Unknown. 6118-4
"How I loved/Witness, ye days and nights..." John Dryden. 6317-9
"How I regret my fallen friends". Emperor Gotoba [or Toba II]. 6852-9
How I walked alone in the jungles of Heaven. Vachel Lindsay. 6032-3
How I wish I was single again. Unknown. 6058-7
How I won my wife. W.A. Eaton. 6417-5
How Iacke Cade traiterously rebelling... Unknown. 6586-4
"How history repeats itself". Can't. Harriet Prescott Spofford. 6946-0,6820-0
"How I am held within a tranquil shell". The woman with child. Muredach J. Dooher. 6930-4
"How I bawled 'ship, ahoy!'". The pilot, fr. A tiny trip. Joseph Ashby Sterry. 6770-0
"How I loved you in your sleep". Memory. Laurence (Adele Florence Nicolson) Hope. 6856-1
"How ill doth he deserve a lover's name". Song ("How ill"). Thomas Carew. 6562-7
"How ill doth he deserve a lover's name". Thomas Carew. 6187-7,6935-5
"How ill doth he deserve a lovers name". Eternity of love protested. Thomas Carew. 6341-1,6933-9
"How in heaven's name did Columbus get over". Columbus. Arthur Hugh Clough. 6820-0
"How infamous that men should raise". Thomas A. Hendricks's appeal. Eugene Field. 6949-5
"How is it I can eat bread here and cut meat". Evening meal in the twentieth century. John Holmes. 6761-1
"How is it that before mine eyes". To my own portrait. Felicia Dorothea Hemans. 6973-8
"How is it you and I". Rondel. John Cameron Grant. 6770-0
How is the gold become dim, fr. Lamentations of Jeremiah. Bible. 6125-7
"How is the grass set free?". The grass. May Lewis. 6979-7, 6039-0
"How is't each bough a several music yields?". Nature's accord. Ben Jonson. 6943-6
How it happened. George Colman the Younger. 6302-0
How it happened. Colonel John Hay. 7041-8
How it happened. John Hay. 6620-8,6004-8
How it happened. James Whitcomb Riley. 6892-8
How it happened. James Whitcomb Riley. 6992-4
"How it happened, who can tell". Zaidee of the golden west, fr. The Tuscan princess. Gay H. Narramore. 7030-2
How it is done. Unknown. 6530-9
"How it sings, sings, sings". The song of the sea wind. Unknown. 6928-2
How it strikes a contemporary. Robert Browning. 6657-7
How Jack found that beans may go back on a chap. Guy Wetmore Carryl. 6026-9
How Jamie came home. Will Carleton. 6406-X
How John quit the farm. James Whitcomb Riley. 6991-6
"How joyous his neigh!". Song of the horse. Unknown (Navaho Indian). 7039-6
"How joyous the spring is!". David and Bathshua. Charles William Cayzer. 6848-0
How kindly hast thou led me! T. Grinfield. 6219-9
How King Edward and his menge met with the Spaniards... Laurence Minot. 6378-0
"How know I, love, that thou art true?". Love. Elena Vossen Greenfield. 6841-3
How knows he summer comes? Unknown. 6936-3
How Kuloskap conquered Aklibimo, the great bullfrog. Unknown (Algonquin Indian) 6864-2
How Kuloskap fought the giant sorcerers at Saco. Unknown (Algonquin Indian) 6864-2
How Kuloskap granted gifts and favors to many Indians. Unknown (Algonquin Indian) 6864-2
How Kuloskap left the world. Unknown (Algonquin Indian) 6864-2
How Kuloskap named the animals. Unknown (Algonquin Indian)

HOW

    6864-2
How Kuloskap sailed through the cavern of darkness. Unknown (Algonquin Indian) 6864-2
How Kuloskap was conquered by the babe. Unknown (Algonquin Indian) 6864-2
How Kuloskap went whale-fishing. Unknown (Algonquin Indian) 6864-2
How Larry sang the 'Angus'. Jeannie Pendleton Ewing. 6928-2
"How lang shall our land thus suffer distress". Our ain bonny laddie. William Meston. 6859-6
"How large that thrush looks on the..thorntree". Winter. Dante Gabriel Rossetti. 6793-X
"How larger is remembrance than desire". Ebbtide at sundown. Michael (Katherine Bradley & Edith Cooper) Field. 6844-8
"How lightly leaps the youthful chamois". The glad young chamois. Burges Johnson. 6861-8
"How like a fawning publican...", fr. The merchant... William Shakespeare. 6392-6
"How like a golden dreame you met and parted". To the most illvstrivos and mighty. Thomas Campion. 6794-8
"How like a mighty picture, tint by tint". To W.H.H. Paul Hamilton Hayne. 7017-5
"How like a winter hath my absence been". Sonnet 097 ("How like a winter"). William Shakespeare. 6208-3,6271-7, 6436-1,6250-4,6560-0
"How like a winter hath my absence been". William Shakespeare. 6198-2
How like a woman. Caroline and Alice Duer. 6441-8,6652-6
How Lisa loved the king. George (Mary Ann Cross) Eliot. 6679-8
"How like the eternity doth nature seem". The constancy of nature contrasted with...human life. Richard Henry Dana. 6752-2
"How like the leper, with his own sad cry". The buoy-bell. Charles Tennyson Turner. 6833-2,6656-9
"'How like your mother, child!' I said". Echo. Walter De La Mare. 6905-3
"How little flattering is a woman's love". Sir Henry Taylor. 6238-5
How little it costs. Mary Dow Brine. 6654-2
How little Katie knows the next door neighbor. Unknown. 6155-9
How little Tom was saved. Alexander ("Surfaceman") Anderson. 6167-2,6652-6
"How little recks it where men die". Where man should die. Unknown. 6910-X
"How little we think, as we go our way". Making faces. Mary Lydia Carpenter. 6799-9
"How lonely the delicate sound" Sojin Takei. 6981-9
How long. Louise Chandler Moulton. 7041-8
"How long false hope, wilt thou mislead myne eyes." Unknown. 6563-5
"How long in stealthy silence...". Paulus Silentiarius. 6251-2
"How long is the night, brother". Day and night. Henry Van Dyke. 6961-4
How long it once was. Unknown. 6453-1
"How long must women wait in vain". From the innocent impostors. Thomas Shadwell. 6867-7
"How long shall I endure without reply". Satirical lines on Dryden. Thomas Shadwell. 6867-7
"How long shall man's imprison'd spirit groan". Life. Caleb C. Colton. 6980-0,6214-8
"How long since you last stood so reflective". The political lobbyist waits to leave the capitol. Stephan Chan. 7018-3
"How long the echoes love to play". The after-echo. Henry Van Dyke. 6961-4
"How long the singing voices in my heart". Lost songs. Nina Salaman. 6778-6
How long this night is. Unknown. 6881-2
How long will you remain? Emily Bronte. 6655-0
"How long wilt thou sleep, o sluggard?...". Proverbs. Bible. 6958-4
"How long, and slim, and straight thou liest..". Comparison. Helen Hoyt. 6880-4
"How long, boys? Unknown. 6149-4
"How long, great God, how long must I". The aspiration. John Norris. 6931-2
"How long, o God, how long". How long. O God. James Abraham Martling. 6952-5
"How long, O God, shall men be ridden down". Poland. Alfred Lord Tennyson. 6867-7
"How long, O Lord, shall this, my country, be". Australia infelix. William Gay. 6784-0
"How long, O Lord? The voice is sounding still". Democracy downtrodden. William Michael Rossetti. 7015-9
"How long, O sister, how long". The bells at midnight. Thomas Bailey Aldrich. 6946-0
How long, o Lord! Hall Caine. 6954-1
How long, O Lord?. Robert Palmer. 6650-X
How long. O God. James Abraham Martling. 6952-5
"How long/Shall I be strong". Adolescence. Melba Williams. 6906-1
How long? Horatius Bonar. 6385-3
How long? Ferner R. Nuhn. 6542-2
How love looked for hell. Sidney Lanier. 6753-0
How love looked for hell. Sidney Lanier. 6008-0,6126-5
How love looked for hell. Sidney Lanier. 6753-0
How Lucy backslid. Paul Laurence Dunbar. 6692-5
"How lovely are the waters of Babylon". Ultimate exile, sels. Ralph Nixon Currey. 6788-3
"How lovely are thy dwellings fair". Psalm 084. Bible. 6848-0
"How many a mighty mind is shut". Germs of greatness. Eliza Cook. 6923-1
"How many a mighty ship". The star of the sea. Adelaide Anne Procter. 6957-6
"How many a rainbow dream has thinned to air!". Illusions. Robert Haven Schauffler. 6764-6
"How many ages of my lean forebears". Grass heritage. Helen Molyneaux Salisbury. 6782-4
"How many an acorn falls to die". Compensation. John Banister Tabb. 7017-5
"How many are the scenes he limned". Unfading pictures. Louella C. Poole. 6762-X
How many bards. John Keats. 6110-9,6199-0
"How many bards gild the lapses of time" John Keats. 6828-6
"How many between east and west". To Miss Creuze on her birthday. William Cowper. 6814-6
"How many blessed groups this hour are bending". Sabbath sonnet. Felicia Dorothea Hemans. 6973-8
"How many clouds must wraithlike rise...ocean". Sonnet ("How many clouds"). Conrad Aiken. 6783-2
"How many days has my baby to play?" Mother Goose. 6452-3
"How many equal...", fr. Epistle to Elizabeth... Ben Jonson. 6726-3
"How many flowers are gently met". George Sterling. 6338-1
How many heavens... Edith Sitwell. 6357-8
"How many hopes were borne upon thy bier". The tomb of Madame Langhans. Felicia Dorothea Hemans. 6973-8
"How many humble hearts have dipped". Christopher Morley. 6289-X
"How many miles I've seen". From an old boat. Edward H. Butler. 6983-5
"How many miles is it to Babylon?" Unknown. 6904-5
"How many miles to Babylon?". Mother Goose. 6363-2
"How many miles to baby-land?". Baby-land. George Cooper. 6273-3,6452-3,6131-1,6627-5,6078-1
"How many miles to Babylon". Nursery rhyme ("How many miles"). Unknown. 6179-6
"How many months, how many a weary year". Life unlived. John Payne. 7015-9
"How many more thousand miles" Sojin Takei. 6981-9
How many new years have grown old. Unknown. 6182-6
"How many now are dead to me". To the dead. John Gardiner Calkins Brainard. 6752-2
"How many paltry, foolish, painted things". Idea, sels. Michael Drayton. 6879-0
"How many paltry, foolish, painted things" Michael Drayton. 6182-6,6586-4
"How many saucy airs we meet". The barley-mow and the dunghill. John Gay. 6972-X
How many seconds in a minute? Christina Georgina Rossetti. 6963-0
"How many sing of wars". Ode to Richard Martin, Esquire. Thomas Hood. 6974-6

"How many sons, how many generations". Rizpah. Algernon Charles Swinburne. 6828-6
"How many spring flowers blossom late!". The new name. Luella D. Smith. 6799-9
"How many strive to force a way". Forcing a way. Unknown. 6902-9
"How many things have oft been sung or said". In praise of sleep. Passeroni. 6787-5
"How many thousand of my poorest subjects". Henry IV, part 002 William Shakespeare. 6958-4
"How many thousands are wakening now!". The wakening. Felicia Dorothea Hemans. 6973-8
"How many time do I love thee, dear". Song ("How many times"). Thomas Lovell Beddoes. 6512-0
"How many times do I love thee. Thomas Lovell Beddoes. 6240-7,6328-4,6429-9,6620-8,6246-6,6383 ,6226-1,6219-1, 6321-7
"How many times from life away I fled". You and my song. Prisca Paul. 6799-9
"How many times my thoughOs have turned to you". Letter from a sanatorium: To J.M.S. Charles Whitby. 6994-0
"How many times night's silent queen". Sonnet ("How many times"). William Drummond of Hawthornden. 6908-8
"How many times, as through the rooms I hasten". Ellen M.H. Gates. 6238-5
"How many verticals there are!". Verticals. Helen Danforth Prudden. 6818-9
How many voices gaily sing. Walter Savage Landor. 6110-9, 6092-7,6199-0,6301-2
"How many voices gaily sing" Walter Savage Landor. 6828-6, 6874-X
"How many voices must be echoing in heaven...". You should listen closely, God. Martha A.M. Thoms. 6750-6
"How many will say 'forgive' and find". Alfred Lord Tennyson. 6238-5
How Margrave Rudeger was slain, fr. The Nibelungen lied. Unknown (German) 6372-1
"How many years to Bethlehem?". Christmas, 1940. Ogden Nash. 6761-1
How marigolds came yellow. Robert Herrick. 6125-7
How Maud kept watch. Unknown. 6713-1
How McClellan took Manassas. Unknown. 6946-0
"How menacing the howl is" Keiho Soga. 6981-9
How Mickey got kilt in the war. Unknown. 6922-3
How Mikchik the turtle was false to the master. Unknown (Algonquin Indian) 6864-2
How moracles abound. Clinton Scollard. 6374-8
"How mournful is the silence of night". 'Sean Dana,' sels. Unknown. 6873-1
"How mournfully this burial ground". Lines written in a lonely burial ground... Christopher (John Wilson) North. 6980-0
"How mournfully this burial-ground". Lines written in a lonely burial grounds in...highlands. Christopher (John Wilson) North. 6997-5
"How much am I bid for a proud old wall". Auction. Leone Rice Grelle. 6750-6
"How much do I love thee?". How much do you love me. Mary Ashley Townsend. 7041-8
"How much I loved that way you had". Song of Zahir-u-Din (2). Laurence (Adele Florence Nicolson) Hope. 6856-1
How much do you love me. Mary Ashley Townsend. 7041-8
How much do you love me?. Mary Ashley Townsend. 6226-1
How much of godhood. Louis Untermeyer. 6102-8,6556-2,6250-4,6076-5,6393-4
"How much of memory dwells amidst thy bloom". A thought of the rose. Felicia Dorothea Hemans. 6973-8
"How much so ever in this life's mutations". Unknown. 6238-5
"How much turmoil do you intend to cause me, oh Krnsa" Unknown (Newari) 7013-2
"How much, egregious Moore, are we". To Mr. John Moore. Alexander Pope. 6760-3
"How my heart aches for you". Remembrance ("How my heart aches for you"). Mary Eva (Mrs. Kevin O"Doherty) Kelly. 6174-5
How my song of her began. Philip Bourke Marston. 6656-9
"How nakedly an animal". Humiliation. Winifred Welles. 6880-4
"How near am I now to a happiness." Thomas Middleton. 6317-9
How near to good is what is fair! Ben Jonson. 6600-3,6438-8,6250-4,6189-3
How Nixat made animals. Eda Lou Walton. 6628-3
How Nixat made the ocean. Eda Lou Walton. 6628-3
"How nice a month on moors to pass". Triolets ("How nice"). Cotsford Dick. 6770-0
How no age is content with his own estate. Henry Howard, Earl of Surrey. 6182-6,6586-4,6315-2,6543-0
"How now, Shylock...", fr. The merchant of Venice. William Shakespeare. 6392-6
"How now, shepherd, what means that?". The willow tree. Unknown. 6874-X
"How Oedipous departed, who may tell". The passing of Oedipous, fr. Oedipus. Sophocles. 6987-8
How of the virgin mother shall I sing? Ennodius. 6282-2
"How oft do they tell us that, ah, there's". Blood of our fathers. Brian ("Korongo") Brooke. 6938-X
How oft has the banshee cried. Thomas Moore. 7039-6
"How oft in schoolboy-days, from the school's sway". Frederick Goddard Tuckerman. 6333-0
"How oft some passing word will tend". Mother. Unknown. 6097-8
"How oft the strange magnetic glamour of..sea". The sea-spell. William ("Fiona Macleod") Sharp. 6997-5
"How oft when are at the point of death", fr. Romeo... William Shakespeare. 6879-0
"How oft when men...", fr. Romeo and Juliet. William Shakespeare. 6339-X
"How oft when thou art my music, music play'st". Sonnet 128 ("How oft when thou"). William Shakespeare. 6438-8
"How oft, in my tear-flowing momments...sorrow". Stanzas ("How oft, in my tear-flowing..."). Charles W. Denison. 6755-7
"How oft, when thou, my music, music play'st". William Shakespeare. 6182-6,6198-2,6122-2,6339-X
How often. Ben King. 6089-7,6440-X
"How often have I prayed that I might cease". Moon-wrought tides. Charlotte Blake Loring. 6799-9
"How often I have watched an ocean wave". Limitless supply. Alice Troxwell McCoun. 6799-9
"How often sit I, poring o'er". Arthur Hugh Clough. 6246-5
"How often we forget all time, when alone". Stanzas ("How often"). Edgar Allan Poe. 6333-0
"How often, in this cold and bitter world". Bitter experience. Letitia Elizabeth ("L.E.L.") Landon. 6980-0
"How often, when life's summer day". Friends. Walter Savage Landor. 6832-4
"How often, when life's summer day" Walter Savage Landor. 6828-6
How ofter sit I, fr. Blank misgivings. Arthur Hugh Clough. 6199-0
How old Brown took Harper's Ferry. Edmund Clarence Stedman. 6753-0
How old Brown took Harper's Ferry. Edmund Clarence Stedman. 6008-0,6288-1,6431-0
How old Brown took Harper's Ferry. Edmund Clarence Stedman. 6753-0
How old I have become. David Baker. 6860-X
"How one loves them". The plains. Laurence (Adele Florence Nicolson) Hope. 6856-1
How one winter came in the lake region. William Wilfred Campbell. 6446-9
How one-thumb Willie got his name. John L. Seller. 6870-7
How Oswald dined with God. Edwin Markham. 6162-1,6478-7, 6419-1
"How orient is thy beauty!". Sonnet ("How orient"). Francis Quarles. 6271-7
"How out of whack the city seems". A Vermont appreciation. Daniel L. Cady. 6989-4
"How passing sad! Listen, it sings again". To the nightingale. Frances Anne Kemble. 6980-0
How peace came. Alice Cary. 6865-0;6969-X
How Pearl street was paved. Arthur Guiterman. 6773-5
How Persimmons took cah ob der baby. Unknown. 6913-4
How Persimmons took cah oh der baby. Unknown. 6692-5
"How petty then, the me above you". Sonnet ("How petty"). Clement Wood. 6393-4

HOW
748

"How pitiful are little folk". Willard Wattles. 6289-X
"How pleas'd within my native bowers". The landskip. William Shenstone. 6831-6
"How pleasant is this flowery plain and grove!" Unknown. 6933-9
"How pleasant it is at the end of the day". The way to be happy. Ann and Jane Taylor. 7028-0
How pleasant to know Mr. Lear. Edward Lear. 6722-0,6125-7, 6633-X
"How pleasant to know Mr. Lear!". Lines to a young lady. Edward Lear. 6902-9
"How precious is that one desire". Psalm 027 Bible. 6848-0
"How pretty and neat". Unknown. 6364-0
"How prosperous is this good prince!". The song of the Egyptian minstrel. Unknown (Egyptian). 6879-0
"How pure at heart and sound in head", fr. In memoriam. Alfred Lord Tennyson. 6867-7
"How pure his spirit", fr. The excursion. William Wordsworth. 6867-7
How pussy and mousie kept house. A.C. Kish. 6699-2
How pussy bathes. Unknown. 6699-2
"How quick the change from joy to woe". Written after leaving her at New Burns. William Cowper. 6814-6
"How quiet is the trysting-place". Lily of the valley. William White. 6868-5
"How radiant glow the huge fir-trees there". O Switzerland, how art so fair! Unknown. 6952-5
"How rare the solitude-hour!". Solitude. Edwin E. Deal. 6799-9
"How readily the dreaming mind forgets". Sonnet ("How readily"). Florence Kilpatrick Mixter. 6347-0
How red the rose that is the soldier's wound. Wallace Stevens. 6666-6
How Robin Hood rescued the widow's three sons. Unknown. 6188-5
"How rich the wave, in front, imprest". Lines written near Richmond, upon Thames, at evening. William Wordsworth. 6932-0
"How rich the world in beauty of good dreams!". Good dreams. Owen R. Washburn. 7030-2
"How richly glows the water's breast". Evening by the Thames. William Wordsworth. 6980-0
How roses came red. Robert Herrick. 6198-2,6125-7,6723-9
"How royal is the May time!". May. Staub. 6952-5
"How sacred and how innocent". A country life. Katherine Philips. 6934-7
"How sad and dismal sound the farewells which". Platonic lovers. Sir William Davenant. 6867-7
How sad and gloomy is the world. Do-in. 6852-9
"How sad and solitary now (alas!)". The lamentations of Jeremiah. George Wither. 6848-0
"How sad the note of that funeral drum". On the death of Commodore Oliver H. Perry. John Gardiner Calkins Brainard. 6946-0
"How sad to reflect, when called far away". The soldier's soliloquy. Edward R. Huxley. 6885-5
"How sad's a scorch'd louers fate." Unknown. 6563-5
How Salty win out. Eugene Field. 6949-5
How Salvator won. Ella Wheeler Wilcox. 6671-2,6964-9
How Samson bore away the gates of Gaza. Vachel Lindsay. 6032-3
"How schweed to dhink of home". Home again. Unknown. 6791-3,6823-5
"How season shall be known in...doomed cities". Season in the doomed cities. Edward Weismiller. 6761-1
"How seldom, friend! a good great man inherits". The good' great man. Samuel Taylor Coleridge. 6828-6
"How shall a man fore-doom'd to lone estate". Sonnet ("How shall a man"). Hartley Coleridge. 6545-7
"How shall a man fore-doomed to lone estate" Hartley Coleridge. 6380-2
"How shall I build". Wilfrid Scawen Blunt. 6292-X, 6172-9
How shall I come, sweet love, to thee? Thomas Campion. 6315-2
"How shall I describe my suffering, oh my beloved!" Unknown (Newari) 7013-2
How shall I go? Muriel Strode. 6102-8,6076-5
"How shall I know thee in the sphere which keeps". William Cullen Bryant. 6238-5
"How shall I report". John Skelton. 6187-7

How shall I sing? Frederick C. Boden. 6542-2
"How shall a man or woman pass unstirred?". A shilling each. Norman Gale. 6785-9
"How shall I dare to speak of her". 'My lady of the south'. Sannie Metelerkamp. 6800-6
"'...How shall I find you, oh, my dear?'". The way. Coletta Ryan. 6799-9
"How shall I fitly delineate Jimmy". J. K. Berton Braley. 6853-7
"How shall I learn to live with...strange love". Sonnet ("How shall I"). Florence Kilpatrick Mixter. 6347-0
"How shall I report". In praise of Johanna Scroope. John Skelton. 6830-8
"How shall I say good-bye to you...". Envoi. Edward de Stein. 7029-9
"How shall I say it when we have never had...". Message. Sarah Litsey. 6761-1
"How shall I weave what spires in my breast". Kirman weaves the first prayer-rug. Ethel M. Feuerlicht. 6847-2
"How shall I woo thee, sweetest...?". To health, fr. Contemplation. Richard Gifford. 6934-7
"How shall the harp of poesy regain". The scared harp. Felicia Dorothea Hemans. 6973-8
"How shall the heart measure its rich content". Life. E. DeVilliers-Hertzler. 6818-9
How shall they sleep? Eloise Hamilton. 6224-5
How shall we honor them? Edwin Markham. 6420-5
"How shall we know it is the last good-bye?". The last good-bye. Louise Chandler Moulton. 7041-8
"How shall we open the door of spring". The door of spring. Ethelwyn Wetherald. 6797-2
How shall we rise to greet the dawn? Osbert Sitwell. 6730-1
"How shall we say 'God rest him!'". Of him who loved not rest. Helen Gray Cone. 6995-9
How shall we tell an angel. Gertrude Hall. 6431-0
"How shall you ever know the adoration". For a word. William Alexander Percy. 6777-8
How she cured him. Unknown. 6744-1,6167-2
"How she would have loved". Lament. Thomas Hardy. 6879-0
"How short, sweet flower, have..thy beauties..". On a rose. Felicia Dorothea Hemans. 6973-8
How should I be so pleasant? Sir Thomas Wyatt. 6315-2,6584-3
"How should I catch, O birch, your...grace". White birch. Gertrude Darling. 6764-6
"How should I praise theise sug'red plenties." Unknown. 6563-5
How should I your true love know. Sir Walter Raleigh. 6934-7
"How should I your true love know", fr. Hamlet. William Shakespeare. 6134-6,6187-7,6271-7,6328-4,6189-3,6153
How Siegfried was slain, fr. Nibelungen lied. Unknown (Middle High German) 6679-8
"How should my lord come home to his lands?". Dirge. Maurice Hewlett. 6872-3
"How silent are the trees in winter's grasp!". Dover road - midnight. John Starie. 6764-6
How silent they who die. Milan Dedinac. 6068-4
"How silently, how silently." Phillips Brooks. 6225-3
How Sir Richard died. George Walter Thornbury. 6980-0
"How simple in their grandeur are the forms". Lines written at Needles Hotel, Alum Bay, Isle of Wight. Sir Thomas Noon Talfourd. 6980-0
How sleep the brave. William Collins. 6186-9,6424-8,6102-8, 6328-4,6502-3,6114 ,6304-7,6421-3,6131-1,6219-9,6301-2,6601 ,6240-7,6395-0,6323-3,6340-3,6427-2,6479-5, 6504-X,6302-0,6385-3,6239-3,6889-8
How sleep the brave. William H. Monk. 6889-8
"How sleep the brave who sink to rest". Ode ("How sleep the brave"). William Collins. 6228-8,6271-7,6250-4, 6430-2,6438-4,6242 ,6024-2,6473-6,6315-2
'How sleep the brave'. Walter De La Mare. 7026-4
"How slow yon tiny vessel ploughs the main!". The Pilgrims. Lydia Huntly Sigourney. 6752-2
"How small a tooth hath mined the season's...". Frost. Edith Matilda Thomas. 7041-8
How soap was first made. Unknown. 6684-4
"How soon hath time the subtle thief of youth." John

Milton. 6187-7,6536-8,6430-2,6301-2,6645-3
"How soon hath time the subtle thief of youth". Sonnet ("How soon hath time"). John Milton. 6315-2,6563-5, 6383-7,6023-4,6214-8
"How soon the prophet stars decree". The danger. Norman Gale. 6872-3
"How spoke the ing, in his crucial hour...". King of the Belgians. Marion Couthouy Smith. 6946-0
How spring came to New York. Hermann Hagedorn. 6032-3
How spring comes at Craigville. Edmund H. Garrett. 6798-0
How spring comes in Georgia. Thomas Caldecot Chubb. 6042-0
How springs came first. Robert Herrick. 6092-7
How springs comes to Shasta Jim. Henry Van Dyke. 6961-4
How stands the glass around. James Wolfe. 6088-9
How stands the glass around? Unknown. 6328-4,6271-7
How stands the glass around? James Wolfe. 6753-0
"How stealthily their feet upon the floor". The dance. Edna St. Vincent Millay. 6959-2
"How stern is March, with blasts that warn...". March. Edgar Fawcett. 6965-7
"How still earth lies! - behind the pines". The reaper. James Matthewes Leagre. 7017-5
"How still it is! I seem to hear the heart". Sarah Litsey. 6761-1
"How still the sea! behold; how calm the sky!". Pastoral landscape. Ambrose Philips. 6932-0
"How strange a fate in love is mine!". Sonnet ("How strange a fate"). Luis de Camoens [or Camoes]. 6973-8
"How strange a thing is bread". Unknown. 6149-4
"How strange if it should fall to you". Palestine. Katharine (Hinkson) Tynan. 7029-9
"How strange it is that I can live to-day". Death's jest book, sel. Thomas Lovell Beddoes. 6958-4
How strange it will be. Frank E. Holliday. 6620-8
"How strange that the nature of light...". The constellation, fr. Texas. Henry Van Dyke. 6961-4
"How strange the sculptures...", fr. Divina commedia. Henry Wadsworth Longfellow. 6536-8
"How strange today has been, at least, today". Portrait of an afternoon. Joyce Lancaster. 6850-2
How strange you are, fr. Paterson. William Carlos Williams. 6399-3
"How sweet 'tis to stroll by...Demurrer". Trills for term-time. Unknown. 6878-2
"How sweet I roam'd from field to field". William Blake. 6187-7,6208-3,6733-6
"How sweet and lovely dost thou make the shame". Sonnet 095 ("How sweet and lovely"). William Shakespeare. 6560-0
"How sweet I roamed from field to field". Song ("How sweet"). William Blake. 6086-2,6430-2,6560-0,6659-3, 6383-7,6371 ,6086-2,6383-7,6371-3,6659-3,6560-0,6430 ,6102-8,6232-6,6423-X,6726-3,6125-7,6195
"How sweet in winter time we feign the spring". Unknown. 6238-5
"How sweet is the season, the sky how serene". Song ("How sweet is the season..."). Jonathan Odell. 6753-0
How sweet is the shepherd's sweet lot. William Blake. 6228-8
How sweet it is. William Wordsworth. 6328-4
"How sweet only yo delight in lambs". Sonnet ("How sweet"). Rex E. Warner. 6317-9
"How sweet she sprawls...a living animal". A good sight of Andromeda. Milton Acorn. 6767-0
"How sweet that valley, clothed in...green". At the convent near Saint Gall. James Cochrane. 6749-2
How sweet the answer echo makes. Thomas Moore. 6328-4
"How sweet the moonlight...", fr. Merchant of Venice. William Shakes eare. 6138-9,6183-9,6395-0,6501-5, 6214-8
"How sweet the name of Jesus sounds!" John Newton. 6302-0, 6219-9
"How sweet the tuneful bells responsive peal". Ostend. William Lisle Bowles. 7015-9
"How sweet the tuneful bells' responsive peal!". Sonnet at Ostend, June 22, 1787. William Lisle Bowles. 6932-0
How sweet this lone vale. Andrew Erskine. 6180-X
"How sweet to mark the softened ray". Sea piece by moonlight. Felicia Dorothea Hemans. 6973-8

"How sweet to softly-cushioned baby ears". Always with song. Mary B. Ward. 6750-6
"How sweetly doth my master sound! My master!". The odour. George Herbert. 6933-9
"How sweetly on the wood-girt town". Pentucket. John Greenleaf Whittier. 6753-0,6946-0
"How sweetly shines through azure skies". Oscar of Alva. George Gordon, 6th Baron Byron. 6945-2
"How swift and silent pass the ages". A word for each month. Clark Jillson. 6913-4
"How swift, in the white of night...". Night driving. Valentine Ackland. 6761-1
"How swiftly pass a thousand years". The ages. John Sterling. 6980-0
How swiftly the bright coins of thought. Amory Hare. 6347-0
"How tears became a water". Mary of Magdala. Geraldine Little. 6822-7
"How tender was the step, fair day". Yesterday. Edward Farquhar. 6939-8
"How that vast heaven intitled first is rolled." William Drummond of Hawthornden. 6182-6
How the age of children is the happiest... Henry Howard, Earl of Surrey. 6533-3
How the babies grow. Jennie Carroll. 6629-1
How the bees came by their sting. Carlotta Perry. 6923-1
How the brook went to mill. Benjamin Franklin Taylor. 6815-4
How the cats went to boarding school. Unknown. 6410-8
How the Christ-flower bloomed. Nora Archibald Smith. 6807-3
".How the cry of a bird can stir us," fr. Sonnets to Orpheus. Rainer Maria Rilke. 6068-4
How the Cumberland went down. Silas Weir Mitchell. 6074-9
How the daughters came at Dunoon. Henry Cholmondeley-Pennell. 6089-7
How the dimples came. Unknown. 6629-1
How the drunkard goes down to the tomb. Unknown. 6716-6
How the fifty-first took the bridge. Jeff. H. Nones. 6923-1
How the flowers grow. Gabriel (Thomas Nicoll Hepburn) Setoun. 6132-X
How the flowers grow. Unknown. 6720-4
How the gates came ajar. Helen Louise Barron Bostwick. 6404-3,6682-8,8889-8
How the gates came ajar. Unknown. 6127-3,6424-8
How the gentlemen do after marriage. Unknown. 6408-6
How the great guest came. Edwin Markham. 6214-8,6072-2
How the great master showed himself a great smoker. Unknown (Algonquin Indian) 6864-2
How the Indians lost their power. Unknown (Algonquin Indian) 6864-2
"How the hot revel's fever dies". Under the stars, fr. Studies for pictures. Bayard Taylor. 6976-2
How the king lost his crown. John Townsend Trowbridge. 6921-5
How the laurel went to church. Emily A. Braddock. 6965-7
How the lawyers got a patron saint. John Godfrey Saxe. 6878-2
How the lawyers got a patron saint. John Godfrey Saxe. 6064-1,6414-0
How the leaves came. Sarah ("Susan Coolidge") Woolsey. 6135-4,6639-9
How the leaves came down. Sarah ("Susan Coolidge") Woolsey. 6049-8,6373-X,6479-5,6519-8
How the little kite learned to fly. Katharine Pyle. 6638-0
How the little kite learned to fly. Unknown. 6401-9
How the master found the summer. Unknown (Algonquin Indian) 6864-2
How the mighty have fallen, fr. Samuel. Bible. 6665-8
How the Mohawks set out for Medoctec. Sir Charles George Douglas Roberts. 6591-0,6592-9
"How the mountains talked together". A farewell to Agassiz. Oliver Wendell Holmes. 6753-0
How the old horse won the bet. Oliver Wendell Holmes. 6142-7,6392-6,6288-1,6126-5,6419-1,6288-1
How the organ was paid for. Kate A. Bradley. 6672-0
How the parson broke the sabbath. Unknown. 6414-0
"How the people held their breath when they heard...". Unknown. 6059-5

HOW

How the question came home. Unknown. 6745-X
How the ransom was paid. Unknown. 6451-5
How the refugees were saved. Ellen Knight Bradford. 6928-2
How the revival came. Margaret J. Bidwell. 6680-1
"How the river cools your blood is...". Autobiography, chapter XVII: floating the big piney. Jim Barnes. 7005-1
How the soul doth exercise her powers in the body. Sir John Davies. 6584-8
How the water comes down at Lodore. Robert Southey. 6543-0
How the water comes down at Lowdore, sels. William Wordsworth. 6484-1
How the week goes. Kate West. 6529-5
How the wind blows. Unknown. 6373-X
How the women will stop war, fr. Lysistrata. Aristophanes. 6658-8,6665-8
"How then the winged splendours round us tower". Sonnet ("How then the winged"). Conrad Aiken. 6783-2
How they brought the good news from Ghent to Aix. Robert Browning. 6014-5,6101-X,6133-8,6136-2,6228-8,6239-, 6046-3,6102-8,6110-9,6131-1,6197-4,6419 ,6134-6,6198-2,6332-2,6478-7,6610-0,6657-,6219-9,6263-6,6267-9, 6396-9,6510-4,6585 ,6242-3,6271-7,6302-0,6385-3,6339-X,6401-,6438-8,6424-8,6518-X,6543-0,6560-0,6655 , 6425-6,6457-4,6473-6,6479-5,6501-5,6504-,6196-6,6383-7,6371-3,6639-9,6656-9,6512-0,6521-X,6534-1,6552-X, 6606-2,6732-
How they caught the panther. Alfred J. Hough. 6674-7
How they died at Thansi. Miss Murray. 6591-0,6592-9
"How they go hurrying/How they go scurrying!". The ski-journey. Bjornstjerne Bjornson. 7035-3
How they pop the question. Unknown. 6064-1
How they sleep. Unknown. 6452-3,6135-4
"How this uncouth enchanted" Edward Estlin Cummings. 6531-7
How Thomas Wolsey did arise vnto great authority... Unknown. 6586-4
How three were made one. Unknown. 6936-3
How time consumeth all earthly things. Thomas Proctor. 6182-6,6125-7
"How tired I am! I sink down all alone". An out-worn Sappho. James Whitcomb Riley. 6992-4
How to ask and have. Samuel Lover. 6089-7
How to be a great writer. Charles Bukowski. 6998-3
"How to bring light into this spider-world?". Thers is no one still living who remembers where... James Pendergast. 6821-9
How to catch a bird. Leland B. Jacobs. 6510-4
How to catch unicorns. William Rose Benet. 6162-1
How to cure a cough. Unknown. 6064-1,6408-6
How to deal with new-laid eggs. Unknown. 6629-1
How to eat a watermelon. Frank Lebby Stanton. 6089-7,6719-4
How to find Easter. Unknown. 6720-4
How to find your way home. Mario Petaccia. 6870-7
How to go and forget. Edwin Markham. 6250-4
"How to labour and find it sweet". Labour and life. James Herbert Morse. 7041-8
How to live. Horatius Bonar. 6240-7
How to look when speaking. Elizabeth Turner. 6105-2
How to make a man of consequence. Mark Lemon. 6089-7
How to make a novel. Lord Charles Neaves. 6996-7
How to make a whistle. Unknown. 6047-1,6049-8,6684-4
How to remember Easter date. Fannie E. Newberry. 6720-4
How to serve my country. Louise Pollock. 6523-6
How to take off your clothes at a picnic. Bill Manhire. 7018-3
How to tell the wild animals. Carolyn Wells. 6534-1
How to tell the wild flowers. Carolyn Wells. 6739-5
How to the singer comes the song? Richard Watson Gilder. 6730-1
"How to weave your web of medicinal flesh...". Big fine woman from Ruleville. Jayne Cortez. 6898-7
How to write a letter. Elizabeth Turner. 6105-2
How Tom saved the train. George Birdseye. 6672-0
"How trifling shall these gifts appear". With two spoons for two spoons. Eugene Field. 6949-5
"How troublesome is day!". Proemium of an epic. Thomas Love Peacock. 6802-2
How two birdies kept house in a shoe. Unknown. 6314-4

"How vain, the world's artillery of words". Verba de verbo vitae. Armel O'Connor. 6799-9
"How vainly men themselves amaze" Andrew Marvell. 7020-5
"How vastly pleasing is my tale". Blessings on Doneraile. Patrick O'Kelly. 6930-4
How very modern. Thomas Moore. 6083-8
"How very sad it is to think". Poor brother. Unknown. 6902-9
How violets came blue. Robert Herrick. 6194-X
"How was it that you came to be". Queries. Clara Keck Heflebower. 6906-1
"How was it then with nature when the soul". The death of Bryant. Edmund Clarence Stedman. 7041-8
How we beat the captain's colt. Campbell Rae-Brown. 6681-X
How we beat the favourite. Adam Lindsay Gordon. 6427-2, 6518-X,6656-9,6681-X
How we became a nation. Harriet Prescott Spofford. 6946-0
How we burned the "Philadelphia". Barrett Eastman. 6062-5, 6274-1
How we celebrated. Zitella Cocke. 6715-8
How we fought the fire. Will Carleton. 7002-7
How we harnassed the horse. Maria Louise Pool. 6686-0
How we kept the day. Will Carleton. 6155-9
How we killed the rooster. Unknown. 6926-0
How we learn. Horatius Bonar. 6240-7,6214-8
How we papooses plant flowers. Vachel Lindsay. 6206-7
"How we photographed/ourselves". Reflections. Miriam Waddington. 6767-0
How we played King William. Jeannie Pendleton Ewing. 6928-2
How we ran in the black warrigal horse... E.G. Millard. 6768-9
"How well my eyes remember the dim path". Elegy ("How well"). Robert Bridges. 6487-6
"How well the soul responds". Friend. Marjorie Dugdale Ashe. 6799-9
"How well those words recall the yarn". 'And seven more redskins bit the dusts' Quincy Kilby. 7007-8
"How wild, how witch-like weird that life...". The wonder of it. Harriet Monroe. 6897-9
How will it seem?. Charles Hanson Towne. 6653-4,6542-2
"How will you manage". Princess Daihaku. 7039-6
"How winneth liberty? By sword and brand". Liberty. Edith M. Thomas. 7022-1
How wise are the flowers! Ethel Romig Fuller. 6750-6
"How wonderful is death". Death and sleep. Percy Bysshe Shelley. 6980-0
"How wonderful is death". Percy Bysshe Shelley. 6407-8
"How wonderful is death,/Death and his...". The daemon of the world, sel. Percy Bysshe Shelley. 6958-4
How wonderful thou art! Frederick William Faber. 6461-2
"How wondrously the next-door man has grown". Town garden. Dorothy Roberts. 6776-X
How worlds and seasons turn. Elinor Lennen. 6316-0
"How would Willie like to go". The land of thus-and-so. James Whitcomb Riley. 7002-7
"How would you have us, as we are?". To America, sel. James Weldon Johnson. 6954-1
"How wretched is he borne or taught." Unknown. 6563-5
"How wretched is the fate of those who write!". Prologue to The pilgrim, revived.. our author's benefit. John Dryden. 6970-3
"How wretched is ye state wee all are in." Unknown. 6563-5
"How young you look! It was not long ago". On a photograph of myself as a boy. J.R. Ackerley. 6776-X
"How! butler, how!". Fill the bowl, butler! Unknown. 6881-2
'How' and 'how'. Vachel Lindsay. 6206-7
The 'how' and the 'why'. Alfred Lord Tennyson. 6977-0
How's my boy? Sydney Dobell. 6097-8,6136-2,6239-3,6302-0, 6385-3,6627-5,6656-9,6543-0,6102-8,6424-8
How's my boy? Sydney Dobell. 6833-2,6910-X
How's my boy?. Sydney Dobell. 6097-8,6344-6
"'How's things? says I'". The way to do. Edgar A. Guest. 6862-6

How, Louis
    A silly song. 6441-8

How, William Walsham
    Behold, I stand at the door and knock. 6219-9
    For all the saints. 6337-3

Funeral hymn. 6730-1
Lord Jesus, when stand afar. 6144-3
O word of God incarnate. 6337-3
We give thee but thine own. 6337-3
"How, my dear Mary, are you critic-bitten". The witch of
    Atlas. Percy Bysshe Shelley. 6828-6
"How/many/years/after". Copyright. Erich Fried. 6769-7
"How/Then/Distinquish". Query. Unknown. 6750-6
How?. Lee Spencer. 6954-1
Howard Lamson. Edgar Lee Masters. 6300-4,6375-6
Howard, Blanche Willis
The popular poplar tree. 6049-8
Howard, Clara M.
The ghost of lone rock. 6675-5
Howard, Elizabeth F.
The way. 6461-2
Howard, Frances Minturn
Foundation. 6979-7
Martyr. 6979-7
Wrist watch. 6879-0
Howard, Geoffrey
The beach road by the wood. 7026-4
"Gratias ago." 6374-8
Howard, Gordon
Spring. 6850-2
Howard, Henry. See Surrey, Earl of
Howard, Hugh
Brandy and soda. 6273-3
Howard, Joy
For the frozen girl, Jean Hilliard, and Wally Nelson...
    6900-2
Howard, Katharine
The little god. 6338-1
Sweet peas. 6143-5
Howard, Mary
Autumn hunter. 6857-X
Howard, Miss
Jepthah's rash vow. 6407-8
Howard, Norman
A Christmas-tide shadow. 6925-8
Howard, Philip
Hymn ("O Christ, the glorious crown.") 6022-6
Howard, Robert E.
Earth-born. 6218-0
The sands of time. 6218-0
Howard, Sara Alice
Sonnet to Shakespeare. 6750-6
Howard, Sir Robert
The conjurer's song, fr. The Indian queen. 6328-4
I attempt from love's sickness, fr. The Indian queen.
    6328-4
To the unconstant Cynthia. 6563-5
Howard, Susan E.
The jubilee of the flowers. 6677-1
Howard, W. S.
A Purim retrospect. 6848-0
Howard, William
A letter from Santa Claus. 6147-8
Howard; 1st Earl of Arundel, Philip
A lament for Our Lady's shrine at Walsingham. 6641-0
"Through thy cross and passion." 6489-2
Howarth, Ellen Clementine
Thou wilt never grow old. 6304-7
Howarth, George R.
Room for you. 6411-6
Howarth, R.G.
Elegy. 6349-7
Howath, Ellen C.
'Tis but a little faded flower. 6632-1
Howdy, Mr. Winter. Wilbur Dick Nesbit. 6401-9
The howe o' the mearns. Violet Jacob. 6395-0
Howe remembraunce made his epytaphy on his grave. Stephen
    Hawes. 6193-1
"Howe'er I turn, or whereso'er I tread". Reproof: a
    satire. Tobias George Smollett. 6975-4
"Howe'er it be, it seems to me". Alfred Lord Tennyson.
    6889-8
"Howe'er it be, it seems to me." Alfred Lord Tennyson.
    6225-3
"Howe'er the uneasy world is vexed...",fr. Casa Guidi.

Elizabeth Barrett Browning. 6123-0
Howe, Charles H.
Accompanied thus. 6799-9
Howe, D.N.
The good shepherd. 6964-9
Howe, Ed
Instead of loving your enemies. 6736-0
Howe, Joseph
Our fathers. 6433-7
Howe, Julia Ward
Battle hymn of the republic. 6014-5,6102-8,6134-6,6165-
    6,6243-4,6302-,6077-3,6113-3,6239-3,6240-7,6337-3,
    6459-,6260-1,6427-2,6471-X,6552-X,6600-3,6605-,6289-
    X,6340-3,6385-3,6399-3,6418-3,6437-,6473-6,6486-8,
    6496-5,6552-X,6589-9,6623-,6610-0,6632-1,6693-3,6730-
    1,6732-8,6735-,6470-1,6088-9,6431-0,6560-0,6250-4,
    6008-0,6016-2,6288-1,6442-6,6214-8,6219-9,6736-0,
    6300-4,6114-1,6121-4,6737-9,6214-8,6219-9,6263-6,
    6267-9,6309-8,6639-9,6304-7,5668-6,6424-8,6438-8,
    6076-5,6309-8,6639-9,6304-7,5668-6,6424-8,6438-8,
    6076-5
The city of my love. 6331-4,6439-6
Crown his bloodstained pillow. 6305-5,6524-4
The dead Christ. 6271-7
The flag. 6223-7,6438-8
Hamlet at the Boston. 6358-6
Ideals for our country. 6461-2
J.A.G. 6946-0
Lincoln ("Through the dim pageant of the years"). 6465-
    5,6524-4
The message of peace. 6386-1
Our country. 6473-6
Our orders. 6735-2
Pardon. 6524-4
Parricide. 6524-4
Robert E. Lee. 6074-9,6465-5,6265-2
The royal guest. 6085-4,6302-2,6385-3
The summons. 6735-2
A tribute to a servant, sels. 6600-3
Howe, M.A. DeWolfe
At the heart. 6051-X
A birthday verse. 6006-4
Fire of apple-wood. 6051-X
The helmsman. 6051-X
The known soldier. 6051-X,6542-2
Pacifists. 6051-X
Pocket and steeple. 6722-0
The sailor-man. 6443-4
A treasure house. 6051-X
Vale-atque salve. 6051-X
The valiant. 6006-4
Howe, Martha C.
The knight and the page. 7002-7
Howe, William Walsham
Funeral hymn. 6214-8
Howel's song. Felicia Dorothea Hemans. 6973-8
Howel, Laurence
Moses' song. 6848-0
Howell, Elizabeth Lloyd
Milton's prayer. 6337-3
Milton's prayer for peace. 6730-1,6735-1
Milton's prayer in blindness. 6600-3
Milton's prayer of patience. 6219-9
Howell, James
Of London Bridge. 6125-7
Opinion. 6294-6
Stanzas for Lent. 6528-7
Upon black eyes, and becoming frowns. 6563-5
Upon Dr. Davies' British grammar. 6528-7
Words ("Words are the soul's ambassadors, who go").
    6294-6
Howell, John
Cantata, sels. 6768-9
Howell, Laurence
Deborah's triumphant song. 6848-0
Howell, Margery
Mine is the choice. 6761-1
Howell, Pansy E.
The cost. 6799-9
Howell, Thomas

HOWELL

Manslyfe likened to a stage play. 6586-4
Of misery. 6182-6
Of the golden worlde. 6586-4
Rewarde doth not alwayes aunswere deserte. 6586-4
The rose ("Whenas the mildest month"). 6182-6,646-1, 6528-7
To the reader. 6586-4
When he thought himself condemned. 6182-6
Who would have thought. 6182-6
A winter's morning muse. 6586-4

Howells, Mildred
God's will. 6027-7
Going too far. 6331-4,6496-5,6439-6
A moral in Sevres. 6441-8
"Oh, little country of my heart." 6331-4,6439-6
"Oh, tell me how my garden grows." 6338-1,6649-6
There is pansies. 6266-0

Howells, William Dean
Avery. 7041-8
The battle in the clouds. 6113-3
Before the gate. 6429-9,6600-3,6670-4,6321-7
The bewildered guest. 6102-8,6076-5
By the sea. 6997-5
Calvary. 6144-3
Caprice. 6429-9,6026-9,6321-7,6652-6
Change. 6431-0
Dead. 7041-8
Earliest spring. 6007-2,6437-X
Experience. 6006-4
Faith. 6337-3,6730-1
Forlorn. 7041-8
From generation to generation. 6467-1
Gone. 6066-8
Heredity. 6102-8,6732-8,6076-5
Hope. 6431-0
If. 6309-8,6431-0
In August. 6239-7,6243-1,6465-5
In earliest spring. 6467-1
Judgment day. 6467-1
Louise, the slave. 6706-9
The mysteries. 6240-7
The passengers of a retarded submersible. 7026-4
The pilot's story. 6412-4,6550-3
The poets friends. 7041-8
prayer ("Lord, for the erring"). 6303-9,6418-3,6730-1
Saint Christopher. 6624-0
Society. 6954-1
Sometimes, when after spirited debate. 6300-4
The song the oriole sings. 6597-X
Thanksgiving. 6006-4
Thanksgiving. 7041-8
The thorn. 6004-8
Through the meadow. 7041-8
The undiscovered country. 6337-3,6214-8
What shall it profit? 6309-8

"The hower is come in wch I must resigne." Unknown. 6563-5
"The hower of sleepy night decayes apace". The mountebank's mask, sel. Thomas Campion. 6958-4

Howerton, Virgie Rucker
The autumn stroll. 6906-1
Love keeps strange time. 6906-1
prayer ("O Holy Father"). 6906-1
They tell me of you. 6906-1
When the pregnant earth shall hold me. 6906-1

Howes, Barbara
L'Ile du Levant: the nudist colony. 6388-8
The triumph of chastity. 6388-8
The triumph of death. 6388-8

Howes, Grace Clementine
Winged mariner. 6833-2

"However much man may philander". Monogamy. Berton Braley. 6853-7
"However we wrangled with Britain awhile". Literary importation. Philip Freneau. 6753-0
"However, I still think, will all due deference". George Gordon, 6th Baron Byron. 7025-6

Howie, Robert G.
The tanker. 6237-7

Howitt, Mary
April. 6456-6
The barley-mowers' song. 6334-9
The beaver. 6510-4
Birds in summer. 6496-5,6519-8,6304-7,6135-4,6131-1, 6156-6
Birds in summer, sels. 6334-9,6156-6
The broom flower. 6271-7,6302-0,6385-3,6424-8
Buttercups and daisies. 6127-3,6479-5,6529-5,6638-0, 6135-4,6114-1,6131-1
The camel. 6131-1
The child's hymn. 6502-3
The children's appeal. 6502-3
The coming of spring. 6242-3,6530-9
Corn-fields. 6127-3,6271-7,6519-8,6597-X,6656-9
The dragon-fly. 6131-1
The fairies of the caldon low. 6127-3,6132-X,6242-3, 6271-7,6356-X,6496-5,6424-8,6131-1,6219-9,6456-6, 6639-9,6638-0,6249-0,6502-3,6519-8,6614-3,6623-2
Father is coming. 6078-1,6127-3,6459-0,6131-1
The flax flower. 6373-X,6519-8
"Heart's ease! One could look for half a day..." 6049-8
The heron. 6639-9
The humming bird. 6466-3,6459-0,6135-4
The lion. 6131-1
Little children. 6519-8
Little streams. 6271-7
Mabel on midsummer day. 6502-3,6131-1
The monkey. 6239-3,6373-X,6529-5
Mountain children. 6233-4
The northern seas. 6502-3
"O life! what after-joy hast thou." 6066-8
The oak tree. 6049-8,6456-6
Old Christmas. 6239-3,6502-3,6456-6,6131-1,6424-8
The rich and the poor. 7009-4
The sea fowler. 6656-9
The sea-gull. 6242-3
September. 6135-4
The silkworm. 6131-1
The sparrow's nest. 6134-6,6242-3,6373-X,6131-1,6456-6
The spider and the fly. 6459-0,6639-9,6638-0,6424-8, 6304-7,6105-2,6127-3,6242-3,6373-X,6401-9,6497-3, 6131-1,6456-6,6131-1
Spring. 6304-7
The squirrel. 6131-1
Summer woods. 6373-X,6623-2,6131-1
Sweet summer. 6529-5
Tibbie Inglis. 6600-3
The use of flowers. 6049-8,6302-0,6373-X,6385-3,6502-3, 6219-9,6304-7,6131-1,6629-1
The voice of spring. 6519-8
The voice of the grass. 6183-4,6373-X,6456-6
The voyage with the Nautilus. 6518-X
The wood-mouse. 6638-0,6510-4

Howitt, Mary (tr.)
The heavenly dove. Frederika Bremer, 6424-8
A little brawl. Frederika Bremer, 6424-8

Howitt, William
The birthday of Washington ever honored. 6171-0,6712-3
The departure of the swallow. 6302-0,6385-3,6600-3,6656-9
The grey squirrels. 6638-0
The northern seas. 6239-3,6639-9
A summer moon. 6385-3
The wind in a frolic. 6114-1,6131-1,6105-2,6242-3,6496-5,6519-8,6502-3

"Howl, ye ships of Tarshish". Ululate naves. Bible. 6830-8

Howland, Louis
Fleet Street. 6793-X

Howland, Mary Woolsey
First spring flowers. 6385-3
In the hospital. 6243-1,6337-3,6471-X
"Now I lay me down to sleep." 6078-1,6385-3
The picket guard. 6403-5
Rest. 6240-7,6424-8,6737-9

Howling of the witches. Charles Godfrey Leland. 6696-8
"The howling, shrieking, wild north wind". The north wind. Lucile S. Kappeler. 6906-1

Howslister, Mary
There are many flags. 6158-3

The Hoyden.. Elizabeth Turner. 6105-2

Hoyland, John S.

For the new year. 6490-6
A prayer for brotherhood. 6337-3
A prayer for family love 6337-3
Prayer for our home. 6337-3
Hoyle, W.
I'll take what father gives. 6408-6,6617-8
Hoyne, Henry William
The kings. 6542-2
Hoynton, John
Why the cows came late. 6672-0
Hoyt, Charles Sumner
The Bowery. 6736-0
Is this the time to halt? 6335-7,6337-3
Hoyt, Helen
The bride and the matron. 6038-2
Comparison. 6880-4
The dancer. 6959-2
Day's end. 6777-8
Difference. 6628-3
Ellis Park. 6101-X,6374-8,6476-0,6497-3,6556-2,6336-5,
  6653-4,6628-3,6497-3,6556-2,6101-X,6374-8,6476-0,
  6497-3,6556-2
Flirtation. 6628-3
Gravid. 6038-2
Green shadows. 7030-2
Hands. 6628-3
Homage. 6019-6,6393-4
In the park. 6019-6
The inextinguishable. 6628-3
Lamp posts. 6808-1
Let me be a star. 6628-3
Let me keep your hand. 6628-3
Like a cloud, like a mist. 6019-6
The lover sings of a garden. 6880-4
The lover sings of a garden. 6897-9
Menaia. 6880-4
The new-born. 6102-8,6102-8,6076-5
October letter. 6628-3
October letter. 6777-8
The office building. 6628-3
Old. 6302-0,6385-3,6632-1
Pine-cones burning. 6628-3
Poem to be danced. 6959-2
Rain at night. 6628-3
Red cloud of dawning. 6628-3
Rune of the forest fire. 6628-3
The sense of death. 6619-4
Since I have felt the sense of death. 6897-9
Telephoning. 6628-3
To Helen of Troy. 6781-6
Two love poems. 6777-8
Weather. 6880-4
Wonder and joy. 6102-8
Your father walked these hills. 6628-3
Hoyt, Jacqueline
Ancient night. 6850-2
Envy. 6850-2
From a lover. 6850-2
To you. 6850-2
Hoyt, Ralph
Snow - a winter sketch. 6302-0,6385-3
The tour of St. Nicholas. 6131-1
The world for sale. 6409-4,6606-2
Hoyt, W. F.
To the spectroscope. 6818-9
Hrolf's thrall, his song. Willard Wattles. 6761-1
Hrolf's thrall-his song. Willard Wattles. 6032-3,6556-2
Hryciuk, Marshall
On the passing of Heidegger. 6767-0
Hsi, Shu
Hot cake. Arthur Waley (tr.). 6106-0
The hub. Oscar Williams. 6337-3
Hubbard, Elizabeth Ingram
The Catholic psalm. 6411-6
Hubbard, Marion
"Blyther than the burnie." 6116-8
Hubbell, Lindley Williams
Advice. 6039-0
Never believe. 6039-0
Nightmare, with moral. 6751-4

Poem ("I wish for a poem"). 6751-4
So for the little while. 6039-0
Hubbell, Rose Strong
If I could dis like a rabbit. 6338-1
The mangroves dance. 6374-8
Hubbub in Hub. Laurence McKinney. 6722-0
Hubenette, Jackie
On pines and needles. 6857-X
Huch, Ricarda
Deep in the heavens. 6643-7
Huckel, Oliver
Peace hymn for the American republic. 6143-5
Peace hymn for the American republics. 6143-5
Huckfield, Leyland
Avon memories. 6033-1
The sons of Dan. 7007-8
Huddesford, J.
The obedient dog. 6018-8
"Huddled chimneys grey, forlorn". Gardens of Babylon.
Laura Benet. 6880-4
"Huddled there on the sidewalk is heartbreak". Evicted.
Beatrice M. Murphy. 7024-8
Hudeburg, C.E.
At colon. 6640-2
October Coney Island. 6640-2
Passage of spring. 6640-2
Poem ("So sleep"). 6640-2
Recluse. 6640-2
Till death. 6640-2
Trinity churchyard. 6640-2
Hudgins, Andrew
Late spring in the nuclear age. 7032-9
Hudibras and the Presbyterians, fr. Hudibras. Samuel
Butler. 6637-2
Hudibras' sword and dagger. Samuel Butler. 6302-0;6385-3
Hudibras' weapon and charger, fr. Hudibras. Samuel Butler.
6637-2
Hudibras, sels. Samuel Butler. 6637-2,6102-8,6188-5,6198-2,
6208-3,6315-2,6562-,6192-3,6195-0,6152-4,6637-2,6378-
0,6732
Hudnut Jr., William H.
No prisoner of time. 6144-3
Hudnut Sr., William H.
"In him ye are made full." 6144-3
Hudson. Arthur Guiterman. 6773-5
Hudson River. Thomas William Parsons. 6484-1
Hudson's cove. John Maher Murphy. 6017-X
Hudson's voyage. Arthur Guiterman. 6503-1
Hudson, Addie Cropsey
The land where the cowboy crows. 6836-7
Other men's dogs. 6836-7
The singing trail. 6836-7
The vision and the pen. 6836-7
Hudson, H.R.
The newsboy's debt. 6914-2
Hudson, S.A.
Truant. 6373-X
Hudson, Thomas
Jack Robinson. 6547-3
Hudson, W.H.
Peach blossoms. 6253-9
The Hudson. Oliver Wendell Holmes. 6126-5
Hue and cry after Chloris. Unknown. 6250-4
Hue and cry after Christmas. Unknown. 6145-1
A hue and cry after fair Amoret. William Congreve. 6932-0
A hue and cry after fair amoret. William Congreve. 6732-8
Huerta, Efrain
Recollection of love. Dudley Fitts (tr.). 6759-X
The sounds of dawn. Dudley Fitts (tr.). 6759-X
Huestis, Annie Campbell
Aldaran. 6115-X
Her wishes. 6796-X
The little white sun. 6115-X
On the stair. 6115-X
The will-o'-the-wisp. 6115-X
Huey, Maud Morrison
The builder. 6818-9
The dream. 6818-9
The world was surely made for me. 6818-9
Huff, William Hrper

A Christmas reverie. 6799-9
Hug me tight. J.K. ("Dum-Dum") Kendall. 6722-0
"A huge boulder!". Boulder. Morris Zwart. 6850-2
"The huge bridge did not lead to you". Wind on the halfmoon. Eugenio Montale. 6803-0
"Huge images of death lurk in my brain". Poem, 1933. Richard Goodman. 6985-1
The huge leviathan, fr. Visions of the world's vanity. Edmund Spenser. 6125-7
"The huge red-buttressed mesa over yonder". Rain in the desert, fr. Arizona poems. Arthur Davison Ficke. 6897-9
"Huge upon the hazy plain". Pastoral. Archibald MacLeish. 6808-1
"A huge upthrust of turreted, white stone". Water tower at Waldo. Daisy Marita Bishop. 6818-9
"Huge, fleecy clouds, like stately ships...". Buzzard's point. George M. Vickers. 6921-5

Huggard, Ethel Florence
Sunrise in Wallkill. 6847-2

Huggins and Duggins. Thomas Hood. 6802-2
Huggins and Duggins. Thomas Hood. 6974-6
Hugh Gordon's iron mill. Horace B. Durant. 6922-3
Hugh Latimer. Henry Augustin Beers. 7041-8
"Hugh McAfee, of Boston town". Commonwealth vs. McAfee. C.P. Greenough. 6878-2
Hugh of Lincoln. Unknown. 6055-2,6056-0,6098-6,6022-6,6518-4,6067
Hugh Selwyn Mauberley, sels. Ezra Pound. 6399-3
Hugh song. Elizabeth Shane. 6872-3
Hugh Spencer's feats in France. Unknown. 6185-0
Hugh Sutherland's pansies. Robert Buchanan. 6669-0
Hugh Thorndyke. Alice Cary. 6969-X
"Hugh! I cannot bear to see thee". The cradle-song of the poor. Adelaide Anne Procter. 6957-6

Hugh, Ricarda
Einmal vor manchem Jahre. 6253-9

Hugh, the carter, tarries. Willard Wattles. 6441-8

Hughes (atr), Henry
"Art thou in loeu? it cannot be." 6563-5
"Behold great Neptunes risen from ye deep." 6563-5
"O I am sick, I am sick to death, tis soe." 6563-5

Hughes, Annie
Pussey's better nature. 6681-X

Hughes, Barbara
Hamden Provision co. 6792-1
How clouds move. 6792-1

Hughes, Daniel
The Damascus road. 6144-3

Hughes, Dorothy Berry
The hand. 6979-7

Hughes, E.A.
The two armies. 6685-2

Hughes, F.E.
Morning after the barrage at El Alamein. 6468-X

Hughes, Henry
Chloris, a constant comfort. 6563-5

Hughes, Hugh J.
The kings. 6846-4
Pards. 6476-0

Hughes, J.
Combat between Fitz James and Roderick Dhu. 6148-6
The ungrateful Cupid. 6133-8

Hughes, James D.
My son. 6443-4

Hughes, John
The court of Neptune. 6833-2
The picture. 6831-6
Sonnet ("I die"). 6023-4

Hughes, Langston
Acceptance. 6388-8
Air raid: Barcelona. 6761-1
April rain song. 6554-X
As I grew older. 6628-3
Barrel house: industrial city. 6561-9
Being walkers with the dawn. 6954-1
The bitter river. 6561-9
The black man speaks. 6561-9
Cross. 6619-4,6491-4
Dear lovely death. 6879-0
Dear Mr. President. 6561-9
Death in Harlem. 6042-0
Dimout in Harlem. 6561-9
Dream variation. 6102-8,6076-5,6628-3
Drum. 6879-0
Early evening quarrel. 6751-4
Epilogue. 6628-3
Fantasy in purple. 6619-4
For Billie Holiday. 6178-8
From Selma. 6178-8
Good morning, Stalingrad. 6561-9
The gypsy. 6628-3
A house in Taos, sels. 6531-7
I, too. 6954-1
Imagine. 6803-0
Jazzonia. 6628-3
Late corner. 6388-8
Mississippi levee. 6751-4
Moon, fr. A house in Taos. 6531-7
Moonlight in Valencia: civil war. 6561-9
Mother to son. 6538-4,6281-4
The Negro speaks of rivers. 6464-7
The negro. 6954-1
The Negro. 6102-8,6076-5
Our land. 6628-3
Poem-to the black beloved. 6628-3
Proem. 6628-3
Proem and epilogue. 6527-9
Question. 6561-9
Rain, fr. A house in Taos. 6531-7
Refugee in America. 6516-3
Roar China! 6761-1
Sanse Africaine. 6538-4
Silhouette. 6561-9
Sun, fr. A house in Taos. 6531-7
Testament. 6388-8
Two somewhat different epigrams. 6388-8
Two things. 6879-0
The underground. 6561-9
"We have tomorrow, fr. 'The crisis'" 6954-1
The weary blues. 6538-4
Where? When? Which? 6388-8
Wind, fr. A house in Taos. 6531-7
Wisdom and war. 6178-8
Young gal's blues. 6108-7
Young sailor. 6628-3

Hughes, Langston (tr.)
Cantaliso in a bar. Nicolas Guillen, 6759-X
Dead soldier. Nicolas Guillen, 6759-X
Guinea. Jacques Roumain, 6759-X
Opinions of the new student. Regino Pedroso, 6759-X
Wake for Papa Montero. Nicolas Guillen, 6759-X
When the tom-tom beats. Jacques Roumain, 6759-X

Hughes, Lois Royal
I could not know. 6178-8
Like unto a rose. 6178-8
Rendezvous. 6178-8

Hughes, M.W.
To grammar. 6072-2

Hughes, Mabel E.
Madonna at Palos. 6674-4

Hughes, Richard
A doubt. 6302-0,6385-3
Ecstatic ode on vision. 6250-4
Lover's reply to good advice. 6069-2
Poets, painters, puddings. 6776-X
Travel-piece. 6071-4
Unicorn mad. 6070-6

Hughes, Rupert
For Decoration Day. 6340-3
The martyrs of the Maine. 6741-X
With a first reader. 6476-0

Hughes, Russell
The ballet school. 6959-2

Hughes, T.S.
Belshazzar's feast. 6606-2

Hughes, Thomas Smart
Belshazzar's feast. 6848-0

Hughes, William
Rufeno, the Mexicano boy. 6149-4

Hughie Graham. Unknown. 6055-2,6185-0,6322-5
Hughie refuses to emigrate. James Logie ("Hugh Haliburton") Robertson. 6819-7
Hughie takes his ease in his inn. James Logie ("Hugh Haliburton") Robertson. 6819-7
Hughie's advice to his younger brother John. James Logie ("Hugh Haliburton") Robertson. 6819-7
Hughie's indignation at the conduct of the...elder. James Logie ("Hugh Haliburton") Robertson. 6819-7
Hughie's monument. James Logie ("Hugh Haliburton") Robertson. 6819-7
Hughie's winter excuse for a dram. James Logie ("Hugh Haliburton") Robertson. 6819-7
Hugley Steeple. Alfred Edward Housman. 6655-0
Hugo the bastard. Robert Buchanan. 7007-8
Hugo, Victor
    A la belle imperieuse. 6801-4
    After six thousand years. Selden Rodman (tr.). 6665-8
    After the battle. 6351-9
    The age is great and strong. 6730-1
    At the barricade. 7022-1
    "Be like a bird, that, halting in her flight." 6238-5
    Booz endormi. 6801-4
    Cain. 6102-8
    Cassandre. 6801-4
    Chanson d'autrefois. 6801-4
    Child at play. Eugene Field (tr.). 6949-5
    The children of the poor. 6954-1
    Choses du soir. 6801-4
    Civil war - an episode of the commune. Lucy H. Hooper (tr.). 6924-X
    Completion. 6351-9
    The djinns. 6732-8
    Ecrit en exil. 6801-4
    Envy and avarice. 6610-0
    Epitaph. Cora Fabri (tr.). 6876-6
    An extravaganza. 6066-8
    Faith. 6351-9
    The faith of the poet. 6102-8
    The father's curse. 6610-0
    The feast of freedom. 6102-8
    Flower to butterfly. Eugene Field (tr.). 6949-5
    "France, a l'heure ou tu te prosternes" 6801-4
    Fraternity. 6351-9
    The genesis of butterflies. Andrew Lang (tr.). 6771-9, 7039-6
    Good night. 6109-5,6466-3,6623-2,6424-8
    The grave and the rose. Andrew Lang (tr.). 6771-9,7039-6
    Gros temps la nuit. 6801-4
    Guitare. 6677-1
    Guitare. 6801-4
    Her name. 6732-8
    The hireling Swiss regiment. 6344-6
    House and home. 6337-3
    How good are the poor. 6424-8
    June nights. 6351-9
    L'ange qui veille. 6691-7
    La chanson de Fantine. 6801-4
    La chanson de Joss. 6801-4
    La coccinelle. 6801-4
    La terre: hymne. 6801-4
    Le chasseur noir. 6801-4
    Le rouet d'omphale. 6801-4
    Les miserables, sel. 6954-1
    Lion and prince. 6716-9
    The lions. Mrs. Newton Crosland (tr.). 6848-0
    The lonely peak. 6351-9
    Marie Tudor, sels. 6351-9
    Mazeppa. 6801-4
    More strong than time. Andrew Lang (tr.). 6771-9
    More strong than time. Andrew Lang (tr.). 7039-6
    More strong than time. Andrew Lang (tr.). 6879-0
    Moses on the Nile. Walter Hart Blumenthal (tr.). 6848-0
    My two daughters. Alan Conder (tr.). 6317-9
    "O gouffre! l'ame plonge et rapporte le doute" 6801-4
    "Oh! je sais qu'ils feront des mensonges sans nombres" 6801-4
    On a barricade. 6707-7
    "Parfois, lorsque tout dort, je m'assieds plein..." 6801-4
    Patria. 6102-8
    The poet's simple faith. 6261-X,6730-1
    Pool in the forest. Eugene Field (tr.). 6949-5
    The poor children. 6102-8
    The poor children. Algernon Charles Swinburne (tr.). 7039-6
    Poor fisher folk. H.W. Alexander (tr.). 6102-8,6344-6, 6385-3
    The poor fisher folk, sels. W.H. Alexander (tr.). 6849-9
    Poor litte children. 6424-8
    Poor little children. 6424-8
    Premier Janvier. 6801-4
    A recollection of childhood. Sir George Young (tr.). 6484-1
    Republic of the world. 6337-3
    The rose and the grave. 6102-8
    Since May all aflower. 6351-9
    Soir. 6801-4
    Song of the Fabiani, sels. 6351-9
    The sower. 6102-8
    A sunset. Francis Thompson (tr.). 7039-6
    To a woman. W.J. Robertson (tr.). 6732-8
    To L. 6351-9
    Torquemada. 6848-0
    Transfiguration. 6351-9
    Trois ans apres. 6801-4
    The universal republic. 6386-1,6420-5,6461-2
    The universal republic. 6954-1
    'Where goest thou?' 6337-3
    Where you may rest. 6351-9
    "Who art thou, shadowy passer-by?" 6238-5
    The wild face at the windows. 6102-8
    Wings. 6351-9,6337-3,6461-2
The **Huguenot's** farewell. Felicia Dorothea Hemans. 6973-8
A **Huguenot**. Mary Elizabeth Coleridge. 6477-9,6437-X,6250-4, 6639-9
Huhner, Leon
    Abraham Lincoln. 6887-1
    "Gigantic figure of a mighty age" 6995-9
    Milton, John. 6585-6
    Quentin Roosevelt. 6887-1
    Theodore Roosevelt. 6336-5
Huidobro, Vicente
    The art of poetry. Milton Ben Davis (tr.). 6759-X
    "Bewitching drowned what time it is". Joseph Staples (tr.). 6759-X
    "Bring games". Joseph Staples (tr.). 6759-X
    Emigrant to America. H.R. Hays (tr.). 6642-9
    "I am partly moon and partly traveling salesman". Joseph Staples (tr.). 6759-X
    In. H.R. Hays (tr.). 6642-9
    Nature vive. Dudley Fitts (tr.). 6759-X
    Nature vive. H.R. Hays (tr.). 6642-9
    Prelude to hope. H.R. Hays (tr.). 6642-9
    Round. Donald Devenish Walsh (tr.). 6759-X
    Serenade of laughing life. H.R. Hays (tr.). 6642-9
    She. Dudley Fitts (tr.). 6759-X
    Time of waiting. H.R. Hays (tr.). 6642-9
    "You have never known the tree of tenderness..." Joseph Staples (tr.). 6759-X
Huiginn, E.J.V.
    Saint Columbkille. 6762-X
    The weaver. 6030-7
Hulda. See Benediktdottir, Unnur
The **hulk**. Maimie A. Richardson. 6269-5
Hulks. Alice Glasgow. 6847-2
Hull, Eleanor
    The fairies' lullaby. 6090-0
    The flower of nut-brown maids. 6090-0
    The old woman of Beare. 6873-1
    She. 6090-0
    Youth and age. 6090-0,
Hull, Eleanor (tr.)
    Consecration. Muiredach O'Daly, 6090-0
    Four prayers. Unknown, 6930-4
    Hymn to the Virgin Mary. Conal O'Riordan, 6282-2
    I lie down with God. Unknown, 6244-X
    Mary's vision. Unknown, 6282-2

HULL

    A prayer. Unknown, 6930-4
    Roisin dubh. Owen (atr.) Roe Mac Ward, 6930-4
Hull, Mary H.
    Sun or satellite? 6274-1
Hullo! Sam Walter Foss. 6085-4,6260-1,6707-7,6964-9
"Hullo, my man, what do you do here...". Coward. Brian ("Korongo") Brooke. 6938-X
Hulme, Edward Maslin
    A twilight song. 6274-1
Hulme, T.E.
    Above the dock. 6209-1
    Autumn. 6315-2,6209-1,6491-4
    Conversion. 6315-2,6209-1
    The embankment. 6209-1
    Mana aboda. 6209-1
Hult, Gottfried
    I dreamed that dream was quenched. 6327-6
"The hum of the motor and whir of the wheel". The call of the countryside. J. M. Meador. 6818-9
Humaine cares. Nathaniel Wanley. 6933-9
Human. Richard Burton. 6027-7
The human abstract. William Blake. 6831-6
The human alarm clock. Edgar A. Guest. 6869-3
Human and divine. Phoebe Cary. 6969-X
Human being - limited. Margaret Medland. 6761-1
Human body lesson in rhyme. Anna E. Badlam. 6314-4
Human cares. Nathaniel Wanley. 6563-5
The human cry, fr. De profundis. Alfred Lord Tennyson. 6655-0
The human cry. Alfred Lord Tennyson. 6977-0
The human equation. Louis Stoddard. 6761-1
The human firewood piano. Douglas Blazek. 6792-1
Human frailty. William Cowper. 6271-7
Human frailty. William Drummond of Hawthornden. 6304-7
Human histories. Siegfried Sassoon. 6879-0
Human imperfection. Simonides. 6435-3
Human life. Matthew Arnold. 6199-0,6828-6
Human life. Aubrey Thomas De Vere. 6172-9,6292-X,6656-9
Human life. John Dryden. 6543-0
Human life. William Hurrell Mallock. 6022-6,6292-X
Human life. Edward de Vere, 17th Earl of Oxford. 6930-4
Human life. Pindar. 6435-3
Human life. William Shakespeare. 6438-8
Human life. Mrs. J.M. Winton. 6412-4
Human life, sels. Samuel Rogers. 6832-4
Human life, sels. Samuel Rogers. 6543-0
Human love. Mary Brotherton. 6785-9
Human nature. Eugene Field. 6949-5
Human nature. Katie F. Nichols. 6764-6
Human nature. William Shakespeare. 6543-0
Human nature. Unknown. 6018-8
Human oppression, fr. The task. William Cowper. 6195-0
The human outlook. John Addington Symonds. 6730-1
Human race. Robert Clairmont. 6751-4
The human race comes to be judged. Cynewulf. 6489-2
The human race. Edward R. Huxley. 6885-5
The human seasons. John Keats. 6138-9,6246-6,6482-5,6669-0, 6543-0,6086-2,6110-9,6737-9
The human soul speaks. William Langland. 6489-2
"The human spirits saw I on a day". The questioning spirit. Arthur Hugh Clough. 6828-6
Human throne. Alfred Kreymborg. 6979-7
The human touch. Richard Burton. 6266-0,6309-8
The human touch. Spencer Michael Free. 6337-3,6482-5
The human tragedy, sels. Alfred Austin. 6997-5
The human trinity. Granville Lowther. 6818-9
Human worms. Anaxilas. 6435-3
Human, all too human!. Andre Spire. 6351-9
The humane mikado. Sir William Schwenck Gilbert. 6026-9
Humane thought. Rebecca McCann. 6736-0
Humaner letters. Samuel Daniel. 6935-5
Humanitad, sels. Oscar Wilde. 6466-3
Humanity. William Cowper. 6302-0,6385-3,6410-8
Humanity. Richard Watson Dixon. 6199-0
Humanity. Eugene Field. 6949-5
Humanity. Royall Snow. 6906-1
"Humanity and valor, wisdom, faith". Epitaph. Hermann Hagedorn. 6944-4
Humble and unnoticed virtue. Hannah More. 6409-4
The humble horse. George Dillon. 6039-0

A humble prayer. Helen Plavnicky. 6894-4
Humble smile. Ruth Pitter. 6893-6
The humble throng. Edgar A. Guest. 6748-4
The humble-bee. Ralph Waldo Emerson. 6006-4,6102-8,6239-3, 6299-7,6473-6,6597 ,6076-5,6153-2,6121-4,6510-4,6265-2,6126 ,6486-8,6632-1,6732-8,6735-2,6396-9,6723 , 6219-9,6288-1,6431-0,6004-8,6307-1,6250 ,6008-0
"Humbly the city bears the strain". Rain. Doris Trahagen De Aragon. 6906-1
Humbug steamship company. Unknown. 6281-4
Hume, Alexander
    Of the day estivall, sels. 6194-X
    The story of a summer day. 6302-0,6385-3
    A summer day. 6134-6,6315-2,6600-3
Hume, Helen Gross
    Beeches. 6847-2
    Four tunes. 6847-2
Hume, Isobel
    Whiteness. 6776-X
Hume, Tobias
    Fain would I change that note. 6204-0,6150-8
Humiliation. Winifred Welles. 6880-4
Humility. Anita Scott Coleman. 6178-8
Humility. Amory Hare. 7038-8
Humility. Robert Herrick. 6623-2,6424-8
Humility. Richard Monckton Milnes; 1st Baron Houghton. 6438-8
Humility. James Montgomery. 6135-4
Humility. Unknown. 6385-3
Humility. Unknown. 6914-2
Humility and doubt, sels. William Blake. 6545-7
"Humility is the base of every virtue". Philip James Bailey. 6238-5
Humility, fr. God's two dwellings. Thomas Washbourne. 6337-3
Humming bird. Padraic Colum. 6253-9
The humming bird ("Dancer of air"). Ednah Proctor (Clarke) Hays. 6073-0,6597-X
Humming bird ("It would take an angel's eye..."). Robert P. Tristram Coffin. 6073-0
The humming bird ("When languorous noons entreat..."). Ivan Swift. 6073-0
The humming bird. Padraic Colum. 6096 X
A humming bird. Edgar Fawcett. 6073-0
The humming bird. Louise Driscoll. 7038-8
The humming bird. Mary Howitt. 6466-3,6459-0,6135-4
The humming bird. Jessica Lewis. 6316-0
The humming birds. Alfred Noyes. 6151-6
The humming of the wires. Edward A. Rand. 6273-3
The humming stair. Joseph Payne Brennan. 6218-0
The humming top. Eugene Field. 6835-9,6949-5
Humming-bird. Robert P. Tristram Coffin. 7040-X
Humming-bird. Hilda Conkling. 6368-3
Humming-bird. David Herbert Lawrence. 6246-6;6357-8
Humming-bird. Myra A. Shattuck. 6715-8
The humming-bird ("A flash of harmless lightning,"). John Banister Tabb. 6597-X
Humming-bird song. Frank Dempster Sherman. 6311-X
The hummingbird.. Hermann Hagedorn. 6338-1
The hummingbird.. Harry Kemp. 6607-0,6250-4
Humn to Horus. Mathilde Blind. 6437-X
Humor of the day. Unknown. 6548-1
Humoresque. Alice Corbin. 6897-9
Humoresque. Eden Phillpotts. 6253-9
'Humoresque.'. Constance Ann Hall. 6750-6
The humorist.. Keith Preston. 6083-8;6722-0
A humorous description of the author's journey... Horace. 6814-6
The humours of Donnybrook fair. Charles O'Flaherty. 6930-4
The humours of Donnybrook fair. Unknown. 6930-4
Humphrey, F.A.
    A mercantile transaction. 6426-4
Humphrey, L.H. (tr.)
    The ilse. Heinrich Heine, 6484-1
Humphreys, Aletha
    Arachnida, female. 6218-0
    Party bid. 6218-0
Humphreys, David
    The happiness of America, sels. 6008-0
    Mount Vernon. 6484-1

On disbanding the army. 6946-0
Humphries et al., Rolfe (tr.)
    Israelite graveyard. Cesar Tiempo, 6759-X
Humphries, Emyr
    1536-1936.Fift. 6360-8
    A nonconformist. 6360-8
    Sympathy explained. 6360-8
    Unloading hay. 6360-8
Humphries, Rolfe
    California. 6038-2
    Dream. 6071-4
    Eternal recurrence. 6880-4
    A gay people. 6761-1
    He visits a hospital. 6619-4
    Heresy for a class room. 6527-9
    Heresy for a classroom. 6817-0
    Homo additus naturae. 6072-2
    One flesh. 6039-0
    Polo grounds. 6527-9
    Rational man. 6039-0
    To an unhappy Negro. 6880-4
    To the greatest city in the world. 6038-2
    Words to be flung up a stairway. 6039-0
Humphries, Rolfe (tr.)
    After twenty years. Louis Aragon, 6068-4
    Ballad of love and blood. Angel Miguel Queremel, 6759-X
    City. Jaime Torres Bodet, 6759-X
    Dance. Jaime Torres Bodet, 6759-X
    Epitaph for my tomb. Alfonsina Storni, 6759-X
    Far over yonder. Rafael Maya, 6759-X
    The moment. German Pardo Garcia, 6759-X
    The night was going... Raul Otero Reiche, 6759-X
    Noon. Jaime Torres Bodet, 6759-X
    Rainy night. Juana de Ibarbourou, 6759-X
    Remoteness. German Pardo Garcia, 6759-X
    Romanza of the guitarrist. Raul Otero Reiche, 6759-X
Humpty Dumpty. Adeline Dutton (Train) Whitney. 6632-1
Humpty Dumpty. Adeline Dutton (Train) Whitney. 6917-7
Humpty Dumpty recitation. Charles Lutwidge ("Lewis Carroll") Dodgson. 6089-7,6125-7
"Humpty Dumpty sat on a wall." Mother Goose. 6452-3,6279-2
The hun with the gun. Will P. Snyder. 6443-4
A Hun. Vincent Godfrey Burns. 6542-2
Hunc, said he. Unknown. 6125-7
The hunchback in the park. Dylan Thomas. 6357-8,6390-X, 6210-5
The hunchback, sels. James Sheridan Knowles. 6677-1
The hunchback. Edward Augustus Blount Jr. 6482-5
The hunchback. Phoebe Cary. 6060-9
"The hunchback? A poor wretch...". In the land of magic, sel. Henri Michaux. 6758-1
The hunchbacked singer. Unknown. 6923-1
"The hunched camels of the night". Francis Thompson. 6187-7
"A hundred autumns he has wheeled". Crow. Mark Van Doren. 6778-6
The hundred best books. Mostyn T. Pigott. 6089-7;6724-7
A hundred collars. Robert Frost. 6538-4,6736-0
The hundred Louis d'Or. Unknown (French) 6166-4
"A hundred miles from the longship's light". 'Leave her, Johnnie!' Cicely Fox Smith. 7031-0
A hundred noble wishes. Charles Francis Richardson. 6337-3
The hundred pipers. Carolina Oliphant, Baroness Nairne. 6153-2
"A hundred thousand northmen". Wait for the wagon. Unknown. 6946-0
"A hundred wings are dropt as soft as one". On startling some pigeons. Charles Tennyson Turner. 7015-9,6943-6
A hundred years ago. Unknown. 6742-5
A hundred years from now. Mary A. Ford. 6215-6
A hundred years from now. Mary A. Ford. 6914-2
"A hundred years in silence I dwelt in the pit". Ostrava. Petr Bezruc. 6763-8
A hundred years to come. C.F. Brown. 6912-6
A hundred years to come. William Goldsmith Brown. 6240-7, 6219-9
A hundred years to come. Hiram Ladd Spencer. 7030-2
A hundred years to come. Unknown. 6302-0
"A hundred years to live," fr. Hastings' sonnets. Sir Egerton Brydges. 6980-0

"A hundred, a thousand to one; even so". In the round tower at Jhansi. Christina Georgina Rossetti. 6828-6
The hundred-yard dash. William Lindsey. 6396-9
"Hundreds of stars in the pretty sky". Mother. George Cooper. 6466-3,6937-1
Hundreds!. Unknown. 6629-1
The hundredth psalm. Richard Corbet. 6427-2
Hung, William (tr.)
    Overnight in the apartment by the river. Tu Fu, 6125-7
Hunger. Julia Ross Alden. 6906-1
Hunger. Lyle Bartscher. 6799-9
Hunger. Laurence Binyon. 6625-9
Hunger. Gamaliel Bradford. 6762-X
Hunger. Dana Burnet. 6320-9
Hunger. Mary Carolyn Davies. 6979-7
Hunger. Francis M. Foster. 6178-8
Hunger. Hermann Ford Martin. 6038-2
Hunger inn. Jessica Nelson North. 6036-6
"Hunger points a bony finger". The little children. Francis Ledwidge. 6812-X
Hunger striker. William ("Wild Bill") Franklin. 6870-7
"Hunger that strivest in the restless arms". Evolution. Emily Ffeiffer. 7015-9
Hungerford, Alys
    A toi. 6784-0
    A summer nocturne. 6784-0
Hungerford, M.C.
    Oh, for a man! 6924-X
    Old King Cole. 6415-9,6167-2
Hungering hearts. Unknown. 6303-9
Hungering hearts. Unknown. 6889-8
Hungry master and hungry cat. Abu Shamaqmaq. 6511-2
"The hungry north wind whines". Farewell, farewell, old year. Clinton Scollard. 6875-8
The hungry one. Nikolay Nekrasov. 6103-6
Hungry winter. Vladimir Mayakovsky. 6546-5
"Hungry, little fellow?". Famine on a schedule. Helen Hardman. 6750-6
The hungry. Caroline Giltinan. 6954-1
The hungry. David Greenhood. 6808-1
Hunneman, Carleton
    College days. 6116-8
Hunnis, William
    Happy shepherds, sit and see. 6198-2
    "A nosegay always sweet, for lovers to send." 6182-6
    "A nosegay, lacking flowers fresh." 6181-8
    The shipmen. 6436-1
Hunt. Kay Boyle. 6781-6
"Hunt half a day for a forfgotten dream". Hart-leap well, sels. William Wordsworth. 6867-7
The hunt is up! William Gray (atr) 6153-2
The hunt is up. ? Gray. 6328-4
The hunt is up. Unknown. 6134-6,6334-9,6189-3
'The hunt of Sliabh Truim,' sels. Unknown. 6930-4
A 'hunt up'. Unknown. 6334-9
Hunt, Albert E.
    An evening doze. 6417-5
Hunt, Belle
    But -. 6675-5
Hunt, Ella Orndorff
    Groping. 6906-1
    Loveliness. 6906-1
Hunt, Evelyn Hazlett
    Mutability. 6799-9
    Pride. 6799-9
Hunt, Helen. See Jackson, Helen Hunt
Hunt, J. Ray
    That maple on the hill. 7019-1
Hunt, James B.
    Back-log moods. 6983-5
Hunt, James Henry Leigh. See Hunt, Leigh
Hunt, Josie R.
    Katie Lee and Willie Grey. 6142-7
Hunt, Leigh
    Abou Ben Adhem. 6101-X,6102-8,6109-5,6134-6,6136-2,6138-,6133-8,6392-6,6600-3,6732-8,6186-9,6198-2,6236-9,6239-3,6242-3,6260-,6271-7,6291-1,6294-6,6302-0,6332-2,6337-,6339-X,6370-5,6385-3,6401-9,6418-9,6426-,6437-X,6451-5,6457-4,6459-0,6473-6,6478-,6479-5,6481-7,6486-8,6501-5,6502-3,6503-,6504-X,6534-1,6605-2,

HUNT

6614-3,6623-2,6730-,6723-9,6737-9,6424-8,6419-1,6639-9,6301-2,6131-1,6219-9,6212-1,6104-4,6199-0,6383-7,6250-4,6135-4,6461-2,6192-3,6155-9,6560-0,6102-8,6304-7,6808-1,6214-8,6438-8,6421-3,6543-0
Abraham and the fire-worshipper. 6848-0
Agolanti and his lady, fr. The legend of Florence. 6980-0
An angel in the house. 6737-9,6219-9,6321-7,6543-0,6271-7,6429-9,6600-3
Ariadne, sels. 6980-0
Better things. 6620-8,6066-8
Captain sword. 6239-3,6046-3
Chorus of flowers. 6271-7,6219-9
Christmas: a song for the young & the wise, sels. 6334-9
Cupid drowned. 6479-5
Cupid swallowed. 6102-8,6280-6,6302-0,6385-3,6737-9,6219-9,6576-7,6585-6
The dearest poets. 6102-8
Dirge. 6934-7
Dirge. 6250-4
Dirge. 6934-7
A domestic scene, fr. The legend of Florence. 6980-0
Fairies' song. 6198-2,6302-0,6385-3,6026-9
Fancy. 6980-0
The fancy concert. 6358-6
The fatal passion. 6980-0
The fish, the man, and the spirit, sels. 6258-X,6199-0,6545-7
The fish, the man, and the spirit. 6125-7
Flowers. 6502-3
"For there are two heavens, sweet." 6066-8
The garden and summer-house, fr. The story of Rimi. 6649-6
A garden, fr. The story of Rimini. 6198-2
The glove and the lions. 6543-0,6571-6,6131-1,6458-2,6219-9,6419-1,6424-8,6543-0,6571-6,6131-1,6458-2,6219-9,6419-1,6424-8,6087-0,6105-2,6136-2,6165-6,6198-2,6211-,6134-6,6302-0,6385-3,6527-9,6552-X,6614-,6239-3,6242-3,6407-8,6479-5,6499-X,6512-
The grasshopper and the cricket. 6850-2
The grasshopper and the cricket. 6250-4
The grasshopper and the cricket. 6850-2
A heaven upon earth. 6980-0
Hero and Leander. 6410-8
His poets. 6297-0
Jaffar. 6085-4,6102-8,6133-8,6271-7,6294-6,6302-,6370-5,6385-3,6552-X,6605-4,6614-3,6661-,6732-8,6424-8,6639-9
Jennie kissed me. 6014-5,6289-X,6385-3,6732-8,6085-4,6102-8,6240-7,6260-1,6271-7,6339-,6395-0,6413-2,6429-9,6437-X,6501-5,6512-,6219-9,6312-7,6226-1,6104-4,6092-9,6026-9,6383-7,6301-2,6230-X,6424-8,6585-6,6737-9,6219-9,6312-7,6226-1,6104-4,6092-7,6026-9,6383-7,6301-2,6230-X,6424-8,6585-6,6737-9
The jovial priest's confession. 6089-7,6278-4,6089-7
Joy of spring. 6049-8
Just as a mother. 6097-8
Kosciusko. 6980-0
The legend of Florence, sels. 6980-0
Lilies. 6049-8,6383-7
Love letters made of flowers. 6302-0,6385-3
Madame d'Albret's laugh. 6026-9
Mahmoud. 6133-8,6385-3,6407-8
May. 6049-8,6385-3
Morning at Ravenna. 6543-0
"My heart and mind and self never in tune." 6238-5
"Next came Walter Scott", fr. The feast of the poets. 6996-7
Nile, sels. 6369-1
The Nile. 6104-4
The nun. 6089-7,6271-7,6437-X,6026-9,6219-9,6089-7,6271-7,6437-X
The poets ("Were I to name, out of the times gone by). 6483-3
The poets. 6483-8
Poppies. 6383-7
Power and gentleness. 7009-4
Power and greatness. 6980-0
Ravenna. 6624-0

The Ravenna pine forest. 6980-0
Rondeau ("Jennie kissed me when we met"). 6122-2,6198-2,6228-8,6332-2,6473-6,6724 ,6652-6,6646-1,6560-0,6153-2,6371-3
Rondeau ("Jenny kissed me when we met") 6875-8
St. Valentine's day. 6787-5
Sneezing. 6385-3
Song of fairies. 6219-9
Song of the cloud nymphs. 6334-9
Song to Ceres. 6438-8
Songs and chorus of the flowers. 6047-1
Spring in Ravenna. 6980-0
Stolen fruit. 6652-6
The story of Rimi, sels. 6649-6
The story of Rimini, sels. 6198-2,6196-6,6649-3
To a child during sickness. 6271-7,6302-0,6385-3
To J.H. - Four years old. 6242-3,6271-7
To John Keats. 6483-3
To June. 6456-6
To Lord Byron. 6980-0
To Percy Shelley on the degrading notions of deity. 7009-4
To T.L.H. 6219-9
To the grasshopper and the cricket. 6102-8,6239-3,6271-7,6302-0,6369-1,6385-,6328-4,6395-0,6473-3,6512-0,6604-6,6660-7,6199-0,6383-7,6129-1,6301-2
Trio and chorus of stout heart... 6334-9
The trumpets of Doolkarnein. 6302-0,6385-3
Two heavens. 6239-3
"Various the trees and passing foliage here..." 6049-8
Vaucluse. 6484-1
Violets. 6049-8
"We the fairies, blithe and antic." 6105-2
Hunt, Leigh (tr.)
"Clear, fresh, and dulcet streams". Francesco Petrarch, 6325-X
A love-lesson. Clement Marot, 7039-6
Madame D'Albert's laugh. Clement Marot, 7039-6
Montepulciano wine. Francesco Redi, 6624-0
Nimrod and the monsters of hell. Dante Alighieri, 6102-8
Nimrod and the monsters of hell. Dante Alighieri, 6102-8
Ode to the golden age. Torquato Tasso, 6732-8
On the death of Binon, the herdsman of love. Theocritus, 6732-8
Paulo and Francesca, fr. Inferno. Dante Alighieri, 6659-3
Priam appeals to Achilles. Homer, 6102-8
The seat under the tree. Theocritus, 6732-8
Spring. Giovanni Battista Guarini, 7039-6
The story of Cyllarus and Hylonome. Ovid, 6732-8
The true king. Seneca, 6605-2,6424-8
Hunt, Sarah Keables
The two little stockings. 6314-4,6964-9
The **hunt**. Adolf von Hatzfeld. 6160-5
The **hunt**. Gertrude McGiffert. 6510-4
"**Hunter** and soldier stalwart to the core". The president. Harry Kemp. 6995-9
"A **hunter** learns a soldier's trade". Unknown. 6435-3
The **hunter** man. Howard Nutt. 6017-X
"The **hunter** of dragon flies". Chiyo. 6850-2
The **hunter** of the prairies. William Cullen Bryant. 6271-7,6484-1,6219-9
The **hunter** sees what is there. Edgar Jackson. 6870-7
Hunter song. Unknown. 6952-5
"The **hunter** squints". The hunter sees what is there. Edgar Jackson. 6870-7
Hunter trials. Sir John Betjeman. 6339-X
A **hunter's** dream. George Edward Hoag. 6342-X
The **hunter's** last ride. Unknown. 6916-9
Hunter's morning. Harold Littlebird. 7005-1
A **hunter's** requiem. Brian ("Korongo") Brooke. 6938-X
Hunter's song. Bryan Waller ("Barry Cornwall") Procter. 6302-0,6328-4,6385-3,6239-9,6656-9
The **hunter's** song. William Basse. 6563-5
The **hunter's** song. Bryan Waller ("Barry Cornwall") Procter. 6424-8
The **hunter's** vision. William Cullen Bryant. 6271-7,6648-8
The **hunter's** wife. Phoebe Cary. 6969-X

Hunter, Anne
  Elegy. 6908-8
  Indian death-song. 6271-7,6385-3
  The lot of thousands. 6219-9
  My mother bids me bind my hair. 6180-X,6086-2
  Remembrance. 6086-2
  Song ("The season"). 6908-8
Hunter, John
  Dreams and deeds. 6144-3,6337-3
Hunter, Lisa
  Larry Rivers self-portrait. 6900-2
Hunter, Mary Kate
  Ashes. 6799-9
Hunter, Minnie S.
  Wings. 6799-9
Hunter, Polly
  Gratitude. 6249-0
Hunter, Ralph W.
  Prison etching. 6750-6
Hunter, Thomas
  Fort Donelson. 6847-2
  To the toiler. 6847-2
Hunter, William Elijah
  As on a hidden voyage. 6800-6
  Aspiration. 6800-6
  Death's silence. 6800-6
  Margaret. 6800-6
  Origen's dream. 6800-6
  Spring. 6800-6
The hunter, tiring of the chase. Edmund Vance Cooke. 6995-9
Hunter-Duvar, John
  Adieu to France, fr. De roberval. 6795-6
  Brawn of England's lay. 6656-9
  De Roberval, sels. 6656-9
  The emigration of the fairies, sels. 6795-6
  The fairies in Prince Edward Island. 6795-6
  Mermaid's song. 6433-7
  Twilight song. 6433-7
The hunter. Brian ("Korongo") Brooke. 6938-X
The hunter. Christopher (John Wilson) North. 6980-0
The hunter. Clinton Scollard. 7041-8
The hunter. Eleanor Glenn Wallis. 6388-8
The hunters of Kentucky. Unknown. 6946-0
"The hunters went out with guns". Good grease. Mary TallMountain. 7005-1
The hunters. Ernest Thompson Seton. 7035-3
Hunting a madman. John F. Nicholls. 6924-X
Hunting ballad. Unknown. 6826-1
Hunting dogs. Winifred Welles. 6037-4
Hunting horns. Guillaume Apollinaire. 6343-8
The hunting of Shumba. Kingsley Fairbridge. 6591-0,6592-9
The hunting of Shumba. Kingsley Fairbridge. 6800-6
The hunting of the cheviot. Unknown. 6055-2,6185-0,6198-2, 6056-0,6430-2,6193-1,6518-4
The hunting of the gods. Walter Wasse. 6563-5
The hunting of the snark, sels. Charles Lutwidge ("Lewis Carroll") Dodgson. 6656-9
The hunting of the snark. Charles Lutwidge ("Lewis Carroll") Dodgson. 6722-0,6089-7,6732-8
A hunting rhyme. Adam Lindsay Gordon. 6951-7
The hunting season. Thomas Haynes Bayly. 7025-6
Hunting song. Samuel Taylor Coleridge. 6132-X,6519-8
Hunting song. John Dryden. 6195-0
Hunting song. Henry Fielding. 6334-9,6152-4
Hunting song. Gene Fowler. 6792-1
Hunting song. Richard Hovey. 6374-8,6121-4
Hunting song. Sir Walter Scott. 6075-7,6478-7,6136-2,6138-9,6180-X,6239 ,6242-3,6289-X,6552-X,6604-6,6183-4, 6543
Hunting song. Unknown. 6136-2
Hunting song. Unknown (American Indian) 6396-9
Hunting song. Raymond W. Walker. 6118-4
Hunting song. Paul Whitehead. 6932-0
Hunting song (made for King Henry VIII). Unknown. 6334-9
Hunting song, fr. King Arthur. Richard Hovey. 6890-1
Hunting song, fr. Music. Henry Van Dyke. 6961-4
A hunting song. Adam Lindsay Gordon. 6951-7
A hunting song. Francis Hopkinson. 6121-4
Hunting tower. Unknown. 6676-3

Hunting, Eunice M.
  Life. 6764-6
Hunting, Florence Kreeger
  Autumn at Anoka. 6342-X
Hunting, G.F.
  Help one another. 6466-3
"The hunting-hound of Midas...". Antipater. 6251-2
Hunting-song. Unknown (Navaho Indian) 7039-6
Huntingdon, D.
  The religious cottage. 6752-2
  The treasure that waxeth not old. 6752-2
Huntington, Emily
  The little housekeepers. 6530-9
Huntington, George
  America and England. 6711-5
  Hymn of world peace. 6889-8
  International hymn. 6337-3
Huntington, M.H.
  Little acorn. 6049-8
Huntington, Mary Clarke
  A legend of the Christ-child. 6807-3
Huntley, Stanley
  Annabel Lee. 6089-7,6280-6,6440-X
Huntress, H.P.
  Ballad of the afternoon tea. 6118-4
  A class-day Hamlet. 6118-4
Huntress, K.G.
  Gunning off clapboard. 6761-1
"The huntsman, Epicydes, across the mountains..." Callimachus. 6251-2
Huntsman, rest!, fr. Lady of the lake. Sir Walter Scott. 6328-4
"Huntsman, that on the hills above". Avetis Isahakian. 6050-1
The huntsmen's chorus. Algernon Charles Swinburne. 6844-8
The huntsmen. Walter De La Mare. 6527-9
A huproar. Ernest Radford. 6875-8,6770-0
Hurd, Harry Elmore
  Abraham Lincoln. 6761-1
  Black and white shuffle. 6722-0
  Edwin Arlington Robinson. 6042-0
  Speak to humble things. 6461-2
  This apple. 6761-1
Hurd, Honora Carroll
  The Madonna of the plains. 6750-6
Hurdis, James
  A bird's nest. 6385-3
  Home-making. 6943-6
The hurdlers. Henry de Montherlant. 6351-9
Hurdy-gurdy. Glenn Ward Dresbach. 6750-6
Hurdy-gurdy days. Martha Haskell Clark. 6891-X
"Hurl down, harsh hills, your bitterness". Invocation. Thomas Moult. 6884-7
Hurley, Morris
  Eternal dream. 6799-9
Hurley, Thomas Henry
  Tennyson. 6656-9
Hurra, Germania! Ferdinand Freiligrath. 6842-1
Hurrah for Scotland's heroes brave. William Shearer-Aitkin. 7009-4
Hurrah for the flag. Unknown. 6373-X
"Hurrah for the forest--the wild pine-wood...". A winter song for the sleigh. C.P. Traill. 7035-3
"Hurrah for the ski! and the taut snowshoe". A northern winter's welcome. C. Turner. 7035-3
"Hurrah! 'tis done - our freedom's won". Song of the volunteers of 1782. Thomas Osborne Davis. 6858-8
"Hurrah! for old Cape Cod". A lay of Cape Cod. Daniel Barker Ford. 6798-0
"Hurrah! hurrah! avoid the...avenging childe". The avenging childe. Unknown (Spanish). 6757-3
"Hurrah! the season's past at last". The last despatch. Austin Dobson. 6760-3
Hurrahing in harvest. Gerard Manley Hopkins. 6317-9,6354-3, 6125-7
Hurricane. Gertrude Callaghan. 6096 X
The hurricane. William Cullen Bryant. 6302-0,6457-4
The hurricane. Philip Freneau. 6121-4
Hurry. Octavio Paz. 6758-1
"The hurry of the times affects us so". Earnestness. Ella

HURRY

Wheeler Wilcox. 6956-8
"Hurry, little laughing girls". Hurdy-gurdy. Glenn Ward Dresbach. 6750-6
"Hurrying along the path from the fateful...". Bells toll. Vojislav Ilic Jr.. 6765-4
Hurst, Cynthia
    Reflections. 6764-6
Hurst, Nellie
    The war rosary. 6846-4
Hurt. Florence P. Newell. 6764-6
Hurt child. Witter Bynner. 6761-1
Hurt hawks. Robinson Jeffers. 6077-3,6491-4
Hurt no living thing. Christina Georgina Rossetti. 6565-5, 6466-3
'The hurt that honour feels'. Sir Owen Seaman. 6996-7
Hurt, Walter
    Rabbi Isaac M. Wise. 6848-0
Hurts of time. George Gordon, 6th Baron Byron. 6438-8
Hurwitz, Hyman
    Israel's lament. Samuel Taylor Coleridge (tr.). 6848-0
    The tears of a grateful people. Samuel Taylor Coleridge (tr.). 6848-0
Husband and heather. Sam Walter Foss. 6089-7
Husband and wife. Edward Harry William Meyerstein. 6317-9
"Husband and wife for fourteen years!". Chums. Edgar A. Guest. 6862-6
"A husband is a fellow that a wife must drag..". Husbands. Edgar A. Guest. 6748-4
The husband of Lady Godiva. Frances Wierman. 6039-0
Husband shoveling snow from the roof. William Meissner. 6821-9
"The husband thus reprov'd his wife". The scold and the parrot. John Gay. 6972-X
The husband to his sick wife. Charles W. Denison. 6755-7
"Husband! I am just a woman!". Angry admonition. Dorothy Jane Deuell. 6750-6
The husband's and wife's grave. Richard Henry Dana. 6302-0;6385-3
The husband's complaint. Unknown. 6787-5
The husband's petition. William Edmonstoune Aytoun. 6278-4
Husband, John Dillon
    Conclusion. 6761-1
    Reluctant heart. 6761-1
    Sons. 6839-1
    White heron. 6761-1
The husband. Leon Gellert. 6784-0
The husbandman. John Sterling. 6271-7,6302-0
The husbandmen, fr. Old and new art. Dante Gabriel Rossetti. 6110-9
Husbandry. William Hammond. 6563-5
Husbands. Edgar A. Guest. 6748-4
Husbands over seas. Lloyd Roberts. 6115-X
Huse, Raymond
    O God quiet woodlands. 6764-6
Husenbeth, Frederick C.
    The ruins of Babylon. 6409-4
Hush. Adelaide Anne Procter. 6677-1
"Hush harlequin brain, wild brain!". An Easter poem for all the year. Herbert Edward Palmer. 6777-8
Hush now. Dorothy C. Parrish. 7024-8
The hush of eventide. Leona Lakeman. 6894-4
"Hush thee, hush thee, little son". The vrigin's lullaby. Nora Hopper. 6807-3
"Hush thee, my babby/Lie still with daddy." Unknown. 6452-3
"Hush thee, my baby". Lullaby ("Hush thee, my baby.") Unknown (Zulu). 6711-5
"Hush thee, my baby-boy...". A lullaby ("Hush thee"). Alexander ("Nether Lochaber") Stewart. 6180-λ
"Hush thee, sw et baby". Lullaby ("Hush thee, sweet baby"). Thomas Davidson. 7022-1
"Hush ye! Hush ye! My babe is sleeping". At even. Frederick Manning. 6897-9
"Hush! 'tis a holy hour - the quiet room". Evening prayer, at a girls' school. Felicia Dorothea Hemans. 6973-8
"Hush! 'tis a holy hour...". Bernard Barton. 6402-7
"Hush! hear you how the night wind keens...". A lay to the famine. Unknown. 6930-4
"Hush! I cannot bear to see thee". Cradle song of the poor. Adelaide Anne Procter. 6772-7

"Hush! I hear the nightingale's pure notes". Ode to a nightingale. Cora Fabri. 6876-6
"Hush! my dear, lie still and slumber". Cradle song, sels. Isaac Watts. 6931-2
"Hush! oh ye billows". Hymn, fr. Beatrice. Joseph Sheridan Le Fanu. 6930-4
"Hush! silence in school - not a noise!". The schoolmaster's motto. Thomas Hood. 6974-6
"Hush! silence in school--not a noise!". The schoolmaster's motto. Thomas Hood. 6760-3
"Hush! speak low; tread softly". Too late. Adelaide Anne Procter. 6957-6
"Hush! the waves are rolling in". Gaelic lullaby. Unknown. 6132-X
"Hush'd are the winds, and still the...gloom". On the death of a young lady. George Gordon, 6th Baron Byron. 6945-2
Hush'd be the camps today. Walt Whitman. 6126-5,6305-5, 6524-4
"Hush'd is each busy shout". Prelude ("Hush'd"). Arthur Christopher Benson. 6301-2
"Hush'd is the din of tongues...", fr. Childe... George Gordon, 6th Baron Byron. 6395-0
"Hush'd was the evening hymn". 'Speak, Lord, for thy servant heareth' James Drummond Borthwick. 6848-0
Hush, all ye sounds of war. William H. Draper. 6144-3
"Hush, baby mine, and weep no more". The lullaby ("Hush, baby mine..."). Owen Roe O'Sullivan. 6858-8
"Hush, bonnie, dinna greit". Balow, my bonnie. Eugene Field. 6949-5
"Hush, hush, baby mine". Lullaby ("Hush, hush, baby mine.") Unknown (Swedish). 6711-5
"Hush, hush, hush! Be wakeful with delight!". Christmas carol. Unknown. 6952-5
"Hush, little one, and fold your hands". Oh, little child (Sicilian lullaby). Eugene Field. 6949-5
"Hush, little ones don't make a noise". Literary mother. Edgar A. Guest. 6862-6
Hush, my dear, lie still and slumber. Isaac Watts. 6456-6
"Hush, my little sleepyhead, the stars...trees". Lullaby ("Hush my little sleepyhead..."). Bert Cooksley. 6750-6
"Hush, thee, hush". Lullaby ("Hush thee, hush.") R.D. H.. 6118-4
"Hush, woman, do not speak to me!". The tryst after death. Unknown. 6930-4
"Hush-a-ba, birdie, croon, croon". Lullaby ("Hush-a-ba, birdie"). Unknown. 6179-6
Hush-a-by twentieth century baby. Mrs. Charles Gay. 6711-5
"Hush-a-bye, baby, life's just a blight". Modern lullaby. Eleanor Stanley Lockwood. 6750-6
"Hush-a-bye, baby, on the tree-top." Mother Goose. 6452-3, 6262-8
"Hush-hush! it is the charm of nothingness". Silence. Joseph Ellis. 7015-9
"Hushaby, baby, thy cradle is green." Mother Goose. 6424-8
Hushaby, sweet my own. Eugene Field. 6834-0;6949-5
A hushaby. Eugene Field. 6949-5
"Hushed are the mourner's sobs: their...". Dead Hector. James Abraham Martling. 6952-5
"Hushed are those lips, their earthly song...". My mother's hymns. Emily Greene Wetherbee. 6925-8
Hushed is the voice of Judah's mirth. Unknown. 6752-2
"Hushed is the world in night and sleep". Invocation. Felicia Dorothea Hemans. 6973-8
"A hushed spring evening in the Plaza de Mayo". Rhythm of the palms: Plaza de Mayo (2). Winifred Huff Gill. 6789-1
"Hushed were his Gertrude's lips, but still...". The Oneyda's death-song, fr. Gertrude of Wyoming. Thomas Campbell. 6832-4
"Husheen, the herons are crying". Lullaby ("Husheen"). Seumas (James Starkey) O'Sullivan. 6236-9,6930-4
Hushing song. William ("Fiona Macleod") Sharp. 6242-3
"Hushy baby, my doll, I pray you don't cry". Unknown. 6904-5
The huskers. John Greenleaf Whittier. 6254-7,6497-3,6288-1, 6126-5,6121-4
The huskin'.. Will F. McSparran. 6744-
The huskin'.. Will F. McSparran. 6922-3

Husking corn in Vermont. Daniel L. Cady. 6989-4
Husking song. A.W. Bellaw. 6682-8
Huskins, Jay
    "Once in a fog/I came upon a bog." 6750-6
"The husks in leady mould lie deep". Spanish chestnuts.
    Seumas (James Starkey) O'Sullivan. 6893-6
Hussey, Dyneley
    Courage. 7026-4
    Things that were yours. 6474-4
Hussey, Ruth Anne
    Little rain men. 6466-3
Husted, Margaret
    Bright hours. 6922-3
Husted, William Colburne
    The highway. 6579-1
Husting glamblers. Unknown. 6826-X
Hustle and grin. Unknown. 6260-1
Huston, Frances B.
    Beware the hawk. 6799-9
Huston, Francis
    Forty years ago. 6085-4
Huswifery. Edward Taylor. 6333-0,6399-3
The hut by the black swamp, sels. Henry Clarence Kendall.
    6768-9
The hut by the black swamp. Henry Clarence Kendall. 6591-0,
    6592-9
The hut on the flat. Thomas Henry. 6768-9
"A hut, and a tree". Diogenes. Max Eastman. 6897-9
Hutchens, Mary K.
    A Christmas hymn. 6799-9
Hutchenson, Ellen Mackay. See Cortissoz...
Hutcheson, Helen Thayer
    In the hay-loft. 6692-2,
Hutchinson, Ellen Mackay. See Cortissoz,Ellen
Hutchinson, Henry William
    Sonnets ("I see across ..."). 6650-X
Hutchinson, Kathyrn
    The strike is on. 6149-4
Hutchinson, Nelly M.
    The world and I. 6273-3
Hutchinson, Percy Adams
    'Bottoms up' ad finem. 6118-4
    Little Big-horn. 6327-6
    The swordless Christ. 6027-7,6027-7,6542-2
Hutchinson, R.K.
    The burial of the cat. 6314-4
Hutchison, Hazel Collister
    A tree may be laughter in the spring. 6039-0
Hutchison, Percy
    Columbus. 6833-2
Hutchman, Laurence
    Nelligan. 6767-0
Huthwaite, Pauline
    Memories. 6782-4
"Huts like white-plumed birds in bevies stud". Moravian
    village. Petr Bezruc. 6763-8
Hutt, Frank Walcott
    The Christmas light. 6807-3
    Fourth of July wish. 6715-8
    Singing soldiers. 6583-X
Hutton, Joseph
    The tomb of the brave. 6946-0
Hutton, Linda
    Stranger at the gate. 6857-X
Huxley, Aldous
    Anniversaries. 6872-3
    Arabia infelix. 6779-4
    By the fire. 6320-9,
    Doors of the temple. 6532-5,6250-4
    Fifth philosopher's song. 6633-X
    First philosopher's song. 7039-6
    Jonah. 6125-7
    Male and female created he them. 6026-9
    Mole. 6872-3
    September. 6477-9
    Song of the poplars. 6477-9
    Villiers de l'isle-Adam. 6250-4
Huxley, Aldous (tr.)
    L'apres-midi d'un faune. Stephane Mallarme, 6343-8
Huxley, Edward R.

Abraham Lincoln. 6885-5
Advent of spiritualism. 6885-5
Adverse desires. 6885-5
Ancestral caste. 6885-5
Angel guidance. 6885-5
Angel hosts. 6885-5
The angel mother. 6885-5
Animality of man. 6885-5
Aunt Sophy's notable experiment. 6885-5
The bachelor's regret. 6885-5
Baneful paths. 6885-5
The banner of love. 6885-5
Be vigilant. 6885-5
The bigot's garb. 6885-5
The bridge o'er the river of death. 6885-5
Brotherhood of man. 6885-5
Christian Science. 6885-5
Christopher Columbus. 6885-5
The comic valentine. 6885-5
The conservative man. 6885-5
The cosmopolite. 6885-5
Creation. 6885-5
The demon of our land. 6885-5
Earth's joys. 6885-5
The earth. 6885-5
An entreaty for peace. 6885-5
Equal rights. 6885-5
Equality of man. 6885-5
Essential requirements. 6885-5
Evolution of man. 6885-5
Fog-land. 6885-5
Fogy themes. 6885-5
Folk-lore. 6885-5
Friendship. 6885-5
Gossipers. 6885-5
Growth of the soul. 6885-5
Habit. 6885-5
Harmony is heaven. 6885-5
Home. 6885-5
The human race. 6885-5
In solitude. 6885-5
An infidel. 6885-5
Innocent pleasures. 6885-5
Isms. 6885-5
Jealousy. 6885-5
Kindly deeds. 6885-5
Knowledge. 6885-5
Known by their fruits. 6885-5
Labor and leisure. 6885-5
Labor Day. 6885-5
Lamp of reason. 6885-5
The latent cause. 6885-5
Liberty. 6885-5
Life. 6885-5
Life's booklet. 6885-5
Life's record. 6885-5
Life's sunset. 6885-5
Look within. 6885-5
Man's inante powers. 6885-5
Man's progression. 6885-5
Man's unfoldment. 6885-5
Man: whence and whither. 6885-5
Meditation at a picnic. 6885-5
The miser's will. 6885-5
The mocking bird. 6885-5
The morning glory. 6885-5
A mother's love. 6885-5
My boyhood days upon the farm. 6885-5
My wife and I. 6885-5
Nature's unfoldment. 6885-5
Nature's work. 6885-5
Needful amendments. 6885-5
The new comer. 6885-5
Not one soul lost. 6885-5
Occult healing. 6885-5
Oh, do not say that I am dead. 6885-5
Our angel daughter. 6885-5
Our lives reflect. 6885-5
Our Lyceum picnic. 6885-5
Our neighbor's hens. 6885-5

HUXLEY

    Our object in life. 6885-5
    Our swimming hole. 6885-5
    Our widowed mother is left alone. 6885-5
    Paddle your own canoe. 6885-5
    Parent's solace. 6885-5
    The parson's guest. 6885-5
    Past, present and future. 6885-5
    Problematic. 6885-5
    Promoter of health. 6885-5
    Providence. 6885-5
    Reformation. 6885-5
    Religion. 6885-5
    Riddance. 6885-5
    The river of life. 6885-5
    St. Valentine's Day. 6885-5
    Search for truth. 6885-5
    The seeds we sow. 6885-5
    Self conviction. 6885-5
    The ship of Zion. 6885-5
    The soldier's soliloquy. 6885-5
    A square deal for every man. 6885-5
    The still small voice. 6885-5
    Superstition. 6885-5
    They say I'm getting old. 6885-5
    This mundane career. 6885-5
    Thought. 6885-5
    The thunder storm. 6885-5
    Toil and slothfulness. 6885-5
    A tramp's lament. 6885-5
    The trend of modern research. 6885-5
    A trubute to the morn. 6885-5
    A trustworthy guide. 6885-5
    Union of thought. 6885-5
    The universe. 6885-5
    Wall Street bulls and bears. 6885-5
    Wayward mortals. 6885-5
    Wealth a delusion. 6885-5
    Wealth's desire. 6885-5
    Wedlock's course. 6885-5
    What and where. 6885-5
    What need you care. 6885-5
    Where is heaven. 6885-5
    With the times keep pace. 6885-5
    The world moves. 6885-5
    The world's excursion. 6885-5
    You are not alone. 6885-5
    Your mansion above. 6885-5
    A youth's adieu. 6885-5
    Youthful aspirations. 6885-5
    Youthful guidance. 6885-5
Huxley, Julian
    Flower and fruit. 6781-6
Huxley, Mildred
    Subalterns. 7027-2
    Subalterns: a song of Oxford. 7031-0
    To my godson. 7027-2
"Huzza for our liberty, boys". Terrapin war. Unknown. 6946-0
"Huzza! Hodgson, we are going". To Mr. Hodgson. George Gordon, 6th Baron Byron. 6874-X
"Huzza, my Jo Bunkers! no taxes we'll pay". A radical song of 1786. St. John Honeywood. 6946-0
Hvitadal, Stefan fra
    You women. Erl. G. Gillies (tr.). 6854-5
Hwang, Sun-won
    Longing for home. 6775-1
Hy-Brasail—the isle of the blest. Gerald Griffin. 6090-0, 6174-5,6244-X
"hyacinth-/hue". Poikilos. Thomas Meyer. 7003-5
Hyacinths to feed thy soul. Sadi [or Saadi] (Mushlih-ud-Din) 6337-2
Hyannis by the sea. Isabella Harris. 6798-0
Hybrias
    "My golden hoard is spear and sword." F.L. Lucas (tr.). 6251-2
    A soldier's riches. Thomas Campbell (tr.). 6435-3
Hyde Park. Florence Hoatson. 6804-9
Hyde, Clara
    Acquisition. 6750-6
    The sewing lesson. 683-1
    Under a garden stone. 6750-6
Hyde, Douglas
    The breedyen. 6873-1
    Christmas hymn. 6090-0
    Cold, sharp lamentation. 6244-X
    Columbkille's farewell. 6090-0
    The cooleen. 6437-X
    Death lament of John O'Mahony. 6174-5
    The druid. 6174-5
    Happy 'tis, thou blind, for thee. 6090-0
    Happy it is. 6174-5
    I shall not die for thee. 6873-1
    Little child, I call thee. 6090-0
    The monk and his white cat. 6090-0
    My grief on the sea. 6437-X
    My love, oh! she is my love. 6174-5
    Nelly of the top-knots. 6873-1
    On the flightiness of thought. 6090-0
    Ringeleted youth of my love. 6174-5,6506-6
    Were you on the mountain? 6090-0
    Will you be as hard? 6244-X
Hyde, Douglas (tr.)
    Blessed be the holy will of God. Unknown, 6930-4
    Christmas hymn. Unknown, 6090-0
    Farewell to Ireland. Colum-Cille (atr), 7039-6
    I am Raftery. Anthony Raftery, 6930-4,7039-6,6244-X
    I shall not die for thee. Unknown, 6873-1
    The Joyce's repentance. Unknown, 6244-X
    My grief on the sea. Unknown, 6930-4
    "My grief on the sea". Unknown, 6244-X,6258-X
    My love, oh, she is my love. Unknown, 6244-X
    The mystery. Amergin (atr.), 6930-4
    O King of the Friday. Unknown, 6244-X
    O youth of the bound black hair. Unknown, 6244-X
    A poem to be said on hearing the birds sing. Unknown (Irish), 7039-6
    The priests and the friars. Unknown, 6244-X
    The red man's wife. Unknown, 6930-4
    The red man's wife. Unknown, 6244-X
    Ringleted youth of my love. Unknown, 6930-4
    This weariness and grief. Unknown, 6244-X
    Though riders be thrown. Unknown, 6244-X
    The troubled friar. Unknown, 6244-X
Hyde, Fillmore
    A philosophical poem on cats. 6120-6
Hyde, George
    Lent. 7021-3
Hyde, Henry M.
    The chop-house in the alley. 6274-1
Hyde, Lewis (tr.)
    A gentleman living alone. Pablo (Neftali Ricardo Reyes Basualto) Neruda, 6803-0
Hyde, Robin
    The people, sels. 6043-9
Hyde, W.S.
    The great immortal Washington. 6712-3
Hyde, William De Witt
    Creation's Lord, we give thee thanks. 6337-3
Hyder Iddle. Unknown. 6089-7
Hydrographic poem. Jorge Carrera Andrade. 6642-9
Hydrographic poem. Jorge Carrera Andrade. 6642-9
Hydrographic report. Frances Frost. 6833-2
Hyett, Ernest
    Les miserables de luxe. 6818-9
Hyla brook. Robert Frost. 6348-9
Hylas. Apollonius Rhodius. 6435-3
Hylas. Robert P. Tristram Coffin. 7040-X
Hylas. Georgiana Goddard King. 6252-0
Hylas. Louis Alexander Mackay. 6021-8
Hylas. Marion M. Miller. 6983-5
Hylas. Bayard Taylor. 6271-7
Hylas, fr. Idyll xiii. Theocritus. 6435-3
Hylas, I hear you calling. Pierre Vivante. 6777-8
The hylas. Celia Thaxter. 6612-7
Hyman, Melanie
    Balance. 6515-5
    "What forms of anguish might this pattern show." 6515-5
A hymb of faith. James Whitcomb Riley. 6892-8
Hymen. Joseph Rutter. 6563-5
"Hymen hath together tyed." Unknown. 6563-5

Hymen's triumph, sels. Samuel Daniel. 6827-8
Hymn. Sarah Flower Adams. 6656-9
Hymn. Joseph Addison. 6543-0
Hymn. Patrick Cary. 6943-6
Hymn. Paul Laurence Dunbar. 6653-4
Hymn. George Edward Hoffman. 6337-3
Hymn. James Abraham Martling. 6952-5
Hymn. Edgar Allan Poe. 6126-5
Hymn. John Greenleaf Whittier. 6126-5
Hymn ("A hymn of glory"). The Venerable Bede. 6730-1
Hymn ("A mighty"). Martin Luther. 6418-3,6730-1
Hymn ("A slant of sun on dull brown walls"). Stephen Crane. 6102-8,6076-5
Hymn ("At morn - at noon - at twilight dim"). Edgar Allan Poe. 6753-0
Hymn ("At morn, at noon, at twilight dim.") Edgar Allan Poe. 6214-8,6288-1
Hymn ("At morn, at noon, at twilight dim"). Edgar Allan Poe. 6282-2
Hymn ("Borne by the tempest, on we sail"). John Pierpont. 6752-2
Hym ("By the rude bridge that arched the flood.") Ralph Waldo Emerson. 6102-8,6176-1,6286-5,6632-1,6503-1, 6076 ,6442-6
Hymn ("Come down, O Lord..."). Phoebe Cary. 6865-0;6969-X
Hymn ("Drop, drop, slow tears") Phineas Fletcher. 6182-6, 6271-7,6315-2,6106-0,6562-7,6150-8,6219-9,6315-2, 6106-0,6562-7
Hymn ("Father, thy paternal care"). Sir John Bowring. 6600-3
Hymn ("God moves in a mysterious way") William Cowper. 6150-8
Hymn ("God moves in a mysterious way.") William Cowper. 6179-6
Hymn ("Great God!..."). Felicia Dorothea Hemans. 6973-8
Hymn ("Hast thou a charm to stay the morning-star"). Samuel Taylor Coleridge. 6331-4
Hymn ("Hast thou a charm to stay.") Samuel Taylor Coleridge. 6214-8
Hymn ("Hear me, O God!") Ben Jonson. 6189-3
Hymn ("How are thy servants blest"). Joseph Addison. 6219-9,6271-7
Hymn ("How dare I..."). Phoebe Cary. 6969-X
Hymn ("Hush! oh ye billows"), fr. Beatrice. Joseph Sheridan Le Fanu. 6174-5
The hymn ("It was the winter wild,"). John Milton. 6198-2;6562-7
Hymn ("Lord, the people of the land"). Unknown. 6286-5
Hymn ("Lord, when I quit this earthly stage."). Isaac Watts. 6438-8
Hymn ("Lord, with glowing heart I praise thee.") Francis Scott Key. 6219-9
Hymn ("My God, I love thee, not because.") Saint Francis Xavier. 6730-1
Hymn ("Nurse of the pilgrim sires..."). Ebenezer Elliott. 6980-0
Hymn ("O Christ, the glorious crown.") Philip Howard. 6022-6
Hymn ("O God of mercy!..."). Felicia Dorothea Hemans. 6973-8
Hymn ("O God! who dost the nations lead"). Jones Very. 6524-4
Hymn ("O God, who guid'st the fate of nations.") Gunnar Wennerberg. 6045-5
Hymn ("O heart of mine..."). Martin Luther. 6949-5
Hymn ("O li'l' lamb out in de col'). Paul Laurence Dunbar. 6266-0,6076-5,6102-8
Hymn ("O painter of the fruits and flowers"). John Greenleaf Whittier. 6049-8
Hymn ("O thou of soul and sense and breath."). Oliver Wendell Holmes. 6305-5,6524-4
Hymn ("O thou who camest from above"). Charles Wesley. 6932-0
Hymn ("O Thou who givest life.") Abner Cheney Goodell Jr. 6524-4
Hymn ("O unseen spirit!..."). John Sterling. 6600-3
hymn ("O, fly my soul!..."). James Shirley. 6830-8
Hymn ("Our God, our help in ages past.") Isaac Watts. 6179-6
Hymn ("She loved her Savior..."). Unknown. 6752-2

Hymn ("Sing, my tongue, the Saviour's glory.") Saint Thomas Aquinas. 6730-1
A hymn ("These, as they change, Almighty Father"). James Thomson. 6122-2,6600-3
Hymn ("Thou hidden love of God, whose height"). John Wesley. 6152-4
Hymn ("Through all the changing scenes of life"). Nahum Tate. 6867-7
Hymn ("Through nature's realm..."). Louis J. Magee. 7004-3
Hymn ("When all thy mercies"). Joseph Addison. 6271-7
Hymn ("When by the marbled lake I lie and listen"). Wathen Mark Wilks Call. 6437-X
Hymn ("When gathering clouds"). Sir Robert Grant. 6271-7
Hymn ("When rising from the bed"). Joseph Addison. 6271-7
Hymn ("When the angels..."). Nicholas Breton. 6271-7
Hymn ("When the world..."). Phoebe Cary. 6865-0;6969-X
Hymn ("Whilest I beheld the neck o' the dove"). Patrick Carey. 6563-5
Hymn ("Ye golden lamps of heav'n, farewell") Philip Doddridge. 6152-4
Hymn 001, fr. Hymns of a hermit. John Sterling. 6980-0
Hymn 002, fr. Hymns of a hermit. John Sterling. 6980-0
Hymn 003, fr. Hymns of a hermit. John Sterling. 6980-0
Hymn 004, fr. Hymns of a hermit. John Sterling. 6980-0
Hymn 005, fr. Hymns of a hermit. John Sterling. 6980-0
Hymn 006, fr. Hymns of a hermit. John Sterling. 6980-0
Hymn against pestilence. St. (atr.) Colmon. 6930-4
Hymn before action. Rudyard Kipling. 6701-8
Hymn before sunrise in the vale of Chamouni. Samuel Taylor Coleridge. 6302-0,6385-3,6240-7,6198-2,6600-3,6332 , 6271-7,6484-1,6730-1,6102-8,6337-3,6424 ,6086-2,6110-9,6219-9,6252-0,6543-0
Hymn before sunrise, in the vale of Chamouni. Samuel Taylor Coleridge. 6192-3,6430-2,6560-0
Hymn by the Euphrates. Henry Hart Milman. 6980-0
Hymn for a household. Daniel Henderson. 6144-3,6335-7,6337-3
Hymn for All-Saints Day in the morning. Henry Alford. 6980-0
A hymn for America. Susie M. Best. 6926-6
A hymn for Arbor Day. Henry Hanby Hay. 6047-1
Hymn for Christmas. Felicia Dorothea Hemans. 6145-1,6239-3
Hymn for Christmas day. John Byrom. 6337-3
A hymn for Christmas day. Thomas Chatterton. 6337-3
A hymn for Christmas day. Jeremy Taylor. 6334-9,6746-8
Hymn for Christmas-day. Charles Wesley. 6024-2
Hymn for epiphany. Reginald Heber. 6747-6
Hymn for family worship. Henry Kirke White. 6219-9
Hymn for grief. Margaret Widdemer. 6532-5
Hymn for harvest-time. William H. Hamilton. 6269-5
Hymn for Lammas-day. Ernest Jones. 7009-4
Hymn for laudes feast of our lady of good counsel. Unknown. 6282-2
Hymn for memorial day. Henry Timrod. 6113-3,6340-3
Hymn for Mother's Day. Emily S. Coit. 6461-2
A hymn for Mother's Day. Marion Franklin Ham. 6143-5
Hymn for Pentecost. Jehuda [or Judah] Halevi. 6214-8
Hymn for second vespers. Unknown. 6282-2
Hymn for Thanksgiving Day. Shaemas O'Sheel. 6143-5
Hymn for the African colonization society. John Pierpont. 6752-2
Hymn for the church militant. Gilbert Keith Chesterton. 6931-2
A hymn for the conquered. W.W. S. 6523-6
Hymn for the day. Gabriela (Lucila Godoy Alcayaga) Mistral. 6337-3
Hymn for the dead. Sir Walter Scott. 6075-7,6086-2,6543-0
Hymn for the feast of the Annunciation. Aubrey Thomas De Vere. 6282-2
Hymn for the Massachusetts Charitable Association. John Pierpont. 6752-2
Hymn for the mother. George Macdonald. 6097-8;6600-3;6627-5
Hymn for the Nativity. Edward Thring. 6145-1
A hymn for the new age. William Steward Gordon. 6337-3
A hymn for the pact of peace. Robert Underwood Johnson. 6420-5
Hymn for the second centennial anniversary of...Boston. John Pierpont. 6752-2
Hymn for the sixteenth Sunday after Trinity. enry Hart

HYMN   764

Milman. 6656-9
Hymn for the two hundred annoversary...Charlestown. John Pierpont. 6752-2
Hymn for the use of the Sunday school at Olney. William Cowper. 6814-6
Hymn for the victorious dead. Hermann Hagedorn. 6051-X, 6449-3
Hymn in adoration of the blessed sacrament. Richard Crashaw. 6341-1
Hymn in contemplation of sudden death. Dorothy L. Sayers. 6532-5
A hymn in honor of Saint Teresa. Richard Crashaw. 6208-3, 6489-2,6562-7,6285-7,6730-1,6022 ,6341-1,6641-0,6563-5,6430-2,6150-8
An hymn in honour of beauty, sels. Edmund Spenser. 6198-2, 6194-X,6586-4,6189-3
A hymn in praise of Neptune. Thomas Campion. 6189-3,6421-3, 6639-9,6794-8,6334-9
A hymn in praise of the natural world. Ellen Beauchamp. 6049-8
Hymn IX, fr. In the spring. Paul Fort. 6351-9
Hymn of a child. Charles Wesley. 6127-3,6131-1
Hymn of Apollo. Percy Bysshe Shelley. 6423-X,6430-2,6250-4, 6383-7,6252-0
The hymn of Armageddon. George Sylvester Viereck. 6327-6
Hymn of at-one-ment. John Haynes Holmes. 6337-3
The hymn of Cleanthes (or, Hymn to Zeus). Cleanthes. 6337-3
A hymn of contentment, sels. Thomas Parnell. 6198-2,6543-0
Hymn of Empedocles. Matthew Arnold. 6437-X
A hymn of empire. Frederick George Scott. 6591-0,6592-9
A hymn of freedom. Mary Perry King. 6846-4,6431-0
Hymn of gladness. Thomas Mair. 6747-6
"A hymn of glory let us sing". Hymn ("A hymn of glory"). The Venerable Bede. 6730-1
A hymn of glory let us sing. Beda. 6065-X
Hymn of Halsted Street. Brent Dow Allinson. 6954-1
A hymn of hate against England, sels. Ernest Lissauer. 6427-2
The hymn of hate. Joseph Dana Miller. 6420-5
An hymn of heavenly beauty, sels. Edmund Spenser. 6198-2, 6189-3
Hymn of joy. Henry Van Dyke. 6337-3
The hymn of King Olaf the Saint. Unknown (Icelandic) 6948-7
The hymn of liberated nations. Percy Bysshe Shelley. 7009-4
The hymn of light, sels. Abraham Cowley. 6385-3
Hymn of love. Saint Francis of Assisi. 6543-0
A hymn of love. Richard Hope. 7031-0
Hymn of man. Algernon Charles Swinburne. 6828-6
Hymn of man. Algernon Charles Swinburne. 6655-0
The hymn of man, sels. Algernon Charles Swinburne. 6730-1
Hymn of nature. William Oliver Bourne Peabody. 6600-3
A hymn of nature, sels. Robert Bridges. 6487-6
Hymn of our first parents. John Milton. 6606-2
Hymn of Pan. Percy Bysshe Shelley. 6086-2,6110-9,6430-2, 6250-4,6639-9,6543 ,6102-8,6331-4,6339-X,6369-1,6423-X,6252
Hymn of Pan, sels. Percy Bysshe Shelley. 6395-0
Hymn of peace. Oliver Wendell Holmes. 6302-0
A hymn of peace. Ernest Bourner Allen. 6337-3
Hymn of progress. Byrdie L. Martin. 6799-9
Hymn of Saint Thomas in adoration of..blessed sacrament. Richard Crashaw. 6489-2
The hymn of Saint Thomas in adoration... Richard Crashaw. 6933-9
Hymn of Sivaite Puritans. Unknown. 6730-1
A hymn of Thanksgiving. Marion Franklin Ham. 6143-5
Hymn of the Alamo. Reuben M. Potter. 6580-5
Hymn of the Cherokee Indians. Isaac McLellan Jr. 6752-2
Hymn of the church yard. John Bethune. 6271-7
Hymn of the city. William Cullen Bryant. 6077-3,6288-1, 6126-5,6121-4
Hymn of the Curetes. Unknown (Greek) 6435-3
Hymn of the earth. William Ellery Channing. 6176-1,6288-1
Hymn of the Hebrew maid. Sir Walter Scott. 6271-7,6600-3
A hymn of the incarnation. Unknown. 6881-2
Hymn of the Knights Templars. John Hay. 6735-2
Hymn of the Moravian nuns. Henry Wadsworth Longfellow.
6752-2
Hymn of the Moravian nuns of Bethlehem. Henry Wadsworth Longfellow. 6946-0
Hymn of the mothers of our volunteers. Horatio Nelson Powers. 6113-3
Hymn of the mountain Christian. Felicia Dorothea Hemans. 6014-5
Hymn of the nativity. Richard Crashaw. 6933-9
Hymn of the Nativity. Richard Crashaw. 6191-5,6341-1
Hymn of the nativity. Richard Crashaw. 6933-9
A hymn of the nativity, sels. Richard Crashaw. 6144-3
Hymn of the new world. Percy MacKaye. 6465-5,6449-3
Hymn of the Polish exiles. Harriet Martineau. 7009-4
A hymn of the Resurrection. William Dunbar. 6881-2
A hymn of the sea. William Cullen Bryant. 6258-X,6302-0
Hymn of the traveller's household on his return. Felicia Dorothea Hemans. 6973-8
Hymn of the unemployed. Thomas Tiplady. 6337-3
Hymn of the Vaudois moutaineers in times of persecution. Felicia Dorothea Hemans. 6973-8
Hymn of the west. Edmund Clarence Stedman. 6946-0
The hymn of the world within, fr. Psalm 103. Bible. 6730-1
Hymn of the world without, fr. Psalm 104. Bible. 6730-1
Hymn of trust. Oliver Wendell Holmes. 6008-0,6126-5,6121-4, 6007-2,6337-3,6303-9,6288-1,6723-9
Hymn of victory: Thyutmose III. Amon-Re. 6665-8
Hymn of world peace. George Huntington. 6889-8
Hymn on solitude. James Thomson. 6152-4,6816-2
Hymn on the morning of Christ's nativity. John Milton. 6186-9,6138-9,6365-9,6145-1,6600-3,6153-2,6424-8, 6627-5
Hymn on the morning of Christ's nativity, sels. John Milton. 6216-4;6427-2;6726-3
Hymn on the Nativity. John Milton. 6189-3
A hymn on the nativity of my Saviour. Ben Jonson. 6145-1, 6328-4,6734-4,6608-9
Hymn on the power of God. James Thomson. 6816-2
Hymn on the seasons. James Thomson. 6302-0,6385-3,6219-9
Hymn sung at the completion of the Concord monument. Ralph Waldo Emerson. 6008-0
Hymn to Abraham Lincoln. William Wilberforce Newton. 6524-4
Hymn to adversity. Thomas Gray. 6975-4
Hymn to adversity. Thomas Gray. 6246-6,6122-2,6732-8,6543-0,6086-2,6152 ,6195-0,6150-8,6219-9
Hymn to adversity, sels. Thomas Gray. 6934-7
Hymn to Amen Ra, the sun god. Unknown (Egyptian) 6730-1
A hymn to Aphrodite. John B.L. Warren, 3d Baron De Tabley. 6046-3
Hymn to Apollo. Sir Philip Sidney. 6198-2
Hymn to Apollo ("Sing to Apollo, god of day"). John Lyly. 6198-2,6250-4,6189-3
Hymn to Astarte, sels. John B.L. Warren, 3d Baron De Tabley. 6301-2
Hymn to charity and humility. Henry More. 6931-2
Hymn to Christ. Mrs. Miles. 6600-3
Hymn to Christ. Wade Robinson. 6014-5
A hymn to Christ, at the author's last going...Germany. John Donne. 6931-2
"A hymn to Christ, at the avthors last going...". John Donne. 6562-7,6430-2
A hymn to Christ. John Donne. 6208-3,6438-8
Hymn to colour. George Meredith. 6186-9
Hymn to Comus. Ben Jonson. 6182-6,6430-2
A hymn to contentment. Thomas Parnell. 6152-4,6195-0,6219-9
Hymn to Cynthia. Ben Jonson. 6597-X,6252-0
Hymn to darkness. John Norris. 6597-X,6737-9
Hymn to death. William Cullen Bryant. 6126-5,6288-1,6753-0
Hymn to death. William Herbert; Earl of Pembroke. 6980-0
Hymn to Demeter, fr. A Sicilian idyl. Louis V. Ledoux. 6027-7,6300-4
Hymn to Diana. Ben Jonson. 6052-8,6246-6,6192-3,6560-0, 6125-7,6153 ,6189-3,6421-3,6371-3,6639-3,6737-9,6723 ,6075-7,6102-8,6182-6,6138-9,6186-7,6328 ,6339-X, 6395-0,6533-3,6558-9,6634-8,6726 ,6732-8,6102-8
Hymn to Diana ("Hail, beauteous Dian, queen of shades") Thomas Heywood. 6182-6
Hymn to Diana, sels. Ben Jonson. 6289-X
Hymn to earth. Elinor Wylie. 6536-8

Hymn to Earth the mother of all. Unknown (Greek) 7039-6, 6879-0,6435-3
Hymn to God. Arthur Symons. 6532-5
A hymn to God in time of stress. Max Eastman. 6532-5
Hymn to God the father. Samuel Wesley. 6931-2
A hymn to God the father. John Donne. 6192-3,6341-1,6154-0, 6189-3,6645-3,6660-7,6737-9,6198-2,6418-3,6634-8, 6315-2,6527-9,6562-7
A hymn to God the father. Ben Jonson. 6337-3
Hymn to God, my God, in my sickness. John Donne. 6315-2, 6438-8,6425-7,6150-8,6438-8
A hymn to happiness. James William Foley. 6291-1
Hymn to intellectual beauty. Percy Bysshe Shelley. 6110-9, 6199-0,6214-8,6560-0,6250-4,6196-6,6640-2,6102-8, 6122-2,6154-0,6198-2,6271-7,6086
A hymn to Jesus. Richard of Caistre. 6881-2
Hymn to labor. Angela Morgan. 6337-3
Hymn to liberty. Dionysios Solomos. 6352-7
Hymn to light. Abraham Cowley. 6341-1,6250-4
Hymn to light. Edward J. O'Brien. 6032-3
A hymn to light. John Milton. 6052-8
Hymn to love. Lascelles Abercrombie. 6437-X
Hymn to Lucifer. John Farrar. 7030-2
Hymn to man. Royall Snow. 7019-1
Hymn to Marduk. Unknown (Assyrian) 6730-1
A hymn to Mary. William Dunbar. 6881-2
A hymn to Mary. Unknown. 6881-2
Hymn to Moloch. Ralph Hodgson. 6943-6
A hymn to my God in a night of my late sickness. Sir Henry Wotton. 6052-8,6341-1
Hymn to Neptune. Albert Pike. 6219-9
Hymn to night. George Washington Bethune. 6385-3
Hymn to night. Melville Cane. 6979-7
A hymn to night. Max Michelson. 6897-9
A hymn to no one body. James Palmer Wade. 6375-6
Hymn to ocean. Richard Chenevix Trench. 6997-5
Hymn to Pan. Francis Beaumont and John Fletcher. 6099-4
Hymn to Pan. John Fletcher. 6102-8,6191-5
Hymn to Pan. Ben Jonson. 6189-3
Hymn to Pan. John Keats. 6271-7,6378-0,6634-8,6732-8,6196-6,6086-2,6102-8,6110-9,6199-0,6543-0
Hymn to passion. Kostes Palamas. 6352-7
Hymn to peace. Joel Barlow. 6176-1
Hymn to Poseidon. Arion. 6435-3
A hymn to Proserpine. Algernon Charles Swinburne. 6508-2, 6110-9,6430-2,6395-0,6437-X,6655-0,6657-7,6726-3
Hymn to Saint Patrick. John E. Barrett. 6840-5
Hymn to science. Mark Akenside. 6152-4
Hymn to sleep. Herve-Noel Le Breton. 6873-1
Hymn to Sophia: the wisdom of God. Christopher M. ("Hugh MacDiarmid") Grieve. 6641-0
Hymn to St. Theresa. Richard Crashaw. 6931-2
Hymn to texture. Ruth Herschberger. 6390-X
Hymn to the belly. Ben Jonson. 6733-2
Hymn to the creation. Joseph Addison. 6820-0
A hymn to the cross. Unknown. 6881-2
Hymn to the dairymaids on Beacon Street. Christopher Morley. 6029-3
An hymn to the evening. Phillis Wheatley. 6077-3
Hymn to the flowers. Horace Smith. 6049-8,6271-7,6302-0, 6385-3,6600-3,6304-7,6543-0,6219-9
Hymn to the flowers. Horace Smith. 6910-X
Hymn to the guardian angel. J. Corson Miller. 6292-X
Hymn to the harvest moon. Erik Axel Karlfeldt. 6045-5
Hymn to the holy spirit. Saint Maelisu. 6090-0
Hymn to the holy spirit. Unknown. 6090-0
Hymn to the holy spirit. Richard Wilton. 6931-2
Hymn to the morning. Phillis Wheatley. 6077-3,6008-0
Hymn to the name of Jesus. Richard Crashaw. 6301-2
Hymn to the Nativity. John Milton. 6579-1
Hymn to the night. Henry Wadsworth Longfellow. 6014-5,6142-7,6077-3,6176-1,6289-X,6299 ,6585-6,6008-0,6300-4, 6431-0,6396-9,6126 ,6102-8,6076-5,6121-4,6250-4,6302-3,6385-3,6315-2,6726-3
Hymn to the north star. William Cullen Bryant. 6457-4
An hymn to the omnipresence. John Byrom. 6152-4
Hymn to the perfect. Edith Lovejoy Pierce. 6144-3
A hymn to the Pillory, sels. Daniel Defoe. 6380-2
Hymn to the sea. Sir William Watson. 6833-2
Hymn to the sea. Anne Whitney. 6006-4

A hymn to the sea, sels. Richard Henry Stoddard. 6997-5
A hymn to the sea. Richard Henry Stoddard. 6833-2
Hymn to the spirit of nature. Percy Bysshe Shelley. 6246-6, 6271-7,6737-9
Hymn to the sun. Amen-Hotep IV. 6879-0
Hymn to the sun. Charles M. Doughty. 6210-5
Hymn to the sun. Thomas Hood. 6974-6
Hymn to the sun. Alfred Lord Tennyson. 6252-0
Hymn to the sun god, Ra. Unknown. 6732-8
Hymn to the sunrise. Unknown. 6902-9
Hymn to the virgin. Sir Walter Scott. 6732-8,6543-0
Hymn to the Virgin Mary. Conal O'Riordan. 6282-2
Hymn to the winds. Joachim Du Bellay. 6253-9
Hymn to the winds. Joachim Du Bellay. 6771-9
Hymn to Venus. Edith Sitwell. 6209-1
Hymn to Zeus. Cleanthes. 6730-1
Hymn to Zeus ("Most glorious of immortals..."). Cleanthes. 6435-3
Hymn to Zeus, fr. Agamemnon. Aeschylus. 6730-1
Hymn" midnight hour. Eugene Field. 6949-5
Hymn, by the sick-bed of a mother. Felicia Dorothea Hemans. 6973-8
Hymn, fr. Beatrice. Joseph Sheridan Le Fanu. 6930-4
A hymn, sels. Gilbert Keith Chesterton. 6427-2
A hymn-O God of earth and altar. Gilbert Keith Chesterton. 6532-5
Hymn: crucifixus pro nobis. Patrick Carey. 6931-2
Hymn: to light. Abraham Cowley. 6933-9
A hymn. Gilbert Keith Chesterton. 6250-4
A hymne ("Drop, drop, slow tears"). Phineas Fletcher. 6933-9
An hymne in honour of...charitie and humilitie. Henry More. 6933-9
An hymne of the ascension. William Drummond of Hawthornden. 6933-9
Hymne to God my God, in my sicknesse. John Donne. 6208-3, 6562-7,6430-2,6341-1
Hymns and anthems sung at Wellesley College, sels. Caroline Hazard. 6762-X
Hymns for childhood, sels. Felicia Dorothea Hemans. 6973-8
Hymns of a hermit. John Sterling. 6980-0
Hymns of the marshes. Sidney Lanier. 7017-5
Hymnus. Unknown. 6125-7
Hymnus sanctae Mariae, sels. Ennodius. 6282-2
Hynd horn. Unknown. 6055-2,6239-3,6290-3,6613-5,6067-6, 6319
Hynson, George B.
   The last charge. 6919-3
   Old glory. 6443-4
Hypatia. Edmund Clarence Stedman. 6735-2
Hypatia, sels. Charles Kingsley. 6046-3
The hyperboreans. Pindar. 6435-3
Hyperion. John Keats. 6138-9,6186-9,6536-8,6110-9,6199-0, 6430
Hyperion's arrival. John Keats. 6543-0
Hyperion, sel. John Keats. 6958-4
Hyperion, sel. John Keats. 6935-5
Hyperion, sels. John Keats. 6049-8,6179-6,6378-0,6122-2, 6198-2,6289 ,6196-6,6541-4,6102-8,6645-3,6369-1,6138 ,6726-3,6208-3
Hypnosis. Alkman. 6847-2
Hypochondriacus. Charles Lamb. 6802-2
Hypocrisy. Samuel Butler. 6089-7,6092-7,6278-4
The hypocrite.. ? Pollok. 6294-6
The hypocrites. Ibn al-Batti. 6362-4
Hyslop, James
   The Cameronian's dream. 6271-7,6383-7
Hysteria. Daisy Arnold Maude. 6841-3
Hywel ab Owain Gwynedd
   Ode to a chosen girl. Gwyn Williams (tr.). 6528-7
Hywel and Blodwen. Idris Davies. 6360-8

"I 'most lost my humor". My husband's famous pup. Estella Moul Miller. 6906-1
"I abide and abide and better abide". Sonnet ("I abide"). Sir Thomas Wyatt. 6584-8
"I ain' anybody in particular". Love on the half shell.

I

David Law ("Pegleg Arkwright") Proudfit. 6914-2
I ain't dead yet. Edgar A. Guest. 7033-7
"I ain't, ner don't p'tend to be". My philosofy. James Whitcomb Riley. 6892-8
I almost had forgotten. Christopher Morley. 6619-4
"I almost received her heart into my own". The pet lamb, sels. William Wordsworth. 6867-7
"I always hoped the world would slowly drift". Not Eliot's whimper. Alice Mackenzie Swaim. 6857-X
"I always loved this solitary hill". Infinity. Giacomo Leopardi. 6879-0
"I always loved to call my lady Rose". Madrigal. Unknown. 6182-6
"I always think of mother, when". The lilacs. Edgar A. Guest. 6862-6
"I always thought of them as potted flowers". Cinerarias. Dorothy Lowry Dolan. 6789-1
I always thought that love would be. Norma Paul Ruedi. 6799-9
"I always wanted to make up poems". No more poems. Hannah Kahn. 6979-7
I am. John Clare. 6208-3,6641-0,6513-9,6726-3
I am. Walter De La Mare. 6905-3
"I am 25 years old/black female poet". My poem. Nikki Giovanni. 7024-8
"I am a blessed Glendoveer". The rebuilding. James Smith. 6802-2
"I am a bold Republican, James Ervin is my name". Unknown. 6059-5
I am a boy again. James Abraham Martling. 6952-5
"I am a child of the universe/Like the...". Soliloquy. Ema Helen Perry. 6799-9
"I am a clerk. I read the papers". The ghost of the clerk. Archibald Fleming. 6761-1
"I am a cunning little elf". The frost-elf. Francis Saltus Saltus. 6965-7
"I am a faded leaf, and you a flower". Minor note 002, fr. In Tuscany. Cora Fabri. 6876-6
"I am a faithless Columbine". Lament of Columbine. Lucy Winn. 6818-9
"I am a feather on the bright sky". The delight song of Tsoai-Talee. N. Scott Momaday. 7005-1
"I am a ferry boat./You're my passenger". The ferry boat and the passenger. Yong-woon Han. 6775-1
"I am a flame". Inspiration. Georgia H. Cooper. 6850-2
"I am a friar of orders gray". The friar of orders gray. John O'Keefe. 6930-4
"I am a friar of orders gray." John O'Keefe. 6271-7,6302-0, 6385-3,6219-9
"I am a garden of red tuli ps". Prayer ("I am a garden"). Richard Aldington. 6649-6
"I am a goddess of the ambrosial courts". Artemis prologuizes. Robert Browning. 6980-0
"I am a gold lock." Mother Goose. 6452-3
I am a grown man. Franz Werfel. 6643-7
I am a little church (no great cathedral). Edward Estlin Cummings. 6388-8
"I am a little world made cunningly". John Donne. 6369-1, 6562-7
"I am a lover yet was never loved." Unknown. 6563-5
"I am a maid in sorrow, in sorrow to complain". Unknown. 6059-5
"I am a merchant's only son; my age it is twenty-two". Unknown. 6059-5
"I am a monarch born". The wail of atlas. James Abraham Martling. 6952-5
"I am a monarch, the king of trees". John Dryden. 6376-4
"I am a namer of words". Talent. Marion D. Kendall. 6818-9
I am a parcel of vain strivings tied. Henry David Thoreau. 6333-0,6208-3
"I am a peevish student, I". Melancholia. Unknown. 6902-9
"I am a Puritan proud to be dancing". Lyric ("I am a Puritan"). Pricilla Heath. 6764-6
"I am a poor tiler in simple array" Unknown. 6182-6
"I am a poore & harmless mayde." Unknown. 6563-5
"I am a regular New York guy". Song of a regular New York guy. Morton. 6817-0
"I am a roaming gambler". Unknown. 6059-5
"I am a shell out of the Asian sea". The shell. Herbert Trench. 6877-4

"I am a small boy again". Game. Robert Davis. 6855-3
"I am a spring". The well. Thomas Edward Brown. 6809-X
"I am a spruce tree tall and strong". The spruce tree. Dorothy Choate Herriman. 6797-2
"I am a tongue for beauty". Sonnet ("I am a tongue"). Clement Wood. 6250-4
"I am a trek-ox weakly, stubborn I may be too". 'Through other eyes'. Brian ("Korongo") Brooke. 6938-X
"I am a wandering black-a-moor". The wandering black-a-moor. Julious C. Hill. 6799-9
"I am a washer-woman". Washer-woman. Constance Crane. 6750-6
"I am a weakling. God, who made". The weakling. Arthur Adams. 6784-0
"I am a willing captive in your hands". Captive. Fay Slobod Greenfield. 6799-9
"I am a woful suitor to your honor". William Shakespeare. 6409-4
"I am a woman, and am proud of it". Woman's power, fr. Joseph and his breathen. Charles Jeremiah Wells. 6934-7
"I am a woman-therefore I may not". A woman's thought. Richard Watson Gilder. 7041-8
"I am a young girl, and my fortune is sad". Unknown. 6059-5
"I am a/Man/I am a/Poet". But. A.D. Winans. 6901-0
"I am Ah-woa-te, the hunter". No answer is given. Constance Lindsay Skinner. 6897-9
"I am all alone and the visions that play". Thomas Kibble Hervey. 6980-0
"I am all bent to glean the golden ore". Madrigal: To his lady Selvaggia Vergiolesi. Cino da Pistoia. 7039-6
"I am alone - Oh be thou near to me". The prayer of a lonely heart. Frances Anne Kemble. 6980-0
"I am alone in the cloister of the falling...". The cloister of the falling snow. Sylvia Hortense Bliss. 7030-2
"I am alone in the forest". The Maine woods. Crea W. Hobart. 6906-1
"I am always bewailing the desolate fair". A lament for Adam. Benjamin Franklin Taylor. 6815-4
"'I am always corrected/correcting'". The lament of the poet. James Reaney. 6767-2
"I am always happy to see you, Allen Ginsberg". Ten years before the blast(an after dinner...) Charles Plymell. 6998-3
"I am an Eskimo". Magic word. Edgar Jackson. 6870-7
"I am an acme of things...", fr. Walt Whitman. Walt Whitman. 6597-X
I am an American. Elias Lieberman. 6337-3,6265-2,6464-7
"I am an American!" Unknown. 6715-8
'I am an elocutionist.' Unknown. 6719-0
"I am an inter-citian, I am Black as you...see". Making of a militant. II), Yillie Bey (William Manns. 7024-8
"I am an unadventurous man". De Gustibus— St. John Hankin. 6760-3
"I am angry at myself said the mirror". Love poem without anyone in it. Neeli Cherkovski. 6792-1
"I am any man's suitor". The 'how' and the 'why'. Alfred Lord Tennyson. 6977-0
"I am as I am and so will I be." Sir Thomas Wyatt. 6584-8
"I am as a field of grass". When love is gone. Nancy Telfair. 6841-3
"I am as light as any roe". Women are worthy. Unknown. 6881-2
"I am as shallow". A river in drouth. Lydia Gibson. 6880-4
"I am at the door of the closed room". The closed room. Benjamin De Casseres. 7007-8
"I am aware, this night of spring". Lilacs. Evelyn Grace Flynn. 6847-2
"I am booming, brother, booming". Cold consolation. Eugene Field. 6949-5
"I am born from the womb of the cloud". Iris. Bayard Taylor. 6976-2
"I am brooding over a nest of red plums and...". Still life. Betsy Bering. 6966-5
I am brown. Oralee Brown Harris. 6750-6
I am but a little girl. Unknown. 6713-1
"I am but an hour in your heart". Clock stop. Evelyn Hudson Rowley. 6799-9

"I am but dust". 'Though he slay'. Albion W. Tourgee. 7022-1
"I am called Chyldhod, in play is all my mynde" Thomas Moore. 6380-2
"I am called childhood, in play is all my mind". A pageant of human life. Sir Thomas More. 6935-5
"I am caught in the new power". Custer must have learned to dance. Elizabeth Woody. 7005-1
"I am come intol my garden, my sister..spouse". Veni in hortum. Bible. 6830-8
"I am Constantine Kanaris". Epitaph of Constantine Kanaris. Wilhelm Muller. 6948-7
I am content. Unknown. 6277-6,6707-7,6552-X
"I am copying down in a book from my heart's..". The mercy of God. Jessica Powers. 6839-1
"I am crawling through the forest...". The fall of the mighty. Brian ("Korongo") Brooke. 6938-X
"I am Edgar, an Eskimo". Self-portrait. Edgar Jackson. 6870-7
"I am dead, but I wait...". Unknown. 6251-2
I am desert-born. Vaida Stewart Montgomery. 6979-7
I am dying. Unknown. 6910-X
"I am dying. Egypt, dying" fr. Antony and Cleopatra. William Shakespeare. 6879-0
"I am dying...", fr. Antony and Cleopatra. William Shakespeare. 6339-X
"I am entrapped, my dear, by...illusion". Krsna. Unknown (Newari). 7013-2
"I am Eve, great Adam's wife". Eve's lament. Unknown. 6930-4
"I am fading from you". The old year's blessing. Adelaide Anne Procter. 6957-6
"I am feeling ache-and-ouchy". Behind the muzzle. W. Livingston Larned. 7008-6
"I am fond of the swallow - I learn from her..". The swallow. Madame De la Mothe Guion. 6814-6
"I am footsore and very weary". A tryst with death. Adelaide Anne Procter. 6957-6
"I am for ever haunted by one dread". Vale. Maurice Baring. 6785-9
"I am four monkeys/One hangs from a limb". The tree. Alfred Kreymborg. 6861-8
"I am free! I have burst through my...chain". The broken chain. Felicia Dorothea Hemans. 6973-8
"I am free, I've broken the halter". Defiance. John W. Boldyreff. 6818-9
"I m freed from the burdens of the sea". Trilice, sels. Cesar Vallejo. 6803-0
I am from Ireland. Unknown. 6881-2
"I am from Ireland,/The sad country". Dispossessed poet. Monk Gibbon. 6930-4
"I am from Rasainen./That is where you...". On the Jewish dealer A.S. Johannes Bobrowski. 6758-1
"I am glad I'm who I am". Jessie Orton Jones. 6999-1
"I am glad to think." Jean Ingelow. 6225-3
"I am going to tell you now what happened...". The little boy kidnapped by the bear. Unknown (Algonquin Indian). 6864-2
"I am he that walks", fr. Song of myself. Walt Whitman. 6332-2,6125-7,6252-0
"I am he who knows not where to set his feet". While I sang my song. Jacinto Fombona Pachano. 6759-X
"I am here for thee". To fancy. Richard Watson Dixon. 6844-8
"I am here, I have traversed the tomb". He cometh forth into the day. Unknown (Egyptian). 7039-6
"I am hhll-born and have not sailed the sea". On the fossil ridge. Dorothy Stott Shaw. 6836-7
"I am his highness' dog at Kew". Unknown. 6289-X
I am in love with high far-seeing places. Arthur Davison Ficke. 6509-0,6556-2,6431-0,6393-4
"I am in love with high far-seeing places", fr.Sonnets. Arthur Davison Ficke. 6897-9
"I am in Rome". Samuel Rogers. 6331-4,6631-3
I am Ireland. Padraic Pearse. 6244-X
"I am in love with the sea, but I do not trust". The sea-captain. Gerald Gould. 6833-2
"I am jealous,/Of the trees and birds". Jaelousy. Trang Thai. 6883-9
"I am Jesu that cum to fight". Undo your heart. Unknown. 6881-2
"I am just two and two, I am warm, I am cold". Riddle. William Cowper. 6814-6
"I am leaving, too./Shall I just pine away...". The departing boat. Yong-chul Park. 6775-1
"I am like a flag unfurled in space". Presaging. Rainer Maria Rilke. 7039-6
I am lonely. James Abraham Martling. 6952-5
I am lonely, fr. The Spanish Gypsy. George (Mary Ann Cross) Eliot. 6239-3
"I am lonely, so lonely". I am lonely. James Abraham Martling. 6952-5
"I am looking for a nosegay". Which shall I choose? Delle Bloss Davenport. 6818-9
"I am lying in the grasses". With the linnets. Cora Fabri. 6876-6
"I am lying in the tomb, love". Lament for a little child. Roden Noel. 6873-1
"I am making songs for you!". A God for you, fr. Songs for Sally. Marion Strobel. 6778-6
I am man. Tomi Caroly Tinsley. 6178-8
"I am monarch of all I survey". Verses ("I am monarch"). William Cowper. 6486-8
"I am Nicholas Tachinardi, hunchbacked...". The hunchbacked singer. Unknown. 6923-1
I am my beloved's, and his desire is toward me. Francis Quarles. 6933-9
"I am my mammie's ae bairn." Robert Burns. 6317-9
"I am no chieftain, fit to lead". El Khalil. Bayard Taylor. 6976-2
"I am no gentleman, not I!". The working man's song. John Stuart Blackie. 6819-7
"I am no pet who can set." Patric Dickinson. 6317-9
"I am no poet, so the critics say...". The juggler. Mary McNeil Fenollosa. 7038-8
"I am no subject unto fate". Unknown. 6933-9
"I am no trumpet, but a reed". A reed. Elizabeth Barrett Browning. 6980-0
"I am not a shaman". Untitled. Robert J. Conley. 7005-1
I am not a-mused. Lani Steele. 6857-X
"I am not ambitious at all". The ballade of the incompetent ballade-monger. James Kenneth Stephen. 6875-8
I am not bound to win. Abraham Lincoln. 6337-3
"I am not concern'd to know". True riches. Isaac Watts. 6932-0,6831-6,6932-0,6831-6
"I am not covetous for gold". Henry's address to his army, fr. King Henry V. William Shakespeare. 6934-7
"I am not dead, I have only become inhuman". Inscription for a gravestone. Robinson Jeffers. 6879-0
"I am not dead, I live again!". My hero. Ethel Mae Artz. 6799-9
I am not flattered. Robert Francis. 6761-1
"I am not here! Nor life nor". Don Marquis. 6850-2
"I am not of those miserable males". George Meredith. 6508-2
"I am not of those miserable males" George Meredith. 6828-6
I am not old. Unknown. 6412-4
"I am not one who much or oft...", fr. Personal talk. William Wordsworth. 6122-2
I am not ready yet. Alice Polk Hill. 6836-7
"I am not sure if I knew the truth". Youth. Laurence (Adele Florence Nicolson) Hope. 6856-1
"I am not surprised". On a clear day I can see forever. Alex Kuo. 6790-5
"I am not what I was". Last prayers. Mary Ann Browne. 6752-2
"I am not yet defeated; I refuse". The devil prompts a sonnet. Ronald Walker Barr. 6906-1
"I am Ojistoh, I am she, the wife". Ojistoh. Emily Pauline ("Tekahionwake") Johnson. 6837-5
"I am numb from too much feeling" Georgia Kunz. 6899-5
I am of Ireland. Unknown. 6930-4
I am of Ireland. William Butler Yeats. 6375-6
'I am of Ireland' William Butler Yeats. 6930-4
"I am old/Days of gold". An ancient stutters. Charles Monroe Walker. 6764-6
"I am on Tom Tiddler's ground". A song ("I am on"). Joan Coster. 6262-8

"I am only a cog in a giant machine...". Ammunition column. Gilbert Frankau. 7027-2
"I am only a faded primrose, dying...". A bunch of primroses. George Robert Sims. 6928-2
"I am pagan, so are you". To April. David Innes. 6750-6
"I am Policeman 12,004.". The policeman's story. George Birdseye. 6917-7
"I am partly moon and partly traveling salesman". Vicente Huidobro. 6759-X
"I am pleased, and yet I'm sad". Henry Kirke White. 6543-0
"I am poor brother Lippo, by your leave!". Fra Lippo Lippi. Robert Browning. 6828-6
"I am prescient by the very hope". Elizabeth Barrett Browning. 6238-5
I am Raftery. Anthony Raftery. 6930-4,7039-6,6244-X
I am Raftery. Anthony Raftery. 6930-4
"I am primarily engaged to myself". Public servant of the gods. Ralph Waldo Emerson. 6954-1
"I am quite sure he thinks I am God". 'Cluny' William Croswell Doane. 7008-6
"I am Raferty the poet". I am Raftery. Anthony Raftery. 6930-4,7039-6,6244-X
"I am Raftery the poet". I am Raftery. Anthony Raftery. 6930-4
"I am reading out of the book of my own evil". The book and the cup. Jessica Powers. 6839-1
I am ready, fr. The bard of the Dimbovitza. Unknown. 6552-X
"I am resilient and in love". Etruscan vase. Jean Nuchtern. 6857-X
"I am resting by the aloes, where the summer..". The dying Kafir. George Blair. 6800-6
"I am saying this to you as you lie asleep". 'Listen, son.' Unknown. 6750-6
I am seven and can sew. Mary Lydia Bolles Branch. 6713-1
"I am shadow. My burden is sorrow". Shadow. John Robert Henderson. 6836-7
"I am she whose ramparts, ringed with..swords". Serbia to the Hohenzollerns. Cecil Chesterton. 7031-0
"I am sitting alone by the desolate hearth...". Cherished letters. Mrs. Alexander McVeigh Miller. 6923-1
"I am sitting here". The poor girl's meditation. Padraic Colum. 6776-X
"I am sitting in my room". House arrest. George Tsongas. 6792-1
"I am so conscious of the girl". The two-seater. Kenneth H. Ashley. 6785-9
"I am so farre from pittying thee" Unknown. 6380-2
"'I am so happy', she said". A joyous little maid. L.C. Whiton. 6965-7
"I am so high on a hill". Hill magic. Estelle Rooks. 6850-2
"I am so well--I am so well/That my bones...". Laughing bones. Alice Carter Cook. 6799-9
"I am somethin' of a vet'ran...". Too progressive for him. Laurana W. Sheldon. 6924-X
"I am stone of many colors" Frank LaPena Tauhindauli. 7005-1
I am sure of it. Jimmy Santiago Baca. 6870-7
"I am surprised you have not heard me bleeding" Ronald R.W. Lightbourne. 6898-7
"I am tenant of nine feet by four". Verses. Horace Twiss. 6802-2
"I am the autumn.". The nutter. Herbert Trench. 6877-4
"I am the beggar who cries for life". Beggar. Dorothy Grey Smith. 6799-9
"I am the bending of the moon". Essence. Raine Stryder. 6857-X
I am the best thing they did. John Rolfe. 6761-1
"I am the birgin; from this granite ledge". The way-side virgin. Langdon Elwyn ("John Philip Varley") Mitchell. 7041-8
"I am the boy with his hands raised over...". The house that fear built: Warsaw, 1943 Jane Flanders. 6803-0
"I am the cool, green earth where lovers lie". Return to earth. Ina Draper DeFoe. 6750-6
"I am the crazy woman". Birthright. Geraldine Kudaka. 6790-5
I am the cr ss. William L. Stidger. 6144-3,6335-7
I am the cry. Muriel Strode. 6102-8,6076-5

"I am the dancer of the wood". The spirit of the birch. Arthur Ketchum. 6891-X
"I am the doll that Nancy broke!". Nancy's nightmare. Laura E. Richards. 6937-1
I am the door. Richard Crashaw. 6430-2
"I am the dreamless dark of the mines". Mine song. E. Falkowski. 6954-1
"I am the first of the Teschen people". I, sels. Petr Bezruc. 6763-8,6886-3
"I am the flower of the field", fr. Canticles. Unknown. 6282-2
"I am the giant Hesperus!". The song of Hesperus. James Abraham Martling. 6952-5
I am the gilly of Christ. Joseph ("Seosamh MacCathmhaoil") Campbell. 6872-3,6930-4
"I am the giver of all gifts, and I". Time. Esther Valck Georgns. 6799-9
"I am the god Thor". The challenge of Thor. Henry Wadsworth Longfellow. 6850-2
"I am the god Thor/I am the war god". The musician's tale. Henry Wadsworth Longfellow. 6753-0
I am the immigrant. Unknown. 6954-1
"I am the luring Vivien". Woman. Zora Cross. 6784-0
"I am the man/who picks your food". To people who pick food. Wilfredo Q. Castano. 6998-3
"I am the monument of fair things slain". Rhodanthe; on herself, grown old. Rosamund Marriott ("Graham R. Tomson") Watson. 6785-9
"I am the Negro/Black as the night is black". The negro. Langston Hughes. 6954-1
"I am the mother of fair love", fr. Ecclesiasticus. Unknown. 6282-2
I am the mountainy singer. Joseph ("Seosamh MacCathmhaoil") Campbell. 6332-2,6102-8,6292-X,6506-6
I am the mule. Will Chamberlain. 6510-4
"I am the one who loved her as my life". The legend of Qu'Appelle valley. Emily Pauline ("Tekahionwake") Johnson. 6837-5
I am the only being whose doom. Emily Bronte. 6317-9,6380-2,6655-0
I am the plow. A. Heinrich. 6662-3
"I am the plow that turns the sod". The breaking plow. Nixon Waterman. 6889-8
"I am the pure lotus". He is like the lotus. Unknown (Egyptian). 7039-6
"I am the reality of things that seem". Poetry. Ella Crosby Heath. 6607-0,6730-1
"'I am the resurrection and the life'.". The only true life. Horace B. Durant. 6921-5
"I am the rose of Sharon". Ego flos campi. Bible. 6830-8
I am the rose of Sharon. Catherine Winkworth. 6065-X
I am the rose of Sharon, fr. Song of Solomon. Bible. 6125-7
"I am the sister of him". Little. Dorothy Aldis. 6850-2
"I am the spirit of the morning sea". Ode. Richard Watson Gilder. 7041-8
"I am the spirit that dwells in the flower". The flower spirit. Unknown. 6752-2
"I am the stage, impassive, mute and cold". Nature. Alfred de Vigny. 7039-6
"I am the tomb of Crethon; here you read". The tomb of Crethon. Leonidas of Tarentum. 7039-6,6879-0
"I am he true companion all will find". Faith. Carolyn Renfrew. 6789-1
"I am the voice of the city". The city speaks. Clara Byrnes. 6847-2
'I am the way, and the truth, and the life'. Unknown. 6752-2
"I am the way." Alice Meynell. 6337-3,6335-7,6096-X,6508-2, 6022-X,6292-X,6250-4,6172-9
I am the wind. Zoe Akins. 6019-6,6076-5,6102-8
"I am the wind - my wing stoops low". The wind. Harold Fehrsen Sampson. 6800-6
"I am the wind that breathes upon the sea". The mystery. Amergin (atr.). 6930-4
"I am the wind which breathes upon the sea". The mystery of Amergin. Unknown. 6873-1
"I am the world.o.unveil this face". I am. Walter De La Mare. 6905-3

"I am thinking of thee, O, quaint little town". O, quaint little town. Mary Matthews Bray. 6798-0
"I am this fountain's god. Below". The river god. John Fletcher. 6935-5
"I am thy father's spirit", fr. Hamlet. William Shakespeare. 6406-X
"I am thy soul, Nekoptis. I have watched". The tomb at Akr Caar. Ezra Pound. 6754-9
I am tired. Fernando Pessoa. 6758-1
"I am tired of London". London, August. Charles Ould. 6800-6
"I am tired of planning and toiling", The cry of the dreamer. John Boyle O'Reilly. 7012-4
"I am tired of the everlasting wrinkled..river". July madness. Nancy Telfair. 6841-3
"I am tired of this!". A variation. James Whitcomb Riley. 6992-4
"I am tired tonight, and something". Tired. Ella Wheeler Wilcox. 6956-8
"I am tired, that is clear". I am tired. Fernando Pessoa. 6758-1
I am to have a child. Edith Livingston Smith. 6097-8
"I am to you all things majestical". Anna Bromberger. 6847-2
"I am told, sir, you're keeping an eye on...". The careful husband. Unknown. 6930-4
"I am too little for a grand eternity". Heaven. Katharine Haviland Taylor. 6750-6
"I am troubled tonight with a curious pain". Misalliance. Ella Wheeler Wilcox. 6956-8
"I am two brothers with one face". The brothers. Dante Gabriel Rossetti. 6802-8
"I am Ulala,/Priestess and Princess". The prophecy of Ulala! James Abraham Martling. 6952-5
"I am Umbawa,/Prince of Mpauqwa!". The curse of Umbawa. James Abraham Martling. 6952-5
I am undone. Virginia Moore. 6619-4
"I am undone/taken down". Today, prison won. Jessica Scarbrough. 6870-7
I am waitin' on the levee. Unknown. 6609-7
"I am waiting in the desert, looking out...". Ojira, to her lover. Laurence (Adele Florence Nicolson) Hope. 6856-1
"I am warm and humane". This prowling zoo. Marge Piercy. 6803-0
I am weary of being bitter. Arthur Davison Ficke. 6374-8, 6509-0,6723-9
"I am weary of lying within the chase". Ballade de Marguerite. Unknown (French). 7039-6
"I am weary of the working". To solitude. Alice Cary. 6969-X
"I am weary, such repose". Prayer ("I am weary"). Luise Hensel. 6259-8
"I am weary- I am weary". Despair. James Abraham Martling. 6952-5
"I am wedded to the greenwood". Solitaire. Muriel F. Hochdorf. 6850-2
I am weeping, mother. Roden Noel. 6097-8
I am with you always. Edwin Henry Nevin. 6065-X
"I am work". Work. Anna H. Gillmore. 6764-6
"I am writing this to you...". A son's letter to his dead father. Unknown. 6750-6
I am writing to you from a far-off country. Henri Michaux. 6758-1
"I am yısterday, to-day, and to-morrow". He walketh by day. Unknown (Egyptian). 7039-6
I am young. George Frederick Cameron. 6115-X
"I am your big trimmer". The big trimmer, fr. Ogesa Ondo. Ronald P. Tanaka. 6790-5
I am your wife. Unknown. 6260-1
"I am, saith the Lord...", fr. The mystery...saints. Charles Peguy. 6351-9
"I am; my maker made me". Lenten Musings. Ida Walden Thomas. 6818-8
"I analyzed the fragile bas-relief". To Justin, drowned. Francis J. Mathues. 6839-1
"I and my body" Konrad Bayer. 6769-7
I and my joy. Edward Carpenter. 6320-9
"I and my white Pangur". The monk and his pet cat. Unknown. 6930-4
"I and new love, in all its living bloom". New and old. Ella Wheeler Wilcox. 6956-8
"I and Pangur ban my cat". Pangur ban. Unknown. 6930-4
"I and the bird/And the wind together". A trio. Arthur Christopher Benson. 6793-X
I and you. Nikolai Gumilev. 6103-6
I announce the kingdom of the star. Jacinto Fombona Pachano. 6642-9
I announce the kingdom of the stars. Jacinto Fombona Pachano. 6642-9
I anonymous. Eve Merriam. 6761-1
"I arise from dreams of thee." Percy Bysshe Shelley. 6240-7,6302-0,6385-3
"I arrive/in the unbearable heat". Song for my father. Jessica Hagedorn. 6790-5
I ask. John Galsworthy. 6888-X
I ask but this. Nova Dornin. 6750-6
"I ask no organ's soulless breath". The meeting, sels. John Greenleaf Whittier. 6934-7
"I ask no other vengeance, love, from you". Angelo Poliziano. 6325-X
"I ask not for riches". A humble prayer. Helen Plavnicky. 6894-4
I ask not for those thoughts that suddenly leap. James Russell Lowell. 6126-5
"I ask not Gyges' riches". Unknown (Greek) 6251-2
"I ask not wealth, but power to take". A prayer ("I ask not wealth..."). Phoebe Cary. 6969-X
"I ask not your silver, I want not your gold". Gifts. Lillian M. Hagar. 6818-9
"I ask one boon of heaven; I have indeed". Forgetfulness. R.A. Thorpe. 7015-9
"I ask that when my spirit quits this shell...". 'He done his damdest' E. Bell Guthrey. 7012-4
"I ask you dear, if I should die". Suppose. Zilla Vollmer Tietgen. 6799-9
"I ask/But an hour of music". An hour. Dorothy Curran. 6750-6
I asked a thief. William Blake. 6733-6
"I asked for peace". Digby Mackworth Dolben. 6931-2
"I asked no other thing". Emily Dickinson. 6339-X,6646-1
"I asked of Echo, t'other day". Echo. John Godfrey Saxe. 6089-7,6277-6,6302-0,6385-3,6613-2,6732-,6724-7,6964-9
"I asked of my muse, had she any objection". Sfere. Morris Rosenfeld. 7011-6
"I asked the angels in my prayer". The pure in heart. Alice Cary. 6969-X
"I asked the sun." Unknown. 6238-5
"I ate a philopena". Give and take. R. Priestley Hayes. 6936-3
"I ate at Ostendorff's, and saw a dame". Traumerei at Ostendorff's. William Laird. 6897-9
I attempt from love's sickness, fr. The Indian queen. Sir Robert Howard. 6328-4
"I awakened to dryness and the ferns were dead". The tragedy of the leaves. Charles Bukowski. 6792-1
"I awoke one morning early". Cheer up. Laura Neary. 6764-6
"I bade thee stay". Song ("I bade thee stay"). Sarah Helen Whitman. 6271-7
"I bathe in the lush of the moon". Bacchante. Alice Louise Jones. 6959-2
"I be parewld most of prise". A lady of high dgeree. Unknown (French). 6771-9
"I be'en a-kindo' 'musin', as the feller says". Romancin'. James Whitcomb Riley. 6991-6
"I bear the banner of the sun at noon". Wind of the west. Eden Phillpotts. 6793-X
"I bear thee flowers shrined in my heart...". Thistledown. Cora Fabri. 6876-6
"I beg of you, I beg of you, my brothers". A beggar. Adelaide Anne Procter. 6957-6
"I beg your pardon, misters". Up thar behind the sky! J.M. Munyon. 6922-3
"I begin through the grass once again...". Reconciliation. George William ("A.E.") Russell. 6872-3
"I beheld a dream last night". Unknown. 6050-1
"I beheld my love this morning...". Sayat Nova. 6050-1
"I believe in stillness". Blessing myself. David Ignatow. 6803-0

I

"I believe in the omnipotent idea which bestow". Thirsting amphora. Rafael Heliodoro Valle. 6759-X
I believe thy precious blood. John Wesley. 6065-X
"I bend above my broom, doggedly as doom". Sweeping. Bertha L. Gibbons. 6906-1
"I bend o'er the wheel at my sewing". From dawn to dawn. Morris Rosenfeld. 7011-6
I bended unto me. Thomas Edward Brown. 6809-X
"I bequeath my turtle dove". Unknown. 6187-7
"I bet God understands about givin up five" Yasmeen Jamal. 6870-7
"I bid farewell" Muin Ozaki. 6981-9
"I bid you, mock not Eros". Of a child that had fever. Christopher Morley. 6777-8
"I bide my time, for, soon or late, the hour". The dream of the multi-millionaire. Charles Whitby. 6994-0
I bind my heart. Lauchlan MacLean Watt. 6337-3
"I bind your heart with love-made twine". To my valentine. Aileen Voight. 6850-2
"I blasphemed/Fate for scanty". The birthplace. Elisabeth Kuskulis. 6836-7
"I bore with thee, long, weary days". Christina Georgina Rossetti. 6065-X
"I bought at the plaza". Unknown. 6364-0
I bought me a wife. Unknown. 6003-X
I bow my forehead. John Greenleaf Whittier. 6503-1
"I bowed my soul before the cross". Transfigured. William White. 6868-5
"I breathe but, Oh!" Moritake. 6027-7
"I breathe into you". The sinew of our dreams. Edgar Jackson. 6870-7
"I bring fresh showers for the thirsting flowers". The cloud. Percy Bysshe Shelley. 6122-2,6154-0,6183-4, 6271-7,6289-X,6302 ,6198-2,6239-3,6332-2,6423-X,6466-3,6610 ,6385-3,6457-4,6552-X,6604-6,6621-6,6661 , 6473-6,6499-X,6536-8,6597-X,6623-2,6102 ,6677-1,6639-9,6660-7,6543-0,6396-9,6304 ,6421-3,6371-3,6252-0, 6219-9,6250-4,6199-0,6153 ,6086-2,6438-8,6196-6,6430-2,6110-9,6560
"I bring fresh showers for the...flowers". The cloud, sels. Percy Bysshe Shelley. 6934-7
I bring no prayers on coloured silk. Kwan-ke. 6852-9
I bring you silence, my beloved. Nellie Burget Miller. 6836-7
I broke the spell that held me long. William Cullen Bryant. 6732-8,6288-1,6431-0
"I brought her from the sand-dunes". My little Cape Cod maiden. Katherine Finnigan Anderson. 6818-9
"I brought in these to make her kitchen sweet". The singer's muse. Francis Ledwidge. 6812-X
"I built a tiny garden". Sanctum. Beulah B. Malkin. 6750-6
"I built a yatch, to call it Nell". The reason. H.F. Covington. 6983-5
"I built myself a castle". A castle in the air. Adelaide Anne Procter. 6957-6
"I bundled it up and tucked it in bed". My grief. Elena Vossen Greenfield. 6841-3
"I burnt for England with a living flame". Poem ("I burnt"). Gervase Stewart. 6666-6
"I bury you here by the edge of the lands". Burial. Kingsley Fairbridge. 6800-6
"I buy a hamburger/at a plexiglass coffeeshop". Revelation of the bare ass. Douglas Blazek. 6792-1
I call and I call. Robert Herrick. 6125-7
"I call her the red lily. Lo! She stands". The red lily. Paul Hamilton Hayne. 7041-8
"I call on Zeus...", fr. Agamemnon. Aeschylus. 6435-3
I call the swallows. Toyohiko Kagawa. 6027-7
"I call thee blest!-though now the voice..fled". The image in the heart. Felicia Dorothea Hemans. 6973-8
"I call you hard", fr. Aurora Leigh. Elizabeth Barrett Browning. 6123-0
"I called my mother in 1979". Collect calls. Diana Bickston. 6870-7
"I called you by sweet names by wood and linn". Ireland. Francis Ledwidge. 6812-X
"I came across 'em, by the stair". At her wedding. Edgar A. Guest. 6869-3
"I came at morn--'twas spring. I smiled,". Mary Pypher. 6083-8

"I came by night to Tehlus wood". Thelus wood. Muriel Stuart. 6884-7
I came down from Lebanon. Clinton Scollard. 6732-8
"I came from out the shiny pack". Song of the ace. Unknown. 6983-5
"I came in to find". A love that was. Margaret Haynes Foster. 7016-7
"I came into this world to see the sunlight" Konstantin Balmont. 6103-6
"I came the Womack Road from Sandy Bridge". Young Kentucky. Jesse Stuart. 7017-5
"I came to thee enraptured, and I found". The message of nature. A. Bernard Miall. 6785-9
"I came to town a happy man". Miss Fanny's farewell flowers. Thomas Hood. 6974-6
"I came to town the other day". My daughter Jane. Sarah L. Flowers. 6916-9
"I came tonight because each corner of my room". Conscience. Evana Llynn. 6906-1
"I came upon a yellow hickory wood". Autumn hickory trees. George A. Scarborough. 6761-1
"I came, but they had passed away". The weary soul. Unknown. 6911-8
I can and I will. Idella Campbell Betts. 6461-2
"I can climb our apple tree". Jessie Orton Jones. 6999-1
"I can count my francs an' santeems". When Private Mugrums parley vous. Charles Divine. 6846-4
"I can love both faire and brown". John Donne. 6187-7
"I can plow upon the hill". Field plowing. William Roehrick. 6850-2
"I can recall that once we knew". Happy days. Robert E. Bernhard. 6894-4
"I can remember days when time". Tempo change. H. Totman. 6750-6
"I can see him now/smiling". My grandfather was a quantum physicist. Duane Big Eagle. 7005-1
"I can sing of myself a true song...". Unknown. 6258-X
"I can sweep a broom". Trash. Earl Gene Box. 6870-7
I can tell de world. Gus Joiner. 6149-4
I can wade grief. Emily Dickinson. 6908-8
"I can't be talkin' of love, dear". Song ("I can't be talkin'"). Esther Matthews. 6324-1
"I can't conceive why God, whose will devine". New England Mayflower. Vileta Nelson Chartier. 6764-6
"I can't forget a gaunt grey barn". Country road. Marie Louise Hersey. 6762-X
"I can't make up my mind". Handgrenades in my grapefuit. Douglas Blazek. 6998-3
"I can't remember how, or when, or where". Fantasia. Joseph Freeman. 6880-4
"I can't see into your eyes". On a gestapo photograph purported to be of the... F.W. Watt. 6767-0
"I can't tell much about the thing, 'twas done...". The railroad crossing. Hezekiah Strong. 6744-1,6964-9, 6918-5
I can't think what he sees in her. Sir Alan Patrick Herbert. 6637-2,6633-X
"I can't" and "I can" William Allen Butler. 6629-1
"I can't". Unknown. 6530-9
I can't, I won't, and I will. Unknown. 6682-8
"I cannot assuage your terror". The fatties. Ann Menebroker. 6998-3
"I cannot call my mistress fayre." Unknown. 6563-5
I cannot change. John Wilmot, 2d Earl of Rochester. 6830-8
"I cannot change as others do". Song ("I cannot change"). John Wilmot, 2d Earl of Rochester. 6562-7
"I cannot change, as others do". Constancy. A song. John Wilmot, 2d Earl of Rochester. 6933-9
"I cannot choos but think upon the time". Brother and sister. George (Mary Ann Cross) Eliot. 6772-7
"I cannot eat my porridge". A piteous plaint. Eugene Field. 6949-5
"I cannot ever feel alone/Or lonely, where...". Quietus. Luna Craven Osburn. 6799-9
"I cannot forget a gaunt grey barn". Country road. Marie Louise Hersey. 6798-0
I cannot forget with what fervid devotion. William Cullen Bryant. 6121-4,6288-1
"I cannot forget with what fervid devotion". William Cullen Bryant. 6753-0

770

"I cannot forget/The sight of that straight...". Kevin Barry. Terence Ward. 6930-4
I cannot grieve. Josephine B. Granducci. 6906-1
"I cannot hope that sorrow's feet forever...". The villages. Martha Haskell Clark. 6764-6
"I cannot keep a grief so long". Impermanence. Lizette Woodworth Reese. 6782-4
I cannot know that other men exist. Clement Wood. 6619-4
"I cannot let lost lives with lost years go". Unknown. 6238-5
"I cannot live with you". Emily Dickinson. 6399-3
"I cannot pray, as Christians use to pray". Credo. Seumas (James Starkey) O'Sullivan. 6930-4
I cannot put you away. Herbert S. Gorman. 6034-X
"I cannot reach it; and my striving eye". Childhood. Henry Vaughan. 6931-2
"I cannot reach it; and my striving eye" Henry Vaughan. 6935-5
"I cannot read, I cannot rest". Nocturne. Louis Untermeyer. 6875-8
"I cannot reap a profit's gain". Compassion. Ralph E. Webber. 6799-9
"I cannot remember the names of roads & hills". The way to the arbutus. Catherine Cate Coblentz. 7030-2
I cannot see. Iraqi. 6448-5
"I cannot see the stars and flowers". St. George's Day, sels. John Davidson. 6954-1
"I cannot separate my brothers from myself". Soul's harbor. Ann Caroline Kabel. 6857-X
"I cannot sleep, the night is hot and empty". Absence. Sara Teasdale. 6777-8
"I cannot sound the depths of my own soul". The miracle. Mabel Hill. 6799-9
I cannot tell. Phoebe Cary. 6969-X
"I cannot tell my joy, when o'er a lake". Kingfishers. Percy Bysshe Shelley. 6943-6
"I cannot tell the spell that binds thine image" Anne Chambers-Ketchum. 6226-1
"I cannot tell the spell that binds thing image." Annie Chambers Ketchum. 6066-8
"I cannot tell what you say, green leaves". Dartside. Charles Kingsley. 6793-X
"I cannot tell when first I saw her face". Unveiled. Paul Hamilton Hayne. 6753-0
"I cannot tell you how it was". May. Christina Georgina Rossetti. 6980-0,6980-0,6828-6
"I cannot tell you how it was". Christina Georgina Rossetti. 6187-7
"I cannot think but God must know." Helen Hunt Jackson. 6066-8
"I cannot think of any word". Old Saul. Lizette Woodworth Reese. 7017-5
'I cannot turn the key and my bairn outside'. Unknown. 6920-7
"I cannot vouch my tale is true". The romance of Nick Van Stann. John Godfrey Saxe. 6909-6,6566-X,6964-9
"I cannot write, I cannot think". Midsummer day. John Davidson. 6785-9
"I cannot, sweetest mother". Sappho. 6251-2
I care nobody, not I, fr. Love in a village. Isaac Bickerstaffe. 6934-7
I care not for these ladies. Thomas Campion. 6733-6,6181-1,6430-2
"I care not for these ladies that must be wooed". Song ("I care not"). Thomas Campion. 6436-1
"I care not how men trace their ancestry", sels. James Russell Lowell. 6047-1
"I care not what the world may say". My window to the sky. Mary Cromwell Low. 6847-2
"I care not who the man may be". The fellowship of books. Edgar A. Guest. 7033-7
"I care not, fortune, what you me deny". Indifference to fortune, fr. The caste of indolence. James Thomson. 6932-0
"I cared not for autumn weather". Love in the autumn. P. R. Minahan. 6818-9
"I caught a fella last in the South Pacific". Radio. Harriet Monroe. 6782-4
"I caught but a glimpse of him.Summer was here". A glimpse of Pan. James Whitcomb Riley. 6993-2

"I celebrate America". Song of the answerer. Helene Magaret. 6761-1
I celebrate myself, fr. Song of myself. Walt Whitman. 6399-3
"I chaffered in the marts today". Interlude. Bert Leach. 6906-1
"I chanced to walk, not long ago". The wedding feast. Johann Wolfgang von Goethe. 6948-7
"I chanced, one afternoon, to pass". When I was young. Unknown. 7002-7
"I chant endure the stoopid, wude". The unpardonable sin. Unknown. 6922-3
"I charge you, lady young and fair". He charges her to lay aside her weapons. Pierce Ferriter. 6930-4
"I chose to anchor on a shifting stone". Sea weed. William Roehrick. 6850-2
"I chuckle as I see her in her...party dress". Little battered legs grows up. Edgar A. Guest. 6748-4
"I clamored for a star/That shone above...". Gesture. Elisabeth Clarke. 6818-9
"I clap a hand upon a hand". Pigeons. Wilfrid Thorley. 6782-4
"I class'd and counted once". Loved once. Elizabeth Barrett Browning. 6980-0
"I climb a mountain path". Mountain path. Ju-dong Yang. 6775-1
"I climb the black rock mountain". Where mountainlion laid down with deer. Leslie Silko. 7005-1
"I climb the majestic mountain to its summit". Sublimity. Lucius M. Fall. 6799-9
"I climb the mossy bank of the glade". Robert Bridges. 6487-6
"I climbed a sheltered hillside, till the sea". A breath. William Lindsey. 6798-0
"I climbed the roofs at break fo day". The southern Alps. Alfred Lord Tennyson. 6749-2
"I close my eyes and I seem to see". Of such as these. Marion L. Bertrand. 6799-9
"I closed my eyes, and laid the paper down". The child-dancers. Percy MacKaye. 6959-2
"I closed my hands upon a moth". Beware. Dora Sigerson Shorter. 6844-8
"I closed the book of verse where sorrow wept". The visitation of peace. Francis Ledwidge. 6812-X
"I comb your hair, I wash your face". For Ninette. Mimi [pseud].. 6817-0
"I come down from Mount Vernon and ride the". Territorial retreat. Tanya Tyler. 6899-5
"I come down from the hills alone". The wanderer. Schmidt von Lubeck. 6973-8
"I come for the grain!- the grain!". The reaper. James Abraham Martling. 6952-5
"I come from a wet land". For my brother and sister southwestern indian poets. Geary Hobson. 7005-1
"I come from busy haunts of men". The cynic in the woods. Arthur Patchett Martin. 6768-2
"I come from haunts...", fr. The brook. Alfred Lord Tennyson. 6339-X
"I come from heaven to tell". Ane sang of the birth of Christ. Unknown. 6756-5
"I come from mountains under other stars". A voice from the Nile. James Thomson. 6828-6
"I come from nothing; but from where". A song of derivations. Alice Meynell. 6879-0
"I come of the seed of the people, the...". The rebel. Padraic Pearse. 6930-4
I come singing. Joseph Auslander. 6034-X,6336-5
"I come to bury Caesar...", fr. Julius Caesar. William Shakespeare. 6601-1
"I come to thee, O earth!". The song of night. Felicia Dorothea Hemans. 6973-8
"I come to you grown weary of much laughter". The return. Theodosia Garrison. 7038-8
I come up out uv Egypt. Unknown. 6609-7
"I come upon it suddenly, alone". A country fairway. James Whitcomb Riley. 6993-2
"I come, I come! ye have called me long". Voice of spring. Felicia Dorothea Hemans. 6392-6,6720-4,6479-5,6529-5, 6018-8,6304 ,6543-0,6964-9
I come, I come, ye have called me long. Felicia Dorothea

Hemans. 6304-7
"I come, I make my place, I stay". Overheard. Gertrude Huntington McGiffert. 6838-3
"I confess I pray with words". Prayer ("I confess"). Gertie Stewart Phillips. 6100-1
I could. Elizabeth Warren Jones. 6799-9
"I could be well content, allow'd the use". The four ages. William Cowper. 6814-6
"I could believe that I am here alone". Solipsism. George Santayana. 6754-9
"I could follow thee, O my father". Heredity. Edward Farquhar. 6939-8
"I could go back, to stand again". To four friends. William Roehrick. 6850-2
"I could have stemmed misfortune's tide". The wife. Unknown. 6752-2
"I could live riotously/From sun to sun". I could. Elizabeth Warren Jones. 6799-9
"I could not be a fashion plate". Careless. Edgar A. Guest. 6869-3
"I could not bear". Post mortem. Rose Koralewsky. 6764-6
"I could not bear these sultry summer days". Sultry days. Thekla N. Berstecher. 6906-1
"I could not even think". Rapunzel. William Morris. 7034-5
"I could not even think". Rapunzel. William Morris. 6828-6
"I could not know". Man's road. Enrique Pena Barrenechea. 6759-X
I could not know. Lois Royal Hughes. 6178-8
"I could not love my life, or you". Exhilaration. Joyce Lancaster. 6850-2
I could not sleep for thinking of the sky. John Masefield. 6339-X,6393-4
"I could not think him dead until I saw". A friend of mine. John E. Barrett. 6840-5
I could not through this burning day. Dollie Radford. 6301-2
I could not understand. Berthal Lanier. 6799-9
"I could resign that eye of blue". Resignation. Thomas Moore. 7025-6
I could snatch a day. Sara Teasdale. 6778-6,6038-2
"I could write the psalms again". James Oppenheim. 6007-2
"I count it true which sages teach". In memoriam technicam. Thomas Hood Jr. 6802-2
"I count my blessings o'er in years". Living. Emma Hally Hammond. 6799-9
'I count my times by times that I meet thee'. Richard Watson Gilder. 6429-9,6431-0,6309-8,6321-7
"I count that friendship little worth". Rendezvous. Henry Van Dyke. 6961-4
"I count this thing to be grandly true". Josiah Gilbert Holland. 6238-5
"I crave an ambler, worthier sphere". Anno 1829. Heinrich Heine. 7039-6
"I crossed the gangway in the winter's rain". Stowaway. Bill Adams. 6833-2
"I cry aloud, and ye shall hear my call". Carlo Maria Maggi. 6973-8
"I cry out to find something else-what is it?". 'A person, a Mexican' Lorri Martinez. 6870-7
"I cry to thee in the day, love me!". Arab song. Hermann Hagedorn. 6944-4
"I cry to you through the night, towers!". The crier in the night. Hermann Hagedorn. 6944-4
"I cry your mercy- pity-love!- aye, love!". To Fanny. John Keats. 6268-6,6086-2
I cry: Love, love!, fr. The vision of the three daughters. William Blake. 6545-7
"I curse the time, wherein these lips of mine." Thomas Watson. 6317-9
I dare believe. Rose Mills Powers. 6102-8,6076-5
"I dare not ask a kiss". Robert Herrick. 6187-7
"I dare not hope my lady-love". Fujiwara Kore-tada (Prince Ken-toku) 6852-9
"I dared not mourn". Dirge. Muriel F. Hochdorf. 6850-2
"I decked my flesh with tinsel gems". Vision. Grace Holbrook Blood. 6764-6
"I declare from this hill". From a hill top. Angela Morgan. 6861-8
"I declare that it's nothing but ignorant stuf". A popular error. John Starkie. 6917-7

"I desired thy garments, O my hope, were grey". Hope overtaken. Dante Gabriel Rossetti. 6832-4
"I des so weak en sinful". An unfortunate. Frank Lebby Stanton. 6807-3
"I despise my friends more than you". To an enemey. Maxwell Bodenheim. 6897-9
I did but look. Thomas Otway. 6737-9
"I did but prompt the age...". John Milton. 6659-3
I did hear you talk far above singing. Francis Beaumont and John Fletcher. 6066-8
I did it-not, "I done it". Unknown. 6314-4
"I did not dream that love would stay". Villanelle ("I did not"). Rosamund Marriott ("Graham R. Tomson") Watson. 6770-0
"I did not heed that spring was here." John Richard Moreland. 6326-8
"I did not know". Resignation. Nora Lane. 6750-6
"I did not know till he had gone". A discovery. Gertrude Huntington McGiffert. 6838-3
"I did not know you till one day last year". Sonnet ("I did not know"). Mary Lovell Cope. 6841-3
"I did not know, the day I nailed". Resurrection. Lloyd Frank Merrell. 6144-3
"I did not live until this time". Katherine Philips. 6187-7
"I did not raise mine eyes to hers". Et sunt commercia coeli. Herbert P. Horne. 6844-8
"I did not see the crown". Faith. Donald Earl Edwards. 6144-3
"I did not write my songs last spring". The poet's garden. Lida Wilson Turner. 6841-3
I didn't like him. Harry Bache Smith. 6089-7
"I didn't realize you were going to follow...". Following. Gene Frumkin. 6803-0
I die aliue. Robert Southwell. 6586-4
'I die daily.' Phil J. Fisher. 6337-3
I die for thy sweet love. Bryan Waller ("Barry Cornwall") Procter. 6980-0
"I die of thirst beside the fountain's brim". Ballade. Francois Villon. 6227-X
"I die with too transporting joy". Sonnet ("I die"). John Hughes. 6023-4
I die, being young. David Gray. 6656-9
I died for beauty. Emily Dickinson. 6726-3,6008-0,6348-9, 6380-2,6488-4,6527-9,6536-8,6726-
"I died in very flow'r...". Robert Bridges. 6487-6
"I dig, under the earth I dig". The pitman. Petr Bezruc. 6886-3
"I dim my eyes (to shut them could be...)". Birthday on deathrow. Harold LaMont Otey. 6870-7
"I discovered, one day, while taking a walk". The old hitching post. Constance Entwhistle Hoar. 6750-6
"I do believe". George Gordon, 6th Baron Byron. 6238-5
I do confess thou'rt smooth and fair. Sir Robert Ayton. 6092-7
'I do like to be beside the seaside', fr. Facade. Edith Sitwell. 7000-0
"I do not ask my life to be the measured tread". Liceat me ministrare. Selma Hamann. 6818-9
"I do not ask that God will keep all storms away". A song ("I do not ask"). Robert Burns Wilson. 6620-8
"I do not believe that heaven and hell...". No discharge. Arthur Waley. 6761-1
"I do not doubt that it was said before". Sonnet ("I do not doubt"). Charles Lafayette Todd. 6042-0
I do not fear. Robert Louis Stevenson. 6508-2
"I do not fear for Margaret". Old nuns' talk. Sister Margaret. 6750-6
"I do not fear to die". The fear, fr. Battle. Wilfred Wilson Gibson. 6897-9
"I do not fear what life may bring to me". I fear not life. Avis Turner French. 6764-6
"I do not go to the fields today". Unknown. 6364-0
"I do not grudge them; Lord, I do not grudge". The mother. Padraic Pearse. 6930-4
I do not know. Yong-woon Han. 6775-1
I do not know. Unknown. 6109-5
"I do not know if you will know." Frances Crawford. 6515-5
"I do not know when I shall go on- on.". Faith. Grace Evelyn Brown 6818-9

"I do not know why at times". Traces. Rafael Estrada. 6759-X
I do not like a roof tonight. Grace Noll Crowell. 6608-9
"I do not like the other sort". An ulsterman. Lynn Doyle. 6930-4
"I do not love a wanton...". Rufinus. 6251-2
"I do not love my empire's foes". Piet. Rudyard Kipling. 6810-3
I do not love thee. Caroline Elizabeth Sarah Sheridan Norton. 6092-7
"I do not love thee for that fair." Thomas Carew. 6302-0;6385-3,6737-9
"I do not love thee less for what is done". Henry Wadsworth Longfellow. 6066-8
I do not love thee, Doctor Fell. Thomas (Tom) Brown. 6722-0,6396-9
"I do not love thee, Dr. Fell". Non amo te. Martial. 7039-6
"I do not love this merciless husband of mine!" Unknown (Newari) 7013-2
I do not love to see your beauty fire. John Hall Wheelock. 6250-4
"I do not mind your telling me". Speaking of driving, fr. Matrimonial melodies. Berton Braley. 6853-7
"I do not pray for peace". A prayer ("I do not pray"). Theodosia Garrison. 6291-1
"I do not question woman's place". Samuel Hoffenstein. 6817-0
"I do not rise to waste the night in words". Catiline's defiance. George Croly. 6909-6
"I do not say bequeath unto my soul". Memory. Letitia Elizabeth ("L.E.L.") Landon. 6980-0
I do not seek, I find, fr. Sighing for retirement. John Clare. 6545-7
"I do not think the providence unkind". Thorns. Alice Cary. 6969-X
"I do not want to be your weeping woman". Poem ("I do not want"). Alison Boodson. 6379-9
"I do not waste what is wild". Empty kettle. Louis (LittleCoon) Oliver. 7005-1
"I do not weep for days that now are past". Lines on reaching maturity. Leith Shackel. 6799-9
I do remember you. Roberta Teale Swartz. 6019-6
"I do' wanna wander, I do' wanna go". A non-wander song. Berton Braley. 6853-7
"I doe confess I love thee." Unknown. 6563-5
"I doe confesse that thou art faire." Unknown. 6563-5
"I don'd lofe you now von schmall little bit". Go vay, Becky Milley, go vay! Unknown. 6918-5
"I don'd vas preaching voman's righdts". Der oak und der vine. Charles Follen Adams. 6505-8,7920-7
"I don't attempt the stuff that makes 'em cry". The modest bard. A. S.. 6817-0
"I don't believe (although I've sometimes..).". Against a romantic interpretation. John Chamberlain. 6761-1
"I don't believe I can ever do it!". The valentine. S.A. (Sarah Annie Shield) Frost. 6851-0
"I don't care if friends never view". In memory. Amoretta Fitch. 6906-1
"I don't care if you're arried I still...". Big fun. Diane Burns. 7005-1
'I don't care.' L.E. Tiddeman. 6018-8
"I don't hate your color". Explanation. Valerie Tarver. 7024-8
'I don't kiss boys.' Unknown. 6707-7
"I don't know how it happened: All I know." Nova Dornin. 6750-6
"I don't know much philosophy". This I know. J.T. Cotton Noe. 6789-1
"I don't know the story of my blue bottles". The blue bottles. Delia Dominguez. 7036-1
"I don't know what it's all about...". Me and ouija board. Edgar A. Guest. 7033-7
I don't know what you want. Lyn Lifshin. 6998-3
"I don't know who they are". The pointed people. Rachel (Lyman) Field. 6891-X
"I don't know why I came; it haunts me so!". Haunted house. Edythe Hope Genee. 6750-6
I don't like beetles. Rose Fyleman. 6044-7
"I don't like my pillow - now". Soft feathers spurned. Ruth Carroll. 6750-6
"I don't lofe you now von schmall little bit". Go vay, Becky Miller, go vay! Unknown. 6791-3,6823-5,6823-5
"I don't mind the cooking, I don't mind the...". Cliff Dweller lyrics. Berton Braley. 6853-7
"I don't mind the training, the hard". A scene from 5th avenue. Reginald E. McLaurin. 6898-7
"I don't say that the fates were actuated". The poet. Herman Charles Bosman. 6788-3
"I don't see any need for any law of any". Freedom. Eve Lott. 6880-4
"I don't want a dog that is wee and effiminate". Dog wanted. Margaret Mackprang Mackay. 6750-6
"I don't want a pipe and I don't want a watch". What I want. Edgar A. Guest. 6748-4
I don't want no more army. Unknown. 6237-7
"I don't want to be equal". ERA. Christine Christian. 6857-X
"I don't want to close my eyes". Camp fire. Martha M. Boutwell. 6764-6
"I done it - I killed 'im". My bug Amos. Virginia Ellis. 6750-6
I doubt a lonely thing is dead. Neil Tracy. 6021-8
I doubt it. Unknown. 6116-8
"I doubt, I doubt, my fire is out". Unknown. 6904-5
"I dove down deeply into the dark". Finale. Josephine A. Meyer. 6847-2
"I drank at a spring, time was, where dark...". Theognis. 6251-2
I dreaded that first robin so. Emily Dickinson. 6288-1
"I dream a dream of far off lands". Dreamland. Josie McNamara Lydon. 6836-7
I dream a war. Ricardo Weeks. 6178-8
"I dream of a little wee house". My dream house. Grace Hosmer Robinson. 6764-6
"I dream of a red-rose tree". Women and roses. Robert Browning. 6828-6
"I dream of a white hart that through..meadows". Hardwick arras. Wilfred Rowland Childe. 6780-8
I dream of all things free. Felicia Dorothea Hemans. 6973-8
"I dream of my lost glasses". Lost glasses. Walt Curtis. 7003-5
"I dream of pinks". A vision. Alexander Karanikas. 6764-6
"I dream that I am Tarzan and I wear no...". The jungle book. Gerald Locklin. 6998-3
"I dream that on far heaven's steep". The spectral army. Gretchen O. Warren. 7027-2
I dream'd a dream. Walt Whitman. 6337-3,6288-1,6126-5
"I dream'd that as I wander'd by the way". Shelley's lists. Percy Bysshe Shelley. 7020-5
"I dream'd there was an emperor...", fr. Antony and... William Shakespeare. 6339-X
"I dreamed (God pity babes at play).". In time of war. Lesbia Thanet. 7031-0
"I dreamed a dream in the midst of my slumbers". The old bachelors' sale. Unknown. 6889-8
"I dreamed a dream in the midst of...slumbers". The bachelor sale. Unknown. 6916-9
"I dreamed a dream: I dreamt that I espied". The shadow. Arthur Hugh Clough. 6832-4
"I dreamed I had a plot of ground". A dream. Alice Cary. 6969-X
"I dreamed I read from off the city wire". A copyreader's dream of fair women. Long John Silver [pseud.]. 6817-0
"I dreamed I stood by a beautiful river". Out of the silence. S. Minerva Boyce. 7030-2
"I dreamed I was in a desert and because I...". The tablets. Nicanor Parra. 6758-1
"I dreamed last night I stood with God on high". Sonnet ("I dreamed"). Snow Longley Hough. 6501-5,6648-8, 6214-8
"I dreamed of a highway". Workday morning. Stephanie Komkov. 6857-X
"I dreamed of Sappho on a summer night". Nocturne: In Anjou. Bliss Carman and Richard Hovey. 6890-1
"I dreamed one night I came". A heterodoxy. Edward John Plunkett, 18th Baron Dunsany. 6930-4
"I dreamed that as I wandered by the way". A dream of

spring. Percy Bysshe Shelley. 6935-5
"I dreamed that I was dead and crossed heavens". A dream. Helen Hunt Jackson. 6754-9
"I dreamed that I went to the city of gold". No Vermonters in heaven. Ernest F. Johnstone. 7030-2
I dreamed that dream was quenched. Gottfried Hult. 6327-6
"I dreamed that overhead". The army of the dead. Barry Pain. 7029-9,7027-2
"I dreamed that somewhere in the shadowy place". Lost in Hades. Andrew Lang. 6771-9
"I dreamed that youth returned,-the...". From far. Charles Pelham Mulvaney. 7041-8
"I dreamed that, as I wandered by the way". A dream. Percy Bysshe Shelley. 6793-X
"I dreamed we had escaped from our own graves". The diggers. Paula R. Sharp. 6900-2
"I dreamed. Now God appeared to me". A dream. John Galsworthy. 6888-X
"I dreamt (no 'dream' awake - a dream indeed).". In sleep. Alice Meynell. 6955-X
"I dreamt a dream the other night." Unknown. 6317-9
"I dreamt a dream, a dazzling dream...". A dream of the future. Denis Florence McCarthy. 6858-8
"I dreamt I climbed to a high, high plain". The pitcher. Yuan Chen. 7039-6
"I dreamt it! such a funny thing". What the Prince of I dreamt. Henry Cholmondeley-Pennell. 6902-9
"I dreamt last night of you, John-John". John-John. Thomas MacDonagh. 6872-3
I dreamt that I dwelt in marble halls. Michael W. Balfe. 6706-9
"I drew a moonbeam from the night". The fisherman. William V.V. Stephens. 6841-3
"I drew a stake from out of the hedge...". Unknown. 6059-5
"I drew it from its china tomb". A dead letter. Austin Dobson. 6676-3,6094-3,6508-2,6656-9
"I drift to another time and space when". All that jazz. Yasmeen Jamal. 6870-7
I drink nod trink to-nighd. Unknown. 6175-5
"I drink to the valiant who combat". The patriot brave. Richard Dalton Williams. 7009-4
"I drive my chariot up to the eastern gate". Years vanish like the morning dew. Mei Sheng. 6879-0
"I dug beneath the cypress shade". The grave of love. Thomas Love Peacock. 6830-8
I dunno and I knowit. Sam Walter Foss. 6312-8
"I dunno what's th' reason thet about...season". Just about these days. A.T. Worden. 6929-0
"I dusted a room so clean today". Home. Nellie Eldora Gould. 6764-6
"I dwell alone- I dwell alone, alone". Autumn. Christina Georgina Rossetti. 6828-6
"'I dwell among mine own' - oh, happy thou!". The reply of the Shunamite woman. Felicia Dorothea Hemans. 6973-8
"'I dwell among mine own.'- Oh! happy thou!". The reply of the Shunamite woman. Felicia Dorothea Hemans. 6848-0
I dwell on trifles, fr. The flitting. John Clare. 6545-7
"I dwell with love in loneliness". Solitude. Edward Harry William Meyerstein. 6893-9
"I edged back against the night". High-tide. Jean Starr Untermeyer. 6850-2
"I employ the blind mandolin player". A music. Wendell Berry. 6803-0
"I enlisted in the infantry last summer". The woes of a rookie. William L. Colestock. 6846-4
"I enter and I see thee in the gloom", fr. Commedia. Henry Wadsworth Longfellow. 6536-8
"I enter thy garden of roses". Romaic song. Unknown. 6945-2
"I entered a garden at midnight". Spirit. Chester Anders Fee. 6799-9
I entreat you, Alfred Tennyson. Walter Savage Landor. 6430-2
"I envy every flower that blows". A lover's envy. Henry Van Dyke. 6961-4
"I envy not Endymion now no more" Sir William Alexander; Earl of Stirling. 6182-6
"I envy not in any moods," fr. In memoriam. Alfred Lord Tennyson. 6543-0,6646-1
"I ever at college/From commoners shrank. The man with a tuft. Thomas Haynes Bayly. 6760-3
")I exist in a real world-made real by...)". Lamentation. Harold LaMont Otey. 6870-7
"I fain would ask thee to forget". Elizabeth Barrett Browning. 6238-5
"I fain would know Clarissa's mind". Rondeau. Unknown. 6983-5
I fear no power a woman wields. Ernest McGaffey. 6309-8
"I fear not henceforth death." William Drummond of Hawthornden. 6317-9
I fear not life. Avis Turner French. 6764-6
"I fear the mount that grimly lies". Inter vias. Charles Fletcher Allen. 6836-7
"'I fear thee, ancient mariner!'". Part the fourth. Samuel Taylor Coleridge. 6943-6
"I fear thy kisses". To - ("I fear thy kisses.") Percy Bysshe Shelley. 6110-9
I fear thy kisses. Percy Bysshe Shelley. 6240-7,6246-6, 6302-0,6328-4,6560-0,6226-1,6737-9
"I fear thy kisses, gentle maiden" Percy Bysshe Shelley. 6828-6
"I fear to me such fortune be assign'd". Sonnet ("I fear"). William Drummond of Hawthornden. 6380-2
"I feared that time would unreel in frames...". Backwards. Nancy Lee Couto. 6900-2
"I feared the lonely dead, so old were they". The dead. Sigourney Thayer. 7027-2
"I feed a flame within". Song ("I feed a flame"). John Dryden. 6195-0
"I feed a flame within, which so torments me". The maiden queen, sels. John Dryden. 6970-3
"I feed a flame within, which so torments me." John Dryden. 6317-9,6150-8
"I feel a breath from other planets blowing". Rapture. Stefan George. 7039-6
"I feel a newer life in every gale". May. James Gates Percival. 6752-2
"I feel content that you would grin with me". At the funeral of --. Kristjan N. ("K.N.") Julius. 6854-5
"I feel love, oh my jewel, I also feel love for you". Unknown (Newari) 7013-2
"I feel no airs". The quivering gum. Sir John Ernest Adamson. 6800-6
"I feele my selfe endaungered beyond reason". Sonnet ("I feele"). Thomas Lodge. 6482-5
"I fell in love with Pin Oak Hall". Pin Oak Hall. Mabel Hall Goltra. 6789-1
"I fell in love with you". Song for the mountains. Kit Blomer. 6883-9
"I felt a funeral in my brain". Emily Dickinson. 6348-9
I felt a spirit of love begin to stir. Dante Alighieri. 6527-9
"I felt the world a-spinning on its nave". The last journey, fr. The testament of John Davidson. John Davidson. 6845-6
"I felt/What independent solaces were mine". William Wordsworth. 6867-7
I fight against you. Comtesse de Noailles. 6351-9
I fill my pipe. A.M. S. 6118-4
I find my God, fr. Solitude. Victoria Mary Sackville-West. 6532-5
"I find myself holding/my heart". Naivete. Traci Teas. 6883-9
"I find no peace and bear no arms for war". Francesco Petrarch. 6325-X
"I find no peace, and all my war is done". Love's inconsistency. Francesco Petrarch. 7039-6
"I find the door standing open". Entering the room. Roger Pfingston. 6966-5
"I fled him, down the nights and down the days". The hound of heaven. Francis Thompson. 6301-2,6655-0,6161-3, 6214-8,6245-8,6153 ,6172-9,6430-2,6250-4,6292-X,6102-8,6199 ,6096-X,6332-2,6427-2,6489-2,6022-6,6052 , 6315-2,6337-3,6418-3,6488-4,6507-4,6527 ,6726-3,6730-1,6732-8,6723-9,6646-1,6508 ,6828-6
"I flung me round him,/I drew him under". 'The water-nymph and the boy,' sels. Roden Noel. 6873-1
"I followed him to the poplars by the river". The siblings. Gail Rixen. 6857-X
"I followed once a fleet and mighty serpent". A

subterranean city. Thomas Lovell Beddoes. 6980-0
I found a beggar starving. Morris Abel Beer. 6347-0
I found God. Mary Afton Thacker. 6337-3
"I found a calf in the goldenrod". Calf in the goldenrod. Julia Van der Veer. 6850-2
"I found a flat rock by a brook". Retreat. Joyce Lancaster. 6850-2
"I found a little bird's house to-day". A bird's house. Anna F. Burnham. 6965-7
"I found a little old elfin man". The dandelion. Katharine Pyle. 6820-0
"I found a little tealeaf". A wish. B.R. M. 6937-1
"I found a nameless stream among the hills". The nameless stream. Thomas Pringle. 6960-6,6800-6
"I found a rapier once, in Spain". Inscriptions. James Barnes. 6983-5
"I found a treasure one sunny day". My treasure. Gertrude Palmer Vaughan. 6764-6
"I found an indian arrow hear". An indian arrow head. Arthur S. Bourniot. 6797-2
"I found at daybreak yester morn". Song ("I found at daybreak..."). Unknown (French). 7039-6
"I found her out there." Thomas Hardy. 6317-9
"I found him in a shell-hole". 'Frenchie'. Frank C. McCarthy. 7008-6
"I found in Innisfail the fair". Aldfrid's itinerary through Ireland. Flann (atr.) Fionn. 6930-4
"I found in the fair Inisfail". Aldfrid's itinerary through Ireland. Flann (atr.) Fionn. 6930-4
"I found it deep in granny's trunk". Granny's receipt. Hazel Golding. 6750-6
"I found it on a morning when the wings". Lost valley. Glenn Ward Dresbach. 6750-6
"I found me glory, and I told the sea". Ecce homo! Edith Albert. 6847-2
"I found the holy spirit in the noise of...". The society of men. Raymond Kresensky. 6954-1
I found the phrase. Emily Dickinson. 6754-9
"I found them in a book last night". A souvenir. Philip C. Reilly. 6929-0
"I found to-day out walking". Robert Bridges. 6487-6
"I found you/sugared with sand". Shellbound. Sheila C. Forsyth. 6857-X
"I found your letter, love. How kind". The love-letter. Coventry Patmore. 6980-0
"I freely confess there are good friends..mine". A family row. Edgar A. Guest. 7033-7
"'I fumbled', said the sad-eyed lad". What makes the game. Edgar A. Guest. 6869-3
"I gaed to spend a week in Fife". The annuity. George Outram. 6878-2,6912-6
"I gathered in my rod and line." Toyo. 6027-7
"I gave her cakes; I gave her ale". Unknown. 6187-7,6317-9
"I gave my heart to a mountaineer". Singsong. Martha Keller. 6761-1
I gave my life for thee. Frances Ridley Havergal. 6656-9
I gave my love. Lexie Dean Robertson. 6441-8
"I gave my love a silver ring". Song ("I gave my love..."). Elizabeth Vera Loeb. 6847-2
"I gazed on the mountains". Scene in Lebanon. Robert Needham Cust. 6848-0
"I gazed sadly from my window". Evanescent love. Eugene Redmond. 7024-8
I gazed upon the cloudless moon. Emily Bronte. 6125-7
"I gazed, and lo! Afar and near". Battle of Somerset. Cornelius C. Cullen. 6946-0
"I get along without you very well". Except...sometimes. Victoria Adelaide Harvey. 6750-6
I give. W.W. Christmas. 6662-3
I give immortal praise. Isaac Watts. 6219-9
I give my heart to thee. Standish O'Grady. 6090-0;6174-5
I give my heart to thee. Ray Palmer. 6065-X
"I give my soldier boy a blade!" Unknown. 6946-0
'I give my soldier boy a blade'. H.M. L. 6074-9
I give thanks. Grace Fallow Norton. 6897-9
I give thee eternity. Michael Drayton. 6737-9
"I give you my house and my lands...". Marriage thoughts: by Morsellin Khan. Laurence (Adele Florence Nicolson) Hope. 6856-1
"I give you the end of a golden string". Epigram ("I give"). William Blake. 6179-6
"I go a-hunting a Copper Fly". Unknown. 6435-3
"I go by road, I go by street". The joyous wanderer. Catulle Mendes. 6955-X
I go by the road. Catulle Mendes. 7039-6
I go fishin'. Richard Stillman Powell. 6281-4
"I go forth from my dwelling". Ode ("I go forth"). Jules Romains. 6351-9
I go home for lunch. Edgar A. Guest. 6748-4
I go my gait. Emily Pfeiffer. 6770-0
"I go my way complacently". You. Florence Kiper Frank. 6897-9
"I go to knit two clans together". The wedding of the clans. Aubrey Thomas De Vere. 6858-8
I go to prove my soul, fr. Paracelsus. Robert Browning. 6337-3
I go to this window. Edward Estlin Cummings. 6375-6
"I go to this window" Edward Estlin Cummings. 6531-7
I go to whiskey bars. Raymond Thompson. 6870-7
"I go, I go! and must mine image fade". The boon of memory. Felicia Dorothea Hemans. 6973-8
I go, nor know wither. Karel Babanek. 6763-8
I go, sweet friends. Felicia Dorothea Hemans. 6973-8
I go, sweet friends! Felicia Dorothea Hemans. 6085-4
"I go, sweet sister! yet,my heart would linger". The sisters. Felicia Dorothea Hemans. 6973-8
"I got a robe, you got a robe". Negro spiritual ("I got a robe"). Unknown. 6176-1
"I got me flowers to straw thy way". George Herbert. 6187-7
"I got myself a bus". The lore of diminishing returns, fr. On the fault line. Russell Haley. 7018-3
I got to go to school. Nixon Waterman. 6964-9
"I got to thinkin' of her - both her parents..". How it happened. James Whitcomb Riley. 6992-4
"I got to thinkin' of her - both her parunts..". How it happened. James Whitcomb Riley. 6892-8
"I grab a slice of moon". Toward tenses two moons. George Rachow. 6870-7
"I grant corruption sways mankind". The jackal, leopard, and other beasts. John Gay. 6972-X
"I grant thou were not married to my muse". Sonnet 082 ("I grant"). William Shakespeare. 6447-7
I grant your eyes are much more bright. John Bulteel. 6563-5
"I grasped at/a straw". Soap bubbles. Erich Fried. 6769-7
"I grew old the other day." Timothy Otis Paine. 6274-1
I grieve for beauty wasted. Grace Noll Crowell. 6326-8
I grieve not that ripe knowledge. James Russell Lowell. 6288-1
"I grieve, and dare not show my discontent." Elizabeth I; Queen of England. 6317-9
I grieved for Bonaparte. William Wordsworth. 6110-9
I grieved for Buonaparte. William Wordsworth. 6828-6
"I guess it is only human to be". Politics. Jonathan Holden. 6803-0
"I ha'e nae kith, I ha'e nae kin". Unknown. 6859-6
"I had a beautiful garment". Moth-eaten. Margaret Elizabeth Sangster. 6916-9
"I had a boon companion". The boon companion. Johann Ludwig Uhland. 6952-5
"I had a cock and a cock loved me". Unknown. 6334-9
I had a dog. O. R. 7008-6
I had a dove. John Keats. 6086-2,6114-1
"I had a dove and the sweet dove died". Song ("I had"). John Keats. 6861-8
"I had a dovem and the sweet dove died". Song ("I had a dove"). John Keats. 6133-8,6519-8,6131-1
I had a dream. Edith Foster. 6799-9
"I had a dream - the summer beam". Fragment ("I had a dream..."). Thomas Hood. 6974-6
"I had a dream and I awoke with it". At daybreak. Walter Conrad Arensberg. 6897-9
"I had a dream of Lethe, of the brink". Lethe. Eugene Lee-Hamilton. 7015-9
"I had a dream of poverty by night". Poverty. Rosa Mulholland; Lady Gilbert. 7037-X
I had a fair young son. Sara Bard Field. 6628-3
"I had a feeling in my neck". Mumps. Elizabeth Madox Roberts. 6891-X

"I had a friend once, and she was to me". Unknown. 6238-5
"I had a gig-horse, and I called him Pleasure". Allegory. Thomas Hood. 6974-6
"I had a little dog, and they called him Buff". Unknown. 6363-2
"I had a little doggy that used to sit and beg." Unknown. 6452-3,6510-4
"I had a little doggy that used to sit and beg". My doggy. M.L. Elliot. 6937-1
"I had a little hen, the prettiest ever seen". Unknown. 6904-5
"I had a little hen, the prettiest ever seen". My little hen. Unknown. 6937-1
"I had a little hobby-horse". My hobby-horse. Unknown. 6937-1
"I had a little horse, his name was Dapple Grap". Unknown. 7028-0
"I had a little husband". Unknown. 6363-2,6452-3
"I had a little kitten-cat". Sagacity. Harriet Doktor. 6850-2
"I had a little moppet". Unknown. 6363-2
"I had a little nut-tree". My little nut-tree. Unknown. 6937-1
"I had a little nut-tree...". Mother Goose. 6363-2
"I had a little pony". Dapple-grey. Unknown. 6937-1
"I had a little pony." Mother Goose. 6363-2,6452-3,6466-3, 6510-4
"I had a little sister/And she was pink...". Lament. Amanda Benjamin Hall. 7038-8
"I had a little tea-party". Three guests. Jessica Nelson North. 6937-1
"I had a little yellow bird". Unknown. 6049-8
"I had a lovely dream today/I climbed...". I had a dream. Edith Foster. 6799-9
"I had a message to send her". Sent to heaven. Adelaide Anne Procter. 6889-8
"I had a piece of pie". Sally Gooden. Unknown. 6826-X
"I had a task last New Year's Eve...". Unknown. 6059-5
"I had a thought. My eager fingers reached". Life. Gertrude W. Robinson. 6906-1
"I had a true love, if ever a girl had one". The tri-colored ribbon. Peadar Kearney. 6930-4
"I had a vision in that solemn hour". The continents. Bayard Taylor. 6976-2
"I had a vision: evening sat in gold". Rebellion. George Croly. 6980-0
"I had a willow whistle". The piper. Rachel (Lyman) Field. 6454-X,6554-X
"I had a young pupil called Ned". Limerick:"I had a young pupil called Ned". H.G. Dixey. 6811-1
"I had been ill; and when I saw". Recovery from mental illness. Herman Charles Bosman. 6788-3
"I had been wanting things again". Last night. Jon Bracker. 7003-5
"I had built me a lofty city". Credo. Edith Albert. 6847-2
"I had forgotten it could rain like this". All day rain. Larry Gould. 6750-6
"I had four brothers over the sea". Unknown. 6059-5
"I had gone clothed in tatters all my days". The prodigal son. Sadie Fuller Seagrave. 6799-9
"I had love dreams and dreams of glory". Broken dreams. Celestin Pierre Cambiaire. 6826-X
"I had no heart to march for war". Going to the front. Hardwicke Drummond Rawnsley. 7027-2
I had no time to hate. Emily Dickinson. 6288-1
"I had not known the price of heaven". A revealing prayer. Henry C. Fellow. 6799-9
"I had not thought to have unlockt my lips". Temperance and virginity, fr. Comus. John Milton. 6933-9
"I had one small glimpse". Memory. Helen Hooper. 6750-6
"I had outstripped him on the moorland wide". The pursuit. Arthur Christopher Benson. 6785-9
"I had over-prepared the event". Villanelle: the psychological hour. Ezra Pound. 6897-9
"I had passed/The night in dancing..", fr. The prelude. William Wordsworth. 6867-7
"I had ridden over hurdles up the country...". The open steeplechase. Unknown. 6924-X
I had seen death come down. E.L. Mayo. 6751-4
"I had seen you at Endion, thosr years before". Endyion.

Witter Bynner. 6780-8
"I had six Moorish nurses, but the seventh...". The Moor Calaynos. Unknown (Spanish). 6757-3
"I had sworn to be a bachelor, she...a maid". Platonic. William B. Terrett. 6910-X
"I had thought patience would come in...". La pucelle. Sister Mary Irma. 6761-1
"I had thought that I could sleep". Climax. Gladys Oaks. 6880-4
"I had three sons, a' young stout, and bauld". The old man's lament. Unknown. 6859-6
"I had to laugh". Montana wives. Gwendolen Haste. 6776-X
"I had told him, Christmas morning". Little Bennie. Annie C. Ketchum. 6909-6
"I had two pigeons". My two pigeons. Unknown. 6937-1
"I had waited long for love". The answer. Josephine A. Meyer. 6847-2
"I had written him a letter which I had...". Clancy of the overflow. Andrew Barton Paterson. 6784-0
I hae laid a herring in saut. James Tytler. 6089-7
"I hail you, 'dreamers'! I pick you out of...". The dreamer. Hugh Francis Blunt. 6954-1
"I hardly know one flower that grows". Ignorance of botany. Walter Savage Landor. 6874-X
"I hardly know you, and already I say...". Etude. Carlos Pellicer. 6759-X
I has a little brother. Unknown. 6017-X
"I hasten from the land of snows". The rose and the iceberg. Eugene Field. 6949-5
"I hastened thro' the world, and lo". Love. Winifred Lucas. 6785-9
"I hate my geography lesson!". The geography demon. Unknown. 6925-8
"I hate that drum's discordant sound". The drum. John Scott (of Amwell). 6932-0
"I hate the clamours of the smoky towns". Of a country life. James Thomson. 6816-2
"I hate the cold unfriendly moon". Nibu No Tadamine. 6852-9
"I hate the common, vulgar herd!". In praise of contentment. Horace. 6949-5
"I hate the dreadful hollow...", fr. Maud. Alfred Lord Tennyson. 6122-2
"I hate the man who builds his name". The poet and the rose. John Gay. 6972-X
"I hate the money-lending avarice". Sonnet ("I hate"). Joachim Du Bellay. 6227-X
"I hate the Persian's costly pride". To his attendant, fr. Ode 038. Horace. 6973-8
"I hate the very name of box". Boxiana. Unknown. 6787-5
"I hate thee, death!". Mors, morituri salutamus! Francis Coutts. 6785-9
"I hate this city, seated on the plain". This month almonds bloom at Kandahar. Laurence (Adele Florence Nicolson) Hope. 6856-1
"I hate to sing your hackneyed birds". A panegyric on geese. Francis Sylvester ("Father Prout") Mahony. 6930-4
"I haue a gentil cook." Unknown. 6378-0
"I haue a yong suster." Unknown. 6378-0
"I have a beautiful structure in my heart". The astronaut. Cecilia Bustamante. 7036-X
"I have a bitter thought, a snake". From 'Phantastes', fr. Borrowed thoughts. Adelaide Anne Procter. 6957-6
"I have a black, black mind!". The song. James Stephens. 6943-6
"I have a boy of five years old". Anecdote for fathers. William Wordsworth. 6867-7,6828-6
"I have a child; so fair". Sappho. 6435-3
"I have a conversation book...". French in the trenches. William J. Robinson. 6846-4
"I have a dream - that some day I shall go". My dream. Henry Dawson Lowry. 6793-X
"I have a feeling for those ships". The stone fleet. Herman Melville. 6833-2
"I have a fine dog, his name is Jerry". My dog Jerry. H. Denlinger. 6799-9
"I have a friend whose wit can shake". Two friends. Ernest G. Moll. 6761-1
"I have a friend, a policeman". My policeman. B.R. M..

6937-1
"I have a garden of my own". Song ("I have a garden"). Thomas Moore. 6232-6
"I have a gentil cok". Unknown. 6733-6
"I have a gentle cock". I have a noble cock. Unknown. 6881-2
I have a gentle cock. Unknown. 6380-2
"I have a heavenly home". The spiritual body. Phoebe Cary. 6969-X
"I have a king who does not speak". Emily Dickinson. 6348-9
I have a life in Christ to live. Unknown. 6335-7
I have a life with Christ to live. John Campbell Shairp. 6337-3
"I have a little boy at home". My boy. Morris Rosenfeld. 7011-6
"I have a little curly-head". Please, it's only me. Walter J. Mathams. 6772-7
"I have a little kinsman". The discoverer. Edmund Clarence Stedman. 6889-8
"I have a little puppy, and he often runs...". A stern story. F. Conquest. 6804-9
I have a little sister. Unknown. 6114-1
"I have a little sister, she's called Peep-peep". Unknown. 7028-0
"I have a little sister, they call her Peep, Peep". Unknown. 6904-5
I have a little son. Flossie Deane Craig. 6662-3
"I have a love has golden hair". Song ("I have"). Langdon Elwyn ("John Philip Varley") Mitchell. 7041-8
"I have a love on the other side of the world". The other side of the world. Charles Julian Downey. 6836-7
"I have a mirror from Halab..." Unknown (Newari) 7013-2
"I have a mistress, for perfections rare". Thomas Randolph. 6187-7
"I have a new bonnet". The new bonnet. Margaret Buller Allen. 6937-1
I have a new garden. Unknown. 6881-2
I have a noble cock. Unknown. 6881-2
"I have a notion tonight, that the earth and I". Dancers. James Oppenheim. 6959-2
"I have a pretty titmouse". A catch. William Wager. 6861-8
"I have a proud flag flying/Though none may...". Pride. Evelyn Hazlett Hunt. 6799-9
"I have a reason. Madness does have limits". Logic. Calvin Murry. 6870-7
I have a rendezvous with death. Alan Seeger. 6051-X,6077-3, 6102-8,6211-3,6224-5,6289 ,6332-2,6337-3,6474-4,6506-6,6509-0,6556 ,6476-0,6732-8,6653-4,6396-9,6393-4, 6650 ,6161-3,6107-9,6076-5,6646-1,6300-4,6336 ,6250-4,6439-6,6464-7,6467-1,6431-0,6666
I have a rendezvous with life. Countee Cullen. 6337-3,6589-9
"I have a secret I would tell". The secret. Robert Norwood. 6797-2
"I have a secret way of steering". Columbus at night. Maggie Helwig. 6767-0
I have a share in Flanders fields. Elizabeth Dimon Preston. 6836-7
I have a son. Emory Pottle. 6649-3
"I have a suit of new clothes in this happy...". 'When I think of the hungry people' O-Shi-O. 6954-1
"I have a thing to say. But how to say it?". A plea for Egypt, fr. The wind and the whirlwind. Wilfrid Scawen Blunt. 7009-4
"I have a thousand pictures of the sea". There are but words... Muna Lee. 6776-X
"I have a tree, a graft of love". Arbor amorsis. Francois Villon. 6771-9
"I have a winter guest". The chickadee. Sara V. Prueser. 6906-1
"I have a word I fain would say...". Sayat Nova. 6050-1
I have a young sister. Unknown. 6881-2
"I have all the sudden quietness". A wintering moon. R. Wayne Hardy. 6870-7
"I have an orchard, fr. The tragedy of Dido. Christopher Marlowe. 6125-7
"I have an uncle I don't like". Manners. Marianna Griswold Van Rensselaer. 6891-X
"I have another lover loving me". Two lovers (II). Agnes Mary F. ("Madame Duclaux") Robinson. 7015-9
"I have awakened.../but there are no memories". Reading sign. Jack L. Anderson. 6870-7
"I have become as quiet as the ground beneath". Peace. Risa Alice Lowie. 6847-2
"I have become without desire". Twoborn. Rokwaho. 7005-1
"I have been every nighy, whether empty...". To E. Simpson, Esq., fr. Croaker papers. Fitz-Greene Halleck and Joseph Rodman Drake. 6753-0
"I have been fed on honeyed dreams so long". Unnamed sonnet. Muriel F. Hochdorf. 6850-2
I have been in love and in debt. Alexander Brome. 6328-4, 6026-9
"I have been in this garden of unripe fruit". First love. Christopher M. ("Hugh MacDiarmid") Grieve. 6893-6
"I have been little used to frame". A prayer ("I have been little"). Alice Cary. 6303-9,6969-X
"I have been out to-day in field and wood". 'Field preaching'. Phoebe Cary. 6969-X,6600-3
"I have been sure of three things". Sonnet ("I have been sure"). Clement Wood. 6250-4
I have been through the gates. Charlotte Mew. 6019-6
"I have been wandering in enchanted ground". On Miss Helen Faucit's Juliet. William Edmonstoune Aytoun. 6948-7
"I have black moments of despair, long hours". In some wide place. Robert Donaldson. 6836-7
"I have borne the anguish of love". Ode 011. Hafiz. 7039-6
"I have broken the panes of the night". The night was going... Raul Otero Reiche. 6759-X
"I have broken the rainbow". Pamphlet. Luis Munoz Martin. 6759-X
"I have builded your towns and cities". A song of labor. Will M. Maupin. 6954-1
I have cared for you, moon. Grace Hazard Conkling. 6607-0
I have cast the world. Yone Noguchi. 6897-9
"I have climbed into silence trying for...". Recuerdo. Paula Gunn Allen. 7005-1
"I have come back to Princeton three days...". Hanging scroll. Gerald Stern. 6966-5
"I have come from a mystical land of light". The strange country. Robert Buchanan. 6873-1
"I have come home to thee". Abdiel-the-Syrian's chant of the kiss. Hermann Hagedorn. 6944-4
"I have come into the desert because my soul..". Prologue, fr. The poet in the desert, sels. Charles Erskine Scott Wood. 6897-9
"I have composed the sun to my belief". The poet. John Macy. 6037-4
I have desired to go. Gerard Manley Hopkins. 6258-X,6153-2
"I have desired to go, where springs not fail". Surcease. Gerard Manley Hopkins. 7007-8
"I have desired to go/Where springs not fail". Heavenhaven. Gerard Manley Hopkins. 6828-6
"I have done my bit of carving". The old figurehead carver. H.A. Cody. 6833-2
"I have done the state some service", fr. Othello. William Shakespeare. 6934-7
I have drank my last glass. Unknown. 6964-9,6910-X
"I have dreamed of joyous springtime". Ila, sels. Hattie Horner Louthan. 6836-7
"I have drunk it in". My own city. Frederick Mortimer Clapp. 6808-1
"I have drunk the sea's good wine". A pagan hymn. John Runcie. 6800-6
"I have dug a hole and put him in the ground". Prayer for the little'un. Phyllis Livingston. 6750-6
I have earned a dollar, fr. Working gang poems. Byron Herbert Reece. 6761-1
"I have examined and do find". To a friend before taking a journey. Katherine Philips. 6935-5
"I have felt a presence," fr. Tintern abbey. William Wordsworth. 6337-3
"I have forebodings of Thee. Time is going" Alexander Blok. 6103-6
"I have fought no mighty fight." John McClure. 6326-8
"I have fought something all my life". German mother. Kaye Starbird. 6761-1
"I have found out a gift for my fair". A geological madrigal. Francis Bret Harte. 6802-2
"I have found the quillback rockfish...". Unchartered.

Keith Vacha. 7003-5
"I have freed me of my moorings, I am...". The freedman. Viola Gerard Garvin. 7007-8
"I have gathered luss/At the wane of the moon". The herb-leech. Joseph ("Seosamh MacCathmhaoil") Campbell. 6930-4
I have golden shoes. Lesbia Harford. 6349-7
"I have gone down to the ground". 4 1/2 point 5 Ed Lipman. 6870-7
"I have grown weary of the open sea". The wanderer. William Alexander Percy. 7017-5
"I have guarded my soul from that which would defile." al-Buhturi. 6766-2
"I have had courage to accuse". The crowning gift. Gladys Cromwell. 6979-7
"'I have had four sons', said the old woman". The old woman with four sons. Phyllis McGinley. 6761-1
I have had great pity. Willard Wattles. 6032-3
"I have had nothing to do to-day". A busy day. Marguerite Wilkinson. 6880-4
"I have had one fear in my life". Virgins, fr. Songs of deliverance. Orrick Johns. 6897-9
"I have had playmates, I have had companions". Charles Lamb. 6187-7
"I have hailed you". Recordition. Marx G. Sabel. 6776-X
"I have heard great tales of their kindly ways". Men she could have married. Edgar A. Guest. 6748-4
"I have heard men for a palace but I want no". The old sheep wagon. Arthur Chapman. 7008-2
"I have heard that a certain princess". The jonquils. Allen Upward. 6897-9
"I have heard the curlew crying". Wild geese. Katharine (Hinkson) Tynan. 6873-1
"I have heard the oak leaves". Charmed voices. Joshua Freeman Crowell. 6798-0
"I have heard the voice of the Lord". El Mahdi to the tribes of the Soudan. Edna Dean Proctor. 7041-8
"I have it in my heart to serve God so". Sonnet: Of his lady in heaven. Jacopo la Lentino. 7039-4
"I have jest about decided". Old winters on the farm. James Whitcomb Riley. 6991-6
"I have kissed/Mountbatten's killers". Fenians all. Brian O'Riordan. 6767-0
I have known beauty. Isabel Brown Shurtleff. 6270-9
"I have known deep, enveloping darkness". Fog: in time of war. Charles Hanson Towne. 6761-1
I have known laughter. Wade Oliver. 7014-0
"I have known love and hate and work and fight". To a photographer. Berton Braley. 6853-7
"I have known the green trees and skies...". Satisfied with life. Edgar A. Guest. 7033-7
"I have known the wizardry of ghostly beaches". Coasts. Clark B. Firestone. 7007-8
"I have known villages where brooding hills". Chelsea. Lillian M. Ainsworth. 7030-2
"I have known/The rush of sweet spring showers". Experience. Edna Davis Romig. 6836-7
"I have learn'd/To look on nature, not as in the hour" William Wordsworth. 6138-9,6289-X
"I have led her home...", fr. Maud. Alfred Lord Tennyson. 6122-2,6102-8,6110-9
"I have left you an empty room" Joyce Odam. 6792-1
"I have lighted a fire on my hearth for you". The fires that glow. Della Hudmon Willien. 6789-1
I have lighted the candles, Mary. Kenneth Patchen. 6734-4
I have lived and I have loved. Unknown. 6541-4
"I have lived long, and watched out many days". Actaeon. Sir Charles George Douglas Roberts. 7041-8
"I have lived this life as the skeptic lives..". Conversion. Ella Wheeler Wilcox. 6956-8
"I have lived! Enough of weeping!". The last bumper. Charles Whitby. 6994-0
I have looked inward, sels. Don Marquis. 6467-1
"I have lost my shoes". Number 026. Constantino Suasnavar. 6759-X
I have loved flowers that fade. Robert Bridges. 6187-7, 6232-6,6246-6,6317-9,6487-6,6507 ,6102-8,6250-4,6396-9,6508-2,6655-0
"I have loved your winsome face". Unknown. 6050-1
"I have lyric aspiration". The curse of faint praise.
Irwin [pseud].. 6817-0
"I have made for you a song". To Thomas Atkins. Rudyard Kipling. 6810-3
"I have made my choice, have lived my poems...". Oscar Wilde. 6238-5
"I have met an old lover!". My old lover. Zola Monk. 6906-1
"I have neither plums nor cherries". Nicholas Breton. 6187-7
"I have never cared for fashion". The cosmis urge. P. W.. 6817-0
I have never known the winter's blast. Josiah Gilbert Holland. 6238-5
"I have never seen the heather". Heart of the gael. Marie Mancino. 6799-9
"I have no brothers and no peers". Ralph Waldo Emerson. 6753-0
"I have no comeliness of frame". The lay of the humble. Richard Monckton Milnes; 1st Baron Houghton. 6980-0
"I have no dread of loneliness". Dread aloe. Hildegarde Flanner. 6808-1
"I have no folded flock to show". The battle flag of Earl Sigurd. Unknown. 6889-8
"I have no foolish fad for pets". The fad obsolete. Maude Andrews. 7021-3
"I have no heart for any other joy". An end. Sara Teasdale. 6778-6
"I have no joy in strife". The peaceful warrior. Henry Van Dyke. 6961-4
"I have no love save beauty". Confession. Jackson Holland Patterson. 6841-3
"I have no moan to make". Waiting the change. Phoebe Cary. 6969-X
"I have no need for water of the sea". Sonnet ("I have no need"). Halley W. Groesbeck. 6906-1
"I have no patience with the man who says". The conqueror. Morris Abel Beer. 6861-8
'I have no ring'. Bernard Gilbert. 6474-4
"I have no soul; this evening I". To - ("I have"). Georgia H. Cooper. 6850-2
'I have no spring', she saith. Cora Fabri. 6876-6
"I have no temple and no creed". Robert Norwood. 6796-4
"I have no wife/much less a son, to lament...". To the old masters. Wing Tek Lum. 6790-5
"I have no will to weep if love should leave". Ballade of a dream addict. Virginia Scott. 6750-6
"I have not brought my Odyssey". A letter from the trenches. Charles Hamilton Sorley. 7027-2
"I have not read a rotten page". A ballade of a book-revviewer. Gilbert Keith Chesterton. 6875-8
"I have not seen that maples grieve the fall". Sonnet. M. Walthall Jackson. 6799-9
"I have not spent the April of my time" Bartholomew Griffin. 6182-6,6586-4
"I have not wept when I have seen". Back to London: a poem of leave. Joseph Johnston Lee. 7027-2,7031-0
"I have often played...", fr. The mystery...saints. Charles Peguy. 6351-9
"I have often, in my learnings". The spy. Edward Farquhar. 6939-8
"I have one fervent prayer". The last bugle. Maude (Emogene Boyce Smith) Meredith. 7030-2
I have overcome the world. Laura Simmons. 6144-3,6335-7
"I have pondered currents, sweeping waves". Sea love. Esther M. Leiper. 6857-X
"I have prayed for you, prayed that your path". For a novice. Sister Mary Edwardine. 6761-1
"I have quaffed the gall and vinegar...". The world goes by. Marie Tello Phillips. 7038-8
"I have read in some old volume, full of...". To-morrow. William E. Pabor. 6836-7
"I have read the review; it is learned & wise". On a review condemnne Thelyphthora. William Cowper. 6814-6
"I have received jewels of conspicuous beauty". On a pair of shes presented to him, sels. Egan O'Rahilly. 6930-4
"I have scribbled in verse and in prose". Ballade of neglected merit. Andrew Lang. 6987-8
"I have seen a French impressionist...". Birc tree. Yung-

gul Lee. 6775-1
"I have seen a thousand/Orchids in a jungle". Song ("I have seen a thousand"). Daniel Whitehead Hicky. 6761-1
"I have seen an old street weeping". La Rue de la Montagne Sainte-Genevieve. Dorothy Dudley. 6897-9
"I have seen beauty; I have sensed her rhythms". Looking on beauty. Walter John Coates. 7030-2
"I have seen clifts that met the ocean foe". St. Bee's head. Thomas Edward Brown. 6809-X
"I have seen four span of dappled Percherons". Tug-of-war. A.M. Sullivan. 6761-1
I have seen higher, holier things than these. Arthur Hugh Clough. 6430-2
"I have seen lace-makers in Madeira". Grisaille. Terence Heywood. 6788-3
"I have seen many things". Miser. Harold Vinal. 6750-6
"I have seen some good friends". Because San Quentin killed two more today. Ed Lipman. 6870-7
"I have seen the cliffs of Dover". The song of an exile. William Hamilton. 6800-6
I have seen the mountains. Horace Gregory. 6761-1
"I have seen the proudest stars". Song ("I have seen..."). Helen Dudley. 6897-9
"I have seen the world's great cities". The land-call. Francis Ernley Walrond. 6800-6
"I have seen this life of tears". La convalescence d'Ezechias. Jean Baptiste Rousseau. 6848-0
"I have seen". Unknown. 6240-7
"'I have seen', said the maid...". The ideal and the real. I. Edgar Jones. 6915-0
"I have seen/A curious child". The sea shell, fr. The excursion. William Wordsworth. 6832-4
"I have seen/A curious child...". A child with a shell. William Wordsworth. 6980-0
"I have shed tears many, many, o sorrow". Departure from home. H. Von Fallersleben. 6952-5
"I have sinned, I have sinned, before thee...". Peccavi. Phoebe Cary. 6969-X
"I have slipped my brown arms around him". Two friends. Dennis Cooper. 7003-5
"I have so much to live for". Unknown. 6109-5
"I have so often". Fate. Harold Monro. 6776-X
"I have some dainty pussies here". Pussy willows. Mary E. Plummer. 6891-X
I have some friends. Robert Service. 6159-1
"I have sought long with steadfastness." Sir Thomas Wyatt. 6584-8
"I have sought thirty years". Song ("I have sought"). Maurice Maeterlinck. 6351-9
"I have still a vision of him". Ragged rover. Leslie Clare Manchester. 7008-6
"I have surprised young beauty, when she fled". Limitations. Elisabeth Kuskulis. 6836-7
"I have taken the woman of beauty". The bear's song. Unknown (Haida Indian). 7039-6
I have the courage to be gay. Jean Ingelow. 6066-8
"I have threatened Theology...", fr. Piers Plowman. William Langland. 6489-2
"I have today to undergo what is written in my karman" Unknown (Newari) 7013-2
I have trod. Robert Louis Stevenson. 6655-0
I have twelve oxen. Unknown. 6125-7,6645-3
"I have walked close to death/And felt his...". The return. Marguerite Hill. 6799-9
"I have walked over frozen ground". Canon. Jackson Holland Patterson. 6841-3
"I have wandered many miles to-day". Growing old. Mrs. M.W. Chase. 6929-0
"I have wandered to a spring." Edna Wahlert McCourt. 6019-6
"I have watched the unseen artist". The cape in June. Sarah A. Dixon. 6798-0
"I have witnesses the great ovation". The Roman boy's trophies - A.D. 61. Margaret Junkin Preston. 6965-7
"I have wondered, when the moon hung low". Borderland. Ellen M. Carroll. 7016-7
I have woven a necklace. Mildred Maralyn Mercer. 6906-1
"I have written a hundred poems in the last...". Tut tut! Julia Copeland. 6799-9

"I have written high school teachers..savants". Chant royal from a copydesk for Bob Garst. Rufus Terral. 6850-2
"I have your regard, as you say". Esteem and love. Steingrimur Thorsteinsson. 6854-5
"I haven't had such jolly fun for 40000 years". Pa shaved off his whiskers. Unknown. 6889-8
I haven't much religion. J.L. Scott. 6926-6
I hear a call. Avis H. Grant. 6906-1
"I hear a cricket at my window sill". Touch. Joseph Auslander. 6850-2
I hear a dear, familiar tone. Alice Cary. 6066-8
"I hear a low voice in the sunset woods". Sonnet ("I hear"). Frances Anne Kemble. 7037-X
"I hear a mighty people asking now". To Theodore Roosevelt. Sir William Watson. 6995-9
"I hear a river thro' the valley wander". Trumbull Stickney. 6380-2
"I hear a voice exceeding rare". The voice of a soul. Marguerite E. Lougee. 6799-9
"I hear a voice you cannot hear". Thomas Tickell. 6238-5
"I hear abroad/The exultation of...earth". Benina to Belshazzar. Henry Hart Milman. 6980-0
I hear along our street. Henry Wadsworth Longfellow. 6747-6
I hear America singing. Walt Whitman. 6006-4,6154-0,6162-1, 6466-3,6496-5,6527 ,6512-0,6464-7,6421-3,6265-2,6371-3,6126-5,6288-1,6107-0,6736-0
I hear an army charging. James Joyce. 6244-X,6581-3,6375-6
"I hear an old song of my youth". London Bridge. Daniel I. Gross. 6799-9
I hear and see not strips of cloth alone. Walt Whitman 6665-8
"I hear it is charged against me that I...". The dear love of comrades, fr. 'Calamus' Walt Whitman. 6954-1
I hear it was charged against me. Walt Whitman. 7014-0
"I hear it was charged against me". Walt Whitman. 6085-4, 6332-2,6008-0,6560-0,6288-1,6126
"I hear it's gone out with". The buddy system (...a release for my cynicism...) Terri Jewell. 6899-5
"I hear leaves drinking rain". Rain. William Henry Davies. 6338-1,6466-3,6371-3,6393-4
"I hear my mother whose highs have". Violets for mother. Lonny Kaneko. 6790-5
"I hear no voice behind the veil". A song of faith. Arthur E.J. Legge. 6785-9
"I hear some say, 'This man is not in love.'" Michael Drayton. 6317-9
"I hear the cries of evening". Stephen Spender. 6536-8
"I hear the distant, far retreat". The Rachmaninoff prelude. Gertrude Huntington McGiffert. 6838-3
"I hear the noise about thy keel", fr. Memroiam. Alfred Lord Tennyson. 6536-8
"I hear the rushing of the sea of time". At midnight of All Souls. Mary Cowden Clarke. 6997-5
"I hear the stag's pathetic call". Saru Maru. 6852-9
"I hear the throbbing music down the lanes...". A little town in Senegal. Will Thompson. 6846-4
"I hear the tinkling of the cattle bell". August 1918. Maurice Baring. 7029-9
"I hear the water singing". The creek. Bert Leach. 6906-1
I hear the wave. Unknown. 6930-4
"I hear the woodlands calling..." Madison Cawein. 6478-7
"I hear them say, 'By all this stir'.". The right above the wrong. William Cox Bennett. 7009-4
"I hear them..the crickets". Owl. Rokwaho. 7005-1
"I hear thou art as modest as". Fujiwara Sadakata. 6852-9
"I hear thy spirit calling unto me". Burdens of unrest. Thomas Holley Chivers. 7017-7
"I hear thy voice, dear Lord". The divine lullaby. Eugene Field. 6949-5
"I hear your familiar footsteps all about me". Second life of my mother. Jorge Carrera Andrade. 6759-X
"I hear/You weeping still". Echo. Louise Fischer. 6850-2
"I heard a fly buzz when I died". Dying. Emily Dickinson. 6754-2
"I heard a fly buzz when I died". Emily Dickinson. 6348-9, 6536-8
"I heard a gentle maiden, in the spring". Time, hope, and memory. Thomas Hood. 6974-6

I heard a linnet courting. Robert Bridges. 6339-X,6487-6
I heard a maid with her guitar. Clinton Scollard. 6770-0
I heard a mess of merry shepherds. Unknown. 6756-5
I heard a soldier. Herbert Trench. 6083-8,6250-4,6301-2, 6464-7
"I heard a song upon the wandering wind". Genius singing to love. Felicia Dorothea Hemans. 6973-8
"I heard a sound of voices from the hill". Children on a hill. Marion Ethel Hamilton. 6979-7
"I heard a story the other day...". A city tale. Alfred H. Miles. 6927-4
"I heard a voice among the olive-trees". Minor note 012, fr. In Tuscany. Cora Fabri. 6876-6
"I heard a voice at early morning say". The voice. Esther Trowbridge Catlin. 6799-9
"I heard a voice say 'Look...,", fr. Penthesperon. Christopher Hassall. 6317-9
"I heard a voice that cried...". The march. Sir John Collings ("Solomon Eagle") Squire. 6872-3
I heard an angel. William Blake. 6502-3,6659-3
"I heard an old farm-wife". The son. (Frederick) Ridgely Torrence. 6861-8
"I heard an old man say today". the tragedy of age. Edgar A. Guest. 6862-6
"I heard her whisper." Ruth Guthrie Harding. 6648-8
I heard Immanuel singing. Vachel Lindsay. 6532-5;6619-4, 6641-0
"I heard him faintly, far away". The corncrake. James H. Cousins. 6930-4
"I heard him fall. He's lying". The secret. Lonny Kaneko. 6790-5
"I heard him in the autumn winds". Life in death. Ellice Hopkins. 7037-X
"I heard how, to the beat of some quick tune". The dancer, fr. the Bustan. Sadi [or Saadi] (Mushlih-ud-Din). 7039-6
"I heard men say that roses turn to dust". Care I for roses so? Arthur Forbes. 6761-1
"I heard my ancient sea-blood say". A life. George Edward Woodberry. 6833-2
"I heard of a duke in Rimini". The duke's layde. Hermann Hagedorn. 6944-4
"I heard or seemed to hear the chiding sea". Seashore. Ralph Waldo Emerson. 6753-0
"I heard the bells on Christmas day". Gifts of peace. D. Isabelle Millar. 6799-9
"I heard the drums a-rolling". Shiloh. Thomas Lynn. 6857-X
"I heard the gay spring coming". Idle. Alice Cary. 6969-X
"I heard the long roar and surge of history...". The age-long war, fr. Towards democracy. Edward Carpenter. 7009-4
"I heard the pipes go by". Bagpipes. haemaS O'Sheel. 6979-7
"I heard the poor old woman say". The blackbirds. Francis Ledwidge. 6812-X
"I heard the radio proclaim/The wonder of a...". The Christmas radio. Mary P. Denny. 6799-9
"I heard the rumbling guns. I saw the smoke". The return. John Freeman. 7026-4,7029-9
"I heard the slender fingers of the rain". An April shower. Nellie Burget Miller. 6836-7
"I heard the spring wind whisper". Earth voices. Bliss Carman. 6115-X,6843-X
I heard the voice of Jesus say. Horatius Bonar. 6065-X, 6337-3
"I heard the voice of murmuring multitudes". Reality. Charles Whitby. 6994-0
I heard the voice of the woods. Edward Carpenter. 6252-0
"I heard the wind all day". Watching by a sick-bed. John Masefield. 6897-9
"I heard them talk about this changing day". Cloister hymn. Emily Hanson Obear. 6799-9
"I heard them talking and praising...French...". To the mother. Katharine (Hinkson) Tynan. 6793-X
"I heard this morning/'Neath my window sill". A tribute. V. Louise Beach. 6799-9
"I heard three brithers resonen". Unknown. 6059-5
I heard your heart's soft tears. Helen C. Harris. 6178-8
"I heard, O Polypaides, I heard the bird's shrill...". Theogns. 6251-2

"I heare the whistling plough-man all day long". On the plough-man. Francis Quarles. 6933-9
"I heed not that my earthly lot". To - ("I heed not"). Edgar Allan Poe. 6126-5,6288-1
"I held a fiddle in my hand again". Note to fiddler's farewell. Leonora Speyer. 6979-7
"I held a jewel in my fingers". Emily Dickinson. 6726-3
"I held her hand" Walter Savage Landor. 6828-6
"I held her hand, the pledge of bliss". Songlet ("I held her hand..."). Walter Savage Landor. 6830-8
"I held her hand, the pledge of bliss" Walter Savage Landor. 6874-X
"I held her hand, the pledge of bliss." Walter Savage Landor. 6110-9
"I held in my hand a wonder - a hymn...". The skylark. Benjamin Franklin Taylor. 6815-4
"I held it truth, with him who sings,", fr. In memoriam. Alfred Lord Tennyson. 6646-1
"I held it truth, with with who sings", fr.In memoriam. Alfred Lord Tennyson. 6867-7
"I here swear/Eterne Apollo!...". The moon. John Keats. 6980-0
"I here; you there". Elegy under the stars. Anne Morrow Lindbergh. 6979-7
"I hereby prophesy that in spite of war & men". Announcement. Harry Brown. 6761-1
"I hereby swear that to uphold your house". Elinor Wylie. 6536-8
"I hid my heart in a nest of roses". A ballad of dreamland. Algernon Charles Swinburne. 6770-0
I hid my love. John Clare. 6380-2
"I hide her in my heart, my May". Love's captive. C. H. Waring. 6770-0
"I hinted in my posthumous, or last". Of the necessity of going down. Sir Owen Seaman. 6785-9
"I hoed and trenched and weeded" Alfred Edward Housman. 6828-6
"I hold as faith." Unknown. 6563-5
"I hold him great, who for love's sake". Adelaide Anne Procter. 6238-5
"I hold him, verily of mean emprise". Canzone: He perceives his rashness in love... Guido Guinicelli. 7039-6
"I hold it truth with him who sings." Alfred Lord Tennyson. 6225-3,6238-5
"I hold it truth with him who sweetly sings". A ballade of death and time. Bert Leston Taylor. 6875-8
I hold still. Julius Sturm. 6344-6
I hold still. Unknown. 6240-7
"I hold them close against my heart". Gold beads. Maude Wheeler Pierce. 7030-2
"I hold your heart!". The bird. Max Michelson. 6897-9
"'I hope it is in good plain verse'". Dipsychus. Arthur Hugh Clough. 6828-6
"I hope our quaint old tavern stands". Vermont 'tavern stands'. Daniel L. Cady. 6988-6
"I hope that she who stole my place". Rival. Rubye Mae Fisher. 6850-2
"I hope that the streets of heaven". Streets of gold. Earl Bigelow Brown. 6954-1
"I hope the sun will shine to-day". Fat cattle in trucks near the Fairfield crane (Glasgow) George Dickson. 6778-6
"I hope there's no soul". True blue. Unknown. 6859-6
"I hunger for life's savory dishes-every one". The jest, fr. Thumb nail sketches. Mary H. Cabaniss. 6841-3
"I hurry through the lot behind the meat...". Hamden Provision co. Barbara Hughes. 6792-1
I hwove a colored altar cloth. Daisy Lee Ervin. 6906-1
"I imagine a good deal of smoke at the funeral". Death and return in January. Roger Lipsey. 6821-9
I in the greyness rose. Stephen Phillips. 6301-2,6102-8
"I in the greyness rose". Stephen Phillips. 6732-8
I in thee, and thou in me. Christopher Pearse Cranch. 6288-1
"I intend to fight it out on this line". Ulysses S. Grant. 6623-2
"I intended an ode". Urceus exit, fr. Rose-leaves. Austin Dobson. 6770-0,6527-9,6250-4
"I intended an ode", fr. Rose-leaves. Austin Dobson. 6850-

"I into life so full of love was sent". My heritage. Ella Wheeler Wilcox. 6956-8
"I invoke the land of Ireland". Invocation to Ireland. Amergin (atr.). 6930-4
"I jogged along the footpath way". 'A merry heart goes all the day'. Unknown. 7031-0
"I journey on an endless quest". The heart of the road. Anna Hempstead Branch. 7012-4
"I journey through a desert" Unknown. 6271-7
I journeyed south to meet the spring. Robert Underwood Johnson. 6441-8
"I journeyed south to meet the spring". Robert Underwood Johnson. 6652-6
"'I joy to see you' one I knew". Pentholatry. Edward Farquhar. 6939-8
"I judge all the Dagoes by Tony Cattini". Provincialism. Aubert Edgar Bruce. 6954-1
"I just fold my wings at nightfall." N.V. W. 6225-3
I just lightning. Maria Sabina. 7036-1
"I keep a candle burning for each friend". Candle and cup. Helen T.D. Robinson. 6799-9
"I keep finding seeds". How clouds move. Barbara Hughes. 6792-1
"I keep neat my virginity". Song ("I kept neat"). Glyn Johns. 6379-9
I keep wondering. Hilda Conkling. 6467-1
"I kept alive by man's due breath of air". Fifine at the fair, sels. Robert Browning. 6997-5
"I kept having to shoo off". Editor. Glenna Luschei. 6792-1, 6998-3
"I killed a gopher/in my garden". Summer. Ernesto Trejo. 6792-1
"I killed a robin.". Remorse. Sydney Dayre. 6820-0
"I killed her? Ah, why do they cheer?". Out. Ernest Radford. 6875-8,6770-0
I kilt er cat. Virginia Frazer Boyle. 6120-6
"I kin saw yo·, you shly leedle raskel". Dot shly leedle raskel. Unknown. 6791-3
"I kissed her hand and it smelt of soap". Clean clothes. Rafael Arevalo Martinez. 6759-X
"I kissed the bride; while the other men". Her wedding. Unknown. 6921-5
I kissed the cook. Unknown. 6687-9
"I kneel by the window tonight". Priedieu. Margaret Haynes Foster. 7016-7
"I kneel upon the soggy ground". Life. Hazel M. Irish. 6764-6
"I knell not now to pray that thou". Prayer ("I kneel not now"). Harry Kemp. 6730-1
"I knew a man - I know him still". One of many (2). Alice Cary. 6969-X
"I knew a man who name was Horner". Grumble corner and thanksgiving street. Unknown. 6923-1
I knew a woman. Theodore Roethke. 6388-8
"I knew by the smoke that so gracefully curled." Thomas Moore. 6302-0,6620-8,6219-9
I knew he would come if I waited. Horace G. Williamson. 6277-6,6280-6
"I knew her first as food and warmth and rest". My mother. Amelia Josephine Burr. 6847-2
"I knew his face the moment that he passed". The one. Unknown. 6889-8
"I knew I should be here". In the tunnel. E.L. Mayo. 6751-4
"I knew it the first of summer". Platonic. Ella Wheeler Wilcox. 6863-4
"I knew not faith nor sought her by the way". The one of three. Francis Charles McDonald. 6983-5
"I knew somethin' was up as soon's I see". Night rider. Carl Carmer. 6887-1
"I knew that an essence, close". The moment. German Pardo Garcia. 6759-X
"I knew the tree where slept the crows". Myself. Harriet Ellen (Grannis) Arey. 7030-2
"I knew thee not! then wherefore gaze". To a profile. Bernard Barton. 6980-0
"I knew you never asked a worldly thing". Recompense. Amy Forbes King. 6818-9
"I knew you wouldn' mind if I sat upon..fence". Small help. Verna Tomlinson. 6750-6
"I knit, I knit, I pray, I pray". The war rosary. Nellie Hurst. 6846-4
I know. Elsa Barker. 6019-6
I know. Grace Lowe Broadhead. 6906-1
I know. Robert L. Wolfe. 6817-0
"I know 'tis but a loom of land". Land, ho! Thomas Edward Brown. 6809-X
"I know a bank whereon the wild-thyme blows". William Shakespeare. 6047-1
"I know a beach road". The beach road by the wood. Geoffrey Howard. 7026-4
"I know a blackfoot chief". Ballad of Jasper road. Katherine (Amelia Beers Warnock Garvin) Hale. 6797-2
"I know a certain tune that my life plays". The tune. Sara Teasdale. 6778-6
"I know a dear old lady". My mother. William Lawrence Chittenden. 6097-8
I know a freshman. Charles Irvin Junkin. 6936-3
"I know a funny little man". Mr. Nobody. Unknown. 6937-1
"I know a garden where gay tulips grow". Tulips. Vesta C. Westfall. 6799-9
"I know a grove". A grove. Samuel Taylor Coleridge. 6793-X
"I know a lady (you know a lady).". Dust. Elizabeth Hollister Frost. 6979-7
"I know a little boy named Jim". Wasted opportunities. Carolyn Wells. 6882-0
"I know a little damsel". A confession. Alice Cary. 6865-0;6969-X
"I know a little garden close". Song ("I know a little"), fr. Jason. William Morris. 6438-8
"I know a little garden-close". William Morris. 6187-7, 6289-X,6508-2,6655-0
I know a little town. Winifred F. Ticer. 6799-9
"I know a little zigzag boy". The zigzag boy and girl. Unknown. 6889-8
"I know a man.../No,/I mean a real man". Some chicks just can't tell a Cezanne from a Sears. Gordon Kirkwood Yates. 6792-1
I know a name. Unknown. 6335-7,6337-3
"I know a patient, nobly-curving hill". A farmer's woman. John Reed. 6880-4
"I know a Persian carpet". The cranberry bog. Sarah A. Dixon. 6798-0
"I know a place where a river wide". Under the old oak tree - Agarland. Harriet E. Durfee. 6927-4
"I know a place where the rainbows go". Open sesame. Edna Davis Romig. 6836-7
I know a quiet vale. Thomas S. Jones Jr. 6347-0,6653-4
I know a road. Carl Vinton Herron. 6335-7
I know a secret. Christopher Morley. 6891-X
"I know a secret fairyland". Child secret. Sylvia Lapidus. 6850-2
"I know a surgeon calm and wise". The drawback. Edgar A. Guest. 6869-3
"I know a weaver and his wife". Octaves. Thomas Edward Brown. 6809-X
I know a wood. Joshua Freeman Crowell. 6798-0
I know all this when gipsy fiddles cry. Vachel Lindsay. 6184-2,6010-2
I know I am but summer to your heart. Edna St. Vincent Millay. 6010-2
I know I am deathless, fr. Song of myself. Walt Whitman. 6337-3
"I know an old man of Durazzo". Limerick:"I know an old man of Durazzo". Unknown. 6811-7
"I know an old New England covered bridge". New England covered bridge. Adelbert M. Jakeman. 6894-4
"I know at length the truth, my friend". The end. Henry Glassford Bell. 6960-6
"I know her by her angry air". Kate. Alfred Lord Tennyson. 6977-0
"I know him, February's thrush". The thrush in February. George Meredith. 6828-6,7020-5
"I know I am a mystery/A mystery for sure". The mystery. C.E. Deal. 6799-9
"I know it must be". Stanzas ("I know"). Winthrop Mackworth Praed. 6980-0
"I know it so of a truth". Vere scio. Bible. 6830-8
"I know it/as if I had been" Thomas Sessler. 6769-7

"I know moon-rise, I know star-rise." Unknown. 6375-6
"I know my body's of frail a kind". Man [or I knew myself a man]. Sir John Davies. 6182-6,6108-2,6737-9
"I know my wife weeps tears of blood". The drunkard's thirst. Unknown. 6919-3
I know myself a man, fr. Nosce teipsum. Sir John Davies. 6125-7
"I know myself the best beloved of all." Alice Wellington Rollins. 6066-8,6226-1
"I know no greater joys than these". True delight. Edgar A. Guest. 6869-3
"I know no word of the quarrel, the...". The riding camel. William Henry Ogilvie. 7010-8
I know not how it falls on me. Emily Bronte. 6655-0
"I know not how some men can lie". Action. Robert Loveman. 6941-X
"I know not how the right may be". doubt. Henry Alford. 6980-0
"I know not how to comfort thee". The sisters. Aubrey Thomas De Vere. 6980-0
"I know not too well how I found my home in". David's journey after comforting Saul. Robert Browning. 7020-5
"I know not what 'twas o'er me stole". To a new morning. Jaromir Borecky. 6763-8
"I know not what it presages". The Lorelei. Heinrich Heine. 6805-7
"I know not what my secret is." Andrew Lang. 6138-9
"I know not what shall befall me". Not knowing. Mary Gardner Brainard. 6303-9,6632-1,6889-8
"I know not what the world may be". In despair. Alice Cary. 6969-X
I know not where. William L. Stidger. 6461-2
"I know not where she be, and yet". The maid in low-moon land. Francis Ledwidge. 6812-X
"I know not whether I am proud." Walter Savage Landor. 6110-9
"I know not which I love the most" Phoebe Cary. 6049-8
I know not why. Camille Mauclair. 6351-9
I know not why. Morris Rosenfeld. 6310-1
"I know not why, but all this weary day". Sonnet ("I know not"). Henry Timrod. 6753-0
"I know not why, but all this weary day". Henry Timrod 6008-0
"I know not, little Ella, what the flowers". Little Ella. Edward Bulwer-Lytton; Baron Lytton. 6772-7
"I know of a pleading silver-tongued bell". The shepherd in the dell. William Fred Sachs. 6906-1
"I know of a street on the edge of town". Marigold lane. M.E. W. 7021-3
"I know of an owl". 'Twelve o'clock, and all's well!' M.S.E. P.. 6965-7
"I know only this gentleman. I do not know any other". Unknown (Newari) 7013-2
I know that all beneath the moon decays. William Drummond of Hawthornden. 6194-X,6250-4
"I know that all the moon decays". Sonnet ("I know that"). William Drummond of Hawthornden. 6301-2
"I know that Edgar's kind and good". Edgar's wife. Phoebe Cary. 6865-0;6969-X
"I know that I am dying, mate...". Out at sea. J.S. Fletcher. 6695-X,6923-1
I know that any weed can tell. Louis Ginsberg. 6619-4
I know that he exists. Emily Dickinson. 6754-9
"I know that mortal men have angel neighbors". Angel neighbors. James Abraham Martling. 6952-0
I know that my redeemer liveth. Virginia Frazer Boyle. 6065-X
"I know that perfect self-esteem". Self-esteem. Edward Coote Pinkney. 7017-5
"I know that somewhere under the sun". Consolation. George Villiers, 2d Duke of Buckingham. 6778-6
"I know that the setting sun will quench..fear". Reverie. Antonin Sova. 6763-8
"I know that there is order in the earth". The way of things. Alice Todd. 6764-6
"I know that this world - that the great big..". The under dog. Unknown. 6889-8
"I know that thou will come when time is right". Resurrection. Amoretta Fitch. 6906-1

"I know that what you say is true, and yet". Second wife. Emily Dawson Crain. 6750-6
"I know the dearest little girl...". A funny little girl. Carolyn Wells. 6882-0
"I know the deep-browed peace of canyon walls". Canyon walls. Iris Sparks. 6799-9
"I know the drifting dust lies on the hill". Silver edge. Constance Deming Lewis. 6841-5
"I know the gun/its handle is made to fit...". The foreman's wife. Jeff Tagami. 6790-5
"I know the hand that is guiding me through...". Unknown. 6238-5
"I know the secrets of thy streams". From the building of the bridge. Barry Straton. 7041-8
"I know the smell of warfare in a trench". A thought on peace conferences. G.B. Birrel. 6880-4
"I know the sound o' these noises". Silence broken. Hjalmar Jonsson. 6854-5
"I know the sun's a glowing, yellow rose". Blind. Isabel Beulah Schein. 6847-2
I know the way of the wild blush rose. Willard Emerson Keyes. 6274-1
"I know thee, truth, my queen alone". The coming. Edward Farquhar. 6939-8
"I know there is no meaning in the mist". Eternity. Irwin Edman. 6879-0
I know there will be peace. Carol Gridley. 6662-3
"I know this young poet who writes". Excuse the harshness excuse the grime but... A.D. Winans. 6998-3, 6901-0
"I know well I am mortal...". Ptolemaeus. 6251-2
"'I know what you're going to say', she said". Candor. Unknown. 6927-4
"I know where I'd get". Asses. Padraic Colum. 6779-4
"I know where I'm going." Unknown. 6317-9,6732-8
"I know where there is honey in a jar". Ad Dorotheam. Edward Verrall Lucas. 6772-7
"I know why the yellow forsythia". Spring song. Edna St. Vincent Millay. 6808-1
"I know you are always by my side". Border-land. Phoebe Cary. 6969-X
"I know you lawyers can with ease". Poor Richard's opinion. Benjamin Franklin. 6878-2
"I know you lawyers can, with ease". The dog and the fox. To a lawyer. John Gay. 6972-X
"I know you, lion of grey Saint Mark". To the lion of Saint Mark. Joaquin Miller. 7041-8
"I know you, rose; I see you there". Poor little rose. Robert Loveman. 6941-X
"I know you: solitary griefs". The precept of silence. Lionel Johnson. 6861-8
I know your heart, O seal. Cale Young Rice. 6653-4
"I know yt my redeemer liues & I." Unknown. 6563-5
"I know, I shouldn't have been standing there". I shouldn't have been standing there. Markey Sullivan. 6750-6
"I knowed a man, which he lived in Jones". More in the man than in the land. Unknown. 6927-4
"I known not whether I am proud" Walter Savage Landor. 6828-6
"I labored on the anvil of my brain". Farewell to mathematics. Frederick Victor Branford. 6884-7
"I lately saw, what now I sing". The sparrow and diamond. Matthew Green. 6831-6,6968-1,6943-6
"I lately thought no man alive". On mending his thoughts. Dr. Barnard; Bishop of Limerick. 6874-X
"I lately vowed, but 'twas in haste." John Oldmixon. 6092-7
"I laugh at each dull bore, taste's parasite". Fresco-sonnet to Christian Sethe (1). Heinrich Heine. 7039-6
"I laugh to see them pray". War. Eloise Robinson. 6031-5
"I laved my hands". Ballad: Lost for a rose's sake. Unknown (French). 7039-6
"I lay a sdead, but scarce chained were my...". A dream of immortality. William Drummond of Hawthornden. 6935-5
"I lay and listened to the long lisping sigh". The voice of the wheat. Jack Lindsay. 6895-2
"I lay close down upon the rocks". Premonition. Witter Bynner. 6037-4
"I lay down my fresh morning paper". Missing. Jefferson

Toombs. 6995-9
"I lay down to sleep only to find I can't...". Prison walls-red brick crevices. Terri Meyette Wilkins. 6870-7
"I lay here naked in/the cold room". A one-winged bird. Bernard Finney. 6898-7
"I lay in my bedroom at Peebles". Peebles. Alexander Smith. 6960-6
"I lay in my tent at mid-day". The crossing at Frederimksburg. George Henry Boker. 6946-0
I lay in sorrow deep distressed. Charles Mackay. 6219-9, 6543-0
"I lay in unrest - old thoughts of pain". The dream of John Macdonnell. Unknown (Irish). 6858-8
"I lay me down and slumber," fr. More poems. Alfred Edward Housman. 6828-6
"I lay my branch of laurel down". To Lord Thurlow. George Gordon, 6th Baron Byron. 6945-2
I lay my sins on Jesus. Horatius Bonar. 6065-X
"I lay on deck, fast bound...", fr. William Tell. Johann C. Friedrich von Schiller. 6606-2
"I lay on that rock where the storms...". The rock of Cader Idris. Felicia Dorothea Hemans. 6973-8
"I lay on the rocks and watched the sea". By the sea. Unknown. 6926-6
"I lay upon the sofa after dinner". A dream. James Abraham Martling. 6952-5
"I lay upon the solemn plain". The sleeper of Marathon. Felicia Dorothea Hemans. 6973-8
"I leaned out from my window yesternight". Moon-shadows. Cora Fabri. 6876-6
"I leaned out my window." Jean Ingelow. 6019-6
"I learn, as the years roll onward". From shadow - sun. Agnes L. Pratt. 6925-8
I learned to know. Mary Cromwell Low. 6847-2
"I learned today the world is round". The road to China. Olive Beaupre Miller. 6891-X
"I learned while in my teens of notes..chords". Portrait of a poet. Alpheus Butler. 6178-8
"I learnt soon after I was born". Planting corn in Vermont. Daniel L. Cady. 6988-6
"I leave behind me the elm-shadowed square". Outward bound. Thomas Bailey Aldrich. 6833-2
"I leave the fields with all their...flowers". Minor note 011, fr. In Tuscany. Cora Fabri. 6876-6
"I leave the world to-morrow". Farewell. Enid Derham. 6784-0
"I leave thee now, my spirit's love". To Myra. Thomas Kibble Hervey. 6980-0
"I left all world to you when I died". Testament (1). Anne Morrow Lindbergh. 6783-2
"I left my darling lying here". A coineachan-a highland lullaby. Unknown. 6873-1
"I left my home for travelling". Distant voices. Dora Sigerson Shorter. 6785-9
"I left my house white". Unknown. 6364-0
"I left the crowded cities". The clover field. Louise Morey Bowman. 6797-2
"I left the little town behind". The circus boy. A.A. Vyvyan Thomson. 6925-8
"I left the throng whose laughter made". A straggler. Edgar Fawcett. 7041-8
I left ye, Jeanie. Hew Ainslie. 6180-X
"I lie alone, beneath the almond blossoms". 'Lost delight', after the Hazara war. Laurence (Adele Florence Nicolson) Hope. 6856-1
I lie down with God. Unknown. 6244-X
"I lie in the summer meadows". In the meadows. Bayard Taylor. 6976-2
I lie on the chilled stones of the great wall. Stephen Shu Ning Liu. 6790-5
"I lie out under a heather sod". The Moor grave. John Galsworthy. 6888-X
"I lie tonight beside the quiet sea". Corona borealis. Inez Barclay Kirby. 6799-9
"I lie upon my bed and hear and see". The largest life. Archibald Lampman. 6843-X
"I lift mine eyes...", fr. Divina commedia. Henry Wadsworth Longfellow. 6536-8
I lift my gaze. John Hall Wheelock. 6337-3

"I lift these hands with iron fetters banded". South Carolina to the states of the north. Paul Hamilton Hayne. 6946-0
I lika da peoples to speeck. Anne Acton Welborn. 6270-9
I like. Esther Webster Skillman. 6750-6
"I like a guy to pull the caveman stuff". Sonnet ("I like a guy"). Unknown. 6817-0
"I like a look of agony". Emily Dickinson. 6380-2
I like Americans. Nancy Boyd. 6736-0
"I like butter creamy yellow". Do you like butter? L. Dickerson-Watkins. 6937-1
"I like cigars". Ella Wheeler Wilcox. 6453-1
"I like clean windows, - those". Clean windows. Effie B. Collins. 6764-6
"I like doors, small friendly doors". Doors. Ruby McDonald. 6799-9
"I like fun - and I like jokes". Thoughts on a pore joke. James Whitcomb Riley. 6892-8
"I like Nantucket". Song for John Howard Payne week. J. Q.. 6817-0
I like little pussy. Jane Taylor. 6102-6,6132-X,6452-3, 6510-4,6262-8,6131
I like little pussy. Unknown. 6937-1
"I like no other garden smell". A Vermont spring smudge. Daniel L. Cady. 6989-4
"I like noise". Noise. J. Pope. 6804-9
"I like not tears in tune, nor will I prize". On the memory of Mr. Edward King, drown'd... John Cleveland. 6933-9
"I like October, but it brings to me". Unbidden mood. Margaret E. Bruner. 6789-1
"I like polks dots. And molasses...". I like. Esther Webster Skillman. 6750-6
"I like that scripture line that says". Harvest time in Vermont. Daniel L. Cady. 6988-6
"I like the Anglo-Saxon speech". 'Good-by - and God bless you!' Eugene Field. 6949-5
"I like the boss' daughter". Number 017. Constantino Suasnavar. 6759-X
"I like the Chinese laundry man". Mar Quong, Chinese laundryman. Christopher Morley. 6891-X
"I like the dream days best of all". The dream days. Edgar A. Guest. 6862-6
"I like the fall". The mist and all. Dixie Willson. 6891-X
"I like the homes where a teddy bear". The homes of joy. Edgar A. Guest. 6862-6
"I like the man who faces what he must". The inevitable. Sarah Knowles Bolton. 6260-1,6337-3,6512-0,6730-1, 6924-X
"I like the music even of my dreams". Music. Orville Gould Wheeler. 7030-2
"I like the nickel shiny". Realization. E. May Livingston. 6894-4
"I like the soft,dark eyelids..tired shopgirls". Velvet dust. Evana Llynn. 6906-1
"I like to fish/an old habit". The big one. Luis Cabalquinto. 6790-5
"I like to hear the cricket in the grass". Jessie Orton Jones. 6999-1
"I like to put on rubber boots". Springtime. Marian Osborne. 6797-2
I like to quote. Mitchell D. Follansbee. 6722-0
"I like to see a brand new lot". Vermont haying tools. Daniel L. Cady. 6989-4
"I like to see a thing I know". New sights. Edith King. 6937-1
"I like to see it lap the miles". The locomotive. Emily Dickinson. 6891-X
"I like to see it lap the miles". Emily Dickinson. 6536-8, 6464-7,6491-4
I like to think of Shakespeare. E.K. Chambers. 6477-9
"I like to think of you as winging forth". In memoriam: W.L.W. Pearl Randall Wasson. 7030-2
"I like to tiptoe round her when she's..asleep". Sleeping child. Edgar A. Guest. 6869-3
"I like to wake up early by myself". Desire under the pines. Tim Dlugos. 7003-5
"I like to walk along the street". Accent on paths. Mary Ernestine Clark. 6789-1
"I like Vermont's old-fashioned flowers". Old-fashioned

Vermont flowers. Daniel L. Cady. 6988-6
I like words. Margaret Caskey. 6488-4
"I like you, Mrs. Fry! I like your name!". A friendly address to Mrs. Frey, in Newgate. Thomas Hood. 6974-6
"I like you, though I feel your scorn". To the younger generation. Lee Wilson Dodd. 6817-0
"I like/the feel of your pulsating fibers". Love poem. Yuri Kageyama. 6790-5
I liked but never loved before. Unknown. 6563-5
"I lingered listening 'neath the tree". Overheard. Robert Loveman. 6941-X
"I listen - but no faculty of mine". On hearing the 'Ranz des Vaches' or... of St.Gotthard. William Wordsworth. 6749-2
"I listen to my parent's language". When father came home for lunch. Jim Mitsui. 6790-5
"I listen to this/86 year old". Look back. Carroll Arnett Gogisgi. 7005-1
"I listened most attentively". Please. Josephine Sievers Birt. 6906-1
"I listened to the phantom by Ontario's shore". As I sat alone by blue Ontario's shore, sels. Walt Whitman. 6753-0
"I live (sweetie love) whereas the gentle winde," Giles (the Elder) Fletcher. 6586-4
"I live alone, like pith in a tree". 'Michaelangelo' the elder. Bob Kaufman. 6901-0
"I live and breathe, I eat and drink". What do you want at sixty-three? John Hollingshead. 7012-4
I live for thee. Alfred Lord Tennyson. 6412-4,6304-7
"I live for those that love me". Johann Wolfgang von Goethe. 6238-5
I live for those who love me. George Linnaeus Banks. 6456-6
I live in great sorrow. Unknown. 6881-2
"I live within the shadow--Hall of Fame". Daybreak over the hall of fame. Leon Loiselle. 6799-9
"I live," fr. Morpheus. Hilda ("H.D.") Doolittle. 6012-9
I lived with visions for my company. Elizabeth Barrett Browning. 6430-2
"I lived, one time, in the strangest house". The tenant. Edward Farquhar. 6939-8
"I lived/Two lives apart...". The death of Themistocles, sels. John Nichol. 6819-7
I lo'ed ne'er a laddie but ane. Hector MacNeill. 6180-X, 6086-2
"I loathe a man that's evil. My face in my veil...". Theognis. 6251-2
"I loathe bards' commonplaces." Callimachus. 6251-2
"I loathe, o Lord, this life below". A complaint on the miseries of life. James Thomson. 6816-2
"I loathed you, Spoon River...". Archibald Higbie. Edgar Lee Masters. 6897-9
"I long for some intenser life". Longings. Eugene Field. 6949-5
"I long have had a quarrel set with time". The two highwaymen. Wilfrid Scawen Blunt. 6879-0
"I long to gaze on stately pines that grow". On my life's design. M. Florence DeLuca. 6894-4
"I look around/The hushed darkness". At the volcano internment camp. Muin Ozaki. 6981-9
"I look at them on buses". U.F.O. 8s. David MacLean. 7003-5
I look into my glass. Thomas Hardy. 6210-5
"I look into my glass". Thomas Hardy. 6187-7,6317-9
I look into the stars. Jane Draper. 6037-4
"I look into your face". Haunted. Renee Roper. 6899-5
I look not back. Annie Johnson Flint. 6065-X
"I look to-day far down the aisles of memory's". The old school-house. H. Elliott McBride. 6919-3
"I look up hotels". Number 030. Constantino Suasnavar. 6759-X
"I look'd upon his brow, no sign". Crescentius. Letitia Elizabeth ("L.E.L.") Landon. 6980-0
"I lookd vpon my true loues eye." Unknown. 6563-5
"I looked and saw a splendid pageantry". Society. William Dean Howells. 6954-1
"I looked at me one day, one day". Discovery. Carol Phillips. 6750-6
"I looked for Christ on Madison street". Christ on Madison street. Raymond Kresensky. 6954-1
"I looked in the brook and saw a face". The brook. Eugene Field. 6949-5
"I looked on the field where the battle was...". The battle-field. Felicia Dorothea Hemans. 6973-8
I looked out into the morning, fr. Sunday up the river. James ("B.V.") Thomson. 6655-0
"I looked up just now". The cloud across the moon. E.O. De Camp. 6906-0
"I looked upon a plain of green". Prose and song. John Sterling. 6980-0
"I lost him - I, who should have been...guide". Lost - a boy. Kate Bringhurst Joor. 6750-6
"I lost my heart ye other day." Unknown. 6563-5
"I lost my love long years ago". Song ("I lost my love long years ago"). Ernest Hartley Coleridge. 6785-9
I lost the love of heaven. John Clare. 6246-5,6545-7,6315-2,6441-0
"I loue but dare not show it for why." Unknown. 6563-5
"I loue thee for thy ficklenes." Unknown. 6563-5
"I lov'd thee once, I'll love no more". Sir Robert Ayton. 6933-9
I love a flower. Thomas Phillips (atr) 6881-2
"I love a poem with a swing". Queer. Elsie Bentley Malin. 6799-9
I love a storm. Grace Turner Smith. 6270-9
"I love all beauteous things" Robert Bridges. 6339-X,6477-9,6487-6,6507-4,6625-9,6655 ,6250-4,6301-2,6508-2, 6581-3
"I love all waves and lovely water in motion". Five degrees south. Francis Brett Young. 6833-2
"I love at early morn...", fr. Summer images. John Clare. 6187-7
"I love daffodils". Spring song. Hilda Conkling. 6891-X
I love everything. Sister Maris Stella. 6761-1
"I love her face". Jenny. Walter De La Mare. 6905-3
I love her still. William White. 6868-5
"I love him so for all the good". A tribute to Charles Dickens. Carmen Sylva. 6889-8
"I love him, I love him, father". Caughnawaga song. Unknown (Caughnawaga Indian). 6795-4
"I love it, I love it; and who shall dare". The old arm-chair. Eliza Cook. 6919-3
I love life. Ruth A. Hartzell. 6799-9
I love little pussy. Jane Taylor. 6183-4,6466-3,6623-2, 6135-4,6456-6
"I love little pussy". Unknown. 6363-2,6459-0
"I love moist eve by riverside". By riversides. Antonin Sova. 6886-3
"I love my country's pine-clad hills". The land of liberty. Unknown. 6917-7
I love my fellow man. Inez Foote. 6799-9
I love my Jean. Robert Burns. 6075-7,6239-3,6152-4
"I love my fellow man/I love my fellow man everyday". I love my fellow man. Inez Foote. 6799-9
"I love my garden of friends". My garden of friends. Nettie Stephenson Bowen. 6799-9
"I love my hour of wind and light". Swallow flight. Sara Teasdale. 6897-9
"I love my lady's eyes". Song ("I love my lady's"). Robert Bridges. 6487-6
I love my love. Charles Mackay. 6219-9
I love my love in the morning. Gerald Griffin. 6096-X,6022-6
"I love my love so well, I would". Jealousy. Phoebe Cary. 6969-X
I love my love with a kiss. Alexander MacLean. 6274-1
"I love my love with an A, because he's Agreeable". Unknown. 6363-2
"I love my lover; on the heights above me". Two lovers (I). Agnes Mary F. ("Madame Duclaux") Robinson. 7015-9
"I love my prairies, they are mine". My prairies. Hamlin Garland. 6964-9
"I love my wife, I love my baby". Pretty little black-eyed Susan. Unknown. 6826-X
"I love old sidewalks, laid in faded brick". Old sidewalks. Lena B. Ellingwood. 6764-6
I love old things. Wilson MacDonald. 6723-9,6843-X
"I love sea words". Sea words. Mary Sinton Leitch. 6833-2

"I love sixpence, pretty little sixpence". Mother Goose. 6363-2
"I love sweet features...", sels. Oliver Wendell Holmes. 66601-1
"I love the attic, dim, mysterious". The attic, fr. The homestead. Gertrude Huntington McGiffert. 6838-3
"I love the deep quiet - all buried in leaves". Contradiction. Alice Cary. 6865-0;6969-X
"I love the evenings, passionless and fair...". A sunset. Victor Hugo. 7039-6
"I love the fair lilies and roses so gay", sels. Dora Read Goodale. 6601-1
"I love the fitful gust that shakes". Autumn. John Clare. 6466-3
"I love the fitful gust...", fr. Summer images. John Clare. 6187-7
"I love the flowers that come...with spring". The field sweet-brier. Alice Cary. 6969-X
I love the friendly faces of old sorrows. Karle Wilson Baker. 6501-5
"I love the hills and mountains". Rugged faces. Mary R. Hartman, 6818-9
"I love the hoss from hoof to head". The Kentucky thoroughbred. James Whitcomb Riley. 7010-8
"I love the hour that comes, with dusky hair". Moving bells, fr. Three Alpine sonnets. Henry Van Dyke. 6961-4
"I love the jocund dance". Song ("I love the jocund dance.") William Blake. 6086-2
"I love the lad no longer; I have spurned...". Theognis. 6251-2
"I love the lazy southern spring". The first julep. Bliss Carman and Richard Hovey. 6890-1
"I love the little bookshop/The cosy little...". Ivory, coral, brass. Jessie Welborn Smith. 7038-8
"I love the little hill farms best". The hill farms. Agnes Bardin Dustin. 6764-6
"I love the Lord because my voice". Psalm 116 Bible. 6848-0
"'I love the Lord', is still the strain". Love increased by suffering. Madame De la Mothe Guion. 6814-6
"I love the lyric muse!". The lyric muse. Horace. 6949-5
"I love the old New England ways". New England return. Wilbert Snow. 6761-1
"I love the pretty things you say". Something in common. Irma Terr. 6850-2
"I love the roads that have not at their edges". Pastel (to Julius Zeyer). Jaroslav Vrchlicky. 6886-3
"I love the smell of burning brush in spring". Jessie Stuart. 6761-1
"I love the sound of the horn in the..woodland". The sound of the horn. Alfred de Vigny. 7039-6
"I love the springtime blossoms". Autumn. Josephine Hoshaw. 6906-1
I love the storm. Ruby Tyrone Roberts. 6799-9
"I love the tiers of wooded mountains". A mountain-girded garden at Asheville. Lavinia R. Clark. 6750-6
"I love the tree line of the sky". The benediction line. Mildred Maralyn Mercer. 6906-1
"I love the wet-lipped wind that stirs...hedge". To my best friend. Francis Ledwidge. 6812-X
"I love the wind and the rain!". The wind and the rain. Vileta Nelson Chartier. 6764-6
"I love the winds that sing of roaring sails". Things I love. Cristel Hastings. 6750-6
I love thee. Thomas Hood. 6328-4,6066-8,6226-1,6543-0
"I love thee in the spring." William Jewett Pabodie. 6049-8
"I love thee! Oh, the strife, the pain". Forbidden love. Bryan Waller ("Barry Cornwall") Procter. 6980-0
"I love thee, dear, and knowing mine own heart". In deep places. Amelia Josephine Burr. 6019-6,6464-7,6847-2
"I love thee, gracious Lord". C.C. Cox. 6065-X
I love thee, Lord. Connie Calenberg. 6065-X
"I love thee, my beloved". Constancy. Alice Campbell. 6764-6
"I love thee, O storm o'er the wold...". The storm. Hannes Hafstein. 6854-5
"I love thee, Oberlin!- thy classic halls!". Oberlin in 1849 James Abraham Martling. 6952-5

"I love thee, sweet, when fade". Words for music. Grace Louise Egbert. 6847-2
"I love this grey old church, the low...nave". The four bridges. Jean Ingelow. 6940-1
"I love thy kingdom Lord". Psalm 137. Bible. 6121-4
I love thy kingdpm Lord. Timothy Dwight. 6288-1,6219-9
"I love to hail the mild, balmy hour". Sonnet ("I love to hail"). Felicia Dorothea Hemans. 6973-8
"I love to hear thine earnest voice", sels. Oliver Wendell Holmes. 66601-1
I love to hear you whistle. Irene McMillan Glanville. 6583-X
"I love to kiss thy feet". Wastwater to Scawfell. Thomas Edward Brown. 6809-X
I love to love. Marion Ward. 6527-9
"I love to rove o'er history's page". Shakespeare. Felicia Dorothea Hemans. 6973-8
"I love to search the little sgtreets". The little streets. Ethel May Ericson. 6847-2
"I love to see the old heath's withered brake". Emmonsail's heath in winter. John Clare. 6943-6
"I love to sit where there are ships". Land-fettered. J. Allan Dunn. 7007-8
"I love to start out arter night's begun". Mason and Slidell, fr. The Bigelow papers. James Russell Lowell. 6753-0
"I love to steal away while". Retirement. Unknown. 6752-2
I love to still awhile away. Phoebe Hinsdale Brown. 6525-2
"I love to top a ridge on wild, clear days". The ridge. George A. Scarborough. 6761-1
"I love to watch the world from here, for all". Youth, fr. Two moods from the hill. Ernest Benshimol. 6762-X
I love you. Celestin Pierre Cambiaire. 6826-X
"I love you dearly, O my sweet!". Rondel. Justin Huntly McCarthy. 6850-2,6875-8
"I love you dearly, o my sweet!". Rondel. Justin Huntly McCarthy. 6770-0
"'I love you not only for what you are...'". To a friend. Unknown. 6750-6
"I love you well, my steel-white dagger". Dagger. Mikhail Lermontov. 7039-6
"I love you with a melancholy ardor". Twilight. Jovan Ducic. 6765-4
I love you, dear. George W. Crofts. 6620-8,6066-8
"'I love you, mother' said little John". Which loved best? Unknown. 6889-8
"'I love you,' he whispered low". A betrothal. Frank Dempster Sherman. 7041-8
"I love you. Words are small." Dinah Maria Mulock Craik. 6066-8
"I love you/Not only for what you are". Love ("I love you"). Unknown. 6337-3
"I love, I love, and whom love ye?". I love a flower. Thomas Phillips (atr). 6881-2
"I love, and have some cause." Francis Quarles. 6302-0
I love, and he loves. Ben Jonson. 6328-4
"I love, loved, and so doth she." Sir Thomas Wyatt. 6584-8
"I love, thou little chirping thing". On listening to a cricket. Andrews Norton. 6752-2
"I loved a child as we should love". Francie. Rose Hawthorne Lathrop. 7041-8
"I loved a lad with summer eyes". Stardust. Alice Wilbur. 6750-6
"I loved a lass, a fair one". A love sonnet. George Wither. 6182-6,6562-7
"I loved a lass, a fair one." George Wither. 6302-0,6385-3, 6317-9,6733-6,6092-7,6513
"I loved a woman. The stars fell from heaven". Near Perigord, sels. Ezra Pound. 6897-9
"I loved her, for that she was beautiful". Angela. Philip James Bailey. 6980-0
"I loved him once. So steady was in me". Loving him once. Melrose Pitman. 6906-1
"I loved him so; his voice had grown". The grandsire. Eugene Field. 6949-5
I loved the jocund dance. William Blake. 6187-7,6328-4
"I loved thee when thou wert but young and coy". An afterthought. Unknown. 6936-3
I loved thee, Atthis, in the long ago. Sappho. 6102-8
"I loved thee, Atthis, in the long ago." Bliss Carman.

I

6433-7
"I loved thee, beautiful and kind" Robert Nugent, Earl Nugent. 6874-X
"I loved you for you loving ways". To my brother. Corinne Roosevelt Robinson. 6995-9
"I loved you once, in in my soul maybe" Alexander Pushkin. 6103-6
"I loved you, Atthis, once, long, long ago...". Sappho. 6435-3
"I loved, I kissed...". Unknown. 6251-2
"I made a bit of a garden". God in a garden. Frances Stockwell Lovell. 7030-2
"I made a house of houselessness". Rose O'Neill. 6102-8, 6076-5
"I made a mountain brook my guide". The Spanish chapel. Felicia Dorothea Hemans. 6973-8
"I made a posie, while the day ran by". Life. George Herbert. 6014-5,6562-7
"I made a vow once, one only". Make no vows. Grace Fallow Norton. 6897-9
I made another garden. Arthur O'Shaughnessy. 6232-6,6658-5
"I made another garden, yea". The new love and the old. Arthur O'Shaughnessy. 6844-8
"I made another song". Robert Bridges. 6487-6
"I made me a beautiful castle". Foundations. Martha M. Schultze. 6922-3
"I made my choice:/'Twas children or my voice". An old prima donna speaks. Helen Wieand Cole. 6799-9
"I made my cross each day". My calvary. Grace H. Amers. 6818-9
"I make a very modest plea". By degrees. Berton Braley. 6853-7
"I make an elephant/from the little". The elephant. Carlos Drummond de Andrade. 6758-1
"I' make appraisal of the maiden moon". Apprisals. Richard Eugene Burton. 7041-8
"I make my shroud, but no one know". Song ("I make my shroud"). Adelaide Crapsey. 6030-7,6556-2
"I make not my division of the hour". Patrick Moloney. 6784-0
"I many times thought peace had come". Peace. Emily Dickinson. 6250-4,6309-8
I march with you! Clara Keck Heflebower. 6906-1
"'I mark the hours that shine', so runs...". Bright hours. Margaret Husted. 6922-3
"I marked all kindred powers the heart finds". Love enthroned, fr. The house of liofe. Dante Gabriel Rossetti. 6828-6
"I marked the young mimosa gaily dight". The mimosa. William Selwyn. 6800-6
"I married me a scolding wife some twenty years ago". Unknown. 6059-5
"I married with a scolding wife". The joyful widower. Robert Burns. 6760-3
I marvel at the ways of God. Elwyn Brooks White. 6722-0
"I marvel how mine eye, ranging the night". Sonnet ("I marvel"). Sidney Lanier. 6753-0
"I marvel oft at interweave of things". Correlations. Erwin F. Smith. 7014-0
"I marvel when they pass you by". Octette (005). Edward Sandford Burgess. 6847-2
"I maun tae the sea, gang doon I maun tae the sea". Unknown. 6325-X
"I may be a miser". The single error. Vivian Pike Boles. 6750-6
I may never believe, fr. A midsummer night's dream. William Shakespeare. 6934-7
"I may not be as clever as my neighbor...". A father's job. Edgar A. Guest. 6869-3
"I may not fo to-night to Bethlehem". Christmastide. Emily Pauline ("Tekahionwake") Johnson. 6837-5
"I may not reach the heights I seek". I will be worthy of it. Ella Wheeler Wilcox. 6956-8
"I may not scale the mountain top". What we are. Pearle Moore Stevens. 6818-9
"I may not speak in words, dear, but let my...". Jacqueminots. John Boyle O'Reilly. 7041-8
"I may save a million pounds". The big game. Alex. C. D. Noe. 6818-9
"I may sing of a may". The five joys. Unknown. 6756-5

"I may sit in my wee croo house". When the king comes o'er the water. Unknown. 6859-6
I meant to do my work to-day. Richard Le Gallienne. 6232-6, 6338-1,6374-8,6503-1,6478-7
I meant to have but modest needs. Emily Dickinson. 6288-1
"I meant to win you with a queen's proud ways". A proud lady surrenders. Janet Newmane Preston. 6841-3
I measure every grief I meet. Emily Dickinson. 6908-8
I measure my love to show you. Unknown. 6826-X
I measure time. William Lindsey. 6320-9
"I meet her on the dust street" Henry Timrod. 6066-8
"I met a little maid one day". The flower of love lies bleeding. Richard Henry Stoddard. 6753-0,6004-8
I met a maiden to-day. William Ernest Henley. 6226-1
I met a man. Thomas Hardy. 7014-0
"I met a man away down east". Massachusetts sends greeting. Benjamin Franklin Taylor. 6815-4
"I met a man when night was nigh". I met a man. Thomas Hardy. 7014-0
"I met a smart damsel at Copenhagen". Limerick:"I met a smart damsel at Copenhagen". Unknown. 6811-1
"I met a woman on life's way". The way we walked. Cy Warman. 6836-7
"I met a youth whose brow was sad". The rarest pearl. S.F. Fiester. 6921-5
"I met Louisa in the shade". Louisa. William Wordsworth. 6828-6
I met at eve. Walter De La Mare. 6423-X,6808-1,6596-1,6421-3
"I met some children in a wood". Arcady in England. Victoria Mary Sackville-West. 6785-9
"I met that image on a mirthful day". On a remembered picture of Christ. Felicia Dorothea Hemans. 6973-8
"I met the love-talker one eve in the glen". The love-taler. Ethna (Anna Johnson MacManus) Carbery. 6090-0, 6102-8,6930-4
I met the master face to face. Unknown. 6065-X
"I met the silent wandering man". Thro' bogac ban. Francis Ledwidge. 6812-X
"I met three children on the road". Three children near Clonmel. Eileen Shanahan. 6930-4
"I met with the kingfisher down by the bridge". King fisher. Stella Sharpley. 6804-9
"I met withe death in his country". Song from an evil wood. Edward John Plunkett, 18th Baron Dunsany. 6872-3
"I might have been a hawk's scream, harsh...". Sonnet ("I might have"). James Playsted Wood. 6750-6
"I might have been rich if I'd wanted the gold". Looking back. Edgar A. Guest. 7033-7
"I might have lived inside a shell". Homes. M.K. Westcott. 6937-1
"I might not, if I could". Lines by a medium. Unknown. 6902-9
"I might-unhappy word!-oh me, I might". Sir Philip Sidney. 6181-8
"I mind me o' my father's broo". The light of other days. John Clark. 6800-6
"I mind me of a promise gleaned". The elf's lament. Daniel Martin Karcher. 6936-3
I miss thee, my mother. Eliza Cook. 6097-8
"I miss you, neighbor, as the days go by". Remembering. Grace Stuart Orcutt. 6764-6
"I missed the painted tea set". Sweet Virginia. Lida Wilson Turner. 6841-3
I morgante maggiore, sels. Luigi Pulci. 6088-9
I mount where he has led. John Henry, Cardinal Newman. 6303-9
I mun be married a Sunday. Nicholas Udall. 6182-6,6052-9
I murder hate by field or flood. Robert Burns. 6380-2
"I must be mad, or very tired". Meeting-house hill. Amy Lowell. 6984-3
I must come back. Charles Badger Clark Jr. 6042-0
I must come out next spring. Thomas Haynes Bayly. 6652-6
"I must complain, yet do enjoy my love". Song ("I must complain"). Thomas Campion. 6026-9
"I must complain, yet doe enjoy my loue" Thomas Campion. 6794-8
"I must complayne she doth enioye my loue." Unknown. 6563-5

"I must depart, but like to his last breath". Parted souls. Edward Herbert, 1st Baron Herbert of Cherbury. 6908-8
"I must do as you do? Your way, I own". Advice. Ella Wheeler Wilcox. 7041-8
"I must find in life". Necessity. Warren Ariail. 7016-7
I must forget. Katharine Rebecca Adams. 7016-7
"I must get out to the woods again". The call of the woods. Edgar A. Guest. 7033-7
I must go walk the wood. Unknown. 6881-2
I must go walk the wood so wild. Unknown. 6380-2
"I must grant you, my son, the right to think". For an open mind. Vera White. 6750-6
"I must have candles". Candles. Harriet Holman. 7016-7
"I must laugh and dance and sing". Youth. A. W. 6891-X
"'I must leave here', sighed Lady de Vere". Limerick:"'I must leave here'...". A.E. Page. 6811-1
I must light a candle. Gertrude Hanson. 6144-3
"I must not gaze at them although". The barrier. Clyde McKay. 6880-4
"I must not grieve my Love, whose eyes would read" Samuel Daniel. 6182-6
"I must not tease my mother". Lydia Huntley Sigourney. 6459-0
"I must not yield." Nora May French. 6019-6
I must out and play again. Kathleen Millay. 6374-8
"I must possess you utterly". Possession. Richard Aldington. 6985-1
I must to prayer. Frank Buchanan. 6532-5
"I must unlearn my early modes of praise". Sonnet ("I must unlearn"). Theodore Maynard. 6184-2
"I must watch over this day". Prayer for each awakening. Luis Cane. 6759-X
I must write. Hattie Horner Louthan. 6836-7
"I mustn't look up from the compass-card...". The quartermaster. Klaxon (John Graham Bower). 7031-0
"I ne'er could any lustre see". Richard Brinsley Sheridan. 6092-7
"I need not any hearing tire". Adonis. John Keats. 6980-0
"I need not go". Thomas Hardy. 6187-7,6437-X
I need thee. George Macdonald. 6337-3
I need thee. Frederick Whitfield. 6065-X
I need thee, precious Jesus. Unknown. 6065-X
"I need to go away with you, my dear". Invitation to a husband. Annette Patton Cornell. 6750-6
"I needs must meet him, for he hath beset". Obviam. Thomas Edward Brown. 6809-X
"I needs must turn to earliest days". To Eva. Celinda Bishoprick Abbot. 6789-1
"I never call that gentle name". My mother. George Washington Bethune. 6097-8,6395-9
"I never cast a flower away". Caroline Anne Bowles Southey. 6238-5
"I never clasped his hand". A woman speaks to Theodore Roosevelt's sister. Corinne Roosevelt Robinson. 6995-9
"I never could any lustre see". Song ("I never could"). Richard Brinsley Sheridan. 6226-1
I never did git to go to Omaha. Alice Mary Kimball. 6817-0
"I never dreamed such treasure lay in snow". The unemployed speak of snow. Estelle Rooks. 6850-2
I never even suggested it. Ogden Nash. 6637-2
"I never gave a lock of hair." Elizabeth Barrett Browning. 6250-4
"I never had a schooner/With pink...". The poet. Kathryn Worth. 6861-8
"I never had a title-deed". My tenants. Helen Hunt Jackson. 7041-8
"I never had an orchid in all my life". Wealth. Marion Schmidt. 6750-6
"I never have got the bearings quite". The flag; an incident of Strain's expedition. James Jeffrey Roche. 6946-0
"I never hear the word 'escape'". Emily Dickinson. 6380-2
"I never hear/The growling diapason of a plane". A little prayer; for the man in the air. John Oxenham. 7014-0
I never knew a night so black. John Kendrick Bangs. 6337-3
"I never knew him, for he never grew". Jimmy. Edgar A. Guest. 6862-6
"I never knew how dear thou wert". Song ("I never knew"). Catharine M. Warfield. 6226-1
"I never knew I had a soul until". Thoughts on taking an anaesthetic. Marjorie DeGraff. 6850-2
I never knew it was you. Wendy Wood. 6900-2
"I never knew it, love, till now." Juan II; King of Castile. 6066-8
"I never knew such a man in my life". Tommy big-eyes. Thomas Edward Brown. 6809-X
"I never knew that one could find in flour". She said to me. Theressa M. DeFosset. 6906-1
"I never knew you save as all men know". Rupert Brooke (in memoriam). Moray Dalton. 7026-4
"I never knowed". William T. Croasdale. 6274-1
"I never laie me downe to rest." Unknown. 6563-5
I never loved ambitiously to climb. Thomas Nashe. 6934-7
"I never prayed for Dryads". An invocation. William Johnson Cory. 6423-X,6437-X,6383-7
I never saw a moor. Emily Dickinson. 6473-6,6723-9
"I never saw an angel". Earth's angels. Unknown. 6918-5
"I never saw that you did painting need". Sonnet 083 ("I never saw"). William Shakespeare. 6447-7
"I never saw you, madam, lay apart." Henry Howard, Earl of Surrey. 6584-8
"I never see the brown earth". Remembrance. Melba Williams. 6906-1
"I never see the red rose crown the year". John Masefield. 6289-X
"I never seen no 'red gods'...". How springs comes to Shasta Jim. Henry Van Dyke. 6961-4
"I never shall furgit the night...". The spellin' bee. Paul Laurence Dunbar. 6887-1
I never shall love the snow again. Robert Bridges. 6477-9, 6487-6,6430-2,6508-2,6655-0
"I never swung a staff and deep, oh deep". Roy Daniells. 6446-9
"I never think of you on sunlit days". Shadow friend. Anderson M. Scruggs. 6780-8
"I never thought again to hear". The Oxford thrushes. Henry Van Dyke. 6961-4
"I never thought my husband, Jimmie Speed". The happy ending. Alice Mary Kimball. 6880-4
"I never thought that strange romantic war". James Miles Langstaff. 6796-4
"I never used to think myself so fine". Michelangelo Buonarroti. 6325-X
"I never was a favourite". Thomas Haynes Bayly. 6980-0
"I never went in for a car". Pantoum of a cadger. George Steele Seymour. 6789-1
"I never wholly feel that summer is high". High summer. Ebenezer Jones. 6958-4,7015-9
"I never will forget that day". Triolet 003, fr. Thistledown. Cora Fabri. 6876-6
"I never would, 'ave done it if I'd known...". Mules. Cicely Fox Smith. 6846-4
I nod in company. Alexander Pope. 6125-7
"I not through sex in darkness as a mole". Common ground. Duncan Mitchel. 7003-5
"I note this morning". Retrospection. Garnet B. Freeman. 6273-3
"I notice in my car, when nearing". Vermont Morgans. Daniel L. Cady. 6988-6
"I notice when they're playing house...". Playing father. Edgar A. Guest. 6869-3
"I noticed as soon as I oprned the door". The trick. Edgar A. Guest. 6748-4
"I now think love is rather deaf than blind". The poet-wooer. Ben Jonson. 6935-5
"I observed a locomotive in the railroad yards". Sand. Unknown. 6925-8
"I offer wrong to my beloved saint". Fulke Greville; 1st Baron Brooke. 6380-2
"I offer you the chance to forgive your wounds". Song from the maker of totems. Duane Niatum. 7005-1
"I often does a quiet read". Ballade. William Ernest Henley. 6724-7
"I often have been told". The Constitution and the Guerriere. Unknown. 6946-0
"I often look when the moon is low". Low-moon land. Francis Ledwidge. 6812-X
"I often say my prayers". Prayer ("I often say"). John

Burton. 6337-3
"I often see in moony moods". Vermont buckwheat batter. Daniel L. Cady. 6988-6
"I often think each tottering form". Youth and age. Unknown. 6910-X
"I often wonder mother loves to creep". Of blessed memory. Eugene Field. 6949-5
"I often wonder, dear/If in the day". To Katharine. William Cary Sanger Jr.. 6799-9
"I often, musing, wander back to days long...". Uncle Ned's tale. John Boyle O'Reilly. 7041-8
"I on the thighs of God, as the leaf...willow!". Indian spring. Constance Lindsay Skinner. 6979-7
"I once did know a charming lad whose name...". Unknown. 6059-5
"I once did know a farmer". Unknown. 6059-5
"I once had a sweet little doll, dears". Song of Madame Do-as-you-would-be..,fr.The water babies. Charles Kingsley. 6832-4
"I once had a sweetheart, but now I have none". Unknown. 6059-5
"I once knew a gard'ner whose aunt". Limerick:"I once knew a gard'ner whose aunt". H.G. Dixey. 6811-1
"I once knew a man". Pre-eminence. Murdock Pemberton. 6817-0
"I once loved nature so that man was nought". Nature and art. Thomas Edward Brown. 6809-X
"I once sat astride on a runaway rhyme". The runaway rhyme. Rudolph Chambers Lehmann. 6760-3
"I once stood silent, aloof and free". A singing tree. Lloyd Roberts. 6797-2
"I once took a fancy to fathom the brains". Fathoming brains. Stockton Bates. 6923-1
"I once was a maid...", fr. The jolly beggars. Robert Burns. 6733-6
"I only gave him/Directions for his road". Smile was my only fault. Dong-hwan Kim. 6775-1
"I only heard the loud ebb on the sand". The death of Leag, Cuchulain's charioteer. Francis Ledwidge. 6812-X
"I open an eye and the trees outside my...". Sicktime. Hugh Fox. 6998-3
I ought to weep. Unknown. 6881-2
"I owe you life. Would I had owed you too". Daughter to mother. Walter De La Mare. 6905-3
"I own a dog who is a gentleman". A gentlemen. Unknown. 7008-6
I own a dream. Will Smallwood. 6178-8
"I own a spot in northern France". I have a share in Flanders fields. Elizabeth Dimon Preston. 6836-7
"I own I am shock'd at the purchase of slaves". Pity for poor Africans. William Cowper. 6814-6
"I own I like not Johnson's turgid style". Lines on Dr. Johnson. John ("Peter Pindar") Wolcott. 6787-5
"I pace beside my books and hear the". Prayer beside a lamp. Yvor Winters. 6808-1
"I paced the grove an hour/My spirit ill at...". Token. Charles J. Schuster. 6799-9
"I paid $3.00 to see Bukowski read" A.D. Winans. 6998-3, 6901-0
"I paid a visit first to Ukenheim". Famine in a besieged city, fr. Philip Van Artevelde. Henry Taylor. 6980-0
I paint what I see. Elwyn Brooks White. 6399-3,6375-6
I pant for the music. Percy Bysshe Shelley. 6328-4
I pass a lighted window. Clement Wood. 6033-1,6556-2
"I pass all my hours in a shady old grove". Song ("I pass all"). Charles II; King of England. 6563-5
I pass all my hours in a shady old grove. Charles II; King of England. 6328-4
"I pass along the public street". Incognito. Mildred Focht. 6847-2
"I pass through/City Hall Park". Gratitude. Arturo [pseud.]. 6817-0
"I passed a tree whose ripe fruit lay". Bitter fruit. Margaret E. Bruner. 6789-1
"I passed her in the factory room". The factory girl. Charles W. Denison. 6755-7
"I passed St. Luke's upon the hill, to-night". The haunted room. Hedwig W.D. Hilker. 6847-2
"I passed the door of the operating room". Alfred Noyes. 6298-9

"I passed the palace in the park". Bayonet and chisel. Shirley Brooks. 6760-3
"I passed the plate in church". The collection. Ernest Howard Crosby. 6954-1
"I passed today along a quiet street". Old Flemish street. Beulah May. 6789-1
"I pause and ponder as I pass the fields". Vermont memory tracks - summer. Leonard Twynham. 7030-2
"I pause not to speak of Raleigh's dreams". John Smith's approach to Jamestown. James Barron Hope. 6946-0
"I peddles pencils on Broadway". The peddler. Hermann Hagedorn. 6944-4,7007-8
"I peer into myself". Island. Wilberto L. Canton. 6759-X
"I picked a primrose, pale as death." Phyllis M. Lubbock. 6317-9
"I picked the little rosebud/I held it in...". Miniature rose bud. Zella Spilka. 6799-9
"I picked this quarrel, D'Avanne, with thee". Hugo the bastard. Robert Buchanan. 7007-8
"I picture her in the quaint old room". Dreaming in the trenches. William Gordon McCabe. 7017-5
"I pile the chill sea-shingle...". Zonas. 6251-2
"I pity him, who, at no small expense". Epistle to a student of dead languages. Philip Freneau. 6753-0
"I pity kings, whom worship waits upon". Table talk, sels. William Cowper. 6831-6
"I pity those who have not been". At Lac Labelle. Susan ("Seranus") Frances. 6797-2
"I pity you. It would be different". To a neglected book. Helen M. Richards. 6764-6
"I place an off'ring at thy shrine". The perfect sacrifice. Madame De la Mothe Guion. 6814-6
"I placed the silver in her palm". Gracie Og Machree. John Keegan Casey. 6873-1
"I plant a tree whose leaf". Romaunt of Margret. Elizabeth Barrett Browning. 6980-0
"I plant corn four years". Corn-planter. Maurice Kenny. 7005-1
"I plant the simple flowers, marigolds". Gardening. T.S. Wallace. 6857-X
I planted flowers today. Mrs. Pope Brooks. 7016-7
I planted little trees to-day. James B. Carrington. 6449-3
"I play a reed flute". Reed flute. Ha-woon Han. 6775-1
"I play for seasons, not eternities!" George Meredith. 6828-6
"I play for seasons," fr. Modern love. George Meredith. 6199-0
"I play the game, as they may play". Song of the defeated. Nellie Burget Miller. 6836-7
"I played I was two polar bears". The bear hunt. Margaret Widdemer. 6891-X
"I played with you 'mid cowslips growing". Love and age. Unknown. 6911-X
"I pledge allegiance to a false symbol". Valerie Tarver. 7024-8
"I plucked for thee the wilding rose". Song ("I plucked..."). Bayard Taylor. 6976-2
"I plucked thee in life's morning, ribboned...". Sonnet. Wellington Brezee. 6799-9
"I pore upon the message brief". Killed in action. John Lomax. 6800-6
"I poured out a tumbler of claret". A tumbler of claret. Ella Wheeler Wilcox. 6928-2
"I pr'ythee leave this peevish fashion". To a coy lady. Alexander Brome. 6874-X
"I praise the tender flower". Robert Bridges. 6187-7,6487-6
I pray. Rose Linda Baldwin. 6799-9
"I pray for peace; yet peace is but a prayer". Sonnet ("I pray for peace"). George Edward Woodberry. 7026-4
"I pray for you, and yet I do not frame". A prayer ("I pray for you"). Mary Dixon Thayer. 6337-3
"I pray that I may never miss". I pray. Rose Linda Baldwin. 6799-9
"I pray thee let me weep to-night". Letitia Elizabeth ("L.E.L.") Landon. 6980-0
"I pray you make me humble, Lord". A little prayer. Ellen Mae Nichols. 6799-9
"I pray you pardon, Elsie". How it happened. Colonel John Hay. 7041-8

"I pray you to say what a mother can do". An appeal. Jessie Scott. 6965-7
I pray you, be merry and sing with me. Unknown. 6756-5
"I pray you, do not turn your head...". In an artist's studio. Thomas Bailey Aldrich. 6887-1
"I pray you, in this hour's confusion, go". In this hour. Arthur Davison Ficke. 6761-1
"I pray you, in your letters", fr. Othello. William Shakespeare. 6289-X
"I pray you, what is't o'clock?" William Shakespeare. 7020-5
"I pressed mine ear close to the warm...earth". The soul's awakening. John Edward Colburn. 7030-2
"I pressed my hand behind the shape of yours". To Katherine Mansfield. Jane Culver. 6781-6
"I prithee send me back my heart". Song ("I prithee"). Sir John Suckling. 6226-1,6383-7
"I prithee send me back my heart". Sir John Suckling. 6099-4,6302-0,6385-3,6563-5,6092-7
"I prithee sweet to me be kind." Unknown. 6563-5
I prithee, leave me. Unknown. 6328-4
"I proclaim thee great and wonderful". Psalm. Murilo Mendes. 6759-X
I promised Sylvia. John Wilmot, 2d Earl of Rochester. 6092-7
"I purposed once to take my pen and write". Sonnet ("I purposed"). Henry Clarence Kendall. 6768-9
"I put aside the branches". The night. Herbert Trench. 6877-4
I put my heart in a fortress. Marian Buxton Clark. 6906-1
"I put my heart to school". School. Henry Van Dyke. 6961-4
"I put my trust in God my king!". Psalm 011. Bible. 6848-0
"I question what poetry will tremble the...". An ordinary composure. James L. White. 7003-5
"I ran down stairs and out the door". Nightmare, with moral. Lindley Williams Hubbell. 6751-4
"I ran down the queerest and tiniest street". Market day. Gladys H. Cooper. 6850-2
"I ransack'd, for a theme of song". Annus memorabilis, 1789. William Cowper. 6814-6
"I reach out with my barbaric hands...". God. Gonzalo Escudero. 6759-X
"I reached the highest place in Spoon River". Henry C. Calhoun. Edgar Lee Masters. 6897-9
"I reached the middle of the mount". Drige ("I reached the middle of the mount"). Ralph Waldo Emerson. 6753-0
"I read a legend of a monk who painted". A legend. Unknown. 6918-5
I read fortunes in dreams. Delia Dominguez. 7036-1
"I read his book: it pictured life to me". The vision and the pen. Addie Cropsey Hudson. 6836-7
"I read it in the restroom, in pink nail...". You're sorry, your mother is crazy, & I'm a Chinese... Deborah Lee. 6790-5
"I read not long ago, how all the tide". The Ganges. Mary McGuire. 6920-7
"I read of the Emperor Conrad the Third". Love's strategy. R.S. Sharpe. 6924-X
"I read somewhere that a swan, snow-white". The watch of a swan. Sarah Morgan Bryan Piatt. 7041-8
"I read the Christabel". Versicles. George Gordon, 6th Baron Byron. 6945-2
"I read the sentence or heard it spoken". The prime of life. Ella Wheeler Wilcox. 6920-7
"I read the story of the Saxon knight". The Count of Gleichen. Bayard Taylor. 6976-2
"I read, dear friend". Robert Louis Stevenson. 6085-4
"I reads aboudt dot vater mill dot runs". Der vater-mill. Charles Follen Adams. 6920-7,7041-8
"I reads in Yawcob's shtory book". Der spider and der fly. Charles Follen Adams. 6924-X
"I really take it very kind". Domestic asides; or, truth in parenthesis. Thomas Hood. 6974-6
"I rebel/Not because of poverty". Why I rebel. Robert J. Sye. 7024-8
"I reckon when the world we leave". When we understand the plan. Edgar A. Guest. 7033-7
I remember. Jayne Cortez. 6898-7
I remember. William White. 6868-5
I remember. Fay M. Yauger. 6979-7

"I remember - why, yes! God bless me!". At a meeting of friends. Oliver Wendell Holmes. 6753-0
"I remember a gloomy room in the old home". The elderly. Molly Dong. 6883-9
"I remember a house I left behind". Empty house. Rosario Castellanos. 7036-1
"I remember a house where all were good." Gerard Manley Hopkins. 6187-7
"I remember a song whose numbers throng". The old sweet song. Unknown. 6914-2
"I remember an April day". The voice of the chestnut tree. Mary Frances Butts. 6965-7
I remember homestead Sundays. Lola Beall Graham. 6857-X
"I remember it all so very well...". An inventor's wife. Jeannie Pendleton Ewing. 6930-0
"I remember it all so very well..married life". An inventor's wife. Jeannie Pendleton Ewing. 6927-4
"I remember little/of the trip there". October hill. R. Wayne Hardy. 6870-7
"I remember lovely things". Spell. Margaret Moore Muettman. 6750-6
"I remember mother/you picked a fragile flower". Down home. Randolph Outlaw. 6870-7
"I remember some words my father said". Zu der edlen jagd, fr. Ye wearie wayfarer. Adam Lindsay Gordon. 6951-7
"I remember that you grew". A degenerate of the pink family. Mary E. Hough. 6764-6
I remember the block party. Oscar Williams. 6761-1,6389-6
"I remember the day". Rice and rose bowl blues. Diane Mei Lin Mark. 6790-5
"I remember the indian hospital". Birthplace. Duane Big Eagle. 7005-1
"I remember the lowering wintry morn". By flood and field, fr. Ye wearie wayfarer. Adam Lindsay Gordon. 6951-7
I remember the only wise thing I ever did. Philip James Bailey. 6066-8
I remember the time ere his temples were grey. Walter Savage Landor. 6092-7
"I remember through remains". I remember. Jayne Cortez. 6898-7
"I remember when a boy that my mother used...". Neighboring. Edgar A. Guest. 6869-3
"I remember when in boyhood". Playing hookey. Unknown. 6889-8
I remember, I remember. Phoebe Cary. 6440-X,6652-6
I remember, I remember. Thomas Hood. 6075-7,6481-7,6512-0, 6127-3,6233-4,6240 ,6192-3,6250-4,6104-4,6219-9,6658-5,6241-7,6328-4,6337-3,6369-1,6370-5,6457 ,6452-4, 6639-9,6424-8,6737-9,6302-0,6385-3,6459-0,6479-5, 6486-8,6504-X,6519-8,6583-X,6732
I remember, I remember, sels. Thomas Hood. 6601-1
"I remember/One time she walked within...". Fleur de lys. Corinne Huntington Jackson. 6799-9
"I remember/The dark night you came". So-and-so. Jim Waters. 6782-4
I renounce the dream. Arthur Davison Ficke. 6879-0
I resolve. Charlotte Perkins Stetson Gilman. 6260-1
"I rest my hopes on thee". Saviour mine. William White. 6868-5
I rest with thee, O Jesus. Unknown. 6292-X
"I rest with thee, o Jesus". Four prayers. Unknown. 6930-4
"I return from a past that will never enter...". Back from London. David Meltzer. 6792-1, 6998-3
"I ride in a gloomy land". The guests of night. Bayard Taylor. 6976-2
"I ride through forest and I ride through dale". Minor note 005, fr. In Tuscany. Cora Fabri. 6876-6
"I rise, & greiue." Unknown. 6563-5
"I roamed the woods to-day and seemed to hear". A fear. Francis Ledwidge. 6812-X
"I rode out one cold winter night". Cold winter night. Unknown. 6826-X
"I roofed my roof-tree at the wane of the moon". The horn of the moon. Herbert Trench. 6877-4
"I run a boarding house all winter long". Boarding the birds. Edgar A. Guest. 6748-4
"I run my left hand". The bird nest is transparent by Qudrat. Jeff Jentz. 6900-2
"I s'pose that young folks anywheres". 'Hopping mad' in Vermont. Daniel L. Cady. 6988-6

"I said 'I'll go my road alone'.". The way in Africa. Arthur Shearly Cripps. 6800-6
"I said I splendidly loved you; it is not true". Sonnet ("I said"). Rupert Brooke. 6508-2
"I said I stood upon thy grave". Arisen at last. John Greenleaf Whittier. 6753-0
"I said I would? Well, I hardly know". Betsy Lee. Thomas Edward Brown. 6809-X
"I said in my heart". Spring. Richard Hovey. 6047-1,6374-8
"I said in the cutting off of my days...". In dimido dierum. Bible. 6830-8
"I said it was a wilful, wayward thing". Love's artifice. James Sheridan Knowles. 6980-0
"I said one day that I would leave the town". Manhattan, sel. Charles Hanson Towne. 7014-0
"I said one year ago". The new-year ledger. Amelia E. Barr. 6921-5
"I said sometimes with tears". Samuel Crossman. 6931-2
"I said the sun had never burned for you". Design for a perfect world. Louis Untermeyer. 6880-4
"I said this morning, as I leaned and threw". Response. Ella Wheeler Wilcox. 6956-8
"I said to a man of Norwich". Limerick:"I said to a man of Norwich". H.G. Dixey. 6811-1
'I said to love'. Thomas Hardy. 6657-7
"I said to love". Thomas Hardy. 6655-0
"I said to my heart, between sleeping & waking". Chloe. Charles Mordaunt; Earl of Peterborough. 6152-4,6932-0
"I said to my heart, between sleeping and waking". Song by a person of quality. Charles Mordaunt; Earl of Peterborough. 6874-X
"I said to myself at the dawn". Joy walks in the morning. Nellie Burget Miller. 7038-8
"I said to myself one morning". Waking. Annie Higgins. 6880-4
"I said to sorrow's awful storm". The soul's defiance. Unknown. 6752-2
"I said to the brown, brown thrush", sels. Dinah Maria Mulock Craik. 6601-1
"I said to young Allan M'Ilveray". Discontent, fr. The road to Avernus. Adam Lindsay Gordon. 6951-7
"I said you'd better go away". Stupidity. Mildred M. Hott. 6750-6
"I said, for love was laggard,O, love was slow". Indifference. Edna St. Vincent Millay. 6986-X
"I said, if I might go back again". A woman's conclusions. Phoebe Cary. 6969-X
I said, this misery must end. Christopher J. Brennan. 6384-5
"I said, when the word came, 'She will break".". Of little faith. Harold Trowbridge Pulsifer. 6833-2
"I said, when the word came, 'She will break'.". Of little faith. Harold Trowbridge Pulsifer. 6979-7
I sail in the fall. David Stefansson. 6283-0
"I sailed/Upon a maiden trip, long, long ago". Dextera excelsi. A. Souby. 6818-9
"I salute the aplomb of animals". Walt Whitman: Goosey, goosey, gander. Charles Powell. 6982-7
"I sang a song of love one day". To my beloved. Lola Greenfield Lawrence. 6799-9
"I sat alone in Coimbra,the town myself..ta'en". The murder of the master. Unknown (Spanish). 6757-3
"I sat alone in thought, quite drowned". Melody in black. Joyce Lancaster. 6850-2
"I sat alone with my conscience". Conscience and future judgement. Unknown. 6294-6,6964-9
I sat among the green leaves. Marjorie L.C. Pickthall. 6232-6,6102-8,6393-4,6019-6
"I sat at my window in silence". Spring. Bertha Merena Mauermann. 6789-1
"I sat at noontide in my tent". The Bechuana boy. Thomas Pringle. 6980-0
"I sat at the opera - round me there floated". A drama of three. Unknown. 6917-7
"I sat at the wheezy organ". The old organ. Helen Booth. 6922-3
"I sat beneath an olive's branches gray". Corcyra. John Henry, Cardinal Newman. 6980-0
"I sat beside the glowing grate, fresh heaped". A meditation on Rhode Island coal. William Cullen Bryant. 6484-1,6753-0
"I sat beside the sleeping child". Innocence asleep. Florence Orndorff. 6906-1
"I sat by the side of my fire, alone on Kapiti". A hunter's requiem. Brian ("Korongo") Brooke. 6938-X
"I sat down on a bumble bee". Suffering. Nathalia Crane. 6861-8
"I sat in my sorrow a-weary alone". The window just over the street. Alice Cary. 6865-0;6969-X
"I sat in the church, sweet Marion Lee". Marion Lee. James Abraham Martling. 6952-5
"I sat in the gathering twilight". For the master's sake. Minnie Mason Beebe. 6818-9
"I sat me weary on a pillar's base", fr. The city.." James ("B.V.") Thomson. 6508-2
"I sat on a cliff where the seas ever rave". By the sea. Steingrimur Thorsteinsson. 6854-5
"I sat on the doorstone of heart's desire". Guerdon. Lena L. Jennings. 6799-9
"I sat to-day beneath the pine". A lover's test. Bayard Taylor. 6976-2
I sat with love upon a woodside well. Dante Gabriel Rossetti. 6560-0
"I sat within the temple of her heart". Sonnet ("I sat"). Charles Sangster. 6115-X
"I saunter by the shore and lose myself". A hymn to the sea, sels. Richard Henry Stoddard. 6997-5
"I sauntered down through Europe". The jackpot. Eugene Fitch Ware. 7012-4
"I sauntered lately through the street". A weird warble. H. Chance Newton. 6927-4
I saw a chapel all of gold. William Blake. 6154-0,6488-4
I saw a delicate flower had grown up 2 feet high. Henry David Thoreau. 6333-0
"I saw a fair maiden sit and sing". Lullay, mine liking, my dear son, mine sweeting. Unknown. 6756-5
"I saw a fair maiden". Unknown. 6187-7,6334-9
"I saw a fallen sparrow". Whose eye is on the sparrow. Byron Herbert Reece. 6979-7
I saw a fish-pond all on fire. Unknown. 6125-7
"I saw a fisher bold yestreen". 'Not willing to stay'. Thomas Edward Brown. 6809-X
"I saw a golden aeroplane". Romance a-wing. Nancy Telfair. 6841-3
"I saw a grave beneath a cypress-tree". Minor note 009, fr. In Tuscany. Cora Fabri. 6876-6
"I saw a little child at play". Truditur dies die. William Charles Scully. 6800-6
"I saw a little stream to-day". Gob-ny-ushtey (Water's mouth). Thomas Edward Brown. 6809-X
I saw a maiden. Unknown. 6282-2
I saw a man. Stephen Crane. 6102-8,6076-5,6464-7
I saw a man. Horace L. Traubel. 6076-5
"I saw a man on a horse". Mirage. Richard Church. 6779-4
I saw a monk of Charlemaine. William Blake. 6378-0
"I saw a mother working:/She gave her home...". Mother love. L.M. Zimmerman. 6799-9
"I saw a mushroom grow up to the clouds". Giant mushrooms. Dan Lemke. 6883-9
I saw a new world. William Brighty Rands. 6656-9
I saw a peacock. Unknown. 6861-8
I saw a peacock with a fiery tail. Unknown. 6125-7
"I saw a peacock with a fiery tail". Unknown. 6904-5
"I saw a phoenix in the wood alone." Edmund Spenser. 6125-7
"I saw a pretty cottage stand". What I saw. J. Milton Akers. 6913-4
"I saw a priest rise to declaim". Morus-multicaulis; a satire...American silk speculators. Charles W. Denison. 6755-7
"I saw a proud, mysterious cat". The mysterious cat. Vachel Lindsay. 6891-X
"I saw a reindeer, strayed from the...". The lost dream. Fannie Stearns Davis. 7038-8
"I saw a ruler take his stand". The three rulers. Adelaide Anne Procter. 6957-6
I saw a ship a-sailing. Mother Goose. 6132-X,6452-3,6114-1, 6554-X,6262-8
"I saw a sickly cellar plant". The incentive. arah N.

Cleghorn. 6954-1
"I saw a small, white sea-gull". Heinrich Heine. 6876-6
"I saw a snail". Little snail. Hilda Conkling. 6891-X
"I saw a snowflake in the air". A snowflake in May. Clinton Scollard. 6770-0,6875-8
"I saw a stable, low and very bare". Mary Elizabeth Coleridge. 6931-2
I saw a sweet and silly sight. Unknown. 6756-5
"I saw a thousand...", fr. King Richard III. William Shakespeare. 6547-3
"I saw a tract of ocean locked inland". A poet's wife. Alice Meynell. 6955-X
"I saw a vision yesternight". Song ("I saw a vision"). John Cleveland. 6324-1
"I saw a vision". Jean Ingelow. 6648-8
"I saw a young bride, in her beauty and pride". Passing under the rod. Mary S.B. Dana. 6219-9,6913-4,6260-1
"I saw above a sea of hills", fr. Berkshire notes. Sara Teasdale. 6778-6
"I saw along the lifeless sea". The mist. Robert Kelley Weeks. 7041-8
"I saw an aged beggar in my walk". The old Cumberland beggar. William Wordsworth. 6866-9
"I saw an armed champion ride". The two champions. Unknown. 6919-3
"I saw an idler on a summer day". The worlds. Martha Gilbert Dickinson Bianchi. 6762-X
"I saw an infant cherub -- soft it lay". 'I thought it slept'. Henry Pickering. 6752-2
"I saw an infant, marble cold". Hebrew dirge. Lydia Huntley Sigourney. 6848-0
"I saw an old dame weaving". The weaving of the Tartan. Alice C. Macdonell. 6873-1
"I saw ants/Tugging, pushing, lifting". Fate. J. P. Zimmerman. 6861-8
"I saw below me", fr. The lifting of the veil. Robert Buchanan. 6997-5
I saw death slain. William Capell. 6144-3
I saw Duluth. Dorothy Bladin Hill. 6342-X
"I saw eternity the other night". The world. Henry Vaughan. 6931-2,7014-0
"I saw fair Chloris walk alone". William Strode. 6187-7
"I saw faire Chloris walke alone". On Chloris walking in the snow. Robert Herrick 6827-8
I saw from the beach. Thomas Moore. 6244-X,6258-X,6543-0
I saw God wash the world. William L. Stidger. 6337-3
"I saw her coming through the flowery grass". Spring love. Francis Ledwidge. 6812-X
"I saw her crop a rose", fr. Summer images. John Clare. 6187-7,6317-9
"I saw her first abreast the Boston Light". The William P. Frye. Jeanne Robert Foster. 6946-0,7026-4
"I saw her first on a day in spring". An idyl. Charles Gurdon Buck. 7025-6,6675-5
"I saw her form before a book-store window...". Desire. Edith Haskell Tappan. 6764-6
"I saw her loose from the anchored quay". The storm spirit's tale of The Lexington. Charles W. Denison. 6755-7
I saw her once. Richard Henry Dana. 6077-3
"I saw her once - so freshly fair". Time's changes. Winthrop Mackworth Praed. 6980-0
"I saw her shadow on the grass". Vestigia. Arthur Symons. 6770-0,6875-8
"I saw her walk the white and sandy beach". Inland woman. Barbara Young. 7038-8
"I saw him 'neath a tropic sky". The runaway. Edgar A. Guest. 6748-4
"I saw him at his sport erstwhile". The child reading the Bible. Felicia Dorothea Hemans. 6973-8
"I saw him dead, a leaden slumber lyes". A poem on the death of Oliver Cromwell, sels. Andrew Marvell. 6933-9
"I saw him do down to the water to bathe". The bather. Bliss Carman and Richard Hovey. 6890-1
"I saw him floating on the stream of time". The sailor. Charles W. Denison. 6755-7
"I saw him in Hollywood yesterday and I asked". Dick Powell. Ronald Koertge. 6792-1, 6998-3
"I saw him on a topmost limb...". Love affair. Edgar A. Guest. 6748-4
"I saw him on his throne, far in the north". Winter. Frances Anne Kemble. 7037-X
"I saw him once before". The last leaf. Oliver Wendell Holmes. 6753-0,6176-1,6243-1,6332-2,6473-6,6486-8, 6583 ,6092-7,6250-4,6126-5,6723-9,6646-1,6424 ,6271-7,6289-X,6302-0,6385-3,6437-X,6441 ,6467-1,6304-7, 6396-9,6300-4,6309-8,6219 ,6457-4,6459-0,6478-7,6481-7,6497-3,6610 ,6230-X,6126-5,6121-4,6265-2,6431-0, 6560 ,6733-6,6735-2,6601-1,6077-3,6101-X,6142 ,6004-8,6307-1,6092-7,6008-0,6288-1,6732 ,6753-0
"I saw him sensitive in frame". Stanzas in memory of Edward Quillinan. Matthew Arnold. 6947-9
"I saw him standing in a barren field". The mule. J.T. Cotton Noe. 6750-6
I saw in Louisiana a live-oak growing. Walt Whitman. 6047-1,6085-4,6236-9,6332-2,6253-9,6126-5,6265-2,6560-0
"I saw in dreams a dim bleak heath". The meeting. Edgar Fawcett. 7041-8
"I saw in my dream a wonderful stream". Pitiless faith Alice Cary. 6865-0;6969-X
"I saw in rift of cloud a beaming light". Judea. Charles M. Wallington. 6848-0
"I saw it in a shell-torn town". The cross. Donald Earl Edwards. 6144-3
"I saw love die! Not slowly, but at once". Bereavement. Viola Bailey Wilson. 6750-6
"I saw my lady by a cool, fresh stream". Lorenzo de' Medici. 6325-X
"I saw my lady weep". Madrigal. Unknown. 6830-8
"I saw my lady weep". Unknown. 6181-8,6182-6,6187-7,6317-9, 6194-X,6250-4,6189-3
I saw my soul. Milton S. Rose. 6836-7
"I saw my soul at rest upon a day". Sestina. Algernon Charles Swinburne. 6850-2,6770-0,6875-8
"I saw my soul throw wide its venturesome...". I saw my soul. Milton S. Rose. 6836-7
"I saw Nelson at the Battle of the Nile". Limerick:"I saw Nelson at the Battle of the Nile." Unknown. 6308-X
"I saw New England coast - its granite rock". New England coast. Herbert Elliott. 6761-1
"I saw night leave her halos down". The lure. Francis Ledwidge. 6812-X
"I saw no doctor..." Unknown (Greek) 6722-0
"I saw old autumn in the misty morn". Ode - autumn. Thomas Hood. 6974-6
I saw old general at bay. Walt Whitman. 6126-5,6288-1
"I saw old wizened wisdom" Ronald W. Povey. 7014-0
"I saw one radiant star". Hope. Avis H. Grant. 6906-1
"I saw pale Dian sitting by the brink". Sonnet written in Keats' Endymion. Thomas Hood. 6974-6
I saw that shadowed thing. Leonard Bacon. 6619-4
"I saw the ages backward roll'd". Rome. William Sotheby. 6980-0
I saw the beauty go. Mary Gilmore. 6384-5
"I saw the blue smoke rising...". Evening smoke. Edgar A. Guest. 6869-3
"I saw the bowman bend his straining arc". The archer. Crawford Williams. 6750-6
"I saw the Connaught rangers...". The Connaught rangers. Winifred M. Letts. 7027-2
I saw the clouds. Hervey White. 6897-9
"I saw the day lean o'er the world's...edge". Sunset. Ella Wheeler Wilcox. 6956-8
"I saw the day's white rapture". Song ("I saw the day's"). Charles Hanson Towne. 6431-0
"I saw the eyes, where Amor took his place". Guido Cavalcanti. 6325-X
"I saw the figure of a lovely maid." William Wordsworth. 6317-9
"I saw the flaring plummet drop". Realization. William Roehrick. 6850-2
"I saw the flowering earth we left spread...". First flight. Elford Caughey. 6761-1
"I saw the great bronze Lincoln, strong". The consoler. Marion Couthouy Smith. 6995-9
"I saw the little quiet town". The sister. Francis Ledwidge. 6812-X
'I saw the morning break'. Sir Owen Seaman. 6224-5
"I saw the night caught, as by a wizard's...". Night. H.

I

Duncan Hall. 6784-0
"I saw the object of my pining thought" Thomas Watson. 6182-6
"I saw the old man pause, then turn his head". The old conservative. L. Frank Tooker. 6833-2
"I saw the ramparts of my native land". Sonnet: Death warnings. Francisco de Quevedo y Villegas. 7039-6
"I saw the stars swept through ethereal space". Ab astris. Anne C. Lynch Botta. 7030-2
"I saw the sun burn in the blue". The missel thrush. Ralph Hodgson. 6943-6
"I saw the sun climb over the sky". Migration. Elena Vossen Greenfield. 6841-3
"I saw the tired city fall in the arms of...". Manhattan, sel. Charles Hanson Towne. 7014-0
I saw the vision of armies. Walt Whitman. 6665-8
"I saw thee on a summer's day". The western sea. Edmond Gore Alexander Holmes. 6997-5
"I saw thee on thy bridal day". To - ("I saw thee"). Edgar Allan Poe. 6126-5,6288-1,6753-0
"I saw thee weep - the big bright tear". George Gordon, 6th Baron Byron, 6945-2
"I saw thee." Ray Palmer. 6385-3
"I saw them sitting in the shade". The maniac. Ella Wheeler Wilcox. 6863-4
I saw three ships. L.R. Gribble. 6490-6
I saw three ships. Unknown. 6756-5,6022-6,6424-8,6383-7, 6135-4,6608-9,6216-4,6258-X,6334-9,6519-8,6668-2, 6747
I saw three witches. Walter De La Mare. 6254-7,6596-1
I saw thy form in youthful prime. Thomas Moore. 6543-0
"I saw time in his workshop carving faces". Time. F.G. Scott. 7041-8
"I saw two clouds at morning." John Gardiner Calkins Brainard. 6240-7,6302-0,6385-3
"I saw two sowers in life's field at morn". Recompense. John McCrae. 7014-0
"I saw two women weeping by the tomb". Easter eve. Henry Alford. 7015-9
"I saw where whitest daisies grew". The daisy. Gertrude Alger. 6798-0
"I saw Wisconsin's eagle borne". Wisconsin. Benjamin Franklin Taylor. 6815-4
"I saw you and I named a flower". The sylph. Francis Ledwidge. 6812-X
"I saw you rise into the sun, trim-lined". Apostrophe to a fighter plane. Virginia Taylor McCormick. 6979-7
"I saw you sink in the golden west". Sunset. Grace Stuart Orcutt. 6764-6
"I saw you toss the kites on high". The wind. Robert Louis Stevenson. 6135-4,6104-4,6456-6,6132-X,6239-3,6466-3, 6533-3,6401-9,6623
"I saw you we lived". Tolusa. Luis Salinas. 6792-1
"I saw you when you were a tiny thing". To a bud. To a leaf. To a tree. Barney T. Clarke. 6894-4
"I saw your eyes tonight, deep blue". Diamond. Douglas V. Le Pan. 6761-1
"I saw your hands lying at peace". Torchbearer. Humbert Wolfe. 6778-6
"I saw your thought wavering". To a rebel. Roberto Vargas. 6998-3
I saw, I saw the lovely child. Frederick W.H. Myers. 6656-9
"I saw/my face". A coffeepot face. Aileen Fisher. 6891-X
"I say I am quite done," fr. Let Zeus record. Hilda ("H.D.") Doolittle. 6011-0
"I say to thee, do thou repeat". The kingdom of God, sels. Richard Chenevix Trench. 6934-7
"I say you'd ought to read this Aldiss". Conversation piece. Jim Holmes. 7003-5
"I say, little boy at the nore". The boy at the nore. Thomas Hood. 6760-3,6974-6
"I say, mamma, are you awake?". Some morning orders. Sarah Morgan Bryan Piatt. 6965-7
"I scarcely grieve, O nature! at the lot". Sonnet ("I scarcely grieve"). Henry Timrod. 6753-0
"'I scheme. You correct'". Saint Mark. James Reaney. 6767-0
"I search among the flowers in the grass". Minor note 001, fr. In Tuscany. Cora Fabri. 6876-6

792

"I search ephemeral Agaricus". Autumn hunter. Mary Howard. 6857-X
"I search/the iridescent faces". Looking for equality. Herman L. McMillan. 7024-8
"I searched in the shops of song". Out of my poverty. Sister Mary Therese. 6839-1
"I searched thro' memory's lumber-room". An old desire. Francis Ledwidge. 6812-X
"I see a dainty butterfly". The coquetts. Eugenia Bragg Smith. 6818-9
"I see a look upon her face". A far country. Alister Mackenzie. 6781-6
"I see a spirit by thy side". A false genius. Adelaide Anne Procter. 6957-6
"I see across the chasm of flying years". Sonnets ("I see across ..."). Henry William Hutchinson. 6650-X
"I see across the lofty table-lands". Morning - the mountain family at their devotions. James Logie ("Hugh Haliburton") Robertson. 6819-7
"I see an eagle winging to the sun". On the death of a kinsman. James Matthewes Leagre. 7017-5
"I see black dragons mount the sky". Shapes and signs. James Clarence Mangan. 6930-4
"I see flashes of cities pass in the night". Christmas day. Art Cuelho. 6998-3
"I see her face in the distance". Love on the links. G.M. Winter. 7021-3
"I see her lying in the moonlight there". Vision. Arthur Goebel. 6850-2
"I see him part the careless throng". Song ("I see him..."). Phoebe Cary. 6969-X
"I see him still, as erst of yore". The village doctor. Samuel Slayton Luce. 7030-2
I see his blood upon the rose. Joseph M. Plinkett. 6172-9
I see his blood upon the rose. Joseph Mary Plunkett. 6477-9,6292-X,6628-3,6250-4,6393-4,6090-0,6144-3,6335-7, 6337-3,6730-1
"I see his pudgy/kid form". Ryan. Lynne Chambers. 6857-X
"I see how she doth see". The lover refused of his love. Unknown. 6830-8
"I see it". Dahomean song for the dead. Unknown. 6879-0
"I see it all again; fair vision she". A reminiscence. Unknown. 6983-5
"I see life rage before my eyes". In an evil time. Evelyn Grace Flynn. 6847-2
I see men's judgment. William Shakespeare. 6438-8
I see my plaint. Sir John Harington. 6182-6
I see she flies me. Unknown. 6328-4
"I see small difference". Music. Bryan Waller ("Barry Cornwall") Procter. 6980-0
"I see that chance hath chosen me." Sir Thomas Wyatt. 6584-8
"I see the Boston papers say". Shall Vermonters raise sheep? Daniel L. Cady. 6988-6
"I see the deep's untrampled floor". Percy Bysshe Shelley. 6997-5
"I see the pickets of the spring...". April. Benjamin Franklin Taylor. 6815-4
"I see the worlds of earth and sky". The palsy of the heart. Richard Monckton Milnes; 1st Baron Houghton. 6980-0
"I see them glimmer where the waters lag". The fire-flies, sels. Charles Mair. 6797-2
"I see them in their beauty once again". Thank God for mountains. Achsa W. Sprague. 7030-2
"I see two boys square off defiantly". Father of the man. Granville Paul Smith. 6761-1
"I see weapons/waiting behind pointless trees". James Gerard. Paul D. Shiplett. 6870-7
"I see you are so steep and high". Bigelow mountain. Norman W. Sturtevant. 6799-9
I see you crowned. Charles Whitby. 6994-0
"I see you sitting in the sungleams there". Old war. Arthur L. Phelps. 7027-2
"I see you there, my garden". Winter's garden. Lucy Wilson Buxton. 7016-7
"I see you, Mister Bawsy-brown". To Robin Goodfellow. Eugene Field. 6949-5
"I see you/in the darkest recess". Letters from Kazuko (Kyoto, Japan-sumemr 1980) Alan Chong Lau. 690-5

"I seek the mountain cleft; alone". The summit of Mount Sinai. James Montgomery. 6848-0
I seek thee in the heart alone. Herbert Trench. 6730-1
"I seem as nothing, source of nature, now". King Konkaput's apostrophe upon Pike'a Peak. Thomas Nelson Haskell. 6836-7
"I seem to be chasing a will-o-the-wisp". Facing the wall. R.A. Medlam. 6799-9
"I seen 'im squattin' there". Jis' knowin' Thomas G. Nickens. 6870-7
"I sell the best brandy and shery". O'Tuomy's drinking song. John O'Tuomy. 6930-4
"I send a garland to my love". The lover's posy. Rufinus. 7039-6
"I send a shell from the ocean beach". With a Nantucket shell. Charles Henry ("John Paul") Webb. 7041-8
I send our lady. Sister Mary Therese. 6282-2
"I send thee, Rhodocleia...". Rufinus. 6251-2
"I send you here a sort of allegory". To - ("I send"). Alfred Lord Tennyson. 6657-7
"I send you here a wreath of blossoms blown". Roses. Pierre de Ronsard. 6771-9,7039-6
"I send, transmit, consign, convey". A suggestion. Berton Braley. 6853-7
"I sent a message to my dear". The miracles. Rudyard Kipling. 6810-3
I sent my soul through the invisible, fr. Rubaiyat. Omar Khayyam. 7039-6
"I serve a mistress whiter than snow". Anthony Munday. 6181-8,6182-6,6317-9
"I serve you not, if you I follow". Etienne de La Boece. Ralph Waldo Emerson. 6753-0
I served in a great cause. Horace L. Traubel. 6300-4
"I served in a great cause", sels. Horace L. Traubel. 6102-8,6076-5
"I set a lighted candle". The still return. Hazel Hall. 6880-4
"I shake my hair in the wind of morning". Triumph of the singer. John Hall Wheelock. 6897-9
"I shake the snow on the ground below", sels. E.L. B. 6601-1
"I shall be a cat, pawing the streets". Fourth declamation (police of the dead day) Jean Garrigue. 6803-0
I shall be loved as quiet things. Karle Wilson Baker. 6250-4,6332-2,6506-6,6619-4
I shall be satisfied. Martin Behemb. 6065-X
I shall be satisfied. Unknown. 6240-7
I shall break a heavy bough. Gertrude Callaghan. 6619-4
"I shall carve a vision". Sculptor. Gilbert O'Connor. 6850-2
"I shall come back, by God, even though my sons". Eternal recurrence. Rolfe Humphries. 6880-4
"I shall discover; I shall know". The soul speaks. Sara Adler Rosalsky. 6750-6
I shall fare forth. Eugene Dimon Preston. 6836-7
"I shall go among faces and virile voices". Cattle show. Christopher M. ("Hugh MacDiarmid") Grieve. 6845-6
I shall go back. Julia Daingerfield Glass. 6799-9
I shall go back. Joyce Lancaster. 6850-2
I shall go singing. Anna Blake Mezquida. 6461-2
"I shall have a little house". A garden of posies. Georgia H. Cooper. 6850-2
I shall laugh purely. Robinson Jeffers. 6390-X,6666-6
"I shall lie quiet, quiet". Rachel. E. Berlein. 6800-6
I shall live to be old. Sara Teasdale. 6037-4
"I shall look back, when on the main". Remembrance. William Lisle Bowles. 6980-0
"I shall lose your face in the flickering...". Elegy. George Dillon. 6808-1
I shall make beauty. Sir John Collings ("Solomon Eagle") Squire. 6320-9
"I shall never forget you, never. Never escape". Reminiscence of Mahomed Akram. Laurence (Adele Florence Nicolson) Hope. 6856-1
"I shall not ask Jean Jacques Rousseau". Pairing time anticipated. William Cowper. 6814-6
I shall not be afraid. Aline Kilmer. 6292-X,6096-X,6102-8, 6320-9,6653-4,6076-5,6464-7
I shall not call. Anne Singelton. 6808-1

I shall not care. Sara Teasdale. 6104-4,6396-9,6327-6,6467-1,6102-8,6289-X,6310-1,6732-8,6076-5
I shall not die for thee. Douglas Hyde. 6873-1
I shall not die for thee. Unknown. 6244-X
"I shall not give his name, for what...matter?". 'For the sake of a joke'. Brian ("Korongo") Brooke. 6938-X
"I shall not go back to the place that I love". Sara Teasdale. 6777-8
'I shall not go back'. Sara Teasdale. 6038-2
I shall not live in vain. Emily Dickinson. 6303-9
"I shall not make a garment of my grief." Roselle Mercier Montgomery. 6326-8
"'I shall not march', said the major". The Armistice Day parade. Nancy Boyd. 6817-0
I shall not pass again. W.R. Fitch. 6303-9
I shall not pass again this way. Unknown. 6260-1,6335-7
'I shall not pass again this way.' Ellen H. Underwood. 6337-3
I shall not pass this way again. Eva Rose York. 6337-3, 6336-5
"I shall not read you yet (Some say I should).". Sonnet to Shakespeare. Sara Alice Howard. 6750-6
"I shall not see the faces of my friends". The dying reservist. Maurice Baring. 6785-9
"I shall not see thee, nay, but I shall know". Metempsychosis. Andrew Lang. 6771-9
"I shall not see you for a hundred days". Parting. Robert Gittings. 6202-4
"I shall perform arati before...Ghana.". Buddha. Unknown (Newari). 7013-2
"I shall pick your blossoms now...". Blossoms. Jewell Bothwell Tull. 7038-8
"I shall recall this day when I am old". From Mount Mansfield. Bettie Margot Cassie. 6750-6
"I shall remember until I die". Can you hear me? Katherine Hunter Coe. 6906-1
"I shall say what inordinat love is". Inordinate love. Unknown. 6881-2
"I shall see a star tonight". Star thought. Frances Shaw. 6897-9
"I shall sing a song to-day". You will know. Bertye Young Williams. 6906-1
"I shall tell you in rhyme how, once on a time". The three tailors. Eugene Field. 6949-5
"I shall turn to the hills...". The hills. Daniel Smythe. 6761-1
"I shall vent my bitterness not by...speech". Words for a solitude. Daniel Smythe. 6761-1
"I shall write verses if I get to heaven". Celestial Rhymes. Fannie Stearns Davis. 7038-8
"I shall you tell a great marvel". What, heard ye not, the King of Jerusalem is now born. Unknown. 6756-5
"I shall, perhaps a thousand years from now". Sonnet ("I shall"). Evana Llynn. 6906-1
"I shan't forget how much I learnt". Vermont housekeeping. Daniel L. Cady. 6988-6
"I shiver, spirit fierce and bold". At the grave of Burns. William Wordsworth. 6198-2,6483-3,6110-9,6828-6
"I shot him where the Rio flows". Marta of Milrone. Herman Scheffauer. 7010-8
"I should be busy about the place". Absence. Edgar A. Guest. 6748-4
"I should be content". Content. David Ignatow. 6803-0
"I should grieve to desperation". Anacreon to the sophist. B. H.. 6817-0
"I should have called it insult". To a lost idol. Margaret Haynes Foster. 7016-7
"I should have deem'd it once an effort vain". On receiving Heyne's Virgil from Hayley. William Cowper. 6814-6
"I should have met your tentative caress". Interval of flame. Sylvia Gardiner Lufburrow. 6750-6
"I should have sold him when he left...mother". The fatted calf. Henry Duncan Chisholm. 6761-1
"I should like a great lake of ale". The feast of Saint Brigid of Kildare. St. (atr.) Brigid. 6930-4
"I should like to be in the black lake now". Black lake. George Abbe. 6761-1
' I should like to die', said Willie. Unknown. 6260-1
"I should like to go". Rest. W.A. Barton Jr.. 7016-7

"I should like to see the heavenly light". Divine drama. Bess Foster Smith. 6799-9
"I should like to write a story". The common little things. Hilda Shutts Farquhar. 6799-9
"I should not choose the scorpion". The rock scorpion. Margaret Whiting Spilhaus. 6800-6
"I should not want the quarried slate". Fit remembrance. I.L. Salomon. 6979-7
I shouldn't have been standing there. Markey Sullivan. 6750-6
"I shouldn't like to-day, I'm sure". A song ("I shouldn't like"). George A. Baker. 6517-1
"I show you my bayberry dips". Bayberry dips. Ellen Vane. 6817-0
"I show, by my distressful tones". The susceptible widow. Eugene Field. 6949-5
"I shudder/Lest some dark minister be near...". A demon's false description of his race... James Abraham Hillhouse. 6752-2
I sigh all the night. Edward Ravenscroft. 6563-5
I sigh for the land of the cypress and pine. Samuel Henry Dickson. 7017-5
"I sigh'd and own'd my love". Unknown. 6187-7
"I sigh, as sure to weare the fruit" Unknown. 6380-2
"I sighed as the soul of April fled" Inconstancy. Francis Charles McDonald. 6983-5
"I sike when I singe". The crucifixion. Unknown. 6881-2
"I simply say that she is good." Joaquin Miller. 6066-8
"I sing a song of rowing". The crew song. Clayton Fotterall McMichael. 6936-3
"I sing a song of sixpence, and rye". An ode ("I sing a song"). Anthony C. Deane. 6440-X
"I sing a song of the west land". A song of settlement. Sir Henry Howarth Bashford. 6793-X
"I sing no idle songs". Prelude ("I sing"). Robert Service. 6159-1
'I sing no more'. Fannie Stearns Davis. 6607-0
"I sing no out-of-date matter". Timotheus. 6251-2
"I sing no song of urban life". The elusive motif. Dunton. 6817-0
"I sing of a journey to Clifton". The distressed travellers; or, labour in vain. William Cowper. 6814-6
"I sing of a maiden". As dew in April. Unknown. 6756-5
I sing of a maiden. Martin Shaw. 6608-9
I sing of a maiden. Unknown. 6106-0,6187-7,6334-9,6339-X, 6625-9,6282 ,6430-2
"I sing of Dionysus, an old story". Homer. 6435-3
I sing of Olaf. Edward Estlin Cummings. 6666-4
"I sing of the Gordons". Lament for the Gordons. David Martin. 6895-2
"I sing of the old-fashioned carver...". The carver. Edgar A. Guest. 6869-3
"I sing that charming thing". The sloth. Ruth Kimball-Gardiner. 7021-3
"I sing that graceful toy, whose waving play". The fan. John Gay. 6972-X
I sing the battle. Harry Kemp. 6327-6
"I sing the family party that once we used...". The family party. Edgar A. Guest. 6862-6
"I sing the hands of labor:". The hands, sels. Anna Spencer Twitchell. 6836-7
"I sing the man who Judahs scepter...", fr. Davideis. Abraham Cowley. 6562-7
"I sing the name which none can say". The name above every name. Richard Crashaw. 6830-8
"I sing the oyster! (Virgin theme!).". An apostrophe to the oyster. J.W. Gesnard. 6919-3
"I sing the sailor of the sail- breed of...". The sailor of the sail. Thomas Fleming Day. 7012-4
"I sing the sofa. I, who lately sang". The sofa, fr. The task. William Cowper. 6814-6
"I sing to him that rests below," fr. In memoriam. Alfred Lord Tennyson. 6646-1
"I sing you a song of Canadian winter". Canadian winter song. William Wye Smith. 7035-3
"I sing you a song to-night, my lads". Tally-ho. Samuel M. Baylis. 7035-3
"I sink my piers to the solid rock". The song of the builder. Edgar A. Guest. 7033-7

"I sit alone and listen." Kijo. 6027-7
"I sit and beat the wizard's magic drum". The wizard's chant. Unknown (Algonquin Indian). 6864-2
"I sit and close my eyelids and I dream I...". The foxhunter's dream. G. C. Scheu. 7010-8
I sit and look out, fr. Leaves of grass. Walt Whitman. 6337-3
I sit as I have always sat. Holger Drachmann. 6555-4
"I sit at the kitchen tabled with sickness". Breath. Arthur Smith. 6792-1
"I sit beneaih the linden's". Where we are. Lucien Stryk. 7032-9
"I sit beside the brazier's glow". Battle. Wilfred Wilson Gibson. 7031-0
"I sit by the fire this cold winter morning". Musing. James Abraham Martling. 6952-5
"I sit by the window and watch and wait". Hoping. Pearl G. Dollear. 6799-9
"I sit down to write a poem of our fighting...". The anxious anthemist. Guy Forrester Lee. 6846-4
"I sit enthroned 'mid icy wastes afar". King Boreas. Clinton Scollard. 6770-0,6875-8
"I sit in my kingly howdah". The engineer's ride. James Abraham Martling. 6952-5
"I sit in the attic tasting forgotten". Ubi Sunt. Patricia Ann Jarrell. 6900-2
"I sit in the early twilight". A lifetime. William Cullen Bryant. 6126-5,6288-1,6753-0
"I sit on the ground". Place-of-many-swans. Charlotte DeClue. 7005-1
"I sit on the lonely headland". On the headland. Bayard Taylor. 6976-2
"I sit on wood floor boards". Autumn moon. Marcia G. Kester. 6857-X
"I sit, I sleep, I wait". The snake. Morton Marcus. 6792-1
"I sleep, but my heart waketh: it is the...". Song of Solomon. Bible. 6958-4
"I sleep. The panoply os sense". Fragment ("I sleep..."). Herbert Trench. 6877-4
"I slept awhile, then woke. The night was wild". Old Testament. John Freeman. 6778-6
"I slept while he died". Her husband's death. Roberta Santlofer Danowsky. 6857-X
"I slept, when Venus entr'd: to my bed". Moschus. 6814-6
"I smell of camphor. My sheets precise...". The rooms. Susan Donnelly. 6822-7
"I sold my soul to Satan for a price". The bargain. Claire Stewart Boyer. 6818-9
"I sometimes have strange fancies in...spring". Minor note 010, fr. In Tuscany. Cora Fabri. 6876-6
I sometimes hold it half a sin. Alfred Lord Tennyson. 6543-0
"I sometimes think that never blows so red". Edward Fitzgerald. 6187-7
"I sometimes think that never blows so red"fr.Rubaiyat. Omar Khayyam. 6317-9
I sometimes think that never blows so red, fr. Rubaiyat. Omar Khayyam. 7039-6
"I sometimes think, when watching...flowers". Winter dreams. Besse Schiff. 6906-1
"I sometimes turn me from the page of glory". Enoch the immortal. Unknown. 6848-0
I sometimes wonder. Amory Hare. 6347-0
"I sometimes wonder if it's really true". Hill-born, fr. Battle. Wilfred Wilson Gibson. 6897-9
"I sometimes wonder of the Grecian men". Israel and Hellas. Thomas Edward Brown. 6809-X
"I sought a soul in the sea". Jalal [or Jelal] ed-din Rumi. 6448-5
"I sought at morn the beechen bower". The broken appointment. John Kenyon. 6980-0
"I sought him and found him". The Christian's confidence. Charles H. McLean. 6799-9
I sought my soul. Unknown. 6337-3
I sought the living God. John Calvin Slemp. 6144-3
I sought the Lord. Unknown. 6337-3
I sought you. John Hall Wheelock. 6039-0
"I speak for the ladies of American birth". Our knight. Hope Harding Davis. 7019-1
"I speak not,I trace not,I breath not thy ame". Stanzas

for music ("I speak not"). George Gordon, 6th Baron Byron. 6945-2
"I speak this elegy now". Elegy. Charles Norman. 6042-0
"I speak this poem now with grave...voice". Immortal autumn. Archibald MacLeish. 6780-8
"I speak with a proud tongue of the people...". Dedication. Patrick MacGill. 6930-4
"I speak, none listens; but I hear". The challenge. Walter De La Mare. 6905-3
I spend my days vainly. Frank Kendon. 6491-4
"I spoke the sea, that reaches green". Gray shore. James Rorty. 6833-2
"I sprang to the saddle and Joris and he". The ride from Ghent to Aix. Irwin Beaumont. 7021-3
"I squander dollars while you save the pence". Another man's poison. Constance Milton. 6750-6
"I staid the night for shelter at a farm". The witch of Coos. Robert Frost. 6776-X
"I stand alone at midnight on the deck". On leaving the coast of Nova Scotia. George Frederick Cameron. 6795-6
"I stand among the dark-gray stones". 'Man giveth up the ghost, and where is he?' Unknown. 6752-2
"I stand and watch the panting lake". The path of the just. James Abraham Martling. 6952-5
"I stand before the book of Ballymote". Disinherited. J. Patrick Byrne. 6761-1
"I stand before the window that opens". Street kid. Duane Niatum. 7005-1
"I stand before you, friends, tonight". The jester, to his audience. Jamie Sexton Holme. 6836-7
"I stand behind the waterfall". The bushman's cave, sels. William Charles Scully. 6800-6
"I stand below the gun tower". The ritual. Paul David Ashley. 6870-7
"I stand beside my little daughter". Presence. Juanita Havill. 6857-X
I stand corrected. Margaret Fishback. 6722-0
"I stand her by my window every night". Beyond the wall. J.J. Maloney. 6870-7
"I stand in a still, damp churchyard". An atom of celestial beauty. Lorna Greene. 7030-2
"I stand in endless space and see". The awakening. Bernard Welland. 6799-9
"I stand in line". Santa Fe internment camp. Muin Ozaki. 6981-9
"I stand in my door and look over the low...". The widow of Drynam. Patrick MacDonough. 6930-4
"I stand in the dark; I beat on the door". The cry of Rachel. Lizette Woodworth Reese. 6848-0
"I stand in the doorway & wait for his coming". My lover. Florence McCurdy. 6921-5
"I stand in the fog". First stand on the mainland. Muin Ozaki. 6981-9
"I stand in the mirror". Mirror. Drew Mauro. 6883-9
"I stand not here in judgment, haughty priest". The mother's plea. William Herbert; Earl of Pembroke. 6980-0
"I stand on Zion's mount." Charles Swain. 6302-0
"I stand on a peak at Verdun...". Here at Verdun. Chester M. Wright. 6846-4
"I stand on Hiram's tomb". Hiram's tomb. Robert Needham Cust. 6848-0
"I stand on the crest of the mountain, lifted". Compass berg. William Charles Scully. 6800-6
"I stand upon my island home". Nobody in town. Dollie Radford. 6785-9
"I stand upon the busy street". The city. James Abraham Martling. 6952-5
"I stand upon the threshold stone". The Huguenot's farewell. Felicia Dorothea Hemans. 6973-8
"I stared the moon down first, and then". Lyric ("I stared"). Pricilla Heath. 6764-6
"I start with a prayer". Joan of Arc. Elizabeth Burns. 6900-2
"I started early, took my dog". Emily Dickinson. 6380-2
"I started off along the shore". Yamabe No Akahito. 6852-9
"I started on a journey just about a week ago". I want to go to morrow. Unknown. 6963-0
"I started to paint quite by accident...". The moon is my uncle, sel. Nahum Tschacbasov. 6803-0
"I staun at the winnock, the sea-faem blins my een". Unknown. 6325-X
"I still do not know your name. I feel...". Letter to two strangers. Octavio Paz. 6758-1
"I still have a sister in Guang Dung". The landlord's wife. Marilyn Chin. 6790-5
"I still think he looks like his father". Dialogue between a proud young mother and a neighbor. Jane Gray Ward. 6850-2
"I still will sing". These remain. Mary Lowrey Babcock. 6847-2
I stole bass. Unknown. 6125-7
"I stole forth dimly in the dripping pause". Moon compass. Robert Frost. 6764-6
"I stood alone where sleep the dead". Lest we forget. Robert Bryan Flanary. 6799-9
"I stood at dawn and watched the morning leap". At dawn. Warren Ariail. 7016-7
"I stood beside a hill". February twilight, fr. Berkshire notes. Sara Teasdale. 6778-6
"I stood beside my window one stormy winter day". Caroline Leslie. 6238-5
"I stood beside the grave of him who blazed". Churchill's grave. George Gordon, 6th Baron Byron. 6945-2,6828-6
"I stood by the couch of my darling". 'It will all be right in the morning'. John Whitaker Watson. 6774-3
I stood in Venice, on the bridge of sighs. George Gordon, 6th Baron Byron. 6484-1
"I stood in gladness - for life's highest joy". Lift's weaving. Millie Colcord. 6926-6
"I stood in the center of a ring of faces". I turned my back. David Ignatow. 6803-0
"I stood in Venice, on the Bridge of Sighs". Venice. George Gordon, 6th Baron Byron. 6624-0,6439-6,6543-0, 6242-8
"I stood on a mound of clay". Created clay. Virgil Browne. 6799-9
"I stood on a tower in the wet". 1865-1866. Alfred Lord Tennyson. 6977-0
"I stood on Brocken's sovran height, and saw". Lines. Samuel Taylor Coleridge. 6828-6
"I stood on the crest in the sunlight". Timber line. Surville J. DeLan. 6920-7
"I stood on the crest of a hill". Distance. E.O. De Camp. 6906-1
"I stood on the frozen river". The skaters. John Whitaker Watson. 6774-3
"I stood on the hill of time when the sun...". Deidre wedded. Herbert Trench. 6877-4
"I stood still and was a tree amid the wood". The tree. Ezra Pound. 6754-9
"I stood them up beside the closet door". Old shoes. Jeanette Marshall Hazen. 6764-6
I stood tiptoe upon a little hill. John Keats. 6395-0,6503-1
I stood tiptoe upon a little hill, sels. John Keats. 6369-1,6196-6
"I stood upon a hill at noon". Escape. Maye DeWeese Porter. 6906-1
"I stood upon a shore, a pleasant shore". The shell's song. John Keats. 6833-2
"I stood upon the hills, when heaven's...arch". Sunrise on the hills. Unknown. 6752-2
"I stood upon the peak, amid the air". Pike's Peak. Eugene Field. 6949-5
"I stood upon the threshold". Prayer ("I stood"). George Sylvester Viereck. 6102-8,6076-5
"I stood where the lip of song lay low". Written after visiting a tomb. Felicia Dorothea Hemans. 6973-8
"I stood within a vision's spell". Niagara. Unknown. 6916-9
I stood within the heart of God. William Vaughn Moody. 6076-5
"I stood within the heart of God". William Vaughn Moody. 6102-8,6076-5
"I stood, to-day, in a temple". Rosh-Hashanah. Joseph K. Foran. 6848-0
"I stop the world for moments-its charade-". Another kind of autumn. Patricia M. Johnson. 6857-X

I store the memories. Mary Weeden. 6761-1
"I strike matches again and again". Evening wind. Un-kyo Kang. 6775-1
"I strive to keep me in the sun". This my life. John Vance Cheney. 7012-4
"I strolled in peace through a beautiful wood". The autumn stroll. Virgie Rucker Howerton. 6906-1
"I strolled into a courtroom not many miles...". Unknown. 6059-5
"I strolled last eve across the lonely down". A picture. Ella Wheeler Wilcox. 6956-8
"I strolled over the lawn at sunrise". Morning strolls. Lillian Hinton. 6818-9
"I strove with none". Epigram. Walter Savage Landor. 6230-X
I strove with none. Walter Savage Landor. 6332-2,6339-X, 6289-X,6187-7,6301-2,6196-6,6383-7,6125-7,6153-2, 6052-8
"I strove with none; for none was worth my". On his seventy-fifth birthday. Walter Savage Landor. 6828-6
"I study wise themes with rigid care". Ballade of wisdom and folly. Carolyn Wells. 6875-8
I stumbled upon happiness. DuBose Heyward. 6326-8
I sue for damages. Unknown. 6910-X
"I suffer fruitless anguish day by day". The vicissitudes experienced in the Christian life. Madame De la Mothe Guion. 6814-6
"I suppose it just depends on where...". The Mallee fire. Charles Henry Souter. 6784-0
"I suppose you have heard of all the talking". Unknown. 6059-5
"I surprise girlhood/in you face: I know". I want Aretha to set this to music. Shirley Williams. 6998-3
"I swear these trees come from before". Sitka spruce. Robert Hedin. 6855-3
"I sweare to thee I will begone." Unknown. 6563-5
"I swept the fallen leaves up yesterday". Leaf burning. Virginia Eaton. 6750-6
"I swing to the sunset land". Prairie greyhounds. Emily Pauline ("Tekahionwake") Johnson. 6837-5
I take 'em and like 'em. Margaret Fishback. 6722-0
I take back everything I've said. Nicanor Parra. 6758-1
"I take four devils with me when I ride". Poem ("I take"). Gervase Stewart. 6666-6
"I talked with a stalwart young seaman...". A brave woman. John F. Nocholls. 6923-1
I taste a liquor never brewed. Emily Dickinson. 6332-2, 6488-4,6399-3,6491-4
"I tell him how it used to be in Paguate". After the pow-wow, sel. Harold Littlebird. 7005-1
"I tell it to the freshmen". Style 5. William Wantling. 6792-1
I tell thee, Dick, where I have been. Sir John Suckling. 6328-4
I tell thee, priest. George Gascoigne. 6087-0
"I tell this blackguy/who sits down at the...". Four wolves. Stan Rice. 6901-0
"I tell you again that I discovered silence". The sounds of dawn. Efrain Huerta. 6759-x
"I tell you what I'd rather do". My ruthers. James Whitcomb Riley. 6892-8
"I tell you, Kate, that Lovejoy cow". Let down the bars. Unknown. 6927-4
"I tend my garden". Note. Helmut Zenker. 6769-7
I thank thee, God. Elaine M. Livingston. 6799-9
I thank Thee, God! for weal and woe. Eliza Cook. 6303-9
I thank thee, God, for beauty. Ruth N. Potts. 6214-8
"I thank you, Mr. President, you've kindly...". Meeting of the alumni of Harvard College. Oliver Wendell Holmes. 6753-0
"I that in health was and gladness". Dunbar's lament when he was sick. William Dunbar. 6830-8
"I that in heill was and gladness". Timor mortis conturbat me, fr. The lament...Makaris... William Dunbar. 6934-7
"I that in heill wes, and gladnes". The fear of death confounds me. William Dunbar. 6881-2
"I the unsated sea, that saw thy beauty". The sea-goddess restores the rapt Shelley. Edward Sandford Burgess. 6847-2

"I think a time will come when you..understand". For my father. Paul Potts. 6895-2
"I think continually of those who were truly great". Stephen Spender. 6208-3,6337-3,6354-3,6666-6,6375-6, 6125-7,6464-7,6150-8,6645-3
I think Delilah had a heart. George Dillon. 6039-0
I think I know no finer things than dogs. Hally Carrington Brent. 6107-9
I think I thought a lie. D. Gatewood Thomas. 6178-8
"I think from mortal breast/No truer warmth...". No truer warmth has leapt. Mary Irene Warner. 6799-9
"I think I hear the sound of horses' feet". The watcher. Ella Wheeler Wilcox. 6863-4
"I think I knew, beloved". On your twenty-fifth birthday. Adrian F. Nader. 6750-6
"I think I know now why an angel's wings". Angel wings. Harriet Holman. 7016-7
"I think I'll/crawl into the". Saturday night. Mary Ann Lowry. 6857-X
"I think I've read about enough". Nature fakirs in Vermont. Daniel L. Cady. 6988-6
"I think if I lay dying in some land". The harbour. Winifred M. Letts. 6887-1
"I think if thou couldst know". If thou couldst know. Adelaide Anne Procter. 6957-6
"I think mice". Mice. Rose Fyleman. 6891-X
"I think of blue confetti, amusement parks". Saturday's child. Delmore Schwartz. 6850-2
"I think of grey and gray". Grey. Fray Angelico Chavez. 6761-1
I think of him as one who fights. Anna Hempstead Branch. 6184-2
"I think of the summer cottage and the joys...". Hail and farewell. Edgar A. Guest. 6748-4
"I think of the tribes: the women prized...". The tribes. Roy Fuller. 6788-3
I think of thee. Elizabeth Barrett Browning. 6199-0
I think of thee. Thomas Kibble Hervey. 6656-9
I think of thee. Kate Goldsboro McDowell. 6274-1
"I think of thee when golden sunbeams glimmer". Love's nearness. Johann Wolfgang von Goethe. 6961-4
"I think of thee whene'er the sun is glowing". Separation. Johann Wolfgang von Goethe. 6948-7
"I think perhaps we'll never know". Innocence. Edgar A. Guest. 6869-3
"I think she sleeps, it must be sleep..," fr. Modern love. George Meredith. 6659-3
"I think that God must be in these blind hands". The barnacles. Robert P. Tristram Coffin. 7040-X
"I think that I should like to be". Black sheep. Margaret Ballard McCann. 6764-6
"I think that many a soul has God within". My creed. Alice Stead. 6847-2
"I think that only childhood lives". Childhood. E.H. Visiak. 6893-6
"I think that the bitterest sorrow or pain". Desolation. Ella Wheeler Wilcox. 6956-8
"I think the dead do speak". They speak to us. Helen Mae Johnson. 6894-4
"I think the sun when he turns at night." Bliss Carman. 6433-7
"I think true love is never blind". True love. Phoebe Cary. 6969-X
I think we had the chief of all love's joys. George (Mary Ann Cross) Eliot. 6066-8
"I think we shall have callers, Mattie dear". Morning calls. S.A. (Sarah Annie Shield) Frost. 6851-0
"I think whatever mortals crave". The chaunt of the brazen head. Winthrop Mackworth Praed. 6874-X
I think when I read that sweet story of old. Jemima Thompson Luke. 6337-3,6466-3,6424-8
"I thou survive my well-contented day". William Shakespeare. 6198-2
I thought I had outlived my pain. Elisabeth Scollard. 6619-4
"I thought I saw a fallen flower." Moritake. 6027-7
"I thought about Arkansas, Arkansas being". Looking for Johnny Cash. Miller Williams. 6860-X
"I thought I saw two starlings lightly fall". Vision. Leslie Rubin. 6850-2

"I thought I'd catch up with my tasks today". Tasks. Irma Louise Ehrensberger. 6750-6
'I thought it slept'. Henry Pickering. 6752-2
"I thought maybe I could stay on the job". A sailor gropes for words. John V.A. Weaver. 6778-6
"I thought my heart had lost the power" Alexander Pushkin. 6103-6
"I thought my net was full of shining fish." Oto. 6027-7
"I thought myself indeed secure". At the door. Eugene Field. 6772-7
"I thought myself, indeed, secure". At the door. Eugene Field. 6834-0;6949-5
"I thought of Chatterton, the marvellous boy". Chatterton. William Wordsworth. 6980-0
"I thought of life, the outer and the inner". Scarlett Rocks. T. E. Brown. 7020-5
"I thought of thee, my partner and my guide". Sonnet ("I thought of thee"). William Wordsworth. 6150-8
"I thought once how Theocritus had sung". Sonnet ("I thought once"). Elizabeth Barrett Browning. 6154-0, 6604-6,6197-4
"I thought once how Theocritus had sung". Elizabeth Barrett Browning. 6204-0,6246-6,6430-2,6560-0,6396-9, 6199 ,6088-9
"I thought our love at full, but I did err". James Russell Lowell. 6126-5
"I thought to deal the death-stroke", fr. Three stages. Christina Georgina Rossetti. 6828-6
"I thought to die that night in the solitude". The edge. Lola Ridge. 6930-4
"I thought to find some healing clime". Answered. Phoebe Cary. 6969-X,6461-2
"I thought to track a world-disdaining light". Crowned. John Nichol. 7015-9
"I thought to work for Him. "Master!" I said". Paul Fleming. 6238-5
"I thought today as I/Walked slowly down". Redbud. Ethel Emily Fels. 6906-1
"I thought, for once and all I had fixed...". Militant. Edward Farquhar. 6939-8
"I thought/but I know her so well". Rosy ear. Zbigniew Herbert. 6758-1
"I thrill beneath the lovelight in your eyes". A sonnet to you. Nellie Davis Hancock. 6799-9
"I thrilled to hear the heavenly." Yaha. 6027-7
"I thrist, but not as once I did". My soul thirsteth for God. William Cowper. 6814-6
"I throw off my covers, afraid". A man about to dream. David Posner. 6803-0
"I throw on my clothes, and wait for the moon." Unknown (Chinese) 6545-7
I tol' yer so. John Langdon Heaton. 6277-6
I told my love. William Blake. 6934-7
"I told you April soon would tire". April ways. Lucile S. Kappeler. 6906-1
I told you so. Unknown. 6693-3
"I told you that I loved you". The real you. Eva Louise Zoller. 6818-9
I too. Constance Fenimore Woolson. 6240-7
"I too 'hate war,' for I have understood". I too hate war. Ida Flood Dodge. 6799-9
"I too could inject gasoline" Hermann Gail. 6769-7
I too hate war. Ida Flood Dodge. 6799-9
"I too have dreamed of dark titanic roses". Sonnets in summer heat. Gilbert Keith Chesterton. 6780-8
"I too remember distant golden days". Reincarnation. Edward Wyndham Tennant. 7027-2
"I too, dislike it: there are things...". Poetry. Marianne Moore. 6375-6,6527-9,6733-6
"I took a little good seed in my hand". Over-payment. Phoebe Cary. 6969-X
"I took a reed and blew a tune". The find. Francis Ledwidge. 6812-X
"I took a task on New Year's Eve". Unknown. 6059-5
"I took a year out of my life and story". A dead year. Jean Ingelow. 6940-1
I took my love. Robert Crawford. 6269-5
"I took my sin to market". Par. Clifton E. Blake. 7030-2
"I took my soul, and walked the wide world...". My alter ego. Jeannette Eugenie Cushing. 6818-9

"I tossed away my". Impatience. Olive Clair. 6850-2
"I tossed my golden anchor to the bsea". Sonnet ("I tossed"). Idris Davies. 6360-8
"I touched - amid the blood". Core. Jaime Torres Bodet. 6759-X
"I touched the heart that loved me as a player". A shattered lute. Alice Meynell. 6955-X
"I touched the heart that loved me...". Without him. Alice Meynell. 7015-9
"I traced your name in sand beside the sea". Consolation. Hazel Reese Collins. 6799-9
"I trailed for four days". Do texans kiss after sex? David Emerson Smith. 7003-5
"I tramped the pavement, cursing God". Comrade Jesus. Ralph Cheyney. 6954-1
"I travel to thee with the sun's first rays". Robert Bridges. 6186-9,6487-6
I traveled among unknown men. William Wordsworth. 6122-2, 6154-0,6246-6,6625-9,6634-8,6199 ,6737-9,6560-0,6086-2,6110-9,6250-4,6430-2,6723-9
"I traveled on the C.V. line". 'Working up the woodpile' in Vermont. Daniel L. Cady. 6988-6
I tremble to think. Oliver St. John Gogarty. 6482-5
"I tried on a new bonnet/It really was...". 1938 bonnets. Erma Haaland. 6799-9
"I tried to be a doughboy, but they said...". In the front-line desks. Elmer Franklin Powell. 6846-4
"I tripped on black shadows". Weather. Helen Hoyt. 6880-4
"I troubled in my dream. I knew". Dreams. Charles Weekes. 6873-1
"I trow that gude ending". Bruce consults his men. John Barbour. 6845-6
"I trowe men would deem it negligence". Description of the lists built by Theseus for the... Geoffrey Chaucer. 6935-5
"I try to capture rhythm with". Futility. Mary S. Hawling. 6782-4
"I turn the key and enter there, the house...". Identity. Edla Park Peck. 6836-7
"I turn the lea-green down". Ploughman. Patrick Kavanagh. 6780-8
"I turn the pages and recall". The mountains of Berne. Samuel Longfellow. 6749-2
"I turn the pages with delight". On first looking into Stedman's American anthology. George Meason Whicher. 6847-2
"I turn to thee in time of need". Thomas Haynes Bayly. 6980-0
"I turned from the weary road". Dream of the beggar-woman. Maurice Reidy. 6761-1
I turned my back. David Ignatow. 6803-0
"I turned to see; upon the shelf a vase of...". Dream roses. Heloise M.B. Hawkins. 6836-7
"I twined a wreath of heather white". Corona inutilis. James Lister Cuthbertson. 6784-0
"I understand the heartbreak of the wind". Cold harvest. Frances Taylor Patterson. 6761-1
"I used to be so lonely when I waked at...". Sentry-go. Amelia Josephine Burr. 6861-8
"I used to believe I wouldn't live past 16". Fan. Walter Lew. 6790-5
"I used to go to grandma's house, so many...". Grandma's house. Olivia Everett. 6857-X
"I used to go to St. John's Wood". Marx and Heine and Dowlais. Idris Davies. 6895-2
"I used to have to be so good". Modern youth. Ruth Vivian Kidwell. 6750-6
"I used to hear a large amount". Choir troubles in Vermont. Daniel L. Cady. 6989-4
"I used to laugh silently as I watched him". Someone gave him some plastic flowers once. Dennis Shady. 6870-7
"I used to like the lowery days". New Vermont names. Daniel L. Cady. 6988-6
"I used to look at with disgust". Falling down to bed. Nila NorthSun. 7005-1
"I used to lose my temper an' git mad...". The deeds of anger. Edgar A. Guest. 7033-7
"I used to think it would be nice". The onlooker, fr. Songs from an invalid chair. Josephine A. Meyer. 6847-2

"I used to think our trees all died in winter". Jessie Orton Jones. 6999-1
I used to wear a gown of green. Katherine (Amelia Beers Warnock Garvin) Hale. 6115-X
"I used to work in the kitchen". Unknown. 6059-5
"I uster own the Chickabee farm". Tornado blues. Unknown. 6826-X
I usually sit at the window in the room facing the road. Unknown (Newari) 7013-2
"I vanquished the angel of sleep...". Nocturnal collection. Pablo (Neftali Ricardo Reyes Basualto) Neruda. 6759-X
"I vant some invormashun, shust so qvickly". Der coming man. Charles Follen Adams. 6565-1,6921-5
'I venerate a carpenter' Amanda Benjamin Hall. 7038-8
I vex me not with brooding o'er the years. Thomas Bailey Aldrich. 6847-2
I vex me not with brooding on the years. Thomas Bailey Aldrich. 6648-8,6431-0
"I visited the squirming second grade". Of such... Alice Dougan Gass. 6750-6
I volunteer. Edgar A. Guest. 6748-4
"I volunteered to Texas". The soldier boy. Unknown. 6826-X
I vow to thee, my country. Sir Cecil Spring-Rice. 6386-1, 6420-5,6477-9
I vow to thee, my country. Spring-Rice. Sir Cecil. 6639-9
"I vow'd to keep my waies upright". Psalm 039. Bible. 6848-0
"I wage not any feud with death", fr. Memoriam. Alfred Lord Tennyson. 6536-8,6108-7
I wait my lord. Unknown (Chinese) 7039-6
"I wait to tangle fear around my hand". Night along the Mackinac bridge. Roberta Hill Whiteman. 7005-1
"I waited meekly for the Lord". Psalm 040 Bible. 6848-0
"I waited on a mountain's midmost side". The chant of the children of the mist. Emily Pfeiffer. 6770-0,6875-8
I waited till the twilight. Charles Swain. 6226-1
"I wake and feel the fell of dark, not day". Sonnet ("I wake"). Gerard Manley Hopkins. 6489-2
"I wake and feel the fell of dark." Gerard Manley Hopkins. 6536-8,6655-0,6430-2,6508-2,6645-3
"I wake from a daytime slumber". From memory. Yun-sung Kim. 6775-1
"I wake in a tangle of sheets". June @! 21/84* a poem with mistakes included. Eli Mandel. 6767-0
"I wake in the night with..uncertain gladness". 'The girl takes her place among the mothers'. Marya Alexandrovna Zaturenska. 6777-8
"I wake to see the morning". Morning and myself. Nia Francisco. 7005-1
I wake up screaming. Carlyle B. Hall. 6178-8
"I wake up/what was I dreaming about?". Lunch at Helen Frankenthaler's. Barbara Guest. 6803-0
"I wake-up/I have nothing else to do". March nine. Americo Casiano. 6898-7
"I wake. Ah! would that I could sleep again". Montebelle. 6238-5
I walk alone. Cy Warman. 6836-7
"I walk alone among the leafless trees". Prelude. Margaret Lee Hope. 6799-9
"I walk as happy in your winter garden". To Anita the gardener. Anna Wickham. 6893-6
"I walk in the dusk through the mowing field". Walking in the dusk. Luna Craven Osburn. 6764-6
I walk on the river at dawn. Joanne Hart. 6966-5
"I walk these cold, gray streets". A chant on the terrible highway. Hermann Hagedorn. 6944-4
"I walk unseen". John Milton. 6395-0
"I walk upon the rocky shore". My mother. Josephine Rice Creelman. 6097-8
"I walk'd and did a little mole-hill view". The vanity of human wishes, fr. The day of doom. Michael Wigglesworth. 6753-0
"I walk'd at sunset by the lonely waves". The haunted shore. Wathen Mark Wilks Call. 7015-9
"I walk, a stranger, in my heart". To an outgoing tenant. Mary Carolyn Davies. 6880-4
"I walk, as in a dream". The Neva. Bayard Taylor. 6976-2
"I walked a green-edged path that led". The soul of a promise. E. Dorcas Palmer. 7030-2

"I walked a little street at night". Street scene. Edgar A. Guest. 6748-4
"I walked a little way/One day". In West Yarmouth. Elizabeth K. Folsom. 6798-0
"I walked alone to my calvary". Calvary. Jessie B. Rittenhouse. 6850-2
"I walked beside a dark gray sea". Sea-mews in winter time. Jean Ingelow. 6929-0
"I walked from our wild north country once". A walk through the snow. Alice Cary. 6969-X
"I walked in loamy Wessex lanes afar". The pity of it. Thomas Hardy. 7031-0
"I walked out once by moonlight." Roy Helton. 6037-4
I walked the other day, to spend my hour. Henry Vaughan. 6563-5
I walked the road of the dawn. Dionysios Solomos. 6352-7
"I walked through Ballinderry in the...". Lament for the death of Thomas Davis. Sir Samuel Ferguson. 6930-4
"I walked today, along a city street". On seeing a picture of Christ in a junk shop. Marion W. Wildman. 6954-1
"I walked up to a taxi, and the man who drove". Plato in a taxi. Edgar A. Guest. 6748-4
"I walked with her I love by the sea". By the sea. William Dean Howells. 6997-5
"I walked with Paul in starlight". Frustration. Anne Scott. 6750-6
"I walked with poets in my youth". Envoi. William Roscoe Thayer. 6762-X
"I walked within the autumn woods". In autumn. Charles Hanson Towne. 6778-6
"I wander all night in my vision". The sleepers, sel. Walt Whitman. 6958-4
"I wander and weep in the forest". Heinrich Heine. 6876-6
"I wander away to my little secluded brook". My scrapbook. M. Annette Papayanakos. 6799-9
"I wander sometimes in a land". The land of dreams. William Archer Way. 6800-6
"I wander thro' each chartered street." William Blake. 6317-9
"I wander'd by the brook-side". Song ("I wander'd"). Richard Monckton Milnes; 1st Baron Houghton. 6133-8
"I wanderd/alone in my". Sailor. Bill Bissett. 7003-5
I wandered by the brookside. Richard Monckton Milnes; 1st Baron Houghton. 6744-1
"I wandered forth this moonlight night". Murasaki Shikibu. 6852-9
"I wandered in a woodland-". Our father's care. Iva Temple Cartwright. 6818-9
"I wandered lonely as a cloud". Daffodils. William Wordsworth. 6047-1,6102-8,6136-2,6232-6,6236-9,6240 ,6246-6,6337-3,6478-7,6481-7,6501-5,6529 ,6271-7,6302-0,6385-3,6328-4,6339-X,6401 ,6291-1,6332-2,6600-3, 6634-8,6134-6,6142 ,6498-1,6503-1,6512-0,6558-9,6597-X,6239 ,6732-8,6456-6,6543-0,6737-9,6668-2,6464 , 6639-9,6219-9,6585-6,6304-7,6114-1,6153 ,6135-4,6192-3,6560-0,6104-4,6438-8,6458
"I wandered lonely as a cloud". William Wordsworth. 6075-7, 6052-8,6289-X,6527-9,6604-6,6315 ,6187-7,6101-X,6122-2,6154-0,6198-2,6423 ,6473-6,6479-5,6484-1,6488-4, 6726-3,6250 ,6645-3,6604-7,6723-9,6631-3,6646-1,6491 ,6396-9,6371-3,6301-2,6421-3,6197-6,6252 ,6199-0, 6430-2,6110-9,6086-2,6196-6,6018-8,6023-4
"I wandered lonely where the pine-trees made". The trailing arbutus. John Greenleaf Whittier. 6049-8, 6006-4,6176-1,6499-X,6288-1,6126
I wandered out. George Wither. 6563-5
"I wandered out one rainy day". Quail's nest. John Clare. 6943-6
"I wandered through Scoglietto's far retreat". Sonnet ("I wandered"). Oscar Wilde. 6624-0
"I wandered through the summer woods". Orange elf-cups. Dorothy Choate Herriman. 6797-2
"I want a boy, a small boy". Cry of a lonely heart. E. Pearl Dancey. 6750-6
"'I want a chance to show what I can do'". His chance. Edgar A. Guest. 6862-0
"I want a poem, I want". Death over the air. Jacinto Fombona Pachano. 6759-X
I want an epitaph. John Bennett. 6764-6
I want Aretha to set this to music. Shirley Williams. 6998-

I want Mama. Unknown. 6314-4
"I want that rose the wind took yesterday". A child's mood. Juliet C. Marsh. 6965-7
"I want the flags torn loose from the thunder". Message to the United Nations. Dan Propper. 6901-0
I want to be a cowboy. Unknown. 6003-X
"I want to be a highbrow". Ambition. Berton Braley. 6887-1
I want to be an angel. Julia Gill. 6131-1
I want to be married and cannot tell how. Unknown. 6930-4
'I want to better myself.' Edgar A. Guest. 6748-4
"I want to breathe the salt wind from the sea". Nocturnes: II. Alice E. Gillington. 7037-X
"I want to dance!". To dance. Margaret B. McGee. 6959-2
"I want to gaze at the skies all day long". Sunlight whispering to stone-wall. Yung-rang Kin. 6775-1
I want to go home! Unknown. 6237-7
I want to go to morrow. Unknown. 6963-0
I want to go wandering. Vachel Lindsay. 6345-4,6602-X,6345-4,6253-9
"I want to know, judge". Is freedom a lie? J.M. Munyon. 6925-8
"I want to roam through Russian hills". To - ("I want"). Georgianna Livinston. 6906-1
"I want to sing a little song to please you". A midsummer song. Mary E. (Freeman) Wilkins. 6965-7
I want to sit next to Emily. Ogden Nash. 6089-7
"I want to take a ship and go". Samuel Hoffenstein. 6817-0
"I want you to stop, think and say a prayer". Formula. Carolyn J. Ogletree. 7024-8
"I wanted her to stop". Woman guard. Pancho Aguila. 6870-7
"I wanted to write". For Saundra. Nikki Giovanni. 7024-8
"I wanted/ to write the ultimate". The birth poem. Sharon Berg. 6767-0
"I wanted/to talk". A typical conversation. Susan Shogren. 6883-9
"I was a boy when I heard red words a thousand". Threes. Carl Sandburg. 6880-4
I was a bustle-maker once, girls. Patrick Barrington. 6722-0
I was a child. Rainer Maria Rilke. 6643-7
"I was a citizen, once of a great city". A Londoner in New England, 1941. Jan (Joyce A. Maxtone Graham) Struther. 6761-1
"I was a dissolute young blade". Wills without lawyers. Unknown. 6878-2
"I was a dreamer: I dreamed". The dream-teller. Padraic Gregory. 6930-4
"I was a grovelin creature once". Lively hope, and gracious fear. William Cowper. 6814-6
"I was a joke at dinners...". Revenge to come. Sextus Propertius. 7039-6
"I was a king of beasts, and he, all valor". The lion that Roosevelt shot. Isabel Fiske Conant. 6995-9
"I was a labourer in the smoky valley". I was a labourer, fr. Cycle: seven war poems. Sean Jennett. 6930-4
"I was a mother, and I weep". The Armenian mother. Eugene Field. 6949-5
"I was a reed in the stilly stream." Bliss Carman. 6433-7
"I was a timid little antelope". The rocks, fr. The ghazul. William Makepeace Thackeray. 6802-2
"I was a wandering sheep". Horatius Bonar. 6065-X
"I was a wretched rambling boy". The wretched rambling boy. Unknown. 6826-X
"I was afraid". Madhouse poem. Carlos Oquendo de Amat. 6759-X
"I was again beside thee in a dream". Love's completeness. Mathilde Blind. 7037-X
"I was an exile from my own country & wandered". France. Armentier Ohanian. 6846-4
"I was angry with my friend". William Blake. 6187-7
"I was blest", fr. The prelude. William Wordsworth. 6867-7
"I was born a hundred thousand years ago". Unknown. 6059-5
"I was born and bred in Boston, that city...". Unknown. 6059-5
"I was born and raised in Covington". Botany bay. Unknown. 6826-X
"I was born and raised in Knoxville...". Unknown. 6059-5
"I was born in a stall". Shall I, mother, shall I, shall I do so? Unknown. 6756-5

"I was born in Belfast between the mountain...". Carrickfergus. Louis MacNeice. 6930-4
"I was born in the century of the death..rose". Biography for the use of the birds. Jorge Carrera Andrade. 6759-X
I was born ten thousand years ago. Unknown. 6237-7
"I was born under a kind star". Katharine (Hinkson) Tynan. 6187-7
"I was brought up in Sherfield, not of a low degree". Unknown. 6059-5
"I was easy, a somnambulist, as I climbed". On Pali lookout. Stephen Shu Ning Liu. 6790-5
"I was forced to take". A catch-22 test. John L. Seller. 6870-7
"I was foretold, your rebell sex". A deposition from love. Thomas Carew. 6341-1,6378-0,6430-2,6194-X,6150-8, 6933
"I was going to make something of it". Testimony. Richard Eberhart. 7032-9
"I was having dinner, but had not yet eaten half..." Unknown (Newari) 7013-2
"I was hoein' my corn-field, on a spring day". Farmer and wheel; or, the new Lochinvar. Will Carleton. 6919-3
"I was in heaven one day when all the prayers". The prayers. Thomas Edward Brown. 6809-X
"I was in Margate last July...". Misadventures at Margate. Richard Harris ("Thomas Ingoldsby") Barham. 7025-6
"I was in the harbor". Resolution. Wiolar [pseud].. 6817-0
"I was ina the garden chatting". An afterthought. Samuel Minturn Peck. 7041-8
"I was June, and I was twenty". When I was twenty. Bliss Carman and Richard Hovey. 6890-1
"I was just a little thing". Ganderfeather's gift. Eugene Field. 6834-6;6949-5
"I was just coming in from the garden". Old Clo'. Francis Ledwidge. 6812-X
"I was lying in the dappled shade". First variation on a theme by George Peele. Sacheverell Sitwell. 6985-1
"I was made erect and lone". Henry David Thoreau. 6208-3
I was made of this and this. Gertrude Robinson Ross. 6037-4,6069-2
"I was mighty good-lookin' when I was young". 'Specially Jim.' Unknown. 6682-8,6964-9
"I was no earth/he travelled upon". Pilgrimage. Aaron Shurin. 7003-5
"I was not born to Helicon, nor dare". Gratulatory to Mr. Ben. Johnson for his adopting of him. Thomas Randolph. 6933-9
"I was not meant to stand in a sea-edge garden". Figurehead. Dorothy Paul. 6833-2
"I was not ready for your return". Maturity. Elydia Shipman. 6799-9
"I was not trained in academic bowers". Written at Cambridge (1819). Charles Lamb. 6934-7
"I was of late a barren plant". On the reed. Unknown (Greek). 6814-6
"I was on the Merrimac." Unknown. 6692-5
"I was on the drive in 'sixty, working...". Silver Jack's religion. John Percival Jones. 7007-8
"I was on the margin of a plain". The song of the thrush. Rhys Goch Ap Rhiccart. 6873-1
"I was on the mountain, wandering, wandering". Hill-fantasy. Fannie Stearns Davis. 6762-X
"I was out early to-day, spying about". A letter from the front. Sir Henry Newbolt. 7026-4
"I was peeling new potatoes". Two poems on love. William Roehrick. 6850-2
"I was put aboard a western train...". Unknown. 6059-5
"I was put in irons, oh shame!". In irons. Milan Rakic. 6765-4
"I was readin' sore/sonia niki don l.". What good is a poet? Lanners. x.l.. 6792-1
"I was reading my paper, dully enough, when...". The sailing list. Berton Braley. 6853-7
"I was recently there". Past either and through both. Marvin Cohen. 6803-0
"I was riding on the B & O". Harper's Ferry floating away. Thomas Hornsby Ferril. 6761-1
"I was seized with an ambition to appear...". My first recital. W.A. Eaton. 6925-8

"I was sent to buy purple silk". A little shopper. Mary
    Frances Butts. 6965-7
"I was sitting alone, toward the twilight". The voice in
    the twilight. Mrs. Herrick Johnson. 6889-8
"I was sitting at my writing desk". Revisiting v8
    nostalgia. Peter Olds. 6998-3
I was sitting in McSorley's. Edward Estlin Cummings. 6491-
    4
"I was sitting in my study". Papa's letter. Unknown. 6142-
    7,6370-5,6964-9,6914-2
"I was sitting with my microscope, upon my...". Nux
    postcoenatica. Oliver Wendell Holmes. 7014-0
"I was sitting with my microscope...", sels. Oliver
    Wendell Holmes. 66601-1
"I was sleepless, and I passed the night keeping vigil. al-
    Khansa. 6766-2
"I was so chill, and overworn, and sad". Song ("I was so
    chill"). Anna Wickham. 6153-2
"I was so small they lifted me to see". Then and now. Mary
    McGuire. 6922-3
"I was so tired of Jack, poor boy". Jack and I. Unknown.
    6929-0
"I was somewhere near the Tana...". 'Bush versus London'.
    Brian ("Korongo") Brooke. 6938-X
"I was strolling one day down the Lawther Arcade". The tin
    gee gee. Fred Cape. 6964-9
"I was the moon./A shadow hid me". Dead. Rhoda Coghill.
    6930-4
"I was the staunchest of our fleet". The derelict. Rudyard
    Kipling. 6810-3
"I was trapped in the wretched net of love..." Unknown
    (Newari) 7013-2
"I was upon the high and blessed mound". Sonnet: Of the
    grave of Selvaggia... Cino da Pistoia. 7039-6
"I was very cold". Song ("I was very cold") George
    Macdonald. 6875-8
"I was very cold/In the summer weather". Song ("I was very
    cold"). George Macdonald. 6770-0
"'I was with Grant' the stranger said". The aged stranger.
    Francis Bret Harte. 6889-8
'I was with Grant.' Francis Bret Harte. 6406-X,6552-X
"I was working on 'The Daily News'". Pavlowa. Murdock
    Pemberton. 6959-2
"I was yesterday in Ben Dorain...". Last leave of the
    hills. Duncan Ban MacIntyre. 6845-6
"I wash the dishes every night at home". Thoughts while
    washing dishes. Bernadetta Nichols. 6850-2
"I watch the dancer,/Bending,/Lithely stooping". The
    dancer. Mary Carolyn Davies. 6959-2
"I watch the golden billows awaiting...". The harvest.
    Unknown. 6923-1
I watch the ships. Arthur Wentworth Hamilton Eaton. 6115-X
"I watch the snowflakes falling". Snowflakes. Josephine
    Hoshaw. 6906-1
"I watch'd a white-hair'd figure like a breeze". Fantasia
    on claviers at night. Herbert Trench. 6877-4
"I watch, and long have watched, with...regret". Sonnet
    ("I watch"). William Wordsworth. 6867-7
"I watched a candle burning at a banquet...". Burning
    candle. Edgar A. Guest. 6748-4
"I watched a little child one day". Childhood. Alice
    Stettiner. 6818-9
"I watched a sail until it dropped from sight". 'Tis life
    beyond. Unknown. 6889-8
"I watched her in the sleeper dressing room". The limit,
    limited. Noemie [pseud].. 6817-0
"I watched him at the banquet wait". Lazarus. Arthur
    Shearly Cripps. 6788-3
"I watched him in the blazing field". The farm hand. Edgar
    A. Guest. 6869-3
"I watched him swinging down the street". Laurel and
    cypress. J. Napier Milne. 7031-0
I watched spring. Joan Andrews. 6764-6
"I watched the children today". Kindergarten. Anna Spencer
    Twitchell. 6836-7
"I watched them from the windows...". City pigeons. Edgar
    A. Guest. 6748-4
"I watched two/barn swallows swoop". Last May. Carroll
    Arnett Gogisgi. 7005-1
"'I wear a cross of bronze', he said". The cross. Leon
    Gellert. 6784-0
"I wear a shamrock in my heart". Shamrocks. Rosa
    Mulholland; Lady Gilbert. 6858-8
"I weep a sight which was not seen". Doom-devoted. Louis
    Golding. 6776-X
"I weep for Adonais – he is dead!". Adonais. Percy Bysshe
    Shelley. 6660-7,6560-0,6430-2,6196-6,6199-0,6250 ,
    6245-8,6102-8,6192-3,6150-8,6110-9,6219 ,6660-7,6560-
    0,6430-2,6196-6,6199-0,6250 ,6245-8,6102-8,6192-3,
    6150-8,6110-9,6219 ,6023-4,6086-2,6424-8,6122-2,6154-
    0,6198-2,6315-2,6332-2,6483 ,6536-8,6604-6,6641-0,
    6726-3,6732-8,6543
"I weep for Adonais – he is dead", fr. Adonais. Percy
    Bysshe Shelley. 6879-0
"I weep, for I am weary – no faint dreaming". To the west!
    Alice E. Gillington. 6997-5
"I weigh the piles of Babylon". Civilization. Wilfred
    Rowland Childe. 6893-9
'I went and washed, and I received sight'. Unknown. 6752-2
I went down into the desert to meet Elijah. Vachel
    Lindsay. 6730-1
"I went down the Painted Desert trail last...". White
    night. Byrdie L. Martin. 6799-9
"I went down to the beach to play". Vanishing joy. Roy
    Walter James. 6818-9
"I went in to the deserts of dim sleep". Fragment ("I
    went"). Percy Bysshe Shelley. 6958-4,6545-7
"I went into a public-'ouse to get a pint o' beer". Tommy.
    Rudyard Kipling. 6507-4,6964-9
I went into the fields. John Masefield. 6477-9
"I went out last night to make my round". Little Sadie.
    Unknown. 6826-X
"I went out on an April morning". Morning. Sara Teasdale.
    6897-9
"I went out only once with my bow last year". Hunter's
    morning. Harold Littlebird. 7005-1
"I went riding through the rain". A ballad of trees.
    Robert Norwood. 6797-2
"I went to a dance last night". Dance. Alfred Kreymborg.
    6959-2
"I went to call on the Lord in His house ...". Unknown.
    6532-5
"I went to her who loveth me no more". Song ("I went to
    her"). Arthur O'Shaughnessy. 6271-7
I went to the fair at Bonlaghy. Unknown. 6058-7
"I went to the wood and got it." Mother Goose. 6452-3
"I went to turn tghe grass once after one". The tuft of
    flowers. Robert Frost. 6850-2
"I went up one pair of stairs". Unknown. 6904-5
"I went up to town". Unknown. 6364-0
"I went upon a journey". The journey. Grace Fallow Norton.
    7026-4
"I went upon a meadow bright with gold". A chill in
    summer. George Augustus Simcox. 7015-9
"I whisper it to the sea!". The rhapsody of Abdiel-the
    Syrian for his beloved. Hermann Hagedorn. 6944-4
'I whisper' Cheri Lynn. 6857-X
"I who erst while ye worlds sweet aire did draw." Unknown.
    6563-5
"I who sit quietly: my listless hand". To a bride. Lilian
    White Spencer. 6836-7
"I who was born to walk the virgin grass". He laments to
    no purpose. William Thomas Walsh. 6761-1
"I who, conceived beneath another star". Liebstod. Alan
    Seeger. 7029-9
"I will always miss the feeling". Poem for Viet nam. Ray
    A. Young Bear. 7005-1
"I will arise and go hence to the west". A Connaught
    lament. Nora Hopper. 6872-3
"I will arise and go now, and go to Innisfree". The lake
    isle of Innisfree. William Butler Yeats. 6861-8
'I will arise.' Richard Le Gallienne. 6720-4
'I will be glad in the Lord'. Unknown. 6752-2
"I will be silent/E'en though her words". To my wife. J.
    Edward Raiser. 6799-9
I will be worthy of it. Ella Wheeler Wilcox. 6956-8
"I will build up a wall for freedom to dwell..". The high
    wall. W.R. Titterton. 6884-7
"I will call her when she comes to me". On the sea. Alice
    Cary. 6865-0;6969-X

"I will come no more awhile". Song-time is over. Francis Ledwidge. 6812-X
"I will convert/This tear to a gem...". The tear. Nahum Tate. 6867-7
"I will cross that bridge". Prevision. Ruth Lambert Jones. 6979-7
"I will die cheering, if I needs must die". On the Italian front, MCMXVI. George Edward Woodberry. 7026-4
"I will die mortal/that is to say having...". Heels over head with life. aaria Mercedes Carranza. 7036-1
I will forget. Alice Furlong. 6090-0,6096-X,6096 X
"I will give my love an apple". Folk song. Unknown. 6179-6
"I will go back again to where". Marching song for the coming year. Muriel F. Hochdorf. 6850-2
"I will go back to the great sweet mother". Algernon Charles Swinburne. 6508-2
"I will go forth 'mong men, not mailed in scorn". Alexander Smith. 6238-5
"I will go hence, and seek her, my old love". Rondeau redouble. Rosamund Marriott ("Graham R. Tomson") Watson. 6770-0,6875-8
I will go with my father a-ploughing. Seosamh Maccathmhaoil. 6873-1
"I will go with my father a-ploughing" Joseph ("Seosamh MacCathmhaoil") Campbell. 6478-7,6292-X
"I will have a little house". The little house. Katharine (Hinkson) Tynan. 6872-3
"I will let myself go, forget, not try to...". Amours de voyage, sel. Arthur Hugh Clough. 7014-0
"I will lift up mine eyes unto the hills". Psalm ("I will lift"). Bible. 6466-3
I will lift up mine eyes, fr. Proverbs. Bible. 6132-X
"I will make you brooches. Robert Louis Stevenson. 6253-9, 6161-3,6395-0,6477-9,6634-8,6668-2,6508-2
"I will make you brooches and toys". Romance. Robert Louis Stevenson. 6123-0,6180-X,6427-2,6437-X,6250-4,6301, 6861-8
"'I will neuer eate nor drinke,' Robin Hood said". Unknown. 6111-7
"I will not bring you songs from off a tip...". Handkerchief song. Evana Llynn. 6906-1
"I will not dance:/I say I will not dance". The dancer. James Stephens. 6959-2
"I will not drink..." John Wrigglesworth. 6685-2
"I will not give thee all my heart" Grace Hazard Conkling. 6019-6
I will not hasten. Barbara Young. 7007-8
I will not hear the sea. Maimie A. Richardson. 6269-5
"I will not hear thee speak". William Shakespeare. 6601-1
I will not hurry. Ralph Spaulding Cushman. 6337-3
"I will not let thee go. Robert Bridges. 6320-9,6477-9,6487-6,6508-2,6656-9
"I will not pass through the world as a...". The conqueror. May C. ([Mary] Gillington) Byron. 7014-0
"I will not perturbate". To the dead cardinal of Westminster. Francis Thompson. 6942-8
"I will not rail, or grieve when torpid eld". Age. Richard Garnett. 7015-9
"I will not shut me from my kind", fr. In memoriam. Alfred Lord Tennyson. 6867-7
"I will not tread on the golden grass". Pilgrimage. Laura Campbell. 6028-5
"I will not weep, for 'twere as great a sin". Henry King. 6187-7
"I will o'ertake thee...", fr. Antony and Cleopatra. William Shakespeare. 6339-X
"I will paint her as I see her". A portrait ("I will paint"). Elizabeth Barrett Browning. 6239-3,6302-9
"I will paint you a sign, rum-seller". A sign-board. Unknown. 6914-2
I will praise the lord at all times. William Cowper. 6152-4
"I will praise thee every day". O Lord, I will praise thee. William Cowper. 6814-6
"I will put enmities", fr. Genesis. Bible. 6282-2
"I will repat you for your tenderness". Song ("I will repay"). Grace Hazard Conkling. 6320-9
"I will return to dig". Archaeology. Babette Deutsch. 7014-0
I will send the comforter. (Frederick) Ridgely Torrence.

6030-7
"I will sing a song of heroes". Abraham. John Stuart Blackie. 6848-0
"I will sing high-hearted Moses". Moses. John Stuart Blackie. 6848-0
"I will sing the son of Jesse". David. John Stuart Blackie. 6848-0
"I will sing unto the Lord...". Cantemus domino. Bible. 6830-8
"I will stand up and loudly sing". Greater than. Margaretta Schuyler. 6880-4
"I will take me out to the autumn woods". Autumn alchemy. Luna Craven Osburn. 6799-9
"I will tell ye of the hunter, if ye listen...". The hunter. Brian ("Korongo") Brooke. 6938-X
"I will tell you a tale that will make you...". The gambler's tale. Will Victor McGuire. 6923-1
"I will tell you of a brisk young farmer". Unknown. 6059-5
"I will tell you of a fellow...". Unknown. 6059-5,6003-X
"I will tell you the way I have heard some say". Unknown. 6059-5
"I will that men pray everywhere." Henry Ware Jr. 6385-3
"I will think as thinks the rabbit". A child's make-believe. George Macdonald. 6965-7
"I will think of water-lilies". Before quiet, fr. Songs of farewell. Hazel Hall. 6778-6
I will trust. Jean Ingelow. 6337-3
"I will turn away from all sweet-scented place". To John Hall Wheelock. Helene Mullins. 6850-2
"I will write a poem". Without figures. Eda Lou Walton. 6778-6
"I will, give thanks unto thee, o Lord". Psalm 009. Bible. 6848-0
I wish I was a little sparrow. Unknown. 6826-X
I wish I was single again. Unknown. 6003-X
I wish I were by that dim lake. Thomas Moore. 6737-9
"I wish I were where Helen lies". Unknown. 6317-9
"I wish for a poem". Poem ("I wish for a poem"). Lindley Williams Hubbell. 6751-4
"I wish for rain - and I wish for snow". Nearing Cold-dale. Hannes Hafstein. 6854-5
"I wish I lived a thowsen year ago". On steam. Thomas Hood. 6974-6
"I wish I were at home in the world". The exile. Anna Wickham. 6893-6
"I wish my mother could see me now...". M.I. Rudyard Kipling. 6810-3
I wish my tongue were a quiver. Louis Alexander Mackay. 6733-6
"I wish she'd open wide the door". The door. Florence Hinds. 6799-9
"I wish that Easter eggs would do". If Easter eggs would hatch. Douglas Malloch. 6891-X
"I wish that I could have my wish to-night". Shakespeare. Henry Ames Blood. 7041-8
I wish that I could run away. John Whitaker Watson. 6774-3
"I wish that I could think of something...". The lonely man. Edgar A. Guest. 6748-4
"I wish that I could trade this spring for one". Spring in Manhattan. Don Wahn. 6750-6
"I wish that I had been awake last night". Knife of nostalgia. Avanelle Wilmeth Blair. 6750-6
"I wish that I might set this day". This day. Marian Buxton Clark. 6906-1
"I wish that my big brother's here". My big brother. Unknown. 6929-0
"I wish that my room had a floor". Limerick:"I wish that my room had a floor." Gelett Burgess. 6308-X
"I wish that my room had a floor". Gelett Burgess. 6026-9, 6722-0
"I wish that whoever it is inside of me". I wish... Bob Kaufman. 6998-3, 6901-0
"I wish there were some wonderful place". Land of beginning again. Louisa Fletcher Tarkington. 6714-X, 6964-9
"I wish thy lot, now bad, still worse...". To a friend in distress. John Owen. 6814-6
"I wish to tell in humble rhyme". The drunkard's wife. Ruth Cooper. 6919-3
"I wish to tune my quivering lyre". Anacreon. 6945-2

"I wish you happiness". Three wishes. Kathleen Gardner. 6750-6
"I wish't I lived away down east". A western boy's lament. Eugene Field. 6949-5
"I wish, I wish I were a ish". Unless. Frederic Edward Weatherley. 6937-1
"I wish, o son of the living God". The hermit's song. Unknown. 6930-4
I wish... Bob Kaufman. 6998-3, 6901-0
"I woke, and we were sailing on". Part the sixth. Samuel Taylor Coleridge. 6943-6
"I won't be my father's Jack". Unknown. 6363-2
"I won't have none of your weevily wheat". Weevily wheat. Unknown. 6826-X
"I won't slide down that metal". Sisyphus angers the gods of condescension. Calvin Murry. 6870-7
I wonder. Elizabeth Colwell. 6880-4
I wonder. Stephen Crane. 6121-4
I wonder. Elva R. Ray. 6750-6
I wonder. Unknown. 6918-5
I wonder. Unknown. 6014-5,6413-2,6654-2
"I wonder could I dare to trace". A Christmas legend. Unknown. 6926-6
"I wonder did you ever count". For the future. Adelaide Anne Procter. 6957-6
"I wonder ef all wimmin air". Lizzie. Eugene Field. 6949-5
"I wonder have you noticed them...". Roadside table. Edgar A. Guest. 6748-4
"I wonder if ever the angel of death". The nameless guest. James Clarence Harvey. 6920-7
'I wonder if he knows it' Wilbur Dick Nesbit. 6995-9
"I wonder if in the far isle". Braddan vicarage. Thomas Edward Brown. 6809-X
"I wonder if life is kind or callous". Close of play. Kenneth H. Ashley. 6785-9
"I wonder if Mary, heavy with child". Two Marys. Vivian Yeiser. 6750-6
"I wonder if old Santa Claus will come tonight". Little Jo. Mary McGuire. 6922-3
"I wonder if the name is right". Unknown. 6466-3
"I wonder if the old crow died or not". The question. Wilfred Wilson Gibson. 7029-9
"I wonder if there ever was". 'Having the thrashers' in Vermont. Daniel L. Cady. 6988-6
I wonder if there'll be a river? Lalla Adams Stark. 7016-7
"I wonder if you've ever heard". How Barre, Vermont, was named. Daniel L. Cady. 6988-6
"I wonder if, some future day". My great-aunt's portrait. Unknown. 7022-1
"I wonder if, sunning in Eden's vales". Ballade of the ancient wheeze. Newman Levy and Nate Salsbury. 6875-8
"I wonder in what isle of bliss" Justin Huntly McCarthy. 6875-8
I wonder not that youth remains. Walter Savage Landor. 6110-9
"I wonder was she fair to see". Gypsy blood. Edgar A. Guest. 6748-4
I wonder what became of Rand, McNally.... Newman Levy. 6722-0
I wonder what Maud will say? Samuel Minturn Peck. 6695-X
"I wonder what day of the week". An untimely thought. Thomas Bailey Aldrich. 6887-1
"I wonder what remembering mind". Farmers' teas in Vermont. Daniel L. Cady. 6989-4
"I wonder what she looked like/Mother sweet...". Full heart. Glory E. Scott. 6799-9
"I wonder what spendthrift chose to spill". March. Celia Thaxter. 6612-7,6623-2,6368-3,6456-6
"I wonder what that great pine said to you". To Emily Dickinson in her garden. Frances Wright Turner. 6789-1
"I wonder what the mischief was in her". St. Patrick's martyrs. Unknown. 6916-9
"I wonder what the trees will say". The lonely garden. Edgar A. Guest. 6846-4
"I wonder what the world beyond can hold...". Eternal spring. Edgar A. Guest. 6748-4
"I wonder what's become of them". 'Butchering in the fall' in Vermont. Daniel L. Cady. 6988-6

"I wonder where the railroad starts". Christmas-land. Unknown. 6807-3
I wonder why. Irene Davis Grueninger. 6906-1
I wonder why. Unknown. 6922-3
"I wonder why that scene comes back to-night". Pilate remembers. William E. Brooks. 6779-4
"'I wonder', says little Hope, with a tear...". 'Tatts'. Annie L. Jack. 6965-7
"I wonder, by my troth, what thou and I". John Donne. 6187-7
"I wonder, dear, if you'll be there". In the nude. Idabel Williams. 6906-1
"I wonder, does the breath". Meditation. Joyce Lancaster. 6850-2
"I wonder, wayward child of mine". The wanderer. V. O. Wallingford. 6818-9
"I wonder, when our little lives are through". Winter afternoon. Helen G. Ladd. 6764-6
"I wonder, will the guelder-roses bloom". Villanelle. Richard Mount. 6032-3
"I wondered if I were a chair myself". Interior. Willard Johnson. 6808-1
"I wondered why in Libya there were". Snow leopards. Dawad Philp. 6899-5
"I work at night, surrounded by city". Burial in the east. Pablo (Neftali Ricardo Reyes Basualto) Neruda. 6759-X
"I work with the tide the wind and the sea". The clam digger. Sarah A. Dixon. 6798-0
I wot full well that beauty cannot last. George Turberville. 6641-0
I would ask this. Alise Williams Whitelaw. 6789-1
"I would be eyes for one/Who ne'er beheld...". The joy of service. Heloise M.B. Hawkins. 6836-7
"I would be left alone with this great love". The cloister. Richard Le Gallienne. 6872-3
I would be true. Howard Arnold Walter. 6211-3,6337-3
"I would be true...". My creed. Harold Arnold Walters. 6889-8
"I would before thy bosom's shrine sink low". My deity. Otakar Aurednicek. 6763-8
"I would feed them bread in the morning". Gulls. George Kuttner. 6900-2
"I would forego," fr. Morpheus. Hilda ("H.D.") Doolittle. 6354-3
I would forget. Elizabeth Dimon Preston. 6836-7
"I would forgo." Hilda ("H.D.") Doolittle. 6317-9
"I would give thee, my love, fair things". The cheerful giver. John McMaster. 6817-0
"I would give two shillings this day...". The old woman of Meath. Jessica Powers. 6761-1
I would go back. Mary M. Curchod. 6144-3
"I would I might forget that I am I." George Santayana. 6310-2
I would I were a careless child. George Gordon, 6th Baron Byron. 6945-2
"I would I were a child". George Macdonald. 6819-7
"I would I were a damask rose". Unknown. 6435-3
I would I were Actaeon. Unknown. 6182-6
"I would I were an excellent devine." Nicholas Breton. 6302-0
"I would have loved:there are no mates..heaven". In an iiluminated missal. Charles Kingsley. 6793-X
"I would have taken 'olden stars from the sky". To the unattainable: lament of Mahomed Akram. Laurence (Adele Florence Nicolson) Hope. 6856-1
"I would I had thrust my hands of flesh". Edmund Pollard. Edgar Lee Masters. 6754-9,6879-0
"I would I were a famous sonneteer". A sonnet to a sonnet. Edwin Chamberlin. 6906-1
"I would I were that portly gentleman". Sonnet: The poet expresses his feelings... Robert Southey. 6802-2
"I would I were the little flower". Valentine. Charles G. Blanden. 6820-0
"I would if I could". Unknown. 6363-2
"I would keep rendezvous with you". My rendezvous. Ann Hope. 6841-3
"I would like to visit my grandfather". Moose Lake state hospital. Dennis Shady. 6870-7
I would like you for a comrade. Edward Abbott Parry. 6242-

3,6466-3,6639-9,6638-0
I would live in your love. Sara Teasdale. 6393-4
"I would live, if I had my will". My will. Arthur Christopher Benson. 6793-X
I would love to be a shepherd. Kostas Krystallis. 6352-7
"I would make a fiddle cry". Bessie Becker. 6847-2
"I would my days had been in other times". N.A. Andrew Lang. 6987-8
"'I would my gift were worthier!' sighed...". A blemished offering. Margaret Junkin Preston. 7041-8
"I would my master were a wat (a hare)". Unknown. 6105-2
"I would my sight were formed to stare". To W.H. Davies. Geoffrey Scott. 6985-1
"I would not be a bird". Poem ("I would not"). Frank Prewett. 6070-6
"I would not be a servingman to carry...". Merrythough's song (1). John Fletcher. 6933-9
"I would not be too wise - so very wise". The simple things. Edgar A. Guest. 7033-7
"I would not die in May". October. Benjamin Franklin Taylor. 6815-4
I would not enter on my list of friends, fr. The task. William Cowper. 6934-7
"I would not even ask my heart to say". Patria. Henry Van Dyke. 6961-4
"I would not have thee warm when I am cold". After death. Louise Chandler Moulton. 7041-8
"I would not have this perfect love of ours". James Russell Lowell. 6753-0
"I would not have you back on earth". The comforting. Margaret E. Bruner. 6750-6
"I would not hcoose my son anothe portion". Early piety. James Abraham Martling. 6952-5
"I would not lift my eyes again". Pledge of faith. Nelda Wood Martin. 6750-6
"I would not like to tell how oft I raced". The back stairs, fr. The homestead. Gertrude Huntington McGiffert. 6838-3
"I would not live alway." William Augustus Muhlenberg. 6302-0,6240-7,6600-3,6219-9,6304-7,6917
'I would not live always'. B.B. Thatcher. 6752-2
"I would not play it the hog's way". Man. Edgar A. Guest. 6748-2
"I would not question your aloofness, nor". Lest the spirit die. Mary Pauline Richardeon. 6789-1
"I would not sing his greatness". When he died. Ethel Brooks Stillwell. 6995-9
"I would not, if I could, repeat". Onward! John Greenleaf Whittier. 6793-X
"I would poise my arm for the discus throwing". Warum? Anna Batchelder. 7030-2
I would remember constant things. J.U. Nicholson. 6619-4
"I would sail upon the tropic seas". Jean Ingelow. 6997-5
"I would swathe thee in huesof the orient". Song ("I would swathe thee"). Thomas Keohler. 6174-5
I would tell. Unknown. 6712-3
"I would that all men my hard case might know". Behold the deeds! Henry Cuyler Bunner. 6770-0
"I would that I alone could sing". My song. Eva Fidler. 6847-2
"I would that even now". Princess Shoku. 7039-6
"I would that free from sickness...". Mimnermus. 6251-2
I would that I were like a tree. Leila Chamberlain Deane. 6799-9
'I would that she were dead'. John Whitaker Watson. 6774-3
I would that wars should cease. Alfred Lord Tennyson. 6051-X
I would thou wert not fair. Nicholas Breton. 6182-6,6189-3
"I would to God that I might be". Desire. Georgianna Livinston. 6906-1
"I would to God, that mine old age might have". His wish to God. Robert Herrick. 6931-2
"I would wake at the hour of dawning in May...". Song of the vine. Herbert Trench. 6877-4
I would walk the ways of the busy town. Ella Colter Johnston. 6906-1
I would we had not met again. Felicia Dorothea Hemans. 6973-8
I would, dear Jesus. John D. Long. 6260-1
"I woulde witen of sum wis wight". The world an illusion. Unknown. 6881-2
"I wouldn't be too free with my kisses". Kisses. Berton Braley. 6853-7
I wouldn't have an old man. Unknown. 6058-7
"I wouldn't marry an old man". Unknown. 6059-5
"I wouldna gie a copper plack". Mary A. Barr. 6102-8
I wouldne gie a copper plack. Mary A. Barr. 6102-8
"I wove a tapestry of colored lies". Vincit omnia veritas. Ronald Walker Barr. 6906-1,6779-4
"I wrap each gift in cellophane". Coup d'etat. Dorothy Howells Walker. 6750-6
"I wrap the morning shift round me..muffler". Morning shift. Honor Arundel. 6895-2
"I wrastled wid Satan, I wrastled wid sin." Unknown. 6375-6
"I write this as a plane drones overhead". Dead man's glory. David Martin. 6895-2
"I write to soothe that inward grief alone". Vittoria Colonna. 6325-X
I write to tell. Comtesse de Noailles. 6351-9
"I wrote a satire of a man". Human nature. Katie F. Nichols. 6764-6
"I wrote some lines once upon a time". The height of the ridiculous. Oliver Wendell Holmes. 6102-8,6385-3, 6732-8,6288-1,6307-1,6739 ,6102-8,6385-3,6732-8,6265-2,6300-4,6464 ,6176-1,6290-3,6332-2,6486-8,6722-0, 6089 ,6076-5,6026-9,6107-9,6736-0,6126-5,6121 ,6505-8,6964-9,6278-4
"I wrote the truest, tend'rest song". My masterpiece. Arthur Macy. 7041-8
"I wrote you a letter". Dennis List. 7018-3
I wudrknot dye in wintur. Unknown. 6273-3
I wuz borned on the rivuh. Unknown. 6609-7
"I youst to bin a doketor vonce". A doketor's drubbles. George M. Warren. 6912-6
"I' b'en a-kindo' 'musin', as the feller says". Romancin'. James Whitcomb Riley. 6892-8
"I' got no patience with blues at all!". A dos't o' blues. James Whitcomb Riley. 6892-8
I' saddest when I sing. Thomas Haynes Bayly. 6980-0
"I' the glooming light". Song ("I' the glooming light"). Alfred Lord Tennyson. 6977-0
I'd be a butterfly. Thomas Haynes Bayly. 6874-X
I'd be a butterfly. Thomas Haynes Bayly. 6652-6
"I'd be a butterfly born in a bower". I'd be a butterfly. Thomas Haynes Bayly. 6874-X
"I'd be a lawyer gifted with power". The vision and the reality. Joel (and 'A Lady') Parker. 6878-2
'I'd be a parody', fr. Bailey ballads. Thomas Hood. 6974-6
I'd be--wouldn't you? Unknown. 6629-1
"I'd been away from her three years...". The faithful lovers. Unknown. 6910-X
"I'd been taking things for granted...". Valentine. Edgar A. Guest. 6748-4
I'd give my love. Helen Consuelo Feldman. 6847-2
I'd give my love. Mollie Rebecca Golomb. 6847-2
"I'd laugh today, today is brief". Today. Unknown. 6889-8
"I'd like to be a bank clerk, and sit ...". The bank clerk. Edgar A. Guest. 6862-6
I'd like to be a bee. Torquato Tasso. 6325-X
"I'd like to be a cowboy an' ride a...horse". The limitations of youth. Eugene Field. 6949-5
I'd like to be a white girl. Alice Barkley. 6789-1
"I'd like to be the lightning". Remembering the dar. Rosalie Goodyear. 6750-6
"I'd like to give the beauty of the stars..you". Love song. Virginia Wuerfel Slayton. 6906-1
"I'd like to go out/after the night". Ash Wednesday. Thomas Bernhard. 6769-7
"I'd like to go wandering over the land". Homecoming. Anna Hansen Hayes. 6836-7
"I'd like to hunt the Injuns 't roam the...plain". I got to go to school. Nixon Waterman. 6964-9
"I'd like to keep a book-shop in some...". My book-shop. Helen Cowles Le Cron. 7038-8
"I'd like to lie beneath a growing tree". Secret ways. Marie Louise Allen. 6906-1
"I'd like to live a slower lif". The weather. John Newlove. 6767-0
"I'd like to love him". Because. Helen Eikamp. 6857-X

I'D
804

"I'd like to own a waterfall". Symbol. Marie Louise Allen. 6906-1
"I'd like to see our store again". New goods at a Vermont store. Daniel L. Cady. 6989-4
"I'd like to steal a day and be". The three me's. Edgar A. Guest. 7033-7
"I'd like to weave a pretty rhyme". In praise of pie. Eugene Field. 6949-5
I'd love to a fairy's child. Robert Graves. 6368-3
"I'd make my heart a harp to play for you". To Eilish of the fair hand. Francis Ledwidge. 6812-X
I'd rather be a failure. Edgar A. Guest. 7033-7
"'I'd rather be blind than see this place'". Another life. Philip Levine. 6792-1,6998-3
"I'd rather be the willing horse that people..". The willing horse. Edgar A. Guest. 7033-7
I'd rather be you, little wide-eyed boy. Florence Davidson Strother. 6750-6
"I'd rather fail than have it said". Success. Edgar A. Guest. 6862-6
"I'd rather have fingers than toes". Goop rhymes. Gelett Burgess. 6861-8
I'd rather have fingers than toes. Gelett Burgess. 6534-1, 6724-7
"I'd rather live in bohemia than in any...". In Bohemia. John Boyle O'Reilly. 7041-8
"I'd rid from far-back Texas in..spring o' 49.". In the elevator. Robert C.V. Meyers. 6925-8
"I'd weave a wreath for those who fought". Through fire in Mobile Bay. Unknown. 6946-0
"I'd wed you without herds, without money...". Cashel of Munster. William English. 6930-4
"I'd write a poem if I could". The old woman's war work. Helen Bosanquet. 7042-6
"I'll be the goodest little girl". Dolly's christening. Unknown. 6772-7
I'll be your epitaph. Leonora Speyer. 6037-4
"I'll bid my hyacinth to blow". Caroline. Thomas Campbell. 6980-0
"I'll clean my desk up bye and bye". System, fr. Matrimonial melodies. Berton Braley. 6853-7
I'll follow June. Robert Kirkland Kernighan. 6591-0,6592-2
"I'll follow you down to the spring". The spring. Luis Fabio Xammar. 6759-X
"I'll frame, my Heliodora! a garland for thy.". A garland for Heliodora. Meleager. 7039-6
"I'll give thee, good fellow, a twelvemonth...". The barefooted friar, fr. Ivanhoe. Sir Walter Scott. 6828-6
"I'll give to you a paper of pins". Unknown. 6059-5
"I'll go into the country now". Love's plans. William Henry Davies. 6779-4
"I'll have the window southward" Sang-yong Kim. 6775-1
"I'll keep a little tavern". Tavern. Edna St. Vincent Millay. 6986-X
"'I'll lend you for a little time a child...'". To all parents. Edgar A. Guest. 6748-4
I'll live in this poor rime. William Shakespeare. 6634-8
I'll love no more. Sir Robert Ayton. 6934-7
"I'll never be a nun, I trow". Nightingale weather. Andrew Lang. 6771-9
I'll never get drunk any more. Unknown. 6930-4
I'll never love thee more. James Graham; Marquess of Montrose. 6429-9,6600-3,6321-7,6737-9,6429-9,6180-X, 6438-8
I'll never take a single drop. Unknown. 6691-7
I'll never use tobacco. Unknown. 6715-8
I'll not confer with sorrow. Thomas Bailey Aldrich. 6431-0
"I'll not grow old in spite of years". Youth. Edwin Garnet Riley. 6799-9
I'll not marry at all. Unknown. 6003-X
"I'll not reveal my true-love's name". The lady of Albany's lament of King Charles. Unknown (Irish). 6858-8
"I'll not weep that thou art going". Stanzas ("I'll not weep"). Emily Bronte. 6123-0,6315-2
"I'll obey them in the winter when the doctors". Cherry pie. Edgar A. Guest. 6748-4
I'll put it off. Unknown. 6629-1
"I'll put you myself, my baby! to slumber". Irish lullaby.

Unknown (Irish). 6858-8
"I'll sail upon the dog star". Song ("I'll sail"). Thomas D'Urfey. 6179-6
"I'll see it through, whate'ver the danger be". Determination. Edgar A. Guest. 6869-3
"I'll sing a song of kings and queens". The fall. Eden Phillpotts. 6884-7
"I'll sing my children's death-song, though". The lamentation of Felix M'Carthy. Unknown (Irish). 6858-8
"I'll sing of heroes". Love. Abraham Cowley. 6339-X
"I'll sing you a ditty that needs no apology". A song of geology, fr. Musa Burschicosa. John Stuart Blackie. 6819-7
"I'll sing you a good old song." Unknown. 6385-3
"I'll sing you a song". Unknown. 6904-5
"I'll sing you a song, if you'll hear me...". A song of Scottish heroes. John Stuart Blackie. 7009-4
"I'll sing you a gong, my brave boys". On the act of succession (1703). Unknown. 6859-6
"I'll sing you now a Dietchen song...". The fine old Dutch gentleman. Unknown. 6791-3
"I'll sing, I'll sing of ancient days". Adam and Eve. Eleazar Dexter. 7030-2
I'll take what father gives. W. Hoyle. 6408-6,6617-8
I'll tell her. George Granville; Baron Lansdowne. 6563-5
"I'll tell her the next time, said I". Song ("I'll tell her"). George Granville; Baron Lansdowne. 6562-7
"'I'll tell thee,' said the old man...". Age and youth. Letitia Elizabeth ("L.E.L.") Landon. 6980-0
"I'll tell you a sad story". Oma Wise. Unknown. 6826-X
"I'll tell you a story that not's in Tom Moore". Come with the ring. Thomas Hood. 6917-7
"I'll tell you a story". Unknown. 6363-2
"I'll tell you a story, a story anon". Unknown. 6059-5
"I'll tell you a story/About Mary Morey." Unknown. 6452-3
"I'll tell you a tale of a wee little elf". Courtship's end. Edgar A. Guest. 6748-4
"I'll tell you how the sun rose". Emily Dickinson. 6299-7, 6288-1
"I'll tell you of a wild Colloina boy, Jack...". Unknown. 6059-5
"I'll tell you what 'twas fun to do". Stock and Vermont punkins. Daniel L. Cady. 6988-6
"I'll tell you what a tank is". There's nothing polite about a tank. John Paul Minarik. 6870-7
"I'll tell you whence the Rose did first grow red". William Strode. 6187-7
I'll tell you where they were! Unknown. 6237-7
"I'll tell you, friend, what sort of wife". A castle in the air. C. Frisbie. 6752-2
"I'll think, there's not one world above",fr How clear. Emily Bronte. 6123-0
"I'll touch you not, you much abus-ed rag". To a country hotel towel. Elmer C. Adams. 6750-6
I'll try. Unknown. 6452-3
I'll try and I can't. Emma Celia & Lizzie J. Rook. 6137-0
"I'll undo the world by dying." John Donne. 6637-2
"I'm 'ere in a ticky ulster...". 'Back to the army again'. Rudyard Kipling. 6810-3
"I'm a calm and placid person and my temper...". The fighting word. Berton Braley. 6853-7
I'm a celebrated bum. Unknown. 6149-4
I'm a cranky old Yank in a clanky old tank. Hoagy Carmichael. 6237-7
"I'm a friend to your theatre...". To Mr. Simpson, fr. Croaker papers. Fitz-Greene Halleck and Joseph Rodman Drake. 6753-0
"I'm a gay tra, la, la". Swiss air. Francis Bret Harte. 6902-9
I'm a good old rebel. Innes Randolph. 7017-5
"I'm a grandchild of the gods". The complaint of New Amsterdam. Jacob Steendam. 6946-0
"I'm a heartbroken raftsman, from Greenville I came". Unknown. 6059-5
"I'm a lad that's forced an exile". Green upon the cape. Dion Boucicault. 6858-8
I'm a lil' rough rider. George V. Hobart. 6721-2
I'm a mirror. Claribel Alegria. 7036-1
"I'm a showman by purfession, gents...". The penny

showman. H. Chance Newton. 6925-8
I'm a shrimp! Robert Barnabas Brough. 6802-2
"I'm a sober polyp in a coral prison". By my own sweat. Alex R. Schmidt. 6750-6
I'm a tight little Irishman. Unknown. 6058-7
"I'm a true child" Konrad Bayer. 6769-7
I'm Alabama bound. Unknown. 6609-7
"I'm after axin', Biddy dea ". Diffidence. Unknown. 6915-0
"I'm allus glad when my Pa gets back". When Pa gets back. Edgar A. Guest. 6862-6
"I'm an extremely charitable man...". A charity sermon. Thomas Hood. 6974-6
"I'm at Yaddo sheltering myself from the drizz". Name-dropping. Robert Sward. 6767-0
"I'm bidden, little Mary, to write verses...". Lines to little Mary. Caroline Anne Bowles Southey. 6772-7
"I'm bin a-visitun 'bout a week". A very youthful affair. James Whitcomb Riley. 6992-4
I'm black and blue. Heinrich Heine. 7039-6
"I'm burning the well-known midnight oil". Futility. Charlotte Blaising. 6750-6
"I'm calling you--calling". Cushlamochree. Frances Wright Turner. 6799-9
"I'm Captain Jnks of the horse marines". Captain Jinks. Unknown. 6826-X
"I'm capable of loving" Walter Buchebner. 6769-7
"I'm carving lilies on the Cross". Craftsman. Edna Bendig. 6750-6
"I'm fifty, I'm fair, an without a gray hair". Widder Budd. Unknown. 6917-7
"I'm fond of partridges - I'm fond of snipes". Sonnet to Lord Wharncliffe on his game bill. Thomas Hood. 6974-6
"I'm for the happy man every time". The man I'm for. Edgar A. Guest. 6862-6
"I'm free again!/Young Man, I'm new!". On the jail steps. Agnes Lee. 7038-8
"I'm getting better, Miriam, though it tires..". Arthur's wife. Phoebe Cary. 6969-X
I'm glad. Unknown. 6274-1,6291-1
"I'm glad I have a wife at home". Why I'm glad. Edgar A. Guest. 6862-6
"I'm glad I walk'd. How fresh the meadows look". Walking to the mail. Alfred Lord Tennyson. 6977-0
I'm glad he knows. Thomas (Tom) Brown. 6680-1
I'm glad I am a little girl. Unknown. 6713-1
"I'm glad my eyes may see the sun". Song ("I'm glad"). Rebecca Turner. 6662-3
"I'm glad our house is a little house". Song for a little house. Christopher Morley. 6891-X
I'm glad you are casually interested in why I was an... Lynne Savitt. 6998-3
I'm goin' down the rivuh. Unknown. 6609-7
I'm goin' down the rivuh, baby. Unknown. 6609-7
"'I'm goin' to die!' says the Widder Green". Widder Green's last words. Unknown. 6913-4
I'm goin' to ship on the Mike Davis. Unknown. 6609-7
"I'm goin' to start next Saturday". Comin' Christmas morn. Ben King. 6807-2
I'm goin' up the rivuh. Unknown. 6609-7
"I'm going softly all my years in wisdom if...". Babylon. Viola Gerard Garvin. 7007-8
I'm going to Bombay. Thomas Hood. 6974-6
"I'm going to make a million some night". Madrigal. Nicanor Parra. 6758-1
"I'm going to school tomorrow, just". Patrick goes to school. Alicia Aspinwall. 6891-X
'I'm going to, anyway'. Strickland Gillilan. 6889-8
I'm growing old. John Godfrey Saxe. 6219-9
"I'm growing old; I've sixty years". Carcassonne. Unknown. 7002-7
"I'm growing very old. This weary head". St. John the aged. Unknown. 6917-7
"I'm hiding, I'm hiding". Hiding. Dorothy Aldis. 6891-X
"I'm home again in late July". After a year in the city. Risa Alice Lowie. 6847-2
"'I'm hungry, man, hungry/My clothes are...'". Reminiscence. Lyle Bartscher. 6799-9
'I'm hurried, child.' Unknown. 6713-1
"I'm in a fairway to go mad". Company. Berton Braley. 6853-7
"I'm in love, but I never told her". Margery Daw. Frederic Edward Weatherley. 6917-7
"I'm like Archimedes for science and skill". Fragment of an oration. George Canning. 6874-X
"I'm longing for a hillside". Longing. Harriet Holman. 7016-7
"I'm looking for a fellow Pan". Poem ("I'm looking"). Chard Powers Smith. 6041-2
"I'm looking westward now, and seeing things". Westward. Mrs. Pope Brooks. 7016-7
"I'm losted here, 'cause I runned away". A deep revenge. Thornton W. Burgess. 6798-0
"I'm mightily fond of Manhattan". The main drag. Berton Braley. 6853-7
"I'm my daddy's little girl". Daddy's little girl. Lindamichellebaron. 6899-5
"I'm never quite alone, for Pierre La Noue". Pierre and I. Chapman J. Milling. 7016-7
"I'm never too weary to sing you a song". A song. Edgar A. Guest. 6862-6
"I'm no more to converse with the swains". To the most honourable the Earl of Oxford... John Gay. 6972-X
"I'm nobody! Who are you". Emily Dickinson. 6380-2,6501-5, 6726-3,6107-9,6736-0,6396-9
"I'm nobody's fool" Josef Mayer-Limberg. 6769-7
"I'm not a bit afraid of the Atlantic". The original slacker. E. Adelaide Hahn. 6847-2
"I'm not a chicken; I have seen". The September gale. Oliver Wendell Holmes. 6165-6,6610-0,6964-9
"I'm not a crack salesman - I don't look..part". Salesmanship. Naomi Rogin. 6850-2
I'm not a single man. Thomas Hood. 6680-1,6646-1
"I'm not here," fr. Halcyon. Hilda ("H.D.") Doolittle. 6012-9
I'm not myself at all! Samuel Lover. 6858-8
"I'm not sentimental, heaven knows". To J. E. Pearl Dancey. 6750-6
"I'm nothing./I'll always be nothing". Tobacco shop. Fernando Pessoa. 6758-1
"I'm notified, fair neighbor mine". The lawyer's valentine. John Godfrey Saxe. 6878-2
"'I'm of no school', I hear one say". To the originals, fr. Gedichte. Johann Wolfgang von Goethe. 7042-6
"I'm often ask'd by plodding souls". The toper's apology. Charles Morris. 6874-X
I'm on the sea. Bryan Waller ("Barry Cornwall") Procter. 6484-1
"I'm one of the wandering dead". Exile. Ingeborg Bachmann. 6769-7
"I'm only four score year, my sons, and a few". Daniel Boone's last look westward. Cale Young Rice. 7017-5
I'm owre young to marry yet. Robert Burns. 6180-X
"I'm rather slow at extravaganzas". Schnapps. Selber. 6787-5
"I'm reaaly not ready to die of benign neglect". Benign neglect. Lindamichellebaron. 6899-5
"I'm ready for the party". Bessie's first party. Belle Marshall Locke. 6927-4
I'm scared of it all. Robert Service. 6159-1
"I'm sending you a valentine". Valentine for my mother. Harry Lee. 6891-X
"I'm sick of books, - the weary pro and con". Ennui. Henry Thornton Craven. 6936-3
"I'm sick of fog and yellow gloom". Homesick. Dorothy Frances McCrae. 6784-0
"I'm sick of school an' sick of home". Childhood. Berton Braley. 6853-7
"I'm sick of the Mongol and Tartar". The exile. Berton Braley. 6853-7
"I'm sitting alone by the fire". Her letter. Francis Bret Harte. 6370-5,6165-6,6289-X,6409-4,6499-X,6630 ,6004-8,6652-6,6219-9,6438-8,7041-8,6732-8,6385-3,6706-9
"I'm sitting alone on the camping ground...". The great adventure. Brian ("Korongo") Brooke. 6938-X
"I'm sitting here with all my words intact". Silence near an ancient stone. Rosario Castellanos. 7036-1
"I'm sleeping all alone, and hear". Go-kyo-goku. 6852-9
"I'm so afraid - I should be brave". Changeling. Josephine Sievers Birt. 6906-1

"I'm sorry for a fellow if he cannot look..see". The grate fire. Edgar A. Guest. 7033-7
"I'm sorry that I spelt the word". John Greenleaf Whittier. 6066-8
"I'm still retaining my slenderness, my...". The shadow of the years. Berton Braley. 6853-7
"I'm sure 'twould give the world relief". Vermont dried beef. Daniel L. Cady. 6988-6
"I'm talking to you out in the American desert". Drought. Robert Gessner. 6761-1
"I'm tellin' this jest ez I heard it, y' know". Davy and Goliar. William Edward Penney. 6923-1
"I'm the best pal that I ever had". Myself and me. George M. Cohan. 6889-8
"I'm the ghost of an old continental". The ghost of an old continental. Fred Emerson Brooks. 6920-7
"I'm the little red stamp." Sam Walter Foss. 6712-3
I'm the man that kin raise so long. Unknown. 6609-7
"I'm the ugly, early". Moor swan. John Logan. 6966-5
"I'm thinking Charles, 'tis just a year". The wife's appeal. Sara J. ("Grace Greenwood") Lippincott. 6918-5
"I'm thinking just now of nobody". Nobody. Unknown. 6787-5
"I'm thinking of the wooing". Old Spanish song. Unknown (Spanish). 6949-5
"I'm thist a little cripple boy...". The happy little cripple. James Whitcomb Riley. 6990-8
"I'm three I'm balancing". This is my death-dream. Ralph Salisbury. 7005-1
"I'm tired of being sensible". The rebel. Vera Evelyn (Doyle) Willard. 7030-2
"I'm tired of cities with churches and schools". Nostalgia. Elizabeth Lineback Ledig. 6799-9
"I'm tired of patience and stop signs". Decade of rain. Richard Solly. 6857-X
"I'm tired of work, I'm tired of play". Samuel Hoffenstein. 6817-0
"I'm tired!--just tired!/I'm hungry for a...". Just tired! Jessie Ward-Haywood. 6799-9
"I'm tired.../I spoke to the trees". Tired. Thomas Bernhard. 6769-7
"I'm told by good authority". The youngest child. Edgar A. Guest. 6748-4
"I'm travellin' down the Castlereagh...". A bushman's song. Andrew Barton Paterson. 6784-0
"I'm utterly sick of this hateful alliance". The husband's complaint. Unknown. 6787-5
I'm very happy where I am. Dion Boucicault. 6858-8
I'm very young. Unknown. 6312-8,6629-1
"I'm weary of my part". John Dryden. 6238-5
"I'm weary of this weather and I hanker...". A dream of springtime. Eugene Field. 6949-5
I'm with you once again. George Pope Morris. 6183-4;6142-7;6392-6
"I'm wondering what secret of dead days". A potsherd. Jean Milne Gower. 6836-7
I'm wukin' my way back home. Unknown. 6609-7
"I'm yearning again for those hours". Yearning. Janet Muriel Montgomery. 6799-9
I'r hen iaith a'i chaneuon. Walter Dowding. 6360-8
"I's reckon Cap'n Fallet". Cap'n & me. Leon Baker. 6870-7
"I've a geranium, I have a star". A bedroom on the East River. Edith Ballinger Price. 6861-8
"I've a head like a concertina...". Cells. Rudyard Kipling. 6810-3
"I've a head like a violin-case; I've a jaw...". Bolts. Unknown. 7010-8
"I've a mistress, passing fair". To Narcissa. E.P. Train. 7021-3
"I've a pal called Billy Peg-leg...". Peg-leg's fiddle. Bill Adams. 6107-9,6833-2
"I've a rare bit of news for you, Mary Malone". Mulligan's gospel. Annie Herbert. 6912-6
"I've a-got a stocking". The old woman looks in the glass. Ruth Manning-Sanders. 6778-6
"I've allays wanted to travel ever since". I never did git to go to Omaha. Alice Mary Kimball. 6817-0
"I've always been a poor girl, my fortune..bad". Loving Nancy. Unknown. 6826-X
"I've always heard/The good die young". Biography. Anna Lovelace Gorsuch. 6750-6
"I've always known the man-in-the-moon". Milady moon. Ethel M. Merritt. 6764-6
"I've always loved lies and fairytales". Night muse. Nancy McCleery. 6855-3
"I've been a hopeless sinner, but I understand". Hunger. Gamaliel Bradford. 6762-X
"I've been away, to far Chicago". To a girl, upon returning. George Jester. 6817-0
"I've been called sway". It's in the name. Kitty Tsui. 6790-5
"I've been meeting men with big cocks lately". Men. Keith Vacha. 7003-5
I've been roaming. George Darley. 6658-5
"I've been round". A-visitin' the school. Unknown. 6927-4
"I've been thinking some, Keziah". Patchwork philosophy. Unknown. 6917-0
"I've been to Quaker meeting, wife...". The simple church. Unknown. 6921-5
I've been wandering. Emily Bronte. 6253-9
"I've been where the mountains majestically stand". Recompense. Lora Evans Sauer. 6270-9
"I've bin a member most my days...". The meetin'-house is split. Louis Eisenbeis. 6926-6
"I've calmly lived my sunny little life". The hothouse violet speaks. Robert ("Droch") Bridges. 6983-5
"I've conned the daintiest of poets lyrical". To a modern girl. Archibald Douglas. 7021-3
"I've divided" Walther Nowotny. 6769-7
"I've drunk Sicilia's crimson wine!". Sicilian wine. Bayard Taylor. 6976-2
"I've dug a million trenches and I've...". Echoes from camp Upton. Irving Brenner. 7007-8
"I've followed the trail/For many a year". Life's venture. Jesse Sill. 6799-9
"I've given all that I can ever give". Renunciation. Anna Hansen Hayes. 6836-7
I've got a dog. Ethel M. Kelley. 6512-0
"I've got a letter, parson, from my son away..west ". Bill's in the legislature. Unknown. 6964-9
"I've got a letter, parson, from my son...". Bill's in trouble. James Barton Adams. 6889-8
I've got them calves to veal. Holman F. Day. 6510-4
"I've had a heap of fun and I've had a heap of". The contented man. Edgar A. Guest. 6862-6
"I've had a vacancy for years". Room - to let. Rae Angelo Ockerman. 6750-6
"I've had the saddest dream", fr. The borderers. William Wordsworth. 6958-4
"I've heard a dozen farmers say". Getting up the winter wood in Vermont. Daniel L. Cady. 6988-6
"I've heard a good joke of an emerald Pat". Pat and his musket. Unknown. 6825-1
"I've heard a half a dozen times". 'And she is spoke'. Unknown. 6846-4
"I've heard all about musicians". Saxophonetyx. Cyn. Zarco. 6790-5
"I've heard in old times that a sage used to say". Song ("I've heard"). Joseph Stansbury. 6589-9
"I've heard in old times that a sage used..say". Let us be happy as long as we can. Unknown. 6753-0
"I've heard of folks that joined our church". A happy Vermonter. Daniel L. Cady. 6989-4
"I've heard so much of Holstein stock". An old Vermont red cow. Daniel L. Cady. 6989-4
"I've heard that whilst the war was on". Simple remedies in Vermont. Daniel L. Cady. 6989-4
"I've heard the poets praise the spring". Miss Anthrope's ode to spring. Morris Shumiatcher. 6799-9
"I've just bin down ter Thompson's boys". Mother's doughnuts. Charles Follen Adams. 6920-7
"I've just got a letter from ma". Our widowed mother is left alone. Edward R. Huxley. 6885-5
"I've kep' summer boarders for years". Uncle Jotham's boarder. Annie Trumbulll Slosson. 6927-4
"I've known the glaze and glamour". Age. Berton Braley. 6853-7
I've learned to sing. Georgia Douglas Johnson. 6178-8
"I've left Ballymornach a long way behind me". Norah M'Shane. Eliza Cook. 7037-X

"I've left my own old home of homes". The flitting. John Clare. 7020-5
"I've lived to bury my desires." Alexander Pushkin. 6103-6
"I've looked for you/in every wet suit...". The problem with loving a ghost of a sailor. Thylias Moss. 6900-2
"I've made a vow - I'll keep it true". The maiden's vow. Carolina Oliphant, Baroness Nairne. 6960-6
"I've named my clam, Irene, although". Misappellation. Stephanie L. Binckli. 6750-6
"I've never been a president and what I write". Club presidents. Edgar A. Guest. 6748-4
"I've never known a dog to wag". The dog. Edgar A. Guest. 6869-3
"I've never seen a Yankier thing". A Vermont horseshed talk. Daniel L. Cady. 6989-4
"I've never seen such playful, prankish aspens". In happy canon. Jean Milne Gower. 6836-7
"I've not said this before". Failure. Jean Nuchtern. 6857-X
"I've not the heart to pick the violets." Naojo. 6027-7
I've often laughed. Morris Rosenfeld. 7011-6
"I've often thought how sweet 'twould be". Love and science. J. Merritt Matthews. 6936-3
"I've often told you". Whims. A.V. Bower. 6918-5
"I've often wish'd that I could write a book". Proem to a national work, by Wm. & Robt. Whistlecraft. John Hookham Frere. 6980-0
"I've panned from Peru to Point Barrow". The miner. Unknown. 7007-8
"I've passed the grim and threatening warders". L'envoi ("I've passed the grim..."). Bayard Taylor. 6976-2
"I've plucked the berry from the bush". 'Sing on, blithe bird' William Motherwell. 6861-8
"I've put me on my old blue coat I wore...". A veteran. Robert C.V. Meyers. 6926-6
I've put some/ashes in my papa's bed. Unknown. 6375-6
"I've reached my three score years and ten". Life's sunset. Edward R. Huxley. 6885-5
"I've read the settlers, bless their souls". Early days in Vermont. Daniel L. Cady. 6988-6
"I've ren about lately with folk intellectual". Apostacy. Berton Braley. 6853-7
"I've roamed amongst the eternal Alps...". The Alps. Bryan Waller ("Barry Cornwall") Procter. 6749-2
"I've sailed in 'ookers plenty...". The ballad of the 'Eastern crown'. Cicely Fox Smith. 7031-0
"I've sat at banquet tables with the greatest". Best of all meals. Edgar A. Guest. 6748-4
I've searched the year. Konstantin Simenov. 6546-5
"I've seen a dying eye". Emily Dickinson. 6348-9
"I've seen an old man die". Dying leaves. Preston Paine Foster. 6906-1
" 'I've seen some great sights in my life,". Unknown. 6083-8
"I've seen strangers". Parole board. Derek Butler. 6870-7
"I've seen such rolling down". Two rivers and two ships. Benjamin Franklin Taylor. 6815-4
"I've seen thee but a few short hours". Kwoka Mon-in No Betto. 6852-9
"I've seen them in the morning light". Red poppies in the corn. W. Campbell Galraith. 7031-0
"I've set in court on many a day". Beaver Brook, West Windsor, Vermont. Daniel L. Cady. 6989-4
"I've shivered in Saskatchewan...". A story-teller's chantey. Samuel Merwin. 6817-0
"I've sojourned here some sixty years or more". Equality of man. Edward R. Huxley. 6885-5
"I've something of the bulldog in my breed". To A. Patchen Martin. Adam Lindsay Gordon. 6951-7
"I've stood in Margate, on a bridge of size". Margate. Richard Harris ("Thomas Ingoldsby") Barham. 6802-2
"I've taken the police squad outline from...". The immigration act of 1924 Laureen Mar. 6790-5
"I've thought at gentle and ungentle hour". Power and gentleness. Leigh Hunt. 7009-4
I've thought of thee,- I've thought of thee. Nathaniel Parker Willis. 6226-1
"I've thought, at gentle and ungentle hour". Power and greatness. Leigh Hunt. 6980-0
I've travelled far in many lands. Hinton White. 6337-3

"I've travelled in heaps of countries...". The red, red west. Eugene Field. 6949-5
"I've trudged life's highway up and down". When we're all alike. Edgar A. Guest. 7033-7
"I've voyaged on uplifting seas like wine". 'Harbors only entered in the night' Felix Riesenberg. 7007-8
"I've walked with you on the way of the moon". The way of the moon. Jean Milne Gower. 6836-7
"I've wander'd east and west". The old soldier in the Gareloch head. John Stuart Blackie. 6873-1
"I've wandered 'round the world a bit". A Vermont train of cars. Daniel L. Cady. 6989-4
I've wandered in the sunny south. John F. McDonnell. 6591-0,6592-2
"I've wandered to the village, Tom...". Twenty years ago. Unknown. 6909-6
"I've watched you now". To a butterfly ("I've watched you now"). William Wordsworth. 6086-2
"I've won the race". On the jail steps. Agnes Lee. 6897-9
"I've won the two tosses from Prescot". Ten paces off, fr. The road to Avernus. Adam Lindsay Gordon. 6951-7
"I've wondered all my life how 'tis". 'Farming it' in Vermont. Daniel L. Cady. 6988-6
I've worked for a silver shilling. Charles W. Kennedy. 6038-2
"I've worked in the field all day, a plowin'..". Gone with a handsomer man. Will Carleton. 6911-8
"I, as a boy in school—a wondering child". Portraits. Thomas Hornsby Ferril. 6836-7
"I, at Eleusis, saw the finest sight". At Eleusis. Ella Wheeler Wilcox. 6956-8
"I, Atilla, am buried here. No man". Lament of Attila. Katherine Kelley Taylor. 6906-1
I, being born a woman... Edna St. Vincent Millay. 6026-9
"I, Denys of Tarsus, lie dead". Unknown. 6435-3
"I, Epicetus, was a slave...". Unknown. 6251-2
I, Jim Rogers. Stanley Burnshaw. 6042-0
"I, catching fevers that I could not quench". Epitaph for a hospital nurse. Edmund Wilson. 6880-4
"I, conning my missal, o'erheard today". Maid Cicely's steeple-cap - A.D. 1480. Margaret Junkin Preston. 6965-7
"I, from a window where the Meuse is wide". Sedan. Hilaire Belloc. 7031-0,7027-2
"I, Joseph, wonder how this may be". 'Marvel not Joseph, on Mary mild'. Unknown. 6756-5
I, sels. Petr Bezruc. 6763-8,6886-3
"I, the France of the Marseillaise". The barricades. Walter Adolphe Roberts. 6880-4
"I, the great muse, singing a song". How knows he summer comes? Unknown. 6936-3
"I, the poet, mussed my hair". Advice. L.L. H.. 7021-3
I, too. Langston Hughes. 6954-1
"I, too, for light the world explore". Fleet Street Eclogues. John Davidson. 6954-1
"I, too, have a rendezvous with death". Rendezvous. Winifred Stoddard LeBar. 6750-6
"I, too, sing America". I, too. Langston Hughes. 6954-1
"I, who fade with the lilacs". William Griffith. 6102-8, 6076-5,6034-X
"I, who know nothing of water and ships". Prelude to mystery. Vincent Starrett. 7007-8
I, who laughed my youth away. William Griffith. 6034-X
"I, who was always counted, they say". Over the hill from the poor-house. Will Carleton. 6964-9
"I, with whose colours Myra dress'd her head". Fulke Greville; 1st Baron Brooke. 6181-8,6187-7
"I- tearless in my sorrow- dumb and tearless". Desolate. James Abraham Martling. 6952-5
I-have and Oh-had-I. ? Langheim. 6424-8
I.,B.
  The garland of the blessed Virgin Marie. 6563-5
I.,W.F.E.
  Twilight's hour. 6273-3
I.H.B. William Winter. 6431-0
I.M. 'Hamish,' a Scotch terrier. Hilton Brown. 6269-5
I.M. Margaritae Sororis. William Ernest Henley. 6653-4
"I?/Why?". Philosophical poem. Unknown. 6850-2
"Iacchus high in glory, thou whose day". The happy dancer. Aristophanes. 6959-2

IACKE

"Iacke and Ione they thinke no ill" Thomas Campion. 6794-8
Iambicum trimetrum. Edmund Spenser. 6182-6
Iannoula. Unknown (Greek) 6771-9
Ianthe. Walter Savage Landor. 6134-6,6186-9,6208-3,6086-2, 6110-9,6250-4,6658-5
Ianthe's shell. Walter Savage Landor. 6092-7
Ianthe, sleeping. Percy Bysshe Shelley. 6302-0,6385-3,6543-0
Ianthe, the lovely. Unknown. 6328-4
Ibanez, Roberto
　Elegy for the drowned men who return. Lloyd Mallan & Donald Devenish Walsh (tr.). 6759-X
Ibant obscurae. Thomas Edward Brown. 6809-X
Ibarbourou, Juana de
　Rainy night. Rolfe Humphries (tr.). 6759-X
Ibis. Unknown. 6073-0
Ibis ad crucem. William White. 6868-5
Iblis and Abraham. Sir Edwin Arnold. 6848-0
Ibn 'Unain
　"Ask the backs of horses on the day of battle". A.J. Arberry (tr.). 6766-2
Ibn A'isha
　The apricot tree. A.J. Arberry (tr.). 6362-4
　Violet. A.J. Arberry (tr.). 6362-4
Ibn Abd Rabbihi
　Favourites. A.J. Arberry (tr.). 6362-4
　Modest blush. A.J. Arberry (tr.). 6362-4
　Ritual. A.J. Arberry (tr.). 6362-4
Ibn Abdul Ghafur
　Coat of mail. A.J. Arberry (tr.). 6362-4
Ibn Abdun
　Fate. A.J. Arberry (tr.). 6362-4
　Poor lodgings. A.J. Arberry (tr.). 6362-4
Ibn Abdus
　A white horse with a crimson flash. A.J. Arberry (tr.). 6362-4
Ibn Abi Bishr
　Sunshine. A.J. Arberry (tr.). 6362-4
Ibn Abi Ruh
　Night of joy. A.J. Arberry (tr.). 6362-4
Ibn Abi l Khayal
　Alchemy. A.J. Arberry (tr.). 6362-4
Ibn Adha
　On taking up a humble place at court. A.J. Arberry (tr.). 6362-4
Ibn al-Abbar
　Gilliflower. A.J. Arberry (tr.). 6362-4
　Jessamine. A.J. Arberry (tr.). 6362-4
　The wheel. A.J. Arberry (tr.). 6362-4
Ibn al-Arabi
　Beauty in rags. A.J. Arberry (tr.). 6362-4
　Sand. A.J. Arberry (tr.). 6362-4
Ibn al-Attar
　White and black. A.J. Arberry (tr.). 6362-4
Ibn al-Bain
　Storm. A.J. Arberry (tr.). 6362-4
　Virgin earth. A.J. Arberry (tr.). 6362-4
Ibn al-Batti
　Eye and heart. A.J. Arberry (tr.). 6362-4
　The hypocrites. A.J. Arberry (tr.). 6362-4
Ibn al-Faras
　Moon of beauty. A.J. Arberry (tr.). 6362-4
Ibn al-Farid
　"We drank upon the remembrance of the beloved". A.J. Arberry (tr.). 6766-2
Ibn al-Haddad
　Apology. A.J. Arberry (tr.). 6362-4
　Compliment. A.J. Arberry (tr.). 6362-4
Ibn al-Hajj
　The beard. A.J. Arberry (tr.). 6362-4
　Clemency. A.J. Arberry (tr.). 6362-4
　Odi et amo. A.J. Arberry (tr.). 6362-4
Ibn al-Hammara
　Eyelashes. A.J. Arberry (tr.). 6362-4
　The house. A.J. Arberry (tr.). 6362-4
　On the death of his wife. A.J. Arberry (tr.). 6362-4
Ibn al-Imam
　Hopes. A.J. Arberry (tr.). 6362-4
Ibn al-Khabbaza
　The king who died young. A.J. Arberry (tr.). 6362-4
　The striking of the tent. A.J. Arberry (tr.). 6362-4
Ibn al-Khaiyat
　"This pretty, twanging boy poured out for me". A.J. Arberry (tr.). 6766-2
Ibn al-Labbana
　Patronage. A.J. Arberry (tr.). 6362-4
Ibn al-Missisi
　Fragment ("Praise not"). A.J. Arberry (tr.). 6362-4
Ibn al-Mu'tazz
　"When the horizon burst forth with light". A.J. Arberry (tr.). 6766-2
Ibn al-Qabila
　Gazelle. A.J. Arberry (tr.). 6362-4
Ibn al-Qabturnu
　The hawk. A.J. Arberry (tr.). 6362-4
　The party. A.J. Arberry (tr.). 6362-4
Ibn al-Qaffun
　Family tree. A.J. Arberry (tr.). 6362-4
Ibn al-Qutiya
　Lilies and roses. A.J. Arberry (tr.). 6362-4
　The walnut. A.J. Arberry (tr.). 6362-4
Ibn al-Ra'i'a
　The fountain. A.J. Arberry (tr.). 6362-4
Ibn al-Rumi
　"Sweet sleep has been barred from my eyes". A.J. Arberry (tr.). 6766-2
Ibn al-Sabuni
　The mirror. A.J. Arberry (tr.). 6362-4
　The red gown. A.J. Arberry (tr.). 6362-4
Ibn al-Talla
　The artichoke. A.J. Arberry (tr.). 6362-4
Ibn al-Tarawa
　A saki refusing to drink wine. A.J. Arberry (tr.). 6362-4
Ibn al-Yamani
　Wings of wine. A.J. Arberry (tr.). 6362-4
Ibn al-Zaqqaq
　The bloody sword. A.J. Arberry (tr.). 6362-4
　Exposure. A.J. Arberry (tr.). 6362-4
　Frankicense. A.J. Arberry (tr.). 6362-4
　Night of bliss. A.J. Arberry (tr.). 6362-4
　The portent. A.J. Arberry (tr.). 6362-4
　Rose-petals. A.J. Arberry (tr.). 6362-4
　Star flowers. A.J. Arberry (tr.). 6362-4
Ibn Alalaf Alnaharwany
　To a cat. J.D. Carlyle (tr.). 6511-2
Ibn Ammar
　In praise of the king. A.J. Arberry (tr.). 6362-4
　Poet's pride. A.J. Arberry (tr.). 6362-4
　Ransom. A.J. Arberry (tr.). 6362-4
　Spare. A.J. Arberry (tr.). 6362-4
Ibn Atiya
　The night traveller. A.J. Arberry (tr.). 6362-4
Ibn Baqi
　Bacchanal. A.J. Arberry (tr.). 6362-4
　The champion. A.J. Arberry (tr.). 6362-4
　Love's evidence. A.J. Arberry (tr.). 6362-4
Ibn Bassam
　Mist. A.J. Arberry (tr.). 6362-4
Ibn Billita
　Dawn. A.J. Arberry (tr.). 6362-4
　Drunken beauty. A.J. Arberry (tr.). 6362-4
　Marguerite. A.J. Arberry (tr.). 6362-4
　Sails. A.J. Arberry (tr.). 6362-4
Ibn Burd
　Blue and gold. A.J. Arberry (tr.). 6362-4
　Daybreak. A.J. Arberry (tr.). 6362-4
　Moon in mist. A.J. Arberry (tr.). 6362-4
Ibn Darraj
　Lilies. A.J. Arberry (tr.). 6362-4
　Night and day. A.J. Arberry (tr.). 6362-4
　Ship in storm. A.J. Arberry (tr.). 6362-4
Ibn Darraj al-Andalusi
　The wing of separation. J.B. Trend (tr.). 7039-6
Ibn Faddal
　The young pilgrim. A.J. Arberry (tr.). 6362-4
Ibn Faraj
　Continence. A.J. Arberry (tr.). 6362-4
Ibn Farsan
　Battle song. A.J. Arberry (tr.). 6362-4

Ibn Ghaiyath
  White hair. A.J. Arberry (tr.). 6362-4
Ibn Haiyun
  Inverted eyelids. A.J. Arberry (tr.). 6362-4
  Moles. A.J. Arberry (tr.). 6362-4
Ibn Hamdin
  Ebony and ivory. A.J. Arberry (tr.). 6362-4
Ibn Hamdis
  Early pleasure. A.J. Arberry (tr.). 6362-4
  Flowing stream. A.J. Arberry (tr.). 6362-4
  Moon in eclipse. A.J. Arberry (tr.). 6362-4
  Night visitor. A.J. Arberry (tr.). 6362-4
  Water-lilies. A.J. Arberry (tr.). 6362-4
Ibn Hani
  Aspiration. A.J. Arberry (tr.). 6362-4
  Aubade. A.J. Arberry (tr.). 6362-4
  Royal bounty. A.J. Arberry (tr.). 6362-4
  Victory. A.J. Arberry (tr.). 6362-4
Ibn Hariq
  The galley. A.J. Arberry (tr.). 6362-4
Ibn Hazm
  Absent friends. A.J. Arberry (tr.). 6362-4
  Mutability. A.J. Arberry (tr.). 6362-4
  Slander. A.J. Arberry (tr.). 6362-4
Ibn Iyad
  Beardless youth. A.J. Arberry (tr.). 6362-4
  The glance. A.J. Arberry (tr.). 6362-4
Ibn Jakha
  Serpent curls. A.J. Arberry (tr.). 6362-4
Ibn Khafaja
  Carousal. A.J. Arberry (tr.). 6362-4
  Lovely maid. A.J. Arberry (tr.). 6362-4
  Lovely river. A.J. Arberry (tr.). 6362-4
  "Oft-times a guest of a phantom of one". A.J. Arberry (tr.). 6766-2
  The roan. A.J. Arberry (tr.). 6362-4
  The swimmer. A.J. Arberry (tr.). 6362-4
  Treachery. A.J. Arberry (tr.). 6362-4
Ibn Kharuf
  Aleppo. A.J. Arberry (tr.). 6362-4
  The dancer. A.J. Arberry (tr.). 6362-4
  The tailor's apprentice. A.J. Arberry (tr.). 6362-4
  Wages. A.J. Arberry (tr.). 6362-4
Ibn Lubbal
  The inkstand. A.J. Arberry (tr.). 6362-4
  Schooners. A.J. Arberry (tr.). 6362-4
Ibn Maimun
  Immunity. A.J. Arberry (tr.). 6362-4
Ibn Malik (of Granada)
  Algeciras seen over a stormy sea. A.J. Arberry (tr.). 6362-4
  Sister sun. A.J. Arberry (tr.). 6362-4
Ibn Malik (of Murcia)
  In the mosque. A.J. Arberry (tr.). 6362-4
Ibn Mujbar
  Departure. A.J. Arberry (tr.). 6362-4
  Red wine in a black glass. A.J. Arberry (tr.). 6362-4
Ibn Munakhkhal
  Dialogue. A.J. Arberry (tr.). 6362-4
Ibn Muqana
  Dawn. A.J. Arberry (tr.). 6362-4
Ibn Qadi Mila
  Fruit tree. A.J. Arberry (tr.). 6362-4
  The lute. A.J. Arberry (tr.). 6362-4
Ibn Quzman
  The radish. A.J. Arberry (tr.). 6362-4
Ibn Rashig
  Rain at festival. A.J. Arberry (tr.). 6362-4
Ibn Rashiq
  Continuing love. A.J. Arberry (tr.). 6362-4
  Debauch. A.J. Arberry (tr.). 6362-4
  The down. A.J. Arberry (tr.). 6362-4
  Pretences. A.J. Arberry (tr.). 6362-4
  Rain at festival. A.J. Arberry (tr.). 6362-4
Ibn Sa'id (of Alcala La Real)
  Amulet. A.J. Arberry (tr.). 6362-4
  Archery. A.J. Arberry (tr.). 6362-4
  Betrayal. A.J. Arberry (tr.). 6362-4
  A black horse with a white breast. A.J. Arberry (tr.). 6362-4
  Changes. A.J. Arberry (tr.). 6362-4
  The comely warrior. A.J. Arberry (tr.). 6362-4
  Courtship. A.J. Arberry (tr.). 6362-4
  The crow. A.J. Arberry (tr.). 6362-4
  Dawn song. A.J. Arberry (tr.). 6362-4
  The guardians. A.J. Arberry (tr.). 6362-4
  The knights. A.J. Arberry (tr.). 6362-4
  Love's storm. A.J. Arberry (tr.). 6362-4
  My miser. A.J. Arberry (tr.). 6362-4
  Noblesse oblige. A.J. Arberry (tr.). 6362-4
  The nuptials. A.J. Arberry (tr.). 6362-4
  The old toper. A.J. Arberry (tr.). 6362-4
  The Palanquins. A.J. Arberry (tr.). 6362-4
  The river. A.J. Arberry (tr.). 6362-4
  Royal bounty. A.J. Arberry (tr.). 6362-4
  Sea of night. A.J. Arberry (tr.). 6362-4
  The setting sun. A.J. Arberry (tr.). 6362-4
  The stolen penknife. A.J. Arberry (tr.). 6362-4
  Strategy. A.J. Arberry (tr.). 6362-4
  Sunlight on the sea. A.J. Arberry (tr.). 6362-4
  The tale of battle. A.J. Arberry (tr.). 6362-4
  The virgin. A.J. Arberry (tr.). 6362-4
  Wave wing. A.J. Arberry (tr.). 6362-4
  The wind. A.J. Arberry (tr.). 6362-4
  Wine at dawn. A.J. Arberry (tr.). 6362-4
  A yellow horse with a blaze and a black mane. A.J. Arberry (tr.). 6362-4
  A yellow horse with a blaze. A.J. Arberry (tr.). 6362-4
Ibn Sa'id (of Seville)
  Invitation. A.J. Arberry (tr.). 6362-4
Ibn Saad al-Khair
  Water. A.J. Arberry (tr.). 6362-4
Ibn Safar
  Almeria. A.J. Arberry (tr.). 6362-4
  Carousal. A.J. Arberry (tr.). 6362-4
  Flow and ebb. A.J. Arberry (tr.). 6362-4
  The ship. A.J. Arberry (tr.). 6362-4
  Wine at morning. A.J. Arberry (tr.). 6362-4
Ibn Sahl
  "The earth had put on a green robe". A.J. Arberry (tr.). 6766-2
Ibn Sara
  Aubergines. A.J. Arberry (tr.). 6362-4
  The benefactor. A.J. Arberry (tr.). 6362-4
  Fire. A.J. Arberry (tr.). 6362-4
  Oranges. A.J. Arberry (tr.). 6362-4
  The quince. A.J. Arberry (tr.). 6362-4
  The youth. A.J. Arberry (tr.). 6362-4
Ibn Shakil
  Ugliness. A.J. Arberry (tr.). 6362-4
Ibn Sharaf
  Chess. A.J. Arberry (tr.). 6362-4
  Concert. A.J. Arberry (tr.). 6362-4
  The protector. A.J. Arberry (tr.). 6362-4
Ibn Shuhaid
  Rain and lightning. A.J. Arberry (tr.). 6362-4
  Stolen pleasure. A.J. Arberry (tr.). 6362-4
  Sword and lance. A.J. Arberry (tr.). 6362-4
Ibn Wahbun
  Fate's malignity. A.J. Arberry (tr.). 6362-4
  On hearing al-Mutanabbi praised. A.J. Arberry (tr.). 6362-4
Ibn Zaidun
  Cruel masters. A.J. Arberry (tr.). 6362-4
  Fidelity. A.J. Arberry (tr.). 6362-4
  Flirtation. A.J. Arberry (tr.). 6362-4
  "Indeed I remembered you yearningly". A.J. Arberry (tr.). 6766-2
Ibn Zakur
  "Pass round the cups of the wine of the lips' deep red. A.J. Arberry (tr.). 6766-2
Ibn Zuhr
  "Resign the affair to destiny". A.J. Arberry (tr.). 6766-2
Ibsen, Henrik
  Ase's death, fr. Peer Gynt. 6585-6
  Brand speaks. 6730-1
  In the orchard. Sir Edmund Gosse (tr.). 7039-6
  The petrel. 6732-8
  Solveig's song. 6732-8

The swan. 6732-8
Ibycus
An epilogue to Polycrates. Cecil Maurice Bowra (tr.). 6435-3
In the spring. Walter Headlam (tr.). 6435-3
Love. Cecil Maurice Bowra (tr.). 6435-3
"Only in spring do the quince-flowers quiver". F.L. Lucas (tr.). 6251-2

Icarus. Evelyn Ahrend. 6850-2
Icarus. James Wallis Eastburn (atr.) 6752-2
Icarus. Valentin Iremonger. 6930-4
Icarus. Harry Lyman Koopman. 6861-8
Icarus. Earl B. Marlatt. 7001-9
Icarus. Bayard Taylor. 6976-2
Icarus. Unknown. 6186-9
"Icarus has stirred beneath his mouldering...". 'We' James H. S. Melville. 7019-1
Icarus in November. Alec Brock Stevenson. 7017-5
"Icarus is fallen here, the marvelous boy". A sonnet ("Icarus"). Philippe Desportes. 6978-9
"Icarus made himself wings". Icarus. Earl B. Marlatt. 7001-9
Icarus, sels. Unknown. 6317-9
Ice. Stephen Spender. 6209-1
"Ice built, ice bound, and ice bounded!". Alaska. Joaquin Miller. 6946-0
"Ice has been cracking all day". Spring. Michael Hogan. 6870-7
The ice palace. William Cowper. 6438-8
The ice, fr. Thoroughfares. Wilfred Wilson Gibson. 6199-0
"The ice, weeping, breaks". The ghost whose lips were warm. Edith Sitwell. 7000-0
The ice-cart. Wilfred Wilson Gibson. 6395-0,6476-0,6668-2
The ice-cream man. Orgill Cogie. 6269-5
Ice-fishing. Denise Pendleton. 6900-2
Ice-fishing in winter. John Harrington Keene. 7035-3
The iceberg. Edgar Fawcett. 6358-6
The iceberg. J.O. Rockwell. 6752-2
Icebergs. William Prescott Foster. 6833-2
Icebergs. Henri Michaux. 6758-1
Icebergs. Estelle Rooks. 6850-2
"Icebergs, without guardrail, without...". Icebergs. Henri Michaux. 6758-1
The iceboat. Alice Ward Bailey. 7035-3
The icebound swans. Sean O'Faolain. 6582-1
Iceland. Jonas Hallgrimsson. 6854-5
Iceland. Bjarni Thorarensen. 6854-5
Iceland. Steingrimur Thorsteinsson. 6854-5
Iceland first seen. William Morris. 6828-6
Iceland first seen. William Morris. 6110-9
Iceland first seen, sels. William Morris. 6123-0;6179-6
"Iceland! gracious Fron". Iceland. Jonas Hallgrimsson. 6854-5
Iceland's song. Grimur Thomsen. 6854-5
Iceland's song. Grimur Thomsen. 6283-0
"Ices- programmes- lemonade!". Transpontine. Ernest Radford. 6770-0
"Ices-programmes-lemonade!". Transpontine. Ernest Radford. 6875-8
"Ich am of Irlaunde". I am from Ireland. Unknown. 6881-2
'Ich bin dein'. Unknown. 6724-7
"Ich glaube, dass die schone Welt regiere". Mein glaube. Carl Friedrich Kayser. 6847-2
"Ich have house and land...". Unknown. 6334-9
"Ich stand auf hohen Berge". Unknown. 6547-3
Ichabod. John Greenleaf Whittier. 6006-4,6102-8,6176-1, 6271-7,6302-0,6385 ,6243-1,6632-1,6735-2,6219-9,6121-4,6212 ,6126-5,6088-1,6250-4,6076-5,6288-1,6513 , 6438-8,6309-8,6396-9
"Icham of Irlaunde". I am of Ireland. Unknown. 6930-4
The ichneumon. Oppian. 6435-3
'Ici repose.' Bernard Freeman Trotter. 6337-3
Icicle drops. Arthur John Lockhart. 6795-6
An icicle. Irene Meybert. 6396-9
Icicles. William White. 6868-5
Icicles on trees. Catherine L. Finley. 6178-8
Icilius on Virginia's seizure. Thomas Babington Macaulay, 1st Baron Macaulay. 6606-2
"Ickity, pickity, ally gadaw". Unknown. 7028-0
Icon. Mark Osaki. 6790-5

Iconoclast. Mary Brent Whiteside. 6841-3
The iconoclast.. Rose Terry Cooke. 6600-3
The iconoclasts. Terry B. Dinkel. 6906-1
Ida Red. Unknown. 6609-7
Idas and Marpessa, sels. Howard Vigne Sutherland. 6836-7
The idea of ancestry. Etheridge Knight. 6870-7
An idea of wealth. Christopher Marlowe. 6102-8
The idea realised. John Donne. 6935-5
Idea, sels. Michael Drayton. 7039-6
Idea, sels. Michael Drayton. 6879-0
Idea, sels. Michael Drayton. 6198-2,6317-9,6378-0,6194-X, 6430-2
An idea. Januario Puruganan. 6799-9,6906-1
The idea. Agnes Mary F. ("Madame Duclaux") Robinson. 6648-8
Ideal. Padraic Pearse. 6096-X,6292-X,6172-9
Ideal. Padraic Pearse. 7039-6
Ideal. William Wordsworth. 6322-5
"Ideal although our homage be and vain". Gordon (I). Sir William Watson. 7015-9
Ideal and real. Unknown. 6698-4
The ideal and the real. I. Edgar Jones. 6915-0
Ideal beauty. E.S. Hall. 6768-9
An ideal future. T.A. Harcourt. 6273-3
The ideal general. Archilochus. 6435-3
The ideal girl. A.W. Curtis. 6523-6
The ideal husband to his wife. Sam Walter Foss. 6089-7
The ideal India. Fred Shelley Ryman. 6919-3
The ideal is the real. Ann Preston. 6925-8
Ideal love. Michelangelo Buonarroti. 6321-7,6429-9
Ideal memory. William James Dawson. 6656-9
An ideal with a Roman nose. Unknown. 6916-9
The ideal young man. Unknown. 6523-6
An ideal. Adelaide Anne Procter. 6957-6
The ideal. Gertrude Alger. 6798-0
The ideal. Katharine Lee Bates. 6798-0
The ideal. William Peter. 6980-0
The ideal. Percy Bysshe Shelley. 6087-0
The ideal. Unknown. 6109-5,6572-4
Idealism and realism. Gustaf Froding. 6045-5
The idealist. Robert Service. 6159-1,6583-X
Idealists. Katharine Lee Bates. 7001-9
Idealists. Alfred Kreymborg. 6102-8,6338-1,6556-2,6393-4, 6076-5,6030-7,6161-3
Ideality. Hartley Coleridge. 6656-9
Ideals. Louis J. Magee. 7004-3
Ideals for our country. Julia Ward Howe. 6461-2
Ideas. Geoffrey Winthrop Young. 6233-4
Ideas mirrour, sel. Michael Drayton. 6958-4
Ideas mirrour, sels. Michael Drayton. 6378-0
Ideas of good and evil, auguries of innocence. William Blake. 6198-2,6254-0
Idees Napoleoniennes. William Edmonstoune Aytoun. 6278-4
Idem Latine redditum. William Cowper. 6814-6
Idem Latine redditum. William Cowper. 6814-6
Identity. Thomas Bailey Aldrich. 6076-5,6102-8,6464-7,6468-8,7041-8
Identity. Mary Sinton Leitch. 6042-0
Identity. Gertrude Huntington McGiffert. 6838-3
Identity. Edla Park Peck. 6836-7
Identity card. Yannis Ritsos. 6803-0
Idiot. Allen Tate. 6209-1,6375-6
The idiot boy, sels. William Wordsworth. 6369-1
The idiot boy. Robert Southey. 6344-6,6385-3
The idiot boy. Unknown. 6406-X
The idiot lad. Robert Overton. 6924-X,6744-1
An idiot's gallantry. John F. Nicholls. 6921-5
The idiot. Frederick Victor Branford. 6778-6
The idiot. Frederick Victor Branford. 6070-6
The idiot. David Osborne Hamilton. 6036-6
The idiot. Frederick Peterson. 6482-5
"Idiots will prate and prate of suicide". Leonard Bacon. 6619-4
Idle. Alice Cary. 6969-X
Idle Charon. Eugene Lee-Hamilton. 7015-9
Idle Charon. Eugene Lee-Hamilton. 6301-2
Idle Charon. Eugene Lee-Hamilton. 7015-9
Idle fears. Alice Cary. 6969-X
The idle flowers. Robert Bridges. 6487-6,6125-7
Idle Fyn. Unknown. 6125-7

Idle hands. Neva DuMont. 6799-9
"Idle I dreamed and dreamed and dreamed of old". Retribution. Gertrude Huntington McGiffert. 6838-3
The idle lake. Edmund Spenser. 6501-5
The idle life I lead. Robert Bridges. 6187-7,6339-X,6487-6
"An idle poet, here and there". Coventry Patmore. 6187-7
The idle shepherd-boys. William Wordsworth. 6502-3
The idle singer. William Morris. 6385-3,6102-8,6560-0
Idle to grieve. Duncan Campbell Scott. 6501-5
Idle verse. Henry Vaughan. 6378-0,6430-2
Idle words. Unknown. 6752-2
Idleness. George Gordon, 6th Baron Byron. 6294-6
Idleness. Silas Weir Mitchell. 6431-0
Idleness. Thomas Sturge Moore. 6477-9
"An idler is a watch that wants both hands". An idler. William Cowper. 6861-8
The idler. Jones Very. 6309-8
The idler. H.E. Warner. 6385-3
The idlers. Emily Pauline ("Tekahionwake") Johnson. 6837-5
"Idles the night wind through the...firs". Moonset. Emily Pauline ("Tekahionwake") Johnson. 6837-5
"Idly, rajah, dost thou reason thus". Freedom of the will. Robert Southey. 6867-7
The idol-maker prays. Arthur Guiterman. 6556-2,6250-4
The idol. Louise Driscoll. 6076-5,6102-8
Idols. Clara T. Brown. 6906-1
Idyl. Amanda Benjamin Hall. 6607-0
Idyl. Alfred Mombert. 7039-6
Idyl (1). Bion. 6949-5
Idyl (2). Bion. 6949-5
Idyl 008, sels. Theocritus. 6484-1
Idyl 009, sels. Theocritus. 6484-1
An idyl of the farm. Thomas O'Hagan. 6115-X
Idyl of the ocean. Marion Short. 6707-7
An idyl of the period. George A. Baker. 6517-1,6392-6
An idyl of the strap. Arthur Hobson Quinn. 6936-3
Idyl, fr. In Tuscany. Cora Fabri. 6876-6
An idyl. Charles Gurdon Buck. 7025-6,6675-5
An idyl. Henry Hunter Welsh. 6936-3
An idyll of Platte and Leene. Unknown. 6089-7,6440-X
Idyll of the rose. Decimus Magnus Ausonius. 6649-6
An idyll. Padraic Colum. 6320-9
An idyll. Opal Louise Jackson. 6249-0
Idylls. Henry Tyrrell. 7041-8
The idylls of the king, sels. Alfred Lord Tennyson. 6154-0, 6657-7,6123-0,6669-0,6264-4,6655
Idyls of the king. Alfred Lord Tennyson. 6977-0
Iedgarj
  Sable theology. 6139-7
Iesu. George Herbert. 6933-9
If. Carolyn Sherwin Bailey. 6466-3
If. Mortimer Collins. 6337-3,6427-2,6440-X
If. Mortimer Collins. 6802-7
If. Emily Dickinson. 6473-6
If. H.C. Dodge. 6089-7,6652-6
If. Cora Fabri. 6876-6
If. Isabella Howe Fiske. 6130-3
If. William Dean Howells. 6309-8,6431-0
If. J. 6118-4
If. Rudyard Kipling. 6138-9,6337-3,6427-2,6476-0,6534-1, 6291 ,6102-8,6107-9,6104-4,6464-7,6655-0,6634 ,6421-3
If. James Jeffrey Roche. 6652-6
If. Alexey Tolstoy. 6732-8
If. Unknown. 6902-9
If. Unknown. 6913-4
If. Unknown. 6861-8
If. Unknown. 6089-7,6226-1
If. Unknown. 6690-9
If. Ella Wheeler Wilcox. 6583-X
"If '80's scribe had to express". To Vice-President Roosevelt. Frederic Almy. 6995-9
"If 'tis sweet to have the record". Lines written in an album (1). James Abraham Martling. 6952-5
"If 'Trane had only seen/her body". Number 25. Doughtry ("Doc") Long Jr.. 7024-8
If ("If I were fire I'd seek the frozen north"). John Kendrick Bangs. 6291-1
"If a daughter you have, she's the plague". Song ("If a daughter"). Richard Brinsley Sheridan. 6152-4

"If a feller's been a-straddle". When you're throwed. Unknown. 7010-8
If a man die. Florence Hamilton. 6337-3
If a man die shall he live again?, fr. A blue wave... John Richard Moreland. 6337-3;6144-3
"If a man who turnips cries". Unknown. 6363-2
"If Adam fell in the days of innocency". William Shakespeare. 6238-5
"If a stranger passed the ten of Hoseyn, he...". Muleykeh. Robert Browning. 7010-8
"If all be true that I do think". A catch. Henry Aldrich. 6933-9
If all be true that I do think. Thomas Bailey Aldrich. 6563-5
"If all our thoughts were silver". The ship o' dreams. Frances Evertson. 6799-9
"If all the land were apple-pie". If. Unknown. 6902-9
"If all the lands that stretch to the side...". To - (2). Georgianna Livinston. 6906-1
"If all the pens that ever poets held" Christopher Marlowe. 6935-5
If all the pens that ever poets held, fr. Tamburlaine. Christopher Marlowe. 6125-7
"If all the seas were one sea". Unknown. 6904-5
"If all the ships I have at sea". My love ship. Ella Wheeler Wilcox. 6963-0
If all the skies. Henry Van Dyke. 6730-1
"If all the tears thou madest mine". Margaret L. Woods. 6844-8
If all the voices of men. Horace L. Traubel. 6102-8,6076-5
"If all the women in the town were bundled...". The agricultural Irish girl. Unknown. 6930-4
If all the world. Dollie Radford. 6656-9
"If all the world and love were young". The shepherdess replies. Sir Walter Raleigh. 6830-8
"If all the world and love were young". Sir Walter Raleigh. 6181-8
"If all the world was apple-pie". Unknown. 6904-5
If all the world were apple pie. Mother Goose. 6135-4
If all the world were apple pie, fr. Mother Goose. Unknown. 6133-8,6363-2,6401-9,6466-3,6452-3
"If all the world were apple-pie". If. Unknown. 6861-8
"If all the world were paper". Unknown. 6228-8,6315-2,6563-5
"If all the world were playing holidays". Suppose. William Shakespeare. 6861-8
"If all the year was summertime". An answer. Ella Wheeler Wilcox. 6956-7
If all the young maidens. Patrick Joseph McCall. 6090-0
"If all the young maidens were blackbirds...". Ballade of colleens. Hamish Maclaren. 6779-4
If all who hate would love us. James Newton Matthews. 6260-1;6583-X
"If amorous faith, a heart of guileless ways". Signs of love. Francesco Petrarch. 7039-6
"If an apple seed" Richard George-Murray. 7003-5
If and if. Alice Cary. 6969-X
"If any hath the heart to kill" Thomas Campion. 6794-8
"If any man would come after me" Edwin McNeill Poteat. 6144-3
"If any stranger thinks Vermont". That's Vermont. Daniel L. Cady. 6988-6
"If any woman of us all". Magdalen. Harriet Prescott Spofford. 7041-8
If anybody's friend be dead. Emily Dickinson. 6288-1
"If anywhere in the world". Tower beyond tragedy, sels. Robinson Jeffers. 6808-1
"If at least this pain helped". The shriek. Renata Pallotini. 7036-1
If aught can make me seek. Philip James Bailey. 6066-8
"If aught of history you've been told". Pompey's Christmas. Carolyn Wells. 6882-0
"If aught of oaten stop, or pastoral song". William Collins. 6187-7
"If aught of worth be in my psalms". Envoi. Arthur Shearly Cripps. 6800-6
"If aught that stumbles in my speech". Abstemia. Gelett Burgess. 6902-9
"If Bethlehem were here today". Christmas morning. Elizabeth Madox Roberts. 6891-X
If beauty came to you. William Kean Seymour. 6884-7

IF

"If being morticed with a dream" Edward Estlin Cummings. 6531-7
"If breezes on Inaba's peak". Ariara No Yuki-hira. 6852-9
"If but with my pen I could draw him". The pale operator. Morris Rosenfeld. 7011-6
"If by chance you should look...". The conservative man. Edward R. Huxley. 6885-5
"If care do cause men cry, why do I not complain?" Henry Howard, Earl of Surrey. 6584-8
"If chance assign'd." Sir Thomas Wyatt. 6584-8
"If chance some pensive stranger hither led". Matilda. William Lisle Bowles. 6980-0
"If chaste and pure deoution of my youth." Michael Drayton. 6586-4
"If chaste and pure devotion of my youth". Sonnet ("If chaste"). Michael Drayton. 6436-1
"If courage thrives on reeking slaughter". The soldier speaks. John Galsworthy. 7027-2
If crossed with all mishaps be my poor life. William Drummond of Hawthornden. 6194-X
If Cynthia be a queen. Sir Walter Raleigh. 6584-8
"If daffodils could only blow". If only. Geoffrey Johnson. 6761-1
"If Dante breathes on me his awful breath". Dante and Ariosto. Thomas Edward Brown. 6809-X
"If death had come here with me, to New Haven". Nocturne in which death speaks. Xavier Villaurrutia. 6759-X
If death were good. May C. [Mary] Gillington) Byron. 6800-6
"If deep within your heart there's a care". Nature's balm. Blanche H. Griffin. 6894-4
"If doughty deeds my lady please." Robert (Cunningham) Graham. 6302-0,6385-3,6246-6,6328-4,6639-9,6732
If Easter be not true. Henry H. Barstow. 6337-3
If Easter eggs would hatch. Douglas Malloch. 6891-X
"If England to itself do rest but true," fr. King John. William Shakespeare. 6934-7
"If down his throat a man should choose". An unsuspected fact. Edward Cannon. 6902-9
"If e'er again my spirit be allowed". Hope of future communion with nature. Felicia Dorothea Hemans. 6973-8
"If e'er for human bliss or woe". To my mother. Felicia Dorothea Hemans. 6973-8
"If echoes from the fitful past". Abstrosophy. Gelett Burgess. 6902-9
"If Elphie had been slow to think". The elephant tries to rescue the jackass. Marshal E. Grover. 6799-9
If ever I marry, I'll marry a maid. Unknown. 6182-6
If ever I see. Lydia Maria Child. 6373-X,6452-3,6456-6, 6510-4
"If ever a sailor was fond of good sport". Jack's fidelity. Charles Dibdin. 6833-2
"If ever chance or choice thy footsteps lead". The flying tailor. James Hogg. 6802-2
"If ever happiness hath lodged with man". Poetic communion. William Wordsworth. 7020-5
"If ever I in Rome should dwell". Rome. Bessie Parkes. 6624-0
"If ever I shall go to hell". To a girl with two eyes. George Jester. 6817-0
"If ever in the sylvan shade". To his lute. Horace. 6949-5
"If ever justice with her iron hand". The eighth ode of the second book of Horace imitated. Thomas Warton (the Elder). 6962-2
"If ever man might him avaunt." Sir Thomas Wyatt. 6584-8
"If ever sorrow spoke from soul that loves." Henry Constable. 6182-6,6586-4
If ever time shall come. Alison [or Allison] Brown. 6449-3
"If ever you come to Phthia...". Unknown. 6251-2
If ever you should walk away. Lucia M. Pitts. 6178-8
"If every critic, without stint". Aging poet, fr. Poetical sketches. Robert Hillyer. 6761-1
"If every person saw like me". Just like me. Dorothy Lewis Maddox. 6799-9
"If faithfull soules be alike glorifi'd". John Donne. 6562-7
"If fancy do not all deceive". A day dream. Phoebe Cary. 6969-X
"If Faraday's or Liebig's art". The counsel's tear. Unknown. 6878-2
"If fancy would favour." Sir Thomas Wyatt. 6584-8
"If fathers knew but how to leave". Unknown. 6182-6,6187-7
"If for your oath broken, or word lightly...". To Barine. Horace. 6949-5
"If fortune, with a smiling face". Unknown. 6109-5
"If from the sea of passion, this all...". 'If' Winthrop M. Crowell. 6798-0
"If from your own the dimpled hands had...". When Bessie died. James Whitcomb Riley. 7041-8
"If Gideon's fleece, which drench'd with dew". To a young friend on his arriving at Cambridge wet. William Cowper. 6814-6
"If God should come and say to me". A wish. Edgar A. Guest. 6862-6
"If God would turn to gold the tears". To Iceland. Sigurdur Julius Johannesson. 6854-5
"If Granada bells were ringing". The first Thanksgiving. Hezekiah Butterworth. 7002-7
If gold could lenthen life. Unknown. 6328-4
If Gray had had to write his elegy in the cemetery... Sir John Collings ("Solomon Eagle") Squire. 6722-0
If grief for grief can touch thee. Emily Bronte. 6908-8
"If haloed Christ still walked to-day". Old Ellen. Isabel Fiske Conant. 7038-8
"If happiness has not her seat". Robert Burns. 6238-5
"If he could only stay a little boy". Prayer for a boy with a kite. Dorothy P. Albaugh. 6750-6
If he should come. Lilith Lorraine. 6144-3,6337-3
If he should come. Edwin Markham. 6144-3;6335-7
"If he should come again..." Maurice Maeterlinck. 6343-8
"If he that erst the form so lively drew." Henry Howard, Earl of Surrey. 6584-8
"If hearts were not so infinite". Reflection. Katharine Rebecca Adams. 7016-7
"If heat of youth, 'tis heat suppressed". My prologue. Bayard Taylor. 6976-2
"If heaven's bright halls are very far..sea". A starry night at sea, fr. The coming of love. Theodore Watts-Dunton. 6997-5
"If Homer ne'er had sung; if Socrates". Antigone. John Reade. 7041-8
"If honest, candid people knew". Riddance. Edward R. Huxley. 6885-5
If hope of a laurel. Raymond de la Tailhede. 6351-9
If I am but the water. Christopher La Farge. 6761-1
"If I am not a fool in prophecy". Sophocles. 6435-3
If I am sitting close to you. Jessie Downs Belknap. 6799-9
"If I be lifted up" E.P. Dickie. 6144-3
If I can stop one heart from breaking. Emily Dickinson. 6006-4,6162-1
"If I can stop one heart from breaking". Unknown. 6109-5
If I come back. Julia Ross Alden. 6906-1
If I come back. Victor Starbuck. 6326-1
If I could dis like a rabbit. Rose Strong Hubbell. 6338-1
"If I could do so, lovely girl of mine". Unknown. 6325-X
If I could grasp a wave from the great sea. John Richard Moreland. 6833-2
"If I could hold my grief." Corinne Roosevelt Robinson. 6030-7
If I could lay my hand. May Riley Smith. 6097-8
If I could love. John Gardiner Calkins Brainard. 6441-8
If I could shut the gate. Unknown. 6182-6,6315-2
If I desire with pleasant songs. Thomas Burbidge. 6271-7, 6302-0,6620-8,6627-5,6656-9
If I ever have time for things that matter. Vilda Sauvage Owens. 6089-7
If I forget thee. Sarah N. Cleghorn. 7038-8
"If I forget thee, Jerusalem" Yehuda Amichai. 6758-1
If I freely may discover. Ben Jonson. 6092-7
"If I freely may discover". Ben Jonson. 6187-7,6733-6
If I had a broomstick. Patrick Reginald Chalmers. 6044-7, 6638-0,6639-9
If I had a hatchet. Charles Phillips. 6529-5
If I had an eagle's wing. Eliza Sproat Turner. 6097-8
If I h-d but two little wings. Samuel Taylor Coleridge. 6479-5
"If I had but two little wings" Samuel Taylor Coleridge. 6935-5
If I had known in the morning. Margaret Elizabeth

Sangster. 6461-2
If I had loved you more. Aline Kilmer. 6096 X
"If I had made thy proffered arm". Suwo No Naishi. 6852-9
If I had the time. Unknown. 6260-1
If I had though thou couldst have died. Charles Wolfe. 6090-0,6486-8
If I had thought thou couldst have died. Charles Wolfe. 6174-5
If I had youth. Edgar A. Guest. 6476-0
If I have made, my lady, intricate. Edward Estlin Cummings. 6375-6
"If I have sinn'd in act, I may repent" Hartley Coleridge. 6380-1
"If I have too austerely...", fr. The tempest. William Shakespeare. 6661-5
"If I have wronged you in the days". Trumbull Stickney. 6380-2
If I hope, I pine. Thomas Campion. 6328-4
If I knew. Unknown. 6583-X,6605-4
"If I leave all for thee, wilt thou exchange". Elizabeth Barrett Browning. 6238-5
If I might choose. John Anster. 6930-4
"If I seeke t'enjoy ye fruit of my paine." Unknown. 6563-5
If I should die. Rupert Brooke. 6538-4
If I should die. Ella Wheeler Wilcox. 6956-8
If I should die to-night. Ben King. 6089-7,6083-8,6291-1, 6732-8,6274-1,6440 ,6300-4,6736-0,6698-4
If I should die to-night. Robert C.V. Meyers. 6920-7
If I should die to-night. Arabella Eugenia Smith. 6464-7, 6567-8,6273-3,6486-8,6211-3,6085-4,6732-8
"If I should die to-night". Robert C.V Myers. 6102-8,6076-5
"If I should die to-night". Unknown. 6238-5,6260-1,6155-9
'If I should ever by chance'. Edward Thomas. 6331-4,6161-3, 6650-X
If I should learn, in some quite casual way. Edna St. Vincent Millay. 6339-X
If I should lose you. Pearl Goldsmith Philbrick. 6764-6
"If I should pray this lady pitiless". Guido Cavalcanti. 6325-X
If I should wake. Emily Huntington Miller. 6274-1
"If I shouldn't be alive". Emily Dickinson. 6348-9,6513-9
If I sit silent. Lansing Christman. 6761-1
If I were a cat. Unknown. 6120-6
If I were a fairy. Charles Buxton Going. 6338-1
If I were a little baby! M.E. B. 6965-7
If I were a man, a young man. Ella Wheeler Wilcox. 6211-3
If I were a pig. Elizabeth Rendall. 6262-8
"If I were a poet." Albert Ulrik Baath. 6045-5
If I were a sunbeam. Lucy Larcom. 6373-X,6129-X,6456-6
If I were a voice. Charles Mackay. 6211-3,6260-1,6742-5, 6304-9
If I were dead. Coventry Patmore. 6122-2,6198-2,6172-9, 6655-0,6508-2,6022-6,6292-X
If I were fair. Marian Osborne. 6115-X
If I were king. William Ernest Henley. 6423-X,6453-1
If I were king. Justin Huntly McCarthy. 6875-8
If I were king. Justin Huntly McCarthy. 6260-1,6320-9,6301-2
If I were Santa Claus. Edgar A. Guest. 6862-6
If I were Santa Claus. Rosamund Livingstone McNaught. 6807-3
If I were the lord God. Claudia Cranston. 6653-4
"If I were to tell of our labours, our hard lodging." Aeschylus. 6665-8
If I were you. Amoretta Fitch. 6906-1
If I were you. George H. Murphy. 6889-8
If I were you. Unknown. 6530-9
"If I'd as much money as I could spend". Unknown. 6363-9
"If hunger had not been so fierce in me". Confession. Gertrude Joan Buckman. 6850-2
"If hush'd the loud whirlwind that ruffled...". The pilot that weathered the storm. George Canning. 6793-X, 6934-7
"If I am taken from this patchwork life". Any soldier son to his mother. N.G. H. 7031-0
"If I can find a loveliness". Song of a quiet life. Marion Kilroy. 6750-6
"If I could be old Santa Claus". If I were Santa Claus. Rosamund Livingstone McNaught. 6807-3

"If I could change these words to flow'rs". The offering. Anita Gray Chandler. 6799-9
"If I could choose a gift for thee, dear heart". Minor note 003, fr. In Tuscany. Cora Fabri. 6876-6
"If I could climb to heavenly heights". Inspiration. Unknown. 6109-5
"If I could come again to that dear place". Sonnet ("If I could"). Herbert P. Horne. 6301-2
"If I could drive a yoke of steers". Driving oxen in Vermont. Daniel L. Cady. 6989-4
"If I could feel my hand, dear Lord, in thine". Faith. Sarah Knowles Bolton. 6303-9,6525-2
"If I could forge you verses that would ring". 'He is all ours' Wendell Phillips Stafford. 6995-9
"If I could forget the needless pain". Consideration. Basil C. Hammond. 6799-9
"'If I could forget', she said...". Jane Reed. Bayard Taylor. 6976-2
"If I could help myself to wings". Wanted wings. Francia Holliday. 6799-9
"If I could know that thought of mine". To Eugene Field. Harriet L. Wason. 6836-7
"If I could lay my head upon your heart". Faith. E. DeVilliers-Hertzler. 6818-9
"If I could paint the beauty of a rose". Lines to the elite. Donald J. Paquette. 6783-2
"If I could paint the colors of the sea". The sea. Marguerite E. Wetzel. 6799-9
"If I could see thee- if twere mine". Written in Katie's album. James Abraham Martling. 6952-5
"If I could sing the song of the dawn". Song ("If I could sing"). Leonora Speyer. 6034-X
"If I could steal God's insight and break...". Reality. Francis Ernley Walrond. 6800-6
"If I could touch with Petrarch's pen...". Christmas sonnet to J.L.G. Bayard Taylor. 6976-2
"If I could wish for you one wish today". On her wedding day. Monica Williams. 6799-9
"If I die in the spring/Don't put anything". Christmas burial. Margaret Hazelwood. 6799-9
"If I don't drive around the park". Observation. Dorothy Parker. 6817-0
"If I dressed up in a feather". The weathercock on the moor. Geoffrey Scott. 6985-1
"If I find spread out upon a chair". The boy in the house. Robert P. Tristram Coffin. 7040-X
"If I freely may discover". Song ("If I freely"). Ben Jonson. 6182-6
"If I had a bit of the rainbow". May miracles. Mary Frances Butts. 6965-7
"If I had a path, I'd keep it open". The path. Clement Wood. 6761-1
"If I had but two little wings". Something childish but very natural. Samuel Taylor Coleridge. 6874-X
"If I had known how narrow a prison is love". Liadain to Curithir. Moireen Fox. 6897-9
"If I had known in the morning". Our own. Margaret Elizabeth Sangster. 6226-1,6964-9,6260-1,6066-8,6304-7,6568-6,6964-9,6913-4
"If I had lived ere seer or prince unveiled". Immortality. John Westland Marston. 7015-9
"If I had only loved your flesh". Song ("If I had only..."). Victoria Mary Sackville-West. 6777-8
"If I had wealth and I had health". What to do. Edgar A. Guest. 6862-6
"If I have erred in showing all my heart". Without disguise. Henry Van Dyke. 6961-4
"If I have ever dimmed with tears". To 'him that's awa'. Mrs. J.O. Arnold. 7031-0
"If I have him only,/Is he only mine". The saviour. Novalis. 6952-5
"If I have made, my lady, intricate". Sonnet ("If I have made"). Edward Estlin Cummings. 6506-6
"If I have seen the universe condense". Thought for pausing and considering. Dorothy E. Reid. 6906-1
"If I have sinned in act, I may repent". Sin. Hartley Coleridge. 7015-9
"If I kissed my lover". On feeling surrounded. Jack Veasey. 7003-5
"f I knew a better country in this...world...". No better

land than this. Edgar A. Guest. 7033-7
"If I leave all for thee, wilt thou exchange". Sonnet ("If I leave"). Elizabeth Barrett Browning. 6604-6
"If I live to be old, for I find I go down". The old man's wish. Walter Pope. 6092-7,6933-9,6157-5,6562-7,6219-9
"If I might choose where my tired limbs...". If I might choose. John Anster. 6930-4
"If I might meet her in the lane". King's daughter. Victoria Mary Sackville-West. 6780-8
"If I might only love my God and die". If only. Christina Georgina Rossetti. 6931-2
"If I might write of you in flame". Memorial in flame. Flora Shufelt Rivola. 6750-6
"If I shoot any more I'll be shot". Shooting pains. Thomas Hood. 6974-6
"If I should borrow lips from other lovers". Sonnet: the old song. A. Wolseley Russell. 6781-6
"If I should carefully each petal tear". To -. Samuel Goldman. 6818-9
"If I should chance to live and see". Revolution. Anne Herendeen. 6880-4
"If I should die while some fierce battle rage". Old age: 1916. Helen Bosanquet. 7042-6
"If I should ever wed, it would not be". Ana, Zipporah, Huldah. James Abraham Martling. 6952-5
"If I should quit thee, sacrifice, forswear". Unlinked. Alice Meynell. 6955-X
"If I should see". As ye would. Edith Virginia Bradt. 6928-2
"If I should sing of love a thousand years". Sonnet ("If I should sing"). Phyllis Reid. 6659-3
"If I should steal a little kiss". Under the rose. Samuel Minturn Peck. 6875-8,6770-0
"If I should wish to hold and neatly phrase". Gladioli. Ann Bryant. 6750-6
"If I should write a valentine". Supposing. Laura Ledyard. 6965-7
"If I sit in half the house". One Christmas day. Stephan Chan. 7018-3
"If I sole ma ole blind trotter...". Dieudonne. William Henry Drummond. 6843-X
"If I think music". Music. Hilda Conkling. 6891-X
"If I thins night, at set of sun". I wonder. Unknown. 6918-5
"If I to-night were lying dead". When I am dead. Unknown. 6924-X
"If I vrge my kinde desires". A booke of Ayres (IV). Thomas Campion. 6794-8
"'If I was a judge', said the Kid Kokomo". Kokomo arraigned. Ralph E. Goll. 6880-4
"If I were a bird". If. Cora Fabri. 6876-6
"If I were a hotel waiter". In the subjunctive. Berton Braley. 6853-7
"If I were a modest violet". My secret sin. Marguerite Young. 6750-6
"If I were a painter, I could paint". If and if. Alice Cary. 6969-X
"If I were a scabious". Scabious time. Teresa Hooley. 6804-9
"If I were asked to give a thought...". My mother. Unknown. 6889-8
"If I were fire, I'd burn the world away". Sonnet: Of all he would do. Cecco Angiolieri da Siena. 7039-6
"If I were God but for a day". His way. John Travers Moore. 6906-1
"If I were hanged on the highest hill". Mother o' mine. Rudyard Kipling. 6211-3,6337-3,6365-9,6627-5,6097-8, 6964
"If I were in the middle of the Atlantic". When drowning. Grace Paley. 6803-0
"If I were king-ah, love, if I were king!". If I were king. Justin Huntly McCarthy. 6875-8
"If I were only Adam,I would not stay confined". Waiting room: maternity ward. Louis J. Sanker. 6839-1
"If I were running a factory". The better job. Edgar A. Guest. 7033-7
"If I were Santa Claus this year". A Christmas bit. Edgar A. Guest. 6869-3
"If I were to see". Grandmother. Ray A. Young Bear. 7005-1

"If I were told that I must die to-morrow". When. Sarah ("Susan Coolidge") Woolsey. 6910-X
"If I were you, when ladies at the play, sir". Tu quoque. Austin Dobson. 6887-1
"If I write not to you". Letter in verse. William Cowper. 6814-6
"If I'm allowed, some day I'll write". On spring poems. Richard Hallberg. 6850-2
"If I'm at church these days". Rondel. Christine de Pisan. 6227-X
"If I, who only sing, in other ways". The new physician. Stephen Chalmers. 7014-0
"If Il Penseroso's mood prevail". Envoi. J. Ernest Whitney. 6836-7
"If ifs and ands". Unknown. 6363-2
"If in the fight my arm was strong". The warrior to his dead bride. Adelaide Anne Procter. 6957-6
"If in the fullness of my years". Climax. Alice Harrod Muir. 6799-9
"If in the silence of this lonely eve". An evening guest. Dinah Maria Mulock Craik. 6980-0
"If in the summer of thy bright regard". To M. William Gay. 6784-0
If in the world there be more woe. Sir Thomas Wyatt. 6182-6,6187-7,6584-8
"If in this troubled world of ours". Emperor Sanjo. 6852-9
"If in thy glorious home above". Ecologue 015, sels. Luis de Camoens [or Camoes]. 6973-8
"If in your confusion/you could have seen...". Animula. David Wevill. 6767-0
If it ain't Bill. Fred W. Leu. 6906-1
"If it all be for nought". Resurrection. Unknown. 6144-3
If it be destined. Francesco Petrarch. 7039-6
"If it be sad to speak of treasres gone". To the memory of Heber. Felicia Dorothea Hemans. 6973-8
"If it be true that any beauteous thing". Sonnet ("If it be true"). Michelangelo Buonarroti. 6271-7,6302-0, 6385-3,6066-8
"If it be true that those beloved of heaven". The early dead. Charles W. Denison. 6755-7
"If it do come to pass", fr. As you like it. William Shakespeare. 6395-0
"If it is thou whose casual hand withdraws." Arthur Hugh Clough. 6110-9
"If it must be; if it must be, O God!". Sonnet ("If it must be"). David Gray. 6180-X
"If it rained tonight, I should retreat". Cesar Vallejo. 6759-X
'If it was not for the drink'. A.L. Westcombe. 6922-3
"If it were done...", fr. Macbeth. William Shakespeare. 6726-3,6424-8
"If it were not for the poetic" William Blake. 7014-0
If Jesus came back today, sels. Vincent Godfrey Burns. 6144-3
"If Jove would give the leafy bowers..." Clodia. 6049-8
"If it were not for woman's care". The feminine touch. Edgar A. Guest. 6748-4
"If it were so, how truly good 't would seem". Folk-lore. Edward R. Huxley. 6885-5
"If it's flattery you want, you must always...". Flatterers. Edgar A. Guest. 6748-4
"If it's only just a shelter from the rain...". Home ingredients. Edgar A. Guest. 6748-4
"If Jesus Christ is a man". A song ("If Jesus Christ"). Richard Watson Gilder. 6102-8,6076-5
"If John marries Mary, and Mary alone". Impromptu on reading the chapter on polygamy... William Cowper. 6814-6
"If Lake Champlain was ten times smaller". Too much Lake Champlain in Vermont. Daniel L. Cady. 6988-6
"If lavish Dryden so profusely writ". The wife of Bath. John Gay. 6972-X
"If learned in other things you be," fr. Resolved... Abraham Cowley. 6317-9
"If life be but getting and keeping". Life's underpay. William Lindsey. 6798-0
"If life be gone, fresh life to you". Jalal [or Jelal] ed-din Rumi. 6448-5
"If life be nothing but a fight". The things eternal. Edgar A. Guest. 6748-4

"If life were never bitter". If. Mortimer Collins. 6802-2
"If life were rosy and skies were blue". The benefit of trouble. Edgar A. Guest. 6862-6
"If light of life outlive the set of sun", fr. Sunset. Algernon Charles Swinburne. 6123-0
If like you. Louise Goodson Tennyson. 6316-0
"If livelihood by knowledge were endowed". Mesnevi, fr. the Gulistan. Sadi [or Saadi] (Mushlih-ud-Din). 7039-6
"If loue loues truth, then women doe not loue" Thomas Campion. 6794-8
"If love be life, I long to die". Dispraise of love. Unknown. 6830-8
"If love be life, I long to die." Unknown. 6317-9
If love be love, fr. Idylls of the king. Alfred Lord Tennyson. 6934-7
If love be true. Samuel Waddington. 6770-0
If love could last. Louise Chandler Moulton. 6875-8
"If love has never thrilled the heart". Ritterhaus. 6523-6
If love his arrows shoot. Unknown. 6328-4
"If love make me forsworn, how shall I swear..". Biron's canzonet, fr. Love's labour's lost. William Shakespeare. 6827-8
If love should come again. Bayard Taylor. 6976-2
If love should faint. Sir Edmund Gosse. 6770-0
"If love should faint, and half decline". Rondeau. Sir Edmund Gosse. 6875-8
"If love were but a little thing". Song ("If love"). Florence Earle Coates. 6310-1
If love's a sweet passion. Unknown. 6328-4
If love, for love of long time had. John Heywood. 6182-6
If Lucy should be dead. William Wordsworth. 6634-8
"If man might know/The ill he must undergo". The advantage of foreknowledge. Sir John Suckling. 6874-X
"If March can hold six weeks of cold". 'Settled going' in Vermont. Daniel L. Cady. 6989-4
If men be worlds. John Donne. 6438-8
"If men could still be holy anywhere". Towers of silence. Robert P. Tristram Coffin. 7040-X
"If men whom men condemn as ill". Judge not. Joaquin Miller. 6889-8
"If might made right, life were a wild-beasts'". Might and right. Henry Van Dyke. 6961-4
If mother would listen. Margaret Elizabeth Sangster. 6183-4
If Mr. Masefield had written 'Casaianca'. Sir John Collings ("Solomon Eagle") Squire. 6506-6
"If music be the food of love". Food of love. Harry Romaine. 7021-3
If music be the food of love. William Shakespeare. 6102-8
If music be the food of love. Unknown. 6328-4
If my dark grandam had but known. Grace Fallow Norton. 7038-8
"If my dear love were but the child of state". Sonnet 124 ("If my dear love"). William Shakespeare. 6447-7
"If my eyes might see thee". An Andalusian folk song. Richard Lawson Gales. 6950-9
"If my peculiar pulchritude in Paris...". An intermezzo for the fourth act. William Allen White. 6817-0
"If my valentine caused you sorrow". The comic valentine. Edward R. Huxley. 6885-5
"If nature, for a favorite child". Matthew. William Wordsworth. 6086-2,6110-9,6383-7,6828-6
If needs be. Charlotte Mansfield. 6085-4
"If neither brass, nor marble, can withstand". The power of time. Jonathan Swift. 7014-0
If not quite true, it ought to be. Margaret Eytinge. 6713-1
"If of us two might only one be glad". The greatest gift. Blanche Edith Baughan. 6784-0
"If on a day it should befall". Dirge. Theodore Maynard. 6884-7
"If on a spring mnight I went by". A prayer ("If on a spring"). John Galsworthy. 6532-5
"If on my grave the summer grass were growing". How long. Louise Chandler Moulton. 7041-8
If on some balmy summer night. Edith (Bland) Nesbit. 6301-2
"If on the book itself we cast our view". The scriptures, fr. Religio laici. John Dryden. 6933-9

"If on the closed curtain of my sight". Portrait and reality. Henry Van Dyke. 6961-4
"If once I could gather in song". Song ("If once."). Wilfred Wilson Gibson. 6437-X
"If one dies owning an estate". Rules of descent in the United States. T.W. Davidson. 6878-2
"If one had never seen the full completeness". Plea for charity. Alice Cary. 6865-0;6969-X
If one has failed. William J. Lampton. 6211-3
"If one is sick the case is plain". Secundem artem. James Abraham Martling. 6952-5
If one might live. Ethelwyn Wetherald. 6115-X
"If one of the comedy-makers of old had attempted...". Aristophanes. 6435-3
If one should come. Mahlon Leonard Fisher. 6029-3
"If one were sound-proof, like some...". Machines- or men? Elizabeth Newport Hepburn. 7014-0
If only. Mary Dillingham Frear. 6799-9
If only. Geoffrey Johnson. 6761-1
If only. Christina Georgina Rossetti. 6931-2
If only. Christina Georgina Rossetti. 6123-0
If only. Christina Georgina Rossetti. 6931-2
"If only dreams came true, my dear". Orison. Ruth Jeffery. 6818-9
"If only I can feel your love/Wrapping me...". If only. Mary Dillingham Frear. 6799-9
"If only I were Santa Claus I'd travel...". If I were Santa Claus. Edgar A. Guest. 6862-6
If only the dreams abide. Clinton Scollard. 6309-8
"If only the glow would not fade...". Brief pledge. Clarissa Hall. 6789-1
If only thou art true. George Barlow. 6656-9
If only you were here. Hester A. Benedict. 6226-1
"If only you would not forgive". Accusation against the forgiving friend. Francis D. Clare. 6839-1
"If origin had lived in these births". Daybreak. Phillip Yellowhawk Minthorn. 7005-1
"If our love may fail, Lily". 'The pity of it' Roden Noel. 6873-1
"If our own life is the life of a flower". A Rhine-land drinking song. Unknown (German). 6949-5
"If oxen, or lions, or horses had hands like men...". Xenophanes. 6251-2
If Phyllis denies me relief. Unknown. 6328-4
"If plants were human, 'twere a merry group!". In the garden. Milton S. Rose. 6836-7
If poisonous minerals..., fr. Holy sonnets. John Donne. 6154-0,6324-1
If Robert Herrick had been Dorothy Parker. Eric Divine. 6850-2
If Roosevelt had been bad. Jack Crawford. 6995-9
"If privilege were mine to name the time". Let it be springtime. Nelle Loraine Milroy. 6799-9
"If rest is sweet at shut of day". A roundel of rest. Arthur Symons. 6770-0
"If Rome so great, and in her wisest age". To Edward Allen (Alleyne). Ben Jonson. 6933-9
If scors are worth the keeping. Glenn Ward Dresbach. 6619-4
"If seeing all the fiends rebel". The terms. Porsteinn Erlingsson. 6854-5
"If she be made of white and red". The rhyme of white and red, fr. Love's labour's lost. William Shakespeare. 6827-8
"If she be made of white and red". Herbert P. Horne. 6656-9
"If she be not as kind as fair". Song ("If she be not"). Sir George Etherege. 6544-9,6733-6,6152-4
If she be not as kind as fair. Sir George Etherege. 6563-5
If she but knew. Arthur O'Shaughnessy. 6226-1
If she forsake me. Thomas Campion. 6328-4
"If she had been beautiful, even". Of a woman, dead young. Dorothy Parker. 6879-0
"If she knew that I am Cupid". D.D. P. 7021-3
"If sleep and death be truly one". In memoriam, sel. Alfred Lord Tennyson. 6958-4
If sleep and death be truly one. Alfred Lord Tennyson. 6488-4
If so tommorrow saves. Christina Georgina Rossetti. 6501-5
"If some day this body of mine were burned. Thoughts:

Mahomed Akram. Laurence (Adele Florence Nicolson) Hope. 6856-1
"If some day you come back". Some day. So-wol Kim. 6775-1
If some true maiden's love were mine. Samuel Minturn Peck. 6770-0
If sometimes in the haunts of man. George Gordon, 6th Baron Byron. 6543-0
"If spring has maids of honor". Arbutus. Helen Hunt Jackson. 6049-8
"If spring should come again". Promise. Martha Simonton. 6799-9
"If sweethearts were sweethearts always". Sweethearts always. Daniel O'Connell. 6889-8
"If talk were fire - 'twould burn the town". Talk. Anna Jane Granniss. 6761-1
If that high world. George Gordon, 6th Baron Byron. 6014-5, 6543-0
"If that my hand, like yours, dear George...". Christmas sonnet to G.H.B. Bayard Taylor. 6976-2
If that were true! Frances Brown. 6271-7
If the Christ you mean. Richard Watson Gilder. 6303-9
"If the best merit be to lose life well". Epitaph on the Athenian dead at Plataea. Simonides. 6879-0
"If the bird/Had no list'ner, wrapt, adoring". Song ("If the bird"). Cora Fabri. 6876-6
"If the bowl be of gold and the liquor...". The boys who never grew up. Charles Law Watkins. 7012-4
"If the call comes, who answers?". Problem of immortality. Theodore Spencer. 6751-4
"If the dark mantle of infinity". The sea, fr. Nightfall. Lady Margaret Sackville. 6785-9
"If the deep sighs of an afflicted breast". Madrigal. Michael Drayton. 6908-8
"If the dread day that calls thee hence". Life in death and death in life. Adelaide Anne Procter. 6957-6
"If the dull substance of my flesh were thought". Sonnet 044 ("If the dull substance"). William Shakespeare. 6369-1,6447-7
"If the great king, Henri Quatre". 'Si le roy m'avait donne'. Richard Lawson Gales. 6950-9
If the heart be homeless. Annemarie Ewing. 6388-8
"If the heart break like a wineskin...=". Protocol. Francis Sweeney. 6839-1
If the kitten had flown. Harold Willard Gleason. 7019-1
"If the led striker call it a strike". An American. Rudyard Kipling. 6810-3
If the man who turnips cries. Samuel Johnson. 6089-7,6722-0,6092-7
"If the meteor mind, swift-ranger". To a dead poet. Herbert Trench. 6877-4
If the moonbeam. Unnur ("Hulda") Benediktdottir. 6854-5, 6283-0
"If the mules were in a patient mood", fr. The boys... Mary B. Plummer. 6149-4
"If the Oak is out before the Ash". Unknown. 6047-1
If the owl calls again. John Haines. 6855-3
"If the rope is folded". Unknown. 6364-0
"If the rose in meek duty". Dedication to Wilfird and Alive Meynell. Francis Thompson. 6942-8
"If the sea were one great ink-pot". Song ("If the sea were one..."). Unknown (Spanish). 7039-6
If the seas dry. Clement Wood. 6076-5
"If the song I have to sing". Songs of gloom. Edgar A. Guest. 6862-6
"If the strife in this case is...perverse". Owen Kerr vs. Owen Kerr. Unknown. 6878-2
"If the wild bowler thinks he bowls". Brahma. Andrew Lang. 6802-2
"If the woodland and the heath". Love's palace. Arthur Maquarie. 6784-0
"If the young folk build an altar to the..true". The black hound bays. George Sterling. 6880-4
"If then at last this ordeal shall be done". Arizona summer. Eleanor Baldwin. 6750-6
"If there are any bounds to any man". Christopher M. ("Hugh MacDiarmid") Grieve. 6893-6
"If there be a tear unshed". On the right honourable Charles, Lord Herbert... William Browne. 6908-8
"If there be leaves on the forest floor". The divine forest. Charles R.Murphy. 6762-X

"If there be memory in the world to come". The star's monument. Jean Ingelow. 6940-1
"If there be memory in the world to come". Jean Ingelow. 6238-5
"If there be nothing new, but that which is". Sonnet 059 ("If their be"). William Shakespeare. 6208-3
"If there be one whose thoughts delight". Psalm 133 Bible. 6848-0
"If there be some weaker one." John Greenleaf Whittier. 6225-3
"If there be time enough". Poem ("If there be time"). Wyn Griffith. 6360-8
"If there exists a hell, the case is clear". To Sir Toby. Philip Freneau. 6753-0
"If there should be a sound of song". Earth love. John Drinkwater. 6875-8
"If there should come a time, as well there may". Unknown. 6238-5
If there were dreams to sell. Thomas Lovell Beddoes. 6187-7,6328-4
"If there were dreams to sell" Louise Chandler Moulton. 7041-8
'If there were dreams to sell.' Louise Chandler Moulton. 6006-4
"If there's no other life above". Agnostic. Helen G. Ladd. 6764-6
"If there's silence in summer". Falling day. Christy MacKaye. 6799-9
"If they could view us now, that...throng". Luxurys' children. Elaine Pierce McCreless. 6750-6
If they forget to see. Edith Lombard Squires. 6461-2
"If they hint, o musician, the piece that...". The ballad of imitation. Austin Dobson. 6770-0
If they meant all they said. Alice Duer Miller. 6089-7
If they still live. Edith M. Thomas. 6431-0
"If they want me to be a mystic, fine.So I'm a mystic" Fernando Pessoa. 6758-1
'If things were only sich!' B.P. Shillaber. 6911-8
"If this be dreaming, may I never wake". Sonnet ("If this be"). Hazel S. Marshall. 6761-1
If this be good-bye. Ruby Berkle Goodwin. 6178-8
"If this be love, to draw a weary breath". Sonnet ("If this be love"). Samuel Daniel. 6436-1
"If this fair rose offend thy sight". The white rose. Unknown. 6874-X
If this great world of joy and pain. William Wordsworth. 6110-9,6199-0,6828-6
"If this has been a nightmare hour". Conclusion. John Dillon Husband. 6761-1
"If this morning, I lead rain". No. 8 Rochelle DuBois. 6898-7
"If this old place". Mary Kolars. 6292-X,6096-X
"If this our little life is but a day". A sonnet to heavenly beauty. Joachim Du Bellay. 7039-6,6771-9
"If this shall be the last time". Last prelude. Sara Teasdale. 6879-0
If this should change. Stephen Vincent Benet. 6761-1
"If this should fail, why,then I scarcely know". The love-letter. Austin Dobson. 6996-7
If this were all. Edgar A. Guest. 7033-7
If this were faith. Robert Louis Stevenson. 6508-2,6102-8, 6123-0,6337-3,6477-9,6501-5,6730-1,6732
"If this world's friends might see but once". The seed growing secretly. Henry Vaughan. 6931-2
"If those entwined in nuptial rights". Wedlock's course. Edward R. Huxley. 6885-5
"If those who wield the rod forget". The poet and the critics. Austin Dobson. 6996-7
"If thou a reason dost desire to know". Sir Francis Kynaston. 6187-7
"If thou are sleeping, maiden". Song ("If thou art sleeping..."). Gil Vicente. 7039-6
"If thou art blest." Ann [or Annie E.] Hamilton. 6225-3
"If thou couldst empty all thyself of self". Indwelling. Thomas Edward Brown. 6809-X
If thou couldst know. Adelaide Anne Procter. 6957-6
"If thou dist ever hold...", fr. Hamlet. William Shakespeare. 6289-X
"If thou doest not loue sacke." Unknown. 6563-5
'If thou dost bid thy friend farewell". William

Shakespeare. 6238-5
"If thou dost loue me as thou sayst." Unknown. 6563-5
"If thou dost loue." Unknown. 6563-5
"If thou hadst died at midnight". Atonement. Bayard Taylor. 6976-2
If thou hast crushed a flower. Felicia Dorothea Hemans. 6973-8
"If thou hast lost a friend". Charles Swain. 6980-0
"If thou hast seen the standard dim". Abi, viator--. Unknown. 7031-0
"If thou in surety safe wilt sit". Jasper Heywood. 6181-8
If thou indeed derive thy light from heaven. William Wordsworth. 6110-9,6199-0,6828-6
"If thou indeed derive thy light from heaven". The poet. William Wordsworth. 6867-7
"If thou long'st so much to learne (sweet boy)..." Thomas Campion. 6794-8
If thou must love me. Elizabeth Barrett Browning. 6337-3, 6339-X,6646-1,6513-9,6585-6,6250 ,6019-6,6153-2,6199-0
"If thou must love me, let it be for nought". Sonnet ("If thou must"). Elizabeth Barrett Browning. 6154-0
"If thou shouldst ever come by choice..chance". Ginerva, fr. Italy. Samuel Rogers. 6832-4
"If thou survive my well contented day". William Shakespeare. 6204-0,6182-6,6246-6
"If thou survive my well-contented day". Sonnet 032 ("If thou survive"). William Shakespeare. 6085-4,6436-1
If thou wert by my side. Reginald Heber. 6271-7,6600-3, 6620-8,6302-0,6385-3,6438
"If thou wert by my side, my love". Verses to Mrs. Heber. Reginald Heber. 6980-0
"If thou wilt ease thine heart". Dirge. Thomas Lovell Beddoes. 6317-7,6328-4
"If thou wilt ease thine heart". Thomas Lovell Beddoes. 6187-7,6385-3
"If thou wilt mighty be, flee from the rage." Sir Thomas Wyatt. 6584-8
"If thou would'st view fair Melrose aright". Sir Walter Scott. 6934-7
If thou wouldst read. Robert Loveman. 6941-X
If thou'lt be mine. Thomas Moore. 6328-4
"If thou'lt play me fair play". Highland laddie. Unknown. 6859-6
"If thought can reach to heaven". The rabbi's song. Rudyard Kipling. 6844-8
"If thro' this roar o' the guns one prayer...". Before the assault. Robert Ernest Vernede. 7029-9
"If through its precepts you are growing". Religion. Edward R. Huxley. 6885-5
"If thus thy fallen grandeur I behold". Genoa mia! Pastorini. 6973-8
"If thy Mrs be too coy." Unknown. 6563-5
"If thy sad heart, pinning for human love". Sonnet ("If thy sad"). Sarah Helen Whitman. 6102-8
"If thy soul check thee that I come so near". Sonnet 136 ("If thy soul"). William Shakespeare. 6447-7
"If time and nature serve us both alike". Re-union. William Henry Davies. 6778-6
"If to be sprong of hgih and princely blood". To the right noble and verutous Theophilus Howard... Thomas Campion. 6794-8
"If to grumbling you're inclined". On lying down. Edgar A. Guest. 6748-4
"'If to ripe old age you'd live.'". Ripe old age. Edgar A. Guest. 6748-4
"If to the sighing breeze of summer-hours". Francesco Petrarch. 6973-8
"If trampled grass gives perfume, if the bowl". Sorrow. Isa Blagden. 7037-X
"If trees be women, marry one and die". The words of the excited boy. Harry Brown. 6761-1
If truth in hearts that perish. Alfred Edward Housman. 6723-9
"If unto marble statues thou had'st spoken". To an eloquent advocate of Indian rights. William Lloyd Garrison. 7009-4
"If unto marble statues thou hadst spoken". To the Hon. Theodore Frelinghuysen. William Lloyd Garrison. 6752-2

If war be kind. Stephen Crane. 6732-8,6102-8,6076-5,6542-2
If war should come. Benjamin Francis Musser. 6420-5
"If we could but silence the gongs...". Memorial for 1940. John Gould Fletcher. 6783-2
"If we could go to slumber town...". The way to slumber town. Lucy Maud Montgomery. 6797-2
It we could hear with God. Brother X (pseud.) 6662-3
"If we could hold the moment, hold the light". Only a little longer. Reba Jane Tyson. 6761-1
"If we could meet in privacy". Michimasa. 6852-9
If we could only be!. Lee Shippey. 6449-3
"If we could only spin a top". Raising Hubbard squash in Vermont. Daniel L. Cady. 6988-6
"If we could speak today to all our dead". Decoration Day. Louis Stoddard. 6761-1
If we didn't have to eat. Nixon Waterman. 6089-7
"If we dreamed that we loved her aforetime". To San Francisco. S.J. Alexander. 6946-0
"If we had a keg of whiskey, we'd roll it along". Unknown. 6059-5
If we had but a day. Unknown. 6523-6
If we had but known. Unknown. 6910-X
If we had met. Edmund Blunden. 6655-0
If we had the time. Richard Burton. 6887-1
If we knew. Virginia May Haynard. 6925-8
If we knew. May Riley Smith. 6097-8,6211-3,6273-3
If we knew. Unknown. 6909-6,6260-1,6303-9,6337-3
If we knew the woe and heartache. Unknown. 6304-7
If we only knew. Unknown. 6274-1
"If we part - as inevitably we must". My dreams go with you always. Ralph Douberly. 6841-3
If we return. Frederick W. Harvey. 7029-9
"If we shadows have offended". Epilogue ("If we shadows"). William Shakespeare. 6436-1
"If we should be shipwrecked together". Chums. James William Foley. 6964-9
"If we should see one sowing seed". To my friend. Alice Cary. 6865-0;6969-X
"If we sit down at set of sun". At set of sun. Unknown. 6914-2
If we understood. Unknown. 6964-9
"If we were all alike, what a dreadful world..". The world and Bud. Edgar A. Guest. 7033-7
"If we with earnest effort could succeed". Sonnet ("If we"). Richard Chenevix Trench. 6214-8
If we would. Unknown. 6407-8
"If we're to be anywhere at all". The torch. Greg Forker. 6870-7
"If when I come to paradise". A sealess world. Joan Campbell. 7020-5
If when I die. William Fowler. 6182-6
"If when the sun at noon displays". Thomas Carew. 6187-7
"If when the sun at noone displayes". A beautifull mistress. Thomas Carew. 6933-9
"If when thy children, O my friend". In his arms. Phoebe Cary. 6865-0;6969-X
"If wine and music have the power". A song ("If wine"). Matthew Prior. 6315-2,6634-8,6152-4
If winter come. Grace Blackburn. 6115-X
If wishes were horses! M.E. B. 6965-7
"If wishes were horses." Mother Goose. 6363-2,6452-3
"If with complaint the pain might be express'd." Sir Thomas Wyatt. 6584-8
"If with pleasure you are viewing any work...". Do it now. Berton Braley. 6853-7
If women could be fair. Edward de Vere, 17th Earl of Oxford. 6182-6
"If women could be fair." Unknown. 6302-0,6385-3,6430-2
"If ye've been up ayont Dundee". A fragment. George Outram. 6878-2
"If yet there be a few that take delight". Prologue. John Dryden. 6970-3
"If yonder children asleep beneath the dawn...". Before the coming of the planes that burn the cities. Otto D'Sola. 6759-X
"If you a reformation would begin". Reformation. Edward R. Huxley. 6885-5
"If you a wrinkle on the sea haue seene." Unknown. 6563-5
If you are a mousie. Vachel Lindsay. 6206-7
"If you are anybody's wife". Vermont freestones. Daniel L.

IF

Cady. 6989-4
"If you are beside me when the sirens go". Letter VII. Randall Swingler. 6895-2
"If you are down with the blues...". Remedies for trouble. Unknown. 6889-8
"If you are good, for goodness' sake be...". Of courtesy, fr. Proverbs. Arthur Guiterman. 6861-8
"If you can dress to make yourself attractive". An 'if' for girls. Elizabeth Lincoln Otis. 6964-9
"If you can finde a hart sweet loue to kill." Unknown. 6563-5
If you can hear my hooves. Harold Littlebird. 7005-1
"If you can take your dreams into the classroom". The teacher's 'if'. R.J. Gale. 6964-9
"If you can tell the number". Unknown (Greek) 6251-2
"If you can't go over or under, go round. Joseph Morris. 6291-1
"If you climb to the top of the highest...". The spell of provincetown. Lilybell Bates. 6798-0
"If you could drink with me, I say, beware". Christmas at the officers' mess. John Streeter Manifold. 6895-2
"If you could go back to the forks of the road". Which road? Unknown. 6923-1
"If you could lie upon this berth...". Through a porthole. Leon Gellert. 6784-0
"If you for orders, and a gown design". A satyr address'd to a friend..., sels. John Oldham. 6933-9
If you had a friend. Robert Service. 6159-1
"If you have a carrier-dove". The carrier-dove. James Thomson. 6943-6
If you have a friend. Unknown. 6211-3
"If you have a friend worth loving". A sermon in rhyme. Unknown. 6964-9,6918-5
"If you have a friend worth loving". Unknown. 6109-5,6260-1
If you have a little boy. Oma Carlyle Anderson. 6750-6
"If you have gentle words and looks, my friends". Unknown. 6238-5
"If you have hard work to do". Now. Unknown. 6889-8
"If you have not read the Slavic poets". To Robinson Jeffers. Czeslaw Milosz. 6758-1
If you have seen. Thomas Moore. 6089-7
"If you have somewhere". Inspiration. Celestin Pierre Cambiaire. 6826-X
"If you have tears...", fr. Julius Caesar. William Shakespeare. 6339-X,6601-1
"If you hold a blue rock to your ear". Why stone does not sing by itself. Anita Endrezze-Danielson. 7005-1
"If you join St. Michael's ring". Unknown. 6364-0
If you love me. Samuel Hoffenstein. 6026-9
"If you love me, pop and fly". Unknown. 6904-5
"If you loved me as I love you". For the charming Miss I.F.'s album. Eugene Field. 6949-2
"If you mark, my lord". Justin Huntly McCarthy. 6238-5
"If you never write verses yourself". Dear reader. Ernest Radford. 6875-8,6770-0
"If you see a tall fellow ahead of the crowd". Forget it. Unknown. 6889-8
"If you see a tall fellow ahead of the crwod". Forget it. Unknown. 6889-8
"If you should go to La Bassee". The belfries. Alys Fane Trotter. 7029-9
"If you should let me wrap you in my love". Robe, fr. Once again the Eden. Noel Hudson Stearn. 6789-1
"If you should lightly, as I've known you, come". Trumbull Stickney. 6380-2
If you should return. Maye DeWeese Porter. 6906-1
If you should tire of loving me. Margaret Widdemer. 6441-8, 6556-2,6431-0
"If you sit down at set of sun". A day well spent. Unknown. 6930-0
"If you sneeze on Monday, you sneeze for danger." Mother Goose. 6452-3
If you stick a stock of liquor. Newman Levy. 6026-9
"If you turn west from the sunken river". Old roads. G.S. Bryan. 6764-6
If you want a kiss, why, take it. Unknown. 6273-3,6280-6, 6652-6
"If you want a proud foe to 'make tracks'.". Limerick:"If you want a proud foe..." Sir William Schwenck Gilbert. 6811-1
"If you want to get to the heaven". Litany of the little bourgeois. Nicanor Parra. 6758-1
"If you want to know who I am, I shall tell...". What Michael said to the census taker. James Rorty. 6880-4
If you were. Unknown. 6583-X
"If you were a Chinese born in America...". A Chinaman's chance. Marilyn Chin. 6790-5
"If you were coming in the fall". Emily Dickinson. 6299-7, 6429-9,6321-7
If you were here. Philip Bourke Marston. 6656-9
"If you were so innocent". Survival in a stone maze. George Rachow. 6870-7
"If you will listen to me, boys, I will sing you...". Unknown. 6059-5
"If you will love know such to be." Unknown. 6563-5
"If you wish to win bright laurels". Lucette. 6238-5
"If you would do good, then do it to-day". Generosity. Steingrimur Thorsteinsson. 6854-5
If you would hold me. Sister Mary Madeleva. 6096-X
"If you would know a happy man". The happy man. Edgar A. Guest. 7033-7
"If you would know the love I you bear". Sonnet ("If you would"). Sir John Davies. 6584-8
"If you would know why men dread nonchalance". The king of Spain. Maxwell Bodenheim. 6779-4
"If you would learn to love the night". Go to the barn with a lantern. Robert P. Tristram Coffin. 7040-X
"If you would live free from sin". The still small voice. Edward R. Huxley. 6885-5
"If you would work one small miracle". Prison. Paul David Ashley. 6870-7
"If you'd help the world a bit". Unknown. 6109-5
If you've anything good to say. Unknown. 6260-1
"If you've essayed to find the maid". The Pennsylvania girl. Edward W. Mumford. 6936-3
"If you've ever stole a pheasant-egg...". Loot. Rudyard Kipling. 6810-3
"If your hair were as white as the cool...snow". Love song. Ethel M. Brainerd. 6906-1
"If your health is not quite right". A panacea. R.O. Ryder. 6117-6
"If your purse no longer bulges...". Plant a garden. Edgar A. Guest. 6869-3
"If youth be thine". Juventa perennis. Thomas Edward Brown. 6809-X
"If youth were all- fleet-footed, gay with...". Privilege. Ruth Miller Red. 6818-9
"If yt I for thy sweet sake." Unknown. 6563-5
An 'if' for girls. Elizabeth Lincoln Otis. 6964-9
'If'. Winthrop M. Crowell. 6798-0
"If, after all". Communion. David McCord. 6761-1
"If, as I have, you also do" John Donne. 6935-5
"If, as they tell in stories old". The eye of the beholder. James Lionel Michael. 6784-0
"If, for silver or for gold". Epigram. Rulhieres. 6945-2
If, in the garden. B.R. M. 6937-1
If, Lord, thy love for me is strong. Saint Theresa of Avila. 7039-6
"If, in the month of dark December". Written after swimming from Sestos to Abydos. George Gordon, 6th Baron Byron. 6089-7,6026-9,6464-7,6278-6,6945-2
"If, my religion safe, I durst embrace". To Sir Henrie Savile upon his translation of Tacitus. Ben Jonson. 6933-9
"If, of a wretched state and all forlorn." Leonard Digges. 6317-9,6562-7
If, on account of the political situation. Wystan Hugh Auden. 6666-6
"If, sitting with his little worn-out shoe". If. Unknown. 6690-9
"If, sitting with this little worn-out shoe". If. Unknown. 6913-4
"If, through some wondrous miracle of grace". 'Without are the dogs' Edward A. Church. 7008-6
"If, when I'm a boy." Unknown. 6715-8
If-two miles after Kipling. Helen Rowland. 6537-6
"If/Being wronged, you have not". On being wronged. Elisabeth Kuskulis. 6836-7

"If/Thou hast known anywhere amid a storm". Chamouni.
      Sydney Dobell. 6832-4
Ifs. Louise Barrett. 6249-0
Ifs. Caroline Elizabeth Sarah Sheridan Norton. 7037-X
Ignata, Sister Mary
   On a certain nun. 6285-7
Ignatius of Loyola, Saint
   Anima Christi. 6543-0
Ignatius, Sister Mary
   Our lady of the libraries. 6282-2
Ignatow, David
   Blessing myself. 6803-0
   Content. 6803-0
   I turned my back. 6803-0
   No theory. 6803-0
   Simultaneously. 6803-0
   With the door open. 6803-0
Ignorance. Ken LaMere. 6883-9
Ignorance. John Masefield. 6320-9
Ignorance of botany. Walter Savage Landor. 6874-X
The ignorance of man. James Merrick. 6931-2
Iloihmation. Thomas Edward Brown. 6809-X
"Ignorant tyrants, reckless and uncouth". To congress
      concerning...for universal military service. Robert
      Hillyer. 6880-4
Ignoto
   Phillida's love-call. 6191-5
   Phillis. 6191-5
"Ih that my lungs could bleat like butter'd...". Nonsense.
      Unknown. 6902-9
Ijajee's story. Charlotte DeClue. 7005-1
Ike Walton's prayer. James Whitcomb Riley. 6358-6
Ikeda, Patricia Y.
   A card game: kinjiro sawada. 6790-5
   Recovery. 6790-5
   Translations. 6790-5
Il bacio. Paul Verlaine. 6652-6
"Il boite affreusement, ce vieux cheval de...". Mourir,
      dormir. Theodore de Banville. 6801-4
'Il est Cocu--le chef de gare'. H.S. MacKintosh. 6722-0
"Il est au fond des bois, il est une peuplade".
      Invocation. Auguste Brizeux. 6801-4
"Il est dans l'atrium, le beau rouet d'ivoire". Le rouet
      d'omphale. Victor Hugo. 6801-4
"Il est des coeurs epris du triste amour du...". Ribeira.
      Theophile Gautier. 6801-4
"Il est temps que je me repose". Trois ans apres. Victor
      Hugo. 6801-4
"Il est un air pour qui je donnerais". Fantaisie. Gerard
      de Nerval. 6801-4
"Il est un vieil air populaire". Variations sur le
      carnaval de Venise. Theophile Gautier. 6801-4
Il etait un bergere. Unknown. 6120-6
"Il etait un homme de Madere". Limerick:"Il etait un homme
      de Madere". George Du Maurier. 6811-1,6811-1,6308-X
"Il etait une jeune fille de Tours". Limerick:"Il etait
      une jeune fille de Tours". Unknown. 6811-1
Il fior degli eroici furori. John Addington Symonds. 6656-
   9
"Il m'aima. C'est alors que sa voix adoree". L'attente.
      Marceline Desbordes-Valmore. 6801-4
"Il naquit pres de Choisy-le-Roi". Limerick:"Il naquit
      pres de Choisy-le-Roi." Unknown. 6308-X
Il penseroso. John Milton. 6102-8,6122-2,6138-9,6186-9,
      6198-2,6246 ,6129-9,6639-9,6660-7,6301-2,6192-3,6194
      ,6203-0,6385-3,6332-2,6369-1,6473-6,6536 ,6197-4,
      6560-0,6250-4,6152-3,6723-9,6543 ,6604-6,6634-8,6726-
      3,6023-4,6189-3,6438-8,6491-4
Il penseroso, sels. John Milton. 6501-5,6597-X
Il pleut doucement sur la ville. Paul Verlaine. 6513-9
Il pleut doucement sur la ville. Paul Verlaine. 7039-6
"Il y avait une jeunne fille de Tours". Limerick:"Il y
      avait une jeunne fille de Tours." Unknown. 6308-X
Ila, sels. Hattie Horner Louthan. 6836-7
Ilia's dream. Unknown (Latin) 6948-7
Iliad. Humbert Wolfe. 6506-6
Iliad, sel. Homer. 7014-0
The Iliad, sels. Homer. 6435-3,6605-2,6732-8,6679-8
The Iliad, sels. Homer. 6487-6
The Iliad, sels. Homer. 6372-1,6610-0
The Iliad, sels. Homer. 6562-7,6194-X
The Iliad, sels. Homer. 6289-X
The Iliad, sels. Homer. 6251-2
The Iliad, sels. Homer. 6289-X,6543-0
The Iliad. Homer. 6198-2
The Iliad. Frances Halley Newton. 6118-4
Ilic Jr., Vojislav
   Bells toll. 6765-4
   From a walk. 6765-4
   Night music. 6765-4
Ilic, Vojislav
   Gypsy. 6765-4
   Late fall. 6765-4
   On the river Vardar. 6765-4
   "The sky is grey and gloomy. For days now" 6765-4
   "With eyses spend and unseeing" 6765-4
Ilicet. Algernon Charles Swinburne. 6828-6
Ilicet. Algernon Charles Swinburne. 6655-0
Ilicet, sels. Algernon Charles Swinburne. 6472-8
Ilion, Ilion. Alfred Lord Tennyson. 6315-2
Ill. Bernard Spencer. 6379-9
"Ill canst thou bide in alien lands like these". Ivy.
      Edgar Fawcett. 7041-8
"Ill fares the land, to hastening ills a prey". The
      deserted village, sel. Oliver Goldsmith. 6954-1
Ill humour. Jorge Carrera Andrade. 6759-X
Ill requited. Eugene Field. 6949-5
Ill thrift. Sir Thomas More. 6383-7
The ill wind. Unknown. 6787-5
"Ill-fated heart! and can it be". On a Cornelian heart
      which was broken. George Gordon, 6th Baron Byron.
      6945-2
The ill-natured briar. Anna Bache. 6131-1
Ill-tempered lover, sels. Louis Alexander Mackay. 6021-8
The ill-tempered man. Edgar A. Guest. 6748-4
Illan-na-gila. Frederick Robert Higgins. 6781-6
Illileo. James Whitcomb Riley. 6992-4
Illimitable. Gamaliel Bradford. 6036-6,6619-4
The illimitable God, fr. A death in the desert. Robert
      Browning. 6337-3
Illinois. C.H. Chamberlain. 6465-5
Illinois farmer. Beulah Jackson Charmley. 6750-6
Illness. Po Chu-I. 6357-8
Illogical. Ella Wheeler Wilcox. 6863-4
"Ills fits the abstemious muse a crown...weave". Webster.
      Ralph Waldo Emerson. 6753-0
The illuminated canticle. Florence Wilkinson. 6467-1
The illuminated city. Felicia Dorothea Hemans. 6973-8
Illumination for victories in Mexico. Sara J. ("Grace
      Greenwood"') Lippincott. 6946-0
The illumination of George Jr. Gerald Cable. 6855-3
An illumination. Joshua Freeman Crowell. 6130-3
The illuminations of St. Peter's. Richard Monckton Milnes;
      1st Baron Houghton. 6624-0
Illumined. Tom McInnes. 6115-X
Illusion. Sir William Alexander; Earl of Stirling. 6180-X
Illusion. Jean Cocteau. 6351-9
Illusion. Nicholas Flood Davin. 6433-7
Illusion. Ralph Waldo Emerson. 7014-0
Illusion. Alfred Hayes. 6785-9
Illusion. Adelaide Anne Procter. 6957-6
Illusion. George William ("A.E.") Russell. 6659-3
Illusion. Nevah Trebor. 6501-5
Illusion. Ella Wheeler Wilcox. 6730-1
Illusion, fr. Four songs, after Verlaine. Alfred Noyes.
      6151-2
Illssions. Robert Underwood Johnson. 6632-1
Illusions. Robert Haven Schauffler. 6764-6
Illusive month. Hildegarde Flanner. 6628-3
The illustrated world. Cesar Moro. 6759-X
"Illustrious Cook, Columbus of our shore". Australasia.
      William Charles Wentworth. 6768-9
"Illustrious monarch of Iberia's soil". Columbus to
      Ferdinand. Philip Freneau. 6946-0
Illvstrissimo, poetentissimoqve principi, Fredrico...
      Thomas Campion. 6794-8
"Illyrian woodlands, echoing falls". To E.L., on his
      travels in Greece. Alfred Lord Tennyson. 6977-0
Ilmarinen's wedding feast, fr. The Kalevala. Unknown
      (Finnish) 6372-1

Ilott, Percy
   John and Molly. 6937-1
   Mary Keltie Craig. 6937-1
   The point of view. 6937-1
"Ils ont passe dans la nuit bleue". Fuite en Angleterre. Emile Cammaerts. 6785-9
The ilse. Heinrich Heine. 6484-1
Image. Gustave Kahn. 6801-4
Image in a lilac tree. Terence Tiller. 6379-9
The image in lava. Felicia Dorothea Hemans. 6973-8
The image in the forum. Robert Buchanan. 6144-3
The image in the heart. Felicia Dorothea Hemans. 6973-8
The image of death. Thomas, 2nd Baron Vaux. 6245-8
The image of delight. William Ellery Leonard. 6754-9
The image of God. Francisco de Aldana. 6730-1
"The image of earth/in winter". The year of winter. Frank LaPena Tauhindauli. 7005-1
"Image of her whom I love, more than she". Elegie 010, The dreame. John Donne. 6958-4
"An image of Lenthe". The coming of war: Actaeon. Ezra Pound. 6897-9
"Image of one, who lived of yore!". Incognita. James Montgomery. 6980-0
The image repetition. Douglas Barbour. 6767-0
Image, Selwyn
   Her confirmation. 6656-9
   A meditation for Chriatmas day. 6747-6
   A prayer ("Dear, let me dream"). 6274-1,6656-9
   The protestation. 6656-9
"An image-dance of change". Poetry. Siegfried Sassoon. 6071-4
Images. Richard Aldington. 6102-8
Images of disaster. Dunstan Thompson. 6391-8
Images of patriarchal life. Felicia Dorothea Hemans. 6973-8
Images, sels. Valery Larbaud. 6351-9
The images. Richard Lawson Gales. 6950-9
Imaginary dialogue. Dudley Fitts. 6641-0
The imaginary invalid, sels. Moliere (Jean Baptiste Poquelin) 6637-2
Imagination, fr. Midsummer night's dream. William Shakespeare. 6302-0;6385-3
The imaginative crisis. Unknown. 6089-7
Imaginative sympathy with nature. George Gordon, 6th Baron Byron. 6240-7
Imagine. Langston Hughes. 6803-0
"Imagine a town where no one walks the...". Hopper's 'Nighthawks' (1942). Ira Sadoff. 6966-5
"Imagine a world of people whose motto is" Ronald James Dessus. 6870-7
Imagine the south. George Woodcock. 6379-9
"Imagine!/They are afraid of you". Imagine. Langston Hughes. 6803-0
"An imagined footfall/like a sudden memory". The missing person. Theodora Todd. 6900-2
Imagined happiness. Erik Axel Karlfeldt. 6045-5
Imagiste love lines. Unknown. 6089-7
"Imbre lachrymarum largo." Unknown. 6563-5
Imbrie, Frank Morgan
   District no. 9. 6681-X
Imbs, Bravig
   Jenny was a jewel. 6039-0
Imelda, fr. Records of woman. Felicia Dorothea Hemans. 6973-8
Imitated. Thomas Warton (the Elder) 6962-2
Imitation. Anthony C. Deane. 6089-7
Imitation ("Calm and implacable"). Anthony C. Deane. 6089-7,6440-X
Imitation ("My love she leans from the window"). Henry Cuyler Bunner. 6440-X
Imitation of Christ. Wilma C. Ludlow. 6144-3
An imitation of Dr. Watts. Eugene Field. 6949-5
The imitation of Faust. Alfred Hayes. 6389-6
Imitation of Horace. John Dryden. 6654-2
Imitation of Robert Browning. James Kenneth Stephen. 6440-X
An imitation of some French verses. Thomas Parnell. 6975-4
Imitation of Southey. George Canning and John Hookham Frere. 6092-7
An imitation of Spencer. John Armstrong. 6968-1

Imitation of Spenser. John Keats. 6110-9
Imitation of the style of [Percy]. Samuel Johnson. 6975-4
Imitation of Walt Whitman ("Who am I?"). Judy [pseud]. 6440-X
An imitation of Wordsworth. Catherine Maria Fanshawe. 6089-7
Imitation to Spenser. John Keats. 6828-6
Imitations of Horace (satires & epistles): To Augustus. Alexander Pope. 6152-4
Imitations of Shakespeare. John Armstrong. 6968-1
Imitations of Walt Whitman. Unknown. 6089-7
Imitatrix ales. Archias. 6435-3
Immaculata, Sister Mary
   Altar boy. 6839-1
The Immaculate Conception. John Banister Tabb. 6282-2
Immaculate palm. Joseph Joel Keith. 6282-2
Immanence. Edmond Gore Alexander Holmes. 6337-3
Immanence. Richard Hovey. 6730-1
Immanence. Thomas Durley Landels. 6337-3
Immanence. Evelyn Underhill. 6303-9,6337-3,6477-9,6532-5
Immanent. Walter De La Mare. 6905-3
Immanuel. Orgill Cogie. 6269-5
"Immensitie cloysterd in thy deare wombe". Nativitie. John Donne. 6933-9
Immensity. John Hall Wheelock. 6102-8,6076-5
"Immersed in loneliness and dripping dark". Return to town. David Morton. 6839-1
"Immersed in the haven of beef flesh". Hamburger Mary's. Todd S.J. Lawson. 6792-1, 6998-3
The immigrant Madonna. Helen Dwight Fisher. 6954-1
The immigrant. Frank Kendon. 6339-X
Immigrants. Genevieve Louise Lynch. 6070-6
Immigrants. Nancy Byrd Turner. 6464-7
The immigrants. Alfred Noyes. 6151-6
The immigration act of 1924 Laureen Mar. 6790-5
Immolation. Robert Farren. 6930-4
The immolation of Constance de Beverley. Sir Walter Scott. 6302-0
The immoral arctic. Morris Bishop. 6722-0
Immortal. Florence Earle Coates. 6337-3
Immortal. Sara Teasdale. 6730-1
Immortal. Mark Van Doren. 6464-7
Immortal autumn. Archibald MacLeish. 6780-8
Immortal Autumn. Archibald MacLeish. 6536-8
"Immortal babe, who this dear day". For Christmas day. Bishop Hall. 6756-5
Immortal babe, who this dear day. Joseph Hall. 6747-6
The immortal dead. Algernon Charles Swinburne. 6461-2
"Immortal eyes, why do they never die?". The poet betrayed. Louis Untermeyer. 6875-8
"Immortal Imogen, crown'd queen above". The two swans. Thomas Hood. 6974-6
An immortal guest. Hannah More. 6211-3
The immortal hour. Humbert Wolfe. 6779-4
Immortal living. Harold Trowbridge Pulsifer. 6337-3
'Immortal love'. George Edward Woodberry. 6007-2,6031-5
"Immortal love, author of this great frame." George Herbert. 6645-3
Immortal love, forever full. John Greenleaf Whittier. 6490-6,6143-5
"The immortal mind craves objects that endure". Those words were uttered, sels. William Wordsworth. 6867-7
"Immortal Newton never spoke". On the above lines. Philip Dormer Stanhope, 4th Earl of Chesterfield. 6874-X
The immortal mind. George Gordon, 6th Baron Byron. 6600-3, 6730-1
Immortal morn. Hezekiah Butterworth. 6465-5,6143-5,6449-3
Immortal morning. Rosa Mulholland; Lady Gilbert. 6174-5
Immortal nature. Erasmus Darwin. 6879-0
Immortal nature, fr. The economy of vegetation. Erasmus Darwin. 6932-0
"Immortal Newton never spoke". Philip Dormer Stanhope, 4th Earl of Chesterfield. 6289-X
The immortal part. Alfred Edward Housman. 6508-2
The immortal residue. Adelaide Crapsey. 6337-3
Immortal sails. Alfred Noyes. 6151-6
"Immortal sorrow, that with the spirit of God". Ode to sorrow. Frederick Victor Branford. 6777-8
Immortal tent. William Blake. 6978-9
Immortal words. Aline Badger Carter. 6144-3

The immortal. William Blake. 6315-2
The immortal. Marjorie L.C. Pickthall. 6591-0,6592-9
The immortal. Cale Young Rice. 6266-0,6374-8,6653-4
Immortalia ne speres. Alcaeus. 6435-3
Immortality. Joseph Addison. 6461-2
Immortality. Matthew Arnold. 6337-3,6110-9,6250-4,6199-0, 6354-3,6373 ,6655-0
Immortality. W.A. Barton Jr. 7016-7
Immortality. Arthur S. Bourinot. 6796-4
Immortality. Richard Henry Dana. 6240-7
Immortality. Emily Dickinson. 6179-6
Immortality. William H. Hamilton. 6269-5
Immortality. Joseph Jefferson. 6303-9,6889-8,6798-0
Immortality. Leo Konopka. 6249-0
Immortality. John Westland Marston. 7015-9
Immortality. Gertrude Huntington McGiffert. 6838-3
Immortality. Gertrude Huntington McGiffert. 6320-9
Immortality. Susan L. Mitchell. 6930-4
Immortality. Frederick W.H. Myers. 6656-9
Immortality. Lizette Woodworth Reese. 6102-8,6476-0,6607-0, 6300-4,6396-9,6076
Immortality. William Shakespeare. 6214-8
Immortality. Sir Philip Sidney. 6436-1
Immortality. William Wordsworth. 6438-8
Immortality ("Age cannot reach me..."). Susan L. Mitchell. 6244-X;6174-5
Immortality ("For me--to have made one soul"). Edwin Hatch. 6303-9
Immortality ("Past ruin'd Ilion Helen lives"). Walter Savage Landor. 6186-9
Immortality ("We must pass like smoke..") George William ("A.E.") Russell. 6244-X,6730-1,6659-3,6656-9
Immortality conferred in vain. Theognis. 6435-3
Immortality in books. John Florio. 6934-7
Immortality in song. Michael Drayton. 6092-7,6250-4,6102-8
The immortality of love. Robert Southey. 6097-8,6412-7, 6627-5,6627-5
The immortality of verse. Horace. 7039-6
Immortality, fr. Job. Bible. 6730-1
Immortality, fr. Lycidas. John Milton. 6337-3,6214-8
An immortality. Ezra Pound. 6431-0
Immortals. David Morton. 6083-8
Immortals in exile. Arthur Davison Ficke. 6467-1
The immortals. Isaac Rosenberg. 6210-5
Immunity. Ibn Maimun. 6362-4
Immunity. Thomas a Kempis. 6144-3,6335-7
Immunity of beauty. Clarence L. Haynie. 6841-3
Immutable. Berton Braley. 6853-7
Imogen. Richard Henry Stoddard. 6753-0,6288-1
The imp of spring-time. Bayard Taylor. 6976-2
The impassable.. William Wilkins. 6174-5
Impatience. Phoebe Cary. 6969-X
Impatience. Olive Clair. 6850-2
Impatience. Ella Wheeler Wilcox. 6956-8
The impatient lover. Sir Philip Sidney. 6250-4,6383-7
The impatient maid. George Peele. 6733-6
Impatient with desire. George Granville; Baron Lansdowne. 6563-5
"Impatient women, as you wait". Happy women. Phoebe Cary. 6969-X,6006-4
The impecunious fop. Joseph Hall. 6200-8
Impenitentia ultima. Ernest Dowson. 6507-4,6508-2,6655-0
Imperative. Josephine Miles. 6640-2
Imperatrix. Gustav Davidson. 6619-4
The impercipient. Thomas Hardy. 6337-3,6657-7,6730-1,6430-2,6508-2
Imperfect beauty. Clarence L. Haynie. 6841-3
Imperfection. Edgar Fawcett. 7041-8
Imperfection. James Abraham Martling. 6952-5
Imperial airways. Louis Untermeyer. 7014-0
"Imperial gem of floral fame". The morning glory. Edward R. Huxley. 6885-5
"Imperial Persia bowed to his wise". Daniel. Richard Wilton. 6848-0
An imperial rescript. Rudyard Kipling. 6810-3
Imperialism. Bertrand Shadwell. 6542-2
"Imperiled stands the day.Up the bright street". For the undefeated. Eleanor Wells. 6761-1,6783-2
The imperious angler, fr. A session with... James Whitcomb Riley. 6091-9

Imperious design. Maureen Cobb Mabbott. 6979-7
Impermanence. Lizette Woodworth Reese. 6782-4
"Impertinence at first is born". the hound and the huntsman. John Gay. 6972-X
Impertinent poems, sels. Edmund Vance Cooke. 6291-1,6337-3, 6260-1,6274-1
An impetuous resolve. James Whitcomb Riley. 6990-8
An impetuous resolve. James Whitcomb Riley. 6018-8
Impetutous Samuel. Harry ("Col. D. Streamer") Graham. 6902-9
'Imph-m'.. Unknown. 6277-6
"The impious monarch sat upon his throne". The plague of hailstones. Edwin Atherstone. 6848-0
Implacable tower, fr. Two gentlemen in bonds. John Crowe Ransom. 6011-0
"Implacables as are thy artic floes". Russia. Elliott Napier. 6784-0
Implora pace. Bayard Taylor. 6976-2
An important discovery. Carolyn Wells. 6882-0
Importune me no more. Elizabeth I; Queen of England. 6182-6
Impossibility. Jamye H. Coleman. 6178-8
The impossible fact. Christian Morgenstern. 6643-7
Impossible to trust women. Unknown. 6881-2
Impossibly, motivated by midnight. Edward Estlin Cummings. 6375-6
Impregnable. Frederick George Scott. 6224-5
Impress of the Crucifix. Mother Mary Alphonsa. 6285-7
Impression. Sir Edmund Gosse. 6507-4,6732-8,6102-8,6301-2
Impression. Clark Ashton Smith. 6250-4
Impression at Reno. C.R. Holmes. 6515-5
Impression de voyage. Oscar Wilde. 6331-4
Impression du nuit: London. Lord Alfred Bruce Douglas. 6439-6
Impression of autumn. Rachel Annand Taylor. 6180-X
An impression of old Cape Cod from a motor car. Eva Macey Watson. 6798-0
Impressionistic. Unknown. 6118-4
Impressions. Harold Monro. 6102-8
Impressions. Jean Mutter. 6799-9
Impressions 004. Edward Estlin Cummings. 6808-1
Impressions of Bermuda. Madeline B. Foster. 6799-9
Impressions of Paris. Norma Paul Ruedi. 6750-6
Impressions of the Rockies. Katherine Hunter Coe. 6906-1
"Imprimis: I forgot all day your face". Sonnet ("Imprimis"). Conrad Aiken. 6012-9
Imprisoned. Thomas Bernhard. 6769-7
Imprisoned. John Hall Wheelock. 6441-8
The imprisoned soul. Walt Whitman. 6730-1
Impromptu. John Gould Fletcher. 6010-2
Impromptu. Thomas Gray. 6369-1,6380-2
Impromptu. Rossiter W. Raymond. 6385-3
An impromptu fairy-tale. James Whitcomb Riley. 6091-9
Impromptu on Charles II. John Wilmot, 2d Earl of Rochester. 6125-7
Impromptu on hearing Mrs Thrale consulting with..friend. Samuel Johnson. 6975-4
Impromptu on reading the chapter on polygamy... William Cowper. 6814-6
Impromptu on writing a letter without...anything to say. William Cowper. 6814-6
Impromptu, in reply to a friend. George Gordon, 6th Baron Byron. 6945-2
Impromtu. George Gordon, 6th Baron Byron. 6110-9
Improved "Enoch Arden". Unknown. 6273-3
Improvement in the forties. Thomas Barnard. 6092-7
"'Improvement' puts old times to rout". The cider mill. Benjamin Franklin Taylor. 6815-4
Improvident. Hesper Le Gallienne. 6347-0
Improvisation. Louis Gilmore. 6070-2
Improvisation. Paul S. Nickerson. 6037-4
"An improvisation on One glimpsed in passing." Maurice Kelley. 6397-7
Improvisations. Bayard Taylor. 6976-2
Improvising. Louise Townsend Nicholl. 6388-8
Impu Mon-in No Osuke
  "The fisher's clothes, though cheap, withstand".
  William N. Porter (tr.). 6852-9
Impulse. Archibald MacLeish. 6070-6
Impulse. Robert Southey. 6867-7

"The impulse of all love is to create". Creation. Ella
    Wheeler Wilcox. 6956-8
The impulse, fr. The hill wife. Robert Frost. 6030-7
The impulse. Robert Frost. 6317-9,6030-7
Imputantur. Bible. 7020-5
In. Vicente Huidobro. 6642-9
In "The Book of loves". Jose Maria de Heredia. 6351-9
In 1732. Unknown. 6158-3
"In 1855/one hundred and sixty-seven boys". State school.
    Paul D. Shiplett. 6870-7
In 1929. Stephen Spender. 6354-3
"In a 'bus queue a Jueue, bound for Kueue". Limerick:"In a
    'bus queue a Jueue, bound for Kueue". Unknown. 6811-
    1
"In a blue valley far from me". The willow. Harold Fehrsen
    Sampson. 6800-6
In a boarding house. Frances Rogers Upton. 6764-6
In a boat. Hilaire Belloc. 6282-2
"In a bowl to sea went wise men three". The wise men of
    gotham. Thomas Love Peacock. 6802-2
In a burying ground. Sara Teasdale. 6032-3
In a bye-canal. Herman Melville. 6333-0
In a cafe. Francis Ledwidge. 6812-X
In a canoe. Richard R. Kirk. 6548-1
"In a cart of no memory". Run-Run went north. Violeta
    Parra. 7036-1
In a cathedral city. Thomas Hardy. 6908-8
"In a certain fair island, for commerce renown". Elessde.
    Unknown. 6787-5
In a chair. Sir John Collings ("Solomon Eagle") Squire.
    6250-4
"In a chamber, grand and gloomy, in the shadow". The
    stigma. Francis De Haes Janvier. 6912-6
"In a chariot of light from the regions of day". Liberty
    tree. Thomas Paine. 6753-0,6946-0
In a child's album. William Wordsworth. 6239-3,6466-3
In a churchyard. Walter De La Mare. 6905-3
In a city square. Eleanor Glenn Wallis. 6388-8
In a class of moral theology. Francis Sweeney. 6839-1
In a clear starry night. George Wither. 6271-7
In a closed universe. James Hayford. 6388-8
In a coffee pot. Alfred Hayes. 6640-2
In a convex mirror. Rosemary Dobson. 6349-7
In a copy of Browning. Bliss Carman and Richard Hovey.
    6890-1
In a copy of Omar Khayyam. James Russell Lowell. 6126-5
"In a cottage far away where the twilight...". Just a
    cottage, quaint and old. Katherine Call Simonds.
    6764-6
In a country churchyard. Edmund Blunden. 6072-2
In a dance. Jessica Nelson North. 6070-6
"In a dark and dismal alley where sunshine...". Tommy's
    prayer. John F. Nicholls. 6919-3
"In a dark and dismal alley where the sunshine...".
    Tommy's prayer. John F. Nicholls. 6964-9
"In a Devonshire lane, as I trotted along". The Devonshire
    lane. Unknown. 6787-5
In a dark hour. Gertrude Hall. 6097-8
In a darkening garden. Sara Teasdale. 6649-6
"In a dimly lighted room a woman". Lost thoughts. Jane M.
    Stern. 6799-9
"In a dirty old house lived a dirty old man". The dirty
    old man. William Allingham. 6358-6,6512-0,6927-4
In a dream. Heinrich Heine. 6842-1
In a dream. James Oppenheim. 6345-4
"In a dream late as I lay". By-by, lullaby. Unknown. 6756-
    5
"In a dream, I wandered lightly". A dream. Gertrude Alger.
    6798-0
In a drear-nighted December. John Keats. 6122-2,6134-6,
    6187-7,6102-8,6110-9,6086-2,6371-3,6199-0
In a factory. Annette Wynne. 6032-3
In a fair garden. Thomas Edward Brown. 6809-X
"In a fair summer's radiant morn". The entail. Horace
    Walpole; 4th Earl of Orford. 6874-X
"In a fairy boat on a fairy sea". Rondels of childhood
    ('In a fairy boat') Bernard Weller. 6770-0
"In a fairy-like bower/I found a sweet flower". The fatal
    rose. Lillian Mack. 6799-9
"In a far country that I cannot name". The proud king fr.

The earthly paradise. William Morris. 7034-5
In a forest. Andrew Marvell. 6935-5
In a forest. Robert Southey. 6049-8
"In a forest, far away". Pax vobiscum. Thomas Bracken.
    6784-0
In a forgotten burying-ground. Ruth Guthrie Harding. 6027-
    7
In a friendly sort o' way. James Whitcomb Riley. 6260-1
In a friendly sort o' way. Unknown. 6085-4,6211-3
In a garden. Pauline B. Barrington. 6241-5
In a garden. Livingston L. Biddle. 6338-1
In a garden. Josephine Sievers Birt. 6906-1
In a garden. Bliss Carman and Richard Hovey. 6890-1
In a garden. Horace Holley. 6338-1
In a garden. Theda Kenyon. 6374-8
In a garden. Louise Chandler Moulton. 6677-1
In a garden. Leslie Rubin. 6850-2
In a garden. Stephen Spender. 6645-3
In a garden. Algernon Charles Swinburne. 6519-8,6084-6,
    6655-0
In a garden. Arthur Symons. 6649-6
In a garden of Granada. Thomas Walsh. 6331-4,6338-1
In a garret. Elizabeth Akers Allen. 6300-4
"In a gay jar upon his shoulder". The amphora. Fedor
    Sologub. 7039-6
In a girls' school. David Morton. 6478-7;6465-5
"In a glass amphora the color of swimming-pool". Bridled.
    Cynthia Ozick. 6803-0
"In a glorious garden grene". Unknown. 6187-7,6649-6
In a gondola. Robert Browning. 6186-9,6204-0,6437-X,6657-7,
    6199-0,6439 ,6110-9,6655-0,6656-9
In a gondola. Joaquin Miller. 6066-8
In a gondola. John Todhunter. 6331-4,6631-3
"In a goodly night, as in my bede I laye". Waking alone.
    Unknown. 6881-2
In a graveyard. Unknown. 6273-3
In a graveyard. Theodore Watts-Dunton. 7015-9,6785-9
In a Greek garden. Bernice Lesbia Kenyon. 6037-4
"In a great elm against the winter sky". Song of
    starlings. Ruth Lechlitner. 6979-7
"In a great land, a new land, a land full...". Longfellow.
    Henry Van Dyke. 6961-4
In a green garden. Angelo Poliziano. 6649-6
"In a grove most rich of shade". Sir Philip Sidney. 6430-2
In a hall bedroom. Aline Kilmer. 6232-6
In a hard shell. Otto Laaber. 6769-7
In a herber green. Robert Weever. 6958-4
"In a herber green, asleep whereas I lay". R. Wever. 6187-
    7
In a hermitage. William Whitehead. 6086-2
In a hospital corridor. Anne-Elise Roane Winter. 6270-9
In a June garden. May Lewis. 6232-6
In a lady's album. Marcus Clarke. 6784-0
'In a lady's album'. Marcus Clarke. 6768-9
"In a land of many waters, by a sun-forsaken..". Oine.
    Roderick Kidston. 6784-0
In a latticed balcony. Sarojini Naidu. 6320-9
In a lecture-room. Arthur Hugh Clough. 6657-7,6110-9,6199-
    0
In a London square. Arthur Hugh Clough. 6123-0,6110-9,6199-
    0
"In a little chapel lowly/Kneels a child...". Our lady of
    the rosary. Catherine McAleese. 6799-9
"In a little German village". The blacksmith of Ragenbach.
    frank Murray. 6912-6
"In a little roadside cottage...". The rusty sword. George
    M. Vickers. 6926-6
"In a little theater, in the jewry of the". A tragedy of
    to-day. Richard Watson Gilder. 6848-0
"In a long valley of the hemlock ranges". If I forget
    thee. Sarah N. Cleghorn. 7038-8
"In a mansion grand, just over the way". Dell and I. Ella
    Wheeler Wilcox. 6863-4
"In a Mexican mission bells toll no mark". Going back.
    George Rachow. 6870-7
In a maple grove. Amos F. Stalcup Jr. 6799-9
In a meadow. John Swinnerton Phillimore. 6096 X
"In a moonlit room sitting alone". A beautiful unknown.
    Celestin Pierre Cambiaire. 6826-X
In a museum. Anne Elizabeth Wilson. 6120-6

In a music hall, sels. John Davidson. 6819-7
In a mysterious way. William Cowper. 6461-2
In a mystery veiled. Mamie Ozburn Odum. 6799-9
'In a night of midsumme.' Richard Watson Gilder. 6177-X
In a Persian garden. Eve Gilbert Swift. 6585-6
"In a patch of clearing, scarcely more". The settler's Christmas eve. Alice Cary. 6969-X
"In a pioneer's cabin out West, so they say". Betty and the bear. Unknown. 6909-6
"In a place of the mountains of Edom". Peniel. Lizette Woodworth Reese. 6848-0
In a powder closet. Amy Lowell. 6072-2
In a province. Frank Templeton Prince. 6788-3
"In a queer old Irish village". The strange request. Annie R. Johnson. 6921-5
In a quiet neighborhood. Unknown. 6274-1
"In a quiet water'd land, a land of roses". The dead at Clonmacnois. Angus O'Gillan. 6930-4
"In a quiet watered land, a land of roses". The dead at Clonmacnois. Thomas William Rolleston. 6873-1
In a railway carriage. Alfred Noyes. 6151-6
In a railway station. Mary Sinton Leitch. 6038-2
In a restaurant. Wilfred Wilson Gibson. 6464-7
"In a room of the palace". Black Mrs. Behemoth, fr. Facade. Edith Sitwell. 7000-0
In a rooming house. Nell H. Royse. 6799-9
In a September night. F. Wyville Home. 6656-9
"In a shady nook one moonlit night". The leprahaun. Robert Dwyer Joyce. 6930-4
In a shop window. Margaret Elizabeth Sangster. 6510-4
"In a sky of methylene blue". Fantasia. Carlos Drummond de Andrade. 6759-X
In a sloping field of clover". The little brook. L.C. Whiton. 6965-7
In a slum. A. Stodart Walker. 6474-4
"In a small cabin, lit by a single lamp". Alfred Noyes. 6298-9
"In a small cabin, lit by a single port-hole". Alfred Noyes. 6298-9
"In a small chamber, friendless and unseen". To W.L. Garrison. James Russell Lowell. 6934-7
"In a small town in Scotland they sell...". Instructions on or rather examples of how to be afraid. Julio Cortazar. 6758-1
"In a small, quiet country town". The two stammerers. Unknown. 6915-0
In a snowstorm. Gertrude Alger. 6798-0
In a southern garden. Dorothea MacKellar. 6784-0
In a Staffordshire churchyard. Unknown. 6722-0
"In a stately hall at Brentford...". The last meeting of Pocahontas and the great captain. Margaret Junkin Preston. 6946-0
In a station of the metro, sels. Ezra Pound. 6289-X
In a storm. Harry Kemp. 6467-1
In a strange land. James Thomas Fields. 6240-7
In a Sudan village. Isabel Anderson. 6894-4
"In a subdued voice". Psaume sur une voix. Paul Valery. 6761-1
"In a sunny little corner". My garden corner. Maybelle Mayne Porter. 6841-3
In a sunny nook. Hans Vilhelm Kaalund. 6555-4
In a sweatshop. Richard Burton. 6954-1
"In a sweet, sweet dream, at dead of night". In a dream. Heinrich Heine. 6842-1
"In a swoon I can see it" Ken Wrinio. 6901-0
"In a tabernacle of a toure". Quia amore langueo. Unknown. 6881-2
"In a tangled knot of humanity" Thomas Sessler. 6769-7
In a theater. Capua. 6610-0
In a thunderstorm. Unknown. 6952-5
In a time of flowers. Sarojini Naidu. 6266-0
In a troubled dream. Stanton A. Coblentz. 6648-8
In a troubled world. Stanton A. Coblentz. 6144-3
In a two million dollar chapel. Richard M. Steiner. 6954-1
"In a vacant mood the phrase came to me". Ballade of the lost refrain. Christopher Morley. 6875-8
"In a vale among the herdsmen". The maiden from a far country. Johann C. Friedrich von Schiller. 6842-1
"In a valley, centuries ago". The petrified fern. Mary Lydia Bolles Branch. 6304-7,6523-6,6600-3,6621-6, 6964-9,6006-4,6049-8,6183-4,6385-3,6162-1,6478
"In a very humble cot". The washerwoman's song. Eugene F. Ware. 6889-8
In a waiting-room. Thomas Hardy. 6331-4
In a wife I would desire. William Blake. 6733-6
"In a winter of the 1600s...(it matters...)". The envoy from Dubrovnik. Jovan Ducic. 6765-4
"In a withered banana peel". The boy. Hertha Kraftner. 6769-7
"In Afric's fabled fountains I have panned...". The alien. Charles Murray. 6800-6
"In Agamemnon's tomb the poppy blows". Mycenae. C.R.R.. 6799-9
In a woman's face. Richard Church. 6317-9
In a wood. Thomas Hardy. 6289-X,6430-2,6508-2
In a year. Robert Browning. 6271-7,6302-0,6385-3,6543-0, 6655-0,6219 ,6102-8,6199-0
In absence. Avenzoar. 6362-4
In absence. Phoebe Cary. 6969-X
In absence. Benedikt Grondal. 6283-0
In absence. Josephine Johnson. 6042-0
In absence. Archibald Lampman. 6620-8
In absence. James Russell Lowell. 6077-3
In absence. Robert Cameron Rogers. 6441-8
In absence. Gaspara Stampa. 6325-X
In absence. John Banister Tabb. 6243-1,6737-9
In absence. Arthur Weir. 7041-8
In acceptance lieth peace. Amy Carmichael. 6337-3
In action. Unknown. 6340-3,6471-X
In adversity. Brian ("Korongo") Brooke. 6938-X
In Aesop's vain. W.H. Mitchell. 6505-8
In Africa. Roy Fuller. 6788-3
In after days. George Frederick Cameron. 6021-8,6115-X
In after days. Austin Dobson. 6301-2,6655-0,6653-4,6646-1, 6123-0,6289-X,6476-0,6656-9,6250-4,6508-2,6046-3, 6102-8,6153-2,6301-2
In after time. Walter Savage Landor. 6086-2
In age of science. Thomas Curtis Clark. 6039-0,6337-3
In air, fr. Two gentlemen in bonds. John Crowe Ransom. 6011-0
"In all earth's boundless beauty here revealed". Old rice-fields. Edith L. Fraser. 7016-7
"In all except a heart, and a black shade". Agolanti and his lady, fr. The legend of Florence. Leigh Hunt. 6980-0
"In all great Shushan's palaces was there". Vashti. Helen Hunt Jackson. 6848-0
In all the argosy of your bright hair. Dunstan Thompson. 6666-6
"In all the eastern hemisphere". The fall of J.W. Beane. Oliver Herford. 7021-3
"In all the land, range up, range down". Langley lane. Robert Buchanan. 6925-8
"In all the world there is not anything". Paris. Lydia Gibson. 6880-4
In all things, victory. Nagata. 6027-7
In Ampezzo. Trumbull Stickney. 6380-2
In Amsterdam. Eugene Field. 6735-2
"In all thy humors, whether grave or mellow". Temperament. Martial. 7039-6
"In Allah's name, the ever merciful". Shakh Ahnaf's letter from Baghdad. Bayard Taylor. 6848-0
In age of fops and toys, fr. Voluntaries. Ralph Waldo Emerson. 6212-1
In an Alameda field. Anna Catherine Markham. 6102-8,6076-5, 6241-5
In an Alameda field. Edwin Markham. 6076-5
"In an arboure of green may". Unknown. 6563-5
In an artist's studio. Thomas Bailey Aldrich. 6887-1
In an artist's studio. Christina Georgina Rossetti. 6123-0, 6508-2,6430-2,6655-0
In an atelier. Thomas Bailey Aldrich. 6358-6
"In an attic bare and cheerless, Jim..dying lay". The dying newsboy. Emily Thornton. 6964-9
In an auction room. Christopher Morley. 6431-0
In an Egyptian garden. Clinton Scollard. 6338-1
In an evil time. Evelyn Grace Flynn. 6847-2
In an iiluminated missal. Charles Kingsley. 6793-X
In an island garden. Alfred Noyes. 6782-4
In an Italian garden. Gertrude Hutington McGiffert. 6838-

3

In an old cemetery. Mary S. Boutwell. 6764-6
"In an old chamber softly lit". During a chorale by Cesar Franck, fr. To Celia. Witter Bynner. 6897-9
"In an old city by the storied shores". Opportunity. Edwin Markham. 6291-1;6478-7
"In an old faded photograph". Rabbit hunting no. 7. Jechun Park. 6775-1
In an old garden. Madison Cawein. 6649-6,6232-6,6338-1
In an old garden. Terry B. Dinkel. 6906-1
In an old garden. Frank Dempster Sherman. 6649-6
In an old garden forgotten. Arthur Wallace Peach. 7030-2
In an old nursery. Patrick Reginald Chalmers. 6653-4
In an old southern garden. Hallie Hall. 6799-9
"In an old story, dear to pilgrim-soul". Valiant-fortruth. Louise Manning Hodgkins. 7001-9
In an omnibus. Arthur Symons. 6507-4
In an orient barque. Charles Van Lerberghe. 6351-9
In an Oriental harbour. Cale Young Rice. 6653-4
In an oriental shop. Norreys Jephson O'Conor. 6184-2
In an Oxford garden. Arthur Upson. 6338-1
In an unknown tongue. John White Chadwick. 6321-7
In ancient Greece. Henry Felton. 6934-7
"In ancient days when wizard power was great". The wizard's hunting. Unknown (Algonquin Indian). 6864-2
"In ancient days, as the old stories run". Oriental mysticism. Unknown (Persian). 6752-2
"In ancient times a castle stood, so proud...". The minstrel's curse. Johann Ludwig Uhland. 6903-7
"In and out we watch your winding". To a Kaffir footpath. Louis Sordell. 6800-6
"In anger I flung out my hand/Against the...". I could not understand. Berthal Lanier. 6799-9
"In Aprell and in May". Besse Bunting. Unknown. 6881-2
"In April mortal's eye hath seen". October. Robert Loveman. 6941-X
"In April/He shows his bill". Cuckoo lore. Unknown. 6943-6
"In Arcady, wherever that may be". The fall of Corydon. W.B. A.". 7021-3
In answer. Rose Hartwick Thorpe. 6414-0
In answer to a lady who advised retirement. Lady Mary Wortley Montagu. 6932-0
In Apia Bay. Sir Charles George Douglas Roberts. 6062-5
In apple-time. Ernest Neal Lyon. 6721-2
In April. Emily Gail Arnold. 6449-3
In April. Margaret Lee Ashley. 6027-7,6431-0
In April. Winifred Virginia Jackson. 6036-6
In April. Minna Keyser. 6789-1
In April. John Richard Moreland. 6039-0,6326-8
In Arcadia. Lawrence Durrell. 6209-1
In Arcadia. James Russell Lowell. 6004-8
In Arcadie. Josephine A. Cass. 6084-6
In Arcadie. Helen M. Merrill. 6115-X
In Arcadie. John Robert Moses. 6936-3
In Arcady by moonlight. Kendall Banning. 6347-0
In Arlington. Edna Mead. 6542-2
In August. William Dean Howells. 6239-7,6243-1,6465-5
"In art some hold themselves content". The two painters. Austin Dobson. 7014-0
"In asking how I came to choose". Love's secret springs. Alice Cary. 6865-0;6969-X
"In Augusta, Montana: prairie dovetailed". Silos. Paul Zarzyski. 7032-9
In autumn. Robert Loveman. 6941-X
In autumn. Alice Meynell. 6955-X
In autumn. George Sterling. 6007-2,6648-8
In autumn. Arthur Symons. 6507-4
In autumn. Charles Hanson Towne. 6778-6
In autumn fields. Helen Merrill Egerton. 6797-2
In autumn tones. Margaret Perkins Briggs. 6039-0
"In autumn/the barren trees'". Lost love. Herman L. McMillan. 7024-8
"In awe/Before life's penny show". Poet. Nat Henry. 6462-0
"In baby carriage I begin my drive". Driven. Mary V. Traeger. 6857-X
"In Babylon and Nineveh". Skyscrapers. Charles Hanson Towne. 6761-1
"In Babylon they sat and wept". The tombs of the fathers. James Montgomery. 6848-0
"In Babylon, high Babylon". Beyond the breakers, sels.

George Sterling. 6954-1
In bachelor's hall. Clarence W. Peabody. 6116-8
"In Bainbridge town there dwelt of late". Unknown. 6059-5
In Ballyshannon. Robert J. Kerr. 6090-0
"In ballades things always contrive to get...". A ballade of ballade-mongers. Augustus M. Moore. 6770-0,6875-8
In barracks. Siegfried Sassoon. 6210-5
In battle. Abul Hasan (of Badajoz) 6362-4
In battle. Wallace Stevens. 6897-9
In Bay Chaleur. Hezekiah Butterworth. 6273-3,6670-4
In bed, not dead, fr. Two gentlemen in bonds. John Crowe Ransom. 6011-0
In beechen shade. Rosamund Marriott ("Graham R. Tomson") Watson. 6770-0,6875-8
In Berkshire. Richard Hengist Horne. 6793-X
In Bethlehem, that noble place. Unknown. 6747-6,6756-5
"In beechen shade the hours are sweet". In beechen shade. Rosamund Marriott ("Graham R. Tomson") Watson. 6770-0,6875-8
"In Bethlehem, in that fair city". To bliss God brings us, all and some. Unknown. 6756-5
"In Bethlehem, that fair city". To bliss God bring us all and some. Unknown. 6756-5
In between time (transcience). Marsha Ann Jackson. 7024-8
In Bibberley town. Unknown. 6549-X
"In billowy bloom the apple trees wave". April. Anne Wolf. 6750-6
"In Bodenstown churchyard there is a green...". Tone's grave. Thomas Osborne Davis. 6930-4
"In Bond Street buildings, on a winter's night". The gouty merchant and the stranger. Unknown. 6787-5
"In Bone county,/men and women live alone". Bone county. Jane M. Fink. 6900-2
In black and white: winter etchings, sels. John Addington Symonds. 7015-9
In blossom time. Ina D. Coolbrith. 6336-5,6478-7
"In body alone was Zosime". Damascius. 6251-2
In Bohemia. John Boyle O'Reilly. 7041-8
In Bohemia. John Boyle O'Reilly. 6166-4,6732-8,6307-1
In bonds. Alice Cary. 6865-0;6969-X
"In bonnie, blithe, and fair Scotland". Unknown. 6059-5
In Bourbon Street. John McClure. 6397-7
"In bowre and field he sought, where any tuft". Eve, fr. Paradise lost. John Milton. 6933-9
"In boyhood's days I loved the mellow earth". Old, old trees. John Girdler. 6836-7
"In boyhood's morn I sat me oft". The sawmill. John W. Garvin. 6797-2
"In boyish days 'twas fun to watch". Closing a trade in Vermont. Daniel L. Cady. 6989-4
In bozen of a Sunday. Amelia Josephine Burr. 6847-2
In Brittany. Charles Weekes. 6930-4
"In briery dell or thicken brown". Love and liberty. Royall Tyler. 7030-2
"In Britain's isle and Arthur's days". A fairy tale in the ancient English style. Thomas Parnell. 6975-4
"In Brittany I lost my way". In Brittany. Charles Weekes. 6930-4
"In Brooklyn, Abe Schwartz installs". News of the neighborhoods. Otto Paul Gonzalez. 6898-7
"In Bruges town is many a street". An incident at Bruges. William Wordsworth. 6980-0
"In Bruton town there lived a farmer". Bruton town. Unknown. 6829-4
"In Bruxelles Emperor Charles abode...". The abdication of Charles V. Sir William Stirling-Maxwell. 6960-6
"In Bunhill Row, some years ago". Jarvis and Mrs. Cope. Thomas Hood. 6974-6
"In Cagliostro's mirror the magician keeps...". Picasso's women. Olga Cabral. 6966-5
"In Camelot how grey and green". Rondeauz of the galleries. Andrew Lang. 6875-8
In broken images. Robert Graves. 6150-8,6354-3
In cabined ships at sea. Walt Whitman. 6154-0,6258-X,6008-0,6288-1,6560-0
In cabined ships, fr. Ships. John Masefield. 6258-X
"In cadenced mirrors fall the sudden notes". William ("Fiona Macleod") Sharp. 6997-5
In calm content. Unknown. 6274-1
In camp. William Haines Lytle. 6074-9

In cap and gown. Unknown. 6116-8
In Carmel Bay. Madge Clover. 6241-5
In castle land. Louis J. Magee. 7004-3
In Castyle there lived a lady. Unknown. 6061-7
"In certain brains, there is an inborn might". Genius. Elmer Ruan Coates. 6920-7
"In Chepstow stands a castle". The silver music. Ford Madox (Hueffer) Ford. 6785-9
"In Cherbourg Roads the pirate lay". The eagle and the vulture. Thomas Buchanan Read. 6946-0
In chains, fr. Sonnets from Moabite prison. Albrecht Haushofer. 6643-7
In change unchanging. Henry Ward Beecher. 6177-X
In Chartres cathedral. James Rennell Rodd; 1st Baron Rennell. 6271-7
In Cheltenham. Idris Davies. 6895-2
In cherry lane. William Livingston. 6292-X
"In childhood's bright and halcyon hours". The spirit-hand and voice. Charles W. Denison. 6755-7
In childhood's kingdom. Ernest Howard Crosby. 6274-1
In China. Carolyn Wells. 6882-0
In Christmas land. Unknown. 6274-1
"In childhood's lively days, when sleep". Wonderland. Frederick Charles Kolbe. 6800-6
"In childhood, when with eager eyes". The trance of time. John Henry, Cardinal Newman. 6931-2
"In Christian world Mary the garland wears?". A sonnet on Christian names. Charles Lamb. 6934-7
In church. Thomas Hardy. 6637-2,6491-4
In city streets. Ada Smith. 6083-8,6374-8,6423-X,6477-9
In class we create ourselves- having been told to... P.K. Page. 6767-0
In Clementina's artless mien. Walter Savage Landor. 6092-7
"In clay the statue stood complete". The torso. Bayard Taylor. 6976-2
"In clear cold blue Itasca Lake". Mississippi-Missouri. Charles H. Tiffany. 6818-9
"In clear, deep pools". Odyssey, sixth book. Hess. M. Whitcomb. 6839-1
"In Clementina's artless mien". Clementina and Lucilla. Walter Savage Landor. 6874-X
In cloak of grey. Alfred Noyes. 6320-9
"In cloudy legends of the dawn of years". The burden of time. Charles Lotin Hildreth. 7041-8
In clover. Elisabeth G. Palmer. 6662-3
"In Cnidus born, the consort I became". Heraclides. 6814-6
"In cock-wattle sunset or grey". Nostalgia. Louis MacNeice. 6930-4
"In Collins Street standeth a statue tall". Gone. Adam Lindsay Gordon. 6951-7,6784-0
"In coma now/With no apparent breath". Last incident. Grace Mansfield. 6750-6
"In comes the captain's daughter". The boys of Wexford. Robert Dwyer Joyce. 6858-8
In commendation of George Gascoigne's Steel glass(1576) Sir Walter Raleigh. 6584-8
In common things. Minot Judson Savage. 6109-5
"In concert with friends, on a bright June day". Meditation at a picnic. Edward R. Huxley. 6885-5
In conjunction. Charles Madge. 6209-1,6379-9
"In contemplation of pleasures in store". Our Lyceum picnic. Edward R. Huxley. 6885-5
"In Copeman's ear this truth let Echo tell". Thanks for a gift of pheasants. William Cowper. 6814-6
"In Cornish I was born, not of a low degree". Farewell, lovely Polly. Unknown. 6826-X
In convertendo. Bible. 6830-8
In cool, green haunts. Mahlon Leonard Fisher. 6510-4
"In country lanes the robins sing". The redbreast. Charles Henry Luders. 6770-0
In course of time. Wilfred Wilson Gibson. 6488-4
In coventry. James J. Daly. 6096 X
"In crystal towers and turrets ri hly set" Unknown. 6935-5
"In Cyprus springs-whereas dame Venus dwelt." Henry Howard, Earl of Surrey. 6584-8
"In crystal towns and turrets richly set". Song ("In crystal towns"). William Byrd. 6022-6
"In Cupid's court when suit is brought". Nonsuited. T.H.E. Printer [pseud].. 6878-2
"In cycles past, when here on earth before". Affinity. Unknown. 7021-3
In dark hour. Seumas MacManus. 6730-1,622-X,6172-9
"In darkness let me dwell, the ground shall...". John Cooper's funeral teares. Unknown. 6908-8
In days gone by. Lilla Cabot Perry. 6274-1
"In days gone by, St. Valentine". To St. Valentine. Madeleine Reese. 7021-3
In days like these. Thomas H. Stacy. 6340-3,6741-X
"In days of ease, when now the weary sword". The court of Charles II, fr. Epistle to Augustus. Alexander Pope. 6932-0
"In days of old, as we are told". Ben Franklin, Esq. Charles Irvin Junkin. 6936-3
"In days of old, there lived of mighty fame". Palamon and Arcite; or, the knight's tale. Geoffrey Chaucer. 6970-3
"In days of old, when Arthur fill'd the throne". The wife of Bath. Geoffrey Chaucer. 6970-3
"In days of old, when Enlishment were ––". Italian opera. James Miller. 6932-0
"In days of yore some Indians were". The p'mula or air-demon. Unknown (Algonquin Indian). 6864-2
"In days that were- no matter when". An old road. Arthur Guiterman. 6773-5
In de mawnin'. Unknown. 6274-1
"In death he lives to read his wondrous dream". The living dead. Frank Lebby Stanton. 7001-9
In death the eyes are still. Randall Swingler. 6985-1
"In debt, deserted, and forlorn". The ill wind. Unknown. 6787-5
"In December, the earth slams shut". Circling. Ann Leventhal. 6822-7
"In deep distress I oft have cry'd". Psalm 120. Bible. 6848-0
In deep places. Amelia Josephine Burr. 6019-6,6464-7,6847-2
In defence of the advertising muse. Richard Kendall Munkittrick. 6274-1
In defence of the bush. Andrew Barton Paterson. 7012-4
In defense of humanism. David Gascoyne. 6391-8
In defense of the Royal Society. Abraham Cowley. 6250-4
In degree. Paul Hamilton Hayne. 6889-8
"In delta junction/the only poet is the wind". The stone harp. John Haines. 6803-0
"In dense forest/yet within sight of the...". In the cranberry gardens. Ann Chandonnet. 6855-3
"In depth of night the furnace flame". The city of Scranton. John E. Barrett. 6840-5
In der fremde. Robert Bridges. 6487-6
In der shweed long ago. Unknown. 6175-3
In derision of a country life. Edward Ravenscroft. 6563-5
In description. Ann Louise Hayes. 6515-5
In deserto. Arthur Shearly Cripps. 6800-6
In despair. Alice Cary. 6969-X
In die nativitatis. Unknown. 6756-5
In die nativitatis. Unknown. 6756-5
"In different contexts different words". H.B Mallalieu. 6052-8
"In digging up your bones, Tom Paine". Epigram, fr. Tom Paine. George Gordon, 6th Baron Byron. 6945-2
"In digging up your bones, Tom Paine". George Gordon, 6th Baron Byron. 6088-9
In dimido dierum. Bible. 6830-8
In distrust of merits. Marianne Moore. 6465-5,6391-8,6666-6,6665-8
In Donegal. Irene Haugh. 6782-4
In doubt. Sarah Morgan Bryan Piatt. 7041-8
In dou t of doubt, fr. BishoptBlougram's apology. Robert Browning. 6337-3
"In Dublin's fair city, where the girls are so pretty" Unknown. 6317-9
"In dreams I crossed a barren land". Ballade of broken c   flutes. Edwin Arlington Robinson. 6875-8
"In dreams of thee, sweetheart of old". My first love. Grace Reynolds Parrish. 6799-9
"In dublin's fair city,/Where the girls are...". Cockles and mussels. Unknown. 6930-4
In ducli iubilo. John Wedderburn. 6756-5
In dulci jubilo. Unknown (German) 6125-7
In durance. Babette Deutsch. 6070-6

"In each land the sun doth visit". Selection, fr. Wilhelm Meister. Johann Wolfgang von Goethe. 7014-0
In earliest spring. William Dean Howells. 6467-1
"In earliest times, long ere the day". The punishment. Felix E. Schelling. 6936-3
"In early hours, of the starry dew". Morning and afternoon. Edward Farquhar. 6939-8
In early spring. Alice Meynell. 6423-X
In Egypt, sels. Virna Sheard. 6115-X
In England. May O'Rourke. 7031-0
"In early spring I watched two sparrows build". The rape of the nest. Francis Adams. 6510-4,6943-6
"In early spring-time, after their tea". En famille. Edith Sitwell. 6985-1
"In early summer moonlight I have strayed". The sedge-warbler. Ralph Hodgson. 7020-5
"In early years our valiant fight began". The happy warrior. Thomas Curtis Clark. 6995-9
"In eaves sole sparrowe sitts not more alone". Psalm 102, verses 6 and 7. Bible. 6848-0
"In eerie lights beneath the sky". Bells from out of the past. Joellen Ingram. 6799-9
"In Egypt's centre, when the world was young". The head of Memnon. Horace Smith. 6980-0
"In either hand the hastening angel". The departure from paradise. John Milton. 6848-0
"In England the leaves are falling...". Lines written in captivity. F.J. Patmore. 7029-9
In envy of cows. Joseph Auslander. 6037-4,6777-8
"In eternum I was once determed." Sir Thomas Wyatt. 6378-0, 6584-8
In ethics. E.H. W. 6118-4
In every home. Unknown. 6097-8
"In every little crooked path that leads". Where shall I go? Miriam Wolfson. 6850-2
"In every sound, I think I hear her feet". Villanelle. May Probyn. 7037-X,6770-0
In evil long I took delight. John Newton. 6337-3
"In evil long I took delight". John Newton. 6931-2
In excelsis. Lord Alfred Bruce Douglas. 6778-6
In excelsis. Arthur Cecil Hillier. 6507-4
In excelsis. Thomas S. Jones Jr. 6556-2
In excelsis. Amy Lowell. 6010-2
"In excelsis gloria". Unknown. 6145-1,6747-6,6424-8
In exile. Mary Elizabeth Blake. 6309-8
In exile. Andrew Marvell. 6322-5
In exitu. Henry Longan Stuart. 6096-X
In explanation. Walter Learned. 6875-8
In explanation. Walter Learned. 6309-8
"In extended observation of the ways...of man". Et dona ferentes. Rudyard Kipling. 6810-3
In extremis. Fray Angelico Chavez. 6839-1
In extremis. Mildred D. Harding. 6857-X
In extremis. Vera Larminie. 6532-1
In extremity. Phoebe Cary. 6969-X
In fact. Judson Crews. 6998-3
"In fair Naples, just at noonday". The flower girl. Edith Wordsworth. 6925-8
"In fair Provence, the land of lute and rose". Sestina. Sir Edmund Gosse. 6770-0,6289-X
"In fairest garden wandered". The dream. Johann Ludwig Uhland. 6948-7
In fairy land. Lucy Larcom. 6129-X
"In fairyland are purple cats". Fairyland. Doris V. Lecky. 6850-2
"In faith I wot not what to say." Sir Thomas Wyatt. 6584-8
"In faith, I do not love thee with mine eyes". William Shakespeare. 6204-0
In Falmouth harbour, sels. Lionel Johnson. 6508-2
"In faith, I do not love thee with mine eyes". Sonnet 141 ("In faith"). William Shakespeare. 6447-7
"In fancy these scenes I often review". Aunt Sophy's notable experiment. Edward R. Huxley. 6885-5
In favor of tobacco. Samuel Rowlands. 6453-1
In February. Alice Meynell. 6955-X
In February. John Addington Symonds. 6519-8,6556-6
"In fear of death". Poem ("In fear"). John Prichard. 6360-8
"In Finisterre, between two winding bays". St. Pol de Leon, fr. Pictures by the way. John Nichol. 6819-7

In fervent praise of picnics. James Whitcomb Riley. 6091-9
"In fir tar is". Unknown. 6904-5
In Fisherrow. William Ernest Henley. 6250-4,6653-4
In Flanders. Eugene Field. 6949-5
In Flanders. James Norman Hall. 6420-5
In Flanders field: an answer. C.B. Galbreath. 6963-0
In Flanders fields. John McCrae. 6465-5,6506-6,6021-8,6211-3,6224-5,6289 ,6446-9,6646-1,6542-2,6250-4,6104-4, 6161 ,6331-4,6332-2,6337-3,6427-2,6443-4,6476 ,6301-2,6449-3,6102-8,6396-9,6650-X,6639 ,6482-5,6496-5, 6509-0,6732-8,6474-4,6631
In Flanders now. Edna Jaques. 6337-3
In Florence. Cora Fabbri. 6331-4,6631-3
"In five-score summers! All new eyes". 1967. Thomas Hardy. 6879-0
"In Flanders fields the cannon boom". In Flanders field: an answer. C.B. Galbreath. 6963-0
"'In Flanders fields, where poppies blow'.". Our soldier dead. Annette Kohn. 6846-4
"In Fleet-street dwelt, in days of yore". The magpie. Unknown. 6924-X
In for it. Somerville Gibney. 6652-6
"In former times my numerous rhymes". The doings of Delsarte. Eugene Field. 6949-5
"In forty years we've changed the world...". Sleigh bells. Edgar A. Guest. 6748-4
In fountain court. Arthur Symons. 6477-9,6508-2,6655-0
In France. Frances Cornford. 6044-7,6506-6
In France. Francis Ledwidge. 6812-X,7029-9,6812-X,7029-9
In France. Clinton Scollard. 6542-2
In friendship false, implacable in hate," fr. Absalom. John Dryden. 6637-2
"In front between the gaping heights". Coventry Patmore. 6997-5
In Galilee. Mary Frances Butts. 6848-0
In Gallipoli. Eden Phillpotts. 7027-2
"In Georgia City where I did dwell...". Unknown. 6059-5
In Gethsemane. Giles (the Younger) Fletcher. 6337-3
In Gethsemane. Crawford Trotter. 6335-7
"In front the awful Alpine track". Stanzas in memory of the author of Obermann. Matthew Arnold. 6046-3,6199-0,6250-4,6947-9
"In gayer hours, when high my fancy run". The bastard's lot. Richard Savage. 6932-0
"In genial mood/While at our pastoral banquet". Twin peaks of the valley, fr. The excursion. William Wordsworth. 6832-4
"In Genoa, when the sunset gave". Night-scene in Genoa. Felicia Dorothea Hemans. 6973-8
"In Gettysburg at break of day". The charge of Pickett's brigade. Unknown. 6964-9
"In going to my naked bed...". The falling out of faithful friends. Richard Edwards. 6934-7
"In good King Charles's golden days". Unknown. 6932-0
In good old colony times. Unknown. 6003-X
In Grantan wood. Joyce Lancaster. 6850-2
"In graceful windings, trailing their white..". Sky writers. William Rose Benet. 6978-9
"In grappled ships around The Victory". The last three from Trafalgar. Dante Gabriel Rossetti. 6793-X
In green old gardens. Violet Fane; Baroness Currie. 6656-9, 6649-6
"In green old gardens, hidden away". Rest. Violet Fane; Baroness Currie. 7037-X
In greenwood glen. Clinton Scollard. 6770-0
In Gremio. Thomas Edward Brown. 6809-X
"In greenwood glen, where greedy bees". In greenwood glen. Clinton Scollard. 6770-0
In grey days. Emily Pauline ("Tekahionwake") Johnson. 6837-5
In guernsey. Algernon Charles Swinburne. 6770-0
In Guernsey. Algernon Charles Swinburne. 6110-9,6252-0, 6655-0
"In guilty night & hid in false disguise." Unknown. 6563-5
"In halls of sleep you wandered by". Among shadows. Arthur Davison Ficke. 6897-9
"In Hampton Roads, the airs of March...bland". The attack. Thomas Buchanan Read. 6946-0
In happy canon. Jean Milne Gower. 6836-7
"In happy hour doth he receive". Carmen triumphale, sels.

Robert Southey. 6867-7
In harbor. Paul Hamilton Hayne. 6102-8,6076-5,6288-1,6309-8,6464-7
In harmony with nature. Matthew Arnold. 6337-3,6430-2,6199-0,6655-0
"'In harmony with nature?' Restless fool". To an independent preacher. Matthew Arnold. 6947-9,6828-6
In haste. Alfred Edward Housman. 6084-6
"In haste the sons of Achaea...", fr. The Iliad. Homer. 6251-2
"In health and ease am I". Francis Davison. 6187-7
In heaven. Thomas Westwood. 6385-3
In heaven I'll rock thee to sleep. Unknown. 6911-8
In Heaven they say. Joseph Morris. 6303-9
"In heaven-high musings and many". Chorus, fr. Alcestis. Euripides. 7039-6
In heavenly love abiding. Anna Laetitia Waring. 6337-3
In Hebrid seas. Unknown. 6873-1
"In her body's perfect sweet". Isabel. Richard Hovey. 7006-X
"In her dark cabin, the stricken mother knelt". Alfred Noyes. 6298-9
"In her dim cabin, above the unconscious child". Alfred Noyes. 6298-9
"In her master's yard once came a pig". Chovronja-the pig. Florence Randal Livesay. 6797-2
"In her order of consecration". The latest nun. Edward Farquhar. 6939-8
In her paths. Francis Thompson. 6655-0
"In her spirit the sunny high places". Song ("In her spirit"). Milton S. Rose. 6836-7
"In her the whole world's womanhood". A daughter of Israel. Robert Burns Wilson. 6848-0
"In here/the gods have lost all their words". Isolation cell poem. J. Charles Green. 6870-7
"In Hester Street, hard by a telegraph post". The candle seller. Morris Rosenfeld. 7011-6
"In high Jehovah's praise, my strain". Ode to Jehovah. John Leyden. 6980-0
In him. James Vila Blake. 6730-1
In Him confiding. William Cowper. 6337-3
In him we live. Henry More. 6337-3
"In him ye are made full." William H. Hudnut Sr. 6144-3
In his arms. Phoebe Cary. 6865-0;6969-X
"In his arms thy silly lamb". Triolet ("In his arms"). George Macdonald. 6770-0
"In his bed, bolt upright". 'Napoleon's midnight review'. Thomas Hood. 6974-6
'In his blanket on the ground'. Caroline H. Gervais. 6074-9
"In his great cushioned chair by the fender". Grandpa's Christmas. Ella Wheeler Wilcox. 6863-4
In his lady's praise. Henry Howard, Earl of Surrey. 6830-8
"In his last binn Sir Peter lies." Thomas Love Peacock. 6092-7
"In his lodge beside a river". The white man's foot, fr. The song of Hiawatha. Henry Wadsworth Longfellow. 6753-0
"In his tower sat the poet". The rose. James Russell Lowell. 6917-7
In his utter wretchedness. John Audelay. 6881-2
"In his white room/between white sheets". Familiar sheets. Ulalume Gonzalez de Leon. 7036-1
'In his will.' Howard Mumford Jones. 6326-8
"In his wshitening years his country store". Signal. Arthur Wallace Peach. 6761-1
In hoc signo. Godfrey Fox Bradby. 6337-3
In Holland. Eugene Field. 6949-5
In honor of Taffy Topaz. Christopher Morley. 6120-6,6510-1
In honour of America, 1917. Alice Meynell. 6955-X
In honour of Christmas. Unknown. 6881-2
In honour of St. David's day. Unknown. 6528-7
In honour of the city of London. William Dunbar. 6331-4,6150-8,6439-6
In hood of blue. Unknown. 6116-8
In hospital. James Elroy Flecker. 7014-0
In hospital. Gertrude Huntington McGiffert. 6838-3
In hospital. Annie Rothwell. 6795-6
In hospital, sels. William Ernest Henley. 6250-4
In hospital-music. William Ernes Henley. 6123-0

In hospital: Poona. Alun Lewis. 6357-8,6379-9
In hospital: Poona. Alun Lewis. 6895-2
"In humble dwelling born, retired, remote". The author's account of himself. Robert Pollock. 6980-0
"In Hydaspia, by Howzen". Oak leaves are hands. Wallace Stevens. 6751-4
"In Ipswich nights are cool and fair". Ipswich. Eugene Field. 6949-5
"In Ireland 'tis evening...". Song of an exile. James Orr. 6858-8
"In Ispwich town, not far from the sea". Heartbreak hill. Celia Thaxter. 6912-6
In idol-smashing land. C.L. Edson. 6615-1
In imitation of Anacreon. Matthew Prior. 6152-4
In imitation of Pope, fr. A pipe of tobacco. Isaac Hawkins Browne. 6932-0
In imitation of Shakespeare. William Cowper. 6814-6
In imitation of Spenser, fr. The school-mistress. William Shenstone. 6198-2
In imitation of Young, fr. A pipe of tobacco. Isaac Hawkins Browne. 6932-0
In immemoriam. Cuthbert (Edward Bradley) Bede. 6440-X
In impressions of hawk feathers willow leaves shadow. Elizabeth Woody. 7005-1
In Iona. Katharine (Hinkson) Tynan. 6174-5
In Ireland, fr. Reflexions. Alice Meynell. 6955-X
In Irish rain. Martha Haskell Clark. 6762-X
In irons. Milan Rakic. 6765-4
In Italy. Bayard Taylor. 6976-2
"In Jersey City where I did dwell". Unknown. 6059-5
"In Jersey City where....a butcher boy I loved...". Unknown. 6059-5
"In its color, shade and shine". A wraith of summertime. James Whitcomb Riley. 6993-2
"In its summer pride array'd". Funeral on the death of the Princess Charlotte. Robert Southey. 6832-4
"In its summer pride arrayed". Funeral song for the Princess Charlotte of Wales, sels. Robert Southey. 6867-7
"In January, when down the dairy the cream...". Country sleighing. Edmund Clarence Stedman. 6915-0
"In Japanese,/two charachers combins". Definitions of the word gout. Tina Koyama. 6790-5
In jest. Olive W. Sevens. 6894-7
In June. Denis Aloysius McCarthy. 6478-7
In June. Nora Perry. 6597-X;6600-3;6632-1
In June. Edward William Thomson. 6433-7
"In June and gentle oven". Anne Wilkinson. 6446-9
"In joy, in pain, in sorrow". Kyrie Eleison. Adelaide Anne Procter. 6957-6
"In Judah God is known; his name". Psalm 076. Bible. 6848-0
"In July, when the bees swarmed thick...". The battle of Sempach. George Walter Thornbury. 6749-2
"In jungles where the bushmaster lay grim". The humming bird. Louise Driscoll. 7038-8
"In just-/spring when the world...". Chansons innocentes I. Edward Estlin Cummings. 6808-1
"In Kalamazoo, in Kalamazoo". Why I no longer travel. Laura E. Richards. 6891-X
In just-spring when the world. Edward Estlin Cummings. 6324-1
In Kerry. John Millington Synge. 7039-6
In Kew Gardens. Isadore Elizabeth Flanders. 6789-1
In Lady Street. John Drinkwater. 6336-5,6668-2
In Laleham churchyard. Sir William Watson. 6046-3,6250-4
"In language warm as could be breath'd..penn'd". On receiving Hayley's picture. William Cowper. 6814-6
"In lapse to God though thus the world remains". True knowledge and its use. Fulke Greville; 1st Baron Brooke. 6935-5
In last year's camp. Mary Adair-Macdonald. 7031-0
In later days. Arthur L. Salmon. 6780-8
In laudem amoris. Unknown. 6189-3
In Leinster. Louise Imogen Guiney. 6437-X,6467-1
"In law an infant, and in years a boy". Damaetas. George Gordon, 6th Baron Byron. 6945-2
"In leathern volume, old and quaint". The knight and the page. Martha C. Howe. 7002-7
"In Leonardo's painting, she studies". The annunciation.

Margot Kriel. 6966-5
"In life, Manes the slave...". Anyte. 6251-2
"In light of sunrise and sunsetting". Fairy land. Andrew Lang. 6771-9
In lighter vain. Robert Loveman. 6941-X
"In lilac-time (which means in May) I made...". Alfred Noyes: Ride a cock-horse. Charles Powell. 6982-7
"In limbo, floating". Where you came up. Norma Warren. 6857-X
"In Liquorpond Street,as is well known to many". The barber's nuptials. Unknown. 6787-5
In liquor. Unknown. 6699-2
"In little towns I fancy still the factory...". I go home for lunch. Edgar A. Guest. 6748-4
"In London I never know what I'd be at". The contrast. Charles Morris. 6874-X
"In London town men love and hate". Love in London. Justin Huntly McCarthy. 6875-8,6770-0
In London town the lights are low". Zepp days. P.H.B. Lyon. 7029-9
In loco. Peter Jackson. 6788-3
In loco parentis. James Abraham Martling. 6952-5
"In London city was Bicham born". Unknown. 6111-7
In London on Saturday night. Robert Buchanan. 6092-7
"In London there lived a blacksmith by trade". Unknown. 6059-5
In London town. Mary Elizabeth Coleridge. 6861-8
"In London's fair city a lady did dwell". Unknown. 6059-5
In London, September, 1802. William Wordsworth. 6332-2, 6337-3
"In lonely solitude I dwell". Gyoson. 6852-9
In Loring park. Eleanor Rothenberger. 6342-X
"In loopy links the canker crawls". Indifference. Unknown. 6902-9
"In loue with you I all things elce doe hate." Unknown. 6563-5
In Louisiana. John William De Forest. 6016-2
In Louisiana. Albert Bigelow Paine. 6484-1
In love. Thomas Campion. 6935-5
"In love with home, I rose and eyed", fr. Tamerton. Coventry Patmore. 6123-0
'In love's disport' Walter Crane. 6770-0,6875-8,6770-0, 6875-8
In love's own time. Michelangelo Buonarroti. 6321-7,6429-9
In love, if love be love, fr. Merlin and Vivien. Alfred Lord Tennyson. 6023-4,6250-4,6543-0
"In love, if love be love, if love be ours". If love be love, fr. Idylls of the king. Alfred Lord Tennyson. 6934-7
In love, if love be true, fr. The princess. Alfred Lord Tennyson. 6655-0
"In loving thee thou know'st I am forsworn". Sonnet 152 ("In loving thee"). William Shakespeare. 6732-8
"In low dark rounds the arches hung". The trial of Constance. Sir Walter Scott. 6980-0
"On lowly dale, fast by a river's side". The land of indolence, fr. The castle of indolence. James Thomson. 6932-0
"In Lyons, in the mart of that French town". The signer's alms. Unknown. 6914-2
"In Mark Twain's birthplace there's a...". Roundabout. Glenn D. Whisler. 7019-1
In luceum tranitus, October, 1892. Henry Van Dyke. 6104-4
In lyric season. Bliss Carman. 6795-6
In mamma's day. Curley (pseud). 7021-3
In Manchester. Francis Ledwidge. 6812-X
In Manchester Square. Alice Meynell. 6955-X
In manor. John Veitch. 6819-7
"In marble walls as white as milk." Mother Goose. 6452-3, 6114-1
In March. Max Eastman. 6897-9
In March. Susan Frances ("Seranus") Harrison. 6115-X
In March. Archibald Lampman. 6115-X
In March. Harriet Monroe. 6850-2
In March. William Wordsworth. 6502-3,6456-6
In May. Duncan Campbell Scott. 6396-9
In May. Edwin M. Stern. 6688-7
In May. Robert Kelley Weeks. 6597-X
In May and in the green Chaucerian meadow. Chad Walsh. 6839-1

In May, fr. Songs of joy. William Henry Davies. 6234-2, 6253-9
"In massive gothic majesty it stands". Profit or loss. William B. Gilbert. 6954-1
"In matrial sports I had my cunning tried". Sonnet ("In martial sports"). Sir Philip Sidney. 6271-7
"In matters intellectual she's somewhat...". Nobody home. Berton Braley. 6853-7
"In matters of commerce, the fault of the...". A political despatch. Right Hon. George Canning. 6874-X
"In maudlin spite let Thracians fight". Let us have peace. Horace. 6949-5
"In May, at the break of dawn". Archipelagoes. Bartolo Cattafi. 6803-0
"In May, when sea-winds pierced our solitudes". The rhodora. Ralph Waldo Emerson. 6049-8,6077-3,6374-8, 6176-1,6239-3,6737 ,6332-2,6300-0,6385-3,6726-3,6473-6,6585 ,6008-8,6212-1,6735-2,6047-1,6102-8,6232 , 6250-4,6288-1,6431-0,6214-8,6219-9,6121 ,6300-4,6265-2,6076-5,6126-5,6104-4,6396 ,6639-9,6964-9,6250-4, 6288-1,6431-0,6214-8,6219-9,6121 ,6300-4,6265-2,6076-5,6126-5,6104-4,6396
"In May/Back in the islands". Blue tropic. Luis Cabalquinto. 6790-5
"In meantime flew our ships...", fr. The Odyssey. Homer. 6547-3
"In mediaeval Rome, I know not where", fr. Morituri. Henry Wadsworth Longfellow. 6165-6
In medio tuoissimus ibis. Robert J. Burdette. 6588-0
"In meetinge-time I watched you well". Salem. Edmund Clarence Stedman. 6946-0
In memoriam. Joseph Auslander. 6879-0
In memoriam. Theodore Howard Banks Jr. 6347-0
In memoriam. Cuthbert (Edward Bradley) Bede. 6089-7
In memoriam. Dorothy Wardell Boice. 6662-3
In memoriam. Thomas Edward Brown. 6655-0
In memoriam. Thomas Edward Brown. 6809-X
In memoriam. Laura M. Carter. 6764-6
In memoriam. Lee Wilson Dodd. 6817-0
In memoriam. George Douglass. 6995-9
In memoriam. Martin Feinstein. 6531-7
In memoriam. A.M. Fleming. 6799-9
In memoriam. Josephine Franco. 6850-2
In memoriam. Clarence S. Jarvis. 6799-9
In memoriam. Alan Mackintosh. 6542-2
In memoriam. Louis J. Magee. 7004-3
In memoriam. Eric Sutherland Robertson. 7015-9
In memoriam. Frederick George Scott. 6433-7
In memoriam. Sir Walter Scott. 6322-5
In memoriam. Stephen Spender. 6390-X
In memoriam. Sir William Stirling-Maxwell. 6180-X
In memoriam. Charles Russell Wakeley. 7001-9
In memoriam. Harriet L. Wason. 6836-7
In memoriam ("Canadian soldiers-valorous and true"). Irene Chapman Benson. 6224-5
In memoriam ("On the bosom of a river"). George Denison Prentice. 6408-6
In memoriam ("Rest, though the clamorous surge of war") Edward John. 6474-4
In memoriam - Alfred, Lord Tennyson. Thomas Herbert Warren. 6046-3
In memoriam - Jockie. John Veitch. 6819-7
In memoriam A.H.H. Alfred Lord Tennyson. 6122-2,6085-4, 6473-6,6641-0,6655-0,6657 ,6084-6
In memoriam A.H.H., sels. Alfred Lord Tennyson. 6154-0, 6047-1,6144-3,6320-9,6332-2,6339 ,6179-6,6725-3,6597-X,6271-7,6123-0,6246 ,6216-4,6315-2,6335-7,6532-5, 6536-8,6634 ,6302-0,6385-3,6198-2,6208-3,6317-9,6484 ,6604-6,6730-1,6110-9,6668-2,6560-0,4672 ,6199-0, 6430-2,6046-3,6102-8,6649-6,6196 ,6107-9,6110-9,6192-3,6177-X,6150-8,6219 ,6250-4,6746-8,6648-8,6639-9, 6646-1,6301-2,6304-7,6491-4,6660-7
In memoriam A.M.W. Gordon Bottomley. 6250-4,6301-2
In memoriam E.A.M. Theodore Maynard. 6761-1
In memoriam F.O.S. Sara Teasdale. 6897-9
In memoriam of October 25, 1854. John Reade. 6433-7
In memoriam technicam. Thomas Hood Jr. 6089-7
'In memoriam'. Henry Van Dyke. 6961-4
In memoriam, A.H. Maurice Baring. 6096 X
In memoriam, sel. Alfred Lord Tennyson. 6958-4

In memoriam, sel. Alfred Lord Tennyson. 6958-4
In memoriam, sel. Alfred Lord Tennyson. 6958-4
In Memoriam-- P. W. Peter Baker. 6475-2
In memoriam-A. Lincoln. Emily J. Bugbee. 6392-6
In memoriam-Theodore Roosevelt. Annette Kohn. 6995-9
In memoriam: A.F. Thomas Edward Brown. 6809-X
In memoriam: Abraham Lincoln. James Thompson McKay. 6524-4
In memoriam: Cardinal Newman. H.D. Pearson. 6260-1
In memoriam: Charles P. Krauth. Edwin Ford Schively. 6936-3
In memoriam: F.R.H. [Frederick Higgins]. William Jeffrey. 6783-2
In memoriam: Henry Kendall. J. Howlett Ross. 6768-9
In memoriam: Henry La Barre Jayne. Alfred Noyes. 6151-6
In memoriam: Ingvald Bjorndal. Malcolm Boden Lowry. 6761-1
In memoriam: J. Macmeikin. Thomas Edward Brown. 6809-X
In memoriam: James Abram Garfield. William White. 6868-5
In memoriam: John Cookson. Harold Douglas. 6761-1
In memoriam: John Davidson. Ronald Campbell Macfie. 6845-6
In memoriam: Lady Blessington. Walter Savage Landor. 6641-0
In memoriam: Leo. a yellow cat. Margaret Sherwood. 6120-6
In memoriam: Lydia F. Wadleigh. Helen Gray Cone. 6847-2
In memoriam: Paul Bridson. Thomas Edward Brown. 6809-X
In memoriam: Roy Campbell. Ralph Nixon Currey. 6788-3
In memoriam: S.M. Theodore Maynard. 6839-1
In memoriam: Samuel Coleridge-Taylor. Alfred Noyes. 6151-6
In memoriam: T.S.K. William Allen Butler. 6903-7
In memoriam: those killed in the north-west, 1885. Frederick George Scott. 6795-6
In memoriam: W.G. Ward. Alfred Lord Tennyson. 6867-7
In memoriam: W.L.W. Pearl Randall Wasson. 7030-2
In memorian technicam. Thomas Hood Jr. 6802-2
In memorium ("Timothy Corsellis"). Patricia Ledward. 6475-2
In memory. Marjorie W. Brachlow. 6342-X
In memory. Amoretta Fitch. 6906-1
In memory. Richard Realf. 6113-3
In memory. Pearl C. Trimble. 6270-9
In memory Garcia Lorca. Eldon Grier. 6446-9
In memory of a British aviator. Alfred Noyes. 6151-6
In memory of a dumb friend. Amelia Josephine Burr. 6510-4
In memory of Abraham Lincoln. Oliver Wendell Holmes. 6871-5
In memory of Ann Jones. Dylan Thomas. 6360-8,6379-9,6391-8
In memory of Arden Davis: smokejumper 1966 David McElroy. 6855-3
In memory of Charles Dickens. Sue M. Remak. 6404-3
In memory of Edward Wilson. James Clerk Maxwell. 6722-0
In memory of Eva Gore-Booth and Con Markiewicz. William Butler Yeats. 6641-0
In memory of F.C.C. Francis Turner Palgrave. 7015-9
In memory of James T. Fields. John Greenleaf Whittier. 6437-X
In memory of Jean Rhys. Bill Olsen. 6900-2
In memory of John Greenleaf Whittier. Oliver Wendell Holmes. 6126-5
In memory of Lewis Carroll. Unknown. 6465-5
In memory of Major Robert Gregory. William Butler Yeats. 6641-0
In memory of Meredith. Alfred Noyes. 6151-6
In memory of my dear grandchild Ann Bradstreet... Anne Bradstreet. 6077-3
In memory of my father. Clara Gordon. 6799-9
In memory of my friend Joyce Kilmer, poet and soldier. Vachel Lindsay. 6607-0
In memory of Nancy Hanks. William J. Lampton. 7010-8
In memory of Richard Jebb, aged 8. Unknown. 6396-9
In memory of Sigmund Freud. Wystan Hugh Auden. 6209-1
In memory of Swinburne. Alfred Noyes. 6151-6,6250-4
In memory of the late John Thornton, Esq. William Cowper. 6814-6
In memory of the moon.(A killing.) Charlotte DeClue. 7005-1
In memory of the Pilgrims. Grenville Mellen. 6678-X
In memory of Vachel Lindsay. Sara Teasdale. 6782-4
In memory of W.B. Yeats. Wystan Hugh Auden. 6125-7,6389-6, 6645-3,6491-4
In memory of W.B. Yeats, sels. Wystan Hugh Auden. 6210-5
In memory of Walter Savage Landor. Algernon Charles Swinburne. 6828-6
In memory of Walter Savage Landor. Algernon Charles Swinburne. 6483-3,6110-9,6250-4,6560-0,6508-2,6655-0, 6656-9
In memory's garden. Thomas Walsh. 6338-1
In memory, sels. Lionel Johnson. 6208-3
In men whom men condemn. Joaquin Miller. 6102-8,6337-3, 6076-5
"In men whom men pronounce as ill". Joaquin Miller. 6238-5
In Mercer street: a piper. Seumas (James Starkey) O'Sullivan. 6477-9;6496-5;6506-6
In merry mood, sels. Nixon Waterman. 6260-1
In mesa land. Arthur Chapman. 6836-7
In Michigan. Ivan Swift. 6484-1
"In mesa land the sand dunes stretch afar". In mesa land. Arthur Chapman. 6836-7
"In middle row, some years ago". The ghost. Thomas Hood. 6974-6
In midsummer. L.C. Whiton. 6965-7
"In minds pure glasse when I my selfe behold". Sonnet 024 ("In minds pure glasse..."). William Drummond of Hawthornden. 6933-9
"In mirth he mocks the other birds at noon". The mocking-bird. Henry Van Dyke. 6961-4
In misty blue. Laurence Binyon. 6477-9
In Monmouth. Eve Gilbert Swift. 6270-9
In Moreh's wood. Winifred Virginia Jackson. 6038-2
"In moments to delight devoted". Tu me chamas. Unknown (Portuguese). 6945-2
"In moonlight reposing, its charms..disclosing". Campus song. Louis J. Magee. 7004-3
"In morning light my damson showed". The plum tree by the house. Oliver St. John Gogarty. 6985-1
"In most cases/it is the old woman". Who makes the journey. Cathy Song. 6790-5
"In most men's eyes one virtue, alone, is worth...". Theognis. 6251-2
In mother's room. Joseph Crosby Lincoln. 6119-2
In Mott Street. Evelyn Grace Flynn. 6847-2
"In mountain morn, at silver dawn". The flowers. John Galsworthy. 6888-X
In mourning. Anna F. Burnham. 6965-7
In musical Boston. Unknown. 6694-1
"In my attic all alone". Alone in the big town she dreams. Frank (Michael O'Donovan) O'Connor. 6779-4,6096-X
"In my cool white body, peace". Song heard by St. Anthony. Robert L. Wolf. 6880-4
In my craft or sullen art. Dylan Thomas. 6379-9
"In my distress to thee I cried, oh Lord!". The prayer of Jonah. George Wither. 6848-0
"In my dream" Taisanboku Mori. 6981-9
In my father's house. Robert Freeman. 6461-2
In my father's house. Patricia M. Johnson. 6857-X
"In my former days of bliss". On the muse of poetry. George Wither. 6935-5
"In my garden there are flowers". Flowers. H. W. Sloan. 6818-9
In my hammock. Laura Vandivier. 6799-9
"In my head the juxtapositions". A vision of labor. William Carlos Williams. 6761-1
In my heart. John Reade. 6433-7
"In my journey down the river of life". Paddle your own canoe. Edward R. Huxley. 6885-5
In my library. Edla Park Peck. 6836-7
"In my life, so dark and dreary". Heinrich Heine. 6876-6
In my lifetime. James Welch. 7005-1
"In my lost childhood old folks said to me". Idle fears. Alice Cary. 6969-X
"In my mind's eye a temple, like a cloud". A vision. William Wordsworth. 6980-0
In my mother's garden. Margaret Widdemer. 6338-1,6649-6
In my old verses. Charles Guerin. 6351-9
In my own album. Charles Lamb. 6086-2
"In my own hands my want and weakness are." Bayard Taylor. 6225-3
"In my own land, and hunting through the hills". A meeting of magicians. George Croly. 6980-0
"In my own shire, if I was sad" Alfred Edward Housman. 6828-6
"In my poor mind it is most sweet to muse". Childhood.

Charles Lamb. 6772-7
In my room. Max Eastman. 6880-4
"In my sleep I was fain of their fellowship...". Sunrise-a hymn of the marshes. Sidney Lanier. 7041-8
"In my soul the bells are ringing". Love's melody. Barbara M. Booth. 6799-9
"In my unfinished cellar". The mortuary. Mary Mullis Hinricks. 6857-X
In my vineyard. Bayard Taylor. 6976-2
"In my walled garden". Moonlight in St. Augustine. Florence Ralston Werum. 6906-1
In my workshop. Unknown. 6461-2
In Naishapur. Robert Loveman. 6941-X
In Nazareth. Leslie Savage Clark. 6144-3
In New Orleans. Eugene Field. 6949-5
In New York. Mary Elizabeth Mahnkey. 6662-3
In New York. William Vaughn Moody. 6300-4
In New York. William Alexander Percy. 6619-4
In New York: On Sunday morning. William Alexander Percy. 6532-5
"In my youth I lived for a time in the...". The tunnel. Nicanor Parra. 6758-1
"In nature's bright blossoms not always repose". Memory's river. Ella Wheeler Wilcox. 6863-4
"In Northport town the sun goes down". Northport town. Robert Loveman. 6941-X
"In Norton wood the sun was bright". Norton wood, fr. Clevedon verses. Thomas Edward Brown. 6809-X
"In Nottamun town not a soul would look up". Folk song. Unknown. 6179-6
"In November I lost my food stamps, the...". In November. Harold Norse. 6792-1
"In Oberhausen, on a time". Gosling stew. Eugene Field. 6949-5
"In Oklahoma an old man died, long ago". Elf night. Ronald Rogers. 7005-1
In nicotina. Rena Carey Sheffield. 6750-6
"In nineteen twenty-eight my father's office boy". David Wright. 6788-3
In no man's land. Ewart Alan Mackintosh. 6650-X
In no strange land. Francis Thompson. 7020-5
In no strange land. Francis Thompson. 6144-3,6730-1,6214-8, 6150-8,6102-8
In November. Harold Norse. 6792-1
In November. Susan Kelly Phillips. 6183-4,6618-6,6456-6
In November. Duncan Campbell Scott. 6656-9
In obitum M.S. X May 1614. William Browne. 6182-6,6562-7, 6250-4,6153-2
In October. L.C. Whiton. 6965-7
"In old Pekin a monarch reigned". The street of doctors. Thomas Walsh. 7014-0
In old Rouen. Antoinette De Coursey Patterson. 6331-4,6439-6,6631-3
In olden days. Xavier de Magellon. 6351-9
In olden style. W.F. Barron. 6118-4
In olden time. Charles Francis Dunn. 6983-5
In olden time. Robert Loveman. 6941-X
In Olivia's garden. William Shakespeare. 6094-3
"In olden times a castle stood...". The minstrel's curse. Johann Ludwig Uhland. 6913-4
"In Olinda, if you go out with a magnifying...". Hidden cities 001. Italo Calvino. 6758-1
"In one dread night our city saw, and sighed". Address spoken at the opening..Drury-Lane Theatre,1812. George Gordon, 6th Baron Byron. 6945-2
In one spring night. William White. 6868-5
In Orknay. William Fowler. 6845-6
In Othello, fr. Reflexions. Alice Meynell. 6955-X
"In one who felt as once he felt". On finding a fan. George Gordon, 6th Baron Byron. 6945-2
"In open field King Solomon". Solomon and the sower. Friedrich Ruckert. 6848-0
"In order to escape you". Love. Jaime Torres Bodet. 6759-X
"In Ortygia the dawn land the old gods dwell". Ortygia. Jessie MacKay. 6784-0
"In other days I sang of simpler things". From the Somme. Leslie Coulson. 7029-9
"In other men we faults can spy". The turkey and the ant. John Gay. 6972-X
In our boat. inah Maria Mulock Craik. 6240-7

"In our garden there's a pool". My boats. Alice Barkley. 6789-1
"In our hill-country of the north". God's hills. William Noel Hodgson. 7027-2
"In our ignorance/we are flying low beneath". Ignorance. Ken LaMere. 6883-9
"In our museum galleries". The burden of Nineveh. Dante Gabriel Rossetti. 6828-6
"In our old shipwrecked days there was an hour". Sonnet 016 ("In our old"), fr. Modern love. George Meredith. 6560-0
"In our old shipwrecked days there was an hour." George Meredith. 6122-2;6317-9
In our time. Huw Menai. 6337-3
In our time. Michael Roberts. 6666-6
In our yard. William Alexander Percy. 6031-5,6421-3
In pace. Arthur Reed Ropes. 6271-7,6656-9
In Palestine. George W. Carlin. 6144-3
In Panther Gorge. William James. 6253-9
"In painted plumes suberbly drest". The parrot. Vincent Bourne. 6814-6
"In Paris all look'd hot and like to fade". Rachel. Matthew Arnold. 6848-0
"In Paris sits the lady..be Sir Roland's bride". Lady Alda's dream. Unknown (Spanish). 6757-3
"In Paris town, in Paris town...". Infantry. Patrick Reginald Chalmers. 7027-2
In parenthesis. Frank Dempster Sherman. 6441-8
In Paris. Thomas MacDonagh. 6930-4
"In parting from a dear old friend for months". On station farewells. Edgar A. Guest. 6862-6
"In passing through this primal state". Essential requirements. Edward R. Huxley. 6885-5
"In pastures green? Not always; sometimes he". Psalm 023 (He leadeth me). Bible. 6848-0
In patris mei memoriam. John Myers O'Hara. 6556-2
In Pennsylvania's praise. Edward S. Dunn. 6936-3
In Perdita's garden, fr. The winter's tale. William Shakespeare. 6649-6
"In peace, love tunes the shepherd's reed". Love, fr. The lay of the last minstrel. Sir Walter Scott. 6934-7
"In peaceful dells and woodland glades". Song of a wood nymph. Felicia Dorothea Hemans. 6973-8
"In perfect peace thou, Lord wilt keep". Hymn. James Abraham Martling. 6952-5
"In Picardy the shadows creep". Where heroes sleep. Eleanor Voswinkel. 6799-9
In perpetuum. Unknown. 6118-4
In perpetuum mobile. David Gascoyne. 6985-1
In Phaeacia. James Elroy Flecker. 6250-4,6541-4
In Philistia. Bliss Carman. 6026-9
"In pilgrim land one sabbath day". The captain's drum. Benjamin Franklin Taylor. 6815-4
In plague time. Thomas Nashe. 6436-1
In Portugal, 1912. Alice Meynell. 6955-X
In Portugal, 1912. Alice Meynell. 6931-2
"In poems/I hide behind". Method a. Helmut Zenker. 6769-7
In postures that call. Oscar Williams. 6666-6
In poverty street. Elliott Flower. 6274-1
In praesepio. Richard Lawson Gales. 6216-4
In praise of a beggar's life. A. W. 6182-6
In praise of a girl. Huw Morus. 6528-7
In praise of a harp. Osborn Bergin. 6582-1
In praise of abrigada. Leonora Speyer. 6036-6
In praise of ale. Thomas Bonham. 6563-5,6026-9
In praise of ale. Unknown. 6423-X,6562-7
In praise of Bombyca. Theocritus. 6435-3
In praise of common things. Lizette Woodworth Reese. 6303-9,6326-8
In praise of contentment. Horace. 6949-5
In praise of death. Walt Whitman. 6006-4
In praise of Elisa, queen of shepherds. Edmund Spenser. 6935-5
In praise of Fidelia. Mildmay Fane, 2d Earl of Westmorland. 6563-5
In praise of Gilbert White, fr. The paradise of birds. William James Courthope. 6656-9
In praise of Grattan. Edward Lysaght. 7009-4
In praise of his Daphnis. Sir John Wotton. 6182-6
In praise of his lady. Matthew Grove. 6182-6

In praise of his mistress. Thomas Carew. 6827-8
In praise of hunting. Unknown (Greek) 6435-3
In praise of Isabel Pennell. John Skelton. 6830-8
In praise of ivy. Unknown. 6881-2
In praise of Johanna Scroope. John Skelton. 6830-8
In praise of Johnny Appleseed. Vachel Lindsay. 6465-5,6036-6,6010-2
In praise of Mary. Unknown. 6881-2
In praise of May. Fionn MacCumhaill. 6253-9
In praise of melancholy. John Fletcher. 6830-8
In praise of pie. Eugene Field. 6949-5
In praise of righteous war. Walter Malone. 6443-4
In praise of sailors. Unknown. 6134-6
In praise of sleep. Passeroni. 6787-5
In praise of the king. Ibn Ammar. 6362-4
In praise of the Royal Scots Fusiliers. John Buchan. 6476-0
In praise of the sun. A. W. 6436-1
In praise of the Turk. George Gordon, 6th Baron Byron. 6633-X
In praise of trees. Edmund Spenser. 6304-7
In praise of trees. Kazimierz Wierzynski. 6068-4
In praise of trees, fr. The fairie queen. Edmund Spenser. 6049-8
In praise of truth and simplicity in song. Eugene Field. 6949-5
In praise of unfamous men. Francis Meynell. 6339-X
In praise of wine. Unknown. 6273-3
In praise of women. Unknown. 6383-7
In praise of Wyatt's psalms. Henry Howard, Earl of Surrey. 6584-8
"In pride of May". Song ("In pride of May.") Unknown. 6436-1
"In pride of wit, when high desire of fame." Michael Drayton. 6586-4
In prison. Sir Roger L'Estrange. 6600-3
In prison. William Morris. 6110-9
In prison. Frederick Peterson. 6441-8
In prison. Tamiko Yamamuro. 6027-7
"In prisonyou put on your clothes". Rehabilitative report: we can still laugh. Daniel Berrigan. 6870-7
"In Pumpkintown there lived a girl as fair...". A mournful tale. H. Elliott McBride. 6925-8
In prize. Cicely Fox Smith. 6722-9
In process of a noble alliance. John Crowe Ransom. 6037-4, 6581-3
In prospect of death. William Freeland. 7015-9
In Provincetown bay. Roger C. Dickey. 6798-0
"In purple pools, half dry". Trevone. Song II: Major key. Lilian Sauter. 7023-X
"In quaint old Talmud's pages". The sabbath eve. Samuel Willoughby Duffield. 6848-0
In quantity. Alfred Lord Tennyson. 6977-0
In Quebec. Rudyard Kipling. 6861-8
"In rail transportation the old-fashioned...". The warmth of memory. Berton Braley. 6853-7
"In Reno, Nevada the old ladies play slot". Reno Nevada. Richard Morris. 6998-3
"In railway halls." Stephen Spender. 6209-1
In re Solomon Warshawer. Abraham M. Klein. 6761-1
"In regal quiet deep." Jean Ingelow. 6225-3
In remembrance of Cork. Norreys Jephson O'Conor. 6331-4
In remembrance of Joseph Sturge. John Greenleaf Whittier. 6219-9
In remembrance of the Hon. Edward Ernest Villiers. Sir Henry Taylor. 6271-7
In repudiation. William Foster Elliott. 6070-6
In response to executive order 9066... Dwight Okita. 6790-5
"In retrospective paths of man we find". The human race. Edward R. Huxley. 6885-5
In return for some prairie birds. Thomas William Parsons. 6004-9
"In revel and carousing". Theodosia Burr: the wrecker's story. John Williamson Palmer. 6946-0
"In reverence will we speak of those that woo". Prayer ("In reverence will we speak..."). Richard Monckton Milnes; 1st Baron Houghton. 6980-0
"In Richard's days, when lost his...plain". The country justice. John Langhorne. 6866-9

In reverie. Harriet McEwen Kimball. 6632-1
In Romney marsh. John Davidson. 6873-1
In Romney marsh. John Davidson. 6246-5,6258-X,6477-9,6501-5
"In rigorous hours, when down the iron lane". Winter. Robert Louis Stevenson. 6123-0,6558-9
"In robes of Tyrian blue the king was drest". The vain king. Henry Van Dyke. 6961-4
"In rooms too-often let, too-meanly furnished". Week-end love. Henry Morton Robinson. 6979-7
In rotten row. William Ernest Henley. 6453-1
"In round round rooms of our wanderings". Hiroshima exit. Joy Kogawa. 6790-5
"In S Street trod the phantom guard". The warrior passes. Hubert Kelley. 7001-9
"In sable clad, Urania came". Ode on the passion. Thomas Warton (the Elder). 6962-2
"In Salisbury by the beach". Salisbury by the beach, put your finger in my sea... Walt Curtis. 7003-5
In salutation to the eternal peace. Sarojini Naidu. 6607-0
In Samarcand. Laura E. Richards. 6554-X
In San Lorenzo. Algernon Charles Swinburne. 6624-0
In sano corpore. E. E. 6817-0
In Santa Claus land. Ada Stewart Shelton. 6745-X
In Santa Claus time. Frank Lebby Stanton. 6807-3
"In Scarlet town, where I was born." Unknown. 6317-9
"In scenery sublime and rude". The Alpine shepherd. Felicia Dorothea Hemans. 6973-8
In school day's. Unknown. 6616-X
In school days. John Greenleaf Whittier. 6127-3,6142-7, 6499-X,6512-0,6473-6,6486 ,6621-6,6623-2,6732-8,6419-1,6585-6,6126 ,6004-8,6092-7,6084-6,6155-9,6288-1, 6104
"In Scotland I was bred and born". Unknown. 6059-5
"In Scotland there was a babie born". Unknown. 6111-7
"In schools of wisdom all the day was". The lent jewels. Richard Chenevix Trench. 6848-0
"In Scotland's cause, for Scotland's gude". The battle-word. Robert Nicoll. 7009-4
"In secret place, this hindir nicht". The man of valour to his lady fair. William Dunbar. 6881-2
In seditionem horrendam. William Cowper. 6814-6
In September. Francis Ledwidge. 6096-X
In September. Unknown. 6373-X
In service. J.E. Evans. 6443-4
In service. Winifred M. Letts. 6162-1,6266-0,6476-0,6506-6, 6653-4
In Seville. George Gordon, 6th Baron Byron. 6484-1
"In seventeen hundred and seventy-five". The bombardment of Bristol. Unknown. 6946-0
In shadowland. Sir Joseph Noel Paton. 6873-1
In Shakespeare land. Robert Loveman. 6941-X
"In shadowy calm the boat". Hope. Phillips Stewart. 7041-8
"In shantung suits we whites are cool". The devil-dancers. William Plomer. 6788-3
"In Sharon's vale some roses grew". Rose, lily, and may-flower. Benjamin Franklin Taylor. 6815-4
"In Sherwood lived stout Robin Hood". Song ("In Sherwood"). Unknown. 6436-1
In shimmering robes. Virginia Spates. 6818-9
In sickness. Jonathan Swift. 6024-2,6152-4
In sickness. William White. 6868-5
In silence. Bliss Carman and Richard Hovey. 6890-1
In silence. Lorenzo Mavilis. 6352-7
"In silent gaze the tuneful choir among". To Richard Bentley. Thomas Gray. 6935-5
In silk attire. Susanna Blamire. 6086-2,6383-7
"In silks and satins the ladies went". Chemin des dames. Crosbie Garstin. 7029-9
"In Sligo the country was soft; there were...". County Sligo. Louis MacNeice. 6930-4
In sleep. Alice Meynell. 6955-X
"In smoky lamplight of a Smyrna cafe". The cakewalk. Wilfred Wilson Gibson. 6959-2
In snow time. Unknown. 6273-3
In soapsuds street. Manuel Bandeira. 6759-X
"In solemn night when throught he blue abysses". Midnight worship. James Abraham Martling. 6952-5
In solitude. Edward R. Huxley. 6885-5
WIn solitude. Clinton Scollard. 6632-1

In solitude. Virna Sheard. 6433-7,6115-X
"In some dead age a pioneer". The Tennessee river. Benjamin Franklin Taylor. 6815-4
"In some green nook upon Mount Latmos lies". Endymion. Marion M. Miller. 6983-5
"In some strange place". Her waiting face. James Whitcomb Riley. 6992-4
In some time hence. Isabelle McClellan Taylor. 6178-8
In some wide place. Robert Donaldson. 6836-7
"In somer, when pe shawes be sheyne". Unknown. 6111-7
"In sooth, I know not why I am so sad". Unknown. 6392-6
"In sooth, the dust on insects' wings". As precious stone... Jaroslav Vrchlicky. 6886-3
In sorrow. Thomas Hastings. 6735-2,6219-9
In sorrow. Clement Wood. 6039-0
"In sorrow and in nakedness of soul". Exile. Thomas Edward Brown. 6809-X
"In sorrowes drown'd I wast my weary dayes." Unknown. 6563-5
In southern California. Alfred Noyes. 6151-6
"In southern Missouri, it was". Polio memoir. Lloyd Henley. 6860-X
In space the one great ornament. Louise Townsend Nicholl. 6979-7
In Spain. Sir Thomas Wyatt. 6436-1
"In space, unlimited and wide". west, The. Pearl V. Doddridge. 6799-9
"In speaking of a person's faults". Be careful what you say. Unknown. 6928-2
"In spite of my torpor, my squinting eyes...". Hurry. Octavio Paz. 6758-1
"In spite of rice, in spite of wheat". Epigram on the poor of Boston employed..paving streets. Unknown. 6946-0
In spite of sorrow. Adoniram Judson. 6337-3
In spite of this. Lionel Wiggam. 6640-2
In spite of war. Angela Morgan. 6162-1;6556-2
In spring. Ianthe Jerrold. 6777-8
In spring. Aline Kilmer. 6032-3
In spring. Unknown. 6118-4
In spring. Unknown. 6983-5
In spring. Julius Zeyer. 6763-8
"In spring a young man's fancy". In spring. Unknown. 6983-5
"In spring and summer winds may blow". Walter Savage Landor. 6844-8
"In spring and summer winds may blow". Walter Savage Landor. 6513-9
"In spring, when the green gets back in..trees". When the green gits back in the trees. James Whitcomb Riley. 6993-2
"In spring, when the green gits back in..trees". When the green gits back in the trees. James Whitcomb Riley. 6991-4
In spring-time. William Henry Davies. 6374-8
In spring: Santa Barbara. Sara Teasdale. 6345-4
In Springfield mountain. Unknown. 6281-4
In springtime. Rudyard Kipling. 6649-6
In springtime. Lewis Morris. 6820-0
"In springtime by the sunny woods". Wild flowers. Olive Boda Brown. 6818-9
In state. Forceythe Willson. 6074-9,6113-3,6240-7,6438-8
"In stature perfect, and in every gift". 'Of such is the kingdom of God'. Hartley Coleridge. 6772-7
"In steering across the down, I came to a...". The Avon valley. William Cobbett. 7020-5
"In step with my young mind". The withered thorn. Stella Gibbons. 6893-6
"In Steyermark - green Steyermark". Steyermark. Bayard Taylor. 6976-2
"In Steyermark, green Steyermark". The Styrian Alps. Bayard Taylor. 6749-2
"In Stockton town did plaintiff hold". Hopkins vs. W.P.R.R. Co. Unknown. 6878-2
"In still midsummer night". Robert Bridges. 6487-6
In stratis viarum. Arthur Hugh Clough. 6655-0
"In strong battalions marching heavenward". The wanderers. Helen Bosanquet. 7042-6
In submersionem navigii cui Georgius regale nomen... William Cowper. 6814-6
"In such a night", fr. The merchant of Venice. William Shakespeare. 6339-X,6125-7
In such an age! Angela Morgan. 6954-1
In sugarin'-time. Helen M. Winslow. 7030-2
In summer. Trumbull Stickney. 6380-2
"In summer on the sunny wall the yellow cat& I". The yellow cat. Madeleine Nightingale. 6937-1
In summer time. William W. Caldwell. 6385-3
In summer time. Unknown. 6134-6,6328-4
"In summer when the rose-bushes". Perrine, fr. Country cousin. Edith Sitwell. 7000-0
In summer when the vales are clear. Herbert Trench. 6877-4
In summer-time when Mary bathes. Herbert Trench. 6877-4
In Swanage bay. Dinah Maria Mulock Craik. 6669-0
In Swarthmore college ethics class. John Oliver Simon. 6792-1, 6998-3
"In sunset's light o'er Afric thrown". The traveller at the source of the Nile. Felicia Dorothea Hemans. 6980-0
"In sunset's light, o'er Afric thrown". The traveller at the source of the Nile. Felicia Dorothea Hemans. 6973-8
"In surety and obscurity twice mailed". Not always. Edwin Arlington Robinson. 6778-6
"In Swarthmore college ehtics class in 1961...". In Swarthmore college ethics class. John Oliver Simon. 6792-1, 6998-3
"In Tarbolton, ye ken, there are proper...". The Ronalds of the Bennals. Robert Burns. 6760-3
In swimming-time. James Whitcomb Riley. 6993-2
In tall grass. Carl Sandburg. 6031-5
"' The style of dress In teacup-times!'". A rondeau to Ethel. Austin Dobson. 6770-0
"In tears, the heart opprest with grief". Pietro Metastasio. 6973-8
In Tehachapi. David Starr Jordan. 6241-5
In tempore senectutis. Ernest Dowson. 6250-4
In temptation. Charles Wesley. 6152-4
In Tenebris. Thomas Hardy. 6208-3,6657-7,6491-4
In Texas. May Sarton. 6761-1
"In tempus old, a hero lived". A mixture. Unknown. 6983-5
"In terror of its own delight". The golden leopard. Gustav Davidson. 6979-7
"In that blest age when never care annoyed". Pity; an allegory, versified. Felicia Dorothea Hemans. 6973-8
"In that dear distant homeland". To Mrs. von U. Louis J. Magee. 7004-3
"In that desolate land and lone". The revenge of Rain-in-the-face. Henry Wadsworth Longfellow. 6946-0
"In that forgotten land from which I came". In the desert. Beatrice Allhusen. 6800-6
"In that last hour when earthly hope has fled". The saints gone home. William White. 6868-5
In that new world which is old. George A. Mackenzie. 6115-X
"In that pale hour taken". An eye. Joseph Auslander. 6779-4
"In that soft mid-land where the breezes bear". Rodney's ride. Elbridge Streeter Brooks. 6922-3
"In that strange city". Hunger. Mary Carolyn Davies. 6979-7
"In that tranced hush when sound sank awed...". Mine. John Westland Marston. 7015-9
"In that Valhalla where the heroes go". The heroes. M. Forrest. 7027-2
"In that, O queen of queens, thy birth was free." Henry Constable. 6181-8
In the "state of McDowell" Orville J. Jenks. 6149-4
In the air. Lucy Larcom. 6066-8
"In the air picketed by hours with missing minutes" Pete Winslow. 6998-3
In the album of Lucy Barton. Charles Lamb. 6297-0
In the Alps. Samuel Rogers. 6749-2
In the ambulance. Wilfred Wilson Gibson. 6732-8,6102-8, 6542-2
In the Antwerp gallery. Mary Atwater Taylor. 6039-0
"In the ancestral presence of the dead". Necessity. Letitia Elizabeth ("L.E.L.") Landon. 6980-0
"In the ancient kingly hall". The drink from a jack-boot. Pfarrius. 6842-1
In the arena. Anthero de Quental. 6648-8

In the art museum. Gertrude Hall. 6431-0
In the autumn. Han-mo Chung. 6775-1
In the autumn. Harriet F. Payn. 6272-5
"In the autumn/Let me pray...". Prayer in autumn. Hyun-sung Kim. 6775-1
In the backs. Frances Cornford. 6659-3
"In the barn the tenant cock". Day: a pastoral. John Cunningham. 6932-0
In the bath. Ethel M. Kelley. 6266-0
In the battell hemlocks. Frederick Lewis Pattee. 7030-2
In the bay. Algernon Charles Swinburne. 6102-8,6152-4
In the beginning. William D. Barney. 6218-0
In the beginning. Angela Morgan. 6211-3
In the beginning. Robert Wolf. 6039-0
In the beginning was the bird. Henry Treece. 6666-6,6360-8
In the beginning was the word. Anna Hempstead Branch. 6619-4,6393-4
"In the beginning was the word geography". The death of geography. Eve Merriam. 6783-2
"In the beginning was the word next to God". Francesca of Rimini, fr. The divine comedy. Dante Alighieri. 6945-2
"In the beginning?- Slowly grope we back". The origin of life. Alfred Noyes. 7014-0
In the belfry of the Nieuwe Kerk. Thomas Bailey Aldrich. 6484-1
In the black country. Olive Tilford Dargan. 6036-6
In the black forest. Celia Thaxter. 6612-7
"In the black night, along the mud-deep roads". Outside London. Francis W.L. Adams. 7009-4
"In the bleak mid-winter". Christina Georgina Rossetti. 6931-2
In the bleak midwinter. Christina Georgina Rossetti. 6747-6
"In the blind alley". Blind alley. Tae-jin Park. 6775-1
"In the blonde room the lustrous-limbed piano". Soiree. Babette Deutsch. 6780-8
"In the blossom-land Japan". An old song. Yehoash (Solomon Bloomgarden). 7039-6
"In the blue dreamlight, the blue dreamlight". Blue dreamlight Shaman song. Tom Lowenstein. 6855-3
In the blue heaven. Henry Van Dyke. 6961-4
"In the book of the iron angels there is...". Of the beloved caravan. Conny Hannes Meyer. 6769-7
In the bottom drawer. Unknown. 6744-1
"In the breast of a bulb." William L. Stidger. 6750-6
"In the breeze, on a bough that is asking" Boris Pasternak. 6103-6
"In the burgh town of Arras". Pipes in Arras. Neil Munro. 7031-0,7027-2
In the candle light. Golda M. Goldman. 6847-2
In the carpenter shop. Unknown. 6144-3
In the catacombs. Harlan House Ballard. 6089-7,6415-9,6736-0
In the cathedral close. Edward Dowden. 6244-X
"In the cathedral vault with the great...gums". Cafeteria afternoon. Oscar Williams. 6761-1
"In the cavern's lonely hall". The poet's home. John Sterling. 6980-0
"In the cedarn shadow sleeping". The new sirens: a palinode. Matthew Arnold. 6947-9
"In the Christmas times of the long ago". The Christmas gift for mother. Edgar A. Guest. 7033-7
In the cemetery of the sun. Wilfred Watson. 6446-9
In the character of a Hampshire farmer. James Smith. 6802-2
In the children's hospital. Joseph Joel Keith. 6761-1
In the children's hospital. Alfred Lord Tennyson. 6255-5,6683-6
In the choir. Roy Farrell Greene. 7021-3
"In the church of Capistrano--tarnished...". Easter chimes. Virginia Donaghe McClurg. 6836-7
In the churchyard. Charles Lamb. 6304-7
In the churchyard at Tarrytown. Henry Wadsworth Longfellow. 6126-5
In the city. Hattie Horner Louthan. 6836-7
In the city. Israel Zangwill. 6730-1
"In the city without classes, white". Birdseye. Charles Madge. 6985-1
"In the clatter of the train". Villanelle ("In the clatter"). William Ernest Henley. 6875-8
In the cloister. William J. Fischer. 6285-7
In the closet. Laura E. Richards. 6137-0,6131-1
"In the cloud-gray mornings". Hoar-frost. Amy Lowell. 6897-9
In the coach. Thomas Edward Brown. 6809-X
In the coach, sels. Thomas Edward Brown. 6508-2
"In the cold ocean only whales are warm...". Mean mother metaphor. David McElroy. 6855-3
"In the cold wind, towers grind round". On the vanity of human aspirations. Edith Sitwell. 7000-0
In the cold, bright wind. William Alexander Percy. 6036-6
In the confessional, about 1200, A.D. Katherine Oliver. 6039-0
In the cool of the evening. Alfred Noyes. 6266-0;6473-6;6498-1
In the cool of the evening, fr. The hill of vision. James Stephens. 6234-2,6339-X
"In the cool tender twilight hour". My guest. Frances Moyes. 6799-9
"In the cool, calm palace of prayer". A modern scholar to a mediaeval man. Joel Elias Spingarn. 6880-4
"In the coppice, where leaves are decaying". Promenade. Antonin Sova. 6886-3
"In the corner of the living room was an...". The dead in frock coats. Carlos Drummond de Andrade. 6758-1
"In the cosy twilight hid". Tellin' what the baby did. Sam Walter Foss. 6772-7
In the country. William Henry Davies. 6102-8
"In the county of Antrim, near the town of Gallow". Unknown. 6059-5
"In the county of Derry where I was bred and born". Unknown. 6059-5
In the cove. Mary Fanny Youngs. 6995-9
In the cradle of the deep. Emma Hart Willard. 6431-0
In the cradle-boat. George Cooper. 6965-7
In the cranberry gardens. Ann Chandonnet. 6855-3
In the cross of Christ I glory. Sir John Bowring. 6251-X,6337-3,6730-1,6214-8
"In the damp and dim-lit room". The old mill. W.W. Christman. 6761-1
In the dark. Lucy Wilson Buxton. 7016-7
In the dark. Sophie ("Ellen Burroughs") Jewett. 6309-8
In the dark (1). Alice Cary. 6969-X
In the dark (2). Alice Cary. 6969-X
"In the dark and peace of my final bed". Little pagan rain song. Frances Shaw. 6897-9
"In the dark caverns of the night". Poem ("In the dark"). Henry Treece. 6379-9
In the dark city. John Hall Wheelock. 6036-6
"In the dark days I have striven for..useful". 'Today I am in chains'. S.H. Vatsyayasna. 6761-1
"In the dark days, the early evenings...". The bell-ringers. James Rorty. 6979-7
"In the dark night,from sweet refreshing sleep". Floods. Ella Wheeler Wilcox. 6956-9
"In the dark Thuringian forest stood a castle". The wizard's spell. Letitia Virginia Douglas. 6923-1
"In the dark pine wood", fr. Chamber music. James Joyce. 6536-8
"In the darkness he signs of the dawning". The poet. Mary Sinton Leitch. 6037-4,6088-9,6326-8
In the dawn. Odell Shepard. 6730-1
"In the dawn of the day when the sea &..earth". The kingdom of love. Ella Wheeler Wilcox. 6863-4
In the dawn, sels. Odell Shepard. 6337-3
In the day of the east wind. Elizabeth Craigmyle. 6997-5
In the day's work. Jessie Litchfield. 6349-7
"In the days my hands had". A song to Sally, fr. Songs for Sally. Marion Strobel. 6778-6
In the days o' Langsyne. Robert Gilfillan. 6543-0
"In the days of childish troubles". Mother's boy. Unknown. 6097-9
In the days of crinoline. Thomas Hardy. 6722-0
"In the days of long ago every lady had toknow". Hand-painted china days. Edgar A. Guest. 6748-4
"In the days of my youth". Triolet ("In the days"). Justin Huntly McCarthy. 6770-0
"In the days of my youth I've been...". Good old things. John Collins. 6874-X

In the days of old, fr. Crotchet castle. Thomas Love Peacock. 6934-7
"In the days to come, some remittance chum". 'Magadi'. Brian ("Korongo") Brooke. 6938-X
"In the days when my mother, the earth...young". Question? Joaquin Miller. 6753-0
In the days when the cattle ran. Hamlin Garland. 6497-3
"In the dead av the night, acushla". Exile. Arthur Stringer. 6797-2
"In the dead of night". Dead of night. Manuel Bandeira. 6759-X
"In the dead of night to the dead-house". The dead-house. Alice Cary. 6865-0;6969-X
"In the dead unhappy midnight". Gerald Massey. 6648-8
"In the deep cave of the heart, far down...". In the deep caves of the heart, fr. 'Towards democracy' Edward Carpenter. 6954-1
"In the deep hour of dreams". The Italian girl's hymn to the Virgin. Felicia Dorothea Hemans. 6973-8
"In the deep wilderness unseen she prayed". The prayer in the wilderness. Felicia Dorothea Hemans. 6973-8
In the delta. William Alexander Parcy. 6421-3
In the dense woods. Unknown. 6061-7
In the depot...refugees. Nancy Cardozo. 6761-1
In the depths. Arthur Hugh Clough. 6828-6
In the depths. Arthur Hugh Clough. 6110-9
In the desert. Beatrice Allhusen. 6800-6
In the desert. Alice Corbin. 6506-6
In the desert. Joseph Joel Keith. 6783-2
In the desert of the holy land. Unknown. 6271-7
In the desert to-day. L. Challoner. 6468-X
"In the deserted moon-blanched street". A summer night. Matthew Arnold. 6199-0,6430-2,6560-0,6828-6
"In the dim and lofty vis,as". Dwells a maiden. Thomas Noel Wrenn. 6983-5
"In the dim conservatory". Procrastination. Unknown. 6923-1
"In the din and dust of the street". The cry of the uncreated. Arthur Henry Goodenough. 7030-2
"In the distance tree-fringed valleys and...". Going back at evening. Jim Thomas. 6860-X
In the doorway. Robert Browning. 6380-2
In the doorway. Louise C. Custice. 6078-1
In the down-hill of life. John Collins. 6219-9
In the Duke of York's garden, fr. King Richard II. William Shakespeare. 6649-6
In the dumps. Unknown. 6902-9
In the dusk. Francis Ledwidge. 6812-X
"In the dusky distance of the heaven". The stars. Unknown. 6952-5
"In the dust by the wayside...wherever it...". Hidden beauty. Isabelle Ruby Owen. 6799-9
"In the dusty, dusty hall". On a late edition of Webster. Unknown. 6936-3
"In the earliest time on the greatest mountain". The scarlet tanager and the leaf. Unknown (Algonquin Indian). 6864-2
"In the early chilled morning". Seacliff at dawn. Peter Olds. 7018-3
"In the early morn, ere the break of dawn". The missing something. Brian ("Korongo") Brooke. 6938-X
In the early morning. Adelaide G. Waters. 6965-7
"In the early morning I saw". A test of competence. Greg Forker. 6870-7
"In the early spring,..the nights grow shorter". Charles's wain. Sir Alfred Comyn Lyall. 6793-2
"In the early spring-time, after their tea". En famille. Edith Sitwell. 7000-0
"In the early white of a February morning...". Poem for John my brother. William Aberg. 6870-7
'In the early, pearly morning': song by Valgovind. Laurence (Adele Florence Nicolson) Hope. 6856-1
In the elevator. Robert C.V. Meyers. 6925-8
In the elk season. Erik Axel Karlfeldt. 6045-5
"In the elm-woods and the oaken". Euripides. 6395-0
In the end, fr. The dark cup. Sara Teasdale. 6531-7
In the Esplanade des Invalides. George O'Neil. 6808-1
In the Etrurian valley. Edward Bulwer-Lytton; Baron Lytton. 6385-3
"In the endless nights, from my bed, where...". Mater tenebrarum. James Thomson. 6828-6
In the evening. Hamilton Aide. 6226-1
"In the evening after supper". When mother quilted. Hazel Grant Fisher. 6799-9
"In the evening the dusk". The poet is dead. William Everson. 6792-1, 6998-3
"In the face of death, they say, he joked...". A cross in Flanders. George Rostrevor Hamilton. 7031-0,7026-4
In the factory. Morris Rosenfeld. 7011-6
"In the faint tuberose fragrances, oblivion...". Tuberoses. Jiri Karascek ze Lvovic. 6763-8
"In the fair picture". Sonnet ("In the fair picture.") Arthur Davison Ficke. 6250-4
"In the famed Scottish castle of Glamis". Limerick:"In the famed Scottish castle of Glamis". Louis P. Berlyn. 6811-1
"In the far distant times of legend and story". The legend of King Nilus. Edith Wordsworth. 6926-6
"In the far old time". The story of Nipon the summer. Unknown (Algonquin Indian). 6864-2
"In the farmhouse porch the farmer sat". Two of them. Unknown. 6889-8
In the fern, fr. Australian transcripts. William ("Fiona Macleod") Sharp. 6768-9
In the field. Otto Laaber. 6769-7
In the fields. Charlotte Mew. 6354-3,6253-9
"In the fields like an Indian mazery". Rose. Edith Sitwell. 7000-0
"In the fields near the convent of San Raphael". The dance of the nuns. Angel Guimera. 6959-2
In the fields of love. Rachel Annand Taylor. 6628-3
"In the fields where, long ago". A Christmas hymn. Unknown. 6916-9
"In the fierce rhythmn of love we two...swung". Severance. Babette Deutsch. 6880-4
In the fight. Alfred Lord Tennyson. 6438-8
In the firelight. Eugene Field. 6949-5
In the firelight. Eugene Field. 6273-3,6303-9
"In the first place of my life" Ray A. Young Bear. 7005-1
"In the first year of freedom's second dawn". George Gordon, 6th Baron Byron. 6289-X
"In the fold/Out the wold". The little young lambs. Patrick Reginald Chalmers. 6804-9
In the forest. R. Grant Brown. 6591-0,6592-9
In the forest. Gerhard Fritsch. 6769-7
In the forest. Jules Supervielle. 6343-8
In the forest. Oscar Wilde. 6253-9
In the forrest of Fontainebleau. Christopher Pearse Cranch. 6331-4
In the foundry. Hubert Nicholson. 6895-2
In the front-line desks. Elmer Franklin Powell. 6846-4
"In the full tide of melody and mirth". Stanzas to the memory of —. Felicia Dorothea Hemans. 6973-8
In the galleries of the Louvre. Charles Lewis Slattery. 6331-4,6439-6,6631-3
"In the gap of Dunlo". Paddy Blake's echo. Samuel Lover. 6825-1,6916-9
In t e garb of old Gaul. Sir Henry Erskine. 6180-X
In the garden. Arthur Christopher Benson. 6649-6
In the garden. Emily Dickinson. 6232-6,6008-0,6649-6
In the garden. Richard Eberhart. 6388-8
In the garden. Thomas S. Jones Jr. 6331-4
In the garden. Edna Davis Romig. 6836-7
In the garden. Milton S. Rose. 6836-7
In the garden. Pai Ta-Shun. 6338-1
In the garden. Unknown. 6337-3
"In the garden I remember". Written garden. Ulalume Gonzalez de Leon. 7036-1
In the garden at Swainston. Alfred Lord Tennyson. 6437-X, 6655-0,6657-7
In the garden of the Lord. Helen Keller. 6337-3,6007-2, 6730-4,6214-8
In the garden, fr. The road to Avernus. Adam Lindsay Gordon. 6951-7
In the garden, sels. Robert Buchanan. 6066-8
In the garden-close at Mezra. Clinton Scollard. 6338-1
In the gardens. Arthur Vine Hall. 6800-6
"In the garment factory where I work". Cultural exchange. Al Masarik. 6792-1
'In the garret are our boys'. Unknown. 6915-0

"In the glittering wet, by new pools". Apple wine. Elizabeth Grey Stewart. 6761-1
In the gloaming. James C. Bayles. 6902-9
In the gloaming. Charles Stuart Calverley. 6440-X
In the glorious assumption of our blessed lady. Richard Crashaw. 6315-2
In the golden birch. Jane Elizabeth Gostwycke Roberts. 6656-9
In the golden morning of the world. Thomas Westwood. 6656-9
"In the golden summer morning". Heinrich Heine. 6876-6
In the grass. Hamlin Garland. 6476-0,6309-8
In the grass. Sir Edmund Gosse. 6770-0
In the graveyard. Macdonald Clarke. 6481-7
"In the gray beginning of years, in the...". Hymn of man. Algernon Charles Swinburne. 6828-6
"In the gray, dim light where time is not". The beacon-light. Murray Ketcham Kirk. 6995-9
"In the great house, and in the house of fire". He holdeth fast to the memory of his identity. Unknown (Egyptian). 7039-6
In the great metropolis. Arthur Hugh Clough. 6828-6
In the great metropolis. Arthur Hugh Clough. 6655-0
In the great morning of the world. Percy Bysshe Shelley. 6383-7
"In the green garden the nightingale" Ivan Surikov. 6103-6
"In the green gardens stretched by...river". The swan. James E. Warren Jr.. 6979-7
"In the grey wastes of dread". Horses on the Camargue. Roy Campbell. 6625-9,6780-8,6985-1
"In the grim, greyish light of the...night". In adversity. Brian ("Korongo") Brooke. 6938-X
"In the grove sings the throstle". In spring. Julius Zeyer. 6763-8
"In the growing haste of the world...". Sails. George Sterling. 6833-2
In the hall. Unknown. 6928-2
"In the hallway/behind the stairs". Derelict. Henry Johnson. 6870-7
In the hammock. Unknown. 6273-3
In the harbor. George Robert Sims. 6917-7
"In the hard winter of the world". The happy night. Richard Lawson Gales. 6776-X
In the haunts of bass and bream. James Maurice Thompson. 6006-4,6597-X,6623-2
"In the hawthorn country". The strong fortress. Hamish Maclaren. 6893-6
In the hay-loft. Helen Thayer Hutcheson. 6692-2,
In the heart of a garden. Rosamund Marriott ("Graham R. Tomson") Watson. 6232-6
In the heart of contemplation. Cecil Day Lewis. 6209-1
In the heart of the hills. Bliss Carman. 6433-7
In the heart of the hills, sels. Albert Durrant Watson. 6796-4
In the heat of the day, sels. Louis J. Magee. 7004-3
In the Hebrites. F.L. Lucas. 6782-4
In the hedgeback. Christopher M. ("Hugh MacDiarmid") Grieve. 6379-9
In the Henry James country. William Abrahams. 6666-6
In the highlands. Robert Louis Stevenson. 6123-0,6395-0, 6250-4,6301-2,6508-2,6439 ,6246-6,6331-4,6477-9,6339-X,6423-X,6437
"In the hills' embraces holden". The cemetery nightingale. Morris Rosenfeld. 7011-6
"In the hoar years ere from the earth". From the north. James Abraham Martling. 6952-5
In the holy nativity [of our Lord God]. Richard Crashaw. 6198-2,6334-9,6562-7
In the home stretch. Robert Frost. 6030-7
In the honour of Christes birth, sing we all with joy. Unknown. 6756-5
"In the horizon, from a sultry cloud". Summer evening lightning. Carlos Wilcox. 6752-2
In the hospital. Arthur Guiterman. 6027-7,6303-9,6337-3, 6556-2,6607-0,6653-4,6730-1
In the hospital. Mary Woolsey Howland. 6243-1,6337-3,6471-X
In the hospital courtyard. Stan Rice. 6901-0
In the hospital ward. Unknown. 6670-4
"In the hot malodorous pen". Goat-pen. Luis L. Franco. 6759-X
In the hour of my distress. Robert Herrick. 6337-3
In the hours of darkness. James Flexner. 6891-X
In the house of Idiedaily. Bliss Carman. 6437-X,6467-1
"In the huge and glassy room". The avenue, fr. Facade. Edith Sitwell. 7000-0
In the humpbacked sky. Nikolai Tikhonov. 6546-5
In the Jacquerie. Mrs. Simcox. 6046-3
"In the hush and the lonely silence". Autumn leaves. Angelina Wray. 6964-9
"In the hysterical hour of war". The prospect for peace. David Boyd. 6789-1
In the joint of his armour. Marie Van Vorst. 7038-8
"In the jolly winters". Old man's nursery rhyme. James Whitcomb Riley. 6991-6
In the key of blue. Nelson Antrim Crawford. 6033-1
In the king's english. Berton Braley. 6853-7
In the king's garden. Abbie Farwell Brown. 7022-1
"In the kingdom of sham". The kingdom of sham. I. Edgar Jones. 6926-6
In the kitchen. Carolyn Wells. 6882-0
"In the land of Brittany, and long ago". Only a Jew. Unknown. 6915-0,6848-0
In the land of magic, sel. Henri Michaux. 6758-1
"In the land where ever-blooming lotus". Nofertete. Caroline Sparks. 6799-9
In the land where we were dreaming. Daniel B. Lucas. 6113-3
In the lane. Leonard Alfred George Strong. 6257-1
In the lanes of Nazareth. Earl B. Marlatt. 6335-7
In the lap o' the bog. Cahir Healy. 6174-5
"In the last trench of all". Foch. Frederick George Scott. 6797-2
"In the leaf-strewn cavern...". Theocritus. 6251-2
In the leaves the raindrops gently. Alexey Tolstoy. 6103-6
"In the leveled guns' uncertain stammer". Bird on the rifle range. Daniel Smythe. 6761-1
In the library. Anne C. Lynch Botta. 7030-2
In the library. Clinton Scollard. 6297-0
"In the light of the moon, by the side...water". My daughter Louise. Homer Greene. 6917-7
"In the li ht of the silent stars that...". The loom of years. Alfred Noyes. 7014-0
"In the light, in the shade". Triolet. Walter Crane. 6875-8
"In the light, in the shade,/This is time...". Triolet ("In the light"). Walter Crane. 6770-0
In the lilac-bush. Celia Thaxter. 6612-7
In the lists. Bayard Taylor. 6976-2
"In the little country meeting". A-Maying. Irwin Shupp Jr.. 6936-3
"In the little town of Wellsboro". Unknown. 6059-5
"In the living room Walter Cronkite". Trying to sleep late on a saturday morning in November. Richard Eberhart. 6803-0
In the long run. Victor F. Murray. 6269-5
In the Longhouse, Oneida museum. Roberta Hill Whiteman. 7005-1
"In the long silence of the sea, the seaman". Seven twilights, sels. Conrad Aiken. 6798-0
"In the long time ago". How the master found the summer. Unknown (Algonquin Indian). 6864-2
"In the Maine woods I shot a white-tailed deer". The wounded deer leaps highest. Donald Junkins. 6803-0
In the looking glass. Priscilla Leonard. 6928-2
In the Louvre. John Todhunter. 7015-9
"In the lower lands of day". Algernon Charles Swinburne. 6187-7
In the manner of Spencer. Samuel Taylor Coleridge. 6967-3
In the mansion yard. William Hervey Woods. 7008-6
In the mantle of God. Harold Trowbridge Pulsifer. 6320-9
"In th market of Clare, so cheery the glare". Clare market. Eugene Field. 6949-5
In the market-place. George Sterling. 6954-1
"In the marsh...", sels. Sarah F. Davis. 6601-1
In the May. Katharine (Hinkson) Tynan. 6174-5
In the meadow. Frank Dempster Sherman. 6311-X
In the meadow. Unknown. 6373-X
In the meadows. Bayard Taylor. 6976-2
In the meadows at Mantua. Artur Symons. 6477-9,6624-0

In the Mediterranean - going to the war. Francis Ledwidge. 6812-X
In the Mediterranean- going to the war. Francis Ledwidge. 7014-0
"In the meadows near life's highway". Friendship town. Elizabeth Abbey Everett. 6799-9
"In the merry hay-time..." C.K. Paul. 6046-3
"In the merry month of May". Pastoral. Nicholas Breton. 6830-8
"In the merry month of May". Nicholas Breton. 6181-8,6187-7
"In the middle of our porridge plates". Butterfly laughter. Katherine Mansfield. 6777-8
In the middle of the night. Duncan Mitchel. 7003-5
"In the middle of the night when the...". Night music. Vojislav Ilic Jr.. 6765-4
"In the Middle West there's a place of...". Fishing for water buckets in the cistern. A.M. Fleming. 6799-9
"In the middle part of Britain there is a hideous fen" Dugdale. 7020-5
"In the midnight of darkness and terror". Delilah. Ella Wheeler Wilcox. 6956-8
"In the midnight, in the rain". The last rally. John Gould Fletcher. 7027-2
In the midst of death is life. Clive Sansom. 6475-2
"In the midst of life..." Dora Sigerson Shorter. 6244-X
"In the midst of my garden". The palm tree. Abr-ar-Rahman I. 7039-6
"In the midst of them" Margaret Bell Merrill. 6478-7
In the mining town. Rose Hartwick Thorpe. 6215-6
In the mist. Sarah ("Susan Coolidge") Woolsey. 6240-7,6600-3
In the modern manner. Dorothy Parnall. 6490-6
In the Mohave. Patrick Orr. 6393-4,6252-0
In the Mojave. Charles F. Lummis. 6241-5
"In the moment of his glory". Lincoln slain. Edwin Markham. 6871-5
In the monastery. Norreys Jephson O'Conor. 6556-2
"In the month of Beaver". Ts'eekkaayah. Mary TallMountain. 7005-1
In the month of February. Unknown. 6904-5
In the mood of Blake. William Soutar. 6257-1
In the moonlight. Thomas Hardy. 6154-0,6102-8,6301-2
In the moonlight. Jens Peter Jacobsen. 6555-4
In the moonlight. David McKee Wright. 6784-0
"In the moonlight, in this night". Clair de Lune. Luis Pales Matos. 6759-X
In the morgue, fr. Pictures of women. Agnes Lee. 6033-1
"In the morn he sat at meat". The willow. Karel Jaromir Erben. 6763-8
"In the morn of the holy sabbath". Dear little heads in the pew. Margaret Elizabeth Sangster. 6889-8
In the morning. Paul Laurence Dunbar. 6714-X
In the morning. Klaxon (John Graham Bower) 7031-0
In the morning. Patrick MacGill. 7027-2
In the morning. Emma Celia & Lizzie J. Rook. 6741-7
In the morning. Ernst Stadler. 6160-5
"In the morning she jumped out of bed very...". Three tropisms. Nathalie Sarraute. 6803-0
In the morning, fr. Studies for pictures. Bayard Taylor. 6976-2
In the mosque. Ibn Malik (of Murcia) 6362-4
In the mountains. James Abraham Martling. 6952-5
"In the mountains/you tell me". Three songs. Edgar Jackson. 6870-7
"In the mud of the Cambrian main". A ballade of evolution. Grant Allen. 6770-0,6875-8
In the mulberry leaves. Frederic Mistral. 6102-8
"In the muses paths I stray", fr. The spleen. Anne Finch, Countess of Winchilsea. 6934-7
In the mushroom meadows. Thomas Walsh. 6556-2
In the naked bed, in Plato's grave. Delmore Schwartz. 6389-6
In the name of God, the compassionate, the merciful. Koran. 6679-8
In the Neolithic age. Rudyard Kipling. 6810-3
In the Neolithic age, sels. Rudyard Kipling. 6427-2
"In the name of the empress of India, make way". The overland mail. Rudyard Kipling. 6924-X
In the night. C. Bain. 6216-4

In the night. Stephen Crane. 6121-4
In the night. Unknown. 6902-9
"In the night again I go". Felix Vexler. 6847-2
In the night watches. Sir Charles George Douglas Roberts. 6446-9
In the night watches. Alice Wellington Rollins. 6097-8
"In the night when all the sky was lit". The first frost. Thornton W. Burgess. 6798-0
"In the night, when the sea-winds take...". Night movement - New York. Carl Sandburg. 6808-1
In the nude. Idabel Williams. 6906-1
In the nursery. Jean Ingelow. 6683-6
"In the nurserywas burning a fire, warm and...". I am not ready yet. Alice Polk Hill. 6836-7
In the ol' tobacker patch. S.Q. Lapius. 6453-1
"In the old age black was not counted fair". Sonnet 127 ("In the old age"). William Shakespeare. 6447-7
"In the old back streets o' Pimlico". The rambling sailor. Charlotte Mew. 6985-1,6776-X
In the old church choir. Lowell Otus Reese. 6486-8
"In the old church, thro' Gothic windows...". Quis ut deus? Jaroslav Vrchlicky. 6886-3
"In the old familiar nursery". The new nursery. Sarah ("Susan Coolidge") Woolsey. 6772-7
"In the old hash-house at college...". U.P. cafe. Mary Hibbs Geisler. 6936-3
In the old home. Arthur O'Shaughnessy. 6250-4
"In the old house there is a chamber high". The bower, fr. The old Scotch house. William Bell Scott. 6819-7
"In the old marble town of Kilkenny". Ninety-eight. ? Campion. 6918-5
"In the old old times". A fable, for Henricus D., Esq., Jr. Thomas Edward Brown. 6809-X
"In the old rabbinical stories". The treasure of Abram. John Boyle O'Reilly. 6848-0
In the olden time. Sir Walter Scott. 6145-1
"In the oldest of our alleys". The banished Bejant. Robert Fuller Murray. 7025-6
In the orchard. Henrik Ibsen. 7039-6
In the orchard. Frank Dempster Sherman. 6311-X
In the orchard. Muriel Stuart. 6269-5,6019-6,6070-6,6069-2
In the orchard. Algernon Charles Swinburne. 6732-8,6659-3
In the orchard. George Weatherly. 6770-0
In the orchard path. Homer Green. 6260-1
In the other world. Harriet Beecher Stowe. 6909-6
"In the outer court I was singing". The inner chamber. Adelaide Anne Procter. 6957-6
"In the outermost borders of Blue Ash town". The old-fashioned garden club. Clara Degman Hook. 6906-1
In the park. Helen Hoyt. 6019-6
In the pass. Clinton Scollard. 6619-4
In the piazza of San Petronio. Giosue Carducci. 6624-0
"In the picture/they sit". Dying old and dying young. Susan L. Williams. 6857-X
In the pine forest of the Cascine. Percy Bysshe Shelley. 6624-0
In the pinewoods. Eva Gore-Booth. 6174-5
In the pioneer camp. Anna Akhmatova. 6546-5
In the Place de la Bastille. Richard Burton. 6102-8,6076-5
"In the place to which I go". Reveille. Ronald Lewis Carton. 7027-2
In the plain words of an ordinary man. Paul Potts. 6895-2
"In the pleasant spring-time weather". Epithalamium. Alice Cary. 6865-0;6969-X
"In the pleasant time of Pentecost". The red flower. Henry Van Dyke. 6961-4
In the poppy field, fr. The hill of vision. James Stephens. 6234-2,6668-2,6116-3,6393-4
"In the primitive days of our grandfather's...". The hole in the floor. Lizzie Clark Hardy. 6916-9
In the procession. Unknown. 6274-1
"In the profound and dreadful calm of night". To my beloved dead. Ethel Ashton Edwards. 6777-8
In the proscenium. Gene Derwood. 6390-X
"In the proud old fanes of England". The brother's dirge. Felicia Dorothea Hemans. 6973-8
In the province of Shantung. Bertye Young Williams. 7038-8
In the public ward. Florence Randal Livesay. 6115-X
"In the quiet house/a lamp is burning". Listening in October. John Haines. 6855-3

"In the quiet nursery chambers". Prayers of children. Unknown. 6910-X
"In the rags of a wind". Encounter. John Peale Bishop. 6979-7
"In the Rhine, that beautiful river". Song ("In the Rhine"). Heinrich Heine. 6484-1
In the rain. William Wetmore Story. 6735-2
In the ranges. William ("Fiona Macleod") Sharp. 6768-9
In the ravine. W.W. Eustace Ross. 6446-9
In the Roman amphitheatre, Verona. Herbert Trench. 6877-4
"In the rift of the rock he has covered..head". The rift of the rock. Annie Herbert. 6914-2
"In the ripples of your books". To Edna St. Vincent Millay. Witter Bynner. 6817-0
"In the Roman dungeon sighing". The gospel for the poor. Benjamin Franklin Taylor. 6815-4
In the room. James ("B.V.") Thomson. 6437-X
"In the room below the young man sat". The young man waited. Edmund Vance Cooke. 6929-0,6930-0
"In the rosy red of the dawning your hoof...". Remounts. William Henry Ogilvie. 7010-8
In the round tower at Jhansi. Christina Georgina Rossetti. 6828-6
In the Royal Academy. Austin Dobson. 6683-6
"In the royal path/Came maidens rob'd in...". The triumph of Joseph. Charles Jeremiah Wells. 6848-0
"In the rude age when scyence was not so rife" Henry Howard, Earl of Surrey. 6380-4
"In the rugged limestone pasture". Deathless. William Douw Lighthall. 6796-4
"In the sad cafes that are our lives". Cafes. Robert B. Smith. 6870-7
"In the sad louthwest, iJ the mystical sunland". Homes of the cliff dwellers. Stanley Wood. 6836-7
"In the scarlet town where I was born". Barbara Allen. Unknown. 6826-X
In the school assembly hall. G.H. McGaw. 6764-6
"In the school of coquettes". Circe, fr. Rose-leaves. Austin Dobson. 6770-0
In the sea. Hiram Rich. 6240-7,6600-3
In the season. Robert Louis Stevenson. 6732-8,6655-0,6656-9
In the servants' quarters. Thomas Hardy. 6506-6,6532-5
In the seven woods. William Butler Yeats. 6315-2
"In the shade of the cloister, long ago". St. Bernard of Clairvaux. Phoebe Cary. 6969-X
"In the shade/Of a grey granite boulder...". Noontide. Madeline Holland. 6800-6
In the shadow. William Canton. 6250-4
"In the shadow of a tomb". To 'an amiable child'. Mabel N. Lawson. 6750-6
In the shadows. David Gray. 6102-8
In the shadows. Emily Pauline ("Tekahionwake") Johnson. 6115-X,6591-0,6592-2
In the shadows. Francis Ledwidge. 6812-X
"In the shadows of the pyramid". The burial in the desert. Felicia Dorothea Hemans. 6973-8
In the shadows, sels. David Gray. 6960-6
"In the shadowy passageway". The girl with the blue lamp. Jose Maria Eguren. 6759-X
"In the sheltered garden, pale beneath...moon". Pierrot goes to war. Gabrielle Elliot. 7027-2
In the silence. Eleanor Bichnell Forbes. 6799-9
In the silence. Josephine Preston Peabody. 6532-5
In the Simplon pass. William Wordsworth. 6749-2
"In the silence and grandeur of midnight...". The cross of the south. Felicia Dorothea Hemans. 6973-8
"In the silence I am listening". In the silence. Eleanor Bichnell Forbes. 6799-9
"In the silence of my chamber". The buried flower. William Edmonstoune Aytoun. 6948-7
"In the silence of the midnight". The Indian with his dead child. Felicia Dorothea Hemans. 6973-8
"In the silent cloister garden". The nun. Johann Ludwig Uhland. 6903-7
In the s;tting room of the opera. Criss E. Cannady. 6966-5
In the sixties. Roba Beatrice Ward. 6342-X
"In the sky the moon shines bright". Lullaby ("In the sky"). Unknown (Spanish). 6711-5
"In the sky/the sun looks back". The sun looks back. Delia Dominguez. 7036-1
"In the slow Mexican air I watched the bull...". The priest and the matador. Charles Bukowski. 6792-1
"In the slums" Friederike Mayrocker. 6769-7
In the small canals. John Addington Symonds. 6624-0
In the small stove. Aleksey Surkov. 6546-5
In the snow, fr. The four winds. Ralph Cheever Dunning. 6531-7
"In the snowing and the blowing". Spring. Mary Mapes Dodge. 6049-8
"In the soft shoots of lilac,...quick of green". The quick of the green. Maurice Carpenter. 6895-2
"In the solemn midnight watches...". The warders of the seas. Agnes Maule Machar. 6796-4
"In the sorrow and the terror of the nations". The mother. Nettie Palmer. 6784-0
In the south. James Whitcomb Riley. 6993-2
"In the south of white rooms and young men...". Dialogue on the panning of Zelda Sayre Fitzgerald. Kaye McDonough. 6901-0
In the south seas. Peter Gray Wolf. 6478-7
In the spring. William Barnes. 6545-7
In the spring. Ibycus. 6435-3
In the spring. Eva Wilder McGlasson. 6682-8
In the spring. Meleager. 7039-6
"In the spring a fuller crimson comes...". Locksley hall, sels. Alfred Lord Tennyson. 6934-7
In the spring, sels. Paul Fort. 6351-9
In the springtime (1). Horace. 6949-5
In the springtime (2). Horace. 6949-5
"In the stagnant pride of an outworn race". Santiago. Thomas A. Janvier. 6946-0
In the stagnant pride of an outworn race. Thomas A. Janvier. 6946-0
In the states. Robert Louis Stevenson. 6122-2,6123-0,6241-5,6655-0,6656-9
"In the still black water". The swamp road, fr. Roads in the lowlands. Marie W. Reddy. 6841-3
"In the still insantiy/of the forest where". Serronydion. Jack Hirshman. 6792-1
"In the still jungle of the senses lay". The tiger. Ella Wheeler Wilcox. 6956-8
"In the stillness o' the night." William Barnes. 6302-0, 6383-7
In the stillness of the night. Margaret F. Pirigyi. 6894-4
In the storm. Stanton A. Coblentz. 6144-3
In the Strand. Havelock Ellis. 6482-5
"In the stormy waters of Gallaway". The ferry of Gallaway. Alice Cary. 6969-X
In the strange isle. Michael Roberts. 6209-1
In the street. Francois Coppee. 6351-9
In the street of by-and-by. Mrs. ? Abdy. 6916-9
In the street of lost time. Humbert Wolfe. 6777-8
In the studio. Agnes Maule Machar. 7041-8
In the subjunctive. Berton Braley. 6853-7
"In the subtraction of my yeares." Unknown. 6563-5
In the subway. Florence Ripley Mastin. 6880-4
In the subway. Louis Untermeyer. 6464-7
"In the sudden downpour" Muin Ozaki. 6981-9
In the sultan's garden. Clinton Scollard. 6770-0
In the sultan's garden. Clinton Scollard. 6289-X,6488-4
"In the summer even". Ballad ("In the summer"). Harriet Prescott Spofford. 6243-1,6309-8
In the summer of sixty. Unknown. 6003-X,6281-4
"In the summer of the north-land". The good man's evening. James Abraham Martling. 6952-5
"In the sunny orchard". In the orchard. Henrik Ibsen. 7039-6
"In the surround of snow-touched mountains". A circle begins. Harold Littlebird. 7005-1
"In the sweet morn of life, when health & joy". Serenity of childhood. John Leyden. 6980-0
In the swing. Eudora S. Bumstead. 6373-X
In the temple. Richard Crashaw. 6250-4
"In the temple's midst." Alfred Mombert. 6160-5
"In the tent the lamps were bright". The pavilion. Agnes Mary F. ("Madame Duclaux") Robinson. 6770-0
In the tenth circle. Unknown. 6118-4
In the third year of the war. Henry Treece. 6666-6
In the tidal marshes. obert Hillyer. 6781-6

"In the tides of the warm south wind it lay". Verazzano at Rhodes and Rhode Island. Hezekiah Butterworth. 6946-0
"In the time before forever". Sky-boy. Edward P. Gilchrist. 6750-6
In the time of strife. Frank Lebby Stanton. 6741-X,6223-7
"In the town where wondrous Merlin". The house of Hendra. Ernest Rhys. 6873-1
In the trades. Cicely Fox Smith. 6833-2
In the train. Clifford Bax. 6090-6,6250-4
In the train. Bodil Bech. 6555-4
In the train. James ("B.V.") Thomson. 6331-4,6512-0
In the tree-top. Lucy Larcom. 6078-1,6129-X
In the trench. Leon Gellert. 6349-7
In the trenches. Richard Aldington. 6542-2
In the trenches. Katherine (Amelia Beers Warnock Garvin) Hale. 6115-X
In the trenches. Maurice Hewlett. 7026-4
In the trenches. F. Whitmore. 6053-6
In the trolley car. Ruth Baldwin Chenery. 6762-X
In the tunnel. Francis Bret Harte. 6062-5
In the tunnel. E.L. Mayo. 6751-4
In the twilight. George Cotterell. 6656-9
In the twilight. James Russell Lowell. 6006-4,6732-8,6560-0,6126-5,6243-1,6288
"In the twilight, silent smiled". A lament. Thomas Lovell Beddoes. 6908-8
"In the two-minute TV spot". Brand loyalty. Dennis Schmitz. 7032-9
In the vale of Glamorgan. Huw Menai. 6360-8
In the valley. Yone Noguchi. 6241-5
In the valley of Cauteretz. Alfred Lord Tennyson. 6437-X, 6655-0,6250-4,6199-0,6110-9,6648-8,6657-7
In the VanGogh room. Traise Yamamoto. 6790-5
"In the valley of Craft, a dressmaker lived". A happy couple. H. Elliott McBride. 6920-7
In the vast and dim cathedral. Mary Cromwell Low. 6847-2
"In the very olden time". What Kuloskap did for the Indians. Unknown (Algonquin Indian). 6864-2
"In the village church where a child she was..". Wedded, fr. Dovecote mill. Phoebe Cary. 6865-0;6969-X
"In the village of Mont Cheri". The wedding gift. Unknown. 6929-0
"In the wake of the moon is one faithful...". Lyric. Howard Vigne Sutherland. 6836-7
"In the walled world of darkness and his fever". Child with malaria. Clark Mills. 6751-4,6761-1
"In the warm, black mill-pool winking". Song ("In the warm"). Owen (Edward Bulwer-Lytton, Earl Lytton) Meredith. 6980-0
"In the warm-flushded heart of the...west". My queen of dreams. Philip J. Holdsworth. 6768-9
In the water. Algernon Charles Swinburne. 6875-8
In the water, fr. A midsummer holiday. Algernon Charles Swinburne. 6110-9,6655-0
"In the water-blue of the wide sky-bowl". A solar myth. Delphine Harris Coy. 6836-7
In the way of peace. Lauchlan MacLean Watt. 6144-3,6335-7
In the wayland willows. Bliss Carman and Richard Hovey. 6890-1
"In the west hath arisen a light". al-Shidyaq. 6766-2
In the wheat. Paul Fort. 6351-9
In the wheat-field. Paul Hamilton Hayne. 6006-4
"In the white cabin at the foot of the...". Love song. Unknown. 6873-1
"In the white-flower'd...", fr. The earthly paradise. William Morris. 6187-7
"In the wild deluge where the world...drown'd". To his sacred majesty Charles the Second. John Dryden. 6970-3
In the wilderness. Robert Graves. 6246-6,6634-8
In the wilderness. Morris Rosenfeld. 7011-6
"In the wind-blown wrack when the night..black". The song of the seven seas. Adele Jordan Tarr. 6789-1
"In the winter bleak and bare". The birches. William White. 6868-5
In the winter woods. Frederick George Scott. 6115-X
"In the wintertime/at night". Toe'osh: a Laguna coyote story. Leslie Silko. 7005-1
In the womb. George William ("A.E.") Russell. 6338-1

"In the wondrous breastplate golden". Aaron's breastplate. Anna Shipton. 6848-0
In the wood. Herbert Edwin Clarke. 6656-9
In the wood. Adelaide Anne Procter. 6957-6
In the wood. William Kean Seymour. 6884-7
In the wood. Sara Teasdale. 6501-5
"In the woods". I love you. Celestin Pierre Cambiaire. 6826-X
In the woods. Ralph Waldo Emerson. 6253-9
In the woods. Frederick George Scott. 6433-7
In the woods in November. Sir John Collings ("Solomon Eagle") Squire. 6781-6
In the workshop. Richard Hovey. 7006-X
"In the worst inn's worst room...". The Duke of Buckingham, fr. Of the ueses of riches. Alexander Pope. 6932-0
"In the wrackes of Walsingam" Robert Southwell. 6586-4
"In the wrackes of Walsingam" Unknown. 6380-2
"In the yard choking". Without names. Jeff Tagami. 6790-5
In the year that's come and gone. William Ernest Henley. 6429-9,6226-1,6321-7
In the Yosemite. Robert Loveman. 6941-X
"In the years that now are dead and gone". My neighbor's house. Phoebe Cary. 6865-0;6969-X
In the zoo. George T. Marsh. 6510-4
"In thee, I fondly hoped to clasp". To D--. George Gordon, 6th Baron Byron. 6945-2
"In these ambiguous photos, their faces gaze". A Nisei picnic. David Mura. 6790-5
"In these deep shades a floweret blows". Fable of the wood rose and the laurel. Unknown. 6752-2
In these our winter days. Cecil Day Lewis. 6625-9
"In these prosaic days/Of politics and trade". Where are the pipes of Pan? Oscar Fay Adams. 6770-0
"In these sad hours, a prey to ceaseless pain". R.S.S. Written in a fit of illness. William Cowper. 6814-6
"In these years that I have hunted under stone". The hungry. David Greenhood. 6808-1
In thine image. Fania Kruger. 6532-5
In thine own heart. Angelus Silesius. 6144-3,6337-3
"In this autumnal ecstasy". Incised to change. Phil Eisenberg. 6857-X
"In this beloved marble view". On the bust of Helen by Canova. George Gordon, 6th Baron Byron. 6945-2,6828-6
"In this brown seed, so dry and hard". Resurrection. Agnes W. Storer. 6144-3,6335-7
"In this cold country". Angels of snow. Lorna Crozier. 6767-0
"In this country/the sign outlives the...". Americana, sels. Carl Rakosi. 6803-0
"In this dark, weed-grown wilderness". A gentleman of Somerset. W.G. Hole. 6793-X
"In this desolate field" Sojin Takei. 6981-9
"In this distant land of dust-covered olives". Memory. Annette Betz. 6799-9
"In this flat land, far from any home". Nebraska, U.S.A. Philip Booth. 6803-0
"In this fox hole I am writing". 'Fill that cookie jar, ma'. Emilia Edwards. 6894-4
"In this free Pantheon of the air and sun". Shakespeare's statue. Bayard Taylor. 6976-2
In this gray season. Ralph Friedrich. 6761-1
In this great world of joy and pain. William Wordsworth. 6086-2
"In this green valley where the Ouse". Cowper in Bedfordshire. Sylvia Lynd. 6779-4
"In this high rock-crowned vale the air..still". Still life. Lilian Sauter. 7023-X
In this hour. Arthur Davison Ficke. 6761-1
"In this hour of pure sunlight". Brazil. Ronald de Carvalho. 6759-X
"In this imprisoned congo beserk suns". War factory. Hubert Nicholson. 6895-2
"In this lane/near Jama Masjid". The butcher. Agha Shahid Ali. 6900-2
"In this last hour, before the bugles blare". Morituri te salutant. P.H.B. L.. 7031-0,6846-4
"In this life/Of error, ignorance, and strife." Percy Bysshe Shelley. 6317-9
"I this marble, buried lies". Epitaph. Thomas Jordan.

6563-5
"In this mimic form of a matron in years". Denner's old woman. Vincent Bourne. 6814-6
"In this savage place the sun stands still". Lustration of the winter tree, sels. Margaret Allonby. 6788-3
"In this secluded place I kneel". Where god walked in the calm of day. Gordon Cooper. 6818-9
"In this secluded, sheltered life". Domesticity. Eleanor Goodson Mitchell. 6750-6
"In this solemn year,let us omit giving thanks". Anathema. Josephine Hancock Logan. 6789-1
In this stern hour. Josephine Johnson. 6337-3
"In this still place, remote from men". Glen-Almain, the narrow glen. William Wordsworth. 6850-2,6935-5,6867-7
"In this Stygian age of lust for power". The grimace of death. Josephine Hancock Logan. 6789-1
"In this this high room,my room of quiet space". In my room. Max Eastman. 6880-4
"In this time Christ hath us sent". Man, be glad in hall and bower. Unknown. 6756-5
"In this time God hath sent". Make we merry in hall and bower, this time is born... Unknown. 6756-5
"In this time of Christmas". In the honour of Christes birth, sing we all with joy. Unknown. 6756-5
"In this tremendous quiet hall men can read...". Men reading: New York Public Library. John Chamberlain. 6761-1
"In this vale of wretchedness". Pray for us that we saved we, protomartyr Stephane. Unknown. 6756-5
"In this week's history of the fair". Big Thursday. Eugene Field. 6949-5
"In this world, O scattered man". An island. John Schaffner. 6979-7
"In this, o nature, yield, I pray, to me". The scientist's prayer. Sir Ronald Ross. 7014-0
"In those ages bright but olden". Song of the golden lyre. Jesse Walker. 7030-2
"In those cold regions which no summers cheer". To his royal highness,...appearance at Duke's theatre. John Dryden. 6970-3
In three days. Robert Browning. 6204-0,6429-9,6110-9,6199-0,6321-7
"In thy cavern-hall". Echo-song. Felicia Dorothea Hemans. 6973-8
In thy clear eyes. Arlo Bates. 6770-0,6875-8,6770-0,6875-8
"In thy fair domain/Yes, my lov'd Albion!...". Landscape, fr. The English garden. William Mason. 6932-0
"In thy great strength, o God". Psalm 021. Bible. 6848-0
"In thy time, and times of mourning". Remember. Alice Cary. 6969-X
In time. Robert Graves. 6339-X
In time. Kathleen Raine. 6379-9
In time like a glass. Walter James Turner. 6324-1,6375-6
In time of 'the breaking of nations'. Thomas Hardy. 6844-8
In time of 'The breaking of nations'. Thomas Hardy. 6315-2, 6659-3,6581-3,6102-8,6153-2,6655 ,6625-9,6052-8,6186-9,6634-8
In time of darkness. Raymond F. Roseliep. 6218-0
In time of grief. Lizette Woodworth Reese. 6309-8,6467-1
In time of invasion. Audrey Alexandra Brown. 6224-5
In time of mistrust, XIII. Robert Hillyer. 6532-5
In time of mourning. Algernon Charles Swinburne. 6110-9, 6655-0
In time of peace. Robert J. Burdette. 6588-0
In time of peace. Michael Roberts. 6354-3
In time of pestilence. Thomas Nashe. 6339-X,6179-6,6150-8, 6197-4
In time of pestilence, fr. Oedipus tyrannus. Sophocles. 6435-3
In time of snow. Dorothy Brown Thompson. 6979-7
In time of suspense. Laurence Whistler. 6475-2
In time of war. Lesbia Thanet. 7031-0
In time of war I sing. Allen Crafton. 6032-3
"In time we rode that trail". Thanksgiving at Snake Butte. James Welch. 7005-1
In time's swing. Lucy Larcom. 6129-X
In Tintagel. Andrew Lang. 6987-8
In Tir-na'n-og. Ethna (Anna Johnson MacManus) Carbery. 6292-X,6172-9

"In times o'ergrown with rust and ignorance". Priestcraft and private judgement, fr. Religio laici. John Dryden. 6933-9
"In times prehistoric, when lovers' fond ways". The regular story. Berton Braley. 6853-7
In town. Austin Dobson. 6652-6
In town. Louis J. Magee. 7004-3
In Trafalgar Square. Francis W.L. Adams. 7009-4
In Trinity church-yard. Thomas S. Jones Jr. 6653-4
"In tropic lands where nature is sensously...". Rhythm of the palms. Winifred Huff Gill. 6789-1
In trouble. Josephine Pollard. 6682-8
"In troublous days of anguish and rebuke". Elijah in Horeb. John Keble. 6848-0
"In truth O Love, with what a boyish kind" Sir Philip Sidney. 6182-6
"In truth, we might have known it from..start". Field of honor. Sara Henderson Hay. 6750-6
"In Tuscany the Apennines lie low". Fair places. Mabel Hall Goltra. 6789-1
In tuaim inbhir. Robin Flower. 6641-0
In Tuaim Inbhir. Unknown. 6244-X
In tune with the infinite, fr. The merchant of Venice. William Shakespeare. 6337-3
In Tuscany. Eric Mackay. 6624-0,6656-9
In Tuscany, sels. Cora Fabri. 6876-6
"In twilight of the longest day". The fortunate islands. Andrew Lang. 6987-8
In two cities. John Lehmann. 6042-0
In two months now. George Dillon. 6232-6
In two poets, fr. Reflexions. Alice Meynell. 6955-X
"In two things(right honorable) it is...". To the right noble and worthily honourd, the Lord... Thomas Campion. 6794-8
In twos. William Channing Gannett. 6429-9,6066-8,6321-7
"In tyme the strong and statelie turrets fall," Giles (the Elder) Fletcher. 6586-4
In Umbria. Helen J. Sanborne. 6624-0
In utrumque paratus. Matthew Arnold. 6378-0;6655-0,6430-2
In utrumque paratus, fr. Ye wearie wayfarer. Adam Lindsay Gordon. 6951-7
In vain. Alice Cary. 6969-X
In vain. Rose Terry Cooke. 6300-4
In vain. C.F. McClumpha. 6983-5
In vain. Marion Short. 6700-X
"In vain I lament what is past". Owed to my creditors. Unknown. 6787-5
"In vain I look around". To the memory of a lady. George Lyttelton, Baron Lyttelton. 6932-0
In vain love, sels. Abraham Cowley. 6317-9
"In vain the future snaps his fangs". Hughie's monument. James Logie ("Hugh Haliburton") Robertson. 6819-7
"In vain the morning trims her brows". The shadow (1). Alice Cary. 6865-0;6969-X
"In vain through history we search". Old Tennant Church. George W. Bungay. 6922-3
"In vain to live from age to age". Lines written...collection of handwritings & signatures. William Cowper. 6814-6
"In vain to me the smiling mornings shine". Sonnet ("In vain"). Thomas Gray. 6024-2
"In vain to-day I scrape and blot". 'In vain to-day' Austin Dobson. 6770-0
"In vain ye woo me to your harmless joys". Love faithful in the absence of the beloved. Madame De la Mothe Guion. 6814-6
"In vain you tell your parting lover". A song ("In vain"). Matthew Prior. 6198-2
"In vain you tell your parting lover" Matthew Prior. 6874-X
In vain, mine eyes. Sir Philip Sidney. 6584-8
"In vale of Thirlemere, once on a time". The curse of the laureate. James Hogg. 6802-2
"In Vanity fair, as we bow and smile". Vanity fair. Ella Wheeler Wilcox. 6863-4
"In Vietnam/eels live in the water". Militerotics. Charles Ortleb. 7003-5
"In Visionshire the sky is blue". In Visionshire. Edwin Meade Robinson. 6875-8
In valleys green and still Alfred Edward Housman. 6210-5

In Vanity Fair. Florence Tylee. 6920-7
In Venice. Robert Loveman. 6941-X
In Venice, Dipsychus speaks, fr. Dipsychus. Arthur Hugh Clough. 6832-4
"In very wantonness of childish mirth". Thomas Babington Macaulay, 1st Baron Macaulay. 6088-9
In Visionshire. Edwin Meade Robinson. 6875-8
In war. Ivan Adair. 7031-0
In war time. Wystan Hugh Auden. 6645-3
In war time. Katharine (Hinkson) Tynan. 7031-0
In war-time. Florence Earle Coates. 7026-4
In war-time, fr. In war time. Wilfred Wilson Gibson. 6884-7
"In warlike pomp, with banners flowing". The fall of the leaves. Henry Van Dyke. 6961-4
In wartime. Mrs. Schuyler Van Rensselaer. 6443-4
In wartime, a prayer of the understanding. Sydney Dobell. 6198-2
"In ways of beauty...", fr. A hymn of nature. Robert Bridges. 6487-6
In welcome to the president. W.H. Anderson. 7001-9
In West Yarmouth. Elizabeth K. Folsom. 6798-0
In Westminster Abbey. Thomas Bailey Aldrich. 6484-1
In Westminster Abbey. Francis Beaumont. 6322-5
"In well-devised battle array". The march of the faerie host. Unknown. 6873-1
"In western climes where the bright god of day". The story of Chephisa. John Gay. 6972-X
"In Westminster Hall it is darkness all". The demise of Doe and Roe. Unknown. 6878-2
"In what divine ideal, what lofty sphere". Francesco Petrarch. 6325-X
"In what dry mountain ravine can I disarm...". Thomas Merton. Neeli Cherkovski. 6901-0
"In what far land you dwelt before you came". To my infant son. Arlo Bates. 7041-8
In what manner the soul is united to the body. Sir John Davies. 6584-8
"In what torn ship soever I embark". A hymn to Christ, at the author's last going...Germany. John Donne. 6931-2
In which a toal eclipse of the moon is eclipsed by... John Morgan. 6855-3
In which Roosevelt is compared to Saul? Vachel Lindsay. 6995-9
In whom we live and have our being. James Rhoades. 6337-3
In Windsor Castle. Henry Howard, Earl of Surrey. 6436-1
"In winds that leave man's spirit cold". 'Advance, America'. John Helston. 7027-2
In winter. Bernice Lesbia Kenyon. 6880-4
In winter. Louise Chandler Moulton. 6770-0,6875-8
In winter. Booth Tarkington. 6983-5
In winter. Bayard Taylor. 6976-2
In winter. R.N.D. Wilson. 6071-4
"In winter's just return, when Boreas gan his reign." Henry Howard, Earl of Surrey. 6584-8
"In winter, in my room." Emily Dickinson. 6348-9
"In winter, once, an honest traveler wight". The guide post. Unknown. 6924-X
"In Worcester, when the sun was low". Luther vs. Worcester. C.P. Greenough. 6878-2
"In Wouter Van Twiller's manorial pale". How Pearl street was paved. Arthur Guiterman. 6773-5
"In Xanadu did Kubla Khan". The sacred river, fr. Kubla Khan. Samuel Taylor Coleridge. 7020-5
"In winter, when the dismal rain". Alexander Smith. 6960-6
In wintry midnight. Francesco Petrarch. 6125-7
In wintry midnight. Unknown (Welsh) 6125-7
In woman's praise. Sheppard Barclay. 6878-2
In wonted walks. Sir Philip Sidney. 6328-4
In woods and meadows. James Stephens. 6234-2
In woods near the frontline. Mikhail Isakovsky. 6546-5
In wreaths of smoke. Frank Newton Holman. 6453-1
In Yosemite Valley. Joaquin Miller. 6008-0,6241-5
"In yon dense wood full oft a bell". The lost church. Robert Tilney. 6914-2
"In yon small field, that dimly steals...". The destruction of the Pequods, fr. Greenfield hill. Timothy Dwight. 6753-0
"In yonder old cathedral". The two coffins. Eugene Field. 6949-5
"In your amphitheatres of flood-worn rock". Ode at Assouan on the Nile. Herbert Trench. 6877-4
"In your arms was still delight". Retrospect. Rupert Brooke. 6897-9
"In your house/in your absence". Animus. Mary Baron. 6855-3
In your life we shall live. George Allen. 6761-1
"In your little armored bed". Lullaby ("In your little armored bed"). Elya Bresler. 6761-1
In your sleep, sels. Vittorio Sereni. 6803-0
"In your window there are pies". To a bakery. Alice Levy. 6850-2
"In your/Curled petals what ghosts". Blue hyacinths. Adelaide Crapsey. 6850-2
"In youth he wrought, with eyes ablur". The wife-blessed. James Whitcomb Riley. 6992-4
In youth is pleasure. R. Wever. 6125-7,6383-7
"In youth my wings were strong...". Edgar Lee Masters. 6289-X
"In youth we love the darksome lawn". Sonnet, fr. Ode to Lycoris. William Wordsworth. 6867-7
"In youth we raised our brows on high". Summer causerie. Jan Svatopluk Machar. 6763-7
"In youthful minds to wake the ardent flame". Vision of Columbus, sels. Joel Barlow. 6753-0
"In Zorah dwells no youth like him". The young Samson. Edgar Fawcett. 6848-0
Inada, Lawson Fusao
  Since when as ever more. 6790-5
The inalienable bond. Lucy Larcom. 6085-4
The inalienable. Rabindranath Tagore. 6339-X
Inamorata. Francis Ledwidge. 6812-X
Inanimates. Dorothy Aldis. 6808-1
"Inanity of living palls on me". Ennui. Frances Fuerst Quick. 6799-9
Inarime. Henry Wadsworth Longfellow. 6624-0
Inarticulate. Eva Riehle. 6750-6
Inarticulate. Eleanor Preston Watkins. 6789-1
Inasmuch. S.V.R. Ford. 6417-5,6964-9
'Inasmuch'.. Wallace Bruce. 6139-7
Inaugural verses for the woman's club of Denver, Virginia Donaghe McClurg. 6836-7
Inauguration day. Richard Watson Gilder. 6465-5
An inavlid's plea. Alice Cary. 6969-X
Inb Mujbar
  Red wine in a black glass. A.J. Arberry (tr.). 6362-4
Inber, Vera
  Dawn in besieged Leningrad. Jack Lindsay (tr.). 6546-5
  Five days and nights. Jack Lindsay (tr.). 6546-5
  Leningrad: 1943, fr. The Pulkovo meridian. Dorothe Prall Radin and A. Kauh (tr.). 6665-8
  Mayakovsky memory. Jack Lindsay (tr.). 6546-5
Inborn royalty. William Shakespeare. 6438-8
Inbound. Burnham Eaton. 6218-0
Inbrothered. Edwin Markham. 6861-8
Incantation. John Dryden. 6195-0
Incantation. Edward A. Richards. 6761-1
Incantation. Marguerite Wilkinson. 6019-6
Incantation for healing. Constance Lindsay Skinner. 6393-4
Incantation from the sorceress. Theocritus. 6102-8
Incantation of Kolpo, fr. The story of Baladeadro. George Gordon McCrae. 6768-9
Incantation, fr. Manfred. George Gordon, 6th Baron Byron. 6438-8
Incantation, fr. Oedipus. Sophocles. 6189-3
Incantation: Sabrina fair. John Milton. 6189-3
The incantation. Amergin (atr.) 6930-4
The incantation. Theocritus. 7039-6
Incarnate love. Christina Georgina Rossetti. 6144-3,6337-3
Incarnation. Maurine Halliburton. 6648-8
Incarnation. Edith Lovejoy Pierce. 6337-3
The incarnation of Sirius. James McAuley. 6349-7
Incense. Leslie Savage Clark. 6144-3
Incense. Louise Townsend Nicholl. 6388-8
"The incense at the altar slowly burns". Zabelle Essayan. 6050-1
The incense burner. Abus Salt. 6362-4
The incentive. Sarah N. Cleghorn. 6954-1
"An incessantly rumbling avalance". Intuition. Albert

Paris Gutersloh. 6769-7
"Incest represented by a frockcoated gentleman". Vision of moth-eaten pianos falling to pieces. Cesar Moro. 6759-X
"Inch by inch and a foot is gained". Little by little. Edgar A. Guest. 6748-4
Inchbold, J.W.
   One dead. 7015-9
The Inchcape rock. Robert Southey. 6014-5,6239-3,6302-0, 6385-3,6479-5,6661 ,6242-3,6271-7,6370-5,6413-2,6459-0,6502 ,6499-X,6558-9,6600-3,6133-8,6134-6,6136 , 6552-X,6614-3,6424-8,6543-0,6304-7,6219 ,6131-1,612 - 7,6419-1,6086-2,6639-9,6808
Incident. Countee Cullen. 6538-4
Incident. Edgar A. Guest. 6869-3
Incident at Bethlehem. Edgar A. Guest. 6748-4
An incident at Bruges. William Wordsworth. 6980-0
An incident at Ratisbon. Robert Browning. 6424-8
Incident characteristic of a favourite dog. William Wordsworth. 6133-8
An incident in a railway car. James Russell Lowell. 6632-1, 6250-4,6126-5,6304-7
Incident of the French camp. Robert Browning. 6861-8
Incident of the French camp. Robert Browning. 6123-0,6183-4,6198-2,6239-3,6242-3,6271-,6046-3,6102-8,6263-6, 6110-9,6267-9,6560 ,6302-0,6332-2,6385-3,6395-0,6410-8,6473-,6107-9,6199-0,6419-1,6421-3,6371-3,6560 , 6550-3,6552-X,6614-3,6625-9,6732-8,6479-1,6131-1,6197-4,6219-9,6464-7,6656-9
An incident of the Johnstown flood. Monnie Moore. 6166-4
An incident of the rebellion. Unknown. 6451-5
An incident of the war. Harry W. Kimball. 6744-1
An incident of the war. M.W. W. 6008-0
An incident of the west. Unknown. 6274-1
An incident of war. Maurice Thomson. 6062-5
An incident. Agnes Macdonell. 6690-9
Incidental. Hazel Hall. 6036-6
Incidents in Playfair house. Nicholas Moore. 6379-9
Incidents in the life of my Uncle Arly. Edward Lear. 6722-0,6633-X
'Incipit vita nova'. Phyllis Megroz. 6777-8
Incised to change. Phil Eisenberg. 6857-X
Inclusions. Elizabeth Barrett Browning. 6437-X
Inclusiveness, fr. The house of life. Dante Gabriel Rossetti. 6122-2,6198-2,6380-2,6604-6,6646-1,6656-0, 6660-7
Inclyti Israel. Bible. 6830-8
Incognita. James Montgomery. 6980-0
The incognita of Raphael. William Allen Butler. 6735-2
Incognito. Mildred Focht. 6847-2
The incoming tide. Arthur Hugh Clough. 7020-5
The incoming tide. William ("Fiona Macleod") Sharp. 6997-5
An incomparable kiss. Unknown. 6562-7,6563-5
An incomplete revelation. Richard A. Jackson. 6415-9
Incompleteness. Adelaide Anne Procter. 6303-9
Incomprehensibility of God. Elizabeth Townsend. 6752-2
The incomprehensible. Isaac Watts. 6730-1,6152-4
Inconsistencies. Michelle Roberts. 6870-7
The inconsistent sex. John Langdon Heaton. 6632-1
Inconstancy. Phoebe Cary. 6865-0;6969-X
Inconstancy. Joseph Rodman Drake. 6441-8
Inconstancy. Francis Charles McDonald. 6983-5
Inconstancy. Rene Francois Armand Sully-Prudhomme. 6351-9
Inconstancy reproved. Sir Robert Ayton. 6180-X
Inconstancy, fr. Much ado about nothing. William Shakespeare. 6827-2
Inconstant. Amy Buford Cooke. 6750-6
Inconstant. Unknown. 6910-X
Incontrovertible facts. Unknown. 6724-7
Incorporeal. Loretto Troy. 6906-1
Incorrect speaking. Charles and Mary Lamb. 6295-4
"Incredible Huns! vile Goths!-under God's ban". Ode: September and October, 1939. Herbert Edward Palmer. 6783-2
The incubus of time. Clark Ashton Smith. 6218-0
Incurable. Dorothy Parker. 6441-8
Incursio. Ruth H. Hausman. 6850-2
An incursion of the Danes. Anna F. Burnham. 6965-7
Indebted. Edgar A. Guest. 6869-3
Indecision. Unknown. 6273-3,6672-0,6652-6

"Indeed I love thee". Alfred Lord Tennyson. 6066-8
"Indeed I remembered you yearningly". Ibn Zaidun. 6766-2
Indeed the idols I have loved so long, fr. Rubaiyat. Omar Khayyam. 7039-6
"Indeed, it will soon be over. I shall be done". Intimations of mortality. Phyllis McGinley. 6761-1
"Indeed, my Caeli, 'tis in vain". Song ("Indeed, my Caeli"). Sir John Henry Moore. 6317-9
Independence. Tobias George Smollett. 6240-7,6543-0
Independence. Henry David Thoreau. 6176-1
Independence. Unknown. 6753-0
Indépendence bell. Unknown. 6142-7,6451-5,6552-X,6621-6, 6706-9,6554 ,6286-5,6449-3,6565-1,6088-9
Independence Day. William Lloyd Garrison. 7009-4
Independence day. Edgar A. Guest. 6862-6
Independence Day. Royall Tyler. 6176-1
Independence Day to-day. Margaret Elizabeth Sangster. 6449-3
Independence Square, Christmas 1783 Arthur Guiterman. 6449-3
Indestructible. H. Stanley Haskins. 6750-6
India. Walter James Turner. 6625-9
"India became his jasmined youth, Goa". The man of grass, sels. Roy Macnab. 6788-3
India to England. Nizamat Jung. 6224-5,6474-4
India, fr. Geography. Edward Verrall Lucas. 6018-8
The Indiaman. Thomas Edward Brown. 6809-X
Indian America. Mah-do-ge Tohee. 7005-1
The Indian and the trout. Eugene Field. 6949-5
The Indian Army. Robert Ernest Vernede. 7029-9
An indian arrow head. Arthur S. Bourniot. 6797-2
The Indian attack. John Brownjohn. 6580-5
Indian bearers. Katharine Lee Bates. 6798-0
Indian blood. Mary TallMountain. 7005-1
The Indian brave. Francis S. Smith. 6743-3
The Indian burying gound. Philip Freneau. 6396-9,6008-0, 6288-1,6431-0,6121-4,6077-3,6176-1,6333-0,6641-0, 6309-8,6648-8,6008-0,6288-1,6431-0,6121-4
The Indian burying ground. Philip Freneau. 6265-2
The Indian chief. Charles W. Denison. 6755-7
The Indian chieftan. Unknown. 6302-0,6410-8
Indian children. Annette Wynne. 6466-3
The Indian city, fr. Records of woman. Felicia Dorothea Hemans. 6973-8
The Indian corn planter. Emily Pauline ("Tekahionwake") Johnson. 6796-4,6837-5
Indian dancers. Sarojini Naidu. 6959-2
Indian death-song. Philip Freneau. 6302-0
Indian death-song. Anne Hunter. 6271-7,6385-3
Indian drums. Isabel Winslow. 6799-9
Indian education. Adrian C. Louis. 7005-1
Indian emperor, sels. John Dryden. 6208-3
Indian fevers. Sir Ronald Ross. 6482-5
"Indian fingers/Sinewy red Indian fingers". Sea and singing country. Robert L. Roe. 6781-6
The Indian gipsy. Sarojini Naidu. 6591-0,6592-9
Indian girl. Emilio Vasquez. 6759-X
Indian giver. Josephine Johnson. 6039-0
Indian graveyard--Montauk. Isabel Fiske Conant. 7038-8
Indian guys at the bar. Simon J. Ortiz. 7005-1
The Indian hunter. Henry Wadsworth Longfellow. 6678-X
An Indian hymn of thanks to Mother Corn. Unknown. 6466-3
The Indian lady. John Keats. 6830-8
The Indian lass. Unknown. 6057-9
Indian legend. Robert J. Eaton. 6249-0
Indian love song. Gertrude Alger. 6798-0
Indian love-song. Owen (Edward Bulwer-Lytton, Earl Lytton) Meredith. 6732-8,6656-9
Indian lullaby. Charles Myall. 6132-X
An Indian lullaby. Unknown. 6490-6
Indian macho. Louis (LittleCoon) Oliver. 7005-1
Indian maiden at Lake Harriet. Ada Greiner Marks. 6342-X
Indian names. Edith Colby Banfield. 6836-7
Indian names. Phebe T. Chamberlain. 6798-0
Indian names. Lydia Huntley Sigourney. 6102-8,6077-3,6465-5,6600-3,6101-X,6385 ,6465-5,6396-9,6304-7,6076-5, 6219-9,6300
The Indian names of Acadia. De Mille (atr). 6795-6
The Indian names of Canada. De Mille. 6134-6
The Indian pipe. Agnes Maule Machar. 6591-0,6592-9

INDIAN

Indian pipes. Winifred Welles. 6036-6
Indian prayer. Joseph Strongwolf. 6461-2
Indian rbellion. Jorge Carrera Andrade. 6642-9
Indian rebellion. Jorge Carrera Andrade. 6642-9
Indian revelry. Bartholomew Dowling. 6219-9
The Indian serenade. Percy Bysshe Shelley. 6102-8,6198-2, 6204-0,6332-2,6481-7,6122 ,6154-0,6315-2,6328-4,6732-8,6513-9,6371 ,6086-2,6646-1,6723-9,6110-9,6197-9, 6737 ,6196-6,6430-2,6250-4,6560-0
The indian sign. Berton Braley. 6853-7
Indian sleep-song. Edwin Arlington Robinson. 6036-6
An Indian song. William Butler Yeats. 6656-9
Indian spring. Constance Lindsay Skinner. 6979-7
The Indian student. Unknown. 6651-8
Indian Summer. N.R. Baker. 6799-9
Indian summer. Eudora S. Bumstead. 6618-6
Indian summer. William Wilfred Campbell. 6021-8,6795-6
Indian summer. Helena Coleman. 6115-X
Indian summer. Clinton H. Collester. 6118-4
Indian summer. Emily Dickinson. 6374-8,6253-9,6646-1
Indian summer. Dallett Fuguet. 6936-3
Indian summer. John J. Haining. 6857-X
Indian summer. Mary Louisa Hellings. 6799-9
Indian summer. J.P. Irvine. 6597-X
Indian summer. Kenneth C. Kaufman. 6397-7
Indian summer. Richard R. Kirk. 6118-4
Indian summer. William Ellery Leɪnard. 6506-6;6556-2
Indian summer. Jeannette Marks. 6036-6
Indian summer. J. Corson Miller. 6761-1
Indian summer. Susanna Strickland Moodie. 6433-7
Indian summer. Nyleen Morrison. 6764-6
Indian summer. Dorothy Parker. 6637-2
Indian summer. Lydia Huntley Sigourney. 6077-3
Indian summer. John Banister Tabb. 6006-4
Indian summer. Sara Teasdale. 6338-1
Indian summer. Unknown. 6302-0;6385-3
Indian summer. Henry Van Dyke. 6653-4
Indian summer ("I see"). Benjamin Franklin Taylor. 6815-4
Indian summer ("Then past"). Benjamin Franklin Taylor. 6815-4
"Indian summer camps in the hills". Indian drums. Isabel Winslow. 6799-9
An Indian summer carol. Fidelis [pseud]. 6795-6
Indian summer, fr. The eve of election. John Greenleaf Whittier. 6466-3,6481-7,6302-0,6623-2
The Indian summer. John Gardiner Calkins Brainard. 6752-2
The Indian summer. John Howard Bryant. 6618-6
The Indian trader. Chapman J. Milling. 7016-7
Indian tribes. Unknown. 6724-7
An Indian upon God. William Butler Yeats. 6244-X,6730-1, 6508-2,6659-3
"The Indian war was over". The captive's hymn. Edna Dean Proctor. 6946-0
The Indian warrior's last song. J. Howard Wert. 6678-X
"The Indian weed withered quite". A religious use of taking tobacco. Robert Wisom (atr.). 6933-9
"The Indian weed, withered quite". Tobacco. George Wither. 6453-1
The Indian weed. Ralph Erskine. 6230-X
Indian wife. Gertrude Claytor. 6979-7
An Indian wind song. Peter McArthur. 6115-X
The Indian with his dead child. Felicia Dorothea Hemans. 6973-8
Indian woman's death-song, fr. Records of woman. Felicia Dorothea Hemans. 6973-8
The Indian woman. Walt Whitman. 6134-6,6466-3
The Indian's grave. G.J. Mountain. 6433-7
The Indian's prayer. Unknown. 6486-8
The Indian's revenge. Felicia Dorothea Hemans. 6973-8
The Indian's tale. John Greenleaf Whittier. 6752-2
The indian's welcome to the pilgrim fathers. Lydia Huntley Sigourney. 6820-0
An Indian-summer reverie. James Russell Lowell. 6008-0
Indiana. Lori Lubeski. 6857-X
Indiana dusk. Carl Sandburg. 6345-4
Indians. Haniel Long. 6396-9
Indians. Charles Sprague. 6239-3,6385-3,6438-8
Indians at the Guthrie. Gerald Vizenor. 7005-1
The Indians come down from Mixco. Miguel Angel Asturias. 6759-X

"The indians laugh in their sleep". Men in New Mexico, sel. David Herbert Lawrence. 6958-4
Indians!. Leonora Speyer. 6072-2
Indictment. Dorothy C. Parrish. 7024-8
Indifference. Matthew Arnold. 6271-7
Indifference. Louise Driscoll. 6510-4
Indifference. Harry ("Col. D. Streamer") Graham. 6633-X
Indifference. Edna St. Vincent Millay. 6986-X
Indifference. G.A. Studdert-Kennedy. 6144-3,6337-3,6532-5, 6335-7
Indifference. Unknown. 6902-9
Indifference. Unknown. 6089-7
Indifference. Marya Alexandrovna Zaturenska. 6880-4
Indifference to fortune, fr. The caste of indolence. James Thomson. 6932-0
The indifference. Sir Charles Sedley. 6152-4
The indifferent. Francis Beaumont. 6182-6
The indifferent. John Donne. 6198-2,6430-2,6194-X
An indignant male. A.B. Ross. 6891-X
Indignant Polly Wog. Margaret Eytinge. 6670-4
"Indignantly he spoke...", fr. The Odyssey. Homer. 6435-3
Indignation of a high-minded Spaniard. William Wordsworth. 6142-7,6543-0
Indigo bird. Stephen Crombie. 6073-0
The indigo bird. Ethelwyn Wetherald. 6433-7,6115-X,6253-9, 6591-0,6592-9
The indigo glass in the grass, fr. Pecksniffiana. Wallace Stevens. 6531-7
Indirection. Richard Realf. 6102-8,6240-7,6260-1,6337-3, 6411-6,6076-5,6431-0,6241-5,6309-8
Individuality. Ella Wheeler Wilcox. 6956-8
Individuality, fr. Hymns of the marshes. Sidney Lanier. 7017-5
Indolence. Robert Bridges. 6487-6
Indolence. Vernon Watkins. 6210-5
"Indolent and kitten-eyed". Cheetah. Charles Eglinton. 6788-3
"An indolent vicar of Bray". Limerick:"An indolent vicar of Bray". L. R.. 6811-1
The indoor woman. Margaret Winters. 6270-9
Inducement. Ira South. 7007-8
The induction to the mirror for magistrates, sels. Thomas Sackville; 1st Earl of Dorset. 6198-2,6194-X,6726-3
The induction to the mirror for magistrates, Thomas Sackville; 1st Earl of Dorset. 6436-1
The induction, fr. The vision of Piers Plowman. William Langland. 6489-2
The induction, sels. Thomas Sackville; 1st Earl of Dorset. 6194-X
Industrial poems. A.M. Sullivan. 6839-1
Industry and prayer. Carlos Wilcox. 6752-2
Indwelling. Thomas Edward Brown. 6655-0
Indwelling. Thomas Edward Brown. 6809-X
The indwelling God. Frederick L. Hosmer. 6007-2,6337-3, 6730-1
The inebriate. Richard Harris ("Thomas Ingoldsby") Barham. 6302-0
Inebriates. Philip Brasfield. 6870-7
Inebriety. George Crabbe. 6802-2
Inevitability. Robert N. Perry Jr. 6178-8
Inevitable. Selma Hamann. 6906-1
Inevitable. Unknown. 6983-5
Inevitable. Ella Wheeler Wilcox. 6078-1
Inevitable change. John Addington Symonds. 7015-9
The inevitable road. Eldon George McLean. 6178-8
The inevitable. Sarah Knowles Bolton. 6260-1,6337-3,6512-0, 6730-1,6924-X
Inexorable death. Aeschylus. 6435-3
The inexorable. Huw Menai. 6360-8
Inexperience. June Breining. 6396-9
The inextinguishable. Helen Hoyt. 6628-3
"The inextinquishable sun; a sky". The Amazons. Yvonne Ffrench. 6782-X
Inez de Castro, fr. The lusiad. Luis de Camoens [or Camoes]. 6372-1
Infancy. Edith Colby Banfield. 6836-7
Infancy. Hugh Downman. 6482-5
Infancy and childhood, fr. The song of Hiawatha. Henry Wadsworth Longfellow. 6616-X
The infant Heracles. Pindar. 6435-3

"The infant camel felt depressed". A medical opinion. J.G.
    Francis. 6786-7
Infant innocence. Alfred Edward Housman. 6722-0,6125-7
Infant joy. William Black. 6424-8
Infant joy. William Blake. 6078-1,6102-8,6134-6,6186-9,
    6233-4,6242-,6086-2,6301-2,6737-9,6315-2,6339-X,6502-
    3,6519-8,6533-3
The infant Moses. Max Jacob. 6343-8
Infant Noah. Vernon Watkins. 6379-9
"An infant on its mother's breast". Life. Unknown. 6919-3
Infant sorrow. William Blake. 6078-1,6086-2,6208-3,6233-4,
    6533-3
Infant spring. Fredegond Shove. 6070-6
"Infant! I envy thee". Life's pilgrimage. Robert Nicoll.
    6960-6
Infant's funeral hymn. Charles W. Denison. 6755-7
The infant, fr. Lucretius. John Dryden. 6867-7
Infantry. Patrick Reginald Chalmers. 7027-2
The infantry - kings of the highway. R.J. Burt Sr. 6237-7
The infantry. Unknown. 6237-7
The infants plead their case. Michael Wigglesworth. 6121-4
"Infatuating is the appearance of Buddha...". The
    Tatagata. Unknown (Newari). 7013-2
Infatuation. W.A. Barton Jr. 7016-7
Infection. Louis de Louk. 6889-8
Infelicissime. Unknown. 6402-7
Inferential. Edwin Arlington Robinson. 6034-X
The inferno, sels. Dante Alighieri. 6732-8
Infida's song. Robert Greene. 6436-1
An infidel. Edward R. Huxley. 6885-5
The infidel. Hermann Hagedorn. 6944-4
Infidelity. Robert Service. 6159-1
"The infidels, a motley band'. 'We're building two a day!'
    Alfred J. Hough. 6919-3
"The infinite always is silent". The infinite. John Boyle
    O'Reilly. 6930-4
"Infinite Portugal, June eleventh...". Salutation to Walt
    Whitman. Fernando Pessoa. 6758-1
"The infinite power essenciall". Mary, queen of heaven.
    Unknown. 6881-2
The infinite shining heavens. Robert Louis Stevenson. 6252-
    0
"The 'infinite'. Word horrible! at feud". Legem tuam
    dilexi. Coventry Patmore. 6931-2
The infinite. John Boyle O'Reilly. 6930-4
The infinite. John Boyle O'Reilly. 6648-8
"An infinitely good-natured Newfoundland puppy". Humanity.
    Royall Snow. 6906-1
Infinitude. Hattie Meyers. 6799-9
Infinity. Edwin N. Ackerman. 6750-6
Infinity. Giacomo Leopardi. 6879-0
Infinity. Philip Henry Savage. 6309-8
Infinity. Louisa Carroll Thomas. 6789-1
Infinity, sels. Walt Whitman. 6467-1
Infir taris. Unknown. 6125-7
Infirm. Edward Sandford Martin. 6441-8,6026-9,6652-6
The inflatable globe. Theodore Spencer. 6389-6,6666-6
InFlorence, fr. In Tuscany. Cora Fabri. 6876-6
Influence. Joseph Norris. 6337-3
Influence. Robert Haven Schauffler. 6118-4
Influence. Robert Haven Schauffler. 6983-5
Influence. John Banister Tabb. 6006-4
Influence. Unknown. 6337-3
Influence. Unknown. 6211-3
Influence ("Drop a pebble in the water,"). Joseph Morris.
    6211-3
Influence of music. William Shakespeare. 6271-7,6219-9
Influence of natural objects. William Wordsworth. 6271-7,
    6315-2,6332-2,6086-2,6196-6,6197-4,6252-0,6110-9
Influence of time on grief. William Lisle Bowles. 6086-2
The influence of woman. Edgar A. Guest. 6862-6
Influence of...time on national looks, fr. Jonas Fisher.
    James Carnegie; Earl of Southesk. 6819-7
Influence, fr. The friend of a prince. Frank Moore
    Jeffery. 6789-1
The information bureau. Vachel Lindsay. 6206-7
The informing spirit. Ralph Waldo Emerson. 6730-1,6288-1,
    6126-5
Ingalla, John James
    The ballad of bouillabaisse. 6026-9,6439-6,6652-6,6656-
        9,6092-7
    Opportunity. 6274-1,6260-1,6615-4,6702-6,6481-7,6732
Ingalls, John James
    Opportunity. 6735-2,6291-1,6309-8,6585-6,6104-4,6076-5,
        6736-0,6102-8
Ingamells, Rex
    Ship from Thames. 6349-7
Inge, Charles
    "A certain young gourmet of Crediton". 6722-0
    Limerick:"..madame called Tussaud". 6811-1
    Limerick:"A certain young gourmet of Crediton". 6811-1,
        6811-1,6308-X
    Limerick:"This very remarkable man". 6811-1
    Limerick:"Your verses, dear Fred. I surmise". 6811-1
Inge, W.R.
    Limerick:"..good canon of Durham". 6811-1
Inge, the boy king, sels. Hjalmar Hjorth Boyesen. 7002-7
Ingelow, Jean
    Afternoon at a parsonage. 6940-1
    Afternoon at a parsonage, sels. 6934-7
    An ancient chess king. 7015-9
    An ancient chess king. 7015-9,7037-X
    An ancient chess king. 7015-9
    An ancient chess king. 7015-9,7037-X
    "And still I changed; I was a boy no more". 6238-5
    Apprenticed. 6437-X
    The awakening, fr. Lily and lute. 6689-5
    The better way. 6240-7
    Binding sheaves. 6543-0
    The brides of Enderby. 6479-5,6403-5
    Brothers, and a sermon. 6940-1
    "The coming in of the 'Mermaiden'". 6543-0
    A cottage in Chine. 6940-1
    A dead year. 6940-1
    Divided. 6271-7,6385-3,6438-8,6066-8,6304-7
    Dominion. 6543-0
    Eagles, fr. Songs of the voices of birds. 6105-2
    Echo and the ferry. 6183-4,6669-0,6574-0,6114-1
    The entrance into the ark. 6848-0
    For Exmoor. 6437-X
    The four bridges. 6940-1
    Goldilocks. 6438-8
    Heigh-ho! daises and buttercups. 6304-7
    The high tide at Lincolnshire. 6605-4,6239-3,6427-2,
        6600-3,6134-6,6228-8,6250-4,6424-8,6102-8,6438-8
    The high tide on the coast of Lincolnshire (1571). 6656-
        9,6304-7,6219-9,6344-6,6246-6,6302-0,6385-3,6518-X,
        6732-8,6179
    High tide; or, the brides of Enderby (1571). 6566-X,
        6964-9
    Honors I: A scholar is musing on his want of success.
        6940-1
    Honors II: The answer. 6940-1
    "I am glad to think." 6225-3
    I have the courage to be gay. 6066-8
    "I leaned out my window." 6019-6
    "I saw a vision". 6648-8
    I will trust. 6337-3
    "I would sail upon the tropic seas". 6997-5
    "If there be memory in the world to come". 6238-5
    "In regal quiet deep." 6225-3
    In the nursery. 6683-6
    Kinsman. 6337-3
    "Learn that to love is the one way to know." 6066-8
    The letter L. 6940-1
    Like a laverock in the lift. 6240-7,6385-3,6620-8,6543-
        0
    The long white seam. 6239-3,6737-9,6656-9,6658-5
    Longing for home. 6240-7,6730-1
    Love. 6066-8,6383-7
    "Love not told". 6238-5
    Love's thread of gold. 6066-8
    Lovers. 6066-8
    A maiden with a milking-pail. 6302-0,6385-3
    "Man lives apart but not alone". 6238-5
    A mother showing the portrait of her child. 6940-1
    The noble tuck-man. 6902-9
    Oh, my lost love, fr. Supper at the mill. 6934-7
    The old fisherman's prayer. 6294-6,6344-6
    On the borders of Cannock Chase. 6669-0

Over the green downs. 6304-7
Persephone. 6677-1
Playing on the virginals, fr. Supper at the mill. 6934-7
Reflections. 6940-1
Regret. 6569-4
Regret. 6914-2
Remonstrance. 6980-0
Requiescat in pace! 6940-1
Sailing beyond seas. 6605-4,6648-8,6656-9
Scholar and carpenter. 6940-1
Sea mews in winter time. 6980-0
A sea song. 6940-1
Sea-mews in winter time. 6929-0
Sea-nurtured. 6833-2
"The sea/Was filled with light...". 6997-5
Seven times four. 6097-8,6373-X,6385-3,6600-3,6627-5
Seven times one. 6424-8,6131-1,6456-6,6127-3,6132-X, 6242-3,6249-0,6373-X,6466-,6519-8,6737-9,6639-9,6638-0,6135-4
Seven times seven. 6600-3
Seven times six. 6097-8,6385-3
Seven times three. 6385-3
Seven times two. 6239-3,6424-8
"Shall not the fashioner command his work?" 6225-3
A singing lesson. 6706-9,6212-1,6304-7,6424-8
The singing lesson. 6820-0
The singing-lesson. 6131-1
Song for a babe. 6078-1
Song of a nest. 6943-6
Song of Margaret. 6219-9
Song of the going away. 6980-0
Songs of seven. 6148-6,6473-6,6219-9
Songs of the voices of birds, sels. 6105-2
Sorrows humanize our race. 6303-9,6337-3,6730-1
The star's monument. 6940-1
A story of life. 6917-7
Strife and peace. 6940-1
Supper at the mill. 6940-1
Sweet is childhood. 6658-5
Take joy home. 6304-7
"They are poor". 6238-5
To bear, to nurse, to rear, fr. Songs of seven. 6934-7
A weak white girl. 6066-8
A wedding song. 6940-1
When sparrows build. 6683-6,6383-7
When the sea gives up the dead. 6094-3
Winstanley. 6502-3,6438-8,6304-7
Work. 7037-X
Wreck of the 'Grace' of Sunderland. 6385-3,6438-8
Wrong seraph and right bird. 6943-6
Ingeman, Bernard S.
The pilgrim's song. Sabine Baring-Gould (tr.). 6214-8, 6730-1
Ingemann, B.S.
Dannebrog. Charles Wharton Stork (tr.). 6555-4
Lovely the earth is. Charles Wharton Stork (tr.). 6555-4
The two days. Charles Wharton Stork (tr.). 6555-4
Ingemann, Bernard
Pilgrim's song. 6214-8
"An **ingenious** man named Abiram Barr". A queer voyage. Carolyn Wells. 6882-0
"**Ingenuous** student, who with curious eye". Tuft v. Warman. Unknown. 6878-2
Ingersoll, Marian C.
Marjorie. 6155-9
Ingersoll, Robert G.
Cheers for the living-tears for the dead. 6449-3
Hope sees a star. 6889-8
Life is a narrow vale. 6076-5,6732-8
Ingham, D.H.
Reciprocity. 6274-1
Ingham, John Hall
George Washington. 6946-0
Love in Italy, sels. 6624-0
Phillips Brooks. 6820-0
"True love should overwhelm...," fr. Love in Italy. 6624-0
"Under the shadow...," fr. Love in Italy. 6624-0

Ingin summer. Eva Wilder McGlasson. 6453-1;6703-4
Inglis, Jeffrey
The laird. 6331-4,6439-6
Ingoldsby, Thomas. See Barham, Richard
Ingraham, Charles Anson
Frightening death. 6482-5
Value of elemental remedies. 6482-5
Ingram, Joellen
Bells from out of the past. 6799-9
Ingram, John Kells
A fragment ("Noble warrior"). 6174-5
The memory of the dead. 6858-8
The memory of the dead. 6090-0,6174-5,6244-X,6323-3, 6271-7,6244-X,6771-7,6656-9
The memory of the dead. 6858-8
Memory of the Irish dead. 6714-X
The men of 'ninety-eight. 7009-4
The men of 'ninety-eight. 6793-X
A monition. 6793-X
A nation's wealth. 6793-X
National presage. 6174-5
The social future. 6174-5
The social future. 6930-4
To A.F. 6174-5
Winged thoughts. 6174-5
Ingram, Paula Sylva
Kitten Jim. 6799-9
Ingrateful beauty threatened. Thomas Carew. 6198-2,6317-9, 6562-7,6150-8,6153-2,6341-1
Ingratitude. William Shakespeare. 6479-5,6107-9,6543-0
Inheritance. Anna Hempstead Branch. 6619-4
Inheritance. Mary Thacher Higginson. 6309-8
Inheritance. Edna Jaques. 6224-5
Inheritance. George William ("A.E.") Russell. 6199-0
An **inhibited** person. Richard Hart. 6120-6
Inhibition. Margery Swett Mansfied. 6761-1
Inhospitality. Celia Thaxter. 6612-7
The **inhuman** wolf and the lamb sans gene. Guy Wetmore Carryl. 6026-9
The **inimitable** lovers. Alfred Noyes. 6151-6
Inis fal. Egan O'Rahilly. 6244-X
Inisfail. George Arthur Greene. 6174-5
Inisgallun. Darrell Figgis. 6930-4
Inish Fay. Jane Barlow. 6793-X
Inishowen. Sir Charles Gavan Duffy. 6858-8
"**Initials** carved from tenderloin days". Wicked lady of Gough street. Todd S.J. Lawson. 6792-1
"**Initiate** soul drunken with deity". To Francis Thompson in paradise. Charles Whitby. 6994-0
Initiation. Laurence Binyon. 6253-9
Initiation. Laurent Tailhede. 6351-9
'The **Injun**'.. John E. ("Barry Dane") Logan. 6795-6
Injunction. Henry Bryan Binns. 6506-6
Injunction. Jean Starr Untermeyer. 6012-9
The **injunction.** Christopher Bursk. 7032-9
"**Injured,** hopeless, faint, and weary". Hagar in the desert. Mary Tighe. 6848-0
"**Injurious** charmer". A song ("Injurious charmer"). John Wilmot, 2d Earl of Rochester. 6544-9
Injustice. Alfred Edward Housman. 6954-1
Injustice. Sheldon Shepard. 6144-3
"The **ink** grows pale upon the page". Margaretta's book 1816. Katherine Van der Veer. 6750-6
Inke, Lillian V.
Autumn: allegro con fuoco, fr. Time is a dream. 6640-2
Early spring: adagio, fr. Time is a dream. 6640-2
Prelude to autumn, fr. Time is a dream. 6640-2
Time is a dream, sels. 6640-2
Winter: menuetto, fr. Time is a dream. 6640-2
Inkermann. Charles Mackay. 6676-3
The **inkstand.** Ibn Lubbal. 6362-4
The **inky** mouth. Al-Barraq. 6362-4
Inland. Edna St. Vincent Millay. 6034-X
Inland. Joan Dareth Prosper. 7038-8
Inland. Joan Dareth Prosper. 6039-0
The **inland** city. Edmund Clarence Stedman. 6484-1
Inland woman. Barbara Young. 7038-8
Inman, Arthur Crew
At the dance. 6959-2
Desert. 6037-4

The deserted barn. 6037-4
Paths across the sea. 6036-6
A picture ("Long surges of the summer sea"). 6031-5
A picture. 6031-5
River song. 6036-6
"Inmate of a mountain-dwelling". To - [Miss Blackett] on her first ascent..Helvellyn. William Wordsworth. 6832-4
The inn o' the sword: a song of youth and war. Unknown. 7031-0
The inn of Apollo. Alfred Noyes. 6151-6
The inn of care. Samuel Waddington. 6437-X,6656-9
The inn of life. John Oxenham. 6335-7
The inn of the five chimes. Clinton Scollard. 6030-7
The inn: an old epitaph. Arthur Guiterman. 6773-5
The inn. John Presland. 6653-4
Innamorata. William Force Stead. 6780-8
Inner brother. Stephen Stepanchev. 6666-6
The inner calm. Horatius Bonar. 6418-3,6600-3,6219-9
The inner chamber. Adelaide Anne Procter. 6957-6
"An inner cry/is carried across". The wind carries me free. Dennis Shady. 6870-7
The inner light, fr. Saint Paul. Frederick W.H. Myers. 6337-3,6730-1,6102-8,6301-2,6660-7
The inner light. John Milton. 6291-1;6337-3
The inner passion. Alfred Noyes. 6151-6
The inner silence. Harriet Monroe. 6897-9
Inner song while watching a song dance, sels. Thomas Hornsby Ferril. 6751-4
The inner vision, sels. William Wordsworth. 6122-2,6208-3
The inner vision. Maude Freeman Osborne. 6836-7
The inner vision. William Wordsworth. 6246-6,6302-0,6385-3, 6737-9
The inner voice. Anthero de Quental. 6648-8
Innes, David
    To April. 6750-6
Innocence. George S. Chappell. 6736-0
Innocence. Francois Coppee. 6351-9
Innocence. Edgar A. Guest. 6869-3
Innocence. Charles Lamb. 7015-9
Innocence. Charles Mair. 6433-7
Innocence ("But that which most I wonder at..."). Thomas Traherne. 6533-3
Innocence asleep. Florence Orndorff. 6906-1
Innocent child and snow-white flower. Unknown. 6530-9
The innocent country-maid's..., or A description... Unknown. 6157-5
Innocent fears. Gerasimos Markoras. 6352-7
The innocent ones who come after. Walter Rauschenbusch. 6954-1
Innocent play. Isaac Watts. 6459-0
Innocent pleasures. Edward R. Huxley. 6885-5
Innocent sleep! William Shakespeare. 6238-5
The innocent thief. Vincent Bourne. 6814-6
"The innocent, sweet day is dead". Night and day. Sidney Lanier. 6753-0
The innocent. Gene Derwood. 6666-6
Innocents' day. Harriet Eleanor Hamiliton (Baille) King. 6772-7
The innocents.. Elinor Wylie. 6038-2,6012-9
Innominatus. Sir Walter Scott. 6503-1
"Innumerable beauties, thou white haire". Sonnet ("Innumerable beauties"). Edward Herbert, 1st Baron Herbert of Cherbury. 6106-0
Inopportune. Thomas H. Briggs Jr. 6274-1
Inordinate love. Unknown. 6881-2
"Inordinately fond am I". My favorites. Esther Wollam. 6750-6
An inovcation. Charles Whitby. 6994-0
Inquest - not extraordinary. Unknown. 6278-4
The inquest. Francis Coutts. 6785-9
Inquiry. John Henrik Clarke. 6178-8
The inquiry, fr. At Casterbridge fair. Thomas Hardy. 6828-6
The inquiry.. Charles Mackay. 6165-6,6554-6,6567-8
The inquiry. Thomas Carew. 6874-X
The inquiry. John Dyer. 6968-1
The inquiry. Charles Mackay. 6403-5
The inquisitor. Olive Tilford Dargan. 6037-4
An inqvisition vpon fame and honovr. Fulke Greville; 1st Baron Brooke. 6586-4
Insanity. William Roehrick. 6850-2
The insatiable sex. Wilfred J. Funk. 6732-8
Insatiableness. Thomas Traherne. 6931-2
"Insatiate brute, whose teeth abuse". The small silver-coloured bookworm. Thomas Parnell. 6930-4
Inscho, Ruth
    Poverty. 6750-6
    Requital. 6750-6
Inscribed on the collar of a dog. Alexander Pope. 6466-3
'Inscribed: 'To whom 'tis due'. Curtis Hidden Page. 6850-2
Inscription. Lascelles Abercrombie. 6879-0
Inscription. Mark Akenside. 6932-0
Inscription. George Canning and John Hookham Frere. 6802-2
Inscription. Ann [or Annie E.] Hamilton. 6037-4
Inscription. Leslie Nelson Jennings. 6032-3
Inscription. Alfred Noyes. 6151-6
Inscription. Sir William Watson. 6396-9
An inscription ("Grass of levity") Unknown. 6182-6
Inscription (anti-Jacobin). Unknown. 6278-4
Inscription at Mount Vernon. Unknown. 6465-5,6265-2
An inscription by the sea. Glaucus. 7039-6,6879-0
An inscription by the sea. Edwin Arlington Robinson. 6125-7
Inscription for a book. W.A. Barton Jr. 7016-7
Inscription for a bust of Homer. William Cowper. 6814-6
Inscription for a cavern that overlooks the river Avon. Robert Southey. 6867-7
Inscription for a clock. Frank Berchenko. 6396-9
Inscription for a fountain. Stephen Lucius Gwynn. 6244-X
Inscription for a fountain. Bryan Waller ("Barry Cornwall") Procter. 6543-0
Inscription for a fountain on a heath. Samuel Taylor Coleridge. 6196-6,6421-3,6430-2,6332-2
Inscription for a garage door. Doris V. Lecky. 6850-2
Inscription for a garden gate. Ruth H. Hausman. 6850-2
Inscription for a garden gate (2). Ruth H. Hausman. 6850-2
Inscription for a garden wall. Doris V. Lecky. 6850-2
Inscription for a gravestone. Robinson Jeffers. 6879-0
Inscription for a hermitage. Felicia Dorothea Hemans. 6973-8
Inscription for a hospital. E.O. Laughlin. 6482-5
Inscription for a mirror in a deserted dwelling. William Rose Benet. 6641-0
Inscription for a moss-house in the shrubbery at Weston. William Cowper. 6814-6
Inscription for a prayer book. Edith Ella Davis. 6214-8
Inscription for a seat in the groves of Coleorton. William Wordsworth. 6980-0
Inscription for a statue of Chaucer at Woodstock. Mark Akenside. 6219-9
Inscription for a stone (1). William Cowper. 6814-6
Inscription for a stone (2). William Cowper. 6814-6
Inscription for a sundial. Daniel Whitehead Hicky. 6841-3, 6780-8
Inscription for a tablet on the banks of a stream. Robert Southey. 6932-0
Inscription for a tobacco jar. Unknown. 6453-1,6719-0
Inscription for a tomb in England. Henry Van Dyke. 6961-4
An inscription for all council-chambers, fr. Eth. Nic. Aristotle. 7042-6
Inscription for an entrance to a wood. William Cullen Bryant. 6047-1,6049-8,6077-3,6332-2,6333-0,6288 6008-0,6121-4,6126-5
Inscription for an hermitage in the author's garden. William Cowper. 6814-6
Inscription for an old bed. William Morris. 6668-2
Inscription for an old goblet. Jaroslav Vrchlicky. 6886-3
Inscription for an old tomb. Clive Sansom. 6475-2
Inscription for an old well. John Fallon. 6482-5
Inscription for Brownrigg's cell. George Canning. 6302-0
Inscription for Henry Marten's cell. Robert Southey. 6302-0
Inscription for my little son's silver plate. Eugene Field. 6452-3
Inscription for the Hermitage, sels. William Wordsworth. 6867-7
Inscription for the scabbard of a sword of honour. Herbert Trench. 6877-4
Inscription for the tomb of Mr. Hamlton. William Cowper.

INSCRIPTION

      6814-6
Inscription in a garden. George Gascoigne. 6436-1
Inscription in a hermitage. Thomas Wharton, 1st Marquess of Wharton. 6271-7
Inscription in a library. W.G. Wendell. 6722-0
Inscription in Faversham church. Unknown. 6385-3
Inscription on a fountain. Edward Lovibond. 6086-2
Inscription on a ruin. Thomas MacDonagh. 6096 X
Inscription on a sea shell. Walter Savage Landor. 6438-8
Inscription on a wall in St. Edmund's Church...London. Unknown. 6191-5
Inscription on an ancient bell. Unknown. 6282-2
Inscription on Melrose Abbey. Unknown. 6191-5,6385-3
Inscription on the monument of a Newfoundland dog. George Gordon, 6th Baron Byron. 6945-2,6510-4,6945-2
Inscription on the Statue of Liberty. Emma Lazarus. 6465-5
The inscription on the tomb of the Lady Mary Wentworth. Thomas Carew. 6933-9,6933-9,6150-8
Inscription opn a grot. Samuel Rogers. 6932-0
Inscription proposed for a soldiers' and sailors' monument. James Russell Lowell. 6126-5
Inscription, to the mistress of Cedarcroft. Bayard Taylor. 6976-2
Inscriptions. Richard Aldington. 6581-3,6780-8
Inscriptions. James Barnes. 6983-5
Inscriptions. Fydell Edmund Garrett. 6224-5,6625-9,6800-6
Inscriptions at the city of brass. Edward Powys Mathers. 6513-9
Inscriptions at the city of brass. Unknown (Arabic) 6665-8
Inscriptions at the city of brass, fr. 1000 & 1 nights. Unknown (Arabian) 6879-0
Inscriptions for a house. Henry Van Dyke. 6478-7
Inscriptions, sels. William Wordsworth. 6867-7
[Inscription] For a grotto. Mark Akenside. 6152-4,6195-0
Inscrutable. William Carman Roberts. 6433-7
"An inscrutable/Little minor tune...". Adolescence. Bernard K. Kay. 6764-1
Insects. Isidor Schneider. 6396-9
Insensibility. Douglas Gibson. 6475-2
Insensibility. Wilfred Owen. 6150-8,6210-5,6666-6
"Insensible to high heroic deeds". William Wallace. Joanna Baillie. 6813-8
'Insets' in 'All fellows' Laurence Housman. 6102-8
Inside a prison cell at count time. Daniel L. Klauck. 6870-7
Inside and out. Romina Morse. 6883-9
Inside of King's College chapel, Cambridge. William Wordsworth. 6122-2,6154-0,6337-3,6625-9,6631-3,6371 6199-0,6086-2,6110-9,6196-6,6430-2,6219-9,6639-9
"Inside the heart of/our in egumental waste". Storybook fossils, sels. George J. Honecker. 6803-0
"Inside this green cafeteria, a woman in blue". Sunlight in a cafeteria. Criss E. Cannady. 6966-5
"Inside this vast hotel the prairie". Lethbridge, Alberta; Thursdday evening, November 25... Stephen Scobie. 6767-2
The inside track. Robert J. Burdette. 6588-0
Inside you insdie me. Gary Glickman. 6857-X
Insight. David Wadsworth Cannon Jr. 6178-8
Insight. Mary Goose. 7005-1
Insight. Sir William Watson. 6737-9
Insignificance. Rena Rosenthal. 6396-9
Insignificant existence. Isaac Watts. 6302-0;6385-3
Insignificant needs. Yannis Ritsos. 6758-1
Insomnia. Ella Colter Johnston. 6906-1
Insomnia. Dante Gabriel Rossetti. 6110-9
Insomnia. Robert Service. 6159-1
Inspect us. Edith Daniell. 6089-7
Inspection. Wilfred Owen. 6666-6
Inspiration. Robert Burns. 6438-8
Inspiration. Celestin Pierre Cambiaire. 6826-X
Inspiration. Georgia H. Cooper. 6850-2
Inspiration. Abbotte McKinnon Downing. 6799-9
Inspiration. Wilfred Wilson Gibson. 6730-1
Inspiration. Per Hallstrom. 6045-5
Inspiration. Hilda Mary Hooke. 6796-4
Inspiration. Samuel Johnson. 6730-1
Inspiration. Henry Wadsworth Longfellow. 7020-5
Inspiration. Robert Loveman. 6941-X
Inspiration. William Shakespeare. 6150-8

Inspiration. Sir Philip Sidney. 6092-7,6250-4
Inspiration. John Banister Tabb. 6730-1
Inspiration. Henry David Thoreau. 6007-2,6600-3,6641-0, 6730-1,6438-8,6288 ,6431-0,6309-8,6300-4,6250-4
Inspiration. Unknown. 6109-5
The inspiration of quiet. William Wordsworth. 6793-X
Inspiration point. Jean Milne Gower. 6836-7
Inspiration, fr. Solomon. Unknown. 6730-1
The inspiration, fr. The West Indies. James Montgomery. 6946-0
Inspiration, sels. Henry David Thoreau. 6337-3,6102-8
An inspiration... Ella Wheeler Wilcox. 6211-3,6730-1
"Inspire my spirit, spirit of De Foe". Ode to the treadmill. Charles Lamb. 6787-5
"Inspiring and romantic Switzer's land". The statue of Arnold von Winkelried, Stanz. Thomas Campbell. 6749-2
Inspiring music. Marianne Clarke. 6789-1
Installation hymn. John Pierpont. 6752-2
Instans tyrannus. Robert Browning. 6473-6,6655-0
Instant out of time. Amanda Benjamin Hall. 6979-7
"The instant splendour". Prothalmion. Terence Tiller. 6379-9
"Instantly, quietly, with no remembering". Epithalamion. Robert Kelly. 6803-0
"Instead of a pound or two, spending a mint". Epigram on his garden shed (2). William Cowper. 6814-6
Instead of features. Jim Moore. 6966-5
Instead of loving your enemies. Ed Howe. 6736-0
Instead of neat inclosures, fr. An ode of the birth..Saviour. Robert Herrick. 6125-7
Instinct. Cesare Pavese. 6803-0
Instructions for a ballet. Maxwell Bodenheim. 6036-6
Instructions for my funeral. H. M. 6817-0
Instructions on how to wind a watch. Julio Cortazar. 6758-1
Instructions on or rather examples of how to be afraid. Julio Cortazar. 6758-1
The instructor. Rudyard Kipling. 6810-3
Insubordination. Margaret Evelyn Singleton. 6144-3
An insubstantial pageant. William Shakespeare. 6191-5
Insufficiency. Elizabeth Barrett Browning. 6123-0,6019-6
Insulting beauty. John Wilmot, 2d Earl of Rochester. 6092-7
The insulting letter. William Ellery Leonard. 6250-4
Intangible. Max Holzer. 6769-7
Intangible influence. Leonard Gray. 6764-6
Integer vitae. Thomas Campion. 6732-8,6102-8,6513-9
Integrity. William L. Stidger. 6144-3
Intellectual limitations. James Whitcomb Riley. 6091-9
The intellectual memory. Sir John Davies. 6584-8
Intellectual powers. Felicia Dorothea Hemans. 6973-8
The intellectual powers of the soul. Sir John Davies. 6584-8
Intellectual powers, fr. Thoughts during sickness. Felicia Dorothea Hemans. 6980-0
"Intelligence in man conceived". Eternal dream. Morris Hurley. 6799-9
Intelligence test. Cedric Adams. 6491-4
Intelligent cat. Grace Bacon Holway. 6699-2
The intelligent sheep-man. William Carlos Williams. 6388-8
Intemperance. Clarice Ellsworth. 6397-7
Intemperance, fr. Isaiah. Bible. 6337-3
Intempestiva. Henry Longan Stuart. 6292-X
Intended for Sir Isaac Newton. Alexander Pope. 6208-3,6430-2
Intends to be post-office man. F. Louise Walworth. 6715-8
"Intensity abstracted in air, ready to break." Frances Crawford. 6515-5
Intentions. John Richard Moreland. 6347-0
Inter solades. William Ernest Henley. 6230-X
Inter vias. Charles Fletcher Allen. 6836-7
Inter-mintry. Eugene Field. 6834-0;6949-5
Interceding. Opal Leonore Gibbs. 6065-X
The intercepted salute. Thomas Edward Brown. 6508-2
The intercepted salute. Thomas Edward Brown. 6809-X
Intercession. Cordelia Cox. 6799-9
Intercession. Louis Untermeyer. 6345-4
"The interest on the mortgage on the house..." Indebted. Edgar A. Guest. 6869-3

Interesting. Henry Cuyler Bunner. 6652-6
Interferin'. Olive Tilford Dargan. 7038-8
Interfusion. Han-mo Chung. 6775-1
Interim. Edna St. Vincent Millay. 6986-X
Interim. Sydney King Russell. 6069-2
Interior. Ronald de Carvalho. 6759-X
Interior. Willard Johnson. 6072-2
Interior. Willard Johnson. 6808-1
Interior. Josephine Miles. 6640-2
An interior. Edward Dowden. 7015-9
Interlude. Maxwell Bodenheim. 6348-9
Interlude. Idris Davies. 6360-8
Interlude. William Griffith. 6232-6,6029-3
Interlude. Bert Leach. 6906-1
Interlude. Scudder Middleton. 6102-8,6556-2,6076-5,6393-4
Interlude. Keidrych Rhys. 6360-8
Interlude. Lilian White Spencer. 6836-7
Interlude. Ella Wheeler Wilcox. 6309-8
Interlude, for a solitary flute, sels. Samuel Hoffenstein. 6532-5
Interlude: do not stuff them with children's songs. Vachel Lindsay. 6206-7
An interlude. Algernon Charles Swinburne. 6092-7,6732-8, 6092-7
Intermezzo. Monalinda Evigan. 6857-X
Intermezzo. Clem Portman. 6857-X
An intermezzo for the fourth act. William Allen White. 6817-0
Intermezzo: noon in the bazaar cafe. Gerald Bisinger. 6769-7
"The interminable ocean lay beneath". Sunrise at sea. Edwin Atherstone. 6833-2
Intermission, please! Irwin Edman. 6722-0
Intermittent fever. Walter De La Mare. 6905-3
Internal harmony. George Meredith. 6199-0
The international band. Oliver Harper. 6926-6
The International Brigade arrives at Madrid. Pablo (Neftali Ricardo Reyes Basualto) Neruda. 6665-8
The international brigades. Norman Rosten. 6561-9
International copyright. James Russell Lowell. 6288-1
An international episode. Caroline Duer. 6274-1
An international episode. Caroline Duer. 6946-0
"International hotel-in the mongo heart...". Rapping with one millin carabaos in the dark. Al Robles. 6792-1, 6998-3
International hymn. George Huntington. 6337-3
The internationale. Eugene Pottier. 6954-1
The internationalist. Louis Ginsberg. 6420-5,6542-2
The internationalists. Philip M. Harding. 6542-2
The interne. Maxwell Bodenheim. 6897-9
An internee mourns for his son who died in Italy. Sojin Takei. 6981-9
Interpretation. Louis J. Magee. 7004-3
Interpretation. Sheldon Shepard. 6144-3
Interpretations. Alfred Noyes. 6151-6
Interpretations. Ralph Duffield Small. 6983-5
The interpreter.. Orrick Johns. 6031-5,6556-2,6467-1
The interpreters. Algernon Charles Swinburne. 6110-9
Interracial. Georgia Douglas Johnson. 6178-3
"Interred beneath this marble stone". An epitaph. Matthew Prior. 6089-7,6633-X
Interrogation. Walter G. Arnold. 6178-8
The interrogations. Michael Knoll. 6870-7
Interrogativa cantilena. Unknown. 6562-7
An interrupted proposal. Robert C.V. Meyers. 6924-X
Interruption. Robert Graves. 6391-8
"Intersections/1/the late october sun". White earth reservation 1980 Gerald Vizenor. 7005-1
Interval. Joseph Auslander. 6070-6
Interval of flame. Sylvia Gardiner Lufburrow. 6750-6
Intervals. Beatrice Ravenel. 6619-4
Interview. Dorothy Parker. 6817-0
Interview with Lazarus. Joseph Auslander. 6879-0
An interview with Miles Standish. James Russell Lowell. 6457-4
An interview. Philip Brasfield. 6870-7
"Intery, mintery, cutery corn". Unknown. 7028-0
"Intery, mintery, cutery-corn". Mother Goose. 6363-2,6466-3
"Intice not me with thy alluringe eye." Unknown. 6563-5

Intimate apparel. Irene Wilde. 6750-6
Intimations. Alice Cary. 6865-0;6969-X
Intimations of immortality. Richard Henry Dana. 6014-5
Intimations of immortality. William Wordsworth. 6302-0, 6385-3,6600-3,6634-8,6543-0,6125-7,6143-5,6424-8
Intimations of mortality. Phyllis McGinley. 6761-1
Intimations of mortality. Alice Meynell. 6955-X
"Into a tube, with mirrors lined". The kaleidoscope. Edward Willard Watson. 6936-3
"Into a ward of the whitewashed halls". Somebody's darling. Marie La Conte (or La Coste). 6471-X,6074-9, 6113-3,6016-2,6964-9
"Into a ward of the whitewashed walls". Somebody's darling. Marie Lacost. 6889-8
Into battle. Julian Grenfell. 6044-7,6224-5,6315-2,6427-2, 6474-4,6477-9,6650-X,6665-8
"'Into each life some rain must fall'". Reflections, sels. Frances E. ("Fanny Fales") Swift. 6798-0
"Into her chamber went". The child's prayer. Hodges Reed. 6927-4
"Into her lying down head". Poem ("Into her lying"). Dylan Thomas. 6389-6
Into his house. Mary Cromwell Low. 6847-2
Into life. Stephen Spender. 6645-3
"Into my heart an air that kills". Alfred Edward Housman. 6138-9,6125-7,6508-2,6723-9
"Into silence of the morning's splendor". In midsummer. L.C. Whiton. 6965-7
Into the battalions of death. George Allan England. 7007-8
"Into the cold unknown". The victor. Helen Gray Cone. 7019-1
"Into the dust of the making of man". The builders. Henry Van Dyke. 6961-4
Into the endless night. Lilith Lorraine. 6648-8
"Into the green heart of a wave". Curiosity. Carrie Ward Lyon. 6861-8
"Into the house ran Lettice". The young soldier. Alice Cary. 6969-X
"Into the inmost temple...", fr. The faerie queen. Edmund Spenser. 6726-3
"Into the land of dreams I went". The dear white hand. Henry Van Dyke. 6983-5
"Into the mountains climb I, and below me". In the mountains. James Abraham Martling. 6952-5
Into the noiseless country. Thomas William Parsons. 6300-4
"Into the path of sin". Unknown. 6238-5
"Into the pewter cup of life/Pour agony". Mutability. Evelyn Hazlett Hunt. 6799-9
Into the poet's life. Robert Loveman. 6941-X
"Into the rescued world newcomer". Beyond knowledge. Alice Meynell. 6955-X
"Into the rose gold westland...". The happy hunting grounds. Emily Pauline ("Tekahionwake") Johnson. 6837-5
Into the silence. William Hamilton Hayne. 6995-9
"Into the silent waiting east". Christmas carol. Juliet C. Marsh. 6965-7
Into the sunbeam's keeping. Jennie D. Moore. 6048-X
Into the sunrise. Percy MacKaye. 7001-9
Into the sunset. Unknown. 6928-2
Into the sunset. S. Hall Young. 6461-2
"Into the thick of the fight he went, pallid". Wheeler at Santiago. James Lindsay Gordon. 6946-0
"Into the town of Conemaugh". The man who rode to Conemaugh. John Eliot Bowen. 7041-8,6062-5
Into the twilight. William Butler Yeats. 6477-9,6252-0, 6508-2,6723-9,6199-0,6501-5,6507-4
"Into the twilight of Trafalgar Square". Bacchanal, fr. In war time. Wilfred Wilson Gibson. 6884-7
"Into the vineyard I went with Bill". The vineyard. Eugene Field. 6949-5
"Into the west they are marching!...". The Indian Army. Robert Ernest Vernede. 7029-9
"Into the woods I wandered". Realization. Beth Cheney-Nichols. 6954-1
"Into the woods three huntsmen came". White stag. Johann Ludwig Uhland. 6949-5
Into the world and out. Sarah Morgan Bryan Piatt. 6240-7

"Into these loues, who but for passion lookes." Michael Drayton. 6586-4
"Into this quiet town the young men swarm". Fort town. Kathleen Sutton. 6761-1
Into this universe, and why not knowing, fr. Rubaiyat. Omar Khayyam. 7039-6
Into this world now is come. Unknown. 6756-5
"Into this world, and a cry in the night". Humility. Amory Hare. 7038-8
"Into this world, this day did come". I pray you, be merry and sing with me. Unknown. 6756-5
"Into thy hands." Loren W. Burch. 6144-3
Into wind...against the polar star. James E. Warren Jr. 6761-1
Intolerance. Molly Anderson Haley. 6337-3
Intolerance. John Richard Moreland. 6144-3
Intolerance. Winthrop Mackworth Praed. 6337-3
Intorduction, fr. Songs of captivity. Felicia Dorothea Hemans. 6973-8
The intoxicated poet. Allen Upward. 6897-9
"Intoxicatingly/Her eyes across the...". To a dancer. Arthur Symons. 6959-2
Intoxication. Emily Dickinson. 6076-5,6102-8
Intra muros. May C. ([Mary] Gillington) Byron. 6481-7
Intra, mintra, cutra, corn. Unknown. 6913-4
Intra, mintra, cutra, corn. Unknown. 6304-7
Intramural aestivation. Oliver Wendell Holmes. 6125-7
"Intrepid spirits of St. Louis". The spirits of St. Louis. Eva M. Campbell. 7019-1
The intro.. C.J. Dennis. 6722-0
Introduction ("Weeping Philosophers there were of old") Unknown. 6064-1
Introduction to the last book: To Chaucer. William Morris. 6828-6
Introduction to the last fruit off an old tree. Walter Savage Landor. 6604-6
Introduction to the true-born Englishman. Daniel Defoe. 6200-8
Introduction, fr. A rhymed lesson. Oliver Wendell Holmes. 6753-0
Introduction, fr. Poetry. Oliver Wendell Holmes. 6753-0
Introduction, fr. Songs of innocence. William Blake. 6219-9,6371-3,6543-0,660-7,6024-2,6198-2,6315-2,6488-4,6604-6,6634-
Introduction, fr. The house of life. Dante Gabriel Rossetti. 6656-9
Introduction, fr. The testament of beauty. Robert Bridges. 6487-6
Introduction, fr. Yamoyden. Robert C. Sands. 6752-2
Introduction: "Piping down the valleys." William Blake. 6271-7
The introduction. Al-Dhahabi. 6362-4
Introductory verses, fr. Hymns for childhood. Felicia Dorothea Hemans. 6973-8
Introspection. John M. Dean. 7001-9
Introspection. Ruth D. McGinnis. 6750-6
Introspective reflection. Ogden Nash. 6722-0
Introversion. Evelyn Underhill. 6337-3,6730-1
Intruder. Walter De La Mare. 6905-3
The intruder. Richard Church. 6072-2
The intruders. James Rorty. 6037-4
"Intruding hopes what make you heere." Unknown. 6563-5
Intrusion. Kathleen Hewitt. 6659-3
Intuition. Marie Louise Allen. 6906-1
Intuition. R.H. Grenville. 6218-0
Intuition. Albert Paris Gutersloh. 6769-7
Intuition, fr. In memoriam. Alfred Lord Tennyson. 6337-3
"Inty, minty, dibbity, fig". Unknown. 7028-0
The invaders. Jocelyn Macy Sloan. 6218-0
Invalid. Audrey McGaffin. 6388-4
Invalided. Edward Shillito. 7027-2
Invasion of weather. Douglas Newton. 6379-9
'The invasion', sels. Gerald Griffin. 6174-5
Invective. Pearce Young. 6515-5
An invective against love. Unknown. 6385-3
Invective against swans. Wallace Stevens. 6808-1
An invective written ...against Mr. Ben Johnson. George Chapman. 6200-8
The inventin'est man. J.B. H. 6281-4
Invention. Sir William Watson. 6250-4

"The invention all admired, and each how he". Paradise lost, sel. John Milton. 7014-0
The invention of New Jersey. Jack Anderson. 6803-0
An invention. Charles Godfrey Leland. 6983-5
Inventions. Samuel Butler. 6278-4
The inventor's wife, Mrs. E.T. Corbett. 6139-7,6416-7,6964-9
An inventor's wife. Jeannie Pendleton Ewing. 6930-0
An inventor's wife. Jeannie Pendleton Ewing. 6927-4
Inventory. Fydell Edmund Garrett. 6800-6
Inventory. Louis J. Magee. 7004-3
Inverberg. J.F. Hendry. 6379-9
Inversnaid. Gerard Manley Hopkins. 6828-6
Inversnaid. Gerard Manley Hopkins. 6022-6,6200-1,6253-9
The Inversnaid inn. William Allen Butler. 6903-7
Inverted eyelids. Ibn Haiyun. 6362-4
The inverted torch. Edith M. Thomas. 6310-1
Invictus. William Ernest Henley. 6289-X,6427-2,6481-7,6732-8,6123-0,6291 ,6153-2,6161-3,6102-8,6560-0,6461-2,6250 ,6332-2,6337-3,6437-X,6476-0,6498-1,6501 ,6104-4,6107-9,6214-8,6301-2,6371-3,6396 ,6503-1,6507-4,6512-0,6534-1,6589-9,6726 ,6464-7,6655-0,6737-9,6723-9,6653-4
The invincible armada. Johann C. Friedrich von Schiller. 6424-8
The invincible vanquished. Kathryn Wright. 6954-1
Invincible, fr. A lover's diary. Gilbert Parker. 6656-9
The invisible bride. Edwin Markham. 6310-1,6250-4,6431-0
The invisible bridge. Gelett Burgess. 6089-7
"Invisible hands from summer lands". Song of spring. John Vance Cheney. 6965-7
Invisible history. Walta Borawski. 7003-5
"The invisible moths of time, concealed in air". Dust storm. David Morton. 6783-2
Invisible painter. Alfred Dorn. 6218-0
The invisible playmate. Margaret Widdemer. 6891-X
The invisible rain. Alfred Edgar Coppard. 6071-4
"The invisible telephones of the wind are ringing" Pete Winslow. 6998-3
"The invisible wheels go softly round and...". A power-plant. Harriet Monroe. 7014-0
The invisible. Richard Watson Gilder. 6730-1
Invita Minerva. Oliver Wendell Holmes. 6126-5
Invita Minerva. James Russell Lowell. 6753-0
Invitation. Al-Mutawakkil. 6362-4
Invitation. Heathcote William Garrod. 6785-9
Invitation. Ibn Sa'id (of Seville) 6362-4
Invitation. Hattie Horner Louthan. 6836-7
Invitation. William Roehrick. 6850-2
Invitation. Lucille Schmedtje. 6850-2
Invitation. (Frederick) Ridgely Torrence. 6466-3
Invitation. Unknown. 6529-5
The invitation (to Tom Hughes) Charles Kingsley. 6092-7
Invitation to a husband. Annette Patton Cornell. 6750-6
Invitation to eternity. John Clare. 6380-2,6641-0,6648-8
Invitation to fancy, fr. Ode to fancy. Joseph Warton. 6932-0
Invitation to Isaac Walton. Charles Cotton. 6219-9
Invitation to Izaak Walton. Charles Cotton. 6240-7
Invitation to Juno. William Empson. 6209-1
An invitation to Maecenas. Horace. 6949-5
An invitation to sleep. Eugene Field. 6949-5
Invitation to tea. Myrna St. John. 6750-6
Invitation to the country, fr. Spring. Robert Bridges. 6487-6
An invitation to the country. William Cullen Bryant. 6047-1,6049-8,6597-X
Invitation to the dance. Unknown. 6959-2
Invitation to the dance. Unknown (Latin) 6879-0
The invitation to the gondola. John Addington Symonds. 6631-3
An invitation to the Oxford pageant, July 1907. Robert Bridges. 6487-6
An invitation to the poor tenants. Thomas Rowley. 7030-2
Invitation to the redbreast. Vincent Bourne. 6814-6
An invitation to the zoological gardens. Unknown. 6089-7, 6412-4,6724-7
The invitation, fr. The sun's darling. Thomas Dekker. 6827-8
An invitation. William Browne. 6191-5

An invitation. Theophile Gautier. 6652-6
An invitation. James Russell Lowell. 6385-3
An invitation. James Clarence Mangan. 7009-4
An invitation. James Abraham Martling. 6952-5
The invitation. Thomas Godfrey. 6288-1,6072-2
The invitation. George Herbert. 6641-0
The invitation. Robert Herrick. 6430-2
The invitation. Donagh MacDonagh. 6930-4
The invitation. Goronwy Owen. 6528-7
The invitation. Percy Bysshe Shelley. 6246-6,6423-X,6501-5, 6597-X,6732-8,6543-0,6219-9,6252-0
The invitation. Unknown. 6931-2
The invitation. Nathaniel Wanley. 6562-7
Inviting a friend to supper. Ben Jonson. 6198-2,6315-2, 6733-6,6562-7,6430-2,6194 ,6092-7
Inviting a friend to supper. Martial. 7039-6
Invocatio ad Mariam, fr. prologue to the 2nd nun's tale. Geoffrey Chaucer. 6282-2
Invocation. Berton Braley. 7007-8
Invocation. Auguste Brizeux. 6801-4
Invocation. Alice Cary. 6969-X
Invocation. Charles De Kay. 7041-8
Invocation. Reuel Denney. 6640-2
Invocation. S.A. Dethall. 6542-2
Invocation. John Drinkwater. 6250-4
Invocation. William Drummond of Hawthornden. 6301-2
Invocation. Max Eastman. 6102-8,6730-1,6393-4,6076-5,6161-3
Invocation. Felicia Dorothea Hemans. 6973-8
Invocation. Horace. 7039-6
Invocation. Philip Massinger. 6830-8
Invocation. Francesca Falk Miller. 6449-3
Invocation. Thomas Moult. 6884-7
Invocation. William Alexander Percy. 7014-0
Invocation. Pearl Goldsmith Philbrick. 6764-6
Invocation. David George Plotkin. 6954-1
Invocation. Sydney King Russell. 6979-7
Invocation. Caelius Sedulius. 6930-4
Invocation. Percy Bysshe Shelley. 6134-6,6246-6,6543-0
Invocation. Marya Alexandrovna Zaturenska. 6034-X
Invocation ("Ancestral Spirit, hidden from my sight") Eli Edwards. 6032-3
Invocation ("Answer me, burning stars of night!...") Felicia Dorothea Hemans. 6606-2
Invocation ("Comrade of ·olitude, Spirit of Joy"). Charles Wharton Stork. 6607-0
Invocation ("I am he that walks with the tender..."). Walt Whitman. 6423-X
Invocation ("Lord, from far several climes we come"). John Hay. 6486-8
Invocation ("O Glass-Blower of time"). Clara Shanafelt. 6556-2
Invocation ("O Thou whose equal purpose runs"). Wendell Phillips Stafford. 6337-3,6473-6,6250-4,6029-3
Invocation ("O Thou, Creator from original chaos"). George Rostrevor Hamilton. 6532-3
Invocation ("Oh! glen of mine"). Mary E. Boyle. 6269-5
Invocation ("Spain, the body"). Norman Rosten. 6561-9
Invocation ("We, children of the free"). Parr Harlow. 6049-8
Invocation (for Arbor Day). Parr Harlow. 6171-0
Invocation and promise. Verner von Heidenstam. 6045-5
An invocation in a library. Helen Gray Cone. 6847-2
The invocation of Comus, fr. Comus. John Milton. 6933-9
Invocation of Isis, fr. Metamorphoses. Apuleius. 6987-8
Invocation of silence. Richard Flecknoe. 6563-5
Invocation of the dawn. Kalidasa. 6879-0
An invocation to a water-nymph. Thomas Warton (the Elder) 6962-2
Invocation to Chaucer, fr. The life and death of Jason. William Morris. 6110-9
Invocation to Ireland. Amergin (atr.) 6930-4
Invocation to light. John Milton. 6302-0,6385-3,6150-8
Invocation to misery. Percy Bysshe Shelley. 6828-6
Invocation to misery. Percy Bysshe Shelley. 6102-8,6250-4
Invocation to nature. Percy Bysshe Shelley. 6240-7,6199-0
Invocation to Pegasus. Marietta Thompson Sprague. 6316-0
An invocation to poesy. Charles Mackay. 6273-3
Invocation to rain in summer. William Cox Bennett. 6239-3, 6302-0,6385-3,6771-7

The invocation to Sabrina. John Milton. 6830-8
Invocation to sleep. Francis Beaumont and John Fletcher. 6099-4,6302-0,6385-3
Invocation to sleep. John Fletcher. 6198-2,6533-3,6726-3, 6189-3
Invocation to the African muse, fr.The flaming terrapin. Roy Campbell. 6788-3
Invocation to the earth. William Wordsworth. 6543-0
Invocation to the genius of Greece. Mark Akenside. 6932-0
Invocation to the morning star. Unknown (American Indian) 6396-9
Invocation to the power of love, fr. Endymion. John Keats. 6110-9
Invocation to the social muse. Archibald MacLeish. 6399-3, 6375-6
Invocation to the spirit of Achilles. George Gordon, 6th Baron Byron. 6086-2
Invocation to tobacco. Henry James Mellen. 6453-1
Invocation to Urania, fr. Paradise lost. John Milton. 6933-9
Invocation to youth. Laurence Binyon. 6437-X
Invocation, fr. Christ unconquered. Arthur J. Little. 6282-2
Invocation, fr. Don Juan. George Gordon, 6th Baron Byron. 6315-2,6543-0
Invocation, fr. Female characters of scripture. Felicia Dorothea Hemans. 6973-8
Invocation, fr. John Brown's body. Stephen Vincent Benet. 6891-X
Invocation, fr. John Brown's body. Stephen Vincent Benet. 6984-3
Invocation, fr. Music. Henry Van Dyke. 6961-4
Invocation, fr. Paradise lost. John Milton. 6610-0,6543-0
An invocation, fr. Remorse. Samuel Taylor Coleridge. 6828-6
Invocation, fr. The American village. Charles W. Denison. 6755-7
Invocation, fr. the prologue of The prioress's tale. Geoffrey Chaucer. 6282-2
An invocation, sels. John Addington Symonds. 6337-3
An invocation. Ambrose Bierce. 6076-5,6102-8
An invocation. Samuel Taylor Coleridge. 6430-2
An invocation. William Johnson Cory. 6423-X,6437-X,6383-7
An invocation. John Addington Symonds. 6418-3,6730-1
The invocation. Abraham Cowley. 6385-3
The invocation. Felicia Dorothea Hemans. 6973-8
The inward clarion. Wallace B. Nichols. 7031-0
The inward light. Henry Septimus Sutton. 6730-1
The inward morning. Henry David Thoreau. 6333-0
Inward music. John Keble. 6600-3
Inward peace, fr. Lines written in Kensington gardens. Matthew Arnold. 6337-3
The inward voice. Charles Whitby. 6994-0
Io. Aeschylus. 6435-3
Io. James Shirley. 6562-7,6563-5
"Io ritornai dalla santissima onda" Leonard Bacon. 6217-2, 6250-4
"Io triumphe! Lo, thy certain art". Icarus. Bayard Taylor. 6976-2
Io victis. William Wetmore Story. 6211-3,6730-1,6214-8
Io victis, sels. William Wetmore Story. 6144-3
'Io vidi'. Vittoria Aganoor Pompilj. 6050-1
"Io! Paean!sIo! ing". Triumph of the whale. Charles Lamb. 6833-2
Iolanthe, sels. Sir William Schwenck Gilbert. 6732-8
Iolaus restor'd to youth. John Gay. 6972-X
Ion at the entrance of a forest. Sir Thomas Noon Talfourd. 6980-0
Ion described by Agenor. Sir Thomas Noon Talfourd. 6980-0
Ion receiving the sacrificial knife from Ctesiphon. Sir Thomas Noon Talfourd. 6980-0
"Ion, our sometime darling, whom we prized". Ion described by Agenor. Sir Thomas Noon Talfourd. 6980-0
Ion, sels. Sir Thomas Talfourd. 6109-5
Ionian holiday. Unknown (Greek) 6435-3
Ionian song. Constantine P. Cavafy. 6352-7
Ionicus. Sir Henry Newbolt. 6793-X
Iotis dying. Unknown (Greek) 6948-7
Iowa. Maurice Morris. 6036-6
Iowa summer. Richard Eberhart. 6803-0

Ipecacuanha. George Canning. 6125-7
Iphigeneia and Agamemnon. Walter Savage Landor. 6473-6, 6199-0,6110-9,6543-0
Iphigenia. Alfred Lord Tennyson. 6087-0
Iphigenia in Aulis. Charles Phillips. 6241-5
The Ipighenia in tauris, sels. Euripides. 6334-9
Ippolito di Este, sels. Walter Savage Landor. 6980-0
Ipsa quae. Nicholas Breton. 6436-1
Ipsissimus. Eugene Lee-Hamilton. 6102-8,6670-4
Ipswich. Eugene Field. 6949-5
Ipswich bar. Esther Bates and Brainard Bates. 6053-6
Ipswich town. J.A. Morgan. 6484-1
Iqbal
    Community. A.J. Arberry (tr.). 6448-5
Ira and Kate. W.W. Christman. 6662-3
Iraj
    Epitaph. A.J. Arberry (tr.). 6448-5
    Mother. A.J. Arberry (tr.). 6448-5
Iraqi
    Gamble. A.J. Arberry (tr.). 6448-5
    I cannot see. Sir Denison Ross (tr.). 6448-5
    Mystic cups. E.G. Browne (tr.). 6448-5
The irate bee. Ida L. Padleford. 6818-9
Ireland. G.A.J. C. 6474-4
Ireland. Stephen Lucius Gwynn. 6090-0,6174-5
Ireland. Walter Savage Landor. 6733-6
Ireland. Edmund Leamy. 6292-X
Ireland. Francis Ledwidge. 6812-X
Ireland. Denis Florence MacCarthy. 6302-0;6385-3
Ireland. John James Piatt. 6309-8
Ireland. Dora Sigerson Shorter. 6096-X,6437-X,6331-4,6244-X,6174-5,6102-8,6301-2,6628-3
Ireland [pseud]., Baron
    Apex. 6722-0
    To a new-born infant. 6817-0
Ireland to-day. Shane Leslie. 6174-5
Ireland was never contented. Walter Savage Landor. 6092-7
Ireland weeping. William Livinston. 6845-6
Ireland, 1924. George William ("A.E.") Russell. 6070-6
Ireland, Mary E.
    Sunday school truant. 6715-8
Ireland, mother of priests. Shane Leslie. 6096-X,6172-9, 6292-X
Ireland, oh, my country! Frances Isabel Parnell. 6714-X
Iremonger, Valentin
    Icarus. 6930-4
    Recollection in autumn. 6930-4
    Spring stops me suddenly. 6930-4
Irene. Margaret Elizabeth Sangster. 6486-8
Iris. Michael (Katherine Bradley & Edith Cooper) Field. 6656-9
Iris. Roberta Holloway. 6628-3
Iris. Hilda Mary Hooke. 6843-X
Iris. Hilda Mary Hooke. 6797-2
Iris. C.E.D. Phelps. 6274-1
Iris. Bayard Taylor. 6976-2
Iris. Unknown (Japanese) 6891-X
Iris [pseud].
    Missing. 6846-4
"Iris by athe riverside". Iris. Hilda Mary Hooke. 6797-2
"Iris by the riverside". Iris. Hilda Mary Hooke. 6843-X
Iris flowers. Mary McNeil Fenollosa. 6338-1
Iris, Scharmel
    After the martyrdom. 6144-3,6337-3
    Early nightfall. 6897-9
    A fisherman speaks. 6144-3,6335-7
    The friar of Genoa. 6292-X,6172-9
    Iteration. 6897-9
    Lament. 6897-9
Iris, fr. Music. Henry Van Dyke. 6961-4
Iris, sels. Oliver Wendell Holmes. 6317-9
An Irish airman foresees his death. William Butler Yeats. 6666-6,6209-1
Irish astronomy. Charles G. ("Miles O'Reilly") Halpine. 6302-0,6165-6,6505-8
The Irish avatar. George Gordon, 6th Baron Byron. 6945-2
Irish bachelor. Thomas Augustine Daly. 6714-X
"The Irish brigade" at Fontenoy. Bartholomew Dowling. 6404-3
Irish coquetry. Unknown. 6825-1

Irish coquetry. Unknown. 6917-7
Irish coquetry. Unknown. 6139-7
The Irish council bill, 1907 Unknown. 6930-4
The Irish drummer. Unknown. 6064-1
The Irish drummer. Unknown. 6825-1
The Irish emigrant. Helen Selina Sheridan; Lady Dufferin. 6014-5,6600-3
An Irish face. George William ("A.E.") Russell. 6090-0
An Irish fantasy. John Franklin Blunt. 6799-9
The Irish harper and his dog. Thomas Campbell. 6891-X
An Irish headland. Robinson Jeffers. 6628-3
The Irish hurrah. Thomas Osborne Davis. 6930-4
Irish love song. Margaret Widdemer. 6556-2
An Irish love song. John Todhunter. 6873-1
Irish love-song. Katharine (Hinkson) Tynan. 6090-0
Irish lullaby. Unknown. 6090-0
Irish lullaby. Unknown (Irish) 6858-8
An Irish lullaby. Alfred Perceval Graves. 6078-1,6442-3
The Irish maiden's song. John Banim. 6858-8
Irish melodies. John Todhunter. 6090-0
An Irish melody. Denis Aloysius McCarthy. 6805-7
An Irish melody. John Francis Waller. 6271-7
Irish memories. George Arthur Greene. 6090-0
Irish Molly. Unknown. 6858-8
The Irish mother's lament. Cecil Frances Alexander. 6090-0
Irish particular. Unknown. 6278-4
The Irish peasant girl. Charles Joseph Kickham. 6292-X, 6174-5
Irish peasant song. Louise Imogen Guiney. 6310-1,6331-4, 6431-0
The Irish peasant to his mistress. Thomas Moore. 6022-6
The Irish picket. Robert Henry ("Orpheus C. Kerr") Newell. 6404-3,6630-5
The Irish rapparees. Sir Charles Gavan Duffy. 6858-8
The Irish rapparees. Sir Charles Gavan Duffy. 6656-9
The Irish rapparees. Sir Charles Gavan Duffy. 6858-8
The Irish reaper's harvest hymn. John Keegan. 6174-5
The Irish sailor. Unknown. 6858-8
The Irish schoolmaster. Thomas Hood. 6802-2,6974-6
The Irish schoolmaster. James A. Sidey. 6630-5
The Irish schoolmaster. James A. Sidney. 6089-7
Irish song. Helen Coale Crew. 6776-X
Irish song. Helen Coale Crew. 6331-4
The Irish spinning-wheel. Alfred Perceval Graves. 6174-5, 6255-5
Irish stew, fr. The poetical cookbook. Unknown. 6278-4
An Irish thing in rhyme. Elsa Keeling. 6249-0
The Irish traveler. Unknown. 6825-1
Irish war-song. Edward Walsh. 6858-8
Irish wide-awake quickstep song. Unknown. 6709-3
The Irish widow to her son. Ellen Forrester. 6927-4
Irish widow's message to her son in America. Ellen Forrester. 6090-0
The Irish wife. Thomas D'Arcy McGee. 6656-9
The Irish wolf-hound. Denis Florence MacCarthy. 6597-X, 6090-0,6510-4,6656-9
The Irish wolf-hound. Denis Florence. 6090-0
Irish, Hazel M.
    Life. 6764-6
Irish, Marie
    Pennant drill for Washington's birthday. 6248-2
Irish, Robert J.
    Sapping time. 6764-6
    A slumber story. 6818-9
The Irish. Francis Carlin. 6292-X
The Irishman and the lady. William Maginn. 6089-7,6656-9
"An Irishman traveling, though not for delight". The Irish traveler. Unknown. 6825-1
An Irishman's christening. Unknown. 6930-4
The Irishman. William Maginn. 6219-9
The Irishman. James Orr. 6090-0,6174-5,6820-0
The Irishwoman's letter. Unknown. 6554-6,6304-7
The Irishwoman's letter. Unknown. 6909-6
Irma, Sister Mary
    La pucelle. 6761-1
    Letter from a postulant. 6285-7
Irmeline rose. Jens Peter Jacobsen. 6555-4
"Iron birds floating in the sky". Aeroplanes. Walter James Turner 7029-9
The iron crown. Alfred Noyes. 6151-6

Iron fare, fr. Bread out of iron. Marjorie Allen Seiffert. 6531-7
The iron gate. Oliver Wendell Holmes. 6411-6,6126-5
The iron grays. Fitz-Greene Halleck. 6753-0
The iron music. Ford Madox (Hueffer) Ford. 6393-4
"Iron plates, barbells/black as a moonless...". The field's retention. Jose Y. Teran Jr.. 6870-7
Iron-silver-gold. Unknown. 6314-4
Ironin' day. Amanda Benjamin Hall. 6538-4
Ironquill. See Ware, Eugene Fitch
Irons, Genevieve M.J
   Easter. 6177-X
Irons, William J. (tr.)
   Dies irae. Thomas of Celano, 6219-9
Irony. Louis Untermeyer. 6897-9,6879-0
Irony. Mary Frances Ward. 6818-9
Irony of fate. Grace Jervis Smith. 6270-9
"The irony of fate so tragic is". Fate. Ethel M. Brainerd. 6906-1
The irony of fate; or, why she was jilted. Langford Reed. 6811-1
Irony of God. Eva Warner. 6144-3,6335-7
Irradiations. John Gould Fletcher. 6299-7,6348-9
Irradiations, sels. John Gould Fletcher. 6300-4
Irregular ode, on the death of Lord Byron. Caleb C. Colton. 6980-0
An irrepressible boy. Unknown. 6691-7
Irresistable time. Henry Kirke White. 6543-0
Irresolute resolution. Unknown. 6675-5
The irreverent Brahmin. Arthur Guiterman. 6303-9,6307-1
Irrevocable. Mary Wright Plummer. 6260-1;6730-1
Irrigation. Naomi Rogin. 6850-2
Irvine, J.P.
   An August afternoon. 6597-X
   Indian summer. 6597-X
   Summer drought. 6597-X
Irvine, John
   One haunted night. 6648-8
   The swans. 6648-8
Irvine, Lyn Lloyd
   Lines on growing old. 6072-2
Irvine, Mabel V.
   During sickness. 6269-5
   Love in absence. 6269-5
   To a new baby. 6269-5
Irving, Henry
   'Said I to myself, said I.' 6721-2
Irving, Minna
   Americans all. 6449-3
   And she cried. 6277-6
   Betsy's battle flag. 6274-1,6356-X,6465-5,6449-3
   The bugle. 6471-X
   A Christmas minuet. 6807-3
   El Camilo. 6670-4
   Grandmother's valentine. 6274-1
   Lost bonnet-lost heart. 6720-4
   Marching still. 6471-X
   New Fourth of July. 6714-X
   The old Virginia reel. 6694-1
   The parade. 6443-4
   A Thanksgiving wooing. 6703-4
   A veteran. 6690-9
   Wearing of the green. 6694-1
Irving, Washington
   Album verses. 6240-7,6004-8
   The Alhambra, sels. 6484-1
   Catskill Mountains. 6484-1
   A certain young lady. 6280-6,6441-8,6004-8,6652-6,6585-6
   The falls of the Passaic. 6484-1
   Mother-love. 6461-2
Irwin [pseud].
   The curse of faint praise. 6817-0
   Greek temples. 6817-0
   Ragged days. 6817-0
Irwin, Richard D.
   Only a volunteer. 6443-4
Irwin, Thomas Caulfield
   The faerie's child. 6174-5
   The faerie's child. 6930-4

Minnie. 6090-0
   The minstrel's appointment, sels. 6174-5
   The potato digger's song. 6090-0
   The troubadour's pilgrimage. 6174-5
   The vine song, fr. The minstrel's appointment. 6174-5
Irwin, Wallace
   At the Stevenson fountain. 6476-0,6241-5
   The ballad of Grizzly Gulch. 6995-9
   The ballad of Sagamore hill. 6995-9
   Blow my eyes! 6083-8,6089-7
   The constant cannibal maiden. 6083-8,6089-7
   Da strit pianna. 6280-6
   From Romany to Rome. 6732-8
   A grain of salt. 6089-7,6722-0
   He entereth America by the front door, fr. The Teddysee. 6995-9
   A nautical extravagance. 6499-X
   Song for a cracked voice. 6724-7,6732-8,6396-9
   "This fever called living." 6280-6
   To what we love and dread. 6717-4
   The Vassar girl. 6277-6,6718-2
Irwin, Will
   Heroic ballad 1976. 6817-0,6732-8
Iry and Billy and Jo. James Whitcomb Riley. 6689-5
Is 5, sels. Edward Estlin Cummings. 6736-0
"Is a short string of beautiful". My past. Dennis Cooper. 7003-5
"Is anything so good as to return". The library, fr. The homestead. Gertrude Huntington McGiffert. 6838-3
"Is death more cruel from a private dagger". King John, sels. Colley Cibber. 6867-7
"Is death so great a gamester, that he throws". An elegy. William Browne. 6908-8
"Is every day a separate life to a bird?". A bird's life. May Swenson. 6803-0
Is freedom a lie? J.M. Munyon. 6925-8
Is he dead? Francis Carco. 6351-9
"Is he indeed provoked to anger in high places". The unregretting. Anne Goodwin Winslow. 6777-8
Is he not fair? Horatius Bonar. 6848-0
Is he true? William White. 6868-5
Is is raining, little flower? Unknown. 6291-1
Is it a dream? G.A. Studdert-Kennedy. 6337-3,6420-5,6461-2
"Is it a sea on which the souls embark". Lollingdon Downs: XV. John Masefield. 6879-0
Is it amavi or is it amo? Thomas Edward Brown. 6809-X
Is it anybody's business? Unknown. 6045-1
"Is it because of some dear grace". South sun and brimming sea. Louis Golding. 6778-6
"Is it because that lad is dead". Vision. Frank Sidgwick. 7029-9
"Is it come?" Frances Brown. 6271-7,6219-9
"Is it deep sleep, or is it rather death?". One dead. J.W. Inchbold. 7015-9
Is it far to go? Cecil Day Lewis. 6246-5
"'Is it far to the town?', said the poet". The coming poet. Francis Ledwidge. 6812-7
"Is it for fear to wet a widow's eye". Sonnet 009 ("Is it for fear"). William Shakespeare. 6447-7
"Is it good-bye for ever". Vale atque ave. Ewart Alan Mackintosh. 6785-9
Is it good-bye? William Ernest Henley. 6226-1
"Is it her face that looks from forth...glare". Hotwells. Thomas Edward Brown. 6809-X
"Is it his daily toil that wrings". The chain. John Pierpont. 7009-4
"Is it indeed so? If I lay here dead." Elizabeth Barrett Browning. 6560-0
"Is it ironical, a fool enigma". Dartmoor: sunset at Chagford: Homo loqvitvr. Thomas Edward Brown. 6809-X
Is it love? Unknown. 6680-1
"Is it more than yestreen since I played...". The young mother. James Abraham Martling. 6952-5
"Is it naught? Is it naught". Cuba. Edmund Clarence Stedman. 6946-0
Is it not better. Walter Savage Landor. 6110-9
"Is it not better at an early hour" Walter Savage Landor. 6828-6
"Is it not possible to believe without...fight". This faith, this violence. Robert Nathan. 6761-1

"Is it not sure a deadly pain". Unknown. 6187-7
"Is it not sweet to die? for, what is death". Sweet to die. Thomas Lovell Beddoes. 6980-0
Is it nothing to you? L. James Kindig. 6065-X
Is it nothing to you? Unknown. 6913-4
"Is it nothing to you?" May Probyn. 6172-9,6656-9
"Is it possible" Johann C. Friedrich von Schiller. 6606-2
Is it possible? Sir Thomas Wyatt. 6315-2
"Is it safe to lie so lonely when the summer..". Song by Gulbaz. Laurence (Adele Florence Nicolson) Hope. 6856-1
"Is it so small a thing". Empedocles on Etna, sels. Matthew Arnold. 6879-0
"Is it so sudden? Then did you believe, dear". After a proposal. Edgar A. Guest. 6862-6
"Is it strange that we should be". March. Sally Bruce Kinsolving. 6818-9
Is it success? Susie M. Best. 6109-5
"Is it that black star". Day's black star. William Henry Davies. 6943-6
"Is it the beauty of the rose". The reversible metaphor. Troubadour [pseud].. 6817-0
"Is it the blood-red sun that divides our...". On Henri Rousseau's 'Virgin forest at sunst...' Wade Newman. 6900-2
"Is it the tramp of men to battle". Heartsick! Mary Elizabeth Blake. 7041-8
"Is it the wind of the dawn that I hear...". Duet from Becket, fr. Locksley Hall. Alfred Lord Tennyson. 6867-7
"Is it the wind, the many-tongued, the weird". The draft riot. Charles De Kay. 6946-0
Is it this sky's vast vault or ocean's sound. Dante Gabriel Rossetti. 6560-0
"Is it this you call home rule?". The Irish council bill, 1907 Unknown. 6930-4
"Is it thy will thy image should keep open." William Shakespeare. 6317-9
"Is it thy will thy image should keep open". Sonnet 061 ("Is it thy will"). William Shakespeare. 6150-4,6560-0
"Is it to labor for wealth and fame". Our object in life. Edward R. Huxley. 6885-5
"Is it true that she is dead". May. Mary McKinley Cobb. 6841-3
"Is it well that while we range with...". Locksley hall fifty years after, sel. Alfred Lord Tennyson. 6954-1
"Is it where the spiral stairway". Heaven. M. Sophie Holmes. 6909-6
"Is it worth while that we jostle a brother". Joaquin Miller. 6238-5;6523-6;6260-1
"Is it you, that preach'd in the chapel...". Despair. Alfred Lord Tennyson. 6977-0
"Is Kuloskap living yet?". The master and the final day. Unknown (Algonquin Indian). 6864-2
Is it you? Emma Celia & Lizzie J. Rook. 6137-0
"Is it, then, regret for buried time", fr. In memoriam. Alfred Lord Tennyson. 6867-7
"Is John Smith within?". Mother Goose. 6363-2
Is life worth living, sels. Alfred Austin. 6337-3
Is life worth living? Alfred Austin. 6793-X,6322-5
"Is life worth living?" Thomas Wilson Brown. 6109-5
Is love blind? Unknown. 6118-4
Is love worth learning? John Davidson. 6819-7
"Is love, then, so simple, my dear". Song ("Is love"). Irene Rutherford McLeod. 6320-9
Is love, then, so simple? Irene Rutherford McLeod. 6726-3, 6102-8
'Is missus. Gordon Malherbe Hillman. 6032-3
"Is my child aware that I/Fear and worry...". The mother. Francis J. Preston. 6799-9
"Is my darling tired already". True honors. Adelaide Anne Procter. 6965-7,6957-6
Is my lover on the sea? Bryan Waller ("Barry Cornwall") Procter. 6833-2
Is my team ploughing. Alfred Edward Housman. 6872-3,6527-9, 6536-8,6726-3,6513-9,6655-0
"Is night near spent?". The captives. A tragedy. John Gay. 6972-X
"Is not man's greatest heart's desire". Omnia vanitas. Unknown (Gaelic). 6845-6
"Is not the contrast fortunate?". Old lovers. Louis J. Magee. 7004-3
"Is not the messenger returned?". Marino Faliero, doge of Venice. George Gordon, 6th Baron Byron. 6945-2
"Is not the oak beside the sea". The oak by the sea. Sylvester Baxter. 6798-0
"Is not this the merry month of May". May. Edmund Spenser. 6935-5
"Is not thy heart far off amidst the wood". The child of the forests. Felicia Dorothea Hemans. 6973-8
"Is someone who knew you". What keeps us alive. Jacqueline J. Johnson. 6899-5
"Is that oft uttered adage true". Old and new. William Allen Butler. 6903-7
"Is that star dumb, or am I deaf?". Venus. William Henry Davies. 6778-6
"Is that you, death? Hello, old skate!". Indestructible. H. Stanley Haskins. 6750-6
"Is that you, Peggy? my goodness me!". Peggy's wedding. Thomas Edward Brown. 6809-X
"Is the house on fire". Destruction of the house. Ann L. Zoller. 6857-X
Is the moon made of green cheese? Nicholas Nichols. 6131-1
Is the pathetic fallacy true? Elizabeth Brewster. 6767-0
Is there a Santa Claus? F.P. Church. 6145-1
Is there a Santa Claus? Francis Pharcellus Church. 6449-3
Is there a Santa Claus? Edgar A. Guest. 6862-6
"Is there a bard whom genius fires". The persian, the sun and the cloud. John Gay. 6972-X
"Is there a crim ". Caesar in Egypt, sels. Colley Cibber. 6867-7
"Is there a genie in this marble vase". Child at the library. Kalfus Kurtz. 6761-1
"Is there a lost child crying in the night". The lost heart. Herbert S. Gorman. 6033-1,6880-4
"Is there a man, that, from some lofty steep". Christopher Columbus. Joanna Baillie. 6980-0,6813-8,6813-8
"Is there a pleasure can with this compare?". 'Paa Heja': life on the heights. James Logie ("Hugh Haliburton") Robertson. 6819-7
"'Is there a Santa Claus?' she asked". Is there a Santa Claus? Edgar A. Guest. 6862-6
'Is there any word from the Lord?' John Vance Cheney. 6848-0
"Is there but emptiness from sky to sky". Today. Lizette Woodworth Reese. 7017-5
Is there for honest poverty. Robert Burns. 6180-X,6604-6, 6195-0,6250-4,6660-7
Is there more than one St. Nick? Unknown. 6715-8
"Is there no fading of thy central fire". A lament for Percy Bysshe Shelley. William Edmonstoune Aytoun. 6948-7
"Is there no grand, immortal sphere". Art thou living yet? James G. Clarke. 6913-4
"Is there no hope? the sick man said". The sick man and the angel. John Gay. 6996-7,6972-X
"Is there no music in the trees". Unknown. 6902-9
Is there not faith enough? Alfred Kreymborg. 6042-0
Is there room in angel land? Unknown. 6912-6
Is there some spirit sighing? Felicia Dorothea Hemans. 6973-8
"Is there virtue in the sweet medium". Poem ("Is there virtue"). John Prichard. 6360-7
Is this a dagger?. William Shakespeare. 6424-8
"Is this a holy thing to see". Holy Thursday. William Blake. 7009-4
"Is this a time to be gloomy". Spring. Unknown. 6392-6
"Is this a truly church, do you ask?". A truly church. Charlotte M. Packard. 6965-7
Is this all. Horatius Bonar. 6302-0
"Is this all the love that he bore me, my". Queen Vashti's lament. John Edmund Reade. 6848-0,6574-0
"Is this old autumn standing here". Old autumn. William Henry Davies. 6780-8
Is this presumption? Louise H. Toness. 6144-3
"Is this some glowering titan, inly bright". Stanzas to Tolstoy in his old age. Herbert Trench. 6877-4
Is this the lark! Joseph Auslander. 6464-7,6581-3,6776-X
"Is this the office of Cupid's Express". Traced. Layton

Brewer. 7021-3
"Is this the price of beauty! Fairest, thou". Charleston. Richard Watson Gilder. 6946-0
"Is this the sky, and this the very earth". Youth and nature. Philip Bourke Marston. 7015-9
"Is this the tel'graph office?". A message for mama in heaven. Unknown. 6929-0
Is this the time to halt? Charles Sumner Hoyt. 6335-7,6337-3
"Is this the way Attica was". Folsom, August 11th: a question of races. Pancho Aguila. 6792-1, 6998-3
"Is this thy tomb, amid the mournful shades". The tomb of Absalom. Lydia Huntley Sigourney. 6848-0
"Is this your faith, then, Fanny!". To Fanny. Thomas Hood. 6974-6
"Is this/The moonlight on". Apple blossom. Estelle Rooks. 6850-2
"Is thy cruse of comfort failing?" Mrs. Charles. 6238-5
"Is thy face like thy mother's my fair child!". Childe Harold's pilgrimage. George Gordon, 6th Baron Byron. 6198-2,6088-9,6828-2
"Is thy face like thy mother's, my fair child!". Harold the wanderer, fr. Chile Harold's Pilgrimage. George Gordon, 6th Baron Byron. 6832-4
"Is thy servant a dog?". John Banister Tabb. 6292-X,6172-9
"Is thy servant a dog?" John Banister Tabb. 6510-4
Is yo' lamps gone out? Unknown. 6609-7
Isaac. John Henry, Cardinal Newman. 6980-0
Isaac and Archibald. Edwin Arlington Robinson. 6333-0,6153-2
Isaac Ashford. George Crabbe. 6600-3
Isaac La Bissoniere, at eighty, recalls October of 1841 Emma M. Larson. 6342-X
Isaac Walton's prayer. D.L. James. 6118-4
Isabel. Richard Hovey. 7006-X
Isabel. John Skelton. 6383-7
Isabel. Alfred Lord Tennyson. 6977-0
Isabel Clare, sels. John Francis Waller. 6174-5
Isabella, or the pot of basil. John Keats. 6679-8,6086-2, 6110-9
Isabella, sels. John Keats. 6648-8
Isabelle. James Hogg. 6802-2
Isadora. Witter Bynner. 6959-2
Isadora Duncan. Johnra Collier. 6959-2
Isadora Duncan. Max Eastman. 6880-4
Isadora Duncan. Max Eastman. 6959-2
Isadora Duncan dancing. Joel Elias Springarn. 6959-2
Isadora Duncan dancing. Louis Untermeyer. 6959-2
Isadora Duncan dancing. Louis Untermeyer. 6959-2
Isadore. Thomas Holley Chivers. 7017-5
Isahakian, Avetis
"Do not trust black eyes, but fear them". 6050-1
"Huntsman, that on the hills above". 6050-1
"The sun went down behind the hill". 6050-1
"The wind is howling through the winter night". 6050-1
"Ye mountain bluebells, weep with me". 6050-1
Isaiah 035 John Gardiner Calkins Brainard. 6848-0
Isaiah 046: 9 Hartley Coleridge. 6848-0
Isaiah 060: 15-20 William Cowper. 6848-0
Isaiah Beethoven. Edgar Lee Masters. 6393-4
Isaiah LII, sels. Bible. 6334-9
Isaiah XL. Bible. 6490-6
Isaiah XXXV. John Gardiner Calkins Brainard. 6752-2
Isaiah, sels. Bible. 6334-9,6134-5
"Isaiah, the country-boy,marched against..jazz". Babylon, Babylon, Baybylon the great. Vachel Lindsay. 6871-5
Isaias, sels. Unknown. 6282-2
Isakovsky, Mikhail
He saw her home. Jack Lindsay (tr.). 6546-5
In woods near the frontline. Jack Lindsay (tr.). 6546-5
Maiden meditation. Jack Lindsay (tr.). 6546-5
Twelve blades of grass. Jack Lindsay (tr.). 6546-5
Isas
"All day/The bird sits in his cage." Lois J. Erickson (tr.). 6027-7
Isaura. Ella Wheeler Wilcox. 6956-8
Isbell, Bernetta L.
Courage. 6799-9
Isbell, Hugh O.
Crucifixion ("Golgotha's journey is an ancient way")
6144-3,6420-5
Faith. 6144-3
"Iscariot, never more thy stricken name". Military necessity. Josephine Preston Peabody. 7027-2
Ise, Lady
"The double cherry trees, which grew". William N. Porter (tr.). 6852-9
Ise, Princess
"Short as the joints of bamboo reeds". William N. Porter (tr.). 6852-9
Isenhour, Walter E.
Golden October. 6799-9
Ish-Kishor, Sulamith
Birth. 6847-2
Shakespeare. 6847-2
Ishigaki, Rin
Cliffs. Harold P. Wright (tr.). 6803-0
Living. Harold P. Wright (tr.). 6803-0
Ishii
His grace. Lois J. Erickson (tr.). 6027-7
Ishmael. Louis Untermeyer. 6031-5
Isiah XIV, sels. Bible. 6472-8
Isidorus
On a fowler. William Cowper (tr.). 6850-2,6814-6
Sea trade. Sir William Marris (tr.). 6435-3
Isidorus Aegeates
"To far-off shores as merchant...". F.L. Lucas (tr.). 6251-2
Isis wanderer. Kathleen Raine. 6209-1
Island. Wilberto L. Canton. 6759-X
Island (the sea cave) George Gordon, 6th Baron Byron. 6438-8
Island battlefield. C.R. Holmes. 6515-5
Island born. Harold Vinal. 6347-0
The island cemetery. Wystan Hugh Auden. 6388-8
Island dogs. Charles G. Bell. 6388-8
"An island etched on a silver sky." Basho (Matsuo Basho) 6027-7
An island fisherman. Katharine (Hinkson) Tynan. 6507-4
The island hawk. Alfred Noyes. 6151-6
"The island lies nine leagues away". Description of the quiet island, fr. The buccaneer. Richard Henry Dana. 6752-2
The island of Blest. Pindar. 6435-3
The island of home. Ira J. Bailey. 6416-7
The island of shadows. Richard Garnett. 6656-9
The island of Skyros. John Masefield. 6474-4
The island of sleep. William Butler Yeats. 6090-0
The island of the blest, fr. Odes. Pindar. 6932-0
The island of the Scots. William Edmonstoune Aytoun. 6948-7,7022-1
Island on the lake. William Wordsworth. 6484-1
Island rose, fr. Two island songs. Hamish Maclaren. 6269-5
An island song. Marjorie L.C. Pickthall. 7012-4
Island tea. William Aspenwall Bradley. 6441-8
Island, E.H.L.
Penny whistle blues. 6287-3
The island, fr. The land. Victoria Mary Sackville-West. 6649-6
The island.. Christopher Morley. 6331-4
The island.. Unknown. 6087-0
An island. John Schaffner. 6979-7
An island. Shawn Wong. 6790-5
The island. George Gordon, 6th Baron Byron. 6945-2,6438-8, 6945-2
The island. Richard Henry Dana. 6385-3,6600-3
The island. Alfred Domett. 6591-0,6592-9
The island. Glenn Ward Dresbach. 6761-1
The island. George Woodcock. 6379-9
The islanders. Rudyard Kipling. 6810-3
Islands of mist. Lauchlan MacLean Watt. 6269-5
The islands of the sea. George Edward Woodberry. 6946-0
The islands. Hilda ("H.D.") Doolittle. 6619-4,6217-2,6019-6,6034-X,6513-9
"Isle after isle with grey empurpled rocks". Charles Mackay. 6997-5
The isle of Achilles. Robert Bridges. 6487-6
"Isle of a summer sea". Cuba. Harvey Rice. 6946-0
"The isle of Imbros, set in turquoise blue". From 'W' beach. Geoffre Dearmer. 7029-9

ISLE

The isle of apple-trees. Fritz S. Burnell. 6784-0
Isle of beauty. Thomas Haynes Bayly. 6543-0,6744-1
The isle of demons, fr. Marguerite. George Martin. 6795-6
The isle of Founts, fr. Lays of many lands. Felicia Dorothea Hemans. 6973-8
The isle of Heather. Murdo Macleod. 6180-X
The isle of Ione. Walter De La Mare. 6596-1
The isle of long ago. Benjamin Franklin Taylor. 6142-7, 6212-1,6565-1,6964-9
The isle of lost dreams. William ("Fiona Macleod") Sharp. 6656-9
The isle of memories. Alfred Noyes. 6151-6
Isle of my heart. Donald A. Mackenzie. 6134-6
The isle of Portland. Alfred Edward Housman. 6491-4
"The isle was barren. Far as hawk may scan". The man digging. Herbert Trench. 6877-4
The isles of Greece. George Gordon, 6th Baron Byron. 6186-9,6208-3,6331-4,6339-X,6481-7,6484-,6301-2,6125-7, 6383-7,6192-3,6199-0,6110 ,6726-3,6023-4,6086-2,6104-4,6252-0,6212 ,6439-6,6639-9,6668-2,6543-0,6723-9
The isles of the blessed, fr. Odes. Pindar. 6987-8
The isles of the sirens. John Henry, Cardinal Newman. 6980-0
The isles: an ode. Sir Charles George Douglas Roberts. 7041-8
The isles. Sir Charles George Douglas Roberts. 6656-9
The islesman's home. Thomas Pattison. 6180-X
Islet the Dachs. George Meredith. 6230-X
The islet. Alfred Lord Tennyson. 6977-0
Islwyn
    The storm, sels. Gwyn Williams (tr.). 6528-7
Ismail. Michael Roberts. 6783-2
Isms. Edward R. Huxley. 6885-5
"Isn't God upon the ocean just the same..." Unknown. 6629-1
"Isn't is a lovely thing". The garden. Clara T. Brown. 6906-1
"Isn't it funny--this fight over money?". Isn't it true! Bernice Gibbs Anderson. 6799-9
"'Isn't this Joseph's son?' -ay, it is he". Jesus the carpenter. Catherine C. Liddell. 6479-5,6656-9,6820-0
Isolate. Portia Martin. 6039-0
Isolation. Matthew Arnold. 6437-X,6110-9,6250-4,6383-7, 6655-0
Isolation. Arthur Hugh Clough. 6437-X
Isolation. Albert Teodor Gellerstedt. 6045-5
Isolation cell poem. J. Charles Green. 6870-7
The isolation of genius. George Gordon, 6th Baron Byron. 6543-0
Isolationist. Alfred Kreymborg. 6561-9
"Isolde, in the story old". A ballade of irresolution. Bert Leston Taylor. 6875-8
Isolt of the white hands, fr. Tristram. Edwin Arlington Robinson. 6984-3
Isosceles [pseud].
    Le derniere chanson. 6817-0
    To Maurya. 6817-0
Israel. John Hay. 6848-0
Israel. William Ellery Leonard. 6532-5
Israel and Hellas. Thomas Edward Brown. 6809-X
Israel Freyer's bid for gold. Edmund Clarence Stedman. 6946-0
"Israel in ancient days". Old-Testament gospel. William Cowper. 6814-6
Israel's lament. Hyman Hurwitz. 6848-0
Israelite graveyard. Cesar Tiempo. 6759-X
Israfel. Edgar Allan Poe. 6527-9,6673-9,6726-3,6732-8,6126-5,6121 ,6008-0,6250-4,6560-0,6288-1,6076-5,6300 , 6467-1,6646-1,6309-8,6006-4,6243-1,6333 ,6077-3,6102-8,6176-1
Israfel. Karl Shapiro. 6483-3
Israfiddlestrings. Unknown. 6089-7,6724-7
Issa
    "Cherry flowers." Lois J. Erickson (tr.). 6027-7
    "Dear little one." Lois J. Erickson (tr.). 6027-7
    "These cherry flowers." Lois J. Erickson (tr.). 6027-7
    "The tree will soon be hewn." Lois J. Erickson (tr.). 6027-7
Issa, sels. Robert Norwood. 6232-6

"Issaker, I'd like to know, what's come across". The church kitten. Louis Eisenbeis. 6924-X
Isthmian ode III. Pindar. 6527-9
It. Albert Bigelow Paine. 6713-1
"It 'pears to me we oughter see". An 'over the mountain' Vermont frock. Daniel L. Cady. 6989-4
"It ain' the ringing of the bell". Back to school. Edgar A. Guest. 6862-6
"It ain't the funniest thing a man can do". The first settler's story. Will Carleton. 6281-4,7041-8,6413-2, 6550-3,6740-9
"It ain't the kid that's sittin' over there". The champion. Berton Braley. 6853-7
"It all began/with my fingers pressing". Loss. Alex Kuo. 6790-5
"It all begins at the end". So it was done. Barry Callaghan. 6767-0
"It autumne was, and on our hemisphere". Song 002 ("It autumne was..."). William Drummond of Hawthornden. 6933-9
"It befell at Martinmas". Unknown. 6111-7,6518-X
"It befell at Martynmas". Captain Car, or Edom O Gordon. Unknown. 6907-X
"It began to snow/'you suspect my silence". Snowfall. Barry Callaghan. 6767-0
"It blew in on the telephone". Private hurricaine. Elizabeth Bartlett. 6792-1
"It calls - it calls to me". The rune of the forest. Gertrude Huntington McGiffert. 6838-3
"It came and went so lightly". The happy pair. Johann Wolfgang von Goethe. 6948-7
"It came so quietly". Resurrection. Ida Norton Munson. 6144-3
It came upon the midnight clear. Edmund Hamilton Sears. 6466-3,6337-3,6129-9,6304-7,6608-9
"It can't be understood" Alfred Kolleritsch. 6769-7
It cannot be. F.E. Maitland. 7031-0
"It cannot be that men who are the seed". Our first century. George Edward Woodberry. 6946-0
"It chanced to me upon a time to sail". My native land. John Boyle O'Reilly. 6858-8
"It chanced when the dance was pealing" Alexey Tolstoy. 6103-6
"It chanceth once to every soul". On the bridge of sighs. Elizabeth Stuart Phelps Ward. 7041-8
"It clings to pine and hemlock boughs". Twilight snow. Rosemary Farrar. 6761-1
It couldn't be done. Edgar A. Guest. 6291-1,6736-0
"It didn't seem important when it happened...". Memory. Edgar A. Guest. 6748-4
"It does not comes/crawling on little cat's...". 27 years of madness. Laurel Ann Bogen. 6998-3
"It does not matter who we love or what we...". Inconsistencies. Michelle Roberts. 6870-7
"It dropped into the well one evening". Lament for lost love. Genaro Estrada. 6759-X
"It embraces the river". Fog. Sylvia Adelman. 6850-2
"It ended, and the morrow brought the task" George Meredith. 6828-6
"It fell about the Lammas tide". Unknown. 6518-X
"It fell about the Martinmas time". Unknown. 6111-7
"It fell on a day, and a bonny summer day". Unknown. 6111-7
"It fell upon the August month". The queen in France. William Edmonstoune Aytoun. 6948-7
"It fell upon us like a crushing blow". Colonel Ellsworth. Richard Henry Stoddard. 6946-0
It finished him. Unknown. 6312-8
"It flatters and deceives thy view". To Demosthenis. Unknown (Greek). 6814-6
"It follows me/fifteen miles-eyes catching...". Lac Courte Orielles: 1936 Phyllis Wolf. 7005-1
"It fortifies my soul to know". With whom is no variableness, neither shadow of turning. Arthur Hugh Clough. 6828-6
It fortifies my soul to know. Arthur Hugh Clough. 6430-2
"It fries in the pan:/the white so tender". Fried egg. N.M. Hoffman. 6857-X
"It fronts upon the city street". The St. Louis slave pen. James Abraham Martling. 6952-5

"It glistened like silver, so sparkling and bright". Ned Harrigan. 6149-4
"It goeth forth, an instrument of power". The newspaper. Thomas Wade. 7009-4
"It got beyond all orders an'..beyond all 'ope". That day. Rudyard Kipling. 6810-3
"It grows in gladness, fair and green". The growing of the Christmas tree. John E. Barrett. 6840-5
"It hangs 'mong a hundred others". The story of the picture. Unknown. 6889-8
"It happened aboot the Middlemas time". Unknown. 6059-5
"It happened in the angel's shadow" Jutta Schutting. 6769-7
"It happened like this - to get..to talking". "The thing that I knew'. Brian ("Korongo") Brooke. 6938-X
It happens often. Edwin Meade Robinson. 6102-8,6076-5
"It has been said, the mind of every man". The swinging branch. Everest Lewin. 6778-6
It has been such a day as that, thou knowest. Philip James Bailey. 6066-8
"It has come at last!". 'Let me into the darkness again'. Gertrude Huntington McGiffert. 6838-3
"It has dawned on me". Flash. Stephen Todd Booker. 6870-7
"It has flowered - fragrant joy". Van Riebeck's rose, sels. Francis Carey ("Jan van Avond") Slater. 6800-6
"It hath come, good Sohemus. 'T hath". Herod and Mariamne. Amelie ("Princess Pierre Troubetzkoy") Rives. 6848-0
"It hath crashed down-the mighty oak". The mighty oak. Theodosia Garrison. 6995-9
"It hath passed, my daughter; fare thee well!". The bride. Unknown. 6752-2
"It holds warmth and security". The flame. Michelle Lee. 6883-9
It hurts! Makeda Zulu. 6883-9
"It is a beauteous evening". Sonnet ("It is a beauteous evening"). William Wordsworth. 6315-2,6129-9
It is a beauteous evening [calm and free]. William Wordsworth. 6122-2,6258-X,6154-0,6332-2,6488-4,6536, 6726-3,6723-9,6645-3,6646-1,6214-8,6252,6371-3,6125-7,6560-0,6199-0,6250-4,6110-9,6196-6,6430-2
"It is a beauteous evening, calm and free". Holy calm. William Wordsworth. 7020-5
"It is a common fate - a woman's lot". The common lot. Ella Wheeler Wilcox. 6956-8
"It is a dreary evening". My journal. Adelaide Anne Procter. 6957-6
"It is a fair death, fighting in the front of battle". Tyrtaeus of Sparta. 6251-2
"It is a fascination she has". Women have their idols goldplated... Anne Donovan. 7018-3
"It is a fearful night". Sonnet ("It is a fearful night"). Semedo. 6732-8
"It is a fearful stake the poet casts". The poet's first essay. Letitia Elizabeth ("L.E.L.") Landon. 6980-0
"It is a huge spider that cannot crawl farther". The spider. Cesar Vallejo. 6759-X
"It is a maxim of much weight". William Cowper. 6814-6
"It is a promise unfulfilled". Fujiwara No Mototoshi. 6852-9
"It is a secret sorrow." Frances Crawford. 6515-5
"It is a small freedom". Minimum security. James Lewisohn. 6870-7
"It is a sorry slight to leave out there". Saint Francis in winter. Ruth Knowles. 6799-9
"It is a summer's gloaming, faint and sweet". Summer gloaming. Charles Tennyson Turner. 7015-9
It is a sweet thing. Percy Bysshe Shelley. 6085-4
"It is a window round and square". Collage of us in May windows. Paul Fericano. 6901-0
"It is a wraith - no mortal haunts my way". Walter De La Mare. 6905-3
"It is almost forgotten - the steeping down...". Death of the grandmother. Gwendolen Haste. 6979-7
"It is alone in solitude we feel". A fragment. Sir Humphry Davy. 6980-0
"It is an aunciert waggonere". The rime of the aunciere waggonere. William Maginn. 6802-2
"It is an autumn in my heart". Recompense. Anna M. Spencer. 6270-9
"It is an honourable thought". Emily Dickinson. 6187-7, 6348-9
It is an illusion, fr. Amours de voyage. Arthur Hugh Clough. 6199-0
"It is as true as strange, else trial feigns" John Davies of Hereford. 6182-6
"It is at morning, twilight they expire". After midnight. Charles Vildrac. 7039-6
"It is best to me that it be so". The pool of pilate. Unknown. 6873-1
"It is better to die, since death comes surely". Sir Hugo's choice. James Jeffrey Roche. 7041-8
"It is but lost labour that ye haste to...". Psalm 127, sel. Bible. 6958-4
"It is Christmas day in the workhouse". Christmas day in the workhouse. George Robert Sims. 6964-9
"It is Christmas Day on the river". Christmas Day at sunset. Jane Broad Cole. 6764-6
"It is cold, dark midnight, yet listen". Homeless. Adelaide Anne Procter. 6957-6
It is coming. M. Florence Mosher. 6617-8
It is common. Unknown. 6273-3
"It is difficult to read". Noisy place. Edgar A. Guest. 6869-3
"It is done. My kettle shall be overturned...". An old man's lamentations. Selma Hamann. 6906-1
It is enough. Esther Freshman. 6750-6
"It is enough of honour for one lifetime". The beloved. Sara Teasdale. 6777-8
"It is enough to love you. Let me be". To Tamaris. Theo. Marzials. 6875-8,6770-0
"It is enough, dear God". Adequacy, fr. Mother-songs. Marian Williams McGaw. 6906-1
"It is God's will". Rebel. Margaret Haynes Foster. 7016-7
It is finished. Horatius Bonar. 6065-X
It is finished. Barney Bush. 7005-1
It is finished. Jonathan Evens. 6065-X
It is finished. Sir Henry Watson. 6065-X
"It is finished". Christina Georgina Rossetti. 6656-9
"It is full strange to him", fr. The city of dreadful-James ("B.V.") Thomson. 6819-7
"It is good to see your face, Brother Skull!". On the study table. Edward Farquhar. 6939-8
It is great for our country to die. James Gates Percival. 6219-9
It is I, be not afraid. Albert Benjamin Simpson. 6065-X
"It is hard oft' times to be good". Look within. Edward R. Huxley. 6885-5
"It is hardly sensuous, but having". How to take off your clothes at a picnic. Bill Manhire. 7018-3
"It is I that am under sorrow at this time". Another song. William Ross. 6845-6
"It is I, America, calling!". A call to arms. Mary Raymond Shipman Andrews. 6946-0
"It is in battle, Antietam, some". The colonel's story. Robert Cameron Rogers. 7022-1
"It is Indiana and we are crying". Indiana. Lori Lubeski. 6857-X
It is known. Unknown. 6530-9
It is late, I can wait. Marianne Moore. 6516-3,6391-8
"It is late, I said: there will be a cold rain". The funeral. Marguerite Young. 6979-7
It is later than you think. Robert Service. 6159-1
"It is like getting married in the rain". Getting rid of the ego. Ken Wainio. 6998-3,6901-0
"It is long since knighthood was in flower". Nineteen-seventeen. Susan Hooker Whitman. 6846-4
"'It is long since we met", she said". One end of love. James Branch Cabell. 7017-5
"It is May among the blossoms but November...". 'And forbid them not'. Benjamin Franklin Taylor. 6815-4
"It is May morning and the birds are singing". Inhibition. Margery Swett Mansfied. 6761-1
It is long waiting. Philip Henry Savage. 6006-4
"It is May - and I am blind". Margery Swett Mansfield. 6839-1
"It is midnight. Hark! the old clock whirs". The dying child. George M. Vickers. 6918-5
"It is midnight.And the mountains that all day". Dunmore. Charles Malam. 7030-2
"It is mighty good to feel". A harvest stiff comes back to

town. Keene Wallis. 6880-4
It is more blessed. Rose Terry Cooke. 6303-9
"It is more blessed." Rose Terry Cooke. 6304-7
"It is morning and I am kneeling". Nunc dimittis. Patrick Lane. 6767-0
"It is morning, Senlin, says, and in..morning". Morning song of Senlin. Conrad Aiken. 6153-2,6808-1,6393-4
"It is most true that eyes are form'd to serve." Sir Philip Sidney. 6645-3
"It is my dream to have you here with me". A voice from the farm. James Whitcomb Riley. 6993-2
"It is my joy in life to find". A prayer ("It is my joy"). Frank Dempster Sherman. 6266-0,6476-0,6654-2
It is my own invention. Charles Lutwidge ("Lewis Carroll") Dodgson. 6732-8
"It is nearly a hundred years ago". The romance of a rose. Nora Perry. 7041-8
"It is never so cold there is no warmth..woods". Winter woods. Anderson M. Scruggs. 6841-3
It is no dream of mine. Henry David Thoreau. 6333-0
"It is no dream! yet haunting visions come". Shadows of recollection. William Edmonstoune Aytoun. 6948-7
"It is no favour, and no charity". Woman's plea for suffrage. Lilian Sauter. 7023-X
"Ut is no longer/that heaviness" Paul Celan. 6769-7
"It is not alone while we live in the light". To Mary. Bernard Barton. 6980-0
"It is not always the doing well". Unknown. 6109-5
"It is not anything he says". Kavin again. Bliss Carman and Richard Hovey. 6890-1
"It is not beauty I demand". George Darley. 6187-7,6046-3
It is not beauty I demand, sels. George Darley. 6545-7
"It is not beauty I demand". Unknown. 6385-3
"It is not death". Sonnet ("It is not death"). Thomas Hood. 6315-2
"It is not death that is bitter...". Unknown. 6251-2
It is not death to die. H. Malan. 6065-X
"It is not death, that sometime in a sigh". Death. Thomas Hood. 6980-0
"It is not death, that sometime in a sigh". Thomas Hood. 6187-7
"It is not death, that sometimes in a sigh". Death. Thomas Hood. 7015-9
"It is not easy for me/to remove my eyes". Borderline. Paul Fericano. 6901-0
"It is not enough". Two motions. A. R. Ammons. 6803-0
It is not finished, Lord. G.A. Studdert-Kennedy. 6144-3, 6335-7
"It is not from his form, in which we trace". Tirocinium: or, a review of schools. William Cowper. 6814-6
"It is not good for man to be alone". Companionship. Mabel W. Arnold. 6799-9
It is not growing like a tree. Ben Jonson. 6134-6,6107-9, 6125-7,6328-4,6473-6,6138-9,6208-3
"It is not Lord the sound of many words". Henry Lok. 6586-4
"It is not in being careful, as mothers are". The going forth. Conrad Aiken. 6761-1
"It is not in her azure eyes". Love's colours. John Kendall. 6760-3
"It is not just because you might be fair". Mother to daughter. Marguerite Steffan. 6750-6
"It is not pleasant to wander". Artist and model, sels. Robert Buchanan. 6934-7
"It is not right for you to know...". Ad leuconoen. Horace. 7039-6
"It is not so much what you say". The tone of the voice. Unknown. 6924-X
"It is not streets where proud-roofed mansions stand". Alcaeus of Mytilene. 6251-2
"It is not sweet content, be sure". In the depths. Arthur Hugh Clough. 6828-6
"It is not that the magnolia tree is not...". The magnolia tree. Marjorie Meeker. 6979-7
"It is not the deep-heaving sigh". The test of friendhsip. James Abraham Martling. 6952-5
"It is not the fear of death". Andre's request to Washington. Nathaniel Parker Willis. 6946-0
"It is not thought. There is not room for...". Last pipe at night. John Maher Murphy. 6761-1

"It is not to be thought of that the flood. William Wordsworth. 6122-2,6323-3,6337-3,6473-6,6086-2,6371-3,6110-9,6250-4,6199-0
"It is not to be thought of that the flood". The British heritage. William Wordsworth. 6793-X
"It is not tragedy to fail, nor yet". Almost attained. John Girdler. 6836-7
"It is not true, this tale". Unknown. 6435-3
"It is not vertue, wisdom, valour, wit". Woman, fr. Samson Agonistes. John Milton. 6933-9
"It is not weariness that lines this face". Beet farmer. Mark Mirich. 6750-6
"It is not what we say or sing". All here. Oliver Wendell Holmes. 6753-0
"It is not with a hope my feeble praise". Hero and Leander. Thomas Hood. 6974-6
It is not yours, O mother, to complain. Robert Louis Stevenson. 6097-8
"It is not/better to be dead". Antother letter to Joseph Bruchac. Jack L. Anderson. 6870-7
"It is of a handsome lady who lived by the seaside". Unknown. 6059-5
"It is of a pretty female". Unknown. 6059-5
"It is only a little twig". The poem. Amy Lowell. 6880-4
"It is only death/That awakens us". Journey. Raymond Thompson. 6870-7
"It is pleasant Easter morning". Easter - 1947. Gladys McKee. 6839-1
"It is pleasant in the forest". Angling. Ada E. Hall. 6818-9
"It is quick, leaping change of Norhthern...". What is the sonnet? Milan E. Hawkins. 6799-9
"It is raining - Wait, do not sleep". Rainy night. Juana de Ibarbourou. 6759-2
It is raining again. Apostolos Melachrinos. 6352-7
"It is raining./The night quietly spreads...". Sound of rain. Yo-han Chu. 6775-1
"It is sad today/And the winds blow wild". Birthday thoughts. Mabel Celia Saunders. 6799-9
"It is said that Miguel de Cervantes". Variation on an old theme. M. A.. 6817-0
"It is she alone that matters". Bouquet of belle scavoir. Wallace Stevens. 6761-1
"It is snowing through the mouth of this...". The library is on fire. Rene Char. 6803-0
"It is so common to be dead". Triolet. Winifred Lucas. 6274-1
"It is so hard that men grow gray". Nothing changes with the birds. Robert P. Tristram Coffin. 7040-X
"It is so long a way that I must go". The pilgrim. Charles M. Luce. 6266-0,6359-4
"It is so long ago; and men well-nigh". The departing of Clote Scarp. Sir Charles George Douglas Roberts. 6795-6
"It is so still that I can hear". Hour before light. Josephine Johnson. 6761-1
It is spring and all is well. Charles Erskine Scott Wood. 6467-1
"It is strange perhaps to think of...". 'Nature'. Brian ("Korongo") Brooke. 6938-X
"It is success that colors all in life". Success ("It is success"). J. Thomson. 6294-6
"It is sultry hot in the chamber small". A night of spring. ? Storm. 6842-1
"It is Sunday afternoon on the Grand Canal...". Seurat. Ira Sadoff. 6966-5
"It is tattered and old, a bunch of shreds". A mother's treasure. John E. Barrett. 6840-5
"It is that death by which we may be...". The night is come. Sir Thomas Browne. 6958-4
"It is the best, erely and late". Be true to your condition in life. John Audelay. 6881-2
"It is the brave that first forget". Soldiers of peace. Bayard Taylor. 6976-2
"It is the caus ,eit is the cause...", fr. Othello. William Shakespeare. 6339-X
It is the day when he was born. Alfred Lord Tennyson. 6543-0
"It is the evening hour; the rapid sky". Francesco Petrarch. 6325-X

"It is the fairest sigh in nature's realms". Morning. Charles Tennyson Turner. 6980-0
It is the following. Ruth Knowles. 6799-9
"It is the hour when from the boughs". Parisina. George Gordon, 6th Baron Byron. 6945-2
"It is the hush of night, and all between". Night, fr. Childe Harold's pilgrimage. George Gordon, 6th Baron Byron. 6315-2
"It is the law of crystals and of souls". Whittier's 'eternal goodness' James Abraham Martling. 6952-5
"It is the little rift within the lute". Alfred Lord Tennyson. 6238-5
"It is the midnight hour - the beauteous sea". Calm as the cloudless heaven. Christopher (John Wilson) North. 6833-2
It is the miller's daughter. Alfred Lord Tennyson. 6187-7, 6328-4,6226-1
"It is the pain, it is the pain, endures". Villanelle. William Empson. 6985-1
"It is the poet Uhland, from whose wreathings". Uhland. William Allen Butler. 6903-7
"It is the Rhine! our mountain vineyards...". Rhine song of the German soldiers after victory. Felicia Dorothea Hemans. 6973-8
"It is the road, the chart". Faith. John Richard Moreland. 6144-3,6039-0,6326-8
It is the season. Robert Louis Stevenson. 6508-2
"It is the season of the sweet wild rose" George Meredith. 6828-6
"It is the small familiar things that hurt". Any wife. Albertine H. Miller. 6750-6
"It is the smoke that makes mine eyelids red". Falstaff's sister. Dorothy Margaret Stuart. 6779-4
"It is the thirty-first of March". Peter Bell: a lyrical ballad. John Hamilton Reynolds. 6802-2
"It is the true star" Cecil Day Lewis. 6072-2
"It is the twilight hour" Twilight. Caroline Elizabeth Sarah Sheridan Norton. 6980-0
"It is thy voice that floats above the din". Sarah Doudney. 6238-5
It is time. Frantisek Halas. 6068-4
It is time to build. Elias Lieberman. 6337-3
"It is time to summon the workers". Summon the workers. Clara Lambert. 6891-X
"It is told in old traditions". How Kuloskap sailed through the cavern of darkness. Unknown (Algonquin Indian). 6864-2
"It is told, in Buddhi-theosophic schools". Transcendentalism. Unknown. 6902-9
It is toward evening. Unknown. 6065-X
"It is true that you say the gods are more use". The choice. Ezra Pound. 6897-9
"It is up with the dawn". Moo bhuachailin ban. Ralph Varian. 6858-8
"It is very aggravating". The truth about Horace. Eugene Field. 6449-5
It is well we cannot see the end. Unknown. 6045-1
It is well with the child. Mrs. Schuyler Van Rensselaer. 6443-4
"It is well, may be so, to bear losses". Joaquin Miller. 6238-5
"It is wisest when the flutes are playing". Nocturne. Patricia Peart. 6764-6
"It is written on the rose". Passing away. Felicia Dorothea Hemans. 6973-8
"It is youth, when the thing that we hear &see". Youth. Edward Farquhar. 6939-8
"It is, methinks, a morning full of fate". Lines, fr. Catiline. Ben Jonson. 6867-7
"It isn't enough that when I go off for...". Alpha the dog. Robert Sward. 6767-0
"It isn't only where the tall wood ferns". Third Avenue. Gordon Lawrence. 6979-7
"It isn't raining rain to me". A song for April. Robert Loveman. 6889-8
"It isn't that I've got a thing agin' you...". The reason why. Katharine H. Terry. 6922-3
"It isn't the thing you do, dear". Margaret Elizabeth Sangster. 6066-8,6226-1
"It isn't the thing you do, my dear". The sin of omission. Margaret Elizabeth Sangster. 6260-1,6303-9,6337-3.6964-9
"It keeps eternal whisperings around". Sonnet ("It keeps"). John Keats. 6547-3
"It kindles my soul." Casimir the Great; King of Poland. 6385-3
"It knows but will not tell". Intimations of mortality. Alice Meynell. 6955-X
"It lay upon a pillow white". A bit of lace. Arthur Hobson Quinn. 6936-3
"It lies around us like a cloud". In the other world. Harriet Beecher Stowe. 6909-6
"It lies not in our power...", fr. Hero and Leander. Christopher Marlowe. 6726-3
"It lies, unwept, between two crowding hills". The deserted city. Edwin Chamberlin. 6906-1
"It listens, huddled in a clump of trees". Old house. Margaret Perkins Briggs. 7038-8
"It looks as if in dreams the soul was free". Dreams. Thomas Edward Brown. 6809-X
"' Josiah said to us It looks like snow,'". Old Josiah predicts. Esther Houghtaling. 6799-9
"It makes a cat-o'-nine-tails simply smile". The cat-o'-nine-tails. J.G. Francis. 6786-7
"It matters not that time has shed". To my father. William Hamilton Hayne. 7017-5
"It matters not to me how rich or poor he be". The friend. Edgar A. Guest. 6869-3
It may be. Percy ("Percy Hemingway") Addleshaw. 6656-9
It may be. Samuel Ellsworth Kiser. 6291-1
"It may be dramatic, it doubtless is dear". A digest of Lord's ---'s evidence. G. J.. 6878-2
"It may be I'm old-fashioned, but the times...". When friends drop in. Edgar A. Guest. 7033-7
"It may be glorious to write". James Russell Lowell. 6238-5
"It may be good, like it who list." Sir Thomas Wyatt. 6584-8
"It may be just the way you have of talking". Confession. Fritz [pseud].. 6817-0
It may be mine. Unknown. 6109-5
"It may be so, good sir, it may be so". To a certain gentleman. Alice Duer Miller. 6880-4
"It may be so; but let the unknown be". Sonnet ("It may be so"). John Masefield. 6338-1
"It may be that he sits so still". Communion. Dorothy P. Albaugh. 6750-6
"It may be that in future years". Lyric ("It may"). Arthur K. Sabin. 6884-7
"It may be that the words I spoke". The heartening. Winifred Webb. 6964-9
"It may be that yours is a powerful land". The heritage. Porsteinn Erlingsson. 6854-5
It may be weeds. Unknown. 6453-1
It may be, mother mine. Roden Noel. 6097-8
"It may not be, because this tranquil hour". Malbay sands, fr. Atlantic coast scenery. Sir Aubrey De Vere. 6997-5
It might have been. A.A. Hopkins. 6407-8
It might have been. Unknown. 6240-7
It must be abstract. Wallace Stevens. 6399-3
"It must be fine to go a fishing". Fishing. Sarah A. Dixon. 6798-0
"It must be havenly to be mysterious". Envy. Winifred White. 6764-6
"It must be magic". Red white & another ism. Harold LaMont Otey. 6870-7
"It must be so - Plato, thou reason'st well", fr. Cato. Joseph Addison. 6934-7
"It must be so - Plato, thou reason'st well". Cato, sels. Joseph Addison. 6879-0
"It must be v ry hard to live to die". To die. John Harolde. 7016-7
"It must have been for one of us, my own". Not thou but I. Philip Bourke Marston. 6879-0
It must have eeen for one of us, my own. Philip Bourke Marston. 6301-2
"It needs all the gaiety/We can give...". They who laugh. Mary Carolyn Davies. 7038-8
"It never comes again." Richard Henry Stoddard. 6302-0,

6358-6,6385-3,6304-7
It never dies. E.O. Jewell. 6097-8
It never pays. Unknown. 6294-6,6530-9
It never rains, but it pours. S.A. (Sarah Annie Shield) Frost. 6851-0
"It often comes into my head". Walter Savage Landor. 6052-8
"It pleased the Lord of Angels". A legend of service. Henry Van Dyke. 6961-4
It rained in the night. Jorge Carrera Andrade. 6759-X
"It rains on my friends' faces". Rain on a battlefield. Yehuda Amichai. 6758-1
'It rains'. Lucy S. Ruggles. 6629-1
"It rests my weary aching eyes." Phoebe Cary. 6225-3
"It rose before us". The wave. Andrew Charles Wehner. 6258-X
"It seemed a paradox, that she whose placid day". Paradox. Magdelen Eden Boyle. 6750-6
"It seemed corrival of the world's great prime". A fallen yew. Francis Thompson. 6828-6,6942-8
"It seemed poor beyond all mockery". The city park. Melrose Pitman. 6906-1
"It seemed so strange to her dead heart". Agnes Miegel. 6643-7
"It seems a marvel when a simple strain". Dixie. Daisy Arnold Maude. 6841-3
It seems but yesterday. William E. Marshall. 6433-7
"It seems but yesterday, my love...". To William - wtitten by a bereaved father. William Oliver Bourne Peabody. 6752-2
"It seems like a dream - that sweet wooing...". Bachelor hall. Eugene Field. 6949-5
"It seems so lonely in the nest". The first fledgling. Emma Tuttle. 6772-7
"It seems that somehow the straps, the...". Losing touch. John L. Kirkhoff. 6857-X
"It seems the snow is falling deeper than God". The lifeguard in the snow. Eugene Ruggles. 6901-0
It seems to me. Edna L. Anderson. 6178-8
"It seems to me a year's revolving". Imperfection. James Abraham Martling. 6952-5
"It seems to me but yesterday". How we played King William. Jeannie Pendleton Ewing. 6928-2
"It semes white and is rede". The sacrament of the altar. Unknown. 6881-2
"It shall be ended, and no victory". You have looked upon the sun. Anne Singleton. 6808-1
"It shall be said I died for Coelia!" William Percy. 6182-6
It shall not be again. Thomas Curtis Clark. 6465-5,6449-3
It shall not matter. Frederic Prokosch. 6781-6
"It should be brief; if lengthy, it will steep". A model sermon. Unknown. 6787-5
t singeth low in every heart. John White Chadwick. 6303-9, 6889-8
"It smells like the stale air in". Cowardliness is a dull black. Kim Fitzgerald. 6883-9
"It snowed today". Fallen riches. Francis H. Deter. 6906-1
It snows. Hannah Flagg Gould. 6131-1
It snows! It snows. Unknown. 6373-X,6131-1
"It so happens I am tired of being a man". Walking around. Pablo (Neftali Ricardo Reyes Basualto) Neruda. 6759-X
"'It so happens that I was born in Cork'". An Irish fantasy. John Franklin Blunt. 6799-9
"It sometimes happens that two friends will meet". Unknown. 6238-5
"It sounds like stories from the land of spirits". Samuel Taylor Coleridge. 6238-5
"It squats in awkward fashion on a china dish". To an heirloom. Ethel Greenfield. 6850-2
"It stands upon a strident thoroughfare". Beauty shop. Mary Brent Whiteside. 6841-3
"It stands where northern willows weep". The queen of Prussia's tomb, fr. Records of woman. Felicia Dorothea Hemans. 6973-8
It started. Jimmy Santiago Baca. 6870-7
"It started early, the attacking trek". Dieppe. Joyce Rowe. 6895-2
"It stood in the cellar low and dim". The apple-barrel.

Edwin L. Sabin. 6820-0
"It surely does you good". The University of Vermont service flag - 1517 stars. Daniel L. Cady. 6988-6
"It takes a crew of fifteen men". Sleepers. E. Merrill Moot. 6880-4
"It takes a heap o' living t' make it home". Home. Edgar A. Guest. 6732-8,6964-9
"It takes a smile to pull you through". A smile and a tear. Stephen Praisner. 6799-9
It takes courage. Charlotte Perkins Stetson Gilman. 6583-X
It takes so little. Ida G. Morris. 6583-X
"It takes two for a kiss". Grief and joy. Frederic Lawrence ("R.L. Paget") Knowles. 6889-8
"It thundered in my dormant heart today". Catastrophic. Clarence LaFayette Stocks. 6799-9
"It tis hir voice, deare mis, sweetest hart." Unknown. 6563-5
"It took three weeks to make them friends". The child and the wren. Edwin John Pratt. 6797-2
"It tossed its head at the wooing breeze". The rose. James Whitcomb Riley. 6992-4
"It trailed on a sheltered hillside". The arbutus. Unknown. 6373-X
"It used to be all so simple". TGG. Jim Holmes. 7003-5
"It vas der goot schkiff Hezberus". 'Der wreck of der Hezberus' before Longfellow. Esse Phoster. 6791-3, 6823-5
"It vas in a half-starved garret-house...". Dot loaf of bread. Carl Pretzel [pseud]. 6791-3
'It war crackit afore.' Gath Brittle. 6687-9
"It was a beauty that I saw". Ben Jonson. 6562-7,6563-5, 6052-8
"It was a bird of paradise". In London town. Mary Elizabeth Coleridge. 6861-8
"It was a brave and jolly wight". The sub-marine. Thomas Hood. 6974-6
"It was a bright and lovely summer's morn". Two pictures. Unknown. 6273-3,6474-4,6964-9
"It was a cold night, I was sleeping". Opportunity. Celestin Pierre Cambiaire. 6826-X
"It was a cough that carried him off,". Unknown. 6722-0
"It was a cove, a huge recess". A mountain solitude. William Wordsworth. 6980-0
"It was a den...", fr. Hyperion. John Keats. 6726-3
"It was a dull day in February". The first maple. Maybelle McLaurin Kinsey. 7016-7
"It was a gallant cavalier". The cavalier's choice. Johann Wolfgang von Goethe. 6948-7
It was a goodly co. Edward Estlin Cummings. 6666-6
"It was a gruesome butcher". The ballad of a butcher and the dear little children. Unknown. 6916-9
"It was a heavenly time of life". The quest. Ellen Mackay Hutchinson Cortissoz. 6873-1
"It was a hunter's tale that rolled like wind". The tall men, sels. Donald Davidson. 7017-5
"It was a jolly mariner!". The sea-spell. Thomas Hood. 6974-6
"It was a jolly miller lived on the river Dee". The jolly miller. James Whitcomb Riley. 6990-8
"It was a king of Yvetot". The king of Yvetot. Pierre Jean de Beranger. 6787-5
"It was a little tonsil". The tonsil's coming-out party. Jean Graham. 6797-2
"It was a Lusitanian lady, and she was lofty..". The departure of King Sebastian. Unknown (Spanish). 6757-3
"It was a lording's ...", fr. The passionate pilgrim. William Shakespeare. 6182-6
"It was a lover and his lass," fr. As you like it. William Shakespeare. 6246-6,6315-2,6395-0,6182-6,6194-X,6191,6317-9,6488-4,6733-6,6138-9,6328-4,6187
It was a May morning. Georges Duhamel. 6351-9
"It was a maid lay sick of love". The sudden burial. Unknown (Greek). 6771-9
"It was a merry company". The wee man. Thomas Hood. 6974-6
"It was a Moorish maiden was sitting by a well". The broken pitcher. William Edmonstoune Aytoun. 6948-7
"It was a most wonderful poem". Crowned. Mary Frances Hill. 6799-9

"It was a night in harvest time". A country courtship. Francis O'Connor. 6916-9
"It was a noble Roman". On Fort Sumter. Unknown. 6946-0
"It was a pretty song of spring". With a difference. Carlone Mischka Roberts. 6889-8
"It was a railway passenger/And he lept out...". Striking. Charles Stuart Calverley. 6440-X,6228-8,6760-3
"It was a robber's daughter, and her name was". Gentle Alice Brown. Sir William Schwenck Gilbert. 6902-9
"It was a robber's daughter...". Gentle Alice Brown. Sir William Schwenck Gilbert. 6911-8
"It was a sad, ay, 'twas a sad farewell". An elegy on parting. James Thomson. 6816-2
"It was a sandy level wherein stood". A fragment ("It was a sandy..."). Alice Cary. 6865-0;6969-X
"It was a sergeant old and gray". Picciola. Robert Henry ("Orpheus C. Kerr") Newell. 6964-9
"It was a silver day". Silver day. Talma Windle Wolfe. 6857-X
"It was a silver sky. Silver". Anatomy of melancholy. Ralph Gustafson. 6767-0
It was a special treat. Luci Tapahonso. 7005-1
"It was a still autumnal day". We walked among the whispering pines. John Henry Boner. 7041-8
"It was a sultry day of summer-time". The Shunamite. Nathaniel Parker Willis. 6848-0
"It was a temple, such as mortal hand". The revolt of Islam, sel. Percy Bysshe Shelley. 6980-0
"It was a time for unravelling". The weaving. V. Valiska Gregory. 6821-9
"It was a time of sadness, and my heart". The changed cross. Unknown. 6909-6
"It was a time when they were afraid of him". Ancestor. Jimmy Santiago Baca. 6870-7
"It was a village built in a green rent". Brothers, and a sermon. Jean Ingelow. 6940-1
"It was a well/Of whitest marble...". The fountain. Samuel Rogers. 6980-0
"It was a white chrysanthemum". Oshi-kochi No Mistune. 6852-9
"It was a' for our rightfu' king". A' for our rightfu' king. Robert Burns. 6934-7
It was a' for our rightfu' king. Robert Burns. 6024-2,6180-X,6086-2
"It was a' for our rightfu' king". Unknown. 6859-6
"It was about the feast of Christmas-tide". The angel. Unknown. 6920-7
"It was after his skull lodged down". The distrust of logic. Toi Derricotte. 7032-9
"It was after the din of the battle". After the battle. V. Stuart Mosby. 6744-1,6167-2,6922-3
It was an April morning. William Wordsworth. 6828-6
"It was an amateur dram. Ass". The amateur Orlando. George Thomas Lanigan. 7025-6
"It was an April morning: fresh and clear". It was an April morning. William Wordsworth. 6828-6
"It was an English ladye bright". Song of Albert Graeme, fr. The lay of the last minstrel. Sir Walter Scott. 6828-6
"It was an early day of spring" Alexey Tolstoy. 6103-6
It was an English lady bright. Sir Walter Scott. 6328-4, 6371-3
"It was an hour of grief and fear". The Cid's deathbed. Felicia Dorothea Hemans. 6973-8
"It was an icy day". Complete destruction. William Carlos Williams. 6808-1
"It was an old, old lady". 'One, two, three'. Henry Cuyler Bunner. 7022-1
"It was an old, old, old, old lady". One, two, three. Henry Cuyler Bunner. 6183-2,6242-3,6289-X,6466-3, 6519-8,6534 ,6135-4,6004-8,6368-3,6456-6,6639-9,6638 ,6632-1,6701-8,6732-8,6964-9
"It was as calm as calm could be". Becalmed. Samuel K. Cowan. 6919-3
"It was as fine a spectacle as any one...see". The Ballotville female convention. Unknown. 6914-2
"It was at a pow wow". Future generation. Nila NorthSun. 7005-1
"It was before Elkin Matthews published...". Rioperoux re-visited. Humbert Wolfe. 6761-1
"It was between two rigs of rye". Unknown. 6059-5
"It was but now their sounding clamours sung". On the crucifixion. Giles (the Younger) Fletcher. 6931-2
"It was but yesterday the children swung". Deserted swing. Gladys Verville Deane. 6764-6
"It was Captain Pierce of the Lion...". The first Thanksgiving. Clinton Scollard. 6946-0
"It was Christmas eve in the year 'fourteen'.". Under the snow. Robert Collyer. 6928-2
"It was Christmas in the city; people hurried". The Christmas angel's message. Clare Beatrice Coffey. 6929-0
"It was dark and cold in the cottage". A legend of the Christ-child. Mary Clarke Huntington. 6807-3
"It was dark in the hall". Phew! Unknown. 6936-3
"It was difficult to work with;..stubborn clay". Garden experience. Edgar A. Guest. 6869-3
"It was down in yonder lowlands a fair damsel...". Unknown. 6059-5
"It was dreary and desolate weather". Childless. Ben Wood Davis. 6918-5
"It was Earl Haldan's daughter". Ballad ("It was Earl Haldan's"). Charles Kingsley. 6239-3
"It was early Sunday morning, in the year..'64". Kearsarge and Alabama. Unknown. 6946-0
"It was early in the season, in the fall...". Unknown. 6059-5
"It was eve in the winter- her reign in the...". The convert's meeting. James Abraham Martling. 6952-5
'It was good for the Hebrew children..." Gilbert Maxwell. 6979-7
"It was in a grocer's window". A simple sign. Unknown. 6922-3
"It was in and about the Martinmas time". Unknown. 6111-7
"It was in London city a rich merchant did dwell". Unknown. 6059-5
"It was in eighteen-hundred — yes — and nine". The benediction. Francois Coppee. 6411-6,6451-5,6576-7, 6610-0,6550-3,6692
"It was in old times...trees composed rhymes". The thistle and the rose. Unknown. 6859-6
"It was in pleasant Derbyshire". Iloihmation. Thomas Edward Brown. 6809-X
"It was in the Californias - beauteous...". Alameda. Mary Stewart. 6928-2
"It was in the days when Culverhouse". Jamie Douglas. Unknown. 6185-0,6410-8,6726-3,6964-9
"It was in the Indian summer-time...". The masher. Charles Godfrey Leland. 7025-6
"It was in the month of November". Fairies and flowers. Celestin Pierre Cambiaire. 6826-X
"It was in the night of a winter mild". Innocents' day. Harriet Eleanor Hamiliton (Baille) King. 6772-7
"It was in the paper years ago; one summer...". A not uncommon case· a melodrama. Jack Anderson. 7003-5
"It was in the town of Liverpool,...month of May' Unknown. 6317-9
"It was just a very". The pixy people. James Whitcomb Riley. 6990-8
"It was just late of Oxford city". Unknown. 6059-5
"It was kept out in the kitchen...". The wood-box. Joseph Crosby Lincoln. 6260-1,6964-9
"It was known by the arduous pupils of...". Cyclical night. Jorge Luis Borges. 6803-0
"It was late summer, and the grass again". The aftermath. Samuel Waddington. 7015-9
"It was late when I came to you, America". American prelude. Axton Clark. 6761-1
"It was less than two thousand we numbered". With corse at Allatoona. Samuel H.M. Byers. 6946-0
"It was like that year and it is the same now". Love song. Harold Vinal. 6761-1
"It was Lilith the wife of Adam". Eden bower. Dante Gabriel Rossetti. 6828-6
"It was many and many a year ago". Andrew M'Crie. Robert Fuller Murray. 6802-2
"It was midnight when I listened". The tyrant and the captive. Adelaide Anne Procter. 6957-6
It was my blood, fr. Lament for my brother. Hans Egon

Holthusen. 6643-7
"It was my choice, it was no chance." Sir Thomas Wyatt. 6584-8
"It was my first/time in Kula". Kula...a homecoming. Diane Mei Lin Mark. 6790-5
"It was my lot of late to travel far". Golden stars. Henry Van Dyke. 6961-4
"It was nearly twelve o'clock...". A finger and a huge, thick thumb. James Norman Hall. 7027-2
"It was needless to say 'twas a glorious day". McFeeter's Fourth. James Whitcomb Riley. 6993-2
"It was night on the deep,and the dancing wave". What the diver saw. Horace B. Durant. 6921-5
"It was no dull though lonely strand". Abertawy. Walter Savage Landor. 6828-6
"It was not anything she said." Unknown. 6225-3
"It was not by vile loitering in ease". The praise of industry, fr. The caste of indolence. James Thomson. 6932-0
"It was not day, and was not night". Ruth and I. Alice Cary. 6969-X
"It was not death, for I stoop up". Emily Dickinson. 6348-9
"It was not in the winter". Ballad ("It was not in the winter"). Thomas Hood. 6271-7,6423-X
It was not in winter. Thomas Hood. 6737-9
"It was not Zeus, I think, made this decree". Sophocles. 6435-3
"It was not like your great and gracious ways!". The angel in the house. Coventry Patmore. 6908-8
"It was not pleasant shoveling the dung". Evening after manure hauling. Byron Herbert Reece. 6761-1
"It was on a September eve". September dream. Celestin Pierre Cambiaire. 6826-X
"It was on July the first". Rough riding at El Caney. John Paul Bocock. 6995-9
"It was on a day when the heather was bloomin'". Unknown. 6059-5
"It was on a Maundy Thursday that our Lord rose". Unknown. 6111-7
"It was on a Monday's morning in eighteen hundred...". Unknown. 6059-5
"It was on a New Year's morning...". Unknown. 6059-5
"It was on last Tuesday's evening at the theater..." Unknown. 6059-5
"It was on the seventeenth, by break of day". The battle of Bunker Hill. Unknown. 6946-0
"It was one of those swell stone churches, Jim". Two boys. Mary E. (Freeman) Wilkins. 6965-7
"It was only a simple ballad". Only a song. Unknown. 6921-5
"It was Pablo who saw him most clearly". Write, do write. Marilyn Chin. 6790-5
"It was Private Blair, of the regulars". Private Blair of the regulars. Clinton Scollard. 6946-0
"It was sad enough, weak enough, mad enough". The going of the battery. Thomas Hardy. 6793-X
"It was sad weather when you went away". At parting. Katharine (Hinkson) Tynan. 7027-2
"It was silent in the street". The mobilization in Brittany. Grace Fallow Norton. 7026-4
"It was so narrow, that two butterflies". The hazel path. Jaroslav Vrchlicky. 6886-3
"It was so quiet you could hear". Walls breathe. Paul Mariah. 6870-7
"It was so still.../Up at dawn and chores...". Tumble-weeds. Nellie Burget Miller. 7038-8
"It was so sweet to see her". A dream. Gertrude Huntington McGiffert. 6838-3
"It was spring". Spring. Rubye Arnold. 7016-7
"It was star-time when he died". Feast of the epiphany. Marion Couthouy Smith. 6995-9
"It was that time of year when green things...". Spring and the angel. Charles Hanson Towne. 6777-8
"It was the calm and silent night!". A Christmas hymn. Alfred Domett. 6820-1
It was the cat, fr. H.M.S. Pinafore. Sir William Schwenck Gilbert. 6120-6
"It was the closing of a summer's day". Karl the martyr. Unknown. 6915-0

"It was the day- the awful day". Sergeant Kirkland. James Abraham Martling. 6952-5
"It was the eve of Christmas day". The snow man. Graham Hill. 6772-7
"It was the evening of the second day". Second evening. Bayard Taylor. 6976-2
"It was the high midsummer, and the sun...". Bullington. Cicely Fox Smith. 6846-4
"It was the kind of house where passersby". House of eyes. Robert P. Tristram Coffin. 7040-X
"It was the king of the goblin crew". King of the goblins. Marian Osborne. 6797-2
"It was the little leaves beside the road". The sceptics. Bliss Carman. 6006-4,6996-7
"It was the May when I was born". Love and fame. Edward Bulwer-Lytton; Baron Lytton. 6980-0
"It was the morning of the first of May". Song ("It was the morning..."). Unknown (Italian). 7039-6
"It was the pleasant harvest-time". The witch's daughter. John Greenleaf Whittier. 6334-6,6412-4,6419-1,6964-9
"It was the south: mid-everything". 'The return to nature'. Alice Meynell. 6955-X
"It was the spring-time in its earliest hour". The sleeper. Unknown. 6752-2
"It was the summer and a sabbath day". Light from above. James Abraham Martling. 6952-5
It was the time of roses. Thomas Hood. 6250-4
"It was the time when children bound to meet". The Switzer's wife, fr. Records of woman. Felicia Dorothea Hemans. 6973-8
"It was the twilight hour". An old man's dreams. Eliza M. Sherman. 6964-9
"It was the very heart of peace that thrilled". Louvain. Laurence Binyon. 7031-0
"It was the very witching time of night". The origin of shoes. Edmund J. Burk. 6936-3
"It was the winter wild...", fr. Hymn ...nativity. John Milton. 6726-3
"It was the year that polio raged". The swimming lesson. Carol Kyle. 6821-9
"It was thick with Prussian troopers...". The battle of Belleau Wood. Edgar A. Guest. 6846-4
"It was twenty and a hundred years, O blue...". Marmara. Clara Barton. 7022-1
"It was when from Spain across the main...". The excommunication of the Cid. Unknown (Spanish). 6757-3
"It was when my songs became quiet". How I came to be a graduate student. Wendy Rose. 7005-1
"It was when the King Rodrigo lost his realm..". The penitence of Don Roderick. Unknown (Spanish). 6757-3
"It was when the trees were leafless...". Like decorations in a nigger cemetery, sels. Wallace Stevens. 6751-4
"It was when/he smoked that first cigarette". Paula's story. Judyth Hill. 6821-9
"It was Wopsenonic, the warrior". Wopsenonic. Louise E.V. Boyd. 6927-4
"It was years ago, and no one knows". An old orchard in winter. Florence Boyce Davis. 7030-2
"It was your way, my dear". Without ceremony. Thomas Hardy. 6879-0,6908-8
"It wasn't lovelight". Goose and the gander. Frances Farfone. 6750-6
"It wasn't so very long ago". 'Hailing the doctor' in Vermont. Daniel L. Cady. 6988-6
"It wasn't what he said or did, nor how". Intangible influence. Leonard Gray. 6764-6
"It wasna from a golden throne". A kiss of the king's hand. Sarah Robertson Matheson. 6873-1
"It waved not through an eastern sky". The palm tree. Felicia Dorothea Hemans. 6980-0
"It wes upon a scere Thorsday that oure Lord". Judas sells his Lord. Unknown. 6881-2
"It western Pennsylvania fair". Unknown. 6059-5
"It whistles and flutes in the twilight". The robin in the square. Arthur Stringer. 6797-2
It will all be right in the morning. Benjamin Franklin Taylor. 6815-4
'It will all be rght in the morning'. John Whitaker Watson. 6774-3

It will be a hard winter. Olive Tilford Dargan. 6619-4
It will be a Kansas year. J.B. Edson. 6615-1
"It will be easy to love you when I am dead". Muna Lee. 6102-8
It will be light this evening. Comtesse de Noailles. 6351-9
It will not last. Laurence Whistler. 6475-2
"It winds across a little hill". The little path. Sallie P. FitzHugh. 6799-9
"It would be a blessing to be blind". Rura cano. Robert P. Tristram Coffin. 7040-X
"It would be lots of fun to be". The only poet. Ruth H. Hausman. 6850-2
"It would have been as fine and brave a deed". 'We'. Amelia Josephine Burr. 7019-1
"It would have been better for us both". Blue eyes. Unknown. 6826-X
"It would never be morning, always evening". Memory of brother Michael. Patrick Kavanagh. 6930-4
"It would not be easy to explain". Late for chores. Glenn Ward Dresbach. 6761-1
"It would take an aniel's eye". Humming-bird. Robert P. Tristram Coffin. 7040-X
"It would take so small a fire to burn me". This April. Bernice Lesbia Kenyon. 7038-8
"It would/Be nice to reach". More tangible. Constance Stern. 6850-2
'It', fr. A session with my uncle Sidney. James Whitcomb Riley. 6091-9
"It's 'out of print' they say". My book. Louis J. Magee. 7004-3
"It's a bonnie, bonnie warl' that we're livin'". The palace o' the king. William Mitchell. 6915-0
"It's a box of furniture in a right angle". Where he hangs his hat. Deborah Lee. 6790-5
"It's a cold, cold blows in from the sea". The three false women of Llanlar. Hermann Hagedorn. 6944-4
It's a far far cry. Patrick MacGill. 6653-4
It's a fib. Elspeth (Elspeth MacDuffie O'Hallowran) 6026-9
It's a gay old world. Unknown. 6889-8,6583-X
"It's a high-falutin'title they have handed us". Soldiers of the soil. Everard Jack Appleton. 6846-4
"It's a long hot walk up Fathead mountain". Hiking up Hieizan with Alam Lau/Buddha's birthday 1974. Garrett Kaoru Hongo. 6790-5
It's a long way to Tipperary. Jack Judge and Harry Williams. 6732-8
"It's a month to-day since they brought me". Nellie's prayer. George Robert Sims. 6924-X
"It's a pretty good world when I figure it...". Riches. Berton Braley. 6853-7
It's a queer time. Robert Graves. 6332-2,6102-8,6542-2
"It's a question of bright stars". Dogwood blossoms. Peter Blue Cloud. 7005-1
It's a short life. Unknown. 6237-7
"It's a tiny noise". Sensitive ears. James Tate. 6998-3
"It's a wonderful world when you sum it all up". A wonderful world. Edgar A. Guest. 6862-6
"It's about time someone ought to". Asshole poem. Jim Holmes. 7003-5
"It's all in the way that you look at the...". The way of the world. Edgar A. Guest. 6862-6
"It's all planned and settled.". Wedding plans. Edgar A. Guest. 6869-3
"It's almost like going to heaven". Waking to fall down the stairs. William Meissner. 6821-9
"It's an ill wind". W.L. Kitchel. 6116-8
"It's an old iron bed". Bed. Charles Simic. 6803-0
"It's April and the snow is sifting down". Contrast. O.E. Enfield. 6799-9
"It's an owercome sooth for age an' youth". Robert Louis Stevenson. 6819-7
"It's autumn-time again". Hereafter. Ronald Lewis Carton. 7027-2
"It's bedtime, and we lock the door". Bedtime. Edgar A. Guest. 7033-7
"It's been three years of this". The divorce. Adrianne Marcus. 6792-1
"'It's better to have loved and lost.'". Purchase. Ruth D. McGinnis. 6750-6

"It's cold and raw the north winds blow". the maid that sold her barley. Unknown. 6930-4
"It's curious whut a sight o' good...". A daily motto. Unknown. 6889-8
It's day in Hopi-land. Jean Allard Jeancon. 6836-7
"It's difficult to write". These triolets! Naomi Rogin. 6850-2
It's dowie in the hint o' hairst, fr. Mary. Hew Ainslie. 6180-X
"It's easy enough to sing paeans". Ella Wheeler Wilcox: Little Tom Tucker. Charles Powell. 6982-7
"It's easy to laugh when the skies are blue". The conqueror. Emil Carl Aurin. 6889-8
"It's easy to talk of the patience of Job". The inventor's wife. Mrs. E.T. Corbett. 6139-7,6416-7,6964-9
"It's everywhere that women fair invite...". Grandma's bombazine. Eugene Field. 6949-5
"It's funny 'bout a feller's hat". A feller's hat. Edgar A. Guest. 7033-7
"It's funny how our ancestors". A Vermont 'donation'. Daniel L. Cady. 6988-6
"It's funny when understanding". A truth. Noah Mitchell. 6870-7
"It's Geordie's now come hereabout". The sow's tail to Geordie. Unknown. 6859-6
"It's gettin' bits o' posies". Sweethearts. Mary Gilmore. 6784-0
"It's getting on to Christmas...". Not a man's job. Edgar A. Guest. 6748-4
"It's going to come out all right-do you know?". Caboose thoughts. Carl Sandburg. 6808-1
It's good to have a mother. Unknown. 6629-1
It's good up here. Anna Akhmatova. 6546-5
It's hame and it's hame. Allan Cunningham. 6240-7
It's hame, and it's hame. Allan Cunningham. 6219-9
It's hard to be good. Unknown. 6670-4
It's hard to say. Berton Braley. 6853-7
"It's hard to see/with mace blown in your eyes". Louie. Paul D. Shiplett. 6870-7
"It's hard to think Claude Lackey has passed". Claude Lackey. Lewis Chesser. 6860-X
"It's ho for the holly and laughter and kisses". The Christmas spirit. Edgar A. Guest. 6862-6
"It's human for a woman". A woman's ways. Edgar A. Guest. 6862-6
It's in the name. Kitty Tsui. 6790-5
"It's Lamkin was a mason good". Unknown. 6518-X
It's Lent. Unknown. 6710-7
"It's joy yo churn on Juney morns". Winter churning in Vermont. Daniel L. Cady. 6988-6
"It's June ag'in, an' in my soul I feel...joy". Picnic-time. Eugene Field. 6949-5
"It's like the sea the way she". One year after. Gary Allan Kizer. 6870-7
"It's little I can tell". The echo in the heart. Henry Van Dyke. 6961-4
It's little for glory I care. Charles Lever. 6930-4
"It's lonesome - sorto' lonesome...". Decoration Day on the place. James Whitcomb Riley. 6892-8
"It's my fear that my wake won't be quiet". A Connachtman. Padraic Colum. 6872-3
"It's no go the merry-go-round, it's no go...". Bagpipe music. Louis MacNeice. 6930-4
"It's not so nice here as it looks". Comfort through a window. Sarah Morgan Bryan Piatt. 7041-8
"It's not the perfect picture that I seek". Through loving eyes. Elna Forsell Pawson. 6857-X
It's not yet time to light the candles. Suk-jung Shin. 6775-1
"It's of a lovely fair maid bewailing in love". Unknown. 6059-5
"It's one o' my idees that men ain't all...". Men and the dreamers. Edgar A. Guest. 6862-6
"'It's only a little grave,' they said". The little grave. Unknown. 6910-X
It's only fair. Berton Braley. 6853-7
"It's pouring outside/thunder and lightning...". Pittsburgh. Stephanie Herbst. 6883-9
"It's raining and the apple tree". Codicil to a will. Nancy McCleery. 6855-3

It's raining down in Georgia. Edith L. Nichols. 6083-8
"It's rather nice on Sunday night". Courting in Vermont. Daniel L. Cady. 6989-4
"It's rose-time here..." Muriel Stuart. 7029-9
"It's seldom comes alone. I've noticed this...". Trouble being friends. Edgar A. Guest. 7033-7
"It's singin' in an' out". Marri'd. Mary Gilmore. 6784-0
"It's sometimes tiresome, you see". A point of view. Ethel M. Kelley. 6798-0
"It's spring at home; I know the signs". Spring. F.M.H. D.. 6846-4
"It's spring now!/And I love it more this...". Comparison. Mary Thomasine Downer. 6818-9
"It's spring on the hill". Autumn in spring. John Summers. 7018-3
"It's strange how little boys' mothers". A bird story. M.E. B.. 6965-7
"It's sugar' time up country...". In sugarin'-time. Helen M. Winslow. 7030-2
"It's Sunday & the sun shines". Anne's curls. Stan Rice. 6901-0
"'It's sure a dreadful story,' the captain...". The direful tale of horror. Berton Braley. 6853-7
"It's sweet to be a dreamer, joy to weave". The dreamer. Beatrice Payne Morgan. 6841-3
"It's tellin' my story, ye're askin'?". Kitty Malone. Kate True. 6825-1
"It's that roustabout, born of a fairy mother". April. Janet Norris Bangs. 6799-9
"It's the business of an uncle...". The busines of an uncle. Edgar A. Guest. 6869-3
"It's the curiousest thing in creation". A old played-out song. James Whitcomb Riley. 6892-8
It's the gypsy in me. Frances Bragan Richman. 6750-6
"It's the long road to Guinea". Guinea. Jacques Roumain. 6759-X
It's the other boys who live afraid. Gene Derwood. 6391-8
It's the syme the whole world over. Unknown. 6237-7
"It's the unheard beat of pulsing earth". Heirs of twilight. Buteau Shock. 6799-9
"It's the winter in the park today, and all...". Ecstasy. Frances Dell Moore. 6799-9
"It's true it can only happen". Night atlas. Luke Breitt. 6792-1
It's vera weel. Wallace Dunbar. 6139-7
"It's very cold, dear Chloe, to me". An Arcadian flirtation. Unknown. 7021-3
"It's very hard! and so it is". Number one. Thomas Hood. 6974-6
"It's very hard! Oh, Dick, my boy". The stage-struck hero. Thomas Hood. 6974-6
It's very unwise to kill the goose. Philip H. Rhinelander. 6722-0
"It's when the birds go piping". The happy household. Eugene Field. 6949-5
"It's wiser being good than bad", fr.Apparent failure. Robert Browning. 6123-0,6102-8
"It/was the". On pines and needles. Jackie Hubenette. 6857-X
Ita, Saint (atr.)
    Jesukin. George Sigerson (tr.). 6930-4
    Saint Ita's fosterling. Robin Flower (tr.). 6930-4
Itahaca. Constantine P. Cavafy. 6352-7
Italia. Oscar Wilde. 6624-0
"Italia! oh, no more Italia now!" Alessandro Marchetti. 6973-8
"Italia! thou, by lavish nature graced". Vincenzo da Filicaja. 6973-8
Italia, io ti saluto! Christina Georgina Rossetti. 6331-4, 6437-X,6123-0,6624-0,6508-2,6655
An Italian donkey. Agnes Kendrick Gray. 6841-3
An Italian garden. Agnes Mary F. ("Madame Duclaux") Robinson. 6872-3
The Italian girl's hymn to the Virgin. Felicia Dorothea Hemans. 6973-8
The Italian in England. Robert Browning. 6473-6,6657-7, 6655-0,6110-9,6430-2,6458 ,6419-1
The Italian in England. Robert Browning. 6828-6
Italian opera. James Miller. 6932-0
Italian poems of John Milton, sels. Agnes Tobin. 6096 X

Italian quatrains. Leonora Speyer. 6038-2
Italian rhapsody, sels. Robert Underwood Johnson. 6624-0, 6439-6
Italian song. Samuel Rogers. 6600-3,6086-2,6250-4,6219-9
"Italians, Magyars, aliens all". Under the tan. Lewis Worthington Smith. 6954-1
The italics are George Macdonald's. Marc Connelly. 6817-0
Italy. Joseph Addison. 6543-0
Italy. Richard Church. 6069-2
Italy. A.W. Hare. 6600-3,6631-3
Italy. Samuel Rogers. 6302-0;6385-3
Italy ("The darling of the earth"). Elizabeth Barrett Browning. 6302-0,6624-0
Italy and Bergamo, sels. Samuel Rogers. 6198-2
Italy and Britain. Joseph Addison. 6932-0
Italy and Switzerland. Oliver Goldsmith. 6302-0
Italy in arms. Clinton Scollard. 7026-4
Italy sweet too! John Keats. 6423-X,6484-1
Italy, fr. A litany of nations. Algernon Charles Swinburne. 6624-0
Italy, fr. De Gustibus. Robert Browning. 6934-7
"Italy, loved of the sun". Pandora. Bayard Taylor. 6976-2
"Italy, my Italy!". Italy, fr. De Gustibus. Robert Browning. 6934-7
Italy, sels. Samuel Rogers. 6832-4
Italy, sels. Samuel Rogers. 6198-2,6543-0
Itasca in October. Nellie Manley Buck. 6342-X
Itching heels. Paul Laurence Dunbar. 6714-X
Ite domun saturae, venit Hesperus. Arthur Hugh Clough. 6378-0,6110-9,6655-0,6656-9
Iter supermum. Arthur Sherburne Hardy. 6309-8
Iteration. Scharmel Iris. 6897-9
"Its babyhood, with cheerful grace". Music. Joshua Freeman Crowell. 6798-0
"Its balmly life the infant blest". Epitaph on an infant. Samuel Taylor Coleridge. 6772-7
"Its deepest song the manor sings". In manor. John Veitch. 6819-7
"Its form half buried in the gathered sands". The Egyptian sphynx. James Abraham Martling. 6952-5
"Its friendship and its carelessness". The path to the woods. Madison Cawein. 6887-1
"Its not that I hate you". A prison bi-centennial address. Pancho Aguila. 6792-1
Its past th green margarine now. Bill Bissett. 7003-5
"Its roof among the stars projected". Phantasus. Arno Holz. 7039-9
"Its roots oiled round about eternity". Each root to separate dwellings led, fr. Tree of time. Gertrude Huntington McGiffert. 6838-3
Itylus. Algernon Charles Swinburne. 6073-0,6198-2,6536-8, 6657-7,6726-3,6250-4,6383-7,6125-7,6508-2,6655-0
Iulus. Eleanor Glenn Wallis. 6388-8
Ivan Ivanovitch. Robert Browning. 6669-0
Ivan the csar. Felicia Dorothea Hemans. 6973-8
Ivan the Czar. Felicia Dorothea Hemans. 6928-2
Ivanov, Vyacheslav
    Beauty's nomads. Cecil Maurice Bowra (tr.). 6103-6
    Complaint. Cecil Maurice Bowra (tr.). 6103-6
    The holy rose. Babette Deutsch and Avrahm Yarmolinsky (tr.). 7039-6
    The road to Emmanus. Cecil Maurice Bowra (tr.). 6103-6
Ives. Richard Eberhart. 6803-0
Ives, Alice E.
    Delsarte girl. 6698-4
Ivey, Sam Anthony
    "You came last night." 6750-6
Ivinghow hill. George Robins. 7020-5
The ivory cradle. Auguste Angellier. 6961-4
The ivory crucifix. George Henry Miles. 6674-7
The ivory gate. Mortimer Collins. 6656-9
"An ivory tower leans against the wind". From an ivory tower. Helen Frith Stickney. 6979-7
Ivory, coral, brass. Jessie Welborn Smith. 7038-8
Ivry. Thomas Babington Macaulay, 1st Baron Macaulay. 6552-X,6239-3,6014-5,6087-0,6479-5,6732 ,6656-9,6639-9, 6383-7,6219-9,6263-6,6267
Ivy. Edgar Fawcett. 7041-8
The ivy and the ash. Herbert Read. 6391-8
Ivy chief of trees it is. Unknown. 6756-5

The ivy green. Charles Dickens. 6049-8,6240-7,6302-0,6385-
   3,6479-5,6889 ,6486-8,6250-4,6639-9,6219-9,6457-4,
   6658 ,6934-7
"The ivy is green along the forest path". Landscape. Suk-
   jung Shin. 6775-1
The ivy leaf. Helen Gray Cone. 6847-2
Ivy ode, '89. Edward Christman Knight. 6936-3
Ivy poem. Lo Amy Heater. 6717-4
Ivy poem. Unknown. 6156-7
Ivy song. Felicia Dorothea Hemans. 6973-8
Ivy song. Unknown. 6156-7
"An ivy spray in my hand I hold". The clocks of
   Kenilworth. Hezekiah Butterworth. 7041-8
"Ivy, chefe of trees is". In praise of ivy. Unknown. 6881-
   2
The ivy-song. Felicia Dorothea Hemans. 6973-8
The ivy. Henry Burton. 6049-8
Iyad
   Corn in the wind. A.J. Arberry (tr.). 6362-4
Iye-taka
   "The twilight dim, the gentle breeze". William N.
      Porter (tr.). 6852-9
Izan
   A homeless beggar. Lois J. Erickson (tr.). 6027-5
Izard, Forrest
   The art of our necessities is strange. 6722-0
Izumi Shikibu
   "My life is drawing to a close". William N. Porter
      (tr.). 6852-9

"J'ai dit a mon coeur, a mon faible coeur". Chanson ("J'ai
   dit"). Alfred de Musset. 6801-4
"J'ai perdu ma force et ma vie". Tristesse. Alfred de
   Musset. 6801-4
"J'aime le son du cor, le soir, au fond des...". Le cor.
   Alfred de Vigny. 6801-4
"J'aime le souvenir de ces epoque nues" Charles
   Baudelaire. 6801-4
J'aspire. William Kimball Flaceus. 6396-9
"J'aurais pu dire mon amour". Odelette. Henri de Regnier.
   6801-4
J.
   An elfin cruise. 6116-8
   If. 6118-4
J. K. Berton Braley. 6853-7
J.,A.
   The muffin-man. 6320-X
J.,G.
   A digest of Lord's ---'s evidence. 6878-2
J.,H.
   Sometimes, you stars. 6662-3
J.,W.P.
   The French market. 6676-3
J.A.G.. Julia Ward Howe. 6946-0
J.D.R.. Oliver Wendell Holmes. 6126-5,6288-1
J.S.. W.R. Moses. 6640-2
J.S. Mill. Edmund Clerihew Bentley. 6089-7,6722-0
Jaap, Alexander Hay
   A music lesson. 6656-9
Jabberwocky. Charles Lutwidge ("Lewis Carroll") Dodgson.
   6732-8,6089-7,6488-4,6527-9,6534-1,6375-6,6026-9,
   6301-2,6656-9,6723-9
The jaberwocky of authors. Harry Persons Taber. 6089-7
Jabson, Edith
   Four songs. 6039-0
Jacet Leo XIII. John Banister Tabb. 6096 X
Jacinto, Jaime
   The beads. 6790-5
   The fire breather, Mexico City. 6790-5
   Looking for Buddha. 6790-5
   Reflections on the death of a parrot. 6790-5
Jack. Edward Verrall Lucas. 6423-X
Jack. Frederick George Scott. 6797-2
Jack. F.M. Stanley. 6451-5
Jack. Unknown. 6928-2
Jack a Nory. Mother Goose. 6135-4
Jack a Nory, fr. Mother Goose. Unknown. 6401-9

Jack abroad, and Jill at home. William Brighty Rands. 6134-
   6
Jack and I. Unknown. 6929-0
Jack and Jill. Mother Goose. 6135-4
Jack and Jill ("Here is the tale..."). Anthony C. Deane.
   6440-X
Jack and Jill ("Their pail they must fill"). Charles
   Battell Loomis. 6440-X
Jack and Jill ("What moan is made of the mountain...").
   Elizabeth Cavazza. 6440-X
Jack and Jill in variations. C. N. 6889-8
Jack and Jill went up the hill. Mother Goose. 6363-2,6401-
   9,6452-3,6466-3
Jack and Joan. Matthew Prior. 6278-4
Jack and Joan [they think no ill]. Thomas Campion. 6344-9,
   6339-X,6187-7,6194-X,6250-4,6383-7,6668-2,6228-8
"Jack and Joan they think no ill". Song ("Jack and Joan").
   Thomas Campion. 6436-1
"Jack Newman was in love; a common case". Love and law.
   John Godfrey Saxe. 6878-2
Jack and me. George A. Baker. 6517-1
Jack and Roger. Benjamin Franklin. 6125-7
Jack at the opera. Charles Dibdin. 7025-6
"Jack be nimble". Mother Goose. 6363-2,6466-3
"Jack being weary he hung down his head". Unknown. 6059-5
Jack Creamer. James Jeffrey Roche. 6579-1
Jack Donahue. Unknown. 6057-9,6003-X,6003-X
Jack Frenchman's lamentation. Unknown. 6157-5
Jack Frost. William Cullen Bryant. 6242-3
Jack Frost. Helen Bayley Davis. 6891-X
Jack Frost. Hannah Flagg Gould. 6127-3,6519-8,6456-6
Jack Frost. Cicely E. Pike. 6937-1
Jack Frost. Gabriel (Thomas Nicoll Hepburn) Setoun. 6105-2,
   6132-X,6242-3,6401-9,6135-4
Jack Frost. Celia Thaxter. 6612-7,6623-2
Jack Frost. Unknown. 6312-8,6373-X,6529-5,6706-9
Jack Frost's little sister. Carrie W. Bronson. 6713-1
Jack Grey. Emma Celia & Lizzie J. Rook. 6137-0
Jack Hall. Thomas Hood. 6974-6
Jack Horner. Mother Goose. 6401-9,6452-3,6135-4
Jack Horner [for grown people]. Unknown. 6909-6
Jack in the pulpit. Unknown. 6127-3
Jack in the pulpit. John Greenleaf Whittier. 6049-8,6373-X
Jack London and O'Henry. Carl Sandburg. 6345-4
Jack O'Diamonds. Unknown. 6732-8
Jack Riley. Unknown. 6003-X
Jack Robinson. Thomas Hudson. 6547-3
Jack Sheppard. Unknown. 6057-9
"Jack Sprat could eat no fat". Mother Goose. 6363-2,6466-3,
   6452-3
"Jack Sprat could eat no fat." Mother Goose. 6739-5
Jack Spratt et ux. Winfield Townley Scott. 6017-X
Jack Tar. E. Jacot. 6937-1
"Jack on my queen...Oh dear, I will forget". Solitaire.
   Florence Luft. 6850-2
Jack the Evangelist. Unknown. 6451-5
Jack the piper. Unknown. 6125-7
Jack went a-sailing. Unknown. 6058-7
Jack Williams. Unknown. 6057-9,6058-7,6003-X,6003-X
Jack's fidelity. Charles Dibdin. 6833-2
Jack's second trial. Roy Farrell Green. 6697-6
Jack's valentine. Unknown. 6426-4
Jack, Annie L.
   'Tatts'. 6965-7
Jack, thou'rt a toper. John Fletcher. 6328-4
Jack-o'-lantern. Thomas N. Weaver. 6696-8
The jackal, leopard, and other beasts. John Gay. 6972-X
"The jackals howl, the serpents hiss". Elegy. Arthur
   Guiterman. 6089-7
Jackaro. Unknown. 6281-4
The jackdaw of Rheims. Richard Harris ("Thomas Ingoldsby")
   Barham. 6064-1,6089-7,6290-3,6302-0,6385-3,6473 ,
   6464-7,6656-9,6808-1,6600-3,6732-8
The jackdaw. Vincent Bourne. 6814-6
The jackdaw. William Cowper. 6874-X
The jackdaw. William Cowper. 6473-6,6328-4,6808-1,6092-7,
   6383-7,6153
"Jacke took his pype and began to blowe". The dancing
   friar. Unknown. 6959-2
The jacket of gray. Caroline A. Ball. 6074-9

JACKET

The jacket. Rudyard Kipling. 6810-3
Jackie Faa. Unknown. 6125-7
The jackpot. Eugene Fitch Ware. 7012-4
Jacks, Olive Cecilia
    The offering. 6053-6,6337-3,6053-6,6337-3
Jackson at New Orleans. Wallace Rice. 6946-0
Jackson at New Orleans. Wallace Rice. 6820-0
"Jackson at his counter packing tea". The tea trader. Daniel Henderson. 6750-6
Jackson state prison (with a touch of Shakespeare) Leon Baker. 6870-7
Jackson, A.V. Williams (tr.)
    The dream of Dakiki. Firdusi] (Abul Kasin Mansur) Firdausi [or Firdawsi, 6730-1
    Lament in old age. Rudagi, 6448-5
    Zoraster devoutly questions Ormazd. Zoraster, 6730-1
Jackson, Ada
    Again the story is told. 6337-3
Jackson, Catharine Emma
    Piping. 6032-2,6032-3
Jackson, Corinne Huntington
    Fleur de lys. 6799-9
Jackson, E. Dudley
    Miriam. 6848-0
Jackson, E. Maude
    A floral birthday greeting. 6661-5
Jackson, E. Stanway
    Bo's'n Jack of the "Albatross". 6417-5
    The dynamiter's daughter. 6922-3
    The dynamiter's daughter. 6744-1
    The wreck of the Mary Wiley. 6923-1
Jackson, Edgar
    The hunter sees what is there. 6870-7
    Magic word. 6870-7
    Self-portrait. 6870-7
    The sinew of our dreams. 6870-7
    Three songs. 6870-7
Jackson, Frederick
    Rain song. 6937-1
Jackson, George Anson
    Legend of Iyob the upright. 6848-0
Jackson, Hardy
    The song of the headlight. 6744-1
Jackson, Helen Hunt
    Arbutus. 6049-8
    Ariadne's farewell. 6438-8
    At last. 7041-8
    Avalanches. 7041-8
    Avalanches. 6749-2
    Ballad of the gold country. 6241-5
    Best. 6632-1
    Bon voyage. 7041-8
    Burnt ships. 6066-8
    Cheyenne mountain. 7041-8
    Christmas night in Saint Peter's. 7041-8
    A Christmas symphony. 7041-8
    Coronation. 6431-0,6309-8,6467-1,6385-3,6600-3,6632-1, 6239-3,6243-1,6438-8,6219-9
    Danger. 7041-8
    Danger. 6754-9
    The day-star in the east. 6162-1
    Dedication. 7041-8
    Doubt. 6303-9,6730-1
    Down to sleep. 6239-3,6212-1,6456-6
    A dream. 6754-9
    Emigravit. 6431-0
    Esther. 6848-0
    The fir-tree and the brook. 7041-8
    Forgiven. 6066-8
    Fra Luigi's marriage. 6676-3
    Gondolieds. 6243-1
    Habeas corpus. 7041-8
    Habeas corpus. 6102-8,6730-1,6431-0,6300-4,6076-5
    "I cannot think but God must know." 6066-8
    Joy. 6438-8
    Land. 7041-8
    A last prayer. 7041-8
    A last prayer. 6337-3,6512-0,6431-0
    Last words. 6836-7
    Like God's love. 6097-8
    Love's fulfilling. 6620-8,6066-8
    May. 7041-8
    Mordecai. 6848-0,7041-8
    Morning-glory. 6429-9,6321-7
    My legacy. 6438-8,6240-7,6385-3
    My strawberry. 6243-1,6473-6
    My tenants. 7041-8
    Not as I will. 6836-7
    October's bright blue weather. 6162-1,6239-3,6373-X, 6478-7,6499-X,6623-2,6456-6
    "One day at a time!" 6109-5
    The parable of St. Christopher, fr. The golden legend. 6614-3,6131-1
    The pass of Ampezzo. 6749-2
    The poet's forge. 7041-8
    Poppies in the wheat. 6624-0,6076-5,6431-0,6300-4,6467-1,6102
    Refrain. 7041-8
    Return to the hills. 6836-7
    Sail east, sail west. 6097-8
    Sealed orders. 7041-8
    September. 6449-3,6135-4,6424-8,6456-6,6373-X,6401-9, 6465-5,6519-8,6623-2
    A song of clover. 6239-X,6373-X,6457-4
    Spinning. 6006-4,6162-1,6271-7,6309-8
    Thought. 6438-8
    Thought ("O messenger, art thou the king, or I?"). 6243-1
    Torcello. 6624-0
    Transplanted. 6177-X
    Two truths. 6220-8,6441-8,6632-1,6243-1,6066-8,6321-7, 6429-9,6429-9
    Vanity f vanities. 7041-8
    Vashti. 6848-0
    The way to sing. 6600-3
    "When the baby died" 7041-8
    When the kings come. 7041-8
    "When the tide comes in" 7041-8
    When the baby died. 6632-1
    A woman's death-wound. 6066-8
Jackson, Henry R.
    The live oak. 6049-8
    My wife and child. 6410-8,6481-7
Jackson, Kenneth (tr.)
    Arran. Unknown (Irish), 6125-7
    Winter. Unknown (Welsh), 6528-7
Jackson, Leroy F.
    The candle. 6466-3
    Fun. 6497-3
    The house beside the mill. 6496-5
Jackson, M. Walthall
    Sonnet. 6799-9
Jackson, Marsha Ann
    In between time (transcience). 7024-8
    Tears and a dream. 7024-8
Jackson, Maud Frazer
    Faith. 6337-3
Jackson, Opal Louise
    An idyll. 6249-0
Jackson, Peter
    Afrikaans homestead. 6788-3
    At the grave of Cecil Rhodes. 6788-3
    Dombashawa. 6788-3
    Grey Zimbabwe. 6788-3
    In loco. 6788-3
Jackson, R. M.
    Pyrrhic dancers. 6959-2
Jackson, Richard A.
    An incomplete revelation. 6415-9
Jackson, Schuyler B.
    Funeral. 6777-8
Jackson, Thomas Jonathan ("Stonewall")
    My wife and child. 6385-3
Jackson, Winifred Virginia
    And one is two? 6039-0
    Black Aiken's lot. 6038-2
    Brandy pond. 6039-0
    Cross-currents. 6762-X
    Dust-song. 6037-4
    Earth-breaths. 6038-2

Fallen fences. 6762-X
The farewell. 6762-X
Finality. 6076-5
Hands. 6038-2
Heritage. 6036-6
In April. 6036-6
In Moreh's wood. 6038-2
Makin' rhymes. 6039-0
Midnight at the mill. 6039-0
Miss Doane. 6762-X
The northwest corner. 6036-6
Poor river drivers. 6039-0
The purchase. 6035-8
Red winds. 6037-4
She told Mary. 6038-2
The sin. 6037-4
Strange paths. 6037-4
Tenants. 6039-0
Threads. 6037-4
Under-currents. 6036-6
Wimin's work. 6039-0
"Jacky, come give me thy fiddle". Unknown. 6904-5
Jacob. Phoebe Cary. 6089-7,6440-X
Jacob. Arthur Hugh Clough. 6848-0
Jacob. George Croly. 6848-0
Jacob and Pharaoh. James Grahame. 6848-0
Jacob and Rachel. George Crabbe. 6848-0
Jacob Omnium's hoss. William Makepeace Thackeray. 6278-4
Jacob Tonson, his publisher. John Dryden. 6125-7
Jacob's dream. George Croly. 6980-0
Jacob's dream. S. D. 6848-0
Jacob's ladder. Unknown (Negro spiritual) 6337-3
Jacob's wives. Arthur Hugh Clough. 6848-0
Jacob, Max
    The blind lady. 6351-9
    The infant Moses. Cecily Mackworth (tr.). 6343-8
    Villonelle. 6351-9
Jacob, Violet
    The Gowk. 6477-9
    The howe o' the mearns. 6395-0
    The northern lights. 6269-5
    The rowan. 6269-5
    Tam i the kirk. 6845-6
    Tam i' the Kirk. 6477-9,6269-5,6506-6
    The twa weelums. 6474-4
Jacob, Zerea
    Salutation. F. Baetman (tr.). 6282-2
The **Jacobin** of Paris. Viscount Strangford; George Sydney Smythe. 7009-4
The **Jacobite** on Tower hill. George Walter Thornbury. 6188-5,6656-9
Jacobite song. Algernon Charles Swinburne. 6732-8
Jacobite toast. John Byrom. 6427-2,6733-6,6092-7,6219-9
A **Jacobite**'s epitaph. Thomas Babington Macaulay, 1st Baron Macaulay. 6323-3,6250-4,6153-2,6322-5,6668-2
A **Jacobite**'s exile. Algernon Charles Swinburne. 6427-2,6437-X,6508-2,6322-5
The **Jacobite**'s pledge. Allan Ramsay. 6859-6
Jacobs, David Morrison
    Shall I forget? 6800-6
    Veld, sels. 6800-6
Jacobs, Elise Jean
    A call to youth. 6847-2
    The flame. 6847-2
    Judgment. 6847-2
    Pioneers. 6847-2
Jacobs, Florence B.
    Not wholly chained. 6750-6
Jacobs, Leland B.
    How to catch a bird. 6510-4
Jacobs, Maria
    Just war. 6767-0
Jacobs, P.L.
    Abbreviated rumination. 6870-7
    Electrocution script. 6870-7
    Fish story. 6870-7
    Obligatory love poem. 6870-7
    Old man Hall. 6870-7
    Safety or something. 6870-7
Jacobs, Sarah S.
    The changeless world. 6049-8
Jacobsen, Jens Peter
    Dream! Charles Wharton Stork (tr.). 6555-4
    In the moonlight. Charles Wharton Stork (tr.). 6555-4
    Irmeline rose. Charles Wharton Stork (tr.). 6555-4
    The moment inexpressible. Charles Wharton Stork (tr.). 6555-4
    No more than a dream. Charles Wharton Stork (tr.). 6555-4
    Silken shoe upon golden last. Charles Wharton Stork (tr.). 6555-4
Jacobsen, Josephine
    Augury. 6839-1
    The eyes of children at the brinkof the sea's grasp. 6388-8
    For a dancer. 6979-7
    Midnight Eden. 6979-7
    Mollesse. 6388-8
    Night city. 6761-1
    Short short story. 6388-8
Jacobson, Ethel
    Carefully. 6750-6
Jacoby Jr., Grover I.
    The golden telegram. 6316-0
    Joy's prisoner. 6316-0
    Loud intersection. 6316-0
    The target. 6316-0
Jacopone da Todi (Jacobus de Benedictus)
    Stabat mater. 6730-1,6727-1
    Stabat mater. Aubrey Thomas De Vere (tr.). 6282-2
    Stabat mater dolorosa. Abraham Coles (tr.). 6302-0
    To Jesus. 6337-3
Jacot, E.
    Jack Tar. 6937-1
    The tale of a star. 6937-1
Jacque, George
    The moon and the child. 6743-3
Jacqueminots. John Boyle O'Reilly. 7041-8
Jacqueminots. John Boyle O'Reilly. 6320-9
The **jacquerie**, sels. Sidney Lanier. 6008-0
Jacques Cartier. Thomas D'Arcy McGee. 6433-7,6591-0
Jacques Tahareau, 1530. Andrew Lang. 6771-9
Jacques Tahureau. Andrew Lang. 6879-0
Jacques, Edna
    The Red Cross. 6465-5
Jacques, M.J.
    Great-grandmother's garden. 6373-X
Jacquet, John
    Oh, say, what is truth? 6889-8
Jade and bronze. Robert Conine. 6397-7
A **jade** relents. Francis Paxton. 6397-7
"The **jaded** light of late July". The new millennium. Andrew Lang. 6987-8
Jaeck, Emma Gertrude
    Evening song. 6799-9
    Maytime. 6799-9
Jaelousy. Trang Thai. 6883-9
The **Jaffa** and Jerusalem railway. Eugene Field. 6949-5
Jaffar. Leigh Hunt. 6085-4,6102-8,6133-8,6271-7,6294-6,6302-,6370-5,6385-3,6552-X,6605-4,6614-3,6661-,6732-8,6424-8,6639-9
"A **jagged** line of trees in grayish green". Fugue. Marjorie L. Wolfe. 6818-9
"The **jagged** thorns have stabbed my flesh". Ascent. Melba Williams. 6906-1
Jago, Richard
    Absence. 6102-8,6086-2,6383-7
    The blackbirds: an elegy. 6943-6
    The swallows. 6943-6
    With leaden foot time creeps along. 6092-7
"The **jail** was built by workers for the friends". The county jail. Stanley Boone. 6880-4
Jailhouse lawyers. Robert B. Smith. 6510-4
"**Jailhouse** murder/rarely carries more". Wire monkey. Paul D. Shiplett. 6870-7
Jailless crimes. Unknown. 6178-8
Jaimson, Elizabeth
    The cloud child. 6130-3
Jakeman, Adelbert M.
    New England covered bridge. 6894-4

Jakeway, H.W.
    The autograph book of blue. 6688-7
Jaksic, Djura
    Where I... 6765-4
Jaku-ren
    "The rain, which fell from passing showers". William N. Porter (tr.). 6852-9
The jam-pot.. Rudyard Kipling. 6440-X
Jamaica pond at night. Mary A. Flynn. 6894-4
"Jamais elle ne raille,/Etant un calme esprit". Chanson d'autrefois. Victor Hugo. 6801-4
Jamal, Yasmeen
    All that jazz. 6870-7
    Canteen pimpin' 6870-7
    Did ya hear? 6870-7
    The gate. 6870-7
    "I bet God understands about givin up five" 6870-7
Jamee
    True friendship. William Rounseville Alger (tr.). 6085-4
James I; King of Scotland
    "The azured vault, the crystal circles bright" 6182-6
    The coming of love, fr. The kingis quhair. 6845-6
    The dawn of love. 6180-X
    Description of his prison garden. fr. The king's quair. 6649-6
    Godspeed to his book. 6659-3
    Good counsel. 6180-X
    The great change. 6186-9
    Heaven and earth. 6125-7
    The kingis quair, sels. 6193-1,6378-0,6301-2,6649-6, 6193-1
    The Kingis quair. 6198-2
    A May burden. 6943-6
    Sonnet ("God gives not kings"). 6934-7
James I; King of Scotland (tr.)
    Psalm 029. Bible, 6848-0
James V; King of Scotland
    The Gaberlunzie man. 6328-4
    The jolly beggar. 6157-5,6328-4
James and the shoulder of mutton. Ann and Jane Taylor. 6105-2
James Bird. Unknown. 6058-7,6061-7,6003-X
James Buchanan. James Abraham Martling. 6952-5
James Fitz-James and Ellen. Sir Walter Scott. 6302-0
James Gerard. Paul D. Shiplett. 6870-7
James Grant. Unknown. 6185-0
James Harris (The daemon lover) Unknown. 6058-7,6185-0
James Hatley. Unknown. 6185-0
James Henry in school. Emily Selinger. 6688-7
James IV. Robert Greene. 6186-9
James IV at Flodden. William Edmonstoune Aytoun. 6046-3
James Lee's wife. Robert Browning. 6204-0
James Lee's wife, sels. Robert Browning. 6199-0,6560-0
James McCosh. Robert ("Droch") Bridges. 6983-5
James Melville's child. Mrs. A.S. Menteath. 6219-9
James Munks's confession. Unknown. 6058-7
James Russell Lowell. John Greenleaf Whittier. 6820-0
James Russell Lowell. John Greenleaf Whittier. 6126-5
James Russell Lowell, 1819-1891. Oliver Wendell Holmes. 6126-5
James Russell Lowell, sels. Oliver Wendell Holmes. 6820-0
James Whaland. Unknown. 6281-4
James Whitcomb Riley. Robert J. Burdette. 6588-0
James, Charles
    Arise, ye men of strength and might. 6274-1
    A thought from Nietzsche. 6274-1
    Where the mountain sips the sea. 6274-1
James, D.L.
    Isaac Walton's prayer. 6118-4
James, Fleming
    Johnston at Shiloh. 6062-5
James, Gwennie
    Escape. 6042-0
James, Jennie M.
    My own. 6764-6
James, Judith
    Porphyrogne. 6038-2
James, Mary Belden
    The fishermen sing. 6847-2
    King of a king. 6847-2
    'Yea, a sword shall pierce through thy own soul...' 6847-2
James, Paul Moon
    The beacon. 6385-3
James, Robert
    To the modern battleship. 6274-1
James, Robert W.
    Mother. 6799-9
James, Roy Walter
    Vanishing joy. 6818-9
James, Shirley
    Death the leveller. 6600-3
James, Thomas
    Lines on his companions who died. 6563-5
James, Thomas D.
    What is that to thee. 67441-1,6408-6
James, Tom
    The bottom of the car. 6149-4
    The draped charter. 6149-4
    The man in the big high coal. 6149-4
James, William
    In Panther Gorge. 6253-9
Jameson, Anna
    Take me, mother earth. 6656-9
The Jamestown flood. Unknown. 6003-X
Jami
    Morning air. Sir William Jones (tr.). 6448-5
    Salaman and Absal. Edward Fitzgerald (tr.). 6448-5
    Sequence. A.J. Arberry (tr.). 6448-5
    Solitude. S. Weston (tr.). 6448-5
    Tears. S. Weston (tr.). 6448-5
Jamie. Robert C.V. Meyers. 6415-9,6167-2,6573-2
Jamie Douglas. Unknown. 6185-0,6410-8,6726-3,6964-9
Jamie Telfer in the fair dodhead. Unknown. 6185-0,6180-X
Jamie the rover. Unknown. 6859-6
Jamie's on the stormy sea. David Macbeth Moir. 6385-3
Jamie, the gentleman. Mabel C. Dowd. 6965-7
Jamieson, Iris
    Letter from Alice. 6750-6
    Understanding. 6750-6
Jamieson, Robert
    My wife's a winsome wee thing. 6180-X
    The queen lilt. 6960-6
Jamieson, Robert (tr.)
    Ballad: The mer-man, and Marstig's daughter. Unknown (Danish), 7039-6
Jamison, Elizabeth
    Trouble in the tree-top. 6130-3
Jamison, Roscoe C.
    Negro soldiers. 6031-5
Jammes, Francis
    Amsterdam. Jethro Bithell (tr.). 7039-6
    The child reads an almanac. Ludwig Lewisohn (tr.). 7039-6
    The child reads an almanac. 6351-9
    The dining room. 6351-9
    Prayer that an infant may not die. 6351-9
    Prayer that an infant may not die. Joseph T. Shipley (tr.). 6351-9
    Prayer to go to paradise with the asses. 6351-9
    Prayer to go to paradise with the asses. Jethro Bithell (tr.). 7039-6
    Prayer to go to paradise with the asses. Joseph T. Shipley (tr.). 6351-9
    Prayer to go to paradise with the donkeys. Vernon Watkins (tr.). 6343-8
    That thou art poor. 6102-8
    We see, when autumn comes. 6351-9
    When you elect to call me, God, O call. Alan Conder (tr.). 6317-9
"Jams, and jellies, and juices". A catastrophe. M.E. B.. 6965-7
Jan Ibn Jan. Rena Carey Sheffield. 6102-8,6076-5
Jan Kubelik. Carl Sandburg. 6531-7
Jan. 11, 1865, 3 o'clock p.m. James Abraham Martling. 6952-5
Janda, Victoria
    Winter's last embrace. 6342-X
Jandl, Ernst

Lenin in winter. Milne Holton and Herbert Kuhner (tr.). 6769-7
Once and now. Milne Holton and Herbert Kuhner (tr.). 6769-7
Parting. Milne Holton and Herbert Kuhner (tr.). 6769-7
"To live" Milne Holton and Herbert Kuhner (tr.). 6769-7
Jane. Nora Perry. 6385-3
Jane Addams. Ruth Comfort Mitchell. 6033-1
Jane and Eliza. Ann Taylor. 6459-0
Jane Conquest. Unknown. 6963-0
Jane Conquest. Unknown. 6915-0
Jane dreams. Nancy McCleery. 6855-3
Jane Jones. Ben King. 6926-6,6211-3,6605-4,6260-1,6281-4
Jane Reed. Bayard Taylor. 6976-2
Jane Smith. Rudyard Kipling. 6440-X
Jane's graduation. Mabel Florence Nash. 6260-1
Jane's rescue. Mary Mapes Dodge. 6249-0
Janet. Richard Watson Gilder. 6652-6
Janet Fisher. Agnes Mary F. ("Madame Duclaux") Robinson. 7037-X
"Janet has a pair of rabbits just as white...". Rabbits. Edgar A. Guest. 6869-3
Janet waking. John Crowe Ransom. 6536-8
Janette's hair. Charles G. ("Miles O'Reilly") Halpine. 6240-7
Jangled bells. Unknown. 6717-4
Janie on the moor. Unknown. 6057-9
Janik, Phyllis
  Sleeping peasants. 6966-5
Janis, Elsie
  The modern hinky-dink. 6237-7
  My prayer. 6654-2
Jankin, the clerical seducer. Unknown. 6881-2
Jans, Paul
  A corner fo my heart. 6799-9
"Januar by thys fyre I warme my handys" Unknown. 6380-2
January. Robert Bridges. 6487-6
January. Alice Cary. 6969-X
January. Warren Cheney. 6241-5
January. Henry S. Cornwell. 6632-1
January. Thomas Hornsby Ferril. 6836-7
January. James Russell Lowell. 6465-5,6456-6
January. Frank Dempster Sherman. 6311-X
January. Irwin Shupp Jr. 6936-3
January. Edmund Spenser. 6191-5
January. Unknown. 6394-2
January 1, 1828. Nathaniel Parker Willis. 6077-3
January 1940. Roy Fuller. 6666-6
January 3, 1913, fr. For the feast of St Genevieve... Charles Peguy. 6351-9
January 4, 1913, fr. For the feast of St. Genevieve... Charles Peguy. 6351-9
January 6, 1919 Julian Street. 6995-9
"January brings the snow". The months. Unknown. 6820-0
A January morning. Archibald Lampman. 6021-8,6115-X,6723-9
"January night, quiet and luminous". Rafael Alberto Arrieta. 6759-X
January roses. Benjamin Franklin Taylor. 6815-4
January sunrise. Hattie B. Terril. 6799-9
A January thaw. E.L. Benedict. 6394-2
January wind. Robert Buchanan. 6424-8
January, fr. Caledner. Frances Abbot. 6764-6
January, fr. Sonnets of the months. Folgore da San Gemignano. 6325-X
"January, wan and gray". The year's twelve children. Unknown. 6918-5
Janus!. George R. Wallace. 6983-5
Janvier, Francis De Haes
  God save our president. 6913-4
  God save our president. 6946-0
  The sleeping sentinel. 6402-7,6554-8
  The stigma. 6912-6
  The Union. 6568-6
Janvier, Margaret T. See "Vandegrift, Margaret"
Janvier, Thomas A.
  In the stagnant pride of an outworn race. 6946-0
  Santiago. 6946-0
Japan can teach. Toyohiko Kagawa. 6027-7
Japanese cherries. Katherine Bregy. 6292-X
Japanese hokkus. Yone Noguchi. 6607-0

A Japanese love-song. Alfred Noyes. 6151-6,6437-X,6301-2
Japanese lullabies. John Harsen Rhoades. 6799-9
Japanese lullaby. Eugene Field. 6373-X,6529-5,6627-5,6683-6,6421-3,6456
A Japanese print. Ruth Mason Rice. 6102-8,6076-5,6585-6
The Japanese.. Ogden Nash. 6637-2;6722-0
Japanesque. Oliver Herford. 6724-7
Japonica bush. Josephine Pinckney. 6039-0
Japp, Alexander Hay
  Landor. 6483-3,6656-9
  Memories. 6274-1,6656-9
Jaqueline. George M. Vickers. 6922-3
Jaques, Edna
  In Flanders now. 6337-3
  Inheritance. 6224-5
The jar. Fedor Sologub. 6103-6
The jar. Richard Henry Stoddard. 6300-4,6431-0
Jardin de la Chapelle Expiatoire. Robert Finch. 6446-9
Jardin des fleurs. Charles David Webb. 6388-8
Jardin des Tuileries. John Dos Passos. 6649-6
Jarintzov, Minnie (tr.)
  If. Alexey Tolstoy, 6732-8
Jarl Sigurd's Christmas Eve. Hjalmar Hjorth Boyesen. 6676-3
Jarman, Wrenne
  The neutral. 6475-2
Jarrell, Patricia Ann
  Ubi Sunt. 6900-2
Jarrell, Randall
  The death of the ball-turret gunner. 6666-6,6665-8
  The emancipators. 6666-6
  The head of wisdom. 6751-4
  Losses. 6666-6
  An officers' prison camp seen from a troop-train. 6666-6
  Pictures from a world. 6391-8
  Pictures of a world (Orestes at Tarvis). 6391-8
  A poem ("There I was"). 6390-X
  Prisoners. 6666-6
  Soldier (T.P.) 6666-6
  The soldier walks under the trees of the university. 6666-6
  2nd Air Force. 6666-6
"...Jarring the air with rumour cool". Small fountains. Lascelles Abercrombie. 6861-8
Jarry, Alfred
  Fable. A.L. Lloyd (tr.). 6343-8
  Sonnet ("Across the heath"). Francis Scarfe (tr.). 6343-8
Jarvis and Mrs. Cope. Thomas Hood. 6974-6
Jarvis, Clarence S.
  In memoriam. 6799-9
Jarvis, Mary R.
  John Harding. 6681-X
"Jasmine's tangled in her hair". A Persian dancing girl. Frank Dempster Sherman. 7041-8
Jason and Medea. John Gower. 6022-6
Jason at Corinth. John Gould Fletcher. 6072-2
Jason's sowing and reaping. Apollonius Rhodius. 6435-3
Jasper. Donald Davidson. 6039-0
Jasper's song. Marjorie L.C. Pickthall. 6433-7
Javanese dancers. Arthur Symons. 6508-2
Javier. Jose Y. Teran Jr. 6870-7
Javis, Alexander
  A ship in a pier. 6037-4
Javitz, Alexander
  Hands. 6778-6
The jay walker. Berton Braley. 6853-7
Jay, Marie
  Oh I should live with homely things. 6397-7
  We walked in summer's twilight. 6397-7
Jay, W.M.L.
  "Not for thine own." 6225-3
Jay, William
  "There dwelt the man, the flower of human kind". 6601-1
The jaybird. James Whitcomb Riley. 6091-9
"Jays in the orchard are screaming, and hark". Down in the strawberry bed. Clinton Scollard. 7022-1
The jazz baby. Berton Braley. 6853-7
"Jaz enters/My life". Blues. Mary du Passage. 6899-5

JAZZ

Jazz fantasia. Carl Sandburg. 6488-4,6121-4,6491-4
Jazz on the island. Leonora Speyer. 7038-8
"Jazz poets scream th death of Hernandez". Lady Grace. Jon Adams. 7018-3
"Jazz slips between her fingers". The ugly girl wants to eat an apple. Otto Paul Gonzales. 6898-7
"Jazz/Caught from tortured". Counterfeit. James Gorham. 6850-2
Jazzonia. Langston Hughes. 6628-3
"Je fais souvent ce reve etrange et penetrant". Mon reve familier. Paul Verlaine. 6801-4
The je ne sais quoi. William Whitehead. 6024-2,6317-9,6092-7,6086-2
Je ne veux de personne aupres de ma tristesse. Henri de Regnier. 7039-6
Je suis Americain. Unknown. 6414-0
"Je suis le tenebreux,- le veuf,- l'inconsole". El desdichado. Gerard de Nerval. 6801-4
Je t'aime. Unknown. 6750-6
"Je veux bien vivre; mais vraiment". Dialogue. Jules Laforgue. 6801-4
"Je veux te raconter, o molle enchanteresse!". Le beau navire. Charles Baudelaire. 6801-4
"Je vous entends glisser avec un secret bruit" Jean Moreas. 6801-4
The jealous doll. Rebecca Deming Moore. 6130-3
The jealous lover. Unknown. 6003-X
The jealous rose. Unknown. 6116-8
The jealous wife. Fred Emerson Brooks. 6921-5
Jealous, I own it. Walter Savage Landor. 6828-6
"Jealous, and with love o'erflowing". Love pure and fervent. Madame De la Mothe Guion. 6814-6
"Jealous. I own it, I was once". Jealous, I own it. Walter Savage Landor. 6828-6
Jealousy. Phoebe Cary. 6969-X
Jealousy. Mary Elizabeth Coleridge. 6507-4
Jealousy. Paul Geraldy. 6351-9
Jealousy. William Herbert; Earl of Pembroke. 6980-0
Jealousy. Edward R. Huxley. 6885-5
Jealousy. Ben Jonson. 6543-0
Jealousy. William Shakespeare. 6094-3
Jealousy. Anne Finch, Countess of Winchilsea. 6563-5
Jealousy in the choir. Unknown. 6702-6
The jealousy of the gods. Carol Jordan. 6396-9
Jealousy, the tyrant of the mind. John Dryden. 6219-9
Jeames of Buckley Square. William Makepeace Thackeray. 6760-3
Jean. Robert Burns. 6246-6,6332-2,6560-0,6301-2,6226-1, 6737,6104-4,6219-9,6250-4
Jean. Paul Potts. 6379-9
Jean. George R. Wallace. 6983-5
Jean Anderson, my joy, Jean. Jeremiah Eames Rankin. 6565-1
Jean desprez. Robert Service. 6159-1,6162-1
Jean Richepin's song. Herbert Trench. 6877-4
Jean-Francois Millet. Rosamund Marriott ("Graham R. Tomson") Watson. 6875-8
Jean-Louis. David Slater. 6998-3
Jeancon, Jean Allard
    Good-night in Hopi-land. 6836-7
    It's day in Hopi-land. 6836-7
Jeane. William Barnes. 6317-9
Jeanie Morrison. William Motherwell. 6127-3,6142-7,6302-0, 6385-3,6317-9,6600-3,6094-3,6219-9,6383-7,6438-3
"Jeanie, come tie my". The cravat. Unknown. 6937-1
Jeanne. Remy de Gourmont. 6351-9
Jeanne d'Arc returns. Henry Van Dyke. 6961-4
Jeannette and Jo. Mary Mapes Dodge. 6131-1
Jeannie Marsh. George Pope Morris. 6673-9
Jebb, Richard C. (tr.)
    Antigone, sels. Sophocles, 6527-9
Jefferies, Richard
    Daybreak. 6253-9
Jefferies, Robert D.
    Sonnet. 6857-X
Jeffers, Robinson
    Adjustment. 6012-9
    Age in prospect. 6012-9
    Ante mortem. 6012-9
    Apology for bad dreams. 6399-3,6012-9
    The beach. 6012-9

The bed by the window. 6628-3
Birds ("The fierce musical cries..."). 6073-0
Black-out. 6666-6
Bloody sire. 6389-6
The caged eagle's death dream, fr. Cawdor. 6978-9
A California garden, fr. Emilia. 6649-6
A California vignette, fr. Tamar. 6501-5
Calm and full the ocean. 6666-6
Cassandra. 6666-6
Clouds of evening. 6012-9,6628-3
The coast road. 6527-9
Compensation. 6012-9
The cycle. 6619-4
Eagle valor, chicken mind. 6666-6
Emilia, sels. 6649-6
The excesses of God. 6337-3,6532-5
The eye. 6666-6,6208-3
Fire on the hills. 6628-3
Fog. 6619-4
Fourth act. 6666-6
The giant's ring: Ballylesson, near Belfast. 6879-0
Hands. 6628-3
Haunted country. 6808-1
Hellenistics. 6399-3
Hooded night. 6628-3
Hurt hawks. 6077-3,6491-4
I shall laugh purely. 6390-X,6666-6
Inscription for a gravestone. 6879-0
An Irish headland. 6628-3
Joy. 6250-4
Let us go home to paradise. 6241-5
Love-children. 6012-9
The machine, fr. The trumpet. 6808-1
The maid's thought. 6077-3
May-June, 1940. 6666-6,6389-6
Night. 6726-3,6628-3
Noon. 6012-9
Not our good luck. 6501-5
October evening. 6012-9
Pelicans. 6012-9
The place for no story. 6628-3
Post mortem. 6012-9
Post-mortem. 6012-9
Practical people. 6375-6
Promise of peace. 6012-9
Roan stallion. 6375-6
Salmon fishing. 6501-5
Science. 6808-1
Shakespeare's grave. 6641-0
Shine, perishing republic. 6527-9,6536-8,6375-6,6491-4
The stars go over the lonely ocean. 6391-8,6666-6
The stone axe. 6628-3
Suicide's stone. 6501-5
Summer holiday. 6012-9
To his father. 6808-1
To the children, fr. The trumpet. 6808-1
To the stone cutters. 6501-5,6619-4,6217-2
Tor house. 6315-2
Tower beyond tragedy, sels. 6808-1
The trumpet, sels. 6808-1
Woodrow Wilson. 6628-3
Jeffers, Susan
    "The tired grey body of the fishing vessel" 6857-X
Jefferson D. Henry S. Cornwell. 6946-0
Jefferson Davis. Walker Meriwether Bell. 6946-0,6088-9
Jefferson Davis. Harry Thurston Peck. 6088-9
Jefferson, Floyd W.
    For memory's sake. 6118-4
    Rosemary and rue. 6118-4
Jefferson, Joseph
    Immortality. 6303-9,6889-8,6798-0
Jeffery, Frank Moore
    The dominant sea. 6789-1
    Influence, fr. The friend of a prince. 6789-1
Jeffery, Ruth
    Orison. 6818-9
Jefferys, William Hamilton
    Lights to steer by. 6936-3
Jeffrey, Francis Jeffrey, Lord
    On Peter Robinson. 6722-0,6633-X

Verses ("Why write"). 6086-2
Why write my name. 6092-7
Jeffrey, John
The emancipation of the press. 7009-4
Jeffrey, Rosa Vertner
Owl in church. 6695-X
The phantom bell. 6695-X
Jeffrey, William
Angus remembers. 6269-5
The hollow bone. 6269-5
In memoriam: F.R.H. [Frederick Higgins]. 6783-2
The mechanical age. 6269-5
Ode to evening. 6269-5
Jeffries, Henry A.
Old Jim. 6149-4
Jehanne. Edward Farquhar. 6939-8
"Jehoshaphat reigned over Judah in peace". Jehoshaphat's deliverance. George Lansing Taylor. 6848-0
Jehovah. Israel Zangwill. 6730-1
Jehovah liveth. Edward Everett Hale. 6848-0
Jehovah our righteousness. William Cowper. 6814-6
"Jehovah reigns, the mighty God". Psalm 099. Bible. 6848-0
"Jehovah said unto my Lord". Psalm 110. Bible. 6848-0
Jehovah-Jesus. William Cowper. 6814-6
Jehovah-Jireh. William Cowper. 6814-6
Jehovah-Nissi. William Cowper. 6814-6
Jehovah-nissi, the Lord my banner. William Cowper. 6848-0
Jehovah-Rophi. William Cowper. 6814-6
Jehovah-Shalom. William Cowper. 6814-6
Jehovah-Shammah. William Cowper. 6814-6
Jehu. Louis MacNeice. 6389-6,6666-6
Jekyll, Joseph
Two heads are better than one. 6722-0
Jelinek, Hunus
The song of the heavens, the stars, Schumann & my wife. Paul Selver (tr.). 6763-8
Jellicoe, S. Charles
Advice to a lover. 6174-5
Can you give gladness to me? 6174-5
The destiny of dreams. 6174-5
Erin's plea. 6174-5
Laudator temporis actai. 6174-5
Jellon Grame. Unknown. 6185-0
The jelly-fish. Robert P. Tristram Coffin. 7040-X
Jellyfish. Raquel Jodorowsky. 7036-1
Jem and the shoulder of mutton. Jane Taylor. 6131-1
Jemima. Unknown. 6105-2,6179-6,6242-3
Jemima. Unknown. 6772-7
Jemmy Dawson. William Shenstone. 6086-2
Jemmy Dawson. Unknown. 6859-6
Jemmy the sailor. Francis Hopkinson. 6121-4
Jenkins, Arthur Lewis
Sonnet sequence. 6650-X
Jenkins, B.H.
Cheer de union travelers. 6149-4
Jenkins, Bruce
Fort Macon. 6900-2
Jenkins, Elinor
The last evening. 7029-9
A legend of Ypres. 6474-4
Jenkins, Lucy Dean
Mammy's pickanin'. 6605-4
Jenkins, MacGregor
To Phyllis returned to town. 7021-3
Jenkins, Oliver
Captain's walk. 6764-6
Day on a hill. 6764-6
Love autumnal. 6762-X
New England coast. 6780-8
A ship comes in. 6466-3
A ship comes in. 6764-6
Song ("Let me be great..."). 6762-X
Waterfront. 6833-2
Jenkins, William Vaughan
O God of ours, to thee we bow. 6337-3
Jenks, Edward A.
Going and coming. 6385-3
Jenks, Orville J.
The Bartley explosion. 6149-4
The dying mine brakeman. 6149-4
In the "state of McDowell" 6149-4
John L. Lewis blues. 6149-4
Sprinkle coal dust on my grave. 6149-4
Jenks, Tudor
Boy's great schemes. 6715-8
A Christmas song ("When mother-love makes..."). 6145-1
A complaint. 6690-9
Madcap April. 6820-0
An old bachelor. 6089-7,6307-1
On the road. 6902-9
Small and early. 6512-0
The spirit of the Maine. 6741-X
"Through him the first fond prayers are said." 6225-3
The whirling wheel. 6578-3
Jenkyn, Pattericke
To the sun. 6563-5
Jenkyns, Ruthven
Though lost to sight, to memory dear. 6913-4
Jenner, Arthur E.
Queen of night. 6818-9
Jenner, Edward
Signs of foul weather. 6105-2
Signs of rain. 6133-8,6385-3,6482-5,6519-8
Jennett, Sean
And the dead. 6379-9
Cycle. 6666-6
I was a labourer, fr. Cycle: seven war poems. 6930-4
The quick. 6379-9
Jenney, Florence
Achievement. 6034-X
Jennie. Fred Emerson Brooks. 6670-4
Jennie. Alice Cary. 6865-0;6969-X
Jennie. Phoebe Cary. 6695-X
Jennie. Eugene Field. 6949-5
Jennie. Josephine Pollitt. 6038-2
Jennie kissed me. Leigh Hunt. 6014-5,6289-X,6385-3,6732-8, 6085-4,6102-8,6240-7,6260-1,6271-7,6339-,6395-0,6413-2,6429-9,6437-X,6501-5,6512-,6219-9,6312-7,6226-1, 6104-4,6092-7,6026-9,6383-7,6301-2,6230-X,6424-8, 6585-6,6737-9,6219-9,6312-7,6226-1,6104-4,6092-7, 6026-9,6383-7,6301-2,6230-X,6424-8,6585-6,6737-9
Jennie put the kettle on. Unknown. 6826-X
Jennings, Amy S.
Eros. 6039-0,6072-2
Jennings, Elizabeth
Florence: design for a city. 6257-1
Ghosts. 6339-X
Jennings, Lena L.
Guerdon. 6799-9
Jennings, Leslie Nelson
Astrology. 6072-2
Beyond Rhodope, once. 6038-2
Carpentry. 6979-7
Harborless. 6880-4
Highways. 6031-5,6374-8
Hour of the lizard. 6781-6
Inscription. 6032-3
Keep darkness. 6218-0
Lost harbor. 6619-4
On the line. 6038-2
Stones. 6761-1
Tapestry. 6072-2
The yellow cat. 6218-0
Jennings, Leslie Norton
Castlebar. 6880-4
Jenny. Walter De La Mare. 6905-3
Jenny and Peggy. Allan Ramsay. 6543-0
Jenny dang the weaver. Sir Alexander Boswell. 6180-X
Jenny Dunleath. Alice Cary. 6411-6
Jenny June. Benjamin Franklin Taylor. 6815-4
Jenny Lee. Jack Micheline. 6901-0
Jenny Malone. Unknown. 6413-2
"Jenny is a butterfly". The choice. Berton Braley. 6853-7
"Jenny kiss'd me in a dream". 'Such stuff as dreams' Franklin Pierce Adams. 6875-8
"Jenny Wren and her mate had a spat one day". The power of a song. Besse Schiff. 6906-1
Jenny was a jewel. Bravig Imbs. 6039-0
Jenny wi' the airn teeth. Alexander ("Surfaceman") Anderson. 6819-7

JENNY

Jenny Wren. Walter De La Mare. 6395-0
Jenny Wren. Mother Goose. 6739-5
Jenny Wren. Unknown. 6262-8
Jenny Wren and Robin Redbreast. Unknown. 6424-8
"Jenny Wren fell sick." Mother Goose. 6133-8,6262-8
"Jenny! puir Jenny! the flow'r o' the lea". The process of wakening. George Outram. 6878-2
Jenny's bawbee. Sir Alexander Boswell. 6180-X
Jenny, fr. The house of life. Dante Gabriel Rossetti. 6198-2,6526-0,6508-2,6655-0
Jensen, Frances Greenleaf
  Flying the beam. 6342-X
Jensen, Johannes V.
  A bathing girl. Charles Wharton Stork (tr.). 6555-4
  Denmark song. Charles Wharton Stork (tr.). 6555-4
Jentz, Jeff
  The bird nest is transparent by Qudrat. 6900-2
Jenyns, Soame
  Too plain, dear youth, these tell-tale eyes. 6086-2
Jephcott, Sydney
  The dreamers. 6784-0
  White paper. 6784-0
Jephtha's daughter. George Gordon, 6th Baron Byron. 6438-8, 6543-0,6828-6
Jephtha's daughter. Rose Terry Cooke. 6848-0
Jephtha's daughter. W.W. Marsh. 6675-5
Jephtha's vow. James Grahame. 6848-0
Jephthah's daughter. Alfred Lord Tennyson. 6087-0
Jephthah, judge of Israel. Unknown. 6848-0
Jepthah's rash vow. Miss Howard. 6407-8
"Jerdan, farewell! farewell to all". Ode to W. Jerdan, Esq. Thomas Hood. 6974-6
Jeremiah
  The dancer. 6959-2
Jeremiah's lamentation. Bible. 6143-5
Jeremy, Sister Mary
  Saint in winter. 6839-1
  A sister lights the candles. 6285-7
Jericho. Frank Foxcroft. 6848-0
The Jericho road. Edwin McNeill Poteat. 6144-3;6532-5;6337-3
Jericho, Vermont. Daniel L. Cady. 6988-6
Jerico. Willard Wattles. 6556-2
Jerolamen. C. Grace
  Kitty's lesson. 6699-2
"Jerome again was such another. Once". Sonnet ("Jerome again"). Herbert Corby. 6895-2
Jerrold, Douglas
  Female tenderness. 6279-2
  The helpless gray head. 6411-6
Jerrold, Ianthe
  In spring. 6777-8
  On Epsom Down. 6776-X
Jerrold, Maud F. (tr.)
  "Dear one, I love thine eyes, amazed" Feodor Ivanovich Tyutchev. 6103-6
  "The heavy clouds at length are scattering" Alexander Pushkin. 6103-6
  The nightingale. Alexey Koltsov, 6103-6
  "O Virgin-rose, no blushes". Alexander Pushkin, 6103-6
  "She sat upon the ground; there lay". Feodor Ivanovich Tyutchev, 6103-6
  Three springs. Alexander Pushkin, 6103-6
  "We parted, but my heart still wears" Mikhail Lermontov, 6103-6
Jerry. Mary Lowe Dickinson. 6414-0,6706-9,6574-0
Jerry an' me. H. Rich. 6243-1
"Jerry Hall, he is so small". Unknown. 6363-2
Jerusalem. William Blake. 6228-8,6334-9,6339-X,6395-0,6427-2,6658 ,6107-9,6150-8,6665-8
Jerusalem. John Gardiner Calkins Brainard. 6752-2
Jerusalem. Sir Aubrey De Vere. 7015-9
Jerusalem. John Kebble Hervey. 6848-0
Jerusalem. James Abraham Martling. 6952-5
Jerusalem. Unknown. 6150-8
Jerusalem delivered, sels. Torquato Tasso. 6649-6
Jerusalem delivered, sels. Torquato Tasso. 6372-1
Jerusalem the beautiful. M.L. Hofford. 6921-5
Jerusalem the golden. John Mason Neale. 6481-7
Jerusalem the golden. Unknown (Latin) 6889-8

"Jerusalem! Jerusalem!/Thou art low; thou...". The fall of Jerusalem. Alfred Lord Tennyson. 6848-0
Jerusalem's dayspring. Horatius Bonar. 6848-0
"Jerusalem, my happy home". The heavenly Jerusalem. F.B. P.. 6934-7
Jerusalem, my happy home. F.B. P. 6182-6,6730-1,6337-3
"Jerusalem, rejoice for joy". William Dunbar (atr) 6636-4
Jerusalem, sels. William Blake. 6334-9,6378-0
Jerusalem, the golden. Bernard of Cluny. 6730-1,6304-7, 6214-8
Jerusalem, the golden. Bernard of Cluny. 6337-3
Jervey, Mary
  General Albert Sidney Johnston. 6113-3
The Jervis Bay goes down. Gene Fowler. 6224-5
Jes' only her. John Edward Hazzard. 6707-7
Jes' to be along o' you. Unknown. 6694-1
Jes' whistle up a song. Unknown. 6711-5
Jesenka, Ruzena
  Beneath the mountains. Paul Selver (tr.). 6763-8
  By the ocean. Paul Selver (tr.). 6763-8
Jessamine. Ibn al-Abbar. 6362-4
Jesse James. Unknown. 6289-X,6732-8,6281-4,6736-0,6003-X
Jesse James. Unknown. 6826-X
"Jesse James was a sonofabitch". Rules & men & boundaries. Kell Robertson. 6901-0
Jesse James: American myth. William Rose Benet. 6011-0, 6107-9,6375-6,6464-7,6488-4,6527
Jesse Seligman. Noah Davis. 6848-0
Jesse Welch. Leonard Alfred George Strong. 6633-X
Jesseph, Flora Dingle
  Christmas, 1941. 6789-1
Jessica dances. Eleanor Farjeon. 6959-2
Jessie. Thomas Edward Brown. 6204-0
Jessie. Eugene Field. 6949-5
Jessie. Francis Bret Harte. 6239-3
Jessie Cameron. Christina Georgina Rossetti. 6411-6
Jessie's book. Lucy Larcom. 6129-X
Jessie, the flower o' Dunblane. Robert Tannahill. 6180-X, 6086-2,6219-9
Jessop, George H.
  At the opera. 6414-0
  The siren's wedding-ring. 6415-9
  Telling fortunes. 6672-0
  Yes! (Is it true?-that's the doubtful suggestion"). 6273-3
Jessy. Robert Burns. 6219-9
Jest 'fore Christmas. Eugene Field. 6834-0;6949-5,6891-X, 6820-0
Jest 'fore Christmas. Eugene Field. 6534-1,6486-8,6356-X, 6739-5,6318-7,6608
'Jest a-thinkin' o' you.' Ella Higginson. 6687-9
Jest a-wearyin' fer you. Frank Lebby Stanton. 6583-X
"Jest as atween the awk'ard lines a hand...". 'The old homestead'. Eugene Field. 6949-5
The jest of fate. Sam Walter Foss. 6688-7
"Jest take an apple tree that leans". May in Vermont. Daniel L. Cady. 6989-4
Jest to be happy. Frank Lebby Stanton. 6583-X
The jest, fr. Thumb nail sketches. Mary H. Cabaniss. 6841-3
Jester bee. Frank Dempster Sherman. 6311-X
The jester condemned to death. Horace Smith. 6089-7,6294-6, 6425-6,6523-6,6744-1,6464
The jester conedemned [to death]. Horace Smith. 6909-6
The jester's plea. Frederick Locker-Lampson. 6092-7
The jester's sermon. George Walter Thornbury. 6156-6,6302-0,6385-3,6408-6,6600-3,6102-8,6219-9
Jester, George
  Daphne and Apollo. 6817-0
  To a girl with two eyes. 6817-0
  To a girl, upon returning. 6817-0
  To a lot of girls. 6817-0
"'Jester, spin your silver ball, youth...'". Dream. Ellen M. Acton. 6818-9
The jester, to his audience. Jamie Sexton Holme. 6836-7
The jester. Unknown. 6680-1
Jesu. George Herbert. 6341-1
"Jesu! by that shuddering dread which fell...". Angel of the agony, fr. The dream of Gerontius. John Henry, Cardinal Newman. 6931-2

"Jesu! for thy mercy endelesse". Jesu! send us peace. Unknown. 6881-2
"Jesu, Lord, welcom thou be". A prayer to the sacrament of the altar. Unknown. 6881-2
"Jesu, Lorde, that madest me". A hymn to Jesus. Richard of Caistre. 6881-2
Jesu, as thou art our saviour. Unknown. 6756-5
Jesu, fili Dei. John Trouluffe & Richard Smert. 6756-5
Jesu, fili virgnis, miserere nobis. Unknown. 6756-5
Jesu, lover of my soul. Philip Skelton. 6732-8
"Jesu, lover of my soul". Charles Wesley. 6931-2
Jesu, my strength, my hope. Charles Wesley. 6219-9
"Jesu, that hast me dere iboght". A devout prayer of the passion. Unknown. 6881-2
Jesukin. Saint (atr.) Ita. 6930-4
Jesus. Joseph Eliyia. 6352-7
Jesus. Unknown. 6335-7,6532-5
Jesus. Unknown. 6144-3
Jesus ("The martyred Christ of the working class...") Eugene V. Debs. 6144-3
Jesus and the sinner. Sadi [or Saadi] (Mushlih-ud-Din) 6448-5
Jesus approaches his people. Unknown. 6881-2
Jesus bids man remember. Unknown. 6881-2
Jesus calls us o'er the tumult. Cecil Frances Alexander. 6337-3
Jesus Christ, the same yesterday, to-day, and forever. William White. 6868-5
Jesus comes on clouds triumphant. Godfrey Thring. 6065-X
Jesus comforts his mother. Unknown. 6881-2
Jesus contrasts man and himself. Unknown. 6881-2
Jesus first and Jesus last. Thomas MacKellar. 6065-X
Jesus goin' to make up mah dyin' bed. Unknown. 6594-5
"Jesus hail! enthroned in glory". The feast of the Eucharist. William White. 6868-5
Jesus hasting to suffer. William Cowper. 6814-6
Jesus is calling. Estelle Geraldine Griffen. 6799-9
Jesus is near. Robert Cassie Waterston. 6065-X
Jesus lives, and so shall I. Christian Furchtegott Gellert. 6065-X
Jesus nevuh come in the mornin' Unknown. 6609-7
Jesus of Nazareth. Ernest Cadman Colwell. 6144-3,6532-5, 6337-3
Jesus of Nazareth passes by. George T. Liddell. 6144-3;6335-7
Jesus of Nazareth passeth by. Lydia Huntley Sigourney. 6065-X
Jesus of the scars. Edward Shillito. 6144-3,6335-7,6337-3
Jesus only. Elias Nason. 6065-X
Jesus only. Albert Benjamin Simpson. 6065-X
Jesus praying. Hartley Coleridge. 6337-3
Jesus prays alone. William Bingham Tappan. 6065-X
Jesus reassures his mother. Unknown. 6881-2
"Jesus saviour, pilot me". Prayer of the aviator. Lucy H. King Smith. 6906-1
Jesus shall reign where'er the sun. Isaac Watts. 6065-X, 6271-7,6337-3,6730-1,6214-8
J₂sus the carpenter. Catherine C. Liddell. 6479-5,6656-9, 6820-0
Jesus the carpenter. Charles M. Sheldon. 6144-3,6303-9, 6335-7,6337-3,6473-6
Jesus the comforter, sels. Unknown. 6337-3
Jesus the very thought of thee. Saint Bernard of Clairvaux (atr) 6337-3
Jesus to those who pass by. Unknown. 6881-2
Jesus was a humble man. Raymond Kresensky. 6144-3
"Jesus was born in a manger". A spring Christmas carol. Herbert Edward Palmer. 6779-4
"Jesus was sitting in Moses' chair". The everlasting gospel, sels. William Blake. 6931-2
Jesus wept. Benjamin Beddome. 6219-9
Jesus wept. Francis Brooks. 6274-1
Jesus [or Jesu], lover of my soul. Charles Wesley. 6214-8, 6304-7,6302-0,6521-X,6730-1,6192-3,6129-9,6337-3, 6641-0,6065-X,6260-1,6271-7,6600
"Jesus woundes so wide". The wells of Jesus wounds. Unknown. 6881-2
"Jesus, almighty king of blis". The Nativity. Unknown. 6881-2
Jesu, child and Lord. Frederick William Faber. 6065-X

Jesus, fr. The testament of beauty. Robert Bridges. 6337-3
"Jesus, how much thy name unfolds!". Mary Peters. 6065-X
Jesus, I love thy charming name. Philip Doddridge. 6065-X
Jesus, lover of my soul. Eugene J. Hall. 6417-5
Jesus, lover of my soul. Charles Wesley. 6737-9
"Jesus, loving shepherd". To be kept by Jesus. W. Roche. 6937-1
Jesus, my God and my all. Frederick William Faber. 6065-X
Jesus, my saviour, look on me! John Macduff. 6065-X
Jesus, my sweet lover. Unknown. 6881-2
"Jesus, of a maid thou wouldst be born". Jesu, fili virgnis, miserere nobis. Unknown. 6756-5
Jesus, refuge of the weary. Girolamo Savonarola. 6337-3
Jesus, see a little child. Matthias Barr. 6131-1
Jesus, tender shepherd, hear me. Mary Lundie Duncan. 6466-3
"Jesus, the very thought of thee". Saint Bernard of Clairvaux. 6065-X
Jesus, these eyes have never seen. Ray Palmer. 6337-3
Jesus, thou art the king. Charles Wesley. 6065-X
Jesus, thou divine companion. Henry Van Dyke. 6337-3
Jesus, thou joy of living hearts. Saint Bernard of Clairvaux. 6730-1
Jesus, thou joy of living hearts. Bernard of Cluny. 6730-1
Jesus, thou joy of loving hearts. Unknown (Latin) 6337-3
"Jesus, where'er thy people meet". On opening a place for social prayer. William Cowper. 6814-6
"Jesus, whose blood so freely stream'd". Jehovah-Shalom. William Cowper. 6814-6
"Jesus, whose lot with us was cast". Jesus. Unknown. 6144-3
Jet and snowflake. Unknown. 6699-2
"Jete sur cette boule,/Laid, chetif et...". Ma vocation. Pierre Jean de Beranger. 6801-4
Jethro's pet. Robert P. Tristram Coffin. 6628-3
Jetsam. Herman Montagu Donner. 6327-6
Jevohah's immovable throne, fr. Psalm 93. Bible. 6730-1
"A Jew and a Scotchman, found 'tight'.". Limerick:"A Jew and a Scotchman, found 'tight'". H.V. Abraham. 6811-1
"The Jew has flourished down the ages". The Jew. William Joyce. 6848-0
The Jew of Malta, sels. Christopher Marlowe. 6102-8;6378-0;6726-3
The Jew to Jesus. Florence Kiper Frank. 6144-3,6337-3,6730-1,6393-4
"The Jew wrecked in the German cell" Wystan Hugh Auden. 6666-6
'Jew!'. George Vaux Bacon. 6848-0
The Jew's appeal to the Christian. J. W. Blencowe. 6848-0
the Jew's cemetery on the Lido. John Addington Sydmonds. 6848-0
The Jew's cemetery. John Addington Symonds. 6624-0,6046-3
The Jew's gift. Thomas Bailey Aldrich. 6848-0
The Jew. William Joyce. 6848-0
The Jew. George Alfred Townsend. 6848-0
The jewel of a girl. James Abraham Martling. 6952-5
The jewel of a nose. James Abraham Martling. 6952-5
"The jewel of the secret treasury". Ode 006. Hafiz. 7039-6
Jewel-weed. Florence Earle Coates. 6338-1
Jewell, E.O.
    It never dies. 6097-8
    Things that never die. 6415-9
Jewell, Eleanor S.
    Woman. 6764-6
Jewell, Gertrude Scott
    Cocoons. 7019-1
    Freedom is lonely. 6662-3
    To rise again. 6662-3
Jewell, Terri
    The buddy system (...a release for my cynicism...) 6899-5
    Fear of the dark. 6899-5
    Map. 6899-5
    Studies in heat, 1983 6899-5
The jewelled trees. George Martin. 6795-6
Jewels. George Croly. 6980-0
Jewels. Nancy Byrd Turner. 6861-8
The jewels she lacked. Unknown. 6672-0
The jewels. Marion J. Hext. 6799-9

Jewess. Joaquin Miller. 6848-0
Jewett, Eleanor
    Going west. 6846-4
Jewett, Eleanore Myers
    Down among the wharves. 6833-2
Jewett, Ellen A.
    Grandmother's sermon. 6414-0
Jewett, John H.
    Our boys are marching on. 6471-X
    Those rebel flags. 6741-X,6223-7
    A voice from the old boys left behind. 6741-X
Jewett, Mrs. S.W.
    Tommy and his shilling. 6131-1
Jewett, Sarah Orne
    A caged bird. 6597-X,6073-0
    Discontent. 6519-8,6049-8,6131-1,6639-9,6638-0
    The discontented buttercup. 6742-5
    Flowers in the dark. 6338-1
    Sheltered. 6661-5
Jewett, Sophie ("Ellen Burroughs")
    Communion. 6501-5
    Entre nous. 6620-8
    An exile's garden. 6338-1
    A friendship. 6066-8
    In the dark. 6309-8
    The least of carols. 6006-4,6608-9
    Sleep ("Dear gray-eyed Angel,...") 6501-5
    The soldier. 6501-5
    Thus far. 6309-8
    True-hearted friend of mine. 6085-4
Jewett, Susan
    The little girl's address to the river. 6131-1
    The robin. 6131-1
    Skating. 6131-1
    The two friends. 6131-1
A Jewish apologue. Unknown. 6848-0
The Jewish captives. John M. Leavitt. 6848-0
The Jewish cemetery at Newport. Henry Wadsworth Longfellow. 6176-1,6333-0,6399-3,6484-1
The Jewish conscript. Florence Kiper Frank. 6532-5,6542-2
A Jewish family. William Wordsworth. 6848-0
Jewish hymn in Babylon. Henry Hart Milman. 6980-0,6848-0
The Jewish lady. Unknown. 6003-X
Jewish lullaby. Eugene Field. 6949-5,6848-0
Jewish lullaby. Louis Untermeyer. 6039-0
The Jewish May. Morris Rosenfeld. 7011-6
The Jewish pilgrim. Frances Browne. 6848-0
A Jewish rabbi in Rome. With a commentary by Ben Israel. William Wetmore Story. 6848-0
Jewitt, Sophie
    The soldier. 6861-8
Jewitt, W. H.
    Ballade. 6770-0
The Jews of Bucharest. Edward Sydney Tybee. 6848-0
Jews of no man's land. Joy Davidman. 6761-1
The Jews' return to Jerusalem. W. H. Roberts. 6848-0
The Jews. Edwin Markham. 6848-0
The Jews. Henry Vaughan. 6933-9,6848-0
Jewsbury, Maria Jane
    "And this, O Spain...". 6402-7
    The flight of the Xerxes. 6410-8
Jezebel. Scudder Mi^{X}dleton. 6038-2,6531-7,6619-4,6070-6
A jig. Robert Greene. 6182-6
Jigsaw III. Louis MacNeice. 6257-1
Jillian of Berry. Francis Beaumont. 6182-6
Jillson, Clark
    Wet and dry. 6913-4
    A word for each month. 6913-4
Jim. A.W. Bellaw. 6925-8
Jim. Hilaire Belloc. 6861-8
Jim. Hilaire Belloc. 6096-X,6179-6,6125-7
Jim. Perceval Gibbon. 6788-3
Jim. Francis Bret Harte. 6385-3,6404-3,6279-2,6722-0,6089-7,6735 ,6288-1,6300-4
Jim. George V. Hobart. 6274-1
Jim. Nora Perry. 7022-1
Jim. James Whitcomb Riley. 6505-8
Jim. Robert Service. 6159-1
Jim and Bill. Franklin Pierce Adams. 6307-1
"Jim and George were two grat lords". Unknown. 6904-5

Jim and Mariar. Unknown. 6149-4
Jim Bludso. John Hay. 6014-5,6052-8,6062-5,6077-3,6089-7, 6134 ,6431-0,6281-4,6396-9,6076-5,6121-4,6736 ,6211-3,6260-1,6358-6,6370-5,6481-7,6486 ,6107-9,626502, 6300-4,6464-7,6467-1,6332-2,6358-6,6451-5,6503-1, 6605-4,6550 ,6497-3,6687-9,6732-8,6735-2,6512-0,6102
Jim Bowker. Sam Walter Foss. 6580-5
Jim Brady's big brother. James William Foley. 6964-9
Jim Desterland. Hyam Plutzik. 6218-0
Jim dog. Margaret Elizabeth Sangster. 6548-1
Jim Fellowes. Beatrice Ravenel. 7016-7
Jim Jay. Walter De La Mare. 6162-1,6393-4
Jim Lord's cat. Edward Byron Nicholson. 6687-9
Jim Porter's shanty. Unknown. 6281-4
"Jim had a quaint philosophy". His philosophy. Edgar A. Guest. 6862-6
"Jim Hood was a mellow and genial fellow". All in the family. Berton Braley. 6853-7
"Jim knows things". Jim Fellowes. Beatrice Ravenel. 7016-7
"Jim on the bridge was penetrated by the...". Lord Jim, sel. Joseph Conrad. 6958-4
"Jim wan't no good to fish and shoot". The young musician. Sam Walter Foss. 6929-0
Jim's kids. Unknown. 6414-0
Jim's story. H.S. Tomer. 6687-9
The Jim-jam king of the jou-jous. Alaric Betrand Start. 6505-8
The jim-jam king of the jou-jous. Alaric Bertrand Stuart. 6089-7,6732-6
'Jim.'. Joseph Crosby Lincoln. 6119-2;6707-7
Jimmie Rendal. Unknown. 6061-7
Jimmie's prayer. Unknown. 6139-7
Jimmy. Edgar A. Guest. 6862-6
Jimmy and his own true love. Unknown. 6057-9
Jimmy Doane. Rowland Thirlmere. 7026-4
Jimmy O'Neil. James Abraham Martling. 6952-5
Jimmy's enlisted, or The recruited collier. Unknown. 6157-5
Jimmy's wooing. Will Wallace Harney. 6620-8
"Jimson lives in a new". A call to the wild. Edward John Plunkett, 18th Baron Dunsany. 6930-4
"Jimson weed/has nothing to do". Magnetized. Arthur Sze. 6790-5
Jingle bells. James S. Pierpont. 6736-0
Jingle bells. Unknown. 7035-3
Jingles. Unknown. 6742-5
Jinny. Eva Wilder McGlasson. 6672-0
Jinny the just. Matthew Prior. 6733-6,6152-4,6152-4
Jippy and Jimmy. Laura E. Richards. 6891-X
Jis' blue. Etta Baldwin Oldham. 6490-6
Jis' knowin' Thomas G. Nickens. 6870-7
Jito, Empress
    "The spring has gone, the summer's come". William N. Porter (tr.). 6852-9
Jiyen
    "Unfit to rule this wicked world". William N. Porter (tr.). 6852-9
Jo, the tramp. Edgar M. Chipman. 6413-2
Joab at the battle of Medeba. George Peele. 6848-0
Joab's address to David on death of Absalom. George Peele. 6848-0
Joab's description of David. George Peele. 6848-0
Joachimsen, Caroline C.
    Solomon and the sparrow. 6670-4
Joan. Thekla N. Berstecher. 6906-1
Joan. Mildred Jones Keefe. 6143-5
Joan and Jesus. Ralph Cheyney. 6880-4
Joan d'Arc. John Sterling. 6980-0
Joan of Arc. Elizabeth Burns. 6900-2
Joan of Arc at Domremy. Charles Buxton Going. 6653-4
Joan of Arc in prison. Mrs. L.J.B. Case. 6672-0
Joan of Arc in Rheims, fr. Records of woman. Felicia Dorothea Hemans. 6973-8
Joan of Arc, 1926 Virginia Moore. 6619-4
Joan of Arc, in Rheims. Felicia Dorothea Hemans. 6980-0
Joan of France to an English sister. J.H. S. 6474-4
Joannes Barbucallus
    "Stay not for me, O sailor...". F.L. Lucas (tr.). 6251-2
Job. Mary Ann Carter. 6848-0

Job. Samuel Taylor Coleridge. 6874-X
Job. Samuel Taylor Coleridge. 6089-7
Job. Edward Farquhar. 6939-8
Job. Abraham Rowley. 6848-0
Job. William Sotheby. 6848-0
Job. Unknown. 6724-7
Job 14. Bible. 6732-8
Job 23: 8-10 Charles Wesley. 6848-0
Job longeth for death, fr. Job. Bible. 6472-8
Job reviles. Abraham M. Klein. 6532-5
Job the white. Thomas Edward Brown. 6809-X
Job's comforters, fr. Job. Bible. 6730-1
Job's confession. Edward Young. 6848-0
Job's curse, fr. The book of Job. Bible. 7039-6
Job's entreaty, fr. The book of Job. Bible. 7039-6
Job's luck. Samuel Taylor Coleridge. 6848-0
Job, sels. Bible. 6472-8
Jobe, Gussie Ross
    Covering. 6906-1
    Little brown trunk. 6906-1
    Ye old time valentine. 6906-1
Jobson of the Star. Robert Service. 6159-1
Jobson's amen. Rudyard Kipling. 6508-2
Jocasta's death, fr. Oedipus tyrannus. Sophocles. 6435-3
"Joch. Why was my pray'r accepted?". Moses in the bulrushes. Hannah More. 6848-0
Jochanan Hakkadosh. Robert Browning. 6848-0
Jochen, Lucy A.
    Wonder. 6857-X
Jochumsson, Matthias
    Ecstasy. Charles Wharton Stork (tr.). 6283-0
    Eggert Olafsson. Skuli Johnson (tr.). 6854-5
    The millennial hymn of Iceland. Jakobina Johnson (tr.). 6283-0
    The millennial hymn of Iceland. Jakobina Johnson (tr.). 6854-5
    New Year's hymn. Kemp Malone (tr.). 6283-0
    Providence. Jakobina Johnson (tr.). 6283-0
    Providence. Jakobina Johnson (tr.). 6854-5
Jock Johnstone, the tinkler. James Hogg. 6102-8,6302-0, 6385-3,6577-5
Jock o' Hazledean. Sir Walter Scott. 6242-3,6332-2,6459-0, 6246-6,6497-3,6075 ,6228-8,6271-7,6290-3,6504-X,6604- 6,6732 ,6239-3,6676-3,6086-2,6560-0,6430-2,6250
Jock o' the side. Unknown. 6185-0,6518-4
Jock the leg and the merry merchant. Unknown. 6185-0
"A 'Jock' from the town of Dundee". Limerick:"A 'Jock' from the town of Dundee". Unknown. 6811-1
Jock, Rab and Tam. Alexander Laing. 6233-4
"Jockie, thine hornpipe's dull" Unknown. 6380-2
Jocks, John Waniente (tr.)
    Caughnawaga song. Unknown (Caughnawaga Indian), 6795-6
Jocky fou, Jenny fair. Unknown. 6180-X
"Jocky said to Jenny, Jenny wilt thou do't". A dainty song. Allan Ramsay. 6932-0
"Jocky said to Jenny, Jenny, wilt thou do't?". A dainty sang. Allan Ramsay. 6831-6
Jocosa lyra. Austin Dobson. 6089-7,6289-X,6724-7
Jodorowsky, Raquel
    Jellyfish. Pamela Carmell (tr.). 7036-1
    Poem in every language. Pamela Carmell (tr.). 7036-1
    The power of man. Pamela Carmell (tr.). 7036-1
    Song for vocal chords and instruments of electronic... Pamela Carmell (tr.). 7036-1
Joe. Alice Robbins. 6045-1
Joe and Jack and Jennie. Witter Bynner. 6017-X
Joe and Meg. Unknown. 6689-5
Joe Bowers. Unknown. 6003-X,6088-9
The Joe Fowler blues. Unknown. 6609-7
Joe Jones. Unknown. 6406-X
Joe Pye's counter. Mary J.J. Wrinn. 6850-2
"Joe takes me along his preferred pushcart...". Animal havens, sels. John Varney. 6808-1
Joe, my pard, the parson. S. Blair McBeath. 6680-1
Joe-Pyeweed. Louis Untermeyer. 6338-1
Joe; an etching. Emily Pauline ("Tekahionwake") Johnson. 6837-5
Joel. Bible. 6143-5
Joel Baker. Unknown. 6651-8
Jog Alaskar nordue. Corinne Sickel. 6118-4

Jog on, jog on, fr. The winter's tale. William Shakespeare. 6182-2,6187-7,6239-3,6328-4,6395-0,6138 ,6395-0,6457-4,6383-7,6639-9,6638-0
"Jog on, jog on, the footpath way". Unknown. 6240-7,6125-7
Johannes Agricola in meditation. Robert Browning. 6437-X, 6657-7
Johannes Barbucallus
    A ruined harbour. Sir William Marris (tr.). 6435-3
Johannes Milton, senex. Robert Bridges. 6487-6,6375-6
Johannesburg. William Plomer. 6788-3
Johannesson, Sigurdur Julius
    Sorrow sings. Christopher Johnston (tr.). 6854-5
    To Iceland. Christopher Johnston (tr.). 6854-5
    A wish. Skuli Johnson (tr.). 6854-5
John. Julia Johnson Davis. 6979-7
John. Wendy Wood. 6269-5
"John Adams lies here, of...Southwell". Epitaph on John Adams, of Southwell. George Gordon, 6th Baron Byron. 6945-2
John Alcohol. Unknown. 6926-6
"John Brown and Jeanne at Fountainebleau--". Students in Paris. Florence Wilkinson. 7038-8
"John Brown died on a scaffold for the slave". The president's proclamation. Edna Dean Proctor. 6753-0
"John Brown died on the scaffold for the slave". John Brown. Edna Dean Proctor. 6946-0
"John Brown had lands and gold enough,they say". A shadow from an insane asylum. Horace B. Durant. 6924-X
"John Brown in Kansas settled, like a...farmer". How old Brown took Harper's Ferry. Edmund Clarence Stedman. 6753-0
"John Brown of Ossawatomie spake...dying day". Brown of Ossawatomie. John Greenleaf Whittier. 6946-0
"John Brown's body lies a-mould'ring in..grave". Glory hallelujah, or new John Brown song. Unknown. 6753-0
"John Brown's body lies a-mould'ring...grave". Glory hallelujah! or John Brown's body. Charles Sprague Hall. 6946-0,6753-0
"John Bull for pastime took a prance". Nongtongpaw. Charles Dibdin. 6909-6
"John Bull, Esquire, my jo John". A new song to an old tune. Unknown. 6946-0
John and Molly. Percy Ilott. 6937-1
John and Tibbie Davison's dispute. Robert Leighton. 6914-2
John and Tibbie's dispute. Unknown. 6554-6,6569-4
John Anderson, my jo. Robert Burns. 6246-6,6271-7,6289-X, 6339-X,6395-0,6475 ,6086-2,6195-0,6153-2,6192-3,6301- 2,6491 ,6101-X,6180-X,6198-2,6328-4,6332-2,6337 , 6152-4,6373-9,6668-2,6543-0,6438-8,6560 ,6138-9,6240- 7,6302-0,6385-3,6427-2,6481 ,6250-4,6371-3,6219-9, 6639-9,6646-1,6430 ,6488-4,6536-8,6610-0,6625-9,6726- 5,6634
John Barleycorn. Robert Burns. 6024-2,6089-7,6179-6,6385-3, 6479-5,6502 ,6105-8,6023-4,6518-X,6732-8,6733-6
John Barleycorn. Bible. 6133-8
John Baynham's epitaph. Thomas Dermody. 6930-4
"John Bird, a laborer lies here". Sylvia Townsend Warner. 6850-2
"John Bird, a laborer, lies here,". Unknown. 6083-8
John Bottlejohn. Laura E. Richards. 6215-6
John Brown. Henry Howard Brownell. 6589-9,6121-4
John Brown. William Herbert Carruth. 6615-1
John Brown. Phoebe Cary. 6969-X
John Brown. Vachel Lindsay. 6619-4,6641-0
John Brown. Edna Dean Proctor. 6946-0
John Brown. William Haskell Simpson. 6615-1
John Brown. Allen Tate. 7017-5
John Brown. Eugene Fitch Ware. 6615-1
John Brown at Harper's Ferry. Edmund Clarence Stedman. 6630-5
John Brown of Osawatomie. Edmund Clarence Stedman. 6385-3, 6467-1,6438-8
John Brown's body. Charles S. Hall. 6088-9
John Brown's body. Unknown. 6289-X
"John Brown's body lies a-mouldering in the grave". Stephen Vincent Benet. 6984-3
John Brown's body, sels. Stephen Vincent Benet. 6217-2, 6527-9,6726-3
John Brown: a paradox. Louise Imogen Guiney. 6946-0
John &Bun. Unknown. 6722-0

JOHN

John Burns of Gettysburg. Francis Bret Harte. 6062-5,6113-3,6392-6,6404-3,6471-X,6552 ,6470-1,6442-6,6016-2, 6307-1,6267-9,6808 ,6472-5
John Butler Yeats. Jeanne Robert Foster. 6036-6
John C. Fremont. John Greenleaf Whittier. 6385-3
John Charles Fremont. Charles F. Lummis. 6946-0
John Christian. Walter Hendricks. 6542-2
"John Cook he had a little gray mare". Unknown. 6334-9, 6363-2
John Cooper's funeral teares. Unknown. 6908-8
John Darrow. Donald Davidson. 6037-4
John Davidson. Unknown. 6240-7
John Day. Thomas Hood. 6974-6
John Di Procida, sels. James Sheridan Knowles. 6980-0
John Doe - buck private. Allan P. Thomson. 6846-4
John Dory. Unknown. 6087-0,6185-0,6338-4,6547-3
John Dowland's the second book of songs or airs, sels. Unknown. 6908-8
John Dowland's the third and last book of songs...,sels. Unknown. 6908-8
John Evereldown. Edwin Arlington Robinson. 6431-0
John Filson. William Henry Venable. 6946-0
John Ford. Algernon Charles Swinburne. 7015-9
John Francois. Unknown. 6547-3
John Frost. William Miller. 6466-3
John Funston. Unknown. 6058-7
John Gilbert. Unknown. 6609-7
John Gilpin. William Cowper. 6127-3,6075-7,6133-8,6502-3, 6614-3,6419 ,6136-2,6228-8,6406-X,6478-7,6504-X
John Gorham. Edwin Arlington Robinson. 6348-9,6121-4
John Greenleaf Whittier. Phoebe Cary. 6969-X,6820-0
John Greenleaf Whittier. John Cameron Grant. 6820-0
John Grumlie. Allan Cunningham. 6089-7
John Hancock Otis, fr. Spoon river anthology. Edgar Lee Masters. 6289-X
John Harding. Mary R. Jarvis. 6681-X
John Henry. Unknown. 7017-5
John Henry Jones. Unknown. 6158-3
John Hery tol' his cap'n. Unknown. 6375-6
John Howard Payne. Unknown. 6486-8
John Ireland. Laurene Tibbetts. 6342-X
John Jankin's sermon. Unknown. 6294-6,6407-8,6155-9
John Jenkins. Anthony C. Deane. 6996-7
John Jones at the piano. Algernon Charles Swinburne. 6902-9
John Jones, fr. The heptalogia. Algernon Charles Swinburne. 6430-2
John Keats. George Gordon, 6th Baron Byron. 6102-8
John Keats. Adelaide Crapsey. 6879-2
John Keats. Thomas Augustine Daly. 6464-7
John Keats. Dante Gabriel Rossetti. 6828-6
John Keats. Dante Gabriel Rossetti. 6110-9,6196-6,6199-0
John Kinsella's lament for Mrs. Mary Moore. William Butler Yeats. 6733-6
John L. Lewis blues. Orville J. Jenks. 6149-4
John Landless leads the caravan. Iwan [or Yvan] Goll. 6068-4
John Lind. Alfred J. Davis. 6342-X
John Lothrop Motley. Unknown. 6523-6
John Masefield. Amy Sherman Bridgeman. 6762-X
John Masefield: Jack and Jill. Charles Powell. 6982-7
John Masefielf: Jack and Jill. Charles Powell. 6982-7
John Maynard. Horatio Alger Jr. 6565-1,6964-9
John Maynard. Unknown. 6554-6
John McGoldrick's trial for the Quaker's daughter. Unknown. 6858-8
John Mouldy. Walter De La Mare. 6596-1
"John bullikins, my jo, John". Uncle Sam to John Bull. Arthur Guiterman. 6773-5
"John came back from the sea...". With all of Dublin lookin' on. Louise Snodgrass. 6906-1
"John Davison and Tibbie, his wife". John and Tibbie Davison's dispute. Robert Leighton. 6914-2
"John Huggins was as bold a man". Epping hunt. Thomas Hood. 6974-6
"John loved his young wife...flower loves dew". The jealous wife. Fred Emerson Brooks. 6921-5
"John loved Teresa who loved Raymond". Quadrille. Carlos Drummond de Andrade. 6758-1
"John Smith, a young attorney, just admitted..". The first client. Irwin Russell. 6878-2
"John Tompkins lived in a house of logs". The second concession of deer. William Wye Smith. 6795-6
"John Trot he was as tall a lad". John Trot. Thomas Hood. 6760-3
John o' Badenyon. John Skinner. 6180-X
John o' Lorn. Neil Munro. 6180-X
John of Damascus, Saint
 The day of Resurrection. John Mason Neale (tr.). 6337-3
 Easter hymn. 6065-X
 Risen with healing in his wings. 6065-X
 "Today in Bethlehem hear I". 6065-X,6337-3,6747-6
John of Fornsete
 Cuckoo song. 6150-8
John of Hazelgreen. Unknown. 6185-0
John of Mt. Sinai. A.L. Frisbie. 6922-3
John of Tours. Dante Gabriel Rossetti. 6458-2
John of Tours. Unknown (French) 7039-6
John Paul Jones. Richard Watson Gilder. 6465-5
John Peel. Mark Andrews. 7008-6
John Peel. John Woodcock Graves. 6732-8
John Pegram. William Gordon McCabe. 6074-9
John Pelham. James Ryder Randall. 6074-9,6016-2,6016-2
John Reed. Bayard Taylor. 6976-2
John Riley. Unknown. 6826-X
John S. Crow. Kirke Monroe. 6965-7
John Sevier, fr. The tall men. Donald Davidson. 7017-5
John Smith. Eugene Field. 6949-5
John Smith's approach to Jamestown. James Barron Hope. 6946-0
John Smith's will. B.P. Shillaber. 6411-6
John of the Cross, Saint
 Romance VIII. Allison Peers (tr.). 6282-2
John the Pilgrim. Theodore Watts-Dunton. 6337-3,6656-9
John Thompson's daughter. Phoebe Cary. 6089-7,6440-X,6964-9
John Thomson and the Turk. Unknown. 6185-0,6518-X
John Trot. Thomas Hood. 6760-3
John Trot. Thomas Hood. 6974-6
John Underhill. John Greenleaf Whittier. 6946-0
John Wasson. Edgar Lee Masters. 6299-7
John Webster. Algernon Charles Swinburne. 7015-9
John Webster. Algernon Charles Swinburne. 6483-3,6655-0
John Webster. Algernon Charles Swinburne. 7015-9
John Wesley's rule. Unknown. 6260-1,6466-3
John White's Thanksgiving. Unknown. 6925-8
John White's Thanksgiving. Unknown. 6703-4,6745-X
John Winter. Laurence Binyon. 6258-X,6290-3,6547-3
"John was an honest farmer lad". Somehow. Unknown. 6918-5
"John yor my husbandes'man you knowe." Unknown. 6563-5
John's wife. Wilfred Wilson Gibson. 6850-2
John, Edmund
 Fragment ("Give me"). 6102-8
 Symphonie symbolique. 6102-8
John, Edward
 In memoriam ("Rest, though the clamorous surge of war") 6474-4
John, Romilly
 Transitions. 6782-4
John, Sarah F.
 Mothers. 6894-4
John-John. Thomas MacDonagh. 6872-3
John-John. Thomas Macdonough. 6930-4
Johneen. Patrick Joseph Carroll. 6543-0
Johneen. Moira (Nesta Higginson Skrine) O'Neill. 6242-3
Johnie Faa. Unknown. 6180-X
Johnie Scot. Unknown. 6185-0
Johnie [or Johnnie] Armstrong. Unknown. 6180-X,6185-0,6498-1,6055-2,6067-6,6419
Johnnie Cock. Unknown. 6185-0,6473-6,6193-1
Johnnie Cope. Adam Skirving. 6180-X,6198-2,6086-2,6153-2
Johnnie Cope. Unknown. 6859-6
Johnnie Cope: 2d set. Unknown. 6859-6
Johnnie Courteau. William Henry Drummond. 6433-7,6115-X, 6446-9,6591-0,6592-9
"Johnnie and I, in our Sunday hats". October. Kate Crichton Gredler. 6799-9
Johnnie of Breadislee. Unknown. 6055-2,6518-X
Johnnie [or Johnny] Sands. Unknown. 6058-7,6003-X,6157-5
Johnnie's first moose. William Henry Drummond. 6161-3

Johnny. Christina Georgina Rossetti. 6772-7
Johnny and Betsy. Unknown. 6003-X
Johnny Appleseed. Rosemary and Stephen Vincent Benet. 6891-X
Johnny Appleseed. Edgar Lee Masters. 6607-0,6161-3,6121-4
Johnny Appleseed; a ballad of the old northwest. William Henry Venable. 6946-0
Johnny Barbour. Unknown. 6061-7
Johnny Bartholomew. Thomas Dunn English. 6062-5,6406-X
"Johnny bumped his head". Unknown. 6364-0
Johnny Cox. Alfred Perceval Graves. 6518-X
Johnny Dow. Unknown. 6722-0
Johnny Doyle. Unknown. 6057-9,6058-7
Johnny Faa, the lord of little Egypt. Unknown. 6829-4
Johnny German. Unknown. 6057-9
Johnny Judkins. Charles Follen Adams. 6917-7
Johnny Jumper, fr. Memories. William B. Wilson. 6149-4
"Johnny had a golden head". Johnny. Christina Georgina Rossetti. 6772-7
"Johnny he's risen up in the morn". Johnny of Cockley's well. Unknown. 6829-4
Johnny onions. Mary Sinton Leitch. 6039-0
Johnny Randall. Unknown. 6003-X
Johnny Raw and Polly Clark. Unknown. 6157-5
Johnny Right. Alice Cary. 6969-X
Johnny Scott. Unknown. 6061-7,6518-X
"Johnny shall have a new bonnet". Unknown. 6904-5
Johnny the stout. Unknown. 6743-3
Johnny's hist'ry lesson. Nixon Waterman. 6694-1
Johnny's lesson. Unknown. 6684-4
"Johnny's mad, and I am glad". Unknown. 7028-0
Johnny's opinion of grandmothers. Unknown. 6684-4,6566-X
Johnny's pocket. Unknown. 6743-3
Johnny's the lad I love. Unknown. 6244-X
Johnny, I hardly knew ye. Unknown. 6179-6,6244-X,6733-6, 6665-8
The Johnny-cake. Unknown. 6127-3
The johnnycake. Unknown. 6891-X
Johns, Glyn
    Gold. 6379-9
    Night. 6379-9
    Song ("I kept neat"). 6379-9
Johns, Orrick
    Bess. 6032-3
    Dilemma. 6031-5,6556-2,6300-4
    The door. 6320-9,6619-4
    Failure. 6506-6
    The interpreter. 6031-5,6556-2,6467-1
    The last night. 6441-8,6619-4
    Little things. 6374-8,6556-2,6513-9,6393-4
    No prey am I, fr. Songs of deliverance. 6897-9
    Old youth. 6031-5
    Reality. 6072-2
    Royalty. 7008-6
    Salome. 6959-2
    The sea-lands. 6310-1,6347-0
    Second Avenue. 6102-8,6076-5,6327-6
    Shopping day. 6817-0
    The song of youth, fr. Songs of Deliverance. 6102-8, 6076-5
    Songs of deliverance. 6897-9
    Songs of deliverance, sels. 6102-8,6076-5
    The tree-toad. 6464-7
    Virgins, fr. Songs of deliverance. 6897-9
    Wild plum. 6619-4,6513-9,6300-4,6464-7
Johnson's ghost. Horace Smith. 6802-2
Johnson, Albert E.
    The perjured. 6532-5
Johnson, Annie R.
    The strange request. 6921-5
Johnson, Burges
    The anxious farmer. 6338-1
    Ballade of the little things that count. 6875-8
    Bedtime comes too soon. 6715-8
    Blowing bubbles. 6368-3
    Cookin' things. 6700-X
    Daytime naps. 6715-8
    F I was er horse!?' 6510-4
    The glad young chamois. 6861-8
    The play-sprite. 7030-2
    Remarks to my grown-up pup. 7008-6
    Rhapsody on a dog's intelligence. 7008-6
    A rondeau of remorse. 6875-8
    The service. 6211-3,6527-9,6029-3,6653-4
    To be continued. 6817-0
    Toul. 6033-1
    Where dreams are made. 6368-3
    Why doth a pussy cat? 6089-7
Johnson, Charles Frederick
    The modern Romans. 6255-5,6307-1
Johnson, Donald Goold
    Battle hymn. 6650-X
Johnson, Dorothy Vena
    Epitaph for a bigot. 6178-8
    Post war ballad. 6178-8
    Road to anywhere. 6178-8
    Success. 6178-8
Johnson, E.E.
    Symbols - words. 6488-4
Johnson, Edgar (tr.)
    "Dion of Tarsus, here I lie". Unknown (Greek), 6637-2
    "Her love she vowed was mine fore'er". Meleager, 6637-2
Johnson, Edith L.
    Mutes. 6750-6
Johnson, Edward
    A cry unto the Lord to stay His hand, sels. 6077-3
    The water drinker. 6685-2,6605-2
    Wonder-working providence..Sions saviour in New England, sels. 6008-0
Johnson, Eleanor Noyes
    Evidence. 6764-6
    Games. 6764-6
Johnson, Elvira T.
    Spring in Duluth. 6342-X
Johnson, Emily Pauline ("Tekahionwake")
    'And he said, fight on'. 6837-5
    The archers. 6837-5
    The art of Alma-Tadema. 6837-5
    As red men die. 6115-X
    At Crow's Nest Pass. 6837-5
    At half-mast. 6837-5
    At husking time. 6476-0,6656-9
    At sunset. 6837-5
    At the ferry. 6795-6
    Autumn's orchestra. 6837-5
    The ballad of Yaada. 6797-2
    The ballad of Yaada. 6837-5,6843-X
    Beyond the blue. 6837-5
    The birds' lullaby. 6602-X
    Brandon. 6837-5
    Brier. 6337-3
    Calgary of the plains. 6837-5
    The camper. 6837-5
    Canada. 6837-5
    Canadian born. 6837-5
    The cattle country. 6433-7
    The cattle thief. 6837-5
    Christmastide. 6837-5
    The city and the sea. 6837-5
    Close by. 6837-5
    The corn husker. 6837-5
    A cry from an Indian wife. 6837-5
    Dawendine. 6837-5
    Day dawn. 6837-5
    Easter. 6837-5
    Erie waters. 6837-5
    Fasting. 6837-5
    Fire-flowers. 6837-5
    The flight of crows. 6837-5
    'Give us Barabbas'. 6837-5
    Golden - of the Selkirks. 6837-5
    Good-bye. 6837-5
    Guard of the eastern gate. 6433-7
    The happy hunting grounds. 6837-5
    Harvest time. 6433-7,6591-0
    The homing bee. 6837-5
    The idlers. 6837-5
    In grey days. 6837-5
    In the shadows. 6115-X,6591-0,6592-2
    The Indian corn planter. 6796-4,6837-5

Joe; an etching. 6837-5
The king's consort. 6837-5
Lady icicle. 6837-5
Lady Lorgnette. 6837-5
The legend of Qu'Appelle Valley. 6291-0,6592-2,6648-8
The legend of Qu'Appelle valley. 6837-5
The lifting of the muse. 6837-5
The lost lagoon. 6115-X
Low tide at St. Andrews. 6837-5
Lullaby of the Iroquois. 6433-7
The man in chrysanthemum land. 6837-5
The mariner. 6837-5
Marshlands. 6837-5
Moonset. 6837-5
My English letter. 6837-5
Nocturne. 6837-5
Ojistoh. 6837-5
Overlooked. 6837-5
Penseroso. 6837-5
The pilot of the plains. 6115-X,6458-2
Prairie greyhounds. 6837-5
A prodigal. 6837-5
The quill worker. 6591-0,6592-2
The quill workers. 6837-5
Rainfall. 6837-5,6785-9
Re-voyage. 6837-5
The riders of the plains. 6115-X
Shadow river. 6837-5
Shadow river. 6843-X
Silhouette. 6591-0,6592-2
Silhouette. 6837-5
The sleeping giant. 6837-5
The song my paddle sings. 6255-5,6433-7,6465-5,6476-0, 6115-X,6656
The songster. 6115-X
Thistle-down. 6837-5
'Through time and bitter distance'. 6837-5
A toast. 6837-5
The trail to Lillooet. 6837-5
The train dogs. 6837-5
Under canvas. 6837-5
The vagabonds. 6274-1,6656-9
Wave-won. 6837-5
When George was king. 6837-5
Where leaps the Ste. Marie. 6837-5
The wolf. 6837-5
Wolverine. 6837-5
Workworn. 6266-0
Your mirror frame. 6837-5

Johnson, Esther
Stella. 6317-9

Johnson, Fenton
The lost love. 6032-3

Johnson, Frances A. M.
My boy. 6629-1

Johnson, Frances Ann
Granite state. 6764-6
Lilacs. 6764-6

Johnson, Frances Smith
Black music. 6316-0
Where lilacs stand apart. 6316-0
Woman plowing. 6316-0

Johnson, G.T.
Limerick:"One day I went out to then zoo". 6811-1

Johnson, Geoffrey
All over the world. 6257-1
The autumn fire. 6761-1
Drought. 6257-1
The first of April ("Today the swards of heaven..."). 6465-5
The first of April. 6783-2
Furnace wharf. 6761-1
The heron. 6782-4
If only. 6761-1
The Magi. 6782-4
The mirror. 6042-0
Otherworld. 6781-6
Peat-cutters. 6257-1
The windmill. 6257-1
A winter legend. 6218-0

Johnson, Georgia Douglas
Armor. 6038-2
Black recruit. 6178-8
Escape. 6039-0
I've learned to sing. 6178-8
Interracial. 6178-8
Measure. 6036-6
The riddle. 6039-0
To the mantled. 6031-5

Johnson, H.H.
The old church. 6166-4

Johnson, H.U.
Nicknames of the states. 6923-1
Oh, I'm my grandpa's girl. 6713-1

Johnson, Hannah More
Father at play. 6131-1

Johnson, Helen Mae
They speak to us. 6894-4

Johnson, Henry
The cat and the bird and I. 6552-X
Derelict. 6870-7
The funeral parlor. 6870-7
The journey. 6870-7
Mask of stone. 6870-7
Search for love. 6870-7

Johnson, Herbert Clark
A boy's need. 6761-1

Johnson, Herrick
The voice in the twilight. 6303-9

Johnson, Hilda
Ballade of expansion. 6996-7
Ballade of expansion. 6946-0
The legend of realism. 6440-X
The quest of the purple cow. 6089-7

Johnson, Huldah M.
Charles Lindbergh. 7019-1

Johnson, J.C.
The oaks. 6049-8

Johnson, Jacqueline J.
Does it ever make a difference. 6899-5
March water songs I. 6899-5
The song of the land. 6899-5
What keeps us alive. 6899-5

Johnson, Jakobina (tr.)
At close of day. Stephan G. Stephansson, 6283-0,6854-5
At sunset. Steingrimur Thorsteinsson, 6283-0
Canada. Guttormur J. Guttormsson, 6854-5
A day in spring. Kristinn Stefansson, 6854-5
Death comes riding, fr. Governor Lenhard. Einar Hjorleifsson Kvaran, 6283-0
A drop of brine. Kristinn Stefansson, 6854-5
Evening. Stephan G. Stephansson, 6854-5
Evening. Stephan G. Stephansson, 6283-0
Evening. Porsteinn Erlingsson, 6854-5
Good night. Guttormur J. Guttormsson, 6854-5
Governor Lenhard, sels. Einar Hjorleifsson Kvaran, 6283-0
A greeting. Jonas Hallgrimsson, 6283-0
A greeting. Jonas Hallgrimsson, 6854-5
Greetings to Norway. Johann Sigurjonsson, 6283-0
Iceland's song. Grimur Thomsen, 6854-5
Iceland's song. Grimur Thomsen, 6283-0
A love song. Steingrimur Thorsteinsson, 6283-0
The millennial hymn of Iceland. Matthias Jochumsson, 6283-0
The millennial hymn of Iceland. Matthias Jochumsson, 6854-5
Mountain and hillock, fr. Epigrams. Steingrimur Thorsteinsson, 6283-0
My country lies wounded, fr. Governor Lenhard. Einar Hjorleifsson Kvaran, 6283-0
Nearing cold-dale. Hannes Hafstein, 6283-0
Nearing Cold-dale. Hannes Hafstein, 6854-5
Northern lights. Einar Benediktsson, 6283-0
Northern lights. Einar Benediktsson, 6854-5
Peace on earth, sels. Gudmundur Gudmundsson, 6283-0
Peace on earth, sels. Gudmundur Gudmundsson, 6854-5
Prologue, fr. Peace on earth. Gudmundur Gudmundsson, 6283-0
Providence. Matthias Jochumsson, 6283-0

Providence. Matthias Jochumsson, 6854-5
Regret. Benedikt Grondal, 6283-0
Regret. Benedikt Grondal, 6854-5
The rose. Gudmundur Gudmundsson, 6283-0
Servant of light. Einar Paul Jonsson, 6854-5
Spring. Hannes Hafstein, 6283-0
Surf. Einar Benediktsson, 6854-5
Swansong on the moorlands. Steingrimur Thorsteinsson, 6854-5
Swansong on the moorlands. Steingrimur Thorsteinsson, 6283-0
The tear. Kristjan Jonsson, 6283-0
The tear. Kristjan Jonsson, 6854-5
The terms. Thorsteinn Erlingsson, 6283-0
The terms. Porsteinn Erlingsson, 6854-5
Thorvaldur Thoroddsen. Thorsteinn Gislason, 6854-5
Thorvaldur Thoroddsen. Thorsteinn Gislason, 6283-0
Voice of song. Steingrimur Thorsteinsson, 6854-5
Voice of song. Steingrimur Thorsteinsson, 6283-0
The west wind. Bjarni Thorarensen, 6854-5
'What lack we?', sels. Gudmundur Fridjonsson, 6854-5
'What lack we?' Gudmundur Fridjonsson, 6283-0

Johnson, James Noel
A genius. 6675-5
A strange parent. 6701-8

Johnson, James Weldon
Brothers. 6527-9
The creation. 6337-3,6532-5,6527-9,6736-0,6393-4
The dancing girl. 6959-2
Go down, death. 6337-3,6464-7,6628-3
My city. 6038-2
Prayer at sunrise. 6532-5
To America, sel. 6954-1
The white witch. 6029-3

Johnson, Jodi Ann
The death of a horse. 6900-2

Johnson, Josephine
American scene. 6761-1
The exiled heart. 6839-1
Final autumn. 6375-6
Fool's paradise. 6038-2
Hour before light. 6761-1
In absence. 6042-0
In this stern hour. 6337-3
Indian giver. 6039-0
July. 6818-9
The level way. 6037-4
The lightship. 6042-0
Low country. 6979-7
Ol' Bill. 6761-1
Rebellion. 6039-0
Scents. 6038-2
Supplication. 6532-5
This is the trouble with us all. 6532-5
Tonowanda creek. 6799-9
The unwilling gypsy. 6083-8,6037-4
Year's end, sels. 6532-5

Johnson, Just
Song of desolation. 6750-6

Johnson, Leanna F.
Joy or sorrow. 6178-8
Supremacy. 6178-8

Johnson, Lionel
The age of a dream. 6507-4
Bagley wood. 6655-0
Ballade of the Caxton Head. 6875-8
Beyond. 6250-4
By the statue of King Charles at Charing Cross. 6301-2, 6383-7,6250-4,6102-8,6655-0,6508 ,6044-7,6096-X,6244-X,6437-X,6477-9,6022
Cadgwith. 6096-X,6282-2,6437-X,6292-X,6172-9,6301
Celtic speech. 6090-0
Christmas and Ireland. 6292-X,6172-9
Christmas carol II. 6490-6
The church of a dream. 6096-X,6244-X,6507-4
The dark angel, sels. 6317-9
The dark angel. 6022-6,6096-X,6489-2,6244-X,6726-3,6292 ,6172-9,6508-2,6655-1
The darkness. 6507-4
The day of coming days. 6508-2

Dead. 6208-3,6246-6
Desideria. 6655-0
A dream of youth. 6655-0
Enthusiasts. 6174-5
Escape. 6655-0
A friend. 6292-X,6477-9,6655-0,6172-9,6250-4,6022-6, 6477-9
Friends. 6507-4
Glories. 6641-0,6250-4,6383-7
Hill and vale. 6253-9
In Falmouth harbour, sels. 6508-2
In memory, sels. 6208-3
The last music. 6174-5,6244-X
Lucretius. 6483-3
Magic, sels. 6508-2
Mystic and cavalier. 6244-X,6507-4
Oracles. 6655-0
Our lady of France. 6282-2
Our lady of the May. 6282-2
Our lady of the snows. 6172-9,6292-X
Oxford. 6437-X
Oxford nights. 6331-4
Parnell. 6508-2
The precept of silence. 6102-8,6022-6,6250-4,6301-2, 6477-9,6096-X,6339-X,6507-4,6655-0,6301 ,6250-4
The precept of silence. 6861-8
A proselyte. 6507-4
The red wind. 6174-5
Saint Columba. 6174-5
Sancta silvarum. 6253-9
The statue of King Charles at Charing Cross. 6172-9, 6292-X
A stranger. 6507-4
Sylvan mortfydd. 6655-0
Te martyrum candidatus. 6022-6,6244-X,6292-X,6172-9
To a friend. 6508-2
To a traveller. 6641-0
To Morfydd. 6090-0,6244-X,6507-4,6508-2,6655-0
To Morfydd dead. 6507-4
To my patrons. 6172-9,6292-X
To ocean hazard: gipsy. 6655-0
'To weep Irish'. 6174-5,6655-0
Upon a drawing. 6655-0
Vinum daemonum. 6508-2
Wales ("Mother of holy fire!..."). 6331-4
Ways of war. 6060-0,6244-X
Westward. 6508-2
Winchester. 6437-X

Johnson, Louis
Poem in Karori. 6043-9
Pygmalion. 6043-9

Johnson, M.C.
Swimmin' in the crick. 6548-1

Johnson, M.R.
Fire-bells. 6680-1

Johnson, Margaret
Before the shower. 6965-7
The bull. 6690-9
The child's wonder. 6314-4

Johnson, Margaret E.
Eight o'clock. 6965-7

Johnson, Mary E.C.
Scandal. 6416-7

Johnson, Morton Phillips
The poet. 6270-9

Johnson, Mrs. Herrick
'Faultless'. 6925-8
The voice in the twilight. 6521-X,6571-6,6413-2
The voice in the twilight. 6889-8

Johnson, Negro. James Oppenheim. 6345-4

Johnson, Nick
The sleeping gypsy-a painting by Rousseau. 6966-5

Johnson, Patricia M.
Another kind of autumn. 6857-X
Eleventh floor view. 6857-X
The flea market. 6857-X
In my father's house. 6857-X

Johnson, Philander
The stranger. 6137-0

Johnson, Ray M.

JOHNSON

Johnson, Robert Underwood
    The greatest work. 6337-3
Johnson, Robert Underwood
    "And then?". 6585-6
    The art of the arts. 6585-6
    As I walked forth. 6328-4
    Before the blossom. 6652-6
    Browning at Asolo. 6102-8'6331-4,6624-0,6076-5,6309-8, 6631
    Como in April. 6338-1
    Dewey at Manila. 6062-5,6741-X
    An English mother. 6097-8,6627-5
    Farewell to Italy ("We lingered at Domo d'Ossola-"). 6624-0
    The haunting face. 6029-3
    Hearth-song. 6266-0
    A hymn for the pact of peace. 6420-5
    I journeyed south to meet the spring. 6441-8
    "I journeyed south to meet the spring". 6652-6
    Illusions. 6632-1
    Italian rhapsody, sels. 6624-0,6439-6
    Love in the calendar. 6441-8,6652-6
    Love in [or and] Italy. 6102-8,6331-4,6309-8
    Luck and work. 6585-6
    Markham. 6076-5
    Music and love. 6320-9
    The name writ in water. 6631-3
    The night nurse. 6042-0
    On a candidate accused of youth. 6995-9
    Quality. 6424-8
    Reading Horace. 6030-7
    To Dreyfus vindicated. 6848-0
    To Dreyfus vindicated. 6848-0
    To Italy, fr. Italian rhapsody. 6624-0
    To my countrymen. 6143-5,6461-2
    To Russia new and free. 7026-4
    To the Housatonic at Stockbridge. 6597-X
    To the returning brave. 6946-0
    Towers of remembrance. 7001-9
    Two flags upon Westminster Towers. 7027-2
    The wistful days. 6006-4,6597-X,6047-1,6102-8,6076-5, 6300

Johnson, Rossiter
    Faith's surrender. 7041-8
    Laurence. 6014-5
    Lawrence. 7041-8
    Ninety-nine in the shade. 6089-7,6273-3,6424-8,6656-2
    Over, through, and under. 7019-1
    A soldier poet. 6340-3
    A woman of the war. 6113-3,6016-2

Johnson, Ruth Brownlee
    Chained. 6178-8
    Cords. 6178-8

Johnson, Sally
    The helpful fairy. 6249-0

Johnson, Sam
    We done quit. 6149-4

Johnson, Samuel
    Ambition. 6087-0
    Anacreon, ode ninth. 6975-4
    Autumn. 6975-4
    Boethius. 6641-0
    Burlesque. 6228-8
    Burlesque on the modern versification of ancient..tales. 6975-4
    By poverty depressed, fr. London. 6934-7
    Cardinal Wolsey. 6543-0
    Charles XII. 6543-0,6102-8,6240-7,6302-0,6385-3,6250-4, 6150
    City of God. 6337-3,6730-1
    "Condemn'd to hope's delusive mine,". 6208-3
    Dr. Levett. 6087-0
    Epigram (on Colley Cibber) 6092-7
    Epigram on George II and Colley Cibber, Esq. 6975-4
    Epilogue intended to have been spoken by a lady... 6975-4
    Epitaph for Mr Hogarth. 6975-4
    Epitaph on Claude Phillips. 6975-4
    Epitaph on Sir Thomas Hanmer, Bart. 6975-4
    An epitaph upon the celebrated Claudy Philips..musician. 6932-0
    Evening: an ode (1). 6975-4
    Evening: an ode (2). 6975-4
    Fate of Charles the Twelfth. 6605-2
    Friendship. 6543-0
    Friendship ("Friendship, peculiar boon of heav'n"). 6085-4
    Friendship: an ode. 6975-4
    If the man who turnips cries. 6089-7,6722-0,6092-7
    Imitation of the style of [Percy]. 6975-4
    Impromptu on hearing Mrs Thrale consulting with..friend. 6975-4
    Inspiration. 6730-1
    Letter to the Earl of Chesterfield. 6200-8
    Life's last scene, fr. The vanity of human wishes. 6932-0
    Lines written in ridicule of certain poems...1777. 6975-4
    Lines written under a print...persons skaiting. 6975-4
    London. 6245-8
    London, sels. 6198-2,6195-0,6637-2
    Midsummer. 6975-4
    O'er crackling ice. 7035-3
    On seeing a bust of Mrs Montague. 6975-4
    On some lines of Lopez de Vega. 6278-4
    On the death of Dr. Robert Levet. 6024-2,6600-3,6641-0, 6102-8,6152-4,6086 ,6219-9,6491-4
    On the death of Mr. Robert Levet. 6153-2
    On the death of Mr. Robert Levett. 6975-4
    On the death of Stephen Grey, F.R.S. 6975-4
    One and twenty. 6975-4
    One-and-twenty. 6102-8,6186-9,6732-8,6427-2,6092-7,6301
    Paraphrase of Proverbs, chap. IV, verses 6-11. 6975-4
    Parody of a translation from the Medea of Euripides. 6975-4
    Philips! whose touch harmonious, fr. The festoon. 6328-4
    Poverty. 6250-4
    Poverty in London, fr. London. 6125-7,6150-8,6125-7, 6150-6
    Prayer ("...Where then shall"). 6153-2
    Prayer ("Where then shall hope and fear..."). 6932-0
    Prayer ("Where then"). 6150-6
    Prayer for strength. 6337-3
    Prologue at Drury Lane. 6153-2
    Prologue spoken by Mr. Garrick before the Masque..Comus. 6975-4
    Prologue to Goldsmith's comedy of The good-natured man. 6975-4
    Prologue to the comedy of a word to the wise. 6543-0
    Prologue, fr. Opening of the Drury Lane Theatre, 1747 6543-0
    Prologue, fr. The good-natur'd man. 6315-2
    Prologue, spoken by Mr. Garrick...Theatre Royale. 6378-0,6483-3,6733-6,6152-4,6723-9,6086
    Prologue, spoken by Mr. Garrick...Theatre-Royal, 1747. 6086-2
    The quiet life. 6322-5
    A satire. 6086-2
    The scholar's life, fr. The vanity of human wishes. 6932-0
    Shakespeare and Jonson. 6102-8
    A short song of congratulation. 6315-2
    Spring. 6975-4
    Stella in mourning. 6975-4
    Thales finds fault with life in England's capital. 6637-2
    Thirty-five. 6787-5
    To a friend. 6975-4
    To a young lady on her birthday. 6975-4
    To Lady Firebrace. 6975-4
    To Lyce. 6975-4
    To Miss **** on her playing upon a harpsichord... 6975-4
    To Miss *****, on her giving the author...purse. 6975-4
    To Miss Hickman. 6975-4
    To Mrs. Thrale. 6092-7
    To Mrs. Thrale, on her completing her thirty-fifth year. 6086-2
    To Stella. 6975-4
    To-morrow. 6211-3,6385-3

The vanity of human wishes, sels. 6024-2,6122-2,6198-2, 6378-0,6195-0
The vanity of human wishes. 6219-9,6200-8,6208-3,6271-7, 6315-2,6641-0,6152
Verses written at the request of a gentleman... 6975-4
Wealth. 6211-3
Winter. 6975-4
The wise man's prayer. 6605-2
Wolsey. 6323-3
The young author. 6975-4
Johnson, Samuel (tr.)
Adriano, sels. Pietro Mestastio, 6975-4
Anacreon's dove. Anacreon, 7039-6
Celestial wisdom, fr. The tenth Satire. Juvenal, 7039-6
A hinted wish. Martial, 7039-6
Ode 007. Horace, 6975-4
Ode 022, sels. Horace, 6975-4
Odes, sels. Horace, 6641-0
Pastoral 001 Vergil, 6975-4
Rio verde, rio verde, sels. Unknown, 6975-4
Johnson, Skuli (tr.)
Abba-labba-la. David Stefansson, 6283-0
As from a flower's chalice. Unnur ("Hulda") Benediktdottir, 6854-5
The beggar woman. Gestur Palsson, 6854-5
The bride's slippers. David Stefansson fra Fagraskogi, 6854-5
Eggert Olafsson. Matthias Jochumsson, 6854-5
'Fairy hill'. David Stefansson fra Fagraskogi, 6854-5
Father and son. Gudmundur Fridjonsson, 6854-5
From an address at an Icelandic celebration. Stephan G. Stephansson, 6854-5
Iceland. Bjarni Thorarensen, 6854-5
If the moonbeam. Unnur ("Hulda") Benediktdottir, 6854-5, 6283-0
'Neath 'darksome fells'. Jon Thoroddsen, 6854-5
Night. Benedikt Grondal, 6854-5
Oarage. Gudmundur Magnusson, 6854-5
Old flames amid ashes lie hidden. David Stefansson fra Fagraskogi, 6854-5
On Swine's dale. Jon Thoroddsen, 6854-5
Our native tongue. Kristjan N. ("K.N.") Julius, 6854-5
Remembrance. Grimur Thomsen, 6854-5
The shadow. David Stefansson fra Fagraskogi, 6854-5
A sonnet ("Spring"). Johann Sigurjonsson, 6283-0,6854-5
The soul of the house. Guttormur J. Guttormsson, 6854-5
Spring. Thorsteinn Gislason, 6854-5,6283-0
The storm. Hannes Hafstein, 6854-5
A summer greeting. Pall Olafsson, 6854-5
Sunny Haunts' Sand. Grimur Thomsen, 6854-5
To the 'river's slope'. Bjarni Thorarensen, 6854-5
Venus with blithe eyes is beaming. Jon Thoroddsen, 6854-5
The westland (America). Einar Hjorleifsson Kvaran, 6854-5
A wish. Sigurdur Julius Johannesson, 6854-5
Johnson, Stanley
Argument. 6039-0
Pier. 6037-4
Johnson, Thomas H.
Villanelle. 6320-9
Johnson, Victoria Saffelle
The great blue heron. 6979-7
Johnson, Vlyn
Friends ("I have a friend whose stillness rests me so") 6607-0
Johnson, Wilfred M.
The city. 6857-X
The pinball machine. 6857-X
Johnson, Willard
City birds. 6808-1
City quiet. 6808-1
Interior. 6072-2
Interior. 6808-1
The living root. 6070-6
Johnson, William Martin
On snow-flakes melting on his lady's breast. 6077-3, 6004-8
Johnson, William Samuel
Buttadeus. 6030-7

His day. 6995-9
Prayer for peace. 6209-3,6029-3
Johnson, Willis Fletcher
My books. 6297-0
Johnson, Winston
The armoraider's song. 6237-7
Johnson, Yvette
Ghetto. 7024-8
Reality. 7024-8
Sapling. 7024-8
This is the city. 7024-8
Johnston at Shiloh. Fleming James. 6062-5
Johnston, Charles H.L.
The president. 6964-9
Johnston, Christopher (tr.)
Sorrow sings. Sigurdur Julius Johannesson, 6854-5
To Iceland. Sigurdur Julius Johannesson, 6854-5
Johnston, Ella Colter
Amalfi by the sea. 6906-1
I would walk the ways of the busy town. 6906-1
Insomnia. 6906-1
Song of the sea. 6906-1
Spring song. 6906-1
What is April? 6906-1
Johnston, Emma M.
The boy who went from home. 6406-X
Her old-time song. 6097-8
My mother's song. 6415-9
Thanksgiving day dinner. 6713-1
Johnston, James Nicoll
Abraham Lincoln. 6524-4
Johnston, James Noel
How an engineer won his bride. 6924-X
Johnston, Jean Stephen
First loves. 6750-6
Johnston, John H.
The cross-eyed lovers. 6413-2
Johnston, Laban Thomas
Adobe wall and Indian Joe. 6316-0
Autumnal rhythm. 6316-0
The living ray. 6316-0
Johnston, Mary
The river James. 6037-4
Virginiana. 6776-X
Virginiana. 6509-0,6036-6
Johnston, Thomas
On such a night. 6258-X
Johnston, William
On the downtown side of an uptown street. 6089-7
Johnston, Winifred
Advice to a young man wishing to wed. 6397-7
Eternities. 6397-7
"Let this be read." 6397-7
On reading a portion of Rossetti. 6397-7
One weds. 6397-7
To an old man planting seed. 6397-7
Johnstone, Arthur
A fisher's apology. 6845-6
Johnstone, D.V.
Star of the morning. 6065-X
Johnstone, Ernest F.
No Vermonters in heaven. 7030-2
Johnstone, Henry
A charm to call sleep. 6519-8,6135-4
The fastidious serpent. 6089-7,645-3
The gardener's burial. 6046-3
Good-night prayer for a little child. 6452-3
Guessing song. 6519-8,6368-4
Snake story. 6452-3
Johnstone, Mrs.
A new occasional address. 6064-1
"Johny he has risen up i the morn". Unknown. 6111-7
Join the caroling. Rowena Bastin Bennett. 6608-9
"Join the dance, with step as light". The village coquettes. Charles Dickens. 6959-2
Joined the blues. John Jerome Rooney. 6741-X
Joiner, Gus
I can tell de world. 6149-4
No unions down yonder. 6149-4
A joke versified. Thomas Moore. 6278-4

JOKE,

The joke, fr. Battle. Wilfred Wilson Gibson. 6897-9
A joke. Unknown. 6529-5
The jokesmith's vacation. Don Marquis. 6026-9
Jolas, Eugene
    Coda. 6351-9
    Hallucination. 6351-9
    Rhythms of a maimed springtime. 6351-9
    The voyage. 6351-9
Jolas, Eugene (tr.)
    Aeternae memoriae patris. Leon Paul Fargue, 6343-8
The jolly beggar. James V; King of Scotland. 6157-5,6328-4
The jolly beggar. Unknown. 6134-6
The jolly beggars, sels. Robert Burns. 6733-6
The jolly beggars. Robert Burns. 6732-8,6026-9,6152-4,6430-2
Jolly boatman. Unknown. 6058-7
The jolly curlers. James Hogg. 7035-3
The jolly driver. Unknown. 6157-5
The jolly forester. Unknown. 6383-7
"A jolly friar, black, white, or gray". To the friar's senior society. George Linville Baker. 6936-3
Jolly good ale and old. John Still. 6240-7,6219-9,6301-2
Jolly good ale and old. Unknown. 6052-8,6733-6
"Jolly good fellows who die for the death...". The unmercenaries. Unknown. 7007-8
The jolly goshawk. Unknown. 6055-2
Jolly Jack. William Makepeace Thackeray. 6230-X
Jolly Jankyn. Unknown. 6733-6
A jolly journey. Harriet Nutty. 6130-3
The jolly miller. James Whitcomb Riley. 6990-8
The jolly miller. Unknown. 6134-6
The Jolly old crow. Unknown. 6165-6
"Jolly old fellows the mountains are!". The mountain dance. Wallace E. Mather. 6965-7
The jolly old pedagogue. George Arnold. 6004-8,6219-9,6304-7,6910-X
Jolly old Saint Nicholas. Unknown. 6684-4
The jolly pinder of wakefield. Unknown. 6185-0
The jolly ploughboy. Unknown. 6057-9
Jolly robin. Sir Thomas Wyatt. 6383-7
Jolly sailor's bold. Unknown. 6057-9
Jolly shepherd. Unknown. 6328-4,6383-7
The jolly shepherd, fr. King Lear. William Shakespeare. 6134-6,6466-3
"Jolly shepherd, shepherd on a hill". Sir John Wotton. 6181-8
The jolly shepherd. John Wootton. 6383-7
The jolly testator who makes his own will. Unknown. 6878-2
A jolly wassail-bowl. Unknown. 6756-5
Jolly wee miner men. Unknown. 6149-4
Joly joly wat, sels. Unknown. 6339-X
"Jonadab, the son of Rechab". The father's counsel. Ellen Murray. 6920-7
Jonah. Lydia Gibson. 6880-4
Jonah. Aldous Huxley. 6125-7
Jonah. Unknown. 6022-6
Jonas Fisher: a poem in brown and white, sels. James Carnegie; Earl of Southesk. 6819-7
Jonas, S.A.
    The confederate note. 6074-9
    Only a soldier's grave. 6074-9
Jonathan. Thomas Ewing Jr. 6848-0
Jonathan Bing. B. Curtis Brown. 6512-0,6534-1
Jonathan Smith. Karl N. Llewellyn. 6594-5
"Jonathan loved a wanton lass". Three brothers. Jessie Young Norton. 6841-3
Jonathan to John. James Russell Lowell. 6481-7,6470-1,6016-2,6288-1,6505-8
Jonathan's courtship. Unknown, 6651-8
Jonathan's lullaby. S. Foster Damon. 6761-1
Jonathon and the Englishmen. Unknown. 6064-1
Jone's ride. McLandburgh Wilson. 6724-7
Joner swallerin' a whale. Louis Eisenbeis. 6417-5
Jones
    On the beach in Puerto Angel. 6767-0
Jones (atr), Richard
    The printer to the reader. 6182-6
Jones Jr., Bob
    Worship. 6065-X
Jones Jr., Thomas H.

He giveth his beloved sleep. 6320-9
Jones Jr., Thomas S.
    According to St. Mark. 6335-7
    After all. 6653-4
    April. 6653-4
    As in a rose-jar. 6006-4,6338-1,6347-0,6476-0,6653-4
    At even. 6320-9
    Ave atque vale (I). 6653-4
    Beyond. 6338-1,6619-4
    The birds of Whitby. 6073-0
    The blind nun. 6285-7
    Candle-light. 6653-4
    The cathedral. 6337-3
    Clonard. 6331-4,6653-4
    Clonmacnoise. 6979-7
    Copernicus. 6850-2
    Daphne. 6253-9
    Dusk at sea. 6556-2,6102-8,6431-0,6076-5,6607-0
    Elegy. 6347-0
    Ezekiel. 6532-5
    Forgotten. 6347-0
    Four sonnets. 6556-2
    From the hills. 6300-4
    George Herbert. 6483-3
    The gifts of peace. 6033-1,6607-0
    The great refusal. 6532-5
    The guardian angel. 6648-8
    Henry Vaughan. 6483-3
    The hills. 6030-7
    I know a quiet vale. 6347-0,6653-4
    In excelsis. 6556-2
    In the garden. 6331-4
    In Trinity church-yard. 6653-4
    Joyous-gard. 6007-2,6310-1,6250-4
    May upon ictis. 6619-4
    Michelangelo. 6850-2
    "My soul is like a garden-close." 6338-1,6441-8,6653-4
    Noon-tide. 6653-4
    An old song. 6266-0,6476-0
    The path of the stars. 6144-3,6335-7,6393-4,6730-1,6144-3,6393-4
    The pines. 6607-0
    Pythagorus ("Fair as the seven daughters..."). 6020-X
    Quatrain 005 ("Nothing is judged according to..size"). 6462-0
    Quatrain 011 ("Here upon earth eternity is won"). 6462-0
    Quatrain V. 6850-2
    Quatrain XI. 6850-2
    Richard Crashaw. 6483-3
    A Roman road. 6850-2
    Saint Columbia. 6331-4
    Saint Francis. 6331-4
    Saint Teresa. 6285-7
    Socrates. 6850-2
    Solomon. 6850-2
    Sometimes. 6102-8,6266-0,6337-3,6476-0,6509-0,6583, 6310-1,6473-6,6250-4,6396-9,6076-5,6300
    A song in spring. 6310-1,6476-0
    Sonnets of the saints. 6619-4
    To a Greek statue. 6850-2
    To song. 6347-0,6653-4
    Two songs in spring. 6653-4
    Tycho brahe. 6850-2
    Urbs beata. 6648-8
    The way back. 6653-4
    The white city. 6327-6
    You and I. 6441-8
    Youth. 6102-8,6232-6,6266-0,6076-5
Jones at the barber's shop. Unknown. 6385-3,6278-2
"Jones plays the deuce wuth is grammar." Adam Lindsay Gordon. 6951-7
Jones, ?
    Be humble. 6752-2
Jones, Abner (tr.)
    Psalm 035. Bible, 6848-0
    Psalm 047. Bible, 6848-0
    Psalm 066. Bible, 6848-0
    Psalm 094. Bible, 6848-0
    Psalm 135. Bible, 6848-0

Jones, Alan Pryce
  Said the captain. 6360-8
Jones, Alice Louise
  Bacchante. 6959-2
Jones, Amanda T.
  Abigail Becker. 6274-1,6416-7,6566-X
  Apple blossoms. 6554-6
  Chewink. 6615-1
  Flag of truce. 6113-3
  Panama. 6274-1
  The prophecy of the dead. 6113-3
  The red bird, sels. 6615-1
  The sensitive brier. 6615-1
  The thrush. 6615-1
  We twain. 6240-7
Jones, Andrew McCord
  Escape. 6870-7
  A morning kiss. 6870-7
  A poem of broken pieces. 6870-7
  Snowman. 6870-7
  Somewhere west. 6870-7
Jones, Arthur F.
  Christmas. 6799-9
Jones, Charlene
  "Balling". 7018-3
  "Say you are a poem in me". 7018-3
Jones, Charles C.
  As Jimmie sees it. 6697-6
  'De conjure man.' 6692-5
  World wanderers. 7007-8
Jones, Charles L.S.
  Fort Bowyer. 6946-0
  The hero of Bridgewater. 6946-0
Jones, D.G.
  Death of a hornet. 6446-9
  Musica ficta. 6767-0
  A sort of blues. 6767-0
Jones, David
  The anathemata, sels. 6528-7
  Englynion to his love. 6528-7
  The five unmistakable marks. 6360-8
Jones, Dean
  On the democracy of YAle. 6736-0
Jones, Ebenezer
  A coming cry. 7009-4
  The face. 6656-9
  The hand. 6437-X
  High summer. 6958-4,7015-9
  Rain. 6134-6,6383-7
  A slave's triumph. 7009-4
  Ways of regard, sels. 6378-0
  When the world is burning. 6437-X,6528-7,6383-7
Jones, Edith Harriet
  The bird bath. 6799-9
  Fellowship. 6799-9
Jones, Edward C.
  General Joseph Reed... 6402-7
  Marion's dinner. 6410-8,6678-X
  Soliloquy of Arnold. 6402-7,6678-X
Jones, Elizabeth Warren
  I could. 6799-9
  One woman. 6038-2
  When years have passed. 7001-9
Jones, Eloise M.
  The reason. 6529-5
Jones, Emily Read
  Thanksgiving. 6618-6
Jones, Ernest
  Easter hymn. 7009-4
  Hymn for Lammas-day. 7009-4
  Liberty. 6793-X,7009-4
  Prison fancies. 7009-4
  Song of the 'lower classes.' 6157-5,6437-X,6688-7
  The song of the wage-slave. 7009-4
  "A vote in the law they make!" 6793-X
Jones, Ernest Charles
  Earth's burdens. 6656-9
Jones, Florence A.
  He that has kept clean. 6109-5
  Mud pies. 689-8

Jones, Frederick Scheetz
  On the democracy of Yale. 6089-7,6722-0
Jones, Gary
  Clothespin Robins. 6857-X
Jones, George
  Dis what de union done. 6149-4
  Stand together, boys. 6149-4
Jones, Georgia Holloway
  Enchantment. 6178-8
  To James Weldon Johnson. 6178-8
Jones, Gertrude Manly
  A cat's birthday celebration. 6699-2
Jones, Glyn
  Beach. 6360-8
  Esyllt. 6360-8
  Gull. 6360-8
  Merthyr. 6528-7
  Park. 6360-8
  Sande. 6360-8
Jones, Gwyn (tr.)
  The woman of Lyyn Fan's calls to her cattle. Unknown (Welsh), 6528-7
Jones, H. Bedford
  The winner. 6583-X
Jones, Herbert
  On love. 6785-9
  Stars over London. 6785-9
  To France. 7026-4
Jones, Howard Mumford
  Allegory. 6347-0
  Audiences. 6347-0
  The balloon man. 6039-0
  Examinations. 6506-0
  Heartbreak. 6326-8
  'In his will.' 6326-8
  They that dwell in shadow. 6034-X
Jones, Howard Mumford (tr.)
  The church bell at night. Unknown, 6930-4
  The crucifixion. Unknown, 6930-4
  Encouragement to exile. Petronius Arbiter, 7039-6
  The lonely isle. Claudian, 7039-6
Jones, I. Edgar
  'As it is in heaven'. 6923-1
  The dead leader. 6924-X
  Dream rambles. 6927-4
  The drunkard's death. 6916-9
  Find your level. 6921-5
  Heroes of the mines. 6411-6
  The ideal and the real. 6915-0
  Judge Lynch. 6925-8
  The kingdom of sham. 6926-6
  The landlord's last moments. 6412-4
  The legend of Kalooka. 6920-7
  A nature prayer. 6919-3
  Nickel plated. 6417-5
  On the frontier. 6415-9,6167-2
  Popping the question. 6411-6
  Sable sermon. 6922-3
  Sambo's new year sermon. 6928-2
  Shadows on the snow. 6417-5
  Smoked-American theology. 6918-5
  Sound the reveille. 6920-7
  The sunbeam's mission. 6417-5
  There are none. 6415-9
  Three sunbeams. 6921-5
  'Vanity of vanities'. 6925-8
  The vigilants. 6416-7
Jones, Ione L.
  Lady Flora. 6530-9
  Sleep, baby, sleep. 6629-1
Jones, J.A.
  The gladiator. 6406-X
Jones, Jenkins Lloyd
  Music. 6143-5
Jones, Jessie Orton
  "Ants are the busiest people I know". 6999-1
  "At night I like to snuggle in my pillow". 6999-1
  "A butterfly will find the milkweed plant". 6999-1
  "Did you ever have a chipmunk for a friend?" 6999-1
  "Do you know what tree I love best?" 6999-1

"Do you like secrets?" 6999-1
"Flowers always know what they should do". 6999-1
"Have you ever waked up in the middle of the night?" 6999-1
"Have you seen that strange insect...'walkingstick'?" 6999-1
"How could God think of so many kinds of houses?" 6999-1
"I am glad I'm who I am". 6999-1
"I can climb our apple tree". 6999-1
"I like to hear the cricket in the grass". 6999-1
"I used to think our trees all died in winter". 6999-1
"Lilac bush has no fruit at all". 6999-1
"The milkweed seeds need to go far away for planting". 6999-1
"Outdoors is always fresh and new". 6999-1
"Sometimes I hear God's whisper in the night". 6999-1
"The sun has gone to other lands". 6999-1
"The sun shines through our trees in long white rays". 6999-1
"This little fellow must love his home". 6999-1
"The warm sun is shining on our garden". 6999-1
"We have tulips in our flower bed". 6999-1
"When evening brings darkness to our garden". 6999-1

Jones, John
Come, lovers, bring your cares. 6563-5

Jones, John ("Talhaiarn")
"Rise, rise, thou merry lar." Thomas Oliphant (tr.). 6328-4
War's loud alarms. Thomas Oliphant (tr.). 6385-3
Where are the men. Thomas Oliphant (tr.). 6328-4, 6385-3

Jones, John L.
Alan Seeger. 6799-9

Jones, John Percival
Silver Jack's religion. 7007-8

Jones, John Tracy
W'en ma's away. 6687-9

Jones, Julia Clinton
The silent army of Memorial Day. 6166-4

Jones, K.L.
The St. Lawrence. 6795-6

Jones, Leila
The first word. 6761-1
No final death. 6761-1

Jones, Leslie
Locket for the heart. 6979-7

Jones, Llewellyn (tr.)
Cotton. Harry Martinson, 6420-5

Jones, M. Eloise
The reason. 6529-5

Jones, Mary
The lass of the hill. 6874-X

Jones, Mary E. (tr.)
Spain! John Smith, 6610-0

Jones, Mary Elizabeth
When sunset overtakes me. 6750-6

Jones, Mary Hoxie
Harvest. 6979-7

Jones, Mary M.
Dad of mine. 6799-9

Jones, Minnie Lee
Magic Tulsa. 6799-9

Jones, Mrs. W.R.
Perdita. 6166-4
Zenobia. 6680-1

Jones, Nelle Parker
A summer cycle. 6280-6

Jones, Nina
Great is our grief. 6995-9

Jones, Onolee
Mother duck and her ducklings. 6850-2
Snow. 6850-2

Jones, Ralph Mortimer
Bed-time. 6250-4
Oxen. 6102-8

Jones, Richard
The printer to the reader. 6182-6

Jones, Robert
Fair Oriana. 6328-4
Love winge my hopes. 6328-4

My love. 6191-5
An old lover. 6429-9, 6321-7
When love most secret is. 6429-9, 6321-7, 6226-1

Jones, Rosaline E.
The voice of the wind. 6576-7

Jones, Ruth Lambert
Echoes. 6762-X
Prevision. 6979-7
War pictures. 6762-X

Jones, S.A.
Lines on back of a Confederate note. 6889-8
Only a solider's grave. 6340-3

Jones, Shelley
Cruising the bar. 7003-5
Grace be with them all that love. 7003-5

Jones, Sir William
The babe. 6240-7, 6102-8, 6219-9
The fountain at Vaucluse. 6484-1
A moral tetrastich. 6528-7
A new-born child. 6078-1
Ode ("What constitutes a state"). 6271-7, 6086-2
An ode in imitation of Alcaeus, sels. 6332-2
An ode in imitation of Alcaeus. 6219-9
On parent knees. 6092-7, 6086-2
On parent knees, a naked new-born child. 6641-0
So live. 6233-4
A state. 6087-0, 6383-7, 6301-2
To an infant newly born. 6153-2
A Turkish ode of Mesihi. 6545-7
What constitutes a state? 6102-8, 6240-7, 6386-1, 6498-1, 6732-8, 6238, 6332-2, 6449-3, 6304-7, 6250-4

Jones, Sir William (tr.)
The baby. Kalidasa, 6385-3, 6438-8
Compassion. Sadi [or Saadi] (Mushlih-ud-Din), 6448-5
Morning air. Jami, 6448-5
Naravena, spirit of God. Unknown, 6438-8
Naravena: spirit of God. Unknown, 6191-5
A Persian song. Hafiz, 6528-7, 6543-0
The song of the reed. Jalal [or Jelal] ed-din Rumi, 6448-5

Jones, T. Gwynn
Ystrad fflur. Alun Llwelyn-Williams (tr.). 6528-7

Jones, Thomas
Tobacco. 6453-1

Jones, W.E.
On parting. 6468-X

Jones, W.R.
Perdita! ("I breathe, I move, I live!") 6166-4

Jones, W.S. Handley
He is not risen. 6337-3

Jones, Wex
My bull terrier. 7008-6

Jongleurs. Bliss Carman and Richard Hovey. 6890-1
Jonne Armstrong. Unknown. 6501-5
The **jonquils.** Allen Upward. 6897-9

Jonson, Ben
Aeglamour seeks his shepherdess. 6150-8
Aeglamour's lament. 6191-5
The alchemist, sels. 6317-9, 6369-1, 6378-0
All your fortunes we can tell ye, fr. Masque of gipsies. 6125-7
An angel describes truth. 6933-9
Answer to Master Wither's song, 'Shall I, wasting...' 6089-7, 6440-X
Apollo's song. 6315-2
The banquet of sense, fr. The poetaster. 6827-8
Begging another, on colour of mending the former. 6317-9
Begging epistle to the chancellor of the exchequer. 6867-7
Ben invites a friend. 6230-X
Break, fancy, from thy cave. 6328-4
Buzz and hum. 6383-7
Buzz! quoth the blue-fly. 6189-3
The case is altered, sels. 6317-9
A catch. 6182-6
Catiline to his army, near Faesulae. 6606-2
A celebration of Charis, sels. 6179-6, 6562-7, 6228-8, 6317-9, 6208-3, 6645
A celebration of Charis. 6240-7, 6430-2

Celia. 6226-1
Charis. 6830-8
Charis' triumph. 6189-3
Chivalry. 6438-8
Chorus in a masque. 6563-5
Clerimont's song. 6315-2,6527-9,6491-4
"Come, leave the loathed stage,", fr. Ode to himself. 6198-2
Come, my Celia, let us prove. 6645-3,6182-6,6208-3,6181-8,6187-7,6536-8,6726
Corvino offers his wife..., fr. Volpone. 6637-2
Courage ("A valiant man"). 6211-3
Cupid. 6089-7,6652-6
Cynthia's revels, sels. 6179-6,6378-0,6239-3,6208-3, 6301-2,6645
Discourse with Cupid. 6271-7
The dreame. 6958-4
"Drink to me only with thine eyes." 6328-4,6187-7,6289-X,6536-8,6208-3,6645
Earine. 6191-5
Echo's dirge for Narcissus. 6153-2
Echo's lament for NArcissus. 6737-9,6189-3
Echo's song. 6099-4,6315-2
An elegy ("Since you"). 6315-2
An elegy ("Though beauty"). 6186-9
An elegy. 6194-X
Epicoene, sels. 6083-8
Epigram. 6438-8
Epigram 101. 6369-1
Epigram on Sir Francis Drake. 6219-9,6424-8
An epigram to King Charles. 6430-2
Epigrams. 6430-2
Epistle to a friend to persuade hiim to the wars. 6438-8
Epistle to Elizabeth, countess of Rutland, sels. 6726-3
An epistle to Lady Rutland. 6208-3
An epistle to Sir Edward Sackville, now Earl of Dorset. 6380-2
An epistle. 6430-2
Epitaph ("Underneath this sable"). 6438-8
Epitaph ("Underneath this stone"). 6438-8
Epitaph on Elizabeth, L. H. 6122-2,6271-7,6186-9,6600-3, 6182-6,6198 ,6194-X,6250-4,6291-0,6562-7,6726-3
Epitaph on Margaret Ratcliffe. 6867-7
Epitaph on Master Philip Gray, fr. Underwoods. 6867-7
Epitaph on my first daughter. 6867-7
Epitaph on Salathiel Pavy. 6092-7
Epitaph on S[alomon] P[avy], a child... 6315-2,6122-2, 6737-9,6645-3,6320-X,6291 ,6430-2,6150-8,6153-2,6562-7,6181-8,6182-6,6208-3,6052-8,6198
Epitaph on the Countess of Pembroke. 6102-8,6302-0,6385-3,6369-1,6291-9,6737
An epithalamium, sels. 6301-2
Epithalamy. 6830-8
Epode. 6194-X
Every man in his humour, Act I. 6186-9
The fairy beam upon you. 6189-3
Fame. 6438-8
Fantasy. 6385-3,6438-8
A fit of rime against rime. 6378-0
"Follow a shadow, it still flies you." 6385-3,6328-4, 6026-9
Fools. 6182-6
For love's sake. 6328-4
For what is life? 6087-0
The forest, sels. 6301-2
A fragment ("Boast not these titles..."). 6867-7
Freedom in dress. 6302-0,6385-3,6737-9,6438-8
The ghyrlond ef the blessed virgin Marie. 6282-2
Gipsy songs. 6563-5
The glove. 6182-6
Good and fair. 6385-3
Good and great God! 6931-2
The good wife's ale. 6733-6
Greatness in littleness, fr. Ode to Sir Lucius Cary... 6102-8
Halfway in love. 6935-5
Happiness. 6867-7
"Have you seen but a bright lily grow". 6187-7,6339-X
He teaches her to kiss. 6659-3

Hear me, O God. 6732-8
Her man described by her own dictamen. 6378-0,6194-X
Her triumph, fr. A celebration of Charis... 6182-7,6562-7,6645-3
Her triumph, fr. Underwoods. 6023-4
"Here lies one box within another." 6722-0
Hesperus' song, fr. Cynthia's revels. 6239-3
Hesperus's hymn to Cynthia. 6315-2
His excuse for loving, fr. A celebration of Charis... 6562-7
Honour in bud. 6322-5
"How many equal...", fr. Epistle to Elizabeth... 6726-3
How near to good is what is fair! 6600-3,6438-8,6250-4, 6189-3
Hymn ("Hear me, O God!") 6189-3
A hymn on the nativity of my Saviour. 6145-1,6328-4, 6734-4,6608-9
Hymn to Comus. 6182-6,6430-2
Hymn to Cynthia. 6597-X,6252-0
Hymn to Diana. 6052-8,6246-6,6192-3,6560-0,6125-7,6153 , 6189-3,6421-3,6371-3,6639-3,6737-9,6723 ,6075-7,6102-8,6182-6,6138-9,6186-7,6328 ,6339-X,6395-0,6533-3, 6558-9,6634-8,6726 ,6732-8,6102-8
Hymn to Diana, sels. 6289-X
A hymn to God the father. 6337-3
Hymn to Pan. 6189-3
Hymn to the belly. 6733-6
I love, and he loves. 6328-4
If I freely may discover. 6092-7
"If I freely may discover". 6187-7,6733-6
Inviting a friend to supper. 6198-2,6315-2,6733-6,6562-7,6430-2,6194 ,6092-7
It is not growing like a tree. 6134-6,6107-9,6125-7, 6328-4,6473-6,6138-9,6208-3
"It was a beauty that I saw". 6562-7,6563-5,6052-8
Jealousy. 6543-0
Karol's kiss. 6191-5
Karolin's song. 6315-2
"Kiss me, sweet: the wary lover," fr. The forest. 6317-9,6328-4
The kiss, fr. Cynthia's revels. 6934-7
The kiss, fr. Cynthia's revels. 6827-8
The kiss. 6830-8
"Lady, it is to be presumed". 6088-9
Life's measure. 6552-X
Lines on the portrait of Shakespeare. 6219-9
Lines, fr. Catiline. 6867-7
Lines, fr. The sad shepherd. 6867-7
Love. 6226-1
Love and death. 6563-5
Love's chariot. 6383-7
Love's chariot, sels. 6102-8,6301-2
Mab the mistress-fairy. 6182-6
Masque of pleasure and virtue. 6438-8
May. 6438-8
The measure of the perfect life. 6189-3
Middle-age overtakes him. 6659-3
The moon-goddess. 6114-1
Mosca persuades Corbaccio to disinherit..., fr Volpone. 6637-2
Mother Maudlin the witch, fr. The sad shepherd. 6125-7
Nano's song. 6315-2
The Nativity. 6747-6
Nature. 6438-8
Nature's accord. 6943-6
The new cry. 6200-8
The new inn, sels. 6317-9
The noble nature. 6133-8,6246-6,6239-3,6291-1,6332-2, 6479 ,6250-4,6513-9,6104-4,6424-8,6737-9,6543 ,6457-4,6600-3,6732-8,6639-9,6496-5,6558-9,6337-3,6410-8, 6302-0,6385
A nymph's passion. 6191-5
"O, do wanton with those eyes". 6830-8
O, that joy so soon should waste! 6328-4
An ode to himself. 6099-4,6198-2,6099-4,6562-7,6208-3, 6562 ,6430-2,6150-8,6438-8,6219-9,6378-0,6099-4,6198-2,6099-4,6562-7,6208-3,6562 ,6430-2,6150-8,6438-8, 6219-9,6378-0
An ode to Sir Lucius Cary and Sir H. Morrison, sels. 6102-8,6301-2

JONSON

Of his love's beauty. 6737-9
Of kissing. 6935-5
Of life and death. 6527-9
On Banks, the usurer. 6278-4
On Chevril the lawyer. 6278-4
On Don Surly. 6200-8
On English mounsieur. 6733-6
On Giles and Joan. 6194-X
On his first sonne. 6933-9
On Lucy, Countess of Bedford. 6562-7,6600-3,6219-9,6438-8,6430-2
On my first daughter. 6315-2,6562-7
On my first son. 6182-6,6198-2,6215-2,6641-0,6208-3, 6562 ,6430-2,6194-X,6472-8
On the portrait of Shakespeare. 6250-4,6301-2
"On the twenty-second of June". 6722-0
On truth. 6867-7
"One woman reads another's character". 6083-8
Pans anniversarie. 6933-9
Pans anniversarie. 6190-7
The parasite. 6150-8,6150-6
Patrico's song. 6016-0,6315-2,6106-0,6315-2
Perfect beauty. 6737-9
The perfect life, fr. An ode. 6242-3,6668-2
The picture of the mind. 6250-4
A Pindaric ode, sels. 6879-0
A Pindaric ode. 6122-2,6194-X,6198-2,6646-1
Plays and masques, sels. 6430-2
The pleasures of heaven. 6302-0,6385-3
The poet-wooer. 6935-5
The poetaster, sels. 6378-0
Proportion, fr. A Pindaric ode. 6208-3
"Queen and huntress, chaste and fair." 6181-8,6194-X, 6246-6
Robin Goodfellow. 6249-0,6254-7,6385-3,6696-8
The sad shepherd, sels. 6369-1
See the chariot at hand. 6328-4,6438-8
She, fr. Love's Chariot. 6102-8
The shepherd's holiday. 6099-4,6191-5
The shepherd's love. 6240-7
The silent woman, sels. 6317-9
Simplex munditiis. 6153-2,6301-2,6646-1,6723-9,6102-8, 6604-6,6083-8,6660-7,6194-X,6250
Simplicity. 6634-8
Slow slow fresh font. 6250-4,6383-7,6023-4,6125-7
Slow slow fresh fount. 6052-8,6182-6,6726-3,6187-7,6181-8
So sweet is she, fr. 'The triumph of Charis'. 6239-3
Song ("Beauties"). 6430-2
Song ("Follow a shadow"). 6219-9
Song ("If I freely"). 6182-6
A song ("Oh doe not wanton with those eyes"). 6933-9
Song ("Oh, do not wanton..."). 6827-8
Song ("Queene and huntresse.") 6430-2
Song ("Roome, roome"). 6562-7
Song ("Slow, slow"). 6430-2
Song ("Spring all"). 6438-8
Song ("Still to be neat"). 6219-9,6430-2
Song ("The owl is abroad.") 6438-8
Song ("Though I am young.") 6430-2
Song of Echo. 6438-8
Song of Hesperus. 6600-3,6543-0
Song of night. 6383-7
Song to Celia. 6189-3,6250-4,6396-9,6052-8,6198-2,6733-6,6604-6,6289-X,6491
Song to Celia ("Come, my Celia, let us prove"). 6122-2, 6194-X
Song to Celia ("Drink to me only with thine eyes") 6122-2,6182-6,6192-X,6250-4
Song to Celia ("Kiss me, sweet; the wary lover") 6182-6
Song to Cynthia. 6604-6,6660-7
Sonnets, sels. 6600-3
Still to be neat. 6092-7
"Still to be neat, still to be dressed". 6271-7,6182-6, 6328-4,6181-8,6536-8,6187
"Still to be neat, still to be dressed." 6026-9,6383-7, 6197-4,6150-8
Stray thoughts, sels. 6867-7
The sweet neglect. 6543-0,6099-4,6600-3
That women are but men's shadows. 6182-6,6208-3,6092-7

Those eyes. 6302-0;6385-3
Though I am young, fr. The sad shepherd. 6328-4,6383-7
"'Tis not to be told," fr. The case is altered. 6317-9
To a glove, fr. Cytnhia's revels. 6827-8
To brainhardy. 6278-4
To Celia. 6026-9,6464-7,6543-0,6646-1,6737-9,6723 ,6099-4,6371-3,6438-8,6073-4,6560-0,6194 ,6102-8,6153-2, 6197-4,6219-9,6230-X,6094 ,6092-7,6104-4,6513-9,6659-3
To Cynthia. 6219-9
To Diana. 6830-8
To Doctor Empiric. 6089-7,6278-4
To Edward Allen. 6430-2
To Edward Allen (Alleyne). 6933-9
To fine grand. 6278-4
To Francis Beaumont. 6483-3,6562-7,6430-2
To heaven. 6122-2,6315-2,6214-8
To himself. 6563-5
To John Donne. 6483-3,6562-7,6430-2
To King James. 6430-2
To Lady Mary Wroth. 6933-9
To Lucy, Countesse of Bedford, with Mr. Donne's satyres. 6562-7,6084-6
To my book. 6430-2
To my bookseller. 6194-X,6297-0
To my worthy and honoured friend, Mr. George Chapman... 6483-3
To Penshurst. 6315-2,6562-7
To Penshurst, sels. 6208-3
To Sir Henrie Savile upon his translation of Tacitus. 6933-9
To Sir Henry Goodyere. 6297-0
To Sir Robert Wroth. 6194-X
To Sir Samuel Fuller. 6278-4
To the Countess of Rutland. 6438-8
To the ghost of Martial. 6430-2
To the immortall memorie, and friendship... 6562-7
To the memory of my beloved master William Shakespeare. 6430-2,6194-X,6250-4,6245-8,6219-9,6301-2,6723-9, 6102-8,6186-9,6562-7,6154-0,6198-2,6641 ,6726-3,6122-2,6604-6,6483-3,6645-3,6660
To the memory of my beloved...Shakespeare, sels. 6125-7
To the reader. 6430-2
To Thomas Lord Chancellor. 6933-9
To William Camden. 6369-1,6562-7
To William Roe. 6933-9
To William Stanley, on his birthday. 6438-8
The triumph of Charis, sels. 6239-3,6194-X
The triumph of Charis. 6052-8,6271-7,6198-2,6122-2,6315-2,6604 ,6726-3,6219-2,6660-7,6092-7
The triumph. 6150-8,6250-4,6513-9
True balm. 6322-5
The true growth. 6385-3
Truth. 6250-4,6513-9
"Underneath this ancient pew". 6722-0
Underwoods. 6369-1
Unspotted from the world. 7020-5
Venetian song, fr. Volpone, or the fox. 6827-8
Venus' runaway. 6737-9
Verses at the Devil Tavern. 6230-X
Viamus. 6092-7
A vision of beauty. 6302-0;6385-3
Volpone's song: to Celia. 6527-9
Volpone, sels. 6378-0,6637-2
Why I write not of love. 6430-2
A wish. 6465-5,6424-8
Witches' charm. 6182-6,6315-2,6645-3,6383-7,6194-X,6634
"Wretched and foolish jealousy." 6317-9

Jonson, Ben (tr.)
"The dear good angel of the spring". Sappho, 6435-3
"Drink to me only with thine eyes." Philostratus, 6302-0;6385-3
Epigram on Drake. Abraham Cowley, 6438-8
Epigram on Drake. William Cowley, 6438-8
Epigram on Francis Drake. Abraham Cowley, 6867-7
Inviting a friend to supper. Martial, 7039-6
The nightingale. Sappho, 6435-3
To Celia. Caius Catallus, 7039-6

Jonsson, Einar Paul
Servant oflight. Jakobina Johnson (tr.). 6854-5

Jonsson, Hjalmar
   Deaths. Gudmund J. Gislason (tr.). 6854-5
   Feyman's fate. Gudmund J. Gislason (tr.). 6854-5
   Senility. Gudmund J. Gislason (tr.). 6854-5
   Silence broken. Gudmund J. Gislason (tr.). 6854-5
Jonsson, Kristjan
   The cataract. Runolfur Fjeldsted (tr.). 6854-5
   The grave. Gudmund J. Gislason (tr.). 6854-5
   The tear. Jakobina Johnson (tr.). 6283-0
   The tear. Jakobina Johnson (tr.). 6854-5
   The waterfall (Dettifoss). Runolfur Fjeldsted (tr.). 6283-0
Joor, Kate Bringhurst
   Lost - a boy. 6750-6
Jorasse. Samuel Rogers. 6302-0;6385-3
Jordan. George Herbert. 6208-3,6528-7,6641-0,6431-1,6150-8, 6208-3,6528-7,6641-0
Jordan (atr), Thomas
   "By all thy gloryes willingly I goe." 6563-5
Jordan [1]. George Herbert. 6562-7
Jordan [2]. George Herbert. 6562-7
Jordan, Carol
   The jealousy of the gods. 6396-9
Jordan, Charlotte Brewster
   A poem for Arbor Day: what trees speak? 6130-3
   Polly's discovery. 6807-3
   Real 'new' woman. 6715-8
Jordan, D.M.
   Late October. 6273-3
   October. 6273-3
Jordan, David Starr
   Altruism ("The God of things as they are"). 6473-6
   And so at last. 6337-3,6461-2
   In Tehachapi. 6241-5
   Men told me, Lord. 6337-3,6730-1
Jordan, Ethel Blair
   World friendship for boys and girls. 6386-1
Jordan, June
   Who would be free, themselves must strike the blow. 7032-9
Jordan, Thomas
   The careless gallant. 6563-5,6092-7
   A cavalier's lullaby for his mistress. 6563-5
   Coronemus nos rosis antequam marcescant. 6733-6
   Epitaph. 6563-5
   Let us drink and be merry. 6934-7
   Particular acrostic. 6724-7
   Pyms anarchy. 6933-9
Jordan, Travis Tuck
   Silver sandals. 6818-9
Jorgensen, Johannes
   Meseemed there called--. Charles Wharton Stork (tr.). 6555-4
   'Twas at the burial time of flowers. Charles Wharton Stork (tr.). 6555-4
Jortin, Dr.
   On the shortnes of human life. William Cowper (tr.). 6814-6
Jortin, John
   Epitaphium felis. Seumas (James Starkey) O'Sullivan (tr.). 6511-2
Jose, Arthur W.
   Freedom the goddess. 6784-0
   Pioneers. 6784-0
   The sum of things. 6784-0
Joseph. John Henry, Cardinal Newman. 6980-0
Joseph (Chief Joseph)
   War. 6396-9,6542-2
Joseph and his breathen, sels. Charles Jeremiah Wells. 6934-7
Joseph and his breathren, sels. Charles Jeremiah Wells. 6656-9
Joseph and Mary, fr. Forty-two poems. James Elroy Flecker. 6234-2
Joseph being an aged man. Unknown. 6756-5
Joseph Hergesheimer. Daisy Arnold Maude. 6841-3
Joseph in Bethlehem. Pamela Travers. 6985-1
Joseph Mary Plunkett. Wilfrid Meynell. 6282-2
Joseph of Arimathea. Edgar A. Guest. 6869-3
Joseph Rodman Drake. Fitz-Greene Halleck. 6240-7,686-8, 6302-0,6385-3,6076-5
Joseph Sturge. John Greenleaf Whittier. 6087-0
Joseph of the Stadium, Saint
   The finished course. John Mason Neale (tr.). 6730-1
"**Joseph** was an old man". The cherry-tree carol. Unknown. 6756-5
"**Joseph** was an old man". Unknown. 6111-7
"**Joseph!** did you hear the king", fr. Richelieu. Owen (Edward Bulwer-Lytton, Earl Lytton) Meredith. 6416-7
"**Joseph!** they say thou'st left the stage". Ode to Joseph Grimaldi, Senior. Thomas Hood. 6974-6
Joseph's reform. Berton Braley. 6853-7
Joseph's suspicion. Rainer Maria Rilke. 6223-7,6734-4
Joseph, Jesus and Mary. Unknown. 6806-5
Joseph, Michael
   To a Siamese cat. 6511-2
Josephine. Winthrop Mackworth Praed. 6980-0
"**Josephine,** Jo, or Sugar she says she's called". La Cubana. Otto Paul Gonzalez. 6898-7
Josephson, Ernst
   The cello. Charles Wharton Stork (tr.). 6045-5
Joses, the brother of Jesus. Harry Kemp. 6337-3
Joshua and the suicide. Theodore Spencer. 6389-6
Joshua fit de battle ob Jerico. Unknown. 6527-9,6375-6
The **joshua** tree. Harry Noyes Pratt. 6628-3
"**Joshua** was 'the child at old man Allen's,'". Come by chance. Harriet Plimpton. 6799-9
"**Josie** gave to me a rose". Unknown. 6364-0
Jospeh's dream. George Crabbe. 6848-0
Josui
   The cuckoo's song. 6891-X
Jot [or Tot] Jr., Joe
   Country dancing. 6426-4
   The country dance. 6913-4
   Pat's love. 6744-1
   A smooth day. 6917-7
   A smooth day. 6744-1
Jottings for sportsmen. Alice Cary. 6861-8
Jottings for sportsmen. George Herbert. 6861-8
Jottings for sportsmen. George Herbert. 6861-8
Jottings for sportsmen. James Russell Lowell. 6861-8
Jottings for sportsmen. William Shakespeare. 6861-8
Jourdain, Margaret (tr.)
   Nature. Alfred de Vigny, 7039-6
Journal entries written by light through a Princeton... Geraldine Little. 7032-9
Journal of an airman, sels. Wystan Hugh Auden. 6978-9
Journalism. Morris Rosenfeld. 7011-6
A **journalist's** communion. J. L. Garvin. 7020-5
Journee d'hiver. Leon Dierx. 6801-4
Journey. Sul-joo Lee. 6775-1
Journey. Edna St. Vincent Millay. 6506-6,6653-4
Journey. Harold Monro. 6228-8
Journey. Salvador Novo. 6759-X
Journey. Raymond Thompson. 6870-7
The **journey** . Walter De La Mare. 6628-3
A **journey** ends. Don Blanding. 6337-3
Journey from Copenhagen to Skodsborg. Klabund. 6160-5
A **journey** from Patapsco in Maryland to Annapolis. R. Lewis. 6753-0
The **journey** into France. Unknown. 6157-5
Journey of the Magi. Thomas Stearns Eliot. 6179-6,6246-5, 6536-8,6641-0,6734-4,6209 ,6645-3
The **journey** onwards. Thomas Moore. 6246-6,6543-0,6737-9
Journey through hell. Nicanor Parra. 6758-1
A **journey** to Exeter. John Gay. 6398-5
Journey to the sea. Francis Maguire. 6839-1
Journey's end. Witter Bynner. 6320-9
Journey's end. Jack Conroy. 6906-1
Journey's end. Evelyn H. Healey. 6337-3
Journey's end. Alfred Noyes. 6779-4
The **journey's** end. Alfred Noyes. 6169-9
The **journey's** end. Henry Lee Smith. 6482-5
The **journey..** Charles Churchill. 6200-8
The **journey..** Scudder Middleton. 6607-0,6250-4
The **journey..** Unknown. 6109-5
A **journey.** M. Coleman Harris. 6654-2
The **journey.** Thomas Curtis Clark. 6337-3,6461-2
The **journey.** Henry Johnson. 6870-7
The **journey.** Henry Herbert Knibbs. 7012-4

JOURNEY

The **journey**. James Abraham Martling. 6952-5
The **journey**. Grace Fallow Norton. 6542-2
The **journey**. Grace Fallow Norton. 7026-4
The **journey**. Sir John Collings ("Solomon Eagle") Squire. 6320-9
The **journey**. Feodor Ivanovich Tyutchev. 6622-4
The **journeyman**: blue wooden day. Joel Cox. 6860-X
Journeymen. Louise Townsend Nicholl. 6039-0
Journeys. Agnes MacCarthy Hickey. 6818-9
Journeys to go. William Young. 6032-3
Jouve, Pierre Jean
    The two witnesses. David Gascoyne (tr.). 6343-8
    Woman and earth. David Gascoyne (tr.). 6343-8
Jove and the souls. Jonathan Swift. 6438-8
"**Jove** descends in sleet and snow". The storm. Alcoeus. 7039-6
The **jovial** beggar. Unknown. 6105-2,6133-8,6179-6,6271-7, 6302-0,6219-9,6424-8
The **jovial** cobbler of Saint Helen's. Unknown. 6105-2
The **jovial** marriner, or The sea-man's renown. John Playford. 6157-5
The **jovial** priest's confession. Leigh Hunt. 6089-7,6278-4, 6089-7
Jowett, J.H.
    God's ferns. 6232-6
"**Jowler,** they have taxed you, honest friend!". To my dog, Jowler. Jonathan Dorr Bradley. 7030-2
Joy. Elizabeth Barrett Browning. 6134-6
Joy. William Henry Davies. 6508-2
Joy. Walter De La Mare. 6761-1
Joy. Helen Hunt Jackson. 6438-8
Joy. Robinson Jeffers. 6250-4
Joy. Coventry Patmore. 6737-9
Joy. Beatrice St. Leger. 6800-6
Joy. Sara Teasdale. 6538-4,6029-3
Joy. Unknown. 6134-6
Joy. Anne Whitney. 6006-4
Joy ("Joy is not a thing you can see.") Hilda Conkling. 6501-5
Joy ("Let a joy keep you.") Carl Sandburg. 6102-8,6501-5, 6300-4,6076-5
Joy and duty. Henry Van Dyke. 6961-4
Joy and grief. Edward S. Stevens. 6585-6
Joy and peace in believing. William Cowper. 6219-9,6271-7
Joy and sorrow. Sadi [or Saadi] (Mushlih-ud-Din) 6448-5
"**Joy** be your watchword, O soldiers of..future". Soldiers of the future. Marguerite Weed. 6847-2
"**Joy** comes and goes; hope ebbs and flows". To Fausta. Matthew Arnold. 6947-9,6828-6
Joy days. Ella Stevens. 6149-4
"**Joy** holds her court in great Belshazzar's". Belshazzar's feast. Thomas Smart Hughes. 6848-0
Joy in martyrdom. Madame De la Mothe Guion. 6814-6
"**Joy** in rebel Plymouth town, in...sicty-four". 'Albemarle' Cushing. Herman Melville. 6946-0
"**Joy** in rebel Plymouth town, in...sixty-four". 'Albemarle' Cushing. Herman Melville. 6946-0
The **joy** in sorrow. Charles Hare Townshend. 6656-9
Joy in the corn belt. J.B. Edson. 6615-1
Joy is my name. William Blake. 6328-4
"The **joy** is so short, alas, the pain so near." Sir Thomas Wyatt. 6584-8
"**Joy** is the sunshine of the soul". Unknown. 6109-5
"**Joy** is upon the lonely seas". The breeze from shore. Felicia Dorothea Hemans. 6973-8
"**Joy** like a stream flows through the Christmas...". Sonnet ("Joy like a stream"). Alexander Smith. 6960-6
Joy may kill. Michelangelo Buonarroti. 7039-6
Joy meets laughter. Ella Wheeler Wilcox. 6698-4
"**Joy** now hath reached her utmost goal". Inspiration. Robert Loveman. 6941-X
The **joy** o'life. Theodosia Garrison. 6732-8
The **joy** of battle. John Gould Fletcher. 6322-5
The **joy** of being poor. Robert Service. 6159-1
The **joy** of church fellowship rightly attended. Edward Taylor. 6333-0
The **joy** of doing good. Marianne Farningham. 6523-6
Joy of Easter morning. Unknown. 6720-4
The **joy** of incompleteness. Unknown. 6273-3,6303-9
The **joy** of life. Euripides. 6102-8

The **joy** of life. Euripides. 6732-8
The **joy** of little things. Robert Service. 6159-1
The **joy** of living. Gamaliel Bradford. 6291-1
"**Joy** of my life! while left me here". Henry Vaughan. 6933-9
The **joy** of pedigree. W. Livingston Larned. 7008-6
The **joy** of service. Heloise M.B. Hawkins. 6836-7
Joy of spring. Leigh Hunt. 6049-8
The **joy** of the cross. Madame De la Mothe Guion. 6814-6
The **joy** of the hills. Edwin Markham. 6310-1,6473-6,6476-0, 6490-6,6336-5,6241-5
Joy of the morning. Edwin Markham. 6073-0,6465-5,6478-7, 6309-8,6421-3
The **joy** of the springtime. Sarojini Naidu. 6338-1
Joy or sorrow. Leanna F. Johnson. 6178-8
The **joy** ride. Warren Gilbert. 6531-7,6071-4
"**Joy** stayed with me a night". Light of love. Dorothy Parker. 6817-0
"**Joy** to great congress, joy an hundred fold". The congratulation. Jonathan Odell. 6753-0
Joy to you. Francis Carlin. 6607-0,6467-1
Joy walks in the morning. Nellie Burget Miller. 6037-4
Joy walks in the morning. Nellie Burget Miller. 7038-8
"**Joy** was in the halls of Troia". Kassandra. Johann C. Friedrich von Schiller. 6842-1
"**Joy**! joy! the day is come at last...". The muster of the north. Sir Charles Gavan Duffy. 6858-8
"**Joy**! the lost one is restored!". Hymn of the traveller's household on his return. Felicia Dorothea Hemans. 6973-8
Joy's peak. Robert Farren. 6282-2
Joy's prisoner. Grover I. Jacoby Jr. 6316-0
Joy, Jennie
    Co' bossy. 6670-4
    Saved. 6045-1
Joy, fr. Humanitad. Oscar Wilde. 6466-3
"**Joy,** mighty heralds of our Father's love". Christianity in the apostles. Edward Farquhar. 6939-8
"**Joy,** perch above". Epitaph ("Joy"). Lady Margaret Sackville. 6778-6
Joy, shipmate, joy! Walt Whitman. 6006-4,6087-0,6134-6, 6332-2,6466-3,6126-5,6177-X,6288-1,6252-0,6250-4
Joy, sorrow and happiness. Axel Juel. 6555-4
"**Joy,** sweetest lifeborn joy, where dost thou dwell". Robert Bridges. 6487-6
"**Joy,** thou spark of flame divinest". To joy, or freedom, fr. Gedichte. Johann C. Friedrich von Schiller. 7042-6
"**Joy,** wild joy o'er the mountains ran". Joy. Beatrice St. Leger. 6800-6
The **Joyce's** repentance. Unknown. 6244-X
Joyce, James
    All day I hear. 6491-4
    All day I hear the noise of waters. 6930-4
    "Because your voice was at my side",fr. Chamber Music. 6536-8
    Bid adieu to girlish days. 6174-5
    Bid adieu, adieu, adieu. 6244-X
    "Bright cap and streamers", fr. Chamber Music. 6536-8
    Chamber Music, sels. 6536-8
    Ecce puer. 6536-8
    Goldenhair. 6125-7,6301-2
    The holy office. 6210-5
    I hear an army charging. 6244-X,6581-3,6375-6
    "In the dark pine wood", fr. Chamber music. 6536-8
    "Now, O now, in this brown land", fr. Chamber music. 6536-8
    "O sweetheart, hear you", fr. Chamber music. 6536-8
    On the beach at Fontana. 6317-9,6491-4
    She weeps over Rahoon. 6320-9
    Simples. 6396-9
    Song ("O it was out"). 6437-X
    Song ("Who goes"). 6320-9
    Strings in the earth. 6153-2
    Strings in the earth and air. 6090-0,6174-5,6244-X,6253-9,6250-4
    The twilight turns from amethyst. 6491-4
    What counsel has the hooded moon. 6174-5
Joyce, John A.
    Our fame. 6486-8

Joyce, Mabel
    My dog. 6249-0
Joyce, Robert Dwyer
    The blacksmith of Limerick. 6858-8
    The boys of Wexford. 6858-8
    Crossing the blackwater. 6656-9
    The Drynan Dhun. 6090-0,6174-5
    Fair maidens' beauty will soon fade away. 6244-X
    Finneen O'Driscoll the rover. 6174-5,6292-X
    The green dove and the raven. 6518-X
    Kilbrannon. 6518-X
    The leprahaun. 6930-4
    Mairgread ban. 6174-5
    Song of the forest fairy. 6174-5
    The wind that shakes the barley. 6090-0
Joyce, William
    The Jew. 6848-0
A joyful mother of children. Unknown (Greek) 6435-3
A joyful new ballad. Thomas Deloney. 6157-5
The joyful widower. Robert Burns. 6760-3
Joynes, James Leigh
    The roll-call of the ages. 7009-4
"Joyous days speed quickly, woeful hours delay". Fast or slow time. Sarah A. Athearn. 6764-6
A joyous little maid. L.C. Whiton. 6965-7
"A joyous springtide shower of rain". April. Karel Toman. 6886-3
The joyous wanderer. Catulle Mendes. 6955-X
Joyous-gard. Thomas S. Jones Jr. 6007-2,6310-1,6250-4
Joys. Georgianna Livinston. 6906-1
"The joys of April fifty years ago?". Sulphur 'n' m'lasses. J. Waldo Sampson. 6761-1
The joys of a summer morning. Henry A. Wise Wood. 6338-1
The joys of art. Rachel Annand Taylor. 6437-X
The joys of earth. Edgar A. Guest. 6862-6
The joys of home. Edgar A. Guest. 7033-7
The joys of Jamaica. Henry Shirley Bunbury. 6591-0,6592-9
"The joys of life are colourful, but frail". Finale. Beatrice Payne Morgan. 6841-3
"The joys of living wreathe my face". The circling year. Ramona Graham. 6964-9
The joys of marriage. Charles Cotton. 6089-7,6724-7
The joys of the road. Bliss Carman. 6374-8,6437-X,6079-X, 6458-2,6252-0,6423-X,6006-4
The joys of wedlock. Edward Moore. 6874-X
"The joys of youth were mine". Under the four corners' elm. W.W. Christman. 6761-1
The joys we miss. Edgar A. Guest. 7033-7
Juan II; King of Castile
    Cancion ("O love..."). George Ticknor (tr.). 7039-6
    "I never knew it, love, till now." 6066-8
Juan and Haidee, fr. Don Juan. George Gordon, 6th Baron Byron. 6094-3,6196-6,6199-0
Juan Cabrillo. Winifred Davidson. 6039-0
Juan De Pareja. William Brighty Rands. 6134-6
Juan Quintana. Alice Corbin. 6076-5,6102-8
"Juan de Juni the priest said". Red Hugh. Thomas McGreevy. 6930-4
Juana. Alfred de Musset. 7039-6,6732-8
Juana, fr. Records of woman. Felicia Dorothea Hemans. 6973-8
Jubilance. William Blake. 6943-6
Jubilate. George Arnold. 6833-2
Jubilate. Unknown. 6273-3
Jubilate agno, sels. Christopher Smart. 6380-2,6545-7
The jubilee of 1850. Adelaide Anne Procter. 6957-6
The jubilee of Melbounre. J.F. Daniell. 6768-9
The jubilee of the flowers. Susan E. Howard. 6677-1
Jubilee song. Unknown. 6693-3
The jubilee. James Grahame. 6848-0
Jubili, jubilo!, fr. John Brown's body. Stephen Vincent Benet. 6984-3
Jubilo. Allen Tate. 6391-8,6666-6
Judah. Col. Wetmore. 6848-0
Judah Ha-levi. See Halevi, Judah
'Judah's hallowed bards.' Sir Aubrey De Vere. 6848-0
Judaism. John Henry, Cardinal Newman. 6022-6,6096-X
Judas. Howard McKinley Corning. 6144-3
Judas. Edward Davidson. 6393-4
Judas. Gerhard Fritsch. 6769-7
Judas. Jessie Holt. 6789-1
Judas. Unknown. 6185-0
Judas. Harold Vinal. 6102-8,6076-5
Judas Iscariot. Robert Buchanan. 6437-X,6301-2
Judas Iscariot. Margaret Nickerson Martin. 6144-3
Judas Maccabaeus. Henry Wadsworth Longfellow. 6848-0
Judas sells his Lord. Unknown. 6881-2
Judd, Abbie F.
    Midsummer ("Behold the flood-tide of the year"). 6049-8
Judd, Marion
    Man portrait. 6750-6
Judd, Sylvester
    Light of the world. 6065-X
Judea. Charles M. Wallington. 6848-0
Judean hills are holy. William L. Stidger. 6144-3,6335-7, 6337-3
Judge Lynch. I. Edgar Jones. 6925-8
Judge and Harry Williams, Jack
    It's a long way to Tipperary. 6732-8
Judge me, O Lord. Sarah N. Cleghorn. 6337-3
Judge me, O Lord! Sarah N. Cleghorn. 6144-3,6337-3
Judge Not. John Francis Glynn. 6954-1
"Judge me, o Lord, for I have walk'd". Psalm 026 Bible. 6848-0
Judge not. Joaquin Miller. 6889-8
Judge not. Adelaide Anne Procter. 6957-6
Judge not. Unknown. 6912-6,6273-3,6260-1
Judge not the preacher, fr. The church porch. Edward Herbert, 1st Baron Herbert of Cherbury. 6934-7
"Judge not; the workings of his brain". Adelaide Anne Procter. 6238-5;6600-3
The judge of Bellinzona. J.J. Reithard. 6918-5
The judge pronounceth the sentence of condemnation. Michael Wigglesworth. 6121-4
"The judge removed, though he's no more my lord". Prologue to Don Sebastian. John Dryden. 6970-3
A judge's temperance lecture. Unknown. 6744-1
The judgement of God. William Morris. 6508-2
"The judges all agree that I'm". His good points. W. Livingston Larned. 7008-6
The judges of the little box. Vasko Popa. 6758-1
"A judgeship is vacant". Opportunity. Unknown. 6691-7
Judging by appearances. Anne Emilie Poulsson. 6891-X
Judging by appearances. Unknown. 6279-2
Judging from the tracks. Thomas Hornsby Ferril. 6836-7
Judgment. William Rose Benet. 6076-5
Judgment. Leslie Coulson. 6650-X
Judgment. Hortense Flexner. 6069-2
Judgment. Elise Jean Jacobs. 6847-2
Judgment. Fernand Mazade. 6351-9
Judgment. Gertrude Huntington McGiffert. 6838-3
Judgment. Kenneth W. Porter. 6144-3
Judgment and mercy, fr. The devil to pay. Dorothy L. Sayers. 6337-3
Judgment day. William Dean Howells. 6467-1
A judgment in heaven. Francis Thompson. 6661-5
The judgment of Paris, fr. Goddesses three. Unknown. 6427-2
The judgment of the poets. William Cowper. 6814-6,6874-X
"Judgment was over; all the world redeem'd". The vision of the man accurst, fr. The book of Orm. Robert Buchanan. 6819-7
The judgment-book.. Clarence Urmy. 6274-1
The judgment. Dora Read Goodale. 6300-4
Judith. Thomas Bailey Aldrich. 6848-0
Judith. Eugene Lee-Hamilton. 7015-9
Judith. James Whitcomb Riley. 6992-4
Judith. Swithun (atr.); Bishop of Winchester. 6848-0
Judith. Unknown. 6193-1
Judith 16. Bible. 6732-8
Judith of Bethulia. John Crowe Ransom. 7017-5
Judith of Bethulia. John Crowe Ransom. 6209-1,6326-8
Judson, Adoniram
    In spite of sorrow. 6337-3
Judson, Carmen
    What is a poem? 6750-6
Judson, Emily
    Ministering angels. 6404-3
    Samson. 6848-0
Judson, Emily Chubbuck

My bird. 6078-1,6385-3,6627-5
Watching. 6385-3,6271-7
Judtih and Holofernes. Fanny E. Lacey. 6848-0
Judy [pseud].
  The bells. 6440-X
  Imitation of Walt Whitman ("Who am I?"). 6440-X
  A loss. 6453-1
  Remember. 6440-X
  Sarah's halls. 6440-X
Juel, Axel
  Joy, sorrow and happiness. Charles Wharton Stork (tr.). 6555-4
Juggernaut. Leonora Speyer. 6037-4
"A **juggler** long through all the town". The jugglers. John Gay. 6972-X
The **juggler** of Touraine, sels. Edwin Markham. 6849-9
The **juggler**, sels. Bliss Carman. 6076-5,6102-8
The **juggler**. Bliss Carman. 6162-1,6309-8
The **juggler**. Mary McNeil Fenollosa. 7038-8
The **juggler**. Frank Dempster Sherman. 6311-X
The **jugglers**. John Gay. 6972-X
Juggling Jerry. George Meredith. 6198-2,6477-9,6634-8,6657-7,6732-8,6660 ,6199-0,6419-1,6508-2,6655-0,6656-9,6430
Jugurtha. Henry Wadsworth Longfellow. 6288-1
Julia. Samuel Taylor Coleridge. 6278-4
Julia. Robert Herrick. 6240-7
Julia. Wendy Rose. 7005-1
Julia's bed. Robert Herrick. 6092-7
Julia's commencement day. Benjamin Franklin Taylor. 6815-4
Julian. Edward Farquhar. 6939-8
Julian and Maddalo, sels. Percy Bysshe Shelley. 6484-1
Julian Grenfell. Maurice Baring. 7029-9
Julian the apostate. Ernest Denny. 6532-5
Juliana. Unknown (Spanish) 6757-3
Julianus [or Julian the Egyptian]
  "Anastasia, fair blossom...". F.L. Lucas (tr.). 6251-2
  "Just as she was, the painter...". F.L. Lucas (tr.). 6251-2
  "Oft and often I sang it...". F.L. Lucas (tr.). 6251-2
  An old fishing net. A.J. Butler (tr.). 6435-3
  An old fishing net. J.A. Pott (tr.). 6435-3
  "Queen of the phantom..." F.L. Lucas (tr.). 6251-2
  "A Spartan, his companion slain". William Cowper (tr.). 6814-2
Juliet. Edmund Blunden. 6659-3
Juliet protests. Wendy Marsh. 6799-9
Julius Caesar. William Shakespeare. 6087-0
Julius Caesar, sel. William Shakespeare. 6958-4
Julius Caesar, sels. William Shakespeare. 6378-0,6102-8, J148-6,6183-4,6260-1,6339 ,6732-8,6250-4,6104-4,6585-6,6409-4,6479-5,6601-1,6606-2,6610-0,6726
Julius Polyaenus
  Deceitful hope. H. Macnaghten (tr.). 6435-3
  Prayer for home-coming. Walter Leaf (tr.). 6435-3
  "Though Thine ears be filled...". F.L. Lucas (tr.). 6251-2
Julius, Kristjan N. ("K.N.")
  At the funeral of —. Bogi Bjarnason (tr.). 6854-5
  Our native tongue. Skuli Johnson (tr.). 6854-5
  Tale of the wayside. Gudmund J. Gislason (tr.). 6854-5
Julot the apache. Robert Service. 6159-1
Julson, Tiffany
  The knight of yesteryear. 6883-9
July. John Clare. 6219-9,6271-7
July. Austin Dobson. 6770-0
July. Mahlon Leonard Fisher. 6029-3
July. Josephine Johnson. 6818-9
July. Frank Dempster Sherman. 6311-X
July. Susan Hartley Swett. 6239-3,6465-5,6497-3,6456-6
July 4, 1870 James Abraham Martling. 6952-5
"**July** 4th, 1981 and all is hell". Elegy for the forgotten oldsmobile. Adrian C. Louis. 7005-1
"**July** and June brought flowers and love". Love and wisdom. Andrew Lang. 6771-9
July avenue. Jorge Luis Borges. 6642-9
July dawn. Louise Bogan. 6388-3
July dawning. Unknown. 6600-3
July Fourth, 1886. Benjamin Franklin Taylor. 6815-4
July fugitive. Francis Thompson. 6477-9

"**July** in my native village". Grapes. Yuk-sa Lee. 6775-1
July madness. Nancy Telfair. 6841-3
July midnight. Amy Lowell. 6338-1
"**July** the twenty-second day". The descent on Middlesex. Peter St. John. 6946-0
July, fr. Calendar. Frances Abbot. 6764-6
July, fr. Love's calendar. Max Dauthendey. 6160-5
The **jumblies**. Edward Lear. 6089-7,6496-5,6427-2,6132-X, 6242-3,6501 ,6125-7,6150-8,6371-3,6656-9,6861-8
"**Jumbo** asleep!". Lullaby for Jumbo, fr. Facade. Edith Sitwell. 7000-0
Jun-toku, Emperor
  "My ancient palace I regret". William N. Porter (tr.). 6852-9
June. William Cullen Bryant. 6240-7,6735-2,6288-1,6126-5
June. John Clare. 6649-6
June. Ellen Mackay Hutchinson Cortissoz. 6873-1
June. Betty Alice Erhard. 6662-3
June. Susan Grant. 6118-4
June. Nora Hopper. 6396-9
June. Francis Ledwidge. 6244-X,6506-6,6153-2,6161-3,6464-7, 6393-7,6653-4
June. Emanuel Leseticky z Lesehradu. 6763-8
June. James Russell Lowell. 6820-0
June. James Russell Lowell. 6240-7,6260-1,6385-3,6465-5, 6479-5,6250-4,6107-9,6104-4,6421-3,6456-6,6481-7, 6575-9,6585-6
June. Douglas Malloch. 6338-1;6476-0
June. James Abraham Martling. 6952-5
June. John Russell McCarthy. 6030-7
June. Harrison Smith Morris. 6102-8,6076-5
June. Fred Passmore. 6397-7
June. James Whitcomb Riley. 6993-2,6991-6
June. Isabel Beulah Schein. 6847-2
June. Frank Dempster Sherman. 6311-X
June. Edmund Spenser. 6191-5
June. Benjamin Franklin Taylor. 6815-4
June 21st. George Birdseye. 6505-8
June @! 21/84* a poem with mistakes included. Eli Mandel. 6767-4
June Bracken and Heather. Alfred Lord Tennyson. 6655-0
June dawn. Constance Deming Lewis. 6841-3
A **June** day. John Todhunter. 6890-1
June fourteenth. Caroline Bowers Tombo. 6654-2
June has brought loveliness to birth. Ellen M. Carroll. 6818-9
June in January. Richard Kendall Munkittrick. 6632-1
June in Wiltshire. Geoffrey Grigson. 6666-6
"**June** leaves are green, pink is the rose". Who knows. James Herbert Morse. 7041-8
A **June** morning. Benjamin Franklin Taylor. 6260-1
June night in Washington. Bliss Carman and Richard Hovey. 6890-1
June nights. Victor Hugo. 6351-9
June rapture. Angela Morgan. 6338-1
June thunder. Louis MacNeice. 6246-6
"**June** was not over,/Though past the full". Another way of love. Robert Browning. 6828-6
June weather. James Russell Lowell. 6239-3
June, fr. The earthly paradise. William Morris. 6657-7, 6076-5,6102-8,6110-9,6655-0,6660 ,6508-2
June, fr. Vision of Sir Launfal. James Russell Lowell. 6963-0
June, sels. William Cullen Bryant. 6934-7
Jung, Nizamat
  India to England. 6224-5,6474-4
Jungfrau. William Wordsworth. 6749-2
The **jungfrau's** cry. Stopford Augustus Brooke. 6656-9
Jungle. Edward Farquhar. 6939-8
The **jungle** book. Gerald Locklin. 6998-3
The **jungle** pest. Roland Young. 6089-7
"The **jungle** wallah, he lives alone". The jungle wallah. Berton Braley. 6853-7
The **jungle**, sels. Archibald Fleming. 6375-6
The **jungle**. Louis Dudek. 6446-9
Junia
  Ballade of a summer hotel. 6722-0
The **junior** God. Robert Service. 6159-1
"The **junior** fellow's vows were said". Lines on the death of a college cat. Frederick Pollock. 6760-3

A **junior** partner wanted. M.E. Sandford. 6744-1
Junior public library. Lilian White Spencer. 6836-7
The **junior's** foxy friends. Raymond W. Walker. 6118-4
Juniors' farewell to the senior class. Edith Putnam Painton. 6718-2
Juniper. Laurie Lee. 6379-9
The **juniper** tree. Wilfred Watson. 6446-9
Junipero Serra. Richard Edward White. 6920-7
Junius
    To the king. 6200-8
Junkermann, Katharine Eggleston
    A union. 6691-7
'**Junkets**,' immortal. William Rose Benet. 6331-4
Junkin, Charles Irvin
    Awful hazardous. 6274-1
    Ben Franklin, Esq. 6936-3
    I know a freshman. 6936-3
Junkins, Donald
    The wounded deer leaps highest. 6803-0
"**Juno**, that on her head loves liverie carried". Fulke Greville; 1st Baron Brooke. 6380-2
Jupiter Amans. Unknown. 6278-4
Jupiter and ten. James Thomas Fields. 6344-6,6575-9
The **Jura** mountains. George Gordon, 6th Baron Byron. 6749-2
Jurica, Alice B.
    Good Friday ("'The Son of God am I,' he humbly said") 6144-3
Juror number six. Unknown. 6878-2
Jury trial in the days of Edward I. John Gibson Lockhart (atr) 6878-2
The **jury-law** victim. Unknown. 6878-2
A **juryman's** story. Emilia Aylmer Blake. 6924-X
Just & unjust. Charles Synge Bowen, Baron Bowen. 6722-0
"**Just** a bit of a girl". To a bit of a girl. Ethel M. Brainerd. 6906-1
Just a boy. Edgar A. Guest. 7033-7
Just a cottage, quaint and old. Katherine Call Simonds. 6764-6
"**Just** a gnarled mass of roots". Gnarled roots. Ethel H. Kleppinger. 6857-X
"**Just** a little baby". Parental pride. Edgar A. Guest. 6869-3
Just a little girl. Unknown. 6248-2
Just a love-letter. Henry Cuyler Bunner. 6735-2
Just a mannish custom. Clement Gelezumas. 6799-9
Just a smack at Auden. William Empson. 6210-5
"**Just** a wee little scrap of a laddie, so fair". His name. Pauline Frances Camp. 6995-9
"**Just** about the time the clouds are blackest". Buckle in. Edgar A. Guest. 6862-6
Just about these days. A.T. Worden. 6929-0
"**Just** above the ancient doorway were". 'Think and thank' Mary Secor Meserole. 6848-2
"**Just** after supper sheets were passed out". I am sure of it. Jimmy Santiago Baca. 6870-7
"**Just** a ter thefsunset, yesterday". chapel, fr. Pictures by the way. John Nichol. 6819-7
Just an old man. Mary Goose. 7005-1
"**Just** an ordinary man, eight and forty to..day". The ordinary folks. Edgar A. Guest. 6869-3
"**Just** another little farmhouse". Geranium in the window. Elinor Gibney Kibbee. 6764-6
"**Just** are the ways of God". The transcedence of God, fr. Samson Agonistes. John Milton. 6933-9
"**Just** as I thought I was growing old". The prime of life. Walter Learned. 7041-8
Just as a mother. Leigh Hunt. 6097-8
Just as I am. Charlotte Elliot. 6219-9
"**Just** as I am." Unknown. 6302-0
"**just** as of yore with friendlt rain". Mater dolorosa. Elliott Napier. 6784-0
"**Just** as she was, the painter...". Julianus [or Julian the Egyptian]. 6251-2
"**Just** as that wild animal, the sea". The lives we invite to flower aaong us flower beyond us. Wendy Battin. 6900-2
"**Just** as the dawn of love was breaking". Fate knows no tears. Laurence (Adele Florence Nicolson) Hope. 6856-1
"**Just** as the hour was darkest". The ballad of New Orleans.
    George Henry Boker. 6946-0
"**Just** as the plum-tree lifts its ivory flower". Life. Elkanah East Taylor. 6818-9
"**Just** as the sun is dismissing the day". The matriarch. Josephine Hancock Logan. 6789-1
"**Just** at the edge of the night and ...". Little miss six o'clock. Edgar A. Guest. 6862-6
"**Just** at the point/Of facing death in...". Last days of Byron. Charlotte Fiske Bates. 7041-8
"**Just** at the time when jasmins bloom...". Song of Faiz Ulla. Laurence (Adele Florence Nicolson) Hope. 6856-1
Just before the battle, mother. George F. Root. 6074-9, 6121-4
"**Just** before the creek gets ready". Tonowanda creek. Josephine Johnson. 6799-9
Just between friends. De France. 6818-9
Just California. John Steven McGroarty. 6241-5
"**Just** beyond the words/floats an elusive". Nebula. Petronella Helen Urasky-Chapp. 6799-9
"**Just** beyond this field of clover...". A sermon in flowers. Addie F. Davis. 6927-4
"**Just** drifting on together". He and I. James Whitcomb Riley. 6992-4,6993-2
"**Just** eighteen years ago this day". Nahum Fay on the loss of his wife. Unknown. 6787-5
"**Just** for a 'scrap of paper'.". A scrap of paper. Herbert Kaufman. 6846-4
Just for a minute. F.J.H. Sutton. 6983-5
"**Just** for the handful of silver he left us". The lost leader. Robert Browning. 6828-6
Just for to-day. Samuel Wilberforce. 6656-9
Just for today. Blanche McElhiney. 6799-9
Just for today. Sybil F. Partridge. 6337-3
Just for today. Eunice Ward. 6130-3
"**Just** for today, dear Lord, give me the faith". Christmas. Esther Bergman Narey. 6799-9
"**Just** God! - and these are they". Clerical oppressions. John Greenleaf Whittier. 7009-4
"**Just** God! and these are they". Clerical oppressors. John Greenleaf Whittier. 6946-0
"**Just** in the gray of the dawn...". Expedition to Wessagusset, fr. The courtship..Standish. Henry Wadsworth Longfellow. 6946-0
"**Just** in the hush before the dawn". Verses: Faiz Ulla. Laurence (Adele Florence Nicolson) Hope. 6856-1
Just like a man. Unknown. 6928-2
Just like me. Dorothy Lewis Maddox. 6799-9
Just like Washington. Unknown. 6712-3
"**Just** look'ee here, Mr. Preacher, you're...". Told to the missionary. George Robert Sims. 7008-6
"**Just** look, Manetto, at that wry-mouth'd minx". Sonnet: To an ill-favored lady. Guido Cavalcanti. 7039-6
"**Just** now I think, I'd like to be". Dreaming. Edgar A. Guest. 6862-6
"**Just** now there was a word: a silver fox". Poet's hunting song. Helen Frazee-Bower. 6750-6
"**Just** one cast more! how many a year". The last cast. Andrew Lang. 6987-8
"**Just** one more bride has passed before". Wedding feast. Amy Bower. 6750-6
Just one more spring. Nicephorus Vrettakos. 6352-7
Just one signal. Unknown. 6946-0
Just one signal. Unknown. 6741-X
Just our dog. Unknown. 7008-6
"**Just** out of the window". A York music box. Sarah D. Clarke. 6965-7
Just over the way. Unknown. 6917-7
Just plain cat. Jeannie Pendleton Ewing. 6692-2
Just plain yellow. Anna Hadley Middlemas. 7008-6
Just smile. Mrs. Zell Struthers. 6270-9
Just so. Unknown. 6889-8
Just so. Unknown. 6583-X
Just tell them so. John T. Hinds. 6583-X
"**Just** that glimpse of the table rock". A Cape homestead. Lance Fallaw. 6800-6
"**Just** the airiest, fairiest slip of a thing". discouraging model. James Whitcomb Riley. 6992-4
"**Just** the clanking of switch engines...". A day as a wage. Keene Wallis. 6880-4

"**Just** think of it! You are ten today". To a little girl of ten. John E. Barrett. 6840-5
Just think! Robert Service. 6159-1
Just thinkin'. Hudson Hawley. 6443-4,6589-9
Just thinking. Hudson Hawley. 6846-4
"**Just** this I ask, an eye to see". Prayer. John Girdler. 6836-7
Just this minute. Unknown. 6303-9
Just tired! Jessie Ward-Haywood. 6799-9
Just to be glad. James Whitcomb Riley. 6260-1,6291-1
Just to be tender. Unknown. 6109-5,6260-1
"**Just** to give up, and trust". Bitter-sweet. Henry Van Dyke. 6961-4
"**Just** to please my Bonnie belle". Bonnie belle. Samuel Minturn Peck. 6770-0
"**Just** to walk among the roses". Among the roses. Thornton W. Burgess. 6798-0
Just war. Maria Jacobs. 6767-0
"**Just** what the bushmen told,while raging rains". Station hunting on the Warrego. Philip J. Holdsworth. 6768-9
"**Just** when he said the tornado". The tornado. Norman H. Russell. 7005-1
"**Just** when the red June roses blow". Three roses. Adelaide Anne Procter. 6957-6
"**Just** where the treasury's marble front". Pan in Wall street. Edmund Clarence Stedman. 7041-8
Just whistle. Frank Lebby Stanton. 6291-1
Justice. Samuel Daniel. 6935-5
Justice. Ralph Waldo Emerson. 6302-0,6385-3
Justice. William Shakespeare. 6499-X
Justice. Jessie M. Wood. 7021-3
Justice and the lawyer. Edward Moore. 6878-2
Justice for womankind. William Dudley Foulke. 6954-1
Justice in Leadville-1878. Helen Hinsdale Rich. 6415-9
Justice protects the dead. Aeschylus. 6435-3
Justice to Scotland. Unknown. 6089-7,6724-7
Justice, fr. Australian transcripts. William ("Fiona Macleod") Sharp. 6768-9
A **justiciary** opera. James Boswell. 6787-5
A **justified** fear. Edward Lear. 6396-9
The **justified** mother of men. Walt Whitman. 6097-8
Justina's temptation. Pedro de la Barca Calderon. 6102-8
Justine, you love me not. John Godfrey Saxe. 6441-8
Justine, you love me not! John Godfrey Saxe. 6652-6
Justus quidem tu es, domine. Gerard Manley Hopkins. 6844-8
Justus, May
 A garden path. 6466-3
The **Jutlander**. Steen Steensen Blicher. 6555-4
Juvenal
 Celestial wisdom, fr. The tenth Satire. Samuel Johnson (tr.). 7039-6
 Umbricius, departing for Cumae, denounces all the vices. 6637-2
Juventa perennis. Thomas Edward Brown. 6809-X
Jvstvm et tenacem. Thomas Campion. 6935-5
"**Jwohnny,** git oot!" Unknown. 6302-0

K
 How firm a foundation. 6337-3
"**K'in-K'in**– the bells peal on". The dance of delight. Unknown. 6959-2
K.,A.E.
 They two. 6260-1
K.,A.S.
 A.S.K. 6474-4
K.,E.H.
 The city church. 6730-1
K.,G.S.
 Ballade of the table d'hote. 6817-0
K.,M.
 My twentieth birthday. 6674-4
K.,M.E.
 "God never meant that we should call this home". 6238-5
K.,R.K.
 A plea for spring poetry. 6118-4
 The tastes of yesterday. 6118-4
 The white opal. 6118-4

K.,R.R.
 The girl of our town. 6118-4
 Mis' Rose. 6118-4
 A spring rondeau. 6118-4
K.,R.W.
 My sweetheart. 6118-4
K.,W.E.
 A lament from the dead. 7031-0
K.D. of Wirsin (Swedish)
 Love and books. Sir Edmund Gosse (tr.). 6297-0
K.K. - can't calculate. Frances M. Whitcher. 6089-7
The **K.K.K.** disco. Noah Mitchell. 6870-7
K.P. blues. Whitt Highbaugh. 6237-7
Kaalund, Hans Vilhelm
 In a sunny nook. Charles Wharton Stork (tr.). 6555-4
Kabel, Ann Caroline
 Linda Ann, July 16, 1947 6857-X
 Soul's harbor. 6857-X
Kabir
 He cares. 6337-3
 Hope in him while thou livest. 6337-3
 My Lord hides himself. 6337-3
 Songs of Kabir. Rabindranath Tagore (tr.). 6730-1
Kabraji, Fredoon
 A pianoforte recital. 6070-6
Kabraji, Freidon
 A pianoforte recital. 6070-6
Kafir songs, sels. Francis Carey ("Jan van Avond") Slater. 6800-6
Kafka's America. Richard Eberhart. 6390-X
Kafoozelum. Unknown. 6594-5
Kagawa, Toyohiko
 The burden. 6337-3
 Christ liveth in me. Lois J. Erickson (tr.). 6027-7
 Day's end. Lois J. Erickson (tr.). 6337-3
 I call the swallows. Lois J. Erickson (tr.). 6027-7
 Japan can teach. Lois J. Erickson (tr.). 6027-7
 The kingdom of God is within in. Lois J. Erickson (tr.). 6027-7
 The living Christ. Lois J. Erickson (tr.). 6027-7
 Love means adventure. Lois J. Erickson (tr.). 6027-7
 Meditation. 6337-3
 Mirrors. Lois J. Erickson (tr.). 6027-7
 O skylarks, teach Japan to sing. Lois J. Erickson (tr.). 6027-7
 One with the universe. Lois J. Erickson (tr.). 6027-7
 Only a flower. 6337-3
 Penniless. 6337-3
 Sculptor of the soul. 6337-3
 Silence. Lois J. Erickson (tr.). 6027-7
 The simple life. Lois J. Erickson (tr.). 6027-7
 Spring. Lois J. Erickson (tr.). 6027-7
 Waiting for the dawn. Lois J. Erickson (tr.). 6027-7
 Work. Lois J. Erickson (tr.). 6027-7
Kagesue, Kajiwara
 Resolution. 6102-8
Kageyama, Yuri
 A day in a long hot summer. 6790-5
 Disco Chinatown. 6790-5
 Love poem. 6790-5
 My mother takes a bath. 6790-5
 Strings/himo. 6790-5
Kahl, Marjorie
 The weaver of dreams. 6818-9
Kahn, Amy
 Six little sparrows. 6529-5
Kahn, Gustave
 Image. 6801-4
 Pardon. 6351-9
 Pardon. Joseph T. Shipley (tr.). 6351-9
 "Quand le roi vint a sa tour" 6801-4
 Sky of blood. 6351-9
 The voices tell over. 6351-9
 Your kingdom is a fairyland. 6351-9
Kahn, Hannah
 No more poems. 6979-7
Kais declares his love. Nizami. 6448-5
Kais in the desert. Nizami. 6448-5
Kaiser & Co. Alexander Macgregor Rose. 6088-9
The **kaiser** and Belgium. Stephen Phillips. 7026-4

Kaiser and counsellor. Stuart P. Sherman. 7027-2
The **kaiser** and god. Barry Pain. 6474-4
Kaiser dead. Matthew Arnold. 6196-6
The **kaiser's** feast. Felicia Dorothea Hemans. 6973-8
The **Kaiserblumen**. Celia Thaxter. 6612-7
Kaki-no-moto
    "Long is the mountain pheasant's tail". William N. Porter (tr.). 6852-9
Kal. J.K. ("Dum Dum") Kendall. 6591-0,6592-9
Kalakaua; King of the Hawaiian Islands
    Our native land. 6465-5
The **kaleidoscope**. Edward Willard Watson. 6936-3
Kalevala, sels. Unknown (Finnish) 6679-8
The **Kalevala**, sels. Unknown (Finnish) 6372-1
Kali. Unknown (Newari) 7013-2
Kalich, inheritor of tragedy. Ripley Dunlap Saunders. 6848-0
Kalidasa
    Autumn, fr. The seasons. Arthur W. Ryder (tr.). 7039-6
    The baby. Sir William Jones (tr.). 6385-3,6438-8
    Invocation of the dawn. 6879-0
    Woman. Horace W. Wilson (tr.). 6438-8,6385-3
Kallunborg church. John Greenleaf Whittier. 6236-9,6290-3
The **kallyope** yell. Vachel Lindsay. 6027-7
Kaminsky, Bohdan
    Ritournelles. Paul Selver (tr.). 6763-8
Kamp, James R.
    Wing on! 7019-1
Kan-il-lak the singer. Constance Lindsay Skinner. 6030-7
Kanaris. Alexandros Pallis. 6352-7
"**Kanawaki**, - 'by the rapid'.". The Caughnawaga beadwork-seller. William Douw Lighthall. 6795-6
The **Kanawha** striker. Unknown. 6880-4
Kanda
    His will. Lois J. Erickson (tr.). 6027-7
Kandinsky: 'improvisation no. 27' Edward Tick. 6966-5
Kane. Fitz-James O'Brien. 6302-0,6402-7,6219-9
Kane to the king. Unknown. 6859-6
Kane, Douglas V.
    Requiem. 6648-8
Kane, Rubin
    The haunted house. 6799-9
    Life's stairway. 6799-9
Kane, Sara
    To a picture of a lady. 6799-9
Kane, Sherry
    Reminder. 6088-9
Kane, Susan M.
    The vision. 6799-9
Kaneko, Lonny
    Coming home from camp. 6790-5
    Family album. 6790-5
    The secret. 6790-5
    Violets for mother. 6790-5
Kanesuke
    "Oh! rippling river Izumi". William N. Porter (tr.). 6852-9
Kanfer, Allen
    Epistle to a German. 6042-0
Kang, Un-kyo
    Background. 6775-1
    Evening wind. 6775-1
    A spring day. 6775-1
Kang, Woo-shik
    Three quatrains. 6775-1
Kangaroo. David Herbert Lawrence. 6733-6
The **kangaroo.**. Ogden Nash. 6722-0
The **kangaroos**. Thomas Hood. 6974-6
Kansas. Thomas Emmet Dewey. 6615-1
Kansas. Max Eastman. 6880-4
Kansas. Harry Kemp. 6615-1
Kansas. Vachel Lindsay. 6506-6;6615-1
Kansas. Willard Wattles. 6615-1
Kansas and London. Harry Kemp. 6615-1
Kansas boys. Unknown. 6594-5,6281-4
The **Kansas** emigrants. John Greenleaf Whittier. 6121-4
The **Kansas** emigrants. John Greenleaf Whittier. 6946-0
Kansas, mother of us all. Willard Wattles. 6615-1
Kant, Immanuel
    Rule for happiness. 6109-5

Kantor, MacKinlay
    The First Minnesota at Gettysburg. 6628-3
    Lyman Dillon and his plow. 6628-3
    The snow of the Okoboji. 6628-3
    A wife's lament. 6039-0
Kao Shih
    Desolation. 6732-8
The **kapji** blue. H. Woodhouse Neale. 6591-0,6592-9
Kaplan, Mordecai
    God the life of nature. 6532-5
Kappeler, Lucile S.
    April ways. 6906-1
    The north wind. 6906-1
    The playful sun-beam. 6906-1
Kapstein, I.J.
    Lindbergh. 7019-1
The **Karamanian** exile. James Clarence Mangan. 6174-5
Karanikas, Alexander
    Autumn flight. 6764-6
    A vision. 6764-6
Karcher, Daniel Martin
    The elf's lament. 6936-3
    Triolet. 6936-3
Karfeldt, Erik Axel
    Prelude, fr. Fridolin's pleasure garden. Charles Wharton Stork (tr.). 6045-5
Kariotakis, Kostas
    Athens. Rae Dalven (tr.). 6352-7
    Diakos. Rae Dalven (tr.). 6352-7
    Michael. Rae Dalven (tr.). 6352-7
    Prevesa. Rae Dalven (tr.). 6352-7
    Sleep. Rae Dalven (tr.). 6352-7
Karl Radek. Simon Felshin. 6880-4
Karl the martyr. Unknown. 6915-0
Karlene (1). Bliss Carman and Richard Hovey. 6890-1
Karlene (2). Bliss Carman and Richard Hovey. 6890-1
Karlfeldt, Erik Axel
    Dalecarlian march. Charles Wharton Stork (tr.). 6045-5
    Dreams and life. Charles Wharton Stork (tr.). 6045-5
    Flower-songs, sels. Charles Wharton Stork (tr.). 6045-5
    Fridolon's pleasure-garden, sels. Charles Wharton Stork (tr.). 6045-5
    Hymn to the harvest moon. Charles Wharton Stork (tr.). 6045-5
    Imagined happiness. Charles Wharton Stork (tr.). 6045-5
    In the elk season. Charles Wharton Stork (tr.). 6045-5
    The misjudged fiddler. Charles Wharton Stork (tr.). 6045-5
    My forefathers, fr. Songs of nature and love. Charles Wharton Stork (tr.). 6045-5
    Song after harvest. Charles Wharton Stork (tr.). 6045-5
    Time of waiting. Charles Wharton Stork (tr.). 6045-5
    A vagrant. Charles Wharton Stork (tr.). 6045-5
    The Virgin Mary. Charles Wharton Stork (tr.). 6045-5
Karma. William Canton. 6656-9
Karma. Edwin Arlington Robinson. 6038-2,6011-0
Karnosh, Louis J.
    Melancholia. 6482-5
    Paranoia. 6482-5
    These hands of ours. 6482-5
Karol's kiss. Ben Jonson. 6191-5
Karolin's song. Ben Jonson. 6315-2
Karoniaktatie
    'Dead heroes' 7005-1
    Elegy. 7005-1
    The face... 7005-1
    Stone song (Zen Rock) the seer & the unbeliever. 7005-1
The **karroo**, sels. Francis Carey ("Jan van Avond") Slater. 6800-6
Karshish, sels. Robert Browning. 6144-3
Karshish, the Arab physician. Robert Browning. 6730-1
"**Karshish**, the picker-up of learning's crumbs". An epistle. Robert Browning. 6828-6
Karsner, Walta
    Xmas time. 6070-6
Karvounis, Nicholas
    The song of the vanquished. Rae Dalven (tr.). 6352-7
Kasa, The Lady of
    To Otomo No Yackamochi. 6102-8
Kash, Marsha Elaine

Everybody has to go home sometime. 6998-3
Kashiwagi, Hiroshi
  Haircut. 6998-3
Kashmiri song. Laurence (Adele Florence Nicolson) Hope. 6732-8
Kashmiri song by Juma. Laurence (Adele Florence Nicolson) Hope. 6856-1
Kasischke, Laura
  The poem the poet tell me. 6822-7
"**Kaspar**, Balthasar, Melchior". The Magi. Geoffrey Johnson. 6782-4
Kassandra. Johann C. Friedrich von Schiller. 6842-1
Kate. Alfred Lord Tennyson. 6977-0
Kate. Unknown. 6919-3
Kate. Unknown. 6744-1,6576-7
The **Kate** Adams. Unknown. 6609-7
Kate and her horns. Unknown. 6057-9,6059-5
Kate Ketchem. Phoebe Cary. 6406-X
Kate Maloney. Dagonet. 6411-6
Kate of Aberdeen. John Cunningham. 6086-2
Kate of Araglen. Denny Lane. 6174-5
Kate of Garnavilla. Edward Lysaght. 6086-2
Kate Shelly. Eugene J. Hall. 6917-7
Kate Shelly. Eugene J. Hall. 6142-7,6451-5,6478-7
Kate Temple's song. Mortimer Collins. 6656-9
Kate Vane. Thomas Dunn English. 6004-8
Kate's French lesson. Unknown. 6314-4
Kate's mother. Robert Bridges. 6487-6
Kate, Ricketty. See Filson, Mrs. A.J.
"**Kate**, with her great blue eyes and golden...". In loco parentis. James Abraham Martling. 6952-5
Kathaleen Ny-Houlahan. James Clarence Mangan. 6174-5
Katharine. Robert Louis Stevenson. 6123-0
Katharine Fanfarie. Unknown. 6055-2
Katharine Jaffray. Unknown. 6185-0,6289-X
Katharine Janfarie. Unknown. 6056-0,6491-4,6219-9
Katherine. Paul F. Fericano. 6792-1
Katherine Milton. John Milton. 6208-3
Katherine Veitch. Wilfred Wilson Gibson. 6162-1
Kathie Morris. Unknown. 6415-9,6167-2
Kathleen [pseud].
  Martha in meditation. 6817-0
Kathleen ban adair. Francis Davis. 6409-4
Kathleen Mavourneen. Louisa Macartney Crawford. 6732-8, 6250-4
Kathleen O'More. George Nugent Reynolds. 6090-0,6086-2
Katie. Henry Timrod. 6385-3,6243-1
Katie an' me. Edmund Vance Cooke. 6688-7
Katie an' the Jim Lee had a little race. Unknown. 6609-7
Katie an' the Jim Lee had a race. Unknown. 6609-7
Katie Lee and Willie Gray. Unknown. 6165-6,6385-3,6554-6, 6407-8,6742-5,6744 ,6565-1
Katie Lee and Willie Grey. Josie R. Hunt. 6142-7
Katie's answer. William B. Fowle. 6280-6
Katie's answer. Unknown. 6255-5,6277-6,6413-2
Katie's cares. Unknown. 6713-1
Katie's questions. Unknown. 6928-2
Katie's sceret. Unknown. 6003-X
Katrina. Denys Lefebvre. 6800-6
Katrina. Sneyd (pseud). 6591-0,6592-9
Katrina. Unknown. 6745-X
Katrina likes me poody vell. Unknown. 6791-3,6823-5
Katrina likes me poody vell. Unknown. 6277-6
Katrina on the porch. Alice Cary. 6865-0;6969-X
Katrina, sels. Josiah Gilbert Holland. 6066-8
Katscher, Hedwig
  Before night. Milne Holton and Herbert Kuhner (tr.). 6769-7
  "From the bread of life" Milne Holton and Herbert Kuhner (tr.). 6769-7
  The tree. Milne Holton and Herbert Kuhner (tr.). 6769-7
  "Your candle of suffering" Milne Holton and Herbert Kuhner (tr.). 6769-7
Katterhenry, Rose
  Quatrains. 6750-6
Katy's answer. Allan Ramsay. 6152-4
Katy's letter. Helen Selina Sheridan; Lady Dufferin. 6711-5,6744-1
Katydid. Oliver Wendell Holmes. 6165-6,6302-0,6385-3,6629-1,6456-6,6565

The **katydids**. James Whitcomb Riley. 6091-9
Katz, Leslie
  Sestina: Europa and the bull. 6900-2
The **Katzenjammer** Kids. James Reaney. 6446-9
Kauffman, George
  Plant 35. 6761-1
Kauffman, Reginald Wright
  Easter-eggs. 6846-4
  Home. 6846-4
  The nation's David. 6474-4
  Skull and bones. 7007-8
Kauffman, Russell E.
  The Christ of God. 6065-X
Kauffman, Ruth
  Motherhood ("O God, I know his sins are red"). 6097-8
Kauffman, Ruth Wright
  Let there be light! 6846-4
Kaufman, Bob
  Cocoa morning. 6901-0
  Geneology. 6901-0
  Heavy water blues. 6792-1
  Heavy water blues. 6998-3
  I wish... 6998-3, 6901-0
  'Michaelangelo' the elder. 6901-0
  Night song sailor's prayer. 6901-0
  Suicide. 6792-1
Kaufman, George S.
  Advice to worriers. 6026-9,6501-5
Kaufman, Herbert
  The hell-gate of Soissons. 6474-4,6419-1
  The hell-gate of Soissons. 7026-4
  A scrap of paper. 6846-4
  The song of the guns. 6846-4
  "Why in the world do you want to carry". 6109-5
Kaufman, Kenneth C.
  Bittersweet. 6397-7
  The deputy. 6397-7
  Indian summer. 6397-7
  Man-talk. 6397-7
  Rain-in-the-face. 6397-7
  Tame duck. 6464-7
  Wild heart. 6397-7
Kaufmann, Ruth Wright
  The vagabond at home. 6374-8
Kaun, Alexander (tr.)
  Grenada. Mikhail Arkadyevich Svetlov, 6665-8
Kaunas 1941 Johannes Bobrowski. 6758-1
Kavanagh, Jane
  A Christmas story. 6417-5
Kavanagh, Kathleen
  A Christmas chime. 6747-6
Kavanagh, Katie H.
  Treasures. 6675-5
Kavanagh, Patrick
  A glut on the market. 6930-4
  Memory of brother Michael. 6930-4
  Pegasus. 6210-5
  Ploughman. 6780-8
  Sanctity. 6210-5
Kavanagh, Rose
  Lough bray. 6060-0,6174-5
  The northern blackwater. 6858-8
  St. Michan's churchyard. 6090-5,6174-5
  The turn of the tide. 6674-4
The **Kavanagh**. Bliss Carman and Richard Hovey. 6006-4
The **Kavanagh**. Richard Hovey. 6307-1,6309-8
Kavenaugh, Mrs. Russell
  Poetry, prose and fact. 6293-8
  Poor men vs. rich men. 6293-8
  The power of temper. 6293-8
Kavin again. Bliss Carman and Richard Hovey. 6890-1
Kawabuchi
  Thou art. Lois J. Erickson (tr.). 6027-7
Kay, Bernard K.
  Adolescence. 6764-6
  From a sonnet sequence. 6764-6
Kay, Fredrica
  Last gift. 6818-9
Kay, Margaret de
  The courier. 6995-9

Kay, W. (tr.)
    The knight of Toggenburg. Johann C. Friedrich von Schiller, 6675-5
The **kayak**.. Unknown. 6466-3
Kaye-Smith, Sheila
    Lady day in harvest. 6282-2
    The optimist. 6541-4
Kayser, Carl Friedrich
    Ein tag. 6847-2
    Mein glaube. 6847-2
Kayser, Carl Friedrich (into German) (tr.)
    I vex me not with brooding o'er the years. Thomas Bailey Aldrich, 6847-2
Kazantzakis, Galatea
    The laborer. Rae Dalven (tr.). 6352-7
    Sinner. Rae Dalven (tr.). 6352-7
Kazin, Vasili
    The bricklayer. Cecil Maurice Bowra (tr.). 6103-6
Kazin, Vladimir
    Accordionist. Jack Lindsay (tr.). 6546-5
    The match's way. Jack Lindsay (tr.). 6546-5
    Uncle or sun. Jack Lindsay (tr.). 6546-5
Kazinezi, Francis
    Separation. 6226-1
Ke-ni-ga song. Unknown (American Indian) 6891-X
The **ke**. James Abraham Martling. 6952-5
Keagle, Cora L.
    Summer evening. 6799-9
Kearney, Peadar
    The soldier's song. 6930-4
    The tri-colored ribbon. 6930-4
Kearny at Seven Pines. Edmund Clarence Stedman. 6062-5, 6014-5,6113-3,6742-5,6340-3,6471 ,6735-2,6016-2,6470-1
The **Kearsage**. James Jeffrey Roche. 6006-4,6096-X,6274-1, 6459-0,6431-0
Kearsarge. Silas Weir Mitchell. 6946-0
Kearsarge and Alabama. Unknown. 6946-0
Kearsarge and Alabama. Unknown. 6016-2
"**Kearsarge** the red man called me, as he turned". Prologue, fr. The strength of the hills. Enid Bliss Kiernan. 6764-6
Keating, Geoffrey
    Geoffrey Keating to his letter. 6090-0
    Keen thyself, poor wight. Padraic Pearse (tr.). 6930-4
    O woman full of wile. Padraic Pearse (tr.). 6930-4
Keating, George
    'My grief on Fal's proud plain,' sel. Padraic Pearse (tr.). 6930-4
Keats. Edith Albert. 6847-2
Keats. Richard Watson Gilder. 7041-8
Keats. Henry Wadsworth Longfellow. 6333-0,6288-1,6126-5
Keats. Gertrude Huntington McGiffert. 6838-3
Keats. Lizette Woodworth Reese. 6102-8,6076-5
Keats. Arthur Stringer. 6433-7
Keats. Henry Van Dyke. 6961-4
Keats at Teignmouth: 1818. Charles Causley. 6339-X
'**Keats** took snuff'. Unknown. 6453-1
Keats, John
    Addressed to Haydon. 6828-6
    Addressed to Haydon. 6543-0
    Adonis. 6980-0
    Adonis sleeping. 6980-0
    After dark vapors have oppressed our plains. 6110-9, 6371-3,6086-2
    "After dark vapors have oppressed our plains" 6828-6
    "And truly I would rather be struck dumb" 6935-5
    Angel thoughts. 7020-5
    "As heaven and earth are fairer," fr. Hyperion. 6438-X
    As Hermes once took to his feathers light. 6086-2
    Autumn. 6634-8
    "Ay, if a madman could have leave." 6482-5
    Bacchus. 6423-X,6543-0
    The bard speaks, fr. Epistle to my brother George. 6832-4
    Bards of passion and of mirth. 6483-3,6732-8,6086-2, 6102-8
    Beauty ("A thing of beauty is a joy forever"). 6183-4, 6232-6,6610-0,6102-8,6543-0
    Beauty triumphant. 6423-X

Bitter chill. 6083-8
Bright star! would I were steadfast as thou art. 6154-0, 6527-9,6726-3,6198-2,6154-0,6122 ,6246-6,6536-8,6208-3,6737-9,6110-9,6371 ,6122-2,6317-9,6527-9,6726-3, 6198-2,6154 ,6199-0,6196-6,6430-2,6560-0,6464-7,6646 ,6086-2,6491-4,6723-9
Calidore. 6828-6
Coelus to Hyperion. 6543-0
The coming of Dian, fr. Endymion. 6110-9
Cybele drawn by lions, fr. Endymion. 6545-7
Cynthia's bridal evening. 6543-0
The daisy's song, sels. 6047-1
The daisy's song. 6519-8
The dance of the merry damsels. 6959-2
The day is gone. 6086-2
December. 6239-3
Dedication to Leigh Hunt, Esq. 6250-4
"Deep in the shady sadness of a vale", fr. Hyperion. 6122-2,6289-X
The Devon maid. 6086-2
Diana. 6102-8
The dove. 6424-8
A dream, after reading Dante's episode of Paolo... 6483-3
Dreaming oaks. 6793-X
Endymion. 6186-9,6527-9,6543-0
Endymion, sels. 6122-2,6198-2,6332-2,6369-1,6732-8,6513 ,6110-9,6430-2,6196-6,6250-4,6199-0
Epistle to Charles Cowden Clarke. 6943-6,6828-6
Epistle to George Felton Mathew. 6828-6
Epistle to J.H. Reynolds. 6092-7
Epistle to my brother George. 6828-6
Epistle to Reynolds, fr. On imagination. 6199-0
Eve of St. Agnes, sels. 6289-X,6501-5,6317-9
The eve of St. Agnes, sels. 6301-2
The eve of St. Agnes. 6052-8,6600-3,6198-2,6369-1,6473-6,6536 ,6291-9,6646-1,6660-7,6199-0,6196-6,6430 , 6122-6,6154-0,6271-7,6302-0,6385-3,6488 ,6560-0,6192-3,6250-4,6102-8,6245-8,6153 ,6527-9,6604-6,6726-3, 6732-8,6723-9,6645 ,6023-4,6086-2,6110-9,6371-3
The eve of St. Agnes. 6828-6
The eve of St. Mark. 6186-9,6378-0,6726-3,6086-2,6110-9
A fairy scene, fr. Endymion. 6980-0
Fairy song ("Shed no tear! O shed no tear!"). 6254-7, 6271-7,6302-0,6385-3,6479-5,6291 ,6219-9,6424-8,6737-9
The fall of hyperion, a dream. 6958-4
The fall of the Titans, fr. Hyperion. 6935-5
Fancy. 6271-7,6315-2,6486-8,6501-5,6219-9,6199 ,6086-2, 6110-9,6196-6,6230-X
Fancy. 6828-6
The fear of death. 6737-9
The feast of Dian, fr. Endymion. 6086-2,6110-9
Fingal's cave. 6484-1
The flight. 6543-0
The forest. 6102-8
Fragment of an ode to Maia. 6086-2,6250-4,6430-2
Fragment of an ode to Maia, written on May Day, 1818 6828-6
"Freshest breeze I caught", fr. Epistle to my brother. 6997-5
From the bridge. 6466-3
Goldfinches. 6239-3
The grasshopper and cricket. 6198-2,6232-6,6302-0,6385-3,6304-7,6102-8,6639-9
Great spirits now on earth are sojourning. 6110-9,6086-2
Happy insensibility. 6246-6,6429-9,6321-7
Happy is England. 6934-7
He saw far in the concave green of the sea. 6833-2
"Here lies one whose name was writ in water." 6083-8
His last sonnet ("Bright star!"). 6186-9,6315-2
Hope ("And as, in sparkling majesty, a star"). 6583-X
How many bards. 6110-9,6199-0
"How many bards gild the lapses of time" 6828-6
The human seasons. 6138-9,6246-6,6482-5,6669-0,6543-0, 6086-2,6110-9,6737-9
Hymn to Pan. 6271-7,6378-0,6634-8,6732-8,6196-6,6086-2, 6102-8,6110-9,6199-0,6543-0
Hyperion. 6138-9,6186-9,6536-8,6110-9,6199-0,6430

KEATS

Hyperion's arrival. 6543-0
Hyperion, sel. 6958-4
Hyperion, sel. 6935-5
Hyperion, sels. 6049-8,6179-6,6378-0,6122-2,6198-2,6289 ,6196-6,6541-4,6102-8,6645-3,6369-1,6138 ,6726-3, 6208-3
I had a dove. 6086-2,6114-1
I stood tiptoe upon a little hill. 6395-0,6503-1
I stood tiptoe upon a little hill, sels. 6369-1,6196-6
Imitation of Spenser. 6110-9
Imitation to Spenser. 6828-6
In a drear-nighted December. 6122-2,6134-6,6187-7,6102-8,6110-9,6086-2,6371-3,6199-0
The Indian lady. 6830-8
Invocation to the power of love, fr. Endymion. 6110-9
Isabella, or the pot of basil. 6679-8,6086-2,6110-9
Isabella, sels. 6648-8
"It was a den...", fr. Hyperion. 6726-3
Italy sweet too! 6423-X,6484-1
"Keen, fitful gusts are whisp'ring here and there" 6828-6
Keen, fitful gusts are whispering here and there. 6122-2,6110-9,6430-2
Keen, fitful gusts are whispering here and there, sels. 6369-1
King Stephen. 6188-5
King Stephen, sels. 6610-0
La belle dame sans merci. 6052-8,6122-2,6134-6,6138-9, 6154-0,6339 ,6023-4,6086-2,6102-8,6150-8,6110-9,6645 ,6075-7,6133-8,6196-6,6430-2,6560-0,6199 ,6192-3, 6613-5,6250-4,6107-9,6396-9,6659 ,6186-9,6198-2,6204-0,6236-9,6246-6,6254 ,6125-7,6153-2,6219-9,6301-2, 6513-9,6419 ,6289-X,6302-0,6315-2,6317-9,6328-4,6332 ,6252-0,6319-5,6371-3,6639-9,6646-1,6723 ,6369-1, 6395-0,6427-2,6459-0,6473-6,6527 ,6518-X,6660-7,6668-2,6536-8,6604-6,6610-0,6634-8,6726-3,6732
Lamia. 6199-0,6430-2,6198-2,6430-2,6199-0
Lamia, sel. 6958-4
Lamia, sels. 6196-6
Last sonnet. 6604-6,6634-8,6086-2,6301-2,6102-8,6252-0, 6543-0,6660-7
Life. 6634-8
Lines on seeing a lock of Milton's hair. 6641-0
Lines on the Mermaid Tavern. 6122-2,6154-0,6198-2,6315-2,6527-9,6733 ,6102-8,6430-2,6491-4,6543-0,6371-3, 6250 ,6086-2,6110-9,6219-9,6199-0
Lines supposed to have been addressed to Fanny Brawne. 6380-2
Madeline on St. Agnes' eve. 6634-8
Marigolds. 6047-1
Meg Merrilies. 6134-6,6138-9,6236-9,6254-7,6465-5,6466 , 6496-5,6519-8,6558-9,6179-6,6086-2,6383
The Mermaid Tavern. 6246-6,6732-8,6737-6,6230-X,6092-7
Minnows. 6239-3,6510-4
"The Moon lifting her silver rim". 6395-0
The moon. 6980-0
Morning. 6239-3
"Mother of Hermes and still youthful Maia!" 6935-5
Mother of Hermes, and still youthful Maia. 6196-6
Music, fr. Hyperion. 6438-8
Nature's delights. 6240-7
The nightingale. 6438-8
The Nile. 7015-9
"No, no, go not to Lethe, neither twist". 6187-7
O sleep a little while. 6958-4
O solitude. 6199-0
"The ocean, with its vastness, its blue green". 6997-5
Oceanus. 6543-0
Ode. 6585-6
Ode ("Bards"). 6122-2,6198-2,6527-9,6271-7,6110-9,6430-2,6199-0,6219-9,6371-3
Ode on a Grecian urn. 6052-8,6122-2,6138-9,6154-0,6198-2,6208 ,6439-2,6464-7,6639-9,6646-1,6491-4,6543 , 6255-5,6271-7,6289-X,6302-0,6385-3,6315 ,6585-6,6660-7,6723-9,6645-3,6424-8,6430 ,6331-4,6501-5,6634-8, 6332-2,6339-X,6358 ,6023-4,6086-2,6102-8,6153-2,6110-9,6301 ,6423-X,6473-6,6481-7,6484-1,6488-4,6527 , 6196-6,6250-4,6199-0,6252-0,6219-9,6560 ,6536-8,6604-6,6625-9,6726-3,6732-8,6371 ,6150-8,6192-3,6219-9
Ode on a grecian urn. 6828-6

Ode on a Grecian urn, sels. 6369-1
Ode on indolence. 6110-9,6645-3,6086-2
Ode on melancholy. 6122-2,6154-0,6208-3,6317-9,6527-9, 6536 ,6196-6,6430-2,6250-4,6560-0,6086-2,6371 ,6102-8,6110-9,6645-3
Ode on the poets. 6246-6,6230-X
Ode to a nightingale. 6052-8,6726-3,6073-0,6083-8,6138-9,6154 ,6153-2,6086-2,6023-4,6646-1,6645-3,6723 , 6122-2,6198-2,6219-9,6639-9,6371-3,6660 ,6197-4,6430-2,6196-6,6192-3,6560-0,6110 ,6186-9,6208-3,6232-6, 6236-9,6240-7,6246 ,6102-8,6250-8,6199-0,6150-8,6301-2,6464 ,6271-7,6302-0,6385-3,6315-2,6328-4,6332 , 6491-4,6543-0,6339-X,6423-X,6427-2,6473-6,6488-4, 6501 ,6527-9,6536-8,6558-9,6597-X,6604-6,6732
Ode to Apollo. 6142-7
Ode to autumn. 6138-9,6246-6,6315-2,6328-4,6332-2,6339 , 6143-5,6430-2,6560-0,6102-8,6196-6,6668 ,6597-X,6618-6,6732-8,6138-9,6246-6,6315-2,6328-4,6332-2,6339 , 6143-5,6430-2,6560-0,6102-8,6196-6,6668 ,6597-X,6618-6,6732-8
Ode to Maia, sels. 6102-8
Ode to Psyche. 6315-2,6726-3,6086-2,6110-9,6430-2,6645 , 6301-2,6102-8,6250-4,6199-0,6315-2,6726-3,6086-2, 6110-9,6430-2,6645 ,6301-2,6102-8,6250-4,6199-0
Ode to Psyche, sels. 6317-9
Ode to Pysche. 6199-0
On a picture of Leander. 6110-9,6086-2
On death. 6486-8
On fame. 6380-2,6086-2,6110-9,6199-0
On first looking into Chapman's Homer. 6052-8,6187-7, 6075-7,6122-2,6138-9,6154 ,6585-6,6645-3,6737-9,6491-4,6543-0,6646 ,6186-9,6198-2,6208-3,6239-3,6246-6, 6271 ,6464-7,6660-7,6424-8,6639-9,6304-7,6301 ,6289-X,6315-2,6332-2,6473-6,6478-7,6479 ,6421-3,6230-X, 6252-0,6219-9,6153-2,6438 ,6483-3,6488-4,6527-9,6536-8,6604-6,6634 ,6125-7,6150-8,6197-4,6199-0,6104-4, 6212 ,6726-3,6732-8,6560-0,6371-3,6110-9,6102 ,6196-6,6430-2,6192-3,6541-4,6250-4,6052-8,6187-7,6075-7, 6122-2,6138-9,6154 ,6585-6,6645-3,6737-9,6491-4,6543-0,6646 ,6186-9,6198-2,6208-3,6239-3,6246-6,6271 , 6464-7,6660-7,6424-8,6639-9,6304-7,6301 ,6289-X,6315-2,6332-2,6473-6,6478-7,6479 ,6421-3,6230-X,6252-0, 6219-9,6153-2,6438 ,6483-3,6488-4,6527-9,6536-8,6604-6,6634 ,6125-7,6150-8,6197-4,6199-0,6104-4,6212 , 6726-3,6732-8,6560-0,6371-3,6110-9,6102 ,6196-6,6430-2,6192-3,6541-4,6250-4
On first looking into Chapman's Homer, sels. 6369-1, 6086-2,6023-4
On imagination, sels. 6199-0
On melancholy. 6301-2,6383-7
On Oxford. 6802-2
On seeing the Elgin marbles. 6122-2,6726-3,6086-2,6110-9,6560-0
On sitting down to read King Lear once again. 6483-3, 6196-6
On the grasshopper and cricket. 6239-3,6271-7,6289-X, 6395-0,6604-6,6154 ,6086-2,6424-8,6110-9,6199-0,6197-4,6219 ,6473-6,6543-0,6421-3,6660-7,6371-3,6219
On the sea. 6052-8,6122-2,6198-2,6332-2,6488-4,6527 , 6086-2,6110-9,6199-0,6383-7,6439-6,6421 ,6371-3,6645-3
"One day thou wilt be blest". 6238-5
A party of lovers. 6585-6
Peerless poesy. 6634-8
The penitent, fr. The eve of St. Agnes. 6240-7
The poetry of earth. 6669-0
A portrait. 6089-7,6440-X,6110-9
A pot of basil. 6110-9
Proem ("A thing of beauty"). 6086-2
Proem, fr. Endymion. 6110-9,6196-6,6086-2,6196-6,6428-0
The realm of fancy. 6246-6,6302-0
Regalities. 6980-0
Robin Hood. 6122-2,6186-9,6228-8,6323-5,6358-6,6558 , 6512-0,6304-7,6424-8,6421-3,6458-2,6212 ,6086-2,6110-9,6199-0,6212-1
Roundelay, fr. Endymion. 6110-9
The sacrifice to Pan. 6102-8
Saturn. 6315-2,6543-0
Saturn, as he walked into the midst, fr. Hyperion. 6438-8

'Say, doth the dull soil...' 6943-6
Scenes of boyhood. 6980-0
The sea. 6138-9,6560-0
"Season of mists and mellow fruitfulness". 6187-7
The seasons of man. 7020-5
The shell's song. 6833-2
The sigh of silence. 6239-3
Sleep. 6732-8,6102-8
Sleep and poetry. 6828-6
Sleep and poetry. 6110-9
Sleep and poetry, sel. 6958-4
Sleep and poetry, sels. 6289-X,6369-1
Solitude. 6304-7
Song ("I had"). 6861-8
Song ("I had a dove"). 6133-8,6519-8,6131-1
A song about myself. 6541-4
Song of sorrow. 6383-7
Song of the Indian maid, fr. Endymion. 6086-2
Song of the shepherds of Latmos. 6334-9
Song, fr. Endymion. 6315-2
Sonnet. 6828-6
Sonnet. 6828-6
Sonnet. 6828-6
Sonnet ("Bright star"). 6052-8,6204-0,6659-3
Sonnet ("It keeps"). 6547-3
Sonnet ("Keen fitful guests"). 6179-6
Sonnet ("To one"). 6315-2,6604-6,6660-7,6219-9
Sonnet ("When I have fears"). 6250-4,6472-8
Sonnet ("Why did I laugh"). 6378-0,6023-4
Sonnet on 'A lover's complaint.' 6250-4
Sonnet on the sea. 6833-2
Sonnet to Homer. 6641-0,6250-4
Sonnet to Mrs. Reynold's cat. 6120-6
Sonnet to sleep. 6250-4
Sonnet: On a picture of Leander. 6832-4
Sovereignty of love. 6980-0
Specimen of an induction to a poem. 6828-6
Spenserian stanzas on Charles Brown. 6659-3
Squirrels. 7020-5
Stanzas. 6250-4
Stanzas on Charles Armitage Brown. 6802-2
Sweet peas. 6047-1,6239-3,6466-3,6456-6
The terror of death. 6246-6
Thea, fr. Hyperion. 6438-8
There was a naughty boy. 6633-X
"A thiang of beauty is a joy for ever" 6935-5
"A thing of beauty is a joy forever." 6138-9,6332-2, 6238-5,6122-2,6498-1,6337 ,6732-8,6107-9,6199-0,6396-9
Time's sea hath been five years at its slow ebb. 6086-2
To a cat. 6511-2
To a nightingale. 6634-8,6125-7,6252-0
To Ailsa rock. 6258-X,6110-9
To autumn. 6219-9,6396-9,6110-9,6464-7,6639-9,6660 ,
6023-4,6086-2,6153-2,6491-4,6114-1,6645 ,6646-1,6723-9,6737-9,6219-9,6396-9,6110-9,6464-7,6639-9,6660 ,
6023-4,6086-2,6153-2,6491-4,6114-1,6645 ,6646-1,6723-9,6737-9,6052-8,6154-0,6179-6,6186-9,6252-0,6301 ,
6122-2,6108-7,6250-4,6199-0,6659-3,6150 ,6198-2,6208-3,6228-8,6077-1,6369-1,6395 ,6423-X,6473-6,6488-4,
6536-8,6604-6,6726
To Byron. 6483-3
To Chatterton. 6483-3
To Fanny. 6828-6,6086-2
To Homer. 6380-2,6483-3,6086-2,6383-7,6110-9
To Homer, sels. 6501-5
To hope. 6980-0
To Leigh Hunt, Esq. 6110-9
To Leigh Hunt, esq. 6828-6
To Maia. 6199-0
To my brothers. 6828-6
"To one who has been long in city pent." 6086-2,6110-9, 6250-4,6138-9,6154-0,6332-2,6501-5,6560-0
To Psyche. 6830-8
To sleep. 6086-2,6110-9,6125-7,6199-0,6659-3,6430 ,6198-2,6315-2,6536-8,6726-3,6501-5,6533
to solitude. 6828-6
To solitude. 6086-2,6110-9
To the adventurous. 6322-5
To the poets. 6830-8

Two sonnets on fame. 6828-6
The wayfarer. 6138-9
What is life? 6138-9
When I have fears that I may cease to be. 6086-2,6110-9, 6301-2,6646-1,6371-3,6196-6,6153-2,6199-0,6482-5,
6198-2,6332-2,6122-2,6154-0,6337 ,6488-4,6527-9,6726-3,6536-8,6645-3,6560
World outside the world, fr. Lines written in the highlands . 6545-7
Written in disgust of vulgar superstition. 7009-4
Written in disgust of vulgar superstition. 6879-0
Written in January, 1817. 6543-0
Written in January, 1818. 6543-0
Written on the day that Mr. Leigh Hunt left prison. 7009-4

Keats, John (tr.)
Fragment of a sonnet. Pierre de Ronsard, 6102-8
Fragment of a sonnet. Pierre de Ronsard, 7039-6

Keble, John
Address to the poets. 6980-0
Advent Sunday. 6980-0
All Saints' Day. 6543-0
All things beautiful. 6131-1,6449-3
April. 6271-7
As we pray. 6303-9,6337-3,6214-8
Balaam. 6848-0
Balaam. 6437-X
Bathing. 6459-0
Champions of the truth. 6980-0
Children's Christmas Eve. 6747-6
Christmas bells. 6424-8
Christmas day. 6046-3
Dimness. 6980-0
Easter day. 6177-X
The effect of example. 6337-3,6478-7
The elder scripture. 6271-7
Elijah in Horeb. 6848-0
Evening hymn. 6065-X,6337-3,6291-9
Example. 6303-9,6385-3
Fifteenth Sunday after Trinity. 6543-0
"Fill high the bowl, and spice it well, and pour". 6931-2
First Sunday after Epiphany. 6046-3
First Sunday after Trinity. 6046-3
Flowers. 6219-9
The flowers of the field. 6980-0
Forest leaves in autumn. 6980-0
The gathering of the church. 6046-3
Happiness. 6014-5,6424-8
Holy matrimony. 6337-3,6656-9
Hopes in the wilderness. 6848-0
Inward music. 6600-3
Morning. 6600-3
Morning hymn. 6219-9
Naaman's servant. 6848-0
The nightingale. 6980-0
November. 6437-X
Oh, timely happy, timely wise. 6087-0
The rainbow. 6133-8,6424-8
"Red o'er the forest peers the setting sun". 6931-2
Saint Matthew. 6046-3
St. Peter's day. 6271-7
St. Thomas the apostle. 6198-2
Second Sunday after Easter. 6046-3
Second Sunday after Trinity. 6046-3
Seed time hymn. 6656-9
The snowdrop, sels. 5558-9
Sun of my soul. 6304-7
Sweet nurslings, fr. The Christian year. 6934-7
Third Sunday in Advent. 6046-3
Third Sunday is lent. 6543-0
Twentieth Sunday after Trinity. 6046-3
Twenty-first Sunday after Trinity. 6046-3
United States. 6122-2
The waterfall, sels. 6198-2
The waterfall, sels. 6832-4
We need not bid, for cloistered cell. 6214-8
Who ever saw, fr. The Christian year. 6934-7
Who runs may read. 6656-9

Kebra Nagast, sel. Unknown. 7014-0

KEEFE

Keefe, Mildred Jones
    Communion. 6143-5
    Friendship. 6143-5
    Joan. 6143-5
    Starlight. 6143-5
Keegan, Cathleen
    Fulfillment. 6648-8
Keegan, John
    Bouchalleen bawn. 6174-5
    Caoch the piper. 6174-5,6451-5,6404-3,6518-X
    'The dark girl' by the 'holy well'. 6090-0,6174-5
    The Irish reaper's harvest hymn. 6174-5
Keeler, Charles Augustus
    The bells of San Juan Capistrano. 6241-5
    Black sailor's chanty. 6833-2
    The child heart. 6241-5
    Cleaning ship. 6833-2
    An ocean lullaby. 6833-2
    On the dedication of a drinking fountain. 6510-4
    Our brothers of the fields and trees. 6510-4
    Pescadero pebbles. 6102-8,6076-5,6241-5,6076-5,6102-8
    To an Alaskan glacier. 6597-X
Keeler, Clyde E.
    Shanghai insect market. 6799-9
Keeler, Florence M.
    Twin beds. 6750-6
Keeler, Francis L.
    No matter. 6097-8
    Some mother's child. 6365-9,6409-4
Keeler, Julia
    His Matisses, 1938 6767-0
Keeley, Edmund (tr.)
    Among the blind. Yannis Ritsos, 6803-0
    the cheap apartment building. Yannis Ritsos, 6803-0
    Compulsory assent. Yannis Ritsos, 6803-0
    Eleven poems, sels. Yannis Ritsos, 6803-0
    The end of the performance. Yannis Ritsos, 6803-0
    Identity card. Yannis Ritsos, 6803-0
    Miniature. Yannis Ritsos, 6758-1
    Momentary immobility. Yannis Ritsos, 6803-0
    Out of place. Yannis Ritsos, 6803-0
    Sad cunning. Yannis Ritsos, 6803-0
Keeling, Elsa
    An Irish thing in rhyme. 6249-0
Keen. Edna St. Vincent Millay. 6777-8
"Keen as the breath". Portraits. Babette Deutsch. 6035-8
"Keen fitful guests are whispering here and there". Sonnet ("Keen fitful guests"). John Keats. 6179-6
"Keen is the clear deep vault of night". December. Luman R. Bowdish. 6799-9
"The ke n sharp escent of the sea comes...". Sea-breeze, fr. In Tuscany. Cora Fabri. 6876-6
Keen thyself, poor wight. Geoffrey Keating. 6930-4
Keen, Paul F.
    Solidity. 6799-9
"Keen, fitful gusts are whisp'ring here and there" John Keats. 6828-6
Keen, fitful gusts are whispering here and there. John Keats. 6122-2,6110-9,6430-2
Keen, fitful gusts are whispering here and there, sels. John Keats. 6369-1
Keenan's charge. George Parsons Lathrop. 6113-3,6610-0, 6340-3,6471-X,6062-5,6467 ,6016-2,6431-0,6470-1,7917-7,7041-8
Keenan, Deborah
    Folds of a white dress/shaft of light. 6966-5
Keenan, Florence Gibbs
    Henry Benjamin Whipple. 6342-X
Keenan, J.G.
    Menagerie diet. 6719-0
Keene (atr), Robert
    How firm a foundation. 6730-1
Keene, E.H.
    "And there are hearts like richest wines". 6109-5
Keene, John Harrington
    Ice-fishing in winter. 7035-3
Keene; or, lament of an Irish mother over her son. Felicia Dorothea Hemans. 6973-8
The keening of Mary. Unknown. 6282-2
Keep a good tongue in your head for. Martin Parker. 6157-5

Keep a little moment. J. Franklin Babb. 6764-6
Keep a smile on your lips. Nixon Waterman. 6583-X
Keep a stiff upper lip. Phoebe Cary. 6060-9
Keep a stiff upper lip. Unknown. 6211-3,6294-6
Keep a-goin'. Frank Lebby Stanton. 6109-5,6291-1,6277-6, 6527-9,6697-6,6143
Keep a-plugging away. Paul Laurence Dunbar. 6332-2
Keep a-trying. Nixon Waterman. 6211-3
Keep away. Harriet Nutty. 6130-3
"Keep back the one word more". Lizette Woodworth Reese. 6850-2
Keep cheering some one on. Folger McKinsey. 6583-X
Keep climbing. Elizabeth Cushing Taylor. 6270-9
Keep darkness. Leslie Nelson Jennings. 6218-0
"Keep heart, O comrade, God may be delayed." Walt Whitman. 6107-9
Keep hustling. George Loarts. 6109-5
"Keep my memory green." Unknown. 6385-3
"Keep not thou silence, O God". Deus, quis similis. Bible. 6830-8
Keep on just the same. Sam Walter Foss. 6280-6
Keep on keepin' on. Unknown. 6291-1
"Keep on your mask and hide your eye." Unknown. 6317-9
"Keep open house; dabble in bricks and mortar". Unknown. 6435-3
Keep sweet. Strickland Gillilan. 6291-1
"Keep sweet and keep movin'". Robert J. Burdette. 6260-1
Keep the bright side out. Samuel Ellsworth Kiser. 6109-5
Keep the glad flag flying. Unknown. 6583-X
Keep the record clean! Harriet W. Requa. 6685-2
Keep them rolling. Gerald Griffin. 6237-7
"Keep thou/Thy tearless watch". Anguish. Adelaide Crapsey. 6850-2
Keep thy tongue. Unknown. 6334-9
"Keep thy tongue from evil", fr. Psalms. Bible. 6623-2
Keep to the line. Ellen Murray. 6927-4
Keep to the right. Edgar A. Guest. 6862-6
Keep trying. Unknown. 6530-9
"Keep tuned to this station for the latest...". Sunday broadcast: transcribed. Christopher La Farge. 6761-1
Keep up with the times. Arthur J. Burdick. 6928-2
"Keep upon your tongue pure speech". A message to boys. C.E. Walker. 6799-9
Keep your face. George Tsongas. 6792-1,6998-3
Keep your grit. Louis E. Thayer. 6109-5,6583-X
"Keep your lamp of reason burning". Lamp of reason. Edward R. Huxley. 6885-5
"Keeper of my soul tonight". A prayer ("Keeper"). Clyde Wood Sneed. 6270-9
"Keeper of promises made in spring". Ballade a double refrain. Edwin Meade Robinson. 6850-2,6875-8
"Keeper of the keys of heaven". Hymn to sleep. Herve-Noel Le Breton. 6873-1
Teep keeper of the lock. Agnes Lee. 6030-7
Keeper of the orchards. Hilda ("H.D.") Doolittle. 6232-6, 6076-5,6102-8,6076-5
The keeper of the wall. Frederick W. Branch. 6764-6
The keeper. Arthur Stringer. 6337-3,6115-X
The keepers of the light. Letitia Virginia Douglas. 6417-5
The keepers of the nation. Hermann Hagedorn. 6944-4
The keepers of the pass. Sir Charles George Douglas Roberts. 6656-9
Keeping a heart. Arthur O'Shaughnessy. 6094-3,6226-1,6250-4
Keeping an ancient custom. Callie L. Bonney. 6720-4
Keeping his word. Unknown. 6142-7
Keeping his word. Allie Wellington. 6404-3
Keeping on. Arthur Hugh Clough. 6114-1
Keeping store. Mary Frances Butts. 6452-3,6466-3,6135-4
Keeping their world large. Marianne Moore. 6666-6
Keepsake. Albert Samain. 6351-9
Keepsakes. Unknown. 6688-7
Kees, Weldon
    White collar ballad. 6389-6
Keese, Will L.
    Old dobbin. 6690-9
Keese, William L.
    After the wedding. 6693-3
    Captain Joe. 6451-5
    On the Avon. 6451-5

Kehama, sels. Robert Southey. 6867-7,6832-4
Kehama, sels. Robert Southey. 6543-0
Keith of Ravelston. Sydney Dobell. 6600-3,6660-7,6383-7, 6518-X,6250-4
Keith, Joseph Joel
    Bedtime tales. 6218-0
    Child wife. 6218-0
    Flogged child. 6218-0
    Immaculate palm. 6282-2
    In the children's hospital. 6761-1
    In the desert. 6783-2
    Let us answer this query. 6761-1
    Like a boy. 6761-1
    Mr. Lerner. 6218-0
    Nightmare in Morganza. 6218-0
    Old Meg of Kitrann. 6218-0
    The old place. 6761-1
    Only the eyes. 6761-1
    Party line. 6218-0
    The prodigals. 6761-1
    Salems of oppression. 6218-0
    She walks. 6282-2
    Sunday edition. 6218-0
    Telling tall tales. 6761-1
    Though she slumbers. 6282-2
    250 Willow Lane Two h. 6218-0
    Wolf and tiger dining, A.B.. 6218-0
    Woman telephoning. 6218-0
Keller, Gottfried
    Waldied. 6253-9
Keller, H.S.
    Resistless march of girl graduates. 6718-2
Keller, Helen
    In the garden of the Lord. 6337-3,6007-2,6730-1,6214-8
Keller, Horace S.
    The village doctor. 6260-1
Keller, Leonard
    'Temporary escape' 6792-1
Keller, Martha
    Appeasement. 6761-1
    Center square. 6761-1
    Herbs and simples. 6218-0
    Singsong. 6761-1
    Warsaw - Poland. 6761-1
    Widow. 6761-1
    Wilderness road. 6218-0
Kelley, Ethel M.
    I've got a dog. 6512-0
    In the bath. 6266-0
    Letter from the farm. 6715-8
    Oh, lady mine. 6118-4
    A point of view. 6798-0
    A simple quartrain. 6798-0
    The Sunday little boys. 6798-0
    Susie to her ex-young man. 6817-0
    The telephone. 6798-0
    This year. 6118-4
    Wail of a waitress. 6702-6
    Whose little girl? 6266-0
Kelley, Francis Clement
    The throne of the king. 6172-9,6292-X
Kelley, Hubert
    The warrior passes. 7001-9
Kelley, J. Liddell
    The Moa. 6591-0,6592-9
    Old New Zealand. 6591-0,6592-9
    Tahiti. 6591-0,6592-9
    The Taniwha. 6591-0,6592-9
Kelley, Maurice
    "Compunction." 6397-7
    "An improvisation on One glimpsed in passing." 6397-7
    "The mourners." 6397-7
    Peer Gynt. 6397-7
    "Quest." 6397-7
Kellgren, Johan Henrik
    The art of succeeding. Charles Wharton Stork (tr.). 6045-5
Kellock, Harold
    April flower-song. 6118-4
    Arma virumque. 6118-4

Kellogg, Anita M.
    Dot's version of the text. 6670-4
    Molly. 6166-4
Kellogg, E.
    A modest wit. 6402-7
Kellogg, James H.
    A song to mother earth. 6049-8
Kellogg, Kate
    Lady moon. 6452-3
Kellogg, Robert James
    To a dead bird. 6116-8
Kelly of the legion. Robert Service. 6159-1
Kelly the pirate. Unknown. 6057-9
Kelly's Ferry. Benjamin Franklin Taylor. 6815-4
Kelly, Anne V.
    Alibi. 6249-0
Kelly, Blanche Mary
    Brother juniper. 6292-X,6172-9
    Horizons. 6096-X
    The housewife's prayer. 6292-X,6172-9,6727-1,6096-X
    Swallow song. 6096 X
Kelly, Dennis
    Albert. 7003-5
    Ballad of the imperial goldfish. 7003-5
    Gunslinger. 7003-5
    Legs. 7003-5
    Let the boy walk naked. 7003-5
Kelly, John Liddell
    arrival and welcome, fr. Tahiti. 6768-9
    Tahiti: the land of love and beauty, sels. 6768-9
Kelly, Mary Eva (Mrs. Kevin O"Doherty)
    Remembrance ("How my heart aches for you"). 6174-5
    Tipperary. 6656-9,6858-8
    To Erin. 6174-5
Kelly, Maurice
    Quest. 6397-7
Kelly, Patrick
    Light shoes. 6292-X
    The sally ring. 6244-X
Kelly, Robert
    Epithalamion. 6803-0
Kelly, Samuel Walter
    A meditation. 6482-5
Kelly, Sarah Hammond
    Hagar. 6880-4
Kelly, Thomas
    The cross and the crown. 6337-3
    Good tidings to Zion. 6848-0
    A newsboy in church. 6929-0
    We sing the praise of him who died. 6219-9
Kelly, William D.
    Country courtship. 6682-8
    The twilight of Thanksgiving. 6618-6
The kelpie of Corrievreckan. Charles Mackay. 6613-5
Kelso, Hugh
    The old wood. 6049-8
Kelton, Charlotte
    Quest. 6799-9
Kelvin grove. Thomas Lyle. 6180-X
Kemble, Frances Anne
    Absence. 6219-9,6226-1,6066-8,6045-1,6271-7,6302-0,6385-3,6358-6,6620
    Art thou weary? 6046-3
    "Better trust all and be deceived". 6238-5
    The black wall-flower. 6656-9
    Dream land. 6437-X
    Evening. 6046-3
    Faith. 6385-3,6437-X,6600-3,6438-8,6219-9,6303-9,6656-9
    Fragment ("Walking by moonlight on the golden margin"). 6980-0
    Fragment ("Walking by moonlight"). 6980-0
    Lines written in London. 6980-0
    On a forget-me-not. 6980-0
    On a musical box. 6980-0
    Onward, upward. 6889-8
    The prayer of a lonely heart. 6980-0
    A promise. 6980-0
    Sonnet ("Art thou already"). 7037-X
    Sonnet ("I hear"). 7037-X
    To the nightingale. 6980-0

KEMBLE

Trust. 6337-3,6412-4
The vision of life. 6980-0
Winter. 7037-X
A wish. 6980-0
Woman's heart, sels. 6365-9
Kemp Owyne. Unknown. 6154-0,6185-0,6518-X,6067-6,6193-1, 6613-5,6192-3
Kemp, Harry
Alienation. 6102-8,6076-5
Blind. 6076-5,6250-4,6467-1,6102-8,6338-1,6374-8,6476-0, 6556-2
The call. 7007-8
The conquerors. 6300-4,6542-2,6102-8,6335-7,6144-3,6337-3,6732-8
Diminution. 6042-0
The dunes. 6038-2
Every time I see a ship. 6798-0
Farewell. 6374-8
Fickleness. 6441-8
Fisherman. 6798-0
The fountain. 6338-1,6347-0
God the architect. 6303-9,6337-3,6730-1,6250-4,6214-8
Going down in ships. 6374-8
The going of his feet. 6374-8,6532-5
Good morning, America!. 6449-3
He did not know. 6730-1,6034-X
Helen in hades. 6347-0
Hesperides. 6374-8
The hummingbird. 6607-0,6250-4
I sing the battle. 6327-6
In a storm. 6467-1
Joses, the brother of Jesus. 6337-3
Kansas. 6615-1
Kansas and London. 6615-1
The land that God forgot. 6615-1
Lincoln: a retrospect. 6524-4
The new ally. 7027-2
On rereading Catullus. 6039-0
Our thirty pieces. 6619-4
The passing flower. 6250-4
Prayer ("I kneel not now"). 6730-1
A prayer, sels. 6076-5,6102-8,6337-3,6076-5
The president. 6995-9
Prithee, strive not. 6300-4,6441-8
The remedy. 6476-0
Shakespeare and later. 6354-3
Tell all the world. 6374-8,6607-0
Thanks, sels. 6732-8
The tide. 6619-4
To the kings. 6542-2
A tramp's prayer. 6532-5
The unknown ("Here, under sacred ground"). 6051-X,6542-2
The voice of Christmas. 6335-7,6337-3,6476-0
A whaler's confession. 6393-4
A wheat-field fantasy. 6615-1
A wind's life. 6374-8
You talk of this and that. 6034-X
Zenobia. 6880-4
Kemp, Lysander (tr.)
Vrindaban. Octavio Paz, 6758-1
Kempe, Mary Louise
The wagon-maker. 6042-0
Kempion. Unknown. 6055-2,6056-0
Ken, Thomas
An anodyne ("As in the night I restless lie"). 6533-3
An anodyne. 6931-2
"Awake, my soul". 6931-2
Evening hymn. 6302-0,6337-3
Glory to thee this night. 6065-X
Heroism. 6337-3
Midnight hymn. 6219-9
Morning hymn. 6600-3,6219-9
A morning hymne. 6933-9
Now. 6931-2
Kendall, C.P.
A poem defined. 6764-6
Woodland fantasy. 6764-6
Kendall, Guy
To my pupils, gone before their day. 7027-2

Kendall, Harriett
Synariss, 'Queen of Babylon.' 6716-6
Kendall, Henry Clarence
After many years. 6768-9,6591-0,6592-9
Arakoon. 6997-5
Bell birds. 6768-9,6784-0
Beyond Kerguelen. 6784-0
Christmas Creek. 6591-0,6592-9
Coogee. 6656-9
Coogee, sels. 6997-5
Cooranbean, sels. 6768-9
The curse of mother flood. 6768-9
The hut by the black swamp, sels. 6768-9
The hut by the black swamp. 6591-0,6592-9
The last of his tribe. 6656-9
Leichhardt. 6768-9
Mooni. 6784-0,6437-X
Mooni, sels. 6768-9
Orara. 6768-9,6784-0
September in Australia. 6768-9,6437-X,6656-9
"Set your face toward the darkness...". 6768-9
"The songs austere of the forests drear". 6768-9
Sonnet ("I purposed"). 6768-9
Sonnet ("So take"). 6768-9
To a mountain. 6384-5,6656-9
The voice in the wild oak. 6656-9
The warrigal. 6768-9,6591-0,6592-9
Kendall, J.K. ("Dum Dum")
Kal. 6591-0,6592-9
The shores of nothing. 6591-0,6592-9
Kendall, J.K. ("Dum-Dum")
Circumstance without pomp. 6722-0
Hug me tight. 6722-0
My last illusion. 6722-0
Pipes in the sty. 6722-0
The problem of the Poles. 6722-0
A soldier of weight. 6722-0
Kendall, John
Love's colours. 6760-3
Ode to the back of my head. 6760-3
Kendall, Marion D.
Talent. 6818-9
Kendall, May
A board school pastoral. 6274-1,6656-9
Education's martyr. 7037-X
A legend. 6274-1,6656-9
The page of Lancelot. 6656-9
A pure hypothesis. 6656-9
Success. 6274-1
Woman's future. 7037-X
Kendall, Mrs. E.D.
Wink. 6742-5
Kendall, Timothy
To his bed. 6958-4
Kendall, Timothy (tr.)
A dead child. Lucian, 6435-3
Kendim, Ben
The New Zealander. 7027-2
Kendler, Joel
Miser. 6850-2
Kendon, Frank
Child to whom all words. 6777-8
The crane in Bloomsbury. 6072-2
I spend my days vainly. 6491-4
The immigrant. 6339-X
Now to the world. 6785-9
Ophelia. 6785-9
Sonnet 016 ("To that great day how slowly..."). 6785-9
The wind and the corn. 6781-6
Kendrick, Green
Very felis-itous. 6724-7
Kendrick, Hephzibah Elizabeth Spencer
America's peace cry. 6799-9
Kendrick, John
A fable: the mice and felis. 6120-6
Kendrick, Lucile
Not all the crosses. 6144-3,6335-7
Kenealy, Edward
Dreams of my youth, sels. 6545-7
Love's warning. 6518-X

Sweet castle Hyde. 6545-7
Kenmure's on and awa'. Robert Burns. 6271-7
Kennack sands. Laurence Binyon. 6793-X
Kennealy, J.J.
    Tsar Oleg. 6922-3,6744-1
Kennedy, B.H.
    On Christopher Wordsworth, Master of Trinity. 6733-6
Kennedy, Charles Rann
    Ambition. 6980-0
    The church. 6490-6
    Domestic bliss. 6980-0
    The merry bells of England. 6980-0
    The terrible meek, sels. 6144-3,6420-5,6542-2
Kennedy, Charles W.
    I've worked for a silver shilling. 6038-2
Kennedy, Charles W. (tr.)
    The approach of Pharaoh, fr. Genesis. Caedmon, 6665-8
    The seafarer. Unknown, 6833-2
    Sole survivor. Beowulf, 6879-0
Kennedy, Crammond
    Greenwood cemetery. 6302-0;6385-3
Kennedy, Joseph
    Limerick:"Says the Frenchman..."). 6811-1
Kennedy, Leo
    Bitter stream. 6021-8
    Mad boy's song. 6021-8
    Mole talk. 6021-8,6446-9
    Of one dead. 6446-9
    Rite of spring. 6021-8
    Words for a resurrection. 6021-8,6446-9
Kennedy, Margaret D.
    Lester park. 6342-X
Kennedy, Marion
    Tribute to our soldiers. 6449-3
Kennedy, Mary
    One of the Sidhe. 6218-0
Kennedy, Sarah Beaumont
    Battle of Manila. 6580-5
    Mommie. 6792-1
    The prayer rug. 6653-4
    With little boy blue. 6964-9
Kennedy, Susie E.
    Miss willow. 6373-X
Kennedy, Terry
    For my sister on her 5th wedding anniversary. 6998-3
Kennedy, Walter
    The praise of age. 6250-4,6226-1,6383-7
Kennedy, William Sloane
    Shadows. 6597-X
Kennedy, X. J.
    The medium is the message. 6803-0
Kennedy, X.J. (tr.)
    At world's end. Robert Desnos, 6803-0
Kennedy-Fraser, Marjory
    Kishmul's galley. 6873-1
    Land of heart's desire. 6873-1
    Ossian's midsummer day-dream. 6873-1
Kenney, James
    The green leaves all turn yellow. 6174-5
    The old story over again. 6930-4
Kenny, A.A.
    The cat and the broom. 6804-9
Kenny, Maurice
    Boston tea party. 7003-5
    Corn-planter. 7005-1
    December. 7005-1
    Going home. 7005-1
    They tell me I am lost. 7005-1
    Two radio interview. 7003-5
    Wild strawberry. 7005-1
Keno! M.J. Neville. 6175-3
Kenrick, Daniel
    To Celia. 6563-5
Kenry, James
    The old story over again. 6874-X
Kensal green. Alexander Drake. 6632-1
Kensington Gardens, fr. The gardens. Abbe de Lille. 6649-6
Kensington Gardens, sels. Thomas Tickell. 6649-6
Kensington Gardens, sels. Humbert Wolfe. 6069-2,6649-6
Kensington, A.B.

Limerick:"..young lady of Malta". 6811-1
Kent, A.F.
    Kneel at no human shrine. 6402-7
Kent, Charles
    Pope at Twickenham. 6483-3,6656-9
Kent, E.
    Parting words. 6913-4
Kent, Henry S.
    Questions. 6915-0
    True contentment. 6926-6
Kent, Lucy
    Winter overture. 6979-7
Kent, Ruth Norris
    Twentieth Century Limited. 6750-6
Kent, W.H. (tr.)
    The Annunciation ("Mary, Mother of our Maker"). Saint Nerses, 6282-2
    Christmas hymn, sels. Saint Ephrem, 6282-2
    Virgin truly full of wonder. Saint Ephrem, 6282-2
Kent, William
    The peace of Christ. 6807-3
"Kentish Sir Byng stood for his king". Cavalier tunes. Robert Browning. 6828-6
Kenton, Dorothy McGraw
    America is free. 6789-1
Kentucky babe. Richard Henry Buck. 6006-4,6078-1,6132-X, 6732-8
Kentucky belle. Constance Fenimore Woolson. 6568-6
Kentucky belle. Constance Fenimore Woolson. 6912-6
Kentucky belle. Constance Fenimore Woolson. 6074-9,6249-0, 6370-5,6521-X,6554-6,6706
Kentucky mountain farm. Robert Penn Warren. 7017-5
Kentucky mountaineer. Jesse Stuart. 6464-7
Kentucky philosophy. Harrison Robertson. 6281-4
Kentucky philosophy. Harrison Robertson. 6917-7
Kentucky Rye. Sir Walter Scott. 6149-4
The **Kentucky** thoroughbred. James Whitcomb Riley. 7010-8
Kenyon, Bernice Lesbia
    Answer to a timid lover. 6036-6
    Ballerina. 7038-8
    Cat's world. 6120-6
    The city dweller. 6509-0
    Conversation. 6042-0
    Defiance to false gods. 6619-4
    Homecoming in storm. 6036-6
    In a Greek garden. 6037-4
    In winter. 6880-4
    The love-song. 6019-6
    Night of rain. 6347-0
    Nocturne. 6036-6
    Old age. 6723-9
    Premonition. 6036-6
    Premonition. 6036-6
    Quiet. 6780-8
    Return. 6393-4
    The shadow. 6723-9
    Sleepless night. 6038-2
    This April. 7038-8
    To a violinist. 6038-2
    Two cats on the hearth. 6120-6
    Unrest. 6880-4
Kenyon, Doris
    Foreknown. 6648-8
    The play. 6347-0
Kenyon, James Benjamin
    At sunset. 6347-0
    A colonial garden. 6338-1,6649-6
    The cricket. 6006-4,6309-8
    Quatrain. 7041-8
    The racers. 6309-8
    The reconciliation. 6441-8
    Sympathy. 6648-8
    Syrinx. 7041-8
    The tyrian's memory. 7041-8
    The unseen world. 6347-0
    We shall attain. 6461-2
    When clover blooms. 6006-4
    When clover blooms. 7041-8
Kenyon, John
    The broken appointment. 6980-0

KENYON

Champagne rose. 6271-7,6437-X,6656-9
Monument at Lucerne. 6331-4,6631-3,6331-4
To the moon. 6980-0
Kenyon, S.C.
　The spirit of summer. 6118-4
Kenyon, Theda
　Heredity. 6732-8
　In a garden. 6374-8
　Relinquishing. 6051-X
　Stacking the needles. 6051-X
　Wealth. 6861-8
Keohler, Thomas
　Song ("I would swathe thee"). 6174-5
　Supplication. 6174-5
　The town beyond the trees. 6174-5
　Wind and sea. 6174-5
Keough, Hugh Edmund
　The lay of the hospital race. 7010-8
Keown, A.G.
　Reported missing. 7031-0
Keplinger, Walter S.
　Scipio. 6744-1
　'Scipio'. 6922-3
Keppel, Francis
　The silver tree. 6073-0
Keppel, Lady Caroline
　Robin Adair. 6102-8,6385-3,6732-8
"Keppel, returning from afar". On the trial of Admiral Keppel. William Cowper. 6814-6
Kept for Jesus. Edith E. Cherry. 6065-X
Kept in. Ethel Lynn Beers. 6424-8
Kept in. Mary Corona Schoff. 6249-0
Kera Phrosini. Aristote Valaoritis. 6352-7
Keramos. Henry Wadsworth Longfellow. 6333-0,6250-4,6541-4
Kernahan, Coulson
　Limerick:"A poodle was charged by the law". 6811-1
　Of skating. 7035-3
　With good steel ringing. 7035-3
Kernahan, Mary
　LimericK: A tale of tragedy. 6811-1
　A tale of tragedy. 6811-1
Kernan, Will Hubbard
　Agatha. 6670-4
Kerner, Andreas
　The king and the poet. 6424-8
　The richest prince. H.W. Dulcken (tr.). 6614-3
Kerner, Justinus
　Home-sickness. 6648-8
Kernighan, Robert Kirkland
　Bairnies, cuddle doon. 6797-2
　Be merciful to horses. 6591-0,6592-2
　The Canadian west. 6797-2
　I'll follow June. 6591-0,6592-2
　Lady Lilac. 6797-2
　My summer fallow. 6591-0,6592-2
　The perfume of the sods. 6797-2
Kerr, Hazel M.
　New gethsemane. 6144-3
Kerr, Hugh Thomson
　Come thou my light. 6337-3
　God of our life. 6337-3
　Thy will be done. 6337-3
Kerr, Joe
　Over behind der moon. 6247-4
　That littul orfun brat. 6247-4
　Unawares. 6247-4
　Voices of the night. 6247-4
　'You git up!' 6247-4,6277-6,6671-2
Kerr, Minnie Markham
　Avowal. 6750-6
Kerr, Orpheus C. See Newell, Robert
Kerr, Robert J.
　In Ballyshannon. 6090-0
Kerr, Walter H.
　Curtains for a spinster. 6388-8
　The dignity of man-Lesson #1 6388-8
　The hanged thing. 6218-0
　Prenatal fanstasy. 6218-0
　Prenatal fantasy. 6218-0
　The proud trees. 6388-8

　The stone. 6218-0
　Trap. 6218-0
　Vampire. 6218-0
　Villanelle. 6388-8
Kerr, Watson
　The ancient thought. 6730-1
Kerrighan, Robert Kirkland
　Hear ye his voice. 6796-4
The Kerry cow. Winifred M. Letts. 6331-4,6510-4
The kerry dance. James Lyman Molloy. 6930-4
The Kerry lads. Theodosia Garrison. 6331-4
Kersh, Gerald
　A soldier-his prayer. 6532-5
Kershner, Ivan
　August. 6857-X
Kessler, Elizabeth Porter
　Santy isn't Santy Claus. 6750-6
Kessler, Johnnie Ruth
　A prayer. 6818-9
Kester, Marcia G.
　Autumn moon. 6857-X
　Woman at the fruit stand. 6857-X
The Kestrels. Sidney Keyes. 6209-1
"Ket folly praise that fancy loves...". A child my choice. Robert Southwell. 6931-2
Ketcham, Howard
　Limerick:"This bird is the keel-billed toucan." 6308-X
Ketchum, Alfred
　An old song. 6320-9
Ketchum, Annie C.
　Little Bennie. 6909-6
Ketchum, Annie Chambers
　Benny. 6385-3
　The bonnie blue flag. 6015-3,6113-3,6223-7
　"I cannot tell the spell that binds thing image." 6066-8
　Sea-weeds. 6074-9
Ketchum, Arthur
　The bygone year. 6747-6
　Candle-lighting song. 6478-7,6607-0
　Candlemas. 6053-6
　Countersign. 6607-0
　My lady goes to the play. 6441-8
　The name. 6320-9
　An old song. 6762-X
　The road to Granada. 6439-6
　Roadside rest. 6762-X
　The sea-wind. 6374-8
　The spirit of the birch. 6338-1,6368-3
　The spirit of the birch. 6891-X
　Traveller's joy. 6331-4,6374-8,6631-3
Kethe, William
　Old hundreth. 6337-3
　Scotch te deum. 6730-1
Kethe, William (tr.)
　Psalm 100. Bible, 6848-0
Kett, George
　Autumn leaves. 6800-6
　The divine comedy, sels. 6800-6
　The spoilers, sels. 6800-6
"The kettle on the fire". The singer. Alice Levy. 6850-2
Kettle, Thomas M.
　Cancel the past. 6244-X
　The lady of life. 6022-6,6292-X
　Parnell's memory. 6022-6,6292-X
　To my daughter Betty, the gift of God. 6096-X,6650-X
Kevin Barry. Terence Ward. 6930-4
Kew in lilac-time. Alfred Noyes. 6473-6
The key of the kingdom. Unknown. 6334-9,6427-2
"The key set me" Mike Bursaw. 6883-9
Key, Francis Scott
　Greenwood cemetery. 6302-0;6385-3
　Hymn ("Lord, with glowing heart I praise thee.") 6219-9
　Life. 6219-9
　On a young lady's going into a shower bath. 6736-0
　Our rock. 6065-X
　The star-spangled banner. 6642-6,6470-1,6223-7,6135-4,6107-9,6121 ,6212-1,6449-3,6736-0,6131-1,6219-9,6304 ,6267-9,6424-8,6639-9,6223-7,6101-X,6156-7,6183-4, 6240-7,6271-7,6289 ,6302-0,6385-3,6337-3,6401-9,6404-

3,6457 ,6465-5,6632-1,6732-8,6356-X,6300-4,6088 ,
6471-X,6481-7,6260-1,6503-1,6074-9,6176 ,6479-5,6486-
8,6623-2,6735-2,6015-2,6077
    With glowing heart I'd praise thee. 6461-2
The key. John Oxenham. 6065-X
The key. Muriel Rukeyser. 6391-8
The key. Gretchen O. Warren. 6320-9
The keyboard. Anne Campbell. 6799-9
Keyes, Edward Livingston
    Cleopatra's protest. 6671-2
Keyes, Julia L.
    Only one killed. 6074-9
    The soldier in the rain. 6074-9
Keyes, Sidney
    Alexander Pope at Stanton Harcourt. 6210-5
    Early spring. 6209-1
    Elegy. 6209-1,6666-6
    Glaucus. 6209-1
    The grail. 6210-5
    Holstenwall. 6210-5
    The Kestrels. 6209-1
    Moonlight night on the port. 6472-8
    Pheasant. 6257-1
    Remember your lovers. 6666-6
    The snow. 6379-9
    War poet. 6339-X
    The wilderness. 6379-9
    William Wordsworth. 6246-6
Keyes, Willard Emerson
    I know the way of the wild blush rose. 6274-1
Keyes-Becker, Mrs.
    Fiftieth milestone of class. 6717-4
The keynote.. James Rennell Rodd; 1st Baron Rennell. 6331-4
The keys of heaven. Unknown. 6058-7,6134-6
Keyser, Minna
    In April. 6789-1
The keystone. Margaret Clyde Robertson. 6836-7
Kezhyn, Bronislav
    On Volga banks. Jack Lindsay (tr.). 6546-5
Keziah. William Wilfred Campbell. 7041-8
Khall, Sheloh
    Who killed Christ. 6894-4
Khama, sels. David John Darlow. 6800-6
Khamsin. Clinton Scollard. 6309-8
Khan Zada's song on the hillside. Laurence (Adele Florence Nicolson) Hope. 6856-1
Khan [pseud]., The
    The stuttering umpire. 6277-6
Khanlari
    The eagle. A.J. Arberry (tr.). 6448-5
    Night the plunderer. A.J. Arberry (tr.). 6448-5
Khansa
    Tears. R.A. Nicholson (tr.). 7039-6
Khartoum. Sir Charles George Douglas Roberts. 7041-8
Khartoum. Sir Charles George Douglas Roberts. 6591-0,6592-9
Khemnitzer
    The rich man and the poor. Sir John Bowring (tr.). 6606-2
Khodasevich, Vladislav
    Temptation. Cecil Maurice Bowra (tr.). 6103-6
Khomyakov, Alexey
    The labourer. Sir Bernard Pares (tr.). 6103-6
Khusrau, Amir
    Goddess. J.H. Hindley (tr.). 6448-5
Khusrau, Nasir-i
    Message ("Bear from me to Khurasan, Zephyr..."). E.G. Browne (tr.). 6448-5
Khustina - the kerchief. Unknown (Ukrainian) 6115-X
The ki-wi song. Unknown. 6237-7
Kibbee, Elinor Gibney
    Geranium in the window. 6764-6
Kibby, William Judson
    Appreciation. 6085-4,6291-1
    Helpin' out. 6291-1
The kick under the table. Edgar A. Guest. 7033-7
Kickham, Charles Joseph
    The Irish peasant girl. 6292-X,6174-5
    Patrick Sheehan. 6858-8

Rory of the hill. 6174-5
Kicking against the pricks. Unknown (Greek) 6435-3
The kid has gone to the colors. William Herschell. 6846-4, 6443-4
Kidder, Isabel Alden
    Afternoon class. 6764-6
    Sonnet 003, fr. Sonnet sequence. 6764-6
    Sonnet 006, fr. Sonnet sequence. 6764-6
Kidder, Martha A.
    'Satiabor, cum apparuerit tua Gloria' 6818-9
Kidder, Mary A.
    The bright side. 6260-1,6583-X,6404-3
    Don't go in. 6527-9,6685-2
    Less than cost. 6410-8
    Mother, watch! 6424-8
    What became of a lie. 6745-X
The kidnapping of Sims. John Pierpont. 6946-0
Kids. Witter Bynner. 6891-X,6887-1
"The kids here know the wino". A cathouse in Cincinnati. Al Masarik. 6901-0
"Kids in the street". This is the city. Yvette Johnson. 7024-8
"The kids outside are breaking bottles". American woods. Harvey Shapiro. 6803-0
Kidston, Roderick
    Oine. 6784-0
Kidwell, Lorna Tallent
    Late love. 6750-6
    What our eyes behold. 6799-9
Kidwell, Ruth Vivian
    Modern youth. 6750-6
Kieffer, Paul
    Limerick:"Yes, theirs was a love that was tidal." 6308-X
Kiernan, Enid Bliss
    Epilogue, fr. The strength of the hills. 6764-6
    Prologue, fr. The strength of the hills. 6764-6
Kii, Lady
    "The sound of ripples on the shore". William N. Porter (tr.). 6852-9
Kijo
    "I sit alone and listen." Lois J. Erickson (tr.). 6027-7
Kijov. Petr Bezruc. 6886-3
Kikaku
    "A darting dragon-fly - but lo!" Curtis Hidden Page (tr.). 6850-2
    Evening. 6102-8
    Fairies. 6891-X
"Kilbarchan now may say, alas!". The life and death of the piper of Kilbarchan. Robert Sempill. 6933-9
Kilbrannon. Robert Dwyer Joyce. 6518-X
Kilby, Quincy
    'And seven more redskins bit the dusts' 7007-8
Kilchurn castle, sels. William Wordsworth. 6867-7
Kildee. John Banister Tabb. 7017-5
Kildrostan, sels. Walter Chalmers Smith. 6819-7
Kilimandjaro. Bayard Taylor. 6976-2
The Kilkenny cats. Unknown. 6089-7,6120-6
Kill, Colum
    On leaving Ireland. 6484-1
Killarkey. Harold Faller. 6042-0
Killarney. Charles Kingsley. 6722-0
Killarney. Edmund ("Edmund Falconer") O'Rourke. 6858-8
Killary. Herbert Trench. 6090-0
Killed. George Weatherly. 6744-1
Killed at Fredericksburg. Chauncey Hickox. 6113-3
Killed at the ford. Henry Wadsworth Longfellow. 6113-3, 6320-5,6126-5,61-7-9,6288-1
Killed in action. John Lomax. 6800-6
Killed in action. Isabel Ecclestone Mackay. 6796-4
Killed in action. Terence Tiller. 6379-9
Killers. Carl Sandburg. 6628-3
Killicrankie. Unknown. 6859-6
Killicrankie. William Wordsworth. 6323-3
Killicrankie - second set. Unknown. 6859-6
Killigrew, Sir William
    Beauty paramount. 6563-5
    Come, come, thou glorious object. 6328-4
Killiney far away. Francis A. Fahy. 6858-8

KILLINEY

Killiney far away. Francis A. Fahy. 6873-1
The **killing** pace. Edgar A. Guest. 6862-6
Killyburn brae. Unknown. 6930-4
Kilmeny. James Hogg. 6180-X,6302-0,6385-3,6271-7,6114-1, 6219 ,6086-2,6438-8,6613-5
Kilmeny. Alfred Noyes. 6151-6;6289-X;6476-0
Kilmeny, sels. James Hogg. 6395-0,6427-2
Kilmer, Aline
    After grieving. 6607-0
    Against the wall. 6393-4
    Age invading. 6031-5
    Ambition. 6031-5,6556-2,6307-1,6727-1
    Atonement. 6250-4
    An autumn walk with Deborah. 6033-1
    Diagonals. 6019-6
    Favete Linguis. 6096 X
    For all ladies of Shalott. 6619-4
    The gift. 6393-4,6161-3
    A guest speaks. 6478-7
    Haunted. 6250-4
    The heart knoweth its own bitterness. 6153-2,6300-4
    High heart. 6032-3
    Hill-country. 6250-4
    I shall not be afraid. 6292-X,6096-X,6102-8,6320-9,6653-4,6076-5,6464-7
    If I had loved you more. 6096 X
    In a hall bedroom. 6232-6
    In spring. 6032-3
    Light lover. 6300-4
    The mother's helper. 6320-9
    My mirror. 6250-4,6393-4
    Olim meminisse juvabit. 6292-X,6096-X,6252-4
    One shall be taken and the other left. 6619-4,6300-4
    Prevision. 6250-4,6556-2,6250-4
    Sanctuary. 6776-X
    Sanctuary. 6300-4
    Shards. 6467-1
    Song against children. 6509-0,6421-3,6161-3
    Things. 6332-2,6506-6
    To a young aviator. 6250-4
    To Aphrodite: with a mirror. 6096-X,6250-4,6396-9
    To Sappho, about her apple. 6102-8,6300-4,6076-5
    To two little sisters of the poor. 6285-7
    Tribute ("Deborah and Christopher brought..."). 6619-4
    Two lovers. 6019-6
    Victory. 6337-3
    Violin song. 6033-1
    A wind rose in the night. 6556-2
Kilmer, Joyce
    As winds that blow against a star. 6096 X
    Ballade of my lady's beauty. 6310-1,6320-9,6441-8,6300-4
    A blue valentine. 6031-5,6096-X,6292-X,6282-2,6307-1
    Citizen of the world. 6335-7
    Dave Lilly. 6292-X,6300-4
    Delicatessen. 6498-1
    Easter. 6850-2,6897-9,6891-X
    Father Gerard Hopkins, S.J. 6483-3
    Gates and doors. 6162-1,6236-9,6266-0,6478-7,6532-5, 6143-5,6214-8,6746-8,6653-4,6608-9
    God is at the organ. 6303-9
    His laureate. 6335-7
    The house with nobody in it. 6478-7,6497-3,6964-9
    The house with nobody in it. 6891-X
    Kings. 6543-0
    Lionel Johnson. 6483-3
    Main street. 6292-X
    Martin. 6102-8,6310-1,6653-4,6336-5,6464-7,6467 ,6076-5, 6161-3,6250-4,6327-6,6393-4,6431
    Memorial Day. 6337-3,6650-X
    Multiplication. 6543-0
    The new school. 7027-2
    Old poets. 6300-4
    The peacemaker. 6337-3
    Poets. 6556-2,6730-1,6250-4,6336-5
    Prayer of a soldier in France. 6032-2,6542-2,6556-2, 6303-9
    A prayer of busy hands. 6303-9
    Princess ballade. 6875-8
    The robe of Christ. 6096-X
    Roofs. 6266-0,6653-4
    Rouge bouquet. 6033-1,6162-1,6556-2,6431-0,6393-4,6467-1,6542-2
    The servant girl and the grocer's boy. 6307-1,6736-0, 6650-X
    The singinig girl. 6292-X
    Thanksgiving. 6337-3,6607-0,6303-9
    Theology. 6421-3
    To a younger poet who killed himself. 6096-X
    To certain poets. 6650-X
    Trees. 6431-0,6104-4,6250-4,6300-4,6650-X,6393 ,6076-5, 6161-3,6214-8,6449-3,6646-1,6654 ,6491-4,6510-4,6631-3,6653-4,6431-0,6104-4,6250-4,6300-4,6650-X,6393 , 6076-5,6161-3,6214-8,6449-3,6646-1,6654 ,6491-4,6510-4,6631-3,6653-4,6027-7,6292-X,6077-3,6101-X,6102-8, 6162 ,6211-3,6232-6,6266-0,6289-X,6332-2,6337 ,6418-3,6473-6,6499-X,6503-1,6506-6,6509 ,6556-2,6730-1, 6732-8,6338-1,6476-0,6723
    Wealth. 6300-4
    The white ships and the red. 6162-1,6474-4,6023-9,6650-X
Kilmer, Kenton
    Love and fear. 6042-0
Kilroy, Marion
    Song of a quiet life. 6750-6
"**Kilrudden** ford, Kilrudden dale". Lal of Kilrudden. Bliss Carman and Richard Hovey. 6890-1
The **Kilruddery** hunt. Thomas Mozeen. 6090-0
Kilvany. John Hay. 6424-8
Kim, Chun-soo
    Blossom. 6775-1
Kim, Dong-hwan
    Smile was my only fault. 6775-1
Kim, Dong-myung
    My mind. 6775-1
    Night. 6775-1
    Plantain. 6775-1
Kim, Hyun-sung
    Plane tree. 6775-1
    Prayer in autumn. 6775-1
Kim, Jong-han
    Poem of the old garden. 6775-1
Kim, Kwang-kyun
    Gaslight. 6775-1
Kim, Kwang-sup
    My mind. 6775-1
    Senses of life. 6775-1
    Songbook doves. 6775-1
    Summer morning after a rain. 6775-1
Kim, Kyu-dong
    The truth about the incident. 6775-1
    The vacuum conference. 6775-1
Kim, Nam-jo
    Daytime slumber. 6775-1
Kim, Sang-yong
    "I'll have the window southward" 6775-1
Kim, So-wol
    Azalea flowers. 6775-1
    Cannot forget. 6775-1
    Cuckoo. 6775-1
    Evocation. 6775-1
    Flowers on the hills. 6775-1
    Golden turf. 6775-1
    Mother, sister. 6775-1
    Parting. 6775-1
    Some day. 6775-1
Kim, Yun-sung
    From memory. 6775-1
Kim, Yung-rang
    "Till peonies bllom" 6775-1
Kimball, Alice Mary
    The happy ending. 6880-4
    I never did git to go to Omaha. 6817-0
Kimball, Hannah Parker
    Sun, cardinal, and corn flowers. 6338-1
Kimball, Harriet McEwen
    All's well. 6385-3,6600-3
    The blessed task. 6065-X
    "The Christ who came of old to his own." 6225-3
    The crickets. 6597-X,6600-3,6006-4,6632-1

An evening prayer ("The day is ended. Ere I sink..."). 6303-9
The guest. 6680-1
In reverie. 6632-1
Undowered. 6273-3,6652-6
Kimball, Harry W.
An incident of the war. 6744-1
Soul incubation. 6894-4
Kimball, Mather D.
Mariar in heaven. 6928-2
Ol' Pickett's Nell. 6166-4,6505-8
Kimball-Gardiner, Ruth
The sloth. 7021-3
Kimber, Thomas
Moonrise on the prairies. 7016-7
Westward the course of empire takes it way. 7016-7
Kimmel, Stanley
Niggers. 6781-6
Kin. Carl Sandburg. 6102-8,6076-5
"A **kin** am I this hour to winds that sing". Rhapsody. Rene Albourne dePender. 6818-9
Kin to sorrow. Edna St. Vincent Millay. 6986-X
'**Kin** unknown'. Alexander Louis Fraser. 6796-4
Kin, Yung-rang
Sunlight whispering to stone-wall. 6775-1
Kinchinjunga. Cale Young Rice. 6310-1
Kincora. Mac (atr.) Liag. 6930-4
Kincora. James Clarence Mangan. 6174-5
Kincora. Unknown. 6244-X
"**Kind** are her answers". Song ("Kind are her answers.") Thomas Campion. 6436-1
"**Kind** are her answers". Thomas Campion. 6187-7,6181-8,6328-4,6250-4
The **kind** boy. Mrs. Frederick W. Pender. 6692-2
Kind fortune smiles, fr. The tempest. William Shakespeare. 6328-4
"**Kind** friends that gather on this natal day". September 8th. Louis J. Magee. 7004-3
"**Kind** friends, I'm glad to meet you here". What whiskey did to me. Edward Carswell. 6916-9
Kind hearts. Unknown. 6529-5
"**Kind** heaven, assist the trembling muse". The Wyoming massacre. Uriah Terry. 6946-0
The **kind** lady's furs. Strickland Gillilan. 6510-4
A **kind** lady. Carolyn Wells. 6882-0
A **kind** little girl. Eva Lovett. 6529-5
The **kind** look. Willard Maas. 6389-6
"**Kind** lovers, love on". Song ("Kind lovers"). John Crowne. 6-26-9,6563-5
The **kind** moon. Sara Teasdale. 6266-0
Kind of an ode to duty. Ogden Nash. 6637-2;6722-0
A **kind** of truth. Theodore Spencer. 6761-1
"The **kind** old friendly feelings". Charles Swain. 6980-0
Kind Robin lo'es me. Carolina Oliphant, Baroness Nairne. 6086-2
"**Kind** reader! take your choice to cry or laugh". Substitute for an epitaph. George Gordon, 6th Baron Byron. 6945-2
Kind sleep. Isabel Fiske Conant. 6501-5
"**Kind** souls! who strive what pious hand..bring". Epitaph on a poet in a Welsh courtyard. Walter Savage Landor. 6980-0
"**Kind** to my frailities still, Eumenes, hear". Of benevolence: an epistle to Eumenes. John Armstrong. 6968-1
Kind words. Unknown. 6049-8,6312-8
"**Kinde** in vnkindnesse, when will you relent". A booke of Ayres (XIX). Thomas Campion. 6794-8
"**Kinder** like to see the bright side". The bright side. Edgar A. Guest. 6862-6
Kindergarten. Anna Spencer Twitchell. 6836-7
The **kindergarten** miss. Edgar A. Guest. 6862-6
The **kindergarten** tot. Fred Emerson Brooks. 6702-6
Kindig, L. James
Is it nothing to you? 6065-X
Kindled from deep darkness. Louis Golding. 6777-8
Kindlemarsh, M.
For Whitsunday, fr. The Paradise of Dainty Devices. 6586-4
Kindly advice. Unknown. 6089-7

A **kindly** deed. Fred W. Leu. 6906-1
Kindly deeds. Edward R. Huxley. 6885-5
The **kindly** neighbor, sels. Edgar A. Guest. 6337-3
The **kindly** neighbor. Edgar A. Guest. 6461-2
The **kindly** screen. Belle Chapman Morrill. 6337-3
Kindly vision. Otto Julius Bierbaum. 7039-6
Kindly winter. Charles Mackay. 6980-0
Kindly words. Unknown. 6629-1
Kindness. Thomas Sturge Moore. 6844-8
Kindness. Sir Thomas Noon Talfourd. 6980-0
Kindness to animals. Joseph Ashby-Sterry. 6902-9
Kindness to animals. Unknown. 6105-2,6242-3,6452-3,6459-0, 6135-4,6510
Kindred. Abbie Farwell Brown. 6006-4
Kindred. George Sterling. 6121-4,6431-0
Kindred hearts. Felicia Dorothea Hemans. 6385-3,6600-3, 6084-6
Kindred quacks. Unknown. 6281-4
Kindred souls. Edward Sims Vanzile. 7019-1
Kinds of trees to plant, sels. Edmund Spenser. 6047-1
The **kine** of my father. Dora Sigerson Shorter. 6174-5
Kinfolk. Kate Whiting Patch. 6338-1
King Ailill's death. Whitley Stokes. 6090-0,6174-5
"**King** Alexander led the van". Allegro. McM [pseud].. 6817-0
"**King** Almanzor of Granada, he had bid...". The bull-fight of Gazul. Unknown (Spanish). 6757-3
"**King** Arthur made new knights to fill the gap". Pelleas and Ettarre. Alfred Lord Tennyson. 6977-0
"**King** Arthur, growing very tired indeed". Salad: hair. Mortimer Collins. 6802-2
King alcohol's soliloquy. Harriet Adams Sawyer. 6685-2
King Alfred and the shepherd. Unknown. 6613-5
King Alfred answers the Danes. Gilbert Keith Chesterton. 6931-2
King Alfred the harper. John Sterling. 6614-3
King and Zoe Elliot, Stoddard
There's a long, long trail. 6732-8
King and hermit. Unknown. 6090-0
King and queen. Unknown. 6623-2
The **king** and queen of hearts. Charles and Mary Lamb. 6295-4
King and slave. Adelaide Anne Procter. 6620-8,6226-1
The **king** and the child. Eugene J. Hall. 6743-3,6964-9
The **king** and the countryman. Unknown. 6518-X
The **king** and the miller of Mansfield. Unknown. 6302-0,6614-3
The **king** and the poet. Andreas Kerner. 6424-8
The **king** and the pope. Charles Henry ("John Paul") Webb. 6632-1,6004-4
King Arthur. Layamon. 6301-2
King Arthur. Alfred Lord Tennyson. 6634-8
King Arthur. Unknown. 6089-7
King Arthur and King Cornwall. Unknown. 6185-0
King Arthur's death. Unknown. 6022-6,6271-7
King Arthur's dream. Unknown. 6022-6
King Arthur's tomb. William Morris. 7034-5
King Arthur's waes-hael. Robert Stephen Hawker. 6022-6, 6282-2,6096-X,6437-X,6172-9,6608 ,6292-X
King Arthur, sels. John Dryden. 6970-3
King Arthur, sels. Richard Hovey. 6890-1
King Bell. Frank Dempster Sherman. 6311-X
King Blaabhein. Robert Buchanan. 6819-7
King Boreas. Clinton Scollard. 6770-0,6875-8
King Bruce and the spider. Eliza Cook. 6018-8
King Canute. William Makepeace Thackeray. 6136-2,6732-8, 6610-0,6188-5,6614-3,6079
King Canute and his nobles. John ("Peter Pindar") Wolcott. 6344-6
King Charles upon the scaffold, fr. An Horatian ode... Andrew Marvell. 6125-7
King Christian. Johannes Evald. 7039-6
King Christian the Dane. Unknown. 6742-5
King Christmas. Unknown. 66601-1
King Coal to Uncle Sam. Robert Burns. 6741-X
King Cophetua and the beggar-maid. Unknown. 6098-6
"The **king** bowed low on his brazen". Consecration of the temple. Gulielma A. Wheeler Baker. 6848-0
"**King** Crack was the best of all possible kings". King Crack and his idols. Thomas Moore. 6874-X

KING

"King Cupid sang his song of love". Cupid's Easter
    composition. Unknown. 7021-3
King cotton, sels. Sir Leo Money. 6337-3
King Crack and his idols. Thomas Moore. 6874-X
King David. Stephen Vincent Benet. 6037-4,6069-2,6531-7
King David. Walter Stanley ("Stanley Vestal") Campbell.
    6397-7
King David. George Peele. 6848-0
King death. Bryan Waller ("Barry Cornwall") Procter. 6658-5
"King death sped forth in his dreaded power". The
    mourners. Eliza Cook. 6980-0
"King Ferdinand alone did stand one day...hill". Garci
    Perez de Vargas. Unknown (Spanish). 6757-3
"King Frederick, of Prussia, grew nervous...". The court
    of Berlin. Unknown. 6921-5
The king dying on the battlefield. Alexander Smith. 6102-8
King Edward the fourth and a tanner of Tamworth. Unknown.
    6185-0
King Edward the second. Christopher Marlowe. 6188-5
King Edward the third. Christopher Marlowe. 6188-5
King Edward VII. Sir William Watson. 6323-3
King Edwin's feast. John White Chadwick. 6614-3,6424-8
The king enjoys his own again. Martin Parker. 6933-9
King Erik. Count Carl Snoilsky. 6045-5
King Estmere. Unknown. 6185-0
The king eternal. James Montgomery. 6337-3
King fisher. Stella Sharpley. 6804-9
"The king from his council chamber". The king's picture.
    Helen B. Bostwick. 6889-8,6912-6
King goodheart. Sir William Schwenck Gilbert. 6026-9
King Grover craves pie, fr. The white house ballads.
    Eugene Field. 6949-5
King Hal and the cobbler. Unknown. 6079-X
King Henry. Unknown. 6185-0,6518-X
King Henry as Rosamond. Michael Drayton. 6436-1
King Henry before the field of Saint Crispian, fr. Henry
    V. William Shakespeare. 6107-9
King Henry Fifth's conquest of France. Unknown. 6185-0
King Henry IV, sels. William Shakespeare. 6102-8,6185-4,
    6291-1,6369-1,6427-2,6637
King Henry the Eighth. Unknown. 6188-5
King Henry the Eighth ("The imperial stature..."). William
    Wordsworth. 6188-5
King Henry to fair Rosamond. Michael Drayton. 6543-0
King Henry V, sels. William Shakespeare. 6188-5,6239-1,
    6323-3,6369-1,6395-0,6473 ,6291-1,6726-3,6610-0,6438-
    8,6107-9,6301-2,6250-4
King Henry V. and the hermit of Dreux. Robert Southey.
    6188-5
King Henry VI, sels. William Shakespeare. 6188-5
King Henry VI, sels. William Shakespeare. 6228-8,6323-3,
    6392-6,6104-4
King Henry VII and the shipwrights. Rudyard Kipling. 6458-2
King Henry VIII, sels. William Shakespeare. 6242-3,6323-3,
    6102-8,6239-3,6402-7,6606 ,6430-2,6250-4
King Henry's ambition. William Shakespeare. 6191-5
King Henry's speech before the battle of Agincourt.
    William Shakespeare. 6543-0
King Horn. Unknown. 6198-2
"A king had proudly walked within my garden". In the
    garden. Edna Davis Romig. 6836-7
"King Hancock sat in regal state". A song about
    Charleston. Unknown. 6946-0
"King Hassan, well beloved, was wont to say". Tomorrow.
    James Buckham. 7030-2
"The king have called the Devon lads...". The Devonshire
    mother. Marjorie Wilson. 7027-2
"King Henry the Fourth/Was a monarch of worth". Lay of
    Gascoigne justice. John William Smith. 6878-2
A king in disguise. Lillie E. Barr. 6523-6
The king in his beauty. James G. Deck. 6065-X
The king in Thule. Johann Wolfgang von Goethe. 6948-7
The king is cold. Robert Browning. 6385-3
The king is cold. Richard Henry Stoddard. 6753-0
A king is dead, fr. King Henry VI. William Shakespeare.
    6125-7
The king is dead, long live the king. Louise Chandler
    Moulton. 6676-3

King James and Brown. Unknown. 6185-0
King James II. John Dryden. 6022-6
King James the First and the tinkler. Unknown. 6613-5
King James the First of Scotland, sels. Robert Bain. 6269-5
King John. William Shakespeare. 6188-5
King John and the abbot. Unknown. 6055-2,6089-7,6518-X,
    6278-4
King John and the abbot of Canterbury. Unknown. 6056-0,
    6105-2,6133-8,6136-2,6239-3,6242 ,6271-7,6290-3,6385-
    3,6498-1,6614-3,6669 ,6328-4,6067-6,6421-3,6808-1,
    6438-8
King John and the bishop. Unknown. 6185-0
King John, sels. Colley Cibber. 6867-7
King John, sels. William Shakespeare. 6102-8,6323-3,6395-0,
    6250-4,6472-8,6585
King Konkaput's apostrophe upon Pike'a Peak. Thomas Nelson
    Haskell. 6836-7
King Lear and his three daughters. Unknown. 6133-8
King Lear's wife. Gordon Bottomley. 6234-2
King Lear, sels. William Shakespeare. 6052-8,6179-6,6378-0,
    6677-1,6102-8,6339 ,6634-8,6637-2,6726-3,6466-3,6585-
    6,6438 ,6472-8,6250-4
King Leir and his three daughters. Unknown. 6098-6,6105-2
"The king looked on him kindly, as on a vassal". Bavieca.
    Unknown (Spanish). 6757-3
"The king looked on him kindly, as on a...". Bavieca. John
    Gibson Lockhart. 7010-8
"King Louis on his bridge is he". Ballad: Le pere severe.
    Unknown (French). 7039-6
"A king may knight a knave, but God." Susie M. Best. 6225-3
King Midas. Celia Thaxter. 6612-7
The King o' Spain's daughter. Jeanne Robert Foster. 6102-8,
    6076-5
King of a king. Mary Belden James. 6847-2
The King of Aragon. Unknown (Spanish) 6757-3
The king of Arragon's lament for his brother. Felicia
    Dorothea Hemans. 6973-8
The king of Brentford's testament. William Makepeace
    Thackeray. 6278-4,6219-9
The king of Brentford. William Makepeace Thackeray. 6934-7
The king of China's daughter, fr. Facade. Edith Sitwell.
    7000-0
The king of China's daughter. Edith Sitwell. 6654-X
The king of Denmark's ride. Caroline Elizabeth Sarah
    Sheridan Norton. 6239-3,6410-8,6271-7,6498-1,6732-8,
    6742 ,6107-9,6656-9,6219-9
The king of dreams. Clinton Scollard. 6083-8
The king of Erin's daughter. Norah M. Holland. 6843-X,6115-X
A king of France and the fair lady. John ("Peter Pindar")
    Walcott. 6278-4
"The King of France went up the hill". Unknown. 6363-2
"The King of France, and four thousand men." Unknown. 6452-3
The king of glory. Bible. 6373-X
The king of Ireland's son. Nora Hopper. 6244-X
King of kings. Herbert Edwin Clarke. 7015-9
"King of kings! and lord of lords!". Chorus ("King").
    Henry Hart Milman. 6980-0
The king of kings. James Shirley. 6322-5
The King of kings. Lon Woodrum. 6065-X
The King of love. Henry W. Baker. 6065-X,6337-3
The king of Spain and the horse. John ("Peter Pindar")
    Walcott. 6278-4
The king of Spain. Maxwell Bodenheim. 6779-4
King of the Belgians. Marion Couthouy Smith. 6946-0
The king of the crocodiles. Robert Southey. 6133-8
The king of the doctors, sels. Joseph Rodman Drake. 6482-5
King of the goblins. Marian Osborne. 6797-2
The king of Thule. Johann Wolfgang von Goethe. 7039-6
The king of Thule. Johann Wolfgang von Goethe. 6385-3
The king of Yvetot. Pierre Jean de Beranger. 6102-8,6732-8
The king of Yvetot. Pierre Jean de Beranger. 6787-5
The king of Yvetot. Pierre Jean de Beranger. 7039-6
The king of Yvetot. Pierre Jean De Beranger. 6996-7
"King of the lionmen/come dancing in my tube". Ming the
    merciless. Jessica Hagedorn. 6790-5
The king on the tower. William Makepeace Thackeray. 6437-X

King Orfeo. Unknown. 6185-0
King or Henry King, John
    My midnight meditation. 6563-5
King or Sir John Eaton, Phillip
    Song ("Tell me not"). 6563-5
The king over the water. Unknown. 6793-X
'King Pandion, he is dead' Don Marquis. 6875-8
The king passes. Anne Hunter Temple. 6335-7,6144-3
King Philip's last stand. Clinton Scollard. 6946-0
"King Pippin he built a fine new hall". Unknown. 6363-2
King Raedwald. Helen Gray Cone. 6847-2
King Richard II, sels. William Shakespeare. 6179-6,6186-9, 6323-3,6392-6,6395-0,6634 ,6228-8,6649-6,6250-4,6102-8,6188-5,6250
King Richard III, sels. William Shakespeare. 6188-5,6258-X, 6339-X,6547-3,6395-0,6250
King Richard in Sherwood Forest. Alfred Lord Tennyson. 6188-5
King Richard's soliloquy. William Shakespeare. 6438-8
King Robert of Sicily. Henry Wadsworth Longfellow. 6410-8, 6473-6,6605-4,6661-5,6706-9,6419-1,6458-2,6614-3
King Robert of Sicily. Unknown. 6742-5
"The king rode out throught the palace gate". The king. Edgar A. Guest. 6748-4
"The king said, 'Come/Sweet son...'.". The sorrow of Buddha. Sir Edwin Arnold. 6929-0
"King Siegfried sat in his lofty hall". The three songs. Johann Ludwig Uhland. 6903-7
"King Sigfrid sat in his palace-hall". The three songs. Johann Ludwig Uhland. 6842-1
"King Solomon drew merchantmen". The merchantmen. Rudyard Kipling. 6810-3
"King Solomon stood in the house of the Lord". The dead Solomon. John Aylmer Dorgan. 6848-0
"King Solomon was old-/The cares of his...". The king's friend. W. H. Woods. 6848-0
"King Solomon, before his palace gate". Azrael. Henry Wadsworth Longfellow. 6848-0
"The king sits in Dumferling toun". Unknown. 6111-7,6518-X
King Solomon. Owen (Edward Bulwer-Lytton, Earl Lytton) Meredith. 6473-6,6102-8
King Solomon and the ants. John Greenleaf Whittier. 6457-4, 6212-1
King Solomon and the bees. John Godfrey Saxe. 6064-1,6614-3
King Stephen. John Keats. 6188-5
King Stephen, sels. John Keats. 6610-0
King Sverrir. Grimur Thomsen. 6854-5,6283-0
King Volmer and Elsie. John Greenleaf Whittier. 6413-2
"The king stood still". David's lament over Absalom. Nathaniel Parker Willis. 6889-8
"A king there was in days of old". The man born to be king, fr. The earthly paradise. William Morris. 7034-5
"A king there was in Thule". The king in Thule. Johann Wolfgang von Goethe. 6948-7
"The king was faint with battle; and he stood". The well of Bethlehem. John Stuart Blackie. 6848-0
"The king was on his throne". Vision of Belshazzar. George Gordon, 6th Baron Byron. 6848-0,6134-6,6395-0,6552-X, 6614-3,6438-8,6192
The king who died young. Ibn al-Khabbaza. 6362-4
King William thanks his God. James Russell Lowell. 6404-3
King William's march. Unknown. 6859-6
King Witlaf's drinking-horn. Henry Wadsworth Longfellow. 6747-6
"The king will come this way, I said". Beggar maid. Lillie Hall. 7016-7
"King Winter's last carousal came as March". Bravado. Marie M. Mott. 6799-9
The king's and mine. H.A. Cody. 6224-5
The king's anthem. Unknown. 6859-6
The king's bastion. Frederick George Scott. 6433-7
The king's breakfast. Alan Alexander Milne. 6534-1
King's bridge. Frederick William Faber. 6980-0
King's College chapel, Cambridge. William Wordsworth. 6138-9,6634-8,6659-3
The king's consort. Emily Pauline ("Tekahionwake") Johnson. 6837-5
King's daughter. Victoria Mary Sackville-West. 6780-8
A king's daughter. Gertrude Hall. 6431-0
The king's daughter. M.L. Henderson. 6505-8
The king's daughter. Algernon Charles Swinburne. 6518-X, 6526-0
The king's daughter. Unknown (French) 6134-6
The king's decree. Dorothy Adele Shoemaker. 6579-1
The king's diary. John White Chadwick. 6424-8
The king's disguise and friendship with Robin Hood. Unknown. 6185-0
The king's dochter lady Jean. Unknown. 6185-0
The king's envy of a shepherd's life. William Shakespeare. 6543-0
The king's friend. W. H. Woods. 6848-0
The king's hand. Al-Mu'tamid. 6362-4
The king's highway. John Steven McGroarty. 6374-8;6476-0
The king's highway. Sir Henry Newbolt. 7031-0
The king's horses. Herbert H. Longfellow. 6038-2
The king's jewels. Phoebe Cary. 6865-0;6969-X
The king's joy-bells. Kate A. Bradley. 6674-4
The king's kisses. Arthur Lewis Tubbs. 6579-1
King's landing. M. Travis Lane. 6767-0
"The king's men, when he had slain the boar". How the king lost his crown. John Townsend Trowbridge. 6921-5
A king's merry Christmas. Sarah Morgan Bryan Piatt. 6965-7
The king's messengers. Ronald A. Hopwood. 7029-9
The king's missive. John Greenleaf Whittier. 6946-0
The king's own regulars &..triumph over the irregulars. Unknown. 6946-0
The king's picture. Helen Louise Barron Bostwick. 6273-3
The king's picture. Unknown. 6294-6
The king's picture. Helen B. Bostwick. 6889-8,6912-6
The king's progress. Unknown. 6250-4
King's ransom. Elinor Wylie. 6038-2,6070-6,6011-0
The king's ride. Lucy H. Hooper. 6165-6
The king's ring. Theodore Tilton. 6552-X,6424-8,6964-9
The king's ships. Caroline Spencer. 6273-3
"The king's son walks in the garden fair". The little handmaiden. Archibald Lampman. 6797-2
The king's son. Thomas Boyd. 6090-0,6244-X
The king's son. Richard Hovey. 7006-X
"King's Sutton is a pretty town". Unknown. 6904-5
The king's temple. Unknown. 6911-8
"The king's three daughters stood on..terrace". Expectation. Adelaide Anne Procter. 6957-6
The king's three questions. Unknown. 6061-7
The king's tragedy, sels. Dante Gabriel Rossetti. 6560-0
The king's tragedy. Dante Gabriel Rossetti. 6122-2,6188-5, 6657-7,6661-5,6110-9,6199-0,6655-0
The king's visit, fr. The earthly paradise. William Morris. 6656-9
King, Amabel
    Alloquy. 6224-5
King, Amy Forbes
    Recompense. 6818-9
King, Annie Bronson
    Our flag at Apia. 6621-6
King, Ben
    But then. 6211-3,6707-7
    Comin' Christmas morn. 6807-3
    The cow slips away. 6732-8
    Dat's right, ain't it? 6274-1
    De Cushville hop. 6166-2
    Gittin' inter shape. 6303-9
    How often. 6089-7,6440-X
    If I should die to-night. 6089-7,6083-8,6291-1,6732-8, 6274-1,6440 ,6300-4,6736-0,6698-4
    Jane Jones. 6926-6,6211-3,6605-4,6260-1,6281-4
    Mary had a cactus plant. 6583-X
    Nothing to do but work. 6260-1
    The pessimist. 6026-9,6089-7,6291-1,6605-4,6732-8,6287
    St, Patrick's Day. 6576-7
    The sum of life. 6274-1
    That cat. 6083-8,6699-2
King, Byron W.
    What should a young maid do? 6670-4
King, Edith
    The beetle. 6262-8
    The holly. 6216-4
    New sights. 6937-1
    To the bat. 6937-1
    Veld pans. 6800-6

KING

King, Edward
    Captain Loredan. 6467-1
    A woman's execution. 6300-4
King, Francis
    Conscripts ("Related to the picnic..."). 6475-2
    Portrait of a friend. 6475-2
    Portrait of a friend. 6475-2
King, Georgiana Goddard
    Hylas. 6252-0
    Peregrino's song. 6252-0
    Song ("Something calls"). 6374-8
King, Harriet Eleanor Hamiliton (Baille)
    Baron Giovanni Nicotera. 7037-X
    The bride reluctant. 6096 X
    The children. 6772-7
    The crocus. 6597-X,6656-9
    A dream maiden. 6543-0
    The garden of the holy souls. 6022-6,6292-X
    A haunted house. 6543-0
    Innocents' day. 6772-7
    Palermo. 6484-1,6656-9
King, Henry
    An acknowledgment. 6150-8
    Against weeping. 6935-5
    The anniverse. 6378-0
    "Brave flowers, that I could gallant it like you". 6187-7
    A contemplation upon flowers. 6933-9
    A contemplation upon flowers. 6513-9,6341-1,6737-9,6315-2,6562-7,6563-5,6194-X,6250-4
    Death of a beautiful wife. 6302-0;6385-3
    A dirge. 6934-7
    The dirge. 6302-0,6385-3,6250-4
    The double rock. 6378-0
    Elegy. 6600-3,6250-4
    An elegy upon..incomparable King Charles the First, sels. 6933-9
    An epitaph on his most honored friend, Richard, Earl... 6908-8
    Exequy on his wife. 6102-8,6250-4
    The exequy to his matchlesse never to be forgotten... 6908-8
    The exequy, sels. 6317-9
    The exequy. 6208-3,6102-8,6562-7,6317-9,6271-7,6315 , 6341-1,6150-8,6023-4,6563-5,6726-3
    Go thou, that vainly dost mine eyes invite. 6563-5
    "I will not weep, for 'twere as great a sin". 6187-7
    Life. 6271-7,6302-0,6737-9
    "Like to the falling of a star". 6187-7,6334-9
    Of human life. 6472-8
    Paradox, sels. 6317-9
    A renunciation. 6186-9
    A requiem. 6737-9
    Sic vita. 6219-9,6250-4,6383-7,6302-0,6385-3,6334-9, 6412-4,6600-3
    "Since thou hast view'd some Gorgon...". 6106-0
    Sonnet ("Tell me"). 6378-0,6341-1
    The surrender. 6317-9,6'50-8,6737-9
    "Tell me no more how fair she is". 6562-7,6563-5,6187-7, 6023-4
    Upon the death of my ever constant friend Doctor Donne. 6378-0
    The vow-breaker. 6562-7
King, Herman Stowell
    Evocation. 6218-0
"A king, I ween, it must have been". A song of the ski. Unknown. 7035-3
King, Joshua
    Hosanna! 6629-1
King, Mary
    Mary of Bethlehem. 6282-2
King, Mary Perry
    A hymn of freedom. 6846-4,6431-0
King, Mary R.
    Still waters. 6799-9
King, Mrs. Hamilton. See King, Harriet E.
King, Polly
    The night. 6249-0
King, Stafford
    Hang out the flag. 6342-X

King, Stoddard
    Commissary report. 6026-9
    Etude geographique. 6722-0,6218-4
King, William
    You say you love. 6563-5
King, William James
    1918-1942. 6224-5
The king.. Alfred Lord Tennyson. 6087-0
A king. Robert Browning. 6438-8
The king. Skipwith Cannell. 6897-9
The king. Mary Elizabeth Coleridge. 6437-X
The king. Edgar A. Guest. 6748-4
The king. Rudyard Kipling. 6289-X
The king. James Whitcomb Riley. 6993-2,7041-8
Kingcups. Eleanor Farjeon. 6236-9
Kingdom. Sir Edward Dyer. 6315-2,6436-1
The kingdom come. Albert Benjamin Simpson. 6065-X
The kingdom of God is with6n in. Toyohiko Kagawa. 6027-7
The kingdom of God, sels. Richard Chenevix Trench. 6934-7
The kingdom of God. Francis Thompson. 6477-9,6489-2,6536-8, 6634-8,6337-3,6339 ,6507-4,6641-0,6161-3,6508-2,6199-0,6655-9,6723-9
The kingdom of God. Richard Chenevix Trench. 6303-9,6600-3, 6219-9
The kingdom of love. Ella Wheeler Wilcox. 6863-4
The kingdom of man. John Kendrick Bangs. 6291-1
The kingdom of sham. I. Edgar Jones. 6926-6
"A kingdom that was mighty once". An hebraic lamentation. Swithin Saint Swithaine. 6848-0
The kingdom within. Percy Clough Ainsworth. 6337-3
The kingdom. Thomas Curtis Clark. 6144-3,6337-3
The kingdom. Elizabeth Doten. 6344-6
Kingdoms. John Gould Fletcher. 6345-4
Kingdoms. Charles Oluf Olsen. 6461-2
Kingdoms. Unknown. 6144-3
The kingfisher, fr. Upon Arlington house. Andrew Marvell. 6125-7
The kingfisher. Charles Lee Barnes. 6795-6
The kingfisher. William Henry Davies. 6073-0,6044-7,66234-2,6246-5,6395-0,6253-9,6250-4
The kingfisher. Celia Thaxter. 6612-7
Kingfishers. Percy Bysshe Shelley. 6943-6
"Kinght-errant of the never-ending quest". Shelley. Henry Van Dyke. 6961-4
The kingis quair, sels. James I; King of Scotland. 6193-1, 6378-0,6301-2,6649-6,6193-1
The Kingis quair. James I; King of Scotland. 6198-2
"A kingly soul is dumb within the". Our lost captain. William Dudley Foulke. 6995-9
"The kingly sun hath westward sped". Her majesty. Robert Loveman. 6941-X
Kings. Euripides. 6954-1
Kings. Joyce Kilmer. 6543-0
Kings. John Richard Moreland. 6144-3;6337-3
Kings. Bryan Waller ("Barry Cornwall") Procter. 6980-0
Kings and courtiers. John ("Peter Pindar") Walcott. 6278-4
Kings and queens. Walter De La Mare. 6334-9
Kings and seals. Thomas Moore. 6278-4
"The kings are dying! In blood and flame". The kings. Hugh J. Hughes. 6846-4
The kings are passing deathward. David Morton. 6347-0;6556-2
Kings bow their heads. Robert Liddell Lowe. 6640-2
"Kings do not touch doors". The pleasures of the door. Francis Ponge. 6758-7
The kings from the east. Alexander Gray. 6845-6
The kings from the east. Heinrich Heine. 6125-7
"The kings go by with jewelled crowns". The choice. John Masefield. 7027-2
The kings go by. John Masefield. 6464-7
The kings good-night. Thomas Campion. 6794-8
"The kings have trod/Near lands and far". The travellers. Richard Lawson Gales. 6950-9
The kings of Europe. Robert Dodsley. 6152-4
"The kings of old have shrine and tomb". The graves of martyrs. Felicia Dorothea Hemans. 6973-8
The kings of the east. Katharine Lee Bates. 6144-3,6337-3, 6730-1,6608-9
The kings of Troy, fr. Andromache. Euripides. 6435-3
"The kings sits in Dumfermline town". Unknown. 6258-X

The **kings**. Louise Imogen Guiney. 6464-7,6431-0,6250-4,6336-5,6026-5,6243-1,6266-0,6501-5
The **kings**. Henry William Hoyne. 6542-2
The **kings**. Hugh J. Hughes. 6846-4
Kingsbury, H.T.
    The mark of the rose. 6116-8
Kingship. William Shakespeare. 6935-5
Kingsley, Charles
    Airly beacon. 6123-0,6204-0,6658-5,6737-9
    Alton Locke's song. 6123-0
    Andromeda and the sea-nymphs. 6656-9
    Bad squire, sel. 6954-1
    The bad squire. 6934-7
    Ballad ("Are you ready"). 6661-5
    Ballad ("It was Earl Haldan's"). 6239-3
    Ballad of Earl Haldan's daughter. 6136-2,6518-X
    "Be good, my dear, let who will be clever". 6238-5
    A boat song, fr. Hypatia. 6832-4
    Buccaneer. 6732-8
    Christmas carols everywhere. 6747-6
    Christmas day, 1868. 6747-6
    Clear and cool. 6239-3,6501-5,6604-6,6660-7
    Crusader chorus, sels. 6334-9
    Dartside. 6793-X
    Dhe day of the Lord. 6271-7,6102-8,6660-7
    The dead church. 6568-6
    "Deep in the warm vale...", fr. The saint's tragedy. 6123-0
    "Do noble things, not dream them all day long." 6225-3
    Do the work that's nearest. 6337-3
    Dolcino to Margaret. 6123-0,6620-8
    Drifting away. 6123-0
    Drifting away, sels. 6931-2
    Earl Haldan's daughter. 6980-0
    Earl Haldan's daughter. 6613-5
    Earl Haldan's daughter. 6980-0
    Easter week. 6123-0,6177-X
    Farewell advice. 6424-8
    A farewell. 6479-5,6737-9,6461-2,6656-9,6304-7,6046-3,6102-8,6135-4,6219-9,6131-1,6658 ,6240-7,6670-4,6123-0,6239-3,6473-6,6429 ,6623-2,6242-3,6249-0,6459-0,6732-8
    The find. 6423-X
    The fisherman. 6165-6,6271-7,6302-0,6737-9
    "Friends, in this world of hurry." 6225-3
    The great physician. 6337-3
    Guta's song. 6541-4
    Helping lame dogs. 6303-9
    Hey, nonny! 6437-X
    "High among the lonely hills",fr. The saint's tragedy. 6123-0
    Home comfort. 6429-9,6321-7
    A hope. 6123-0
    Hypatia, sels. 6046-3
    In an iiluminated missal. 6793-X
    The invitation (to Tom Hughes) 6092-7
    Killarney. 6722-0
    The knight's leap. 6087-0,6136-2,6271-7,6512-0,6808-1,6639
    A lament ("The merry, merry lark was up and singing"). 6123-0
    The last buccaneer ("On England is a pleasant..."). 6547-3,6332-2,6258-X,6808-1,6197-4,6219-9,6656-9
    Last poem. 6490-6
    Longings, fr. Saint's tragedy. 6123-0
    Lorraine. 6413-2,6732-8,6370-5,6424-8,6656-9
    Lorraine Loree. 6107-9
    Lorraine, Lorainee, lorree. 6518-X
    The lost doll. 6132-X,6623-2,6242-3,6249-0,6519-8,6131-1,6135-4,6424-8,6456-6,6638-0,6639
    A march. 6123-0
    Margaret to Dolcino. 6123-0
    The merry Christmas Eve. 6147-8
    The merry lark. 6302-0,6385-3,6737-9
    My childhood's love. 6688-7
    My little doll. 6123-0,6092-7
    A myth ("A floating, a floating"). 6239-3
    A myth. 6600-3
    A myth. 6656-9
    The night bird. 6123-0
    "O Mary, go and call the cattle home." 6302-0,6457-4
    Ode to the north-east wind. 6228-8,6334-9,6473-6,6661-5, 6639-9,6239-3,6250-4,6018-8,6228-8,6334-9,6473-6, 6661-5,6639-9,6239-3,6250-4,6018-8
    "Oh, that we two were Maying." 6066-8
    The old buccaneer. 6114-1
    The old song. 6437-X,6513-9
    The old, old song. 6737-9,6337-3,6104-4,6396-6,6543-0,6197-4
    On the death of a certain journal. 7009-4
    On the death of a certain journal. 6102-8
    On the death of a certain journal. 7009-4
    On the death of Leopold, King of the Belgians. 6123-0
    The oubit. 6089-7
    Palas in Olympus. 6153-2
    Pallas in Olympus. 6153-2
    People's song, 1849 6954-1
    The pleasant isle of Aves. 6322-5
    The poetry of a root crop. 6123-0,6315-2
    The red king. 6188-5,6323-3
    The river. 6134-6,6252-0
    A rough rhyme on a rough matter. 6302-0,6385-3,6102-8
    Saint's tragedy, sels. 6123-0,6656-9
    The sands of Dee. 6656-9,6723-9,6737-9,6102-8,6639-9, 6668-2,6648-8,6658-5,6046-3,6212-1,6219-9,6301-2, 6518-X,6560 ,6656-9,6723-9,6737-9,6102-8,6639-9,6668-2,6648-8,6658-5,6046-3,6212-1,6219-9,6301-2,6518-X, 6560 ,6114-1,6153-2,6131-1,6613-5,6543-0,6396 ,6123-0,6186-9,6236-9,6239-3,6332-2,6479 ,6133-8,6459-0, 6385-3,6711-5,6240-7,6490 ,6258-X,6502-3,6534-1,6604-6,6732-8,6660 ,6600-3,6605-4,6132-X,6134-6,6138-9, 6242
    Sappho. 6123-0
    September 21, 1870. 6123-0
    Sing heigh-ho! 6026-9,6094-3
    Song ("O Mary"). 6271-7
    Song ("Oh! that we two"). 6604-6
    Song of Madame Do-as-you-would-be..,fr.The water babies. 6832-4
    Song of the river. 6334-9,6597-X,6334-9,6219-9,6421-3
    The south wind. 6423-X
    The starlings. 6134-6
    The summer sea. 6123-0
    There sits a bird. 6236-9
    The three fishers. 6102-8,6560-0,6107-9,6104-4,6424-8, 6304 ,6131-1,6219-9,6301-2.6646-1,6656-9,6567 ,6133-8,6328-4,6332-2,6552-X,6290-3,6240 ,6385-3,6409-4, 6457-4,6459-0,6481-7,6490 ,6604-6,6692-5,6732-8,6543-0,6658-5,6639
    The tide river. 6018-8
    To G. 6123-0
    To Miss Mitford. 6123-0
    Twin stars aloft. 6226-1
    Valentine's day. 6820-0
    Valentine's day. 6242-3
    Valentine's song. 6328-4
    The water babies, sels. 6332-2,6486-8,6490-6,6239-3
    The weird lady. 6518-X
    Welcome wind, fr. Ode to the north-east wind. 7020-5
    A welcome. 6322-5
    When all the world is young, lad. 6304-7,6579-1
    Wild oats. 6670-4
    "The world goes up, and the world goes down". 6109-5,6583-X
    The world's age. 6123-0
    "Yet ere we part, one lesson I can leave you". 6109-5
    Young and old. 7012-4
    Young and old. 6123-0,6211-3,6289-X,6473-6,6332-2
Kingsley, Henry
    At Glastonbury. 6339-X
    The blackbird's song, fr. The boy in grey. 6518-X
    Magdalen. 6337-3,6437-X
Kingsway, Lydia
    Old tenants. 6799-9
The **Kinkaiders'** song. Unknown. 6003-X
Kinkel, ?
    Petrus. Elizabeth Craigmyle (tr.). 6842-1
Kinmont Willie. Sir Walter Scott. 6473-6,6438-8,6110-9
Kinmont Willie. Unknown. 6055-2,6056-0,6075-7,6180-X,6185-0,6395 ,6518-X,6322-5,6197-4,6153-2,6067-6

Kinnaird head. George Bruce. 6379-9
Kinnan, Marjorie
    The monastery. 6887-1
Kinnell, Galway
    Full moon. 6388-8
    Leaping falls. 6388-8
    Near Barbizon. 6388-8
    Old arrivals. 6803-0
    Told by seafarers. 6388-8
Kinnell, Galway (tr.)
    River of lead. Iwan [or Yvan] Goll, 6803-0
Kinney, Charlotte Conkright
    Song for friendship. 6461-2
Kinney, Coates
    The patter of rain. 6093-5,6097-8,6260-1
    The patter of the rain. 6260-1
    Rain on the roof. 6403-5,6964-9,6240-7,6271-7,6273-3, 6302-0,6385-3,6554
Kinney, Elizabeth Clementine
    To the boy. 6006-4
Kinnison, Charles S.
    Faith. 6303-9
    My Sunday nap (?). 6583-X
    Near-sighted eyes. 6583-X
Kino Tomonori
    "The spring has come, and once again". William N. Porter (tr.). 6852-9
Kino Tsura-yuki
    "The village of my youth is gone". William N. Porter (tr.). 6852-9
Kinsey, Maybelle McLaurin
    Ambition. 7016-7
    Beauty awake. 7016-7
    The first maple. 7016-7
    Little blue shoes. 7016-7
    Now and then. 7016-7
Kinship. Angela Morgan. 6266-0
Kinship. Wade Oliver. 6482-5
Kinship. Edward H.S. Terry. 6337-3
Kinsman. Jean Ingelow. 6337-3
"Kinsman belov'd, and as a son, by me!". To John Johnson. William Cowper. 6814-6
Kinsmen all. Rose Mills Powers. 7019-1
Kinsolving, Sally Bruce
    Adventure. 6102-8
    April. 6039-0
    Go down, Moses. 6979-7
    March. 6818-9
    Time. 6039-0
    White iris. 6232-6
Kinto
    "This waterfall's melodious voice". William N. Porter (tr.). 6852-9
Kintsune (Nyudo Saki Daijodaijin)
    "This snow is not from blossoms white". William N. Porter (tr.). 6852-9
Kinwelmersh, Francis
    For Christmas day. 6328-4
    For Christmas day. 6756-5
Kip. Dennis Cooper. 7003-5
Kiper, Florence
    The tired. 6327-6
Kipling, Alice Macdonald
    At the dawn. 6337-3
Kipling, John Lockwood
    Beast and man in India. 6510-4
Kipling, Rudyard
    An American. 6810-3
    Amour de voyage. 6652-6
    Anchor song. 6507-4
    The answer. 6810-3
    'Back to the army again'. 6810-3
    The ballad of Boh Da Thone. 6810-3
    A ballad of east and west. 6419-1,6656-9,6322-5,6107-9, 6161-3,6660 ,6675-5,6473-6,6337-3,6101-X,6395-0,6476
    The ballad of Fisher's boarding-house. 6518-X
    The ballad of The Bolivar. 6810-3
    The ballad of the Clampherdown. 6479-5
    The ballad of the king's jest. 6236-9
    The ballad of the king's jest. 6810-3

    The ballad of the king's mercy. 6810-3
    The bee-boy's song. 6655-0
    Before a midnight breaks in storm. 6810-3
    The bell buoy. 6508-2
    Belts. 6810-3
    The betrothed. 6453-1,6732-8,6688-7,6576-7
    Beyond the path of the outmost sun. 7012-4
    Bill 'Awkins. 6810-3
    Birds of prey march. 6542-2
    Boots. 6726-3
    Boxing, fr. Verses on games. 6427-2
    Bridge-guard in the Karroo. 6810-3,6788-3
    The broken men. 6810-3
    The Buddha at Kamakura. 6315-2
    The burial ("When that great Kings return to clay"). 6625-9
    The camel's hump. 6242-3
    The captive. 6655-0
    Cells. 6810-3
    Certain maxims of Hafiz, sels. 6427-2
    Chant-pagan. 6810-3
    A charm. 6427-2
    The children's song. 6478-7,6639-9
    The choice. 7026-4
    Cholera camp. 6810-3
    Christmas in India. 6747-6
    "Cities and thrones and powers". 6208-3,6339-X,6246-6, 6150-8,6250-4,6508
    'Cleared'. 6810-3
    The coastwise lights. 6331-4
    Cold iron. 6532-5,6655-0
    Columns. 6810-3
    Commonplaces. 6089-7,6440-X
    The conundrum of the workshops. 6507-4,6102-8,6656-9
    Cruisers. 6810-3
    Danny Deever. 6150-8,6371-3,6569-0,6723-9,6560-0,6289-X, 6332-2,6396-3,6656-9,6301-2,6491
    The dawn wind. 6476-0,6607-0
    Dedication, fr. Barrack room ballads. 6810-3
    A dedication. 6337-3,6437-X,6102-8
    The deep-sea cables. 6331-4
    The derelict. 6810-3
    The destroyers. 6810-3
    Dirge of the dead sisters. 6810-3
    Divided destinies. 6089-7
    The dove of Dacca. 6239-3
    The dykes. 6810-3
    The 'eathen. 6810-3
    Eddi's service. 6655-0
    England's answer. 6810-3
    England, fr. The return. 6427-2
    The English flag. 6473-6,6479-5
    English irregular: '99-'02. 6138-9,6153-2
    Estunt the griff. 6440-X
    Et dona ferentes. 6810-3
    Evarra and his gods. 6810-3
    The explanation. 6810-3
    The explorer. 6887-1
    The explorer. 6507-4,6726-3,6396-9
    The fairies' siege. 6427-2,6655-0
    The fall of Jock Gillespie. 6518-X
    The feet of the young men. 6465-5,6236-9,6427-2,6732-8
    The female of the species. 6083-8,6427-2,6655-0
    Files on parade. 6683-6
    The files. 6810-3
    The first chantey. 6810-3
    Five war epitaphs. 6210-5
    The flag of England. 6322-5
    The flight of the bucket. 6440-X
    The flowers. 6224-5,6477-9,6437-X
    'Follow me 'ome'. 6810-3
    For all we have and are. 6224-5,6289-X,6290-3
    For to admire. 6395-0
    Ford o' Kabul river. 6210-5,6508-2
    Frankie's trade. 6833-2
    The frist friend. 6891-X
    Fuzzy-wuzzy. 6162-1,6332-2,6079-X,6655-0,6656-9
    The galley-slave. 7007-8
    Gehazi. 6427-2
    General Joubert. 6810-3

General summary. 6996-7
Gentlemen-rankers. 6810-3
Gertrude's prayer. 6208-3
Gethsemane. 6210-5
The gift of the sea. 6810-3
The gipsy trail. 6289-X,6374-8,6732-8,6655-0
Gipsy vans. 6427-2,6655-0
The glory of the garden. 6655-0
Great heart. 6732-8
Great-heart. 6995-9
Gunga Din. 6211-3,6162-1,6332-2,6451-5,6499-X,6107-9, 6396-9,6964-9
Half-ballad of Waterval. 6810-3
Harp song of the Dane women. 6208-3
Hymn before action. 6701-8
If. 6138-9,6337-3,6427-2,6476-0,6534-1,6291 ,6102-8, 6107-9,6104-4,6464-7,6655-0,6634 ,6421-3
An imperial rescript. 6810-3
In Quebec. 6861-8
In springtime. 6649-6
In the Neolithic age. 6810-3
In the Neolithic age, sels. 6427-2
The instructor. 6810-3
The islanders. 6810-3
The jacket. 6810-3
The jam-pot. 6440-X
Jane Smith. 6440-X
Jobson's amen. 6508-2
King Henry VII and the shipwrights. 6458-2
The king. 6289-X
Kitchener's school. 6810-3
L'envoi. 6337-3,6437-X,6479-5,6730-1,6301-2,6104-4,6214-8
The ladies. 6589-9,6732-8,6026-9,6491-4
The lament of the border cattle thief. 6810-3
Land of our birth. 6337-3
The last chantey. 6427-2,6473-6,6258-X,6437-X,6547-3, 6102-8,6199-0,6508-2,6371-3,6655-0,6656
The last of the light brigade. 6670-4
The last rhyme of True Thomas. 6427-2
The last Suttee. 6810-3
The law for the wolves. 6656-9
The legends of evil, sels. 6339-X
The legends of evil. 6810-3
The lesson. 6810-3
Lest we forget! 6702-6
Lichtenberg. 6810-3
Limerick:"..young boy of Quebec". 6811-1
The liner she's a lady. 6810-3
Little mother of mine. 6691-7
The long trail. 6427-2,6732-8,6508-2,6655-0
The looking glass. 6210-5
Loot. 6810-3
The lost legion. 6810-3
The love song of Har Dyal. 6204-0,6236-9,6427-2
The lover's litany. 6652-6
"Lukannon." 6510-4
M.I. 6810-3
McAndrew's hymn. 6427-2,6732-8
McAndrew's hymn, sels. 6258-X
The maid of the meerschaum. 6440-X
Mandalay. 6255-5,6583-X,6605-4,6732-8,6301-2,6046-3, 6655-0,6723-9,6660-7
The married man. 6810-3
The Mary Gloster. 6427-2
'Mary, pity women!' 6810-3
Maxim, fr. Certain maxims of Hafiz. 6427-2
"The men that fought at Minden". 6810-3
The merchantmen. 6810-3
The mine-sweepers. 7026-4
The miracles. 6810-3
Mother o' mine. 6211-3,6337-3,6365-9,6627-5,6097-8,6964
The mother-lodge. 6810-3
Mulholland's contract. 6810-3
Municipal. 6722-0
My boy Jack. 6427-2
My new-cut Ashlar. 6508-2
My rival. 6255-5,6610-0,6672-0,6633-X
Naaman's song. 6427-2
The native-born. 6810-3

Natural theology. 6633-X
O Mary pierced with sorrow, fr. Song before action. 6282-2
The old issue. 6810-3
The old men. 6810-3
The only son. 6655-0
Oonts! 6719-0
Our lady of the snows. 6810-3
The overland mail. 6162-1,6478-7,6479-5
The overland mail. 6924-X
The palace. 6810-3
Pan in Vermont. 6722-0
The parting of the columns. 6810-3
The peace of Dives. 6810-3
Pharoah and the sergeant. 6810-3
Piet. 6810-3
Playing Robinson Crusoe. 6479-5
The post that fitted. 6672-0
The power of the dog. 7008-6
Predestination. 6315-2
Puck's song. 6508-2,6625-9
Quaeritur. 6724-7
The rabbi's song. 6844-8
Rahere. 6655-0
Rebirth. 6315-2
Recessional. 6101-X,6161-1,6211-3,6239-3,6255-5,6260 , 6274-1,6289-X,6323-3,6332-2,6337-3,6418 ,6437-X,6457-4,6476-0,6479-5,6604-6,6655 ,6726-3,6730-1,6473-6, 6486-8,6634-8,6605 ,6197-4,6214-8,6161-3,6104-4,6212-1,6107 ,6199-0,6250-4,6560-0,6102-8,6371-3,6301 , 6396-9,6639-9,6646-1,6653-4,6542-2,6579 ,6660-7,6737-9,6723-9
The reformers. 6810-3
The return, sels. 6247-2
The return. 6810-3
The rhyme of the three captains. 6810-3
Rhyme of the three sealers. 6810-3
Rimmon. 6810-3
Road-song of the bandar-log. 6393-4,6655-0
Route marchin'. 6810-3
The sacrifice of Er-Heb. 6810-3
A St. Helena lullaby. 6427-2
Sappers. 6810-3
Screw-guns. 6810-3
The sea and the hills. 6427-2
The sea-wife. 6810-3
Seal lullaby. 6519-8,6393-4
The second voyage. 6810-3
The sergeant's weddin'. 6810-3
Sestina of the tramp royal. 6331-4,6427-2,6507-4
The settler. 6810-3
Shillin' a day. 6810-3
Shiv and the grasshopper. 6242-3,6655-0
The shut-eye sentry. 6810-3
Sir Richard's song. 6427-2
The sleepy sentinel. 6958-4
'Snarleyow'. 6810-3
'Soldier an' sailor too'. 6810-3
Soldier, soldier. 6810-3
Song before action, sels. 6282-2
The song of Diego Valdez. 6427-2
The song of the banjo. 6427-2,6732-8,6507-4,6655-0,6723-9
The song of the banjo. 6810-3
The song of the cities. 6810-3
The song of the dead. 6810-3
A song of the English, sels. 6258-X
A song of the English. 6810-3
song of the Fifth River. 6848-0
Song of the galley-slaves. 6125-7
The song of the sons. 6810-3
Song of the wise children. 6810-3
The sons of Martha. 6730-1,6732-8,6199-0
The sons of the widow. 6687-9
South Africa. 6810-3
Stellenbosh. 6810-3
The story of Ung. 6810-3
The story of Uriah. 6301-2
Study of an elevation, in Indian ink. 6089-7
Sussex. 6810-3

KIPLING

Sussex. 6423-X,6477-9,6625-9,6634-8,6250-4,6508-2,6655-0
That day. 6810-3
Theodore Roosevelt. 6088-9
"There was once a small boy in Quebec". 6083-8
The three-decker. 6810-3
To the city of Bombay. 6810-3
To the true romance. 6810-3
To Thomas Atkins. 6810-3
To-day. 6138-9
Tomlinson. 6507-4,6655-0
Tomlinson, sels. 6427-2
Tommy. 6507-4,6964-9
Tommy Atkins. 6681-X
Toomai of the elephants. 6510-4
Troppin'. 6810-3
The truce of the bear. 6810-3
True royalty. 6479-5,6669-0,6421-3
Two kopjes. 6810-3
Ubique. 6810-3
The undertaker's horse. 7010-8
Vampire. 6719-0,6102-8,6301-2
Verses on games, sels. 6427-2
The voortrekker. 7012-4
The wage-slaves. 6810-3
The way through the woods. 6228-8,6332-2,6246-6,6395-0, 6437-X,6509
The wet litany. 6641-0
"What happened." 6046-3
When 'Omer smote 'is bloomin' lyre. 6427-2
When earth's last picture is painted. 6291-1,6476-0, 6655-0,6102-8
White horses. 6810-3
The white man's burden. 6289-X,6692-5,6591-0
The wide, wide world, fr. In the Neolithic age. 6427-2
The widow's party. 6810-3
'Wilful-missing'. 6810-3
The window at Windsor. 6810-3
The wishing-caps. 6427-2
With Scindia to Delhi. 6810-3
The young British soldier. 6810-3
The young queen. 6810-3

Kirby, Elizabeth
A song of fairies. 6338-1

Kirby, Inez Barclay
Corona borealis. 6799-9
Strange promise. 6648-2
Tides. 6750-6

Kirby, Patrick F.
Sequel to finality. 6337-3

Kirby, W.
Thunderstorm in August. 6433-7

Kirby, William
Niagara, fr. 'The U.E.' 6795-6
Sonnet: for the hairs of your head are all numbered. 6796-4
Spina Christi. 6795-6

Kirchberg, Conrad
The merry month of may. 6490-6

Kirchwey, Freda
To a soap-box orator. 6880-4

Kirk, Betty
Lesson. 6397-7
Realistic. 6397-7

Kirk, Eleanor
'Bob white'. 6314-4
The other side of the case. 6183-4

Kirk, Murray Ketcham
The beacon-light. 6995-9

Kirk, Richard
Explaining the bitterness of the wind. 6039-0
The stone-cutter. 6039-0

Kirk, Richard R.
Brother Toper. 6118-4
Cock-a-doodle-doo! 6326-8
The comforter. 6118-4
A conversational neighbor. 6326-8,6396-9
The faithful servant. 6326-8
In a canoe. 6548-1
Indan summer. 6118-4
The mice. 6326-8,6396-9
My wine. 6118-4
Old people. 6326-8
There may, of course, be mice. 6326-8
Thrice blessed. 6326-8
We visit my estate. 6326-8,6396-9
Where are you sleeping, lady fair? 6118-4

Kirk, William F.
Ballade of the fan. 6274-1
Giving. 6337-3
The goldfish. 6307-1
The lumberyak. 6281-4
Sonnet on stewed prunes. 6722-0

Kirkbride. Robert Reid. 6395-0

Kirkconnell, Watson
Ode on the burial of Marshal Joseph Pilsudski. 6021-8
The road to Bethlehem. 6337-3

Kirkconnell, Watson (tr.)
The cathedral in Trondheim. Jakob Thorarensen, 6283-0
Desert dangers. Jakob Thorarensen, 6283-0
The golden plover. Jonas Hallgrimsson, 6283-0
The happy valley. Pall Olafsson, 6283-0
The harp. Jakob Johannesson Smari, 6283-0
I sail in the fall. David Stefansson, 6283-0
In absence. Benedikt Grondal, 6283-0
Lament ("Snows cloaked"). Gudmundur Gudmundsson, 6283-0
Lilies of white. Unnur ("Hulda") Benediktdottir, 6283-0
Lines to Sigrun. Bjarni Thorarensen, 6283-0
Rain. Einar Benediktsson, 6283-0

Kirkham, B.W.
The last wish. 6915-0

Kirkham, Kate
Old woman. 6799-9

Kirkhoff, John L.
A little later on. 6857-X
Losing touch. 6857-X

Kirkman, Audrey Lee
An empty little bed. 6799-9

Kirkpatrick, Elenita Thompson
Beneath the sanctuary lamp. 6285-7

Kirkup, James
A correct compassion. 6210-5
La bete humaine. 6379-9
Mortally. 6379-9
The pavement artist. 6257-1

Kirkup, James (tr.)
Candle-light. Jules Supervielle, 6343-8
Everything is dark. Pierre Reverdy, 6343-8
In the forest. Jules Supervielle, 6343-8
Whisper in agony. Jules Supervielle, 6343-8
Women's loveliness. Paul Verlaine, 6343-8

Kirkwood, Marie
The convent garden. 6285-7

Kirkwood, Worrell
Woodrow Wilson. 7001-9

Kirman weaves the first prayer-rug. Ethel M. Feuerlicht. 6847-2

Kirov is with us. Nikolai Tikhonov. 6546-5

Kirsanov, Semyon
Simplicity. Jack Lindsay (tr.). 6546-5
Wishes. Jack Lindsay (tr.). 6546-5

Kirschblute bie nacht. Barthold Heinrich Brockes. 6253-9

Kirsopp, Catherine
To one who revisited an old garden. 6779-4

Kirtle gaol. Unknown. 6057-9
Kirtle red. W.H. Bellamy. 6652-6

Kirwan, M.
"Look not upon me, seek no more to stay me." 6317-9
"These are my tears that now you see." 6317-9

Kisa-gotami. Arthur Davison Ficke. 6327-6

Kiser, Samuel Ellsworth
A bargain sale. 6583-X
Blessing of toil. 6449-3
The boy next door. 6846-4
Boy with pony. 6715-8
A boy's king. 6690-9
The certain victory. 6211-3
December 31. 6291-1
Don't wait. 6109-5
Faith. 6291-1

The fighter. 6291-1
Getting to be a man. 6687-9
Golf and life. 6274-1
His new suit. 6340-3,6741-X
Horse, dog, and man. 7008-6
It may be. 6291-1
Keep the bright side out. 6109-5
Lincoln. 6524-4
A little prayer. 6291-1,6337-3
The man who cooks the grub. 6274-1
Maud Muller a-wheel. 6274-1
Meditations of Johnny. 6700-X
Memorial Day 1889. 6340-3,6449-3
My creed. 6291-1
The passing of the horse. 7010-8
Peace. 6274-1
Peace. 6274-1
A profitable day. 6583-X
She never was a boy. 6692-5
The soldier boy for me. 6471-X
Still in the fight. 6583-X
Tolerance. 6303-9
Unsubdued. 6291-1,6337-3
Visiting Laura Belle. 6690-9
When clouds are dark. 6303-9
When doctors disagree. 6714-X
When grandma comes to our house. 6715-8
When Pa was a boy. 6277-6,6697-6
Why be a rainy day? 6583-X
The yankee dude'll do. 6995-9
The Yankee dude'll do. 6274-1
Your mother. 6097-8

Kish, A.C.
How pussy and mousie kept house. 6699-2

Kishineff and Port Arthur. Edward Sydney Tybee. 6848-0
'Kishinex'. Strickland Gillilan. 6848-0
Kishmul's galley. Marjory Kennedy-Fraser. 6873-1
Kismet. Rosamund Marriott ("Graham R. Tomson") Watson. 7029-9
A **kiss** ("Hark, happy lovers, hark!") William Drummond of Hawthornden. 6182-6
The **kiss** ("I saw you take his kiss..."). Coventry Patmore. 6339-X,6501-5,6092-7,6026-9
A **kiss** - by mistake. Joel Benton. 6652-4
A **kiss** at the door. Unknown. 6406-X
The **kiss** deferred. Unknown. 6920-7
Kiss her. Thomas Augustine Daly. 6702-6
The **kiss** in school. William Pitt Palmer. 6279-2
A **kiss** in the dark. Milton Thompson. 6921-5
A **kiss** in the dark. John G. Watts. 6681-X
A **kiss** in the rain. Unknown. 6273-3
A **kiss** in the rain. Samuel Minturn Peck. 6089-7,6632-1, 6226-1,6505-8
The **kiss** in the street. John Whitaker Watson. 6774-3
The **kiss** in the tunnel. Unknown. 6925-8
Kiss me. Bjarni Thorarensen. 6854-5
"**Kiss** me good night, remembrance dear". The last wish. Victor Sampson. 6800-6
Kiss me softly. John Godfrey Saxe. 6240-7,6302-0,6385-3, 6226-1,6066-8
"**Kiss** me, and say good-bye". Good-bye. Andrew Lang. 6771-9
"**Kiss** me, dearest maid, and then". The parting. James Abraham Martling. 6952-5
"**Kiss** me, sweet: the wary lover". To Celia. Caius Catallus. 7039-6
"**Kiss** me, sweet: the wary lover," fr. The forest. Ben Jonson. 6317-9,6328-4
"**Kiss** me, sweetheart, the spring is here". Rondel. John Payne. 6850-2,6770-0,6875-8
"'**Kiss** me, Will', sang Marguerite". No kiss. Madge Elliott. 6919-3
The **kiss** of Allah. Celestin Pierre Cambiaire. 6826-X
The **kiss** of god. John White Chadwick. 6848-0
A **kiss** of the king's hand. Sarah Robertson Matheson. 6873-1
"A **kiss** that is blown to the wind, a quirk...". Your fecund breath. Harvey C. Grumbine. 6799-9
Kiss the dear old mother. Josephine Pollard. 6097-8;6274-1
"**Kiss** the maid and pass her round". In a cafe. Francis Ledwidge. 6812-X

"The **kiss,** dear maid! thy lips have left". On parting. George Gordon, 6th Baron Byron. 6945-2
"The **kiss,** dear maid." George Gordon, 6th Baron Byron. 6302-0;6385-3
The **kiss,** fr. Cynthia's revels. Ben Jonson. 6934-7
The **kiss,** fr. Cynthia's revels. Ben Jonson. 6827-8
A **kiss,** fr. Rose-leaves. Austin Dobson. 6770-0
"A **kiss,** one of the sacred things". Why? Rubye Arnold. 7016-7
A **kiss.** Austin Dobson. 6289-X,6026-9,6153-2,6646-1
A **kiss.** Alfred Domett. 6658-5
A **kiss.** Charles Henry Luders. 6770-0
A **kiss.** Bernard Freeman Trotter. 7027-2
The **kiss.** Milutin Bojic. 6765-4
The **kiss.** Samuel Taylor Coleridge. 6967-3
The **kiss.** Robert Herrick. 6302-0,6385-3,6737-9
The **kiss.** Ben Jonson. 6830-8
The **kiss.** Einar Hjorleifsson Kvaran. 6854-5
The **kiss.** Thomas Masson. 6089-7
The **kiss.** Thomas Moore. 6278-4
The **kiss.** Comtesse de Noailles. 6351-9
The **kiss.** Lizette Woodworth Reese. 6037-4
The **kiss.** Siegfried Sassoon. 6506-6,6393-4
The **kiss.** Claude Clayton Smith. 6966-5
The **kiss.** Unknown. 6022-6
The **kiss.** Unknown. 6930-4
"**Kissed** before? My memory replies". First kiss. Christie Lund. 6750-6
Kissed his mother. Eben Eugene Rexford. 6450-7
Kisses. Berton Braley. 6853-7
Kisses. Thomas Campion. 6182-6,6436-1
Kisses. William Strode. 6219-9
Kisses. Arthur Symons. 6655-0
Kisses. Esaias Tegner. 6045-5
Kisses. Unknown. 6078-1
Kissin'.. Unknown. 6260-1
Kissing and bussing. Robert Herrick. 6430-2
Kissing bridge. Arthur Guiterman. 6773-5
Kissing cup's race. Campbell Rae Brown. 6451-5
Kissing Cup's race. Campbell Rae-Brown. 6924-X
Kissing her hair. Algernon Charles Swinburne. 6302-0,6429-9,6321-7,6737-9
"**Kissing** her hair sat against her feet". Rondel. Algernon Charles Swinburne. 6875-8
"**Kissing** me, each one's lips paired". Party boy. Fred W. Wright Jr.. 6857-X
The **kissing** of the bride, fr. The white house ballads. Eugene Field. 6949-5
Kissing time. Eugene Field. 6318-7
Kissing's no sin. Unknown. 6302-0,6385-3,6652-6
The **kissing-gate..** Alma Frances McCollum. 6433-7
Kit Carson's ride. Joaquin Miller. 6344-6,6407-8,6744-1, 6288-1,6265-2,6396-9,6484-1,6567-8
Kit's cradle. Juliana Horatia Ewing. 6120-6,6808-1
Kit, W.
The cowboy's tale. 6505-8
Kitchel, Mary Eva
So runs our song. 6144-3
Kitchel, W.L.
"It's an ill wind". 6116-8
Old letters. 6116-8
The **kitchen** clock. John Vance Cheney. 6724-7,6089-7,6732-8, 6166-4,6451-5,6567
Kitchen garden. Rupert Croft-Cooke. 6649-6
Kitchen may-day song. Unknown. 6820-0
Kitchen police. Unknown. 6237-7
Kitchener. John Helston. 7026-7
Kitchener. Unknown. 6474-4
Kitchener of Khartoum. Robert J.C. Stead. 6474-4
Kitchener's march. A.J. B. 7031-0
Kitchener's march. Amelia Josephine Burr. 6224-5
Kitchener's school. Rudyard Kipling. 6810-3
The **kitchie-boy.** Unknown. 6185-0
"A **kite,** while devouring a skylark, complained". The stupid kite. Allen Upward. 6897-9
A **kite..** Unknown. 6466-3
A **kite.** Irene Davis Grueninger. 6906-1
The **kite.** Alan Sullivan. 6115-X
Kithen, Laura
'Sign of the times' 6857-X

KITTEN

The **kitten** and falling leaves. William Wordsworth. 6861-8
Kitten and firefly. Marie Grimes. 6120-6
Kitten and the mouse. Unknown. 6699-2
The **kitten** at play. William Wordsworth. 6135-4
Kitten gossip. Thomas Westwood. 6742-5,6808-1,6131-1
Kitten Jim. Paula Sylva Ingram. 6799-9
Kitten of the regiment. James Buckram. 6699-2
The **kitten** of the regiment. James Buckham. 6621-6
Kitten that never grew old. Unknown. 6692-2
The **kitten's** eclogue. Ruth Ritter. 6511-2
Kitten's night thoughts. Oliver Herford. 6891-X
Kitten's view of life. Thomas Westwood. 6692-2
"A **kitten**, a fish and a butterfly". The three wishes. Carolyn Wells. 6882-0
"A **kitten**, a kite and a kangaroo". A call on a ball. Carolyn Wells. 6882-0
The **kitten**, and falling leaves. William Wordsworth. 6075-7, 6133-8,6385-3,6120-6,6519-8,6692 ,6092-7,6131-7,6511-2,6808-1,6219-9,6424
The **kitten**.. Ogden Nash. 6722-0
The **kitten**. Joanna Baillie. 6120-6,6219-9,6511-2
Kittens. Catherine Parmenter. 6120-6
Kittens and babies. Lizzie M. Hadley. 6921-5
Kittens and babies. Lizzie M. Hadley. 6426-4
Kittens and babies. Lzzie M. Hadley. 6426-4
Kittens' blind-man's-buff. Unknown. 6692-2
Kittens' dancing lesson. Stanley Schell. 6692-2
The **kittens'** fright. Unknown. 6692-2
Kittens' promenade. Unknown. 6699-2
The **kittens**. Emma Celia & Lizzie J. Rook. 6741-7
"The **kittiwake** hangs on the seaward cliff". Vigil. May C. ([Mary] Gillington) Byron. 6997-5
The **kittiwakes**. Celia Thaxter. 6612-7
Kittredge, Herman Eugene
    Miriam. 6327-6
    Reality. 6648-8
Kittredge, Walter
    Tenting on the old camp ground. 6589-9,6121-4
    We're tenting tonight. 6074-9
Kitty. Marian (Annie D.G. Robinson) Douglas. 6127-3,6131-1, 6424-8
Kitty. Elizabeth Payson Prentiss. 6114-1
Kitty. Emma Celia & Lizzie J. Rook. 6137-0
Kitty. Unknown. 6279-2,6629-1,6699-2
"**Kitty** Hawk is a Caesar among monuments". The structure of the plane. Muriel Rukeyser. 6978-9
Kitty and I. Emma Celia & Lizzie J. Rook. 6137-0
Kitty at school. Kate Ulmer. 6699-2
Kitty Bhan. Edward Walsh. 6022-6
Kitty Clover. Carrie W. Thompson. 6670-4
Kitty didn't mean to. Emma Celia & Lizzie J. Rook. 6137-0
Kitty in the basket. Eliza Lee Follen. 6502-3,6131-1,6456-6
Kitty Malone. Kate True. 6825-1
Kitty Neil. John Francis Waller. 6858-8
Kitty Neil. John Francis Waller. 6090-0,6174-5,6414-0,6656-9
Kitty Neil. John Francis Waller. 6858-8
Kitty of Coleraine. Edward Lysaght. 6089-7,6733-6,6092-7
Kitty of Coleraine. Charles Dawson Shanly. 6083-8,6332-2, 6255-5,6302-0
Kitty of Coleraine. Unknown. 6090-0,6174-5,6385-3
Kitty of the Sherragh Vane. Thomas Edward Brown. 6809-X
Kitty wants to write. Gelett Burgess. 6089-7,6732-8
Kitty Wells. Unknown. 6003-X
Kitty's graduation. Thomas Augustine Daly. 6718-2
Kitty's lesson. Jerolamen. C. Grace. 6699-2
Kitty's prayer. Unknown. 6919-3
Kitty's summering. Henry Cuyler Bunner. 6652-6
Kitty's wish. Emma Celia & Lizzie J. Rook. 6137-0
Kitty: how to treat her. Unknown. 6114-1
Kitty: what she thinks of herself. William Brighty Rands. 6114-1
Kittycat and the milkman. Unknown. 6699-2
Kiumers. Firdusi] (Abul Kasin Mansur) Firdausi [or Firdawsi. 6448-5
"**Kiver** up yo' haid". Lullaby ("Kiver up"). Paul Laurence Dunbar. 6580-5
Kivers. Ann Cobb. 6034-X
Kiyowara

"Pure, and fragile and pale". Lois J. Erickson (tr.). 6027-7
Kiyowara Fukuyabu
    "Because river-fog". Arthur Waley (tr.). 7039-6
Kiyowara No Fuka-yabu
    "To short the lovely summer night". William N. Porter (tr.). 6852-9
Kiyowara No Moto-suke
    "Our sleeves, all wet with tears, attest". William N. Porter (tr.). 6852-9
Kizen
    "My home is near the capital". William N. Porter (tr.). 6852-9
Kizer, Carolyn
    Afterthoughts of Donna Elvira. 6388-8
    To my friend, behind walls. 6388-8
    What the bones know. 6388-8
Kizer, Gary Allan
    The boxer turned bartender. 6870-7
    Even the best. 6870-7
    Oil and blood. 6870-7
    One year after. 6870-7
    Skyhook. 6870-7
Klabund
    Fever. Babette Deutsch (tr.). 6160-5
    Journey from Copenhagen to Skodsborg. Babette Deutsch (tr.). 6160-5
    The poet to his beloved. Babette Deutsch (tr.). 6160-5
    The wind strode wildly. Babette Deutsch (tr.). 6160-5
Klan song. Morrie [pseud]. 6817-0
Klare von Reuter. Jorge Carrera Andrade. 6759-X
Klastersky, Ant.
    The cloister garden. Paul Selver (tr.). 6763-8
Klauck, Daniel L.
    Catwalk. 6870-7
    Eulogy for a tough guy. 6870-7
    Inside a prison cell at count time. 6870-7
    Visits. 6870-7
Klaxon (John Graham Bower)
    America comes in. 6224-5
    Destroyers. 7029-9,6846-4
    In the morning. 7031-0
    Old women. 7031-0
    'Our annual'. 7031-0
    The quartermaster. 7031-0
    Sky signs. 7031-0
    Submarines. 7029-9
    'That have no doubts'. 7031-0
Klebnikov, Viktor
    Hey, lads. Jack Lindsay (tr.). 6546-5
Klein, Abraham M.
    Biography. 6042-0
    Design for mediaeval tapestry. 6021-8
    Elijah. 6042-0
    Heirloom. 6042-0,6446-9
    In re Solomon Warshawer. 6761-1
    Job reviles. 6532-5
Klein, Abraham Moses
    Bread. 6446-9
    Psalm 006, fr. The psalter of Avram Haktani. 6446-9
    Psalm 009. 6532-5
    Psalm 012, fr. The psalter of Avram Haktani. 6446-9
    The rocking chair. 6446-9
    The still small voice. 6446-9
Klein, Ruth
    Full bloom. 6850-2
    Late chrysanthemums. 6850-2
Klein, Ruth H.
    Progress. 6850-2
Kleiner, Rheinhart
    Light the old pipe. 7007-8
Kleinert, Deborah
    The lake. 6847-2
Kleinschmidt, Gustav A.
    Christmas, today and yesterday. 6799-9
Kleinschmidt, Mildred
    Breath of pines. 6397-7
    F.C. 6397-7
    Minutes. 6397-7
Kleiser, Grenville

The bridge you'll never cross. 6337-3,6583-X
My daily prayer. 6337-3
Song of the subway. 6277-6
Kleisoura. Angelos Sikelianos. 6352-7
Klemm, Wilhelm
The battle of the Marne. Babette Deutsch (tr.). 6160-5
Night. Babette Deutsch (tr.). 6160-5
The poet to his beloved. Babette Deutsch and Avrahm Yarmolinsky (tr.). 6160-6
Reflections. Babette Deutsch (tr.). 6160-5
Kleppinger, Ethel H.
Gnarled roots. 6857-X
The **kleptomaniac.** Leonora Speyer. 6037-4
Klier, Helenbelle
Origin of the Mayo clinic. 6342-X
Klinger, Kurt
Variations on death. Milne Holton and Herbert Kuhner (tr.). 6769-7
Klingle, George. See Holmes, Georgiana Klingle
Klingsor, Tristan
The curtain. 6351-9
Love's inspiration. 6351-9
The wicker chair. 6351-9
The **Klondike.** Edwin Arlington Robinson. 6946-0
The **Klondike.** Edwin Arlington Robinson. 7012-4
Klopstock, Friedrich Gottlieb
Hermann and Thusnelda. Charles Timothy Brooks (tr.). 6302-0;6385-3
The lake of Zurich. 6749-2
The resurrection. 6177-X
Knapp, Charles R.
A woodsman goes to sea. 6281-4
Knapp, Lewis M.
Apples for sale. 6039-0
Knapp, Lillian E.
Arbor day poem ("Listen! the grand old forests..."). 6049-8
Knapweed. Arthur Christopher Benson. 6656-9
Knee deep. Robert McIntyre. 6836-7
Knee-deep in June. James Whitcomb Riley. 6006-4,6550-3, 6605-4,6732-8
Knee-songs. Unknown. 6078-1
"Kneedy knife-grinder! whither are you going?". The friend of humanity and the knife-grinder. Unknown. 6874-X
Kneel at no human shrine. A.F. Kent. 6402-7
"Kneele then with me, fall worm-like on the...". The shadow of night, sel. George Chapman. 6958-4
"Kneeling, white-robed, sleepy eyes". Little Margery. Unknown. 6912-6
"Knees are pretty important". A nine-year-old boy's definition of knees. Sara D. Lewis. 6750-6
Knell. George Chapman. 6337-3
"The **knell** it has sounded". Toll the bells. Grace D. Vanamee. 6995-9
"**Knell** nor deep minute-gun gave the". Cid of the west. Edna Dean Proctor. 6995-9
The **knell** shall sound once more. Unknown. 6074-9
Knevet, Ralph
".Now of all fashions, she thinks change the best, "fr.Rhodon. 6088-9
Rhodon and Iris, sels. 6088-9
Knibbs, Henry Herbert
Braves of the hunt. 6510-4
Burro. 6506-2
Chance. 7008-6
The dog-star pup. 7008-6
The glorious fool. 7012-4
The journey. 7012-4
Largo. 7010-8
The little fires. 7012-4
The long road west. 6281-4
The lost trail. 7008-6
Names. 6506-6
The Oro stage. 6281-4
Out there somewhere. 6732-8
The outcast. 6510-4
Riders of the stars. 7010-8
Roll a rock down. 6467-1
Songs of men. 7007-8
The sun-worshipers. 6607-0

Sunlight. 7010-8
That roan cayuse. 7010-8
The trail makers. 6431-0
Trail song. 7007-8
The valley that God forgot. 6512-0
The walking man. 7012-4
Kniel, S.M.
For decoration day. 6314-4
A **knife** and belt. Woodson Tyree. 6397-7
The **knife** of boyhood. Louise S. Upham. 6744-1
Knife of nostalgia. Avanelle Wilmeth Blair. 6750-6
"A **knife**, dear girl, cuts love, they say". To his wife, with a knife. Samuel Bishop. 6874-X
The **knife-grinder.** George Canning. 6089-7,6102-8,6279-2, 6732-8
knife-thrower/The. Violet McDougal. 7038-8
The **knife.** J. R. 6349-7
"A **knight** and a lady once met in a grove". Sympathy. Reginald Heber. 6919-3
The **knight** and shepherd's daughter. Unknown. 6185-0
The **knight** and the lady. Richard Harris ("Thomas Ingoldsby") Barham. 6302-0,6089-7,6045-7
The **knight** and the lady. Robertson Trowbridge. 6671-2
The **knight** and the page. Martha C. Howe. 7002-7
The **knight** errant. Louise Imogen Guiney. 6096 X
"**Knight** had hunted long, and twilight closed". The lady of the tree. Unknown (Spanish). 6757-3
The **knight** in the bower. Unknown. 6125-7
The **knight** in the wood. John B.L. Warren, 3d Baron De Tabley. 6380-2
"The **knight** knock'd at the castle gate". William Cornish. 6187-7
A **knight** of Bethlehem. Henry Neville Maugham. 6144-3,6114-1,6337-3
The **knight** of Liddesdale. Unknown. 6185-0
The **knight** of old Japan. Alfred Noyes. 6151-6
The **knight** of Saint George. Johann Ludwig Uhland. 6903-7
Knight of the lofty blue. Louise Custis Minetree. 7019-1
The **knight** of Toggenburg. Johann C. Friedrich von Schiller. 6675-5
"The **knight** of yesteryear, a". The knight of yesteryear. Tiffany Julson. 6883-9
The **knight** strained from battle. William Herbert; Earl of Pembroke. 6881-2
"A **knight** ther was, and that a worthy man". The perfect knight, fr. The Canterbuty tales. Geoffrey Chaucer. 6934-7
The **knight's** ghost. Unknown. 6185-0
The **knight's** leap. Charles Kingsley. 6087-0,6136-2,6271-7, 6512-0,6808-1,6639
The **knight's** toast. Unknown. 6165-6,6450-7
The **knight's** toast. John Godfrey Saxe. 6404-3
The **knight's** toast. Sir Walter Scott. 6365-9,6512-0,6614-3, 6304-7,6964-9
The **knight's** tomb. Sir Walter Scott. 6087-0
The **knight's** tomb. Samuel Taylor Coleridge. 6828-6
The **knight's** tomb. Samuel Taylor Coleridge. 6239-3,6102-8, 6219-9,6301-2,6639-9,6199 ,6023-4,6383-7,6302-0,6385-3,6134-4,6395-0,6732-8
The **knight's** vow. J. Beaufoy Lane. 6414-0
Knight, Arthur Winfield
Anniversary. 6998-3
Knight, Camilla J.
The clothes-pin dollies. 6130-3
Cough and coiffure. 6698-4
Knight, Edward Christman
Ivy ode, '89. 6936-3
Knight, Etheridge
For freckle-faced Gerald. 6870-7
Hard Rock returns to prison from the hospital for... 6870-7
"He sees through stone" 6870-7
The idea of ancestry. 6870-7
Prison graveyard. 6870-7
Knight, Henry Cogswell
Cradled 'mid the oxen. 6747-6
Lunar stanzas. 6089-7
A summer's day, sels. 6008-0
Knight, Katharine
Roads. 6639-9

KNIGHT

Knight, Matthew Richey
   Dream and deed. 7041-8
   A song of failure. 7041-8
Knight, Nellie
   Mary ("On the first Easter, ere the harbinger"). 6335-7, 6144-3
Knight, Signalman H. G.
   Christmas in Tobruk. 6468-X
Knight, William Blackstone
   A lawyer's farewell to his muse. 6878-2
Knight, death and devil. Jeffery Beam. 7003-5
The knight, fr. the Canterbury tales. Geoffrey Chaucer. 6197-4,6424-8
Knight-Adkin, J.A.
   The loom. 7031-0
Knight-Adkin, J.H.
   Dead man's cottage. 7027-2
   No man's land. 6332-2,6542-2,6443-4
   The patrol. 6332-2
   Will Adams. 6793-X
Knight-Adkin, James H.
   No man's land. 6846-4
   'On les aura'. 7026-X
A knight-errant. Adelaide Anne Procter. 6957-6
The knight. Sister Maryanna. 6543-0
The knightes tale. Geoffrey Chaucer. 6245-8
The knighting of the sirloin of beef by Charles.... Unknown. 6145-1
The knighting of the sirloin of beef. Unknown. 6424-8
Knighting the loin of beef. Unknown. 6370-5
The knightly guerdon. William Makepeace Thackeray. 6802-2
"Knightly rider of the knee". The rider of the knee. James Whitcomb Riley. 6990-8
A knightly welcome. S.K. Cox. 6920-7
The knights in the ruby windowpane. Mildred Plew Meigs. 6083-8
The knights in the ruby windowpane. Mildred Plew Merryman. 6496-5
Knights of the cross. A.L.O. E. 6131-1
The knights to Chrysola. Rachel Annand Taylor. 6437-X
Knights-errant. S.M. M. 6032-3
The knights; or, both right and both wrong. Unknown. 6064-1
The knights. Ibn Sa'id (of Alcala La Real) 6362-4
Knightsbridge of Libya. Sorley Maclean. 6379-9
Knister, Raymond
   Boy remembers in the field. 6021-8
   Change. 6646-9
   Feed. 6021-8,6446-9
   Late harvest. 6021-8
   The ploughman [or plowman]. 6021-8,6446-9,6081-1
   The roller. 6021-8
   Stable talk. 6021-8
   Windfalls for cider, sels. 6021-8
"Knit thyself close, memorial grass". To the grave of an unknown British soldier. Alan Sullivan. 6796-4
Knittin' at the 'stockin'. A.W. Bellaw. 6505-8
Knitting. J.S. Cutter. 6672-0
Knitting. Mary Kyle Dallas. 6680-1
Knitting socks. Unknown. 6846-4
The knitting. Margaret Barber. 6750-6
Knocked about. Daniel Connolly. 6045-1,6344-6
"Knolege, aquayntance, resort, favour with grace" John Skelton. 6380-2
Knoll, Michael
   A dangerous music. 6870-7
   The interrogations. 6870-7
   An overture. 6870-7
   Prison letter. 6870-7
   Vigil. 6870-7
   Vivaldi on the far side of the bars. 6870-7
The knoll, fr. The homestead. Gertrude Huntington McGiffert. 6838-3
Knoop, Jeanne Showers
   The camper. 6342-X
Knorr, Nell Barnes
   Narcissus. 6818-9
The knot of blue and gray. Unknown. 6449-3
A knot of blue. Samuel Minturn Peck. 7041-8
"Knots of anger/fears of frustration". Success. Karin McGowan. 6883-9
Knott, John Olin
   Life's unfolding. 6799-9
Knotting. Charles Sackville; 6th Earl of Dorset. 6544-9
The knotting song. Sir Charles Sedley. 6563-5
"Know by the thread of music woven through". Autumn's orchestra. Emily Pauline ("Tekahionwake") Johnson. 6837-5
"Know lady yt my life depends." Unknown. 6563-5
"Know that the age of Pyrrha is long passed". Patrick Moloney. 6784-0
"Know then thyself, presume not God to scan." Alexander Pope. 6138-9;6339-X;6337-3
"Know then, my breathen". Song ("Know then"). Unknown. 6733-6
Know thyself. Angela Morgan. 6291-1
"Know ye in ages past that tower". Babel. Caroline Elizabeth Sarah Sheridan Norton. 7037-X
Know ye not that lovely river. Gerald Griffin. 6930-4
"Know ye not when our dead". The shade of Thesueus. Felicia Dorothea Hemans. 6973-8
Know ye the land?, fr. The bride of Abydos. George Gordon, 6th Baron Byron. 6198-2,6332-2,6543-0
"Know ye the red cloud - red cloud of Afric". The red cloud. Kingsley Fairbridge. 6800-6
"Know ye what ye will meet in the city?". The plague in the city. Christopher (John Wilson) North. 6980-0
"Know ye, fair folk who dwell on earth". Epitaph. Iraj. 6448-5
"Know'st thou the land where bloom the citron". Mignon's song. Johann Wolfgang von Goethe. 6973-8
"Know'st thou where that kingdom lies?". Journey's end. Alfred Noyes. 6779-4
"Know'st thou yon stream". Pompeii. John Edmund Reade. 6624-0
"Know'st thou, dear mother, of the golden sun". To mm mother, sels. Jan Neruda. 6763-9
"Know, 'twas well said, that spirits are too high". Sir Francis Kynaston. 6187-7
"Know, Celia, since thou art so proud". Ungrateful beauty. Thomas Carew. 6102-8,6092-7,6543-0,6827-8
"Know, Celia, since thou art so proud". Thomas Carew. 6187-7
"Knowed him more 'n twenty year". Greetings for two. F.W. Foley. 6887-1
The knowers. Reuel Denney. 6516-3
"Knowest thou all the stars that hover". God supreme. Wilhelm Hey. 6952-5
Knowest thou the land. Johann Wolfgang von Goethe. 6328-4
"Knowest thou the land where bloom the lemon..". Mignon. Johann Wolfgang von Goethe. 7039-X
Knowing. Christopher Pearse Cranch. 6304-7
Knowing. Julia C.R. Dorr. 6632-1
Knowing the heart of man is set to be. Samuel Daniel. 6438-8
Knowledge. Archilochus. 6435-3
Knowledge. Francis S. Cook. 6750-6
Knowledge. Theodosia Garrison. 6085-4
Knowledge. Edward R. Huxley. 6885-5
Knowledge. Archibald Lampman. 7041-8
Knowledge. Archibald Lampman. 6433-7
Knowledge. Camille Mauclair. 6351-9
Knowledge. John Henry, Cardinal Newman. 6046-3
Knowledge. F.G. Scott. 7041-8
Knowledge. Frederick George Scott. 6656-9
Knowledge. Jan (Joyce A. Maxtone Graham) Struther. 6532-5
Knowledge. Henry David Thoreau. 6423-X
Knowledge after death. Henry Charles Beeching. 6447-X,6656-9
Knowledge and doubt. Edgar A. Guest. 6748-4
"Knowledge and poer are reciprocal," fr. Novum organum. Sir Francis Bacon. 7014-0
Knowledge and reason. Sir John Davies. 6436-1
Knowledge and wisdom. Bible. 6574-0
Knowledge of age. Margaret Avison. 6446-9
Knowledge through suffering. George Wallace Briggs. 6337-3
Knowledge, power, honor. Malvina Liebermann. 6717-4
Knowles, Frederic Lawrence ("R.L. Paget")
   Columbia. 6286-5,6471-X
   A funeral. 6116-8

Grief and joy. 6889-8
Hail, America. 6471-X,6223-7
Laus mortis. 6250-4
Life. 6144-3,6337-3
Love triumphant. 6006-4,6310-1,6441-8,6732-8,6102-8, 6076-5,6250-4
Love's entrance. 6116-8
The man in the white house. 6995-9
Nature: the artist. 6250-4
The new age. 6337-3
The new patriot. 6954-1
The new patriot. 6335-7,6420-5,6143-5
On a fly-leaf of Burn's songs. 6310-1,6250-4
A pasture. 6117-6
Royalty. 6116-8
A soap-bubble. 6116-8
A song of content. 6441-8
A song of desire. 6374-8
Soul shadow. 6116-8
To a football. 6116-8
To mother nature. 6250-4
To the American poet. 6471-X
The victory which is peace. 6088-9

Knowles, Herbert
Lines written in Richmond churchyard, Yorkshire. 6271-7, 6408-6,6385-3,6600-3,6219-9,6438

Knowles, James Sheridan
Alfred the Great to his men. 6621-6,6606-2
Artifice disowned by love. 6980-0
The growth of love. 6980-0
"The honey-bee that wanders all day long". 6402-7
The hunchback, sels. 6677-1
John Di Procida, sels. 6980-0
Lost freedom of Switzerland. 6980-0
Love's artifice. 6980-0
"Once Switzerland was free! With what a pride" 6606-2
Pride of rank. 6980-0
St. Pierre to Ferrardo. 6404-3,6606-2
Switzerland. 6302-0;6385-3
Tell among the mountains. 6980-0
Tell on his native hills. 6554-6,6567-8,6304-7
Tell on Switzerland. 6402-7
Tell's address to the alps. 6392-6
Virginius in the Forum. 6980-0
William Tell among the mountains. 6606-2,6425-6,6014-5, 6610-0
William Tell on Switzerland. 6425-6
"Ye crags and peaks...". 6402-7

Knowles, Marjorie
Mushroom caves. 6342-X

Knowles, Ruth
It is the following. 6799-9
Saint Francis in winter. 6799-9
Say not alone. 6799-9

Knowles, Sarah Knowles
Left on the battle-field. 6302-0;6385-3

Knowles, Sheridan
Helen and Modus. 6382-9
Known and unknown. Alfred Lord Tennyson. 6252-0
Known by their fruits. Edward R. Huxley. 6885-5
Known in vain, fr. The house of life. Dante Gabriel Rossetti. 6122-2,6198-2,6110-9
The known soldier. M.A. DeWolfe Howe. 6051-X,6542-2
Known unto God. Constance Faunt LeRoy Runcie. 6670-4
"Known you before? Yes aeons we have known". Waiting on the quay. Eva Hammond Churchill. 6818-9
Knowning what time it is at night. Louise Townsend Nicholl. 6979-7
"Knows't thou the land where citron-flowers...". The song of Mignon. Johann Wolfgang von Goethe. 6976-2

Knox, A.D. (tr.)
A visit from wealth. Hipponax, 6435-3

Knox, E.V.
Limerick:"..old man who said, 'Please'". 6811-1
Limerick:"..young curate of Hants". 6811-1

Knox, Edmund George Valpy
The old silent house. 6633-X
A polite protest. 6633-X
To the god of love. 6026-9
The water zoo. 6228-8

Knox, Isa Craig
Ballad of the brides of Quair. 6518-X,6600-3
Ode on the centenary of Burns. 6219-9
The woodruffe. 6656-9

Knox, J. Mason
Co-operation. 6291-1,6736-0

Knox, John
The Lord is my shepherd. 6065-X

Knox, Kathleen
A lost land. 7027-2

Knox, Mrs. O.N.
Sunday - a calm at sea. 6997-5

Knox, Ronald
Limerick:"..man who said, 'God'." 6811-1
Limerick:"Evangelical vicar in want". 6811-1,6811-1, 6308-X
Limerick:"O God, for as much as without thee". 6811-1

Knox, Ronald Arbuthnott
Absolute and Abitofhell. 6096 X
"A clergyman, in want". 6722-0
Limerick"..young man of Devizes". 6811-1

Knox, Ronald Arbuthnott (tr.)
"Rome, from thy queenly walls lest glory die." Unknown (Greek), 6435-3

Knox, Thomas
"Though scoffers ask, where is your gain?" 6238-5

Knox, William
The atheist. 6045-1
The curse of Cain. 6606-2
Dirge of Rachel. 6848-0
The field of Gilboa. 6848-0
Gilboa. 6848-0
Harp of Zion. 6848-0
Mortality. 6271-7,6337-3,6479-5
O why should the spirit of mortal be proud? 6211-3,6732- 8,6102-8,6543-0,6219-9,6304 ,6418-3,6730-1,6260-1, 6481-7,6486-8,6585 ,6600-3,6302-0,6385-3,6459-0,6706- 9,6402
The wooer's visit. 6960-6
The knuckles. H.W. Green. 6591-0,6592-9
Knute Nelson. Marie Dugas. 6342-X
Ko-Ko's song. Sir William Schwenck Gilbert. 6512-0,6108-7, 6534-1

Ko-shikibu No Naishi
"So long and dreary is the road". William N. Porter (tr.). 6852-9

Kobbe, Gustave
Homeward. 6274-1
Kochia. Thomas Hornsby Ferril. 6388-8

Koehler, G. Stanley
Ground swell. 6388-8
New construction: bath iron works. 6388-8
Siciliana: the landings at Gela. 6388-8

Koehn-Heine, Lala
Letter to an exile. 6767-0

Koertge, Ronald
Dick Powell. 6792-1, 6998-3
The whore were taking vitamins. 6998-3

Kogawa, Joy
Ancestors' graves in Kurakawa. 6790-5
Dream after touring the Tokyo Tokei. 6790-5
Fish poem. 6767-0
Hiroshima exit. 6790-5
Minerals from stone. 6767-0
On meeting the clergy of the Holy Catholic Church... 6790-5
Woodtick. 6790-5

Koh, Chang-soo
Chuang-Tze's butterfly. 6775-1
View from the window. 6775-1

Kohei
"A band of beggars out to view." Lois J. Erickson (tr.). 6027-7

Kohn, Annette
Epitaph for the unknown soldier. 6846-4
In memoriam-Theodore Roosevelt. 6995-9
Our soldier dead. 6846-4

Kohn, Shyrlee
Retort to time. 6850-2

ohner, Howard

KOHNER

Avarice. 6850-2
Kohut, George Alexander
Prelude. 6848-0
Kohut, George Alexander (tr.)
Abraham and the idolater. Sadi [or Saadi] (Mushlih-ud-Din), 6848-0
Koila, fr. The purple island. Phineas Fletcher. 6194-X
Koina ta ton Philon. John Addington Symonds. 6437-X
"Koko Head nears" Sojin Takei. 6981-9
Kokomo arraigned. Ralph E. Goll. 6880-4
Kolars, Mary
"If this old place". 6292-X,6096-X
Kolbe, Frederick Charles
'Out of the strong came forth sweetness'. 6800-6
A rainbow at Victoria Falls. 6800-6
South Africa's serenade to poesy. 6800-6
To a lady of my own age. 6800-6
Wonderland. 6800-6
Kollar, Jan
Prelude, fr. The daughter of Slava. Paul Selver (tr.). 6763-8
Kolleritsch, Alfred
"It can't be understood" Milne Holton and Herbert Kuhner (tr.). 6769-7
"Occasionally you catch up with yourself" Milne Holton and Herbert Kuhner (tr.). 6769-7
"When one writes" Milne Holton and Herbert Kuhner (tr.). 6769-7
"Where were you" Milne Holton and Herbert Kuhner (tr.). 6769-7
Kolorkor's threat, fr. The story of Baladeadro. George Gordon McCrae. 6768-9
"**Kolorkor's** vengeance nigh complete". The death of Baladeadro, fr. The story of Baladeadro. George Gordon McCrae. 6768-9
Kolorkor's wooing, fr. The story of Balladeadro. George Gordon McCrae. 6768-9
Kolorkor, fr. The story of Balladeadro. George Gordon McCrae. 6768-9
Koltsov, Alexey
"Do not rustle, rye" Cecil Maurice Bowra (tr.). 6103-6
A hawk's thoughts. 6103-6
The nightingale. Maud F. Jerrold (tr.). 6103-6
Old man's song. Cecil Maurice Bowra (tr.). 6103-6
Song ("Sing not"). Cecil Maurice Bowra (tr.). 6103-6
Woman's song. 6103-6
Komani. Perceval Gibbon. 6800-6
Komia, Gonnoske
Hoh-shuku-sei-ten. 6070-6
Komkov, Stephanie
Workday morning. 6857-X
Konopak, Farona
Largo. 6979-7
Konopka, Leo
Captives. 6249-0
Immortality. 6249-0
The wind knocks at my window. 6249-0
Konrick, Vera Bishop
Erda. 6218-0
Kookaburra, sels. T. Inglis Moore. 6384-5
Koon, S. P.
the faithful servant. 6818-9
Koonsen, Mabelle Fay
The healing ministry of Jesus. 6799-9
Koopman, Harry Lyman
The death of Guinevere. 6682-8
Icarus. 6861-8
Kopis'taya (a gahtering of spirits) Paula Gunn Allen. 7005-1
Koralewsky, Rose
November twilight. 6764-6
Post mortem. 6764-6
Koran
Concerning usury. 6954-1
Dhoulkarnain. 6679-8
In the name of God, the compassionate, the merciful. 6679-8
Kore. Ezra Pound. 6315-2
Korner, Karl [or Charles] Theodore
Battle hyn. 6606-2

Battle prayer. Eugene Field (tr.). 6949-5
Good night. Charles Timothy Brooks (tr.). 6302-0;6385-3
The sword song. 6358-6,6263-6
The sword song. Charles Timothy Brooks (tr.). 6302-0, 6385-3
Sword-song. Elizabeth Craigmyle (tr.). 6842-1
Korongo. See Brooke, Brian
Korosta Katzina song. Unknown (American Indian) 6396-9
Korosta katzina song. Unknown (Hopi Indian) 7039-6
Korsor. Adam Gottlob Oehlenschlager. 6555-4
Korte, Mary Norbert
Every day shaggy man mushroom. 6792-1
Letter 60 6792-1
Kortrecht, Augusta
A naughty girl. 6713-1
Sick-bed promises. 6715-8
Kosciusko. Leigh Hunt. 6980-0
Kosmark, Katharine
Sunrise. 6036-6
Kossuth. James Russell Lowell. 6087-0
Kossuth. John Greenleaf Whittier. 6753-0
Kossuth and the Hungarians. Wathen Mark Wilks Call. 7009-4
Kotri, by the river. Laurence (Adele Florence Nicolson) Hope. 6856-1
Kouchak, Nahabed
"My heart is turned into a wailing child". 6050-1
"O night, be long...". 6050-1
"On the morning of thy birth". 6050-1
"Kowards who kover their faces". Ku Klux. Arthur Guiterman. 6817-0
Koyama, Tina
Definitions of the word gout. 6790-5
Grape daiquiri. 6790-5
Next. 6790-5
Ojisan after the stroke: three notes to himself. 6790-5
The **kraals..** June Daly. 6625-9
Kraftner, Hertha
The boy. Milne Holton and Herbert Kuhner (tr.). 6769-7
The hangman's wife. Milne Holton and Herbert Kuhner (tr.). 6769-7
Litany. Milne Holton and Herbert Kuhner (tr.). 6769-7
"The sky turned as yellow as cheap paper" Milne Holton and Herbert Kuhner (tr.). 6769-7
With early cattails. Milne Holton and Herbert Kuhner (tr.). 6769-7
The **kraken.** Alfred Lord Tennyson. 6052-8,6246-6,6378-0, 6655-0
Kramer, Aaron
Barcelona celebrates three years of Franco. 6561-9
Berlin air raid. 6561-9
Garcia Lorca. 6561-9
Guernica. 6561-9
Natchez. 6561-9
Stalingrad. 6561-9
United Nations' cantata. 6561-9
Kramer, Arthur F.
Shadows. 6038-2
Kramer, Edgar Daniel
Cargoes. 7007-8
Good Friday ("You drove the nails in His white..."). 6335-7
New-year prayer. 6449-3
Tall trees. 6449-3
Youth's thankfulness. 6449-3
Krantzor, Douglas B.
Dress model. 6083-8
Krapf, Norbert
Durer's piece of turf. 6966-5
A gloomy day. 6966-5
Harvesting wheat. 6966-5
Returning from the hung. 6966-5
Rural lines after Breughel, sels. 6966-5
Krasnohorska, Eliska
And far away, the azure peaks. Paul Selver (tr.). 6763-8
Krause, Anna Jirak
God's masterpiece, us humans. 6799-9
Kremnitzer
The rich and the poor man. Sir John Bowring (tr.). 6996-7

Kresensky, Raymond
    Afternoon in a church. 6144-3,6335-7
    At the workers' benches. 6954-1
    Christ on Madison street. 6954-1
    Comrade, remember. 6420-5
    The feast. 6017-X
    Golgotha's cross. 6144-3
    Jesus was a humble man. 6144-3
    Men follow Simon. 6144-3,6335-7
    Mothers and walls. 6461-2
    Patriotism. 6542-2
    The society of men. 6954-1
    The suffering God. 6144-3
    To the tomb. 6144-3
    Voices. 6954-1
Kreuttner, John Daniel
    To Woodrow Wilson. 7001-9
Kreymborg, Alfred
    Adagio: a duet. 6010-2
    Advertisement. 6069-2
    America. 6897-9
    And she said and I said. 6070-6
    Ants. 6348-9
    Arabs. 6348-9
    Ballad of the common man. 6561-9
    Ballad of the Lincoln penny. 6736-0
    A barker incites an old man..., fr. Old and new New York. 6012-9
    The beggar and burglar..., fr. Old and new New York. 6012-9
    Bloom. 6776-X
    Bubbles. 6010-2
    Cake on Sunday, fr. Old and new New York. 6012-9
    Call him high Shelley now. 6619-4
    Cezanne. 6102-8,6076-5
    Chipmunks. 6184-2
    Circe. 6348-9
    City chap, fr. Seven movements. 6011-0
    Cloudy drop. 6071-4
    Colophon. 6010-2
    Convention. 6348-9
    Credo. 6076-5
    Dance. 6959-2
    Democracy. 6012-9
    Destroy a day. 6781-6
    Die kuche. 6010-2
    Dirge. 6010-2
    The ditty the city sang, fr. Old and new New York. 6012-9
    Donkey. 6012-9
    Dorothy. 6034-X
    Earth wisdom. 6030-7
    Ego's dream. 6348-9
    Empire, fr. Old and new New York. 6012-9
    Factories, fr. Old and new New York. 6012-9
    Hermit thrush, fr. Seven movements. 6011-0
    Human throne. 6979-7
    Idealists. 6102-8,6338-1,6556-2,6393-4,6076-5,6030-7, 6161-3
    Is there not faith enough? 6042-0
    Isolationist. 6561-9
    A man besmitten so. 6619-4
    Manikin and minikin. 6348-9
    Neapolitan. 6331-4,6439-6
    Neighbors, fr. Seven movements. 6011-0
    New Year's Eve and NEw Year's day, fr. Old and new New York . 6012-9
    Nun snow. 6033-1,6348-9
    Old and new New York, sels. 6012-9
    Old manuscript. 6102-8,6509-0,6556-2,6076-5,6161-3,6300
    Overheard in an asylum. 6474-4
    Pain. 6010-2
    Parallels. 6011-0
    Parasite. 6897-9
    Peasant. 6011-0
    Pebble, song and water fall. 6887-1
    Peewee, fr. Seven movements. 6011-0
    Pianissimo. 6531-7
    The poll-tax blues. 6561-9
    Rain. 6010-2
    Rain inters Maggiore. 6037-4,6217-2
    Remember Wake Island. 6561-9
    Robin, fr, Seven movements. 6011-0
    Savanrola burning. 6037-4
    September 1939. 6561-9
    Seven movements. 6011-0
    Six movements. 6038-2
    Song sparrow, fr. Seven movements. 6011-0
    Springtime. 6348-9
    Still in the cradle. 6561-9
    A Sunday in Central Park, 1900, fr. Old and new New York. 6012-9
    Swallows, fr. Seven movements. 6011-0
    They are not dead yet. 6561-9
    They are not yet dead. 6783-2
    Threnody ("I have been with a snob to-day"). 6348-9
    To the old south. 6561-9
    To the tune of a hurdy-gurdy, fr. Old and new New York. 6012-9
    Tobacco smoke. 6072-2
    The tree. 6102-8
    The tree. 6861-8
    Trinity Churchyard, 1927, fr. Old and new New York. 6012-9
    Truck drivers. 6069-2
    Under glass. 6348-9
    Vista. 6348-9
    White crepe on the door, fr. Old and new New York. 6012-9
    Yearning. 6348-9
Kriel, Margot
    The annunciation. 6966-5
Kriloff, Ivan Andreevich
    The peasant and the sheep. C. Fillingham Coxwell (tr.). 7039-6
Kringle, George
    To-morrow's news. 6632-1
    Why mother is proud. 6632-1
Krinken. Eugene Field. 6479-5,6104-4
Krishna. George William ("A.E.") Russell. 6659-3
Kriss Kringle. Thomas Bailey Aldrich. 6747-6
Kriss Kringle. Susie M. Best. 6147-8
Kriss Kringle. Frank Dempster Sherman. 6311-X
Kriss Kringle. Unknown. 6272-5
Kriss Kringle's visit. Unknown. 6745-X
Kristensen, Tom
    Diminuendo. Charles Wharton Stork (tr.). 6555-4
Krogmann, Dorothy A.
    A mountain lodge. 6818-9
Krotz, Lillias Hays
    New England winter. 6894-4
Krout, Mary Hannah
    Little brown hands. 6127-3,6136-2,6215-6,6424-8,6912-6
Krsna. Unknown (Newari) 7013-2
Krsna and Sudaman. Unknown (Newari) 7013-2
Krug, Terry
    Trilogy. 6799-9
Kruger, Charlotte M.
    Beautiful saviour. 6065-X
Kruger, Fania
    German Jewess prays. 6042-0
    In thine image. 6532-5
    Passover eve. 6532-5
    Since I have seen death's face. 6648-8
    Wandering child. 6979-7
Krumley. Alice Cary. 6600-3
Krummacher, Friedrich Adolf
    Alpine heights. Charles Timothy Brooks (tr.). 6302-0;6385-3
    Mountain and valley. 6749-2
Kruna (pseud.)
    Corregio. 6680-1
Kruppism. Percy MacKaye. 6542-2
Kruszewska & M.M. Coleman, A. (tr.)
    In praise of trees. Kazimierz Wierzynski, 6068-4
Krystallis, Kostas
    The embroidery on the kerchief. Rae Dalven (tr.). 6352-7
    I would love to be a shepherd. Rae Dalven (tr.). 6352-7
    To the imperial eagle. Rae Dalven (tr.). 6352-7

KRYSTALLIS

The vintage. Rae Dalven (tr.). 6352-7
Ku Klux. Madison Cawein. 6309-8,7017-5
Ku Klux. Arthur Guiterman. 6817-0
Ku Klux Klanthem. Seymour Barnard. 6880-4
Kubla Khan. Samuel Taylor Coleridge. 6154-0,6424-8,6639-9, 6543-0,6464-7,6646 ,6491-4,6645-3,6634-8,6536-8,6430-2,6726 ,6179-6,6198-2,6358-6,6369-1,6501-5,6527 , 6052-8,6075-7,6102-8,6138-9,6238-4,6271 ,6186-9,6187-7,6208-3,6228-8,6236-9,6239 ,6086-2,6560-0,6192-3, 6199-0,6125-7,6252 ,6110-9,6150-8,6153-2,6219-9,6114-1,6438 ,6301-2,6396-6,6196-6,6289-X,6302-0,6315 , 6332-2,6339-X,6395-0,6423-X,6427-2,6473 ,6481-7,6488-4
Kubleh. Bayard Taylor. 6673-9
Kuby, Lolette
　The trade. 6821-9
Kudaka, Geraldine
　Birthright. 6790-5
　Death is a second cousin dining with us tonight. 6790-5
　Giving up butterflies. 6790-5
　"Okinawa Kanashii Monogatari" 6790-5
　On writing Asian-American poetry. 6790-5
Kuhn et al. vs. Jewett, receiver. William B. Gourley. 6878-2
Kuhn, Orville Lawrence
　Come to him. 6799-9
　The good samaritan. 6799-9
Kuhns, Oscar
　Future full of cheer. 6717-4
Kula...a homecoming. Diane Mei Lin Mark. 6790-5
Kulnasatz, my reindeer. Unknown. 6271-7
Kuloskap and the beaver. Unknown (Algonquin Indian) 6864-2
Kuloskap and the fool. Unknown (Algonquin Indian) 6864-2
Kuloskap and the loons. Unknown (Algonquin Indian) 6864-2
Kuloskap and the turtle. Unknown (Algonquin Indian) 6864-2
Kuloskap and the wise wishers. Unknown (Algonquin Indian) 6864-2
Kuloskap and the witch. Unknown (Algonquin Indian) 6864-2
Kuloskap and the witch called 'The Pitcher'. Unknown (Algonquin Indian) 6864-2
Kuloskap and Winpe; or, the master's first victory. Unknown (Algonquin Indian) 6864-2
Kuloskap and Wucho'sen, the wind-eagle. Unknown (Algonquin Indian) 6864-2
"Kuloskap was first/First and greatest". The creation of man and the animals. Unknown (Algonquian Indian). 6864-2
"Kung walked/by the dynastic temple". Canto 013 ("Kung walked"). Ezra Pound. 6209-1
Kung's wisdom, sels. Ezra Pound. 6354-3
Kunitz, Stanley J.
　Careless love. 6666-6
　The hemorrhage. 6666-6
　Lovers relentlessly. 6250-4
　Reflections by a mailbox. 6666-6
Kunz, Georgia
　Haiku. 6899-5
　"I am numb from too much feeling" 6899-5
　"Was it planned, wind?" 6899-5
Kuo Ch'en
　Clouds by night. Arthur Waley (tr.). 6072-2
Kuo, Alex
　Did you not see. 6790-5
　An early Illinois winter. 6790-5
　Loss. 6790-5
　On a clear day I can see forever. 6790-5
　There is something I want to say. 6790-5
Kurt, Kim
　Runaway. 6388-8
　The sun-bather. 6388-8
　Vernal paradox. 6388-8
　Woodlore. 6388-8
Kurtz, Babette
　Ann Curtis. 6850-2
　To my grandmother. 6850-2
Kurtz, Kalfus
　Child at the library. 6761-1
Kurz, Isolde
　The first night. 6643-7
Kuskulis, Elisabeth

The birthplace. 6836-7
Content. 6836-7
The fog-girl. 6836-7
Generation unto generation. 6836-7
Limitations. 6836-7
Ode to beauty. 6836-7
On being wronged. 6836-7
On the altar. 6836-7
Sanctuary. 6836-7
A sonnet of hate. 6836-7
Kuthiyir
　The raven. A.J. Arberry (tr.). 6362-4
Kuttner, George
　Gulls. 6900-2
Kuznets, George
　Realization. 6850-2
Kvapil, Fr.
　Spring song. Paul Selver (tr.). 6763-8
Kvaran, Einar Hjorleifsson
　Death comes riding, fr. Governor Lenhard. Jakobina Johnson (tr.). 6283-0
　Governor Lenhard, sels. Jakobina Johnson (tr.). 6283-0
　The kiss. Runolfur Fjeldsted (tr.). 6854-5
　My country lies wounded, fr. Governor Lenhard. Jakobina Johnson (tr.). 6283-0
　The orphan. Mekkin Sveinson Perkins (tr.). 6283-0
　The westland (America). Skuli Johnson (tr.). 6854-5
Kwan-ke
　I bring no prayers on coloured silk. William N. Porter (tr.). 6852-9
Kwannon, the compassionate. Isabel Fiske Conant. 6850-2
Kwasind: his death, fr. The song of Hiawatha. Henry Wadsworth Longfellow. 6018-8
Kwasind: his strength, fr. The song of Hiawatha. Henry Wadsworth Longfellow. 6018-8
Kwoka Mon-in No Betto
　"I've seen thee but a few short hours". William N. Porter (tr.). 6852-9
Kwoko, Emperor
　"Mother, for thy sake I have been". William N. Porter (tr.). 6852-9
Kyarlina Jim. A.C. Gordon. 6139-7
Kyarlina Jim. Unknown. 6914-2
Kyd, Thomas
　Of fortune. 6182-6
"The kye had been milkit,the milk had been set". Robin and Meg. Jane Leck. 7037-X
Kyjov. Petr Bezruc. 6763-8
Kyle, Carol
　Garage sale. 6821-9
　The swimming lesson. 6821-9
Kyle, Grace O.
　The acorn. 6529-5
　The apple. 6529-5
　The corn. 6529-5
　The hickory-nut. 6529-5
Kynaston, Herbert (tr.)
　Hymn to Poseidon. Arion, 6435-3
Kynaston, Sir Francis
　"Dear Cynthia, though thou bear'st the name". 6187-7
　"Do not conceal thy radiant eyes". 6187-7
　"If thou a reason dost desire to know". 6187-7
　"Know, 'twas well said, that spirits are too high". 6187-7
　To Cynthia. 6023-4
　To Cynthia on concealment of her beauty. 6317-9,6562-7, 6563-5
　To Cynthia on her being an incendiary. 6380-2,6341-1
　To Cynthia on her embraces. 6317-9,6380-2
　To Cynthia on his love after death. 6562-7
　To Cynthia, on her changing. 6563-5
Kynd Kittock in heaven. William Dunbar. 6733-6
Kynge David, hys lamente over the bodyes of Kynge... Sir Philip Sidney. 6848-0
The kynge's balade. Henry VIII; King of England. 6328-4
Kyohaku
　"There are no gloomy days." Lois J. Erickson (tr.). 6027-7
Kyoko
　"Far beyond/White lilies, wild around my feet." Lois J.

Erickson (tr.). 6027-7
Kyoroku
"Above white clouds I hear sweet." Lois J. Erickson (tr.). 6027-7
Kyoshi
"The butterflies can scarcely find." Lois J. Erickson (tr.). 6027-7
Kyrie Eleison. Adelaide Anne Procter. 6957-6
"Kyrie, so kryie". Jankin, the clerical seducer. Unknown. 6881-2
Kyrielle. John Payne. 6770-0

L'Abbate. William Wetmore Story. 6735-2
L'Estrange, Sir Roger
    In prison. 6600-3
    The liberty of the imprisoned royalist. 6934-7
    Loyalty confin'd. 6933-9
    Mr. Le Strange. 6563-5
L'allegro. John Milton. 6102-8,6122-2,6138-9,6142-7,6186-9, 6198 ,6491-4,6639-9,6646-1,6543-0,6301-2,6304 ,6246-6,6302-0,6385-3,6315-2,6332-2,6369 ,6424-8,6152-3, 6189-3,6197-4,6219-9,6560 ,6423-X,6473-6,6488-4,6536-8,6604-6,6634 ,6250-4,6659-3,6192-3,6438-8,6194-X, 6723 ,6661-5,6726-3,6732-8
L'allegro, sels. John Milton. 6934-7
L'allegro, sels. John Milton. 6239-3;6501-5
L'allegro, sels. John Milton. 6934-7
L'amitie est l'amour sans ailes. George Gordon, 6th Baron Byron. 6945-2
L'amour sans ailes. Charles Fenno Hoffman. 6441-8
"L'amour, panique/De la raison". A la belle imperieuse. Victor Hugo. 6801-4
L'an trentiesme de mon eage. Archibald MacLeish. 6641-0;6619-4
L'ange qui veille. Victor Hugo. 6691-7
L'apres. Eve Brodlique Summers. 6796-4
L'apres-midi. Thomas Meyer. 7003-5
L'apres-midi d'un faune. Stephane Mallarme. 6343-8
L'arret a la lisiere des bois par un soir de neige. Edouard Roditi. 6527-9
L'attente. Marceline Desbordes-Valmore. 6801-4
L'eau dormante. Thomas Bailey Aldrich. 6004-8
L'emoi forestier. Paul Fort. 6253-9
"L'enfant ayant apercu". A David, statuaire. Charles Augustin Sainte-Beuve. 6801-4
L'enthousiasme. Alphonse Marie Louis de Lamartine. 6801-4
L'envoi. Sir Henry Howarth Bashford. 7007-8
L'envoi. Thomas Lovell Beddoes. 6317-9
L'envoi. Robert Buchanan. 6639-9
L'envoi. Willa Sibert Cather. 6274-1,6347-0,6274-1,6320-9
L'envoi. Rudyard Kipling. 6337-3,6437-X,6479-5,6730-1,6301-2,6104-4,6214-8
L'envoi. Henry Wadsworth Longfellow. 6126-5
L'envoi. Beatrice Lowenstein. 6847-2
L'envoi. Dorothea Lawrence Mann. 6033-1
L'envoi. Virginia Donaghe McClurg. 6836-7
L'Envoi. Herman Melville. 6176-1
L'envoi. Nellie Burget Miller. 6836-7
L'envoi. William Morris. 6657-7,6660-7
L'envoi. John G. Neihardt. 6337-3
L'Envoi. Edward Bliss Reed. 6116-8,6652-6
L'envoi. Edwin Arlington Robinson. 6723-9
L'envoi. Mary Muriel Rochester. 6847-2
L'envoi. Robert Service. 6159-1
L'envoi. Bayard Taylor. 6121-4
L'envoi. Unknown. 6811-1
L'envoi. Unknown. 6145-1
L'envoi. Unknown. 6811-1
L'envoi. Unknown (Algonquin Indian) 6864-2
L'envoi ("I've passed the grim..."). Bayard Taylor. 6976-2
L'envoi ("May-time and August..."). Bayard Taylor. 6976-2
L'envoi ("My job is done..."). Robert Service. 6159-1
L'envoi ("Once more my sheaf of songs I tie"). Robert Service. 6159-1
L'envoi ("Unto the desert..."). Bayard Taylor. 6976-2
L'envoi ("We talked of yesteryears, of trails..."). Robert Service. 6159-1

L'envoi ("We've finished up the filthy war"). Robert Service. 6159-1
L'envoi (To-night on Madagascan..."). Hermann Hagedorn. 6944-4
L'envoi to E.W.G. Andrew Lang. 6987-8
L'envoi, fr. The earthly paradise. William Morris. 6110-9
L'Envoi-leave her Johnny. Unknown. 6547-3
L'envoie. Martyn Summerbell. 6798-0
L'envoy. Mathilde Blind. 7037-X
L'envoy. ? Randolph. 6273-3
L'envoy to W. L. H. Ainsworth, esq. Francis Sylvester ("Father Prout") Mahony. 6930-4
L'escargot d'or. Robert Service. 6159-1
L'etat c'est moi, fr. Two gentlemen in bonds. John Crowe Ransom. 6011-0
L'habitude. Auguste Angellier. 6801-4
"L'heureux n'est pas le vrai, le droit...". Ecrit en exil. Victor Hugo. 6801-4
L'homme machine. Helen Seaman. 6954-1
L'hymne de la nuit. Alphonse Marie Louis de Lamartine. 6801-4
L'Ile du Levant: the nudist colony. Barbara Howes. 6388-8
L'Ile Sainte Croix. Arthur Wentworth Hamilton Eaton. 6115-X,6591-0,6592-2
"L'immense mer sommeille.". Sacra fames. Charles Marie Leconte de Lisle. 6801-4
L'inconnue. Oliver Wendell Holmes. 6077-3,6092-7,6250-4, 6126-5
L'inconnue. Winthrop Mackworth Praed. 6424-8
L'inconnue. Harold Fehrsen Sampson. 6800-6
L'infinito. Giacomo Leopardi. 7039-6
L'irreparable. Charles Baudelaire. 6801-4
L'isolement. Alphonse Marie Louis de Lamartine. 6801-4
L'oiseau bleu. Mary Elizabeth Coleridge. 6253-9
L'ordre de bon atemps. Arthur Weir. 7041-8
L'ordre de bon temps. Arthur Wentworth Hamilton Eaton. 7041-8
L.
    Battery Park. 6817-0
    The bluefinch. 6084-6
    Nazareth. 6846-4
    Vigil. 6817-0
L. E. L. Christina Georgina Rossetti. 6828-6
L. of G.'s purport. Walt Whitman. 6126-5,6288-1
L.,H.
    What I like. 6453-1
L.,H.M.
    'I give my soldier boy a blade'. 6074-9
L.,J.G.
    Platonic friendship. 6084-6
L.,J.O.
    Triolet. 6817-0
L.,L.
    The graves of Gallipoli. 6846-4
L.,O.
    Prayer of the satirist. 6118-4
    Prayer of the satyrist. 6118-4
    The river of commerce. 6118-4
    Verse ("A melancholy Prussian.") 6118-4
L.,P.H.B.
    Morituri te salutant. 7031-0,6846-4
L.,R.
    Autobiography in fourteen chapters. 6662-3
L.,R.A.
    Under false colours. 6118-4
L.,U.A.
    Watchin' out for subs. 6846-4
L.,W.
    The casualty list. 7031-0
L.E.L. See Landon, Letitia Elizabeth
La Bassee Road. Patrick MacGill. 6443-4
La Conte (or La Coste), Marie
    Somebody's darling. 6471-X,6074-9,6113-3,6016-2,6964-9
La Coste, Maria. See La Conte, Maria
La Farge, Christopher
    Grandfather. 6761-1
    If I am but the water. 6761-1
    Sunday broadcast: transcribed. 6761-1
La Fontaine, Jean de
    The castle-builder. 6105-2

LA

The cat and the fox. Sir Edward Marsh (tr.). 6511-2
The cat changed into a woman. 6120-6
The cock and the fox. Elizur Wright Jr. (tr.). 6732-8
The council held by the rats. 6120-6,6679-8
Dissatisfied with a Log for King, the frogs get a
   crane. Elizur Wright Jr. (tr.). 6637-2
The drunkard and his wife. 6064-1
Each satisfied with himself, the animals criticize...
   Elizur Wright Jr. (tr.). 6637-2
The fox hoaxes the raven out of his cheese. 6637-2
The monkey and the cat. 6120-6
The old cat and the young mouse. 6120-6
The wise cock fools the fox. 6637-2
La Moille, T.G.
   Only a tramp. 6215-6
   Thanksgiving. 6215-6
   "39"Thirty. 6215-6
La Trobe, John Antes
   The peace of Christ. 6065-X
La beatrice. Charles Baudelaire. 6801-4
La beaute. Charles Baudelaire. 7039-6
"La beaute, dans la femme, est une melodie". La melodie et
   l'accompagnement. Theophile Gautier. 6801-4
La bella donna del mia mente. Oscar Wilde. 6732-8
La belle confidente. Thomas Stanley. 6208-3,6341-1
La belle dame sans merci. John Keats. 6052-8,6122-2,6134-6,
   .6138-9,6154-0,6339 ,6023-4,6086-2,6102-8,6150-8,6110-
   9,6645 ,6075-7,6133-8,6196-6,6430-2,6560-0,6199 ,
   6192-3,6613-5,6250-4,6107-9,6396-9,6659 ,6186-9,6198-
   2,6204-0,6236-9,6246-6,6254 ,6125-7,6153-2,6219-9,
   6301-2,6513-9,6419 ,6289-X,6302-0,6315-2,6317-9,6328-
   4,6332 ,6252-0,6319-5,6371-3,6639-9,6646-1,6723 ,
   6369-1,6395-0,6427-2,6459-0,6473-6,6527 ,6518-X,6660-
   7,6668-2,6536-8,6604-6,6610-0,6634-8,6726-3,6732
La bete humaine. James Kirkup. 6379-9
La Blanchisseuse. Isabella Valancy Crawford. 6591-0,659 -2
"La bise tourne et la brise". Ronde finale. Francis Viele-
   Griffin. 6801-4
"La Chapelle, little village". La Chapelle-St. Remy.
   Eugene Dimon Preston. 6836-7
"La Gitanilla! Tall dragoons". Carmen. Madison Cawein.
   7041-8
La caporal. Daniel Carman McArthur. 6796-4
La chanson de Fantine. Victor Hugo. 6801-4
La chanson de Joss. Victor Hugo. 6801-4
La Chapelle-St. Remy. Eugene Dimon Preston. 6836-7
La chute des etoiles. Charles Marie Leconte de Lisle. 6801-
   4
La chute des feuilles. Charles Millevoye. 6801-4
La coccinelle. Victor Hugo. 6801-4
La colline. Henri de Regnier. 6801-4
La colombe. Louis Bouilhet. 6801-4
La convalescence d'Ezechias. Jean Baptiste Rousseau. 6848-
   0
La Corona. John Donne. 6933-9
La Cubana. Otto Paul Gonzalez. 6898-7
La curee. Auguste Barbier. 6801-4
'La decouverte du Mississipi' Louis Flechette. 7041-8
La devastation du musee et des monuments. Casimir
   Delavigne. 6801-4
La Fayette. Samuel Taylor Coleridge. 6828-6
La Fayette. Samuel Taylor Coleridge. 6110-9
La Fayette. Dolly Madison. 6946-0
La Fayette's lands. Hervey Allen. 6421-3
La figlia che piange. Thomas Stearns Eliot. 6527-9,6393-4,
   6210-5
La fraisne. Ezra Pound. 6513-9
La fraisne. Ezra Pound. 6897-9
A 'La France' rose. Robert Loveman. 6941-X
L' giostra, simonetta. Angelo Poliziano. 6325-X
La gitana. John Curtis Underwood. 6029-3
La gloire de Voltaire. Robert Bridges. 6487-6
La grande ivresse. Paul Fort. 6253-9
La grele. Auguste Angellier. 6801-4
La Grisette. Oliver Wendell Holmes. 6126-5,6288-1
La la, fr. The waste land. Thomas Stearns Eliot. 6531-9
La maison d'or. Oliver Wendell Holmes. 6126-5
La maison du Berger. Alfred de Vigny. 6801-4
La marche des machines. Arthur Seymour John Tessimond.
   634-3

La Melinite: Moulin-Rouge. Arthur Symons. 6508-2
La melodie et l'accompagnement. Theophile Gautier. 6801-4
La menace. Henri de Regnier. 6801-4
La montagne. Theodore de Banville. 6801-4
La mort d'Arthur. William Edmonstoune Aytoun. 6948-7
La mort d'un chene. Victor de Laprade. 6801-4
La mort du loup. Alfred de Vigny. 6801-4
La musica trionfante. Thomas William Parsons. 6693-3
La nuit de Decembre. Alfred de Musset. 6801-4
La Paloma in London. Claude McKay. 6036-6
La Petite Fiancee. Virginia Taylor McCormick. 6038-2
La preciosa. Thomas Walsh. 6096-X,6282-2
La prierede nostre dame. Geoffrey Chaucer. 6282-2
La promessa sposa. Walter Savage Landor. 6874-X
La pucelle. Sister Mary Irma. 6761-1
La ronde. Paul Fort. 6134-6
La ronde du diable. Amy Lowell. 6010-2
La Rue de la Montagne Sainte-Genevieve. Dorothy Dudley.
   6897-9
La Saisiaz. Robert Browning. 6828-6
"La sainte verite qui m'echauffe et m'inspire". La
   devastation du musee et des monuments. Casimir
   Delavigne. 6801-4
La saisiaz, sels. Robert Browning. 6110-9
"La sottise, l'erreur, le peche, la lesine". Preface.
   Charles Baudelaire. 6801-4
La terre. Frank Oliver Call. 6021-8
La terre: hymne. Victor Hugo. 6801-4
La tour d'Auvergne. Maida Buon. 6417-5
"La tranquille habitude aux mains silencieuses".
   L'habitude. Auguste Angellier. 6801-4
La tricoteuse. George Walter Thornbury. 6102-8
La vesuviana. Rebe S. Webb. 6116-8
"La vie est une voie estroite". A deux. Eugene Aubert.
   6847-2
La2villa Adrienne. Casimir Delavigne. 6801-4
La vision. Alfred de Musset. 6801-4
La vita nuova, sels. Dante Alighieri. 7039-6
Laaber, Otto
   The drum. Milne Holton and Herbert Kuhner (tr.). 6769-7
   In a hard shell. Milne Holton and Herbert Kuhner (tr.).
      6769-7
   In the field. Milne Holton and Herbert Kuhner (tr.).
      6769-7
   Like the wind. Milne Holton and Herbert Kuhner (tr.).
      6769-7
   Who says. Milne Holton and Herbert Kuhner (tr.). 6769-7
Labaree, Mary Fleming
   Blind clay. 6036-6
Labe, Louise
   Elegy, sels. Ralph Nixon Currey (tr.). 6227-X
   Povre ame amoureuse. Robert Bridges (tr.). 6958-4,6487-
      6
   Sonnet ("As soon"). Ralph Nixon Currey (tr.). 6227-X
Labor. George W. Bungay. 6920-7
Labor. Orville Dewey. 6449-3
Labor. Frances Sargent Osgood. 6465-5,6294-6,6600-3
Labor. Edith Thomas. 6880-4
Labor. Unknown. 6523-6,6449-3
Labor and leisure. Edward R. Huxley. 6885-5
Labor Day. Edward R. Huxley. 6885-5
Labor is worship. Frances Sargent Osgood. 6406-X,6304-7
Labor song. Denis Florence MacCarthy. 6302-0;6385-3
Labor song. Unknown. 6167-2,6738-7
Labor, fr. A glance behind the curtain. James Russell
   Lowell. 6337-3
Laborare est orare. Francis Albert Rollo Russell. 6337-3
The laboratory. Robert Browning. 6052-8,6154-0,6437-X,6657-
   7,6677-1,6655 ,6153-2,6196-6,6541-2
Labore est orare. Frances Sargent Osgood. 6569-4,6219-9
"A laborer in Christian England". Bad squire, sel. Charles
   Kingsley. 6954-7
The laborer's noonday hymn. William Wordsworth. 6271-7
The laborer. John Clare. 6385-3,6219-9,6438-8
The laborer. Richard Dehmel. 7039-6
The laborer. William Davis Gallagher. 6344-6,6407-8,6632-1,
   6304-7
The laborer. Jose Maria de Heredia. 7039-6
The laborer. Galatea Kazantzakis. 6352-7
Laborers. Charles Gustav Girelius. 6143-5

Laborers. Kostes Palamas. 6352-7
Laborious writers. Samuel Butler. 6278-4
Labour and life. James Herbert Morse. 7041-8
Labour and love. Sir Edmund Gosse. 7014-0
The labourer in the vineyard. Stephen Spender. 6379-9
The labourer. Alexey Khomyakov. 6103-6
The labours of Hercules. Marianne Moore. 6751-4
Labuntur, fr. Canto I. George Gordon, 6th Baron Byron. 6110-9
Lac Courte Orielles: 1936 Phyllis Wolf. 7005-1
Lac qui parle. Gertrude Hanson. 6342-X
Lace. Doris V. Lecky. 6850-2
Lace shroud. Winifred Welles. 6038-2
Lacedaemon. Unknown (Greek) 6435-3
"Lacedaemon, land unconquered...". Unknown. 6251-2
Lacey, Fanny E.
    Judtih and Holofernes. 6848-0
Lacey, Maria
    Loveliness. 6743-3
Lachicotte, Virginia Wilson
    The deer. 7016-7
    The fawn. 7016-7
    Happiness. 7016-7
    Rain. 7016-7
    White herons. 7016-7
Lachin y Gair. George Gordon, 6th Baron Byron. 6110-9,6196-6,6438-3,6859-6,6945-2
Lachrimae musarum, sels. Sir William Watson. 6289-X
Lachrymae. David Gascoyne. 6106-0
Lachrymae musarum (6th October, 1892). Sir William Watson. 6656-9
The lachrymatory. Charles Tennyson Turner. 6219-9
Lachrymose writers. Horace Smith. 6606-2
Lack of steadfastness. Geoffrey Chaucer. 6489-2
Lackey, Alexander M.
    Lightless Susan. 6037-4
"Lacking my love, I go from place to place". Sonnet 078 ("Lacking my love"), fr. Amoretti. Edmund Spenser. 6182-6
"Lackyng my loue, I go from place to place". Amoretti, sels. Edmund Spenser. 6908-8
Lacon and Thyrsis. Robert Herrick. 6191-5
Lacost, Marie
    Somebody's darling. 6889-8
Lacrimae musarum, sels. Sir William Watson. 6793-X
Lacrimae rerum. Palladas. 6435-3
Lacrimae rerum. Lambros Porphyras. 6352-7
Lacy, Mattie Hallam
    Carved sandal-wood. 6750-6
The lad frae Cockpen. Unknown. 6878-2
A lad that is gone. Robert Louis Stevenson. 6723-9
"A lad that was a fowler...". Bion. 6251-2
Lad's epitaph. Albert Payson Terhune. 7008-6
The lad's return. Paul Fort. 6490-9
Lad, have you things to do? Alfred Edward Housman. 6473-6
"The lad, of all-sufficient merit". The cur, the horse, and the shepherd's dog. John Gay. 6972-X
"Lad, you took the soul of me/That long had...". Lindbergh. Angela Morgan. 7019-1
A lad. Laura E. Richards. 6937-1
Ladd, Frederic P.
    Petronius. 7008-6
Ladd, Helen G.
    Agnostic. 6764-6
    Thought. 6764-6
    Winter afternoon. 6764-6
Ladd, Marie S.
    Taking aim. 6530-9
The ladder of St. Augustine. Henry Wadsworth Longfellow. 6142-7,6219-9,6288-1,6121-1,6126-5,6964
The ladder, sels. Henry Wadsworth Longfellow. 6260-1
The ladder. Leonora Speyer. 6102-8,6619-4,6732-8,6250-4,6513-9,6076
Ladders. Loton Rogers Pitts. 6761-3
Ladders through the blue. Hermann Hagedorn. 6501-5
Laddie. Katharine Lee Bates. 6476-0,6510-4
"Laddie! laddie! laddie! somewhere in France..". Over the hills of the home, sels. Lilian Leveridge. 6796-4
Laddie's long sleep. James Clarence Harvey. 7008-6
Laddies. Edgar A. Guest. 6509-0

"The laddies plague me for a sang". When we were at the schule. Thomas Carstairs Latto. 6960-6
Laddy blue eyes. Minna Caroline Smith. 6629-1
"Laden with spoil of the south...". The death of Admiral Blake. Sir Henry Newbolt. 6844-8
Ladies and gentlemen this little girl. Edward Estlin Cummings. 6751-4
"The ladies men admire, I've heard". Interview. Dorothy Parker. 6817-0
The ladies of Saint James's. Austin Dobson. 6331-4,6639-9,6658-5,6458-2,6301-2,6508-2,6655-0,6656-9
The ladies' aid. Unknown. 6714-X
Ladies' eyes serve Cupid both for darts and fire. A. W. 6436-1
Ladies' gard. William Morris. 6102-8,6649-6
The ladies' whist club. Unknown. 6694-1
Ladies, farewell! Henry Howard, Earl of Surrey. 6563-5
"Ladies, have you no reward for one whose actions". Abu Firas. 6766-2
"Ladies, though to your conqu'ring eyes". Song ("Ladies"). Sir George Etherege. 6544-9
"Ladies, though to your conquering eyes." Sir John Etherege. 6317-9
The ladies. Rudyard Kipling. 6589-9,6732-8,6026-9,6491-4
The lads in their hundreds. Alfred Edward Housman. 6527-9,6655-0,6491-4
The lads of Wamphray. Unknown. 6185-0
Lady Alda's dream. Unknown (Spanish) 6757-3
Lady Alice. Unknown. 6133-8,6185-0
"Lady Anne Dewhurst on a crimson couch". Mater domina, fr. Olrig grange. Walter Chalmers Smith. 6819-7
"Lady Astor, M.P., for sobriety". Limerick:"Lady Astor, M.P., for sobriety". A.E. Halliday. 6811-1
"Lady Clara Vere de Vere"˙ The wedding. Thomas Hood Jr.. 6802-2
Lady alone. Phyllis McGinley. 6042-0
The lady analyst & the little green room. Jana Harris. 6901-0
A lady and an ape. Sir William Schwenck Gilbert. 6236-9
Lady and crocodile. Charles Burgess. 6388-8
The lady and the dame. Ella Wheeler Wilcox. 6863-4
The lady and the farmer's son. Unknown. 6061-7
The lady and the wasp. John Gay. 6972-X
Lady Ann Bothwell's lament. Unknown. 6302-0,6385-3,6271-7,6219-9
Lady Anne Bothwell's lament, sels. Unknown. 6934-7
Lady Anne's meditations during divine service. Margaret Tod Ritter. 6039-0
"A lady asks for me". Guido Cavalcanti. 6325-X
The lady at sea. Thomas Hood. 6271-7
A lady at the opera. Emma Gray Trigg. 6039-0
Lady Barbara. Alexander Smith. 6600-3
"A lady bug". Joshua Freeman Crowell. 6130-3
Lady button-eyes. Eugene Field. 6949-5
Lady Clara Vere de Vere. Alfred Lord Tennyson. 6410-8,6486-8,6521-X,6438-8,6219-9,6543
Lady Clare. Alfred Lord Tennyson. 6142-7,6242-3,6136-2,6392-6,6404-3,6478 ,6370-5,6479-5,6497-3,6610-3,6290-3,6486 ,6457-4,6419-1,6639-9,6219-9,6438-8,6319-5,6304-7,6613-5,6131-1
Lady day in harvest. Sheila Kaye-Smith. 6282-2
Lady day in Ireand. Patrick J. Carrol. 6292-X
Lady day in Ireland. Patrick Joseph Carroll. 6172-9
Lady diamond. Unknown. 6185-0
"The lady did, it is true, once signalise...". Maid Marian. Thomas Love Peacock. 7020-5
A lady dying in childbed. Robert Herrick. 6187-7
The lady Elgin. Unknown. 6003-X
Lady Elspat. Unknown. 6055-2,6185-0,6067-6
Lady fair. Francis Ledwidge. 6812-X
Lady Flora. Ione L. Jones. 6530-9
"A lady from Madagascar/Fell in love...". Limerick:"A lady from Madagascar". Unknown. 6811-1
"The Lady Mary Villiers lies". Epitaph on Lady Mary Villiers (I) Thomas Carew. 6908-8
The lady from the west. Robert C.V. Meyers. 6926-6
Lady Geraldine's courtship. Elizabeth Barrett Browning. 6271-7,6677-1,6438-8,6219-9
Lady golden-rod. Carrie W. Bronson. 6049-8,6629-1
Lady Grace. Jon Adams. 7018-3

LADY

Lady Griseld Baillie. Joanna Baillie. 6813-8
The lady Hildegarde. Unknown (German) 6674-7
A lady I know. Countee Cullen. 6337-3
Lady icicle. Emily Pauline ("Tekahionwake") Johnson. 6837-5
Lady in a limousine. Lucia Trent. 6441-8
"Lady ird, lady bird, fly away home". Unknown. 6363-2
Lady Isabel. Unknown. 6185-0
Lady Isabel and the elf knight. Unknown. 6057-9,6058-7, 6185-0,6056-0,6430-2,6067-6,6518-4,6185-0
The Lady Jacqueline. Phoebe Cary. 6969-X
Lady Jane. Sir Arthur Quiller-Couch. 6440-X,6722-0
Lady Jane. Unknown. 6417-5
Lady Jane Grey. John Webster. 6188-5
Lady Jane Grey, sels. Nicholas Rowe. 6867-7
The lady Judith's vision. Mrs. E.V. Wilson. 6575-9
Lady Laburnam. Ffrida Wolfe. 6558-9
Lady Lilac. Robert Kirkland Kernighan. 6797-2
"A lady lived in Lancaster". Unknown. 6059-5
Lady Lorgnette. Emily Pauline ("Tekahionwake") Johnson. 6837-5
Lady lost. John Crowe Ransom. 6072-2
Lady lost in the wood. John Milton. 6385-3
Lady Maisry. Unknown. 6185-0
Lady Margaret and King William. Unknown. 6061-7
Lady Margaret's song. Edward Dowden. 6090-0
"Lady Marjorie, Lady Marjorie". Unknown. 6518-X
Lady Marjory. Phoebe Cary. 6969-X
Lady Mary. Henry Alford. 6046-3
Lady Mary Ann. Robert Burns. 6518-X
Lady Mary Ann. Unknown. 6600-3
Lady Mary Villiers. Thomas Carew. 6659-3
Lady Maud's oath. Re. Henry. 6923-1
Lady mine. H.E. Clarke. 6089-7
Lady mine. Herbert Edwin Clarke. 6652-6
Lady moon. Terry B. Dinkel. 6906-1
Lady moon. Kate Kellogg. 6452-3
Lady moon. Richard Monckton Milnes; 1st Baron Houghton. 6242-3,6127-3,6132-X,6466-3,6519-8,6623 ,6131-1,6424-8,6456-6
Lady moon. Christina Georgina Rossetti. 6105-2,6134-6,6466-3,6724-7
Lady Nasturtium. M. Marie Thyng. 6764-6
"A lady non-suited at Diss". Lim_rick:"A lady non-suited at Diss". Unknown. 6811-1
The lady of Albany's lament of King Charles. Unknown (Irish) 6858-8
The lady of Arngosk. Unknown. 6185-0
"The Lady of Belmont looked out to the east". Mary Murray of Murray Hill. Arthur Guiterman. 6773-5
Lady of Castlenoire. Thomas Bailey Aldrich. 6319-5
The lady of Gedo. Unknown (Hungarian). 6670-4
"Lady of heaven and earth, and therewithal". His mother's service to our lady. Dante Gabriel Rossetti. 6875-8
A lady of high dgeree. Unknown (French) 6771-9
The lady of La Garaye, sels. Caroline Elizabeth Sarah Sheridan Norton. 6046-3
Lady of letters. Raymond F. Roseliep. 6282-2
Lady of Lidice. Fray Angelico Chavez. 6282-2
The lady of life. Thomas M. Kettle. 6022-6,6292-X
Lady of O. James J. Galvin. 6282-2
Lady of peace. Fray Angelico Chavez. 6282-2
The lady of Provence. Felicia Dorothea Hemans. 6973-8
The lady of Shalott. Alfred Lord Tennyson. 6154-0,6271-7, 6332-2,6498-1,6657-7,6122 ,6228-8,6726-3,6186-9,6236-9,6473-6,6198 ,6249-0,6239-3,6605-4,6437-X,6488-4, 6655 ,6732-8,6102-8,6110-9,6250-4,6613-5,6383 ,6419-1,6543-0,6723-9,6301-2,6219-9,6252 ,6153-2,6079-X, 6114-1,6560-0,6199-0,6196-6,6430-2
The lady of snows. C.N. Buzzard. 7035-3
"Lady of sorrow! What though laughing blue". Grey. Archibald T. Strong. 6784-0
The lady of the apples. Mildred Whitney Stillman. 6232-6
The lady of the castle, fr. Portrait gallery. Felicia Dorothea Hemans. 6973-8
The lady of the castle. Unknown. 7022-1
The lady of the lake, sels. Sir Walter Scott. 6049-8,6102-8,6198-2,6282-2,6558-5,6605 ,6726-3,6732-8,6180-X, 6484-1,6239-3,6250
The lady of the lake. Unknown. 6057-9

The lady of the lambs. Alice Meynell. 6249-0,6423-X,6301-2
The lady of the land, fr. The earthly paradise. William Morris. 6122-2,6198-2,6473-6,6655-0
A lady of the snows. Harriet Monroe. 6338-1
The lady of the tree. Unknown (Spanish) 6757-3
The lady of vain delight. Giles (the Elder) Fletcher. 6679-8
The lady poverty. Alice Meynell. 6477-9,6250-4,6508-2
The lady poverty. Evelyn Underhill. 6161-3
The lady prayeth the return of her lover... Unknown. 6182-6
"The lady she walk'd in yon wild wood". The bonnie bairns. Allan Cunningham. 6960-6
Lady slippers. Grace A. Schaefer. 6342-X
"A lady somewhat dowdy as to dress". Boston. Berton Braley. 6853-7
Lady sweet pea. M.B. Hill. 6710-7
"A lady that was so fair and bright". Enixa est puerpera. Unknown. 6756-5
"A lady that was so fair...". Unknown. 6334-9
"The lady thus address'd her spouse". Mutual forebearance necessary to...the married state. William Cowper. 6814-6
A lady to a lover. Roden Noel. 6437-X
The lady to her guitar. Emily Bronte. 6123-0
The lady to the lover. Alice Cary. 6865-0;6969-X
The lady turned serving-man. Unknown. 6133-8
Lady Vere De Vere. Alfred Lord Tennyson. 6732-8
Lady Wentworth. Henry Wadsworth Longfellow. 6744-1
"Lady who hold'st on me dominion!". 'Manus animam pinxit'. Francis Thompson. 6942-8
"The lady who intervenes/In the Trinity...". Virgin. Padraic Fallon. 6930-4
"A lady who lived by the Thames". Carolyn Wells. 6724-7
The lady who offers her looking-glass for Venus. Matthew Prior. 6092-7
The lady whose offers her looking-glass to Venus. Matthew Prior. 6934-7
"Lady wind, my lady wind". Unknown. 6363-2
The lady with a train. Unknown. 6675-5
Lady with arrows. Margaret Marks. 6042-0
The lady with the sewing-machine. Edith Sitwell. 6393-4
A lady without paragon. Geoffrey Chaucer. 6881-2
"Lady! helpe, Jesu! mercy! In his utter wretchedness. John Audelay. 6881-2
"Lady! if for the cold and cloudy clime". The prophecy of Dante. George Gordon, 6th Baron Byron. 6945-2
"Lady! it cannot be, but that thine eyes". Sonnet ("Lady! it cannot"). John Milton. 6814-6
"Lady! you ask of me a strain". Reply of the harp. Charles W. Denison. 6755-7
A lady's adieu to her tea-table. Unknown. 6753-0
The lady's dream. Thomas Hood. 6358-6,6219-9
The lady's dressing room. Jonathan Swift. 6380-2
The lady's fan. Unknown. 6057-9
The lady's lamentation. John Gay. 6024-2,6733-6,6092-7
The lady's looking glass. Matthew Prior. 6302-0;6385-3
The lady's receipt for a beau's dress. Unknown. 6157-5
The lady's song. John Dryden. 6315-2,6191-5
The lady's song. John Milton. 6543-0
The lady's third song. William Butler Yeats. 6210-5
The lady's yes. Elizabeth Barrett Browning. 6123-0,6302-0, 6385-3,6438-8,6219-9
"Lady, I bid thee to a sunny dome". Arthur Henry Hallam. 6980-0
"A lady, an expert on skis". Limerick:"A lady, an expert on skis". Unknown. 6811-1
"Lady, around thy throat/Gleameth the one...". Ballade-Lilith. John Cameron Grant. 6770-0
"Lady, how can it chance - yet this we see". To Vitorria Colonna. Michelangelo Buonarroti. 6879-0
"Lady, it is to be presumed". Ben Jonson. 6088-9
"Lady, lady, should you meet". Social note. Dorothy Parker. 6817-0
"Lady, let the rolling drums". Song ("Lady, let the rolling drums"). Alfred Lord Tennyson. 6977-0
"Lady, that in the prime of earliest youth". John Milton. 6122-2
"Lady, the silly flea of all disdained" Unknown. 6380-2
"Lady, through grasses stiff with rime". A winter song.

Herbert Trench. 6877-4
"**Lady,** up to your high and shining crown". Michelangelo Buonarroti. 6325-X
"**Lady,** when I behold the roses sprouting". Unknown. 6187-7, 6189-3
"**Lady,** wouldst thou heiress be". To a cold beauty. Thomas Hood. 6980-0,6974-6
"**Lady,** you are with beauties so enriched". Song ("Lady"). Francis Davison. 6182-6
"**Lady,** your head is on upside down". After Chagall. Rene Wenger. 6966-5
"**Lady,** your heart has turned to dust". Lament. Scharmel Iris. 6897-9
The **lady-bird** and the ant. Lydia Huntley Sigourney. 6131-1
"**Lady-bird,** lady-bird, fly away home." Unknown. 6452-3
The **lady-bug** and the ant. Unknown. 6165-6
Lady-probationer, fr. In hospital. William Ernest Henley. 6250-4
A **lady.** Amy Lowell. 6102-8,6076-5,6464-7,6348-9,6556-2, 6348-9
A **lady.** Edgar Lee Masters. 6033-1
The **lady.** Elizabeth J. Coatsworth. 6861-8
Ladybird. Caroline Anne Bowles Southey. 6132-X,6623-2,6131-1,6373-X,6424-8
Ladybird's race. Campbell Rae-Brown. 6681-X
"**Ladybird,** ladybird, fly away home". The ladybird. Unknown. 6937-1
Ladybug, ladybug. Unknown. 6373-X
Ladye Chapel at Eden Hall. Eleanor C. Donnelly. 6172-9
Ladye Maude. Cora Fabri. 6876-6
The **ladye's** rock. E.J. Armstrong. 6518-X
"**Ladyes,** you yt seeme soe nice." Unknown. 6563-5
Laertes, fr. The Odyssey. Homer. 6435-3
Lafler, Henry Andersen
    The white feet of Atthis. 6252-0
Laforgue, Jules
    Albums. 6351-9
    Complaint of forgetting the dead. 6351-9
    Complaint of the lad with heart-disease. 6351-9
    Complainte. 6801-4
    Dialogue. 6801-4
    Dialogue before sunrise. 6351-9
    Gulf lightning. 6351-9
    Lament at the day's end. Cecily Mackworth (tr.). 6343-8
    Lament of the forgetfulness of the dead. Cecily Mackworth (tr.). 6343-8
    Our little helpmeet. 6351-9
Lagerlof, Selma
    The child of peace. Charles Wharton Stork (tr.). 6045-5
"The **laggard** winter ebbed so slow". Flood-tide of flowers in Holland. Henry Van Dyke. 6961-4
The **laggards..** Edwin Arlington Robinson. 6038-2
Lago Varese. Sir Henry Taylor. 6624-0
"**Laid** on thine altar, O Lord divine!" Unknown. 6238-5
Laidlaw, Louise Burton
    Ours is the song. 6042-0
    Rise Damocles. 6761-1
Laidlaw, William
    Her bonnie black e'e. 6960-6
    Lucy's flittin'. 6180-X,6219-9,6240-7,6600-3
The **laidley** worm o' Spindleston-Heighs. Unknown. 6613-5
Laight, Frederick E.
    Soliloquy. 6021-8
Laight, Herbert
    "Sence Sally's been to Europe." 6687-9
Laighton, Albert
    Autumn. 6373-X;6529-5
    The missing ships. 6688-7
    Under the leaves. 6597-X
Laighton, Oscar
    The clover blossoms. 6066-8
Laili disconsolate. Nizami. 6448-5
The **laily** worm and the machrel of the sea. Unknown. 6154-0, 6485-2,6125-7
The **laily** worm. Unknown. 6315-2
Laing, Alexander
    Alone. 7019-1
    David today. 6979-7
    Ae happy hour. 6180-X
    Jock, Rab and Tam. 6233-4

    My ain wife. 6627-5,6656-9
    The standard on the braes o' Mar. 6180-X
The **laird** o Drum. Unknown. 6185-0
The **laird** o' Cockpen. Carolina Oliphant, Baroness Nairne. 6089-7,6086-2,6219-9,6518-X
The **laird** o' Cockpen. Unknown. 6328-4
The **laird** o' drum. Unknown. 6055-2,6056-0,6518-X
The **laird** o' Logie. Unknown. 6185-0,6518-X
The **laird** o'cockpen (additional stanzas) Susan Ferrier. 6760-3
The **laird** of Schelynlaw. John Veitch. 6656-9
The **laird** of Waristoun. Unknown. 6185-0,6518-X
Laird, William
    Traumerei at Ostendorff's. 6897-9
    A very old song. 6897-9
The **laird.** Jeffrey Inglis. 6331-4,6439-6
Lais. Hilda ("H.D.") Doolittle. 6010-2
Lais growing old. Plato. 6732-8
Lais' mirror. Plato. 6435-3
Lak of steadfastnesse. Geoffrey Chaucer. 6150-8
The **lake** -- To ---. Edgar Allan Poe. 6176-1,6641-0,6333-0, 6288-1
"A **lake** and a fairy boat". Song for music. Thomas Hood. 6974-6
"A **lake** and a fairy book". Song ("A lake"). Thomas Hood. 6075-7,6271-7,6466-3,6421-3
The **lake** at Zurich. James Cochrane. 6749-2
Lake Como. Walter Malone. 6624-0
Lake Como. William Wordsworth. 6749-2
Lake Como (2). William Wordsworth. 6749-2
Lake Coriskin. Sir Walter Scott. 6543-0
Lake Coriskin, fr. The lord of the isles. Sir Walter Scott. 6832-4
"The **lake** beneath, and the city". Lucerne, fr. Pictures by the way. John Nichol. 6819-7
"The **lake** comes throbbing in with voice of...". A lake memory, fr. The century. William Wilfred Campbell. 6656-9,7041-8
Lake garden. Hamish Maclaren. 6893-6
Lake George. Arthur Cleveland Coxe. 6484-1
Lake Glamour. Vincent O'Sullivan. 6174-5
The **lake** has burst. Bryan Waller ("Barry Cornwall") Procter. 6980-0
Lake Huron. William Wilfred Campbell. 6591-0,6592-2
"The **lake** has drawn the last gold from the sun". Marsh twilight. Daniel Whitehead Hicky. 6841-3
"The **lake** is black". Ed's boots. Brad Gooch. 7003-5
"The **lake** is calm; and, calm, the skies". The heart and nature. Owen (Edward Bulwer-Lytton, Earl Lytton) Meredith. 6844-8
The **lake** island of Innisfree. William Butler Yeats. 6044-7, 6174-5,6236-9,6311-4,6477-9,6507 ,6289-X,6437-X,6476-0,6484-1,6501-5,6527 ,6332-2,6423-X,6473-6,6634-8, 6138-9,6154 ,6726-3,6732-8,6723-9,6655-0,6508-2,6252 ,6439-6,6639-9,6301-2,6102-8,6581-3,6250
The **lake** isle of Innisfree. William Butler Yeats. 6861-8
Lake Itasca. Gertie M. Orcutt. 6342-X
Lake Leman. George Gordon, 6th Baron Byron. 6331-4,6385-3, 6196-6
Lake Leman and Chillon. Henry Morford. 6749-2
Lake Leman, fr. Before dawn. Harold Monro. 6234-2;6331-4
Lake Maggiore. William Wordsworth. 6749-2
Lake Mahopac-Saturday night. George A. Baker. 6187-7
A **lake** memory, fr. The century. William Wilfred Campbell. 6656-9,7041-8
Lake of Como. William Wordsworth. 6624-0,6631-3
The **lake** of Constance. Gustave Schwab. 6749-2
The **lake** of Gaube. Algernon Charles Swinburne. 6655-0
The **lake** of Geneva. George Gordon, 6th Baron Byron. 6600-3, 6543-0,6631-3
The **lake** of Geneva. Samuel Rogers. 6749-2
The **lake** of Geneva. Samuel Rogers. 6484-1
The **lake** of Geneva. Samuel Rogers. 6749-2
The **lake** of Geneva. James Thomson. 6749-2
"A **lake** of sapphire lies on Evans' height". Sempiternal. Maude Freeman Osborne. 6836-7
The **lake** of the dismal swamp. Thomas Moore. 6302-0,6385-3, 6438-8,6484-1,6219-9
The **lake** of the fallen moon. Frank Ernest Hill. 6039-0
Lake of the isles. Ethlyn Wightman Whittier. 6342-X

LAKE

Lake of the woods. Natalie Fitz-Patrick. 6342-X
The lake of Van. Raffi. 6050-1
The lake of Zurich. Friedrich Gottlieb Klopstock. 6749-2
Lake Ozatonka. Madeline Weaver. 6342-X
Lake Pepin. Nell Mabey. 6342-X
Lake Saganaga. Leslie L. Code. 6342-X
Lake Saratoga. John Godfrey Saxe. 6415-9,6484-1
Lake scene. Mary Bradley Bramhall. 6764-6
Lake scene in western Canada. E.J. Chapman. 6591-0,6592-2
Lake Superior. Samuel G. Goodrich. 6752-2
Lake Superior fishermen. Helen Jenswold Dahle. 6342-X
Lake Uri. William Wordsworth. 6749-2
"The lake with placid depth of calm". The deserted mountain way. William White. 6868-5
"The lake's sail-speckled blue expanse". Contentment. Richard Lawson Gales. 6950-9
Lake, George Burt
    Birth. 6482-5
    Overflow. 6789-1
    Too swift the night. 6789-1
The lake-dweller. Cale Young Rice. 6184-2
Lake-song. Jean Starr Untermeyer. 6019-6
The lake. Matthew Arnold. 6947-9
The lake. Helen Birch-Bartlett. 6037-4
The lake. Deborah Kleinert. 6847-2
The lake. Ena Limebeer. 6072-2
The lake. Caroline Elizabeth Sarah Sheridan Norton. 6331-4;6374-8
The lake. Sir John Collings ("Solomon Eagle") Squire. 6250-4
The lake. Charles Tennyson Turner. 7015-9
Lakeman, Leona
    The hush of eventide. 6894-4
The lakeside. John Greenleaf Whittier. 6126-5
Lal of Kilrudden. Bliss Carman and Richard Hovey. 6890-1
"Lala, 'sana lwam!". Francis Carey ("Jan van Avond") Slater. 6591-0,6592-9
Lalila, to the Ferengi lover. Laurence (Adele Florence Nicolson) Hope. 6856-1
Lalla rookh, sels. Thomas Moore. 6049-8,6198-2,6232-6,6469-6,6196-6
Lallay, my child, and weep no more. Unknown. 6756-5
Lally, Michael
    "For some of us" 7003-5
Lamartine, Alphonse Marie Louis de
    Adieux au college de Belley. 6718-2
    "Beaute, secret d'en haut, rayon, divin embleme" 6801-4
    The cedars of Lebanon. Tom Dutt (tr.). 7039-6
    "Eh! qui m'emportera sur des flots..." 6801-4
    L'enthousiasme. 6801-4
    L'hymne de la nuit. 6801-4
    L'isolement. 6801-4
    Le lac. 6801-4
    Le soir. 6801-4
Lamb et al., Thelma (tr.)
    Second dream. Bernardo Ortiz de Montellano, 6759-X
"Lamb of God, who takest away". Little Saint Caecilia. Margaret Holmes. 6924-X
Lamb, Cecelia Slawik
    Celestial food. 6249-0
Lamb, Charles
    Acrostic ("Go, little poem"). 6724-7
    A child. 6934-7
    Childhood. 6772-7
    Choosing a name. 6242-3
    Death of Coleridge. 6304-7
    Epicedium - going or gone. 6802-2
    The family name. 6980-0
    A farewell to tobacco, sels. 6934-7
    A farewell to tobacco. 6092-7,6219-9,6278-4,6089-7;6200-8;6453-1;6302-0;6385-3;6732
    The frugal snail. 6529-5
    The grandame. 6086-2
    Harmony in unlikeness. 6086-2
    Hester. 6385-3,6246-6,6315-2,6600-3,6250-4,6301-2,6092-7,6086-2,6737-9,6641-0
    Hester, sels. 6317-9
    The housekeeper. 6302-0;6385-3;6498-1;6597-X;6600-3,6421-3,6424-8,6639-9,6457-4
    Hypochondriacus. 6802-2
    "I have had playmates, I have had companions". 6187-7
    In my own album. 6086-2
    In the album of Lucy Barton. 6297-0
    In the churchyard. 6304-7
    Innocence. 7015-9
    Lines on the celebrated picture by Leonardo Da Vinci... 6282-2
    Newton's Principia. 6302-0
    Nonsense verses. 6089-7;6732-8
    Ode to the treadmill. 6787-5
    The old familiar faces. 6122-2;6240-7;6246-6;6302-0;6385-3;6481 ,6086-2,6102-8,6199-0,6396-9,6513-9,6186-9;6198-2;6473-6;6486-8;6600-3;6085 ,6219-9,6301-2,6304-7,6250-4,6464-7,6732-8,6723-9,6543-0,6737-9,6560-0,6084 ,6122-2;6240-7;6246-6;6302-0;6385-3;6481 ,6086-2,6102-8,6199-0,6396-9,6513-9,6186-9;6198-2;6473-6;6486-8;6600-3;6085 ,6219-9,6301-2,6304-7,6250-4,6464-7,6732-8,6723-9,6543-0,6737-9,6560-0,6084
    On an infant dying as soon as born. 6102-8,6102-8,6086-2,6246-6,6365-9
    On rising with the lark. 6304-7
    On the disappointment of the Whig associates... 6278-4
    Parental recollections. 6078-1,6092-7
    Patience with love. 6078-1
    Penny pieces. 6295-4
    Pindaric ode to the treadmill. 6760-3
    Prince Dorus. 6295-4,6808-1,6018-8
    Sonnet ("We were two"). 6980-0
    A sonnet on Christian names. 6934-7
    The three friends. 6502-3
    To Hester. 6604-6
    To Hester Savory. 6874-X
    To John Lamb, Esq. 6385-3
    Triumph of the whale. 6833-2
    A vision of repentance. 6086-2
    We cherish dreams. 6304-7
    Work. 6832-4
    Written at Cambridge (1819). 6934-7
Lamb, Charles and Mary
    The beasts in the tower. 6295-4
    Beauty and the beast. 6295-4
    A birthday thought. 6295-4
    The blackbird. 6242-3
    The boy and the skylark. 6459-0
    Charity. 6295-4
    Cleanliness. 6519-8
    Clock striking. 6295-4
    The coffee slips. 6295-4
    The confidant. 6295-4
    Conquest of prejudice. 6295-4
    Crumbs to the birds. 6018-8
    David. 6295-4
    David in the cave of Adullam. 6295-4
    The dessert. 6295-4
    Eyes. 6295-4
    The fairy. 6295-4
    Feigned courage. 6233-4;6239-3;6105-2
    The force of habit. 6295-4
    Going into breeches. 6233-4;6242-3;6519-8;6105-2
    Good temper. 6295-4
    The great grandfather. 6295-4
    Home delights. 6295-4
    Incorrect speaking. 6295-4
    The king and queen of hearts. 6295-4
    The magpie's nest. 6519-8
    Moderation in diet. 6295-4
    My birthday. 6295-4
    The new-born infant. 6233-4
    On a picture of the finding of Moses... 6295-4
    The orange. 6459-0
    Parental recollections. 6233-4,6078-1
    The peach. 6295-4
    Penny pieces. 6295-4,6295-2
    Prince Dorus. 6295-4,6808-1
    Queen Oriana's dream. 6295-4
    The rainbow. 6295-4
    The Spartan boy. 6295-4;6502-3
    Thoughtless cruelty. 6295-4
    Time spent in dress. 6295-4

To a young lady, on being too fond of music. 6295-4
Why not do it, sir, to-day? 6295-4
Lamb, Louis Albert
  Beth-El. 6274-1
Lamb, Mary
  A child ("A child's a plaything for an hour"). 6533-3, 6086-2
  The children and the snake. 6134-6
  Choosing a name. 6078-1,6127-3,6240-7,6302-0,6101-1, 6424-8,6808-1
  Choosing a profession. 6105-2
  Feigned courage. 6772-7
  Maternal lady with the virgin grace. 6282-2
  The new-born infant. 6772-7
Lamb, William. See Melbourne, Viscount
The lamb-child. John Banister Tabb. 6216-4,6608-9
The lamb. William Blake. 6024-2,6075-7,6078-1,6102-8,6 34-6,6154 ,6086-2,6104-4,6152-4,6195-0,6114-1,6131 , 6183-4,6216-4,6242-3,6315-2,6337-3,6339 ,6371-3,6430-2,6424-8,6456-6,6510-X,6454 ,6418-3,6481-7,6519-8, 6604-6,6726-3,6730 ,6630-7,6639-9,6543-0,6638-0,6645-3,6723 ,6634-8,6964-9
The lamb. Kate Greenaway. 6452-3,6135-4
Lambert, Clara
  Skyscraper is a city's house. 6891-X
  Summon the workers. 6891-X
Lambkins. Christina Georgina Rossetti. 6937-1
Lambro's return. George Gordon, 6th Baron Byron. 6302-0
Lambs. Katharine (Hinkson) Tynan. 6244-X
Lambs at play. Robert Bloomfield. 6302-0;6385-3
Lambs in the meadow. Laurence Alma Tadema. 6519-8
A lame beggar. John Donne. 6491-4
The lame boy and the fairy. Vachel Lindsay. 6421-3
The lame shepherd. Katharine Lee Bates. 6746-8,6608-9
"Lame, impotent conclusion to youth's dreams". Vanitas vanitatis. Wilfrid Scawen Blunt. 7015-9
Lamennais, Robert de
  Brotherhood. 6420-5
LaMere, Ken
  Army. 6883-9
  Ignorance. 6883-9
  The way it is. 6883-9
Lament. Wilfred Wilson Gibson. 6102-8
Lament. Amanda Benjamin Hall. 7038-8
Lament. Thomas Hardy. 6879-0
Lament. Scharmel Iris. 6897-9
Lament. Walter Savage Landor. 6102-8
Lament. Denis Florence MacCarthy. 6090-0;6096-X
Lament. Frances Mayo. 6895-2
Lament. Edna St. Vincent Millay. 6538-4,6300-4,6464-7
Lament. Jacqueline Edith Morand. 6764-6
Lament. John Richard Moreland. 6039-0
Lament. Theodore Morrison. 6879-0
Lament. Roden Noel. 6097-8,6656-9
Lament. Eden Phillpotts. 7007-8
Lament. Pablo de (Carlos Diaz Loyola) Rokha. 6642-9
Lament. Douglas Stewart. 6349-7
Lament ("Chaste maids which haunt..."). William Drummond of Hawthornden. 6315-2
Lament ("Day droops..."). Francis Carey ("Jan van Avond") Slater. 6800-6
Lament ("He is gone with his blue eyes.") Isabella Holt. 6030-7
Lament ("I loved him not;..."). Walter Savage Landor. 6600-3
A lament ("It's hard to be a turnip") Mrs. A.J. Wirtz. 6270-9
Lament ("Lo, now he shineth yonder.") Hugh Holland. 6472-8
Lament ("Mild is the parting year, and sweet"). Walter Savage Landor. 6102-8
Lament ("My man is a bone ringed with weed") Brenda Chamberlain. 6379-9
A lament ("O world! O life! O time!"). Percy Bysshe Shelley. 6102-8,6339-X,6122-2,6315-2,6328-4,6726 , 6271-7,6154-0,6604-6,6634-8,6138-9,6246 ,6302-0,6385-3,6430-2,6250-4,6192-3,6199 ,6153-2,6219-9,6543-0
Lament ("Snows cloaked"). Gudmundur Gudmundsson. 6283-0
A lament ("The dream is over"). Denis Florence MacCarthy. 6174-5
A lament ("The merry, merry lark was up and singing"). Charles Kingsley. 6123-0
Lament ("The Sioux are singing songs"). Unknown (American Indian) 6396-9
Lament ("We who are left, how shall we look again"). Wilfred Wilson Gibson. 6477-9,6542-2
Lament ("When the folk of my household.") Edward Walsh. 6437-X
Lament ("When twilight falls..."). Francis Carey ("Jan van Avond") Slater. 6800-6
A lament ("Youth's bright palace.") Denis Florence MacCarthy. 6090-0
Lament at the day's end. Jules Laforgue. 6343-8
Lament for a dead cow. Francis Carey ("Jan van Avond") Slater. 6625-9
Lament for a dead crow. Francis Carey ("Jan van Avond") Slater. 6788-3
Lament for a little child. Roden Noel. 6873-1
Lament for a lover. Maurice Carpenter. 6895-2
Lament for a sailor. Paul Dehn. 6666-6
Lament for Absalom. Nathaniel Parker Willis. 6304-7
A lament for Adam. Benjamin Franklin Taylor. 6815-4
Lament for Adonis. Bion. 6435-3
Lament for Astrophel. Mary Sidney Herbert, Countess of Pembroke. 6935-5
Lament for Astrophel (Sir Philip Sidney). Matthew Royden. 6600-3
Lament for Banba. Egan O'Rahilly. 7039-6
Lament for better or worse. Gene Baro. 6218-0
Lament for Bion. Moschus. 7039-6
Lament for Bion. Moschus. 6385-3
Lament for Cael. Sean O'Faolain. 6582-1
Lament for Chaucer. Thomas Hoccleve. 6483-3,6659-3
Lament for Corc and Niall of the nine hostages. Torna (atr.) 6930-4
Lament for Culloden. Robert Burns. 6188-5,6246-6,6088-9
Lament for Flodden. Jane [or Jean] Elliot. 6188-5,6246-5, 6600-3
Lament for Glasgerion. Elinor Wylie. 6531-7
Lament for Glencairn. Robert Burns. 6304-7
A lament for Ireland ("I do not know of anything...") Shemus Cartan. 6244-X
Lament for James, Earl of Glencairn. Robert Burns. 6438-8
Lament for Lafayette. Unknown. 6486-8
Lament for lost love. Genaro Estrada. 6759-X
Lament for Macleod of Raasay. Neil Munro. 6269-5
A lament for Meliboeus. Thomas Watson. 6191-5
Lament for my brother, sels. Hans Egon Holthusen. 6643-7
A lament for Our Lady's shrine at Walsingham. Philip Howard; 1st Earl of Arundel. 6641-0
A lament for our lady's shrine at Walsingham. Unknown. 6282-2
Lament for Pasiphae. Robert Graves. 6210-5
A lament for Percy Bysshe Shelley. William Edmonstoune Aytoun. 6948-7
Lament for Prince Henry. Thomas Campion. 6641-0
Lament for Robin Hood. Anthony Munday. 6334-9
Lament for Spain. Jessica Powers. 6761-1
Lament for summer. Mabel Crehore Greene. 6841-3
Lament for tabby. Unknown. 6120-6
A lament for tall ships. Robert L. Miller. 6662-3
Lament for the death of Eoghan Ruadh (Owen Roe) O'Neil. Thomas Osborne Davis. 6858-8
Lament for the death of Eoghan Ruadh O'Neill. Thomas Osborne Davis. 6244-X
Lament for the death of Thomas Davis. Sir Samuel Ferguson. 6930-4
Lament for the Gordons. David Martin. 6895-2
Lament for the great yachts. Patric Dickinson. 6257-1
Lament for the Lord Maxwell. Unknown. 6859-6
The lament for the Makaris quhen he was seik, sels. William Dunbar. 6934-7
Lament for the Makaris... William Dunbar. 6150-8,6586-4, 6022-6,6430-2,6472-8,6125-9,6023
Lament for the Milesians. Thomas Osborne Davis. 6858-8
Lament for the poets: 1916 Francis Ledwidge. 6930-4
Lament for the poets: 1916. Francis Ledwidge. 6872-3,7039-6
Lament for the poets: 1916. Francis Ledwidge. 6292-X
A lament for the priory of Walsingham. Unknown. 6125-7
A lament for the red earl. Richard Mahony. 6090-0

LAMENT 926

Lament for the sailing of the crusade. Rinaldo D'Aquino. 6325-X
A lament for the summer. Adelaide Anne Procter. 6957-6
A lament for the Tyronian and Tyrconnellian... James Clarence Mangan. 6174-5
Lament for Thomas Davis. Sir Samuel Ferguson. 6090-0,6244-X
A lament from the dead. W.E. K. 7031-0
A lament in exile (Psalm 137) Bible. 6153-2
Lament in old age. Rudagi. 6448-5
A lament in spring. Thomas Lodge. 6191-5
Lament of a foresaken cat. Elizabeth Harcourt Mitchell. 6699-2
The lament of a left-over doll. Unknown. 6629-1
Lament of a man for his son. Unknown (Paiute Indian) 7039-6,6602-X
Lament of a neglected boss. Eugene Field. 6949-5
Lament of a New England art student. Lee Wilson Dodd. 6506-6
Lament of a Swiss minstrel over the ruins of Goldau. John Neal. 6752-2
Lament of Adonis, sels. Bion. 7039-6
The lament of Aideen for Oscar. John Todhunter. 6174-5
Lament of Attila. Katherine Kelley Taylor. 6906-1
Lament of Columbine. Lucy Winn. 6818-9
The lament of David over Saul and Jonathan. Bible. 6228-8, 6396-9
The lament of David, fr. Samuel. Bible. 6334-9
The lament of Edward Blastock. Edith Sitwell. 7000-0
The lament of Eve. Unknown. 6022-6
Lament of Fand at parting from Cuchulain. Unknown. 6090-0
The lament of Flora Macdonald. James Hogg. 6180-X,6088-9
Lament of granite. David Ross. 6513-9
The lament of Ian the Proud. William ("Fiona Macleod") Sharp. 6655-0
The lament of Jacob Gray. H. Elliott McBride. 6045-1
The lament of Llywarch Hen [Llywarch the Aged]. Felicia Dorothea Hemans. 6973-8
The lament of Maev Leith-Dherg. Unknown. 6930-4
Lament of Mary, Queen of Scots, on the approach of spring. Robert Burns. 6188-5,6438-8,6088-9,6543-0
Lament of Morian Shehone for Miss Mary Bourke. Unknown. 6174-5
Lament of O'Sullivan Bear. Unknown (Irish) 6244-X
The lament of Queen Maev. Unknown. 6873-1
Lament of Richard during his imprisonment. Richard I; King of England. 6188-5
The lament of Tasso. George Gordon, 6th Baron Byron. 6980-0,6945-2,6828-6
The lament of the border cattle thief. Rudyard Kipling. 6810-3
Lament of the border widow. Unknown. 6180-X,6395-0,6153-2, 6219-9,6067-6,6737 ,6271-7,6302-0,6385-3,6055-2,6518-X,6098
The lament of the damned in hell. Edward Young. 6931-2
The lament of the deer. Angus Mackenzie. 6873-1
Lament of the evicted Irish peasant. Unknown. 6858-8
The lament of the flowers. Jones Very. 6333-0
Lament of the forgetfulness of the dead. Jules Laforgue. 6343-8
Lament of the frontier guard. Li Po. 6665-8
Lament of the Irish emigrant. Helen Selina Sheridan; Lady Dufferin. 6302-0,6328-4,6328-4,6434-X,6656-9,6240-7, 6244-X,6402-7,6486-8,6219-9,6543-0,6658-5
Lament of the Irish maiden. Denny Lane. 6090-0,6174-5
Lament of the mangaire sugach. Andrew Magrath. 6930-4
The lament of the mole-catcher. Osbert Sitwell. 6872-3
Lament of the old magician. Frederic Prokosch. 6782-4
Lament of the old woman remembering her youth. Francois Villon. 6227-X
The lament of the Outalissi. Thomas Campbell. 6543-0
Lament of the peri for hinda. Thomas Moore. 6630-5
Lament of the players. Roland Burke Hennessy. 7001-9
The lament of the poet. James Reaney. 6767-0
Lament of the steam shovel. Pier Paolo Pasolini. 6803-0
Lament of the veld. Beatrice Marian Bromley. 6800-6
Lament of the Wazir Dandan for Prince Sharkan. Unknown (Arabic) 7039-6
Lament of the widowed inebriate. Augustine Joseph Hickey Duganne. 6685-2

The lament of Thel. William Blake. 6634-8
Lament of Tumadir Al-Khanasa for her brother. Unknown (Arabic) 7039-6
Lament of Virginius. John Webster. 6385-3
Lament over Saul, fr. Samuel. Bible. 6087-0
Lament over Sir Phillip Sidney. Unknown. 6087-0
Lament over the heroes fallen in the battle... Karekin Srvanstian. 6050-1
"Lament, fair hearted...", fr. Ode to music. Robert Bridges. 6487-6
Lament, fr. Cymbeline. William Shakespeare. 6208-3
"Lament, lament, Sir Isaac Heard". Epitaph on a tufthunter. Thomas Moore. 6760-3
A lament. Thomas Lovell Beddoes. 6908-8
A lament. William Drummond of Hawthornden. 6737-9
A lament. Denis Florence MacCarthy. 6292-X
A lament. Thomas Nashe. 6935-5
A lament. Percy Bysshe Shelley. 6935-5
A lament. Percy Bysshe Shelley. 6125-7
The lamentable ballad of the bloody brook. Edward Everett Hale. 6946-0
The lamentable ballad of the foundling of Shoreditch. William Makepeace Thackeray. 6278-4
Lamentation. Harold LaMont Otey. 6870-7
Lamentation. Lynette Roberts. 6360-8
Lamentation for Celin. Unknown. 6271-7
The lamentation for Celin. Unknown (Spanish) 6757-3,7039-6
The lamentation of Aga. William Waterfield. 6591-0,6592-9
The lamentation of Beckles. Unknown. 6586-4
The lamentation of Chloris. Unknown. 6157-5
Lamentation of David over Saul and Jonathan. George Sandys. 6848-0
The lamentation of David over Saul and Jonathan his son. George Wither. 6848-0
The lamentation of Don Roderick. Unknown (Spanish) 6757-3
The lamentation of Felix M'Carthy. Unknown (Irish) 6858-8
The lamentation of Hugh Reynolds. Unknown. 6174-5
Lamentation over Jerusalem. Henry Hart Milman. 6980-0
A lamentation. Thomas Campion. 6179-6
The lamentations of Jeremiah. George Wither. 6848-0
The lamentations, fr. The Iliad. Homer. 6435-3
Lamia. John Keats. 6199-0,6430-2,6198-2,6430-2,6199-0
Lamia, sel. John Keats. 6958-4
Lamia, sels. John Keats. 6196-6
Lamilia's song. Robert Greene. 6436-1
Lamkin. Unknown. 6055-2,6056-0,6058-7,6185-0,6067-6,6518
Lamkin, Eleanore Randall
    To Stephen Collins Foster. 6750-6
Lamont, Alexander
    The round of life. 6414-0
Lamont, Margaret I.
    Protest. 6879-0
    To Elisabeth Morrow Morgan. 6879-0
The lamp flower. Margaret Cecilia Furse. 6477-9
"The lamp must be replenished, but even then". Manfred. George Gordon, 6th Baron Byron. 6110-9,6196-6,6438-3, 6828-6
The lamp of Greece. Laurence Binyon. 6783-2
The lamp of life. Amy Lowell. 6337-3
The lamp of poor souls. Marjorie L.C. Pickthall. 6115-X
Lamp of reason. Edward R. Huxley. 6885-5
"The lamp of valor flickered low". Alone. Alexander Laing. 7019-1
The lamp on the prairie. Phoebe Cary. 6969-X
Lamp posts. Helen Hoyt. 6808-1
lamp's shrine, fr. The house of life. Dante Gabriel Rossetti. 6250-4
The lamp. Sara Teasdale. 6289-X,6250-4,6393-4
The lamp. Henry Vaughan. 6563-5
The lamp. Charles Whitehead. 6437-X
Lampert, Jack
    Great-granddad. 6594-5
Lamplight. May Wedderburn Cannan. 7029-9
"The lamplight's shaded rose". Homes. Margaret Widdemer. 7027-2
The lamplighter.. Robert Louis Stevenson. 6105-2,6132-X, 6242-3,6421-3,6639-9,6638
The lamplighter. Walter De La Mare. 6596-1
The lamplighter. Seumas (James Starkey) O'Sullivan. 6072-2
The lamplighter. Robert Louis Stevenson. 6891-

Lampman, Archibald
  After rain. 6115-X
  Among the millet. 6433-7
  April in the hills. 6115-X,6253-9
  April night. 6115-X
  Between the rapids. 7041-8
  Clouds. 6795-6
  Comfort. 7041-8
  A forest path in winter. 7035-3
  The frogs. 6433-7
  Heat. 6021-8,6433-7,6115-X,5446-9,6656-9
  Heat. 7041-8
  In absence. 6620-8
  In March. 6115-X
  A January morning. 6021-8,6115-X,6723-9
  Knowledge. 7041-8
  Knowledge. 6433-7
  The larger life. 6433-7
  The largest life. 6843-X
  The largest life. 6115-X
  Life and nature. 6021-8,6446-9
  The little handmaiden. 6797-2
  Midnight. 6021-8,6446-9
  Midsummer night. 6433-7;6501-5
  Morning on the Lievre. 6797-2
  Morning on the Lievre. 6115-X
  Oeccavi, domine. 6337-3
  On the companionship with nature. 6510-4
  One day. 7041-8
  Outlook. 7041-8
  Perfect love. 6620-8
  A prayer ("O earth"). 6433-7
  A prayer. 6433-7
  The railway station. 7041-8
  The railway station. 6115-X
  September. 6433-7,6446-9
  Snowbirds. 6433-7
  The spirit of the house. 6620-8
  A summer evening. 6021-8,6446-9
  There is a beauty. 6337-3
  The truth. 6433-7,6115-X
  War. 6115-X
  The weaver. 7041-8
  Winter evening. 6115-X
  Winter recalled. 7035-3
  Winter uplands. 7035-3
Lamprocles
  A national anthem. Cecil Maurice Bowra (tr.). 6435-3
Lamps. Alfred Noyes. 6151-6
Lamps. Unknown. 6706-9
Lamps and lanterns. E.H. Visiak. 6884-7
"The lamps gleamed out along the well-screened decks". Alfred Noyes. 6298-9
"The lamps were thick; the air was hot". In the morning, fr. Studies for pictures. Bayard Taylor. 6976-2
"Lamps, lamps! Lamps ev'rywhere!". Street lamps. John Galsworthy. 6888-X
Lampson, Robin
  Even the bitter and difficult. 6042-0
  Sometimes I envy the blind. 6761-1
  Young laughter. 6750-6
Lampton, William J.
  Castles in the air. 6274-1
  Cupid's casuistry. 6277-6
  Fallen. 6698-4
  A final day dialogue. 7021-3
  If one has failed. 6211-3
  In memory of Nancy Hanks. 7010-8
  A lightening story. 6415-9
  Lincoln. 6708-5
  The new version. 6089-7;6440-X
  Once. 6682-8
  Opportunity talks. 6274-1
Lamson, Lina R.
  Spring is on its way. 6764-6
  You ask for peace. 6764-6
Lan Nguyen: the uniform of death 1971 David Mura. 6790-5
The lanawn shee. Francis Ledwidge. 6812-X
A Lancashire doxology. Dinah Maria Mulock Craik. 6219-9
Lancashire lads. Unknown. 6157-5

A Lancaster doxology. Dinah Maria Mulock Craik. 6302-0;6385-3
Lancaster, A.E.
  The little church round the corner. 6045-1;6273-3
Lancaster, Joyce
  Absence. 6850-2
  At the edge of the garden. 6850-2
  Barriers. 6850-2
  Exhilaration. 6850-2
  Harvest. 6850-2
  I shall go back. 6850-2
  In Grantan wood. 6850-2
  Late blossom. 6850-2
  Meditation. 6850-2
  Melody in black. 6850-2
  Night mood. 6850-2
  Past and future. 6850-2
  Portrait of an afternoon. 6850-2
  Preference. 6850-2
  Retreat. 6850-2
  Romance is gone. 6850-2
  Snow ghosts. 6850-2
  To Emily Dickinson. 6850-2
  To K.E.R. 6850-2
  Tryst. 6850-2
  The untrodden road. 6850-2
Lancelot and Elaine, fr. Idylls of the king. Alfred Lord Tennyson. 6208-3,6473-6,6657-7,6264-4,6655-0
Lances. C.T. Lanham. 6039-0
Land. Helen Hunt Jackson. 7041-8
The land (spring). Victoria Mary Sackville-West. 6354-3
A land across the sea, fr. The earthly paradise. William Morris. 6656-9
Land and sea. Unknown (Greek) 6435-3
The land beyond the sea. Frederick William Faber. 6271-7
A land dirge. John Webster. 6228-8,6246-6,6315-2,6737-9
The land God forgot. Robert Service. 6159-1
"The land for which our valiant fahters whilom". July 4, 1870 James Abraham Martling. 6952-5
Land grant. Josephine Miles. 6640-2
The land horse compared to the sea horse. Vachel Lindsay. 6345-4
"The land is in gloom and the cloud-banks...". My kingdom. Jon Olafsson. 6854-5
"The land it is the landlord's". The song of the wage-slave. Ernest Jones. 7009-4
The land o' dreams. Marian Osborne. 6797-2
The land o' the leal. Carolina Oliphant, Baroness Nairne. 6089-7,6302-0,6385-3,6192-3,6560-0,6219 ,6102-8,6138-9,6732-8,6600-3,6332-2,6138 ,6271-7,6198-2,6019-6, 6543-0,6737-9,6086 ,6302-0,6385-3,6337-3,6486-8,6246-6,6075
Land of beginning again. Louisa Fletcher Tarkington. 6714-X,6964-9
The land of beyond. Robert Service. 6159-1
The land of Biscay. Alfred Edward Housman. 6536-8
The land of Cokaygne. Unknown. 6930-4
The land of counterpane. Robert Louis Stevenson. 6242-3, 6466-3,6732-8,6656-9
"A land of deathful sleep, where fitful dreams". Namaqualand. William Charles Scully. 6800-6
"Land of departed fame! whose classic plains". The restoration of the works of art to Italy. Felicia Dorothea Hemans. 6973-8
Land of destiny. Catherine Parmenter. 6449-3
"A land of dreams and sleep, a poppied land!". Nubia. Bayard Taylor. 6976-2
The land of dreams. William Blake. 6134-6,6186-9,6233-4, 6533-3,6086-2,6114
The land of dreams. Felicia Dorothea Hemans. 6973-8
The land of dreams. William Archer Way. 6800-6
The land of eternal summer. John Milton. 6189-3
The land of faery. Edmund Spenser. 6793-X
The land of fancy. Ethel Ursula Foran. 6789-1
The land of France. Sir Edmund Gosse. 6331-4
"Land of gold! thy sisters greet thee". California. Lydia Huntley Sigourney. 6946-0
Land of heart's desire. Marjory Kennedy-Fraser. 6873-1
The land of heart's desire, sels. William Butler Yeats. 6289-X,611-3,6393-4

LAND

The **land** of heart's desire. William Butler Yeats. 6250-4
"A **land** of homing; the homing of sea winds...". Mattakese. Joshua Freeman Crowell. 6798-0
"**Land** of immortal life, whose death reveres!". Egypt. Edward Farquhar. 6939-8
The **land** of indolence, fr. The castle of indolence. James Thomson. 6932-0
The **land** of lands. Alfred Lord Tennyson. 6385-3
The **land** of liberty. Unknown. 6917-7
"The **land** of love, the land of light". Carcassonne. Robert Loveman. 6941-X
"**Land** of lyric splendor, glorious and free". Our New Hampshire. Allen Eastman Cross. 6764-6
"**Land** of mine, where I was bred" Alexey Tolstoy. 6103-6
The **land** of Muravia. Aleksandr Tvardovsky. 6546-5
"**Land** of my fathers! - though no mangrove here". Teviotdale. John Leyden. 6980-0
"**Land** of my heart,/What future is before...". Ad patriam, sel. William Dudley Foulke. 6954-1
The **land** of nod. Lucy Marion Blinn. 6682-8
The **land** of nod. Robert Louis Stevenson. 6459-0, 6732-8, 6655-0, 6656-9
The **land** of nod. Ella Wheeler Wilcox. 6577-5
The **land** of nowhere. Ella Wheeler Wilcox. 6682-8
Land of our birth. Rudyard Kipling. 6337-3
Land of plenty. George D. Craig. 6342-X
The **land** of song. Dwight Willison Marvin. 6118-4
The **land** of story-books. Robert Louis Stevenson. 6459-0, 6519-8, 6135-4, 6114-1, 6368-3, 6456
"A **land** of streams! some, like ...", fr. Lotos-eaters. Alfred Lord Tennyson. 6123-0
Land of the afternoon. Unknown. 6919-3
The **land** of the blest. William Oliver Bourne Peabody. 6752-2
"**Land** of the desolate, mother of tears". To Belgium in exile. Sir Owen Seaman. 7026-4
Land of the drowsyhead. James Thomson. 6634-8
The **land** of the evening mirage. Unknown (Sioux Indians) 6730-1
Land of the free. Sister Mary Honora. 6388-8
"**Land** of the martyrs - of the martyred dead". To Russia new and free. Robert Underwood Johnson. 7026-4
"**Land** of the prophet, from whose rugged...". Arabia. James Abraham Martling. 6952-5
"**Land** of the purple heather, where, much to...". Adieu to Argyll. Charles Larcom Graves. 6760-3
"**Land** of the undimmed heaven! where the earth". Colorado. J. Ernest Whitney. 6836-7
Land of the wilful gospel, fr. Psalm of the west. Sidney Lanier. 6946-0
The **land** of thus-and-so. James Whitcomb Riley. 7002-7
The **land** of used-to-be. James Whitcomb Riley. 6459-0
Land on your feet. Sam Walter Foss. 6692-2
Land poor. J.W. Donovan. 6408-6
"The **land** shimmers in silence and in sun". White heron. John Dillon Husband. 6761-1
Land song of the west country. John Galsworthy. 6888-X
The **land** that God forgot. Harry Kemp. 6615-1
"A **land** that is lonelier than ruin". By the North Sea. Algernon Charles Swinburne. 6828-6
Land that we love. Richard Watson Gilder. 6386-1
The **land** war. Seumas (James Starkey) O'Sullivan. 6244-X
"The **land** was broken in despair". Come back again, Jeanne d'Arc. Henry Van Dyke. 6961-4
The **land** we love. Wendell Phillips Stafford. 7030-2
"The **land** where I was born sits by the seas". The morganna maggiore, sels. Luigi Pulci. 6945-2
The **land** where hate should die. Denis Aloysius McCarthy. 6478-7, 6250-4, 6964-9
The **land** where I was born. John Shaw Neilson. 6784-0
"A **land** where one may pray with cursed intent". Satire on the Scots. John Cleveland. 6996-7
"**Land** where the bones of our fathers..sleeping". The missionaries' farewell. Unknown. 6752-2
The **land** where the columbines grow. Arthur J. Fynn. 6836-7
The **land** where the cowboy crows. Addie Cropsey Hudson. 6836-7
The **land** where the rainbow ends. G.A. Studdert-Kennedy. 6558-9
"The **land** which freemen till". Alfred Lord Tennyson. 6238-5
T **th land** which no mortal may know. Bernard Barton. 6014-5
The **land** which no one knows. Ebenezer Elliott. 6934-7
A **land** without ruins. Abram Joseph Ryan. 7017-5
Land's end. Sara Teasdale. 6777-8
Land's end (Point Lobos, California). Stanton A. Coblentz. 6833-2
"The **land**, boys, we live in." Unknown. 6302-0
Land, ho! Thomas Edward Brown. 6809-X
The **land**, sels. Victoria Mary Sackville-West. 6649-6
The **land**-call. Francis Ernley Walrond. 6800-6
Land-fettered. J. Allan Dunn. 7007-8
The **land**.. Struthers Burt. 6031-5, 6051-X
The **land**.. Walter James Turner. 6532-5
Landels, Thomas Durley
    At eighty-three, sels. 6045-1; 6337-3
    Immanence. 6337-3
    Pilate remembers, fr. Pontius Pilate. 6337-3
Lander F.W.
    Rhode Island to the south. 6015-3
"A **landholdOng** freeman, a burgher of pith". Borger Joris's hammer. Arthur Guiterman. 6773-5
Landing of the pilgrim fathers. Felicia Dorothea Hemans. 6014-5, 6452-4, 6240-7, 6239-3, 6260-1, 6486 , 6457-4, 6424-8, 6263-6, 6304-7, 6219-9, 6131 , 6271-7, 6504-X, 6049-8, 6337-3, 6552-X, 6198 , 6088-9, 6267-9, 6438-8, 6102-8, 6323-3, 6465-5, 6478-7, 6479-5, 6623-2, 6732 , 6473-6, 6498-1, 6466-3, 6302-0, 6385-3, 6459
The **landlady**'s daughter. Eugene Parsons. 6215-6
The **landlady**'s daughter. Johann Ludwig Uhland. 6302-0
The **landlady**'s daughter. Johann Ludwig Uhland. 6903-7
Landlocked. Charles Buxton Going. 6653-4
Landlocked. Celia Thaxter. 6121-4, 6253-9
Landlord and tenant. Edgar A. Guest. 6869-3
The **landlord** of "The blue hen". Phoebe Cary. 6410-8
"The **landlord** wouldn't paint the place". Landlord and tenant. Edgar A. Guest. 6869-3
The **landlord**'s last moments. I. Edgar Jones. 6412-4
The **landlord**'s visit. De Witt Clinton Lockwood. 6918-5
The **landlord**'s visit. DeWitt C. Lockwood. 6744-1
The **landlord**'s wife. Marilyn Chin. 6790-5
The **landmark**, fr. The house of life. Dante Gabriel Rossetti. 6198-2, 6110-9, 6199-0
"The **landmarks** by me cherished". My town, sels. N.S. E.. 6798-0
Landon, Letitia Elizabeth ("L.E.L.")
    Affection. 6980-0
    Age and youth. 6980-0
    The ancestress, sels. 6066-8
    Awakening of Endymion. 6219-9
    Bitter experience. 6980-0
    Bonds of affection. 6014-5
    Calypso watching the ocean. 6980-0
    "Can you forget me? I who have so cherished". 6980-0
    The carrier-pigeon returned. 6980-0
    The castle of Chillon. 6749-2
    Crescentius. 6219-9
    Crescentius. 6980-0
    Death and the youth. 6385-3; 6600-3
    Despondency. 6980-0
    Experience. 6980-0
    The factory. 6102-8
    The factory. 6980-0
    The farewell. 6980-0
    The feast of life. 6980-0
    Felicia Hemans. 6046-3
    The female convict. 6302-0; 6385-3
    "I pray thee let me weep to-night". 6980-0
    Little Red Riding Hood. 6302-0
    long while ago<A. 6980-0
    Memory. 6980-0
    The minstrel's monitor. 6980-0
    Necessity. 6102-8
    Necessity. 6980-0
    "Oh! if thou lovest and art a woman". 6238-5
    The old times. 6980-0
    The poet's first essay. 6980-0
    Resolves. 6980-0
    She was sent forth. 6066-8
    The shepherd-boy. 6600-3

Stanzas ("Oh, no"). 6980-0
Success alone seen. 6980-0
"We might have been! these are but common words". 6980-0
The wind 6519-8
The wrongs of love. 6980-0

Landon, Rufus Clark
A lazy boy's idea. 6529-5

Landon, Ruth
Dreams. 6396-9

Landor. John Albee. 6300-4

Landor. Alexander Hay Japp. 6483-3,6656-9

Landor, Walter Savage
Abertawy. 6828-6
Absence. 6086-2
Acon and Rhodope; or, inconstancy, sels. 6198-2,6110-9
Aeschylos and Sophocles. 6102-8,6110-9,6102-8,6483-4
An aged man who loved to doze away. 6110-9,6086-2
Ah, what avails the sceptered race. 6604-6,6196-6,6660-7,6187-7,6328-4
Alas, how soon. 6110-9,6199-0
"Alas, how soon the hours are over" 6828-6
An ancient rhyme. 6092-7
"And small are the white-crested that play". 6997-5
The appeal. 6086-2
An Arab to his mistress. 6980-0
Around the child. 6934-7,6102-8
Autumn. 6086-2
"Away my verse; and never fear." 6086-2,6110-9
Before a saint's picture. 6233-4
"Behold what homage to his idol paid". 6289-X
Behold, O Aspasia! I send you verses. 6315-2
Botany. 6092-7
The brier. 6980-0
"The burden of an ancient rhyme." 6513-9
"But I have sinuous shells of pearly blue". 6997-5
Byron and the rest. 6186-9
The casket. 6874-X
A cathedral scene. 6980-0
Child of a day. 6086-2,6656-9,6737-9,6097-8,6233-4,6250-4,6656-9,6110-9
Children. 6097-8,6627-5,6219-9
Children playing in a church-yard. 6772-7
Children playing in a churchyard. 6832-4,6874-X
The chrysolites and rubies. 6828-6
The chrysolites and rubies. 6110-9,6199-0
The cistus. 6092-7
Clementina and Lucilla. 6874-X
Cleone to Aspasia. 6086-2,6110-9
Clifton. 6980-0
Commination. 6026-9
A copy of verses sent by Cleone to Aspasia. 6315-2
Corinna to Tanagra, from Athens. 6086-2,6110-9
Corinna, from Athens, to Tanagra, fr. Pericles... 6832-4
Count Julian, sels. 6980-0
A critic. 6125-7
Daniel Defoe. 6380-2
"The day returns, my natal day" 6828-6
The day returns, my natal day. 6110-9,6086-2
Death. 6250-4
The death of Artemidora. 6122-2,6196-6,6199-0,6656-9,6543-0
The death of Chrysaor, fr. The hellenics. 6828-6
Death of the day. 6641-0
Death stands above me. 6289-X,6337-3,6339-X,6086-2,6396-9,6153 ,6052-8,6086-2,6023-4,6199-0,6110-9,6110 ,6396-9,6668-2,6430-2
Destiny uncertain. 6874-X
Different graces. 6233-4
Dirce. 6430-2,6150-8,6102-8,6301-2,6656-9,6086-2,6092-7,6122-2;6208-3;6315-2,6339-X;6722-3;6726
"Do you remember me? or are you proud?" 6246-6,6086-2,6110-9
The dragon fly. 6092-7
The dying fire. 6186-9
The effects of age. 6874-X
The end. 6328-4
Envoi. 6208-3
Epigram. 6230-X

Epitaph on a poet in a Welsh courtyard. 6980-0
Farewell to Italy ("I leave thee, beauteous Italy..."). 6624-0,6656-9,6110-9,6086-2
Feathers. 6874-X
A Fiesolan idyl. 6198-2,6086-2,6110-9,6196-6,6430-2,6543-0,6656-9
Finis. 6102-8,6102-8,6560-0,6501-5
For a gravestone in Spain. 6641-0
For an epitaph at Fiesole. 6110-9,6086-2,6624-0,6656-9
Friends. 6832-4
Gebir. 6208-3,6110-9
The genius of Greece. 6828-6
The Georges. 6125-7
Gifts returned. 6089-7,6092-7
Give me the eyes. 6110-9,6199-0
"Give me the eyes" 6828-6
God scatters beauty. 6153-2,6199-0
"God scatters beauty as he scatters flowers" 6828-6
"Gone down the tide". 6997-5
"The grateful heart for all things blesses" 6874-X
The Hamadryad, fr. The hellenics. 6828-6
The Hamadryad. 6153-2,6196-6,6199-0
Heart's-ease. 6086-2,6110-9,6396-9
Helen and Corythos. 6315-2
Her lips. 6874-X
The honeymoon. 6089-7
Household gods. 6092-7
How many voices gaily sing. 6110-9,6092-7,6199-0,6301-2
"How many voices gaily sing" 6828-6,6874-X
"How often, when life's summer day" 6828-6
I entreat you, Alfred Tennyson. 6430-2
"I held her hand" 6828-6
"I held her hand, the pledge of bliss" 6874-X
"I held her hand, the pledge of bliss." 6110-9
"I know not whether I am proud." 6110-9
"I known not whether I am proud" 6828-6
I remember the time ere his temples were grey. 6092-7
I strove with none. 6332-2,6339-X,6289-X,6187-7,6301-2,6196-6,6383-7,6125-7,6153-2,6052-8
I wonder not that youth remains. 6110-9
Ianthe. 6134-6,6186-9,6208-3,6086-2,6110-9,6250-4,6658-5
Ianthe's shell. 6092-7
Ignorance of botany. 6874-X
Immortality ("Past ruin'd Ilion Helen lives"). 6186-9
In after time. 6086-2
In Clementina's artless mien. 6092-7
In memoriam: Lady Blessington. 6641-0
"In spring and summer winds may blow". 6844-8
"In spring and summer winds may blow." 6513-9
Inscription on a sea shell. 6438-8
Introduction to the last fruit off an old tree. 6604-6
Iphigeneia and Agamemnon. 6473-6,6199-0,6110-9,6543-0
Ippolito di Este, sels. 6980-0
Ireland. 6733-6
Ireland was never contented. 6092-7
Is it not better. 6110-9
"Is it not better at an early hour" 6828-6
"It often comes into my head". 6052-8
Jealous, I own it. 6828-6
La promessa sposa. 6874-X
Lament. 6102-8
Lament ("I loved him not;..."). 6600-3
Lament ("Mild is the parting year, and sweet"). 6102-8
Late leaves. 6086-2
"Lately our poets loitered in green lanes". 6832-4
Lately our songsters loitered. 6086-2,6110-9,6199-0
"Lately our songsters loitered in green lanes" 6828-6
Leaf after leaf drops off. 6232-6,6737-9
"The leaves are falling: so am I". 6187-7
Let love remain. 6086-2
Little Aglae. 6086-2,6110-9
Love is enough. 6732-9
The love of other years. 6122-2
A lyric. 6102-8,6732-8
Macaulay. 6302-0
"The maid I love ne'er thought of me." 6092-7,6199-0
The maid's lament. 6014-5,6302-0,6385-3,6543-0,6737-9,6086-2,6541-4,6656-9,6110-9,6219-9
Masar. 6315-2

LANDOR

Memory. 6828-6
Memory and pride. 6122-2
Menelaus and Helen at Troy. 6110-9
Mild is the parting year, and sweet. 6122-2,6513-9,6196-6,6110-9,6153-2,6604-6,6660-7
Milton in Italy. 6186-9,6631-3
Morning. 6980-0
Music ("Many love music but for music's sake"). 6186-9
My hopes retire. 6828-6
My serious son. 6934-7
Nancy's hair. 6641-0
New style ("I very much indeed approve.") 6092-7
Night airs and moonshine. 6125-7
No doubt thy little bosom beats. 6934-7
No fear of death. 6461-2
No word for fear. 6211-3
"No, my own love of other years." 6092-7,6110-9
Of Clementina. 6086-2
Old style ("Aurelius, sire of hungrinesses.") 6092-7
On 'The Hellenics.' 6110-9,6199-0
On Catullus. 6483-3,6086-2,6250-4
On death. 6154-0,6198-2
On his own Agamemnon and Iphigeneia. 6828-6
On his own Iphigeneia and Agamemnon. 6110-9
On his seventy-fifth birthday. 6122-2,6154-0,6198-2,6337-2,6527-9,6726 ,6430-2,6199-0,6150-8,6110-9,6023-4,6046 ,6086-2,6396-9,6668-2,6723-9,6646-1
On his seventy-fifth birthday. 6828-6
On living too long. 6086-2
On Lucretia Borgia's hair. 6110-9,6122-2,6732-8,6102-8
On man. 6641-0
On music. 6110-9,6086-2,6641-0
On observing a vulgar name on the plinth of...ancient statue. 6278-4
On one in illness. 6874-X
On receiving a monthly rose. 6331-4
On seeing a hair of Lucretia Borgia. 6536-8,6430-2
On Southey's death. 6832-4
On Southey's death. 6874-X
On Sunium's height. 6250-4
On the dead. 6641-0
On the death of M. D'Ossoli & his wife, Margaret Fuller. 6946-0
On the death of Southey. 6110-9,6153-2,6641-0
On the hellenics. 6828-6
On the smooth brow. 6086-2,6110-9,6199-0
"On the smooth brow and clustering hair" 6828-6
On timely death. 6122-2
The one gray hair. 6302-0,6385-3,6250-4,6219-9
"One year ago my path was green." 6110-9,6086-2,6092-7
An open grave. 6641-0
Past ruined Ilion. 6246-6,6315-2,6536-8,6122-2,6317-9, 6488 ,6110-9,6430-2,6199-0,6153-2
Persistence. 6086-2,6211-3,6656-9,6086-2,6211-3
"The place where soon" 6828-6
Plays. 6086-2,6102-8,6250-4,6086-2,6093-5,6102-8,6150-4, 6396-9
Pleasure! why thus desert the heart. 6086-2,6110-9
"Pleasure! why thus desert the heart." 6110-9,6086-2
"Pleasure! Why thus desert" 6828-6
Prayers, fr. Gebir. 6832-4
Progress of evening. 6201-6
Proud word you never spoke. 6934-7,6110-9,6153-2,6199-0, 6934-7,6086-2,6092-7,6110-9,6153-2,6199-0,6256
"Proud word you never spoke" 6828-6
"Proud word you never spoke, but you will speak" 6874-X
Quatrain ("It is not better at an early hour.") 6110-9
Quatrain ("My hopes retire.")" 6110-9
Quatrain ("Various the roads of life.") 6110-9
Quatrains ("On the smooth brow ans clusterin hair"). 6110-9
Regeneration. 6110-9,6086-2
Remain, ah not in youth alone. 6102-8
Repentance of King Roderigo. 6980-0
A reply to lines by Thomas Moore. 6125-7
Resignation. 6250-4
A retrospect. 6874-X
Robert Browning. 6197-4,6250-4
Rose Aylmer. 6052-8,6102-8,6154-0,6186-9,6204-0,6208 , 6246-8,6289-X,6315-2,6317-9,6527-9,6726 ,6732-8,6658-5,6737-9,6560-0,6656-9,6430 ,6153-2,6383-7,6668-2, 6371-3,6646-1,6197-4,6192-3,6110-9,6199 ,6023-4,6153-2,6086-2,6250-4,6301-2,6102
Rose Aylmer's hair, given by her sister. 6110-9,6086-2, 6641-0
Rose's birthday. 6092-7
Roses and thorns. 6250-4,6383-7
Rosina. 6233-4
Rubies. 6226-1,6658-5
Sacrifice. 6322-5
Sappho to Hesperus. 6110-9,6086-2
Separation. 6204-0,6086-2,6250-4
The shades of Agamemnon and Iphigenia. 6110-9
Shakespeare and Milton. 6483-3,6086-2,6110-9
The shells. 6102-8,6258-X,6543-0
The shortest day. 6874-X
Sixteen. 6980-0
Sixteen. 6233-4,6383-7,6219-9,6658-5
So then, I feel not deeply. 6110-9,6199-0
"So then, I feel not deeply!" 6828-6
The society of children. 6233-4
Some of Wordsworth. 6125-7
Songlet ("I held her hand..."). 6830-8
Songlet ("Mild is the parting year..."). 6830-8
Songlet ("No, my own love..."). 6830-8
Songlet ("Pleasure!...). 6830-8
"Soon, O Ianthe! life is o'er." 6110-9
"Stand close around, ye Stygian set". 6187-7,6246-6, 6153-2,6023-4,6125-7
Stanzas ("Say ye"). 6980-0
Sweet was the song that youth once sang. 6250-4
Sympathy. 6250-4,6383-7
Sympathy in sorrow. 6874-X
Tamar and the nymph, fr. Gebir. 6832-4
Tamar relates to Gebir his first encounter with...nymph. 6980-0
The tamed dormouse. 6980-0
Tears. 6874-X
Ternissa! you are fled. 6208-3,6315-2,6219-9
The test. 6086-2
"There are some wishes that may start." 6092-7
There are who say. 6199-0
"There are who say we are but dust". 6832-4
Theseus and Hyppolyta. 6110-9
Thou needst not. 6199-0
"Thou needst not pitch upon my hat" 6828-6
Thrasymedes and Eunoe. 6110-9
Thrasymedes and Eunoe, fr. The hellenics. 6828-6
The three roses. 6828-6
The three roses. 6110-9,6086-2
Time to be wise. 6086-2
To a bride. 6828-6
To a bride. 6110-9,6086-2
To a cyclamen. 6110-9,6086-2
To a dead child. 6980-0
To a fair maiden. 6874-X
To a painter. 6828-6
To age. 6122-2,6086-2,6110-9,6196-6,6199-0,6656
To age. 6828-6
To Alfred Tennyson. 6092-7
To Corinth. 6980-0
To E. Arundell. 6092-7
To E.F. ("No doubt thy little bosom beats.") 6092-7
"To his young Rose an old man said" 6874-X
To Ianthe. 6980-0
To Ianthe. 6086-2,6219-9
To Ianthe. 6086-2
To Joseph Ablett. 6828-6
To Joseph Ablett. 6110-9
To Leigh Hunt. 6092-7
To Macaulay. 6302-0;6385-3
To Mary Lamb. 6110-9
To my nineth decade. 6086-2,6110-9
"To my ninth decade I have tottered on" 6828-6
To one in grief. 6874-X
To Robert Browning. 6102-8,6604-6,6086-2,6199-0,6660-7, 6723 ,6122-2,6154-0,6110-9,6430-2,6301-2,6198-2;6289-X;6332-2;6465-5;6483-3;6527
To Robert Browning, sels. 6369-1
To Rose. 6641-0

To Southey, 1833. 6483-3
To Tacaea. 6832-4
To the sister of Elia. 6641-0,6086-2,6219-9
To Verona. 6624-0
To Wordsworth. 6828-6
To Wordsworth. 6110-9
To youth. 6828-6
To youth. 6199-0,6250-4
Twenty years hence. 6250-4,6383-7,6513-9
"Twenty years hence" 6828-6
Tyrannicide. 7009-4
Upon a sweet-briar. 6086-2,6110-9
"Various the roads of life" 6828-6
Verse. 6102-8
Verse ("Past ruined Ilion"). 6102-8
Very true, the linnets sing. 6250-4
"The vessel that rests here at last." 6092-7
Walter Savage Landor's favorite cat, Chinchinillo. 6699-2
Well I remember. 6315-2,6092-7,6102-8,6110-9
Well I remember how you smiled. 6086-2
"Well I remember how you smiled" 6828-6
"Wert thou but blind, O fortune, then perhaps." 6513-9
"When Helen first saw wrinkles in her face." 6110-9
Where are sighs. 6874-X
"While thou wert by" 6874-X
Why. 6198-2
"Why do our joys depart" 6828-6
Why repine, my friend? 6085-4,6211-3,6199-0,6301-2,6110-9
With an album. 6086-2,6196-6
With Petrarch's sonnets. 6874-X
"With rosy hand a little girl pressed down." 6110-9, 6199-0
"With rosy hand" 6828-6
Worship God only. 6980-0
Wrinkles. 6086-2
"Ye who have toiled uphill to reach the summit". 6832-4
Years. 6086-2
Years, many parti-colored years. 6110-9
Yes, I write verses. 6092-7,6110-9,6199-0
Yes! I write verses. 6604-4
You smiled, you spoke. 6125-7,6430-2
"You smiled, you spoke" 6828-6
"You smiled, you spoke, and I believed". 6832-4
"You smiled, you spoke, and I believed" 6874-X
"Your pleasures spring lie daisies in the grass" 6828-6
Your pleasures spring like daisies. 6199-0
Youth. 6092-7
Youth and age. 6186-9
Landor, Walter Savage (tr.)
   Mother, I cannot mind my wheel. Sappho, 6187-7,6430-2, 6513-9,6092-7,6086-2,6110 ,7039-6
   True or false. Caius Catallus, 7039-6
Landore. George Woodcock. 6360-8
Landscape. Ralph Nixon Currey. 6788-3
Landscape. Suk-jung Shin. 6775-1
Landscape. Challis Silvay. 6039-0
Landscape. Alfred Lord Tennyson. 6438-8
Landscape. Jaroslav Vrchlicky. 6886-3
Landscape. Robert Wells. 6339-X
A **landscape** by Courbet. Algernon Charles Swinburne. 6123-0
The **landscape** fading. Goronwy Rees. 6360-8
"The **landscape** lies within my head". Gervase Stewart. 6665-8
A **landscape** near an aerodrome. Stephen Spender. 6179-6
Landscape of evil. Tristan Corbiere. 6343-8
Landscape of my heart, fr. The brothers. Charles Abraham Elton. 6545-7
The **landscape** of the heart. Geoffrey Grigson. 6666-6
"The **landscape** that doesn't want to end". August (2). Andreas Okopenko. 6769-7
Landscape with children. Sister Maris Stella. 6761-1
Landscape with figure. Norman Rosten. 6561-9
Landscape with ruins. R.N.D. Wilson. 6072-2
Landscape, fr. The English garden. William Mason. 6932-0
"The **landscape,** like the awed face of a child". The shower. James Whitcomb Riley. 6993-2
A **landscape,** sels. John Cunningham. 6545-7
A **landscape.** WilliamBrowne. 6191-5

A **landscape.** John Cunningham. 6152-4
Landscapes. Louis Untermeyer. 6300-4,6336-5
Landsdowne, Lord. See Granville, George
Landshoff and J.T. Latouchie, R. (tr.)
   Yes, I live in a dark age. Bert Brecht, 6068-4
The **landskip.** William Shenstone. 6831-6
The **landsman.** Moschus. 6435-3
"**Landsmen** at sea know loneliness". To a figurehead at a farmhouse door. Katherine Drayton Simons. 7016-7
Landward. Richard Henry Stoddard. 6600-3
The **Lane** County bachelor. Unknown. 6594-5
Lane, Denny
   Kate of Araglen. 6174-5
   Lament of the Irish maiden. 6090-0,6174-5
Lane, J. Beaufoy
   The knight's vow. 6414-0
Lane, M. Travis
   Farther north. 6767-0
   King's landing. 6767-0
Lane, M.A.L.
   Hilda's Christmas. 6623-2
Lane, Nora
   Resignation. 6750-6
Lane, Patrick
   Dante's angels. 6767-0
   Nunc dimittis. 6767-0
Lane, Richard
   O master workman. 6461-2
The **lane.** Andrew Young. 6257-1
Laneer. Hermann Hagedorn. 6944-4
"The **lanes** are long, and home is far". Land song of the west country. John Galsworthy. 6888-X
The **lanes** of boyhood. Edgar A. Guest. 6862-6
Laneve, Elizabeth
   Summer. 6894-4
Lang (fr. the French of M. Fauriel), Andrew (tr.)
   The brigand's grave. Unknown (Greek), 6771-9
   The sudden burtal. Unknown (Greek), 6771-9
"**Lang** Jock Maclean, the toozie loon". Bowl aboot. Alexander ("Surfaceman") Anderson. 6819-7
Lang Johnny More. Unknown. 6185-0
Lang et al., Andrew (tr.)
   Ajax on the decks, fr. The Iliad. Homer, 6435-3
   The last fight, fr. The Iliad. Homer, 6435-3
Lang, Andrew
   A la belle Helene. 6771-9
   Advance, Australia. 6323-3
   Aesop. 6732-8,6656-9
   Almae matres. 6269-5,6508-2
   Another way. 6180-X
   April on Tweed. 6180-X
   Art's martyr. 6987-8
   Ballad of the gibbet. 6875-8
   Ballade dedicatory to Mrs. Elton of White Staunton. 6987-8
   Ballade des pendus (gringoire) 6875-8
   Ballade for the laureate. 6770-0,6875-8
   Ballade of Aucassin. 6850-2
   Ballade of blue china. 6732-8,6102-8,6424-8,6656-9
   Ballade of Christmas ghosts. 6145-1,6608-9
   Ballade of cricket. 6802-2,6687-8,6770-0
   Ballade of dead cities. 6875-8
   Ballade of dead ladies. 6875-8
   Ballade of his own country. 6331-4
   Ballade of literary fame. 6987-8,6996-7
   Ballade of middle age. 6770-0,6850-2
   Ballade of middle age. 6301-2
   Ballade of middle age. 6850-2,6987-8
   Ballade of neglected merit. 6987-8
   Ballade of old plays. 6875-8
   Ballade of primitive man. 6770-0,6875-8
   Ballade of railway novels. 6987-8
   Ballade of summer. 6987-8,6770-0
   Ballade of the book-hunter. 6186-9,6297-0,6656-9,6186-9
   The Ballade of the book-man's paradise. 6987-8
   Ballade of the bookworm. 6226-1
   Ballade of the Girton girl. 6987-8
   Ballade of the Girton girl. 6875-8
   Ballade of the primitive jest. 6089-7
   Ballade of the real and ideal. 6875-8

Ballade of the southern crosse. 6289-X
Ballade of the unattainable. 6875-8
Ballade of true wisdom. 6297-0
Ballade of Yule. 6770-0
Ballade to Theocritus, in winter. 6289-X,6501-5,6656-9,
 6543-0
Ballade of sleep. 6770-0
Ballades des pendus. 6770-0
The barbarous bird-gods: a savage parabasis. 6987-8
Brahma. 6802-2
Cameos. 6987-8
Circe's island revisited. 6771-9
Clevedon church. 6845-6
Colinette. 6771-9
Colonel Burnaby. 7015-9
Culloden. 6793-X
The death of Mirandola, 1494. 6771-9
The departure from Phaeacia. 6771-9
Desiderium: in memoriam, S.F.A. 6987-8
Double ballade of primitive man. 6089-7;6732-8
Dreams. 6771-9
England. 6819-7
Fairy land. 6771-9
The fortunate islands. 6987-8
Francois Villon, 1450. 6771-9
From the east to the west. 6987-8
'Gaily the troubadour'. 6802-2
Gerard de Nerval. 6771-9
Good-bye. 6771-9
Hesperothen. 6771-9
Homeric unities. 7015-9
Homeric unity. 6987-8
"I know not what my secret is." 6138-9
In Tintagel. 6987-8
Jacques Tahareau, 1530. 6771-9
Jacques Tahureau. 6879-0
L'envoi to E.W.G. 6987-8
The last cast. 6987-8
The last chance. 6269-5
The last Maying. 6987-8
"The level sands and grey". 6997-5
The limit of lands. 6771-9
Lone places of the deer. 6269-5
Lost in Hades. 6771-9
Lost love. 6320-9,6102-8,6301-2
A lost path. 6771-9
Love and wisdom. 6771-9
Love the vampire. 6987-8
Love's Easter. 6987-8
Love's miracle. 6771-9
Man and the Ascidian. 6987-8
Martial in town. 6483-3,6508-2
Melville and Coghill. 6793-X
Melville and Coghill. 6180-X
Melville and Coghill. 6793-X
Metempsychosis. 6771-9
"Mowers, weary and brown and blythe". 6205-9
N.A. 6987-8
A nativity of Sandro Botticelli. 6771-9
The new millennium. 6987-8
Nightingale weather. 6771-9
The Odyssey. 6186-9,6427-2,6246-6,6315-2,6483-3,6732 ,
 6102-8,6230-X,6543-0,6301-2,6464-7,6656 ,6726-3,6653-
 4,6508-2,6186-9,6427-2,6246-6,6315-2,6483-3,6732 ,
 6102-8,6230-X,6543-0,6301-2,6464-7,6656 ,6726-3,6653-
 4,6508-2
'Oh, no, we never mention her'. 6802-2
An old prayer. 6771-9
One flower. 6771-9
The palace of bric-a-brac. 6802-2,6987-8
Pen and ink. 7012-4
Penthesilea. 6094-3
Pierre Ronsard, 1560. 6771-9
Pisidice. 6987-8
Proem: Ballade of the bookworm. 6063-3
Romance. 6396-9
Rondeaux of the galleries. 6987-8
Rondeauz of the galleries. 6875-8
Rondel (Francois Villon) 6875-8
Rondel, Charles d'Orleans. 6875-8

Ronsard. 6483-3
Ronsard's grave. 6987-8
St. Andrews Bay at night. 6269-5
San Terenzo. 6624-0,6656-9,6631-3
Scythe song. 6239-3,6597-X,6250-4,6457-4,6656-9,6464-7,
 6508-2
The seekers for Phaeacia. 6771-9
The shade of Helen. 6771-9
A song of life and golk. 6269-5
A song of Phaeacia. 6771-9
Sonnet of the sirens (1). 6771-9
Sonnet of the sirens (2). 6771-9
Sonnets to poets, sels. 6771-9
The spinet. 6987-8
Spring. 6047-1,6653-4
Spring (Charles d'Orleans) 6875-8
A star in the night. 6771-9
Summer's ending. 6771-9
A sunset of Watteau. 6771-9
A sunset on Yarrow. 6771-9
Sylvie et Aurelie. 6771-9
They hear the sirens for the second time. 6771-9
Three portraits of Prince Charles. 6188-5,6656-9
To the gentle reader. 6760-3
Triolet to her husband. 6875-8
Triolets after Moschus. 6987-8,6879-0,6875-8
Trout-fishing on Tweed. 6476-0
Twilight. 6987-8
Twilight on Tweed. 6819-7
Twilight on Tweed. 6180-X
Two homes. 6771-9
Valentine in form of ballade. 6770-0
A very woeful ballade of the art critic. 6987-8
A very woful ballade of the art critic. 6875-8
Villanelle. 6875-8
Villanelle. 6875-8,6770-0
Villanelle, to Mr. Joseph Boulmier. 6987-8
The white pacha. 6323-3,6322-5
Woman and the weed. 6661-5
Zimbabwe. 6625-9

Lang, Andrew (tr.)
Amaryllis, fr. Idylls. Theocritus, 6987-8
April. Remy Belleau, 6771-9
Arbor amorsis. Francois Villon, 6771-9
A ballad of departure. Unknown (Greek), 6771-9
Ballad of the gibbet. Francois Villon, 6771-9,7039-6
Ballad: Le pere severe. Unknown (French), 7039-6
Ballad: Lost for a rose's sake. Unknown (French), 7039-6
Ballade of a friar. Clement Marot, 6987-8
The bridge of death. Unknown (French), 6771-9
The cannibal Zeus. Unknown (Greek), 6987-8
The cloud chorus. Aristophanes, 6987-8
Colonus, fr. Oedipus. Sophocles, 6987-8
The coming of Isis, fr. Metamorphoses. Apuleius, 6987-8
Criticism of life, fr. Hippolytus. Euripides, 6987-8
Deadly kisses. Pierre de Ronsard, 6771-9
Death. Aeschylus, 6987-8,6879-0
Dewy garlands. Asclepiades, 6819-7
A domestic event. F. Fertiault, 6297-0
The fisherman's tomb. Leonidas of Tarentum, 6819-7
The genesis of butterflies. Victor Hugo, 6771-9,7039-6
The grave and the rose. Victor Hugo, 6771-9,7039-6
Helen on the walls, fr. The Iliad. Homer, 6987-8
Heliodora. Meleager, 6435-3
His book's patron. Martial, 6297-0
His bookseller's address. Martial, 6297-0
His lady's death. Pierre de Ronsard, 6771-9
His lady's tomb. Pierre de Ronsard, 6771-9,7039-6
Hymn to the winds. Joachim Du Bellay, 6253-9
Hymn to the winds. Joachim Du Bellay, 6771-9
Iannoula. Unknown (Greek), 6771-9
In the spring. Meleager, 7039-6
Invocation of Isis, fr. Metamorphoses. Apuleius, 6987-8
The isles of the blessed, fr. Odes. Pindar, 6987-8
Juana. Alfred de Musset, 7039-6,6732-8
A lady of high dgeree. Unknown (French), 6771-9
Le pere Severe. Unknown (French), 6771-9
Lost for a rose's sake. Unknown (French), 6771-9
Love in her hair. Unknown (Greek), 6435-3

Love in May. Jean Passerat, 6771-9
The milk white doe. Unknown (French), 6771-9
Moonlight. Jacques Tahureau, 6771-9
More strong than time. Victor Hugo, 6771-9
More strong than time. Victor Hugo, 7039-6
More strong than time. Victor Hugo, 6879-0
Musette. Henri Murger, 6771-9
Nysa. Aeschylus, 6987-8
Nysa. Sophocles, 6987-8
The Odyssey, sels. Homer, 6250-4
Of his lady's old age. Pierre de Ronsard, 6732-8,6102-8
Of his lady's old age. Pierre de Ronsard, 7039-6
Old loves. Henri Murger, 6771-9
An old tune. Gerard de Nerval, 6771-9,7039-6
On his lady's waking. Pierre de Ronsard, 6771-9
The passing of Oedipous, fr. Oedipus. Sophocles, 6987-8
Rondel. Francois Villon, 6771-9
Rondel. Francois Villon, 7039-6
Rondel. Charles, Duc d' Orleans, 6850-2
Rondel: To his mistress. Charles, Duc d' Orleans, 6771-9
The rose. Pierre de Ronsard, 6771-9,6879-0
Roses. Pierre de Ronsard, 6771-9,7039-6
"The sacred keep of Ilion is rent." Homer, 6383-7
Shadows of his lady. Jacques Tahureau, 6771-9
A sonnet to heavenly beauty. Joachim Du Bellay, 7039-6, 6771-9
The spinning woman. Leonidas of Tarentum, 7039-6
Spring. Charles, Duc d' Orleans, 6771-9
Spring. Charles, Duc d' Orleans, 7039-6
Spring in the student's quarter. Henri Murger, 6771-9
The stingy friend. Martial, 6297-0
The taming of Tyro. Sophocles, 6987-8
The tell-tales. Unknown (Greek), 6771-9
The three captains. Unknown (French), 6771-9
To Artemis, fr. Hippolytus. Euripides, 6987-8
To his book. Caius Catallus, 6297-0
To his book. Horace, 6297-0
To his friend in Elysium. Joachim Du Bellay, 6771-9, 6039-6
To his young mistress. Pierre de Ronsard, 6771-9
To the moon. Pierre de Ronsard, 6771-9
A traitor. F. Fertiault, 6297-0
A vow to heavenly Venus. Joachim Du Bellay, 6771-9
The wayside well. Leonidas of Tarentum, 6819-7
"Whether I find thee bright with fair". Unknown, 6435-3

Lang, David
Harley's rose. 6857-X

Langbridge, Frederick
The parson's comforter. 6273-3
Quite by chance. 6089-7
Sent back by the angels. 6687-9
Sent back by the angels. 6922-3
A song for the girl I love. 6273-3
The vision of Rabbi Nathan. 6848-0

Langbridge, Rosamond
Phosphorescence. 6541-4

Langdon Jr., W.C.
The unseen depths. 6116-8

Langemarck at Ypres. William Wilfred Campbell. 6443-4

Langford, Charles
De union growin' strong. 6149-4
Union boys are we. 6149-4
We shall not be moved. 6149-4

Langford, Dorothy J.
On top of troubled waters. 6065-X
The only name given under heaven. 6065-X

Langford, Gary
Horse loose in city. 7018-3
Our house. 7018-3
Zoo. 7018-3

Langheim, ?
I-have and Oh-had-I. 6424-8

Langhorne, Charles Hartley
Theocritus. 6483-3,6656-9

Langhorne, John
Apology for vagrants, fr. The country justice. 6932-0
The child of misery, fr. The country justice. 6934-7
The country justice. 6866-9
The dead. 6600-3
The evening primrose. 6932-0
A farewell hymn to the valley of Irwan. 6251-4
Hope. 6086-2
To a redbreast. 6502-3

Langhorne, John (tr.)
"Wail'd the sweet warbler...". Francesco Petrarch, 6545-7

Langland, William
Avarice. 6489-2
The average man. 6489-2
The confession of gluttony. 6733-6
A dream. 6150-8
Eighth Passus, fr. Pier's Plowman's vision. 6200-8
The glutton. 6022-6
Gluttony. 6150-8
Holy church speaks. 6489-2
The human soul speaks. 6489-2
"I have threatened Theology...", fr. Piers Plowman. 6489-2
The induction, fr. The vision of Piers Plowman. 6489-2
Love we as brothers. 6489-2
The palace of truth. 6022-6
The palmer. 6022-6
Piers Plowman. 6186-9,6198-2
Piers Plowman, sels. 6369-1,6187-7,6198-2
Pilgrimage in search of do-well. 6200-8
Poverty not all loss. 6489-2
Prayer for the poor. 6489-2
Preaching and not doing. 6489-2
Providence ("'No', said the Patience patiently"). 6489-2
The sufferings of the poor. 6489-2
"This I trow be truth...". 6187-7
The vision of Jesus. 6022-6
The vision of Piers Plowman. 6489-2
The vision of Piers the Plowman, sels. 6102-8,6200-8, 6732-8

Langley lane. Robert Buchanan. 6925-8
Langley lane. Robert Buchanan. 6183-4,6242-3,6344-6,6219-9

Langley, Eve
Native-born. 6384-5

A **langorous** waltz beside the river. Victor Victorovitch Hofman. 6959-2

Langstaff, James Miles
"I never thought that strange romantic war". 6796-4

Langsyne, beside the woodland burn. Robert Tannahill. 6960-6
"**Langsyne,** when life was bonnie". Alexander ("Surfaceman") Anderson. 6819-7

Language. Frances Frost. 7030-2
The **language** of cats. Unknown. 6699-2
Language of music. Esther Eugenia Davis. 6799-9
Language of nature's fragrancy, fr. The coming of love. Theodore Watts-Dunton. 6997-5
The **language** of the eyes. Edward Bulwer-Lytton; Baron Lytton. 6980-0
The **language** of the eyes. Edward Bulwer-Lytton; Baron Lytton. 6543-0
The **language** of the eyes. Edward Bulwer-Lytton; Baron Lytton. 6980-0
Language of the learned. Samuel Butler. 6278-4
"The **languid** lady next appears in state". Satire V: Of women, fr. Love of fame. Edward Young. 6831-6
The **languid** lady, fr. Characters of women. Edward Young. 6932-0
"The **languid** sunset, mother of roses". A song of Phaeacia. Andrew Lang. 6771-9
"**Languid,** and sad, and slow, from day to day". Sonnet ("Languid, and sad"). William Lisle Bowles. 6152-4
"**Languish** and dispaire my hart." Unknown. 6563-5
Languor. Stephane Mallarme. 6343-8

Lanham, C.T.
Aesthetics. 6039-0
Lances. 6039-0
Neurosis. 6039-0

Lanier, Berthal
I could not understand. 6799-9

Lanier, Clifford
Edgar Allan Poe. 6465-5
Friar Servetus. 6674-7

Lanier, Clifford and Sidney
   The power of prayer. 6240-7,6255-5
Lanier, Sidney
   Acknowledgment. 6153-2,6250-4,6753-0
   Baby Charley. 6078-1
   A ballad of trees and the master. 6121-4,6467-1,6730-1, 6723-9,6250-4,6288-1,6431-0,6104 ,6047-1,6077-3,6144-3,6337-3,6465-5,6478 ,6299-7,6333-0,6335-7,6423-X, 6473-6,6006 ,6501-5,6509-0,6632-1,6309-8,6464-7,6727
   Barnacles. 6479-5,6288-1
   The battle of Lexington. 6240-7,6267-9,6470-1
   The bee. 6753-0
   Centennial meditation of Columbia. 6385-3
   The centennial ode, sels. 6239-3;6386-1
   Clover. 6753-0
   Corn. 6299-7,6333-0,6673-9,6121-4
   The cross. 6065-X
   The crystal Christ, fr. The crystal. 6337-3
   The crystal, sels. 6144-3;6335-7;6065-X
   The crystal. 7041-8
   The crystal. 6483-3
   Dear land of all my love, fr. The centennial ode. 6239-3;6386-1
   The dying words of Stonewall Jackson. 6753-0,6946-0
   Evening song. 6102-8,6126-5,6250-4,6288-1,6431-0,6300 , 6240-7,6243-1,6320-9,6481-7,6726-3,6513 ,6066-8,6102-8,6076-5,6309-8,6464-7
   From the flats. 6126-5,6288-1
   Heartstrong south and headstrong north, fr. Psalm... 6753-0
   How love looked for hell. 6753-0
   How love looked for hell. 6008-0,6126-5
   How love looked for hell. 6753-0
   Hymns of the marshes. 7017-5
   Individuality, fr. Hymns of the marshes. 7017-5
   The jacquerie, sels. 6008-0
   Land of the wilful gospel, fr. Psalm of the west. 6946-0
   Lexington, fr. Psalm of the west. 6946-0
   Marsh song - at sunset. 6753-0
   Marsh song - at sunset. 6126-5
   Marsh song - at sunset. 6753-0
   Marsh song - at sunset, fr. Hymns of the marshes. 7017-5
   The marshes of Glynn, sels. 6102-8,6467-1,6214-8,6484-1, 6337-3,6732
   The marshes of Glynn. 6047-1,6303-9,6332-2,6333-0,6473-6,6735 ,6300-4,6646-1,6250-4,6008-0,6288-1,6513 , 6501-5,6726-3,6374-8,61-7-9,6126-5,6076 ,6102-8,6730-1
   The mocking bird ("Superb and sole..."). 6073-0,6265-2, 6288-1,6126-5,6723-9
   My springs. 6126-5
   Night and day. 6753-0
   Night and day. 6126-5
   Night and day. 6753-0
   Nirvana. 6077-3
   On the shore. 6632-1
   Opposition. 6754-9
   Opposition. 6431-0
   Owl against robin. 6299-7
   Psalm of the west, sels. 6753-0,6447-7,6126-5
   Remonstrance. 6753-0
   The revenge of Hamish. 6052-8,6255-5,6399-3,6126-5
   Song for The Jacquerie. 7017-5
   Song of the Chattahoochee. 6126-5,6300-4,6736-0,6484-1, 6964-9,6250-4,6288-1,6464-7,6371-3,6396-9,6421 ,6183-4,6243-1,6255-5,6299-7,6332-2,6735 ,6498-1,6289-X, 6459-0,6431-0,6560-0,6121
   Song of the chattahoochee. 7041-8
   Sonnet ("'Twixt this and dawn..."). 6753-0
   Sonnet ("Columbus"). 6753-0
   Sonnet ("Ere we Gomera"). 6753-0
   Sonnet ("I marvel"). 6753-0
   Sonnet ("My dawn"). 6753-0
   Sonnet ("Next drive"). 6753-0
   Sonnet ("Now speaks"). 6753-0
   Sonnet ("Or, haply"). 6753-0
   Sonnet ("So when"). 6753-0
   Sonnets on Columbus, fr. Psalm of the west. 6753-0
   Sonnets on Columbus, sels. 6126-5
   The stirrup-cup. 6102-8,6431-0,6288-1,6076-5,6126-5, 6309 ,6726-3,6583-X,6424-8,6371-3,6467-1
   The story of Vinland, fr. Psalm of the west. 6946-0
   Sunrise. 6006-4,6126-5,6121-4,6265-2
   A sunrise song. 6126-5
   Sunrise, sels. 6047-1,6208-3
   Sunrise-a hymn of the marshes. 7041-8
   'The symphony,' sel. 7041-8
   The symphony. 6753-0,7017-5
   Tampa robins. 6465-5,6498-1,6126-5,6484-1
   Thou crystal Christ, fr. The crystal. 6335-7
   To Bayard Taylor. 6126-5
   The tournament. 6113-3;6479-5
   Trade, fr. The symphony. 6324-1
   The trees and the master. 6374-8,6304-7
   The triumph, fr. Psalm of the west. 6946-0
   Tyranny. 6333-0
   The waving of the corn. 6126-5
Lanigan, George Thomas
   The Ahkoond of swat. 6021-8,6089-7,6732-8,6505-8
   The amateur Orlando. 7025-6
   Dirge of the moola of Kotal. 6089-7
   Quatrain. 6722-9
   A threnody. 6083-8,6583-X,6307-1,6300-4,6446-9
Lanigan, R.W.
   Charity. 6674-7
Lankford, Frances Stoakley
   Grace for a spring morning. 6839-1
   Prayer at a nursery window. 6839-1
   Sermon. 6761-1
Lanners. x.l.
   What good is a poet? 6792-1
Lanning, Jane McKay
   Lent. 6337-3
Lansdowne, Baron. See Granville, George
The lantern out of doors. Gerard Manley Hopkins. 6931-2, 6828-6
Lanterns. Alfred Noyes. 6169-9
"The lanterns and the gondolas have vanished". Bitter serenade. Herbert Trench. 6877-4
Lanthier, Kateri
   Dream scars. 6767-0
The lanthorn. Ruth Eede. 6906-1
Lanty Leary. Samuel Lover. 6089-7
Lanty Leary. Unknown. 6125-7
"Lanty was in you, you see". Won't you follow me. Samuel Lover. 6928-2
Lanyon, Carla
   One generation to another. 6541-4
Lanyon, Helen
   Haunted. 6244-X
   The hill o' dreams. 6090-0
Lao-tzu
   The philosopher. Arthur Waley (tr.). 6722-0
Laocoon. Don Gordon. 6665-8
Laocoon. Donald Hall. 6388-8
Laocoon. Paul Hamilton Hayne. 6121-4
Laodamia. William Wordsworth. 6198-2,6271-7,6438-8,6086-2, 6110-9,6430-2,6199-0,6543-0
Laodamia, sels. Audrey Alexandra Brown. 6021-8
Laodamia, sels. William Wordsworth. 6867-7
Laodicea. Henry Longan Stuart. 6039-0
The laodiceans. Marion Couthouy Smith. 7038-8
Laon and Cythna, sels. Percy Bysshe Shelley. 6369-1
Lape, Fred
   From this the strength. 6761-1
   Summer nights. 6761-1
The lapful of nuts. Sir Samuel Ferguson. 6668-2
The lapful of nuts. Unknown. 6244-X
Lapidus, Sylvia
   Child secret. 6850-2
   Plea. 6850-2
   Prisoned. 6850-2
   Triolet. 6850-2
Lapis. Shawn Wong. 6790-5
Lapis luzuli. William Butler Yeats. 6210-5
Lapius, S.Q.
   In the ol' tobacker patch. 6453-1
Lapooka. Charles Sangster. 6796-4

"**Lappilatawan**, fair tree-fungus". The song of Lappilatwan, the singer in the dusk. Unknown (Algonquin Indian). 6864-2
"**Lappilatwan/Lappilatwan/Gray** singer of...dusk". The last Wabanaki. Hermann Hagedorn. 6944-4
Lappin, Margaret Redding
    Snow on Lake Harriet. 6342-X
Laprade, Victor de
    La mort d'un chene. 6801-4
Lapraik, John
    When I upon thy bosom lean. 6086-2
A **lapse** of time and a word of explanatin. Robert Service. 6159-1
"The **lapse** of time and rivers is the same". A comparison. William Cowper. 6814-6
The **lapse** of time, fr. Night thoughts. Edward Young. 6102-8
The **lapse** of time. William Cullen Bryant. 6077-3
Lapsus calami-to R.K. James Kenneth Stephen. 6656-9
Lapsus linguae. Keith Preston. 6722-0
Lapus calami. James Kenneth Stephen. 6732-8
The **lapwing**. William Blake. 6545-7
Lara. George Gordon, 6th Baron Byron. 6945-2
Laramore, Vivian Yeiser. See Yeiser, Vivian
Larbaud, Valery
    Alma perdida. 6351-9
    "Between Cordova and Seville", fr. Images. 6351-9
    Images, sels. 6351-9
    "One day, in Kharkov...", fr. Images. 6351-9
The **larceny**. Elliott Flower. 6274-1
Larch hill. Leslie Daiken. 6930-4
"The **larch** hs donned its rosy plumes". Rondel. Richard Wilton. 6770-0
Larcom, Lucy
    Across the river. 6407-8
    And in that twilight. 6066-8
    At nightfall. 6129-X
    At Queen Maude's banquet. 6129-X
    Baby's day. 6129-X
    The baby's thoughts. 6129-X
    The barn window. 6129-X
    Berrying song. 6129-X
    Bring back my flowers. 6129-X
    The brook that ran into the sea. 6129-X
    The brown thrush. 6449-3,6510-4,6638-0,6049-8,6623-2, 6127-3,6452-3,6135-2,6129
    By the fireside. 6385-3;6600-3
    Calling the violet. 6891-X
    Calling the violet. 6129-X
    Canticle de profundis. 6340-3
    Cat-life. 6699-2
    Cat-questions. 6129-X
    Christmas green. 6129-X
    A Christmas thought. 6147-8
    The clock-tinker. 6129-X
    Do something. 6273-3
    Dumpy ducky. 6129-X
    A face in the tongs. 6129-X
    Farther on. 6129-X
    The flag. 6820-0
    Flower-girls. 6129-X
    "For an empty crown is a bauble". 6109-5
    A friend in heaven. 6085-4
    A friend. 6066-8
    Gipsy children's song. 6129-X
    Gowns of gossamer. 6129-X
    Grace and her friends. 6127-3,6639-9
    Grace's friends. 6129-X
    Hal's birthday. 6129-X
    Hannah binding shoes. 6240-7,6344-6,6408-6,6239-3,6459-0,6735 ,6219-9,6304-7,6424-8,6484-1,6571-6,6744
    A harebell. 6129-X
    If I were a sunbeam. 6373-X,6129-X,6456-6
    In fairy land. 6129-X
    In the air. 6066-8
    In the tree-top. 6078-1,6129-X
    In time's swing. 6129-X
    The inalienable bond. 6085-4
    Jessie's book. 6129-X
    The last flower of the year. 6129-X

The lily of the resurrection. 6177-X
A lily's word. 6129-X
Lincoln's passing bell. 6524-4
The little bird. 6530-9
The little brown cabin. 6620-8,6066-8
A little cavalier. 6129-X
Little nannie. 6373-X,6129-X
The little tambourine girl. 6129-X
A loyal woman's no. 6438-8
Manitou's garden. 6129-X
March. 6466-3,6623-2,6639-9
Moonshine. 6129-X
A mountain pastoral. 6260-1
My children. 6129-X
The national flower. 6049-8,6373-X
Nature's Easter music. 6177-X
New Year's wishes. 6129-X
New-year song. 6129-X
The nineteenth of April, 1861. 6340-3,6113-3,6678-X
On the stairway. 6129-X
Our Christ. 6335-7,6337-3
Peepsy. 6129-X
Plant a tree. 6047-1,6049-8,6304-7,6401-9
Plant a tree. 6820-0
Playthings. 6129-X
Prince Hal. 6129-X
Prince Hall. 6129-X
The proof. 6177-X
Pussy clover. 6129-X,6530-9
Rain. 6374-8
Re-enlisted. 6340-3
Red sandwort. 6129-X
Red-top and Timothy. 6129-X
Ring, happy bells. 6171-0
The rivulet. 6519-8,6135-4,6129-X,6368-3,6639-9
The roadside pracher. 6129-X
The robin. 6530-9
A sea-glimpse. 6997-5
Shared. 6374-8,6461-2
The sing-away bird. 6215-6
Singing on a birch-tree. 6129-X
The sinking of the Merrimac. 6946-0
Sir robin. 6891-X
Sir Robin. 6129-X,6368-3
Sister and bluebirds. 6129-X
Snow song. 6129-X
Song of the brown thrush. 6530-9,6456-6
Spring whistles. 6129-X
Starlight. 6129-X
A strip of blue, sels. 6337-3
A strip of blue. 6240-7,6374-8,6418-3,6597-X,6600-3, 6632 ,6309-8,6461-2,6431-0
A strip of blue. 6730-1
The sun-beam. 6530-9
Swing away. 6129-X
A thanksgiving. 6408-6,6570-8
Tolling. 6305-5,6524-4
The trees. 6374-8,6461-2
Two festivals. 6618-6
The violet. 6529-5
Violets. 6047-1
What shall we wrap the baby in? 6078-1
What the train run over. 6129-X
Who plants a tree. 7022-1
Woman's Easter. 6177-X
"A **large** cannon cracker stood upon a shelf". The false firecracker. Carolyn Wells. 6882-0
"**Large** clusters of lilacs hum in full bloom". A love poem. Milan Rakic. 6765-4
A **large** edition. Unknown. 6083-8,6260-1,6579-1
Large eternal fellows. Sam Walter Foss. 6303-9
A **large** evening at the club. Berton Braley. 6853-7
".**Large** glooms were gathered in the mighty fane",fr.The city. James ("B.V.") Thomson. 6508-2
"The **large** porcupine breathes smaller ones". There won't be another. Diane Glancy. 7005-1
Large was his soul, fr. On the death of Willam Harvey. Abraham Cowley. 6934-7
The **larger** hope, fr. In memoriam. Alfred Lord Tennyson. 6337-3,6600-3,6730-1

The larger life. Archibald Lampman. 6433-7
The larger prayer. Ednah D. Cheney. 6303-9
The largess. Richard Eberhart. 6390-X
The largest life. Archibald Lampman. 6843-X
The largest life. Archibald Lampman. 6115-X
Largo. Henry Herbert Knibbs. 7010-8
Largo. Farona Konopak. 6979-7
Largo. Sidney Goodsir Smith. 6379-9
Largo. Dunstan Thompson. 6391-8,6666-6
Lariat Bill. Unknown. 6277-6
Laris, Ethel A.
    A new birth. 6799-9
Lark. Myra A. Shattuck. 6715-8
The lark and the rook. Unknown. 6242-3,6519-8,6563-5,6424-8,6131-1
The lark ascending. George Meredith. 6073-0,6122-2,6315-2,6477-9,6560-0,6430-2,6199-0,6508-2,6656-9
Lark descending. Edmund Blunden. 6354-3
"The lark had left the evening cloud". The lovely lass of Preston Mill. Allan Cunningham. 6960-6
"The lark has sung his carol in the sky". The four eras. Samuel Rogers. 6980-0
The lark in autumn. Alfred Hayes. 6785-9
"A lark in the mesh of the tangled vine". Kyrielle. John Payne. 6770-0
The lark in the morning. Unknown. 6125-7
"The lark now leaves his watery nest". Sir William Davenant. 6187-7,6198-2,6562-7,6726-3
"The lark now leaves his watery nest". Song ("The lark now leaves"). Sir William Davenant. 6219-9,6431-1
"The lark now leaves his watry nest". Sir William D'Avenant. 6208-3
"The lark now leaves his wintry nest". Song ("The lark now leaves his wintry nest"). Sir William Davenant. 6933-9
A lark singing in the city. George Roberts. 6174-5
A lark went singing. Ruth Guthrie Harding. 6648-8
The lark's grave. Thomas Westwood. 6334-9,6639-9,6638-0
The lark's song, fr. In Mercer street. Seumas (James Starkey) O'Sullivan. 6073-0;6395-0
"Lark, in the glow of eve". Song ("Lark, in the glow of eve"). Irma Geisslova. 6763-8
"Lark, lark, I call thee". To a skylark. Edward J. O'Brien. 6798-0
"The lark, whose instinct/Reaches high". Wings. Anna Streeter Wood. 6799-9
"The lark". Song ("The lark"). Hartley Coleridge. 6271-7
The lark. Wilfred Wilson Gibson. 6488-4
The lark. James Hogg. 6271-7,6597-X,6629-1
The lark. Lizette Woodworth Reese. 6073-0,6374-8,6653-4
The lark. Robert Service. 6510-4
The lark. John Banister Tabb. 6943-6
The lark. Unknown. 6933-9
Larkin, Frances S.
    Desire. 6799-9
Larkin, John D.
    'Some day.' 6714-X
Larkin, Margaret
    Goodbye - to my mother. 6093-5
    Nikral I. 6808-1
    Nikral II. 6808-1
Larkin, Philip
    At grass. 6257-1
    Born yesterday. 6257-1
    Church going. 6257-1
    First sight. 6339-X
Larks. Robert Bridges. 6487-6
Larks. Saint-Paul Roux. 6351-9
Larks. Katharine (Hinkson) Tynan. 6244-X,6253-X
Larks and nightingales. Nathan Haskell Dole. 6505-8
Larkspur. Marjorie Meeker. 6232-6
Larkspur. James Oppenheim. 6338-1
"Larkspur and mignonette! Well does she know". Old-fashioned valentine. Jessie Wilmore Murton. 6750-6
"Larkspur, thistle, these her eyes". Triolet. Muriel F. Hochdorf. 6850-2
Larkyn, Harry
    Who can tell? 6303-9
Larminie, Vera
    In extremis. 6532-5

Larminie, William
    Consolation. 6174-5
    'Fand', sels. 6174-5
    'Moytura', sels. 6174-5
    The nameless doon. 6174-5;6244-X
    The nameless ruin. 6930-4
    Sunset at Malinmore. 6174-5
    The sword of Tethra. 6930-4
Larned, Augusta
    The homage of beasts. 6510-4
Larned, Frank Madison
    Oblivion's gate. 6116-8
Larned, W. Livingston
    Behind the muzzle. 7008-6
    Fame--fame--fame. 6274-1
    His good points. 7008-6
    The joy of pedigree. 7008-6
Larrabee, Harold A.
    Professors. 6287-3
    The very model of a modern college president. 6722-0
Larrie O'Dee. William W. Fink. 6089-7,6416-7,6167-2,6505-8,6573-2
"The Larry Rivers on your wall". Larry Rivers self-portrait. Lisa Hunter. 6900-2
Larry kisses the right way. Jennie E.T. Dowe. 6702-6
Larry McGee. Unknown. 6057-9
Larry McHale. Charles Lever. 6174-5
Larry O'Toole. William Makepeace Thackeray. 6802-2
Larry Rivers self-portrait. Lisa Hunter. 6900-2
Larry's on the force. Irwin Russell. 6139-7,6412-4
Lars, Claudia
    Heads and tails. Donald Devenish Walsh (tr.). 6759-X
    Sketch of the frontier woman. Donald Devenish Walsh (tr.). 6759-X
Lars: a pastoral of Norway. Bayard Taylor. 6976-2
Larson, Emma M.
    Isaac La Bissoniere, at eighty, recalls October of 1841 6342-X
Larsson, Raymond Ellsworth
    An arrangement for an inquiring oboe of philosphic bent. 6038-2
    Ballad: the spring rain. 6783-2
    The contemplation of the word. 6779-4
    Philosophic bent. 6038-2
    <u>Swan song arranged for two pianos. 6778-6</u>
    To our lady, the ark of the covenants. 6282-2
Larvae. Adeline Dutton (Train) Whitney. 6127-3
Las Sierpes Street. Oliverio Girondo. 6759-X
"Las du triste hopital et de l'encens fetide". Les fenetres. Stephane Mallarme. 6801-4
"Las' July - and, I presume". The way it wuz. James Whitcomb Riley. 6892-8
"Las' time 'at Uncle Sidney come". The boys' candidate. James Whitcomb Riley. 6990-8
Lasca. F. Desprez. 6392-6,6414-0
Lasca. Unknown. 6605-4
The lash of the northland. Andrew F. Underhill. 7035-3
"Lashed to his flagship's mast". Blaine of Maine. Eugene Fitch Ware. 6820-0
Lasker-Schuler, Else
    End of the world. Babette Deutsch (tr.). 6160-5
    My love song. Babette Deutsch (tr.). 6160-5
    My people. Babette Deutsch (tr.). 6160-5
    Palm song. Babette Deutsch (tr.). 6160-5
    Reconciliation. Babette Deutsch (tr.). 6160-5
    Sphinx. Babette Deutsch (tr.). 6160-5
    To you. Babette Deutsch (tr.). 6160-5
Lass Dorothy. Unknown. 6674-7
The lass o' Arranteenie. Robert Tannahill. 6180-X,6086-2
The lass o' Arranteenie. Robert Tannahill. 6960-6
The lass o' Ballochmyle. Robert Burns. 6180-X,6271-7
The lass o' Gowrie. Carolina Oliphant, Baroness Nairne. 6086-2
The lass of Islington. Unknown. 6157-5
The lass of Lochroyan. Unknown. 6180-X,6547-3
The lass of Lynn's new joy, for finding a father... Unknown. 6157-5
The lass of Mohee. Unknown. 6057-9
The lass of Mohee. Unknown. 6595-3
The lass of Patie's mill. Allan Ramsay. 6180-X,6271-7,6385-

3,6219-9
The lass of Richmond Hill. James Upton. 6302-0;6385-3
The lass of Roch Royal. Unknown. 6185-0
The lass of the hill. Mary Jones. 6874-X
The lass with the delicate air. Unknown. 6328-4
The lass with the golden locks. Christopher Smart. 6545-7
Lass, gin ye lo'e me. James Tytler. 6086-2
"A lassie has a watering-pot". A little song of angels. Marjorie L.C. Pickthall. 6797-2
Lassie wi' the lint-white locks. Robert Burns. 6191-5,6545-7
The lassie's decision. H.D. McAthol. 6670-4
Lassie, what mair wad ye ha'e? Alexander Gray. 6845-6
"Lassie, with the lips sae rosy". Madchen mit dem rothen mundchen. Heinrich Heine. 7039-6
"Last All Saints' holy-day, even now gone by". Sonnet: Of Beatrice d' Portinari, on All Saints' Day. Dante Alighieri. 7039-6
The last abbot of Gloucester. Wilfred Rowland Childe. 6096X
The last aboriginal. William ("Fiona Macleod") Sharp. 6656-9
The last act. Phoebe Cary. 6969-X
The last ally. William Rose Benet. 6464-7
The last ancestor. Gene Fowler. 6792-1
Last and best. Alice Cary. 6969-X
"The last and greatest herald of heavens king". For the Baptiste. William Drummond of Hawthornden. 6933-9
"A last and lonely thrush is calling". Too late to light the lamps. Robert P. Tristram Coffin. 7040-X
The last antelope. Edwin Ford Piper. 6861-8
The last antelope. Edwin Ford Piper. 6510-4
Last antiphon: to Mary. James J. Donohue. 6282-2
A last appeal. Frederick W.H. Myers. 6337-3,6656-9
The last appendix to Yankee Doodle. Unknown. 6278-4
The last appendix to Yankee Doodle. Unknown. 6946-0
The last arrival. George Washington Cable. 6273-3
"Last at first the question rings". Last chorus, fr. The dynasts. Thomas Hardy. 7014-0
The last banquet of Antony and Cleopatra. Felicia Dorothea Hemans. 6973-8
The last banquet. Edward Renaud. 6915-0
The last battle. Ellen Murray. 6925-8
The last bed. Phoebe Cary. 6969-X
The last bison. Charles Mair. 6795-6
The last bison. Charles Mair. 6115-X
The last bison. Charles Mair. 6795-6
"The last bit of snow". The last snowflake. Margarethe Herzele. 6769-7
The last bob white. Whitney Montgomery. 6073-0
The last booke of the ocean to Scinthia, sels. Sir Walter Raleigh. 6208-3
The last buccaneer ("On England is a pleasant..."). Charles Kingsley. 6547-3,6332-2,6258-X,6808-1,6197-4, 6219-9,6656-9
The last buccaneer. Thomas Babington Macaulay, 1st Baron Macaulay. 6473-6,6322-5,6547-3,6478-7
The last bugle. Maude (Emogene Boyce Smith) Meredith. 7030-2
The last bumper. Charles Whitby. 6994-0
The last call. Etta Miller. 6799-9
Last cargo. Silence Buck Bellows. 6833-2
The last cast. Andrew Lang. 6987-8
The last chance. Andrew Lang. 6269-5
The last chantey. Rudyard Kipling. 6427-2,6473-6,6258-X, 6437-X,6547-3,6102-8,6199-0,6508-2,6371-3,6655-0, 6656
The last charge at Appomattox. Henry Jerome Stockard. 6074-9
The last charge. George B. Hynson. 6919-3
Last chorus, fr. Hellas. Percy Bysshe Shelley. 6832-4
Last chorus, fr. Medea. Euripides. 6867-7
Last chorus, fr. The dynasts. Thomas Hardy. 7014-0
The last chrysanthemum. Helene Magaret. 6042-0
The last cigar. Unknown. 6440-X
Last cigarette. Wayne Miller. 6901-0
The last communion. Leo Ward. 6096-X
A last confession, sels. Dante Gabriel Rossetti. 6526-0
A last confession. Dante Gabriel Rossetti. 6380-2
A last confession. William Butler Yeats. 6317-9

Last confessional. John Drinkwater. 6250-4
The last conqueror. James Shirley. 6246-6,6219-9
The last Constantine. Felicia Dorothea Hemans. 6973-8
The last cowboy. Glenn Ward Dresbach. 6265-2
The last cradle song. James Hogg. 6233-8
Ther last crusader. Edward Bulwer-Lytton; Baron Lytton. 6980-0
The last cup of canary. Helen Gray Cone. 6467-1
The last dance. May Riley Smith. 6102-8,6076-5
The last day of Jerusalem. George Croly. 6848-0
The last day of the year. Alexander Smart. 6466-3,6131-1
The last day. Richard A. Porter. 6883-9
Last days of Byron. Charlotte Fiske Bates. 7041-8
The last days of Herculaneum, sels. Edwin Atherstone. 6570-8
Last days of Queen Elizabeth. Edward Bulwer-Lytton; Baron Lytton. 6980-0
The last days. George Sterling. 6506-6,6161-3,6121-4,6241-5,6253-9,6250 ,6431-0,6393-4
The last defile. Amy Carmichael. 6337-3
A last desire. Rose M. Burdick. 6818-9
The last despatch. Austin Dobson. 6760-3
The last ditch. Edith (Bland) Nesbit. 6652-6
The last dream. Ray A. Young Bear. 7005-1
The last drunkard. Unknown. 6685-2
The last dying speech and confession of poor puss. Ann and Jane Taylor. 6105-2
Last dying speech and confession of poor puss. Jane Taylor. 6131-1
The last dying words of Bonnie Heck. William (of Gilbertfield) Hamilton. 6180-X
Last eve. Dora Sigerson Shorter. 6174-5
The last eve of summer. John Greenleaf Whittier. 6126-5
"Last eve the earth was calm, the heavens...". After the tornado. Paul Hamilton Hayne. 7041-8
The last evening before eternity. James Abraham Hillhouse. 6752-2
The last evening. Elinor Jenkins. 7029-9
The last evening. Rainer Maria Rilke. 6665-8
The last evening. Clinton Scollard. 6320-9
The last exploit of Samson. John Milton. 6625-4
The last fairy-tale. Lambros Porphyras. 6352-7
The last fairy. Rosamund Marriott ("Graham R. Tomson") Watson. 6437-X
The last farewell. Edward Bliss Emerson. 6438-8
The last faring. Hermann Hagedorn. 6944-4
"The last few days feeling I". Tuesday. Lyn Lifshin. 6998-3
The last fierce charge. Unknown. 6058-7
The last fight, fr. The Iliad. Homer. 6435-3
The last fight. Lewis Frank Tooker. 6340-3,6255-5
The last fire. Herbert S. Gorman. 6036-6,6250-4
The last flower of the year. Lucy Larcom. 6129-X
The last frontiersman. Marion Lockwood Ferguson. 7019-1
Last generation. Michelle Roberts. 6870-7
Last gift. Fredrica Kay. 6818-9
The last Gloucesterman. Gordon Grant. 6833-2
The last good-bye. Louise Chandler Moulton. 7041-8
The last good-bye. Louise Chandler Moulton. 6309-8
The last harper. J. Corson Miller. 6096-X,6039-0
The last heifer. Mary Linda Bradley. 6894-4
The last hero. Gilbert Keith Chesterton. 6427-2
The last hero. George William ("A.E.") Russell. 7027-2
Last hill. Edith Mirick. 6144-3,6335-7
The last hour. Ethel Clifford. 6374-8
The last hours of Faustus. Christopher Marlowe. 6153-2
Last hymn. Emily Bronte. 6424-8
The last hymn. Marianne Farningham. 6486-8,6569-4
The last hymn. Marianne Farningham Hearn. 6303-9
The last hymn. Marianne Farningham. 6914-2
The last hymn. Blanche Lee. 6818-9
The last hymn. Unknown. 6451-5
Last incident. Grace Mansfield. 6750-6
The last inn. Grantland Rice. 6303-9
Last instructions. Virginia Moore. 6781-6
The last invocation. Walt Whitman. 6007-2,6246-6,6337-3, 6399-3,6288-1,6126-5,6214-8,6309-8
Last journey. Gretelle Suzanne LeGron. 6857-X
The last journey of the wooers, fr. The Odyssey. Homer. 6435-3

LAST

The **last** journey, fr. Antigone. Sophocles. 6435-3
The **last** journey, fr. The testament of John Davidson. John Davidson. 6845-6
The **last** journey. John Davidson. 7012-4
The **last** journey. Richard Lawson Gales. 6950-9
The **last** journey. Leonidas of Tarentum. 7039-6
The **last** journey. Caroline Anne Bowles Southey. 6271-7
Last judgment. Stanton A. Coblentz. 6337-3
The **Last** Judgment. John Crowe Ransom. 6039-0
The **last** kick of Fop's alley. Unknown. 6278-4
The **last** labour. Charles R. Murphy. 6037-4
The **last** lamp of the alley. William Maginn. 6802-2
"The **last** leaf has its resting place". November. Sara V. Prueser. 6906-1
The **last** leaf. Oliver Wendell Holmes. 6753-0,6176-1,6243-1, 6332-2,6473-6,6486-8,6583 ,6092-7,6250-4,6126-5,6723-9,6646-1,6424 ,6271-7,6289-X,6302-0,6385-3,6437-X, 6441 ,6467-1,6304-7,6396-9,6300-4,6309-8,6219 ,6457-4,6459-0,6478-7,6481-7,6497-3,6610 ,6230-X,6126-5, 6121-4,6265-2,6431-0,6560 ,6733-6,6735-2,6601-1,6077-3,6101-X,6142 ,6004-8,6307-1,6092-7,6008-0,6288-1, 6732 ,6753-0
The **last** leap. Adam Lindsay Gordon. 6951-0,6784-0
Last leave of the hills. Duncan Ban MacIntyre. 6845-6
The **last** letter. Frank Dempster Sherman. 6066-8
"The **last** light lingers in the west". Influence. Robert Haven Schauffler. 6983-5
Last lines. Richard Harris ("Thomas Ingoldsby") Barham. 6437-X
Last lines. Emily Bronte. 6090-0,6123-0,6186-9,6337-3,6339-X,6418 ,6102-8,6250-4,6383-7,6150-8,6543-0,6301 , 6437-X,6501-5,6726-3,6730-1,6723-9,6214
Last lines. Robert E. Sterling. 6650-X
A **last** look. George Robert Sims. 6416-7,6744-1
Last love. James Elroy Flecker. 6320-9
Last love. Feodor Ivanovich Tyutchev. 6622-4
The **last** love. Edward Farquhar. 6939-8
The **last** lullaby. Henry Bataille. 6351-9
The **last** man. Thomas Campbell. 6075-7,6086-2,6219-9,6648-8, 6600-3,6910
The **last** man. Thomas Hood. 6378-0,6545-7
The **last** man. Thomas Hood. 6974-6
Last May. Carroll Arnett Gogisgi. 7005-1
Last May a braw wooer. Robert Burns. 6024-2,6545-7,6518-X, 6195-0
The **last** Maying. Andrew Lang. 6987-8
The **last** meeting of Pocahontas and the great captain. Margaret Junkin Preston. 6946-0
The **last** memory. Arthur Symons. 6507-4,6250-4
The **last** mile-stones. Pearl Rivers. 6910-X
The **last** mobilization. George Herbert Clarke. 6224-5,6184-2
"The .**last** month of the winter was the for the most part..." Unknown (Chinese) 6545-7
The **last** music. Lionel Johnson. 6174-5,6244-X
"**Last** New Year's Eve, I had a task..." Unknown. 6059-5
Last news about the little box. Vasko Popa. 6758-1
Last night. Jon Bracker. 7003-5
Last night. George Darley. 6244-X
Last night. Mildred Ann Hobbs. 6662-3
Last night. Theophile Marzials. 6656-9
Last night. Warren Pease. 6274-1
Last night. Clement Scott. 6681-X
Last night. Hervey White. 6897-9
Last night - and this. James Whitcomb Riley. 6992-4
"**Last** night I dreamed we parted once again". Frederick Goddard Tuckerman. 6333-3
"**Last** night a zealous Irishman in town". Neophyte. Eugene Fitch Ware. 7025-0
"**Last** night at Bon Odori the drums of...". Letter to Tina Koyama from Elliot Bay Park. Jim Mitsui. 6790-5
"**Last** night I asked the stars to stop...". Turning once to look back. Ross Leckie. 6767-0
"**Last** night I built a dream house". My dream house. Helen G. Stephenson. 6799-9
"**Last** night I could not rest...". An aurora borealis. George Croly. 6980-0
"**Last** night I crept across the snow". Prayer ("Last night"). John Chipman Farrar. 6746-8
"**Last** night I did not fight for sleep". In hospital: Poona. Alun Lewis. 6895-2
"**Last** night I dreamed". Prewar. Thomas Brasch. 7032-9
"**Last** night I dreamed of mystic isles". A dream. Mary Enola Rudolph. 6799-9
"**Last** night I had a dream: I woke". A dream of one dead. A. Bernard Miall. 6785-9
"**Last** night I has a sweet, sweet dream". You're as welcome as the flowers in May. Unknown. 6826-X
"**Last** night I said I loved you". Confession. Evelyne Love Cooper. 6850-2
"**Last** night I saw a horse above". Letter to an exile. Lala Koehn-Heine. 6767-0
"**Last** night I saw an April moon". Silver sandals. Travis Tuck Jordan. 6818-9
"**Last** night I saw the Pleiades again". The Pleiades. Arthur Adams. 6784-0
"**Last** night I single handed fought a gang...". Doughnuts and cider. Edgar A. Guest. 6862-6
"**Last** night I stood in a tawdry place". When we play the fool. Edgar A. Guest. 7033-7
"**Last** night I stood in the castle hall". My castle. Alma G. Wallace. 6750-6
"**Last** night in blue my little love was dressed". Charles Henry ("John Paul") Webb. 6429-9,6321-7
Last night in Sisseton, S.D. Mary Goose. 7005-1
"**Last** night in memory's boughs aswing". Villanelle. William Henry Ogilvie. 6875-8
"**Last** night in sleep I seemed a king". Voltaire (Francois Marie Arouet) 6088-9
"**Last** night ma said to pa: 'My dear'.". When ma wants something new. Edgar A. Guest. 7033-7
"**Last** night my fayre resolu'd to goe." Unknown. 6563-5
The **last** night of winter. Winifred Welles. 6036-6
"The **last** night that she lived". Emily Dickinson. 6246-5
"**Last** night the moon flamed with a...fire". Star ghosts. Tessa Sweazy Webb. 6906-1
"**Last** night the moon poked a long". And the winner is. Greg Forker. 6870-7
"**Last** night the mother said to me". I volunteer. Edgar A. Guest. 6748-2
"**Last** night the sea-wind was to me". Changed voices. Sir William Watson. 6997-5
"**Last** night the seeking wind sang". Song ("Last night"). Ben H. Smith. 6662-3
"**Last** night the tempter came to me, and said". The voice of the tempter. Bayard Taylor. 6976-2
"**Last** night there came a messenger to mine ear". The night's message. Ernest Myers. 7015-9
"**Last** night they held a meetin'...". The deacon, me and him. Louis Eisenbeis. 6923-1
"**Last** night when the moon was free". Phantom. Guanetta Gordon. 6750-6
"**Last** night, ah, yesternight, betwixt her lips". Non sum qualis eram bonae sub regno Cynarae. Ernest Dowson. 6785-9
"**Last** night, as my dear babe lay dead". The dead babe. Eugene Field. 6949-5
"**Last** night, by the side of the mountain lake". The lost shoe. Norah M. Holland. 6797-2
"**Last** night, dear Lord, he dreamed he was tall". Proposed pact. Jessie Farnham. 6750-6
"**Last** night, I saw a documentary". Losing track. Cathy Song. 6790-5
"**Last** night, I wept". Defenceless. Grace Holbrook Blood. 6764-6
"**Last** night, it must have been a ghost at best". Morning, fr. Parted love. William Bell Scott. 6819-7
"**Last** night, quite late". Disguise. Evana Llynn. 6906-1
"**Last** night, the shadows dark'ning in my room". Shadows. Isabel R. Boyer. 6818-9
"**Last** night, when the sweet young moon shone..". The fickle day. PWoebe Cary. 6865-0;6969-X
"**Last** night, when weary silence fell on all". The two spirits. Adelaide Anne Procter. 6957-6
"**Last** night, within our little town". The return. Lady Margaret Sackville. 6884-7
"**Last** night/I reached out the window". Les etoiles. Mildred Potter. 6750-6
The **last** night. Orrick Johns. 6441-8,6619-4
The **last** night. Virna Woods. 6680-1

The last of all. Grantland Rice. 7012-4
The last of his tribe. Henry Clarence Kendall. 6656-9
The last of May in Vermont. Daniel L. Cady. 6988-6
The last of the Bohemians. Jack Micheline. 6901-0
The last of the books. Alfred Noyes. 6169-9
The last of the choir. Unknown. 6744-1,6167-2
The last of the Eurydice. Sir Joseph Noel Paton. 6656-9
The last of the flock. William Wordsworth. 6133-8,6134-6
The last of the light brigade. Rudyard Kipling. 6670-4
The last of the pippins. Clara Doty Bates. 6965-7
The last of the snow. Alfred Noyes. 6151-6
The last oracle. Algernon Charles Swinburne. 6036-6,6102-8
"'Last pa said to ma: 'My dear, it's gettin'". Cleaning the furnace. Edgar A. Guest. 7033-7
The last pagan mourns for dark Rosaleen. Joseph Payne Brennan. 6218-0
The last party. Katherine Hunter Coe. 6906-1
The last party. Jesse H. Wilson Jr. 6118-4
The last pilot. Duncan Tovey. 6476-0
Last pipe at night. John Maher Murphy. 6761-1
The last pipe. Unknown. 6453-1
The last piper. Edward J. O'Brien. 6556-2,6029-3,6102-8, 6076-5
Last plea. Jean Starr Untermeyer. 6012-9
Last poem. Charles Kingsley. 6490-6
Last poems, sels. Alfred Edward Housman. 6828-6
The last portage. William Henry Drummond. 6433-7
The last portage. Wilson MacDonald. 6337-3
The last post. Robert Graves. 7027-2
The last prairie-dog town. Kenneth W. Porter. 6042-0
Last prayer. Christina Georgina Rossetti. 6437-X
Last prayer of Mary Queen of Scots. W.G. Clarke. 6408-6
Last prayer of Mary, Queen of Scots. Willis Gaylord Clark. 6572-4
A last prayer. Helen Hunt Jackson. 7041-8
A last prayer. Helen Hunt Jackson. 6337-3,6512-0,6431-0
The last prayer. William Wilfred Campbell. 6115-X
Last prayers. Mary Ann Browne. 6752-2
Last prelude. Sara Teasdale. 6879-0
The last prospect. Edmund Waller. 6189-3
The last quarrel. Charles Mackay. 6980-0
The last race. Ernest Harold Baynes. 6039-0
The last raft. Joseph V. Adams. 6799-9
Last rally. Clifford J. Laube. 6761-1
The last rally. John Gould Fletcher. 7027-2
The last redoubt. Alfred Austin. 6744-1
The last regiment. Joaquin Miller. 6113-3
The last renegade. Mykki Verlyn Culver. 6899-5
The last request. Philetas. 6435-3
The last reservation. Walter Learned. 6632-1,6484-1
"The last resort of kings are we...". 'That have no doubts'. Klaxon (John Graham Bower). 7031-0
The last resort. Charles G. ("Miles O'Reilly") Halpine. 6278-4
The last rhyme of True Thomas. Rudyard Kipling. 6427-2
The last ride together. Robert Browning. 6196-6,6301-2, 6655-0,6154-0,6198-2,6315-2,6437-X,6726-3,6723 ,6102-8,6110-9,6153-2,6250-4,6430-2,6560
The last ride together. James Kenneth Stephen. 6089-7,6440-X
Last rites. Felicia Dorothea Hemans. 6973-8
The last rose of summer. Thomas Moore. 6930-4
The last rose of summer. Thomas Moore. 6102-8,6479-5,6232-6,6527-9,6383-7,6250-4,6304-7
The last scab of Harworth. John Streeter Manifold. 6895-2
The last scene at Fotheringay. Algernon Charles Swinburne. 6323-3
The last scene from Mordred. William Wilfred Campbell. 6433-7
The last sigh of the moor. Theophile Gautier. 6484-1
The last sleep of Tristram and Iseult. Algernon Charles Swinburne. 6997-5
The last sleep. Charles Hanson Towne. 6619-4,6653-4
The last snowflake. Margarethe Herzele. 6769-7
Last song. James Guthrie. 6269-5
Last song in an opera. Robert Nichols. 6607-0
Last song of Callicles. Matthew Arnold. 6655-0
The last song of Sappho. Felicia Dorothea Hemans. 6973-8
Last song to a girl of the waterfront. Otto D'Sola. 6759-X
Last song to a poet. Marjorie Meeker. 6039-0

Last song: from exile. Guido Cavalcanti. 6325-X
Last sonnet. John Keats. 6604-6,6634-8,6086-2,6301-2,6102-8,6252-0,6543-0,6660-7
"The last specks of sunlight". Returning from the hung. Norbert Krapf. 6966-5
Last speech to the court. Bartolomeo Vanzetti. 6375-6
"Last spring this summer may be autumn styl'd". Threnodia on Samuel Stone. Edward Bulkley (atr.). 6753-0
The last spring. R. D. 6118-4
The last string. Gustav Hartwig. 6670-4
"Last Sunday at St. James's prayers" Unknown. 6874-X
Last supper. Elinor Wylie. 6531-7
The Last supper, by Leonardo da Vinci. William Wordsworth. 6484-1,6624-0,6631-3
Last supper: Jesus to Judas. S. Foster Damon. 6619-4
The last supper. Oscar Williams. 6390-X
The last Suttee. Rudyard Kipling. 6810-3
"The last tall son of Lot and Bellicent". Gareth, fr. Garth and Lynette. Alfred Lord Tennyson. 7022-1
"Last Thursday, down by Slipshod Hill". Making soap in Vermont. Daniel L. Cady. 6988-6
Last taps. Theodore Goodridge Roberts. 6690-9
The last Taschastas, sels. Joaquin Miller. 6753-0
The last three from Trafalgar. Dante Gabriel Rossetti. 6793-X
The last time I met Lady Ruth. Owen (Edward Bulwer-Lytton, Earl Lytton) Meredith. 6683-6
The last time I the well woke. Unknown. 6380-2
"The last time that we quarrell'd, love". The last quarrel. Charles Mackay. 6980-0
Last token. W.A. Eaton. 6710-7
The last tournament, fr. Idylls of the King. Alfred Lord Tennyson. 6657-7
The last trail. J. Corson Miller. 7012-4
Last trams, sels. Kenneth Slessor. 6349-7
The last tree of the forest. Felicia Dorothea Hemans. 6973-8
The last trek. Fydell Edmund Garrett. 6800-6
The last trial. Unknown. 6436-1
The last Tudor. Annie M.L. Hawes. 6926-6
Last Valentine's day. Unknown. 6328-4
Last verses. Thomas Chatterton. 6086-2,6102-8
Last verses. Edmund Waller. 6931-2,6659-3
The last visitor. John Bennett. 6764-6
The last voyage of Sir Francis Drake, and Sir John... Charles Fitz-Geffrey. 6547-3
The last voyage. Katharine (Hinkson) Tynan. 6777-8
The last Wabanaki. Hermann Hagedorn. 6944-4
The last walk in autumn. John Greenleaf Whittier. 6126-5, 6288-1
"Last week - I heard a man speak". Pride and prejudice. Linwood Daggette Smith Jr.. 7024-8
"Last week - Jhe Lord be praised for all...". Letter. John Greenleaf Whittier. 6753-0
Last week of February, 1890. Robert Bridges. 6487-6,6508-2
"Last week/The moon was only a bud". Full bloom. Ruth Klein. 6850-2
The last whiskey cup. Paul Engle. 6736-0
The last will and testament of the grey mare. Unknown. 6334-9
The last will and testament of William Ruffell, Esq. Unknown. 6878-2
A last will and testament. Unknown. 6881-2
A last wish. Unknown. 6752-2
The last wish. Felicia Dorothea Hemans. 6973-8
The last wish. B.W. Kirkham. 6915-0
The last wish. Owen (Edward Bulwer-Lytton, Earl Lytton) Meredith. 6437-X
The last wish. Victor Sampson. 6800-6
A last word. Ernest Dowson. 6507-4,6655-0,6507-4
The last word. Matthew Arnold. 6052-8,6208-3,6271-7,6337-3, 6378-0,6437-,6102-8,6110-9,6250-4,6513-9,6543-0,6737 ,6371-3,6655-0
The last word. Louis J. Magee. 7004-3
Last words. Helen Hunt Jackson. 6836-7
Last words. Robert Nichols. 6506-6
Last words. Unknown. 6167-2
Last words of Byron. George Chapman. 6150-8
The last words of juggling Jerry. George Meredith. 6122-2
Last words over a little bed at night. Sarah Morgan Bryan

LAST

Piatt. 6772-7
Last words to a dumb friend. Thomas Hardy. 6511-2
The **last** words. Maurice Maeterlinck. 7039-6
Last year's dead. Benjamin Franklin Taylor. 6815-4
"The **last**, forever still the last!". The unregarded. Edward Farquhar. 6939-8
"**Last-born** of Babel men". July Fourth, 1886. Benjamin Franklin Taylor. 6815-4
"**Lastly** came winter cloathed all in frize". Winter. Edmund Spenser. 6239-3
Lastra a signa. Sarah D. Clarke. 6624-0
The **lasy** day. Daniel Sargent. 6723-9
"**Lat** no man booste of conning nor vertu". Transient as a rose. John Lydgate. 6881-2
"**Lat** noman booste of konnyng nor vertu." John Lydgate. 6378-0
Lat take a cat, fr. The maunciples tale. Geoffrey Chaucer. 6125-7
Latchaw, Gladys
    My yoke is easy. 6144-3;6335-7;6337-3
Latches. Charles N. Sinnett. 6924-X
Late. Ilse Aichinger. 6769-7
Late acquaintance. Leigh Buckner Hanes. 6042-0
Late afternoon doves. Jutta Schutting. 6769-7
"**Late** at een, drinkin the wine". Unknown. 6111-7
Late August. Mary Gilchrist Powell. 6396-9
"**Late** at night/I hear her whispering". The beads. Jaime Jacinto. 6790-5
Late autumn. Andrew Young. 6257-1
"**Late** autumn gale" Keiho Soga. 6981-9
"**Late** autumn, and an arrowhead of geese". Indian summer. John J. Haining. 6857-X
Late blossom. Joyce Lancaster. 6850-2
Late chrysanthemums. Marjorie DeGraff. 6850-2
Late chrysanthemums. Ruth Klein. 6850-2
Late chrysanthemums. Marie Tello Phillips. 6850-2
Late chrysanthemums. Muriel Slater. 6850-2
Late corner. Langston Hughes. 6388-8
Late days. Ilse Brem. 6769-7
"The **late** Dr. Jartin/Had the good fortune". William Cowper. 6814-6
"**Late** days-short days". Late days. Ilse Brem. 6769-7
"**Late** even now, and overclouded skies". Twilight - Normandy, fr. Sea pictures. James Rennell Rodd; 1st Baron Rennell. 6997-5
Late fall. Vojislav Ilic. 6765-4
Late February days. William Morris. 6793-X
"A **late** fall leaf sways guidelessly down". Yet to be named. C.G. Thompson. 7016-7
Late for chores. Glenn Ward Dresbach. 6761-1
Late harvest. Raymond Knister. 6021-8
"**Late** in September came our corn-crops home". Harvest-home. Charles Tennyson Turner. 6980-0
"**Late** in the month a rough east wind had sway". The charming of the east wind. Charles Tennyson Turner. 6980-0
"A **late** lark twitters from the quiet skies". The happy passing. William Ernest Henley. 6793-X
A **late** lark twitters. William Ernest Henley. 6123-0,6073-0, 6473-6,6301-2,6508-2,6655
Late leaves. Walter Savage Landor. 6086-2
"**Late** lingers Cleophantis...". Paulus Silentiarius. 6251-2
Late love. Lorna Tallent Kidwell. 6750-6
The **late** massacre. John Milton. 6322-5
Late November morning. Madison Cawein. 6396-9
Late October. D.M. Jordan. 6273-3
"**Late** on me weeping did this whisper fall." Henry Septimus Sutton. 6225-3
Late one night. Unknown. 6609-7
A **late** passer. William Wilkins. 6174-5
Late plowing. Louise Driscoll. 6607-0
Late spring evening. Robert Bridges. 6487-6
Late spring in the nuclear age. Andrew Hudgins. 7032-9
Late spring, sur coast. Naomi Clark. 6792-1, 6998-3
The **late** spring. Louise Chandler Moulton. 6240-7;6385-3;6600-3
Late summer. William Rose Benet. 6979-7
Late summer in the country. fr. Idyll vii. Theocritus. 6435-3
Late testament. Erick Brenstrum. 7018-3

A **late** walk. Robert Frost. 6338-1,6649-6
Late when the autumn evening fell, fr. Waverley. Sir Walter Scott. 6180-X
Late winter. J.P. McAuley. 6384-5
Late winter. Philip Henry Savage. 6466-3
Late wisdom. George Crabbe. 6250-4
Late! J.G. Francis. 6786-7
"**Late**, from this western shore, that morning..". The western world. William Cullen Bryant. 6752-2
The **late**, last rook. Ralph Hodgson. 6477-9
Late, late, so late! Alfred Lord Tennyson. 6328-4,6122-2, 6304-7
"**Late**, my grandson", fr. Locksley hall. Alfred Lord Tennyson. 6867-7
"**Lately** Manzi herded kine". Manzi. Francis Carey ("Jan van Avond") Slater. 6800-6
"**Lately** our poets loitered in green lanes". Walter Savage Landor. 6832-3
Lately our songsters loitered. Walter Savage Landor. 6086-2,6110-9,6199-0
"**Lately** our songsters loitered in green lanes" Walter Savage Landor. 6828-6
Lately, alas, I knew a gentle boy. Henry David Thoreau. 6333-0
The **latent** cause. Edward R. Huxley. 6885-5
Latent life. Alice Cary. 6969-X
Later. Willard Huntington Wright. 6027-7
Later life, sels. Christina Georgina Rossetti. 7037-X
Later life, sels. Christina Georgina Rossetti. 6656-9
Later ter glory. Emmeline Lowe. 6750-6
"**Later**, the planes were seen as they came...". Air raid, old style. Helen Bryant. 6761-1
The **lateshow** diorama. Christopher Dewdney. 6767-0
"**Latest** born of Jesse's race". The call of David. John Henry, Cardinal Newman. 6848-0
The **latest** convert. F.W. Littleton Hay. 6453-1
The **latest** decalogue. Arthur Hugh Clough. 6123-0,6437-X, 6730-1,6092-7,6110-9,6125 ,6150-8,6655-0,6430-2,6199-0,6427-7,6657 ,6315-2,6527-9,6732-8,6733-6
The **latest** decalogue. Arthur Hugh Clough. 6199-0
The **latest** nun. Edward Farquhar. 6939-8
The **latest** toast. Raymond W. Walker. 6118-4
Latest verses. George Gordon, 6th Baron Byron. 6302-0;6385-3
"**Latest**, earliest, of the year". Primroses. Alfred Austin. 6198-2,6102-8,6437-X
Lathbury, Mary Artemisia
    Break thou the bread of life. 6337-3
    The day is dying in the west. 6418-3
    A deep sea dream. 6965-7
    Easter song. 6143-5
    Release. 6965-7
    Snowdrops, lilies, and butterflies. 6720-4
    Song of hope. 6337-3
    A song of to-day. 6473-6
    A spring snow storm. 6965-7
    "There was once a little maiden". 6965-7
Lathrap, Mary T. See Lathrop, Mary T.
Lathrop [or Lathrap], Mary T.
    Day dawn of the heart. 6144-3;6335-7
    Will it pay? 6685-2
    A woman's answer to a man's question. 6689-5
Lathrop, George Parsons
    The cavalry charge. 6552-X,6673-9
    Charity. 6292-X
    The child's wish granted. 6292-X
    The flown soul. 6632-1
    Keenan's charge. 6113-3,6610-0,6340-3,6471-X,6062-5, 6467 ,6016-2,6431-0,6470-1,7917-7,7041-8
    Marthy Virginia's hand. 6074-9;6632-1;6672-0
    The name of Washington. 6820-0
    The phoebe bird. 6632-1
    The phoebe-bird. 7041-8
    Remembrance. 6096-X,6300-4
    The song-sparrow. 6597-X
    "The sunshine of thine eyes" 7041-8
    The sunshine of thine eyes. 6441-8,6309-8
Lathrop, Lena
    A woman's question. 6963-0
Lathrop, Mary T.

The dead march. 7002-7
Lathrop, Ona Freeman
    A mother's reward. 6337-3
Lathrop, Rose Hawthorne
    The clock's song. 6172-9,6292-X
    Dorothy. 7041-8
    Francie. 7041-8
    Looking backward. 7041-8
    The out-going race. 7041-8
    A song before grief. 6006-4,6096-X,6172-9,6292-X
Latimer and Ridley, burned at the stake in Oxford,1851. William Edmonstoune Aytoun. 6948-7
Latimer, Mrs. E.W.
    Saint Anthony. 6674-4
Latin. Unknown. 6125-7
The **Latin** tongue. James J. Daly. 6096 X
Latter day warnings. Oliver Wendell Holmes. 6399-3,6512-0, 6126-5,6288-1
The **latter** day. Thomas Hastings. 6735-2
The **latter** rain. Jones Very. 6271-7,6302-0,6385-3
The **lattice** at sunrise. Charles Tennyson Turner. 6437-X, 6656-9
Lattimore, Richard
    The father. 6388-8
    Ship bottom. 6388-8
Lattimore, Richard (tr.)
    "Achaians have got Troy, upon this very day". Aeschylus, 6665-8
    Achilles to Lycaon, fr. The Iliad. Homer, 6665-8
    The Aftermath, fr. Iphigenia in Aulis. Euripides, 6665-8
    "The god of war, money changer of dead bodies". Aeschylus, 6665-8
    Hektor to Andromache, fr. The Iliad. Homer, 6665-8
    Sarpedon to Glaukos, fr. The Iliad. Homer, 6665-8
    We have paid enough long since in our own blood, fr.Georgics. Vergil, 6665-8
Lattin, Pauline
    Prayer of the homesteader. 6662-3
Latto, Thomas Carstairs
    When we were at the schule. 6960-6
Latvian songs. Johannes Bobrowski. 6758-1
Latvinia, fr. The seasons (Autumn). James Thomson. 6932-0
Lau, Alan Chong
    Crossing Portsmouth bridge. 6790-5
    Day of the parade. 6790-5
    "Father takes to the road and lets his hair down" 6790-5
    Letters from Kazuko (Kyoto, Japan-sumemr 1980) 6790-5
    Living in the world. 6790-5
Laube, Clifford J.
    Ave, vita nostra. 6282-2
    Bidden word. 6042-0
    Cobwebs. 6839-1
    Cry out of Babylon. 6761-1
    Last rally. 6761-1
    To fear. 6292-X
Laubenheimer, Milicent
    The heart, defenseless of shield. 6640-2
    A memory. 6799-9
Lauda Sion. Saint Thomas Aquinas. 6543-0
Laudabo. Seumas (James Starkey) O'Sullivan. 6071-4
Laudabunt Alii. Ernest Currie. 6793-X
Laudamus. Adam Lindsay Gordon. 6951-7
Laudate dominum. Bible. 6125-7
Laudate dominum. Bible. 6830-8
Laudator temporis actai. S. Charles Jellicoe. 6174-5
Laudauer, Hortense
    For boldness. 6640-2
    For Emily Dickinson. 6640-2
    Two towers. 6640-2
"**Laude,** honor, praisingis, thankis infinite". The difficulties of translation, fr. Aeneid. Vergil. 6845-6
Laudenheimer, Milicent
    The pattern. 6640-2
    Preludes to fairytales. 6640-2
Laudo puellam. H.A. Richmond. 6116-8
Laufenberg, Heinrich von
    Solothurn. 6749-2

Laugh. Wilbur Dick Nesbit. 6583-X
Laugh a little bit. Edmund Vance Cooke. 6291-1
Laugh and be jolly. Nancy Byrd Turner. 6861-8
Laugh and be merry. John Masefield. 6477-9;6501-5;6583-X
Laugh and grow fat. Winthrop Mackworth Praed. 6408-6
A **laugh** in church. Unknown. 6690-9,6964-9,7008-6
Laugh it off. Bolton Hall. 6880-4
"**Laugh** not fond foole cause I a face." Unknown. 6563-5
"**Laugh** out, O stream, from your bed of greens". Song ("Laugh out..."). Phoebe Cary. 6969-X
Laugh, and the whole world laughs with you. Ella Wheeler Wilcox. 6102-8,6694-1,6732-8,6076-5
"**Laugh,** and the world laughs with you". Solitude. Ella Wheeler Wilcox. 6006-4,6291-1,6632-1,6736-0,6300-4, 6964 ,7041-8
"**Laugh,** and the world laughs with you" Unknown. 6621-6
"**Laugh,** my friends, and without blame". To my friends who ridiculed a tender leave-taking. Matthew Arnold. 6947-9
A **laugh.** Ripley Dunlap Saunders. 6461-2,6654-2
The **laugh.** Thomas Edward Brown. 6809-X
The **laughers..** Louis Untermeyer. 6474-4,6029-3,6336-5,6542-2
Laughing bones. Alice Carter Cook. 6799-9
Laughing boy. George Cooper. 6706-9
A **laughing** chorus. Unknown. 6249-0,6373-X,6964-9
Laughing corn. Carl Sandburg. 6583-X,6121-1
"**Laughing** faces/serious hearts beat". Tomorrow's dream. Sheila Hertel. 6883-9
"**Laughing** mountain waters rush". Wild gooseberries-- Colorado. Lilian White Spencer. 6836-7
Laughing song. James Whitcomb Riley. 6993-2
A **laughing** song. William Blake. 6334-9,6466-3,6585-6,6454-X,6153-2,6668 ,6086-2
The **laughing** willow. Oliver Herford. 6089-7
Laughing woman. Anna Elizabeth Bennett. 6640-2
Laughlin, E.O.
    The doctor. 6482-5
    Inscription for a hospital. 6482-5
    The unknown ("I do not understand"). 6051-X
Laughlin, James
    A letter to Hitler. 6666-6
Laughlin, James (tr.)
    The fourth eclogue. Vergil, 6734-4
    Litany of the little bourgeois. Nicanor Parra, 6758-1
Laughter. Isabella Valancy Crawford. 6433-7
Laughter. James Oppenheim. 6030-7
Laughter. Robert Service. 6159-1
Laughter. Mary Craig Sinclair. 6954-1
Laughter. Unknown. 6916-9
Laughter and death. Wilfrid Scawen Blunt. 6102-8
"**Laughter** and song and mirth". The joys of earth. Edgar A. Guest. 6862-6
Laughter and tears. Tertius Van Dyke. 6337-3
"**Laughter** and tears to you the gods once gave". To Catullus. Ewart Alan Mackintosh. 6875-8
Laughter in heaven. Sister Mary Angeline. 6285-7
Laughter of the waves. Aeschylus. 7020-5
"**Laughter** trills down from the blossoming...". Swing high, swing low. Marjorie Coles Smith. 6799-9
"**Laughter!** 'tis the poor man's plaster". Laughter. Unknown. 6916-9
Laughtertown. Katherine Devereux Blake. 6847-2
Laughton, Freda
    Rain on a cottage roof. 6930-4
Laughton, James L.
    She would be a mason. 6277-6;6706-9
Launa Dee. Richard Hovey. 6735-2
Launch out into the deep. Joseph W. Arnett. 6799-9
"**Launch** out into the deep" Ida Norton Munson. 6144-3
"'**Launch** out into the deep'". Launch out into the deep. Joseph W. Arnett. 6799-9
The **launch..** Alice Meynell. 6477-9
The **launch.** Henry Wadsworth Longfellow. 6385-3
The **launching** of a ship. Thomas Caldecot Chubb. 6781-6
The **launching** of the ship. Henry Wadsworth Longfellow. 6142-7,6554-6,6404-3,6425-6,6565-1
Laura. Thomas Campion. 6186-9,6436-1,6182-6,6934-7
Laura. Bernard Raymund. 6880-4
Laura. Robert Tofte. 6182-6

LAURA

Laura Ann Phillips. June Curley. 6850-2
Laura Secord. Agnes Maule Machar. 6591-0,6592-9
Laura sleeping. Charles Cotton. 6208-3,6563-5,6189-3,6315-2
Laura's song. Oliver Madox Brown. 6437-X,6656-9
Laura, my darling. Edmund Clarence Stedman. 6429-9,6620-8, 6321-7
Laurana's song. Richard Hovey. 7006-X
Laurance, Ray
    The hollyhocks. 6374-8
Laureame: the marble dream. Emma Dunning Banks. 6426-4
The **laureate** of dulness. John Dryden. 6150-8
The **laureate's** bust at Trinity. Tom Taylor. 6802-2
A **laureate's** log. Unknown. 6440-X
The **laureate**. William Edmonstoune Aytoun. 6996-7
The **laureate**. Robert Graves. 6210-5
The **laureate**. William Whitehead. 6867-7
"**Laurel** and bay/Decked that poor shed". Twelfth night. Richard Lawson Gales. 6950-9
Laurel and cypress. J. Napier Milne. 7031-0
"The **laurel** crown". Fame. Lady Margaret Sackville. 6778-6
Laurel in the Berkshires. Adelaide Crapsey. 6850-2
Laurel Mountain, fr. Blue Juanita. Malcolm Cowley. 6531-7
"The **laurel** wreath of glory". A soldier's offering. George M. Vickers. 6920-7
The **laurel** wreath. Lizzie M. Hadley. 6268-7
The **laurels** are felled. Theodore de Banville. 6351-9
"**Laurels** for song! And nobler bays". 'To Louis honore Frechette' Sir Charles George Douglas Roberts. 6770-0
"**Laurels** may flourish round...conqu'or's tomb". Epitaph on Mrs. M. Higgins, of Weston. William Cowper. 6814-6
Laurence. Rossiter Johnson. 6014-5
Laurie, William
    Answer to 'I am dying'. 6910-X
Laurse, Ross
    The death penalty. 6792-1
Laus Deo. Robert Bridges. 6487-6,6641-0
Laus Deo. John Greenleaf Whittier. 6006-4,6176-1,6302-0, 6385-3,6600-3,6605 ,6641-0,6288-1,6126-5,6121-4
Laus deo! Theodore Maynard. 6884-7
Laus infantium. William Canton. 6250-4,6656-9,6274-1
Laus mortis. Frederic Lawrence ("R.L. Paget") Knowles. 6250-4
Laus veneris. Louise Chandler Moulton. 6431-0
Laus veneris. Algernon Charles Swinburne. 6828-6
Lausanne. Thomas Hardy. 6641-0,6657-7,6210-5
Lauterbrunnen. Thomas Gold Appleton. 6749-2
Lauterbrunnen. Samuel Rogers. 6749-2
Lauth. Robert Burns. 6510-4
Lautreamont, Comte de (Isidore L. Ducasse).
    The song of Maldoror, sels. John Rodker (tr.). 6343-8
    The songs of Maldoror, sels. 6351-9
Laval: noble educator. John Daniel Logan. 6115-X
Lavant, Christine
    "Behind the back of our time" Milne Holton and Herbert Kuhner (tr.). 6769-7
    "From the sunken road a rain frog croaks" Milne Holton and Herbert Kuhner (tr.). 6769-7
    "Through the steely air" Milne Holton and Herbert Kuhner (tr.). 6769-7
    "You have taken me from all joy" Milne Holton and Herbert Kuhner (tr.). 6769-7
Lavater, Louis
    The barrier. 6349-7
    Courage ("If in the past should brooding sorrow ..."). 6211-3
    Courage ("Two kinds of courage..."). 6784-0
    Mopoke. 6384-5
    Ocean. 6784-0
Lavazzi, Thomas G.
    Two women. 6860-X
Lavelle, Thomas
    The county of Mayo. George Fox (tr.). 6858-8,6858-8, 6244-X
Lavender. Archie Austin Coates. 6032-3
Lavender. W.W. Blair Fish. 6338-1
Lavender. Alfred Noyes. 6266-0,6653-4
Lavender. Unknown. 6273-3
Lavender and flame. Virginia Spiker. 6042-0

The **lavender** beds. William Brighty Rands. 6114-1
"**Lavender** breath of the sea". The fog-girl. Elisabeth Kuskulis. 6836-7
"**Lavender's** blue, dilly dilly, lavender's green". Unknown. 6363-2,6732-8
Lavengro, sels. George Borrow. 6107-9
Law. James Beattie. 6302-0,6385-3,6410-8
The **law** against lovers, sels. Sir William Davenant. 6472-8
A **law** agin it. Mrs. G. Archibald. 6920-7
Law and liberty. Elbridge Jefferson Cutler. 6964-9
Law at our boarding-house. A.C. Gordon. 6878-2
A **law** case. William Cowper. 6424-8
The **law** for the wolves. Rudyard Kipling. 6656-9
Law like love. Wystan Hugh Auden. 6210-5
"The **law** of God is one, as God is one...". The spirit of brotherhood. Joseph Mazzini. 6954-1
The **law** of averages. Troubadour [pseud]. 6817-0
The **law** of death. Sir Edwin Arnold. 6573-2
The **law** of liberty. Alice Cary. 6969-X
The **law** of love. Richard Chenevix Trench. 6654-2
The **law** of love. Richard Chenevix Trench. 6848-0
The **law** of the Yukon. Robert Service. 6159-1,6433-7,6115-X
"The **law** the lawyers know about" H. D. C. Peplar. 7014-0
The **law** the lawyers know about. Douglas Pepler. 6096-X;6044-7
The **law** west of the Pecos. S. Omar Barker. 6281-4
The **law** within, fr. Psalm 19. Bible. 6337-3
Law, R.H.
    Euthanasy. 7031-0
Law, T. (tr.)
    My bosom grac'd. Hafiz, 6448-5
    A Persian song. Hafiz, 6448-5
Law, a comic song. Unknown. 6878-2
Law-love. Unknown. 6878-2
The **law**. Samuel Butler. 6278-4
"The **Lawd** is dead". On philosophy. Barbara Marshall. 7024-8
"**Lawd**, tis harder by the day". And 'I know why the caged bird sings': a villanelle. Geroge Mosby Jr.. 6870-7
Lawes, Henry
    Anacreon's ode. 6328-4
    The captive lover. 6328-4
    A caution to fair ladies. 6328-4
    Love and music. 6328-4
    No constancy in man. 6328-4
    The reformed lover. 6328-4
    A smile or a frown. 6328-4
    'Tis true, fair Celia. 6328-4
    'Tis wine that inspires. 6328-4
    To Celia singing. 6328-4
    To his mistress upon going to travel. 6328-4
    Upon a crowned heart sent to a cruel mistress. 6328-4
Lawful wine. Hafiz. 6448-5
The **lawgiver's** boast. Sappho. 6435-3
The **lawgiver's** boast. Solon. 6435-3
The **lawlands** o' Holland. Unknown. 6055-2,6056-0,6075-7, 6258-X
Lawless, Emily
    After aughrim. 6244-X
    An appeal. 6090-0
    An appeal. 6090-0
    Clare coast. 6244-X
    Dirge of the munster forest. 6244-X
    An exile's mother. 6174-5
    Fontenoy 1745. 6090-0;6174-5
    Fontenoy, 1745, I. 6090-0
    Fontenoy, 1745, II. 6090-0
    From the burren. 6090-0
    The stranger's grave. 6174-5
Lawless, Margaret H.
    'Bring out your dead.' 6690-9
    Fightin fire. 6924-X
Lawlor, William T. (tr.)
    La Cubana. Otto Paul Gonzalez, 6898-7
    News of the neighborhoods. Otto Paul Gonzalez, 6898-7
    The ugly girl wants to eat an apple. Otto Paul Gonzales, 6898-7
"**Lawn** as white as driven snow", fr. The winter's tale. William Shakespeare. 6182-6,6302-0,6328-4,6668-2
"The **lawn** is set for vacation". The Afghani nomad coat

(part V) Rita Dove. 7032-9
Lawn order. William ("Wild Bill") Franklin. 6870-7
Lawner, Lynee (tr.)
    Lament of the steam shovel. Pier Paolo Pasolini, 6803-0
Lawrence. Rossiter Johnson. 7041-8
"**Lawrence** of vertuous Father vertuous Son". John Milton. 6562-7
"**Lawrence** of vertuous father vertuous son". Sonnet 017 ("Lawrence of vertuous father..."). John Milton. 6933-9
Lawrence, Abbott
    Before and behind. 6685-2
Lawrence, Annie M.
    Ben Isaac's vision. 6411-6
Lawrence, C.E.
    The daytime moon. 6069-2
Lawrence, David Herbert
    All of roses. 6301-2
    A baby asleep after pain. 6958-4
    A baby asleep after pain. 6872-3
    Ballad of another Orphelia. 6125-7
    Bare almond trees. 6354-3
    Bavarian gentians. 6641-0,6209-1
    Brooding grief. 6315-2
    The collier's wife. 6257-1
    Cruelty and love. 6234-2
    Dreams old and nascent. 6730-1
    The elephant is slow to mate. 6375-6
    End of another home holiday. 6209-1
    The evening land. 6069-2
    Fate and the younger generation. 6722-0
    Fireflies in the corn. 6393-4
    Fireflies in the corn. 6897-9
    Gloire de Dijon. 6872-3
    Green. 6897-9
    Green. 6354-3
    Grief. 6897-9
    How beastly the bourgeois is. 6125-7
    Humming-bird. 6246-6;6357-8
    Kangaroo. 6733-6
    Let us be men. 6357-8
    Meeting among the mountains. 6234-2
    Men in New Mexico, sel. 6958-4
    Moonrise. 6641-0
    Mountain lion. 6257-1,6354-3
    Nostalgia. 6872-3
    The optimist. 6357-8
    Pax. 6337-3
    Piano. 6150-8,6150-6
    The sea ("You, you are all unloving..."). 6258-X,6375-6
    Service of all the dead. 6234-2
    The ship of death, sels. 6375-6
    The ship of death. 6315-2,6210-5
    Slopes of Etna. 6184-2
    Snake. 6315-2,6357-8,6538-4,6510-4,6209-1,6108-2,6107-9, 6150-8
    The snapdragon. 6234-2
    Song of a man who has come through. 6209-1
    Song of death. 6879-0
    Sphinx. 6354-3
    Tortoise family connections. 6257-1
    The triumph of the machine. 6780-8
    Tropic. 6184-2
    A woman and her dead husband. 6897-9
    Work. 6354-3
Lawrence, Gordon
    Museum piece. 6979-7
    Prayer ("Lord-great Leviathan"). 6041-2
    Third Avenue. 6979-7
Lawrence, Jonathan
    Look aloft. 6425-6,6632-1,,6403-5
Lawrence, Kate
    The bed-post doll. 6965-7
    A little boy's wants. 6530-9
Lawrence, Lola Greenfield
    Heirloom lace. 6799-9
    To my beloved. 6799-9
Lawrence, N. Margaret Myers
    From my window. 6342-X
Lawrence, Patricia A.
    Uplifted spirit. 6857-X
Lawrence, Robert
    Barra. 6767-0
Lawrence, S. St. G.
    An answer. 6510-4
    A safe attachment. 7021-3
Lawrence, Thomas Edward ("Shaw") (tr.)
    The dog Argos, fr. The Odyssey. Homer, 6435-3
    Nausicaa, fr. The Odyssey. Homer, 6435-3
    Phaeacian nights – Demodocus, fr. The Odyssey. Homer, 6435-3
    The vision of Theoclymenus, fr. The Odyssey. Homer, 6435-3
Lawrence, Virginia
    Query. 6441-8
    Wisdom. 6441-8
Lawrence: the last crusade, sels. Selden Rodman. 6375-6
"**Laws** and governments are to the political...". The preface, fr. The fable of the bees. Bernard Mandeville. 6831-6
The **laws** of God, the laws of men. Alfred Edward Housman. 6532-5
"The **laws** of equilibrium". Lyric ("The laws of equilibrium"). John Smith [pseud]. 6751-4
The **laws** of verse. Alice Meynell. 6955-X
Lawson, Clarence
    A young man to his wife. 6761-1
Lawson, Henry
    The great grey plain. 6784-0
    The roaring days. 6384-5
    The sliprails and the spur. 6274-1
    The teams. 6384-5
Lawson, M.J. Katzmann
    The battle of Grand Pre. 6795-6
Lawson, Mabel N.
    To 'an amiable child'. 6750-6
Lawson, Richard
    Coal buckin' misery. 6149-4
    Don't want to work for nothing. 6149-4
Lawson, Todd S.J.
    For James Earl Carter. 6901-0
    Hamburger Mary's. 6792-1, 6998-3
    "On the fifth day of Easter" 6901-0
    "On the first day of Easter" 6901-0
    "On the fourteenth day of Easter" 6901-0
    "On the twenty-first day of Easter" 6901-0
    Wicked lady of Gough street. 6792-1
Lawton, David
    Life's purpose. 6617-8
Lawton, William C. (tr.)
    The Athenian monument, fr. Platea. Simonides, 6435-3
    "Straight is the downward journey, tho' it be". Unknown, 6435-3
    The way to hades. Unknown (Greek), 6435-3
    Whence and whither? Macedonius, 6879-0
"A **lawyer** of Brittany , once on a time". How the lawyers got a patron saint. John Godfrey Saxe. 6878-2
A **lawyer's** daughter. J.H. Thacher. 7021-3
A **lawyer's** farewell to his muse. William Blackstone Knight. 6878-2
The **lawyer's** farewell to his muse. Sir William Blackstone. 6889-8,6219-9
The **lawyer's** invocation to spring. Henry Howard Brownell. 6089-7,6240-7,6302-0,6385-3,6441-8,6505 ,6219-9,6652-6
The **lawyer's** lullaby. F.H. Coggswell. 6001-3
A **lawyer's** poem to spring. Henry Howard Brownell. 6629-1
Lawyer's prayer. Unknown. 6878-2
The **lawyer's** stratagem. Unknown. 6878-2
The **lawyer's** suit. John Godfrey Saxe. 6878-2
The **lawyer's** valentine. John Godfrey Saxe. 6878-2
A **lawyer's** will. Unknown. 6878-2
The **lawyers** know too much. Carl Sandburg. 6034-X,6736-0
"**Lay** a garland in my hearse". Song ("Lay a garland"). Francis Beaumont and John Fletcher. 6219-9
Lay a garland on my hearse. Francis Beaumont and John Fletcher. 6430-2
Lay a garland on my hearse. John Fletcher. 6052-8,6182-6, 6726-3,6181-3
"**Lay** a garland on my hearse of the dismal yew". Aspatia's

song. Francis Beaumont. 6933-9
"Lay aside phrases; speak as in the night". This is not
    death. Humbert Wolfe. 6782-4
"Lay by the weekly, Betsey, it's old like you". The fast
    mail and the stage. John H. Yates. 6912-6
"Lay by your pleading, love lies a-bleeding." Unknown.
    6317-9
Lay me down on the hill-top. Charles Erskine Scott Wood.
    6628-3
Lay me low. Unknown. 6273-3
"Lay me low, my work is done". Valedictory poem. Adam
    Lindsay Gordon. 6951-2
Lay me to sleep. William ("Fiona Macleod") Sharp. 6252-0
"Lay not your pencill'd cheek where love..read". Even as
    the grass. Ruth Enck Engle. 6750-6
Lay of ancient Rome. Thomas Russell Ybarra. 6118-4,6274-1,
    6089-7,6307-1,6722-0
A lay of Cape Cod. Daniel Barker Ford. 6798-0
Lay of eggs. Unknown. 6720-4
The lay of Elena. Henry Taylor. 6980-0
Lay of Gascoigne justice. John William Smith. 6878-2
The lay of Havelock the hur's court, fr. Sir Gawain.
    Unknown. 6193-1
The lay of macaroni. Bayard Taylor. 6440-X
The lay of Mr. Colt. William Edmonstoune Aytoun. 6948-7
A lay of real life. Thomas Hood. 6408-6
A lay of real life. Thomas Hood. 6974-6
The lay of St. Cuthbert. Richard Harris ("Thomas
    Ingoldsby") Barham. 6427-2
A lay of St. Gengulphus. Richard Harris ("Thomas
    Ingoldsby") Barham. 6278-4
A lay of the conscription. Unknown (Russian) 6681-X
A lay of the Derby sweep. M.C. Conway Poole. 6591-0,6592-9
Lay of the deserted influenzaed. Henry Cholmondeley-
    Pennell. 6724-7,6089-7
A lay of the early rose. Elizabeth Barrett Browning. 7037-
    X
Lay of the forlorn. George Darley. 6930-4
Lay of the grateful patient. F. D. 7021-3
The lay of the hospital race. Hugh Edmund Keough. 7010-8
The lay of the humble. Richard Monckton Milnes; 1st Baron
    Houghton. 6980-0
Lay of the imprisoned huntsman. Sir Walter Scott. 6600-3,
    6543-0
Lay of the Irish famine. Rosa Mulholland; Lady Gilbert.
    6696-8
The lay of the laborer. Thomas Hood. 6656-9
The lay of the laborer. Thomas Hood. 6820-0
The lay of the last minstrel, sels. Sir Walter Scott. 6260-
    1,6289-X,6395-0,6486-8,6623-2,6484 ,6239-3,6439-6,
    6301-2,6104-4,6430-2,6107
The lay of the last minstrel. Sir Walter Scott. 6198-2
The lay of the legion. William Edmonstoune Aytoun. 6948-7
The lay of the Levite. William Edmonstoune Aytoun. 6092-7
The lay of the Levite. William Edmonstoune Aytoun. 6948-7
The lay of the lovelorn. Sir Theodore Martin. 6802-2
The lay of the lover's friend. William Edmonstoune Aytoun.
    6278-4
Lay of the madman. Isaac Hinton Brown. 6014-5
Lay of the madman. Unknown. 6294-6,6408-6
The lay of the rose. Elizabeth Barrett Browning. 6980-0
A lay of the twaddle school. Unknown. 6787-5
"Lay on the fire their ancient hold". Burning the bee-
    tree. Ruth Pitter. 6893-6
"Lay out the earth in a sheet of snow". Thanksgiving.
    Benjamin Franklin Taylor. 6815-4
The lay preacher ponders. Idris Davies. 6210-5
"Lay the hand on the breast". An old-fashioned song. Ruth
    Pitter. 6893-6
A lay to the famine. Unknown. 6930-4
"Lay your sleeping head, my love". Wystan Hugh Auden. 6208-
    3
Lay, E. Elizabeth
    Margaret's guest. 6921-5
Lay, Elizabeth Stanton
    Query. 6750-6
Layamon
    King Arthur. 6301-2
Layamon, fr. The Brut. Unknown. 6198-2
Layde Maude. Cora Fabbri. 6682-8

"Laying here alone tonight". Rebirth. A.D. Winans. 6792-1
The layman. Edgar A. Guest. 6869-3
Layne, Castle
    Love's caramels lost. 6926-6
Lays of ancient Rome, sels. Thomas Babington Macaulay, 1st
    Baron Macaulay. 6554-6,6046-3
Lays of many lands, sels. Felicia Dorothea Hemans. 6973-8
Lays of the Scottish cavaliers. William Edmonstoune
    Aytoun. 6948-7
Lays of tom-cat Hiddigeigei. J.V. Scheffel. 6511-2
Layton, Irving
    Boschka Layton 1921-1984 6767-0
    Dionysians in a bad time. 6767-0
Lazarus. Alfred Cochrane. 7012-4
Lazarus. Arthur Shearly Cripps. 6788-3
Lazarus. Unknown. 6518-X,6549-X
Lazarus, Emma
    The banner of the Jew. 7041-8
    The banner of the Jew. 6431-0
    The crowing of the red cock. 7041-8
    The crowing of the red cock. 6006-4,6431-0
    The feast of lights. 6214-8
    Gifts. 6702-6,6214-8,6424-8,6730-1
    Inscription on the Statue of Liberty. 6465-5
    A masque of Venice. 6624-0
    A masque of Venice. 7041-8
    Mater amabilis. 6097-8
    The new colossus. 6337-3,6396-9,6585-6
    On the proposal to erect a monument...to Lord Byron.
        6309-8
    Raschi in Prague. 6673-9
    Venus of the Louvre. 6309-8
Lazarus, sels. John Gould Fletcher. 6011-0
Lazenby, Charles A.
    Myself. 6433-7
"Lazily, cloudlets, over the moon". The moonlight sonata.
    Henry Sambrooke Leigh. 6760-3
Laziness. Robert Service. 6159-1
Lazy. Benjamin Franklin Taylor. 6815-4
A lazy boy's idea. Rufus Clark Landon. 6529-5
Lazy daisy. Unknown. 6743-3
'Lazy folks take the most pains.' Unknown. 6713-1
"The lazy man, before his task is done". Of order, fr.
    Proverbs. Arthur Guiterman. 6861-8
The lazy roof. Gelett Burgess. 6089-7
"A lazy sea came washing in". Portsmouth bells. Unknown.
    7031-0
"The lazy Tapook raised his head". The Tapook's
    reception..., fr. The story of Balladeadro. George
    Gordon McCrae. 6768-9
The lazy writer. Bert Leston Taylor. 6026-9
"The lazy, sleepy Cape/Basking in the sun". An impression
    of old Cape Cod from a motor car. Eva Macey Watson.
    6798-0
Le Ber, N. Gordon
    Forgotten acres. 6042-0
Le Braz, Anatole
    The song of the oaks. Morys Gascoyen (tr.). 6232-6
Le Breton, Herve-Noel
    The burden of lost souls. 6873-1
    Hymn to sleep. 6873-1
Le Clerq, J.G. Clemenceau. See "Tanaquil, Paul"
Le Compte, Calvin
    The visitation. 6282-2
Le Cron, Helen Cowles
    Experience. 7038-8
    My book-shop. 7038-8
Le Fanu, Joseph Sheridan
    Abhain au bhuideil. 6174-5
    Beatrice, sels. 6174-5
    A drunkard's address to a bottle of whiskey. 6090-0
    A drunkard to his bottle. 6930-4
    A drunkard's address to a bottle of whiskey. 6090-0
    Hymn ("Hush! oh ye billows"), fr. Beatrice. 6174-5
    Hymn, fr. Beatrice. 6930-4
    The legend of the Glaive, sels. 6174-5
    Shamus O'Brien. 6385-3,6605-4,6344-6,6255-5
    The song of the spirits. 6930-4
Le Gallienne, Hesper
    Improvident. 6347-0

Le Gallienne, Richard
    After the war. 6946-0,7027-2
    All sung. 6785-9
    April night. 6252-0
    As in the woodland I walk. 6162-1
    Ballad of Amaryllis in the shade. 6029-3
    A ballad of London. 6507-4,6102-8,6439-6
    A ballade of old sweethearts. 6770-0
    Ballade against the enemies of France. 6875-8
    A ballade catalogue of lovely things. 6490-6
    Ballade of old laughter. 6875-8
    A ballade of old sweethearts. 6875-8
    Ballade of queen's lace. 6162-1
    Ballade of the hanging gardens of Babylon. 6875-8
    Ballade of the hanging gardens of Babylon. 6732-8
    Ballade of the junk-man. 6732-8
    Ballade of the road unknown. 6162-1
    Ballade of the things that remain. 6875-8
    Ballade of the unchanging beauty. 6488-4
    A ballade-catalogue of lovely things. 6476-0,6607-0, 6509-0,6153-2,6161-3
    Beatus vir. 6253-9
    Beauty accurst. 6507-4
    A caravan from China comes. 6310-1;6499-X;6509-0
    A child's evensong. 6242-3
    The cloister. 6872-3
    The cuckoo. 6073-0
    Desiderium. 6027-7,6581-3
    The destined maid: a prayer. 6875-8
    Dream tryst. 6879-0
    The eternal play. 6030-7
    The eternal way. 6289-X
    Flos aevorum. 6232-6,6266-0,6102-8,6250-4,6309-8,6320
    The happy smoking-ground. 6453-1
    I meant to do my work to-day. 6232-6,6338-1,6374-8,6503-1,6478-7
    'I will arise.' 6720-4
    London beautiful. 6331-4,6439-6
    The lonely dancer. 6250-4
    May is building her house. 6027-7,6232-6,6310-1,6338-1, 6503-1,6336-5,6509-0,6476-0
    A Melton mowbray pork-pie. 6089-7;6440-X
    Noon. 6162-1
    November. 6872-3
    The palaces of the rose. 6884-7
    The passionate reader to his poet. 6250-4
    A plea for the old music. 7014-0
    Regret. 6656-9
    Sacred idleness. 6607-0
    The second crucifixion. 6335-7,6337-3,6730-1
    Shadow. 6327-6
    "Small men at grapple with a mighty hour" 6995-9
    Song ("She's somewhere"). 6310-1,6250-4
    A song of bread and honey. 6466-3
    Songs for Fragoletta. 6078-1,6266-0
    Spirit of sadness. 6250-4
    Sunset in the city. 7014-0
    To a bird at dawn. 6073-0,6266-0,6250-4,6371-3,6102-8
    To a mountain spring. 6162-1
    To my wife, Mildred. 6046-3
    War. 6337-3,6490-6
    War poem. 6471-X
    What of the darkness? 6309-8
    When I am very old. 6732-8
    The wife from fairyland. 6310-1
    With pipe and book. 6453-1
    Wood flower. 6253-9
Le Gallienne, Richard (tr.)
    Comrades, the morning breaks. Hafiz, 6253-9
    Harvest. Hafiz, 6448-5
    Love's language. Hafiz, 6448-5
    Nostalgia. Hafiz, 6102-8
Le H, F.A.
    "This mortal body that I wear." 6273-3
Le Pan, Douglas V.
    Diamond. 6761-1
Le Prade, Ruth
    The lost joy, sel. 6954-1
Le Row, Caroline
    'Scallywag.' 6687-9,6577-5

Le Vayer, Francois La Mothe
    Epitaph on the Duchess of Maine's cat. Sir Edmund Gosse (tr.). 6511-2
Le bazar. Emile Verhaeren. 6801-4
Le beau navire. Charles Baudelaire. 6801-4
Le bonheur de ce monde. Plantin. 7020-5
"Le brouillard est froid, la bruyere est grise". Choses du soir. Victor Hugo. 6801-4
"Le cabaret est plein de panses". Image. Gustave Kahn. 6801-4
Le chasseur noir. Victor Hugo. 6801-4
"Le choeur. Elle est fille de roi.- Mais sa...". Cassandre. Victor Hugo. 6801-4
Le coeur de l'Immaculee. Benjamin Francis Musser. 6543-0
Le cor. Alfred de Vigny. 6801-4
Le depart. G.R. Wallace. 6116-8
"Le dernier jour d'un Condamne". George A. Baker. 6004-8, 6187-7,6632-1,6652-6
Le dernier ocean. Jean Richepin. 6801-4
Le derniere chanson. Isosceles [pseud]. 6817-0
Le docteur Fiset. William Henry Drummond. 6591-0,6592-2
'Le drapeau anglais' Louis Frechette. 7041-8
"Le galop de la houle ecume a l'horizon". Apparition. Henri de Regnier. 6801-4
Le glaive. Emile Verhaeren. 6801-4
"Le grand fleuve dormait couche dans la savane". 'La decouverte du Mississipi' Louis Flechette. 7041-8
Le houx. Remy de Gourmont. 6253-9
Le jardin. Oscar Wilde. 6244-X,6649-6
Le Jardin des Tuileries. Oscar Wilde. 6292-X,6649-6
Le jeune Barbaroux. John ("Evelyn Douglas") Barlas. 7009-4
Le jeune homme caressant sa chimere. John Addington Symonds. 6437-X
"Le jour s'eteint sur tes collines". L'hymne de la nuit. Alphonse Marie Louis de Lamartine. 6801-4
Le lac. Alphonse Marie Louis de Lamartine. 6801-4
Le lit. Jose Maria de Heredia. 6801-4
"Le luxe des Persans, O garcon, je deteste". Persicos odi, puer, apparatus. E. Adelaide Hahn. 6847-2
Le marais du cynge. John Greenleaf Whittier. 6615-1
Le mauvais larron. Rosamund Marriott ("Graham R. Tomson") Watson. 6671-2,6656-9
Le medecin malgre lui. William Carlos Williams. 6482-5
Le mistral. Maimie A. Richardson. 6269-5
Le monocle de mon oncle. Wallace Stevens. 6348-9
Le parti pris des choses, sels. Francis Ponge. 6803-0
Le passage de la barre. Eugene Aubert. 6847-2
Le pere Severe. Unknown (French) 6771-9
Le petit chat. Edmond Rostand. 6511-2
Le petit homme rouge. Pierre Jean de Beranger. 6801-4
Le plus doux moment. Ethelyn Alice Stoddard. 6836-7
'Le poilu de Carcassonne'. Unknown. 7031-0
Le printemps empoissone. Frances Westgate Butterfield. 6979-7
Le recit d'une soeur. Aubrey Thomas De Vere. 6046-3
Le repos en Egypte: the sphinx. Agnes Repplier. 6022-6, 6096-X,6282-2,6172-9
Le roi est mort. Agnes Mary F. ("Madame Duclaux") Robinson. 6437-X,6543-0
"Le Roman de la rose." Austin Dobson. 6652-6
Le rouet d'omphale. Victor Hugo. 6801-4
Le sacre de Paris. Charles Marie Leconte de Lisle. 6801-4
Le soir. Alphonse Marie Louis de Lamartine. 6801-4
"Le soleil dans les flots avait noye ses...". Les hurleurs. Charles Marie Leconte de Lisle. 6801-4
"Le sombre ciel lacte se voute en forme d'arche" Charles Guerin. 6801-4
Le vase brise. Rene Francois Armand Sully-Prudhomme. 6801-4
"Le vent hurle, la rafale/Sort, ruisselante...". Gros temps la nuit. Victor Hugo. 6801-4
Le vierge, le vivace et le bel aujourd'hui. Stephane Mallarme. 6106-0
"Le vierge, le vivace et le bel aujourd'hui". Sonnet. Stephane Mallarme. 6801-4
"Le vieux a gueule de bandit". Regard de pauvre. Jean Richepin. 6801-4
Le vieux caporal. Pierre Jean de Beranger. 6801-4
Le vin de l'assassin. Charles Baudelaire. 6801-4
The **lea** rig. Robert Fergusson. 6960-6

LEA

Lea, Fanny Heaslip
    The dead faith. 6730-1
Lea, Jocelyn C.
    The fly in church. 6249-0
Lea, Peter A.
    Actions speak louder. 6249-0
The lea-rig. Robert Burns. 6180-X
Leach, Bert
    The creek. 6906-1
    Interlude. 6906-1
    October. 6906-1
    Voices. 6906-1
    Wisdom. 6906-1
Leach, Grace W.
    The skaters. 7035-3
Leach, Marcia Lewis
    To Noel Davis. 7014-0
Leach, Virginia LePorin
    An ode to a mountain. 6799-9
Leacock, Stephen
    Melpomenus Jones. 6277-6
"Lead me in gently to my mother's arms". The dying convict. Charles W. Denison. 6755-7
Lead on, O king eternal. Ernest Warburton Shurtleff. 6337-3
"Lead thou me on. My path is steep". Divine guidance. Edward Hartley Dewart. 6796-4
Lead ye me on, O God. Cleanthes. 6435-3,6251-2
Lead, kindly light. John Henry, Cardinal Newman. 6001-3, 6014-5,6260-1,6407-8,6481-7,6289 ,6291-9,6304-7,6654-2,6737-9,6102-8,6192 ,6369-1,6459-0,6479-5,6498-1, 6238-5,6250 ,6104-4,6197-4,6723-9
Leaded glass saint. Israel Newman. 6072-2
"The leaden drops that in their stupor lie". Sonnet. James Abraham Martling. 6952-5
The leaden echo and the golden echo ("Recension"). Thomas Sturge Moore. 6536-8
The leaden echo and the golden echo. Gerard Manley Hopkins. 6246-6,6315-2,6334-9,6527-9,6536-8,6657 ,6655-0
"The leaden years have dragged themseles away". Pierrot at the war. Osbert Sitwell. 7029-9
The leaden-eyed. Vachel Lindsay. 6954-1
The leaden-eyed. Vachel Lindsay. 6337-3,6339-X,6375-6,6393-4,6464-7
Leader Haughs. Minstrel Burn. 6075-7
Leader of men. Robert Gordon Anderson. 6995-9
Leader of the gang. Edgar A. Guest. 7033-7
Leader-haughs and Yarrow. Unknown. 6180-X
The leader. Bible. 6512-0
The leader. Thomas Curtis Clark. 7001-9
Leaders, fr. Marmion. Sir Walter Scott. 6427-2
The leaders. Edith M. Thomas. 6121-4
Leadership. Edward Farquhar. 6939-8
Leading. Mary Carolyn Davies. 6461-2
Leading. Nagata. 6027-7
Leading the choir. Edith M. Norris. 6687-9
The leadsman's song. Unknown. 6258-X,6547-3
Leadville Jim. William W. Fink. 6920-7
Leaf after leaf drops off. Walter Savage Landor. 6232-6, 6737-9
Leaf and limb. Edward Farquhar. 6939-8
The leaf and the tree. Edna St. Vincent Millay. 6879-0
Leaf burning. Virginia Eaton. 6750-6
A leaf falls upon the grass. Imogen Merrill. 6397-7
"A leaf quietly wafts through the autumn". In the autumn. Han-mo Chung. 6775-1
Leaf, Walter (tr.)
    Archedike. Simonides, 6435-3
    Cenotaph. Glaucus, 6435-3
    Country gods. Plato, 6435-3
    A decoy partridge. Simias, 6435-3
    Euripides. Thucydides, 6435-3
    Lacrimae rerum. Palladas, 6435-3
    Lawful wine. Hafiz, 6448-5
    The lion over the tombs of Leonidas. Unknown, 6850-2
    The lion over the tomb of Leonidas. Unknown (Greek), 7039-6
    Lost at sea. Simonides, 6435-3
    The lyre and the crown. Marcus Argentarius, 6435-3
    Mycene. Pompeius, 6435-3
    A On a garden by the sea. Paulus Silentiarius, 6649-6
    On himself. Meleager, 6435-3
    An ox past service. Addaeus, 6435-3
    Pan and Daphnis. Glaucus, 6435-3
    Passing away. Lucian, 6435-3
    Prayer for home-coming. Julius Polyaenus, 6435-3
    The rest is silence. Palladas, 6435-3
    The ruins of Corinth. Antipater of Sidon, 6435-3
    A rule of life. Lucian, 6435-3
    Sophocles' tomb. Simias, 6435-3
    "A strange land holds thy bones...", fr. Lost at sea. Simonides, 6435-3
    Swimming. Hafiz, 6448-5
    A tomb by the sea. Asclepiades, 6435-3
    Unseen riches. Bianor, 6435-3
    Zeus too is a victim. Asclepiades, 6435-3
Leaf-burning. Karle Wilson Baker. 6607-0
The leaf-picking. Frederic Mistral. 7039-6
A leaf-treader. Robert Frost. 6042-0
A leaf.. John McGovern. 6274-1
The leaf. William Carson Fagg. 6870-7
The leaf. John Williams. 6388-8
"Leafless trees stand cold and stiff and stark". A sonnet ("The leafless trees"). F.L. Drummond. 6983-5
The leaflets. Kate Louise Brown. 6373-X
The leafy dead. Humbert Wolfe. 6780-8
A leafy welcome. Mary Jane Dew. 6818-9
Leagcies. Ethelwyn Wetherald. 6337-3,6115-X
Leagh's summons to Cuchulain. Unknown. 6090-0
Leagre, James Matthewes
    Flowers in ashes. 7017-5
    Haw-blossoms. 7017-5
    On the death of a kinsman. 7017-5
    The reaper. 7017-5
    To a lily. 7017-5
"League after league of sunshine, and a face". The gladness of the sea. Hardwicke Drummond Rawnsley. 6997-5
"A league and a league from the trenches...". Headquarters. Gilbert Frankau. 7026-4
The league of love in action. Edwin Markham. 6449-3
League of Nations. Nancy Byrd Turner. 6051-X,6542-2
The League of Nations. Mary Siegrist. 6946-0
The league of the Alps; or..meeting on field of Grutli. Felicia Dorothea Hemans. 6973-8
Leagued with death. Unknown. 6370-5
"Leagues north, as fly the gull and auk". The Palatine. John Greenleaf Whittier. 6833-2
Leahy, A.H.
    The song of the fairies. 6090-0
    The song of the fairies. 6090-0
Leahy, A.H. (tr.)
    Song of the fairies. Unknown, 6930-4
Leahy, W.A.
    Riding to the hunt. 6116-8
The leak in the dike. Phoebe Cary. 6451-5,6614-3,6569-4, 6865-0,6969-X
The leak in the dyke. Alice Cary. 6267-9
"The leakiest roof in all Vermont". Vermont farming tools. Daniel L. Cady. 6988-6
Leaming, Charlotte
    Plowers. 6799-9
Leamy, Edmund
    Gethsemane. 6172-9,6461-2,6292-X
    Ireland. 6292-X
    My lips would sing. 6292-X
    'My lips would sing-'. 6292-X,6607-0
    The ticket agent. 6331-4,6478-7,6499-X,6037-4
    Visions. 6107-9,6172-9,6292-X
"Lean down...lean down...and you will see". Sweeter than rain. Sara Van Alstyne Allen. 6761-1
"The lean gray rats of hunger". The lean gray rats. Skipwith Cannell. 6954-1
"Lean not on one mind constantly". Owen (Edward Bulwer-Lytton, Earl Lytton) Meredith. 6238-5
Lean street. George S. Fraser. 6379-9
Leanard tarries along. Sir Walter Scott. 6737-9
Leander's death. Musaeus. 6435-3
Leande, Richard

Moonlight on the Riviera. Robert Haven Schauffler (tr.). 6624-0
Leaners of lifters. Ella Wheeler Wilcox. 6337-3
"The **leaning** Dryad! See, her breast is pure". On a picture of trees by O.H. Gotch. Edward Harry William Meyerstein. 6779-4
"**Leaning** on the table with my head". Report card. Andy Roberts. 6883-9
"**Leaning** over a wall made up of numberless...". The vacuum conference. Kyu-dong Kim. 6775-1
A **leap** for lie. Walter Colton. 6552-X
A **leap** for life. George Pope Morris. 6211-3
"**Leap** from the crags, brave boy!". The dhoon. Thomas Edward Brown. 6809-X
The **leap** of Curtius. George Aspinall. 6912-6
The **leap** of Roushan Beg. Henry Wadsworth Longfellow. 6478-7,6498-1,6079-X
"**Leap** out of the wild terror of the pines...". Black funnel spouting black. Michael Roberts. 6985-1
"**Leap** out, chill water, over reeds and brakes". The river god. Sacheverell Sitwell. 6985-1
Leap year in the village with one gentleman. Unknown. 6276-8
A **leap-year** episode. Eugene Field. 6652-6
A **leap-year** lament. Eugene Field. 6949-5
The **leap**. Dana Chambers. 7019-1
Leaping falls. Galway Kinnell. 6388-8
The **leaping** poll. Hervey Allen. 6037-4
Leapor, Mary
　Mira's song. 6086-2
"**Leaps** the little river, and laughs at fetters". Sapphics. Don Marquis. 6850-2
Lear. Thomas Hood. 6656-9
Lear's prayer. William Shakespeare. 6385-3,6102-8
Lear, Edward
　A was an ant. 6452-3
　A. Apple pie. 6452-3
　The Ahkond of swat. 6089-7,6026-9
　An animal alphabet ("A-the absolutely abstemious..."). 6724-7
　At Dingle Bank. 6722-0
　The author of the "Pobble". 6105-2
　Calico pie. 6891-X,6722-0
　The dong with a luminous nose. 6290-3,6125-7
　The duck and the kangaroo. 6459-0,6454-X
　How pleasant to know Mr. Lear. 6722-0,6125-7,6633-X
　Incidents in the life of my Uncle Arly. 6722-0,6633-X
　The jumblies. 6089-7,6496-5,6427-2,6132-X,6242-3,6501 6125-7,6150-8,6371-3,6656-9,6861-8
　A justified fear. 6396-9
　Limerick:"..young lady of Norway". 6861-8
　Limerick:"..young lady whose eyes". 6861-8
　Limerick:"..old man in a tree". 6861-8
　Limerick:"..old man of Cape Horn". 6861-8
　Limerick:"..old man who said...". 6861-8
　Limerick:"..old man with a beard". 6861-8
　Limerick:"..old man who said 'Hush!'" 6739-5
　Limerick:"..an old man in a tree". 6724-7
　Limerick:"..old man in a tree." 6308-X;6083-8
　Limerick:"..old man of Lyme." 6527-9
　Limerick:"..old man of the Cape." 6811-1,6811-1,6308-X
　Limerick:"..old man of the coast." 6308-X
　Limerick:"..old man of the west". 7028-0
　Limerick:"..old man of Thermopylae." 6308-X,6739-5
　Limerick:"..old man of Vesuvius." 6308-X
　Limerick:"..old man who supposed." 6308-X
　Limerick:"..old man with a beard." 6308-X,6125-7
　Limerick:"..old person of Anerly." 6308-X
　Limerick:"..old person of Dean." 6466-3
　Limerick:"..old person of Ware." 6308-X;6466-3
　Limerick:"..young girl of Majorca." 6308-X
　Limerick:"..young lady of Wales". 6811-1
　Limerick:"..young lady whose bonnet." 6466-3
　Limerick:"..young lady whose chin". 6811-1,6811-1,7028-0
　Limerick:"..young lady whose nose". 7028-0
　Limerick:"..young person of Smyrna". 6811-1
　Limerick:"Although at the lim'ricks of Lear". 6811-1
　Limerick:"Said a foolish young lady of Wales". 6811-1
　Limericks by the limerick's inventor. 6861-8
　Lines to a young lady. 6902-9
　M ("M was once a little mouse"). 6722-0
　The new vestments. 6089-7
　Nonsense pictures in rhyme. 6891-X
　Nonsense rhymes. 6534-1
　The nutcrackers and the sugar-tongs. 6861-8
　The nutcrackers and the sugar-tongs. 6026-9
　The owl and the pussy cat. 6089-7,6127-3,6427-2,6466-3, 6479-5,6623 ,6135-4,6739-5,6104-4,6301-2,6638-0,6614 ,6722-0,6339-X,6401-9,6459-0,6490-6,6519 ,6424-8, 6454-X,6639-9,6732-8,6120-6,6132
　The pobble who has no toes. 6134-6,6135-4,6179-6,6289-X, 6356-X,6401-9,6089-7,6861-8
　The quangle wangle's hat. 6132-X,6496-5,6454-X,6964-9
　Says I to myself. 6722-0
　The table and the chair. 6452-3;6466-3
　There was a young lady of Corsica. 6125-7
　There was an old man of the Dargle. 6125-7
　There was an old person of Gretna. 6125-7
　There was an old person of Skye. 6125-7
　The two old bachelors. 6089-7;6290-3
　The yonghy-bonghy-bo. 6089-7,6739-5
Lear, Oscar H.
　The wide open spaces. 6817-0
Learn a little every day. Unknown. 6601-1
"**Learn** that to love is the one way to know." Jean Ingelow. 6066-8
"**Learn** to dissemble wrongs...". Ulysses. Nicholas Rowe. 6867-7
"**Learn** to live, and live to learn". To my daughter. Bayard Taylor. 6976-2
Learn to smile. Edgar A. Guest. 7033-7
Learn to wait. Unknown. 6273-3
Learn truly. Stepan Shepipachov. 6546-5
Learn your lesson. Alexander Smart. 6131-1
"**Learn,** all time's vagrants, where to look". The cosmopolitan. Alan Porter. 6776-X
"**Learn,** ye nations of the earth". On the death of the vice-chancellor, a physician. John Milton. 6814-6
The **learned** Negro. Unknown. 6911-8
The **learned** Negro. Unknown. 6089-7,6505-8
"A **learned** man, whom once a week". A fragment of science, fr. Hudibras. Samuel Butler. 6787-5
Learned women. Sir John Vanbrugh. 6943-6
Learned, Leila Sprague
　To my son, four days old. 6365-9
Learned, Walter
　Consolation. 6632-1
　Cupid's kiss. 6004-8
　Eheu! Fugaces. 7041-8
　Eheu! fugaces. 6004-8
　An explanation. 6273-3,6026-9
　Five little white heads. 6552-X;6632-1
　Growing old. 6083-8,6300-4
　In explanation. 6875-8
　In explanation. 6309-8
　The last reservation. 6632-1,6484-1
　Marjorie's kisses. 7041-8
　On a fly leaf of a book of old plays. 6632-1,6230-X, 6297-0
　Ona the fly-leaf of a book of old plays. 7041-8
　The prime of life. 7041-8
　The prime of life. 6274-1
　The song of the vane. 6632-1
　Time's revenge. 6004-8
　To critics. 6004-8
　Triolet, after Catullus. 6770-0
　The wayside well. 6632-1
　With a spray of apple blossoms. 6047-1
"The **learned,** full of inward pride". The two monkeys. John Gay. 6972-X
Learning. Mary Fullerton. 6384-5
Learning their letters. Unknown. 6713-1
Learning to be patient. Unknown. 6303-9
Learning to play. Abbie Farwell Brown. 6452-3
Learning to pray. Mary E. Dodge. 6045-1
Learning to sew. Unknown. 6684-4
Learning to walk. Unknown. 6312-8
Leary, T. Edwin
　Maud Rosihue's choice. 6451-5

LEAST

"The least flower, with a brimming cup...", sels. Elizabeth Barrett Browning. 6601-1
The least of carols. Sophie ("Ellen Burroughs") Jewett. 6006-4,6608-9
The leather bottel. Unknown. 6328-4
The leather bottel. John Wade. 6563-5
Leather, Robinson Kay
  Advice to a boy. 6301-2
Leatherland, J.A.
  Song ("Base oppressors"). 7009-4
  Song ("Base oppressors..."). 7009-4
Leaue leaue to weepe ornone, & now, moue. Unknown. 6563-5
"Leaue prolonging thy distresse" Thomas Campion. 6794-8
Leave a kiss within the cup. Agathias Scholasticus. 6435-3
"Leave God to order all thy ways". George Newman. 6238-5
'Leave her, Johnnie!' Cicely Fox Smith. 7031-0
Leave her, Johnny. Unknown. 6258-X,6732-8
"Leave him now quiet by the way". Trumbull Stickney. 6380-2
Leave it all quietly to God, fr. Psalm 62. Bible. 6337-3
"Leave it to the ministers, &..church will die". The layman. Edgar A. Guest. 6869-3
"Leave me alone here, proudly, with my dead". Somewhere in France, 1918. Almon Hensley. 6846-4
Leave me not yet. Felicia Dorothea Hemans. 6973-8
"Leave me not yet, through rosy skies from far". Felicia Dorothea Hemans. 6980-0
Leave me to my own. Lew Sarett. 6300-4
"Leave me to wither here by this dark pool". Syrinx. James Benjamin Kenyon. 7041-8
"Leave me, O love which reachest but to dust". Sir Philip Sidney. 6181-8,6182-6,6187-7,6634-8,6726-3,6194-X, 6430-2
"Leave me, all sweet refrains my lips...made". Sonnet ("Leave me"). Luis de Camoens [or Camoes]. 7039-6
"Leave me, O love, which reachest to dust". Sonnet ("Leave me, O love"). Sir Philip Sidney. 6150-8,6102-8
"Leave me, oh, leave me! - unto all below". Parting words. Felicia Dorothea Hemans. 6973-8
"Leave not Britannia's isle,since Pope is fled". Ode to taste. Thomas Warton (the Elder). 6962-2
"Leave the dull present, to seek awhile". The pirate's spuke. Arthur Guiterman. 6773-5
"Leave the lady, Willy, let the racket rip". Willy and the lady. Gelett Burgess. 7007-8
Leave the liquor alone. Unknown. 6617-8
"Leave the lovely words unsaid". Bird of passion. Rollo Britten. 6897-9
"Leave the main road". An old wagon road, fr. Roads in the lowlands. Marie W. Reddy. 6841-3
"Leave the thirsting cattle". Harvest home. (Frederick) Ridgely Torrence. 6979-7
"Leave the young hearts to nature and to God". Unknown. 6238-5
"Leave thine own home, O youth...". Encouragement to exile. Petronius Arbiter. 7039-6
"Leave this gawdy guilded stage". A Song ("Leave this"). John Wilmot, 2d Earl of Rochester. 6544-9
"Leave, arrive--leave, arrive". Time table. Fanny de Groot Hastings. 6799-9
"Leave, Caelia, leave the woods to chase". On his mistris that lov'd hunting. Unknown. 6933-9
Leave, fr. In war time. Wilfred Wilson Gibson. 6884-7
Leave-taking. Mary L. Viger. 6799-9
A leave-taking. Arno Holz. 7039-6
A leave-taking. Algernon Charles Swinburne. 6208-3,6196-6, 6430-2,6655-0
The leaven.. Henry Longan Stuart. 6096-X
Leaves. Richard Caldwell. 6397-7
Leaves. Jessie Stuart. 6761-1
Leaves. Sara Teasdale. 6393-4
The leaves and the wind. George Cooper. 6632-1,6131-1,6394-2,6143-5
"Leaves are clean trumpets blurting...". Leaves. Jessie Stuart. 6761-1
"The leaves are falling fast/Every tree...". Autumn. Jean J. Eastly. 6799-9
"The leaves are falling one by one". Autumn. Edgar A. Guest. 6862-6
"The leaves are falling: so am I". Walter Savage Landor. 6187-7

"The leaves are many under my feet". In autumn. Alice Meynell. 6955-X
"The leaves are sere, and on the ground". The leaves are sere. William Ernest Henley. 6770-0
Leaves at play. Frank Dempster Sherman. 6311-X
"Leaves blowing, and the young girls blowing". Campus. Ted Olson. 6761-1
"Leaves blown over water/By a wind after...". Reflection. Grace Mary Seeley Coryell. 6799-9
"The leaves floated down, crisp, brown". His Matisses, 1938 Julia Keeler. 6767-0
Leaves from fatherland. T.W. Handford. 6629-1
Leaves from the anthology. Lewis Parke Chamberlayne. 6030-7
"Leaves have not yet gone; then why do ye come". Unseasonable snows. Alfred Austin. 7015-9
"Leaves have their time to fall". Felicia Dorothea Hemans. 6238-5
Leaves of grass, sels. Walt Whitman. 6047-1,6255-5,6317-9, 6597-X,6560-0
The leaves of life. Edith (Bland) Nesbit. 6303-9
"Leaves of the lilac mingle with the flowers". Spring. Vincent O'Sullivan. 6174-5
"The leaves of trees". After the rain. Arthur A. Greve. 6857-X
Leaves on the Capitol grass. James Dawson. 6640-2
"The leaves on the ground". October augury. Ernest Rhys. 6782-4
The leaves). Unknown. 6049-8
"The leaves, once more dying". The sutumn has come. Jaroslav Vrchlicky. 6763-8
"Leaves/early morning". D.S. Long. 7018-3
The leaves. William Barnes. 6125-7
Leavetaking. Sir William Watson. 6023-4,6250-4
Leaving Barra. Louis MacNeice. 6536-8
Leaving England. Lena Whittaker Blakeney. 6397-7
'Leaving it out' in Vermont. Daniel L. Cady. 6989-4
Leaving Raiford. Mario Petaccia. 6870-7
Leaving Seoul: 1953 Walter Lew. 6790-5
Leaving smoke's. Gordon Henry. 7005-1
Leaving the homestead. Unknown. 6411-6,6964-9
Leavitt, John M.
  The Jewish captives. 6848-0
Leavitt, Mary Clement
  The birthday of Abraham Lincoln. 6524-4
LeBar, Winifred Stoddard
  "And thou would'st not!" 6144-3
  Rendezvous. 6750-6
Lechlitner, Ruth
  Dirge for civilization. 6490-6
  Only the years. 6979-7
  Song of starlings. 6979-7
Leck, Jane
  Robin and Meg. 7037-X
Leckie, Ross
  Turning once to look back. 6767-0
Lecky, Doris V.
  Cemetery. 6850-2
  Fairyland. 6850-2
  Forsythia. 6850-2
  Hawthorn for hope. 6850-2
  Inscription for a garage door. 6850-2
  Inscription for a garden wall. 6850-2
  Lace. 6850-2
  Night moth. 6850-2
  Palm Sunday. 6850-2
  The road. 6850-2
Lecky, William Edward Hartpole
  Early thoughts. 6174-5
  Homeward bound. 6250-4
  Love and sorrow. 6174-5
  Of an old song. 6730-1
  Old age. 6174-5
  On an old song. 6046-3
  Say not that the past is dead. 6199-0
  To - ("'Twas not"). 6250-4
  Unconscious cerebration. 6250-4
  Voices of the evening. 6174-5
LeClaire, Gordon

Chameleon. 6833-2
A half-caste prays. 6750-6
Lecompton's black brigade. Charles G. ("Miles O'Reilly") Halpine. 6946-0
Leconte de Lisle, Charles Marie
    The black panther. 6873-1
    The elves. 6351-9
    La chute des etoiles. 6801-4
    Le sacre de Paris. 6801-4
    Les hurleurs. 6801-4
    Les montreurs. 6801-4
    Les plaintes du cyclope. 6801-4
    Midi. 6801-4
    Sacra fames. 6801-4
    The spring. 6873-1
Leconte, Sebastien Charles
    Sappho. 6351-9
A **lecture** on avant-garde art. Jack Anderson. 7003-5
A **lecture** upon the shadow. John Donne. 6562-7
The **lecture.** Mrs. E.T. Corbett. 6928-2
The **lecturer.** Unknown. 6983-5
"Led on through many years to my last hours". Michelangelo Buonarroti. 6325-X
Leda. John Minczeski. 6966-5
Leda. Muriel Stuart. 6776-X
Leda. W. Wesley Trimpi. 6515-5
Leda. William Butler Yeats. 6071-4
Leda and the swan. Alice R. Friman. 6966-5
Leda and the swan. Oliver St. John Gogarty. 6930-4
Leda and the swan. William Butler Yeats. 6208-3,6150-8, 6491-4,6645-3
Ledig, Elizabeth Lineback
    Nostalgia. 6799-9
Ledoux, Louis V.
    The gift. 6556-2
    Hymn to Demeter, fr. A Sicilian idyl. 6027-7,6300-4
    Mater dolorosa. 6556-2,6102-8,6030-7,6076-5
    The only way. 6310-1
    Persephone (singing). 6076-5,6102-8
    Semper resurgens. 6331-4
    Slumber song. 6556-2,6653-4
    A threnody. 6027-7
    The unknown brothers. 6327-6
    We who were lovers o. 6030-7
    Whip-poor-will. 6033-1
Ledoux, Sidney
    Persephone (singing). 6076-5,6102-8
Ledward, Patricia
    Air-raid casualties: Ashridge hospital. 6475-2
    Evening in camp. 6666-6
    In memorium ("Timothy Corsellis"). 6475-2
    Maturity. 6475-2
Ledwidge, Francis
    After. 6812-X
    After court martial. 6812-X
    After my last song. 6812-X
    All-Hallows eve. 6812-X
    Ardan mor. 6244-X
    At a poet's grave. 6812-X
    At Currabwee. 6812-X
    An attempt at a city sunset. 6812-X
    August. 6812-X
    Autumn. 6812-X
    Autumn evening in Serbia. 6812-X,7027-2
    Before the tears. 6812-X
    Before the war of Cooley. 6812-X
    Behind the closed eye. 6266-0,6332-2,6653-4
    The blackbirds. 6812-X
    Bound to the mast. 6812-X
    The broken tryst. 6812-X
    By Faughan. 6812-X
    Ceol sidhe. 6812-X
    The coming poet. 6812-X
    Crewbawn. 6812-X
    Crocknaharna. 6331-4
    Dawn. 6812-X
    The dead kings. 6812-X
    The death of Ailill. 6812-X
    The death of Ailill. 6930-4
    The death of Leag, Cuchulain's charioteer. 6812-X

    The death of Sualtem. 6812-X
    The departure of Proserpine. 6812-X
    Desire in spring. 6506-6,6161-3,6393-4,6653-4
    A dream dance. 6812-X
    A dream of Artemis. 6812-X
    Evening clouds. 6812-X
    Evening clouds. 7027-2
    Evening in England. 6332-2,6102-8,6439-6
    Evening in February. 6812-X
    Evening in May. 6812-X
    Fairies. 6812-X
    Fate. 6812-X
    A fear. 6812-X
    The find. 6812-X
    The gardener. 6812-X
    God's remembrance. 6244-X
    Growing old. 6090-0,6301-2
    Had I a golden pound. 6812-X,6292-X,6812-X
    The herons. 6930-4,6812-X
    The herons. 6253-9,6022-6
    The herons. 6812-X
    The hills. 6812-X
    Home. 6812-X
    The homecoming of the sheep. 6331-4,6477-9,6478-7,6653-4
    In a cafe. 6812-X
    In France. 6812-X,7029-9,6812-X,7029-9
    In Manchester. 6812-X
    In September. 6096-X
    In the dusk. 6812-X
    In the Mediterranean - going to the war. 6812-X
    In the Mediterranean- going to the war. 7014-0
    In the shadows. 6812-X
    Inamorata. 6812-X
    Ireland. 6812-X
    June. 6244-X,6506-6,6153-2,6161-3,6464-7,6393-7,6653-4
    Lady fair. 6812-X
    Lament for the poets: 1916 6930-4
    Lament for the poets: 1916. 6872-3,7039-6
    Lament for the poets: 1916. 6292-X
    The lanawn shee. 6812-X
    A little boy in the morning. 6332-2
    A little boy in the morning. 6930-4
    The little children. 6812-X
    The lost ones. 6096-X;6234-2
    The lost ones. 6846-4
    Low-moon land. 6812-X
    The lure. 6812-X
    The maid in low-moon land. 6812-X
    May. 6812-X
    A memory. 6812-X
    A mother's song. 6812-X,6833-2
    Music on water. 6812-X
    My mother. 6812-X,6873-1
    Nocturne. 6812-X
    Old Clo'. 6812-X
    An old desire. 6812-X
    An old pain. 6812-X
    On an oaten straw. 6812-X
    On dream water. 6812-X
    Pan. 6812-X,6861-8
    The passing of Caoilte. 6812-X
    The place. 6812-X,7027-2
    A rainy day in April. 6234-2
    The resurrection. 6812-X
    The rushes. 6812-X
    The shadow people. 6332-2,6891-X,6254-7,6466-0,6476-0, 6506-6,6466-3,6653
    The ships of Arcady. 6812-X
    The ships of Arcady. 6833-2
    The singer's muse. 6812-X
    The sister. 6812-X
    Soliloquy. 6812-X
    song ("My heart has flown on wings..."). 6812-X
    Song ("Nothing but sweet music wakes"). 6812-X
    Song ("The winds are scented..."). 6812-X
    A song of April. 6812-X
    Song-time is over. 6812-X
    The sorrow of Findebar. 6812-X
    Spring. 6338-1,6253-9

Spring and autumn. 6812-X
Spring love. 6812-X
The sylph. 6812-X
Thomas MacDonagh. 6244-X
Thoughts at the trysting stile. 6812-X
Thro' bogac ban. 6812-X
To a distant one. 6320-9
To a linnet in a cage. 6943-6,6930-4,6812-X
To a linnet in a cage. 6510-4,6635-6
To a linnet in a cage. 6812-X
To a sparrow. 6073-0,6653-9
To an old quill of Lord Dunsany's. 6812-X
To Eilish of the fair hand. 6812-X
To Lord Dunsany. 6812-X
To Mr. McG. 6812-X
To my best friend. 6812-X
To one dead. 6812-X
To one weeping. 6812-X
To one who comes now and then. 6812-X
A twilight in middle march. 6244-X;6726-3
A twilight in middle March. 6930-4
Una Bawn. 6812-X
The vision on the brink. 6812-X
The visitation of peace. 6812-X
Waiting. 6812-X
The wedding morning. 6812-X
When love and beauty wander away. 6812-X
The wife of Llew. 6234-2,6477-9,6301-2
With flowers. 6812-X
Youth. 6812-X

Ledyard, Laura
Shopping. 6965-7
Supposing. 6965-7

Ledyard, Ray
Boat-building in Spain. 6116-8

Lee. Kate Langley Bosher. 6184-2
Lee. Archibald Rutledge. 6326-8

Lee (atr), Arthur
A prophecy. 6946-0

Lee at the wilderness. Mary [or Mollie] Evelyn Moore Davis. 6074-9
Lee in the mountains. Donald Davidson. 7017-5
The lee shore. Thomas Hood. 6383-7
Lee to the rear. John Reuben Thompson. 7017-5
Lee to the rear. John Reuben Thompson. 6113-3,6340-3,6062-5,6074-9,6016-2
Lee's parole. Marion Manville. 6946-0
Lee's parole. Marion Manville. 6074-9

Lee, Agnes
Bark-bound, fr. Pictures of women. 6033-1
The broken tie, fr. Pictures of women. 6033-1
The changeling. 6347-0
Cloud and flower. 6338-1
Convention. 6102-8,6556-2,6076-5,6396-9
The doll. 6031-5
Her going. 6897-9
In the morgue, fr. Pictures of women. 6033-1
Teep keeper of the lock. 6030-7
Motherhood ("Mother of Christ long slain..."). 6097-8,6627-5,6102-8,6393-4,6076-5
November 11, 1918. 6347-0
Old Lizette on sleep. 6034-X
An old woman with flowers, fr. Pictures of women. 6033-1
On the jail steps. 6897-9
On the jail steps. 7038-8
Peace. 6076-5,6102-8,6556-2
A peasant of Assisi. 6331-4
Pictures of women. 6033-1
Pictures of women, sels. 6033-1
Red pearls. 6030-7
A Roman doll. 6027-7
Shakespeare. 6347-0
The singer of the shadows. 6184-2
The slacker, fr. Pictures of women. 6033-1
A statue in the garden. 6232-6,6029-3
The sweeper, fr. Pictures of women. 6033-16102-8,6076-5
A sweet-eyed child. 6274-1
To a poet. 6266-0
To Robert Browning. 6327-6

Two canals. 6033-1

Lee, Alexander
The soldier's tear. 6087-0

Lee, Annabelle
Her hat. 6799-9

Lee, Benjamin
Brimiga's woe. 6936-3

Lee, Blanche
The last hymn. 6818-9

Lee, Deborah
Taking care of it. 6790-5
Where he hangs his hat. 6790-5
Women open cautiously. 6790-5
Words from a bottle. 6790-5
You're sorry, your mother is crazy, & I'm a Chinese... 6790-5

Lee, Dennis
Excerpts from 'Riffs' (a work in progress) 6767-0

Lee, Ed
Blend. 6178-8
Freedom's snare. 6178-8
Man. 6178-8
Southern justice. 6178-8
Tragedy. 6178-8

Lee, Frances H.
The happiest time of a woman's life. 6889-8

Lee, Frank
"He'll see it when he wakes." 6113-3,6340-3

Lee, Franklyn W.
House-cleaning. 6690-9

Lee, Guy
The first pager. 6995-9

Lee, Guy Forrester
The anxious anthemist. 6846-4

Lee, Harry
Angeline. 6607-0
The awakening. 6761-1
The bells of Califon. 6083-8
Home lights. 6320-9
The library at Hyannis. 6798-0
Madness. 6337-3
My master. 6144-3;6335-7;6337-3
Valentine for my mother. 6891-X

Lee, Holme
Lost on the shore. 6416-7

Lee, Jang-hi
The chirping cricket. 6775-1
"Snow falls" 6775-1
The spring is a cat. 6775-1

Lee, Joseph Johnston
Back to London: a poem of leave. 7027-2,7031-0
The drum. 6846-4
The gate of departure. 6269-5
German prisoners. 6337-3,6542-2,7031-0

Lee, Laurie
April rise. 6246-6
Day of these days. 6209-1
Juniper. 6379-9
Milkmaid. 6210-5
Poem ("The evening...") 6783-2
The three winds. 6209-1
The wild trees. 6246-6

Lee, Lawrence
For a poet growing old. 6619-4
For any lady's birthday. 6619-4
Subway builders. 6808-1
Subway builders. 7014-0
When Mars was near the Earth. 6761-1

Lee, Mary. See Chudleigh, Lady

Lee, Michelle
The flame. 6883-9

Lee, Muna
As Helen once. 6619-4
August. 6038-2
Behind the house is the millet plot. 6556-2
The carnival. 6397-7
Choice. 6619-4,6393-4
The drug-store. 6397-7
The duelist. 6397-7
Gifts. 6102-8,6076-5

"It will be easy to love you when I am dead". 6102-8
Prairie sky. 6038-2,,6038-2
The revival. 6397-7
There are but words... 6776-X
Tropical pool. 6393-4
Voters. 6397-7
"When we shall be dust." 6019-6
Lee, Muna (tr.)
Andean crossing. Alejandro Peralta, 6759-X
Clean clothes. Rafael Arevalo Martinez, 6759-X
Core. Jaime Torres Bodet, 6759-X
Cradle song to put a Negro baby to sleep. Ildefonso Pereda Valdes, 6759-X
Dregs. Cesar Vallejo, 6759-X
Elegy to the invented woman. Xavier Abril, 6759-X
Goat-pen. Luis L. Franco, 6759-X
The guest. Jorge Carrera Andrade, 6759-X
The illustrated world. Cesar Moro, 6759-X
It rained in the night. Jorge Carrera Andrade, 6759-X
"January night, quiet and luminous". Rafael Alberto Arrieta, 6759-X
Klare von Reuter. Jorge Carrera Andrade, 6759-X
The little girl that lost a finger. Gabriela (Lucila Godoy Alcayaga) Mistral, 6759-X
Love. Jaime Torres Bodet, 6759-X
Man's road. Enrique Pena Barrenechea, 6759-X
Mob of mountains. Jose Verallanos, 6759-X
The mocking-bird. Jose Santos Chocano, 6102-8
Nativity. Martin Adan, 6759-X,6734-4
Number 009. Constantino Suasnavar, 6759-X
Number 026. Constantino Suasnavar, 6759-X
Number 030. Constantino Suasnavar, 6759-X
On someone's death. Eugenio Florit, 6759-X
Pamphlet. Luis Munoz Martin, 6759-X
Proletarians. Luis Munoz Martin, 6759-X
Reaping the barley. Jorge Carrera Andrade, 6759-X
Second life of my mother. Jorge Carrera Andrade, 6759-X
Sierra. Jorge Carrera Andrade, 6759-X
Song to the glory of the sky in America. Emilio Oribe, 6759-X
The spring. Luis Fabio Xammar, 6759-X
Stroke of one. Jorge Carrera Andrade, 6759-X
Sunday. Jorge Carrera Andrade, 6759-X
Telegraph pole. Enrique Bustamante y Ballivian, 6759-X
Thirsting amphora. Rafael Heliodoro Valle, 6759-X
Vision of moth-eaten pianos falling to pieces. Cesar Moro, 6759-X
Vocation of the mirror. Jorge Carrera Andrade, 6759-X
Lee, Nathaniel
Blush not redder than the morning. 6563-5
"The Blush not redder thaought of me." 6092-7
Brutus and Titus. 6606-2
Thy genius, lo!, fr. The massacre of Paris. 6328-4
Lee, Sang
Mirror. 6775-1
Lee, Sang-hwa
Does spring come to a lost land. 6775-1
To my bedchamber. 6775-1
Lee, Sul-joo
Journey. 6775-1
Lee, Sylvia
Freedom. 6818-9
Lee, Virginia
Dying summer. 6764-6
Lee, William J.
Shelter. 6911-8
Lee, Yuk-sa
Grapes. 6775-1
Lee, Yung-gul
Birch tree. 6775-1
River village. 6775-1
Lee-Hamilton, Eugene
Baudelaire. 6301-2
The death of Puck. 6473-6
Elfin skates. 6473-6
Idle Charon. 7015-9
Idle Charon. 6301-2
Idle Charon. 7015-9
Ipsissimus. 6102-8,6670-4
Judith. 7015-9

Lethe. 7015-9
Mimma bella. 6473-6
My own hereafter. 6730-1
Oh, bless the law. 6250-4
The phantom ship. 7015-9,6997-5,7015-9,6997-5
Prince Charlie's weather-vane. 6793-X
The rise of Faustus. 6250-4
Sea-shell murmurs. 7015-9
Sea-shell murmurs. 6997-5
Sea-shell murmurs. 7015-9
Sea-shell murmurs. 6997-5
Sunken gold. 6274-1,6656-9,6380-2,6543-0
What the sonnet is. 6250-4
The **leech-gatherer**. William Wordsworth. 6138-9
Leedle Yawcob Strauss. Charles Follen Adams. 6505-8,6739-5
Leesome brand. Unknown. 6185-0
Leeson, Jane Eliza
Saviour, teach me. 6337-3
Leetla Giorgio Washeenton. Thomas Augustine Daly. 6891-X
Leetla Joe. Thomas Augustine Daly. 6486-8
Leetle Bateese. William Henry Drummond. 6266-0,6433-7,6476-0,6719-0,6102-8,6591 ,6592-9,6964-9
Lefebvre, Denys
Drought. 6800-6
Katrina. 6800-6
Moonlight. 6800-6
Oom Paul. 6625-9
Oom Paul. 6800-6
Silhouette. 6800-6
The voortrekker. 6625-9
The Voortrekker. 6800-6
Lefevre, Edwin
Quatrains of idlesness. 6274-1
Lefevre, Lily Alice
Mavis. 6797-2
Song of the St. Lawrence. 6797-2
The spirit of the carnival. 7035-3
Lefroy, Edward Cracroft
A football player. 6396-9
Love's delay. 6274-1
O love, o love, how long? 6274-1
On a dull dog. 6274-1
On the beach in November. 7015-9,6997-5
A Philistine. 6274-1
A philistine. 6274-1
Rataplan. 6097-8,6274-1
Something lost. 7015-9
Suburban meadows. 7015-9
A thought from Pindar. 7015-9
Two thoughts. 6793-X
Lefroy, Edward Cracroft (tr.)
Cleonicos. Theocritus, 7039-6
The grave of Hipponax. Theocritus, 7039-6
The monument of Cleita. Theocritus, 7039-6,6879-0
A Sylvan revel. Theocritus, 7039-6
Left alone. Unknown. 6260-1,6715-8
Left alone at eighty. Alice Robbins. 6406-X
Left on the battle-field. Sarah Tittle Bolton. 6016-2
Left on the battle-field. Sarah Knowles Knowles. 6302-0;6385-3
"Left to the saviour's conquering foes". Ther last crusader. Edward Bulwer-Lytton; Baron Lytton. 6980-0
"Left!/Left!/Had a good girl when I". A marching soliloquy. Unknown. 6846-4
The **leg** in the subway. Oscar Williams. 6389-6
"Leg over leg". Unknown. 6363-2
Legacy. Alta Booth Dunn. 6662-3
Legacy. Ruth Winant Wheeler. 6144-3
A legacy. Karl Gustaf of Leopold. 6045-5
The legacy. Thomas Moore. 6830-8
Legal fiction. William Empson. 6150-8,6354-3,6391-8
Legare, James Matthews
Ahab Mohammed. 6459-0
LeGear, Laura Lourene
Water mocassin. 6979-7
Legem tuam dilexi. Coventry Patmore. 6931-2
Legem tuam dilexi. Coventry Patmore. 6489-2
Legem tuam dilexi. Coventry Patmore. 6931-2
Legend. George Dillon. 6039-0
Legend. Davd Morton. 6850-2

LEGEND

Legend. Adul Tima [pseud]. 6817-0
Legend. (Frederick) Ridgely Torrence. 6833-2
Legend. John V.A. Weaver. 6506-6,6736-0,6467-1
A legend ("Christ, when a child..."). Peter Ilich Tschaikovsky. 6608-9
Legend and truth. John Holmes. 6042-0
The legend beautiful. Henry Wadsworth Longfellow. 6661-5, 6706-9,6419-1,6114-1,6964-9
Legend for library door. Chapman J. Milling. 7016-7
Legend from Cabell. Myrril [pseud]. 6817-0
The legend of a shirt. Richard Harris ("Thomas Ingoldsby") Barham. 6302-0
The legend of Aino, fr. Kalevala. Unknown (Finnish) 6679-8
A legend of Arabia. Unknown. 6671-2
The legend of Bishop Hatto. Robert Southey. 6136-2,6479-5, 6496-5
The legend of boastful Bill. Charles Badger Clark Jr. 7010-8
A legend of Bregenz. Adelaide Anne Procter. 6142-7,6344-6, 6554-6,6610-0,6661-5,6263-6,6267-9
Legend of Crystal Spring. Henry W. Austin. 6920-7
The legend of Easter eggs. Fitz-James O'Brien. 6614-3;6171-0
The legend of Easter eggs. Unknown. 6928-2
The legend of Fergus Leideson. Sir Samuel Ferguson. 6090-0
The legend of Florence, sels. Leigh Hunt. 6980-0
The legend of ghost lagoon, sels. Joseph Schull. 6021-8
The legend of Glooscap. Arthur Wentworth Hamilton Eaton. 7041-8,6797-2
The legend of good women, sels. Geoffrey Chaucer. 6193-1, 6378-0,6193-1
The legend of Heinz von Stein. Charles Godfrey Leland. 6083-8;6089-7
A legend of Hinemoa. Margaret A. Sinclair. 6591-0,6592-9
The legend of Innisfallen. Minnie D. Bateham. 6415-9
Legend of Iyob the upright. George Anson Jackson. 6848-0
The legend of Jubal. George Eliot. 6848-0
The legend of Kalooka. I. Edgar Jones. 6920-7
The legend of King Nilus. Edith Wordsworth. 6926-6
A legend of Lake Okeefinokee. Laura E. Richards. 6554-X
A legend of Madrid. Unknown (Spanish) 6951-7
A legend of Maiden Lane. Arthur Guiterman. 6773-5
The legend of manor hall. Thomas Love Peacock. 6760-3
A legend of Navarre. Thomas Hood. 6974-6
The legend of Ogre castle. Thomas Dunn English. 6672-0
A legend of paradise. Benjamin Ward Richardson. 6848-0
A legend of Provence. Adelaide Anne Procter. 6661-5
The legend of Qu'Appelle Valley. Emily Pauline ("Tekahionwake") Johnson. 6291-0,6592-2,6648-8
The legend of Qu'Appelle valley. Emily Pauline ("Tekahionwake") Johnson. 6837-5
The legend of Rabbi Ben Levi. Henry Wadsworth Longfellow. 6848-0
The legend of Rabbi Ben Levi. Henry Wadsworth Longfellow. 6077-3,6236-9
Legend of Ramapo mountains. Jennie M. Palen. 6218-0
The legend of realism. Hilda Johnson. 6440-X
A legend of rose Sunday. Emma Dunning Banks. 6426-4
Legend of secret guilt. Otakar Brezina. 6886-3
A legend of service. Henry Van Dyke. 6961-4
The legend of Siwash rock. A.M. Stephen. 6797-2
Legend of St. Christopher. Unknown. 6304-7
The legend of St. Christopher. Mary Fletcher. 6416-7,6669-0
The legend of St. Freda. Sarah D. Hobart. 6922-3
A legend of St. Valentine. George A. Baker. 6187-7
The legend of Tawhaki, fr. Ranolf and Amohia. Alfred Domett. 6768-9
Legend of the aspen. Unknown. 6049-8
Legend of the bewitched nunnery. Max Herrmann-Neisse. 6160-5
The legend of the Bronx. Arthur Guiterman. 6773-5
A legend of the Christ-child. Mary Clarke Huntington. 6807-3
The legend of the Christmas rose. Florence Boyce Davis. 6449-3
Legend of the Corrievrechan. George Macdonald. 6819-7
The legend of the dead lambs. Owen (Edward Bulwer-Lytton, Earl Lytton) Meredith. 6848-0
The legend of the dead lambs. Owen (Edward Bulwer-Lytton, Earl Lytton) Meredith. 6656-9
A legend of the dove. George Sterling. 6300-4
The legend of the first cam-u-el. Arthur Guiterman. 6089-7, 6102-8,6076-5,6026-9,6464-7
The legend of the fleur-de-lis. Mabel Cronise. 6925-8
The legend of the forget-me-not. Unknown. 6889-8
legend of the ghost lagoon. Joseph Schull. 6264-4
The legend of the Glaive, sels. Joseph Sheridan Le Fanu. 6174-5
Legend of the heather. Unknown. 6674-4
The legend of the lily. Annie Wall. 6674-7
A legend of the northland. Phoebe Cary. 6135-4,6964-9,6060-9
The legend of the organ builder. Julia C.R. Dorr. 6917-7
The legend of the organ-builder. Julia C.R. Dorr. 6486-8, 6610-0
The legend of the organ-builder. Unknown. 6215-6,6742-5
The legend of the Tawhaki. Alfred Domett. 6591-0,6592-9
A legend of the true. Marietta F. Cloud. 6675-5
Legend of the valley lilies. Alma Frances McCollum. 6797-2
A legend of the west highlands, fr. Ticonderoga. Robert Louis Stevenson. 6805-7
Legend of the willow-pattern plate. Unknown. 6671-2
A legend of the wise king. James A. McCreedy. 6848-0
A legend of three missions. Lee C. Harby. 6674-7
The legend of thunder. H.R.A. Pocock. 6795-6
A legend of Toledo. Richard Chenevix Trench. 6614-3
The legend of Walbach tower. George Houghton. 6946-0
The legend of Waukulla. Hezekiah Butterworth. 6946-0
The legend of woman. Milutin Bojic. 6765-4
A legend of Ypres. Elinor Jenkins. 6474-4
A legend.. May Kendall. 6274-1,6656-9
A legend. Nathan Haskell Dole. 6144-3
A legend. Rose A. Hannon. 6894-4
A legend. Rose Osborne. 6225-3
A legend. Adelaide Anne Procter. 6172-9
A legend. Richard Henry Stoddard. 6424-8
A legend. Unknown. 6918-5
A legend. Unknown. 6337-3
Legends for trees. Emily Vanderbilt Hammond. 6585-6
The legends of evil, sels. Rudyard Kipling. 6339-X
The legends of evil. Rudyard Kipling. 6810-3
Legge, Arthur E.J.
Blossom and bird. 6793-X
Charles Kingsley. 6793-X
The losing side. 6253-9
On Exmoor. 6793-X
A song of faith. 6785-9
Leggett, Benjamin F.
The quest of the Magi. 6807-3
Leggett, William
Love and friendship. 6600-3,6226-1
LeGron, Gretelle Suzanne
Last journey. 6857-X
Questions to an image. 6857-X
The legion of honor. Henry Lynden Flash. 6074-9
The legion of iron. Lola Ridge. 6375-6
"'The legion that never was listed'". The tropics. Charles Johnson Post. 7007-8
"The legions of Lee, all exultant of manner". The flag at Gettysburg. John E. Barrett. 6840-5
Legislators. Bible. 6954-1
The legless man. Robert Service. 6159-1
Legs. Dennis Kelly. 7003-5
The legs without the man. William Cowper. 6634-8
"Legs, hips, breasts, immersion". Bennington lake. Gene Fendt. 6857-X
The legs. Robert Graves. 6257-1,6354-3,6391-8
Lehman, Suzanne
Grievous words. 6249-0
Lehmann, John
In two cities. 6042-0
A little distance off. 6354-3
This excellent machine. 6354-3
Lehmann, Rudolph Chambers
At Putney. 6785-9
Ave Caesar! 7008-6
The bath. 7008-6
The dancer. 6959-2
Easy. 6155-9

The first child. 6233-4
The old gray mare. 7010-8
The runaway rhyme. 6760-3
To Rufus, a spaniel. 6423-X
Lehmer, Derrick
Riches. 6076-5,6102-8,6102-8
Lehmer, Eunice Mitchell
Armistice. 6420-5,6461-2,6542-2
The watchman. 7001-9
Lehmer, Verona Watson
Puerto Rico. 6270-9
Leicester chambermaid. Unknown. 6157-5
Leichhardt. Henry Clarence Kendall. 6768-9
"**Leif** was a man's name". Saga of Leif the lucky, sels. Hervey Allen. 6833-2
Leigh, Felix
The old doll to the new one. 6684-4
Leigh, Henry S.
Getting up. 6920-7
Leigh, Henry Sambrooke
The ballad of baby bunting. 6078-1
Chateaux d'Espagne. 6802-2
Cossimbazar. 6089-7
Maud. 6089-7
The moonlight sonata. 6760-3
My after-dinner cloud. 6453-1
My love and my heart. 6089-7,6120-6,6652-6
My three loves. 6453-1
A nursery legend. 6089-7
Only seven. 6089-7;6385-3;6440-X
Romantic recollections. 6724-7
The romaunt of Humpty Dumpty. 6089-7
'Thus ever thus. 6089-7;6440-X
The twins. 6219-9,6464-7,6089-7,6290-3,6280-6,6356-X, 6385-3
Leigh, Richard
Her window. 6562-7,6563-5
Sleeping on her couch. 6208-3
Leighton, Louise
St. Louis river. 6342-X
Leighton, Mary
Palm Beach. 6818-9
Leighton, Robert
John and Tibbie Davison's dispute. 6914-2
Scotch words. 6279-2
Leila. George Hill. 6176-1
Leinster. Louise Imogen Guiney. 6022-6,6292-X
Leiper, Esther M.
Sea love. 6857-X
Leipsydrion. Unknown (Greek) 6435-3
Leirioessa kalyx. Maurice Baring. 6437-X
Leishman and S. Spender, J.B. (tr.)
The second duino elegy. Rainer Maria Rilke, 6068-4
Leishman, J.B. (tr.)
The death of the poet. Rainer Maria Rilke, 6879-0
Leisure. William Henry Davies. 6464-7, 6508-2,6427-2,6477-9,6501-5,6726-3,6102-8,6250-4,6668-2,6371-3,6421-3, 6639-9
Leisure. Rosemary Farrar. 6761-1
The **leisure** classes. Unknown. 6274-1
"**Leisure** the serfs will not forget". Reading Tolstoy. John Peter. 6788-3
Leitch, Mary Sinton
April. 6326-8
Before. 6954-1
Charlemagne. 6331-4,6631-3
Clues. 6039-0,6326-8
Failure. 6144-3;6335-7
Glacier. 6102-8
He who has known a river. 6619-4
He who loves the ocean. 6979-7
Identity. 6042-0
In a railway station. 6038-2
Johnny onions. 6039-0
Lines to a dictator. 6761-1
Mallows of the marshes. 7038-8
My instant. 6326-8
Nightfall on the Lynnhaven. 6039-0
One rose. 6441-8,6037-4
The pagan. 6326-8
Pity the great. 6326-8
The poet. 6037-4,6088-9,6326-8
The poet. 6326-8
Point of view. 6211-3
The proffered cup. 6039-0
The road to London. 7038-8
Sea words. 6833-2
The secret. 6326-8
Shelter. 6320-9
Ship of the years. 6347-0
Snowfall in the wood. 6038-2
Statue inscribed 'Lee,' Richmond. 6326-8
To a city man. 6750-6
To my mother ("Your form is dim..."). 6097-8
To the little jessamine. 6038-2
The voice. 6038-2
When spring came to Nazareth. 6144-3
Leith races. Robert Fergusson. 6086-2
Leitner
The crusade. Louis J. Magee (tr.). 7004-3
A **Leitrim** woman. Lyle Donaghy. 6930-4
Leland & John Dyneley Prince, Charles Godfrey (tr.)
How Kuloskap conquered Aklibimo, the great bullfrog. Unknown (Algonquin Indian), 6864-2
How Kuloskap granted gifts and favors to many Indians. Unknown (Algonquin Indian), 6864-2
Kuloskap and the beaver. Unknown (Algonquin Indian), 6864-2
Kuloskap and the fool. Unknown (Algonquin Indian), 6864-2
Kuloskap and the loons. Unknown (Algonquin Indian), 6864-2
Kuloskap and the wise wishers. Unknown (Algonquin Indian), 6864-2
Kuloskap and the witch. Unknown (Algonquin Indian), 6864-2
Kuloskap and the witch called 'The Pitcher'. Unknown (Algonquin Indian), 6864-2
Kuloskap and Winpe; or, the master's first victory. Unknown (Algonquin Indian), 6864-2
The sable and the serpent. Unknown (Algonquin Indian), 6864-2
The song of the stars. Unknown (Algonquin Indian), 6864-2
The three brothers who became trees. Unknown (Algonquin Indian), 6864-2
Leland, Charles Godfrey
A ballad of charity. 6089-7,6508-8
Ballad of Hans Breitmann. 6089-7
Ballad of the mermaid. 7025-6,6760-3
Carey, of Carson. 7025-6
Eva. 6004-8
The fisher's cottage. 6302-0
Hans Breitmann and the Turners. 6791-3,6823-5
Hans Breitmann's party. 6089-7,6240-7,6302-0,6300-4, 6307-1,6092-7,6155-9,6505-8
Howling of the witches. 6696-8
An invention. 6983-5
The legend of Heinz von Stein. 6083-8;6089-7
The masher. 7025-6
Maud Miller [in Dutch]. 6175-3
Mine own. 6600-3
The music-lesson of Confucius. 6600-3
Out and fight. 6946-0
The proclamation. 6524-4
The riddler. 6165-6
Ritter Hugo. 6385-3
Romany song. 6321-7
Schnitzerl's philosopede. 6791-3,6823-5
Schnitzerl's velocipede [or philosopede]. 6155-9
Theleme! 6004-8
There's a time to be jolly. 6441-8,6652-6
To a friend studying German. 6791-3
The two friends. 6309-8
The water fay. 6302-0
Leland, Charles Godfrey (tr.)
Almansor. Heinrich Heine, 6484-1
birth of Kuloskap, the lord of beasts and men...The. Unknown (Algonquian Indian), 6864-2
The blind boy. Unknown (Algonquin Indian), 6864-2

The creation of man and the animals. Unknown
 (Algonquian Indian), 6864-2
The dance of old age. Unknown (Algonquin Indian), 6864-2
The fisher's cottage. Heinrich Heine, 6271-7
How a witch sought to cajole the master. Unknown
 (Algonquin Indian), 6864-2
How a witch sought to cajole the master. Unknown
 (Algonquin Indian), 6864-2
How Kuloskap fought the giant sorcerers at Saco.
 Unknown (Algonquin Indian), 6864-2
How Kuloskap left the world. Unknown (Algonquin Indian),
 6864-2
How Kuloskap named the animals. Unknown (Algonquin
 Indian), 6864-2
How Kuloskap sailed through the cavern of darkness.
 Unknown (Algonquin Indian), 6864-2
How Kuloskap was conquered by the babe. Unknown
 (Algonquin Indian), 6864-2
How Kuloskap went whale-fishing. Unknown (Algonquin
 Indian), 6864-2
How Mikchik the turtle was false to the master. Unknown
 (Algonquin Indian), 6864-2
How the great master showed himself a great smoker.
 Unknown (Algonquin Indian), 6864-2
How the Indians lost their power. Unknown (Algonquin
 Indian), 6864-2
How the master found the summer. Unknown (Algonquin
 Indian), 6864-2
Kuloskap and the turtle. Unknown (Algonquin Indian),
 6864-2
Kuloskap and Wucho'sen, the wind-eagle. Unknown
 (Algonquin Indian), 6864-2
Lox, the Indian devil. Unknown (Algonquin Indian), 6864-2
The master and the final day. Unknown (Algonquin
 Indian), 6864-2
The origin of rattlesnakes. Unknown (Algonquian Indian),
 6864-2
The partridge and the spring. Unknown (Algonquin
 Indian), 6864-2
The scarlet tanager and the leaf. Unknown (Algonquin
 Indian), 6864-2
Sleep, little darling. Unknown (German), 6233-4
The song of Lappilatwan, the singer in the dusk.
 Unknown (Algonquin Indian), 6864-2
The story of Nipon the summer. Unknown (Algonquin
 Indian), 6864-2
The water fay. Heinrich Heine, 6271-7,6302-0
What Kuloskap did for the Indians. Unknown (Algonquin
 Indian), 6864-2
The woman and the serpent. Unknown (Algonquin Indian),
 6864-2
Leland, Marian
A sonnet to that great mother Schumann-Heink. 6365-9
Lelant. E.K. Chambers. 6477-9
Lemaitre, Jules
A cat. 6120-6
Lemarr, D.F.
The roving rebel. 6074-9
LeMieux, Dotty
Poem for Robert Creeley. 6998-3
A **lementable** new ballad upon the Earle of Essex...
 Unknown. 6157-5
Lemke, Dan
Giant mushrooms. 6883-9
Lemke, E.
A rhyme of musicians. 6089-7,6724-7
The **lemmings.** John Masefield. 6491-4
The **lemmings.** Donald A. Stauffer. 6666-6
Lemoine, G.
Blacksmith's song (no. 2). 6711-5
The blacksmith. 6701-8
Lemon, Mark
Abraham Lincoln. 6304-7
How to make a man of consequence. 6089-7
Old time and I. 6273-3
Lemont, Jessie
Diana remembers Actaeon. 6979-7
Snake. 6232-6

Snake. 6782-4
LeNart, Marie
Atonement. 6144-3
Litany. 6144-3;6335-7
Lemont, Jessie (tr.)
Presaging. Rainer Maria Rilke, 7039-6
Lemuel's song. George Wither. 6219-9
Lenachan's farewell. Unknown. 6859-6
Lend a hand. Edward Everett Hale. 6337-3
"**Lend** me your ears, thou man of law". To -, the lawyer.
 Unknown. 6878-2
Length of days. Alice Meynell. 6096 X
Length of life. Hesiod. 6435-3
The **length** of life. Amos R. Wells. 6461-2
Lenigrad: 1943, fr. The Pulkovo meridian. Inberm Vera.
 6665-8
Lenin. MacKnight Black. 6880-4
Lenin in winter. Ernst Jandl. 6769-7
"**Lenin**". Josef Mayer-Limberg. 6769-7
Leningrad: 1943, fr. The Pulkovo meridian. Vera Inber.
 6665-8
Lenna's dream. Unknown. 6740-9
"**Lennavan-mo**". Lullaby ("Lennavan-mo"). William ("Fiona
 Macleod") Sharp. 6873-1
Lennen, Elinor
Before a trophy case. 6316-0
A caller for Samuel Taylor Coleridge. 6316-0
Fellowship. 6144-3
Geometry discredited. 6316-0
Harvest. 6316-0
How worlds and seasons turn. 6316-0
'No quiet'. 6420-5
Pilgrimage ("Discord and darkness, but the song...").
 6463-9
Lenngren, Anna Maria
The boy and his playthings. Charles Wharton Stork
 (tr.). 6045-5
Castle and cottage. Charles Wharton Stork (tr.). 6045-5
The portraits. Charles Wharton Stork (tr.). 6045-5
The portraits. Charles Wharton Stork (tr.). 6045-5
Leno, John Bedford
The name of liberty. 7009-4
Lenora. August Burger. 6675-5
Lenore. Gottfried A. Berger. 6842-1
Lenore. Edgar Allan Poe. 6102-8,6358-6,6726-3,6732-8,6250-4,6076-5,6288-1,6560-0,6126-5,6121-4
"**Lenore** she woke at morning-red". Lenore. Gottfried A.
 Berger. 6842-1
Lenox, Opal Blaisdell
Milady knits. 6750-6
Lens. Anne Wilkinson. 6446-9
Lent. Miriam LeFevre Crouse. 6144-3
Lent. George Hyde. 7021-3
Lent. Jane McKay Lanning. 6337-3
Lent. William Robert Rodgers. 6379-9
"**Lent** gathers up her cloak of sombre shading". Easter.
 Emily Pauline ("Tekahionwake") Johnson. 6837-5
The **lent** jewels. Richard Chenevix Trench. 6848-0
The **lent** lily. Alfred Edward Housman. 6465-5,6478-7
Lent, Emma A.
Marching away. 6443-4
Unawares. 6303-9,6964-9
A **Lenten** call. Hilda Johnson Wise. 6652-6
Lenten is come with love to toune. Unknown. 6881-2
Lenten is come with love to town. Unknown. 6383-7
Lenten lines to Lydia. Sennett Stephens. 6441-8
Lenten Musings. Ida Walden Thomas. 6818-9
The **Lenten** offering. Sylvia Townsend Warner. 6985-1
Lentino, Jacopo la
Sonnet: Of his lady in heaven. Dante Gabriel Rossetti
 (tr.). 7039-6
Lenton, Francis
Beauties eclipsed. 6328-4
Leo Frank and Mary Phagan. Unknown. 6058-7
Leo XIII, Pope
War cry:to Mary. Raymond F. Roseliep (tr.). 6282-2
Leo to his mistress. Henry Dwight Sedgwick. 6120-6
Leo-Kermorvan
The return of Taliesen. 6873-1
"**Leoffricus** the noble earl". Unknown. 6518-X,6518-4

Leolin and Edith, fr. Aylmer's field. Alfred Lord Tennyson. 6239-3,6084-6
Leona. James G. Clarke. 6406-X
Leonainie. James Whitcomb Riley. 6083-8
Leonard, Dorothy
Alone. 6039-0
The message. 6509-0
Leonard, H.C. (tr.)
The end of being. Seneca, 6337-3
The good parson, fr. The Canterbury tales. Geoffrey Chaucer, 6337-3,6730-1
Leonard, Priscilla
In the looking glass. 6928-2
The lost key. 6337-3
The making of man. 6337-3
The starting-point. 6583-X
The tide will win. 6337-3
What man may choose. 6337-3
Leonard, S.G.
The mistress. 6360-8
Moron. 6360-8
Leonard, William Ellery
The cat, the raven, and the public. 6887-1
Compensation. 6556-2
The duck and the nightingale. 6887-1
Flight of crows. 6184-2
For a forest walker. 6253-9
The geese of Athabasca. 6887-1
The heretics. 6880-4
The image of delight. 6754-9
Indian summer. 6506-6;6556-2
The insulting letter. 6250-4
Israel. 6532-5
Saecla ferarum. 6051-X
The shepherd boy and the wolf. 6891-X
Sonnet ("We act"), fr. Two lives. 6217-2
Sonnets, fr. Two lives. 6619-4
To the dead doughboys. 6051-X
Tom Mooney. 6527-9
Two lives, sels. 6076-5,6102-8
Two lives, sels. 6102-8
Leonard, William Ellery (tr.)
The ass in the lion's skin. Aesop, 7039-6
The divine philosopher. Empedocles, 6435-3
Forever dead. Sappho, 7039-6
Full moon. Sappho, 7039-6
Round about me. Sappho, 7039-6
Sappho. Caius Catallus, 7039-6
The shepherd-boy and the wolf. Aesop, 7039-6
The swan and the goose. Aesop, 7039-6
Leonard: 'The sun upon the lake is low,' Sir Walter Scott. 6828-6
Leonardo de Argensola, Bartolome
Mary Magdalen. William Cullen Bryant (tr.). 6752-2
Leonardo's Monna Lisa. Edward Dowden. 6656-9
"**Leonardo's** angel/looked out and beyond the...". Verrocchio. Richard Harrison. 6767-0
Leonatus. Richard Henry Stoddard. 6008-0,6125-7,6288-1
Leong, George
A sometimes love poem. 6790-5
"This is our music" 6790-5
Leonhardt, Rudolf
The dead Liebknecht. Babette Deutsch (tr.). 6160-5
Leonidas. George Croly. 6980-0
Leonidas. George Croly. 6271-7,6263-6
Leonidas. Ellen Murray. 6416-7
Leonidas of Alexandria
Menodotis. Richard Garnett (tr.). 6850-2
Menodotis. Richard Garnett (tr.). 7039-6
Leonidas of Tarentum
The fisherman's tomb. Andrew Lang (tr.). 6819-7
The last journey. Charles Merivale (tr.). 7039-6
The mother's strategem. Samuel Rogers (tr.). 6302-0;6385-3
An only son. Edwyn R. Bevan (tr.). 6435-3
Shepherd. Edwyn R. Bevan (tr.). 6435-3
The spinning woman. Andrew Lang (tr.). 7039-6
Time. Edwyn R. Bevan (tr.). 6435-3
The tomb of Crethon. John Hermann Merivale (tr.). 7039-6,6879-0

A wayside grave. Edwyn R. Bevan (tr.). 6435-3
The wayside well. Andrew Lang (tr.). 6819-7
The **leonids.** Margaret S. Hosmer. 6316-0
Leontius
Picture of a physician. T.F. Higham (tr.). 6435-3
Plato, a musician. A.J. Butler (tr.). 6435-3
Plato, to a musician. J.A. Pott (tr.). 6435-3
Leopardi, Giacomo
A se stesso. Lorna de' Lucchi (tr.). 7039-6
Infinity. Lorna de' Lucchi (tr.). 6879-0
L'infinito. Lorna de' Lucchi (tr.). 7039-6
To himself. Lorna de' Lucchi (tr.). 6879-0
To Italy. 6624-0
Lepanto. Gilbert Keith Chesterton. 6732-8,6052-8,6102-8, 6161-3,6393-4,6331 ,6427-2,6501-5,6109-X,6476-0,6506-6,6509-0,6726-3,6491-4
The **leper** cleansed. John Collop. 6102-8
The **leper** of London. Herman Scheffauer. 6102-8,6076-5
The **leper.** Algernon Charles Swinburne. 6317-9,6655-0
The **leper.** Nathaniel Parker Willis. 6183-4,6255-5,6302-0, 6385-3,6425-6,6632 ,6621-6,6730-1,6571-6
The **lepracaun** or fairy shoemaker. William Allingham. 6090-0
The **leprahaun.** Robert Dwyer Joyce. 6930-4
Leprechauns and cluricauns. Denis Aloysius McCarthy. 6762-X
"A **leprecuan-fairy** was pegging some shoes". The wish. Isabel Ecclestone Mackay. 6797-2
Leprohon, J.L.
Winter in Canada. 7035-3
Leprohon, Mrs.
A Canadian summer evening. 6795-6
Lerberghe, Charles Van
In an orient barque. 6351-9
The lord spoke. 6351-9
My sister, the rain. 6351-9
Through the dark. 6351-9
Toward you. 6351-9
With her there. 6351-9
Lerch, Mary F.
The epic. 7019-1
Lermontov, Mikhail
The angel. Vivian de Sola Pinto (tr.). 6103-6
Circassian song. John Swinnerton Phillimore (tr.). 6103-6
Clouds. 6103-6
Cossack cradle=song. Cecil Maurice Bowra (tr.). 6103-6
The crag. Vivian de Sola Pinto (tr.). 6103-6
The cup of life. Cecil Maurice Bowra (tr.). 6103-6
Dagger. Max Eastman (tr.). 7039-6
"Do you remember how together" Cecil Maurice Bowra (tr.). 6103-6
Dream. 6103-6
Farewell. Vladimir Nabokov (tr.). 6622-4
Gratitude. Cecil Maurice Bowra (tr.). 6103-6
Hope. Cecil Maurice Bowra (tr.). 6103-6
"Lone, I wander where the pathway glistens" John Swinnerton Phillimore (tr.). 6103-6
The mountain. Max Eastman (tr.). 7039-6
My country. John Swinnerton Phillimore (tr.). 6103-6
My native land. Vladimir Nabokov (tr.). 6622-4
"No, not for you, for you, does my love flame". Cecil Maurice Bowra (tr.). 6103-6
The novice, sels. Babette Deutsch (tr.). 6879-0
"Oh gloomy and dreary! and no one to stretch out..." Cecil Maurice Bowra (tr.). 6103-6
Prayer ("When life's"). Cecil Maurice Bowra (tr.). 6103-6
The prophet ("Thou eternal justice"). John Swinnerton Phillimore (tr.). 6103-6
The prophet. John Swinnerton Phillimore (tr.). 6103-6
The reed. J.J. Robbins (tr.). 7039-6
A sail. Cecil Maurice Bowra (tr.). 6103-6
A sail. Max Eastman (tr.). 7039-6
The testament. Maurice Baring (tr.). 6103-6
The triple dream. Vladimir Nabokov (tr.). 6622-4
The veteran's grave. John Swinnerton Phillimore (tr.). 6103-6
"We parted, but my heart still wears" Maud F. Jerrold (tr.). 6103-6

"When o'er the yellowing corn a fleeting shadow..."
  W.A. Morison (tr.). 6103-6
Why. J. Pollen (tr.). 6103-6
Lerner, Laurence David
  The desert travellers. 6788-3
  14 July 1956. 6788-3
  Senchi ferry: gold coast. 6788-3
Lersch, Heinrich
  Brothers. 6643-7
'Les belles roses sans mercie.' Arthur Shearly Cripps. 6437-X
Les bohemiens. Pierre Jean de Beranger. 6801-4
Les chantiers. Susan Frances ("Seranus") Harrison. 6115-X
Les enfants perdus. George A. Baker. 6517-1
Les etoiles. Mildred Potter. 6750-6
Les fenetres. Stephane Mallarme. 6801-4
Les grand allies. Charles E. Waterman. 6818-9
Les grands mutiles. Robert Service. 6159-1
Les hiboux. Charles Baudelaire. 7039-6
Les hurleurs. Charles Marie Leconte de Lisle. 6801-4
"Les legers grelons de la grele". La grele. Auguste Angellier. 6801-4
Les malheurs des immortels, sels. Paul Eluard. 6803-0
Les matelots. Theophile Gautier. 6253-9
Les miserables de luxe. Ernest Hyett. 6818-9
Les miserables, sel. Victor Hugo. 6954-1
Les montreurs. Charles Marie Leconte de Lisle. 6801-4
Les morts vont vite. Henry Cuyler Bunner. 6770-0
Les morts vont vite. Henry Cuyler Bunner. 6875-8
Les morts vont vite. Brander Matthews. 6875-8
Les Papillottes. Gertrude Hall. 6652-6
"Les morts vont vite! Ay for a little space". Les morts vont vite. Henry Cuyler Bunner. 6770-0
"Les morts vont vite! Ay, for a little space". Les morts vont vite. Henry Cuyler Bunner. 6875-8
"Les morts vont vite: the dead go fast!". Les morts vont vite. Brander Matthews. 6875-8
"Les nuages couraient sur la lune enflammee". La mort du loup. Alfred de Vigny. 6801-4
Les plaintes du cyclope. Charles Marie Leconte de Lisle. 6801-4
Les roses mortes. Rosamund Marriott ("Graham R. Tomson") Watson. 6875-8
Les savants ne sont pas curieux. Merrill Moore. 6482-5
Les sept viellards. Charles Baudelaire. 6106-0
Les silhouettes. Oscar Wilde. 6174-5,6258-X,6655-0
Les souvenirs du peuple. Pierre Jean de Beranger. 6732-8
Les tours au bord de la mer. Emile Verhaeren. 6801-4
Les vaches. Arthur Hugh Clough. 6430-2
Lesbia. Richard Aldington. 6897-9
Lesbia. William Congreve. 6102-8
Lesbia. James Stephens. 6628-3
"Lesbia forever on me rails". Lesbia railing. Caius Catallus. 7039-6
Lesbia hath a beaming eye. Thomas Moore. 6328-4,6092-7, 6086-2,6196-6,6543-0
Lesbia on her sparrow. William Cartwright. 6874-X
Lesbia railing. Caius Catallus. 7039-6
"Lesbia! since far from you I've ranged". To Lesbia. George Gordon, 6th Baron Byron. 6945-2
The lesbian maid. Thomas Moore. 6328-4
Lese-majeste. Herbert S. Gorman. 6102-8,6076-5,6037-2
Lesehradu, Emanuel Leseticky z
  Blue evening. Paul Selver (tr.). 6763-8
  June. Paul Selver (tr.). 6763-8
Lesemann, Maurice
  Storm gathering. 6070-6
Leslie [pseud], J.W.
  The ripple's request. 6983-5
Leslie, Caroline
  "Each in his hidden sphere of joy or woe". 6238-5
  "I stood beside my window one stormy winter day". 6238-5
Leslie, Kenneth
  By stubborn stars, sels. 6021-8
  Escapade. 6833-2
  Halibut cover harvest. 6021-8
Leslie, Lutie Price
  Prayer ("Guide me"). 6270-9
Leslie, Sarabeth

  Listen! 6799-9
Leslie, Shane
  Epitaphs for aviators. 6506-6
  The exiles speak to Ireland. 6174-5
  Fleet Street. 6096-X,6477-9,6439-6
  The four winds. 6930-4
  Ireland to-day. 6174-5
  Ireland, mother of priests. 6096-X,6172-9,6292-X
  Monaghan. 6930-4
  Rebel mother's lullaby. 6090-0,6174-5
  Requiem. 6174-5
  The two mothers. 6282-2
Leslie, Shane (tr.)
  Epigrams ("On our lady of Blachernae"). Unknown, 6282-2
  Epigrams ("On the Annunciation"). Unknown, 6282-2
  Epigrams("To the most holy mother of God"). Unknown, 6282-2
Lesperance, John T.
  Empire first. 6433-7
Less disturbing. Miriam Vedder. 6880-4
Less than cost. Mary A. Kidder. 6410-8
Less than kin. Isabel Fiske Conant. 6072-2,6178-8
Less than the dust. Laurence (Adele Florence Nicolson) Hope. 6732-8,6019-6
"Less than the dust". Laurence (Adele Florence Nicolson) Hope. 6856-1
The lesser children. (Frederick) Ridgely Torrence. 6073-0, 6310-1
Lessing, Gotthold Ephraim
  The dead miser. 6278-4
  Fritz. 6278-4
  Mendax. 6089-7,6278-4
  A nice point. 6278-4
  Niger. 6278-4
  On Dorilis. 6278-4
  On two beautiful one-eyed sisters. 6278-4
  The opal ring, fr. Nathan the wise. Sara S. Rice (tr.). 6166-4
  The per contra, or matrimonial balance. 6278-4
  The ring. 6344-6
  Specimen of the laconic. 6278-4
  To a liar. 6278-4
  To a slow walker and quick eater. 6089-7
  The wise child. 6278-4
Lesson. Lillie Hall. 7016-7
Lesson. Betty Kirk. 6397-7
Lesson. J. Whitebird. 6901-0
A lesson (1). Alice Cary. 6865-0;6969-X
A lesson (2). Alice Cary. 6969-X
A lesson for Mama. Sydney Dayre. 6105-2,6242-3,6713-1
Lesson for mamma. Unknown. 6684-4
The lesson for today. Robert Frost. 6391-8,6666-6
A lesson from a bell. Walter S. Smith. 6919-3
A lesson from history. Joseph Morris. 6291-1
A lesson in mythology. Eliza Calvert Hall. 6273-3
Lesson in natural history. Theodore Spencer. 6761-1
Lesson in poetry. Ruth Evelyn Henderson. 6038-2
A lesson in weighing. Charles R. Talbot. 6674-4
The lesson of a tree. Walt Whitman. 6510-4
Lesson of history. Edward Farquhar. 6939-8
A lesson of mercy. George Murray. 6274-1,6656-9
A lesson of mercy. Alice Cary. 6060-9,6456-6
A lesson of obedience. Emma Dunning Banks. 6426-4
The lesson of the flowers. Hafiz. 6448-5
The lesson of the grave. Charles W. Denison. 6755-7
Lesson of the leaves. Unknown. 6049-8
The lesson of the rose. Gertrude Fitzpatrick. 6789-1
The lesson of the war, 1855. Adelaide Anne Procter. 6957-6
The lesson of Waterloo. Unknown. 6411-6
Lesson that Easter teaches. Adelle E. Burch. 6720-4
A lesson to lovers. Moschus. 6435-3
A lesson to my ghost. John Drinkwater. 6184-2
Lesson with the fan. Unknown. 6277-6,6681-X
The lesson.. Arthur Wallace Peach. 6583-X
The lesson.. Elizabeth Turner. 6105-2
A lesson. Unknown. 6373-X
A lesson. William Wordsworth. 6134-6,6246-6,6150-8,6737-9
The lesson. Wystan Hugh Auden. 6209-1
The lesson. Rudyard Kipling. 6810-3
The leson. Anne Goodwin Winslow. 6326-8

Lessons. Sallie Neill Roach. 6918-5
Lessons. Sara Teasdale. 6501-5
Lessons for a boy. Samuel Taylor Coleridge. 6512-0
Lessons from the gorse. Elizabeth Barrett Browning. 6123-0
The **lessons** of nature. William Drummond of Hawthornden. 6246-5,6246-5,6250-4,6543-0
Lessons of the war: judging distances. Henry Reed. 6209-1
Lessons on cruelty. William Blake. 6134-6
"**Lessons** sweet of spring returning". The nightingale. John Keble. 6980-0
Lest I learn. Witter Bynner. 6027-7
"**Lest** any of life's harvest should be lost". Gleaners. Helen Bosanquet. 7042-6
"**Lest** heaven be thronged with grey-beards...". Flower of youth. Katharine (Hinkson) Tynan. 7029-9
"**Lest** I hould think your sun was...shining". Good-bye. May C. ([Mary] Gillington) Byron. 6800-6
"**Lest** some sweet thought all unaware". The vigil. Robert Loveman. 6941-X
"**Lest** the great glory from on high". Mercies. Alice Cary. 6969-X
Lest the spirit die. Mary Pauline Richardson. 6789-1
"**Lest** to evil ways I run". The golden mean. Alice Cary. 6969-X
Lest we forget. Robert Bryan Flanary. 6799-9
Lest we forget. Curtis Wheeler. 6051-X
Lest we forget! Rudyard Kipling. 6702-6
Lest you forget. Emmanuel Litvinoff. 6475-2
"**Lest** you should think that verse shall die". The immortality of verse. Horace. 7039-6
"**Lestenyt**, lordynges, both elde and yinge". Of a rose, a lovely rose, of a rose is alm myn song. Unknown. 6931-2
Lester
    An epic of Gotham. 6817-0
Lester park. Margaret D. Kennedy. 6342-X
Lester, C.F.
    On the stair. 6929-0
Let. John Galsworthy. 6888-X
"**Let** all men living on earth take heed". The ballade of the summer-boarder. Henry Cuyler Bunner. 6770-0,6875-8
"**Let** all the fish that swim the sea". Herring is king. Alfred Perceval Graves. 6873-1
"**Let** Bacchus's sons be not dismayed". Garryowen. Unknown. 6858-8,6930-4
Let all things pass away. William Butler Yeats. 6125-7
"**Let** be! the crest of summer turns and breaks". Acceptance. Marie Emilie Gilchrist. 6906-1
"**Let** children hear the mighty deeds". Psalm 077. Bible. 6848-0
"**Let** crowded city pavements be your school". To a student. E.K. Biddle. 6954-1
"**Let** dew the flowers fill". Dirge. Thomas Lovell Beddoes. 6908-8
"**Let** dogs delight to bark and bite". Against quarelling and fighting. Isaac Watts. 6932-0
Let dogs delight to bark and bite. Isaac Watts. 6142-2, 6479-5,6459-0,6131-1
Let down the bars. Unknown. 6927-4
"**Let** drum to trumpet speak". Grant. Melville W. Fuller. 6922-3
"**Let** each man think himself an act of God". Philip James Bailey. 6402-7
"**Let** Erin remember the days of old." Thomas Moore. 6302-0;6385-3;6328-4
"'**Let** earth give thanks', the deacon said". Give thanks for what? W.F. Croffut. 6917-7
"**Let** every day be Mother's Day!". Mother's Day. Edgar A. Guest. 6097-8
"**Let** every honest British soul". The chevalier's birthday. Unknown. 6859-6
"**Let** Exeter Change lament its change". On the removal of a menagerie. Thomas Hood. 6974-6
Let everyone sweep before his own door. Unknown. 6407-8
"**Let** fate do her worst, there are moments of joy". Thomas Moore. 6407-8
"**Let** fate do her worst, there are relics of joy". Thomas Moore. 6238-5
"**Let** fate do her worst;there are relics of joy". The scent of the roses. Thomas Moore. 6889-8
"**Let** fire not turn". Sepulcralis. Marion Smith. 6764-6
"**Let** folly smile, to view the names". To E--. George Gordon, 6th Baron Byron. 6945-2
"'**Let** go aft'...and out she slides". War risks. Cicely Fox Smith. 7031-0
"**Let** go of the unicorn's reins". The beast that rode the unicorn. Conny Hannes Meyer. 6769-7
"**Let** God, the God of battle, rise". Psalm 068 Bible. 6848-0
'**Let** go!'. W.A. Blackwell. 6274-1
Let her depart. Felicia Dorothea Hemans. 6973-8
Let her slide. Unknown. 6260-1
"**Let** him dream a little, God". A mother's prayer. Virginia Wuerfel Slayton. 6906-1
"**Let** him how wishes seek pomp and honor, follow". Lorenzo de' Medici. 6325-X
"**Let** him kiss me with the kisses of his mouth". Osculetur me. Bible. 6830-8
"**Let** him on me the balmy kiss bestow". The song of songs. Ann Francis. 6848-0
"**Let** him that will be free and keep his...". A booke of Ayres (VI). Thomas Campion. 6794-8
"**Let** him that will, ascend the tottering seat". Free from the world. Sir Matthew Hale. 6793-X
"**Let** him who will go running for the lights...". Achievement. Edgar A. Guest. 6869-3
"**Let** idlers despair!there is hope for the wise". Song ("Let idlers despair"). Ebenezer Elliott. 7009-4
"**Let** Israel their avenger's glory raise". Deborah's triumphant song. Laurence Howell. 6848-0
"**Let** it be forgotten, as a flower is forgotten". Song ("Let it be forgotten"). Sara Teasdale. 6034-X
"**Let** it be forgotten." Sara Teasdale. 6077-3,6102-8,6538-4, 6513-9,6153-2
Let it be springtime. Nelle Loraine Milroy. 6799-9
Let it be you. Sara Teasdale. 6039-0
"**Let** it idly droop, or sway". The flag. Lucy Larcom. 6820-0
"**Let** it no longer be a forlorne hope". Richard Crashaw. 6562-7
"**Let** it not be forgotten". Sara Teasdale. 6076-5,6161-3
Let it pass. Unknown. 6530-9
"**Let** jarring realms, and Europe's doubtful...". The banish'd beauty. John Gay. 6972-X
Let life be royal. Katharine Lee Bates. 7038-8
Let love remain. Walter Savage Landor. 6086-2
"**Let** man serve law for man" Ralph Waldo Emerson. 6954-1
Let me be a giver. Mary Carolyn Davies. 6461-2
Let me be a star. Helen Hoyt. 6628-3
"**Let** me be a woman in this world of beauty". A woman's cycle of prayer. Delphine Harris Coy. 6836-7
"**Let** me be done for good and all with news". Good news. Tertius Van Dyke. 6954-1
"**Let** me be glad, be glad; arise". Sonnet ("Let me be glad"). Sir Cecil Spring-Rice. 6607-0
"**Let** me be great, as stars are great". Song ("Let me be great..."). Oliver Jenkins. 6762-X
Let me be like a tree. John Freeman. 6461-2
"**Let** me be the inspiration." Eleanor Vincent Pricer. 6750-6
Let me be with thee. Charlotte Elliot. 6656-9
"**Let** me but do my work from day to day". Work, fr. The three best things. Henry Van Dyke. 6961-4
"**Let** me but feel thy look's embrace". Love in a look. Henry Van Dyke. 6961-4
"**Let** me but live my life from year to year". Life, fr. The three best things. Henry Van Dyke. 6961-4
"**Let** me but love my love without disguise". Love, fr. The three best things. Henry Van Dyke. 6961-4
"**Let** me close my lids". Prayer for a dampened spirit. Grace M. Graves. 6750-6
"**Let** me confess that we two must be twain". Sonnet 036 ("Let me confess"). William Shakespeare. 6430-2,6560-0
"**LEt** me contemplate thee (fair soul), and...Ha". Elegies on George Talbot, esq. William Habington. 6935-5
"**Let** me count my treasures". Treasures. Adelaide Anne Procter. 6957-6
"**Let** me die on the trail, with my face to...". The last

call. Etta Miller. 6799-9
Let me die working. S. Hall Young. 6337-3
Let me do it my way! Milan Curcin. 6765-4
"Let me do my work each day". A prayer ("Let me do my work each day"). Max Ehrmann. 6750-6
Let me embrace you. Rosalea Schonbar. 6799-9
Let me enjoy. Thomas Hardy. 6655-0
Let me forget. Oma Carlyle Anderson. 6750-6
Let me forget. Unknown. 6118-4
Let me go down to dust. Lew Sarett. 6619-4,6253-9
"Let me go forth to run amid the gale". Wind in the hills. Stanton A. Coblentz. 6789-1
Let me go warm. Luis de Gongora. 7039-6
Let me go where'er I will. Ralph Waldo Emerson. 6374-8, 6252-0
"Let me go where'er I will". Ralph Waldo Emerson. 6753-0
"Let me hate fools as I could once". Prayer for strength to hate fools. Robert Louis Burgess. 6880-4
"Let me have no shame". Prelude. Dong-ju Yun. 6775-1
'Let me into the darkness again'. Gertrude Huntington McGiffert. 6838-3
Let me keep your hand. Helen Hoyt. 6628-3
'Let me kiss him for his mother'. Unknown. 6074-9
Let me laugh. Unknown. 6563-5
Let me lean hard. Ella Wheeler Wilcox. 6956-8
"Let me lift Jesus, Lord". Jo Gardner. 6065-X
"Let me linger a few days more". I store the memories. Mary Weeden. 6761-1
Let me live for a time way back from the road. C.G. Farnum. 6482-5
"Let me live in God's great out-of-doors". Solitude. Grace Shuster Vallancourt. 6799-9
Let me live out my years. John G. Neihardt. 6291-1,6337-3, 6347-0,6501-5,6602-X,6619-4,6102-8,6076-5,6736-0
Let me live out my years in New Hampshire. Estrella Lake Montgomery. 6894-4
Let me love bright things. A. Newberry Choyce. 6776-X
Let me no more a mendicant. Arthur Colton. 6310-1
"Let me not deem that I was made in vain". Not in vain. Hartley Coleridge. 7015-9
"Let me not die before I've done for Thee". Unknown. 6238-5
"Let me not have this gloomy view". George Crabbe. 6980-0
"Let me not know so much of books". After discussion. Agnes Ryan. 6764-6
"Let me not to the marriage of true minds". Sonnet 116 ("Let me not"). William Shakespeare. 6192-3,6250-4, 6430-2,6560-0,6558-9,6438 ,6085-4,6208-3,6332-2,6436-1,6337-3,6604 ,6154-0,6102-8,6271-7,6317-9,6315-2, 6102 ,6732-8,6660-7,6646-1,6189-3,6197-4,6301
"Let me not to the marriage of true minds". William Shakespeare. 6099-4,6488-4,6600-3,6181-8,6186-9,6187 ,6198-2,6204-0,6240-7,6246-6,6339-X,6473 ,6726-3, 6536-8,6182-6,6527-9,6122-2,6371
"Let me not to the marriage of true minds." William Shakespeare. 6513-9,6094-3,6219-9
"Let me pause here, both tongue and foot...". A rural retreat. George Darley. 6980-0
"Let me pick a case and demolish it". A grudg against Boston. Charles Potts. 6998-3
Let me praise once your body. Jason Bolles. 6042-0
Let me remember. Florence Crow. 6042-0
"Let me remember how I saved a man". Ariel and the suicide. Thomas Hood. 6980-0
"Let me remember you or dream you". The wall. Octavio Paz. 6759-X
"Let me set sail for strange harbors...". Strange harbors. Edith Chandler Haubold. 6750-6
"Let me shake off the gray dust of the road". Wings aloft. Constance Deming Lewis. 6841-3
Let me sleep. Christina Georgina Rossetti. 6501-5
"Let me stand still upon the height of life". Forward. Sarah ("Susan Coolidge") Woolsey. 6918-5
"Let me tell you, boys, of a run we made". The peril of the passenger train. Mrs. A.D. Gillet. 6921-5
"Let me today do something that shall take". Because of some good act. Unknown. 6889-8
Let me unloose. Clement Wood. 6039-0
Let me walk with the men in the road. Walter J. Gresham. 6964-9

"Let me, oh God, from sinners be defended". Psalm 140. Bible. 6848-0
Let mine eyes see thee. Saint Theresa of Avila. 7039-6
Let minions marshal every hair. Unknown. 6026-9
"Let misers tremble o'er their wealth". Unknown. 6859-6
"Let mournful Britons now deplore". The clans are all away. Unknown. 6859-6
"Let my road be the plain road". The plain road. Edgar A. Guest. 6869-3
"Let my voice ring out and over the earth". Song ("Let my voice"). James ("B.V.") Thomson. 6337-3
"Let my voice ring out and over the earth". James ("B.V.") Thomson. 6508-2,6655-0
Let nature be your teacher, fr. The tables turned. William Wordsworth. 6337-3
Let never day nor night. William Shakespeare. 6214-8
Let no charitable hope. Elinor Wylie. 6052-8,6619-4,6581-3, 6036-6,6250-4,6300-4,6393-4
"Let no cold marble o'er my body rise". Epitaph ("Let no cold marble"). Unknown. 6453-1
"Let no man ask thee of anything". Soothsay. Dante Gabriel Rossetti. 6828-6
"Let no man come into this hall". Make we merry, both more and less, for now is Christmas. Unknown. 6756-5
"Let no one awaken". Deep sleep. Gabriela (Lucila Godoy Alcayaga) Mistral. 6759-X
"Let no one curse him. If he bear". James Buchanan. James Abraham Martling. 6952-5
"Let no profane ignoble foot tread neer". An epitaph on his most honored friend, Richard, Earl... Henry King. 6908-8
"Let not Chloris think, because". Song ("Let not Chloris"). Unknown. 6436-1
"Let not a woman e'er complain." Robert Burns. 6302-0;6385-3
"Let not my death be long". Leonora Speyer. 6102-8,6076-5
"Let not my love be called idolatry". Sonnet 105 ("Let not my love"). William Shakespeare. 6447-7
"Let not pearl of laughter". Talisman. Mary Hume Mills. 7016-7
"Let not the sluggish sleep". Song ("Let not"). William Byrd. 6022-6
"Let not the sluggish sleep". Unknown. 6931-2
"Let not the white, hot metal of your desire". Counsel for youth. A.M. Sullivan. 6979-7
"Let not young souls be smothered out before". The leaden-eyed. Vachel Lindsay. 6954-1
Let not your heart be troubled. Alice Mortenson. 6065-X
"Let nothing disturb thee". Henry Wadsworth Longfellow. 6109-5
Let Oliver now be forgotten. Unknown. 6328-4
"Let others of the world's decaying tell". Sir William Alexander; Earl of Stirling. 6181-8,6182-6
"Let others praise analysis". Ballade of railway novels. Andrew Lang. 6987-6
"Let others quail and, trembling, force the...". A complacent rondeau redouble. Louis Untermeyer. 6875-8
"Let others sing of knights and paladins" Samuel Daniel. 6182-6,6436-1
"Let our great James come over". Unknown. 6859-6
Let our love be. Samuel Hoffenstein. 6441-8
"Let poets and bards the loveliness of spring". Spring song. Rubye Mae Fisher. 6850-2
"Let poets rhyme of what they will". Tobacco. Thomas Jones. 6453-1
"Let poets scrawl satirick rhymes". Eulogy on the times. Thomas Green Fessenden. 7030-2
"Let sailors watch the waning Pleiades". Cleonicos. Theocritus. 7039-6
"Let scholars furnish their needy spirits". Only one way. Elsa Gidlow. 6880-4
"Let school-masters puzzle their brain". Song ("Let school-masters"). Oliver Goldsmith. 6430-2
Let some great joys pretend to find. Thomas Shadwell. 6430-2
Let something good be said. James Whitcomb Riley. 6211-3, 6260-1,6337-3
Let Spain's proud traders. Isaac Watts. 6328-4
"Let star-wheels and angel-wings, with their holy...".

Elizabeth Barrett Browning. 6238-5
"Let that which is to come be as it may". Sonnet ("Let that which"). John Masefield. 6879-0
"Let the bells ring, and let the boys sing". Song ("Let the bells ring..."). John Fletcher. 6933-9
"Let the bestow on ev'ry airth a limb". On himself, upon hearing what was his sentence. James Graham; Marquess of Montrose. 6933-9
"Let the bird of loudest lay". William Shakespeare. 6181-8
Let the boat go. Kostes Hatzopoulos. 6352-7
Let the boy walk naked. Dennis Kelly. 7003-5
"Let the brown lark fly". Close to the earth. Margaret Emerson Bailey. 6780-8
"Let the Catholic Church be now arrayed". Bishop Butler of Kilcash. Unknown. 6930-4
"Let the cold fire break out in happy men". The new story. John Pudney. 6895-2
"Let the coward shrink aside". Our own again. Thomas Osborne Davis. 6858-8
"Let the damned ride their earwigs to hell...". Rock pilgrim. Herbert Edward Palmer. 6893-6
"Let the day perish wherein I was born". Job's curse, fr. The book of Job. Bible. 7039-6
"Let the day perish wherein I was born", fr. Job. Bible. 6879-0
"Let the farmer praise his grounds". A cruiscin lan. Unknown. 6858-8
"Let the full leaf expand". Entreaty. Irene M. Ward. 6782-4
Let the gay ones and great. David Garrick. 6328-4
Let the ghosts in black Erebus roar. Unknown. 6328-4
"Let the leaders of nations". We pass. Beatrice M. Murphy. 7024-8
"Let the little birds sing". Edna St. Vincent Millay. 6986-X
Let the little ones come unto me. May Riley Smith. 6097-8
"Let the music play,/I would dance alway". The dance. Grace Denio Litchfield. 6959-2
"Let the Nile cloak his head in the clouds...". On the discoveries of Captain Lewis. Joel Barlow. 6946-0
"Let the nymph still avoid and be deaf...". Song ("Let the nymph..."). Tobias George Smollett. 6975-4
"Let the old fire blaze". Safe at home. Edgar A. Guest. 7033-7
"Let the r(evolution) come. uh". U name this one. Carolyn Rodgers. 7024-8
"Let the red dawn surmise." Bliss Carman. 6433-7
"Let the reign of hate cease". Peace. Samuel Ellsworth Kiser. 6274-1
"Let the rich man fill his belly". Song ("Let the rich man..."). Unknown (Spanish). 7039-6
"Let the saint forgo his world". Soliloquy. Babette Deutsch. 7038-8
"Let the spring sun creep close to those". Prayer for spring. Sylvia Hill. 6954-1
Let the toast pass, fr. The school for scandal. Richard Brinsley Sheridan. 6527-9,6717-4
"Let the toper regale in his tankard of ale". A pipe of tobacco. John Usher. 6453-1
"Let the trim tapers burn exceedingly bright". The bride. Thomas Wade. 6980-0
"Let the vain courier waste his days". Lope de Vega Carpio. 6973-8
Let the warm air condense on the window. Ivan Hargrave. 6475-2
Let the waves beat. Nina Willis Walter. 6316-0
"Let the yellow mead shine for the sons..brave". Grufydd's feast. Felicia Dorothea Hemans. 6973-8
"Let them bury your big eyes". Elegy. Edna St. Vincent Millay. 6102-8,6289-X,6076-5,6396-9
Let them come to us. Lucia M. Pitts. 6178-8
"Let them say to my lover". Amor mysticus. Sister Marcela de Carpio de San Felix. 7039-6
Let there be dreams to-day. Clinton Scollard. 6327-6
Let there be kites again. Glenn Ward Dresbach. 6761-1
Let there be light. John Pierpont. 6D24-4
Let there be light! Ruth Wright Kauffman. 6846-4
"'Let there be light!' - When from on high". Installation hymn. John Pierpont. 6752-2
"'Let there be light'!-God's voice was heard". In memoriam-Theodore Roosevelt. Annette Kohn. 6995-9
"Let there be many windows to your soul". Progress. Ella Wheeler Wilcox. 6956-8
"Let there be years of laughter". Renewal. Dorothy O'Gara. 6764-6
"Let this be read." Winifred Johnston. 6397-7
"Let this good-bye of ours - this last goodbye". Renunciation. Unknown. 6750-6
"Let this place be sweet with flowers". Prescience, fr. Songs for Sally. Marion Strobel. 6778-6
"Let those who are in favor with their stars" William Shakespeare. 6122-2,6198-2
"Let Tobias bless charity...", fr. Jubilate agno. Christopher Smart. 6380-2
"Let those who are in favour with their stars". Sonnet 025 ("Let those"). William Shakespeare. 6085-4,6271-7, 6436-1
"Let those who will hang rapturously". 'Judah's hallowed bards.' Sir Aubrey De Vere. 6848-0
"Let thy tears, Le Vayer, let them flow". To Monsieur De La Mothe Le Vayer. Moliere (Jean Baptiste Poquelin). 6879-0,7039-6
"Let us admit freely, as a business people...". The lesson. Rudyard Kipling. 6810-3
Let us all be unhappy together. Charles Dibdin. 6996-7
"Let us alone, you beggarly knaves!". Noli me tangere. James Abraham Martling. 6952-5
"Let us alone." Henry Howard Brownell. 6302-0,6385-3,6505-8
Let us answer this query. Joseph Joel Keith. 6761-1
Let us be happy as long as we can. Joseph Stansbury. 6288-1
Let us be happy as long as we can. Unknown. 6753-0
Let us be kind. W. Lomax Childress. 6303-9,6964-9
Let us be men. David Herbert Lawrence. 6357-8
"Let us be still and think on air". Approach. Grace Fallow Norton. 6761-1
"Let us begin and carry up this corpse". A grammarian's funeral. Robert Browning. 6828-6
"Let us begin and portion out these sweets". A Girtonian funeral. Unknown. 6802-2
"Let us begin, dear love, where we left off". Reunited. Ella Wheeler Wilcox. 6956-8
"Let us believe in the flesh, the hope made...". Poem for use. Hildegarde Flanner. 6761-1
Let us break down the barriers. Osmond Thomas. 6360-8
"Let us consider, cats and men, what would...". If the kitten had flown. Harold Willard Gleason. 7019-1
Let us construct a god. Roberta Holloway. 6072-2
Let us depart. Felicia Dorothea Hemans. 6848-0
Let us depart! Felicia Dorothea Hemans. 6973-8
Let us drink and be merry. Thomas Jordan. 6934-7
"Let us dry our tears now, laddie". Daddy knows. James William Foley. 6889-8
Let us forget. James Whitcomb Riley. 6992-4
Let us forget. Agnes Mary F. ("Madame Duclaux") Robinson. 6726-3
"Let us give over now the thought of snowlight". Prelude for spring. Sarah Litsey. 6761-1
Let us give thanks. Marianne Farningham. 6449-3
Let us go back. Thomas Curtis Clark. 6461-2
"Let us go hence, my songs; she will not hear". Algernon Charles Swinburne. 6187-7
Let us go home to paradise. Robinson Jeffers. 6241-5
Let us go on. Johann Wolfgang von Goethe. 6461-2
Let us go to no more museums. T.C. Wilson. 6640-2
"Let us go, oh queen, we shall worship the god!" Unknown (Newari) 7013-2
Let us have hope. Frederick W.H. Myers. 6461-2
Let us have peace. Horace. 6949-5
Let us have peace. Nancy Byrd Turner. 6337-3,6461-2,6542-2
Let us keep Christmas. Grace Noll Crowell. 6337-3
Let us keep faith. Lucia Trent. 6461-2
"Let us live then and be glad". Gaudeamus igitur. Unknown (Latin). 6879-0
"Let us look at the little things...". Let us answer this query. Joseph Joel Keith. 6761-1
"Let us love one another". Charles Swain. 6980-0
"Let us not fear for the creative word". Libertie, egalite, fraternite. Florence Converse. 6761-1

LET

"Let us not think of our departed dead". An epitaph. Edwin Markham. 6303-9;6337-3
Let us now praise famous men, fr. Ecclesiasticus. Bible. 6087-0,6334-9,6625-9,6125-7
"'Let us pass over!' We were far astray". Unknown. 6238-5
"Let us praise God for the dead...". The British army of 1914. Alfred W. Pollard. 6846-4
"Let us pray by means of song". A song for the unpopular folk. Mabel Grant Sund. 6750-6
"Let us quarrel for these reasons". Quarrel. Elinor Wylie. 6776-X
"Let us reflect now, since we had forgotten". Audit, September 1939. James Walker. 6783-2
"Let us rejoice and sing". The conception of Christ. John Wedderburn (atr). 6756-5
"Let us remember how we came". For remembrance. Edward Shanks. 6872-3
"Let us ride together-/blowing mane and hair". Riding song. Unknown. 7010-8
"Let us roll back the world on its axle..fire". An old-time picture. Benjamin Franklin Taylor. 6815-4
"Let us royster with the oyster". A song of the oyster. Unknown. 6922-3
Let us see Jesus. Anna B. Warner. 6337-3
"Let us sing of the babe that was born to-day". At Bethlehem. N.W. Rand. 6926-6
"Let us sing then for my friend not a dirge...". A time to dance, sels. Cecil Day Lewis. 6879-0
Let us smile. Unknown. 6109-5,6260-1,6583-X
"Let us take to our hearts a lesson...". The tapestry weavers. Unknown. 6963-0
"Let us throw more logs on the fire!". The voice of the wind. Adelaide Anne Procter. 6965-7,6957-6
"Let us turn to Chamouny that shields". Chamouny. William Wordsworth. 6749-2
"Let us use time whilst we may". Of beauty. Sir Richard Fanshawe. 6908-8
"Let us visit the shrine of..sri-Lokanantha!". Gorakhanatha and Lokanatha. Unknown (Newari). 7013-2
Let us with a gladsome mind. John Milton. 6337-3,6418-3, 6730-1,6214-8
Let us wreathe the mighty cup. Michael (Katherine Bradley & Edith Cooper) Field. 6658-5
"Let us, with a gladsome mine". Psalm 136. Bible. 6848-1
"Let verse be as a key". The art of poetry. Vicente Huidobro. 6759-X
"Let vs now sing of loues delight". The maskers second daunce. Thomas Campion. 6794-8
"Let who list, for me, advance". The flower of flowers, fr. The mistress of Philarete. George Wither. 6934-7
Let years bring wisdom. Margaret I. Simpson. 6764-6
Let you would be lovers. Frank Ernest Hill. 6039-0
Let Zeus record, sels. Hilda ("H.D.") Doolittle. 6011-0
Let's be brave. Edgar A. Guest. 6211-3
"Let's dance. Let's make our marks first...". Round dance. David Wagoner. 6803-0
Let's go again. Circe Maia. 7036-1
Let's go dancing. Charles Divine. 6959-2
Let's go to bed. Unknown. 6125-7
Let's go to the woods. Unknown. 6003-X
"Let's go, you and I". Adultery at a Las Vegas bookstore. Stephen Shu Ning Liu. 6790-5
Let's have a picnic out-of-doors. Mary Carolyn Davies. 6466-3
"Let's meet again to-night, my Fair", fr. Queen. Thomas Hardy. 6634-8
"Let's see. We believe in wings". Fairies - or fireflies? Sarah Morgan Bryan Piatt. 6965-7
"Let's to the brow of yonder hill". Tender moon. Katharine Kennon Rucker. 6799-9
"Let's travel" Doris Muhringer. 6769-7
"Let's wonder beneath the apple trees". Beneath the apple tree. Delphia L. Hopper. 6906-1
Lethargy. Zoe Akins. 6327-6
Lethargy. Idabel Williams. 6906-1
Lethbridge, Alberta; Thursday evening, November 25... Stephen Scobie. 6767-0
Lethe. Walter De La Mare. 6905-3
Lethe. Hilda ("H.D.") Doolittle. 6536-8,6726-3,6513-9,6153-2

960

Lethe. Eugene Lee-Hamilton. 7015-9
Lethe. Lorenzo Mavilis. 6352-7
Lethe. Edna St. Vincent Millay. 6513-9
Letter. John Greenleaf Whittier. 6753-0
Letter 60 Mary Norbert Korte. 6792-1
Letter after a visit. Haniel Long. 6808-1
A letter and a crown. Jennie M. Burr. 6965-7
A letter and an answer. Unknown. 6278-4
"A letter came in the mail from the vice...". Getting fired or 'Not being retained' Sandra Gilbert. 6792-1
Letter containing a panegyric on Bath. Christopher Anstey. 6932-0
A letter from a candidate for the presidency. James Russell Lowell. 6385-3,6278-4
Letter from a candidate, fr. Bigelow papers. James Russell Lowell. 6787-5
A letter from a girl to her own old age. Alice Meynell. 6245-8
Letter from a missionary. John Greenleaf Whittier. 6288-1
Letter from a postulant. Sister Mary Irma. 6285-7
Letter from a sanatorium: To J.M.S. Charles Whitby. 6994-0
Letter from a sanatorium: To K.J. Charles Whitby. 6994-0
Letter from Alice. Iris Jamieson. 6750-6
A letter from Artemisa in the town, to Cloe..., sels. John Wilmot, 2d Earl of Rochester. 6378-0
Letter from exile. Frederick Ebright. 6761-1
A letter from father. Unknown. 6278-4
A letter from home. John Paul Minarik. 6870-7
A letter from Italy, sels. Joseph Addison. 6831-6
A letter from Italy. Joseph Addison. 6152-4
A letter from Mr. Hosea Biglow, fr. Biglow papers. James Russell Lowell. 6505-8
A letter from Newport. Frederick W.H. Myers. 6656-9
A letter from Rome. Arthur Hugh Clough. 6315-2
Letter from safety. Alex Comfort. 6391-8
Letter from the farm. Ethel M. Kelley. 6715-8
Letter from the front. Angelos Sikelianos. 6352-7
A letter from the front. Sir Henry Newbolt. 7026-4
A letter from the trenches. Charles Hamilton Sorley. 7027-2
A letter fron Santa Claus. William Howard. 6147-8
The letter H's protest to the cockneys. Walter William Skeat. 6724-7
The letter H. Catherine Maria Fanshawe. 6416-7
The letter he did not mail. Unknown. 6714-X
Letter I. Randall Swingler. 6666-6
"A letter in my mailbox says you've made it". To the girl who lives in a tree. Audre Lorde. 6898-7
Letter in verse. William Cowper. 6814-6
The letter L. Jean Ingelow. 6940-1
A letter of advice. Thomas Hood Jr. 6652-6
A letter of advice. Winthrop Mackworth Praed. 6122-2,6722-0,6676-3,6092-7
A letter of authors, fr. The faerie queene. Edmund Spenser. 6430-2
The Letter of Marque. Caroline F. Orne. 6916-9
"The letter ran thus". Nothing for use. Elmer Ruan Coates. 6920-7
Letter to Alex Comfort. Dannie Abse. 6210-5
Letter to an aviator in France. Grace Hazard Conkling. 7027-2
Letter to an exile. Lala Koehn-Heine. 6767-0
Letter to Ben Jonson. Francis Beaumont. 6933-9
A letter to Ben Jonson. Francis Beaumont. 6315-2,6250-4, 6301-2
A letter to her husband, absent upon public employment. Anne Bradstreet. 6333-0,6088-0,6288-1
A letter to his friend, Mu Kow. Christopher Morley. 6538-4
A letter to Hitler. James Laughlin. 6666-6
A letter to Lady Margaret Cavendish Holles-Harley... Matthew Prior. 6186-9,6092-7
Letter to Lord Byron: part V. Wystan Hugh Auden. 6354-3
Letter to Michael from New York. Jody Gladding. 6900-2
A letter to Mother Nature. Sydney Dayre. 6690-9
Letter to my parents. F.W. Watt. 6767-0
Letter to my wife. Roy Fuller. 6379-9
Letter to my wife. Keidrych Rhys. 6666-6
A letter to Peter. Fay Chiang. 6790-5
Letter to R. Willard Maas. 6666-6
A leter to Robert Frost. Robert Hillyer. 6483-3

Letter to Saint Peter. Marion Doyle. 6750-6
Letter to Santa Claus. Unknown. 6312-8
A letter to Sara Hutchinson [Dejection]. Samuel Taylor Coleridge. 6380-2
A letter to Sir George Etherege. John Dryden. 6970-3
Letter to Sir H. Wotton at his going ambassador..Venice. John Donne. 6933-9
A letter to Sir Robert Walpole. Henry Fielding. 6152-4
Letter to the city clerk. Frederick A. Wright. 6979-7,6751-4
Letter to the Earl of Chesterfield. Samuel Johnson. 6200-8
Letter to the front. Muriel Rukeyser. 6666-6
A letter to the Hon. Lady Miss Margaret... Matthew Prior. 6315-2;6634-8
A.letter to the Honourable..Margaret-Cavandish-Holles-Harley. Matthew Prior. 6152-4
Letter to Tina Koyama from Elliot Bay Park. Jim Mitsui. 6790-5
Letter to two strangers. Octavio Paz. 6758-1
Letter to Viscount Cobham. William Congreve. 6315-2
Letter VII. Randall Swingler. 6895-2
Letter VIII. Randall Swingler. 6666-6
"The letter which you wrote me." Heinrich Heine. 6226-1
A letter, fr. The Bigelow papers. James Russell Lowell. 6288-1
The letter-burning. Tristam Livingstone. 6799-9
Letter..to Joseph T. Buckingham, fr. The Bigelow papers. James Russell Lowell. 6753-0
A letter.. Matthew Prior. 6024-2;6634-8
The letter.. Edgar Lee Masters. 6031-5
A letter. Philip James Bailey. 6980-0
A letter. Elizabeth Stuart Phelps. 6620-8,6066-8,6226-1
A letter. Matthew Prior. 6668-2
A letter. Adelaide Anne Procter. 6957-6
A letter. Anne Ridler. 6391-8
A letter. Lynn Riggs. 6397-7
The letter. Al-Mu'tamid. 6362-4
The letter. Henri Barbusse. 6351-9
The letter. Amy Lowell. 6019-6
The letter. Alfred Lord Tennyson. 6977-0
The letter. Elizabeth Turner. 6018-8
The letter. Arthur Waley. 6315-2
The letter. John Hall Wheelock. 6723-9
The lettergae. Charles Murray. 6180-X
Letters. Ralph Waldo Emerson. 6302-0;6385-3
Letters. Bernard Spencer. 6379-9,6666-6
Letters (fudge correspondence). Thomas Moore. 6278-4
The letters at school. Unknown. 6772-7
Letters from God. Walt Whitman. 6153-2
Letters from Kazuko (Kyoto, Japan-sumemr 1980) Alan Chong Lau. 6790-5
Letters to her husband. Anne Bradstreet. 6753-0
The letters. Alfred Lord Tennyson. 6271-7,6402-7,6429-9, 6321-7
Lettice. Dinah Maria Mulock Craik. 6321-7
Lettice. Michael (Katherine Bradley & Edith Cooper) Field. 6274-1,6656-9
Letting the old cat die. Mary Mapes Dodge. 6131-1
Letting the old cat die. Unknown. 6373-X,6410-3,6742-5
Letts, Winifred M.
   Angelic service. 6162-1
   Blessings. 6090-0
   The call to arms in our street. 7031-0
   The call to arms in our street. 7027-2
   Chaplain to the forces. 7031-0,7026-4
   The children's ghosts. 6102-8
   The Connaught rangers. 7027-2
   A dog's grave. 6510-4
   Dreams. 6090-0
   For England's sake men give their lives. 6301-2
   Glorny's weir. 6090-0
   Grandeur. 6266-0,6102-6
   Guinea fowl. 6421-3
   The harbour. 6887-1
   He prayed. 7031-0
   In service. 6162-1,6266-0,6476-0,6506-6,6653-4
   The Kerry cow. 6331-4,6510-4
   The little children in the street. 6303-9
   The monkey's carol. 6162-1
   My blessing be on Waterford. 6090-0,6653-4
   Pensioners. 6510-4
   Quantity and quality. 6162-X,6607-0
   Says she. 6506-6
   Scared. 6887-1
   Screens. 6443-4
   The secrets of the heart. 6887-1
   Shops. 6478-7
   A soft day. 6338-1,6653-4
   A soft day. 6887-1
   Somehow-somewhere-sometime. 6184-2,6102-8
   The spires of Oxford. 6224-5,6331-4,6332-2,6337-3,6631-3,6503-1,6730-1,6102-8,6301-2,6646-1,6653
   Spring, the travelling man. 6090-0,6090-0,6653-4
   Synge's grave. 6872-3
   Tim, an Irish Terrier. 6477-9,6558-9,6639-9
   To a soldier in hospital. 7026-4
   To a solider in hospital. 7031-0
   To Scott - a collie. 7008-6
   To Tim--an Irish terrier. 7008-6
   The winds at Bethlehem. 6331-4
   Wishes for William. 6930-4
Lettsom, William Nanson (tr.)
   How Brunhild was received at Worms, fr. Nibelungen lied. Unknown (German), 6372-1
   How Margrave Rudeger was slain, fr. The Nibelungen lied. Unknown (German), 6372-1
   The Nibelungen lied, sels. Unknown (German), 6372-1
Letty's globe. Charles Tennyson Turner. 6233-4,6437-X,6479-5,6092-7,6199-0,6104-4,6533-0,6656-9,6737-9
Leu, Fred W.
   About 'two'. 6906-1
   If it ain't Bill. 6906-1
   A kindly deed. 6906-1
   My friend. 6906-1
   My mother. 6906-1
   Our poppy. 6906-1
   The sweetpea. 6906-1
Leucadia. George Gordon, 6th Baron Byron. 6484-1
Leukothea. Keith Douglas. 6379-9
Leuville, Marquis de
   The choice of arms. 6681-X
Levate signum. Bible. 6830-8
"Level and lovely in the dawn's dim air". Fog - Spanish phantasy. Agnes Kendrick Gray. 6841-3
The level mind. Alex Comfort. 6475-2
"The level sands and grey". Andrew Lang. 6997-5
"The level sands and grey". Love the vampire. Andrew Lang. 6987-8
The level way. Josephine Johnson. 6037-4
"Level-eyed, serene and knowing". Brenda at thirty. Gertrude Joan Buckman. 6850-2
Leveling. Unknown. 6681-X
The leveller. Bryan Waller ("Barry Cornwall") Procter. 6328-4
Levels. Lena Hall. 6039-0
Leventhal, Ann
   Circling. 6822-7
   Mending time. 6822-7
Lever, Bernice
   As if carbon is nothing. 6767-0
Lever, Charles
   Bad luck to this marching. 6930-4
   It's little for glory I care. 6930-4
   Larry McHale. 6174-5
   The man for Galway. 6174-5
   Mickey Free's song. 6026-9
   The pope. 6089-7,6732-8,6089-7
   The widow Malone. 6089-7;6174-5;6277-6;6174-5;6412-4;6481-,6732-8;6302-0;6385-3
Leveridge, Lilian
   Over the hills of the home, sels. 6796-4
Leveridge, Richard
   The roast beef of old England. 6087-0,6105-2
Levertin, Oscar
   The artist. Charles Wharton Stork (tr.). 6045-5
   Beatrice. Charles Wharton Stork (tr.). 6045-5
   Monica. Charles Wharton Stork (tr.). 6045-5
   An old New-Year's song. Charles Wharton Stork (tr.). 6045-5
   Solomon's hymn to the moon. Charles Wharton Stork

LEVERTIN

    (tr.). 6045-5
Levertov, Denise
    Christmas 1944. 6379-9
    Folding a shirt. 6379-9
    The gulf. 6803-0
    Poem ("Some are too"). 6379-9
    The postcards: a triptych. 6966-5
Levi, Peter
    Second year in a seminary. 6339-X
"Leviathan drives the eyed prow of his face". Leviathan, sels. Peter Quennell. 6985-1
Levicki, Jean
    Barely autumn. 6857-X
Levin, Louis H.
    A tree-tise on nature. 6674-7
Levine, Philip
    Another life. 6792-1,6998-3
    Waiting. 6792-1, 6998-3
Levins, Helen Fisher
    Peace. 6894-4
Levis, S. Virginia
    The woe-begone wiggle-dee. 6130-3
Leviticus Tate. Lloyd Warren. 6178-8
Levy and Nate Salsbury, Newman
    Ballade of the ancient wheeze. 6875-8
Levy, Alban A.
    Poem ("Out of a dust"). 6360-8
Levy, Alice
    The singer. 6850-2
    To a bakery. 6850-2
    With sympathy. 6850-2
Levy, Amy
    Between the showers. 6875-8
    The birch tree at Loschwitz. 6019-6
    The call of the city. 6793-X
    Epitaph. 6872-3
    A reminiscence. 6019-6
    Sonnet ("Most wonderful"). 7037-X
    Straw in the street. 6875-8
    The two terrors. 7037-X
Levy, Mabel Rose
    A picture of the deep south. 6083-8
    A picture of the old south. 6083-8
Levy, Nathan M.
    My books. 6770-0
Levy, Newman
    The belle of the Balkans. 6026-9
    Carmen. 6026-9
    I wonder what became of Rand, McNally.... 6722-0
    If you stick a stock of liquor. 6026-9
    Rain. 6089-7
    Thais. 6089-7
Levy, Norman
    The scandalous tale of Percival and Genevieve. 6722-0
Lew, Walter
    Fan. 6790-5
    Leaving Seoul: 1953 6790-5
    Two handfuls of Waka for Thelonious Sphere Monk... 6790-5
    Urn I: silent for twenty-five. 6790-5
Lewd love is loss. Robert Southwell. 6022-6
Lewes, Mary Ann. See Eliot, George
Lewie Gordon. Alexander Geddes. 6180-X,6086-2
Lewie Gordon. Unknown. 6859-6
Lewin, Everest
    The magic hour. 6779-4
    The swinging branch. 6778-6
Lewin, Frances Sesca
    The story of Abel Tasman. 6768-9
Lewis and Clark. George H. Nixon. 6260-1
Lewis Carroll. Edward Verrall Lucas. 6018-8
Lewis vs. state. Unknown. 6878-2
Lewis, Alonzo
    Death song. 6946-0
    Summer evening at a short distance from the city. 6752-2
    The wanderer of Africa. 6752-2
Lewis, Alun
    Christmas holiday. 6528-7
    Dawn on the east coast. 6209-1
    The defeated. 6528-7,6360-8
    In hospital: Poona. 6357-8,6379-9
    In hospital: Poona. 6895-2
    Mid-winter. 6360-8
    The mountain over Aberdare. 6360-8
    The peasants. 6209-1
    Raiders' dawn. 6783-2
    River Rhondda. 6360-8
    The sentry. 6360-8
    The soldier. 6360-8
    To a comrade in arms. 6210-5
    To Edward Thomas. 6360-8,6666-6
    Troopship in the tropics. 6666-6
    Water music. 6246-6;6339-X
Lewis, C. Day. See Day Lewis, Cecil
Lewis, C.B.
    As the pigeon flies. 6415-9,6167-2
Lewis, Charles M.
    Bijah. 6683-6
Lewis, Charlton M.
    Pro patria. 6031-5
Lewis, Clives Staples
    "Passing today by a cottage, I shed tears." 6317-9
Lewis, Constance Deming
    Dawn on Chateaugay. 6841-3
    June dawn. 6841-3
    Release. 6841-3
    Road! 6841-3
    Silver edge. 6841-3
    Waiting. 6841-3
    Wings aloft. 6841-3
Lewis, David
    Lines to Alexander Pnt. 6438-8
    When none shall rail. 6932-0
Lewis, Dio
    The malcontents. 6178-8
    Time. 6178-8
Lewis, Elsie M.
    Spring blues. 6894-4
Lewis, Ethelreda
    Asleep. 6800-6
    Christmas eve in the Karoo. 6800-6
    The return of Botha. 6800-6
Lewis, George Monk
    The maniac. 6302-0
Lewis, Harriet Rossiter
    Clouds at sunset. 6764-6
Lewis, Isabel
    Tujunga. 6799-9
Lewis, Jessica
    The humming bird. 6316-0
Lewis, Judd Mortimer
    A boy's whistle. 6274-1
    Mamma's dirl. 6260-1
    On Christmas eve. 6807-3
    Resignation. 6303-9
    Up to you ("Life's a bunch of roses in a sky blue..."). 6583-X
Lewis, Laurence (tr.)
    The stone of madness, sels. Fernando Arrabal, 6803-0
Lewis, Marion F.
    Thespian. 6750-6
Lewis, Matthew G.
    The hours. 6874-X
Lewis, Matthew Gregory
    Alonzo the brave and the fair Imogene. 6406-X,6086-2, 6219-9,6518-X
    The maniac. 6385-3;6404-3
Lewis, May
    Days at sea. 6979-7
    The grass. 6979-7,6039-0
    In a June garden. 6232-6
    Passer-by. 6072-2
    Study in vermilion. 6232-6
Lewis, Miriam S.
    Retribution. 6799-9
    Upon looking into my mirror. 6799-9
Lewis, Morris
    The maidens' lake. 6661-5
Lewis, Muriel

Pastoral ("The farmer"). 6349-7
Lewis, R.
  A journey from Patapsco in Maryland to Annapolis. 6753-0
Lewis, Sara D.
  A nine-year-old boy's definition of knees. 6750-6
Lewis, Saunders
  Cafe scene. Gwyn Williams (tr.). 6528-7
Lewis, the lost lover. Sir Thomas More. 6436-1
Lewisohn, James
  Basketball. 6870-7
  The blind man. 6870-7
  The children of the state. 6870-7
  Guernica. 6870-7
  Minimum security. 6870-7
  Poem. 6870-7
Lewisohn, Ludwig
  Saturnalia. 6327-6
  Together. 6619-4
Lewisohn, Ludwig (tr.)
  Autumn. Detlev von Liliencron, 7039-6
  Before the storm. Richard Dehmel, 7039-6
  The child reads an almanac. Francis Jammes, 7039-6
  For, Lord, the crowded cities be. Rainer Maria Rilke, 7039-6
  God's harp. Gustav Falke, 7039-6
  Harvest song. Richard Dehmel, 7039-6
  Idyl. Alfred Mombert, 7039-6
  The lord of the isle. Stefan George, 7039-6
  Oft in the silent night. Otto Julius Bierbaum, 7039-6
  Phantasus. Arno Holz, 7039-6
  The poor. Emile Verhaeren, 7039-6
  The quiet kingdom. Carl Busse, 7039-6
  Rapture. Stefan George, 7039-6
  The sleeper of the valley. Arthur Rimbaud, 7039-6
  Spring song. Hermann Hesse, 7039-6
  Stanzas concerning love. Stefan George, 7039-6
  There is an old city. Karl Bulcke, 7039-6
  The thought eternal. Johann Wolfgang von Goethe, 7039-6, 6879-0
  The two. Hugo von Hofmannsthal, 7039-6
  A Venetian night. Hugo von Hofmannsthal, 7039-6
  Vigil. Richard Dehmel, 7039-6
Lewisohn, Ruth
  At Neponsit. 6847-2
Lewti. Samuel Taylor Coleridge. 6828-6
Lewti, or the Circassian love chant. Samuel Taylor Coleridge. 6110-9
The lex talionis upon Benjamin West. John ("Peter Pindar") Walcott. 6278-4
Lex talionis, fr. Ye wearie wayfarer. Adam Lindsay Gordon. 6951-7
Lexington. Oliver Wendell Holmes. 6552-X, 6735-2
Lexington. Prosper M. Wetmore. 6678-X
Lexington. John Greenleaf Whittier. 6006-4, 6126-5
Lexington, fr. Psalm of the west. Sidney Lanier. 6946-0
Leyden, John
  Changes of home. 6980-0
  The daisy. 6302-0; 6385-3
  The memory of the past. 6980-0
  The mermaid. 6613-5
  A morning scene. 6980-0
  Noontide. 6302-0; 6385-3
  Ode to an Indian gold coin. 6600-3, 6304-7, 6219-9, 6980-0
  Ode to Jehovah. 6980-0
  Portuguese hymn to the virgin. 6980-0
  The sabbath morning. 6302-0, 6385-3, 6219-9
  Serenity of childhood. 6980-0
  Teviotdale. 6980-0
Leys, H.M.
  Crow's-foot. 6804-9
Leys, W.H.
  Shepherd's purse. 6804-9
Lezama Lima, Jose
  Rhapsody for the mule. Donald Devenish Walsh et al. (tr.). 6759-X
Li Hung Chang
  The sad sight of the hungry. 6954-1
Li Po
  The battle to the south of the city. Florence Ayscough and Amy Lowell (tr.). 6102-8
  The cataract of Luh Shan. Shigeyoshi Obata (tr.). 6253-9
  The Ching-Ting mountain. 6102-8
  A farewell song of white clouds. Shigeyoshi Obata (tr.). 6253-9
  Girls on the Yueh River. 6125-7
  Lament of the frontier guard. Ezra Pound (tr.). 6665-8
  The long war. Cheng Yu Sun (tr.). 6665-8
  The moon at the fortified pass. Witter Bynner and Kiang Kangohu (tr.). 6665-8
  On hearing a bamboo flute. Florence Ayscough and Amy Lowell (tr.). 6649-6
  On the banks of Jo-Eh. Lancelot Cranmer-Byng (tr.). 6732-8
  A poem ("The east wind"). Shigeyoshi Obata (tr.). 6649-6
  A poem composed at the imperial command. Shigeyoshi Obata (tr.). 6649-6
  The river-merchant's wife: a letter. Ezra Pound (tr.). 6513-9
  A visit to Yuan-Chiu in the mountains. Shigeyoshi Obata (tr.). 6253-9
  War. Rewi Alley (tr.). 6125-7
Li T'ai-po
  Clearing at dawn. Arthur Waley (tr.). 7039-6
  The river merchant's wife: a letter. Ezra Pound (tr.). 7039-6
Li Tai Po. See Li Po
Li fu-jen. Emperor Wu-ti. 6106-0
Li loenge nostre dame, sels. Unknown. 6282-2
Li'l pickaninny coon. P. H. 6118-4
Li-Tai-Pe
  The dance on the terrace. 6959-2
Liadain and Cuirithir. Frank (Michael O'Donovan) O'Connor. 6582-1
Liadain to Curithir. Moireen Fox. 6897-9
Liag, Mac (atr.)
  Kincora. James Clarence Mangan (tr.). 6930-4
"A liar goes in fine clothes". The liars. Carl Sandburg. 6880-4
Libaire, George
  Limerick:"..young curate of Salisbury." 6308-X
  Limerick:"A half baked potato, named Sue." 6308-X
  Limerick:"These places abound in the old." 6308-X
Libbey, Constance
  My heritage. 6764-6
A libel on D[octor] D[elaney] and a certain great lord. Jonathan Swift. 6380-2
Libera me. Ernest Dowson. 6507-4
Libera nos, domine. Philip Freneau. 6589-9
Liberation. Diane Mei Lin Mark. 6790-5
The liberator. Horace Spencer Fiske. 6524-4
Libertatis sacra fames. Oscar Wilde. 7015-9
Libertie, egalite, fraternite. Florence Converse. 6761-1
Liberty. Abraham Cowley. 6600-3, 6543-0
Liberty. David Greenhood. 6808-1
Liberty. Jennie Scott Griffiths. 6799-9
Liberty. John Hay. 7022-1
Liberty. Felicia Dorothea Hemans. 6973-8
Liberty. Edward R. Huxley. 6885-5
Liberty. Ernest Jones. 6793-X, 7009-4
Liberty. John Milton. 6935-5
Liberty. Morris Rosenfeld. 7011-6
Liberty. Percy Bysshe Shelley. 6383-7
Liberty. Edith M. Thomas. 7022-1
Liberty. James Thomson. 6816-2
Liberty. William Wordsworth. 6438-8
Liberty. Sir Thomas Wyatt. 6436-1
Liberty and America. George Gordon, 6th Baron Byron. 6323-3
"Liberty and Union, now and forever...". Daniel Webster. 6623-2
Liberty bell. Doyle Hennessy. 6839-1
The Liberty bell. Elbridge Streeter Brooks. 6552-X
Liberty elm. Lucia M. Mooney. 6684-4
Liberty enlightening the world. Edmund Clarence Stedman. 6946-0
Liberty enlightening the world. Edmund Clarence Stedman. 7041-8

LIBERTY

'**Liberty** enlightening the world'. Henry Van Dyke. 6961-4, 7026-4
Liberty for all. William Lloyd Garrison. 6286-5
The **liberty** of the imprisoned royalist. Sir Roger L'Estrange. 6934-7
The **liberty** pole satirized. Unknown. 6753-0
The **liberty** pole, fr. M'Fingal. John Trumbull. 6753-0
The **liberty** pole. Unknown. 6946-0
The **liberty** song. John Dickinson. 6008-0
Liberty tree. Thomas Paine. 6753-0,6946-0
Liberty's latest daughter. Bayard Taylor. 6286-5
Library. Harold Vinal. 6761-1
The **library** a glorious court, fr. The elder brother. John Fletcher. 6934-7
The **library** at Hyannis. Harry Lee. 6798-0
The **library** dove. John Russell Hayes. 6510-4
The **library** is on fire. Rene Char. 6803-0
Library note. Eve Merriam. 6761-1
The **library**, fr. The homestead. Gertrude Huntington McGiffert. 6838-3
The **library**, Greatham. George Rostrevor Hamilton. 6783-2
The **library**.. George Crabbe. 6186-9
The **library**. George Crabbe. 6297-0
The **library**. John Godfrey Saxe. 6297-0
The **library**. Frank Dempster Sherman. 6431-0
The **library**. Robert Southey. 6297-0
The **library**. John Greenleaf Whittier. 6297-0
Libration. Edward Estlin Cummings. 6880-4
Libretto in white, fr. Gather these bones. Lewis Turco. 6218-0
Libya. L. Challoner. 6468-X
Libyssa. Edward Farquhar. 6939-8
Liceat me ministrare. Selma Hamann. 6818-9
Licensed to sell; or, thy little blossom. Margaret J. Bidwell. 6567-8
"**Lichens** of green and grey on every side". Under canvas. Emily Pauline ("Tekahionwake") Johnson. 6837-5
Lichtenberg. Rudyard Kipling. 6810-3
Lichtenstein, Alfred
Fog. Babette Deutsch (tr.). 6160-5
icial, sels. Giles (the Elder) Fletcher. 6181-8
Licia: sonnet XLVII. Giles (the Elder) Fletcher. 6198-2
The **liddel** bower. James Hogg. 6086-2
Liddell, Catherine C.
Jesus the carpenter. 6479-5,6656-9,6820-0
Liddell, E. Louise
Out for a high time. 6699-2
Liddell, George T.
The Christ of common folks. 6335-7
Jesus of Nazareth passes by. 6144-3;6335-7
Liddell, Mark H.
The sibyl's response. 6983-5
Lides to baby jade. Unknown. 6409-4
Lides to Bary Jade. Unknown. 6277-6
Lidner, Bengt
Medea, sels. Charles Wharton Stork (tr.). 6045-5
Song of the battle-skald. Charles Wharton Stork (tr.). 6045-5
Spastarar's death, sels. Charles Wharton Stork (tr.). 6045-5
Lido. Richard Monckton Milnes; 1st Baron Houghton. 6631-3
Lido. Percy Bysshe Shelley. 6624-0
"**Lie** at thy rest, brave length of oaken brawn". The backlog. Edward Farquhar. 6939-8
"**Lie** in my arms, Ailsie, my bairn". Ailsie, my bairn. Eugene Field. 6949-5
"'**Lie** there', I said, 'my sorrow!...". A morning walk. Thomas Edward Brown. 6809-X
Lie-awake songs. Amelia Josephine Burr. 6266-0
The **lie**. Sir Walter Raleigh. 6087-0,6436-1,6102-8,6302-0, 6322-3,6436 ,6506-4,6584-8,6732-8,6479-5,6271-7,6125 ,6150-8,6219-9,6192-3,6250-4,6430-2
Lieber, Francis
The ship canal from the Atlantic to the Pacific. 6946-0
Lieber, Rose
Peace. 6396-9
Lieberman, Elias
A abandoned tow-path. 6072-2
The caravels of Columbus. 6336-5
Credo. 6503-1

Dawn after Christmas. 6954-1
I am an American. 6337-3,6265-2,6464-7
It is time to build. 6337-3
Sitting room in a Bowery hotel. 6042-0
To my brothers everywhere. 6979-7
Weary peddlers. 6102-8,6076-5,6102-8
Liebermann, Malvina
Knowledge, power, honor. 6717-4
Liebesweh. Dora Wilcox. 6784-0
Liebstod. Alan Seeger. 7029-9
Liechtenstein, Sir Ulrich von
Love, whose month was ever May. Jethro Bithell (tr.). 7039-6
Lied V. Jose Maria Eguren. 6759-X
Lief's trail. Celestin Pierre Cambiaire. 6826-X
The **liefboat**. George Robert Sims. 6918-5
Lienhard, Siegfried (tr.)
"Alas, alas! Where shall I go to search..my children?" Unknown (Newari), 7013-2
"Alas, where have been, oh husband?..." Unknown (Newari), 7013-2
"Be off, Krnsa! Do not behave like this!..." Unknown (Newari), 7013-2
"Because of love, oh friend, he and I are one". Unknown (Newari), 7013-2
Bhavani. Unknown (Newari), 7013-2
Bhimasena. Unknown (Newari), 7013-2
Bhimasena (2). Unknown (Newari), 7013-2
Buddha. Unknown (Newari), 7013-2
Buddha descends to Lumbini. Unknown (Newari), 7013-2
Buddha Sakyamuni. Unknown (Newari), 7013-2
Cobhara-Lokesvara. Unknown (Newari), 7013-2
"Come, oh friend, let us secretly move around & look". Unknown (Newari), 7013-2
"Destroying obstacles for the benefit of this world". Unknown (Newari), 7013-2
"Do not do what is untoward, oh lord of my life". Unknown (Newari), 7013-2
"Do not hinder me today, Lord Gopala! I am going..." Unknown (Newari), 7013-2
"Do not keep me at home, oh amaju!..." Unknown (Newari), 7013-2
"Do not keep me here, sir, making me suffer". Unknown (Newari), 7013-2
"The eminent Rsi Bhavabhuti came to give away..." Unknown (Newari), 7013-2
"The eyes of the Yogin sitting on the phalica..." Unknown (Newari), 7013-2
"For quite a long time I have worshipped Bhimasea Deva. Unknown (Newari), 7013-2
"Friends: as long as there is food and drink..." Unknown (Newari), 7013-2
"The frog's idea of a joke is to seize the lion's mane" Unknown (Newari), 7013-2
Ganesa. Unknown (Newari), 7013-2
Gorakhanatha and Lokanatha. Unknown (Newari), 7013-2
Guhyakali. Unknown (Newari), 7013-2
"Ha de! May the goddess Sarasvati, whom I invoked.." Unknown (Newari), 7013-2
"Ha de, you nine Nagas and Indra..." Unknown (Newari), 7013-2
"Haughty words, oh girl, do not use these words..." Unknown (Newari), 7013-2
"Having assembled, the Gopis went to the forest..." Unknown (Newari), 7013-2
"Having worshipped the Ganesa..." Unknown (Newari), 7013-2
"How much turmoil do you intend to cause me, oh Krnsa" Unknown (Newari), 7013-2
"How shall I describe my suffering, oh my beloved?" Unknown (Newari), 7013-2
"<u>I do not love this merciless husband of mine!</u>" Unknown (Newari), 7013-2
"I feel love, oh my jewel, I also feel love for you". Unknown (Newari), 7013-2
"I have a mirror from Halab..." Unknown (Newari), 7013-2
"I have today to undergo what is written in my karman" Unknown (Newari), 7013-2
"I kow only this gentleman. I do not know any other".

Unknown (Newari), 7013-2
I usually sit at the window in the room facing the road. Unknown (Newari), 7013-2
"I was having dinner, but had not yet eaten half..." Unknown (Newari), 7013-2
"I was trapped in the wretched net of love..." Unknown (Newari), 7013-2
Kali. Unknown (Newari), 7013-2
Krsna. Unknown (Newari), 7013-2
Krsna and Sudaman. Unknown (Newari), 7013-2
"Let us go, oh queen, we shall worship the god!" Unknown (Newari), 7013-2
Lokanatha. Unknown (Newari), 7013-2
"Look at Krsna's behavior, look!" Unknown (Newari), 7013-2
"Look, oh look, you lovers, it is springtime!" Unknown (Newari), 7013-2
"The man I love has abandoned me". Unknown (Newari), 7013-2
Manjusri. Unknown (Newari), 7013-2
Manjusri (2). Unknown (Newari), 7013-2
Matsyendranatha. Unknown (Newari), 7013-2
Matsyendranatha (2). Unknown (Newari), 7013-2
"My beloved has gone abroad. My heart feels sick". Unknown (Newari), 7013-2
"My heart was like the fragrance of the madhuli-flower. Unknown (Newari), 7013-2
Narayana. Unknown (Newari), 7013-2
"The neighbors came to know that you and I..." Unknown (Newari), 7013-2
"Not permanent in this body. Why?..." Unknown (Newari), 7013-2
Oh aunt, why have I been given away to a child-husband? Unknown (Newari), 7013-2
"Oh beautiful lady, where can I meet you?" Unknown (Newari), 7013-2
"Oh beautiful prince/In vain perished Kavi[ra]kumara". Unknown (Newari), 7013-2
"Oh girl, your hair-knot is as beautiful..." Unknown (Newari), 7013-2
"Oh Gopala, why do you spill my curds?" Unknown (Newari), 7013-2
"Oh Hari, don't be merciless!" Unknown (Newari), 7013-2
"Oh Hari, Hari! Destiny carried away the lord I loved" Unknown (Newari), 7013-2
"Oh Hari, where shall I go, abstaining from..pleasures" Unknown (Newari), 7013-2
"Oh husband, how shall I live, weeping all the time?" Unknown (Newari), 7013-2
"Oh king mind, you are the lord of the entire body". Unknown (Newari), 7013-2
"Oh Krsna, I never imagined you would abandon me". Unknown (Newari), 7013-2
"Oh little Chamchimi, why did you not wake up". Unknown (Newari), 7013-2
"'Oh look aunt', I said, 'I do not like him'". Unknown (Newari), 7013-2
Oh Lord Krsna, send me to the other bank of the Yamuna! Unknown (Newari), 7013-2
"Oh mother Dudhana, save me in time!" Unknown (Newari), 7013-2
"Oh mother Sitala, behold the pious state of..people". Unknown (Newari), 7013-2
"O mother, he is the man who has captured my heart". Unknown (Newari), 7013-2
"Oh my life! What can I do?This is the effect..karmen" Unknown (Newari), 7013-2
"Oh Nagara, be favorable to my request". Unknown (Newari), 7013-2
"Oh you artful little girl with amorously moving eyes" Unknown (Newari), 7013-2
"Oh, here comes the young little girl". Unknown (Newari), 7013-2
"Oh, sri-Bhimasena, grant us the boon of power..." Unknown (Newari), 7013-2
"Queen Bijyalaksmi was brought from outside..." Unknown (Newari), 7013-2
"Rajamti is foolish. If she comes to me..." Unknown (Newari), 7013-2
Saranda. Unknown (Newari), 7013-2

"Seriously, oh friend, tell me a successful means..." Unknown (Newari), 7013-2
"She saw him, when was bathing in the holy Ganges". Unknown (Newari), 7013-2
Siddhartha Gautama addresses Yasodhara. Unknown (Newari), 7013-2
Siva. Unknown (Newari), 7013-2
Svayambhu. Unknown (Newari), 7013-2
The Tatagata. Unknown (Newari), 7013-2
"Tears, oh dear mother, flowed down from the eyes". Unknown (Newari), 7013-2
"That girl seems to me like a minah-bird..." Unknown (Newari), 7013-2
"We women are stupid, alas!" Unknown (Newari), 7013-2
"What alley is that? What alley is this?..." Unknown (Newari), 7013-2
"What sort of comparison should I make?" Unknown (Newari), 7013-2
Yasodhara. Unknown (Newari), 7013-2
"Your big corals are already half-worn out..." Unknown (Newari), 7013-2
"Your mother is frightening. Your father lies weakly". Unknown (Newari), 7013-2
"Lies and gossip" Raymond Ringo Fernandez. 6870-7
Lieutenant Luff. Thomas Hood. 6974-6
"A **lieutenant** who went out to shout". Limerick:"A lieutenant who went out to shoot." Morgan Taylor. 6308-X
"**Lieutenant-Colonel** Roosevelt". The new patriotism. Edmund Wilson. 6880-4
Life. Sir Francis Bacon. 6219-9,6246-6,6560-0
Life. Philip James Bailey. 6461-2
Life. Anna Letitia Barbauld. 6102-8,6198-2,6600-3,6240-7, 6271-7,6260 ,6086-2,6104-4,6438-8,6301-2,6219-9,6737 ,6238-5,6402-7,6530-9,6732-8,6250-4,6543 ,6302-0, 6337-3,6385-3,6481-7,6486-8,6502
Life. Charlotte Becker. 6109-5
Life. William Blake. 6138-9
Life. Paul C. Boomer. 6482-5
Life. Harry Duane Brown. 6396-9
Life. Thomas Edward Brown. 6809-X
Life. Robert Burns. 6302-0
Life. N. C. 6563-5
Life. Alice Cary. 6865-0;6969-X
Life. Richard Coe Jr. 6632-1
Life. Samuel Taylor Coleridge. 6110-9
Life. Caleb C. Colton. 6980-0,6214-8
Life. Joseph Cook. 6889-8
Life. Samuel K. Cowan. 6416-7
Life. Samuel K. Cowan. 6167-2
Life. Abraham Cowley. 6250-4
Life. George Crabbe. 6932-0
Life. Mrs. H.A. Daming. 6260-1,6273-3
Life. Sir Humphry Davy. 6980-0
Life. Margaret Deland. 7041-8
Life. Henry Denison. 7030-2
Life. E. DeVilliers-Hertzler. 6818-9
Life. Emily Dickinson. 6006-4,6077-3,6300-4
Life. Edgar A. Guest. 6862-6
Life. Edgar A. Guest. 6748-4
Life. Amory Hare. 6347-0
Life. Belle R. Harrison. 6274-1
Life. George Herbert. 6302-0,6385-3,6563-5,6733-6,6341-1, 6219-9,6438-8
Life. George Herbert. 6014-5,6562-7
Life. John F.G. Holmes. 6764-6
Life. Eunice M. Hunting. 6764-6
Life. Edward R. Huxley. 6885-5
Life. Hazel M. Irish. 6764-6
Life. John Keats. 6634-8
Life. Francis Scott Key. 6219-9
Life. Henry King. 6271-7,6302-0,6737-9
Life. Frederic Lawrence ("R.L. Paget") Knowles. 6144-3, 6337-3
Life. Elizabeth Mary Little. 6090-0,6090-0;6174-5
Life. L.M. Little. 7037-X
Life. Henry Wadsworth Longfellow. 6820-0
Life. L.F. M. 6118-4
Life. Xavier de Magellon. 6351-9
Life. Joseph Morris. 6211-3

LIFE

Life. Edward Moxon. 6980-0
Life. Victor F. Murray. 6269-5
Life. Edward H. Pfeiffer. 6347-0,6646-8
Life. Genevieve Gray Rawson. 6906-1
Life. Cecil Roberts. 6607-0
Life. Gertrude W. Robinson. 6906-1
Life. Adeline Rubin. 6397-7
Life. Alexander R. Schooler. 6799-9
Life. Sir Walter Scott. 6086-2,6110-9
Life. William Shakespeare. 6102-8,6301-2
Life. Edward Rowland Sill. 6006-4,6620-8,6255-5,6337-3, 6490-6,6291 ,6309-8
Life. Mrs. F.S. Smith. 6270-9
Life. Arthur Stringer. 6785-9
Life. Charles Swain. 6656-9
Life. Elkanah East Taylor. 6818-9
Life. Kathryn Rich Tice. 6799-9
Life. Unknown. 6919-3
Life. Unknown. 6089-7,6724-7,6226-1
Life. W.M. Vories. 6337-3
Life. H.B. Wallace. 6304-7
Life. Metta Elaine Walsh. 6799-9
Life. Tessa Sweazy Webb. 6270-9
Life. John Hall Wheelock. 6310-1
Life. Ella Wheeler Wilcox. 7041-8
Life. Ella Wheeler Wilcox. 6291-1
Life. Richard Henry Wilde. 6302-0;6385-3
Life. T.P. Cameron ("Tipcuca") Wilson. 6653-4
Life ("A busy dream"). Unknown. 6273-3
Life ("Oh! let the soul"). Unknown. 6273-3
Life - what is it? James Newton Matthews. 6482-5
Life a bubble. William Drummond of Hawthornden. 6935-5
Life a cheat. John Dryden. 6102-8,6250-4
Life a voyage. Palladas. 6435-3
The life above, the life on high. Saint Theresa of Avila. 6730-1
Life after death. Pindar. 6435-3
The life after death. Samuel Butler. 6879-0
"Life an enfranchised bird, who wildly springs". Sonnet ("Like an enfranchised"). Caroline Elizabeth Sarah Sheridan Norton. 6980-0
Life and death. Anna Letitia Barbauld. 6291-1
Life and death. Ernest Howard Crosby. 6291-1,6337-3
Life and death. Sir William Davenant. 6933-9
Life and death. Cosmo Monkhouse. 7015-9
Life and death. Omar Khayyam. 6424-8
Life and death. John Oxenham. 6461-2
Life and death. Lilla Cabot Perry. 6723-9
Life and death. Adelaide Anne Procter. 6957-6
Life and death. Christina Georgina Rossetti. 6123-0,6508-2, 6655-0
Life and death. Duncan Campbell Scott. 6656-9
Life and death. William Shakespeare. 6438-8
Life and death. Walter James Turner. 6210-5
Life and death. Unknown. 6271-7,6273-3
The life and death of Dr. Faustus, sels. Christopher Marlowe. 6102-8,6732-8,6301-2
Life and death of Jason, sels. William Morris. 6123-0,6657- 7,6334-9,6526-0,6334-9,6110-9,6508-2,6655-0
The life and death of Jason, sels. William Morris. 6828-6
The life and death of Jason, sels. William Morris. 6110-9
The life and death of the piper of Kilbarchan. Robert Sempill. 6933-9
Life and eternity. Unknown. 6385-3
life and hereafter. Edgar A. Guest. 6862-6
Life and love. Robert Clarkson Tongue. 6116-8
Life and love. Robert Burns Wilson. 7041-8
Life and nature. Archibald Lampman. 6021-8,6446-9
"Life and the universe show spontaneity". The positivists. Mortimer Collins. 6996-7,7025-6
"Life and thought have gone away". The deserted house. Alfred Lord Tennyson. 6980-0
Life beyond the tomb. James Beattie. 6606-2
The life beyond. John Greenleaf Whittier. 6461-2
"The life boat that's kept at Torquay". Limerick:"The life boat that's kept at Torquay." Unknown. 6308-X
The life brigade. Minnie Mackay. 6916-9
"Life burns us up like fire". Life. John Hall Wheelock. 6310-1
"Life comes to us from God each day". Ascending footsteps. Josephine Byington. 6799-9
Life compared to a game of cards. Unknown. 6277-6
"Life ever seems as from its present site". Sonnet ("Life ever seems"). Henry Timrod. 6753-0
Life from death. Horatius Bonar. 6910-X
Life gives to me. Mary Helen Barbie. 7016-7
Life goes on. Mildred Evadne Hickman. 6799-9
"Life grows better every day". Loss and gain. Phoebe Cary. 6969-X
Life half lived. Friedrich Holderlin. 6125-7
"Life has no song more lovely than the one". Autumn in a New Hampshire village. Joan Andrews. 6764-6
"Life has three parts to its day". Life. Alexander R. Schooler. 6799-9
Life hidden. Christina Georgina Rossetti. 6655-0
"Life holds so much variety". All in a lifetime. Edgar A. Guest. 6748-4
"Life hurries on, a frantic refugee". Francesco Petrarch. 6325-X
Life ideal. John Edward Magraw. 6800-6
Life in a love. Robert Browning. 6429-9,6437-X,6655-0,6321- 7,6430-2,6102
Life in death. Ellice Hopkins. 7037-X
Life in death and death in life. Adelaide Anne Procter. 6957-6
"Life in her creaking shoes," fr. Echoes. William Ernest Henley. 6508-2
Life in its spring-time. E.A. Holbrook. 6049-8
"Life in itself, it life to all things gives". Power of the soul. Richard Henry Dana. 6752-2
Life in laconics. Mary Mapes Dodge. 6089-7
Life in the autumn woods. Philip Pendleton Cooke. 6006-4
Life in the chem lab. Henry W. Eliot Jr. 6118-4
Life in the spirit. Maurice Smiley. 6889-8
Life is a feast, they say. Thomas Curtis Clark. 6954-1
"Life is a jailer or a lover". Life. Eunice M. Hunting. 6764-6
"Life is a jest". Life is what we make it. Edgar A. Guest. 7033-7
"Life is a jest, and all things show it". John Gay. 6289-X
"Life is a keyboard/On which we press". The keyboard. Anne Campbell. 6799-9
"Life is a mask that we wear". Masks. Nellie Burget Miller. 6836-7
Life is a narrow vale. Robert G. Ingersoll. 6076-5,6732-8
"Life is a narrow vale...". Hope sees a star. Robert G. Ingersoll. 6889-8
"Life is a poet's fable". Song ("Life is a poet's fable.") Unknown. 6436-1
"Life is a poet's fable". Unknown. 6181-8
"Life is a sad and somber mystery sublet...". The raveling venture, sels. John Harolde. 7016-7
"Life is a seesaw that goes up and down". Life. Joseph Morris. 6211-3
"Life is a voyage of peril..." Palladas. 6251-2
"Life is a work-begin it". Unknown. 6109-5
"Life is but a day". Life. John Keats. 6634-8
"Life is but a joke, you say?". No, never. Bessie Irons Grauch. 6799-9
Life is but losse. Robert Southwell. 6586-4
Life is just a dream. Ernest Pool. 6149-4
"Life is less disturbing than it used to be". Less disturbing. Miriam Vedder. 6880-4
Life is like a river. Frances Archer Walls. 6906-1
"Life is like a sonata, depicting". Life. Metta Elaine Walsh. 6799-9
"'Life is maintenance,' you say". Maintenance. Deborah Pease. 6803-0
Life is more true. Edward Estlin Cummings. 6666-6
"Life is naught but a stairway/For us to go...". Life's stairway. Rubin Kane. 6799-9
"Life is not all for effort; there are hours". Winter recalled. Archibald Lampman. 7035-3
Life is our scene. Victor Sampson. 6800-6
Life is struggle. Arthur Hugh Clough. 6828-6
Life is struggle. Arthur Hugh Clough. 6123-0
Life is the art of drawing. Carolyn J. Ogletree. 7024-8
Life is too short. Ella Wheeler Wilcox. 6956-8
"Life is too short to fuss and fret". Life. Charlotte Becker. 6109-

Life is what we make it. Edgar A. Guest. 7033-7
"Life isn't dreary,/Nor altogether hard". A word about woodpiles. Nancy Byrd Turner. 6861-8
Life lapses by. John Payne. 6770-0
"Life lies between parentheses". (Parentheses]. Ulalume Gonzalez de Leon. 7036-1
Life like a matador goes forth. John Ransom Palmer. 6482-5
"Life lives on life". Walter De La Mare. 6905-3
"Life looked at me and said". Life. Edgar A. Guest. 6748-4
"Life make of him". The poet. Carl John Bostelmann. 6041-2
"Life makes noise within the morning". Yellow butterfly. Ulalume Gonzalez de Leon. 7036-1
The life mask. Virginia Donaghe McClurg. 6836-7
"Life may change, but it may fly not". Choruses from Hellas. Percy Bysshe Shelley. 6828-6
Life may change, fr. Hellas. Percy Bysshe Shelley. 6110-9, 6199-0
Life may to you bring every good. Phoebe Cary. 6066-8
Life not death, fr. The two voices. Alfred Lord Tennyson. 6337-3,6291-1
The life of a beau. James Miller. 6932-0
"The life of a leaf/Is sealed with the year". Autumn leaves. Elizabeth Dimon Preston. 6836-7
The life of god in the soul of man. Richard Henry Dana. 6752-2
The life of Guthlac, sels.. Unknown. 6489-2
Life of life. Alice Cary. 6969-X
"Life of life! thy lips enkindle". Chorus ("Life of life"). Percy Bysshe Shelley. 6315-2
"Life of life! Thy lips enkindle". Life of life, fr. Prometheus unbound. Percy Bysshe Shelley. 6935-5
Life of life! thy lips enkindle. Percy Bysshe Shelley. 6317-9,6328-4,6383-7
Life of life, fr. Prometheus unbound. Percy Bysshe Shelley. 6935-5
The life of man, fr. Atalanta in Calydon. Algernon Charles Swinburne. 6110-9,6102-8
The life of man. Sir Francis Bacon. 6182-6,6726-3,6436-1
The life of man. Barnabe Barnes. 6436-1
The life of man. Keidrych Rhys. 6641-0
The life of man. Algernon Charles Swinburne. 6828-6
Life of men, fr. The birds. Aristophanes. 6545-7
The life of nature, fr. Dejection: an ode. Samuel Taylor Coleridge. 6545-7
Life of our life. Henry Burke Robins. 6337-3
The life of Riley. Berton Braley. 6853-7
Life of Shakespeare. Frank Sidgwick. 6558-9
'Life of St. Cellach of Killala,' sels. Unknown. 6930-4
"The life of the air is stained with darkness". A poem for Captain Cool. Charles Price. 6998-3
The life of the blessed. Luis Ponce de Leon. 6752-2
Life on the farm, sels. Benjamin Franklin Taylor. 6815-4
A life on the ocean wave. Epes Sargent. 6239-3,6240-7,6479-5,6486-8,6735-2,6006 ,6484-1,6732-8,6219-9,6300-4
Life or death. E. B. 6273-3
Life pictures. Unknown. 6523-6
"Life said to me, 'Your days have run'". The sunset hill. Mary Pollard Tymes. 6799-9
"Life seems belittled when a great man". Roosevelt. John Jay Chapman. 6995-9
Life shall live for evermore, fr. In memoriam. Alfred Lord Tennyson. 6337-3
"Life she loved him - she seemed the slave". Life's favorite. Alfred Cochrane. 7031-0
A life story. Sam Walter Foss. 6097-8
The life that counts. Unknown. 6303-9
The life that counts. A.W. S. 6889-8
"A life that whittles passing hours away". Shavings. Frances Archer Walls. 6906-1
Life the beloved. Dante Gabriel Rossetti. 6110-9
Life through death. Richard Chenevix Trench. 6720-4,6177-X
Life unlived. John Payne. 7015-9
Life up your heads, rejoice! Thomas T. Lynch. 6730-1
"Life was to us an amphora of wine". The wine-cup. Richard Aldington. 6872-3
"Life will finish the work you are doing". Fulfilling. MacKnight Black. 6954-1
Life without death. Stephen Teets. 6799-9
Life without freedom. Thomas Moore. 6543-0
"Life would be bleak without the joys". Earth's joys.

Edward R. Huxley. 6885-5
Life!. Dorothy J. Smith. 6764-6
"Life! I know not what thou art". Anna Letitia Barbauld. 6230-X,6396-9,6246-6,6479-5
"Life! we've been long together". The cheerful way. Anna Letitia Barbauld. 6889-8
"Life! we've been long together". Anna Letitia Barbauld. 6238-5,6402-7
"Life!/What hast thou to offer me?". Life! Dorothy J. Smith. 6764-6
"Life's a good thing for sixteen hours-perhaps". Meditation on sleep. Ted Olson. 6761-1
"Life's angel watched a happy child at play". The angel of life. Richard Rowe. 6784-0
Life's battle-an oration. Unknown. 6406-X
Life's booklet. Edward R. Huxley. 6885-5
"Life's but a puppet-play...". Palladas. 6251-2
"Life's but a short chase, our game - content". Richard III, sels. Colley Cibber. 6867-7
Life's circumnavigators. William Robert Rodgers. 6209-1
Life's common things. Alice E. Allen. 6654-2
Life's common things. Unknown. 6274-1,6583-X
Life's conflict. William Whitehead. 6406-X
Life's curtain. Emma Magin Bissell. 6799-9
Life's day. Mary L. Gaddess. 6674-7
Life's end. Edward Young. 6211-3
Life's evening. William Dudley Foulke. 6730-1
Life's favorite. Alfred Cochrane. 7031-0
Life's forest trees. Ella Wheeler Wilcox. 6047-1,6049-8
Life's game of ball. Unknown. 6139-7,6416-7
Life's gifts. George Barlow. 6066-8
Life's good-morning. Anna Letitia Barbauld. 6424-8
Life's greeting. Arthur Leslie Green. 6116-8
Life's hebe. James ("B.V.") Thomson. 6656-9
Life's highway. Edgar A. Guest. 6869-3
Life's incongruities. Egbert Phelps. 6240-7,7030-2
Life's journey. John E. Barrett. 6840-5
Life's journey. Unknown (Greek) 6879-0
Life's last scene, fr. The vanity of human wishes. Samuel Johnson. 6932-0
Life's lesson. Unknown. 6583-X
"Life's loom is set by fate. Stern...kind". Fate. Clara Keck Heflebower. 6906-1
"Life's looms are ever weaving". Weaving. William White. 6868-5
Life's magnet. Ella Wheeler Wilcox. 6451-5
Life's measure. Ben Jonson. 6552-X
Life's medleys. Philetas. 6435-3
Life's mirror. Mary Ainge ("Madeline Bridges") De Vere. 6303-9,6337-3,6654-2,6109-5
Life's mysteries. Alice Cary. 6969-X
Life's mysteries, sels. Alice Cary. 6066-8
Life's mystery. Alice Cary. 6969-X
Life's mystery. Sheldon Darling. 6818-9
Life's nobles heights. Burton W. Lockhart. 7041-8
Life's pageant, fr. The tempest. William Shakespeare. 6634-8
A life's parallels. Christina Georgina Rossetti. 6641-0
"Life's parting beam were in his eye". The hero's death. Felicia Dorothea Hemans. 6973-8
Life's past and future. William Hankins Chitwood. 6799-9
Life's paths. Joseph Crosby Lincoln. 6119-2
Life's pilgrimage. Robert Nicoll. 6960-6
Life's poor play, fr. An essay on man. Alexander Pope. 6932-0
Life's purpose. David Lawton. 6617-8
Life's purpose, fr. The cathedral. James Russell Lowell. 6337-3
"Life's race well run". Unknown. 6109-5
Life's record. Edward R. Huxley. 6885-5
Life's roses. Alice Cary. 6865-0;6969-X
"Life's sadly solemn mystery". Life's mystery. Alice Cary. 6969-X
Life's seesaw. Unknown. 6260-1
Life's shaping moments. James A. Tucker. 6433-7
Life's single standard. Edgar A. Guest. 7033-7
Life's stairway. Rubin Kane. 6799-9
Life's sunset. Edward R. Huxley. 6885-5
Life's tragi-comedy. Sir Walter Raleigh. 6934-7
Life's triumph. Thomas S. Collier. 6273-3

Life's underpay. William Lindsey. 6798-0
Life's unfolding. John Olin Knott. 6799-9
Life's venture. Jesse Sill. 6799-9
Life, a question? Corinne Roosevelt Robinson. 6266-0,6478-7
Life, death, and eternity. John Clare. 6214-8
Life, death, and love. Alexander Gordon Cowie. 6650-X
"Life, deliver up to me/All fate has...". My demand. Marion L. Bertrand. 6799-9
Life, fr. Psalm of life. Henry Wadsworth Longfellow. 6239-3,6438-8
Life, fr. The three best things. Henry Van Dyke. 6961-4
Life, fr. The three best things. Henry Van Dyke. 6337-3
Life, I know not what thou art. Anna Letitia Barbauld. 6964-9
Life, liberty and lager. Unknown. 6791-3,6823-5
"Life, like a page unpenned". For a closing page. Austin Dobson. 7014-0
"Life, like a romping schoolboy full of glee". Life. Ella Wheeler Wilcox. 7041-8
Life, sels. William Blake. 6018-8
"Life, thou art vaguely strangely sweet". Villanelle. James Ashcroft Noble. 6770-0
"Life, you were lovely! Ah, I know it now". Looking back. Blanche Yvonne Mosley. 6761-1
'The life-boat'.. Unknown. 6392-6
The life-boat. Erik Lindorm. 6045-5
"Life-documents are they, enduring seal". The portraits, fr. The homestead. Gertrude Huntington McGiffert. 6838-3
A life-drama, sels. Alexander Smith. 6656-9
Life-drunk. Arthur Stringer. 6501-5
Life-in-love, fr. The house of life. Dante Gabriel Rossetti. 6655-0
A life-lesson. James Whitcomb Riley. 6889-8
A life-lesson. James Whitcomb Riley. 6102-8,6303-9,6632-1,6732-8,6431-0,6066-8,6076-5,6121-4,6300-4,6723-9
The life-lover. Frederic F. Vandewater. 7007-8
The life-mask of Abraham Lincoln. Stuart (Gertrude Bloede) Sterne. 6524-4
The life-saver. Joseph Crosby Lincoln. 6119-2
Life-saving medal. Phillipe Soupault. 6351-9
A life. Bryan Waller ("Barry Cornwall") Procter. 6240-7,6385-3,6219-9,6656-9
A life. George Edward Woodberry. 6833-2
Life?. John Galsworthy. 6888-X
"The lifeboat that's kept in Torquay". Unknown. 6083-8
The lifeboat. George Robert Sims. 6451-5,6575-9
The lifeguard in the snow. Eugene Ruggles. 6901-0
"The lifeless son - the mother's agony". The three Marys at Castle Howard, in 1812 and 1837. Ebenezer Elliott. 6832-4
Lifesaver. Elizabeth Riddell. 6384-5
Lifetime. Winifred Welles. 6653-4
A lifetime. William Cullen Bryant. 6126-5,6288-1,6753-0
Lifshin, Lyn
    I don't know what you want. 6998-3
    Tuesday. 6998-3
"Lift - lift, ye mists, from off the...coast". The lost expedition. Thomas Hood. 6997-5
"Lift a song to Illinois, a song of pride...". A song to Illinois. Horace Spencer Fiske. 6818-9
"Lift me without the tent, I say". The scheik of Sinai in 1830. Ferdinand Freiligrath. 6948-7
"Lift not the painted veil". Sonnet ("Lift not"). Percy Bysshe Shelley. 6208-3,6250-4
Lift not the painted veil. Percy Bysshe Shelley. 6199-0
"Lift not thy trumpet, victory, to the sky". A dirge of victory. Edward John Plunkett, 18th Baron Dunsany. 7029-9
Lift the Prohibition banner. Lilian M. Heath. 6685-2
"Lift up a banner on the lofty hill". The destruction of Babylon. Unknown. 6848-0
Lift up the curtain, fr. The heart of youth. Hermann Hagedorn. 6532-5
"Lift up the shuttered eyelids that were drawn". He is not desecrate. David Morton. 6817-0
Lift up your heads, O ye gates! Bible. 6512-0
"Lift up your heads, great gates, and sing". The ascension. Joseph Beaumont. 6931-2
Lift up your heads, rejoice! Thomas Toke Lynch. 6418-3
"Lift up your heartes and be glad!". What cheer? Good cheer! Be merry and glad this new year. Unknown. 6756-5
"Lift up your heartes and be glad". Unknown. 6334-9
Lift up your hearts! Henry Montague Butler. 6337-3
"Lift up your hearts, old men, afraid...". Psalm before the dark mirror. A.M. Sullivan. 6783-2
"Lift vp to heau'n, sad wretch, thy heauy spright" Thomas Campion. 6794-8
"Lift ye up a banner upon the high mountain". Levate signum. Bible. 6830-8
"Lift your voice and thankful sing". Psalm 118 Bible. 6848-0
Lift's weaving. Millie Colcord. 6926-6
Lifting and leaning. Ella Wheeler Wilcox. 6461-2
"Lifting dark beside the trail". Ophida. Gwendolen Haste. 6979-7
The lifting of the muse. Emily Pauline ("Tekahionwake") Johnson. 6837-5
Liggett, Carr
    Helen. 7007-8
"Lighg ebbs from off the earth...". Evening, near the sea. Edward Dowden. 6997-5
Light. Francis William Bourdillon. 6219-9,6654-2,6371-3,6737-9,6226-1,6273-3,6477-9,6486-8,6620-8
Light. Alice Cary. 6865-0;6969-X
Light. Phoebe Cary. 6969-X
Light. M. Elizabeth Crouse. 6274-1
Light. Pascal D'Angelo. 6776-X
Light. Paul Fort. 6351-9
Light. Zona Gale. 6007-2
Light. Hermann Hagedorn. 6761-1
Light. George Macdonald. 6656-9
Light. John Milton. 6424-8
Light. William Pitt Pammer. 6910-X
Light. John J. Procter. 6433-7
Light. Aimee Paul Thomas. 6270-9
Light. Adelene Kissam Watt. 6750-6
Light ("Mistress of my days..."). Xavier de Magellon. 6351-9
Light after darkness. Edward Wyndham Tennant. 7027-2
Light after darkness. Edward Wyndham Tennant. 6650-X
Light and darkness. Alice Cary. 6969-X
Light and love. Francis William Bourdillon. 6337-3
Light and love. Unknown. 6273-3
Light and shade. Edmond Gore Alexander Holmes. 6997-5
Light and shade. Adelaide Anne Procter. 6957-6
Light and shadow. Robert E. Brittain. 6397-7
The light and the glory of the word. William Cowper. 6814-6
"Light as a leaf on the lifting swell". Under the Palisades. Arthur Guiterman. 6773-5
Light between the trees. Henry Van Dyke. 6961-4
Light breaks where no sun shines. Dylan Thomas. 6209-1, 6389-6
"A light broke in upon my soul". George Gordon, 6th Baron Byron. 66601-1
"Light do I see within my Lady's eyes". Guido Cavalcanti. 6325-X
"Light ebbs from off the earth...". Evening, near the sea. Edward Dowden. 7015-9
"Light flicks across the fence". Stopping by a sundial. Paul Evison. 7018-3
"Light flows our war of mocking words". The buried life. Matthew Arnold. 6199-0,6250-4,6430-2,6655-0,6828-6
"Light for the dreary vales". Missions. Lydia Huntley Sigourney. 6752-2
Light from above. James Abraham Martling. 6952-5
Light from an eminent S.S.C. Unknown. 6878-2
The light from within. Jones Very. 6730-1
"Light graceful clouds across the sky". Ships of the north. William Talbot Allison. 7035-3
"Light green of grass and richer green of bush". The guns in Sussex. Sir Arthur Conan Doyle. 7031-0,7027-2
"Light has flown!". Twilight. Andrew Lang. 6987-8
"A light heart had the Irish lad". Goldsmith's whistle. Harriet Prescott Spofford. 7041-8
The light hearted fairy. Unknown. 6466-3,6639-9
The light in mother's eyes. Lucy Maud Montgomery. 609-

8;6274-1
A **light** in the window. Joseph Morris. 6303-9
"**Light** is holy as the bees". Unholy light. Robert P. Tristram Coffin. 7040-X
"The **light** is like a spider". Tattoo. Wallace Stevens. 6754-9
"The **light** is shining through the window-pane". Out in the streets. Thomas Dunn English. 6909-6
Light love. Charles Hanson Towne. 6441-8
Light lover. Aline Kilmer. 6300-4
The **light** of Asia, sels. Sir Edwin Arnold. 6046-3
The **light** of Bethlehem. John Banister Tabb. 6144-3,6337-3, 6465-5,6746-8,6172-9
The **light** of Christmas. Norval Clyne. 6747-6
The **light** of days gone by. Alice Cary. 6969-X
The **light** of faith. George Santayana. 6143-5
"The **light** of freedom beameth!". Freedom's dawning. James Abraham Martling. 6952-5
The **light** of freedom. Robert Buchanan. 7009-4
The **light** of God is falling. Louis FitzGerald Benson. 6337-3
The **light** of home. Mrs. Hale. 6752-2
The **light** of life. Charles W. Denison. 6755-7
Light of love. Dorothy Parker. 6817-0
The **light** of love. John Hay. 6226-1
Light of morning. Bill Adams. 7007-8
The **light** of other days. Thomas Moore. 6186-9,6464-7,6383-7,6212-1,6104-4,6086-2,6383-7,6737-9
The **light** of other days. John Clark. 6800-6
The **light** of stars. Henry Wadsworth Longfellow. 6126-5, 6271-4
The **light** of the Haram, fr. Lalla Rookh. Thomas Moore. 6832-4
The **light** of the harem, sels. Thomas Moore. 6198-2
The **light** of the house. Louise Imogen Guiney. 7041-8
"**Light** of the soul". Unknown. 6065-X
Light of the world. Sylvester Judd. 6065-X
"The **light** of the world is of gold". By Lough-na-Gar: green light. Arthur Symons. 6793-X
Light of the world, how long the quest. Edwin McNeill Poteat. 6337-3
The **light** on deadman's bar. Eben Eugene Rexford. 7022-1
"**Light** on the brow". The light of freedom. Robert Buchanan. 7009-4
"**Light** on the green glass on the mantel-piece". Sunday morning. Hal Saunders White. 6808-1
"**Light** over hills from purple skies". Noel, fr. Mother-songs. Marian Williams McGaw. 6906-1
"The **light** passes". Evening. Hilda ("H.D.") Doolittle. 6315-2,6209-1
"**Light** ripples lace, glitters from the eaves". Still lives. Emilie Buchwald. 6966-5
Light shining out of darkness. William Cowper. 6154-0,6271-7,6337-3,6730-1,6023-4,6219 ,6214-8,6723-9,6418-3
Light shoes. Patrick Kelly. 6292-X
Light song. Lola Ridge. 6217-2
The **light** that is felt. John Greenleaf Whittier. 6575-9
The **light** that lies. Thomas Moore. 6104-4
"**Light** the bayberry candle". The bayberry candle. Samuel W. Hallett. 6798-0
"**Light** the hills! till heaven is glowing". The mountain fires. Felicia Dorothea Hemans. 6973-8
Light the lamps up, lamplighter! Eleanor Farjeon. 6421-3
Light the old pipe. Rheinhart Kleiner. 7007-8
"**Light** thickens; and the crow", fr. Macbeth. William Shakespeare. 6392-6
"**Light** to the eye and music to the ear". Iris, fr. Music. Henry Van Dyke. 6961-4
"**Light** up those homes, Columbia". Illumination for victories in Mexico. Sara J. ("Grace Greenwood") Lippincott. 6946-0
A **light** upon the mountains. Henry Burton. 6337-3
"The **light** was low in the school-room". The silent children. Elizabeth Stuart Phelps. 6965-7
A **light** woman. Robert Browning. 6023-4
The **light** yoke and easy burden. Charles Wesley. 6065-X
"The **light** young man who was to die". Saint Catherine of Siena. Alice Meynell. 6955-X
The **light'odd** fire. John Henry Boner. 7041-8
The **light'ood** fire. John Henry Boner. 6006-4

"**Light's** glittering morn bedecks the sky". John Mason Neale. 6931-2
Light, fr. Paradise lost. John Milton. 6933-9
"**Light**, like a closing flower, covers to earth". Summer night. Laurence Housman. 6884-7
"**Light**, so low upon earth". Marriage morning. Alfred Lord Tennyson. 6977-0
"**Light**, then darkness". A night on the town. Charles Price. 6998-3
"**Light**, warmth, and sprouting greenness". Pictures. John Greenleaf Whittier. 6753-0
The **light-bringer**. Witter Bynner. 6542-2
Light-footed Iphiclus. Hesiod. 6435-3
The **light-house**.. Unknown. 6523-6
The **light-house**. Thomas Moore. 6409-4
The **light-keeper**. Joseph Crosby Lincoln. 6119-2
The **light-o'-love**. Howard Vigne Sutherland. 6836-7
The **light-ship**.. Wolstan Dixey. 6523-6
Light-winged smoke, Icarian bird. Henry David Thoreau. 6333-0
Lightbourne, Ronald R.W.
  "Astonished children" 6898-7
  "I am surprised you have not heard me bleeding" 6898-7
  "Something keeps" 6898-7
A **lighted** open door. Robert P. Tristram Coffin. 7040-X
"**Lighten**, heauy hart, thy spright" Thomas Campion. 6794-8
A **lightening** story. William J. Lampton. 6415-9
"The **lightening** stricken giant gum". The wood-swallows, fr. Australian transcripts. William ("Fiona Macleod") Sharp. 6768-9
"**Lighter** and sweeter/Let your song be". Song ("Lighter"). Greville Ewing Matheson. 6861-8
"**Lightest** foam, straightest spray". Waters of the sea. Cecil Goldbeck. 6833-2
Lightfoot Larry. Berton Braley. 6853-7
Lighthall, William Douw
  All hail to a night. 7035-3
  The battle of La Prairie. 6433-7,6656-9
  Canada not last. 6795-6
  Canada not last. 7041-8
  The Caughnawaga beadwork-seller. 6795-6
  The confused dawn. 6433-7,6656-9
  Deathless. 6796-4
  Eben Picken, bookseller. 6433-7
  Homer. 7041-8
  Montreal. 6433-7,6656-9
  My England. 6224-5
  National hymn. 7041-8
Lighthall, William Douw (tr.)
  A la Claire Fontaine. Unknown (French Canadian), 6795-6
Lighthouse May. E. Faxton. 6571-6
"The **lighthouse** keeper's daughter looked out..". The light on deadman's bar. Eben Eugene Rexford. 7022-1
The **lighthouse** of love. Sir William Watson. 6780-8
The **lighthouse**.. Sir Walter Scott. 6466-3,6623-2
The **lightkeeper's** daughter. Myra A. Goodwin. 6410-8,6744-1, 6744-1
A **lightkeeper**. Charles Poole Cleaves. 6764-6
Lightless suburb. Pablo (Neftali Ricardo Reyes Basualto) Neruda. 6642-9
Lightless Susan. Alexander M. Lackey. 6037-4
"**Lightly** as two shell-gatherers we went down". Harborless. Leslie Nelson Jennings. 6880-4
"**Lightly** now the frosted leaf". Indian summer. Nyleen Morrison. 6764-6
"**Lightly** she slept, that splendid mother mine". Mother and mate. Gilbert Frankau. 7027-2
"**Lightly** the breath of the spring wind blows". By wood and wold. Adam Lindsay Gordon. 6784-0
"**Lightly**, alpine rover/Tread the mountains...". The boy of the Alps. Thomas Moore. 6749-2
"**Lightly**, lightly/Summer breezes playing." Bokujin. 6027-7
"The **lightning** flashed, and lifted". The thunder-shower. John Hall Wheelock. 6897-9
"The **lightning** is a yellow fork". Emily Dickinson. 6399-3
"The **lightning** witch is mad again!". Windy night. Chris Real. 6750-6
The **lightning-rod** dispenser. Will Carleton. 6630-5
The **lightning**. Minamoto No Jun. 6732-8
Lights. Mabel Cleland Ludlum. 6478-7

LIGHTS

Lights. Mary Lanier Magruder. 6653-4
Lights along the mile. Alfred Chandler. 6784-0
Lights and shades. Felicia Dorothea Hemans. 6409-4
Lights and shades. Felicia Dorothea Hemans. 6973-8
"The lights and shadows fly!". On the hill. Alfred Lord Tennyson. 6977-0
"The lights are dim on the steerage deck". The dance in the steerage. Joseph Warren Beach. 6959-2
The lights o' London. George Robert Sims. 6917-7
"The lights of cities belie much of darkness". Nocturne. Marie de L. Welch. 6761-1
The lights of home. Alfred Noyes. 6151-6,6177-X
The lights of Lawrence. Ernest Warburton Shurtleff. 6621-6
The lights of London Town. George Robert Sims. 6083-8
Lights out. Edward Thomas. 6246-6,6634-8,6354-3,6150-8
Lights out. Henry Van Dyke. 6961-4
"Lights that have been on all day in offices". Home is where. Louis Hasley. 6761-1
Lights to steer by. William Hamilton Jefferys. 6936-3
"The lights/From out the fleet". The message. James Gorham. 6850-2
The lights. John Joy Bell. 6242-3
The lights. Unknown (American Indian) 6396-9
The lightship. Josephine Johnson. 6042-0
"Like a black enamoured king whispering low...". Dunedin in the gloaming. Jessie MacKay. 6784-0
Like a boy. Joseph Joel Keith. 6761-1
"Like a breath that comes and goes". The wild mare. William ("Fiona Macleod") Sharp. 6819-7
"Like a child that is lost". A penitent's plea. Alice Cary. 6969-X
Like a cloud, like a mist. Helen Hoyt. 6019-6
"Like a crumpled paper cutout". Days ago. Dianne Hai-Jew. 6790-5
"Like a dear old lady". A portrait. Caroline Giltinan. 6039-0,6649-6
"Like a dog/I am commanded". At the Sand island camp. Keiho Soga. 6981-9
"Like a dream, it all comes o'er me as I hear..bell". A Christmas long ago. Unknown. 6964-9
"Like a dusky cave, the barn looms high...". Barn sounds. Daniel Smythe. 6761-1
"Like a fire about to extinguish". A gloomy day. Norbert Krapf. 6966-5
"Like a foundling in slumber...summer day lay". Jenny June. Benjamin Franklin Taylor. 6815-4
"Like a genie selling suckers". Boxer shorts named champion. Melvin Douglass Brown. 6870-7
"Like a god I hoped to". Crying Cupid. Josephine Sievers Birt. 6906-1
"Like a great rock, far out at sea". Lady Sanuki. 7039-6
"Like a great seagull lost and flying blind". Fog off Brunswick Sound. Daniel Whitehead Hicky. 6783-2
"Like a grey shadow lurking in the light". The wolf. Emily Pauline ("Tekahionwake") Johnson. 6837-5
"Like a hawk that hangs in mid-heavens". Road! Constance Deming Lewis. 6841-3
Like a laverock in the lift. Jean Ingelow. 6240-7,6385-3, 6620-8,6543-0
"Like a lean robber on life's bleak highway". The outcast. H.J. Cleugh. 6778-6
Like a little child. George Macdonald. 6429-9,6321-7
"Like a long arrow through the dark...". Fire-fly city. Henry Van Dyke. 6961-4
"Like a Ponsonby native". On probation. Peter Olds. 7018-3
Like a midsummer rose, fr. The fall of princes. John Lydgate. 6150-8
"Like a musician that with flying finger". William Caldwell Roscoe. 7015-9
"Like a pearl dropped...". Trumbull Stickney. 6380-2
"Like a pool of sunny sea". Washing dishes. Marcene Stoops. 6799-9
"Like a queen enchanted who may not laugh...". A ballad of bath. Algernon Charles Swinburne. 6770-0,6875-8
"Like a rose that is blooming in beauty so...". Love. Howard Phillips. 6799-9
Like a shadow. David Coy. 6860-X
"Like a shower of rain," fr. Annales. Ennius. 6665-8
"Like a sick child. Elizabeth Barrett Browning. 6097-8
"Like a skein of loose silk blown against...". The garden. Ezra Pound. 6897-9
"Like a small boy counting". Return to war. George Allen. 6761-1
"Like a star whose brightness grows". Unknown. 6050-1
"Like a stone toppled from an endless hill". The fall of Satan, fr. The flaming terrapin. Roy Campbell. 6788-3
'Like a thief in the night'. Sister Mary St. Virginia. 6839-1
"Like a wing, wong, waddle". The swapping song. Unknown. 6826-X
"Like an adventurous seafarer am I". Michael Drayton. 6258-X,6586-4
Like an island in a river. Philip James Bailey. 6543-0
"Like an ocean is this world". Hovhannes Erzingatzi. 6050-1
Like angels' visits. John Norris. 6934-7
".Like as a ship, that through the ocean wide," fr. Amoretti. Edmund Spenser. 6645-3
"Like as a star/That maketh not hast." Unknown. 6225-3
"Like as the bird in the cage enclosed." Sir Thomas Wyatt. 6584-8
Like as the Damask rose. Francis Quarles. 6315-2
"Like as the culver, on the bared bough". Sonnet ("Like as the culver"). Edmund Spenser. 6219-9
"Like as the damask rose you see". Man's mortality. Unknown (Irish). 6914-2
"Like as the damaske rose you see". Verses of mans mortalitie, with an other of the hope... Unknown. 6933-9
Like as the dove. Sir Philip Sidney. 6584-8
"Like as the dumb solsequium, with care...". The solsequium. Alexander Montgomerie. 6845-6
"Like as the swan towards her death." Sir Thomas Wyatt. 6584-8
"Like as the waves make toward the pebbled shore." William Shakespeare. 6125-7
"Like as the waves make towards the pebbled shore". William Shakespeare. 6122-2,6219-9,6198-2,6488-4, 6204-0,6246-6,6536-8,6182-
"Like as the waves make towards the pebbled shore". Sonnet 060 ("Like as the waves"). William Shakespeare. 6208-3,6660-7,6645-3,6150-4,6560-0,6189-3,6301-2
"Like as to make our appetites more keen". Sonnet 118 ("Like as to make"). William Shakespeare. 6447-7
"Like barley bending," fr. Sea sand. Sara Teasdale. 6161-3, 6345-4
"Like beryl which some mighty alchemist". Sea birds. Katharine Lee Bates. 6798-0
"Like brands ye laid us nightly in red heat". The place of heroes, fr. Tree of time. Gertrude Huntington McGiffert. 6838-3
"Like cameos carved on a purple sky". White worlds. H. Gandy. 7035-3
"Like cans with all the labels mixed". Lottery. Lucile Enlow. 6841-3
"Like chipped pearl". Car six. Americo Casiano. 6898-7
"Like coral insects multitudinous". Work. Jean Ingelow. 7037-X
Like decorations in a nigger cemetery, sels. Wallace Stevens. 6751-4
"Like dew on the blossoms". Rainbow. Jean Mutter. 6799-9
"Like Dian, her trim ankles seen". My lady of the links. Unknown. 7021-3
"Like dreary prison walls". Over the mountain. Adelaide Anne Procter. 6957-6
"Like elfin wraiths/That dance grotesquely...". Slum children. Florence Orndorff. 6906-1
"Like everything else but this is all". Poetry. Al Masarik. 6792-1
"Like fashioned rock". Clocks. Tessa Sweazy Webb. 6750-6
"Like flocks of sheep celestial...". Easter. Benjamin Franklin Taylor. 6815-4
"Like God's own heart". The shadow. David Stefansson fra Fagraskogi. 6854-5
Like flowers we spring. Unknown. 6182-6
Like God's love. Helen Hunt Jackson. 6097-8
"Like him who met his own eyes in the river". The love of Narcissus. Alice Meynell. 6955-X
Like him whose spirit. Arthur Dvison Ficke. 6897-9

Like his mother used to make. James Whitcomb Riley. 6097-8, 6273-3
"**Like** lightning's flash/Upon the foe". We are free. Robert Nicoll. 7009-4
"**Like** liquid gold the wheat field lies". Collor in the wheat. Hamlin Garland. 6964-9
Like magic. James Oppenheim. 6345-4
"**Like** Memnon's rock, touched with the rising sun" Giles (the Elder) Fletcher. 6182-6
"**Like** many a one, when you had gold". The old story. Marcus Argentarius. 7039-6
"**Like** merry Momus,while the gods were quaffing". Eulogy on laughing. Jonathan Mitchell Sewall. 6787-5
"**Like** mountain honey, richly red". Honey boy. Billie Marie Crabb. 6750-6
Like music. John Hall Wheelock. 6897-9
Like one I know. Nancy Campbell. 6090-0,6172-9
"**Like** one vast sapphire flashing light". Gerald Massey. 6997-5
"**Like** one who leaves the trampled street". The chapel. Bayard Taylor. 6976-2
"**Like** other men, you fly from adjectives". Finalities. Maxwell Bodenheim. 6776-X
"**Like** other tyrants, death delights to smite". Death ("Like other tyrants"). Unknown. 6294-6
"**Like** pearls that lie hid 'neath the ocean's..". Our sweet unexpressed. W.F. Fox. 6912-4
"**Like** pebbles tossed by careless gods". Fantasy. Doris Trahagen De Aragon. 6906-1
"**Like** Perdita, who heard the swift March run". To an old man gone. Janet Newmane Preston. 6841-3
"**Like** pretty birds/Melodious words". An hour with you. Celestin Pierre Cambiaire. 6826-X
"**Like** question-marks the ferns lift up..heads". Adolescence. Alice M. Shepard. 6764-6
"**Like** sand in an hourglass". From the other side. Alejandra Pizarnik. 7036-1
"**Like** shadows, old things came to him...night". He remembered. Florence Crocker Comfort. 6789-1
"**Like** silver dew the tears of love". Epitaph. Alfred Edgar Coppard. 6072-2
"**Like** silver shafts imprisoned in a fine". Love. Grace Imogen Duffy. 6818-9
"**Like** small curled feathers white and soft". While shepherds watched their flocks by night. Margaret Deland. 7041-8
"**Like** some cathedral spire that cleaves". To Noel Davis. Marcia Lewis Leach. 7014-0
"**Like** some dim echo of the pristine sea". 'The spell' Rudolph Hill. 6818-9
"**Like** some great rock that stands securely...". The rock. Helen Bosanquet. 7042-6
"**Like** some old wanderer out of the past". Captain's walk. Oliver Jenkins. 6764-6
"**Like** some raw sophister that mounts...pulpit". Epilogue to The husband his own cuckold. John Dryden. 6970-3
"**Like** South-Sea Stock, expressions rise & fall". Time's changes. James Bramston. 6932-0
"**Like** some small hungry bird that sees and hears". Vittoria Colonna. 6325-X
"**Like** spectral hounds across the sky". Minot's lodge. Fitz-James O'Brien. 6912-6
"**Like** stars/Which sparkle". Your eyes. Ethel Emily Fels. 6906-1
'**Like** the Idalian Queene'. William Drummond of Hawthornden. 6208-3,6182-6,6562-7,6153-2,6737-9,6092
"**Like** the battalions of Europe now". Spring offensive. J.C. Hall. 6783-2
"**Like** the ears of wheat in a wheat-field...". Epilog, fr. The North Sea. Heinrich Heine. 7039-6
"**Like** the ghost of a dear friend dead". Time long past. Percy Bysshe Shelley. 6828-6
"**Like** the Idalian queene". Madrigal 003 ("Like the Idaliane que ne"). William Drummond of Hawthornden. 6933-9
"**Like** the life beyond the tomb". May Day. John E. Barrett. 6840-4
"**Like** the music of triumph and joy". Return to the hills. Helen Hunt Jackson. 6836-7
"**Like** the shadows in the stream". Hymn of the Cherokee Indians. Isaac McLellan Jr.. 6752-2

"**Like** the snail who on his back". Creeper. Percy MacKaye. 6799-9
"**Like** the south flying swallows". Song ("Like the south").. Marion Delcomyn. 6327-6
"**Like** the sun frozen/Still in the faded sky". Walls of ice. Janet Campbell Hale. 7005-1
"**Like** the sweeping sound of a new-bought broom". Poem ("Like the sweeping sound..."). Arthur K. Smart. 6764-6
"**Like** the sweet apple which reddens upon". One girl. Sappho. 7039-6
"**Like** the tribes of Israel". Sherman's in Savannah. Oliver Wendell Holmes. 6946-0
"**Like** the will o' the wisp was her hair". Gold. Florence Luft. 6850-2
Like the wind. Otto Laaber. 6769-7
"**Like** thee I once have stemm'd". An epitaph. James Beattie. 6339-X
"**Like** thee to die, thou sun!my boyhood's dream". The soldier's deathbed. Felicia Dorothea Hemans. 6973-8
"**Like** those pale stars of tempest-hours...". The women of Jerusalem at the cross. Felicia Dorothea Hemans. 6973-8
"**Like** tired lids the leaves drop down". October. Edith Brownell. 6820-0
"**Like** to a hermit poor, in place obscure." Sir Walter Raleigh. 6187-7,6584-8,6181-8,6586-4
"**Like** to a silkworm of one year". William Browne. 6334-9
"**Like** to a spreading tree am I", fr. Songs of evening. Viteslav Halek. 6763-8
"**Like** to an eye which sleep doth chain". William Strode. 6334-9
"**Like** to an hermit poor, in place obscure" Unknown. 6182-6
"**Like** to be a god he seems to me". Sappho. Caius Catallus. 7039-6
"**Like** to that little homely flower". Miriam. Alice Cary. 6865-0;6969-X
"**Like** to the Arctick needle, that does guide". Francis Quarles. 6562-7
'**Like** to the Artic needle,' sels. Francis Quarles. 6337-3
"**Like** to the artick needle, that doth guide". I am my beloved's, and his desire is toward me. Francis Quarles. 6933-9
"**Like** to the clear in highest sphere". Rosaline. Thomas Lodge. 6935-5
"**Like** to the falling of a star". Henry King. 6187-7,6334-9
'**Like** to the falling of a star" Francis Beaumont. 6935-5
"**Like** to the grass that's newly sprung...". Simon Wastell. 6334-9
"**Like** to the rolling of an eye". Unknown. 6334-9
"**Like** to the seely fly". Francis Davison. 6187-7
Like to the thundering tone. Richard Corbet. 6089-7
"**Like** truthless dreams, so are my joys expired". Sir Walter Raleigh. 6181-8
"**Like** two proud armied marching in the field". Song ("Like two proud"). Unknown. 6436-1
Like unto a rose. Lois Royal Hughes. 6178-8
Like Washington. Clara J. Denton. 6712-3
"**Like** us the lightning fires". Empedocles on Etna, sels. Matthew Arnold. 6934-7
"**Like** Venus/My spin is retrograde". Sputin. Ishmael Reed. 6792-1
"**Like** violets pale i' the spring o' the year". Song ("Like violets"). James ("B.V.") Thomson. 6437-X
Like weary elephants. Sarah Bixby Smith. 6628-3
"**Like** windy leaves borne here and there". Gypsies. Elizabeth Voss. 6906-1
"**Like** wine grown stale, the street-lamp's pallor...". Sonnet ("Like wine"). Maxwell Bodenheim. 6034-X
"**Like** wretched sores". The damned. Manuel Moreno Jimeno. 6759-X
"**Like** your window that does not exist". The illustrated world. Cesar Moro. 6759-X
"**Like** [or Lyke] as a huntsman after weary chase". Sonnet 067 ("Like as a huntsman"), fr. Amoretti. Edmund Spenser. 6248-4,6645-3
"**Like** [or Lyke] as a ship, that through the ocean". Sonnet 034 ("Like as a ship"), fr. Amoretti. Edmund Spenser. 6536-8,6645-3,6189-3
"**Likeness** of heaven!". The ocean. John Augustus Shea. 6833-

LIKENESS

2
A likeness. Robert Browning. 6378-0,6110-9
A likeness. Willa Sibert Cather. 6027-7
The likeness. William Henry Davies. 6339-X
The likeness. Unknown. 6408-6
Liking and loving. Oliver Marble. 6274-1
"Lil bro,/pain done caught me". Haywood. Harold LaMont Otey. 6870-7
A lil' ol' porterhouse steak. T. P. McEvoy. 7007-8
"lilac bush has no fruit at all". Jessie Orton Jones. 6999-1
Lilac dusk. Lizette Woodworth Reese. 6653-4
Lilac light. Mabel Posegate. 6906-1
Lilac time. Georgiana T. Moore. 6764-6
Lilac time. Frederick Lewis Pattee. 6764-6
The lilac. Clara Doty Bates. 6049-8,6373-X,6529-5
The lilac. Walter Prichard Eaton. 6762-X
The lilac. Humbert Wolfe. 6374-8,6368-3
'The lilace are in bloom' George Moore. 6770-0
Lilacs. Evelyn Grace Flynn. 6847-2
Lilacs. Frances Ann Johnson. 6764-6
Lilacs. Amy Lowell. 6299-7,6506-6,6619-4,6396-9,6121-4, 6153-2,6288-1,6010-2,6464-7
Lilacs. Gertrude Parthenia McBrown. 6178-8
Lilacs. Elizabeth Dimon Preston. 6836-7
Lilacs ("After lilacs come out"). Hilda Conkling. 6619-4
"Lilacs along the strap iron fence". At Billings' bridge graveyard. Robert Billings. 6767-0
"Lilacs blossom just as sweet". Threnody. Dorothy Parker. 6817-0
Lilacs in the city. Brian Hooker. 6347-0
"Lilacs of springtime". For one who was lovely. Bertye Young Williams. 6750-6
The lilacs. William Faulkner. 6039-0
The lilacs. Edgar A. Guest. 6862-6
Lilford, Lord F.Z.S.
    Poet and naturalist. 7020-5
Lili's park. Johann Wolfgang von Goethe. 6948-7
Lilian. Alfred Lord Tennyson. 6198-2,6219-9,6652-6,6655-0
Lilian Adelaide Neilson. Clement Scott. 6656-9
Lilie, Mai Elmendorf
    Consolator. 6335-7
Liliencron, Detlev von
    Acherontic chill. Babette Deutsch (tr.). 6160-5
    After partridge shooting. Babette Deutsch (tr.). 6160-5
    Autumn. Ludwig Lewisohn (tr.). 7039-6
    The birch tree. Babette Deutsch (tr.). 6160-5
    Death in the corn. C.F. MacIntyre (tr.). 6665-8
    Deep longing. Babette Deutsch (tr.). 6160-5
    Early spring at the woods' edge. Babette Deutsch (tr.). 6160-5
    Parting and return. Margarete A. Munsterberg (tr.). 6259-8
    Sphinx among the roses. Babette Deutsch (tr.). 6160-5
    Storm. Babette Deutsch (tr.). 6160-5
    Time. Babette Deutsch (tr.). 6160-5
    Winter scene. Babette Deutsch (tr.). 6160-5
Lilienthal, Joseph
    A full edition. 6118-4;6274-1
Lilies. Leigh Hunt. 6049-8,6383-7
Lilies. Ibn Darraj. 6362-4
Lilies. Ronald Campbell Macfie. 6269-5
Lilies. Don Marquis. 6089-7
Lilies. Caroline May. 6529-5
Lilies and roses. Ibn al-Qutiya. 6362-4
Lilies are white. Unknown. 6134-6
The lilies in the field. Wilhelm Greef. 6952-5
"The lilies lie in my lady's bower". Oh! weary motherr. Barry Pain. 6902-9
The lilies of the field. Daniel Henderson. 6335-7,6337-3
The lilies of the field. Felicia Dorothea Hemans. 6973-8
Lilies of the valley. Jo Gardner. 6065-X
Lilies of white. Unnur ("Hulda") Benediktdottir. 6283-0
Lilies without, lilies within. George Wither. 6250-4
The lilies.. George Edward Woodberry. 6338-1
Lilith. E.T. F. 6433-7
Lilith. Dante Gabriel Rossetti. 6250-4
Lilith, Lilith. Herbert S. Gorman. 6034-X
Lilium regis. Francis Thompson. 6292-X,6730-1,6172-9,6723-9

Lill' angels. Beatrice Ravenel. 6036-6,6326-8,6776-X
Lillard, R.W.
    America's answer. 6476-0,6548-1,6449-3
Lille, Abbe de
    Advice to gardeners, fr. The gardens. 6649-6
    The gardens at Versaille, fr. The gardens. 6649-6
    The gardens, sels. 6649-6
    Kensington Gardens, fr. The gardens. 6649-6
    Vaucluse, fr. The gardens. 6649-6
Lillian's reading. Edgar A. Guest. 6862-6
Lilliat, John
    False love. 6436-1
    Song ("When love on time"). 6182-6
Lillibulero. Unknown. 6858-8
Lilliput levee. William Brighty Rands. 6861-8
Lilliput levee. Unknown. 6742-5
Lillo, George
    The sweet and blushing rose. 6328-4
A lilt in fall. Arthur Guiterman. 6773-5
"Lilting leaflets, dappled with April light". The masked knight. Bertha L. Gibbons. 6906-1
Lily ("O lily, be a token true for me.") Unknown. 6720-4
Lily Adair. Thomas Holley Chivers. 7017-5
The lily and the linden. Fred Crosby. 6273-3
The lily and the rose. William Cowper. 6086-2
The lily bed. Isabella Valancy Crawford. 6446-9
"The lily cheek, the 'purple light of love'.". To Mary Wolstonecraft. Robert Southey. 6867-7
The lily confidante. Henry Timrod. 6008-0
"The lily holds its flower high". To a pansy. Waters Dewess Roberts. 6936-3
"Lily O'Grady/Silly and shady". Popular song. Edith Sitwell. 7000-0
The lily of Nithsdale. Allan Cunningham. 6438-8
The lily of the resurrection. Lucy Larcom. 6177-X
The lily of the vale. Felicia Dorothea Hemans. 6973-8
Lily of the valley. William White. 6868-5
The lily of the valley. Thomas Lovell Beddoes. 6187-7
The lily of the valley. James Gates Percival. 6373-X
The lily of the west. Unknown. 6058-7
The lily of Yorrow. Henry Van Dyke. 6961-4
The lily pond. Virna Sheard. 6115-X
The lily princess. Unknown (Japanese) 6891-2
Lily's ball. Unknown. 6165-6,6373-X,6502-3,6131-1
The lily's thanksgiving. Mrs. Dawson M. Phelps. 6171-0;6618-6
A lily's word. Lucy Larcom. 6129-X
Lily, John. See Lyly, John
The lily-pool and the cow. Thomas Edward Brown. 6339-X
The lily-white rose. Unknown. 6881-2
The lily. Mary Tighe. 6543-0
The lily. Albert Durrant Watson. 6115-X
Lim, Genny
    Departure. 6790-5
    Sweet 'n sour. 6790-5
    Visiting father. 6790-5
    Wonder woman. 6790-5
Lima, Jorge de
    The big mystical circus. Dudley Poore (tr.). 6759-X
    The bird. Dudley Poore (tr.). 6759-X
    Christian's poem. Dudley Poore (tr.). 6759-X
    Daddy John. Dudley Poore (tr.). 6759-X
    Paraclete. Dudley Poore (tr.). 6759-X
    Poem of any virgin. Dudley Poore (tr.). 6759-X
Lima, Robert (tr.)
    Cyclical night. Jorge Luis Borges, 6803-0
Limbo. Samuel Taylor Coleridge. 6378-0
"Limbs abare, icy stare". Quatrains. Rose Katterhenry. 6750-6
Lime street. Thomas Edward Brown. 6809-X
Limebeer, Ena
    The lake. 6072-2
Limeratomy. Anthony Euwer. 6861-8
"A limerick packs laughs anatomical". Limerick:"A limerick packs laughs anatomical." Unknown. 6308-X
"Limerick"..young man of Devizes". Ronald Arbuthnott Knox. 6811-1
Limerick: A tale of tragedy. Mary Kernahan. 6811-1
Limerick: The irony of fate. Langford Reed. 6811-1
Limerick:"'I must leave here'...". A.E. Page. 6811-1

Limerick:"..an old man in a tree". Edward Lear. 6724-7
Limerick:"..Arabian sheik". Unknown. 6811-1
Limerick:"..archdeacon who said". Unknown. 6811-1
Limerick:"..bad schoolboy who baited". R. Norman. 6811-1
Limerick:"..bonnie Scotch laddie". Unknown. 6811-1
Limerick:"..bonnie Scotch laddie." Unknown. 6308-X
Limerick:"..brave damsel of Brighton". Unknown. 6811-1
Limerick:"..Buff Orpington hen". Unknown. 6811-1
Limerick:"..certain Miss Gale". Mildred Mocatta. 6811-1
Limerick:"..certain young girl of the east". Unknown. 6811-1
Limerick:"..combative young artist named Whistler". Dante Gabriel Rossetti. 6811-1
Limerick:"..creator named God." James Abbott McNeill Whistler. 6308-X
Limerick:"..dear lady of Eden." Unknown. 6308-X
Limerick:"..diarist named Pepys". Hugh Powell. 6811-1
Limerick:"..dull painter, named Wells". Dante Gabriel Rossetti. 6811-1
Limerick:"..fair maid from Decatur." Unknown. 6308-X
Limerick:"..faith-healer of Deal". Unknown. 6811-1,6811-1, 6308-X
Limerick:"..fellow of Trinity". Unknown. 6811-1
Limerick:"..gay damsel of Lynn." Unknown. 6308-X
Limerick:"..girl of New York." Cosmo Monkhouse. 6308-X
Limerick:"..good canon of Durham". W.R. Inge. 6811-1
Limerick:"..intelligent hippopotamus". Langford Reed. 6811-1
Limerick:"..lad of Bagdad". Unknown. 6811-1
Limerick:"..lady of Erskine". Unknown. 6811-1
Limerick:"..madame called Tussaud". Charles Inge. 6811-1
Limerick:"..maid fair to the sight". Langford Reed. 6811-1
Limerick:"..man of Calcutta". Unknown. 6811-1,6811-1,6308-X
Limerick:"..man who said, 'God'." Ronald Knox. 6811-1
Limerick:"..man who said, How." Unknown. 6308-X
Limerick:"..man with a fad". Mrs. Charles Harris. 6811-1
Limerick:"..mechalnwick of Alnwick". Unknown. 6811-1
Limerick:"..old bore of Torbay". Unknown. 6811-1
Limerick:"..old buffer of Bath". Unknown. 6811-1
Limerick:"..old dame of Dunbar". Unknown. 6811-1
Limerick:"..old dame of Nicaragua". Unknown. 6811-1
Limerick:"..old dame of Tip'rary". Unknown. 6811-1
Limerick:"..old fellow of Clewer". Langford Reed. 6811-1
Limerick:"..old fellow of Cosham". Unknown. 6811-1
Limerick:"..old fellow of Croydon". Sir Gilbert Parker. 6811-1
Limerick:"..old fellow of Lynn." Unknown. 6308-X
Limerick:"..old fellow of Spain". Unknown. 6811-1
Limerick:"..old fellow of Tonga". Unknown. 6811-1
Limerick:"..old fellow of Trinity." Unknown. 6308-X
Limerick:"..old fellow of Tyre". Unknown. 6811-1
Limerick:"..old fellow of Wilton". Unknown. 6811-1
Limerick:"..old hag of Malacca". Unknown. 6811-1
Limerick:"..old lady of Bicester". Unknown. 6811-1
Limerick:"..old lady of Harrow". Unknown. 6811-1
Limerick:"..old lady of Herm". Unknown. 6811-1
Limerick:"..old lady of Leith". Langford Reed. 6811-1
Limerick:"..old lady of Russia". Unknown. 6811-1
Limerick:"..old lady of Rye". Unknown. 6811-1
Limerick:"..old lady of Tooting". Unknown. 6811-1
Limerick:"..old lady of Wales". John H. More. 6811-1
Limerick:"..old lady who said". Mrs. Charles Harris. 6811-1
Limerick:"..old maid of Vancouver". Unknown. 6811-1
Limerick:"..old man in a tree". Edward Lear. 6861-8
Limerick:"..old man in a tree." Edward Lear. 6308-X;6083-8
Limerick:"..old man of Bath". Unknown. 6811-1
Limerick:"..old man of Blackheath". Unknown. 6811-1
Limerick:"..old man of Bombay". Langford Reed. 6811-1
Limerick:"..old man of Boulogne". Unknown. 6811-1
Limerick:"..old man of Cape Horn". Edward Lear. 6861-8
Limerick:"..old man of Denton". Unknown. 6811-1
Limerick:"..old man of Hawaii". Unknown. 6811-1
Limerick:"..old man of Khartoum." Unknown. 6308-X
Limerick:"..old man of Lyme". Edward Lear. 6527-9
Limerick:"..old man of Madrid". Unknown. 6811-1
Limerick:"..old man of Nantucket." Unknown. 6308-X
Limerick:"..old man of Peru". Unknown. 6811-1
Limerick:"..old man of Peru". Unknown. 6811-1

Limerick:"..old man of Sheerness". Unknown. 6811-1
Limerick:"..old man of St. Bees". Sir William Schwenck Gilbert. 6811-1
Limerick:"..old man of Tarentum". Unknown. 6811-1,6811-1, 6308-X
Limerick:"..old man of the Cape". Edward Lear. 6811-1,6811-1,6308-X
Limerick:"..old man of the coast." Edward Lear. 6308-X
Limerick:"..old man of the Nore". Unknown. 6811-1
Limerick:"..old man of the west". Edward Lear. 7028-0
Limerick:"..old man of Thermopylae." Edward Lear. 6308-X, 6739-5
Limerick:"..old man of Tobago". Langford Reed. 6811-1,6811-1,6308-X
Limerick:"..old man of Tralee". Unknown. 6811-1
Limerick:"..old man of Vesuvius." Edward Lear. 6308-X
Limerick:"..old man of Wisbeach". Mrs. Charles Harris. 6811-1
Limerick:"..old man who said 'Hush!'" Edward Lear. 6739-5
Limerick:"..old man who said, 'Do'". Unknown. 6308-X
Limerick:"..old man who said, 'Motion'". J. St. Joe Strachey. 6811-1
Limerick:"..old man who said, 'Please'". E.V. Knox. 6811-1
Limerick:"..old man who said...". Edward Lear. 6861-8
Limerick:"..old man who supposed". Edward Lear. 6308-X
Limerick:"..old man with a beard". Edward Lear. 6861-8
Limerick:"..old man with a beard." Edward Lear. 6308-X, 6125-7
Limerick:"..old monk of Siberia." Unknown. 6308-X
Limerick:"..old Negress named Hannah". Unknown. 6811-1
Limerick:"..old party of Lyme". Unknown. 6811-1
Limerick:"..old person of Anerly." Edward Lear. 6308-X
Limerick:"..old person of Dean." Edward Lear. 6466-3
Limerick:"..old person of Florida". Langford Reed. 6811-1
Limerick:"..old person of Tring." Unknown. 6308-X
Limerick:"..old person of Ware." Edward Lear. 6308-X;6466-3
Limerick:"..old prelate of Brittany". Unknown. 6811-1
Limerick:"..old stupid who wrote." Walter Parke. 6308-X
Limerick:"..old womam of Honiton". Unknown. 6811-1
Limerick:"..old woman of Churston". Unknown. 6811-1
Limerick:"..old woman of Clewer". Unknown. 6811-1
Limerick:"..old woman of Thrace". Unknown. 6811-1
Limerick:"..olf man of Saxmundham". Unknown. 6811-1
Limerick:"..painter named Scott". Dante Gabriel Rossetti. 6811-1
Limerick:"..party of Negroes". Unknown. 6811-1
Limerick:"..person of Benin." Unknown. 6308-X
Limerick:"..pious young priest". Unknown. 6811-1
Limerick:"..plesiosaurus".. Unknown. 6811-1
Limerick:"..popular crooner." M.B. Thornton. 6308-X
Limerick:"..professor of Caius". Unknown. 6811-1
Limerick:"..publishing party, named Ellis". Dante Gabriel Rossetti. 6811-1
Limerick:"..sculptor named Phidias". Unknown. 6811-1,6811-1,6308-X
Limerick:"..some learned M.D.'s. Oliver Herford. 6308-X, 6724-7
Limerick:"..some learned M.D.'s. Unknown. 6811-1
Limerick:"..spinster of Ealing". Unknown. 6811-1
Limerick:"..sweet maiden sublime". Langford Reed. 6811-1
Limerick:"..trim maiden named Wood." William A. Lockwood. 6308-X
Limerick:"..two young ladies of Birmingham". Unknown. 6811-1
Limerick:"..very mean man of Belsize". Unknown. 6811-1
Limerick:"..young 'feller' called Broke". Unknown. 6811-1
Limerick:"..young angler of Worthing". Unknown. 6811-1
Limerick:"..young artist named Whistler." Dante Gabriel Rossetti. 6308-X
Limerick:"..young belle of old Natchez." Unknown. 6308-X
Limerick:"..young Birton B.A." T.H. Bryant. 6811-1
Limerick:"..young boy of Quebec". Rudyard Kipling. 6811-1
Limerick:"..young cashier of Calais". Unknown. 6811-1
Limerick:"..young curate of Hants". E.V. Knox. 6811-1
Limerick:"..young curate of Kidderminster". Unknown. 6811-1
Limerick:"..young curate of Salisbury." George Libaire. 6308-X
Limerick:"..young curate, named Stone". F.H. Cozens. 6811-

1

Limerick:"..young dancer of Ipswich". Unknown. 6811-1
Limerick:"..young dandy of Bute". Unknown. 6811-1
Limerick:"..young farmer of Limerick". Unknown. 6811-1
Limerick:"..young fellow from Fife." Thomas Russell Ybarra. 6308-X
Limerick:"..young fellow named Dice." Unknown. 6308-X
Limerick:"..young fellow named Fisher". Unknown. 6811-1
Limerick:"..young fellow named Hatch." Unknown. 6308-X
Limerick:"..young fellow named Sydney." Don Marquis. 6308-X
Limerick:"..young fellow of Beaulieu". Unknown. 6811-1
Limerick:"..young fellow of Boston". Unknown. 6811-1
Limerick:"..young fellow of Bristol". Unknown. 6811-1
Limerick:"..young fellow of Gloucester". Unknown. 6811-1
Limerick:"..young fellow of Herts". Unknown. 6811-1
Limerick:"..young fellow of Lyme." Unknown. 6308-X
Limerick:"..young fellow of Magdalen". Unknown. 6811-1
Limerick:"..young fellow of Perth". Unknown. 6811-1
Limerick:"..young fellow of Spa". Langford Reed. 6811-1
Limerick:"..young fellow, named Vaughan". Unknown. 6811-1
Limerick:"..young girl named Bianca". Unknown. 6811-1
Limerick:"..young girl of Asturias". Unknown. 6811-1
Limerick:"..young girl of Australia". Unknown. 6811-1
Limerick:"..young girl of Kilkenny". Unknown. 6811-1
Limerick:"..young girl of Majorca." Edward Lear. 6308-X
Limerick:"..young girl of Uttoxeter". Unknown. 6811-1
Limerick:"..young girl of West Ham". Unknown. 6811-1
Limerick:"..young lady at Bingham." Unknown. 6308-X
Limerick:"..young lady from Joppa." Unknown. 6811-1
Limerick:"..young lady named Kate". R.F. Wells. 6811-1
Limerick:"..young lady named Psyche". Unknown. 6811-1
Limerick:"..young lady named Sheila". Unknown. 6811-1
Limerick:"..young lady named Wemyss". Unknown. 6811-1
Limerick:"..young lady of Bandon". Unknown. 6811-1
Limerick:"..young lady of Byde." Unknown. 6308-X
Limerick:"..young lady of Cheadle". Unknown. 6811-1
Limerick:"..young lady of Cheltenham". Unknown. 6811-1
Limerick:"..young lady of Cirencester". Bishop Blomfield. 6811-1
Limerick:"..young lady of Crewe". Unknown. 6811-1
Limerick:"..young lady of Diss". Unknown. 6811-1
Limerick:"..young lady of Ealing". Unknown. 6811-1
Limerick:"..young lady of Ealing". Unknown. 6811-1
Limerick:"..young lady of Ealing". Unknown. 6811-1
Limerick:"..young lady of Ealing". Unknown. 6811-1
Limerick:"..young lady of Eton". Unknown. 6308-X
Limerick:"..young lady of Flint". Unknown. 6811-1
Limerick:"..young lady of Florence". Unknown. 6811-1
Limerick:"..young lady of Glasgow". Unknown. 6811-1
Limerick:"..young lady of Gloucester". Unknown. 6811-1
Limerick:"..young lady of Harwich". Langford Reed. 6811-1
Limerick:"..young lady of Jarrow". Wilkie Bard. 6811-1
Limerick:"..young lady of Joppa". Unknown. 6811-1
Limerick:"..young lady of Keighley". Unknown. 6811-1
Limerick:"..young lady of Kent". Unknown. 6308-X
Limerick:"..young lady of Lancashire". Unknown. 6811-1
Limerick:"..young lady of Luton". Mrs. Charles Harris. 6811-1
Limerick:"..young lady of Lynn". Unknown. 6811-1
Limerick:"..young lady of Lynn." Unknown. 6308-X,6811-1
Limerick:"..young lady of Malta". A.B. Kensington. 6811-1
Limerick:"..young lady of Malta". Unknown. 6811-1
Limerick:"..young lady of Michigan". Unknown. 6811-1
Limerick:"..young lady of Munich". Unknown. 6811-1
Limerick:"..young lady of Niger". Unknown. 6308-X,6739-5
Limerick:"..young lady of Norway". Edward Lear. 6861-8
Limerick:"..young lady of Prague". Athene Seyler. 6811-1
Limerick:"..young lady of Riga". Unknown. 6811-1
Limerick:"..young lady of Rio". Unknown. 6811-1
Limerick:"..young lady of Ryde". Unknown. 6811-1
Limerick:"..young lady of Savanah". Unknown. 6811-1
Limerick:"..young lady of Skye". Unknown. 6811-1
Limerick:"..young lady of Slough". Langford Reed. 6811-1
Limerick:"..young lady of Stornoway". Unknown. 6811-1
Limerick:"..young lady of Tahiti". Unknown. 6811-1
Limerick:"..young lady of Tenby". Unknown. 6811-1
Limerick:"..young lady of Tottenham". Unknown. 6811-1
Limerick:"..young lady of Twickenham". Unknown. 6811-1
Limerick:"..young lady of Twickenham." Oliver Herford. 6308-X,6722-0
Limerick:"..young lady of Venice". Unknown. 6811-1,6811-1, 6308-X
Limerick:"..young lady of Wales". Edward Lear. 6811-1
Limerick:"..young lady of Warwick". Unknown. 6811-1
Limerick:"..young lady of Wilts". Unknown. 6811-1
Limerick:"..young lady of Woosester." Unknown. 6308-X
Limerick:"..young lady of Zenda". Seymour Hicks. 6811-1
Limerick:"..young lady whose bonnet". Edward Lear. 6466-3
Limerick:"..young lady whose chin". Edward Lear. 6811-1, 6811-1,7028-0
Limerick:"..young lady whose eyes". Edward Lear. 6861-8
Limerick:"..young lady whose nose". Edward Lear. 7028-0
Limerick:"..young lady, named Maud". Unknown. 6811-1
Limerick:"..young lady, named Perkins". Unknown. 6811-1
Limerick:"..young maid of Aberystwyth". Unknown. 6811-1
Limerick:"..young maid of Japan". Unknown. 6811-1
Limerick:"..young maid of Ostend". Gordon Selfridge. 6811-1
Limerick:"..young maid of Tralee". Unknown. 6811-1
Limerick:"..young maid who said, Why?" Unknown. 6308-X, 6739-5
Limerick:"..young maiden, a Sioux." Unknown. 6308-X
Limerick:"..young man at St. Kitts." Unknown. 6308-X
Limerick:"..young man at the war office". J.W. Churton. 6811-1
Limerick:"..young man from Japan." Unknown. 6308-X
Limerick:"..young man from Kilbride". Unknown. 6811-1
Limerick:"..young man from New York". Unknown. 6811-1
Limerick:"..young man from Quebec." Unknown. 6308-X
Limerick:"..young man from the west". Unknown. 6811-1
Limerick:"..young man of Bengal". Unknown. 6811-1
Limerick:"..young man of Bow Bells". Langford Reed. 6811-1
Limerick:"..young man of Bulgaria". Unknown. 6811-1
Limerick:"..young man of Cadiz". J. St. Joe Strachey. 6811-1
Limerick:"..young man of Fort Blainy." Unknown. 6308-X
Limerick:"..young man of Havana". J.E.C. Welldon. 6811-1
Limerick:"..young man of Herne Bay". Unknown. 6811-1
Limerick:"..young man of Hong Kong." Unknown. 6308-X
Limerick:"..young man of Japan". Unknown. 6811-1
Limerick:"..young man of Lugano". H.G. Dixey. 6811-1
Limerick:"..young man of Madrid." Unknown. 6308-X
Limerick:"..young man of Montrose". Arnold Bennett. 6811-1
Limerick:"..young man of Ostend". Unknown. 6308-X
Limerick:"..young man of St. Bees." Sir William Schwenck Gilbert. 6308-X
Limerick:"..young man of the Tyne". Unknown. 6811-1
Limerick:"..young man of the veldt". Unknown. 6811-1
Limerick:"..young man who said, Damn!" Unknown. 6308-X
Limerick:"..young man who said, God." Unknown. 6308-X
Limerick:"..young man who said, Run." Unknown. 6308-X
Limerick:"..young man who was bitten". Unknown. 6811-1
Limerick:"..young man who was bitten." Walter Parke. 6308-X
Limerick:"..young monk of Siberia". Unknown. 6811-1
Limerick:"..young mother of Devonport". Unknown. 6811-1
Limerick:"..young native of Java". Unknown. 6811-1
Limerick:"..young person named Tate". Unknown. 6811-1,6811-1,6308-X
Limerick:"..young person of Smyrna". Edward Lear. 6811-1
Limerick:"..young plumber of Leigh". Arnold Bennett. 6811-1
Limerick:"..young poet of Kew". Marchioness of Townshend. 6811-1
Limerick:"..young poet of Thusis. Unknown. 6811-1
Limerick:"..young seedsman of Leeds". Unknown. 6811-1
Limerick:"..young servant at Drogheda". P.L. Mannock. 6811-1
Limerick:"..young student of Queen's". Unknown. 6811-1
Limerick:"..young swell of Saltash". Unknown. 6811-1
Limerick:"..young tenor of Tring". Unknown. 6811-1
Limerick:"..young typist in Oldham". Unknown. 6811-1
Limerick:"..young warrior of Parma". Unknown. 6811-1
Limerick:"..young woman named Bright." Unknown. 6308-X
Limerick:"..young woman of Ayr". Unknown. 6811-1
Limerick:"..young woman of Twickenham". Unknown. 6811-1
Limerick:"..young woman of Welwyn". Unknown. 6811-1
Limerick:"..young woman whose jaw". Langford Reed. 6811-1
Limerick:"..young yokel of Beaconsfield". Unknown. 6811-1

Limerick:"A 'Jock' from the town of Dundee". Unknown. 6811-1
Limerick:"A bad-tempered bully of Thurso". Langford Reed. 6811-1
Limerick:"A bald-headed judge called Beauclerk". Unknown. 6811-1
Limerick:"A barber who lived in Batavia". Unknown. 6811-1
Limerick:"A beautiful lady named Psyche." Unknown. 6308-X
Limerick:"A beautiful maid of Madrid". Unknown. 6811-1
Limerick:"A Benedict youth known as Rutters". Edward Minshall. 6811-1
Limerick:"A book and a jug and a dame." Unknown. 6308-X
Limerick:"A canner remarkably canny." Unknown. 6308-X
Limerick:"A cannibal bold of Penzance." Unknown. 6308-X
Limerick:"A canny old codger at Yalta." Unknown. 6308-X
Limerick:"A canny Scotch lad of Pitlochry". Langford Reed. 6811-1
Limerick:"A certain young fellow named Bobbie." Unknown. 6308-X
Limerick:"A certain young gourmet of Crediton". Charles Inge. 6811-1,6811-1,6308-X
Limerick:"A charming old lady of Settle". Unknown. 6811-1
Limerick:"A charming young lady named Nelly". Charles Coburn. 6811-1
Limerick:"A cheery old lady of Reading". Celia C. Stevens. 6811-1
Limerick:"A clergyman out in Dumont." Morris Bishop. 6308-X
Limerick:"A comical camel, named Bert". Langford Reed. 6811-1
Limerick:"A Conservative, out on his motor". A.W. Webster. 6811-1
Limerick:"A corpulent spinster of Crewe". Unknown. 6811-1
Limerick:"A cynic of much savoir-faire". Mrs. Charles Harris. 6811-1
Limerick:"A decrepit old gasman, named Peter." Unknown. 6308-X
Limerick:"A fellow who lisped went to Merthyr". Unknown. 6811-1
Limerick:"A flea and a fly in a flue." Unknown. 6308-X
Limerick:"A fly and a flea in a flue". Unknown. 6811-1
Limerick:"A foolish young anarchist". H.G. Dixey. 6811-1
Limerick:"A Frenchman went up to St. John's". M. Strickland. 6811-1
Limerick:"A giddy young fellow of Sparta". Unknown. 6811-1
Limerick:"A girl who weighs many an oz". P.T. Mannock. 6811-1
Limerick:"A half baked potato, named Sue." George Libaire. 6308-X
Limerick:"A historial painter, named Brown". Dante Gabriel Rossetti. 6811-1
Limerick:"A homely young heiress of Beccles". Unknown. 6811-1
Limerick:"A Jew and a Scotchman, found 'tight'". H.V. Abraham. 6811-1
Limerick:"A lady from Madagascar". Unknown. 6811-1
Limerick:"A lady non-suited at Diss". Unknown. 6811-1
Limerick:"A lady, an expert on skis". Unknown. 6811-1
Limerick:"A lieutenant who went out to shoot." Morgan Taylor. 6308-X
Limerick:"A limerick packs laughs anatomical." Unknown. 6308-X
Limerick:"A maiden at college, named Breeze". Mrs. Warren. 6811-1
Limerick:"A major, with wonderful force". Unknown. 6811-1
Limerick:"A man to whom illness was chronic." Unknown. 6308-X
Limerick:"A menagerie came to our place". H.G. Dixey. 6811-1
Limerick:"A motorist, out on a spree". James Benyon. 6811-1
Limerick:"A nice old lady named Tweedle." Unknown. 6308-X
Limerick:"A persistent young fellow of Bootle". Unknown. 6811-1
Limerick:"A pony, renowned for his sauce". Langford Reed. 6811-1
Limerick:"A poodle was charged by the law". Coulson Kernahan. 6811-1
Limerick:"A Potsdam les totaux absteneurs." Unknown. 6308-X

Limerick:"A pretty young actress, a stammerer". Eille Norwood. 6811-1
Limerick:"A pretty young school-mistress...Beauchamp". Unknown. 6811-1
Limerick:"A railway official at Crewe". H.G. Dixey. 6811-1
Limerick:"A rapid young couple, named Ord". K.C. Spiers. 6811-1
Limerick:"A rare old bird is the pelican". Dixon Merritt. 6811-1
Limerick:"A rather polite man of Hawarden". Unknown. 6811-1
Limerick:"A rheumatic old man in White Plains." Unknown. 6308-X
Limerick:"A right-handed man named Wright". Unknown. 6811-1
Limerick:"A sawyer named Esau, from Dee". Edward Milligan. 6811-1
Limerick:"A sawyer named Esau, from Dee". Unknown. 6811-1
Limerick:"A scraggy old spinster of Bude". Unknown. 6811-1
Limerick:"A silly young fellow named Hyde." Unknown. 6308-X
Limerick:"A singer who thought he could charm". Edward Milligan. 6811-1
Limerick:"A singular Yankee of Wis". Langford Reed. 6811-1
Limerick:"A small boy who lived in Iquique". Unknown. 6811-1
Limerick:"A stateman, who lived near Isis". Unknown. 6811-1
Limerick:"A strong silent man on a ranch". Langford Reed. 6811-1
Limerick:"A thoughtful old man of Lahore". Mrs. Charles Harris. 6811-1
Limerick:"A thrifty young fellow of Shoreham". Unknown. 6811-1
Limerick:"A tiger, by taste anthropophagous". Unknown. 6811-1
Limerick:"A trader, named Sandy M'Veetie". F.J. Smith. 6811-1
Limerick:"A traveller once, to his sorrow". H.G. Dixey. 6811-1
Limerick:"A tutor who taught on a flute". Unknown. 6811-1
Limerick:"A tutot who tooted a flute." Carolyn Wells. 6308-X
Limerick:"A wonderful bird is the pelican." Unknown. 6308-X
Limerick:"A wonderful family is Stein." Unknown. 6308-X
Limerick:"A writer who worshipped Nijinski". Unknown. 6811-1
Limerick:"A young man from Madere arose". George Du Maurier. 6811-1
Limerick:"A young man on a journey had met her." Unknown. 6308-X
Limerick:"A youthful beer-packer named Young". Unknown. 6811-1
Limerick:"All young men should take note of the case." M.B. Thornton. 6308-X
Limerick:"Although at the lim'ricks of Lear". Edward Lear. 6811-1
Limerick:"An amorous M.A." Unknown. 6308-X
Limerick:"An angry young husband called Bicket". John Galsworthy. 6811-1
Limerick:"An athletic young lady of Clewer". Unknown. 6811-1
Limerick:"An author who laid down the law". Helen Taylor. 6811-1
Limerick:"An author, by name Gilber St. John". P.T. Mannock. 6811-1
Limerick:"An authoress, living at Trim". Unknown. 6811-1
Limerick:"An eccentric old lady of Rhyl". Unknown. 6811-1
Limerick:"An eccentric old person of Slough". George Robey. 6811-1
Limerick:"An epicure dining at Crewe." Unknown. 6308-X, 6811-1
Limerick:"An epicure, dining at Crewe". Unknown. 6811-1
Limerick:"An heiress of Abergravenny". Unknown. 6811-1
Limerick:"An indolent vicar of Bray". L. R. 6811-1
Limerick:"An obstinate lady of Leicester". Unknown. 6811-1
Limerick:"An old vivisector, who'd died". Langford Reed. 6811-1
Limerick:"An old-fashioned 'pills and red-flannellist'"

LIMERICK:"AN

Unknown. 6811-1
Limerick:"An optimist living at Datchet". Langford Reed. 6811-1
Limerick:"An unfortunate dumb man of Kew". Unknown. 6811-1
Limerick:"An unpopular youth of Cologne". Unknown. 6811-1
Limerick:"An unskhylful rider from Rhyl". Unknown. 6811-1
Limerick:"And those two young ladies of Birmingham." Unknown. 6308-X
Limerick:"As a beauty I am not a star". Woodrow Wilson. 6811-1
Limerick:"As a critic, the poet, Buchanan". Dante Gabriel Rossetti. 6811-1
Limerick:"Certain pairs who had banns...". Unknown. 6811-1
Limerick:"Cleopatra, who thought they maligned her." Unknown. 6308-X
Limerick:"Dear sir: your astonishment's odd." Unknown. 6308-X
Limerick:"Eustace K. Bonehead...". Langford Reed. 6811-1
Limerick:"Evangelical vicar in want". Ronald Knox. 6811-1, 6811-1,6308-X
Limerick:"For a naughty nabob of Nigeria". Unknown. 6811-1
Limerick:"Has our government quite lost its wits". Unknown. 6811-1
Limerick:"I had a young pupil called Ned". H.G. Dixey. 6811-1
Limerick:"I know an old man of Durazzo". Unknown. 6811-1
Limerick:"I met a smart damsel at Copenhagen". Unknown. 6811-1
Limerick:"I once knew a gard'ner whose aunt". H.G. Dixey. 6811-1
Limerick:"I said to a man of Norwich". H.G. Dixey. 6811-1
Limerick:"I saw Nelson at the Battle of the Nile." Unknown. 6308-X
Limerick:"I wish that my room had a floor." Gelett Burgess. 6308-X
Limerick:"If you want a proud foe..." Sir William Schwenck Gilbert. 6811-1
Limerick:"Il etait un homme de Madere". George Du Maurier. 6811-1,6811-1,6308-X
Limerick:"Il etait une jeune fille de Tours". Unknown. 6811-1
Limerick:"Il naquit pres de Choisy-le-Roi." Unknown. 6308-X
Limerick:"Il y avait une jeunne fille de Tours." Unknown. 6308-X
Limerick:"In a 'bus queue a Jueue, bound for Kueue". Unknown. 6811-1
Limerick:"In the famed Scottish castle of Glamis". Louis P. Berlyn. 6811-1
Limerick:"Lady Astor, M.P., for sobriety". A.E. Halliday. 6811-1
Limerick:"Miss Minnie McFinney of Butte." Carolyn Wells. 6308-X
Limerick:"Mrs. James Simpson.. ". Langford Reed. 6811-1
Limerick:"Mussolini's pet marshal, Graziani." Thomas Russell Ybarra. 6308-X
Limerick:"No matter how grouchy you're feeling." Unknown. 6308-X
Limerick:"O God, for as much as without thee". Ronald Knox. 6811-1
Limerick:"O God, inasmuch as without Thee." Unknown. 6308-X
Limerick:"Oh, my name is John Wellington Wells". Unknown. 6811-1
Limerick:"One day I went out to then zoo". G.T. Johnson. 6811-1
Limerick:"Our vicar is good Mr. Inge". Unknown. 6811-1
Limerick:"Pa followed the pair to Pawtucket." Unknown. 6308-X
Limerick:"Rebecca, a silly young wrench". G. Herbert Thring. 6811-1
Limerick:"Said a constable stern, on his beat". Unknown. 6811-1
Limerick:"Said a crow to a pelican...". Langford Reed. 6811-1
Limerick:"Said a fair-haired young Jewess... Unknown. 6811-1
Limerick:"Said a foolish young lady of Wales". Edward Lear. 6811-1
Limerick:"Said a girl from beyond Pompton Lakes." Morris Bishop. 6308-X
Limerick:"Said a gleeful young man of Torbay". Unknown. 6811-1
Limerick:"Said a great Congregational preacher." Unknown. 6308-X
Limerick:"Said a lively young nurse out in Padua". Unknown. 6811-1
Limerick:"Said a man to his wife, down in Sydenham". P.L. Mannock. 6811-1
Limerick:"Said a scholarly fellow of Siam". Unknown. 6811-1
Limerick:"Said a stern-faced young man, 'It is plain'". Langford Reed. 6811-1
Limerick:"Said a zealous young student named Coles". F.C. Wilson. 6811-1
Limerick:"Said an elephant travelling by train". Langford Reed. 6811-1
Limerick:"Said I to my friend, Mrs. Lee". Edgar Bateman. 6811-1
Limerick:"Said Nero to one of his train." Unknown. 6308-X
Limerick:"Said old Peeping Tom of Fort Lee." Unknown. 6308-X
Limerick:"Said the chancellor of Britain's exchequer". Unknown. 6811-1
Limerick:"Said the Reverend Jabez McCotton." James Montgomery Flagg. 6308-X
Limerick:"Says the Frenchman..."). Joseph Kennedy. 6811-1
Limerick:"She was peeved..." Unknown. 6811-1
Limerick:"Should a plan we suggest, just that minute." R.K. B. 6308-X
Limerick:"Some amateur players, most brave". Unknown. 6811-1
Limerick:"Some charming selections from Strauss". Unknown. 6811-1
Limerick:"The bottle of perfume that Willie sent". Unknown. 6811-1
Limerick:"The cautious collapsible cow." Unknown. 6308-X
Limerick:"The complaints of the beasts in the ark". Unknown. 6811-1
Limerick:"The life boat that's kept at Torquay". Unknown. 6308-X
Limerick:"The reverend Henry Ward Beecher". Oliver Wendell Holmes. 6811-1
Limerick:"The styles that at present are regnant." Unknown. 6308-X
Limerick:"Then the pair followed Pa to Manhasset." Unknown. 6308-X
Limerick:"There is a poor sneak called Rossetti". Dante Gabriel Rossetti. 6811-1
Limerick:"There lived a young lady named Geoghegan". W.S. Webb. 6811-1
Limerick:"There was a young hopeful called Daniel". H.G. Dixey. 6811-1
Limerick:"There's a 'don-cher-know'...Cholmondeley. Unknown. 6811-1
Limerick:"There's a place...called Westcliff-on-Sea". Herbert C. Sergeant. 6811-1
Limerick:"There's a vaporish maiden in Harrison." Morris Bishop. 6308-X
Limerick:"These places abound in the old." George Libaire. 6308-X
Limerick:"This bird is the keel-billed toucan." Howard Ketcham. 6308-X
Limerick:"This very remarkable man". Charles Inge. 6811-1
Limerick:"To London there came, from Corea. Langford Reed. 6811-1
Limerick:"Tut-Ankh-Amen, best known as old Tankh". Elsie Ridgewell. 6811-1
Limerick:"Twin houris who dwelt by the Bosphorus". Unknown. 6811-1
Limerick:"Two gluttonous youngsters of Streatham". Unknown. 6811-1
Limerick:"Un vieux duc (le meilleur des epoux)." Unknown. 6308-X
Limerick:"We thought him an absolute lamb". Unknown. 6811-1
Limerick:"When a jolly young fisher named Fisher." Unknown. 6308-X
Limerick:"When the war was concluded in Hanover". Unknown. 6811-1

Limerick:"When Tommy first saw Colonel Beak". H. Cripps. 6811-1
Limerick:"When you think of the hosts without no". Unknown. 6811-1
Limerick:"With railways not being content". H.G. Dixey. 6811-1
Limerick:"Yelled a communist, 'down with the pope'. Unknown. 6811-1
Limerick:"Yes, theirs was a love that was tidal." Paul Kieffer. 6308-X
Limerick:"You remember that pastoral frolic." R.K. B. 6308-X
Limerick:"Your verses, dear Fred. I surmise". Charles Inge. 6811-1
Limerick:"Your verses, dear friend, I surmise." Unknown. 6308-X
Limericks. Unknown. 6497-3
Limericks. Carolyn Wells. 6089-7
Limericks ('There was a young lady of Niger') Cosmo Monkhouse. 6861-8
Limericks by the limerick's inventor. Edward Lear. 6861-8
Limit of fate. John Dryden. 6867-7
The limit of lands. Andrew Lang. 6771-9
The limit, limited. Noemie [pseud] 6817-0
Limitation. Douglas Mackintosh. 7016-7
Limitations. Elisabeth Kuskulis. 6836-7
Limitations of genius. James Whitcomb Riley. 6128-1
The limitations of greatness. Edgar A. Guest. 6862-6
The limitations of knowledge. Empedocles. 6435-3
The limitations of youth. Eugene Field. 6949-5
Limitless supply. Alice Troxwell McCoun. 6799-9
"A limousine pulled up to Paradise pictures". Stars in my eyes. Edward Field. 6803-0
"Limpid dewdrops on the plants". Dewdrops. Bertha Merena Mauermann. 6789-2
"Limpopo and Tugela churned". The scorpion. William Plomer. 6788-3
'Limpy Tim.' T. Harley. 6744-1
Lin Yutang (tr.)
  Weapons of evil, fr. The Tao Teh king. Unknown, 6337-3
"Lina, rival of the linnet". To Lina. Johann Wolfgang von Goethe. 6948-7
Lincoln. John E. Barrett. 6840-5
Lincoln. John E. Barrett. 6524-4
Lincoln. George Henry Boker. 6305-5,6524-4
Lincoln. John Vance Cheney. 6305-5,6524-4,6449-3
Lincoln. James G. Clark. 6524-4,6708-5
Lincoln. Thomas Curtis Clark. 6036-6,6076-5,6102-8
Lincoln. Paul Laurence Dunbar. 6305-5
Lincoln. Lydia Landon Elliot. 6524-4
Lincoln. Lydia Lando Elliott. 6524-4
Lincoln. John Gould Fletcher. 6299-7,6556-2,6465-5,6458-2, 6653-4,6030
Lincoln. Clyde Walton Hill. 6449-3
Lincoln. Samuel Ellsworth Kiser. 6524-4
Lincoln. William J. Lampton. 6708-5
Lincoln. Richard Linthicum. 6524-4
Lincoln. James Russell Lowell. 6820-0
Lincoln. Thomas MacKellar. 6524-4
Lincoln. Silas Weir Mitchell. 6946-0
Lincoln. Silas Weir Mitchell. 6524-4
Lincoln. Harriet Monroe. 6871-5
Lincoln. Wilbur Dick Nesbit. 6524-4
Lincoln. Robert Henry ("Orpheus C. Kerr") Newell. 6524-4
Lincoln. Benjamin S. Parker. 6524-4
Lincoln. James Larkin Pearson. 6102-8,6076-5
Lincoln. Edna Dean Proctor. 6305-5
Lincoln. James Whitcomb Riley. 6524-4
Lincoln. Corinne Roosevelt Robinson. 6337-3
Lincoln. B.F.M. Sours. 6524-4
Lincoln. George Taylor. 6708-5
Lincoln. James Maurice Thompson. 6449-3
Lincoln. John Townsend Trowbridge. 6305-5,6524-4
Lincoln. Nancy Byrd Turner. 6891-X
Lincoln. Henry Tyrrell. 6449-3
Lincoln. Unknown. 6524-4,6248-2,6524-4
Lincoln. Richard Wightman. 6524-4
Lincoln ("Through the dim pageant of the years"). Julia Ward Howe. 6465-5,6524-4
Lincoln (Lincoln! When men would name a man"). Unknown.

6309-8
Lincoln - the boy. James Whitcomb Riley. 6524-4
Lincoln and Davis. Stephen Vincent Benet. 6542-2
Lincoln and his psalm. Benjamin Franklin Taylor. 6524-4
Lincoln as man and boy. Unknown. 6708-5
Lincoln at Gettysburg. Mary M. Adams. 6524-4
Lincoln at Gettysburg. Bayard Taylor. 6074-9
The Lincoln boulder. Louis Bradford Couch. 6524-4
A Lincoln campaign song. Unknown. 6524-4
Lincoln centenary ode. Percy MacKaye. 6524-4
Lincoln in bronze. Robertus Love. 6524-4
Lincoln memorial. R.L. Duffus. 6143-5
Lincoln Memorial. Thomas Hornsby Ferril. 6781-6
The Lincoln Memorial. Alma Adams Wiley. 6449-3
Lincoln slain. Edwin Markham. 6871-5
Lincoln the great commoner. Edwin Markham. 6239-3
Lincoln triumphant. Edwin Markham. 6465-5
"Lincoln was a long man". Abraham Lincoln. Rosemary and Stephen Vincent Benet. 6871-5
Lincoln's birthday. Nathan Haskell Dole. 6524-4
Lincoln's birthday. Richard Henry Stoddard. 6465-5
Lincoln's birthday. Ida Vose Woodbury. 6305-5,6524-4,6449-3
Lincoln's burial. James Thompson McKay. 6708-5
Lincoln's dream. John Jerome Rooney. 6708-5
Lincoln's dream. (Frederick) Ridgely Torrence. 6871-5
Lincoln's grave. James Maurice Thompson. 6395-5,6524-4
Lincoln's heart. Hezekiah Butterworth. 6260-1
Lincoln's humour. Unknown. 6248-2
Lincoln's last dream. Hezekiah Butterworth. 6524-4
Lincoln's motherless kittens. Mrs. Frederick W. Pender. 6699-2
Lincoln's passing bell. Lucy Larcom. 6524-4
Lincoln's picture. Unknown. 6248-2
Lincoln, 1865-1915. Wendell Phillips Stafford. 6029-3
Lincoln, Abraham
  Address at Gettysburg. 6503-1
  America's task, fr. The second inaugural address. 6386-1
  The bulwark of liberty. 6337-3;6420-5
  The Gettysburg address. 6337-3;6503-1
  I am not bound to win. 6337-3
  Memory. 6709-3
  The prose-poetry of Lincoln. 6093-5
  The second inaugural address, sels. 6386-1
  The ultimate justice of the people. 6954-1
  A wild bear chase didst never see? 6708-5
  With malice toward none. 6337-3
Lincoln, Elliott C.
  Wheel-tracks. 7007-8
Lincoln, J.R.
  Don't go down in the mine. 6149-4
Lincoln, James
  England. 6188-5
  Simon de Montfort, Earl of Leicester. 6188-5
Lincoln, Joseph Crosby
  The ant and the grasshopper. 6119-2
  At eventide. 6119-2
  'Aunt 'Mandy.' 6119-2
  The ballad of McCarthy's trombone. 6119-2
  The ballade of the dream-ship. 6119-2
  The best spare room. 6119-2
  Birds'-nesting time. 6119-2
  The bullfrog serenade. 6119-2
  Circle day. 6119-2
  The cod-fisher. 6119-2
  A college training. 6119-2
  The croaker. 6119-2
  A crushed hero. 6119-2
  The cuckoo clock. 6119-2
  'The evening hymn.' 6119-2
  'The fift' ward j'int debate.' 6119-2
  Fireman O'Rafferty. 6119-2
  Friday evening meetings. 6119-2
  Grandpa's 'summer sweets.' 6119-2
  The hand-organ ball. 6119-2
  Her first husband. 6707-7
  Hezekiah's art. 6119-2
  His new brother. 6119-2;6166-4
  In mother's room. 6119-2

LINCOLN 978

'Jim.' 6119-2;6707-7
Life's paths. 6119-2
The life-saver. 6119-2
The light-keeper. 6119-2
Little bare feet. 6119-2
'The little feller's stockin'.' 6119-2
The little feller's stockin'. 6807-3
The little old house by the shore. 6119-2
Matildy's beau. 6119-2
May memories. 6119-2
The Mayflower. 6119-2
The meadow road. 6119-2
Midsummer. 6119-2
The minister's wife. 6119-2
A modern Washington. 6712-3
My old gray cat and I. 6692-2
My old gray nag. 6119-2
Ninety-eight in the shade. 6119-2
Novermber's come. 6119-2
O'Reilly's billy-goat. 6119-2
The old carryall. 6119-2
The old daguerreotypes. 6119-2
The old sword on the wall. 6119-2
The old-fashioned garden. 6119-2
Our first firecrackers. 6119-2
The parson's daughter. 6119-2
The popular song. 6119-2
A rainy day. 6119-2
"The reg'lar army man." 6119-2
'Sary Emma's photygraphs.' 6119-2
The school-committee man. 6119-2
'September mornin's.' 6119-2
Sermon time. 6119-2
Sister Simmons. 6119-2
'Sister's best feller.' 6119-2;6702-6
The song of the sea. 6119-2
The story-book boy. 6119-2
Summer nights at grandpa's. 6119-2
Sunday afternoons. 6119-2
The Sunday-school picnic. 6119-2
Sunset land. 6119-2
The surf along the shore. 6119-2
Susan Van Doozen. 6119-2
'Takin' boarders.' 6119-2
A Thanksgiving dream. 6119-2
Through the fog. 6119-2
The tin peddler. 6119-2
The village oracle. 6119-2;6274-1
Wasted energy. 6119-2
The watchers. 6119-2
When Nathan led the choir. 6119-2
When papa's sick. 6119-2;6697-6
When the minister comes to tea. 6119-2;6451-5,6451-5
When the tide goes out. 6119-2
'The widder Clark.' 6119-2
The wind's song. 6119-2
The winter nights at home. 6119-2
The wood-box. 6260-1,6964-9
'Yap.' 6119-2
Lincoln, Kitty
Troubles of a wife. 6911-8
Troubles of a wife. 6167-2
Lincoln, the greatest. Unknown. 6248-2
Lincoln, the man of the people. Edwin Markham. 6102-8,6162-1,6310-1,6332-2,6476-0,6486 ,6393-4,6300-4,6396-6,6265-2,6161-3,6336 ,6708-5,6509-0,6732-6,6464-7,6467-1,6250 ,6076-5,6305-5,6524-4,6653-4,6964-9
Lincoln, the man of the people, sels. Edwin Markham. 6337-3
Lincoln, the martyr chief. James Russell Lowell. 6304-7
The **Lincoln-child.** James Oppenheim. 6524-4
Lincoln: a retrospect. Harry Kemp. 6524-4
A **Lincolnshire** landscape. Alfred Lord Tennyson. 6793-X
The **Lincolnshire** poacher. Unknown. 6105-2,6228-8,6328-4
Lincolnshire remembered. Frances Cornford. 6257-1
A **Lincolnshire** tale. Sir John Betjeman. 6218-0
Lind, L.R.
Flowering quince: for Rosa. 6325-X
Lind, L.R. (tr.)
"Arms and the leader I sang whose piety". Torquato Tasso, 6325-X
The cats of Santa Anna. Torquato Tasso, 6325-X
Desperate. Cino da Pistoia, 6325-X
"Eyes that without a tongue can speak to me". Angelo Poliziano, 6325-X
"Give me, full-handed, lilies, give me the rose". Matteo Maria Boiardo, 6325-X
"How fruitless is each human hope, how vain". Lorenzo de' Medici, 6325-X
"I ask no other vengeance, love, from you". Angelo Poliziano, 6325-X
"I saw my lady by a cool, fresh stream". Lorenzo de' Medici, 6325-X
"I write to soothe that inward grief alone". Vittoria Colonna, 6325-X
I'd like to be a bee. Torquato Tasso, 6325-X
"If I could do so, lovely girl of mine". Unknown, 6325-X
"Let him how wishes seek pomp and honor, follow". Lorenzo de' Medici, 6325-X
"Like some small hungry bird that sees and hears". Vittoria Colonna, 6325-X
"More than honey the words you speak are sweet". Unknown, 6325-X
"O sweetest sleep, come now at last to stay". Lorenzo de' Medici, 6325-X
On the death of the Emperor Henry VII. Cino da Pistoia, 6325-X
"Once in good hour there came in company". Matteo Maria Boiardo, 6325-X
Portrait. Francesco Berni, 6325-X
Praise of diseases. Jacopone da Todi, 6325-X
"Royal spouse, the season is now at hand." Torquato Tasso, 6325-X
"She held my stirrup". Unknown, 6325-X
"Sing with me, you little amorous birds". Matteo Maria Boiardo, 6325-X
Sonnet for Selvaggia. Cino da Pistoia, 6325-X
The swallow. Torquato Tasso, 6325-X
"This little girl's so gay and fidgety". Angelo Poliziano, 6325-X
To the princesses of Ferrara. Torquato Tasso, 6325-X
Welcome to May. Angelo Poliziano, 6325-X
"What a fine life is the farmer's in the open air". Unknown, 6325-X
"When, these eyes closed in death, you look on me". Angelo Poliziano, 6325-X
"Would it had pleased the Lord that I never was born". Unknown, 6325-X
Linda Ann, July 16, 1947 Ann Caroline Kabel. 6857-X
Linda to Hafed. Thomas Moore. 6302-0;6385-3
Lindamichellebaron
...And free. 6899-5
Benign neglect. 6899-5
Daddy's little girl. 6899-5
Lindberg, Anne Morrow
Remembrance. 6850-2
Lindberg, J.C.
What shall endure? 6083-8
Lindbergh. William Rose Benet. 7019-1
Lindbergh. Theodore Best. 7019-1
Lindbergh. Witter Bynner. 7019-1
Lindbergh. E.R. Coe. 7019-1
Lindbergh. Robert Peter Tristam Coffin. 7019-1
Lindbergh. Mary Carolyn Davies. 7019-1
Lindbergh. Helen Byrom Griggs. 7019-1
Lindbergh. Georgiana Hodgkins. 7019-1
Lindbergh. I.J. Kapstein. 7019-1
Lindbergh. Mary Hume Mills. 7019-1
Lindbergh. Harriet Monroe. 7019-1
Lindbergh. Angela Morgan. 7019-1
Lindbergh. Melissa W. Nash. 7019-1
Lindbergh. Edna Stimson. 7019-1
Lindbergh. Arthur Van Meter. 7019-1
Lindbergh. Anna E. Wimmer. 7019-1
Lindbergh. Hilda Ziegler. 7019-1
'**Lindbergh** flies alone' Cornelia Fulton Crary. 7019-1
"**Lindbergh** is that maple/That maple on the...". That maple on the hill. J. Ray Hunt. 7019-1
Lindbergh's lay. Elias Gartman. 7019-1

Lindbergh, Anne Morrow
    Elegy under the stars. 6979-7
    A final cry. 6761-1
    Testament (1). 6783-2
    Testament (2). 6879-0
"**Lindbergh,** our clamorous times had need of...". The leap. Dana Chambers. 7019-1
"**Lindbergh,** viking of the air!". The hero. Edmund Vance Cooke. 7019-1
Lindbergh—alone!. Byron Cooney. 7019-1
Linden, Anna
    A reformed man's lament. 6916-9
Lindesay, Sir David
    A carman's account of a law suit. 6089-7
Lindisfarne. Herbert Trench. 6877-4
Lindner, Breta
    Pilgrimage to Calvary. 6761-1
Lindorm, Erik
    The life-boat. Charles Wharton Stork (tr.). 6045-5
Lindsay, ?
    Palus the lawyer. 6278-4
Lindsay, Alexander Hynd
    North lake. 6799-9
Lindsay, Alison
    The toll-payers. 7031-0
Lindsay, Jack
    Berneval. 6895-2
    Exercises. 6895-2
    Out of the dark. 6895-2
    Requiem mass. 6895-2
    Squadding. 6895-2
    The two pulls. 6895-2
    Verengeville again. 6895-2
    The voice of the wheat. 6895-2
    Withdrawal. 6895-2
    The wrung heart. 6339-X
Lindsay, Jack (tr.)
    Accordionist. Vladimir Kazin, 6546-5
    Address to tragedy. Olga Berggolts, 6546-5
    Afterthoughts. Unknown (Greek), 6435-3
    Alyona. Alexsandr Yashin, 6546-5
    Aphrodite on Ida. Unknown (Greek), 6435-3
    At night. Sergei Smirnov, 6546-5
    The ballad of nails. Nikolai Tikhonov, 6546-5
    Before the Aragava at night. Nikolai Tikhonov, 6546-5
    Biography. Aleksey Nedogonov, 6546-5
    Black hussars. Nikolai Aseyev, 6546-5
    "The bow of Zeus has twanged...", fr. Agamemnon. Aeschylus, 6435-3
    The bridge. Nikolai Tikhonov, 6546-5
    "But this may not be. Age is shrouding you...". Homer, 6435-3
    Childhood. Boris Pasternak, 6546-5
    "The clear-toned swan, to the beating of his wings". Homer, 6435-3
    Coming of winter. Boris Pasternak, 6546-5
    Confession of a hooligan. Sergei Esenin, 6546-5
    Dawn in besieged Leningrad. Vera Inber, 6546-5
    Dawn in London. Nikolai Ushakov, 6546-5
    The death of Lenin. Vladimir Mayakovsky, 6546-5
    Definition of creativeness. Boris Pasternak, 6546-5
    Dictionary. Samuel Marshak, 6546-5
    Drawing. Sergei Mikhalkov, 6546-5
    Duel. Stepan Shepipachov, 6546-5
    Endpiece. Olga Berggolts, 6546-5
    The epoch. Nikolai Tikhonov, 6546-5
    The fire in the noose. Nikolai Tikhonov, 6546-5
    The five ages. Hesiod, 6435-3
    Five days and nights. Vera Inber, 6546-5
    Flanders roses. Nikolai Ushakov, 6546-5
    For the signboards. Vladimir Mayakovsky, 6546-5
    From Gombor. Nikolai Ushakov, 6546-5
    Girl's song. Aleksey Surkov, 6546-5
    The goddess of the hearth. Unknown (Greek), 6435-3
    Gorgo and Praxinoa, fr. Idyll xv. Theocritus, 6435-3
    Granada. Mikhail Arkadyevich Svetlov, 6546-5
    Guitar. Iosif Utkin, 6546-5
    He saw her home. Mikhail Isakovsky, 6546-5
    "Hestia, wherever homes shelter...". Homer, 6435-3
    Hey, lads. Viktor Klebnikov, 6546-5
    Hungry winter. Vladimir Mayakovsky, 6546-5
    "I call on Zeus...", fr. Agamemnon. Aeschylus, 6435-3
    I've searched the year. Konstantin Simenov, 6546-5
    In the humpbacked sky. Nikolai Tikhonov, 6546-5
    In the pioneer camp. Anna Akhmatova, 6546-5
    In the small stove. Aleksey Surkov, 6546-5
    In woods near the frontline. Mikhail Isakovsky, 6546-5
    It's good up here. Anna Akhmatova, 6546-5
    Kirov is with us. Nikolai Tikhonov, 6546-5
    The land of Muravia. Aleksandr Tvardovsky, 6546-5
    Learn truly. Stepan Shepipachov, 6546-5
    The long road blossoms. Samuel Marshak, 6546-5
    Long was the road. Nikolai Tikhonov, 6546-5
    Maiden meditation. Mikhail Isakovsky, 6546-5
    The man seven years standing. Vladimir Mayakovsky, 6546-5
    Marriage. Hesiod, 6435-3
    The match's way. Vladimir Kazin, 6546-5
    Mayakovsky memory. Vera Inber, 6546-5
    Mowers in the line of fire. Valery Bryusov, 6456-5
    "Muse, tell of Pan, the dear seed of Hermes...". Homer, 6435-3
    The muses' gift. Hesiod, 6435-3
    My mother. Nikolai Tikhonov, 6546-5
    My voice. Demyan Byedny, 6546-5
    Native land. Andrei Byely, 6546-5
    Nazim hikmet. Yaroslav Smelyakov, 6546-5
    Nelly. Nikolai Tikhonov, 6546-5
    None knew. Demyan Byedny, 6546-5
    Not vain the winds. Sergei Esenin, 6546-5
    The nurse. Iosif Utkin, 6546-5
    On the Altai. Alexsandr Yashin, 6546-5
    On Volga banks. Bronislav Kezhyn, 6546-5
    Pandora. Hesiod, 6435-3
    Parting. Olga Berggolts, 6546-5
    Prometheus in the earthquake. Aeschylus, 6435-3
    Rainbow. Konstantin Simenov, 6546-5
    Reckless devil-may-care. Nikolai Tikhonov, 6546-5
    Remote in a closed space. Valery Bryusov, 6456-5
    The rider. Mikhail Arkadyevich Svetlov, 6546-5
    The rye unharvested. Yulia Drunina, 6546-5
    The Scythians. Aleksandr Blok, 6665-8
    Simaetha, fr. Idyll ii. Theocritus, 6435-3
    Simplicity. Semyon Kirsanov, 6546-5
    Snow of the crane. Nikolai Ushakov, 6546-5
    Soldier's tale. Aleksey Nedogonov, 6546-5
    Song of Babek. Ilya Selvinsky, 6546-5
    Song of the Cossack girl. Ilya Selvinsky, 6546-5
    Songs of the Spanish children. Olga Berggolts, 6546-5
    The sons of our sons. Ilya Ehrenburg, 6546-5
    "Then Aphrodite, the lover of laughter, was clad". Homer, 6435-3
    Three love poems. Stepan Shepipachov, 6546-5
    To a shining falcon. Nikolai Asyev, 6546-5
    To Apollo. Unknown (Greek), 6435-3
    To comrade intellectuals. Valery Bryusov, 6456-5
    To my fellow writers. Alexsandr Yashin, 6546-5
    To Pan. Unknown (Greek), 6435-3
    Tragic tale. Boris Pasternak, 6546-5
    The trance. Konstantin Simenov, 6546-5
    Tryst. Stepan Shepipachov, 6546-5
    Twelve blades of grass. Mikhail Isakovsky, 6546-5
    Twenty years old. Aleksey Surkov, 6546-5
    Uncle or sun. Vladimir Kazin, 6546-5
    Vorobeyev hills. Boris Pasternak, 6546-5
    Wake me tomorrow. Sergei Esenin, 6546-5
    When the crane flies south, fr. The farmer's year. Hesiod, 6435-3
    Wine. Nikolai Ushakov, 6546-5
    Wishes. Semyon Kirsanov, 6546-5
    You remember, Alyosha. Konstantin Simenov, 6546-5
    Zeus and the titans. Hesiod, 6435-3
Lindsay, Lady Anne
    Auld robin gray. 6024-2,6240-7,6271-7,6302-0,6385-3, 6600 ,6086-2,6153-2,6438-8,6491-4,6560-0,6019-6,6102-8,6139-9,6180-X,6219-9,6410 ,6134-6,6138-9,6198-2, 6228-8,6246-6,6732 ,6102-8,6543-0
    Carol of the three kings. 6747-6
    Carol, carol, tenderly. 6747-6
    East coast lullaby. 6833-2

LINDSAY

    Happy shepherds. 6747-6
    Old French carol. 6747-6
    A Provencal noel. 6747-6
Lindsay, Maud
    Far away. 6304-7
    New song of 'Dixie.' 6711-5
Lindsay, Sir David
    The dreme, sels. 6180-X
Lindsay, Vachel
    Abraham Lincoln walks at midnight. 6088-9,6375-6,6431-0, 616-3,6542-2,6449-3,6653-4,6289-X,6299-7,6332-2,6337-3,6347-0,6465 ,6474-4,6538-4,6556-2,6583-X,6108-7, 6641
    Address to a canoe-birch. 6206-7
    Aladdin and the jinn. 6619-4,6393-4
    The Anglo-Saxon language. 6345-4
    Babylon, Babylon, Bayblon the great. 6871-5
    Behind Mount Spokane, the beehive mountain. 6206-7
    Beside her carriage. 6206-7
    Beware of the silver grizzly. 6206-7
    The book-path, fr. The five seals in the sky. 6206-7
    The breakfast and dinner trees. 6206-7
    The broncho that would not be broken of dancing. 6031-5, 6299-7,6162-1,6619-4,6732-8,6393 ,6102-8,6076-5,6107-9,6161-3,6510-4,6467
    The building of Springfield. 6473-6
    Butterfly picture-writing. 6206-7
    The calico cat. 6206-7
    The cauliflower worm. 6206-7
    The Chinese nightingale. 6348-9,6531-7,6556-2,6029-3, 6288-1,6646
    A Christ child book. 6206-7
    The circus called 'The universe', fr. My lady... 6206-7
    The clocks that I like best. 6206-7
    Concerning a western mountain shaped like a whale. 6206-7
    The Congo, sels. 6527-9,6732-8,6300-4
    The Congo. 6332-2,6726-3,6102-8,6076-5,6464-7,6467
    The conscientious deacon. 6339-X
    The dandelion. 6228-8;6338-1
    Daniel. 6602-X,6125-7
    A dirge for a righteous cat. 6120-6;6334-9
    The dreamer. 6310-1,6250-4
    The druid Christmas, fr. my lady, dancer... 6206-7
    The druid-harp, fr. My lady, dancer for the universe. 6206-7
    The eagle hen. 6206-7
    The eagle that is forgotten. 6102-8,6076-5,6581-3,6288-1,6161-3,6121 ,6289-X,6310-1,6602-X,6726-3,6732-8, 6300 ,6464-7,6467-1
    The empire of China is crumbling down. 6033-1
    Euclid. 6375-6,6736-0
    Every soul is a circus. 6206-7
    Excuse me if I cry into my handkerchief. 6206-7
    An explanaton of the grasshopper. 6466-3,6554-X
    "The eyes of Queen Esther and how they conquered..." 6032-3
    Factory windows are always broken. 6375-6
    The fairy circus. 6265-2
    The fern called: 'the grasshopper's grandma'. 6206-7
    The five seals in the sky, sels. 6206-7
    The flower of mending. 6556-2,6431-0,6300-4
    The flower-fed buffaloes. 6315-2,6011-0,6125-7
    The flying papooses are boys and girls with wings. 6206-7
    Foreign missions in battle array. 6337-3;6532-5
    Forest-mirrors, fr. My lady, dancer for the universe. 6206-7
    The Freer gallery, Washington, D.C. 6012-9
    Friend forest-horse. 6206-7
    From the Santa-Fe trail. 6299-7
    The fur-backed skate fish. 6206-7
    General William Booth enters into heaven. 6076-5,6102-8, 6396-9,6464-7,6628-3,6730 ,6153-2,6209-1,6288-1,6300-4,6354-3,6431 ,6723-9,6399-3,6337-3,6531-7,6077-3, 6556-2,6732
    The ghosts of the buffaloes. 6490-6;6527-9
    The glacial flea. 6206-7
    Hamlet. 6345-4
    The heart-beat, fr. The song of my fiftieth birthday. 6206-7

    A high-school national song. 6206-7
    How I walked alone in the jungles of Heaven. 6032-3
    How Samson bore away the gates of Gaza. 6032-3
    How we papooses plant flowers. 6206-7
    'How' and 'how'. 6206-7
    I heard Immanuel singing. 6532-5;6619-4,6641-0
    I know all this when gipsy fiddles cry. 6184-2,6010-2
    I want to go wandering. 6345-4,6602-X,6345-4,6253-9
    I went down into the desert to meet Elijah. 6730-1
    If you are a mousie. 6206-7
    In memory of my friend Joyce Kilmer, poet and soldier. 6607-0
    In praise of Johnny Appleseed. 6465-5,6036-6,6010-2
    In which Roosevelt is compared to Saul? 6995-9
    The information bureau. 6206-7
    Interlude: do not stuff them with children's songs. 6206-7
    John Brown. 6619-4,6641-0
    The kallyope yell. 6027-7
    Kansas. 6506-6;6615-1
    The lame boy and the fairy. 6421-3
    The land horse compared to the sea horse. 6345-4
    The leaden-eyed. 6954-1
    The leaden-eyed. 6337-3,6339-X,6375-6,6393-4,6464-7
    The lion. 6228-8;6534-1
    Litany of the heroes, sels. 6871-5
    The little turtle. 6466-3
    The locomotive dragon-hippogriff. 6206-7
    The long street lifts. 6206-7
    Look you, I'll go pray. 6581-3
    Meeting ourselves. 6206-7
    Mice. 6880-4
    Mike Whaler and the parrot. 6206-7
    A million singing circuses. 6206-7
    Mister chipmunk. 6206-7,6143-5
    The Mohawk in the sky. 6206-7
    The moon is a floating sea-shell. 6206-7
    The moon's the north wind's cooky. 6228-8,6545-X
    The moon-path, fr. The five seals in the sky. 6206-7
    The mountain cat. 6069-2
    The mouse that gnawed the oak tree down. 6228-8,6458-2, 6464-7
    My brothers of the poet-trade. 6206-7
    My lady is compared to a young tree. 6488-4
    My lady, dancer for the universe, sels. 6206-7
    My tree toad. 6206-7
    The mysterious cat. 6891-X
    The mysterious cat. 6125-7
    Nancy Hanks, mother of Abraham Lincoln. 6871-5
    A net to snare the moon light. 6253-9
    Niagara. 7027-2
    O'er the ramparts we watch, fr. The song...birthday. 6206-7
    O. Henry. 6327-6
    On entering a solemn forest. 6206-7
    On porcupine ridge. 6206-7
    On the building of Springfield. 6289-X,6310-1,6726-3, 6375-6
    On the garden wall. 6421-3
    One of the first families of Carmi. 6345-4
    Our mother Pochahontas. 6184-2
    perilous whisper, fr. The song of my...birthday. 6206-7
    The pet elk. 6206-7
    Poems about the moon. 6348-9
    The pontoon bridge miracle. 6206-7,6315-2
    The pontton bridge miracle. 6315-2
    The potatoes' dance. 6891-X
    The powerful squirrel. 6206-7
    Prologue to Rhymes to be traded for bread. 6299-7
    The proud mysterious cat. 6334-9
    The queen of bubbles. 6253-9
    Quite enchanted. 6206-7
    The ranger's hound dog. 6206-7
    Red eagle - the mountain with wings. 6393-4
    The red Indian witch girl. 6206-7
    A remarkable story from Kokomo. 6012-9
    Returning to Springfield. 6012-9
    The rim rock of Spokane. 6206-7
    Robinson Crusoe's monkey. 6206-7

Robinson Crusoe's parrots. 6206-7
Sacajawea and Chief Joseph, fr. The song...birthday. 6206-7
The Sante Fe Trail - a humoresque. 6161-3,6288-1,6253-9, 6464-7,6393-4,6628 ,6509-0,6602-X,6334-9,6162-1,6228-8
Sante Fe Trail, sels. 6538-4
Sew the flags together. 6051-X;6386-1;6420-5
The sick eagle, fr. My lady, dancer for the universe. 6206-7
Simon Legree: a Negro sermon. 6375-6,6458-2
The smoke lion. 6206-7
A snail parade. 6206-7
Song for Hilda, sels. 6538-4
The song of my fiftieth birthday, sels. 6206-7
The spacious days of Roosevelt. 6995-9
Stanzas, fr. A litany of heroes. 7001-9
Star of my heart. 6746-8
The sun-up dance, fr. The song of my fiftieth birthday. 6206-7
Sunrise, fr. The five seals in the sky. 6206-7
Sunset, fr. The five seals in the sky. 6206-7
A swan is like a moon to me. 6206-7
The ten plagues, fr. The song of my fiftieth birthday. 6206-7
The thirsty puppy's dream. 6206-7
Thomas Jefferson rules, fr. The song...birthday. 6206-7
Three red Indians. 6206-7
To a golden haired girl. 6345-4
The traveller heart. 6253-9
The traveller. 6345-4
The tree-climbing fish. 6206-7
Twenty years ago. 6206-7
The unpardonable sin. 6337-3,6532-5,6542-2
The Virginians are coming again. 6206-7
The voyage. 6206-7,6011-0
The war-path, fr. The five seals in the sky. 6206-7
The waterfall that sings like a bacchante. 6206-7
The whale we saw. 6206-7
What is the Mohawk?. 6206-7
What the beach hen said when the tide came in. 6206-7
What the clown said. 6345-4
When Lincoln came to Springfield. 6012-9,6871-5
When Peter Jackson preached in the old church. 6607-0
When the sun rose from the mariposa lily. 6206-7
When we plugne into the wilderness. 6206-7
Where my lady sleeps. 6012-9
The whistling marmot. 6206-7
The wicked old tree. 6206-7
The wicked pouter pigeon. 6206-7
Wild cats. 6012-9
The wild forest duck. 6206-7
With a rose, to Brunhilde. 6338-1
The wood-squeak. 6206-7
Writing wills, and so forth. 6345-4

Lindsey, Therese
The man Christ. 6065-X,6335-7,6144-3,6337-3
Radio. 6076-5,6102-8,6102-8

Lindsey, William
A breath. 6798-0
En garde, messieurs. 6798-0
En garde, messieurs. 6300-4
Have you forgotten that juggler - fate. 6347-0
The hundred-yard dash. 6396-9
I measure time. 6320-9
Life's underpay. 6798-0
An old world melody. 6798-0
A rhyme of a cedar shell. 6798-0
A sad story. 6798-0
Two roses. 6338-1
The waves' confessional. 6798-0

Line after line. Peter Baker. 6475-2
Line in the morning. Joanne Dimmick. 6761-1
"The line of Aaron has not yet been run". Altar boy. Sister Mary Immaculata. 6839-1
The line of beauty. Arthur O'Shaughnessy. 6174-5
The line of beauty. Arthur O'Shaughnessy. 6930-4
Line to my mother, sels. Phillips Stewart. 6433-7
Line up, brave boys. Hamlin Garland. 6597-X,6252-0
The line-gang. Robert Frot. 6421-3

A line-up.. Unknown. 6466-3
Linen and lace. Edgar A. Guest. 6869-3
"The linen on my pilow". Perhaps. Julia Glasgow. 6817-0
The liner she's a lady. Rudyard Kipling. 6810-3
Lines. Joseph Addison. 6648-8
Lines. Emily Bronte. 6648-8
Lines. George Gordon, 6th Baron Byron. 6828-6
Lines. Samuel Taylor Coleridge. 6828-6
Lines. William Hurrell Mallock. 6096-X,6292-X,6022-6
Lines. George Meredith. 6737-9
Lines. Sir Walter Raleigh. 6737-9
Lines. Percy Bysshe Shelley. 6380-2
Lines. Henry Van Dyke. 6983-5
Lines ("A slumber"). William Wordsworth. 6315-2
Lines ("Clear had the day"). Michael Drayton. 6315-2
Lines ("Five years"). William Wordsworth. 6634-8
Lines ("Mine ears"). Sir John Collings ("Solomon Eagle") Squire. 6722-0
Lines ("Nay, traveller"). William Wordsworth. 6828-6,6332-2
Lines ("Shall earth"). Emily Bronte. 6315-2
Lines ("The cold earth"). Percy Bysshe Shelley. 6315-2
Lines ("The mountains"). Richard Chenevix Trench. 6624-0
Lines ("The sights"). Aubrey Thomas De Vere. 6102-8
Lines ("This day"). John Greenleaf Whittier. 6049-8
Lines ("Though the night"). Arthur Spayd Brooke. 6936-3
Lines ("When the lamp is shattered"). Percy Bysshe Shelley. 6371-3,6153-2,6110-9,6199-0
Lines ("When the lamp"). Percy Bysshe Shelley. 6154-0,6198-2,6102-8,6315-2,6122-2,6732
Lines ("When youthful faith"). John Gibson Lockhart. 6046-3
Lines addressed to --- on the 29th of September... Unknown. 6089-7
Lines addressed to a friend, in answer to..melancholy letter. Samuel Taylor Coleridge. 6967-3
Lines addressed to a seagull. Gerald Griffin. 6930-4
Lines addressed to a young lady. George Gordon, 6th Baron Byron. 6945-2
Lines addressed to Dr. Darwin. William Cowper. 6814-6
Lines addressed to Messrs. Dwight and Barlow. John Trumbull. 6753-0
Lines addressed to my children. Robert Bloomfield. 6543-0
Lines addressed to the Rev. J.T. Becher. George Gordon, 6th Baron Byron. 6945-2
Lines after tea at Grasmere. William Wordsworth. 6334-9
Lines after the manner of Homer,...opening of a hamper. William Cowper. 6814-6
Lines against worry. Margery Swett Mansfield. 6232-6
Lines and couplets. Alexander Pope. 6302-0,6385-3
The lines around Petersburg. Samuel Davis. 6074-9
Lines by a fond lover. Unknown. 6902-9
Lines by a lady of fashion, sels. Richard Brinsley Sheridan. 6649-6
Lines by a medium. Unknown. 6902-9
Lines by a person of quality. J.B.B. Nichols. 6656-9
Lines by a person of quality. Alexander Pope. 6902-9
Lines by an old fogy. Unknown. 6083-8,6089-7,6273-3,6280-6
Lines by Claudia. Emily Bronte. 6648-8
Lines by Taj Mahomed. Laurence (Adele Florence Nicolson) Hope. 6856-1
Lines composed a few miles above Tintern Abbey. William Wordsworth. 6052-8,6154-0,6315-2,6331-4,6332-2,6527 , 6198-2,6645-3,6723-9,6660-7,6153-2,6110 ,6378-0,6488-4,6604-6,6726-3,6730-1,6122 ,6250-4,6199-0,6560-0, 6192-3,6576-6,6086-2,6430-2
Lines composed a few miles above Tintern Abbey, sels. William Wordsworth. 6102-8,6208-3,6501-5,6301-2,6439-6,6648
Lines composed at Clevedon. Samuel Taylor Coleridge. 6967-3
Lines composed for a memorial of Ashley Cowper, Esq. William Cowper. 6814-6
Lines composed upon Westminster bridge. William Wordsworth. 6289-X
Lines fer Isaac Bradwell, of Indianapoolis, Ind. James Whitcomb Riley. 6892-8
Lines for a bed at Kelmscott Manor. William Morris. 6228-8
Lines for a drawing of our lady of the night. Francis Thompson. 6282-2,6650-0,6508-2

LINES

Lines for a feast of our lady. Sister Maris Stella. 6282-2
Lines for a sun-dial. Alfred Noyes. 6151-6
Lines for a sundial. Thomas Herbert Warren. 6437-X
Lines for a tomb. Donald Davidson. 6072-2
Lines for an internment. Archibald MacLeish. 6337-3;6536-8;6488-4
Lines for an old man. Thomas Stearns Eliot. 6399-3,6210-5
Lines for the hour. Hamilton Fish Armstrong. 6034-X,6076-5, 6102-8,6337-3
Lines from an alcoholic ward. Eugene Ruggles. 6998-3, 6901-0
Lines from Catullus. Sir Walter Raleigh. 6584-8
Lines given to a friend. William Motherwell. 6980-0
Lines in a young lady's album. Thomas Hood. 6026-9
Lines in dispraise of dispraise. Ogden Nash. 6375-6
Lines in memory of Edmund Morris, sels. Duncan Campbell Scott. 6115-X
Lines in the traveller's book at Orchomenus. George Gordon, 6th Baron Byron. 6945-2
Lines inscribed upon a cup formed from a skull. George Gordon, 6th Baron Byron. 6545-7,6945-2
Lines inspired by the muskrat's house. Grace E. Wheeler. 6270-9
Lines left at Mr. Theodore Hook's house in June, 1834 Richard Harris ("Thomas Ingoldsby") Barham. 6874-X
Lines left upon a seat in a yew-tree. William Wordsworth. 6110-0,6199-0
Lines occasioned by hearing a little boy mock...clock.. Lydia Maria Child. 6752-2
The lines of the hand. Julio Cortazar. 6758-1
Lines on a bill of mortality, 1790. William Cowper. 6931-2
Lines on a canary singing to an electric beater. Amy Lee Spencer. 6750-6
Lines on a grasshopper. Unknown. 6273-3
Lines on a lap dog, sels. John Gay. 6501-5
Lines on a late hospicious event. William Makepeace Thackeray. 6278-4
Lines on a Moslem garden gate. Unknown (Arabian) 6232-6
Lines on a Moslem garden gate. Unknown (Arabic) 6232-6
Lines on a rereading of parts of the Old Testament. William Wilfred Campbell. 6433-7
Lines on a ring. Loren M. Luke. 6983-5
Lines on a skeleton. William Wilfred Campbell. 6433-7
Lines on a skeleton. Unknown. 6271-7,6583-X
Lines on an autumnal evening. Samuel Taylor Coleridge. 6110-9
Lines on an X-ray portrait of a lady. Lawrence K. Russel. 7021-3
Lines on back of a Confederate note. S.A. Jones. 6889-8
Lines on death, and ballade of the women of the past. Francois Villon. 6227-X
Lines on Dr. Johnson. John ("Peter Pindar") Wolcott. 6150-8
Lines on Dr. Johnson. John ("Peter Pindar") Wolcott. 6787-5
Lines on growing old. Lyn Lloyd Irvine. 6072-2
Lines on hearing the death of Garafilia Mohalbi. Lydia Huntley Sigourney. 6752-2
Lines on hearing that Lady Byron was ill. George Gordon, 6th Baron Byron. 6945-2
Lines on his companions who died. Thomas James. 6563-5
Lines on Isabella Markham. Sir John Harrington. 6219-9
Lines on leaving Europe. Nathaniel Parker Willis. 6438-8
Lines on leaving Italy. Adam Gottlob Oehlenschlager. 6624-0
Lines on Leigh Hunt. Thomas Moore. 6200-8
Lines on marblefield. James Thomson. 6816-2
Lines on Naples. Thomas Moore. 6165-6
Lines on observing a blossom. Samuel Taylor Coleridge. 6967-3
Lines on passing the grave of my sister. Micah P. Flint. 6752-2
Lines on reaching maturity. Leith Shackel. 6799-9
Lines on reading D.H. Lawrence, Sherwood Anderson,et al. John Haynes Holmes. 6817-0
Lines on receiving his mother's picture, sels. William Cowper. 6339-X
Lines on revisiting the country. William Cullen Bryant. 6484-1
Lines on Rose. Charles Battell Loomis. 6724-7

Lines on seeing a lock of Milton's hair. John Keats. 6641-0
Lines on seeing my wife and two children sleeping... Thomas Hood. 6974-6
Lines on the antiquity of microbes. Strickland Gillilan. 6527-9
Lines on the birthday of Sir Thomas White. Richard Harris ("Thomas Ingoldsby") Barham. 6018-8
Lines on the celebrated picture by Leonardo Da Vinci... Charles Lamb. 6282-2
Lines on the common saying that love is blind. Sara Coleridge. 7037-X
Lines on the death of a college cat. Frederick Pollock. 6760-3
Lines on the death of baby. B. H. 6486-8
Lines on the death of his son Charles. Daniel Webster. 6486-8
Lines on the death of S.O. Torrey. John Greenleaf Whittier. 6735-2
Lines on the death of Sheridan. Thomas Moore. 6090-0;6174-5
Lines on the execution of Charles I. James Graham; Marquess of Montrose. 6845-6
Lines on the Mermaid Tavern. John Keats. 6122-2,6154-0, 6198-2,6315-2,6527-9,6733 ,6102-8,6430-2,6491-4,6543-0,6371-3,6250 ,6086-2,6110-9,6219-9,6199-0
Lines on the monument of Mazzini at Genoa. Algernon Charles Swinburne. 6655-0
Lines on the portrait of Shakespeare. Ben Jonson. 6219-9
Lines on the tombs in Westminster. Francis Beaumont and John Fletcher. 6197-4
Lines on the tombs in Westminster. Francis Beaumont. 6198-2,6337-3,6189-3,6543-0
Lines on Tintern Abbey. William Wordsworth. 6245-8
Lines prefixed to St John of Damascus. Douglas Ainslie. 6046-3
Lines printed under the engraved portrait of Milton. John Dryden. 6152-4
Lines sent to George Lyttelton. James Thomson. 6816-2
Lines sent with two coxcombs to Miss Green. William Cowper. 6814-6
Lines suggested by the fourteenth of February. Charles Stuart Calverley. 6026-9
Lines sung at the dinner given to Charles Kemble... J. Hamilton Reynolds. 6874-X
Lines supposed to have been addressed to Fanny Brawne. John Keats. 6380-2
Lines to a beautiful spring in a village. Samuel Taylor Coleridge. 6967-3
Lines to a child on his voyage to France... Henry Ware Jr. 6752-2
Lines to a critic. Percy Bysshe Shelley. 6199-0
Lines to a dictator. Mary Sinton Leitch. 6761-1
Lines to a disconsolate buddy. Unknown. 6589-X
Lines to a don. Hilaire Belloc. 6427-2,6633-X
Lines to a dreamer. Harriet Holman. 7016-7
Lines to a friend at Cobham. Thomas Hood. 6974-6
Lines to a friend who died of a frenzy fever. Samuel Taylor Coleridge. 6967-3
Lines to a garden hose. Unknown. 6274-1
Lines to a lady. Djuna Barnes. 6032-3
Lines to a lady. Thomas Hood. 6974-6
Lines to a lady of great musical talent. Lydia Maria Child. 6752-2
Lines to a lady: who asked of him how long... Sir George Etherege. 6187-7
Lines to a late lamented rabbit. Billie Marie Crabb. 6750-6
Lines to a milkweed. Galdys Higbee Polinske. 6799-9
Lines to a mule. Robert J. Burdette. 6588-0
Lines to a philanderer. Berta G. Guirk. 6750-6
Lines to a seagull. Gerald Griffin. 6174-5
Lines to a skeleton. Unknown. 6889-8
Lines to a transfer check. Unknown. 6118-4
Lines to a young lady. Edward Lear. 6902-9
Lines to accompany a flagon of Georgia's famous product... Eugene Edmund Murphey. 6723-9
Lines to Alexander Pnt. David Lewis. 6438-8
Lines to an anti-semite. Edward Sydney Tybee. 6848-0
Lines to an Indian air. Percy Bysshe Shelley. 6246-6,6271-

7,6543-0,6226-1,6219-9,6301
Lines to Bessy. Unknown. 6878-2
Lines to Cape Cod. Martyn Summerbell. 6798-0
Lines to Ellen. Ralph Waldo Emerson. 6126-5,6288-1
Lines to Garrick. William Whitehead. 6867-7
Lines to J.S., sels. Alfred Lord Tennyson. 6867-7
Lines to John Lapraik, sels. Robert Burns. 6198-2
Lines to John Webster. John Ford. 6369-1
Lines to Joseph Cottle. Samuel Taylor Coleridge. 6967-3
Lines to Kate. Unknown. 6743-3
Lines to little Mary. Caroline Anne Bowles Southey. 6772-7
Lines to Mary, fr. Bailey ballads. Thomas Hood. 6974-6
Lines to Miss Floremce Huntingdon. Unknown. 6089-7
Lines to Mr. Hodgson. George Gordon, 6th Baron Byron. 6092-7
Lines to my mother's picture. William Cowper. 6600-3,6627-5
Lines to perfesser John Clark Ridpath. James Whitcomb Riley. 6892-8
Lines to Ratclif. Henry Howard, Earl of Surrey. 6584-8
Lines to Sigrun. Bjarni Thorarensen. 6283-0
Lines to the blessed sacrament. Jeremiah [or James] Joseph Callanan. 6930-4
Lines to the Des Moines river. Eugene Parsons. 6215-6
Lines to the elite. Donald J. Paquette. 6783-2
Lines to the honourable Charles Townsend, sels. William Whitehead. 6867-7
Lines to the memory of Annie. Harriet Beecher Stowe. 6302-0;6385-3
Lines to the stormy petrel. Unknown. 6302-0;6385-3
Lines to the western mummy. W.E. Gallaudet. 6752-2
Lines upon hearing a political convention... Alice Fawley. 6662-3
Lines written ("by request") for a dinner ... Sir Owen Seaman. 6440-X
Lines written above Tintern Abbey. William Wordsworth. 6107-9
Lines written after a battle. Unknown. 6089-7,6278-4
Lines written after a very severe tempest,... Mercy Warren. 6077-3
Lines written after the discovery..germ of yellow fever. Sir Ronald Ross. 6337-3,6464-7
Lines written among the Euganean hills. Percy Bysshe Shelley. 6110-9
Lines written among the Euganean Hills, sels. Percy Bysshe Shelley. 6102-8,6198-2,6086-2
Lines written at Cambridge, to W.R., Esquire. Phineas Fletcher. 6182-6
Lines written at Elbingerode. Samuel Taylor Coleridge. 6484-1,6086-2
Lines written at Needles Hotel, Alum Bay, Isle of Wight. Sir Thomas Noon Talfourd. 6980-0
Lines written at the approach of death. Thomas Dudley. 6008-0
Lines written at the King's Arms, Ross. Samuel Taylor Coleridge. 6967-3
Lines written at the temple of the holy sepulchre. Unknown. 6065-X
Lines written beneath a picture. George Gordon, 6th Baron Byron. 6945-2
Lines written beneath an elm in the churchyard...Harrow. George Gordon, 6th Baron Byron. 6945-2
Lines written by a death-bed. Matthew Arnold. 6947-9
Lines written by a death-bed, sels. Matthew Arnold. 6934-7
Lines written by one in the tower. Chidiock Tichborne. 6302-0,6385-3,6219-9
Lines written during a period of insanity. William Cowper. 6378-0
Lines written for a wife. Elaine V. Emans. 6750-6
Lines written for the album at Rosanna. Felicia Dorothea Hemans. 6973-8
Lines written in a country parson's orchard. Leslie Daiken. 6930-4
Lines written in a fire-trench. W.S.S. Lyon. 7027-2
Lines written in a hermitage on the seashore. Felicia Dorothea Hemans. 6973-8
Lines written in a highland glen. Christopher (John Wilson) North. 6980-0
Lines written in a lady's album. Daniel Webster. 6438-8
Lines written in a lonely burial groud... Christopher (John Wilson) North. 6980-0
Lines written in a lonely burial grounds in...highlands. Christopher (John Wilson) North. 6997-5
Lines written in a moment of vibrant ill-health. Morris Bishop. 6722-0
Lines written in an album. Willis Gaylord. 6385-3
Lines written in an album (1). James Abraham Martling. 6952-5
Lines written in an album (2). James Abraham Martling. 6952-5
Lines written in an album (3). James Abraham Martling. 6952-5
Lines written in an album at Malta, sels. George Gordon, 6th Baron Byron. 6289-X
Lines written in August 1847. Thomas Babington Macaulay, 1st Baron Macaulay. 6046-3
Lines written in captivity. F.J. Patmore. 7029-9
Lines written in early spring. William Wordsworth. 6047-1, 6332-2,6473-6,6597-X,6153-2,6196 ,6110-9,6430-2,6199-0,6513-9,6252-0
Lines written in her breviary. Saint Theresa of Avila. 6337-3
Lines written in Illinois. Margaret Fuller Ossoli. 6484-1
Lines written in Kensington Gardens. Matthew Arnold. 6046-3,6199-0,6110-9,6649-6,6604-6;6655 ,6110-9,6196-6, 6660-7
Lines written in Kensington Gardens, sels. Matthew Arnold. 6301-2
Lines written in London. Frances Anne Kemble. 6980-0
Lines written in March. William Wordsworth. 6623-2
Lines written in memory of Elizabeth Smith. Felicia Dorothea Hemans. 6973-8
Lines written in Richmond churchyard, Yorkshire. Herbert Knowles. 6271-7,6408-6,6385-3,6600-3,6219-9,6438
Lines written in ridicule of certain poems...1777. Samuel Johnson. 6975-4
Lines written in Rousseau's Letters of an Italian nun.. George Gordon, 6th Baron Byron. 6945-2
Lines written in Surrey, 1917. George Herbert Clarke. 7026-4
Lines written near Richmond, upon Thames, at evening. William Wordsworth. 6932-0
Lines written on a blank leaf of The pleasures...memory. George Gordon, 6th Baron Byron. 6945-2
Lines written on a garden seat. George Gascoigne. 6232-6, 6649-6
Lines written on a page of the Monthly Review... William Cowper. 6814-6
Lines written on a window-shutter at Weston. William Cowper. 6814-6
Lines written on hearing an argument in court. Joseph Story. 6878-2
Lines written on the night of the 30th of July, 1847 Thomas Babington Macaulay, 1st Baron Macaulay. 6219-9
Lines written on the roof of Milan cathedral. John Addington Symonds. 6624-0,6631-3
Lines written on tidings...death of Charles James Fox. William Wordsworth. 6438-8
Lines written the night before his execution. Sir Walter Raleigh. 6302-0,6385-3,6177-X,6219-9
Lines written to accompany the gift of a distaff... Theocritus. 6435-3
Lines written to his wife. Reginald Heber. 6219-9
Lines written under a print...persons skaiting. Samuel Johnson. 6975-4
Lines written under the portrait of John Milton. John Dryden. 6198-2,6302-0,6385-3,6129-9
Lines written...collection of handwritings & signatures. William Cowper. 6814-6
Lines, composed at Grasmere. William Wordsworth. 6867-7
Lines, fr. a letter to C.P. Esq., ill with rheumatism. William Cowper. 6814-6
Lines, fr. Catiline. Ben Jonson. 6867-7
Lines, fr. The sad shepherd. Ben Jonson. 6867-7
Lines, written on the window of the Globe tavern, Dumfries. Robert Burns. 6723-9
Lines: "The cold earth slept below" Percy Bysshe Shelley. 6828-6
Linette. Florence Folsom. 6688-7

"Ling-Tso Ah Sin, on murderer's flat". Justice, fr. Australian transcripts. William ("Fiona Macleod") Sharp. 6768-9
"Linger of light in the pale clear west". Beagles at twilight. Edward A. Briggs. 6761-1
"'Linger', I cried, 'O radiant time!...'". Past and present. Adelaide Anne Procter. 6957-6
Linger, O gentle time. Adelaide Anne Procter. 6957-6
"Lingering fade the rays of daylight...". Philip and Mildred. Adelaide Anne Procter. 6957-6
Lingering latimer. Unknown. 6742-5
"Lingers long as time". Lost child. August Derleth. 6979-7
Lingg, ?
    Attila's sword. Elizabeth Craigmyle (tr.). 6842-1
"Liniments for horses". The little country drug store. Edgar A. Guest. 6869-3
"Link by link we forge the loyal chain". Class song. Eleanor Guiterman. 6847-2
Link, Carolyn Wilson
    Apology to my heirs. 6979-7
    Sleeping beauty. 6839-1
Link, Seymour Gordden
    Communion song. 6042-0
    The deaf. 6979-7
    Sadist child. 6420-5
Linklater, E.R.R.
    A farewell. 6269-5
    Sea moon. 6269-5
"Links interwoven/the cold damn steel". Indian education. Adrian C. Louis. 7005-1
The links of chance. Edward Rowland Sill. 6467-1
The links of love. Sir Owen Seaman. 6274-1
Links with heaven. Adelaide Anne Procter. 6097-8
Linley, George
    Song ("Tho' lost to sight"). 6085-4
Linn, Edith Willis
    The downy owl. 6073-0
    The festival of the year. 6268-7
    Persephone. 6347-0
    Restless heart, don't worry so. 6109-5
"The linnet in the rocky dells". Song ("The linnet in the rocky dells"). Emily Bronte. 6123-0,6430-2
'A linnet who had lost her way' James Elroy Flecker. 7007-8
The linnet. Robert Burns. 6943-6
The linnet. Walter De La Mare. 6250-4,6073-0,6315-2,6102-8, 6250-4
Linnie. Stella Reinhardt. 6397-7
Linos. Unknown (Greek) 6435-3
Linota Rufescens. Lyle Donaghy. 6930-4
Linser, Paul W.
    Pulp writing. 6857-X
Linsley, Edna E.
    My zoological flame. 6118-4
Linthicum, Richard
    Lincoln. 6524-4
    Recessional. 7001-9
Linton, Lulu
    Watch the corners. 6260-1;6583-X
Linton, William James
    The brave women of Tann. 6087-0
    The coming day. 7009-4
    Definitions. 6600-3
    The happy land. 7009-4
    Heart and will. 7009-4
    Midwinter. 6600-3
    Nature's gentleman. 6087-0
    Patience. 7009-4
    Robin Hood. 6087-0
    The torch-dance of liberty. 7009-4
"The lintwhite and the throstlecock". Song ("The lintwhite..."). Alfred Lord Tennyson. 6977-0
Lion and lioness. Edwin Markham. 6083-8,6309-8
Lion and prince. Victor Hugo. 6716-6
Lion and swine, fr. Epigrams. Steingrimur Thorsteinsson. 6283-0
The lion and the cub. John Gay. 6133-8,6239-3,6459-0,6424-8
The lion and the mouse. Jeffreys Taylor. 6401-9,6459-0, 6135-4

The lion and the unicorn. Mother Goose. 6132-X
"A lion emerged from his lair". The lion in the barber-shop. J.G. Francis. 6786-7
Lion fountain. Al-Tutili. 6362-4
The lion house. John Hall Wheelock. 6102-8,6509-0,6619-4, 6076-5,6037-4,6250
The lion in the barber-shop. J.G. Francis. 6786-7
"The lion oft hungers, and yet". Lions and swine. Steingrimur Thorsteinsson. 6854-5
The lion over the tomb of Leonidas. Unknown (Greek) 7039-6
The lion over the tombs of Leonidas. Unknown. 6850-2
The lion path. Charlotte Perkins Stetson Gilman. 6291-1
The Lion Tavern. Felix E. Schelling. 6936-3
The lion that Roosevelt shot. Isabel Fiske Conant. 6995-9
The lion's club. James Maurice Thompson. 7012-4
A lion's dream. Herbert Price. 6800-6
The lion's ride. Ferdinand Freiligrath. 6271-7
The lion's skeleton. Charles Tennyson Turner. 6656-9
The lion's whelps. Unknown. 6224-5
"Lion-hunger, tiger-leap!". The way of Cape Race. Edwin John Pratt. 6833-2
The lion.. Walter James Turner. 6625-9
A lion. Joseph G. Francis. 6891-X
The lion. Mary Howitt. 6131-1
The lion. Vachel Lindsay. 6228-8;6534-1
The lion. Ogden Nash. 6339-X
Lionel Johnson. Joyce Kilmer. 6483-3
Lions and ants. Walt Mason. 6291-1
Lions and swine. Steingrimur Thorsteinsson. 6854-5
"The lions of the hill are gone". Deirdre's lament for the sons of Usnach. Unknown. 6873-1
The lions. Victor Hugo. 6848-0
The lip and the heart. John Quincy Adams. 6004-8,6026-9, 6307-1
Lip service. Helen G. Quigless. 7024-8
Lip-stick Liz, fr. Five frivolous songs. Robert Service. 6159-1
"The lipless grin is nsothing but an...". Knight, death and devil. Jeffery Beam. 7003-5
Lipman, Ed
    Because our past lives every day. 6870-7
    Because San Quentin killed two more today. 6870-7
    4 1/2 point 5 6870-7
    Matrix III. 6870-7
    Nights primarily III. 6870-7
    Poem for Rupert Weber, 85 years too late. 6792-1, 6998-3
"Lippetty, lappetty, shipetty shop". Mr. Frog. B.R. M.. 6937-1
Lippincott, Sara J. ("Grace Greenwood")
    The horseback ride. 6344-6
    "How hardly doth the cold and careless world". 6996-7
    Illumination for victories in Mexico. 6946-0
    A mother's excuse. 6127-3
    The poet of to-day. 6385-3,6600-3
    Song for tree-planting. 6049-8,6171-0
    The wife's appeal. 6918-5
Lippmann, Julie Mathilde
    A song of the road. 7041-8
    Time. 7041-8
The lips of April. Arthur Henry Goodenough. 7030-2
"The lips of the Christ-child are like to twin leaves". Saint Gregory of Narek. 6050-1
"Lips sealed in iron stillness...". Paulus Silentiarius. 6251-2
"The lips so apt for deeds of passion". Portrait. Wystan Hugh Auden. 6072-2
The lips that touch liqour shall never touch mine. Harriet A. Glazebrook. 6617-8
The lips that touch liquor must never touch mine. George W. Young. 6963-0,6915-0
"Lips too red/Hair like a crow's wing". Flame. E.L.F. Van Dyke. 6750-6
The lips will part. David Morton. 6783-2
Lipsey, Roger
    Death and return in January. 6821-9
Liquor & longevity. Unknown. 6722-0
The liquor-seller's dream. Ellen Murray. 6925-8
Lisa's message to the king. George (Mary Ann Cross) Eliot. 6543-0

The Lisbon packet. George Gordon, 6th Baron Byron. 6278-4
Liscannor bay. Edmond Gore Alexander Holmes. 6997-5
Lisle, Charles M.Leconte de. See Leconte de..
Lisle, Rouget de. See Rouget de Lisle, Claude
Lisle, Samuel
    When Orpheus went down, fr. Orpheus and Eurydice. 6328-4,6026-9
Lisp. Unknown. 6277-6
Lissauer, Ernest
    A hymn of hate against England, sels. Barbara Henderson (tr.). 6427-2
A list of our presidents. Unknown. 6745-X
List, Dennis
    Bears' bones. 7018-3
    "I wrote you a letter". 7018-3
"List, all that love light mirth, light tears". Francois Villon, 1450. Andrew Lang. 6771-9
"List, viper, in thy sulky cell". Exportulation. Edward Farquhar. 6939-8
Listen. Edward Estlin Cummings. 6665-8
Listen. Ogden Nash. 6761-1
Listen. James Oppenheim. 6007-2
"Listen all ye, 'tis the feast o' St. Stephen". Feast o' St. Stephen. Ruth Sawyer. 6806-5
"Listen and learn what manner of god I am". Unknown. 6435-3
"Listen in to thrilling music". Inspiring music. Marianne Clarke. 6789-1
"'Listen my child,' said the old pine tree...". The old pine tree. William Henry Drummond. 7035-3
"Listen to me, as when ye heard our father". The Canadian boat song. J. Wilson. 6934-7
"Listen to me, listen to me, my dear!". Morning Sonnet. Grace Hazard Conkling. 7038-8
"Listen to the kitchen clock!". The old kitchen clock. Ann ("Aunt Effie") Hawkshawe. 6135-4,6937-1
"Listen to the mournful drums of a funeral". A strange funeral in Braddock. Michael Gold. 6880-4
"Listen to the rippling waters/Whispering...". The waters of the lake. Nellie E. Fealy. 6799-9
"Listen to the tawny thief". Bacchus. Frank Dempster Sherman. 7041-8
"Listen to the wind howl across our...". Late fall. Vojislav Ilic. 6765-4
"Listen to the wind, fellows". On to cube! Franklin McDuffee. 7035-3
"Listen what a sudden rustle". Persephone. Margaret Junkin Preston. 7041-8
"Listen when I call de figgers! Watch de...". Terpsichore in the quarters. John Alfred Macon. 6959-2
"Listen where thou art sitting". Sabrina fair, fr. Comus. John Milton. 6239-3;6563-5;6187-7
Listen!. Sarabeth Leslie. 6799-9
"Listen! The mother". The poet. Louise Imogen Guiney. 7041-8
"Listen! in my breezy moan", sels. Felicia Dorothea Hemans. 6601-1
"Listen! The wind is rising" Humbert Wolfe. 7020-5
"Listen! the somber foliage of the pine". The pine's mystery. Paul Hamilton Hayne. 7017-5
"Listen, fair maid, my song shall tell". Unknown (German) 6973-8
"Listen, friend, and I will tell you". Dream-life. Adelaide Anne Procter. 6957-6
"Listen, Ithuriel. Do you hear...weeping?". Converse of angels. Hermann Hagedorn. 6944-4
"Listen, my boy, and you shall know". How we killed the rooster. Unknown. 6926-6
"Listen, my children, and you shall hear". Paul Revere's ride. Henry Wadsworth Longfellow. 6861-8
"Listen, my colleague traduced (nothing I...". Dead languages. Jay Macpherson. 6767-0
"Listen, my love, to these words so sincere...". The ewer. Milan Rakic. 6765-4
Listen, pigeon, bend an ear. H.W. Haenigsen. 6722-0
Listen, put on morning. William Sydney Graham. 6210-5
'Listen, son.' Unknown. 6750-6
"Listen, sweetheart, to my plea". The atavistic maid. Berton Braley. 6853-7
"Listen. The wind is still". Spring thunder. Mark Van Doren. 6984-3
The listeners, sels. Walter De La Mare. 6234-2,6102-8
The listeners.. Walter De La Mare. 6653-4,6464-7,6639-9, 6723-9,6234-2,6246-5,6339-X,6395-0,6427-2,6477-9, 6107-9,6375-6,6150-8,6153-2,6301-2,6371-3,6648-8, 6653-4,6693-4,6490-6,6527-9,6488-4,6726-3,6648-8
"Listeneth, lordings, both great and small". A, a, a, a, nunc gaudet ecclsia. Unknown. 6756-5
Listening. Don Marquis. 6761-1
Listening. Unknown (American Indian) 6396-9
Listening angels. Adelaide Anne Procter. 6957-6
Listening for God. William Channing Gannett. 6600-3
Listening for trains. Sibbie O'Sullivan. 6822-7
Listening in October. John Haines. 6855-3
Listening in, sels. Annie Charlotte Dalton. 6843-X
"Listening now to the tide in its broad-flung...roar". Alfred Lord Tennyson. 6997-5
Listening to a broadcast. John Streeter Manifold. 6666-6
Listening to storms. Robert Southey. 6980-0
Listening to the wind. Egbert Sandford. 6558-9
"Listless palm-trees catch the breeze above". There is no breeze to cool the heat of love. Laurence (Adele Florence Nicolson) Hope. 6856-1
Liston, James K.
    Songs of the Canadian winter. 7035-3
"Lists all white and blue in the skies". Heartstrong south and headstrong north, fr. Psalm... Sidney Lanier. 6753-0
Lisy's parting with her cat. James Thomson. 6120-6,6511-2
Lita. Estelle Rooks. 6850-2
Litanies of the rose. Remy de Gourmont. 6351-9
Litany. Jane M. Fink. 6900-2
Litany. Sir Robert Grant. 6271-7,6385-3,6219-9
Litany. Allebe Gregory. 6846-4
Litany. Hertha Kraftner. 6769-7
Litany. Marie LeNart. 6144-3;6335-7
Litany. John Samuel Bewley Monsell. 6656-9
Litany for dictatorships. Stephen Vincent Benet. 6375-6
Litany for Halloween. Unknown. 6465-5
A litany for latter-day mystics. Cale Young Rice. 6730-1
A litany for peace. Pearce Young. 6515-2
Litany in war time. J.W. A. 7031-0
Litany of beauty, sels. Thomas MacDonagh. 6873-1
The litany of nations, sels. Algernon Charles Swinburne. 6334-9,6624-0
Litany of our lady. Richard Lawson Gales. 6950-9
The litany of the comfortable. Viola Chittenden White. 6032-3,6532-5
The litany of the dark people. Countee Cullen. 6532-5,6337-3,6393-4,6608-9,6746-8
Litany of the heroes, sels. Vachel Lindsay. 6871-5
Litany of the little bourgeois. Nicanor Parra. 6758-1
Litany to our lady. Caryll Houselander. 6282-2
Litany to the holy spirit. Robert Herrick. 6186-9,6271-7, 6641-0,6438-8,6371-3
Litany, fr. A hymn. Gilbert Keith Chesterton. 6427-2
The litany, sels. John Donne. 6214-3
A litany.. Sir Philip Sidney. 6436-1,6150-8
A litany. Phineas Fletcher. 6931-2
A litany. Gertrude M. Hort. 7012-4
The litany. Robert Herrick. 6189-3,6250-4
Litchfield, Grace Denio
    Caged. 6510-4
    The dance. 6959-2
    Good-by ("We say it for an hour or for years"). 6273-3, 6085-4
    To a hurt child. 6431-0
Litchfield, Jessie
    In the day's work. 6349-7
Literary advertisement. Thomas Moore. 6760-3
Literary and literal. Thomas Hood. 6974-6
A literary curiosity. Unknown. 6693-3
Literary importation. Philip Freneau. 6753-0
Literary importation. Philip Freneau. 6288-1
Literary importation. Philip Freneau. 6753-0
Literary incident. Helen Goldbaum. 6640-2
The literary lady. Richard Brinsley Sheridan. 6089-7,6278-4
Literary landscape with dove and poet. Phyllis McGinley. 6388-8

LITERARY

Literary lottery. John Albert Macy. 6118-4
A literary miss. Oliver Marble. 6274-1
Literary mother. Edgar A. Guest. 6862-6
A literary poet to his patron. Alexander Pope. 6138-9
The literary vampire. Unknown. 6118-4
Literature and nature. Samuel Waddington. 6297-0
"Lithe stripling of the stock of pioneers". To C.A.L. Gladys M. Cripps. 7019-1
Litle dandelion. Helen Louise Barron Bostwick. 6132-X,6127-3,6502-3,6519-8,6135-4,6131
Litsey, Edwin Carlile
   Wild geese go over. 6750-6
Litsey, Edwin Carlisle
   The dreams ahead. 6211-3;6260-1
Litsey, Sarah
   Alchemy. 6750-6
   Come of age. 6761-1
   "How still it is! I seem to hear the heart". 6761-1
   Message. 6761-1
   Prelude for spring. 6761-1
   The roads. 6042-0
   Skunk cabbage rising in March. 6979-7
   So is he made. 6750-6
   Song for the old cities. 6761-1
Litte Ah. Unknown. 6280-6
"A litte bird sat on a twig of a tree". Why little birds hop, and other birds walk. L.J. Bates. 6965-7
Littell, Philip
   Not a swarrow falleth. 6880-4
Little. Dorothy Aldis. 6850-2
Little acorn. M.H. Huntington. 6049-8
Little Aglae. Walter Savage Landor. 6086-2,6110-9
Little all-aloney. Eugene Field. 6949-5
Little and (or, but) Charles Mackay. 6583-X,6639-9
Little and great. Unknown. 6165-6
Little and lonely under the evening star. George Brandon Saul. 6619-4
Little angel. Unknown. 6713-1
The little angel. Elizabeth Payson Prentiss. 6424-8
A little April fool. C.L. C. 6965-7
The little artist. Unknown. 6373-X
Little Assunta. Celia Thaxter. 6612-7
Little ballads. Norman Rosten. 6561-9
Little bare feet. Joseph Crosby Lincoln. 6119-2
Little bare feet. Unknown. 6629-1
Little barefoot. Unknown. 6413-2
"A little basket cradle-bed". Life. Samuel K. Cowan. 6167-2
"Little bat, little bat". To the bat. Edith King. 6937-1
Little battered legs grows up. Edgar A. Guest. 6748-4
The little beach bird. Richard Henry Dana. 6121-4,6219-9, 6300-4,6309-8,6176-1,6006-4,6385-3,6597-X,6073-0
"A little bear lives in the zoo". Difference. William Reohrick. 6850-2
"A little bee in search of sweets". The death of the bee. John Russell Hayes. 6936-3
"Little Belinda Bumble". Belinda Bumble. Carolyn Wells. 6882-0
Little bell. Thomas Westwood. 6127-3,6239-3,6271-7,6302-0, 6385-3,6131-1,6219-9,6424-8,6638-0,6543-0
The little bells of Sevilla. Dora Sigerson Shorter. 6331-4, 6478-7,6636-1
Little Bennie. Annie C. Ketchum. 6909-6
Little Benny. Unknown. 6742-5
Little Bessie. Unknown. 6414-0
"Little Betty Blue". Mother Goose. 6363-2
"Little Betty Winckle she had a pig". Unknown. 6363-2
Little Big Horn. Ernest McGaffey. 6946-0
Little Big-horn. Percy Adams Hutchinson. 6327-6
Little Billee. William Makepeace Thackeray. 6089-7,6732-8, 6132-X,6240-7,6242-3,6249 ,6258-X,6302-0,6385-3,6479-5,6486-8,6497 ,6639-9,6371-3,6153-2,6219-9,6808-1, 6739
"The little betrothed has washed her linen". Whiteness. Isobel Hume. 6776-X
"The little biplane that has the river-meadow". The machine, fr. The trumpet. Robinson Jeffers. 6808-1
Little bird. Madison Cawein. 6510-4
Little bird blue. Elizabeth M. Thomas. 6529-5
A little bird I am. Jeanne Marie Bouvier de la Motte Guyon. 6730-1,6214-8
"A little bird flew my window by". Over the hills and far away. Dinah Maria Mulock Craik. 6980-0
"A little bird sat on a low swinging bough". A pinch of salt. Norman Ault. 6937-1
The little bird's complaint to his mistress. Jane Taylor. 6131-1
A little bird. Ellen M. Huntington Gales. 6510-4
The little bird. Walter De La Mare. 6421-3
The little bird. Lucy Larcom. 6530-9
The little bird. Martin Luther. 6424-8
The little bird. Unknown. 6312-8,6529-5
Little birdie. Alfred Lord Tennyson. 6127-3,6132-X,6242-3, 6183-4,6078-1,6502 ,6131-1,6424-8,6456-6
Little birdie. Unknown. 6049-8
A little birdie in a cage. Alice Barkley. 6789-1
Little birds. Charles Lutwidge ("Lewis Carroll") Dodgson. 6722-0
"Little birds when spring arrives". A bird wooing. Herbert Price. 6800-6
A little bit of home. Katherine J. Ball Putney. 6799-9
"A little bit of woman came". Dedication, fr. Second book of verse. Eugene Field. 6949-5
"'A little bit queer' - my Mary!". Sent back by the angels. Frederick Langbridge. 6922-3
">'A little bit queer' - my Mary". Sent back by the angels. Unknown. 7002-7
The little black ass. Michael Scot. 6893-6
Little black boy. Barbara Marshall. 7024-8
The little black boy. William Blake. 6102-8,6228-8,6233-4, 6249-0,6271-7,6369-,6086-2,6152-4,6430-2,6219-9,6150-8,6214 ,6395-9,6627-5,6737-9
"A little black man ran through the town". A little black man. Alexander Blok. 7014-0
Little black man with a rose in his hat. Audrey Wurdemann. 6739-0
A little black man. Alexander Blok. 7014-0
"The little black rose shall be red at last". The little black rose. Aubrey Thomas De Vere. 6930-4
The little black rose. Aubrey Thomas De Vere. 6022-6
A little black train. Unknown. 6149-4
The little black-eyed rebel. Will Carleton. 6267-9,6470-1
The little blacksmith. Alice Cary. 6969-X
The little blades of grass. Stephen Crane. 6396-9
Little blue pigeon. Eugene Field. 6639-9
Little blue ribbons. Austin Dobson. 6669-0
"Little blue shoes". Blue shoes. Kate Greenaway. 6891-X
Little blue shoes. Maybelle McLaurin Kinsey. 7016-7
Little Bo-Peep. Mother Goose. 6363-2,6401-9,6452-3,6466-3, 6456-6,6135
Little Bo-Peep and Little Boy Blue. Samuel Minturn Peck. 6632-1;6695-X
'Little boatie'. Henry Van Dyke. 6961-4
The little boats of Britain. Sara Carsley. 6224-5
"The little boom they said was in vain". Mr. Holman's farewell. Eugene Field. 6949-5
A little bow to books on how to. Irwin Edman. 6722-0
"The little box gets her first teeth". The little box. Vasko Popa. 6758-1
"The little box which contains the world". Last news about the little box. Vasko Popa. 6758-1
The little box. Vasko Popa. 6758-1
Little boy. William Bell Scott. 6233-4
The little boy and the locomotive. Benjamin R.C. Low. 6473-6
The little boy and the sheep. Ann Taylor. 6529-5,6131-1
The little boy and the stars. Ann ("Aunt Effie") Hawkshawe. 6131-1
Little boy blue. Guy Wetmore Carryl. 6026-9
Little Boy Blue. Eugene Field. 6006-4,6101-X,6102-8,6242-3, 6303-9,6365 ,6653-4,6723-9,6288-1,6309-8,6304-7,6464 ,6401-9,6486-8,6501-5,6509-0,6512-0,6534 ,6161-3, 6431-0,6104-4,6076-5,6632-1,6732
Little Boy Blue. Unknown. 6680-1
"Little Boy Blue, come blow your horn". Mother Goose. 6271-7,6452-3,6466-3,6452-3,6363-2
Little boy bubble. Marion Short. 6707-7
The little boy found. William Blake. 6086-2
A little boy in the morning. Francis Ledwidge. 6332-2
A little boy in the morning. Francis Ledwidge. 6930-4

"A little boy just half-past three". Beyond understanding. Marion Walley. 6750-6
The little boy kidnapped by the bear. Unknown (Algonquin Indian) 6864-2
A little boy lost, fr. Songs of Innocence. William Blake. 6430-2,6086-2,6152-4
The little boy lost, fr. Songs of innocence. William Blake. 6086-2
The little boy lost. Stevie Smith. 6210-5
The little boy next door. Helen Mallory Schrader. 6750-6
The little boy that died. J.D. Robinson. 6344-6,6406-X
The little boy who ran away. Susan Teall Perry. 6684-4
"A little boy whose name was Tim". Ballad of the jelly-cake. Eugene Field. 6949-5
Little boy's baby prayer. S. Marie Talbot. 6585-6
The little boy's baby prayer. S. Maria Talbot. 6280-6
Little boy's first recitation. Unknown. 6312-8,6314-4
The little boy's goodnight. Eliza Lee Follen. 6135-4
The little boy's lament. Unknown. 6743-3
A little boy's lecture. Julia M. Thayer. 6629-1
A little boy's pocket. Unknown. 6452-3,6530-9
The little boy's prayer. S. Maria Talbot. 6451-5
A little boy's reasons. Unknown. 6684-4
A little boy's speech. Unknown. 6314-4
A little boy's talk with God. James W. Stanistreet. 6249-0
A little boy's troubles. Carlotta Perry. 6743-3
Little boy's wants. Unknown. 6312-8
Little boy's wants. Kate Lawrence. 6530-9
Little boy's wish. Idac M.C. Clarke. 6715-8
A little boy's wonder. Unknown. 6314-4
"Little boy/Full of joy". Song ("Little boy"). William Blake. 6233-4
A little boy. Susan Miles. 6070-6
Little boys take warning. Unknown. 6724-7
A little brawl. Frederika Bremer. 6424-8
A little breath I'll borrow. Thomas Campion. 6482-5
Little breeches. John Hay. 6014-5,6089-7,6302-0,6481-7, 6583-X,6605 ,6431-0,6214-8,6505-8,6260-1,6732-8,6294
"A little breeze blew over the sea". Sampan song. Laurence (Adele Florence Nicolson) Hope. 6856-1
"The little brook behind our house". Our brook in winter. Lovina E. Overlock. 6894-4
"Little brook! Little brook!". The brook-song. James Whitcomb Riley. 6991-6
"Little brook, laughing brook, how do you know". Ned's wonderings. Emma K. Brown. 6965-7
The little brook. L.C. Whiton. 6965-7
Little brother. Unknown. 6684-4
Little brother's secret. Katherine Mansfield. 6777-8
Little brother's secret. Katherine Mansfield. 6503-1
The little brother. Alice Cary. 6127-3
The little brother. William Brighty Rands. 6502-3
Little brothers of the ground. Edwin Markham. 6006-4;6597-X
Little brown baby. Paul Laurence Dunbar. 6078-1,6694-1, 6505-8
"Little brown bear". Up-stream. Katherine Kelley Taylor. 6750-6
A little brown bird. Unknown. 6502-3
"Little brown brother,oh! little brown brother". Seed song. Edith (Bland) Nesbit. 6793-X
"Little brown bulb in a litle brown bowl". Narcissus. Nell Barnes Knorr. 6818-9
Little brown bushy-tail. Astley H. Baldwin. 6629-1
The little brown cabin. Lucy Larcom. 6620-8,6066-8
"A little brown cottage, sheltered by trees". A deserted cottage. James H. Fitzpatrick. 6894-4
The little brown curl. Unknown. 6415-9
Little brown hands. Mary Hannah Krout. 6127-3,6136-2,6215-6,6424-8,6912-6
Little brown hands. Unknown. 6260-1,6312-8,6629-1
The little brown seed in the furrow. Ida W. Benham. 6049-8
Little brown trunk. Gussie Ross Jobe. 6906-1
Little builder. Unknown. 6312-8
"Little bunny long-ears". Brother bunnies. B.R. M.. 6937-1
Little buttercup, fr. H.M.S. Pinafore. Sir William Schwenck Gilbert. 6732-8
Little by little. Luella Clark. 6131-1
Little by little. Edgar A. Guest. 6748-4
Little by little. Unknown. 6049-8,6109-5,6260-1,6373-X, 6413-2,6459 ,6530-9,6743-3,6601-1,6167-2,6456-6
"Little Callimachus harsh death bore...". Lucian. 6251-2
"Little by little we subtract". Observation. Samuel Hoffenstein. 6780-8
"A little cabbage here is seen". A saucy cabbage. Carolyn Wells. 6882-0
Little cambric tamales. Claribel Alegria. 7036-1
"Little candles glistening". The feast of lights. Morris Rosenfeld. 7011-6
"The little cares that fretted me". Out in the fields with God. Unknown. 6889-8
Little caribou makes big talk. Lew Sarett. 6034-X
The little cart. Arthur Waley. 6315-2
The little cat angel. Leontine Stanfield. 6120-6
A little cavalier. Lucy Larcom. 6129-X
"'A little chamber,' built 'upon the wall'". Elisha's chamber. Richard Wilton. 6848-0
"A little changeling spirit". A changeling. Adelaide Anne Procter. 6957-6
"A little child in manger lay". Bell carol. Louise Morey Bowman. 6797-2
A little child shall lead them. Unknown. 6917-7
"A little child soul/Once forlorn". The child's soul ward. Samuel Dunievitz. 6799-9
A little child there is yborn. Unknown. 6756-5
"A little child with sunny, floating hair". The child angel. L.C. Whiton. 6965-7
A little child's faith. Unknown. 6303-9
A little child's hymn. Francis Turner Palgrave. 6627-5, 6656-9
A little child, a limber elf. Samuel Taylor Coleridge. 6315-2
A little child, fr. Christable. Samuel Taylor Coleridge. 6934-7
Little child, I call thee. Douglas Hyde. 6090-0
The little child. Albert Bigelow Paine. 6144-3;6337-3
Little children. Alice Cary. 6060-9
Little children. Mary Howitt. 6519-8
Little children. Unknown. 6629-1
"Little children in our care". God's jewels. Estella Moul Miller. 6906-1
The little children in the street. Winifred M. Letts. 6303-9
"Little children ought to be". About children. Edgar A. Guest. 6869-3
"Little children sleeping lie". Asleep. Ethelreda Lewis. 6800-6
"Little children, don't you know". Warning to children. Edgar A. Guest. 6869-3
Little children, love one another. Aunt Mary (pseud) 6131-1
The little children. Irwin Granich. 6337-3
The little children. Francis Ledwidge. 6812-X
The little children. Unknown. 6772-7
Little Christ child. Elsie M. Fowler. 6465-5
The little Christ. Laura Spencer Portor. 6053-6
Little Christel. Mary Emily Bradley. 6744-1
Little Christel. William Brighty Rands. 6519-8,6131-1
Little Christel. Unknown. 6127-3,6131-1
Little Christian Scientist. Unknown. 6715-8
The little Christian. Theodosia Garrison. 6732-8
The little Christmas tree. Sarah ("Susan Coolidge") Woolsey. 6147-8,6820-0
The little church round the corner. A.E. Lancaster. 6045-1;6273-3
The little clock. Emma Celia & Lizzie J. Rook. 6137-0
A little cloud. Bible. 7020-5
The little cloud. John Howard Bryant. 6302-0;6385-3
The little coat. James Whitcomb Riley. 6260-1
"A little cock-sparrow sat on a tree". Mother Goose. 6363-2
The little conqueror. Unknown. 6273-3
Little cookie-hookie. H.L. Piner. 6680-1
Little cookie-hookie. Unknown. 6689-5
The little Cossack. Laura E. Richards. 6554-X
"The little cottage/I see in my dream". My dream house. M. Pearl Gillespie. 6894-4
"The little Count of Lemonade". Look out for the snake! Luis Pales Matos. 6759-X
The little country drug store. Edgar A. Guest. 6869-3

LITTLE

The little coward. Ann and Jane Taylor. 6233-4
"Little cowboy, what have you heard". The lupracaun, or fairy shoemaker. William Allingham. 6930-4
The little cowslip. Unknown. 6629-1
"A little crisp are the ages". Lesson of history. Edward Farquhar. 6939-8
The little crooked garden. Agnes Kendrick Gray. 6232-6
"A little cross,/To tell my loss". Robin's cross. George Darley. 6930-4
"Little Cupid one day on a sunbeam...floating". Love and the flimsies. Thomas Love Peacock. 6802-2
"Little Daisy smiling wakes". Gathering blackberries. Phoebe Cary. 6969-X
The little cup-bearer. Unknown. 6411-6
Little Cyrus. Alice Cary. 6969-X
The little dago girl. Robert C.V. Meyers. 6417-5
Little Dame Crump. Unknown. 6466-3,6530-9
The little dancers. Laurence Binyon. 6395-0,6437-X,6477-9, 6507-4
The little dancers. Laurence Binyon. 6959-2
The little dark rose. Owen (atr.) Roe Mac Ward. 6930-4
Little Dick and the clock. James Whitcomb Riley. 6091-9, 6683-6
"Little Dicky Dilver". Unknown. 6363-2
"A little demon in defense". My fox terrier. Unknown. 7008-6
"The little dimpled baby-girl". As she says. Joseph Bert Smiley. 6926-6
A little distance off. John Lehmann. 6354-3
Little dog of amusement zoo. Alice Jean Cleator. 6510-4
The little dog's day. Rupert Brooke. 6228-4
Little Dorothy's sayings. George P. Bible. 6579-1
Little Dot. Unknown. 6744-1,6167-2
The little doves. Unknown. 6373-X,6452-3,6502-3
The little dreamer. Unknown. 6502-3,6629-1,6684-4
The little dreams. Joseph Mills Hanson. 6589-9
"A little drop from a rose's cup". The drop. James Abraham Martling. 6952-5
Little drops. Unknown. 6314-4
"Little drops of water". Little things. Frances Sargent Osgood. 6889-8
The little drummer. Richard Henry Stoddard. 6062-5,6131-1
A little Dutch garden. Harriet Whitney Durbin. 6368-3
A little Dutch Garden. Hattie Whitney. 6585-6
"A little elbow leans upon your knee". Tired mother. Unknown. 6772-7
Little elegy. Elinor Wylie. 6879-0
The little elf man. John Kendrick Bangs. 6466-3
The little elf. John Kendrick Bangs. 6135-4,6401-9,6519-8
Little Ella. Edward Bulwer-Lytton; Baron Lytton. 6772-7
A little envious gossip in heaven. Lucian. 6637-2
"Little eyelids, cease your winking". An invitation to sleep. Eugene Field. 6949-5
The little fair soul. Menella Bute Smedley. 6656-9,6543-0
Little fairy child! Helen C. Willis. 6818-9
The little family. Unknown. 6058-7
The little farm. Witter Bynner. 6030-7
"Little fat boy on the floor". City songs 004. Mark Van Doren. 6808-1
"Little Fay, than a bird more tender". Fay. Thomas Ashe. 6772-7
The little fay. Robert Buchanan. 6424-8
Little feet. Unknown. 6385-3
'The little feller's stockin'.' Joseph Crosby Lincoln. 6119-2
The little feller's stockin'. Joseph Crosby Lincoln. 6807-3
A little feller. Unknown. 6277-6
A little feller. Unknown. 6925-8
"A little fellow, brown with wind". Reuben boy. Harold Crawford Stearns. 6762-X
The little fighting chance. Unknown. 6057-9
"A little fir grew in the midst of the wood". The foolish fir-tree. Henry Van Dyke. 6961-4
The little fir-trees. Evaleen Stein. 6964-9
The little fireman. John F. Nicholls. 6919-3
The little fires. Henry Herbert Knibbs. 7012-4
The little fish that would not do as it was bid. Ann and Jane Taylor. 6242-3
The little fisherman. Ann and Jane Taylor. 6105-2

Little fishes. Max Eastman. 6880-4
"Little fishwife of the stars". Star market. Pierre Loving. 6880-4
The little flags. John Clair Minot. 6449-3
Little Flo's letter. Emma Celia & Lizzie J. Rook. 6137-0
"A little flame breaks out". An October fire. Unknown. 7020-5
"A little flock of clouds do down to rest". Evening clouds. Francis Ledwidge. 6812-X
"A little flock of clouds go down to rest". Evening clouds. Francis Ledwidge. 7027-2
The little flower strewers. Matthew Russell. 6174-5
"Little flower, I hold you here" William Henry Davies. 7020-5
The little flower. Leonard Feeney. 6285-7
The little flower. Gerald Massey. 6529-5
The little flutes. Denis O'Sullivan. 6090-0
"Little fluttering beauteous fly". To a butterfly. Felicia Dorothea Hemans. 6973-8
"The little French doll was a dear little doll". The doll's wooing. Eugene Field. 6949-5
Little folk. Carrie Ward Lyon. 6254-7
Little folks in the grass. Annette Wynne. 6490-6
"The little fox, the wolf and bear made peace". Unknown. 6050-1
Little foxes. Unknown. 6629-1
Little foxes and little hunters. Unknown. 6314-4
The little foxes. Frances Dickenson Pindar. 6761-1
A little French for a little girl. Unknown. 6314-4
"A little fresh went out to swim". Warning to freshmen. Clayton Fotterall McMichael. 6936-3
Little friends in fairyland. Edith M. Thomas. 6510-4
Little garaine. Sir Gilbert Parker. 6519-8
"The little garden plot I tread". Flower courage. Edgar A. Guest. 6869-3
A little garden. Amy Lowell. 6236-9,6266-0
The little gate to God. Walter Rauschenbusch. 6337-3,6532-5
Little Geffen. Francis Orrery Ticknor. 6016-2,6288-1,6431-0,6088-9,6419-1
The little gentleman. Unknown. 6233-4
A little geste of Robin Hood and his meynie. Unknown. 6186-9
The little ghost who died for love. Edith Sitwell. 6339-X, 6634-8,6354-3
The little ghost who died for love. Edith Sitwell. 7000-0
The little ghost. Edna St. Vincent Millay. 6338-1
Little Gidding. Thomas Stearns Eliot. 6208-3
Little Giffen. Francis Orrery Ticknor. 6211-3,6512-0,6482-5,6113-3,6499-X,6589 ,6552-X,6678-X,6074-9,6062-5, 6121-4
Little Giffin of Tennessee. Unknown. 6260-1
Little girl. Edgar A. Guest. 6862-6
A little girl and Washington. Unknown. 6158-3
"A little girl asked some kittens to tea". The tea-party. J.G. Francis. 6786-7
Little girl at home. Unknown. 6714-X
A little girl in school. Frances Viola Holden. 6274-1
Little girl of long ago. Joe Cone. 6274-1
"A little girl of three". The oak. John E. Barrett. 6840-5
The little girl that grew up. Unknown. 7022-1
The little girl that lost a finger. Gabriela (Lucila Godoy Alcayaga) Mistral. 6759-X
The little girl's address to the river. Susan Jewett. 6131-1
A little girl's declaration. Unknown. 6314-4
A little-girl's fancies. Unknown. 6127-3,6131-1
A little girl's hopes. Unknown. 6314-4
The little girl's lament. Dora Greenwell. 6502-3
A little girl's letter. Unknown. 6502-3,6131-1
A little girl's questions. Unknown. 6629-1
Little girl's request. Unknown. 6713-1
A little girl's song of autumn. Unknown. 6529-5
A little girl's songs. Hilda Conkling. 6338-1
A little girl's wish. Libbie C. Baer. 6684-4
"Little girl, little girl, where have you been?" Unknown. 6904-5
A little girl. Frederick A. Hinckley. 6798-0
A little girl. Ella Wheeler Wilcox. 6629-1
The little girl. Nicholas Moore. 6379-9

Little girls. Edgar A. Guest. 6135-4
Little girls. Laurence Alma Tadema. 6242-3
Little girls are best. Edgar A. Guest. 7033-7
"Little girls". Unknown. 6364-0
The little god. Katharine Howard. 6338-1
The little gods. Abigail Cresson. 6396-9
Little golden hair. Will Carleton. 6413-2
Little goldenhair. F. Burge Smith. 6273-3,6304-7,6567-8
Little goldenhair. Unknown. 6014-5,6165-6,6344-6,6385-6
A little goose. Eliza Sproat Turner. 6089-7,6127-3,6502-3, 6131-1,6424-8
The little gopher man. Nancy Bockius Scott. 6466-3
Little Gottlieb. Phoebe Cary. 6638-0
Little Gottlieb's Christmas. Phoebe Cary. 6574-0
The little grand lama. Thomas Moore. 6669-0,6278-4
"The little granite church upholds". Sheepstor. Leonard Alfred George Strong. 6777-8
The little grave. Unknown. 6910-X
The little grave. Unknown. 6523-6
"The little gray cat was walking prettily". The little white cat. Unknown. 6930-4
"'Little Haly! Little Haly!' chirps the robin". On the death of little Mahala Ashcraft. James Whitcomb Riley. 6892-8
The little gray lamb. Archibald Beresford Sullivan. 6608-9
Little gray songs from St. Joseph's. Grace Fallow Norton. 6310-1
Little gray songs: number 3. Grace Fallow Norton. 6509-0
Little green Bermuda poem. Hilda Conkling. 6776-X
The little green orchard. Walter De La Mare. 6508-2
The little grenadier. Unknown. 6215-6
Little Gretchen. Hans Christian Andersen. 6131-1
Little Gretchen. Unknown. 6409-4
Little grey water. William Henry Ogilvie. 6804-9
A little grimy-fingered girl. Lee Wilson Dodd. 6846-4
Little Gunver. Johannes Ewald. 6555-4
Little Gustava. Celia Thaxter. 6132-X,6519-8,6612-7,6623-2, 6135-4,6510
Little Hal. ? Colton. 6889-8
Little hand. Cora Fabri. 6876-6
A little hand. Frank Lebby Stanton. 6486-8,6576-7
TIe little handmaiden. Archibald Lampman. 6797-2
Little hands. Laurence Binyon. 6233-4,6320-9,6337-3
The little hare. Ann ("Aunt Effie") Hawkshawe. 6018-8
Little Harry Huston. Unknown. 6061-7
The little hatchet story. R.N. Burdette. 6570-8
A little hatchet. Unknown. 6712-3
Little heart within thy cage. Edward Carpenter. 6879-0
"Little hedge-birds, pick these brittle sticks". Vineyard song. Fray Angelico Chavez. 6783-2
Little helper. Pauline Frances Camp. 6713-1
Little helpers. Emma Celia & Lizzie J. Rook. 6137-0
Little helpers. Unknown. 6740-9,6131-1
The little hero. Unknown. 6913-4
The little hero. Unknown. 6742-5
The little hill. Edna St. Vincent Millay. 6331-4
The little holdfast. Unknown. 6134-6
The little home paper. Charles Hanson Towne. 6846-4
Little Homer's slate. Eugene Field. 6834-0;6949-5
"Little honey baby, shet yo' eyes up tight". A southern lullaby. Virna Sheard. 6797-2
The little house on the hill. Alice Cary. 6969-X
The little house. Grace Noll Crowell. 7038-8
The little house. John Richard Moreland. 6326-8
The little house. Katharine (Hinkson) Tynan. 6872-3
The little housekeepers. Emily Huntington. 6530-9
The little hunchback. James Whitcomb Riley. 6744-1
A little hymn to Mary. Unknown. 6881-2
"A little ink more or less!" Stephen Crane. 6996-7
"Little inmate, full of mirth". The cricket. Vincent Bourne. 6814-6,6271-7
"Little Jaqueline sat 'neath an old oaken tree". Jaqueline. George M. Vickers. 6922-3
Little interlopers. James C. Melody. 6761-1
Little ivory figures pulled with string. Amy Lowell. 6348-9,6375-6
Little Jack Frost. Unknown. 6132-X,6452-3,6135-4
Little Jack Horner. Anthony C. Deane. 6440-X
Little Jack Horner. Mother Goose. 6466-3,6363-2
'Little Jack janitor'. James Whitcomb Riley. 6128-1

Little Jack Pumpkin face. Unknown. 6466-3
Little Jack two-sticks. Marion Manville. 6417-5
Little Jerry, the miller. John Godfrey Saxe. 6004-8
Little Jesus. Francis Thompson. 6337-3,6508-2,6653-4
The little Jew. Dinah Maria Mulock Craik. 6848-0
Little Jim. Edward Farmer. 6772-7
Little Jim. Frank J. Hayes. 6149-4
Little Jim. George Robert Sims. 6918-5,6682-8
Little Jim. Unknown. 6554-6,6403-5
Little Jo. Mary McGuire. 6922-3
Little Joe. Robert C.V. Meyers. 6927-4
Little Joe-Johnny. Gustaf Froding. 6045-5
Little John and the red friar. William Edmonstoune Aytoun. 6948-7
Little John Bottlejohn. Laura E. Richards. 6772-7
"The little jay town, says Ed Vance Cook". A few left. Berton Braley. 6853-7
Little joke. Elinor Wylie. 6307-1
Little jumping Joan. Unknown. 6937-1
"The little kindergarten miss". The kindergarten miss. Edgar A. Guest. 6862-6
The little kings and queens. Unknown. 6772-7
A little kiss when no one sees. Samuel Minturn Peck. 6527-9
Little Kit. John G. Watts. 6131-1
The little kittens. Unknown. 6373-X,6699-2,6456-6
Little Kitty. Elizabeth Payson Prentiss. 6120-6,6424-8
Little kitty. Unknown. 6314-4,6699-2,6692-2
Little knight-errant. Margaret A. Richard. 6715-8
A little knot of blue. Samuel Minturn Peck. 6226-1
Little Lac Grenier. William Henry Drummond. 6266-0,6433-7, 6252-0
A little lad's answer. Unknown. 6097-8
"Little lad, little lad, and who's for...". '--a scotch terrier Hamish' C. Hilton Brown. 7008-6
"Little lady icicle is dreaming in..north-land". Lady icicle. Emily Pauline ("Tekahionwake") Johnson. 6837-5
"The little lady old and gray". The lovely smile. Edgar A. Guest. 6869-3
Little lady riches. Edgar A. Guest. 6869-3
The little lady-bird. Caroline Anne Bowles Southey. 6680-1
The little lady. James Whitcomb Riley. 6091-9
The little lake. Bedros Tourian. 6050-1
Little lamb. William Blake. 6502-3
"Little lamb, who made thee?". The lamb. William Blake. 6024-2,6075-7,6078-1,6102-8,6134-6,6154 ,6086-2,6104-4,6152-4,6195-0,6114-1,6131 ,6183-4,6216-4,6242-3, 6315-2,6337-3,6339 ,6371-3,6430-2,6424-8,6456-6,6510-X,6454 ,6418-3,6481-7,6519-8,6604-6,6726-3,6730 , 6630-7,6639-9,6543-0,6638-0,6645-3,6723 ,6634-8,6964-9
"The little lamp that lit my room". Death stirs the arras. Eleanor Sands Smith. 6979-7
The little land. Robert Louis Stevenson. 6132-X,6135-4, 6639-9,6638-0
"The little lanes of England". Oh, to be in England, now that April's there. Vilda Sauvage Owens. 7038-8
The little lark. Ann and Jane Taylor. 6242-3
The little lark. Jane Taylor. 6183-4,6456-6
"Little lass of Plymouth, gentle, shy, and sweet". Boy and girl of Plymouth. Helen L. Smith. 6964-9
"A little later on, I'll gather wisdom like". A little later on. John L. Kirkhoff. 6857-X
The little lazy cloud. Unknown. 6373-X
"A little learning is a dangerous thing". Alexander Pope. 6238-5,6102-8,6125-7
"Little leaves that dance so softly". Guess. George Elliston. 6906-1
The little leaves. George Cooper. 6373-X
"A little less returned for him each spring". Anglais mort a Florence. Wallace Stevens. 6751-4
.'The little less' Ruby Clarke McIntyre. 6847-2
A little lesson. James Whitcomb Riley. 6509-0
"Little lichen, fondly clinging", sels. R.M. E. 6601-1
The little light. Unknown. 6743-3,6167-2
Little lights. Unknown. 6312-8
Little lonesome soul. Frances Shaw. 6031-5
A little longer. Adelaide Anne Procter. 6957-6
Little lost pup. Arthur Guiterman. 6512-0,6107-9,6510-4

LITTLE 990

Little lost pup. Unknown. 7008-6
Little Lottie's grievance. Paul Hamilton Hayne. 6965-7
"Little loue serues my time." Unknown. 6563-5
"The little love-god lying once asleep". Sonnet 154 ("The little love-god"). William Shakespeare. 6447-4
"Little Madonna hanging on the wall". Studio. Keith Sterling. 6780-8
"Little Maggie sitting in the pew". Dunoon. Thomas Edward Brown. 6809-X
Little lover. Leonora Speyer. 6102-8,6076-5,6037-4
Little Lucy. Anson D.F. Randolph. 6131-1
Little Mack. Eugene Field. 6949-5
Little Mag's victory. George L. Catlin. 6411-6,6744-1
Little Maia. Zakarias Topelius. 6045-5
Little maid and the speckled hen. E.W. Dennison. 6688-7
"A little maid climbed upon an old man's knee". After the ball. Unknown. 6826-X
The little maid for me. A.L. Smith. 6530-9
"A little maid of Astraken". The divan. Richard Henry Stoddard. 6004-8,6753-0
Little maid of far Japan. Annette Wynne. 6891-X
Little maid-o'-dreams. James Whitcomb Riley. 6772-7
The little maiden and the little bird. Lydia Maria Child. 6242-3,6131-1
The little maiden and the little bird. Unknown. 6127-3
"Little maiden dressed in mourning". Unknown. 6364-0
"A little maiden met me in the lane". The intercepted salute. Thomas Edward Brown. 6809-X
"Little Maud, my queen!". Maud. Thomas Westwood. 6980-0
Little mamma. Charles Henry ("John Paul") Webb. 6089-7, 6632-1,6424-8,6505-8,7041-8
Little man. Unknown. 6097-8
"Little man, old and weird". Unknown. 6364-0
Little Margery. Unknown. 6912-6
Little Martha Washington. Mrs. Royal A. Bristol. 6712-3
The little martyr. Unknown. 6408-6
Little Mary Cassidy. Francis A. Fahy. 6090-0
Little Mary Fagan. Unknown. 6826-X
"Little Mary Phagan". Unknown. 6059-5
Little Mary's wish. Lucy Marion Blinn. 6406-X
Little Matthy Groves. Unknown. 6003-X
Little Mattie. Elizabeth Barrett Browning. 6014-5,6134-6
Little Maud. Unknown. 6415-9
Little May. Emily Huntington Miller. 6502-3;6632-2
"A little meal of frozen cake". The sparrow. Albert Durrant Watson. 6797-2
Little memories. Louise Owen. 6764-6
Little men. Daniel Whitehead Hicky. 6761-1
"The little men in the park". Men in the park. Preston Paine Foster. 6906-1
"The little mice are playing". Finger play. Unknown. 6937-1
Little midget. Unknown. 6312-8,6629-1
A little milkmaid. Anna Boynton Averill. 6965-7
The little milliner. Robert Buchanan. 6302-0;6385-3
Little mischief. Sister Maris Stella. 6713-1
Little mischief. Annie H. Streater. 6530-9
Little Miss Bragg. Eugene Field. 6834-0;6949-5
Little Miss Dandy. Eugene Field. 6949-5
Little Miss Muffet. Mother Goose. 6135-4,6052-8,6363-2, 6401-9,6466-3,6440-X,6452
Little miss six o'clock. Edgar A. Guest. 6862-6
Little Mistress Sans-Merci. Eugene Field. 6949-5
"Little mistress mine, good-bye!". Villanelle ("Little"). Sir Edmund Gosse. 6770-0,6875-8
Little moccasins. Robert Service. 6159-1,6115-X
Little moments. Unknown. 6424-8
"Little monitor, by thee". Verses in a watch. William Czar Bradley. 7030-2
A little more heart. Unknown. 6109-5
"A little more of loving, a little less of...". Our little needs. Edgar A. Guest. 6862-6
"A little more, a little less!". To the fortune seeker. Morris Rosenfeld. 7011-6
Little mother. M.P. D. 6449-8
Little mother of mine. Rudyard Kipling. 6691-7
A little mother's trials. Bessie B. McClure. 6697-6
"Little mother, hold her tightly!". To a young mother. Helen Darby Berning. 6750-6
The little mothers. Emma Celia & Lizzie J. Rook. 6137-0

The little mud-sparrows. Elizabeth Stuart Phelps. 6608-9
Little Musgrave and Lady Barnard. Unknown. 6057-9,6058-7, 6185-0,6055-2,6067-2,6281 ,6185-0
Little Nan. Unknown. 6340-3,6451-5,6579-1
Little Nancy Etticoat. Unknown. 6904-5
"Little my lacking fortunes show". Expenses. Adelaide Crapsey. 6897-9
"The little naked brown boy!". The swimming hole. Thornton W. Burgess. 6798-0
"Little Nancy Etticoat". The candle. Unknown. 6937-1
Little nannie. Lucy Larcom. 6373-X,6129-X
Little Ned. Robert Buchanan. 6302-0
Little Nell's funeral, fr. Old curiosity shop. Charles Dickens. 6909-6
Little Nellie in the prison. Paul Hamilton Hayne. 6413-2
Little Nellie's pa. Alma Frances McCollum. 6115-X
"Little new neighbor, have you come to be". Welcome. Rose Waldo. 6891-X
"The little new soul is come to earth". The child. Ethel Clifford. 6793-X
A little night music. Felix Stefanile. 6218-0
The little nurse. Madame Tastu. 6424-8
The little nurse. Unknown. 6127-3
Little nut people. E.J. Nicholson. 6373-X
The little old Cupid. Walter De La Mare. 6649-6
The little old house by the shore. Joseph Crosby Lincoln. 6119-2
The little old log cabin. Robert Service. 6159-1
"A little old man lived up in a cloud". The cloud house. Adrian Mott. 6262-8,6937-1
The little old road. Gertrude Palmer Vaughan. 7031-0
The little old sod shanty on the claim. Unknown. 6615-1, 6003-X,6281-4
"The little old tailor that came from Mayo". The tailor that came from Mayo. Denis A. McCarthy. 6930-4
"A little old woman lived lone on a hill". Auto-suggestion. Georgette Agnew. 6804-9
The little old women. Charles Baudelaire. 6102-8
"The little old-fashioned church, with the...". The little old-fashioned church. Edgar A. Guest. 6862-6
The little one smiles. Oscar Stjerne. 6045-5
The little one's land. Unknown. 6130-3
Little one's speech. Unknown. 6312-8,6314-4
"Little one, come to my knee!". A night with a wolf. Bayard Taylor. 6127-3,6239-3,6242-3,6639-9,6638-0, 6964 ,6084-6,6131-1
"Little one, I lie i' the dark". A dream-child. Dinah Maria Mulock Craik. 6772-7
The little one-star flag. (Alfred) Damon Runyon. 6443-4
The little orator. Thaddeus Mason Harris. 6314-4,6673-9
Little Orphant Annie. James Whitcomb Riley. 6121-4,6424-8, 6723-9,6739-5,6467-1,6076 ,6102-8,6132-X,6254-7,6478-7,6479-5,6486 ,6496-5,6583-X,6732-8,6808-1,6431-0
"Little orphan Teddy(s come to our". Little orphant Teddy. John Kendrick Bangs. 6995-9
The little outcast's plea. Unknown. 6450-7,6579-1
Little pagan rain song. Frances Shaw. 6897-9
A little page's song. William Alexander Percy. 6030-7
"Little pansy faces/Your loveliness erases". Pansy faces. Anne Pauline Clark. 6818-9
A little parable. Anne Reeve Aldrich. 6076-5,6102-8,6300-4, 6309-8,6337-3
Little Pat and the parson. Unknown. 6914-2
Little Pat and the parson. Unknown. 6742-5
Little patch o' blue. Gazelle S. Sharp. 6799-9
"Little patch, who made thee?". The patch. Elizabeth Mary Prew. 6847-2
"Little Penelope Socrates". Christmas chimes in Boston, Philadelphia, New York... Unknown. 6929-0
The little path. Sallie P. FitzHugh. 6799-9
The little patriot. Emma Celia & Lizzie J. Rook. 6137-0
The little peach. Eugene Field. 6273-3,6735-2,6089-7,6732-8
The little peach. Unknown. 6902-9
The little peddler. Unknown. 6530-9
The little people of the snow. William Cullen Bryant. 6126-5
The little people. Nathaniel Parker Willis. 6772-7
The little peoples. Claude McKay. 6033-1
The little peoples. B. Paul Neuman. 7031-0

Little Phil. Helen Hinsdale Rich. 6014-5,6273-3,6917-7
The little philosopher. Unknown. 6530-9
A little philosophy. Douglas Leader Durkin. 6796-4
"A little pig found a fifty-dollar note". Unknown. 6363-2
The little piggy-wig. D'Arcy W. Thompson. 6262-8
A little pilgrim. Unknown. 6924-X
A little pilgrim. Unknown. 6674-4
The little pine tree. Unknown (German) 6373-X,6049-8
The little piou-piou. Robert Service. 6159-1
"The little pitiful, worn, laughing faces". The beggars. Margaret Widdemer. 6897-9
The little plant. Kate Louise Brown. 6143-5,6177-X
A little planter. Unknown. 6049-8
Little poem. Narihira. 6879-0
Little poem for evening. Frances Frost. 7030-2
"Little Polly Flinders". Mother Goose. 6363-2
Little Polly Perkins. Grace May North. 6130-3
"Little pony, little pony". Unknown. 6364-0
A little prayer; for the man in the air. John Oxenham. 7014-0
A little prayer. Samuel Ellsworth Kiser. 6291-1,6337-3
A little prayer. Ellen Mae Nichols. 6799-9
A little prayer. Anne Steele. 6889-8
A little pretty bonny lass. Unknown. 6182-6,6380-2
"The little pretty nightingale". Unknown. 6187-7,6328-4, 6383-7
"The little priest of Felton." Unknown. 6452-3
The little Princes. William Shakespeare. 6188-5
"The little princess whose hair was the...". The little princess. Jovan Ducic. 6765-4
The little progress. Mary Atwater Taylor. 6979-7
"hittle puddles have a way". Puddles. Ruth Eckman. 6750-6
"Little Robert Robin sat on a leafless vine". On St. Valentine's Day. Mary B.C. Slade. 6965-7
"Little Rose, be not sad for all that hath". The little dark rose. Owen (atr.) Roe Mac Ward. 6930-4
"Little Sarah she stood by her grandmother's..". The johnnycake. Unknown. 6891-X
Little puddleton. Robert Service. 6159-1
Little puss. Unknown. 6302-0;6385-3
Little pussy (I like little pussy). Jane Taylor. 6692-2
The little Quaker sinner. Lucy Maud Montgomery. 6249-0
Little queen. Ella Wheeler Wilcox. 6956-8
Little rain. Elizabeth Madox Roberts. 6554-X
Little rain drops. Unknown. 6312-8,6373-X,6135-4,6131-1
Little rain men. Ruth Anne Hussey. 6466-3
The little raindrops. Ann ("Aunt Effie") Hawkshawe. 6018-8, 6937-1
The little reader. Unknown. 6742-5
The little rebel. Joseph Ashby-Sterry. 6656-9
The little red bullock. Herbert Tremaine. 6510-4
The little red god. Unknown. 7012-4
The little red lark. Katharine (Hinkson) Tynan. 6476-0
Little red leaves. Unknown. 6937-1
The little red ribbon. James Whitcomb Riley. 6993-2
Little Red Riding Hood. Thomas Hood. 6167-2
Little Red Riding Hood. Letitia Elizabeth ("L.E.L.") Landon. 6302-0
Little Red Riding-Hood. Unknown. 6744-1,6131-1
The little red sled. Jocelyn Bush. 6466-3
Little responsory for a republican hero. Cesar Vallejo. 6642-9
The little rift within the lute. Alfred Lord Tennyson. 6094-3,6654-2
Little roach poem. C.W. Truesdale. 6966-5
The little roads. Alfred Noyes. 6151-6;6607-0
Little Robin Adair. Fannie E. Robinson. 6965-7
"Little Robin Redbreast jump'd upon". Unknown. 6363-2
"Little robin redbreast sat upon a rail". Unknown. 6904-5
"Little robin redbreast sat upon a tree". Unknown. 6904-5
Little Rocket's Christmas. Marc Eugene ("Vandyke Brown") Cook. 6410-8,6744-1,6410-8,6744-1,6573-2
The little rose is dust, my dear. Grace Hazard Conkling. 6431-0
Little Sadie. Unknown. 6826-X
"A little said and truly said". William Wordsworth. 6238-5
The little sailor-man. Joseph Morris. 6078-1
Little Saint Caecilia. Margaret Holmes. 6924-X
The little salamander. Walter De La Mare. 6102-8
A little schoolma'am. Unknown. 6314-4

"The little screech-owl sits polite". The warning. Robert P. Tristram Coffin. 7040-X
A little seamstress. Unknown. 6314-4,6484-4
The little seamstress. Emma Celia & Lizzie J. Rook. 6137-0
Little senorita. Charles Divine. 6891-X
The little servant. Sophia Mavroidi Papadaky. 6352-7
The little shade. Edwina Stanton Babcock. 6076-5,6102-8
The little shepherd's song. William Alexander Percy. 6249-0;6476-0;6607-0
Little ships in the air. Edward A. Rand. 6639-9
"Little ships of whitest pearl". A mother's song. Francis Ledwidge. 6812-X,6833-2
The little ships. Hilton Brown. 6269-5
The little ships. Unknown. 7031-0
A little shoe. Unknown. 6889-8,6916-9
The little shoes did it. Unknown. 6917-7
The little shoes. Charles Sangster. 6433-7
A little shopper. Mary Frances Butts. 6965-7
The little sick girl. Edgar A. Guest. 6748-4
Little Sigrid. Hjalmar Hjorth Boyesen. 6676-3
Little sinnerc repents. Unknown. 6713-1
Little sister. Unknown. 6090-0
The little sister of Mercy. Helen Booth. 6922-3
A little sister's story. M.E. B. 6965-7
Little snail. Hilda Conkling. 6638-0
Little snail. Hilda Conkling. 6891-X
Little snowflakes. M. M. 6373-X
Little snowflakes. Ella M. Powers. 6147-8
Little snowflakes. Unknown. 6373-X
The little soldier. James Lyman Molloy. 6074-9
The little son. May C. ([Mary]) Gillington) Byron. 6800-6
The little son. Moira (Nesta Higginson Skrine) O'Neill. 6266-0
"A little song I tried to sing...summer's day". Autumn song. Lydia Gibson. 6880-4
Little song in the air. Genaro Estrada. 6759-X
A little song of angels. Marjorie L.C. Pickthall. 6797-2
A little song of life. Lizette Woodworth Reese. 6266-0, 6473-6,6478-7,6501-5,6396-9
A little song. Duncan Campbell Scott. 6433-7
A little song. L. Alma Tadema. 6937-1
A little song. Robert Grosseteste. 6282-2
A little song. Duncan Campbell Scott. 6656-9
A little song. Unknown. 6137-0
Little sorrow. Marian (Annie D.G. Robinson) Douglas. 6127-3,6639-9,6638-0
"Little soul, for such brief space...". A dead baby. Dinah Maria Mulock Craik. 6980-0
A little speech. Emma Celia & Lizzie J. Rook. 6741-7
The little star. Unknown. 6089-7,6529-5,6724-7,6131-1
Little Steenie. Anna L. Ruth. 6911-8
"A little state-funded barrack". It started. Jimmy Santiago Baca. 6870-7
Little stitcher. Unknown. 6530-9,6721-2
Little stitches. Unknown. 6273-3
The little stones. Barbara Young. 6542-2
A little story. Hester A. Benedict. 6131-1
Little straight tree. Adeline Rubin. 6397-7
"A little stray lamb crept into my fold". Lottie. James Abraham Martling. 6952-5
"A little stream had lost its way". A deed and a word. Charles Mackay. 6889-8
Little streams. Mary Howitt. 6271-7
The little street. Herbert H. Hines. 6214-8
The little streets. Ethel May Ericson. 6847-2
The little streets. Edgar A. Guest. 6748-4
"Little strokes/Fell great oaks". Unknown. 7028-0
Little sweet pea. Robert Palfrey Utter. 6131-1
"Little sweetfern-bordered paths that lead...". Beach trails. Martha Haskell Clark. 6798-0
A little swirl of vers libra. Thomas Russell Ybarra. 6089-7
"Little tail wf a pig". Anacreontic to a little pig's tail. Isaac Story. 6787-5
The little tambourine girl. Lucy Larcom. 6129-X
The little tavern. Edna St. Vincent Millay. 6607-0
The little teacher. Sophie E. Eastman. 6684-4
Little tee-hee. William W. Fink. 6416-7
The little telltale. Unknown. 6142-7
"The little tender blades of grass". The little things,

LITTLE

sels. John Frushard Waddington. 6796-4
A little thankful song. Frank Lebby Stanton. 6291-1
A little the best of it. Edgar A. Guest. 6862-6
The little theatre. Gwendolen Haste. 6037-4
"Little thing!/I would sing/Lofty song". The man-mountain's answer to the lilliputian verses. John Gay. 6972-X
Little things. Mary Helen Barbie. 7016-7
Little things. Ebenezer Cobham Brewer. 6479-5
Little things. Julia A. Fletcher Carney. 6356-X,6401-9
Little things. Julia Fletch Carney. 6135-4
Little things. Polly Chase. 6039-0
Little things. Kate Clyde. 6530-9
Little things. Orrick Jo^hns. 6374-8,6556-2,6513-9,6393-4
Little things. Frances Sargent Osgood. 6889-8
Little things. James Stephens. 6777-8,6339-X,6464-7,6628-3
Little things. Unknown. 6049-8,6314-4,6623-2,6629-1,6424-8,6456
"Little things of which we lately chattered". 'The soul of a nation'. Sir Owen Seaman. 7031-0
The little things, sels. John Frushard Waddington. 6796-4
The little things. Gerald Gould. 6844-8
"Little think'st thou, poor flower". Foreknowledge. John Donne. 6935-5
Little think'st thou, poor flower. John Donne. 6317-9
Little Thornback. John Runcie. 6591-0,6592-9
The little tin cup. Thomas Frost. 6674-7
A little tin plate. Garnet Walch. 6768-9,6681-X
Little Titian's palette. Margaret Junkin Preston. 6965-7
"Little Tom Tucker/Sings for his supper." Mother Goose. 6452-3
Little Tommy Tiddler. Paul Edmonds. 6937-1
"Little Tommy Tittlemouse". Unknown. 6363-2
Little Tommy Tucker. Unknown. 6363-2,6466-3
"Little toddlin' sweetheart". About 'two'. Fred W. Leu. 6906-1
"Little tortillas, little tortillas". Unknown. 6364-0
The little tower. William Morris. 6508-2
A little town in Senegal. Will Thompson. 6846-4
"A little town lies by the sea". Hyannis by the sea. Isabella Harris. 6798-0
The little town o' Tailholt. James Whitcomb Riley. 6484-1
The little town. Clara T. Brown. 6906-1
The little town. Clinton Scollard. 6608-9
Little towns at dusk. Brother X (pseud.) 6662-3
The little towns. Irene Maryl Davidson. 6265-2
The little toy land of the Dutch. Unknown. 6891-X
Little toy-dog. John Kendrick Bangs. 6714-X
"Little tree-top lover". To a warbling vireo. Josie Eppert. 6906-1
The little tree. Dorothy Margaret Stuart. 6776-X
Little trotty wagtail. John Clare. 6179-6,6466-3,6668-2
"Little tube of mighty power", fr. A pipe of tobacco. Isaac Hawkins Browne. 6092-7
The little turkey gobbler. Unknown. 6703-4
Little turncoats. Georgia A. Peck. 6920-7
Little turncoats. Georgia A. Peck. 6699-2
The little turtle. Vachel Lindsay. 6466-3
Little tyrant. Unknown. 6014-5,6629-1
The little vagabond. William Blake. 6089-7,6271-7,6328-4,6733-6,6152-4
A little valentine. Elizabeth Winton. 6466-3
A little verse for Holy Week. Delphine Schmitt. 6490-6
A little visitor. Helen Standish Parkins. 6579-1
The little vulgar boy. Richard Harris ("Thomas Ingoldsby") Barham. 6279-2
"Little wat ye wha's coming". The chevalier's muster-roll. Unknown. 6859-6
The little waves of Breffny. Eva Gore Booth. 6423-X,6477-9
The little waves of Breffny. Eva Gore-Booth. 6090-0,6174-5,6331-4,6266-0,6090-0,6476,6161-3,6639-9
"A little way below her chin". On some buttercups. Frank Dempster Sherman. 7041-8
"A little way, more soft and sweet". First footsteps. Algernon Charles Swinburne. 6828-6
A little way. Frank Lebby Stanton. 6309-8,6431-0
"Little we know what stranger enters here". Birth. Stanton A. Coblentz. 6750-6
"A little while I fain would linger yet". Paul Hamilton Hayne. 6753-0

A little while I fain would linger yet. Paul Hamilton Hayne. 7017-5,6008-0,6288-1,6431-0
"A little while ago". A winter piece. Cora Fabri. 6876-6
"A little while the rose". Roseleaf. Unknown (Greek). 6961-4
A little while to love and rave. Samuel Hoffenstein. 6026-9
"A little while", fr. The dark cup. Sara Teasdale. 6531-7
"A little while, a little while". Emily Bronte. 6123-0,6244-X,6430-2
"A little while, a little while". The weary task. Emily Bronte. 6828-6
A little while. Horatius Bonar. 6271-7,6219-9,6656-9
A little while. Janice M. Goodrich Doten. 7030-2
A little while. Dante Gabriel Rossetti. 6110-9
The little white angel of Connemaugh. Miller Hageman. 6686-0
The little white beggars. Helen W. Ludlow. 6166-4
The little white cat. Unknown. 6930-4
The little white hearse. James Whitcomb Riley. 6486-8
Little white lily. George Macdonald. 6127-3,6519-8,6133-8,6356-X,6459-0,6502-3,6135-4,6131-1,6456-6,6479-5
The little white sun. Annie Campbell Huestis. 6115-X
"Little wife/If you find". To V –. Louis J. Magee. 7004-3
"The little Will comes naked to its world". The head of wisdom. Randall Jarrell. 6751-4
"Little Willie hung his sister". Little Willie. Unknown. 6902-9
The little wife. Kate Greenaway. 6262-8
Little Willie. Charles Grant. 6518-X
Little Willie. Gerald Massey. 6980-0,6772-7
Little Willie. Unknown. 6902-9
"Little Willie from his mirror". Unknown. 6722-0
Little Willie's hearing. Unknown. 6964-9
"A little wind blew over the sky". Fireflies. Gertrude Alger. 6798-0
Little windows. Charles G. Blanden. 6036-6
Little wit. Unknown. 6134-6
Little woman. Unknown. 6630-5
"A little woman's voice". To V. Louis J. Magee. 7004-3
A little woman. Eugene Field. 6451-5
The little woman. M.C. Barnes. 6576-7
"A little word in kindness spoken". Daniel Clement Colesworthy. 6238-5
The little word. Unknown. 6109-5
A little word. Daniel Clement Colesworthy. 6654-2
Little words. Mary Mapes Dodge. 6004-8
The little words. Edith Daley. 6076-5,6102-8
"A little work, a little play". George Du Maurier. 6109-5
"A little work, a little play". A little. George Du Maurier. 6889-8
The little world. Jan (Joyce A. Maxtone Graham) Struther. 6782-4
Little worries. George Robert Sims. 6923-1
Little wrangles. Edgar A. Guest. 7033-7
A little wrinkled soul of loveliness. William Byron Charles. 6750-6
Little ye, Sister-Nine, fr. Contemplation. Richard Gifford. 6934-7
"Little you know what ghosts are hidden here". Inscription for a garden wall. Doris V. Lecky. 6850-2
The little young lambs. Patrick Reginald Chalmers. 6804-9
Little, Arthur J.
  Christ unconquered, sels. 6282-2
  Invocation, fr. Christ unconquered. 6282-2
Little, Elizabeth Mary
  Life. 6090-0,6090-0;6174-5
  A whisper. 6174-5
Little, Geraldine
  The breakfast table, August 5, 1945 7032-9
  Journal entries written by light through a Princeton... 7032-9
  Mary of Magdala. 6822-7
Little, L.M.
  Life. 7037-X
  Remembrance. 7037-X
Little, Noah
  The fate of Mackay. 6695-X
Little, Philip Francis
  The blue hills. 6244-X

The three poplars. 6244-X,6253-9
To a dead infant. 6096-X,6244-X
"Little, airy, hateful thing". To a mosquito. Unknown. 6983-5
"Little, one, come to my knee!". A wolf story. Bayard Taylor. 6861-8
"A little, tiny, pretty, witty,". Lucretius. 6083-8
Little-girl-two-little-girls. James Whitcomb Riley. 6091-9
The Little-neck clam. Henry Van Dyke. 6961-4
Little-of-dear. Eugene Field. 6949-5
Little-oh-dear. Eugene Field. 6835-9
A little. George Du Maurier. 6889-8
Littlebird, Harold
    After the pow-wow, sel. 7005-1
    A circle begins. 7005-1
    Coming home in March. 7005-1
    Hunter's morning. 7005-1
    If you can hear my hooves. 7005-1
Littledale, Richard Frederick
    The well of Bethlehem. 6848-0
Littlefield, Dorcas
    The gay green fairy. 6249-0
Littlefield, Walter
    The pipe critic. 6453-1
Littlejohn, William
    Mad. 6924-X
"The littles leaves, ah me!". Loves of leaves and grasses. John Vance Cheney. 7041-8
Littlewood, W.E.
    The heart of God. 6065-X
Liturgy of my legs. Pablo (Neftali Ricardo Reyes Basualto) Neruda. 6759-X
Litvinoff, Emmanuel
    All ruin is the same. 6666-6
    The conscripts. 6475-2
    Garrison town. 6666-6
    Lest you forget. 6475-2
    Not revenge...but these. 6475-2
    Poem for the atomic age. 6379-9
    Rededication. 6666-6
    See the wasted cities! 6475-2
    Thoughts on the eve. 6475-2
    War swaggers. 6666-6
Liu Fang-p'ing
    Spring heart-break. Witter Bynner (tr.). 6232-6
Liu, Stephen Shu Ning
    Adultery at a Las Vegas bookstore. 6790-5
    I lie on the chilled stones of the great wall. 6790-5
    My father's martial art. 6790-5
    On Pali lookout. 6790-5
    A pair of fireflies. 6790-5
Live a-humble. Unknown. 6594-5
Live and help live. Edwin Markham. 6337-3
"Live and love". Elizabeth Barrett Browning. 6402-7
"Live and love; live and love". Differences. Valerie Tarver. 7024-8
Live blindly. Trumbull Stickney. 6310-1
Live Christ. John Oxenham. 6144-3;6335-7
Live each day. Johann Wolfgang von Goethe. 6461-2
Live for eternity. Carlos Wilcox. 6752-2
Live for something. Robert Whitaker. 6583-X
"Live here, great heart; and love & dy & kill". The flaming heart, sels. Richard Crashaw. 6933-9
Live in the present. Sarah Knowles Bolton. 6461-2
Live it down. Unknown. 6109-5
"Live not, poore bloome, but perish" Unknown. 6380-2
The live oak. Henry R. Jackson. 6049-8
"A live spring sparkles in the bosky gloom". The spring. Charles Marie Leconte de Lisle. 6873-1
"Live thou in nature! Live". 'Live thou in nature' Richard Watson Gilder. 6995-9
Live thy life. Florence Earle Coates. 6607-0
"Live thy life,/Young and old". The oak. Alfred Lord Tennyson. 6828-6
Live today. Sarah Knowles Bolton. 6337-3
"Live unlamenting though obscure remaining". To J.S. Collis. Ruth Pitter. 6931-2
"'Live while you live', the epicure would say". Philip Doddridge. 6931-2
"Live you by love confined." Cecil Day Lewis. 6317-9,6354-3
"Lived a woman wonderful". South Africa. Rudyard Kipling. 6810-3
Lively hope, and gracious fear. William Cowper. 6814-6
Livermore, C.P.
    A love poem. 6764-6
Livermore, Mary A.
    "With white wings spread she bounded o'er the deep". 6238-5
The Liverpool packet. Unknown. 6732-8
Liverpoor girls. Unknown. 6258-X
Lives. Cyril Dabydeen. 6790-5
"Lives nobly ended make the twilights long". Twilights. Benjamin Franklin Taylor. 6815-4
"Lives of great men all remind us". Henry Wadsworth Longfellow. 6109-5
"Lives of great men all reming us". Life. Henry Wadsworth Longfellow. 6820-0
"Lives there a man whose sole delights". To Lady Fleming. William Wordsworth. 6867-7
The lives we invite to flower among us flower beyond us. Wendy Battin. 6900-2
Livesay, Dorothy
    The ancestors. 6767-0
    The fallow mind. 6021-8
    Poem ("Nights of armor"). 6081-1
    Prelude for spring. 6021-8,6446-9,6081-1
Livesay, Florence Randal
    Butterfly weed - Indian fire. 6115-X
    Chovronja-the pig. 6797-2
    Cowbells at midnight. 6797-2
    The golden touch. 6797-2
    In the public ward. 6115-X
    Pansy royal. 6796-4
    Tim, the fairy. 6115-X
    Violin calls. 6115-X
    The well-brought-up dog. 6797-2
Livesay, Florence Randal (tr.)
    Khustina - the kerchief. Unknown (Ukrainian), 6115-X
Livezey, Herman
    Chi Lien Chang. 6249-0
    Magnolia tree. 6249-0
    Rain on a tin roof. 6249-0
Living. Emma Hally Hammond. 6799-9
Living. Rin Ishigaki. 6803-0
Living. Harold Monro. 6209-1
Living. Daisy Covin Walker. 6799-9
"Living alone in a catamaran". The fish's wish. Carolyn Wells. 6882-0
A living and a dead faith. William Cowper. 6814-6
"Living and dying, hoping and despairing". Elegy. Frederic Prokosch. 6389-6
Living bread. Eva Weaver Sefton. 6065-X
Living by faith. Phoebe Cary. 6969-X
The living Christ. Toyohiko Kagawa. 6027-7
"Living child or pictured cherub". A mother showing the portrait of her child. Jean Ingelow. 6940-1
The living dead. Ralph Chaplin. 6880-4
The living dead. Helena Coleman. 6796-4
The living dead. Frank Lebby Stanton. 7001-9
The living epitaph. Berton Braley. 6085-4,6303-9
The living God. Charlotte Perkins Stetson Gilman. 6303-9, 6730-1
The living god. Oracle of Serapis. 6435-3
Living I shall live. Daniel Berrigan. 6839-1
Living in the world. Alan Chong Lau. 6790-5
The living line. Harold Begbie. 7031-0
The living lost. William Cullen Bryant. 6219-9
The living lustres. Horace Smith. 6802-2
The living present. Alice Cary. 6969-X
The living ray. Laban Thomas Johnston. 6316-0
The living root. Willard Johnson. 6070-6
Living stones. Unknown. 6925-8
The living temple. Oliver Wendell Holmes. 6473-6,6600-3, 6730-1,6288-1,6121-4,6300 ,6304-7
The living temple. Oliver Wendell Holmes. 6126-5
The living tithe. Mabel Munns Charles. 6144-3
Living unto Thee. John Ellerton. 6303-9
Living water. Madame De la Mothe Guion. 6814-6
Living water. Ruth M. Williams. 6065-X

LIVING

Living waters. Ethel M. Feuerlicht. 6847-2
Living waters. Caroline Spencer. 6302-0;6385-3
"Living, thou dost not live", sels. Oliver Wendell Holmes. 6601-1
The living. Marie de L. Welch. 6628-3
Livingston, E. May
  Realization. 6894-4
Livingston, Elaine M.
  I thank thee, God. 6799-9
Livingston, Phyllis
  Prayer for the little'un. 6750-6
Livingston, Robert
  Planting. 6338-1
Livingston, S.T.
  At church. 6116-8
  Hidden. 6116-8
Livingston, Thomas B.
  The blessed trail. 6799-9
Livingston, William
  Hail, wedlock! 6719-0
  In cherry lane. 6292-X
  The wife. 6077-3
Livingstone. Francis Brooks. 6274-1
Livingstone, Sir Richard (tr.)
  The power of love. Sophocles, 6435-3
Livingstone, Tristam
  The letter-burning. 6799-9
Livinston, Georgianna
  At the Cafe de la Paix. 6906-1
  Desire. 6906-1
  Joys. 6906-1
  Night to dawn. 6906-1
  Question. 6906-1
  To - ("I want"). 6906-1
  To - (2). 6906-1
Livinston, William
  Ireland weeping. Christopher M. ("Hugh MacDiarmid") Grieve (tr.). 6845-6
  Message to the bard. Christopher M. ("Hugh MacDiarmid") Grieve (tr.). 6845-6
Livy
  "As soon as woman begins to be ashamed". 6083-8
"Livy, thou shouldst be living at this hour". Unknown. 6847-2
Lixey. Unknown. 6824-3
Liz. Robert Buchanan. 6934-7
A Liz-town humorist. James Whitcomb Riley. 6281-4
Liza Ann's lament. Mary Flammer. 6675-5
"The lizard sat on my finger". Grey him. Paul Mariah. 6870-7
The lizard. Edwin Markham. 6510-4
Lizie Lindsay. Unknown. 6055-2,6056-0,6185-0
Lizie Wan. Unknown. 6185-0
Lizzie. Helen B. Cruickshank. 6269-5
Lizzie. Eugene Field. 6949-5
Lizzie. Robert C.V. Meyers. 6920-7
Lizzie and I are one. Unknown. 6916-9
Lizzie Borden. Unknown. 6089-7
Lizzie Lindsay. Unknown. 6180-X,6518-X
The llama. Hilaire Belloc. 6089-7
Llewellyn and his dog. Robert Southey. 6502-3
Llewellyn and his dog. William Robert Spencer. 6242-3,6290-3
Llewellyn, Karl N.
  Jonathan Smith. 6594-5
Llewelyn's chariot. Vernon Watkins. 6360-8
Llewelyn, Mrs. M.C. (tr.)
  The Saxons of Flint. Lewys Glyn Cothi, 6528-7
Llorens, David
  A resonant silence. 7024-8
  Wayward child. 7024-8
Lloyd, A.L. (tr.)
  Fable. Alfred Jarry, 6343-8
  The smoked herring. Charles Cros, 6343-8
Lloyd, Alfred H.
  Modulation. 6045-1
Lloyd, Anne
  Delphiniums. 6232-6
  The treetop child. 7019-1
  Two powers. 6979-7

Lloyd, D.M. (tr.)
  On Christians, mercy will fall. Unknown (Welsh), 6528-7
Lloyd, Elizabeth
  A holiday acrostic. 6268-7
  Milton's prayer of patience. 6406-X,6304-7
Lloyd, Henry Demarest
  The new church, fr. 'Man the social creator' 6954-1
Lloyd, J. William
  Anywhere, nowhere. 6799-9
Lloyd, Robert
  The critic's rules. 6932-0
  The milkmaid. 6133-8
  Spirit of contradiction. 6787-5
  To Chloe. 6934-7
LLoyd, W.
  A song without a name. 6453-1
Lloyd, William
  A reflection on the course of human life. 6528-7
Lluellyn, Martin
  Cock-throwing. 6563-5
Llwelyn-Williams, Alun (tr.)
  Ystrad fflur. T. Gwynn Jones, 6528-7
Llyn-y-dreiddiad-vrawd (The pool of the living friar) Thomas Love Peacock. 6092-7,6518-X
Llyn-y-dreiddiad-vrawd, the pool of the diving...sels. Thomas Love Peacock. 6427-2
Llynn, Evana
  Conscience. 6906-1
  Disguise. 6906-1
  Handkerchief song. 6906-1
  Sonnet ("I shall"). 6906-1
  Tryst. 6906-1
  Velvet dust. 6906-1
  Wishes for him. 6906-1
Llywarc's Hen
  The gorwynion. 6873-1
  The tercets of Llywarc'h. 6873-1
Llywelyn-Williams, Alun
  When I was young. Gwyn Williams (tr.). 6528-7
"Lo from our loitering ship a new land...",fr.Iceland. William Morris. 6123-0
"Lo! Fancy from her magic realm". Unknown. 6902-9
Lo! He comes, with clouds descending. Thomas Olivers. 6219-9
"Lo! He would lift the burden" William Dudley Foulke. 6995-9
"Lo! all in silence, all in order stand". Books, fr. The library. George Crabbe. 6932-0
"Lo! here is our comrade - he's racing along". The treacherous maid of the mill. Johann Wolfgang von Goethe. 6948-7
"Lo! here the gentle lark...", fr. Venus and Adonis. William Shakespeare. 6328-4,6726-3,6125-7
"Lo! Lord, I sit in thy wide space." George Macdonald. 6225-3
"Lo! here we come a-reaping, a-reaping". Song ("Lo! here"). George Peele. 6436-1
"Lo! how much grander for a human being". Better walk than ride. Unknown. 6787-5
"Lo! I must tell a tale of chivalry". Specimen of an induction to a poem. John Keats. 6828-6
"Lo! in corruption's lumber-room". The fate of a broom: an anticipation. Thomas Love Peacock. 6874-X
"Lo! in the vales, where wandering rivulets...". A morning scene. John Leyden. 6980-0
Lo! new-born Jesus. Christina Georgina Rossetti. 6747-6
"Lo! one wayfaring on a devious track". The life mask. Virginia Donaghe McClurg. 6836-7
"Lo! steadfast and serene". The old man. James Whitcomb Riley. 6892-8
"Lo! the dream of life is o'er". The song of a seraph. Felicia Dorothea Hemans. 6973-8
"Lo! the king's son hath taken prisoner". The hostage. Helen Booth. 6920-7
"Lo! The unbounded sea!". The ship starting. Walt Whitman. 7014-0
"Lo! there he lies, our patriarch poet,dead!". Bryant dead. Paul Hamilton Hayne. 6820-0
"Lo! they come, they come!". Ancient song of victory. Felicia Dorothea Hemans. 6973-8

"Lo! Venice, gay with colour, lights and song". Canada not last. William Douw Lighthall. 7041-8
"Lo! Venice, gay with colour, lights, and song". Canada not last. William Douw Lighthall. 6795-6
"Lo! we answer! see, we come". Union hymn. Unknown. 7009-4
"Lo! where Euphrates, in his tranquil bed". Psalm 137. The Jewish captive. Bible. 6848-0
"Lo! where the gaily vestur'd throng". Ode ("Lo! where the gaily vestur'd throng"). Catherine Maria Fanshawe. 6802-2
"Lo! where the rosy-bosomed hours". Ode to the spring. Thomas Gray. 6934-7
"Lo! where this silent marble weeps". Epitaph on Mrs Jane Clarke. Thomas Gray. 6975-4
"Lo, a silver pulse in a crystal vein". The garden thermometer. Benjamin Franklin Taylor. 6815-4
"Lo, a sonata is a flower enchanted". Music. Karel Selepa. 6763-8
"Lo, as a careful housewife runs to catch". Sonnet 143 ("Lo, as a careful"). William Shakespeare. 6430-2
"Lo, Caesar's legioned army, victor-led". Zenobia. Harry Kemp. 6880-4
Lo, as a dove when up she springs. Alfred Lord Tennyson. 6543-0
"Lo, far on the horizon's verge reclined". Paestum. John Edmund Reade. 6624-0
"Lo, from our loitering ship a new land at...". Iceland first seen. William Morris. 6828-6
"Lo, how I seek and sue to have." Sir Thomas Wyatt. 6584-8
Lo, I am with you always. John Charles Earle. 6144-3
Lo, I am with you always. Martha Snell Nickolson. 6065-X
"Lo, how impatiently upon the tide". Lines to a child on his voyage to France... Henry Ware Jr.. 6752-2
"Lo, I who erst beneath a tree". Prologue. John Gay. 6972-X
"Lo, in storms, the triple-headed". Arakoon. Henry Clarence Kendall. 6997-5
"Lo, in the orient when the gracious light". Sonnet 007 ("Lo, in the orient"). William Shakespeare. 6447-7
"Lo, Joseph dreams his dream again". The League of Nations. Mary Siegrist. 6946-0
"Lo, lilies fade, before the roses show". Song ("Lo, lilies"). William Clerke. 6563-5
"Lo, love again with glancing eyes". Love. Ibycus. 6435-3
"Lo, mine heart indites good matter". Psalm 045. Bible. 6848-0
"Lo, moving o'er chaotic waters". Chants of life. Mathilde Blind. 7037-X
"Lo, my heart, so sound asleep". Triolet ("Lo, my heart"). Justin Huntly McCarthy. 6770-0
"Lo, now is come the joyfull'st feast!" Unknown. 6272-5
"Lo, that small office! there th' incautious..". Sly lawyers. George Crabbe. 6996-7
"Lo, there were giants in old days". Museum piece. Gordon Lawrence. 6979-7
"Lo, thus, as prostrate, 'in the dust I write". The city of dreadful night. James Thomson. 6828-6
"Lo, we are side by side. One dark arm furls". Antony in arms. Robert Buchanan. 6889-8
Lo, what is it to love. Alexander Scott. 6383-7
Lo, where the multitude mourned... Etta May Van Tassel. 6839-1
"Lo, where the war-god leads...dance of death". The dance of death. Unknown (Greek). 7042-6
Lo-yang. Ch'ien Wen-ti. 7039-6
Load. John Hewitt. 6930-4
"A load of furniture once at my doorway stood". A little girl. Frederick A. Hinckley. 6798-0
"Loaded with gallant soldiers". Ready. Phoebe Cary. 6969-X
The loadstone of his love. Charles Wesley. 6065-X
Loafin' time. Ernest Neal Lyon. 6721-2
Loam. Carl Sandburg. 6556-2,6393-4
The loan of a stall. James Leo Duff. 6282-2
The loan. Sabine Baring-Gould. 6848-0
Loarts, George
    Keep hustling. 6109-5
Lob lie-by-the-fire. Walter De La Mare. 6162-1
The lobster quadrille. Charles Lutwidge ("Lewis Carroll")

Lobster salad, fr. The poetical cookbook. Unknown. 6278-4
The lobsters. Unknown. 6278-4
Loca senta situ. Henry Charles Beeching. 6785-9
Local color. Lois Randolph. 6818-9
Local lives, sel. Millen Brand. 6803-0
Locarno. Earl B. Marlatt. 6420-5
Locarno. William Wordsworth. 6749-2
Loch Erroch side. James Tytler. 6086-2
Loch Fiodiag. Angela Gordon. 6253-9
A loch in the hills. Hugh P.F. McIntosh. 6269-5
Loch-long. Samuel Rogers. 6980-0
Lochaber no more. Neil Munro. 6542-2
Lochaber no more. Allan Ramsay. 6219-9,6383-7
'Lochaber no more!' Neil Munro. 7027-2
Lochaber, Nether. See Stewart, Alexander
Lochhead, Marion
    Christmas night. 6337-3
Lochiel's farewell. Unknown. 6859-6
Lochiel's warning. Thomas Campbell. 6302-0,6385-3,6438-8, 6219-9,6606-2,6086-2,6148-6,6271-7,6409-4,6606-2, 6601
"Lochiel, Lochiel, my brave Lochiel". The fate of Charlie. Unknown. 6859-6
Lochinvar's ride. Sir Walter Scott. 6521-X,6566-X
Lochinvar, fr. Marmion. Sir Walter Scott. 6105-2,6134-4, 6136-2,6165-6,6242-3,6271 ,6198-2,6427-2,6473-6,6552-X,6267-9,6219 ,6289-X,6332-2,6512-0,6726-3,6101-X, 6102 ,6302-0,6339-X,6358-6,6370-5,6401-9,6457 ,6479-5,6497-3,6502-3,6534-1,6552-X,6606 ,6625-9,6661-5, 6706-9,6732-8,6239-3,6180
Lochmaben gate. Unknown. 6859-6
The lochmaben harper. Unknown. 6185-0
The lock ascends to heaven, fr. Rape. Alexander Pope. 6637-2
Lock the door, Lariston. James Hogg. 6180-X,6395-0,6086-2
"Lock up, fair lids, the treasure of my heart". Sir Philip Sidney. 6182-6,6187-7
"Lock up, faire liddes, the treasure of my...". Sweet sleepe. Sir Philip Sidney. 6958-4
Locke, Addie I.
    A song ("She sat alone"). 6116-8
Locke, Belle Marshall
    Bessie's first party. 6927-4
Locke, D.R. ("Petroleum V. Nasby")
    Hannah Jane. 6889-8
Locke, John
    Dawn on the Irish coast. 6671-2
    The or dawn on the Irish coast exile's return. 7007-8
Locker-Lampson, Frederick
    The angora cat. 6760-3
    At her window. 6301-2
    Baby mine. 6078-1,6429-9,6321-7
    The bear pit. 6760-3
    Circumstance. 6089-7
    From the fly-leaf of the Rowfant Montaigne. 6297-0
    Geraldine and I. 6661-5
    The jester's plea. 6092-7
    The lord of Butrago. 6385-3
    Loulou and her cat. 6026-9
    Mrs. Smith. 6089-7
    My life is a— 6760-3
    My love is always near. 6102-8
    My mistress's boots. 6122-2,6289-X,6089-7,6652-6
    A nice correspondent. 6429-9,6652-6,6226-1,6321-7,6066-8,6092
    The old cradle. 6233-4
    The old cradle. 6772-7
    On a sense of humor. 6089-7
    On an old muff. 6092-7
    Our photographs. 6026-9
    Piccadilly. 6092-7
    The reason why. 6473-6
    A rhyme of one. 6076-1,6233-4,6429-9,6321-7
    The rose and the ring. 6046-3
    Rotten row. 6026-9
    St. George's, Hanover Square. 6429-9,6321-7
    St. James's Street. 6331-4,6320-X,6439-7,6092-7
    Some ladies. 6089-7

LOCKER-LAMPSON

    A terrible infant. 6089-7,6233-4,6722-0,6026-9,6652-6,
      6633
    To my grandmother. 6122-2,6198-2,6732-8,6543-0,6656-9,
      6046-3,6092-7,6026-9
    To my mistress. 6732-8
    To my mistress's boots. 6092-7
    Unfortunate Miss Bailey. 6802-2
    The unrealised ideal. 6198-2,6301-2,6383-7,6250-4
    The widow's mite. 6097-8,6233-4,6627-5,6214-8,6656-9,
      6737
    Zara's ear-rings. 6385-3
Locket for the heart. Leslie Jones. 6979-7
Lockhart (atr), John Gibson
    Jury trial in the days of Edward I. 6878-2
Lockhart (pseud.), Lucia
    Verses to Mary. 6324-1
Lockhart, Arthur John
    Frost-work. 7041-8
    Guilt in solitude. 7041-8
    Icicle drops. 6795-6
    The vale of the Gaspereau, fr. Gaspereau. 6795-6
Lockhart, Burton W.
    Life's nobles heights. 7041-8
    Song ("Slope"). 7041-8
Lockhart, John Arthur
    Service. 6796-4
Lockhart, John Gibson
    The avenging childe. 6344-6
    Bavieca. 7010-8
    Bernardo and Alphonso. 6242-3,6403-5
    Beyond. 6337-3
    The broadswords of Scotland. 6302-0,6219-9
    Captain Paton's lament. 6960-6
    Captain Paton. 6787-5
    Captain Paton's lament. 6180-X
    Lines ("When youthful faith"). 6046-3
    "My ornaments are arms". 6187-7
    When youthful faith had fled. 6934-7
Lockhart, John Gibson (tr.)
    The admiral Guarinos. Unknown (Spanish), 6757-3
    The avenging childe. Unknown (Spanish), 6757-3
    The avenging childe. Unknown (Spanish), 6676-3
    Bavieca. Unknown (Spanish), 6757-3
    Bernardo and Alphonso. Unknown (Spanish), 6757-3
    Bridal of Andalla. Unknown (Spanish), 6438-8,6219-9
    The bridal of Andalla. Unknown (Spanish), 6757-3
    The bull-fight of Gazul. Unknown (Spanish), 6757-3
    The captive knight and the blackbird. Unknown (Spanish),
      6757-3
    The Cid and the five Moorish kings. Unknown (Spanish),
      6757-3
    The Cid and the leper. Unknown (Spanish), 6757-3
    The Cid's courtship. Unknown (Spanish), 6757-3
    The Cid's wedding. Unknown (Spanish), 6757-3
    The complaint of the Count of Saldana. Unknown
      (Spanish), 6757-3
    Count Alarcos and the infanta Solisa. Unknown (Spanish),
      6757-3
    Count Arnaldos. Unknown (Spanish), 6757-3
    The death of Don Pedro. Unknown (Spanish), 6757-3
    The death of Queen Blanche. Unknown (Spanish), 6757-3
    The death vow of Don Alonzo of Aguilar. Unknown
      (Spanish), 6757-3
    The departure of King Sebastian. Unknown (Spanish),
      6757-3
    Dragut, the corsair. Unknown (Spanish), 6757-3
    The escape of Count Fernan Gonzalez. Unknown (Spanish),
      6757-3
    The escape of Gayferos. Unknown (Spanish), 6757-3
    The excommunication of the Cid. Unknown (Spanish), 6757-
      3
    The flight from Granada. Unknown (Spanish), 6757-3
    The funeral of the Count of Saldana. Unknown (Spanish),
      6757-3
    Garci Perez de Vargas. Unknown (Spanish), 6757-3
    Garcia Perez de Vargas. Unknown (Spanish), 6438-8,6126-
      5
    Juliana. Unknown (Spanish), 6757-3
    The King of Aragon. Unknown (Spanish), 6757-3
    Lady Alda's dream. Uknown (Spanish), 6757-3

    The lady of the tree. Unknown (Spanish), 6757-3
    The lamentation for Celin. Unknown (Spanish), 6757-3,
      7039-6
    The lamentation of Don Roderick. Unknown (Spanish),
      6757-3
    The lord of Butrago. Unknown (Spanish), 6424-8
    The Lord of Butrago. Unknown (Spanish), 6757-3
    The maiden tribute. Unknown (Spanish), 6757-3
    The march of Bernardo del Carpio. Unknown (Spanish),
      6757-3
    Melisendra. Unknown (Spanish), 6757-3
    The Moor Calaynos. Unknown (Spanish), 6757-3
    The murder of the master. Unknown (Spanish), 6757-3
    The penitence of Don Roderick. Unknown (Spanish), 6757-
      3
    The pounder. Unknown (Spanish), 6757-3
    The proclamation of King Henry. Unknown (Spanish), 6757-
      3
    Serenade. Unknown (Spanish), 6757-3
    The seven heads. Unknown (Spanish), 6757-3
    Song for the morning of St. John the Baptist. Unknown
      (Spanish), 6757-3
    The song of the galley. Unknown (Spanish), 6757-3
    Valladolid. Unknown (Spanish), 6757-3
    The vengeance of Mudara. Unknown (Spanish), 6757-3
    The vow of Reduan. Unknown (Spanish), 6757-3
    The wandering knight's song. Unknown (Spanish), 6125-7
    The wandering knight's song. Unknown (Spanish), 6757-3
    The wedding of the Lady Theresa. Unknown (Spanish),
      6757-3
    Ximena demands vengeance. Unknown (Spanish), 6757-3
    The young Cid. Unknown (Spanish), 6757-3
    Zara's ear-rings. Unknown (Spanish), 6385-3
    Zara's ear-rings. Unknown (Spanish), 6757-3
    The Zegri's bride. Unknown (Spanish), 6757-3
Lockhead, Marion
    Nox est perpetua. 6317-9
The **lockless** door. Robert Frost. 6345-4
Locklin, Gerald
    The jungle book. 6998-3
    Peanuts. 6792-1
Lockout Mountain, 1863 - Beutelsbach, 1880. George L.
    Catlin. 6791-3
Locksley Hall. Alfred Lord Tennyson. 6302-0,6385-3,6122-2,
    6271-7,6657-7,6726 ,6370-5,6473-6,6198-2,6604-6,6655-
    0,6732 ,6542-2,6660-7,6196-6,6430-2,6560-0,6450 ,
    6149-0,6461-2,6110-9,6102-8,6219-9,6438
Locksley hall fifty years after, sel. Alfred Lord
    Tennyson. 6954-1
Locksley Hall sixty years after. Alfred Lord Tennyson.
    6657-7,6655-0
Locksley hall, sel. Alfred Lord Tennyson. 7014-0
Locksley hall, sel. Alfred Lord Tennyson. 6954-1
Locksley hall, sels. Alfred Lord Tennyson. 6934-7
Locksley Hall, sels. Alfred Lord Tennyson. 6123-0,6420-5,
    6088-9
Lockung. Count Joseph von Eichendorff. 6252-0
Lockwood, De Witt Clinton
    The landlord's visit. 6918-5
Lockwood, DeWitt C.
    The landlord's visit. 6744-1
Lockwood, Eleanor Stanley
    Modern lullaby. 6750-6
    Temperament. 6750-6
Lockwood, Jane E.W.
    A tribute to music. 6799-9
Lockwood, William A.
    Limerick:"..trim maiden named Wood." 6308-X
Locock, C.D. (tr.)
    A peasant's garden. Anders Osterling, 6649-6
    A peasant's garden. Andras Osterling, 6649-6
Locomotion. Dawad Philip. 6899-5
The **locomotive** dragon-hippogriff. Vachel Lindsay. 6206-7
The **locomotive** to the little boy. Benjamin R.C. Low. 6607-
    0
The **locomotive.** Emily Dickinson. 6891-X
The **locomotive.** Unknown. 6215-6
Locomotives. Mary Pollard Tynes. 6270-9
The **locust** cloud. Robert Southey. 6980-0
"The **locust** drones along the drowsy noon". Bush goblins.

H.M. Green. 6784-0
The **locust** hunt. Philip Murray. 6388-8
"**Locust,** locust, playing a flute". The coyote and the locust. Unknown (Zuni Indian). 7039-6
The **locust.** Leonora Speyer. 6034-X
The **locvsts,** or apolyonists, sels. Phineas Fletcher. 6562-7
Lodge, George Cabot
    Day and dark. 6754-9
    Death. 7007-8
    Essex. 6762-X
    Exordium. 6310-1
    Primavera. 6338-1
    Song ("Out of one heart..."). 6762-X
    A song of the wave. 6833-2
    The song of the wave. 6762-X
    Trumbull Stickney. 6310-1
Lodge, Thomas
    Armistice. 6436-1
    Beauty, alas, where wast thou born. 6182-6
    A blith and bonny country lass. 6026-9
    Carpe diem, fr. Robert, second duke of Normandy. 6436-1
    The contents of the scedule... 6586-4
    The deceitful mistress. 6827-8
    Do me right, and do me reason. 6827-8
    Down a down, fr. Rosalynde. 6328-4
    "The earth, late chok'd with showers". 6181-8;6182-6;6586-4
    Fair Rosalynd. 6250-4
    The fair shepherdess. 6383-7
    A fancy. 6182-6;6436-1;6315-2;6436-1
    Fidelity. 6436-1
    "First shall the heavens want starry light". 6181-8;6328-4
    For pity, pretty eyes, surcease. 6182-6
    The harmony of love. 6189-3
    Her rambling. 6315-2;6436-1
    A lament in spring. 6191-5
    Love. 6383-7
    Love and Phillis. 6191-5
    "Love guards the roses of thy lips". 6187-7;6182-6
    "Love in my bosom like a bee". 6181-8;6187-7
    Love's protestation. 6022-6
    Love's wantonness. 6827-8
    Love's witchery. 6182-6
    A lover's vow. 6830-8
    Melancholy. 6436-1
    Montanus' sonnet. 6191-5
    "My mistress when she goes". 6187-7
    "My Phillis hath the morning sun". 6181-8
    "Not causeless were you christen'd, gentle flowers". 6181-8
    "O shady vales, O fair enriched meads" 6182-6
    Ode ("Now I find"). 6436-1;6586-4;6182-6
    Of Rosalynd. 6489-2
    Old Damon's pastoral. 6436-1;6586-4
    On Phillis' sickness. 6191-5
    Phillis. 6315-2,6436-1,6182-6,6191-5,6250-4,6022
    Phillis, sels. 6586-4
    "Pluck the fruit and taste the pleasure." 6181-8,6182-6
    A poet's vow. 6191-5
    A poet;s vow. 6191-5
    A praise of Rosalind. 6830-8
    Rosader's second sonnetto, fr. Golden legacie. 6328-4
    Rosader's sonnet. 6436-1
    Rosalind. 6182-6,6302-0,6385-3,6317-9,6246-6,6438-8, 6737-9
    Rosalind's complaint. 6302-0,6385-3,6543-0
    Rosalind's description. 6189-3,6436-1,6189-3
    Rosalind's madrigal. 6219-9,6122-2.6732-8,6198-2,6182-6, 6186-9,6315 ,6099-4,6436-1,6328-4,6208-3,6586-4,6189-3,6174-9,6194-X,6026-9,6652-6,6219-9,6301-2
    Rosalind's song. 6830-8
    Rosaline. 6935-5
    The rose. 6436-1
    The solitary shepherd's song. 6191-5
    Sonetto. 6586-4
    Song ("Now I see"). 6315-2
    Sonnet ("I feele"). 6482-5
    Sonnet ("O shady vales"). 6436-1

    Spring and melancholy. 6099-4
    To love. 6934-7
    To love. 6102-8
    To Phyllis. 6934-7
    To Phyllis, the fair sheperdess. 6153-2
    "When I admire the rose". 6181-8
    Whilst youthful sports are lasting. 6189-3
The **lodge,** fr. The lady of the lake. Sir Walter Scott. 6049-8
Lodged. Robert Frost. 6102-8,6232-6,6070-6,6012-9,6076-5
Lodging with the old man of the stream. Po Chu-I. 7039-6
Lodgings for single gentlemen. George Colman the Younger. 6787-5,6760-3,6064-1
"**Loe,** when backe mine eye" Thomas Campion. 6794-8
Loeb, Elizabeth Vera
    Song ("I gave my love..."). 6847-2
Loeb, Oscar
    Prayer of the satirist. 6936-3
The **Loehrs** and the Hammonds. James Whitcomb Riley. 6128-1
"**Loevedy,** ic thonke thee". Thanks and a plea to Mary. Unknown. 6881-2
Loewen (atr), Arnulf
    O sacred head, now wounded. Paul Gerhardt & J.W.Alexander (tr.). 6337-3
<u>**Loffins, Caspar Friedrich**</u>
    The good rich man. James Abraham Martling (tr.). 6952-5
"A **loft** with a ruckle of twisted rafters...". Dead man's cottage. J.H. Knight-Adkin. 7027-2
A **loftier** peace. John Addington Symonds. 6337-3,6386-1
A **loftier** race. John Addington Symonds. 6879-0
A **loftier** race. John Addington Symonds. 6954-1
Lofton, Blanche DeGood
    Scrap iron...for the Yen Maru. 6750-6
    Skyline trails. 6750-6
"**Lofty** and enduring is...monument I've reared". To Melopomene. Horace. 6949-5
Lofty faith. Unknown. 6407-8
"A **lofty** ship from Salcombe came". The pirate of high Barbary. Unknown. 6833-2
"**Lofty** vision of thornless sleep". Heads and tails. Claudia Lars. 6759-X
Logan at Peach Tree Creek. Hamlin Garland. 6946-0
Logan braes. Robert Burns. 6365-9,6545-7
Logan braes. John Mayne. 6180-X,6198-2,6086-2
Logan braes, sels. John Mayne. 6934-7
Logan, John
    Bird on a rock. 6966-5
    The braes of Yarrow. 6180-X,6086-2,6219-9,6438-8,6246-6
    The cuckoo. 6127-3,6808-1
    Dawn and a woman. 6803-0
    Moor swan. 6966-5
    Ode to the cuckoo. 6133-8
    Spirit bird. 6966-5
    Three poems on Morris Graves' paintings, sels. 6966-5
    "Thy braes were bonny." 6302-0;6385-3
    To the cuckoo. 6102-8,6250-4,6219-9,6301-2,6302-0,6385-3,6481-7,6597-X,6600-3,6385-3
    Yarrow stream. 6600-3
Logan, John Daniel
    Brock: valiant leader. 6115-X
    Cartier: dauntless discoverer. 6115-X
    Champlain: first Canadian. 6115-X
    The heavenly runaway. 6797-2
    Heliodore fled. 6433-7
    Laval: noble educator. 6115-X
    The over-song of Niagara. 6115-X
    Rainbow row in heaven. 6797-2
    Renouncement. 6433-7
    A soldier's shrines. 6796-4
    <u>Winifred Waters. 6115-X</u>
Logan, John E. ("Barry Dane")
    A blood-red ring hung round the moon. 6274-1,6656-9
    'The Injun'. 6795-6
    The nor'west courier. 6795-6
    The squaw's lament. 6433-7
Logan, Josephine Hancock
    Anathema. 6789-1
    The grimace of death. 6789-1
    Love's withery. 6789-1
    The matriarch. 6789-1

The old skipper. 6789-1
What saw I upon the desert's floor. 6789-1
Logau, Friedrich von
Retribution. Henry Wadsworth Longfellow (tr.). 6302-0;6385-3;6337-3
The **logger**. Robert Service. 6159-1
Logic. Calvin Murry. 6870-7
Logic. Unknown. 6089-7,6466-3,6652-6
The **logic** of Hudibras. Samuel Butler. 6302-0;6385-3
Logical English. Unknown. 6089-7
A **logical** story--the deacon's masterpiece... Oliver Wendell Holmes. 6102-8,6076-5,6300-4
Logicians. Samuel Butler. 6278-4
The **logicians** refuted. Oliver Goldsmith. 6200-8
The **logicians**. Thomas Hood. 6974-6
Logie o' Buchan. George Halket. 6086-2
Logie of Buchan. Unknown. 6180-X
Logos. Herbert Read. 6985-1
Logos. George William ("A.E.") Russell. 6780-8
Lohengrin. Barbara Henderson. 7019-1
Loines, Russell Hillard
On a magazine sonnet. 6089-7;6501-5
"Scorn not the sonnet...". 6289-X
Loiselle, Leon
Daybreak over the hall of fame. 6799-9
"**Loitering** with a vacant eye" Alfred Edward Housman. 6828-6
Lok, Henry
"It is not Lord the sound of many words". 6586-4
"Words may well want, both inke and paper faile". 6586-4
Lokanatha. Unknown (Newari) 7013-2
Loki bound. Louise Alexander Alexander. 6021-8
"**Lokk** out! Look out!". Jack Frost. Cicely E. Pike. 6937-1
Lokk to the blowing rose about us, fr. Rubaiyat. Omar Khayyam. 7039-6
Lola wears lace. Helen Birch-Bartlett. 6037-4
Lollai, lollai, litil child. Unknown. 6095-1
"**Lollay**, lollay, little child, why wepestou...". An adult lullaby. Unknown. 6881-2
Lollingdon Downs: XV. John Masefield. 6879-0
Lollocks. Robert Graves. 6125-7
"**Lolo** died yesterday" Cyn. Zarco. 6790-5
Lom, Iain. See MacDonald, John
Lomax, John
Killed in action. 6800-6
They held the wood. 6800-6
Lomax, John A.
Cow-puncher's song. 6711-5
The cowboy's life. 6891-X
A home on the range. 6465-5
They held the wood. 6224-5
Whoopee ti yi yo, git along, little dogies. 6891-X
Lomin, M.
"Then, too, I love thee". 6238-5
LonCoke, Eunice Mildred
Silver swans. 6761-1
London. William Blake. 6086-2,6152-4,6208-3,6378-0,6150-8,6125 ,6491-4,6645-3,6250-4
London. John Davidson. 6477-9,6656-9
London. William Dunbar. 6934-7
London. Francis Stewart Flint. 6872-3
London. Samuel Johnson. 6245-8
London. Irene Rutherford McLeod. 6653-4
London. Alan Alexander Milne. 6783-2
London. Peter Anthony Motteux. 6563-5
London. John Nichol. 7015-9
London. T.P. Cameron ("Tipcuca") Wilson. 6653-4
London ("The shadowy slender footfalls of the past"). Esther Alida Phillips. 6331-4
"**London** Journal said some three years since". An invention. Charles Godfrey Leland. 6983-5
London beautif l. Richard Le Gallienne. 6331-4,6439-6
London bells. Josephine Young Case. 6761-1
London bells. Unknown. 6724-7,6125-7
The **London** Bobby. Arthur Guiterman. 6331-4,6439-6
London Bridge. Daniel I. Gross. 6799-9
London Bridge. Unknown. 6459-0,6466-3,6262-8,6125-7
London bridge. Frederic Edward Weatherley. 6656-9
London bridge; or, capital and labor. James Abraham Martling. 6952-5
London churches. Richard Monckton Milnes; 1st Baron Houghton. 6302-0,6385-3,6737-9
A **London** clock. Unknown. 6466-3
London during plague. George Wither. 6958-4
London feast. Ernest Rhys. 6656-9
London fog. Henry Luttrell. 6134-6
London girl. Louise Snodgrass. 6906-1
A **London** idyll. Arthur Hugh Clough. 6123-0
A **London** idyll. John Presland. 6653-4
London is a fine town. Unknown. 6157-5
The **London** lackpenny [or, lyckpenny, or, lackpenny]. John Lydgate. 6200-8,6198-2,6245-8,6193-1
London lickpenny. Unknown. 6157-5,6125-7,6636-4
London literature and society, fr. Canto XI. George Gordon, 6th Baron Byron. 6110-9
London night. Kathleen Raine. 6379-9
The **London** prentice. Unknown. 6157-5
London river. Frederic Edward Weatherley. 6639-9
London sad London. Unknown. 6933-9
"**London** shall perish - arch and tower and wall". Lines to a dictator. Mary Sinton Leitch. 6761-1
London snow. Robert Bridges. 6154-0,6186-9,6315-2,6395-0, 6473-6,6477 ,6125-7,6135-2,6487-6,6507-4,6464-7,6655
The **London** sparrows. Edward Verrall Lucas. 6018-8
London spring. Lilian Sauter. 7023-X
London squares. Osbert Sitwell. 6872-3
London to Paris. Ronald Gorell Barnes, Lord Gorell. 6723-9
London to Paris by air. Ronald Gorell Barnes, Lord Gorell. 6228-8,6723-9
London town. John Masefield. 6154-0,6427-2,6631-3
London town. Unknown. 6466-3
London troops. Unknown. 7031-0
London tube station. Nancy Head. 6761-1
London types, sels. William Ernest Henley. 6507-4
London under bombardment. Greta Briggs. 6427-2
The **London** University. Richard Harris ("Thomas Ingoldsby") Barham. 6278-4
London voluntaries. William Ernest Henley. 6507-4
London voluntaries, sels. William Ernest Henley. 6301-2
London, 1802. William Wordsworth. 6122-2,6198-2,6385-3, 6332-2,6527-9,6625 ,6645-3,6660-7,6371-3,6199-0,6086-2,6192 ,6250-4,6110-9,6196-6,6430-2,6560-0,6646-1, 6737-9,6723-9,6246-6,6138-9,6154-0,6289-X,6473-6, 6536-8,6604-
London, 1940. Alan Alexander Milne. 6337-3;6224-5
London, 1940. Alan Rook. 6475-2
London, after midnight. Henry Ellison. 7015-9
London, August. Charles Ould. 6800-6
London, fr. Don Juan. George Gordon, 6th Baron Byron. 6439-6
London, fr. The human image. William Blake. 6125-7
"**London**, my beautiful". London. Francis Stewart Flint. 6872-3
London, sels. Samuel Johnson. 6198-2,6195-0,6637-2
"**London**, thou art of townes a per se". London. William Dunbar. 6934-7
London, thou hast accused me. Henry Howard, Earl of Surrey. 6430-2
"**London**, to wit: Hereby complains". Craft vs. Boite. R.H. Thornton. 6878-2
A **Londoner** in New England, 1941. Jan (Joyce A. Maxtone Graham) Struther. 6761-1
The **Londoner** in the country. Richard Church. 6257-1
The **Londoner's** chariot. Wilfrid Thorley. 6777-8
Londroche, A. Phil
Reads landing. 6342-X
"**Lone** and forgotten". The lonely. George William ("A.E.") Russell. 7039-9
"**Lone** and forgotten/Through a long sleeping". The lonely. George William Russell. 6930-4
The **lone** biker. R. Wayne Hardy. 6870-7
Lone dog. Irene Rutherford McLeod. 6044-7,6332-2,6478-7, 6102-8,6639-9
Lone gentleman. Pablo (Neftali Ricardo Reyes Basualto) Neruda. 6759-X
The **lone** hand. Cicely Fox Smith. 7031-0
"**Lone** house shakes, the wild waves leap....The". Storm and calm. Robert Buchanan. 6997-5
"**Lone** in the heart of his continent sleeping". Cecil John

Rhodes. William Blane. 6800-6
"**Lone** in the wilderness, her child and she". Hagar. Hartley Coleridge. 6848-0
The **lone** man. Unknown. 6489-2
"**Lone** mountaineer/Scaling those virgin heights". Aspiration. William Elijah Hunter. 6800-6
"A **lone** peak where/Pine pollen flies". April. Mok-wol Park. 6775-1
Lone places of the deer. Andrew Lang. 6269-5
The **lone** sentry. James Ryder Randall. 6074-9
"**Lone** shadows move". In the wood. William Kean Seymour. 6884-7
The **lone** star of Cuba. David Graham Adee. 7022-1
The **lone** star, fr. Texas. Henry Van Dyke. 6961-4
Lone swan. Rose Mills Powers. 6073-0
The **lone** trail. Robert Service. 6159-1
Lone wolf lament. Tom MacInnes. 6797-2
The **lone** woman. Robert A. Christie. 7031-0
"**Lone**, 'neath San Gabriel and Sierra Madre". The message. James Abraham Martling. 6952-5
"**Lone**, I wander where the pathway glistens" Mikhail Lermontov. 6103-6
"**Lone**, mid the loftier wonders of the past". Euripides. Edward Bulwer-Lytton; Baron Lytton. 6980-0
Lone-land. John Banister Tabb. 6007-2
"The **loneliest** night of all the lonely year". Christmas guests. Lindsay (Cloud) Duncan. 6768-9
"The **loneliest** night of all the year". The Chirstmas guests. Lindsay Duncan. 6924-X
Loneliness. Sylvia Adelman. 6850-2
Loneliness. Ina D. Coolbrith. 6347-0
Loneliness. Edwin Essex. 6096-X,6292-X
Loneliness. Nikolai Gumilev. 6103-6
Loneliness. William Hamilton Hayne. 6632-1
"**Loneliness** is a forlorn bird". Loneliness. Sylvia Adelman. 6850-2
"**Loneliness** leapt in the mirrors, but all week". Departure's girlfriend. W. S. Merwin. 6803-0
"**Loneliness** lies just there beyond heartbreak". Soliloquy. Dorothy C. Parrish. 7024-8
"The **loneliness** of it all dampens". Alone. Jamie Tobias. 6883-9
Loneliness, fr. The Hill Wife. Robert Frost. 6102-8,6208-3
Lonely. Edgar A. Guest. 7033-7
Lonely. Andre Spire. 7039-6
"**Lonely** and bare and desolate". From Albert to Bapaume. Alec Waugh. 7029-9
"**Lonely** and cold and fierce I keep my way". Gulf stream. Sarah ("Susan Coolidge") Woolsey. 6833-2
"**Lonely** and still are now thy marble halls". The Abencerrage. Felicia Dorothea Hemans. 6973-8
"**Lonely** and wild it rose". The mysterious music of ocean. Unknown. 6752-2,6833-2
The **lonely** bather. Max Eastman. 6880-4
Lonely beauty. Samuel Daniel. 6436-1
The **lonely** bird. Harrison Smith Morris. 6597-X
The **lonely** bird. Felicia Dorothea Hemans. 6973-8
"The **lonely** blood/searches through its halls". For Barbara. Andrew Brooks. 6767-0
"A **lonely** boy, far venturing from home". A storm on the mountains. Charles Harper. 6768-9
The **lonely** bugle grieves. Grenville Mellen. 6102-8,6286-5, 6076-5,6300-4,6396-9,6723
Lonely burial. Stephen Vincent Benet. 6076-5,6102-8,6556-2
The **lonely** child. Ernest Briggs. 6384-5
"A **lonely** child/deserted streets". Alone. Kit Blomer. 6883-9
The **lonely** child. James Oppenheim. 6300-4
The **lonely** Christ. Edward Shillito. 6144-3
The **lonely** crib. Leonard Feeney. 6543-0
The **lonely** dancer. Richard Le Gallienne. 6250-4
The **lonely** death. Adelaide Crapsey. 6556-2
Lonely flowers. John Todhunter. 6383-7
Lonely for the country. Bronwen Wallace. 6767-0
The **lonely** garden. Edgar A. Guest. 6846-4
The **lonely** garden. Virginia Taylor McCormick. 6347-0
The **lonely** god, fr. The hill of vision. James Stephens. 6234-2
"A **lonely** grave above the rock-rimmed sea". Sonnet on a Phoenician tomb. Kerr Rainsford. 6799-9

"**Lonely** I wait, asking the world for you". L'inconnue. Harold Fehrsen Sampson. 6800-6
Lonely harbor. Helen Evelyn Williams. 6799-9
The **lonely** host. Leonie Adams. 6012-9
The **lonely** house. Emily Dickinson. 6467-1
The **lonely** hunter. William ("Fiona Macleod") Sharp. 6628-3
Lonely I go faring'/' Unknown. 7008-6
"**Lonely** is my garden dear." Unknown. 6203-2
The **lonely** isle. Claudian. 7039-6
The **lonely** land. Arthur James Marshall Smith. 6021-8
Lonely Louisa. Unknown. 6058-7
The **lonely** man. Thomas Butler Feeney. 6761-1
The **lonely** man. Edgar A. Guest. 6748-4
"The **lonely** margin of the sea". Charles Mackay. 6997-5
Lonely maturity. Richard Monckton Milnes; 1st Baron Houghton. 6980-0
The **lonely** month. Ruthven Todd. 6379-9
The **lonely** mountain. John Banister Tabb. 6943-6
The **lonely** night. Darius Earl Maston. 6083-8
The **lonely** peak. Victor Hugo. 6351-9
"A **lonely** pond in age-old stillness sleeps". Basho (Matsuo Basho) 7039-6
The **lonely** road. Virna Sheard. 6115-X
"A **lonely** rock uprose above the sea". Growth. Sarah Williams. 7037-X
The **lonely** rose. Philip Bourke Marston. 6965-7
The **lonely** street. William Carlos Williams. 6808-1
The **lonely** tree. Wilfred Wilson Gibson. 6228-8,6509-0,6723-9
The **lonely** unicorn. Frederic Prokosch. 6782-4
The **lonely** woman. M. Forrest. 6784-0
"**Lonely**, lonely lay the hill". As rivers of water in a dry place. Anna Bunston De Bary. 6776-X,6253-9
"**Lonely**, save for a few faint stars, the sky". The little dancers. Laurence Binyon. 6959-2
A **lonely**, swimming bird. Robert P. Tristram Coffin. 7040-X
The **lonely**. George William Russell. 6930-4
The **lonely**. George William ("A.E.") Russell. 7039-6
Lonely? Maybe. Cecil Perkins. 6750-6
Lones to a friend. James Berry Bensel. 6358-6
Lonesome. Arthur S. Blodgett. 6764-6
Lonesome. Paul Laurence Dunbar. 6465-5
A **lonesome** cow-puncher. Unknown. 7007-8
Lonesome dove. Unknown. 6826-X
Lonesome little girl. Unknown. 6713-1
A **lonesome** place. Rollin J. Wells. 6889-8
Lonesome water. Roy Helton. 6628-3
The **lonesome** wave. Hilda Conkling. 6607-0
Long Jr., Doughtry ("Doc")
  Number 20. 7024-8
  Number 25. 7024-8
  Number 28. 7024-8
  Number 4. 7024-8
Long after midnight. Jack Micheline. 6998-3
Long ago. Libbie C. Baer. 6674-4
Long ago. Mrs. L.A. Bradbury. 6268-7
Long ago. Eugene Field. 6004-8
Long ago. Emma Celia & Lizzie J. Rook. 6137-0
"**Long** ago Apollo called to Aristaeus...". The white bees. Henry Van Dyke. 6961-4
"**Long** ago I blazed a trail". The pioneer. Arthur Guiterman. 6861-8
"**Long** ago in fair, old, far-famed Venice". The face divine. Ethelyn Alice Stoddard. 6836-7
"**Long** ago some river-elves were living near...". A tale of the river-elves. Unknown (Algonquin Indian). 6864-2
"**Long** ago, in the young moonlight". Song, fr. Mater. Percy MacKaye. 6897-9
"**Long** ago, when violets were blooming". The leaves) Unknown. 6049-8
The **long** ago. Margaret Wilson McCutchen. 6118-4
The **long** ago. Benjamin Franklin Taylor. 6304-7
"**Long** and final passage over the..height". To Rafael Cansinos Assens. Jorge Luis Borges. 6759-X
"**Long** and hard were the lessons studied...". Arithmetic in life. M. Truesdell Cooper. 6926-6
"**Long** and lone this night to me". Unknown. 6050-1
Long and lovely. Arthur Davison Ficke. 6979-7
"**Long** are the hours the sun is above." Robert Bridges. 6187-7,6317-9,6487-6,6508-2

LONG

"Long as I can call to mind". A childish game. Sir Reinmar von Hagenau. 7039-6
"Long as ever". Unknown. 6364-0
"Long autumn rain;/White mists which choke...". Autumn song. Edward Dowden. 6930-4
"Long betwixt love and fear Phillis tormented". John Dryden. 6562-7
"The long blue river was a painter's stroke". The oarsman. Charles Edward Eaton. 6803-0
"The long canoe". Lullaby ("The long canoe"). Robert Hillyer. 6490-6
"Long centuries ago a holy man". Rheims cathedral. McLandburgh Wilson. 7031-0
"The long day is closing". Parting song. Alice Cary. 6969-X
"The long delight and early". To my mother. Genevieve Taggard. 6761-1
"Long did I toil. John Quarles & Henry F. Lyte. 6337-3
"Long distance is expensive". For Avi killed in Lebanon. Mark Osaki. 6790-5
The long dream. Marie Emilie Gilchrist. 6906-1
"Long ere Kuloskap the master". How Kuloskap granted gifts and favors to many Indians. Unknown (Algonquin Indian). 6864-2
"Long ere the shores of green America". Mon-da-min; or, the romance of maize. Bayard Taylor. 6976-2
"Long expected one and twenty". One and twenty. Samuel Johnson. 6975-4
"Long fed on boundless hopes, O race of man". Anti-desperation. Matthew Arnold. 6947-9
Long feud. Louis Untermeyer. 6012-9
"The long grass burned brown". The prairie on fire. Phoebe Cary. 6969-X
Long guns. Carl Sandburg. 6345-4
"Long had I loved this 'Attic shape',the brede". To Julia Marlowe. Henry Van Dyke. 6961-4
"Long had our dull fore-fathers slept supine". An account of the greatest English poets. Joseph Addison. 6831-6
"Long had Panthea felt love's secret smart". Panthea. John Gay. 6972-X
Long haiku no. 7 Louis Cuneo. 6792-1
"Long has grown my night through the love of one". Bashshar ibn Burd. 6766-2
"Long has that portrait hung there on the wall". In the school assembly hall. G.H. McGaw. 6764-6
Long has the furious priest. William Byrd. 7017-5
"Long hast thou borne the burden of the day". On the death of Stephen Grey, F.R.S. Samuel Johnson. 6975-4
"Long hast thou, friend been absent from...". Manuscript draft of part of the welcome to pope. John Gay. 6972-X
"Long hast thou, fri nd! been absent from Greece. John Gay. 6932-0
"Long hast thou, friend! been absent from thy soil ". Mr. Pope's welcome from Greece, sels. John Gay. 6483-3
"Long haue mine eies gaz'd with delight". A booke of Ayres (X). Thomas Campion. 6794-8
"Long have I heard the rhythm of the sea". Go down, Moses. Sally Bruce Kinsolving. 6979-7
"Long have I lived by the side of the sea". Anticipation. Jonathan Slocum. 6817-0
"Long have I searched the earth for liberty". Sonnet ("Long have I"). Wilfrid Scawen Blunt. 7009-4
"Long have the poets vaunted, in their lays". Old and new. Ella Wheeler Wilcox. 6956-8
"Long have we,safe,time's envious fury scorn'd". To the Reverend Dr. Bentley. Lawrence Eusden. 6867-7
The long hill. Sara Teasdale. 6108-7,6345-4,6034-X
Long I have loved to stroll. T'ao Yuan-Ming. 6125-7
"Long is the day without Usnagh's children". Deirdre's lament. Unknown. 6930-4
"Long is the mountain pheasant's tail". Kaki-no-moto. 6852-9
Long is the night. Robert Burns. 6328-4
Long John Brown and little Mary Bell. William Blake. 6633-X
The long joke. R. T. Smith. 7005-1
"The long langoons lie white and still". Black swans..Murray lagoons, fr. Australian transcripts.

William ("Fiona Macleod") Sharp. 6768-9
The long last mile. Lauchlan MacLean Watt. 6337-3
"Long lay the ocean-paths from man conceal'd". The inspiration, fr. The West Indies. James Montgomery. 6946-0
"Long legs, crooked thighs." Mother Goose. 6452-3
"Long life hath taught me many things & shown". Criticism of life, fr. Hippolytus. Euripides. 6987-8
"Long life to thee, long virtue, long delight". To Sylvia. Alice Meynell. 6955-X
"The long lithe wave/Now white fringed..." Alfred Austin. 6997-5
Long live life. Jacques Baron. 6351-9
"Long live the man whose heart is fresh",fr track news. W.H. Wilson. 6109-5
The long look. Albert Durrant Watson. 6797-2
Long narrow roadway. Kim Maltman. 6767-0
"The long neck makes him a sad creature". Deer. Chun-myung No. 6775-1
Long of Louisiana. Vashti R. Stopher. 6465-5
"Long on Golconda's shore a diamond lay". The value of education. Unknown. 6927-4
Long past Moncada. Muriel Rukeyser. 6391-8
"Long past the age for speaking". Childhood of a scientist. A.F. Moritz. 6767-0
Long person. Gladys Cardiff. 7005-1
"Long plung'd in sorrow, I resign". The joy of the cross. Madame De la Mothe Guion. 6814-6
Long pond. Daniel Wing. 6798-0
"The long red flats stretch open to the sky". Low tide at St. Andrews. Emily Pauline ("Tekahionwake") Johnson. 6837-5
"The long resounding marble corridors...". The hotel. Harriet Monroe. 6897-9
"long resounding marble corridors...The". The hotel. Harriet Monroe. 6808-1
The long road blossoms. Samuel Marshak. 6546-5
The long road west. Henry Herbert Knibbs. 6281-4
The long sermon. Unknown. 6629-1
The long shadow of Lincoln. Carl Sandburg. 6871-5
"A long shot of silver in the dull blue sky". A song for Lindbergh. Mary A. O'Connor. 7019-1
"Long since the sorrows of the nightingales". From generation to generation. John Drinkwater. 7029-9
The long sleep. Simonides. 6879-0
"The long slow swell of the still sea". Moonrise at sea. William ("Fiona Macleod") Sharp. 6997-5
"Long steel grass". Trio for two cats and a trombone, fr. Facade. Edith Sitwell. 7000-0
A long story. Thomas Gray. 6092-7
The long street lifts. Vachel Lindsay. 6206-7
The long street. Donald Davidson. 6808-1
"A long swaying branch". Val d'Annivier. Michael Guttenbrunner. 6769-7
"Long the great God patient waited". The belated Christ. Gertrude Huntington McGiffert. 6838-5
"Long the road on either side". Cotton fever. Fred Ross. 6783-2
"Long the tyrant of our coast". On the capture of the Guerriere. Philip Freneau. 6946-0
"Long thy fair cheek was pale". Eire a ruin. Sliabh Cuilinn. 6858-8
"Long time a child, and still a child, when years". Hartley Coleridge. 6980-0,6380-2
"Long time a child, and still a child...". Sonnet ("Long time"). Hartley Coleridge. 6832-4
Long time ago. Leon Black. 6237-7
Long time ago. Elizabeth Payson Prentiss. 6132-X
Long time ago. Unknown. 6937-1
"A long time ago lived Procrustes. The same". Procrustes' bed. Carlotta Perry. 6919-3
"A long time ago, in a land far away". A Christmas party. Carolyn Wells. 6882-0
A long time ago. Unknown. 6132-X,6547-3,6639-9,6638-0
The long trail. Rudyard Kipling. 6427-2,6732-8,6508-2,6655-0
The long trail. Minnie Mills Neal. 6799-9
Long view. Genevieve Taggard. 6761-1
The long voyage. Malcolm Cowley. 6324-1,6236-9
The long war. Li Po. 6665-8

"Long was the great Figg by...fighting swains". Extempore verses upon a trial of skill...Figg & Sutton. John Byrom. 6932-0
"Long was the great Figg..prize fighting swain". Extempore verses ("Long was"). John Byrom. 6831-6
Long was the road. Nikolai Tikhonov. 6546-5
"Long weeks you have stood in...yielding sand". The border land. Marie L. Moffatt. 6919-3
"A long while ago - you the date must suppose". The Gottinger barber. J.E. Carpenter. 6918-5
"Long while I sought to what I might compare". Sonnet 009 ("Long while"), fr. Amoretti. Edmund Spenser. 6645-3
long while ago<A. Letitia Elizabeth ("L.E.L.") Landon. 6980-0
The long white seam. Jean Ingelow. 6239-3,6737-9,6656-9, 6658-5
"Long years ago (how youth to-day).". A school episode. Emma Shaw. 6923-1
"Long years ago he looked at her...". Incident at Bethlehem. Edgar A. Guest. 6748-4
"Long years ago, in that gum-tree's shade". The proclamation tree. J. Sadler. 6768-9
"Long years ago, two lovely Indian girls". The wizard snake. Unknown (Algonquin Indian). 6864-2
"Long years agone a southern artisan". The story of some bells. Hezekiah Strong. 6918-5
"Long years! it tries the thrilling frame...". The lament of Tasso. George Gordon, 6th Baron Byron. 6980-0, 6945-2,6828-6
Long, D.S.
    "Leaves/early morning". 7018-3
    A poem. 7018-3
    "Two of us". 7018-3
    The warehouse. 7018-3
Long, F.C.
    The bridal feast. 6404-3;6554-6
Long, Haniel
    After a city winter. 6039-0
    At parting. 6033-1
    A book of economics. 6102-8,6076-5
    The cause of this I know not. 6032-3
    Dead men tell no tales. 6032-3;6289-X;6332-2;6501-5
    Girl-athletes. 6038-2
    The herd boy. 6509-0
    His deaths. 6102-8
    History. 6039-0
    Indians. 6396-9
    Letter after a visit. 6808-1
    Navajos. 6396-9
    Song ("Poppies paramour"). 6032-3,6300-4
Long, Howard W.
    On the river. 6919-3
Long, John C.
    The soldier's grave. 6799-9
Long, John D.
    I would, dear Jesus. 6260-1
Long, Lily A.
    His reverie. 6620-8
    The yellow bowl. 6053-6
Long, R.H.
    City of God. 6784-0
    The skylark's nest. 6784-0
    The super-lark. 6784-0
Long, Ray
    Puppy love. 6149-4,6148-6
Long, William J.
    The chimney drummer-boy. 6807-3
Long, William Stapleton
    Charlie Lucas. 6761-1
Long, black line. L. Zack Gilbert. 6178-8
"The long, blue evening brings the golden moon". Visitor. David Morton. 6850-2
"The long, bright day of harvest toil is past". Rizpah. Lucy Blins. 6848-0
"The long, cool curve of evening". Peace: an interlude - 1945. George A. McCauliff. 6839-1
"Long, graceful, curving lines of...beach". New England. Elizabeth Mae Crosby. 6894-4
"A long, green swell/slopes soft to the sea". Chill of the eve. James Stephen. 6930-4

"Long, hatchet face, black hair...". Robert Louis Stevenson. B. Paul Neuman. 6793-X
Long, long ago. Unknown. 6806-5
Long, long ago. Unknown. 6891-X
"Long, long ago I heard a little song". Dulcis memoria. Henry Van Dyke. 6961-4
"Long, long ago in the olden day". Michael's mallet. Margaret Junkin Preston. 6965-7
"Long, long ago the Indians believed..witches". The measuring worm. Unknown (Algonquin Indian). 6864-2
"Long, long ago, and as far away as Norroway". The animals' fair. Carolyn Wells. 6882-0
"Long, long ago, ere yet our race began". A Servian legend. Ella Wheeler Wilcox. 6863-4
"Long, long and dreary is the night". The long sleep. Simonides. 6879-0
The long, long dances. Euripides. 6959-2
"The long, long day, in eons long ago". Love's response. James Abraham Martling. 6952-5
"A long, long sleep, a famous sleep". Emily Dickinson. 6380-2
"Long, O Protesilaus, long shall thy fame...". Antiphilus. 6251-2
"Long, long years ago". Wizard warfare. Unknown (Algonquin Indian). 6864-2
"Long, long, long the trail". Light between the trees. Henry Van Dyke. 6961-4
"Long, subtle-floating, the choir". Daughters of joy. Herbert Trench. 6877-4
Long, too long America. Walt Whitman. 6126-5
The long-ago. Richard Monckton Milnes; 1st Baron Houghton. 6219-9
Long-eared bat. Unknown. 6312-8
The long-felt want. Unknown. 6691-7
"Long-idling spring may come". 'Why, the come in...' Walter De La Mare. 6905-3
Long-legged fly. William Butler Yeats. 6208-3,6210-5
"A long-tailed pig, or a short-tailed pig". Unknown. 6363-2
"The longed-for moment near at hand". Reunion. Lida Bell. 6906-1
"The longed-for summer goes". Now. Walter De La Mare. 6905-3
The longer life the more offence. Sir Thomas Wyatt. 6543-0
"The longer life, the more offence". Upon consideration of the state of this life...death. Unknown. 6830-8
"Longer than thine, than thine". The two Shakespeare tercentaries. Alice Meynell. 6955-X
"Longer to muse." Sir Thomas Wyatt. 6584-8
The longest day, sels. William Wordsworth. 6867-7
The longest journey, fr. Epipsychidion. Percy Bysshe Shelley. 6427-2
Longevity. Robert Service. 6159-1
Longfellow. Craven Langstroth Betts. 6820-0
Longfellow. James Whitcomb Riley. 6820-0
Longfellow. James Whitcomb Riley. 6465-5
Longfellow. Henry Van Dyke. 6961-4
Longfellow's alphabet. Unknown. 66601-1
Longfellow's Minnesota. Gertrude Olson. 6342-X
Longfellow, Henry Wadsworth
    Aftermath. 6333-0
    "Age is oppurtunity". 6109-5
    "All common things, each day's events". 6238-5
    Amalfi. 6624-0,6631-3
    America. 6337-3
    "And in haste the refluent ocean". 6997-5
    "And the night shall be filled with music". 6238-5
    The angel and the child, fr. Jean Reboul. 6772-7
    April. 6047-1
    An April day. 6049-8
    The arrow and the song. 6431-0,6560-0,6135-4,6250-4, 6300-4,6006-4,6102-8,6288-1,6076-5,6304-7,6461 ,6060-1,6623-2,6337-3,6401-9,6501-5,6632 ,6085-4,6605-4, 6479-5,6176-1,6291-1,6486 ,6107-9,6457-4,6104-4,6126-5,6457-4,6639
    The arsenal at Springfield. 6176-1,6481-7,6332-2,6473-6, 6735-2,6240 ,6420-5,6610-0,6560-0,6484-1,6585-6
    The arsenal at Springfield. 6665-8,6250-4,6288-1,6126-5, 6219-9
    Autumn. 6077-3,6558-9,6456-6

LONGFELLOW

Azrael. 6848-0
Azrael. 6396-9
Baby reigns supreme. 6078-1
A ballad of the French fleet. 6473-6,6552-X,6126-5,6484-1
A ballad of the French fleet. 6946-0
The battle of Lovell's pond. 6946-0
"The battle of our life is brief". 6238-5
The beleaguered city. 6641-0,6121-4,6648-8,6288-1,6126-5,6133
The belfry of Bruges. 6331-4,6126-5,6648-8,6288-1,6121-4,6126-5,6439-6,6631-3
The belfy of Bruges, sels. 6288-1
Belisarius. 6077-3,6631-3
The bell of Atri. 6478-7,6498-1,6623-2,6419-1,6510-4,6614
The bells of Lynn. 6006-4,6484-1
The bells of San Blas. 6288-1
Beware. 6083-8,6441-8,6004-8,6560-0,6652-6
The birch canoe, fr. The song of Hiawatha. 6252-0
The birds of Killingworth. 6510-4,6288-1,6458-2,6212-1
Birds of passage. 6753-0
Blessings of peace. 6719-0
Blind Bartimeus. 6144-3;6335-7
The bridge. 6006-4,6732-8,6554-6,6597-X,6142-7,6215 , 6457-4,6457-4,6858-6,6126-5,6304-7,6706-9,6288-1,6560-0
"Build me straight, O worthy master". 66601-1
The builders. 6498-1,6523-6,6337-3,6457-4,6571-6,6126-5,6104-4,6560-0,6288-1
The building of the canoe. 6136-2
The building of the Long Serpent. 6833-2
The building of the ship, sels. 6753-0
The building of the ship, sels. 6258-X,6265-2
The building of the ship. 6049-8,6176-1,6499-X,6457-4,6126-5,6322-5,6250-4,6288-1,6736-0,6121-4
Burial of the Minnisink. 6299-7,6502-3,6126-5,6008-0
Cadenabbia. 6331-4,6624-0,6631-3
Captain Kempthorn, fr. John Endicott. 6382-9
Carillon. 6302-0;6385-3
Castles in Spain. 6331-4,6439-6,6631-3
Catawba wine. 6004-8,6307-1
The challenge of Thor. 6623-2
The challenge of Thor. 6850-2
Challenge to youth, fr. The castle builder. 6337-3
The chamber over the gate. 6632-1,6333-0,6431-0
Charlemagne. 6624-0
Charles D'Orleans, sels. 6047-1
Chaucer. 6121-4,6126-5,6153-2,6300-4,6230-X,6176-1,6333-0,6483-3,6288-1,6431-0
Children. 6456-6,6585-6,6008-0,6288-1,6126-5,6049-8,6233-4,6008-0,6288-1,6126-5
The children of the Lord's supper. 6680-1,6066-8
The children's hour. 6219-9,6321-7,6126-5,6438-8,6288-1,6008-0,6131-1,6135-4,6136-2,6127-3,6014-5,6176-1,6299-7,6429 ,6385-3,6401-9,6478-7,6534-1,6570-8,6230 ,6486-8,6498-1,6356-X,6623-2,6240-7,6302
Chimes. 6431-0
Chorus of Oreades, fr. The masque of Pandora. 6334-9
Christmas bells. 6144-3,6145-7,6272-5,6314-4,6337-3,6465 ,6457-4,6746-8,6457-4,6608-9
Christus, sels. 6144-3;6335-7
Chrysaor. 6006-4
Come back! ye friends. 6085-4
Coplas de manrique, sels. 6144-3;6335-7
The courtship of Miles Standish. 6498-1,6503-1,6732-8,6126-5,6503-1
The crew of the Long Serpent, fr. King Olaf. 6105-2
The cross of snow. 6333-0,6337-3,6300-4,6288-1,6126-5,6641
The Cumberland. 6088-9,6263-6,6126-5,6267-9,6062-5,6113-3,6735-2,6471-X,6552-X,6322 ,6403-5,6484-1,6016-2,6438-8,6470-1,6288
Curfew. 6323-3,6332-2,6692-5,6560-0,6126-5
Dante. 6077-3,6333-0,6536-8,6288-1,6126-5,6371
The day is done. 6934-7
The day is done. 6102-8,6457-4,6654-2,6219-9,6300-4,6513 ,6183-4,6176-1,6014-5,6243-1,6332-2,6498 ,6260-1,6735-2,6337-3,6373-X,6374-8,6527 ,6610-0,6632-1,6304-7,6639-9,6575-9,6457

The day is done. 6934-7
The day is done. 6008-0,6461-2,6560-0,6250-4,6976-5,6104-4,6126-5,6288-1,6723-9,6585-6
Daybreak. 6134-8,6302-0,6385-3,6490-6,6502-3,6597 ,6623-2,6126-5,6421-3
Decoration Day. 6340-3,6574-0
Dedication. 6333-0
The discoverer of the North Cape. 6176-1,6531-4,6396-9,6322-5,6808-1
Divina commedia. 6302-0,6385-3,6483-3,6488-4,6008-0,6461 ,6641-0,6309-8,6126-5,6121-4,6104-4,6250 ,6560-0,6288-1,6371-3,6723-9,6737-9,6513
Divina commedia, sels. 6536-8
"Do thy duty, that is best." 6225-3
A Dutch picture. 6006-4,6105-2,6732-8,6322-5,6467-1,6004-8,6431-0,6114-1
Earth, with her thousand voices, praises God. 6752-2
Elegiac. 6077-3
The embarkation, fr. Evangeline. 6946-0
Emma and Eginhard. 6255-5
The emperor's bird's-nest. 6502-3
The emperors' bird's-nest. 6502-3,6614-3
Endymion. 6006-4,6735-2,6288-1,6126-5
The equinox, fr. Seaweed. 6833-2
The eternal word. 6144-3;6335-7
Evangeline. 6503-1,6673-9,6250-4,6126-5,6094-3
Evangeline in the prairie. 6302-0;6385-3
Evangeline, sels. 6753-0,6208-3,6066-8,6008-0,6288-1,6431-0,6288-1,6484-1,6395-0,6365-9,6732-8,6550-3,6077-3,6289-X
Excelsior. 6014-5,6211-3,6402-7,6498-1,6735-2,6964 ,6304-7,6566-X,6291-9,6126-5,6560-0,6457-4,6212-1,6135-4,6288-1,6457-4
The exile of the Acadians. 6552-X
Expedition to Wessagusset, fr. The courtship..Standish. 6946-0
The famine, fr. The song of Hiawatha. 6077-3,6616-X,6142-7,6554-6,6370-5,6008-0,6288-1,6567-8,6402-7
The fate of the prophets, fr. The divine tragedy. 6730-1
The fifieth birthday of Agassiz. 6233-4,6385-3,6431-0,6126-5,6585-6
Finale of Christus. 6126-5
The fire of driftwood. 6243-1,6333-0,6085-4,6288-1,6309-8
Florence Nightingale. 6793-X
Flowers ("Spake full well, in language..."). 6047-1,6049-8,6577-5,6219-9
The foe within. 6337-3
Footsteps of angels. 6302-0,6303-9,6735-2,6121-4,6219-9,6126-5,6288-1,6304-7
"For the structure that we raise." 6225-3
The four princesses at Wilna. 6320-9
The four winds, fr. The song of Hiawatha. 6623-2
Gaspar Becerra. 6126-5
The ghosts, fr. The song of Hiawatha. 6254-7,6315-2,6696-8,6566-X
Giotto's tower. 6624-0,6288-1,6126-5,6309-8,6631-3
God's-acre. 6302-0,6385-3,6465-5,6486-8,6214-8,6304
The golden legend, sels. 6282-2
The golden mile-stone. 6429-9,6321-7,6659-3,6641-2
The hanging of the crane. 6288-1
The happiest land. 6424-8
Haroun Al Raschid. 6934-7
The harvest moon. 6239-3;6333-0
Hawthorne. 6126-5,6385-3,6600-3,6333-0,6600-3,6380-2,6385-3,6288-1,6304 ,6641-0
'He that doeth the will', fr. Christus. 6144-3;6335-7
"The heights by great men reached and kept". 6238-5;6260-1;6601-1
The hemlock tree. 6049-8
Henry W. Longfellow's funniest poem. 6889-8
Hermes Trismegistus. 6431-0
Hiawatha and Mudjekeewis, fr. The song of Hiawatha. 6288-1
Hiawatha and the pearl-feather, fr. The song of Hiawatha. 6018-8
Hiawatha's brothers. 6466-3,6510-4
Hiawatha's chickens. 6466-3,6510-4
Hiawatha's childhood, fr. The song of Hiawatha. 6105-2,

6127-3,6479-5,6132-X,6242-3,6176 ,6008-0,6288-1,6121-4,6639-9,6454-X,6623
Hiawatha's departure, fr. The song of Hiawatha. 6753-0
Hiawatha's departure, fr. The song of Hiawatha. 6288-1
Hiawatha's departure, fr. The song of Hiawatha. 6753-0
Hiawatha's fasting. 6396-9
Hiawatha's fasting, fr. The song of Hiawatha. 6753-0
Hiawatha's fishing, fr. The song of Hiawatha. 6228-8, 6496-5,6552-X,6008-0
Hiawatha's friends, fr. The song of Hiawatha. 6496-5
Hiawatha's sailing, fr. The song of Hiawatha. 6105-2, 6466-3,6496-5,6623-2,6288-1,6107-9,6121-4,6639-9
Hiawatha's wooing, fr. The song of Hiawatha. 6014-5, 6402-7,6585-6,6288-1,6121-4
Hiawatha, sels. 6077-3,6616-X,6254-7,6289-X,6315-2,6484
Holidays. 6109-5,6429-9,6465-5,6321-7
Home song. 6239-3,6135-4,6570-8
"Honor to those whose words or deeds". 6601-1
The household sovereign. 6385-3
"How beautiful is youth! how bright it gleams". 6238-5
"How strange the sculptures...", fr. Divina commedia. 6536-8
Hymn of the Moravian nuns. 6752-2
Hymn of the Moravian nuns of Bethlehem. 6946-0
Hymn to the night. 6014-5,6142-7,6077-3,6176-1,6289-X, 6299 ,6585-6,6008-0,6300-4,6431-0,6396-9,6126 ,6102-8,6076-5,6121-4,6250-4,6302-3,6385-3,6315-2,6726-3
"I do not love thee less for what is done". 6066-8
"I enter and I see thee in the gloom", fr. Commedia. 6536-8
I hear along our street. 6747-6
"I lift mine eyes...", fr. Divina commedia. 6536-8
"In mediaeval Rome, I know not where", fr. Morituri. 6165-6
In the churchyard at Tarrytown. 6126-5
Inarime. 6624-0
The Indian hunter. 6678-X
Infancy and childhood, fr. The song of Hiawatha. 6616-X
Inspiration. 7020-5
The Jewish cemetery at Newport. 6176-1,6333-0,6399-3, 6484-1
Judas Maccabaeus. 6848-0
Jugurtha. 6288-1
Keats. 6333-0,6288-1,6126-5
Keramos. 6333-0,6250-4,6541-4
Killed at the ford. 6113-3,6320-5,6126-5,61-7-9,6288-1
King Robert of Sicily. 6410-8,6473-6,6605-4,6661-5,6706-9,6419-1,6458-2,6614-3
King Witlaf's drinking-horn. 6747-6
Kwasind: his death, fr. The song of Hiawatha. 6018-8
Kwasind: his strength, fr. The song of Hiawatha. 6018-8
L'envoi. 6126-5
The ladder of St. Augustine. 6142-7,6219-9,6288-1,6121-1,6126-5,6964
The ladder, sels. 6260-1
Lady Wentworth. 6744-1
The launch. 6385-3
The launching of the ship. 6142-7,6554-6,6404-3,6425-6, 6565-1
The leap of Roushan Beg. 6478-7,6498-1,6079-X
The legend beautiful. 6661-5,6706-9,6419-1,6114-1,6964-9
The legend of Rabbi Ben Levi. 6848-0
The legend of Rabbi Ben Levi. 6077-3,6236-9
"Let nothing disturb thee". 6109-5
Life. 6820-0
Life, fr. Psalm of life. 6239-3,6438-8
The light of stars. 6126-5,6271-7
"Lives of great men all remind us". 6109-5
Lost youth. 6258-X,6547-3
Love and hate, fr. Christus. 6337-3
The lover's errand, fr. The courtship of Miles Standish. 6753-0
Lullaby of Nokomis. 6466-3
Mad River. 6964-9
Maidenhood. 6302-0,6385-3,6600-3,6473-6,6735-2,6219-9, 6250-4,6288-1,6126-5
The manuscripts of God. 6337-3
The masque of Pandora, sels. 6334-9,6049-8,6334-9
The meeting. 6085-4

Mezzo cammin. 6288-1
Michael Angelo, sels. 6333-0,6066-8
Midnight mass for the dying year. 6465-5,6747-6
Miles Standish. 6552-X
Milton. 6176-1,6333-0,6483-3,6288-1,6126-5
Monte Cassino. 6624-0,6631-3
Morituri salutamus. 6333-0,6288-1,6126-5
Morituri salutamus, sels. 6165-6
Mr. Finney's turnip. 6249-0
The musician's tale. 6753-0
My books. 6063-0,6297-0
My cathedral. 6077-3,6421-3,6510-4
My lost youth. 6006-4,6176-1,6186-9,6246-6,6299-7,6396 , 6121-4,6300-4,6464-7,6309-8,6560-0,6431 ,6332-2,6333-0,6395-0,6473-6,6735-2,6467 ,6076-5,6102-8,6008-0, 6288-1,6126-5,6484
My lost youth, sels. 6102-8
"My work is finished; I am strong", fr. Christus. 6335-7
A nameless grave. 6113-3,6288-1
Nature. 6097-8,6176-1,6303-9,6337-3,6365-9,6243 ,6126-5, 6153-2,6300-4,6214-8,6464-7,6723 ,6627-5,6726-3,6473-6,6250-4,6288-1,6431 ,6491-4,6737-9
A new household. 6239-3
Night. 6288-1
The Norman baron. 6323-3
Nuremberg. 6385-3,6735-2,6288-1,6631-3,6126-5,6439
"O star of morning and of liberty". 6289-X,6536-8
"Oft have I seen at some cathedral door",fr. Commedia. 6289-X,6536-8,6646-1
The old bridge at Florence. 6077-3,6331-4,6624-0,6424-8, 6439-6,6631
The old clock on the stairs. 6473-6,6732-8,6183-4,6459-0,6610-0,6632 ,6008-8,6560-0,6288-1,6212-1,6656-X, 6484 ,6457-4,6126-5,6219-9,6566-X,6473-6,6732-8,6183-4,6459-0,6610-0,6632 ,6008-8,6560-0,6288-1,6212-1, 6656-X,6484 ,6457-4,6126-5,6219-9,6566-X
Oliver Basselin. 6006-4
Omaway! awake, beloved!, fr. Song of Hiawatha. 6328-4
On the fifieth birthday of Agassiz. 6438-8
"Only through suffering are we reconciled." 6225-3
"Other hope had she none, nor wish in life..." 6225-3
"Our lives are rivers, gliding free". 6407-8
"Out of the shadows of night". 6109-5
Paul Revere's ride. 6015-3,6142-7,6600-3,6732-8,6062-5, 6077 ,6136-2,6286-5,6370-5,6385-3,6401-9,6565 ,6496-5,6623-2,6706-9,6076-5,6102-8,6079 ,6421-3,6449-3, 6442-6,6107-9,6263-6,6736 ,6419-1,6568-6,6403-5,6219-9,6126-5,6121 ,6267-9,6470-1,6088-9
Paul Revere's ride. 6861-8
Peace in Acadie. 6302-0,6385-3
Peace on earth. 6747-6
Peace through prayer. 6337-3
The peacepipe, fr. The song of Hiawatha. 6288-1
Pegasus in pound. 6478-7,6552-X,6306-3
Picture-writing. 6496-5
Plea for the birds. 6385-3
"Poet! I come to touch thy lance with mine." 6238-5
The poets ("O ye dead poets who are living still"). 6288-1
The poets. 6288-1
Poor sad humanity. 6261-X
Possibilities. 6006-4,6126-5,6435-3
Prelude. 7020-5
Prelude to Tales of a wayside inn. 6126-5
Prelude, fr. Tales of the Wayside Inn. 6300-1
Prelude, fr. Voices in the night. 6302-0
President Garfield. 6946-0
Primeval forest. 6376-4,6385-3
Primeval forest, sels. 6601-1
Priscilla's wedding. 6677-1
The proclamation, fr. John Endicott. 6946-0
Prologue, fr. Evangeline. 6732-8
Prologue, fr. Giles Corey of the Salem farms. 6946-0
Prologue, fr. John Endicott. 6946-0
A psalm of life. 6077-3,6479-5,6600-3,6134-6,6732-8, 6735 ,6087-0,6176-1,6291-1,6294-6,6473-6,6486 ,6260-1,6499-X,6302-0,6385-3,6328-4,6488 ,6527-9,6610-0, 6632-1,6102-8,6076-5,6008 ,6560-0,6461-2,6288-1,6126-5,6214-8,6121 ,6457-4,6639-9,6396-9,6403-5,6304-7,

LONGFELLOW

6219,6300-4,6461-2
Rain in summer. 6077-3,6133-8,6239-3,6302-0,6385-3,6466,6499-X,6597-X,6018-8
The rainy day. 6260-1,6176-1,6499-X,6554-6,6583-X,6337,6373-X,6632-1,6457-4,6565-1,6219-9,6212,6008-0,6560-0,6964-9,6018-8,6126-5,6121-4,6288-1,6008-0,6491
The reaper and the flowers. 6232-6,6303-9,6302-0,6385-3,6502-3,6300-4,6304-7,6214-8,6212-1,6288-1
The republic. 6286-5,6730-1
Resignation. 6260-1,6302-0,6337-3,6385-3,6486-8,6303,6600-3,6610-0,6632-1,6735-2,6304-7,6126-5,6121-4,6219-9
Resignation, sels. 6934-7
return of spring, fr. Charles D'Orleans. 6047-1,6126-5
The revenge of Rain-in-the-face. 6946-0
The revenge of Rain-in-the-Face. 6107-9
Robert Burns. 6483-3,6126-5,6631-3
The ropewalk. 6333-0
The saga of King Olaf, sels. 6105-2,6732-8
St. Francis' sermon to the birds. 6614-3
The Saint Gotthard pass. 6749-2
St. John's, Cambridge. 6435-4
Salem witchcraft. 6552-X
Sandalphon. 6142-3,6176-1,6392-6,6521-X,6661-5,6692,6344-6,6250-4,6288-1,6431-0,6585-6
Santa Filomena. 6465-5,6610-0,6735-2,6438-8,6126-5,6449
Santa Teresa's book-mark. 6641-0
Sea memories. 6114-1
Sea-weed. 6302-0,6385-3,6610-0,6735-2,6288-1
Sea-weed, sels. 6997-5
Seaweed, sels. 6334-9
The secret of the sea. 6499-X,6808-1,6114-1,6288-1
Serenade ("Stars of the summer night"), fr. Spanish... 6315-2,6121-4,6396-9,6481-7,6008-0,6288-1,6126-5,6300-4
The sermon of St. Francis. 6624-0,6631-3
Shakespeare. 6333-0,6288-1,6126-5
The ship of state. 6337-3,6479-5,6732-8,6478-7,6552-X,6104-4,6470-1,6442-6
"Ships that pass in the night". 6793-X
The Sicilian's tale. 6753-0
Simon Danz. 6395-0
The singers. 6304-7
Sir Humphrey Gilbert. 6087-0,6134-6,6243-1,6323-3,6473-6,6552-X,6639-9
Sir Humphrey Gilbert, sels. 6258-X
The skeleton in armor. 6503-1,6732-8,6176-1,6332-2,6473-6,6498,6610-0,6735-2,6479-5,6632-1,6358-6,6288,6358-6,6503-1,6300-4,6319-5,6396-9,6484
The slave's dream. 6242-3,6523-6,6339-X,6288-1,6126-5
Snow-flakes. 6176-1,6302-0,6385-3,6333-0,6466-3,6623,6107-9,6125-7,6394-2,6737-9
" .So these lives that that had run thsu far in separate..." 6066-8
"So, when a good man dies". 6238-5
Song. 6006-4
Song ("Stay, stay at home"). 6138-9,6126-5
The song of Hiawatha, sels. 6105-2,6732-8,6176-1,6623-2,6008-0,6288
Song of the silent land. 6735-2,6300-4
Sonnet ("Oft have I seen"). 6331-4
The sound of the sea. 6850-2
The sound of the sea. 6288-1,6431-2
The sound of the sea. 6850-2
The south wind. 6249-0,6571-6
The Spanish student, sels. 6008-0,6250-4,6288-1
The spirit of poetry. 6049-8,6288-1,6126-5
Stars of the summer night. 6339-X,6732-8,6328-4,6104-4
The story of "Hiawatha" 6049-8
The story of the monk Felix. 6661-5
"Study yourselves, and most of all note well". 66601-1
Sunrise. 6134-6
Sunrise on the hills. 6049-8
Suspiria. 6486-8
A tale of Acadie, fr. Evangeline. 6753-0
"There are two angels, that attend unseen." 6225-3
"There is no death! what seems so is transition". 6238-5
There was a little girl. 6249-0
They that die in the Lord. 6039-0

This is indeed the blessed Mary's land, fr. gol legend. 6282-2
Thou, too, sail on! 6396-9
Three friends of mine. 6077-3,6333-0,6288-1,6126-5,6121-4
The three kings. 6145-1,6236-9,6496-5,6745-X,6239-3,6496
The three silences of Molinos. 6288-1
The tide rises, the tide falls. 6176-1,6243-1,6333-0,6006-4,6288-1
'To a child', sels. 6208-3
To one alone, fr. Coplas de Manrique. 6335-7
To the driving cloud. 6208-3,6125-7
To the river Charles. 6560-0
To the river Rhone. 6331-4,6631-3
To the silent river. 6304-7
Travels by the fireside. 6331-4,6230-X,6631-3
The trial, fr. Giles Corey of Salem farms. 6946-0
Twilight. 6753-0
The two angels. 6461-2,6964-9
Ultima Thule. 6258-X
Venice ("White swan of cities, slumbering in thy nest") 6624-0,6126-5,6631-3
Victor and vanquished. 6126-5
Victor Galbraith. 6288-1
The village blacksmith. 6132-X,6014-5,6176-1,6243-1,6303-9,6459,6242-3,6479-5,6732-8,6486-8,6623-2,6735,6302-0,6385-3,6008-0,6135-4,6560-0,6456
Voices of the forest, fr. The masque of Pandora. 6334-9,6049-8
Voices of the night. 6049-8
Voices of the waters, fr. The masque of Pandora. 6334-9
Voices of the winds, fr. The masque of Pandora. 6334-9
Walter von de Vogelweid. 6485-X
Wapentake. 6483-3,6126-5
The war-token, fr. The courtship of Miles Standish. 6946-0
The warden of the Cinque ports. 6331-4,6385-3,6726-3,6735-2,6288-1,6126-5,6439-6,6438-8,6424-8
The warning. 6661-5
Weariness. 6078-1,6008-0,6288-1,6126-5
The wedding day, fr. The courtship of Miles Standish. 6753-0
"Were half the power that fills the world with terror" 6238-5
When war shall be no more, fr. Arsenal at Springfield. 6337-3,6386-1,6461-2
"When'er a noble deed is wrought". 6238-5,6601-1,6225-3
The white man's foot, fr. The song of Hiawatha. 6753-0
The wind over the chimney. 6753-0
The windmill. 6105-2,6356-X,6639-9
Winter and spring, fr. The song of Hiawatha. 6623-2
"With snow white veil and garments...", fr. Commedia. 6536-8
Woods in winter. 6333-0
The wooing, fr. The song of Hiawatha. 6616-X
The wreck of the Hesperus. 6126-5,6131-1,6153-2,6304-7,6419-1,6132-X,6239-3,6243-1,6290-3,6554-6,6142,6370-5,6425-6,6632-1,6742-5,6484-1,6457,6614-3,6639-9,6008-0,6288-1,6560-0,6212,6479-5,6134-6,6459-0,6478-7,6133-8,6242
"You call them thieves and pillagers...", sels. 66601-1

Longfellow, Henry Wadsworth (tr.)
Ballad: The elected knight. Unknown (Danish), 7039-6
Beware! Unknown (German), 6004-8,6288-1,6560-0
The castle by the sea. Johann Ludwig Uhland, 6271-7
The child asleep. Clotilde de Surville, 6271-7
Childhood. Jens Baggesen, 7039-6
Dante. Michelangelo Buonarroti, 7039-6
Dante. Michelangelo Buonarroti, 6325-X
Eyes so tristful. Diego de Saldana, 7039-6
Frithiof's farewell. Esaias Tegner, 7039-6
The good shepherd ("Shepherd! that with thine..."). Lope De Vega, 6065-X
The image of God. Francisco de Aldana, 6730-1
King Christian. Johannes Evald, 7039-6
Let me go warm. Luis de Gongora, 7039-6
Lines written in her breviary. Saint Theresa of Avila, 6337-3
The luck of Edenhall. Johann Ludwig Uhland, 6613-5

Malbroock. Unknown (French), 6787-5
"O'er all the hill-tops", fr. Wanderer's night-songs. Johann Wolfgang von Goethe, 6289-X
The passage. Johann Ludwig Uhland, 6385-3
Praise of little women. Juan Ruiz de Hita, 6279-2
Retribution. Friedrich von Logau, 6302-0;6385-3;6337-3
The sea hath its pearls. Heinrich Heine, 7039-6
She is a maid. Gil Vincente, 6271-7
Some day, some day. Cristobal de Castillejo, 7039-6, 6879-0
Song ("If thou art sleeping..."). Gil Vicente, 7039-6
Song of the silent land. Johann Gaudenz von Salis, 6271-7
"Thou that from the heavens...", fr. Wanderer's... Johann Wolfgang von Goethe, 6289-X
To Vitorria Colonna. Michelangelo Buonarroti, 6879-0
To Vittoria Colonna. Michelangelo Buonarroti, 7039-6
Tommorrow. Lope De Vega, 6102-8
Th two locks of hair. Gustav P. Fizer, 6066-8
Wanderer's night songs. Johann Wolfgang von Goethe, 6484-1
Wanderer's night songs, sels. Johann Wolfgang von Goethe, 6289-X
Wanderer's night-songs. Johann Wolfgang von Goethe, 7039-6
The widow. Christian Furchtegott Gellert, 6916-9
Longfellow, Herbert H.
　The fishers. 6038-2
　The king's horses. 6038-2
　Mirrors. 6036-6
　Resurgat. 6036-6
Longfellow, Isabella Bryans
　The answer. 6750-6
　Sons. 6750-6
Longfellow, Samuel
　April. 6597-X
　"Beneath the shadow of the cross". 6065-X
　The Christian life. 6418-3,6730-1
　The church universal. 6337-3,6730-1
　God of the earth, the sky, the sea. 6337-3
　The golden sunset. 6600-3
　The mountains of Berne. 6749-2
　November. 6597-X
　Peace on earth. 6386-1,6463-9
　To a daughter on her marriage. 6429-9,6321-7
A longford legend. Unknown. 6930-4
Longford, Earl of (tr.)
　The careful husband. Unknown, 6930-4
　He charges her to lay aside her weapons. Pierce Ferriter, 6930-4
　The kiss. Unknown, 6930-4
Longing. Matthew Arnold. 6226-1,6430-2
Longing. George Gordon, 6th Baron Byron. 6086-2
Longing. Johann Wolfgang von Goethe. 6948-7
Longing. Johann Wolfgang von Goethe. 6328-4
Longing. Harriet Holman. 7016-9
Longing. James Russell Lowell. 7022-1
Longing. Blanche Kendall McKey. 6818-9
Longing. Arthur Wallace Peach. 6097-8
Longing. Melba Williams. 6906-1
Longing. Christian Winther. 6555-4
Longing. Clement Wood. 6619-4
Longing. Chi-hwan Yu. 6775-1
Longing for heaven. Anne Bradstreet. 6008-0
Longing for home. Sun-won Hwang. 6775-1
Longing for home. Jean Ingelow. 6240-7,6730-1
Longing for reunion with the dead. William Wordsworth. 6980-0
Longing for the old plantation. Addison H. Hinman. 6118-4
Longing to be with Christ. William Cowper. 6814-5
Longings. Eugene Field. 6949-5
Longings, fr. Saint's tragedy. Charles Kingsley. 6123-0
Longitudes. Allen Tate. 6039-0
Longley, Snow. See Hough, Snow Longley
The longshoreman's view of it. Margaret Junkin Preston. 6798-0
Lonnie Kramer. Geary Hobson. 7005-1
Lonsdale, Mark
　Three poor fishermen's song. 6997-5
Loo-wit. Wendy Rose. 7005-1

"Look above thee-never eye". Sir John Bowring. 6238-5
Look ahead. Unknown. 6486-8
Look aloft. Jonathan Lawrence. 6425-6,6632-1,,6403-5
"Look at Krsna's behavior, look!" Unknown (Newari) 7013-2
"Look at her - there she sits upon her throne". The turbine. Harriet Monroe. 6897-9
"Look at her- there she sits upon her throne". The turbine. Harriet Monroe. 7014-0
"Look at it now". Tongueless lines. Pat Mernagh. 6750-6
"Look at me, sun, ere thou set". Song ("Look at me..."). Thomas Edward Brown. 6809-X
Look at the clock. Richard Harris ("Thomas Ingoldsby") Barham. 6278-4,6219-9
"Look at the clock. Richard Harris ("Thomas Ingoldsby") Barham. 6302-0
"Look at the little darlings in the corn". Fireflies in the corn. David Herbert Lawrence. 6897-9
"Look at the sun. Look at the rising...". To the sun's arms. Du-jin Park. 6775-1
"Look at this ancient house; it has survived". A house in war time. Richard Church. 6783-2
Look away/look away. Stephen Todd Booker. 6870-7
Look back. Carroll Arnett Gogisgi. 7005-1
"'Look cautiously and far ahead.'". Exception. Elaine V. Emans. 6750-6
Look down fair moon. Walt Whitman. 6288-1
"Look down, dear eyes, look down", fr Hawthorn. William Ernest Henley. 6123-0
"Look down, o Lord, look down. Are the...". How long, o Lord! Hall Caine. 6954-1
Look ere you leap. Jasper Heywood. 6182-6,6328-4
Look for me on England. H.B. Mallalieu. 6666-6
Look for no pity. Elizabeth Grey Stewart. 6761-1
Look for the best. Alice Cary. 6523-6
"Look forth, beloved, from thy mansion high". A day in March. Bayard Taylor. 6976-2
"Look from the ancient mountains down". The English boy. Felicia Dorothea Hemans. 6973-8
"Look here, ye pedants, who deserve that name". On the Spectator's critique of Milton. Lawrence Eusden. 6867-7
Look home. Robert Southwell. 6935-5
"Look how it sparkles, see it greet". A diamond. Robert Loveman. 6941-X
"Look how the golden ocean shines above". On receiving a gift. Thomas Hood. 6974-6
"Look how the lark soars upward and is gone". False poets and true. Thomas Hood. 6974-6
Look in my face; my name is Might-have-been. Dante Gabriel Rossetti. 6560-2
"Look in the salon des refuses of most periods". A lecture on avant-garde art. Jack Anderson. 7003-5
The look in their eyes. Robert Haven Schauffler. 6051-X
"Look in thy glass, and tell the face thou viewest". William Shakespeare. 6187-7
"Look in thy glass, and tell the face thou viewest ". Sonnet 003 ("Look in thy glass"). William Shakespeare. 6436-1
Look in thy heart and write. Sir Philip Sidney. 6092-7, 6102-8,6250-4
A look into the gulf. Edwin Markham. 6309-8
A look into water. Alfred Edward Housman. 6102-8
"Look long upon this daylight. Soon, too soon". Words before twilight. Daniel William Hicky. 6850-2
"Look not thou on beauty's charming". Two ideals. Sir Walter Scott. 6935-5
"Look not thou on beauty's charms". Sir Walter Scott. 6934-7
"Look not upon me, seek no more to stay me." M. Kirwan. 6317-9
"Look not upon the wine when it is red". Nathaniel Parker Willis. 6752-2
"The look of sympathy, the gentle word". Unknown. 6238-5
Look on me with thy cloudless eyes. Felicia Dorothea Hemans. 6973-8
"Look on the ever-changing blue above". Our privilege. Adelma H. Burd. 6847-2
"Look on the white Alps round!". Swiss song, fr. Lays of many lands. Felicia Dorothea Hemans. 6973-8
"Look on this cast, and know the hand". The hand of

LOOK

Lincoln. Edmund Clarence Stedman. 7041-8
"**Look** on who will in apathy, and stifle...can". On the capture of certain fugitive slaves...Washington. James Russell Lowell. 7009-4
"**Look** once more e're...", fr. Paradise regain'd. John Milton. 6562-7
"**Look** once more ere we leave this...mount". Athens, fr. Paradise regained. John Milton. 6933-9
"**Look** our ransomed shores around". Additional verses to Hail Columbia. Oliver Wendell Holmes. 6946-0
Look out for the snake! Luis Pales Matos. 6759-X
"'**Look** out!', she exclaimed". Man portrait. Marion Judd. 6750-6
Look out, bright eyes. Francis Beaumont and John Fletcher. 6219-9
Look pleasant. Unknown. 6109-5
"**Look** there! the hour is written in the sky". Astrology. George Croly. 6980-0
"**Look** thou yonder, look and tremble". An Arab to his mistress. Walter Savage Landor. 6980-0
"**Look** thro' mine eyes...", fr. The miller's daughter. Alfred Lord Tennyson. 6123-0
Look to this day. Unknown (Sanskrit) 6750-6,6461-2,6750-6
"**Look** to this day!". Invocation of the dawn. Kalidasa. 6879-2
"**Look** up and not down". Edward Everett Hale. 6109-5,6225-3, 6211-3
Look up! John Jarvis Holden. 6274-1
Look up! Unknown. 6260-1
Look up, not down. Unknown. 6523-6
"'**Look** up, not down!' Do you see...". Four mottoes. Alice Freeman Palmer. 6926-6
"**Look** up." Martha Snell Nickolson. 6065-X
"**Look** up/From bleakening hills". Snow. Adelaide Crapsey. 6850-2
"**Look** what immortal floods the sunset pours". The sea - in calm. Bryan Waller ("Barry Cornwall") Procter. 7015-9,6997-5
"**Look** where my dear Hamilla smiles". On Mrs. A. H. at a concert. William Crawford. 6874-X
Look within. Edward R. Huxley. 6885-5
Look you, I'll go pray. Vachel Lindsay. 6581-3
"**Look**! On the great great bronze bell." Buson. 6027-7
"**Look**, Delia, how we esteem the half-blown rose". Samuel Daniel. 6182-6,6436-1,6726-3
"**Look**, Delia, how we esteem the halfblown rose". A supplication. Samuel Daniel. 6830-8
Look, Henry M.
  The rescue of Chicago. 6045-1
"**Look**, I have thrown all right". Louis Alexander Mackay. 6446-9
"**Look**, how he glows for heat!". Christ in the garden, fr. Hymn: crucifixus pro nobis. Patrick Carey. 6931-2
"**Look**, how he shakes for cold!". Christ in the cradle, fr. Hymn: crucifixus pro nobis. Patrick Carey. 6931-2
"**Look**, look! I see - I see my love appear!". Of a scholar and his mistress. John Dryden. 6970-3
"**Look**, my countrymen". Sophocles. 6435-3
"**Look**, oh look, you lovers, it is springtime!" Unknown (Newari) 7013-2
Look, stranger, at this island now. Wystan Hugh Auden. 6354-3
"**Look**, these are all". Turbines. MacKnight Black. 6808-1
"**Look**, they tear down the tenements". Song ("Look"). Clark Mills. 6640-2
"**Look**, when a painter would surpass the life". A picture. William Shakespeare. 7010-8
"'**Look**. See. It's there again'". Star Phoenix. Steve Semler. 6883-9
The **look**.. John Bunker. 6096 X
The **look**. Elizabeth Barrett Browning. 6337-3
The **look**. Sara Teasdale. 6441-8,6473-6,6026-9
"**Lookatitthisway**: I have seen some". Where have all the indians gone? Janet Campbell Hale. 7005-1
Looke how the pale queene. Charles Best. 6833-2
"**Looke** well about, ye that lovers be". Against women. Unknown. 6881-2
Looke, John
  A famous sea-fight. 6157-5
Lookin' back. Moira (Nesta Higginson Skrine) O'Neill. 6046-3

'**Lookin'** back'. Moira (Nesta Higginson Skrine) O'Neill. 6793-X
"**Lookin'** back, I think I see". Looking back. Edgar A. Guest. 6862-6
"**Looking** at Morris Graves' spirit bird". Spirit bird. John Logan. 6966-5
Looking at the cross. John Newton. 6065-X
"**Looking** at these roses". Roses. Ilse Brem. 6769-7
"**Looking** at you I feel the same hushed pain". Beauty, fr. Once again the Eden. Noel Hudson Stearn. 6789-1
Looking back. Edgar A. Guest. 7033-7
Looking back. Edgar A. Guest. 6862-6
Looking back. Blanche Yvonne Mosley. 6761-1
Looking back. John Addington Symonds. 6624-0
"**Looking** back a hundred years". Then and now, 1776-1876. F.W. Fish. 6912-6
Looking backward. Rose Hawthorne Lathrop. 7041-8
"**Looking** down on quaint New London". Mt. Kearsarge. Eunice Worthen. 6764-6
Looking for a happy smile. Jesse Sill. 6799-9
Looking for Buddha. Jaime Jacinto. 6790-5
Looking for equality. Herman L. McMillan. 7024-8
Looking for Johnny Cash. Miller Williams. 6860-X
Looking for my old indian grandmother in the summer... Diane Glancy. 7005-1
Looking for the innr life in 100 mile. Bill Bissett. 6767-0
Looking foreward. Charles Whitby. 6994-0
Looking forward. Edgar A. Guest. 6748-4
Looking forward. Christina Georgina Rossetti. 6828-6
Looking forward. Robert Louis Stevenson. 6655-0
The **looking** glass. Rudyard Kipling. 6210-5
Looking in both directions from inside the covered... David Baker. 6860-X
"**Looking** into the windows that doom has broken". Sonnet ("Looking into"). George Woodcock. 6379-9
Looking on beauty. Walter John Coates. 7030-2
Looking on the bright side. Le Touche Hancock. 6109-5
Looking out into the night. John Godfrey Saxe. 7030-2
"**Looking** out on the bay/the old wharf". The view from JB's window. J. Whitebird. 6901-0
Looking over Vermont town resorts. Daniel L. Cady. 6988-6
Looking seaward. Robert Loveman. 6941-X
Looking unto Jesus. Unknown. 6752-2
Looking up. Hiromi. 6027-7
"**Looking** up at the stars, connecting the dots". In the hospital courtyard. Stan Rice. 6901-0
"**Looking** upward every day." Unknown. 6225-3
Looking upward in a storm. William Cowper. 6814-6
The **looking-glass** world. Charles Lutwidge ("Lewis Carroll") Dodgson. 6368-3
The **looking-glass**. James Shirley. 6317-9
Lookout Mountain. George L. Catlin. 6572-4
Lookout Mountain. Benjamin Franklin Taylor. 6815-4
The **lookout**. William Collins. 6833-2
"**Looks** as though a cyclone hit him". The homely man. Edgar A. Guest. 7033-7
The **looks** of a lover enamoured. George Gascoigne. 6182-6
"**Looks** that love not are silver-cold-". Love. C. H. Waring. 6770-0
Loom o' lights. Mary Garbarini. 6789-1
The **loom** of dreams. Arthur Symons. 6507-4
The **loom** of life. Unknown. 6923-1
The **loom** of time. Unknown. 6337-3,6654-2
The **loom** of years, sels. Alfred Noyes. 6337-3
The **loom** of years. Alfred Noyes. 7014-0
The **loom**.. Edgar Lee Masters. 6031-5;6619-4
The **loom**. J.A. Knight-Adkin. 7031-0
Loomis, Adelaide
  The willow-ware pattern. 6397-7
Loomis, Charles Battell
  A classic ode. 6902-9
  The evolution of a 'name'. 6996-7
  Grace's choice. 7021-3
  Jack and Jill ("Their pail they must fill"). 6440-X
  Lines on Rose. 6724-7
  O-U-G-H. A fresh hack at an old knot. 6089-7,6724-7
  Propinquity needed. 6089-7,6440-X,6287-3,6089-7,6440-X
  A song of sorrow. 6089-7,6724-7

Timon of Archimedes. 6902-9
Loomis, E.S.
  Reason off duty. 6685-2
Loomis, Payson (tr.)
  The aviator. Alexander Blok, 6978-9
The **loon** ("A lonely lake, a lonely shore"). Lew Sarett. 6073-0,6102-8,6619-4,6076-5,6034-X
Loon river anthology. L.W. D. 6817-0
The **loon**. Amelia Josephine Burr. 6510-4
The **loon**. Alfred Billings Street. 6073-0
Loons at night. Leona Bishop Mealey. 6316-0
Loop head. Edmond Gore Alexander Holmes. 6997-5
"**Loose** him and let him go!". The titan, sel. Angela Morgan. 6954-1
"**Loose** the sail, rest the oar, float away down". A boat song, fr. Hypatia. Charles Kingsley. 6832-4
"**Loose-hearted** Ovid yet could find". The rape of virtue. Edward Farquhar. 6939-8
"**Loose-veined** and languid as the yellow mist". The lonely bather. Max Eastman. 6880-4
Loot. Rudyard Kipling. 6810-3
The **loot** of Luxor. Laurence Housman. 6778-6
Lope de Vega Carpio
  "Let the vain courier waste his days". Felicia Dorothea Hemans (tr.). 6973-8
  A song of the Virgin Mother, fr. Los pastores de Belen. Ezra Pound (tr.). 7039-6
  A song of the Virgin Mother. Ezra Pound (tr.). 6292-X
Lopez Merino, Francisco
  "My cousins, on Sundays, come to cut roses". Richard O'Connell (tr.). 6759-X
  Song for afterwards. Richard O'Connell (tr.). 6759-X
Lopez, Luis Carlos
  "Country girl, don't stay away from the market". Donald Devenish Walsh (tr.). 6759-X
  The mayor. H.R. Hays (tr.). 6642-9
  Old maids. H.R. Hays (tr.). 6642-9
  Rubbish, IV. H.R. Hays (tr.). 6642-9
  Rubbish, VII. H.R. Hays (tr.). 6642-9
  Tropic siesta. Donald Devenish Walsh (tr.). 6759-X
  Vespers. Donald Devenish Walsh (tr.). 6759-X
  Village night. Donald Devenish Walsh (tr.). 6759-X
Loquitur William Lyon Mackenzie. W. Stewart Wallace. 6433-7
Lord Arnaldos. James Elroy Flecker. 7007-8
Lord Arnold. Unknown. 6061-7
Lord Bakeman. Unknown. 6061-7
"**Lord** Bateman was a noble lord". Unknown. 6059-5
Lord Bayham. Unknown. 6003-X
Lord Beichan and Susie Pye. Unknown. 6239-3
Lord Chancellor's song, fr. Iolanthe. Sir William Schwenck Gilbert. 6512-0,6108-7,6732-8
"The **Lord** above, in tender love". Thanksgiving hymn. Unknown. 6946-0
"The **Lord** at need vouchsafe thee grace". Psalm 020. Bible. 6848-0
"**Lord** b'ess papa, mamma, Daisy". The baby's prayer. Elizabeth Stuart Phelps. 6965-7
"The **Lord** came near, a kingdom in each hand". Adam's choice. Edward Farquhar. 6939-8
The **lord** chancellours villanies..., or His rise... Unknown. 6157-5
Lord Clive. Edmund Clerihew Bentley. 6089-7,6722-0
Lord Clive. Unknown. 6166-4
Lord Daniel. Unknown. 6826-X
Lord Delamere. Unknown. 6185-0
Lord Derwentwater. Unknown. 6185-0,6518-X
The **Lord** does care. Unknown. 6303-9
Lord Donald. Unknown. 6518-X
"**Lord** Erskine, on woman presuming to rail" Richard Brinsley Sheridan. 6874-X
'The **Lord** God planted a garden'. Dorothy Frances Gurney. 6338-1,6730-1
Lord Guy. George F. Warren. 6089-7
Lord Hervey. Alexander Pope. 6150-8
"The **Lord** doth raigne, whereat ye earth". Psalm 097. Bible. 6848-0
"The **Lord** employed a quaint disguise". Bachelors' landlady. Hyde Clayton. 6750-6
"**Lord** God almighty! great, and full of fear". The prayer of Daniel. George Wither. 6848-0
"**Lord** God of heav'n! who only art". The prayer of Nehemiah. George Wither. 6848-0
"**Lord** God of Israel, hear our prayer". Solomon's prayer. Mary H. Cutts. 7030-2
"**Lord** God thy praise I will declare". Psalm 030. Bible. 6848-0
"**Lord** God! This was a stone". The stone. Thomas Vaughan. 6933-9
"**Lord** God, ere yet our drums are rolled". Prayer before war. W.G. Hole. 7031-0
"**Lord** God, that dost me save and keep". Psalm 088. Bible. 6848-0
"**Lord** God, whay may we think of thee". Ritual. William Rose Benet. 6887-1
"**Lord** Harry has written a novel". A fashionable novel. Thomas Haynes Bayly. 6874-X
"The **Lord** hath anointed me to preach good...". 'Good tidings unto the meek' Bible. 6954-1
Lord high admiral's song, fr. H.M.S. Pinafore. Sir William Schwenck Gilbert. 6732-8
Lord Ingram and Chiel Wyet. Unknown. 6185-0,6067-6
"**Lord** how are my foes increast". Psalm 003. Bible. 6848-0
"**Lord** I would own thy tender care". Praise for mercies. Unknown. 6131-1
The **Lord** is a man of war, fr. Exodus. Bible. 6665-8
The **Lord** is my light, fr. Psalms. Bible. 6805-7
The **Lord** is my light. Oliver Wendell Holmes. 6303-9
The **Lord** is my shepherd, fr. Psalm 23 Bible. 6183-4,6132-X, 6337-3,6527-9
"The **Lord** is my shepherd; I shall not want". Psalm 023. Bible. 7039-6,6143-5,6373-X,6418-3,6464-7,6534-1, 6565 ,6501-5,6503-1,6654-2,6623-2,6732-8,6491 ,6585-6
The **Lord** is my shepherd. John Knox. 6065-X
"The **Lord** is our ruler- Jehoval alone". A psalm of Thanksgiving. James Abraham Martling. 6952-5
"The **lord** is residing happily on the..mountain". Manjusri (2). Unknown (Newari). 7013-2
"**Lord** Jesus! with what sweetness and delights". Ascension day. Henry Vaughan. 6931-2
The **Lord** is risen. Charles Wesley. 6219-9
Lord Jesus, when stand afar. William Walsham How. 6144-3
Lord Jim, sel. Joseph Conrad. 6958-4
Lord John of the east. Joanna Baillie. 6813-8
Lord John Russell. Edward Bulwer-Lytton; Baron Lytton. 6046-3
Lord Kitchener. Robert Bridges. 7029-9,7026-4
Lord Livingston. Unknown. 6185-0
Lord Lovel. Unknown. 6058-7,6185-0,6271-7,6059-5,6136-2, 6003-X,6319-5,6067-6,6613-5,6219-9
Lord Maxwell's good-night. Unknown. 6180-X
Lord Maxwell's last goodnight. Unknown. 6185-0
Lord Melbourne. Edward Bulwer-Lytton; Baron Lytton. 6046-3, 6389-6
The **Lord** Nann and the fairy. Unknown. 6873-1
Lord North's recantation. Unknown. 6946-0
"The **Lord** made clay of spittle and". Epitaph to a man. Robert Reedburg. 7024-8
"**Lord** Malcolm of Ruthven mounts his steed". Lady Maud's oath. Re. Henry. 6923-1
"'The **Lord** my maker, forming me of". Adam's complaint. Theophanes. 6848-0
"The **Lord** my pasture shall prepare". Pastoral hymn. Joseph Addison. 6932-9
"**Lord** never grant me what I ask for". The unforeseen. Conrado Nale Roxlo. 6759-X
"**Lord** of Athene's holy hill". Bacchylides. 6251-2
"**Lord** of Athens' holy ground", fr. Theseus. Bacchylides. 6435-3
The **lord** of Burleigh. Alfred Lord Tennyson. 6133-8,6479--5, 6416-7,6370-5,6219-9,6419
The **lord** of Butrago. Frederick Locker-Lampson. 6385-3
The **lord** of Butrago. Unknown (Spanish) 6424-8
The **lord** of Butrago. Unknown (Spanish) 6757-3
Lord of Eden. Marie de L. Welch. 6628-3
The **Lord** of heaven to earth came down. Kathryn Blackburn Peck. 6065-X
Lord of himself. Sir Henry Wotton. 6322-5
The **lord** of lorn and the false steward. Unknown. 6185-0

LORD

The **lord** of misrule. Alfred Noyes. 6151-6
Lord of my heart's elation. Bliss Carman. 6250-4,6252-0, 6393-4,6310-1,6509-0
"**Lord** of my love, to whom in vassalage". Sonnet 026 ("Lord of my love"). William Shakespeare. 6447-7
"**Lord** of the celtic dells". To Joseph Ablett. Walter Savage Landor. 6828-6
Lord of the city. Dana Burnet. 7014-0
The **Lord** of the Dunderberg. Arthur Guiterman. 6773-5
The **lord** of the isle. Stefan George. 7039-6
The **lord** of the isles, sels. Sir Walter Scott. 6188-5,6250-4
Lord of the quiet heart. Arthur Wallace Peach. 6461-2
"**Lord** of the summer, come up from the south!". Lord of the city. Dana Burnet. 7014-0
"**Lord** Oswald comes to make me grace". Is he true? William White. 6868-5
"**Lord** Pam in the church". Epigram (Lord Pam"). Jonathan Swift. 6380-2
"**Lord** of the winds, I cry to thee". Mary Elizabeth Coleridge. 6931-2
Lord of us all. Donald Hankey. 6337-3
"**Lord** Phoebus, when our Lady, the gracious...". Theognis. 6251-2
"The **Lord** possessed me," fr. Proverbs. Bible. 6282-2
Lord Randal. Unknown. 6058-7,6133-8,6154-0,6179-6,6185-0, 6198 ,6236-9,6271-7,6289-X,6290-3,6315-2,6488 ,6499-X,6527-9,6061-7,6645-3,6668-2,6646 ,6079-X,6458-2, 6067-6,6153-2
Lord Rendal. Unknown. 6829-4
Lord Ronald. Unknown. 6055-2,6056-0,6319-5
Lord Ronald's ride. Edward Bulwer-Lytton; Baron Lytton. 6677-1
Lord Saltoun and Auchanachie. Unknown. 6185-0
Lord Shaftesbury. John Dryden. 6315-2
"The **Lord** proclaims his grace abroad!". The covenant. William Cowper. 6814-6,6848-0
"The **Lord** receives his highest praise". A living and a dead faith. William Cowper. 6814-6
"The **Lord** reigns, cloth'd with majesty". Psalm 093. Bible. 6848-0
"The **Lord** shall slay or the Lord shall save!". Laudamus. Adam Lindsay Gordon. 6951-7
"**Lord** Thomas he was a gay young man". Lord Thomas. Unknown. 6826-X
The **lord** spoke. Charles Van Lerberghe. 6351-9
The **Lord** the creator. Sir John Bowring. 7020-5
Lord Thomas. Unknown. 6003-X,6057-9
Lord Thomas. Unknown. 6826-X
Lord Thomas and fair Annet. Unknown. 6055-2,6056-0,6057-9, 6058-7,6185-0,6111 ,6518-X,6193-1,6067-6,6518-4
Lord Thomas and ₊air Ellinor. Unknown. 6138-8,6055-2
Lord Thomas and Lady Margaret. Unknown. 6185-0
Lord Thomas Stuart. Unknown. 6185-0
Lord Thomasine and fair Ellinnor. Unknown. 6676-3
"**Lord** thou hast cast us off". Psalm 060. Bible. 6848-0
"The **Lord** turned, and looked upon Peter" Elizabeth Barrett Browning. 6144-3
Lord Ullin's daughter. Thomas Campbell. 6134-6,6370-5,6502-3,6552-X,6614-3,6646 ,6136-2,6196-6,6131-1,6560-0, 6668-2,6419 ,6079-X,6219-9,6319-5,6396-9,6543-0,6518 ,6239-3,6242-3,6246-5,6478-7,6479-5,6486 ,6086-2, 6600-3,6639-9,6675-5
Lord Vyet. Arthur Christopher Benson. 6437-X
Lord Walter's wife. Elizabeth Barrett Browning. 6302-0, 6385-3,6671-1
Lord Waterford. Unknown. 6125-7
"**Lord** when the wise men came from afar". Wise men and shepherds. Sidney Godolphin. 6931-2
"**Lord** when the wise men came from afar". Sidney Godolphin. 6933-9
Lord when the wise men came from farr. Sidney Godolphin. 6341-1
"The **Lord** will happiness divine". William Cowper. 6931-2
Lord William. Robert Southey. 6086-2
Lord William and Lady Margaret. Unknown. 6061-7
Lord William, or, Lord Lundy. Unknown. 6185-0
Lord Willoughby. Unknown. 6157-5
"**Lord**! in the temple of thy love". Song of adoration to God. Thomas Holley Chivers. 7017-5

Lord! it is not life to live. Augustus Montague Toplady. 6337-3
"**Lord**! it is not life to live". Augustus Montague Toplady. 6931-2
"**Lord**! we would put aside". Unknown. 6238-5
"**Lord**! when those glorious lights I see." George Wither. 6302-0;6385-3
The **lord's** Marie. Allan Cunningham. 6960-6
The **Lord's** prayer, ₊r. St. Matthew. Bible. 6337-3,6418-3
The **Lord's** prayer. Alice Meynell. 6955-X
The **Lord's** prayer. Martin Farquhar Tupper. 6543-2
"The **Lord's** triumphant name let all rehearse". Moses' song. Laurence Howel. 6848-0
Lord, Caroline A.
  A song of street labor. 6820-0
Lord, Caroline M.
  When to speak. 6764-6
Lord, Phillips H.
  Your church and mine. 6337-3
Lord, William Wilberforce
  On the defeat of Henry Clay. 6946-0
"**Lord,** be my guide through the day". A prayer. Edgar A. Guest. 6862-6
"**Lord,** chide not when thou wroth shalt be". Psalm 038. Bible. 6848-0
Lord, come away! Jeremy Taylor. 6337-3
Lord, dismiss us with Thy blessing. Walter Shirley. 6219-9
Lord, dost thou look. Christina Georgina Rossetti. 6199-0
"**Lord,** for the erring thought". prayer ("Lord, for the erring"). William Dean Howells. 6303-9,6418-3,6730-1
"**Lord,** give the mothers of the world". A prayer ("Lord, give"). Ella Wheeler Wilcox. 6097-8
"**Lord,** give us strength!". Invocation. David George Plotkin. 6954-1
"**Lord,** God of peace, my spirit's high ideal". Peace on earth, sels. Gudmundur Gudmundsson. 6854-5
"**Lord,** grant our little family". The Family prayer for difficult days. Edgar A. Guest. 6869-3
Lord, grant us calm. Christina Georgina Rossetti. 6199-0
"**Lord,** grant us eyes to see". Prayer ("Lord, grant"). Christina Georgina Rossetti. 6214-8,6144-3
Lord, have mercy on us. Thomas Nashe. 6125-7
'**Lord,** I ask a garden'. R. Arevalo Martinez. 6338-1
'**Lord,** I owe thee a death'. Alice Meynell. 6955-X
'**Lord,** I owe thee a death' Alice Meynell. 7029-9
"**Lord,** hear my pray'r and to my cry". Psalm 143. Bible. 6848-0
"**Lord,** how can he be dead?". Missing. Beatrice Ravenel. 7027-2
"**Lord,** how can man preach thy eternall word?". The church windows. George Herbert. 6933-9
"**Lord,** how long, how long wilt thou". Psalm 013. Bible. 6848-0
"**Lord,** I have sinn'd, and the black number swells". The penitent. Jeremy Taylor. 6931-2,6933-9
"**Lord,** I love the habitation". A song of mercy and judgment. William Cowper. 6814-6
"**Lord,** I will sing to thee". The second song of Esai. George Wither. 6848-0
Lord, if Thou art not present. John Gray. 6096 X
"**Lord,** if some little children of our day". The mother's prayer. Kathleen Norris. 6817-0
"**Lord,** in my silence how do I despise". Frailty. George Herbert. 6931-2
"**Lord,** in thy wrath reprove me not". Psalm 006. Bible. 6848-0
Lord, it belongs not to my care. Richard Baxter. 6931-2, 6337-3,6931-2
"**Lord,** judge thou me and plead my right". Psalm 043. Bible. 6848-0
"'**Lord,** let me know mine end, and of my days". The end of David. Unknown. 6848-0
"**Lord,** let me know mine end...", fr. The Bible. Unknown. 6416-7
"**Lord,** let me live like a regular man". A prayer ("Lord, let me"). Berton Braley. 6211-3
"**Lord,** let me never 'settle down'!". Invocation. Berton Braley. 7007-8
"**Lord,** let the golden bells ring out". Prayer (Lord, let"). Julian [or Juljan] Tuwi. 6068-4

"Lord, make me quick to see." R.M. Offord. 6225-3
"Lord, many times I am aweary quite". Richard Chenevix Trench. 6065-X
"Lord, may I be a wandering star". A prayer ("Lord, may"). Marion Couthouy Smith. 6331-4
"Lord, my soul with pleasure springs". True pleasures. William Cowper. 6814-6
"Lord, not for light in darkness do we pray". A prayer ("Lord, not"). John Drinkwater. 6303-9,6532-5,6108-2, 6214-8,6337-3,6359
"Lord, now the prodigal son returns". The prodigal's return. Edgar A. Guest. 6869-3
"Lord, oft I come". Lizette Woodworth Reese. 6007-2
Lord, speak to me, that I may speak. Frances Ridley Havergal. 6337-3,6461-2
"Lord, strive with them that take the". Psalm 035. Bible. 6848-0
Lord, teach a little child. Unknown. 6249-0,6502-3
"Lord, the Roman hyacinths are blooming...". A song for Simeon. Thomas Stearns Eliot. 6931-2
"Lord, thou hast been our refuge. Psalm 90. Bible. 6472-8
"Lord, thou hast crushed thy tender ones...". Messina, 1908. Alice Meynell. 6955-X
"Lord, thy answer I did hear". The prayer of Habakkuk. George Wither. 6848-0
"Lord, we've had our little wrangles...". Little wrangles. Edgar A. Guest. 7033-7
"Lord, what a change within us one short hour". Prayer ("Lord, what"). Richard Chenevix Trench. 6337-3,6303-9,6730-1,6143-5
"Lord, what a change within us, one short hour". Unknown. 6238-5
"Lord, what am I? a worm, dust, vapour,nothing". Anthem. Joseph Hall. 6830-8
"Lord, what can I ask of thee". Beggarly. Josephine A. Meyer. 6847-2
"Lord, what unvalued pleasures crown'd". The invitation. Unknown. 6931-2
"Lord, when I find at last thy paradise". She asks for new earth. Katharine (Hinkson) Tynan. 6776-X
"Lord, when the sense of thy sweet grace". A song ("Lord, when"). Richard Crashaw. 6641-0,6214-8
Lord, when we leave the world. Francis Quarles. 6102-8
Lord, while for all mankind we pray. John R. Wreford. 6337-3
"Lord, who am I to teach the way". The teacher. Leslie Pinckney Hill. 6818-9
Lord, who art merciful. Unknown (Persian) 6337-3
"Lord, who hast suffer'd all for me". Prayer for patience. William Cowper. 6814-6
"Lord, who's the happy man that may". Psalm 015. Bible. 6848-0
"Lord, with what body do they come". Thou knowest. Phoebe Cary. 6969-X
"The Lord- a mighty God is he". El monte- hymn. James Abraham Martling. 6952-5
The lord-chamberlain tells of a famous meeting. Robert Graves. 6069-2
"Lord-great Leviathan". Prayer ("Lord-great Leviathan"). Gordon Lawrence. 6041-2
Lorde, Audre
  Progress report. 6898-7
  To the girl who lives in a tree. 6898-7
  Touring. 6898-7
"Lordings, listen to our lay". Anglo-Norman carol. Unknown. 6756-5
"The lordly genius blooms for all to see". In degree. Paul Hamilton Hayne. 6889-8
The lordly ones. William ("Fiona Macleod") Sharp. 6558-9
"Lords and ladies all bydene". A new carol of Our Lady. Unknown. 6756-5
"Lords had sighed, and princes prayed". Saint Adelaide. Edward Farquhar. 6939-8
Lords of the main. Joseph Stansbury. 6753-0
The lords of the main. Joseph Stansbury. 6288-1
The lords of Thule. Unknown. 6271-7,6424-8
"Lords of the seas' great wilderness". Watchmen of the night. Cecil Roberts. 7027-2
The Lords welcome, sung before the kings goodnight. Thomas Campion. 6794-8

Lordsburg internment camp. Sojin Takei. 6981-9
Lore. Edna Ethel Davis. 6144-3
"Lore large-hearted of life's ways". The researcher, fr. Gedichte. Johann Wolfgang von Goethe. 7042-6
The lore of diminishing returns, fr. On the fault line. Russell Haley. 7018-3
The Lorelei. Thomas Bailey Aldrich. 6439-6
The Lorelei. Heinrich Heine. 6484-1,6102-8
The Lorelei. Heinrich Heine. 6805-7
The Lorelei. Heinrich Heine. 6271-7
Loreley. Heinrich Heine. 6732-8
Lorena. J.P. Webster. 6074-9
Lorentz, Pare
  The river, sels. 6375-6
Lorenzini, Francesco
  "Sylph of the breeze! whose dewy pinions light". Felicia Dorothea Hemans (tr.). 6973-8
Loring Jr., Charles G.
  To Peggy. 6118-4
Loring, Charlotte Blake
  Moon-wrought tides. 6799-9
Loring, Frederick Wadsworth
  The crimson and the blue. 6370-5
  The fair millinger. 6089-7
  The old professor. 6004-8
  Tildy. 6687-9
Loring, Phyllis A.
  Spirit's deity. 6894-4
Lorraine. Charles Kingsley. 6413-2,6732-8,6370-5,6424-8, 6656-9
Lorraine Loree. Charles Kingsley. 6107-9
Lorraine, Lilith
  Alien to the earth. 6648-8
  Beyond the final breath. 6648-8
  If he should come. 6144-3,6337-3
  Into the endless night. 6648-8
  Not made with hands. 6144-3
  The stalker of dreams. 6648-8
  What will the stars remember? 6144-3
  When planes outsoar the spirit. 6337-3
  Who are the dead? 6648-8
Lorraine, Lorainee, lorree. Charles Kingsley. 6518-X
Lorris, Guillaume de
  The garden, fr. The romance of the rose. F.S. Ellis (tr.). 6649-6
  The romaunt of the rose, sels. F.S. Ellis (tr.). 6649-6
Los Angeles. James Abraham Martling. 6952-5
Los mineros. Edward Dorn. 6803-0
"'Lose and love', is love's first art". A song by the shore. Richard Hovey. 7006-X
Loses restored. William Shakespeare. 6084-6
Losing a friend. William Stafford. 6803-0
The losing side. Arthur E.J. Legge. 6253-9
Losing touch. John L. Kirkhoff. 6857-X
Losing track. Cathy Song. 6790-5
Loss. Mary Bradley Bramhall. 6764-6
Loss. Stephen Coleridge. 6785-9
Loss. Julia Johnson Davis. 6037-4
Loss. Hilda ("H.D.") Doolittle. 6250-4
Loss. Edgar A. Guest. 6748-4
Loss. Alex Kuo. 6790-5
Loss and gain. Phoebe Cary. 6969-X
Loss and gain. Bessie Rayner Parkes. 6303-9
Loss and gain. Steingrimur Thorsteinsson. 6854-5
Loss from the least. Robert Herrick. 6198-2
Loss in delay. Robert Southwell. 6436-1,6586-4
"Loss is a word of ache and smart". Loss. Edgar A. Guest. 6748-4
The loss of love. Countee Cullen. 6072-2
The loss of the Birkenhead. Sir Francis Hastings Doyle. 6242-3,6233-6,6656-9
The loss of the coffee pump. Richard Bradford Coolidge. 6118-4
The loss of the hornet. Unknown. 6344-6
Loss of the Royal George. William Cowper. 6246-5,6504-X, 6133-8,6138-9,6328-4,6552 ,6131-1,6438-8,6639-9,6600-3,6726-3,6732
A loss.. Judy [pseud]. 6453-1
Losse in delayes. Robert Southwell. 6586-4
Losses. Frances Brown. 6001-3,6271-7

LOSSES

Losses. Frances Browne. 6914-2
Losses. Frances Browne. 6600-3,6543-0
Losses. Randall Jarrell. 6666-6
Lost. Iris Barry. 6071-4
Lost. L.M. Cunard. 7002-7
Lost. James Whitcomb Riley. 6670-4
Lost. Carl Sandburg. 6154-0,6536-8,6726-3,6531-7,6581-3, 6653
Lost. George A. Scarborough. 6761-1
Lost. Robert Service. 6159-1
Lost. Mabel Stafford. 6750-6
Lost. Celia Thaxter. 6452-3,6490-6,6612-7
Lost. Unknown. 6166-4
Lost - a boy. Kate Bringhurst Joor. 6750-6
Lost acres. Robert Graves. 6209-1
Lost anchors. Edwin Arlington Robinson. 6333-0
Lost and found. Hamilton Aide. 6304-7,6370-5,6744-1,6569-4, 6911-8
Lost and found. Thomas B. Appleget. 6567-8
Lost and found. George Macdonald. 6337-3,6730-1,6155-9
Lost and given over. E.J. Brady. 6784-0
The lost angel. Al-Kasad. 6362-4
The lost ape. J.H.G. W. 6440-X
The lost arts. Unknown. 6294-6
Lost at sea. Simonides. 6435-3
Lost at sea. Simonides. 6435-3
Lost at sea. Simonides. 6435-3
Lost at sea, sels. Simonides. 6435-3
The lost babies. Unknown. 6273-3
The lost babies. Unknown. 6914-2
The lost battle. Alfred Noyes. 6151-6
The lost bell. Celia Thaxter. 6612-7
Lost bonnet-lost heart. Minna Irving. 6720-4
The lost bower. Elizabeth Barrett Browning. 6114-1
Lost but found. Horatius Bonar. 6656-9
Lost cabin. Delphine Harris Coy. 6836-7
The lost caryatid. Bayard Taylor. 6976-2
The lost cat. Lilian Whiting. 6120-6
Lost child. August Derleth. 6979-7
A lost child. Henry Cuyler Bunner. 6441-8
The lost child. Unknown. 6621-6,6629-1,6585-6
"Lost children, and hurt dogs...". From the train window. Grace Mansfield. 6750-6
The lost children. Richard Eberhart. 6388-8
A lost chord found. Willard Holcomb. 6926-6
A lost chord. Adelaide Anne Procter. 6142-7,6478-7,6486-8, 6260-1,6418-3,6730 ,6304-7,6658-5,6543-9,6214-8,6046-3,6521
The lost Christ ("Where have we laid him now") Franklin D. Elmer Jr. 6144-3
The lost Christ ("Your skill has fashioned...") Thomas Curtis Clark. 6144-3
The lost Christ. Estella Moul Miller. 6906-1
The lost church. Robert Tilney. 6914-2
The lost church. Johann Ludwig Uhland. 6648-8
The lost church. Johann Ludwig Uhland. 6271-7
The lost colors. Mary A. Barr. 6621-6
The lost crown. Bayard Taylor. 6976-2
Lost Cupid. Moschus. 6949-5
The lost day. E.O. De Camp. 6906-1
The lost day. Charles Mackay. 6543-0
Lost days, fr. The house of life. Dante Gabriel Rossetti. 6198-2,6337-3,6339-X,6378-0,6380-2,6385 ,6473-6,6122-2,6726-3,6250-4,6110-9,6560 ,6199-0,6508-2,6192-3, 6430-2
'Lost delight', after the Hazara war. Laurence (Adele Florence Nicolson) Hope. 6856-1
Lost dog. Frances Rodman. 6465-5,6396-9
Lost dog. Frances Todman. 6088-3
The lost doll. Charles Kingsley. 6132-X,6623-2,6242-3,6249-0,6519-8,6131-1,6135-4,6424-8,6456-6,6638-0,6639
The lost doll. Unknown. 6629-1
The lost dream. Fannie Stearns Davis. 7038-8
The lost elixir. Austin Dobson. 6123-0
The lost expedition. Thomas Hood. 6997-5
Lost for a rose's sake. Unknown (French) 6771-9
The lost found. Unknown. 6417-5
Lost freedom of Switzerland. James Sheridan Knowles. 6980-0
A lost friend. Paton H. Hoge. 6085-4

A lost friend. John Boyle O'Reilly. 6085-4;6243-1
The lost friend. Norman Gale. 6105-2,6084-6
A lost game. Thompson Seiser Westcott. 6936-3
The lost garden. Ella Wheeler Wilcox. 6956-0
The lost garden. Ella Wheeler Wilcox. 7041-8
Lost gardens. Louise Driscoll. 6649-6
The lost genius. John James Piatt. 6431-0
Lost glasses. Walt Curtis. 7003-5
A lost God, sels. Francis William Bourdillon. 6730-1
Lost harbor. Leslie Nelson Jennings. 6619-4
The lost heart. Herbert S. Gorman. 6033-1,6880-4
A lost heifer. Austin Clarke. 6071-4,6581-3
The lost heifer. Austin Clarke. 6071-4
The lost heir. Thomas Hood. 6302-06385-3,6407-8,6279-2, 6219-9
The lost hellas. Hjalmar Hjorth Boyesen. 7041-8
The lost heritage. William Alexander Percy. 6039-0
Lost hope. Alfred Lord Tennyson. 6977-0
The lost ideal of the world. Eric Sutherland Robertson. 7015-9
Lost in France. Ernest Rhys. 6250-4
Lost in Hades. Andrew Lang. 6771-9
"Lost in a timeless dream the sycamores...". American scene. Josephine Johnson. 6761-1
Lost in the Mallee. Charles Allan Sherard. 6768-9
Lost in the snow. Sir Walter Scott. 6394-2
Lost in the snow. James Thomson. 6438-8
"Lost is my quiet for ever". Song ("Lost is my quiet"). Unknown. 6563-5
The lost jewel. Emily Dickinson. 6121-4
The lost joy, sel. Ruth Le Prade. 6954-1
The lost key. Priscilla Leonard. 6337-3
The lost kiss. James Whitcomb Riley. 6632-1,6691-7
Lost kitten at the door. Emily Templeton. 6750-6
The lost lady found. Unknown. 6057-9
The lost lagoon. Emily Pauline ("Tekahionwake") Johnson. 6115-X
The lost lamb. Thomas Westwood. 6132-X,6466-3,6808-1
A lost land: to Germany. Unknown. 7031-0
A lost land. Kathleen Knox. 7027-2
The lost leader. Robert Browning. 6828-6
The lost leader. Robert Browning. 6154-0,6246-6,6271-7, 6289-X,6328-4,6483-,6046-3,6084-6,6438-8,6424-8,6560-0,6219 ,6198-2,6332-2,6427-2,6600-3,6657-7,6683-, 6102-8,6110-9,6197-4,6304-7,6219-4,6250 ,6196-6,6655-0,6656-9.6543-0,6723-9,6199 ,6092-7,6552-X
A lost legend. Francis William Bourdillon. 6610-0
The lost legion. Rudyard Kipling. 6810-3
A lost letter. Clement Scott. 6273-3,6681-X
Lost lilies. Alice Cary. 6969-X
"Lost lord of song - who grandly gave". The disinterment. Bartholomew Simmons. 6980-0
The lost lotus. Unknown. 6453-1
Lost love. Robert Graves. 6339-X
Lost love. Andrew Lang. 6320-9,6102-8,6301-2
Lost love. Herman L. McMillan. 7024-8
Lost love. Unknown. 6873-1
The lost love. Edward Farquhar. 6939-8
The lost love. Fenton Johnson. 6032-3
The lost love. William Wordsworth. 6246-6,6302-0,6385-3, 6226-1
Lost lovely things. Cecil E.C. Hodgson. 6316-0
The lost lyon. Lewis Spence. 6269-5
The lost master. Robert Service. 6159-1,6583-X
The lost May. Bayard Taylor. 6976-2,6049-8
The lost mistress. Robert Browning. 6828-6
The lost mistress. Robert Browning. 6023-4,6208-3,6437-X, 6371-5,6543-0,6737 ,6655-0
The lost mittens. Unknown. 6699-2
Lost Mr. Blake. Sir William Schwenck Gilbert. 6406-X
"Lost now are the homes...". Alpheus. 6251-2
The lost nymph. George Sterling. 6269-5
The lost occasion. John Greenleaf Whittier. 6126-5,6288-1, 6964-9
Lost on both sides. Dante Gabriel Rossetti. 6110-9
Lost on the prairie. Rose Terry Cooke. 6127-3
Lost on the shore. Holme Lee. 6416-7
The lost ones. Francis Ledwidge. 6096-X;6234-2
The lost ones. Francis Ledwidge. 6846-4
The lost ones. Unkown. 6589-9

1010

The lost orchard. Edgar Lee Masters. 6299-7
The lost page. Unknown. 6926-6
A lost path. Andrew Lang. 6771-9
The lost path. James Whitcomb Riley. 6992-4
The lost penny. Unknown. 6744-1
Lost pins. Agnes Carr. 6965-7
The lost playmate. Abbie Farwell Brown. 6242-3,6607-0
The lost pleiad. Felicia Dorothea Hemans. 6980-0
The lost Pleiad. Felicia Dorothea Hemans. 6973-8
The lost Pleiad. William Gilmore Simms. 7017-5
The lost pleiad. William Gilmore Simms. 6431-0
The lost pudding. Elizabeth Turner. 6105-2,6134-6
The lost puppy. Henry Firth Wood. 6249-0,6577-5
The lost sheep. Sally Pratt McLean. 6273-3
The lost sheep. Elizabeth Cecilia Clephane. 6214-8
The lost shepherd. Louise Morey Bowman. 6843-X
The lost shipmate. Theodore Goodridge Roberts. 6843-X
The lost shipmate. Theodore Goodridge Roberts. 6115-X
Lost ships. Thomas Hornsby Ferril. 6833-2
The lost shoe. Norah M. Holland. 6797-2
The lost singer. Scudder Middleton. 6033-1,6542-2
The lost sister. Lydia Huntley Sigourney. 6302-0;6385-3
"Lost somewhere today in the red-headed clover". My out-of-door cricket. Benjamin Franklin Taylor. 6815-4
Lost songs. Nina Salaman. 6778-6
The lost spectacles. Unknown. 6089-7
Lost spirits. H. Gandy. 7035-3
The lost star. William ("Fiona Macleod") Sharp. 6507-4
The lost steamship. Fitz-James O'Brien. 6914-2
A lost talisman. Ray Clarke Rose. 6274-1
Lost thoughts. Jane M. Stern. 6799-9
Lost Tommy. Julia M. Dana. 6743-3
The lost trail. Henry Herbert Knibbs. 7008-6
The lost trail. Frank Lillie Pollock. 7035-3
The lost traveller's dream. Eva Gore-Booth. 7029-9
Lost twilight. Robert Hillyer. 6761-1
Lost valley. Glenn Ward Dresbach. 6750-6
The lost valley. Stanton A. Coblentz. 6628-3
Lost voice on this hill. Burnham Eaton. 6218-0
A lost voice. Francis William Bourdillon. 6658-5
The lost war-sloop. Edna Dean Proctor. 6678-X
The lost watch. Unknown. 6915-0
The lost watch. Unknown. 6167-2
A lost word of Jesus. Henry Van Dyke. 6730-1
The lost word. Charles Henry ("John Paul") Webb. 6440-X
The lost world of Adonis. Praxilla. 6435-3
Lost youth. Sir Roger Casement. 6292-X
Lost youth. Henry Wadsworth Longfellow. 6258-X,6547-3
"Lost, lost! yet come". Songs from Paracelsus. Robert Browning. 6828-6
Lost—a soul. Anna Spencer Twitchell. 6836-7
Lost—an April. Mary Brent Whiteside. 6619-4
Lost—three little robings. Unknown. 6820-0
The lost.. Jones Very. 6333-0
Lost: three little robins. Unknown. 6304-7,6449-3
The lost. William Hester. 6017-X
The lot of thousands. Anne Hunter. 6219-9
Lot Skinner's elegy. James Thomas Fields. 6505-8
Lot's wife. Elizabeth Morrow. 6102-8,6076-5
Lot's wife. Mary Sylvester Paden. 6836-7
The lot. Gamaliel Bradford. 6039-0
Lothian, A. (tr.)
    To Pan. Unknown (Greek), 6435-3
    "Twy-horn Pan, the ridgy hills". Unknown, 6435-3
The lotos-eaters, sel. Alfred Lord Tennyson. 6958-4
The lotos-eaters, sels. Alfred Lord Tennyson. 6123-0,6395-0,6501-5,6726-3,6541-4,6102 ,6543-0,6645-3,6383-7,6656-9,6245-0,6199
The lotos-eaters. Alfred Lord Tennyson. 6479-5,6657-7,6154-0,6479-5,6423-X,6657-7,6478-7,6547 ,6332-2,6271-7,6536-8,6655-0,6732-8,6491 ,6646-1,6639-9,6301-2,6252-
Lott, Eve
    Freedom. 6880-4
Lottery. Lucile Enlow. 6841-3
Lottie. James Abraham Martling. 6952-5
Lottie Dougherty. Dwight Williams. 6414-0,6744-1
Lottie Mae. Stanley McNail. 6218-0
Lotty's message. Alexander G. Murdoch. 6692-5,6923-1
Lotus. Unknown (Japanese) 6027-7

The lotus eaters. Donald Finkel. 6803-0
The lotus of the Nile. Arthur Wentworth Hamilton Eaton. 6115-X
The lotus-eaters, sels. Alfred Lord Tennyson. 6430-2,6560-0,6110-9,6196-6,6125-7
The lotus. Wiley G. Hosier. 6799-9
"Loud across the world it ringeth...". The voice of freedom. Fred Henderson. 7009-4
"Loud alleluias sing!". Alleluia. William White. 6868-5
"Loud and wild the storm is howling". Old letters. William J. Benners Jr.. 6923-1
"The loud black flight of the storm diverges". A ballade of Calypso. Sir Charles George Douglas Roberts. 6770-0
The loud call. Unknown. 6294-6
"Loud drums are rolling, the mad trumpets blow". Battle cry. William Henry Venable. 6946-0
"Loud from its wicker cage the thrush yet sing". The thrush. Alfred Henry Haynes Bell. 6800-6
Loud intersection. Grover I. Jacoby Jr. 6316-0
"Loud is the vale! the voice is up". Lines, composed at Grasmere. William Wordsworth. 6867-7
Loud jazz horns. Carter Webster. 6178-8
"Loud o'er thy savage child". Hymn for the Massachusetts Charitable Association. John Pierpont. 6752-2
The loud silence. Susie M. Best. 6750-6
"Loud the horns and sweet the strings". Dance. Raymond Peckham Holden. 6959-2
"Loud the wind leaps through the night...". The spell. Edmund Blunden. 6777-8
"Loud through the still November air". The church of the revolution. Hezekiah Butterworth. 6946-0
"Loud without the wind was roaring". Emily Bronte. 6123-0
Loud, Ethel Godfrey
    War. 6799-9
Loud, John J.
    Parting of the ways. 6718-2
"Loudly roared the English cannon...". The captured flag. Arthur Weir. 6795-6
Loudon Hill, or Drumclog. Unknown. 6185-0
Loudoun's bonnie woods and braes. Robert Tannahill. 6086-2
"Loue chill'd wth cold & missing in ye skyes." Unknown. 6563-5
"Loue I obey shoot home thy dart." Unknown. 6563-5
"Loue throwes more dangerous darts yn death I spy." Unknown. 6563-5
"Loue whets the dullest wittes, his plagues...". Canto quarto. Thomas Campion. 6794-8
The louer comforteth himselfe with the worthinesse... Henry Howard, Earl of Surrey. 6586-4
Loues seruile lot. Robert Southwell. 6586-4,6022-6
Lougee, F. Marion
    Moonlight fantasy. 6799-9
Lougee, Marguerite E.
    The voice of a soul. 6799-9
Lough bray. Rose Kavanagh. 6060-0,6174-5
Lough bray. Standish O'Grady. 6174-5
Lough bray, II. Standish O'Grady. 6090-0
Louie. Paul D. Shiplett. 6870-7
Louis Napoleon's address to his army. William Edmonstoune Aytoun. 6278-4
Louis Tikas, Ludlow martyr. Francis Gibson Richard. 6149-4
Louis XV. Christopher (John Wilson) North. 6302-0;6385-3
Louis XV. John Sterling. 6219-9
Louis, Adrian C.
    Captivity narrative: September 1981 7005-1
    Elegy for the forgotten oldsmobile. 7005-1
    The Hemingway syndrome. 7005-1
    Indian education. 7005-1
    The Walker river night. 7005-1
Louis, Louise
    Chameleon. 6750-6
    Festival. 6799-9
    Night solitude. 6750-6
Louisa. William Wordsworth. 6828-6
Louisa May Alcott. Louise Chandler Moulton. 6820-0
Louisbourg. Francis Hopkinson. 6753-0
Louisburg. Unknown. 6946-0
Louise Hedeen. Edgar Lee Masters. 6300-4
Louise Scheper (1). Felicia Dorothea Hemans. 6973-8

LOUISE

Louise Schelper (2). Felicia Dorothea Hemans. 6973-8
"**Louise,** have you forgotten yet". Old loves. Henri Murger. 6771-9
Louise, the slave. William Dean Howells. 6706-9
Louisiana. K. O. Hass. 6818-9
Louk, Louis de
    Infection. 6889-8
Loulou and her cat. Frederick Locker-Lampson. 6026-9
Lounsbery, G. Constant
    The tempest. 6327-6
A **louse** crept out of my lady' shift. Gordon Bottomley. 6125-7
Louse song. Unknown. 6237-7
The **louse-catchers.** Arthur Rimbaud. 6343-8
Lousy Peter. Osbert Sitwell. 6257-1
Louthan, Hattie Horner
    Delusion. 6836-7
    Desert love song. 6836-7
    I must write. 6836-7
    Ila, sels. 6836-7
    In the city. 6836-7
    Invitation. 6836-7
    Songs of Ila, sels. 6836-7
Louther, Hal
    Yes or no. 6255-5
Louvain. Laurence Binyon. 7031-0
Louvre. Rhys Davies. 6360-8
Louÿs, Pierre
    The flute. 6351-9
    The nymph. 6351-9
    The pastoral. Joseph T. Shipley (tr.). 6351-9
    The pastoral. 6351-9
    Second epitaph. 6351-9
The **lovable** child. Anne Emilie Poulsson. 6891-X
Love. Sarah Flower Adams. 6656-9
Love. Anacreon. 6435-3
Love. Joseph Beaumont. 6933-9
Love. Anne C. Lynch Botta. 6600-3
Love. Elizabeth Barrett Browning. 6123-0
Love. Samuel Butler. 6563-5,6737-9
Love. George Gordon, 6th Baron Byron. 6066-8
Love. Charles Stuart Calverley. 6026-9
Love. Reita M. Clapsaddle. 6799-9
Love. John Clare. 6125-7
Love. Samuel Taylor Coleridge. 6246-5,6676-3,6732-8,6271-7, 6086-2,6110 ,6219-9,6543-0,6301-2,6430-2,6560-0,6110-9,6199-0,6250-4
Love. Samuel Taylor Coleridge. 6315-2
Love. Abraham Cowley. 6513-9
Love. Abraham Cowley. 6339-X
Love. Grace Noll Crowell. 6750-6
Love. Samuel Daniel. 6438-8
Love. Samuel Daniel. 6830-8
Love. Emily Dickinson. 6077-3
Love. John Donne. 6438-8
Love. Grace Imogen Duffy. 6818-9
Love. John Galsworthy. 6888-X
Love. Stella Gibbons. 6893-6
Love. Kahlil Gibran. 6979-7
Love. Walker Gibson. 6388-8
Love. Elizabeth D. Gongaware. 6799-9
Love. Elena Vossen Greenfield. 6841-3
Love. Edgar A. Guest. 6862-6
Love. Mary Henderson. 6750-6
Love. George Herbert. 6198-2,6187-7,6341-1,6125-7,6150-8, 6153-2,6189-3,6737-9,6335-7,6208-3,6317-9,6337-3, 6488-4,6563-,6562-7,6339-X,6726-3,6473-6,6625-9,6122-
Love. Thomas Kibble Hervey. 6302-0;6385-3
Love. Charles Lotin Hildreth. 7041-8
Love. Thomas Hood. 6980-0
Love. Thomas Hood. 6974-6
Love. Ibycus. 6435-3
Love. Jean Ingelow. 6066-8,6383-7
Love. Ben Jonson. 6226-1
Love. Thomas Lodge. 6383-7
Love. James Russell Lowell. 6620-8,6066-8
Love. Winifred Lucas. 6785-9
Love. Robert MacGowan. 6461-2
Love. Alma Frances McCollum. 6115-X
Love. Thomas Moore. 6889-8

Love. Edward Moxon. 6980-0
Love. Anthony Munday. 6436-1
Love. Frank (Michael O'Donovan) O'Connor. 6072-2
Love. Frederick L. Paxson. 6936-3
Love. George Peele. 6436-1
Love. Howard Phillips. 6799-9
Love. Richard Rolle. 6102-8,6022-6,6383-7
Love. Sappho. 6435-3
Love. William Shakespeare. 6304-7
Love. Percy Bysshe Shelley. 6980-0
Love. Edmund Spenser. 6436-1
Love. William Wetmore Story. 6429-9,6226-1,6321-7
Love. Charles Swain. 6620-8
Love. Algernon Charles Swinburne. 6302-0;6385-3
Love. Alfred Lord Tennyson. 6977-0
Love. Henry David Thoreau. 6176-1,6437-X
Love. Jaime Torres Bodet. 6759-X
Love. Herbert Trench. 6337-3
Love. C. H. Waring. 6770-0
Love. Charles Wells. 6102-8
Love. Helen Welshimer. 6750-6
"**Love** & I of late did parte." Unknown. 6563-5
"**Love** 'mid the flowers is softly singing". Spring song. Fr. Kvapil. 6763-8
Love ("I love you"). Unknown. 6337-3
Love above beauty. Henry Reynolds. 6328-4
Love abused. William Cowper. 6814-6
Love affair. Edgar A. Guest. 6748-4
Love after death. Arthur O'Shaughnessy. 6244-X
Love against love. David Atwood Wasson. 6302-0,6385-3,6438-8,6429-9,6321-7,6429
Love aglow. Blanche Chalfant Tucker. 6270-9
"**Love** all the senses doth beguile". Of love. James Sandford. 6182-6
Love among the clover. Odell Shepard. 6441-8
Love among the ruins. Robert Browning. 6828-6
Love among the ruins. Robert Browning. 6154-0,6204-0,6320-9,6332-2,6437-X,6473-,6196-6,6199-0,6430-2,6655-0, 6560-0,6541 ,6110-9,6371-3,6066-8,6543-0,6723-9,6657
Love among the ruins, sels. Robert Browning. 6123-0
Love an evil. George Croly. 6980-0
Love and a day. Madison Cawein. 6441-8
Love and absence. James Ashcroft Noble. 6226-1
Love and age. Thomas Love Peacock. 6030-7,6046-3,6092-7
Love and age. Unknown. 6911-8
Love and art. Jean Starr Untermeyer. 6345-4
Love and art. Francis Ernley Walrond. 6800-2
Love and beauty. Edgar Lee Masters. 6778-6
Love and books. K.D. of Wirsin (Swedish) 6297-0
Love and death. Caius Catallus. 7039-6
Love and death. John Ford. 6219-9
Love and death. Ben Jonson. 6563-5
Love and death. Rosa Mulholland; Lady Gilbert. 6656-9
Love and death. Victor F. Murray. 6269-5
Love and death. Alfred Lord Tennyson. 6328-4,6066-8
Love and death. Unknown. 6429-9,6321-7
"**Love** and death once ceased their strife". The explanation. Rudyard Kipling. 6810-3
Love and debt. Sir John Suckling. 6092-7
Love and duty. Alfred Lord Tennyson. 6046-3
Love and fame. Edward Bulwer-Lytton; Baron Lytton. 6980-0
Love and fear. Kenton Kilmer. 6042-0
Love and fortune. Fulke Greville; 1st Baron Brooke. 6436-1
Love and friendship. Emily Bronte. 6246-6
Love and friendship. William Leggett. 6600-3,6226-1
"**Love** and harmony combine". Song ("Love and harmony"). William Blake. 6943-6
Love and hate, fr. Christus. Henry Wadsworth Longfellow. 6337-3
Love and honour. Fulke Greville; 1st Baron Brooke. 6436-1
Love and hope. Francis Brooks. 6274-1
Love and hope. Thomas Moore. 6543-0
Love and humility. Henry More. 6438-8
Love and infinity. Cale Young Rice. 6266-0
Love and jealousy. Robert Greene. 6182-6
Love and jealousy. Sir Philip Sidney. 6584-8
Love and joy come to you. Unknown. 6082-X,6747-6
Love and labor. Unknown. 6273-3,6303-9
Love and law. John Godfrey Saxe. 68782
Love and liberation. John Hall Wheelock. 6509-0

Love and liberty. Royall Tyler. 7030-2
Love and life. Abraham Cowley. 6562-7
Love and life. John Wilmot, 2d Earl of Rochester. 6092-7,
    6195-0,6152-4,6189-3,6315-2,6198-2,6208-3,6328-4,
    6563-5,6562-7,6544
Love and life. Sarah ("Susan Coolidge") Woolsey. 6066-8
Love and love's mates. Algernon Charles Swinburne. 6828-6
Love and love's mates, fr. Atalanta in Calydon. Algernon
    Charles Swinburne. 6110-9
Love and loyalty. Sir Charles Lucas. 6328-4
Love and lust. William Shakespeare. 6543-0
Love and May. Unknown. 6250-4
Love and murder. Unknown. 6279-2
Love and music. Henry Lawes. 6328-4
Love and music. Philip Bourke Marston. 6656-9
Love and music. Meleager. 6102-8
Love and night. Henry Van Dyke. 6961-4
Love and opportunity. Thomas Love Peacock. 6934-7
Love and Phillis. Thomas Lodge. 6191-5
Love and philosophy. George Chapman. 6436-1
Love and pity. Unknown. 6273-3
Love and prudence. William Wetmore Story. 6429-9,6321-7
Love and reason. Arthur Hugh Clough. 6655-0
Love and reason. Thomas Moore. 6092-7
Love and reason. Matthew Prior. 6932-0
Love and reverence. Thomas Randolph. 6102-8
Love and sacrifice. Bernard O'Dowd. 6784-0
Love and science. J. Merritt Matthews. 6936-3
Love and science. Unknown. 6440-X
Love and sleep. Arthur Symons. 6655-0
Love and sorrow. William Edward Hartpole Lecky. 6174-5
Love and sorrow. Alfred Lord Tennyson. 6977-0
Love and sorrow, fr. The sisters. Algernon Charles
    Swinburne. 6508-2
Love and the child. William Brighty Rands. 6519-8
Love and the child. Francis Thompson. 6655-0
Love and the flimsies. Thomas Love Peacock. 6802-2
Love and the poet. William Shakespeare. 6150-8
Love and the sea. Robert Etheridge Gregg. 6116-8
Love and the stars. William Aspenwall Bradley. 6320-9
Love and the universe, sels. Albert Durrant Watson. 6115-X
Love and theology. Unknown. 6672-0
Love and time. Thomas Moore. 6874-X
Love and time. Sir Walter Raleigh. 6584-8
Love and war. Arthur Patchett Martin. 6274-1,6656-9
Love and weariness. Mark Andre Raffalovitch. 7015-9
Love and wine. Hafiz. 6448-5
Love and wisdom. Andrew Lang. 6771-9
Love armed. Aphra Behn. 6563-5
Love as the interest of the poets. Sir Walter Scott. 6543-0
Love at ebb, fr. Chastelard. Algernon Charles Swinburne.
    6110-9
Love at first sigh. Alfred Henry Haynes Bell. 6800-6
Love at first sight. Francis Beaumont and John Fletcher.
    6438-8
Love at first sight. Owen (Edward Bulwer-Lytton, Earl
    Lytton) Meredith. 6226-1
Love at first sight. Christopher Morley. 6078-1;6320-9
Love at first sight, fr. Smith: a tragedy. John Davidson.
    6819-7
Love at sea. Theophile Gautier. 6732-8
Love at sea. Algernon Charles Swinburne. 6123-0,6110-9,
    6560-0,6655-0,6656-9
Love autumnal. Oliver Jenkins. 6762-X
"Love bade me welcome; yet my soul drew back". Love.
    George Herbert. 6198-2,6187-7,6341-1,6125-7,6150-8,
    6153-2,6189-3,6737-9,6335-7,6208-3,6317-9,6337-3,
    6488-4,6563-,6562-7,6339-X,6726-3,6473-6,6625-9,6122-
Love banished heaven. Michael Drayton. 6543-0
Love beleaguered. Katherine Garrison Chapin. 6979-7
Love between brothers and sisters. Isaac Watts. 6479-5
Love beyond change. Fulke Greville; 1st Baron Brooke. 6194-X
Love brings warning of natura maligns,fr.Coming of love.
    Theodore Watts-Dunton. 6997-5
"Love built a stately house;where fortune came". The
    world. George Herbert. 6933-9
Love came back at fall o' dew. Lizette Woodworth Reese.
    6102-8,6310-1,6347-0,6019-6,6076-5,6393
Love can never lose its own. John Greenleaf Whittier. 6461-2
Love cannot die. Phoebe Cary. 6865-0;6969-X
Love cannot live. Unknown. 6182-6
Love ceremonious. Coventry Patmore. 6429-9,6321-7
Love comes. Ernest Howard Crosby. 6542-2
Love comfortless. Katharine (Hinkson) Tynan. 6174-5
Love constraining to obedience. William Cowper. 6814-6
Love crucified. William White. 6868-5
Love defiant. Alfred Lord Tennyson. 7015-9
Love devine, all love excelling. Augustus Montague
    Toplady. 6600-3
Love diademed on earth. William White. 6868-5
"Love died here". Love's Easter. Andrew Lang. 6987-8
Love disappointed. Ralph Douberly. 6841-3
Love dissembled, fr. As you like it. William Shakespeare.
    6302-0;6385-3
Love ditty. R. Grant Brown. 6591-0,6592-9
Love divine. Isabelle Noyes. 6818-9
Love divine. Charles Wesley. 6337-3
Love divine. William White. 6868-5
"Love doth again." Sir Thomas Wyatt. 6584-8
Love doth to her eyes repair. James Freeman Clarke. 6321-7
Love doth to her eyes repair. Friedrich Ruckert. 6226-1
'Love doth to her eyes repair'. James Freeman Clarke. 6429-9
The love elegies of Abel Shufflebottom. Robert Southey.
    6278-4
Love elegies, sels. James Hammond. 6152-4
Love elegy. Tobias George Smollett. 6975-4
Love enthroned. Aphra Behn. 6830-8
Love enthroned, fr. The house of life. Dante Gabriel
    Rossetti. 6110-9,6250-4,6655-0
Love enthroned, fr. The house of liofe. Dante Gabriel
    Rossetti. 6508-2
Love epigram. Sean O'Faolain. 6582-1
Love ever green. Henry VIII; King of England (atr) 6881-2
A love extravaganza. Charles Mackay. 6066-8
Love faithful in the absence of the beloved. Madame De la
    Mothe Guion. 6814-6
"Love flew by! Young wedding day". Rose and yew. John
    Galsworthy. 6888-X
Love for a beautiful lady. Unknown. 6881-2
"The love for fatherland was deep". Sleep, weary child.
    Carl Plough. 6916-9
Love for love's sake. Elizabeth Barrett Browning. 6094-3,
    6321-7
Love for love, sels. William Congreve. 6562-7
A love for Patsy. John Thompson Jr. 6666-6
"Love for such a cherry lip". Song ("Love for such").
    Thomas Middleton. 6182-6
"Love for such a cherry lip". Thomas Middleton. 6187-7
"Love forged for me a golden chain". Wildness. Blanche
    Shoemaker Wagstaff. 6776-X
Love forsworn, fr. measure for measure. William
    Shakespeare. 6332-2,6560-0
Love found me. Richard Chenevix Trench. 6337-3
"Love found them sitting in a woodland place". Love's
    secret. John Boyle O'Reilly. 7041-8
Love from the north. Christina Georgina Rossetti. 6518-X
"Love gave a light kiss". Song ("Love gave"). Florence
    Hamilton. 6324-1
"Love gives every gift,whereby we long to live". Echoes of
    love's house. William Morris. 6844-8
Love goes a-hawking, fr. The bride's tragedy. Thomas
    Lovell Beddoes. 6656-9
"Love growne proude governe me." Unknown. 6563-5
"Love grows dumb". Ase's death. Gertrude Huntington
    McGiffert. 6838-3
"Love guards the roses of thy lips". To love. Thomas
    Lodge. 6934-7
"Love guards the roses of thy lips". Thomas Lodge. 6187-7;6182-6
"Love guides the roses of thy lips". Love's wantonness.
    Thomas Lodge. 6827-8
"Love had left her. The years". Paradox. Elydia Shipman.
    6799-9
"Love has been dragged too often through..mire". Love.
    Grace Noll Crowell. 6750-6
"Love has been sung a thousand ways". Songs ascending, fr.
    To Celia. Witter Bynner. 6897-9

LOVE

"Love has gone and left me...". Ashes of life. Edna St. Vincent Millay. 6986-X
"Love has gone. Ah, my love has gone". Love's silence. Yong-woon Han. 6775-1
Love has not eyes. Thomas Hood. 6974-6
Love has shining eyes. Fannie Stearns Davis. 6320-9
"Love has unbound my limbs". Love. Sappho. 6435-3
Love hath a language, fr. To my son. Helen Selina Sheridan; Lady Dufferin. 6934-7
Love hath no physic for a grief too deep. Robert Nathan. 6619-4,6036-6
Love hath no years. William White. 6868-5
"Love hath wept till he is blind". Blind love. Rosamund Marriott ("Graham R. Tomson") Watson. 6875-8
A love idyl, fr. The song of songs. Bible. 6153-2
A love idyll. Anna C. Bowen. 6799-9
Love importunate. Laurence Housman. 6507-4
Love in a cottage. Nathaniel Parker Willis. 6077-3,6441-8, 6661-5,6661-5,6735-2,6307-1,6278-4,6652-6,6004-8, 6505-8
Love in a life. Robert Browning. 6429-9,6437-X,6430-2,6199-0,6655-0,6321 ,6102-8,6110-9
Love in a look. Henry Van Dyke. 6961-4
Love in absence. Mabel V. Irvine. 6269-5
Love in absence. Edmund Spenser. 6543-0
Love in action. Coventry Patmore. 6187-7
Love in age. Ethel Anderson. 6349-7
Love in age. Charles G. Bell. 6388-8
Love in Arcady. Robert Greene. 6830-8
Love in dreams. John Addington Symonds. 6250-4
Love in exile, sels. Mathilde Blind. 6656-9
Love in fantastic triumph (sat) Aphra Behn. 6092-7,6430-2
"Love in fantastic triumph sate". Love enthroned. Aphra Behn. 6830-8
"Love in fantastic triumph [sate].". Song ("Love in fantastic"). Aphra Behn. 6191-5
"Love in fantastique triumph sat". Song. Love arm'd. Aphra Behn. 6933-9
'Love in her eyes sits playing'. John Gay. 6208-3
Love in her hair. Unknown (Greek) 6435-3
Love in her sunny eyes. Abraham Cowley. 6543-0
Love in Italy, sels. John Hall Ingham. 6624-0
Love in June. Mary Genevieve Manahan. 6818-9
Love in Lent. Unknown. 6697-6
Love in London. Justin Huntly McCarthy. 6875-8,6770-0
"Love in her sunny eyes does basking play". The change. Abraham Cowley. 6933-9
Love in marriage. Struthers Burt. 6320-9
Love in May. Jean Passerat. 6771-9
Love in my arms lies sleeping. Dora Sigerson Shorter. 6174-5
"Love in my bosom like a bee". Rosalind's song. Thomas Lodge. 6830-8
"Love in my bosom like a bee". Thomas Lodge. 6181-8;6187-7
Love in old age. William Force Stead. 6776-X
Love in spring. Meleager. 6435-3
Love in spring-time, fr. As you like it. William Shakespeare. 6332-2,6560-0
Love in the autumn. P. R. Minahan. 6818-9
Love in the calendar. Robert Underwood Johnson. 6441-8, 6652-6
Love in the dark, sels. Sir Francis Fane. 6562-7,6563-5
Love in the desert. Gertrude Huntington McGiffert. 6838-3
Love in the kitchen. David Law ("Pegleg Arkwright") Proudfit. 6825-1
"Love in the middle as we go 'round". Susie Brown. Unknown. 6826-X
Love in the valley. George Meredith. 6828-6
Love in the valley. George Meredith. 6023-4,6199-0,6508-2, 6660-7,6219-9,6301 ,6122-2,6192-6,6657-7,6655-0,6102-8,6250
Love in the valley, sels. George Meredith. 6179-6,6204-0, 6246-6,6634-8,6726-3,6477-9,6491-4
Love in the winds. Richard Hovey. 6753-0
Love in the winds. Richard Hovey. 6250-4,6300-4,6737-9
Love in the winds. Richard Hovey. 6753-0
Love in thy youth. Unknown. 6250-4
Love in thy youth, fair maid, be wise. Unknown. 6187-7
"Love in thy youth, fair maid; be wise". Madrigal. Unknown. 6830-8

"Love in thy youth, fair maid; be wise." Unknown. 6187-7, 6317-9,6250-4
Love in [or and] Italy. Robert Underwood Johnson. 6102-8, 6331-4,6309-8
Love increased by suffering. Madame De la Mothe Guion. 6814-6
Love is a babel. Unknown. 6328-4
Love is a bog. Unknown. 6328-4
"Love is a circle, that doth restless move". Love what it is. Robert Herrick. 6874-X
"Love is a day of golden beams". Psychoanalyzed; or the erotic motive in contribbing. R.N. S.. 6817-0
Love is a hunter-boy. Thomas Moore. 6328-4,6226-1
Love is a law. Unknown. 6182-6
Love is a law, fr. The Thracian wonder. John Webster and William Rowley. 6934-7
"Love is a rose that blooms/Just for a day". Love in June. Mary Genevieve Manahan. 6818-9
"Love is a shield to hold against the dark". Avowal. Minnie Markham Kerr. 6750-6
"Love is a shining vital thing". Love. Elizabeth D. Gongaware. 6799-9
Love is a sickness. Samuel Daniel. 6092-7
"Love is a sickness full of woes". Love. Samuel Daniel. 6830-8
"Love is a sickness full of woes." Samuel Daniel. 6513-9, 6430-2,6219-9,6737-9,6385-3,6317-9,6315-2,6436-1, 6182-6,6302-2
Love is a terrible thing. Grace Fallow Norton. 6556-2,6076-5,6464-7,6393-4,6102-8,6019-6,6467-1
Love is always here. Edmund Clarence Stedman. 6053-6
"Love is and was my lord and king", fr. In memoriam. Alfred Lord Tennyson. 6536-8,6634-8
Love is as strong as death. Christina Georgina Rossetti. 6337-3,6641-0
Love is blind. Unknown. 6673-9
"Love is come with a song a smile". Alfred Lord Tennyson. 6066-8
"Love is cruel, love is sweet". Song ("Love is cruel"). Thomas MacDonagh. 6090-0,6022-6
Love is dead. Sir Philip Sidney. 6198-2
Love is enough. Walter Savage Landor. 6732-8
Love is enough. William Morris. 6123-0,6320-9,6301-2,6655-0,6102-8,6199-0,6250-4
Love is enough. Ella Wheeler Wilcox. 6620-8,6238-5
Love is enough, sels. William Morris. 6110-9
Love is eternal. Carlotta Perry. 6066-8
Love is idle, fr. Danae. Euripides. 6435-3
Love is life. Alice Cary. 6969-X
"Love is like a charming rose". The rose and the thorn. Mary Frances Ward. 6818-9
Love is like a dizziness. James Hogg. 6089-7,6240-7
"Love is like tomato soup". Evaporation. Rosalie Maher. 6850-2
"Love is my sin and thy dear virtue hate". Sonnet 142 ("Love is my sin"). William Shakespeare. 6447-7
"Love is not a feeling to pass away". Song ("Love is not"). Charles Dickens. 6066-8
"Love is not a toy". Waiting. Rubye Arnold. 7016-7
"Love is not love". William Shakespeare. 6238-5
Love is not to be reasoned down or lost. Joseph Addison. 6066-8
Love is not winged. Eubulus. 6435-3
Love is of God. Horatius Bonar. 6337-3
"Love is the blossom where there blows." Giles (the Elder) Fletcher. 6317-9
"Love is the lord whom I obey". Divine love endures no rival. Madame De la Mothe Guion. 6814-6
Love is the only good in the world. Robert Browning. 6066-8
"Love is the peace whereto all thoughts do strive". Fulke Greville; 1st Baron Brooke. 6181-8
"Love is the sunne it selfe from whence." Unknown. 6563-5
"Love is too young to know what conscience is". Sonnet 151 ("Love is too young"). William Shakespeare. 6447-7
Love keeps strange time. Virgie Rucker Howerton. 6906-1
Love knocks at the door. John Hall Wheelock. 6310-1
The love knot. Nora Perry. 6089-7,6385-3,6014-5,6620-8, 6632-1,6004-8,6226-1,6219-9,6652-6,6694-1
Love language of a merry young soldier. Thomas Hood. 6633-

X
Love letter from an impossible land. William Meredith. 6666-6
A love letter. Unknown. 6881-2
Love letters. Elizabeth Barrett Browning. 6737-9
Love letters made of flowers. Leigh Hunt. 6302-0,6385-3
"Love lies a-sleeping: maiden, softly sing". Love's going. Charles W. Coleman. 6770-0
"Love lies beyond the tomb". Song ("Love lies"). John Clare. 6437-X
Love lies bleeding. Christina Georgina Rossetti. 7015-9, 7037-X,7015-9,7037-X
"Love lies bleeding in the bed whereover". Flower-pieces. Algernon Charles Swinburne. 6875-8
Love lightens labor. Unknown. 6045-1,6344-6,6385-3,6620-8, 6219-9
'Love lightly'. Laurence (Adele Florence Nicolson) Hope. 6856-1
The love lights of home. Frank Lebby Stanton. 6620-8
Love lights the fire. William Henry Davies. 6781-6
Love like a boy. Sir Philip Sidney. 6634-8
Love lives beyond the tomb. John Clare. 6545-7
"Love lives beyond the tomb." John Clare. 6208-3,6246-5
Love lyric. Max Michelson. 6897-9
A love lyric. Robert Bridges. 6487-6
"Love me a little, Lord, or let me go". Zira: in captivity. Laurence (Adele Florence Nicolson) Hope. 6856-1
Love me again. Unknown. 6182-6
"Love me and leave me; what love bids...". John Jones at the piano. Algernon Charles Swinburne. 6902-9
Love me and never leave me. Ronald McCuaig. 6349-7
Love me at last. Alice Corbin. 6320-9,6102-8,6109-6,6076-5
"Love me because I am lost". Song ("Love me"). Louise Bogan. 6019-6
Love me little, love me long. Robert Herrick. 6732-8
Love me little, love me long. Unknown. 6889-8,6182-6,6271-7,6302-0,6385-3,6328-4
"Love me not for comely grace". Unknown. 6102-8,6187-7, 6395-0,6250-4,6513-9,6652-6,6737-9
"Love me not, love, for that I first loved thee". Richard Watson Gilder. 6429-9,6094-3,6321-7,6429-9
"Love me or not, love her I must or die." Thomas Campion. 6182-6,6328-4,6794-8
'Love me, love my dog' Isabella Valancy Crawford. 6797-2
Love means adventure. Toyohiko Kagawa. 6027-7
Love much. Ella Wheeler Wilcox. 6066-8
Love music, fr. Romeo and Juliet. William Shakespeare. 6328-4
Love new and old. Charles Mackay. 6250-4
Love not. Caroline Elizabeth Sarah Sheridan Norton. 6271-7, 6219-9,6656-9,6543-0
Love not me. Unknown. 6182-6,6271-7
Love not me for comedy. Unknown. 6527-9
"Love not me for comely grace". Madrigal. Unknown. 6830-8
Love not me for comely grace. Unknown. 6096-9,6083-3,6092-7,6083-8,6302-0,6385-3,6317-9,6246-6,6226-1,6219-9
Love not me for comely grace. John Wilbye. 6328-4,6026-9, 6153-2
"Love not told". Jean Ingelow. 6238-5
Love notes. William Ernest Henley. 6066-8
The love of a boy-today. Richard Hovey. 6004-8
The love of a boy. Richard Hovey. 6441-8
Love of beauty. Edgar A. Guest. 6869-3
Love of children. Mahlon Leonard Fisher. 6032-3
Love of country and home. James Montgomery. 6605-2
The love of country, fr. The lay of the last minstrel. Sir Walter Scott. 6552-X,6589-9,6602-2,6104-4
The love of country. Sir Walter Scott. 6543-0
Love of England. George Gordon, 6th Baron Byron. 6438-8
Love of England. William Cowper. 6315-2
Love of fame, the universal passion, sels. Edward Young. 6195-0
Love of fatherland, fr. The lay of the last minstrel. Sir Walter Scott. 6242-3,6639-9
Love of God and man. Philip James Bailey. 6543-0
The love of God supreme. John Wesley. 6385-3
The love of God the end of life. Madame De la Mothe Guion. 6814-6
The love of God, fr. The provencal. Bernard Rascas. 6730-1

The love of God, fr. The provencal. Bernard Rascas. 6385-3
The love of God. William Cullen Bryant. 6461-2
The love of God. Eliza Scudder. 6385-3,6600-3
The love of God. Unknown (French) 6385-3
"The love of field and coppice". My country. Dorothea MacKellar. 6784-0
The love of his life. Unknown. 6918-5
Love of home. Unknown. 6294-6
The love of Jesus. William White. 6868-5
The love of King David and fair Bathsebe, sels. George Peele. 6301-2
Love of liberty. William Cowper. 6240-7
Love of life. John W. Streets. 6650-X
Love of life. Tertius Van Dyke. 6027-7
The love of Narcissus. Alice Meynell. 6955-X
Love of nature, fr. The seasons (Autumnm). James Thomson. 6932-0
The love of nature. John Clare. 6545-7
The love of nature. William Wordsworth. 6049-8
The love of other years. Walter Savage Landor. 6122-2
The love of swans. Leonard Mann. 6349-7
The love of the past. Unknown. 6273-3
The love of the world reproved, or hypocrisy detected. William Cowper. 6278-4
The love of the world reproved; or, hypocrisy detected. William Cowper. 6814-6
Love on deck. George Barlow. 6066-8
"Love on my heart from heaven fell". Robert Bridges. 6487-6
Love on the Cross. J. Grimstone. 6636-4
Love on the half shell. David Law ("Pegleg Arkwright") Proudfit. 6914-2
Love on the links. G.M. Winter. 7021-3
Love on the mountain. Thomas Boyd. 6244-X
Love on the ocean. Unknown. 6278-4
Love one another. Bedros Tourian. 6050-1
Love or death. Paulus Silentiarius. 6435-3
Love pagan. Arthur Shearly Cripps. 6800-6
Love passed by. Unknown. 6710-7
"Love peering at me". Transparence. Rosa Zagnoni Marinoni. 6750-6
Love planted a rose. Katharine Lee Bates. 6338-1,6653-9
A love playnt. Godfrey Turner. 6089-7
A love poe-um. Arthur T. Wilson. 6899-5
Love poem. William Sydney Graham. 6209-1
Love poem. Yuri Kageyama. 6790-5
Love poem. Kathleen Raine. 6379-9
Love poem ("Less the dog begged to die...") George Barker. 6379-9
Love poem ("My joy, my jockey, my Gabriel"). George Barker. 6379-9
Love poem ("O tender under her right breast") George Barker. 6379-9
Love poem ("They like the ship at rest in the bay.") George Barker. 6209-1
Love poem without anyone in it. Neeli Cherkovski. 6792-1
A love poem. C.P. Livermore. 6764-6
A love poem. Milan Rakic. 6765-4
Love pure and fervent. Madame De la Mothe Guion. 6814-6
Love reigns forever. Ralph Waldo Emerson. 6461-2
Love returned. Bayard Taylor. 6976-2
Love rides the lion. Karl Gjellerup. 6555-4
Love scorned by pride. John Clare. 6545-7
Love scorns degrees. Paul Hamilton Hayne. 6240-7,6385-3, 6066-8
"Love seeketh not itself to please". True and false love. William Blake. 6935-5
"Love seeketh not itself to please." William Blake. 6317-9, 6066-8
Love serviceable, fr. The angel in the house. Coventry Patmore. 6337-3,6560-0
"Love shall not end except in quietness". For the hour after love. Anne Singleton. 6808-1
"Love so great my soul amazes". The love of Jesus. William White. 6868-5
Love song. Ethel M. Brainerd. 6906-1
Love song. Robert Burns. 6625-9
Love song. Mary Carolyn Davies. 6019-6
Love Song. Adam Drinan. 6379-9
Love song. Heinrich Heine. 6949-5

LOVE

Love song. James Abraham Martling. 6952-5
Love song. Dorothy McFarlane. 6750-6
Love song. Harriet Monroe. 6019-6,6431-0,6581-3
Love song. Ellen Otis. 6798-0
Love song. Sophia Mavroidi Papadaky. 6352-7
Love song. Rossiter W. Raymond. 6302-0
Love song. George Brandon Saul. 6038-2,6619-4
Love song. Constance Lindsay Skinner. 6102-8
Love song. Virginia Wuerfel Slayton. 6906-1
Love song. Henry Treece. 6337-3
Love song. Unknown. 6873-1
Love song. Unknown (American Indian) 6021-8
Love song. Unknown (Haida Indian) 7039-6
Love song. Unknown (Papago Indian) 7039-6
Love song. Harold Vinal. 6761-1
Love song. Ella Wheeler Wilcox. 6956-8
Love song ("The deer stand still now ..."). Rudolph G. Binding. 6643-7
Love song from New England. Winifred Welles. 6019-6
The love song of Har Dyal. Rudyard Kipling. 6204-0,6236-9, 6427-2
A love song of Henri Quatre. Sir Edwin Arnold. 6658-5
The love song of J. Alfred Prufrock. Thomas Stearns Eliot. 6102-8,6076-5,6488-4,6399-3,6527-9,6348-9,6536-8, 6150 ,6300-4,6491-4
Love song, fr. The bloody brother. Francis Beaumont and John Fletcher. 6208-3
Love song, fr. The cyclops. Euripides. 7039-6
Love song, fr. Valentinian. Francis Beaumont and John Fletcher. 6208-3
A love song. Steingrimur Thorsteinsson. 6283-0
A love song. Eliza Cook. 6980-0
A love song. Theodosia Garrison. 6556-2,6431-0
A love song. Jonathan Swift. 6874-X,6440-X
A love song. Jonathan Swift. 6278-4
A love song. Jonathan Swift. 6787-5
A love song. Unknown. 6562-7
A love song. Unknown. 6563-5
A love song. Unknown. 6435-3
A love song. Unknown (Greek) 6435-3
Love songs. Isabel Jones Campbell. 6397-7
Love songs. Sara Teasdale. 6777-8,6556-2
A love sonnet. George Wither. 6182-6,6562-7
"Love spake to me and said". 'Oh, no, we never mention her'. Andrew Lang. 6802-2
"Love still is a boy and oft a wanton is". Sir Philip Sidney. 6187-7,6369-1
"Love still has something of the sea". Song ("Love still"). Sir Charles Sedley. 6383-7,61508,6052-8, 6198-2,6378-0,6544-9,6562-7
"Love still has something of the sea". Sir Charles Sedley. 6208-3,6315-2,6563-5,6250-4,6195-0,6023-4,6152-4, 6219-9
A love story. Robert Graves. 6210-5
"Love strong as death-nay, stronger". Unknown. 6238-5
Love strong in death. Ebenezer Elliot. 6543-0
"Love suffereth all things". Sacrifice. Frederick Manning. 6897-9
"Love suffereth long" Sara Henderson Hay. 6144-3
A love symphony. Arthur O'Shaughnessy. 6320-9,6620-8,6655-0,6094-3,6649-6,6066-8,6226-1,6658-5
Love tapped upon my lattice. Annie M.L. Hawes. 7021-3
A love test. Carl Herlozsohn. 6652-6
Love that asketh love again. Dinah Maria Mulock Craik. 6226-1
"Love that holdeth firm in fee". Vis erotis. Clinton Scollard. 6770-0,6875-8
"Love that is dead and buried, yesterday". Love lies
l b eeding. Christina Georgina Rossetti. 7015-9,7037-X, 7015-9,7037-X
"Love that is hoarded, moulds at last". Song ("Love that is hoarded"). Harold Cornelius Sandall. 6337-3,6461-2
"The love that knots you unzips its black cape". Conversions/winter solstice. Aaron Shurin. 7003-5
The love that lives for aye. Samuel Minturn Peck. 6226-1
"Love that liveth and reigneth in my thought." Henry Howard, Earl of Surrey. 6584-8
'Love that never told can be.' John Erskine. 6118-4
A love that was. Margaret Haynes Foster. 7016-7

Love the archer. Rufinus. 6435-3
Love the foe. Sadi [or Saadi] (Mushlih-ud-Din) 6448-5
Love the Lord of all. Sir Walter Scott. 6094-3
Love the rascal. Meleager. 6435-3
Love the vampire. Andrew Lang. 6987-8
Love thee, dearest? Love thee?. Thomas Moore. 6226-1
"'Love thee?' Thou canst not ask of me". A woman's answer. Phoebe Cary. 6969-X
"Love thou art sweet in the spring-time of...". Ballade. John Cameron Grant. 6770-0
Love thou thy land. Alfred Lord Tennyson. 6655-0,6657-7, 6199-0,6110-9
Love thou thy land, sels. Alfred Lord Tennyson. 6867-7
"Love thy bright monarchy I now defy." Unknown. 6563-5
Love thy mother, little one. Thomas Hood. 6629-1
"Love thy mother, little one!". To a child embracing his mother. Thomas Hood. 6974-6
Love thyself last. Ella Wheeler Wilcox. 6303-9,6337-3
"Love thyself last;cherish thou hearts that hate thee" William Shakespeare. 6238-5
"Love to Love calleth", fr. Ode to music. Robert Bridges. 6487-6
Love to my Lord. Louisa van Plettenhaus. 6065-X
Love to the church. Timothy Dwight. 6735-2
A love token. Adelaide Anne Procter. 6957-6
Love took me softly by the hand. Walter R. Cassels. 6066-8
Love triumphant. Frederic Lawrence ("R.L. Paget") Knowles. 6006-4,6310-1,6441-8,6732-8,6102-8,6076-5,6250-4
Love triumphant. Unknown. 6630-5
Love triumphant, sels. John Dryden. 6970-3
Love unaccountable. Richard Brome. 6092-7
Love under difficulties. Unknown. 6744-1
Love under the ledger. Macdonald Clarke. 6632-1
Love unlike love. Unknown. 6881-2
Love unseen, fr. Child Harold's pilgrimage. George Gordon, 6th Baron Byron. 6545-7
Love versus the bottle. Edward Lysaght. 6858-8
"Love wake and weeps/While beauty sleeps". Cleveland's song: 'Love wake and weeps,' fr. The pirate. Sir Walter Scott. 6828-6
"Love was primeval; from forgotten time". Love. Charles Lotin Hildreth. 7041-8
Love was the worm. John Hall. 6475-2
"Love was true to me". Song ("Love was true"). John Boyle O'Reilly. 6022-6
Love was true to me. John Boyle O'Reilly. 6096-X;6244-X
Love we as brothers. William Langland. 6489-2
"Love wears so many guises". On love. Herbert Jones. 6785-9
"Love weepeth always-weepeth for the past". Alfred Lord Tennyson. 6238-5
Love what it is. Robert Herrick. 6874-X
Love which is here a care. William Drummond of Hawthornden. 6931-2
Love who will. William Browne. 6563-5
Love will find out the way. Unknown. 6328-4,6512-0,6563-5, 6600-3,6239-3,6153-2,6219-9
'Love will find out the way'. Charles Mackay. 6980-0
Love winged my hopes. Robert Jones. 6328-4
Love winged my hopes. Unknown. 6181-8,6182-6
"Love winged my hopes and taught me how to fly". Song ("Love winged"). Unknown. 6436-1
'Love with a witness', fr. Bailey ballads. Thomas Hood. 6974-6
"Love with me still, and all the measures". The invitation, fr. The sun's parting. Thomas Dekker. 6827-8
"Love with shut wings, a little ungrown love". Rizzio's love-song. Algernon Charles Swinburne. 6875-8
Love within the lover's breast. George Meredith. 6094-3
Love without hope. Robert Graves. 6125-7
"'Love you?' said I, then I sighed...". Ferdinando and Elvira, or the gentle pieman. Sir William Schwenck Gilbert. 6902-9
Love your neighbor as yourself. George A. Baker. 6568-6
"Love your own, kiss your own". Unknown. 6904-5
"Love! I am freer than the strong white wings". A Norse love song. Kenneth S. Goodman. 6983-5
Love! blessed love! if we could hang our walls. Alice Cary. 6066-8
"Love! if thy destin'd sacrfice am I". The acquiesence

of pure love. Madame De la Mothe Guion. 6814-6
"Love". Loren Stream. 6883-9
"Love's a flower, is born and broken". A mood. John
    Galsworthy. 6888-X
Love's a jest. Peter Anthony Motteux. 6562-7
Love's aforetime. William White. 6868-5
Love's alchemy. John Donne. 6430-2
Love's anguish. Marian Osborne. 6115-X
Love's argument. Father Andrew. 6337-3
"Love's arms were wreathed about the neck of hope". Alfred
    Lord Tennyson. 6238-5
Love's artifice. James Sheridan Knowles. 6980-0
Love's assize. Guido Cavalcanti. 6325-X
Love's autograph. John Banister Tabb. 6396-9
Love's autumn. Paul Hamilton Hayne. 6620-8
Love's autumn. John Payne. 6656-9
Love's belief. Unknown. 6273-3
Love's bird. Katharine (Hinkson) Tynan. 6174-5
Love's birth and becoming. Samuel Daniel. 6189-3
Love's blindness. Alfred Austin. 7015-9
Love's burial. Heinrich Heine. 6842-1
"Love's but the frailty...", fr. The way of the world.
    William Congreve. 6562-7
Love's calendar. Thomas Bailey Aldrich. 6226-1
Love's calendar. William Bell Scott. 6819-7
Love's calendar. Unknown. 6691-7
Love's calendar, sels. Max Dauthendey. 6160-5
Love's call. Fred Berman. 6841-3
Love's capriciousness, fr. Epigrams. Callimachus. 6435-3
Love's captive. C. H. Waring. 6770-0
Love's caramels lost. Castle Layne. 6926-6
Love's change. Anne Reeve Aldrich. 6019-6, 6309-8
Love's chariot. Ben Jonson. 6383-7
Love's chariot, sels. Ben Jonson. 6102-8,6301-2
Love's code. Mutarrif. 6362-4
Love's college. John Lyly. 6827-8
Love's colours. John Kendall. 6760-3
Love's coming. John Shaw Neilson. 6349-7
Love's coming. Ella Wheeler Wilcox. 6620-8,6066-8
Love's completeness. Mathilde Blind. 7037-X
Love's confession. Charles Swain. 6226-1
Love's consolation, sels. Richard Watson Dixon. 6317-9
Love's constancy. John Clare. 6943-6
Love's cup.Robert Cameron Rogers. 6274-1
Love's deity. John Donne. 6182-6,6198-2,6339-X,6369-1,6527-
    9,6430-2,6726-3
Love's delay. Edward Cracroft Lefroy. 6274-1
Love's delights. Nahum Tate. 6563-5
Love's depth. Laura S. Bevington. 7015-9
Love's despair. John Dryden. 6022-6
Love's despair. Richard Lynch. 6182-6
Love's despair. Dermot O'Curnan. 6244-X
Love's detective. Gamaliel Bradford. 6441-8
Love's disguise. John Alan Hamilton. 6116-8
Love's disguises. Matthew Prior. 6737-9
Love's duet, fr. Romeo and Juliet. William Shakespeare.
    6634-8
Love's Easter. Andrew Lang. 6987-8
Love's ecstasy. Thomas Heywood. 6827-8
Love's emblems. John Fletcher. 6182-6,6198-2,6733-6,6189-3,
    6301-2
Love's enchantment. Marian Osborne. 6115-X
Love's ending. Unknown. 6436-1
Love's entrance. Frederic Lawrence ("R.L. Paget") Knowles.
    6116-8
Love's epiphany. Agnes Mary F. ("Madame Duclaux")
    Robinson. 6543-0
Love's epitaph. Genevieve Gray Rawson. 6906-1
"Love's equinoctial gales are past, the path". Winter.
    Maurice Craig. 6930-4
Love's errand. Thomas Carew. 6830-8
Love's eternity. Edward Herbert, 1st Baron Herbert of
    Cherbury. 6189-3
Love's evidence. Ibn Baqi. 6362-4
Love's farewell. Michael Drayton. 6246-5,6560-0,6226-1,
    6543-0,6737-9
Love's farewell. Unknown. 6014-5
Love's fidelity. Francesco Petrarch. 7039-6
Love's final powers. George Barlow. 6066-8
Love's first kiss. Frank Lebby Stanton. 6702-6
Love's fool. Unknown. 6383-7
"Love's footsteps shall not fail nor faint". Triolet
    ("Love's footsteps"). Rosamund Marriott ("Graham R.
    Tomson") Watson. 6770-0
Love's fragility. Alan Porter. 6780-8
Love's Franciscan. Henry Constable. 6022-6
Love's fulfilling. Helen Hunt Jackson. 6620-8,6066-8
Love's garland. Meleager. 6423-X
Love's gifts. Marian Osborne. 6115-X
Love's glory. Fulke Greville; 1st Baron Brooke. 6436-1
Love's going. Charles W. Coleman. 6770-0
Love's grave. Thomas Watson. 6436-1
Love's Hallowe'en. Clarence L. Haynie. 6841-3
Love's harmony. Edmund Spenser. 6094-3
"Love's height is easy scaling; skies allure". Love's
    depth. Laura S. Bevington. 7015-9
Love's helplessness. Alexander Young. 6178-8
Love's hour-glass. Johann Wolfgang von Goethe. 6948-7
Love's immortality. William Byrd (atr) 6153-2
Love's immortality. Robert Southey. 6094-3,6226-1
Love's imperfections. Unknown. 6189-3
Love's inconsistency. Francesco Petrarch. 7039-6
Love's inconsistency. Francesco Petrarch. 6527-9
Love's infinite made finite. Henry Bernard Carpenter. 7041-
    8
Love's inspiration. Tristan Klingsor. 6351-9
Love's island. Doku-Ho. 6032-3
Love's island. Ian Oliver. 6607-0
Love's jealousy. Richard Watson Gilder. 7041-8
Love's justification. Michelangelo Buonarroti. 6321-7,6429-
    9
Love's justification. Michelangelo Buonarroti. 7039-6
Love's labor's lost, sels. William Shakespeare. 6083-8,
    6332-2,6369-1,6512-0,6239-3,6634 ,6154-0,6179-6,6242-
    3,6122-2,6182-6,6198 ,6208-3,6527-9,6466-3,6560-0,
    6250-4,6378
Love's labour lost. Robert Tofte. 6182-6
Love's land. Isabella Valancy Crawford. 6433-7
Love's language. Hafiz. 6448-5
Love's language. Francis Turner Palgrave. 6980-0
Love's language. Francis Turner Palgrave. 6066-8
Love's language. Francis Turner Palgrave. 6980-0
Love's language. Ella Wheeler Wilcox. 6956-8
Love's last adieu. George Gordon, 6th Baron Byron. 6945-2
Love's last gift. Dante Gabriel Rossetti. 6110-9
Love's last messages. Thomas Lovell Beddoes. 6980-0
Love's last request. John MacGregor. 6269-5
Love's last shift, sels. Colley Cibber. 6867-7
Love's last suit. Thomas Davidson. 6960-6
Love's legend. Daniel Henderson. 6320-9
Love's lesson. Jean Blewett. 6796-4
Love's letter-box. Helen J. Wood. 6681-X
A love's life. Unknown. 6273-3
Love's light is strange to you? Ah me! Alice Cary. 6066-8
Love's logic. Unknown. 6116-8,6273-3
Love's longings. Thomas Osborne Davis. 6858-8
Love's lovers, fr. The house of life. Dante Gabriel
    Rossetti. 6828-6
Love's lovers, fr. The house of life. Dante Gabriel
    Rossetti. 6110-9
Love's loyalty. Frances Tyrrell Gill. 6768-9
Love's meaning. Carlotta Perry. 6429-9,6620-8,6226-1,6321-
    7
Love's meinie. Francis William Bourdillon. 6658-5
Love's melody. Barbara M. Booth. 6799-9
Love's memory, fr. All's well that ends well. William
    Shakespeare. 6302-0;6385-3
Love's miracle. Andrew Lang. 6771-9
Love's miracle. James Abraham Martling. 6952-5
Love's miracle. Lucy Maud Montgomery. 6337-3
Love's moods and senses. Unknown. 6089-7,6277-6,6724-7
Love's mortality. Richard Middleton. 6726-3
Love's music. Philip Bourke Marston. 6656-9
Love's nearness. Johann Wolfgang von Goethe. 6961-4
Love's nightingale. Richard Crashaw. 6315-2
Love's nobleness. Edmund Spenser. 6094-3
Love's nocturn. Dante Gabriel Rossetti. 6122-2,6110-9
Love's not time's fool. William Shakespeare. 6634-8
Love's old sweet song. Unknown. 6732-8
Love's omnipresence. Joshua Sylvester. 6246-6,6429-9,6737-

LOVE'S

9,6219-9,6321-7,6153 ,6226-1
"Love's on the highroad". Song ("Love's on the highroad") Dana Burnet. 6266-0,6320-9,6441-8,6476-0,6653-4
Love's outset, fr. A lover's diary. Gilbert Parker. 6656-9
Love's palace. Arthur Maquarie. 6784-0
Love's parting. Michael Drayton. 6153-2
Love's perjuries. William Shakespeare. 6246-6
Love's philosophy. Percy Bysshe Shelley. 6240-7,6246-6, 6271-7,6302-0,6385-3,6328 ,6732-8,6219-9,6197-4,6668-2,6543-0,6250 ,6092-7,6110-9,6023-4,6086-2,6659-3, 6737 ,6199-0,6430-2,6560-0,6066-8,6513-9
Love's pilgrim. John Killick Bathurst. 6433-7
Love's pilgrims. Thomas Campion. 6436-1
Love's plans. William Henry Davies. 6779-4
Love's power. Josephine Pollard. 6226-1
Love's prayer. John Hay. 6066-8
Love's prayer. Lucy Maud Montgomery. 6796-4
Love's precinct. Mnasalcas. 6102-8
Love's prime. Thomas May. 6563-5
Love's priority. Jorge Luis Borges. 6759-X
Love's prisoner. William Blake. 6250-4
"**Love's** progress", sels. John Donne. 6733-6
Love's protestation. Thomas Lodge. 6022-6
Love's proving. Frederic Edward Weatherley. 6226-1
Love's quest. Austin Dobson. 7014-0
Love's realities. Unknown. 6189-3
Love's reaon. Henry Van Dyke. 6961-4
Love's reasons. William Browne. 6189-3
Love's rebel. Henry Howard, Earl of Surrey. 6436-1
Love's recompense. Phoebe Cary. 6969-X
Love's redemption, fr. The house of life. Dante Gabriel Rossetti. 6123-0
Love's reminiscences. Mary Kyle Dallas. 6671-2
Love's request. Thomas Campion. 6827-8
Love's response. James Abraham Martling. 6952-5
Love's resurrection day. Louise Chandler Moulton. 6300-4
Love's retrospect. Isabell Sherrick Wardell. 6836-7
Love's return. Minot Judson Savage. 6620-8
Love's ritual. Charles Hanson Towne. 6310-1
Love's sacrifice. Unknown. 7021-3
Love's secret. William Blake. 6102-8,6198-2,6427-2,6250-4, 6513-9,6153 ,6464-7,6737-9
Love's secret. John Boyle O'Reilly. 7041-8
Love's secret name. John Arthur Blaikie. 6274-1,6656-9
Love's secret springs. Alice Cary. 6865-0;6969-X
Love's silence. Yong-woon Han. 6775-1
Love's silence. Sir Philip Sidney. 6302-0;6385-3
Love's silence. Augusta Webster. 6620-8
Love's slavery. John Sheffield; Duke of Buckingham. 6152-4
Love's song. Gerald Griffin. 6226-1
Love's song. Wealthy Sheetz. 6270-9
Love's spite. Aubrey Thomas De Vere. 6656-9
Love's springtide. Frank Dempster Sherman. 6310-1
Love's storm. Ibn Sa'id (of Alcala La Real) 6362-4
Love's strategy. R.S. Sharpe. 6924-X
Love's strength. Unknown. 6337-3
Love's supremacy. Alfred Austin. 6094-3
Love's telepathy. Angela Morgan. 6274-1
Love's testament, fr. The house of life. Dante Gabriel Rossetti. 6110-9
Love's thread of gold. Jean Ingelow. 6066-8
Love's transfiguration. Unknown. 6273-3
Love's Trappist. Gilbert Keith Chesterton. 6320-9
Love's trinity. Alfred Austin. 6437-X
Love's victory. David Atwood Wasson. 6429-9,6321-7
Love's vision. Edward Carpenter. 6730-1
Love's vision. William Cavendish; Duke of Newcastle. 6317-9
Love's wantonness. Thomas Lodge. 6827-8
Love's warning. Edward Kenealy. 6518-X
Love's wisdom. Alfred Austin. 7015-9
Love's witchery. Thomas Lodge. 6182-6
Love's witchery. Josephine Hancock Logan. 6789-1
Love's without reason. Alexander Brome. 6562-7
Love's witness. Unknown (Greek) 6948-7
Love's young dream. George A. Baker. 6517-1
Love's young dream. Thomas Moore. 6302-0,6385-3,6198-2, 6744-1,6543-0,6086-2,6094-3,6226-1,6438-8
Love, Adelaide
   For a materialist. 6337-3

No more than this. 6461-2
Thy nearness. 6461-2
A woman speaks across the years. 6750-6
Word to a dictator. 6337-3
Love, Katherine Neal
   Spring. 6799-9
Love, Robertus
   The appreciation of Lincoln. 6524-4
   At Lincoln's tomb. 6524-4
   Lincoln in bronze. 6524-4
   One of Lincoln's roommates speaks. 6708-5
Love, a thousand sweets distilling. James Shirley. 6562-7, 6563-5
Love, and never fear. Thomas Campion. 6634-8
"**Love**, brave vertues younger brother". Loves horoscope. Richard Crashaw. 6933-9
"**Love**, by that loosed hair." Bliss Carman. 6433-7
"**Love, by that loosened hair**". Song ("Love, by that loosened hair"). Bliss Carman. 6076-5,6102-8
"**Love**, dearest lady, such as I would speak". Love. Thomas Hood. 6980-0
"**Love**, do not count your labour lost". Sullen moods. Robert Graves. 6872-3
"**Love**, drink, and debt. Alexander Brome. 6427-2
"**Love**, forget me when I'm gone". Love's last suit. Thomas Davidson. 6960-6
Love, fr. Corinthians. Bible. 6179-6
Love, fr. Earth's immortalities. Robert Browning. 6655-0
Love, fr. Love's labour lost. William Shakespeare. 6634-8
Love, fr. Once again the Eden. Noel Hudson Stearn. 6789-1
Love, fr. The faerie queene. Edmund Spenser. 6436-1
Love, fr. The lay of the last minstrel. Sir Walter Scott. 6934-7
Love, fr. The merchant of Venice. William Shakespeare. 6385-3
Love, fr. The prelude. William Wordsworth. 6545-7
Love, fr. The song of Solomon. Bible. 6153-2,6337-3
Love, fr. The three best things. Henry Van Dyke. 6961-4
"**Love, give me one thy dear hands to hold**". Rest. Unknown. 6273-3
Love, give me the feel of to-morrow. Ralph Cheyney. 6051-X
Love, give me the feel of tomorrow. Ralph Cheyney. 6542-2
"**Love**, harken how the boughs o'erhead". Alone in Arcady. Clinton Scollard. 6875-8
"**Love**, I am jealous of a worthless man". Sonnet ("Love, I am jealous"). Thomas Hood. 6974-6
Love, hope and memory. Alfred Lord Tennyson. 6094-3
Love, hope, and patience in education. Samuel Taylor Coleridge. 6086-2
"**Love**, if I weep it will not matter". The dream. Edna St. Vincent Millay. 6986-X
"**Love**, if a god thou art". Francis Davison. 6187-7
"**Love**, let me thank you for this!". Palm trees by the sea. Laurence (Adele Florence Nicolson) Hope. 6856-1
Love, let the wind cry. Sappho. 6732-8,6102-8
Love, lift me up. Edmund Spenser. 6328-4
"**Love**, like a cautious...", fr. The happy pair. Sir Charles Sedley. 6544-9
"**Love**, love me only". Song ("Love, love me..."). Robert Crawford. 6784-0
Love, murder, and almost matrimony. Unknown. 6403-5
Love, not duty. Arthur Hugh Clough. 6655-0
"**Love**, out of the depth of things". Two preludes. Algernon Charles Swinburne. 6875-8
Love, pride, and forgetfulness. Alfred Lord Tennyson. 6977-0
Love, reason, hate. Sir John Suckling. 6380-2
"**Love**, see thy lover humbled at thy feet". Sonnet ("Love, see thy lover"). Thomas Hood. 6974-6
Love, sels. Samuel Taylor Coleridge. 6317-9
"**Love**, shall I liken thee unto the rose". Scent o' pines. Hugh McCulloch. 6873-1
"**Love**, sleep light tonight, for the bombs...". Barcelona. Vincent Sheehan. 6761-1
"**Love**, that looks still on your eyes". Song ("Love, that looks"). William Browne. 6187-7
Love, the best monument. Unknown. 6919-3
Love, the musician. Francesco Redi. 6066-8
Love, the mystic thread. Emma G. Southwick. 6799-9
Love, the pilgrim. Hamilton Aide. 6658-5

"Love, thou art absolute sole lord". Hymn to St. Theresa. Richard Crashaw. 6931-2
"Love, thou art best of human joys". A song ("Love, thou art best"). Anne Finch, Countess of Winchilsea. 6562-7
"Love, though I die, and dying lave". Roundel ('Love, though I die, and dying lave') D. F. Blomfield. 6770-0
Love, unrequited, fr. Twelfth night. William Shakespeare. 6302-0;6385-3
"Love, was it yesternoon, or years agone". The king's consort. Emily Pauline ("Tekahionwake") Johnson. 6837-5
Love, weeping, laid this song. Lizette Woodworth Reese. 6326-8
Love, what art thou? Lady Mary Wroath. 6563-5
Love, whose month was ever May. Sir Ulrich von Liechtenstein. 7039-6
"Love, why so long away" Clinton Scollard. 6875-8
Love, youth, song. John Jarvis Holden. 6274-1
Love-children. Robinson Jeffers. 6012-9
Love-ending, sels. Rose O'Neill. 6102-8,6076-5
Love-in-idleness. William Shakespeare. 7020-5
The love-knot. Unknown. 6414-0
A love-lesson. Clement Marot. 7039-6
The love-letter, fr. The house of life. Dante Gabriel Rossetti. 6655-0
The love-letter.. Dante Gabriel Rossetti. 6429-9,6655-0, 6110-9,6321-7
The love-letter. Austin Dobson. 6996-7
The love-letter. Coventry Patmore. 6980-0
The love-letter. Christina Georgina Rossetti. 6226-1
Love-letters. Arthur Wentworth Hamilton Eaton. 7041-8
Love-lily. Dante Gabriel Rossetti. 6828-6
Love-lily. Dante Gabriel Rossetti. 6508-2,6110-9
Love-music. Mabel Christian Forbes. 6269-5
Love-sight [or, Lovesight], fr. The house of love. Dante Gabriel Rossetti. 6122-2,6198-2,6437-X,6655-0,6250-4, 6508 ,6123-0,6186-9,6208-3,6246-6,6473-6,6526 ,6726-3,6110-9,6656-9,6430-2
A love-song by a lunatic. Unknown. 6902-9
The love-song of Drostan. William ("Fiona Macleod") Sharp. 6320-9
A love-song. Gustaf Froding. 6045-5
A love-song. Norman Gale. 6301-2
The love-song. Bernice Lesbia Kenyon. 6019-6
Love-sweetness, fr. The house of life. Dante Gabriel Rossetti. 6122-2,6198-2,6110-9,6199-0,6655-0,6430-2, 6508-2
The love-taler. Ethna (Anna Johnson MacManus) Carbery. 6090-0,6102-8,6930-4
A love-triology, sels. Mathilde Blind. 6656-9
"Love? I will tell thee". Love. Charles Swain. 6620-8
The loved and lost. Unknown. 6909-6
Loved once. Elizabeth Barrett Browning. 6980-0
The loved one ever near. Johann Wolfgang von Goethe. 6066-8,6508-2
"Loved ones" Mykki Verlyn Culver. 6899-5
Loveday, Percy
    Rosemary. 6818-9
The lovejoy cow. Unknown. 6682-8
Lovejoy, George Newell
    Easter carol. 6144-3,6177-X
    The mother. 6097-8,6143-5
Lovejoy, Mrs. F.J.
    Goldenrod. 6373-X
Lovejoy, Ritchie
    The swamp. 6761-1
Lovelace, Richard
    An anniversary. 6315-2
    Elinda's glove. 6933-9
    Female glory. 6369-1
    The glove. 6187-7,6026-9
    Going to the warres. 6933-9
    Going to the wars. 6197-4,6322-5
    The grasshopper, sels. 6198-2
    The grasshopper. 6933-9
    The grasshopper. 6052-8,6099-4,6563-5,6438-8,6341-1, 6315-7,6562-7,6733-3,6208-3
    Gratiana dancing. 6959-2

LOVELY

    Gratiana dancing and singing. 6315-2,6565-7,6092-7,6430-2,6341-1,6230 ,6563-5
    Gratiana daunsing and singing. 6933-9
    The merit of inconstancy. 6092-7
    On the death of Mrs. Elizabeth Filmer. 6934-7
    The rose ("Sweet, serene, sky-like flower"). 6122-2, 6187-7,6189-3
    The scrutinie. 6933-9
    The scrutiny. 6187-7,6562-7,6317-9,6341-1
    Song ("Why should you swear"). 6089-7
    Strive not, vain lover, to be fine. 6430-2
    To Althea, from prison. 6341-1,6219-9,6639-9,6652-6, 6646-1,6023-4,6092-7,6102-8,6104-4,6194-X,6430 ,6192-3,6189-3,6660-7,6322-5,6371-3,6197 ,6337-3,6645-3, 6438-8,6301-2,6230-X,6737 ,6099-4,6138-9,6102-8,6563-5,6604-6,6543 ,6122-2,6188-5,6240-7,6291-1,6302-0, 6385 ,6154-0,6395-0,6481-7,6473-6,6634-8,6459 ,6198-2,6208-3,6562-7,6726-3,6560-0,6250 ,6246-6,6315-2, 6332-2,6339-X,6501-5,6527
    To Amarantha, that she would dishevel her hair. 6317-9, 6328-4,6187-7,6092-7,6194-X
    To Fletcher reviv'd. 6483-3
    To Lucasta. 6302-2,6385-3,6122-2,6600-3,6321-7,6668 , 6429-9,6459-0,6726-3,6226-1,6438-8
    To Lucasta, going beyond the seas. 6099-4,6563-5,6641-0, 6737-9,6219-9,6208-3,6258-X,6122-2,6481-7,6634-8, 6186 ,6315-2,6317-9,6328-4,6562-7,6341-1,6430
    To Lucasta, on going to the wars. 6102-8,6250-4,6430-2, 6194-X,6192-3,6341 ,6026-9,6114-1,6150-8,6152-3,6301-2,6322 ,6646-1,6660-7,6737-9,6543-0,6321-7,6396 , 6094-3,6219-9,6424-8,6023-4,6092-7,6639 ,6104-4,6560-0,6328-4,6246-6,6138-9,6228-8,6246-6,6289 ,6099-4, 6102-8,6138-9,6563-5,6604-6,6645 ,6154-0,6732-8,6562-7,6186-9,6198-2,6315 ,6302-0,6385-3,6332-2,6473-6, 6733-6,6491
    To the grasshopper. 6935-5
"Loveliest dream girl". To Laura. Clara Elizabeth Vester. 6789-1
"The loveliest flower that I know". The coral vine. Lillie Mae Lumpkin. 6799-9
Loveliest of trees. Alfred Edward Housman. 6476-0,6534-1, 6645-3,6723-9,6655-0,6153-2,6125-7,6161-3,6253-9, 6250-4,6396-9,6464-7,6430-2,6581-3,6371-3,6102-8, 6508-2
"The loveliest", sels. Unknown. 6601-1
Lovelilts. Marion Hill. 6089-7,6724-7
Loveliness. Ella Orndorff Hunt. 6906-1
Loveliness. Maria Lacey. 6743-3
Loveliness. Unknown. 6629-1
Loveliness. Unknown (Japanese) 6027-7
The loveliness of love. George Darley. 6246-5
The loveliness of love. Unknown. 6302-0,6385-3,6219-9
"The loveliness of water, its faery ways". Ballade of the things that remain. Richard Le Gallienne. 6875-8
Lovell, Arthur
    A warning. 6453-1
Lovell, Bertha Chase
    When daylight dies. 6118-4
Lovell, Frances Stockwell
    God in a garden. 7030-2
Lovelocks. Walter De La Mare. 6596-1
"Lovely and loved". Acrostics ("Lovely"). ? Bogart. 6724-7
"Lovely autumn flower". Late chrysanthemums. Muriel Slater. 6850-2
The lovely banks of Boyne. Unknown. 6057-9
"Lovely boy, thou art not dead". Epitaph ("Lovely"). Francis Davison. 6436-1
"Lovely butterfly!/You're like a fleeting...". Inspiration. Abbotte McKinnon Downing. 6799-9
"Lovely Cape Cod, strong arm of the state". An ode to Cape Cod. Samuel W. Hallett. 6798-0
Lovely chance. Sara Teasdale. 6161-3
"Lovely courier of the sky". Anacreon's dove. Anacreon. 7039-6
"Lovely courier of the sky!". Anacreon, ode ninth. Samuel Johnson. 6975-4
"A lovely form there sate beside my bed". Phantom or fact. Samuel Taylor Coleridge. 6828-6
"Lovely frocks hung in a row". Loveliness. Ella Orndorff Hunt. 6906-1

LOVELY

Lovely in decay, fr. Remorse. Samuel Taylor Coleridge. 6545-7
"Lovely is the rose; and yet...". Theocritus. 6251-2
"Lovely kind and kindly loving". Song ("Lovely kind"). Nicholas Breton. 6317-9
Lovely kind and kindly loving. Nicholas Breton. 6189-3
"A lovely lady sat and sange". Mary and her child. Unknown. 6931-2
The lovely lass of Inverness. Robert Burns. 6180-X,6323-3, 6086-2
The lovely lass of Inverness. Allan Cunningham. 6859-6
The lovely lass of Preston Mill. Allan Cunningham. 6960-6
A lovely lass to a friar came. John Wilmot, 2d Earl of Rochester. 6157-5
Lovely maid. Ibn Khafaja. 6362-4
Lovely Mary Donnelly. William Allingham. 6271-7,6543-0, 6656-9,6658-5,6438-8,6219
Lovely Maryanne. Michael Hogan. 6858-8
Lovely Nan. Charles Dibdin. 6543-0
"Lovely maid, with rapture swelling". Lines by a fond lover. Unknown. 6902-9
"Lovely Semiramis/Closes her slanting eyes". Eventail. Edith Sitwell. 6884-7
Lovely river. Ibn Khafaja. 6362-4
A lovely scene. Unknown. 6116-8,6414-0
The lovely smile. Edgar A. Guest. 6869-3
"Lovely space of tranquil sea". The crab-catchers. Celia Thaxter. 6965-7
"Lovely ter of lovely eiye". Christ's tear breaks my heart. Unknown. 6881-2
Lovely the earth is. B.S. Ingemann. 6555-4
Lovely things. Unknown (Japanese) 6027-7
"The lovely things museums hold". Beauty. Edgar A. Guest. 6748-4
"A lovely thought...". It is enough. Esther Freshman. 6750-6
The lovely village fair, or I dont mean to tell you... Unknown. 6157-5
"Lovely was the death/Of him whose life was...". A desultory poem, written on the Christmas eve of 1794. Samuel Taylor Coleridge. 6828-6
"Lovely wings of gold and green". In the Mediterranean - going to the war. Francis Ledwidge. 6812-X
A lovely woman. William Henry Davies. 6210-5
"A lovely young lady". An epitaph. George John Cayley. 6092-7
"The lovely young Latvinia once had friends". Latvinia, fr. The seasons (Autumn). James Thomson. 6932-0

Loveman, Robert
    Action. 6941-X
    Adown the years. 6941-X
    The angelus. 6941-X
    April. 6941-X
    April rain. 6102-8,6368-3,6396-6,6076-5,6300-4,6108, 6232-6,6374-8,6337-3,6356-0,6476-0,6583
    Before the storm. 6941-X
    Bohemia. 6941-X
    Carcassonne. 6941-X
    Charlotte Corday. 6941-X
    Cleopatra. 6941-X
    A comforter. 6941-X
    Creed and deed. 6335-7,6337-3
    Darkness. 6941-X
    The dawn. 6941-X
    A derelict. 6941-X
    A diamond. 6941-X
    A dreamer. 6941-X
    Dreams. 6941-X
    Emancipation. 6941-X
    Faith. 6941-X
    The freebooter. 6941-X
    From far Japan. 6941-X
    From foreign lands. 6941-X
    The galaxy. 6941-X
    Georgia. 6465-5
    Good-by. 6941-X
    He is not old. 6941-X
    Her. 6941-X
    Her majesty. 6941-X
    Her soul is pure. 6941-X
    Hobson and his men. 6946-0
    The home-coming. 6941-X
    If thou wouldst read. 6941-X
    In autumn. 6941-X
    In lighter vain. 6941-X
    In Naishapur. 6941-X
    In olden time. 6941-X
    In Shakespeare land. 6941-X
    In the Yosemite. 6941-X
    In Venice. 6941-X
    Inspiration. 6941-X
    Into the poet's life. 6941-X
    A 'La France' rose. 6941-X
    Looking seaward. 6941-X
    A lyric. 6941-X
    Man. 6941-X
    March. 6941-X
    The mob. 6941-X
    The muse. 6941-X
    The musician. 6941-X
    My Josephine. 6941-X
    Niagara. 6941-X
    Night. 6941-X
    Northport town. 6941-X
    Not thou. 6941-X
    O Israel! 6941-X
    O mother mine! 6941-X
    October. 6941-X
    On the fly-leaf. 6941-X
    Over the way. 6941-X
    Overheard. 6941-X
    The paralytic. 6941-X
    The play is o'er! 6941-X
    The poet (2). 6941-X
    The poet. 6941-X
    Poetry. 6941-X
    Poor little rose. 6941-X
    <u>A prayer ("Not faith"). 6941-X</u>
    Purity. 6941-X
    Quatrain ("God made the night..."). 6941-X
    Quatrain ("The night..."). 6941-X
    Quatrain ("Weak from its war..."). 6941-X
    The quatrain. 6941-X
    Rain song. 6461-2
    The rain. 6941-X
    Repentance. 6941-X
    Resolution. 6941-X
    Riches. 6266-0
    Romeo and Juliet. 6941-X
    Rose is the girl. 6941-X
    The sanctum sanctorum. 6941-X
    Serenade. 6941-X
    She is. 6941-X
    So dark, so dear. 6941-X
    Sole empress. 6941-X
    Some words. 6941-X
    Somewhere, afar. 6941-X
    Song ("A sunshine heart"). 6266-0,6478-7
    A song for April. 6889-8
    Sonnet ("Drunk with delight"). 6941-X
    Spring. 6941-X
    A stormy night. 6941-X
    A sunrise. 6941-X
    A sunset. 6941-X
    Sweet are the names. 6941-X
    This winter night. 6941-X
    A thought. 6941-X
    To lift men up. 6941-X
    To London town. 6941-X
    To my mother. 6941-X
    To-day's resolve. 6941-X
    Trouble town. 6941-X
    The truant. 6941-X
    Up to the realm. 6941-X
    Upon a crutch. 6941-X
    Verlaine, Villon, Baudelaire. 6941-X
    The vigil. 6941-X
    When my dear muse. 6941-X
    When the mood is on. 6941-X
    Where dream-boats drift. 6941-X

Wherefore? 6941-X
The wind. 6941-X
Words. 6941-X
Yon star. 6941-X
The lover abused renounceth love. George Turberville. 6182-6
The lover and birds. William Allingham. 6437-X
Lover and echo. Carroll O'Daly. 6930-4
Lover and philosopher. Sir William Davenant. 6022-6
The lover and the beloved. Francis Quarles. 6830-8
The lover beseecheth his mistress not to forget... Sir Thomas Wyatt. 6317-9,6194-X
The lover bids all passionate women mourn. Shaemas O'Sheel. 6096-X
The lover comforteth himself with the worthiness of... Henry Howard, Earl of Surrey. 6935-5
The lover compareth his state. Sir Thomas Wyatt. 6194-X
The lover complaineth the unkindness of his love. Sir Thomas Wyatt. 6430-2,6182-6,6106-0,6198-2,6208-3, 6641-0
The lover envies an old man. Shaemas O'Sheel. 6556-2
The lover exhorteth his lady to be constant. Unknown. 6436-1
A lover for death. Ralph Cheyney. 6619-4
The lover having dreamed of enjoying his love... Sir Thomas Wyatt. 6198-2,6726-3
A lover I am. Unknown. 6328-4,6563-5
The lover in liberty smileth at them in thraldom... Unknown. 6182-6
The lover in winter plaineth for the spring. Unknown. 6830-8
A lover left alone. Unknown. 6881-2
The lover like to a ship tossed on the sea. Sir Thomas Wyatt. 6833-2
Lover loquitur. Louise Imogen Guiney. 6441-8
"Lover of beauty, walking on the height". Milton. Henry Van Dyke. 6961-4
The lover of his country. Andreas Calvos. 6352-7
A">"lover of late was I. Unknown. 6874-X
The lover refused of his love. Unknown. 6830-8
The lover rejoiceth... Sir Thomas Wyatt. 6208-3
The lover showeth how he is forsaken. Sir Thomas Wyatt. 6108-7,6182-6,6430-2,6189-3,6208-3
The lover sings of a garden. Helen Hoyt. 6880-4
The lover sings of a garden. Helen Hoyt. 6897-9
A lover speaks. Elizabeth Greene Thomas. 7016-7
The lover tells of the rose in his heart. William Butler Yeats. 6507-4,6250-4,6508-2
A lover to his betrothed. David Macbeth Moir. 6980-0
A lover to his doubting lady. Mary J.J. Wrinn. 6850-2
A lover to his lady-love. Mary Wilhelmina Hastings. 6118-4
The lover to his lady. George Turberville. 6436-1,6586-4, 6250-4,6189-3
The lover to his love having forsaken him and... Unknown. 6943-6
Lover to lover. David Morton. 6250-4
The lover to the Thames of London to favour his lady... George Turberville. 6182-6,6436-1,6125-7
The lover urges the better thrift. Alice Meynell. 6955-X
"The lover who, across a gulf". Frost in harvest. Coventry Patmore. 6980-0
The lover with his loved one sailed the sea. Sir Edwin Arnold. 6066-8
A lover without arms. Henry Davenport. 6702-6,6505-8
A lover's anger. Matthew Prior. 6317-9;6563-5
The lover's appeal. Sir Thomas Wyatt. 6246-6,6732-8
A lover's choice. William Bedingfield. 6874-X
A lover's chronicle. Abraham Cowley. 6787-5
Lover's complaint. Unknown. 6118-4
A lover's complaint. William Shakespeare. 6198-2,6380-2
A lover's complaint. Meleager. 6102-8
A lover's dark fancy. William Wordsworth. 6659-3
The lover's despair. William Shakespeare. 6560-0
A lover's dream. Sir Thomas Wyatt. 6659-3
A lover's envy. Henry Van Dyke. 6961-4
The lover's errand, fr. The courtship of Miles Standish. Henry Wadsworth Longfellow. 6753-0
The lover's ghost. Louis Simpson. 6218-0
A lover's greeting. William Browne. 6830-8
The lover's interdict. Alice Cary. 6969-X

A lover's lament. R. Grant Brown. 6591-0,6592-9
A lover's lament. Francis M. Foster. 6178-8
A lover's lament. William Shakespeare. 6543-0
A lover's lament. Unknown (Tewa Indian) 7039-6,6396-9
Lover's lane, Saint Jo. Eugene Field. 6441-8
A lover's legacy. Unknown. 6563-5
The lover's litany. Rudyard Kipling. 6652-6
A lover's lullaby. George Gascoigne. 6830-8
The lover's melancholy, sels. John Ford. 6198-2,6369-1, 6472-8
The lover's night thoughts. William Shakespeare. 6429-9, 6321-7,6226-1
A lover's oath. George Croly. 6980-0
The lover's posy. Rufinus. 7039-6
The lover's progress, sels. John Fletcher. 6908-8
A lover's quarrel. Robert Browning. 6204-0
Lover's reply to good advice. Richard Hughes. 6069-2
The lover's resolution. George Wither. 6122-2,6186-9,6395-0,6560-0,6513-9,6301
The lover's return. Unknown. 6003-X
The lover's sacrifice. Unknown. 6411-6
The lover's song. Edward Rowland Sill. 6735-2
The lover's song. Alfred Austin. 6437-X
The lover's tale, sels. Alfred Lord Tennyson. 6655-0
The lover's tale. Alfred Lord Tennyson. 6977-0
The lover's tears, fr. Love's labour's lost. William Shakespeare. 6827-8
A lover's test. Bayard Taylor. 6976-2
A lover's vow. Thomas Lodge. 6830-8
Lover's walk. Edward Farquhar. 6939-8
The lover's walk, fr. The house of life. Dante Gabriel Rossetti. 6250-4,6430-2
Lover, Samuel
   The angel's whisper. 6219-9,6424-8,6658-5,6543-0,6078-1, 6174-5,6302-0,6385-3,6502-3,6519
   Barney O'Hea. 6930-4
   The birth of Saint Patrick. 6089-7,6165-6,6412-4,6465-5, 6219-9
   The birth of St. Patrick. 6825-1
   Blarney Castle. 6331-4,6484-1,6439-6
   Carolan and Bridget Cruise. 6518-X
   Carolan and Bridget Cruise. 6858-8
   Dermot O'Dowd. 6825-1
   The fairy boy. 6174-5,6459-0
   The fairy tempter. 6613-5
   Father land and mother tongue. 6165-6,6302-0,6385-3
   Father Molloy. 6089-7
   Father Molloy. 6825-1,6915-0
   Father Roach. 6825-1,6914-2
   The haunted spring. 6502-3
   How to ask and have. 6089-7
   I'm not myself at all! 6858-8
   Lanty Leary. 6089-7
   The low-backed car. 6090-0,6174-5,6498-1,6605-4,6166-4, 6302 ,6129-9,6385-3,6744-1
   The low-backed car. 6921-5
   The maiden's request. 6279-2
   Molly Carew. 6001-3
   My mother dear. 6459-0
   My place in childhood. 6097-8
   Never despair. 6605-2
   Paddy Blake's echo. 6424-8
   Paddy Blake's echo. 6825-1,6916-9
   Paddy O'Rafther. 6089-7
   Paddy O'Rafther. 6825-1
   The pope. 6230-X
   Putting up o' the stove. 6402-7
   The Quaker and the robber. 6407-8
   The Quaker's meeting. 6089-7
   Rory O'More. 6219-9,6656-9,6240-7,6413-2,6552-X,6089 , 6174-5,6240-7,6255-5,6302-0,6385-3,6358
   St. Kevin. 6825-1,6930-4
   Shamus O'Brien, the bold boy of Glingall. 6402-7,6554-6
   The war ship of peace. 6946-0
   A way out of it. 6280-6
   What will you do, love? 6930-4
   The whistlin' thief. 6174-5
   Widow Machree. 6174-5,6656-9,6302-0,6385-3,6732-8
   Won't you follow me. 6928-2
The lover, fr. The angel in the house. Coventry Patmore.

LOVER,

6123-0,6600-3,6383-7
"The **lover**, in melodious verses". No sorrow peculiar to the sufferer. Vincent Bourne. 6814-6
The **lover**, whose mistress feared a mouse... George Turberville. 6511-2
The **lover**: a ballad. Lady Mary Wortley Montagu. 6317-9, 6092-7,6152-4
A **lover**. Alfred Edward Coppard. 6780-8
A **lover**. Plato. 6732-8
A **lover**. William Wordsworth. 6980-0
The **lover**. John Crowe Ransom. 6326-8
Lovers. Matthew Arnold. 6066-8
Lovers. Jean Ingelow. 6066-8
Lovers. Unknown. 6429-9,6321-7
"**Lovers** 'tis said are blind...". On a gentleman whose mistress had an ill breath. Thomas Warton (the Elder). 6962-2
Lovers and sweethearts. Phoebe Cary. 6969-X
Lovers how they come and part. Robert Herrick. 6317-9
Lovers in a garden. Unknown. 6649-6
Lovers in a garden. Unknown (Arabian) 6232-6
Lovers infinitenesse. John Donne. 6208-3,6562-7,6182-6, 6341-1,6194-X
Lovers meeting. William Shakespeare. 6094-3,6560-0
Lovers rejoyce, fr. Cupid's revenge. Francis Beaumont and John Fletcher. 6208-3
Lovers relentlessly. Stanley J. Kunitz. 6250-4
"**Lovers** spark/In the dark". Silhouettes. Arthur Hobson Quinn. 6936-3
A **lovers'** estrangement. Antonin Sova. 6886-3
The **lovers'** flight. Alfred Noyes. 6151-6
"**Lovers'** hands caressed these bits". A necklace in a museum. Nancy Telfair. 6841-3
Lovers' quarrel. Sir Edmund Gosse. 6770-0
A **lovers'** quarrel. Austin Dobson. 6481-7
"**Lovers**, a little of this your happy time". To the lovers that come after us. John Drinkwater. 6879-0
Lovers, and a reflection. Charles Stuart Calverley. 6092-7, 6633-X,6722-0,6089-7,6440-X
"**Lovers**, avoid the shafts that fly". Song ("Lovers, avoid"). Charles, Duc d' Orleans. 6227-X
Lovers, rejoice! Francis Beaumont. 6182-6
Lovers, rejoice! John Fletcher. 6182-6
The **lovers**. Phoebe Cary. 6240-7,6385-3
The **lovers**. Alex Comfort. 6379-9
The **lovers**. Edward Davison. 6317-9
The **lovers**. Emily Dickinson. 6008-0
The **lovers**. A. S. 6817-0
Loves deitie. John Donne. 6562-7
Loves growth. John Donne. 6378-0
Loves his daddy best. Myrtle B. Carpenter. 6715-8
Loves horoscope. Richard Crashaw. 6933-9
Loves horoscope. Richard Crashaw. 6341-1
Loves horoscope. Richard Crashaw. 6933-9
'The **loves** of every day' Witter Bynner. 6875-8
Loves of leaves and grasses. John Vance Cheney. 7041-8
The **loves** of the lions. Charles Madge. 6354-3
Loves of the plants. Erasmus Darwin. 6240-7
The **loves** of the triangles. John H. Frere; George Canning & George Ellis. 6802-2
Loves usury. John Donne. 6562-7
Loves victory. Aurelian Townsend. 6341-1
Lovesight. Dante Gabriel Rossetti. 6737-9
Lovest thou me? William Cowper. 6024-2,6378-0,6641-0,6219-9
Lovett, Eva
    A kind little girl. 6529-5
    The wisest fool. 7022-1
Lovett, Robert
    Forbidden drink. 6722-0
Lovewell's fight. Unknown. 6015-3
Lovewell's fight (1). Unknown. 6946-0
Lovewell's fight (2). Unknown. 6946-0
Lovibond, Edward
    Inscription on a fountain. 6086-2
    A monument in Arcadia. 6934-7
Loving and beloved. Sir John Suckling. 6208-3,6562-7
"A **loving** atmosphere surrounds this day of...". Christmas day. Caroline Eleanor Wilkinson. 6799-9
Loving beauty is loving God. Isabelle McClellan Taylor.

6178-8
Loving Henry. Unknown. 6826-X
Loving him once. Melrose Pitman. 6906-1
"**Loving** in truth, and fain in verse my love to". Sir Philip Sidney. 6187-7,6536-8,6645-3,6023-4,6536-8
"**Loving** in truth, and fain in verse my love to show". Sonnet ("Loving in truth"). Sir Philip Sidney. 6301-2
The **loving** little girl. Emma Celia & Lizzie J. Rook. 6314-4
Loving mad Tom. Unknown. 6829-4
Loving Nancy. Unknown. 6826-X
"**Loving** man, I have wearied of the ways of man". Redemption. Thomas Curtis Clark. 6954-1
Loving you. Unknown. 6750-6
Loving, Pierre
    Star market. 6880-4
"**Low** and brown barns thatched and repatched...". The wife of Flanders. Gilbert Keith Chesterton. 7029-9
"**Low** and brown barns, thatched and repatched..". The wife of Flanders. Gilbert Keith Chesterton. 7031-0,7026-4
"A **low** and quiet voice calls". Spring rain. Yung-ro Brun. 6775-1
Low barometer. Robert Bridges. 6487-6
"The **low** bay melts into a ring of silver". The shore. Muriel Stuart. 6884-7
Low country. Josephine Johnson. 6979-7
Low doun in the broom. Unknown. 6845-6
"A **low** full sweep of instrumental string". Sonnet ("A low full sweep"). Unknown. 6118-4
"**Low** lies the land upon the sea". The lookout. William Collins. 6833-2
Low life. Helen Bosanquet. 7042-6
The **low** lintel. Margaret A. Sinclair. 6591-0,6592-9
"**Low** on a sick bed she helplessly lay". Her vision. Unknown. 6923-1
"**Low** on the breezy hill-side grew". The dandelion. Gertrude Alger. 6798-0
"**Low** on the marble floor I lie". Christmas night in Saint Peter's. Helen Hunt Jackson. 7041-8
"**Low** she lies, who blest our eyes". The mourners. Caroline Elizabeth Sarah Sheridan Norton. 6980-0
"**Low** soft rustle of/Wind through leaves". Barnyard symphony. Marie Emilie Gilchrist. 6906-1
"**Low** sounds of night that drip upon the ear". A memory. Francis Ledwidge. 6812-X
Low tide. Lynette Roberts. 6379-9
Low tide at St. Andrews. Emily Pauline ("Tekahionwake") Johnson. 6837-5
Low tide on Grand-Pre. Bliss Carman. 6115-X,6446-9,6021-8, 6433-7
A **low** trade, fr. Mime. Herodas. 6435-3
Low voices. Edwin Ford Piper. 6506-6
"**Low** walks the sun, and broadens by de-", fr. Summer. James Thomson. 6122-2
"**Low** warblings, now, and solitary harps". Evening music of the angels. James Abraham Hillhouse. 6752-2
"**Low** was our pretty cot: our tallest rose". Reflections on having left a place of retirement. Samuel Taylor Coleridge. 6828-2
"A **low** white house at the end of a lane". New Hampshire homestead. Priscilla Alden Wolfe. 6764-6
Low, Benjamin R.C.
    Due north. 6833-2
    Due north. 6266-0
    Even-song. 6607-0
    For the dedication of a toy theatre. 6029-3
    The little boy and the locomotive. 6473-6
    The locomotive to the little boy. 6607-0
    These United States. 6031-5
Low, John W.
    He hated sham. 6995-9
Low, Mary Cromwell
    I learned to know. 6847-2
    In the vast and dim cathedral. 6847-2
    Into his house. 6847-2
    Merry Christmas. 6747-6
    My window to the sky. 6847-2
    Singin' pays. 6847-2
Low, Samuel

To a segar. 6004-8
"The **low**, large moon lies in the liquid sky". Summer, fr. Thistledown. Cora Fabri. 6876-6
"**Low**, low, low/Low I crouch in the grass". The herd-boy in the rain. May C. ([Mary] Gillington) Byron. 6800-6
"**Low**, the woods/Bow their hoar heads". A fall of snow. James Thomson. 6793-X
The **low-backed** car. Samuel Lover. 6090-0,6174-5,6498-1, 6605-4,6166-4,6302 ,6129-9,6385-3,6744-1
The **low-backed** car. Samuel Lover. 6921-5
"**Low-browed** school-house, silver-sided". The old school-house. Benjamin Franklin Taylor. 6815-4
Thu **low-down** white. Robert Service. 6159-1
"**Low-flowing** breezes are roaming...". Elegiacs. Alfred Lord Tennyson. 6977-0
Low-moon land. Francis Ledwidge. 6812-X
Lowater, Ninette M.
    Easter bells. 6171-0
    The happy wind. 6130-3
    The song of labor. 6260-1
A **lowden** sabbath morn. Robert Louis Stevenson. 6819-7
Lowe, Emmeline
    Later ter glory. 6750-6
Lowe, John
    Mary's dream. 6180-X,6302-0;6385-3,6481-7
Lowe, Martha P.
    The brook behind the Waumbek house. 6965-7
Lowe, Robert Liddell
    Beauty and sorrow. 6640-2
    God's hands. 6640-2
    Kings bow their heads. 6640-2
    On a singing girl. 6640-2
    On a singing girl. 6780-8
    This glittering grief. 6640-2
    Woman plowing. 6954-1
Lowe, Titus
    Mother. 6097-8,6274-1
Lowe; Viscount Sherbrooke, Robert
    A horse's epitaph. 6510-4
Lowell & Florence Ayscough, Amy (tr.)
    The excursion. Tu Fu, 7039-6
Lowell, Amy
    After hearing a waltz by Bartok. 6959-2
    Afterglow. 6984-3
    Anticipation. 6300-4
    Apology. 6556-2,6019-6,6431-0,6653-9
    Autumn and death. 6619-4
    A bather. 6031-5
    Battledore and shuttlecock. 6030-7
    The bombardment. 6029-3
    The book of hours of Sister Clotilde. 6754-9
    Chinoiseries, sels. 6897-9
    The city of falling leaves. 6348-9,6030-7
    Convalescence. 7027-2
    The cornucopia of red and green comfits. 6032-3,6393-4
    A critical fable, sels. 6483-3
    Crowned. 6250-4
    A decade. 6488-4,6536-8
    Dolphins in blue water. 6299-7
    The dusty hour-glass. 6338-1
    Easel picture: Decoration Day. 6069-2
    The emperors' garden. 6649-6
    The enchanted castle. 6184-2
    Evelyn Ray. 6531-7
    Exercise in logic. 6070-6
    Falling snow. 6897-9
    The flute. 6033-1,6538-4
    Fragment. 6730-1
    Free fantasia on Japanese themes. 6032-3,6538-4
    Frimaire. 6034-X
    Fringed gentians. 6338-1
    The fruit garden path. 6338-1
    The fruit shop. 6029-3
    Funeral song for the Indian chief Blackbird. 6345-4
    The garden by moonlight. 6647-X
    Gavotte in D minor. 6034-X
    A gift. 6300-4,6102-8
    The giver of stars. 6320-9
    Granadilla. 6345-4
    The gravestone. 6779-4
    Guns as keys: and the great gate swings. 6031-5
    Hoar-frost. 6897-9
    In a powder closet. 6072-2
    In excelsis. 6010-2
    July midnight. 6338-1
    La ronde du diable. 6010-2
    A lady. 6102-8,6076-5,6464-7,6348-9,6556-2,6348-9
    The lamp of life. 6337-3
    The letter. 6019-6
    Lilacs. 6299-7,6506-6,6619-4,6396-9,6121-4,6153-2,6288-1,6010-2,6464-7
    A little garden. 6236-9,6266-0
    Little ivory figures pulled with string. 6348-9,6375-6
    Madonna of the evening flowers. 6032-3,6077-3,6538-4, 6556-2,6581-3,6431-0,6464-7
    Malmaison. 6030-7
    Meeting-house hill. 6984-3
    Meeting-house hill. 6345-4
    Memorandum confided by a yucca to a passion vine, sels. 6538-4
    Merchandise. 6299-7,6348-9
    Merely statement. 6034-X
    New heavens for old. 6345-4
    Night clouds. 6345-4,6102-8,6345-4,6076-5,6527-9,6726-3
    Nuit blanche. 6619-4
    Obligation. 6607-0
    Old snow. 6345-4
    On a certain critic. 6031-5
    On looking at a copy fo Alice Meynell's poems... 6483-3
    Once Jericho. 6345-4
    1777. 6348-9
    An opera house. 6162-1
    Orientation. 6776-X
    The painter of silk. 6162-1
    The paper windmill. 6161-3
    Pastime. 6011-0
    Patterns. 6077-3,6154-0,6232-6,6320-9,6393-4,6527-9, 6536-8,6556-2,6476-0,6474-4,6076-5,6102-8,6491-4, 6506-6,6509-0,6029-3,6431-0,6723-9,6581-3,6288-1
    Planning the garden. 6649-6
    The poem. 6880-4
    The precinct - Rochester. 6431-0
    The precinct, Rochester. 6431-0
    Prime. 6010-2
    Purple grackles. 6073-0,6162-1,6288-1,6161-3
    Red slippers. 6897-9
    Reflections. 6338-1
    A rhyme of the motley. 6619-4
    Roads. 6253-9
    A Roxbury garden. 6299-7
    Sea shell. 6466-3,6478-7,6114-1
    Solitaire. 6299-7,6348-9
    A sprig of rosemary. 6607-0
    Summer. 6320-9
    Summer night piece. 6984-3
    Summer night piece. 6649-6
    Sunshine. 6052-8
    The swans. 6010-2
    The taxi. 6019-6
    Texas. 6289-X
    To John Keats. 6483-3
    To two unknown ladies. 6033-1
    A tulip garden. 6338-1,6347-0,6510-4,6653-4
    Twenty-four hokku on a modern theme. 6010-2
    Venus transiens. 6556-2,6250-4,6431-0
    Vernal equinox. 6348-9
    Vespers. 6010-2
    Violin sonata by Vincent d'Indy. 6538-4
    Wind and silver. 6536-8,6345-4,6345-4
    A winter ride. 6310-1,6583-X,6253-9
    Winter's turning. 6162-1,6538-4,6607-0
Lowell, James Russell
    Abraham Lincoln. 6302-0,6385-3,6552-X,6442-6,6470-1, 6304-7,6396-9
    After the burial. 6600-3,6126-5,6076-5,6723-9,6102-8, 6304 ,6076-5,6288-1
    After the burial, sels. 6102-8
    Agassiz. 6126-5
    Agro-dolce. 6429-9,6321-7,6226-1
    Al fresco. 6049-8

LOWELL

Aladdin. 6077-3,6136-2,6243-1,6331-4,6473-6,6478 ,6496-5,6583-X,6631-3,6421-3,6396-9,6288-1,6126-5,6371-3, 6004-8,6212-2,6107-9
Ambrose. 6600-3
America's gospel. 6337-3
"And the voice that was softer...", fr. The vision... 6335-7
"And they who do their souls no wrong." 6225-3
Appledore in a storm. 6344-6
Auf wiedersehen! 6302-0,6385-3,6735-2,6441-8,6077-3, 6004-8,6092-7,6126-5,6219-9,6288-1,6226-1,6560-0
Auf wiedersehen, sels. 6732-8
Auspex. 6243-1,6288-1,6126-5,6153-2,6309-8
"Be noble, and the nobleness that lies." 6225-3,6238-5
"Be not simply good, but good for something." 6225-3
"Beauty and truth and all that these contain." 6225-3
Beaver brook. 6008-0,6288-1
The beggar. 6502-3
"Beloved, in the noisy city here". 6126-5
Bibliolatres. 6288-1
The Biglow papers, sels. 6176-1,6600-3,6008-0,6288-1, 6542-2
The Biglow papers. 6597-X
The Biglow papers. 6126-5,6739-5
The birch-tree. 6077-3,6049-8
"Blessing she is; God make her so." 6225-3
The bobolink. 6073-5
Boyhood of Columbus. 6624-0
The brook in winter, fr. The vision of Sir Launfal. 6239-3
The candidate's creed. 6089-7,6736-0,6278-4
The cathedral, sels. 6144-3,6335-7
The cathedral. 6333-0
The changeling. 6078-1,6127-3,6126-5
A Chippewa legend. 6077-3
A Christmas carol. 6144-3,6145-1,6623-2,6478-7,6457-4, 6147-8,6608-9,6746-8
Columbus. 6678-X,6087-0,6126-5
Commemoration ode. 6600-3,6438-8,6424-8,6263-6,6250-4, 6309
Commemoration ode, sels. 6113-3
A contrast. 6288-1
The courtin'. 6008-0,6083-8,6092-7,6219-9,6265-2,6307 , 6121-4,6396-9,6281-4,6126-5,6288-1,6964 ,6823-5,6302-0,6385-3,6279-2,6089-7,6332-2,6473 ,6600-3,6696-8, 6732-8,6735-2,6176-1,6404 ,6610-0,6505-8,6438-8,6419-1,6431-0,6278
Credidimus Jovem Regnare. 6735-2
The darkened mind. 6333-0
Das ewig-weibliche. 6641-0
A day in June. 6242-3,6265-2,6464-7
The dead house. 6126-5
The debate in the sennit. 6946-0
Disappointment. 6304-7
Doctor lobster. 6787-5
E.G. de R. 6230-X
Elegy on the death of Dr. Channing, sels. 6337-3
An ember picture. 6691-7,6288-1,6004-8,6230-X,6126-5
Emerson, fr. A fable for critics. 6399-3
Extreme unction. 6632-1
A fable for critics, sels. 6959-2
A fable for critics, sels. 6753-0
A fable for critics, sels. 6008-0,6121-4,6399-3,6483-3, 6176-1,6288-1,6126-5
The fatherland. 6087-0,6239-3,6337-3,6386-1,6420-5,6465-5,6143-5
The finding of the lyre. 6457-4,6503-1,6212-1,6457-4, 6639-9,6964
The first snow fall. 6459-0,6632-1,6219-9,6288-1,6560-0, 6104-4,6126-5,6302-0,6385-3,6078-1,6332-2,6127-3
Flawless his heart. 6946-0
The foot-path. 6126-5
For an autograph. 6289-X,6337-3,6126-5
For an autograph, sels. 6332-2
"For this true nobleness I seek in vain". 6753-0
A foreboding. 6429-9,6226-1,6321-7
The fountain. 6519-8,6466-3,6623-2,6077-3,6133-8,6134-6, 6135-4,6131-1,6424-8,6639-9,6136-2,6356-X,6692-5
Fourth of July ode. 6465-5
Freedom. 6176-1,6250-4

Freedom ("Are we, then, wholly fallen?"). 6486-8
Freedom ("We are not free: Freedom doth not consist"). 6087-0
General Grant. 6552-X
God is not dumb, fr. Bibliolatres. 6337-3,6418-3,6730-1
"God sends his teachers unto every age", fr. Rhoecus. 6934-7
"Goe, little booke." 6304-7
The gracious past. 6085-4
Hand in hand. 6304-7
The Harvard commemoration ode, sels. 6340-3,6305-5, 65244,6467-1
He gives nothing, fr. The vision of Sir Launfal. 6337-3
He spoke of Burns, fr. An incident in a railroad car. 6934-7
Hebe. 6243-1,6732-8,6288-1,6126-5
Her fittest triumph is to show that good"." 6226-1
The heritage. 6457-4,6499-X,6219-9,6304-7,6457-4,6481-7, 6407-8,6486-8,6600-3,6732-8,6964
A hero new. 6708-5
His throne is with the outcast. 6144-3,6335-7
Hosea Bigelow's lament. 6438-8
I ask not for those thoughts that suddenly leap. 6126-5
"I care not how men trace their ancestry", sels. 6047-1
I grieve not that ripe knowledge. 6288-1
"I thought our love at full, but I did err". 6126-5
"I would not have this perfect love of ours". 6753-0
In a copy of Omar Khayyam. 6126-5
In absence. 6077-3
In Arcadia. 6004-8
In the twilight. 6006-4,6732-8,6560-0,6126-5,6243-1, 6288
An incident in a railway car. 6632-1,6250-4,6126-5,6304-7
An Indian-summer reverie. 6008-0
Inscription proposed for a soldiers' and sailors' monument. 6126-5
International copyright. 6288-1
An interview with Miles Standish. 6457-4
Invita Minerva. 6753-0
An invitation. 6385-3
"It may be glorious to write". 6238-5
January. 6465-5,6456-6
Jonathan to John. 6481-7,6470-1,6016-2,6288-1,6505-8
Jottings for sportsmen. 6861-8
June. 6820-0
June. 6240-7,6260-1,6385-3,6465-5,6479-5,6250-4,6107-9, 6104-4,6421-3,6456-6,6481-7,6575-9,6585-6
June weather. 6239-3
June, fr. Vision of Sir Launfal. 6963-0
King William thanks his God. 6404-3
Kossuth. 6087-0
Labor, fr. A glance behind the curtain. 6337-3
A letter from a candidate for the presidency. 6385-3, 6278-4
Letter from a candidate, fr. Bigelow papers. 6787-5
A letter from Mr. Hosea Biglow, fr. Biglow papers. 6505-8
A letter, fr. The Bigelow papers. 6288-1
Letter..to Joseph T. Buckingham, fr. The Bigelow papers. 6753-0
Life's purpose, fr. The cathedral. 6337-3
Lincoln. 6820-0
Lincoln, the martyr chief. 6304-7
Longing. 7022-1
Love. 6620-8,6066-8
The maple. 6047-1
The martyr chief, fr. Ode recited at..Harvard commemoration. 6304-7
Masaccio. 6631-3
Mason and Slidell. 6438-8,6126-5
Mason and Slidell, fr. The Bigelow papers. 6753-0
Monna Lisa. 6126-5
Mr. Hosea Bigelow speaks. 6946-0
Mr. Hosea Bigelow to the editor of the Atlantic Monthly. 6385-3
Mr. Hosea Bigelow to the editor..., fr. Bigelow papers. 6753-0
My country. 6461-2
My love. 6243-1,6250-4,6288-1,6126-5,6639-9,6219-9,6309

8,6243-1,6219-9,6271-7
"My love, I have no fear that thou shouldst die". 6753-0
New England spring, fr. The Biglow Papers. 6600-3
The new-come chief, fr. Under the old elm. 6946-0
The nightingale in the study. 6004-8,6288-1,6126-5
"No man is born into the world whose work". 6238-5
The nobler lover. 6126-5
O mother state. 6087-0,6250-4
O what is so fair as a day in June. 6304-7
The oak. 6047-1,6049-8
An ode for the Fourth of July, 1876 6126-5
An ode of thanks for certain cigars. 6453-1
Ode recited at the Harvard commemoration. 6006-4,6074-9,6333-0,6473-6,6735-2,6008-8,6288-1,6126-5,6121-4
Ode recited at the Harvard commemoration, July 21, 1865. 6006-4
Ode to freedom. 6385-3
On board the '76. 6126-5
On the capture of certain fugitive slaves...Washington. 7009-4
On the death of a friend's child, sels. 6337-3
Once to every man and nation. 6304-7
The origin of didactic poetry. 6753-0
The origin of didactic poetry. 6288-1
The origin of didactic poetry. 6753-0
Our country saved. 6286-5,6344-6
"Our earth is not a fading earthly flower". 6753-0
Our lives should widen. 6304-7
Our love is not a fading, earthly flower. 6008-0,6288-1
Out of doors. 6304-7
Over his keys. 6465-5
Palinode. 6735-2,6288-1,6126-5
A parable. 6144-3,6335-7,6337-3
Peace on earth. 6304-7
The petition. 6004-8,6441-8,6735-2
Phoebe. 6126-5,6435-3
"Phoebus, sitting one day in a laurel tree's shade". 6850-2
The pioneer. 7009-4
The pious editor's creed, fr. The Bigelow papers. 6126-5,6176-1,6288-1
The poor and the rich. 7002-7
A prayer ("God! do not let"). 6486-8
The pregnant comment. 6126-5,6321-7,6429-9
Prelude, fr. The vision of Sir Launfal. 6176-1,6102-8
The present crisis, sel. 6954-1
The present crisis, sels. 6934-7
The present crisis, sels. 6334-9,6076-5,6102-8
The present crisis, sels. 6934-7
The present crisis. 6143-5,6371-3,6288-1,6219-9,6260-1,6359 ,6617-8,6678-X,6260-1,6102-8,6076-5,6126 ,6211-3,6337-3,6473-6,6486-8,6605-4,6735
The protest. 6429-9,6441-8,6321-7,6652-6
A requiem. 6486-8
A revolutionary hero. 6278-4
Rhoecus. 6332-2,6473-6,6008-0,6288-1,6126-5,6304
"Right forever on the scaffold; wrong forever..." 6238-5
The rose. 6917-7
St. Michael the weigher. 6754-9
St. Michael, the weigher. 6431-0
The search. 6337-3
A second letter from B. Sawin, Esq. 6126-5
The secret. 6288-1
She came and went. 6006-4,6078-1,6243-1,6102-8,6076-5, 6288 ,6737-9,6309-8,6300-4,6250-4,6126-5,6121
She came and went, sels. 6102-8
"She doeth little kindnesses". 6623-2
The shepherd of King Admetus, sels. 6934-7
The shepherd of King Admetus. 6473-6,6479-5,6499-X,6136-2,6401-9,6478 ,6288-1,6126-5,6304-7,6431-0
Shipwreck. 6250-4
Si descendero in Infernum, Ades. 6077-3
The singing leaves. 6239-3,6079-X,6613-5,6126-5,6319-5,6419
Sir Launfal and the leper, fr. 'The vision of Sir...' 6239-3,6614-3
Sixty-eighth birthday. 6126-5
Song ("O moonlight"). 6735-2,6126-5

Sonnet ("My friend"). 6085-4
Sonnet: Scottish border. 6126-5
Sonnets. 6302-0;6385-3
A soul in grass and flowers, fr. Vision of Sir Launfal. 6049-8
The sovereign emblem, fr. The cathedral. 6335-7,6337-3
Sphinx. 6304-7
Spring, fr. Sunthin' in the pastoral line. 6332-2
Spring, fr. The vision of Sir Launfal. 6260-1
A stanza on freedom. 6732-8,6265-2
Stanzas on freedom. 6051-X,6239-3,6337-3,6386-1,6623-2, 6288-1,6126-5,6396-9
Stealing. 6337-3
"Still o'er the earth hastes opportunity" 7014-0
The street. 6102-8,6250-4
Sub pondere crescit. 6337-3
"Such was he, our Martyr-Chief", sels. 6289-X
Summer storm. 6302-0;6385-3
Sunthin' in the pastoral line, sels. 6332-2,6288-1,6126-5,6121-4,6288-1,6467
Telepathy. 6429-9,6735-2,6126-5,6226-1,6321-7
"There never yet was flower fair in vain..." 6049-8
'Tis sorrow builds the shining ladder up. 6418-3,6214-8, 6730-1
To a pine tree. 6049-8,6484-1
To a recruiting Sergeant, fr. The Biglow Papers. 6176-1
To C.F. Bradford. 6453-1,6230-X
To Henry Wadsworth Longfellow. 6302-0,6385-3,6483-3, 6126-5
To the dandelion. 6126-5,6049-8,6008-0,6288-1,6121-4, 6396 ,6006-4,6243-1,6374-8,6459-0,6473-6,6481 ,6499-X,6597-X,6632-1,6639-8,6304-7,6431
To the dandelion, sels. 6047-1,6239-3
To the memory of Hood. 6483-3
To the spirit of Keats. 6077-3,6126-5,6288-1
"To those who died for her on land...". 6289-X
To W.L. Garrison. 6934-7
To Washington. 6385-3
To Whittier. 6126-5
To William Lloyd Garrison. 6250-4
The token. 6304-7
Tribute to Lincoln. 6499-X
True love. 6337-3
Truth and love abide, fr. Elegy..death of Dr. Channing. 6337-3
Turner's old temeraire. 6126-5
Under the old elm. 6049-8
Under the old elm, sels. 6239-3,6332-2
Under the willows. 6049-8
"Under the yaller pines I house" 6049-8
The unreturning brave. 6240-7
Unwasted days, fr. Under the old elm. 6332-2
Villa Franca. 6385-3
The violet. 6049-8
The vision of Sir Launfal, sel. 6954-1
The vision of Sir Launfal, sels. 6753-0
The vision of Sir Launfal, sels. 6337-3,6144-3,6335-7, 6732-8,6176-1,6239 ,6102-8,6730-1,6104-4,6107-9,6431-0,6076 ,6008-0,6560-0,6182-2,6049-8
The vision of Sir Launfal. 6332-2,6673-9,6288-1,6126-5, 6300-4,6304
War. 6337-3
The washers of the shroud. 6126-5,6470-1,6113-3,6735-2, 6438-8,6008-0,6288-1
Washington, fr. 'Under the old elm'. 6239-3,6143-5,6396-9
Wendell Phillips. 6008-0,6288-1
What is so rare as a day in June. 6396-9
What Mr. Robinson thinks. 6760-3
What Mr. Robinson thinks. 6076-5,6102-8,6505-8,6307-1, 6126-5,6288-1,6281-4,6736-0,6219-9,6300-4,6302-0, 6385-3,6089-7,6735-2,6176-1
What Mr. Robinson thinks, sels. 6732-8,6102-8
What Rabbi Jehosa said. 6076-5,6102-8
What Rabbi Jehosha said. 6102-8
Whittier, fr. A fable for critics. 6176-1
William Lloyd Garrison. 6385-3
The wind-harp. 6126-5
A winter evening hymn to my fire. 6453-1
winter morning, fr. The vision of Sir Launfal. 6239-3

LOWELL

Winter pictures, fr. The Vision of Sir Launfal. 6385-3, 6102-8,6076-5
Winter's evening hymn to my fire. 6302-0;6385-3
With an armchair. 6423-X
"With my love this knowledge too was given". 6385-3
Without and within. 6126-5,6219-9,6747-6,6089-7,6441-8, 6735-2,6092-7,6004-8
Yussouf. 6302-0,6385-3,6134-4,6087-0,6499-X,6614-3,6107-9,6396-9,6639-9

Lowell, Maria White
The Alpine sheep. 6600-3
The morning glory. 6302-0,6385-3,6014-5,6078-1,6127-3
An opium fantasy. 6754-9
Song ("O bird"). 6309-8

Lowell, Robert
Christ is here. 6065-X
The Massachusetts line. 6015-3
The Quaker graveyard in Nantucket. 6399-3

Lowell, Robert Traill Spence
The relief of Lucknow. 6385-3,6344-6,6554-6,6425-6,6385-3,6550-3,6614 ,6267-9,6263-3,6438-8,6424-8,6565-1

Lowenstein, Beatrice
L'envoi. 6847-2

Lowenstein, Tom
Blue dreamlight Shaman song. 6855-3
Tlingit beauty. 6855-3

The **lower** bough. Conde Benoist Pallen. 6096 X
Lower court. Carolyn Baxter. 6870-7
The **lower** Rhine. Louis J. Magee. 7004-3
"**Lower** him gently, gently, now...". Sea burial. Robina Monkman. 6833-2
The **lowest** place. Christina Georgina Rossetti. 6198-2,6337-3,6657-7
'The **lowest** trees have tops'. Sir Edward Dyer. 6208-3

Lowie (to German), Risa Alice (tr.)
Choric song of the lotos eaters. Alfred Lord Tennyson, 6847-2

Lowie, Risa Alice
After a year in the city. 6847-2
Peace. 6847-2

The **lowland** country. John Hall Wheelock. 6421-3
Lowland lassie. Unknown. 6859-6
A **lowland** witch ballad. William Bell Scott. 6518-X
Lowlands. Unknown. 6057-9,6547-3,6125-7
Lowlands a-ray. Unknown. 6328-4
The **lowlands** low. Unknown. 6003-X
The **lowlands** o' Holland. Unknown. 6547-3
The **lowlands** of Holland. Unknown. 6061-7,6290-3,6134-6, 6180-X,6547-3,6067-6,6153-2
The **lowlands**. Edith L. Fraser. 7016-7
"The **lowliest** combatants are we". Unmentioned in dispatches. Helen Hester Colvill. 7031-0
"**Lowliest** of owmen, and most glorified!". The annunciation. Felicia Dorothea Hemans. 6973-8
"A **lowly** hut, stone piled and redly stained". Lauterbrunnen. Thomas Gold Appleton. 6749-2

Lowrey, Booth
De prodjeckin' son. 6281-4
Miss Hen. 6281-4
Ole Billy William. 6281-4

Lowrey, Perry Holmes
The cowboys pass. 7007-8

Lowry, Henry Dawson
Art and life. 6793-X
My dream. 6793-X
Waiting. 6793-X

Lowry, Lillian
Peace. 6270-9

Lowry, Malcolm Boden
In memoriam: Ingvald Bjorndal. 6761-1

Lowry, Mary Ann
Saturday night. 6857-X

Lowth, Bishop (tr.)
"How beautiful appear on the mountains", fr. The Bible. Unknown, 6606-2

Lowther, Granville
The human trinity. 6818-9

Lox, the Indian devil. Unknown (Algonquin Indian) 6864-2
Loyal effusion. Horace Smith. 6802-2
The **loyal** fisher. Unknown. 6016-2

1026

The **loyal** general, sels. Nahum Tate. 6867-7
A **loyal** song. Henry Carey. 6934-7
A **loyal** woman's no. Lucy Larcom. 6438-8
The **loyalists**. Sarah Anne Curzon. 6795-6,6433-7
Loyalties. Walter A. Cutter. 6143-5
Loyalty. John Barbour. 6180-X
Loyalty. Allan Cunningham. 6322-5,6239-3
Loyalty confin'd. Sir Roger L'Estrange. 6933-9
Loyalty confined. Arthur Lord Capel. 6874-X
Loyalty hymn. Edith Lovejoy Pierce. 6144-3;6337-3
Loyalty to God. Elizabeth Jane Bancroft. 6894-4

Loyson, Paul Hyacinth
'For a scrap of paper'. Sir James Fraser (tr.). 7031-0
'Lt. -- R.F.C., missing believed killed'. Hartley Munro Thomas. 6796-4

Lu Yu
The herd boy. Arthur Waley (tr.). 6125-7

Luallen, C.L.
Fraterville mine explosion. 6149-4

Luath, fr. 'The twa dogs' Robert Burns. 7008-6
Lubber breeze. Thomas Sturge Moore. 6228-8

Lubbock, Phyllis M.
"I picked a primrose, pale as death." 6317-9

Lubeck, Schmidt von
The wanderer. Felicia Dorothea Hemans (tr.). 6973-8

Lubeski, Lori
Indiana. 6857-X

Luca and Andrea Della Robbia. Gertrude Huntington McGiffert. 6838-3

Lucan
Brundisium. Nicholas Rowe (tr.). 6624-0
Cato's address to his troops in Lybia, fr. Pharsalia. Nicholas Rowe (tr.). 6932-0
The coracle, fr. Pharsalia. Sir Walter Raleigh (tr.). 6125-7
The good will, fr. Pharsalia. Bernard Bosanquet (tr.). 7042-6
The Po. Joseph Addison (tr.). 6624-0
Pompey and Cornelia, fr. Pharsalia. Nicholas Rowe (tr.). 6932-0

Lucas, Daniel B.
In the land where we were dreaming. 6113-3

Lucas, Edward Verrall
Ad Dorotheam. 6772-7
Anticipations. 6793-X
The barber. 6018-8
The blacksmith. 6018-8
Brittany, fr. Geography. 6018-8
The bullfinch. 6018-8
The cat's cleanliness, fr. The nature of the cat. 6018-8
The cat's conscience, fr. The nature of the cat. 6018-8, 6120-6
The cat's cruelty, fr. The nature of the cat. 6018-8
The cat's friends, fr. The nature of the cat. 6018-8
The cat's greediness, fr. The nature of the cat. 6018-8
The cat's sleeplessness, fr. The nature of the cat. 6018-8
The chemist. 6018-8
Chocolate cream, fr. Counsel to those that eat. 6018-8, 6089-7
The conjurer. 6018-8
Counsel to those that eat, sels. 6018-8
The cricket ball sings. 6423-X
The debt. 6474-4
The gamekeeper. 6018-8
The gardener. 6018-8
Geography, sels. 6018-8
Germany, fr. Geography. 6018-8
Hands across the sea. 6018-8
Holland, fr. Geography. 6018-8
Hot potatoes, fr. Counsel to those that eat. 6018-8
India, fr. Geography. 6018-8
Jack. 6423-X
Lewis Carroll. 6018-8
The London sparrows. 6018-8
Mr. Coggs. 6018-8
Mr. Coggs, watchmaker. 6891-X
Normandy, fr. Geography. 6018-8
Oranges, fr. Counsel to those that eat. 6018-8

Randolph Caldecott. 6018-8
The shipbuilder. 6018-8
A song against speed. 7020-5
Spain, fr. Geography. 6018-8
The turkey. 6018-8
The visit to the zoo. 6018-8
Wales, fr. Geography. 6018-8
The windmill. 6018-8

Lucas, F.L.
Beleagured cities. 6257-1
In the Hebrites. 6782-4
Modernity. 6317-9
The pipe of peace. 6257-1,6257-9
Spain, 1809. 6257-1
To the graces. 6780-8

Lucas, F.L. (tr.)
"Achaemenides once, Menippus now...". Unknown, 6251-2
"Ah lonely isles, fragments...". Antipater of Thessalonica, 6251-2
"Ah me, once Archeades pressed...". Asclepiades, 6251-2
"Ah voices sweet as honey, ah maiden songs divine". Alcman, 6251-2
"Ah with what heart of wonder...". Oppian, 6251-2
"Ah, misty Gereneia, ill cragg, thou shouldst...". Simonides, 6251-2
"Ah, what is life?-what is joy?-but Aphrodite...". Mimnermus, 6251-2
"Alas for grim old age! Alas for youth...". Theognis, 6251-2
"All the women tell me". Unknown (Greek), 6251-2
"All things thou bringest, Hesper...". Sappho, 6251-2
"All's dust, all's laughter...". Glycon, 6251-2
"Although beneath this grave-mound...". Simonides, 6251-2
"Among the mad, none madder...". Theognis, 6251-2
"Amyntichus the aged, when his fisheo's days...". Macedonius, 6251-2
"Anastasia, fair blossom...". Julianus [or Julian the Egyptian], 6251-2
"And by her side went Eros, and Passion...". Hesiod, 6251-2
"And dirge to dirge than answers...". Unknown, 6251-2
"Aphrodite, daughter of Zeus, undying". Sappho, 6251-2
"Ares, in might surpassing...". Unknown, 6251-2
"Aristion, so swift once...". Thyillus, 6251-2
"As on the fiery lightning followeth the thunder". Solon, 6251-2
"As the hyacinth high on the mountains...". Sappho, 6251-2
"As the sweet apple reddens, high up against the sky". Sappho, 6251-2
"As towering through the height". Bacchylides, 6251-2
"As when from his mountain-outlook...", fr. The Iliad. Homer, 6251-2
"As when the deep lies heaving...", fr. The Iliad. Homer, 6251-2
"As when, high up...", fr. The Iliad. Homer, 6251-2
"Atthis, our own loved Anactoria". Sappho, 6251-2
Autumn. Hesiod, 6251-2
Autumn ploughing. Hesiod, 6251-2
"Be like the twisted polyp that coiling round...". Theognis, 6251-2
"Beside the grey sea-shingle...". Anyte, 6251-2
"Beyond Ortygia there lies an isle", fr. The Odyssey. Homer, 6251-2
"Bid him to dine that loves thee, leave him...". Hesiod, 6251-2
"The black earth's always drinking". Unknown (Greek), 6251-2
"A branch of myrtle in her happiness". Archilochus, 6251-2
"But Achilles, by the breakers...", fr. The Iliad. Homer, 6251-2
"But Alcimus and Automedon...", fr. The Iliad. Homer, 6251-2
"But as bees or supple-waisted...", fr. The Iliad. Homer, 6251-2
"But as in a garden a poppy...", fr. The Iliad. Homer, 6251-2
"But as o'er some parched ountain...", fr. The Iliad. Homer, 6251-2
"But as on a day in winter...", fr. The Iliad. Homer, 6251-2
"But as some star of bale...", fr. The Iliad. Homer, 6251-2
"But as they talked, laid near...", fr. The Odyssey. Homer, 6251-2
"But far astern of Argo her whitening wake...". Apollonius, 6251-2
"But her knees at his words...", fr. The Odyssey. Homer, 6251-2
"But now a herald...", fr. The Odyssey. Homer, 6251-2
"But now Zeus throned in...", fr. The Iliad. Homer, 6251-2
"But now-as ravening wolves...", fr. The Iliad. Homer, 6251-2
"But to tell the white-armed...", fr. The Iliad. Homer, 6251-2
"But up soon swims our mullet...". Oppian, 6251-2
"But when came early morning...", fr. The Odyssey. Homer, 6251-2
"But when the bands were mustered...", fr. The Iliad. Homer, 6251-2
"But when through Troy's wide...", fr. The Iliad. Homer, 6251-2
"But when we were come...", fr. The Odyssey. Homer, 6251-2
"By the vats of Dionysus...". Unknown, 6251-2
"Cythere the Bithynian...". Antipater of Thessalonica, 6251-2
"Damis the Nysaean of a little bark...". Antipater, 6251-2
"Dead you shall lie, for ever...". Sappho, 6251-2
"Dear Earth, within Thy bosom grant rest...". Unknown, 6251-2
"Dear Zeus, at thy ways I wonder...". Theognis, 6251-2
"Desolate is my station...". Unknown, 6251-2
"Dionysius, of Tarsus, here doth rot". Unknown, 6251-2
"Drink deep when the winejar's opened...". Hesiod, 6251-2
"Drink on, love on, not always lover...". Strato, 6251-2
"Drink, drink, Asclepiades...". Asclepiades, 6251-2
"Earth bare the long-ridged mountains...". Hesiod, 6251-2
"Easily as a child that plays...", fr. The Iliad. Homer, 6251-2
"Evil to choose is easy, of her thou canst find...". Hesiod, 6251-2
"The exile has never a friend of loyal...". Theognis, 6251-2
The fall of man and the early ages of the earth. Hesiod, 6251-2
"Farewell, now, Hope and Fortune...". Unknown, 6251-2
"Ferryman that rowest the barge...". Zonas, 6251-2
"First by Andromache the women's...", fr. The Iliad. Homer, 6251-2
"First, of the Heliconian Muses be my song". Hesiod, 6251-2
"Fling yourself here...". Unknown, 6251-2
"The flowery spring-I heard her, coming upon her way". Alcaeus of Mytilene, 6251-2
"For Crethis the teller of stories..." Callimachus, 6251-2
"For Death we all are nurtured...". Palladas, 6251-2
"For it is the Archer Apollo, and the Muses...". Hesiod, 6251-2
"For me my spear is kneaded bread...". Archilochus, 6251-2
"' For nine days then we were...", fr. The Odyssey. Homer, 6251-2
"Give me a mattress...". Antiphilus, 6251-2
"God from the first created diversely". Semonides, 6251-2
"The Gods held me in Egypt...", fr. The Odyssey. Homer, 6251-2
"Hades laid hand upon me...". Unknown, 6251-2
"Hand me the sweet cup...". Zonas, 6251-2
"Have you come then, O my darling...". Theocritus, 6251-2
"Health is the best tht Heaven sends". Simonides, 6251-

2

"Heart, my heart, with cares past curing thou...". Archilochus, 6251-2
"A hen hman sworn of Ares, Lord God of war, I live". Archilochus, 6251-2
"Here Brotachus of Gortyna, a Cretan born, is laid". Simonides, 6251-2
"Here I stand, the gravestone...". Unknown, 6251-2
"Here it was once Leander crossed...". Antipater of Thessalonica, 6251-2
"Here lies one that made shipwreck...". Theodoridas [or Theodorides], 6251-2
"Here, a maiden of bronze, I stand on Midas' grave." Cleobulus of Lindus, 6251-2
Hero and Leander. Musaeus, 6251-2
"Hesper, thou golden light...". Bion, 6251-2
"High up the mountain-meadow...". Satyrus, 6251-2
"Him I hold as happy as god in heaven". Sappho, 6251-2
"His the seat of honour at every celebration". Xenophanes, 6251-2
"His yoke-ox, growing feeble...". Addaeus, 6251-2
"Homer and Hesiod fathered on the Gods' divinity". Xenophanes, 6251-2
"Homeward from earth's far ends thou art returned". Alcaeus of Mytilene, 6251-2
A hound. Simonides, 6435-3
"How long in stealthy silence...". Paulus Silentiarius, 6251-2
"The hunting-hound of Midas...". Antipater, 6251-2
"The huntsman, Epicydes, across the mountains..." Callimachus, 6251-2
"I am dead, but I wait...". Unknown, 6251-2
"I ask not Gyges' riches". Unknown (Greek), 6251-2
"I cannot, sweetest mother". Sappho, 6251-2
"I do not love a wanton...". Rufinus, 6251-2
"I drank at a spring, time was, where dark...". Theognis, 6251-2
"I heard, O Polypaides, I heard the bird's shrill...". Theognis, 6251-2
"I know well I am mortal...". Ptolemaeus, 6251-2
"I loathe a man that's evil. My face in my veil...". Theognis, 6251-2
"I loathe bards' commonplaces." Callimachus, 6251-2
"I love the lad no longer; I have spurned...". Theognis, 6251-2
"I loved, I kissed...". Unknown, 6251-2
"I pile the chill sea-shingle...". Zonas, 6251-2
"I send thee, Rhodocleia...". Rufinus, 6251-2
"I sing no out-of-date matter". Timotheus, 6251-2
"I would that free from sickness...". Mimnermus, 6251-2
"I, Epicetus, was a slave...". Unknown, 6251-2
"If ever you come to Phthia...". Unknown, 6251-2
"If oxen, or lions, or horses had hands like men...". Xenophanes, 6251-2
"If you can tell the number". Unknown (Greek), 6251-2
The Iliad, sels. Homer, 6251-2
"In body alone was Zosime". Damascius, 6251-2
"In haste the sons of Achaea...", fr. The Iliad. Homer, 6251-2
"in life, Manes the slave...". Anyte, 6251-2
"In most men's eyes one virtue, alone, is worth...". Theognis, 6251-2
"In the leaf-strewn cavern...". Theocritus, 6251-2
"It is a fair death, fighting in the front of battle". Tyrtaeus of Sparta, 6251-2
"It is not death that is bitter...". Unknown, 6251-2
"It is not streets where proud-roofed mansions stand". Alcaeus of Mytilene, 6251-2
"Just as she was, the painter...". Julianus [or Julian the Egyptian], 6251-2
"Lacedaemon, land unconquered...". Unknown, 6251-2
"A lad that was a fowler...". Bion, 6251-2
"Late lingers Cleophantis...". Paulus Silentiarius, 6251-2
Lead ye me on, O God. Cleanthes, 6435-3,6251-2
"Life is a voyage of peril...". Palladas, 6251-2
"Life's but a puppet-play...". Palladas, 6251-2
"Lips sealed in iron stillness...". Paulus Silentiarius, 6251-2
"Little Callimachus harsh death bore...". Lucian, 6251-

2

"Long, O Protesilaus, long shall thy fame...". Antiphilus, 6251-2
"Lord of Athene's holy hill". Bacchylides, 6251-2
"Lord Phoebus, when our Lady, the gracious...". Theognis, 6251-2
"Lost now are the homes...". Alpheus, 6251-2
"Lovely is the rose; and yet...". Theocritus, 6251-2
"A Lydian I, a Lydian slave...". Dioscorides, 6251-2
"Maidens, in Thebes Athene loved once.." Callimachus, 6251-2
"Make merry, heart within me. Others shall come...". Theognis, 6251-2
"Many a trick the wise fox knows". Archilochus, 6251-2
"Mariner, ask not whose these ashes be". Unknown, 6251-2
"Maybe now you remember my solemn warning...". Thymocles, 6251-2
Medea's resolve, fr. Medea. Euripides, 6435-3
"Memphis, the snub-nosed dancer...". Palladas, 6251-2
"Moon's set, and Pleiads". Sappho, 6251-2
"Much I guzzled, much I tippled...". Simonides, 6251-2
"My golden hoard is spear and sword." Hybrias, 6251-2
"'My name was--.' Does it matter...". Paulus Silentiarius, 6251-2
"Naked I came on earth...". Palladas, 6251-2
"Nature gave horns to cattle". Unknown (Greek), 6251-2
"Ne'er yet from the root of a squill...". Theognis, 6251-2
"Never again rejoicing in the surges...". Anyte, 6251-2
"No day released from labour...". Mimnermus, 6251-2
"No more shall stones nor oakwoods...". Antipater, 6251-2
"Nod a sod hath Erasippus...". Glaucus, 6251-2
"Not all the Isle of Pelops...". Theocritus, 6251-2
"Not to be born at all is the happiest lot...". Theognis, 6251-2
"Not, Nicias, as we dreamed...". Theocritus, 6251-2
"Now at his hour Love rises, while all the earth...". Theognis, 6251-2
"Now fall the height of Heaven in headlong ruin...". Theognis, 6251-2
"Now Hermes of Cyllene...", fr. The Odyssey. Homer, 6251-2
"Now if a man shall show him in speed of foot...". Xenophanes, 6251-2
"Now is the time to surrender our hearts...". Theognis, 6251-2
"Now night drew darkness...". Apollonius, 6251-2
"Now shall my song remember Apollo...". Unknown, 6251-2
"Now to my prayer in season, O Zeus of Olympus...". Theognis, 6251-2
"Now you are buried, Timon..." Callimachus, 6251-2
"Now, all ye nymphs...". Glaucus, 6251-2
"Now, of the ways of dolphins...". Oppian, 6251-2
"O caves of the nymphs fresh..." Crinagoras, 6251-2
"O father Zeus, if ever among...", fr. The Iliad. Homer, 6251-2
"Oh lucky you, cicada". Unknown (Greek), 6251-2
"O man, keep in remembrance how thy father...". Palladas, 6251-2
"O man, on thyself have mercy...". Automedon, 6251-2
"O noble heart, Sabinus...". Unknown, 6251-2
"O sweet is snow to June...". Asclepiades, 6251-2
The Odyssey, sels. Homer, 6251-2
"Of him that had for mother the glorious Semele". Mimnermus, 6251-2
"Of the dear son of Hermes, O Muse, sing now to me". Unknown, 6251-2
"Of the Gods and these other matters none knows...". Xenophanes, 6251-2
"Of the Golden Aphrodite tell to me...". Unknown, 6251-2
"Of the wreath of the son...", fr. The Iliad. Homer, 6251-2
"Oft and often I sang it...". Julianus [or Julian the Egyptian], 6251-2
"Often the birds of mere or main...". Aratus, 6251-2
"Once I am dead, let earth go...". Unknown, 6251-2
"Once in the ear of Apollo said envy..." Callimachus,

6251-2
"Once in the hours of midnight". Unknown (Greek), 6251-2
"Once Love among the roses". Unknown (Greek), 6251-2
"Once the sacker of towns...". Bacchylides, 6251-2
"Once with his sling Ariston...". Unknown, 6251-2
"One carpenter hates another, potter hates potter...". Hesiod, 6251-2
"One noble heart, one only...". Quintus Smyrnaeus, 6251-2
"One told me, Heraclitus." Callimachus, 6251-2
"Only in spring do the quince-flowers quiver". Ibycus, 6251-2
"Out of the jug we drank...". Hipponax, 6251-2
"Pass with all men's approval through life...". Theognis, 6251-2
Plutocracy. Theognis, 6251-2
Poverty. Theognis, 6251-2
"Queen of the phantom..." Julianus [or Julian the Egyptian], 6251-2
A ram or a stallion, Cyrnus, of good stock... Theognis, 6251-2
"Says this gravestone sorrow-laden...". Philitas, 6251-2
"See from yon looming summit the beacon...". Theognis, 6251-2
"She, too, whom men call 'Iris' is but a mist...". Xenophanes, 6251-2
"Sheer through his neck's...", fr. The Iliad. Homer, 6251-2
Shifting fortune, fr. Medea. Euripides, 6435-3
"Sleeps Charidas beneath you..." Callimachus, 6251-2
"A small ship-thou mayst praise her...". Hesiod, 6251-2
"So Ajax spoke and the others...", fr. The Iliad. Homer, 6251-2
"So flashing-eyed Athene spoke...", fr. The Odyssey. Homer, 6251-2
"So he spoke in her honour...". Apollonius, 6251-2
"So Hector; and loud the Trojans...", fr. The Iliad. Homer, 6251-2
"So on both sides they battled...", fr. The Iliad. Homer, 6251-2
"So saying he passed from Thetis...", fr. The Iliad. Homer, 6251-2
"So saying she came from her cavern...", fr. The Iliad. Homer, 6251-2
"So saying, to Olympus with...", fr. The Iliad. Homer, 6251-2
"So spoke Priam's noble son...", fr. The Iliad. Homer, 6251-2
"So spoke the noble Achilles...". Homer, 6251-2
"So Telemachus spoke. But Pallas...", fr. The Odyssey. Homer, 6251-2
"So Telemachus spoke...gay", fr. The Odyssey. Homer, 6251-2
"So the fugitives of the Trojans...", fr. The Iliad. Homer, 6251-2
"So the noble Odysseus wakened...", fr. The Odyssey. Homer, 6251-2
"So the old nurse took a basin...", fr. The Odyssey. Homer, 6251-2
"So then the noble Odysseus...", fr. The Odyssey. Homer, 6251-2
"So thence with heavy hearts...", fr. The Odyssey. Homer, 6251-2
"So without voice, without murmur...". Apollonius, 6251-2
"So young, the little Callaeschrus...". Unknown, 6251-2
"So, as we lay there resting...". Theocritus, 6251-2
"Some Thracian now goes strutting with the shield...". Archilochus, 6251-2
"Soon of the shock of battle...", fr. The Iliad. Homer, 6251-2
"Speak fair to him that hates thee...". Theognis, 6251-2
Spring plowing. Hesiod, 6251-2
"Stay not for me, O sailor...". Joannes Barbucallus, 6251-2
"Steadfast they stood, as mists...", fr. The Iliad. Homer, 6251-2

"Still we behold Troy city...". Alpheus, 6251-2
"Still, as each night dwindles...". Palladas, 6251-2
Summer. Hesiod, 6251-2
"Sweet is the whisper, goatherd...". Theocritus, 6251-2
"Swiftly as dart the thoughts...", fr. The Iliad. Homer, 6251-2
"Take care to keep thy name untouched of ill report". Hesiod, 6251-2
Take my overcoat and hold it...".." Hipponax, 6251-2
"Take word to Lacedaemon, passer-by". Simonides, 6251-2
"Terse-tongued and sparely worded...". Antipater, 6251-2
"Than love there's nothing sweeter...". Nossis, 6251-2
"Then close at hand came Athene...", fr. The Odyssey. Homer, 6251-2
"Then hearkened the Argus-slayer...", fr. The Odyssey. Homer, 6251-2
Then in the field the Trojans...", fr. The Iliad. Homer, 6251-2
Then indeed had the sons...", fr. The Iliad. Homer, 6251-2
"Then Menelaus, shaking...", fr. The Iliad. Homer, 6251-2
"Then on his arm he settled...", fr. The Iliad. Homer, 6251-2
"Then seeing him the noble Achilles...", fr. The Iliad. Homer, 6251-2
"Then the white-armed goddess...", fr. The Iliad. Homer, 6251-2
"Then up sprang storm-foot Iris...", fr. The Iliad. Homer, 6251-2
"These men, to set a crown of ever quenchless glory". Simonides, 6251-2
"They found Odysseus dear...", fr. The Iliad. Homer, 6251-2
"They say that men whose veins...". Paulus Silentiarius, 6251-2
"This man that is mean...". Bianor, 6251-2
"Thou gavest me birth...". Macedonius, 6251-2
"Thou hast but foreign earth, O Cleisthenes...". Simonides, 6251-2
"Thou hast stolen again-I know it-on the path...". Theognis, 6251-2
"Though Thine ears be filled...". Julius Polyaenus, 6251-2
"Thracian filly, why so heartless...". Anacreon, 6251-2
"Thronged now the shrines with revel...". Bacchylides, 6251-2
"Thus I revealed to my comrades...", fr. The Odyssey. Homer, 6251-2
"Timarete, ere she wedded...". Unknown, 6251-2
"Timocritus fought well. This is his grave". Anacreon, 6251-2
"To far-off shores as merchant...". Isidorus Aegeates, 6251-2
"To Hades' gate the road runs...". Unknown, 6251-2
"To spirits thrice ten thousand by God's will...". Hesiod, 6251-2
"To the Winnowing Demeter...". Zonas, 6251-2
"To thee, my love, for ever I have given wings...". Theognis, 6251-2
"Traveller the long way wearies...". Nicias, 6251-2
"Two days a woman's best...". Hipponax, 6251-2
"Up leapt Achilles dear to Zeus...", fr. The Iliad. Homer, 6251-2
Vengeance, fr. Medea. Euripides, 6435-3
"The voice of Heraclitus...". Unknown, 6251-2
"We died in eth glen of Dirphys...". Simonides, 6251-2
"We men of Hellas live...". Palladas, 6251-2
"Wed, above all, a woman that dwells not far away". Hesiod, 6251-2
"Weep, wooded glens; weep...". Unknown, 6251-2
"Well my heart warns me...". Unknown, 6251-2
What a piece of work is a man, fr. Antigone. Sophocles, 6435-3
"What is my fate to suffer, my Cyrnus...". Theognis, 6251-2
"Whatever the worth of a man, yet poverty...". Theognis, 6251-2
"When she was set in her carven chest". Simonides, 6251-

2
"When two men hate, my Cyrnus, they find traps...".
Theognis, 6251-2
"Where are my leaves of laurel...". Theocritus, 6251-2
"Where are the towers that crowned...". Antipater, 6251-2
"Why, then, let Pholegandros or Sikinos be my city".
Solon, 6251-2
Winter. Hesiod, 6251-2
"With Hermione the witching as I played...".
Asclepiades, 6251-2
"With joy he saw that city...". Nonnus, 6251-2
"Wonders are many, but there is no wonder". Sophocles, 6435-3
"Ye Naiads, ye high pastures...". Unknown, 6251-2
"You with the smooth round belly...". Unknown, 6251-2
"You, my dearest swallow". Unknown (Greek), 6251-2
"Your maidenhead-you grudge it...". Asclepiades, 6251-2
"Zeus spake; and storm-foot Iris...", fr. The Iliad.
Homer, 6251-2

Lucas, Frank Laurence. See Lucas, F.L.
Lucas, June
Blind. 6954-1
Lucas, Sir Charles
Love and loyalty. 6328-4
Lucas, St. John
The curate thinks you have no soul. 7008-6
Mr. Lang's fairy books. 6018-8
To a child. 6233-4
Lucas, Winifred
A grave. 6785-9
Love. 6785-9
Nature. 6274-1
The playmate. 6785-9
Triolet. 6274-1
Lucchi, Lorna de' (tr.)
A se stesso. Giacomo Leopardi, 7039-6
Infinity. Giacomo Leopardi, 6879-0
L'infinito. Giacomo Leopardi, 7039-6
Sonnet ("As I approach"). Francesco Petrarch, 6879-0
To Dante. Vittorio Alfieri, 7039-6
To himself. Giacomo Leopardi, 6879-0
What art thou, death? Vincenzo Monti, 6879-0
Luce, Charles M.
The pilgrim. 6266-0,6359-4
Luce, Samuel Slayton
The village doctor. 7030-2
"Lucent wave/Flash in sparkling bells". To a wave. J. Pierce. 6997-5
Lucerna pietatis. L. Steni. 6781-6
Lucerne. William Lisle Bowles. 6749-2
Lucerne. Samuel Rogers. 6749-2
Lucerne. William Wordsworth. 6749-2
Lucerne, fr. Pictures by the way. John Nichol. 6819-7
Lucette
"If you wish to win bright laurels". 6238-5
Lucia Joyce. Miriam Plevin. 6821-9
Lucian
A dead child. Timothy Kendall (tr.). 6435-3
Diogenes dresses down a proud monarch. 6637-2
"Little Callimachus harsh death bore...". F.L. Lucas (tr.). 6251-2
A little envious gossip in heaven. 6637-2
Old Polystratus tells the tender passions he inspired. 6637-2
Passing away. Walter Leaf (tr.). 6435-3
A rule of life. Walter Leaf (tr.). 6435-3
Three divine beauties strive to overreach one another. 6637-2
Lucianus
Artificial beauty. William Cowper (tr.). 7039-6
Lucid interval. George O'Neil. 6619-4,6039-0
Lucifer. Norman Cameron. 6339-X
Lucifer. Joost van den Vondel. 6848-0
Lucifer in starlight. George Meredith. 6655-0,6301-2,6646-1,6655-0,6656-9,6660 ,6052-8,6198-2,6315-2,6339-X, 6102-8,6430 ,6199-0,6250-4,6153-2,6252-0,6508-2,6491 ,6477-9,6488-4,6536-8,6634-8,6657-7,6250
Lucifer sings in secret. Elinor Wylie. 6007-2
Lucifer's defiance. Joost van den Vondel. 6102-8
Lucifer's feast. Alfred Noyes. 6151-6,6542-2
Lucifer's song. Philip James Bailey. 6102-8
Lucile. Owen (Edward Bulwer-Lytton, Earl Lytton) Meredith. 6198-2
Lucile, sels. Owen (Edward Bulwer-Lytton, Earl Lytton) Meredith. 6260-1,6046-3
Lucilius
Anticipation. William Cowper (tr.). 6850-2
A dead song-writer. Humbert Wolfe (tr.). 6435-3
On an old woman. William Cowper (tr.). 6850-2
Lucille. Robert Service. 6159-1
Lucinda. Unknown. 6563-5
Lucinda Matlock. Edgar Lee Masters. 6077-3,6102-8,6299-7, 6332-2,6365-9,6506 ,6076-5,6161-3,6393-4,6646-1
"Lucinda wink or vaile those eyes." Unknown. 6563-5
Lucinda's fan. Frank Lebby Stanton. 7022-1
Luck. Wilfred Wilson Gibson. 6258-X
Luck. Dare Stark. 6241-5
Luck and work. Robert Underwood Johnson. 6585-6
"Luck had a favor to bestow". The lucky man. Edgar A. Guest. 7033-7
The luck in the square stone, sels. Herman Charles Bosman. 6788-3
The luck of Edenhall. Johann Ludwig Uhland. 6613-5
Lucky. Cathy Song. 6790-5
The lucky call. Unknown. 6911-8
The lucky horseshoe. Unknown. 6523-6
The lucky horseshoe. James Thomas Fields. 6414-0
Lucky Jim. Unknown. 6682-8
The lucky man. Edgar A. Guest. 7033-7
"Lucrative offices are seldom lost". Absence of occupation, fr. Retirement. William Cowper. 6932-0
Lucrece and Nara. Laura Riding. 6209-1
Lucretia Borgia's last letter. Antoinette De Coursey Patterson. 6036-6
Lucretia sleeping. William Shakespeare. 6543-0
Lucretius
Against the fear of death. John Dryden (tr.). 7039-6
Death. William Hurrell Mallock (tr.). 6102-8
Earth-wonder. William Hurrell Mallock (tr.). 6102-8
"A little, tiny, pretty, witty,". 6083-8
"Meantime when thoughts of death disturb thy head". John Dryden (tr.). 6879-0
No single thing abides. William Hurrell Mallock (tr.). 7039-6
No single thing abides, sels. William Hurrell Mallock (tr.). 6513-9
"No single thing abides; but all things flow". William Hurrell Mallock (tr.). 6879-0
On the nature of things, sels. John Dryden (tr.). 6879-0
On the nature of things, sels. William Hurrell Mallock (tr.). 6879-0
Primitive man. William Hurrell Mallock (tr.). 6102-8
"Thy wife, thy home, the child that climbed thy knee". William Hurrell Mallock (tr.). 6879-0
Void and atoms. William Hurrell Mallock (tr.). 6102-8
"What has this bugbear death to frighten man". John Dryden (tr.). 6879-0
Lucretius. Lionel Johnson. 6483-3
Lucretius. Trumbull Stickney. 6006-4
Lucretius. Alfred Lord Tennyson. 6483-3,6657-7,6655-0
Lucy. William Wordsworth. 6134-6,6138-9,6204-0,6228-8,6239-3,6240 ,6271-7,6315-2,6317-9,6385-3,6479-5,6625 , 6732-8,6424-8,6543-0,6737-9,6301-2,6102 ,6219-9,6438-8,6808-1,6150-8
Lucy ("Strange fits"). William Wordsworth. 6828-6
Lucy Ashton's song, fr. The bride of Lammermoor. Sir Walter Scott. 6138-9,6175-7,6395-0,6180-X,6427-2
Lucy Gray; or, solitude. William Wordsworth. 6127-3,6132-X, 6133-8,6134-6,6142-7,6502 ,6242-3,6108-7,6075-7,6154-0,6198-2,6419 ,6249-0,6271-7,6459-0,6473-6,6497-3, 6519 ,6131-1,6153-2,6199-0,6146-6,6430-2,6110 ,6086-2,6219-9,6639-9,6646-1,6543-0
Lucy Lake. Newton Mackintosh. 6089-7;6440-X
Lucy Locket. Unknown. 6937-1
"Lucy Locket lost her pocket." Mother Goose. 6363-2,6452-3,6466-3
The Lucy poems, sels. William Wordsworth. 6199-0
Lucy's birthday. William Makepeace Thackeray. 6980-0

Lucy's flittin'. William Laidlaw. 6180-X,6219-9,6240-7,
    6600-3
"Lucy, don't you hear the voices...in the air". To my
    wife. Benjamin Franklin Taylor. 6815-4
Lucy, sels. William Wordsworth. 6102-8
Luders, Charles Henry
    A corsage bouquet. 6441-8,6652-6
    A coursage bouquet. 6770-0
    The dead nymph. 7041-8
    The four winds. 6006-4,6243-1,6431-0,6212-1,6309-8
    The haunts of the halcyon. 6936-3
    A kiss. 6770-0
    My maiden aunt. 6441-8,6004-8
    An old thought. 6936-3
    The passing show. 6672-0
    The redbreast. 6770-0
    To Q(uintus) H(oratius) F(laccus) 6770-0
    Triolet: 6770-0
Ludlow, Fitzhugh
    The school. 6127-3
    Too late. 6089-7,6385-3,6486-8,6424-8
    Too late. 6913-4
Ludlow, Helen W.
    The little white beggars. 6166-4
Ludlow, Wilma C.
    Imitation of Christ. 6144-3
Ludlum, J.K.
    Edith's secret. 6314-4
Ludlum, Mabel Cleland
    Lights. 6478-7
Ludmilla. Ernest W. Thiele. 6722-0
"Luer, Faulkners! give warning to the feild" Unknown. 6380-2
Lufburrow, Sylvia Gardiner
    Interval of flame. 6750-6
Luft, Florence
    Gold. 6850-2
    Solitaire. 6850-2
Lugano, August 1937. H.L.R. Edwards. 6360-8
Lugete o veneres cupidinesque. Godfrey Elton. 6541-4
The luggie, sels. David Gray. 7035-3
"Lugh made a stir in the air". Fate. Francis Ledwidge. 6812-X
Lugnaquillia. George F. Savage-Armstrong. 6174-5
Lugubrious villanelle of platitudes. Louis Untermeyer. 6875-8
The lugubrious whing-whang. James Whitcomb Riley. 6736-0
Luhrs, Marie
    Murderous weapons. 6070-6
    Sonnet ("Time, of all"). 6039-0
    Women dream. 6781-6
Luhrs, Mary
    New York. 6038-2
Lui Chi
    A poet thinks. Edward Powys Mathers (tr.). 7039-6,6513-9
"Luicifer fell headlong down". Fire in New Orleans:
    December 2, 1972, sels. Norman Simms. 7018-3
Luis de Camoes. Roy Campbell. 6210-5
Lukanin beach I. Richard Dauenhauer. 6855-3
"Lukannon.". Rudyard Kipling. 6510-4
Luke Havergal. Edwin Arlington Robinson. 6333-0,6641-0,
    6300-4,6467-1
"Luke tells us how Jesus". The temple. Clifford Dyment.
    6783-2
Luke, Jemima Thompson
    The child's desire. 6502-3,6459-0,6131-1
    I think when I read that sweet story of old. 6337-3,
    6466-3,6424-8
Luke, Loren M.
    Lines on a ring. 6983-5
    The rose's tomb. 6983-5
Luke, sels. Bible. 6282-2
Lukovic, Stevan
    The autumnal rain song. 6765-4
Lulham, Habberton
    Before battle. 7031-0
    Gifts of the dead. 7031-0
    His only way. 6474-4
    A meeting and a memory. 6482-5

The old doctor. 6482-5
Lull. Rhea B. Zehr. 6270-9
Lullaby. Thomas Dekker. 6634-8,6634-8,6131-1,6189-3,6219-9,
    6737-9
Lullaby. Paul Laurence Dunbar. 6006-4,6309-8,6653-4
Lullaby. Seumas MacManus. 6096-X
Lullaby. Thomas Sturge Moore. 6477-9
Lullaby. Seumas (James Starkey) O'Sullivan. 6639-9
Lullaby. Alfred Lord Tennyson. 6737-9
Lullaby ("A song for the baby"). Shirley Dare. 6131-1
Lullaby ("Baby wants") William Brighty Rands. 6452-3
A lullaby ("Baby, baby". Laurence Alma Tadema. 6242-3
Lullaby ("Baloo, loo"). Carolina Oliphant, Baroness
    Nairne. 6078-1,6424-8
Lullaby ("Be still"). John Phillip. 6182-6
A lullaby ("Because some men"). G.R. Glasgow. 7031-0
Lullaby ("Bedtime's come"). Paul Laurence Dunbar. 6891-X
Lullaby ("Beloved"). William Butler Yeats. 6210-5
A lullaby ("Close to the heart"). Willis Walton Franz.
    6097-8
Lullaby ("Come sleep"). Florence Kilpatrick Mixter. 6036-6
Lullaby ("Dream"). Patience Worth [pseud.]. 6030-7
Lullaby ("Fair is"). Eugene Field. 7041-8
Lullaby ("Girl with eyes"). Max Harris. 6349-7
Lullaby ("Golden slumbers"). Thomas Dekker. 6179-6,6233-4,
    6182-6,6315-2,6533-3,6633-X,6194-X
Lullaby ("Hush my little sleepyhead..."). Bert Cooksley.
    6750-6
A lullaby ("Hush thee"). Alexander ("Nether Lochaber")
    Stewart. 6180-X
Lullaby ("Hush thee, hush.") R.D. H. 6118-4
Lullaby ("Hush thee, my baby.") Unknown (Zulu) 6711-5
Lullaby ("Hush thee, sweet baby"). Thomas Davidson. 7022-1
The lullaby ("Hush, baby mine..."). Owen Roe O'Sullivan.
    6858-8
Lullaby ("Hush, hush, baby mine.") Unknown (Swedish) 6711-5
Lullaby ("Hush-a-ba, birdie"). Unknown. 6179-6
Lullaby ("Husheen"). Seumas (James Starkey) O'Sullivan.
    6236-9,6930-4
Lullaby ("In the sky"). Unknown (Spanish) 6711-5
Lullaby ("In your little armored bed"). Elya Bresler. 6761-1
Lullaby ("Kiver up"). Paul Laurence Dunbar. 6580-5
Lullaby ("Lennavan-mo"). William ("Fiona Macleod") Sharp.
    6873-1
Lullaby ("Lullaby, oh, lullaby!"). Christina Georgina
    Rossetti. 6623-2
A lullaby ("Moon-fingers steal adown the night").
    Elizabeth Greene Thomas. 7016-7
Lullaby ("My little one..."). Harriet Monroe. 6897-9
Lullaby ("Night time"). Cheri Fein. 6822-7
A lullaby ("O saftly sleep"). Alexander A. Ritchie. 6233-4,
    6180-X
Lullaby ("Peaceful slumb'ring..."). Unknown. 6983-5
Lullaby ("Rockaby, baby, thy cradle is green"). Unknown.
    6415-9,6629-1
Lullaby ("Row, row"). Unknown (Norwegian) 6711-5
Lullaby ("Ruin falls..."). Marya Alexandrovna Zaturenska.
    6984-3
A lullaby ("Sich a li'l feller"). Frank Lebby Stanton.
    6078-1
The lullaby ("Sing lullabies"). George Gascoigne. 6383-7
Lullaby ("Sleep like a lily bud"). Mary Lovell Cope. 6841-3
Lullaby ("Sleep, my angels"). Norman Gale. 6233-4
Lullaby ("Sleep, my baby"). Unknown (Arabic) 6711-5
A lullaby ("Sleep, my darling"). Celia Thaxter. 6612-7
A lullaby ("Sleep, my dear one"). George Edgar Montgomery.
    6078-1
Lullaby ("Sleep, sleep"). Walter De La Mare. 6596-1
Lullaby ("Sleep, sleep, little mouse.") Unknown (Danish)
    6711-5
Lullaby ("Sleepy little"). James William Foley. 6964-9
Lullaby ("Sleepy stars..."). Kathleen Wallace Cunningham.
    6764-6
Lullaby ("Slumber, Jesu"). Unknown. 6282-2
Lullaby ("Slumber, slumber"). Frank Dempster Sherman. 6311-X
Lullaby ("Snail, snail"). Unknown (Chinese) 711-5

LULLABY

Lullaby ("Sweet and low"). Alfred Lord Tennyson. 6123-0, 6271-7,6302-0,6401-9,6135-4,6424
lullaby ("Sweet baby, sleep! what ails my dear"). William Austin. 6931-2
Lullaby ("The golden dreamboat's ready"). Edgar A. Guest. 6401-9,6135-4
Lullaby ("The long canoe"). Robert Hillyer. 6490-6
Lullaby ("The maple strews..."). James Whitcomb Riley. 6993-2
Lullaby ("The rooks' nests"). William Barnes. 6242-3,6533-3
Lullaby ("The spotted snakes..."). William Shakespeare. 6772-7
A lullaby ("The stars are twinkling..."). Eugene Field. 6949-5
Lullaby ("The wind's in the pine tree"). Mary Lovell Cope. 6841-3
Lullaby ("The world"). George O'Neil. 6581-3
Lullaby ("Though the world"). Edith Sitwell. 6391-8,6666-6
Lullaby ("Through sleepy-land"). Elizabeth Cavazza. 6373-X
Lullaby ("Upon my lap"). Richard Rowlands. 6233-4,6533-3, 6732-8,6078-1
Lullaby ("Weep not"). Robert Greene. 6078-1
Lullaby ("Weep you no more"). John Dowland (atr) 6153-2
Lullaby ("Weep you"). Unknown. 6250-4
Lullaby for a violent death. Margaret Widdemer. 6042-0
A lullaby for Christmas. John Addington Symonds. 6747-6
Lullaby for Jumbo, fr. Facade. Edith Sitwell. 7000-0
Lullaby for Titania, fr. A midsummer's night's dream. William Shakespeare. 6133-8,6239-3,6334-9,6490-6, 6457-4,6623
Lullaby in undertones. Fedor Sologub. 6103-6
Lullaby of a lover. George Gascoigne. 6099-4,6182-6,6586-4, 6189-3
The lullaby of a lover. Unknown. 6581-3
Lullaby of an infant chief. Sir Walter Scott. 6138-9,6242-3,6078-1,6087-0,6136-2,6459 ,6466-3,6519-8,6627-5, 6502-3,6105-2,6639
Lullaby of Nokomis. Henry Wadsworth Longfellow. 6466-3
Lullaby of the catfish and the crab. William Rose Benet. 6722-0
Lullaby of the Iroquois. Emily Pauline ("Tekahionwake") Johnson. 6433-7
A lullaby of the Nativity. Unknown. 6881-2
Lullaby of the Virgin. Alma Strettell. 6095-1
Lullaby of the woman of the mountain. Padraic Pearse. 6930-4
Lullaby to a dream. James (Nakisaki) Christopher. 6178-8
A lullaby, fr. Kafir songs. Francis Carey ("Jan van Avond") Slater. 6800-6
A lullaby, fr. The triumph of beauty. James Shirley. 6827-8
Lullaby, fr. The woman-hater. Francis Beaumont and John Fletcher. 6208-3
Lullaby, mine liking. Unknown. 6334-9
Lullaby, O lullaby. William Cox Bennett. 6078-1
Lullaby, oh, lullaby! Christina Georgina Rossetti. 6490-6
Lullaby, rest. Ellen Russell Manchester. 6118-4
"Lullay myn lyking my dere sone myn swetyng." Unknown. 6378-0
Lullay, Jesu, lullay, lullay. Unknown. 6756-5
"Lullay, lullay, la, lullay". Jesus reassures his mother. Unknown. 6881-2
"Lullay, lullay, litel child". Unknown. 6931-2
Lullay, lullay, thou little tiny child. Unknown. 6756-5
Lullay, mine liking, my dear son, mine sweeting. Unknown. 6756-5
"Lullay, my liking, my dere son". A lullaby of the Nativity. Unknown. 6881-2
"Lully lullay, lully lullay". Unknown. 6187-7
"Lully, lulla, thou little tiny child". The Coventry carol. Unknown. 6881-2
Lully, lulley. Unknown. 6315-2,6383-7
"Lully, lulley, lulley, lulley". Unknown. 6198-2,6378-0, 6383-7
"Lully, lulley, lully, lulley". The Corpus Christi carol. Unknown. 6881-2
"Lully, lulley; lully, lulley". The falcon. Unknown. 6931-2
Lully, lully...the falcon hath borne my make away.

Unknown. 6756-5
'Lulu'.. Carrie W. Thompson. 6273-3
Lum, Wing Tek
   At a Chinaman's grave. 6790-5
   Chinatown games. 6790-5
   The poet imagines his grandfather's thoughts on the... 6790-5
   To the old masters. 6790-5
   Translations. 6790-5
Lumberman's alphabet. Unknown. 6061-7
The lumberman's life. Unknown. 6057-9
The lumbermen.. John Greenleaf Whittier. 6087-0,6134-6
The lumberyak. William F. Kirk. 6281-4
Lummis, Charles F.
   Arizona Jim. 6670-4
   The empty pocket. 6670-4
   The fellow in greasy jeans. 6686-0
   In the Mojave. 6241-3
   John Charles Fremont. 6946-0
   Mastery. 6102-8
   My cigarette. 6273-3
   My meerschaums. 6453-1
   A poe'-em of passion. 6089-7
   A poe-'em of passion. 6089-7
Lumpkin, Henry
   The challenge. 6396-9
Lumpkin, Lillie Mae
   The coral vine. 6799-9
Luna. Gerald Miller. 6069-2
Lunae custodiens. Lin Carter. 6218-0
Lunar eclipse. Diane Glancy. 7005-1
Lunar eclipse. Jessica Scarbrough. 6870-7
Lunar stanzas. Henry Cogswell Knight. 6089-7
"The lunatic, the lover...", fr. A midsummer night's... William Shakespeare. 6289-X
A lunatic. Mokichi Saito. 6482-5
Lunch at Helen Frankenthaler's. Barbara Guest. 6803-0
The lunch. Thomas Bailey Aldrich. 6652-6
Lund, C.N.
   At rest in the National Cathedral. 7001-9
Lund, Christie
   Bride's mother. 6750-6
   First kiss. 6750-6
Lund, Margaret Deming
   Sister's parting. 6017-X
Lundbergh, Holger
   When a gull falls. 6979-7
Lundy. Frank Ernest Hill. 6037-4
The lunger. Robert Service. 6159-1,6211-3
Lunsford, M. Rosser
   Go young man. 6857-X
Lunt, George
   Pilgrim song. 6600-3
   Requiem. 6431-0
Luper Jr., Luther George
   Sonnet spiritual. 6178-8
The lupracaun, or fairy shoemaker. William Allingham. 6930-4
The lure o' life. Arthur Stringer. 6115-X
The lure of little voices. Robert Service. 6159-1,6115-X
"The lure of sailors". Lyttleton. Anne Donovan. 7018-3
"Lure of the Orient". First loves. Jean Stephen Johnston. 6750-6
The lure of the buttercup. Eleanor Stimmel. 6270-9
The lure of the road. Crea W. Hobart. 6906-1
The lure of the trail. Floyd Meredith. 6478-7
The lure, fr. It is not beauty I demand. George Darley. 6545-7
The lure, sels. John Hall. 6317-9
The lure.. John Boyle O'Reilly. 6083-8
The lure. Francis Ledwidge. 6812-X
Lurline; or, the knight's visit to the mermaids. Richard Harris ("Thomas Ingoldsby") Barham. 6669-0
Luschei, Glenna
   Editor. 6792-1, 6998-3
   Prairie schooner poem. 6792-1
Lushington, Henry
   The morn of Inkerman. 6541-4
   The road to the trenches. 6541-4
   To the memory of Pietro d'Alessandro. 6046-3

Lushington, Sir Franklin
    Alma. 6046-3
    The fleet under sail. 6046-3
    No more words. 6113-3,6471-X
The **lusiad**, sels. Luis de Camoens [or Camoes]. 6372-1
The **'lusive** fairy. Betty Solliday. 6249-0
The **lust** of gold, fr. The West Indies. James Montgomery. 6946-0
Luster, Helen
    February letter to Jack Spicer. 6792-1
"**Lustily**, lustily, let us sail...". Unknown. 6334-9
Lustration of the winter tree, sels. Margaret Allonby. 6788-3
The **lusty** fryer of Flanders. John Wilmot, 2d Earl of Rochester. 6157-5
Lusty Juventus. Charles Madge. 6209-1
Lusty May. Unknown. 6830-8
Lute and furrow. Olive Tilford Dargan. 6619-4,6326-8
The **lute** obeys. Sir Thomas Wyatt. 6436-1
Lute song of the lady Heloise. Herbert Edward Palmer. 6780-8
The **lute-player**. Bayard Taylor. 6302-0;6385-3
The **lute**. Ibn Qadi Mila. 6362-4
Lutea Allison. Sir John Suckling. 6659-3
Lutgen, Grace Welsh
    A prairie miracle. 6270-9
Luther vs. Worcester. C.P. Greenough. 6878-2
Luther, Martin
    Ane sang of the birth of Christ. John Wedderburn (tr.). 6125-7
    Away in a manger. 6337-3
    A Christmas carol for children. 6145-1,6747-6,6608-9
    Cradle hymn ("Away in a manger, no crib for a bed"). 6216-4,6466-3,6519-8,6747-6,6456-6
    Easter. 6177-X
    Hymn ("A mighty"). Frederick Henry Hedge (tr.). 6418-3, 6730-1
    Hymn ("O heart of mine..."). Eugene Field (tr.). 6949-5
    The little bird. 6424-8
    The martyrs' hymn. W.J. Fox (tr.). 6302-0;6385-3
    "A mighty fortress is our God." 6527-9,6214-8
    "A mighty fortress is our God." Frederick Henry Hedge (tr.). 6302-0,6385-3,6337-3
    A New Year's carol. 6747-6
Luther, and Thomas Carlyle, Martin (tr.)
    Psalm 046 Bible, 6848-0
Luttrell, Henry
    Burham-beeches. 6086-2,6092-7
    Death. 6874-X
    London fog. 6134-6
    On Miss Maria Tree. 6385-3
    On Samuel Rogers' seat in the garden at Holland house. 6874-X
    On the distinguished singer, Miss Ellen Tree. 6874-X
Lutz, Gertrude May
    Concept. 6979-7
    Golgotha. 6979-7
A **luve** ron. Thomas De Hales. 6198-2
Lux aeterna. Irwin Edman. 6619-4
Lux est umbra dei. John Addington Symonds. 6656-9
Lux in tenebris. Katharine (Hinkson) Tynan. 6244-X
Lux lucet in Tenebris. William White. 6868-5
"**Lux** my fair falcon, and your fellows all". Epigram ("Lux"). Sir Thomas Wyatt. 6584-8
Luxury. Edgar A. Guest. 6748-4
"The **luxury** derived in doing good". A grain of truth. George M. Vickers. 6921-5
Luxurys' children. Elaine Pierce McCreless. 6750-6
Luzader, Malcolm M.
    The bachelor's hope. 6924-X
Lvovic, Jiri Karascek ze
    The burden of eternity. Paul Selver (tr.). 6763-8
    Tuberoses. Paul Selver (tr.). 6763-8
Lyall, Jennie L.
    Child's fancies. 6713-1
Lyall, Sir Alfred Comyn
    After the skirmish. 6046-3
    Charles's wain. 6793-X
    A hindoo's search for truth. 6240-7
    Meditations of a Hindu prince. 6656-9,6730-1
    A night in the Red Sea. 6046-3
    Retrospection. 6661-5
    Theology in extremis. 6322-5
Lyall, Sir Charles (tr.)
    His camel. Alqamah, 7039-6
    His children. Hittan of Tayyi, 7039-6
"**Lyce**, the gods have heard my prayers". An appeal to Lyce. Horace. 6949-5
Lycidas. John Milton. 6102-8,6122-2,6138-9,6154-0,6198-2, 6208 ,6084-6,6150-8,6152-3,6191-5,6645-3,6660 ,6246-6,6315-2,6332-2,6369-1,6385-3,6423 ,6023-4,6125-7, 6194-X,6192-3,6250-4,6560 ,6473-6,6527-9,6536-8,6562-7,6604-6,6641 ,6219-9,6301-2,6322-5,6430-2,6543-0, 6659 ,6491-4,6438-8,6646-1,6726-3;6730-1;6732 ,6723-9
Lycidas, sels. John Milton. 6047-1,6339-X,6501-5,6472-8
Lycius. Aubrey Thomas De Vere. 6980-0
"**Lycius**, the Cretan prince, of race divine". The wine-cup. Unknown. 6913-4
Lycoris, the nymph, her sad song. Thomas Morley. 6328-4
Lycosa the spider. Annie Charlotte Dalton. 6021-8
Lycus, the centaur. Thomas Hood. 6974-6
Lydgate, John
    Against women's fashions. 6022-6
    A ballad warning men to beware of deceitful women, sels. 6317-9
    The child Jesus to Mary the rose. 6282-2
    Description of a medieval schoolboy. 6186-9
    The duplicity of women. 6881-2
    The fall of princes, sels. 6483-3
    "Lat noman booste of konnyng nor vertu." 6378-0
    Like a midsummer rose, fr. The fall of princes. 6150-8
    The London lackpenny [or, lyckpenny, or, lackpenny]. 6200-8,6198-2,6245-6,6193-1
    The story of Thebes. 6198-2
    Tarye no lenger; toward thyn herytage. 6931-2
    To the virgin. 6489-2,6022-6
    Transient as a rose. 6881-2
    "Wher is now David the moost worthy kyng." 6378-0
Lydia. Madison Cawein. 6441-8
Lydia. Lizette Woodworth Reese. 6431-0
Lydia Dick. Eugene Field. 6735-2
Lydia Dick. Eugene Field. 6949-5
"**Lydia** is gone this many a year". Lizette Woodworth Reese. 6006-4,6236-9,6732-8
Lydia Pinkham. Unknown. 6237-7
Lydia's ride. Thomas Frost. 6576-7
"A **Lydian** I, a Lydian slave...". Dioscorides. 6251-2
Lydon, Josie McNamara
    Dreamland. 6836-7
    Grays Peak in winter. 6836-7
    Weavers. 6836-7
Lying. Thomas Moore. 6083-8;6089-7
"**Lying** a-dying/Such sweet things untasted". Young death. Christina Georgina Rossetti. 6828-6
"**Lying** along the wide branch". Tiger people. Geary Hobson. 7005-1
"**Lying** asleep in the golden light". The blue lake - Mount Gambier. Agnes Neale. 6768-9
Lying awake. Gertrude Kurzenknabe Shaffer. 6270-9
"**Lying** by the fireside". Fire pictures. Emma Rounds. 6891-X
"**Lying** half-awake/I watch the sky grow saffron". Poe's mother. Beatrice Ravenel. 6326-8,7016-7
Lying in the grass. Sir Edmund Gosse. 6186-9,6477-9,6437-X, 6656-9,6543-0
"**Lying** on the window frame". To a dead moth. W.A. Barton Jr.. 7016-7
Lying spring. Laura Riding. 6039-0
"**Lyke** Memnons rocke toucht, with the rising Sunne," Giles (the Elder) Fletcher. 6181-8,6586-4
A **lyke-wake** carol. Arthur Shearly Cripps. 6477-9
Lyke-wake dirge. Unknown. 6055-2,6056-0,6102-8,6180-X,6228-8,6315 ,6385-3.6472-8,6067-6,6125-7,6153-2,6438
A **lyke-wake** dirge. Unknown. 6560-0
Lyksett, Frances
    Runstone saga. 6342-X
Lyle, Thomas
    Kelvin grove. 6180-X
Lyle, William

LYLE

    A' aboot it. 6166-4
    The bonny wee hoose. 6695-X
    Our wee laddie. 6687-9
    A Sottish ballad. 6672-0
    Tit for tat. 6929-0
Lyly, John
    Apelles' song. 6052-8,6189-3,6660-7,6192-3,6186-9,6198 , 6604-6
    Apelles' song ("Cupid and my Campaspe played"). 6092-7
    Apollo's song ("My Daphne's hair is twisted gold"). 6092-7,6250-4
    Arrows for love. 6827-8
    Bird-songs. 6558-9
    Campaspe. 6935-5
    Cards and kisses. 6102-8,6328-4,6732-8
    Cupid and Campaspe. 6301-2,6104-4,6543-0,6102-8,6182-6, 6240-7,6246-6,6302-0,6385-3,6726
    Cupid and my Campaspe played. 6479-5,6634-8,6181-8,6536-8,6219-9,6652 ,6099-4,6430-2,6250-4,6371-3,6737-9
    Cupid arraigned, fr. Galatea. 6827-8
    Cupid's indictment. 6182-6
    Daphne. 6182-6
    The fairy frolic. 6134-6,6466-3,6383-7,6301-2
    Fairy revels. 6198-2,6189-3
    A fairy song. 6436-1
    Friendship and love. 6085-4
    Hymn to Apollo ("Sing to Apollo, god of day"). 6198-2, 6250-4,6189-3
    Love's college. 6827-8
    "My shag-hair Cyclops, come, let's ply". 6181-8
    "O Cupid! monarch over kings". 6181-8,6182-6
    "O yes, O yes, if any maid". 6181-8
    "O! for a bowl of fat canary". 6181-8
    Pan's song. 6102-8,6436-1,6150-8,6186-9
    "Pan's Syrinx was a girl indeed". 6181-8
    Sapho's song. 6436-1
    Sappho's song, fr. Sappho and Phao. 6934-7
    A serving men's song. 6436-1,6026-9
    Sleepe, deathes alye. 6958-4
    The song in making of the arrows. 6315-2,6436-1
    Song of Accius and Silena. 6436-1
    Song of Apelles. 6436-1,6026-9,6194-X
    A song of Daphne to the lute. 6436-1
    A song of Diana's nymphs. 6436-1
    Song to Apollo. 6436-1
    Songs of the faieries. 6334-9,6219-9,6430-2,6737-9
    Spring's welcome. 6102-8,6189-3,6102-8,6383-7,6198-2, 6332-6,6334-9,6732-8
    The spring. 6339-X,6737-9
    Syrinx. 6315-2,6182-6,6726-3,6383-7,6315-2
    To Apollo, fr. Midas. 6934-7
    Trico's song. 6436-1
    Vulcan's song. 6182-6
    "What bird so sings, yet does so wail?" 6099-4,6194-X
    "What bird so sings, yet so does wail". 6187-7,6182-6, 6328-4
Lyly, John M.
    The urchins' dance. 6959-2
Lyman Dillon and his plow. MacKinlay Kantor. 6628-3
Lyman, Florence Van Fleet
    The way of it. 6039-0
Lyman, Frederick, and Jim. Eugene Field. 6949-5
Lynch, ?
    Silence. 6273-3
Lynch, Annie Charlotte
    On a picture. 6385-3
Lynch, Genevieve Louise
    Immigrants. 6070-6
Lynch, John W.
    A woman wrapped in silence. 6282-2
Lynch, P.J.
    Arise ye Nova Scotia slaves. 6149-4
Lynch, Richard
    Love's despair. 6182-6
Lynch, Stanislaus
    Blue Peter. 6930-4
Lynch, Thomas T.
    Life up your heads, rejoice! 6730-1
Lynch, Thomas Toke
    Holy spirit, dwell with me. 6337-3

    Lift up your heads, rejoice! 6418-3
    Where is thy God, my soul? 6337-3
Lynched. Stephen Todd Booker. 6870-7
The lynching. Isabelle McClellan Taylor. 6178-8
Lynd, Sylvia
    Beauty and the beast. 6781-6
    Cowper in Bedfordshire. 6779-4
    Farewell in February. 6776-X
    A fine night in winter. 6779-4
    The happy hour. 6320-9
    R.A.F. 6224-5
    The return of the goldfinches. 6943-6
    To Sheila playing Haydn. 6778-6
    To Sheila playing Haydn. 6317-9
    Virgin gold. 6044-7
Lyndsay, Sir David
    Ane satire of the three estaitis, sels. 6845-6
    Ane supplication in contemplation of syde taillis. 6845-6
    A carman's account of a lawsuit. 6240-7
    Complaint of the common weill of Scotland. 6845-6
    The dreme, sels. 6180-X
    Satire on the syde taillis. 6200-8
Lynes, Alfred W.
    Old Winter, esquire. 6745-X
Lynmouth. Arthur O'Shaughnessy. 6331-4
A Lynmouth widow. Amelia Josephine Burr. 6102-8,6556-2, 6019-6,6076-5,6393-4
Lynn, Cheri
    'I whisper' 6857-X
Lynn, J.W. (tr.)
    A cry from the ghetto. Morris Rosenfeld, 7011-6,6102-8
Lynn, Thomas
    Credo. 6857-X
    For all I knew. 6857-X
    Shiloh. 6857-X
Lynton verses. Thomas Edward Brown. 6423-X
Lyon. Henry Peterson. 6471-X,6016-2
Lyon, Carrie Ward
    Curiosity. 6861-8
    Hallow even. 6254-7
    Halloween ("Walk into the dark room"). 6254-7
    Little folk. 6254-7
Lyon, Ernest Neal
    Aim high. 6701-8
    In apple-time. 6721-2
    Loafin' time. 6721-2
Lyon, Jud
    Fresh vistas. 6764-6
Lyon, Leslie Clyde
    She told me this. 6936-3
Lyon, Lilian Bowes
    Duchess. 6257-1
Lyon, Lilian Bowes. See Bowes-Lyon, Lilian
Lyon, Mabel
    Refugees. 6761-1
Lyon, P.H.B.
    "Now to be still and rest..." 7029-9
    Zepp days. 7029-9
Lyon, W.S.S.
    Easter at Ypres: 1915. 7027-2
    Lines written in a fire-trench. 7027-2
The lyon, the fox, and the geese. John Gay. 6972-X
The lyon, the tyger, and the traveller. John Gay. 6972-X
"A lyon, tir'd with state affairs". The lyon, the fox, and the geese. John Gay. 6972-X
Lyonesse. Godfrey Fox Bradby. 6541-4
Lyons, J. Gilbourne
    The tempest stilled. 6606-2
    Triumphs of the English language. 6409-4
Lyons, John P.
    Bagged the wrong bird. 7021-3
Lyons, Martha E.
    A thing born of darkness. 6178-8
Lyons, Norbert
    The cochero and the horse. 7010-8
Lyons, Richard
    Dogdog. 6803-0
Lyra incantata. Theodore Tilton. 6889-8
Lyra Modulata, sels. Sir Ronald Ross. 6234-2

The lyre and flower. Felicia Dorothea Hemans. 6973-8
The lyre and the crown. Marcus Argentarius. 6435-3
"A lyre its plaintive sweetness poured". The lyre and flower. Felicia Dorothea Hemans. 6973-8
The lyre of Anacreon. Oliver Wendell Holmes. 6126-5
The lyre of life. William Wilfred Campbell. 6433-7
The lyre's lament. Felicia Dorothea Hemans. 6973-8
"A lyre-bird sang a low melodious song". The bell-birds. William ("Fiona Macleod") Sharp. 6768-9
The lyre. Charles Swain. 6980-0
Lyric. Al-Barraq. 6362-4
Lyric. Alice Cary. 6969-X
Lyric. Warren Gilbert. 6070-6
Lyric. Pricilla Heath. 6764-6
Lyric. Howard Vigne Sutherland. 6836-7
Lyric. Edith M. Thomas. 6431-0
Lyric ("I am a Puritan"). Pricilla Heath. 6764-6
Lyric ("I stared"). Pricilla Heath. 6764-6
Lyric ("It may"). Arthur K. Sabin. 6884-7
Lyric ("She came"). Arthur K. Sabin. 6884-7
Lyric ("The birds are quiet..."). Arthur K. Sabin. 6884-7
Lyric ("The laws of equilibrium"). John Smith [pseud]. 6751-4
Lyric ("When old Anacreon..."). Arthur K. Sabin. 6884-7
Lyric 025. Wendell Phillips Stafford. 7030-2
"The lyric April time is forth". In lyric season. Bliss Carman. 6795-6
The lyric argument. Robert Herrick. 6383-7
The lyric deed. John G. Neihardt. 6619-4
A lyric from a play. Unknown. 6881-2
Lyric intermezzo. Heinrich Heine. 6949-5
Lyric love, fr. The ring and the book. Robert Browning. 6437-X
The lyric muse. Horace. 6949-5
Lyric of action. Paul Hamilton Hayne. 6211-3,6577-5
Lyric of doubt. Donald Wandrei. 6218-0
Lyric stanzas from Empedocles. Matthew Arnold. 6110-9
Lyric to the isles. Charles Sangster. 6115-X
Lyric XXVII, fr. Animula vagula. Leonard Bacon. 6393-4
Lyric, fr. The fire-bringer. William Vaughn Moody. 6077-3;6473-6;6399-3
"A lyric, love, for you, my love". A lyric. Robert Loveman. 6941-X
A lyric. Walter Savage Landor. 6102-8,6732-8
A lyric. Robert Loveman. 6941-X
A lyric. Lorenzo de' Medici. 7039-6
A lyrical epigram. Edith Wharton. 6501-5,6607-0,6396-9
The lyrical lackey. James and Horace Smith. 6760-3
The lyrical poem. Richard Garnett. 6656-9
Lyricism. Bong-gun Chun. 6775-1
Lyrick for legacies. Robert Herrick. 6933-9
Lyrics. Sara Teasdale. 6778-6
"Lyrics is gold/Shapes untold". Back-log moods. James B. Hunt. 6983-5
Lysaght, Edward
    Ambition. 6086-2
    Garnyvillo. 6174-5
    In praise of Grattan. 7009-4
    Kate of Garnavilla. 6086-2
    Kitty of Coleraine. 6089-7,6733-6,6092-7
    Love versus the bottle. 6858-8
    The man who led the van of Irish volunteers. 6174-5
    Our dear native island. 6858-8
Lysaght, Sidney Royse
    A deserted home. 6477-9
    The penalty of love. 6090-0,6476-0,6174-5
    The secret of the deeps. 6833-2
    To my comrades. 6174-5
    The unexplored. 6090-0,6174-5
Lyster, Frederic
    At the tunnel's mouth. 6166-4
    The wreck of the Solent. 6674-4
Lyster, Mrs. Henry F.
    Michigan, my Michigan! 6465-5
Lyte, Henry Francis
    Abide with me. 6730-1,6219-9,6656-9,6102-8,6214-8,6238-5,6014-5,6001-3,6240-7,6418-2,6732-8,6337-3,6479-5
    David's three mighty ones. 6848-0
    Forgiveness. 6065-X
    The officer's grave. 6934-7

The unknown God. 6337-3
Lyte, Henry Francis (tr.)
    Psalm 084. Bible, 6219-9
A lytell geste of Robyn Hode. Unknown. 6055-2
Lytle, Andrew Nelson
    Edward Graves. 6039-0
Lytle, William Haines
    Antony and Cleopatra. 6370-5,6408-6,6273-3,6481-7,6385-3,6486 ,6735-2,6732-8,6431-0,6219-9
    In camp. 6074-9
    The siege of Chapultepec. 6946-0
    The volunteers. 6946-0
The Lyttel boy. Eugene Field. 6300-4
Lyttelton, George Lyttelton, Baron
    "None, without hope, e'er loved the brightest fair" 6874-X
    Song ("When Delia"). 6932-0,6024-2,6086-2
    "Tell me, my heart, if this be love." 6302-0;6385-3
    To the memory of a lady. 6932-0
Lyttelton, Lucy
    Simon the Cyrenian. 6335-7
Lyttleton. Anne Donovan. 7018-3
Lyttleton, Lucy
    Quod semper. 6350-0
Lytton, Edward George. See Bulwer-Lytton, Baron
Lytton, Edward Robert, Earl. See Meredith, Owen
"The lytyll, prety nyghtynale". Unknown. 6198-2,6430-2

M. Philip Bourke Marston. 7015-9
M ("M was once a little mouse"). Edward Lear. 6722-0
M and A and R and I. Unknown. 6756-5
M'Fingal, an epic poem. John Trumbull. 6121-4
M'Fingal, sels. John Trumbull. 6753-0,6008-0,6288-1,6753-0
M'hm. Unknown. 6260-1
M'Liss and Louie. Carl Sandburg. 6778-6
M'sieu. Wilson MacDonald. 6797-2
M'sieu Smit'; the adventures of an Englishman in...Canadian William Henry Drummond. 6633-X
M-day's child is fair of face. Muriel Rukeyser. 6761-1
M. Bird's set songs, sels. M. Bird. 6198-2
M. Crashaws answer for hope. Richard Crashaw. 6933-9
M. Crashaws answer for hope, sels. Richard Crashaw. 6208-3
M. E. Medley. J. Broome. 6468-X
M. Edwards. M.A.Y. fr. The Paradise of Dainty Devices. Unknown. 6586-4
"M. quarrels with N., for M. wrote a book". On Madan's answer to Newton's comments on Thelyphtora. William Cowper. 6814-6
M., B.R.
    The fly. 6937-1
M.,A.E.
    To be continued. 6817-0
M.,B.
    'Spacially Jim. 6273-3
M.,B.R.
    Brother bunnies. 6937-1
    If, in the garden. 6937-1
    Mr. Frog. 6937-1
    My policeman. 6937-1
    Oh, for a drop of rain. 6937-1
    Rose Mary. 6937-1
    The starling. 6937-1
    The thumb march. 6937-1
    Up and down. 6937-1
    A wish. 6937-1
M.,C.L.
    Truthful Dottie. 6131-1
M.,E.B.
    What the circus did. 6965-7
M.,E.J.
    To a bookworm. 6817-0
M.,G.B.
    To be continued. 6817-0
M.,H.
    Instructions for my funeral. 6817-0
M.,H. (tr.)
    The setting sun. Stesichorus, 6435-3

M.

M.,H.J.
    The rivers of France. 6963-0,6846-4
M.,J.W.
    Battle-ship and torpedo-boat. 6471-X
M.,L.F.
    Life. 6118-4
M.,M.
    A Christmas eve adventure. 6743-3
    Little snowflakes. 6373-X
M.,M.W.
    An incident of the war. 6008-0
M.,N.
    Nursery gardening. 6724-7
    Optimism. 6724-7
M.,O.
    Master and pupil. 6474-4
M.,P.S.
    Dawn. 6332-2
    Dawn. 7031-0
M.,R.
    The thyroid gland. 6440-X
M.,S.M.
    Knights-errant. 6032-3
    Surrender. 6172-9
    To my favorite author. 6032-3
M.,W.W.
    To peace. 6542-2
M.I.. Rudyard Kipling. 6810-3
The M.P.. Unknown. 6237-7
M.T.W.. Thomas Edward Brown. 6809-X
Ma. Alter Bordy. 6033-1
Ma and pa, not Polly, needed educatin'. Keene Thompson. 6693-3
Ma cailin donn. George Sigerson. 6873-1
"Ma femme est morte, je suis libre!". Le vin de l'assassin. Charles Baudelaire. 6801-4
A ma future. Sir Edwin Arnold. 6226-1
"Ma she's home - An' I'm 'way here". A Christmas memory. James Whitcomb Riley. 7021-3
Ma vocation. Pierre Jean de Beranger. 6949-5
Ma vocation. Pierre Jean de Beranger. 6801-4
Ma's physical culture. Unknown. 6249-0
Ma's tools. Unknown. 6889-8
Ma, what's a banker? or, hush, my child. Ogden Nash. 6628-3
"Ma-hican-ittuck!/River to the mountains". Hudson. Arthur Guiterman. 6773-5
Maas, Willard
    For an unborn child. 6042-0
    The kind look. 6389-6
    Letter to R. 6666-6
    The marble head. 6389-6
    The secret on the urn. 6389-6
Mab the mistress-fairy. Ben Jonson. 6182-6
Mabbe, James
    Now sleep, and take thy rest. 6563-5
Mabbott, Maureen Cobb
    Imperious design. 6979-7
Mabel. Raymond Macdonald Alden. 6936-3
Mabel. Unknown. 6672-0
Mabel Martin. John Greenleaf Whittier. 6077-3
Mabel on midsummer day. Mary Howitt. 6502-3,6131-1
Mabel's way. Robert Meacham Davis. 6118-4
Mabel, in New Hampshire. James Thomas Fields. 6441-8,6652-6,6004-8
Mabey, Nell
    Lake Pepin. 6342-X
Mabie, Hamilton Wright
    Christmas eve. 6145-1
Mac Flecknoe. John Dryden. 6200-8,6483-3,6536-8,6562-7, 6660-7,6645 ,6152-4,6192-3,6430-2,6195-0,6491-4,6637
Mac Flecknoe, sels. John Dryden. 6733-6,6197-4,6646-1
Mac Kenna's dream. Unknown. 6858-8
MacAlpine, James
    To an Irish blackbird. 6073-0
"MacGaradh! MacGaradh! red face of the tay". The gathering of the Hays. Unknown. 6859-6
Macabre. James Waldo Fawcett. 6036-6
Macalister and Eoin MacNeill, R.A.S. (tr.)
    Invocation to Ireland. Amergin (atr.), 6930-4

MacCarthy, Denis Florence (tr.)
    Justina's temptation. Pedro de la Barca Calderon, 6102-8
MacColl, D.S. (tr.)
    Cats. Charles Baudelaire, 6511-2
MacDonagh, Thomas (tr.)
    Ideal. Padraic Pearse, 7039-6
    Lullaby of the woman of the mountain. Padraic Pearse, 6930-4
    The stars stand up in the air. Unknown, 6244-X
    To his ideal. Padraic Pearse, 6301-2
    The yettlow bittern. Cathal Buidhe MacElguin, 6930-4
MacDonald, Dwight (tr.)
    Paris-am-Seine. Jean Malaquais, 6343-8
MacGregor, Marshall (tr.)
    "Fiercely, methinks, will he rage in his heart...". Aristophanes, 6435-3
    "Nay, I'll not chip and scratch them line by line". Aristophanes, 6435-3
MacIntyre, C.F. (tr.)
    Caesar. Paul Valery, 6665-8
    Death in the corn. Detlev von Liliencron, 6665-8
    Joseph's suspicion. Rainer Maria Rilke, 6223-7,6734-4
    The last evening. Rainer Maria Rilke, 6665-8
    O Strassburg. Unknown (German), 6665-8
    Prelude. Stefan George, 6665-8
McCalla and the widdy. Unknown. 6744-1
Macandrew, Barbara Miller
    Ezekiel. 6848-0
    The Hebrew mother. 6848-0
    The man of God from Judah. 6848-0
MacArthur, Elinor
    Sanctuary. 6073-0
    Sea-birds ("Birds that float upon a wave"). 6073-0
    Winter birds. 6073-0
MacArthur, Irene Cole
    The unknown soldier speaks. 6750-6
MacArthur, Ruth Brown
    When Daddy's ship comes in. 6799-9
Macarius the monk. John Boyle O'Reilly. 6294-6
Macaronic Mother Goose. Unknown. 6724-7
Macartney, F.T.
    Bargain basement. 6349-7
    You'll know love. 6349-7
Macaulay. Walter Savage Landor. 6302-2
Macaulay, Rose
    The continental boat basin. 6633-X
    The devourers. 6477-9
    Driving sheep. 6477-9
    Many sisters to many brothers. 6477-9
    The new year. 6875-8
    Old year. 6875-8
    Peace. 6884-7
    Recovery. 6542-2
Macaulay, Rose E.
    Ballade of dreams. 6875-8
Macaulay, Thomas Babington Macaulay, 1st Baron
    The armada, sels. 6427-2,6239-3
    The armada. 6087-0,6232-3,6290-3,6186-9,6669-0,6188 ,6459-0,6732-8,6322-5,6639-9,6046-3,6263-6,6808-1, 6079-X
    The battle of Lake Regillus. 6250-4
    Battle of Ivry. 6554-6,6240-7,6604-6,6045-1,6240-7,6328 ,6606-2,6610-0,6425-6,6570-8,6660-7,6424
    The battle of Naseby, sels. 6395-0
    The battle of Naseby. 6192-3,6197-4,6419-1,6560-0,6639-9,6554-6,6188-5,6323-3,6504-X,6228-8,6656
    The battle of the Lake Regillus, sels. 6427-2,6648-8
    The battle. 6087-0
    The cavalier's march to London. 6980-0
    "The consul's brow was sad..." 6606-2
    The country clergyman's trip to Cambridge. 6874-X
    The county clergyman's trip to Cambridge. 6200-8,6092-7
    The death of Herminius, fr. The battle...Lake Regillus. 6427-2,6610-0
    England's standard, fr. The armada. 6427-2
    Epitaph on a Jacobite. 6138-9,6732-8,6046-3,6656-9
    Fate of Virginia. 6706-9,6304-7
    The fight at the bridge, fr. Horatius. 6427-2
    The fight in the ceetre, r.The battle...Lake Regillus.

End of Volume I